Profiles
of
Illinois

2014
Fourth Edition

Profiles
of
Illinois

A UNIVERSAL REFERENCE BOOK

Grey House
Publishing

PUBLISHER: Leslie Mackenzie
EDITORIAL DIRECTOR: Laura Mars
SENIOR EDITOR: David Garoogian
MARKETING DIRECTOR: Jessica Moody

Grey House Publishing, Inc.
4919 Route 22
Amenia, NY 12501
518.789.8700
FAX 845.373.6390
www.greyhouse.com
e-mail: books @greyhouse.com

While every effort has been made to ensure the reliability of the information presented in this publication, Grey House Publishing neither guarantees the accuracy of the data contained herein nor assumes any responsibility for errors, omissions or discrepancies. Grey House accepts no payment for listing; inclusion in the publication of any organization, agency, institution, publication, service or individual does not imply endorsement of the editors or publisher.

Errors brought to the attention of the publisher and verified to the satisfaction of the publisher will be corrected in future editions.

First edition published 2005
Printed in the Canada

ISBN: 978-1-61925-282-0

Table of Contents

Introduction

This is the fourth edition of *Profiles of Illinois—Facts, Figures & Statistics for 1,491 Populated Places in Illinois.* As with the other titles in our *State Profiles* series, it was built with content from Grey House Publishing's award-winning *Profiles of America*—a 4-volume compilation of data on more than 42,000 places in the United States. We have updated and included the Illinois chapter from *Profiles of America,* and added several new chapters of demographic information and ranking sections, so that *Profiles of Illinois* is the most comprehensive portrait of the state of Illinois ever published.

Profiles of Illinois provides data on all populated communities and counties in the state of Illinois for which the US Census provides individual statistics. This edition also includes profiles of 128 unincorporated places based on US Census data by zip code and, for the first time, includes communities that span multiple zip codes.

This premier reference work includes five major sections that cover everything from **Education** to **Ethnic Backgrounds** to **Climate**. All sections include **Comparative Statistics** or **Rankings**. New to this edition is a section called **About Illinois** at the front of the book, comprised of detailed narrative and colorful photos and maps. Here is an overview of each section:

1. About Illinois
This **NEW** 4-color section gives the researcher a real sense of the state and its history. It includes a Photo Gallery, and comprehensive sections on Illinois's Government, Land and Natural Resources, and Demographic Maps. With charts and maps, these 34 pages help to anchor the researcher to the state, both physically and politically.

2. Profiles
This section, organized by county, gives detailed profiles of 1,491 places plus 102 counties, based on Census 2010 and the 2008-2012 American Community Survey. **NEW** to this edition is data on Health Insurance and Homeowner/Rental Vacancy Rates. Together with current government statistics and original research, these profiles pull together statistical and descriptive information on every Census-recognized place in the state. Major fields of information include:

Geography	*Housing*	*Education*	*Religion*
Ancestry	*Transportation*	*Population*	*Climate*
Economy	*Industry*	*Health*	

In addition to place profiles, this section includes an **Alphabetical Place Index** and **Comparative Statistics** that compare Illinois's 100 largest communities by dozens of data points.

3. Education
This section begins with an **Educational State Profile,** summarizing number of schools, students, diplomas granted and educational dollars spent. Following the state profile are **School District Rankings** on 16 topics ranging from *Teacher/Student Ratios* to *High School Drop-Out Rates.* Following these rankings are statewide *National Assessment of Educational Progress (NAEP)* results and data from the *Illinois State Report Card—* an overview of student performance by subject, grade, and demographic.

4. Ancestry and Ethnicity
This section provides a detailed look at the ancestral, Hispanic and racial makeup of Illinois's 200+ ethnic categories. Profiles are included for the state, for all counties with 100,000 or more residents, and for all places with 50,000 or more residents. In the ranking section, data is displayed three ways: 1) by number, based on all places regardless of population; 2) by percent, based on all places regardless of population; 3) by percent, based on places with populations of 50,000 or more. You will discover, for example, that Glen Ellyn has the greatest number of Afghans in the state (305), and that 100.0% of the population of Paderborn are of Germans ancestry.

5. Climate

This section includes a State Summary, three colorful maps and profiles of both National and Cooperative Weather Stations. In addition, you'll find Weather Station Rankings with hundreds of interesting details, such as Kaskaskia River at Navigation Lock & Dam reporting the highest annual extreme maximum temperature (109° F) and Antioch reporting the highest nnual snowfall (39.2 inches)

This section also includes Significant Storm Event data from January 2000 through December 2009. Here you will learn that 100 mph thunderstorm wind caused more than $175 million in property damage in Williamson County in May 2009 and that a F3 tornado was responsible for eight deaths and seven injuries in La Salle County in April 2004.

Note: The extensive **User's Guide** that follows this introduction is segmented into four sections and examines, in some detail, each data field in the individual profiles and comparative sections for all chapters. It provides sources for all data points and statistical definitions as necessary.

User's Guide: Profiles

Places Covered

All 102 counties.

1,298 incorporated municipalities and minor civil divisions. Comprised of 300 cities, 16 towns, and 982 villages.

65 Census Designated Places (CDP). The U.S. Bureau of the Census defines a CDP as "a statistical entity, defined for each decennial census according to Census Bureau guidelines, comprising a densely settled concentration of population that is not within an incorporated place, but is locally identified by a name. CDPs are delineated cooperatively by state and local officials and the Census Bureau, following Census Bureau guidelines.

128 unincorporated communities. The communities included have statistics for their ZIP Code Tabulation Area (ZCTA) available from the Census Bureau. They are referred to as "postal areas." A ZCTA is a statistical entity developed by the Census Bureau to approximate the delivery area for a US Postal Service 5-digit or 3-digit ZIP Code in the US and Puerto Rico. A ZCTA is an aggregation of census blocks that have the same predominant ZIP Code associated with the mailing addresses in the Census Bureau's Master Address File. Thus, the Postal Service's delivery areas have been adjusted to encompass whole census blocks so that the Census Bureau can tabulate census data for the ZCTAs. ZCTAs do not include all ZIP Codes used for mail delivery and therefore do not precisely depict the area within which mail deliveries associated with that ZIP Code occur. Additionally, some areas that are known by a unique name, although they are part of a larger incorporated place, are also included as "postal areas."

For a more in-depth discussion of geographic areas, please refer to the Census Bureau's Geographic Areas Reference Manual at http://www.census.gov/geo/www/garm.html.

Important Notes

- *Profiles of Illinois* uses the term "community" to refer to all places except counties. The term "county" is used to refer to counties and county-equivalents. All places are defined as of the 2010 Census.
- In each community profile, only school districts that have schools that are physically located within the community are shown. In addition, statistics for each school district cover the entire district, regardless of the physical location of the schools within the district.
- Special care should be taken when interpreting certain statistics for communities containing large colleges or universities. College students were counted as residents of the area in which they were living while attending college (as they have been since the 1950 census). One effect this may have is skewing the figures for population, income, housing, and educational attainment.
- Some information (e.g. unemployment rates) is available for both counties and individual communities. Other information is available for just counties (e.g. election results), or just individual communities (e.g. local newspapers).
- Some statistical information is available only for larger communities. In addition, the larger places are more apt to have services such as airports, hospitals, colleges, etc.
- For the most complete information on any community, you should also check the entry for the county in which the community is located. In addition, more information and services will be listed under the larger places in the county.

Information for Incorporated Communities and Census Designated Places

PHYSICAL CHARACTERISTICS

Place Type: Lists the type of place (city, town, village, borough, special city, CDP, township, plantation, gore, district, grant, location, reservation, or postal area). *Source: U.S. Census Bureau, Census 2010 and U.S. Postal Service, City State File.*

Land and Water Area: Land and water area in square miles. *Source: U.S. Census Bureau, Census 2010.*

Latitude and Longitude: Latitude and longitude in degrees. *Source: U.S. Census Bureau, Census 2010.*

Elevation: Elevation in feet. *Source: U.S. Geological Survey, Geographic Names Information System (GNIS).*

HISTORY

History: Historical information. *Source: Columbia University Press, The Columbia Gazetteer of North America; Original research.*

POPULATION

Population: 1990, 2000 and 2010 figures are a 100% count of population. *Source: U.S. Census Bureau, Census 2010.*

Race/Hispanic Origin: Figures include the U.S. Census Bureau categories of White alone; Black/African American alone; Asian alone; American Indian/Alaska Native alone; Native Hawaiian/ Other Pacific Islander alone; Some Other Race alone; Two or More Races; and Hispanic of any race. Alone refers to the fact that these figures are not in combination with any other race. *Source: American Community Survey, 2008-2012 Five-Year Estimates.*

The concept of race, as used by the Census Bureau, reflects self-identification by people according to the race or races with which they most closely identify. These categories are socio-political constructs and should not be interpreted as being scientific or anthropological in nature. Furthermore, the race categories include both racial and national-origin groups.

- **White:** A person having origins in any of the original peoples of Europe, the Middle East, or North Africa. It includes people who indicated their race(s) as "White" or reported entries such as Irish, German, Italian, Lebanese, Arab, Moroccan, or Caucasian.
- **Black/African American:** A person having origins in any of the Black racial groups of Africa. It includes people who indicated their race(s) as "Black, African Am., or Negro" or reported entries such as African American, Kenyan, Nigerian, or Haitian.
- **Asian:** A person having origins in any of the original peoples of the Far East, Southeast Asia, or the Indian subcontinent, including, for example, Cambodia, China, India, Japan, Korea, Malaysia, Pakistan, the Philippine Islands, Thailand, and Vietnam. It includes people who indicated their race(s) as "Asian" or reported entries such as "Asian Indian," "Chinese," "Filipino," "Korean," "Japanese," "Vietnamese," and "Other Asian" or provided other detailed Asian responses.
- **American Indian/Alaska Native:** A person having origins in any of the original peoples of North and South America (including Central America) and who maintains tribal affiliation or community attachment. This category includes people who indicated their race(s) as "American Indian or Alaska Native" or reported their enrolled or principal tribe, such as Navajo, Blackfeet, Inupiat, Yup'ik, or Central American Indian groups or South American Indian groups.
- **Native Hawaiian/Other Pacific Islander:** A person having origins in any of the original peoples of Hawaii, Guam, Samoa, or other Pacific Islands. It includes people who indicated their race(s) as "Pacific Islander" or reported entries such as "Native Hawaiian," "Guamanian or Chamorro," "Samoan," and "Other Pacific Islander" or provided other detailed Pacific Islander responses.
- **Some Other Race:** Includes all other responses not included in the race categories described above. Respondents reporting entries such as multiracial, mixed, interracial, or a Hispanic, Latino, or Spanish group (for example, Mexican, Puerto Rican, Cuban, or Spanish) in response to the race question are included in this category.

- **Two or More Races:** People may choose to provide two or more races either by checking two or more race response check boxes, by providing multiple responses, or by some combination of check boxes and other responses. The race response categories shown on the questionnaire are collapsed into the five minimum race groups identified by OMB, and the Census Bureau's "Some Other Race" category.

- **Hispanic:** The data on the Hispanic or Latino population were derived from answers to a question that was asked of all people. The terms "Spanish," "Hispanic origin," and "Latino" are used interchangeably. Some respondents identify with all three terms while others may identify with only one of these three specific terms. Hispanics or Latinos who identify with the terms "Spanish," "Hispanic," or "Latino" are those who classify themselves in one of the specific Spanish, Hispanic, or Latino categories listed on the questionnaire ("Mexican," "Puerto Rican," or "Cuban") as well as those who indicate that they are "other Spanish/Hispanic/Latino." People who do not identify with one of the specific origins listed on the questionnaire but indicate that they are "other Spanish/Hispanic/Latino" are those whose origins are from Spain, the Spanish-speaking countries of Central or South America, the Dominican Republic, or people identifying themselves generally as Spanish, Spanish-American, Hispanic, Hispano, Latino, and so on. All write-in responses to the "other Spanish/Hispanic/Latino" category were coded. Origin can be viewed as the heritage, nationality group, lineage, or country of birth of the person or the person's parents or ancestors before their arrival in the United States. People who identify their origin as Spanish, Hispanic, or Latino may be of any race.

Population Density: Total population divided by the land area in square miles. *Source: U.S. Census Bureau, American Community Survey, 2008-2012 Five-Year Estimates.*

Average Household Size: Number of persons in the average household. *Source: U.S. Census Bureau, American Community Survey, 2008-2012 Five-Year Estimates.*

Median Age: Median age of the population. *Source: U.S. Census Bureau, American Community Survey, 2008-2012 Five-Year Estimates.*

Male/Female Ratio: Number of males per 100 females. *Source: U.S. Census Bureau, American Community Survey, 2008-2012 Five-Year Estimates.*

Marital Status: Percentage of population never married, now married, widowed, or divorced. *Source: U.S. Census Bureau, American Community Survey, 2008-2012 Five-Year Estimates.*

The marital status classification refers to the status at the time of enumeration. Data on marital status are tabulated only for the population 15 years old and over. Each person was asked whether they were "Now married," "Widowed," "Divorced," or "Never married." Couples who live together (for example, people in common-law marriages) were able to report the marital status they considered to be the most appropriate.

- **Never married.** Never married includes all people who have never been married, including people whose only marriage(s) was annulled.
- **Now married.** All people whose current marriage has not ended by widowhood or divorce. This category includes people defined as "separated."
- **Widowed.** This category includes widows and widowers who have not remarried.
- **Divorced.** This category includes people who are legally divorced and who have not remarried.

Foreign Born: Percentage of population who were not U.S. citizens at birth. Foreign-born people are those who indicated they were either a U.S. citizen by naturalization or they were not a citizen of the United States. *Source: U.S. Census Bureau, American Community Survey, 2008-2012 Five-Year Estimates.*

Ancestry: Largest ancestry groups reported (up to five). The data includes persons who report multiple ancestries. For example, if a person reported being Irish and Italian, they would be included in both categories. Thus, the sum of the percentages may be greater than 100%. *Source: U.S. Census Bureau, American Community Survey, 2008-2012 Five-Year Estimates.*

The data represent self-classification by people according to the ancestry group or groups with which they most closely identify. Ancestry refers to a person's ethnic origin or descent, "roots," heritage, or the place of birth of the person, the person's parents, or their ancestors before their arrival in the United States. Some ethnic identities, such as Egyptian or Polish, can be traced to geographic areas outside the United States, while other ethnicities such as Pennsylvania German or Cajun evolved in the United States.

The ancestry question was intended to provide data for groups that were not included in the Hispanic origin and race questions. Therefore, although data on all groups are collected, the ancestry data shown in these tabulations are for non-Hispanic and non-race groups. *See* Race/Hispanic Origin for information on Hispanic and race groups.

ECONOMY

Unemployment Rate: Unemployment rate as of April 2014. Includes all civilians age 16 or over who were unemployed and looking for work. *Source: U.S. Department of Labor, Bureau of Labor Statistics, Local Area Unemployment Statistics.*

Total Civilian Labor Force: Total civilian labor force as of April 2014. Includes all civilians age 16 or over who were either employed, or unemployed and looking for work. *Source: U.S. Department of Labor, Bureau of Labor Statistics, Local Area Unemployment Statistics.*

Employment by Occupation: Percentage of the employed civilian population 16 years and over in management, professional, service, sales, farming, construction, and production occupations. *Source: U.S. Census Bureau, American Community Survey, 2008-2012 Five-Year Estimates.*

- Management, business, and financial occupations include:
  Management occupations
  Business and financial operations occupations

- Computer, engineering, and science occupations include:
  Computer and mathematical occupations
  Architecture and engineering occupations
  Life, physical, and social science occupations

- Education, legal, community service, arts, and media occupations include:
  Community and social service occupations
  Legal occupations
  Education, training, and library occupations
  Arts, design, entertainment, sports, and media occupations

- Healthcare practitioners and technical occupations include:
  Health diagnosing and treating practitioners and other technical occupations
  Health technologists and technicians

- Service occupations include:
  Healthcare support occupations
  Protective service occupations:
      Fire fighting and prevention, and other protective service workers including supervisors
      Law enforcement workers including supervisors
  Food preparation and serving related occupations
  Building and grounds cleaning and maintenance occupations
  Personal care and service occupations

- Sales and office occupations include:
  Sales and related occupations
  Office and administrative support occupations

- Natural resources, construction, and maintenance occupations include:
  Farming, fishing, and forestry occupations
  Construction and extraction occupations
  Installation, maintenance, and repair occupations

- Production, transportation, and material moving occupations include:
  Production occupations
  Transportation occupations
  Material moving occupations

Single-Family Building Permits Issued: Building permits issued for new single-family housing units in 2013. *Source: U.S. Census Bureau, Manufacturing and Construction Division.*

Multi-Family Building Permits Issued: Building permits issued for new multi-family housing units in 2013. *Source: U.S. Census Bureau, Manufacturing and Construction Division.*

Statistics on housing units authorized by building permits include housing units issued in local permit-issuing jurisdictions by a building or zoning permit. Not all areas of the country require a building or zoning permit. The statistics only represent those areas that do require a permit. Current surveys indicate that construction is undertaken for all but a very small percentage of housing units authorized by building permits. A major portion typically get under way during the month of permit issuance and most of the remainder begin within the three following months. Because of this lag, the housing unit authorization statistics do not represent the number of units actually put into construction for the period shown, and should therefore not be directly interpreted as "housing starts."

Statistics are based upon reports submitted by local building permit officials in response to a mail survey. They are obtained using Form C-404 const/www/c404.pdf, "Report of New Privately-Owned Residential Building or Zoning Permits Issued." When a report is not received, missing data are either (1) obtained from the Survey of Use of Permits (SUP) which is used to collect information on housing starts, or (2) imputed based on the assumption that the ratio of current month authorizations to those of a year ago should be the same for reporting and non-reporting places.

Homeowner Vacancy Rate: Proportion of the homeowner inventory that is vacant "for sale." It is computed by dividing the number of vacant units "for sale only" by the sum of the owner-occupied units, vacant units that are "for sale only," and vacant units that have been sold but not yet occupied, and then multiplying by 100. This measure is rounded to the nearest tenth. *Source: U.S. Census Bureau, American Community Survey, 2008-2012 Five-Year Estimates.*

Rental Vacancy Rate: Proportion of the rental inventory that is vacant "for rent." It is computed by dividing the number of vacant units "for rent" by the sum of the renter-occupied units, vacant units that are "for rent," and vacant units that have been rented but not yet occupied, and then multiplying by 100. This measure is rounded to the nearest tenth. *Source: U.S. Census Bureau, American Community Survey, 2008-2012 Five-Year Estimates.*

INCOME

Per Capita Income: Per capita income is the mean income computed for every man, woman, and child in a particular group. It is derived by dividing the total income of a particular group by the total population in that group. Per capita income is rounded to the nearest whole dollar. *Source: U.S. Census Bureau, American Community Survey, 2008-2012 Five-Year Estimates.*

Median Household Income: Includes the income of the householder and all other individuals 15 years old and over in the household, whether they are related to the householder or not. The median divides the income distribution into two equal parts: one-half of the cases falling below the median income and one-half above the median. For households, the median income is based on the distribution of the total number of households including those with no income. Median income for households is computed on the basis of a standard distribution and is rounded to the nearest whole dollar. *Source: U.S. Census Bureau, American Community Survey, 2008-2012 Five-Year Estimates.*

Average Household Income: Average household income is obtained by dividing total household income by the total number of households. *Source: U.S. Census Bureau, American Community Survey, 2008-2012 Five-Year Estimates.*

Percent of Households with Income of $100,000 or more: Percent of households with income of $100,000 or more. *Source: U.S. Census Bureau, American Community Survey, 2008-2012 Five-Year Estimates.*

Poverty Rate: Percentage of population with income below the poverty level. Based on individuals for whom poverty status is determined. Poverty status was determined for all people except institutionalized people, people in military group quarters, people in college dormitories, and unrelated individuals under 15 years old. *Source: U.S. Census Bureau, American Community Survey, 2008-2012 Five-Year Estimates.*

TAXES

Total City Taxes Per Capita: Total city taxes collected divided by the population of the city. *Source: U.S. Census Bureau, State and Local Government Finances, 2011.*

Taxes include:
- Property Taxes
- Sales and Gross Receipts Taxes

- Federal Customs Duties
- General Sales and Gross Receipts Taxes
- Selective Sales Taxes (alcoholic beverages; amusements; insurance premiums; motor fuels; pari-mutuels; public utilities; tobacco products; other)
- License Taxes (alcoholic beverages; amusements; corporations in general; hunting and fishing; motor vehicles motor vehicle operators; public utilities; occupation and business, NEC; other)
- Income Taxes (individual income; corporation net income; other)
- Death and Gift
- Documentary & Stock Transfer
- Severance
- Taxes, NEC

Total City Property Taxes Per Capita: Total city property taxes collected divided by the population of the city. *Source: U.S. Census Bureau, State and Local Government Finances, 2011.*

Property Taxes include general property taxes, relating to property as a whole, taxed at a single rate or at classified rates according to the class of property. Property refers to real property (e.g. land and structures) as well as personal property; personal property can be either tangible (e.g. automobiles and boats) or intangible (e.g. bank accounts and stocks and bonds). Special property taxes, levied on selected types of property (e.g. oil and gas properties, house trailers, motor vehicles, and intangibles) and subject to rates not directly related to general property tax rates. Taxes based on income produced by property as a measure of its value on the assessment date.

EDUCATION

Educational Attainment: Figures show the percent of population age 25 and over with:

- **High school diploma (including GED) or higher:** Includes people whose highest degree is a high school diploma or its equivalent, people who attended college but did not receive a degree, and people who received a college, university, or professional degree.
- **Bachelor's degree or higher:** Includes people who received a bachelor's, master's, doctorate, or professional degree.
- **Master's degree or higher:** Includes people who received a master's, doctorate, or professional degree. *Source: U.S. Census Bureau, American Community Survey, 2008-2012 Five-Year Estimates.*

School Districts: Lists the name of each school district, the grade range (PK=pre-kindergarten; KG=kindergarten), the student enrollment, and the district headquarters' phone number. In each community profile, only school districts that have schools that are physically located within the community are shown. In addition, statistics for each school district cover the entire district, regardless of the physical location of the schools within the district. *Source: U.S. Department of Education, National Center for Educational Statistics, Directory of Public Elementary and Secondary Education Agencies, 2010-11.*

Four-year Colleges: Lists the name of each four-year college, the type of institution (private or public; for-profit or non-profit; religious affiliation; historically black), the total estimated student enrollment in 2012, the general telephone number, and the annual tuition and fees for full-time, first-time undergraduate students (in-state and out-of-state). *Source: U.S. Department of Education, National Center for Educational Statistics, IPEDS College Data, 2012-13.*

Two-year Colleges: Lists the name of each two-year college, the type of institution (private or public; for-profit or non-profit; religious affiliation; historically black), the total estimated student enrollment in 2012, the general telephone number, and the annual tuition and fees for full-time, first-time undergraduate students (in-state and out-of-state). *Source: U.S. Department of Education, National Center for Educational Statistics, IPEDS College Data, 2012-13.*

Vocational/Technical Schools: Lists the name of each vocational/technical school, the type of institution (private or public; for-profit or non-profit; religious affiliation; historically black), the total estimated student enrollment in 2012, the general telephone number, and the annual tuition and fees for full-time students. *Source: U.S. Department of Education, National Center for Educational Statistics, IPEDS College Data, 2012-13.*

HOUSING

Homeownership Rate: Percentage of housing units that are owner-occupied. *Source: U.S. Census Bureau, American Community Survey, 2008-2012 Five-Year Estimates.*

Median Home Value: Median value of all owner-occupied housing units as reported by the owner. Figures shown are 2010 estimates. *Source: U.S. Census Bureau, American Community Survey, 2008-2012 Five-Year Estimates.*

Median Rent: Median monthly contract rent on specified renter-occupied and specified vacant-for-rent units. Specified renter-occupied and specified vacant-for-rent units exclude 1-family houses on 10 acres or more. Contract rent is the monthly rent agreed to or contracted for, regardless of any furnishings, utilities, fees, meals, or services that may be included. For vacant units, it is the monthly rent asked for the rental unit at the time of enumeration. *Source: U.S. Census Bureau, American Community Survey, 2008-2012 Five-Year Estimates.*

Median Year Structure Built: Year structure built refers to when the building was first constructed, not when it was remodeled, added to, or converted. For mobile homes, houseboats, RVs, etc, the manufacturer's model year was assumed to be the year built. The data relate to the number of units built during the specified periods that were still in existence at the time of enumeration. *Source: U.S. Census Bureau, American Community Survey, 2008-2012 Five-Year Estimates.*

HEALTH INSURANCE

Private: Percent of the civilian noninstitutionalized population with private health insurance. A person may report that they have both public and private health insurance, thus, the sum of the percentages may be greater than 100%. *Source: U.S. Census Bureau, American Community Survey, 2008-2012 Five-Year Estimates.*

Public: Percent of the civilian noninstitutionalized population with public health insurance. A person may report that they have both public and private health insurance, thus, the sum of the percentages may be greater than 100%. *Source: U.S. Census Bureau, American Community Survey, 2008-2012 Five-Year Estimates.*

None: Percent of the civilian noninstitutionalized population with no health insurance. *Source: U.S. Census Bureau, American Community Survey, 2008-2012 Five-Year Estimates.*

HOSPITALS

Lists the hospital name and the number of licensed beds. *Source: Grey House Publishing, Directory of Hospital Personnel, 2011.*

SAFETY

Violent Crime Rate: Number of violent crimes reported per 10,000 population. Violent crimes include murder, forcible rape, robbery, and aggravated assault. *Source: Federal Bureau of Investigation, Uniform Crime Reports 2012*

Property Crime Rate: Number of property crimes reported per 10,000 population. Property crimes include burglary, larceny-theft, and motor vehicle theft. *Source: Federal Bureau of Investigation, Uniform Crime Reports 2012*

TRANSPORTATION

Commute to Work: Percentage of workers 16 years old and over that use the following means of transportation to commute to work: car; public transportation; walk; work from home. *Source: U.S. Census Bureau, American Community Survey, 2008-2012 Five-Year Estimates.*

The means of transportation data for some areas may show workers using modes of public transportation that are not available in those areas (e.g. subway or elevated riders in a metropolitan area where there actually is no subway or elevated service). This result is largely due to people who worked during the reference week at a location that was different from their usual place of work (such as people away from home on business in an area where subway service was available) and people who used more than one means of transportation each day but whose principal means was unavailable where they lived (e.g. residents of non-metropolitan areas who drove to the fringe of a metropolitan area and took the commuter railroad most of the distance to work).

Travel Time to Work: Travel time to work for workers 16 years old and over. Reported for the following intervals: less than 15 minutes; 15 to 30 minutes; 30 to 45 minutes; 45 to 60 minutes; 60 minutes or more. *Source: U.S. Census Bureau, American Community Survey, 2008-2012 Five-Year Estimates.*

Travel time to work refers to the total number of minutes that it usually took the person to get from home to work each day during the reference week. The elapsed time includes time spent waiting for public transportation, picking up passengers in carpools, and time spent in other activities related to getting to work.

Amtrak: Indicates if Amtrak rail or bus service is available. Please note that the cities being served continually change. *Source: National Railroad Passenger Corporation, Amtrak National Timetable, 2014*

AIRPORTS

Lists the local airport(s) along with type of service and hub size. *Source: U.S. Department of Transportation, Bureau of Transportation Statistics*

ADDITIONAL INFORMATION CONTACTS

The following phone numbers are provided as sources of additional information: Chambers of Commerce; Economic Development Agencies; and Convention & Visitors Bureaus. Efforts have been made to provide the most recent area codes. However, area code changes may have occurred in listed numbers. *Source: Original research.*

Information for Unincorporated Communities (Postal Areas)

PHYSICAL CHARACTERISTICS

Zip Code: The statistics that follow cover the corresponding ZIP Code Tabulation Area (ZCTA). A ZCTA is a statistical entity developed by the Census Bureau to approximate the delivery area for a US Postal Service 5-digit or 3-digit ZIP Code in the US and Puerto Rico. A ZCTA is an aggregation of census blocks that have the same predominant ZIP Code associated with the mailing addresses in the Census Bureau's Master Address File. Thus, the Postal Service's delivery areas have been adjusted to encompass whole census blocks so that the Census Bureau can tabulate census data for the ZCTAs. ZCTAs do not include all ZIP Codes used for mail delivery and therefore do not precisely depict the area within which mail deliveries associated with that ZIP Code occur. Additionally, some areas that are known by a unique name, although they are part of a larger incorporated place, are also included as "postal areas." *Source: U.S. Census Bureau, Census 2010 and U.S. Postal Service, City State File.*

Land and Water Area: Land and water area in square miles. *Source: U.S. Census Bureau, Census 2010.*

Latitude and Longitude: Latitude and longitude in degrees. *Source: U.S. Census Bureau, Census 2010.*

Elevation: Elevation in feet. *Source: U.S. Geological Survey, Geographic Names Information System (GNIS).*

POPULATION

Population: Figures are a 100% count of population. *Source: U.S. Census Bureau, Census 2010.*

Population Density: Total population divided by the land area in square miles. *Source: U.S. Census Bureau, Census 2010.*

Race/Hispanic Origin: Figures include the U.S. Census Bureau categories of White alone; Black/African American alone; Asian alone; American Indian/Alaska Native alone; Native Hawaiian/ Other Pacific Islander alone; Some Other Race alone; Two or More Races; and Hispanic of any race. Alone refers to the fact that these figures are not in combination with any other race. *Source: U.S. Census Bureau, Census 2010.*

The concept of race, as used by the Census Bureau, reflects self-identification by people according to the race or races with which they most closely identify. These categories are socio-political constructs and should not be interpreted as being scientific or anthropological in nature. Furthermore, the race categories include both racial and national-origin groups.

- **White:** A person having origins in any of the original peoples of Europe, the Middle East, or North Africa. It includes people who indicated their race(s) as "White" or reported entries such as Irish, German, Italian, Lebanese, Arab, Moroccan, or Caucasian.

- **Black/African American:** A person having origins in any of the Black racial groups of Africa. It includes people who indicated their race(s) as "Black, African Am., or Negro" or reported entries such as African American, Kenyan, Nigerian, or Haitian.

- **Asian:** A person having origins in any of the original peoples of the Far East, Southeast Asia, or the Indian subcontinent, including, for example, Cambodia, China, India, Japan, Korea, Malaysia, Pakistan, the Philippine Islands, Thailand, and Vietnam. It includes people who indicated their race(s) as "Asian" or reported entries such as "Asian Indian," "Chinese," "Filipino," "Korean," "Japanese," "Vietnamese," and "Other Asian" or provided other detailed Asian responses.

- **American Indian/Alaska Native:** A person having origins in any of the original peoples of North and South America (including Central America) and who maintains tribal affiliation or community attachment. This category includes people who indicated their race(s) as "American Indian or Alaska Native" or reported their enrolled or principal tribe, such as Navajo, Blackfeet, Inupiat, Yup'ik, or Central American Indian groups or South American Indian groups.

- **Native Hawaiian/Other Pacific Islander:** A person having origins in any of the original peoples of Hawaii, Guam, Samoa, or other Pacific Islands. It includes people who indicated their race(s) as "Pacific Islander" or reported entries such as "Native Hawaiian," "Guamanian or Chamorro," "Samoan," and "Other Pacific Islander" or provided other detailed Pacific Islander responses.

- **Some Other Race:** Includes all other responses not included in the race categories described above. Respondents reporting entries such as multiracial, mixed, interracial, or a Hispanic, Latino, or Spanish group (for example, Mexican, Puerto Rican, Cuban, or Spanish) in response to the race question are included in this category.

- **Two or More Races:** People may choose to provide two or more races either by checking two or more race response check boxes, by providing multiple responses, or by some combination of check boxes and other responses. The race response categories shown on the questionnaire are collapsed into the five minimum race groups identified by OMB, and the Census Bureau's "Some Other Race" category.

- **Hispanic:** The data on the Hispanic or Latino population were derived from answers to a question that was asked of all people. The terms "Spanish," "Hispanic origin," and "Latino" are used interchangeably. Some respondents identify with all three terms while others may identify with only one of these three specific terms. Hispanics or Latinos who identify with the terms "Spanish," "Hispanic," or "Latino" are those who classify themselves in one of the specific Spanish, Hispanic, or Latino categories listed on the questionnaire ("Mexican," "Puerto Rican," or "Cuban") as well as those who indicate that they are "other Spanish/Hispanic/Latino." People who do not identify with one of the specific origins listed on the questionnaire but indicate that they are "other Spanish/Hispanic/Latino" are those whose origins are from Spain, the Spanish-speaking countries of Central or South America, the Dominican Republic, or people identifying themselves generally as Spanish, Spanish-American, Hispanic, Hispano, Latino, and so on. All write-in responses to the "other Spanish/Hispanic/Latino" category were coded. Origin can be viewed as the heritage, nationality group, lineage, or country of birth of the person or the person's parents or ancestors before their arrival in the United States. People who identify their origin as Spanish, Hispanic, or Latino may be of any race.

Average Household Size: Number of persons in the average household. *Source: U.S. Census Bureau, Census 2010.*

Median Age: Median age of the population. *Source: U.S. Census Bureau, Census 2010.*

Male/Female Ratio: Number of males per 100 females. *Source: U.S. Census Bureau, Census 2010.*

Homeownership Rate: Percentage of housing units that are owner-occupied. *Source: U.S. Census Bureau, Census 2010.*

Information for Counties

PHYSICAL CHARACTERISTICS

Physical Location: Describes the physical location of the county. *Source: Columbia University Press, The Columbia Gazetteer of North America and original research.*

Land and Water Area: Land and water area in square miles. *Source: U.S. Census Bureau, Census 2010.*

Time Zone: Lists the time zone. *Source: Original research.*

Year Organized: Year the county government was organized. *Source: National Association of Counties*

County Seat: Lists the county seat. If a county has more than one seat, then both are listed. *Source: National Association of Counties*

Metropolitan Area: Indicates the metropolitan area the county is located in. Also lists all the component counties of that metropolitan area. The Office of Management and Budget (OMB) defines metropolitan and micropolitan statistical areas. The most current definitions are as of February 2013. *Source: U.S. Census Bureau.*

Climate: Includes all weather stations located within the county. Indicates the station name and elevation as well as the monthly average high and low temperatures, average precipitation, and average snowfall. The period of record is generally 1980-2009, however, certain weather stations contain averages going back as far as 1900. *Source: Grey House Publishing, Weather America: A Thirty-Year Summary of Statistical Weather Data and Rankings, 2010.*

POPULATION

Population: 1990, 2000 and 2010 figures are a 100% count of population. *Source: U.S. Census Bureau, Census 2010.*

Race/Hispanic Origin: Figures include the U.S. Census Bureau categories of White alone; Black/African American alone; Asian alone; American Indian/Alaska Native alone; Native Hawaiian/ Other Pacific Islander alone; Some Other Race alone; Two or More Races; and Hispanic of any race. Alone refers to the fact that these figures are not in combination with any other race. *Source: American Community Survey, 2008-2012 Five-Year Estimates.*

The concept of race, as used by the Census Bureau, reflects self-identification by people according to the race or races with which they most closely identify. These categories are socio-political constructs and should not be interpreted as being scientific or anthropological in nature. Furthermore, the race categories include both racial and national-origin groups.

- **White:** A person having origins in any of the original peoples of Europe, the Middle East, or North Africa. It includes people who indicated their race(s) as "White" or reported entries such as Irish, German, Italian, Lebanese, Arab, Moroccan, or Caucasian.

- **Black/African American:** A person having origins in any of the Black racial groups of Africa. It includes people who indicated their race(s) as "Black, African Am., or Negro" or reported entries such as African American, Kenyan, Nigerian, or Haitian.

- **Asian:** A person having origins in any of the original peoples of the Far East, Southeast Asia, or the Indian subcontinent, including, for example, Cambodia, China, India, Japan, Korea, Malaysia, Pakistan, the Philippine Islands, Thailand, and Vietnam. It includes people who indicated their race(s) as "Asian" or reported entries such as "Asian Indian," "Chinese," "Filipino," "Korean," "Japanese," "Vietnamese," and "Other Asian" or provided other detailed Asian responses.

- **American Indian/Alaska Native:** A person having origins in any of the original peoples of North and South America (including Central America) and who maintains tribal affiliation or community attachment. This category includes people who indicated their race(s) as "American Indian or Alaska Native" or reported their enrolled or principal tribe, such as Navajo, Blackfeet, Inupiat, Yup'ik, or Central American Indian groups or South American Indian groups.

- **Native Hawaiian/Other Pacific Islander:** A person having origins in any of the original peoples of Hawaii, Guam, Samoa, or other Pacific Islands. It includes people who indicated their race(s) as "Pacific Islander" or reported entries such as "Native Hawaiian," "Guamanian or Chamorro," "Samoan," and "Other Pacific Islander" or provided other detailed Pacific Islander responses.

- **Some Other Race:** Includes all other responses not included in the race categories described above. Respondents reporting entries such as multiracial, mixed, interracial, or a Hispanic, Latino, or Spanish group (for example, Mexican, Puerto Rican, Cuban, or Spanish) in response to the race question are included in this category.

- **Two or More Races:** People may choose to provide two or more races either by checking two or more race response check boxes, by providing multiple responses, or by some combination of check boxes and other responses. The race response categories shown on the questionnaire are collapsed into the five minimum race groups identified by OMB, and the Census Bureau's "Some Other Race" category.

- **Hispanic:** The data on the Hispanic or Latino population were derived from answers to a question that was asked of all people. The terms "Spanish," "Hispanic origin," and "Latino" are used interchangeably. Some respondents identify with all three terms while others may identify with only one of these three specific terms. Hispanics or Latinos who identify with the terms "Spanish," "Hispanic," or "Latino" are those who classify themselves in one of the specific Spanish, Hispanic, or Latino categories listed on the questionnaire ("Mexican," "Puerto Rican," or "Cuban") as well as those who indicate that they are "other Spanish/Hispanic/Latino." People who do not identify with one of the specific origins listed on the questionnaire but indicate that they are "other Spanish/Hispanic/Latino" are those whose origins are from Spain, the Spanish-speaking countries of Central or South America, the Dominican Republic, or people identifying themselves generally as Spanish, Spanish-American, Hispanic, Hispano, Latino, and so on. All write-in responses to the "other Spanish/Hispanic/Latino" category were coded. Origin can be viewed as the heritage, nationality group, lineage, or country of birth of the person or the person's parents or ancestors before their arrival in the United States. People who identify their origin as Spanish, Hispanic, or Latino may be of any race.

Population Density: Total population divided by the land area in square miles. *Source: U.S. Census Bureau, American Community Survey, 2008-2012 Five-Year Estimates.*

Average Household Size: Number of persons in the average household. *Source: U.S. Census Bureau, American Community Survey, 2008-2012 Five-Year Estimates.*

Median Age: Median age of the population. *Source: U.S. Census Bureau, American Community Survey, 2008-2012 Five-Year Estimates.*

Male/Female Ratio: Number of males per 100 females. *Source: U.S. Census Bureau, American Community Survey, 2008-2012 Five-Year Estimates.*

RELIGION

Religion: Lists the largest religious groups (up to six) based on the number of adherents divided by the population of the county. Adherents are defined as "all members, including full members, their children and the estimated number of other regular participants who are not considered as communicant, confirmed or full members." *Source: American Religious Bodies, 2010 U.S. Religion Census: Religious Congregations & Membership Study*

ECONOMY

Unemployment Rate: Unemployment rate as of April 2014. Includes all civilians age 16 or over who were unemployed and looking for work. *Source: U.S. Department of Labor, Bureau of Labor Statistics, Local Area Unemployment Statistics.*

Total Civilian Labor Force: Total civilian labor force as of April 2014. Includes all civilians age 16 or over who were either employed, or unemployed and looking for work. *Source: U.S. Department of Labor, Bureau of Labor Statistics, Local Area Unemployment Statistics.*

Leading Industries: Lists the three largest industries (excluding government) based on the number of employees. *Source: U.S. Census Bureau, County Business Patterns 2012.*

Farms: The total number of farms and the total acreage they occupy. *Source: U.S. Department of Agriculture, National Agricultural Statistics Service, 2012 Census of Agriculture.*

Companies that Employ 500 or more persons: The numbers of companies that employ 500 or more persons. Includes private employers only. *Source: U.S. Census Bureau, County Business Patterns 2012*

Companies that Employ 100-499 persons: The numbers of companies that employ 100 to 499 persons. Includes private employers only. *Source: U.S. Census Bureau, County Business Patterns 2012*

Companies that Employ 1-99 persons: The numbers of companies that employ 1 to 99 persons. Includes private employers only. *Source: U.S. Census Bureau, County Business Patterns 2012*

Black-Owned Businesses: Number of businesses that are majority-owned by a Black or African-American person(s). Majority ownership is defined as having 51 percent or more of the stock or equity in the business. Black or African American is defined as a person having origins in any of the black racial groups of Africa, including those who consider themselves to be "Haitian." *Source: U.S. Census Bureau, 2007 Economic Census, Survey of Business Owners: Black-Owned Firms, 2007*

Asian-Owned Businesses: Number of businesses that are majority-owned by an Asian person(s). Majority ownership is defined as having 51 percent or more of the stock or equity in the business. *Source: U.S. Census Bureau, 2007 Economic Census, Survey of Business Owners: Asian-Owned Firms, 2007*

Hispanic-Owned Businesses: Number of businesses that are majority-owned by a person(s) of Hispanic or Latino origin. Majority ownership is defined as having 51 percent or more of the stock or equity in the business. Hispanic or Latino origin is defined as a person of Cuban, Mexican, Puerto Rican, South or Central American, or other Spanish culture or origin, regardless of race. *Source: U.S. Census Bureau, 2007 Economic Census, Survey of Business Owners: Hispanic-Owned Firms, 2007*

Women-Owned Businesses: Number of businesses that are majority-owned by a woman. Majority ownership is defined as having 51 percent or more of the stock or equity in the business. *Source: U.S. Census Bureau, 2007 Economic Census, Survey of Business Owners: Women-Owned Firms, 2007*

Single-Family Building Permits Issued: Building permits issued for new, single-family housing units in 2013. *Source: U.S. Census Bureau, Manufacturing and Construction Division*

Multi-Family Building Permits Issued: Building permits issued for new, multi-family housing units in 2013. *Source: U.S. Census Bureau, Manufacturing and Construction Division*

Statistics on housing units authorized by building permits include housing units issued in local permit-issuing jurisdictions by a building or zoning permit. Not all areas of the country require a building or zoning permit. The statistics only represent those areas that do require a permit. Current surveys indicate that construction is undertaken for all but a very small percentage of housing units authorized by building permits. A major portion typically get under way during the month of permit issuance and most of the remainder begin within the three following months. Because of this lag, the housing unit authorization statistics do not represent the number of units actually put into construction for the period shown, and should therefore not be directly interpreted as "housing starts."

Statistics are based upon reports submitted by local building permit officials in response to a mail survey. They are obtained using Form C-404 const/www/c404.pdf, "Report of New Privately-Owned Residential Building or Zoning Permits Issued." When a report is not received, missing data are either (1) obtained from the Survey of Use of Permits (SUP) which is used to collect information on housing starts, or (2) imputed based on the assumption that the ratio of current month authorizations to those of a year ago should be the same for reporting and non-reporting places.

INCOME

Per Capita Income: Per capita income is the mean income computed for every man, woman, and child in a particular group. It is derived by dividing the total income of a particular group by the total population in that group. Per capita income is rounded to the nearest whole dollar. *Source: U.S. Census Bureau, American Community Survey, 2008-2012 Five-Year Estimates.*

Median Household Income: Includes the income of the householder and all other individuals 15 years old and over in the household, whether they are related to the householder or not. The median divides the income distribution into two equal parts: one-half of the cases falling below the median income and one-half above the median. For households, the median income is based on the distribution of the total number of households including those with no income. Median income for households is computed on the basis of a standard distribution and is rounded to the nearest whole dollar. *Source: U.S. Census Bureau, American Community Survey, 2008-2012 Five-Year Estimates.*

Average Household Income: Average household income is obtained by dividing total household income by the total number of households. *Source: U.S. Census Bureau, American Community Survey, 2008-2012 Five-Year Estimates.*

Percent of Households with Income of $100,000 or more: Percent of households with income of $100,000 or more. *Source: U.S. Census Bureau, American Community Survey, 2008-2012 Five-Year Estimates.*

Poverty Rate: Percentage of population with income below the poverty level. Based on individuals for whom poverty status is determined. Poverty status was determined for all people except institutionalized people, people in military group quarters, people in college dormitories, and unrelated individuals under 15 years old. *Source: U.S. Census Bureau, American Community Survey, 2008-2012 Five-Year Estimates.*

Bankruptcy Rate: The personal bankruptcy filing rate is the number of bankruptcies per thousand residents in 2013. Personal bankruptcy filings include both Chapter 7 (liquidations) and Chapter 13 (reorganizations) based on the county of residence of the filer. *Source: Federal Deposit Insurance Corporation, Regional Economic Conditions*

TAXES

Total County Taxes Per Capita: Total county taxes collected divided by the population of the county. *Source: U.S. Census Bureau, State and Local Government Finances, 2011*

Taxes include:
* Property Taxes
* Sales and Gross Receipts Taxes
* Federal Customs Duties
* General Sales and Gross Receipts Taxes
* Selective Sales Taxes (alcoholic beverages; amusements; insurance premiums; motor fuels; pari-mutuels; public utilities; tobacco products; other)
* License Taxes (alcoholic beverages; amusements; corporations in general; hunting and fishing; motor vehicles motor vehicle operators; public utilities; occupation and business, NEC; other)
* Income Taxes (individual income; corporation net income; other)
* Death and Gift
* Documentary & Stock Transfer
* Severance
* Taxes, NEC

Total County Property Taxes Per Capita: Total county property taxes collected divided by the population of the county. *Source: U.S. Census Bureau, State and Local Government Finances, 2011*

Property Taxes include general property taxes, relating to property as a whole, taxed at a single rate or at classified rates according to the class of property. Property refers to real property (e.g. land and structures) as well as personal property; personal property can be either tangible (e.g. automobiles and boats) or intangible (e.g. bank accounts and stocks and bonds). Special property taxes, levied on selected types of property (e.g. oil and gas properties, house trailers, motor vehicles, and intangibles) and subject to rates not directly related to general property tax rates. Taxes based on income produced by property as a measure of its value on the assessment date.

EDUCATION

Educational Attainment: Figures show the percent of population age 25 and over with:

* **High school diploma (including GED) or higher:** Includes people whose highest degree is a high school diploma or its equivalent, people who attended college but did not receive a degree, and people who received a college, university, or professional degree.
* **Bachelor's degree or higher:** Includes people who received a bachelor's, master's, doctorate, or professional degree.
* **Master's degree or higher:** Includes people who received a master's, doctorate, or professional degree. *Source: U.S. Census Bureau, American Community Survey, 2008-2012 Five-Year Estimates.*

HOUSING

Homeownership Rate: Percentage of housing units that are owner-occupied. *Source: U.S. Census Bureau, American Community Survey, 2008-2012 Five-Year Estimates.*

Median Home Value: Median value of all owner-occupied housing units as reported by the owner. Figures shown are 2010 estimates. *Source: U.S. Census Bureau, American Community Survey, 2008-2012 Five-Year Estimates.*

Median Rent: Median monthly contract rent on specified renter-occupied and specified vacant-for-rent units. Specified renter-occupied and specified vacant-for-rent units exclude 1-family houses on 10 acres or more. Contract rent is the monthly rent agreed to or contracted for, regardless of any furnishings, utilities, fees, meals, or services that may be included. For vacant units, it is the monthly rent asked for the rental unit at the time of enumeration. *Source: U.S. Census Bureau, American Community Survey, 2008-2012 Five-Year Estimates.*

Median Year Structure Built: Year structure built refers to when the building was first constructed, not when it was remodeled, added to, or converted. For mobile homes, houseboats, RVs, etc, the manufacturer's model year was assumed to be the year built. The data relate to the number of units built during the specified periods that were still in existence at the time of enumeration. *Source: U.S. Census Bureau, American Community Survey, 2008-2012 Five-Year Estimates.*

HEALTH AND VITAL STATISTICS

Birth Rate: Estimated number of births per 10,000 population in 2013. *Source: U.S. Census Bureau, Annual Components of Population Change, July 1, 2010 - July 1, 2013*

Death Rate: Estimated number of deaths per 10,000 population in 2013. *Source: U.S. Census Bureau, Annual Components of Population Change, July 1, 2010 - July 1, 2013*

Age-adjusted Cancer Mortality Rate: Number of age-adjusted deaths from cancer per 100,000 population in 2011. Cancer is defined as International Classification of Disease (ICD) codes C00 - D48.9 Neoplasms. *Source: Centers for Disease Control, CDC Wonder*

Age-adjusted death rates are weighted averages of the age-specific death rates, where the weights represent a fixed population by age. They are used because the rates of almost all causes of death vary by age. Age adjustment is a technique for "removing" the effects of age from crude rates, so as to allow meaningful comparisons across populations with different underlying age structures. For example, comparing the crude rate of heart disease in Virginia to that of California is misleading, because the relatively older population in Virginia will lead to a higher crude death rate, even if the age-specific rates of heart disease in Virginia and California are the same. For such a comparison, age-adjusted rates would be preferable. Age-adjusted rates should be viewed as relative indexes rather than as direct or actual measures of mortality risk.

Death rates based on counts of twenty or less (≤ 20) are flagged as "Unreliable". Death rates based on fewer than three years of data for counties with populations of less than 100,000 in the 2000 Census counts, are also flagged as "Unreliable" if the number of deaths is five or less (≤ 5).

Air Quality Index: The percentage of days in 2013 the AQI fell into the Good (0-50), Moderate (51-100), Unhealthy for Sensitive Groups (101-150), Unhealthy (151-199), and Very Unhealthy (200-299) ranges. Data covers January 2013 through December 2013. *Source: AirData: Access to Air Pollution Data, U.S. Environmental Protection Agency, Office of Air and Radiation*

The AQI is an index for reporting daily air quality. It tells you how clean or polluted your air is, and what associated health concerns you should be aware of. The AQI focuses on health effects that can happen within a few hours or days after breathing polluted air. EPA uses the AQI for five major air pollutants regulated by the Clean Air Act: ground-level ozone, particulate matter, carbon monoxide, sulfur dioxide, and nitrogen dioxide. For each of these pollutants, EPA has established national air quality standards to protect against harmful health effects.

The AQI runs from 0 to 500. The higher the AQI value, the greater the level of air pollution and the greater the health danger. For example, an AQI value of 50 represents good air quality and little potential to affect public health, while an AQI value over 300 represents hazardous air quality. An AQI value of 100 generally corresponds to the national air quality standard for the pollutant, which is the level EPA has set to protect public health. So, AQI values below 100 are generally thought of as satisfactory. When AQI values are above 100, air quality is considered to be unhealthy- at first for certain sensitive groups of people, then for everyone as AQI values get higher. Each category corresponds to a different level of health concern. For example, when the AQI for a pollutant is between 51 and 100, the health concern is "Moderate." Here are the six levels of health concern and what they mean:

- "Good" The AQI value for your community is between 0 and 50. Air quality is considered satisfactory and air pollution poses little or no risk.

- "Moderate" The AQI for your community is between 51 and 100. Air quality is acceptable; however, for some pollutants there may be a moderate health concern for a very small number of individuals. For example, people who are unusually sensitive to ozone may experience respiratory symptoms.

- "Unhealthy for Sensitive Groups" Certain groups of people are particularly sensitive to the harmful effects of certain air pollutants. This means they are likely to be affected at lower levels than the general public. For example, children and adults who are active outdoors and people with respiratory disease are at greater risk from exposure to ozone, while people with heart disease are at greater risk from carbon monoxide. Some people may be sensitive to more than one pollutant. When AQI values are between 101 and 150, members of sensitive groups may experience health effects. The general public is not likely to be affected when the AQI is in this range.

- "Unhealthy" AQI values are between 151 and 200. Everyone may begin to experience health effects. Members of sensitive groups may experience more serious health effects.

- "Very Unhealthy" AQI values between 201 and 300 trigger a health alert, meaning everyone may experience more serious health effects.

- "Hazardous" AQI values over 300 trigger health warnings of emergency conditions. The entire population is more likely to be affected.

Number of Physicians: The number of active, non-federal physicians (MDs and DOs) per 10,000 population in 2011. *Source: Area Resource File (ARF) 2012-2013. U.S. Department of Health and Human Services, Health Resources and Services Administration, Bureau of Health Professions, Rockville, MD.*

Number of Hospital Beds: The number of hospital beds per 10,000 population in 2010. *Source: Area Resource File (ARF) 2012-2013. U.S. Department of Health and Human Services, Health Resources and Services Administration, Bureau of Health Professions, Rockville, MD.*

Number of Hospital Admissions: The number of hospital admissions per 10,000 population in 2010. *Source: Area Resource File (ARF) 2012-2013. U.S. Department of Health and Human Services, Health Resources and Services Administration, Bureau of Health Professions, Rockville, MD.*

ELECTIONS

Elections: 2012 Presidential election results. *Source: Dave Leip's Atlas of U.S. Presidential Elections.*

NATIONAL AND STATE PARKS

Lists National and State parks located in the area. *Source: U.S. Geological Survey, Geographic Names Information System.*

ADDITIONAL INFORMATION CONTACTS

The following phone numbers are provided as sources of additional information: Chambers of Commerce; Economic Development Agencies; and Convention & Visitors Bureaus. Efforts have been made to provide the most recent area codes. However, area code changes may have occurred in listed numbers. *Source: Original research.*

User's Guide: Education

School District Rankings

Number of Schools: Total number of schools in the district. *Source: U.S. Department of Education, National Center for Education Statistics, Common Core of Data, Public Elementary/Secondary School Universe Survey: School Year 2011-2012.*

Number of Teachers: Teachers are defined as individuals who provide instruction to pre-kindergarten, kindergarten, grades 1 through 12, or ungraded classes, or individuals who teach in an environment other than a classroom setting, and who maintain daily student attendance records. Numbers reported are full-time equivalents (FTE). *Source: U.S. Department of Education, National Center for Education Statistics, Common Core of Data, Local Education Agency (School District) Universe Survey: School Year 2011-2012.*

Number of Students: A student is an individual for whom instruction is provided in an elementary or secondary education program that is not an adult education program and is under the jurisdiction of a school, school system, or other education institution. *Sources: U.S. Department of Education, National Center for Education Statistics, Common Core of Data, Local Education Agency (School District) Universe Survey: School Year 2011-2012 and Public Elementary/Secondary School Universe Survey: School Year 2011-2012*

Individual Education Program (IEP) Students: A written instructional plan for students with disabilities designated as special education students under IDEA-Part B. The written instructional plan includes a statement of present levels of educational performance of a child; statement of annual goals, including short-term instructional objectives; statement of specific educational services to be provided and the extent to which the child will be able to participate in regular educational programs; the projected date for initiation and anticipated duration of services; the appropriate objectives, criteria and evaluation procedures; and the schedules for determining, on at least an annual basis, whether instructional objectives are being achieved. *Source: U.S. Department of Education, National Center for Education Statistics, Common Core of Data, Local Education Agency (School District) Universe Survey: School Year 2011-2012*

English Language Learner (ELL) Students: Formerly referred to as Limited English Proficient (LEP). Students being served in appropriate programs of language assistance (e.g., English as a Second Language, High Intensity Language Training, bilingual education). Does not include pupils enrolled in a class to learn a language other than English. Also Limited-English-Proficient students are individuals who were not born in the United States or whose native language is a language other than English; or individuals who come from environments where a language other than English is dominant; or individuals who are American Indians and Alaskan Natives and who come from environments where a language other than English has had a significant impact on their level of English language proficiency; and who, by reason thereof, have sufficient difficulty speaking, reading, writing, or understanding the English language, to deny such individuals the opportunity to learn successfully in classrooms where the language of instruction is English or to participate fully in our society. *Source: U.S. Department of Education, National Center for Education Statistics, Common Core of Data, Local Education Agency (School District) Universe Survey: School Year 2011-2012*

Students Eligible for Free Lunch Program: The free lunch program is defined as a program under the National School Lunch Act that provides cash subsidies for free lunches to students based on family size and income criteria. *Source: U.S. Department of Education, National Center for Education Statistics, Common Core of Data, Public Elementary/Secondary School Universe Survey: School Year 2011-2012*

Students Eligible for Reduced-Price Lunch Program: A student who is eligible to participate in the Reduced-Price Lunch Program under the National School Lunch Act. *Source: U.S. Department of Education, National Center for Education Statistics, Common Core of Data, Public Elementary/Secondary School Universe Survey: School Year 2011-2012*

Student/Teacher Ratio: The number of students divided by the number of teachers (FTE). See Number of Students and Number of Teachers above for for information.

Student/Librarian Ratio: The number of students divided by the number of library and media support staff. Library and media support staff are defined as staff members who render other professional library and media services; also includes library aides and those involved in library/media support. Their duties include selecting, preparing, caring for, and making available to instructional staff, equipment, films, filmstrips, transparencies, tapes, TV programs, and similar materials maintained separately or as part of an instructional materials center. Also included are activities in the audio-visual center, TV studio, related-work-study areas, and services provided by audio-visual personnel.

Numbers are based on full-time equivalents. *Source: U.S. Department of Education, National Center for Education Statistics, Common Core of Data, Local Education Agency (School District) Universe Survey: School Year 2011-2012.*

Student/Counselor Ratio: The number of students divided by the number of guidance counselors. Guidance counselors are professional staff assigned specific duties and school time for any of the following activities in an elementary or secondary setting: counseling with students and parents; consulting with other staff members on learning problems; evaluating student abilities; assisting students in making educational and career choices; assisting students in personal and social development; providing referral assistance; and/or working with other staff members in planning and conducting guidance programs for students. The state applies its own standards in apportioning the aggregate of guidance counselors/directors into the elementary and secondary level components. Numbers reported are full-time equivalents. *Source: U.S. Department of Education, National Center for Education Statistics, Common Core of Data, Local Education Agency (School District) Universe Survey: School Year 2011-2012.*

Current Spending per Student: Expenditure for Instruction, Support Services, and Other Elementary/Secondary Programs. Includes salaries, employee benefits, purchased services, and supplies, as well as payments made by states on behalf of school districts. Also includes transfers made by school districts into their own retirement system. Excludes expenditure for Non-Elementary/Secondary Programs, debt service, capital outlay, and transfers to other governments or school districts. This item is formally called "Current Expenditures for Public Elementary/Secondary Education."

Instruction: Includes payments from all funds for salaries, employee benefits, supplies, materials, and contractual services for elementary/secondary instruction. It excludes capital outlay, debt service, and interfund transfers for elementary/secondary instruction. Instruction covers regular, special, and vocational programs offered in both the regular school year and summer school. It excludes instructional support activities as well as adult education and community services. Instruction salaries includes salaries for teachers and teacher aides and assistants.

Support Services: Relates to support services functions (series 2000) defined in Financial Accounting for Local and State School Systems (National Center for Education Statistics 2000). Includes payments from all funds for salaries, employee benefits, supplies, materials, and contractual services. It excludes capital outlay, debt service, and interfund transfers. It includes expenditure for the following functions:

- Business/Central/Other Support Services
- General Administration
- Instructional Staff Support
- Operation and Maintenance
- Pupil Support Services
- Pupil Transportation Services
- School Administration
- Nonspecified Support Services

Values shown are dollars per pupil per year. They were calculated by dividing the total dollar amounts by the fall membership. Fall membership is comprised of the total student enrollment on October 1 (or the closest school day to October 1) for all grade levels (including prekindergarten and kindergarten) and ungraded pupils. Membership includes students both present and absent on the measurement day. *Source: U.S. Department of Education, National Center for Education Statistics, Common Core of Data, School District Finance Survey (F-33), Fiscal Year 2011.*

Drop-out Rate: A dropout is a student who was enrolled in school at some time during the previous school year; was not enrolled at the beginning of the current school year; has not graduated from high school or completed a state or district approved educational program; and does not meet any of the following exclusionary conditions: has transferred to another public school district, private school, or state- or district-approved educational program; is temporarily absent due to suspension or school-approved illness; or has died. The values shown cover grades 9 through 12. *Note: Drop-out rates are no longer available to the general public disaggregated by grade, race/ethnicity, and gender at the school district level. Beginning with the 2005–06 school year the CCD is reporting dropout data aggregated from the local education agency (district) level to the state level. This allows data users to compare event dropout rates across states, regions, and other jurisdictions. Source: U.S. Department of Education, National Center for Education Statistics, Common Core of Data, Local Education Agency (School District) Universe Survey Dropout and Completion Data, 2008-2009; U.S. Department of Education, National Center for Education Statistics, Common Core of Data, State Dropout and Completion Data File, 2009-2010*

Average Freshman Graduation Rate (AFGR): The AFGR is the number of regular diploma recipients in a given year divided by the average of the membership in grades 8, 9, and 10, reported 5, 4, and 3 years earlier, respectively. For example, the denominator of the 2008–09 AFGR is the average of the 8th-grade membership in 2004–05, 9th-grade membership in 2005–06, and 10th-grade membership in 2006–07. Ungraded students are prorated into

these grades. Averaging these three grades provides an estimate of the number of first-time freshmen in the class of 2005–06 freshmen in order to estimate the on-time graduation rate for 2008–09.

Caution in interpreting the AFGR. Although the AFGR was selected as the best of the available alternatives, several factors make it fall short of a true on-time graduation rate. First, the AFGR does not take into account any imbalances in the number of students moving in and out of the nation or individual states over the high school years. As a result, the averaged freshman class is at best an approximation of the actual number of freshmen, where differences in the rates of transfers, retention, and dropping out in the three grades affect the average. Second, by including all graduates in a specific year, the graduates may include students who repeated a grade in high school or completed high school early and thus are not on-time graduates in that year. *Source: U.S. Department of Education, National Center for Education Statistics, Common Core of Data, Local Education Agency (School District) Universe Survey Dropout and Completion Data, 2008-2009; U.S. Department of Education, National Center for Education Statistics, Common Core of Data, State Dropout and Completion Data File, 2009-2010*

Number of Diploma Recipients: A student who has received a diploma during the previous school year or subsequent summer school. This category includes regular diploma recipients and other diploma recipients. A High School Diploma is a formal document certifying the successful completion of a secondary school program prescribed by the state education agency or other appropriate body. *Note: Diploma counts are no longer available to the general public disaggregated by grade, race/ethnicity, and gender at the school district level. Source: U.S. Department of Education, National Center for Education Statistics, Common Core of Data, Local Education Agency (School District) Universe Survey Dropout and Completion Data, 2008-2009; U.S. Department of Education, National Center for Education Statistics, Common Core of Data, State Dropout and Completion Data File, 2009-2010*

Note: n/a indicates data not available.

State Educational Profile

Please refer to the District Rankings section in the front of this User's Guide for an explanation of data for all items except for the following:

Average Salary: The average salary for classroom teachers in 2013-2014. *Source: National Education Association, Rankings & Estimates: Rankings of the States 2013 and Estimates of School Statistics 2014*

College Entrance Exam Scores:

Scholastic Aptitude Test (SAT). *Note: Data covers all students during the 2013 school year. The College Board strongly discourages the comparison or ranking of states on the basis of SAT scores alone. Source: The College Board*

American College Testing Program (ACT). *Note: Data covers all students during the 2013 school year. Source: ACT, 2013 ACT National and State Scores*

National Assessment of Educational Progress (NAEP)

The National Assessment of Educational Progress (NAEP), also known as "the Nation's Report Card," is the only nationally representative and continuing assessment of what America's students know and can do in various subject areas. As a result of the "No Child Left Behind" legislation, all states are required to participate in NAEP.

For more information, visit the U.S. Department of Education, National Center for Education Statistics at http://nces.ed.gov/nationsreportcard.

User's Guide: Ancestry and Ethnicity

Places Covered

The ancestry and ethnicity profile section of this book covers the state, all counties with population of 100,000 or more, and all places with population of 50,000 or more. Places included fall into one of the following categories:

Incorporated Places. Depending on the state, places are incorporated as either cities, towns, villages, boroughs, municipalities, independent cities, or corporations. A few municipalities have a form of government combined with another entity (e.g. county) and are listed as special cities or consolidated, unified, or metropolitan governments.

Census Designated Places (CDP). The U.S. Census Bureau defines a CDP as "a statistical entity," defined for each decennial census according to Census Bureau guidelines, comprising a densely settled concentration of population that is not within an incorporated place, but is locally identified by a name. CDPs are delineated cooperatively by state and local officials and the Census Bureau, following Census Bureau guidelines.

Minor Civil Divisions (called charter townships, districts, gores, grants, locations, plantations, purchases, reservations, towns, townships, and unorganized territories) for the states where the Census Bureau has determined that they serve as general-purpose governments. Those states are Connecticut, Maine, Massachusetts, Michigan, Minnesota, New Hampshire, New Jersey, New York, Pennsylvania, Rhode Island, Vermont, and Wisconsin. In some states incorporated municipalities are part of minor civil divisions and in some states they are independent of them.

Note: Several states have incorporated municipalities and minor civil divisions in the same county with the same name. Those communities are given separate entries (e.g. Burlington, New Jersey, in Burlington County will be listed under both the city and township of Burlington). A few states have Census Designated Places and minor civil divisions in the same county with the same name. Those communities are given separate entries (e.g. Bridgewater, Massachusetts, in Plymouth County will be listed under both the CDP and town of Bridgewater).

Source of Data

The ethnicities shown in this book were compiled from two different sources. Data for Race and Hispanic Origin was taken from Census 2010 Summary File 1 (SF1) while Ancestry data was taken from the American Community Survey (ACS) 2006-2010 Five-Year Estimate. The distinction is important because SF1 contains 100-percent data, which is the information compiled from the questions asked of all people and about every housing unit. ACS estimates are compiled from a sampling of households. The 2006-2010 Five-Year Estimate is based on data collected from January 1, 2006 to December 31, 2010.

The American Community Survey (ACS) is a relatively new survey conducted by the U.S. Census Bureau. It uses a series of monthly samples to produce annually updated data for the same small areas (census tracts and block groups) formerly surveyed via the decennial census long-form sample. While some version of this survey has been in the field since 1999, it was not fully implemented in terms of coverage until 2006. In 2005 it was expanded to cover all counties in the country and the 1-in-40 households sampling rate was first applied. The full implementation of the (household) sampling strategy for ACS entails having the survey mailed to about 250,000 households nationwide every month of every year and was begun in January 2005. In January 2006 sampling of group quarters was added to complete the sample as planned. In any given year about 2.5% (1 in 40) of U.S. households will receive the survey. Over any 5-year period about 1 in 8 households should receive the survey (as compared to about 1 in 6 that received the census long form in the 2000 census). Since receiving the survey is not the same as responding to it, the Bureau has adopted a strategy of sampling for non-response, resulting in something closer to 1 in 11 households actually participating in the survey over any 5-year period. For more information about the American Community Survey visit http://www.census.gov/acs/www.

Ancestry

Ancestry refers to a person's ethnic origin, heritage, descent, or "roots," which may reflect their place of birth or that of previous generations of their family. Some ethnic identities, such as "Egyptian" or "Polish" can be traced to geographic areas outside the United States, while other ethnicities such as "Pennsylvania German" or "Cajun" evolved in the United States.

The intent of the ancestry question in the ACS was not to measure the degree of attachment the respondent had to a particular ethnicity, but simply to establish that the respondent had a connection to and self-identified with a particular

ethnic group. For example, a response of "Irish" might reflect total involvement in an Irish community or only a memory of ancestors several generations removed from the respondent.

The Census Bureau coded the responses into a numeric representation of over 1,000 categories. Responses initially were processed through an automated coding system; then, those that were not automatically assigned a code were coded by individuals trained in coding ancestry responses. The code list reflects the results of the Census Bureau's own research and consultations with many ethnic experts. Many decisions were made to determine the classification of responses. These decisions affected the grouping of the tabulated data. For example, the "Indonesian" category includes the responses of "Indonesian," "Celebesian," "Moluccan," and a number of other responses.

Ancestries Covered

Afghan	Palestinian	French, ex. Basque	Scottish
African, Sub-Saharan	Syrian	French Canadian	Serbian
African	Other Arab	German	Slavic
Cape Verdean	Armenian	German Russian	Slovak
Ethiopian	Assyrian/Chaldean/Syriac	Greek	Slovene
Ghanaian	Australian	Guyanese	Soviet Union
Kenyan	Austrian	Hungarian	Swedish
Liberian	Basque	Icelander	Swiss
Nigerian	Belgian	Iranian	Turkish
Senegalese	Brazilian	Irish	Ukrainian
Sierra Leonean	British	Israeli	Welsh
Somalian	Bulgarian	Italian	West Indian, ex.
South African	Cajun	Latvian	Hispanic
Sudanese	Canadian	Lithuanian	Bahamian
Ugandan	Carpatho Rusyn	Luxemburger	Barbadian
Zimbabwean	Celtic	Macedonian	Belizean
Other Sub-Saharan African	Croatian	Maltese	Bermudan
Albanian	Cypriot	New Zealander	British West Indian
Alsatian	Czech	Northern European	Dutch West Indian
American	Czechoslovakian	Norwegian	Haitian
Arab	Danish	Pennsylvania German	Jamaican
Arab	Dutch	Polish	Trinidadian/
Egyptian	Eastern European	Portuguese	Tobagonian
Iraqi	English	Romanian	U.S. Virgin Islander
Jordanian	Estonian	Russian	West Indian
Lebanese	European	Scandinavian	Other West Indian
Moroccan	Finnish	Scotch-Irish	Yugoslavian

The ancestry question allowed respondents to report one or more ancestry groups. Generally, only the first two responses reported were coded. If a response was in terms of a dual ancestry, for example, "Irish English," the person was assigned two codes, in this case one for Irish and another for English. However, in certain cases, multiple responses such as "French Canadian," "Scotch-Irish," "Greek Cypriot," and "Black Dutch" were assigned a single code reflecting their status as unique groups. If a person reported one of these unique groups in addition to another group, for example, "Scotch-Irish English," resulting in three terms, that person received one code for the unique group (Scotch-Irish) and another one for the remaining group (English). If a person reported "English Irish French," only English and Irish were coded. If there were more than two ancestries listed and one of the ancestries was a part of another, such as "German Bavarian Hawaiian," the responses were coded using the more detailed groups (Bavarian and Hawaiian).

The Census Bureau accepted "American" as a unique ethnicity if it was given alone or with one other ancestry. There were some groups such as "American Indian," "Mexican American," and "African American" that were coded and identified separately.

The ancestry question is asked for every person in the American Community Survey, regardless of age, place of birth, Hispanic origin, or race.

Although some people consider religious affiliation a component of ethnic identity, the ancestry question was not designed to collect any information concerning religion. Thus, if a religion was given as an answer to the ancestry question, it was listed in the "Other groups" category which is not shown in this book.

Ancestry should not be confused with a person's place of birth, although a person's place of birth and ancestry may be the same.

Hispanic Origin

The data on the Hispanic or Latino population were derived from answers to a Census 2010 question that was asked of all people. The terms "Spanish," "Hispanic origin," and "Latino" are used interchangeably. Some respondents identify with all three terms while others may identify with only one of these three specific terms. Hispanics or Latinos who identify with the terms "Spanish," "Hispanic," or "Latino" are those who classify themselves in one of the specific Spanish, Hispanic, or Latino categories listed on the questionnaire ("Mexican," "Puerto Rican," or "Cuban") as well as those who indicate that they are "other Spanish/Hispanic/Latino." People who do not identify with one of the specific origins listed on the questionnaire but indicate that they are "other Spanish/Hispanic/Latino" are those whose origins are from Spain, the Spanish-speaking countries of Central or South America, the Dominican Republic, or people identifying themselves generally as Spanish, Spanish-American, Hispanic, Hispano, Latino, and so on. All write-in responses to the "other Spanish/Hispanic/Latino" category were coded.

Hispanic Origins Covered

Hispanic or Latino	Salvadoran	Argentinean	Uruguayan
Central American, ex. Mexican	Other Central American	Bolivian	Venezuelan
Costa Rican	Cuban	Chilean	Other South American
Guatemalan	Dominican Republic	Colombian	Other Hispanic or Latino
Honduran	Mexican	Ecuadorian	
Nicaraguan	Puerto Rican	Paraguayan	
Panamanian	South American	Peruvian	

Origin can be viewed as the heritage, nationality group, lineage, or country of birth of the person or the person's parents or ancestors before their arrival in the United States. People who identify their origin as Hispanic, Latino, or Spanish may be of any race.

Ethnicities Based on Race

The data on race were derived from answers to the Census 2010 question on race that was asked of individuals in the United States. The Census Bureau collects racial data in accordance with guidelines provided by the U.S. Office of Management and Budget (OMB), and these data are based on self-identification.

The racial categories included in the census questionnaire generally reflect a social definition of race recognized in this country and not an attempt to define race biologically, anthropologically, or genetically. In addition, it is recognized that the categories of the race item include racial and national origin or sociocultural groups. People may choose to report more than one race to indicate their racial mixture, such as "American Indian" and "White." People who identify their origin as Hispanic, Latino, or Spanish may be of any race.

Racial Groups Covered

African-American/Black	Crow	Spanish American Indian	Korean
Not Hispanic	Delaware	Tlingit-Haida *(Alaska Native)*	Laotian
Hispanic	Hopi	Tohono O'Odham	Malaysian
American Indian/Alaska Native	Houma	Tsimshian *(Alaska Native)*	Nepalese
Not Hispanic	Inupiat *(Alaska Native)*	Ute	Pakistani
Hispanic	Iroquois	Yakama	Sri Lankan
Alaska Athabascan *(Ala. Nat.)*	Kiowa	Yaqui	Taiwanese
Aleut *(Alaska Native)*	Lumbee	Yuman	Thai
Apache	Menominee	Yup'ik *(Alaska Native)*	Vietnamese
Arapaho	Mexican American Indian	**Asian**	**Hawaii Native/Pacific Islander**
Blackfeet	Navajo	*Not Hispanic*	*Not Hispanic*
Canadian/French Am. Indian	Osage	*Hispanic*	*Hispanic*
Central American Indian	Ottawa	Bangladeshi	Fijian
Cherokee	Paiute	Bhutanese	Guamanian/Chamorro
Cheyenne	Pima	Burmese	Marshallese
Chickasaw	Potawatomi	Cambodian	Native Hawaiian
Chippewa	Pueblo	Chinese, ex. Taiwanese	Samoan
Choctaw	Puget Sound Salish	Filipino	Tongan
Colville	Seminole	Hmong	**White**
Comanche	Shoshone	Indian	*Not Hispanic*
Cree	Sioux	Indonesian	*Hispanic*
Creek	South American Indian	Japanese	

African American or Black: A person having origins in any of the Black racial groups of Africa. It includes people who indicated their race(s) as "Black, African Am., or Negro" or reported entries such as African American, Kenyan, Nigerian, or Haitian.

American Indian or Alaska Native: A person having origins in any of the original peoples of North and South America (including Central America) and who maintains tribal affiliation or community attachment. This category includes people who indicated their race(s) as "American Indian or Alaska Native" or reported their enrolled or principal tribe, such as Navajo, Blackfeet, Inupiat, Yup'ik, or Central American Indian groups or South American Indian groups.

Asian: A person having origins in any of the original peoples of the Far East, Southeast Asia, or the Indian subcontinent, including, for example, Cambodia, China, India, Japan, Korea, Malaysia, Pakistan, the Philippine Islands, Thailand, and Vietnam. It includes people who indicated their race(s) as "Asian" or reported entries such as "Asian Indian," "Chinese," "Filipino," "Korean," "Japanese," "Vietnamese," and "Other Asian" or provided other detailed Asian responses.

Native Hawaiian or Other Pacific Islander: A person having origins in any of the original peoples of Hawaii, Guam, Samoa, or other Pacific Islands. It includes people who indicated their race(s) as "Pacific Islander" or reported entries such as "Native Hawaiian," "Guamanian or Chamorro," "Samoan," and "Other Pacific Islander" or provided other detailed Pacific Islander responses.

White: A person having origins in any of the original peoples of Europe, the Middle East, or North Africa. It includes people who indicated their race(s) as "White" or reported entries such as Irish, German, Italian, Lebanese, Arab, Moroccan, or Caucasian.

Profiles

Each profile shows the name of the place, the county (if a place spans more than one county, the county that holds the majority of the population is shown), and the 2010 population (based on 100-percent data from Census 2010 Summary File 1). The rest of each profile is comprised of all 218 ethnicities grouped into three sections: ancestry; Hispanic origin; and race.

Column one displays the ancestry/Hispanic origin/race name, column two displays the number of people reporting each ancestry/Hispanic origin/race, and column three is the percent of the total population reporting each ancestry/Hispanic origin/race. The population figure shown is used to calculate the value in the "%" column for ethnicities based on race and Hispanic origin. The 2006-2010 estimated population figure from the American Community Survey (not shown) is used to calculate the value in the "%" column for all other ancestries.

For ethnicities in the ancestries group, the value in the "Number" column includes multiple ancestries reported. For example, if a person reported a multiple ancestry such as "French Danish," that response was counted twice in the tabulations, once in the French category and again in the Danish category. Thus, the sum of the counts is not the total population but the total of all responses. Numbers in parentheses indicate the number of people reporting a single ancestry. People reporting a single ancestry includes all people who reported only one ethnic group such as "German." Also included in this category are people with only a multiple-term response such as "Scotch-Irish" who are assigned a single code because they represent one distinct group. For example, the count for German would be interpreted as "The number of people who reported that German was their only ancestry."

For ethnicities based on Hispanic origin, the value in the "Number" column represents the number of people who reported being Mexican, Puerto Rican, Cuban or other Spanish/Hispanic/ Latino (all written-in responses were coded). All ethnicities based on Hispanic origin can be of any race.

For ethnicities based on race data the value in the "Number" column represents the total number of people who reported each category alone or in combination with one or more other race categories. This number represents the maximum number of people reporting and therefore the individual race categories may add up to more than the total population because people may be included in more than one category. The figures in parentheses show the number of people that reported that particular ethnicity alone, not in combination with any other race. For example, in Alabama, the entry for Korean shows 8,320 in parentheses and 10,624 in the "Number" column. This means that 8,320 people reported being Korean alone and 10,624 people reported being Korean alone or in combination with one or more other races.

Rankings

In the rankings section, each ethnicity has three tables. The first table shows the top 10 places sorted by ethnic population (based on all places, regardless of total population), the second table shows the top 10 places sorted by percent of the total population (based on all places, regardless of total population), the third table shows the top 10 places sorted by percent of the total population (based on places with total population of 50,000 or more).

Within each table, column one displays the place name, the state, and the county (if a place spans more than one county, the county that holds the majority of the population is shown). Column one in the first table displays the state only. Column two displays the number of people reporting each ancestry (includes people reporting multiple ancestries), Hispanic origin, or race (alone or in combination with any other race). Column three is the percent of the total population reporting each ancestry, Hispanic origin or race. For tables representing ethnicities based on race or Hispanic origin, the 100-percent population figure from SF1 is used to calculate the value in the "%" column. For all other ancestries, the 2006-2010 five-year estimated population figure from the American Community Survey is used to calculate the value in the "%" column.

Alphabetical Ethnicity Cross-Reference Guide

Afghan *see* Ancestry–Afghan
African *see* Ancestry–African, Sub-Saharan: African
African-American *see* Race–African-American/Black
African-American: Hispanic *see* Race–African-American/Black: Hispanic
African-American: Not Hispanic *see* Race–African-American/Black: Not Hispanic
Alaska Athabascan *see* Race–Alaska Native: Alaska Athabascan
Alaska Native *see* Race–American Indian/Alaska Native
Alaska Native: Hispanic *see* Race–American Indian/Alaska Native: Hispanic
Alaska Native: Not Hispanic *see* Race–American Indian/Alaska Native: Not Hispanic
Albanian *see* Ancestry–Albanian
Aleut *see* Race–Alaska Native: Aleut
Alsatian *see* Ancestry–Alsatian
American *see* Ancestry–American
American Indian *see* Race–American Indian/Alaska Native
American Indian: Hispanic *see* Race–American Indian/Alaska Native: Hispanic
American Indian: Not Hispanic *see* Race–American Indian/Alaska Native: Not Hispanic
Apache *see* Race–American Indian: Apache
Arab *see* Ancestry–Arab: Arab
Arab: Other *see* Ancestry–Arab: Other
Arapaho *see* Race–American Indian: Arapaho
Argentinean *see* Hispanic Origin–South American: Argentinean
Armenian *see* Ancestry–Armenian
Asian *see* Race–Asian
Asian Indian *see* Race–Asian: Indian
Asian: Hispanic *see* Race–Asian: Hispanic
Asian: Not Hispanic *see* Race–Asian: Not Hispanic
Assyrian *see* Ancestry–Assyrian/Chaldean/Syriac
Australian *see* Ancestry–Australian
Austrian *see* Ancestry–Austrian
Bahamian *see* Ancestry–West Indian: Bahamian, except Hispanic
Bangladeshi *see* Race–Asian: Bangladeshi
Barbadian *see* Ancestry–West Indian: Barbadian, except Hispanic
Basque *see* Ancestry–Basque
Belgian *see* Ancestry–Belgian
Belizean *see* Ancestry–West Indian: Belizean, except Hispanic
Bermudan *see* Ancestry–West Indian: Bermudan, except Hispanic
Bhutanese *see* Race–Asian: Bhutanese
Black *see* Race–African-American/Black
Black: Hispanic *see* Race–African-American/Black: Hispanic
Black: Not Hispanic *see* Race–African-American/Black: Not Hispanic
Blackfeet *see* Race–American Indian: Blackfeet
Bolivian *see* Hispanic Origin–South American: Bolivian
Brazilian *see* Ancestry–Brazilian
British *see* Ancestry–British

British West Indian *see* Ancestry–West Indian: British West Indian, except Hispanic
Bulgarian *see* Ancestry–Bulgarian
Burmese *see* Race–Asian: Burmese
Cajun *see* Ancestry–Cajun
Cambodian *see* Race–Asian: Cambodian
Canadian *see* Ancestry–Canadian
Canadian/French American Indian *see* Race–American Indian: Canadian/French American Indian
Cape Verdean *see* Ancestry–African, Sub-Saharan: Cape Verdean
Carpatho Rusyn *see* Ancestry–Carpatho Rusyn
Celtic *see* Ancestry–Celtic
Central American *see* Hispanic Origin–Central American, except Mexican
Central American Indian *see* Race–American Indian: Central American Indian
Central American: Other *see* Hispanic Origin–Central American: Other Central American
Chaldean *see* Ancestry–Assyrian/Chaldean/Syriac
Chamorro *see* Race–Hawaii Native/Pacific Islander: Guamanian or Chamorro
Cherokee *see* Race–American Indian: Cherokee
Cheyenne *see* Race–American Indian: Cheyenne
Chickasaw *see* Race–American Indian: Chickasaw
Chilean *see* Hispanic Origin–South American: Chilean
Chinese (except Taiwanese) *see* Race–Asian: Chinese, except Taiwanese
Chippewa *see* Race–American Indian: Chippewa
Choctaw *see* Race–American Indian: Choctaw
Colombian *see* Hispanic Origin–South American: Colombian
Colville *see* Race–American Indian: Colville
Comanche *see* Race–American Indian: Comanche
Costa Rican *see* Hispanic Origin–Central American: Costa Rican
Cree *see* Race–American Indian: Cree
Creek *see* Race–American Indian: Creek
Croatian *see* Ancestry–Croatian
Crow *see* Race–American Indian: Crow
Cuban *see* Hispanic Origin–Cuban
Cypriot *see* Ancestry–Cypriot
Czech *see* Ancestry–Czech
Czechoslovakian *see* Ancestry–Czechoslovakian
Danish *see* Ancestry–Danish
Delaware *see* Race–American Indian: Delaware
Dominican Republic *see* Hispanic Origin–Dominican Republic
Dutch *see* Ancestry–Dutch
Dutch West Indian *see* Ancestry–West Indian: Dutch West Indian, except Hispanic
Eastern European *see* Ancestry–Eastern European
Ecuadorian *see* Hispanic Origin–South American: Ecuadorian
Egyptian *see* Ancestry–Arab: Egyptian
English *see* Ancestry–English
Eskimo *see* Race–Alaska Native: Inupiat
Estonian *see* Ancestry–Estonian
Ethiopian *see* Ancestry–African, Sub-Saharan: Ethiopian
European *see* Ancestry–European
Fijian *see* Race–Hawaii Native/Pacific Islander: Fijian
Filipino *see* Race–Asian: Filipino
Finnish *see* Ancestry–Finnish
French (except Basque) *see* Ancestry–French, except Basque
French Canadian *see* Ancestry–French Canadian
German *see* Ancestry–German
German Russian *see* Ancestry–German Russian
Ghanaian *see* Ancestry–African, Sub-Saharan: Ghanaian
Greek *see* Ancestry–Greek
Guamanian *see* Race–Hawaii Native/Pacific Islander: Guamanian or Chamorro
Guatemalan *see* Hispanic Origin–Central American: Guatemalan
Guyanese *see* Ancestry–Guyanese
Haitian *see* Ancestry–West Indian: Haitian, except Hispanic
Hawaii Native *see* Race–Hawaii Native/Pacific Islander
Hawaii Native: Hispanic *see* Race–Hawaii Native/Pacific Islander: Hispanic

Hawaii Native: Not Hispanic *see* Race–Hawaii Native/Pacific Islander: Not Hispanic
Hispanic or Latino: *see* Hispanic Origin–Hispanic or Latino (of any race)
Hispanic or Latino: Other *see* Hispanic Origin–Other Hispanic or Latino
Hmong *see* Race–Asian: Hmong
Honduran *see* Hispanic Origin–Central American: Honduran
Hopi *see* Race–American Indian: Hopi
Houma *see* Race–American Indian: Houma
Hungarian *see* Ancestry–Hungarian
Icelander *see* Ancestry–Icelander
Indonesian *see* Race–Asian: Indonesian
Inupiat *see* Race–Alaska Native: Inupiat
Iranian *see* Ancestry–Iranian
Iraqi *see* Ancestry–Arab: Iraqi
Irish *see* Ancestry–Irish
Iroquois *see* Race–American Indian: Iroquois
Israeli *see* Ancestry–Israeli
Italian *see* Ancestry–Italian
Jamaican *see* Ancestry–West Indian: Jamaican, except Hispanic
Japanese *see* Race–Asian: Japanese
Jordanian *see* Ancestry–Arab: Jordanian
Kenyan *see* Ancestry–African, Sub-Saharan: Kenyan
Kiowa *see* Race–American Indian: Kiowa
Korean *see* Race–Asian: Korean
Laotian *see* Race–Asian: Laotian
Latvian *see* Ancestry–Latvian
Lebanese *see* Ancestry–Arab: Lebanese
Liberian *see* Ancestry–African, Sub-Saharan: Liberian
Lithuanian *see* Ancestry–Lithuanian
Lumbee *see* Race–American Indian: Lumbee
Luxemburger *see* Ancestry–Luxemburger
Macedonian *see* Ancestry–Macedonian
Malaysian *see* Race–Asian: Malaysian
Maltese *see* Ancestry–Maltese
Marshallese *see* Race–Hawaii Native/Pacific Islander: Marshallese
Menominee *see* Race–American Indian: Menominee
Mexican *see* Hispanic Origin–Mexican
Mexican American Indian *see* Race–American Indian: Mexican American Indian
Moroccan *see* Ancestry–Arab: Moroccan
Native Hawaiian *see* Race–Hawaii Native/Pacific Islander: Native Hawaiian
Navajo *see* Race–American Indian: Navajo
Nepalese *see* Race–Asian: Nepalese
New Zealander *see* Ancestry–New Zealander
Nicaraguan *see* Hispanic Origin–Central American: Nicaraguan
Nigerian *see* Ancestry–African, Sub-Saharan: Nigerian
Northern European *see* Ancestry–Northern European
Norwegian *see* Ancestry–Norwegian
Osage *see* Race–American Indian: Osage
Ottawa *see* Race–American Indian: Ottawa
Pacific Islander *see* Race–Hawaii Native/Pacific Islander
Pacific Islander: Hispanic *see* Race–Hawaii Native/Pacific Islander: Hispanic
Pacific Islander: Not Hispanic *see* Race–Hawaii Native/Pacific Islander: Not Hispanic
Paiute *see* Race–American Indian: Paiute
Pakistani *see* Race–Asian: Pakistani
Palestinian *see* Ancestry–Arab: Palestinian
Panamanian *see* Hispanic Origin–Central American: Panamanian
Paraguayan *see* Hispanic Origin–South American: Paraguayan
Pennsylvania German *see* Ancestry–Pennsylvania German
Peruvian *see* Hispanic Origin–South American: Peruvian
Pima *see* Race–American Indian: Pima
Polish *see* Ancestry–Polish
Portuguese *see* Ancestry–Portuguese
Potawatomi *see* Race–American Indian: Potawatomi

Pueblo *see* Race–American Indian: Pueblo
Puerto Rican *see* Hispanic Origin–Puerto Rican
Puget Sound Salish *see* Race–American Indian: Puget Sound Salish
Romanian *see* Ancestry–Romanian
Russian *see* Ancestry–Russian
Salvadoran *see* Hispanic Origin–Central American: Salvadoran
Samoan *see* Race–Hawaii Native/Pacific Islander: Samoan
Scandinavian *see* Ancestry–Scandinavian
Scotch-Irish *see* Ancestry–Scotch-Irish
Scottish *see* Ancestry–Scottish
Seminole *see* Race–American Indian: Seminole
Senegalese *see* Ancestry–African, Sub-Saharan: Senegalese
Serbian *see* Ancestry–Serbian
Shoshone *see* Race–American Indian: Shoshone
Sierra Leonean *see* Ancestry–African, Sub-Saharan: Sierra Leonean
Sioux *see* Race–American Indian: Sioux
Slavic *see* Ancestry–Slavic
Slovak *see* Ancestry–Slovak
Slovene *see* Ancestry–Slovene
Somalian *see* Ancestry–African, Sub-Saharan: Somalian
South African *see* Ancestry–African, Sub-Saharan: South African
South American *see* Hispanic Origin–South American
South American Indian *see* Race–American Indian: South American Indian
South American: Other *see* Hispanic Origin–South American: Other South American
Soviet Union *see* Ancestry–Soviet Union
Spanish American Indian *see* Race–American Indian: Spanish American Indian
Sri Lankan *see* Race–Asian: Sri Lankan
Sub-Saharan African *see* Ancestry–African, Sub-Saharan
Sub-Saharan African: Other *see* Ancestry–African, Sub-Saharan: Other
Sudanese *see* Ancestry–African, Sub-Saharan: Sudanese
Swedish *see* Ancestry–Swedish
Swiss *see* Ancestry–Swiss
Syriac *see* Ancestry–Assyrian/Chaldean/Syriac
Syrian *see* Ancestry–Arab: Syrian
Taiwanese *see* Race–Asian: Taiwanese
Thai *see* Race–Asian: Thai
Tlingit-Haida *see* Race–Alaska Native: Tlingit-Haida
Tohono O'Odham *see* Race–American Indian: Tohono O'Odham
Tongan *see* Race–Hawaii Native/Pacific Islander: Tongan
Trinidadian and Tobagonian *see* Ancestry–West Indian: Trinidadian and Tobagonian, except Hispanic
Tsimshian *see* Race–Alaska Native: Tsimshian
Turkish *see* Ancestry–Turkish
U.S. Virgin Islander *see* Ancestry–West Indian: U.S. Virgin Islander, except Hispanic
Ugandan *see* Ancestry–African, Sub-Saharan: Ugandan
Ukrainian *see* Ancestry–Ukrainian
Uruguayan *see* Hispanic Origin–South American: Uruguayan
Ute *see* Race–American Indian: Ute
Venezuelan *see* Hispanic Origin–South American: Venezuelan
Vietnamese *see* Race–Asian: Vietnamese
Welsh *see* Ancestry–Welsh
West Indian *see* Ancestry–West Indian: West Indian, except Hispanic
West Indian (except Hispanic) *see* Ancestry–West Indian, except Hispanic
West Indian: Other *see* Ancestry–West Indian: Other, except Hispanic
White *see* Race–White
White: Hispanic *see* Race–White: Hispanic
White: Not Hispanic *see* Race–White: Not Hispanic
Yakama *see* Race–American Indian: Yakama
Yaqui *see* Race–American Indian: Yaqui
Yugoslavian *see* Ancestry–Yugoslavian
Yuman *see* Race–American Indian: Yuman
Yup'ik *see* Race–Alaska Native: Yup'ik
Zimbabwean *see* Ancestry–African, Sub-Saharan: Zimbabwean

User's Guide: Climate

Sources of the Data

The National Climactic Data Center (NCDC) has two main classes or types of weather stations; first-order stations which are staffed by professional meteorologists and cooperative stations which are staffed by volunteers. All National Weather Service (NWS) stations included in this book are first-order stations.

The data in the climate section is compiled from several sources. The majority comes from the original NCDC computer tapes (DSI-3220 Summary of Month Cooperative). This data was used to create the entire table for each cooperative station and part of each National Weather Service station. The remainder of the data for each NWS station comes from the International Station Meteorological Climate Summary, Version 4.0, September 1996, which is also available from the NCDC.

Storm events come from the NCDC Storm Events Database which is accessible over the Internet at http://www4.ncdc.noaa.gov/ cgi-win/wwcgi.dll?wwevent~storms.

Weather Station Tables

The weather station tables are grouped by type (National Weather Service and Cooperative) and then arranged alphabetically. The station name is almost always a place name, and is shown here just as it appears in NCDC data. The station name is followed by the county in which the station is located (or by county equivalent name), the elevation of the station (at the time beginning of the thirty year period) and the latitude and longitude.

The National Weather Service Station tables contain 32 data elements which were compiled from two different sources, the International Station Meteorological Climate Summary (ISMCS) and NCDC DSI-3220 data tapes. The following 13 elements are from the ISMCS: maximum precipitation, minimum precipitation, maximum snowfall, maximum 24-hour snowfall, thunderstorm days, foggy days, predominant sky cover, relative humidity (morning and afternoon), dewpoint, wind speed and direction, and maximum wind gust. The remaining 19 elements come from the DSI-3220 data tapes. The period of record (POR) for data from the DSI-3220 data tapes is 1980-2009. The POR for ISMCS data varies from station to station and appears in a note below each station.

The Cooperative Station tables contain 19 data elements which were all compiled from the DSI-3220 data tapes with a POR of 1980-2009.

Weather Elements (NWS and Cooperative Stations)

The following elements were compiled by the editor from the NCDC DSI-3220 data tapes using a period of record of 1980-2009.

The average temperatures (maximum, minimum, and mean) are the average (see Methodology below) of those temperatures for all available values for a given month. For example, for a given station the average maximum temperature for July is the arithmetic average of all available maximum July temperatures for that station. (Maximum means the highest recorded temperature, minimum means the lowest recorded temperature, and mean means an arithmetic average temperature.)

The extreme maximum temperature is the highest temperature recorded in each month over the period 1980-2009. The extreme minimum temperature is the lowest temperature recorded in each month over the same time period. The extreme maximum daily precipitation is the largest amount of precipitation recorded over a 24-hour period in each month from 1980-2009. The maximum snow depth is the maximum snow depth recorded in each month over the period 1980-2009.

The days for maximum temperature and minimum temperature are the average number of days those criteria were met for all available instances. The symbol ≥ means greater than or equal to, the symbol ≤ means less than or equal to. For example, for a given station, the number of days the maximum temperature was greater than or equal to 90°F in July, is just an arithmetic average of the number of days in all the available Julys for that station.

Heating and cooling degree days are based on the median temperature for a given day and its variance from 65°F. For example, for a given station if the day's high temperature was 50°F and the day's low temperature was 30°F, the median (midpoint) temperature was 40°F. 40°F is 25 degrees below 65°F, hence on this day there would be 25 heating degree days. This also applies for cooling degree days. For example, for a given station if the day's high temperature was 80°F and the day's low temperature was 70°F, the median (midpoint) temperature was 75°F. 75°F is 10 degrees above 65°F, hence on this day there would be 10 cooling degree days. All heating and/or cooling degree

days in a month are summed for the month giving respective totals for each element for that month. These sums for a given month for a given station over the past thirty years are again summed and then arithmetically averaged. It should be noted that the heating and cooling degree days do not cancel each other out. It is possible to have both for a given station in the same month.

Precipitation data is computed the same as heating and cooling degree days. Mean precipitation and mean snowfall are arithmetic averages of cumulative totals for the month. All available values for the thirty year period for a given month for a given station are summed and then divided by the number of values. The same is true for days of greater than or equal to 0.1", 0.5",and 1.0" of precipitation, and days of greater than or equal to 1.0" of snow depth on the ground. The word trace appears for precipitation and snowfall amounts that are too small to measure.

Finally, remember that all values presented in the tables and the rankings are averages, maximums, or minimums of available data (see Methodology below) for that specific data element for the last thirty years (1980-2009).

Weather Elements (NWS Stations Only)

The following elements were taken directly from the International Station Meteorological Climate Summary. The periods of records vary per station and are noted at the bottom of each table.

Maximum precipitation, minimum precipitation, maximum snowfall, maximum snow depth, maximum 24-hour snowfall, thunderstorm days, foggy days, relative humidity (morning and afternoon), dewpoint, prevailing wind speed and direction, and maximum wind gust are all self-explanatory.

The word trace appears for precipitation and snowfall amounts that are too small to measure.

Predominant sky cover contains four possible entries: CLR (clear); SCT (scattered); BRK (broken); and OVR (overcast).

Inclusion Criteria—How Stations Were Selected

The basic criteria is that a station must have data for temperature, precipitation, heating and cooling degree days of sufficient quantity in order to create a meaningful average. More specifically, the definition of sufficiency here has two parts. First, there must be 22 values for a given data element, and second, ten of the nineteen elements included in the table must pass this sufficiency test. For example, in regard to mean maximum temperature (the first element on every data table), a given station needs to have a value for every month of at least 22 of the last thirty years in order to meet the criteria, and, in addition, every station included must have at least ten of the nineteen elements with at least this minimal level of completeness in order to fulfill the criteria. We then removed stations that were geographically close together, giving preference to stations with better data quality.

Methodology

The following discussion applies only to data compiled from the NCDC DSI-3220 data tapes and excludes weather elements that are extreme maximums or minimums.

The data is based on an arithmetic average of all available data for a specific data element at a given station. For example, the average maximum daily high temperature during July for any given station was abstracted from NCDC source tapes for the thirty Julys, starting in July, 1980 and ending in July, 2009. These thirty figures were then summed and divided by thirty to produce an arithmetic average. As might be expected, there were not thirty values for every data element on every table. For a variety of reasons, NCDC data is sometimes incomplete. Thus the following standards were established.

For those data elements where there were 26-30 values, the data was taken to be essentially complete and an average was computed. For data elements where there were 22-25 values, the data was taken as being partly complete but still valid enough to use to compute an average. Such averages are shown in **bold italic** type to indicate that there was less than 26 values. For the few data elements where there were not even 22 values, no average was computed and 'na' appears in the space. If any of the twelve months for a given data element reported a value of 'na', no annual average was computed and the annual average was reported as 'na' as well.

Thus the basic computational methodology used is designed to provide an arithmetic average. Because of this, such a pure arithmetic average is somewhat different from the special type of average (called a "normal") which NCDC procedures produces and appears in federal publications.

Perhaps the best outline of the contrasting normalization methodology is found in the following paragraph (which appears as part of an NCDC technical document titled, CLIM81 1961-1990 NORMALS TD-9641 prepared by Lewis France of NCDC in May, 1992):

Normals have been defined as the arithmetic mean of a climatological element computed over a long time period. International agreements eventually led to the decision that the appropriate time period would be three consecutive decades (Guttman, 1989). The data record should be consistent (have no changes in location, instruments, observation practices, etc.; these are identified here as "exposure changes") and have no missing values so a normal will reflect the actual average climatic conditions. If any significant exposure changes have occurred, the data record is said to be "inhomogeneous," and the normal may not reflect a true climatic average. Such data need to be adjusted to remove the nonclimatic inhomogeneities. The resulting (adjusted) record is then said to be "homogeneous." If no exposure changes have occurred at a station, the normal is calculated simply by averaging the appropriate 30 values from the 1961-1990 record.

In the main, there are two "inhomogeneities" that NCDC is correcting for with normalization: adjusting for variances in time of day of observation (at the so-called First Order stations data is based on midnight to midnight observation times and this practice is not necessarily followed at cooperative stations which are staffed by volunteers), and second, estimating data that is either missing or incongruent.

The editors had some concerns regarding the comparative results of the two methodologies. Would our methodology produce strikingly different results than NCDC's? To allay concerns, results of the two processes were compared for the time period normalized results are available (1971-2000). In short, what was found was that the answer to this question is no. Never the less, users should be aware that because of both the time period covered (1980-2009) and the methodology used, data is not compatible with data from other sources.

Potential Cautions

First, as with any statistical reference work of this type, users need to be aware of the source of the data. The information here comes from NOAA, and it is the most comprehensive and reliable core data available. Although it is the best, it is not perfect. Most weather stations are staffed by volunteers, times of observation sometimes vary, stations occasionally are moved (especially over a thirty year period), equipment is changed or upgraded, and all of these factors affect the uniformity of the data. The editors do not attempt to correct for these factors, and this data is not intended for either climatologists or atmospheric scientists. Users with concerns about data collection and reporting protocols are both referred to NCDC technical documentation.

Second, users need to be aware of the methodology here which is described above. Although this methodology has produced fully satisfactory results, it is not directly compatible with other methodologies, hence variances in the results published here and those which appear in other publications will doubtlessly arise.

Third, is the trap of that informal logical fallacy known as "hasty generalization," and its corollaries. This may involve presuming the future will be like the past (specifically, next year will be an average year), or it may involve misunderstanding the limitations of an arithmetic average, but more interestingly, it may involve those mistakes made most innocently by generalizing informally on too broad a basis. As weather is highly localized, the data should be taken in that context. A weather station collects data about climatic conditions at that spot, and that spot may or may not be an effective paradigm for an entire town or area.

About Illinois

Governor	**Patrick Joseph "Pat" Quinn III (D)**
Lt Governor	**Sheila J. Simon (D)**
State Capital	Springfield
Date of Statehood	December 3, 1818 (21st state)
State Nickname	Land of Lincoln (official); The "Prairie State"
Largest City	Chicago
Highest Point	Charles Mound (1,235 feet)
Lowest Point	Confluence of Mississippi River & Ohio River (280 ft)
State Amphibian	Eastern Tiger Salamander *(Ambystoma tigrinum)*
State Bird	Northern Cardinal *(Cardinalis cardinalis)*
State Butterfly	Monarch Butterfly *(Danaus plexippus)*
State Folk Dance	Square Dance
State Fish	Bluegill *(Lepomis macrochirus)*
State Flower	Violet *(Viola sororia)*
State Snack Food	Popcorn *(Zea mays averta)*
State Fruit	Gold Rush Apple *(Malus xdomestica)*
State Fossil	Tully Monster *(Tullimonstrum gregarium)*
State Prairie Grass	Big Bluestem *(Andropogon gerardii)*
State Animal	White-tailed Deer *(Odocoileus virginianus)*
State Mineral	Fluorite *(Calcium fluoride)*
State Motto	"State Sovereignty, National Union"
State Reptile	Painted Turtle *(Chrysemys picta)*
State Soil	Drummer Silty Clay Loam *(Mesic typic endoaquoll)*
State Song	"Illinois"
State Tree	White Oak *(Quercus alba)*

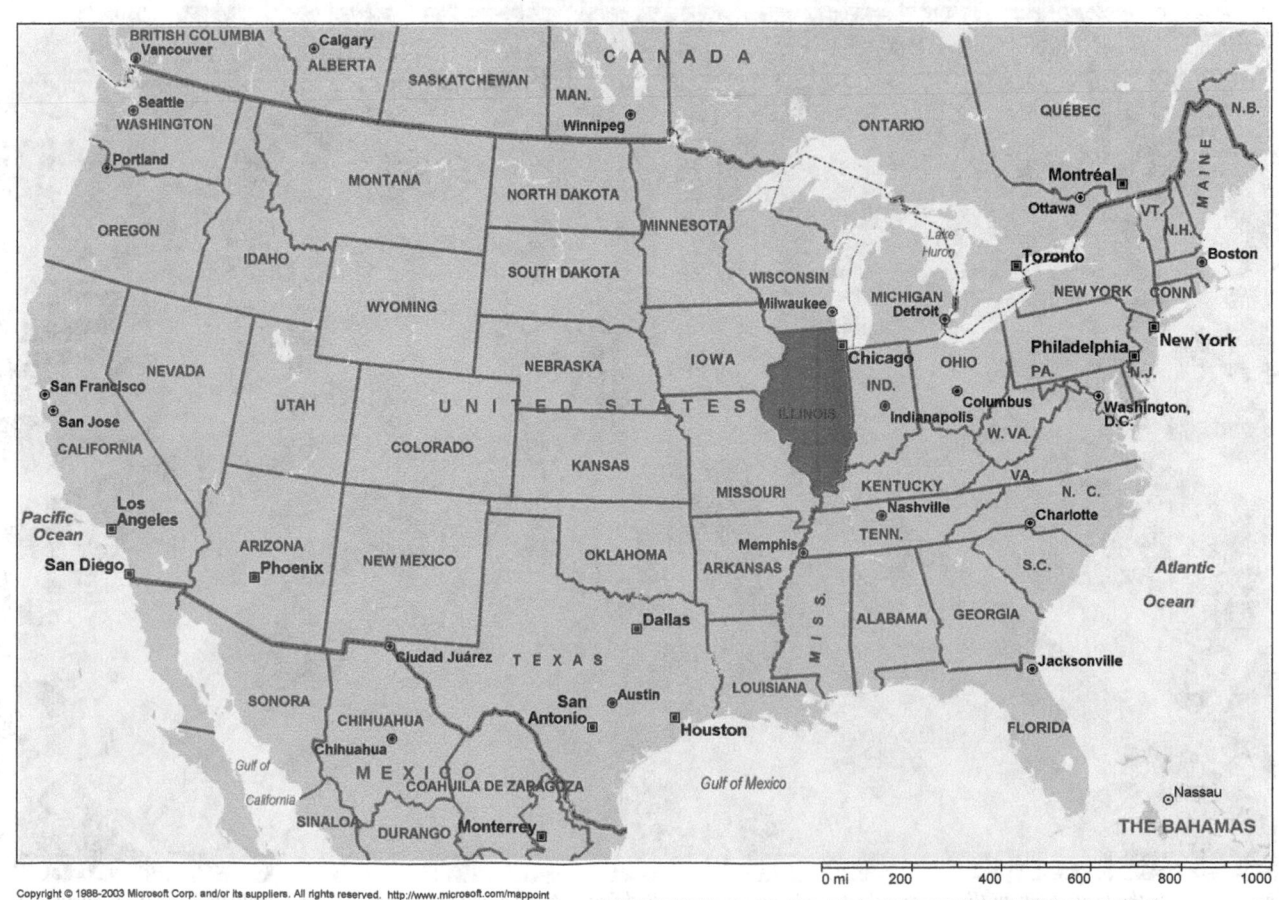

Chicago, top, is the largest city in Illinois and the third largest in the United States. It sits along the shores of Lake Michigan. The lake is home to Navy Pier, which was built 1916 in downtown Chicago and combines warehousing, docking for passenger steamers, and public entertainment, including the Navy Pier Ferris Wheel, pictured bottom. Today, Navy Pier is the city's number one tourist attraction

Garden of the Gods Wilderness, above, within the Shawnee National Forest in southern Illinois, was created by the uplifting of a sandstone plateau that was never covered by glaciers, unlike much of Illinois. In 1990, the Illinois Wilderness Act designated seven parcels of land in the Shawnee Forest as wilderness areas, including the Garden of the Gods Wilderness, the most-visited wilderness area in the state.

Peoria City Hall, top. Established in 1691, Peoria is Illinois' oldest European settlement. Nicknamed "The River City," it's the largest city on the Illinois River, the seventh largest in the state, and headquarters for Caterpillar, one of 30 companies composing the Dow Jones Industrial Average. Upper LaSalle Waterfall at Starved Rock State Park, bottom, is located in Utica, in north central Illinois, and is a major local attraction.

Illinois corn field in summer, above. The state's major agriculture crops are corn, soybeans, hogs, cattle, dairy products, and wheat. Illinois often ranks first or second in U. S. soybean production and consistently ranks second, to Iowa, in corn production. Illinois is considered a leader in the country's food manufacturing and meat processing industries.

Madonna della Strada Chapel, Loyola University's main campus in Chicago, top. Founded in 1870, it is the largest Jesuit university in the United States with over 15,000 students. It's been dubbed the "Miracle along the Lake" with six campuses in Chicago and one overseas in Rome, Italy. DuPage County Courthouse in Wheaton, bottom, is one of the only Richardsonian Romanesque buildings in Northern Illinois. Originally built in 1868, it was replaced in 1896 and is on the National Register of Historic Places.

A Brief History of Illinois

Early Illinois History

Before Illinois became a State, it was known as the Illinois Territory. In early 1818, the General Assembly of the Illinois Territory sent a petition to the United States Congress asking to be admitted into the Union. Part of the process for being admitted as a State was for Illinois to adopt its own constitution.

The word Illinois comes from the French word meaning Illini or Land of Illini. It is an Algonquin word meaning Men or Warriors. Illinois was discovered in 1673, settled in 1720 and entered the Union on December 3, 1818. Illinois is surrounded by bodies of water on nearly every border: the Mississippi River on the west; the Ohio and Wabash Rivers in the south, and Lake Michigan in the North. The States that border Illinois are: Kentucky, Iowa, Wisconsin, Missouri, and Indiana. The first Railroad train crossed the Mississippi River on the river's first bridge in Rock Island, Illinois on April 21, 1856. The highest point in Illinois is Charles Mound in JoDaviess County, elevation, 1,235 feet, and the lowest point is in Cairo, Alexander county at the Mississippi River, elevation 279 feet.

Thousands of years before the French reached Illinois, Paleo-Indians, a nomadic people, and their descendants, archaic Indians, had explored Illinois. The culture of these hunters, dated before 5000 BC, can be studied at the Modoc Rock Shelter in Randolph County. Woodland Indians were their descendants. By 900 AD, Middle Mississippi Indians, who succeeded the Woodland Indians, built large earthen mounds and developed complex urban areas. These cities disappeared possibly because of overpopulation, disease, and exhaustion of resources. The descendants of the Mississippians were the Illiniwek tribes of the 17th, 18th, and 19th centuries. After years of losing land and wars to other Indian groups and European colonists, the Illiniweks were moved to a Kansas reservation.

The French controlled areas along the Mississippi River valley in the American Bottoms between Cahokia and Kaskaskia. Their occupation, from about 1675 to 1763, left few lasting marks, as did the ineffective British rule. European control was ended by the U.S. militia of George Rogers Clark in 1778, whereupon Virginia claimed Illinois as within its territory.

The Northwest Ordinance of 1787 charted this region and organized counties, and in 1809 the Territory of Illinois was created. During the early years of settlement by fur trappers, southern Illinois was the focus of migration to the area, especially along the Mississippi River valley and the Wabash and Ohio rivers. Granting of statehood in 1818 was controversial. The population numbered less than the required 60,000. Moreover, in order to include the Chicago port area, territorial representatives induced the U.S. Congress to draw the Illinois border 51 miles to the north of the original boundary as delimited by the Northwest Ordinance. The first capital was Kaskaskia, followed by Vandalia, along the Kaskaskia River, which held the position for 20 years. After strong pressure from Abraham Lincoln, the capital was moved to Springfield by an 1837 legislative vote.

Early Illinois Statehood

Early statehood problems engulfed Illinois. The state population in 1830 was 157,445. By then the state was near bankruptcy because of government financing of canals and railroad construction. The Black Hawk War in 1832 was fought by the Indians and newly arrived settlers over possession of Illinois land.

In 1833 Chicago was founded, and the final Indian treaty pertaining to Illinois land, the Treaty of Chicago, was concluded with the Potawatomi, Chippewa, and Ottawa tribes. Also, the first higher education institution for women in Illinois, the Jacksonville Female Seminary, was opened.

In 1839, the state capital was moved to Springfield, while the population in Illinois had grown to nearly 500,000. The first railroad, The Northern Cross, started running from the Illinois River to Springfield. Later in 1844, the Mormon prophet Joseph Smith and his brother Hyrum were killed by a mob at Carthage, prompting the Mormons to move out of Illinois by 1848. The Illinois and Michigan Canal opened the same year. By that time, the population was nearly one million.

By 1860, debates were held in seven Illinois communities. The state's population was 1,711,951. In 1861, Abraham Lincoln of Springfield is inaugurated as president. The Civil War caused mixed loyalties among Illinoisans, many of whom were first- or second-generation Southerners; however, many took pride in the fact that the Union was led by a native son, Lincoln, and the state provided 250,000 soldiers to the Union army. Illinois also was the weapons manufacturer, supplier of iron products, and major grain and meat supplier for the North. The Civil War ended in 1865, and Lincoln was assassinated.

In 1867, the Illinois Industrial University (later the University of Illinois) was established. In 1868, a new statehouse was authorized and construction began, but would not be completed for 20 years. By 1870, the state's population is 2,539,891.

By 1880, Illinois had become the fourth most populous state. It was a leader in grain production and manufacturing. Large-scale European immigration provided labor to mine coal, run steel mills, and enhance the economy and culture of the state. Its leadership was achieved despite the economic slumps of the 1880s, 1890s, and early 1900s; the labor disputes in coal mining and railroading; the Chicago fire of 1871. By 1890, the state's population was 3,836,352, and Chicago became a metropolis of 1,099,850.

By 1910, the state's population was 5,638,591. In 1911, Starved Rock State park became the first state park in Illinois. In 1912, Poetry magazine was founded in Chicago by Harriet Monroe, and it helped to launch the careers of Vachel Lindsay, Carl Sandburg, and other notable poets. In 1913, the Women's Suffrage Act was passed, extending voting rights for Illinois women. In 1917, the United States entered World War I, in which 314,504 Illinois men participated. In 1918, Illinois celebrated its centennial. Also, an influenza epidemic killed thousands of Illinois residents and more than 600,000 people nationwide.

Modern Day Illinois
By 1920, Illinois was counted among the foremost states in nearly every significant growth variable-coal mining, industry, farming, urbanization, transportation, and wholesaling. WWII saw Illinois send thousand of its residents to fight in Europe and the Pacific.

The post-World War II era was a time of industrial modification for the production of consumer goods. Even though meat-packing companies began to move away from Chicago and East Saint Louis, in part because of obsolete physical plants, Illinois farms were being mechanized and upgraded for increased output. The use of hybrid seed, chemical fertilizer, herbicides, and insecticides resulted in larger crop yields. Post-World War II Illinois experienced rapid population growth. The rising number of school-age children brought public school reform, rural school consolidations, and huge suburban educational plants. Migration streams of blacks from the South, Hispanics from Mexico and Puerto Rico, and whites from Appalachia reshaped neighborhoods in Chicago, its suburbs, and other large Illinois cities.

Illinois Historical Timeline

1673—Louis Jolliet and Father Marquette arrive in Illinois
1699—Cahokia is founded, the oldest town in Illinois
1717—Illinois becomes part of French Louisiana
1763—England receives Illinois at the end of the French and Indian War
1778—George Rogers Clark captures Kaskaskia from the British
1787—Illinois becomes part of the Northwest Territory
1804—Lewis and Clark expedition starts near Wood River
1809—Illinois Territory is created
1818—Illinois becomes the 21st state
1830—Abraham Lincoln moves to Illinois
1837—Chicago incorporated as a city
1848—The Illinois & Michigan Canal completed
1853—First Illinois State Fair is held
1861—Abraham Lincoln inaugurated as the 16th President of the United States
1863—Emancipation Proclamation
1871—Fire consumes much of Chicago
1888—Present-day State Capitol built
1893—Chicago World's Fair
1900—Completion of the Chicago Sanitary and Ship Canal
1908—Chicago Cubs win their second World Series
1958—Illinois tollway opens
1959—The St. Lawrence Seaway opens
1970—New state constitution adopted
1986—Chicago Bears win Super Bowl XX
1992—Carol Moseley Braun becomes the first black woman in the Senate
1998—The Chicago bulls win their sixth NBA championship
2001—Abraham Lincoln Presidential Library and Museum is dedicated
2005—Abraham Lincoln Presidential Library and Museum opens
2005—Chicago White Sox win their third World Series
2007—Illinois Senator Barack Obama announces bid for U.S. President
2008—Barack Obama elected U.S. President; Governor Rod Blagojevich is charged with trying to sell Barack Obama's Senate seat.
2009—Governor Blagojevich is impeached for abuse of power
2010—Chicago Blackhawks win Stanley Cup
2011—Former White House chief of staff, Rahm Emanuel, elected major of Chicago
2012—Ex-governor Blagojevich begins a 14-year prison sentence after being convicted of 18 counts of Federal corruption
2013—Governor Pat Quinn signs landmark legislation to reform the state's underfunded pension system
2014—Illinois is allowed to issue marriage licenses to same-sex couples

Source: State of Illinois, www.illinois.gov; Original research

An Introduction to Illinois Government

State Constitution

The Constitution of the State of Illinois, the governing document of the state, was first adopted in 1818 after Illinois was admitted to the Union as the 21st state.

The current version of the Illinois Constitution, adopted in 1970, extended anti-discrimination and health environment rights, granted home-rule rights to larger cities and counties to tax and rule without state authorization, and gave line-item veto power to the Governor to eliminate specific provisions in legislation.

Branches: Like the federal government, Illinois government consists of Executive, Legislative and Judicial Branches to check and balance each other's powers.

The Governor heads the Executive Branch and shares authority with five other elected constitutional officers: Lieutenant Governor, Attorney General, Secretary of State, Comptroller and Treasurer. As chief executive, the Governor controls the state budget, appoints department administrators and reports to the General Assembly annually on the condition of the state.

The General Assembly heads the Legislative Branch, made up of the 59-member Senate and the 118-member House of Representatives. The General Assembly introduces and passes legislation involving policy and administration of state and local affairs, taxes and spending.

The Supreme Court heads the Judicial Branch, which comprises five Appellate Court districts and 24 judicial circuits. The seven-member Supreme Court interprets the Illinois Constitution and laws and hears final arguments in certain legal cases.

Local Governments: The powers and responsibilities of local governments, including their ability to raise revenue and enter into debt, are dependent on state statutes. Illinois has 6,968 units of local government, more than any other state.

General purpose units, the main form of local government, have multiple functions and provide basic services such as police, fire, roads, sewer, water and public health services. These local government units include county (102); municipal, including cities, villages and towns (1,298); and township (1,431 in 85 counties).

Unlike general purpose units, special purpose districts (4,137) are dedicated to a single purpose and their boundaries cross the boundaries of other local governments.

School districts (905) may be the most familiar, but special districts provide many other types of services such as parks and recreation, library facilities, soil and water conservation, hospitals and mass transit.

Political Party System: The two major political parties<197>Republican and Democrat<197>are responsible for the conduct of public affairs in the state as well as the nation. Political parties were not established by the U.S. or Illinois Constitutions, but by 1870 the basic party names and structures were established and have continued to this day.

Executive Branch

Office of the Governor

The Governor is the chief executive of the state, responsible for the administration of all areas of the Executive Branch. The Governor appoints administrators and department directors, subject to approval by the Senate, and holds general administrative responsibility over several semi-independent boards and commissions. The Governor annually presents a proposed state budget to the General Assembly and reports on the condition of the state, setting priorities and direction. The Governor also grants pardons and reprieves; calls special legislative

sessions; approves or vetoes legislation; approves state construction contracts; and serves as commander-in-chief of the state's military forces.

Office of the Lieutenant Governor

The Lieutenant Governor is first in line for the governorship. The office handles a variety of responsibilities delegated by statute and assigned by the Governor. The Lieutenant Governor serves as the Governor's point person on education reform and chairs the Governor's Rural Affairs Council; the Illinois River, Mississippi River, and Wabash and Ohio Rivers Coordinating Councils; and the Interagency Military Base Support and Economic Development Committee. The Lieutenant Governor also serves as ambassador to the Illinois Main Street program.

Office of the Attorney General

The Attorney General is the lawyer for the state and the people of Illinois. The Attorney General acts as an advocate to protect consumers, safeguard children and communities, preserve the environment, uphold Illinois' open government laws, and defend the rights of Illinois' most vulnerable residents.

Office of the Secretary of State

The Secretary of State's office is the largest and most diverse office of its kind in the nation, providing more direct services to Illinois citizens than any other public agency. The office issues vehicle license plates and titles; licenses drivers and maintains driver records; registers corporations; enforces the Illinois Securities Act; and administers the state's organ/tissue donor registry. As State Librarian, the Secretary of State oversees State Library and literacy programs, and as State Archivist maintains records of legal and historical value housed in the Illinois State Archives.

Office of the Comptroller

The Comptroller is the chief fiscal control officer for Illinois government, charged with maintaining the state's central fiscal accounts and ordering payments into and out of the appropriate funds. To fulfill these duties, the Comptroller has established accounting standards for use by all state agencies. Maintaining the official records regarding state government's fiscal affairs, the Comptroller serves as a clearinghouse for financial information.

Office of the Treasurer

The Treasurer is the state's chief investment officer, investing a portfolio of approximately $10 billion in state funds and $5.5 billion for local governments to increase their rates of return. The Treasurer's office also administers the Invest in Illinois linked deposit programs to enhance communities and encourage economic growth. The Unclaimed Property Division aims to reunite more than $1.5 billion in lost and abandoned property with its rightful owners. The office's Financial Education Division conducts conferences and workshops statewide on personal savings, debt reduction and wealth accumulation.

Office of the Auditor General

Through the Illinois Constitution and the Illinois State Auditing Act, the Auditor General is vested with the responsibility of auditing and reviewing the receipt, obligation and use of all State of Illinois funds. As a principal agent of legislative oversight and public disclosure, the Auditor General conducts the Illinois Post Audit Program, which strengthens control over government activity by providing accountability to the people of Illinois and their elected representatives. The Illinois Constitution, the State Auditing Act and the Post Audit Program provide a system to help ensure that the General Assembly, which appropriates funds and sets program and policy goals, has the means to review expenditures and results.

Legislative Branch

To be eligible to serve as a member of the Illinois General Assembly, a person must be a United States citizen, at least 21 years old and reside in the district being represented for at least two years prior to the election or appointment.

Functions and Powers

The legislative power of the State of Illinois is vested in the General Assembly, which is composed of a 59-member Senate and a 118-member House of Representatives. Its principal activities are enacting, amending or repealing laws, passing resolutions, adopting appropriation bills and conducting inquiries on proposed legislation.

It also acts on amendments to the U.S. Constitution when they are submitted by Congress, and proposes and submits amendments to the Illinois Constitution for consideration by voters.

In addition to legislative responsibilities, the Senate is constitutionally delegated the responsibility of advising and consenting on most gubernatorial appointments to state offices, boards and commissions.

The General Assembly may impeach and convict executive and judicial officeholders in the State of Illinois. The House of Representatives has the sole power of impeachment, while the Senate serves as adjudicator. If a majority of the members of the House vote to impeach, the case proceeds to the Senate for trial. No officeholder may be convicted and removed from office without a two-thirds guilty vote from the Senate. The Senate may not, however, impose any punishment on an impeached and convicted officeholder other than removal from office.

Organization and Composition

Each legislative district is composed of one senate district, which is divided into two representative districts. Every two years, one Representative is elected from each representative district for a two-year term.

Members of the General Assembly are elected at the general election in evennumbered years. Senate districts are divided into three groups with one or two groups elected every two years. Senators from one group are elected for terms of four years, four years and two years; another group for terms of four years, two years and four years; and the third group for terms of two years, four years and four years.

In January of the odd-numbered year following the November general election, the Secretary of State presides over the House until the members have elected a Speaker. In the Senate, the Governor presides until the Senators have elected a President. Various other leaders and officers are selected by the Speaker and President as well as minority leaders in both the House and Senate. The General Assembly establishes committees and commissions to concentrate on specific subject areas for the consideration of bills.

Legislative Cycle

The General Assembly convenes each year on the second Wednesday in January.

The Governor's State of the State message to the legislature is delivered early in the session.

Constitutional provisions, formal rules and parliamentary procedures provide basic guidelines and relative stability to both chambers as the General Assembly acts on legislation. Any bill passed after May 31 cannot take effect until June 1 of the following year unless the bill passes both the House and Senate by a three-fifths vote.

The General Assembly adjourns at the end of May and reconvenes for two weeks in October or November to consider the Governor's vetoes.

At other times, special sessions of the General Assembly may be convened by the Governor or by joint proclamation by the presiding officers of both chambers. This proclamation confines legislative deliberation to specific subjects, and no other matters except confirmations of appointments and impeachments may be considered.

How a Bill is Passed

The Legislative Reference Bureau drafts legislation based on requests from legislators, constitutional officers and state agencies. A bill may be introduced in either the House or the Senate, and the procedure is almost identical. Each bill must be read on three different days in each chamber before it is passed.

The first reading introduces the bill. After the first reading, the bill is referred to the appropriate committee for review. The second reading allows for amendments.

At the time of the third reading, the bill is debated and then voted on. A simple majority is needed for a bill to pass. Bills approved on third reading move to the other chamber to follow the same process.

If the second chamber approves the bill as written, it is sent to the Governor. If a bill is amended in the second chamber and then passed, it must return to the chamber where it originated for concurrence. If the second chamber concurs with the changes, it is sent to the Governor.

The Governor may sign the bill into law, veto it with recommendations for changes, veto it absolutely, or allow it to become law without his signature. If a bill is vetoed, the General Assembly may override the veto by a three-fifths majority.

For a complete explanation of how a bill becomes law, visit www.ilga.gov.

Judicial Branch

The Illinois Supreme Court, the highest tribunal in the state, has general administrative and supervisory authority over all courts in Illinois. The Supreme Court hears appeals from the Appellate and Circuit Courts and may exercise original jurisdiction in cases relating to revenue, mandamus, prohibition or habeas corpus.

The Supreme Court has seven justices elected from five judicial districts for 10-year terms.

The Appellate Court hears appeals from administrative agencies and the Circuit Court (trial courts of Illinois). Appellate judges are elected from the five judicial districts for 10-year terms.

The Circuit Court is composed of circuit and associate judges. There are 24 judicial circuits in Illinois, each having one chief judge elected by the circuit judges.

The chief judge has general administrative authority in the circuit, subject to the overall administrative authority of the Supreme Court. Circuit judges may hear any case assigned to them by the chief judge. Associate judges may not preside over felony cases unless authorized by the Supreme Court. Circuit judges are elected for six-year terms and they appoint associate judges who serve four-year terms.

Candidates for elective judgeships are nominated at the primary election and elected at the general election. Any judge previously elected, at the expiration of his or her term, may have his or her name submitted to the voters on a special judicial ballot, without party designation and an opposing candidate, on the sole question of whether the judge shall be retained in office for another term.

The Illinois Courts Commission, composed of one Supreme Court justice, two Appellate judges, two Circuit judges and two citizens, has the authority to remove from office or discipline judges for willful misconduct in office or persistent failure to perform duties, or other conduct that brings the judicial office into disrepute. The commission also may suspend or retire any member of the judiciary who is physically or mentally unable to perform his or her duties.

A Judicial Inquiry Board has the authority to conduct investigations, receive or initiate complaints concerning any member of the judiciary, and file complaints with the Courts Commission.

Source: Illinois Secretary of State, Illinois Handbook of Government, 2013-2014

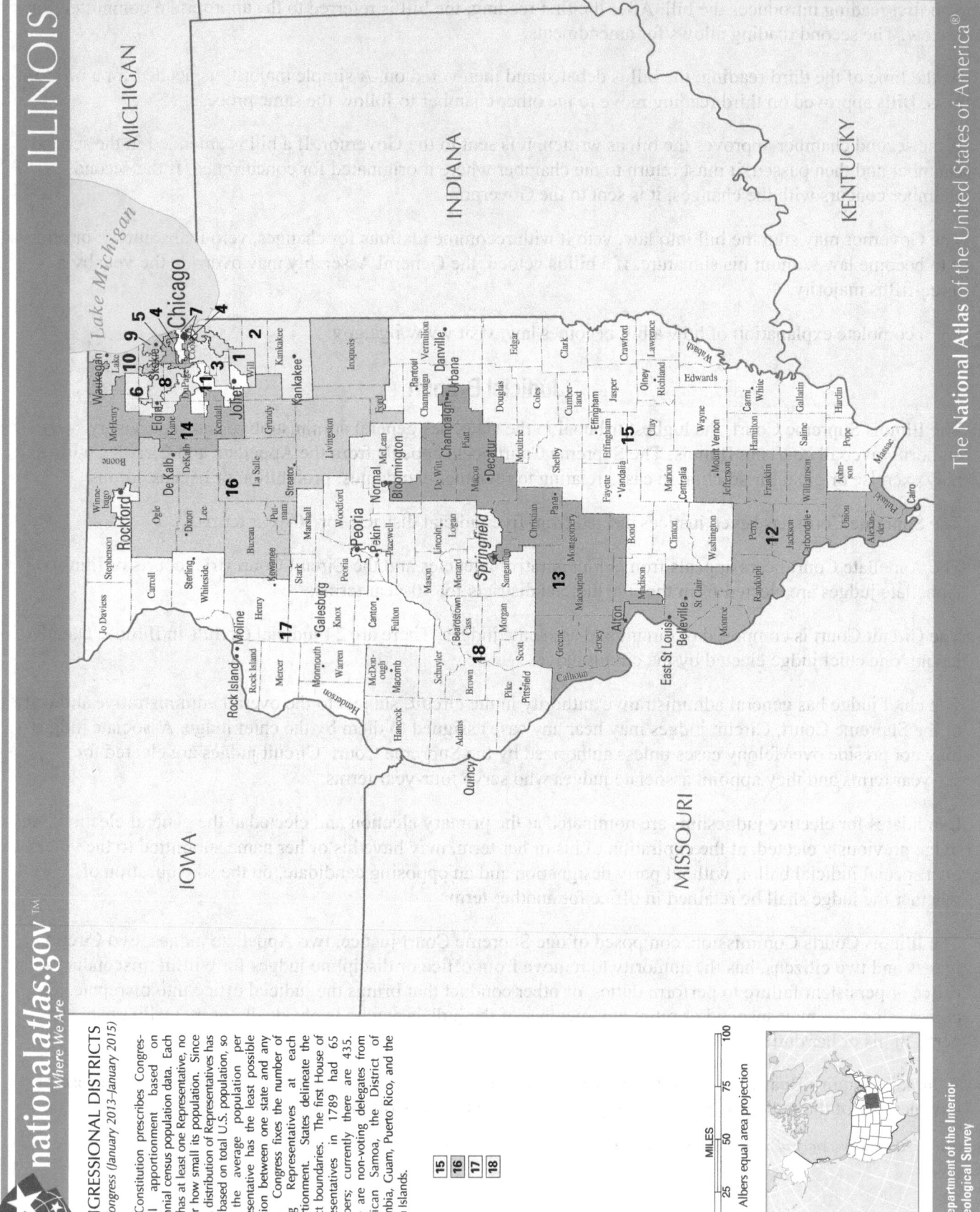

nationalatlas.gov™
Where We Are

CONGRESSIONAL DISTRICTS
113th Congress (January 2013–January 2015)

The Constitution prescribes Congressional apportionment based on decennial census population data. Each state has at least one Representative, no matter how small its population. Since 1941, distribution of Representatives has been based on total U.S. population, so that the average population per Representative has the least possible variation between one state and any other. Congress fixes the number of voting Representatives at each apportionment. States delineate the district boundaries. The first House of Representatives in 1789 had 65 members; currently there are 435. There are non-voting delegates from American Samoa, the District of Columbia, Guam, Puerto Rico, and the Virgin Islands.

U.S. Department of the Interior
U.S. Geological Survey

The **National Atlas** of the United States of America®

MILES
0   25   50   75   100
Albers equal area projection

Percent of Population Who Voted for Barack Obama in 2012

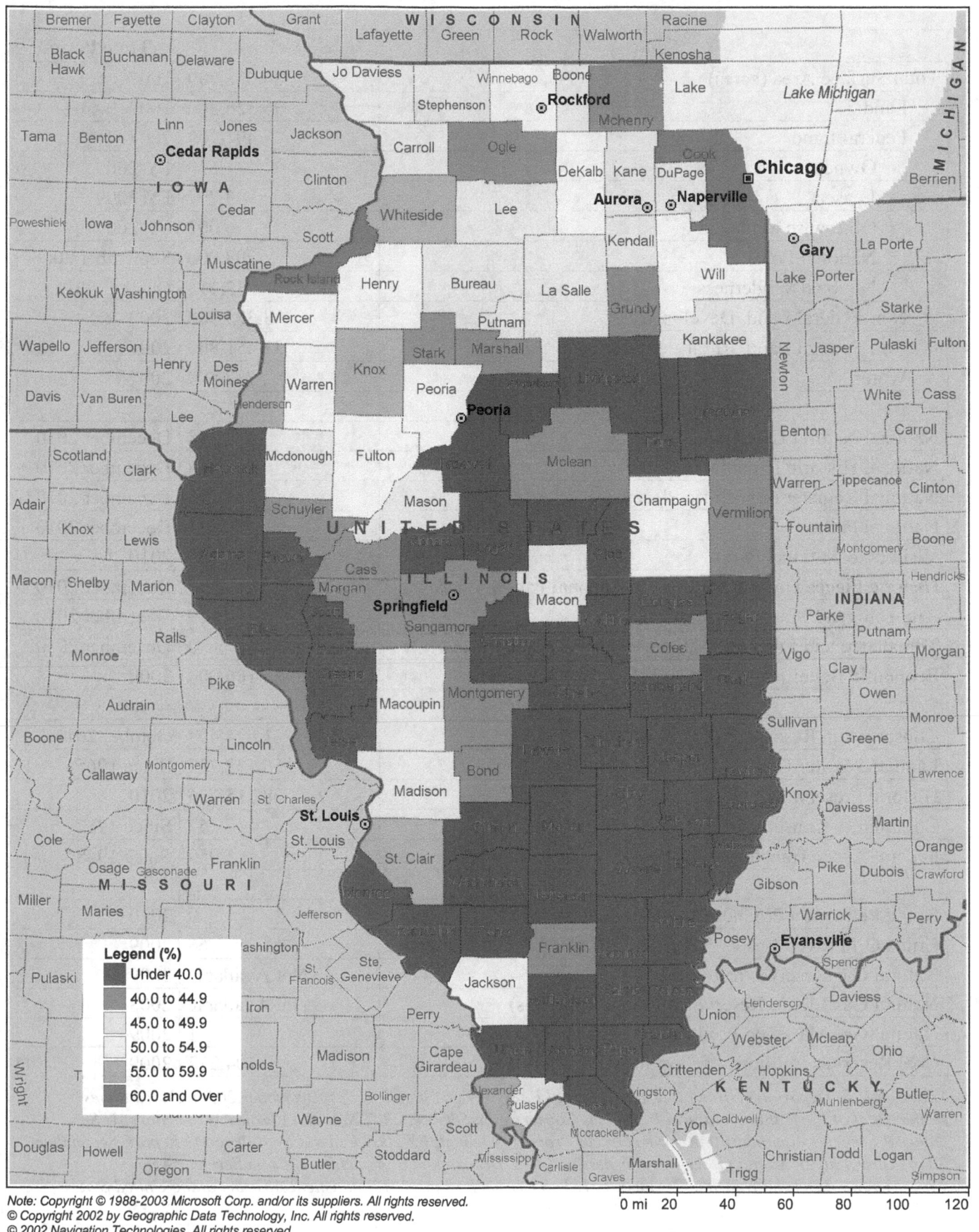

Legend (%)

	Under 40.0
	40.0 to 44.9
	45.0 to 49.9
	50.0 to 54.9
	55.0 to 59.9
	60.0 and Over

0 mi   20   40   60   80   100   120

Land and Natural Resources

Topic	Value	Time Period
Total Surface Area (acres)	36,058,700	2007
Land	35,326,200	2007
Federal Land	491,100	2007
Owned	221,650	FY 2009
Leased	3,797	FY 2009
Otherwise Managed	6,002	FY 2009
National Forest	298,000	September 2006
National Wilderness	32,113	October 2011
Non-Federal Land, Developed	3,383,300	2007
Non-Federal Land, Rural	31,451,800	2007
Water	732,500	2007
National Natural Landmarks	18	December 2010
National Historic Landmarks	85	December 2010
National Register of Historic Places	1,715	December 2010
National Parks	1	December 2010
Visitors to National Parks	354,125	2010
Historic Places Documented by the National Park Service	926	December 2010
Archeological Sites in National Parks	19	December 2010
Threatened and Endangered Species in National Parks	0	December 2010
Economic Benefit from National Park Tourism (dollars)	23,166,000	2009
Conservation Reserve Program (acres)	1,024,409	October 2011
Land and Water Conservation Fund Grants (dollars)	155,159,737	Since 1965
Historic Preservation Grants (dollars)	28,315,736	2010
Community Conservation and Recreation Projects	57	Since 1987
Federal Acres Transferred for Local Parks and Recreation	5,059	Since 1948
Crude Petroleum Production (millions of barrels)	9	2010
Crude Oil Proved Reserves (millions of barrels)	66	2009
Natural Gas Reserves (billions of cubic feet)	Not Available	2009
Natural Gas Liquid Reserves (millions of barrels)	Not Available	2008
Natural Gas Marketed Production (billions of cubic feet)	1	2009
Coal Reserves (millions of short tons)	104,222	2009

Sources: U.S. Department of the Interior, National Park Service, State Profiles, December 2010; United States Department of Agriculture, Natural Resources Conservation Service, 2007 National Resources Inventory; U.S. General Services Administration, Federal Real Property Council, FY 2009 Federal Real Property Report, September 2010; University of Montana, www.wilderness.net; U.S. Department of Agriculture, Farm Services Agency, Conservation Reserve Program, October 2011; U.S Census Bureau, 2012 Statistical Abstract of the United States

Illinois State Energy Profile

Quick Facts

- Illinois is a key transportation hub for crude oil and natural gas moving throughout North America, with over a dozen interstate natural gas pipelines, two natural gas market centers, several petroleum and petroleum product pipelines, and an oil port.
- Illinois leads the Midwest in crude oil refining capacity and ranked fourth in the nation as of January 2013.
- In 2012, Illinois ranked second in the nation in recoverable coal reserves at producing mines.
- With a production capacity of 1.5 billion gallons per year, Illinois is a top producer of ethanol; it ranked third in the United States in 2011.
- Illinois ranked first in the nation in 2013 in both generating capacity and net electricity generation from nuclear power; generation from its nuclear power plants accounted for over 12% of the nation's nuclear power.
- Annually, Illinois households use 129 million Btu of site energy per home, 44 percent more than the U.S. average. Lower utility rates compared to states with a similar climate result in Illinois households only spending 2 percent more for energy than the U.S. average, according to EIA's Residential Energy Consumption Survey.Analysis

Overview

Illinois is a key transportation hub for crude oil and natural gas moving throughout North America.

Located in the center of the nation, Illinois is the most populated and prosperous Midwestern state, ranking 5th in the nation in both population and gross domestic product. Because of its central location and access to major waterways, and rail and aviation hubs, Illinois plays an important role in the nation's economy. The state is a key transportation hub for crude oil and natural gas moving throughout North America. Illinois has fossil fuel resources that include substantial amounts of coal and some crude oil. Despite its large urban population, Illinois has more than 26 million acres of farmland and ranks 6th among the states in the market value of agricultural products sold. Corn, Illinois' most important crop, supplies the state's ethanol plants, making Illinois one of the top ethanol-producing states in the nation. The state also is a leading biodiesel manufacturer and has substantial wind resources.

Although Illinois is a major energy-consuming state, well known for its harsh winters and summer heat waves, its per capita energy consumption is below the national median. Industry is the largest energy-consuming sector, followed by the transportation and residential sectors, which consume almost equivalent amounts of energy. Service industries provide the greatest share of income to the Illinois economy, but machinery, processed foods, and chemicals are the most important manufactured items. Coal is the most important mined product. Illinois has many energy-intensive industries including chemicals, food processing, machinery manufacturing, metal fabrication, and petroleum refining.

Petroleum

Illinois has the largest crude oil refining capacity in the Midwest.

Illinois has the largest crude oil refining capacity in the Midwest and is fourth in the nation after Texas, Louisiana, and California. The state's refineries are supplied with both domestic and foreign crude oil. The largest refinery in the state is the Wood River refinery in Roxana, Illinois near St. Louis. It has a capacity of about 311,000 barrels per calendar day and processes domestic as well as Canadian and other foreign crude oils. The state has two crude oil import sites, one at Chicago on Lake Michigan and another at Peoria, in the center of the state, on the Illinois Waterway that connects Lake Michigan to the Mississippi River. Petroleum products, primarily asphalt and road oil, are also handled at Chicago's port. Illinois is crossed by several crude oil and petroleum product pipelines, as well.

Illinois' own crude oil production and reserves are modest and are located in the southern half of the state. Oil exploration in the state began in the 1850s but commercial production did not occur until 1905. Since that time, tens of thousands of wells have been drilled in the Illinois Basin. Oil production peaked in the middle of the 20th century, but now most of the productive oil wells in the state are stripper wells producing less than 2 barrels of crude oil per day.

Illinois is among the top 10 petroleum-consuming states. Overwhelmingly, petroleum is consumed by the transportation sector. Almost one-half of the petroleum used in the state is consumed as motor gasoline. The only areas in the state that require reformulated gasoline with ethanol are around Chicago to the northeast and near St. Louis to the southwest. However, there are more than 200 stations selling E85, a blend of 85% ethanol and 15% gasoline, across Illinois, more than any of its neighboring states, and second in the nation after Minnesota.

Natural Gas

Illinois is a major energy crossroads, with more than a dozen interstate natural gas pipelines and two natural gas market centers.

Illinois has only few producing natural gas wells and minimal production; however, the state is a major crossroads with more than a dozen interstate natural gas pipelines and two natural gas market centers. Illinois also has 28 natural gas storage fields with a total combined capacity, second only to Michigan, at just less than 1 trillion cubic feet of natural gas.

Natural gas enters Illinois from the west and south primarily by way of Iowa and Missouri, and more than two-thirds of it moves on to Indiana on its way to eastern markets. Illinois is one of the major natural gas-consuming states in the nation, behind Texas, California, Louisiana, Florida, and New York. Almost 1 trillion cubic feet of natural gas per year are consumed in the state. The residential sector consumes the largest share of the natural gas delivered to end users within the state. More than four-fifths of Illinois households use natural gas for home heating. The industrial sector, Illinois' second largest natural gas consuming sector, uses about one-fourth of the natural gas delivered to end users in the state. Although natural gas use by the electric power sector varies from year to year, almost one-tenth of the natural gas consumed within the state in 2012 was used for electric power generation.

Coal

Coal production has a long history in Illinois. The first European discovery of coal in North America was in 1673 along the Illinois River. Currently, there are 24 active mines in Illinois, and coal underlies much of the state in a geologic structure known as the Illinois Basin. Most of the coal is bituminous. Recoverable reserves at producing mines are estimated to be several billion short tons, greater than those of any other state east of the Mississippi River. Those reserves account for about one-eighth of the nation's recoverable coal reserves at producing mines and one-fourth of the nation's bituminous coal reserves.

Illinois' recoverable coal reserves at producing mines are the second largest in the nation.

Illinois' recoverable coal reserves at producing mines are the second largest in the nation after Wyoming, but because of its high-sulfur content, Illinois coal faces stiff competition from low-cost, low-sulfur western coal. Most electric utilities burn Illinois coal in combination with lower sulfur coal from other regions in order to meet the requirements of the Clean Air Act. Illinois coal is shipped by river, rail, and truck to 18 states, and by truck within the state. About one-seventh of the coal produced in Illinois is exported.

The electric power sector is the largest coal-consuming sector in the state and Illinois is routinely among the top three states in the nation in its use of coal for electric power generation. Nine-tenths of the coal received in Illinois comes from Wyoming by rail and is used almost exclusively for electric power generation. In-state shipments of Illinois coal are split almost equally between the electric power sector and industrial users. However, less than one-tenth of coal used in Illinois is consumed by industrial plants, coke plants, and commercial and institutional users.

Electricity

Illinois leads the nation in electricity generation from nuclear power.

Illinois leads the nation in electricity generation from nuclear power. Typically about one-eighth of the nation's nuclear power generation and about one-half of Illinois' net generation are from the state's six nuclear power plants with their 11 reactors. Most of the remainder of Illinois' electricity generation is from coal-fired power facilities. Natural gas and renewable resources, primarily wind, provide the rest of the supply, about one-tenth of all generation. Because Illinois generates considerably more electricity than it consumes, the state supplies the excess to the grid. The state is served by two electrical grids, one of which spans across the northern portion of the state and includes the

major urban areas in and around Chicago. The rest of the state is served by a second grid that includes much of the southeastern portion of the country.

Retail sales of electricity in Illinois are greatest in the commercial sector, followed closely by the residential sector. Although only one-eighth of Illinois households use electricity for home heating, nine-tenths of Illinois households use air conditioning.

Renewable Energy

Although renewable resources contribute only a small amount to Illinois' electric power generation, their contribution has increased dramatically over the past decade. Wind generation is the primary renewable resource for electric power generation in Illinois. The state's wind resource potential is ranked 15th in the nation; however, by the end of 2012, it was one of the top five states in the nation in terms of wind capacity installations with more than 3,500 megawatts of generating capacity online. Almost all of the remaining electricity generated from renewable resources in Illinois comes from biomass, specifically municipal landfills. Despite the state's many rivers, the relatively level terrain of the prairie limits the state's hydroelectric potential, and only a tiny fraction of the state's electricity generation is provided by hydroelectric power.

Biofuels are a major component of Illinois' renewable resources. The state is a leading producer of both ethanol and biodiesel. This fertile prairie state is a leading corn and soybean producer. Corn is the feedstock for Illinois' many ethanol plants and soy is the primary feedstock for biodiesel. Illinois is the third largest producer of ethanol among the states, and biodiesel production capacity in Illinois is second only to Texas.

Illinois' renewable portfolio standard requires that investor-owned electric utilities with more than 100,000 Illinois customers obtain 25% of retail sales from renewable resources by May of 2026, with at least 75% of the requirement from wind and 6% from solar photovoltaics (PV). Alternative retail electric suppliers and investor-owned electric utilities that sell outside of their service territories must comply with the renewable portfolio standard also, but only need to obtain 60% of the annual requirement from wind by 2026. They still must meet the 6% solar PV requirement.

Source: U.S. Energy Information Administration, Illinois State Energy Profile, March 27, 2014

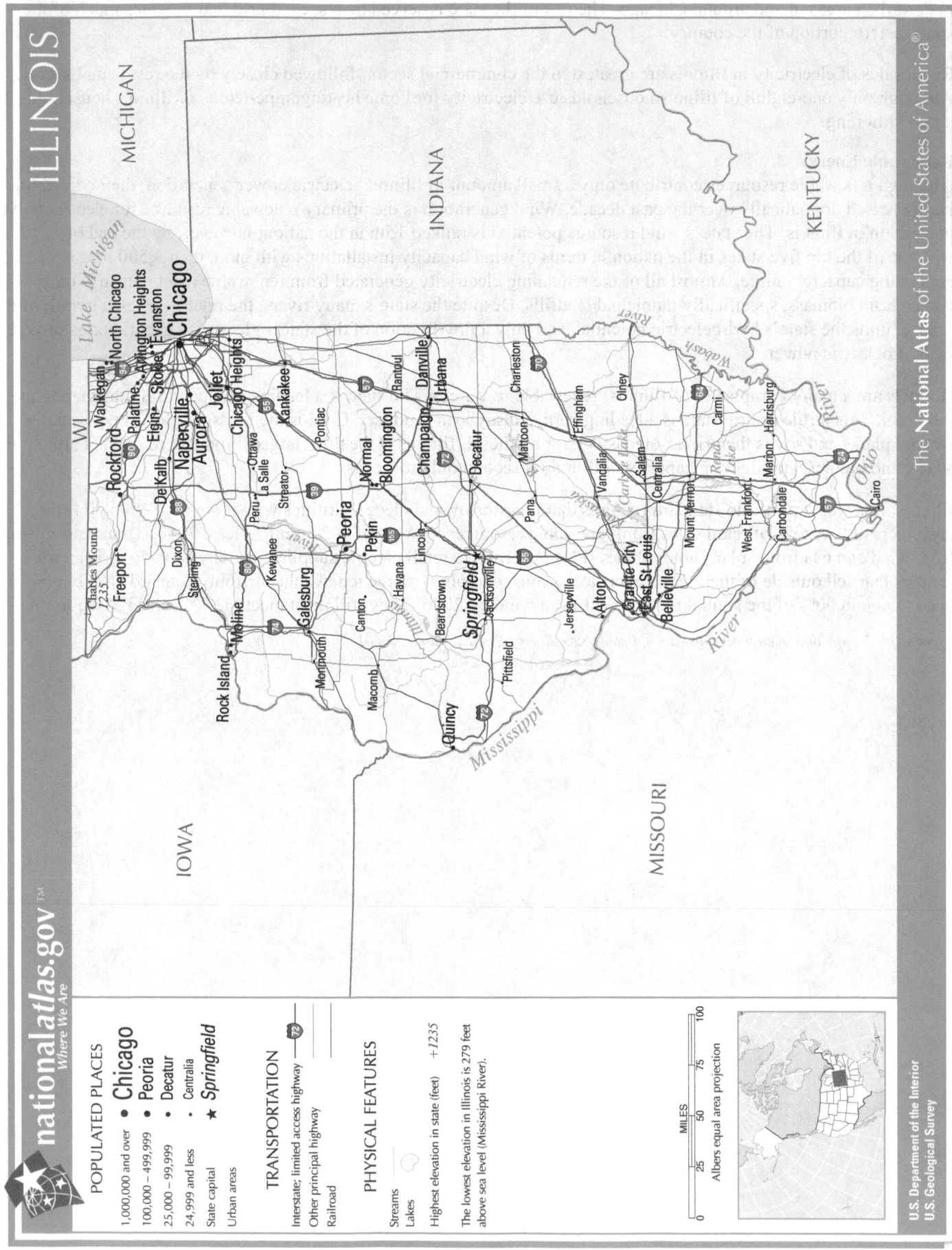

ILLINOIS

nationalatlas.gov™
Where We Are

POPULATED PLACES

1,000,000 and over ● Chicago
100,000 – 499,999 ● Peoria
25,000 – 99,999 ● Decatur
24,999 and less ● Centralia
State capital ★ Springfield
Urban areas

TRANSPORTATION

Interstate; limited access highway
Other principal highway
Railroad

PHYSICAL FEATURES

Streams
Lakes
Highest elevation in state (feet)   +1235

The lowest elevation in Illinois is 279 feet
above sea level (Mississippi River).

MILES
0   25   50   75   100
Albers equal area projection

U.S. Department of the Interior
U.S. Geological Survey

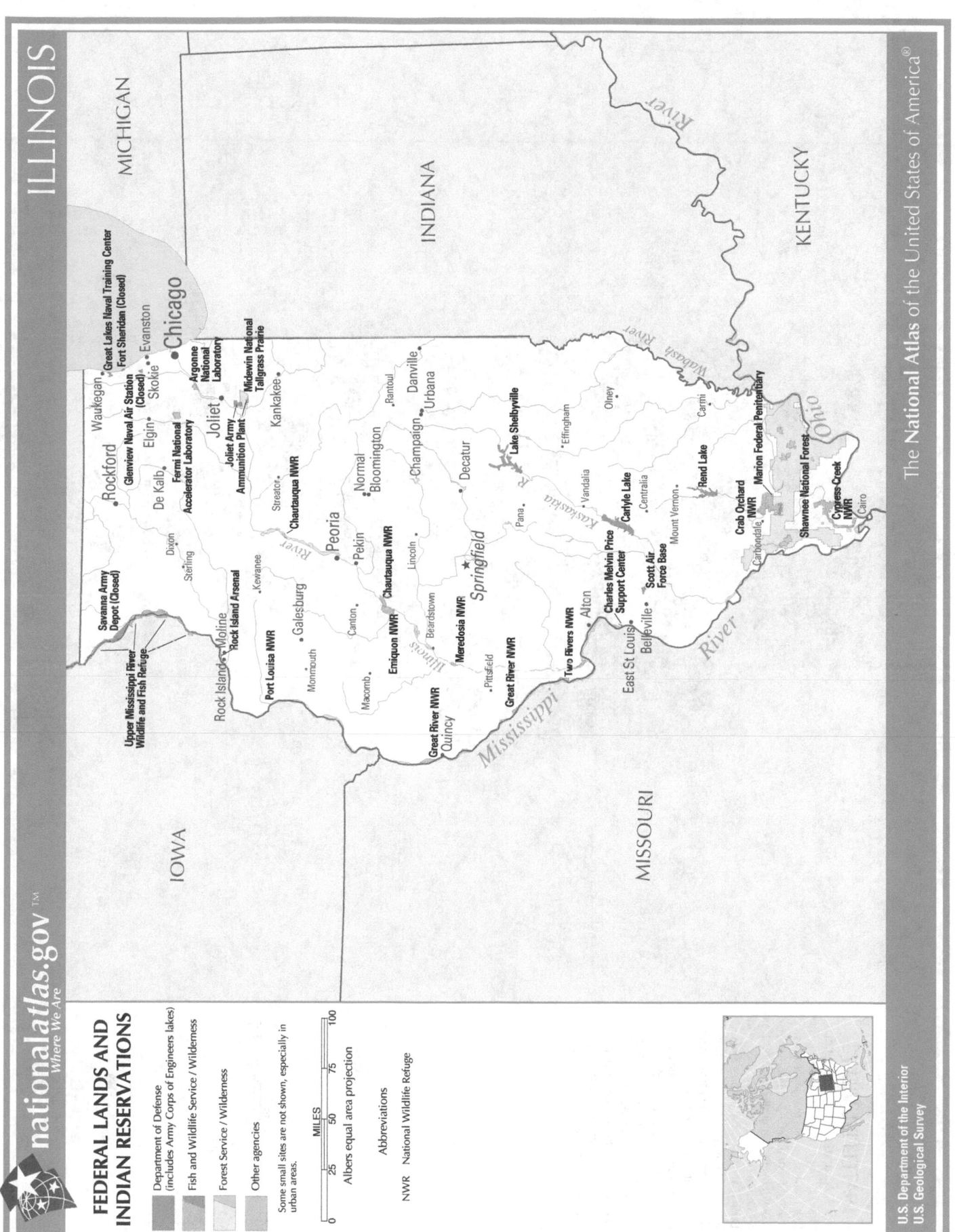

ILLINOIS

FEDERAL LANDS AND INDIAN RESERVATIONS

Department of Defense
(includes Army Corps of Engineers lakes)

Fish and Wildlife Service / Wilderness

Forest Service / Wilderness

Other agencies

Some small sites are not shown, especially in urban areas.

MILES

0   25   50   75   100

Albers equal area projection

Abbreviations

NWR   National Wildlife Refuge

nationalatlas.gov ™
Where We Are

The National Atlas of the United States of America®

U.S. Department of the Interior
U.S. Geological Survey

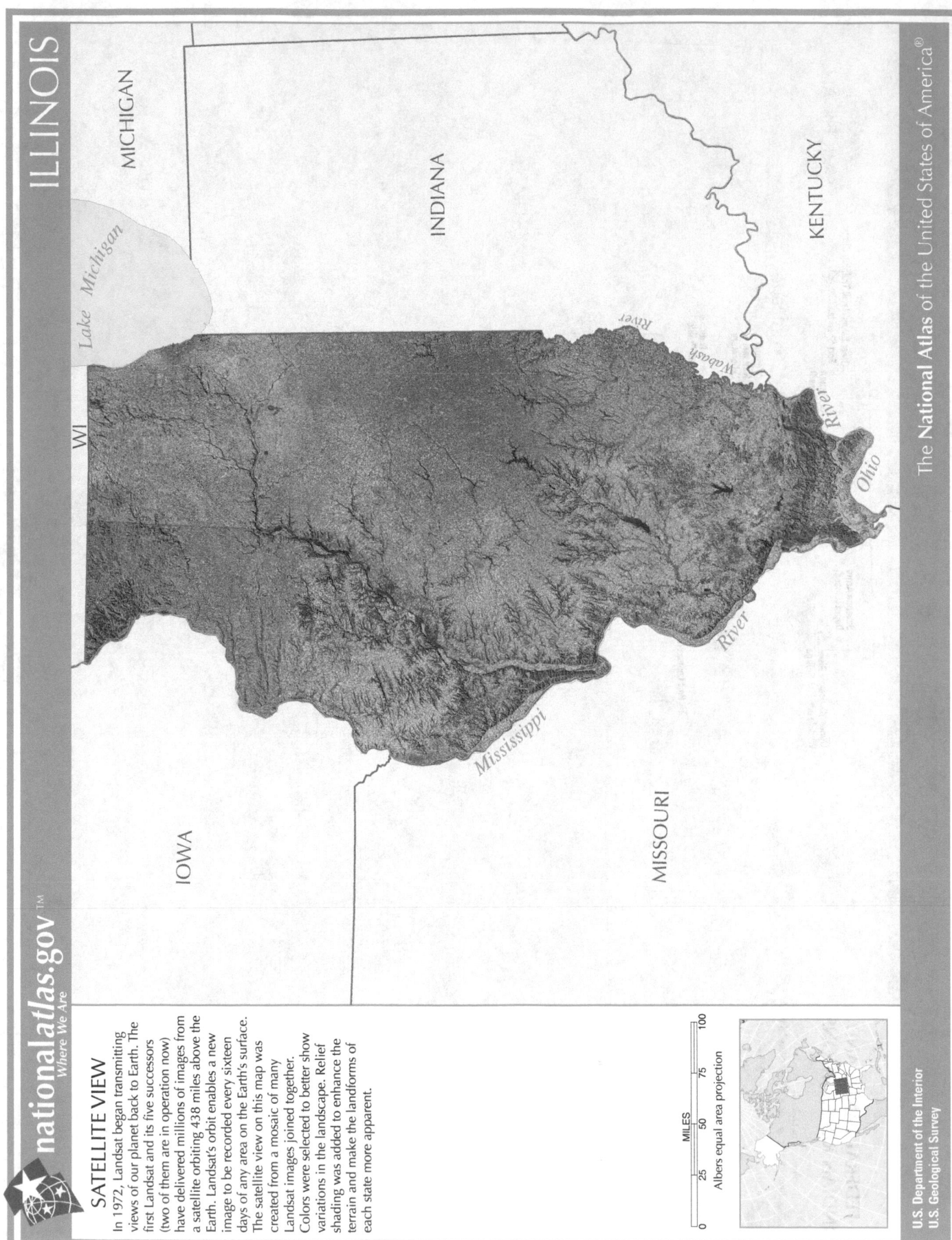

ILLINOIS

MICHIGAN

INDIANA

KENTUCKY

WI

Lake Michigan

IOWA

MISSOURI

Mississippi

River

Ohio

River

Wabash River

nationalatlas.gov™
Where We Are

SATELLITE VIEW

In 1972, Landsat began transmitting views of our planet back to Earth. The first Landsat and its five successors (two of them are in operation now) have delivered millions of images from a satellite orbiting 438 miles above the Earth. Landsat's orbit enables a new image to be recorded every sixteen days of any area on the Earth's surface. The satellite view on this map was created from a mosaic of many Landsat images joined together. Colors were selected to better show variations in the landscape. Relief shading was added to enhance the terrain and make the landforms of each state more apparent.

MILES

0   25   50   75   100

Albers equal area projection

U.S. Department of the Interior
U.S. Geological Survey

The **National Atlas** of the United States of America®

Economic Losses from Hazard Events, 1960-2009

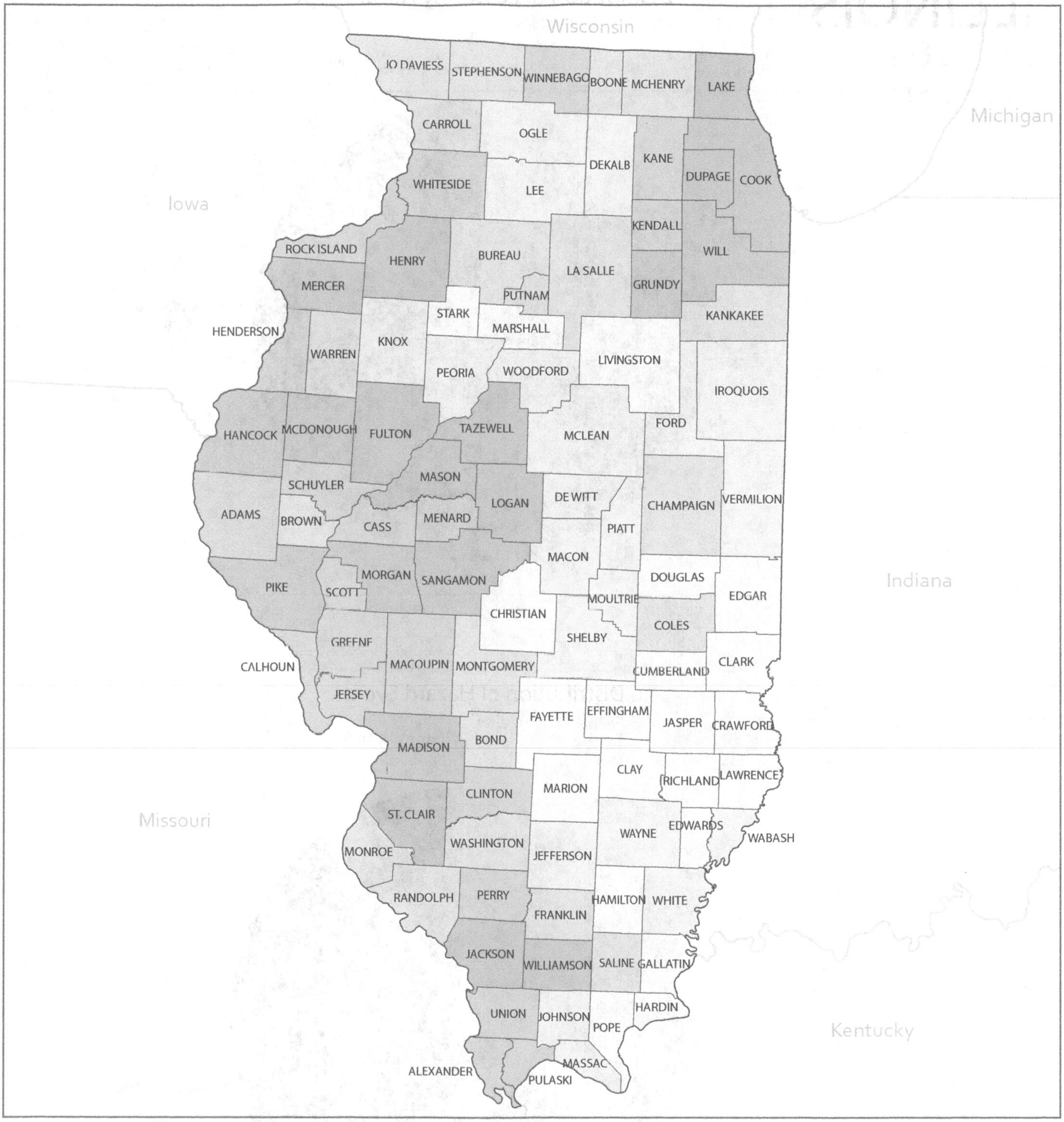

Wisconsin

Michigan

Iowa

JO DAVIESS | STEPHENSON | WINNEBAGO | BOONE | MCHENRY | LAKE

CARROLL | OGLE | DEKALB | KANE | DUPAGE | COOK

WHITESIDE | LEE

ROCK ISLAND | HENRY | BUREAU | LA SALLE | KENDALL | WILL

MERCER | PUTNAM | GRUNDY

HENDERSON | STARK | MARSHALL | KANKAKEE

WARREN | KNOX | PEORIA | WOODFORD | LIVINGSTON | IROQUOIS

HANCOCK | MCDONOUGH | FULTON | TAZEWELL | MCLEAN | FORD

SCHUYLER | MASON | DE WITT | CHAMPAIGN | VERMILION

ADAMS | BROWN | CASS | MENARD | LOGAN | PIATT

MACON

PIKE | SCOTT | MORGAN | SANGAMON | CHRISTIAN | DOUGLAS | EDGAR

MOULTRIE | COLES

GREENE | MACOUPIN | MONTGOMERY | SHELBY | CUMBERLAND | CLARK

CALHOUN | JERSEY | FAYETTE | EFFINGHAM | JASPER | CRAWFORD

MADISON | BOND | CLAY | RICHLAND | LAWRENCE

CLINTON | MARION | WAYNE | EDWARDS | WABASH

ST. CLAIR | WASHINGTON | JEFFERSON

MONROE | RANDOLPH | PERRY | HAMILTON | WHITE

FRANKLIN

JACKSON | WILLIAMSON | SALINE | GALLATIN

UNION | JOHNSON | HARDIN | POPE

ALEXANDER | MASSAC

PULASKI

Indiana

Kentucky

ILLINOIS

Total Losses (Property and Crop)

	7,798,433 - 21,110,928
	21,110,929 - 43,493,360
	43,493,361 - 65,394,087
	65,394,088 - 77,670,873
	77,670,874 - 416,198,985

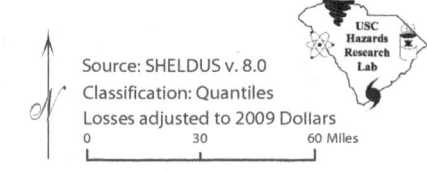

Source: SHELDUS v. 8.0
Classification: Quantiles
Losses adjusted to 2009 Dollars

0   30   60 Miles

USC Hazards Research Lab

ILLINOIS
Hazard Losses
1960-2009

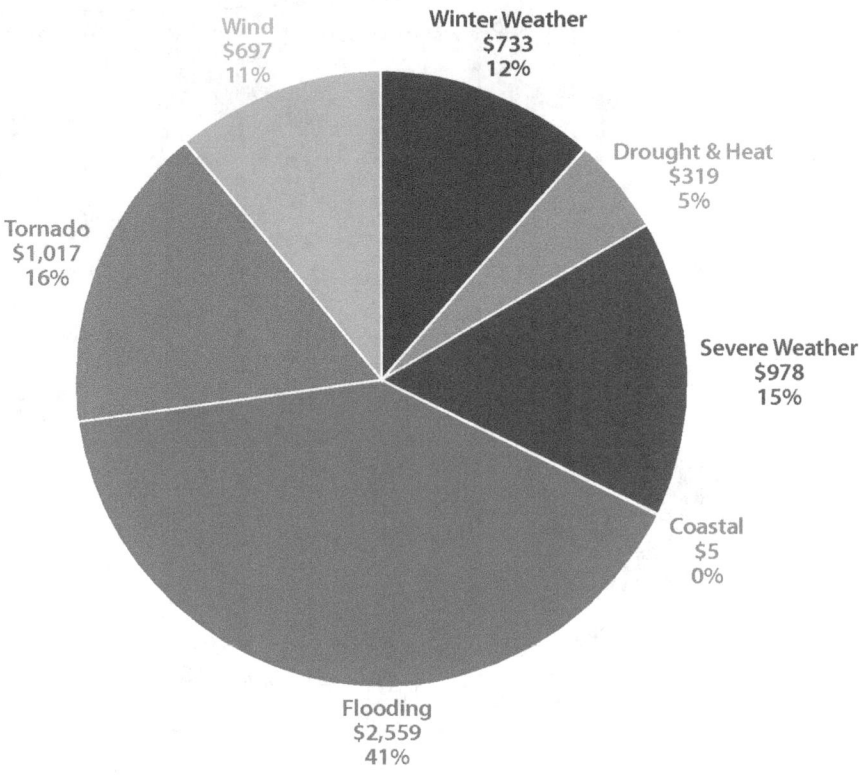

Distribution of Losses by Hazard Type
(in 2009 USD million)

Wind
$697
11%

Winter Weather
$733
12%

Drought & Heat
$319
5%

Severe Weather
$978
15%

Coastal
$5
0%

Tornado
$1,017
16%

Flooding
$2,559
41%

Distribution of Hazard Events
(number of events)

Winter Weather
2,845
8%

Drought & Heat
493
1%

Wind
12,723
35%

Severe Weather
15,795
43%

Tornado
1,328
4%

Flooding
3,305
9%

Coastal
10
0%

Population

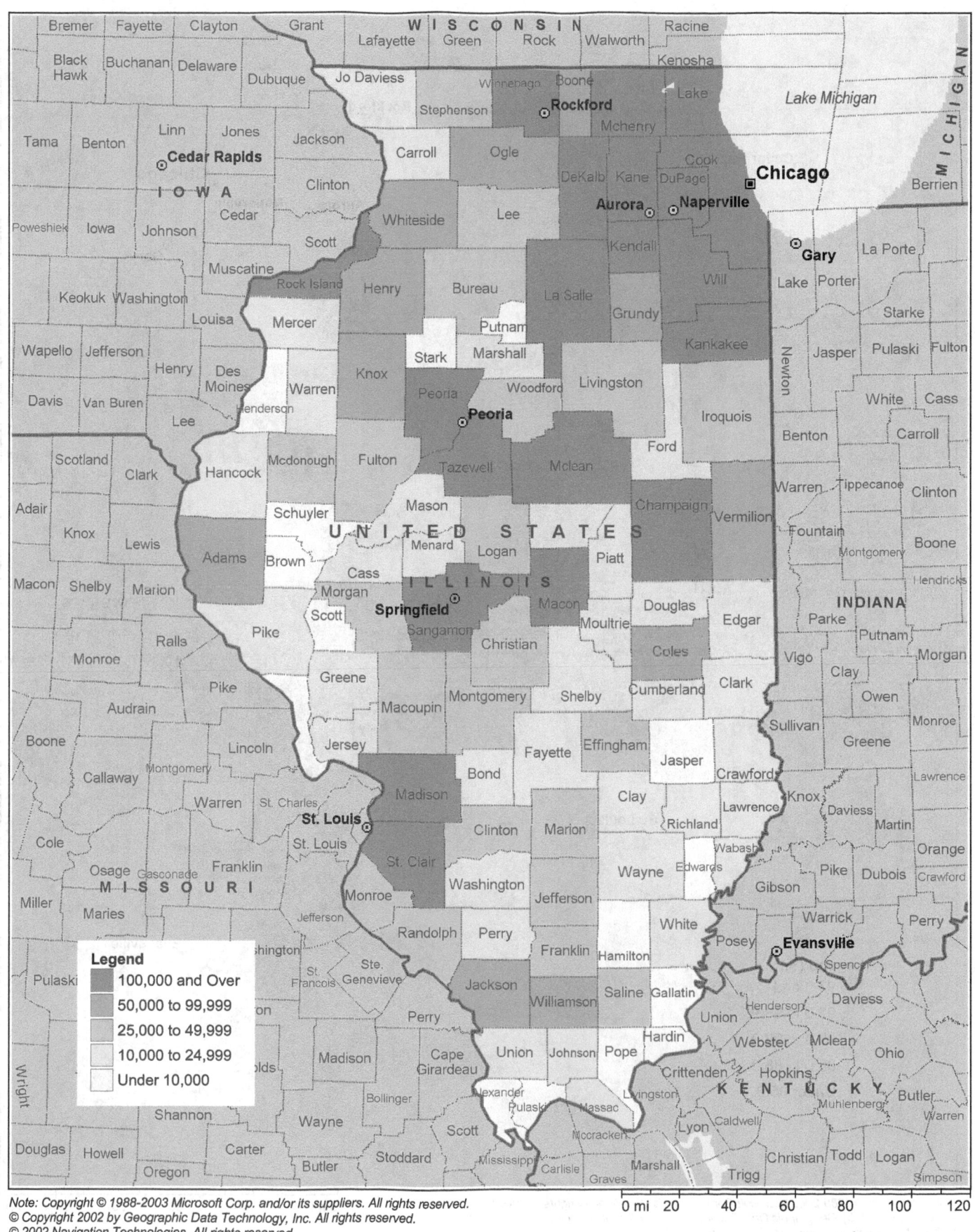

Percent White

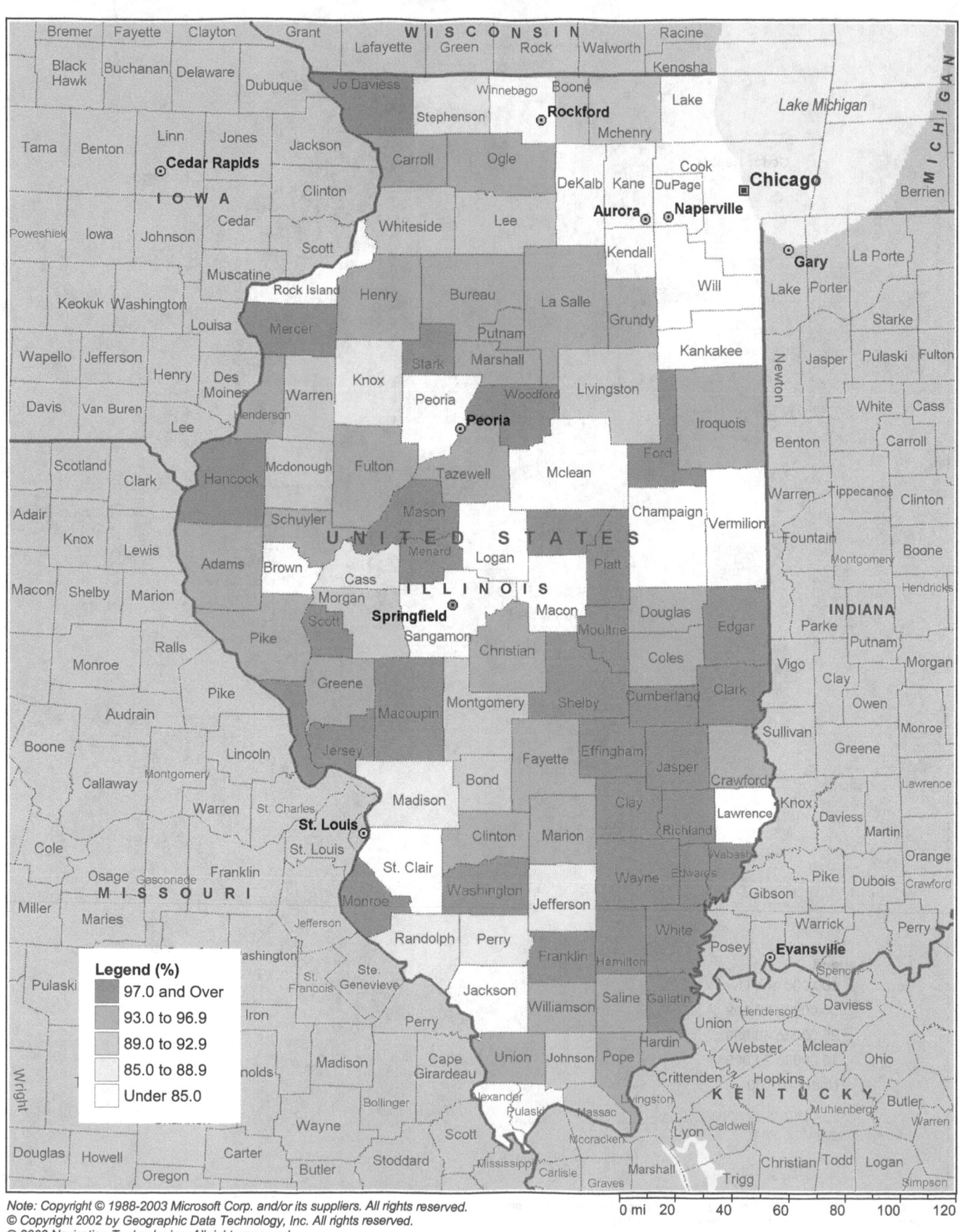

Legend (%)

- 97.0 and Over
- 93.0 to 96.9
- 89.0 to 92.9
- 85.0 to 88.9
- Under 85.0

0 mi 20   40   60   80   100   120

Percent Black

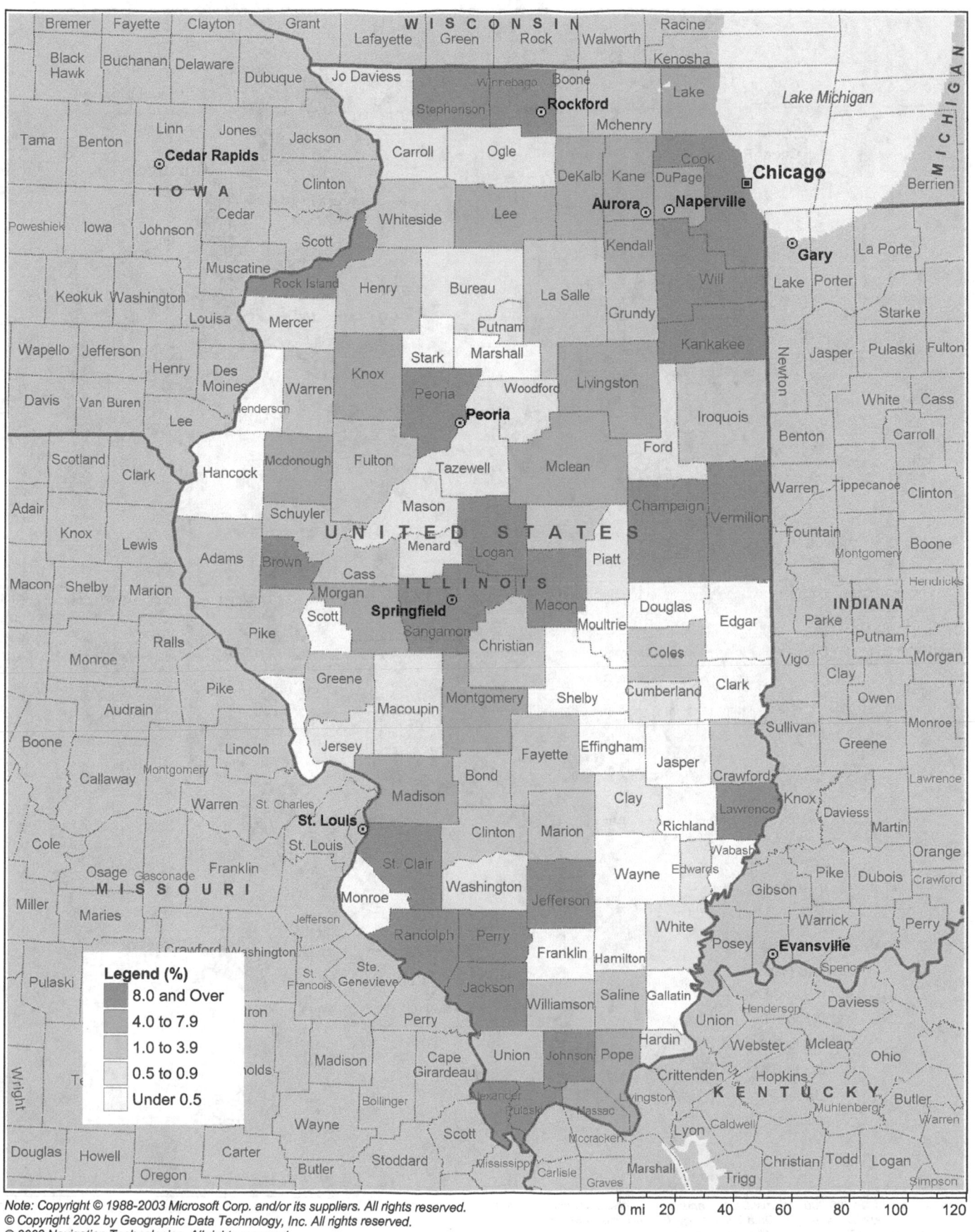

Legend (%)
- 8.0 and Over
- 4.0 to 7.9
- 1.0 to 3.9
- 0.5 to 0.9
- Under 0.5

0 mi   20   40   60   80   100   120

Percent Asian

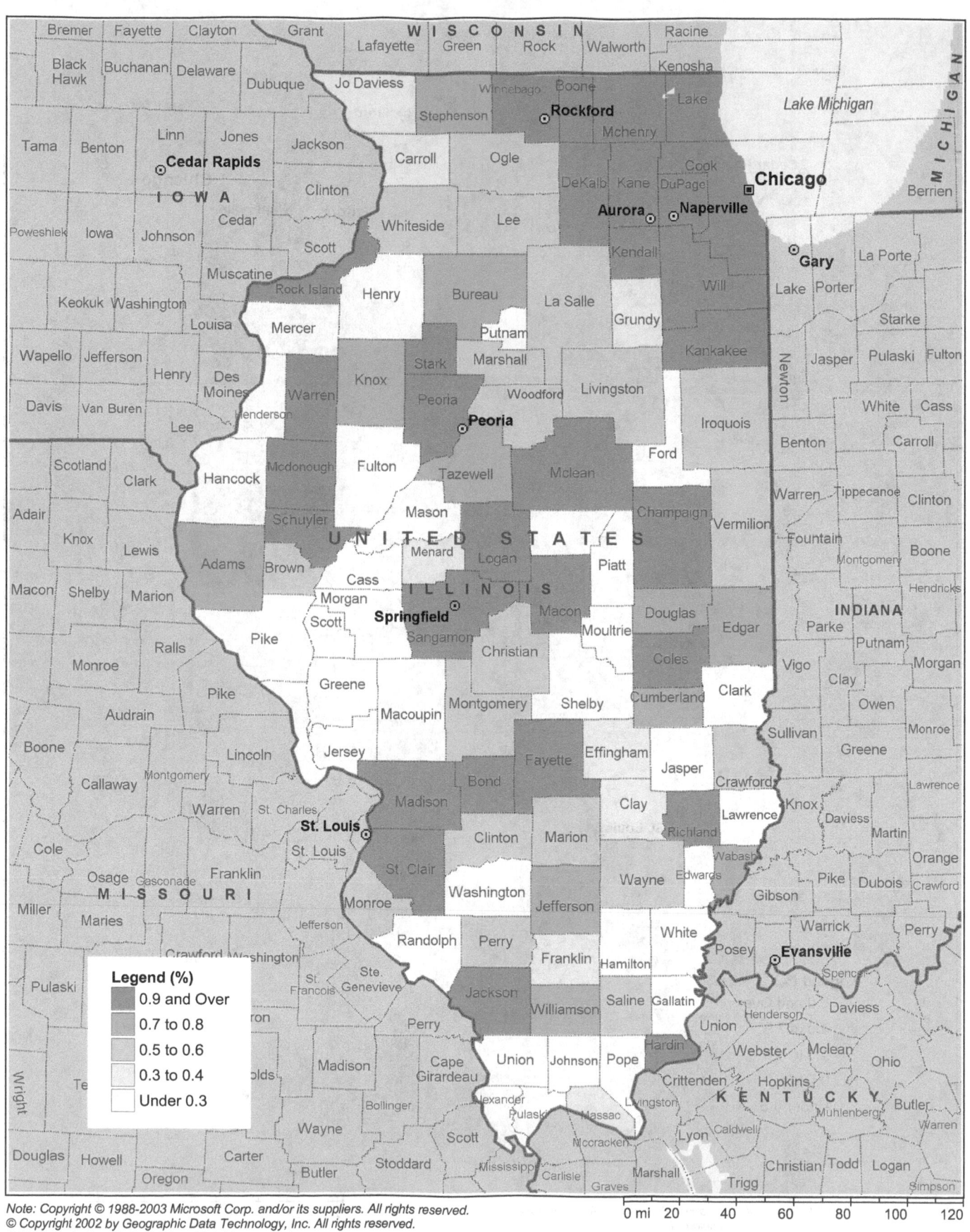

Legend (%)
- 0.9 and Over
- 0.7 to 0.8
- 0.5 to 0.6
- 0.3 to 0.4
- Under 0.3

0 mi   20   40   60   80   100   120

Percent Hispanic

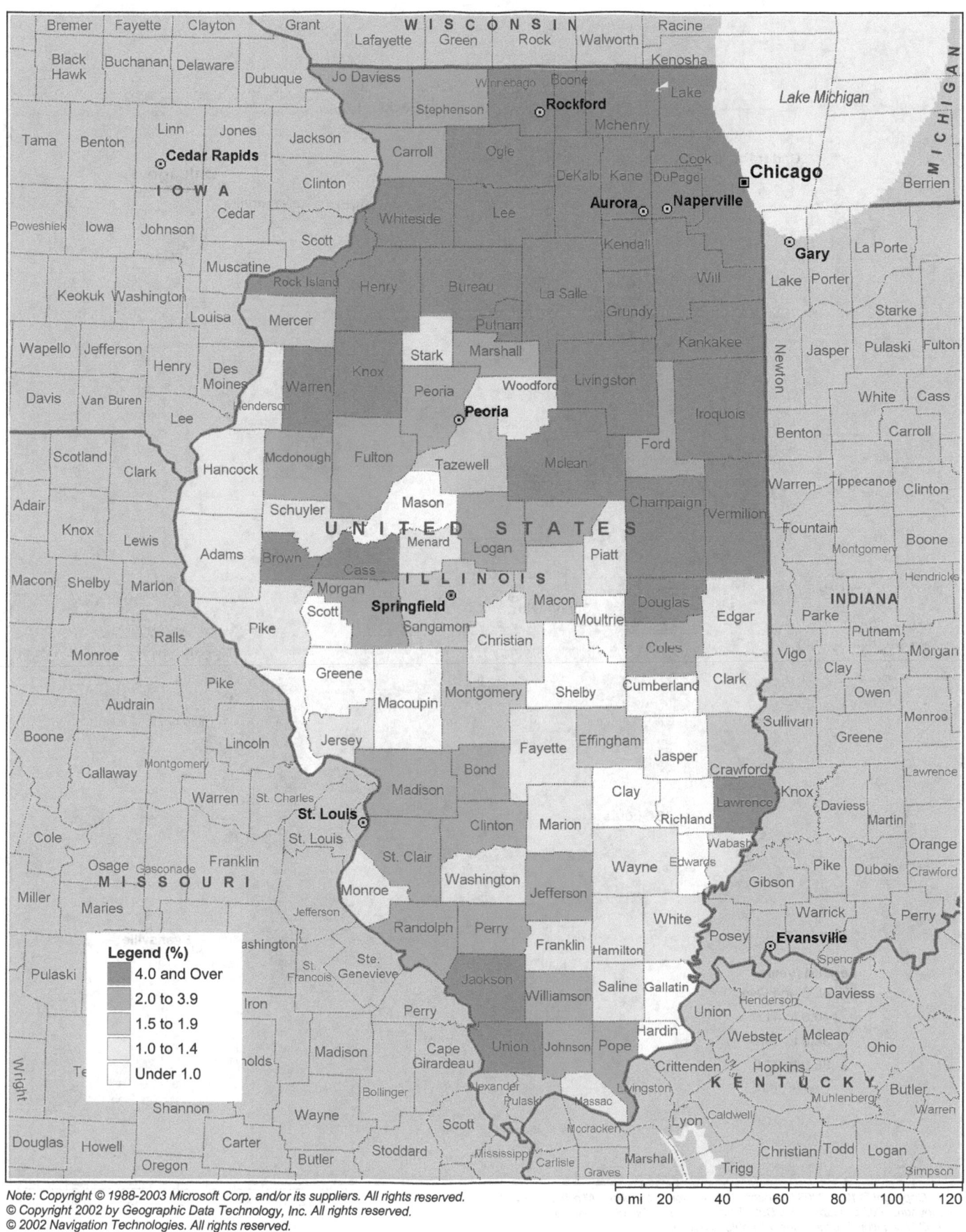

Legend (%)
- 4.0 and Over
- 2.0 to 3.9
- 1.5 to 1.9
- 1.0 to 1.4
- Under 1.0

0 mi   20   40   60   80   100   120

Median Age

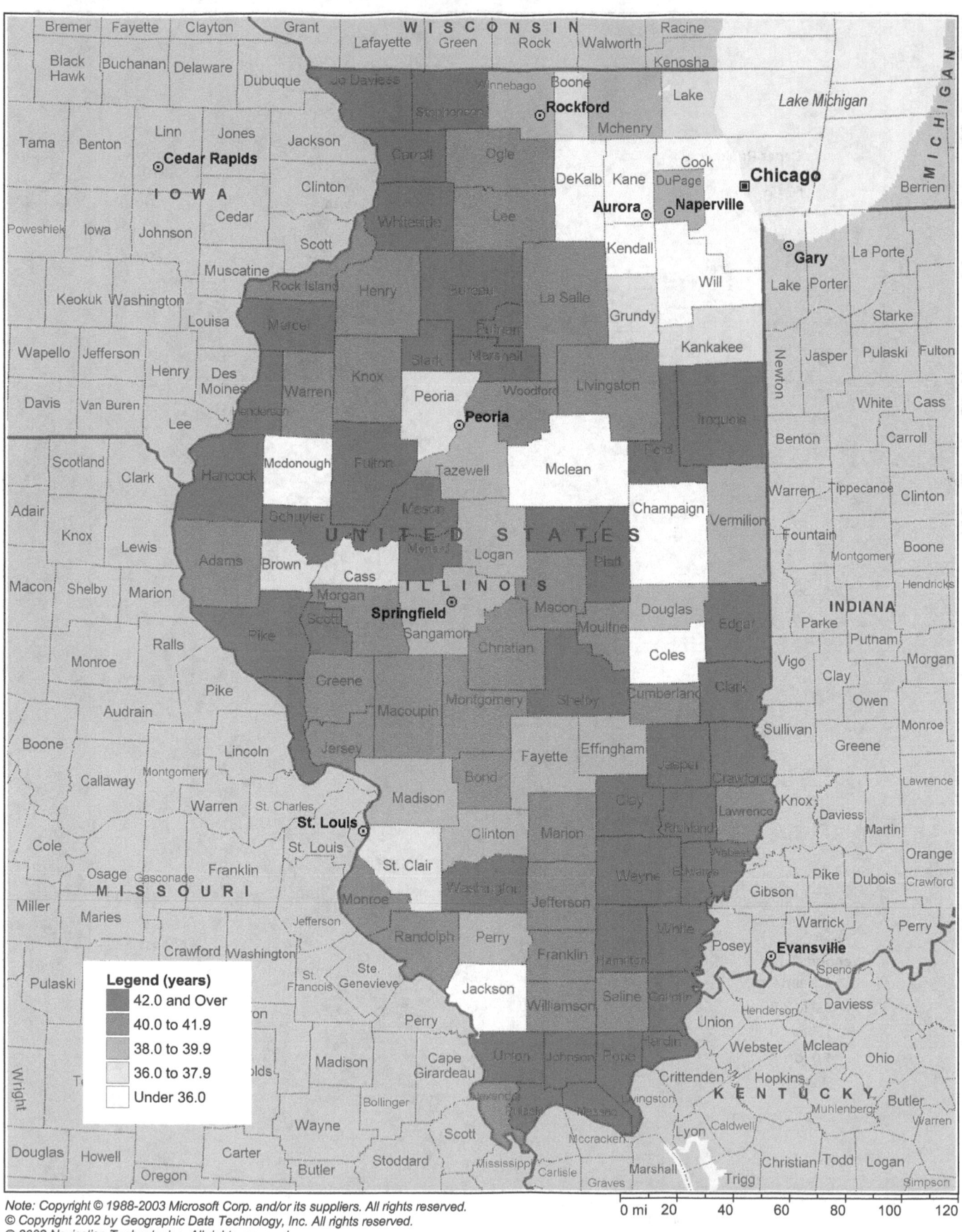

Legend (years)
- 42.0 and Over
- 40.0 to 41.9
- 38.0 to 39.9
- 36.0 to 37.9
- Under 36.0

0 mi   20   40   60   80   100   120

Median Household Income

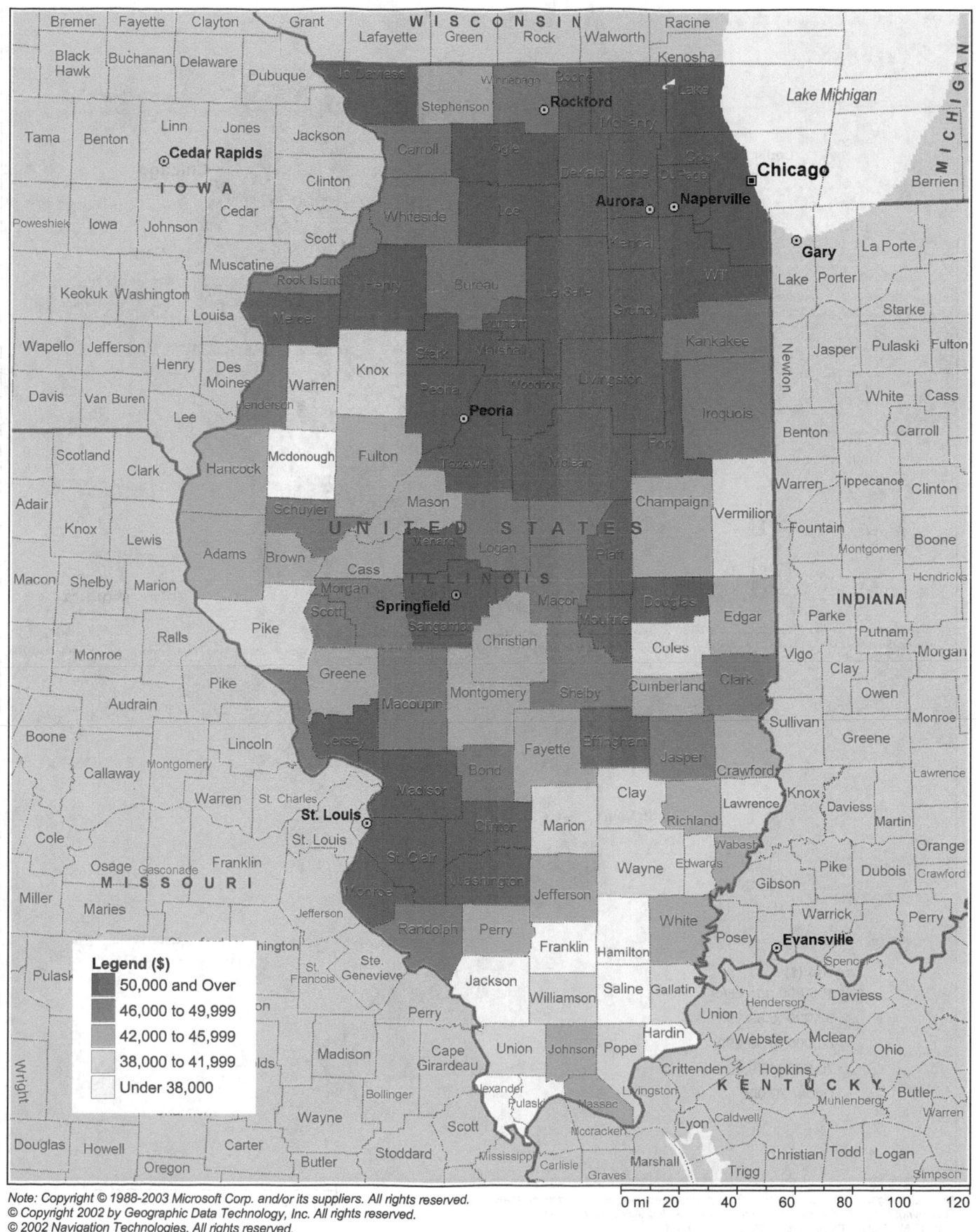

Legend ($)
- 50,000 and Over
- 46,000 to 49,999
- 42,000 to 45,999
- 38,000 to 41,999
- Under 38,000

0 mi   20   40   60   80   100   120

Median Home Value

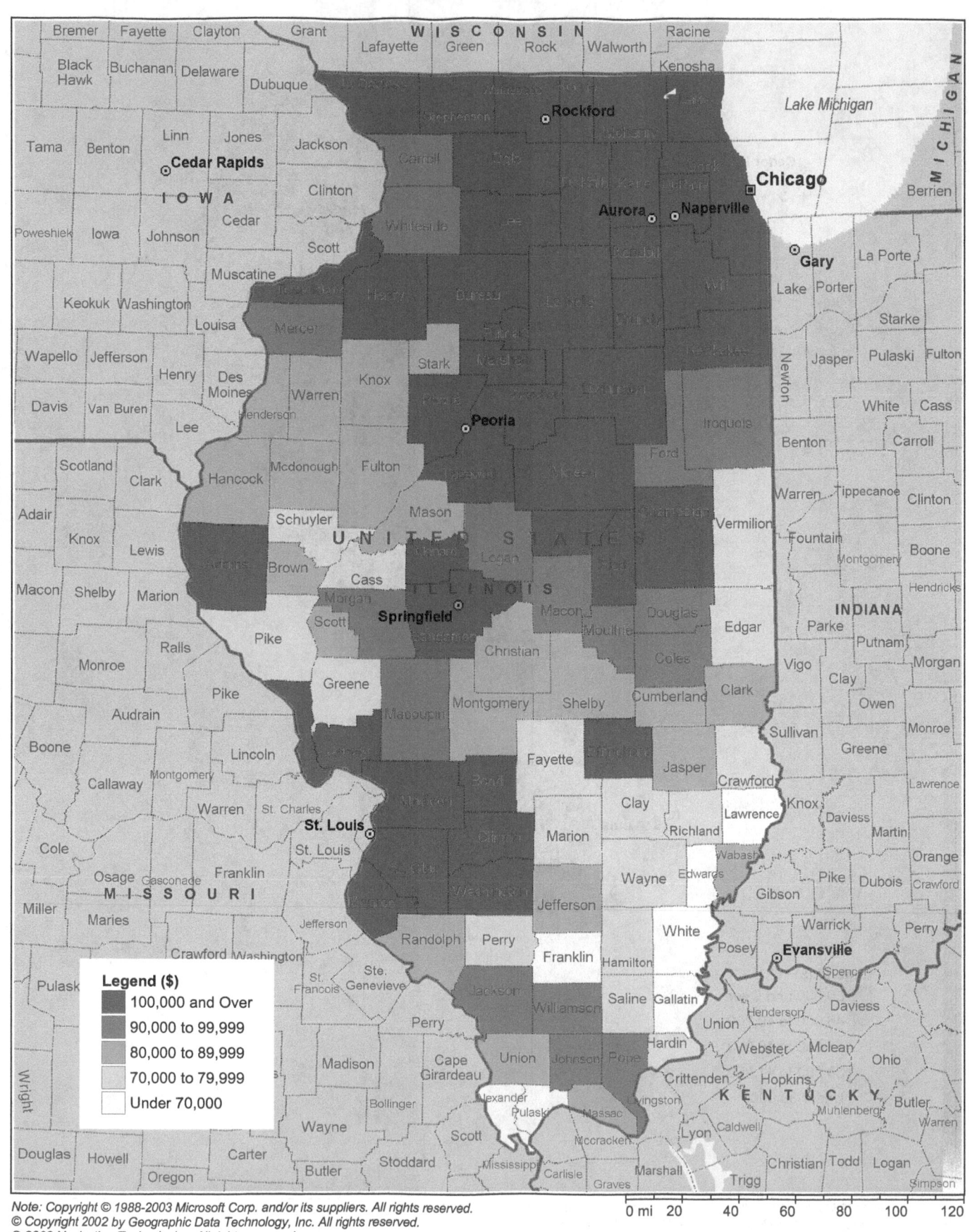

Legend ($)

- 100,000 and Over
- 90,000 to 99,999
- 80,000 to 89,999
- 70,000 to 79,999
- Under 70,000

0 mi   20   40   60   80   100   120

High School Graduates*

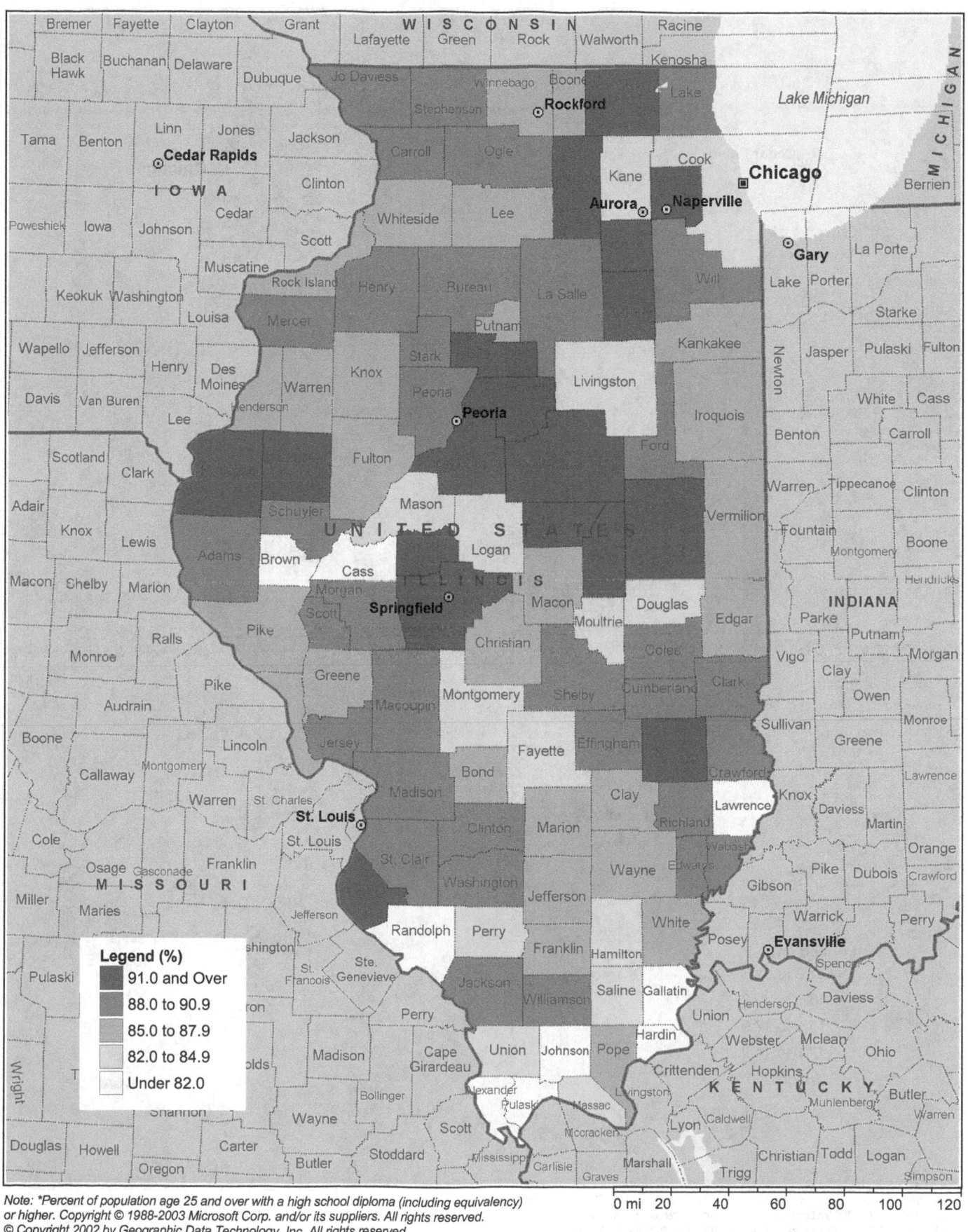

Legend (%)
- 91.0 and Over
- 88.0 to 90.9
- 85.0 to 87.9
- 82.0 to 84.9
- Under 82.0

Note: *Percent of population age 25 and over with a high school diploma (including equivalency) or higher. Copyright © 1988-2003 Microsoft Corp. and/or its suppliers. All rights reserved.
© Copyright 2002 by Geographic Data Technology, Inc. All rights reserved.
© 2002 Navigation Technologies. All rights reserved.

0 mi   20   40   60   80   100   120

College Graduates*

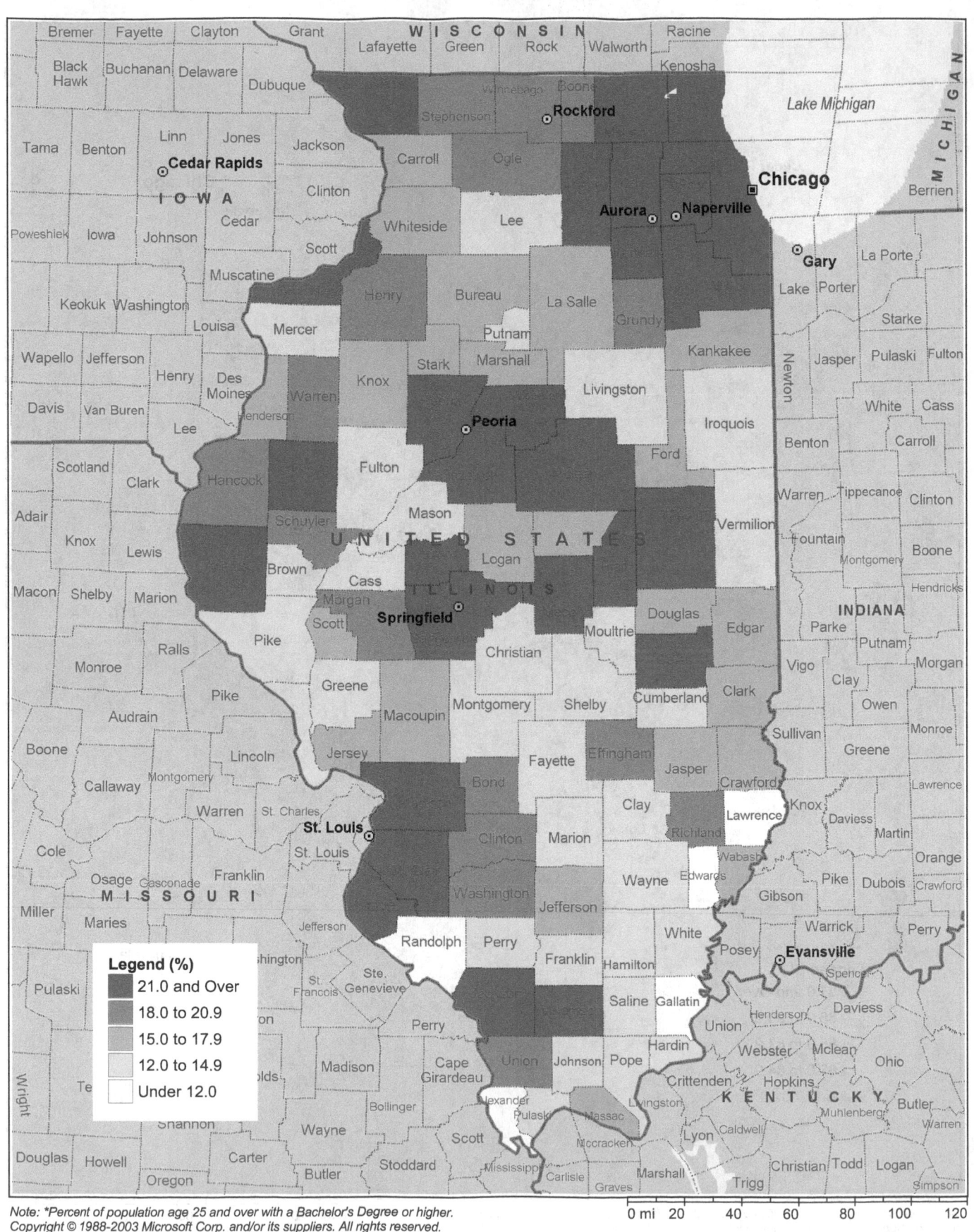

Legend (%)

- 21.0 and Over
- 18.0 to 20.9
- 15.0 to 17.9
- 12.0 to 14.9
- Under 12.0

Note: *Percent of population age 25 and over with a Bachelor's Degree or higher.
Copyright © 1988-2003 Microsoft Corp. and/or its suppliers. All rights reserved.
© Copyright 2002 by Geographic Data Technology, Inc. All rights reserved.
© 2002 Navigation Technologies. All rights reserved.

0 mi   20   40   60   80   100   120

Adams County

Located in western Illinois; bounded on the west by the Mississippi River and the Missouri border. Covers a land area of 855.202 square miles, a water area of 16.136 square miles, and is located in the Central Time Zone at 39.99° N. Lat., 91.19° W. Long. The county was founded in 1825. County seat is Quincy.

Adams County is part of the Quincy, IL-MO Micropolitan Statistical Area. The entire metro area includes: Adams County, IL; Lewis County, MO

Weather Station: Golden   Elevation: 725 feet

	Jan	Feb	Mar	Apr	May	Jun	Jul	Aug	Sep	Oct	Nov	Dec
High	34	38	51	63	74	83	87	85	78	66	50	37
Low	17	20	31	41	52	62	65	63	54	43	32	21
Precip	1.5	1.8	2.5	3.5	5.0	4.5	4.2	4.0	3.1	3.1	3.0	2.1
Snow	5.1	4.2	1.4	0.5	0.0	0.0	0.0	0.0	0.0	tr	0.7	3.8

High and Low temperatures in degrees Fahrenheit; Precipitation and Snow in inches

Weather Station: Quincy Dam 21   Elevation: 482 feet

	Jan	Feb	Mar	Apr	May	Jun	Jul	Aug	Sep	Oct	Nov	Dec
High	35	40	51	64	73	83	87	86	79	66	53	39
Low	18	22	31	42	53	62	67	65	56	44	34	22
Precip	1.4	1.9	2.6	3.6	4.5	3.7	4.0	3.3	2.9	2.7	2.8	2.2
Snow	na	na	1.3	0.3	0.0	0.0	0.0	0.0	0.0	0.0	0.1	2.2

High and Low temperatures in degrees Fahrenheit; Precipitation and Snow in inches

Weather Station: Quincy Muni Baldwin Fld   Elevation: 763 feet

	Jan	Feb	Mar	Apr	May	Jun	Jul	Aug	Sep	Oct	Nov	Dec
High	35	39	51	63	73	82	86	85	77	65	51	38
Low	19	23	32	43	53	62	66	64	56	44	34	22
Precip	1.5	1.9	2.6	3.5	4.6	3.8	3.8	3.7	3.3	3.1	3.0	2.3
Snow	na	na	na	na	na	tr	tr	na	na	na	na	na

High and Low temperatures in degrees Fahrenheit; Precipitation and Snow in inches

Population: 66,090 (1990); 68,277 (2000); 67,103 (2010); Race: 93.5% White, 3.6% Black/African American, 0.8% Asian, 0.1% American Indian/Alaska Native, 0.0% Native Hawaiian/Other Pacific Islander, 2.0% Some other race, 1.4% Two or more races, 1.2% Hispanic of any race (2008-2012 5-year est.); Density: 78.6 persons per square mile (2008-2012 5-year est.); Average household size: 2.44 (2008-2012 5-year est.); Median age: 40.4 (2008-2012 5-year est.); Males per 100 females: 94.4 (2008-2012 5-year est.).

Religion: Six largest groups: 22.6% Catholicism, 16.0% Non-denominational Protestant, 11.9% Baptist, 7.3% Lutheran, 6.3% Pentecostal, 5.0% Methodist/Pietist (2010)

Economy: Unemployment rate: 4.6% (April 2014); Total civilian labor force: 36,403 (April 2014); Leading industries: 17.7% health care and social assistance; 16.4% retail trade; 16.4% manufacturing (2012); Farms: 1,298 totaling 388,747 acres (2012); Companies that employ 500 or more persons: 5 (2012); Companies that employ 100 to 499 persons: 47 (2012); Companies that employ less than 100 persons: 1,791 (2012); Black-owned businesses: n/a (2007); Hispanic-owned businesses: n/a (2007); Asian-owned businesses: 84 (2007); Women-owned businesses: 1,367 (2007); Single-family building permits issued: 44 (2013); Multi-family building permits issued: 0 (2013).

Income: Per capita income: $24,631 (2008-2012 5-year est.); Median household income: $45,691 (2008-2012 5-year est.); Average household income: $59,960 (2008-2012 5-year est.); Percent of households with income of $100,000 or more: 14.2% (2008-2012 5-year est.); Poverty rate: 13.6% (2008-2012 5-year est.); Bankruptcy rate: 2.08% (2013).

Taxes: Total county taxes per capita: $112 (2011); County property taxes per capita: $111 (2011).

Education: Percent of population age 25 and over with: High school diploma (including GED) or higher: 90.1% (2008-2012 5-year est.); Bachelor's degree or higher: 21.0% (2008-2012 5-year est.); Master's degree or higher: 6.6% (2008-2012 5-year est.).

Housing: Homeownership rate: 74.3% (2008-2012 5-year est.); Median home value: $102,500 (2008-2012 5-year est.); Median contract rent: $420 per month (2008-2012 5-year est.); Median year structure built: 1961 (2008-2012 5-year est.)

Health: Birth rate: 121.4 per 10,000 population (2013); Death rate: 116.3 per 10,000 population (2013); Age-adjusted cancer mortality rate: 178.5 deaths per 100,000 population (2011); Number of physicians: 29.3 per 10,000 population (2011); Hospital beds: 50.7 per 10,000 population (2010); Hospital admissions: 2,083.2 per 10,000 population (2010).

Environment: Air Quality Index: 97.4% good, 2.6% moderate, 0.0% unhealthy for sensitive individuals, 0.0% unhealthy (percent of days in 2013)

Elections: 2012 Presidential election results: 31.5% Obama, 66.7% Romney

National and State Parks: Sid Simpson State Park; Siloam Springs State Park

Additional Information Contacts

Adams County Government . . . . (217) 277-2150
http://www.co.adams.il.us

Adams County Communities

CAMP POINT (village). Covers a land area of 1.139 square miles and a water area of 0 square miles. Located at 40.04° N. Lat; 91.07° W. Long. Elevation is 722 feet.

History: Camp Point was settled about 1870 by people of German ancestry.

Population: 1,230 (1990); 1,244 (2000); 1,132 (2010); Density: 1,246.8 persons per square mile (2008-2012 5-year est.); Race: 97.5% White, 0.5% Black/African American, 0.0% Asian, 0.0% American Indian/Alaska Native, 0.0% Native Hawaiian/Other Pacific Islander, 2.0% Some other race, 2.0% Two or more races, 0.8% Hispanic of any race (2008-2012 5-year est.); Average household size: 2.54 (2008-2012 5-year est.); Median age: 38.5 (2008-2012 5-year est.); Males per 100 females: 95.6 (2008-2012 5-year est.); Marriage status: 22.5% never married, 58.5% now married, 8.3% widowed, 10.7% divorced (2008-2012 5-year est.); Foreign born: 1.8% (2008-2012 5-year est.); Ancestry (includes multiple ancestries): 42.1% German, 10.8% Irish, 10.7% American, 7.2% English, 2.7% Scotch-Irish (2008-2012 5-year est.).

Economy: Single-family building permits issued: 1 (2013); Multi-family building permits issued: 0 (2013); Homeowner vacancy rate: 2.6%. Rental vacancy rate: 9.6%. (2008-2012 5-year est.); Employment by occupation: 4.3% management, business, and financial, 0.7% computer, engineering, and science, 10.2% education, legal, community service, arts, and media, 4.0% healthcare practitioners, 14.1% service, 29.3% sales and office, 16.4% natural resources, construction, and maintenance, 21.0% production, transportation, and material moving (2008-2012 5-year est.).

Income: Per capita income: $20,632 (2008-2012 5-year est.); Median household income: $42,467 (2008-2012 5-year est.); Average household income: $51,271 (2008-2012 5-year est.); Percent of households with income of $100,000 or more: 8.7% (2008-2012 5-year est.); Poverty rate: 13.4% (2008-2012 5-year est.).

Education: Percent of population age 25 and over with: High school diploma (including GED) or higher: 90.2% (2008-2012 5-year est.); Bachelor's degree or higher: 8.2% (2008-2012 5-year est.); Master's degree or higher: 1.8% (2008-2012 5-year est.).

School District(s)

Central CUSD 3 (PK-12)
    2011-12 Enrollment: 956 . . . . (217) 593-7116

Housing: Homeownership rate: 76.6% (2008-2012 5-year est.); Median home value: $92,200 (2008-2012 5-year est.); Median contract rent: $281 per month (2008-2012 5-year est.); Median year structure built: 1967 (2008-2012 5-year est.).

Health Insurance: 70.4% Private; 37.0% Public; 8.5% None. (2008-2012 5-year est.)

Transportation: Commute to work: 91.5% car, 0.0% public transportation, 3.1% walk, 3.9% work from home (2008-2012 5-year est.); Travel time to work: 30.0% less than 15 minutes, 27.5% 15 to 30 minutes, 36.6% 30 to 45 minutes, 4.8% 45 to 60 minutes, 1.1% 60 minutes or more (2008-2012 5-year est.)

CLAYTON (village). Covers a land area of 0.869 square miles and a water area of 0.002 square miles. Located at 40.03° N. Lat; 90.96° W. Long. Elevation is 732 feet.

Population: 726 (1990); 904 (2000); 709 (2010); Density: 738.9 persons per square mile (2008-2012 5-year est.); Race: 91.4% White, 8.6% Black/African American, 0.0% Asian, 0.0% American Indian/Alaska Native, 0.0% Native Hawaiian/Other Pacific Islander, 0.0% Some other race, 0.0% Two or more races, 0.6% Hispanic of any race (2008-2012 5-year est.); Average household size: 2.29 (2008-2012 5-year est.); Median age: 40.6 (2008-2012 5-year est.); Males per 100 females: 148.8 (2008-2012 5-year est.); Marriage status: 26.7% never married, 52.4% now married, 6.7% widowed, 14.2% divorced (2008-2012 5-year est.); Foreign born: 0.0% (2008-2012 5-year est.); Ancestry (includes multiple ancestries): 29.0%

German, 14.6% Irish, 14.3% American, 7.9% Swedish, 7.2% English (2008-2012 5-year est.).

Economy: Single-family building permits issued: 0 (2013); Multi-family building permits issued: 0 (2013); Homeowner vacancy rate: 3.2%. Rental vacancy rate: 24.2%. (2008-2012 5-year est.); Employment by occupation: 10.8% management, business, and financial, 1.7% computer, engineering, and science, 4.8% education, legal, community service, arts, and media, 5.2% healthcare practitioners, 23.8% service, 18.2% sales and office, 13.9% natural resources, construction, and maintenance, 21.6% production, transportation, and material moving (2008-2012 5-year est.).

Income: Per capita income: $17,579 (2008-2012 5-year est.); Median household income: $31,771 (2008-2012 5-year est.); Average household income: $40,585 (2008-2012 5-year est.); Percent of households with income of $100,000 or more: 5.2% (2008-2012 5-year est.); Poverty rate: 16.0% (2008-2012 5-year est.).

Education: Percent of population age 25 and over with: High school diploma (including GED) or higher: 75.1% (2008-2012 5-year est.); Bachelor's degree or higher: 2.3% (2008-2012 5-year est.); Master's degree or higher: 0.0% (2008-2012 5-year est.).

Housing: Homeownership rate: 81.3% (2008-2012 5-year est.); Median home value: $54,800 (2008-2012 5-year est.); Median contract rent: $234 per month (2008-2012 5-year est.); Median year structure built: 1942 (2008-2012 5-year est.).

Health Insurance: 62.4% Private; 43.3% Public; 9.9% None. (2008-2012 5-year est.)

Safety: Violent crime rate: 0.0 per 10,000 population; Property crime rate: 28.2 per 10,000 population (2012).

Transportation: Commute to work: 93.1% car, 0.0% public transportation, 3.9% walk, 3.0% work from home (2008-2012 5-year est.); Travel time to work: 29.9% less than 15 minutes, 22.3% 15 to 30 minutes, 37.9% 30 to 45 minutes, 4.0% 45 to 60 minutes, 5.8% 60 minutes or more (2008-2012 5-year est.)

COATSBURG (village). Covers a land area of 0.123 square miles and a water area of 0 square miles. Located at 40.03° N. Lat; 91.16° W. Long. Elevation is 758 feet.

History: Coatsburg was surveyed by R.P. Coates in 1855, and developed as a shipping center for grain and livestock. Coatsburg was incorporated as a village in 1885.

Population: 201 (1990); 226 (2000); 147 (2010); Density: 1,173.9 persons per square mile (2008-2012 5-year est.); Race: 93.8% White, 0.0% Black/African American, 0.0% Asian, 0.0% American Indian/Alaska Native, 0.0% Native Hawaiian/Other Pacific Islander, 6.2% Some other race, 2.8% Two or more races, 6.3% Hispanic of any race (2008-2012 5-year est.); Average household size: 2.82 (2008-2012 5-year est.); Median age: 29.7 (2008-2012 5-year est.); Males per 100 females: 100.0 (2008-2012 5-year est.); Marriage status: 28.9% never married, 47.4% now married, 1.8% widowed, 21.9% divorced (2008-2012 5-year est.); Foreign born: 0.0% (2008-2012 5-year est.); Ancestry (includes multiple ancestries): 37.5% German, 20.8% Irish, 6.9% American, 4.9% English, 2.8% Italian (2008-2012 5-year est.).

Economy: Homeowner vacancy rate: 0.0%. Rental vacancy rate: 0.0%. (2008-2012 5-year est.); Employment by occupation: 4.1% management, business, and financial, 0.0% computer, engineering, and science, 4.1% education, legal, community service, arts, and media, 2.7% healthcare practitioners, 19.2% service, 19.2% sales and office, 20.5% natural resources, construction, and maintenance, 30.1% production, transportation, and material moving (2008-2012 5-year est.).

Income: Per capita income: $19,609 (2008-2012 5-year est.); Median household income: $41,250 (2008-2012 5-year est.); Average household income: $52,265 (2008-2012 5-year est.); Percent of households with income of $100,000 or more: 11.8% (2008-2012 5-year est.); Poverty rate: 9.0% (2008-2012 5-year est.).

Education: Percent of population age 25 and over with: High school diploma (including GED) or higher: 84.9% (2008-2012 5-year est.); Bachelor's degree or higher: 6.5% (2008-2012 5-year est.); Master's degree or higher: 6.5% (2008-2012 5-year est.).

Housing: Homeownership rate: 82.4% (2008-2012 5-year est.); Median home value: $62,200 (2008-2012 5-year est.); Median contract rent: $394 per month (2008-2012 5-year est.); Median year structure built: 1948 (2008-2012 5-year est.).

Health Insurance: 48.6% Private; 34.0% Public; 25.7% None. (2008-2012 5-year est.)

Transportation: Commute to work: 100.0% car, 0.0% public transportation, 0.0% walk, 0.0% work from home (2008-2012 5-year est.);

Travel time to work: 21.9% less than 15 minutes, 50.7% 15 to 30 minutes, 23.3% 30 to 45 minutes, 4.1% 45 to 60 minutes, 0.0% 60 minutes or more (2008-2012 5-year est.)

COLUMBUS (village). Covers a land area of 0.252 square miles and a water area of 0 square miles. Located at 39.99° N. Lat; 91.15° W. Long. Elevation is 722 feet.

History: Vigorously competed with Quincy for seat of Adams county in 19th century.

Population: 88 (1990); 112 (2000); 99 (2010); Density: 428.5 persons per square mile (2008-2012 5-year est.); Race: 80.6% White, 19.4% Black/African American, 0.0% Asian, 0.0% American Indian/Alaska Native, 0.0% Native Hawaiian/Other Pacific Islander, 0.0% Some other race, 0.0% Two or more races, 0.0% Hispanic of any race (2008-2012 5-year est.); Average household size: 2.84 (2008-2012 5-year est.); Median age: 29.6 (2008-2012 5-year est.); Males per 100 females: 86.2 (2008-2012 5-year est.); Marriage status: 31.6% never married, 44.3% now married, 13.9% widowed, 10.1% divorced (2008-2012 5-year est.); Foreign born: 0.0% (2008-2012 5-year est.); Ancestry (includes multiple ancestries): 15.7% German, 6.5% Irish, 6.5% Scottish, 6.5% American, 3.7% Scotch-Irish (2008-2012 5-year est.).

Economy: Homeowner vacancy rate: 16.3%. Rental vacancy rate: 60.0%. (2008-2012 5-year est.); Employment by occupation: 0.0% management, business, and financial, 0.0% computer, engineering, and science, 5.0% education, legal, community service, arts, and media, 10.0% healthcare practitioners, 22.5% service, 22.5% sales and office, 7.5% natural resources, construction, and maintenance, 32.5% production, transportation, and material moving (2008-2012 5-year est.).

Income: Per capita income: $15,931 (2008-2012 5-year est.); Median household income: $40,000 (2008-2012 5-year est.); Average household income: $42,668 (2008-2012 5-year est.); Percent of households with income of $100,000 or more: 5.3% (2008-2012 5-year est.); Poverty rate: 9.3% (2008-2012 5-year est.).

Education: Percent of population age 25 and over with: High school diploma (including GED) or higher: 86.7% (2008-2012 5-year est.); Bachelor's degree or higher: 1.3% (2008-2012 5-year est.); Master's degree or higher: 1.3% (2008-2012 5-year est.).

Housing: Homeownership rate: 94.7% (2008-2012 5-year est.); Median home value: $75,000 (2008-2012 5-year est.); Median contract rent: n/a per month (2008-2012 5-year est.); Median year structure built: 1950 (2008-2012 5-year est.).

Health Insurance: 39.8% Private; 61.1% Public; 15.7% None. (2008-2012 5-year est.)

Transportation: Commute to work: 100.0% car, 0.0% public transportation, 0.0% walk, 0.0% work from home (2008-2012 5-year est.); Travel time to work: 5.3% less than 15 minutes, 57.9% 15 to 30 minutes, 28.9% 30 to 45 minutes, 2.6% 45 to 60 minutes, 5.3% 60 minutes or more (2008-2012 5-year est.)

FOWLER (unincorporated postal area)
Zip Code: 62338
Covers a land area of 36.664 square miles and a water area of 0.079 square miles. Located at 39.98° N. Lat; 91.23° W. Long. Elevation is 732 feet. Population: 1,473 (2010); Density: 40.2 persons per square mile (2010); Race: 98.0% White, 0.8% Black/African American, 0.1% Asian, 0.1% American Indian/Alaska Native, 0.0% Native Hawaiian/Other Pacific Islander, 1.0% Some other race, 0.9% Two or more races, 0.5% Hispanic of any race (2010); Average household size: 2.61 (2010); Median age: 41.9 (2010); Males per 100 females: 99.6 (2010); Homeownership rate: 91.7% (2010)

GOLDEN (village). Covers a land area of 0.627 square miles and a water area of 0 square miles. Located at 40.11° N. Lat; 91.02° W. Long. Elevation is 715 feet.

Population: 565 (1990); 629 (2000); 644 (2010); Density: 1,059.0 persons per square mile (2008-2012 5-year est.); Race: 100.0% White, 0.0% Black/African American, 0.0% Asian, 0.0% American Indian/Alaska Native, 0.0% Native Hawaiian/Other Pacific Islander, 0.0% Some other race, 0.0% Two or more races, 0.0% Hispanic of any race (2008-2012 5-year est.); Average household size: 2.28 (2008-2012 5-year est.); Median age: 42.0 (2008-2012 5-year est.); Males per 100 females: 88.1 (2008-2012 5-year est.); Marriage status: 18.4% never married, 59.3% now married, 11.7% widowed, 10.6% divorced (2008-2012 5-year est.); Foreign born: 0.0% (2008-2012 5-year est.); Ancestry (includes multiple ancestries): 46.2%

German, 9.0% Irish, 9.0% English, 8.9% American, 2.6% Dutch (2008-2012 5-year est.).

Economy: Homeowner vacancy rate: 0.0%. Rental vacancy rate: 0.0%. (2008-2012 5-year est.); Employment by occupation: 13.4% management, business, and financial, 2.3% computer, engineering, and science, 7.0% education, legal, community service, arts, and media, 3.0% healthcare practitioners, 16.1% service, 22.1% sales and office, 12.1% natural resources, construction, and maintenance, 23.8% production, transportation, and material moving (2008-2012 5-year est.).

Income: Per capita income: $22,299 (2008-2012 5-year est.); Median household income: $41,250 (2008-2012 5-year est.); Average household income: $48,552 (2008-2012 5-year est.); Percent of households with income of $100,000 or more: 7.9% (2008-2012 5-year est.); Poverty rate: 7.3% (2008-2012 5-year est.).

Education: Percent of population age 25 and over with: High school diploma (including GED) or higher: 89.9% (2008-2012 5-year est.); Bachelor's degree or higher: 15.9% (2008-2012 5-year est.); Master's degree or higher: 4.8% (2008-2012 5-year est.).

Housing: Homeownership rate: 78.6% (2008-2012 5-year est.); Median home value: $74,700 (2008-2012 5-year est.); Median contract rent: $379 per month (2008-2012 5-year est.); Median year structure built: 1951 (2008-2012 5-year est.).

Health Insurance: 66.2% Private; 39.2% Public; 10.7% None. (2008-2012 5-year est.)

Transportation: Commute to work: 90.5% car, 0.0% public transportation, 3.1% walk, 4.1% work from home (2008-2012 5-year est.); Travel time to work: 30.9% less than 15 minutes, 13.5% 15 to 30 minutes, 39.0% 30 to 45 minutes, 13.8% 45 to 60 minutes, 2.8% 60 minutes or more (2008-2012 5-year est.)

LA PRAIRIE (village). Covers a land area of 0.234 square miles and a water area of 0 square miles. Located at 40.15° N. Lat; 91.00° W. Long. Elevation is 709 feet.

Population: 68 (1990); 60 (2000); 47 (2010); Density: 218.1 persons per square mile (2008-2012 5-year est.); Race: 68.6% White, 0.0% Black/African American, 0.0% Asian, 0.0% American Indian/Alaska Native, 0.0% Native Hawaiian/Other Pacific Islander, 31.4% Some other race, 31.4% Two or more races, 0.0% Hispanic of any race (2008-2012 5-year est.); Average household size: 2.68 (2008-2012 5-year est.); Median age: 24.4 (2008-2012 5-year est.); Males per 100 females: 104.0 (2008-2012 5-year est.); Marriage status: 32.5% never married, 50.0% now married, 5.0% widowed, 12.5% divorced (2008-2012 5-year est.); Foreign born: 0.0% (2008-2012 5-year est.); Ancestry (includes multiple ancestries): 47.1% German, 5.9% Scotch-Irish (2008-2012 5-year est.).

Economy: Homeowner vacancy rate: 0.0%. Rental vacancy rate: 0.0%. (2008-2012 5-year est.); Employment by occupation: 0.0% management, business, and financial, 0.0% computer, engineering, and science, 0.0% education, legal, community service, arts, and media, 0.0% healthcare practitioners, 3.7% service, 48.1% sales and office, 0.0% natural resources, construction, and maintenance, 48.1% production, transportation, and material moving (2008-2012 5-year est.).

Income: Per capita income: $12,237 (2008-2012 5-year est.); Median household income: $37,750 (2008-2012 5-year est.); Average household income: $32,847 (2008-2012 5-year est.); Percent of households with income of $100,000 or more: n/a (2008-2012 5-year est.); Poverty rate: 35.3% (2008-2012 5-year est.).

Education: Percent of population age 25 and over with: High school diploma (including GED) or higher: 60.9% (2008-2012 5-year est.); Bachelor's degree or higher: 13.0% (2008-2012 5-year est.); Master's degree or higher: 13.0% (2008-2012 5-year est.).

Housing: Homeownership rate: 78.9% (2008-2012 5-year est.); Median home value: $37,500 (2008-2012 5-year est.); Median contract rent: n/a per month (2008-2012 5-year est.); Median year structure built: Before 1940 (2008-2012 5-year est.).

Health Insurance: 29.4% Private; 74.5% Public; 0.0% None. (2008-2012 5-year est.)

Transportation: Commute to work: 100.0% car, 0.0% public transportation, 0.0% walk, 0.0% work from home (2008-2012 5-year est.); Travel time to work: 3.7% less than 15 minutes, 33.3% 15 to 30 minutes, 18.5% 30 to 45 minutes, 44.4% 45 to 60 minutes, 0.0% 60 minutes or more (2008-2012 5-year est.)

LIBERTY (village). Covers a land area of 0.379 square miles and a water area of 0 square miles. Located at 39.88° N. Lat; 91.11° W. Long. Elevation is 751 feet.

Population: 541 (1990); 519 (2000); 516 (2010); Density: 1,383.8 persons per square mile (2008-2012 5-year est.); Race: 99.6% White, 0.4% Black/African American, 0.0% Asian, 0.0% American Indian/Alaska Native, 0.0% Native Hawaiian/Other Pacific Islander, 0.0% Some other race, 0.0% Two or more races, 0.0% Hispanic of any race (2008-2012 5-year est.); Average household size: 2.63 (2008-2012 5-year est.); Median age: 36.1 (2008-2012 5-year est.); Males per 100 females: 75.8 (2008-2012 5-year est.); Marriage status: 12.2% never married, 65.0% now married, 10.0% widowed, 12.7% divorced (2008-2012 5-year est.); Foreign born: 0.0% (2008-2012 5-year est.); Ancestry (includes multiple ancestries): 63.0% German, 16.8% English, 4.8% Irish, 3.8% Czech, 3.1% Finnish (2008-2012 5-year est.).

Economy: Homeowner vacancy rate: 1.6%. Rental vacancy rate: 0.0%. (2008-2012 5-year est.); Employment by occupation: 7.7% management, business, and financial, 0.0% computer, engineering, and science, 15.4% education, legal, community service, arts, and media, 5.1% healthcare practitioners, 21.8% service, 24.8% sales and office, 1.3% natural resources, construction, and maintenance, 23.9% production, transportation, and material moving (2008-2012 5-year est.).

Income: Per capita income: $21,364 (2008-2012 5-year est.); Median household income: $48,375 (2008-2012 5-year est.); Average household income: $54,849 (2008-2012 5-year est.); Percent of households with income of $100,000 or more: 19.1% (2008-2012 5-year est.); Poverty rate: 10.3% (2008-2012 5-year est.).

Education: Percent of population age 25 and over with: High school diploma (including GED) or higher: 92.4% (2008-2012 5-year est.); Bachelor's degree or higher: 21.1% (2008-2012 5-year est.); Master's degree or higher: 5.4% (2008-2012 5-year est.).

School District(s)

Liberty CUSD 2 (PK-12)
    2011-12 Enrollment: 661 . . . . (217) 645-3433

Housing: Homeownership rate: 90.5% (2008-2012 5-year est.); Median home value: $87,400 (2008-2012 5-year est.); Median contract rent: $266 per month (2008-2012 5-year est.); Median year structure built: 1971 (2008-2012 5-year est.).

Health Insurance: 78.1% Private; 39.1% Public; 2.1% None. (2008-2012 5-year est.)

Transportation: Commute to work: 91.0% car, 0.0% public transportation, 2.1% walk, 6.8% work from home (2008-2012 5-year est.); Travel time to work: 13.3% less than 15 minutes, 33.0% 15 to 30 minutes, 42.2% 30 to 45 minutes, 11.5% 45 to 60 minutes, 0.0% 60 minutes or more (2008-2012 5-year est.)

LIMA (village). Covers a land area of 0.192 square miles and a water area of 0 square miles. Located at 40.18° N. Lat; 91.38° W. Long. Elevation is 653 feet.

Population: 120 (1990); 159 (2000); 163 (2010); Density: 1,041.9 persons per square mile (2008-2012 5-year est.); Race: 100.0% White, 0.0% Black/African American, 0.0% Asian, 0.0% American Indian/Alaska Native, 0.0% Native Hawaiian/Other Pacific Islander, 0.0% Some other race, 0.0% Two or more races, 5.5% Hispanic of any race (2008-2012 5-year est.); Average household size: 2.63 (2008-2012 5-year est.); Median age: 33.7 (2008-2012 5-year est.); Males per 100 females: 51.5 (2008-2012 5-year est.); Marriage status: 16.0% never married, 60.4% now married, 4.9% widowed, 18.8% divorced (2008-2012 5-year est.); Foreign born: 0.0% (2008-2012 5-year est.); Ancestry (includes multiple ancestries): 37.0% German, 17.5% Dutch, 15.5% Italian, 12.5% Irish, 6.0% English (2008-2012 5-year est.).

Economy: Homeowner vacancy rate: 4.3%. Rental vacancy rate: 0.0%. (2008-2012 5-year est.); Employment by occupation: 20.0% management, business, and financial, 2.9% computer, engineering, and science, 0.0% education, legal, community service, arts, and media, 11.4% healthcare practitioners, 30.5% service, 18.1% sales and office, 0.0% natural resources, construction, and maintenance, 17.1% production, transportation, and material moving (2008-2012 5-year est.).

Income: Per capita income: $16,323 (2008-2012 5-year est.); Median household income: $31,250 (2008-2012 5-year est.); Average household income: $40,511 (2008-2012 5-year est.); Percent of households with income of $100,000 or more: 5.3% (2008-2012 5-year est.); Poverty rate: 18.0% (2008-2012 5-year est.).

Education: Percent of population age 25 and over with: High school diploma (including GED) or higher: 96.7% (2008-2012 5-year est.);

Bachelor's degree or higher: 6.6% (2008-2012 5-year est.); Master's degree or higher: 0.0% (2008-2012 5-year est.).
Housing: Homeownership rate: 86.8% (2008-2012 5-year est.); Median home value: $56,000 (2008-2012 5-year est.); Median contract rent: $292 per month (2008-2012 5-year est.); Median year structure built: 1953 (2008-2012 5-year est.).
Health Insurance: 56.0% Private; 28.0% Public; 24.0% None. (2008-2012 5-year est.)
Transportation: Commute to work: 97.1% car, 0.0% public transportation, 0.0% walk, 0.0% work from home (2008-2012 5-year est.); Travel time to work: 6.7% less than 15 minutes, 47.6% 15 to 30 minutes, 40.0% 30 to 45 minutes, 5.7% 45 to 60 minutes, 0.0% 60 minutes or more (2008-2012 5-year est.)

LORAINE (village). Covers a land area of 0.853 square miles and a water area of 0 square miles. Located at 40.15° N. Lat; 91.22° W. Long. Elevation is 643 feet.

Population: 331 (1990); 363 (2000); 313 (2010); Density: 333.0 persons per square mile (2008-2012 5-year est.); Race: 98.9% White, 0.0% Black/African American, 0.0% Asian, 0.0% American Indian/Alaska Native, 0.0% Native Hawaiian/Other Pacific Islander, 1.1% Some other race, 0.0% Two or more races, 6.0% Hispanic of any race (2008-2012 5-year est.); Average household size: 2.43 (2008-2012 5-year est.); Median age: 44.7 (2008-2012 5-year est.); Males per 100 females: 98.6 (2008-2012 5-year est.); Marriage status: 14.3% never married, 57.1% now married, 11.2% widowed, 17.4% divorced (2008-2012 5-year est.); Foreign born: 0.0% (2008-2012 5-year est.); Ancestry (includes multiple ancestries): 26.1% German, 16.9% American, 13.7% Irish, 5.3% English, 4.2% Scotch-Irish (2008-2012 5-year est.).
Economy: Homeowner vacancy rate: 0.0%. Rental vacancy rate: 0.0%. (2008-2012 5-year est.); Employment by occupation: 1.6% management, business, and financial, 4.9% computer, engineering, and science, 10.7% education, legal, community service, arts, and media, 5.7% healthcare practitioners, 18.0% service, 18.9% sales and office, 9.8% natural resources, construction, and maintenance, 30.3% production, transportation, and material moving (2008-2012 5-year est.).
Income: Per capita income: $16,103 (2008-2012 5-year est.); Median household income: $35,375 (2008-2012 5-year est.); Average household income: $39,162 (2008-2012 5-year est.); Percent of households with income of $100,000 or more: n/a (2008-2012 5-year est.); Poverty rate: 13.4% (2008-2012 5-year est.).
Education: Percent of population age 25 and over with: High school diploma (including GED) or higher: 87.1% (2008-2012 5-year est.); Bachelor's degree or higher: 8.4% (2008-2012 5-year est.); Master's degree or higher: 2.5% (2008-2012 5-year est.).
Housing: Homeownership rate: 83.8% (2008-2012 5-year est.); Median home value: $69,400 (2008-2012 5-year est.); Median contract rent: $305 per month (2008-2012 5-year est.); Median year structure built: 1956 (2008-2012 5-year est.).
Health Insurance: 65.5% Private; 44.4% Public; 8.8% None. (2008-2012 5-year est.)
Transportation: Commute to work: 96.7% car, 0.0% public transportation, 0.0% walk, 1.6% work from home (2008-2012 5-year est.); Travel time to work: 4.2% less than 15 minutes, 55.0% 15 to 30 minutes, 35.0% 30 to 45 minutes, 3.3% 45 to 60 minutes, 2.5% 60 minutes or more (2008-2012 5-year est.)

MENDON (village). Covers a land area of 0.859 square miles and a water area of 0 square miles. Located at 40.09° N. Lat; 91.29° W. Long. Elevation is 761 feet.

Population: 854 (1990); 883 (2000); 953 (2010); Density: 1,013.9 persons per square mile (2008-2012 5-year est.); Race: 98.6% White, 0.7% Black/African American, 0.1% Asian, 0.0% American Indian/Alaska Native, 0.0% Native Hawaiian/Other Pacific Islander, 0.6% Some other race, 0.6% Two or more races, 0.0% Hispanic of any race (2008-2012 5-year est.); Average household size: 2.43 (2008-2012 5-year est.); Median age: 37.5 (2008-2012 5-year est.); Males per 100 females: 99.8 (2008-2012 5-year est.); Marriage status: 27.0% never married, 50.6% now married, 9.3% widowed, 13.2% divorced (2008-2012 5-year est.); Foreign born: 0.0% (2008-2012 5-year est.); Ancestry (includes multiple ancestries): 35.2% German, 17.8% Irish, 12.6% American, 5.1% English, 2.0% Swedish (2008-2012 5-year est.).
Economy: Single-family building permits issued: 2 (2013); Multi-family building permits issued: 0 (2013); Homeowner vacancy rate: 0.0%. Rental vacancy rate: 4.4%. (2008-2012 5-year est.); Employment by occupation:

5.3% management, business, and financial, 0.0% computer, engineering, and science, 7.7% education, legal, community service, arts, and media, 4.8% healthcare practitioners, 24.7% service, 22.3% sales and office, 10.1% natural resources, construction, and maintenance, 25.2% production, transportation, and material moving (2008-2012 5-year est.).
Income: Per capita income: $19,505 (2008-2012 5-year est.); Median household income: $41,528 (2008-2012 5-year est.); Average household income: $47,819 (2008-2012 5-year est.); Percent of households with income of $100,000 or more: 10.1% (2008-2012 5-year est.); Poverty rate: 14.7% (2008-2012 5-year est.).
Education: Percent of population age 25 and over with: High school diploma (including GED) or higher: 88.2% (2008-2012 5-year est.); Bachelor's degree or higher: 9.8% (2008-2012 5-year est.); Master's degree or higher: 3.1% (2008-2012 5-year est.).

School District(s)
CUSD 4 (KG-12)
    2011-12 Enrollment: 714 . . . . (217) 936-2111
Housing: Homeownership rate: 73.7% (2008-2012 5-year est.); Median home value: $83,000 (2008-2012 5-year est.); Median contract rent: $327 per month (2008-2012 5-year est.); Median year structure built: 1962 (2008-2012 5-year est.).
Health Insurance: 71.0% Private; 42.7% Public; 5.4% None. (2008-2012 5-year est.)
Transportation: Commute to work: 92.6% car, 1.7% public transportation, 4.2% walk, 1.5% work from home (2008-2012 5-year est.); Travel time to work: 19.5% less than 15 minutes, 60.4% 15 to 30 minutes, 15.0% 30 to 45 minutes, 3.0% 45 to 60 minutes, 2.0% 60 minutes or more (2008-2012 5-year est.)

PALOMA (unincorporated postal area)
Zip Code: 62359
    Covers a land area of 4.000 square miles and a water area of 0.003 square miles. Located at 40.03° N. Lat; 91.20° W. Long. Elevation is 732 feet. Population: 166 (2010); Density: 41.5 persons per square mile (2010); Race: 99.4% White, 0.0% Black/African American, 0.0% Asian, 0.0% American Indian/Alaska Native, 0.0% Native Hawaiian/Other Pacific Islander, 0.6% Some other race, 0.6% Two or more races, 0.0% Hispanic of any race (2010); Average household size: 2.63 (2010); Median age: 41.8 (2010); Males per 100 females: 78.5 (2010); Homeownership rate: 90.5% (2010)

PAYSON (village). Covers a land area of 1.120 square miles and a water area of 0 square miles. Located at 39.82° N. Lat; 91.24° W. Long. Elevation is 761 feet.

Population: 1,114 (1990); 1,066 (2000); 1,026 (2010); Density: 1,083.1 persons per square mile (2008-2012 5-year est.); Race: 96.7% White, 2.4% Black/African American, 0.0% Asian, 0.9% American Indian/Alaska Native, 0.0% Native Hawaiian/Other Pacific Islander, 0.0% Some other race, 0.0% Two or more races, 0.2% Hispanic of any race (2008-2012 5-year est.); Average household size: 2.78 (2008-2012 5-year est.); Median age: 35.1 (2008-2012 5-year est.); Males per 100 females: 93.5 (2008-2012 5-year est.); Marriage status: 23.5% never married, 52.3% now married, 7.6% widowed, 16.6% divorced (2008-2012 5-year est.); Foreign born: 0.7% (2008-2012 5-year est.); Ancestry (includes multiple ancestries): 43.4% German, 10.9% American, 9.6% Irish, 7.2% English, 5.7% Polish (2008-2012 5-year est.).
Economy: Homeowner vacancy rate: 0.0%. Rental vacancy rate: 7.8%. (2008-2012 5-year est.); Employment by occupation: 8.0% management, business, and financial, 3.4% computer, engineering, and science, 8.0% education, legal, community service, arts, and media, 4.8% healthcare practitioners, 22.0% service, 18.5% sales and office, 10.1% natural resources, construction, and maintenance, 25.2% production, transportation, and material moving (2008-2012 5-year est.).
Income: Per capita income: $21,092 (2008-2012 5-year est.); Median household income: $45,694 (2008-2012 5-year est.); Average household income: $56,342 (2008-2012 5-year est.); Percent of households with income of $100,000 or more: 11.4% (2008-2012 5-year est.); Poverty rate: 6.5% (2008-2012 5-year est.).
Education: Percent of population age 25 and over with: High school diploma (including GED) or higher: 85.0% (2008-2012 5-year est.); Bachelor's degree or higher: 11.0% (2008-2012 5-year est.); Master's degree or higher: 5.4% (2008-2012 5-year est.).

School District(s)
Payson CUSD 1 (PK-12)
    2011-12 Enrollment: 535 . . . . (217) 656-3323

Housing: Homeownership rate: 89.2% (2008-2012 5-year est.); Median home value: $83,500 (2008-2012 5-year est.); Median contract rent: $327 per month (2008-2012 5-year est.); Median year structure built: 1972 (2008-2012 5-year est.).
Health Insurance: 74.4% Private; 26.0% Public; 11.6% None. (2008-2012 5-year est.)
Transportation: Commute to work: 97.6% car, 0.0% public transportation, 0.0% walk, 2.4% work from home (2008-2012 5-year est.); Travel time to work: 11.3% less than 15 minutes, 61.1% 15 to 30 minutes, 24.8% 30 to 45 minutes, 1.6% 45 to 60 minutes, 1.1% 60 minutes or more (2008-2012 5-year est.)

PLAINVILLE (village). Covers a land area of 0.230 square miles and a water area of 0 square miles. Located at 39.78° N. Lat; 91.18° W. Long. Elevation is 692 feet.
Population: 261 (1990); 248 (2000); 264 (2010); Density: 1,522.6 persons per square mile (2008-2012 5-year est.); Race: 100.0% White, 0.0% Black/African American, 0.0% Asian, 0.0% American Indian/Alaska Native, 0.0% Native Hawaiian/Other Pacific Islander, 0.0% Some other race, 0.0% Two or more races, 0.0% Hispanic of any race (2008-2012 5-year est.); Average household size: 2.63 (2008-2012 5-year est.); Median age: 35.0 (2008-2012 5-year est.); Males per 100 females: 79.5 (2008-2012 5-year est.); Marriage status: 19.6% never married, 73.6% now married, 2.5% widowed, 4.3% divorced (2008-2012 5-year est.); Foreign born: 0.0% (2008-2012 5-year est.); Ancestry (includes multiple ancestries): 25.7% German, 14.3% Irish, 12.6% American, 9.7% Italian, 4.6% Dutch (2008-2012 5-year est.).
Economy: Homeowner vacancy rate: 0.0%. Rental vacancy rate: 0.0%. (2008-2012 5-year est.); Employment by occupation: 0.6% management, business, and financial, 0.0% computer, engineering, and science, 3.5% education, legal, community service, arts, and media, 4.7% healthcare practitioners, 16.4% service, 22.8% sales and office, 25.7% natural resources, construction, and maintenance, 26.3% production, transportation, and material moving (2008-2012 5-year est.).
Income: Per capita income: $17,586 (2008-2012 5-year est.); Median household income: $39,375 (2008-2012 5-year est.); Average household income: $46,452 (2008-2012 5-year est.); Percent of households with income of $100,000 or more: 3.8% (2008-2012 5-year est.); Poverty rate: 3.1% (2008-2012 5-year est.).
Education: Percent of population age 25 and over with: High school diploma (including GED) or higher: 88.5% (2008-2012 5-year est.); Bachelor's degree or higher: 5.1% (2008-2012 5-year est.); Master's degree or higher: 3.4% (2008-2012 5-year est.).
Housing: Homeownership rate: 89.5% (2008-2012 5-year est.); Median home value: $64,700 (2008-2012 5-year est.); Median contract rent: $425 per month (2008-2012 5-year est.); Median year structure built: 1947 (2008-2012 5-year est.).
Health Insurance: 56.6% Private; 48.3% Public; 10.3% None. (2008-2012 5-year est.)
Transportation: Commute to work: 89.5% car, 0.0% public transportation, 9.4% walk, 1.2% work from home (2008-2012 5-year est.); Travel time to work: 16.0% less than 15 minutes, 39.1% 15 to 30 minutes, 40.2% 30 to 45 minutes, 3.0% 45 to 60 minutes, 1.8% 60 minutes or more (2008-2012 5-year est.)

QUINCY (city). County seat. Covers a land area of 15.909 square miles and a water area of 0.036 square miles. Located at 39.93° N. Lat; 91.38° W. Long. Elevation is 568 feet.
History: The first settlement at Quincy was called The Bluffs, and centered around the cabin of John Wood. Wood later served as lieutenant governor and governor of Illinois. When Adams County was created in 1825, Quincy was named as the county seat, and the town was platted. In the mid-1800's Quincy was an active shipping center.
Population: 39,681 (1990); 40,366 (2000); 40,633 (2010); Density: 2,555.0 persons per square mile (2008-2012 5-year est.); Race: 90.2% White, 5.5% Black/African American, 1.2% Asian, 0.1% American Indian/Alaska Native, 0.0% Native Hawaiian/Other Pacific Islander, 3.0% Some other race, 2.0% Two or more races, 1.5% Hispanic of any race (2008-2012 5-year est.); Average household size: 2.35 (2008-2012 5-year est.); Median age: 38.5 (2008-2012 5-year est.); Males per 100 females: 88.4 (2008-2012 5-year est.); Marriage status: 30.3% never married, 47.6% now married, 9.4% widowed, 12.7% divorced (2008-2012 5-year est.); Foreign born: 1.6% (2008-2012 5-year est.); Ancestry (includes multiple ancestries): 40.1% German, 11.8% Irish, 10.0% American, 9.7% English, 2.1% French (2008-2012 5-year est.).

Economy: Unemployment rate: 4.8% (April 2014); Total civilian labor force: 21,473 (April 2014); Single-family building permits issued: 43 (2013); Multi-family building permits issued: 0 (2013); Homeowner vacancy rate: 1.8%. Rental vacancy rate: 5.2%. (2008-2012 5-year est.); Employment by occupation: 11.8% management, business, and financial, 2.5% computer, engineering, and science, 8.9% education, legal, community service, arts, and media, 4.8% healthcare practitioners, 22.6% service, 27.2% sales and office, 5.5% natural resources, construction, and maintenance, 16.6% production, transportation, and material moving (2008-2012 5-year est.).
Income: Per capita income: $23,493 (2008-2012 5-year est.); Median household income: $41,239 (2008-2012 5-year est.); Average household income: $55,275 (2008-2012 5-year est.); Percent of households with income of $100,000 or more: 11.0% (2008-2012 5-year est.); Poverty rate: 16.9% (2008-2012 5-year est.).
Taxes: Total city taxes per capita: $340 (2011); City property taxes per capita: $77 (2011).
Education: Percent of population age 25 and over with: High school diploma (including GED) or higher: 89.4% (2008-2012 5-year est.); Bachelor's degree or higher: 21.8% (2008-2012 5-year est.); Master's degree or higher: 7.1% (2008-2012 5-year est.).

School District(s)

Adams/pike Roe (PK-12)
   2011-12 Enrollment: n/a . . . . (217) 277-2080
Central CUSD 3 (PK-12)
   2011-12 Enrollment: 956. . . . . (217) 593-7116
Quincy Area Voc Ctr (11-12)
   2011-12 Enrollment: n/a . . . . (217) 224-3775
Quincy SD 172 (PK-12)
   2011-12 Enrollment: 7,176 . . . . (217) 223-8700

Four-year College(s)

Blessing Rieman College of Nursing (Private, Not-for-profit)
   Fall 2012 Enrollment: 274 . . . . (217) 228-5520
Quincy University (Private, Not-for-profit, Roman Catholic)
   Fall 2012 Enrollment: 1,632 . . . . (217) 222-8020
   2012-13 Tuition: In-state $25,180; Out-of-state $25,180

Two-year College(s)

Blessing Hospital School of Medical Laboratory Technology (Private, Not-for-profit)
   Fall 2012 Enrollment: 4 . . . . (217) 228-2250
Blessing Hospital School of Radiologic Technology (Private, Not-for-profit)
   Fall 2012 Enrollment: 21 . . . . (217) 223-8400
John Wood Community College (Public)
   Fall 2012 Enrollment: 2,172 . . . . (217) 224-6500
   2012-13 Tuition: In-state $7,290; Out-of-state $7,290
Vatterott College-Quincy (Private, For-profit)
   Fall 2012 Enrollment: 155 . . . . (217) 224-0600
   2012-13 Tuition: In-state $11,965; Out-of-state $11,965

Vocational/Technical School(s)

Gem City College (Private, For-profit)
   Fall 2012 Enrollment: 67 . . . . (217) 222-0391
   2012-13 Tuition: $13,975
Housing: Homeownership rate: 66.2% (2008-2012 5-year est.); Median home value: $96,400 (2008-2012 5-year est.); Median contract rent: $432 per month (2008-2012 5-year est.); Median year structure built: 1956 (2008-2012 5-year est.).
Health Insurance: 67.0% Private; 39.3% Public; 9.7% None. (2008-2012 5-year est.)
Hospitals: Blessing Hospital (426 beds)
Safety: Violent crime rate: 46.2 per 10,000 population; Property crime rate: 320.5 per 10,000 population (2012).
Transportation: Commute to work: 90.9% car, 0.7% public transportation, 4.1% walk, 2.9% work from home (2008-2012 5-year est.); Travel time to work: 63.9% less than 15 minutes, 29.4% 15 to 30 minutes, 3.5% 30 to 45 minutes, 1.3% 45 to 60 minutes, 2.0% 60 minutes or more (2008-2012 5-year est.); Amtrak: Train service available.
Airports: Quincy Regional Airport (commercial service–non-primary)
Additional Information Contacts
City of Quincy . . . . (217) 228-4500
   http://www.ci.quincy.il.us
Quincy Area Chamber of Commerce . . . . (217) 222-7980
   http://www.quincychamber.org

URSA (village). Covers a land area of 0.697 square miles and a water area of 0 square miles. Located at 40.07° N. Lat; 91.37° W. Long. Elevation is 610 feet.

Population: 506 (1990); 595 (2000); 626 (2010); Density: 898.7 persons per square mile (2008-2012 5-year est.); Race: 97.1% White, 0.0% Black/African American, 0.6% Asian, 0.0% American Indian/Alaska Native, 0.0% Native Hawaiian/Other Pacific Islander, 2.3% Some other race, 2.2% Two or more races, 1.6% Hispanic of any race (2008-2012 5-year est.); Average household size: 2.21 (2008-2012 5-year est.); Median age: 43.5 (2008-2012 5-year est.); Males per 100 females: 96.2 (2008-2012 5-year est.); Marriage status: 17.8% never married, 64.7% now married, 7.1% widowed, 10.5% divorced (2008-2012 5-year est.); Foreign born: 1.3% (2008-2012 5-year est.); Ancestry (includes multiple ancestries): 37.4% German, 17.3% American, 16.1% Irish, 6.1% English, 4.5% Scotch-Irish (2008-2012 5-year est.).

Economy: Homeowner vacancy rate: 0.0%. Rental vacancy rate: 19.8%. (2008-2012 5-year est.); Employment by occupation: 16.2% management, business, and financial, 2.6% computer, engineering, and science, 3.7% education, legal, community service, arts, and media, 8.0% healthcare practitioners, 10.3% service, 31.9% sales and office, 8.0% natural resources, construction, and maintenance, 19.4% production, transportation, and material moving (2008-2012 5-year est.).

Income: Per capita income: $24,920 (2008-2012 5-year est.); Median household income: $42,159 (2008-2012 5-year est.); Average household income: $56,866 (2008-2012 5-year est.); Percent of households with income of $100,000 or more: 12.0% (2008-2012 5-year est.); Poverty rate: 5.3% (2008-2012 5-year est.).

Education: Percent of population age 25 and over with: High school diploma (including GED) or higher: 91.1% (2008-2012 5-year est.); Bachelor's degree or higher: 18.4% (2008-2012 5-year est.); Master's degree or higher: 3.3% (2008-2012 5-year est.).

School District(s)

CUSD 4 (KG-12)
    2011-12 Enrollment: 714 . . . . (217) 936-2111

Housing: Homeownership rate: 74.2% (2008-2012 5-year est.); Median home value: $107,400 (2008-2012 5-year est.); Median contract rent: $325 per month (2008-2012 5-year est.); Median year structure built: 1974 (2008-2012 5-year est.).

Health Insurance: 80.2% Private; 24.9% Public; 9.6% None. (2008-2012 5-year est.)

Transportation: Commute to work: 94.3% car, 0.0% public transportation, 2.7% walk, 0.6% work from home (2008-2012 5-year est.); Travel time to work: 31.1% less than 15 minutes, 52.7% 15 to 30 minutes, 10.8% 30 to 45 minutes, 3.6% 45 to 60 minutes, 1.8% 60 minutes or more (2008-2012 5-year est.)

Alexander County

Located in southern Illinois; bounded on the west and south by the Mississippi River and the Missouri border, and on the southeast by the Ohio River; includes part of Shawnee National Forest. Covers a land area of 235.509 square miles, a water area of 17.092 square miles, and is located in the Central Time Zone at 37.18° N. Lat., 89.35° W. Long. The county was founded in 1819. County seat is Cairo.

Alexander County is part of the Cape Girardeau, MO-IL Metropolitan Statistical Area. The entire metro area includes: Alexander County, IL; Bollinger County, MO; Cape Girardeau County, MO

Weather Station: Cairo Wso City   Elevation: 313 feet

	Jan	Feb	Mar	Apr	May	Jun	Jul	Aug	Sep	Oct	Nov	Dec
High	43	48	58	69	78	86	89	88	82	70	58	45
Low	27	30	38	48	58	66	70	68	60	48	39	29
Precip	3.3	3.9	4.2	4.9	5.4	3.9	4.5	3.2	3.1	4.3	4.2	4.2
Snow	1.9	2.2	0.6	tr	0.0	0.0	0.0	0.0	0.0	0.1	0.1	0.8

High and Low temperatures in degrees Fahrenheit; Precipitation and Snow in inches

Population: 10,626 (1990); 9,590 (2000); 8,238 (2010); Race: 61.5% White, 34.8% Black/African American, 0.3% Asian, 0.3% American Indian/Alaska Native, 0.0% Native Hawaiian/Other Pacific Islander, 3.1% Some other race, 2.9% Two or more races, 1.9% Hispanic of any race (2008-2012 5-year est.); Density: 32.9 persons per square mile (2008-2012 5-year est.); Average household size: 2.49 (2008-2012 5-year est.); Median age: 41.0 (2008-2012 5-year est.); Males per 100 females: 105.1 (2008-2012 5-year est.).

Religion: Six largest groups: 27.0% Baptist, 5.7% Catholicism, 3.4% Methodist/Pietist, 3.0% Pentecostal, 0.6% Non-denominational Protestant, 0.6% Lutheran (2010)

Economy: Unemployment rate: 9.5% (April 2014); Total civilian labor force: 2,789 (April 2014); Leading industries: 25.5% transportation & warehousing; 21.0% health care and social assistance; 11.7% retail trade (2012); Farms: 144 totaling 62,425 acres (2012); Companies that employ 500 or more persons: 0 (2012); Companies that employ 100 to 499 persons: 2 (2012); Companies that employ less than 100 persons: 109 (2012); Black-owned businesses: n/a (2007); Hispanic-owned businesses: n/a (2007); Asian-owned businesses: n/a (2007); Women-owned businesses: 165 (2007); Single-family building permits issued: 0 (2013); Multi-family building permits issued: 0 (2013).

Income: Per capita income: $14,222 (2008-2012 5-year est.); Median household income: $27,248 (2008-2012 5-year est.); Average household income: $35,518 (2008-2012 5-year est.); Percent of households with income of $100,000 or more: 3.2% (2008-2012 5-year est.); Poverty rate: 31.1% (2008-2012 5-year est.); Bankruptcy rate: 6.98% (2013).

Taxes: Total county taxes per capita: $135 (2011); County property taxes per capita: $135 (2011).

Education: Percent of population age 25 and over with: High school diploma (including GED) or higher: 76.6% (2008-2012 5-year est.); Bachelor's degree or higher: 8.9% (2008-2012 5-year est.); Master's degree or higher: 2.4% (2008-2012 5-year est.).

Housing: Homeownership rate: 65.9% (2008-2012 5-year est.); Median home value: $58,000 (2008-2012 5-year est.); Median contract rent: $281 per month (2008-2012 5-year est.); Median year structure built: 1962 (2008-2012 5-year est.)

Health: Birth rate: 131.1 per 10,000 population (2013); Death rate: 129.8 per 10,000 population (2013); Age-adjusted cancer mortality rate: Unreliable deaths per 100,000 population (2011); Number of physicians: 5.0 per 10,000 population (2011); Hospital beds: 0.0 per 10,000 population (2010); Hospital admissions: 0.0 per 10,000 population (2010).

Elections: 2012 Presidential election results: 56.1% Obama, 42.5% Romney

National and State Parks: Fort Defiance State Park; Horseshoe Lake State Conservation Area

Additional Information Contacts
Alexander County Government . . . . (618) 734-7000

Alexander County Communities

CAIRO (city). County seat. Covers a land area of 6.968 square miles and a water area of 2.116 square miles. Located at 37.01° N. Lat; 89.18° W. Long. Elevation is 322 feet.

History: John G. Comegys, a St. Louis merchant, in 1818 secured the incorporation of the city of Cairo, named because he thought its site resembled Cairo, Egypt. Comegys died before he could carry out his plans, but the name Cairo remained when the Cairo City and Canal Company was formed in 1837 by Darius B. Holbrook. When the Illinois Central Railroad tracks were laid between Cairo and Chicago, Cairo's economy grew. Cairo was a Union headquarters during the Civil War, and received many thousands of Confederate prisoners.

Population: 4,846 (1990); 3,632 (2000); 2,831 (2010); Density: 403.6 persons per square mile (2008-2012 5-year est.); Race: 26.9% White, 69.5% Black/African American, 0.5% Asian, 0.2% American Indian/Alaska Native, 0.0% Native Hawaiian/Other Pacific Islander, 2.9% Some other race, 2.5% Two or more races, 0.3% Hispanic of any race (2008-2012 5-year est.); Average household size: 2.30 (2008-2012 5-year est.); Median age: 34.2 (2008-2012 5-year est.); Males per 100 females: 74.5 (2008-2012 5-year est.); Marriage status: 48.3% never married, 29.2% now married, 14.3% widowed, 8.2% divorced (2008-2012 5-year est.); Foreign born: 2.0% (2008-2012 5-year est.); Ancestry (includes multiple ancestries): 7.2% American, 5.4% German, 4.0% English, 3.6% Irish, 1.2% Italian (2008-2012 5-year est.).

Economy: Single-family building permits issued: 0 (2013); Multi-family building permits issued: 0 (2013); Homeowner vacancy rate: 2.7%. Rental vacancy rate: 7.1%. (2008-2012 5-year est.); Employment by occupation: 6.7% management, business, and financial, 0.4% computer, engineering, and science, 9.9% education, legal, community service, arts, and media, 6.4% healthcare practitioners, 34.6% service, 17.6% sales and office, 8.4% natural resources, construction, and maintenance, 16.1% production, transportation, and material moving (2008-2012 5-year est.).

Income: Per capita income: $10,993 (2008-2012 5-year est.); Median household income: $16,977 (2008-2012 5-year est.); Average household income: $24,022 (2008-2012 5-year est.); Percent of households with income of $100,000 or more: 1.3% (2008-2012 5-year est.); Poverty rate: 50.6% (2008-2012 5-year est.).

Education: Percent of population age 25 and over with: High school diploma (including GED) or higher: 76.2% (2008-2012 5-year est.); Bachelor's degree or higher: 8.4% (2008-2012 5-year est.); Master's degree or higher: 3.2% (2008-2012 5-year est.).

School District(s)

Cairo USD 1 (PK-12)
    2011-12 Enrollment: 510 . . . . (618) 734-4102
Five County Reg Voc System
    2011-12 Enrollment: n/a . . . . (618) 747-2703

Housing: Homeownership rate: 44.9% (2008-2012 5-year est.); Median home value: $33,900 (2008-2012 5-year est.); Median contract rent: $278 per month (2008-2012 5-year est.); Median year structure built: 1946 (2008-2012 5-year est.).

Health Insurance: 29.5% Private; 62.7% Public; 19.1% None. (2008-2012 5-year est.)

Safety: Violent crime rate: 391.3 per 10,000 population; Property crime rate: 764.5 per 10,000 population (2012).

Transportation: Commute to work: 82.0% car, 8.4% public transportation, 3.0% walk, 0.2% work from home (2008-2012 5-year est.); Travel time to work: 42.8% less than 15 minutes, 11.9% 15 to 30 minutes, 19.1% 30 to 45 minutes, 6.3% 45 to 60 minutes, 19.9% 60 minutes or more (2008-2012 5-year est.)

Airports: Cairo Regional Airport (general aviation)

EAST CAPE GIRARDEAU (village). Covers a land area of 1.961 square miles and a water area of 0.034 square miles. Located at 37.29° N. Lat; 89.48° W. Long. Elevation is 341 feet.

Population: 451 (1990); 437 (2000); 385 (2010); Density: 341.2 persons per square mile (2008-2012 5-year est.); Race: 94.6% White, 1.6% Black/African American, 0.1% Asian, 0.6% American Indian/Alaska Native, 0.0% Native Hawaiian/Other Pacific Islander, 3.1% Some other race, 3.0% Two or more races, 0.7% Hispanic of any race (2008-2012 5-year est.); Average household size: 2.83 (2008-2012 5-year est.); Median age: 40.6 (2008-2012 5-year est.); Males per 100 females: 75.6 (2008-2012 5-year est.); Marriage status: 23.5% never married, 42.3% now married, 4.9% widowed, 29.3% divorced (2008-2012 5-year est.); Foreign born: 3.1% (2008-2012 5-year est.); Ancestry (includes multiple ancestries): 26.3% German, 13.5% Irish, 9.7% English, 7.5% American, 2.5% Jamaican (2008-2012 5-year est.).

Economy: Single-family building permits issued: 0 (2013); Multi-family building permits issued: 0 (2013); Homeowner vacancy rate: 0.0%. Rental vacancy rate: 7.2%. (2008-2012 5-year est.); Employment by occupation: 9.2% management, business, and financial, 1.3% computer, engineering, and science, 9.2% education, legal, community service, arts, and media, 6.6% healthcare practitioners, 24.7% service, 21.1% sales and office, 4.9% natural resources, construction, and maintenance, 23.0% production, transportation, and material moving (2008-2012 5-year est.).

Income: Per capita income: $18,681 (2008-2012 5-year est.); Median household income: $37,500 (2008-2012 5-year est.); Average household income: $49,092 (2008-2012 5-year est.); Percent of households with income of $100,000 or more: 11.9% (2008-2012 5-year est.); Poverty rate: 15.2% (2008-2012 5-year est.).

Education: Percent of population age 25 and over with: High school diploma (including GED) or higher: 80.9% (2008-2012 5-year est.); Bachelor's degree or higher: 11.3% (2008-2012 5-year est.); Master's degree or higher: 2.7% (2008-2012 5-year est.).

Housing: Homeownership rate: 72.9% (2008-2012 5-year est.); Median home value: $59,400 (2008-2012 5-year est.); Median contract rent: $501 per month (2008-2012 5-year est.); Median year structure built: 1975 (2008-2012 5-year est.).

Health Insurance: 47.9% Private; 47.1% Public; 16.4% None. (2008-2012 5-year est.)

Transportation: Commute to work: 94.5% car, 0.0% public transportation, 3.3% walk, 0.0% work from home (2008-2012 5-year est.); Travel time to work: 20.8% less than 15 minutes, 58.0% 15 to 30 minutes, 16.0% 30 to 45 minutes, 0.0% 45 to 60 minutes, 5.2% 60 minutes or more (2008-2012 5-year est.)

MCCLURE (village). Covers a land area of 1.528 square miles and a water area of <.001 square miles. Located at 37.31° N. Lat; 89.43° W. Long. Elevation is 341 feet.

History: Incorporated 2004.

Population: n/a (1990); n/a (2000); 402 (2010); Density: 272.2 persons per square mile (2008-2012 5-year est.); Race: 99.8% White, 0.0% Black/African American, 0.0% Asian, 0.0% American Indian/Alaska Native, 0.0% Native Hawaiian/Other Pacific Islander, 0.2% Some other race, 0.2% Two or more races, 0.0% Hispanic of any race (2008-2012 5-year est.); Average household size: 2.48 (2008-2012 5-year est.); Median age: 54.0 (2008-2012 5-year est.); Males per 100 females: 118.9 (2008-2012 5-year est.); Marriage status: 25.9% never married, 58.8% now married, 7.9% widowed, 7.4% divorced (2008-2012 5-year est.); Foreign born: 0.0% (2008-2012 5-year est.); Ancestry (includes multiple ancestries): 21.4% Irish, 20.7% German, 6.0% English, 5.5% American, 3.4% French (2008-2012 5-year est.).

Economy: Homeowner vacancy rate: 6.8%. Rental vacancy rate: 10.0%. (2008-2012 5-year est.); Employment by occupation: 10.1% management, business, and financial, 0.0% computer, engineering, and science, 4.3% education, legal, community service, arts, and media, 4.3% healthcare practitioners, 16.0% service, 25.0% sales and office, 25.0% natural resources, construction, and maintenance, 15.4% production, transportation, and material moving (2008-2012 5-year est.).

Income: Per capita income: $18,834 (2008-2012 5-year est.); Median household income: $35,441 (2008-2012 5-year est.); Average household income: $45,038 (2008-2012 5-year est.); Percent of households with income of $100,000 or more: 10.1% (2008-2012 5-year est.); Poverty rate: 15.6% (2008-2012 5-year est.).

Education: Percent of population age 25 and over with: High school diploma (including GED) or higher: 83.0% (2008-2012 5-year est.); Bachelor's degree or higher: 5.9% (2008-2012 5-year est.); Master's degree or higher: 0.3% (2008-2012 5-year est.).

School District(s)

Shawnee CUSD 84 (KG-12)
    2011-12 Enrollment: 413 . . . . (618) 833-5709

Housing: Homeownership rate: 89.3% (2008-2012 5-year est.); Median home value: $52,700 (2008-2012 5-year est.); Median contract rent: $255 per month (2008-2012 5-year est.); Median year structure built: 1965 (2008-2012 5-year est.).

Health Insurance: 60.3% Private; 43.8% Public; 13.5% None. (2008-2012 5-year est.)

Transportation: Commute to work: 98.9% car, 0.0% public transportation, 1.1% walk, 0.0% work from home (2008-2012 5-year est.); Travel time to work: 16.1% less than 15 minutes, 64.0% 15 to 30 minutes, 9.1% 30 to 45 minutes, 8.1% 45 to 60 minutes, 2.7% 60 minutes or more (2008-2012 5-year est.)

MILLER CITY (unincorporated postal area)

Zip Code: 62962

    Covers a land area of 39.254 square miles and a water area of 8.080 square miles. Located at 37.07° N. Lat; 89.33° W. Long. Elevation is 331 feet. Population: 82 (2010); Density: 2.1 persons per square mile (2010); Race: 97.6% White, 2.4% Black/African American, 0.0% Asian, 0.0% American Indian/Alaska Native, 0.0% Native Hawaiian/Other Pacific Islander, 0.0% Some other race, 0.0% Two or more races, 0.0% Hispanic of any race (2010); Average household size: 2.00 (2010); Median age: 54.0 (2010); Males per 100 females: 105.0 (2010); Homeownership rate: 82.9% (2010)

OLIVE BRANCH (CDP). Covers a land area of 9.642 square miles and a water area of 0.006 square miles. Located at 37.18° N. Lat; 89.35° W. Long. Elevation is 341 feet.

Population: n/a (1990); n/a (2000); 864 (2010); Density: 83.2 persons per square mile (2008-2012 5-year est.); Race: 100.0% White, 0.0% Black/African American, 0.0% Asian, 0.0% American Indian/Alaska Native, 0.0% Native Hawaiian/Other Pacific Islander, 0.0% Some other race, 0.0% Two or more races, 3.6% Hispanic of any race (2008-2012 5-year est.); Average household size: 2.42 (2008-2012 5-year est.); Median age: 52.4 (2008-2012 5-year est.); Males per 100 females: 102.5 (2008-2012 5-year est.); Marriage status: 16.9% never married, 58.8% now married, 10.2% widowed, 14.1% divorced (2008-2012 5-year est.); Foreign born: 0.0% (2008-2012 5-year est.); Ancestry (includes multiple ancestries): 22.2% German, 9.6% French, 9.5% Italian, 8.9% Irish, 8.2% American (2008-2012 5-year est.).

Economy: Homeowner vacancy rate: 0.0%. Rental vacancy rate: 34.8%. (2008-2012 5-year est.); Employment by occupation: 16.7% management, business, and financial, 0.0% computer, engineering, and science, 0.0% education, legal, community service, arts, and media, 17.1% healthcare practitioners, 8.4% service, 25.5% sales and office, 15.9% natural resources, construction, and maintenance, 16.3% production, transportation, and material moving (2008-2012 5-year est.).

Income: Per capita income: $20,077 (2008-2012 5-year est.); Median household income: $40,515 (2008-2012 5-year est.); Average household income: $47,477 (2008-2012 5-year est.); Percent of households with income of $100,000 or more: 3.3% (2008-2012 5-year est.); Poverty rate: 11.0% (2008-2012 5-year est.).

Education: Percent of population age 25 and over with: High school diploma (including GED) or higher: 79.1% (2008-2012 5-year est.); Bachelor's degree or higher: 14.5% (2008-2012 5-year est.); Master's degree or higher: 0.0% (2008-2012 5-year est.).

Housing: Homeownership rate: 81.9% (2008-2012 5-year est.); Median home value: $76,900 (2008-2012 5-year est.); Median contract rent: $347 per month (2008-2012 5-year est.); Median year structure built: 1975 (2008-2012 5-year est.).

Health Insurance: 64.2% Private; 38.8% Public; 14.2% None. (2008-2012 5-year est.)

Transportation: Commute to work: 100.0% car, 0.0% public transportation, 0.0% walk, 0.0% work from home (2008-2012 5-year est.); Travel time to work: 7.6% less than 15 minutes, 42.6% 15 to 30 minutes, 37.1% 30 to 45 minutes, 8.4% 45 to 60 minutes, 4.4% 60 minutes or more (2008-2012 5-year est.)

TAMMS (village). Covers a land area of 2.332 square miles and a water area of 0 square miles. Located at 37.24° N. Lat; 89.27° W. Long. Elevation is 341 feet.

Population: 748 (1990); 724 (2000); 632 (2010); Density: 328.1 persons per square mile (2008-2012 5-year est.); Race: 55.4% White, 34.6% Black/African American, 0.8% Asian, 1.2% American Indian/Alaska Native, 0.0% Native Hawaiian/Other Pacific Islander, 8.0% Some other race, 8.0% Two or more races, 1.0% Hispanic of any race (2008-2012 5-year est.); Average household size: 2.81 (2008-2012 5-year est.); Median age: 34.3 (2008-2012 5-year est.); Males per 100 females: 197.7 (2008-2012 5-year est.); Marriage status: 45.6% never married, 37.2% now married, 10.1% widowed, 7.1% divorced (2008-2012 5-year est.); Foreign born: 0.3% (2008-2012 5-year est.); Ancestry (includes multiple ancestries): 15.7% German, 8.1% English, 6.8% Irish, 4.4% American, 2.6% Polish (2008-2012 5-year est.).

Economy: Homeowner vacancy rate: 6.7%. Rental vacancy rate: 13.5%. (2008-2012 5-year est.); Employment by occupation: 2.1% management, business, and financial, 0.0% computer, engineering, and science, 6.2% education, legal, community service, arts, and media, 0.0% healthcare practitioners, 13.8% service, 15.2% sales and office, 20.0% natural resources, construction, and maintenance, 42.8% production, transportation, and material moving (2008-2012 5-year est.).

Income: Per capita income: $9,571 (2008-2012 5-year est.); Median household income: $21,488 (2008-2012 5-year est.); Average household income: $31,047 (2008-2012 5-year est.); Percent of households with income of $100,000 or more: 0.9% (2008-2012 5-year est.); Poverty rate: 39.1% (2008-2012 5-year est.).

Education: Percent of population age 25 and over with: High school diploma (including GED) or higher: 67.8% (2008-2012 5-year est.); Bachelor's degree or higher: 1.6% (2008-2012 5-year est.); Master's degree or higher: 0.6% (2008-2012 5-year est.).

School District(s)

Egyptian CUSD 5 (PK-12)
    2011-12 Enrollment: 532 . . . . (618) 776-5306
Five County Reg Voc Center (11-12)
    2011-12 Enrollment: n/a . . . . (618) 747-2703
Five County Reg Voc System
    2011-12 Enrollment: n/a . . . . (618) 747-2703

Housing: Homeownership rate: 70.5% (2008-2012 5-year est.); Median home value: $49,800 (2008-2012 5-year est.); Median contract rent: $336 per month (2008-2012 5-year est.); Median year structure built: 1958 (2008-2012 5-year est.).

Health Insurance: 34.7% Private; 65.8% Public; 11.6% None. (2008-2012 5-year est.)

Transportation: Commute to work: 97.8% car, 0.0% public transportation, 2.2% walk, 0.0% work from home (2008-2012 5-year est.); Travel time to work: 52.5% less than 15 minutes, 12.2% 15 to 30 minutes, 27.3% 30 to

45 minutes, 7.2% 45 to 60 minutes, 0.7% 60 minutes or more (2008-2012 5-year est.)

THEBES (village). Covers a land area of 1.745 square miles and a water area of 0.568 square miles. Located at 37.21° N. Lat; 89.45° W. Long. Elevation is 351 feet.

History: Thebes was laid out in 1844, and once served as the seat of Alexander County. The site was earlier known as Sparhawk's Landing.

Population: 461 (1990); 478 (2000); 436 (2010); Density: 274.4 persons per square mile (2008-2012 5-year est.); Race: 60.5% White, 37.8% Black/African American, 0.0% Asian, 0.4% American Indian/Alaska Native, 0.0% Native Hawaiian/Other Pacific Islander, 1.3% Some other race, 1.3% Two or more races, 3.1% Hispanic of any race (2008-2012 5-year est.); Average household size: 2.82 (2008-2012 5-year est.); Median age: 27.5 (2008-2012 5-year est.); Males per 100 females: 116.7 (2008-2012 5-year est.); Marriage status: 45.0% never married, 41.3% now married, 6.7% widowed, 7.0% divorced (2008-2012 5-year est.); Foreign born: 0.0% (2008-2012 5-year est.); Ancestry (includes multiple ancestries): 9.6% Irish, 8.1% German, 5.2% American, 2.9% English, 2.3% Italian (2008-2012 5-year est.).

Economy: Single-family building permits issued: 0 (2013); Multi-family building permits issued: 0 (2013); Homeowner vacancy rate: 0.0%. Rental vacancy rate: 10.0%. (2008-2012 5-year est.); Employment by occupation: 14.0% management, business, and financial, 1.5% computer, engineering, and science, 1.5% education, legal, community service, arts, and media, 0.0% healthcare practitioners, 35.3% service, 11.0% sales and office, 6.6% natural resources, construction, and maintenance, 30.1% production, transportation, and material moving (2008-2012 5-year est.).

Income: Per capita income: $9,871 (2008-2012 5-year est.); Median household income: $23,704 (2008-2012 5-year est.); Average household income: $27,789 (2008-2012 5-year est.); Percent of households with income of $100,000 or more: n/a (2008-2012 5-year est.); Poverty rate: 37.6% (2008-2012 5-year est.).

Education: Percent of population age 25 and over with: High school diploma (including GED) or higher: 68.4% (2008-2012 5-year est.); Bachelor's degree or higher: 1.5% (2008-2012 5-year est.); Master's degree or higher: 0.7% (2008-2012 5-year est.).

Housing: Homeownership rate: 57.6% (2008-2012 5-year est.); Median home value: $48,300 (2008-2012 5-year est.); Median contract rent: $188 per month (2008-2012 5-year est.); Median year structure built: 1969 (2008-2012 5-year est.).

Health Insurance: 21.7% Private; 53.0% Public; 30.3% None. (2008-2012 5-year est.)

Transportation: Commute to work: 99.3% car, 0.0% public transportation, 0.7% walk, 0.0% work from home (2008-2012 5-year est.); Travel time to work: 5.9% less than 15 minutes, 66.9% 15 to 30 minutes, 2.2% 30 to 45 minutes, 18.4% 45 to 60 minutes, 6.6% 60 minutes or more (2008-2012 5-year est.)

Bond County

Located in southwest central Illinois; drained by the Kaskaskia River. Covers a land area of 380.279 square miles, a water area of 2.481 square miles, and is located in the Central Time Zone at 38.89° N. Lat., 89.44° W. Long. The county was founded in 1817. County seat is Greenville.

Bond County is part of the St. Louis, MO-IL Metropolitan Statistical Area. The entire metro area includes: Bond County, IL; Calhoun County, IL; Clinton County, IL; Jersey County, IL; Macoupin County, IL; Madison County, IL; Monroe County, IL; Saint Clair County, IL; Franklin County, MO; Jefferson County, MO; Lincoln County, MO; Saint Charles County, MO; Saint Louis County, MO; Warren County, MO; Saint Louis city, MO

Population: 14,991 (1990); 17,633 (2000); 17,768 (2010); Race: 91.7% White, 2.9% Black/African American, 1.4% Asian, 0.0% American Indian/Alaska Native, 0.0% Native Hawaiian/Other Pacific Islander, 4.0% Some other race, 3.9% Two or more races, 3.1% Hispanic of any race (2008-2012 5-year est.); Density: 46.3 persons per square mile (2008-2012 5-year est.); Average household size: 2.67 (2008-2012 5-year est.); Median age: 40.4 (2008-2012 5-year est.); Males per 100 females: 97.7 (2008-2012 5-year est.).

Religion: Six largest groups: 22.1% Baptist, 13.4% Catholicism, 4.5% Holiness, 4.4% Methodist/Pietist, 1.9% Lutheran, 1.8% Presbyterian-Reformed (2010)

Economy: Unemployment rate: 5.3% (April 2014); Total civilian labor force: 8,206 (April 2014); Leading industries: 21.8% manufacturing; 9.4% retail trade; 8.4% accommodation & food services (2012); Farms: 661 totaling 198,339 acres (2012); Companies that employ 500 or more persons: 1 (2012); Companies that employ 100 to 499 persons: 4 (2012); Companies that employ less than 100 persons: 303 (2012); Black-owned businesses: n/a (2007); Hispanic-owned businesses: n/a (2007); Asian-owned businesses: n/a (2007); Women-owned businesses: 363 (2007); Single-family building permits issued: 11 (2013); Multi-family building permits issued: 2 (2013).

Income: Per capita income: $23,081 (2008-2012 5-year est.); Median household income: $47,705 (2008-2012 5-year est.); Average household income: $60,865 (2008-2012 5-year est.); Percent of households with income of $100,000 or more: 16.3% (2008-2012 5-year est.); Poverty rate: 13.5% (2008-2012 5-year est.); Bankruptcy rate: 2.10% (2013).

Education: Percent of population age 25 and over with: High school diploma (including GED) or higher: 87.1% (2008-2012 5-year est.); Bachelor's degree or higher: 20.2% (2008-2012 5-year est.); Master's degree or higher: 9.4% (2008-2012 5-year est.).

Housing: Homeownership rate: 77.5% (2008-2012 5-year est.); Median home value: $101,900 (2008-2012 5-year est.); Median contract rent: $467 per month (2008-2012 5-year est.); Median year structure built: 1971 (2008-2012 5-year est.)

Health: Birth rate: 84.1 per 10,000 population (2013); Death rate: 91.0 per 10,000 population (2013); Age-adjusted cancer mortality rate: 196.8 deaths per 100,000 population (2011); Number of physicians: 10.7 per 10,000 population (2011); Hospital beds: 84.4 per 10,000 population (2010); Hospital admissions: 817.2 per 10,000 population (2010).

Elections: 2012 Presidential election results: 41.2% Obama, 55.9% Romney

Additional Information Contacts
Bond County Government. . . . . (618) 664-0449
  http://bondcountyil.com

Bond County Communities

GREENVILLE (city). County seat. Covers a land area of 6.188 square miles and a water area of 0 square miles. Located at 38.89° N. Lat; 89.39° W. Long. Elevation is 617 feet.

History: Greenville was settled in 1815, and developed as the seat of Bond County. Early industries were an evaporated milk plant, a glove plant, and a manufacturer of costumes and uniforms.

Population: 4,806 (1990); 6,955 (2000); 7,000 (2010); Density: 1,121.7 persons per square mile (2008-2012 5-year est.); Race: 86.3% White, 4.3% Black/African American, 3.2% Asian, 0.0% American Indian/Alaska Native, 0.0% Native Hawaiian/Other Pacific Islander, 6.2% Some other race, 6.3% Two or more races, 3.3% Hispanic of any race (2008-2012 5-year est.); Average household size: 2.62 (2008-2012 5-year est.); Median age: 28.0 (2008-2012 5-year est.); Males per 100 females: 91.5 (2008-2012 5-year est.); Marriage status: 35.0% never married, 49.2% now married, 8.7% widowed, 7.1% divorced (2008-2012 5-year est.); Foreign born: 3.0% (2008-2012 5-year est.); Ancestry (includes multiple ancestries): 25.8% German, 15.7% English, 9.0% Irish, 6.7% French, 5.3% American (2008-2012 5-year est.).

Economy: Single-family building permits issued: 1 (2013); Multi-family building permits issued: 2 (2013); Homeowner vacancy rate: 3.8%. Rental vacancy rate: 11.8%. (2008-2012 5-year est.); Employment by occupation: 6.9% management, business, and financial, 3.5% computer, engineering, and science, 16.8% education, legal, community service, arts, and media, 5.4% healthcare practitioners, 17.1% service, 24.6% sales and office, 6.6% natural resources, construction, and maintenance, 19.1% production, transportation, and material moving (2008-2012 5-year est.).

Income: Per capita income: $20,139 (2008-2012 5-year est.); Median household income: $44,773 (2008-2012 5-year est.); Average household income: $57,394 (2008-2012 5-year est.); Percent of households with income of $100,000 or more: 8.7% (2008-2012 5-year est.); Poverty rate: 13.4% (2008-2012 5-year est.).

Education: Percent of population age 25 and over with: High school diploma (including GED) or higher: 87.3% (2008-2012 5-year est.); Bachelor's degree or higher: 31.6% (2008-2012 5-year est.); Master's degree or higher: 17.6% (2008-2012 5-year est.).

School District(s)
Bond County CUSD 2 (PK-12)
  2011-12 Enrollment: 1,995 . . . . (618) 664-0170

Four-year College(s)
Greenville College (Private, Not-for-profit, Free Methodist)
  Fall 2012 Enrollment: 1,452 . . . . (618) 664-2800
  2012-13 Tuition: In-state $22,920; Out-of-state $22,920

Housing: Homeownership rate: 61.9% (2008-2012 5-year est.); Median home value: $97,900 (2008-2012 5-year est.); Median contract rent: $473 per month (2008-2012 5-year est.); Median year structure built: 1964 (2008-2012 5-year est.).

Health Insurance: 65.8% Private; 37.5% Public; 8.9% None. (2008-2012 5-year est.)

Hospitals: Greenville Regional Hospital (50 beds)

Safety: Violent crime rate: 2.9 per 10,000 population; Property crime rate: 170.2 per 10,000 population (2012).

Transportation: Commute to work: 81.1% car, 4.9% public transportation, 11.9% walk, 1.5% work from home (2008-2012 5-year est.); Travel time to work: 66.7% less than 15 minutes, 12.9% 15 to 30 minutes, 5.4% 30 to 45 minutes, 9.0% 45 to 60 minutes, 6.0% 60 minutes or more (2008-2012 5-year est.)

Airports: Greenville Airport (general aviation)

Additional Information Contacts
City of Greenville. . . . . (618) 664-1644
  http://www.greenvilleillinois.com
Greenville Chamber of Commerce . . . . (618) 664-9272
  http://www.greenvilleusa.org

KEYESPORT (village). Covers a land area of 0.664 square miles and a water area of 0.017 square miles. Located at 38.74° N. Lat; 89.27° W. Long.

Population: 440 (1990); 481 (2000); 421 (2010); Density: 720.2 persons per square mile (2008-2012 5-year est.); Race: 97.5% White, 0.0% Black/African American, 0.2% Asian, 0.0% American Indian/Alaska Native, 0.0% Native Hawaiian/Other Pacific Islander, 2.3% Some other race, 2.3% Two or more races, 0.0% Hispanic of any race (2008-2012 5-year est.); Average household size: 1.98 (2008-2012 5-year est.); Median age: 52.1 (2008-2012 5-year est.); Males per 100 females: 93.5 (2008-2012 5-year est.); Marriage status: 15.2% never married, 56.7% now married, 18.9% widowed, 9.2% divorced (2008-2012 5-year est.); Foreign born: 1.0% (2008-2012 5-year est.); Ancestry (includes multiple ancestries): 19.7% German, 16.3% Irish, 13.2% American, 10.0% English, 3.3% French (2008-2012 5-year est.).

Economy: Single-family building permits issued: 0 (2013); Multi-family building permits issued: 0 (2013); Homeowner vacancy rate: 0.0%. Rental vacancy rate: 17.0%. (2008-2012 5-year est.); Employment by occupation: 1.6% management, business, and financial, 0.0% computer, engineering, and science, 0.0% education, legal, community service, arts, and media, 20.4% healthcare practitioners, 28.5% service, 12.4% sales and office, 14.5% natural resources, construction, and maintenance, 22.6% production, transportation, and material moving (2008-2012 5-year est.).

Income: Per capita income: $19,406 (2008-2012 5-year est.); Median household income: $25,556 (2008-2012 5-year est.); Average household income: $37,207 (2008-2012 5-year est.); Percent of households with income of $100,000 or more: 7.0% (2008-2012 5-year est.); Poverty rate: 32.3% (2008-2012 5-year est.).

Education: Percent of population age 25 and over with: High school diploma (including GED) or higher: 61.5% (2008-2012 5-year est.); Bachelor's degree or higher: 5.8% (2008-2012 5-year est.); Master's degree or higher: 0.0% (2008-2012 5-year est.).

Housing: Homeownership rate: 81.8% (2008-2012 5-year est.); Median home value: $60,800 (2008-2012 5-year est.); Median contract rent: $273 per month (2008-2012 5-year est.); Median year structure built: 1978 (2008-2012 5-year est.).

Health Insurance: 55.0% Private; 55.2% Public; 15.1% None. (2008-2012 5-year est.)

Transportation: Commute to work: 88.0% car, 0.0% public transportation, 3.8% walk, 7.1% work from home (2008-2012 5-year est.); Travel time to work: 9.4% less than 15 minutes, 24.7% 15 to 30 minutes, 21.8% 30 to 45 minutes, 7.1% 45 to 60 minutes, 37.1% 60 minutes or more (2008-2012 5-year est.)

MULBERRY GROVE (village). Covers a land area of 0.993 square miles and a water area of 0.009 square miles. Located at 38.93° N. Lat; 89.26° W. Long. Elevation is 561 feet.

Population: 660 (1990); 671 (2000); 634 (2010); Density: 793.4 persons per square mile (2008-2012 5-year est.); Race: 95.9% White, 2.8% Black/African American, 0.0% Asian, 0.0% American Indian/Alaska Native,

0.0% Native Hawaiian/Other Pacific Islander, 1.3% Some other race, 0.0% Two or more races, 0.0% Hispanic of any race (2008-2012 5-year est.); Average household size: 2.95 (2008-2012 5-year est.); Median age: 35.8 (2008-2012 5-year est.); Males per 100 females: 106.8 (2008-2012 5-year est.); Marriage status: 31.7% never married, 47.7% now married, 4.7% widowed, 15.9% divorced (2008-2012 5-year est.); Foreign born: 0.4% (2008-2012 5-year est.); Ancestry (includes multiple ancestries): 19.5% German, 13.2% English, 9.6% American, 8.5% Irish, 3.2% Polish (2008-2012 5-year est.).

Economy: Single-family building permits issued: 0 (2013); Multi-family building permits issued: 0 (2013); Homeowner vacancy rate: 3.6%. Rental vacancy rate: 0.0%. (2008-2012 5-year est.); Employment by occupation: 5.2% management, business, and financial, 1.7% computer, engineering, and science, 6.2% education, legal, community service, arts, and media, 0.0% healthcare practitioners, 14.8% service, 28.9% sales and office, 14.1% natural resources, construction, and maintenance, 29.2% production, transportation, and material moving (2008-2012 5-year est.).

Income: Per capita income: $15,791 (2008-2012 5-year est.); Median household income: $37,917 (2008-2012 5-year est.); Average household income: $43,434 (2008-2012 5-year est.); Percent of households with income of $100,000 or more: 7.4% (2008-2012 5-year est.); Poverty rate: 27.6% (2008-2012 5-year est.).

Education: Percent of population age 25 and over with: High school diploma (including GED) or higher: 83.2% (2008-2012 5-year est.); Bachelor's degree or higher: 10.0% (2008-2012 5-year est.); Master's degree or higher: 4.8% (2008-2012 5-year est.).

School District(s)

Mulberry Grove CUSD 1 (PK-12)
    2011-12 Enrollment: 424 . . . . (618) 326-8812

Housing: Homeownership rate: 79.0% (2008-2012 5-year est.); Median home value: $73,300 (2008-2012 5-year est.); Median contract rent: $419 per month (2008-2012 5-year est.); Median year structure built: 1962 (2008-2012 5-year est.).

Health Insurance: 47.0% Private; 44.7% Public; 18.0% None. (2008-2012 5-year est.)

Transportation: Commute to work: 93.4% car, 0.0% public transportation, 0.0% walk, 5.6% work from home (2008-2012 5-year est.); Travel time to work: 28.9% less than 15 minutes, 43.0% 15 to 30 minutes, 9.6% 30 to 45 minutes, 4.4% 45 to 60 minutes, 14.1% 60 minutes or more (2008-2012 5-year est.)

OLD RIPLEY (village). Covers a land area of 0.152 square miles and a water area of 0 square miles. Located at 38.89° N. Lat; 89.57° W. Long. Elevation is 561 feet.

Population: 95 (1990); 127 (2000); 108 (2010); Density: 692.3 persons per square mile (2008-2012 5-year est.); Race: 100.0% White, 0.0% Black/African American, 0.0% Asian, 0.0% American Indian/Alaska Native, 0.0% Native Hawaiian/Other Pacific Islander, 0.0% Some other race, 0.0% Two or more races, 0.0% Hispanic of any race (2008-2012 5-year est.); Average household size: 3.00 (2008-2012 5-year est.); Median age: 40.6 (2008-2012 5-year est.); Males per 100 females: 128.3 (2008-2012 5-year est.); Marriage status: 21.4% never married, 50.0% now married, 7.1% widowed, 21.4% divorced (2008-2012 5-year est.); Foreign born: 0.0% (2008-2012 5-year est.); Ancestry (includes multiple ancestries): 29.5% American, 29.5% German, 12.4% Irish, 5.7% Pennsylvania German, 3.8% French (2008-2012 5-year est.).

Economy: Homeowner vacancy rate: 0.0%. Rental vacancy rate: 0.0%. (2008-2012 5-year est.); Employment by occupation: 7.5% management, business, and financial, 0.0% computer, engineering, and science, 0.0% education, legal, community service, arts, and media, 7.5% healthcare practitioners, 22.5% service, 17.5% sales and office, 17.5% natural resources, construction, and maintenance, 27.5% production, transportation, and material moving (2008-2012 5-year est.).

Income: Per capita income: $16,327 (2008-2012 5-year est.); Median household income: $45,875 (2008-2012 5-year est.); Average household income: $44,863 (2008-2012 5-year est.); Percent of households with income of $100,000 or more: 8.6% (2008-2012 5-year est.); Poverty rate: 27.6% (2008-2012 5-year est.).

Education: Percent of population age 25 and over with: High school diploma (including GED) or higher: 72.9% (2008-2012 5-year est.); Bachelor's degree or higher: 1.4% (2008-2012 5-year est.); Master's degree or higher: 1.4% (2008-2012 5-year est.).

Housing: Homeownership rate: 100.0% (2008-2012 5-year est.); Median home value: $36,300 (2008-2012 5-year est.); Median contract rent: n/a

per month (2008-2012 5-year est.); Median year structure built: 1970 (2008-2012 5-year est.).

Health Insurance: 56.2% Private; 41.9% Public; 20.0% None. (2008-2012 5-year est.)

Transportation: Commute to work: 100.0% car, 0.0% public transportation, 0.0% walk, 0.0% work from home (2008-2012 5-year est.); Travel time to work: 12.8% less than 15 minutes, 41.0% 15 to 30 minutes, 7.7% 30 to 45 minutes, 23.1% 45 to 60 minutes, 15.4% 60 minutes or more (2008-2012 5-year est.)

PIERRON (village). Covers a land area of 0.836 square miles and a water area of 0 square miles. Located at 38.77° N. Lat; 89.60° W. Long. Elevation is 522 feet.

Population: 554 (1990); 653 (2000); 600 (2010); Density: 583.9 persons per square mile (2008-2012 5-year est.); Race: 100.0% White, 0.0% Black/African American, 0.0% Asian, 0.0% American Indian/Alaska Native, 0.0% Native Hawaiian/Other Pacific Islander, 0.0% Some other race, 0.0% Two or more races, 0.8% Hispanic of any race (2008-2012 5-year est.); Average household size: 2.43 (2008-2012 5-year est.); Median age: 47.0 (2008-2012 5-year est.); Males per 100 females: 93.7 (2008-2012 5-year est.); Marriage status: 11.3% never married, 57.7% now married, 14.9% widowed, 16.0% divorced (2008-2012 5-year est.); Foreign born: 0.0% (2008-2012 5-year est.); Ancestry (includes multiple ancestries): 41.2% German, 9.2% Irish, 5.7% Dutch, 5.5% French, 5.1% Polish (2008-2012 5-year est.).

Economy: Single-family building permits issued: 0 (2013); Multi-family building permits issued: 0 (2013); Homeowner vacancy rate: 0.0%. Rental vacancy rate: 0.0%. (2008-2012 5-year est.); Employment by occupation: 1.8% management, business, and financial, 1.2% computer, engineering, and science, 5.3% education, legal, community service, arts, and media, 1.2% healthcare practitioners, 27.8% service, 26.6% sales and office, 16.0% natural resources, construction, and maintenance, 20.1% production, transportation, and material moving (2008-2012 5-year est.).

Income: Per capita income: $18,235 (2008-2012 5-year est.); Median household income: $35,625 (2008-2012 5-year est.); Average household income: $41,972 (2008-2012 5-year est.); Percent of households with income of $100,000 or more: 3.0% (2008-2012 5-year est.); Poverty rate: 8.8% (2008-2012 5-year est.).

Education: Percent of population age 25 and over with: High school diploma (including GED) or higher: 87.6% (2008-2012 5-year est.); Bachelor's degree or higher: 4.3% (2008-2012 5-year est.); Master's degree or higher: 2.9% (2008-2012 5-year est.).

Housing: Homeownership rate: 91.5% (2008-2012 5-year est.); Median home value: $79,400 (2008-2012 5-year est.); Median contract rent: $318 per month (2008-2012 5-year est.); Median year structure built: 1960 (2008-2012 5-year est.).

Health Insurance: 59.0% Private; 56.1% Public; 5.7% None. (2008-2012 5-year est.)

Safety: Violent crime rate: 0.0 per 10,000 population; Property crime rate: 16.7 per 10,000 population (2012).

Transportation: Commute to work: 92.9% car, 0.0% public transportation, 2.4% walk, 4.7% work from home (2008-2012 5-year est.); Travel time to work: 12.4% less than 15 minutes, 47.2% 15 to 30 minutes, 18.0% 30 to 45 minutes, 12.4% 45 to 60 minutes, 9.9% 60 minutes or more (2008-2012 5-year est.)

POCAHONTAS (village). Covers a land area of 0.751 square miles and a water area of 0.021 square miles. Located at 38.82° N. Lat; 89.54° W. Long. Elevation is 561 feet.

History: Pocahontas, named for the legendary Indian princess, began as a stagecoach stop on the Cumberland Road.

Population: 837 (1990); 727 (2000); 784 (2010); Density: 974.7 persons per square mile (2008-2012 5-year est.); Race: 95.5% White, 0.0% Black/African American, 0.0% Asian, 0.4% American Indian/Alaska Native, 0.0% Native Hawaiian/Other Pacific Islander, 4.1% Some other race, 4.1% Two or more races, 2.0% Hispanic of any race (2008-2012 5-year est.); Average household size: 2.74 (2008-2012 5-year est.); Median age: 32.2 (2008-2012 5-year est.); Males per 100 females: 112.8 (2008-2012 5-year est.); Marriage status: 23.1% never married, 45.4% now married, 8.1% widowed, 23.5% divorced (2008-2012 5-year est.); Foreign born: 0.0% (2008-2012 5-year est.); Ancestry (includes multiple ancestries): 14.1% German, 6.3% Irish, 4.5% English, 3.4% French, 1.4% Swedish (2008-2012 5-year est.).

Economy: Single-family building permits issued: 0 (2013); Multi-family building permits issued: 0 (2013); Homeowner vacancy rate: 0.0%. Rental

vacancy rate: 22.9%. (2008-2012 5-year est.); Employment by occupation: 4.1% management, business, and financial, 5.8% computer, engineering, and science, 0.7% education, legal, community service, arts, and media, 5.8% healthcare practitioners, 24.7% service, 21.6% sales and office, 6.8% natural resources, construction, and maintenance, 30.5% production, transportation, and material moving (2008-2012 5-year est.).

Income: Per capita income: $19,604 (2008-2012 5-year est.); Median household income: $40,898 (2008-2012 5-year est.); Average household income: $50,304 (2008-2012 5-year est.); Percent of households with income of $100,000 or more: 12.4% (2008-2012 5-year est.); Poverty rate: 23.6% (2008-2012 5-year est.).

Education: Percent of population age 25 and over with: High school diploma (including GED) or higher: 79.2% (2008-2012 5-year est.); Bachelor's degree or higher: 4.2% (2008-2012 5-year est.); Master's degree or higher: 0.0% (2008-2012 5-year est.).

School District(s)
Bond County CUSD 2 (PK-12)
   2011-12 Enrollment: 1,995 . . . . (618) 664-0170

Housing: Homeownership rate: 76.0% (2008-2012 5-year est.); Median home value: $77,000 (2008-2012 5-year est.); Median contract rent: $477 per month (2008-2012 5-year est.); Median year structure built: 1955 (2008-2012 5-year est.).

Health Insurance: 63.5% Private; 37.3% Public; 14.1% None. (2008-2012 5-year est.)

Transportation: Commute to work: 95.2% car, 0.0% public transportation, 0.0% walk, 3.8% work from home (2008-2012 5-year est.); Travel time to work: 24.9% less than 15 minutes, 40.9% 15 to 30 minutes, 16.0% 30 to 45 minutes, 10.0% 45 to 60 minutes, 8.2% 60 minutes or more (2008-2012 5-year est.)

SMITHBORO (village).
Covers a land area of 0.927 square miles and a water area of 0 square miles. Located at 38.89° N. Lat; 89.34° W. Long. Elevation is 558 feet.

Population: 201 (1990); 200 (2000); 177 (2010); Density: 144.6 persons per square mile (2008-2012 5-year est.); Race: 93.3% White, 0.0% Black/African American, 6.7% Asian, 0.0% American Indian/Alaska Native, 0.0% Native Hawaiian/Other Pacific Islander, 0.0% Some other race, 0.0% Two or more races, 0.0% Hispanic of any race (2008-2012 5-year est.); Average household size: 2.58 (2008-2012 5-year est.); Median age: 50.8 (2008-2012 5-year est.); Males per 100 females: 152.8 (2008-2012 5-year est.); Marriage status: 39.7% never married, 44.3% now married, 9.2% widowed, 6.9% divorced (2008-2012 5-year est.); Foreign born: 6.7% (2008-2012 5-year est.); Ancestry (includes multiple ancestries): 15.7% German, 13.4% Irish, 8.2% Scotch-Irish, 6.7% English, 6.0% Dutch (2008-2012 5-year est.).

Economy: Single-family building permits issued: 0 (2013); Multi-family building permits issued: 0 (2013); Homeowner vacancy rate: 0.0%. Rental vacancy rate: 0.0%. (2008-2012 5-year est.); Employment by occupation: 0.0% management, business, and financial, 0.0% computer, engineering, and science, 0.0% education, legal, community service, arts, and media, 1.5% healthcare practitioners, 13.4% service, 64.2% sales and office, 4.5% natural resources, construction, and maintenance, 16.4% production, transportation, and material moving (2008-2012 5-year est.).

Income: Per capita income: $17,175 (2008-2012 5-year est.); Median household income: $21,250 (2008-2012 5-year est.); Average household income: $37,471 (2008-2012 5-year est.); Percent of households with income of $100,000 or more: 5.8% (2008-2012 5-year est.); Poverty rate: 14.9% (2008-2012 5-year est.).

Education: Percent of population age 25 and over with: High school diploma (including GED) or higher: 89.2% (2008-2012 5-year est.); Bachelor's degree or higher: 18.9% (2008-2012 5-year est.); Master's degree or higher: 0.0% (2008-2012 5-year est.).

Housing: Homeownership rate: 98.1% (2008-2012 5-year est.); Median home value: $57,300 (2008-2012 5-year est.); Median contract rent: n/a per month (2008-2012 5-year est.); Median year structure built: 1953 (2008-2012 5-year est.).

Health Insurance: 49.3% Private; 21.6% Public; 38.1% None. (2008-2012 5-year est.)

Transportation: Commute to work: 85.2% car, 14.8% public transportation, 0.0% walk, 0.0% work from home (2008-2012 5-year est.); Travel time to work: 47.5% less than 15 minutes, 24.6% 15 to 30 minutes, 8.2% 30 to 45 minutes, 9.8% 45 to 60 minutes, 9.8% 60 minutes or more (2008-2012 5-year est.)

SORENTO (village).
Covers a land area of 0.540 square miles and a water area of 0 square miles. Located at 39.00° N. Lat; 89.57° W. Long. Elevation is 584 feet.

Population: 596 (1990); 601 (2000); 498 (2010); Density: 1,279.0 persons per square mile (2008-2012 5-year est.); Race: 96.5% White, 0.0% Black/African American, 3.5% Asian, 0.0% American Indian/Alaska Native, 0.0% Native Hawaiian/Other Pacific Islander, 0.0% Some other race, 0.0% Two or more races, 5.5% Hispanic of any race (2008-2012 5-year est.); Average household size: 3.07 (2008-2012 5-year est.); Median age: 35.8 (2008-2012 5-year est.); Males per 100 females: 100.3 (2008-2012 5-year est.); Marriage status: 30.8% never married, 39.1% now married, 8.6% widowed, 21.5% divorced (2008-2012 5-year est.); Foreign born: 1.4% (2008-2012 5-year est.); Ancestry (includes multiple ancestries): 10.3% English, 9.1% German, 5.4% Irish, 2.5% Scotch-Irish, 2.2% European (2008-2012 5-year est.).

Economy: Single-family building permits issued: 1 (2013); Multi-family building permits issued: 0 (2013); Homeowner vacancy rate: 3.7%. Rental vacancy rate: 0.0%. (2008-2012 5-year est.); Employment by occupation: 5.5% management, business, and financial, 2.2% computer, engineering, and science, 0.4% education, legal, community service, arts, and media, 2.2% healthcare practitioners, 25.5% service, 28.1% sales and office, 21.9% natural resources, construction, and maintenance, 14.2% production, transportation, and material moving (2008-2012 5-year est.).

Income: Per capita income: $14,864 (2008-2012 5-year est.); Median household income: $26,875 (2008-2012 5-year est.); Average household income: $39,559 (2008-2012 5-year est.); Percent of households with income of $100,000 or more: 8.4% (2008-2012 5-year est.); Poverty rate: 32.1% (2008-2012 5-year est.).

Education: Percent of population age 25 and over with: High school diploma (including GED) or higher: 73.9% (2008-2012 5-year est.); Bachelor's degree or higher: 4.2% (2008-2012 5-year est.); Master's degree or higher: 1.9% (2008-2012 5-year est.).

School District(s)
Bond County CUSD 2 (PK-12)
   2011-12 Enrollment: 1,995 . . . . (618) 664-0170

Housing: Homeownership rate: 80.0% (2008-2012 5-year est.); Median home value: $51,600 (2008-2012 5-year est.); Median contract rent: $220 per month (2008-2012 5-year est.); Median year structure built: 1941 (2008-2012 5-year est.).

Health Insurance: 35.2% Private; 50.1% Public; 20.1% None. (2008-2012 5-year est.)

Transportation: Commute to work: 92.1% car, 0.0% public transportation, 1.1% walk, 5.3% work from home (2008-2012 5-year est.); Travel time to work: 12.4% less than 15 minutes, 32.3% 15 to 30 minutes, 28.3% 30 to 45 minutes, 19.9% 45 to 60 minutes, 7.2% 60 minutes or more (2008-2012 5-year est.)

Boone County

Located in northern Illinois; bounded on the north by Wisconsin. Covers a land area of 280.719 square miles, a water area of 1.305 square miles, and is located in the Central Time Zone at 42.32° N. Lat., 88.82° W. Long. The county was founded in 1837. County seat is Belvidere.

Boone County is part of the Rockford, IL Metropolitan Statistical Area. The entire metro area includes: Boone County, IL; Winnebago County, IL

Population: 30,806 (1990); 41,786 (2000); 54,165 (2010); Race: 90.4% White, 2.2% Black/African American, 1.5% Asian, 0.2% American Indian/Alaska Native, 0.0% Native Hawaiian/Other Pacific Islander, 5.7% Some other race, 1.8% Two or more races, 20.2% Hispanic of any race (2008-2012 5-year est.); Density: 191.9 persons per square mile (2008-2012 5-year est.); Average household size: 3.01 (2008-2012 5-year est.); Median age: 36.6 (2008-2012 5-year est.); Males per 100 females: 100.1 (2008-2012 5-year est.).

Religion: Six largest groups: 19.2% Catholicism, 8.5% Lutheran, 4.3% Methodist/Pietist, 2.4% Presbyterian-Reformed, 1.0% Non-denominational Protestant, 0.8% Baptist (2010)

Economy: Unemployment rate: 9.9% (April 2014); Total civilian labor force: 25,411 (April 2014); Leading industries: 49.9% manufacturing; 10.2% retail trade; 7.5% health care and social assistance (2012); Farms: 479 totaling 134,759 acres (2012); Companies that employ 500 or more persons: 2 (2012); Companies that employ 100 to 499 persons: 13 (2012); Companies that employ less than 100 persons: 850 (2012); Black-owned businesses: 45 (2007); Hispanic-owned businesses: n/a (2007);

Asian-owned businesses: n/a (2007); Women-owned businesses: 953 (2007); Single-family building permits issued: 43 (2013); Multi-family building permits issued: 0 (2013).
Income: Per capita income: $26,559 (2008-2012 5-year est.); Median household income: $63,670 (2008-2012 5-year est.); Average household income: $78,434 (2008-2012 5-year est.); Percent of households with income of $100,000 or more: 25.3% (2008-2012 5-year est.); Poverty rate: 10.1% (2008-2012 5-year est.); Bankruptcy rate: 4.72% (2013).
Taxes: Total county taxes per capita: $215 (2011); County property taxes per capita: $163 (2011).
Education: Percent of population age 25 and over with: High school diploma (including GED) or higher: 85.5% (2008-2012 5-year est.); Bachelor's degree or higher: 19.9% (2008-2012 5-year est.); Master's degree or higher: 6.7% (2008-2012 5-year est.).
Housing: Homeownership rate: 84.1% (2008-2012 5-year est.); Median home value: $164,700 (2008-2012 5-year est.); Median contract rent: $577 per month (2008-2012 5-year est.); Median year structure built: 1984 (2008-2012 5-year est.).
Health: Birth rate: 103.4 per 10,000 population (2013); Death rate: 60.8 per 10,000 population (2013); Age-adjusted cancer mortality rate: 166.4 deaths per 100,000 population (2011); Number of physicians: 14.4 per 10,000 population (2011); Hospital beds: 0.0 per 10,000 population (2010); Hospital admissions: 0.0 per 10,000 population (2010).
Elections: 2012 Presidential election results: 46.3% Obama, 52.0% Romney
Additional Information Contacts
Boone County Government . . . . (815) 547-4770
  http://www.boonecountyil.org

Boone County Communities

BELVIDERE (city). County seat. Covers a land area of 12.078 square miles and a water area of 0.232 square miles. Located at 42.26° N. Lat; 88.87° W. Long. Elevation is 781 feet.
History: Belvidere was founded in 1836 as a stop on the Chicago-Galena stagecoach route. The National Sewing Machine Plant was founded here in 1879.
Population: 15,958 (1990); 20,820 (2000); 25,585 (2010); Density: 2,114.8 persons per square mile (2008-2012 5-year est.); Race: 86.7% White, 2.5% Black/African American, 1.4% Asian, 0.0% American Indian/Alaska Native, 0.0% Native Hawaiian/Other Pacific Islander, 9.4% Some other race, 2.5% Two or more races, 33.4% Hispanic of any race (2008-2012 5-year est.); Average household size: 2.99 (2008-2012 5-year est.); Median age: 33.4 (2008-2012 5-year est.); Males per 100 females: 101.0 (2008-2012 5-year est.); Marriage status: 29.5% never married, 54.8% now married, 5.8% widowed, 10.0% divorced (2008-2012 5-year est.); Foreign born: 16.3% (2008-2012 5-year est.); Ancestry (includes multiple ancestries): 18.5% German, 13.0% Irish, 7.7% American, 7.1% English, 5.7% Swedish (2008-2012 5-year est.).
Economy: Unemployment rate: 11.3% (April 2014); Total civilian labor force: 11,908 (April 2014); Single-family building permits issued: 12 (2013); Multi-family building permits issued: 0 (2013); Homeowner vacancy rate: 2.6%. Rental vacancy rate: 4.4%. (2008-2012 5-year est.); Employment by occupation: 8.6% management, business, and financial, 2.7% computer, engineering, and science, 5.3% education, legal, community service, arts, and media, 3.6% healthcare practitioners, 12.8% service, 27.0% sales and office, 10.1% natural resources, construction, and maintenance, 29.8% production, transportation, and material moving (2008-2012 5-year est.).
Income: Per capita income: $20,915 (2008-2012 5-year est.); Median household income: $51,340 (2008-2012 5-year est.); Average household income: $61,179 (2008-2012 5-year est.); Percent of households with income of $100,000 or more: 15.8% (2008-2012 5-year est.); Poverty rate: 13.6% (2008-2012 5-year est.).
Education: Percent of population age 25 and over with: High school diploma (including GED) or higher: 76.4% (2008-2012 5-year est.); Bachelor's degree or higher: 13.5% (2008-2012 5-year est.); Master's degree or higher: 4.2% (2008-2012 5-year est.).
School District(s)
Belvidere CUSD 100 (PK-12)
  2011-12 Enrollment: 8,622 . . . . (815) 544-0301
Boone County Spec Educ Coop (PK-PK)
  2011-12 Enrollment: n/a . . . . (815) 544-9851
Boone/winnebago Roe (PK-12)
  2011-12 Enrollment: n/a . . . . (815) 636-3060

Housing: Homeownership rate: 75.7% (2008-2012 5-year est.); Median home value: $124,200 (2008-2012 5-year est.); Median contract rent: $566 per month (2008-2012 5-year est.); Median year structure built: 1970 (2008-2012 5-year est.).
Health Insurance: 67.7% Private; 29.2% Public; 13.8% None. (2008-2012 5-year est.)
Hospitals: Northwest Suburban Community Hospital (69 beds)
Transportation: Commute to work: 92.1% car, 0.1% public transportation, 2.3% walk, 2.5% work from home (2008-2012 5-year est.); Travel time to work: 29.4% less than 15 minutes, 25.5% 15 to 30 minutes, 20.4% 30 to 45 minutes, 9.7% 45 to 60 minutes, 15.0% 60 minutes or more (2008-2012 5-year est.)
Additional Information Contacts
Belvidere Area Chamber of Commerce . . . . (815) 544-4357
  http://www.belviderechamber.com
City of Belvidere . . . . (815) 544-2612
  http://www.ci.belvidere.il.us

CALEDONIA (village). Aka North Caledonia. Covers a land area of 1.007 square miles and a water area of 0 square miles. Located at 42.37° N. Lat; 88.89° W. Long. Elevation is 928 feet.
Population: n/a (1990); 199 (2000); 197 (2010); Density: 231.4 persons per square mile (2008-2012 5-year est.); Race: 98.3% White, 0.0% Black/African American, 0.0% Asian, 0.0% American Indian/Alaska Native, 0.0% Native Hawaiian/Other Pacific Islander, 1.7% Some other race, 1.7% Two or more races, 12.4% Hispanic of any race (2008-2012 5-year est.); Average household size: 3.28 (2008-2012 5-year est.); Median age: 37.5 (2008-2012 5-year est.); Males per 100 females: 92.6 (2008-2012 5-year est.); Marriage status: 17.0% never married, 70.2% now married, 0.6% widowed, 12.3% divorced (2008-2012 5-year est.); Foreign born: 6.0% (2008-2012 5-year est.); Ancestry (includes multiple ancestries): 37.8% German, 19.3% Irish, 14.2% Swedish, 8.6% Italian, 6.9% Polish (2008-2012 5-year est.).
Economy: Single-family building permits issued: 0 (2013); Multi-family building permits issued: 0 (2013); Homeowner vacancy rate: 0.0%. Rental vacancy rate: 0.0%. (2008-2012 5-year est.); Employment by occupation: 11.0% management, business, and financial, 0.0% computer, engineering, and science, 5.9% education, legal, community service, arts, and media, 3.4% healthcare practitioners, 8.5% service, 38.1% sales and office, 13.6% natural resources, construction, and maintenance, 19.5% production, transportation, and material moving (2008-2012 5-year est.).
Income: Per capita income: $23,533 (2008-2012 5-year est.); Median household income: $64,107 (2008-2012 5-year est.); Average household income: $74,696 (2008-2012 5-year est.); Percent of households with income of $100,000 or more: 25.4% (2008-2012 5-year est.); Poverty rate: 15.9% (2008-2012 5-year est.).
Education: Percent of population age 25 and over with: High school diploma (including GED) or higher: 89.0% (2008-2012 5-year est.); Bachelor's degree or higher: 9.1% (2008-2012 5-year est.); Master's degree or higher: 3.2% (2008-2012 5-year est.).
School District(s)
Belvidere CUSD 100 (PK-12)
  2011-12 Enrollment: 8,622 . . . . (815) 544-0301
Housing: Homeownership rate: 93.0% (2008-2012 5-year est.); Median home value: $153,100 (2008-2012 5-year est.); Median contract rent: $788 per month (2008-2012 5-year est.); Median year structure built: Before 1940 (2008-2012 5-year est.).
Health Insurance: 73.4% Private; 14.6% Public; 18.9% None. (2008-2012 5-year est.)
Transportation: Commute to work: 96.6% car, 0.0% public transportation, 0.9% walk, 1.7% work from home (2008-2012 5-year est.); Travel time to work: 12.3% less than 15 minutes, 50.0% 15 to 30 minutes, 15.8% 30 to 45 minutes, 12.3% 45 to 60 minutes, 9.6% 60 minutes or more (2008-2012 5-year est.)

CAPRON (village). Covers a land area of 0.775 square miles and a water area of <.001 square miles. Located at 42.40° N. Lat; 88.74° W. Long. Elevation is 909 feet.
Population: 682 (1990); 961 (2000); 1,376 (2010); Density: 1,864.9 persons per square mile (2008-2012 5-year est.); Race: 94.8% White, 0.0% Black/African American, 1.2% Asian, 0.0% American Indian/Alaska Native, 0.0% Native Hawaiian/Other Pacific Islander, 4.0% Some other race, 1.7% Two or more races, 27.9% Hispanic of any race (2008-2012 5-year est.); Average household size: 3.11 (2008-2012 5-year est.); Median age: 32.9 (2008-2012 5-year est.); Males per 100 females: 92.4

(2008-2012 5-year est.); Marriage status: 23.8% never married, 56.9% now married, 1.9% widowed, 17.4% divorced (2008-2012 5-year est.); Foreign born: 10.7% (2008-2012 5-year est.); Ancestry (includes multiple ancestries): 33.4% German, 16.4% Irish, 8.2% Italian, 7.5% American, 7.4% Polish (2008-2012 5-year est.).

Economy: Single-family building permits issued: 0 (2013); Multi-family building permits issued: 0 (2013); Homeowner vacancy rate: 2.9%. Rental vacancy rate: 16.0%. (2008-2012 5-year est.); Employment by occupation: 2.6% management, business, and financial, 4.2% computer, engineering, and science, 2.6% education, legal, community service, arts, and media, 1.1% healthcare practitioners, 12.4% service, 26.6% sales and office, 8.7% natural resources, construction, and maintenance, 41.8% production, transportation, and material moving (2008-2012 5-year est.).

Income: Per capita income: $18,953 (2008-2012 5-year est.); Median household income: $51,056 (2008-2012 5-year est.); Average household income: $56,138 (2008-2012 5-year est.); Percent of households with income of $100,000 or more: 9.4% (2008-2012 5-year est.); Poverty rate: 14.1% (2008-2012 5-year est.).

Education: Percent of population age 25 and over with: High school diploma (including GED) or higher: 80.6% (2008-2012 5-year est.); Bachelor's degree or higher: 6.8% (2008-2012 5-year est.); Master's degree or higher: 1.0% (2008-2012 5-year est.).

School District(s)
North Boone CUSD 200 (PK-12)
    2011-12 Enrollment: 1,722 . . . . (815) 765-3322

Housing: Homeownership rate: 85.3% (2008-2012 5-year est.); Median home value: $145,300 (2008-2012 5-year est.); Median contract rent: $563 per month (2008-2012 5-year est.); Median year structure built: 1970 (2008-2012 5-year est.).

Health Insurance: 63.0% Private; 29.1% Public; 13.8% None. (2008-2012 5-year est.)

Transportation: Commute to work: 91.0% car, 0.0% public transportation, 1.7% walk, 6.3% work from home (2008-2012 5-year est.); Travel time to work: 16.9% less than 15 minutes, 25.1% 15 to 30 minutes, 36.0% 30 to 45 minutes, 18.8% 45 to 60 minutes, 3.1% 60 minutes or more (2008-2012 5-year est.)

GARDEN PRAIRIE (village). Covers a land area of 0.906 square miles and a water area of 0.008 square miles. Located at 42.25° N. Lat; 88.71° W. Long. Elevation is 781 feet.

History: Garden Prairie began in 1849 when a station for the Galena & Chicago Union Railroad was built here.

Population: n/a (1990); n/a (2000); 352 (2010); Density: 268.2 persons per square mile (2008-2012 5-year est.); Race: 100.0% White, 0.0% Black/African American, 0.0% Asian, 0.0% American Indian/Alaska Native, 0.0% Native Hawaiian/Other Pacific Islander, 0.0% Some other race, 0.0% Two or more races, 11.1% Hispanic of any race (2008-2012 5-year est.); Average household size: 2.09 (2008-2012 5-year est.); Median age: 47.2 (2008-2012 5-year est.); Males per 100 females: 77.4 (2008-2012 5-year est.); Marriage status: 21.9% never married, 49.6% now married, 1.8% widowed, 26.8% divorced (2008-2012 5-year est.); Foreign born: 2.1% (2008-2012 5-year est.); Ancestry (includes multiple ancestries): 28.8% German, 24.3% American, 12.8% Polish, 11.9% Irish, 9.1% Italian (2008-2012 5-year est.).

Economy: Homeowner vacancy rate: 0.0%. Rental vacancy rate: 0.0%. (2008-2012 5-year est.); Employment by occupation: 4.0% management, business, and financial, 0.0% computer, engineering, and science, 3.2% education, legal, community service, arts, and media, 1.6% healthcare practitioners, 3.2% service, 72.2% sales and office, 3.2% natural resources, construction, and maintenance, 12.7% production, transportation, and material moving (2008-2012 5-year est.).

Income: Per capita income: $28,177 (2008-2012 5-year est.); Median household income: $39,412 (2008-2012 5-year est.); Average household income: $57,741 (2008-2012 5-year est.); Percent of households with income of $100,000 or more: 23.3% (2008-2012 5-year est.); Poverty rate: 12.8% (2008-2012 5-year est.).

Education: Percent of population age 25 and over with: High school diploma (including GED) or higher: 91.4% (2008-2012 5-year est.); Bachelor's degree or higher: 4.3% (2008-2012 5-year est.); Master's degree or higher: 2.1% (2008-2012 5-year est.).

School District(s)
Belvidere CUSD 100 (PK-12)
    2011-12 Enrollment: 8,622 . . . . (815) 544-0301

Housing: Homeownership rate: 69.0% (2008-2012 5-year est.); Median home value: $200,000 (2008-2012 5-year est.); Median contract rent: $416

per month (2008-2012 5-year est.); Median year structure built: 1948 (2008-2012 5-year est.).

Health Insurance: 86.0% Private; 22.6% Public; 7.0% None. (2008-2012 5-year est.)

Transportation: Commute to work: 80.2% car, 0.0% public transportation, 3.2% walk, 16.7% work from home (2008-2012 5-year est.); Travel time to work: 18.1% less than 15 minutes, 44.8% 15 to 30 minutes, 11.4% 30 to 45 minutes, 1.9% 45 to 60 minutes, 23.8% 60 minutes or more (2008-2012 5-year est.)

POPLAR GROVE (village). Covers a land area of 8.029 square miles and a water area of 0.020 square miles. Located at 42.34° N. Lat; 88.84° W. Long. Elevation is 899 feet.

Population: 743 (1990); 1,368 (2000); 5,023 (2010); Density: 732.3 persons per square mile (2008-2012 5-year est.); Race: 88.5% White, 8.0% Black/African American, 0.7% Asian, 0.6% American Indian/Alaska Native, 0.0% Native Hawaiian/Other Pacific Islander, 2.2% Some other race, 2.1% Two or more races, 6.5% Hispanic of any race (2008-2012 5-year est.); Average household size: 3.06 (2008-2012 5-year est.); Median age: 35.7 (2008-2012 5-year est.); Males per 100 females: 86.6 (2008-2012 5-year est.); Marriage status: 19.0% never married, 68.2% now married, 3.8% widowed, 9.0% divorced (2008-2012 5-year est.); Foreign born: 3.4% (2008-2012 5-year est.); Ancestry (includes multiple ancestries): 24.2% German, 18.4% Irish, 11.3% Italian, 11.0% American, 6.1% English (2008-2012 5-year est.).

Economy: Single-family building permits issued: 24 (2013); Multi-family building permits issued: 0 (2013); Homeowner vacancy rate: 1.9%. Rental vacancy rate: 0.0%. (2008-2012 5-year est.); Employment by occupation: 11.0% management, business, and financial, 3.4% computer, engineering, and science, 5.1% education, legal, community service, arts, and media, 4.8% healthcare practitioners, 14.7% service, 27.8% sales and office, 13.1% natural resources, construction, and maintenance, 20.0% production, transportation, and material moving (2008-2012 5-year est.).

Income: Per capita income: $25,733 (2008-2012 5-year est.); Median household income: $57,451 (2008-2012 5-year est.); Average household income: $77,122 (2008-2012 5-year est.); Percent of households with income of $100,000 or more: 23.0% (2008-2012 5-year est.); Poverty rate: 13.3% (2008-2012 5-year est.).

Education: Percent of population age 25 and over with: High school diploma (including GED) or higher: 93.7% (2008-2012 5-year est.); Bachelor's degree or higher: 17.0% (2008-2012 5-year est.); Master's degree or higher: 3.1% (2008-2012 5-year est.).

School District(s)
North Boone CUSD 200 (PK-12)
    2011-12 Enrollment: 1,722 . . . . (815) 765-3322

Housing: Homeownership rate: 88.5% (2008-2012 5-year est.); Median home value: $172,500 (2008-2012 5-year est.); Median contract rent: $887 per month (2008-2012 5-year est.); Median year structure built: 2000 (2008-2012 5-year est.).

Health Insurance: 67.6% Private; 32.7% Public; 12.5% None. (2008-2012 5-year est.)

Transportation: Commute to work: 94.3% car, 0.3% public transportation, 0.0% walk, 2.8% work from home (2008-2012 5-year est.); Travel time to work: 9.1% less than 15 minutes, 31.5% 15 to 30 minutes, 32.8% 30 to 45 minutes, 8.7% 45 to 60 minutes, 18.0% 60 minutes or more (2008-2012 5-year est.)

Airports: Poplar Grove Airport (general aviation)

TIMBERLANE (village). Covers a land area of 1.753 square miles and a water area of 0.019 square miles. Located at 42.34° N. Lat; 88.87° W. Long. Elevation is 840 feet.

Population: n/a (1990); 234 (2000); 934 (2010); Density: 637.6 persons per square mile (2008-2012 5-year est.); Race: 97.9% White, 0.0% Black/African American, 0.2% Asian, 0.0% American Indian/Alaska Native, 0.0% Native Hawaiian/Other Pacific Islander, 1.9% Some other race, 0.6% Two or more races, 4.6% Hispanic of any race (2008-2012 5-year est.); Average household size: 3.29 (2008-2012 5-year est.); Median age: 39.1 (2008-2012 5-year est.); Males per 100 females: 114.6 (2008-2012 5-year est.); Marriage status: 19.5% never married, 70.0% now married, 1.4% widowed, 9.1% divorced (2008-2012 5-year est.); Foreign born: 3.7% (2008-2012 5-year est.); Ancestry (includes multiple ancestries): 34.1% German, 20.5% Irish, 13.7% English, 11.6% American, 7.9% Italian (2008-2012 5-year est.).

Economy: Single-family building permits issued: 2 (2013); Multi-family building permits issued: 0 (2013); Homeowner vacancy rate: 0.0%. Rental

vacancy rate: 0.0%. (2008-2012 5-year est.); Employment by occupation: 16.0% management, business, and financial, 9.6% computer, engineering, and science, 13.0% education, legal, community service, arts, and media, 5.6% healthcare practitioners, 11.4% service, 22.8% sales and office, 10.0% natural resources, construction, and maintenance, 11.6% production, transportation, and material moving (2008-2012 5-year est.).
Income: Per capita income: $38,697 (2008-2012 5-year est.); Median household income: $108,421 (2008-2012 5-year est.); Average household income: $121,450 (2008-2012 5-year est.); Percent of households with income of $100,000 or more: 58.5% (2008-2012 5-year est.); Poverty rate: 1.7% (2008-2012 5-year est.).
Education: Percent of population age 25 and over with: High school diploma (including GED) or higher: 93.3% (2008-2012 5-year est.); Bachelor's degree or higher: 31.0% (2008-2012 5-year est.); Master's degree or higher: 10.6% (2008-2012 5-year est.).
Housing: Homeownership rate: 100.0% (2008-2012 5-year est.); Median home value: $285,700 (2008-2012 5-year est.); Median contract rent: n/a per month (2008-2012 5-year est.); Median year structure built: 2004 (2008-2012 5-year est.).
Health Insurance: 94.5% Private; 7.6% Public; 1.9% None. (2008-2012 5-year est.)
Transportation: Commute to work: 90.7% car, 1.8% public transportation, 0.0% walk, 6.8% work from home (2008-2012 5-year est.); Travel time to work: 11.5% less than 15 minutes, 36.0% 15 to 30 minutes, 18.6% 30 to 45 minutes, 9.0% 45 to 60 minutes, 24.9% 60 minutes or more (2008-2012 5-year est.)

Brown County

Located in western Illinois; bounded on the southeast by the Illinois River, and on the northeast by the La Moine River. Covers a land area of 305.607 square miles, a water area of 1.598 square miles, and is located in the Central Time Zone at 39.96° N. Lat., 90.75° W. Long. The county was founded in 1839. County seat is Mount Sterling.
Population: 5,836 (1990); 6,950 (2000); 6,937 (2010); Race: 80.6% White, 14.4% Black/African American, 0.5% Asian, 0.3% American Indian/Alaska Native, 0.0% Native Hawaiian/Other Pacific Islander, 4.2% Some other race, 4.1% Two or more races, 6.1% Hispanic of any race (2008-2012 5-year est.); Density: 22.6 persons per square mile (2008-2012 5-year est.); Average household size: 2.46 (2008-2012 5-year est.); Median age: 37.2 (2008-2012 5-year est.); Males per 100 females: 179.4 (2008-2012 5-year est.).
Religion: Six largest groups: 24.2% Catholicism, 13.0% Baptist, 3.3% Methodist/Pietist, 1.2% Lutheran, 1.0% Holiness, 0.8% Presbyterian-Reformed (2010)
Economy: Unemployment rate: 3.1% (April 2014); Total civilian labor force: 3,569 (April 2014); Leading industries: 5.5% retail trade; 4.2% accommodation & food services; 1.3% administration, support, waste management, remediation services (2012); Farms: 413 totaling 137,523 acres (2012); Companies that employ 500 or more persons: 1 (2012); Companies that employ 100 to 499 persons: 2 (2012); Companies that employ less than 100 persons: 116 (2012); Black-owned businesses: n/a (2007); Hispanic-owned businesses: n/a (2007); Asian-owned businesses: n/a (2007); Women-owned businesses: n/a (2007); Single-family building permits issued: 0 (2013); Multi-family building permits issued: 0 (2013).
Income: Per capita income: $19,180 (2008-2012 5-year est.); Median household income: $43,915 (2008-2012 5-year est.); Average household income: $56,922 (2008-2012 5-year est.); Percent of households with income of $100,000 or more: 12.9% (2008-2012 5-year est.); Poverty rate: 9.5% (2008-2012 5-year est.); Bankruptcy rate: 1.74% (2013).
Education: Percent of population age 25 and over with: High school diploma (including GED) or higher: 81.9% (2008-2012 5-year est.); Bachelor's degree or higher: 12.7% (2008-2012 5-year est.); Master's degree or higher: 2.9% (2008-2012 5-year est.).
Housing: Homeownership rate: 72.8% (2008-2012 5-year est.); Median home value: $85,400 (2008-2012 5-year est.); Median contract rent: $406 per month (2008-2012 5-year est.); Median year structure built: 1954 (2008-2012 5-year est.).
Health: Birth rate: 68.5 per 10,000 population (2013); Death rate: 83.1 per 10,000 population (2013); Age-adjusted cancer mortality rate: Unreliable deaths per 100,000 population (2011); Number of physicians: 1.5 per 10,000 population (2011); Hospital beds: 0.0 per 10,000 population (2010); Hospital admissions: 0.0 per 10,000 population (2010).
Elections: 2012 Presidential election results: 33.3% Obama, 64.0% Romney

Additional Information Contacts
Brown County Government . . . . (217) 773-3013
  http://www.browncountyil.com

Brown County Communities

MOUND STATION (village). Aka Timewell. Covers a land area of 0.519 square miles and a water area of 0 square miles. Located at 40.01° N. Lat; 90.87° W. Long.
History: Also called Timewell.
Population: 147 (1990); 127 (2000); 122 (2010); Density: 183.2 persons per square mile (2008-2012 5-year est.); Race: 87.4% White, 0.0% Black/African American, 12.6% Asian, 0.0% American Indian/Alaska Native, 0.0% Native Hawaiian/Other Pacific Islander, 0.0% Some other race, 0.0% Two or more races, 0.0% Hispanic of any race (2008-2012 5-year est.); Average household size: 2.71 (2008-2012 5-year est.); Median age: 40.3 (2008-2012 5-year est.); Males per 100 females: 102.1 (2008-2012 5-year est.); Marriage status: 38.2% never married, 52.6% now married, 3.9% widowed, 5.3% divorced (2008-2012 5-year est.); Foreign born: 12.6% (2008-2012 5-year est.); Ancestry (includes multiple ancestries): 24.2% German, 13.7% American, 6.3% English, 4.2% European, 2.1% Irish (2008-2012 5-year est.).
Economy: Homeowner vacancy rate: 0.0%. Rental vacancy rate: 0.0%. (2008-2012 5-year est.); Employment by occupation: 11.7% management, business, and financial, 0.0% computer, engineering, and science, 8.3% education, legal, community service, arts, and media, 0.0% healthcare practitioners, 5.0% service, 35.0% sales and office, 18.3% natural resources, construction, and maintenance, 21.7% production, transportation, and material moving (2008-2012 5-year est.).
Income: Per capita income: $22,829 (2008-2012 5-year est.); Median household income: $44,375 (2008-2012 5-year est.); Average household income: $57,171 (2008-2012 5-year est.); Percent of households with income of $100,000 or more: 14.3% (2008-2012 5-year est.); Poverty rate: 1.1% (2008-2012 5-year est.).
Education: Percent of population age 25 and over with: High school diploma (including GED) or higher: 94.1% (2008-2012 5-year est.); Bachelor's degree or higher: 13.7% (2008-2012 5-year est.); Master's degree or higher: 3.9% (2008-2012 5-year est.).
Housing: Homeownership rate: 91.4% (2008-2012 5-year est.); Median home value: $65,000 (2008-2012 5-year est.); Median contract rent: $313 per month (2008-2012 5-year est.); Median year structure built: Before 1940 (2008-2012 5-year est.).
Health Insurance: 73.7% Private; 21.1% Public; 22.1% None. (2008-2012 5-year est.)
Transportation: Commute to work: 91.7% car, 0.0% public transportation, 3.3% walk, 0.0% work from home (2008-2012 5-year est.); Travel time to work: 65.0% less than 15 minutes, 10.0% 15 to 30 minutes, 10.0% 30 to 45 minutes, 10.0% 45 to 60 minutes, 5.0% 60 minutes or more (2008-2012 5-year est.)

MOUNT STERLING (city). County seat. Covers a land area of 1.108 square miles and a water area of 0 square miles. Located at 39.99° N. Lat; 90.76° W. Long. Elevation is 725 feet.
History: Mount Sterling was settled in 1830 by Robert Curry, who named the village for the "sterling" quality of the soil. Mount Sterling developed as the seat of Brown County.
Population: 1,922 (1990); 2,070 (2000); 2,025 (2010); Density: 2,137.6 persons per square mile (2008-2012 5-year est.); Race: 95.8% White, 2.2% Black/African American, 0.6% Asian, 0.0% American Indian/Alaska Native, 0.0% Native Hawaiian/Other Pacific Islander, 1.4% Some other race, 1.4% Two or more races, 1.4% Hispanic of any race (2008-2012 5-year est.); Average household size: 2.47 (2008-2012 5-year est.); Median age: 36.9 (2008-2012 5-year est.); Males per 100 females: 96.4 (2008-2012 5-year est.); Marriage status: 32.3% never married, 41.5% now married, 12.8% widowed, 13.4% divorced (2008-2012 5-year est.); Foreign born: 1.0% (2008-2012 5-year est.); Ancestry (includes multiple ancestries): 27.5% German, 24.1% American, 14.1% Irish, 7.0% English, 2.7% Norwegian (2008-2012 5-year est.).
Economy: Single-family building permits issued: 0 (2013); Multi-family building permits issued: 0 (2013); Homeowner vacancy rate: 0.0%. Rental vacancy rate: 4.6%. (2008-2012 5-year est.); Employment by occupation: 3.7% management, business, and financial, 2.7% computer, engineering, and science, 4.1% education, legal, community service, arts, and media, 10.6% healthcare practitioners, 23.6% service, 23.3% sales and office,

15.6% natural resources, construction, and maintenance, 16.3% production, transportation, and material moving (2008-2012 5-year est.).

Income: Per capita income: $20,143 (2008-2012 5-year est.); Median household income: $36,052 (2008-2012 5-year est.); Average household income: $46,276 (2008-2012 5-year est.); Percent of households with income of $100,000 or more: 6.8% (2008-2012 5-year est.); Poverty rate: 13.8% (2008-2012 5-year est.).

Education: Percent of population age 25 and over with: High school diploma (including GED) or higher: 85.7% (2008-2012 5-year est.); Bachelor's degree or higher: 17.3% (2008-2012 5-year est.); Master's degree or higher: 3.7% (2008-2012 5-year est.).

School District(s)

Brown County CUSD 1 (PK-12)
    2011-12 Enrollment: 749 . . . . (217) 773-7502
Brown County CUSD 1 (PK-12)
    2011-12 Enrollment: 749 . . . . (217) 773-7502

Housing: Homeownership rate: 70.9% (2008-2012 5-year est.); Median home value: $73,900 (2008-2012 5-year est.); Median contract rent: $296 per month (2008-2012 5-year est.); Median year structure built: 1956 (2008-2012 5-year est.).

Health Insurance: 69.2% Private; 33.7% Public; 11.1% None. (2008-2012 5-year est.)

Safety: Violent crime rate: 20.0 per 10,000 population; Property crime rate: 104.9 per 10,000 population (2012).

Transportation: Commute to work: 91.1% car, 3.8% public transportation, 2.5% walk, 1.6% work from home (2008-2012 5-year est.); Travel time to work: 69.6% less than 15 minutes, 12.3% 15 to 30 minutes, 6.4% 30 to 45 minutes, 1.8% 45 to 60 minutes, 10.0% 60 minutes or more (2008-2012 5-year est.)

Airports: Mount Sterling Municipal Airport (general aviation)

RIPLEY (village). Covers a land area of 0.379 square miles and a water area of 0 square miles. Located at 40.03° N. Lat; 90.64° W. Long. Elevation is 548 feet.

History: Ripley experienced prosperity in the 1830's and 1840's when its pottery kilns were producing.

Population: 103 (1990); 103 (2000); 86 (2010); Density: 155.8 persons per square mile (2008-2012 5-year est.); Race: 100.0% White, 0.0% Black/African American, 0.0% Asian, 0.0% American Indian/Alaska Native, 0.0% Native Hawaiian/Other Pacific Islander, 0.0% Some other race, 0.0% Two or more races, 0.0% Hispanic of any race (2008-2012 5-year est.); Average household size: 2.11 (2008-2012 5-year est.); Median age: 36.8 (2008-2012 5-year est.); Males per 100 females: 103.4 (2008-2012 5-year est.); Marriage status: 4.1% never married, 71.4% now married, 6.1% widowed, 18.4% divorced (2008-2012 5-year est.); Foreign born: 0.0% (2008-2012 5-year est.); Ancestry (includes multiple ancestries): 30.5% German, 13.6% American, 10.2% Norwegian, 8.5% Irish, 6.8% Dutch (2008-2012 5-year est.).

Economy: Single-family building permits issued: 0 (2013); Multi-family building permits issued: 0 (2013); Homeowner vacancy rate: 0.0%. Rental vacancy rate: 0.0%. (2008-2012 5-year est.); Employment by occupation: 3.6% management, business, and financial, 10.7% computer, engineering, and science, 17.9% education, legal, community service, arts, and media, 0.0% healthcare practitioners, 21.4% service, 14.3% sales and office, 25.0% natural resources, construction, and maintenance, 7.1% production, transportation, and material moving (2008-2012 5-year est.).

Income: Per capita income: $13,049 (2008-2012 5-year est.); Median household income: $21,250 (2008-2012 5-year est.); Average household income: $27,396 (2008-2012 5-year est.); Percent of households with income of $100,000 or more: n/a (2008-2012 5-year est.); Poverty rate: 15.3% (2008-2012 5-year est.).

Education: Percent of population age 25 and over with: High school diploma (including GED) or higher: 72.9% (2008-2012 5-year est.); Bachelor's degree or higher: 0.0% (2008-2012 5-year est.); Master's degree or higher: 0.0% (2008-2012 5-year est.).

Housing: Homeownership rate: 71.4% (2008-2012 5-year est.); Median home value: $37,500 (2008-2012 5-year est.); Median contract rent: $650 per month (2008-2012 5-year est.); Median year structure built: 1965 (2008-2012 5-year est.).

Health Insurance: 33.9% Private; 42.4% Public; 28.8% None. (2008-2012 5-year est.)

Transportation: Commute to work: 100.0% car, 0.0% public transportation, 0.0% walk, 0.0% work from home (2008-2012 5-year est.); Travel time to work: 35.7% less than 15 minutes, 17.9% 15 to 30 minutes,

35.7% 30 to 45 minutes, 7.1% 45 to 60 minutes, 3.6% 60 minutes or more (2008-2012 5-year est.)

TIMEWELL (unincorporated postal area)
Zip Code: 62375
    Covers a land area of 44.846 square miles and a water area of 0.017 square miles. Located at 40.00° N. Lat; 90.86° W. Long. Elevation is 755 feet. Population: 369 (2010); Density: 8.2 persons per square mile (2010); Race: 100.0% White, 0.0% Black/African American, 0.0% Asian, 0.0% American Indian/Alaska Native, 0.0% Native Hawaiian/Other Pacific Islander, 0.0% Some other race, 0.0% Two or more races, 0.3% Hispanic of any race (2010); Average household size: 2.37 (2010); Median age: 43.3 (2010); Males per 100 females: 101.6 (2010); Homeownership rate: 82.0% (2010)

VERSAILLES (village). Covers a land area of 0.933 square miles and a water area of 0.005 square miles. Located at 39.88° N. Lat; 90.66° W. Long. Elevation is 633 feet.

Population: 480 (1990); 567 (2000); 478 (2010); Density: 418.9 persons per square mile (2008-2012 5-year est.); Race: 94.9% White, 0.0% Black/African American, 0.0% Asian, 0.0% American Indian/Alaska Native, 0.0% Native Hawaiian/Other Pacific Islander, 5.1% Some other race, 5.1% Two or more races, 0.0% Hispanic of any race (2008-2012 5-year est.); Average household size: 2.11 (2008-2012 5-year est.); Median age: 40.1 (2008-2012 5-year est.); Males per 100 females: 117.2 (2008-2012 5-year est.); Marriage status: 29.2% never married, 56.3% now married, 8.3% widowed, 6.3% divorced (2008-2012 5-year est.); Foreign born: 2.6% (2008-2012 5-year est.); Ancestry (includes multiple ancestries): 28.9% German, 19.2% Irish, 12.0% American, 7.7% English, 3.8% Polish (2008-2012 5-year est.).

Economy: Homeowner vacancy rate: 0.0%. Rental vacancy rate: 0.0%. (2008-2012 5-year est.); Employment by occupation: 6.4% management, business, and financial, 0.0% computer, engineering, and science, 12.4% education, legal, community service, arts, and media, 5.5% healthcare practitioners, 26.1% service, 29.4% sales and office, 14.7% natural resources, construction, and maintenance, 5.5% production, transportation, and material moving (2008-2012 5-year est.).

Income: Per capita income: $24,943 (2008-2012 5-year est.); Median household income: $41,023 (2008-2012 5-year est.); Average household income: $48,876 (2008-2012 5-year est.); Percent of households with income of $100,000 or more: 9.7% (2008-2012 5-year est.); Poverty rate: 0.5% (2008-2012 5-year est.).

Education: Percent of population age 25 and over with: High school diploma (including GED) or higher: 94.6% (2008-2012 5-year est.); Bachelor's degree or higher: 10.9% (2008-2012 5-year est.); Master's degree or higher: 8.0% (2008-2012 5-year est.).

Housing: Homeownership rate: 72.4% (2008-2012 5-year est.); Median home value: $60,400 (2008-2012 5-year est.); Median contract rent: $425 per month (2008-2012 5-year est.); Median year structure built: Before 1940 (2008-2012 5-year est.).

Health Insurance: 82.0% Private; 27.6% Public; 5.2% None. (2008-2012 5-year est.)

Transportation: Commute to work: 87.6% car, 12.0% public transportation, 0.5% walk, 0.0% work from home (2008-2012 5-year est.); Travel time to work: 15.8% less than 15 minutes, 39.2% 15 to 30 minutes, 20.1% 30 to 45 minutes, 7.2% 45 to 60 minutes, 17.7% 60 minutes or more (2008-2012 5-year est.)

Bureau County

Located in northern Illinois; bounded on the southeast by the Illinois River; includes Lake Depue. Covers a land area of 869.031 square miles, a water area of 4.472 square miles, and is located in the Central Time Zone at 41.40° N. Lat., 89.53° W. Long. The county was founded in 1837. County seat is Princeton.

Bureau County is part of the Ottawa-Peru, IL Micropolitan Statistical Area. The entire metro area includes: Bureau County, IL; LaSalle County, IL; Putnam County, IL

Weather Station: Princeton   Elevation: 694 feet

	Jan	Feb	Mar	Apr	May	Jun	Jul	Aug	Sep	Oct	Nov	Dec
High	31	35	48	61	73	82	85	82	76	63	48	34
Low	17	20	30	40	51	61	65	63	55	43	32	20
Precip	2.0	1.9	2.4	3.7	4.5	4.3	na	4.6	3.6	3.0	2.8	2.3
Snow	8.6	6.1	3.3	0.5	tr	0.0	0.0	0.0	0.0	0.1	0.9	7.4

High and Low temperatures in degrees Fahrenheit; Precipitation and Snow in inches

Weather Station: Walnut   Elevation: 689 feet

	Jan	Feb	Mar	Apr	May	Jun	Jul	Aug	Sep	Oct	Nov	Dec
High	30	34	47	61	72	81	84	82	76	64	48	34
Low	13	17	27	38	50	59	63	61	52	40	30	17
Precip	1.3	1.3	2.2	3.2	4.2	4.4	3.8	4.6	3.1	2.8	2.5	1.9
Snow	9.3	7.0	3.3	0.8	tr	0.0	0.0	0.0	0.0	0.1	1.1	9.3

High and Low temperatures in degrees Fahrenheit; Precipitation and Snow in inches

Population: 35,688 (1990); 35,503 (2000); 34,978 (2010); Race: 96.5% White, 0.6% Black/African American, 0.7% Asian, 0.3% American Indian/Alaska Native, 0.0% Native Hawaiian/Other Pacific Islander, 1.9% Some other race, 0.8% Two or more races, 7.8% Hispanic of any race (2008-2012 5-year est.); Density: 39.5 persons per square mile (2008-2012 5-year est.); Average household size: 2.40 (2008-2012 5-year est.); Median age: 42.6 (2008-2012 5-year est.); Males per 100 females: 95.9 (2008-2012 5-year est.).
Religion: Six largest groups: 13.0% Catholicism, 8.0% Methodist/Pietist, 7.7% Lutheran, 4.0% Presbyterian-Reformed, 3.0% Baptist, 1.9% Non-denominational Protestant (2010)
Economy: Unemployment rate: 7.1% (April 2014); Total civilian labor force: 17,781 (April 2014); Leading industries: 22.3% health care and social assistance; 15.2% manufacturing; 12.3% retail trade (2012); Farms: 1,056 totaling 450,132 acres (2012); Companies that employ 500 or more persons: 2 (2012); Companies that employ 100 to 499 persons: 15 (2012); Companies that employ less than 100 persons: 762 (2012); Black-owned businesses: n/a (2007); Hispanic-owned businesses: n/a (2007); Asian-owned businesses: n/a (2007); Women-owned businesses: 837 (2007); Single-family building permits issued: 16 (2013); Multi-family building permits issued: 2 (2013).
Income: Per capita income: $26,259 (2008-2012 5-year est.); Median household income: $48,102 (2008-2012 5-year est.); Average household income: $63,211 (2008-2012 5-year est.); Percent of households with income of $100,000 or more: 15.1% (2008-2012 5-year est.); Poverty rate: 11.1% (2008-2012 5-year est.); Bankruptcy rate: 3.53% (2013).
Education: Percent of population age 25 and over with: High school diploma (including GED) or higher: 88.9% (2008-2012 5-year est.); Bachelor's degree or higher: 16.8% (2008-2012 5-year est.); Master's degree or higher: 6.0% (2008-2012 5-year est.).
Housing: Homeownership rate: 75.4% (2008-2012 5-year est.); Median home value: $103,700 (2008-2012 5-year est.); Median contract rent: $443 per month (2008-2012 5-year est.); Median year structure built: 1950 (2008-2012 5-year est.)
Health: Birth rate: 94.8 per 10,000 population (2013); Death rate: 108.6 per 10,000 population (2013); Age-adjusted cancer mortality rate: 179.0 deaths per 100,000 population (2011); Number of physicians: 12.4 per 10,000 population (2011); Hospital beds: 31.7 per 10,000 population (2010); Hospital admissions: 1,371.4 per 10,000 population (2010).
Elections: 2012 Presidential election results: 48.9% Obama, 49.1% Romney
National and State Parks: Hennepin Canal Parkway State Park; Lake Depue State Fish and Wildlife Area; Miller-Anderson Woods State Nature Preserve
Additional Information Contacts
Bureau County Government . . . . (815) 875-2014
    http://www.bureaucounty.us

Bureau County Communities

ARLINGTON (village). Covers a land area of 0.397 square miles and a water area of 0 square miles. Located at 41.47° N. Lat; 89.25° W. Long. Elevation is 751 feet.
Population: 200 (1990); 211 (2000); 193 (2010); Density: 441.1 persons per square mile (2008-2012 5-year est.); Race: 96.0% White, 0.0% Black/African American, 0.0% Asian, 1.1% American Indian/Alaska Native, 2.3% Native Hawaiian/Other Pacific Islander, 0.6% Some other race, 0.6% Two or more races, 4.0% Hispanic of any race (2008-2012 5-year est.); Average household size: 2.40 (2008-2012 5-year est.); Median age: 40.4 (2008-2012 5-year est.); Males per 100 females: 146.5 (2008-2012 5-year

est.); Marriage status: 27.2% never married, 46.3% now married, 7.5% widowed, 19.0% divorced (2008-2012 5-year est.); Foreign born: 0.0% (2008-2012 5-year est.); Ancestry (includes multiple ancestries): 26.3% German, 16.0% Irish, 16.0% Italian, 9.7% Norwegian, 6.9% English (2008-2012 5-year est.).
Economy: Homeowner vacancy rate: 0.0%. Rental vacancy rate: 15.0%. (2008-2012 5-year est.); Employment by occupation: 7.5% management, business, and financial, 5.0% computer, engineering, and science, 7.5% education, legal, community service, arts, and media, 3.8% healthcare practitioners, 20.0% service, 20.0% sales and office, 7.5% natural resources, construction, and maintenance, 28.7% production, transportation, and material moving (2008-2012 5-year est.).
Income: Per capita income: $21,598 (2008-2012 5-year est.); Median household income: $36,875 (2008-2012 5-year est.); Average household income: $50,104 (2008-2012 5-year est.); Percent of households with income of $100,000 or more: 8.2% (2008-2012 5-year est.); Poverty rate: 14.3% (2008-2012 5-year est.).
Education: Percent of population age 25 and over with: High school diploma (including GED) or higher: 85.5% (2008-2012 5-year est.); Bachelor's degree or higher: 17.1% (2008-2012 5-year est.); Master's degree or higher: 5.1% (2008-2012 5-year est.).
Housing: Homeownership rate: 76.7% (2008-2012 5-year est.); Median home value: $72,500 (2008-2012 5-year est.); Median contract rent: $604 per month (2008-2012 5-year est.); Median year structure built: Before 1940 (2008-2012 5-year est.).
Health Insurance: 73.7% Private; 28.6% Public; 13.7% None. (2008-2012 5-year est.)
Transportation: Commute to work: 100.0% car, 0.0% public transportation, 0.0% walk, 0.0% work from home (2008-2012 5-year est.); Travel time to work: 25.0% less than 15 minutes, 52.5% 15 to 30 minutes, 18.8% 30 to 45 minutes, 3.8% 45 to 60 minutes, 0.0% 60 minutes or more (2008-2012 5-year est.)

BUDA (village). Covers a land area of 1.005 square miles and a water area of 0 square miles. Located at 41.33° N. Lat; 89.68° W. Long. Elevation is 768 feet.
Population: 563 (1990); 592 (2000); 538 (2010); Density: 585.2 persons per square mile (2008-2012 5-year est.); Race: 96.4% White, 0.0% Black/African American, 0.0% Asian, 3.6% American Indian/Alaska Native, 0.0% Native Hawaiian/Other Pacific Islander, 0.0% Some other race, 0.0% Two or more races, 2.7% Hispanic of any race (2008-2012 5-year est.); Average household size: 2.48 (2008-2012 5-year est.); Median age: 40.4 (2008-2012 5-year est.); Males per 100 females: 106.3 (2008-2012 5-year est.); Marriage status: 20.5% never married, 59.2% now married, 8.5% widowed, 11.8% divorced (2008-2012 5-year est.); Foreign born: 0.0% (2008-2012 5-year est.); Ancestry (includes multiple ancestries): 20.9% German, 14.8% Irish, 14.3% American, 11.4% English, 4.6% Swedish (2008-2012 5-year est.).
Economy: Homeowner vacancy rate: 0.0%. Rental vacancy rate: 13.0%. (2008-2012 5-year est.); Employment by occupation: 10.1% management, business, and financial, 0.9% computer, engineering, and science, 3.5% education, legal, community service, arts, and media, 1.6% healthcare practitioners, 20.9% service, 23.1% sales and office, 20.6% natural resources, construction, and maintenance, 19.3% production, transportation, and material moving (2008-2012 5-year est.).
Income: Per capita income: $23,001 (2008-2012 5-year est.); Median household income: $52,688 (2008-2012 5-year est.); Average household income: $52,357 (2008-2012 5-year est.); Percent of households with income of $100,000 or more: 10.1% (2008-2012 5-year est.); Poverty rate: 12.4% (2008-2012 5-year est.).
Education: Percent of population age 25 and over with: High school diploma (including GED) or higher: 87.1% (2008-2012 5-year est.); Bachelor's degree or higher: 9.4% (2008-2012 5-year est.); Master's degree or higher: 1.8% (2008-2012 5-year est.).
School District(s)
Bureau Valley CUSD 340 (PK-12)
    2011-12 Enrollment: 1,154 . . . . (815) 445-3101
Housing: Homeownership rate: 80.2% (2008-2012 5-year est.); Median home value: $58,000 (2008-2012 5-year est.); Median contract rent: $327 per month (2008-2012 5-year est.); Median year structure built: Before 1940 (2008-2012 5-year est.).
Health Insurance: 70.9% Private; 43.4% Public; 4.4% None. (2008-2012 5-year est.)
Transportation: Commute to work: 92.6% car, 0.0% public transportation, 0.0% walk, 0.6% work from home (2008-2012 5-year est.); Travel time to

work: 18.4% less than 15 minutes, 45.3% 15 to 30 minutes, 14.2% 30 to 45 minutes, 7.1% 45 to 60 minutes, 14.9% 60 minutes or more (2008-2012 5-year est.)

BUREAU JUNCTION (village). Aka Bureau. Covers a land area of 1.437 square miles and a water area of 0.066 square miles. Located at 41.29° N. Lat; 89.36° W. Long.

Population: 350 (1990); 368 (2000); 322 (2010); Density: 209.5 persons per square mile (2008-2012 5-year est.); Race: 88.7% White, 0.0% Black/African American, 0.0% Asian, 5.0% American Indian/Alaska Native, 0.0% Native Hawaiian/Other Pacific Islander, 6.3% Some other race, 0.7% Two or more races, 13.0% Hispanic of any race (2008-2012 5-year est.); Average household size: 2.53 (2008-2012 5-year est.); Median age: 44.4 (2008-2012 5-year est.); Males per 100 females: 109.0 (2008-2012 5-year est.); Marriage status: 28.6% never married, 56.0% now married, 4.6% widowed, 10.8% divorced (2008-2012 5-year est.); Foreign born: 6.0% (2008-2012 5-year est.); Ancestry (includes multiple ancestries): 19.6% German, 16.9% Irish, 14.6% American, 10.3% Swedish, 10.0% English (2008-2012 5-year est.).
Economy: Homeowner vacancy rate: 4.0%. Rental vacancy rate: 0.0%. (2008-2012 5-year est.); Employment by occupation: 9.8% management, business, and financial, 3.9% computer, engineering, and science, 0.7% education, legal, community service, arts, and media, 6.5% healthcare practitioners, 17.6% service, 15.7% sales and office, 20.9% natural resources, construction, and maintenance, 24.8% production, transportation, and material moving (2008-2012 5-year est.).
Income: Per capita income: $23,380 (2008-2012 5-year est.); Median household income: $47,083 (2008-2012 5-year est.); Average household income: $57,181 (2008-2012 5-year est.); Percent of households with income of $100,000 or more: 9.2% (2008-2012 5-year est.); Poverty rate: 29.2% (2008-2012 5-year est.).
Education: Percent of population age 25 and over with: High school diploma (including GED) or higher: 82.5% (2008-2012 5-year est.); Bachelor's degree or higher: 6.0% (2008-2012 5-year est.); Master's degree or higher: 2.8% (2008-2012 5-year est.).

School District(s)
Leepertown CCSD 175 (PK-08)
 2011-12 Enrollment: 46 . . . . (815) 659-3191
Housing: Homeownership rate: 80.7% (2008-2012 5-year est.); Median home value: $62,200 (2008-2012 5-year est.); Median contract rent: $330 per month (2008-2012 5-year est.); Median year structure built: 1941 (2008-2012 5-year est.).
Health Insurance: 55.1% Private; 25.6% Public; 25.6% None. (2008-2012 5-year est.)
Transportation: Commute to work: 85.3% car, 2.8% public transportation, 0.0% walk, 2.8% work from home (2008-2012 5-year est.); Travel time to work: 20.1% less than 15 minutes, 51.8% 15 to 30 minutes, 15.8% 30 to 45 minutes, 10.8% 45 to 60 minutes, 1.4% 60 minutes or more (2008-2012 5-year est.)

CHERRY (village). Covers a land area of 0.532 square miles and a water area of 0 square miles. Located at 41.43° N. Lat; 89.21° W. Long. Elevation is 679 feet.

History: Cherry was the scene of a mine fire in 1909 that killed 270 miners.
Population: 487 (1990); 509 (2000); 482 (2010); Density: 639.1 persons per square mile (2008-2012 5-year est.); Race: 97.1% White, 0.0% Black/African American, 1.2% Asian, 0.0% American Indian/Alaska Native, 0.0% Native Hawaiian/Other Pacific Islander, 1.7% Some other race, 1.8% Two or more races, 0.0% Hispanic of any race (2008-2012 5-year est.); Average household size: 2.20 (2008-2012 5-year est.); Median age: 47.2 (2008-2012 5-year est.); Males per 100 females: 86.8 (2008-2012 5-year est.); Marriage status: 16.7% never married, 49.6% now married, 11.3% widowed, 22.3% divorced (2008-2012 5-year est.); Foreign born: 2.9% (2008-2012 5-year est.); Ancestry (includes multiple ancestries): 27.4% German, 22.1% Polish, 15.0% Irish, 9.7% American, 9.4% English (2008-2012 5-year est.).
Economy: Homeowner vacancy rate: 5.6%. Rental vacancy rate: 46.9%. (2008-2012 5-year est.); Employment by occupation: 4.4% management, business, and financial, 0.0% computer, engineering, and science, 3.4% education, legal, community service, arts, and media, 1.5% healthcare practitioners, 20.0% service, 38.5% sales and office, 11.7% natural resources, construction, and maintenance, 20.5% production, transportation, and material moving (2008-2012 5-year est.).

Income: Per capita income: $31,416 (2008-2012 5-year est.); Median household income: $65,625 (2008-2012 5-year est.); Average household income: $70,982 (2008-2012 5-year est.); Percent of households with income of $100,000 or more: 26.2% (2008-2012 5-year est.); Poverty rate: 1.5% (2008-2012 5-year est.).
Education: Percent of population age 25 and over with: High school diploma (including GED) or higher: 86.8% (2008-2012 5-year est.); Bachelor's degree or higher: 15.1% (2008-2012 5-year est.); Master's degree or higher: 3.0% (2008-2012 5-year est.).

School District(s)
Cherry SD 92 (PK-08)
 2011-12 Enrollment: 70 . . . . (815) 894-2777
Housing: Homeownership rate: 88.9% (2008-2012 5-year est.); Median home value: $84,000 (2008-2012 5-year est.); Median contract rent: $421 per month (2008-2012 5-year est.); Median year structure built: Before 1940 (2008-2012 5-year est.).
Health Insurance: 79.4% Private; 28.2% Public; 11.8% None. (2008-2012 5-year est.)
Transportation: Commute to work: 97.1% car, 0.0% public transportation, 0.0% walk, 2.9% work from home (2008-2012 5-year est.); Travel time to work: 22.1% less than 15 minutes, 63.3% 15 to 30 minutes, 3.0% 30 to 45 minutes, 1.5% 45 to 60 minutes, 10.1% 60 minutes or more (2008-2012 5-year est.)

DALZELL (village). Covers a land area of 0.985 square miles and a water area of 0.010 square miles. Located at 41.35° N. Lat; 89.17° W. Long. Elevation is 633 feet.

Population: 587 (1990); 717 (2000); 717 (2010); Density: 752.1 persons per square mile (2008-2012 5-year est.); Race: 97.8% White, 1.5% Black/African American, 0.7% Asian, 0.0% American Indian/Alaska Native, 0.0% Native Hawaiian/Other Pacific Islander, 0.0% Some other race, 0.0% Two or more races, 1.1% Hispanic of any race (2008-2012 5-year est.); Average household size: 2.49 (2008-2012 5-year est.); Median age: 44.6 (2008-2012 5-year est.); Males per 100 females: 88.5 (2008-2012 5-year est.); Marriage status: 16.6% never married, 69.8% now married, 6.0% widowed, 7.6% divorced (2008-2012 5-year est.); Foreign born: 2.7% (2008-2012 5-year est.); Ancestry (includes multiple ancestries): 27.1% Italian, 25.4% German, 17.4% Polish, 11.7% Irish, 8.9% American (2008-2012 5-year est.).
Economy: Single-family building permits issued: 0 (2013); Multi-family building permits issued: 0 (2013); Homeowner vacancy rate: 0.0%. Rental vacancy rate: 19.1%. (2008-2012 5-year est.); Employment by occupation: 10.9% management, business, and financial, 4.6% computer, engineering, and science, 5.9% education, legal, community service, arts, and media, 3.8% healthcare practitioners, 19.3% service, 32.1% sales and office, 5.3% natural resources, construction, and maintenance, 18.1% production, transportation, and material moving (2008-2012 5-year est.).
Income: Per capita income: $25,202 (2008-2012 5-year est.); Median household income: $60,673 (2008-2012 5-year est.); Average household income: $63,845 (2008-2012 5-year est.); Percent of households with income of $100,000 or more: 14.8% (2008-2012 5-year est.); Poverty rate: 4.7% (2008-2012 5-year est.).
Education: Percent of population age 25 and over with: High school diploma (including GED) or higher: 91.6% (2008-2012 5-year est.); Bachelor's degree or higher: 15.0% (2008-2012 5-year est.); Master's degree or higher: 1.9% (2008-2012 5-year est.).

School District(s)
Dalzell SD 98 (KG-08)
 2011-12 Enrollment: 57 . . . . (815) 663-8821
Housing: Homeownership rate: 87.2% (2008-2012 5-year est.); Median home value: $136,700 (2008-2012 5-year est.); Median contract rent: $626 per month (2008-2012 5-year est.); Median year structure built: 1963 (2008-2012 5-year est.).
Health Insurance: 80.4% Private; 31.3% Public; 3.4% None. (2008-2012 5-year est.)
Transportation: Commute to work: 97.4% car, 0.0% public transportation, 1.8% walk, 0.8% work from home (2008-2012 5-year est.); Travel time to work: 49.5% less than 15 minutes, 30.6% 15 to 30 minutes, 7.8% 30 to 45 minutes, 2.3% 45 to 60 minutes, 9.8% 60 minutes or more (2008-2012 5-year est.)

DE PUE (village). Aka Depue. Covers a land area of 2.737 square miles and a water area of 0.259 square miles. Located at 41.33° N. Lat; 89.30° W. Long. Elevation is 472 feet.

Population: 1,729 (1990); 1,842 (2000); 1,838 (2010); Density: 689.3 persons per square mile (2008-2012 5-year est.); Race: 89.7% White, 1.2% Black/African American, 1.9% Asian, 0.0% American Indian/Alaska Native, 0.0% Native Hawaiian/Other Pacific Islander, 7.2% Some other race, 1.7% Two or more races, 60.1% Hispanic of any race (2008-2012 5-year est.); Average household size: 3.02 (2008-2012 5-year est.); Median age: 30.8 (2008-2012 5-year est.); Males per 100 females: 136.8 (2008-2012 5-year est.); Marriage status: 34.2% never married, 51.1% now married, 5.4% widowed, 9.3% divorced (2008-2012 5-year est.); Foreign born: 26.4% (2008-2012 5-year est.); Ancestry (includes multiple ancestries): 10.9% German, 5.7% Irish, 4.5% English, 4.3% Italian, 4.0% Polish (2008-2012 5-year est.).

Economy: Single-family building permits issued: 0 (2013); Multi-family building permits issued: 0 (2013); Homeowner vacancy rate: 2.8%. Rental vacancy rate: 6.8%. (2008-2012 5-year est.); Employment by occupation: 1.6% management, business, and financial, 1.0% computer, engineering, and science, 4.2% education, legal, community service, arts, and media, 3.2% healthcare practitioners, 19.0% service, 19.9% sales and office, 22.1% natural resources, construction, and maintenance, 29.0% production, transportation, and material moving (2008-2012 5-year est.).

Income: Per capita income: $15,617 (2008-2012 5-year est.); Median household income: $37,865 (2008-2012 5-year est.); Average household income: $45,460 (2008-2012 5-year est.); Percent of households with income of $100,000 or more: 7.5% (2008-2012 5-year est.); Poverty rate: 7.7% (2008-2012 5-year est.).

Education: Percent of population age 25 and over with: High school diploma (including GED) or higher: 68.5% (2008-2012 5-year est.); Bachelor's degree or higher: 7.1% (2008-2012 5-year est.); Master's degree or higher: 2.9% (2008-2012 5-year est.).

School District(s)

Depue USD 103 (PK-12)

    2011-12 Enrollment: 482 . . . . (815) 447-2121

Housing: Homeownership rate: 71.3% (2008-2012 5-year est.); Median home value: $67,500 (2008-2012 5-year est.); Median contract rent: $416 per month (2008-2012 5-year est.); Median year structure built: 1942 (2008-2012 5-year est.).

Health Insurance: 61.3% Private; 33.7% Public; 17.0% None. (2008-2012 5-year est.)

Safety: Violent crime rate: 22.0 per 10,000 population; Property crime rate: 98.8 per 10,000 population (2012).

Transportation: Commute to work: 96.7% car, 0.0% public transportation, 1.2% walk, 0.4% work from home (2008-2012 5-year est.); Travel time to work: 34.7% less than 15 minutes, 39.3% 15 to 30 minutes, 15.9% 30 to 45 minutes, 2.8% 45 to 60 minutes, 7.4% 60 minutes or more (2008-2012 5-year est.)

DOVER (village). Covers a land area of 0.264 square miles and a water area of 0 square miles. Located at 41.43° N. Lat; 89.40° W. Long. Elevation is 741 feet.

Population: 163 (1990); 172 (2000); 168 (2010); Density: 499.1 persons per square mile (2008-2012 5-year est.); Race: 100.0% White, 0.0% Black/African American, 0.0% Asian, 0.0% American Indian/Alaska Native, 0.0% Native Hawaiian/Other Pacific Islander, 0.0% Some other race, 0.0% Two or more races, 0.0% Hispanic of any race (2008-2012 5-year est.); Average household size: 2.64 (2008-2012 5-year est.); Median age: 50.5 (2008-2012 5-year est.); Males per 100 females: 61.0 (2008-2012 5-year est.); Marriage status: 11.5% never married, 68.8% now married, 2.1% widowed, 17.7% divorced (2008-2012 5-year est.); Foreign born: 1.5% (2008-2012 5-year est.); Ancestry (includes multiple ancestries): 40.9% German, 29.5% Irish, 22.7% English, 5.3% Swedish, 5.3% Scottish (2008-2012 5-year est.).

Economy: Homeowner vacancy rate: 0.0%. Rental vacancy rate: 0.0%. (2008-2012 5-year est.); Employment by occupation: 5.0% management, business, and financial, 0.0% computer, engineering, and science, 3.3% education, legal, community service, arts, and media, 20.0% healthcare practitioners, 10.0% service, 30.0% sales and office, 5.0% natural resources, construction, and maintenance, 26.7% production, transportation, and material moving (2008-2012 5-year est.).

Income: Per capita income: $14,593 (2008-2012 5-year est.); Median household income: $26,875 (2008-2012 5-year est.); Average household income: $38,690 (2008-2012 5-year est.); Percent of households with

income of $100,000 or more: 6.0% (2008-2012 5-year est.); Poverty rate: 33.3% (2008-2012 5-year est.).

Education: Percent of population age 25 and over with: High school diploma (including GED) or higher: 86.5% (2008-2012 5-year est.); Bachelor's degree or higher: 10.1% (2008-2012 5-year est.); Master's degree or higher: 1.1% (2008-2012 5-year est.).

Housing: Homeownership rate: 92.0% (2008-2012 5-year est.); Median home value: $76,700 (2008-2012 5-year est.); Median contract rent: n/a per month (2008-2012 5-year est.); Median year structure built: Before 1940 (2008-2012 5-year est.).

Health Insurance: 43.9% Private; 58.3% Public; 11.4% None. (2008-2012 5-year est.)

Transportation: Commute to work: 98.3% car, 0.0% public transportation, 0.0% walk, 1.7% work from home (2008-2012 5-year est.); Travel time to work: 52.6% less than 15 minutes, 35.1% 15 to 30 minutes, 7.0% 30 to 45 minutes, 0.0% 45 to 60 minutes, 5.3% 60 minutes or more (2008-2012 5-year est.)

HOLLOWAYVILLE (village). Covers a land area of 0.047 square miles and a water area of 0 square miles. Located at 41.36° N. Lat; 89.29° W. Long. Elevation is 659 feet.

Population: 37 (1990); 90 (2000); 84 (2010); Density: 1,138.2 persons per square mile (2008-2012 5-year est.); Race: 100.0% White, 0.0% Black/African American, 0.0% Asian, 0.0% American Indian/Alaska Native, 0.0% Native Hawaiian/Other Pacific Islander, 0.0% Some other race, 0.0% Two or more races, 0.0% Hispanic of any race (2008-2012 5-year est.); Average household size: 2.57 (2008-2012 5-year est.); Median age: 55.6 (2008-2012 5-year est.); Males per 100 females: 125.0 (2008-2012 5-year est.); Marriage status: 9.6% never married, 82.7% now married, 0.0% widowed, 7.7% divorced (2008-2012 5-year est.); Foreign born: 0.0% (2008-2012 5-year est.); Ancestry (includes multiple ancestries): 35.2% German, 25.9% American, 24.1% English, 18.5% Italian, 11.1% Polish (2008-2012 5-year est.).

Economy: Homeowner vacancy rate: 0.0%. Rental vacancy rate: 100.0%. (2008-2012 5-year est.); Employment by occupation: 17.2% management, business, and financial, 0.0% computer, engineering, and science, 0.0% education, legal, community service, arts, and media, 13.8% healthcare practitioners, 0.0% service, 10.3% sales and office, 10.3% natural resources, construction, and maintenance, 48.3% production, transportation, and material moving (2008-2012 5-year est.).

Income: Per capita income: $28,494 (2008-2012 5-year est.); Median household income: $73,125 (2008-2012 5-year est.); Average household income: $73,162 (2008-2012 5-year est.); Percent of households with income of $100,000 or more: 4.8% (2008-2012 5-year est.); Poverty rate: 0.0% (2008-2012 5-year est.).

Education: Percent of population age 25 and over with: High school diploma (including GED) or higher: 89.4% (2008-2012 5-year est.); Bachelor's degree or higher: 4.3% (2008-2012 5-year est.); Master's degree or higher: 0.0% (2008-2012 5-year est.).

Housing: Homeownership rate: 100.0% (2008-2012 5-year est.); Median home value: $79,000 (2008-2012 5-year est.); Median contract rent: n/a per month (2008-2012 5-year est.); Median year structure built: Before 1940 (2008-2012 5-year est.).

Health Insurance: 81.5% Private; 25.9% Public; 3.7% None. (2008-2012 5-year est.)

Transportation: Commute to work: 100.0% car, 0.0% public transportation, 0.0% walk, 0.0% work from home (2008-2012 5-year est.); Travel time to work: 10.3% less than 15 minutes, 51.7% 15 to 30 minutes, 37.9% 30 to 45 minutes, 0.0% 45 to 60 minutes, 0.0% 60 minutes or more (2008-2012 5-year est.)

KASBEER (unincorporated postal area)

Zip Code: 61328

    Covers a land area of 0.486 square miles and a water area of 0 square miles. Located at 41.49° N. Lat; 89.45° W. Long. Elevation is 741 feet. Population: 42 (2010); Density: 86.3 persons per square mile (2010); Race: 100.0% White, 0.0% Black/African American, 0.0% Asian, 0.0% American Indian/Alaska Native, 0.0% Native Hawaiian/Other Pacific Islander, 0.0% Some other race, 0.0% Two or more races, 0.0% Hispanic of any race (2010); Average household size: 2.63 (2010); Median age: 34.5 (2010); Males per 100 females: 100.0 (2010); Homeownership rate: 81.3% (2010)

LA MOILLE (village). Covers a land area of 1.198 square miles and a water area of 0 square miles. Located at 41.53° N. Lat; 89.28° W. Long. Elevation is 794 feet.

Population: 654 (1990); 773 (2000); 726 (2010); Density: 695.3 persons per square mile (2008-2012 5-year est.); Race: 93.4% White, 0.2% Black/African American, 0.2% Asian, 0.0% American Indian/Alaska Native, 0.0% Native Hawaiian/Other Pacific Islander, 6.2% Some other race, 6.1% Two or more races, 2.9% Hispanic of any race (2008-2012 5-year est.); Average household size: 2.64 (2008-2012 5-year est.); Median age: 35.5 (2008-2012 5-year est.); Males per 100 females: 96.0 (2008-2012 5-year est.); Marriage status: 25.3% never married, 55.2% now married, 6.7% widowed, 12.7% divorced (2008-2012 5-year est.); Foreign born: 0.2% (2008-2012 5-year est.); Ancestry (includes multiple ancestries): 41.2% German, 17.5% Irish, 10.7% English, 6.7% Italian, 5.9% American (2008-2012 5-year est.).

Economy: Homeowner vacancy rate: 0.0%. Rental vacancy rate: 16.1%. (2008-2012 5-year est.); Employment by occupation: 6.4% management, business, and financial, 1.3% computer, engineering, and science, 7.2% education, legal, community service, arts, and media, 3.8% healthcare practitioners, 32.3% service, 22.3% sales and office, 6.6% natural resources, construction, and maintenance, 20.0% production, transportation, and material moving (2008-2012 5-year est.).

Income: Per capita income: $22,090 (2008-2012 5-year est.); Median household income: $49,265 (2008-2012 5-year est.); Average household income: $56,190 (2008-2012 5-year est.); Percent of households with income of $100,000 or more: 9.2% (2008-2012 5-year est.); Poverty rate: 9.0% (2008-2012 5-year est.).

Education: Percent of population age 25 and over with: High school diploma (including GED) or higher: 90.9% (2008-2012 5-year est.); Bachelor's degree or higher: 14.2% (2008-2012 5-year est.); Master's degree or higher: 3.4% (2008-2012 5-year est.).

School District(s)
La Moille CUSD 303 (PK-12)
  2011-12 Enrollment: 261........................ (815) 638-2018
Housing: Homeownership rate: 75.3% (2008-2012 5-year est.); Median home value: $94,500 (2008-2012 5-year est.); Median contract rent: $435 per month (2008-2012 5-year est.); Median year structure built: 1945 (2008-2012 5-year est.).
Health Insurance: 67.5% Private; 34.6% Public; 13.1% None. (2008-2012 5-year est.)
Transportation: Commute to work: 92.3% car, 0.0% public transportation, 3.7% walk, 4.0% work from home (2008-2012 5-year est.); Travel time to work: 24.1% less than 15 minutes, 55.5% 15 to 30 minutes, 11.0% 30 to 45 minutes, 4.1% 45 to 60 minutes, 5.3% 60 minutes or more (2008-2012 5-year est.)

LADD (village). Covers a land area of 1.185 square miles and a water area of 0 square miles. Located at 41.38° N. Lat; 89.21° W. Long. Elevation is 650 feet.
History: Incorporated 1890.
Population: 1,283 (1990); 1,313 (2000); 1,295 (2010); Density: 1,171.7 persons per square mile (2008-2012 5-year est.); Race: 97.3% White, 0.6% Black/African American, 0.9% Asian, 0.1% American Indian/Alaska Native, 0.0% Native Hawaiian/Other Pacific Islander, 1.1% Some other race, 0.9% Two or more races, 4.6% Hispanic of any race (2008-2012 5-year est.); Average household size: 2.35 (2008-2012 5-year est.); Median age: 40.9 (2008-2012 5-year est.); Males per 100 females: 89.9 (2008-2012 5-year est.); Marriage status: 22.1% never married, 59.0% now married, 8.4% widowed, 10.5% divorced (2008-2012 5-year est.); Foreign born: 2.6% (2008-2012 5-year est.); Ancestry (includes multiple ancestries): 32.3% German, 28.0% Italian, 19.6% Irish, 11.1% English, 8.4% American (2008-2012 5-year est.).
Economy: Single-family building permits issued: 1 (2013); Multi-family building permits issued: 0 (2013); Homeowner vacancy rate: 0.0%. Rental vacancy rate: 6.6%. (2008-2012 5-year est.); Employment by occupation: 8.6% management, business, and financial, 1.2% computer, engineering, and science, 16.5% education, legal, community service, arts, and media, 4.4% healthcare practitioners, 15.5% service, 25.4% sales and office, 9.8% natural resources, construction, and maintenance, 18.7% production, transportation, and material moving (2008-2012 5-year est.).
Income: Per capita income: $24,352 (2008-2012 5-year est.); Median household income: $50,063 (2008-2012 5-year est.); Average household income: $56,480 (2008-2012 5-year est.); Percent of households with income of $100,000 or more: 14.1% (2008-2012 5-year est.); Poverty rate: 11.4% (2008-2012 5-year est.).

Education: Percent of population age 25 and over with: High school diploma (including GED) or higher: 92.5% (2008-2012 5-year est.); Bachelor's degree or higher: 23.7% (2008-2012 5-year est.); Master's degree or higher: 8.3% (2008-2012 5-year est.).
School District(s)
Ladd CCSD 94 (KG-08)
  2011-12 Enrollment: 189........................ (815) 894-2363
Housing: Homeownership rate: 75.9% (2008-2012 5-year est.); Median home value: $97,800 (2008-2012 5-year est.); Median contract rent: $581 per month (2008-2012 5-year est.); Median year structure built: 1955 (2008-2012 5-year est.).
Health Insurance: 83.8% Private; 28.3% Public; 4.0% None. (2008-2012 5-year est.)
Transportation: Commute to work: 95.3% car, 0.0% public transportation, 2.5% walk, 1.6% work from home (2008-2012 5-year est.); Travel time to work: 57.8% less than 15 minutes, 29.0% 15 to 30 minutes, 5.6% 30 to 45 minutes, 2.4% 45 to 60 minutes, 5.3% 60 minutes or more (2008-2012 5-year est.)

MALDEN (village). Covers a land area of 0.275 square miles and a water area of 0 square miles. Located at 41.42° N. Lat; 89.37° W. Long. Elevation is 705 feet.
Population: 370 (1990); 343 (2000); 362 (2010); Density: 1,699.3 persons per square mile (2008-2012 5-year est.); Race: 97.4% White, 0.0% Black/African American, 0.0% Asian, 0.0% American Indian/Alaska Native, 0.0% Native Hawaiian/Other Pacific Islander, 2.6% Some other race, 2.6% Two or more races, 4.1% Hispanic of any race (2008-2012 5-year est.); Average household size: 2.83 (2008-2012 5-year est.); Median age: 31.5 (2008-2012 5-year est.); Males per 100 females: 100.4 (2008-2012 5-year est.); Marriage status: 32.4% never married, 55.8% now married, 2.4% widowed, 9.4% divorced (2008-2012 5-year est.); Foreign born: 0.2% (2008-2012 5-year est.); Ancestry (includes multiple ancestries): 35.1% German, 18.6% American, 14.8% Irish, 10.7% English, 7.9% Italian (2008-2012 5-year est.).
Economy: Homeowner vacancy rate: 0.0%. Rental vacancy rate: 0.0%. (2008-2012 5-year est.); Employment by occupation: 6.2% management, business, and financial, 5.3% computer, engineering, and science, 1.8% education, legal, community service, arts, and media, 4.0% healthcare practitioners, 14.1% service, 37.4% sales and office, 4.4% natural resources, construction, and maintenance, 26.9% production, transportation, and material moving (2008-2012 5-year est.).
Income: Per capita income: $19,287 (2008-2012 5-year est.); Median household income: $43,875 (2008-2012 5-year est.); Average household income: $55,770 (2008-2012 5-year est.); Percent of households with income of $100,000 or more: 16.4% (2008-2012 5-year est.); Poverty rate: 12.4% (2008-2012 5-year est.).
Education: Percent of population age 25 and over with: High school diploma (including GED) or higher: 88.6% (2008-2012 5-year est.); Bachelor's degree or higher: 9.5% (2008-2012 5-year est.); Master's degree or higher: 2.9% (2008-2012 5-year est.).
School District(s)
Malden CCSD 84 (PK-08)
  2011-12 Enrollment: 83........................ (815) 643-2436
Housing: Homeownership rate: 77.0% (2008-2012 5-year est.); Median home value: $92,600 (2008-2012 5-year est.); Median contract rent: $419 per month (2008-2012 5-year est.); Median year structure built: 1966 (2008-2012 5-year est.).
Health Insurance: 68.3% Private; 33.2% Public; 12.2% None. (2008-2012 5-year est.)
Transportation: Commute to work: 94.0% car, 0.0% public transportation, 2.3% walk, 1.8% work from home (2008-2012 5-year est.); Travel time to work: 39.0% less than 15 minutes, 38.0% 15 to 30 minutes, 15.0% 30 to 45 minutes, 1.9% 45 to 60 minutes, 6.1% 60 minutes or more (2008-2012 5-year est.)

MANLIUS (village). Covers a land area of 0.306 square miles and a water area of 0 square miles. Located at 41.46° N. Lat; 89.67° W. Long. Elevation is 702 feet.
Population: 365 (1990); 355 (2000); 359 (2010); Density: 1,038.4 persons per square mile (2008-2012 5-year est.); Race: 96.2% White, 0.0% Black/African American, 0.0% Asian, 0.0% American Indian/Alaska Native, 0.0% Native Hawaiian/Other Pacific Islander, 3.8% Some other race, 3.1% Two or more races, 1.3% Hispanic of any race (2008-2012 5-year est.); Average household size: 2.26 (2008-2012 5-year est.); Median age: 43.2 (2008-2012 5-year est.); Males per 100 females: 114.9 (2008-2012 5-year

est.); Marriage status: 22.1% never married, 56.6% now married, 10.7% widowed, 10.7% divorced (2008-2012 5-year est.); Foreign born: 0.6% (2008-2012 5-year est.); Ancestry (includes multiple ancestries): 46.5% German, 10.4% Swedish, 6.3% English, 6.3% Irish, 6.3% American (2008-2012 5-year est.).

Economy: Homeowner vacancy rate: 17.7%. Rental vacancy rate: 0.0%. (2008-2012 5-year est.); Employment by occupation: 8.4% management, business, and financial, 0.0% computer, engineering, and science, 3.5% education, legal, community service, arts, and media, 5.6% healthcare practitioners, 17.5% service, 29.4% sales and office, 11.2% natural resources, construction, and maintenance, 24.5% production, transportation, and material moving (2008-2012 5-year est.).

Income: Per capita income: $18,479 (2008-2012 5-year est.); Median household income: $36,750 (2008-2012 5-year est.); Average household income: $42,212 (2008-2012 5-year est.); Percent of households with income of $100,000 or more: 2.8% (2008-2012 5-year est.); Poverty rate: 30.9% (2008-2012 5-year est.).

Education: Percent of population age 25 and over with: High school diploma (including GED) or higher: 91.9% (2008-2012 5-year est.); Bachelor's degree or higher: 8.6% (2008-2012 5-year est.); Master's degree or higher: 2.4% (2008-2012 5-year est.).

School District(s)

Bureau Valley CUSD 340 (PK-12)

   2011-12 Enrollment: 1,154 . . . . (815) 445-3101

Bureau/henry/stark Roe (06-12)

   2011-12 Enrollment: n/a . . . . (309) 936-7890

Housing: Homeownership rate: 82.3% (2008-2012 5-year est.); Median home value: $75,900 (2008-2012 5-year est.); Median contract rent: $486 per month (2008-2012 5-year est.); Median year structure built: Before 1940 (2008-2012 5-year est.).

Health Insurance: 57.2% Private; 58.5% Public; 5.0% None. (2008-2012 5-year est.)

Transportation: Commute to work: 95.1% car, 0.0% public transportation, 3.5% walk, 0.0% work from home (2008-2012 5-year est.); Travel time to work: 28.7% less than 15 minutes, 55.2% 15 to 30 minutes, 10.5% 30 to 45 minutes, 2.8% 45 to 60 minutes, 2.8% 60 minutes or more (2008-2012 5-year est.)

MINERAL (village). Covers a land area of 0.348 square miles and a water area of 0 square miles. Located at 41.38° N. Lat; 89.84° W. Long. Elevation is 640 feet.

Population: 250 (1990); 272 (2000); 237 (2010); Density: 850.8 persons per square mile (2008-2012 5-year est.); Race: 95.9% White, 0.7% Black/African American, 0.0% Asian, 0.0% American Indian/Alaska Native, 0.0% Native Hawaiian/Other Pacific Islander, 3.4% Some other race, 3.4% Two or more races, 1.7% Hispanic of any race (2008-2012 5-year est.); Average household size: 2.14 (2008-2012 5-year est.); Median age: 37.0 (2008-2012 5-year est.); Males per 100 females: 104.1 (2008-2012 5-year est.); Marriage status: 21.0% never married, 50.4% now married, 10.3% widowed, 18.3% divorced (2008-2012 5-year est.); Foreign born: 0.0% (2008-2012 5-year est.); Ancestry (includes multiple ancestries): 20.3% Belgian, 18.2% German, 15.5% English, 10.8% American, 10.8% Irish (2008-2012 5-year est.).

Economy: Homeowner vacancy rate: 4.6%. Rental vacancy rate: 0.0%. (2008-2012 5-year est.); Employment by occupation: 6.1% management, business, and financial, 14.4% computer, engineering, and science, 0.0% education, legal, community service, arts, and media, 12.1% healthcare practitioners, 3.8% service, 22.0% sales and office, 18.9% natural resources, construction, and maintenance, 22.7% production, transportation, and material moving (2008-2012 5-year est.).

Income: Per capita income: $26,793 (2008-2012 5-year est.); Median household income: $38,333 (2008-2012 5-year est.); Average household income: $56,947 (2008-2012 5-year est.); Percent of households with income of $100,000 or more: 13.0% (2008-2012 5-year est.); Poverty rate: 15.5% (2008-2012 5-year est.).

Education: Percent of population age 25 and over with: High school diploma (including GED) or higher: 87.9% (2008-2012 5-year est.); Bachelor's degree or higher: 12.6% (2008-2012 5-year est.); Master's degree or higher: 9.1% (2008-2012 5-year est.).

Housing: Homeownership rate: 60.1% (2008-2012 5-year est.); Median home value: $57,100 (2008-2012 5-year est.); Median contract rent: $443 per month (2008-2012 5-year est.); Median year structure built: 1954 (2008-2012 5-year est.).

Health Insurance: 74.3% Private; 35.8% Public; 4.1% None. (2008-2012 5-year est.)

Transportation: Commute to work: 97.7% car, 0.0% public transportation, 0.0% walk, 2.3% work from home (2008-2012 5-year est.); Travel time to work: 24.8% less than 15 minutes, 31.8% 15 to 30 minutes, 13.2% 30 to 45 minutes, 27.9% 45 to 60 minutes, 2.3% 60 minutes or more (2008-2012 5-year est.)

NEPONSET (village). Covers a land area of 1.044 square miles and a water area of 0 square miles. Located at 41.30° N. Lat; 89.79° W. Long. Elevation is 830 feet.

Population: 529 (1990); 519 (2000); 473 (2010); Density: 459.8 persons per square mile (2008-2012 5-year est.); Race: 97.5% White, 0.2% Black/African American, 0.8% Asian, 0.0% American Indian/Alaska Native, 0.0% Native Hawaiian/Other Pacific Islander, 1.5% Some other race, 1.5% Two or more races, 5.2% Hispanic of any race (2008-2012 5-year est.); Average household size: 2.36 (2008-2012 5-year est.); Median age: 43.3 (2008-2012 5-year est.); Males per 100 females: 79.1 (2008-2012 5-year est.); Marriage status: 23.2% never married, 59.5% now married, 4.9% widowed, 12.4% divorced (2008-2012 5-year est.); Foreign born: 2.7% (2008-2012 5-year est.); Ancestry (includes multiple ancestries): 26.3% German, 25.2% English, 11.7% Swedish, 11.5% Irish, 9.4% American (2008-2012 5-year est.).

Economy: Single-family building permits issued: 0 (2013); Multi-family building permits issued: 0 (2013); Homeowner vacancy rate: 0.0%. Rental vacancy rate: 0.0%. (2008-2012 5-year est.); Employment by occupation: 17.3% management, business, and financial, 4.8% computer, engineering, and science, 10.1% education, legal, community service, arts, and media, 4.8% healthcare practitioners, 15.7% service, 21.0% sales and office, 5.2% natural resources, construction, and maintenance, 21.0% production, transportation, and material moving (2008-2012 5-year est.).

Income: Per capita income: $40,078 (2008-2012 5-year est.); Median household income: $46,103 (2008-2012 5-year est.); Average household income: $96,502 (2008-2012 5-year est.); Percent of households with income of $100,000 or more: 16.3% (2008-2012 5-year est.); Poverty rate: 10.2% (2008-2012 5-year est.).

Education: Percent of population age 25 and over with: High school diploma (including GED) or higher: 90.5% (2008-2012 5-year est.); Bachelor's degree or higher: 22.9% (2008-2012 5-year est.); Master's degree or higher: 8.9% (2008-2012 5-year est.).

School District(s)

Kewanee CUSD 229 (PK-12)

   2011-12 Enrollment: 1,904 . . . . (309) 853-3341

Housing: Homeownership rate: 87.2% (2008-2012 5-year est.); Median home value: $67,700 (2008-2012 5-year est.); Median contract rent: $350 per month (2008-2012 5-year est.); Median year structure built: Before 1940 (2008-2012 5-year est.).

Health Insurance: 72.5% Private; 28.5% Public; 13.8% None. (2008-2012 5-year est.)

Transportation: Commute to work: 89.3% car, 0.8% public transportation, 1.6% walk, 5.3% work from home (2008-2012 5-year est.); Travel time to work: 25.7% less than 15 minutes, 36.1% 15 to 30 minutes, 16.1% 30 to 45 minutes, 7.8% 45 to 60 minutes, 14.3% 60 minutes or more (2008-2012 5-year est.)

NEW BEDFORD (village). Covers a land area of 0.178 square miles and a water area of 0 square miles. Located at 41.51° N. Lat; 89.72° W. Long. Elevation is 643 feet.

Population: 65 (1990); 95 (2000); 75 (2010); Density: 409.0 persons per square mile (2008-2012 5-year est.); Race: 95.9% White, 0.0% Black/African American, 0.0% Asian, 4.1% American Indian/Alaska Native, 0.0% Native Hawaiian/Other Pacific Islander, 0.0% Some other race, 0.0% Two or more races, 0.0% Hispanic of any race (2008-2012 5-year est.); Average household size: 2.35 (2008-2012 5-year est.); Median age: 46.4 (2008-2012 5-year est.); Males per 100 females: 121.2 (2008-2012 5-year est.); Marriage status: 26.7% never married, 55.0% now married, 11.7% widowed, 6.7% divorced (2008-2012 5-year est.); Foreign born: 1.4% (2008-2012 5-year est.); Ancestry (includes multiple ancestries): 32.9% German, 31.5% Scottish, 9.6% American, 8.2% French, 6.8% Swedish (2008-2012 5-year est.).

Economy: Homeowner vacancy rate: 0.0%. Rental vacancy rate: 0.0%. (2008-2012 5-year est.); Employment by occupation: 0.0% management, business, and financial, 0.0% computer, engineering, and science, 0.0% education, legal, community service, arts, and media, 7.1% healthcare practitioners, 21.4% service, 17.9% sales and office, 39.3% natural resources, construction, and maintenance, 14.3% production, transportation, and material moving (2008-2012 5-year est.).

Income: Per capita income: $18,514 (2008-2012 5-year est.); Median household income: $42,083 (2008-2012 5-year est.); Average household income: $42,248 (2008-2012 5-year est.); Percent of households with income of $100,000 or more: n/a (2008-2012 5-year est.); Poverty rate: 8.2% (2008-2012 5-year est.).
Education: Percent of population age 25 and over with: High school diploma (including GED) or higher: 85.4% (2008-2012 5-year est.); Bachelor's degree or higher: 2.1% (2008-2012 5-year est.); Master's degree or higher: 0.0% (2008-2012 5-year est.).
Housing: Homeownership rate: 100.0% (2008-2012 5-year est.); Median home value: $72,500 (2008-2012 5-year est.); Median contract rent: n/a per month (2008-2012 5-year est.); Median year structure built: Before 1940 (2008-2012 5-year est.).
Health Insurance: 52.1% Private; 60.3% Public; 12.3% None. (2008-2012 5-year est.)
Transportation: Commute to work: 100.0% car, 0.0% public transportation, 0.0% walk, 0.0% work from home (2008-2012 5-year est.); Travel time to work: 0.0% less than 15 minutes, 46.4% 15 to 30 minutes, 42.9% 30 to 45 minutes, 10.7% 45 to 60 minutes, 0.0% 60 minutes or more (2008-2012 5-year est.)

OHIO (village). Covers a land area of 0.803 square miles and a water area of 0 square miles. Located at 41.56° N. Lat; 89.46° W. Long. Elevation is 902 feet.
Population: 426 (1990); 540 (2000); 513 (2010); Density: 601.7 persons per square mile (2008-2012 5-year est.); Race: 98.3% White, 0.0% Black/African American, 0.0% Asian, 0.6% American Indian/Alaska Native, 0.0% Native Hawaiian/Other Pacific Islander, 1.1% Some other race, 0.4% Two or more races, 2.1% Hispanic of any race (2008-2012 5-year est.); Average household size: 2.47 (2008-2012 5-year est.); Median age: 38.4 (2008-2012 5-year est.); Males per 100 females: 81.6 (2008-2012 5-year est.); Marriage status: 27.4% never married, 55.6% now married, 9.1% widowed, 7.8% divorced (2008-2012 5-year est.); Foreign born: 0.0% (2008-2012 5-year est.); Ancestry (includes multiple ancestries): 37.9% German, 23.0% Irish, 11.6% American, 10.1% Polish, 5.4% English (2008-2012 5-year est.).
Economy: Homeowner vacancy rate: 9.6%. Rental vacancy rate: 11.5%. (2008-2012 5-year est.); Employment by occupation: 4.3% management, business, and financial, 0.9% computer, engineering, and science, 6.8% education, legal, community service, arts, and media, 6.8% healthcare practitioners, 17.0% service, 31.5% sales and office, 20.4% natural resources, construction, and maintenance, 12.3% production, transportation, and material moving (2008-2012 5-year est.).
Income: Per capita income: $27,166 (2008-2012 5-year est.); Median household income: $37,159 (2008-2012 5-year est.); Average household income: $66,859 (2008-2012 5-year est.); Percent of households with income of $100,000 or more: 13.8% (2008-2012 5-year est.); Poverty rate: 31.2% (2008-2012 5-year est.).
Education: Percent of population age 25 and over with: High school diploma (including GED) or higher: 89.6% (2008-2012 5-year est.); Bachelor's degree or higher: 13.7% (2008-2012 5-year est.); Master's degree or higher: 2.3% (2008-2012 5-year est.).

School District(s)
Ohio CCSD 17 (KG-08)
    2011-12 Enrollment: 77 . . . . (815) 376-4414
Ohio CHSD 505 (09-12)
    2011-12 Enrollment: 38 . . . . (815) 376-2934
Housing: Homeownership rate: 72.3% (2008-2012 5-year est.); Median home value: $96,600 (2008-2012 5-year est.); Median contract rent: $463 per month (2008-2012 5-year est.); Median year structure built: Before 1940 (2008-2012 5-year est.).
Health Insurance: 69.4% Private; 45.5% Public; 1.5% None. (2008-2012 5-year est.)
Transportation: Commute to work: 91.3% car, 0.9% public transportation, 3.5% walk, 1.3% work from home (2008-2012 5-year est.); Travel time to work: 28.3% less than 15 minutes, 46.5% 15 to 30 minutes, 17.7% 30 to 45 minutes, 4.9% 45 to 60 minutes, 2.7% 60 minutes or more (2008-2012 5-year est.)

PRINCETON (city). County seat. Covers a land area of 7.476 square miles and a water area of 0 square miles. Located at 41.38° N. Lat; 89.47° W. Long. Elevation is 719 feet.
History: Princeton was laid out in 1833 by settlers from Massachusetts. The town grew as an orchard and farming center, and as the seat of Bureau County.

Population: 7,197 (1990); 7,501 (2000); 7,660 (2010); Density: 1,047.4 persons per square mile (2008-2012 5-year est.); Race: 98.1% White, 0.6% Black/African American, 0.2% Asian, 0.1% American Indian/Alaska Native, 0.0% Native Hawaiian/Other Pacific Islander, 1.0% Some other race, 0.5% Two or more races, 2.0% Hispanic of any race (2008-2012 5-year est.); Average household size: 2.15 (2008-2012 5-year est.); Median age: 45.7 (2008-2012 5-year est.); Males per 100 females: 81.4 (2008-2012 5-year est.); Marriage status: 24.5% never married, 50.1% now married, 11.1% widowed, 14.3% divorced (2008-2012 5-year est.); Foreign born: 0.9% (2008-2012 5-year est.); Ancestry (includes multiple ancestries): 34.1% German, 14.3% Irish, 11.1% Swedish, 11.0% English, 8.0% American (2008-2012 5-year est.).
Economy: Single-family building permits issued: 2 (2013); Multi-family building permits issued: 2 (2013); Homeowner vacancy rate: 3.3%. Rental vacancy rate: 12.4%. (2008-2012 5-year est.); Employment by occupation: 11.0% management, business, and financial, 2.2% computer, engineering, and science, 8.3% education, legal, community service, arts, and media, 5.4% healthcare practitioners, 17.2% service, 28.0% sales and office, 11.4% natural resources, construction, and maintenance, 16.7% production, transportation, and material moving (2008-2012 5-year est.).
Income: Per capita income: $29,230 (2008-2012 5-year est.); Median household income: $44,339 (2008-2012 5-year est.); Average household income: $64,337 (2008-2012 5-year est.); Percent of households with income of $100,000 or more: 16.3% (2008-2012 5-year est.); Poverty rate: 14.1% (2008-2012 5-year est.).
Education: Percent of population age 25 and over with: High school diploma (including GED) or higher: 91.8% (2008-2012 5-year est.); Bachelor's degree or higher: 20.4% (2008-2012 5-year est.); Master's degree or higher: 7.5% (2008-2012 5-year est.).
School District(s)
Princeton ESD 115 (PK-08)
    2011-12 Enrollment: 1,297 . . . . (815) 875-3162
Princeton HSD 500 (09-12)
    2011-12 Enrollment: 597 . . . . (815) 875-3308
Housing: Homeownership rate: 69.7% (2008-2012 5-year est.); Median home value: $122,600 (2008-2012 5-year est.); Median contract rent: $468 per month (2008-2012 5-year est.); Median year structure built: 1955 (2008-2012 5-year est.).
Health Insurance: 69.0% Private; 38.4% Public; 11.4% None. (2008-2012 5-year est.)
Hospitals: Perry Memorial Hospital (98 beds)
Safety: Violent crime rate: 17.1 per 10,000 population; Property crime rate: 232.0 per 10,000 population (2012).
Transportation: Commute to work: 91.1% car, 1.2% public transportation, 3.3% walk, 3.1% work from home (2008-2012 5-year est.); Travel time to work: 60.3% less than 15 minutes, 20.7% 15 to 30 minutes, 7.2% 30 to 45 minutes, 3.8% 45 to 60 minutes, 8.1% 60 minutes or more (2008-2012 5-year est.); Amtrak: Train service available.
Additional Information Contacts
City of Princeton . . . . (815) 875-2631
    http://www.princeton-il.com
Princeton Area Chamber of Commerce . . . . (815) 875-2616
    http://www.princetonchamber-il.com

SEATONVILLE (village). Covers a land area of 0.487 square miles and a water area of 0.015 square miles. Located at 41.37° N. Lat; 89.27° W. Long. Elevation is 620 feet.
Population: 259 (1990); 303 (2000); 314 (2010); Density: 577.4 persons per square mile (2008-2012 5-year est.); Race: 98.9% White, 0.0% Black/African American, 0.7% Asian, 0.4% American Indian/Alaska Native, 0.0% Native Hawaiian/Other Pacific Islander, 0.0% Some other race, 0.0% Two or more races, 8.2% Hispanic of any race (2008-2012 5-year est.); Average household size: 2.36 (2008-2012 5-year est.); Median age: 41.7 (2008-2012 5-year est.); Males per 100 females: 89.9 (2008-2012 5-year est.); Marriage status: 21.1% never married, 59.2% now married, 7.5% widowed, 12.3% divorced (2008-2012 5-year est.); Foreign born: 2.5% (2008-2012 5-year est.); Ancestry (includes multiple ancestries): 40.2% German, 22.8% Italian, 15.3% Irish, 12.1% Polish, 7.1% English (2008-2012 5-year est.).
Economy: Single-family building permits issued: 1 (2013); Multi-family building permits issued: 0 (2013); Homeowner vacancy rate: 2.7%. Rental vacancy rate: 0.0%. (2008-2012 5-year est.); Employment by occupation: 3.0% management, business, and financial, 5.3% computer, engineering, and science, 3.0% education, legal, community service, arts, and media, 1.8% healthcare practitioners, 18.9% service, 37.9% sales and office,

8.9% natural resources, construction, and maintenance, 21.3% production, transportation, and material moving (2008-2012 5-year est.).
Income: Per capita income: $23,170 (2008-2012 5-year est.); Median household income: $40,313 (2008-2012 5-year est.); Average household income: $53,137 (2008-2012 5-year est.); Percent of households with income of $100,000 or more: 13.4% (2008-2012 5-year est.); Poverty rate: 8.9% (2008-2012 5-year est.).
Education: Percent of population age 25 and over with: High school diploma (including GED) or higher: 86.2% (2008-2012 5-year est.); Bachelor's degree or higher: 8.2% (2008-2012 5-year est.); Master's degree or higher: 4.1% (2008-2012 5-year est.).
Housing: Homeownership rate: 85.7% (2008-2012 5-year est.); Median home value: $84,000 (2008-2012 5-year est.); Median contract rent: $406 per month (2008-2012 5-year est.); Median year structure built: 1953 (2008-2012 5-year est.).
Health Insurance: 80.1% Private; 25.3% Public; 7.5% None. (2008-2012 5-year est.)
Transportation: Commute to work: 97.0% car, 0.6% public transportation, 1.2% walk, 0.0% work from home (2008-2012 5-year est.); Travel time to work: 30.3% less than 15 minutes, 55.2% 15 to 30 minutes, 9.7% 30 to 45 minutes, 1.2% 45 to 60 minutes, 3.6% 60 minutes or more (2008-2012 5-year est.)

SHEFFIELD (village). Covers a land area of 0.711 square miles and a water area of 0 square miles. Located at 41.36° N. Lat; 89.74° W. Long. Elevation is 689 feet.
Population: 951 (1990); 946 (2000); 926 (2010); Density: 1,436.0 persons per square mile (2008-2012 5-year est.); Race: 99.5% White, 0.0% Black/African American, 0.0% Asian, 0.0% American Indian/Alaska Native, 0.0% Native Hawaiian/Other Pacific Islander, 0.5% Some other race, 0.0% Two or more races, 0.5% Hispanic of any race (2008-2012 5-year est.); Average household size: 2.43 (2008-2012 5-year est.); Median age: 40.2 (2008-2012 5-year est.); Males per 100 females: 100.6 (2008-2012 5-year est.); Marriage status: 30.1% never married, 47.6% now married, 7.5% widowed, 14.8% divorced (2008-2012 5-year est.); Foreign born: 0.0% (2008-2012 5-year est.); Ancestry (includes multiple ancestries): 35.4% German, 18.4% Irish, 12.3% American, 9.6% Belgian, 9.5% English (2008-2012 5-year est.).
Economy: Homeowner vacancy rate: 0.0%. Rental vacancy rate: 0.0%. (2008-2012 5-year est.); Employment by occupation: 7.7% management, business, and financial, 1.7% computer, engineering, and science, 6.8% education, legal, community service, arts, and media, 1.7% healthcare practitioners, 21.2% service, 27.1% sales and office, 11.3% natural resources, construction, and maintenance, 22.4% production, transportation, and material moving (2008-2012 5-year est.).
Income: Per capita income: $21,574 (2008-2012 5-year est.); Median household income: $43,917 (2008-2012 5-year est.); Average household income: $51,943 (2008-2012 5-year est.); Percent of households with income of $100,000 or more: 7.1% (2008-2012 5-year est.); Poverty rate: 12.8% (2008-2012 5-year est.).
Education: Percent of population age 25 and over with: High school diploma (including GED) or higher: 89.8% (2008-2012 5-year est.); Bachelor's degree or higher: 17.9% (2008-2012 5-year est.); Master's degree or higher: 6.4% (2008-2012 5-year est.).

School District(s)
Bureau Valley CUSD 340 (PK-12)
    2011-12 Enrollment: 1,154 . . . . (815) 445-3101
Housing: Homeownership rate: 79.5% (2008-2012 5-year est.); Median home value: $78,700 (2008-2012 5-year est.); Median contract rent: $428 per month (2008-2012 5-year est.); Median year structure built: Before 1940 (2008-2012 5-year est.).
Health Insurance: 57.2% Private; 51.1% Public; 11.6% None. (2008-2012 5-year est.)
Transportation: Commute to work: 92.0% car, 0.0% public transportation, 2.9% walk, 4.2% work from home (2008-2012 5-year est.); Travel time to work: 23.9% less than 15 minutes, 53.6% 15 to 30 minutes, 14.4% 30 to 45 minutes, 4.2% 45 to 60 minutes, 3.9% 60 minutes or more (2008-2012 5-year est.)

SPRING VALLEY (city). Covers a land area of 7.371 square miles and a water area of 0.098 square miles. Located at 41.32° N. Lat; 89.18° W. Long. Elevation is 597 feet.
History: Spring Valley began as a mining operation, but later the economy was based on manufacturing.

Population: 5,246 (1990); 5,398 (2000); 5,558 (2010); Density: 750.2 persons per square mile (2008-2012 5-year est.); Race: 92.1% White, 1.8% Black/African American, 1.0% Asian, 0.4% American Indian/Alaska Native, 0.0% Native Hawaiian/Other Pacific Islander, 4.7% Some other race, 1.5% Two or more races, 13.7% Hispanic of any race (2008-2012 5-year est.); Average household size: 2.35 (2008-2012 5-year est.); Median age: 39.8 (2008-2012 5-year est.); Males per 100 females: 93.7 (2008-2012 5-year est.); Marriage status: 24.9% never married, 50.7% now married, 7.8% widowed, 16.6% divorced (2008-2012 5-year est.); Foreign born: 5.1% (2008-2012 5-year est.); Ancestry (includes multiple ancestries): 22.4% German, 20.2% Italian, 15.0% Irish, 8.7% Polish, 8.0% English (2008-2012 5-year est.).
Economy: Single-family building permits issued: 1 (2013); Multi-family building permits issued: 0 (2013); Homeowner vacancy rate: 0.0%. Rental vacancy rate: 3.6%. (2008-2012 5-year est.); Employment by occupation: 8.3% management, business, and financial, 1.4% computer, engineering, and science, 4.7% education, legal, community service, arts, and media, 6.9% healthcare practitioners, 23.7% service, 20.7% sales and office, 10.3% natural resources, construction, and maintenance, 24.0% production, transportation, and material moving (2008-2012 5-year est.).
Income: Per capita income: $28,305 (2008-2012 5-year est.); Median household income: $46,107 (2008-2012 5-year est.); Average household income: $66,973 (2008-2012 5-year est.); Percent of households with income of $100,000 or more: 13.1% (2008-2012 5-year est.); Poverty rate: 12.1% (2008-2012 5-year est.).
Education: Percent of population age 25 and over with: High school diploma (including GED) or higher: 89.7% (2008-2012 5-year est.); Bachelor's degree or higher: 14.6% (2008-2012 5-year est.); Master's degree or higher: 6.4% (2008-2012 5-year est.).

School District(s)
Hall HSD 502 (09-12)
    2011-12 Enrollment: 401 . . . . (815) 664-4500
Spring Valley CCSD 99 (PK-08)
    2011-12 Enrollment: 802 . . . . (815) 664-4242
Housing: Homeownership rate: 73.0% (2008-2012 5-year est.); Median home value: $102,500 (2008-2012 5-year est.); Median contract rent: $432 per month (2008-2012 5-year est.); Median year structure built: 1953 (2008-2012 5-year est.).
Health Insurance: 66.7% Private; 34.8% Public; 14.4% None. (2008-2012 5-year est.)
Hospitals: St. Margaret's Hospital (155 beds)
Safety: Violent crime rate: 12.7 per 10,000 population; Property crime rate: 205.4 per 10,000 population (2012).
Transportation: Commute to work: 91.5% car, 0.2% public transportation, 5.8% walk, 1.8% work from home (2008-2012 5-year est.); Travel time to work: 53.5% less than 15 minutes, 29.6% 15 to 30 minutes, 7.7% 30 to 45 minutes, 0.4% 45 to 60 minutes, 8.8% 60 minutes or more (2008-2012 5-year est.)
Additional Information Contacts
City of Spring Valley . . . . (815) 664-4221
    http://www.spring-valley.il.us

TISKILWA (village). Covers a land area of 0.455 square miles and a water area of 0 square miles. Located at 41.29° N. Lat; 89.51° W. Long. Elevation is 522 feet.
Population: 830 (1990); 787 (2000); 829 (2010); Density: 1,910.5 persons per square mile (2008-2012 5-year est.); Race: 97.1% White, 0.0% Black/African American, 1.7% Asian, 0.0% American Indian/Alaska Native, 0.0% Native Hawaiian/Other Pacific Islander, 1.2% Some other race, 1.1% Two or more races, 2.2% Hispanic of any race (2008-2012 5-year est.); Average household size: 2.48 (2008-2012 5-year est.); Median age: 37.2 (2008-2012 5-year est.); Males per 100 females: 101.9 (2008-2012 5-year est.); Marriage status: 15.9% never married, 60.7% now married, 9.2% widowed, 14.3% divorced (2008-2012 5-year est.); Foreign born: 1.8% (2008-2012 5-year est.); Ancestry (includes multiple ancestries): 32.5% German, 24.4% Irish, 11.6% English, 10.1% Swedish, 5.4% Norwegian (2008-2012 5-year est.).
Economy: Single-family building permits issued: 0 (2013); Multi-family building permits issued: 0 (2013); Homeowner vacancy rate: 3.6%. Rental vacancy rate: 0.0%. (2008-2012 5-year est.); Employment by occupation: 6.2% management, business, and financial, 1.8% computer, engineering, and science, 6.2% education, legal, community service, arts, and media, 3.3% healthcare practitioners, 20.2% service, 24.9% sales and office, 9.2% natural resources, construction, and maintenance, 28.2% production, transportation, and material moving (2008-2012 5-year est.).

Income: Per capita income: $21,071 (2008-2012 5-year est.); Median household income: $44,375 (2008-2012 5-year est.); Average household income: $52,905 (2008-2012 5-year est.); Percent of households with income of $100,000 or more: 9.4% (2008-2012 5-year est.); Poverty rate: 8.9% (2008-2012 5-year est.).

Education: Percent of population age 25 and over with: High school diploma (including GED) or higher: 94.4% (2008-2012 5-year est.); Bachelor's degree or higher: 11.1% (2008-2012 5-year est.); Master's degree or higher: 2.5% (2008-2012 5-year est.).

School District(s)
Princeton ESD 115 (PK-08)
   2011-12 Enrollment: 1,297 . . . . (815) 875-3162
Housing: Homeownership rate: 84.6% (2008-2012 5-year est.); Median home value: $93,000 (2008-2012 5-year est.); Median contract rent: $425 per month (2008-2012 5-year est.); Median year structure built: Before 1940 (2008-2012 5-year est.).
Health Insurance: 77.1% Private; 39.1% Public; 6.2% None. (2008-2012 5-year est.)
Transportation: Commute to work: 96.9% car, 0.0% public transportation, 2.5% walk, 0.6% work from home (2008-2012 5-year est.); Travel time to work: 21.8% less than 15 minutes, 54.2% 15 to 30 minutes, 10.3% 30 to 45 minutes, 4.4% 45 to 60 minutes, 9.3% 60 minutes or more (2008-2012 5-year est.)

VAN ORIN (unincorporated postal area)
Zip Code: 61374
   Covers a land area of 2.826 square miles and a water area of 0 square miles. Located at 41.54° N. Lat; 89.35° W. Long. Elevation is 801 feet.
   Population: 119 (2010); Density: 42.1 persons per square mile (2010); Race: 99.2% White, 0.0% Black/African American, 0.0% Asian, 0.0% American Indian/Alaska Native, 0.0% Native Hawaiian/Other Pacific Islander, 0.8% Some other race, 0.0% Two or more races, 3.4% Hispanic of any race (2010); Average household size: 2.53 (2010); Median age: 44.6 (2010); Males per 100 females: 95.1 (2010); Homeownership rate: 76.6% (2010)

WALNUT (village).
Covers a land area of 0.825 square miles and a water area of 0 square miles. Located at 41.56° N. Lat; 89.59° W. Long. Elevation is 705 feet.
Population: 1,463 (1990); 1,461 (2000); 1,416 (2010); Density: 1,822.8 persons per square mile (2008-2012 5-year est.); Race: 94.9% White, 0.5% Black/African American, 3.7% Asian, 0.6% American Indian/Alaska Native, 0.0% Native Hawaiian/Other Pacific Islander, 0.3% Some other race, 0.2% Two or more races, 5.3% Hispanic of any race (2008-2012 5-year est.); Average household size: 2.55 (2008-2012 5-year est.); Median age: 38.9 (2008-2012 5-year est.); Males per 100 females: 101.1 (2008-2012 5-year est.); Marriage status: 22.8% never married, 57.2% now married, 8.6% widowed, 11.4% divorced (2008-2012 5-year est.); Foreign born: 5.9% (2008-2012 5-year est.); Ancestry (includes multiple ancestries): 38.2% German, 15.6% Irish, 8.5% English, 7.4% Swedish, 6.8% Polish (2008-2012 5-year est.).
Economy: Single-family building permits issued: 0 (2013); Multi-family building permits issued: 0 (2013); Homeowner vacancy rate: 2.4%. Rental vacancy rate: 0.0%. (2008-2012 5-year est.); Employment by occupation: 15.1% management, business, and financial, 1.1% computer, engineering, and science, 11.1% education, legal, community service, arts, and media, 4.6% healthcare practitioners, 24.1% service, 17.3% sales and office, 11.3% natural resources, construction, and maintenance, 15.3% production, transportation, and material moving (2008-2012 5-year est.).
Income: Per capita income: $23,474 (2008-2012 5-year est.); Median household income: $51,818 (2008-2012 5-year est.); Average household income: $59,912 (2008-2012 5-year est.); Percent of households with income of $100,000 or more: 19.8% (2008-2012 5-year est.); Poverty rate: 9.9% (2008-2012 5-year est.).
Education: Percent of population age 25 and over with: High school diploma (including GED) or higher: 92.7% (2008-2012 5-year est.); Bachelor's degree or higher: 26.2% (2008-2012 5-year est.); Master's degree or higher: 6.9% (2008-2012 5-year est.).

School District(s)
Bureau Valley CUSD 340 (PK-12)
   2011-12 Enrollment: 1,154 . . . . (815) 445-3101
Housing: Homeownership rate: 77.4% (2008-2012 5-year est.); Median home value: $92,800 (2008-2012 5-year est.); Median contract rent: $432 per month (2008-2012 5-year est.); Median year structure built: 1952 (2008-2012 5-year est.).

Health Insurance: 75.7% Private; 26.9% Public; 12.5% None. (2008-2012 5-year est.)
Transportation: Commute to work: 86.8% car, 0.0% public transportation, 8.8% walk, 4.0% work from home (2008-2012 5-year est.); Travel time to work: 47.5% less than 15 minutes, 22.0% 15 to 30 minutes, 20.2% 30 to 45 minutes, 2.8% 45 to 60 minutes, 7.5% 60 minutes or more (2008-2012 5-year est.)
Additional Information Contacts
Walnut Chamber of Commerce . . . . (815) 379-2141
   http://www.villageofwalnut.com/chamber.htm

WYANET (village).
Covers a land area of 0.998 square miles and a water area of 0 square miles. Located at 41.36° N. Lat; 89.58° W. Long. Elevation is 659 feet.
Population: 1,017 (1990); 1,028 (2000); 991 (2010); Density: 1,188.2 persons per square mile (2008-2012 5-year est.); Race: 96.9% White, 0.0% Black/African American, 2.8% Asian, 0.0% American Indian/Alaska Native, 0.0% Native Hawaiian/Other Pacific Islander, 0.3% Some other race, 0.3% Two or more races, 1.8% Hispanic of any race (2008-2012 5-year est.); Average household size: 2.60 (2008-2012 5-year est.); Median age: 39.1 (2008-2012 5-year est.); Males per 100 females: 94.4 (2008-2012 5-year est.); Marriage status: 24.2% never married, 52.9% now married, 6.0% widowed, 16.9% divorced (2008-2012 5-year est.); Foreign born: 3.3% (2008-2012 5-year est.); Ancestry (includes multiple ancestries): 29.6% German, 14.3% Irish, 11.3% English, 10.4% American, 7.5% Swedish (2008-2012 5-year est.).
Economy: Homeowner vacancy rate: 2.7%. Rental vacancy rate: 0.0%. (2008-2012 5-year est.); Employment by occupation: 5.1% management, business, and financial, 1.1% computer, engineering, and science, 1.4% education, legal, community service, arts, and media, 3.4% healthcare practitioners, 22.7% service, 30.3% sales and office, 9.9% natural resources, construction, and maintenance, 26.2% production, transportation, and material moving (2008-2012 5-year est.).
Income: Per capita income: $17,864 (2008-2012 5-year est.); Median household income: $43,920 (2008-2012 5-year est.); Average household income: $46,276 (2008-2012 5-year est.); Percent of households with income of $100,000 or more: 3.7% (2008-2012 5-year est.); Poverty rate: 17.0% (2008-2012 5-year est.).
Education: Percent of population age 25 and over with: High school diploma (including GED) or higher: 89.2% (2008-2012 5-year est.); Bachelor's degree or higher: 4.5% (2008-2012 5-year est.); Master's degree or higher: 1.5% (2008-2012 5-year est.).

School District(s)
Bureau Valley CUSD 340 (PK-12)
   2011-12 Enrollment: 1,154 . . . . (815) 445-3101
Housing: Homeownership rate: 79.6% (2008-2012 5-year est.); Median home value: $79,000 (2008-2012 5-year est.); Median contract rent: $510 per month (2008-2012 5-year est.); Median year structure built: 1949 (2008-2012 5-year est.).
Health Insurance: 67.1% Private; 33.7% Public; 12.2% None. (2008-2012 5-year est.)
Transportation: Commute to work: 94.3% car, 0.0% public transportation, 1.2% walk, 0.4% work from home (2008-2012 5-year est.); Travel time to work: 42.8% less than 15 minutes, 39.3% 15 to 30 minutes, 10.5% 30 to 45 minutes, 2.5% 45 to 60 minutes, 5.0% 60 minutes or more (2008-2012 5-year est.)

Calhoun County

Located in western Illinois; bounded on the west and south by the Mississippi River and the Missouri border, and on the east by the Illinois River, which joins the Mississippi River at the southeastern tip of the county. Covers a land area of 253.825 square miles, a water area of 29.752 square miles, and is located in the Central Time Zone at 39.16° N. Lat., 90.67° W. Long. The county was founded in 1825. County seat is Hardin.

Calhoun County is part of the St. Louis, MO-IL Metropolitan Statistical Area. The entire metro area includes: Bond County, IL; Calhoun County, IL; Clinton County, IL; Jersey County, IL; Macoupin County, IL; Madison County, IL; Monroe County, IL; Saint Clair County, IL; Franklin County, MO; Jefferson County, MO; Lincoln County, MO; Saint Charles County, MO; Saint Louis County, MO; Warren County, MO; Saint Louis city, MO

Population: 5,322 (1990); 5,084 (2000); 5,089 (2010); Race: 98.5% White, 0.1% Black/African American, 0.3% Asian, 0.0% American Indian/Alaska Native, 0.0% Native Hawaiian/Other Pacific Islander, 1.1% Some other race, 1.2% Two or more races, 0.3% Hispanic of any race (2008-2012 5-year est.); Density: 19.8 persons per square mile (2008-2012 5-year est.); Average household size: 2.41 (2008-2012 5-year est.); Median age: 44.6 (2008-2012 5-year est.); Males per 100 females: 101.7 (2008-2012 5-year est.).
Religion: Five largest groups: 56.9% Catholicism, 9.3% Lutheran, 8.4% Baptist, 2.1% Presbyterian-Reformed, 0.5% Methodist/Pietist (2010)
Economy: Unemployment rate: 8.0% (April 2014); Total civilian labor force: 2,503 (April 2014); Leading industries: 26.0% accommodation & food services; 18.3% retail trade; 15.5% health care and social assistance (2012); Farms: 478 totaling 87,750 acres (2012); Companies that employ 500 or more persons: 0 (2012); Companies that employ 100 to 499 persons: 0 (2012); Companies that employ less than 100 persons: 91 (2012); Black-owned businesses: n/a (2007); Hispanic-owned businesses: n/a (2007); Asian-owned businesses: n/a (2007); Women-owned businesses: 82 (2007); Single-family building permits issued: 10 (2013); Multi-family building permits issued: 0 (2013).
Income: Per capita income: $25,822 (2008-2012 5-year est.); Median household income: $47,399 (2008-2012 5-year est.); Average household income: $61,594 (2008-2012 5-year est.); Percent of households with income of $100,000 or more: 16.2% (2008-2012 5-year est.); Poverty rate: 12.9% (2008-2012 5-year est.); Bankruptcy rate: n/a (2013).
Education: Percent of population age 25 and over with: High school diploma (including GED) or higher: 86.9% (2008-2012 5-year est.); Bachelor's degree or higher: 14.6% (2008-2012 5-year est.); Master's degree or higher: 6.5% (2008-2012 5-year est.).
Housing: Homeownership rate: 79.5% (2008-2012 5-year est.); Median home value: $115,600 (2008-2012 5-year est.); Median contract rent: $342 per month (2008-2012 5-year est.); Median year structure built: 1969 (2008-2012 5-year est.)
Health: Birth rate: 100.8 per 10,000 population (2013); Death rate: 116.6 per 10,000 population (2013); Age-adjusted cancer mortality rate: Suppressed deaths per 100,000 population (2011); Number of physicians: 3.9 per 10,000 population (2011); Hospital beds: 0.0 per 10,000 population (2010); Hospital admissions: 0.0 per 10,000 population (2010).
Elections: 2012 Presidential election results: 41.9% Obama, 55.9% Romney
National and State Parks: Batchtown State Fish and Waterfowl Management Area; Diamond-Hurricane Island State Fish and Waterfowl; Fuller Lake State Fish and Waterfowl Management Area; Mark Twain National Wildlife Refuge; Mortland Island State Fish And Waterfowl Man; Reds Landing State Fish And Waterfowl Manage; Rip Rap Landing State Fish and Waterfowl Management Area
Additional Information Contacts
Calhoun County Government . . . . (618) 576-2351

Calhoun County Communities

BATCHTOWN (village). Covers a land area of 1.863 square miles and a water area of 0 square miles. Located at 39.03° N. Lat; 90.65° W. Long. Elevation is 581 feet.
Population: 225 (1990); 218 (2000); 214 (2010); Density: 127.2 persons per square mile (2008-2012 5-year est.); Race: 98.3% White, 0.0% Black/African American, 0.0% Asian, 0.0% American Indian/Alaska Native, 0.0% Native Hawaiian/Other Pacific Islander, 1.7% Some other race, 1.7% Two or more races, 0.8% Hispanic of any race (2008-2012 5-year est.); Average household size: 2.55 (2008-2012 5-year est.); Median age: 40.5 (2008-2012 5-year est.); Males per 100 females: 109.7 (2008-2012 5-year est.); Marriage status: 31.5% never married, 53.2% now married, 5.9% widowed, 9.4% divorced (2008-2012 5-year est.); Foreign born: 1.3% (2008-2012 5-year est.); Ancestry (includes multiple ancestries): 73.0% German, 13.1% Irish, 5.9% American, 2.5% Scotch-Irish, 2.5% English (2008-2012 5-year est.).
Economy: Homeowner vacancy rate: 0.0%. Rental vacancy rate: 0.0%. (2008-2012 5-year est.); Employment by occupation: 3.8% management, business, and financial, 3.8% computer, engineering, and science, 15.0% education, legal, community service, arts, and media, 0.0% healthcare practitioners, 17.3% service, 6.8% sales and office, 24.8% natural resources, construction, and maintenance, 28.6% production, transportation, and material moving (2008-2012 5-year est.).

Income: Per capita income: $28,164 (2008-2012 5-year est.); Median household income: $59,688 (2008-2012 5-year est.); Average household income: $71,428 (2008-2012 5-year est.); Percent of households with income of $100,000 or more: 19.4% (2008-2012 5-year est.); Poverty rate: 7.2% (2008-2012 5-year est.).
Education: Percent of population age 25 and over with: High school diploma (including GED) or higher: 87.3% (2008-2012 5-year est.); Bachelor's degree or higher: 16.4% (2008-2012 5-year est.); Master's degree or higher: 8.5% (2008-2012 5-year est.).
Housing: Homeownership rate: 82.8% (2008-2012 5-year est.); Median home value: $106,700 (2008-2012 5-year est.); Median contract rent: $239 per month (2008-2012 5-year est.); Median year structure built: 1944 (2008-2012 5-year est.).
Health Insurance: 71.3% Private; 24.9% Public; 10.5% None. (2008-2012 5-year est.)
Transportation: Commute to work: 89.6% car, 0.0% public transportation, 5.6% walk, 4.8% work from home (2008-2012 5-year est.); Travel time to work: 12.6% less than 15 minutes, 13.4% 15 to 30 minutes, 4.2% 30 to 45 minutes, 17.6% 45 to 60 minutes, 52.1% 60 minutes or more (2008-2012 5-year est.)

BRUSSELS (village). Covers a land area of 0.558 square miles and a water area of 0 square miles. Located at 38.95° N. Lat; 90.59° W. Long. Elevation is 522 feet.
Population: 125 (1990); 141 (2000); 141 (2010); Density: 270.7 persons per square mile (2008-2012 5-year est.); Race: 96.7% White, 1.3% Black/African American, 0.0% Asian, 0.0% American Indian/Alaska Native, 0.0% Native Hawaiian/Other Pacific Islander, 2.0% Some other race, 2.0% Two or more races, 2.0% Hispanic of any race (2008-2012 5-year est.); Average household size: 2.69 (2008-2012 5-year est.); Median age: 40.1 (2008-2012 5-year est.); Males per 100 females: 65.9 (2008-2012 5-year est.); Marriage status: 25.8% never married, 59.7% now married, 7.3% widowed, 7.3% divorced (2008-2012 5-year est.); Foreign born: 0.0% (2008-2012 5-year est.); Ancestry (includes multiple ancestries): 55.0% German, 16.6% Irish, 6.0% American, 4.0% French, 2.6% Welsh (2008-2012 5-year est.).
Economy: Homeowner vacancy rate: 0.0%. Rental vacancy rate: 0.0%. (2008-2012 5-year est.); Employment by occupation: 14.6% management, business, and financial, 0.0% computer, engineering, and science, 0.0% education, legal, community service, arts, and media, 0.0% healthcare practitioners, 35.4% service, 18.8% sales and office, 22.9% natural resources, construction, and maintenance, 8.3% production, transportation, and material moving (2008-2012 5-year est.).
Income: Per capita income: $14,432 (2008-2012 5-year est.); Median household income: $29,722 (2008-2012 5-year est.); Average household income: $37,639 (2008-2012 5-year est.); Percent of households with income of $100,000 or more: n/a (2008-2012 5-year est.); Poverty rate: 21.9% (2008-2012 5-year est.).
Education: Percent of population age 25 and over with: High school diploma (including GED) or higher: 90.0% (2008-2012 5-year est.); Bachelor's degree or higher: 8.2% (2008-2012 5-year est.); Master's degree or higher: 4.5% (2008-2012 5-year est.).
School District(s)
Brussels CUSD 42 (PK-12)
    2011-12 Enrollment: 115 . . . . (618) 883-2131
Housing: Homeownership rate: 51.9% (2008-2012 5-year est.); Median home value: $83,300 (2008-2012 5-year est.); Median contract rent: $345 per month (2008-2012 5-year est.); Median year structure built: 1947 (2008-2012 5-year est.).
Health Insurance: 43.7% Private; 45.7% Public; 17.9% None. (2008-2012 5-year est.)
Transportation: Commute to work: 97.1% car, 0.0% public transportation, 0.0% walk, 0.0% work from home (2008-2012 5-year est.); Travel time to work: 14.7% less than 15 minutes, 29.4% 15 to 30 minutes, 11.8% 30 to 45 minutes, 2.9% 45 to 60 minutes, 41.2% 60 minutes or more (2008-2012 5-year est.)

GOLDEN EAGLE (unincorporated postal area)
Zip Code: 62036
    Covers a land area of 28.611 square miles and a water area of 4.402 square miles. Located at 38.91° N. Lat; 90.58° W. Long. Elevation is 673 feet. Population: 704 (2010); Density: 24.6 persons per square mile (2010); Race: 99.1% White, 0.0% Black/African American, 0.0% Asian, 0.0% American Indian/Alaska Native, 0.0% Native Hawaiian/Other Pacific Islander, 0.9% Some other race, 0.4% Two or more races, 1.8%

Hispanic of any race (2010); Average household size: 2.39 (2010); Median age: 47.2 (2010); Males per 100 females: 92.3 (2010); Homeownership rate: 86.1% (2010)

HAMBURG (village). Covers a land area of 0.522 square miles and a water area of 0.134 square miles. Located at 39.23° N. Lat; 90.72° W. Long. Elevation is 443 feet.

Population: 150 (1990); 126 (2000); 128 (2010); Density: 310.5 persons per square mile (2008-2012 5-year est.); Race: 93.8% White, 0.0% Black/African American, 6.2% Asian, 0.0% American Indian/Alaska Native, 0.0% Native Hawaiian/Other Pacific Islander, 0.0% Some other race, 0.0% Two or more races, 0.0% Hispanic of any race (2008-2012 5-year est.); Average household size: 2.31 (2008-2012 5-year est.); Median age: 53.4 (2008-2012 5-year est.); Males per 100 females: 82.0 (2008-2012 5-year est.); Marriage status: 9.9% never married, 74.5% now married, 9.9% widowed, 5.7% divorced (2008-2012 5-year est.); Foreign born: 6.2% (2008-2012 5-year est.); Ancestry (includes multiple ancestries): 57.4% German, 13.6% Irish, 11.1% Scotch-Irish, 8.0% Hungarian, 8.0% English (2008-2012 5-year est.).

Economy: Homeowner vacancy rate: 3.6%. Rental vacancy rate: 13.6%. (2008-2012 5-year est.); Employment by occupation: 32.9% management, business, and financial, 0.0% computer, engineering, and science, 0.0% education, legal, community service, arts, and media, 3.8% healthcare practitioners, 30.4% service, 6.3% sales and office, 10.1% natural resources, construction, and maintenance, 16.5% production, transportation, and material moving (2008-2012 5-year est.).

Income: Per capita income: $27,290 (2008-2012 5-year est.); Median household income: $41,667 (2008-2012 5-year est.); Average household income: $61,613 (2008-2012 5-year est.); Percent of households with income of $100,000 or more: 32.9% (2008-2012 5-year est.); Poverty rate: 16.7% (2008-2012 5-year est.).

Education: Percent of population age 25 and over with: High school diploma (including GED) or higher: 86.2% (2008-2012 5-year est.); Bachelor's degree or higher: 6.9% (2008-2012 5-year est.); Master's degree or higher: 0.0% (2008-2012 5-year est.).

Housing: Homeownership rate: 77.1% (2008-2012 5-year est.); Median home value: $85,000 (2008-2012 5-year est.); Median contract rent: $381 per month (2008-2012 5-year est.); Median year structure built: 1966 (2008-2012 5-year est.).

Health Insurance: 75.3% Private; 37.0% Public; 0.0% None. (2008-2012 5-year est.)

Transportation: Commute to work: 89.5% car, 0.0% public transportation, 0.0% walk, 10.5% work from home (2008-2012 5-year est.); Travel time to work: 33.8% less than 15 minutes, 50.0% 15 to 30 minutes, 11.8% 30 to 45 minutes, 0.0% 45 to 60 minutes, 4.4% 60 minutes or more (2008-2012 5-year est.)

HARDIN (village). County seat. Covers a land area of 2.128 square miles and a water area of 0.174 square miles. Located at 39.16° N. Lat; 90.62° W. Long. Elevation is 443 feet.

History: Hardin developed as a distribution center for the surrounding apple-growing region, and as the seat of Calhoun County.

Population: 1,071 (1990); 959 (2000); 967 (2010); Density: 537.5 persons per square mile (2008-2012 5-year est.); Race: 99.9% White, 0.1% Black/African American, 0.0% Asian, 0.0% American Indian/Alaska Native, 0.0% Native Hawaiian/Other Pacific Islander, 0.0% Some other race, 0.0% Two or more races, 0.0% Hispanic of any race (2008-2012 5-year est.); Average household size: 2.37 (2008-2012 5-year est.); Median age: 45.1 (2008-2012 5-year est.); Males per 100 females: 92.3 (2008-2012 5-year est.); Marriage status: 17.5% never married, 60.0% now married, 9.2% widowed, 13.3% divorced (2008-2012 5-year est.); Foreign born: 4.0% (2008-2012 5-year est.); Ancestry (includes multiple ancestries): 45.9% German, 14.4% Irish, 13.0% English, 6.6% French, 5.0% Arab (2008-2012 5-year est.).

Economy: Homeowner vacancy rate: 3.5%. Rental vacancy rate: 7.1%. (2008-2012 5-year est.); Employment by occupation: 9.2% management, business, and financial, 1.3% computer, engineering, and science, 11.0% education, legal, community service, arts, and media, 5.6% healthcare practitioners, 22.8% service, 22.8% sales and office, 9.7% natural resources, construction, and maintenance, 17.6% production, transportation, and material moving (2008-2012 5-year est.).

Income: Per capita income: $24,292 (2008-2012 5-year est.); Median household income: $48,571 (2008-2012 5-year est.); Average household income: $57,351 (2008-2012 5-year est.); Percent of households with

income of $100,000 or more: 13.5% (2008-2012 5-year est.); Poverty rate: 13.9% (2008-2012 5-year est.).

Education: Percent of population age 25 and over with: High school diploma (including GED) or higher: 87.3% (2008-2012 5-year est.); Bachelor's degree or higher: 15.1% (2008-2012 5-year est.); Master's degree or higher: 8.8% (2008-2012 5-year est.).

School District(s)

Calhoun CUSD 40 (KG-12)

    2011-12 Enrollment: 474 . . . . (618) 576-2722

Housing: Homeownership rate: 67.9% (2008-2012 5-year est.); Median home value: $86,900 (2008-2012 5-year est.); Median contract rent: $310 per month (2008-2012 5-year est.); Median year structure built: 1970 (2008-2012 5-year est.).

Health Insurance: 76.5% Private; 37.9% Public; 7.6% None. (2008-2012 5-year est.)

Transportation: Commute to work: 93.0% car, 0.0% public transportation, 0.8% walk, 5.1% work from home (2008-2012 5-year est.); Travel time to work: 45.6% less than 15 minutes, 7.3% 15 to 30 minutes, 9.6% 30 to 45 minutes, 16.9% 45 to 60 minutes, 20.6% 60 minutes or more (2008-2012 5-year est.)

KAMPSVILLE (village). Covers a land area of 1.020 square miles and a water area of 0.220 square miles. Located at 39.30° N. Lat; 90.61° W. Long. Elevation is 433 feet.

Population: 399 (1990); 302 (2000); 328 (2010); Density: 357.9 persons per square mile (2008-2012 5-year est.); Race: 99.5% White, 0.3% Black/African American, 0.3% Asian, 0.0% American Indian/Alaska Native, 0.0% Native Hawaiian/Other Pacific Islander, 0.0% Some other race, 0.0% Two or more races, 0.3% Hispanic of any race (2008-2012 5-year est.); Average household size: 2.13 (2008-2012 5-year est.); Median age: 41.7 (2008-2012 5-year est.); Males per 100 females: 82.5 (2008-2012 5-year est.); Marriage status: 26.5% never married, 47.0% now married, 14.1% widowed, 12.4% divorced (2008-2012 5-year est.); Foreign born: 0.3% (2008-2012 5-year est.); Ancestry (includes multiple ancestries): 44.9% German, 13.4% Irish, 11.0% English, 7.9% French, 3.8% Dutch (2008-2012 5-year est.).

Economy: Homeowner vacancy rate: 12.0%. Rental vacancy rate: 4.0%. (2008-2012 5-year est.); Employment by occupation: 11.9% management, business, and financial, 2.2% computer, engineering, and science, 6.0% education, legal, community service, arts, and media, 0.0% healthcare practitioners, 43.3% service, 23.1% sales and office, 6.7% natural resources, construction, and maintenance, 6.7% production, transportation, and material moving (2008-2012 5-year est.).

Income: Per capita income: $19,095 (2008-2012 5-year est.); Median household income: $30,833 (2008-2012 5-year est.); Average household income: $40,599 (2008-2012 5-year est.); Percent of households with income of $100,000 or more: 7.7% (2008-2012 5-year est.); Poverty rate: 30.7% (2008-2012 5-year est.).

Education: Percent of population age 25 and over with: High school diploma (including GED) or higher: 80.0% (2008-2012 5-year est.); Bachelor's degree or higher: 10.2% (2008-2012 5-year est.); Master's degree or higher: 4.5% (2008-2012 5-year est.).

Housing: Homeownership rate: 61.3% (2008-2012 5-year est.); Median home value: $64,000 (2008-2012 5-year est.); Median contract rent: $297 per month (2008-2012 5-year est.); Median year structure built: 1962 (2008-2012 5-year est.).

Health Insurance: 41.1% Private; 67.4% Public; 8.8% None. (2008-2012 5-year est.)

Transportation: Commute to work: 78.5% car, 0.0% public transportation, 6.9% walk, 7.7% work from home (2008-2012 5-year est.); Travel time to work: 45.8% less than 15 minutes, 30.8% 15 to 30 minutes, 12.5% 30 to 45 minutes, 5.0% 45 to 60 minutes, 5.8% 60 minutes or more (2008-2012 5-year est.)

MICHAEL (unincorporated postal area)

Zip Code: 62065

    Covers a land area of 10.807 square miles and a water area of 1.313 square miles. Located at 39.22° N. Lat; 90.63° W. Long. Elevation is 446 feet. Population: 97 (2010); Density: 9.0 persons per square mile (2010); Race: 100.0% White, 0.0% Black/African American, 0.0% Asian, 0.0% American Indian/Alaska Native, 0.0% Native Hawaiian/Other Pacific Islander, 0.0% Some other race, 0.0% Two or more races, 0.0% Hispanic of any race (2010); Average household size: 2.06 (2010); Median age: 50.1 (2010); Males per 100 females: 110.9 (2010); Homeownership rate: 85.1% (2010)

MOZIER (unincorporated postal area)
Zip Code: 62070
Covers a land area of 1.705 square miles and a water area of 0.033 square miles. Located at 39.29° N. Lat; 90.73° W. Long. Elevation is 446 feet. Population: 37 (2010); Density: 21.7 persons per square mile (2010); Race: 100.0% White, 0.0% Black/African American, 0.0% Asian, 0.0% American Indian/Alaska Native, 0.0% Native Hawaiian/Other Pacific Islander, 0.0% Some other race, 0.0% Two or more races, 0.0% Hispanic of any race (2010); Average household size: 1.76 (2010); Median age: 61.5 (2010); Males per 100 females: 117.6 (2010); Homeownership rate: 90.5% (2010)

Carroll County

Located in northwestern Illinois; bounded on the west by the Mississippi River and the Iowa border; drained by the Plum River and Elkhorn Creek. Covers a land area of 444.807 square miles, a water area of 21.553 square miles, and is located in the Central Time Zone at 42.06° N. Lat., 89.93° W. Long. The county was founded in 1839. County seat is Mount Carroll.

Weather Station: Mount Carroll   Elevation: 640 feet

	Jan	Feb	Mar	Apr	May	Jun	Jul	Aug	Sep	Oct	Nov	Dec
High	30	35	47	60	72	81	84	83	76	63	48	34
Low	10	14	25	35	46	55	59	57	48	36	27	15
Precip	1.4	1.7	2.6	3.7	4.4	4.8	4.3	4.5	3.6	3.1	2.9	2.2
Snow	9.4	7.2	3.5	1.3	tr	0.0	0.0	0.0	tr	0.1	1.3	8.6

High and Low temperatures in degrees Fahrenheit; Precipitation and Snow in inches

Population: 16,805 (1990); 16,674 (2000); 15,387 (2010); Race: 96.3% White, 0.5% Black/African American, 0.4% Asian, 0.1% American Indian/Alaska Native, 0.1% Native Hawaiian/Other Pacific Islander, 2.6% Some other race, 1.9% Two or more races, 2.9% Hispanic of any race (2008-2012 5-year est.); Density: 33.8 persons per square mile (2008-2012 5-year est.); Average household size: 2.23 (2008-2012 5-year est.); Median age: 46.5 (2008-2012 5-year est.); Males per 100 females: 99.2 (2008-2012 5-year est.).
Religion: Six largest groups: 18.0% Methodist/Pietist, 9.8% Catholicism, 8.4% Lutheran, 6.0% Presbyterian-Reformed, 5.1% European Free-Church, 4.3% Non-denominational Protestant (2010)
Economy: Unemployment rate: 7.5% (April 2014); Total civilian labor force: 7,422 (April 2014); Leading industries: 23.8% manufacturing; 14.0% health care and social assistance; 13.1% retail trade (2012); Farms: 643 totaling 256,132 acres (2012); Companies that employ 500 or more persons: 0 (2012); Companies that employ 100 to 499 persons: 5 (2012); Companies that employ less than 100 persons: 403 (2012); Black-owned businesses: n/a (2007); Hispanic-owned businesses: n/a (2007); Asian-owned businesses: n/a (2007); Women-owned businesses: n/a (2007); Single-family building permits issued: 15 (2013); Multi-family building permits issued: 0 (2013).
Income: Per capita income: $27,103 (2008-2012 5-year est.); Median household income: $48,456 (2008-2012 5-year est.); Average household income: $61,372 (2008-2012 5-year est.); Percent of households with income of $100,000 or more: 14.3% (2008-2012 5-year est.); Poverty rate: 12.5% (2008-2012 5-year est.); Bankruptcy rate: 3.13% (2013).
Education: Percent of population age 25 and over with: High school diploma (including GED) or higher: 89.6% (2008-2012 5-year est.); Bachelor's degree or higher: 15.8% (2008-2012 5-year est.); Master's degree or higher: 5.8% (2008-2012 5-year est.).
Housing: Homeownership rate: 76.1% (2008-2012 5-year est.); Median home value: $99,600 (2008-2012 5-year est.); Median contract rent: $395 per month (2008-2012 5-year est.); Median year structure built: 1956 (2008-2012 5-year est.)
Health: Birth rate: 91.2 per 10,000 population (2013); Death rate: 124.7 per 10,000 population (2013); Age-adjusted cancer mortality rate: 224.5 deaths per 100,000 population (2011); Number of physicians: 3.9 per 10,000 population (2011); Hospital beds: 0.0 per 10,000 population (2010); Hospital admissions: 0.0 per 10,000 population (2010).
Elections: 2012 Presidential election results: 49.6% Obama, 48.2% Romney
National and State Parks: Ayers Sand Prairie State Nature Preserve; Mississippi Palisades State Park
Additional Information Contacts
Carroll County Government . . . . (815) 244-0221
   http://carroll-county.net

Carroll County Communities

CHADWICK (village). Covers a land area of 0.311 square miles and a water area of 0 square miles. Located at 42.01° N. Lat; 89.89° W. Long. Elevation is 801 feet.
Population: 557 (1990); 505 (2000); 551 (2010); Density: 1,400.0 persons per square mile (2008-2012 5-year est.); Race: 83.7% White, 0.0% Black/African American, 0.2% Asian, 1.8% American Indian/Alaska Native, 1.8% Native Hawaiian/Other Pacific Islander, 12.5% Some other race, 8.9% Two or more races, 5.5% Hispanic of any race (2008-2012 5-year est.); Average household size: 2.26 (2008-2012 5-year est.); Median age: 48.0 (2008-2012 5-year est.); Males per 100 females: 98.2 (2008-2012 5-year est.); Marriage status: 14.4% never married, 67.6% now married, 5.9% widowed, 12.1% divorced (2008-2012 5-year est.); Foreign born: 0.0% (2008-2012 5-year est.); Ancestry (includes multiple ancestries): 43.3% German, 12.4% Irish, 10.3% American, 7.1% English, 5.3% Italian (2008-2012 5-year est.).
Economy: Homeowner vacancy rate: 7.5%. Rental vacancy rate: 0.0%. (2008-2012 5-year est.); Employment by occupation: 12.7% management, business, and financial, 0.0% computer, engineering, and science, 9.6% education, legal, community service, arts, and media, 5.7% healthcare practitioners, 15.8% service, 31.1% sales and office, 7.5% natural resources, construction, and maintenance, 17.5% production, transportation, and material moving (2008-2012 5-year est.).
Income: Per capita income: $25,416 (2008-2012 5-year est.); Median household income: $50,347 (2008-2012 5-year est.); Average household income: $57,619 (2008-2012 5-year est.); Percent of households with income of $100,000 or more: 9.4% (2008-2012 5-year est.); Poverty rate: 5.3% (2008-2012 5-year est.).
Education: Percent of population age 25 and over with: High school diploma (including GED) or higher: 93.9% (2008-2012 5-year est.); Bachelor's degree or higher: 19.5% (2008-2012 5-year est.); Master's degree or higher: 7.6% (2008-2012 5-year est.).
School District(s)
Chadwick-Milledgeville CUSD 399 (PK-12)
   2011-12 Enrollment: 526 . . . . (815) 684-5191
Housing: Homeownership rate: 89.6% (2008-2012 5-year est.); Median home value: $80,200 (2008-2012 5-year est.); Median contract rent: $389 per month (2008-2012 5-year est.); Median year structure built: 1944 (2008-2012 5-year est.).
Health Insurance: 71.3% Private; 32.6% Public; 12.8% None. (2008-2012 5-year est.)
Transportation: Commute to work: 85.8% car, 1.3% public transportation, 7.5% walk, 1.3% work from home (2008-2012 5-year est.); Travel time to work: 43.0% less than 15 minutes, 18.8% 15 to 30 minutes, 23.3% 30 to 45 minutes, 7.2% 45 to 60 minutes, 7.6% 60 minutes or more (2008-2012 5-year est.)

LANARK (city). Covers a land area of 1.125 square miles and a water area of 0 square miles. Located at 42.10° N. Lat; 89.83° W. Long. Elevation is 879 feet.
History: Lanark developed as a trading center and cannery operation for the surrounding farming community.
Population: 1,382 (1990); 1,584 (2000); 1,457 (2010); Density: 1,435.6 persons per square mile (2008-2012 5-year est.); Race: 96.6% White, 0.0% Black/African American, 0.2% Asian, 0.0% American Indian/Alaska Native, 0.0% Native Hawaiian/Other Pacific Islander, 3.2% Some other race, 2.9% Two or more races, 1.2% Hispanic of any race (2008-2012 5-year est.); Average household size: 2.37 (2008-2012 5-year est.); Median age: 41.1 (2008-2012 5-year est.); Males per 100 females: 94.6 (2008-2012 5-year est.); Marriage status: 24.6% never married, 56.9% now married, 7.8% widowed, 10.7% divorced (2008-2012 5-year est.); Foreign born: 2.5% (2008-2012 5-year est.); Ancestry (includes multiple ancestries): 42.8% German, 12.5% Irish, 11.1% American, 8.5% Dutch, 7.7% English (2008-2012 5-year est.).
Economy: Single-family building permits issued: 0 (2013); Multi-family building permits issued: 0 (2013); Homeowner vacancy rate: 3.2%. Rental vacancy rate: 6.7%. (2008-2012 5-year est.); Employment by occupation: 9.9% management, business, and financial, 2.5% computer, engineering, and science, 8.6% education, legal, community service, arts, and media, 5.0% healthcare practitioners, 15.4% service, 19.4% sales and office, 10.2% natural resources, construction, and maintenance, 29.0% production, transportation, and material moving (2008-2012 5-year est.).

Income: Per capita income: $20,948 (2008-2012 5-year est.); Median household income: $44,276 (2008-2012 5-year est.); Average household income: $50,271 (2008-2012 5-year est.); Percent of households with income of $100,000 or more: 9.2% (2008-2012 5-year est.); Poverty rate: 15.4% (2008-2012 5-year est.).

Education: Percent of population age 25 and over with: High school diploma (including GED) or higher: 88.5% (2008-2012 5-year est.); Bachelor's degree or higher: 14.5% (2008-2012 5-year est.); Master's degree or higher: 3.9% (2008-2012 5-year est.).

School District(s)

Eastland CUSD 308 (PK-12)

    2011-12 Enrollment: 679 . . . . (815) 493-6301

Housing: Homeownership rate: 79.4% (2008-2012 5-year est.); Median home value: $86,300 (2008-2012 5-year est.); Median contract rent: $423 per month (2008-2012 5-year est.); Median year structure built: 1943 (2008-2012 5-year est.).

Health Insurance: 72.8% Private; 38.5% Public; 6.6% None. (2008-2012 5-year est.)

Transportation: Commute to work: 95.6% car, 0.3% public transportation, 1.0% walk, 2.9% work from home (2008-2012 5-year est.); Travel time to work: 39.3% less than 15 minutes, 24.2% 15 to 30 minutes, 24.5% 30 to 45 minutes, 7.2% 45 to 60 minutes, 4.8% 60 minutes or more (2008-2012 5-year est.)

MILLEDGEVILLE (village).

Covers a land area of 0.694 square miles and a water area of 0 square miles. Located at 41.96° N. Lat; 89.77° W. Long. Elevation is 761 feet.

Population: 1,076 (1990); 1,016 (2000); 1,032 (2010); Density: 1,717.0 persons per square mile (2008-2012 5-year est.); Race: 97.6% White, 0.0% Black/African American, 0.5% Asian, 0.0% American Indian/Alaska Native, 0.0% Native Hawaiian/Other Pacific Islander, 1.9% Some other race, 1.8% Two or more races, 4.5% Hispanic of any race (2008-2012 5-year est.); Average household size: 2.44 (2008-2012 5-year est.); Median age: 36.9 (2008-2012 5-year est.); Males per 100 females: 92.7 (2008-2012 5-year est.); Marriage status: 17.5% never married, 67.1% now married, 7.0% widowed, 8.4% divorced (2008-2012 5-year est.); Foreign born: 2.4% (2008-2012 5-year est.); Ancestry (includes multiple ancestries): 39.6% German, 17.7% Irish, 15.9% American, 11.8% English, 5.0% Dutch (2008-2012 5-year est.).

Economy: Single-family building permits issued: 1 (2013); Multi-family building permits issued: 0 (2013); Homeowner vacancy rate: 2.7%. Rental vacancy rate: 14.7%. (2008-2012 5-year est.); Employment by occupation: 9.5% management, business, and financial, 4.5% computer, engineering, and science, 6.5% education, legal, community service, arts, and media, 2.2% healthcare practitioners, 11.4% service, 31.3% sales and office, 11.9% natural resources, construction, and maintenance, 22.7% production, transportation, and material moving (2008-2012 5-year est.).

Income: Per capita income: $24,719 (2008-2012 5-year est.); Median household income: $47,115 (2008-2012 5-year est.); Average household income: $60,534 (2008-2012 5-year est.); Percent of households with income of $100,000 or more: 13.8% (2008-2012 5-year est.); Poverty rate: 7.7% (2008-2012 5-year est.).

Taxes: Total city taxes per capita: $532 (2011); City property taxes per capita: $468 (2011).

Education: Percent of population age 25 and over with: High school diploma (including GED) or higher: 89.6% (2008-2012 5-year est.); Bachelor's degree or higher: 12.0% (2008-2012 5-year est.); Master's degree or higher: 4.7% (2008-2012 5-year est.).

School District(s)

Chadwick-Milledgeville CUSD 399 (PK-12)

    2011-12 Enrollment: 526 . . . . (815) 684-5191

Housing: Homeownership rate: 79.6% (2008-2012 5-year est.); Median home value: $83,500 (2008-2012 5-year est.); Median contract rent: $420 per month (2008-2012 5-year est.); Median year structure built: 1950 (2008-2012 5-year est.).

Health Insurance: 75.7% Private; 37.1% Public; 5.7% None. (2008-2012 5-year est.)

Safety: Violent crime rate: 0.0 per 10,000 population; Property crime rate: 216.1 per 10,000 population (2012).

Transportation: Commute to work: 91.1% car, 0.6% public transportation, 5.6% walk, 1.2% work from home (2008-2012 5-year est.); Travel time to work: 36.0% less than 15 minutes, 38.4% 15 to 30 minutes, 14.5% 30 to 45 minutes, 6.3% 45 to 60 minutes, 4.9% 60 minutes or more (2008-2012 5-year est.)

MOUNT CARROLL (city).

County seat. Covers a land area of 2.017 square miles and a water area of 0 square miles. Located at 42.09° N. Lat; 89.98° W. Long. Elevation is 810 feet.

History: Founded 1843, incorporated 1867.

Population: 1,726 (1990); 1,832 (2000); 1,717 (2010); Density: 963.9 persons per square mile (2008-2012 5-year est.); Race: 93.9% White, 0.7% Black/African American, 0.3% Asian, 0.4% American Indian/Alaska Native, 0.0% Native Hawaiian/Other Pacific Islander, 4.7% Some other race, 4.7% Two or more races, 1.6% Hispanic of any race (2008-2012 5-year est.); Average household size: 2.31 (2008-2012 5-year est.); Median age: 42.8 (2008-2012 5-year est.); Males per 100 females: 82.7 (2008-2012 5-year est.); Marriage status: 20.9% never married, 57.9% now married, 9.9% widowed, 11.4% divorced (2008-2012 5-year est.); Foreign born: 1.2% (2008-2012 5-year est.); Ancestry (includes multiple ancestries): 48.7% German, 14.1% Irish, 10.4% American, 7.2% English, 4.0% Swedish (2008-2012 5-year est.).

Economy: Single-family building permits issued: 0 (2013); Multi-family building permits issued: 0 (2013); Homeowner vacancy rate: 4.7%. Rental vacancy rate: 4.0%. (2008-2012 5-year est.); Employment by occupation: 12.0% management, business, and financial, 0.5% computer, engineering, and science, 12.5% education, legal, community service, arts, and media, 2.7% healthcare practitioners, 22.1% service, 19.8% sales and office, 10.8% natural resources, construction, and maintenance, 19.6% production, transportation, and material moving (2008-2012 5-year est.).

Income: Per capita income: $23,951 (2008-2012 5-year est.); Median household income: $43,015 (2008-2012 5-year est.); Average household income: $55,388 (2008-2012 5-year est.); Percent of households with income of $100,000 or more: 14.7% (2008-2012 5-year est.); Poverty rate: 11.6% (2008-2012 5-year est.).

Education: Percent of population age 25 and over with: High school diploma (including GED) or higher: 89.7% (2008-2012 5-year est.); Bachelor's degree or higher: 21.3% (2008-2012 5-year est.); Master's degree or higher: 8.2% (2008-2012 5-year est.).

School District(s)

West Carroll CUSD 314 (PK-12)

    2011-12 Enrollment: 1,317 . . . . (815) 259-2735

Housing: Homeownership rate: 73.5% (2008-2012 5-year est.); Median home value: $84,200 (2008-2012 5-year est.); Median contract rent: $357 per month (2008-2012 5-year est.); Median year structure built: Before 1940 (2008-2012 5-year est.).

Health Insurance: 70.7% Private; 42.0% Public; 8.0% None. (2008-2012 5-year est.)

Safety: Violent crime rate: 0.0 per 10,000 population; Property crime rate: 188.9 per 10,000 population (2012).

Transportation: Commute to work: 88.1% car, 2.2% public transportation, 2.4% walk, 4.5% work from home (2008-2012 5-year est.); Travel time to work: 41.9% less than 15 minutes, 25.6% 15 to 30 minutes, 13.1% 30 to 45 minutes, 10.5% 45 to 60 minutes, 8.9% 60 minutes or more (2008-2012 5-year est.)

Additional Information Contacts

Mount Carroll Chamber of Commerce . . . . (800) 244-9594
    http://www.mtcarrollil.org

SAVANNA (city).

Covers a land area of 2.619 square miles and a water area of 0.094 square miles. Located at 42.09° N. Lat; 90.14° W. Long. Elevation is 600 feet.

History: Savanna was settled in 1828 as a farming center and river port. The coming of the railroad in 1850 made Savanna a trading town and shipping point for livestock and farm produce.

Population: 3,819 (1990); 3,542 (2000); 3,062 (2010); Density: 1,132.9 persons per square mile (2008-2012 5-year est.); Race: 97.1% White, 0.1% Black/African American, 0.2% Asian, 0.0% American Indian/Alaska Native, 0.0% Native Hawaiian/Other Pacific Islander, 2.6% Some other race, 0.4% Two or more races, 4.1% Hispanic of any race (2008-2012 5-year est.); Average household size: 1.98 (2008-2012 5-year est.); Median age: 45.7 (2008-2012 5-year est.); Males per 100 females: 87.8 (2008-2012 5-year est.); Marriage status: 30.0% never married, 47.3% now married, 10.8% widowed, 11.9% divorced (2008-2012 5-year est.); Foreign born: 4.4% (2008-2012 5-year est.); Ancestry (includes multiple ancestries): 36.4% German, 12.8% American, 12.3% Irish, 10.8% English, 6.2% Italian (2008-2012 5-year est.).

Economy: Single-family building permits issued: 0 (2013); Multi-family building permits issued: 0 (2013); Homeowner vacancy rate: 4.3%. Rental vacancy rate: 0.0%. (2008-2012 5-year est.); Employment by occupation: 6.6% management, business, and financial, 1.0% computer, engineering,

and science, 7.9% education, legal, community service, arts, and media, 2.9% healthcare practitioners, 33.8% service, 10.8% sales and office, 11.8% natural resources, construction, and maintenance, 25.2% production, transportation, and material moving (2008-2012 5-year est.).
Income: Per capita income: $22,848 (2008-2012 5-year est.); Median household income: $36,141 (2008-2012 5-year est.); Average household income: $45,929 (2008-2012 5-year est.); Percent of households with income of $100,000 or more: 10.7% (2008-2012 5-year est.); Poverty rate: 20.4% (2008-2012 5-year est.).
Education: Percent of population age 25 and over with: High school diploma (including GED) or higher: 83.4% (2008-2012 5-year est.); Bachelor's degree or higher: 14.1% (2008-2012 5-year est.); Master's degree or higher: 5.7% (2008-2012 5-year est.).

School District(s)
West Carroll CUSD 314 (PK-12)
    2011-12 Enrollment: 1,317 . . . . (815) 259-2735
Housing: Homeownership rate: 60.5% (2008-2012 5-year est.); Median home value: $67,600 (2008-2012 5-year est.); Median contract rent: $384 per month (2008-2012 5-year est.); Median year structure built: 1942 (2008-2012 5-year est.).
Health Insurance: 60.1% Private; 37.2% Public; 17.4% None. (2008-2012 5-year est.)
Transportation: Commute to work: 87.8% car, 0.1% public transportation, 6.4% walk, 5.7% work from home (2008-2012 5-year est.); Travel time to work: 50.7% less than 15 minutes, 18.9% 15 to 30 minutes, 14.1% 30 to 45 minutes, 9.7% 45 to 60 minutes, 6.5% 60 minutes or more (2008-2012 5-year est.).
Airports: Tri-Township Airport (general aviation)
Additional Information Contacts
Savanna Chamber of Commerce . . . . (815) 273-2722
    http://www.savanna-il.com

SHANNON (village). Covers a land area of 0.479 square miles and a water area of 0 square miles. Located at 42.15° N. Lat; 89.74° W. Long. Elevation is 915 feet.
Population: 887 (1990); 854 (2000); 757 (2010); Density: 1,775.5 persons per square mile (2008-2012 5-year est.); Race: 96.9% White, 0.0% Black/African American, 0.2% Asian, 0.4% American Indian/Alaska Native, 0.0% Native Hawaiian/Other Pacific Islander, 2.5% Some other race, 0.4% Two or more races, 7.2% Hispanic of any race (2008-2012 5-year est.); Average household size: 2.34 (2008-2012 5-year est.); Median age: 41.7 (2008-2012 5-year est.); Males per 100 females: 101.2 (2008-2012 5-year est.); Marriage status: 23.4% never married, 59.5% now married, 8.5% widowed, 8.5% divorced (2008-2012 5-year est.); Foreign born: 3.6% (2008-2012 5-year est.); Ancestry (includes multiple ancestries): 52.3% German, 14.1% American, 8.8% English, 7.8% Irish, 7.2% Dutch (2008-2012 5-year est.).
Economy: Single-family building permits issued: 0 (2013); Multi-family building permits issued: 0 (2013); Homeowner vacancy rate: 1.4%. Rental vacancy rate: 0.0%. (2008-2012 5-year est.); Employment by occupation: 5.3% management, business, and financial, 1.1% computer, engineering, and science, 11.7% education, legal, community service, arts, and media, 2.2% healthcare practitioners, 12.0% service, 30.4% sales and office, 18.7% natural resources, construction, and maintenance, 18.7% production, transportation, and material moving (2008-2012 5-year est.).
Income: Per capita income: $23,619 (2008-2012 5-year est.); Median household income: $53,958 (2008-2012 5-year est.); Average household income: $55,687 (2008-2012 5-year est.); Percent of households with income of $100,000 or more: 8.9% (2008-2012 5-year est.); Poverty rate: 14.3% (2008-2012 5-year est.).
Education: Percent of population age 25 and over with: High school diploma (including GED) or higher: 90.7% (2008-2012 5-year est.); Bachelor's degree or higher: 10.4% (2008-2012 5-year est.); Master's degree or higher: 5.0% (2008-2012 5-year est.).

School District(s)
Eastland CUSD 308 (PK-12)
    2011-12 Enrollment: 679. . . . . (815) 493-6301
Housing: Homeownership rate: 79.1% (2008-2012 5-year est.); Median home value: $96,300 (2008-2012 5-year est.); Median contract rent: $506 per month (2008-2012 5-year est.); Median year structure built: 1956 (2008-2012 5-year est.).
Health Insurance: 70.2% Private; 43.1% Public; 8.7% None. (2008-2012 5-year est.)
Transportation: Commute to work: 96.9% car, 0.0% public transportation, 1.4% walk, 1.4% work from home (2008-2012 5-year est.); Travel time to

work: 25.9% less than 15 minutes, 41.9% 15 to 30 minutes, 22.8% 30 to 45 minutes, 2.0% 45 to 60 minutes, 7.4% 60 minutes or more (2008-2012 5-year est.)
Additional Information Contacts
Shannon Chamber of Commerce . . . .
    http://www.shannonillinois.com/chamberabout.html#

THOMSON (village). Covers a land area of 2.384 square miles and a water area of 0 square miles. Located at 41.97° N. Lat; 90.11° W. Long. Elevation is 597 feet.
Population: 538 (1990); 559 (2000); 590 (2010); Density: 283.1 persons per square mile (2008-2012 5-year est.); Race: 91.1% White, 5.5% Black/African American, 1.3% Asian, 0.0% American Indian/Alaska Native, 0.0% Native Hawaiian/Other Pacific Islander, 2.1% Some other race, 2.1% Two or more races, 7.4% Hispanic of any race (2008-2012 5-year est.); Average household size: 2.34 (2008-2012 5-year est.); Median age: 34.8 (2008-2012 5-year est.); Males per 100 females: 146.4 (2008-2012 5-year est.); Marriage status: 32.2% never married, 51.4% now married, 5.5% widowed, 10.9% divorced (2008-2012 5-year est.); Foreign born: 1.9% (2008-2012 5-year est.); Ancestry (includes multiple ancestries): 36.1% German, 21.9% Irish, 17.0% American, 7.7% English, 7.1% Dutch (2008-2012 5-year est.).
Economy: Single-family building permits issued: 0 (2013); Multi-family building permits issued: 0 (2013); Homeowner vacancy rate: 5.7%. Rental vacancy rate: 0.0%. (2008-2012 5-year est.); Employment by occupation: 4.6% management, business, and financial, 2.3% computer, engineering, and science, 4.6% education, legal, community service, arts, and media, 7.4% healthcare practitioners, 17.6% service, 28.2% sales and office, 13.4% natural resources, construction, and maintenance, 21.8% production, transportation, and material moving (2008-2012 5-year est.).
Income: Per capita income: $20,289 (2008-2012 5-year est.); Median household income: $39,531 (2008-2012 5-year est.); Average household income: $51,210 (2008-2012 5-year est.); Percent of households with income of $100,000 or more: 8.1% (2008-2012 5-year est.); Poverty rate: 18.1% (2008-2012 5-year est.).
Education: Percent of population age 25 and over with: High school diploma (including GED) or higher: 93.1% (2008-2012 5-year est.); Bachelor's degree or higher: 10.7% (2008-2012 5-year est.); Master's degree or higher: 4.7% (2008-2012 5-year est.).

School District(s)
West Carroll CUSD 314 (PK-12)
    2011-12 Enrollment: 1,317 . . . . (815) 259-2735
Housing: Homeownership rate: 60.2% (2008-2012 5-year est.); Median home value: $92,500 (2008-2012 5-year est.); Median contract rent: $461 per month (2008-2012 5-year est.); Median year structure built: 1952 (2008-2012 5-year est.).
Health Insurance: 56.5% Private; 44.7% Public; 13.9% None. (2008-2012 5-year est.)
Transportation: Commute to work: 93.0% car, 0.0% public transportation, 1.9% walk, 4.2% work from home (2008-2012 5-year est.); Travel time to work: 31.7% less than 15 minutes, 39.5% 15 to 30 minutes, 14.6% 30 to 45 minutes, 8.8% 45 to 60 minutes, 5.4% 60 minutes or more (2008-2012 5-year est.)

Cass County

Located in west central Illinois; bounded on the north by the Sangamon River, and on the west by the Illinois River. Covers a land area of 375.818 square miles, a water area of 7.947 square miles, and is located in the Central Time Zone at 39.97° N. Lat., 90.25° W. Long. The county was founded in 1837. County seat is Virginia.
Population: 13,437 (1990); 13,695 (2000); 13,642 (2010); Race: 88.0% White, 3.1% Black/African American, 0.0% Asian, 0.0% American Indian/Alaska Native, 0.0% Native Hawaiian/Other Pacific Islander, 8.9% Some other race, 1.4% Two or more races, 16.7% Hispanic of any race (2008-2012 5-year est.); Density: 35.7 persons per square mile (2008-2012 5-year est.); Average household size: 2.63 (2008-2012 5-year est.); Median age: 37.9 (2008-2012 5-year est.); Males per 100 females: 101.1 (2008-2012 5-year est.).
Religion: Six largest groups: 19.2% Catholicism, 16.9% Lutheran, 12.0% Baptist, 8.4% Methodist/Pietist, 2.6% Holiness, 2.2% Presbyterian-Reformed (2010)
Economy: Unemployment rate: 6.3% (April 2014); Total civilian labor force: 6,904 (April 2014); Leading industries: 11.2% retail trade; 8.7% health care and social assistance; 4.3% accommodation & food services

(2012); Farms: 446 totaling 182,688 acres (2012); Companies that employ 500 or more persons: 1 (2012); Companies that employ 100 to 499 persons: 3 (2012); Companies that employ less than 100 persons: 257 (2012); Black-owned businesses: n/a (2007); Hispanic-owned businesses: n/a (2007); Asian-owned businesses: n/a (2007); Women-owned businesses: n/a (2007); Single-family building permits issued: 6 (2013); Multi-family building permits issued: 0 (2013).

Income: Per capita income: $20,894 (2008-2012 5-year est.); Median household income: $43,180 (2008-2012 5-year est.); Average household income: $53,314 (2008-2012 5-year est.); Percent of households with income of $100,000 or more: 10.1% (2008-2012 5-year est.); Poverty rate: 17.1% (2008-2012 5-year est.); Bankruptcy rate: 2.85% (2013).

Taxes: Total county taxes per capita: $138 (2011); County property taxes per capita: $137 (2011).

Education: Percent of population age 25 and over with: High school diploma (including GED) or higher: 81.6% (2008-2012 5-year est.); Bachelor's degree or higher: 12.0% (2008-2012 5-year est.); Master's degree or higher: 3.7% (2008-2012 5-year est.).

Housing: Homeownership rate: 70.7% (2008-2012 5-year est.); Median home value: $76,400 (2008-2012 5-year est.); Median contract rent: $431 per month (2008-2012 5-year est.); Median year structure built: 1958 (2008-2012 5-year est.).

Health: Birth rate: 129.1 per 10,000 population (2013); Death rate: 98.3 per 10,000 population (2013); Age-adjusted cancer mortality rate: 221.9 deaths per 100,000 population (2011); Number of physicians: 1.5 per 10,000 population (2011); Hospital beds: 0.0 per 10,000 population (2010); Hospital admissions: 0.0 per 10,000 population (2010).

Elections: 2012 Presidential election results: 42.2% Obama, 55.7% Romney

National and State Parks: Meredosia National Wildlife Refuge; Panther Creek State Conservation Area; Sanganois State Conservation Area; Toppers Hole State Conservation Area

Additional Information Contacts

Cass County Government . . . . (217) 452-2277

Cass County Communities

ARENZVILLE (village). Covers a land area of 0.781 square miles and a water area of 0 square miles. Located at 39.88° N. Lat; 90.37° W. Long. Elevation is 505 feet.

Population: 432 (1990); 419 (2000); 409 (2010); Density: 453.3 persons per square mile (2008-2012 5-year est.); Race: 97.5% White, 0.0% Black/African American, 0.0% Asian, 0.0% American Indian/Alaska Native, 0.0% Native Hawaiian/Other Pacific Islander, 2.5% Some other race, 2.5% Two or more races, 7.1% Hispanic of any race (2008-2012 5-year est.); Average household size: 2.28 (2008-2012 5-year est.); Median age: 42.0 (2008-2012 5-year est.); Males per 100 females: 88.3 (2008-2012 5-year est.); Marriage status: 15.3% never married, 55.5% now married, 6.4% widowed, 22.8% divorced (2008-2012 5-year est.); Foreign born: 1.4% (2008-2012 5-year est.); Ancestry (includes multiple ancestries): 40.4% German, 13.6% American, 12.7% English, 11.3% Irish, 2.5% Scottish (2008-2012 5-year est.).

Economy: Homeowner vacancy rate: 3.3%. Rental vacancy rate: 0.0%. (2008-2012 5-year est.); Employment by occupation: 10.5% management, business, and financial, 1.7% computer, engineering, and science, 9.4% education, legal, community service, arts, and media, 5.5% healthcare practitioners, 9.9% service, 29.8% sales and office, 9.4% natural resources, construction, and maintenance, 23.8% production, transportation, and material moving (2008-2012 5-year est.).

Income: Per capita income: $28,850 (2008-2012 5-year est.); Median household income: $48,523 (2008-2012 5-year est.); Average household income: $61,610 (2008-2012 5-year est.); Percent of households with income of $100,000 or more: 14.8% (2008-2012 5-year est.); Poverty rate: 5.1% (2008-2012 5-year est.).

Education: Percent of population age 25 and over with: High school diploma (including GED) or higher: 96.1% (2008-2012 5-year est.); Bachelor's degree or higher: 24.5% (2008-2012 5-year est.); Master's degree or higher: 5.1% (2008-2012 5-year est.).

Housing: Homeownership rate: 76.1% (2008-2012 5-year est.); Median home value: $77,500 (2008-2012 5-year est.); Median contract rent: $350 per month (2008-2012 5-year est.); Median year structure built: 1953 (2008-2012 5-year est.).

Health Insurance: 68.9% Private; 38.7% Public; 9.3% None. (2008-2012 5-year est.)

Transportation: Commute to work: 87.7% car, 0.0% public transportation, 6.7% walk, 1.7% work from home (2008-2012 5-year est.); Travel time to work: 44.3% less than 15 minutes, 31.3% 15 to 30 minutes, 18.8% 30 to 45 minutes, 0.0% 45 to 60 minutes, 5.7% 60 minutes or more (2008-2012 5-year est.)

ASHLAND (village). Covers a land area of 0.735 square miles and a water area of 0 square miles. Located at 39.89° N. Lat; 90.01° W. Long. Elevation is 623 feet.

History: Incorporated 1869.

Population: 1,257 (1990); 1,361 (2000); 1,333 (2010); Density: 2,012.7 persons per square mile (2008-2012 5-year est.); Race: 97.5% White, 0.0% Black/African American, 0.0% Asian, 0.1% American Indian/Alaska Native, 0.0% Native Hawaiian/Other Pacific Islander, 2.4% Some other race, 1.6% Two or more races, 2.0% Hispanic of any race (2008-2012 5-year est.); Average household size: 2.83 (2008-2012 5-year est.); Median age: 36.0 (2008-2012 5-year est.); Males per 100 females: 104.8 (2008-2012 5-year est.); Marriage status: 26.8% never married, 55.5% now married, 9.1% widowed, 8.6% divorced (2008-2012 5-year est.); Foreign born: 0.9% (2008-2012 5-year est.); Ancestry (includes multiple ancestries): 29.3% American, 24.9% German, 14.7% Irish, 6.2% English, 5.0% Swedish (2008-2012 5-year est.).

Economy: Single-family building permits issued: 0 (2013); Multi-family building permits issued: 0 (2013); Homeowner vacancy rate: 0.0%. Rental vacancy rate: 0.0%. (2008-2012 5-year est.); Employment by occupation: 7.8% management, business, and financial, 2.3% computer, engineering, and science, 7.7% education, legal, community service, arts, and media, 4.3% healthcare practitioners, 10.1% service, 31.8% sales and office, 12.1% natural resources, construction, and maintenance, 23.8% production, transportation, and material moving (2008-2012 5-year est.).

Income: Per capita income: $21,736 (2008-2012 5-year est.); Median household income: $49,792 (2008-2012 5-year est.); Average household income: $59,336 (2008-2012 5-year est.); Percent of households with income of $100,000 or more: 17.7% (2008-2012 5-year est.); Poverty rate: 15.0% (2008-2012 5-year est.).

Education: Percent of population age 25 and over with: High school diploma (including GED) or higher: 91.5% (2008-2012 5-year est.); Bachelor's degree or higher: 12.0% (2008-2012 5-year est.); Master's degree or higher: 2.4% (2008-2012 5-year est.).

School District(s)

A-C Central CUSD 262 (PK-12)
    2011-12 Enrollment: 498 . . . . (217) 476-8112

Housing: Homeownership rate: 82.6% (2008-2012 5-year est.); Median home value: $95,000 (2008-2012 5-year est.); Median contract rent: $404 per month (2008-2012 5-year est.); Median year structure built: 1956 (2008-2012 5-year est.).

Health Insurance: 67.6% Private; 37.1% Public; 6.1% None. (2008-2012 5-year est.)

Safety: Violent crime rate: 0.0 per 10,000 population; Property crime rate: 98.0 per 10,000 population (2012).

Transportation: Commute to work: 94.4% car, 1.4% public transportation, 0.3% walk, 3.9% work from home (2008-2012 5-year est.); Travel time to work: 18.6% less than 15 minutes, 20.6% 15 to 30 minutes, 41.6% 30 to 45 minutes, 14.5% 45 to 60 minutes, 4.7% 60 minutes or more (2008-2012 5-year est.)

BEARDSTOWN (city). Covers a land area of 3.567 square miles and a water area of 0.057 square miles. Located at 40.01° N. Lat; 90.43° W. Long. Elevation is 449 feet.

History: Beardstown, first called Beard's Ferry, was settled in 1819 by Thomas Beard, who operated a ferry across the Illinois River. An early commercial fishing and clam industry gave way to farming and shipping. A 1922 flood covered Beardstown with a lake 18 miles wide, prompting the building of a cement sea wall when the waters receded.

Population: 5,270 (1990); 5,766 (2000); 6,123 (2010); Density: 1,736.0 persons per square mile (2008-2012 5-year est.); Race: 75.8% White, 6.3% Black/African American, 0.0% Asian, 0.1% American Indian/Alaska Native, 0.0% Native Hawaiian/Other Pacific Islander, 17.8% Some other race, 2.0% Two or more races, 32.0% Hispanic of any race (2008-2012 5-year est.); Average household size: 2.77 (2008-2012 5-year est.); Median age: 35.6 (2008-2012 5-year est.); Males per 100 females: 107.1 (2008-2012 5-year est.); Marriage status: 30.5% never married, 47.4% now married, 11.0% widowed, 11.2% divorced (2008-2012 5-year est.); Foreign born: 20.0% (2008-2012 5-year est.); Ancestry (includes multiple

ancestries): 16.5% American, 11.2% German, 7.9% Irish, 6.4% English, 1.7% Scottish (2008-2012 5-year est.).

Economy: Single-family building permits issued: 0 (2013); Multi-family building permits issued: 0 (2013); Homeowner vacancy rate: 2.7%. Rental vacancy rate: 7.2%. (2008-2012 5-year est.); Employment by occupation: 7.3% management, business, and financial, 0.5% computer, engineering, and science, 9.4% education, legal, community service, arts, and media, 1.8% healthcare practitioners, 19.6% service, 14.4% sales and office, 11.3% natural resources, construction, and maintenance, 35.8% production, transportation, and material moving (2008-2012 5-year est.).

Income: Per capita income: $17,528 (2008-2012 5-year est.); Median household income: $35,469 (2008-2012 5-year est.); Average household income: $46,474 (2008-2012 5-year est.); Percent of households with income of $100,000 or more: 5.6% (2008-2012 5-year est.); Poverty rate: 26.2% (2008-2012 5-year est.).

Education: Percent of population age 25 and over with: High school diploma (including GED) or higher: 74.1% (2008-2012 5-year est.); Bachelor's degree or higher: 9.5% (2008-2012 5-year est.); Master's degree or higher: 3.3% (2008-2012 5-year est.).

School District(s)
Beardstown CUSD 15 (PK-12)
   2011-12 Enrollment: 1,605 . . . . (217) 323-3099

Housing: Homeownership rate: 55.7% (2008-2012 5-year est.); Median home value: $65,500 (2008-2012 5-year est.); Median contract rent: $441 per month (2008-2012 5-year est.); Median year structure built: 1953 (2008-2012 5-year est.).

Health Insurance: 56.9% Private; 37.3% Public; 15.4% None. (2008-2012 5-year est.)

Safety: Violent crime rate: 37.7 per 10,000 population; Property crime rate: 36.1 per 10,000 population (2012).

Transportation: Commute to work: 92.1% car, 0.4% public transportation, 1.1% walk, 5.2% work from home (2008-2012 5-year est.); Travel time to work: 63.2% less than 15 minutes, 12.3% 15 to 30 minutes, 11.6% 30 to 45 minutes, 3.4% 45 to 60 minutes, 9.6% 60 minutes or more (2008-2012 5-year est.)

Airports: Greater Beardstown Airport (general aviation)

Additional Information Contacts
Beardstown Chamber of Commerce . . . . (217) 323-3271
   http://www.beardstownil.org
City of Beardstown . . . . (217) 323-3110
   http://www.cityofbeardstown.org

BLUFF SPRINGS (unincorporated postal area)
Zip Code: 62622
   Covers a land area of 1.874 square miles and a water area of 0 square miles. Located at 39.97° N. Lat; 90.35° W. Long. Elevation is 492 feet.
Population: 49 (2010); Density: 26.1 persons per square mile (2010); Race: 91.8% White, 0.0% Black/African American, 0.0% Asian, 0.0% American Indian/Alaska Native, 0.0% Native Hawaiian/Other Pacific Islander, 8.2% Some other race, 0.0% Two or more races, 8.2% Hispanic of any race (2010); Average household size: 2.88 (2010); Median age: 37.1 (2010); Males per 100 females: 96.0 (2010); Homeownership rate: 100.0% (2010)

CHANDLERVILLE (village). Covers a land area of 0.865 square miles and a water area of 0 square miles. Located at 40.05° N. Lat; 90.15° W. Long. Elevation is 463 feet.
History: Chandlerville was named for its founder, Dr. Charles Chandler.
Population: 689 (1990); 704 (2000); 553 (2010); Density: 860.0 persons per square mile (2008-2012 5-year est.); Race: 98.9% White, 0.0% Black/African American, 0.0% Asian, 0.0% American Indian/Alaska Native, 0.0% Native Hawaiian/Other Pacific Islander, 1.1% Some other race, 1.1% Two or more races, 1.1% Hispanic of any race (2008-2012 5-year est.); Average household size: 2.60 (2008-2012 5-year est.); Median age: 39.0 (2008-2012 5-year est.); Males per 100 females: 89.8 (2008-2012 5-year est.); Marriage status: 24.0% never married, 67.0% now married, 5.8% widowed, 3.2% divorced (2008-2012 5-year est.); Foreign born: 0.0% (2008-2012 5-year est.); Ancestry (includes multiple ancestries): 40.6% American, 21.5% German, 9.7% Irish, 8.2% English, 1.5% French (2008-2012 5-year est.).
Economy: Single-family building permits issued: 1 (2013); Multi-family building permits issued: 0 (2013); Homeowner vacancy rate: 8.3%. Rental vacancy rate: 0.0%. (2008-2012 5-year est.); Employment by occupation: 3.8% management, business, and financial, 0.0% computer, engineering, and science, 8.7% education, legal, community service, arts, and media,

11.4% healthcare practitioners, 21.7% service, 16.3% sales and office, 12.2% natural resources, construction, and maintenance, 25.9% production, transportation, and material moving (2008-2012 5-year est.).
Income: Per capita income: $18,445 (2008-2012 5-year est.); Median household income: $42,500 (2008-2012 5-year est.); Average household income: $48,925 (2008-2012 5-year est.); Percent of households with income of $100,000 or more: 4.5% (2008-2012 5-year est.); Poverty rate: 11.2% (2008-2012 5-year est.).
Education: Percent of population age 25 and over with: High school diploma (including GED) or higher: 88.5% (2008-2012 5-year est.); Bachelor's degree or higher: 11.1% (2008-2012 5-year est.); Master's degree or higher: 1.2% (2008-2012 5-year est.).

School District(s)
A-C Central CUSD 262 (PK-12)
   2011-12 Enrollment: 498 . . . . (217) 476-8112

Housing: Homeownership rate: 84.3% (2008-2012 5-year est.); Median home value: $53,900 (2008-2012 5-year est.); Median contract rent: $409 per month (2008-2012 5-year est.); Median year structure built: 1962 (2008-2012 5-year est.).
Health Insurance: 75.4% Private; 33.7% Public; 5.5% None. (2008-2012 5-year est.)
Transportation: Commute to work: 95.8% car, 0.0% public transportation, 3.1% walk, 0.0% work from home (2008-2012 5-year est.); Travel time to work: 30.2% less than 15 minutes, 26.7% 15 to 30 minutes, 16.8% 30 to 45 minutes, 20.6% 45 to 60 minutes, 5.7% 60 minutes or more (2008-2012 5-year est.)

VIRGINIA (city). County seat. Covers a land area of 1.177 square miles and a water area of 0.057 square miles. Located at 39.95° N. Lat; 90.21° W. Long. Elevation is 610 feet.
History: Virginia was platted in 1836 by Dr. Henry A. Hall, a former surgeon in the British Navy, and was incorporated as a village in 1842. It developed as a city after 1872.
Population: 1,767 (1990); 1,728 (2000); 1,611 (2010); Density: 1,287.6 persons per square mile (2008-2012 5-year est.); Race: 97.2% White, 0.7% Black/African American, 0.0% Asian, 0.0% American Indian/Alaska Native, 0.2% Native Hawaiian/Other Pacific Islander, 1.9% Some other race, 1.4% Two or more races, 2.0% Hispanic of any race (2008-2012 5-year est.); Average household size: 2.21 (2008-2012 5-year est.); Median age: 45.9 (2008-2012 5-year est.); Males per 100 females: 86.2 (2008-2012 5-year est.); Marriage status: 23.1% never married, 52.7% now married, 7.9% widowed, 16.3% divorced (2008-2012 5-year est.); Foreign born: 1.3% (2008-2012 5-year est.); Ancestry (includes multiple ancestries): 29.2% German, 27.5% American, 15.6% Irish, 13.2% English, 1.6% French (2008-2012 5-year est.).
Economy: Single-family building permits issued: 0 (2013); Multi-family building permits issued: 0 (2013); Homeowner vacancy rate: 1.4%. Rental vacancy rate: 0.0%. (2008-2012 5-year est.); Employment by occupation: 11.3% management, business, and financial, 0.0% computer, engineering, and science, 6.3% education, legal, community service, arts, and media, 5.6% healthcare practitioners, 21.1% service, 28.2% sales and office, 10.0% natural resources, construction, and maintenance, 17.5% production, transportation, and material moving (2008-2012 5-year est.).
Income: Per capita income: $23,476 (2008-2012 5-year est.); Median household income: $43,913 (2008-2012 5-year est.); Average household income: $52,192 (2008-2012 5-year est.); Percent of households with income of $100,000 or more: 8.4% (2008-2012 5-year est.); Poverty rate: 8.0% (2008-2012 5-year est.).
Education: Percent of population age 25 and over with: High school diploma (including GED) or higher: 87.6% (2008-2012 5-year est.); Bachelor's degree or higher: 10.8% (2008-2012 5-year est.); Master's degree or higher: 5.4% (2008-2012 5-year est.).

School District(s)
Virginia CUSD 64 (PK-12)
   2011-12 Enrollment: 339 . . . . (217) 452-3085

Housing: Homeownership rate: 72.8% (2008-2012 5-year est.); Median home value: $70,800 (2008-2012 5-year est.); Median contract rent: $393 per month (2008-2012 5-year est.); Median year structure built: 1960 (2008-2012 5-year est.).
Health Insurance: 67.4% Private; 34.4% Public; 15.6% None. (2008-2012 5-year est.)
Safety: Violent crime rate: 0.0 per 10,000 population; Property crime rate: 0.0 per 10,000 population (2012).
Transportation: Commute to work: 87.8% car, 0.0% public transportation, 4.9% walk, 6.8% work from home (2008-2012 5-year est.); Travel time to

work: 32.5% less than 15 minutes, 30.5% 15 to 30 minutes, 16.7% 30 to 45 minutes, 13.6% 45 to 60 minutes, 6.7% 60 minutes or more (2008-2012 5-year est.)

Champaign County

Located in eastern Illinois; prairie region, drained by the Sangamon, Kaskaskia, and Embarrass Rivers, and by the South Fork of the Vermilion River. Covers a land area of 996.266 square miles, a water area of 2.127 square miles, and is located in the Central Time Zone at 40.14° N. Lat., 88.20° W. Long. The county was founded in 1833. County seat is Urbana.

Champaign County is part of the Champaign-Urbana, IL Metropolitan Statistical Area. The entire metro area includes: Champaign County, IL; Ford County, IL; Piatt County, IL

Weather Station: Rantoul Chanute AFB										Elevation: 754 feet		
	Jan	Feb	Mar	Apr	May	Jun	Jul	Aug	Sep	Oct	Nov	Dec
High	34	38	50	63	74	84	87	85	79	66	51	38
Low	15	19	29	39	50	60	63	61	53	41	31	20
Precip	1.9	2.1	2.9	3.8	4.3	4.0	4.6	4.2	3.1	3.4	3.4	2.6
Snow	3.1	3.5	1.2	0.4	tr	0.0	0.0	0.0	0.0	tr	0.1	1.6

High and Low temperatures in degrees Fahrenheit; Precipitation and Snow in inches

Weather Station: Urbana										Elevation: 743 feet		
	Jan	Feb	Mar	Apr	May	Jun	Jul	Aug	Sep	Oct	Nov	Dec
High	34	38	50	63	74	83	85	84	78	65	51	37
Low	18	22	31	41	52	61	65	63	55	43	33	22
Precip	2.0	2.1	2.9	3.7	4.9	4.2	4.6	4.0	3.2	3.1	3.6	2.7
Snow	6.8	5.9	2.5	0.5	tr	0.0	0.0	0.0	0.0	0.1	1.2	5.8

High and Low temperatures in degrees Fahrenheit; Precipitation and Snow in inches

Population: 173,025 (1990); 179,669 (2000); 201,081 (2010); Race: 74.8% White, 12.6% Black/African American, 9.2% Asian, 0.2% American Indian/Alaska Native, 0.0% Native Hawaiian/Other Pacific Islander, 3.2% Some other race, 2.2% Two or more races, 5.3% Hispanic of any race (2008-2012 5-year est.); Density: 204.2 persons per square mile (2008-2012 5-year est.); Average household size: 2.32 (2008-2012 5-year est.); Median age: 28.9 (2008-2012 5-year est.); Males per 100 females: 99.8 (2008-2012 5-year est.).
Religion: Six largest groups: 7.6% Catholicism, 4.6% Pentecostal, 4.5% Methodist/Pietist, 4.3% Baptist, 3.7% Non-denominational Protestant, 3.0% Lutheran (2010)
Economy: Unemployment rate: 5.8% (April 2014); Total civilian labor force: 101,970 (April 2014); Leading industries: 17.8% health care and social assistance; 15.3% retail trade; 14.3% accommodation & food services (2012); Farms: 1,312 totaling 616,493 acres (2012); Companies that employ 500 or more persons: 8 (2012); Companies that employ 100 to 499 persons: 92 (2012); Companies that employ less than 100 persons: 4,005 (2012); Black-owned businesses: 1,187 (2007); Hispanic-owned businesses: 255 (2007); Asian-owned businesses: n/a (2007); Women-owned businesses: 3,807 (2007); Single-family building permits issued: 261 (2013); Multi-family building permits issued: 364 (2013).
Income: Per capita income: $25,455 (2008-2012 5-year est.); Median household income: $45,088 (2008-2012 5-year est.); Average household income: $63,078 (2008-2012 5-year est.); Percent of households with income of $100,000 or more: 18.3% (2008-2012 5-year est.); Poverty rate: 22.1% (2008-2012 5-year est.); Bankruptcy rate: 1.95% (2013).
Taxes: Total county taxes per capita: $203 (2011); County property taxes per capita: $172 (2011).
Education: Percent of population age 25 and over with: High school diploma (including GED) or higher: 93.3% (2008-2012 5-year est.); Bachelor's degree or higher: 42.2% (2008-2012 5-year est.); Master's degree or higher: 21.3% (2008-2012 5-year est.).
Housing: Homeownership rate: 54.4% (2008-2012 5-year est.); Median home value: $149,000 (2008-2012 5-year est.); Median contract rent: $642 per month (2008-2012 5-year est.); Median year structure built: 1975 (2008-2012 5-year est.).
Health: Birth rate: 115.1 per 10,000 population (2013); Death rate: 60.0 per 10,000 population (2013); Age-adjusted cancer mortality rate: 165.0 deaths per 100,000 population (2011); Number of physicians: 32.6 per 10,000 population (2011); Hospital beds: 26.2 per 10,000 population (2010); Hospital admissions: 1,407.9 per 10,000 population (2010).
Environment: Air Quality Index: 85.2% good, 14.8% moderate, 0.0% unhealthy for sensitive individuals, 0.0% unhealthy (percent of days in 2013)

Elections: 2012 Presidential election results: 52.0% Obama, 45.2% Romney
Additional Information Contacts
Champaign County Government . . . . (217) 384-3720
  http://www.co.champaign.il.us
Champaign County Chamber of Commerce . . . . (217) 359-1791
  http://champaigncounty.org
Champaign County Convention & Visitors Bureau . . . . (217) 351-4133
  http://www.visitchampaigncounty.org

Champaign County Communities

BONDVILLE (village). Covers a land area of 0.247 square miles and a water area of 0 square miles. Located at 40.11° N. Lat; 88.37° W. Long. Elevation is 719 feet.
Population: 354 (1990); 455 (2000); 443 (2010); Density: 2,510.2 persons per square mile (2008-2012 5-year est.); Race: 96.5% White, 1.5% Black/African American, 0.0% Asian, 0.0% American Indian/Alaska Native, 0.0% Native Hawaiian/Other Pacific Islander, 2.0% Some other race, 2.1% Two or more races, 0.0% Hispanic of any race (2008-2012 5-year est.); Average household size: 2.41 (2008-2012 5-year est.); Median age: 40.1 (2008-2012 5-year est.); Males per 100 females: 88.4 (2008-2012 5-year est.); Marriage status: 25.6% never married, 48.7% now married, 5.9% widowed, 19.7% divorced (2008-2012 5-year est.); Foreign born: 0.0% (2008-2012 5-year est.); Ancestry (includes multiple ancestries): 42.1% American, 17.4% German, 13.1% Irish, 4.8% English, 4.0% European (2008-2012 5-year est.).
Economy: Single-family building permits issued: 0 (2013); Multi-family building permits issued: 0 (2013); Homeowner vacancy rate: 0.0%. Rental vacancy rate: 9.6%. (2008-2012 5-year est.); Employment by occupation: 10.6% management, business, and financial, 1.7% computer, engineering, and science, 6.2% education, legal, community service, arts, and media, 5.5% healthcare practitioners, 19.2% service, 28.4% sales and office, 15.1% natural resources, construction, and maintenance, 13.4% production, transportation, and material moving (2008-2012 5-year est.).
Income: Per capita income: $18,120 (2008-2012 5-year est.); Median household income: $36,806 (2008-2012 5-year est.); Average household income: $43,528 (2008-2012 5-year est.); Percent of households with income of $100,000 or more: 7.0% (2008-2012 5-year est.); Poverty rate: 25.2% (2008-2012 5-year est.).
Education: Percent of population age 25 and over with: High school diploma (including GED) or higher: 90.6% (2008-2012 5-year est.); Bachelor's degree or higher: 9.4% (2008-2012 5-year est.); Master's degree or higher: 3.8% (2008-2012 5-year est.).
Housing: Homeownership rate: 63.4% (2008-2012 5-year est.); Median home value: $115,600 (2008-2012 5-year est.); Median contract rent: $533 per month (2008-2012 5-year est.); Median year structure built: 1959 (2008-2012 5-year est.).
Health Insurance: 74.2% Private; 26.1% Public; 9.7% None. (2008-2012 5-year est.)
Transportation: Commute to work: 96.6% car, 0.3% public transportation, 0.0% walk, 2.7% work from home (2008-2012 5-year est.); Travel time to work: 21.1% less than 15 minutes, 50.0% 15 to 30 minutes, 25.0% 30 to 45 minutes, 2.8% 45 to 60 minutes, 1.1% 60 minutes or more (2008-2012 5-year est.)

BROADLANDS (village). Covers a land area of 0.332 square miles and a water area of 0 square miles. Located at 39.91° N. Lat; 88.00° W. Long. Elevation is 679 feet.
Population: 340 (1990); 312 (2000); 349 (2010); Density: 914.7 persons per square mile (2008-2012 5-year est.); Race: 98.7% White, 0.3% Black/African American, 0.3% Asian, 0.0% American Indian/Alaska Native, 0.0% Native Hawaiian/Other Pacific Islander, 0.7% Some other race, 0.7% Two or more races, 0.7% Hispanic of any race (2008-2012 5-year est.); Average household size: 2.53 (2008-2012 5-year est.); Median age: 39.3 (2008-2012 5-year est.); Males per 100 females: 109.7 (2008-2012 5-year est.); Marriage status: 24.9% never married, 54.5% now married, 9.7% widowed, 10.9% divorced (2008-2012 5-year est.); Foreign born: 0.3% (2008-2012 5-year est.); Ancestry (includes multiple ancestries): 31.6% American, 19.1% Irish, 18.4% German, 10.5% English, 3.6% European (2008-2012 5-year est.).
Economy: Single-family building permits issued: 0 (2013); Multi-family building permits issued: 0 (2013); Homeowner vacancy rate: 0.0%. Rental vacancy rate: 33.3%. (2008-2012 5-year est.); Employment by occupation: 12.4% management, business, and financial, 1.4% computer, engineering,

and science, 7.6% education, legal, community service, arts, and media, 4.8% healthcare practitioners, 18.6% service, 17.2% sales and office, 19.3% natural resources, construction, and maintenance, 18.6% production, transportation, and material moving (2008-2012 5-year est.).
Income: Per capita income: $26,761 (2008-2012 5-year est.); Median household income: $55,000 (2008-2012 5-year est.); Average household income: $68,283 (2008-2012 5-year est.); Percent of households with income of $100,000 or more: 13.3% (2008-2012 5-year est.); Poverty rate: 1.0% (2008-2012 5-year est.).
Education: Percent of population age 25 and over with: High school diploma (including GED) or higher: 94.3% (2008-2012 5-year est.); Bachelor's degree or higher: 14.8% (2008-2012 5-year est.); Master's degree or higher: 5.3% (2008-2012 5-year est.).

School District(s)
Heritage CUSD 8 (KG-12)
    2011-12 Enrollment: 527. . . . . (217) 834-3392
Housing: Homeownership rate: 83.3% (2008-2012 5-year est.); Median home value: $82,700 (2008-2012 5-year est.); Median contract rent: $575 per month (2008-2012 5-year est.); Median year structure built: 1944 (2008-2012 5-year est.).
Health Insurance: 83.2% Private; 19.7% Public; 12.2% None. (2008-2012 5-year est.)
Transportation: Commute to work: 87.2% car, 0.0% public transportation, 2.1% walk, 10.6% work from home (2008-2012 5-year est.); Travel time to work: 8.7% less than 15 minutes, 31.7% 15 to 30 minutes, 24.6% 30 to 45 minutes, 24.6% 45 to 60 minutes, 10.3% 60 minutes or more (2008-2012 5-year est.)

CHAMPAIGN (city). Covers a land area of 22.433 square miles and a
water area of 0.027 square miles. Located at 40.12° N. Lat; 88.27° W. Long. Elevation is 738 feet.
History: Champaign came into existence as West Urbana in 1854, built around the railroad station when the Illinois Central Railroad chose a route several miles west of the town of Urbana. Resisting a move to be annexed to Urbana, residents of West Urbana incorporated under the name of Champaign in 1860. Rivalry between the two cities was laid aside when they jointly founded a seminary, later to become the University of Illinois, between them.
Population: 63,502 (1990); 67,518 (2000); 81,055 (2010); Density: 3,614.4 persons per square mile (2008-2012 5-year est.); Race: 69.0% White, 15.3% Black/African American, 12.1% Asian, 0.2% American Indian/Alaska Native, 0.0% Native Hawaiian/Other Pacific Islander, 3.4% Some other race, 2.0% Two or more races, 5.5% Hispanic of any race (2008-2012 5-year est.); Average household size: 2.25 (2008-2012 5-year est.); Median age: 26.3 (2008-2012 5-year est.); Males per 100 females: 104.8 (2008-2012 5-year est.); Marriage status: 53.2% never married, 36.2% now married, 3.0% widowed, 7.6% divorced (2008-2012 5-year est.); Foreign born: 13.7% (2008-2012 5-year est.); Ancestry (includes multiple ancestries): 19.0% German, 11.4% Irish, 11.3% American, 7.6% English, 4.1% Italian (2008-2012 5-year est.).
Economy: Unemployment rate: 5.6% (April 2014); Total civilian labor force: 41,336 (April 2014); Single-family building permits issued: 73 (2013); Multi-family building permits issued: 288 (2013); Homeowner vacancy rate: 2.6%. Rental vacancy rate: 4.8%. (2008-2012 5-year est.); Employment by occupation: 12.1% management, business, and financial, 9.5% computer, engineering, and science, 20.7% education, legal, community service, arts, and media, 4.8% healthcare practitioners, 19.5% service, 21.1% sales and office, 3.9% natural resources, construction, and maintenance, 8.3% production, transportation, and material moving (2008-2012 5-year est.).
Income: Per capita income: $24,855 (2008-2012 5-year est.); Median household income: $41,403 (2008-2012 5-year est.); Average household income: $61,071 (2008-2012 5-year est.); Percent of households with income of $100,000 or more: 17.5% (2008-2012 5-year est.); Poverty rate: 26.3% (2008-2012 5-year est.).
Taxes: Total city taxes per capita: $643 (2011); City property taxes per capita: $314 (2011).
Education: Percent of population age 25 and over with: High school diploma (including GED) or higher: 94.6% (2008-2012 5-year est.); Bachelor's degree or higher: 49.9% (2008-2012 5-year est.); Master's degree or higher: 25.2% (2008-2012 5-year est.).

School District(s)
Champaign CUSD 4 (PK-12)
    2011-12 Enrollment: 9,492 . . . . (217) 351-3800
Champaign/ford Roe (06-12)
    2011-12 Enrollment: n/a . . . . (217) 893-3219

Educ for Employment Sys 330
    2011-12 Enrollment: n/a . . . . (217) 355-1382
Four-year College(s)
University of Illinois at Urbana-Champaign (Public)
    Fall 2012 Enrollment: 44,459 . . . . (217) 333-1000
    2012-13 Tuition: In-state $14,522; Out-of-state $28,664
Two-year College(s)
Parkland College (Public)
    Fall 2012 Enrollment: 8,679 . . . . (217) 351-2200
    2012-13 Tuition: In-state $7,815; Out-of-state $13,305
Vocational/Technical School(s)
Regency Beauty Institute-Champaign (Private, For-profit)
    Fall 2012 Enrollment: 77 . . . . (800) 787-6456
    2012-13 Tuition: $16,425
Housing: Homeownership rate: 47.8% (2008-2012 5-year est.); Median home value: $151,300 (2008-2012 5-year est.); Median contract rent: $687 per month (2008-2012 5-year est.); Median year structure built: 1974 (2008-2012 5-year est.).
Health Insurance: 78.7% Private; 18.6% Public; 10.6% None. (2008-2012 5-year est.)
Hospitals: Pavilion Foundation Hospital (46 beds)
Safety: Violent crime rate: 91.1 per 10,000 population; Property crime rate: 332.0 per 10,000 population (2012).
Transportation: Commute to work: 74.0% car, 5.8% public transportation, 12.1% walk, 4.7% work from home (2008-2012 5-year est.); Travel time to work: 51.5% less than 15 minutes, 40.3% 15 to 30 minutes, 4.2% 30 to 45 minutes, 2.1% 45 to 60 minutes, 2.0% 60 minutes or more (2008-2012 5-year est.); Amtrak: Train service available.
Airports: University of Illinois - Willard Airport (primary service/non-hub)
Additional Information Contacts
Champaign County Chamber of Commerce . . . . (217) 359-1791
    http://champaigncounty.org
Champaign County Convention & Visitors Bureau . . . . (217) 351-4133
    http://www.visitchampaigncounty.org
City of Champaign. . . . . (217) 403-8700
    http://ci.champaign.il.us

DEWEY (unincorporated postal area)
Zip Code: 61840
    Covers a land area of 33.385 square miles and a water area of 0.080 square miles. Located at 40.29° N. Lat; 88.30° W. Long. Elevation is 732 feet. Population: 709 (2010); Density: 21.2 persons per square mile (2010); Race: 97.9% White, 0.7% Black/African American, 0.1% Asian, 0.3% American Indian/Alaska Native, 0.0% Native Hawaiian/Other Pacific Islander, 1.0% Some other race, 0.8% Two or more races, 0.7% Hispanic of any race (2010); Average household size: 2.60 (2010); Median age: 43.1 (2010); Males per 100 females: 99.7 (2010); Homeownership rate: 91.2% (2010)

FISHER (village). Covers a land area of 1.291 square miles and a water
area of 0 square miles. Located at 40.32° N. Lat; 88.35° W. Long. Elevation is 712 feet.
Population: 1,526 (1990); 1,647 (2000); 1,881 (2010); Density: 1,585.4 persons per square mile (2008-2012 5-year est.); Race: 95.5% White, 0.3% Black/African American, 1.3% Asian, 0.0% American Indian/Alaska Native, 0.0% Native Hawaiian/Other Pacific Islander, 2.9% Some other race, 2.1% Two or more races, 3.3% Hispanic of any race (2008-2012 5-year est.); Average household size: 2.68 (2008-2012 5-year est.); Median age: 35.2 (2008-2012 5-year est.); Males per 100 females: 101.9 (2008-2012 5-year est.); Marriage status: 23.2% never married, 63.7% now married, 5.3% widowed, 7.8% divorced (2008-2012 5-year est.); Foreign born: 2.3% (2008-2012 5-year est.); Ancestry (includes multiple ancestries): 32.8% German, 17.9% American, 11.6% English, 11.5% Irish, 4.7% Dutch (2008-2012 5-year est.).
Economy: Single-family building permits issued: 0 (2013); Multi-family building permits issued: 0 (2013); Homeowner vacancy rate: 0.0%. Rental vacancy rate: 14.6%. (2008-2012 5-year est.); Employment by occupation: 10.4% management, business, and financial, 4.3% computer, engineering, and science, 4.7% education, legal, community service, arts, and media, 3.8% healthcare practitioners, 16.1% service, 32.4% sales and office, 14.1% natural resources, construction, and maintenance, 14.2% production, transportation, and material moving (2008-2012 5-year est.).
Income: Per capita income: $26,518 (2008-2012 5-year est.); Median household income: $59,712 (2008-2012 5-year est.); Average household income: $70,689 (2008-2012 5-year est.); Percent of households with

income of $100,000 or more: 19.8% (2008-2012 5-year est.); Poverty rate: 7.3% (2008-2012 5-year est.).

Taxes: Total city taxes per capita: $434 (2011); City property taxes per capita: $378 (2011).

Education: Percent of population age 25 and over with: High school diploma (including GED) or higher: 92.9% (2008-2012 5-year est.); Bachelor's degree or higher: 12.4% (2008-2012 5-year est.); Master's degree or higher: 2.7% (2008-2012 5-year est.).

School District(s)

Fisher CUSD 1 (KG-12)

   2011-12 Enrollment: 618. . . . . (217) 897-6125

Housing: Homeownership rate: 77.1% (2008-2012 5-year est.); Median home value: $126,900 (2008-2012 5-year est.); Median contract rent: $540 per month (2008-2012 5-year est.); Median year structure built: 1970 (2008-2012 5-year est.).

Health Insurance: 77.1% Private; 29.6% Public; 7.9% None. (2008-2012 5-year est.)

Transportation: Commute to work: 90.5% car, 5.9% public transportation, 2.2% walk, 1.3% work from home (2008-2012 5-year est.); Travel time to work: 20.2% less than 15 minutes, 44.0% 15 to 30 minutes, 33.6% 30 to 45 minutes, 1.5% 45 to 60 minutes, 0.6% 60 minutes or more (2008-2012 5-year est.)

FOOSLAND (village). Covers a land area of 0.071 square miles and a water area of 0 square miles. Located at 40.36° N. Lat; 88.43° W. Long. Elevation is 735 feet.

Population: 132 (1990); 90 (2000); 101 (2010); Density: 2,002.7 persons per square mile (2008-2012 5-year est.); Race: 86.0% White, 14.0% Black/African American, 0.0% Asian, 0.0% American Indian/Alaska Native, 0.0% Native Hawaiian/Other Pacific Islander, 0.0% Some other race, 0.0% Two or more races, 7.0% Hispanic of any race (2008-2012 5-year est.); Average household size: 2.39 (2008-2012 5-year est.); Median age: 38.1 (2008-2012 5-year est.); Males per 100 females: 72.3 (2008-2012 5-year est.); Marriage status: 42.9% never married, 30.1% now married, 18.0% widowed, 9.0% divorced (2008-2012 5-year est.); Foreign born: 0.0% (2008-2012 5-year est.); Ancestry (includes multiple ancestries): 23.8% German, 12.6% American, 11.2% English, 9.1% Polish, 8.4% Irish (2008-2012 5-year est.).

Economy: Homeowner vacancy rate: 0.0%. Rental vacancy rate: 66.7%. (2008-2012 5-year est.); Employment by occupation: 1.5% management, business, and financial, 0.0% computer, engineering, and science, 0.0% education, legal, community service, arts, and media, 4.6% healthcare practitioners, 29.2% service, 23.1% sales and office, 26.2% natural resources, construction, and maintenance, 15.4% production, transportation, and material moving (2008-2012 5-year est.).

Income: Per capita income: $14,655 (2008-2012 5-year est.); Median household income: $52,500 (2008-2012 5-year est.); Average household income: $48,421 (2008-2012 5-year est.); Percent of households with income of $100,000 or more: n/a (2008-2012 5-year est.); Poverty rate: 24.7% (2008-2012 5-year est.).

Education: Percent of population age 25 and over with: High school diploma (including GED) or higher: 82.6% (2008-2012 5-year est.); Bachelor's degree or higher: 0.0% (2008-2012 5-year est.); Master's degree or higher: 0.0% (2008-2012 5-year est.).

Housing: Homeownership rate: 92.9% (2008-2012 5-year est.); Median home value: $62,700 (2008-2012 5-year est.); Median contract rent: n/a per month (2008-2012 5-year est.); Median year structure built: Before 1940 (2008-2012 5-year est.).

Health Insurance: 53.8% Private; 13.4% Public; 41.2% None. (2008-2012 5-year est.)

Transportation: Commute to work: 75.4% car, 0.0% public transportation, 24.6% walk, 0.0% work from home (2008-2012 5-year est.); Travel time to work: 27.7% less than 15 minutes, 35.4% 15 to 30 minutes, 16.9% 30 to 45 minutes, 18.5% 45 to 60 minutes, 1.5% 60 minutes or more (2008-2012 5-year est.)

GIFFORD (village). Covers a land area of 0.452 square miles and a water area of 0 square miles. Located at 40.31° N. Lat; 88.02° W. Long. Elevation is 797 feet.

Population: 845 (1990); 815 (2000); 975 (2010); Density: 2,031.4 persons per square mile (2008-2012 5-year est.); Race: 98.0% White, 0.5% Black/African American, 0.0% Asian, 0.0% American Indian/Alaska Native, 0.0% Native Hawaiian/Other Pacific Islander, 1.5% Some other race, 1.0% Two or more races, 1.4% Hispanic of any race (2008-2012 5-year est.); Average household size: 2.68 (2008-2012 5-year est.); Median age: 36.7

(2008-2012 5-year est.); Males per 100 females: 92.9 (2008-2012 5-year est.); Marriage status: 17.9% never married, 61.4% now married, 13.9% widowed, 6.8% divorced (2008-2012 5-year est.); Foreign born: 0.0% (2008-2012 5-year est.); Ancestry (includes multiple ancestries): 43.2% German, 13.7% Irish, 10.3% English, 5.7% Scottish, 5.0% Swedish (2008-2012 5-year est.).

Economy: Single-family building permits issued: 8 (2013); Multi-family building permits issued: 0 (2013); Homeowner vacancy rate: 1.8%. Rental vacancy rate: 6.3%. (2008-2012 5-year est.); Employment by occupation: 10.1% management, business, and financial, 1.2% computer, engineering, and science, 12.9% education, legal, community service, arts, and media, 3.1% healthcare practitioners, 14.1% service, 29.3% sales and office, 14.4% natural resources, construction, and maintenance, 14.9% production, transportation, and material moving (2008-2012 5-year est.).

Income: Per capita income: $24,373 (2008-2012 5-year est.); Median household income: $55,781 (2008-2012 5-year est.); Average household income: $66,379 (2008-2012 5-year est.); Percent of households with income of $100,000 or more: 20.6% (2008-2012 5-year est.); Poverty rate: 6.8% (2008-2012 5-year est.).

Education: Percent of population age 25 and over with: High school diploma (including GED) or higher: 91.6% (2008-2012 5-year est.); Bachelor's degree or higher: 23.7% (2008-2012 5-year est.); Master's degree or higher: 8.9% (2008-2012 5-year est.).

School District(s)

Gifford CCSD 188 (KG-08)

   2011-12 Enrollment: 208. . . . . (217) 568-7733

Housing: Homeownership rate: 85.8% (2008-2012 5-year est.); Median home value: $120,500 (2008-2012 5-year est.); Median contract rent: $419 per month (2008-2012 5-year est.); Median year structure built: 1974 (2008-2012 5-year est.).

Health Insurance: 78.7% Private; 29.9% Public; 6.6% None. (2008-2012 5-year est.)

Safety: Violent crime rate: 10.2 per 10,000 population; Property crime rate: 10.2 per 10,000 population (2012).

Transportation: Commute to work: 96.1% car, 0.0% public transportation, 2.0% walk, 1.5% work from home (2008-2012 5-year est.); Travel time to work: 21.4% less than 15 minutes, 28.9% 15 to 30 minutes, 40.6% 30 to 45 minutes, 7.5% 45 to 60 minutes, 1.5% 60 minutes or more (2008-2012 5-year est.)

HOMER (village). Covers a land area of 0.982 square miles and a water area of 0 square miles. Located at 40.03° N. Lat; 87.96° W. Long. Elevation is 676 feet.

History: Village formerly on Salt Creek to North but moved in 19th century to be on railroad.

Population: 1,264 (1990); 1,200 (2000); 1,193 (2010); Density: 1,092.8 persons per square mile (2008-2012 5-year est.); Race: 97.1% White, 0.4% Black/African American, 1.5% Asian, 0.0% American Indian/Alaska Native, 0.0% Native Hawaiian/Other Pacific Islander, 1.0% Some other race, 1.0% Two or more races, 0.7% Hispanic of any race (2008-2012 5-year est.); Average household size: 2.36 (2008-2012 5-year est.); Median age: 44.3 (2008-2012 5-year est.); Males per 100 females: 86.3 (2008-2012 5-year est.); Marriage status: 16.8% never married, 59.5% now married, 10.4% widowed, 13.3% divorced (2008-2012 5-year est.); Foreign born: 1.9% (2008-2012 5-year est.); Ancestry (includes multiple ancestries): 25.3% German, 23.2% American, 15.8% English, 13.5% Irish, 2.6% Russian (2008-2012 5-year est.).

Economy: Single-family building permits issued: 0 (2013); Multi-family building permits issued: 0 (2013); Homeowner vacancy rate: 7.9%. Rental vacancy rate: 10.6%. (2008-2012 5-year est.); Employment by occupation: 12.6% management, business, and financial, 7.8% computer, engineering, and science, 8.0% education, legal, community service, arts, and media, 2.9% healthcare practitioners, 22.2% service, 19.9% sales and office, 8.8% natural resources, construction, and maintenance, 17.8% production, transportation, and material moving (2008-2012 5-year est.).

Income: Per capita income: $26,636 (2008-2012 5-year est.); Median household income: $49,886 (2008-2012 5-year est.); Average household income: $62,263 (2008-2012 5-year est.); Percent of households with income of $100,000 or more: 12.1% (2008-2012 5-year est.); Poverty rate: 6.9% (2008-2012 5-year est.).

Education: Percent of population age 25 and over with: High school diploma (including GED) or higher: 92.2% (2008-2012 5-year est.); Bachelor's degree or higher: 13.1% (2008-2012 5-year est.); Master's degree or higher: 3.7% (2008-2012 5-year est.).

School District(s)

Heritage CUSD 8 (KG-12)

   2011-12 Enrollment: 527 . . . . (217) 834-3392

Housing: Homeownership rate: 83.3% (2008-2012 5-year est.); Median home value: $93,300 (2008-2012 5-year est.); Median contract rent: $479 per month (2008-2012 5-year est.); Median year structure built: 1945 (2008-2012 5-year est.).

Health Insurance: 82.0% Private; 30.5% Public; 5.5% None. (2008-2012 5-year est.)

Safety: Violent crime rate: 8.4 per 10,000 population; Property crime rate: 58.5 per 10,000 population (2012).

Transportation: Commute to work: 89.5% car, 0.0% public transportation, 2.7% walk, 6.4% work from home (2008-2012 5-year est.); Travel time to work: 17.3% less than 15 minutes, 24.3% 15 to 30 minutes, 47.6% 30 to 45 minutes, 10.2% 45 to 60 minutes, 0.6% 60 minutes or more (2008-2012 5-year est.)

IVESDALE (village). Covers a land area of 0.829 square miles and a water area of 0 square miles. Located at 39.95° N. Lat; 88.46° W. Long. Elevation is 682 feet.

Population: 339 (1990); 288 (2000); 267 (2010); Density: 306.4 persons per square mile (2008-2012 5-year est.); Race: 100.0% White, 0.0% Black/African American, 0.0% Asian, 0.0% American Indian/Alaska Native, 0.0% Native Hawaiian/Other Pacific Islander, 0.0% Some other race, 0.0% Two or more races, 0.0% Hispanic of any race (2008-2012 5-year est.); Average household size: 2.42 (2008-2012 5-year est.); Median age: 43.6 (2008-2012 5-year est.); Males per 100 females: 104.8 (2008-2012 5-year est.); Marriage status: 20.4% never married, 64.1% now married, 5.3% widowed, 10.2% divorced (2008-2012 5-year est.); Foreign born: 0.0% (2008-2012 5-year est.); Ancestry (includes multiple ancestries): 32.3% German, 29.5% American, 27.6% Irish, 5.9% French, 2.8% English (2008-2012 5-year est.).

Economy: Single-family building permits issued: 0 (2013); Multi-family building permits issued: 0 (2013); Homeowner vacancy rate: 0.0%. Rental vacancy rate: 0.0%. (2008-2012 5-year est.); Employment by occupation: 13.9% management, business, and financial, 2.9% computer, engineering, and science, 3.6% education, legal, community service, arts, and media, 2.9% healthcare practitioners, 23.4% service, 25.5% sales and office, 8.0% natural resources, construction, and maintenance, 19.7% production, transportation, and material moving (2008-2012 5-year est.).

Income: Per capita income: $26,806 (2008-2012 5-year est.); Median household income: $53,594 (2008-2012 5-year est.); Average household income: $65,296 (2008-2012 5-year est.); Percent of households with income of $100,000 or more: 12.4% (2008-2012 5-year est.); Poverty rate: 2.5% (2008-2012 5-year est.).

Education: Percent of population age 25 and over with: High school diploma (including GED) or higher: 97.8% (2008-2012 5-year est.); Bachelor's degree or higher: 16.6% (2008-2012 5-year est.); Master's degree or higher: 4.4% (2008-2012 5-year est.).

Housing: Homeownership rate: 89.5% (2008-2012 5-year est.); Median home value: $93,500 (2008-2012 5-year est.); Median contract rent: $488 per month (2008-2012 5-year est.); Median year structure built: Before 1940 (2008-2012 5-year est.).

Health Insurance: 75.6% Private; 28.0% Public; 8.7% None. (2008-2012 5-year est.)

Transportation: Commute to work: 96.2% car, 0.0% public transportation, 0.8% walk, 3.1% work from home (2008-2012 5-year est.); Travel time to work: 17.5% less than 15 minutes, 32.5% 15 to 30 minutes, 38.9% 30 to 45 minutes, 7.1% 45 to 60 minutes, 4.0% 60 minutes or more (2008-2012 5-year est.)

LAKE OF THE WOODS (CDP). Covers a land area of 1.773 square miles and a water area of 0.069 square miles. Located at 40.20° N. Lat; 88.37° W. Long. Elevation is 748 feet.

History: Covered bridge.

Population: 2,748 (1990); 3,026 (2000); 2,912 (2010); Density: 1,706.3 persons per square mile (2008-2012 5-year est.); Race: 97.5% White, 0.0% Black/African American, 0.0% Asian, 0.0% American Indian/Alaska Native, 0.0% Native Hawaiian/Other Pacific Islander, 2.5% Some other race, 1.8% Two or more races, 1.6% Hispanic of any race (2008-2012 5-year est.); Average household size: 2.53 (2008-2012 5-year est.); Median age: 33.0 (2008-2012 5-year est.); Males per 100 females: 90.0 (2008-2012 5-year est.); Marriage status: 29.2% never married, 51.2% now married, 2.3% widowed, 17.3% divorced (2008-2012 5-year est.); Foreign born: 1.9% (2008-2012 5-year est.); Ancestry (includes multiple

ancestries): 28.6% American, 28.4% German, 8.6% English, 7.8% Irish, 4.0% European (2008-2012 5-year est.).

Economy: Homeowner vacancy rate: 4.6%. Rental vacancy rate: 0.0%. (2008-2012 5-year est.); Employment by occupation: 9.6% management, business, and financial, 2.2% computer, engineering, and science, 4.0% education, legal, community service, arts, and media, 4.5% healthcare practitioners, 26.5% service, 33.5% sales and office, 10.0% natural resources, construction, and maintenance, 9.8% production, transportation, and material moving (2008-2012 5-year est.).

Income: Per capita income: $20,936 (2008-2012 5-year est.); Median household income: $38,068 (2008-2012 5-year est.); Average household income: $52,640 (2008-2012 5-year est.); Percent of households with income of $100,000 or more: 12.9% (2008-2012 5-year est.); Poverty rate: 9.2% (2008-2012 5-year est.).

Education: Percent of population age 25 and over with: High school diploma (including GED) or higher: 96.5% (2008-2012 5-year est.); Bachelor's degree or higher: 29.0% (2008-2012 5-year est.); Master's degree or higher: 8.0% (2008-2012 5-year est.).

Housing: Homeownership rate: 85.8% (2008-2012 5-year est.); Median home value: $86,700 (2008-2012 5-year est.); Median contract rent: $621 per month (2008-2012 5-year est.); Median year structure built: 1988 (2008-2012 5-year est.).

Health Insurance: 68.5% Private; 31.4% Public; 15.7% None. (2008-2012 5-year est.)

Transportation: Commute to work: 96.9% car, 0.0% public transportation, 0.0% walk, 1.9% work from home (2008-2012 5-year est.); Travel time to work: 27.6% less than 15 minutes, 56.7% 15 to 30 minutes, 9.6% 30 to 45 minutes, 1.2% 45 to 60 minutes, 4.9% 60 minutes or more (2008-2012 5-year est.)

LONGVIEW (village). Aka Long View. Covers a land area of 0.247 square miles and a water area of 0 square miles. Located at 39.89° N. Lat; 88.07° W. Long. Elevation is 679 feet.

Population: 180 (1990); 153 (2000); 153 (2010); Density: 658.8 persons per square mile (2008-2012 5-year est.); Race: 99.4% White, 0.0% Black/African American, 0.0% Asian, 0.6% American Indian/Alaska Native, 0.0% Native Hawaiian/Other Pacific Islander, 0.0% Some other race, 0.0% Two or more races, 2.5% Hispanic of any race (2008-2012 5-year est.); Average household size: 2.43 (2008-2012 5-year est.); Median age: 41.8 (2008-2012 5-year est.); Males per 100 females: 109.0 (2008-2012 5-year est.); Marriage status: 16.9% never married, 55.1% now married, 8.8% widowed, 19.1% divorced (2008-2012 5-year est.); Foreign born: 2.5% (2008-2012 5-year est.); Ancestry (includes multiple ancestries): 33.7% American, 21.5% English, 11.0% Scottish, 9.8% German, 7.4% French (2008-2012 5-year est.).

Economy: Homeowner vacancy rate: 0.0%. Rental vacancy rate: 0.0%. (2008-2012 5-year est.); Employment by occupation: 9.6% management, business, and financial, 1.4% computer, engineering, and science, 15.1% education, legal, community service, arts, and media, 0.0% healthcare practitioners, 24.7% service, 32.9% sales and office, 11.0% natural resources, construction, and maintenance, 5.5% production, transportation, and material moving (2008-2012 5-year est.).

Income: Per capita income: $20,144 (2008-2012 5-year est.); Median household income: $41,250 (2008-2012 5-year est.); Average household income: $48,460 (2008-2012 5-year est.); Percent of households with income of $100,000 or more: 9.0% (2008-2012 5-year est.); Poverty rate: 12.3% (2008-2012 5-year est.).

Education: Percent of population age 25 and over with: High school diploma (including GED) or higher: 88.7% (2008-2012 5-year est.); Bachelor's degree or higher: 13.9% (2008-2012 5-year est.); Master's degree or higher: 9.6% (2008-2012 5-year est.).

Housing: Homeownership rate: 89.6% (2008-2012 5-year est.); Median home value: $46,700 (2008-2012 5-year est.); Median contract rent: $506 per month (2008-2012 5-year est.); Median year structure built: Before 1940 (2008-2012 5-year est.).

Health Insurance: 66.3% Private; 24.5% Public; 17.2% None. (2008-2012 5-year est.)

Transportation: Commute to work: 100.0% car, 0.0% public transportation, 0.0% walk, 0.0% work from home (2008-2012 5-year est.); Travel time to work: 5.5% less than 15 minutes, 19.2% 15 to 30 minutes, 47.9% 30 to 45 minutes, 24.7% 45 to 60 minutes, 2.7% 60 minutes or more (2008-2012 5-year est.)

LUDLOW (village). Covers a land area of 0.357 square miles and a water area of 0 square miles. Located at 40.39° N. Lat; 88.13° W. Long. Elevation is 774 feet.

Population: 323 (1990); 324 (2000); 371 (2010); Density: 1,034.2 persons per square mile (2008-2012 5-year est.); Race: 93.8% White, 1.4% Black/African American, 0.0% Asian, 0.0% American Indian/Alaska Native, 0.0% Native Hawaiian/Other Pacific Islander, 4.8% Some other race, 4.3% Two or more races, 0.0% Hispanic of any race (2008-2012 5-year est.); Average household size: 2.53 (2008-2012 5-year est.); Median age: 29.4 (2008-2012 5-year est.); Males per 100 females: 98.4 (2008-2012 5-year est.); Marriage status: 37.4% never married, 34.5% now married, 9.0% widowed, 19.1% divorced (2008-2012 5-year est.); Foreign born: 1.1% (2008-2012 5-year est.); Ancestry (includes multiple ancestries): 28.7% American, 15.4% German, 15.2% Irish, 11.7% English, 6.5% Italian (2008-2012 5-year est.).

Economy: Single-family building permits issued: 0 (2013); Multi-family building permits issued: 0 (2013); Homeowner vacancy rate: 9.0%. Rental vacancy rate: 22.7%. (2008-2012 5-year est.); Employment by occupation: 3.6% management, business, and financial, 4.1% computer, engineering, and science, 2.4% education, legal, community service, arts, and media, 1.8% healthcare practitioners, 16.0% service, 20.7% sales and office, 17.2% natural resources, construction, and maintenance, 34.3% production, transportation, and material moving (2008-2012 5-year est.).

Income: Per capita income: $17,455 (2008-2012 5-year est.); Median household income: $35,000 (2008-2012 5-year est.); Average household income: $44,671 (2008-2012 5-year est.); Percent of households with income of $100,000 or more: 6.8% (2008-2012 5-year est.); Poverty rate: 30.7% (2008-2012 5-year est.).

Education: Percent of population age 25 and over with: High school diploma (including GED) or higher: 94.6% (2008-2012 5-year est.); Bachelor's degree or higher: 2.0% (2008-2012 5-year est.); Master's degree or higher: 0.0% (2008-2012 5-year est.).

School District(s)
Ludlow CCSD 142 (PK-08)
   2011-12 Enrollment: 85. . . . . (217) 396-5261

Housing: Homeownership rate: 48.6% (2008-2012 5-year est.); Median home value: $71,800 (2008-2012 5-year est.); Median contract rent: $440 per month (2008-2012 5-year est.); Median year structure built: 1968 (2008-2012 5-year est.).

Health Insurance: 34.4% Private; 53.9% Public; 23.0% None. (2008-2012 5-year est.)

Transportation: Commute to work: 98.2% car, 0.0% public transportation, 1.8% walk, 0.0% work from home (2008-2012 5-year est.); Travel time to work: 24.6% less than 15 minutes, 32.3% 15 to 30 minutes, 33.5% 30 to 45 minutes, 9.0% 45 to 60 minutes, 0.6% 60 minutes or more (2008-2012 5-year est.)

MAHOMET (village). Covers a land area of 9.016 square miles and a water area of 0.066 square miles. Located at 40.19° N. Lat; 88.39° W. Long. Elevation is 732 feet.

Population: 3,103 (1990); 4,877 (2000); 7,258 (2010); Density: 801.9 persons per square mile (2008-2012 5-year est.); Race: 94.3% White, 0.7% Black/African American, 1.7% Asian, 0.5% American Indian/Alaska Native, 0.0% Native Hawaiian/Other Pacific Islander, 2.8% Some other race, 2.8% Two or more races, 2.6% Hispanic of any race (2008-2012 5-year est.); Average household size: 2.69 (2008-2012 5-year est.); Median age: 37.3 (2008-2012 5-year est.); Males per 100 females: 90.1 (2008-2012 5-year est.); Marriage status: 21.8% never married, 68.6% now married, 3.7% widowed, 6.0% divorced (2008-2012 5-year est.); Foreign born: 2.8% (2008-2012 5-year est.); Ancestry (includes multiple ancestries): 31.6% German, 11.3% American, 11.1% English, 8.5% Irish, 7.2% European (2008-2012 5-year est.).

Economy: Single-family building permits issued: 73 (2013); Multi-family building permits issued: 0 (2013); Homeowner vacancy rate: 2.0%. Rental vacancy rate: 0.0%. (2008-2012 5-year est.); Employment by occupation: 19.3% management, business, and financial, 5.4% computer, engineering, and science, 14.5% education, legal, community service, arts, and media, 8.3% healthcare practitioners, 12.4% service, 24.8% sales and office, 8.4% natural resources, construction, and maintenance, 6.8% production, transportation, and material moving (2008-2012 5-year est.).

Income: Per capita income: $37,547 (2008-2012 5-year est.); Median household income: $82,056 (2008-2012 5-year est.); Average household income: $100,479 (2008-2012 5-year est.); Percent of households with income of $100,000 or more: 38.7% (2008-2012 5-year est.); Poverty rate: 4.9% (2008-2012 5-year est.).

Education: Percent of population age 25 and over with: High school diploma (including GED) or higher: 99.2% (2008-2012 5-year est.); Bachelor's degree or higher: 47.2% (2008-2012 5-year est.); Master's degree or higher: 21.8% (2008-2012 5-year est.).

School District(s)
Mahomet-Seymour CUSD 3 (PK-12)
   2011-12 Enrollment: 2,904 . . . . (217) 586-4995

Housing: Homeownership rate: 80.6% (2008-2012 5-year est.); Median home value: $184,000 (2008-2012 5-year est.); Median contract rent: $652 per month (2008-2012 5-year est.); Median year structure built: 1988 (2008-2012 5-year est.).

Health Insurance: 89.0% Private; 17.7% Public; 3.7% None. (2008-2012 5-year est.)

Safety: Violent crime rate: 5.5 per 10,000 population; Property crime rate: 134.5 per 10,000 population (2012).

Transportation: Commute to work: 94.4% car, 0.2% public transportation, 0.9% walk, 4.1% work from home (2008-2012 5-year est.); Travel time to work: 22.2% less than 15 minutes, 55.4% 15 to 30 minutes, 11.1% 30 to 45 minutes, 5.2% 45 to 60 minutes, 6.0% 60 minutes or more (2008-2012 5-year est.)

Additional Information Contacts
Mahomet Area Chamber of Commerce . . . . (217) 586-3165
   http://www.mahometchamberofcommerce.com
Village of Mahomet . . . . (217) 586-4456
   http://www.mahomet.govoffice.com

OGDEN (village). Covers a land area of 0.572 square miles and a water area of 0 square miles. Located at 40.12° N. Lat; 87.96° W. Long. Elevation is 669 feet.

Population: 671 (1990); 743 (2000); 810 (2010); Density: 1,283.6 persons per square mile (2008-2012 5-year est.); Race: 99.5% White, 0.0% Black/African American, 0.0% Asian, 0.3% American Indian/Alaska Native, 0.0% Native Hawaiian/Other Pacific Islander, 0.2% Some other race, 0.3% Two or more races, 0.0% Hispanic of any race (2008-2012 5-year est.); Average household size: 2.65 (2008-2012 5-year est.); Median age: 39.6 (2008-2012 5-year est.); Males per 100 females: 96.3 (2008-2012 5-year est.); Marriage status: 18.4% never married, 61.5% now married, 7.4% widowed, 12.7% divorced (2008-2012 5-year est.); Foreign born: 0.4% (2008-2012 5-year est.); Ancestry (includes multiple ancestries): 35.1% German, 29.4% American, 12.9% Irish, 9.5% English, 7.2% Dutch (2008-2012 5-year est.).

Economy: Single-family building permits issued: 0 (2013); Multi-family building permits issued: 0 (2013); Homeowner vacancy rate: 3.3%. Rental vacancy rate: 0.0%. (2008-2012 5-year est.); Employment by occupation: 13.1% management, business, and financial, 8.4% computer, engineering, and science, 4.1% education, legal, community service, arts, and media, 6.4% healthcare practitioners, 14.6% service, 24.6% sales and office, 15.5% natural resources, construction, and maintenance, 13.4% production, transportation, and material moving (2008-2012 5-year est.).

Income: Per capita income: $27,549 (2008-2012 5-year est.); Median household income: $64,632 (2008-2012 5-year est.); Average household income: $71,734 (2008-2012 5-year est.); Percent of households with income of $100,000 or more: 18.7% (2008-2012 5-year est.); Poverty rate: 2.5% (2008-2012 5-year est.).

Education: Percent of population age 25 and over with: High school diploma (including GED) or higher: 97.4% (2008-2012 5-year est.); Bachelor's degree or higher: 20.3% (2008-2012 5-year est.); Master's degree or higher: 6.5% (2008-2012 5-year est.).

School District(s)
Prairieview-Ogden CCSD 197 (KG-08)
   2011-12 Enrollment: 250. . . . . (217) 583-3300

Housing: Homeownership rate: 91.0% (2008-2012 5-year est.); Median home value: $118,700 (2008-2012 5-year est.); Median contract rent: $538 per month (2008-2012 5-year est.); Median year structure built: 1970 (2008-2012 5-year est.).

Health Insurance: 83.1% Private; 25.9% Public; 3.4% None. (2008-2012 5-year est.)

Transportation: Commute to work: 95.5% car, 0.0% public transportation, 1.0% walk, 2.7% work from home (2008-2012 5-year est.); Travel time to work: 18.8% less than 15 minutes, 52.7% 15 to 30 minutes, 26.0% 30 to 45 minutes, 0.5% 45 to 60 minutes, 2.0% 60 minutes or more (2008-2012 5-year est.)

PENFIELD (CDP). Covers a land area of 0.257 square miles and a water area of 0 square miles. Located at 40.30° N. Lat; 87.94° W. Long. Elevation is 712 feet.
Population: n/a (1990); n/a (2000); 193 (2010); Density: 606.5 persons per square mile (2008-2012 5-year est.); Race: 92.3% White, 0.0% Black/African American, 1.3% Asian, 0.0% American Indian/Alaska Native, 0.0% Native Hawaiian/Other Pacific Islander, 6.4% Some other race, 6.4% Two or more races, 8.3% Hispanic of any race (2008-2012 5-year est.); Average household size: 1.93 (2008-2012 5-year est.); Median age: 41.3 (2008-2012 5-year est.); Males per 100 females: 110.8 (2008-2012 5-year est.); Marriage status: 34.6% never married, 37.6% now married, 12.8% widowed, 15.0% divorced (2008-2012 5-year est.); Foreign born: 1.3% (2008-2012 5-year est.); Ancestry (includes multiple ancestries): 30.8% German, 22.4% American, 19.2% English, 5.1% Irish, 1.9% French (2008-2012 5-year est.).
Economy: Homeowner vacancy rate: 0.0%. Rental vacancy rate: 8.1%. (2008-2012 5-year est.); Employment by occupation: 15.7% management, business, and financial, 0.0% computer, engineering, and science, 5.6% education, legal, community service, arts, and media, 0.0% healthcare practitioners, 17.6% service, 17.6% sales and office, 35.2% natural resources, construction, and maintenance, 8.3% production, transportation, and material moving (2008-2012 5-year est.).
Income: Per capita income: $27,562 (2008-2012 5-year est.); Median household income: $57,679 (2008-2012 5-year est.); Average household income: $52,396 (2008-2012 5-year est.); Percent of households with income of $100,000 or more: 6.2% (2008-2012 5-year est.); Poverty rate: 7.7% (2008-2012 5-year est.).
Education: Percent of population age 25 and over with: High school diploma (including GED) or higher: 87.0% (2008-2012 5-year est.); Bachelor's degree or higher: 2.6% (2008-2012 5-year est.); Master's degree or higher: 0.0% (2008-2012 5-year est.).
Housing: Homeownership rate: 58.0% (2008-2012 5-year est.); Median home value: $73,200 (2008-2012 5-year est.); Median contract rent: $434 per month (2008-2012 5-year est.); Median year structure built: 1943 (2008-2012 5-year est.).
Health Insurance: 75.6% Private; 36.5% Public; 6.4% None. (2008-2012 5-year est.)
Transportation: Commute to work: 92.4% car, 0.0% public transportation, 7.6% walk, 0.0% work from home (2008-2012 5-year est.); Travel time to work: 27.6% less than 15 minutes, 22.9% 15 to 30 minutes, 42.9% 30 to 45 minutes, 6.7% 45 to 60 minutes, 0.0% 60 minutes or more (2008-2012 5-year est.)

PESOTUM (village). Covers a land area of 0.588 square miles and a water area of 0.008 square miles. Located at 39.91° N. Lat; 88.28° W. Long. Elevation is 715 feet.
History: Pesotum developed as a grain storage and shipping center.
Population: 558 (1990); 521 (2000); 551 (2010); Density: 878.0 persons per square mile (2008-2012 5-year est.); Race: 98.4% White, 0.0% Black/African American, 0.0% Asian, 0.0% American Indian/Alaska Native, 0.0% Native Hawaiian/Other Pacific Islander, 1.6% Some other race, 1.6% Two or more races, 1.6% Hispanic of any race (2008-2012 5-year est.); Average household size: 2.16 (2008-2012 5-year est.); Median age: 37.7 (2008-2012 5-year est.); Males per 100 females: 91.1 (2008-2012 5-year est.); Marriage status: 18.4% never married, 64.1% now married, 9.3% widowed, 8.1% divorced (2008-2012 5-year est.); Foreign born: 0.6% (2008-2012 5-year est.); Ancestry (includes multiple ancestries): 37.6% German, 14.7% English, 13.8% American, 11.4% Irish, 5.0% French (2008-2012 5-year est.).
Economy: Single-family building permits issued: 0 (2013); Multi-family building permits issued: 0 (2013); Homeowner vacancy rate: 2.6%. Rental vacancy rate: 0.0%. (2008-2012 5-year est.); Employment by occupation: 8.4% management, business, and financial, 1.9% computer, engineering, and science, 18.6% education, legal, community service, arts, and media, 6.1% healthcare practitioners, 11.0% service, 30.0% sales and office, 19.8% natural resources, construction, and maintenance, 4.2% production, transportation, and material moving (2008-2012 5-year est.).
Income: Per capita income: $28,145 (2008-2012 5-year est.); Median household income: $56,094 (2008-2012 5-year est.); Average household income: $60,801 (2008-2012 5-year est.); Percent of households with income of $100,000 or more: 11.7% (2008-2012 5-year est.); Poverty rate: 3.0% (2008-2012 5-year est.).
Education: Percent of population age 25 and over with: High school diploma (including GED) or higher: 96.0% (2008-2012 5-year est.);

Bachelor's degree or higher: 19.4% (2008-2012 5-year est.); Master's degree or higher: 4.8% (2008-2012 5-year est.).
Housing: Homeownership rate: 93.7% (2008-2012 5-year est.); Median home value: $114,300 (2008-2012 5-year est.); Median contract rent: $509 per month (2008-2012 5-year est.); Median year structure built: 1953 (2008-2012 5-year est.).
Health Insurance: 88.8% Private; 27.5% Public; 2.9% None. (2008-2012 5-year est.)
Transportation: Commute to work: 96.6% car, 0.0% public transportation, 0.0% walk, 1.5% work from home (2008-2012 5-year est.); Travel time to work: 20.8% less than 15 minutes, 47.5% 15 to 30 minutes, 25.9% 30 to 45 minutes, 1.9% 45 to 60 minutes, 3.9% 60 minutes or more (2008-2012 5-year est.)

PHILO (village). Covers a land area of 0.826 square miles and a water area of 0 square miles. Located at 40.00° N. Lat; 88.16° W. Long. Elevation is 735 feet.
Population: 1,028 (1990); 1,314 (2000); 1,466 (2010); Density: 1,898.7 persons per square mile (2008-2012 5-year est.); Race: 98.0% White, 0.0% Black/African American, 1.0% Asian, 0.5% American Indian/Alaska Native, 0.0% Native Hawaiian/Other Pacific Islander, 0.5% Some other race, 0.3% Two or more races, 0.3% Hispanic of any race (2008-2012 5-year est.); Average household size: 2.49 (2008-2012 5-year est.); Median age: 38.4 (2008-2012 5-year est.); Males per 100 females: 109.5 (2008-2012 5-year est.); Marriage status: 18.9% never married, 70.1% now married, 3.7% widowed, 7.3% divorced (2008-2012 5-year est.); Foreign born: 1.1% (2008-2012 5-year est.); Ancestry (includes multiple ancestries): 33.1% German, 24.2% American, 14.7% Irish, 8.9% English, 3.1% European (2008-2012 5-year est.).
Economy: Single-family building permits issued: 0 (2013); Multi-family building permits issued: 0 (2013); Homeowner vacancy rate: 0.0%. Rental vacancy rate: 0.0%. (2008-2012 5-year est.); Employment by occupation: 14.2% management, business, and financial, 9.2% computer, engineering, and science, 11.2% education, legal, community service, arts, and media, 7.7% healthcare practitioners, 17.3% service, 21.4% sales and office, 11.3% natural resources, construction, and maintenance, 7.8% production, transportation, and material moving (2008-2012 5-year est.).
Income: Per capita income: $32,194 (2008-2012 5-year est.); Median household income: $68,750 (2008-2012 5-year est.); Average household income: $79,932 (2008-2012 5-year est.); Percent of households with income of $100,000 or more: 27.4% (2008-2012 5-year est.); Poverty rate: 1.3% (2008-2012 5-year est.).
Education: Percent of population age 25 and over with: High school diploma (including GED) or higher: 97.3% (2008-2012 5-year est.); Bachelor's degree or higher: 34.5% (2008-2012 5-year est.); Master's degree or higher: 12.8% (2008-2012 5-year est.).
School District(s)
Tolono CUSD 7 (PK-12)
    2011-12 Enrollment: 1,690 . . . . (217) 485-6510
Housing: Homeownership rate: 87.5% (2008-2012 5-year est.); Median home value: $143,100 (2008-2012 5-year est.); Median contract rent: $492 per month (2008-2012 5-year est.); Median year structure built: 1973 (2008-2012 5-year est.).
Health Insurance: 87.8% Private; 21.5% Public; 3.4% None. (2008-2012 5-year est.)
Transportation: Commute to work: 93.0% car, 0.0% public transportation, 1.6% walk, 5.2% work from home (2008-2012 5-year est.); Travel time to work: 12.2% less than 15 minutes, 67.9% 15 to 30 minutes, 13.4% 30 to 45 minutes, 1.3% 45 to 60 minutes, 5.2% 60 minutes or more (2008-2012 5-year est.)

RANTOUL (village). Covers a land area of 8.150 square miles and a water area of 0.109 square miles. Located at 40.30° N. Lat; 88.15° W. Long. Elevation is 745 feet.
History: Rantoul was named for Robert Rantoul who was a director of the Illinois Central Railroad.
Population: 17,212 (1990); 12,857 (2000); 12,941 (2010); Density: 1,580.4 persons per square mile (2008-2012 5-year est.); Race: 68.0% White, 22.9% Black/African American, 1.3% Asian, 0.3% American Indian/Alaska Native, 0.0% Native Hawaiian/Other Pacific Islander, 7.5% Some other race, 5.3% Two or more races, 11.9% Hispanic of any race (2008-2012 5-year est.); Average household size: 2.46 (2008-2012 5-year est.); Median age: 33.5 (2008-2012 5-year est.); Males per 100 females: 101.4 (2008-2012 5-year est.); Marriage status: 37.6% never married, 43.3% now married, 6.3% widowed, 12.8% divorced (2008-2012 5-year

est.); Foreign born: 7.5% (2008-2012 5-year est.); Ancestry (includes multiple ancestries): 18.6% German, 14.8% American, 10.3% Irish, 7.4% English, 2.9% Italian (2008-2012 5-year est.).

Economy: Single-family building permits issued: 1 (2013); Multi-family building permits issued: 0 (2013); Homeowner vacancy rate: 4.1%. Rental vacancy rate: 9.5%. (2008-2012 5-year est.); Employment by occupation: 7.6% management, business, and financial, 4.0% computer, engineering, and science, 9.2% education, legal, community service, arts, and media, 2.2% healthcare practitioners, 17.3% service, 31.3% sales and office, 8.0% natural resources, construction, and maintenance, 20.5% production, transportation, and material moving (2008-2012 5-year est.).

Income: Per capita income: $20,492 (2008-2012 5-year est.); Median household income: $37,837 (2008-2012 5-year est.); Average household income: $50,050 (2008-2012 5-year est.); Percent of households with income of $100,000 or more: 8.0% (2008-2012 5-year est.); Poverty rate: 27.1% (2008-2012 5-year est.).

Education: Percent of population age 25 and over with: High school diploma (including GED) or higher: 85.9% (2008-2012 5-year est.); Bachelor's degree or higher: 16.4% (2008-2012 5-year est.); Master's degree or higher: 4.9% (2008-2012 5-year est.).

School District(s)

Rantoul City SD 137 (PK-08)

    2011-12 Enrollment: 1,588 . . . . (217) 893-4171

Rantoul Township HSD 193 (09-12)

    2011-12 Enrollment: 744. . . . . (217) 892-2151

Rural Champaign County Spec Ed Coop

    2011-12 Enrollment: n/a . . . . (217) 892-8877

Housing: Homeownership rate: 50.0% (2008-2012 5-year est.); Median home value: $82,100 (2008-2012 5-year est.); Median contract rent: $485 per month (2008-2012 5-year est.); Median year structure built: 1963 (2008-2012 5-year est.).

Health Insurance: 52.4% Private; 42.3% Public; 17.8% None. (2008-2012 5-year est.)

Safety: Violent crime rate: 86.2 per 10,000 population; Property crime rate: 207.9 per 10,000 population (2012).

Transportation: Commute to work: 91.5% car, 1.8% public transportation, 2.0% walk, 3.1% work from home (2008-2012 5-year est.); Travel time to work: 43.5% less than 15 minutes, 34.0% 15 to 30 minutes, 16.0% 30 to 45 minutes, 2.8% 45 to 60 minutes, 3.7% 60 minutes or more (2008-2012 5-year est.); Amtrak: Train service available.

Airports: Rantoul National Aviation Center (general aviation)

Additional Information Contacts

Rantoul Area Chamber of Commerce . . . . (217) 893-3323

   http://www.rantoulchamber.com

Village of Rantoul . . . . (217) 893-1661

   http://www.village.rantoul.il.us

ROYAL (village). Covers a land area of 0.163 square miles and a water area of 0 square miles. Located at 40.19° N. Lat; 87.97° W. Long. Elevation is 682 feet.

Population: 217 (1990); 279 (2000); 293 (2010); Density: 1,547.3 persons per square mile (2008-2012 5-year est.); Race: 98.4% White, 0.0% Black/African American, 0.0% Asian, 0.0% American Indian/Alaska Native, 0.0% Native Hawaiian/Other Pacific Islander, 1.6% Some other race, 1.6% Two or more races, 2.0% Hispanic of any race (2008-2012 5-year est.); Average household size: 2.17 (2008-2012 5-year est.); Median age: 41.2 (2008-2012 5-year est.); Males per 100 females: 86.7 (2008-2012 5-year est.); Marriage status: 25.6% never married, 58.5% now married, 7.2% widowed, 8.7% divorced (2008-2012 5-year est.); Foreign born: 0.0% (2008-2012 5-year est.); Ancestry (includes multiple ancestries): 59.5% German, 23.0% Irish, 20.6% American, 8.7% English, 4.4% Italian (2008-2012 5-year est.).

Economy: Single-family building permits issued: 1 (2013); Multi-family building permits issued: 0 (2013); Homeowner vacancy rate: 6.7%. Rental vacancy rate: 0.0%. (2008-2012 5-year est.); Employment by occupation: 27.6% management, business, and financial, 0.0% computer, engineering, and science, 6.0% education, legal, community service, arts, and media, 10.3% healthcare practitioners, 17.2% service, 23.3% sales and office, 6.9% natural resources, construction, and maintenance, 8.6% production, transportation, and material moving (2008-2012 5-year est.).

Income: Per capita income: $32,866 (2008-2012 5-year est.); Median household income: $57,083 (2008-2012 5-year est.); Average household income: $69,998 (2008-2012 5-year est.); Percent of households with income of $100,000 or more: 15.5% (2008-2012 5-year est.); Poverty rate: 13.9% (2008-2012 5-year est.).

Education: Percent of population age 25 and over with: High school diploma (including GED) or higher: 91.3% (2008-2012 5-year est.); Bachelor's degree or higher: 20.9% (2008-2012 5-year est.); Master's degree or higher: 3.5% (2008-2012 5-year est.).

School District(s)

Prairieview-Ogden CCSD 197 (KG-08)

    2011-12 Enrollment: 250 . . . . (217) 583-3300

Housing: Homeownership rate: 96.6% (2008-2012 5-year est.); Median home value: $122,500 (2008-2012 5-year est.); Median contract rent: $450 per month (2008-2012 5-year est.); Median year structure built: 1962 (2008-2012 5-year est.).

Health Insurance: 74.2% Private; 34.5% Public; 7.9% None. (2008-2012 5-year est.)

Transportation: Commute to work: 70.7% car, 0.0% public transportation, 0.0% walk, 29.3% work from home (2008-2012 5-year est.); Travel time to work: 18.3% less than 15 minutes, 45.1% 15 to 30 minutes, 35.4% 30 to 45 minutes, 1.2% 45 to 60 minutes, 0.0% 60 minutes or more (2008-2012 5-year est.)

SADORUS (village). Covers a land area of 1.027 square miles and a water area of 0 square miles. Located at 39.97° N. Lat; 88.35° W. Long. Elevation is 692 feet.

Population: 469 (1990); 426 (2000); 416 (2010); Density: 549.0 persons per square mile (2008-2012 5-year est.); Race: 97.3% White, 0.5% Black/African American, 0.0% Asian, 0.0% American Indian/Alaska Native, 0.0% Native Hawaiian/Other Pacific Islander, 2.2% Some other race, 2.1% Two or more races, 0.0% Hispanic of any race (2008-2012 5-year est.); Average household size: 2.61 (2008-2012 5-year est.); Median age: 44.8 (2008-2012 5-year est.); Males per 100 females: 142.1 (2008-2012 5-year est.); Marriage status: 25.8% never married, 64.7% now married, 3.9% widowed, 5.6% divorced (2008-2012 5-year est.); Foreign born: 0.0% (2008-2012 5-year est.); Ancestry (includes multiple ancestries): 48.4% American, 21.1% German, 8.7% Irish, 8.2% English, 2.3% Scottish (2008-2012 5-year est.).

Economy: Single-family building permits issued: 0 (2013); Multi-family building permits issued: 0 (2013); Homeowner vacancy rate: 1.6%. Rental vacancy rate: 12.1%. (2008-2012 5-year est.); Employment by occupation: 5.7% management, business, and financial, 2.7% computer, engineering, and science, 2.4% education, legal, community service, arts, and media, 0.3% healthcare practitioners, 21.0% service, 18.6% sales and office, 13.8% natural resources, construction, and maintenance, 35.6% production, transportation, and material moving (2008-2012 5-year est.).

Income: Per capita income: $22,552 (2008-2012 5-year est.); Median household income: $57,500 (2008-2012 5-year est.); Average household income: $59,196 (2008-2012 5-year est.); Percent of households with income of $100,000 or more: 10.7% (2008-2012 5-year est.); Poverty rate: 10.6% (2008-2012 5-year est.).

Education: Percent of population age 25 and over with: High school diploma (including GED) or higher: 93.5% (2008-2012 5-year est.); Bachelor's degree or higher: 6.5% (2008-2012 5-year est.); Master's degree or higher: 2.2% (2008-2012 5-year est.).

Housing: Homeownership rate: 86.6% (2008-2012 5-year est.); Median home value: $81,400 (2008-2012 5-year est.); Median contract rent: $538 per month (2008-2012 5-year est.); Median year structure built: 1967 (2008-2012 5-year est.).

Health Insurance: 62.4% Private; 31.9% Public; 18.6% None. (2008-2012 5-year est.)

Transportation: Commute to work: 84.0% car, 0.0% public transportation, 13.6% walk, 2.4% work from home (2008-2012 5-year est.); Travel time to work: 26.6% less than 15 minutes, 44.9% 15 to 30 minutes, 24.5% 30 to 45 minutes, 3.1% 45 to 60 minutes, 0.9% 60 minutes or more (2008-2012 5-year est.)

SAINT JOSEPH (village). Covers a land area of 2.120 square miles and a water area of 0.020 square miles. Located at 40.11° N. Lat; 88.04° W. Long. Elevation is 673 feet.

Population: 2,052 (1990); 2,912 (2000); 3,967 (2010); Density: 1,794.6 persons per square mile (2008-2012 5-year est.); Race: 97.9% White, 0.0% Black/African American, 0.4% Asian, 0.0% American Indian/Alaska Native, 0.0% Native Hawaiian/Other Pacific Islander, 1.7% Some other race, 1.3% Two or more races, 3.5% Hispanic of any race (2008-2012 5-year est.); Average household size: 2.64 (2008-2012 5-year est.); Median age: 34.2 (2008-2012 5-year est.); Males per 100 females: 88.8 (2008-2012 5-year est.); Marriage status: 19.8% never married, 61.0% now married, 8.2% widowed, 11.0% divorced (2008-2012 5-year est.);

Foreign born: 5.1% (2008-2012 5-year est.); Ancestry (includes multiple ancestries): 36.4% German, 17.1% Irish, 17.1% American, 8.9% English, 3.0% French (2008-2012 5-year est.).

Economy: Single-family building permits issued: 2 (2013); Multi-family building permits issued: 0 (2013); Homeowner vacancy rate: 0.0%. Rental vacancy rate: 13.3%. (2008-2012 5-year est.); Employment by occupation: 14.3% management, business, and financial, 4.8% computer, engineering, and science, 8.4% education, legal, community service, arts, and media, 8.0% healthcare practitioners, 18.6% service, 21.3% sales and office, 9.8% natural resources, construction, and maintenance, 14.9% production, transportation, and material moving (2008-2012 5-year est.).

Income: Per capita income: $26,345 (2008-2012 5-year est.); Median household income: $67,694 (2008-2012 5-year est.); Average household income: $69,181 (2008-2012 5-year est.); Percent of households with income of $100,000 or more: 17.2% (2008-2012 5-year est.); Poverty rate: 5.3% (2008-2012 5-year est.).

Education: Percent of population age 25 and over with: High school diploma (including GED) or higher: 92.5% (2008-2012 5-year est.); Bachelor's degree or higher: 31.4% (2008-2012 5-year est.); Master's degree or higher: 16.1% (2008-2012 5-year est.).

School District(s)

Saint Joseph CCSD 169 (PK-08)
    2011-12 Enrollment: 915. . . . . (217) 469-2291
Saint Joseph Ogden CHSD 305 (09-12)
    2011-12 Enrollment: 494. . . . . (217) 469-2586

Housing: Homeownership rate: 81.4% (2008-2012 5-year est.); Median home value: $162,400 (2008-2012 5-year est.); Median contract rent: $713 per month (2008-2012 5-year est.); Median year structure built: 1990 (2008-2012 5-year est.).

Health Insurance: 86.2% Private; 20.3% Public; 5.8% None. (2008-2012 5-year est.)

Transportation: Commute to work: 90.0% car, 0.7% public transportation, 4.5% walk, 4.2% work from home (2008-2012 5-year est.); Travel time to work: 24.1% less than 15 minutes, 61.5% 15 to 30 minutes, 11.3% 30 to 45 minutes, 0.0% 45 to 60 minutes, 3.1% 60 minutes or more (2008-2012 5-year est.)

SAVOY (village). Covers a land area of 3.199 square miles and a water area of 0.020 square miles. Located at 40.06° N. Lat; 88.25° W. Long. Elevation is 735 feet.

Population: 2,674 (1990); 4,476 (2000); 7,280 (2010); Density: 2,184.6 persons per square mile (2008-2012 5-year est.); Race: 72.9% White, 7.0% Black/African American, 13.6% Asian, 0.3% American Indian/Alaska Native, 0.0% Native Hawaiian/Other Pacific Islander, 6.2% Some other race, 3.2% Two or more races, 6.4% Hispanic of any race (2008-2012 5-year est.); Average household size: 2.38 (2008-2012 5-year est.); Median age: 33.0 (2008-2012 5-year est.); Males per 100 females: 82.7 (2008-2012 5-year est.); Marriage status: 31.0% never married, 55.6% now married, 6.9% widowed, 6.5% divorced (2008-2012 5-year est.); Foreign born: 21.0% (2008-2012 5-year est.); Ancestry (includes multiple ancestries): 19.2% German, 11.8% American, 8.0% English, 7.3% Irish, 5.6% European (2008-2012 5-year est.).

Economy: Single-family building permits issued: 69 (2013); Multi-family building permits issued: 12 (2013); Homeowner vacancy rate: 0.5%. Rental vacancy rate: 3.4%. (2008-2012 5-year est.); Employment by occupation: 18.2% management, business, and financial, 14.4% computer, engineering, and science, 25.4% education, legal, community service, arts, and media, 7.2% healthcare practitioners, 11.8% service, 13.5% sales and office, 2.2% natural resources, construction, and maintenance, 7.2% production, transportation, and material moving (2008-2012 5-year est.).

Income: Per capita income: $30,415 (2008-2012 5-year est.); Median household income: $53,832 (2008-2012 5-year est.); Average household income: $72,640 (2008-2012 5-year est.); Percent of households with income of $100,000 or more: 28.4% (2008-2012 5-year est.); Poverty rate: 12.6% (2008-2012 5-year est.).

Education: Percent of population age 25 and over with: High school diploma (including GED) or higher: 97.2% (2008-2012 5-year est.); Bachelor's degree or higher: 65.8% (2008-2012 5-year est.); Master's degree or higher: 35.4% (2008-2012 5-year est.).

Housing: Homeownership rate: 51.1% (2008-2012 5-year est.); Median home value: $205,300 (2008-2012 5-year est.); Median contract rent: $775 per month (2008-2012 5-year est.); Median year structure built: 1994 (2008-2012 5-year est.).

Health Insurance: 85.5% Private; 19.4% Public; 7.1% None. (2008-2012 5-year est.)

Transportation: Commute to work: 85.0% car, 6.7% public transportation, 0.8% walk, 6.1% work from home (2008-2012 5-year est.); Travel time to work: 43.8% less than 15 minutes, 45.2% 15 to 30 minutes, 7.1% 30 to 45 minutes, 0.9% 45 to 60 minutes, 2.9% 60 minutes or more (2008-2012 5-year est.)

SEYMOUR (CDP). Covers a land area of 0.090 square miles and a water area of 0 square miles. Located at 40.11° N. Lat; 88.43° W. Long. Elevation is 699 feet.

Population: n/a (1990); n/a (2000); 303 (2010); Density: 2,942.3 persons per square mile (2008-2012 5-year est.); Race: 71.6% White, 17.4% Black/African American, 0.0% Asian, 0.0% American Indian/Alaska Native, 0.0% Native Hawaiian/Other Pacific Islander, 11.0% Some other race, 11.0% Two or more races, 0.0% Hispanic of any race (2008-2012 5-year est.); Average household size: 2.47 (2008-2012 5-year est.); Median age: 19.6 (2008-2012 5-year est.); Males per 100 females: 125.6 (2008-2012 5-year est.); Marriage status: 54.4% never married, 31.7% now married, 7.2% widowed, 6.7% divorced (2008-2012 5-year est.); Foreign born: 0.0% (2008-2012 5-year est.); Ancestry (includes multiple ancestries): 25.4% German, 17.4% English, 11.0% Polish, 4.5% Irish, 4.2% Italian (2008-2012 5-year est.).

Economy: Homeowner vacancy rate: 0.0%. Rental vacancy rate: 48.1%. (2008-2012 5-year est.); Employment by occupation: 10.4% management, business, and financial, 0.0% computer, engineering, and science, 0.0% education, legal, community service, arts, and media, 9.0% healthcare practitioners, 0.0% service, 61.2% sales and office, 0.0% natural resources, construction, and maintenance, 19.4% production, transportation, and material moving (2008-2012 5-year est.).

Income: Per capita income: $11,522 (2008-2012 5-year est.); Median household income: $12,212 (2008-2012 5-year est.); Average household income: $28,138 (2008-2012 5-year est.); Percent of households with income of $100,000 or more: n/a (2008-2012 5-year est.); Poverty rate: 56.1% (2008-2012 5-year est.).

Education: Percent of population age 25 and over with: High school diploma (including GED) or higher: 71.7% (2008-2012 5-year est.); Bachelor's degree or higher: 6.6% (2008-2012 5-year est.); Master's degree or higher: 0.0% (2008-2012 5-year est.).

Housing: Homeownership rate: 60.7% (2008-2012 5-year est.); Median home value: $128,100 (2008-2012 5-year est.); Median contract rent: $136 per month (2008-2012 5-year est.); Median year structure built: 1974 (2008-2012 5-year est.).

Health Insurance: 57.2% Private; 54.5% Public; 4.5% None. (2008-2012 5-year est.)

Transportation: Commute to work: 100.0% car, 0.0% public transportation, 0.0% walk, 0.0% work from home (2008-2012 5-year est.); Travel time to work: 10.4% less than 15 minutes, 89.6% 15 to 30 minutes, 0.0% 30 to 45 minutes, 0.0% 45 to 60 minutes, 0.0% 60 minutes or more (2008-2012 5-year est.)

SIDNEY (village). Covers a land area of 0.624 square miles and a water area of 0.005 square miles. Located at 40.03° N. Lat; 88.07° W. Long. Elevation is 656 feet.

Population: 1,027 (1990); 1,062 (2000); 1,233 (2010); Density: 1,948.1 persons per square mile (2008-2012 5-year est.); Race: 93.6% White, 2.9% Black/African American, 0.7% Asian, 0.0% American Indian/Alaska Native, 0.0% Native Hawaiian/Other Pacific Islander, 2.8% Some other race, 0.7% Two or more races, 2.8% Hispanic of any race (2008-2012 5-year est.); Average household size: 2.53 (2008-2012 5-year est.); Median age: 36.9 (2008-2012 5-year est.); Males per 100 females: 93.2 (2008-2012 5-year est.); Marriage status: 17.8% never married, 63.1% now married, 3.8% widowed, 15.2% divorced (2008-2012 5-year est.); Foreign born: 0.7% (2008-2012 5-year est.); Ancestry (includes multiple ancestries): 27.5% German, 22.6% American, 22.6% Irish, 17.4% English, 3.8% Dutch (2008-2012 5-year est.).

Economy: Single-family building permits issued: 0 (2013); Multi-family building permits issued: 0 (2013); Homeowner vacancy rate: 0.0%. Rental vacancy rate: 0.0%. (2008-2012 5-year est.); Employment by occupation: 16.6% management, business, and financial, 2.5% computer, engineering, and science, 12.0% education, legal, community service, arts, and media, 5.1% healthcare practitioners, 22.5% service, 20.8% sales and office, 9.6% natural resources, construction, and maintenance, 11.0% production, transportation, and material moving (2008-2012 5-year est.).

Income: Per capita income: $26,624 (2008-2012 5-year est.); Median household income: $51,161 (2008-2012 5-year est.); Average household income: $66,520 (2008-2012 5-year est.); Percent of households with

income of $100,000 or more: 19.5% (2008-2012 5-year est.); Poverty rate: 6.8% (2008-2012 5-year est.).

Education: Percent of population age 25 and over with: High school diploma (including GED) or higher: 93.7% (2008-2012 5-year est.); Bachelor's degree or higher: 15.8% (2008-2012 5-year est.); Master's degree or higher: 3.3% (2008-2012 5-year est.).

Housing: Homeownership rate: 69.2% (2008-2012 5-year est.); Median home value: $125,700 (2008-2012 5-year est.); Median contract rent: $559 per month (2008-2012 5-year est.); Median year structure built: 1972 (2008-2012 5-year est.).

Health Insurance: 71.9% Private; 29.0% Public; 10.7% None. (2008-2012 5-year est.)

Transportation: Commute to work: 95.8% car, 0.5% public transportation, 1.9% walk, 0.8% work from home (2008-2012 5-year est.); Travel time to work: 14.6% less than 15 minutes, 61.6% 15 to 30 minutes, 16.1% 30 to 45 minutes, 6.2% 45 to 60 minutes, 1.5% 60 minutes or more (2008-2012 5-year est.)

THOMASBORO (village). Covers a land area of 1.002 square miles and a water area of 0 square miles. Located at 40.24° N. Lat; 88.19° W. Long. Elevation is 732 feet.

Population: 1,250 (1990); 1,233 (2000); 1,126 (2010); Density: 1,079.7 persons per square mile (2008-2012 5-year est.); Race: 94.4% White, 3.1% Black/African American, 0.7% Asian, 0.0% American Indian/Alaska Native, 0.0% Native Hawaiian/Other Pacific Islander, 1.8% Some other race, 1.4% Two or more races, 0.6% Hispanic of any race (2008-2012 5-year est.); Average household size: 2.25 (2008-2012 5-year est.); Median age: 38.7 (2008-2012 5-year est.); Males per 100 females: 106.5 (2008-2012 5-year est.); Marriage status: 23.2% never married, 56.4% now married, 4.6% widowed, 15.9% divorced (2008-2012 5-year est.); Foreign born: 1.8% (2008-2012 5-year est.); Ancestry (includes multiple ancestries): 39.0% German, 18.9% American, 8.0% Irish, 5.8% English, 2.5% Dutch (2008-2012 5-year est.).

Economy: Single-family building permits issued: 1 (2013); Multi-family building permits issued: 0 (2013); Homeowner vacancy rate: 3.3%. Rental vacancy rate: 5.8%. (2008-2012 5-year est.); Employment by occupation: 8.0% management, business, and financial, 1.6% computer, engineering, and science, 3.3% education, legal, community service, arts, and media, 6.2% healthcare practitioners, 20.6% service, 29.7% sales and office, 8.8% natural resources, construction, and maintenance, 21.7% production, transportation, and material moving (2008-2012 5-year est.).

Income: Per capita income: $25,083 (2008-2012 5-year est.); Median household income: $50,682 (2008-2012 5-year est.); Average household income: $56,293 (2008-2012 5-year est.); Percent of households with income of $100,000 or more: 11.8% (2008-2012 5-year est.); Poverty rate: 7.5% (2008-2012 5-year est.).

Education: Percent of population age 25 and over with: High school diploma (including GED) or higher: 93.4% (2008-2012 5-year est.); Bachelor's degree or higher: 10.2% (2008-2012 5-year est.); Master's degree or higher: 4.7% (2008-2012 5-year est.).

School District(s)
Prairieview-Ogden CCSD 197 (KG-08)
   2011-12 Enrollment: 250 . . . . (217) 583-3300
Thomasboro CCSD 130 (PK-08)
   2011-12 Enrollment: 159 . . . . (217) 643-3275

Housing: Homeownership rate: 73.1% (2008-2012 5-year est.); Median home value: $98,300 (2008-2012 5-year est.); Median contract rent: $436 per month (2008-2012 5-year est.); Median year structure built: 1972 (2008-2012 5-year est.).

Health Insurance: 72.2% Private; 27.9% Public; 12.8% None. (2008-2012 5-year est.)

Safety: Violent crime rate: 61.9 per 10,000 population; Property crime rate: 230.1 per 10,000 population (2012).

Transportation: Commute to work: 89.0% car, 0.0% public transportation, 3.3% walk, 3.3% work from home (2008-2012 5-year est.); Travel time to work: 25.1% less than 15 minutes, 65.4% 15 to 30 minutes, 7.3% 30 to 45 minutes, 1.7% 45 to 60 minutes, 0.5% 60 minutes or more (2008-2012 5-year est.)

TOLONO (village). Covers a land area of 2.136 square miles and a water area of 0 square miles. Located at 39.99° N. Lat; 88.26° W. Long. Elevation is 735 feet.

History: The name of Tolono was made up by J.B. Calhoun of the Illinois Central Railroad.

Population: 2,605 (1990); 2,700 (2000); 3,447 (2010); Density: 1,626.3 persons per square mile (2008-2012 5-year est.); Race: 99.1% White, 0.0% Black/African American, 0.4% Asian, 0.0% American Indian/Alaska Native, 0.0% Native Hawaiian/Other Pacific Islander, 0.5% Some other race, 0.5% Two or more races, 3.9% Hispanic of any race (2008-2012 5-year est.); Average household size: 2.61 (2008-2012 5-year est.); Median age: 32.6 (2008-2012 5-year est.); Males per 100 females: 115.1 (2008-2012 5-year est.); Marriage status: 29.8% never married, 51.9% now married, 6.0% widowed, 12.4% divorced (2008-2012 5-year est.); Foreign born: 0.7% (2008-2012 5-year est.); Ancestry (includes multiple ancestries): 33.6% German, 17.0% American, 14.9% Irish, 13.5% English, 8.4% European (2008-2012 5-year est.).

Economy: Single-family building permits issued: 4 (2013); Multi-family building permits issued: 0 (2013); Homeowner vacancy rate: 5.5%. Rental vacancy rate: 11.6%. (2008-2012 5-year est.); Employment by occupation: 14.4% management, business, and financial, 8.8% computer, engineering, and science, 7.3% education, legal, community service, arts, and media, 3.9% healthcare practitioners, 11.8% service, 27.3% sales and office, 12.0% natural resources, construction, and maintenance, 14.5% production, transportation, and material moving (2008-2012 5-year est.).

Income: Per capita income: $23,993 (2008-2012 5-year est.); Median household income: $55,807 (2008-2012 5-year est.); Average household income: $62,300 (2008-2012 5-year est.); Percent of households with income of $100,000 or more: 15.9% (2008-2012 5-year est.); Poverty rate: 6.3% (2008-2012 5-year est.).

Education: Percent of population age 25 and over with: High school diploma (including GED) or higher: 92.0% (2008-2012 5-year est.); Bachelor's degree or higher: 22.9% (2008-2012 5-year est.); Master's degree or higher: 10.1% (2008-2012 5-year est.).

School District(s)
Tolono CUSD 7 (PK-12)
   2011-12 Enrollment: 1,690 . . . . (217) 485-6510

Housing: Homeownership rate: 76.4% (2008-2012 5-year est.); Median home value: $124,100 (2008-2012 5-year est.); Median contract rent: $563 per month (2008-2012 5-year est.); Median year structure built: 1984 (2008-2012 5-year est.).

Health Insurance: 69.9% Private; 31.2% Public; 9.8% None. (2008-2012 5-year est.)

Safety: Violent crime rate: 11.6 per 10,000 population; Property crime rate: 179.1 per 10,000 population (2012).

Transportation: Commute to work: 96.9% car, 0.2% public transportation, 0.0% walk, 2.9% work from home (2008-2012 5-year est.); Travel time to work: 20.2% less than 15 minutes, 58.9% 15 to 30 minutes, 14.7% 30 to 45 minutes, 3.9% 45 to 60 minutes, 2.3% 60 minutes or more (2008-2012 5-year est.)

URBANA (city). County seat. Covers a land area of 11.654 square miles and a water area of 0.040 square miles. Located at 40.11° N. Lat; 88.20° W. Long. Elevation is 728 feet.

History: Urbana was settled in 1822 by Willard Tompkins. Although designated as the county seat in 1833, the loss of the railroad to nearby Champaign in 1854 slowed Urbana's development. When the Illinois Industrial College, later to become the University of Illinois, was sited between Urbana and Champaign in 1867, the character of Urbana was determined.

Population: 36,344 (1990); 36,395 (2000); 41,250 (2010); Density: 3,543.8 persons per square mile (2008-2012 5-year est.); Race: 62.7% White, 17.7% Black/African American, 16.2% Asian, 0.3% American Indian/Alaska Native, 0.0% Native Hawaiian/Other Pacific Islander, 3.1% Some other race, 2.4% Two or more races, 5.2% Hispanic of any race (2008-2012 5-year est.); Average household size: 2.12 (2008-2012 5-year est.); Median age: 24.0 (2008-2012 5-year est.); Males per 100 females: 98.8 (2008-2012 5-year est.); Marriage status: 64.6% never married, 26.1% now married, 3.2% widowed, 6.1% divorced (2008-2012 5-year est.); Foreign born: 18.9% (2008-2012 5-year est.); Ancestry (includes multiple ancestries): 16.4% German, 10.5% American, 9.0% Irish, 7.7% English, 4.1% European (2008-2012 5-year est.).

Economy: Unemployment rate: 6.3% (April 2014); Total civilian labor force: 20,027 (April 2014); Single-family building permits issued: 15 (2013); Multi-family building permits issued: 64 (2013); Homeowner vacancy rate: 3.8%. Rental vacancy rate: 8.8%. (2008-2012 5-year est.); Employment by occupation: 7.3% management, business, and financial, 10.8% computer, engineering, and science, 29.5% education, legal, community service, arts, and media, 3.8% healthcare practitioners, 18.8% service, 21.7% sales and

office, 3.2% natural resources, construction, and maintenance, 4.9% production, transportation, and material moving (2008-2012 5-year est.).
Income: Per capita income: $19,052 (2008-2012 5-year est.); Median household income: $30,313 (2008-2012 5-year est.); Average household income: $47,079 (2008-2012 5-year est.); Percent of households with income of $100,000 or more: 11.7% (2008-2012 5-year est.); Poverty rate: 35.5% (2008-2012 5-year est.).
Taxes: Total city taxes per capita: $582 (2011); City property taxes per capita: $298 (2011).
Education: Percent of population age 25 and over with: High school diploma (including GED) or higher: 92.5% (2008-2012 5-year est.); Bachelor's degree or higher: 54.3% (2008-2012 5-year est.); Master's degree or higher: 32.0% (2008-2012 5-year est.).

School District(s)
Champaign/ford Roe (06-12)
   2011-12 Enrollment: n/a . . . . (217) 893-3219
University of Ill Lab School (08-12)
   2011-12 Enrollment: 315. . . . . (217) 333-2870
Urbana SD 116 (PK-12)
   2011-12 Enrollment: 4,324 . . . . (217) 384-3636

Vocational/Technical School(s)
Concept College of Cosmetology (Private, For-profit)
   Fall 2012 Enrollment: 33 . . . . (217) 344-7550
   2012-13 Tuition: $13,675

Housing: Homeownership rate: 34.2% (2008-2012 5-year est.); Median home value: $151,100 (2008-2012 5-year est.); Median contract rent: $640 per month (2008-2012 5-year est.); Median year structure built: 1973 (2008-2012 5-year est.).
Health Insurance: 77.7% Private; 19.8% Public; 9.0% None. (2008-2012 5-year est.)
Hospitals: Carle Foundation Hospital (305 beds); Provena Covenant Medical Center (268 beds)
Safety: Violent crime rate: 35.6 per 10,000 population; Property crime rate: 347.4 per 10,000 population (2012).
Transportation: Commute to work: 55.4% car, 16.0% public transportation, 16.6% walk, 5.8% work from home (2008-2012 5-year est.); Travel time to work: 55.3% less than 15 minutes, 35.9% 15 to 30 minutes, 5.9% 30 to 45 minutes, 0.8% 45 to 60 minutes, 2.1% 60 minutes or more (2008-2012 5-year est.); Amtrak: Train service available.
Airports: University of Illinois - Willard Airport (primary service/non-hub)
Additional Information Contacts
Champaign County Chamber of Commerce . . . . (217) 359-1791
   http://champaigncounty.org
City of Urbana . . . . (217) 384-2366
   http://urbanaillinois.us

Christian County

Located in central Illinois; bounded on the north by the Sangamon River; drained by the South Fork of the Sangamon River. Covers a land area of 709.377 square miles, a water area of 6.263 square miles, and is located in the Central Time Zone at 39.55° N. Lat., 89.28° W. Long. The county was founded in 1839. County seat is Taylorville.

Christian County is part of the Taylorville, IL Micropolitan Statistical Area. The entire metro area includes: Christian County, IL

Weather Station: Morrisonville | | | | | | | | | | Elevation: 629 feet

	Jan	Feb	Mar	Apr	May	Jun	Jul	Aug	Sep	Oct	Nov	Dec
High	35	39	51	64	74	83	86	85	80	67	52	38
Low	18	22	31	42	52	62	65	63	54	42	33	22
Precip	2.0	1.9	2.7	3.4	4.4	3.5	3.5	3.0	3.2	3.0	3.6	2.6
Snow	6.1	5.0	3.0	0.3	0.0	0.0	0.0	0.0	0.0	0.1	0.8	4.9

High and Low temperatures in degrees Fahrenheit; Precipitation and Snow in inches

Weather Station: Pana 3 E | | | | | | | | | | Elevation: 700 feet

	Jan	Feb	Mar	Apr	May	Jun	Jul	Aug	Sep	Oct	Nov	Dec
High	37	42	53	65	75	84	88	86	80	67	54	40
Low	20	24	33	43	53	62	66	63	55	44	35	23
Precip	2.4	2.1	3.1	4.0	4.5	4.2	3.9	3.0	3.3	3.6	4.0	3.0
Snow	5.6	4.4	3.4	0.7	0.0	0.0	0.0	0.0	0.0	0.1	1.2	4.8

High and Low temperatures in degrees Fahrenheit; Precipitation and Snow in inches

Population: 34,418 (1990); 35,372 (2000); 34,800 (2010); Race: 96.4% White, 1.4% Black/African American, 0.5% Asian, 0.2% American Indian/Alaska Native, 0.0% Native Hawaiian/Other Pacific Islander, 1.5%

Some other race, 0.9% Two or more races, 1.4% Hispanic of any race (2008-2012 5-year est.); Density: 48.8 persons per square mile (2008-2012 5-year est.); Average household size: 2.33 (2008-2012 5-year est.); Median age: 41.6 (2008-2012 5-year est.); Males per 100 females: 102.9 (2008-2012 5-year est.).
Religion: Six largest groups: 15.7% Catholicism, 11.7% Baptist, 8.5% Methodist/Pietist, 3.9% Lutheran, 2.6% Presbyterian-Reformed, 1.8% Non-denominational Protestant (2010)
Economy: Unemployment rate: 7.4% (April 2014); Total civilian labor force: 16,658 (April 2014); Leading industries: 19.7% health care and social assistance; 15.8% retail trade; 12.2% manufacturing (2012); Farms: 816 totaling 373,631 acres (2012); Companies that employ 500 or more persons: 1 (2012); Companies that employ 100 to 499 persons: 15 (2012); Companies that employ less than 100 persons: 717 (2012); Black-owned businesses: n/a (2007); Hispanic-owned businesses: n/a (2007); Asian-owned businesses: n/a (2007); Women-owned businesses: 905 (2007); Single-family building permits issued: 46 (2013); Multi-family building permits issued: 0 (2013).
Income: Per capita income: $23,340 (2008-2012 5-year est.); Median household income: $44,211 (2008-2012 5-year est.); Average household income: $57,270 (2008-2012 5-year est.); Percent of households with income of $100,000 or more: 13.0% (2008-2012 5-year est.); Poverty rate: 15.9% (2008-2012 5-year est.); Bankruptcy rate: 3.38% (2013).
Education: Percent of population age 25 and over with: High school diploma (including GED) or higher: 87.3% (2008-2012 5-year est.); Bachelor's degree or higher: 13.0% (2008-2012 5-year est.); Master's degree or higher: 3.9% (2008-2012 5-year est.).
Housing: Homeownership rate: 74.0% (2008-2012 5-year est.); Median home value: $82,000 (2008-2012 5-year est.); Median contract rent: $412 per month (2008-2012 5-year est.); Median year structure built: 1957 (2008-2012 5-year est.).
Health: Birth rate: 108.8 per 10,000 population (2013); Death rate: 111.7 per 10,000 population (2013); Age-adjusted cancer mortality rate: 215.2 deaths per 100,000 population (2011); Number of physicians: 6.6 per 10,000 population (2011); Hospital beds: 19.3 per 10,000 population (2010); Hospital admissions: 632.8 per 10,000 population (2010).
Elections: 2012 Presidential election results: 37.4% Obama, 60.4% Romney
Additional Information Contacts
Christian County Government . . . . (217) 824-4969
   http://christiancountyil.com/contact.htm

Christian County Communities

ASSUMPTION (city). Covers a land area of 0.880 square miles and a water area of 0 square miles. Located at 39.52° N. Lat; 89.05° W. Long. Elevation is 646 feet.
History: Incorporated 1902.
Population: 1,244 (1990); 1,261 (2000); 1,168 (2010); Density: 1,455.1 persons per square mile (2008-2012 5-year est.); Race: 97.4% White, 1.3% Black/African American, 0.0% Asian, 0.0% American Indian/Alaska Native, 0.0% Native Hawaiian/Other Pacific Islander, 1.3% Some other race, 1.3% Two or more races, 0.7% Hispanic of any race (2008-2012 5-year est.); Average household size: 2.31 (2008-2012 5-year est.); Median age: 39.7 (2008-2012 5-year est.); Males per 100 females: 80.5 (2008-2012 5-year est.); Marriage status: 24.1% never married, 51.4% now married, 9.1% widowed, 15.4% divorced (2008-2012 5-year est.); Foreign born: 0.9% (2008-2012 5-year est.); Ancestry (includes multiple ancestries): 19.6% German, 13.8% American, 12.5% Irish, 8.0% English, 2.8% Dutch (2008-2012 5-year est.).
Economy: Single-family building permits issued: 2 (2013); Multi-family building permits issued: 0 (2013); Homeowner vacancy rate: 1.4%. Rental vacancy rate: 0.0%. (2008-2012 5-year est.); Employment by occupation: 5.8% management, business, and financial, 2.6% computer, engineering, and science, 7.7% education, legal, community service, arts, and media, 2.7% healthcare practitioners, 15.6% service, 21.7% sales and office, 17.1% natural resources, construction, and maintenance, 26.8% production, transportation, and material moving (2008-2012 5-year est.).
Income: Per capita income: $19,903 (2008-2012 5-year est.); Median household income: $39,453 (2008-2012 5-year est.); Average household income: $46,471 (2008-2012 5-year est.); Percent of households with income of $100,000 or more: 5.8% (2008-2012 5-year est.); Poverty rate: 10.2% (2008-2012 5-year est.).
Education: Percent of population age 25 and over with: High school diploma (including GED) or higher: 88.1% (2008-2012 5-year est.);

Bachelor's degree or higher: 8.4% (2008-2012 5-year est.); Master's degree or higher: 1.3% (2008-2012 5-year est.).

School District(s)
Central A & M CUD 21 (PK-12)
  2011-12 Enrollment: 892 . . . . (217) 226-4042
Housing: Homeownership rate: 75.9% (2008-2012 5-year est.); Median home value: $66,000 (2008-2012 5-year est.); Median contract rent: $346 per month (2008-2012 5-year est.); Median year structure built: Before 1940 (2008-2012 5-year est.).
Health Insurance: 68.5% Private; 42.3% Public; 10.9% None. (2008-2012 5-year est.)
Transportation: Commute to work: 89.6% car, 0.0% public transportation, 6.6% walk, 2.2% work from home (2008-2012 5-year est.); Travel time to work: 41.2% less than 15 minutes, 29.4% 15 to 30 minutes, 18.6% 30 to 45 minutes, 6.7% 45 to 60 minutes, 4.1% 60 minutes or more (2008-2012 5-year est.)

BULPITT (village). Covers a land area of 0.068 square miles and a water area of 0 square miles. Located at 39.59° N. Lat; 89.43° W. Long. Elevation is 600 feet.
Population: 206 (1990); 206 (2000); 222 (2010); Density: 4,997.9 persons per square mile (2008-2012 5-year est.); Race: 98.5% White, 0.0% Black/African American, 0.0% Asian, 0.0% American Indian/Alaska Native, 0.0% Native Hawaiian/Other Pacific Islander, 1.5% Some other race, 1.5% Two or more races, 0.0% Hispanic of any race (2008-2012 5-year est.); Average household size: 2.60 (2008-2012 5-year est.); Median age: 28.8 (2008-2012 5-year est.); Males per 100 females: 75.1 (2008-2012 5-year est.); Marriage status: 20.0% never married, 51.2% now married, 7.5% widowed, 21.3% divorced (2008-2012 5-year est.); Foreign born: 0.6% (2008-2012 5-year est.); Ancestry (includes multiple ancestries): 25.4% German, 13.3% American, 11.2% Irish, 7.7% Italian, 4.4% English (2008-2012 5-year est.).
Economy: Single-family building permits issued: 0 (2013); Multi-family building permits issued: 0 (2013); Homeowner vacancy rate: 0.0%. Rental vacancy rate: 0.0%. (2008-2012 5-year est.); Employment by occupation: 7.7% management, business, and financial, 11.0% computer, engineering, and science, 11.0% education, legal, community service, arts, and media, 5.5% healthcare practitioners, 22.0% service, 20.9% sales and office, 9.9% natural resources, construction, and maintenance, 12.1% production, transportation, and material moving (2008-2012 5-year est.).
Income: Per capita income: $16,242 (2008-2012 5-year est.); Median household income: $31,923 (2008-2012 5-year est.); Average household income: $43,752 (2008-2012 5-year est.); Percent of households with income of $100,000 or more: 2.3% (2008-2012 5-year est.); Poverty rate: 35.3% (2008-2012 5-year est.).
Education: Percent of population age 25 and over with: High school diploma (including GED) or higher: 80.0% (2008-2012 5-year est.); Bachelor's degree or higher: 6.8% (2008-2012 5-year est.); Master's degree or higher: 2.6% (2008-2012 5-year est.).
Housing: Homeownership rate: 64.6% (2008-2012 5-year est.); Median home value: $56,300 (2008-2012 5-year est.); Median contract rent: $146 per month (2008-2012 5-year est.); Median year structure built: Before 1940 (2008-2012 5-year est.).
Health Insurance: 36.7% Private; 57.1% Public; 18.3% None. (2008-2012 5-year est.)
Transportation: Commute to work: 95.3% car, 0.0% public transportation, 0.0% walk, 0.0% work from home (2008-2012 5-year est.); Travel time to work: 22.1% less than 15 minutes, 19.8% 15 to 30 minutes, 43.0% 30 to 45 minutes, 9.3% 45 to 60 minutes, 5.8% 60 minutes or more (2008-2012 5-year est.)

EDINBURG (village). Covers a land area of 0.625 square miles and a water area of 0 square miles. Located at 39.66° N. Lat; 89.39° W. Long. Elevation is 591 feet.
Population: 982 (1990); 1,135 (2000); 1,078 (2010); Density: 1,709.9 persons per square mile (2008-2012 5-year est.); Race: 94.7% White, 0.9% Black/African American, 0.4% Asian, 0.0% American Indian/Alaska Native, 0.0% Native Hawaiian/Other Pacific Islander, 4.0% Some other race, 0.7% Two or more races, 3.5% Hispanic of any race (2008-2012 5-year est.); Average household size: 2.47 (2008-2012 5-year est.); Median age: 38.8 (2008-2012 5-year est.); Males per 100 females: 95.1 (2008-2012 5-year est.); Marriage status: 20.1% never married, 53.8% now married, 7.0% widowed, 19.1% divorced (2008-2012 5-year est.); Foreign born: 1.4% (2008-2012 5-year est.); Ancestry (includes multiple

ancestries): 20.5% German, 18.1% English, 9.4% Irish, 7.7% American, 3.6% Scottish (2008-2012 5-year est.).
Economy: Single-family building permits issued: 2 (2013); Multi-family building permits issued: 0 (2013); Homeowner vacancy rate: 2.2%. Rental vacancy rate: 5.6%. (2008-2012 5-year est.); Employment by occupation: 7.9% management, business, and financial, 3.5% computer, engineering, and science, 3.5% education, legal, community service, arts, and media, 4.9% healthcare practitioners, 20.6% service, 36.4% sales and office, 10.2% natural resources, construction, and maintenance, 13.0% production, transportation, and material moving (2008-2012 5-year est.).
Income: Per capita income: $25,678 (2008-2012 5-year est.); Median household income: $62,500 (2008-2012 5-year est.); Average household income: $65,061 (2008-2012 5-year est.); Percent of households with income of $100,000 or more: 17.4% (2008-2012 5-year est.); Poverty rate: 6.7% (2008-2012 5-year est.).
Education: Percent of population age 25 and over with: High school diploma (including GED) or higher: 92.2% (2008-2012 5-year est.); Bachelor's degree or higher: 15.2% (2008-2012 5-year est.); Master's degree or higher: 4.5% (2008-2012 5-year est.).

School District(s)
Edinburg CUSD 4 (PK-12)
  2011-12 Enrollment: 292 . . . . (217) 623-5603
Housing: Homeownership rate: 72.5% (2008-2012 5-year est.); Median home value: $88,100 (2008-2012 5-year est.); Median contract rent: $519 per month (2008-2012 5-year est.); Median year structure built: 1951 (2008-2012 5-year est.).
Health Insurance: 71.2% Private; 31.2% Public; 11.6% None. (2008-2012 5-year est.)
Transportation: Commute to work: 89.9% car, 1.8% public transportation, 2.8% walk, 2.7% work from home (2008-2012 5-year est.); Travel time to work: 19.7% less than 15 minutes, 26.3% 15 to 30 minutes, 45.6% 30 to 45 minutes, 6.0% 45 to 60 minutes, 2.4% 60 minutes or more (2008-2012 5-year est.)

JEISYVILLE (village). Covers a land area of 0.123 square miles and a water area of 0 square miles. Located at 39.58° N. Lat; 89.41° W. Long. Elevation is 581 feet.
Population: 126 (1990); 128 (2000); 107 (2010); Density: 1,291.6 persons per square mile (2008-2012 5-year est.); Race: 100.0% White, 0.0% Black/African American, 0.0% Asian, 0.0% American Indian/Alaska Native, 0.0% Native Hawaiian/Other Pacific Islander, 0.0% Some other race, 0.0% Two or more races, 0.0% Hispanic of any race (2008-2012 5-year est.); Average household size: 2.12 (2008-2012 5-year est.); Median age: 45.0 (2008-2012 5-year est.); Males per 100 females: 91.6 (2008-2012 5-year est.); Marriage status: 9.2% never married, 61.5% now married, 16.9% widowed, 12.3% divorced (2008-2012 5-year est.); Foreign born: 0.0% (2008-2012 5-year est.); Ancestry (includes multiple ancestries): 10.7% German, 8.8% American, 6.3% English, 3.8% French, 3.8% Scottish (2008-2012 5-year est.).
Economy: Homeowner vacancy rate: 7.4%. Rental vacancy rate: 0.0%. (2008-2012 5-year est.); Employment by occupation: 11.5% management, business, and financial, 0.0% computer, engineering, and science, 0.0% education, legal, community service, arts, and media, 3.8% healthcare practitioners, 23.1% service, 15.4% sales and office, 25.0% natural resources, construction, and maintenance, 21.2% production, transportation, and material moving (2008-2012 5-year est.).
Income: Per capita income: $17,301 (2008-2012 5-year est.); Median household income: $32,083 (2008-2012 5-year est.); Average household income: $36,813 (2008-2012 5-year est.); Percent of households with income of $100,000 or more: 2.7% (2008-2012 5-year est.); Poverty rate: 23.9% (2008-2012 5-year est.).
Education: Percent of population age 25 and over with: High school diploma (including GED) or higher: 67.0% (2008-2012 5-year est.); Bachelor's degree or higher: 0.9% (2008-2012 5-year est.); Master's degree or higher: 0.9% (2008-2012 5-year est.).
Housing: Homeownership rate: 84.0% (2008-2012 5-year est.); Median home value: $67,900 (2008-2012 5-year est.); Median contract rent: $617 per month (2008-2012 5-year est.); Median year structure built: Before 1940 (2008-2012 5-year est.).
Health Insurance: 69.2% Private; 45.3% Public; 5.0% None. (2008-2012 5-year est.)
Transportation: Commute to work: 100.0% car, 0.0% public transportation, 0.0% walk, 0.0% work from home (2008-2012 5-year est.); Travel time to work: 36.5% less than 15 minutes, 9.6% 15 to 30 minutes,

13.5% 30 to 45 minutes, 34.6% 45 to 60 minutes, 5.8% 60 minutes or more (2008-2012 5-year est.)

KINCAID (village).
Covers a land area of 0.819 square miles and a water area of 0 square miles. Located at 39.59° N. Lat; 89.42° W. Long. Elevation is 600 feet.

History: Incorporated 1915.

Population: 1,353 (1990); 1,441 (2000); 1,505 (2010); Density: 1,911.8 persons per square mile (2008-2012 5-year est.); Race: 93.4% White, 0.3% Black/African American, 0.3% Asian, 0.0% American Indian/Alaska Native, 0.0% Native Hawaiian/Other Pacific Islander, 6.0% Some other race, 6.0% Two or more races, 0.0% Hispanic of any race (2008-2012 5-year est.); Average household size: 2.27 (2008-2012 5-year est.); Median age: 34.9 (2008-2012 5-year est.); Males per 100 females: 89.7 (2008-2012 5-year est.); Marriage status: 28.8% never married, 49.9% now married, 8.1% widowed, 13.2% divorced (2008-2012 5-year est.); Foreign born: 0.3% (2008-2012 5-year est.); Ancestry (includes multiple ancestries): 12.7% German, 10.9% Irish, 10.1% Italian, 9.6% American, 7.6% English (2008-2012 5-year est.).

Economy: Single-family building permits issued: 0 (2013); Multi-family building permits issued: 0 (2013); Homeowner vacancy rate: 1.9%. Rental vacancy rate: 10.9%. (2008-2012 5-year est.); Employment by occupation: 5.8% management, business, and financial, 1.4% computer, engineering, and science, 7.5% education, legal, community service, arts, and media, 6.1% healthcare practitioners, 29.8% service, 26.9% sales and office, 10.4% natural resources, construction, and maintenance, 12.0% production, transportation, and material moving (2008-2012 5-year est.).

Income: Per capita income: $20,806 (2008-2012 5-year est.); Median household income: $41,667 (2008-2012 5-year est.); Average household income: $47,345 (2008-2012 5-year est.); Percent of households with income of $100,000 or more: 9.3% (2008-2012 5-year est.); Poverty rate: 15.5% (2008-2012 5-year est.).

Education: Percent of population age 25 and over with: High school diploma (including GED) or higher: 89.8% (2008-2012 5-year est.); Bachelor's degree or higher: 11.5% (2008-2012 5-year est.); Master's degree or higher: 4.8% (2008-2012 5-year est.).

School District(s)
South Fork SD 14 (PK-12)
 2011-12 Enrollment: 408 . . . . (217) 237-4333

Housing: Homeownership rate: 75.1% (2008-2012 5-year est.); Median home value: $69,400 (2008-2012 5-year est.); Median contract rent: $406 per month (2008-2012 5-year est.); Median year structure built: 1951 (2008-2012 5-year est.).

Health Insurance: 68.1% Private; 38.6% Public; 11.8% None. (2008-2012 5-year est.)

Safety: Violent crime rate: 26.5 per 10,000 population; Property crime rate: 39.7 per 10,000 population (2012).

Transportation: Commute to work: 96.2% car, 0.0% public transportation, 1.5% walk, 1.3% work from home (2008-2012 5-year est.); Travel time to work: 24.0% less than 15 minutes, 31.0% 15 to 30 minutes, 21.7% 30 to 45 minutes, 13.4% 45 to 60 minutes, 10.0% 60 minutes or more (2008-2012 5-year est.)

LANGLEYVILLE (CDP).
Covers a land area of 0.393 square miles and a water area of 0 square miles. Located at 39.56° N. Lat; 89.36° W. Long. Elevation is 610 feet.

Population: n/a (1990); n/a (2000); 432 (2010); Density: 1,117.3 persons per square mile (2008-2012 5-year est.); Race: 100.0% White, 0.0% Black/African American, 0.0% Asian, 0.0% American Indian/Alaska Native, 0.0% Native Hawaiian/Other Pacific Islander, 0.0% Some other race, 0.0% Two or more races, 0.0% Hispanic of any race (2008-2012 5-year est.); Average household size: 2.60 (2008-2012 5-year est.); Median age: 36.6 (2008-2012 5-year est.); Males per 100 females: 77.7 (2008-2012 5-year est.); Marriage status: 25.1% never married, 57.0% now married, 3.4% widowed, 14.6% divorced (2008-2012 5-year est.); Foreign born: 0.0% (2008-2012 5-year est.); Ancestry (includes multiple ancestries): 29.8% German, 18.2% Irish, 12.1% English, 9.1% American, 3.2% Italian (2008-2012 5-year est.).

Economy: Homeowner vacancy rate: 0.0%. Rental vacancy rate: 0.0%. (2008-2012 5-year est.); Employment by occupation: 12.9% management, business, and financial, 0.0% computer, engineering, and science, 0.0% education, legal, community service, arts, and media, 0.0% healthcare practitioners, 6.0% service, 41.3% sales and office, 18.9% natural resources, construction, and maintenance, 20.9% production, transportation, and material moving (2008-2012 5-year est.).

Income: Per capita income: $19,435 (2008-2012 5-year est.); Median household income: $34,732 (2008-2012 5-year est.); Average household income: $50,924 (2008-2012 5-year est.); Percent of households with income of $100,000 or more: 15.4% (2008-2012 5-year est.); Poverty rate: 26.7% (2008-2012 5-year est.).

Education: Percent of population age 25 and over with: High school diploma (including GED) or higher: 77.7% (2008-2012 5-year est.); Bachelor's degree or higher: 8.9% (2008-2012 5-year est.); Master's degree or higher: 3.0% (2008-2012 5-year est.).

Housing: Homeownership rate: 89.9% (2008-2012 5-year est.); Median home value: $74,800 (2008-2012 5-year est.); Median contract rent: n/a per month (2008-2012 5-year est.); Median year structure built: 1967 (2008-2012 5-year est.).

Health Insurance: 58.2% Private; 25.5% Public; 18.2% None. (2008-2012 5-year est.)

Transportation: Commute to work: 100.0% car, 0.0% public transportation, 0.0% walk, 0.0% work from home (2008-2012 5-year est.); Travel time to work: 49.3% less than 15 minutes, 27.2% 15 to 30 minutes, 7.4% 30 to 45 minutes, 0.0% 45 to 60 minutes, 16.1% 60 minutes or more (2008-2012 5-year est.)

MORRISONVILLE (village).
Covers a land area of 1.035 square miles and a water area of 0 square miles. Located at 39.42° N. Lat; 89.46° W. Long. Elevation is 630 feet.

History: Incorporated 1872.

Population: 1,113 (1990); 1,068 (2000); 1,056 (2010); Density: 952.9 persons per square mile (2008-2012 5-year est.); Race: 98.0% White, 0.0% Black/African American, 2.0% Asian, 0.0% American Indian/Alaska Native, 0.0% Native Hawaiian/Other Pacific Islander, 0.0% Some other race, 0.0% Two or more races, 0.0% Hispanic of any race (2008-2012 5-year est.); Average household size: 2.60 (2008-2012 5-year est.); Median age: 39.3 (2008-2012 5-year est.); Males per 100 females: 103.7 (2008-2012 5-year est.); Marriage status: 24.8% never married, 59.8% now married, 6.7% widowed, 8.7% divorced (2008-2012 5-year est.); Foreign born: 4.3% (2008-2012 5-year est.); Ancestry (includes multiple ancestries): 19.3% German, 16.0% Irish, 13.0% American, 6.5% English, 4.7% Dutch (2008-2012 5-year est.).

Economy: Homeowner vacancy rate: 0.0%. Rental vacancy rate: 12.9%. (2008-2012 5-year est.); Employment by occupation: 6.7% management, business, and financial, 1.0% computer, engineering, and science, 10.9% education, legal, community service, arts, and media, 5.2% healthcare practitioners, 28.2% service, 22.1% sales and office, 9.0% natural resources, construction, and maintenance, 16.9% production, transportation, and material moving (2008-2012 5-year est.).

Income: Per capita income: $21,271 (2008-2012 5-year est.); Median household income: $50,089 (2008-2012 5-year est.); Average household income: $55,515 (2008-2012 5-year est.); Percent of households with income of $100,000 or more: 10.0% (2008-2012 5-year est.); Poverty rate: 14.0% (2008-2012 5-year est.).

Education: Percent of population age 25 and over with: High school diploma (including GED) or higher: 85.3% (2008-2012 5-year est.); Bachelor's degree or higher: 10.4% (2008-2012 5-year est.); Master's degree or higher: 1.9% (2008-2012 5-year est.).

School District(s)
Morrisonville CUSD 1 (PK-12)
 2011-12 Enrollment: 321 . . . . (217) 526-4431

Housing: Homeownership rate: 83.9% (2008-2012 5-year est.); Median home value: $75,900 (2008-2012 5-year est.); Median contract rent: $471 per month (2008-2012 5-year est.); Median year structure built: 1947 (2008-2012 5-year est.).

Health Insurance: 64.9% Private; 43.7% Public; 11.2% None. (2008-2012 5-year est.)

Transportation: Commute to work: 90.8% car, 1.0% public transportation, 1.0% walk, 6.1% work from home (2008-2012 5-year est.); Travel time to work: 31.0% less than 15 minutes, 31.7% 15 to 30 minutes, 18.3% 30 to 45 minutes, 15.4% 45 to 60 minutes, 3.6% 60 minutes or more (2008-2012 5-year est.)

MOUNT AUBURN (village).
Covers a land area of 0.997 square miles and a water area of <.001 square miles. Located at 39.77° N. Lat; 89.26° W. Long. Elevation is 699 feet.

Population: 544 (1990); 515 (2000); 480 (2010); Density: 459.5 persons per square mile (2008-2012 5-year est.); Race: 98.9% White, 0.0% Black/African American, 0.0% Asian, 1.1% American Indian/Alaska Native, 0.0% Native Hawaiian/Other Pacific Islander, 0.0% Some other race, 0.0%

Two or more races, 0.0% Hispanic of any race (2008-2012 5-year est.); Average household size: 2.14 (2008-2012 5-year est.); Median age: 49.1 (2008-2012 5-year est.); Males per 100 females: 89.3 (2008-2012 5-year est.); Marriage status: 19.3% never married, 65.8% now married, 6.8% widowed, 8.1% divorced (2008-2012 5-year est.); Foreign born: 0.0% (2008-2012 5-year est.); Ancestry (includes multiple ancestries): 14.4% German, 12.0% American, 9.6% Irish, 5.5% English, 3.5% Italian (2008-2012 5-year est.).

Economy: Single-family building permits issued: 1 (2013); Multi-family building permits issued: 0 (2013); Homeowner vacancy rate: 3.6%. Rental vacancy rate: 0.0%. (2008-2012 5-year est.); Employment by occupation: 11.5% management, business, and financial, 3.1% computer, engineering, and science, 1.6% education, legal, community service, arts, and media, 2.6% healthcare practitioners, 13.5% service, 27.6% sales and office, 10.9% natural resources, construction, and maintenance, 29.2% production, transportation, and material moving (2008-2012 5-year est.).

Income: Per capita income: $21,243 (2008-2012 5-year est.); Median household income: $41,389 (2008-2012 5-year est.); Average household income: $45,347 (2008-2012 5-year est.); Percent of households with income of $100,000 or more: 4.7% (2008-2012 5-year est.); Poverty rate: 23.6% (2008-2012 5-year est.).

Education: Percent of population age 25 and over with: High school diploma (including GED) or higher: 85.1% (2008-2012 5-year est.); Bachelor's degree or higher: 3.4% (2008-2012 5-year est.); Master's degree or higher: 1.7% (2008-2012 5-year est.).

Housing: Homeownership rate: 87.9% (2008-2012 5-year est.); Median home value: $54,200 (2008-2012 5-year est.); Median contract rent: $273 per month (2008-2012 5-year est.); Median year structure built: 1970 (2008-2012 5-year est.).

Health Insurance: 66.2% Private; 37.8% Public; 12.4% None. (2008-2012 5-year est.)

Transportation: Commute to work: 97.9% car, 0.0% public transportation, 1.6% walk, 0.0% work from home (2008-2012 5-year est.); Travel time to work: 15.3% less than 15 minutes, 13.7% 15 to 30 minutes, 54.2% 30 to 45 minutes, 7.9% 45 to 60 minutes, 8.9% 60 minutes or more (2008-2012 5-year est.)

OWANECO (village). Covers a land area of 0.458 square miles and a water area of 0 square miles. Located at 39.48° N. Lat; 89.19° W. Long. Elevation is 620 feet.

Population: 260 (1990); 256 (2000); 239 (2010); Density: 342.6 persons per square mile (2008-2012 5-year est.); Race: 98.1% White, 0.0% Black/African American, 0.0% Asian, 0.0% American Indian/Alaska Native, 0.0% Native Hawaiian/Other Pacific Islander, 1.9% Some other race, 1.9% Two or more races, 0.6% Hispanic of any race (2008-2012 5-year est.); Average household size: 2.62 (2008-2012 5-year est.); Median age: 44.3 (2008-2012 5-year est.); Males per 100 females: 86.9 (2008-2012 5-year est.); Marriage status: 19.3% never married, 66.7% now married, 8.1% widowed, 5.9% divorced (2008-2012 5-year est.); Foreign born: 0.0% (2008-2012 5-year est.); Ancestry (includes multiple ancestries): 32.5% German, 17.2% American, 10.8% English, 9.6% Irish, 7.6% Dutch (2008-2012 5-year est.).

Economy: Homeowner vacancy rate: 0.0%. Rental vacancy rate: 0.0%. (2008-2012 5-year est.); Employment by occupation: 2.5% management, business, and financial, 3.8% computer, engineering, and science, 13.9% education, legal, community service, arts, and media, 1.3% healthcare practitioners, 21.5% service, 20.3% sales and office, 19.0% natural resources, construction, and maintenance, 17.7% production, transportation, and material moving (2008-2012 5-year est.).

Income: Per capita income: $19,229 (2008-2012 5-year est.); Median household income: $47,500 (2008-2012 5-year est.); Average household income: $53,940 (2008-2012 5-year est.); Percent of households with income of $100,000 or more: 13.3% (2008-2012 5-year est.); Poverty rate: 6.4% (2008-2012 5-year est.).

Education: Percent of population age 25 and over with: High school diploma (including GED) or higher: 84.8% (2008-2012 5-year est.); Bachelor's degree or higher: 12.5% (2008-2012 5-year est.); Master's degree or higher: 1.8% (2008-2012 5-year est.).

Housing: Homeownership rate: 93.3% (2008-2012 5-year est.); Median home value: $58,800 (2008-2012 5-year est.); Median contract rent: $275 per month (2008-2012 5-year est.); Median year structure built: Before 1940 (2008-2012 5-year est.).

Health Insurance: 74.5% Private; 42.7% Public; 5.1% None. (2008-2012 5-year est.)

Transportation: Commute to work: 92.1% car, 0.0% public transportation, 2.6% walk, 0.0% work from home (2008-2012 5-year est.); Travel time to work: 19.7% less than 15 minutes, 36.8% 15 to 30 minutes, 9.2% 30 to 45 minutes, 21.1% 45 to 60 minutes, 13.2% 60 minutes or more (2008-2012 5-year est.)

PALMER (village). Covers a land area of 0.995 square miles and a water area of 0 square miles. Located at 39.46° N. Lat; 89.41° W. Long. Elevation is 623 feet.

Population: 275 (1990); 248 (2000); 229 (2010); Density: 227.1 persons per square mile (2008-2012 5-year est.); Race: 100.0% White, 0.0% Black/African American, 0.0% Asian, 0.0% American Indian/Alaska Native, 0.0% Native Hawaiian/Other Pacific Islander, 0.0% Some other race, 0.0% Two or more races, 0.0% Hispanic of any race (2008-2012 5-year est.); Average household size: 2.63 (2008-2012 5-year est.); Median age: 48.4 (2008-2012 5-year est.); Males per 100 females: 93.2 (2008-2012 5-year est.); Marriage status: 24.6% never married, 44.9% now married, 11.6% widowed, 18.8% divorced (2008-2012 5-year est.); Foreign born: 0.0% (2008-2012 5-year est.); Ancestry (includes multiple ancestries): 13.7% German, 8.8% English, 8.0% Irish, 7.1% American, 5.8% Italian (2008-2012 5-year est.).

Economy: Single-family building permits issued: 0 (2013); Multi-family building permits issued: 0 (2013); Homeowner vacancy rate: 0.0%. Rental vacancy rate: 0.0%. (2008-2012 5-year est.); Employment by occupation: 10.5% management, business, and financial, 0.9% computer, engineering, and science, 3.5% education, legal, community service, arts, and media, 0.0% healthcare practitioners, 16.7% service, 19.3% sales and office, 15.8% natural resources, construction, and maintenance, 33.3% production, transportation, and material moving (2008-2012 5-year est.).

Income: Per capita income: $21,279 (2008-2012 5-year est.); Median household income: $55,000 (2008-2012 5-year est.); Average household income: $55,441 (2008-2012 5-year est.); Percent of households with income of $100,000 or more: 8.1% (2008-2012 5-year est.); Poverty rate: 5.8% (2008-2012 5-year est.).

Education: Percent of population age 25 and over with: High school diploma (including GED) or higher: 77.3% (2008-2012 5-year est.); Bachelor's degree or higher: 2.9% (2008-2012 5-year est.); Master's degree or higher: 0.0% (2008-2012 5-year est.).

Housing: Homeownership rate: 97.7% (2008-2012 5-year est.); Median home value: $70,400 (2008-2012 5-year est.); Median contract rent: $250 per month (2008-2012 5-year est.); Median year structure built: 1948 (2008-2012 5-year est.).

Health Insurance: 65.9% Private; 35.4% Public; 19.0% None. (2008-2012 5-year est.)

Transportation: Commute to work: 69.9% car, 5.3% public transportation, 2.7% walk, 22.1% work from home (2008-2012 5-year est.); Travel time to work: 19.3% less than 15 minutes, 43.2% 15 to 30 minutes, 9.1% 30 to 45 minutes, 12.5% 45 to 60 minutes, 15.9% 60 minutes or more (2008-2012 5-year est.)

PANA (city). Covers a land area of 3.840 square miles and a water area of 0.308 square miles. Located at 39.39° N. Lat; 89.09° W. Long. Elevation is 699 feet.

History: Pana developed as a center for rose cultivation, with acres of greenhouses warmed by steam heat.

Population: 5,796 (1990); 5,614 (2000); 5,847 (2010); Density: 1,523.4 persons per square mile (2008-2012 5-year est.); Race: 97.1% White, 0.2% Black/African American, 0.0% Asian, 0.0% American Indian/Alaska Native, 0.0% Native Hawaiian/Other Pacific Islander, 2.7% Some other race, 2.7% Two or more races, 0.5% Hispanic of any race (2008-2012 5-year est.); Average household size: 2.20 (2008-2012 5-year est.); Median age: 39.3 (2008-2012 5-year est.); Males per 100 females: 88.3 (2008-2012 5-year est.); Marriage status: 20.4% never married, 49.0% now married, 13.9% widowed, 16.7% divorced (2008-2012 5-year est.); Foreign born: 1.2% (2008-2012 5-year est.); Ancestry (includes multiple ancestries): 20.9% German, 9.1% American, 9.0% Irish, 7.4% English, 3.3% Italian (2008-2012 5-year est.).

Economy: Single-family building permits issued: 4 (2013); Multi-family building permits issued: 0 (2013); Homeowner vacancy rate: 4.7%. Rental vacancy rate: 6.2%. (2008-2012 5-year est.); Employment by occupation: 5.2% management, business, and financial, 1.8% computer, engineering, and science, 7.6% education, legal, community service, arts, and media, 7.5% healthcare practitioners, 29.0% service, 20.7% sales and office, 7.4% natural resources, construction, and maintenance, 20.9% production, transportation, and material moving (2008-2012 5-year est.).

Income: Per capita income: $17,880 (2008-2012 5-year est.); Median household income: $29,675 (2008-2012 5-year est.); Average household income: $40,694 (2008-2012 5-year est.); Percent of households with income of $100,000 or more: 7.1% (2008-2012 5-year est.); Poverty rate: 26.8% (2008-2012 5-year est.).

Education: Percent of population age 25 and over with: High school diploma (including GED) or higher: 85.4% (2008-2012 5-year est.); Bachelor's degree or higher: 8.7% (2008-2012 5-year est.); Master's degree or higher: 1.8% (2008-2012 5-year est.).

School District(s)
Pana CUSD 8 (PK-12)
   2011-12 Enrollment: 1,418 . . . . (217) 562-1500

Housing: Homeownership rate: 68.7% (2008-2012 5-year est.); Median home value: $71,100 (2008-2012 5-year est.); Median contract rent: $406 per month (2008-2012 5-year est.); Median year structure built: 1956 (2008-2012 5-year est.).

Health Insurance: 58.8% Private; 51.4% Public; 9.3% None. (2008-2012 5-year est.)

Hospitals: Pana Community Hospital (44 beds)

Safety: Violent crime rate: 8.5 per 10,000 population; Property crime rate: 182.6 per 10,000 population (2012).

Transportation: Commute to work: 96.2% car, 0.6% public transportation, 0.0% walk, 2.6% work from home (2008-2012 5-year est.); Travel time to work: 49.2% less than 15 minutes, 26.1% 15 to 30 minutes, 9.0% 30 to 45 minutes, 12.2% 45 to 60 minutes, 3.4% 60 minutes or more (2008-2012 5-year est.)

Additional Information Contacts
City of Pana. . . . . (217) 562-3109
   http://www.panaillinois.org
Pana Chamber of Commerce . . . . (217) 562-4240
   http://www.panachamber.com

ROSAMOND (unincorporated postal area)
Zip Code: 62083

Covers a land area of 19.550 square miles and a water area of 0 square miles. Located at 39.35° N. Lat; 89.20° W. Long. Elevation is 709 feet.
Population: 295 (2010); Density: 15.1 persons per square mile (2010); Race: 99.7% White, 0.0% Black/African American, 0.0% Asian, 0.0% American Indian/Alaska Native, 0.0% Native Hawaiian/Other Pacific Islander, 0.3% Some other race, 0.3% Two or more races, 2.4% Hispanic of any race (2010); Average household size: 2.92 (2010); Median age: 35.9 (2010); Males per 100 females: 92.8 (2010); Homeownership rate: 88.1% (2010)

STONINGTON (village). Covers a land area of 0.460 square miles and a water area of 0 square miles. Located at 39.64° N. Lat; 89.19° W. Long. Elevation is 610 feet.
History: Incorporated 1885.

Population: 1,006 (1990); 960 (2000); 932 (2010); Density: 1,772.2 persons per square mile (2008-2012 5-year est.); Race: 99.9% White, 0.1% Black/African American, 0.0% Asian, 0.0% American Indian/Alaska Native, 0.0% Native Hawaiian/Other Pacific Islander, 0.0% Some other race, 0.0% Two or more races, 0.6% Hispanic of any race (2008-2012 5-year est.); Average household size: 2.34 (2008-2012 5-year est.); Median age: 40.3 (2008-2012 5-year est.); Males per 100 females: 88.5 (2008-2012 5-year est.); Marriage status: 27.5% never married, 52.5% now married, 6.6% widowed, 13.4% divorced (2008-2012 5-year est.); Foreign born: 0.0% (2008-2012 5-year est.); Ancestry (includes multiple ancestries): 21.0% German, 12.3% American, 10.2% Irish, 7.5% English, 5.0% Italian (2008-2012 5-year est.).

Economy: Single-family building permits issued: 0 (2013); Multi-family building permits issued: 0 (2013); Homeowner vacancy rate: 0.0%. Rental vacancy rate: 0.0%. (2008-2012 5-year est.); Employment by occupation: 8.5% management, business, and financial, 5.0% computer, engineering, and science, 3.7% education, legal, community service, arts, and media, 5.3% healthcare practitioners, 18.5% service, 15.9% sales and office, 16.7% natural resources, construction, and maintenance, 26.5% production, transportation, and material moving (2008-2012 5-year est.).

Income: Per capita income: $22,090 (2008-2012 5-year est.); Median household income: $47,500 (2008-2012 5-year est.); Average household income: $53,232 (2008-2012 5-year est.); Percent of households with income of $100,000 or more: 8.4% (2008-2012 5-year est.); Poverty rate: 12.6% (2008-2012 5-year est.).

Education: Percent of population age 25 and over with: High school diploma (including GED) or higher: 88.9% (2008-2012 5-year est.);

Bachelor's degree or higher: 14.7% (2008-2012 5-year est.); Master's degree or higher: 3.8% (2008-2012 5-year est.).

School District(s)
Taylorville CUSD 3 (PK-12)
   2011-12 Enrollment: 2,768 . . . . (217) 824-4951

Housing: Homeownership rate: 84.5% (2008-2012 5-year est.); Median home value: $71,400 (2008-2012 5-year est.); Median contract rent: $396 per month (2008-2012 5-year est.); Median year structure built: Before 1940 (2008-2012 5-year est.).

Health Insurance: 66.8% Private; 41.3% Public; 9.3% None. (2008-2012 5-year est.)

Safety: Violent crime rate: 10.7 per 10,000 population; Property crime rate: 85.7 per 10,000 population (2012).

Transportation: Commute to work: 93.5% car, 0.0% public transportation, 1.9% walk, 1.3% work from home (2008-2012 5-year est.); Travel time to work: 29.7% less than 15 minutes, 27.5% 15 to 30 minutes, 26.4% 30 to 45 minutes, 12.0% 45 to 60 minutes, 4.4% 60 minutes or more (2008-2012 5-year est.)

TAYLORVILLE (city). County seat. Covers a land area of 9.864 square miles and a water area of 1.910 square miles. Located at 39.56° N. Lat; 89.31° W. Long. Elevation is 627 feet.
History: Incorporated 1881.

Population: 11,133 (1990); 11,427 (2000); 11,246 (2010); Density: 1,193.0 persons per square mile (2008-2012 5-year est.); Race: 95.8% White, 2.0% Black/African American, 1.1% Asian, 0.5% American Indian/Alaska Native, 0.0% Native Hawaiian/Other Pacific Islander, 0.6% Some other race, 0.2% Two or more races, 2.0% Hispanic of any race (2008-2012 5-year est.); Average household size: 2.21 (2008-2012 5-year est.); Median age: 42.3 (2008-2012 5-year est.); Males per 100 females: 105.9 (2008-2012 5-year est.); Marriage status: 24.6% never married, 49.1% now married, 8.2% widowed, 18.1% divorced (2008-2012 5-year est.); Foreign born: 2.1% (2008-2012 5-year est.); Ancestry (includes multiple ancestries): 18.2% German, 15.7% Irish, 11.5% English, 10.2% American, 5.5% Italian (2008-2012 5-year est.).

Economy: Single-family building permits issued: 20 (2013); Multi-family building permits issued: 0 (2013); Homeowner vacancy rate: 2.1%. Rental vacancy rate: 3.5%. (2008-2012 5-year est.); Employment by occupation: 9.8% management, business, and financial, 2.0% computer, engineering, and science, 5.9% education, legal, community service, arts, and media, 7.2% healthcare practitioners, 15.6% service, 29.4% sales and office, 12.0% natural resources, construction, and maintenance, 18.1% production, transportation, and material moving (2008-2012 5-year est.).

Income: Per capita income: $24,392 (2008-2012 5-year est.); Median household income: $42,030 (2008-2012 5-year est.); Average household income: $58,774 (2008-2012 5-year est.); Percent of households with income of $100,000 or more: 10.8% (2008-2012 5-year est.); Poverty rate: 15.5% (2008-2012 5-year est.).

Taxes: Total city taxes per capita: $229 (2011); City property taxes per capita: $138 (2011).

Education: Percent of population age 25 and over with: High school diploma (including GED) or higher: 85.6% (2008-2012 5-year est.); Bachelor's degree or higher: 13.3% (2008-2012 5-year est.); Master's degree or higher: 5.0% (2008-2012 5-year est.).

School District(s)
Taylorville CUSD 3 (PK-12)
   2011-12 Enrollment: 2,768 . . . . (217) 824-4951

Housing: Homeownership rate: 63.8% (2008-2012 5-year est.); Median home value: $81,200 (2008-2012 5-year est.); Median contract rent: $411 per month (2008-2012 5-year est.); Median year structure built: 1956 (2008-2012 5-year est.).

Health Insurance: 67.3% Private; 36.2% Public; 12.5% None. (2008-2012 5-year est.)

Hospitals: Taylorville Memorial Hospital

Safety: Violent crime rate: 28.4 per 10,000 population; Property crime rate: 200.5 per 10,000 population (2012).

Transportation: Commute to work: 91.2% car, 1.6% public transportation, 3.0% walk, 3.7% work from home (2008-2012 5-year est.); Travel time to work: 46.7% less than 15 minutes, 17.2% 15 to 30 minutes, 19.4% 30 to 45 minutes, 12.4% 45 to 60 minutes, 4.4% 60 minutes or more (2008-2012 5-year est.)

Airports: Taylorville Municipal Airport (general aviation)

Additional Information Contacts
City of Taylorville . . . . (217) 824-2101
   http://www.taylorville.net

The Greater Taylorville Chamber of Commerce . . . . (217) 824-4919
http://www.taylorvillechamber.com

TOVEY (village). Aka Humphrey. Covers a land area of 0.224 square miles and a water area of 0 square miles. Located at 39.59° N. Lat; 89.45° W. Long. Elevation is 600 feet.
History: Also known as Humphrey.
Population: 533 (1990); 516 (2000); 512 (2010); Density: 2,196.9 persons per square mile (2008-2012 5-year est.); Race: 99.4% White, 0.0% Black/African American, 0.0% Asian, 0.0% American Indian/Alaska Native, 0.0% Native Hawaiian/Other Pacific Islander, 0.6% Some other race, 0.2% Two or more races, 0.0% Hispanic of any race (2008-2012 5-year est.); Average household size: 2.32 (2008-2012 5-year est.); Median age: 47.7 (2008-2012 5-year est.); Males per 100 females: 96.8 (2008-2012 5-year est.); Marriage status: 23.4% never married, 62.3% now married, 4.4% widowed, 10.0% divorced (2008-2012 5-year est.); Foreign born: 0.4% (2008-2012 5-year est.); Ancestry (includes multiple ancestries): 17.3% American, 16.9% Italian, 14.2% German, 11.6% French, 8.3% Irish (2008-2012 5-year est.).
Economy: Single-family building permits issued: 0 (2013); Multi-family building permits issued: 0 (2013); Homeowner vacancy rate: 0.0%. Rental vacancy rate: 40.6%. (2008-2012 5-year est.); Employment by occupation: 6.1% management, business, and financial, 0.0% computer, engineering, and science, 13.6% education, legal, community service, arts, and media, 9.8% healthcare practitioners, 16.8% service, 23.4% sales and office, 13.6% natural resources, construction, and maintenance, 16.8% production, transportation, and material moving (2008-2012 5-year est.).
Income: Per capita income: $21,011 (2008-2012 5-year est.); Median household income: $37,500 (2008-2012 5-year est.); Average household income: $49,405 (2008-2012 5-year est.); Percent of households with income of $100,000 or more: 8.5% (2008-2012 5-year est.); Poverty rate: 23.0% (2008-2012 5-year est.).
Education: Percent of population age 25 and over with: High school diploma (including GED) or higher: 80.6% (2008-2012 5-year est.); Bachelor's degree or higher: 9.0% (2008-2012 5-year est.); Master's degree or higher: 3.4% (2008-2012 5-year est.).
Housing: Homeownership rate: 91.0% (2008-2012 5-year est.); Median home value: $63,700 (2008-2012 5-year est.); Median contract rent: $357 per month (2008-2012 5-year est.); Median year structure built: 1962 (2008-2012 5-year est.).
Health Insurance: 64.0% Private; 42.5% Public; 7.7% None. (2008-2012 5-year est.)
Transportation: Commute to work: 97.1% car, 1.9% public transportation, 1.0% walk, 0.0% work from home (2008-2012 5-year est.); Travel time to work: 21.5% less than 15 minutes, 24.9% 15 to 30 minutes, 35.4% 30 to 45 minutes, 8.1% 45 to 60 minutes, 10.0% 60 minutes or more (2008-2012 5-year est.)

Clark County

Located in eastern Illinois; bounded on the southeast by the Wabash River and the Indiana border; drained by the North Fork Embarrass River. Covers a land area of 501.418 square miles, a water area of 3.400 square miles, and is located in the Central Time Zone at 39.33° N. Lat., 87.79° W. Long. The county was founded in 1819. County seat is Marshall.
Population: 15,921 (1990); 17,008 (2000); 16,335 (2010); Race: 98.2% White, 0.4% Black/African American, 0.3% Asian, 0.1% American Indian/Alaska Native, 0.0% Native Hawaiian/Other Pacific Islander, 1.0% Some other race, 0.8% Two or more races, 1.1% Hispanic of any race (2008-2012 5-year est.); Density: 32.5 persons per square mile (2008-2012 5-year est.); Average household size: 2.44 (2008-2012 5-year est.); Median age: 42.8 (2008-2012 5-year est.); Males per 100 females: 96.2 (2008-2012 5-year est.).
Religion: Six largest groups: 30.4% Baptist, 11.8% Methodist/Pietist, 5.6% Holiness, 4.8% Catholicism, 4.7% Non-denominational Protestant, 4.1% Presbyterian-Reformed (2010)
Economy: Unemployment rate: 7.4% (April 2014); Total civilian labor force: 7,717 (April 2014); Leading industries: 11.5% retail trade; 11.2% accommodation & food services; 9.1% health care and social assistance (2012); Farms: 677 totaling 266,804 acres (2012); Companies that employ 500 or more persons: 1 (2012); Companies that employ 100 to 499 persons: 5 (2012); Companies that employ less than 100 persons: 332 (2012); Black-owned businesses: n/a (2007); Hispanic-owned businesses: n/a (2007); Asian-owned businesses: n/a (2007); Women-owned

businesses: 311 (2007); Single-family building permits issued: 12 (2013); Multi-family building permits issued: 0 (2013).
Income: Per capita income: $24,652 (2008-2012 5-year est.); Median household income: $47,176 (2008-2012 5-year est.); Average household income: $60,361 (2008-2012 5-year est.); Percent of households with income of $100,000 or more: 15.1% (2008-2012 5-year est.); Poverty rate: 11.5% (2008-2012 5-year est.); Bankruptcy rate: 3.46% (2013).
Education: Percent of population age 25 and over with: High school diploma (including GED) or higher: 88.5% (2008-2012 5-year est.); Bachelor's degree or higher: 17.6% (2008-2012 5-year est.); Master's degree or higher: 5.4% (2008-2012 5-year est.).
Housing: Homeownership rate: 75.9% (2008-2012 5-year est.); Median home value: $86,300 (2008-2012 5-year est.); Median contract rent: $370 per month (2008-2012 5-year est.); Median year structure built: 1966 (2008-2012 5-year est.)
Health: Birth rate: 122.4 per 10,000 population (2013); Death rate: 129.8 per 10,000 population (2013); Age-adjusted cancer mortality rate: 202.1 deaths per 100,000 population (2011); Number of physicians: 4.3 per 10,000 population (2011); Hospital beds: 0.0 per 10,000 population (2010); Hospital admissions: 0.0 per 10,000 population (2010).
Environment: Air Quality Index: 97.1% good, 2.9% moderate, 0.0% unhealthy for sensitive individuals, 0.0% unhealthy (percent of days in 2013)
Elections: 2012 Presidential election results: 33.0% Obama, 65.5% Romney
National and State Parks: Lincoln Trail State Park
Additional Information Contacts
Clark County Government. . . . . (217) 826-8311
http://www.clarkcountyil.org

Clark County Communities

CASEY (city). Covers a land area of 2.158 square miles and a water area of 0 square miles. Located at 39.30° N. Lat; 87.99° W. Long. Elevation is 646 feet.
History: Incorporated 1896. Had oil boom in early 20th cent.
Population: 2,914 (1990); 2,942 (2000); 2,769 (2010); Density: 1,213.4 persons per square mile (2008-2012 5-year est.); Race: 98.9% White, 0.5% Black/African American, 0.3% Asian, 0.0% American Indian/Alaska Native, 0.3% Native Hawaiian/Other Pacific Islander, 0.0% Some other race, 0.0% Two or more races, 0.3% Hispanic of any race (2008-2012 5-year est.); Average household size: 2.28 (2008-2012 5-year est.); Median age: 41.5 (2008-2012 5-year est.); Males per 100 females: 90.8 (2008-2012 5-year est.); Marriage status: 23.9% never married, 48.4% now married, 15.2% widowed, 12.5% divorced (2008-2012 5-year est.); Foreign born: 0.0% (2008-2012 5-year est.); Ancestry (includes multiple ancestries): 21.3% English, 14.7% German, 13.9% Irish, 8.3% American, 2.3% Slovak (2008-2012 5-year est.).
Economy: Homeowner vacancy rate: 6.8%. Rental vacancy rate: 0.0%. (2008-2012 5-year est.); Employment by occupation: 9.3% management, business, and financial, 4.1% computer, engineering, and science, 15.2% education, legal, community service, arts, and media, 3.0% healthcare practitioners, 16.7% service, 28.5% sales and office, 10.0% natural resources, construction, and maintenance, 13.1% production, transportation, and material moving (2008-2012 5-year est.).
Income: Per capita income: $22,367 (2008-2012 5-year est.); Median household income: $37,213 (2008-2012 5-year est.); Average household income: $50,987 (2008-2012 5-year est.); Percent of households with income of $100,000 or more: 13.0% (2008-2012 5-year est.); Poverty rate: 11.4% (2008-2012 5-year est.).
Education: Percent of population age 25 and over with: High school diploma (including GED) or higher: 88.1% (2008-2012 5-year est.); Bachelor's degree or higher: 16.9% (2008-2012 5-year est.); Master's degree or higher: 6.3% (2008-2012 5-year est.).
School District(s)
Casey-Westfield CUSD 4c (PK-12)
2011-12 Enrollment: 1,009 . . . . (217) 932-2184
Housing: Homeownership rate: 62.4% (2008-2012 5-year est.); Median home value: $73,600 (2008-2012 5-year est.); Median contract rent: $316 per month (2008-2012 5-year est.); Median year structure built: 1960 (2008-2012 5-year est.).
Health Insurance: 60.7% Private; 50.3% Public; 8.2% None. (2008-2012 5-year est.)
Safety: Violent crime rate: 113.1 per 10,000 population; Property crime rate: 120.4 per 10,000 population (2012).

Transportation: Commute to work: 89.7% car, 0.0% public transportation, 1.8% walk, 7.7% work from home (2008-2012 5-year est.); Travel time to work: 51.6% less than 15 minutes, 15.0% 15 to 30 minutes, 17.6% 30 to 45 minutes, 12.2% 45 to 60 minutes, 3.5% 60 minutes or more (2008-2012 5-year est.)

Airports: Casey Municipal Airport (general aviation)

Additional Information Contacts

City of Casey . . . . (217) 932-2700
    http://www.cityofcaseyil.org

DENNISON (unincorporated postal area)

Zip Code: 62423

Covers a land area of 23.168 square miles and a water area of 0.016 square miles. Located at 39.46° N. Lat; 87.57° W. Long. Elevation is 581 feet. Population: 724 (2010); Density: 31.2 persons per square mile (2010); Race: 97.8% White, 0.0% Black/African American, 0.7% Asian, 0.3% American Indian/Alaska Native, 0.0% Native Hawaiian/Other Pacific Islander, 1.2% Some other race, 1.0% Two or more races, 1.4% Hispanic of any race (2010); Average household size: 2.54 (2010); Median age: 41.3 (2010); Males per 100 females: 102.8 (2010); Homeownership rate: 87.4% (2010)

MARSHALL (city). County seat. Covers a land area of 3.723 square miles and a water area of 0.016 square miles. Located at 39.40° N. Lat; 87.69° W. Long. Elevation is 640 feet.

History: Marshall was founded by William B. Archer and named by him for Chief Justice John Marshall. The town developed as the seat of Clark County.

Population: 3,555 (1990); 3,771 (2000); 3,933 (2010); Density: 1,069.8 persons per square mile (2008-2012 5-year est.); Race: 97.0% White, 0.7% Black/African American, 0.3% Asian, 0.3% American Indian/Alaska Native, 0.0% Native Hawaiian/Other Pacific Islander, 1.7% Some other race, 1.4% Two or more races, 1.9% Hispanic of any race (2008-2012 5-year est.); Average household size: 2.22 (2008-2012 5-year est.); Median age: 38.4 (2008-2012 5-year est.); Males per 100 females: 80.4 (2008-2012 5-year est.); Marriage status: 23.8% never married, 46.2% now married, 14.8% widowed, 15.2% divorced (2008-2012 5-year est.); Foreign born: 1.5% (2008-2012 5-year est.); Ancestry (includes multiple ancestries): 26.7% German, 10.8% Irish, 9.9% English, 7.8% American, 1.4% French (2008-2012 5-year est.).

Economy: Single-family building permits issued: 12 (2013); Multi-family building permits issued: 0 (2013); Homeowner vacancy rate: 0.5%. Rental vacancy rate: 3.0%. (2008-2012 5-year est.); Employment by occupation: 10.1% management, business, and financial, 4.7% computer, engineering, and science, 7.3% education, legal, community service, arts, and media, 2.6% healthcare practitioners, 24.6% service, 22.2% sales and office, 13.9% natural resources, construction, and maintenance, 14.6% production, transportation, and material moving (2008-2012 5-year est.).

Income: Per capita income: $22,450 (2008-2012 5-year est.); Median household income: $42,875 (2008-2012 5-year est.); Average household income: $51,493 (2008-2012 5-year est.); Percent of households with income of $100,000 or more: 12.7% (2008-2012 5-year est.); Poverty rate: 15.3% (2008-2012 5-year est.).

Education: Percent of population age 25 and over with: High school diploma (including GED) or higher: 86.0% (2008-2012 5-year est.); Bachelor's degree or higher: 17.0% (2008-2012 5-year est.); Master's degree or higher: 5.3% (2008-2012 5-year est.).

School District(s)

Eastern Il Area of Spec Educ (PK-12)
    2011-12 Enrollment: n/a . . . . (217) 348-7700
Marshall CUSD 2c (PK-12)
    2011-12 Enrollment: 1,385 . . . . (217) 826-5912

Housing: Homeownership rate: 62.7% (2008-2012 5-year est.); Median home value: $87,700 (2008-2012 5-year est.); Median contract rent: $429 per month (2008-2012 5-year est.); Median year structure built: 1969 (2008-2012 5-year est.).

Health Insurance: 62.2% Private; 49.4% Public; 6.2% None. (2008-2012 5-year est.)

Transportation: Commute to work: 94.2% car, 0.0% public transportation, 2.7% walk, 0.7% work from home (2008-2012 5-year est.); Travel time to work: 48.1% less than 15 minutes, 28.0% 15 to 30 minutes, 15.0% 30 to 45 minutes, 2.9% 45 to 60 minutes, 6.1% 60 minutes or more (2008-2012 5-year est.)

Additional Information Contacts

Marshall Area Chamber of Commerce . . . . (217) 826-2034
    http://www.marshallilchamber.com

MARTINSVILLE (city). Covers a land area of 2.054 square miles and a water area of 0.030 square miles. Located at 39.34° N. Lat; 87.88° W. Long. Elevation is 610 feet.

History: Martinsville was platted in 1833 by Joseph Martin, and operated as a trading post, stagecoach station, and tavern. A period of growth came in 1904 when oil and gas were discovered, but by 1916 the wells were dry.

Population: 1,161 (1990); 1,225 (2000); 1,167 (2010); Density: 538.1 persons per square mile (2008-2012 5-year est.); Race: 93.3% White, 1.5% Black/African American, 1.6% Asian, 0.4% American Indian/Alaska Native, 0.0% Native Hawaiian/Other Pacific Islander, 3.2% Some other race, 2.0% Two or more races, 4.9% Hispanic of any race (2008-2012 5-year est.); Average household size: 2.33 (2008-2012 5-year est.); Median age: 41.7 (2008-2012 5-year est.); Males per 100 females: 86.0 (2008-2012 5-year est.); Marriage status: 20.8% never married, 58.3% now married, 12.1% widowed, 8.8% divorced (2008-2012 5-year est.); Foreign born: 2.8% (2008-2012 5-year est.); Ancestry (includes multiple ancestries): 21.7% German, 13.3% American, 11.1% English, 10.7% Irish, 2.3% French (2008-2012 5-year est.).

Economy: Homeowner vacancy rate: 4.3%. Rental vacancy rate: 13.2%. (2008-2012 5-year est.); Employment by occupation: 13.8% management, business, and financial, 0.7% computer, engineering, and science, 14.7% education, legal, community service, arts, and media, 0.9% healthcare practitioners, 21.8% service, 19.3% sales and office, 10.3% natural resources, construction, and maintenance, 18.6% production, transportation, and material moving (2008-2012 5-year est.).

Income: Per capita income: $16,380 (2008-2012 5-year est.); Median household income: $30,380 (2008-2012 5-year est.); Average household income: $37,703 (2008-2012 5-year est.); Percent of households with income of $100,000 or more: 2.9% (2008-2012 5-year est.); Poverty rate: 22.4% (2008-2012 5-year est.).

Education: Percent of population age 25 and over with: High school diploma (including GED) or higher: 81.2% (2008-2012 5-year est.); Bachelor's degree or higher: 14.1% (2008-2012 5-year est.); Master's degree or higher: 3.7% (2008-2012 5-year est.).

School District(s)

Martinsville CUSD 3c (PK-12)
    2011-12 Enrollment: 412 . . . . (217) 382-4321

Housing: Homeownership rate: 69.5% (2008-2012 5-year est.); Median home value: $58,700 (2008-2012 5-year est.); Median contract rent: $338 per month (2008-2012 5-year est.); Median year structure built: 1950 (2008-2012 5-year est.).

Health Insurance: 50.9% Private; 52.6% Public; 11.9% None. (2008-2012 5-year est.)

Safety: Violent crime rate: 8.7 per 10,000 population; Property crime rate: 415.9 per 10,000 population (2012).

Transportation: Commute to work: 92.3% car, 0.0% public transportation, 2.6% walk, 3.8% work from home (2008-2012 5-year est.); Travel time to work: 43.4% less than 15 minutes, 22.2% 15 to 30 minutes, 17.7% 30 to 45 minutes, 8.0% 45 to 60 minutes, 8.7% 60 minutes or more (2008-2012 5-year est.)

Additional Information Contacts

Martinsville Chamber of Commerce . . . . (217) 251-5505

WEST UNION (CDP). Covers a land area of 1.583 square miles and a water area of 0 square miles. Located at 39.22° N. Lat; 87.67° W. Long. Elevation is 472 feet.

Population: n/a (1990); n/a (2000); 288 (2010); Density: 255.8 persons per square mile (2008-2012 5-year est.); Race: 96.5% White, 1.5% Black/African American, 0.0% Asian, 0.0% American Indian/Alaska Native, 0.0% Native Hawaiian/Other Pacific Islander, 2.0% Some other race, 2.0% Two or more races, 1.5% Hispanic of any race (2008-2012 5-year est.); Average household size: 2.91 (2008-2012 5-year est.); Median age: 33.1 (2008-2012 5-year est.); Males per 100 females: 85.8 (2008-2012 5-year est.); Marriage status: 31.2% never married, 40.8% now married, 0.0% widowed, 28.0% divorced (2008-2012 5-year est.); Foreign born: 0.0% (2008-2012 5-year est.); Ancestry (includes multiple ancestries): 55.1% German, 14.6% English, 3.0% American, 2.7% Irish (2008-2012 5-year est.).

Economy: Homeowner vacancy rate: 0.0%. Rental vacancy rate: 0.0%. (2008-2012 5-year est.); Employment by occupation: 6.5% management, business, and financial, 0.0% computer, engineering, and science, 0.0% education, legal, community service, arts, and media, 0.0% healthcare

practitioners, 26.6% service, 10.1% sales and office, 2.4% natural resources, construction, and maintenance, 54.4% production, transportation, and material moving (2008-2012 5-year est.).
Income: Per capita income: $20,040 (2008-2012 5-year est.); Median household income: $43,021 (2008-2012 5-year est.); Average household income: $57,524 (2008-2012 5-year est.); Percent of households with income of $100,000 or more: 15.8% (2008-2012 5-year est.); Poverty rate: 7.8% (2008-2012 5-year est.).
Education: Percent of population age 25 and over with: High school diploma (including GED) or higher: 89.4% (2008-2012 5-year est.); Bachelor's degree or higher: 2.1% (2008-2012 5-year est.); Master's degree or higher: 0.0% (2008-2012 5-year est.).
Housing: Homeownership rate: 89.2% (2008-2012 5-year est.); Median home value: $41,800 (2008-2012 5-year est.); Median contract rent: n/a per month (2008-2012 5-year est.); Median year structure built: 1946 (2008-2012 5-year est.).
Health Insurance: 58.0% Private; 27.2% Public; 18.8% None. (2008-2012 5-year est.)
Transportation: Commute to work: 89.9% car, 0.0% public transportation, 0.0% walk, 10.1% work from home (2008-2012 5-year est.); Travel time to work: 0.0% less than 15 minutes, 88.2% 15 to 30 minutes, 5.3% 30 to 45 minutes, 2.6% 45 to 60 minutes, 3.9% 60 minutes or more (2008-2012 5-year est.)

WESTFIELD (village). Covers a land area of 1.001 square miles and a water area of 0 square miles. Located at 39.46° N. Lat; 88.00° W. Long. Elevation is 755 feet.
Population: 676 (1990); 678 (2000); 601 (2010); Density: 596.1 persons per square mile (2008-2012 5-year est.); Race: 99.2% White, 0.0% Black/African American, 0.0% Asian, 0.0% American Indian/Alaska Native, 0.0% Native Hawaiian/Other Pacific Islander, 0.8% Some other race, 0.8% Two or more races, 0.0% Hispanic of any race (2008-2012 5-year est.); Average household size: 2.13 (2008-2012 5-year est.); Median age: 47.5 (2008-2012 5-year est.); Males per 100 females: 66.8 (2008-2012 5-year est.); Marriage status: 16.8% never married, 56.1% now married, 13.9% widowed, 13.3% divorced (2008-2012 5-year est.); Foreign born: 1.0% (2008-2012 5-year est.); Ancestry (includes multiple ancestries): 19.3% German, 18.9% English, 18.6% Irish, 15.1% American, 5.2% Italian (2008-2012 5-year est.).
Economy: Single-family building permits issued: 0 (2013); Multi-family building permits issued: 0 (2013); Homeowner vacancy rate: 2.7%. Rental vacancy rate: 34.1%. (2008-2012 5-year est.); Employment by occupation: 18.7% management, business, and financial, 0.5% computer, engineering, and science, 1.8% education, legal, community service, arts, and media, 4.6% healthcare practitioners, 18.3% service, 22.4% sales and office, 9.6% natural resources, construction, and maintenance, 24.2% production, transportation, and material moving (2008-2012 5-year est.).
Income: Per capita income: $22,316 (2008-2012 5-year est.); Median household income: $31,786 (2008-2012 5-year est.); Average household income: $47,645 (2008-2012 5-year est.); Percent of households with income of $100,000 or more: 4.7% (2008-2012 5-year est.); Poverty rate: 13.4% (2008-2012 5-year est.).
Education: Percent of population age 25 and over with: High school diploma (including GED) or higher: 86.8% (2008-2012 5-year est.); Bachelor's degree or higher: 4.3% (2008-2012 5-year est.); Master's degree or higher: 0.9% (2008-2012 5-year est.).
Housing: Homeownership rate: 90.4% (2008-2012 5-year est.); Median home value: $61,700 (2008-2012 5-year est.); Median contract rent: $375 per month (2008-2012 5-year est.); Median year structure built: 1951 (2008-2012 5-year est.).
Health Insurance: 53.4% Private; 52.1% Public; 16.4% None. (2008-2012 5-year est.)
Transportation: Commute to work: 86.6% car, 0.0% public transportation, 1.9% walk, 11.5% work from home (2008-2012 5-year est.); Travel time to work: 21.6% less than 15 minutes, 45.9% 15 to 30 minutes, 28.6% 30 to 45 minutes, 3.2% 45 to 60 minutes, 0.5% 60 minutes or more (2008-2012 5-year est.)

Clay County

Located in south central Illinois; drained by the Little Wabash River. Covers a land area of 468.316 square miles, a water area of 1.276 square miles, and is located in the Central Time Zone at 38.75° N. Lat., 88.48° W. Long. The county was founded in 1824. County seat is Louisville.

Weather Station: Flora 5 NW										Elevation: 500 feet		
	Jan	Feb	Mar	Apr	May	Jun	Jul	Aug	Sep	Oct	Nov	Dec
High	40	45	56	68	77	85	89	88	81	69	56	43
Low	23	26	34	44	54	62	66	64	56	45	36	26
Precip	2.9	2.6	3.8	4.0	5.1	4.2	3.8	3.4	3.1	3.7	4.2	3.3
Snow	2.8	1.9	0.9	tr	tr	0.0	0.0	0.0	0.0	tr	0.4	2.0

High and Low temperatures in degrees Fahrenheit; Precipitation and Snow in inches

Population: 14,460 (1990); 14,560 (2000); 13,815 (2010); Race: 97.3% White, 0.6% Black/African American, 0.4% Asian, 0.5% American Indian/Alaska Native, 0.0% Native Hawaiian/Other Pacific Islander, 1.2% Some other race, 0.9% Two or more races, 0.4% Hispanic of any race (2008-2012 5-year est.); Density: 29.4 persons per square mile (2008-2012 5-year est.); Average household size: 2.42 (2008-2012 5-year est.); Median age: 42.5 (2008-2012 5-year est.); Males per 100 females: 95.4 (2008-2012 5-year est.).
Religion: Six largest groups: 28.6% Baptist, 16.4% Catholicism, 15.9% Non-denominational Protestant, 7.7% Methodist/Pietist, 4.3% Lutheran, 2.2% Pentecostal (2010)
Economy: Unemployment rate: 8.9% (April 2014); Total civilian labor force: 6,098 (April 2014); Leading industries: 39.9% manufacturing; 14.7% health care and social assistance; 10.4% retail trade (2012); Farms: 774 totaling 270,319 acres (2012); Companies that employ 500 or more persons: 1 (2012); Companies that employ 100 to 499 persons: 6 (2012); Companies that employ less than 100 persons: 353 (2012); Black-owned businesses: n/a (2007); Hispanic-owned businesses: n/a (2007); Asian-owned businesses: n/a (2007); Women-owned businesses: 306 (2007); Single-family building permits issued: 3 (2013); Multi-family building permits issued: 0 (2013).
Income: Per capita income: $21,111 (2008-2012 5-year est.); Median household income: $39,966 (2008-2012 5-year est.); Average household income: $49,257 (2008-2012 5-year est.); Percent of households with income of $100,000 or more: 8.8% (2008-2012 5-year est.); Poverty rate: 14.9% (2008-2012 5-year est.); Bankruptcy rate: 1.82% (2013).
Taxes: Total county taxes per capita: $138 (2011); County property taxes per capita: $138 (2011).
Education: Percent of population age 25 and over with: High school diploma (including GED) or higher: 87.5% (2008-2012 5-year est.); Bachelor's degree or higher: 13.9% (2008-2012 5-year est.); Master's degree or higher: 4.3% (2008-2012 5-year est.).
Housing: Homeownership rate: 77.7% (2008-2012 5-year est.); Median home value: $75,500 (2008-2012 5-year est.); Median contract rent: $330 per month (2008-2012 5-year est.); Median year structure built: 1971 (2008-2012 5-year est.)
Health: Birth rate: 111.3 per 10,000 population (2013); Death rate: 133.4 per 10,000 population (2013); Age-adjusted cancer mortality rate: 236.9 deaths per 100,000 population (2011); Number of physicians: 8.0 per 10,000 population (2011); Hospital beds: 15.9 per 10,000 population (2010); Hospital admissions: 764.4 per 10,000 population (2010).
Elections: 2012 Presidential election results: 26.8% Obama, 70.9% Romney
Additional Information Contacts
Clay County Government . . . . (618) 665-3626
    http://claycountyillinois.org

Clay County Communities

CLAY CITY (village). Covers a land area of 1.744 square miles and a water area of 0 square miles. Located at 38.69° N. Lat; 88.35° W. Long. Elevation is 433 feet.
History: Clay City developed as a shipping and trading center for the surrounding agricultural area when the railroad arrived here. It was built on the site of the first seat of Clay County, called Maysville. Oil was discovered near Clay City in 1937.
Population: 929 (1990); 1,000 (2000); 959 (2010); Density: 517.7 persons per square mile (2008-2012 5-year est.); Race: 99.8% White, 0.0% Black/African American, 0.0% Asian, 0.2% American Indian/Alaska Native, 0.0% Native Hawaiian/Other Pacific Islander, 0.0% Some other race, 0.0% Two or more races, 0.0% Hispanic of any race (2008-2012 5-year est.); Average household size: 2.18 (2008-2012 5-year est.); Median age: 43.6 (2008-2012 5-year est.); Males per 100 females: 88.1 (2008-2012 5-year est.); Marriage status: 24.8% never married, 37.5% now married, 10.1% widowed, 27.6% divorced (2008-2012 5-year est.); Foreign born: 0.0% (2008-2012 5-year est.); Ancestry (includes multiple ancestries): 19.9% German, 12.6% American, 9.4% English, 9.2% Irish, 1.3% Dutch (2008-2012 5-year est.).

Economy: Single-family building permits issued: 0 (2013); Multi-family building permits issued: 0 (2013); Homeowner vacancy rate: 2.3%. Rental vacancy rate: 6.3%. (2008-2012 5-year est.); Employment by occupation: 8.3% management, business, and financial, 0.0% computer, engineering, and science, 2.8% education, legal, community service, arts, and media, 6.6% healthcare practitioners, 18.8% service, 18.8% sales and office, 9.7% natural resources, construction, and maintenance, 34.9% production, transportation, and material moving (2008-2012 5-year est.).
Income: Per capita income: $17,619 (2008-2012 5-year est.); Median household income: $29,625 (2008-2012 5-year est.); Average household income: $36,872 (2008-2012 5-year est.); Percent of households with income of $100,000 or more: 1.9% (2008-2012 5-year est.); Poverty rate: 19.6% (2008-2012 5-year est.).
Education: Percent of population age 25 and over with: High school diploma (including GED) or higher: 81.0% (2008-2012 5-year est.); Bachelor's degree or higher: 7.7% (2008-2012 5-year est.); Master's degree or higher: 1.4% (2008-2012 5-year est.).

School District(s)
Clay City CUSD 10 (PK-12)
    2011-12 Enrollment: 344. . . . . (618) 676-1431
Housing: Homeownership rate: 81.9% (2008-2012 5-year est.); Median home value: $52,100 (2008-2012 5-year est.); Median contract rent: $243 per month (2008-2012 5-year est.); Median year structure built: 1959 (2008-2012 5-year est.).
Health Insurance: 55.0% Private; 41.3% Public; 24.7% None. (2008-2012 5-year est.)
Transportation: Commute to work: 94.2% car, 0.0% public transportation, 2.6% walk, 0.9% work from home (2008-2012 5-year est.); Travel time to work: 50.3% less than 15 minutes, 33.9% 15 to 30 minutes, 7.6% 30 to 45 minutes, 4.1% 45 to 60 minutes, 4.1% 60 minutes or more (2008-2012 5-year est.)

FLORA (city). Covers a land area of 4.727 square miles and a water area of 0.003 square miles. Located at 38.67° N. Lat; 88.47° W. Long. Elevation is 492 feet.
History: Flora was named for the daughter of one of its founders. It developed as an industrial center with a diversity of manufacturing.
Population: 5,054 (1990); 5,086 (2000); 5,070 (2010); Density: 1,061.5 persons per square mile (2008-2012 5-year est.); Race: 95.2% White, 1.5% Black/African American, 1.1% Asian, 0.0% American Indian/Alaska Native, 0.0% Native Hawaiian/Other Pacific Islander, 2.2% Some other race, 2.1% Two or more races, 0.1% Hispanic of any race (2008-2012 5-year est.); Average household size: 2.51 (2008-2012 5-year est.); Median age: 38.3 (2008-2012 5-year est.); Males per 100 females: 84.4 (2008-2012 5-year est.); Marriage status: 26.7% never married, 51.1% now married, 8.9% widowed, 13.3% divorced (2008-2012 5-year est.); Foreign born: 1.1% (2008-2012 5-year est.); Ancestry (includes multiple ancestries): 19.0% German, 15.1% American, 13.9% Irish, 9.5% English, 2.6% British (2008-2012 5-year est.).
Economy: Single-family building permits issued: 3 (2013); Multi-family building permits issued: 0 (2013); Homeowner vacancy rate: 7.6%. Rental vacancy rate: 0.0%. (2008-2012 5-year est.); Employment by occupation: 10.5% management, business, and financial, 4.4% computer, engineering, and science, 5.9% education, legal, community service, arts, and media, 7.0% healthcare practitioners, 19.3% service, 17.2% sales and office, 10.3% natural resources, construction, and maintenance, 25.5% production, transportation, and material moving (2008-2012 5-year est.).
Income: Per capita income: $18,087 (2008-2012 5-year est.); Median household income: $37,746 (2008-2012 5-year est.); Average household income: $44,118 (2008-2012 5-year est.); Percent of households with income of $100,000 or more: 5.0% (2008-2012 5-year est.); Poverty rate: 17.8% (2008-2012 5-year est.).
Taxes: Total city taxes per capita: $256 (2011); City property taxes per capita: $221 (2011).
Education: Percent of population age 25 and over with: High school diploma (including GED) or higher: 91.2% (2008-2012 5-year est.); Bachelor's degree or higher: 16.6% (2008-2012 5-year est.); Master's degree or higher: 8.1% (2008-2012 5-year est.).

School District(s)
Flora CUSD 35 (PK-12)
    2011-12 Enrollment: 1,430 . . . . (618) 662-2412
Housing: Homeownership rate: 65.7% (2008-2012 5-year est.); Median home value: $76,600 (2008-2012 5-year est.); Median contract rent: $340 per month (2008-2012 5-year est.); Median year structure built: 1964 (2008-2012 5-year est.).

Health Insurance: 53.0% Private; 50.3% Public; 11.8% None. (2008-2012 5-year est.)
Hospitals: Clay County Hospital (18 beds)
Safety: Violent crime rate: 7.9 per 10,000 population; Property crime rate: 313.3 per 10,000 population (2012).
Transportation: Commute to work: 89.5% car, 0.0% public transportation, 6.6% walk, 1.3% work from home (2008-2012 5-year est.); Travel time to work: 80.1% less than 15 minutes, 9.3% 15 to 30 minutes, 7.7% 30 to 45 minutes, 1.4% 45 to 60 minutes, 1.5% 60 minutes or more (2008-2012 5-year est.)
Airports: Flora Municipal Airport (general aviation)
Additional Information Contacts
City of Flora. . . . . (618) 662-8313
    http://florail.govoffice2.com
Flora Chamber of Commerce . . . . (618) 662-5646
    http://www.florachamber.com

INGRAHAM (unincorporated postal area)
Zip Code: 62434
    Covers a land area of 26.642 square miles and a water area of 0.042 square miles. Located at 38.84° N. Lat; 88.32° W. Long. Elevation is 486 feet. Population: 330 (2010); Density: 12.4 persons per square mile (2010); Race: 99.4% White, 0.0% Black/African American, 0.0% Asian, 0.0% American Indian/Alaska Native, 0.0% Native Hawaiian/Other Pacific Islander, 0.6% Some other race, 0.6% Two or more races, 0.0% Hispanic of any race (2010); Average household size: 2.37 (2010); Median age: 44.5 (2010); Males per 100 females: 111.5 (2010); Homeownership rate: 92.8% (2010)

IOLA (village). Covers a land area of 0.975 square miles and a water area of 0 square miles. Located at 38.83° N. Lat; 88.63° W. Long. Elevation is 525 feet.
History: Incorporated 1914.
Population: 163 (1990); 171 (2000); 141 (2010); Density: 105.6 persons per square mile (2008-2012 5-year est.); Race: 100.0% White, 0.0% Black/African American, 0.0% Asian, 0.0% American Indian/Alaska Native, 0.0% Native Hawaiian/Other Pacific Islander, 0.0% Some other race, 0.0% Two or more races, 0.0% Hispanic of any race (2008-2012 5-year est.); Average household size: 3.32 (2008-2012 5-year est.); Median age: 35.1 (2008-2012 5-year est.); Males per 100 females: 106.0 (2008-2012 5-year est.); Marriage status: 18.2% never married, 59.7% now married, 11.7% widowed, 10.4% divorced (2008-2012 5-year est.); Foreign born: 0.0% (2008-2012 5-year est.); Ancestry (includes multiple ancestries): 22.3% American, 12.6% German, 5.8% French, 5.8% Celtic, 4.9% Dutch (2008-2012 5-year est.).
Economy: Homeowner vacancy rate: 0.0%. Rental vacancy rate: 0.0%. (2008-2012 5-year est.); Employment by occupation: 0.0% management, business, and financial, 0.0% computer, engineering, and science, 12.2% education, legal, community service, arts, and media, 0.0% healthcare practitioners, 17.1% service, 9.8% sales and office, 29.3% natural resources, construction, and maintenance, 31.7% production, transportation, and material moving (2008-2012 5-year est.).
Income: Per capita income: $11,718 (2008-2012 5-year est.); Median household income: $35,313 (2008-2012 5-year est.); Average household income: $39,461 (2008-2012 5-year est.); Percent of households with income of $100,000 or more: n/a (2008-2012 5-year est.); Poverty rate: 16.5% (2008-2012 5-year est.).
Education: Percent of population age 25 and over with: High school diploma (including GED) or higher: 76.3% (2008-2012 5-year est.); Bachelor's degree or higher: 0.0% (2008-2012 5-year est.); Master's degree or higher: 0.0% (2008-2012 5-year est.).
Housing: Homeownership rate: 87.1% (2008-2012 5-year est.); Median home value: $52,500 (2008-2012 5-year est.); Median contract rent: $500 per month (2008-2012 5-year est.); Median year structure built: 1965 (2008-2012 5-year est.).
Health Insurance: 60.2% Private; 38.8% Public; 14.6% None. (2008-2012 5-year est.)
Transportation: Commute to work: 71.8% car, 0.0% public transportation, 12.8% walk, 15.4% work from home (2008-2012 5-year est.); Travel time to work: 33.3% less than 15 minutes, 33.3% 15 to 30 minutes, 18.2% 30 to 45 minutes, 15.2% 45 to 60 minutes, 0.0% 60 minutes or more (2008-2012 5-year est.)

LOUISVILLE (village). Aka Louis. County seat. Covers a land area of 0.747 square miles and a water area of 0 square miles. Located at 38.77° N. Lat; 88.51° W. Long. Elevation is 479 feet.
Population: 1,098 (1990); 1,242 (2000); 1,139 (2010); Density: 1,575.4 persons per square mile (2008-2012 5-year est.); Race: 98.2% White, 0.6% Black/African American, 0.0% Asian, 0.1% American Indian/Alaska Native, 0.0% Native Hawaiian/Other Pacific Islander, 1.1% Some other race, 1.1% Two or more races, 0.0% Hispanic of any race (2008-2012 5-year est.); Average household size: 2.42 (2008-2012 5-year est.); Median age: 39.7 (2008-2012 5-year est.); Males per 100 females: 85.9 (2008-2012 5-year est.); Marriage status: 27.2% never married, 52.6% now married, 8.3% widowed, 11.9% divorced (2008-2012 5-year est.); Foreign born: 0.7% (2008-2012 5-year est.); Ancestry (includes multiple ancestries): 24.5% German, 12.7% English, 10.4% Irish, 9.0% American, 1.3% Dutch (2008-2012 5-year est.).
Economy: Homeowner vacancy rate: 5.3%. Rental vacancy rate: 0.0%. (2008-2012 5-year est.); Employment by occupation: 5.3% management, business, and financial, 2.7% computer, engineering, and science, 9.0% education, legal, community service, arts, and media, 2.9% healthcare practitioners, 14.8% service, 27.1% sales and office, 10.7% natural resources, construction, and maintenance, 27.5% production, transportation, and material moving (2008-2012 5-year est.).
Income: Per capita income: $17,990 (2008-2012 5-year est.); Median household income: $35,724 (2008-2012 5-year est.); Average household income: $42,755 (2008-2012 5-year est.); Percent of households with income of $100,000 or more: 5.0% (2008-2012 5-year est.); Poverty rate: 21.8% (2008-2012 5-year est.).
Education: Percent of population age 25 and over with: High school diploma (including GED) or higher: 83.9% (2008-2012 5-year est.); Bachelor's degree or higher: 11.4% (2008-2012 5-year est.); Master's degree or higher: 1.5% (2008-2012 5-year est.).

School District(s)

North Clay CUSD 25 (PK-12)
   2011-12 Enrollment: 706 . . . . (618) 665-3358
Housing: Homeownership rate: 73.4% (2008-2012 5-year est.); Median home value: $64,800 (2008-2012 5-year est.); Median contract rent: $256 per month (2008-2012 5-year est.); Median year structure built: 1964 (2008-2012 5-year est.).
Health Insurance: 52.2% Private; 47.5% Public; 12.9% None. (2008-2012 5-year est.)
Transportation: Commute to work: 90.9% car, 1.2% public transportation, 3.3% walk, 2.7% work from home (2008-2012 5-year est.); Travel time to work: 39.4% less than 15 minutes, 25.7% 15 to 30 minutes, 20.9% 30 to 45 minutes, 9.8% 45 to 60 minutes, 4.3% 60 minutes or more (2008-2012 5-year est.)

SAILOR SPRINGS (village). Covers a land area of 0.249 square miles and a water area of 0 square miles. Located at 38.76° N. Lat; 88.36° W. Long. Elevation is 440 feet.
Population: 136 (1990); 128 (2000); 95 (2010); Density: 454.1 persons per square mile (2008-2012 5-year est.); Race: 100.0% White, 0.0% Black/African American, 0.0% Asian, 0.0% American Indian/Alaska Native, 0.0% Native Hawaiian/Other Pacific Islander, 0.0% Some other race, 0.0% Two or more races, 0.0% Hispanic of any race (2008-2012 5-year est.); Average household size: 2.57 (2008-2012 5-year est.); Median age: 45.3 (2008-2012 5-year est.); Males per 100 females: 121.6 (2008-2012 5-year est.); Marriage status: 34.6% never married, 45.2% now married, 11.5% widowed, 8.7% divorced (2008-2012 5-year est.); Foreign born: 0.0% (2008-2012 5-year est.); Ancestry (includes multiple ancestries): 36.3% American, 9.7% Irish, 6.2% Dutch, 2.7% Scottish, 1.8% French (2008-2012 5-year est.).
Economy: Homeowner vacancy rate: 0.0%. Rental vacancy rate: 0.0%. (2008-2012 5-year est.); Employment by occupation: 0.0% management, business, and financial, 0.0% computer, engineering, and science, 0.0% education, legal, community service, arts, and media, 15.6% healthcare practitioners, 34.4% service, 0.0% sales and office, 15.6% natural resources, construction, and maintenance, 34.4% production, transportation, and material moving (2008-2012 5-year est.).
Income: Per capita income: $12,162 (2008-2012 5-year est.); Median household income: $30,000 (2008-2012 5-year est.); Average household income: $31,407 (2008-2012 5-year est.); Percent of households with income of $100,000 or more: n/a (2008-2012 5-year est.); Poverty rate: 11.5% (2008-2012 5-year est.).
Education: Percent of population age 25 and over with: High school diploma (including GED) or higher: 70.7% (2008-2012 5-year est.);

Bachelor's degree or higher: 0.0% (2008-2012 5-year est.); Master's degree or higher: 0.0% (2008-2012 5-year est.).
Housing: Homeownership rate: 100.0% (2008-2012 5-year est.); Median home value: $46,700 (2008-2012 5-year est.); Median contract rent: n/a per month (2008-2012 5-year est.); Median year structure built: 1960 (2008-2012 5-year est.).
Health Insurance: 50.4% Private; 43.4% Public; 23.9% None. (2008-2012 5-year est.)
Transportation: Commute to work: 100.0% car, 0.0% public transportation, 0.0% walk, 0.0% work from home (2008-2012 5-year est.); Travel time to work: 21.9% less than 15 minutes, 40.6% 15 to 30 minutes, 15.6% 30 to 45 minutes, 0.0% 45 to 60 minutes, 21.9% 60 minutes or more (2008-2012 5-year est.)

XENIA (village). Covers a land area of 0.537 square miles and a water area of 0 square miles. Located at 38.64° N. Lat; 88.64° W. Long. Elevation is 541 feet.
Population: 424 (1990); 407 (2000); 391 (2010); Density: 1,002.6 persons per square mile (2008-2012 5-year est.); Race: 99.8% White, 0.0% Black/African American, 0.0% Asian, 0.0% American Indian/Alaska Native, 0.0% Native Hawaiian/Other Pacific Islander, 0.2% Some other race, 0.2% Two or more races, 0.9% Hispanic of any race (2008-2012 5-year est.); Average household size: 2.88 (2008-2012 5-year est.); Median age: 31.8 (2008-2012 5-year est.); Males per 100 females: 104.6 (2008-2012 5-year est.); Marriage status: 35.6% never married, 43.1% now married, 7.7% widowed, 13.6% divorced (2008-2012 5-year est.); Foreign born: 0.6% (2008-2012 5-year est.); Ancestry (includes multiple ancestries): 17.7% German, 13.6% Irish, 8.2% English, 5.2% American, 3.0% Dutch (2008-2012 5-year est.).
Economy: Homeowner vacancy rate: 0.0%. Rental vacancy rate: 21.4%. (2008-2012 5-year est.); Employment by occupation: 7.8% management, business, and financial, 2.0% computer, engineering, and science, 5.4% education, legal, community service, arts, and media, 1.5% healthcare practitioners, 24.4% service, 15.6% sales and office, 16.1% natural resources, construction, and maintenance, 27.3% production, transportation, and material moving (2008-2012 5-year est.).
Income: Per capita income: $15,390 (2008-2012 5-year est.); Median household income: $37,639 (2008-2012 5-year est.); Average household income: $42,319 (2008-2012 5-year est.); Percent of households with income of $100,000 or more: 5.9% (2008-2012 5-year est.); Poverty rate: 23.0% (2008-2012 5-year est.).
Education: Percent of population age 25 and over with: High school diploma (including GED) or higher: 83.6% (2008-2012 5-year est.); Bachelor's degree or higher: 7.9% (2008-2012 5-year est.); Master's degree or higher: 0.0% (2008-2012 5-year est.).

School District(s)

Flora CUSD 35 (PK-12)
   2011-12 Enrollment: 1,430 . . . . (618) 662-2412
Housing: Homeownership rate: 82.4% (2008-2012 5-year est.); Median home value: $59,500 (2008-2012 5-year est.); Median contract rent: $287 per month (2008-2012 5-year est.); Median year structure built: 1965 (2008-2012 5-year est.).
Health Insurance: 54.5% Private; 44.8% Public; 14.5% None. (2008-2012 5-year est.)
Transportation: Commute to work: 93.2% car, 0.0% public transportation, 4.4% walk, 2.4% work from home (2008-2012 5-year est.); Travel time to work: 32.5% less than 15 minutes, 40.5% 15 to 30 minutes, 15.0% 30 to 45 minutes, 6.5% 45 to 60 minutes, 5.5% 60 minutes or more (2008-2012 5-year est.)

Clinton County

Located in southern Illinois; bounded on the south by the Kaskaskia River. Covers a land area of 474.085 square miles, a water area of 29.186 square miles, and is located in the Central Time Zone at 38.61° N. Lat., 89.42° W. Long. The county was founded in 1824. County seat is Carlyle.

Clinton County is part of the St. Louis, MO-IL Metropolitan Statistical Area. The entire metro area includes: Bond County, IL; Calhoun County, IL; Clinton County, IL; Jersey County, IL; Macoupin County, IL; Madison County, IL; Monroe County, IL; Saint Clair County, IL; Franklin County, MO; Jefferson County, MO; Lincoln County, MO; Saint Charles County, MO; Saint Louis County, MO; Warren County, MO; Saint Louis city, MO

Population: 33,944 (1990); 35,535 (2000); 37,762 (2010); Race: 94.3% White, 3.5% Black/African American, 0.5% Asian, 0.2% American Indian/Alaska Native, 0.0% Native Hawaiian/Other Pacific Islander, 1.5% Some other race, 1.3% Two or more races, 2.8% Hispanic of any race (2008-2012 5-year est.); Density: 80.3 persons per square mile (2008-2012 5-year est.); Average household size: 2.54 (2008-2012 5-year est.); Median age: 39.4 (2008-2012 5-year est.); Males per 100 females: 105.6 (2008-2012 5-year est.).

Religion: Six largest groups: 53.8% Catholicism, 4.9% Baptist, 3.8% Lutheran, 3.8% Methodist/Pietist, 2.5% Presbyterian-Reformed, 0.7% Holiness (2010)

Economy: Unemployment rate: 5.4% (April 2014); Total civilian labor force: 19,492 (April 2014); Leading industries: 17.8% health care and social assistance; 17.2% retail trade; 11.5% accommodation & food services (2012); Farms: 915 totaling 285,489 acres (2012); Companies that employ 500 or more persons: 0 (2012); Companies that employ 100 to 499 persons: 11 (2012); Companies that employ less than 100 persons: 848 (2012); Black-owned businesses: n/a (2007); Hispanic-owned businesses: n/a (2007); Asian-owned businesses: n/a (2007); Women-owned businesses: n/a (2007); Single-family building permits issued: 81 (2013); Multi-family building permits issued: 0 (2013).

Income: Per capita income: $27,527 (2008-2012 5-year est.); Median household income: $60,661 (2008-2012 5-year est.); Average household income: $71,616 (2008-2012 5-year est.); Percent of households with income of $100,000 or more: 22.6% (2008-2012 5-year est.); Poverty rate: 7.7% (2008-2012 5-year est.); Bankruptcy rate: 2.23% (2013).

Taxes: Total county taxes per capita: $218 (2011); County property taxes per capita: $217 (2011).

Education: Percent of population age 25 and over with: High school diploma (including GED) or higher: 88.4% (2008-2012 5-year est.); Bachelor's degree or higher: 19.8% (2008-2012 5-year est.); Master's degree or higher: 5.9% (2008-2012 5-year est.).

Housing: Homeownership rate: 82.3% (2008-2012 5-year est.); Median home value: $128,700 (2008-2012 5-year est.); Median contract rent: $503 per month (2008-2012 5-year est.); Median year structure built: 1974 (2008-2012 5-year est.)

Health: Birth rate: 113.2 per 10,000 population (2013); Death rate: 97.1 per 10,000 population (2013); Age-adjusted cancer mortality rate: 158.2 deaths per 100,000 population (2011); Number of physicians: 6.0 per 10,000 population (2011); Hospital beds: 15.1 per 10,000 population (2010); Hospital admissions: 497.9 per 10,000 population (2010).

Elections: 2012 Presidential election results: 34.0% Obama, 64.0% Romney

National and State Parks: Hazlet State Park; South Shore State Park

Additional Information Contacts

Clinton County Government . . . . (618) 594-2464
  https://www.clintonco.illinois.gov

Clinton County Communities

ALBERS (village). Covers a land area of 0.846 square miles and a water area of 0 square miles. Located at 38.55° N. Lat; 89.61° W. Long. Elevation is 440 feet.

Population: 700 (1990); 878 (2000); 1,190 (2010); Density: 1,486.4 persons per square mile (2008-2012 5-year est.); Race: 95.9% White, 2.4% Black/African American, 0.7% Asian, 0.0% American Indian/Alaska Native, 0.0% Native Hawaiian/Other Pacific Islander, 1.0% Some other race, 1.0% Two or more races, 2.6% Hispanic of any race (2008-2012 5-year est.); Average household size: 3.01 (2008-2012 5-year est.); Median age: 34.3 (2008-2012 5-year est.); Males per 100 females: 100.5 (2008-2012 5-year est.); Marriage status: 23.4% never married, 66.4% now married, 4.0% widowed, 6.3% divorced (2008-2012 5-year est.); Foreign born: 2.5% (2008-2012 5-year est.); Ancestry (includes multiple ancestries): 58.6% German, 8.4% American, 6.2% Irish, 5.6% English, 2.1% Danish (2008-2012 5-year est.).

Economy: Single-family building permits issued: 3 (2013); Multi-family building permits issued: 0 (2013); Homeowner vacancy rate: 3.2%. Rental vacancy rate: 0.0%. (2008-2012 5-year est.); Employment by occupation: 18.9% management, business, and financial, 8.0% computer, engineering, and science, 7.2% education, legal, community service, arts, and media, 7.3% healthcare practitioners, 10.2% service, 23.6% sales and office, 10.0% natural resources, construction, and maintenance, 14.9% production, transportation, and material moving (2008-2012 5-year est.).

Income: Per capita income: $28,683 (2008-2012 5-year est.); Median household income: $85,341 (2008-2012 5-year est.); Average household income: $86,471 (2008-2012 5-year est.); Percent of households with income of $100,000 or more: 34.7% (2008-2012 5-year est.); Poverty rate: 2.5% (2008-2012 5-year est.).

Education: Percent of population age 25 and over with: High school diploma (including GED) or higher: 92.7% (2008-2012 5-year est.); Bachelor's degree or higher: 24.4% (2008-2012 5-year est.); Master's degree or higher: 6.3% (2008-2012 5-year est.).

School District(s)

Albers SD 63 (PK-08)
  2011-12 Enrollment: 175 . . . . (618) 248-5146

Housing: Homeownership rate: 87.1% (2008-2012 5-year est.); Median home value: $157,800 (2008-2012 5-year est.); Median contract rent: $565 per month (2008-2012 5-year est.); Median year structure built: 1984 (2008-2012 5-year est.).

Health Insurance: 84.6% Private; 21.1% Public; 5.5% None. (2008-2012 5-year est.).

Safety: Violent crime rate: 0.0 per 10,000 population; Property crime rate: 16.7 per 10,000 population (2012).

Transportation: Commute to work: 93.9% car, 0.9% public transportation, 1.8% walk, 1.9% work from home (2008-2012 5-year est.); Travel time to work: 21.9% less than 15 minutes, 19.7% 15 to 30 minutes, 26.9% 30 to 45 minutes, 21.8% 45 to 60 minutes, 9.7% 60 minutes or more (2008-2012 5-year est.)

AVISTON (village). Covers a land area of 1.468 square miles and a water area of 0 square miles. Located at 38.63° N. Lat; 89.61° W. Long. Elevation is 469 feet.

Population: 924 (1990); 1,231 (2000); 1,945 (2010); Density: 1,330.1 persons per square mile (2008-2012 5-year est.); Race: 97.2% White, 0.0% Black/African American, 0.5% Asian, 0.6% American Indian/Alaska Native, 0.0% Native Hawaiian/Other Pacific Islander, 1.7% Some other race, 1.6% Two or more races, 2.7% Hispanic of any race (2008-2012 5-year est.); Average household size: 2.77 (2008-2012 5-year est.); Median age: 34.8 (2008-2012 5-year est.); Males per 100 females: 111.4 (2008-2012 5-year est.); Marriage status: 23.2% never married, 62.3% now married, 8.3% widowed, 6.2% divorced (2008-2012 5-year est.); Foreign born: 1.5% (2008-2012 5-year est.); Ancestry (includes multiple ancestries): 68.9% German, 7.4% American, 5.9% Irish, 4.9% English, 4.5% Italian (2008-2012 5-year est.).

Economy: Single-family building permits issued: 8 (2013); Multi-family building permits issued: 0 (2013); Homeowner vacancy rate: 0.0%. Rental vacancy rate: 0.0%. (2008-2012 5-year est.); Employment by occupation: 17.7% management, business, and financial, 6.5% computer, engineering, and science, 4.7% education, legal, community service, arts, and media, 5.2% healthcare practitioners, 17.2% service, 24.2% sales and office, 7.6% natural resources, construction, and maintenance, 16.8% production, transportation, and material moving (2008-2012 5-year est.).

Income: Per capita income: $28,859 (2008-2012 5-year est.); Median household income: $78,750 (2008-2012 5-year est.); Average household income: $80,300 (2008-2012 5-year est.); Percent of households with income of $100,000 or more: 31.0% (2008-2012 5-year est.); Poverty rate: 3.1% (2008-2012 5-year est.).

Education: Percent of population age 25 and over with: High school diploma (including GED) or higher: 91.5% (2008-2012 5-year est.); Bachelor's degree or higher: 22.9% (2008-2012 5-year est.); Master's degree or higher: 5.5% (2008-2012 5-year est.).

School District(s)

Aviston SD 21 (PK-08)
  2011-12 Enrollment: 387 . . . . (618) 228-7245

Housing: Homeownership rate: 82.4% (2008-2012 5-year est.); Median home value: $157,700 (2008-2012 5-year est.); Median contract rent: $560 per month (2008-2012 5-year est.); Median year structure built: 1984 (2008-2012 5-year est.).

Health Insurance: 87.8% Private; 20.9% Public; 3.6% None. (2008-2012 5-year est.)

Safety: Violent crime rate: 5.1 per 10,000 population; Property crime rate: 10.2 per 10,000 population (2012).

Transportation: Commute to work: 94.9% car, 0.8% public transportation, 1.6% walk, 2.3% work from home (2008-2012 5-year est.); Travel time to work: 35.5% less than 15 minutes, 18.4% 15 to 30 minutes, 20.8% 30 to 45 minutes, 14.3% 45 to 60 minutes, 10.9% 60 minutes or more (2008-2012 5-year est.)

BARTELSO (village). Covers a land area of 0.384 square miles and a water area of 0 square miles. Located at 38.54° N. Lat; 89.47° W. Long. Elevation is 449 feet.

Population: 412 (1990); 593 (2000); 595 (2010); Density: 1,709.7 persons per square mile (2008-2012 5-year est.); Race: 99.5% White, 0.0% Black/African American, 0.0% Asian, 0.0% American Indian/Alaska Native, 0.0% Native Hawaiian/Other Pacific Islander, 0.5% Some other race, 0.5% Two or more races, 0.6% Hispanic of any race (2008-2012 5-year est.); Average household size: 3.11 (2008-2012 5-year est.); Median age: 29.9 (2008-2012 5-year est.); Males per 100 females: 105.6 (2008-2012 5-year est.); Marriage status: 31.7% never married, 62.5% now married, 4.8% widowed, 1.0% divorced (2008-2012 5-year est.); Foreign born: 0.0% (2008-2012 5-year est.); Ancestry (includes multiple ancestries): 82.9% German, 7.6% American, 5.2% Irish, 3.8% English, 1.2% French (2008-2012 5-year est.).

Economy: Homeowner vacancy rate: 4.8%. Rental vacancy rate: 54.2%. (2008-2012 5-year est.); Employment by occupation: 12.5% management, business, and financial, 7.5% computer, engineering, and science, 7.5% education, legal, community service, arts, and media, 5.5% healthcare practitioners, 8.2% service, 26.2% sales and office, 20.4% natural resources, construction, and maintenance, 12.2% production, transportation, and material moving (2008-2012 5-year est.).

Income: Per capita income: $26,835 (2008-2012 5-year est.); Median household income: $76,875 (2008-2012 5-year est.); Average household income: $79,401 (2008-2012 5-year est.); Percent of households with income of $100,000 or more: 21.8% (2008-2012 5-year est.); Poverty rate: 0.9% (2008-2012 5-year est.).

Education: Percent of population age 25 and over with: High school diploma (including GED) or higher: 92.5% (2008-2012 5-year est.); Bachelor's degree or higher: 21.4% (2008-2012 5-year est.); Master's degree or higher: 7.2% (2008-2012 5-year est.).

School District(s)

Bartelso SD 57 (PK-08)
    2011-12 Enrollment: 144 . . . . (618) 765-2164
Housing: Homeownership rate: 94.8% (2008-2012 5-year est.); Median home value: $145,800 (2008-2012 5-year est.); Median contract rent: $431 per month (2008-2012 5-year est.); Median year structure built: 1970 (2008-2012 5-year est.).
Health Insurance: 92.7% Private; 15.2% Public; 1.4% None. (2008-2012 5-year est.)
Transportation: Commute to work: 98.8% car, 0.0% public transportation, 0.2% walk, 1.0% work from home (2008-2012 5-year est.); Travel time to work: 20.7% less than 15 minutes, 40.3% 15 to 30 minutes, 20.7% 30 to 45 minutes, 8.8% 45 to 60 minutes, 9.6% 60 minutes or more (2008-2012 5-year est.)

BECKEMEYER (village). Covers a land area of 0.613 square miles and a water area of 0 square miles. Located at 38.61° N. Lat; 89.43° W. Long. Elevation is 459 feet.

Population: 1,070 (1990); 1,043 (2000); 1,040 (2010); Density: 1,483.7 persons per square mile (2008-2012 5-year est.); Race: 94.5% White, 0.0% Black/African American, 2.8% Asian, 0.0% American Indian/Alaska Native, 0.0% Native Hawaiian/Other Pacific Islander, 2.7% Some other race, 2.8% Two or more races, 4.3% Hispanic of any race (2008-2012 5-year est.); Average household size: 2.28 (2008-2012 5-year est.); Median age: 37.3 (2008-2012 5-year est.); Males per 100 females: 89.8 (2008-2012 5-year est.); Marriage status: 32.8% never married, 48.1% now married, 7.3% widowed, 11.8% divorced (2008-2012 5-year est.); Foreign born: 2.2% (2008-2012 5-year est.); Ancestry (includes multiple ancestries): 54.7% German, 18.6% Irish, 5.7% Polish, 4.6% English, 3.5% Swiss (2008-2012 5-year est.).

Economy: Single-family building permits issued: 1 (2013); Multi-family building permits issued: 0 (2013); Homeowner vacancy rate: 0.0%. Rental vacancy rate: 0.0%. (2008-2012 5-year est.); Employment by occupation: 2.3% management, business, and financial, 6.0% computer, engineering, and science, 5.2% education, legal, community service, arts, and media, 4.8% healthcare practitioners, 31.0% service, 20.5% sales and office, 8.7% natural resources, construction, and maintenance, 21.7% production, transportation, and material moving (2008-2012 5-year est.).

Income: Per capita income: $24,081 (2008-2012 5-year est.); Median household income: $46,793 (2008-2012 5-year est.); Average household income: $53,053 (2008-2012 5-year est.); Percent of households with income of $100,000 or more: 10.6% (2008-2012 5-year est.); Poverty rate: 6.3% (2008-2012 5-year est.).

Education: Percent of population age 25 and over with: High school diploma (including GED) or higher: 87.0% (2008-2012 5-year est.); Bachelor's degree or higher: 10.6% (2008-2012 5-year est.); Master's degree or higher: 2.9% (2008-2012 5-year est.).

School District(s)

Breese SD 12 (PK-08)
    2011-12 Enrollment: 639 . . . . (618) 526-7128
Housing: Homeownership rate: 89.0% (2008-2012 5-year est.); Median home value: $85,800 (2008-2012 5-year est.); Median contract rent: $569 per month (2008-2012 5-year est.); Median year structure built: 1971 (2008-2012 5-year est.).
Health Insurance: 68.0% Private; 39.3% Public; 11.8% None. (2008-2012 5-year est.)
Transportation: Commute to work: 95.1% car, 1.0% public transportation, 0.0% walk, 3.9% work from home (2008-2012 5-year est.); Travel time to work: 47.5% less than 15 minutes, 23.3% 15 to 30 minutes, 13.1% 30 to 45 minutes, 7.9% 45 to 60 minutes, 8.1% 60 minutes or more (2008-2012 5-year est.)

BREESE (city). Covers a land area of 2.618 square miles and a water area of 0.025 square miles. Located at 38.61° N. Lat; 89.52° W. Long. Elevation is 453 feet.

History: Breese was named for Judge Sidney Breese (1800-1876), an Illinois jurist and resident of the city. King Edward VII, then Prince of Wales, visited Breese in 1860.

Population: 3,567 (1990); 4,048 (2000); 4,442 (2010); Density: 1,835.2 persons per square mile (2008-2012 5-year est.); Race: 98.6% White, 0.2% Black/African American, 0.2% Asian, 0.0% American Indian/Alaska Native, 0.0% Native Hawaiian/Other Pacific Islander, 1.0% Some other race, 1.0% Two or more races, 2.5% Hispanic of any race (2008-2012 5-year est.); Average household size: 2.60 (2008-2012 5-year est.); Median age: 36.0 (2008-2012 5-year est.); Males per 100 females: 89.3 (2008-2012 5-year est.); Marriage status: 25.5% never married, 55.2% now married, 10.7% widowed, 8.6% divorced (2008-2012 5-year est.); Foreign born: 0.2% (2008-2012 5-year est.); Ancestry (includes multiple ancestries): 62.2% German, 11.3% Irish, 7.8% American, 2.5% Italian, 2.1% English (2008-2012 5-year est.).

Economy: Single-family building permits issued: 12 (2013); Multi-family building permits issued: 0 (2013); Homeowner vacancy rate: 0.8%. Rental vacancy rate: 11.1%. (2008-2012 5-year est.); Employment by occupation: 7.6% management, business, and financial, 5.1% computer, engineering, and science, 7.6% education, legal, community service, arts, and media, 6.5% healthcare practitioners, 21.2% service, 22.9% sales and office, 7.7% natural resources, construction, and maintenance, 21.5% production, transportation, and material moving (2008-2012 5-year est.).

Income: Per capita income: $29,483 (2008-2012 5-year est.); Median household income: $64,516 (2008-2012 5-year est.); Average household income: $76,398 (2008-2012 5-year est.); Percent of households with income of $100,000 or more: 28.5% (2008-2012 5-year est.); Poverty rate: 8.7% (2008-2012 5-year est.).

Education: Percent of population age 25 and over with: High school diploma (including GED) or higher: 91.2% (2008-2012 5-year est.); Bachelor's degree or higher: 16.9% (2008-2012 5-year est.); Master's degree or higher: 5.0% (2008-2012 5-year est.).

School District(s)

Breese SD 12 (PK-08)
    2011-12 Enrollment: 639 . . . . (618) 526-7128
Central CHSD 71 (09-12)
    2011-12 Enrollment: 594 . . . . (618) 526-4510
Saint Rose SD 14-15 (PK-08)
    2011-12 Enrollment: 170 . . . . (618) 526-7484
Housing: Homeownership rate: 79.7% (2008-2012 5-year est.); Median home value: $137,700 (2008-2012 5-year est.); Median contract rent: $548 per month (2008-2012 5-year est.); Median year structure built: 1971 (2008-2012 5-year est.).
Health Insurance: 81.7% Private; 27.1% Public; 4.1% None. (2008-2012 5-year est.)
Hospitals: St. Joseph's Hospital (85 beds)
Safety: Violent crime rate: 13.4 per 10,000 population; Property crime rate: 85.1 per 10,000 population (2012).
Transportation: Commute to work: 96.0% car, 1.0% public transportation, 1.7% walk, 0.8% work from home (2008-2012 5-year est.); Travel time to work: 44.3% less than 15 minutes, 9.0% 15 to 30 minutes, 15.5% 30 to 45 minutes, 12.0% 45 to 60 minutes, 19.2% 60 minutes or more (2008-2012 5-year est.)

CARLYLE (city). County seat. Covers a land area of 3.368 square miles and a water area of <.001 square miles. Located at 38.62° N. Lat; 89.38° W. Long. Elevation is 456 feet.

History: Carlyle was sited on the location of John Hill's Fort, built in the early 1800's. Carlyle developed as the seat of Clinton County.

Population: 3,474 (1990); 3,406 (2000); 3,281 (2010); Density: 969.5 persons per square mile (2008-2012 5-year est.); Race: 97.3% White, 1.5% Black/African American, 0.4% Asian, 0.0% American Indian/Alaska Native, 0.0% Native Hawaiian/Other Pacific Islander, 0.8% Some other race, 0.8% Two or more races, 1.0% Hispanic of any race (2008-2012 5-year est.); Average household size: 2.36 (2008-2012 5-year est.); Median age: 42.7 (2008-2012 5-year est.); Males per 100 females: 78.7 (2008-2012 5-year est.); Marriage status: 24.1% never married, 53.7% now married, 9.8% widowed, 12.5% divorced (2008-2012 5-year est.); Foreign born: 0.4% (2008-2012 5-year est.); Ancestry (includes multiple ancestries): 52.9% German, 18.2% Irish, 8.8% English, 5.3% American, 2.1% Italian (2008-2012 5-year est.).

Economy: Single-family building permits issued: 3 (2013); Multi-family building permits issued: 0 (2013); Homeowner vacancy rate: 0.0%. Rental vacancy rate: 12.4%. (2008-2012 5-year est.); Employment by occupation: 11.1% management, business, and financial, 0.0% computer, engineering, and science, 5.7% education, legal, community service, arts, and media, 3.3% healthcare practitioners, 11.0% service, 37.2% sales and office, 14.5% natural resources, construction, and maintenance, 17.2% production, transportation, and material moving (2008-2012 5-year est.).

Income: Per capita income: $31,601 (2008-2012 5-year est.); Median household income: $55,417 (2008-2012 5-year est.); Average household income: $75,759 (2008-2012 5-year est.); Percent of households with income of $100,000 or more: 22.3% (2008-2012 5-year est.); Poverty rate: 8.2% (2008-2012 5-year est.).

Education: Percent of population age 25 and over with: High school diploma (including GED) or higher: 84.2% (2008-2012 5-year est.); Bachelor's degree or higher: 21.8% (2008-2012 5-year est.); Master's degree or higher: 7.0% (2008-2012 5-year est.).

School District(s)
Carlyle CUSD 1 (PK-12)
 2011-12 Enrollment: 1,233 . . . . (618) 594-8283

Housing: Homeownership rate: 69.5% (2008-2012 5-year est.); Median home value: $121,000 (2008-2012 5-year est.); Median contract rent: $505 per month (2008-2012 5-year est.); Median year structure built: 1968 (2008-2012 5-year est.).

Health Insurance: 71.8% Private; 34.7% Public; 11.6% None. (2008-2012 5-year est.)

Safety: Violent crime rate: 21.2 per 10,000 population; Property crime rate: 211.7 per 10,000 population (2012).

Transportation: Commute to work: 95.5% car, 0.0% public transportation, 2.7% walk, 1.8% work from home (2008-2012 5-year est.); Travel time to work: 42.1% less than 15 minutes, 24.0% 15 to 30 minutes, 15.0% 30 to 45 minutes, 14.8% 45 to 60 minutes, 4.1% 60 minutes or more (2008-2012 5-year est.)

Additional Information Contacts
City of Carlyle . . . . (618) 594-2468
 http://carlylelake.com

DAMIANSVILLE (village). Covers a land area of 0.822 square miles and a water area of 0 square miles. Located at 38.51° N. Lat; 89.62° W. Long. Elevation is 430 feet.

Population: 379 (1990); 368 (2000); 491 (2010); Density: 640.2 persons per square mile (2008-2012 5-year est.); Race: 91.1% White, 2.3% Black/African American, 1.3% Asian, 0.8% American Indian/Alaska Native, 0.0% Native Hawaiian/Other Pacific Islander, 4.5% Some other race, 1.1% Two or more races, 11.8% Hispanic of any race (2008-2012 5-year est.); Average household size: 2.42 (2008-2012 5-year est.); Median age: 41.0 (2008-2012 5-year est.); Males per 100 females: 97.7 (2008-2012 5-year est.); Marriage status: 32.5% never married, 56.1% now married, 5.9% widowed, 5.5% divorced (2008-2012 5-year est.); Foreign born: 1.3% (2008-2012 5-year est.); Ancestry (includes multiple ancestries): 54.8% German, 9.7% French, 9.7% American, 4.8% Irish, 4.8% English (2008-2012 5-year est.).

Economy: Single-family building permits issued: 1 (2013); Multi-family building permits issued: 0 (2013); Homeowner vacancy rate: 0.0%. Rental vacancy rate: 0.0%. (2008-2012 5-year est.); Employment by occupation: 13.6% management, business, and financial, 2.2% computer, engineering, and science, 7.9% education, legal, community service, arts, and media, 6.0% healthcare practitioners, 19.6% service, 18.6% sales and office,

16.1% natural resources, construction, and maintenance, 16.1% production, transportation, and material moving (2008-2012 5-year est.).

Income: Per capita income: $26,981 (2008-2012 5-year est.); Median household income: $61,638 (2008-2012 5-year est.); Average household income: $68,846 (2008-2012 5-year est.); Percent of households with income of $100,000 or more: 17.9% (2008-2012 5-year est.); Poverty rate: 11.7% (2008-2012 5-year est.).

Education: Percent of population age 25 and over with: High school diploma (including GED) or higher: 90.9% (2008-2012 5-year est.); Bachelor's degree or higher: 19.4% (2008-2012 5-year est.); Master's degree or higher: 2.7% (2008-2012 5-year est.).

School District(s)
Damiansville SD 62 (PK-08)
 2011-12 Enrollment: 120 . . . . (618) 248-5188

Housing: Homeownership rate: 81.7% (2008-2012 5-year est.); Median home value: $124,600 (2008-2012 5-year est.); Median contract rent: $605 per month (2008-2012 5-year est.); Median year structure built: 1976 (2008-2012 5-year est.).

Health Insurance: 85.7% Private; 18.5% Public; 9.0% None. (2008-2012 5-year est.)

Transportation: Commute to work: 90.8% car, 1.6% public transportation, 6.6% walk, 1.0% work from home (2008-2012 5-year est.); Travel time to work: 24.2% less than 15 minutes, 44.0% 15 to 30 minutes, 20.5% 30 to 45 minutes, 7.3% 45 to 60 minutes, 4.0% 60 minutes or more (2008-2012 5-year est.)

GERMANTOWN (village). Covers a land area of 0.867 square miles and a water area of 0 square miles. Located at 38.56° N. Lat; 89.54° W. Long. Elevation is 430 feet.

Population: 1,167 (1990); 1,118 (2000); 1,269 (2010); Density: 1,382.7 persons per square mile (2008-2012 5-year est.); Race: 99.7% White, 0.3% Black/African American, 0.0% Asian, 0.0% American Indian/Alaska Native, 0.0% Native Hawaiian/Other Pacific Islander, 0.0% Some other race, 0.0% Two or more races, 3.5% Hispanic of any race (2008-2012 5-year est.); Average household size: 2.44 (2008-2012 5-year est.); Median age: 43.0 (2008-2012 5-year est.); Males per 100 females: 110.7 (2008-2012 5-year est.); Marriage status: 31.0% never married, 56.4% now married, 7.2% widowed, 5.4% divorced (2008-2012 5-year est.); Foreign born: 2.2% (2008-2012 5-year est.); Ancestry (includes multiple ancestries): 74.5% German, 5.8% American, 4.2% Irish, 2.4% English, 2.3% French (2008-2012 5-year est.).

Economy: Single-family building permits issued: 1 (2013); Multi-family building permits issued: 0 (2013); Homeowner vacancy rate: 0.0%. Rental vacancy rate: 0.0%. (2008-2012 5-year est.); Employment by occupation: 13.3% management, business, and financial, 3.6% computer, engineering, and science, 5.8% education, legal, community service, arts, and media, 6.1% healthcare practitioners, 17.7% service, 24.0% sales and office, 16.5% natural resources, construction, and maintenance, 13.1% production, transportation, and material moving (2008-2012 5-year est.).

Income: Per capita income: $30,485 (2008-2012 5-year est.); Median household income: $59,875 (2008-2012 5-year est.); Average household income: $73,213 (2008-2012 5-year est.); Percent of households with income of $100,000 or more: 25.1% (2008-2012 5-year est.); Poverty rate: 4.2% (2008-2012 5-year est.).

Education: Percent of population age 25 and over with: High school diploma (including GED) or higher: 89.9% (2008-2012 5-year est.); Bachelor's degree or higher: 19.2% (2008-2012 5-year est.); Master's degree or higher: 5.3% (2008-2012 5-year est.).

School District(s)
Germantown SD 60 (PK-08)
 2011-12 Enrollment: 273 . . . . (618) 523-4253

Housing: Homeownership rate: 87.9% (2008-2012 5-year est.); Median home value: $144,700 (2008-2012 5-year est.); Median contract rent: $407 per month (2008-2012 5-year est.); Median year structure built: 1969 (2008-2012 5-year est.).

Health Insurance: 89.5% Private; 24.5% Public; 2.5% None. (2008-2012 5-year est.)

Safety: Violent crime rate: 0.0 per 10,000 population; Property crime rate: 70.4 per 10,000 population (2012).

Transportation: Commute to work: 94.5% car, 0.0% public transportation, 2.5% walk, 3.0% work from home (2008-2012 5-year est.); Travel time to work: 31.5% less than 15 minutes, 24.0% 15 to 30 minutes, 16.9% 30 to 45 minutes, 17.1% 45 to 60 minutes, 10.5% 60 minutes or more (2008-2012 5-year est.)

HOFFMAN (village). Covers a land area of 0.507 square miles and a water area of 0 square miles. Located at 38.54° N. Lat; 89.26° W. Long. Elevation is 456 feet.

Population: 492 (1990); 460 (2000); 508 (2010); Density: 1,181.7 persons per square mile (2008-2012 5-year est.); Race: 92.3% White, 4.0% Black/African American, 3.0% Asian, 0.0% American Indian/Alaska Native, 0.0% Native Hawaiian/Other Pacific Islander, 0.7% Some other race, 0.7% Two or more races, 0.0% Hispanic of any race (2008-2012 5-year est.); Average household size: 2.80 (2008-2012 5-year est.); Median age: 32.1 (2008-2012 5-year est.); Males per 100 females: 111.7 (2008-2012 5-year est.); Marriage status: 28.2% never married, 56.2% now married, 3.0% widowed, 12.6% divorced (2008-2012 5-year est.); Foreign born: 2.7% (2008-2012 5-year est.); Ancestry (includes multiple ancestries): 50.6% German, 10.9% Irish, 7.2% American, 4.3% Polish, 2.8% English (2008-2012 5-year est.).
Economy: Single-family building permits issued: 0 (2013); Multi-family building permits issued: 0 (2013); Homeowner vacancy rate: 2.1%. Rental vacancy rate: 38.1%. (2008-2012 5-year est.); Employment by occupation: 11.6% management, business, and financial, 1.8% computer, engineering, and science, 9.1% education, legal, community service, arts, and media, 8.5% healthcare practitioners, 20.1% service, 21.3% sales and office, 5.5% natural resources, construction, and maintenance, 22.2% production, transportation, and material moving (2008-2012 5-year est.).
Income: Per capita income: $25,258 (2008-2012 5-year est.); Median household income: $60,962 (2008-2012 5-year est.); Average household income: $68,908 (2008-2012 5-year est.); Percent of households with income of $100,000 or more: 17.8% (2008-2012 5-year est.); Poverty rate: 2.8% (2008-2012 5-year est.).
Education: Percent of population age 25 and over with: High school diploma (including GED) or higher: 86.2% (2008-2012 5-year est.); Bachelor's degree or higher: 19.6% (2008-2012 5-year est.); Master's degree or higher: 4.0% (2008-2012 5-year est.).
Housing: Homeownership rate: 87.9% (2008-2012 5-year est.); Median home value: $85,800 (2008-2012 5-year est.); Median contract rent: $419 per month (2008-2012 5-year est.); Median year structure built: 1962 (2008-2012 5-year est.).
Health Insurance: 85.6% Private; 12.9% Public; 9.0% None. (2008-2012 5-year est.)
Transportation: Commute to work: 84.7% car, 0.3% public transportation, 8.9% walk, 5.5% work from home (2008-2012 5-year est.); Travel time to work: 43.5% less than 15 minutes, 36.0% 15 to 30 minutes, 6.5% 30 to 45 minutes, 7.5% 45 to 60 minutes, 6.5% 60 minutes or more (2008-2012 5-year est.)

HUEY (village). Covers a land area of 0.216 square miles and a water area of 0 square miles. Located at 38.61° N. Lat; 89.29° W. Long. Elevation is 453 feet.

Population: 210 (1990); 196 (2000); 169 (2010); Density: 936.5 persons per square mile (2008-2012 5-year est.); Race: 99.0% White, 0.0% Black/African American, 0.0% Asian, 0.0% American Indian/Alaska Native, 0.0% Native Hawaiian/Other Pacific Islander, 1.0% Some other race, 1.0% Two or more races, 0.0% Hispanic of any race (2008-2012 5-year est.); Average household size: 2.53 (2008-2012 5-year est.); Median age: 42.1 (2008-2012 5-year est.); Males per 100 females: 85.3 (2008-2012 5-year est.); Marriage status: 29.7% never married, 48.4% now married, 11.0% widowed, 11.0% divorced (2008-2012 5-year est.); Foreign born: 0.0% (2008-2012 5-year est.); Ancestry (includes multiple ancestries): 44.6% German, 6.9% English, 6.4% American, 5.4% Polish, 5.4% Slovak (2008-2012 5-year est.).
Economy: Single-family building permits issued: 0 (2013); Multi-family building permits issued: 0 (2013); Homeowner vacancy rate: 0.0%. Rental vacancy rate: 0.0%. (2008-2012 5-year est.); Employment by occupation: 0.0% management, business, and financial, 3.4% computer, engineering, and science, 19.0% education, legal, community service, arts, and media, 5.2% healthcare practitioners, 22.4% service, 22.4% sales and office, 3.4% natural resources, construction, and maintenance, 24.1% production, transportation, and material moving (2008-2012 5-year est.).
Income: Per capita income: $21,701 (2008-2012 5-year est.); Median household income: $43,750 (2008-2012 5-year est.); Average household income: $55,035 (2008-2012 5-year est.); Percent of households with income of $100,000 or more: 10.1% (2008-2012 5-year est.); Poverty rate: 16.8% (2008-2012 5-year est.).
Education: Percent of population age 25 and over with: High school diploma (including GED) or higher: 90.1% (2008-2012 5-year est.);

Bachelor's degree or higher: 14.9% (2008-2012 5-year est.); Master's degree or higher: 1.4% (2008-2012 5-year est.).
Housing: Homeownership rate: 85.0% (2008-2012 5-year est.); Median home value: $84,200 (2008-2012 5-year est.); Median contract rent: $525 per month (2008-2012 5-year est.); Median year structure built: 1960 (2008-2012 5-year est.).
Health Insurance: 67.7% Private; 29.8% Public; 13.6% None. (2008-2012 5-year est.)
Transportation: Commute to work: 94.9% car, 0.0% public transportation, 5.1% walk, 0.0% work from home (2008-2012 5-year est.); Travel time to work: 25.4% less than 15 minutes, 36.4% 15 to 30 minutes, 21.2% 30 to 45 minutes, 6.8% 45 to 60 minutes, 10.2% 60 minutes or more (2008-2012 5-year est.)

NEW BADEN (village). Covers a land area of 1.599 square miles and a water area of <.001 square miles. Located at 38.54° N. Lat; 89.70° W. Long. Elevation is 459 feet.

Population: 2,602 (1990); 3,001 (2000); 3,349 (2010); Density: 2,004.2 persons per square mile (2008-2012 5-year est.); Race: 88.0% White, 6.6% Black/African American, 0.8% Asian, 1.2% American Indian/Alaska Native, 0.0% Native Hawaiian/Other Pacific Islander, 3.4% Some other race, 3.3% Two or more races, 2.6% Hispanic of any race (2008-2012 5-year est.); Average household size: 2.67 (2008-2012 5-year est.); Median age: 39.1 (2008-2012 5-year est.); Males per 100 females: 100.8 (2008-2012 5-year est.); Marriage status: 30.5% never married, 56.0% now married, 6.3% widowed, 7.3% divorced (2008-2012 5-year est.); Foreign born: 2.4% (2008-2012 5-year est.); Ancestry (includes multiple ancestries): 42.7% German, 13.8% English, 7.1% Irish, 3.3% American, 3.1% Italian (2008-2012 5-year est.).
Economy: Single-family building permits issued: 6 (2013); Multi-family building permits issued: 0 (2013); Homeowner vacancy rate: 0.0%. Rental vacancy rate: 0.0%. (2008-2012 5-year est.); Employment by occupation: 11.6% management, business, and financial, 6.3% computer, engineering, and science, 7.2% education, legal, community service, arts, and media, 5.0% healthcare practitioners, 28.0% service, 26.0% sales and office, 8.1% natural resources, construction, and maintenance, 7.8% production, transportation, and material moving (2008-2012 5-year est.).
Income: Per capita income: $25,703 (2008-2012 5-year est.); Median household income: $62,115 (2008-2012 5-year est.); Average household income: $67,378 (2008-2012 5-year est.); Percent of households with income of $100,000 or more: 15.6% (2008-2012 5-year est.); Poverty rate: 11.9% (2008-2012 5-year est.).
Education: Percent of population age 25 and over with: High school diploma (including GED) or higher: 86.8% (2008-2012 5-year est.); Bachelor's degree or higher: 22.6% (2008-2012 5-year est.); Master's degree or higher: 6.6% (2008-2012 5-year est.).

School District(s)

Wesclin CUSD 3 (PK-12)
    2011-12 Enrollment: 1,371 . . . . (618) 224-7583
Housing: Homeownership rate: 79.6% (2008-2012 5-year est.); Median home value: $137,800 (2008-2012 5-year est.); Median contract rent: $564 per month (2008-2012 5-year est.); Median year structure built: 1976 (2008-2012 5-year est.).
Health Insurance: 79.3% Private; 29.2% Public; 6.3% None. (2008-2012 5-year est.)
Transportation: Commute to work: 89.6% car, 0.0% public transportation, 6.1% walk, 1.6% work from home (2008-2012 5-year est.); Travel time to work: 31.2% less than 15 minutes, 38.8% 15 to 30 minutes, 20.0% 30 to 45 minutes, 7.2% 45 to 60 minutes, 2.8% 60 minutes or more (2008-2012 5-year est.)

NEW MEMPHIS (unincorporated postal area)
Zip Code: 62266
    Covers a land area of 1.134 square miles and a water area of 0 square miles. Located at 38.48° N. Lat; 89.67° W. Long. Elevation is 420 feet.
    Population: 254 (2010); Density: 224.0 persons per square mile (2010); Race: 90.2% White, 0.4% Black/African American, 0.4% Asian, 0.8% American Indian/Alaska Native, 0.0% Native Hawaiian/Other Pacific Islander, 8.2% Some other race, 3.9% Two or more races, 14.2% Hispanic of any race (2010); Average household size: 2.79 (2010); Median age: 33.3 (2010); Males per 100 females: 111.7 (2010); Homeownership rate: 71.5% (2010)

TRENTON (city). Covers a land area of 1.312 square miles and a water area of 0 square miles. Located at 38.61° N. Lat; 89.68° W. Long. Elevation is 495 feet.

History: Incorporated 1865.

Population: 2,481 (1990); 2,610 (2000); 2,715 (2010); Density: 2,070.8 persons per square mile (2008-2012 5-year est.); Race: 97.3% White, 0.3% Black/African American, 0.7% Asian, 0.2% American Indian/Alaska Native, 0.0% Native Hawaiian/Other Pacific Islander, 1.5% Some other race, 0.2% Two or more races, 3.6% Hispanic of any race (2008-2012 5-year est.); Average household size: 2.31 (2008-2012 5-year est.); Median age: 42.8 (2008-2012 5-year est.); Males per 100 females: 93.4 (2008-2012 5-year est.); Marriage status: 22.2% never married, 58.0% now married, 9.6% widowed, 10.2% divorced (2008-2012 5-year est.); Foreign born: 2.0% (2008-2012 5-year est.); Ancestry (includes multiple ancestries): 48.6% German, 14.4% Irish, 12.7% English, 6.7% American, 5.4% French (2008-2012 5-year est.).

Economy: Single-family building permits issued: 2 (2013); Multi-family building permits issued: 0 (2013); Homeowner vacancy rate: 0.0%. Rental vacancy rate: 0.0%. (2008-2012 5-year est.); Employment by occupation: 13.9% management, business, and financial, 5.5% computer, engineering, and science, 10.4% education, legal, community service, arts, and media, 7.6% healthcare practitioners, 13.4% service, 22.6% sales and office, 13.1% natural resources, construction, and maintenance, 13.4% production, transportation, and material moving (2008-2012 5-year est.).

Income: Per capita income: $31,322 (2008-2012 5-year est.); Median household income: $65,038 (2008-2012 5-year est.); Average household income: $71,517 (2008-2012 5-year est.); Percent of households with income of $100,000 or more: 22.2% (2008-2012 5-year est.); Poverty rate: 3.8% (2008-2012 5-year est.).

Education: Percent of population age 25 and over with: High school diploma (including GED) or higher: 92.1% (2008-2012 5-year est.); Bachelor's degree or higher: 30.4% (2008-2012 5-year est.); Master's degree or higher: 7.5% (2008-2012 5-year est.).

School District(s)

Wesclin CUSD 3 (PK-12)

    2011-12 Enrollment: 1,371 . . . . (618) 224-7583

Housing: Homeownership rate: 78.8% (2008-2012 5-year est.); Median home value: $129,000 (2008-2012 5-year est.); Median contract rent: $588 per month (2008-2012 5-year est.); Median year structure built: 1963 (2008-2012 5-year est.).

Health Insurance: 90.8% Private; 25.8% Public; 5.7% None. (2008-2012 5-year est.)

Transportation: Commute to work: 95.0% car, 0.5% public transportation, 0.4% walk, 3.1% work from home (2008-2012 5-year est.); Travel time to work: 29.5% less than 15 minutes, 30.2% 15 to 30 minutes, 23.8% 30 to 45 minutes, 8.4% 45 to 60 minutes, 8.0% 60 minutes or more (2008-2012 5-year est.)

Additional Information Contacts

Trenton Chamber of Commerce . . . .
    http://www.trenton-ilchamber.com

WAMAC (city). Covers a land area of 1.406 square miles and a water area of 0.021 square miles. Located at 38.49° N. Lat; 89.15° W. Long. Elevation is 499 feet.

Population: 1,501 (1990); 1,378 (2000); 1,185 (2010); Density: 1,035.2 persons per square mile (2008-2012 5-year est.); Race: 89.7% White, 4.9% Black/African American, 0.0% Asian, 0.3% American Indian/Alaska Native, 0.0% Native Hawaiian/Other Pacific Islander, 5.1% Some other race, 5.1% Two or more races, 2.2% Hispanic of any race (2008-2012 5-year est.); Average household size: 2.48 (2008-2012 5-year est.); Median age: 38.1 (2008-2012 5-year est.); Males per 100 females: 98.2 (2008-2012 5-year est.); Marriage status: 27.9% never married, 44.6% now married, 8.7% widowed, 18.8% divorced (2008-2012 5-year est.); Foreign born: 0.2% (2008-2012 5-year est.); Ancestry (includes multiple ancestries): 19.6% German, 15.0% Irish, 9.3% American, 7.2% English, 3.8% Italian (2008-2012 5-year est.).

Economy: Single-family building permits issued: 0 (2013); Multi-family building permits issued: 0 (2013); Homeowner vacancy rate: 1.0%. Rental vacancy rate: 7.8%. (2008-2012 5-year est.); Employment by occupation: 2.6% management, business, and financial, 0.6% computer, engineering, and science, 4.1% education, legal, community service, arts, and media, 6.2% healthcare practitioners, 32.2% service, 13.7% sales and office, 9.0% natural resources, construction, and maintenance, 31.5% production, transportation, and material moving (2008-2012 5-year est.).

Income: Per capita income: $13,908 (2008-2012 5-year est.); Median household income: $26,285 (2008-2012 5-year est.); Average household income: $34,655 (2008-2012 5-year est.); Percent of households with income of $100,000 or more: 3.2% (2008-2012 5-year est.); Poverty rate: 30.5% (2008-2012 5-year est.).

Education: Percent of population age 25 and over with: High school diploma (including GED) or higher: 73.2% (2008-2012 5-year est.); Bachelor's degree or higher: 2.5% (2008-2012 5-year est.); Master's degree or higher: 1.5% (2008-2012 5-year est.).

Housing: Homeownership rate: 67.3% (2008-2012 5-year est.); Median home value: $24,400 (2008-2012 5-year est.); Median contract rent: $397 per month (2008-2012 5-year est.); Median year structure built: 1970 (2008-2012 5-year est.).

Health Insurance: 32.6% Private; 61.2% Public; 15.5% None. (2008-2012 5-year est.)

Transportation: Commute to work: 87.7% car, 4.2% public transportation, 3.7% walk, 1.5% work from home (2008-2012 5-year est.); Travel time to work: 51.1% less than 15 minutes, 20.8% 15 to 30 minutes, 14.7% 30 to 45 minutes, 4.2% 45 to 60 minutes, 9.2% 60 minutes or more (2008-2012 5-year est.)

Coles County

Located in east central Illinois; drained by the Kaskaskia, Embarrass, and Little Wabash Rivers; includes Paradise Lake. Covers a land area of 508.290 square miles, a water area of 1.786 square miles, and is located in the Central Time Zone at 39.51° N. Lat., 88.22° W. Long. The county was founded in 1830. County seat is Charleston.

Coles County is part of the Charleston-Mattoon, IL Micropolitan Statistical Area. The entire metro area includes: Coles County, IL; Cumberland County, IL

Weather Station: Charleston   Elevation: 680 feet

	Jan	Feb	Mar	Apr	May	Jun	Jul	Aug	Sep	Oct	Nov	Dec
High	37	41	53	65	75	84	87	85	79	67	53	40
Low	21	24	33	44	53	62	66	64	56	45	36	24
Precip	2.4	2.4	3.0	4.2	4.5	3.9	4.2	3.3	3.2	3.9	4.0	3.1
Snow	8.5	3.8	2.1	0.2	tr	0.0	0.0	0.0	0.0	tr	1.0	5.1

High and Low temperatures in degrees Fahrenheit; Precipitation and Snow in inches

Population: 51,644 (1990); 53,196 (2000); 53,873 (2010); Race: 93.2% White, 3.8% Black/African American, 0.9% Asian, 0.1% American Indian/Alaska Native, 0.0% Native Hawaiian/Other Pacific Islander, 2.0% Some other race, 1.7% Two or more races, 2.2% Hispanic of any race (2008-2012 5-year est.); Density: 105.6 persons per square mile (2008-2012 5-year est.); Average household size: 2.31 (2008-2012 5-year est.); Median age: 32.3 (2008-2012 5-year est.); Males per 100 females: 92.5 (2008-2012 5-year est.).

Religion: Six largest groups: 13.4% Baptist, 7.2% Catholicism, 7.0% Non-denominational Protestant, 4.3% Lutheran, 4.2% Methodist/Pietist, 2.4% Presbyterian-Reformed (2010)

Economy: Unemployment rate: 6.0% (April 2014); Total civilian labor force: 26,490 (April 2014); Leading industries: 23.2% health care and social assistance; 15.5% retail trade; 15.4% manufacturing (2012); Farms: 704 totaling 266,773 acres (2012); Companies that employ 500 or more persons: 2 (2012); Companies that employ 100 to 499 persons: 25 (2012); Companies that employ less than 100 persons: 1,179 (2012); Black-owned businesses: 101 (2007); Hispanic-owned businesses: n/a (2007); Asian-owned businesses: n/a (2007); Women-owned businesses: 992 (2007); Single-family building permits issued: 12 (2013); Multi-family building permits issued: 17 (2013).

Income: Per capita income: $22,263 (2008-2012 5-year est.); Median household income: $38,088 (2008-2012 5-year est.); Average household income: $54,393 (2008-2012 5-year est.); Percent of households with income of $100,000 or more: 12.2% (2008-2012 5-year est.); Poverty rate: 22.0% (2008-2012 5-year est.); Bankruptcy rate: 3.17% (2013).

Education: Percent of population age 25 and over with: High school diploma (including GED) or higher: 89.2% (2008-2012 5-year est.); Bachelor's degree or higher: 24.1% (2008-2012 5-year est.); Master's degree or higher: 9.7% (2008-2012 5-year est.).

Housing: Homeownership rate: 62.4% (2008-2012 5-year est.); Median home value: $91,100 (2008-2012 5-year est.); Median contract rent: $465 per month (2008-2012 5-year est.); Median year structure built: 1967 (2008-2012 5-year est.)

Health: Birth rate: 95.2 per 10,000 population (2013); Death rate: 86.2 per 10,000 population (2013); Age-adjusted cancer mortality rate: 139.1 deaths per 100,000 population (2011); Number of physicians: 17.1 per 10,000 population (2011); Hospital beds: 23.8 per 10,000 population (2010); Hospital admissions: 1,245.9 per 10,000 population (2010).

Elections: 2012 Presidential election results: 43.4% Obama, 54.5% Romney

National and State Parks: Fox Ridge State Park; Lincoln Log Cabin State Historic Site

Additional Information Contacts
Coles County Government . . . . (217) 348-0501
   http://www.co.coles.il.us

Coles County Communities

ASHMORE (village). Covers a land area of 0.837 square miles and a water area of 0 square miles. Located at 39.53° N. Lat; 88.02° W. Long. Elevation is 699 feet.

Population: 800 (1990); 809 (2000); 785 (2010); Density: 935.7 persons per square mile (2008-2012 5-year est.); Race: 96.6% White, 0.6% Black/African American, 0.0% Asian, 0.0% American Indian/Alaska Native, 0.0% Native Hawaiian/Other Pacific Islander, 2.8% Some other race, 2.8% Two or more races, 0.0% Hispanic of any race (2008-2012 5-year est.); Average household size: 2.51 (2008-2012 5-year est.); Median age: 39.2 (2008-2012 5-year est.); Males per 100 females: 102.8 (2008-2012 5-year est.); Marriage status: 22.4% never married, 56.3% now married, 6.7% widowed, 14.6% divorced (2008-2012 5-year est.); Foreign born: 0.0% (2008-2012 5-year est.); Ancestry (includes multiple ancestries): 20.9% German, 14.0% American, 8.4% Irish, 7.8% English, 3.4% Polish (2008-2012 5-year est.).

Economy: Single-family building permits issued: 0 (2013); Multi-family building permits issued: 0 (2013); Homeowner vacancy rate: 0.0%. Rental vacancy rate: 0.0%. (2008-2012 5-year est.); Employment by occupation: 12.2% management, business, and financial, 0.5% computer, engineering, and science, 9.1% education, legal, community service, arts, and media, 5.2% healthcare practitioners, 16.8% service, 18.4% sales and office, 17.9% natural resources, construction, and maintenance, 19.9% production, transportation, and material moving (2008-2012 5-year est.).

Income: Per capita income: $21,115 (2008-2012 5-year est.); Median household income: $50,000 (2008-2012 5-year est.); Average household income: $52,251 (2008-2012 5-year est.); Percent of households with income of $100,000 or more: 9.6% (2008-2012 5-year est.); Poverty rate: 11.6% (2008-2012 5-year est.).

Education: Percent of population age 25 and over with: High school diploma (including GED) or higher: 87.7% (2008-2012 5-year est.); Bachelor's degree or higher: 16.3% (2008-2012 5-year est.); Master's degree or higher: 3.3% (2008-2012 5-year est.).
School District(s)
Charleston CUSD 1 (PK-12)
   2011-12 Enrollment: 2,795 . . . . (217) 639-1000

Housing: Homeownership rate: 83.7% (2008-2012 5-year est.); Median home value: $76,700 (2008-2012 5-year est.); Median contract rent: $344 per month (2008-2012 5-year est.); Median year structure built: 1972 (2008-2012 5-year est.).

Health Insurance: 69.7% Private; 30.0% Public; 11.4% None. (2008-2012 5-year est.)

Transportation: Commute to work: 92.9% car, 0.0% public transportation, 0.0% walk, 5.5% work from home (2008-2012 5-year est.); Travel time to work: 27.0% less than 15 minutes, 46.0% 15 to 30 minutes, 21.2% 30 to 45 minutes, 0.8% 45 to 60 minutes, 5.0% 60 minutes or more (2008-2012 5-year est.)

CHARLESTON (city). County seat. Covers a land area of 8.917 square miles and a water area of 0.710 square miles. Located at 39.48° N. Lat; 88.18° W. Long. Elevation is 669 feet.

History: Charleston was the site of the fourth Lincoln-Douglas debate in 1858, when 12,000 people gathered to hear Abraham Lincoln state his views on equality of all people.

Population: 20,398 (1990); 21,039 (2000); 21,838 (2010); Density: 2,461.9 persons per square mile (2008-2012 5-year est.); Race: 89.7% White, 6.6% Black/African American, 1.7% Asian, 0.1% American Indian/Alaska Native, 0.0% Native Hawaiian/Other Pacific Islander, 1.9% Some other race, 1.5% Two or more races, 2.9% Hispanic of any race (2008-2012 5-year est.); Average household size: 2.24 (2008-2012 5-year est.); Median age: 23.3 (2008-2012 5-year est.); Males per 100 females:

96.2 (2008-2012 5-year est.); Marriage status: 61.2% never married, 26.6% now married, 5.0% widowed, 7.1% divorced (2008-2012 5-year est.); Foreign born: 3.2% (2008-2012 5-year est.); Ancestry (includes multiple ancestries): 23.7% German, 16.3% Irish, 10.3% American, 7.8% English, 4.3% Italian (2008-2012 5-year est.).

Economy: Single-family building permits issued: 10 (2013); Multi-family building permits issued: 13 (2013); Homeowner vacancy rate: 0.8%. Rental vacancy rate: 5.6%. (2008-2012 5-year est.); Employment by occupation: 10.4% management, business, and financial, 3.7% computer, engineering, and science, 15.2% education, legal, community service, arts, and media, 3.6% healthcare practitioners, 23.3% service, 26.7% sales and office, 5.1% natural resources, construction, and maintenance, 11.9% production, transportation, and material moving (2008-2012 5-year est.).

Income: Per capita income: $19,404 (2008-2012 5-year est.); Median household income: $28,974 (2008-2012 5-year est.); Average household income: $50,362 (2008-2012 5-year est.); Percent of households with income of $100,000 or more: 10.6% (2008-2012 5-year est.); Poverty rate: 34.3% (2008-2012 5-year est.).

Education: Percent of population age 25 and over with: High school diploma (including GED) or higher: 89.5% (2008-2012 5-year est.); Bachelor's degree or higher: 35.6% (2008-2012 5-year est.); Master's degree or higher: 15.9% (2008-2012 5-year est.).
School District(s)
Charleston CUSD 1 (PK-12)
   2011-12 Enrollment: 2,795 . . . . (217) 639-1000
Four-year College(s)
Eastern Illinois University (Public)
   Fall 2012 Enrollment: 10,417 . . . . (217) 581-5000
   2012-13 Tuition: In-state $10,930; Out-of-state $27,670

Housing: Homeownership rate: 49.8% (2008-2012 5-year est.); Median home value: $95,600 (2008-2012 5-year est.); Median contract rent: $498 per month (2008-2012 5-year est.); Median year structure built: 1972 (2008-2012 5-year est.).

Health Insurance: 75.3% Private; 22.4% Public; 10.1% None. (2008-2012 5-year est.)

Safety: Violent crime rate: 22.9 per 10,000 population; Property crime rate: 58.1 per 10,000 population (2012).

Transportation: Commute to work: 78.2% car, 2.0% public transportation, 13.5% walk, 5.1% work from home (2008-2012 5-year est.); Travel time to work: 64.3% less than 15 minutes, 20.1% 15 to 30 minutes, 8.0% 30 to 45 minutes, 2.0% 45 to 60 minutes, 5.6% 60 minutes or more (2008-2012 5-year est.)

Airports: Coles County Memorial Airport (general aviation)

Additional Information Contacts
Charleston Area Chamber of Commerce . . . . (217) 345-7041
   http://www.charlestonchamber.com
City of Charleston . . . . (217) 345-5650
   http://www.charlestonillinois.org

HUMBOLDT (village). Covers a land area of 0.348 square miles and a water area of 0 square miles. Located at 39.60° N. Lat; 88.32° W. Long. Elevation is 663 feet.

Population: 470 (1990); 481 (2000); 437 (2010); Density: 1,130.9 persons per square mile (2008-2012 5-year est.); Race: 92.6% White, 0.0% Black/African American, 1.3% Asian, 0.0% American Indian/Alaska Native, 0.0% Native Hawaiian/Other Pacific Islander, 6.1% Some other race, 0.0% Two or more races, 17.3% Hispanic of any race (2008-2012 5-year est.); Average household size: 2.49 (2008-2012 5-year est.); Median age: 44.0 (2008-2012 5-year est.); Males per 100 females: 127.7 (2008-2012 5-year est.); Marriage status: 16.0% never married, 64.1% now married, 4.7% widowed, 15.1% divorced (2008-2012 5-year est.); Foreign born: 13.2% (2008-2012 5-year est.); Ancestry (includes multiple ancestries): 17.8% Irish, 14.2% German, 8.4% English, 8.1% American, 2.3% Polish (2008-2012 5-year est.).

Economy: Homeowner vacancy rate: 0.0%. Rental vacancy rate: 0.0%. (2008-2012 5-year est.); Employment by occupation: 8.5% management, business, and financial, 1.5% computer, engineering, and science, 5.5% education, legal, community service, arts, and media, 4.0% healthcare practitioners, 24.1% service, 11.6% sales and office, 15.6% natural resources, construction, and maintenance, 29.1% production, transportation, and material moving (2008-2012 5-year est.).

Income: Per capita income: $21,431 (2008-2012 5-year est.); Median household income: $42,750 (2008-2012 5-year est.); Average household income: $51,940 (2008-2012 5-year est.); Percent of households with

income of $100,000 or more: 12.7% (2008-2012 5-year est.); Poverty rate: 8.6% (2008-2012 5-year est.).

Education: Percent of population age 25 and over with: High school diploma (including GED) or higher: 76.8% (2008-2012 5-year est.); Bachelor's degree or higher: 9.8% (2008-2012 5-year est.); Master's degree or higher: 2.6% (2008-2012 5-year est.).

School District(s)

Eastern Il Area of Spec Educ (PK-12)

  2011-12 Enrollment: n/a . . . . (217) 348-7700

Housing: Homeownership rate: 73.4% (2008-2012 5-year est.); Median home value: $65,500 (2008-2012 5-year est.); Median contract rent: $451 per month (2008-2012 5-year est.); Median year structure built: 1957 (2008-2012 5-year est.).

Health Insurance: 60.6% Private; 33.8% Public; 21.1% None. (2008-2012 5-year est.)

Transportation: Commute to work: 94.3% car, 0.0% public transportation, 4.7% walk, 0.0% work from home (2008-2012 5-year est.); Travel time to work: 36.5% less than 15 minutes, 37.0% 15 to 30 minutes, 15.6% 30 to 45 minutes, 2.6% 45 to 60 minutes, 8.3% 60 minutes or more (2008-2012 5-year est.)

LERNA (village). Covers a land area of 0.117 square miles and a water area of 0 square miles. Located at 39.42° N. Lat; 88.29° W. Long. Elevation is 751 feet.

Population: 301 (1990); 322 (2000); 286 (2010); Density: 3,258.4 persons per square mile (2008-2012 5-year est.); Race: 100.0% White, 0.0% Black/African American, 0.0% Asian, 0.0% American Indian/Alaska Native, 0.0% Native Hawaiian/Other Pacific Islander, 0.0% Some other race, 0.0% Two or more races, 3.1% Hispanic of any race (2008-2012 5-year est.); Average household size: 2.82 (2008-2012 5-year est.); Median age: 32.0 (2008-2012 5-year est.); Males per 100 females: 105.9 (2008-2012 5-year est.); Marriage status: 26.7% never married, 57.7% now married, 7.5% widowed, 8.1% divorced (2008-2012 5-year est.); Foreign born: 0.0% (2008-2012 5-year est.); Ancestry (includes multiple ancestries): 30.2% German, 15.0% Irish, 10.5% American, 5.2% English, 2.4% Dutch (2008-2012 5-year est.).

Economy: Homeowner vacancy rate: 0.0%. Rental vacancy rate: 0.0%. (2008-2012 5-year est.); Employment by occupation: 9.1% management, business, and financial, 0.0% computer, engineering, and science, 6.1% education, legal, community service, arts, and media, 3.7% healthcare practitioners, 18.9% service, 10.4% sales and office, 18.9% natural resources, construction, and maintenance, 32.9% production, transportation, and material moving (2008-2012 5-year est.).

Income: Per capita income: $20,903 (2008-2012 5-year est.); Median household income: $50,750 (2008-2012 5-year est.); Average household income: $55,158 (2008-2012 5-year est.); Percent of households with income of $100,000 or more: 13.3% (2008-2012 5-year est.); Poverty rate: 26.8% (2008-2012 5-year est.).

Education: Percent of population age 25 and over with: High school diploma (including GED) or higher: 89.5% (2008-2012 5-year est.); Bachelor's degree or higher: 6.6% (2008-2012 5-year est.); Master's degree or higher: 2.2% (2008-2012 5-year est.).

School District(s)

Clk/cls/cmbn/dglas/edgr/mltr/shlb

  2011-12 Enrollment: n/a . . . . (217) 348-0151

Housing: Homeownership rate: 74.1% (2008-2012 5-year est.); Median home value: $63,000 (2008-2012 5-year est.); Median contract rent: $414 per month (2008-2012 5-year est.); Median year structure built: 1966 (2008-2012 5-year est.).

Health Insurance: 55.4% Private; 41.2% Public; 14.4% None. (2008-2012 5-year est.)

Transportation: Commute to work: 100.0% car, 0.0% public transportation, 0.0% walk, 0.0% work from home (2008-2012 5-year est.); Travel time to work: 18.2% less than 15 minutes, 45.9% 15 to 30 minutes, 32.1% 30 to 45 minutes, 0.0% 45 to 60 minutes, 3.8% 60 minutes or more (2008-2012 5-year est.)

MATTOON (city). Covers a land area of 10.339 square miles and a water area of 0.004 square miles. Located at 39.48° N. Lat; 88.36° W. Long. Elevation is 735 feet.

History: Mattoon was named for William Mattoon of the Illinois Central Railroad. The town was established in the early 1850's as a railroad station and shipping center.

Population: 18,441 (1990); 18,291 (2000); 18,555 (2010); Density: 1,756.6 persons per square mile (2008-2012 5-year est.); Race: 93.9%

White, 2.9% Black/African American, 0.6% Asian, 0.1% American Indian/Alaska Native, 0.0% Native Hawaiian/Other Pacific Islander, 2.5% Some other race, 2.4% Two or more races, 2.1% Hispanic of any race (2008-2012 5-year est.); Average household size: 2.25 (2008-2012 5-year est.); Median age: 38.5 (2008-2012 5-year est.); Males per 100 females: 84.0 (2008-2012 5-year est.); Marriage status: 28.7% never married, 44.9% now married, 8.9% widowed, 17.5% divorced (2008-2012 5-year est.); Foreign born: 1.1% (2008-2012 5-year est.); Ancestry (includes multiple ancestries): 26.4% German, 16.8% Irish, 9.7% American, 9.5% English, 2.1% French (2008-2012 5-year est.).

Economy: Single-family building permits issued: 2 (2013); Multi-family building permits issued: 4 (2013); Homeowner vacancy rate: 0.9%. Rental vacancy rate: 6.2%. (2008-2012 5-year est.); Employment by occupation: 9.4% management, business, and financial, 2.0% computer, engineering, and science, 9.8% education, legal, community service, arts, and media, 4.0% healthcare practitioners, 19.1% service, 21.0% sales and office, 10.7% natural resources, construction, and maintenance, 24.0% production, transportation, and material moving (2008-2012 5-year est.).

Income: Per capita income: $21,470 (2008-2012 5-year est.); Median household income: $37,609 (2008-2012 5-year est.); Average household income: $48,576 (2008-2012 5-year est.); Percent of households with income of $100,000 or more: 9.2% (2008-2012 5-year est.); Poverty rate: 19.4% (2008-2012 5-year est.).

Education: Percent of population age 25 and over with: High school diploma (including GED) or higher: 87.3% (2008-2012 5-year est.); Bachelor's degree or higher: 16.8% (2008-2012 5-year est.); Master's degree or higher: 5.0% (2008-2012 5-year est.).

School District(s)

Clk/cls/cmbn/dglas/edgr/mltr/shlb

  2011-12 Enrollment: n/a . . . . (217) 348-0151

Eastern Il Area of Spec Educ (PK-12)

  2011-12 Enrollment: n/a . . . . (217) 348-7700

Eastern Il Efe System (09-12)

  2011-12 Enrollment: n/a . . . . (217) 258-6238

Mattoon CUSD 2 (PK-12)

  2011-12 Enrollment: 3,436 . . . . (217) 238-8850

Two-year College(s)

Lake Land College (Public)

  Fall 2012 Enrollment: 6,818 . . . . (217) 234-5253

  2012-13 Tuition: In-state $6,444; Out-of-state $11,701

Housing: Homeownership rate: 58.9% (2008-2012 5-year est.); Median home value: $79,700 (2008-2012 5-year est.); Median contract rent: $423 per month (2008-2012 5-year est.); Median year structure built: 1956 (2008-2012 5-year est.).

Health Insurance: 62.7% Private; 42.1% Public; 12.3% None. (2008-2012 5-year est.)

Hospitals: Sarah Bush Lincoln Health Center (202 beds)

Safety: Violent crime rate: 35.0 per 10,000 population; Property crime rate: 195.9 per 10,000 population (2012).

Transportation: Commute to work: 93.1% car, 0.2% public transportation, 2.2% walk, 2.7% work from home (2008-2012 5-year est.); Travel time to work: 58.6% less than 15 minutes, 25.2% 15 to 30 minutes, 8.9% 30 to 45 minutes, 3.7% 45 to 60 minutes, 3.6% 60 minutes or more (2008-2012 5-year est.); Amtrak: Train service available.

Airports: Coles County Memorial Airport (general aviation)

Additional Information Contacts

City of Mattoon . . . . (217) 235-5654

  http://mattoon.illinois.gov

Mattoon Chamber of Commerce . . . . (217) 235-5661

  http://www.mattoonchamber.com

OAKLAND (city). Covers a land area of 0.826 square miles and a water area of 0.043 square miles. Located at 39.66° N. Lat; 88.03° W. Long. Elevation is 659 feet.

History: Incorporated 1855.

Population: 996 (1990); 996 (2000); 880 (2010); Density: 852.1 persons per square mile (2008-2012 5-year est.); Race: 99.1% White, 0.0% Black/African American, 0.9% Asian, 0.0% American Indian/Alaska Native, 0.0% Native Hawaiian/Other Pacific Islander, 0.0% Some other race, 0.0% Two or more races, 0.3% Hispanic of any race (2008-2012 5-year est.); Average household size: 2.19 (2008-2012 5-year est.); Median age: 49.7 (2008-2012 5-year est.); Males per 100 females: 96.1 (2008-2012 5-year est.); Marriage status: 21.3% never married, 51.3% now married, 12.7% widowed, 14.7% divorced (2008-2012 5-year est.); Foreign born: 0.9% (2008-2012 5-year est.); Ancestry (includes multiple ancestries): 21.0%

German, 18.6% English, 14.3% Irish, 11.8% American, 2.8% European (2008-2012 5-year est.).

Economy: Single-family building permits issued: 0 (2013); Multi-family building permits issued: 0 (2013); Homeowner vacancy rate: 0.0%. Rental vacancy rate: 0.0%. (2008-2012 5-year est.); Employment by occupation: 3.9% management, business, and financial, 2.4% computer, engineering, and science, 9.5% education, legal, community service, arts, and media, 1.2% healthcare practitioners, 19.6% service, 24.1% sales and office, 14.3% natural resources, construction, and maintenance, 25.0% production, transportation, and material moving (2008-2012 5-year est.).

Income: Per capita income: $23,428 (2008-2012 5-year est.); Median household income: $45,179 (2008-2012 5-year est.); Average household income: $50,707 (2008-2012 5-year est.); Percent of households with income of $100,000 or more: 7.4% (2008-2012 5-year est.); Poverty rate: 8.7% (2008-2012 5-year est.).

Education: Percent of population age 25 and over with: High school diploma (including GED) or higher: 81.9% (2008-2012 5-year est.); Bachelor's degree or higher: 10.9% (2008-2012 5-year est.); Master's degree or higher: 3.2% (2008-2012 5-year est.).

School District(s)

Oakland CUSD 5 (PK-12)
    2011-12 Enrollment: 302. . . . . (217) 346-2555

Housing: Homeownership rate: 81.6% (2008-2012 5-year est.); Median home value: $59,700 (2008-2012 5-year est.); Median contract rent: $308 per month (2008-2012 5-year est.); Median year structure built: 1959 (2008-2012 5-year est.).

Health Insurance: 65.6% Private; 41.5% Public; 11.8% None. (2008-2012 5-year est.)

Transportation: Commute to work: 93.0% car, 0.0% public transportation, 0.6% walk, 4.8% work from home (2008-2012 5-year est.); Travel time to work: 32.5% less than 15 minutes, 31.5% 15 to 30 minutes, 27.4% 30 to 45 minutes, 4.8% 45 to 60 minutes, 3.8% 60 minutes or more (2008-2012 5-year est.)

TRILLA (unincorporated postal area)

Zip Code: 62469

Covers a land area of 23.364 square miles and a water area of 0.022 square miles. Located at 39.35° N. Lat; 88.33° W. Long. Elevation is 653 feet. Population: 419 (2010); Density: 17.9 persons per square mile (2010); Race: 96.7% White, 0.0% Black/African American, 1.0% Asian, 0.2% American Indian/Alaska Native, 0.0% Native Hawaiian/Other Pacific Islander, 2.1% Some other race, 1.0% Two or more races, 1.2% Hispanic of any race (2010); Average household size: 2.62 (2010); Median age: 39.5 (2010); Males per 100 females: 99.5 (2010); Homeownership rate: 90.0% (2010)

Cook County

Located in northeastern Illinois; bounded on the east by Lake Michigan and Indiana; crossed by the Chicago and Des Plaines Rivers. Covers a land area of 945.326 square miles, a water area of 689.533 square miles, and is located in the Central Time Zone at 41.89° N. Lat., 87.65° W. Long. The county was founded in 1831. County seat is Chicago.

Cook County is part of the Chicago-Naperville-Elgin, IL-IN-WI Metropolitan Statistical Area. The entire metro area includes: Chicago-Naperville-Arlington Heights, IL Metropolitan Division (Cook County, IL; DuPage County, IL; Grundy County, IL; Kendall County, IL; McHenry County, IL; Will County, IL); Elgin, IL Metropolitan Division (DeKalb County, IL; Kane County, IL); Gary, IN Metropolitan Division (Jasper County, IN; Lake County, IN; Newton County, IN; Porter County, IN); Lake County-Kenosha County, IL-WI Metropolitan Division (Lake County, IL; Kenosha County, WI)

Weather Station: Chicago Botanical Garden   Elevation: 629 feet

	Jan	Feb	Mar	Apr	May	Jun	Jul	Aug	Sep	Oct	Nov	Dec
High	32	36	45	56	67	78	83	81	74	62	49	36
Low	16	19	28	38	47	57	63	62	54	42	33	21
Precip	2.0	1.7	2.5	3.5	4.0	3.6	3.5	4.7	3.5	3.3	3.1	2.4
Snow	10.2	8.1	5.2	0.9	tr	0.0	0.0	0.0	0.0	0.1	1.5	7.8

High and Low temperatures in degrees Fahrenheit; Precipitation and Snow in inches

Weather Station: Chicago Midway Arpt   Elevation: 620 feet

	Jan	Feb	Mar	Apr	May	Jun	Jul	Aug	Sep	Oct	Nov	Dec
High	32	36	47	60	71	81	85	83	76	63	49	36
Low	18	22	31	41	51	61	67	66	57	45	35	23
Precip	2.0	1.9	2.7	3.6	4.1	3.9	3.9	4.1	3.4	3.3	3.4	2.6
Snow	11.6	9.3	5.6	1.1	tr	0.0	tr	0.0	tr	0.1	1.4	8.5

High and Low temperatures in degrees Fahrenheit; Precipitation and Snow in inches

Weather Station: Chicago Ohare Intl Arpt   Elevation: 658 feet

	Jan	Feb	Mar	Apr	May	Jun	Jul	Aug	Sep	Oct	Nov	Dec
High	31	35	46	59	70	80	84	82	75	62	48	35
Low	16	20	29	38	48	58	64	63	54	42	32	21
Precip	1.7	1.8	2.5	3.4	3.6	3.4	3.5	5.1	3.3	3.2	3.1	2.3
Snow	11.4	8.6	5.9	1.4	tr	tr	tr	tr	tr	0.3	1.4	8.3

High and Low temperatures in degrees Fahrenheit; Precipitation and Snow in inches

Weather Station: Park Forest   Elevation: 709 feet

	Jan	Feb	Mar	Apr	May	Jun	Jul	Aug	Sep	Oct	Nov	Dec
High	31	35	46	59	70	80	84	82	75	62	49	35
Low	16	19	29	39	49	59	64	63	54	42	33	20
Precip	2.1	1.8	2.6	3.8	4.4	4.4	4.3	4.1	3.3	3.3	3.5	2.6
Snow	9.4	7.8	4.9	0.8	tr	0.0	0.0	0.0	0.0	0.3	0.9	6.7

High and Low temperatures in degrees Fahrenheit; Precipitation and Snow in inches

Population: 5,105,067 (1990); 5,376,741 (2000); 5,194,675 (2010); Race: 56.5% White, 24.7% Black/African American, 6.3% Asian, 0.2% American Indian/Alaska Native, 0.0% Native Hawaiian/Other Pacific Islander, 12.3% Some other race, 1.9% Two or more races, 24.0% Hispanic of any race (2008-2012 5-year est.); Density: 5,530.4 persons per square mile (2008-2012 5-year est.); Average household size: 2.64 (2008-2012 5-year est.); Median age: 35.3 (2008-2012 5-year est.); Males per 100 females: 93.9 (2008-2012 5-year est.).

Religion: Six largest groups: 37.5% Catholicism, 4.0% Non-denominational Protestant, 3.9% Muslim Estimate, 3.8% Baptist, 1.9% Lutheran, 1.7% Presbyterian-Reformed (2010)

Economy: Unemployment rate: 7.7% (April 2014); Total civilian labor force: 2,571,912 (April 2014); Leading industries: 16.0% health care and social assistance; 10.0% retail trade; 9.6% professional, scientific & technical services (2012); Farms: 127 totaling 8,499 acres (2012); Companies that employ 500 or more persons: 417 (2012); Companies that employ 100 to 499 persons: 3,101 (2012); Companies that employ less than 100 persons: 125,204 (2012); Black-owned businesses: 83,723 (2007); Hispanic-owned businesses: 36,740 (2007); Asian-owned businesses: 35,105 (2007); Women-owned businesses: 165,249 (2007); Single-family building permits issued: 1,396 (2013); Multi-family building permits issued: 3,249 (2013).

Income: Per capita income: $30,048 (2008-2012 5-year est.); Median household income: $54,648 (2008-2012 5-year est.); Average household income: $77,976 (2008-2012 5-year est.); Percent of households with income of $100,000 or more: 24.1% (2008-2012 5-year est.); Poverty rate: 16.4% (2008-2012 5-year est.); Bankruptcy rate: 6.90% (2013).

Taxes: Total county taxes per capita: $358 (2011); County property taxes per capita: $167 (2011).

Education: Percent of population age 25 and over with: High school diploma (including GED) or higher: 84.1% (2008-2012 5-year est.); Bachelor's degree or higher: 34.3% (2008-2012 5-year est.); Master's degree or higher: 13.6% (2008-2012 5-year est.).

Housing: Homeownership rate: 59.0% (2008-2012 5-year est.); Median home value: $244,900 (2008-2012 5-year est.); Median contract rent: $833 per month (2008-2012 5-year est.); Median year structure built: 1957 (2008-2012 5-year est.)

Health: Birth rate: 134.7 per 10,000 population (2013); Death rate: 77.1 per 10,000 population (2013); Age-adjusted cancer mortality rate: 179.8 deaths per 100,000 population (2011); Number of physicians: 42.9 per 10,000 population (2011); Hospital beds: 35.7 per 10,000 population (2010); Hospital admissions: 1,582.3 per 10,000 population (2010).

Environment: Air Quality Index: 35.3% good, 62.2% moderate, 2.5% unhealthy for sensitive individuals, 0.0% unhealthy (percent of days in 2013)

Elections: 2012 Presidential election results: 74.0% Obama, 24.6% Romney

National and State Parks: Chicago Portage National Historic Site; Illinois and Michigan Canal State Trail

Additional Information Contacts

Cook County Government. . . . . (312) 603-5656
    http://blog.cookcountygov.com

Cook County Communities

ALSIP (village). Covers a land area of 6.390 square miles and a water area of 0.104 square miles. Located at 41.67° N. Lat; 87.74° W. Long. Elevation is 623 feet.

Population: 18,227 (1990); 19,725 (2000); 19,277 (2010); Density: 3,014.9 persons per square mile (2008-2012 5-year est.); Race: 74.4% White, 14.7% Black/African American, 2.5% Asian, 0.0% American Indian/Alaska Native, 0.0% Native Hawaiian/Other Pacific Islander, 8.4% Some other race, 1.4% Two or more races, 21.5% Hispanic of any race (2008-2012 5-year est.); Average household size: 2.63 (2008-2012 5-year est.); Median age: 34.5 (2008-2012 5-year est.); Males per 100 females: 91.0 (2008-2012 5-year est.); Marriage status: 34.6% never married, 47.7% now married, 6.3% widowed, 11.4% divorced (2008-2012 5-year est.); Foreign born: 11.8% (2008-2012 5-year est.); Ancestry (includes multiple ancestries): 18.7% Irish, 16.0% Polish, 14.9% German, 6.2% Italian, 3.8% English (2008-2012 5-year est.).

Economy: Single-family building permits issued: 0 (2013); Multi-family building permits issued: 0 (2013); Homeowner vacancy rate: 0.9%. Rental vacancy rate: 6.5%. (2008-2012 5-year est.); Employment by occupation: 10.3% management, business, and financial, 3.0% computer, engineering, and science, 6.6% education, legal, community service, arts, and media, 3.2% healthcare practitioners, 19.3% service, 35.2% sales and office, 9.1% natural resources, construction, and maintenance, 13.3% production, transportation, and material moving (2008-2012 5-year est.).

Income: Per capita income: $24,393 (2008-2012 5-year est.); Median household income: $53,487 (2008-2012 5-year est.); Average household income: $62,233 (2008-2012 5-year est.); Percent of households with income of $100,000 or more: 19.1% (2008-2012 5-year est.); Poverty rate: 9.8% (2008-2012 5-year est.).

Education: Percent of population age 25 and over with: High school diploma (including GED) or higher: 87.5% (2008-2012 5-year est.); Bachelor's degree or higher: 16.1% (2008-2012 5-year est.); Master's degree or higher: 4.2% (2008-2012 5-year est.).

School District(s)

Alsip-Hazlgrn-Oaklwn SD 126 (PK-08)
    2011-12 Enrollment: 1,596 . . . . (708) 389-1900
Atwood Heights SD 125 (PK-08)
    2011-12 Enrollment: 739 . . . . (708) 371-0080
Cook County SD 130 (PK-08)
    2011-12 Enrollment: 3,869 . . . . (708) 385-6800

Housing: Homeownership rate: 64.7% (2008-2012 5-year est.); Median home value: $190,100 (2008-2012 5-year est.); Median contract rent: $785 per month (2008-2012 5-year est.); Median year structure built: 1973 (2008-2012 5-year est.).

Health Insurance: 69.2% Private; 28.4% Public; 13.5% None. (2008-2012 5-year est.)

Safety: Violent crime rate: 18.6 per 10,000 population; Property crime rate: 367.6 per 10,000 population (2012).

Transportation: Commute to work: 85.9% car, 9.5% public transportation, 1.4% walk, 2.0% work from home (2008-2012 5-year est.); Travel time to work: 22.6% less than 15 minutes, 26.4% 15 to 30 minutes, 23.5% 30 to 45 minutes, 12.1% 45 to 60 minutes, 15.4% 60 minutes or more (2008-2012 5-year est.)

Additional Information Contacts

Alsip Chamber of Commerce . . . . (708) 597-2668
    http://www.alsipchamber.org
Village of Alsip . . . . (708) 385-6902
    http://villageofalsip.org

ARLINGTON HEIGHTS (village). Covers a land area of 16.608 square miles and a water area of 0.029 square miles. Located at 42.10° N. Lat; 87.98° W. Long. Elevation is 702 feet.

History: Named for Henry Bennet (1618-1685), 1st Earl of Arlington. Arlington Heights was settled in the 1830's. The Arlington Park Race Track opened here in 1929, drawing many visitors from Chicago.

Population: 75,460 (1990); 76,031 (2000); 75,101 (2010); Density: 4,529.1 persons per square mile (2008-2012 5-year est.); Race: 87.0% White, 1.8% Black/African American, 7.8% Asian, 0.2% American Indian/Alaska Native, 0.0% Native Hawaiian/Other Pacific Islander, 3.2% Some other race, 1.7% Two or more races, 6.4% Hispanic of any race (2008-2012 5-year est.); Average household size: 2.47 (2008-2012 5-year est.); Median age: 42.1 (2008-2012 5-year est.); Males per 100 females: 93.1 (2008-2012 5-year est.); Marriage status: 25.5% never married,

59.9% now married, 6.4% widowed, 8.2% divorced (2008-2012 5-year est.); Foreign born: 18.2% (2008-2012 5-year est.); Ancestry (includes multiple ancestries): 26.7% German, 18.0% Irish, 16.0% Polish, 11.2% Italian, 6.1% English (2008-2012 5-year est.).

Economy: Unemployment rate: 5.5% (April 2014); Total civilian labor force: 42,203 (April 2014); Single-family building permits issued: 55 (2013); Multi-family building permits issued: 0 (2013); Homeowner vacancy rate: 2.0%. Rental vacancy rate: 4.5%. (2008-2012 5-year est.); Employment by occupation: 24.4% management, business, and financial, 8.5% computer, engineering, and science, 12.6% education, legal, community service, arts, and media, 5.2% healthcare practitioners, 10.5% service, 26.2% sales and office, 5.0% natural resources, construction, and maintenance, 7.6% production, transportation, and material moving (2008-2012 5-year est.).

Income: Per capita income: $40,645 (2008-2012 5-year est.); Median household income: $77,121 (2008-2012 5-year est.); Average household income: $99,707 (2008-2012 5-year est.); Percent of households with income of $100,000 or more: 37.8% (2008-2012 5-year est.); Poverty rate: 4.1% (2008-2012 5-year est.).

Taxes: Total city taxes per capita: $859 (2011); City property taxes per capita: $560 (2011).

Education: Percent of population age 25 and over with: High school diploma (including GED) or higher: 95.6% (2008-2012 5-year est.); Bachelor's degree or higher: 51.7% (2008-2012 5-year est.); Master's degree or higher: 20.1% (2008-2012 5-year est.).

School District(s)

Arlington Heights SD 25 (PK-08)
    2011-12 Enrollment: 5,192 . . . . (847) 758-4900
Community CSD 59 (PK-08)
    2011-12 Enrollment: 6,537 . . . . (847) 593-4300
Northwest Suburban Ed To Careers
    2011-12 Enrollment: n/a . . . . (847) 718-6800
Nw Suburban Spec Educ Org
    2011-12 Enrollment: n/a . . . . (847) 463-8100
Township HSD 214 (09-12)
    2011-12 Enrollment: 12,305 . . . . (847) 718-7600
Wheeling CCSD 21 (PK-08)
    2011-12 Enrollment: 6,866 . . . . (847) 537-8270

Vocational/Technical School(s)

Empire Beauty School-Arlington Heights (Private, For-profit)
    Fall 2012 Enrollment: 190 . . . . (800) 920-4593
    2012-13 Tuition: $17,595

Housing: Homeownership rate: 76.9% (2008-2012 5-year est.); Median home value: $343,500 (2008-2012 5-year est.); Median contract rent: $1,057 per month (2008-2012 5-year est.); Median year structure built: 1971 (2008-2012 5-year est.).

Health Insurance: 84.2% Private; 22.7% Public; 6.9% None. (2008-2012 5-year est.)

Hospitals: Northwest Community Hospital (488 beds)

Safety: Violent crime rate: 5.4 per 10,000 population; Property crime rate: 129.6 per 10,000 population (2012).

Transportation: Commute to work: 86.6% car, 5.9% public transportation, 1.6% walk, 5.0% work from home (2008-2012 5-year est.); Travel time to work: 21.9% less than 15 minutes, 33.0% 15 to 30 minutes, 24.4% 30 to 45 minutes, 10.1% 45 to 60 minutes, 10.6% 60 minutes or more (2008-2012 5-year est.)

Additional Information Contacts

Arlington Heights Chamber of Commerce . . . . (847) 253-1703
    http://www.arlingtonhtschamber.com
Village of Arlington Heights . . . . (847) 368-5000
    http://www.vah.com

BARRINGTON (village). Covers a land area of 4.616 square miles and a water area of 0.188 square miles. Located at 42.15° N. Lat; 88.13° W. Long. Elevation is 827 feet.

History: Named for Great Barrington, Massachusetts. Barrington was founded in the 1850's and developed as an agricultural community.

Population: 9,504 (1990); 10,168 (2000); 10,327 (2010); Density: 2,326.4 persons per square mile (2008-2012 5-year est.); Race: 88.7% White, 0.3% Black/African American, 8.2% Asian, 0.1% American Indian/Alaska Native, 0.0% Native Hawaiian/Other Pacific Islander, 2.7% Some other race, 0.7% Two or more races, 8.3% Hispanic of any race (2008-2012 5-year est.); Average household size: 2.70 (2008-2012 5-year est.); Median age: 42.0 (2008-2012 5-year est.); Males per 100 females: 99.9 (2008-2012 5-year est.); Marriage status: 21.4% never married, 65.5% now married, 5.4% widowed, 7.7% divorced (2008-2012 5-year est.);

Foreign born: 10.8% (2008-2012 5-year est.); Ancestry (includes multiple ancestries): 21.7% German, 21.0% Irish, 12.8% Italian, 12.6% English, 10.2% Polish (2008-2012 5-year est.).
Economy: Single-family building permits issued: 11 (2013); Multi-family building permits issued: 0 (2013); Homeowner vacancy rate: 4.0%. Rental vacancy rate: 2.8%. (2008-2012 5-year est.); Employment by occupation: 34.0% management, business, and financial, 4.8% computer, engineering, and science, 17.0% education, legal, community service, arts, and media, 5.6% healthcare practitioners, 9.0% service, 23.5% sales and office, 4.2% natural resources, construction, and maintenance, 2.0% production, transportation, and material moving (2008-2012 5-year est.).
Income: Per capita income: $54,310 (2008-2012 5-year est.); Median household income: $106,127 (2008-2012 5-year est.); Average household income: $145,538 (2008-2012 5-year est.); Percent of households with income of $100,000 or more: 51.8% (2008-2012 5-year est.); Poverty rate: 9.2% (2008-2012 5-year est.).
Taxes: Total city taxes per capita: $676 (2011); City property taxes per capita: $449 (2011).
Education: Percent of population age 25 and over with: High school diploma (including GED) or higher: 96.2% (2008-2012 5-year est.); Bachelor's degree or higher: 62.7% (2008-2012 5-year est.); Master's degree or higher: 27.0% (2008-2012 5-year est.).

School District(s)
Barrington CUSD 220 (PK-12)
   2011-12 Enrollment: 9,088 . . . . (847) 381-6300
Barrington CUSD 220 (PK-12)
   2011-12 Enrollment: 9,088 . . . . (847) 381-6300
Housing: Homeownership rate: 78.1% (2008-2012 5-year est.); Median home value: $460,500 (2008-2012 5-year est.); Median contract rent: $1,176 per month (2008-2012 5-year est.); Median year structure built: 1969 (2008-2012 5-year est.).
Health Insurance: 84.8% Private; 21.5% Public; 5.6% None. (2008-2012 5-year est.)
Hospitals: Advocate Good Shephard Hospital (154 beds)
Safety: Violent crime rate: 1.0 per 10,000 population; Property crime rate: 141.7 per 10,000 population (2012).
Transportation: Commute to work: 75.2% car, 12.0% public transportation, 2.0% walk, 9.1% work from home (2008-2012 5-year est.); Travel time to work: 26.1% less than 15 minutes, 24.4% 15 to 30 minutes, 15.5% 30 to 45 minutes, 16.2% 45 to 60 minutes, 17.8% 60 minutes or more (2008-2012 5-year est.)
Additional Information Contacts
Barrington Area Chamber of Commerce . . . . (847) 381-2525
   http://www.barringtonchamber.com
Village of Barrington . . . . (847) 304-3400
   http://www.barrington-il.gov

BARRINGTON HILLS (village). Covers a land area of 27.425 square miles and a water area of 0.609 square miles. Located at 42.14° N. Lat; 88.20° W. Long. Elevation is 846 feet.
History: Settlers Jesse Miller and William Van Orsdal arrived in 1834; in the 1840's other settlers formed a town called Miller's Grove, later named Barrington Center.
Population: 4,202 (1990); 3,915 (2000); 4,209 (2010); Density: 143.6 persons per square mile (2008-2012 5-year est.); Race: 93.8% White, 0.5% Black/African American, 5.3% Asian, 0.0% American Indian/Alaska Native, 0.0% Native Hawaiian/Other Pacific Islander, 0.4% Some other race, 0.5% Two or more races, 4.5% Hispanic of any race (2008-2012 5-year est.); Average household size: 2.53 (2008-2012 5-year est.); Median age: 49.6 (2008-2012 5-year est.); Males per 100 females: 102.2 (2008-2012 5-year est.); Marriage status: 19.0% never married, 66.7% now married, 3.5% widowed, 10.8% divorced (2008-2012 5-year est.); Foreign born: 11.7% (2008-2012 5-year est.); Ancestry (includes multiple ancestries): 26.2% German, 19.9% Irish, 13.2% English, 12.5% Italian, 9.4% Polish (2008-2012 5-year est.).
Economy: Single-family building permits issued: 11 (2013); Multi-family building permits issued: 0 (2013); Homeowner vacancy rate: 3.0%. Rental vacancy rate: 0.0%. (2008-2012 5-year est.); Employment by occupation: 34.9% management, business, and financial, 2.4% computer, engineering, and science, 10.4% education, legal, community service, arts, and media, 9.5% healthcare practitioners, 12.0% service, 21.3% sales and office, 7.5% natural resources, construction, and maintenance, 2.0% production, transportation, and material moving (2008-2012 5-year est.).
Income: Per capita income: $93,280 (2008-2012 5-year est.); Median household income: $114,213 (2008-2012 5-year est.); Average household

income: $236,133 (2008-2012 5-year est.); Percent of households with income of $100,000 or more: 56.7% (2008-2012 5-year est.); Poverty rate: 8.3% (2008-2012 5-year est.).
Education: Percent of population age 25 and over with: High school diploma (including GED) or higher: 99.9% (2008-2012 5-year est.); Bachelor's degree or higher: 54.5% (2008-2012 5-year est.); Master's degree or higher: 24.0% (2008-2012 5-year est.).
Housing: Homeownership rate: 93.5% (2008-2012 5-year est.); Median home value: $888,000 (2008-2012 5-year est.); Median contract rent: $1,463 per month (2008-2012 5-year est.); Median year structure built: 1977 (2008-2012 5-year est.).
Health Insurance: 93.8% Private; 22.8% Public; 2.5% None. (2008-2012 5-year est.)
Safety: Violent crime rate: 4.7 per 10,000 population; Property crime rate: 94.7 per 10,000 population (2012).
Transportation: Commute to work: 86.2% car, 4.8% public transportation, 0.0% walk, 8.1% work from home (2008-2012 5-year est.); Travel time to work: 25.4% less than 15 minutes, 19.1% 15 to 30 minutes, 23.8% 30 to 45 minutes, 16.9% 45 to 60 minutes, 14.8% 60 minutes or more (2008-2012 5-year est.)

BEDFORD PARK (village). Covers a land area of 5.929 square miles and a water area of 0.106 square miles. Located at 41.77° N. Lat; 87.80° W. Long. Elevation is 617 feet.
Population: 566 (1990); 574 (2000); 580 (2010); Density: 105.2 persons per square mile (2008-2012 5-year est.); Race: 80.3% White, 0.0% Black/African American, 0.3% Asian, 0.0% American Indian/Alaska Native, 0.0% Native Hawaiian/Other Pacific Islander, 19.4% Some other race, 0.5% Two or more races, 33.3% Hispanic of any race (2008-2012 5-year est.); Average household size: 3.01 (2008-2012 5-year est.); Median age: 34.9 (2008-2012 5-year est.); Males per 100 females: 105.3 (2008-2012 5-year est.); Marriage status: 27.7% never married, 62.9% now married, 6.9% widowed, 2.5% divorced (2008-2012 5-year est.); Foreign born: 14.4% (2008-2012 5-year est.); Ancestry (includes multiple ancestries): 15.7% Irish, 14.6% Polish, 13.9% German, 9.1% Italian, 6.6% American (2008-2012 5-year est.).
Economy: Single-family building permits issued: 0 (2013); Multi-family building permits issued: 0 (2013); Homeowner vacancy rate: 0.0%. Rental vacancy rate: 35.7%. (2008-2012 5-year est.); Employment by occupation: 17.1% management, business, and financial, 7.0% computer, engineering, and science, 9.1% education, legal, community service, arts, and media, 4.2% healthcare practitioners, 12.6% service, 20.3% sales and office, 8.4% natural resources, construction, and maintenance, 21.3% production, transportation, and material moving (2008-2012 5-year est.).
Income: Per capita income: $23,797 (2008-2012 5-year est.); Median household income: $63,618 (2008-2012 5-year est.); Average household income: $69,267 (2008-2012 5-year est.); Percent of households with income of $100,000 or more: 21.3% (2008-2012 5-year est.); Poverty rate: 16.2% (2008-2012 5-year est.).
Taxes: Total city taxes per capita: $46,371 (2011); City property taxes per capita: $36,808 (2011).
Education: Percent of population age 25 and over with: High school diploma (including GED) or higher: 80.3% (2008-2012 5-year est.); Bachelor's degree or higher: 15.5% (2008-2012 5-year est.); Master's degree or higher: 7.3% (2008-2012 5-year est.).

School District(s)
Summit SD 104 (PK-08)
   2011-12 Enrollment: 1,832 . . . . (708) 458-0505
Two-year College(s)
Fox College Inc (Private, For-profit)
   Fall 2012 Enrollment: 413 . . . . (708) 444-4500
   2012-13 Tuition: In-state $15,180; Out-of-state $15,180
Vocational/Technical School(s)
Everest College-Bedford Park (Private, For-profit)
   Fall 2012 Enrollment: 901 . . . . (708) 793-4600
   2012-13 Tuition: $18,841
Housing: Homeownership rate: 95.7% (2008-2012 5-year est.); Median home value: $210,200 (2008-2012 5-year est.); Median contract rent: $558 per month (2008-2012 5-year est.); Median year structure built: 1951 (2008-2012 5-year est.).
Health Insurance: 72.9% Private; 18.3% Public; 22.6% None. (2008-2012 5-year est.)
Transportation: Commute to work: 93.6% car, 4.6% public transportation, 1.1% walk, 0.7% work from home (2008-2012 5-year est.); Travel time to work: 36.9% less than 15 minutes, 31.9% 15 to 30 minutes, 10.8% 30 to

45 minutes, 9.3% 45 to 60 minutes, 11.1% 60 minutes or more (2008-2012 5-year est.)

BELLWOOD (village). Covers a land area of 2.398 square miles and a water area of 0 square miles. Located at 41.88° N. Lat; 87.88° W. Long. Elevation is 633 feet.

History: Derived from its original name of Bell's Wood, which was probably named for a landowner. Incorporated 1900.

Population: 20,241 (1990); 20,535 (2000); 19,071 (2010); Density: 7,967.3 persons per square mile (2008-2012 5-year est.); Race: 11.4% White, 75.2% Black/African American, 0.5% Asian, 0.5% American Indian/Alaska Native, 0.0% Native Hawaiian/Other Pacific Islander, 12.4% Some other race, 2.0% Two or more races, 18.8% Hispanic of any race (2008-2012 5-year est.); Average household size: 3.19 (2008-2012 5-year est.); Median age: 35.0 (2008-2012 5-year est.); Males per 100 females: 85.7 (2008-2012 5-year est.); Marriage status: 47.4% never married, 38.7% now married, 4.7% widowed, 9.1% divorced (2008-2012 5-year est.); Foreign born: 8.2% (2008-2012 5-year est.); Ancestry (includes multiple ancestries): 1.3% German, 1.1% African, 1.0% Italian, 0.6% Polish, 0.6% Irish (2008-2012 5-year est.).

Economy: Single-family building permits issued: 5 (2013); Multi-family building permits issued: 0 (2013); Homeowner vacancy rate: 3.5%. Rental vacancy rate: 8.8%. (2008-2012 5-year est.); Employment by occupation: 9.8% management, business, and financial, 1.9% computer, engineering, and science, 5.4% education, legal, community service, arts, and media, 3.4% healthcare practitioners, 15.3% service, 34.1% sales and office, 5.7% natural resources, construction, and maintenance, 24.4% production, transportation, and material moving (2008-2012 5-year est.).

Income: Per capita income: $20,543 (2008-2012 5-year est.); Median household income: $54,047 (2008-2012 5-year est.); Average household income: $61,974 (2008-2012 5-year est.); Percent of households with income of $100,000 or more: 17.2% (2008-2012 5-year est.); Poverty rate: 12.8% (2008-2012 5-year est.).

Taxes: Total city taxes per capita: $1,210 (2011); City property taxes per capita: $997 (2011).

Education: Percent of population age 25 and over with: High school diploma (including GED) or higher: 81.1% (2008-2012 5-year est.); Bachelor's degree or higher: 14.8% (2008-2012 5-year est.); Master's degree or higher: 4.6% (2008-2012 5-year est.).

School District(s)

Bellwood SD 88 (PK-08)
   2011-12 Enrollment: 2,879 . . . . (708) 344-9344
Berkeley SD 87 (PK-08)
   2011-12 Enrollment: 2,838 . . . . (708) 449-3350
Region 06 West Cook Isc 2 (PK-12)
   2011-12 Enrollment: n/a . . . . (708) 544-4890

Housing: Homeownership rate: 75.3% (2008-2012 5-year est.); Median home value: $164,000 (2008-2012 5-year est.); Median contract rent: $860 per month (2008-2012 5-year est.); Median year structure built: 1955 (2008-2012 5-year est.).

Health Insurance: 59.1% Private; 33.2% Public; 17.0% None. (2008-2012 5-year est.)

Safety: Violent crime rate: 72.0 per 10,000 population; Property crime rate: 341.8 per 10,000 population (2012).

Transportation: Commute to work: 82.7% car, 12.1% public transportation, 2.2% walk, 1.4% work from home (2008-2012 5-year est.); Travel time to work: 19.6% less than 15 minutes, 33.5% 15 to 30 minutes, 26.8% 30 to 45 minutes, 9.4% 45 to 60 minutes, 10.6% 60 minutes or more (2008-2012 5-year est.)

Additional Information Contacts

Bellwood Chamber of Commerce & Industry . . . . (630) 747-6785
Village of Bellwood . . . . (708) 547-3500
   http://www.vil.bellwood.il.us

BERKELEY (village). Covers a land area of 1.400 square miles and a water area of 0 square miles. Located at 41.89° N. Lat; 87.91° W. Long. Elevation is 650 feet.

Population: 5,137 (1990); 5,245 (2000); 5,209 (2010); Density: 3,705.6 persons per square mile (2008-2012 5-year est.); Race: 50.1% White, 26.1% Black/African American, 2.9% Asian, 0.1% American Indian/Alaska Native, 0.0% Native Hawaiian/Other Pacific Islander, 20.8% Some other race, 1.6% Two or more races, 30.5% Hispanic of any race (2008-2012 5-year est.); Average household size: 2.80 (2008-2012 5-year est.); Median age: 39.5 (2008-2012 5-year est.); Males per 100 females: 96.6 (2008-2012 5-year est.); Marriage status: 30.0% never married, 52.2%

now married, 6.1% widowed, 11.6% divorced (2008-2012 5-year est.); Foreign born: 19.2% (2008-2012 5-year est.); Ancestry (includes multiple ancestries): 11.0% Irish, 10.6% German, 8.6% Polish, 5.1% English, 5.0% Italian (2008-2012 5-year est.).

Economy: Single-family building permits issued: 1 (2013); Multi-family building permits issued: 0 (2013); Homeowner vacancy rate: 1.9%. Rental vacancy rate: 10.6%. (2008-2012 5-year est.); Employment by occupation: 15.1% management, business, and financial, 8.0% computer, engineering, and science, 9.2% education, legal, community service, arts, and media, 4.6% healthcare practitioners, 12.8% service, 26.1% sales and office, 10.3% natural resources, construction, and maintenance, 14.0% production, transportation, and material moving (2008-2012 5-year est.).

Income: Per capita income: $28,236 (2008-2012 5-year est.); Median household income: $62,644 (2008-2012 5-year est.); Average household income: $77,003 (2008-2012 5-year est.); Percent of households with income of $100,000 or more: 17.3% (2008-2012 5-year est.); Poverty rate: 3.3% (2008-2012 5-year est.).

Education: Percent of population age 25 and over with: High school diploma (including GED) or higher: 83.5% (2008-2012 5-year est.); Bachelor's degree or higher: 21.6% (2008-2012 5-year est.); Master's degree or higher: 4.6% (2008-2012 5-year est.).

School District(s)

Berkeley SD 87 (PK-08)
   2011-12 Enrollment: 2,838 . . . . (708) 449-3350

Housing: Homeownership rate: 85.0% (2008-2012 5-year est.); Median home value: $186,800 (2008-2012 5-year est.); Median contract rent: $831 per month (2008-2012 5-year est.); Median year structure built: 1956 (2008-2012 5-year est.).

Health Insurance: 75.0% Private; 19.7% Public; 16.9% None. (2008-2012 5-year est.)

Safety: Violent crime rate: 19.1 per 10,000 population; Property crime rate: 172.0 per 10,000 population (2012).

Transportation: Commute to work: 88.4% car, 7.8% public transportation, 0.8% walk, 2.1% work from home (2008-2012 5-year est.); Travel time to work: 14.4% less than 15 minutes, 36.9% 15 to 30 minutes, 22.2% 30 to 45 minutes, 14.4% 45 to 60 minutes, 12.0% 60 minutes or more (2008-2012 5-year est.)

Additional Information Contacts

Village of Berkeley. . . . . (708) 449-8840
   http://www.berkeley.il.us

BERWYN (city). Covers a land area of 3.905 square miles and a water area of 0 square miles. Located at 41.84° N. Lat; 87.79° W. Long. Elevation is 617 feet.

History: Named for Berwyn, Pennsylvania. Berwyn was organized in 1890 by Charles E. Piper and Wilbur J. Andrews, realtors who felt that a town would be populated if they built it. Berwyn was incorporated as a village in 1891 and chartered as a city in 1908. It grew as a residential suburb, with many of the people employed in neighboring Cicero, where the Western Electric Company had a plant.

Population: 45,426 (1990); 54,016 (2000); 56,657 (2010); Density: 14,436.9 persons per square mile (2008-2012 5-year est.); Race: 62.3% White, 6.7% Black/African American, 1.8% Asian, 0.4% American Indian/Alaska Native, 0.0% Native Hawaiian/Other Pacific Islander, 28.8% Some other race, 2.3% Two or more races, 58.4% Hispanic of any race (2008-2012 5-year est.); Average household size: 3.05 (2008-2012 5-year est.); Median age: 33.1 (2008-2012 5-year est.); Males per 100 females: 94.5 (2008-2012 5-year est.); Marriage status: 38.9% never married, 46.0% now married, 5.8% widowed, 9.3% divorced (2008-2012 5-year est.); Foreign born: 25.1% (2008-2012 5-year est.); Ancestry (includes multiple ancestries): 8.1% Italian, 7.4% German, 7.2% Irish, 6.8% Polish, 3.4% Czech (2008-2012 5-year est.).

Economy: Unemployment rate: 7.7% (April 2014); Total civilian labor force: 28,330 (April 2014); Single-family building permits issued: 0 (2013); Multi-family building permits issued: 0 (2013); Homeowner vacancy rate: 3.0%. Rental vacancy rate: 6.3%. (2008-2012 5-year est.); Employment by occupation: 8.4% management, business, and financial, 3.1% computer, engineering, and science, 9.0% education, legal, community service, arts, and media, 3.8% healthcare practitioners, 22.0% service, 27.1% sales and office, 8.9% natural resources, construction, and maintenance, 17.7% production, transportation, and material moving (2008-2012 5-year est.).

Income: Per capita income: $21,101 (2008-2012 5-year est.); Median household income: $51,192 (2008-2012 5-year est.); Average household income: $61,487 (2008-2012 5-year est.); Percent of households with

income of $100,000 or more: 16.0% (2008-2012 5-year est.); Poverty rate: 13.8% (2008-2012 5-year est.).

Taxes: Total city taxes per capita: $751 (2011); City property taxes per capita: $552 (2011).

Education: Percent of population age 25 and over with: High school diploma (including GED) or higher: 76.8% (2008-2012 5-year est.); Bachelor's degree or higher: 18.6% (2008-2012 5-year est.); Master's degree or higher: 5.5% (2008-2012 5-year est.).

School District(s)
Berwyn North SD 98 (PK-08)
   2011-12 Enrollment: 3,389 . . . . (708) 484-6200
Berwyn South SD 100 (PK-08)
   2011-12 Enrollment: 3,963 . . . . (708) 795-2300
J S Morton HSD 201 (09-12)
   2011-12 Enrollment: 8,344 . . . . (708) 222-5702

Housing: Homeownership rate: 60.5% (2008-2012 5-year est.); Median home value: $216,200 (2008-2012 5-year est.); Median contract rent: $778 per month (2008-2012 5-year est.); Median year structure built: Before 1940 (2008-2012 5-year est.).

Health Insurance: 57.5% Private; 32.6% Public; 18.5% None. (2008-2012 5-year est.)

Hospitals: MacNeal Hospital (427 beds)

Safety: Violent crime rate: 19.8 per 10,000 population; Property crime rate: 251.3 per 10,000 population (2012).

Transportation: Commute to work: 80.9% car, 11.1% public transportation, 4.7% walk, 2.3% work from home (2008-2012 5-year est.); Travel time to work: 17.0% less than 15 minutes, 29.7% 15 to 30 minutes, 29.6% 30 to 45 minutes, 11.4% 45 to 60 minutes, 12.2% 60 minutes or more (2008-2012 5-year est.)

Additional Information Contacts
Berwyn Development Corporation . . . . (708) 788-8100
   http://www.berwyn.net/chamberservices
City of Berwyn . . . . (708) 788-2660
   http://www.berwyn-il.gov

BLUE ISLAND (city). Covers a land area of 4.071 square miles and a water area of 0.086 square miles. Located at 41.66° N. Lat; 87.68° W. Long. Elevation is 640 feet.

History: Blue Island was named because it looked like an island surrounded by marshes, and a blue haze often hung over its woods. Settlers first came in 1835, and the village was laid out in 1872. Many of the early residents were of German and Italian ancestry.

Population: 21,203 (1990); 23,463 (2000); 23,706 (2010); Density: 5,761.7 persons per square mile (2008-2012 5-year est.); Race: 49.7% White, 32.5% Black/African American, 0.2% Asian, 0.2% American Indian/Alaska Native, 0.0% Native Hawaiian/Other Pacific Islander, 17.4% Some other race, 2.1% Two or more races, 44.9% Hispanic of any race (2008-2012 5-year est.); Average household size: 3.02 (2008-2012 5-year est.); Median age: 31.7 (2008-2012 5-year est.); Males per 100 females: 100.3 (2008-2012 5-year est.); Marriage status: 40.6% never married, 42.9% now married, 6.1% widowed, 10.4% divorced (2008-2012 5-year est.); Foreign born: 20.4% (2008-2012 5-year est.); Ancestry (includes multiple ancestries): 8.3% German, 5.1% Polish, 5.1% Irish, 4.9% Italian, 1.5% English (2008-2012 5-year est.).

Economy: Single-family building permits issued: 0 (2013); Multi-family building permits issued: 0 (2013); Homeowner vacancy rate: 4.9%. Rental vacancy rate: 8.3%. (2008-2012 5-year est.); Employment by occupation: 9.9% management, business, and financial, 1.8% computer, engineering, and science, 5.7% education, legal, community service, arts, and media, 3.5% healthcare practitioners, 20.3% service, 29.3% sales and office, 9.9% natural resources, construction, and maintenance, 19.6% production, transportation, and material moving (2008-2012 5-year est.).

Income: Per capita income: $17,633 (2008-2012 5-year est.); Median household income: $42,721 (2008-2012 5-year est.); Average household income: $50,917 (2008-2012 5-year est.); Percent of households with income of $100,000 or more: 11.1% (2008-2012 5-year est.); Poverty rate: 21.3% (2008-2012 5-year est.).

Taxes: Total city taxes per capita: $568 (2011); City property taxes per capita: $470 (2011).

Education: Percent of population age 25 and over with: High school diploma (including GED) or higher: 75.5% (2008-2012 5-year est.); Bachelor's degree or higher: 12.8% (2008-2012 5-year est.); Master's degree or higher: 4.4% (2008-2012 5-year est.).

School District(s)
CHSD 218 (09-12)
   2011-12 Enrollment: 5,671 . . . . (708) 424-2000
Cook County SD 130 (PK-08)
   2011-12 Enrollment: 3,869 . . . . (708) 385-6800
Vocational/Technical School(s)
Cannella School of Hair Design-Blue Island (Private, For-profit)
   Fall 2012 Enrollment: 62 . . . . (708) 388-4949
   2012-13 Tuition: $12,190
Environmental Technical Institute-Blue Island (Private, For-profit)
   Fall 2012 Enrollment: 132 . . . . (630) 285-9100
   2012-13 Tuition: $13,710

Housing: Homeownership rate: 53.9% (2008-2012 5-year est.); Median home value: $148,600 (2008-2012 5-year est.); Median contract rent: $730 per month (2008-2012 5-year est.); Median year structure built: 1949 (2008-2012 5-year est.).

Health Insurance: 46.0% Private; 39.1% Public; 22.7% None. (2008-2012 5-year est.)

Hospitals: St. Francis Hospital & Health Center (410 beds)

Safety: Violent crime rate: 37.4 per 10,000 population; Property crime rate: 224.6 per 10,000 population (2012).

Transportation: Commute to work: 83.2% car, 10.6% public transportation, 2.7% walk, 1.9% work from home (2008-2012 5-year est.); Travel time to work: 23.5% less than 15 minutes, 27.9% 15 to 30 minutes, 26.3% 30 to 45 minutes, 9.6% 45 to 60 minutes, 12.7% 60 minutes or more (2008-2012 5-year est.)

Additional Information Contacts
Blue Island Area Chamber of Commerce . . . . (708) 388-1000
   http://www.blueislandchamber.org
City of Blue Island . . . . (708) 597-8603
   http://www.blueisland.org

BRIDGEVIEW (village). Covers a land area of 4.153 square miles and a water area of 0 square miles. Located at 41.74° N. Lat; 87.81° W. Long. Elevation is 620 feet.

History: Named for the city's many bridges. Incorporated 1947.

Population: 14,402 (1990); 15,335 (2000); 16,446 (2010); Density: 3,947.9 persons per square mile (2008-2012 5-year est.); Race: 84.2% White, 3.2% Black/African American, 6.4% Asian, 0.0% American Indian/Alaska Native, 0.0% Native Hawaiian/Other Pacific Islander, 6.2% Some other race, 2.8% Two or more races, 16.8% Hispanic of any race (2008-2012 5-year est.); Average household size: 2.82 (2008-2012 5-year est.); Median age: 38.0 (2008-2012 5-year est.); Males per 100 females: 100.0 (2008-2012 5-year est.); Marriage status: 32.4% never married, 48.5% now married, 8.6% widowed, 10.5% divorced (2008-2012 5-year est.); Foreign born: 27.2% (2008-2012 5-year est.); Ancestry (includes multiple ancestries): 25.2% Polish, 16.9% Irish, 13.9% German, 8.0% Italian, 4.6% Other Arab (2008-2012 5-year est.).

Economy: Single-family building permits issued: 0 (2013); Multi-family building permits issued: 0 (2013); Homeowner vacancy rate: 1.7%. Rental vacancy rate: 2.6%. (2008-2012 5-year est.); Employment by occupation: 5.3% management, business, and financial, 1.3% computer, engineering, and science, 6.0% education, legal, community service, arts, and media, 4.2% healthcare practitioners, 21.9% service, 27.6% sales and office, 14.2% natural resources, construction, and maintenance, 19.6% production, transportation, and material moving (2008-2012 5-year est.).

Income: Per capita income: $20,907 (2008-2012 5-year est.); Median household income: $50,727 (2008-2012 5-year est.); Average household income: $57,418 (2008-2012 5-year est.); Percent of households with income of $100,000 or more: 14.5% (2008-2012 5-year est.); Poverty rate: 15.7% (2008-2012 5-year est.).

Taxes: Total city taxes per capita: $766 (2011); City property taxes per capita: $592 (2011).

Education: Percent of population age 25 and over with: High school diploma (including GED) or higher: 79.1% (2008-2012 5-year est.); Bachelor's degree or higher: 13.9% (2008-2012 5-year est.); Master's degree or higher: 3.9% (2008-2012 5-year est.).

School District(s)
Indian Springs SD 109 (PK-08)
   2011-12 Enrollment: 3,108 . . . . (708) 496-8700
Ridgeland SD 122 (PK-08)
   2011-12 Enrollment: 2,342 . . . . (708) 599-5550

Two-year College(s)
Northwestern College-Southwestern Campus (Private, For-profit)
    Fall 2012 Enrollment: 857 . . . . (888) 205-2283
    2012-13 Tuition: In-state $16,215; Out-of-state $16,215
Vocational/Technical School(s)
Tricoci University of Beauty Culture-Bridgeview (Private, For-profit)
    Fall 2012 Enrollment: 166 . . . . (630) 528-3336
    2012-13 Tuition: $18,050
Housing: Homeownership rate: 70.9% (2008-2012 5-year est.); Median home value: $192,000 (2008-2012 5-year est.); Median contract rent: $797 per month (2008-2012 5-year est.); Median year structure built: 1972 (2008-2012 5-year est.).
Health Insurance: 58.1% Private; 33.0% Public; 18.9% None. (2008-2012 5-year est.)
Safety: Violent crime rate: 26.0 per 10,000 population; Property crime rate: 320.1 per 10,000 population (2012).
Transportation: Commute to work: 92.6% car, 2.6% public transportation, 2.2% walk, 1.8% work from home (2008-2012 5-year est.); Travel time to work: 22.7% less than 15 minutes, 30.9% 15 to 30 minutes, 26.7% 30 to 45 minutes, 11.9% 45 to 60 minutes, 7.9% 60 minutes or more (2008-2012 5-year est.)
Additional Information Contacts
Bridgeview Chamber of Commerce . . . . (708) 598-1700
    http://www.bridgeview-il.gov/chamber
Village of Bridgeview. . . . . (708) 594-2525
    http://www.bridgeview-il.gov

BROADVIEW (village). Covers a land area of 1.777 square miles and a water area of 0 square miles. Located at 41.86° N. Lat; 87.86° W. Long. Elevation is 630 feet.
History: Broadview was incorporated as a village in 1910, and developed as a residential community.
Population: 8,713 (1990); 8,264 (2000); 7,932 (2010); Density: 4,465.8 persons per square mile (2008-2012 5-year est.); Race: 20.5% White, 73.1% Black/African American, 0.9% Asian, 0.0% American Indian/Alaska Native, 0.0% Native Hawaiian/Other Pacific Islander, 5.5% Some other race, 0.3% Two or more races, 7.0% Hispanic of any race (2008-2012 5-year est.); Average household size: 2.51 (2008-2012 5-year est.); Median age: 42.7 (2008-2012 5-year est.); Males per 100 females: 98.5 (2008-2012 5-year est.); Marriage status: 35.9% never married, 40.5% now married, 6.7% widowed, 17.0% divorced (2008-2012 5-year est.); Foreign born: 7.7% (2008-2012 5-year est.); Ancestry (includes multiple ancestries): 4.4% Jamaican, 3.4% German, 3.1% Polish, 2.5% English, 2.1% Irish (2008-2012 5-year est.).
Economy: Single-family building permits issued: 0 (2013); Multi-family building permits issued: 0 (2013); Homeowner vacancy rate: 3.6%. Rental vacancy rate: 7.9%. (2008-2012 5-year est.); Employment by occupation: 12.2% management, business, and financial, 3.3% computer, engineering, and science, 8.3% education, legal, community service, arts, and media, 6.0% healthcare practitioners, 18.7% service, 29.0% sales and office, 7.0% natural resources, construction, and maintenance, 15.4% production, transportation, and material moving (2008-2012 5-year est.).
Income: Per capita income: $29,020 (2008-2012 5-year est.); Median household income: $49,750 (2008-2012 5-year est.); Average household income: $70,280 (2008-2012 5-year est.); Percent of households with income of $100,000 or more: 18.7% (2008-2012 5-year est.); Poverty rate: 9.9% (2008-2012 5-year est.).
Taxes: Total city taxes per capita: $1,397 (2011); City property taxes per capita: $1,141 (2011).
Education: Percent of population age 25 and over with: High school diploma (including GED) or higher: 90.3% (2008-2012 5-year est.); Bachelor's degree or higher: 19.4% (2008-2012 5-year est.); Master's degree or higher: 6.3% (2008-2012 5-year est.).
School District(s)
Lindop SD 92 (PK-08)
    2011-12 Enrollment: 530. . . . . (708) 786-6460
Maywood-Melrose Park-Broadview 89 (PK-08)
    2011-12 Enrollment: 5,362 . . . . (708) 450-2460
Housing: Homeownership rate: 64.4% (2008-2012 5-year est.); Median home value: $177,900 (2008-2012 5-year est.); Median contract rent: $730 per month (2008-2012 5-year est.); Median year structure built: 1954 (2008-2012 5-year est.).
Health Insurance: 66.1% Private; 29.5% Public; 13.3% None. (2008-2012 5-year est.)

Safety: Violent crime rate: 35.1 per 10,000 population; Property crime rate: 530.7 per 10,000 population (2012).
Transportation: Commute to work: 87.5% car, 5.2% public transportation, 5.7% walk, 0.3% work from home (2008-2012 5-year est.); Travel time to work: 28.9% less than 15 minutes, 29.4% 15 to 30 minutes, 27.8% 30 to 45 minutes, 10.6% 45 to 60 minutes, 3.3% 60 minutes or more (2008-2012 5-year est.)
Additional Information Contacts
Village of Broadview . . . . (708) 681-3600
    http://www.broadview-il.gov

BROOKFIELD (village). Covers a land area of 3.063 square miles and a water area of 0.007 square miles. Located at 41.83° N. Lat; 87.85° W. Long. Elevation is 623 feet.
History: Named for the many local brooks. Incorporated 1893.
Population: 18,876 (1990); 19,085 (2000); 18,978 (2010); Density: 6,141.5 persons per square mile (2008-2012 5-year est.); Race: 92.1% White, 1.8% Black/African American, 1.6% Asian, 0.2% American Indian/Alaska Native, 0.0% Native Hawaiian/Other Pacific Islander, 4.3% Some other race, 1.2% Two or more races, 15.4% Hispanic of any race (2008-2012 5-year est.); Average household size: 2.67 (2008-2012 5-year est.); Median age: 38.0 (2008-2012 5-year est.); Males per 100 females: 88.2 (2008-2012 5-year est.); Marriage status: 31.7% never married, 51.2% now married, 6.6% widowed, 10.6% divorced (2008-2012 5-year est.); Foreign born: 10.2% (2008-2012 5-year est.); Ancestry (includes multiple ancestries): 27.0% German, 21.6% Irish, 15.9% Italian, 15.0% Polish, 7.5% Czech (2008-2012 5-year est.).
Economy: Single-family building permits issued: 3 (2013); Multi-family building permits issued: 0 (2013); Homeowner vacancy rate: 0.3%. Rental vacancy rate: 6.7%. (2008-2012 5-year est.); Employment by occupation: 15.3% management, business, and financial, 6.2% computer, engineering, and science, 13.8% education, legal, community service, arts, and media, 4.8% healthcare practitioners, 11.5% service, 29.9% sales and office, 6.9% natural resources, construction, and maintenance, 11.7% production, transportation, and material moving (2008-2012 5-year est.).
Income: Per capita income: $31,449 (2008-2012 5-year est.); Median household income: $71,360 (2008-2012 5-year est.); Average household income: $81,895 (2008-2012 5-year est.); Percent of households with income of $100,000 or more: 31.3% (2008-2012 5-year est.); Poverty rate: 7.2% (2008-2012 5-year est.).
Education: Percent of population age 25 and over with: High school diploma (including GED) or higher: 93.6% (2008-2012 5-year est.); Bachelor's degree or higher: 32.6% (2008-2012 5-year est.); Master's degree or higher: 11.5% (2008-2012 5-year est.).
School District(s)
Brookfield Lagrange Park SD 95 (PK-08)
    2011-12 Enrollment: 1,087 . . . . (708) 485-0606
La Grange SD 102 (PK-08)
    2011-12 Enrollment: 3,126 . . . . (708) 482-2400
Lyons SD 103 (PK-08)
    2011-12 Enrollment: 2,486 . . . . (708) 783-4100
Riverside SD 96 (PK-08)
    2011-12 Enrollment: 1,579 . . . . (708) 447-5007
Housing: Homeownership rate: 76.3% (2008-2012 5-year est.); Median home value: $251,900 (2008-2012 5-year est.); Median contract rent: $854 per month (2008-2012 5-year est.); Median year structure built: 1951 (2008-2012 5-year est.).
Health Insurance: 82.7% Private; 18.8% Public; 7.8% None. (2008-2012 5-year est.)
Safety: Violent crime rate: 15.2 per 10,000 population; Property crime rate: 164.1 per 10,000 population (2012).
Transportation: Commute to work: 85.7% car, 7.8% public transportation, 2.9% walk, 2.9% work from home (2008-2012 5-year est.); Travel time to work: 19.3% less than 15 minutes, 32.1% 15 to 30 minutes, 29.2% 30 to 45 minutes, 10.5% 45 to 60 minutes, 8.8% 60 minutes or more (2008-2012 5-year est.)
Additional Information Contacts
Brookfield Chamber of Commerce . . . . (708) 268-8080
    http://brookfieldchamber.net
Village of Brookfield . . . . (708) 485-7344
    http://www.villageofbrookfield.com

BURBANK (city). Aka South Stickney. Covers a land area of 4.172 square miles and a water area of 0 square miles. Located at 41.74° N. Lat; 87.77° W. Long. Elevation is 620 feet.
Population: 27,600 (1990); 27,902 (2000); 28,925 (2010); Density: 6,914.7 persons per square mile (2008-2012 5-year est.); Race: 83.7% White, 0.6% Black/African American, 3.1% Asian, 0.5% American Indian/Alaska Native, 0.0% Native Hawaiian/Other Pacific Islander, 12.1% Some other race, 0.9% Two or more races, 27.2% Hispanic of any race (2008-2012 5-year est.); Average household size: 3.21 (2008-2012 5-year est.); Median age: 36.9 (2008-2012 5-year est.); Males per 100 females: 95.2 (2008-2012 5-year est.); Marriage status: 32.6% never married, 52.6% now married, 7.2% widowed, 7.6% divorced (2008-2012 5-year est.); Foreign born: 30.7% (2008-2012 5-year est.); Ancestry (includes multiple ancestries): 30.5% Polish, 11.2% Irish, 10.9% German, 5.5% Italian, 3.2% Palestinian (2008-2012 5-year est.).
Economy: Unemployment rate: 7.3% (April 2014); Total civilian labor force: 15,053 (April 2014); Single-family building permits issued: 14 (2013); Multi-family building permits issued: 0 (2013); Homeowner vacancy rate: 2.0%. Rental vacancy rate: 6.2%. (2008-2012 5-year est.); Employment by occupation: 8.1% management, business, and financial, 2.6% computer, engineering, and science, 4.6% education, legal, community service, arts, and media, 3.1% healthcare practitioners, 19.9% service, 26.3% sales and office, 12.5% natural resources, construction, and maintenance, 22.8% production, transportation, and material moving (2008-2012 5-year est.).
Income: Per capita income: $21,516 (2008-2012 5-year est.); Median household income: $56,617 (2008-2012 5-year est.); Average household income: $65,599 (2008-2012 5-year est.); Percent of households with income of $100,000 or more: 18.2% (2008-2012 5-year est.); Poverty rate: 11.7% (2008-2012 5-year est.).
Taxes: Total city taxes per capita: $316 (2011); City property taxes per capita: $167 (2011).
Education: Percent of population age 25 and over with: High school diploma (including GED) or higher: 76.3% (2008-2012 5-year est.); Bachelor's degree or higher: 12.1% (2008-2012 5-year est.); Master's degree or higher: 2.9% (2008-2012 5-year est.).

School District(s)
A E R O Spec Educ Coop (PK-12)
 2011-12 Enrollment: n/a . . . . (708) 496-3330
Burbank SD 111 (PK-08)
 2011-12 Enrollment: 3,356 . . . . (708) 496-0500
Reavis Twp HSD 220 (09-12)
 2011-12 Enrollment: 1,785 . . . . (708) 599-7200
Housing: Homeownership rate: 80.0% (2008-2012 5-year est.); Median home value: $210,600 (2008-2012 5-year est.); Median contract rent: $873 per month (2008-2012 5-year est.); Median year structure built: 1963 (2008-2012 5-year est.).
Health Insurance: 62.6% Private; 31.1% Public; 16.9% None. (2008-2012 5-year est.)
Safety: Violent crime rate: 17.9 per 10,000 population; Property crime rate: 197.8 per 10,000 population (2012).
Transportation: Commute to work: 91.4% car, 4.7% public transportation, 1.4% walk, 1.6% work from home (2008-2012 5-year est.); Travel time to work: 22.0% less than 15 minutes, 28.4% 15 to 30 minutes, 23.9% 30 to 45 minutes, 12.9% 45 to 60 minutes, 12.7% 60 minutes or more (2008-2012 5-year est.)
Additional Information Contacts
Burbank Chamber of Commerce . . . . (708) 425-4668
 http://www.burbankilchamber.com
City of Burbank . . . . (708) 599-5500
 http://www.burbankil.gov

BURNHAM (village). Covers a land area of 1.867 square miles and a water area of 0.086 square miles. Located at 41.64° N. Lat; 87.54° W. Long. Elevation is 584 feet.
Population: 3,916 (1990); 4,170 (2000); 4,206 (2010); Density: 2,254.3 persons per square mile (2008-2012 5-year est.); Race: 28.3% White, 64.4% Black/African American, 1.7% Asian, 0.1% American Indian/Alaska Native, 0.0% Native Hawaiian/Other Pacific Islander, 5.5% Some other race, 0.5% Two or more races, 20.9% Hispanic of any race (2008-2012 5-year est.); Average household size: 2.56 (2008-2012 5-year est.); Median age: 38.4 (2008-2012 5-year est.); Males per 100 females: 87.9 (2008-2012 5-year est.); Marriage status: 48.1% never married, 34.7% now married, 5.1% widowed, 12.1% divorced (2008-2012 5-year est.); Foreign born: 11.4% (2008-2012 5-year est.); Ancestry (includes multiple

ancestries): 4.3% Polish, 2.5% German, 2.1% Irish, 1.6% Italian, 1.6% African (2008-2012 5-year est.).
Economy: Single-family building permits issued: 0 (2013); Multi-family building permits issued: 0 (2013); Homeowner vacancy rate: 1.5%. Rental vacancy rate: 7.2%. (2008-2012 5-year est.); Employment by occupation: 5.7% management, business, and financial, 3.8% computer, engineering, and science, 8.5% education, legal, community service, arts, and media, 6.5% healthcare practitioners, 13.0% service, 29.6% sales and office, 8.9% natural resources, construction, and maintenance, 23.9% production, transportation, and material moving (2008-2012 5-year est.).
Income: Per capita income: $19,106 (2008-2012 5-year est.); Median household income: $39,871 (2008-2012 5-year est.); Average household income: $48,833 (2008-2012 5-year est.); Percent of households with income of $100,000 or more: 9.7% (2008-2012 5-year est.); Poverty rate: 19.2% (2008-2012 5-year est.).
Education: Percent of population age 25 and over with: High school diploma (including GED) or higher: 86.0% (2008-2012 5-year est.); Bachelor's degree or higher: 10.2% (2008-2012 5-year est.); Master's degree or higher: 3.2% (2008-2012 5-year est.).

School District(s)
Burnham SD 154-5 (PK-08)
 2011-12 Enrollment: 190 . . . . (708) 862-8636
Housing: Homeownership rate: 61.8% (2008-2012 5-year est.); Median home value: $134,200 (2008-2012 5-year est.); Median contract rent: $773 per month (2008-2012 5-year est.); Median year structure built: 1965 (2008-2012 5-year est.).
Health Insurance: 56.2% Private; 37.4% Public; 16.2% None. (2008-2012 5-year est.)
Safety: Violent crime rate: 26.0 per 10,000 population; Property crime rate: 378.6 per 10,000 population (2012).
Transportation: Commute to work: 89.7% car, 6.7% public transportation, 1.3% walk, 2.0% work from home (2008-2012 5-year est.); Travel time to work: 15.8% less than 15 minutes, 28.7% 15 to 30 minutes, 24.8% 30 to 45 minutes, 16.8% 45 to 60 minutes, 13.9% 60 minutes or more (2008-2012 5-year est.)

CALUMET CITY (city). Covers a land area of 7.185 square miles and a water area of 0.124 square miles. Located at 41.60° N. Lat; 87.54° W. Long. Elevation is 591 feet.
History: Named for the French translation of "straw". Calumet City was platted in 1833, and developed in the 1920's as a residential outgrowth of Hammond, Indiana. Calumet is the French name for the Indian peace-pipe.
Population: 37,840 (1990); 39,071 (2000); 37,042 (2010); Density: 5,159.1 persons per square mile (2008-2012 5-year est.); Race: 23.2% White, 68.8% Black/African American, 0.2% Asian, 0.1% American Indian/Alaska Native, 0.0% Native Hawaiian/Other Pacific Islander, 7.7% Some other race, 1.5% Two or more races, 16.6% Hispanic of any race (2008-2012 5-year est.); Average household size: 2.57 (2008-2012 5-year est.); Median age: 35.9 (2008-2012 5-year est.); Males per 100 females: 78.3 (2008-2012 5-year est.); Marriage status: 42.1% never married, 35.3% now married, 8.3% widowed, 14.3% divorced (2008-2012 5-year est.); Foreign born: 8.8% (2008-2012 5-year est.); Ancestry (includes multiple ancestries): 5.4% Polish, 2.3% German, 2.0% Irish, 2.0% Italian, 1.4% African (2008-2012 5-year est.).
Economy: Unemployment rate: 10.1% (April 2014); Total civilian labor force: 18,081 (April 2014); Single-family building permits issued: 0 (2013); Multi-family building permits issued: 0 (2013); Homeowner vacancy rate: 4.1%. Rental vacancy rate: 9.6%. (2008-2012 5-year est.); Employment by occupation: 8.1% management, business, and financial, 1.6% computer, engineering, and science, 6.7% education, legal, community service, arts, and media, 5.4% healthcare practitioners, 20.6% service, 29.5% sales and office, 6.9% natural resources, construction, and maintenance, 21.3% production, transportation, and material moving (2008-2012 5-year est.).
Income: Per capita income: $20,723 (2008-2012 5-year est.); Median household income: $41,244 (2008-2012 5-year est.); Average household income: $51,358 (2008-2012 5-year est.); Percent of households with income of $100,000 or more: 9.3% (2008-2012 5-year est.); Poverty rate: 20.3% (2008-2012 5-year est.).
Taxes: Total city taxes per capita: $825 (2011); City property taxes per capita: $513 (2011).
Education: Percent of population age 25 and over with: High school diploma (including GED) or higher: 84.7% (2008-2012 5-year est.); Bachelor's degree or higher: 15.2% (2008-2012 5-year est.); Master's degree or higher: 4.8% (2008-2012 5-year est.).

School District(s)

Calumet City SD 155 (PK-08)
 2011-12 Enrollment: 1,361 . . . . (708) 862-7665
Dolton SD 149 (PK-08)
 2011-12 Enrollment: 3,135 . . . . (708) 868-7861
Hoover-Schrum Memorial SD 157 (PK-08)
 2011-12 Enrollment: 935 . . . . (708) 868-7500
Lincoln ESD 156 (PK-08)
 2011-12 Enrollment: 1,132 . . . . (708) 862-6625
Thornton Fractional Twp HSD 215 (09-12)
 2011-12 Enrollment: 3,567 . . . . (708) 585-2309

Four-year College(s)

Westwood College-River Oaks (Private, For-profit)
 Fall 2012 Enrollment: 388 . . . . (708) 832-1988
 2012-13 Tuition: In-state $14,517; Out-of-state $14,517
Housing: Homeownership rate: 59.1% (2008-2012 5-year est.); Median home value: $122,400 (2008-2012 5-year est.); Median contract rent: $749 per month (2008-2012 5-year est.); Median year structure built: 1965 (2008-2012 5-year est.).
Health Insurance: 50.9% Private; 37.7% Public; 20.6% None. (2008-2012 5-year est.)
Transportation: Commute to work: 85.9% car, 8.7% public transportation, 2.3% walk, 1.3% work from home (2008-2012 5-year est.); Travel time to work: 14.5% less than 15 minutes, 28.4% 15 to 30 minutes, 25.3% 30 to 45 minutes, 13.1% 45 to 60 minutes, 18.8% 60 minutes or more (2008-2012 5-year est.)
Additional Information Contacts
Calumet City Chamber of Commerce . . . . (708) 891-5888
 http://www.calumetcitychamber.com
City of Calumet City. . . . . (708) 891-8100
 http://calumetcity.org

CALUMET PARK (village). Covers a land area of 1.112 square miles and a water area of 0.036 square miles. Located at 41.67° N. Lat; 87.66° W. Long. Elevation is 604 feet.

History: Incorporated 1912; name changed from Burr Oak in 1925.
Population: 8,418 (1990); 8,516 (2000); 7,835 (2010); Density: 7,113.6 persons per square mile (2008-2012 5-year est.); Race: 18.3% White, 81.0% Black/African American, 0.0% Asian, 0.0% American Indian/Alaska Native, 0.0% Native Hawaiian/Other Pacific Islander, 0.7% Some other race, 0.6% Two or more races, 12.8% Hispanic of any race (2008-2012 5-year est.); Average household size: 2.63 (2008-2012 5-year est.); Median age: 37.6 (2008-2012 5-year est.); Males per 100 females: 99.1 (2008-2012 5-year est.); Marriage status: 45.8% never married, 34.8% now married, 6.4% widowed, 13.0% divorced (2008-2012 5-year est.); Foreign born: 7.7% (2008-2012 5-year est.); Ancestry (includes multiple ancestries): 2.2% German, 1.7% Russian, 1.5% Irish, 1.0% Haitian, 0.7% African (2008-2012 5-year est.).
Economy: Single-family building permits issued: 0 (2013); Multi-family building permits issued: 0 (2013); Homeowner vacancy rate: 4.7%. Rental vacancy rate: 9.3%. (2008-2012 5-year est.); Employment by occupation: 5.8% management, business, and financial, 1.9% computer, engineering, and science, 10.7% education, legal, community service, arts, and media, 2.5% healthcare practitioners, 22.4% service, 35.5% sales and office, 1.9% natural resources, construction, and maintenance, 19.3% production, transportation, and material moving (2008-2012 5-year est.).
Income: Per capita income: $23,649 (2008-2012 5-year est.); Median household income: $44,874 (2008-2012 5-year est.); Average household income: $59,271 (2008-2012 5-year est.); Percent of households with income of $100,000 or more: 13.4% (2008-2012 5-year est.); Poverty rate: 16.1% (2008-2012 5-year est.).
Education: Percent of population age 25 and over with: High school diploma (including GED) or higher: 86.1% (2008-2012 5-year est.); Bachelor's degree or higher: 12.9% (2008-2012 5-year est.); Master's degree or higher: 5.2% (2008-2012 5-year est.).

School District(s)

Calumet Public SD 132 (PK-08)
 2011-12 Enrollment: 1,168 . . . . (708) 388-8920
Housing: Homeownership rate: 57.8% (2008-2012 5-year est.); Median home value: $138,300 (2008-2012 5-year est.); Median contract rent: $804 per month (2008-2012 5-year est.); Median year structure built: 1959 (2008-2012 5-year est.).
Health Insurance: 55.4% Private; 32.1% Public; 21.8% None. (2008-2012 5-year est.)

Transportation: Commute to work: 80.8% car, 17.0% public transportation, 0.0% walk, 1.4% work from home (2008-2012 5-year est.); Travel time to work: 12.2% less than 15 minutes, 25.2% 15 to 30 minutes, 29.7% 30 to 45 minutes, 10.1% 45 to 60 minutes, 22.9% 60 minutes or more (2008-2012 5-year est.)
Additional Information Contacts
Village of Calumet Park. . . . . (708) 389-0850
 http://www.calumetparkvillage.org

CHICAGO (city). County seat. Covers a land area of 227.635 square miles and a water area of 6.479 square miles. Located at 41.84° N. Lat; 87.68° W. Long. Elevation is 587 feet.

History: The river here was called Checagou by the Indians, meaning something big, strong, or powerful. In 1803 Captain John Whistler and his men built Fort Dearborn on the site that was to become Chicago, where a few cabins occupied by Frenchmen and the Sable trading post already existed. John Kinzie, a Scotch-Canadian trader who took over the trading post, was the first English settler in the community that developed around Fort Dearborn. When Chicago was incorporated as a town in 1833, the population numbered under 200. The projected Illinois & Michigan Canal brought speculators; Chicago was incorporated as a city in 1837 and soon became the world's largest grain market and a major slaughterhouse. The completion of the Illinois & Michigan Canal in 1848 increased the commercial importance of Chicago, as did the many railroad lines that soon radiated from it. The quick ramshackle building of Chicago was halted in 1871 when the fire started in Patrick O'Leary's cow barn destroyed 17,450 buildings in 27 hours. Rebuilding was fast and more permanent.
Population: 2,783,726 (1990); 2,896,016 (2000); 2,695,598 (2010); Density: 11,872.0 persons per square mile (2008-2012 5-year est.); Race: 47.0% White, 32.9% Black/African American, 5.6% Asian, 0.3% American Indian/Alaska Native, 0.0% Native Hawaiian/Other Pacific Islander, 14.2% Some other race, 1.9% Two or more races, 28.4% Hispanic of any race (2008-2012 5-year est.); Average household size: 2.57 (2008-2012 5-year est.); Median age: 33.1 (2008-2012 5-year est.); Males per 100 females: 93.9 (2008-2012 5-year est.); Marriage status: 47.9% never married, 37.6% now married, 5.7% widowed, 8.8% divorced (2008-2012 5-year est.); Foreign born: 21.2% (2008-2012 5-year est.); Ancestry (includes multiple ancestries): 7.6% German, 7.6% Irish, 6.2% Polish, 3.9% Italian, 2.3% English (2008-2012 5-year est.).
Economy: Unemployment rate: 8.4% (April 2014); Total civilian labor force: 1,253,780 (April 2014); Single-family building permits issued: 448 (2013); Multi-family building permits issued: 2,577 (2013); Homeowner vacancy rate: 3.8%. Rental vacancy rate: 7.7%. (2008-2012 5-year est.); Employment by occupation: 15.3% management, business, and financial, 4.7% computer, engineering, and science, 12.8% education, legal, community service, arts, and media, 4.6% healthcare practitioners, 20.1% service, 23.5% sales and office, 5.9% natural resources, construction, and maintenance, 13.1% production, transportation, and material moving (2008-2012 5-year est.).
Income: Per capita income: $28,202 (2008-2012 5-year est.); Median household income: $47,408 (2008-2012 5-year est.); Average household income: $71,020 (2008-2012 5-year est.); Percent of households with income of $100,000 or more: 20.6% (2008-2012 5-year est.); Poverty rate: 22.1% (2008-2012 5-year est.).
Taxes: Total city taxes per capita: $821 (2011); City property taxes per capita: $266 (2011).
Education: Percent of population age 25 and over with: High school diploma (including GED) or higher: 80.5% (2008-2012 5-year est.); Bachelor's degree or higher: 33.6% (2008-2012 5-year est.); Master's degree or higher: 13.5% (2008-2012 5-year est.).

School District(s)

Central Stickney SD 110 (PK-08)
 2011-12 Enrollment: 463. . . . . (708) 458-1152
City of Chicago SD 299 (PK-12)
 2011-12 Enrollment: 403,004 . . . . (773) 553-1000
Dept of Human Services (PK-12)
 2011-12 Enrollment: n/a . . . . (217) 524-1379
Idjj SD 428 (06-12)
 2011-12 Enrollment: 784. . . . . (309) 584-0506
Intermediate Service Center 3
 2011-12 Enrollment: n/a . . . . (312) 263-7767

Four-year College(s)

Adler School of Professional Psychology (Private, Not-for-profit)
 Fall 2012 Enrollment: 978 . . . . (312) 662-4000

American Academy of Art (Private, For-profit)
Fall 2012 Enrollment: 433 . . . . (312) 461-0600
2012-13 Tuition: In-state $27,770; Out-of-state $27,770

Argosy University-Chicago (Private, For-profit)
Fall 2012 Enrollment: 1,336 . . . . (312) 777-7600
2012-13 Tuition: In-state $12,685; Out-of-state $12,685

Catholic Theological Union at Chicago (Private, Not-for-profit, Roman Catholic)
Fall 2012 Enrollment: 420 . . . . (773) 324-8000

Chicago State University (Public)
Fall 2012 Enrollment: 6,107 . . . . (773) 995-2000
2012-13 Tuition: In-state $8,558; Out-of-state $14,654

Chicago Theological Seminary (Private, Not-for-profit, United Church of Christ)
Fall 2012 Enrollment: 224 . . . . (773) 896-2400

Columbia College-Chicago (Private, Not-for-profit)
Fall 2012 Enrollment: 10,783 . . . . (312) 663-1600
2012-13 Tuition: In-state $21,730; Out-of-state $21,730

DePaul University (Private, Not-for-profit, Roman Catholic)
Fall 2012 Enrollment: 24,042 . . . . (312) 362-8000
2012-13 Tuition: In-state $32,295; Out-of-state $32,295

DeVry University-Illinois (Private, For-profit)
Fall 2012 Enrollment: 27,921 . . . . (773) 929-8500
2012-13 Tuition: In-state $15,915; Out-of-state $15,915

East-West University (Private, Not-for-profit)
Fall 2012 Enrollment: 879 . . . . (312) 939-0111
2012-13 Tuition: In-state $17,595; Out-of-state $17,595

Erikson Institute (Private, Not-for-profit)
Fall 2012 Enrollment: 257 . . . . (312) 755-2250

Harrington College of Design (Private, For-profit)
Fall 2012 Enrollment: 616 . . . . (312) 939-4975
2012-13 Tuition: In-state $19,300; Out-of-state $19,300

Illinois College of Optometry (Private, Not-for-profit)
Fall 2012 Enrollment: 626 . . . . (312) 949-7400

Illinois Institute of Technology (Private, Not-for-profit)
Fall 2012 Enrollment: 7,684 . . . . (312) 567-3000
2012-13 Tuition: In-state $37,969; Out-of-state $37,969

Institute for Clinical Social Work (Private, Not-for-profit)
Fall 2012 Enrollment: 94 . . . . (312) 935-4232

International Academy of Design and Technology-Chicago (Private, For-profit)
Fall 2012 Enrollment: 550 . . . . (312) 980-9200
2012-13 Tuition: In-state $14,400; Out-of-state $14,400

Kendall College (Private, For-profit)
Fall 2012 Enrollment: 1,799 . . . . (312) 752-2000
2012-13 Tuition: In-state $24,246; Out-of-state $24,246

Lexington College (Private, Not-for-profit)
Fall 2012 Enrollment: 52 . . . . (312) 226-6294
2012-13 Tuition: In-state $24,700; Out-of-state $24,700

Loyola University Chicago (Private, Not-for-profit, Roman Catholic)
Fall 2012 Enrollment: 15,720 . . . . (773) 274-3000
2012-13 Tuition: In-state $34,578; Out-of-state $34,578

Lutheran School of Theology at Chicago (Private, Not-for-profit, Evangelical Lutheran Church)
Fall 2012 Enrollment: 257 . . . . (773) 256-0700

McCormick Theological Seminary (Private, Not-for-profit, Presbyterian Church (USA))
Fall 2012 Enrollment: 207 . . . . (773) 947-6300

Meadville Lombard Theological School (Private, Not-for-profit, Unitarian Universalist)
Fall 2012 Enrollment: 103 . . . . (773) 256-3000

Midwest College of Oriental Medicine-Chicago (Private, For-profit)
Fall 2012 Enrollment: 118 . . . . (800) 593-2320

Moody Bible Institute (Private, Not-for-profit, Interdenominational)
Fall 2012 Enrollment: 3,723 . . . . (312) 329-4000
2012-13 Tuition: In-state $10,954; Out-of-state $10,954

National Louis University (Private, Not-for-profit)
Fall 2012 Enrollment: 4,681 . . . . (800) 443-5522
2012-13 Tuition: In-state $18,930; Out-of-state $18,930

North Park University (Private, Not-for-profit, Evangelical Covenant Church of America)
Fall 2012 Enrollment: 3,141 . . . . (773) 244-6200
2012-13 Tuition: In-state $22,150; Out-of-state $22,150

Northeastern Illinois University (Public)
Fall 2012 Enrollment: 11,149 . . . . (773) 583-4050
2012-13 Tuition: In-state $8,089; Out-of-state $14,689

Pacific College of Oriental Medicine-Chicago (Private, For-profit)
Fall 2012 Enrollment: 239 . . . . (773) 477-4822
2012-13 Tuition: In-state $12,257; Out-of-state $12,257

Robert Morris University Illinois (Private, Not-for-profit)
Fall 2012 Enrollment: 3,793 . . . . (312) 935-6800
2012-13 Tuition: In-state $22,200; Out-of-state $22,200

Roosevelt University (Private, Not-for-profit)
Fall 2012 Enrollment: 6,493 . . . . (312) 341-3500
2012-13 Tuition: In-state $25,950; Out-of-state $25,950

Rush University (Private, Not-for-profit)
Fall 2012 Enrollment: 2,206 . . . . (312) 942-7100

Saint Augustine College (Private, Not-for-profit)
Fall 2012 Enrollment: 1,683 . . . . (773) 878-8756
2012-13 Tuition: In-state $8,760; Out-of-state $8,760

Saint Xavier University (Private, Not-for-profit, Roman Catholic)
Fall 2012 Enrollment: 4,353 . . . . (773) 298-3000
2012-13 Tuition: In-state $28,110; Out-of-state $28,110

School of the Art Institute of Chicago (Private, Not-for-profit)
Fall 2012 Enrollment: 3,240 . . . . (312) 629-6100
2012-13 Tuition: In-state $39,020; Out-of-state $39,020

Seabury-Western Theological Seminary (Private, Not-for-profit, Protestant Episcopal)
Fall 2012 Enrollment: 22 . . . . (773) 380-6780

Shimer College (Private, Not-for-profit)
Fall 2012 Enrollment: 113 . . . . (312) 235-3500
2012-13 Tuition: In-state $30,780; Out-of-state $30,780

Spertus College (Private, Not-for-profit)
Fall 2012 Enrollment: 246 . . . . (312) 922-9012

Strayer University-Illinois (Private, For-profit)
Fall 2012 Enrollment: 219 . . . . (312) 803-4150
2012-13 Tuition: In-state $14,985; Out-of-state $14,985

Telshe Yeshiva-Chicago (Private, Not-for-profit, Jewish)
Fall 2012 Enrollment: 83 . . . . (773) 463-7738
2012-13 Tuition: In-state $12,000; Out-of-state $12,000

The Chicago School of Professional Psychology at Chicago (Private, Not-for-profit)
Fall 2012 Enrollment: 2,874 . . . . (312) 329-6600

The Illinois Institute of Art-Chicago (Private, For-profit)
Fall 2012 Enrollment: 2,711 . . . . (312) 280-3500
2012-13 Tuition: In-state $17,796; Out-of-state $17,796

The John Marshall Law School (Private, Not-for-profit)
Fall 2012 Enrollment: 1,617 . . . . (312) 427-2737

University of Chicago (Private, Not-for-profit)
Fall 2012 Enrollment: 15,272 . . . . (773) 702-1234
2012-13 Tuition: In-state $45,609; Out-of-state $45,609

University of Illinois at Chicago (Public)
Fall 2012 Enrollment: 27,875 . . . . (312) 996-7000
2012-13 Tuition: In-state $13,122; Out-of-state $25,512

VanderCook College of Music (Private, Not-for-profit)
Fall 2012 Enrollment: 228 . . . . (312) 225-6288
2012-13 Tuition: In-state $24,116; Out-of-state $24,116

Westwood College-Chicago Loop (Private, For-profit)
Fall 2012 Enrollment: 484 . . . . (312) 739-0850
2012-13 Tuition: In-state $14,982; Out-of-state $14,982

Westwood College-O'Hare Airport (Private, For-profit)
Fall 2012 Enrollment: 477 . . . . (773) 380-6800
2012-13 Tuition: In-state $14,517; Out-of-state $14,517

Two-year College(s)

City Colleges of Chicago-Harold Washington College (Public)
Fall 2012 Enrollment: 8,937 . . . . (312) 553-5600
2012-13 Tuition: In-state $5,961; Out-of-state $7,498

City Colleges of Chicago-Harry S Truman College (Public)
Fall 2012 Enrollment: 11,919 . . . . (773) 907-4000
2012-13 Tuition: In-state $5,961; Out-of-state $7,498

City Colleges of Chicago-Kennedy-King College (Public)
Fall 2012 Enrollment: 6,235 . . . . (773) 602-5000
2012-13 Tuition: In-state $5,961; Out-of-state $7,498

City Colleges of Chicago-Malcolm X College (Public)
Fall 2012 Enrollment: 6,530 . . . . (312) 850-7000
2012-13 Tuition: In-state $5,961; Out-of-state $7,498

City Colleges of Chicago-Olive-Harvey College (Public)
Fall 2012 Enrollment: 4,963 . . . . (773) 291-6100
2012-13 Tuition: In-state $5,961; Out-of-state $7,498

City Colleges of Chicago-Richard J Daley College (Public)
Fall 2012 Enrollment: 9,337 . . . . (773) 838-7500
2012-13 Tuition: In-state $5,961; Out-of-state $7,498
City Colleges of Chicago-Wilbur Wright College (Public)
Fall 2012 Enrollment: 12,448 . . . . (773) 777-7900
2012-13 Tuition: In-state $5,961; Out-of-state $7,498
Coyne College (Private, For-profit)
Fall 2012 Enrollment: 885 . . . . (773) 577-8100
Le Cordon Bleu College of Culinary Arts-Chicago (Private, For-profit)
Fall 2012 Enrollment: 1,301 . . . . (312) 944-0882
2012-13 Tuition: In-state $12,912; Out-of-state $12,912
MacCormac College (Private, Not-for-profit)
Fall 2012 Enrollment: 194 . . . . (312) 922-1884
2012-13 Tuition: In-state $12,930; Out-of-state $12,930
Midwestern Career College (Private, For-profit)
Fall 2012 Enrollment: 178 . . . . (312) 236-9000
Northwestern College (Private, For-profit)
Fall 2012 Enrollment: 673 . . . . (773) 777-4220
2012-13 Tuition: In-state $16,215; Out-of-state $16,215
Taylor Business Institute (Private, For-profit)
Fall 2012 Enrollment: 257 . . . . (312) 658-5100
2012-13 Tuition: In-state $13,500; Out-of-state $13,500
The College of Office Technology (Private, For-profit)
Fall 2012 Enrollment: 115 . . . . (773) 278-0042
Tribeca Flashpoint Media Arts Academy (Private, For-profit)
Fall 2012 Enrollment: 493 . . . . (312) 506-0725
2012-13 Tuition: In-state $25,250; Out-of-state $25,250

Vocational/Technical School(s)

Aveda Institute-Chicago (Private, For-profit)
Fall 2012 Enrollment: 78 . . . . (773) 883-1560
2012-13 Tuition: $17,500
BIR Training Center (Private, For-profit)
Fall 2012 Enrollment: 977 . . . . (773) 866-0111
2012-13 Tuition: $11,900
CET-Chicago (Private, Not-for-profit)
Fall 2012 Enrollment: 307 . . . . (408) 287-7924
2012-13 Tuition: $7,437
Cain's Barber College Inc (Private, For-profit)
Fall 2012 Enrollment: 74 . . . . (773) 536-4441
2012-13 Tuition: $11,700
Cannella School of Hair Design-Chicago (Private, For-profit)
Fall 2012 Enrollment: 76 . . . . (773) 221-4700
2012-13 Tuition: $12,190
Cannella School of Hair Design-Chicago (Private, For-profit)
Fall 2012 Enrollment: 127 . . . . (773) 890-0412
2012-13 Tuition: $10,190
Cannella School of Hair Design-Chicago (Private, For-profit)
Fall 2012 Enrollment: 63 . . . . (773) 278-4477
2012-13 Tuition: $10,190
Capri Beauty College (Private, For-profit)
Fall 2012 Enrollment: 92 . . . . (773) 778-0882
2012-13 Tuition: $15,400
Chicago School for Piano Technology (The) (Private, Not-for-profit)
Fall 2012 Enrollment: 11 . . . . (312) 666-7440
2012-13 Tuition: $19,000
Cortiva Institute-Chicago (Private, For-profit)
Fall 2012 Enrollment: 401 . . . . (312) 753-7900
Illinois CareerPath Institute (Private, Not-for-profit)
Fall 2012 Enrollment: 71 . . . . (312) 346-3662
2012-13 Tuition: $8,371
Illinois Center for Broadcastingâ€"Chicago Campus (Private, For-profit)
Fall 2012 Enrollment: 226 . . . . (312) 884-8000
2012-13 Tuition: $16,479
Illinois School of Health Careers (Private, For-profit)
Fall 2012 Enrollment: 591 . . . . (312) 913-1230
2012-13 Tuition: $15,750
Illinois School of Health Careers-O'Hare Campus (Private, For-profit)
Fall 2012 Enrollment: 254 . . . . (773) 444-0300
2012-13 Tuition: $15,250
Larry's Barber College (Public)
Fall 2012 Enrollment: 25 . . . . (773) 779-2100
2012-13 Tuition: $9,900
Mac Daniels Beauty School (Private, For-profit)
Fall 2012 Enrollment: 62 . . . . (773) 883-5100
2012-13 Tuition: $15,000

National Latino Education Institute (Private, Not-for-profit)
Fall 2012 Enrollment: 84 . . . . (773) 247-0707
2012-13 Tuition: $9,725
Northwestern Institute of Health and Technology (Private, Not-for-profit)
Fall 2012 Enrollment: 275 . . . . (877) 908-9969
2012-13 Tuition: $24,875
Paul Mitchell the School-Chicago (Private, For-profit)
Fall 2012 Enrollment: 316 . . . . (312) 733-9285
2012-13 Tuition: $19,500
Pivot Point Academy (Private, For-profit)
Fall 2012 Enrollment: 56 . . . . (773) 463-3121
2012-13 Tuition: $18,345
Rosel School of Cosmetology (Private, For-profit)
Fall 2012 Enrollment: 93 . . . . (773) 508-5600
2012-13 Tuition: $10,600
Soma Institute-The National School of Clinical Massage Therapy (Private, For-profit)
Fall 2012 Enrollment: 352 . . . . (312) 939-2723
Tricoci University of Beauty Culture (Private, For-profit)
Fall 2012 Enrollment: 82 . . . . (630) 528-3336
2012-13 Tuition: $18,050
Tricoci University of Beauty Culture-Chicago (Private, For-profit)
Fall 2012 Enrollment: 165 . . . . (630) 528-3336
2012-13 Tuition: $18,050
University of Aesthetics-Chicago (Private, For-profit)
Fall 2012 Enrollment: 27 . . . . (773) 661-0026
2012-13 Tuition: $10,785

Housing: Homeownership rate: 46.1% (2008-2012 5-year est.); Median home value: $247,800 (2008-2012 5-year est.); Median contract rent: $806 per month (2008-2012 5-year est.); Median year structure built: 1945 (2008-2012 5-year est.).

Health Insurance: 54.3% Private; 32.7% Public; 19.6% None. (2008-2012 5-year est.)

Hospitals: Advocate Bethany Hospital (240 beds); Advocate Illinois Masonic Medical Center (370 beds); Advocate Trinity Hospital; Chicago Lakeshore Hospital (150 beds); Chicago Read Mental Health Center (26 beds); Children's Memorial Hospital (270 beds); Hartgrove Hospital (119 beds); Hazelden Chicago (22 beds); Holy Cross Hospital (244 beds); Jackson Park Hospital & Medical Center (336 beds); John H Stroger, Jr Hospital of Cook County (464 beds); Kindred Chicago Lakeshore (103 beds); La Rabida Childrens Hospital (49 beds); Lincoln Park Hospital (191 beds); Loretto Hospital (189 beds); Mercy Hospital & Medical Center (507 beds); Methodist Hospital of Chicago (198 beds); Michael Reese Hospital (565 beds); Mount Sinai Hospital (432 beds); Neurologic and Orthopedic Insitute of Chicago (78 beds); Northwestern Memorial Hospital (744 beds); Norwegian-American Hospital (200 beds); Our Lady of the Resurrection Medical Center (264 beds); Provident Hospital (243 beds); Rehabilitation Institute of Chicago (155 beds); Resurrection Medical Center (434 beds); Roseland Community Hospital (162 beds); Rush University Medical Center (618 beds); Sacred Heart Hospital (119 beds); Saint Anthony Hospital (183 beds); Saint Bernard Hospital and Health Care Center (183 beds); Saints Mary & Elizabeth Medical Center (387 beds); Schwab Rehabilitation Hospital (85 beds); Shriners Hospital for Children (60 beds); Sinai Community Institute; South Shore Hospital (170 beds); St. Elizabeth's Hospital (276 beds); St. Joseph Hospital (492 beds); Swedish Covenant Hospital (330 beds); Thorek Hospital and Medical Center (218 beds); University of Chicago Comer Children's Hospital (155 beds); University of Chicago Hospitals (662 beds); University of Illinois at Chicago Medical Center (570 beds); Veterans Affairs Lakeside Medical Center (337 beds); Veterans Affairs West Side Medical Center (435 beds); Weiss Memorial Hospital (357 beds)

Safety: Violent crime rate: n/a per 10,000 population; Property crime rate: 415.3 per 10,000 population (2012).

Transportation: Commute to work: 59.9% car, 26.7% public transportation, 6.4% walk, 4.2% work from home (2008-2012 5-year est.); Travel time to work: 13.4% less than 15 minutes, 28.3% 15 to 30 minutes, 29.4% 30 to 45 minutes, 14.0% 45 to 60 minutes, 14.9% 60 minutes or more (2008-2012 5-year est.); Amtrak: Train service available.

Airports: Chicago Midway International Airport (primary service/large hub); Chicago O'Hare International Airport (primary service/large hub)

Additional Information Contacts

America - Israel Chamber of Commerce Chicago . . . . (312) 558-1346
http://www.americaisrael.org
Andersonville Chamber of Commerce . . . . (773) 728-2995
http://www.andersonville.org

Chicago Area Gay & Lesbian Chamber of Commerce .... (773) 303-0167
http://www.glchamber.org
Chicago Chinatown Chamber of Commerce........... (312) 326-5320
http://www.chicagochinatown.org
Chicagoland Chamber of Commerce .... (312) 494-6700
http://www.chicagolandchamber.org
Choose Chicago .... (312) 567-8500
http://www.choosechicago.com
City of Chicago .... (312) 744-5000
http://www.cityofchicago.org
German American Chamber of Commerce of the Midwest . (312) 644-2662
http://www.gaccmidwest.org
Illinois Chamber of Commerce .... (312) 983-7100
http://www.ilchamber.org
Italian American Chamber of Commerce - Midwest ...... (312) 553-9137
http://iacc-chicago.com
Lake View East Chamber of Commerce .... (773) 348-8608
http://www.lakevieweast.com
Latin American Chamber of Commerce .... (773) 252-5211
http://www.laccusa.com
Lincoln Park Chamber of Commerce .... (773) 880-5200
http://www.lincolnparkchamber.com
Logan Square Chamber of Commerce .... (773) 489-3222
http://www.loganchamber.org
Old Town Merchants & Residents Association .... (312) 951-6106
http://www.oldtownchicago.org
Portage Park Chamber of Commerce .... (773) 777-2020
http://www.portageparkchamber.org
Puerto Rico Convention Bureau .... (312) 840-8090
http://www.meetpuertorico.com
South Shore Chamber of Commerce .... (781) 421-3900
http://southshorechamber.org
SouthEast Chicago Chamber of Commerce .... (773) 734-0626
http://southeastchgochamber.org
Streeterville Chamber of Commerce .... (312) 664-2560
http://www.streetervillechamber.org
Turkish American Chamber of Commerce-Midwest ...... (312) 276-5171
http://www.tacci-midwest.org
Wicker Park Bucktown Chamber of Commerce .... (773) 384-2672
http://www.wickerparkbucktown.com

CHICAGO HEIGHTS (city). Covers a land area of 10.075 square miles and a water area of 0.013 square miles. Located at 41.51° N. Lat; 87.63° W. Long. Elevation is 659 feet.

History: Chicago Heights developed at the point where the Hubbard Trail crossed the Sauk Trail, a heavily traveled junction. The first settlement here in the 1830's was called Thorn Grove, but it was renamed Bloom in 1849 by German settlers. In 1890 the Chicago Heights Land Association began encouraging settlers and industry to come here, and the name of the town was changed.

Population: 33,072 (1990); 32,776 (2000); 30,276 (2010); Density: 3,010.2 persons per square mile (2008-2012 5-year est.); Race: 40.6% White, 42.0% Black/African American, 0.2% Asian, 0.5% American Indian/Alaska Native, 0.0% Native Hawaiian/Other Pacific Islander, 16.7% Some other race, 4.0% Two or more races, 34.2% Hispanic of any race (2008-2012 5-year est.); Average household size: 3.09 (2008-2012 5-year est.); Median age: 30.7 (2008-2012 5-year est.); Males per 100 females: 96.9 (2008-2012 5-year est.); Marriage status: 43.3% never married, 40.4% now married, 7.4% widowed, 8.8% divorced (2008-2012 5-year est.); Foreign born: 12.5% (2008-2012 5-year est.); Ancestry (includes multiple ancestries): 8.4% Italian, 6.9% German, 4.3% Polish, 4.3% Irish, 1.8% American (2008-2012 5-year est.).

Economy: Unemployment rate: 11.3% (April 2014); Total civilian labor force: 13,036 (April 2014); Single-family building permits issued: 0 (2013); Multi-family building permits issued: 0 (2013); Homeowner vacancy rate: 3.3%. Rental vacancy rate: 9.9%. (2008-2012 5-year est.); Employment by occupation: 7.8% management, business, and financial, 1.9% computer, engineering, and science, 8.7% education, legal, community service, arts, and media, 5.6% healthcare practitioners, 24.1% service, 22.5% sales and office, 9.9% natural resources, construction, and maintenance, 19.6% production, transportation, and material moving (2008-2012 5-year est.).

Income: Per capita income: $17,452 (2008-2012 5-year est.); Median household income: $42,959 (2008-2012 5-year est.); Average household income: $52,413 (2008-2012 5-year est.); Percent of households with

income of $100,000 or more: 12.4% (2008-2012 5-year est.); Poverty rate: 28.8% (2008-2012 5-year est.).

Taxes: Total city taxes per capita: $686 (2011); City property taxes per capita: $531 (2011).

Education: Percent of population age 25 and over with: High school diploma (including GED) or higher: 79.5% (2008-2012 5-year est.); Bachelor's degree or higher: 14.1% (2008-2012 5-year est.); Master's degree or higher: 5.7% (2008-2012 5-year est.).

School District(s)
Bloom Twp HSD 206 (09-12)
2011-12 Enrollment: 3,406 .... (708) 755-7010
Career Prep Net @ Prairie State
2011-12 Enrollment: n/a .... (708) 709-7903
Chicago Heights SD 170 (PK-08)
2011-12 Enrollment: 3,232 .... (708) 756-4165
Flossmoor SD 161 (PK-08)
2011-12 Enrollment: 2,389 .... (708) 647-7000
Park Forest SD 163 (PK-08)
2011-12 Enrollment: 1,957 .... (708) 668-9400
Speed Seja #802 (PK-12)
2011-12 Enrollment: n/a .... (708) 481-6100

Two-year College(s)
Prairie State College (Public)
Fall 2012 Enrollment: 4,890 .... (708) 709-3500
2012-13 Tuition: In-state $6,600; Out-of-state $7,560

Housing: Homeownership rate: 61.2% (2008-2012 5-year est.); Median home value: $127,300 (2008-2012 5-year est.); Median contract rent: $683 per month (2008-2012 5-year est.); Median year structure built: 1956 (2008-2012 5-year est.).

Health Insurance: 46.7% Private; 42.5% Public; 20.4% None. (2008-2012 5-year est.)

Hospitals: St. James Hospital and Health Center (587 beds)

Safety: Violent crime rate: 82.8 per 10,000 population; Property crime rate: 361.3 per 10,000 population (2012).

Transportation: Commute to work: 89.4% car, 5.9% public transportation, 1.7% walk, 0.6% work from home (2008-2012 5-year est.); Travel time to work: 31.1% less than 15 minutes, 30.2% 15 to 30 minutes, 19.9% 30 to 45 minutes, 8.4% 45 to 60 minutes, 10.4% 60 minutes or more (2008-2012 5-year est.)

Additional Information Contacts
Chicago Heights Chamber of Commerce ....
http://www.chicagosouthlandchamber.com
City of Chicago Heights............................ (708) 756-5300
http://www.cityofchicagoheights.org

CHICAGO RIDGE (village). Covers a land area of 2.254 square miles and a water area of 0 square miles. Located at 41.70° N. Lat; 87.78° W. Long. Elevation is 594 feet.

Population: 13,643 (1990); 14,127 (2000); 14,305 (2010); Density: 6,344.9 persons per square mile (2008-2012 5-year est.); Race: 86.1% White, 3.9% Black/African American, 2.4% Asian, 0.0% American Indian/Alaska Native, 0.0% Native Hawaiian/Other Pacific Islander, 7.6% Some other race, 1.8% Two or more races, 13.1% Hispanic of any race (2008-2012 5-year est.); Average household size: 2.38 (2008-2012 5-year est.); Median age: 36.7 (2008-2012 5-year est.); Males per 100 females: 107.5 (2008-2012 5-year est.); Marriage status: 34.8% never married, 43.2% now married, 6.9% widowed, 15.1% divorced (2008-2012 5-year est.); Foreign born: 19.8% (2008-2012 5-year est.); Ancestry (includes multiple ancestries): 24.5% Irish, 19.2% Polish, 14.2% German, 8.4% Italian, 3.6% Palestinian (2008-2012 5-year est.).

Economy: Single-family building permits issued: 0 (2013); Multi-family building permits issued: 0 (2013); Homeowner vacancy rate: 2.4%. Rental vacancy rate: 10.2%. (2008-2012 5-year est.); Employment by occupation: 10.7% management, business, and financial, 2.2% computer, engineering, and science, 8.7% education, legal, community service, arts, and media, 4.3% healthcare practitioners, 17.7% service, 32.6% sales and office, 8.5% natural resources, construction, and maintenance, 15.3% production, transportation, and material moving (2008-2012 5-year est.).

Income: Per capita income: $23,693 (2008-2012 5-year est.); Median household income: $49,694 (2008-2012 5-year est.); Average household income: $55,153 (2008-2012 5-year est.); Percent of households with income of $100,000 or more: 9.9% (2008-2012 5-year est.); Poverty rate: 11.0% (2008-2012 5-year est.).

Taxes: Total city taxes per capita: $612 (2011); City property taxes per capita: $324 (2011).

Education: Percent of population age 25 and over with: High school diploma (including GED) or higher: 87.6% (2008-2012 5-year est.); Bachelor's degree or higher: 18.9% (2008-2012 5-year est.); Master's degree or higher: 5.1% (2008-2012 5-year est.).

School District(s)

Chicago Ridge SD 127-5 (PK-08)
  2011-12 Enrollment: 1,390 . . . . (708) 636-2000

Housing: Homeownership rate: 52.1% (2008-2012 5-year est.); Median home value: $176,900 (2008-2012 5-year est.); Median contract rent: $795 per month (2008-2012 5-year est.); Median year structure built: 1972 (2008-2012 5-year est.).

Health Insurance: 63.7% Private; 32.2% Public; 15.7% None. (2008-2012 5-year est.)

Safety: Violent crime rate: 20.2 per 10,000 population; Property crime rate: 429.3 per 10,000 population (2012).

Transportation: Commute to work: 89.0% car, 6.2% public transportation, 1.0% walk, 2.0% work from home (2008-2012 5-year est.); Travel time to work: 16.3% less than 15 minutes, 33.7% 15 to 30 minutes, 19.9% 30 to 45 minutes, 14.9% 45 to 60 minutes, 15.1% 60 minutes or more (2008-2012 5-year est.)

Additional Information Contacts

Chicago Ridge/Worth Chamber of Commerce . . . . (708) 923-2050
  http://www.crwchamber.org
Village of Chicago Ridge. . . . . (708) 425-7700
  http://www.chicagoridge.org

CICERO (town). Covers a land area of 5.865 square miles and a water area of 0 square miles. Located at 41.84° N. Lat; 87.76° W. Long. Elevation is 604 feet.

History: Named for Marcus Tullius Cicero, a Roman orator. Cicero was settled in the mid-1800's. The first township election was held in 1857, and Cicero was incorporated as a town in 1867 and as a city in 1869, following an influx of homesteaders during the Civil War. Cicero shrank when parts of it were annexed to Chicago in 1892. During the industrial boom that followed the turn of the century, Al Capone was the proprietor of a row of gambling houses here.

Population: 67,436 (1990); 85,616 (2000); 83,891 (2010); Density: 14,281.8 persons per square mile (2008-2012 5-year est.); Race: 36.8% White, 3.5% Black/African American, 0.3% Asian, 0.4% American Indian/Alaska Native, 0.1% Native Hawaiian/Other Pacific Islander, 58.9% Some other race, 2.0% Two or more races, 86.7% Hispanic of any race (2008-2012 5-year est.); Average household size: 3.89 (2008-2012 5-year est.); Median age: 28.0 (2008-2012 5-year est.); Males per 100 females: 103.8 (2008-2012 5-year est.); Marriage status: 39.0% never married, 50.8% now married, 3.8% widowed, 6.4% divorced (2008-2012 5-year est.); Foreign born: 42.6% (2008-2012 5-year est.); Ancestry (includes multiple ancestries): 2.4% Polish, 2.4% Irish, 2.3% German, 2.0% Italian, 0.9% Czech (2008-2012 5-year est.).

Economy: Unemployment rate: 9.4% (April 2014); Total civilian labor force: 33,280 (April 2014); Single-family building permits issued: 0 (2013); Multi-family building permits issued: 0 (2013); Homeowner vacancy rate: 3.5%. Rental vacancy rate: 6.0%. (2008-2012 5-year est.); Employment by occupation: 6.2% management, business, and financial, 1.2% computer, engineering, and science, 4.1% education, legal, community service, arts, and media, 1.6% healthcare practitioners, 21.6% service, 22.4% sales and office, 11.8% natural resources, construction, and maintenance, 31.1% production, transportation, and material moving (2008-2012 5-year est.).

Income: Per capita income: $14,935 (2008-2012 5-year est.); Median household income: $45,656 (2008-2012 5-year est.); Average household income: $54,480 (2008-2012 5-year est.); Percent of households with income of $100,000 or more: 11.3% (2008-2012 5-year est.); Poverty rate: 18.7% (2008-2012 5-year est.).

Taxes: Total city taxes per capita: $777 (2011); City property taxes per capita: $458 (2011).

Education: Percent of population age 25 and over with: High school diploma (including GED) or higher: 63.1% (2008-2012 5-year est.); Bachelor's degree or higher: 7.6% (2008-2012 5-year est.); Master's degree or higher: 1.4% (2008-2012 5-year est.).

School District(s)

Cicero SD 99 (PK-08)
  2011-12 Enrollment: 13,367 . . . . (708) 863-4856
J S Morton HSD 201 (09-12)
  2011-12 Enrollment: 8,344 . . . . (708) 222-5702
Region 06 West Cook Isc 2 (PK-12)
  2011-12 Enrollment: n/a . . . . (708) 544-4890

Two-year College(s)

Morton College (Public)
  Fall 2012 Enrollment: 5,202 . . . . (708) 656-8000
  2012-13 Tuition: In-state $7,284; Out-of-state $9,332

Vocational/Technical School(s)

Bell Mar Beauty College (Private, For-profit)
  Fall 2012 Enrollment: 52 . . . . (708) 863-6644
  2012-13 Tuition: $10,150

Housing: Homeownership rate: 52.5% (2008-2012 5-year est.); Median home value: $171,000 (2008-2012 5-year est.); Median contract rent: $706 per month (2008-2012 5-year est.); Median year structure built: Before 1940 (2008-2012 5-year est.).

Health Insurance: 41.8% Private; 34.7% Public; 28.4% None. (2008-2012 5-year est.)

Safety: Violent crime rate: 45.0 per 10,000 population; Property crime rate: 263.5 per 10,000 population (2012).

Transportation: Commute to work: 83.3% car, 10.5% public transportation, 3.5% walk, 1.1% work from home (2008-2012 5-year est.); Travel time to work: 14.1% less than 15 minutes, 30.4% 15 to 30 minutes, 31.2% 30 to 45 minutes, 12.1% 45 to 60 minutes, 12.1% 60 minutes or more (2008-2012 5-year est.)

Additional Information Contacts

Cicero Chamber of Commerce & Industry . . . . (708) 863-6000
Town of Cicero . . . . (708) 656-3600
  http://www.thetownofcicero.com

COUNTRY CLUB HILLS (city). Covers a land area of 4.818 square miles and a water area of 0.018 square miles. Located at 41.56° N. Lat; 87.73° W. Long. Elevation is 682 feet.

Population: 15,431 (1990); 16,169 (2000); 16,541 (2010); Density: 3,432.7 persons per square mile (2008-2012 5-year est.); Race: 10.8% White, 86.2% Black/African American, 0.5% Asian, 0.6% American Indian/Alaska Native, 0.0% Native Hawaiian/Other Pacific Islander, 1.9% Some other race, 1.5% Two or more races, 3.3% Hispanic of any race (2008-2012 5-year est.); Average household size: 2.86 (2008-2012 5-year est.); Median age: 42.0 (2008-2012 5-year est.); Males per 100 females: 88.0 (2008-2012 5-year est.); Marriage status: 34.8% never married, 44.1% now married, 7.1% widowed, 13.9% divorced (2008-2012 5-year est.); Foreign born: 1.7% (2008-2012 5-year est.); Ancestry (includes multiple ancestries): 3.0% German, 1.5% Swedish, 1.5% Nigerian, 1.4% English, 1.1% Polish (2008-2012 5-year est.).

Economy: Single-family building permits issued: 0 (2013); Multi-family building permits issued: 0 (2013); Homeowner vacancy rate: 2.7%. Rental vacancy rate: 7.6%. (2008-2012 5-year est.); Employment by occupation: 18.5% management, business, and financial, 4.4% computer, engineering, and science, 12.0% education, legal, community service, arts, and media, 5.6% healthcare practitioners, 17.7% service, 25.2% sales and office, 6.3% natural resources, construction, and maintenance, 10.2% production, transportation, and material moving (2008-2012 5-year est.).

Income: Per capita income: $26,008 (2008-2012 5-year est.); Median household income: $61,944 (2008-2012 5-year est.); Average household income: $71,483 (2008-2012 5-year est.); Percent of households with income of $100,000 or more: 22.4% (2008-2012 5-year est.); Poverty rate: 10.1% (2008-2012 5-year est.).

Education: Percent of population age 25 and over with: High school diploma (including GED) or higher: 93.5% (2008-2012 5-year est.); Bachelor's degree or higher: 30.8% (2008-2012 5-year est.); Master's degree or higher: 10.8% (2008-2012 5-year est.).

School District(s)

Bremen CHSD 228 (09-12)
  2011-12 Enrollment: 5,491 . . . . (708) 389-1175
Country Club Hills SD 160 (PK-08)
  2011-12 Enrollment: 1,328 . . . . (708) 957-6200
Prairie-Hills ESD 144 (PK-08)
  2011-12 Enrollment: 2,796 . . . . (708) 210-2888

Housing: Homeownership rate: 86.6% (2008-2012 5-year est.); Median home value: $154,700 (2008-2012 5-year est.); Median contract rent: $1,193 per month (2008-2012 5-year est.); Median year structure built: 1975 (2008-2012 5-year est.).

Health Insurance: 67.9% Private; 31.6% Public; 12.8% None. (2008-2012 5-year est.)

Safety: Violent crime rate: 37.3 per 10,000 population; Property crime rate: 283.9 per 10,000 population (2012).

Transportation: Commute to work: 85.3% car, 11.1% public transportation, 0.5% walk, 2.8% work from home (2008-2012 5-year est.);

Travel time to work: 8.3% less than 15 minutes, 29.0% 15 to 30 minutes, 25.1% 30 to 45 minutes, 15.9% 45 to 60 minutes, 21.8% 60 minutes or more (2008-2012 5-year est.)

Additional Information Contacts

City of Country Club Hills . . . . (708) 798-2616
  http://www.countryclubhills.org
Country Club Hills Chamber of Commerce . . . . (708) 970-8385
  http://www.cchillschamber.org

COUNTRYSIDE (city).
Covers a land area of 2.878 square miles and a water area of 0 square miles. Located at 41.77° N. Lat; 87.88° W. Long. Elevation is 663 feet.

Population: 5,716 (1990); 5,991 (2000); 5,895 (2010); Density: 2,051.5 persons per square mile (2008-2012 5-year est.); Race: 88.3% White, 2.8% Black/African American, 2.4% Asian, 1.5% American Indian/Alaska Native, 0.0% Native Hawaiian/Other Pacific Islander, 5.0% Some other race, 1.0% Two or more races, 16.9% Hispanic of any race (2008-2012 5-year est.); Average household size: 2.60 (2008-2012 5-year est.); Median age: 41.2 (2008-2012 5-year est.); Males per 100 females: 85.8 (2008-2012 5-year est.); Marriage status: 31.8% never married, 49.0% now married, 9.3% widowed, 9.9% divorced (2008-2012 5-year est.); Foreign born: 15.6% (2008-2012 5-year est.); Ancestry (includes multiple ancestries): 20.5% Irish, 19.1% German, 13.0% Polish, 10.3% Italian, 6.1% Czech (2008-2012 5-year est.).

Economy: Single-family building permits issued: 6 (2013); Multi-family building permits issued: 18 (2013); Homeowner vacancy rate: 2.2%. Rental vacancy rate: 8.1%. (2008-2012 5-year est.); Employment by occupation: 18.3% management, business, and financial, 2.5% computer, engineering, and science, 4.3% education, legal, community service, arts, and media, 3.8% healthcare practitioners, 17.8% service, 34.3% sales and office, 4.3% natural resources, construction, and maintenance, 14.7% production, transportation, and material moving (2008-2012 5-year est.).

Income: Per capita income: $30,048 (2008-2012 5-year est.); Median household income: $60,916 (2008-2012 5-year est.); Average household income: $75,419 (2008-2012 5-year est.); Percent of households with income of $100,000 or more: 25.6% (2008-2012 5-year est.); Poverty rate: 9.0% (2008-2012 5-year est.).

Education: Percent of population age 25 and over with: High school diploma (including GED) or higher: 85.8% (2008-2012 5-year est.); Bachelor's degree or higher: 25.5% (2008-2012 5-year est.); Master's degree or higher: 6.9% (2008-2012 5-year est.).

School District(s)

La Grange SD 105 South (PK-08)
  2011-12 Enrollment: 1,392 . . . . (708) 482-2700
Housing: Homeownership rate: 78.0% (2008-2012 5-year est.); Median home value: $222,100 (2008-2012 5-year est.); Median contract rent: $872 per month (2008-2012 5-year est.); Median year structure built: 1971 (2008-2012 5-year est.).
Health Insurance: 73.3% Private; 29.3% Public; 11.3% None. (2008-2012 5-year est.)
Safety: Violent crime rate: 13.5 per 10,000 population; Property crime rate: 405.2 per 10,000 population (2012).
Transportation: Commute to work: 86.4% car, 7.7% public transportation, 1.1% walk, 4.4% work from home (2008-2012 5-year est.); Travel time to work: 25.8% less than 15 minutes, 33.3% 15 to 30 minutes, 25.9% 30 to 45 minutes, 8.6% 45 to 60 minutes, 6.4% 60 minutes or more (2008-2012 5-year est.)

Additional Information Contacts

City of Countryside . . . . (708) 354-7270
  http://www.countryside-il.org

CRESTWOOD (village).
Covers a land area of 3.046 square miles and a water area of 0.028 square miles. Located at 41.65° N. Lat; 87.74° W. Long. Elevation is 597 feet.

Population: 10,823 (1990); 11,251 (2000); 10,950 (2010); Density: 3,595.2 persons per square mile (2008-2012 5-year est.); Race: 85.2% White, 7.1% Black/African American, 0.4% Asian, 0.3% American Indian/Alaska Native, 0.0% Native Hawaiian/Other Pacific Islander, 7.0% Some other race, 1.4% Two or more races, 11.7% Hispanic of any race (2008-2012 5-year est.); Average household size: 2.24 (2008-2012 5-year est.); Median age: 43.4 (2008-2012 5-year est.); Males per 100 females: 95.2 (2008-2012 5-year est.); Marriage status: 31.3% never married, 43.7% now married, 10.5% widowed, 14.5% divorced (2008-2012 5-year est.); Foreign born: 7.5% (2008-2012 5-year est.); Ancestry (includes

multiple ancestries): 23.6% Irish, 17.7% German, 17.5% Polish, 11.8% Italian, 3.8% Lithuanian (2008-2012 5-year est.).

Economy: Single-family building permits issued: 1 (2013); Multi-family building permits issued: 0 (2013); Homeowner vacancy rate: 3.9%. Rental vacancy rate: 1.1%. (2008-2012 5-year est.); Employment by occupation: 11.6% management, business, and financial, 3.7% computer, engineering, and science, 9.0% education, legal, community service, arts, and media, 4.2% healthcare practitioners, 14.2% service, 30.3% sales and office, 12.6% natural resources, construction, and maintenance, 14.4% production, transportation, and material moving (2008-2012 5-year est.).

Income: Per capita income: $28,520 (2008-2012 5-year est.); Median household income: $55,188 (2008-2012 5-year est.); Average household income: $64,725 (2008-2012 5-year est.); Percent of households with income of $100,000 or more: 20.1% (2008-2012 5-year est.); Poverty rate: 4.3% (2008-2012 5-year est.).

Education: Percent of population age 25 and over with: High school diploma (including GED) or higher: 87.9% (2008-2012 5-year est.); Bachelor's degree or higher: 18.0% (2008-2012 5-year est.); Master's degree or higher: 5.0% (2008-2012 5-year est.).

School District(s)

Cook County SD 130 (PK-08)
  2011-12 Enrollment: 3,869 . . . . (708) 385-6800
Housing: Homeownership rate: 83.7% (2008-2012 5-year est.); Median home value: $169,000 (2008-2012 5-year est.); Median contract rent: $805 per month (2008-2012 5-year est.); Median year structure built: 1975 (2008-2012 5-year est.).
Health Insurance: 76.3% Private; 27.6% Public; 9.9% None. (2008-2012 5-year est.)
Safety: Violent crime rate: 14.5 per 10,000 population; Property crime rate: 498.1 per 10,000 population (2012).
Transportation: Commute to work: 88.2% car, 6.8% public transportation, 1.4% walk, 2.3% work from home (2008-2012 5-year est.); Travel time to work: 22.9% less than 15 minutes, 29.0% 15 to 30 minutes, 25.4% 30 to 45 minutes, 8.3% 45 to 60 minutes, 14.3% 60 minutes or more (2008-2012 5-year est.)

Additional Information Contacts

Oak Forest-Crestwood Area Chamber of Commerce . . . . . (708) 687-4600
  http://oc-chamber.org
Village of Crestwood . . . . (708) 371-4800
  http://www.villageofcrestwood.com

DES PLAINES (city).
Covers a land area of 14.283 square miles and a water area of 0.135 square miles. Located at 42.04° N. Lat; 87.90° W. Long. Elevation is 633 feet.

History: Named for the French translation of "the maples," which are abundant along the nearby river. When Des Plaines was founded in the 1830's it was known as Rand, for its first settler, Socrates Rand. The name was changed in 1869 to that of the river which transverses the town.

Population: 53,223 (1990); 58,720 (2000); 58,364 (2010); Density: 4,081.8 persons per square mile (2008-2012 5-year est.); Race: 78.1% White, 1.0% Black/African American, 12.1% Asian, 0.3% American Indian/Alaska Native, 0.0% Native Hawaiian/Other Pacific Islander, 8.5% Some other race, 1.2% Two or more races, 18.1% Hispanic of any race (2008-2012 5-year est.); Average household size: 2.57 (2008-2012 5-year est.); Median age: 41.5 (2008-2012 5-year est.); Males per 100 females: 94.5 (2008-2012 5-year est.); Marriage status: 28.6% never married, 54.2% now married, 8.5% widowed, 8.7% divorced (2008-2012 5-year est.); Foreign born: 28.5% (2008-2012 5-year est.); Ancestry (includes multiple ancestries): 19.9% German, 15.1% Polish, 13.7% Irish, 9.1% Italian, 3.8% English (2008-2012 5-year est.).

Economy: Unemployment rate: 7.1% (April 2014); Total civilian labor force: 31,005 (April 2014); Single-family building permits issued: 31 (2013); Multi-family building permits issued: 0 (2013); Homeowner vacancy rate: 2.5%. Rental vacancy rate: 7.7%. (2008-2012 5-year est.); Employment by occupation: 17.2% management, business, and financial, 5.4% computer, engineering, and science, 8.7% education, legal, community service, arts, and media, 6.2% healthcare practitioners, 15.3% service, 26.8% sales and office, 8.1% natural resources, construction, and maintenance, 12.3% production, transportation, and material moving (2008-2012 5-year est.).

Income: Per capita income: $31,007 (2008-2012 5-year est.); Median household income: $65,194 (2008-2012 5-year est.); Average household income: $78,317 (2008-2012 5-year est.); Percent of households with income of $100,000 or more: 26.5% (2008-2012 5-year est.); Poverty rate: 7.0% (2008-2012 5-year est.).

Taxes: Total city taxes per capita: $1,004 (2011); City property taxes per capita: $622 (2011).

Education: Percent of population age 25 and over with: High school diploma (including GED) or higher: 87.4% (2008-2012 5-year est.); Bachelor's degree or higher: 32.4% (2008-2012 5-year est.); Master's degree or higher: 10.5% (2008-2012 5-year est.).

School District(s)

CCSD 62 (PK-08)
2011-12 Enrollment: 4,679 . . . . (847) 824-1136
Community CSD 59 (PK-08)
2011-12 Enrollment: 6,537 . . . . (847) 593-4300
East Maine SD 63 (PK-08)
2011-12 Enrollment: 3,628 . . . . (847) 299-1900
Maine Township HSD 207 (06-12)
2011-12 Enrollment: 5,097 . . . . (847) 696-3600
Region 05 North Cook Isc 1 (PK-12)
2011-12 Enrollment: n/a . . . . (847) 824-8300

Two-year College(s)

Oakton Community College (Public)
Fall 2012 Enrollment: 11,431 . . . . (847) 635-1600
2012-13 Tuition: In-state $8,220; Out-of-state $9,907

Housing: Homeownership rate: 80.2% (2008-2012 5-year est.); Median home value: $258,100 (2008-2012 5-year est.); Median contract rent: $903 per month (2008-2012 5-year est.); Median year structure built: 1964 (2008-2012 5-year est.).

Health Insurance: 73.6% Private; 26.4% Public; 12.9% None. (2008-2012 5-year est.)

Hospitals: Holy Family Medical Center (184 beds)

Safety: Violent crime rate: 11.1 per 10,000 population; Property crime rate: 160.5 per 10,000 population (2012).

Transportation: Commute to work: 88.4% car, 6.5% public transportation, 1.0% walk, 3.0% work from home (2008-2012 5-year est.); Travel time to work: 18.8% less than 15 minutes, 36.0% 15 to 30 minutes, 27.5% 30 to 45 minutes, 9.1% 45 to 60 minutes, 8.6% 60 minutes or more (2008-2012 5-year est.)

Additional Information Contacts
City of Des Plaines . . . . (847) 391-5300
  http://www.desplaines.org
Des Plaines Chamber of Commerce & Industry . . . . (847) 824-4200
  http://www.dpchamber.com

DIXMOOR (village). Covers a land area of 1.248 square miles and a water area of 0 square miles. Located at 41.63° N. Lat; 87.67° W. Long. Elevation is 600 feet.

History: Incorporated 1922.

Population: 3,647 (1990); 3,934 (2000); 3,644 (2010); Density: 2,917.9 persons per square mile (2008-2012 5-year est.); Race: 35.0% White, 41.3% Black/African American, 0.0% Asian, 0.4% American Indian/Alaska Native, 0.0% Native Hawaiian/Other Pacific Islander, 23.3% Some other race, 3.5% Two or more races, 45.2% Hispanic of any race (2008-2012 5-year est.); Average household size: 3.02 (2008-2012 5-year est.); Median age: 28.7 (2008-2012 5-year est.); Males per 100 females: 85.7 (2008-2012 5-year est.); Marriage status: 46.1% never married, 39.5% now married, 5.4% widowed, 9.0% divorced (2008-2012 5-year est.); Foreign born: 17.2% (2008-2012 5-year est.); Ancestry (includes multiple ancestries): 4.6% German, 3.5% Polish, 2.2% Italian, 1.7% African, 1.1% French (2008-2012 5-year est.).

Economy: Single-family building permits issued: 0 (2013); Multi-family building permits issued: 0 (2013); Homeowner vacancy rate: 3.0%. Rental vacancy rate: 10.6%. (2008-2012 5-year est.); Employment by occupation: 7.7% management, business, and financial, 0.6% computer, engineering, and science, 8.9% education, legal, community service, arts, and media, 2.1% healthcare practitioners, 27.4% service, 10.4% sales and office, 20.5% natural resources, construction, and maintenance, 22.4% production, transportation, and material moving (2008-2012 5-year est.).

Income: Per capita income: $13,538 (2008-2012 5-year est.); Median household income: $40,594 (2008-2012 5-year est.); Average household income: $38,899 (2008-2012 5-year est.); Percent of households with income of $100,000 or more: 1.8% (2008-2012 5-year est.); Poverty rate: 39.3% (2008-2012 5-year est.).

Education: Percent of population age 25 and over with: High school diploma (including GED) or higher: 72.4% (2008-2012 5-year est.); Bachelor's degree or higher: 8.4% (2008-2012 5-year est.); Master's degree or higher: 1.2% (2008-2012 5-year est.).

School District(s)

W Harvey-Dixmoor PSD 147 (PK-08)
2011-12 Enrollment: 1,409 . . . . (708) 339-9500

Housing: Homeownership rate: 53.3% (2008-2012 5-year est.); Median home value: $45,800 (2008-2012 5-year est.); Median contract rent: $621 per month (2008-2012 5-year est.); Median year structure built: 1970 (2008-2012 5-year est.).

Health Insurance: 31.2% Private; 49.6% Public; 26.4% None. (2008-2012 5-year est.)

Transportation: Commute to work: 89.7% car, 6.2% public transportation, 2.6% walk, 1.4% work from home (2008-2012 5-year est.); Travel time to work: 19.9% less than 15 minutes, 28.6% 15 to 30 minutes, 39.5% 30 to 45 minutes, 0.0% 45 to 60 minutes, 11.9% 60 minutes or more (2008-2012 5-year est.)

DOLTON (village). Covers a land area of 4.565 square miles and a water area of 0.120 square miles. Located at 41.63° N. Lat; 87.60° W. Long. Elevation is 604 feet.

History: Named for Andrew H. Dolton, town founder. Settled 1832. Incorporated 1892.

Population: 23,930 (1990); 25,614 (2000); 23,153 (2010); Density: 5,088.9 persons per square mile (2008-2012 5-year est.); Race: 6.2% White, 91.5% Black/African American, 0.2% Asian, 0.1% American Indian/Alaska Native, 0.0% Native Hawaiian/Other Pacific Islander, 2.0% Some other race, 1.4% Two or more races, 2.1% Hispanic of any race (2008-2012 5-year est.); Average household size: 2.84 (2008-2012 5-year est.); Median age: 34.6 (2008-2012 5-year est.); Males per 100 females: 88.3 (2008-2012 5-year est.); Marriage status: 45.0% never married, 36.8% now married, 5.8% widowed, 12.3% divorced (2008-2012 5-year est.); Foreign born: 2.1% (2008-2012 5-year est.); Ancestry (includes multiple ancestries): 1.6% German, 1.1% Polish, 1.1% American, 1.0% Irish, 1.0% Nigerian (2008-2012 5-year est.).

Economy: Unemployment rate: 10.6% (April 2014); Total civilian labor force: 11,799 (April 2014); Single-family building permits issued: 0 (2013); Multi-family building permits issued: 0 (2013); Homeowner vacancy rate: 3.0%. Rental vacancy rate: 8.5%. (2008-2012 5-year est.); Employment by occupation: 9.5% management, business, and financial, 3.0% computer, engineering, and science, 10.4% education, legal, community service, arts, and media, 5.6% healthcare practitioners, 19.2% service, 29.5% sales and office, 6.1% natural resources, construction, and maintenance, 16.7% production, transportation, and material moving (2008-2012 5-year est.).

Income: Per capita income: $22,519 (2008-2012 5-year est.); Median household income: $53,161 (2008-2012 5-year est.); Average household income: $61,674 (2008-2012 5-year est.); Percent of households with income of $100,000 or more: 14.9% (2008-2012 5-year est.); Poverty rate: 16.7% (2008-2012 5-year est.).

Taxes: Total city taxes per capita: $516 (2011); City property taxes per capita: $300 (2011).

Education: Percent of population age 25 and over with: High school diploma (including GED) or higher: 88.9% (2008-2012 5-year est.); Bachelor's degree or higher: 21.1% (2008-2012 5-year est.); Master's degree or higher: 6.1% (2008-2012 5-year est.).

School District(s)

Dolton SD 148 (PK-08)
2011-12 Enrollment: 2,446 . . . . (708) 841-2290
Dolton SD 149 (PK-08)
2011-12 Enrollment: 3,135 . . . . (708) 868-7861
Exc Children Have Opportunities (KG-12)
2011-12 Enrollment: n/a . . . . (708) 333-7880
Thornton Twp HSD 205 (09-12)
2011-12 Enrollment: 5,283 . . . . (708) 225-4000

Housing: Homeownership rate: 73.9% (2008-2012 5-year est.); Median home value: $129,200 (2008-2012 5-year est.); Median contract rent: $875 per month (2008-2012 5-year est.); Median year structure built: 1964 (2008-2012 5-year est.).

Health Insurance: 58.6% Private; 33.8% Public; 17.8% None. (2008-2012 5-year est.)

Safety: Violent crime rate: 48.6 per 10,000 population; Property crime rate: 613.0 per 10,000 population (2012).

Transportation: Commute to work: 83.2% car, 13.5% public transportation, 0.7% walk, 1.8% work from home (2008-2012 5-year est.); Travel time to work: 10.8% less than 15 minutes, 23.5% 15 to 30 minutes, 27.2% 30 to 45 minutes, 15.1% 45 to 60 minutes, 23.4% 60 minutes or more (2008-2012 5-year est.)

Additional Information Contacts

Dolton Chamber of Commerce . . . . (708) 201-3375
  http://vodolton.org
Village of Dolton . . . . (708) 849-4000
  http://vodolton.org

EAST HAZEL CREST (village). Covers a land area of 0.784

square miles and a water area of 0 square miles. Located at 41.58° N. Lat;
87.65° W. Long. Elevation is 620 feet.
Population: 1,570 (1990); 1,607 (2000); 1,543 (2010); Density: 2,362.6
persons per square mile (2008-2012 5-year est.); Race: 31.1% White,
50.7% Black/African American, 4.3% Asian, 2.0% American Indian/Alaska
Native, 0.0% Native Hawaiian/Other Pacific Islander, 11.9% Some other
race, 0.8% Two or more races, 14.4% Hispanic of any race (2008-2012
5-year est.); Average household size: 2.64 (2008-2012 5-year est.);
Median age: 34.9 (2008-2012 5-year est.); Males per 100 females: 96.9
(2008-2012 5-year est.); Marriage status: 44.3% never married, 37.4%
now married, 6.1% widowed, 12.3% divorced (2008-2012 5-year est.);
Foreign born: 12.7% (2008-2012 5-year est.); Ancestry (includes multiple
ancestries): 9.9% German, 8.2% Polish, 6.9% Irish, 3.6% Italian, 1.5%
English (2008-2012 5-year est.).
Economy: Single-family building permits issued: 0 (2013); Multi-family
building permits issued: 0 (2013); Homeowner vacancy rate: 0.0%. Rental
vacancy rate: 3.3%. (2008-2012 5-year est.); Employment by occupation:
9.7% management, business, and financial, 2.3% computer, engineering,
and science, 5.6% education, legal, community service, arts, and media,
3.5% healthcare practitioners, 17.0% service, 27.6% sales and office,
10.7% natural resources, construction, and maintenance, 23.5%
production, transportation, and material moving (2008-2012 5-year est.).
Income: Per capita income: $20,524 (2008-2012 5-year est.); Median
household income: $44,655 (2008-2012 5-year est.); Average household
income: $52,654 (2008-2012 5-year est.); Percent of households with
income of $100,000 or more: 15.7% (2008-2012 5-year est.); Poverty rate:
23.9% (2008-2012 5-year est.).
Education: Percent of population age 25 and over with: High school
diploma (including GED) or higher: 88.0% (2008-2012 5-year est.);
Bachelor's degree or higher: 13.7% (2008-2012 5-year est.); Master's
degree or higher: 2.3% (2008-2012 5-year est.).
Housing: Homeownership rate: 58.0% (2008-2012 5-year est.); Median
home value: $133,600 (2008-2012 5-year est.); Median contract rent: $871
per month (2008-2012 5-year est.); Median year structure built: 1969
(2008-2012 5-year est.).
Health Insurance: 50.4% Private; 37.3% Public; 20.2% None. (2008-2012
5-year est.)
Transportation: Commute to work: 81.9% car, 11.1% public
transportation, 5.2% walk, 0.4% work from home (2008-2012 5-year est.);
Travel time to work: 25.3% less than 15 minutes, 27.8% 15 to 30 minutes,
22.0% 30 to 45 minutes, 12.9% 45 to 60 minutes, 12.1% 60 minutes or
more (2008-2012 5-year est.)

ELK GROVE VILLAGE (village). Aka Elk Grove. Covers a land

area of 11.343 square miles and a water area of 0.068 square miles.
Located at 42.01° N. Lat; 87.99° W. Long. Elevation is 686 feet.
Population: 33,429 (1990); 34,727 (2000); 33,127 (2010); Density:
2,924.0 persons per square mile (2008-2012 5-year est.); Race: 82.3%
White, 1.3% Black/African American, 8.9% Asian, 0.4% American
Indian/Alaska Native, 0.1% Native Hawaiian/Other Pacific Islander, 7.0%
Some other race, 1.9% Two or more races, 10.4% Hispanic of any race
(2008-2012 5-year est.); Average household size: 2.51 (2008-2012 5-year
est.); Median age: 42.9 (2008-2012 5-year est.); Males per 100 females:
98.2 (2008-2012 5-year est.); Marriage status: 26.7% never married,
57.0% now married, 5.4% widowed, 10.9% divorced (2008-2012 5-year
est.); Foreign born: 19.7% (2008-2012 5-year est.); Ancestry (includes
multiple ancestries): 25.1% German, 20.1% Polish, 18.2% Irish, 12.4%
Italian, 5.6% English (2008-2012 5-year est.).
Economy: Unemployment rate: 5.9% (April 2014); Total civilian labor
force: 19,924 (April 2014); Single-family building permits issued: 0 (2013);
Multi-family building permits issued: 0 (2013); Homeowner vacancy rate:
1.0%. Rental vacancy rate: 2.2%. (2008-2012 5-year est.); Employment by
occupation: 17.7% management, business, and financial, 5.3% computer,
engineering, and science, 10.2% education, legal, community service, arts,
and media, 4.1% healthcare practitioners, 14.3% service, 30.7% sales and
office, 6.8% natural resources, construction, and maintenance, 10.9%
production, transportation, and material moving (2008-2012 5-year est.).
Income: Per capita income: $33,828 (2008-2012 5-year est.); Median
household income: $67,983 (2008-2012 5-year est.); Average household

income: $82,852 (2008-2012 5-year est.); Percent of households with
income of $100,000 or more: 30.1% (2008-2012 5-year est.); Poverty rate:
4.7% (2008-2012 5-year est.).
Taxes: Total city taxes per capita: $1,033 (2011); City property taxes per
capita: $590 (2011).
Education: Percent of population age 25 and over with: High school
diploma (including GED) or higher: 93.5% (2008-2012 5-year est.);
Bachelor's degree or higher: 35.5% (2008-2012 5-year est.); Master's
degree or higher: 9.5% (2008-2012 5-year est.).
School District(s)
Community CSD 59 (PK-08)
  2011-12 Enrollment: 6,537 . . . . (847) 593-4300
Schaumburg CCSD 54 (PK-08)
  2011-12 Enrollment: 14,083 . . . . (847) 357-5000
Township HSD 214 (09-12)
  2011-12 Enrollment: 12,305 . . . . (847) 718-7600
Housing: Homeownership rate: 76.0% (2008-2012 5-year est.); Median
home value: $274,800 (2008-2012 5-year est.); Median contract rent: $914
per month (2008-2012 5-year est.); Median year structure built: 1974
(2008-2012 5-year est.).
Health Insurance: 82.8% Private; 20.5% Public; 8.3% None. (2008-2012
5-year est.)
Hospitals: Alexian Brothers Medical Center (473 beds)
Safety: Violent crime rate: 6.3 per 10,000 population; Property crime rate:
205.2 per 10,000 population (2012).
Transportation: Commute to work: 91.1% car, 3.3% public transportation,
1.2% walk, 3.6% work from home (2008-2012 5-year est.); Travel time to
work: 29.0% less than 15 minutes, 36.0% 15 to 30 minutes, 20.0% 30 to
45 minutes, 8.2% 45 to 60 minutes, 6.8% 60 minutes or more (2008-2012
5-year est.)
Additional Information Contacts
Elk Grove Chamber of Commerce . . . . (877) 355-4768
  http://www.elkgrovechamber.org
Village of Elk Grove Village . . . . (847) 439-3900
  http://elkgrove.com

ELMWOOD PARK (village). Covers a land area of 1.907 square

miles and a water area of 0 square miles. Located at 41.92° N. Lat; 87.82°
W. Long. Elevation is 643 feet.
Population: 23,206 (1990); 25,405 (2000); 24,883 (2010); Density:
13,042.1 persons per square mile (2008-2012 5-year est.); Race: 82.1%
White, 0.9% Black/African American, 3.1% Asian, 0.7% American
Indian/Alaska Native, 0.0% Native Hawaiian/Other Pacific Islander, 13.2%
Some other race, 2.4% Two or more races, 22.3% Hispanic of any race
(2008-2012 5-year est.); Average household size: 2.70 (2008-2012 5-year
est.); Median age: 39.8 (2008-2012 5-year est.); Males per 100 females:
89.8 (2008-2012 5-year est.); Marriage status: 33.6% never married,
49.5% now married, 8.2% widowed, 8.7% divorced (2008-2012 5-year
est.); Foreign born: 29.7% (2008-2012 5-year est.); Ancestry (includes
multiple ancestries): 24.5% Polish, 19.7% Italian, 12.6% German, 11.5%
Irish, 3.1% Ukrainian (2008-2012 5-year est.).
Economy: Unemployment rate: 6.6% (April 2014); Total civilian labor
force: 13,456 (April 2014); Single-family building permits issued: 0 (2013);
Multi-family building permits issued: 0 (2013); Homeowner vacancy rate:
4.7%. Rental vacancy rate: 2.8%. (2008-2012 5-year est.); Employment by
occupation: 12.1% management, business, and financial, 2.9% computer,
engineering, and science, 6.5% education, legal, community service, arts,
and media, 6.0% healthcare practitioners, 18.2% service, 32.0% sales and
office, 10.3% natural resources, construction, and maintenance, 12.0%
production, transportation, and material moving (2008-2012 5-year est.).
Income: Per capita income: $26,709 (2008-2012 5-year est.); Median
household income: $56,396 (2008-2012 5-year est.); Average household
income: $70,106 (2008-2012 5-year est.); Percent of households with
income of $100,000 or more: 23.2% (2008-2012 5-year est.); Poverty rate:
7.1% (2008-2012 5-year est.).
Education: Percent of population age 25 and over with: High school
diploma (including GED) or higher: 86.9% (2008-2012 5-year est.);
Bachelor's degree or higher: 25.3% (2008-2012 5-year est.); Master's
degree or higher: 10.3% (2008-2012 5-year est.).
School District(s)
Elmwood Park CUSD 401 (PK-12)
  2011-12 Enrollment: 2,983 . . . . (708) 583-5831

Vocational/Technical School(s)

Curve Metric School of Hair Design (Private, For-profit)
  Fall 2012 Enrollment: 55 . . . . (708) 453-2020
  2012-13 Tuition: $9,350

Housing: Homeownership rate: 70.5% (2008-2012 5-year est.); Median home value: $241,900 (2008-2012 5-year est.); Median contract rent: $814 per month (2008-2012 5-year est.); Median year structure built: 1952 (2008-2012 5-year est.).

Health Insurance: 65.7% Private; 25.6% Public; 19.2% None. (2008-2012 5-year est.)

Safety: Violent crime rate: 11.6 per 10,000 population; Property crime rate: 179.2 per 10,000 population (2012).

Transportation: Commute to work: 85.3% car, 8.6% public transportation, 2.7% walk, 2.6% work from home (2008-2012 5-year est.); Travel time to work: 18.0% less than 15 minutes, 26.1% 15 to 30 minutes, 31.5% 30 to 45 minutes, 11.5% 45 to 60 minutes, 12.8% 60 minutes or more (2008-2012 5-year est.)

Additional Information Contacts

Grand Corridor Chamber of Commerce . . . . (708) 456-8000
  http://www.grandchamber.org
Village of Elmwood Park . . . . (708) 452-7300
  http://www.elmwoodpark.org

EVANSTON (city).
Covers a land area of 7.779 square miles and a water area of 0.022 square miles. Located at 42.05° N. Lat; 87.69° W. Long. Elevation is 614 feet.

History: Named for John Evans, founder of Northwestern University. Settlement at Evanston began around the harbor formed by the Grosse Pointe bluffs. The town was platted in 1854, and in 1855 Northwestern University was founded by the Methodist Episcopal Church. One of the first professors here was Frances E. Willard, who later founded the Women's Christian Temperance Union. In 1892 Evanston annexed the community of South Evanston and was incorporated as a city. The city was named for John Evans, one of the university founders.

Population: 73,233 (1990); 74,239 (2000); 74,486 (2010); Density: 9,592.1 persons per square mile (2008-2012 5-year est.); Race: 67.7% White, 18.3% Black/African American, 8.6% Asian, 0.0% American Indian/Alaska Native, 0.0% Native Hawaiian/Other Pacific Islander, 5.4% Some other race, 3.1% Two or more races, 10.0% Hispanic of any race (2008-2012 5-year est.); Average household size: 2.36 (2008-2012 5-year est.); Median age: 34.4 (2008-2012 5-year est.); Males per 100 females: 94.5 (2008-2012 5-year est.); Marriage status: 42.7% never married, 43.7% now married, 5.2% widowed, 8.3% divorced (2008-2012 5-year est.); Foreign born: 17.8% (2008-2012 5-year est.); Ancestry (includes multiple ancestries): 16.1% German, 12.6% Irish, 7.9% English, 6.3% Polish, 4.7% Italian (2008-2012 5-year est.).

Economy: Unemployment rate: 5.5% (April 2014); Total civilian labor force: 41,256 (April 2014); Single-family building permits issued: 7 (2013); Multi-family building permits issued: 77 (2013); Homeowner vacancy rate: 2.6%. Rental vacancy rate: 5.6%. (2008-2012 5-year est.); Employment by occupation: 20.3% management, business, and financial, 10.3% computer, engineering, and science, 25.3% education, legal, community service, arts, and media, 5.7% healthcare practitioners, 11.7% service, 19.2% sales and office, 3.2% natural resources, construction, and maintenance, 4.3% production, transportation, and material moving (2008-2012 5-year est.).

Income: Per capita income: $41,725 (2008-2012 5-year est.); Median household income: $68,051 (2008-2012 5-year est.); Average household income: $105,497 (2008-2012 5-year est.); Percent of households with income of $100,000 or more: 35.7% (2008-2012 5-year est.); Poverty rate: 12.8% (2008-2012 5-year est.).

Taxes: Total city taxes per capita: $1,055 (2011); City property taxes per capita: $620 (2011).

Education: Percent of population age 25 and over with: High school diploma (including GED) or higher: 93.9% (2008-2012 5-year est.); Bachelor's degree or higher: 65.4% (2008-2012 5-year est.); Master's degree or higher: 37.0% (2008-2012 5-year est.).

School District(s)

Evanston CCSD 65 (PK-08)
  2011-12 Enrollment: 7,271 . . . . (847) 859-8010
Evanston Dists 65/202 Jnt Agr
  2011-12 Enrollment: n/a . . . . (847) 492-5986
Evanston Twp HSD 202 (09-12)
  2011-12 Enrollment: 3,142 . . . . (847) 424-7220

Four-year College(s)

Garrett-Evangelical Theological Seminary (Private, Not-for-profit, United Methodist)
  Fall 2012 Enrollment: 390 . . . . (847) 866-3900
NorthShore University HealthSystem School of Nurse Anesthesia (Private, Not-for-profit)
  Fall 2012 Enrollment: 62 . . . . (847) 570-1959
Northwestern University (Private, Not-for-profit)
  Fall 2012 Enrollment: 21,370 . . . . (847) 491-3741
  2012-13 Tuition: In-state $43,779; Out-of-state $43,779

Vocational/Technical School(s)

Pivot Point Academy (Private, For-profit)
  Fall 2012 Enrollment: 199 . . . . (800) 886-0500
  2012-13 Tuition: $18,351

Housing: Homeownership rate: 56.6% (2008-2012 5-year est.); Median home value: $367,800 (2008-2012 5-year est.); Median contract rent: $1,039 per month (2008-2012 5-year est.); Median year structure built: 1942 (2008-2012 5-year est.).

Health Insurance: 81.2% Private; 19.4% Public; 8.4% None. (2008-2012 5-year est.)

Hospitals: Evanston Hospital (635 beds); St. Francis Hospital (445 beds)

Safety: Violent crime rate: 30.5 per 10,000 population; Property crime rate: 274.5 per 10,000 population (2012).

Transportation: Commute to work: 55.9% car, 20.3% public transportation, 11.6% walk, 8.1% work from home (2008-2012 5-year est.); Travel time to work: 25.8% less than 15 minutes, 26.0% 15 to 30 minutes, 21.3% 30 to 45 minutes, 16.0% 45 to 60 minutes, 10.9% 60 minutes or more (2008-2012 5-year est.)

Additional Information Contacts

City of Evanston . . . . (847) 448-4311
  http://www.cityofevanston.org
Evanston Chamber of Commerce . . . . (847) 328-1500
  http://www.evchamber.com

EVERGREEN PARK (village).
Covers a land area of 3.161 square miles and a water area of 0 square miles. Located at 41.72° N. Lat; 87.70° W. Long. Elevation is 623 feet.

History: Named for the evergreen trees in the area. Incorporated 1893. St. Xavier College nearby.

Population: 20,874 (1990); 20,821 (2000); 19,852 (2010); Density: 6,279.8 persons per square mile (2008-2012 5-year est.); Race: 72.9% White, 21.1% Black/African American, 1.3% Asian, 0.0% American Indian/Alaska Native, 0.0% Native Hawaiian/Other Pacific Islander, 4.7% Some other race, 1.2% Two or more races, 11.7% Hispanic of any race (2008-2012 5-year est.); Average household size: 2.82 (2008-2012 5-year est.); Median age: 37.5 (2008-2012 5-year est.); Males per 100 females: 88.1 (2008-2012 5-year est.); Marriage status: 34.1% never married, 46.2% now married, 9.2% widowed, 10.5% divorced (2008-2012 5-year est.); Foreign born: 6.6% (2008-2012 5-year est.); Ancestry (includes multiple ancestries): 29.4% Irish, 18.2% German, 9.9% Italian, 9.2% Polish, 5.6% English (2008-2012 5-year est.).

Economy: Single-family building permits issued: 1 (2013); Multi-family building permits issued: 0 (2013); Homeowner vacancy rate: 1.6%. Rental vacancy rate: 7.4%. (2008-2012 5-year est.); Employment by occupation: 14.6% management, business, and financial, 3.4% computer, engineering, and science, 15.6% education, legal, community service, arts, and media, 6.4% healthcare practitioners, 14.0% service, 27.4% sales and office, 7.1% natural resources, construction, and maintenance, 11.5% production, transportation, and material moving (2008-2012 5-year est.).

Income: Per capita income: $29,379 (2008-2012 5-year est.); Median household income: $65,980 (2008-2012 5-year est.); Average household income: $81,021 (2008-2012 5-year est.); Percent of households with income of $100,000 or more: 29.6% (2008-2012 5-year est.); Poverty rate: 8.0% (2008-2012 5-year est.).

Taxes: Total city taxes per capita: $578 (2011); City property taxes per capita: $337 (2011).

Education: Percent of population age 25 and over with: High school diploma (including GED) or higher: 90.3% (2008-2012 5-year est.); Bachelor's degree or higher: 30.9% (2008-2012 5-year est.); Master's degree or higher: 12.1% (2008-2012 5-year est.).

School District(s)

Evergreen Park CHSD 231 (09-12)
  2011-12 Enrollment: 878 . . . . (708) 424-7400
Evergreen Park ESD 124 (PK-08)
  2011-12 Enrollment: 1,838 . . . . (708) 423-0950

Housing: Homeownership rate: 81.8% (2008-2012 5-year est.); Median home value: $214,500 (2008-2012 5-year est.); Median contract rent: $837 per month (2008-2012 5-year est.); Median year structure built: 1955 (2008-2012 5-year est.).

Health Insurance: 78.4% Private; 24.0% Public; 9.0% None. (2008-2012 5-year est.)

Hospitals: Little Company of Mary Hospital & Health Care Centers (487 beds)

Safety: Violent crime rate: 17.0 per 10,000 population; Property crime rate: 287.2 per 10,000 population (2012).

Transportation: Commute to work: 81.4% car, 11.1% public transportation, 2.8% walk, 3.7% work from home (2008-2012 5-year est.); Travel time to work: 22.7% less than 15 minutes, 22.5% 15 to 30 minutes, 25.9% 30 to 45 minutes, 13.0% 45 to 60 minutes, 15.9% 60 minutes or more (2008-2012 5-year est.)

Additional Information Contacts

Evergreen Park Chamber of Commerce . . . . (708) 423-1118
   http://www.evergreenparkchamber.org

Village of Evergreen Park . . . . (708) 422-1551
   http://www.evergreenpark-ill.com

FLOSSMOOR (village). Covers a land area of 3.658 square miles and a water area of 0 square miles. Located at 41.54° N. Lat; 87.69° W. Long. Elevation is 676 feet.

History: Incorporated 1924.

Population: 8,651 (1990); 9,301 (2000); 9,464 (2010); Density: 2,566.4 persons per square mile (2008-2012 5-year est.); Race: 43.2% White, 48.7% Black/African American, 1.9% Asian, 0.1% American Indian/Alaska Native, 0.0% Native Hawaiian/Other Pacific Islander, 6.1% Some other race, 4.8% Two or more races, 1.4% Hispanic of any race (2008-2012 5-year est.); Average household size: 2.70 (2008-2012 5-year est.); Median age: 45.7 (2008-2012 5-year est.); Males per 100 females: 80.3 (2008-2012 5-year est.); Marriage status: 27.3% never married, 58.8% now married, 6.6% widowed, 7.3% divorced (2008-2012 5-year est.); Foreign born: 8.5% (2008-2012 5-year est.); Ancestry (includes multiple ancestries): 12.5% Irish, 12.2% German, 7.6% Polish, 5.4% Russian, 4.8% English (2008-2012 5-year est.).

Economy: Single-family building permits issued: 2 (2013); Multi-family building permits issued: 0 (2013); Homeowner vacancy rate: 4.1%. Rental vacancy rate: 0.0%. (2008-2012 5-year est.); Employment by occupation: 23.4% management, business, and financial, 7.1% computer, engineering, and science, 19.0% education, legal, community service, arts, and media, 13.4% healthcare practitioners, 8.4% service, 18.0% sales and office, 3.9% natural resources, construction, and maintenance, 6.7% production, transportation, and material moving (2008-2012 5-year est.).

Income: Per capita income: $53,616 (2008-2012 5-year est.); Median household income: $106,250 (2008-2012 5-year est.); Average household income: $143,039 (2008-2012 5-year est.); Percent of households with income of $100,000 or more: 52.6% (2008-2012 5-year est.); Poverty rate: 1.6% (2008-2012 5-year est.).

Education: Percent of population age 25 and over with: High school diploma (including GED) or higher: 98.8% (2008-2012 5-year est.); Bachelor's degree or higher: 64.6% (2008-2012 5-year est.); Master's degree or higher: 32.8% (2008-2012 5-year est.).

School District(s)

Flossmoor SD 161 (PK-08)
   2011-12 Enrollment: 2,389 . . . . (708) 647-7000
Homewood Flossmoor CHSD 233 (09-12)
   2011-12 Enrollment: 2,841 . . . . (708) 799-3000

Housing: Homeownership rate: 96.4% (2008-2012 5-year est.); Median home value: $270,800 (2008-2012 5-year est.); Median contract rent: $871 per month (2008-2012 5-year est.); Median year structure built: 1968 (2008-2012 5-year est.).

Health Insurance: 85.0% Private; 24.2% Public; 5.9% None. (2008-2012 5-year est.)

Safety: Violent crime rate: 9.5 per 10,000 population; Property crime rate: 162.0 per 10,000 population (2012).

Transportation: Commute to work: 79.8% car, 11.5% public transportation, 0.9% walk, 6.1% work from home (2008-2012 5-year est.); Travel time to work: 18.3% less than 15 minutes, 21.4% 15 to 30 minutes, 24.1% 30 to 45 minutes, 10.6% 45 to 60 minutes, 25.6% 60 minutes or more (2008-2012 5-year est.)

Additional Information Contacts

Village of Flossmoor . . . . (708) 798-2300
   http://www.flossmoor.org

FORD HEIGHTS (village). Aka East Chicago Heights. Covers a land area of 1.946 square miles and a water area of 0 square miles. Located at 41.51° N. Lat; 87.58° W. Long. Elevation is 663 feet.

Population: 4,259 (1990); 3,456 (2000); 2,763 (2010); Density: 1,431.9 persons per square mile (2008-2012 5-year est.); Race: 1.7% White, 95.6% Black/African American, 0.0% Asian, 0.0% American Indian/Alaska Native, 0.0% Native Hawaiian/Other Pacific Islander, 2.7% Some other race, 2.7% Two or more races, 0.0% Hispanic of any race (2008-2012 5-year est.); Average household size: 3.20 (2008-2012 5-year est.); Median age: 28.8 (2008-2012 5-year est.); Males per 100 females: 79.5 (2008-2012 5-year est.); Marriage status: 60.7% never married, 24.6% now married, 7.7% widowed, 7.0% divorced (2008-2012 5-year est.); Foreign born: 0.0% (2008-2012 5-year est.); Ancestry (includes multiple ancestries): 1.4% German, 1.0% English, 0.9% Irish, 0.7% Jamaican, 0.6% Nigerian (2008-2012 5-year est.).

Economy: Single-family building permits issued: 0 (2013); Multi-family building permits issued: 0 (2013); Homeowner vacancy rate: 0.0%. Rental vacancy rate: 2.1%. (2008-2012 5-year est.); Employment by occupation: 0.8% management, business, and financial, 0.0% computer, engineering, and science, 7.9% education, legal, community service, arts, and media, 12.1% healthcare practitioners, 52.5% service, 14.3% sales and office, 4.2% natural resources, construction, and maintenance, 8.2% production, transportation, and material moving (2008-2012 5-year est.).

Income: Per capita income: $10,755 (2008-2012 5-year est.); Median household income: $21,994 (2008-2012 5-year est.); Average household income: $31,423 (2008-2012 5-year est.); Percent of households with income of $100,000 or more: 4.7% (2008-2012 5-year est.); Poverty rate: 43.1% (2008-2012 5-year est.).

Education: Percent of population age 25 and over with: High school diploma (including GED) or higher: 79.3% (2008-2012 5-year est.); Bachelor's degree or higher: 5.2% (2008-2012 5-year est.); Master's degree or higher: 0.0% (2008-2012 5-year est.).

School District(s)

Ford Heights SD 169 (PK-08)
   2011-12 Enrollment: 450 . . . . (708) 758-1370

Housing: Homeownership rate: 32.2% (2008-2012 5-year est.); Median home value: $80,300 (2008-2012 5-year est.); Median contract rent: $639 per month (2008-2012 5-year est.); Median year structure built: 1965 (2008-2012 5-year est.).

Health Insurance: 28.8% Private; 55.9% Public; 24.5% None. (2008-2012 5-year est.)

Transportation: Commute to work: 84.8% car, 10.2% public transportation, 5.0% walk, 0.0% work from home (2008-2012 5-year est.); Travel time to work: 22.9% less than 15 minutes, 50.1% 15 to 30 minutes, 11.4% 30 to 45 minutes, 3.2% 45 to 60 minutes, 12.4% 60 minutes or more (2008-2012 5-year est.)

FOREST PARK (village). Covers a land area of 2.402 square miles and a water area of 0 square miles. Located at 41.87° N. Lat; 87.82° W. Long. Elevation is 623 feet.

Population: 14,918 (1990); 15,688 (2000); 14,167 (2010); Density: 5,909.9 persons per square mile (2008-2012 5-year est.); Race: 52.1% White, 34.6% Black/African American, 6.9% Asian, 0.1% American Indian/Alaska Native, 0.0% Native Hawaiian/Other Pacific Islander, 6.3% Some other race, 2.9% Two or more races, 11.6% Hispanic of any race (2008-2012 5-year est.); Average household size: 2.03 (2008-2012 5-year est.); Median age: 39.0 (2008-2012 5-year est.); Males per 100 females: 88.6 (2008-2012 5-year est.); Marriage status: 45.0% never married, 38.0% now married, 4.9% widowed, 12.1% divorced (2008-2012 5-year est.); Foreign born: 13.6% (2008-2012 5-year est.); Ancestry (includes multiple ancestries): 12.9% Irish, 12.3% German, 8.0% Italian, 4.9% Polish, 3.7% English (2008-2012 5-year est.).

Economy: Single-family building permits issued: 0 (2013); Multi-family building permits issued: 0 (2013); Homeowner vacancy rate: 4.3%. Rental vacancy rate: 11.5%. (2008-2012 5-year est.); Employment by occupation: 17.1% management, business, and financial, 5.5% computer, engineering, and science, 15.2% education, legal, community service, arts, and media, 6.3% healthcare practitioners, 14.1% service, 27.2% sales and office, 3.1% natural resources, construction, and maintenance, 11.4% production, transportation, and material moving (2008-2012 5-year est.).

Income: Per capita income: $35,231 (2008-2012 5-year est.); Median household income: $50,700 (2008-2012 5-year est.); Average household income: $70,573 (2008-2012 5-year est.); Percent of households with income of $100,000 or more: 16.3% (2008-2012 5-year est.); Poverty rate: 9.9% (2008-2012 5-year est.).

Education: Percent of population age 25 and over with: High school diploma (including GED) or higher: 92.8% (2008-2012 5-year est.); Bachelor's degree or higher: 41.7% (2008-2012 5-year est.); Master's degree or higher: 16.1% (2008-2012 5-year est.).

School District(s)

Forest Park SD 91 (PK-08)
    2011-12 Enrollment: 903 . . . . (708) 366-5700
Proviso Twp HSD 209 (09-12)
    2011-12 Enrollment: 5,122 . . . . (708) 338-5912

Housing: Homeownership rate: 47.4% (2008-2012 5-year est.); Median home value: $224,300 (2008-2012 5-year est.); Median contract rent: $846 per month (2008-2012 5-year est.); Median year structure built: 1956 (2008-2012 5-year est.).

Health Insurance: 72.4% Private; 22.5% Public; 13.9% None. (2008-2012 5-year est.)

Hospitals: Riveredge Hospital (210 beds)

Safety: Violent crime rate: 37.2 per 10,000 population; Property crime rate: 519.1 per 10,000 population (2012).

Transportation: Commute to work: 68.7% car, 22.3% public transportation, 3.8% walk, 4.2% work from home (2008-2012 5-year est.); Travel time to work: 16.6% less than 15 minutes, 31.7% 15 to 30 minutes, 23.8% 30 to 45 minutes, 13.0% 45 to 60 minutes, 15.0% 60 minutes or more (2008-2012 5-year est.)

Additional Information Contacts

Forest Park Chamber of Commerce . . . . (708) 366-2543
    http://www.exploreforestpark.com
Village of Forest Park . . . . (708) 366-2323
    http://www.forestpark.net

FOREST VIEW (village). Covers a land area of 1.067 square miles and a water area of 0.130 square miles. Located at 41.81° N. Lat; 87.77° W. Long. Elevation is 594 feet.

Population: 743 (1990); 778 (2000); 698 (2010); Density: 753.7 persons per square mile (2008-2012 5-year est.); Race: 82.3% White, 0.0% Black/African American, 1.2% Asian, 0.0% American Indian/Alaska Native, 0.0% Native Hawaiian/Other Pacific Islander, 16.5% Some other race, 1.5% Two or more races, 33.1% Hispanic of any race (2008-2012 5-year est.); Average household size: 2.92 (2008-2012 5-year est.); Median age: 42.1 (2008-2012 5-year est.); Males per 100 females: 87.9 (2008-2012 5-year est.); Marriage status: 29.2% never married, 56.8% now married, 12.0% widowed, 2.0% divorced (2008-2012 5-year est.); Foreign born: 13.2% (2008-2012 5-year est.); Ancestry (includes multiple ancestries): 20.3% German, 17.4% Czech, 13.1% Polish, 12.6% Irish, 10.3% Italian (2008-2012 5-year est.).

Economy: Single-family building permits issued: 0 (2013); Multi-family building permits issued: 0 (2013); Homeowner vacancy rate: 5.3%. Rental vacancy rate: 0.0%. (2008-2012 5-year est.); Employment by occupation: 5.3% management, business, and financial, 2.9% computer, engineering, and science, 6.9% education, legal, community service, arts, and media, 6.3% healthcare practitioners, 16.9% service, 33.5% sales and office, 12.7% natural resources, construction, and maintenance, 15.6% production, transportation, and material moving (2008-2012 5-year est.).

Income: Per capita income: $26,186 (2008-2012 5-year est.); Median household income: $65,096 (2008-2012 5-year est.); Average household income: $71,989 (2008-2012 5-year est.); Percent of households with income of $100,000 or more: 24.0% (2008-2012 5-year est.); Poverty rate: 5.1% (2008-2012 5-year est.).

Education: Percent of population age 25 and over with: High school diploma (including GED) or higher: 90.1% (2008-2012 5-year est.); Bachelor's degree or higher: 15.4% (2008-2012 5-year est.); Master's degree or higher: 4.8% (2008-2012 5-year est.).

Housing: Homeownership rate: 91.3% (2008-2012 5-year est.); Median home value: $203,800 (2008-2012 5-year est.); Median contract rent: $1,083 per month (2008-2012 5-year est.); Median year structure built: 1955 (2008-2012 5-year est.).

Health Insurance: 69.3% Private; 32.2% Public; 13.7% None. (2008-2012 5-year est.)

Safety: Violent crime rate: 0.0 per 10,000 population; Property crime rate: 542.9 per 10,000 population (2012).

Transportation: Commute to work: 88.8% car, 5.7% public transportation, 1.4% walk, 3.3% work from home (2008-2012 5-year est.); Travel time to work: 20.1% less than 15 minutes, 31.9% 15 to 30 minutes, 30.2% 30 to 45 minutes, 7.1% 45 to 60 minutes, 10.7% 60 minutes or more (2008-2012 5-year est.)

FRANKLIN PARK (village). Covers a land area of 4.767 square miles and a water area of 0 square miles. Located at 41.94° N. Lat; 87.88° W. Long. Elevation is 643 feet.

Population: 18,485 (1990); 19,434 (2000); 18,333 (2010); Density: 3,845.9 persons per square mile (2008-2012 5-year est.); Race: 78.6% White, 0.8% Black/African American, 3.4% Asian, 0.5% American Indian/Alaska Native, 0.0% Native Hawaiian/Other Pacific Islander, 16.7% Some other race, 1.5% Two or more races, 43.1% Hispanic of any race (2008-2012 5-year est.); Average household size: 2.96 (2008-2012 5-year est.); Median age: 36.8 (2008-2012 5-year est.); Males per 100 females: 94.6 (2008-2012 5-year est.); Marriage status: 32.6% never married, 51.7% now married, 5.8% widowed, 10.0% divorced (2008-2012 5-year est.); Foreign born: 34.7% (2008-2012 5-year est.); Ancestry (includes multiple ancestries): 22.2% Polish, 11.2% German, 10.5% Italian, 8.2% Irish, 2.1% American (2008-2012 5-year est.).

Economy: Single-family building permits issued: 0 (2013); Multi-family building permits issued: 0 (2013); Homeowner vacancy rate: 1.9%. Rental vacancy rate: 4.6%. (2008-2012 5-year est.); Employment by occupation: 7.5% management, business, and financial, 1.7% computer, engineering, and science, 6.6% education, legal, community service, arts, and media, 3.3% healthcare practitioners, 17.4% service, 26.6% sales and office, 13.4% natural resources, construction, and maintenance, 23.6% production, transportation, and material moving (2008-2012 5-year est.).

Income: Per capita income: $22,983 (2008-2012 5-year est.); Median household income: $56,098 (2008-2012 5-year est.); Average household income: $65,226 (2008-2012 5-year est.); Percent of households with income of $100,000 or more: 16.0% (2008-2012 5-year est.); Poverty rate: 12.5% (2008-2012 5-year est.).

Education: Percent of population age 25 and over with: High school diploma (including GED) or higher: 78.1% (2008-2012 5-year est.); Bachelor's degree or higher: 14.6% (2008-2012 5-year est.); Master's degree or higher: 4.0% (2008-2012 5-year est.).

School District(s)

Franklin Park SD 84 (PK-08)
    2011-12 Enrollment: 1,337 . . . . (847) 455-4230
Leyden CHSD 212 (09-12)
    2011-12 Enrollment: 3,500 . . . . (847) 451-3020
Mannheim SD 83 (PK-08)
    2011-12 Enrollment: 2,604 . . . . (847) 455-4413
Region 06 West Cook Isc 2 (PK-12)
    2011-12 Enrollment: n/a . . . . (708) 544-4890
Ridgewood CHSD 234 (09-12)
    2011-12 Enrollment: 857 . . . . (708) 456-4242

Housing: Homeownership rate: 74.9% (2008-2012 5-year est.); Median home value: $204,800 (2008-2012 5-year est.); Median contract rent: $733 per month (2008-2012 5-year est.); Median year structure built: 1954 (2008-2012 5-year est.).

Health Insurance: 59.0% Private; 28.8% Public; 20.5% None. (2008-2012 5-year est.)

Safety: Violent crime rate: 14.7 per 10,000 population; Property crime rate: 200.8 per 10,000 population (2012).

Transportation: Commute to work: 90.8% car, 4.2% public transportation, 2.3% walk, 1.8% work from home (2008-2012 5-year est.); Travel time to work: 24.7% less than 15 minutes, 30.2% 15 to 30 minutes, 28.3% 30 to 45 minutes, 8.8% 45 to 60 minutes, 8.0% 60 minutes or more (2008-2012 5-year est.)

Additional Information Contacts

Franklin Park/Schiller Park Chamber of Commerce . . . . . . (708) 865-9510
    http://www.chamberbyohare.org
Village of Franklin Park . . . . (847) 671-4800
    http://www.villageoffranklinpark.com

GLENCOE (village). Covers a land area of 3.719 square miles and a water area of 0.061 square miles. Located at 42.13° N. Lat; 87.76° W. Long. Elevation is 673 feet.

History: One of the founders of Glencoe was Walter S. Gurnee, and the "coe" part of the town's name came from his wife's maiden name. Glencoe was incorporated as a village in 1869.

Population: 8,499 (1990); 8,762 (2000); 8,723 (2010); Density: 2,346.7 persons per square mile (2008-2012 5-year est.); Race: 94.2% White, 1.2% Black/African American, 3.0% Asian, 0.2% American Indian/Alaska Native, 0.0% Native Hawaiian/Other Pacific Islander, 1.4% Some other race, 1.0% Two or more races, 2.9% Hispanic of any race (2008-2012 5-year est.); Average household size: 2.89 (2008-2012 5-year est.); Median age: 43.4 (2008-2012 5-year est.); Males per 100 females: 97.5

(2008-2012 5-year est.); Marriage status: 17.3% never married, 73.4% now married, 3.6% widowed, 5.7% divorced (2008-2012 5-year est.); Foreign born: 8.5% (2008-2012 5-year est.); Ancestry (includes multiple ancestries): 14.2% German, 13.1% Russian, 10.5% Irish, 9.2% English, 7.7% American (2008-2012 5-year est.).

Economy: Single-family building permits issued: 30 (2013); Multi-family building permits issued: 0 (2013); Homeowner vacancy rate: 2.4%. Rental vacancy rate: 20.3%. (2008-2012 5-year est.); Employment by occupation: 33.5% management, business, and financial, 3.3% computer, engineering, and science, 26.7% education, legal, community service, arts, and media, 6.8% healthcare practitioners, 4.9% service, 20.0% sales and office, 3.3% natural resources, construction, and maintenance, 1.5% production, transportation, and material moving (2008-2012 5-year est.).

Income: Per capita income: $99,036 (2008-2012 5-year est.); Median household income: $184,028 (2008-2012 5-year est.); Average household income: $283,185 (2008-2012 5-year est.); Percent of households with income of $100,000 or more: 70.2% (2008-2012 5-year est.); Poverty rate: 5.3% (2008-2012 5-year est.).

Education: Percent of population age 25 and over with: High school diploma (including GED) or higher: 99.9% (2008-2012 5-year est.); Bachelor's degree or higher: 85.3% (2008-2012 5-year est.); Master's degree or higher: 51.4% (2008-2012 5-year est.).

School District(s)

Glencoe SD 35 (KG-08)
  2011-12 Enrollment: 1,287 . . . . (847) 835-7800

Housing: Homeownership rate: 93.9% (2008-2012 5-year est.); Median home value: $927,400 (2008-2012 5-year est.); Median contract rent: $1,355 per month (2008-2012 5-year est.); Median year structure built: 1954 (2008-2012 5-year est.).

Health Insurance: 93.7% Private; 13.3% Public; 3.3% None. (2008-2012 5-year est.)

Safety: Violent crime rate: 0.0 per 10,000 population; Property crime rate: 107.3 per 10,000 population (2012).

Transportation: Commute to work: 61.4% car, 19.9% public transportation, 2.2% walk, 15.0% work from home (2008-2012 5-year est.); Travel time to work: 17.3% less than 15 minutes, 16.1% 15 to 30 minutes, 26.3% 30 to 45 minutes, 21.2% 45 to 60 minutes, 19.1% 60 minutes or more (2008-2012 5-year est.)

Additional Information Contacts
Glencoe Chamber of Commerce. . . . . (847) 835-3333
  http://www.glencoechamber.org
Village of Glencoe . . . . (847) 835-4111
  http://www.villageofglencoe.org

GLENVIEW (village). Covers a land area of 13.948 square miles and a water area of 0.042 square miles. Located at 42.08° N. Lat; 87.83° W. Long. Elevation is 653 feet.

History: Named to promote the town as a good place to live. Settled 1833. Incorporated 1899.

Population: 37,093 (1990); 41,847 (2000); 44,692 (2010); Density: 3,188.8 persons per square mile (2008-2012 5-year est.); Race: 83.6% White, 1.4% Black/African American, 12.3% Asian, 0.1% American Indian/Alaska Native, 0.0% Native Hawaiian/Other Pacific Islander, 2.6% Some other race, 1.7% Two or more races, 6.4% Hispanic of any race (2008-2012 5-year est.); Average household size: 2.64 (2008-2012 5-year est.); Median age: 45.7 (2008-2012 5-year est.); Males per 100 females: 90.6 (2008-2012 5-year est.); Marriage status: 22.9% never married, 62.1% now married, 8.3% widowed, 6.6% divorced (2008-2012 5-year est.); Foreign born: 20.7% (2008-2012 5-year est.); Ancestry (includes multiple ancestries): 19.6% German, 14.6% Irish, 10.9% Polish, 9.4% Italian, 6.2% Russian (2008-2012 5-year est.).

Economy: Unemployment rate: 4.6% (April 2014); Total civilian labor force: 23,228 (April 2014); Single-family building permits issued: 124 (2013); Multi-family building permits issued: 434 (2013); Homeowner vacancy rate: 1.7%. Rental vacancy rate: 4.5%. (2008-2012 5-year est.); Employment by occupation: 27.0% management, business, and financial, 6.5% computer, engineering, and science, 15.1% education, legal, community service, arts, and media, 7.7% healthcare practitioners, 8.5% service, 25.7% sales and office, 4.8% natural resources, construction, and maintenance, 4.8% production, transportation, and material moving (2008-2012 5-year est.).

Income: Per capita income: $52,227 (2008-2012 5-year est.); Median household income: $99,841 (2008-2012 5-year est.); Average household income: $137,996 (2008-2012 5-year est.); Percent of households with

income of $100,000 or more: 49.9% (2008-2012 5-year est.); Poverty rate: 3.7% (2008-2012 5-year est.).

Taxes: Total city taxes per capita: $1,233 (2011); City property taxes per capita: $884 (2011).

Education: Percent of population age 25 and over with: High school diploma (including GED) or higher: 95.9% (2008-2012 5-year est.); Bachelor's degree or higher: 61.3% (2008-2012 5-year est.); Master's degree or higher: 27.5% (2008-2012 5-year est.).

School District(s)

Avoca SD 37 (PK-08)
  2011-12 Enrollment: 656 . . . . (847) 251-3587
East Maine SD 63 (PK-08)
  2011-12 Enrollment: 3,628 . . . . (847) 299-1900
Glenview CCSD 34 (PK-08)
  2011-12 Enrollment: 4,901 . . . . (847) 998-5005
Northbrook/glenview SD 30 (PK-08)
  2011-12 Enrollment: 1,096 . . . . (847) 498-4190
Northern Suburban Spec Ed Dist (KG-12)
  2011-12 Enrollment: n/a . . . . (847) 831-5100
Northfield Twp HSD 225 (09-12)
  2011-12 Enrollment: 4,750 . . . . (847) 486-4700
West Northfield SD 31 (KG-08)
  2011-12 Enrollment: 890 . . . . (847) 272-6880

Housing: Homeownership rate: 83.6% (2008-2012 5-year est.); Median home value: $494,500 (2008-2012 5-year est.); Median contract rent: $1,439 per month (2008-2012 5-year est.); Median year structure built: 1973 (2008-2012 5-year est.).

Health Insurance: 85.0% Private; 23.8% Public; 5.9% None. (2008-2012 5-year est.)

Hospitals: Glenbrook Hospital (144 beds)

Safety: Violent crime rate: 8.7 per 10,000 population; Property crime rate: 106.7 per 10,000 population (2012).

Transportation: Commute to work: 80.1% car, 11.0% public transportation, 1.3% walk, 6.8% work from home (2008-2012 5-year est.); Travel time to work: 22.1% less than 15 minutes, 27.7% 15 to 30 minutes, 27.6% 30 to 45 minutes, 10.6% 45 to 60 minutes, 12.1% 60 minutes or more (2008-2012 5-year est.); Amtrak: Train service available.

Additional Information Contacts
Glenview Chamber of Commerce . . . . (847) 724-0900
  http://www.glenviewchamber.com
Village of Glenview . . . . (847) 904-4370
  http://www.glenview.il.us

GLENWOOD (village). Covers a land area of 3.123 square miles and a water area of 0 square miles. Located at 41.54° N. Lat; 87.61° W. Long. Elevation is 620 feet.

Population: 9,289 (1990); 9,000 (2000); 8,969 (2010); Density: 2,892.7 persons per square mile (2008-2012 5-year est.); Race: 26.2% White, 70.0% Black/African American, 0.0% Asian, 0.5% American Indian/Alaska Native, 0.0% Native Hawaiian/Other Pacific Islander, 3.3% Some other race, 1.4% Two or more races, 5.6% Hispanic of any race (2008-2012 5-year est.); Average household size: 2.72 (2008-2012 5-year est.); Median age: 38.5 (2008-2012 5-year est.); Males per 100 females: 102.7 (2008-2012 5-year est.); Marriage status: 34.8% never married, 45.6% now married, 5.8% widowed, 13.8% divorced (2008-2012 5-year est.); Foreign born: 2.2% (2008-2012 5-year est.); Ancestry (includes multiple ancestries): 9.4% German, 4.9% Italian, 3.9% Irish, 2.2% French, 2.1% Polish (2008-2012 5-year est.).

Economy: Single-family building permits issued: 0 (2013); Multi-family building permits issued: 0 (2013); Homeowner vacancy rate: 3.1%. Rental vacancy rate: 6.5%. (2008-2012 5-year est.); Employment by occupation: 14.3% management, business, and financial, 7.0% computer, engineering, and science, 10.0% education, legal, community service, arts, and media, 5.9% healthcare practitioners, 13.2% service, 28.5% sales and office, 5.7% natural resources, construction, and maintenance, 15.4% production, transportation, and material moving (2008-2012 5-year est.).

Income: Per capita income: $25,631 (2008-2012 5-year est.); Median household income: $57,092 (2008-2012 5-year est.); Average household income: $68,800 (2008-2012 5-year est.); Percent of households with income of $100,000 or more: 20.3% (2008-2012 5-year est.); Poverty rate: 12.0% (2008-2012 5-year est.).

Education: Percent of population age 25 and over with: High school diploma (including GED) or higher: 91.5% (2008-2012 5-year est.); Bachelor's degree or higher: 25.7% (2008-2012 5-year est.); Master's degree or higher: 7.2% (2008-2012 5-year est.).

School District(s)
Brookwood SD 167 (PK-08)
   2011-12 Enrollment: 1,217 . . . . (708) 758-5190
Housing: Homeownership rate: 83.1% (2008-2012 5-year est.); Median home value: $153,700 (2008-2012 5-year est.); Median contract rent: $879 per month (2008-2012 5-year est.); Median year structure built: 1970 (2008-2012 5-year est.).
Health Insurance: 72.2% Private; 34.3% Public; 13.0% None. (2008-2012 5-year est.)
Safety: Violent crime rate: 24.4 per 10,000 population; Property crime rate: 274.1 per 10,000 population (2012).
Transportation: Commute to work: 83.7% car, 11.6% public transportation, 2.3% walk, 1.5% work from home (2008-2012 5-year est.); Travel time to work: 24.5% less than 15 minutes, 18.8% 15 to 30 minutes, 21.9% 30 to 45 minutes, 16.3% 45 to 60 minutes, 18.5% 60 minutes or more (2008-2012 5-year est.)
Additional Information Contacts
Village of Glenwood . . . . (708) 753-2400
  http://www.villageofglenwood.com

GOLF (village). Covers a land area of 0.448 square miles and a water area of 0 square miles. Located at 42.06° N. Lat; 87.78° W. Long. Elevation is 636 feet.
Population: 454 (1990); 451 (2000); 500 (2010); Density: 1,315.8 persons per square mile (2008-2012 5-year est.); Race: 86.6% White, 1.5% Black/African American, 2.0% Asian, 0.0% American Indian/Alaska Native, 0.0% Native Hawaiian/Other Pacific Islander, 9.9% Some other race, 5.9% Two or more races, 3.7% Hispanic of any race (2008-2012 5-year est.); Average household size: 3.32 (2008-2012 5-year est.); Median age: 40.5 (2008-2012 5-year est.); Males per 100 females: 131.4 (2008-2012 5-year est.); Marriage status: 19.8% never married, 74.8% now married, 5.2% widowed, 0.2% divorced (2008-2012 5-year est.); Foreign born: 12.7% (2008-2012 5-year est.); Ancestry (includes multiple ancestries): 35.8% German, 31.5% Irish, 11.7% English, 11.2% Italian, 10.0% Polish (2008-2012 5-year est.).
Economy: Single-family building permits issued: 0 (2013); Multi-family building permits issued: 0 (2013); Homeowner vacancy rate: 0.6%. Rental vacancy rate: 0.0%. (2008-2012 5-year est.); Employment by occupation: 37.0% management, business, and financial, 3.8% computer, engineering, and science, 20.4% education, legal, community service, arts, and media, 8.9% healthcare practitioners, 3.0% service, 25.1% sales and office, 1.7% natural resources, construction, and maintenance, 0.0% production, transportation, and material moving (2008-2012 5-year est.).
Income: Per capita income: $55,372 (2008-2012 5-year est.); Median household income: $170,577 (2008-2012 5-year est.); Average household income: $191,876 (2008-2012 5-year est.); Percent of households with income of $100,000 or more: 78.2% (2008-2012 5-year est.); Poverty rate: 1.2% (2008-2012 5-year est.).
Education: Percent of population age 25 and over with: High school diploma (including GED) or higher: 94.6% (2008-2012 5-year est.); Bachelor's degree or higher: 75.8% (2008-2012 5-year est.); Master's degree or higher: 35.0% (2008-2012 5-year est.).
Housing: Homeownership rate: 100.0% (2008-2012 5-year est.); Median home value: $837,300 (2008-2012 5-year est.); Median contract rent: n/a per month (2008-2012 5-year est.); Median year structure built: 1953 (2008-2012 5-year est.).
Health Insurance: 94.7% Private; 11.7% Public; 1.2% None. (2008-2012 5-year est.)
Transportation: Commute to work: 49.4% car, 31.5% public transportation, 2.6% walk, 12.3% work from home (2008-2012 5-year est.); Travel time to work: 18.4% less than 15 minutes, 18.4% 15 to 30 minutes, 40.3% 30 to 45 minutes, 18.4% 45 to 60 minutes, 4.4% 60 minutes or more (2008-2012 5-year est.)

HANOVER PARK (village). Covers a land area of 6.329 square miles and a water area of 0.105 square miles. Located at 41.98° N. Lat; 88.14° W. Long. Elevation is 804 feet.
Population: 32,895 (1990); 38,278 (2000); 37,973 (2010); Density: 6,002.6 persons per square mile (2008-2012 5-year est.); Race: 51.5% White, 7.8% Black/African American, 17.9% Asian, 0.0% American Indian/Alaska Native, 0.0% Native Hawaiian/Other Pacific Islander, 22.8% Some other race, 2.5% Two or more races, 36.4% Hispanic of any race (2008-2012 5-year est.); Average household size: 3.49 (2008-2012 5-year est.); Median age: 32.1 (2008-2012 5-year est.); Males per 100 females: 98.7 (2008-2012 5-year est.); Marriage status: 31.3% never married,

58.6% now married, 3.0% widowed, 7.1% divorced (2008-2012 5-year est.); Foreign born: 36.6% (2008-2012 5-year est.); Ancestry (includes multiple ancestries): 13.3% German, 9.8% Polish, 8.5% Irish, 5.8% Italian, 2.8% English (2008-2012 5-year est.).
Economy: Unemployment rate: 7.9% (April 2014); Total civilian labor force: 21,524 (April 2014); Single-family building permits issued: 14 (2013); Multi-family building permits issued: 0 (2013); Homeowner vacancy rate: 2.8%. Rental vacancy rate: 3.6%. (2008-2012 5-year est.); Employment by occupation: 11.0% management, business, and financial, 5.7% computer, engineering, and science, 5.4% education, legal, community service, arts, and media, 3.1% healthcare practitioners, 20.8% service, 27.1% sales and office, 7.3% natural resources, construction, and maintenance, 19.6% production, transportation, and material moving (2008-2012 5-year est.).
Income: Per capita income: $23,338 (2008-2012 5-year est.); Median household income: $70,067 (2008-2012 5-year est.); Average household income: $78,395 (2008-2012 5-year est.); Percent of households with income of $100,000 or more: 25.3% (2008-2012 5-year est.); Poverty rate: 12.9% (2008-2012 5-year est.).
Taxes: Total city taxes per capita: $525 (2011); City property taxes per capita: $356 (2011).
Education: Percent of population age 25 and over with: High school diploma (including GED) or higher: 79.9% (2008-2012 5-year est.); Bachelor's degree or higher: 24.7% (2008-2012 5-year est.); Master's degree or higher: 5.8% (2008-2012 5-year est.).
School District(s)
CCSD 93 (PK-08)
   2011-12 Enrollment: 3,879 . . . . (630) 539-3000
Keeneyville SD 20 (PK-08)
   2011-12 Enrollment: 1,620 . . . . (630) 894-4606
SD U-46 (PK-12)
   2011-12 Enrollment: 40,687 . . . . (847) 888-5000
SD U-46 (PK-12)
   2011-12 Enrollment: 40,687 . . . . (847) 888-5000
Schaumburg CCSD 54 (PK-08)
   2011-12 Enrollment: 14,083 . . . . (847) 357-5000
Vocational/Technical School(s)
Empire Beauty School-Hanover Park (Private, For-profit)
   Fall 2012 Enrollment: 132 . . . . (800) 920-4593
   2012-13 Tuition: $17,595
Housing: Homeownership rate: 80.1% (2008-2012 5-year est.); Median home value: $196,000 (2008-2012 5-year est.); Median contract rent: $939 per month (2008-2012 5-year est.); Median year structure built: 1975 (2008-2012 5-year est.).
Health Insurance: 63.8% Private; 25.5% Public; 15.6% None. (2008-2012 5-year est.)
Safety: Violent crime rate: 11.8 per 10,000 population; Property crime rate: 114.9 per 10,000 population (2012).
Transportation: Commute to work: 90.3% car, 2.9% public transportation, 1.1% walk, 2.6% work from home (2008-2012 5-year est.); Travel time to work: 19.3% less than 15 minutes, 36.6% 15 to 30 minutes, 25.9% 30 to 45 minutes, 8.9% 45 to 60 minutes, 9.3% 60 minutes or more (2008-2012 5-year est.)
Additional Information Contacts
Hanover Park Chamber of Commerce & Industry . . . . (630) 372-2009
  http://www.hanoverparkchamber.com
Village of Hanover Park . . . . (630) 823-5600
  http://www.hanoverparkillinois.org

HARVEY (city). Covers a land area of 6.303 square miles and a water area of 0 square miles. Located at 41.61° N. Lat; 87.65° W. Long. Elevation is 604 feet.
History: Named for Turlington W. Harvey, town founder. The site of Harvey was purchased in 1889 by Turlington W. Harvey, a Chicago lumberman, who organized a village that attracted other settlers and industries.
Population: 29,771 (1990); 30,000 (2000); 25,282 (2010); Density: 3,959.8 persons per square mile (2008-2012 5-year est.); Race: 13.4% White, 76.0% Black/African American, 0.4% Asian, 0.0% American Indian/Alaska Native, 0.0% Native Hawaiian/Other Pacific Islander, 10.2% Some other race, 1.2% Two or more races, 16.7% Hispanic of any race (2008-2012 5-year est.); Average household size: 3.22 (2008-2012 5-year est.); Median age: 30.6 (2008-2012 5-year est.); Males per 100 females: 80.8 (2008-2012 5-year est.); Marriage status: 48.9% never married, 32.4% now married, 8.2% widowed, 10.4% divorced (2008-2012 5-year est.); Foreign born: 8.5% (2008-2012 5-year est.); Ancestry (includes

multiple ancestries): 1.0% African, 1.0% Polish, 0.7% American, 0.6% English, 0.6% German (2008-2012 5-year est.).
Economy: Unemployment rate: 12.4% (April 2014); Total civilian labor force: 9,897 (April 2014); Single-family building permits issued: 0 (2013); Multi-family building permits issued: 0 (2013); Homeowner vacancy rate: 2.3%. Rental vacancy rate: 9.9%. (2008-2012 5-year est.); Employment by occupation: 5.4% management, business, and financial, 1.0% computer, engineering, and science, 7.7% education, legal, community service, arts, and media, 4.2% healthcare practitioners, 29.7% service, 22.8% sales and office, 8.6% natural resources, construction, and maintenance, 20.6% production, transportation, and material moving (2008-2012 5-year est.).
Income: Per capita income: $13,678 (2008-2012 5-year est.); Median household income: $28,123 (2008-2012 5-year est.); Average household income: $40,597 (2008-2012 5-year est.); Percent of households with income of $100,000 or more: 8.5% (2008-2012 5-year est.); Poverty rate: 34.4% (2008-2012 5-year est.).
Education: Percent of population age 25 and over with: High school diploma (including GED) or higher: 76.7% (2008-2012 5-year est.); Bachelor's degree or higher: 10.5% (2008-2012 5-year est.); Master's degree or higher: 2.0% (2008-2012 5-year est.).

School District(s)

Harvey SD 152 (PK-08)
   2011-12 Enrollment: 2,459 . . . . (708) 333-0300
South Holland SD 151 (PK-08)
   2011-12 Enrollment: 1,494 . . . . (708) 339-1516
Thornton Twp HSD 205 (09-12)
   2011-12 Enrollment: 5,283 . . . . (708) 225-4000
W Harvey-Dixmoor PSD 147 (PK-08)
   2011-12 Enrollment: 1,409 . . . . (708) 339-9500

Four-year College(s)

Ingalls Memorial Hospital Dietetic Internship (Private, Not-for-profit)
   Fall 2012 Enrollment: 8 . . . . (708) 915-5723
Housing: Homeownership rate: 51.6% (2008-2012 5-year est.); Median home value: $95,000 (2008-2012 5-year est.); Median contract rent: $718 per month (2008-2012 5-year est.); Median year structure built: 1956 (2008-2012 5-year est.).
Health Insurance: 33.6% Private; 46.0% Public; 28.0% None. (2008-2012 5-year est.)
Hospitals: Ingalls Memorial Hospital (326 beds)
Safety: Violent crime rate: 137.4 per 10,000 population; Property crime rate: 583.8 per 10,000 population (2012).
Transportation: Commute to work: 81.0% car, 11.5% public transportation, 3.6% walk, 2.5% work from home (2008-2012 5-year est.); Travel time to work: 21.2% less than 15 minutes, 27.3% 15 to 30 minutes, 29.3% 30 to 45 minutes, 9.9% 45 to 60 minutes, 12.3% 60 minutes or more (2008-2012 5-year est.)
Additional Information Contacts
City of Harvey . . . . (708) 210-5301
   http://www.cityofharvey.org
Harvey Chamber of Commerce. (708) 596-4222

HARWOOD HEIGHTS (village).
Covers a land area of 0.825 square miles and a water area of 0 square miles. Located at 41.97° N. Lat; 87.81° W. Long. Elevation is 650 feet.
Population: 7,680 (1990); 8,297 (2000); 8,612 (2010); Density: 10,393.8 persons per square mile (2008-2012 5-year est.); Race: 91.7% White, 0.3% Black/African American, 4.4% Asian, 0.0% American Indian/Alaska Native, 0.0% Native Hawaiian/Other Pacific Islander, 3.6% Some other race, 1.5% Two or more races, 7.6% Hispanic of any race (2008-2012 5-year est.); Average household size: 2.40 (2008-2012 5-year est.); Median age: 45.0 (2008-2012 5-year est.); Males per 100 females: 88.9 (2008-2012 5-year est.); Marriage status: 26.2% never married, 52.6% now married, 11.8% widowed, 9.4% divorced (2008-2012 5-year est.); Foreign born: 38.8% (2008-2012 5-year est.); Ancestry (includes multiple ancestries): 30.1% Polish, 17.9% Italian, 11.8% German, 6.2% Irish, 4.9% Serbian (2008-2012 5-year est.).
Economy: Single-family building permits issued: 2 (2013); Multi-family building permits issued: 0 (2013); Homeowner vacancy rate: 2.4%. Rental vacancy rate: 2.0%. (2008-2012 5-year est.); Employment by occupation: 12.2% management, business, and financial, 3.4% computer, engineering, and science, 4.9% education, legal, community service, arts, and media, 4.9% healthcare practitioners, 19.2% service, 27.9% sales and office, 9.7% natural resources, construction, and maintenance, 17.8% production, transportation, and material moving (2008-2012 5-year est.).

Income: Per capita income: $23,570 (2008-2012 5-year est.); Median household income: $46,553 (2008-2012 5-year est.); Average household income: $54,882 (2008-2012 5-year est.); Percent of households with income of $100,000 or more: 14.7% (2008-2012 5-year est.); Poverty rate: 10.7% (2008-2012 5-year est.).
Education: Percent of population age 25 and over with: High school diploma (including GED) or higher: 82.0% (2008-2012 5-year est.); Bachelor's degree or higher: 22.5% (2008-2012 5-year est.); Master's degree or higher: 6.8% (2008-2012 5-year est.).

School District(s)

Union Ridge SD 86 (PK-08)
   2011-12 Enrollment: 604. . . . . (708) 867-5822
Housing: Homeownership rate: 56.4% (2008-2012 5-year est.); Median home value: $287,300 (2008-2012 5-year est.); Median contract rent: $791 per month (2008-2012 5-year est.); Median year structure built: 1961 (2008-2012 5-year est.).
Health Insurance: 67.2% Private; 29.5% Public; 15.1% None. (2008-2012 5-year est.)
Safety: Violent crime rate: 9.2 per 10,000 population; Property crime rate: 146.8 per 10,000 population (2012).
Transportation: Commute to work: 89.0% car, 4.8% public transportation, 1.6% walk, 3.3% work from home (2008-2012 5-year est.); Travel time to work: 13.5% less than 15 minutes, 35.0% 15 to 30 minutes, 31.5% 30 to 45 minutes, 12.8% 45 to 60 minutes, 7.1% 60 minutes or more (2008-2012 5-year est.)
Additional Information Contacts
Village of Harwood Heights . . . . (708) 867-7200
   http://www.harwoodheights.org

HAZEL CREST (village).
Covers a land area of 3.390 square miles and a water area of 0.021 square miles. Located at 41.57° N. Lat; 87.69° W. Long. Elevation is 646 feet.
Population: 13,334 (1990); 14,816 (2000); 14,100 (2010); Density: 4,230.9 persons per square mile (2008-2012 5-year est.); Race: 13.3% White, 82.4% Black/African American, 0.7% Asian, 0.0% American Indian/Alaska Native, 0.0% Native Hawaiian/Other Pacific Islander, 3.6% Some other race, 1.2% Two or more races, 6.5% Hispanic of any race (2008-2012 5-year est.); Average household size: 2.98 (2008-2012 5-year est.); Median age: 36.2 (2008-2012 5-year est.); Males per 100 females: 88.8 (2008-2012 5-year est.); Marriage status: 42.0% never married, 36.8% now married, 8.2% widowed, 13.0% divorced (2008-2012 5-year est.); Foreign born: 3.0% (2008-2012 5-year est.); Ancestry (includes multiple ancestries): 3.8% German, 2.0% Irish, 1.5% African, 1.3% American, 1.2% Polish (2008-2012 5-year est.).
Economy: Single-family building permits issued: 0 (2013); Multi-family building permits issued: 0 (2013); Homeowner vacancy rate: 2.8%. Rental vacancy rate: 8.6%. (2008-2012 5-year est.); Employment by occupation: 10.1% management, business, and financial, 2.9% computer, engineering, and science, 9.2% education, legal, community service, arts, and media, 6.0% healthcare practitioners, 20.2% service, 30.6% sales and office, 6.9% natural resources, construction, and maintenance, 14.2% production, transportation, and material moving (2008-2012 5-year est.).
Income: Per capita income: $21,803 (2008-2012 5-year est.); Median household income: $50,947 (2008-2012 5-year est.); Average household income: $62,185 (2008-2012 5-year est.); Percent of households with income of $100,000 or more: 15.8% (2008-2012 5-year est.); Poverty rate: 18.0% (2008-2012 5-year est.).
Education: Percent of population age 25 and over with: High school diploma (including GED) or higher: 85.5% (2008-2012 5-year est.); Bachelor's degree or higher: 21.3% (2008-2012 5-year est.); Master's degree or higher: 8.4% (2008-2012 5-year est.).

School District(s)

Hazel Crest SD 152-5 (PK-08)
   2011-12 Enrollment: 1,040 . . . . (708) 335-0790
Prairie-Hills ESD 144 (PK-08)
   2011-12 Enrollment: 2,796 . . . . (708) 210-2888
Housing: Homeownership rate: 65.9% (2008-2012 5-year est.); Median home value: $138,200 (2008-2012 5-year est.); Median contract rent: $1,204 per month (2008-2012 5-year est.); Median year structure built: 1970 (2008-2012 5-year est.).
Health Insurance: 61.2% Private; 35.0% Public; 15.8% None. (2008-2012 5-year est.)
Hospitals: Advocate South Suburban Hospital (291 beds)
Safety: Violent crime rate: 40.9 per 10,000 population; Property crime rate: 410.1 per 10,000 population (2012).

Transportation: Commute to work: 82.7% car, 12.0% public transportation, 0.8% walk, 2.5% work from home (2008-2012 5-year est.); Travel time to work: 11.9% less than 15 minutes, 26.6% 15 to 30 minutes, 31.7% 30 to 45 minutes, 12.1% 45 to 60 minutes, 17.8% 60 minutes or more (2008-2012 5-year est.)

Additional Information Contacts
Hazel Crest Chamber of Commerce . . . . (708) 335-9890
Village of Hazel Crest . . . . (708) 335-9600
   http://www.villageofhazelcrest.com

HICKORY HILLS (city).
Covers a land area of 2.827 square miles and a water area of 0 square miles. Located at 41.72° N. Lat; 87.83° W. Long. Elevation is 679 feet.

Population: 13,021 (1990); 13,926 (2000); 14,049 (2010); Density: 5,077.1 persons per square mile (2008-2012 5-year est.); Race: 88.4% White, 2.6% Black/African American, 2.2% Asian, 0.1% American Indian/Alaska Native, 0.0% Native Hawaiian/Other Pacific Islander, 6.7% Some other race, 2.0% Two or more races, 11.3% Hispanic of any race (2008-2012 5-year est.); Average household size: 2.81 (2008-2012 5-year est.); Median age: 36.7 (2008-2012 5-year est.); Males per 100 females: 92.9 (2008-2012 5-year est.); Marriage status: 27.8% never married, 57.0% now married, 5.2% widowed, 10.0% divorced (2008-2012 5-year est.); Foreign born: 28.4% (2008-2012 5-year est.); Ancestry (includes multiple ancestries): 28.0% Polish, 17.1% Irish, 12.1% German, 9.3% Italian, 5.1% Arab (2008-2012 5-year est.).

Economy: Single-family building permits issued: 1 (2013); Multi-family building permits issued: 4 (2013); Homeowner vacancy rate: 3.1%. Rental vacancy rate: 3.3%. (2008-2012 5-year est.); Employment by occupation: 10.7% management, business, and financial, 4.6% computer, engineering, and science, 6.1% education, legal, community service, arts, and media, 4.9% healthcare practitioners, 18.3% service, 25.8% sales and office, 13.3% natural resources, construction, and maintenance, 16.2% production, transportation, and material moving (2008-2012 5-year est.).

Income: Per capita income: $25,946 (2008-2012 5-year est.); Median household income: $56,956 (2008-2012 5-year est.); Average household income: $71,165 (2008-2012 5-year est.); Percent of households with income of $100,000 or more: 24.0% (2008-2012 5-year est.); Poverty rate: 12.7% (2008-2012 5-year est.).

Education: Percent of population age 25 and over with: High school diploma (including GED) or higher: 86.0% (2008-2012 5-year est.); Bachelor's degree or higher: 26.7% (2008-2012 5-year est.); Master's degree or higher: 8.9% (2008-2012 5-year est.).

School District(s)
North Palos SD 117 (PK-08)
   2011-12 Enrollment: 3,005 . . . . (708) 598-5500

Vocational/Technical School(s)
Star Truck Driving School-Hickory Hills (Private, For-profit)
   Fall 2012 Enrollment: 76 . . . . (630) 236-7200
   2012-13 Tuition: $4,595

Housing: Homeownership rate: 72.2% (2008-2012 5-year est.); Median home value: $244,000 (2008-2012 5-year est.); Median contract rent: $814 per month (2008-2012 5-year est.); Median year structure built: 1970 (2008-2012 5-year est.).

Health Insurance: 65.8% Private; 30.8% Public; 14.5% None. (2008-2012 5-year est.)

Safety: Violent crime rate: 10.6 per 10,000 population; Property crime rate: 173.6 per 10,000 population (2012).

Transportation: Commute to work: 91.3% car, 4.6% public transportation, 0.6% walk, 2.6% work from home (2008-2012 5-year est.); Travel time to work: 20.9% less than 15 minutes, 27.9% 15 to 30 minutes, 28.5% 30 to 45 minutes, 10.8% 45 to 60 minutes, 11.9% 60 minutes or more (2008-2012 5-year est.)

Additional Information Contacts
City of Hickory Hills . . . . (708) 598-4800
   http://www.hickoryhillsil.org
Hickory Hills Chamber of Commerce . . . . (708) 364-7739
   http://www.thehillschamber.com

HILLSIDE (village).
Covers a land area of 3.183 square miles and a water area of 0 square miles. Located at 41.87° N. Lat; 87.90° W. Long. Elevation is 656 feet.

History: Incorporated 1905.

Population: 7,672 (1990); 8,155 (2000); 8,157 (2010); Density: 2,556.2 persons per square mile (2008-2012 5-year est.); Race: 32.4% White, 41.5% Black/African American, 3.8% Asian, 0.0% American Indian/Alaska Native, 0.0% Native Hawaiian/Other Pacific Islander, 22.3% Some other race, 2.3% Two or more races, 28.9% Hispanic of any race (2008-2012 5-year est.); Average household size: 2.62 (2008-2012 5-year est.); Median age: 39.8 (2008-2012 5-year est.); Males per 100 females: 99.1 (2008-2012 5-year est.); Marriage status: 37.6% never married, 46.2% now married, 6.9% widowed, 9.2% divorced (2008-2012 5-year est.); Foreign born: 18.2% (2008-2012 5-year est.); Ancestry (includes multiple ancestries): 7.3% German, 5.5% Italian, 4.9% Irish, 4.4% Polish, 1.9% Czech (2008-2012 5-year est.).

Economy: Single-family building permits issued: 0 (2013); Multi-family building permits issued: 0 (2013); Homeowner vacancy rate: 7.5%. Rental vacancy rate: 8.6%. (2008-2012 5-year est.); Employment by occupation: 11.8% management, business, and financial, 3.3% computer, engineering, and science, 6.6% education, legal, community service, arts, and media, 7.6% healthcare practitioners, 16.9% service, 34.8% sales and office, 4.2% natural resources, construction, and maintenance, 14.9% production, transportation, and material moving (2008-2012 5-year est.).

Income: Per capita income: $24,505 (2008-2012 5-year est.); Median household income: $52,395 (2008-2012 5-year est.); Average household income: $62,911 (2008-2012 5-year est.); Percent of households with income of $100,000 or more: 17.5% (2008-2012 5-year est.); Poverty rate: 14.6% (2008-2012 5-year est.).

Taxes: Total city taxes per capita: $1,858 (2011); City property taxes per capita: $1,611 (2011).

Education: Percent of population age 25 and over with: High school diploma (including GED) or higher: 81.7% (2008-2012 5-year est.); Bachelor's degree or higher: 22.1% (2008-2012 5-year est.); Master's degree or higher: 5.9% (2008-2012 5-year est.).

School District(s)
Hillside SD 93 (KG-08)
   2011-12 Enrollment: 477 . . . . (708) 449-7280
Proviso Twp HSD 209 (09-12)
   2011-12 Enrollment: 5,122 . . . . (708) 338-5912

Two-year College(s)
Sanford-Brown College-Hillside (Private, For-profit)
   Fall 2012 Enrollment: 245 . . . . (708) 836-3200
   2012-13 Tuition: In-state $14,555; Out-of-state $14,555

Housing: Homeownership rate: 68.9% (2008-2012 5-year est.); Median home value: $200,600 (2008-2012 5-year est.); Median contract rent: $779 per month (2008-2012 5-year est.); Median year structure built: 1959 (2008-2012 5-year est.).

Health Insurance: 67.7% Private; 26.2% Public; 14.9% None. (2008-2012 5-year est.)

Transportation: Commute to work: 89.7% car, 6.7% public transportation, 1.8% walk, 1.0% work from home (2008-2012 5-year est.); Travel time to work: 19.9% less than 15 minutes, 35.1% 15 to 30 minutes, 29.3% 30 to 45 minutes, 9.2% 45 to 60 minutes, 6.5% 60 minutes or more (2008-2012 5-year est.)

Additional Information Contacts
Hillside-Berkeley Chamber of Commerce . . . . (708) 449-2449
   http://www.hillsideberkeleychamber.com
Village of Hillside . . . . (708) 449-6450
   http://www.hillside-il.org

HINES (unincorporated postal area)
Zip Code: 60141

Covers a land area of 0.413 square miles and a water area of 0 square miles. Located at 41.85° N. Lat; 87.83° W. Long. Elevation is 623 feet. Population: 224 (2010); Density: 541.2 persons per square mile (2010); Race: 64.3% White, 34.8% Black/African American, 0.0% Asian, 0.0% American Indian/Alaska Native, 0.0% Native Hawaiian/Other Pacific Islander, 0.9% Some other race, 0.0% Two or more races, 3.6% Hispanic of any race (2010); Average household size: 1.09 (2010); Median age: 72.5 (2010); Males per 100 females: 376.6 (2010); Homeownership rate: 1.4% (2010)

HODGKINS (village).
Covers a land area of 2.584 square miles and a water area of 0.054 square miles. Located at 41.77° N. Lat; 87.86° W. Long. Elevation is 604 feet.

Population: 1,963 (1990); 2,134 (2000); 1,897 (2010); Density: 930.9 persons per square mile (2008-2012 5-year est.); Race: 88.0% White, 0.0% Black/African American, 0.0% Asian, 0.0% American Indian/Alaska Native, 0.0% Native Hawaiian/Other Pacific Islander, 12.0% Some other race, 2.2% Two or more races, 50.5% Hispanic of any race (2008-2012 5-year est.); Average household size: 3.31 (2008-2012 5-year est.);

Median age: 34.0 (2008-2012 5-year est.); Males per 100 females: 112.6 (2008-2012 5-year est.); Marriage status: 29.3% never married, 52.9% now married, 5.2% widowed, 12.6% divorced (2008-2012 5-year est.); Foreign born: 29.8% (2008-2012 5-year est.); Ancestry (includes multiple ancestries): 19.9% German, 13.4% Irish, 11.1% Polish, 9.8% Italian, 3.7% English (2008-2012 5-year est.).
Economy: Single-family building permits issued: 0 (2013); Multi-family building permits issued: 0 (2013); Homeowner vacancy rate: 7.4%. Rental vacancy rate: 0.0%. (2008-2012 5-year est.); Employment by occupation: 8.0% management, business, and financial, 2.8% computer, engineering, and science, 4.3% education, legal, community service, arts, and media, 2.2% healthcare practitioners, 33.9% service, 20.5% sales and office, 11.6% natural resources, construction, and maintenance, 16.7% production, transportation, and material moving (2008-2012 5-year est.).
Income: Per capita income: $18,392 (2008-2012 5-year est.); Median household income: $45,114 (2008-2012 5-year est.); Average household income: $56,302 (2008-2012 5-year est.); Percent of households with income of $100,000 or more: 19.6% (2008-2012 5-year est.); Poverty rate: 16.9% (2008-2012 5-year est.).
Taxes: Total city taxes per capita: $4,747 (2011); City property taxes per capita: $3,907 (2011).
Education: Percent of population age 25 and over with: High school diploma (including GED) or higher: 72.0% (2008-2012 5-year est.); Bachelor's degree or higher: 5.8% (2008-2012 5-year est.); Master's degree or higher: 2.7% (2008-2012 5-year est.).

School District(s)
La Grange SD 105 South (PK-08)
    2011-12 Enrollment: 1,392 . . . . (708) 482-2700
Housing: Homeownership rate: 65.6% (2008-2012 5-year est.); Median home value: $47,200 (2008-2012 5-year est.); Median contract rent: $717 per month (2008-2012 5-year est.); Median year structure built: 1978 (2008-2012 5-year est.).
Health Insurance: 35.0% Private; 42.2% Public; 36.5% None. (2008-2012 5-year est.)
Safety: Violent crime rate: 31.5 per 10,000 population; Property crime rate: 1,443.6 per 10,000 population (2012).
Transportation: Commute to work: 73.8% car, 4.7% public transportation, 17.2% walk, 0.2% work from home (2008-2012 5-year est.); Travel time to work: 40.4% less than 15 minutes, 31.5% 15 to 30 minutes, 18.1% 30 to 45 minutes, 3.3% 45 to 60 minutes, 6.6% 60 minutes or more (2008-2012 5-year est.)
Additional Information Contacts
West Suburban Chamber of Commerce & Industry . . . . . . (708) 387-7550
    http://www.wscci.org

HOFFMAN ESTATES (village). Covers a land area of 20.796 square miles and a water area of 0.181 square miles. Located at 42.07° N. Lat; 88.15° W. Long. Elevation is 784 feet.
Population: 46,561 (1990); 49,495 (2000); 51,895 (2010); Density: 2,503.7 persons per square mile (2008-2012 5-year est.); Race: 62.8% White, 3.7% Black/African American, 22.3% Asian, 0.1% American Indian/Alaska Native, 0.0% Native Hawaiian/Other Pacific Islander, 11.1% Some other race, 2.0% Two or more races, 15.3% Hispanic of any race (2008-2012 5-year est.); Average household size: 2.90 (2008-2012 5-year est.); Median age: 36.5 (2008-2012 5-year est.); Males per 100 females: 97.0 (2008-2012 5-year est.); Marriage status: 28.3% never married, 59.9% now married, 4.2% widowed, 7.7% divorced (2008-2012 5-year est.); Foreign born: 29.8% (2008-2012 5-year est.); Ancestry (includes multiple ancestries): 16.8% German, 13.2% Polish, 10.4% Irish, 8.6% Italian, 5.2% English (2008-2012 5-year est.).
Economy: Unemployment rate: 5.5% (April 2014); Total civilian labor force: 30,000 (April 2014); Single-family building permits issued: 2 (2013); Multi-family building permits issued: 0 (2013); Homeowner vacancy rate: 1.9%. Rental vacancy rate: 8.7%. (2008-2012 5-year est.); Employment by occupation: 19.1% management, business, and financial, 9.7% computer, engineering, and science, 9.2% education, legal, community service, arts, and media, 4.8% healthcare practitioners, 14.2% service, 28.3% sales and office, 3.8% natural resources, construction, and maintenance, 10.9% production, transportation, and material moving (2008-2012 5-year est.).
Income: Per capita income: $33,456 (2008-2012 5-year est.); Median household income: $81,105 (2008-2012 5-year est.); Average household income: $95,279 (2008-2012 5-year est.); Percent of households with income of $100,000 or more: 37.9% (2008-2012 5-year est.); Poverty rate: 5.7% (2008-2012 5-year est.).

Taxes: Total city taxes per capita: $1,066 (2011); City property taxes per capita: $837 (2011).
Education: Percent of population age 25 and over with: High school diploma (including GED) or higher: 91.2% (2008-2012 5-year est.); Bachelor's degree or higher: 44.8% (2008-2012 5-year est.); Master's degree or higher: 15.4% (2008-2012 5-year est.).

School District(s)
Palatine CCSD 15 (PK-08)
    2011-12 Enrollment: 12,663 . . . . (847) 963-3000
SD U-46 (PK-12)
    2011-12 Enrollment: 40,687 . . . . (847) 888-5000
Schaumburg CCSD 54 (PK-08)
    2011-12 Enrollment: 14,083 . . . . (847) 357-5000
Township HSD 211 (09-12)
    2011-12 Enrollment: 12,593 . . . . (847) 755-6600
Two-year College(s)
Ambria College of Nursing (Private, For-profit)
    Fall 2012 Enrollment: 323 . . . . (847) 397-0300
Housing: Homeownership rate: 77.3% (2008-2012 5-year est.); Median home value: $270,100 (2008-2012 5-year est.); Median contract rent: $988 per month (2008-2012 5-year est.); Median year structure built: 1976 (2008-2012 5-year est.).
Health Insurance: 77.1% Private; 17.9% Public; 11.7% None. (2008-2012 5-year est.)
Hospitals: St. Alexius Medical Center (331 beds)
Safety: Violent crime rate: 12.7 per 10,000 population; Property crime rate: 136.2 per 10,000 population (2012).
Transportation: Commute to work: 90.2% car, 3.3% public transportation, 0.8% walk, 3.7% work from home (2008-2012 5-year est.); Travel time to work: 18.5% less than 15 minutes, 35.7% 15 to 30 minutes, 23.9% 30 to 45 minutes, 10.7% 45 to 60 minutes, 11.1% 60 minutes or more (2008-2012 5-year est.)
Additional Information Contacts
Hoffman Estates Chamber of Commerce & Industry . . . . . (847) 781-9100
    http://www.hechamber.com
Village of Hoffman Estates . . . . (847) 882-9100
    http://www.hoffmanestates.com

HOMETOWN (city). Covers a land area of 0.479 square miles and a water area of 0 square miles. Located at 41.73° N. Lat; 87.73° W. Long. Elevation is 620 feet.
Population: 4,769 (1990); 4,467 (2000); 4,349 (2010); Density: 9,075.0 persons per square mile (2008-2012 5-year est.); Race: 96.6% White, 0.0% Black/African American, 0.0% Asian, 0.0% American Indian/Alaska Native, 0.0% Native Hawaiian/Other Pacific Islander, 3.4% Some other race, 0.3% Two or more races, 18.2% Hispanic of any race (2008-2012 5-year est.); Average household size: 2.43 (2008-2012 5-year est.); Median age: 40.0 (2008-2012 5-year est.); Males per 100 females: 81.5 (2008-2012 5-year est.); Marriage status: 31.5% never married, 44.0% now married, 9.1% widowed, 15.4% divorced (2008-2012 5-year est.); Foreign born: 5.6% (2008-2012 5-year est.); Ancestry (includes multiple ancestries): 28.2% Irish, 26.2% German, 22.2% Polish, 17.2% Italian, 5.3% English (2008-2012 5-year est.).
Economy: Single-family building permits issued: 0 (2013); Multi-family building permits issued: 0 (2013); Homeowner vacancy rate: 2.1%. Rental vacancy rate: 8.0%. (2008-2012 5-year est.); Employment by occupation: 7.2% management, business, and financial, 5.2% computer, engineering, and science, 9.1% education, legal, community service, arts, and media, 3.9% healthcare practitioners, 13.9% service, 33.4% sales and office, 16.0% natural resources, construction, and maintenance, 11.1% production, transportation, and material moving (2008-2012 5-year est.).
Income: Per capita income: $22,894 (2008-2012 5-year est.); Median household income: $49,094 (2008-2012 5-year est.); Average household income: $54,432 (2008-2012 5-year est.); Percent of households with income of $100,000 or more: 10.0% (2008-2012 5-year est.); Poverty rate: 9.4% (2008-2012 5-year est.).
Education: Percent of population age 25 and over with: High school diploma (including GED) or higher: 92.4% (2008-2012 5-year est.); Bachelor's degree or higher: 14.4% (2008-2012 5-year est.); Master's degree or higher: 4.0% (2008-2012 5-year est.).

School District(s)
Oak Lawn-Hometown SD 123 (PK-08)
    2011-12 Enrollment: 3,057 . . . . (708) 423-0150
Housing: Homeownership rate: 80.5% (2008-2012 5-year est.); Median home value: $142,200 (2008-2012 5-year est.); Median contract rent: $286

per month (2008-2012 5-year est.); Median year structure built: 1954 (2008-2012 5-year est.).

Health Insurance: 72.8% Private; 27.5% Public; 14.7% None. (2008-2012 5-year est.)

Safety: Violent crime rate: 4.6 per 10,000 population; Property crime rate: 141.9 per 10,000 population (2012).

Transportation: Commute to work: 92.9% car, 5.1% public transportation, 0.9% walk, 1.0% work from home (2008-2012 5-year est.); Travel time to work: 26.7% less than 15 minutes, 30.5% 15 to 30 minutes, 21.0% 30 to 45 minutes, 11.8% 45 to 60 minutes, 10.1% 60 minutes or more (2008-2012 5-year est.)

HOMEWOOD (village). Covers a land area of 5.210 square miles and a water area of 0.049 square miles. Located at 41.56° N. Lat; 87.66° W. Long. Elevation is 659 feet.

History: Named for Homewood, Pennsylvania. The site of Homewood was laid out in 1852 by James Hart and was first known as Hartford.

Population: 19,278 (1990); 19,543 (2000); 19,323 (2010); Density: 3,747.4 persons per square mile (2008-2012 5-year est.); Race: 57.7% White, 35.0% Black/African American, 0.6% Asian, 0.0% American Indian/Alaska Native, 0.0% Native Hawaiian/Other Pacific Islander, 6.7% Some other race, 2.0% Two or more races, 8.5% Hispanic of any race (2008-2012 5-year est.); Average household size: 2.66 (2008-2012 5-year est.); Median age: 41.3 (2008-2012 5-year est.); Males per 100 females: 91.6 (2008-2012 5-year est.); Marriage status: 31.0% never married, 51.3% now married, 7.6% widowed, 10.1% divorced (2008-2012 5-year est.); Foreign born: 5.0% (2008-2012 5-year est.); Ancestry (includes multiple ancestries): 18.1% German, 17.2% Irish, 8.2% Polish, 8.0% Italian, 5.6% English (2008-2012 5-year est.).

Economy: Single-family building permits issued: 1 (2013); Multi-family building permits issued: 16 (2013); Homeowner vacancy rate: 3.3%. Rental vacancy rate: 1.4%. (2008-2012 5-year est.); Employment by occupation: 16.0% management, business, and financial, 3.3% computer, engineering, and science, 16.8% education, legal, community service, arts, and media, 9.1% healthcare practitioners, 11.8% service, 26.5% sales and office, 5.5% natural resources, construction, and maintenance, 11.0% production, transportation, and material moving (2008-2012 5-year est.).

Income: Per capita income: $31,983 (2008-2012 5-year est.); Median household income: $69,835 (2008-2012 5-year est.); Average household income: $83,882 (2008-2012 5-year est.); Percent of households with income of $100,000 or more: 32.4% (2008-2012 5-year est.); Poverty rate: 7.3% (2008-2012 5-year est.).

Education: Percent of population age 25 and over with: High school diploma (including GED) or higher: 95.4% (2008-2012 5-year est.); Bachelor's degree or higher: 42.2% (2008-2012 5-year est.); Master's degree or higher: 16.5% (2008-2012 5-year est.).

School District(s)

Homewood SD 153 (PK-08)

    2011-12 Enrollment: 1,888 . . . . (708) 799-5661

Housing: Homeownership rate: 84.9% (2008-2012 5-year est.); Median home value: $182,600 (2008-2012 5-year est.); Median contract rent: $905 per month (2008-2012 5-year est.); Median year structure built: 1960 (2008-2012 5-year est.).

Health Insurance: 80.5% Private; 24.0% Public; 7.7% None. (2008-2012 5-year est.)

Safety: Violent crime rate: 12.9 per 10,000 population; Property crime rate: 364.2 per 10,000 population (2012).

Transportation: Commute to work: 82.4% car, 11.9% public transportation, 2.2% walk, 2.6% work from home (2008-2012 5-year est.); Travel time to work: 24.7% less than 15 minutes, 25.5% 15 to 30 minutes, 21.6% 30 to 45 minutes, 13.0% 45 to 60 minutes, 15.2% 60 minutes or more (2008-2012 5-year est.); Amtrak: Train service available.

Additional Information Contacts

Homewood Area Chamber of Commerce . . . . (708) 206-3384
    http://www.homewoodareachamber.com
Village of Homewood . . . . (708) 798-3000
    http://village.homewood.il.us

INDIAN HEAD PARK (village). Covers a land area of 0.931 square miles and a water area of 0.008 square miles. Located at 41.77° N. Lat; 87.90° W. Long. Elevation is 653 feet.

Population: 3,503 (1990); 3,685 (2000); 3,809 (2010); Density: 4,088.4 persons per square mile (2008-2012 5-year est.); Race: 91.8% White, 3.2% Black/African American, 3.2% Asian, 0.0% American Indian/Alaska Native, 0.0% Native Hawaiian/Other Pacific Islander, 1.8% Some other

race, 0.8% Two or more races, 4.2% Hispanic of any race (2008-2012 5-year est.); Average household size: 1.98 (2008-2012 5-year est.); Median age: 53.3 (2008-2012 5-year est.); Males per 100 females: 66.8 (2008-2012 5-year est.); Marriage status: 25.6% never married, 42.5% now married, 17.9% widowed, 14.1% divorced (2008-2012 5-year est.); Foreign born: 14.8% (2008-2012 5-year est.); Ancestry (includes multiple ancestries): 20.6% German, 19.1% Irish, 12.7% Polish, 11.6% Italian, 9.7% English (2008-2012 5-year est.).

Economy: Single-family building permits issued: 1 (2013); Multi-family building permits issued: 0 (2013); Homeowner vacancy rate: 1.1%. Rental vacancy rate: 0.0%. (2008-2012 5-year est.); Employment by occupation: 25.9% management, business, and financial, 3.2% computer, engineering, and science, 10.9% education, legal, community service, arts, and media, 12.4% healthcare practitioners, 6.5% service, 27.2% sales and office, 5.7% natural resources, construction, and maintenance, 8.1% production, transportation, and material moving (2008-2012 5-year est.).

Income: Per capita income: $55,156 (2008-2012 5-year est.); Median household income: $72,978 (2008-2012 5-year est.); Average household income: $110,263 (2008-2012 5-year est.); Percent of households with income of $100,000 or more: 32.9% (2008-2012 5-year est.); Poverty rate: 5.8% (2008-2012 5-year est.).

Education: Percent of population age 25 and over with: High school diploma (including GED) or higher: 91.7% (2008-2012 5-year est.); Bachelor's degree or higher: 49.0% (2008-2012 5-year est.); Master's degree or higher: 19.3% (2008-2012 5-year est.).

Housing: Homeownership rate: 90.3% (2008-2012 5-year est.); Median home value: $277,700 (2008-2012 5-year est.); Median contract rent: $859 per month (2008-2012 5-year est.); Median year structure built: 1978 (2008-2012 5-year est.).

Health Insurance: 84.6% Private; 29.8% Public; 6.1% None. (2008-2012 5-year est.)

Safety: Violent crime rate: 15.7 per 10,000 population; Property crime rate: 75.8 per 10,000 population (2012).

Transportation: Commute to work: 87.7% car, 6.2% public transportation, 0.0% walk, 4.3% work from home (2008-2012 5-year est.); Travel time to work: 20.3% less than 15 minutes, 30.9% 15 to 30 minutes, 25.8% 30 to 45 minutes, 11.4% 45 to 60 minutes, 11.6% 60 minutes or more (2008-2012 5-year est.)

INVERNESS (village). Covers a land area of 6.539 square miles and a water area of 0.163 square miles. Located at 42.12° N. Lat; 88.10° W. Long. Elevation is 843 feet.

History: Incorporated 1962.

Population: 6,503 (1990); 6,749 (2000); 7,399 (2010); Density: 1,140.5 persons per square mile (2008-2012 5-year est.); Race: 90.3% White, 0.2% Black/African American, 7.5% Asian, 0.0% American Indian/Alaska Native, 0.0% Native Hawaiian/Other Pacific Islander, 2.0% Some other race, 1.5% Two or more races, 3.1% Hispanic of any race (2008-2012 5-year est.); Average household size: 2.64 (2008-2012 5-year est.); Median age: 51.1 (2008-2012 5-year est.); Males per 100 females: 104.6 (2008-2012 5-year est.); Marriage status: 14.8% never married, 78.1% now married, 4.1% widowed, 3.0% divorced (2008-2012 5-year est.); Foreign born: 13.0% (2008-2012 5-year est.); Ancestry (includes multiple ancestries): 28.7% German, 17.6% Italian, 16.7% Irish, 11.2% Polish, 10.4% English (2008-2012 5-year est.).

Economy: Single-family building permits issued: 21 (2013); Multi-family building permits issued: 0 (2013); Homeowner vacancy rate: 2.8%. Rental vacancy rate: 0.0%. (2008-2012 5-year est.); Employment by occupation: 36.4% management, business, and financial, 8.6% computer, engineering, and science, 11.9% education, legal, community service, arts, and media, 6.5% healthcare practitioners, 7.2% service, 25.2% sales and office, 0.0% natural resources, construction, and maintenance, 4.3% production, transportation, and material moving (2008-2012 5-year est.).

Income: Per capita income: $77,037 (2008-2012 5-year est.); Median household income: $151,707 (2008-2012 5-year est.); Average household income: $204,517 (2008-2012 5-year est.); Percent of households with income of $100,000 or more: 69.7% (2008-2012 5-year est.); Poverty rate: 1.4% (2008-2012 5-year est.).

Education: Percent of population age 25 and over with: High school diploma (including GED) or higher: 98.1% (2008-2012 5-year est.); Bachelor's degree or higher: 63.1% (2008-2012 5-year est.); Master's degree or higher: 33.1% (2008-2012 5-year est.).

Housing: Homeownership rate: 97.6% (2008-2012 5-year est.); Median home value: $657,000 (2008-2012 5-year est.); Median contract rent:

$2,000+ per month (2008-2012 5-year est.); Median year structure built: 1983 (2008-2012 5-year est.).
Health Insurance: 91.6% Private; 24.9% Public; 1.9% None. (2008-2012 5-year est.)
Safety: Violent crime rate: 0.0 per 10,000 population; Property crime rate: 45.7 per 10,000 population (2012).
Transportation: Commute to work: 83.6% car, 5.0% public transportation, 0.5% walk, 9.8% work from home (2008-2012 5-year est.); Travel time to work: 16.4% less than 15 minutes, 22.7% 15 to 30 minutes, 30.7% 30 to 45 minutes, 13.5% 45 to 60 minutes, 16.7% 60 minutes or more (2008-2012 5-year est.)
Additional Information Contacts
Village of Inverness . . . . (847) 358-7740
   http://www.villageofinverness.org

JUSTICE (village).
Covers a land area of 2.839 square miles and a water area of 0.044 square miles. Located at 41.75° N. Lat; 87.83° W. Long. Elevation is 617 feet.
Population: 11,137 (1990); 12,193 (2000); 12,926 (2010); Density: 4,536.1 persons per square mile (2008-2012 5-year est.); Race: 69.4% White, 21.9% Black/African American, 0.3% Asian, 0.1% American Indian/Alaska Native, 0.0% Native Hawaiian/Other Pacific Islander, 8.3% Some other race, 2.5% Two or more races, 16.8% Hispanic of any race (2008-2012 5-year est.); Average household size: 2.76 (2008-2012 5-year est.); Median age: 31.8 (2008-2012 5-year est.); Males per 100 females: 84.9 (2008-2012 5-year est.); Marriage status: 37.5% never married, 46.9% now married, 4.9% widowed, 10.7% divorced (2008-2012 5-year est.); Foreign born: 21.0% (2008-2012 5-year est.); Ancestry (includes multiple ancestries): 26.3% Polish, 11.4% German, 8.8% Irish, 7.1% Italian, 4.5% American (2008-2012 5-year est.).
Economy: Single-family building permits issued: 0 (2013); Multi-family building permits issued: 0 (2013); Homeowner vacancy rate: 3.3%. Rental vacancy rate: 9.0%. (2008-2012 5-year est.); Employment by occupation: 7.3% management, business, and financial, 2.4% computer, engineering, and science, 7.3% education, legal, community service, arts, and media, 2.5% healthcare practitioners, 19.3% service, 25.0% sales and office, 13.3% natural resources, construction, and maintenance, 22.9% production, transportation, and material moving (2008-2012 5-year est.).
Income: Per capita income: $22,236 (2008-2012 5-year est.); Median household income: $47,387 (2008-2012 5-year est.); Average household income: $58,379 (2008-2012 5-year est.); Percent of households with income of $100,000 or more: 15.9% (2008-2012 5-year est.); Poverty rate: 16.2% (2008-2012 5-year est.).
Education: Percent of population age 25 and over with: High school diploma (including GED) or higher: 85.9% (2008-2012 5-year est.); Bachelor's degree or higher: 16.8% (2008-2012 5-year est.); Master's degree or higher: 4.5% (2008-2012 5-year est.).
School District(s)
Indian Springs SD 109 (PK-08)
   2011-12 Enrollment: 3,108 . . . . (708) 496-8700
Housing: Homeownership rate: 52.9% (2008-2012 5-year est.); Median home value: $202,400 (2008-2012 5-year est.); Median contract rent: $835 per month (2008-2012 5-year est.); Median year structure built: 1976 (2008-2012 5-year est.).
Health Insurance: 54.1% Private; 37.9% Public; 16.8% None. (2008-2012 5-year est.)
Safety: Violent crime rate: 12.3 per 10,000 population; Property crime rate: 107.0 per 10,000 population (2012).
Transportation: Commute to work: 89.7% car, 7.1% public transportation, 0.7% walk, 2.5% work from home (2008-2012 5-year est.); Travel time to work: 17.9% less than 15 minutes, 32.7% 15 to 30 minutes, 21.9% 30 to 45 minutes, 12.2% 45 to 60 minutes, 15.2% 60 minutes or more (2008-2012 5-year est.)
Additional Information Contacts
Justice Chamber of Commerce . . . .
   http://www.villageofjustice.org/chamber_of_commerce
Village of Justice . . . . (708) 458-2520
   http://villageofjustice.org

KENILWORTH (village).
Covers a land area of 0.608 square miles and a water area of 0 square miles. Located at 42.09° N. Lat; 87.71° W. Long. Elevation is 617 feet.
History: Kenilworth was named for the novel by Sir Walter Scott. Many streets in the town are named for places or characters in the book. Kenilworth is the burial place of poet Eugene Field.

Population: 2,402 (1990); 2,494 (2000); 2,513 (2010); Density: 4,386.3 persons per square mile (2008-2012 5-year est.); Race: 97.9% White, 0.6% Black/African American, 1.2% Asian, 0.0% American Indian/Alaska Native, 0.0% Native Hawaiian/Other Pacific Islander, 0.3% Some other race, 0.2% Two or more races, 2.7% Hispanic of any race (2008-2012 5-year est.); Average household size: 3.33 (2008-2012 5-year est.); Median age: 40.7 (2008-2012 5-year est.); Males per 100 females: 94.5 (2008-2012 5-year est.); Marriage status: 20.3% never married, 73.8% now married, 4.6% widowed, 1.3% divorced (2008-2012 5-year est.); Foreign born: 6.1% (2008-2012 5-year est.); Ancestry (includes multiple ancestries): 23.5% Irish, 20.2% German, 18.8% English, 10.7% Italian, 7.9% Polish (2008-2012 5-year est.).
Economy: Single-family building permits issued: 5 (2013); Multi-family building permits issued: 0 (2013); Homeowner vacancy rate: 4.3%. Rental vacancy rate: 0.0%. (2008-2012 5-year est.); Employment by occupation: 40.2% management, business, and financial, 4.0% computer, engineering, and science, 20.3% education, legal, community service, arts, and media, 3.6% healthcare practitioners, 7.2% service, 22.4% sales and office, 0.7% natural resources, construction, and maintenance, 1.7% production, transportation, and material moving (2008-2012 5-year est.).
Income: Per capita income: $96,525 (2008-2012 5-year est.); Median household income: $229,792 (2008-2012 5-year est.); Average household income: $318,383 (2008-2012 5-year est.); Percent of households with income of $100,000 or more: 78.5% (2008-2012 5-year est.); Poverty rate: 1.5% (2008-2012 5-year est.).
Education: Percent of population age 25 and over with: High school diploma (including GED) or higher: 99.1% (2008-2012 5-year est.); Bachelor's degree or higher: 88.2% (2008-2012 5-year est.); Master's degree or higher: 48.5% (2008-2012 5-year est.).
School District(s)
Kenilworth SD 38 (PK-08)
   2011-12 Enrollment: 570 . . . . (847) 853-3803
Housing: Homeownership rate: 94.6% (2008-2012 5-year est.); Median home value: 1 million+ (2008-2012 5-year est.); Median contract rent: $2,000+ per month (2008-2012 5-year est.); Median year structure built: Before 1940 (2008-2012 5-year est.).
Health Insurance: 94.8% Private; 14.9% Public; 1.0% None. (2008-2012 5-year est.)
Safety: Violent crime rate: 0.0 per 10,000 population; Property crime rate: 118.9 per 10,000 population (2012).
Transportation: Commute to work: 56.1% car, 32.3% public transportation, 3.3% walk, 6.4% work from home (2008-2012 5-year est.); Travel time to work: 16.7% less than 15 minutes, 18.7% 15 to 30 minutes, 25.8% 30 to 45 minutes, 23.5% 45 to 60 minutes, 15.3% 60 minutes or more (2008-2012 5-year est.)

LA GRANGE (village).
Covers a land area of 2.523 square miles and a water area of 0 square miles. Located at 41.81° N. Lat; 87.87° W. Long. Elevation is 646 feet.
History: La Grange was founded by W.D. Cossitt and named for Marquis de Lafayette's home in France. An early settlement along the Chicago, Burlington & Quincy Railroad, La Grange was incorporated in 1879.
Population: 15,362 (1990); 15,608 (2000); 15,550 (2010); Density: 6,168.4 persons per square mile (2008-2012 5-year est.); Race: 91.7% White, 4.3% Black/African American, 1.2% Asian, 0.0% American Indian/Alaska Native, 0.0% Native Hawaiian/Other Pacific Islander, 2.8% Some other race, 2.2% Two or more races, 9.7% Hispanic of any race (2008-2012 5-year est.); Average household size: 2.78 (2008-2012 5-year est.); Median age: 39.7 (2008-2012 5-year est.); Males per 100 females: 95.1 (2008-2012 5-year est.); Marriage status: 25.3% never married, 58.9% now married, 7.9% widowed, 8.0% divorced (2008-2012 5-year est.); Foreign born: 7.9% (2008-2012 5-year est.); Ancestry (includes multiple ancestries): 33.5% Irish, 21.1% German, 12.4% Polish, 11.6% Italian, 8.6% English (2008-2012 5-year est.).
Economy: Single-family building permits issued: 20 (2013); Multi-family building permits issued: 0 (2013); Homeowner vacancy rate: 2.4%. Rental vacancy rate: 2.5%. (2008-2012 5-year est.); Employment by occupation: 24.1% management, business, and financial, 5.2% computer, engineering, and science, 17.9% education, legal, community service, arts, and media, 6.8% healthcare practitioners, 8.1% service, 24.7% sales and office, 4.3% natural resources, construction, and maintenance, 8.9% production, transportation, and material moving (2008-2012 5-year est.).
Income: Per capita income: $48,479 (2008-2012 5-year est.); Median household income: $97,425 (2008-2012 5-year est.); Average household income: $136,461 (2008-2012 5-year est.); Percent of households with

income of $100,000 or more: 48.2% (2008-2012 5-year est.); Poverty rate: 5.2% (2008-2012 5-year est.).

Taxes: Total city taxes per capita: $684 (2011); City property taxes per capita: $558 (2011).

Education: Percent of population age 25 and over with: High school diploma (including GED) or higher: 95.4% (2008-2012 5-year est.); Bachelor's degree or higher: 58.8% (2008-2012 5-year est.); Master's degree or higher: 26.3% (2008-2012 5-year est.).

School District(s)

La Grange SD 102 (PK-08)
   2011-12 Enrollment: 3,126 . . . . (708) 482-2400
La Grange SD 105 South (PK-08)
   2011-12 Enrollment: 1,392 . . . . (708) 482-2700
Lyons Twp HSD 204 (09-12)
   2011-12 Enrollment: 3,981 . . . . (708) 579-6451
Pleasantdale SD 107 (PK-08)
   2011-12 Enrollment: 806 . . . . (708) 784-2013

Housing: Homeownership rate: 80.3% (2008-2012 5-year est.); Median home value: $459,200 (2008-2012 5-year est.); Median contract rent: $899 per month (2008-2012 5-year est.); Median year structure built: 1951 (2008-2012 5-year est.).

Health Insurance: 88.3% Private; 17.3% Public; 5.0% None. (2008-2012 5-year est.)

Hospitals: Adventist LaGrange Memorial Hospital (274 beds)

Safety: Violent crime rate: 9.0 per 10,000 population; Property crime rate: 105.6 per 10,000 population (2012).

Transportation: Commute to work: 74.0% car, 14.8% public transportation, 3.9% walk, 5.8% work from home (2008-2012 5-year est.); Travel time to work: 22.7% less than 15 minutes, 26.7% 15 to 30 minutes, 26.5% 30 to 45 minutes, 14.7% 45 to 60 minutes, 9.5% 60 minutes or more (2008-2012 5-year est.); Amtrak: Train service available.

Additional Information Contacts
Village of La Grange . . . . (708) 579-2300
   http://www.villageoflagrange.com
West Suburban Chamber of Commerce & Industry . . . . . . (708) 387-7550
   http://www.wscci.org

LA GRANGE PARK (village). Covers a land area of 2.232 square miles and a water area of 0 square miles. Located at 41.83° N. Lat; 87.87° W. Long. Elevation is 623 feet.

History: Named for the French translation of "the barn". Incorporated 1892.

Population: 12,861 (1990); 13,295 (2000); 13,579 (2010); Density: 6,072.6 persons per square mile (2008-2012 5-year est.); Race: 90.3% White, 6.2% Black/African American, 1.7% Asian, 0.0% American Indian/Alaska Native, 0.0% Native Hawaiian/Other Pacific Islander, 1.8% Some other race, 0.6% Two or more races, 10.3% Hispanic of any race (2008-2012 5-year est.); Average household size: 2.45 (2008-2012 5-year est.); Median age: 42.5 (2008-2012 5-year est.); Males per 100 females: 92.4 (2008-2012 5-year est.); Marriage status: 29.9% never married, 54.2% now married, 10.5% widowed, 5.3% divorced (2008-2012 5-year est.); Foreign born: 9.1% (2008-2012 5-year est.); Ancestry (includes multiple ancestries): 21.6% German, 20.9% Irish, 14.9% Italian, 13.7% Polish, 7.4% English (2008-2012 5-year est.).

Economy: Single-family building permits issued: 10 (2013); Multi-family building permits issued: 0 (2013); Homeowner vacancy rate: 0.4%. Rental vacancy rate: 5.6%. (2008-2012 5-year est.); Employment by occupation: 22.5% management, business, and financial, 5.2% computer, engineering, and science, 13.9% education, legal, community service, arts, and media, 7.5% healthcare practitioners, 9.0% service, 27.1% sales and office, 5.2% natural resources, construction, and maintenance, 9.7% production, transportation, and material moving (2008-2012 5-year est.).

Income: Per capita income: $38,128 (2008-2012 5-year est.); Median household income: $66,826 (2008-2012 5-year est.); Average household income: $92,968 (2008-2012 5-year est.); Percent of households with income of $100,000 or more: 30.9% (2008-2012 5-year est.); Poverty rate: 5.2% (2008-2012 5-year est.).

Education: Percent of population age 25 and over with: High school diploma (including GED) or higher: 94.7% (2008-2012 5-year est.); Bachelor's degree or higher: 44.8% (2008-2012 5-year est.); Master's degree or higher: 17.3% (2008-2012 5-year est.).

School District(s)

Brookfield Lagrange Park SD 95 (PK-08)
   2011-12 Enrollment: 1,087 . . . . (708) 485-0606

La Grange SD 102 (PK-08)
   2011-12 Enrollment: 3,126 . . . . (708) 482-2400

Housing: Homeownership rate: 67.1% (2008-2012 5-year est.); Median home value: $340,000 (2008-2012 5-year est.); Median contract rent: $954 per month (2008-2012 5-year est.); Median year structure built: 1955 (2008-2012 5-year est.).

Health Insurance: 83.4% Private; 24.3% Public; 5.9% None. (2008-2012 5-year est.)

Safety: Violent crime rate: 2.9 per 10,000 population; Property crime rate: 78.4 per 10,000 population (2012).

Transportation: Commute to work: 81.1% car, 11.0% public transportation, 3.1% walk, 3.9% work from home (2008-2012 5-year est.); Travel time to work: 23.4% less than 15 minutes, 30.3% 15 to 30 minutes, 21.2% 30 to 45 minutes, 14.2% 45 to 60 minutes, 10.8% 60 minutes or more (2008-2012 5-year est.); Amtrak: Train service available.

Additional Information Contacts
La Grange Park Chamber of Commerce . . . . (708) 372-2579
   http://lagrangeparkbusinessassociation.com
Village of La Grange Park . . . . (708) 354-0225
   http://www.lagrangepark.org

LANSING (village). Covers a land area of 6.787 square miles and a water area of 0.058 square miles. Located at 41.57° N. Lat; 87.55° W. Long. Elevation is 630 feet.

History: Named for John Lansing (1754-1829), hero of the American Revolution. Lansing was settled in the 1860's by Dutch and German farmers.

Population: 28,086 (1990); 28,332 (2000); 28,331 (2010); Density: 4,165.4 persons per square mile (2008-2012 5-year est.); Race: 61.5% White, 31.4% Black/African American, 0.8% Asian, 0.0% American Indian/Alaska Native, 0.0% Native Hawaiian/Other Pacific Islander, 6.3% Some other race, 2.1% Two or more races, 13.9% Hispanic of any race (2008-2012 5-year est.); Average household size: 2.50 (2008-2012 5-year est.); Median age: 39.3 (2008-2012 5-year est.); Males per 100 females: 85.2 (2008-2012 5-year est.); Marriage status: 34.3% never married, 46.9% now married, 7.4% widowed, 11.4% divorced (2008-2012 5-year est.); Foreign born: 6.4% (2008-2012 5-year est.); Ancestry (includes multiple ancestries): 14.3% German, 13.1% Polish, 10.3% Irish, 8.1% Dutch, 7.0% Italian (2008-2012 5-year est.).

Economy: Unemployment rate: 7.8% (April 2014); Total civilian labor force: 15,002 (April 2014); Single-family building permits issued: 0 (2013); Multi-family building permits issued: 0 (2013); Homeowner vacancy rate: 3.7%. Rental vacancy rate: 9.1%. (2008-2012 5-year est.); Employment by occupation: 9.6% management, business, and financial, 3.4% computer, engineering, and science, 10.7% education, legal, community service, arts, and media, 5.3% healthcare practitioners, 16.1% service, 31.4% sales and office, 10.2% natural resources, construction, and maintenance, 13.3% production, transportation, and material moving (2008-2012 5-year est.).

Income: Per capita income: $25,215 (2008-2012 5-year est.); Median household income: $51,637 (2008-2012 5-year est.); Average household income: $61,426 (2008-2012 5-year est.); Percent of households with income of $100,000 or more: 17.6% (2008-2012 5-year est.); Poverty rate: 11.5% (2008-2012 5-year est.).

Taxes: Total city taxes per capita: $691 (2011); City property taxes per capita: $472 (2011).

Education: Percent of population age 25 and over with: High school diploma (including GED) or higher: 89.6% (2008-2012 5-year est.); Bachelor's degree or higher: 20.4% (2008-2012 5-year est.); Master's degree or higher: 5.6% (2008-2012 5-year est.).

School District(s)

Lansing SD 158 (PK-08)
   2011-12 Enrollment: 2,372 . . . . (708) 474-6700
Sunnybrook SD 171 (PK-08)
   2011-12 Enrollment: 1,021 . . . . (708) 895-0750
Thornton Fractional Twp HSD 215 (09-12)
   2011-12 Enrollment: 3,567 . . . . (708) 585-2309

Housing: Homeownership rate: 74.2% (2008-2012 5-year est.); Median home value: $143,600 (2008-2012 5-year est.); Median contract rent: $814 per month (2008-2012 5-year est.); Median year structure built: 1965 (2008-2012 5-year est.).

Health Insurance: 73.7% Private; 29.3% Public; 10.3% None. (2008-2012 5-year est.)

Safety: Violent crime rate: 32.7 per 10,000 population; Property crime rate: 467.8 per 10,000 population (2012).

Transportation: Commute to work: 90.2% car, 6.5% public transportation, 0.8% walk, 1.5% work from home (2008-2012 5-year est.); Travel time to work: 24.0% less than 15 minutes, 26.2% 15 to 30 minutes, 22.7% 30 to 45 minutes, 12.5% 45 to 60 minutes, 14.7% 60 minutes or more (2008-2012 5-year est.)

Airports: Lansing Municipal Airport (reliver airport)

Additional Information Contacts

Chicago Southland Convention & Visitors Bureau . . . . (708) 895-8200
http://www.visitchicagosouthland.com

Lansing Area Chamber of Commerce. . . . . (708) 474-4170
http://chamberoflansing.com

Village of Lansing . . . . (708) 895-7200
http://www.lansingmunicipal.com

LEMONT (village).

Covers a land area of 7.967 square miles and a water area of 0.384 square miles. Located at 41.67° N. Lat; 87.98° W. Long. Elevation is 607 feet.

History: Named for the French translation of "the mount". Incorporated 1873.

Population: 7,348 (1990); 13,098 (2000); 16,000 (2010); Density: 2,002.5 persons per square mile (2008-2012 5-year est.); Race: 95.9% White, 0.6% Black/African American, 0.8% Asian, 0.0% American Indian/Alaska Native, 0.0% Native Hawaiian/Other Pacific Islander, 2.7% Some other race, 1.3% Two or more races, 6.3% Hispanic of any race (2008-2012 5-year est.); Average household size: 2.91 (2008-2012 5-year est.); Median age: 41.0 (2008-2012 5-year est.); Males per 100 females: 90.3 (2008-2012 5-year est.); Marriage status: 26.1% never married, 61.4% now married, 7.2% widowed, 5.3% divorced (2008-2012 5-year est.); Foreign born: 13.5% (2008-2012 5-year est.); Ancestry (includes multiple ancestries): 26.5% Polish, 20.6% Irish, 17.7% German, 13.4% Italian, 8.2% Lithuanian (2008-2012 5-year est.).

Economy: Single-family building permits issued: 62 (2013); Multi-family building permits issued: 0 (2013); Homeowner vacancy rate: 0.2%. Rental vacancy rate: 11.1%. (2008-2012 5-year est.); Employment by occupation: 19.2% management, business, and financial, 3.8% computer, engineering, and science, 9.4% education, legal, community service, arts, and media, 6.7% healthcare practitioners, 13.9% service, 28.0% sales and office, 9.7% natural resources, construction, and maintenance, 9.2% production, transportation, and material moving (2008-2012 5-year est.).

Income: Per capita income: $37,992 (2008-2012 5-year est.); Median household income: $88,662 (2008-2012 5-year est.); Average household income: $109,852 (2008-2012 5-year est.); Percent of households with income of $100,000 or more: 40.1% (2008-2012 5-year est.); Poverty rate: 1.3% (2008-2012 5-year est.).

Education: Percent of population age 25 and over with: High school diploma (including GED) or higher: 93.2% (2008-2012 5-year est.); Bachelor's degree or higher: 39.3% (2008-2012 5-year est.); Master's degree or higher: 15.9% (2008-2012 5-year est.).

School District(s)

Lemont Twp HSD 210 (09-12)
2011-12 Enrollment: 1,507 . . . . (630) 243-3260

Lemont-Bromberek CSD 113a (PK-08)
2011-12 Enrollment: 2,398 . . . . (630) 257-2286

Lemont-Bromberek CSD 113a (PK-08)
2011-12 Enrollment: 2,398 . . . . (630) 257-2286

Housing: Homeownership rate: 87.6% (2008-2012 5-year est.); Median home value: $354,900 (2008-2012 5-year est.); Median contract rent: $744 per month (2008-2012 5-year est.); Median year structure built: 1992 (2008-2012 5-year est.).

Health Insurance: 88.0% Private; 18.9% Public; 5.9% None. (2008-2012 5-year est.)

Safety: Violent crime rate: 8.7 per 10,000 population; Property crime rate: 146.7 per 10,000 population (2012).

Transportation: Commute to work: 88.8% car, 7.0% public transportation, 1.0% walk, 2.9% work from home (2008-2012 5-year est.); Travel time to work: 14.6% less than 15 minutes, 25.6% 15 to 30 minutes, 31.0% 30 to 45 minutes, 10.8% 45 to 60 minutes, 18.0% 60 minutes or more (2008-2012 5-year est.)

Additional Information Contacts

Lemont Area Chamber of Commerce . . . . (630) 257-5997
http://www.lemontchamber.com

Village of Lemont . . . . (630) 257-1550
http://www.lemont.il.us

LINCOLNWOOD (village).

Covers a land area of 2.691 square miles and a water area of 0 square miles. Located at 42.01° N. Lat; 87.73° W. Long. Elevation is 604 feet.

History: Named for Abraham Lincoln, 16th President of the U.S. Until 1935 called Tessville.

Population: 11,365 (1990); 12,359 (2000); 12,590 (2010); Density: 4,658.4 persons per square mile (2008-2012 5-year est.); Race: 64.4% White, 1.6% Black/African American, 29.9% Asian, 1.4% American Indian/Alaska Native, 0.0% Native Hawaiian/Other Pacific Islander, 2.7% Some other race, 1.7% Two or more races, 6.9% Hispanic of any race (2008-2012 5-year est.); Average household size: 3.00 (2008-2012 5-year est.); Median age: 47.2 (2008-2012 5-year est.); Males per 100 females: 92.9 (2008-2012 5-year est.); Marriage status: 26.8% never married, 60.7% now married, 8.5% widowed, 4.1% divorced (2008-2012 5-year est.); Foreign born: 38.8% (2008-2012 5-year est.); Ancestry (includes multiple ancestries): 7.3% Greek, 6.1% German, 5.8% Russian, 5.8% Polish, 4.7% Assyrian/Chaldean/Syriac (2008-2012 5-year est.).

Economy: Single-family building permits issued: 4 (2013); Multi-family building permits issued: 0 (2013); Homeowner vacancy rate: 2.0%. Rental vacancy rate: 11.4%. (2008-2012 5-year est.); Employment by occupation: 19.0% management, business, and financial, 5.6% computer, engineering, and science, 11.9% education, legal, community service, arts, and media, 11.7% healthcare practitioners, 11.3% service, 29.1% sales and office, 3.8% natural resources, construction, and maintenance, 7.6% production, transportation, and material moving (2008-2012 5-year est.).

Income: Per capita income: $42,967 (2008-2012 5-year est.); Median household income: $91,250 (2008-2012 5-year est.); Average household income: $125,868 (2008-2012 5-year est.); Percent of households with income of $100,000 or more: 46.6% (2008-2012 5-year est.); Poverty rate: 5.9% (2008-2012 5-year est.).

Education: Percent of population age 25 and over with: High school diploma (including GED) or higher: 89.6% (2008-2012 5-year est.); Bachelor's degree or higher: 49.3% (2008-2012 5-year est.); Master's degree or higher: 19.7% (2008-2012 5-year est.).

School District(s)

Lincolnwood SD 74 (PK-08)
2011-12 Enrollment: 1,255 . . . . (847) 675-8234

Housing: Homeownership rate: 85.8% (2008-2012 5-year est.); Median home value: $396,000 (2008-2012 5-year est.); Median contract rent: $1,426 per month (2008-2012 5-year est.); Median year structure built: 1958 (2008-2012 5-year est.).

Health Insurance: 74.5% Private; 31.6% Public; 10.8% None. (2008-2012 5-year est.)

Safety: Violent crime rate: 8.7 per 10,000 population; Property crime rate: 588.8 per 10,000 population (2012).

Transportation: Commute to work: 87.0% car, 6.2% public transportation, 1.5% walk, 5.3% work from home (2008-2012 5-year est.); Travel time to work: 25.9% less than 15 minutes, 27.8% 15 to 30 minutes, 27.7% 30 to 45 minutes, 11.6% 45 to 60 minutes, 7.1% 60 minutes or more (2008-2012 5-year est.)

Additional Information Contacts

Lincolnwood Chamber of Commerce & Industry . . . . (847) 679-5760
http://www.lincolnwoodchamber.org

Village of Lincolnwood . . . . (847) 673-1540
http://www.lincolnwoodil.org

LYNWOOD (village).

Covers a land area of 5.465 square miles and a water area of 0.077 square miles. Located at 41.52° N. Lat; 87.55° W. Long. Elevation is 617 feet.

Population: 6,535 (1990); 7,377 (2000); 9,007 (2010); Density: 1,654.5 persons per square mile (2008-2012 5-year est.); Race: 32.6% White, 63.3% Black/African American, 0.4% Asian, 0.0% American Indian/Alaska Native, 0.0% Native Hawaiian/Other Pacific Islander, 3.7% Some other race, 1.8% Two or more races, 11.6% Hispanic of any race (2008-2012 5-year est.); Average household size: 2.76 (2008-2012 5-year est.); Median age: 36.5 (2008-2012 5-year est.); Males per 100 females: 81.7 (2008-2012 5-year est.); Marriage status: 35.8% never married, 43.7% now married, 6.8% widowed, 13.8% divorced (2008-2012 5-year est.); Foreign born: 6.9% (2008-2012 5-year est.); Ancestry (includes multiple ancestries): 7.6% German, 6.3% Polish, 3.9% Irish, 3.6% Dutch, 3.3% English (2008-2012 5-year est.).

Economy: Single-family building permits issued: 7 (2013); Multi-family building permits issued: 0 (2013); Homeowner vacancy rate: 4.9%. Rental vacancy rate: 12.2%. (2008-2012 5-year est.); Employment by occupation: 9.4% management, business, and financial, 5.0% computer, engineering,

and science, 11.6% education, legal, community service, arts, and media, 7.3% healthcare practitioners, 17.1% service, 31.3% sales and office, 5.0% natural resources, construction, and maintenance, 13.3% production, transportation, and material moving (2008-2012 5-year est.).

Income: Per capita income: $23,581 (2008-2012 5-year est.); Median household income: $53,944 (2008-2012 5-year est.); Average household income: $63,753 (2008-2012 5-year est.); Percent of households with income of $100,000 or more: 21.4% (2008-2012 5-year est.); Poverty rate: 22.3% (2008-2012 5-year est.).

Education: Percent of population age 25 and over with: High school diploma (including GED) or higher: 89.5% (2008-2012 5-year est.); Bachelor's degree or higher: 25.4% (2008-2012 5-year est.); Master's degree or higher: 9.0% (2008-2012 5-year est.).

School District(s)

Sandridge SD 172 (PK-08)
　2011-12 Enrollment: 446 . . . . (708) 895-8339

Housing: Homeownership rate: 79.5% (2008-2012 5-year est.); Median home value: $146,900 (2008-2012 5-year est.); Median contract rent: $783 per month (2008-2012 5-year est.); Median year structure built: 1990 (2008-2012 5-year est.).

Health Insurance: 63.3% Private; 35.0% Public; 13.4% None. (2008-2012 5-year est.)

Transportation: Commute to work: 88.9% car, 7.7% public transportation, 0.0% walk, 1.0% work from home (2008-2012 5-year est.); Travel time to work: 20.6% less than 15 minutes, 28.1% 15 to 30 minutes, 17.9% 30 to 45 minutes, 14.4% 45 to 60 minutes, 18.9% 60 minutes or more (2008-2012 5-year est.)

Additional Information Contacts

Lynwood Chamber of Commerce . . . . (708) 895-6322
　http://www.ynns.com/lcc/location.php
Village of Lynwood . . . . (708) 758-6101
　http://www.lynwoodil.us

LYONS (village).

Covers a land area of 2.185 square miles and a water area of 0.057 square miles. Located at 41.81° N. Lat; 87.82° W. Long. Elevation is 620 feet.

History: Lyons was established near the portage between the Chicago and Des Plaines Rivers, used by Marquette and Jolliet. Lyons developed as a residential community.

Population: 9,828 (1990); 10,255 (2000); 10,729 (2010); Density: 4,875.0 persons per square mile (2008-2012 5-year est.); Race: 83.9% White, 4.0% Black/African American, 2.7% Asian, 0.8% American Indian/Alaska Native, 0.0% Native Hawaiian/Other Pacific Islander, 8.6% Some other race, 2.1% Two or more races, 42.2% Hispanic of any race (2008-2012 5-year est.); Average household size: 2.62 (2008-2012 5-year est.); Median age: 37.2 (2008-2012 5-year est.); Males per 100 females: 117.6 (2008-2012 5-year est.); Marriage status: 32.4% never married, 48.5% now married, 5.7% widowed, 13.4% divorced (2008-2012 5-year est.); Foreign born: 23.0% (2008-2012 5-year est.); Ancestry (includes multiple ancestries): 18.7% Polish, 10.4% Irish, 9.1% German, 8.1% Italian, 4.8% Czech (2008-2012 5-year est.).

Economy: Single-family building permits issued: 1 (2013); Multi-family building permits issued: 0 (2013); Homeowner vacancy rate: 2.5%. Rental vacancy rate: 10.8%. (2008-2012 5-year est.); Employment by occupation: 11.2% management, business, and financial, 3.5% computer, engineering, and science, 5.3% education, legal, community service, arts, and media, 3.3% healthcare practitioners, 17.5% service, 28.4% sales and office, 11.0% natural resources, construction, and maintenance, 19.7% production, transportation, and material moving (2008-2012 5-year est.).

Income: Per capita income: $24,331 (2008-2012 5-year est.); Median household income: $54,685 (2008-2012 5-year est.); Average household income: $61,173 (2008-2012 5-year est.); Percent of households with income of $100,000 or more: 11.6% (2008-2012 5-year est.); Poverty rate: 9.7% (2008-2012 5-year est.).

Education: Percent of population age 25 and over with: High school diploma (including GED) or higher: 85.9% (2008-2012 5-year est.); Bachelor's degree or higher: 19.7% (2008-2012 5-year est.); Master's degree or higher: 4.5% (2008-2012 5-year est.).

School District(s)

Lyons SD 103 (PK-08)
　2011-12 Enrollment: 2,486 . . . . (708) 783-4100
Region 06 West Cook Isc 2 (PK-12)
　2011-12 Enrollment: n/a . . . . (708) 544-4890

Housing: Homeownership rate: 64.9% (2008-2012 5-year est.); Median home value: $197,000 (2008-2012 5-year est.); Median contract rent: $852

per month (2008-2012 5-year est.); Median year structure built: 1956 (2008-2012 5-year est.).

Health Insurance: 65.7% Private; 29.5% Public; 15.0% None. (2008-2012 5-year est.)

Safety: Violent crime rate: 16.7 per 10,000 population; Property crime rate: 177.2 per 10,000 population (2012).

Transportation: Commute to work: 89.8% car, 4.5% public transportation, 1.4% walk, 3.8% work from home (2008-2012 5-year est.); Travel time to work: 20.2% less than 15 minutes, 33.4% 15 to 30 minutes, 24.6% 30 to 45 minutes, 12.3% 45 to 60 minutes, 9.6% 60 minutes or more (2008-2012 5-year est.)

Additional Information Contacts

Village of Lyons . . . . (708) 442-4500
　http://www.villageoflyons-il.net

MARKHAM (city).

Covers a land area of 5.308 square miles and a water area of 0 square miles. Located at 41.60° N. Lat; 87.69° W. Long. Elevation is 620 feet.

History: Named for Charles H. Markham, president of the Illinois Central railroad. Native prairie preserved at Indian Boundaries Prairies. Incorporated 1925.

Population: 13,136 (1990); 12,620 (2000); 12,508 (2010); Density: 2,357.6 persons per square mile (2008-2012 5-year est.); Race: 15.9% White, 78.9% Black/African American, 0.7% Asian, 0.0% American Indian/Alaska Native, 0.0% Native Hawaiian/Other Pacific Islander, 4.5% Some other race, 0.7% Two or more races, 8.4% Hispanic of any race (2008-2012 5-year est.); Average household size: 3.09 (2008-2012 5-year est.); Median age: 37.2 (2008-2012 5-year est.); Males per 100 females: 85.1 (2008-2012 5-year est.); Marriage status: 42.9% never married, 40.1% now married, 7.4% widowed, 9.6% divorced (2008-2012 5-year est.); Foreign born: 6.1% (2008-2012 5-year est.); Ancestry (includes multiple ancestries): 2.9% Irish, 2.6% German, 1.8% Italian, 1.8% Polish, 1.4% English (2008-2012 5-year est.).

Economy: Single-family building permits issued: 11 (2013); Multi-family building permits issued: 0 (2013); Homeowner vacancy rate: 2.6%. Rental vacancy rate: 2.7%. (2008-2012 5-year est.); Employment by occupation: 8.4% management, business, and financial, 1.4% computer, engineering, and science, 10.7% education, legal, community service, arts, and media, 2.8% healthcare practitioners, 23.3% service, 31.7% sales and office, 6.3% natural resources, construction, and maintenance, 15.5% production, transportation, and material moving (2008-2012 5-year est.).

Income: Per capita income: $18,740 (2008-2012 5-year est.); Median household income: $44,730 (2008-2012 5-year est.); Average household income: $54,824 (2008-2012 5-year est.); Percent of households with income of $100,000 or more: 13.6% (2008-2012 5-year est.); Poverty rate: 22.3% (2008-2012 5-year est.).

Education: Percent of population age 25 and over with: High school diploma (including GED) or higher: 81.7% (2008-2012 5-year est.); Bachelor's degree or higher: 14.2% (2008-2012 5-year est.); Master's degree or higher: 4.2% (2008-2012 5-year est.).

School District(s)

Hazel Crest SD 152-5 (PK-08)
　2011-12 Enrollment: 1,040 . . . . (708) 335-0790
Prairie-Hills ESD 144 (PK-08)
　2011-12 Enrollment: 2,796 . . . . (708) 210-2888

Housing: Homeownership rate: 75.6% (2008-2012 5-year est.); Median home value: $111,500 (2008-2012 5-year est.); Median contract rent: $1,071 per month (2008-2012 5-year est.); Median year structure built: 1962 (2008-2012 5-year est.).

Health Insurance: 48.0% Private; 44.8% Public; 18.7% None. (2008-2012 5-year est.)

Transportation: Commute to work: 81.0% car, 12.5% public transportation, 1.0% walk, 4.5% work from home (2008-2012 5-year est.); Travel time to work: 14.4% less than 15 minutes, 32.6% 15 to 30 minutes, 25.9% 30 to 45 minutes, 12.9% 45 to 60 minutes, 14.2% 60 minutes or more (2008-2012 5-year est.)

Additional Information Contacts

City of Markham . . . . (708) 331-4905
　http://cityofmarkham.net

MATTESON (village).

Covers a land area of 9.324 square miles and a water area of 0.034 square miles. Located at 41.51° N. Lat; 87.75° W. Long. Elevation is 692 feet.

Population: 11,378 (1990); 12,928 (2000); 19,009 (2010); Density: 2,004.7 persons per square mile (2008-2012 5-year est.); Race: 14.7%

White, 81.3% Black/African American, 0.6% Asian, 0.1% American Indian/Alaska Native, 0.0% Native Hawaiian/Other Pacific Islander, 3.3% Some other race, 1.4% Two or more races, 2.7% Hispanic of any race (2008-2012 5-year est.); Average household size: 2.77 (2008-2012 5-year est.); Median age: 38.9 (2008-2012 5-year est.); Males per 100 females: 93.8 (2008-2012 5-year est.); Marriage status: 30.4% never married, 52.3% now married, 5.1% widowed, 12.2% divorced (2008-2012 5-year est.); Foreign born: 3.9% (2008-2012 5-year est.); Ancestry (includes multiple ancestries): 5.2% German, 3.2% Irish, 2.2% English, 2.1% American, 2.1% Italian (2008-2012 5-year est.).

Economy: Single-family building permits issued: 6 (2013); Multi-family building permits issued: 0 (2013); Homeowner vacancy rate: 1.0%. Rental vacancy rate: 4.1%. (2008-2012 5-year est.); Employment by occupation: 18.2% management, business, and financial, 3.6% computer, engineering, and science, 13.6% education, legal, community service, arts, and media, 9.9% healthcare practitioners, 12.4% service, 20.7% sales and office, 5.7% natural resources, construction, and maintenance, 16.0% production, transportation, and material moving (2008-2012 5-year est.).

Income: Per capita income: $28,772 (2008-2012 5-year est.); Median household income: $66,847 (2008-2012 5-year est.); Average household income: $77,245 (2008-2012 5-year est.); Percent of households with income of $100,000 or more: 29.1% (2008-2012 5-year est.); Poverty rate: 9.6% (2008-2012 5-year est.).

Taxes: Total city taxes per capita: $880 (2011); City property taxes per capita: $674 (2011).

Education: Percent of population age 25 and over with: High school diploma (including GED) or higher: 92.9% (2008-2012 5-year est.); Bachelor's degree or higher: 30.7% (2008-2012 5-year est.); Master's degree or higher: 11.3% (2008-2012 5-year est.).

School District(s)
ESD 159 (PK-08)
    2011-12 Enrollment: 1,967 . . . . (708) 720-1300
Matteson ESD 162 (PK-08)
    2011-12 Enrollment: 3,180 . . . . (708) 748-0100

Housing: Homeownership rate: 79.4% (2008-2012 5-year est.); Median home value: $183,200 (2008-2012 5-year est.); Median contract rent: $974 per month (2008-2012 5-year est.); Median year structure built: 1983 (2008-2012 5-year est.).

Health Insurance: 73.1% Private; 28.1% Public; 9.7% None. (2008-2012 5-year est.)

Safety: Violent crime rate: 18.3 per 10,000 population; Property crime rate: 405.7 per 10,000 population (2012).

Transportation: Commute to work: 84.6% car, 10.0% public transportation, 0.6% walk, 3.8% work from home (2008-2012 5-year est.); Travel time to work: 13.9% less than 15 minutes, 28.3% 15 to 30 minutes, 27.3% 30 to 45 minutes, 16.0% 45 to 60 minutes, 14.6% 60 minutes or more (2008-2012 5-year est.)

Additional Information Contacts
Matteson Area Chamber of Commerce. . . . . (708) 747-6000
    http://www.macclink.com
Village of Matteson . . . . (708) 283-4900
    http://www.villageofmatteson.org

MAYWOOD (village).
Covers a land area of 2.721 square miles and a water area of 0 square miles. Located at 41.88° N. Lat; 87.84° W. Long. Elevation is 627 feet.

History: Named for May, the daugher of W. T. Nichols, owner of the town site. Maywood developed in the 1880's, when industrial growth in the Chicago area created a need for more residential areas.

Population: 27,139 (1990); 26,987 (2000); 24,090 (2010); Density: 8,885.9 persons per square mile (2008-2012 5-year est.); Race: 13.9% White, 73.7% Black/African American, 0.3% Asian, 0.1% American Indian/Alaska Native, 0.2% Native Hawaiian/Other Pacific Islander, 11.8% Some other race, 1.0% Two or more races, 21.4% Hispanic of any race (2008-2012 5-year est.); Average household size: 3.12 (2008-2012 5-year est.); Median age: 36.4 (2008-2012 5-year est.); Males per 100 females: 90.5 (2008-2012 5-year est.); Marriage status: 44.3% never married, 39.4% now married, 6.4% widowed, 9.8% divorced (2008-2012 5-year est.); Foreign born: 10.7% (2008-2012 5-year est.); Ancestry (includes multiple ancestries): 1.8% American, 1.4% Irish, 1.3% African, 1.3% German, 0.7% Barbadian (2008-2012 5-year est.).

Economy: Unemployment rate: 10.5% (April 2014); Total civilian labor force: 10,973 (April 2014); Single-family building permits issued: 0 (2013); Multi-family building permits issued: 0 (2013); Homeowner vacancy rate: 4.7%. Rental vacancy rate: 13.8%. (2008-2012 5-year est.); Employment by occupation: 8.6% management, business, and financial, 1.4% computer, engineering, and science, 7.7% education, legal, community service, arts, and media, 5.8% healthcare practitioners, 24.5% service, 24.4% sales and office, 5.3% natural resources, construction, and maintenance, 22.3% production, transportation, and material moving (2008-2012 5-year est.).

Income: Per capita income: $19,661 (2008-2012 5-year est.); Median household income: $43,869 (2008-2012 5-year est.); Average household income: $57,710 (2008-2012 5-year est.); Percent of households with income of $100,000 or more: 15.3% (2008-2012 5-year est.); Poverty rate: 18.6% (2008-2012 5-year est.).

Taxes: Total city taxes per capita: $910 (2011); City property taxes per capita: $759 (2011).

Education: Percent of population age 25 and over with: High school diploma (including GED) or higher: 77.1% (2008-2012 5-year est.); Bachelor's degree or higher: 12.6% (2008-2012 5-year est.); Master's degree or higher: 4.4% (2008-2012 5-year est.).

School District(s)
Maywood-Melrose Park-Broadview 89 (PK-08)
    2011-12 Enrollment: 5,362 . . . . (708) 450-2460
Proviso Area Exceptional Child (PK-12)
    2011-12 Enrollment: n/a . . . . (708) 450-2100
Proviso Twp HSD 209 (09-12)
    2011-12 Enrollment: 5,122 . . . . (708) 338-5912

Housing: Homeownership rate: 63.5% (2008-2012 5-year est.); Median home value: $167,200 (2008-2012 5-year est.); Median contract rent: $703 per month (2008-2012 5-year est.); Median year structure built: 1941 (2008-2012 5-year est.).

Health Insurance: 47.4% Private; 37.8% Public; 24.2% None. (2008-2012 5-year est.)

Hospitals: Loyola University Medical Center (589 beds)

Safety: Violent crime rate: 98.3 per 10,000 population; Property crime rate: 408.1 per 10,000 population (2012).

Transportation: Commute to work: 87.3% car, 7.2% public transportation, 1.8% walk, 2.8% work from home (2008-2012 5-year est.); Travel time to work: 21.2% less than 15 minutes, 31.9% 15 to 30 minutes, 28.5% 30 to 45 minutes, 10.5% 45 to 60 minutes, 7.9% 60 minutes or more (2008-2012 5-year est.)

Additional Information Contacts
Maywood Chamber of Commerce. . . . . (708) 345-7077
    http://maywoodchamber.com
Village of Maywood . . . . (708) 450-6300
    http://www.maywood-il.org

MCCOOK (village).
Covers a land area of 2.614 square miles and a water area of 0.021 square miles. Located at 41.80° N. Lat; 87.84° W. Long. Elevation is 617 feet.

Population: 235 (1990); 254 (2000); 228 (2010); Density: 116.3 persons per square mile (2008-2012 5-year est.); Race: 97.0% White, 0.0% Black/African American, 1.6% Asian, 0.0% American Indian/Alaska Native, 0.0% Native Hawaiian/Other Pacific Islander, 1.4% Some other race, 1.3% Two or more races, 17.8% Hispanic of any race (2008-2012 5-year est.); Average household size: 2.62 (2008-2012 5-year est.); Median age: 36.8 (2008-2012 5-year est.); Males per 100 females: 105.4 (2008-2012 5-year est.); Marriage status: 32.4% never married, 43.2% now married, 5.8% widowed, 18.5% divorced (2008-2012 5-year est.); Foreign born: 9.2% (2008-2012 5-year est.); Ancestry (includes multiple ancestries): 27.0% Polish, 26.3% Irish, 17.4% German, 15.1% Croatian, 8.2% Czech (2008-2012 5-year est.).

Economy: Single-family building permits issued: 0 (2013); Multi-family building permits issued: 0 (2013); Homeowner vacancy rate: 0.0%. Rental vacancy rate: 0.0%. (2008-2012 5-year est.); Employment by occupation: 5.5% management, business, and financial, 0.6% computer, engineering, and science, 9.1% education, legal, community service, arts, and media, 6.7% healthcare practitioners, 23.6% service, 21.8% sales and office, 18.2% natural resources, construction, and maintenance, 14.5% production, transportation, and material moving (2008-2012 5-year est.).

Income: Per capita income: $26,388 (2008-2012 5-year est.); Median household income: $59,167 (2008-2012 5-year est.); Average household income: $65,178 (2008-2012 5-year est.); Percent of households with income of $100,000 or more: 22.4% (2008-2012 5-year est.); Poverty rate: 3.6% (2008-2012 5-year est.).

Education: Percent of population age 25 and over with: High school diploma (including GED) or higher: 87.2% (2008-2012 5-year est.);

Bachelor's degree or higher: 22.1% (2008-2012 5-year est.); Master's degree or higher: 10.2% (2008-2012 5-year est.).
Housing: Homeownership rate: 56.0% (2008-2012 5-year est.); Median home value: $241,700 (2008-2012 5-year est.); Median contract rent: $848 per month (2008-2012 5-year est.); Median year structure built: 1954 (2008-2012 5-year est.).
Health Insurance: 72.7% Private; 26.6% Public; 13.5% None. (2008-2012 5-year est.)
Safety: Violent crime rate: 436.7 per 10,000 population; Property crime rate: 1,441.0 per 10,000 population (2012).
Transportation: Commute to work: 84.6% car, 8.0% public transportation, 4.9% walk, 0.6% work from home (2008-2012 5-year est.); Travel time to work: 35.4% less than 15 minutes, 16.1% 15 to 30 minutes, 26.7% 30 to 45 minutes, 14.9% 45 to 60 minutes, 6.8% 60 minutes or more (2008-2012 5-year est.)

MELROSE PARK (village). Covers a land area of 4.238 square miles and a water area of 0 square miles. Located at 41.90° N. Lat; 87.86° W. Long. Elevation is 633 feet.

History: Named for Melrose in Roxburghshire, Scotland. Incorporated 1893.
Population: 20,859 (1990); 23,171 (2000); 25,411 (2010); Density: 5,956.2 persons per square mile (2008-2012 5-year est.); Race: 52.5% White, 6.6% Black/African American, 1.1% Asian, 0.0% American Indian/Alaska Native, 0.0% Native Hawaiian/Other Pacific Islander, 39.8% Some other race, 1.5% Two or more races, 71.1% Hispanic of any race (2008-2012 5-year est.); Average household size: 3.31 (2008-2012 5-year est.); Median age: 30.3 (2008-2012 5-year est.); Males per 100 females: 105.5 (2008-2012 5-year est.); Marriage status: 37.6% never married, 48.5% now married, 5.0% widowed, 8.9% divorced (2008-2012 5-year est.); Foreign born: 38.4% (2008-2012 5-year est.); Ancestry (includes multiple ancestries): 12.2% Italian, 4.1% German, 3.2% Polish, 2.8% Irish, 0.8% American (2008-2012 5-year est.).
Economy: Unemployment rate: 8.0% (April 2014); Total civilian labor force: 12,305 (April 2014); Single-family building permits issued: 0 (2013); Multi-family building permits issued: 0 (2013); Homeowner vacancy rate: 3.7%. Rental vacancy rate: 10.3%. (2008-2012 5-year est.); Employment by occupation: 6.3% management, business, and financial, 1.5% computer, engineering, and science, 3.6% education, legal, community service, arts, and media, 2.7% healthcare practitioners, 20.8% service, 23.7% sales and office, 9.2% natural resources, construction, and maintenance, 32.2% production, transportation, and material moving (2008-2012 5-year est.).
Income: Per capita income: $17,597 (2008-2012 5-year est.); Median household income: $44,691 (2008-2012 5-year est.); Average household income: $55,028 (2008-2012 5-year est.); Percent of households with income of $100,000 or more: 14.6% (2008-2012 5-year est.); Poverty rate: 14.1% (2008-2012 5-year est.).
Taxes: Total city taxes per capita: $960 (2011); City property taxes per capita: $751 (2011).
Education: Percent of population age 25 and over with: High school diploma (including GED) or higher: 67.4% (2008-2012 5-year est.); Bachelor's degree or higher: 9.5% (2008-2012 5-year est.); Master's degree or higher: 2.6% (2008-2012 5-year est.).

School District(s)
Bellwood SD 88 (PK-08)
   2011-12 Enrollment: 2,879 . . . . (708) 344-9344
Mannheim SD 83 (PK-08)
   2011-12 Enrollment: 2,604 . . . . (847) 455-4413
Maywood-Melrose Park-Broadview 89 (PK-08)
   2011-12 Enrollment: 5,362 . . . . (708) 450-2460

Two-year College(s)
Lincoln College of Technology-Melrose Park (Private, For-profit)
   Fall 2012 Enrollment: 1,011 . . . . (708) 344-4700

Vocational/Technical School(s)
Everest College-Melrose Park (Private, For-profit)
   Fall 2012 Enrollment: 635 . . . . (708) 731-4400
   2012-13 Tuition: $18,841

Housing: Homeownership rate: 54.4% (2008-2012 5-year est.); Median home value: $213,900 (2008-2012 5-year est.); Median contract rent: $769 per month (2008-2012 5-year est.); Median year structure built: 1955 (2008-2012 5-year est.).
Health Insurance: 47.3% Private; 35.4% Public; 24.4% None. (2008-2012 5-year est.)

Hospitals: Gottlieb Memorial Hospital (250 beds); Westlake Community Hospital (326 beds)
Safety: Violent crime rate: 22.7 per 10,000 population; Property crime rate: 195.8 per 10,000 population (2012).
Transportation: Commute to work: 88.4% car, 4.8% public transportation, 3.5% walk, 1.7% work from home (2008-2012 5-year est.); Travel time to work: 32.3% less than 15 minutes, 33.4% 15 to 30 minutes, 21.5% 30 to 45 minutes, 7.0% 45 to 60 minutes, 5.8% 60 minutes or more (2008-2012 5-year est.)
Additional Information Contacts
Melrose Park Chamber of Commerce & Industry . . . . (708) 338-1007
   http://www.melroseparkchamber.org
Village of Melrose Park . . . . (708) 343-4000
   http://www.melrosepark.org

MERRIONETTE PARK (village). Covers a land area of 0.375 square miles and a water area of 0 square miles. Located at 41.68° N. Lat; 87.70° W. Long. Elevation is 620 feet.

History: Incorporated 1947.
Population: 2,065 (1990); 1,999 (2000); 1,900 (2010); Density: 5,566.4 persons per square mile (2008-2012 5-year est.); Race: 90.7% White, 5.2% Black/African American, 1.8% Asian, 0.2% American Indian/Alaska Native, 0.0% Native Hawaiian/Other Pacific Islander, 2.1% Some other race, 1.2% Two or more races, 5.7% Hispanic of any race (2008-2012 5-year est.); Average household size: 2.23 (2008-2012 5-year est.); Median age: 43.5 (2008-2012 5-year est.); Males per 100 females: 104.7 (2008-2012 5-year est.); Marriage status: 38.1% never married, 37.9% now married, 7.7% widowed, 16.4% divorced (2008-2012 5-year est.); Foreign born: 5.4% (2008-2012 5-year est.); Ancestry (includes multiple ancestries): 40.7% Irish, 26.7% German, 13.8% Polish, 11.4% Italian, 6.4% English (2008-2012 5-year est.).
Economy: Single-family building permits issued: 0 (2013); Multi-family building permits issued: 0 (2013); Homeowner vacancy rate: 0.0%. Rental vacancy rate: 0.0%. (2008-2012 5-year est.); Employment by occupation: 8.0% management, business, and financial, 4.6% computer, engineering, and science, 6.5% education, legal, community service, arts, and media, 6.5% healthcare practitioners, 21.9% service, 32.5% sales and office, 8.5% natural resources, construction, and maintenance, 11.5% production, transportation, and material moving (2008-2012 5-year est.).
Income: Per capita income: $25,011 (2008-2012 5-year est.); Median household income: $39,071 (2008-2012 5-year est.); Average household income: $52,532 (2008-2012 5-year est.); Percent of households with income of $100,000 or more: 11.5% (2008-2012 5-year est.); Poverty rate: 8.7% (2008-2012 5-year est.).
Education: Percent of population age 25 and over with: High school diploma (including GED) or higher: 91.5% (2008-2012 5-year est.); Bachelor's degree or higher: 17.5% (2008-2012 5-year est.); Master's degree or higher: 5.7% (2008-2012 5-year est.).

School District(s)
Atwood Heights SD 125 (PK-08)
   2011-12 Enrollment: 739 . . . . (708) 371-0080

Vocational/Technical School(s)
Everest College-Merrionette Park (Private, For-profit)
   Fall 2012 Enrollment: 513 . . . . (708) 239-0055
   2012-13 Tuition: $17,471

Housing: Homeownership rate: 72.5% (2008-2012 5-year est.); Median home value: $122,900 (2008-2012 5-year est.); Median contract rent: $753 per month (2008-2012 5-year est.); Median year structure built: 1959 (2008-2012 5-year est.).
Health Insurance: 72.3% Private; 19.7% Public; 17.9% None. (2008-2012 5-year est.)
Safety: Violent crime rate: 21.0 per 10,000 population; Property crime rate: 288.1 per 10,000 population (2012).
Transportation: Commute to work: 85.2% car, 6.3% public transportation, 1.7% walk, 0.0% work from home (2008-2012 5-year est.); Travel time to work: 16.5% less than 15 minutes, 37.1% 15 to 30 minutes, 23.1% 30 to 45 minutes, 10.7% 45 to 60 minutes, 12.6% 60 minutes or more (2008-2012 5-year est.)

MIDLOTHIAN (village). Covers a land area of 2.819 square miles and a water area of 0 square miles. Located at 41.63° N. Lat; 87.72° W. Long. Elevation is 614 feet.

History: Named for the title of a novel by Sir Walter Scott. Incorporated 1927.

Population: 14,372 (1990); 14,315 (2000); 14,819 (2010); Density: 5,245.4 persons per square mile (2008-2012 5-year est.); Race: 77.4% White, 8.5% Black/African American, 2.0% Asian, 0.5% American Indian/Alaska Native, 0.0% Native Hawaiian/Other Pacific Islander, 11.6% Some other race, 5.5% Two or more races, 23.9% Hispanic of any race (2008-2012 5-year est.); Average household size: 2.89 (2008-2012 5-year est.); Median age: 33.9 (2008-2012 5-year est.); Males per 100 females: 103.5 (2008-2012 5-year est.); Marriage status: 37.1% never married, 47.3% now married, 5.2% widowed, 10.3% divorced (2008-2012 5-year est.); Foreign born: 8.2% (2008-2012 5-year est.); Ancestry (includes multiple ancestries): 24.7% Irish, 19.4% German, 14.7% Polish, 10.7% Italian, 4.1% English (2008-2012 5-year est.).
Economy: Single-family building permits issued: 1 (2013); Multi-family building permits issued: 0 (2013); Homeowner vacancy rate: 3.7%. Rental vacancy rate: 9.6%. (2008-2012 5-year est.); Employment by occupation: 12.9% management, business, and financial, 3.0% computer, engineering, and science, 7.6% education, legal, community service, arts, and media, 6.2% healthcare practitioners, 17.3% service, 24.2% sales and office, 12.9% natural resources, construction, and maintenance, 15.9% production, transportation, and material moving (2008-2012 5-year est.).
Income: Per capita income: $23,873 (2008-2012 5-year est.); Median household income: $60,829 (2008-2012 5-year est.); Average household income: $67,106 (2008-2012 5-year est.); Percent of households with income of $100,000 or more: 20.8% (2008-2012 5-year est.); Poverty rate: 16.7% (2008-2012 5-year est.).
Taxes: Total city taxes per capita: $450 (2011); City property taxes per capita: $326 (2011).
Education: Percent of population age 25 and over with: High school diploma (including GED) or higher: 87.5% (2008-2012 5-year est.); Bachelor's degree or higher: 18.9% (2008-2012 5-year est.); Master's degree or higher: 5.0% (2008-2012 5-year est.).

School District(s)
Bremen CHSD 228 (09-12)
   2011-12 Enrollment: 5,491 . . . . (708) 389-1175
Eisenhower Cooperative (PK-08)
   2011-12 Enrollment: n/a . . . . (708) 389-7580
Midlothian SD 143 (PK-08)
   2011-12 Enrollment: 1,984 . . . . (708) 388-6450
Housing: Homeownership rate: 74.2% (2008-2012 5-year est.); Median home value: $169,800 (2008-2012 5-year est.); Median contract rent: $819 per month (2008-2012 5-year est.); Median year structure built: 1965 (2008-2012 5-year est.).
Health Insurance: 67.6% Private; 31.3% Public; 9.2% None. (2008-2012 5-year est.)
Safety: Violent crime rate: 28.2 per 10,000 population; Property crime rate: 182.7 per 10,000 population (2012).
Transportation: Commute to work: 88.8% car, 6.4% public transportation, 1.4% walk, 2.1% work from home (2008-2012 5-year est.); Travel time to work: 23.4% less than 15 minutes, 26.7% 15 to 30 minutes, 26.4% 30 to 45 minutes, 11.7% 45 to 60 minutes, 11.7% 60 minutes or more (2008-2012 5-year est.)
Additional Information Contacts
Midlothian Chamber of Commerce . . . . (708) 389-0020
   http://www.villageprofile.com/illinois/midlothian
Village of Midlothian . . . . (708) 389-0200
   http://www.villageofmidlothian.net

MORTON GROVE (village). Covers a land area of 5.088 square miles and a water area of 0 square miles. Located at 42.04° N. Lat; 87.79° W. Long. Elevation is 623 feet.
History: Named for Marcus Morton, governor of Massachusetts (1840-1843). Incorporated 1895.
Population: 22,408 (1990); 22,451 (2000); 23,270 (2010); Density: 4,558.4 persons per square mile (2008-2012 5-year est.); Race: 63.7% White, 1.0% Black/African American, 28.9% Asian, 0.3% American Indian/Alaska Native, 0.3% Native Hawaiian/Other Pacific Islander, 5.8% Some other race, 4.1% Two or more races, 7.1% Hispanic of any race (2008-2012 5-year est.); Average household size: 2.73 (2008-2012 5-year est.); Median age: 45.1 (2008-2012 5-year est.); Males per 100 females: 93.0 (2008-2012 5-year est.); Marriage status: 25.6% never married, 59.1% now married, 9.1% widowed, 6.3% divorced (2008-2012 5-year est.); Foreign born: 38.8% (2008-2012 5-year est.); Ancestry (includes multiple ancestries): 13.2% German, 10.0% Polish, 8.4% Irish, 6.0% Italian, 4.2% Russian (2008-2012 5-year est.).

Economy: Single-family building permits issued: 4 (2013); Multi-family building permits issued: 0 (2013); Homeowner vacancy rate: 1.7%. Rental vacancy rate: 0.0%. (2008-2012 5-year est.); Employment by occupation: 15.1% management, business, and financial, 6.5% computer, engineering, and science, 12.0% education, legal, community service, arts, and media, 12.6% healthcare practitioners, 13.0% service, 24.0% sales and office, 5.9% natural resources, construction, and maintenance, 10.8% production, transportation, and material moving (2008-2012 5-year est.).
Income: Per capita income: $32,868 (2008-2012 5-year est.); Median household income: $72,204 (2008-2012 5-year est.); Average household income: $87,546 (2008-2012 5-year est.); Percent of households with income of $100,000 or more: 34.5% (2008-2012 5-year est.); Poverty rate: 6.5% (2008-2012 5-year est.).
Education: Percent of population age 25 and over with: High school diploma (including GED) or higher: 89.4% (2008-2012 5-year est.); Bachelor's degree or higher: 42.0% (2008-2012 5-year est.); Master's degree or higher: 15.0% (2008-2012 5-year est.).

School District(s)
East Maine SD 63 (PK-08)
   2011-12 Enrollment: 3,628 . . . . (847) 299-1900
Golf ESD 67 (PK-08)
   2011-12 Enrollment: 574. . . . . (847) 966-8200
Morton Grove SD 70 (PK-08)
   2011-12 Enrollment: 862. . . . . (847) 965-6200
Niles Twp District for Spec Educ (PK-12)
   2011-12 Enrollment: n/a . . . . (847) 965-9040
Skokie SD 69 (PK-08)
   2011-12 Enrollment: 1,721 . . . . (847) 675-7666
Housing: Homeownership rate: 90.5% (2008-2012 5-year est.); Median home value: $327,300 (2008-2012 5-year est.); Median contract rent: $1,149 per month (2008-2012 5-year est.); Median year structure built: 1959 (2008-2012 5-year est.).
Health Insurance: 77.4% Private; 27.5% Public; 9.4% None. (2008-2012 5-year est.)
Safety: Violent crime rate: 1.7 per 10,000 population; Property crime rate: 174.5 per 10,000 population (2012).
Transportation: Commute to work: 86.2% car, 8.4% public transportation, 0.7% walk, 3.8% work from home (2008-2012 5-year est.); Travel time to work: 21.8% less than 15 minutes, 33.4% 15 to 30 minutes, 27.2% 30 to 45 minutes, 8.7% 45 to 60 minutes, 9.0% 60 minutes or more (2008-2012 5-year est.)
Additional Information Contacts
Morton Grove Chamber of Commerce & Industry . . . . (847) 965-0330
   http://www.mgcci.org
Village of Morton Grove. . . . . (847) 965-4100
   http://www.mortongroveil.org

MOUNT PROSPECT (village). Covers a land area of 10.338 square miles and a water area of 0.034 square miles. Located at 42.07° N. Lat; 87.94° W. Long. Elevation is 669 feet.
History: Named for its high location, and for the hope that newcomers would view the town as a good place to settle. Incorporated 1917.
Population: 53,170 (1990); 56,265 (2000); 54,167 (2010); Density: 5,237.1 persons per square mile (2008-2012 5-year est.); Race: 74.6% White, 1.8% Black/African American, 11.7% Asian, 0.2% American Indian/Alaska Native, 0.0% Native Hawaiian/Other Pacific Islander, 11.7% Some other race, 1.8% Two or more races, 16.2% Hispanic of any race (2008-2012 5-year est.); Average household size: 2.66 (2008-2012 5-year est.); Median age: 39.4 (2008-2012 5-year est.); Males per 100 females: 97.4 (2008-2012 5-year est.); Marriage status: 28.6% never married, 58.1% now married, 6.6% widowed, 6.6% divorced (2008-2012 5-year est.); Foreign born: 32.0% (2008-2012 5-year est.); Ancestry (includes multiple ancestries): 20.9% German, 18.2% Polish, 12.5% Irish, 9.5% Italian, 4.1% English (2008-2012 5-year est.).
Economy: Unemployment rate: 5.3% (April 2014); Total civilian labor force: 30,430 (April 2014); Single-family building permits issued: 8 (2013); Multi-family building permits issued: 92 (2013); Homeowner vacancy rate: 2.1%. Rental vacancy rate: 8.3%. (2008-2012 5-year est.); Employment by occupation: 16.2% management, business, and financial, 6.0% computer, engineering, and science, 9.8% education, legal, community service, arts, and media, 6.4% healthcare practitioners, 15.5% service, 24.7% sales and office, 6.4% natural resources, construction, and maintenance, 15.0% production, transportation, and material moving (2008-2012 5-year est.).
Income: Per capita income: $33,054 (2008-2012 5-year est.); Median household income: $68,375 (2008-2012 5-year est.); Average household

income: $86,088 (2008-2012 5-year est.); Percent of households with income of $100,000 or more: 29.8% (2008-2012 5-year est.); Poverty rate: 5.9% (2008-2012 5-year est.).

Taxes: Total city taxes per capita: $775 (2011); City property taxes per capita: $511 (2011).

Education: Percent of population age 25 and over with: High school diploma (including GED) or higher: 88.7% (2008-2012 5-year est.); Bachelor's degree or higher: 38.0% (2008-2012 5-year est.); Master's degree or higher: 13.0% (2008-2012 5-year est.).

School District(s)
Community CSD 59 (PK-08)
   2011-12 Enrollment: 6,537 . . . . (847) 593-4300
Mount Prospect SD 57 (PK-08)
   2011-12 Enrollment: 2,133 . . . . (847) 394-7300
River Trails SD 26 (PK-08)
   2011-12 Enrollment: 1,386 . . . . (847) 297-4120
Township HSD 214 (09-12)
   2011-12 Enrollment: 12,305 . . . . (847) 718-7600
Wheeling CCSD 21 (PK-08)
   2011-12 Enrollment: 6,866 . . . . (847) 537-8270

Four-year College(s)
Christian Life College (Private, Not-for-profit, Other Protestant)
   Fall 2012 Enrollment: 50 . . . . (847) 259-1840
   2012-13 Tuition: In-state $10,590; Out-of-state $10,590
ITT Technical Institute-Mount Prospect (Private, For-profit)
   Fall 2012 Enrollment: 307 . . . . (847) 375-8800
   2012-13 Tuition: In-state $18,048; Out-of-state $18,048

Housing: Homeownership rate: 71.9% (2008-2012 5-year est.); Median home value: $316,300 (2008-2012 5-year est.); Median contract rent: $875 per month (2008-2012 5-year est.); Median year structure built: 1967 (2008-2012 5-year est.).

Health Insurance: 73.4% Private; 25.1% Public; 14.2% None. (2008-2012 5-year est.)

Safety: Violent crime rate: 5.9 per 10,000 population; Property crime rate: 136.9 per 10,000 population (2012).

Transportation: Commute to work: 85.8% car, 6.8% public transportation, 2.7% walk, 2.9% work from home (2008-2012 5-year est.); Travel time to work: 20.7% less than 15 minutes, 34.7% 15 to 30 minutes, 26.1% 30 to 45 minutes, 8.9% 45 to 60 minutes, 9.6% 60 minutes or more (2008-2012 5-year est.)

Additional Information Contacts
Mount Prospect Chamber of Commerce . . . . (847) 398-6616
   http://www.mountprospectchamber.org
Village of Mount Prospect . . . . (847) 392-6000
   http://www.mountprospect.org

NILES (village). Covers a land area of 5.847 square miles and a water area of 0 square miles. Located at 42.03° N. Lat; 87.81° W. Long. Elevation is 636 feet.

History: Named for Niles, New York. Settled 1832. Incorporated 1899. The village has a half size replica of the leaning tower of Pisa. Niles College of Loyola University is here.

Population: 28,284 (1990); 30,068 (2000); 29,803 (2010); Density: 5,083.1 persons per square mile (2008-2012 5-year est.); Race: 75.1% White, 1.1% Black/African American, 18.9% Asian, 0.3% American Indian/Alaska Native, 0.0% Native Hawaiian/Other Pacific Islander, 4.6% Some other race, 1.5% Two or more races, 9.5% Hispanic of any race (2008-2012 5-year est.); Average household size: 2.52 (2008-2012 5-year est.); Median age: 48.5 (2008-2012 5-year est.); Males per 100 females: 92.6 (2008-2012 5-year est.); Marriage status: 28.1% never married, 53.2% now married, 12.0% widowed, 6.8% divorced (2008-2012 5-year est.); Foreign born: 44.2% (2008-2012 5-year est.); Ancestry (includes multiple ancestries): 21.0% Polish, 11.3% German, 7.0% Irish, 6.7% Italian, 4.0% Greek (2008-2012 5-year est.).

Economy: Unemployment rate: 6.1% (April 2014); Total civilian labor force: 14,636 (April 2014); Single-family building permits issued: 5 (2013); Multi-family building permits issued: 0 (2013); Homeowner vacancy rate: 3.6%. Rental vacancy rate: 9.5%. (2008-2012 5-year est.); Employment by occupation: 12.3% management, business, and financial, 5.1% computer, engineering, and science, 6.0% education, legal, community service, arts, and media, 7.1% healthcare practitioners, 20.0% service, 26.3% sales and office, 9.2% natural resources, construction, and maintenance, 14.1% production, transportation, and material moving (2008-2012 5-year est.).

Income: Per capita income: $26,127 (2008-2012 5-year est.); Median household income: $45,546 (2008-2012 5-year est.); Average household

income: $64,462 (2008-2012 5-year est.); Percent of households with income of $100,000 or more: 19.7% (2008-2012 5-year est.); Poverty rate: 10.3% (2008-2012 5-year est.).

Taxes: Total city taxes per capita: $797 (2011); City property taxes per capita: $262 (2011).

Education: Percent of population age 25 and over with: High school diploma (including GED) or higher: 81.0% (2008-2012 5-year est.); Bachelor's degree or higher: 27.9% (2008-2012 5-year est.); Master's degree or higher: 9.1% (2008-2012 5-year est.).

School District(s)
East Maine SD 63 (PK-08)
   2011-12 Enrollment: 3,628 . . . . (847) 299-1900
Niles ESD 71 (PK-08)
   2011-12 Enrollment: 470 . . . . (847) 470-3407
Park Ridge CCSD 64 (PK-08)
   2011-12 Enrollment: 4,317 . . . . (847) 318-4300

Vocational/Technical School(s)
Niles School of Cosmetology (Private, For-profit)
   Fall 2012 Enrollment: 86 . . . . (847) 965-8061
   2012-13 Tuition: $11,095

Housing: Homeownership rate: 76.7% (2008-2012 5-year est.); Median home value: $290,700 (2008-2012 5-year est.); Median contract rent: $911 per month (2008-2012 5-year est.); Median year structure built: 1963 (2008-2012 5-year est.).

Health Insurance: 67.0% Private; 37.5% Public; 15.0% None. (2008-2012 5-year est.)

Safety: Violent crime rate: 8.0 per 10,000 population; Property crime rate: 250.5 per 10,000 population (2012).

Transportation: Commute to work: 84.3% car, 8.6% public transportation, 1.6% walk, 3.4% work from home (2008-2012 5-year est.); Travel time to work: 18.8% less than 15 minutes, 34.6% 15 to 30 minutes, 26.4% 30 to 45 minutes, 10.7% 45 to 60 minutes, 9.5% 60 minutes or more (2008-2012 5-year est.)

Additional Information Contacts
Niles Chamber of Commerce & Industry . . . . (847) 268-8180
   http://www.nileschamber.org
Village of Niles . . . . (847) 588-8000
   http://www.vniles.com

NORRIDGE (village). Covers a land area of 1.810 square miles and a water area of 0 square miles. Located at 41.96° N. Lat; 87.82° W. Long. Elevation is 640 feet.

History: Named for two nearby residential areas, Norwood and Park Ridge. Incorporated 1948.

Population: 14,459 (1990); 14,582 (2000); 14,572 (2010); Density: 8,095.9 persons per square mile (2008-2012 5-year est.); Race: 92.7% White, 0.4% Black/African American, 5.6% Asian, 0.1% American Indian/Alaska Native, 0.0% Native Hawaiian/Other Pacific Islander, 1.2% Some other race, 0.7% Two or more races, 6.4% Hispanic of any race (2008-2012 5-year est.); Average household size: 2.56 (2008-2012 5-year est.); Median age: 46.0 (2008-2012 5-year est.); Males per 100 females: 88.4 (2008-2012 5-year est.); Marriage status: 29.0% never married, 48.9% now married, 13.8% widowed, 8.3% divorced (2008-2012 5-year est.); Foreign born: 38.0% (2008-2012 5-year est.); Ancestry (includes multiple ancestries): 37.8% Polish, 21.0% Italian, 14.1% German, 8.2% Irish, 3.9% Greek (2008-2012 5-year est.).

Economy: Single-family building permits issued: 2 (2013); Multi-family building permits issued: 0 (2013); Homeowner vacancy rate: 3.3%. Rental vacancy rate: 3.8%. (2008-2012 5-year est.); Employment by occupation: 16.7% management, business, and financial, 2.9% computer, engineering, and science, 6.1% education, legal, community service, arts, and media, 3.3% healthcare practitioners, 15.4% service, 25.1% sales and office, 13.2% natural resources, construction, and maintenance, 17.4% production, transportation, and material moving (2008-2012 5-year est.).

Income: Per capita income: $25,628 (2008-2012 5-year est.); Median household income: $55,096 (2008-2012 5-year est.); Average household income: $63,936 (2008-2012 5-year est.); Percent of households with income of $100,000 or more: 17.9% (2008-2012 5-year est.); Poverty rate: 7.3% (2008-2012 5-year est.).

Education: Percent of population age 25 and over with: High school diploma (including GED) or higher: 84.5% (2008-2012 5-year est.); Bachelor's degree or higher: 19.8% (2008-2012 5-year est.); Master's degree or higher: 6.4% (2008-2012 5-year est.).

School District(s)

Norridge SD 80 (PK-08)
   2011-12 Enrollment: 968........................ (708) 583-2068
Pennoyer SD 79 (PK-08)
   2011-12 Enrollment: 392........................ (708) 456-9094
Ridgewood CHSD 234 (09-12)
   2011-12 Enrollment: 857........................ (708) 456-4242

Housing: Homeownership rate: 83.9% (2008-2012 5-year est.); Median home value: $277,700 (2008-2012 5-year est.); Median contract rent: $856 per month (2008-2012 5-year est.); Median year structure built: 1958 (2008-2012 5-year est.).

Health Insurance: 77.4% Private; 30.6% Public; 9.0% None. (2008-2012 5-year est.)

Safety: Violent crime rate: 13.7 per 10,000 population; Property crime rate: 540.2 per 10,000 population (2012).

Transportation: Commute to work: 87.6% car, 3.8% public transportation, 2.2% walk, 5.2% work from home (2008-2012 5-year est.); Travel time to work: 19.2% less than 15 minutes, 28.5% 15 to 30 minutes, 27.4% 30 to 45 minutes, 17.0% 45 to 60 minutes, 7.9% 60 minutes or more (2008-2012 5-year est.)

Additional Information Contacts

Harwood Heights-Norridge Chamber of Commerce ...... (708) 802-1868
   http://www.harwoodnorridgechamber.com
Village of Norridge................................. (708) 453-0800
   http://www.villageofnorridge.com

NORTH RIVERSIDE (village).

Covers a land area of 1.644 square miles and a water area of 0 square miles. Located at 41.85° N. Lat; 87.83° W. Long. Elevation is 617 feet.

Population: 6,005 (1990); 6,688 (2000); 6,672 (2010); Density: 4,210.3 persons per square mile (2008-2012 5-year est.); Race: 82.6% White, 5.5% Black/African American, 1.7% Asian, 0.5% American Indian/Alaska Native, 0.0% Native Hawaiian/Other Pacific Islander, 9.7% Some other race, 3.3% Two or more races, 28.9% Hispanic of any race (2008-2012 5-year est.); Average household size: 2.42 (2008-2012 5-year est.); Median age: 41.6 (2008-2012 5-year est.); Males per 100 females: 82.2 (2008-2012 5-year est.); Marriage status: 31.6% never married, 44.0% now married, 9.3% widowed, 15.0% divorced (2008-2012 5-year est.); Foreign born: 12.0% (2008-2012 5-year est.); Ancestry (includes multiple ancestries): 16.5% German, 15.2% Polish, 13.7% Irish, 13.3% Italian, 9.1% Czech (2008-2012 5-year est.).

Economy: Single-family building permits issued: 0 (2013); Multi-family building permits issued: 0 (2013); Homeowner vacancy rate: 0.0%. Rental vacancy rate: 3.7%. (2008-2012 5-year est.); Employment by occupation: 7.5% management, business, and financial, 8.5% computer, engineering, and science, 12.2% education, legal, community service, arts, and media, 5.0% healthcare practitioners, 14.3% service, 36.2% sales and office, 3.0% natural resources, construction, and maintenance, 13.3% production, transportation, and material moving (2008-2012 5-year est.).

Income: Per capita income: $27,027 (2008-2012 5-year est.); Median household income: $53,630 (2008-2012 5-year est.); Average household income: $64,003 (2008-2012 5-year est.); Percent of households with income of $100,000 or more: 17.0% (2008-2012 5-year est.); Poverty rate: 7.6% (2008-2012 5-year est.).

Education: Percent of population age 25 and over with: High school diploma (including GED) or higher: 86.0% (2008-2012 5-year est.); Bachelor's degree or higher: 23.5% (2008-2012 5-year est.); Master's degree or higher: 7.7% (2008-2012 5-year est.).

School District(s)

Komarek SD 94 (PK-08)
   2011-12 Enrollment: 527........................ (708) 447-8030

Housing: Homeownership rate: 71.6% (2008-2012 5-year est.); Median home value: $254,100 (2008-2012 5-year est.); Median contract rent: $804 per month (2008-2012 5-year est.); Median year structure built: 1955 (2008-2012 5-year est.).

Health Insurance: 73.0% Private; 30.9% Public; 11.0% None. (2008-2012 5-year est.)

Safety: Violent crime rate: 11.9 per 10,000 population; Property crime rate: 898.2 per 10,000 population (2012).

Transportation: Commute to work: 85.7% car, 7.5% public transportation, 2.8% walk, 3.4% work from home (2008-2012 5-year est.); Travel time to work: 25.3% less than 15 minutes, 34.4% 15 to 30 minutes, 21.7% 30 to 45 minutes, 11.1% 45 to 60 minutes, 7.5% 60 minutes or more (2008-2012 5-year est.)

Additional Information Contacts

Village of North Riverside .... (708) 447-4211
   http://www.northriverside-il.org

NORTHBROOK (village).

Covers a land area of 13.190 square miles and a water area of 0.065 square miles. Located at 42.13° N. Lat; 87.84° W. Long. Elevation is 646 feet.

History: Named for the middle forks of the north branch of the Chicago River. It was incorporated as Shermerville in 1901 and was reincorporated as Northbrook in 1923. Once a farming community, Northbrook developed industry after the coming of a railroad in 1871. Settled 1836.

Population: 32,308 (1990); 33,435 (2000); 33,170 (2010); Density: 2,509.2 persons per square mile (2008-2012 5-year est.); Race: 84.4% White, 1.0% Black/African American, 12.9% Asian, 0.0% American Indian/Alaska Native, 0.0% Native Hawaiian/Other Pacific Islander, 1.7% Some other race, 1.2% Two or more races, 1.9% Hispanic of any race (2008-2012 5-year est.); Average household size: 2.67 (2008-2012 5-year est.); Median age: 46.5 (2008-2012 5-year est.); Males per 100 females: 92.8 (2008-2012 5-year est.); Marriage status: 20.6% never married, 64.3% now married, 7.6% widowed, 7.5% divorced (2008-2012 5-year est.); Foreign born: 19.2% (2008-2012 5-year est.); Ancestry (includes multiple ancestries): 16.9% German, 11.3% Irish, 11.1% Russian, 9.3% Polish, 6.6% American (2008-2012 5-year est.).

Economy: Unemployment rate: 5.0% (April 2014); Total civilian labor force: 16,872 (April 2014); Single-family building permits issued: 39 (2013); Multi-family building permits issued: 0 (2013); Homeowner vacancy rate: 1.7%. Rental vacancy rate: 5.2%. (2008-2012 5-year est.); Employment by occupation: 27.3% management, business, and financial, 6.8% computer, engineering, and science, 16.9% education, legal, community service, arts, and media, 8.4% healthcare practitioners, 8.1% service, 27.8% sales and office, 2.0% natural resources, construction, and maintenance, 2.8% production, transportation, and material moving (2008-2012 5-year est.).

Income: Per capita income: $56,077 (2008-2012 5-year est.); Median household income: $109,241 (2008-2012 5-year est.); Average household income: $150,016 (2008-2012 5-year est.); Percent of households with income of $100,000 or more: 54.4% (2008-2012 5-year est.); Poverty rate: 4.0% (2008-2012 5-year est.).

Taxes: Total city taxes per capita: $717 (2011); City property taxes per capita: $485 (2011).

Education: Percent of population age 25 and over with: High school diploma (including GED) or higher: 97.0% (2008-2012 5-year est.); Bachelor's degree or higher: 68.3% (2008-2012 5-year est.); Master's degree or higher: 31.3% (2008-2012 5-year est.).

School District(s)

Northbrook ESD 27 (PK-08)
   2011-12 Enrollment: 1,192 .... (847) 498-2610
Northbrook SD 28 (PK-08)
   2011-12 Enrollment: 1,691 .... (847) 498-7900
Northbrook/glenview SD 30 (PK-08)
   2011-12 Enrollment: 1,096 .... (847) 498-4190
Northern Suburban Spec Ed Dist (KG-12)
   2011-12 Enrollment: n/a .... (847) 831-5100
Northfield Twp HSD 225 (09-12)
   2011-12 Enrollment: 4,750 .... (847) 486-4700
West Northfield SD 31 (KG-08)
   2011-12 Enrollment: 890........................ (847) 272-6880

Housing: Homeownership rate: 88.6% (2008-2012 5-year est.); Median home value: $528,400 (2008-2012 5-year est.); Median contract rent: $1,668 per month (2008-2012 5-year est.); Median year structure built: 1972 (2008-2012 5-year est.).

Health Insurance: 88.1% Private; 22.2% Public; 4.7% None. (2008-2012 5-year est.)

Safety: Violent crime rate: 3.0 per 10,000 population; Property crime rate: 159.9 per 10,000 population (2012).

Transportation: Commute to work: 79.5% car, 9.9% public transportation, 1.7% walk, 8.1% work from home (2008-2012 5-year est.); Travel time to work: 27.5% less than 15 minutes, 26.0% 15 to 30 minutes, 21.8% 30 to 45 minutes, 11.5% 45 to 60 minutes, 13.2% 60 minutes or more (2008-2012 5-year est.)

Additional Information Contacts

Northbrook Chamber of Commerce & Industry .... (847) 498-5555
   http://www.northbrookchamber.org
Village of Northbrook............................. (847) 272-5050
   http://www.northbrook.il.us

NORTHFIELD (village). Covers a land area of 3.214 square miles and a water area of 0 square miles. Located at 42.10° N. Lat; 87.78° W. Long. Elevation is 633 feet.

History: The Village of Northfield was first settled in the mid-1800s by Mary Young and her two daughters near present day Bracken Lane. When the settlers first arrived, Northfield was a remote swamp.

Population: 4,635 (1990); 5,389 (2000); 5,420 (2010); Density: 1,628.4 persons per square mile (2008-2012 5-year est.); Race: 91.5% White, 0.0% Black/African American, 6.3% Asian, 0.0% American Indian/Alaska Native, 0.0% Native Hawaiian/Other Pacific Islander, 2.2% Some other race, 1.8% Two or more races, 1.0% Hispanic of any race (2008-2012 5-year est.); Average household size: 2.51 (2008-2012 5-year est.); Median age: 50.4 (2008-2012 5-year est.); Males per 100 females: 89.6 (2008-2012 5-year est.); Marriage status: 19.6% never married, 68.1% now married, 5.4% widowed, 6.9% divorced (2008-2012 5-year est.); Foreign born: 15.6% (2008-2012 5-year est.); Ancestry (includes multiple ancestries): 25.2% German, 24.1% Irish, 11.6% English, 9.1% Polish, 7.1% Italian (2008-2012 5-year est.).

Economy: Single-family building permits issued: 4 (2013); Multi-family building permits issued: 0 (2013); Homeowner vacancy rate: 0.8%. Rental vacancy rate: 4.8%. (2008-2012 5-year est.); Employment by occupation: 21.2% management, business, and financial, 6.5% computer, engineering, and science, 18.5% education, legal, community service, arts, and media, 6.7% healthcare practitioners, 12.4% service, 25.0% sales and office, 6.7% natural resources, construction, and maintenance, 3.1% production, transportation, and material moving (2008-2012 5-year est.).

Income: Per capita income: $77,471 (2008-2012 5-year est.); Median household income: $116,378 (2008-2012 5-year est.); Average household income: $194,366 (2008-2012 5-year est.); Percent of households with income of $100,000 or more: 57.4% (2008-2012 5-year est.); Poverty rate: 3.2% (2008-2012 5-year est.).

Education: Percent of population age 25 and over with: High school diploma (including GED) or higher: 98.2% (2008-2012 5-year est.); Bachelor's degree or higher: 75.8% (2008-2012 5-year est.); Master's degree or higher: 31.2% (2008-2012 5-year est.).

School District(s)
New Trier Twp HSD 203 (09-12)
    2011-12 Enrollment: 4,234 . . . . (847) 784-6109
Sunset Ridge SD 29 (PK-08)
    2011-12 Enrollment: 495 . . . . (847) 881-9456

Housing: Homeownership rate: 91.4% (2008-2012 5-year est.); Median home value: $641,700 (2008-2012 5-year est.); Median contract rent: $1,730 per month (2008-2012 5-year est.); Median year structure built: 1962 (2008-2012 5-year est.).

Health Insurance: 87.6% Private; 28.8% Public; 4.0% None. (2008-2012 5-year est.)

Safety: Violent crime rate: 3.7 per 10,000 population; Property crime rate: 130.4 per 10,000 population (2012).

Transportation: Commute to work: 73.3% car, 11.0% public transportation, 5.2% walk, 10.4% work from home (2008-2012 5-year est.); Travel time to work: 25.0% less than 15 minutes, 31.7% 15 to 30 minutes, 18.7% 30 to 45 minutes, 15.3% 45 to 60 minutes, 9.2% 60 minutes or more (2008-2012 5-year est.)

Additional Information Contacts
Village of Northfield . . . . (847) 446-9200
    http://www.northfieldil.org
Winnetka-Northfield Chamber of Commerce . . . . (847) 446-4451
    http://www.northfieldchamber.org

NORTHLAKE (city). Aka North Lake. Covers a land area of 3.167 square miles and a water area of 0 square miles. Located at 41.91° N. Lat; 87.91° W. Long. Elevation is 646 feet.

History: St. John Vianney Roman Catholic Church, which is shaped like a fish, has the largest mosaic-tile mural in the Western Hemisphere. Incorporated 1949.

Population: 12,505 (1990); 11,878 (2000); 12,323 (2010); Density: 3,879.2 persons per square mile (2008-2012 5-year est.); Race: 64.1% White, 2.2% Black/African American, 3.3% Asian, 1.0% American Indian/Alaska Native, 0.0% Native Hawaiian/Other Pacific Islander, 29.4% Some other race, 2.6% Two or more races, 58.6% Hispanic of any race (2008-2012 5-year est.); Average household size: 3.28 (2008-2012 5-year est.); Median age: 35.1 (2008-2012 5-year est.); Males per 100 females: 98.5 (2008-2012 5-year est.); Marriage status: 35.4% never married, 48.4% now married, 9.3% widowed, 6.9% divorced (2008-2012 5-year est.); Foreign born: 33.5% (2008-2012 5-year est.); Ancestry (includes multiple ancestries): 9.9% Polish, 9.1% Italian, 8.1% German, 7.9% Irish, 2.4% English (2008-2012 5-year est.).

Economy: Single-family building permits issued: 0 (2013); Multi-family building permits issued: 0 (2013); Homeowner vacancy rate: 4.4%. Rental vacancy rate: 13.4%. (2008-2012 5-year est.); Employment by occupation: 7.0% management, business, and financial, 0.9% computer, engineering, and science, 8.0% education, legal, community service, arts, and media, 1.7% healthcare practitioners, 13.9% service, 27.7% sales and office, 10.6% natural resources, construction, and maintenance, 30.1% production, transportation, and material moving (2008-2012 5-year est.).

Income: Per capita income: $20,168 (2008-2012 5-year est.); Median household income: $56,005 (2008-2012 5-year est.); Average household income: $63,237 (2008-2012 5-year est.); Percent of households with income of $100,000 or more: 15.8% (2008-2012 5-year est.); Poverty rate: 9.5% (2008-2012 5-year est.).

Taxes: Total city taxes per capita: $1,034 (2011); City property taxes per capita: $598 (2011).

Education: Percent of population age 25 and over with: High school diploma (including GED) or higher: 70.7% (2008-2012 5-year est.); Bachelor's degree or higher: 11.8% (2008-2012 5-year est.); Master's degree or higher: 2.0% (2008-2012 5-year est.).

School District(s)
Berkeley SD 87 (PK-08)
    2011-12 Enrollment: 2,838 . . . . (708) 449-3350
Leyden CHSD 212 (09-12)
    2011-12 Enrollment: 3,500 . . . . (847) 451-3020
Mannheim SD 83 (PK-08)
    2011-12 Enrollment: 2,604 . . . . (847) 455-4413

Housing: Homeownership rate: 72.0% (2008-2012 5-year est.); Median home value: $188,100 (2008-2012 5-year est.); Median contract rent: $784 per month (2008-2012 5-year est.); Median year structure built: 1957 (2008-2012 5-year est.).

Health Insurance: 60.1% Private; 30.8% Public; 18.1% None. (2008-2012 5-year est.)

Hospitals: Kindred Hospital-Northlake (94 beds)

Safety: Violent crime rate: 10.5 per 10,000 population; Property crime rate: 288.3 per 10,000 population (2012).

Transportation: Commute to work: 95.0% car, 2.0% public transportation, 1.3% walk, 1.7% work from home (2008-2012 5-year est.); Travel time to work: 29.1% less than 15 minutes, 36.1% 15 to 30 minutes, 20.5% 30 to 45 minutes, 11.2% 45 to 60 minutes, 3.0% 60 minutes or more (2008-2012 5-year est.)

Additional Information Contacts
City of Northlake . . . . (708) 343-8700
    http://www.northlakecity.com
Northlake Chamber of Commerce . . . . (708) 562-4200
    http://northlakecity.com/businesses

OAK FOREST (city). Covers a land area of 5.952 square miles and a water area of 0.048 square miles. Located at 41.61° N. Lat; 87.75° W. Long. Elevation is 673 feet.

History: Named for the many oak trees in the area. In 1911 the Oak Forest Infirmary and Tuberculosis Hospital was established in the town of Oak Forest.

Population: 26,203 (1990); 28,051 (2000); 27,962 (2010); Density: 4,691.6 persons per square mile (2008-2012 5-year est.); Race: 87.0% White, 4.7% Black/African American, 2.9% Asian, 0.5% American Indian/Alaska Native, 0.0% Native Hawaiian/Other Pacific Islander, 4.9% Some other race, 2.8% Two or more races, 14.7% Hispanic of any race (2008-2012 5-year est.); Average household size: 2.92 (2008-2012 5-year est.); Median age: 35.3 (2008-2012 5-year est.); Males per 100 females: 95.1 (2008-2012 5-year est.); Marriage status: 32.3% never married, 53.3% now married, 5.0% widowed, 9.4% divorced (2008-2012 5-year est.); Foreign born: 7.9% (2008-2012 5-year est.); Ancestry (includes multiple ancestries): 24.4% German, 24.3% Irish, 14.8% Polish, 13.0% Italian, 3.7% Dutch (2008-2012 5-year est.).

Economy: Unemployment rate: 7.1% (April 2014); Total civilian labor force: 15,935 (April 2014); Single-family building permits issued: 1 (2013); Multi-family building permits issued: 0 (2013); Homeowner vacancy rate: 1.7%. Rental vacancy rate: 3.1%. (2008-2012 5-year est.); Employment by occupation: 11.2% management, business, and financial, 4.6% computer, engineering, and science, 12.2% education, legal, community service, arts, and media, 4.4% healthcare practitioners, 18.2% service, 26.8% sales and office, 11.4% natural resources, construction, and maintenance, 11.3% production, transportation, and material moving (2008-2012 5-year est.).

Income: Per capita income: $27,745 (2008-2012 5-year est.); Median household income: $69,048 (2008-2012 5-year est.); Average household income: $78,729 (2008-2012 5-year est.); Percent of households with income of $100,000 or more: 28.9% (2008-2012 5-year est.); Poverty rate: 6.7% (2008-2012 5-year est.).

Education: Percent of population age 25 and over with: High school diploma (including GED) or higher: 89.7% (2008-2012 5-year est.); Bachelor's degree or higher: 23.2% (2008-2012 5-year est.); Master's degree or higher: 7.8% (2008-2012 5-year est.).

School District(s)

Arbor Park SD 145 (PK-08)
   2011-12 Enrollment: 1,461 . . . . (708) 687-8040
Bremen CHSD 228 (09-12)
   2011-12 Enrollment: 5,491 . . . . (708) 389-1175
Forest Ridge SD 142 (PK-08)
   2011-12 Enrollment: 1,665 . . . . (708) 687-3334
Prairie-Hills ESD 144 (PK-08)
   2011-12 Enrollment: 2,796 . . . . (708) 210-2888
Southwest Cook Coop Spec Ed (11-12)
   2011-12 Enrollment: n/a . . . . (708) 687-0900
Tinley Park CCSD 146 (PK-08)
   2011-12 Enrollment: 2,408 . . . . (708) 614-4500

Vocational/Technical School(s)

Capri Beauty College (Private, For-profit)
   Fall 2012 Enrollment: 95 . . . . (708) 687-3020
   2012-13 Tuition: $18,100

Housing: Homeownership rate: 80.5% (2008-2012 5-year est.); Median home value: $210,300 (2008-2012 5-year est.); Median contract rent: $855 per month (2008-2012 5-year est.); Median year structure built: 1972 (2008-2012 5-year est.).

Health Insurance: 78.0% Private; 22.3% Public; 10.5% None. (2008-2012 5-year est.)

Hospitals: Oak Forest Hospital of Cook County (600 beds)

Safety: Violent crime rate: 10.3 per 10,000 population; Property crime rate: 159.8 per 10,000 population (2012).

Transportation: Commute to work: 89.5% car, 7.9% public transportation, 0.2% walk, 1.7% work from home (2008-2012 5-year est.); Travel time to work: 18.7% less than 15 minutes, 29.7% 15 to 30 minutes, 24.6% 30 to 45 minutes, 13.0% 45 to 60 minutes, 14.0% 60 minutes or more (2008-2012 5-year est.)

Additional Information Contacts

City of Oak Forest . . . . (708) 687-4050
   http://www.oak-forest.org
Oak Forest-Crestwood Area Chamber of Commerce . . . . . (708) 687-4600
   http://www.oc-chamber.org

OAK LAWN (village). Covers a land area of 8.594 square miles and a water area of <.001 square miles. Located at 41.71° N. Lat; 87.75° W. Long. Elevation is 597 feet.

History: Named for its many oak trees. Incorporated 1909.

Population: 56,182 (1990); 55,245 (2000); 56,690 (2010); Density: 6,576.8 persons per square mile (2008-2012 5-year est.); Race: 89.5% White, 3.8% Black/African American, 1.1% Asian, 0.3% American Indian/Alaska Native, 0.0% Native Hawaiian/Other Pacific Islander, 5.3% Some other race, 1.3% Two or more races, 15.7% Hispanic of any race (2008-2012 5-year est.); Average household size: 2.58 (2008-2012 5-year est.); Median age: 40.8 (2008-2012 5-year est.); Males per 100 females: 90.2 (2008-2012 5-year est.); Marriage status: 30.6% never married, 50.7% now married, 9.0% widowed, 9.7% divorced (2008-2012 5-year est.); Foreign born: 15.0% (2008-2012 5-year est.); Ancestry (includes multiple ancestries): 24.9% Irish, 19.8% Polish, 17.8% German, 10.2% Italian, 4.0% Lithuanian (2008-2012 5-year est.).

Economy: Unemployment rate: 7.8% (April 2014); Total civilian labor force: 28,137 (April 2014); Single-family building permits issued: 6 (2013); Multi-family building permits issued: 0 (2013); Homeowner vacancy rate: 2.1%. Rental vacancy rate: 8.9%. (2008-2012 5-year est.); Employment by occupation: 12.5% management, business, and financial, 2.3% computer, engineering, and science, 10.3% education, legal, community service, arts, and media, 5.5% healthcare practitioners, 17.1% service, 28.8% sales and office, 9.7% natural resources, construction, and maintenance, 13.8% production, transportation, and material moving (2008-2012 5-year est.).

Income: Per capita income: $28,781 (2008-2012 5-year est.); Median household income: $57,428 (2008-2012 5-year est.); Average household income: $72,429 (2008-2012 5-year est.); Percent of households with

income of $100,000 or more: 23.7% (2008-2012 5-year est.); Poverty rate: 8.8% (2008-2012 5-year est.).

Taxes: Total city taxes per capita: $532 (2011); City property taxes per capita: $401 (2011).

Education: Percent of population age 25 and over with: High school diploma (including GED) or higher: 87.7% (2008-2012 5-year est.); Bachelor's degree or higher: 26.4% (2008-2012 5-year est.); Master's degree or higher: 9.4% (2008-2012 5-year est.).

School District(s)

A E R O Spec Educ Coop (PK-12)
   2011-12 Enrollment: n/a . . . . (708) 496-3330
Atwood Heights SD 125 (PK-08)
   2011-12 Enrollment: 739 . . . . (708) 371-0080
CHSD 218 (09-12)
   2011-12 Enrollment: 5,671 . . . . (708) 424-2000
Oak Lawn CHSD 229 (09-12)
   2011-12 Enrollment: 1,889 . . . . (708) 424-5200
Oak Lawn-Hometown SD 123 (PK-08)
   2011-12 Enrollment: 3,057 . . . . (708) 423-0150
Ridgeland SD 122 (PK-08)
   2011-12 Enrollment: 2,342 . . . . (708) 599-5550

Vocational/Technical School(s)

Cameo Beauty Academy (Private, For-profit)
   Fall 2012 Enrollment: 94 . . . . (708) 636-4660
   2012-13 Tuition: $17,425

Housing: Homeownership rate: 82.9% (2008-2012 5-year est.); Median home value: $213,300 (2008-2012 5-year est.); Median contract rent: $846 per month (2008-2012 5-year est.); Median year structure built: 1966 (2008-2012 5-year est.).

Health Insurance: 74.0% Private; 30.1% Public; 9.7% None. (2008-2012 5-year est.)

Hospitals: Advocate Christ Medical Center and Hope Children's Hospital (64 beds)

Safety: Violent crime rate: 14.4 per 10,000 population; Property crime rate: 199.6 per 10,000 population (2012).

Transportation: Commute to work: 87.8% car, 6.9% public transportation, 2.4% walk, 1.7% work from home (2008-2012 5-year est.); Travel time to work: 23.2% less than 15 minutes, 24.4% 15 to 30 minutes, 27.2% 30 to 45 minutes, 12.2% 45 to 60 minutes, 13.0% 60 minutes or more (2008-2012 5-year est.)

Additional Information Contacts

Oak Lawn Chamber of Commerce . . . . (708) 424-8300
   http://www.oaklawnchamber.com
Village of Oak Lawn . . . . (708) 636-4400
   http://www.oaklawn-il.gov

OAK PARK (village). Covers a land area of 4.700 square miles and a water area of 0 square miles. Located at 41.89° N. Lat; 87.79° W. Long. Elevation is 620 feet.

History: Oak Park was settled in 1833 by Joseph Kettlestrings, who came with his wife from Maryland. They named the village for the oak trees growing here. In the 1890's Oak Park was known as Saints' Rest because of its many churches. This was the site of one of Frank Lloyd Wright's early workshops and examples of his architecture graced the village.

Population: 53,648 (1990); 52,524 (2000); 51,878 (2010); Density: 11,016.4 persons per square mile (2008-2012 5-year est.); Race: 68.4% White, 21.0% Black/African American, 5.2% Asian, 0.2% American Indian/Alaska Native, 0.0% Native Hawaiian/Other Pacific Islander, 5.2% Some other race, 2.7% Two or more races, 6.1% Hispanic of any race (2008-2012 5-year est.); Average household size: 2.36 (2008-2012 5-year est.); Median age: 38.5 (2008-2012 5-year est.); Males per 100 females: 86.3 (2008-2012 5-year est.); Marriage status: 33.0% never married, 53.6% now married, 4.0% widowed, 9.4% divorced (2008-2012 5-year est.); Foreign born: 10.4% (2008-2012 5-year est.); Ancestry (includes multiple ancestries): 18.6% German, 18.4% Irish, 9.4% English, 8.2% Italian, 7.6% Polish (2008-2012 5-year est.).

Economy: Unemployment rate: 5.2% (April 2014); Total civilian labor force: 31,442 (April 2014); Single-family building permits issued: 1 (2013); Multi-family building permits issued: 0 (2013); Homeowner vacancy rate: 1.7%. Rental vacancy rate: 11.7%. (2008-2012 5-year est.); Employment by occupation: 21.6% management, business, and financial, 8.9% computer, engineering, and science, 25.5% education, legal, community service, arts, and media, 7.8% healthcare practitioners, 9.0% service, 21.3% sales and office, 2.0% natural resources, construction, and

maintenance, 3.9% production, transportation, and material moving (2008-2012 5-year est.).

Income: Per capita income: $46,386 (2008-2012 5-year est.); Median household income: $75,118 (2008-2012 5-year est.); Average household income: $108,800 (2008-2012 5-year est.); Percent of households with income of $100,000 or more: 38.2% (2008-2012 5-year est.); Poverty rate: 8.0% (2008-2012 5-year est.).

Taxes: Total city taxes per capita: $1,098 (2011); City property taxes per capita: $818 (2011).

Education: Percent of population age 25 and over with: High school diploma (including GED) or higher: 96.5% (2008-2012 5-year est.); Bachelor's degree or higher: 67.2% (2008-2012 5-year est.); Master's degree or higher: 35.3% (2008-2012 5-year est.).

School District(s)

Oak Park - River Forest SD 200 (09-12)
  2011-12 Enrollment: 3,273 . . . . (708) 383-0700
Oak Park ESD 97 (PK-08)
  2011-12 Enrollment: 5,631 . . . . (708) 524-3000
Region 06 West Cook Isc 2 (PK-12)
  2011-12 Enrollment: n/a . . . . (708) 544-4890

Four-year College(s)

Resurrection University (Private, Not-for-profit, Roman Catholic)
  Fall 2012 Enrollment: 481 . . . . (708) 763-6530

Housing: Homeownership rate: 62.2% (2008-2012 5-year est.); Median home value: $369,200 (2008-2012 5-year est.); Median contract rent: $933 per month (2008-2012 5-year est.); Median year structure built: Before 1940 (2008-2012 5-year est.).

Health Insurance: 83.8% Private; 17.4% Public; 6.8% None. (2008-2012 5-year est.)

Hospitals: Rush Oak Park Hospital (296 beds); West Suburban Medical Center (245 beds)

Transportation: Commute to work: 64.1% car, 22.5% public transportation, 3.7% walk, 7.0% work from home (2008-2012 5-year est.); Travel time to work: 16.1% less than 15 minutes, 22.4% 15 to 30 minutes, 34.9% 30 to 45 minutes, 17.8% 45 to 60 minutes, 8.7% 60 minutes or more (2008-2012 5-year est.)

Additional Information Contacts

Oak Park-River Forest Chamber of Commerce . . . . (708) 613-0550
  http://www.oprfchamber.org
Village of Oak Park . . . . (708) 383-6400
  http://www.oak-park.us

OLYMPIA FIELDS (village).

Covers a land area of 2.939 square miles and a water area of 0.004 square miles. Located at 41.52° N. Lat; 87.69° W. Long. Elevation is 692 feet.

History: Olympia Fields was developed in 1926 as a residential community centered around the Olympia Fields Country Club and Golf Course.

Population: 4,248 (1990); 4,732 (2000); 4,988 (2010); Density: 1,641.3 persons per square mile (2008-2012 5-year est.); Race: 30.8% White, 65.4% Black/African American, 1.7% Asian, 0.0% American Indian/Alaska Native, 0.0% Native Hawaiian/Other Pacific Islander, 2.1% Some other race, 1.6% Two or more races, 0.3% Hispanic of any race (2008-2012 5-year est.); Average household size: 2.33 (2008-2012 5-year est.); Median age: 52.3 (2008-2012 5-year est.); Males per 100 females: 83.4 (2008-2012 5-year est.); Marriage status: 24.6% never married, 56.4% now married, 11.0% widowed, 7.9% divorced (2008-2012 5-year est.); Foreign born: 3.4% (2008-2012 5-year est.); Ancestry (includes multiple ancestries): 7.1% German, 6.6% Irish, 3.8% Italian, 3.3% English, 1.9% Polish (2008-2012 5-year est.).

Economy: Single-family building permits issued: 2 (2013); Multi-family building permits issued: 0 (2013); Homeowner vacancy rate: 7.2%. Rental vacancy rate: 0.0%. (2008-2012 5-year est.); Employment by occupation: 20.6% management, business, and financial, 7.1% computer, engineering, and science, 14.9% education, legal, community service, arts, and media, 14.9% healthcare practitioners, 14.4% service, 18.2% sales and office, 2.7% natural resources, construction, and maintenance, 7.2% production, transportation, and material moving (2008-2012 5-year est.).

Income: Per capita income: $45,922 (2008-2012 5-year est.); Median household income: $79,762 (2008-2012 5-year est.); Average household income: $105,833 (2008-2012 5-year est.); Percent of households with income of $100,000 or more: 38.5% (2008-2012 5-year est.); Poverty rate: 8.6% (2008-2012 5-year est.).

Education: Percent of population age 25 and over with: High school diploma (including GED) or higher: 92.6% (2008-2012 5-year est.);

Bachelor's degree or higher: 46.0% (2008-2012 5-year est.); Master's degree or higher: 19.3% (2008-2012 5-year est.).

School District(s)

Matteson ESD 162 (PK-08)
  2011-12 Enrollment: 3,180 . . . . (708) 748-0100
Rich Twp HSD 227 (09-12)
  2011-12 Enrollment: 3,905 . . . . (708) 679-5800

Housing: Homeownership rate: 87.8% (2008-2012 5-year est.); Median home value: $263,000 (2008-2012 5-year est.); Median contract rent: $2,000+ per month (2008-2012 5-year est.); Median year structure built: 1976 (2008-2012 5-year est.).

Health Insurance: 76.2% Private; 40.6% Public; 6.9% None. (2008-2012 5-year est.)

Hospitals: St. James Hospital and Health Center (201 beds)

Safety: Violent crime rate: 14.0 per 10,000 population; Property crime rate: 219.5 per 10,000 population (2012).

Transportation: Commute to work: 80.4% car, 14.1% public transportation, 0.2% walk, 4.3% work from home (2008-2012 5-year est.); Travel time to work: 18.6% less than 15 minutes, 20.9% 15 to 30 minutes, 16.6% 30 to 45 minutes, 23.0% 45 to 60 minutes, 20.9% 60 minutes or more (2008-2012 5-year est.)

Additional Information Contacts

Matteson Area Chamber of Commerce . . . . (708) 747-6000
  http://www.macclink.com

ORLAND HILLS (village).

Aka Westhaven. Covers a land area of 1.142 square miles and a water area of 0.008 square miles. Located at 41.59° N. Lat; 87.84° W. Long. Elevation is 702 feet.

Population: 5,510 (1990); 6,779 (2000); 7,149 (2010); Density: 6,230.6 persons per square mile (2008-2012 5-year est.); Race: 82.4% White, 3.7% Black/African American, 5.5% Asian, 0.0% American Indian/Alaska Native, 0.0% Native Hawaiian/Other Pacific Islander, 8.4% Some other race, 1.9% Two or more races, 10.2% Hispanic of any race (2008-2012 5-year est.); Average household size: 2.83 (2008-2012 5-year est.); Median age: 34.1 (2008-2012 5-year est.); Males per 100 females: 102.9 (2008-2012 5-year est.); Marriage status: 29.5% never married, 59.5% now married, 1.8% widowed, 9.1% divorced (2008-2012 5-year est.); Foreign born: 13.2% (2008-2012 5-year est.); Ancestry (includes multiple ancestries): 26.8% Irish, 19.3% German, 19.0% Polish, 13.3% Italian, 5.7% Arab (2008-2012 5-year est.).

Economy: Single-family building permits issued: 0 (2013); Multi-family building permits issued: 0 (2013); Homeowner vacancy rate: 0.0%. Rental vacancy rate: 0.0%. (2008-2012 5-year est.); Employment by occupation: 13.4% management, business, and financial, 2.2% computer, engineering, and science, 11.1% education, legal, community service, arts, and media, 5.0% healthcare practitioners, 14.2% service, 32.4% sales and office, 13.5% natural resources, construction, and maintenance, 8.1% production, transportation, and material moving (2008-2012 5-year est.).

Income: Per capita income: $29,191 (2008-2012 5-year est.); Median household income: $78,500 (2008-2012 5-year est.); Average household income: $81,764 (2008-2012 5-year est.); Percent of households with income of $100,000 or more: 31.5% (2008-2012 5-year est.); Poverty rate: 5.0% (2008-2012 5-year est.).

Education: Percent of population age 25 and over with: High school diploma (including GED) or higher: 94.8% (2008-2012 5-year est.); Bachelor's degree or higher: 32.0% (2008-2012 5-year est.); Master's degree or higher: 8.6% (2008-2012 5-year est.).

School District(s)

Cons HSD 230 (09-12)
  2011-12 Enrollment: 8,301 . . . . (708) 745-5210

Housing: Homeownership rate: 80.7% (2008-2012 5-year est.); Median home value: $230,000 (2008-2012 5-year est.); Median contract rent: $1,095 per month (2008-2012 5-year est.); Median year structure built: 1985 (2008-2012 5-year est.).

Health Insurance: 80.1% Private; 17.2% Public; 9.3% None. (2008-2012 5-year est.)

Transportation: Commute to work: 93.2% car, 3.6% public transportation, 0.4% walk, 2.8% work from home (2008-2012 5-year est.); Travel time to work: 15.8% less than 15 minutes, 28.8% 15 to 30 minutes, 21.1% 30 to 45 minutes, 18.9% 45 to 60 minutes, 15.4% 60 minutes or more (2008-2012 5-year est.)

Additional Information Contacts

Village of Orland Hills . . . . (708) 349-6865
  http://www.orlandhills.org

ORLAND PARK (village). Covers a land area of 21.878 square miles and a water area of 0.287 square miles. Located at 41.61° N. Lat; 87.86° W. Long. Elevation is 705 feet.

Population: 35,720 (1990); 51,077 (2000); 56,767 (2010); Density: 2,587.4 persons per square mile (2008-2012 5-year est.); Race: 90.9% White, 2.0% Black/African American, 4.7% Asian, 0.0% American Indian/Alaska Native, 0.0% Native Hawaiian/Other Pacific Islander, 2.4% Some other race, 1.2% Two or more races, 5.4% Hispanic of any race (2008-2012 5-year est.); Average household size: 2.63 (2008-2012 5-year est.); Median age: 45.0 (2008-2012 5-year est.); Males per 100 females: 88.8 (2008-2012 5-year est.); Marriage status: 27.3% never married, 56.8% now married, 8.8% widowed, 7.0% divorced (2008-2012 5-year est.); Foreign born: 13.2% (2008-2012 5-year est.); Ancestry (includes multiple ancestries): 23.9% Irish, 18.4% German, 17.1% Polish, 14.4% Italian, 4.4% English (2008-2012 5-year est.).

Economy: Unemployment rate: 6.1% (April 2014); Total civilian labor force: 29,736 (April 2014); Single-family building permits issued: 68 (2013); Multi-family building permits issued: 0 (2013); Homeowner vacancy rate: 1.8%. Rental vacancy rate: 2.5%. (2008-2012 5-year est.); Employment by occupation: 19.0% management, business, and financial, 3.5% computer, engineering, and science, 11.9% education, legal, community service, arts, and media, 7.8% healthcare practitioners, 13.5% service, 28.8% sales and office, 6.3% natural resources, construction, and maintenance, 9.3% production, transportation, and material moving (2008-2012 5-year est.).

Income: Per capita income: $36,374 (2008-2012 5-year est.); Median household income: $77,863 (2008-2012 5-year est.); Average household income: $94,385 (2008-2012 5-year est.); Percent of households with income of $100,000 or more: 36.1% (2008-2012 5-year est.); Poverty rate: 4.9% (2008-2012 5-year est.).

Taxes: Total city taxes per capita: $560 (2011); City property taxes per capita: $329 (2011).

Education: Percent of population age 25 and over with: High school diploma (including GED) or higher: 94.1% (2008-2012 5-year est.); Bachelor's degree or higher: 37.9% (2008-2012 5-year est.); Master's degree or higher: 14.5% (2008-2012 5-year est.).

School District(s)

Cons HSD 230 (09-12)
    2011-12 Enrollment: 8,301 . . . . (708) 745-5210
Kirby SD 140 (PK-08)
    2011-12 Enrollment: 3,735 . . . . (708) 532-6462
Orland SD 135 (PK-08)
    2011-12 Enrollment: 5,213 . . . . (708) 364-3306
Southwest Cook Coop Spec Ed (11-12)
    2011-12 Enrollment: n/a . . . . (708) 687-0900
Tinley Park CCSD 146 (PK-08)
    2011-12 Enrollment: 2,408 . . . . (708) 614-4500

Four-year College(s)

ITT Technical Institute-Orland Park (Private, For-profit)
    Fall 2012 Enrollment: 567 . . . . (708) 326-3200
    2012-13 Tuition: In-state $18,048; Out-of-state $18,048

Housing: Homeownership rate: 89.3% (2008-2012 5-year est.); Median home value: $289,200 (2008-2012 5-year est.); Median contract rent: $925 per month (2008-2012 5-year est.); Median year structure built: 1987 (2008-2012 5-year est.).

Health Insurance: 83.2% Private; 26.2% Public; 6.2% None. (2008-2012 5-year est.)

Safety: Violent crime rate: 2.8 per 10,000 population; Property crime rate: 238.2 per 10,000 population (2012).

Transportation: Commute to work: 87.1% car, 7.6% public transportation, 1.3% walk, 3.7% work from home (2008-2012 5-year est.); Travel time to work: 19.1% less than 15 minutes, 27.0% 15 to 30 minutes, 24.6% 30 to 45 minutes, 10.6% 45 to 60 minutes, 18.7% 60 minutes or more (2008-2012 5-year est.)

Additional Information Contacts

Orland Park Area Chamber of Commerce . . . . (708) 349-2972
    http://www.orlandparkchamber.org
Village of Orland Park . . . . (708) 403-6100
    http://www.orland-park.il.us

PALATINE (village). Covers a land area of 13.617 square miles and a water area of 0.143 square miles. Located at 42.12° N. Lat; 88.04° W. Long. Elevation is 741 feet.

History: Named for the Rhenish Palatinate, Germany, as "palatine" designates a high official. William Rainey Harper College is in Palatine. Incorporated 1869.

Population: 39,253 (1990); 65,479 (2000); 68,557 (2010); Density: 5,018.7 persons per square mile (2008-2012 5-year est.); Race: 79.8% White, 3.2% Black/African American, 11.1% Asian, 0.0% American Indian/Alaska Native, 0.1% Native Hawaiian/Other Pacific Islander, 5.8% Some other race, 1.9% Two or more races, 17.4% Hispanic of any race (2008-2012 5-year est.); Average household size: 2.65 (2008-2012 5-year est.); Median age: 36.3 (2008-2012 5-year est.); Males per 100 females: 97.1 (2008-2012 5-year est.); Marriage status: 30.7% never married, 56.1% now married, 4.5% widowed, 8.7% divorced (2008-2012 5-year est.); Foreign born: 22.2% (2008-2012 5-year est.); Ancestry (includes multiple ancestries): 21.0% German, 14.6% Irish, 14.0% Polish, 9.9% Italian, 5.6% English (2008-2012 5-year est.).

Economy: Unemployment rate: 5.8% (April 2014); Total civilian labor force: 41,546 (April 2014); Single-family building permits issued: 51 (2013); Multi-family building permits issued: 0 (2013); Homeowner vacancy rate: 1.9%. Rental vacancy rate: 10.5%. (2008-2012 5-year est.); Employment by occupation: 20.6% management, business, and financial, 8.2% computer, engineering, and science, 11.2% education, legal, community service, arts, and media, 4.2% healthcare practitioners, 14.8% service, 26.3% sales and office, 4.8% natural resources, construction, and maintenance, 9.9% production, transportation, and material moving (2008-2012 5-year est.).

Income: Per capita income: $35,738 (2008-2012 5-year est.); Median household income: $73,811 (2008-2012 5-year est.); Average household income: $93,179 (2008-2012 5-year est.); Percent of households with income of $100,000 or more: 35.5% (2008-2012 5-year est.); Poverty rate: 8.5% (2008-2012 5-year est.).

Taxes: Total city taxes per capita: $646 (2011); City property taxes per capita: $438 (2011).

Education: Percent of population age 25 and over with: High school diploma (including GED) or higher: 91.0% (2008-2012 5-year est.); Bachelor's degree or higher: 47.9% (2008-2012 5-year est.); Master's degree or higher: 17.1% (2008-2012 5-year est.).

School District(s)

Nw Suburban Spec Educ Org
    2011-12 Enrollment: n/a . . . . (847) 463-8100
Palatine CCSD 15 (PK-08)
    2011-12 Enrollment: 12,663 . . . . (847) 963-3000
Region 05 North Cook Isc 1 (PK-12)
    2011-12 Enrollment: n/a . . . . (847) 824-8300
Township HSD 211 (09-12)
    2011-12 Enrollment: 12,593 . . . . (847) 755-6600

Two-year College(s)

Harper College (Public)
    Fall 2012 Enrollment: 17,306 . . . . (847) 925-6000
    2012-13 Tuition: In-state $9,186; Out-of-state $10,986

Housing: Homeownership rate: 70.7% (2008-2012 5-year est.); Median home value: $290,200 (2008-2012 5-year est.); Median contract rent: $986 per month (2008-2012 5-year est.); Median year structure built: 1977 (2008-2012 5-year est.).

Health Insurance: 76.0% Private; 20.8% Public; 11.7% None. (2008-2012 5-year est.)

Safety: Violent crime rate: 4.2 per 10,000 population; Property crime rate: 129.3 per 10,000 population (2012).

Transportation: Commute to work: 88.2% car, 5.0% public transportation, 1.4% walk, 4.6% work from home (2008-2012 5-year est.); Travel time to work: 21.6% less than 15 minutes, 33.7% 15 to 30 minutes, 26.8% 30 to 45 minutes, 8.7% 45 to 60 minutes, 9.1% 60 minutes or more (2008-2012 5-year est.)

Additional Information Contacts

Palatine Area Chamber of Commerce . . . . (847) 359-7200
    http://www.palatinechamber.com
Village of Palatine . . . . (847) 358-7500
    http://www.palatine.il.us

PALOS HEIGHTS (city). Covers a land area of 3.777 square miles and a water area of 0.098 square miles. Located at 41.66° N. Lat; 87.80° W. Long. Elevation is 623 feet.

History: Named for Palos, Spain. Trinity Christian College is here.

Population: 11,478 (1990); 11,260 (2000); 12,515 (2010); Density: 3,295.0 persons per square mile (2008-2012 5-year est.); Race: 93.0% White, 2.6% Black/African American, 2.7% Asian, 0.0% American Indian/Alaska Native, 0.0% Native Hawaiian/Other Pacific Islander, 1.7% Some other race, 1.3% Two or more races, 3.4% Hispanic of any race (2008-2012 5-year est.); Average household size: 2.42 (2008-2012 5-year

est.); Median age: 51.9 (2008-2012 5-year est.); Males per 100 females: 89.8 (2008-2012 5-year est.); Marriage status: 24.8% never married, 56.1% now married, 11.2% widowed, 7.9% divorced (2008-2012 5-year est.); Foreign born: 8.9% (2008-2012 5-year est.); Ancestry (includes multiple ancestries): 28.7% Irish, 22.8% German, 15.5% Polish, 10.6% Italian, 5.2% Lithuanian (2008-2012 5-year est.).

Economy: Single-family building permits issued: 0 (2013); Multi-family building permits issued: 0 (2013); Homeowner vacancy rate: 4.3%. Rental vacancy rate: 0.0%. (2008-2012 5-year est.); Employment by occupation: 20.6% management, business, and financial, 4.4% computer, engineering, and science, 13.5% education, legal, community service, arts, and media, 10.3% healthcare practitioners, 13.8% service, 28.9% sales and office, 4.9% natural resources, construction, and maintenance, 3.7% production, transportation, and material moving (2008-2012 5-year est.).

Income: Per capita income: $39,788 (2008-2012 5-year est.); Median household income: $76,436 (2008-2012 5-year est.); Average household income: $98,749 (2008-2012 5-year est.); Percent of households with income of $100,000 or more: 38.2% (2008-2012 5-year est.); Poverty rate: 5.9% (2008-2012 5-year est.).

Education: Percent of population age 25 and over with: High school diploma (including GED) or higher: 93.1% (2008-2012 5-year est.); Bachelor's degree or higher: 44.7% (2008-2012 5-year est.); Master's degree or higher: 18.4% (2008-2012 5-year est.).

School District(s)
CHSD 218 (09-12)
  2011-12 Enrollment: 5,671 . . . . (708) 424-2000
Palos CCSD 118 (PK-08)
  2011-12 Enrollment: 1,873 . . . . (708) 448-4800
Palos Heights SD 128 (PK-08)
  2011-12 Enrollment: 759 . . . . (708) 597-9040

Four-year College(s)
Trinity Christian College (Private, Not-for-profit, Interdenominational)
  Fall 2012 Enrollment: 1,369 . . . . (708) 597-3000
  2012-13 Tuition: In-state $23,513; Out-of-state $23,513

Housing: Homeownership rate: 95.3% (2008-2012 5-year est.); Median home value: $292,700 (2008-2012 5-year est.); Median contract rent: $1,402 per month (2008-2012 5-year est.); Median year structure built: 1974 (2008-2012 5-year est.).

Health Insurance: 87.0% Private; 31.0% Public; 3.9% None. (2008-2012 5-year est.)

Hospitals: Palos Community Hospital (436 beds)

Safety: Violent crime rate: 4.8 per 10,000 population; Property crime rate: 98.6 per 10,000 population (2012).

Transportation: Commute to work: 83.8% car, 6.8% public transportation, 2.7% walk, 5.6% work from home (2008-2012 5-year est.); Travel time to work: 23.8% less than 15 minutes, 32.6% 15 to 30 minutes, 15.9% 30 to 45 minutes, 10.2% 45 to 60 minutes, 17.4% 60 minutes or more (2008-2012 5-year est.)

Additional Information Contacts
City of Palos Heights. . . . . (708) 361-1800
  http://www.palosheights.org
Palos Area Chamber of Commerce . . . . (708) 480-3025
  http://palosareachamber.org

PALOS HILLS (city). Covers a land area of 4.248 square miles and a water area of 0.042 square miles. Located at 41.70° N. Lat; 87.83° W. Long. Elevation is 597 feet.

Population: 17,803 (1990); 17,665 (2000); 17,484 (2010); Density: 4,109.3 persons per square mile (2008-2012 5-year est.); Race: 88.6% White, 4.9% Black/African American, 4.1% Asian, 0.0% American Indian/Alaska Native, 0.0% Native Hawaiian/Other Pacific Islander, 2.4% Some other race, 0.5% Two or more races, 6.4% Hispanic of any race (2008-2012 5-year est.); Average household size: 2.42 (2008-2012 5-year est.); Median age: 42.3 (2008-2012 5-year est.); Males per 100 females: 98.1 (2008-2012 5-year est.); Marriage status: 30.8% never married, 47.4% now married, 9.0% widowed, 12.8% divorced (2008-2012 5-year est.); Foreign born: 28.2% (2008-2012 5-year est.); Ancestry (includes multiple ancestries): 21.0% Polish, 13.9% German, 13.3% Irish, 9.7% Italian, 8.4% Arab (2008-2012 5-year est.).

Economy: Single-family building permits issued: 3 (2013); Multi-family building permits issued: 0 (2013); Homeowner vacancy rate: 0.7%. Rental vacancy rate: 5.7%. (2008-2012 5-year est.); Employment by occupation: 15.2% management, business, and financial, 3.4% computer, engineering, and science, 7.5% education, legal, community service, arts, and media, 5.5% healthcare practitioners, 13.4% service, 32.0% sales and office,

9.5% natural resources, construction, and maintenance, 13.5% production, transportation, and material moving (2008-2012 5-year est.).

Income: Per capita income: $28,723 (2008-2012 5-year est.); Median household income: $55,221 (2008-2012 5-year est.); Average household income: $68,026 (2008-2012 5-year est.); Percent of households with income of $100,000 or more: 19.4% (2008-2012 5-year est.); Poverty rate: 9.6% (2008-2012 5-year est.).

Education: Percent of population age 25 and over with: High school diploma (including GED) or higher: 88.5% (2008-2012 5-year est.); Bachelor's degree or higher: 22.0% (2008-2012 5-year est.); Master's degree or higher: 7.8% (2008-2012 5-year est.).

School District(s)
Cons HSD 230 (09-12)
  2011-12 Enrollment: 8,301 . . . . (708) 745-5210
North Palos SD 117 (PK-08)
  2011-12 Enrollment: 3,005 . . . . (708) 598-5500

Two-year College(s)
Moraine Valley Community College (Public)
  Fall 2012 Enrollment: 16,650 . . . . (708) 974-4300
  2012-13 Tuition: In-state $8,256; Out-of-state $9,576

Vocational/Technical School(s)
Hair Professionals Career College (Private, For-profit)
  Fall 2012 Enrollment: 59 . . . . (708) 430-1755
  2012-13 Tuition: $16,950

Housing: Homeownership rate: 79.8% (2008-2012 5-year est.); Median home value: $218,400 (2008-2012 5-year est.); Median contract rent: $905 per month (2008-2012 5-year est.); Median year structure built: 1977 (2008-2012 5-year est.).

Health Insurance: 67.4% Private; 31.8% Public; 15.6% None. (2008-2012 5-year est.)

Safety: Violent crime rate: 3.4 per 10,000 population; Property crime rate: 79.7 per 10,000 population (2012).

Transportation: Commute to work: 92.5% car, 5.6% public transportation, 0.8% walk, 0.8% work from home (2008-2012 5-year est.); Travel time to work: 18.5% less than 15 minutes, 25.9% 15 to 30 minutes, 26.2% 30 to 45 minutes, 15.9% 45 to 60 minutes, 13.5% 60 minutes or more (2008-2012 5-year est.)

Additional Information Contacts
City of Palos Hills . . . . (708) 598-3400
  http://www.paloshillsweb.org
The Hills Chamber of Commerce . . . . (708) 364-7739
  http://www.thehillschamber.com

PALOS PARK (village). Covers a land area of 3.933 square miles and a water area of 0.043 square miles. Located at 41.67° N. Lat; 87.82° W. Long. Elevation is 689 feet.

History: The Village of Palos Park was incorporated in 1914. In the early 1920's, an artist colony emerged and by 1940 the Village had become a center for artists, writers and intellectuals. From early on, the art colony in Palos Park played a pivotal role in the personal and artistic development of our community.

Population: 4,199 (1990); 4,689 (2000); 4,847 (2010); Density: 1,221.8 persons per square mile (2008-2012 5-year est.); Race: 92.3% White, 0.8% Black/African American, 6.0% Asian, 0.0% American Indian/Alaska Native, 0.0% Native Hawaiian/Other Pacific Islander, 0.9% Some other race, 1.0% Two or more races, 1.8% Hispanic of any race (2008-2012 5-year est.); Average household size: 2.30 (2008-2012 5-year est.); Median age: 52.0 (2008-2012 5-year est.); Males per 100 females: 85.7 (2008-2012 5-year est.); Marriage status: 18.3% never married, 57.2% now married, 13.8% widowed, 10.7% divorced (2008-2012 5-year est.); Foreign born: 11.1% (2008-2012 5-year est.); Ancestry (includes multiple ancestries): 23.1% Irish, 19.2% German, 17.1% Polish, 12.0% Italian, 8.7% Lithuanian (2008-2012 5-year est.).

Economy: Single-family building permits issued: 2 (2013); Multi-family building permits issued: 0 (2013); Homeowner vacancy rate: 4.9%. Rental vacancy rate: 0.0%. (2008-2012 5-year est.); Employment by occupation: 26.9% management, business, and financial, 6.8% computer, engineering, and science, 8.1% education, legal, community service, arts, and media, 12.9% healthcare practitioners, 5.2% service, 25.7% sales and office, 5.9% natural resources, construction, and maintenance, 8.3% production, transportation, and material moving (2008-2012 5-year est.).

Income: Per capita income: $49,449 (2008-2012 5-year est.); Median household income: $81,970 (2008-2012 5-year est.); Average household income: $112,947 (2008-2012 5-year est.); Percent of households with

income of $100,000 or more: 43.2% (2008-2012 5-year est.); Poverty rate: 2.6% (2008-2012 5-year est.).

Education: Percent of population age 25 and over with: High school diploma (including GED) or higher: 97.0% (2008-2012 5-year est.); Bachelor's degree or higher: 46.2% (2008-2012 5-year est.); Master's degree or higher: 20.9% (2008-2012 5-year est.).

School District(s)

Palos CCSD 118 (PK-08)

    2011-12 Enrollment: 1,873 . . . . (708) 448-4800

Housing: Homeownership rate: 92.3% (2008-2012 5-year est.); Median home value: $418,800 (2008-2012 5-year est.); Median contract rent: $1,743 per month (2008-2012 5-year est.); Median year structure built: 1973 (2008-2012 5-year est.).

Health Insurance: 80.0% Private; 28.8% Public; 10.4% None. (2008-2012 5-year est.).

Safety: Violent crime rate: 8.2 per 10,000 population; Property crime rate: 82.1 per 10,000 population (2012).

Transportation: Commute to work: 86.8% car, 5.8% public transportation, 0.3% walk, 7.0% work from home (2008-2012 5-year est.); Travel time to work: 16.2% less than 15 minutes, 27.4% 15 to 30 minutes, 25.2% 30 to 45 minutes, 16.3% 45 to 60 minutes, 14.9% 60 minutes or more (2008-2012 5-year est.)

Additional Information Contacts

Palos Area Chamber of Commerce . . . . (708) 480-3025
    http://palosareachamber.org

PARK FOREST (village). Covers a land area of 4.962 square miles and a water area of 0 square miles. Located at 41.48° N. Lat; 87.69° W. Long. Elevation is 712 feet.

Population: 24,656 (1990); 23,462 (2000); 21,975 (2010); Density: 4,519.2 persons per square mile (2008-2012 5-year est.); Race: 31.6% White, 61.0% Black/African American, 2.2% Asian, 0.0% American Indian/Alaska Native, 0.0% Native Hawaiian/Other Pacific Islander, 5.2% Some other race, 3.2% Two or more races, 6.4% Hispanic of any race (2008-2012 5-year est.); Average household size: 2.56 (2008-2012 5-year est.); Median age: 36.2 (2008-2012 5-year est.); Males per 100 females: 90.4 (2008-2012 5-year est.); Marriage status: 42.6% never married, 37.0% now married, 6.9% widowed, 13.4% divorced (2008-2012 5-year est.); Foreign born: 3.6% (2008-2012 5-year est.); Ancestry (includes multiple ancestries): 9.4% German, 7.3% Irish, 4.4% English, 3.0% Italian, 2.5% Polish (2008-2012 5-year est.).

Economy: Unemployment rate: 8.1% (April 2014); Total civilian labor force: 11,886 (April 2014); Single-family building permits issued: 0 (2013); Multi-family building permits issued: 0 (2013); Homeowner vacancy rate: 1.7%. Rental vacancy rate: 10.0%. (2008-2012 5-year est.); Employment by occupation: 9.8% management, business, and financial, 2.2% computer, engineering, and science, 16.0% education, legal, community service, arts, and media, 6.3% healthcare practitioners, 18.8% service, 27.0% sales and office, 5.6% natural resources, construction, and maintenance, 14.3% production, transportation, and material moving (2008-2012 5-year est.).

Income: Per capita income: $21,705 (2008-2012 5-year est.); Median household income: $47,062 (2008-2012 5-year est.); Average household income: $54,512 (2008-2012 5-year est.); Percent of households with income of $100,000 or more: 11.1% (2008-2012 5-year est.); Poverty rate: 17.4% (2008-2012 5-year est.).

Taxes: Total city taxes per capita: $746 (2011); City property taxes per capita: $630 (2011).

Education: Percent of population age 25 and over with: High school diploma (including GED) or higher: 87.2% (2008-2012 5-year est.); Bachelor's degree or higher: 24.5% (2008-2012 5-year est.); Master's degree or higher: 9.7% (2008-2012 5-year est.).

School District(s)

Crete Monee CUSD 201u (PK-12)

    2011-12 Enrollment: 5,136 . . . . (708) 367-8300

Matteson ESD 162 (PK-08)

    2011-12 Enrollment: 3,180 . . . . (708) 748-0100

Park Forest SD 163 (PK-08)

    2011-12 Enrollment: 1,957 . . . . (708) 668-9400

Rich Twp HSD 227 (09-12)

    2011-12 Enrollment: 3,905 . . . . (708) 679-5800

Speed Seja #802 (PK-12)

    2011-12 Enrollment: n/a . . . . (708) 481-6100

Housing: Homeownership rate: 66.8% (2008-2012 5-year est.); Median home value: $98,800 (2008-2012 5-year est.); Median contract rent: $778

per month (2008-2012 5-year est.); Median year structure built: 1956 (2008-2012 5-year est.).

Health Insurance: 62.9% Private; 34.3% Public; 14.4% None. (2008-2012 5-year est.)

Safety: Violent crime rate: 29.9 per 10,000 population; Property crime rate: 316.0 per 10,000 population (2012).

Transportation: Commute to work: 84.3% car, 12.3% public transportation, 0.6% walk, 2.1% work from home (2008-2012 5-year est.); Travel time to work: 21.1% less than 15 minutes, 31.2% 15 to 30 minutes, 23.2% 30 to 45 minutes, 9.2% 45 to 60 minutes, 15.3% 60 minutes or more (2008-2012 5-year est.)

Additional Information Contacts

Matteson Area Chamber of Commerce. . . . . (708) 747-6000
    http://www.macclink.com

Village of Park Forest . . . . (708) 748-1112
    http://www.villageofparkforest.com

PARK RIDGE (city). Covers a land area of 7.090 square miles and a water area of 0.044 square miles. Located at 42.01° N. Lat; 87.84° W. Long. Elevation is 643 feet.

History: Named for its location on a mountain ridge, and the pleasant parklike surroundings. Park Ridge began in 1853 when George Penny started a brickyard and lumberyard. Residents called the town Pennyville, but changed it to Brickton when Penny protested. When the clay from which the bricks were produced was gone and the Chicago & North Western Railway had arrived, Brickton became a commuting suburb and changed its name to Park Ridge.

Population: 36,175 (1990); 37,775 (2000); 37,480 (2010); Density: 5,256.4 persons per square mile (2008-2012 5-year est.); Race: 93.5% White, 1.2% Black/African American, 3.4% Asian, 0.0% American Indian/Alaska Native, 0.0% Native Hawaiian/Other Pacific Islander, 1.9% Some other race, 1.0% Two or more races, 5.4% Hispanic of any race (2008-2012 5-year est.); Average household size: 2.64 (2008-2012 5-year est.); Median age: 44.4 (2008-2012 5-year est.); Males per 100 females: 91.7 (2008-2012 5-year est.); Marriage status: 26.6% never married, 59.0% now married, 7.0% widowed, 7.5% divorced (2008-2012 5-year est.); Foreign born: 15.2% (2008-2012 5-year est.); Ancestry (includes multiple ancestries): 22.3% Irish, 22.2% German, 20.3% Polish, 14.2% Italian, 6.3% English (2008-2012 5-year est.).

Economy: Unemployment rate: 5.6% (April 2014); Total civilian labor force: 19,520 (April 2014); Single-family building permits issued: 24 (2013); Multi-family building permits issued: 0 (2013); Homeowner vacancy rate: 0.4%. Rental vacancy rate: 6.6%. (2008-2012 5-year est.); Employment by occupation: 24.3% management, business, and financial, 6.4% computer, engineering, and science, 13.5% education, legal, community service, arts, and media, 8.1% healthcare practitioners, 11.5% service, 26.3% sales and office, 4.6% natural resources, construction, and maintenance, 5.2% production, transportation, and material moving (2008-2012 5-year est.).

Income: Per capita income: $43,003 (2008-2012 5-year est.); Median household income: $86,621 (2008-2012 5-year est.); Average household income: $113,035 (2008-2012 5-year est.); Percent of households with income of $100,000 or more: 43.9% (2008-2012 5-year est.); Poverty rate: 3.6% (2008-2012 5-year est.).

Taxes: Total city taxes per capita: $803 (2011); City property taxes per capita: $508 (2011).

Education: Percent of population age 25 and over with: High school diploma (including GED) or higher: 95.4% (2008-2012 5-year est.); Bachelor's degree or higher: 53.4% (2008-2012 5-year est.); Master's degree or higher: 23.0% (2008-2012 5-year est.).

School District(s)

Maine Township HSD 207 (06-12)

    2011-12 Enrollment: 5,097 . . . . (847) 696-3600

Park Ridge CCSD 64 (PK-08)

    2011-12 Enrollment: 4,317 . . . . (847) 318-4300

Housing: Homeownership rate: 84.7% (2008-2012 5-year est.); Median home value: $421,800 (2008-2012 5-year est.); Median contract rent: $1,083 per month (2008-2012 5-year est.); Median year structure built: 1957 (2008-2012 5-year est.).

Health Insurance: 85.0% Private; 23.4% Public; 6.4% None. (2008-2012 5-year est.)

Hospitals: Advocate Lutheran General Children's Hospital

Safety: Violent crime rate: 5.8 per 10,000 population; Property crime rate: 121.9 per 10,000 population (2012).

Transportation: Commute to work: 79.0% car, 10.4% public transportation, 3.8% walk, 5.8% work from home (2008-2012 5-year est.);

Travel time to work: 26.5% less than 15 minutes, 27.5% 15 to 30 minutes, 25.0% 30 to 45 minutes, 11.7% 45 to 60 minutes, 9.2% 60 minutes or more (2008-2012 5-year est.)

Additional Information Contacts

City of Park Ridge . . . . (847) 318-5200
  http://www.parkridge.us

Park Ridge Chamber of Commerce . . . . (847) 825-3121
  http://www.parkridgechamber.org

PHOENIX (village). Covers a land area of 0.450 square miles and a water area of 0 square miles. Located at 41.61° N. Lat; 87.63° W. Long. Elevation is 600 feet.

History: Phoenix developed as a residential outgrowth of its neighbor, Harvey.

Population: 2,217 (1990); 2,157 (2000); 1,964 (2010); Density: 4,197.2 persons per square mile (2008-2012 5-year est.); Race: 7.5% White, 88.5% Black/African American, 0.2% Asian, 0.0% American Indian/Alaska Native, 0.0% Native Hawaiian/Other Pacific Islander, 3.8% Some other race, 2.8% Two or more races, 7.3% Hispanic of any race (2008-2012 5-year est.); Average household size: 2.41 (2008-2012 5-year est.); Median age: 39.8 (2008-2012 5-year est.); Males per 100 females: 93.9 (2008-2012 5-year est.); Marriage status: 44.9% never married, 32.0% now married, 12.7% widowed, 10.4% divorced (2008-2012 5-year est.); Foreign born: 4.7% (2008-2012 5-year est.); Ancestry (includes multiple ancestries): 2.4% Italian, 1.5% African, 1.3% Jamaican, 1.1% Canadian, 1.0% German (2008-2012 5-year est.).

Economy: Single-family building permits issued: 0 (2013); Multi-family building permits issued: 0 (2013); Homeowner vacancy rate: 1.7%. Rental vacancy rate: 10.2%. (2008-2012 5-year est.); Employment by occupation: 6.8% management, business, and financial, 1.2% computer, engineering, and science, 15.1% education, legal, community service, arts, and media, 3.8% healthcare practitioners, 21.0% service, 27.4% sales and office, 8.9% natural resources, construction, and maintenance, 15.7% production, transportation, and material moving (2008-2012 5-year est.).

Income: Per capita income: $16,902 (2008-2012 5-year est.); Median household income: $28,289 (2008-2012 5-year est.); Average household income: $38,718 (2008-2012 5-year est.); Percent of households with income of $100,000 or more: 4.6% (2008-2012 5-year est.); Poverty rate: 32.6% (2008-2012 5-year est.).

Education: Percent of population age 25 and over with: High school diploma (including GED) or higher: 78.6% (2008-2012 5-year est.); Bachelor's degree or higher: 10.3% (2008-2012 5-year est.); Master's degree or higher: 5.8% (2008-2012 5-year est.).

School District(s)

South Holland SD 151 (PK-08)
  2011-12 Enrollment: 1,494 . . . . (708) 339-1516

Housing: Homeownership rate: 57.4% (2008-2012 5-year est.); Median home value: $90,000 (2008-2012 5-year est.); Median contract rent: $550 per month (2008-2012 5-year est.); Median year structure built: 1960 (2008-2012 5-year est.).

Health Insurance: 39.8% Private; 51.0% Public; 22.2% None. (2008-2012 5-year est.)

Safety: Violent crime rate: 55.8 per 10,000 population; Property crime rate: 192.6 per 10,000 population (2012).

Transportation: Commute to work: 80.2% car, 8.4% public transportation, 5.9% walk, 2.9% work from home (2008-2012 5-year est.); Travel time to work: 29.5% less than 15 minutes, 26.5% 15 to 30 minutes, 19.9% 30 to 45 minutes, 8.3% 45 to 60 minutes, 15.8% 60 minutes or more (2008-2012 5-year est.)

POSEN (village). Covers a land area of 1.169 square miles and a water area of 0 square miles. Located at 41.63° N. Lat; 87.69° W. Long. Elevation is 600 feet.

History: Posen was settled in 1893 when a Chicago realtor sold 12,000 lots, mostly to Polish immigrants. Posen was incorporated in 1901.

Population: 4,226 (1990); 4,730 (2000); 5,987 (2010); Density: 5,110.7 persons per square mile (2008-2012 5-year est.); Race: 54.4% White, 27.1% Black/African American, 0.0% Asian, 0.5% American Indian/Alaska Native, 0.0% Native Hawaiian/Other Pacific Islander, 18.0% Some other race, 0.5% Two or more races, 47.8% Hispanic of any race (2008-2012 5-year est.); Average household size: 3.38 (2008-2012 5-year est.); Median age: 31.0 (2008-2012 5-year est.); Males per 100 females: 104.0 (2008-2012 5-year est.); Marriage status: 41.5% never married, 48.1% now married, 4.7% widowed, 5.7% divorced (2008-2012 5-year est.); Foreign born: 28.9% (2008-2012 5-year est.); Ancestry (includes multiple

ancestries): 7.2% Polish, 6.3% Irish, 6.2% German, 3.0% Nigerian, 2.2% American (2008-2012 5-year est.).

Economy: Single-family building permits issued: 0 (2013); Multi-family building permits issued: 0 (2013); Homeowner vacancy rate: 0.0%. Rental vacancy rate: 14.4%. (2008-2012 5-year est.); Employment by occupation: 9.4% management, business, and financial, 1.9% computer, engineering, and science, 2.1% education, legal, community service, arts, and media, 1.4% healthcare practitioners, 34.0% service, 17.6% sales and office, 24.0% natural resources, construction, and maintenance, 9.6% production, transportation, and material moving (2008-2012 5-year est.).

Income: Per capita income: $15,912 (2008-2012 5-year est.); Median household income: $49,400 (2008-2012 5-year est.); Average household income: $52,902 (2008-2012 5-year est.); Percent of households with income of $100,000 or more: 12.8% (2008-2012 5-year est.); Poverty rate: 12.8% (2008-2012 5-year est.).

Education: Percent of population age 25 and over with: High school diploma (including GED) or higher: 71.0% (2008-2012 5-year est.); Bachelor's degree or higher: 10.1% (2008-2012 5-year est.); Master's degree or higher: 2.7% (2008-2012 5-year est.).

School District(s)

Posen-Robbins ESD 143-5 (PK-08)
  2011-12 Enrollment: 1,850 . . . . (708) 388-7200

Housing: Homeownership rate: 75.7% (2008-2012 5-year est.); Median home value: $152,900 (2008-2012 5-year est.); Median contract rent: $724 per month (2008-2012 5-year est.); Median year structure built: 1973 (2008-2012 5-year est.).

Health Insurance: 54.2% Private; 31.4% Public; 25.1% None. (2008-2012 5-year est.)

Safety: Violent crime rate: 21.6 per 10,000 population; Property crime rate: 267.6 per 10,000 population (2012).

Transportation: Commute to work: 95.6% car, 3.8% public transportation, 0.6% walk, 0.0% work from home (2008-2012 5-year est.); Travel time to work: 8.6% less than 15 minutes, 23.1% 15 to 30 minutes, 32.8% 30 to 45 minutes, 13.1% 45 to 60 minutes, 22.3% 60 minutes or more (2008-2012 5-year est.)

Additional Information Contacts

Village of Posen . . . . (708) 385-0139
  http://www.villageofposen.org

PROSPECT HEIGHTS (city). Covers a land area of 4.237 square miles and a water area of 0.029 square miles. Located at 42.10° N. Lat; 87.92° W. Long. Elevation is 669 feet.

Population: 15,239 (1990); 17,081 (2000); 16,256 (2010); Density: 3,829.8 persons per square mile (2008-2012 5-year est.); Race: 88.0% White, 1.0% Black/African American, 5.5% Asian, 0.1% American Indian/Alaska Native, 0.0% Native Hawaiian/Other Pacific Islander, 5.4% Some other race, 0.7% Two or more races, 31.0% Hispanic of any race (2008-2012 5-year est.); Average household size: 2.60 (2008-2012 5-year est.); Median age: 38.1 (2008-2012 5-year est.); Males per 100 females: 100.2 (2008-2012 5-year est.); Marriage status: 26.5% never married, 60.7% now married, 5.2% widowed, 7.6% divorced (2008-2012 5-year est.); Foreign born: 40.8% (2008-2012 5-year est.); Ancestry (includes multiple ancestries): 19.1% Polish, 12.1% German, 8.6% Irish, 4.9% Italian, 4.0% English (2008-2012 5-year est.).

Economy: Single-family building permits issued: 16 (2013); Multi-family building permits issued: 0 (2013); Homeowner vacancy rate: 3.8%. Rental vacancy rate: 4.3%. (2008-2012 5-year est.); Employment by occupation: 14.4% management, business, and financial, 5.7% computer, engineering, and science, 6.6% education, legal, community service, arts, and media, 3.8% healthcare practitioners, 20.9% service, 23.7% sales and office, 8.5% natural resources, construction, and maintenance, 16.5% production, transportation, and material moving (2008-2012 5-year est.).

Income: Per capita income: $31,840 (2008-2012 5-year est.); Median household income: $61,500 (2008-2012 5-year est.); Average household income: $80,425 (2008-2012 5-year est.); Percent of households with income of $100,000 or more: 19.7% (2008-2012 5-year est.); Poverty rate: 10.4% (2008-2012 5-year est.).

Education: Percent of population age 25 and over with: High school diploma (including GED) or higher: 85.0% (2008-2012 5-year est.); Bachelor's degree or higher: 35.0% (2008-2012 5-year est.); Master's degree or higher: 12.6% (2008-2012 5-year est.).

School District(s)

Prospect Heights SD 23 (PK-08)
  2011-12 Enrollment: 1,484 . . . . (847) 870-5550

Housing: Homeownership rate: 75.5% (2008-2012 5-year est.); Median home value: $284,600 (2008-2012 5-year est.); Median contract rent: $916 per month (2008-2012 5-year est.); Median year structure built: 1974 (2008-2012 5-year est.).

Health Insurance: 63.8% Private; 29.0% Public; 18.3% None. (2008-2012 5-year est.)

Safety: Violent crime rate: 8.6 per 10,000 population; Property crime rate: 86.9 per 10,000 population (2012).

Transportation: Commute to work: 88.8% car, 2.8% public transportation, 1.6% walk, 6.8% work from home (2008-2012 5-year est.); Travel time to work: 20.6% less than 15 minutes, 36.6% 15 to 30 minutes, 29.4% 30 to 45 minutes, 6.9% 45 to 60 minutes, 6.5% 60 minutes or more (2008-2012 5-year est.)

Airports: Chicago Executive Airport (reliver airport)

Additional Information Contacts

City of Prospect Heights . . . . (847) 398-6070
　http://www.prospect-heights.il.us
Wheeling/Prospect Heights Area Chamber of Commerce & Industr . . (847) 541-0170
　http://www.wphchamber.com

RICHTON PARK (village). Aka Richton. Covers a land area of 3.982 square miles and a water area of 0.012 square miles. Located at 41.48° N. Lat; 87.74° W. Long. Elevation is 725 feet.

Population: 10,523 (1990); 12,533 (2000); 13,646 (2010); Density: 3,407.1 persons per square mile (2008-2012 5-year est.); Race: 13.9% White, 80.2% Black/African American, 2.8% Asian, 0.2% American Indian/Alaska Native, 0.0% Native Hawaiian/Other Pacific Islander, 2.9% Some other race, 1.9% Two or more races, 5.6% Hispanic of any race (2008-2012 5-year est.); Average household size: 2.56 (2008-2012 5-year est.); Median age: 37.6 (2008-2012 5-year est.); Males per 100 females: 79.0 (2008-2012 5-year est.); Marriage status: 41.0% never married, 40.9% now married, 5.0% widowed, 13.2% divorced (2008-2012 5-year est.); Foreign born: 3.8% (2008-2012 5-year est.); Ancestry (includes multiple ancestries): 4.5% German, 3.3% Irish, 2.7% Polish, 1.8% English, 1.1% African (2008-2012 5-year est.).

Economy: Single-family building permits issued: 0 (2013); Multi-family building permits issued: 0 (2013); Homeowner vacancy rate: 1.1%. Rental vacancy rate: 13.4%. (2008-2012 5-year est.); Employment by occupation: 14.7% management, business, and financial, 5.1% computer, engineering, and science, 11.7% education, legal, community service, arts, and media, 8.0% healthcare practitioners, 12.4% service, 28.3% sales and office, 4.6% natural resources, construction, and maintenance, 15.1% production, transportation, and material moving (2008-2012 5-year est.).

Income: Per capita income: $27,636 (2008-2012 5-year est.); Median household income: $60,516 (2008-2012 5-year est.); Average household income: $69,230 (2008-2012 5-year est.); Percent of households with income of $100,000 or more: 22.6% (2008-2012 5-year est.); Poverty rate: 11.7% (2008-2012 5-year est.).

Taxes: Total city taxes per capita: $493 (2011); City property taxes per capita: $359 (2011).

Education: Percent of population age 25 and over with: High school diploma (including GED) or higher: 93.0% (2008-2012 5-year est.); Bachelor's degree or higher: 30.7% (2008-2012 5-year est.); Master's degree or higher: 10.6% (2008-2012 5-year est.).

School District(s)

ESD 159 (PK-08)
　2011-12 Enrollment: 1,967 . . . . (708) 720-1300
Matteson ESD 162 (PK-08)
　2011-12 Enrollment: 3,180 . . . . (708) 748-0100
Rich Twp HSD 227 (09-12)
　2011-12 Enrollment: 3,905 . . . . (708) 679-5800
Southland College Prep (09-12)
　2011-12 Enrollment: 249. . . . . (708) 747-0301

Housing: Homeownership rate: 63.5% (2008-2012 5-year est.); Median home value: $168,600 (2008-2012 5-year est.); Median contract rent: $825 per month (2008-2012 5-year est.); Median year structure built: 1978 (2008-2012 5-year est.).

Health Insurance: 68.0% Private; 28.8% Public; 11.6% None. (2008-2012 5-year est.)

Safety: Violent crime rate: 34.3 per 10,000 population; Property crime rate: 257.5 per 10,000 population (2012).

Transportation: Commute to work: 82.3% car, 9.5% public transportation, 3.2% walk, 0.8% work from home (2008-2012 5-year est.); Travel time to work: 22.7% less than 15 minutes, 26.7% 15 to 30 minutes, 24.1% 30 to

45 minutes, 6.9% 45 to 60 minutes, 19.6% 60 minutes or more (2008-2012 5-year est.)

Additional Information Contacts

Matteson Area Chamber of Commerce . . . . (708) 747-6000
　http://www.macclink.com
Village of Richton Park . . . . (708) 481-8950
　http://www.richtonpark.org

RIVER FOREST (village). Covers a land area of 2.475 square miles and a water area of 0.002 square miles. Located at 41.89° N. Lat; 87.82° W. Long. Elevation is 630 feet.

History: Named for the forest along the Des Plaines River. River Forest was settled in 1836 by the Ashbel Steele family. Another early resident was Daniel Cunningham Thatcher, a Chicago businessman who retired to River Forest in 1854. In 1862 Thatcher persuaded the Chicago & North Western Railway to build a station on his property, which was called Thatcher. For ten years, River Forest was known as Thatcher, but in 1880 the community was organized as the Village of River Forest.

Population: 11,669 (1990); 11,635 (2000); 11,172 (2010); Density: 4,514.3 persons per square mile (2008-2012 5-year est.); Race: 84.5% White, 6.0% Black/African American, 4.9% Asian, 0.1% American Indian/Alaska Native, 0.0% Native Hawaiian/Other Pacific Islander, 4.5% Some other race, 3.2% Two or more races, 4.9% Hispanic of any race (2008-2012 5-year est.); Average household size: 2.68 (2008-2012 5-year est.); Median age: 41.3 (2008-2012 5-year est.); Males per 100 females: 93.3 (2008-2012 5-year est.); Marriage status: 33.2% never married, 55.7% now married, 3.7% widowed, 7.5% divorced (2008-2012 5-year est.); Foreign born: 8.9% (2008-2012 5-year est.); Ancestry (includes multiple ancestries): 28.0% Irish, 24.3% German, 13.2% English, 10.3% Italian, 8.0% Polish (2008-2012 5-year est.).

Economy: Single-family building permits issued: 2 (2013); Multi-family building permits issued: 0 (2013); Homeowner vacancy rate: 3.8%. Rental vacancy rate: 4.0%. (2008-2012 5-year est.); Employment by occupation: 25.4% management, business, and financial, 5.5% computer, engineering, and science, 22.2% education, legal, community service, arts, and media, 11.2% healthcare practitioners, 9.3% service, 22.3% sales and office, 1.0% natural resources, construction, and maintenance, 3.0% production, transportation, and material moving (2008-2012 5-year est.).

Income: Per capita income: $64,856 (2008-2012 5-year est.); Median household income: $121,250 (2008-2012 5-year est.); Average household income: $186,834 (2008-2012 5-year est.); Percent of households with income of $100,000 or more: 55.1% (2008-2012 5-year est.); Poverty rate: 5.6% (2008-2012 5-year est.).

Taxes: Total city taxes per capita: $956 (2011); City property taxes per capita: $738 (2011).

Education: Percent of population age 25 and over with: High school diploma (including GED) or higher: 97.1% (2008-2012 5-year est.); Bachelor's degree or higher: 75.2% (2008-2012 5-year est.); Master's degree or higher: 39.1% (2008-2012 5-year est.).

School District(s)

River Forest SD 90 (PK-08)
　2011-12 Enrollment: 1,338 . . . . (708) 771-8282

Four-year College(s)

Concordia University-Chicago (Private, Not-for-profit, Lutheran Church - Missouri Synod)
　Fall 2012 Enrollment: 5,454 . . . . (708) 771-8300
　2012-13 Tuition: In-state $26,476; Out-of-state $26,476
Dominican University (Private, Not-for-profit, Roman Catholic)
　Fall 2012 Enrollment: 3,589 . . . . (708) 366-2490
　2012-13 Tuition: In-state $27,730; Out-of-state $27,730

Housing: Homeownership rate: 92.7% (2008-2012 5-year est.); Median home value: $583,300 (2008-2012 5-year est.); Median contract rent: $959 per month (2008-2012 5-year est.); Median year structure built: 1940 (2008-2012 5-year est.).

Health Insurance: 91.9% Private; 15.0% Public; 4.6% None. (2008-2012 5-year est.)

Safety: Violent crime rate: 15.1 per 10,000 population; Property crime rate: 269.1 per 10,000 population (2012).

Transportation: Commute to work: 62.7% car, 17.6% public transportation, 6.8% walk, 11.0% work from home (2008-2012 5-year est.); Travel time to work: 26.7% less than 15 minutes, 21.4% 15 to 30 minutes, 26.8% 30 to 45 minutes, 16.2% 45 to 60 minutes, 8.9% 60 minutes or more (2008-2012 5-year est.)

Additional Information Contacts

Oak Park-River Forest Chamber of Commerce .... (708) 613-0550
　http://www.oprfchamber.org
Village of River Forest............................... (708) 366-8500
　http://www.vrf.us

RIVER GROVE (village).
Covers a land area of 2.392 square miles and a water area of 0 square miles. Located at 41.92° N. Lat; 87.84° W. Long. Elevation is 627 feet.

History: Triton College. Incorporated 1888.

Population: 9,961 (1990); 10,668 (2000); 10,227 (2010); Density: 4,274.7 persons per square mile (2008-2012 5-year est.); Race: 84.9% White, 1.7% Black/African American, 4.0% Asian, 0.2% American Indian/Alaska Native, 0.0% Native Hawaiian/Other Pacific Islander, 9.2% Some other race, 1.9% Two or more races, 21.0% Hispanic of any race (2008-2012 5-year est.); Average household size: 2.49 (2008-2012 5-year est.); Median age: 35.7 (2008-2012 5-year est.); Males per 100 females: 90.0 (2008-2012 5-year est.); Marriage status: 32.9% never married, 49.3% now married, 7.2% widowed, 10.6% divorced (2008-2012 5-year est.); Foreign born: 35.5% (2008-2012 5-year est.); Ancestry (includes multiple ancestries): 32.8% Polish, 12.1% Italian, 10.6% German, 8.4% Irish, 2.2% American (2008-2012 5-year est.).

Economy: Single-family building permits issued: 1 (2013); Multi-family building permits issued: 0 (2013); Homeowner vacancy rate: 2.6%. Rental vacancy rate: 8.9%. (2008-2012 5-year est.); Employment by occupation: 8.4% management, business, and financial, 3.3% computer, engineering, and science, 5.6% education, legal, community service, arts, and media, 5.3% healthcare practitioners, 19.9% service, 30.2% sales and office, 14.0% natural resources, construction, and maintenance, 13.3% production, transportation, and material moving (2008-2012 5-year est.).

Income: Per capita income: $23,423 (2008-2012 5-year est.); Median household income: $47,584 (2008-2012 5-year est.); Average household income: $56,261 (2008-2012 5-year est.); Percent of households with income of $100,000 or more: 11.9% (2008-2012 5-year est.); Poverty rate: 11.2% (2008-2012 5-year est.).

Education: Percent of population age 25 and over with: High school diploma (including GED) or higher: 85.4% (2008-2012 5-year est.); Bachelor's degree or higher: 22.8% (2008-2012 5-year est.); Master's degree or higher: 9.0% (2008-2012 5-year est.).

School District(s)
Rhodes SD 84-5 (PK-08)
　2011-12 Enrollment: 684........................ (708) 453-1266
River Grove SD 85-5 (KG-08)
　2011-12 Enrollment: 598........................ (708) 453-6172

Two-year College(s)
Triton College (Public)
　Fall 2012 Enrollment: 13,897 .... (708) 456-0300
　2012-13 Tuition: In-state $8,042; Out-of-state $9,994

Housing: Homeownership rate: 61.5% (2008-2012 5-year est.); Median home value: $205,300 (2008-2012 5-year est.); Median contract rent: $762 per month (2008-2012 5-year est.); Median year structure built: 1959 (2008-2012 5-year est.).

Health Insurance: 56.0% Private; 30.4% Public; 23.4% None. (2008-2012 5-year est.).

Safety: Violent crime rate: 8.8 per 10,000 population; Property crime rate: 219.9 per 10,000 population (2012).

Transportation: Commute to work: 87.6% car, 5.5% public transportation, 3.5% walk, 1.3% work from home (2008-2012 5-year est.); Travel time to work: 19.6% less than 15 minutes, 27.1% 15 to 30 minutes, 31.7% 30 to 45 minutes, 6.5% 45 to 60 minutes, 15.1% 60 minutes or more (2008-2012 5-year est.)

Additional Information Contacts
Grand Corridor Chamber of Commerce .... (708) 456-8000
　http://www.grandchamber.org
River Grove Area Chamber of Commerce .... (708) 452-8259
　http://villageofrivergrove.org/organizations.html
Village of River Grove .... (708) 453-8000
　http://villageofrivergrove.org

RIVERDALE (village).
Covers a land area of 3.574 square miles and a water area of 0.175 square miles. Located at 41.64° N. Lat; 87.64° W. Long. Elevation is 600 feet.

History: Named for its location along the Calumet River, by Frederick C. Schmidt. Riverdale began when George Dolton and J.C. Matthews established a ferry across the Little Calumet River in 1836. The town later became a railroad center and a steel manufacturing area.

Population: 13,671 (1990); 15,055 (2000); 13,549 (2010); Density: 3,791.5 persons per square mile (2008-2012 5-year est.); Race: 5.7% White, 92.5% Black/African American, 0.0% Asian, 0.0% American Indian/Alaska Native, 0.0% Native Hawaiian/Other Pacific Islander, 1.8% Some other race, 1.6% Two or more races, 1.4% Hispanic of any race (2008-2012 5-year est.); Average household size: 2.84 (2008-2012 5-year est.); Median age: 32.1 (2008-2012 5-year est.); Males per 100 females: 79.9 (2008-2012 5-year est.); Marriage status: 53.3% never married, 29.2% now married, 5.4% widowed, 12.1% divorced (2008-2012 5-year est.); Foreign born: 1.4% (2008-2012 5-year est.); Ancestry (includes multiple ancestries): 1.0% African, 0.8% Polish, 0.8% Irish, 0.8% English, 0.8% German (2008-2012 5-year est.).

Economy: Single-family building permits issued: 0 (2013); Multi-family building permits issued: 0 (2013); Homeowner vacancy rate: 4.7%. Rental vacancy rate: 10.4%. (2008-2012 5-year est.); Employment by occupation: 7.4% management, business, and financial, 2.6% computer, engineering, and science, 10.2% education, legal, community service, arts, and media, 5.8% healthcare practitioners, 21.4% service, 28.4% sales and office, 6.3% natural resources, construction, and maintenance, 18.0% production, transportation, and material moving (2008-2012 5-year est.).

Income: Per capita income: $17,143 (2008-2012 5-year est.); Median household income: $40,650 (2008-2012 5-year est.); Average household income: $46,436 (2008-2012 5-year est.); Percent of households with income of $100,000 or more: 7.0% (2008-2012 5-year est.); Poverty rate: 22.6% (2008-2012 5-year est.).

Taxes: Total city taxes per capita: $700 (2011); City property taxes per capita: $571 (2011).

Education: Percent of population age 25 and over with: High school diploma (including GED) or higher: 87.2% (2008-2012 5-year est.); Bachelor's degree or higher: 14.0% (2008-2012 5-year est.); Master's degree or higher: 4.3% (2008-2012 5-year est.).

School District(s)
Dolton SD 148 (PK-08)
　2011-12 Enrollment: 2,446 .... (708) 841-2290
Exc Children Have Opportunities (KG-12)
　2011-12 Enrollment: n/a .... (708) 333-7880
Gen George Patton SD 133 (PK-08)
　2011-12 Enrollment: 430 .... (708) 841-3955

Housing: Homeownership rate: 48.8% (2008-2012 5-year est.); Median home value: $95,800 (2008-2012 5-year est.); Median contract rent: $791 per month (2008-2012 5-year est.); Median year structure built: 1958 (2008-2012 5-year est.).

Health Insurance: 48.2% Private; 39.0% Public; 20.1% None. (2008-2012 5-year est.).

Safety: Violent crime rate: 130.7 per 10,000 population; Property crime rate: 361.4 per 10,000 population (2012).

Transportation: Commute to work: 79.3% car, 15.0% public transportation, 2.9% walk, 2.0% work from home (2008-2012 5-year est.); Travel time to work: 11.6% less than 15 minutes, 25.5% 15 to 30 minutes, 29.7% 30 to 45 minutes, 15.2% 45 to 60 minutes, 18.0% 60 minutes or more (2008-2012 5-year est.)

Additional Information Contacts
Riverdale Chamber of Commerce................... (708) 841-3311
　http://www.district148.net/rcoc
Village of Riverdale............................ (708) 841-2200
　http://www.villageofriverdale.org

RIVERSIDE (village).
Covers a land area of 1.978 square miles and a water area of 0.018 square miles. Located at 41.83° N. Lat; 87.82° W. Long. Elevation is 617 feet.

History: Riverside originated in 1866 with the plan of the Riverside Improvement Company to create an ideal suburb. They commissioned Olmsted and Vaux, New York landscape architects who had designed Central Park. The site for Riverside was selected for its forested terrain, the railroad facilities, and the Des Plaines River whose winding course determined the layout of the town. Incorporated 1923.

Population: 8,774 (1990); 8,895 (2000); 8,875 (2010); Density: 4,477.8 persons per square mile (2008-2012 5-year est.); Race: 87.2% White, 0.3% Black/African American, 2.1% Asian, 0.2% American Indian/Alaska Native, 1.3% Native Hawaiian/Other Pacific Islander, 8.9% Some other race, 1.7% Two or more races, 13.9% Hispanic of any race (2008-2012 5-year est.); Average household size: 2.70 (2008-2012 5-year est.); Median age: 41.6 (2008-2012 5-year est.); Males per 100 females: 97.0 (2008-2012 5-year est.); Marriage status: 28.1% never married, 62.4% now married, 4.4% widowed, 5.1% divorced (2008-2012 5-year est.);

Foreign born: 10.0% (2008-2012 5-year est.); Ancestry (includes multiple ancestries): 22.1% German, 21.0% Irish, 15.1% Polish, 14.4% Italian, 11.1% Czech (2008-2012 5-year est.).

Economy: Single-family building permits issued: 0 (2013); Multi-family building permits issued: 0 (2013); Homeowner vacancy rate: 0.7%. Rental vacancy rate: 12.5%. (2008-2012 5-year est.); Employment by occupation: 21.6% management, business, and financial, 6.7% computer, engineering, and science, 19.0% education, legal, community service, arts, and media, 9.3% healthcare practitioners, 11.4% service, 22.4% sales and office, 4.9% natural resources, construction, and maintenance, 4.7% production, transportation, and material moving (2008-2012 5-year est.).

Income: Per capita income: $48,230 (2008-2012 5-year est.); Median household income: $95,156 (2008-2012 5-year est.); Average household income: $129,270 (2008-2012 5-year est.); Percent of households with income of $100,000 or more: 47.2% (2008-2012 5-year est.); Poverty rate: 3.6% (2008-2012 5-year est.).

Education: Percent of population age 25 and over with: High school diploma (including GED) or higher: 94.5% (2008-2012 5-year est.); Bachelor's degree or higher: 60.5% (2008-2012 5-year est.); Master's degree or higher: 31.7% (2008-2012 5-year est.).

School District(s)

Riverside SD 96 (PK-08)
    2011-12 Enrollment: 1,579 . . . . (708) 447-5007
Riverside-Brookfield Twp SD 208 (09-12)
    2011-12 Enrollment: 1,465 . . . . (708) 442-7500

Housing: Homeownership rate: 81.4% (2008-2012 5-year est.); Median home value: $386,700 (2008-2012 5-year est.); Median contract rent: $825 per month (2008-2012 5-year est.); Median year structure built: Before 1940 (2008-2012 5-year est.).

Health Insurance: 88.2% Private; 17.5% Public; 6.2% None. (2008-2012 5-year est.)

Safety: Violent crime rate: 2.2 per 10,000 population; Property crime rate: 155.8 per 10,000 population (2012).

Transportation: Commute to work: 70.9% car, 16.4% public transportation, 2.6% walk, 8.4% work from home (2008-2012 5-year est.); Travel time to work: 19.7% less than 15 minutes, 30.8% 15 to 30 minutes, 23.6% 30 to 45 minutes, 13.5% 45 to 60 minutes, 12.4% 60 minutes or more (2008-2012 5-year est.)

Additional Information Contacts

Riverside Chamber of Commerce . . . . (708) 447-8510
    http://www.riversidechamberofcommerce.com
Village of Riverside . . . . (708) 447-2700
    http://riverside.il.us

ROBBINS (village). Covers a land area of 1.449 square miles and a water area of 0 square miles. Located at 41.64° N. Lat; 87.71° W. Long. Elevation is 600 feet.

History: Robbins, named for realtor and developer Eugene S. Robbins, was organized as a residential area and incorporated in 1917.

Population: 7,498 (1990); 6,635 (2000); 5,337 (2010); Density: 3,542.1 persons per square mile (2008-2012 5-year est.); Race: 4.7% White, 95.3% Black/African American, 0.0% Asian, 0.0% American Indian/Alaska Native, 0.0% Native Hawaiian/Other Pacific Islander, 0.0% Some other race, 0.0% Two or more races, 0.4% Hispanic of any race (2008-2012 5-year est.); Average household size: 2.47 (2008-2012 5-year est.); Median age: 43.9 (2008-2012 5-year est.); Males per 100 females: 128.0 (2008-2012 5-year est.); Marriage status: 45.5% never married, 26.6% now married, 11.0% widowed, 16.8% divorced (2008-2012 5-year est.); Foreign born: 2.8% (2008-2012 5-year est.); Ancestry (includes multiple ancestries): 2.2% Liberian, 1.8% West Indian, 1.5% English, 1.4% American, 0.8% African (2008-2012 5-year est.).

Economy: Single-family building permits issued: 14 (2013); Multi-family building permits issued: 0 (2013); Homeowner vacancy rate: 0.0%. Rental vacancy rate: 6.7%. (2008-2012 5-year est.); Employment by occupation: 3.8% management, business, and financial, 4.3% computer, engineering, and science, 6.7% education, legal, community service, arts, and media, 4.9% healthcare practitioners, 22.2% service, 20.4% sales and office, 5.0% natural resources, construction, and maintenance, 32.7% production, transportation, and material moving (2008-2012 5-year est.).

Income: Per capita income: $14,579 (2008-2012 5-year est.); Median household income: $21,765 (2008-2012 5-year est.); Average household income: $35,889 (2008-2012 5-year est.); Percent of households with income of $100,000 or more: 3.9% (2008-2012 5-year est.); Poverty rate: 27.6% (2008-2012 5-year est.).

Taxes: Total city taxes per capita: $196 (2011); City property taxes per capita: $121 (2011).

Education: Percent of population age 25 and over with: High school diploma (including GED) or higher: 75.2% (2008-2012 5-year est.); Bachelor's degree or higher: 9.3% (2008-2012 5-year est.); Master's degree or higher: 0.3% (2008-2012 5-year est.).

School District(s)

CHSD 218 (09-12)
    2011-12 Enrollment: 5,671 . . . . (708) 424-2000
Posen-Robbins ESD 143-5 (PK-08)
    2011-12 Enrollment: 1,850 . . . . (708) 388-7200

Housing: Homeownership rate: 47.6% (2008-2012 5-year est.); Median home value: $74,800 (2008-2012 5-year est.); Median contract rent: $622 per month (2008-2012 5-year est.); Median year structure built: 1962 (2008-2012 5-year est.).

Health Insurance: 41.0% Private; 52.5% Public; 17.8% None. (2008-2012 5-year est.)

Transportation: Commute to work: 80.5% car, 13.7% public transportation, 0.0% walk, 4.9% work from home (2008-2012 5-year est.); Travel time to work: 22.0% less than 15 minutes, 35.3% 15 to 30 minutes, 20.3% 30 to 45 minutes, 7.2% 45 to 60 minutes, 15.2% 60 minutes or more (2008-2012 5-year est.)

ROLLING MEADOWS (city). Covers a land area of 5.632 square miles and a water area of 0.005 square miles. Located at 42.07° N. Lat; 88.03° W. Long. Elevation is 719 feet.

History: Named to promote the town as a pleasant place to live. Incorporated 1955.

Population: 22,591 (1990); 24,604 (2000); 24,099 (2010); Density: 4,198.3 persons per square mile (2008-2012 5-year est.); Race: 71.9% White, 2.9% Black/African American, 8.5% Asian, 0.4% American Indian/Alaska Native, 0.0% Native Hawaiian/Other Pacific Islander, 16.3% Some other race, 1.2% Two or more races, 25.2% Hispanic of any race (2008-2012 5-year est.); Average household size: 2.59 (2008-2012 5-year est.); Median age: 36.6 (2008-2012 5-year est.); Males per 100 females: 97.0 (2008-2012 5-year est.); Marriage status: 29.1% never married, 55.9% now married, 5.7% widowed, 9.4% divorced (2008-2012 5-year est.); Foreign born: 27.8% (2008-2012 5-year est.); Ancestry (includes multiple ancestries): 20.4% German, 13.8% Polish, 11.3% Irish, 10.3% Italian, 4.6% English (2008-2012 5-year est.).

Economy: Single-family building permits issued: 7 (2013); Multi-family building permits issued: 0 (2013); Homeowner vacancy rate: 1.2%. Rental vacancy rate: 3.1%. (2008-2012 5-year est.); Employment by occupation: 14.8% management, business, and financial, 6.5% computer, engineering, and science, 8.1% education, legal, community service, arts, and media, 3.4% healthcare practitioners, 20.6% service, 26.4% sales and office, 7.7% natural resources, construction, and maintenance, 12.6% production, transportation, and material moving (2008-2012 5-year est.).

Income: Per capita income: $30,919 (2008-2012 5-year est.); Median household income: $60,409 (2008-2012 5-year est.); Average household income: $78,758 (2008-2012 5-year est.); Percent of households with income of $100,000 or more: 24.3% (2008-2012 5-year est.); Poverty rate: 9.3% (2008-2012 5-year est.).

Taxes: Total city taxes per capita: $963 (2011); City property taxes per capita: $594 (2011).

Education: Percent of population age 25 and over with: High school diploma (including GED) or higher: 86.1% (2008-2012 5-year est.); Bachelor's degree or higher: 30.7% (2008-2012 5-year est.); Master's degree or higher: 10.7% (2008-2012 5-year est.).

School District(s)

Palatine CCSD 15 (PK-08)
    2011-12 Enrollment: 12,663 . . . . (847) 963-3000
Township HSD 214 (09-12)
    2011-12 Enrollment: 12,305 . . . . (847) 718-7600

Housing: Homeownership rate: 72.7% (2008-2012 5-year est.); Median home value: $254,500 (2008-2012 5-year est.); Median contract rent: $966 per month (2008-2012 5-year est.); Median year structure built: 1972 (2008-2012 5-year est.).

Health Insurance: 67.1% Private; 24.1% Public; 18.6% None. (2008-2012 5-year est.)

Safety: Violent crime rate: 8.7 per 10,000 population; Property crime rate: 149.1 per 10,000 population (2012).

Transportation: Commute to work: 89.6% car, 3.9% public transportation, 2.5% walk, 3.1% work from home (2008-2012 5-year est.); Travel time to work: 28.1% less than 15 minutes, 36.8% 15 to 30 minutes, 21.5% 30 to

45 minutes, 6.7% 45 to 60 minutes, 6.9% 60 minutes or more (2008-2012 5-year est.)

Additional Information Contacts

City of Rolling Meadows . . . . (847) 394-8500
  http://www.ci.rolling-meadows.il.us
Rolling Meadows Chamber of Commerce . . . . (847) 398-3730
  http://www.rmchamber.org

ROSEMONT (village). Covers a land area of 1.792 square miles and a water area of 0 square miles. Located at 41.99° N. Lat; 87.87° W. Long. Elevation is 636 feet.

Population: 3,995 (1990); 4,224 (2000); 4,202 (2010); Density: 1,952.3 persons per square mile (2008-2012 5-year est.); Race: 83.9% White, 3.9% Black/African American, 5.8% Asian, 0.0% American Indian/Alaska Native, 0.0% Native Hawaiian/Other Pacific Islander, 6.4% Some other race, 0.1% Two or more races, 18.6% Hispanic of any race (2008-2012 5-year est.); Average household size: 2.17 (2008-2012 5-year est.); Median age: 41.1 (2008-2012 5-year est.); Males per 100 females: 102.7 (2008-2012 5-year est.); Marriage status: 28.4% never married, 52.2% now married, 4.5% widowed, 14.8% divorced (2008-2012 5-year est.); Foreign born: 26.8% (2008-2012 5-year est.); Ancestry (includes multiple ancestries): 17.3% Italian, 13.5% German, 12.2% Polish, 10.0% Irish, 4.1% American (2008-2012 5-year est.).

Economy: Single-family building permits issued: 0 (2013); Multi-family building permits issued: 0 (2013); Homeowner vacancy rate: 0.0%. Rental vacancy rate: 8.8%. (2008-2012 5-year est.); Employment by occupation: 10.7% management, business, and financial, 2.7% computer, engineering, and science, 6.3% education, legal, community service, arts, and media, 2.0% healthcare practitioners, 25.5% service, 27.6% sales and office, 8.3% natural resources, construction, and maintenance, 16.9% production, transportation, and material moving (2008-2012 5-year est.).

Income: Per capita income: $26,121 (2008-2012 5-year est.); Median household income: $35,461 (2008-2012 5-year est.); Average household income: $54,704 (2008-2012 5-year est.); Percent of households with income of $100,000 or more: 12.0% (2008-2012 5-year est.); Poverty rate: 17.1% (2008-2012 5-year est.).

Taxes: Total city taxes per capita: $15,329 (2011); City property taxes per capita: $10,507 (2011).

Education: Percent of population age 25 and over with: High school diploma (including GED) or higher: 86.9% (2008-2012 5-year est.); Bachelor's degree or higher: 14.9% (2008-2012 5-year est.); Master's degree or higher: 3.1% (2008-2012 5-year est.).

School District(s)

Rosemont ESD 78 (PK-08)
  2011-12 Enrollment: 273 . . . . (847) 825-0144

Housing: Homeownership rate: 29.0% (2008-2012 5-year est.); Median home value: $311,500 (2008-2012 5-year est.); Median contract rent: $773 per month (2008-2012 5-year est.); Median year structure built: 1964 (2008-2012 5-year est.).

Health Insurance: 59.0% Private; 33.1% Public; 20.6% None. (2008-2012 5-year est.)

Safety: Violent crime rate: 16.6 per 10,000 population; Property crime rate: 535.0 per 10,000 population (2012).

Transportation: Commute to work: 82.4% car, 3.7% public transportation, 8.0% walk, 2.7% work from home (2008-2012 5-year est.); Travel time to work: 38.2% less than 15 minutes, 27.8% 15 to 30 minutes, 22.4% 30 to 45 minutes, 8.1% 45 to 60 minutes, 3.5% 60 minutes or more (2008-2012 5-year est.)

Additional Information Contacts

Rosemont Chamber of Commerce . . . . (847) 698-1190
  http://www.rosemontchamber.com

SAUK VILLAGE (village). Covers a land area of 3.835 square miles and a water area of 0.038 square miles. Located at 41.49° N. Lat; 87.57° W. Long. Elevation is 653 feet.

Population: 9,926 (1990); 10,411 (2000); 10,506 (2010); Density: 2,730.6 persons per square mile (2008-2012 5-year est.); Race: 30.2% White, 63.8% Black/African American, 0.0% Asian, 0.0% American Indian/Alaska Native, 0.0% Native Hawaiian/Other Pacific Islander, 6.0% Some other race, 2.3% Two or more races, 8.7% Hispanic of any race (2008-2012 5-year est.); Average household size: 3.55 (2008-2012 5-year est.); Median age: 27.8 (2008-2012 5-year est.); Males per 100 females: 95.1 (2008-2012 5-year est.); Marriage status: 47.6% never married, 36.0% now married, 5.7% widowed, 10.7% divorced (2008-2012 5-year est.); Foreign born: 2.3% (2008-2012 5-year est.); Ancestry (includes multiple

ancestries): 9.2% Irish, 7.4% German, 5.2% Polish, 3.0% English, 2.4% Italian (2008-2012 5-year est.).

Economy: Single-family building permits issued: 0 (2013); Multi-family building permits issued: 0 (2013); Homeowner vacancy rate: 5.9%. Rental vacancy rate: 4.4%. (2008-2012 5-year est.); Employment by occupation: 8.7% management, business, and financial, 2.1% computer, engineering, and science, 12.5% education, legal, community service, arts, and media, 2.0% healthcare practitioners, 21.4% service, 29.0% sales and office, 9.0% natural resources, construction, and maintenance, 15.3% production, transportation, and material moving (2008-2012 5-year est.).

Income: Per capita income: $16,938 (2008-2012 5-year est.); Median household income: $50,841 (2008-2012 5-year est.); Average household income: $57,186 (2008-2012 5-year est.); Percent of households with income of $100,000 or more: 16.0% (2008-2012 5-year est.); Poverty rate: 24.3% (2008-2012 5-year est.).

Taxes: Total city taxes per capita: $712 (2011); City property taxes per capita: $590 (2011).

Education: Percent of population age 25 and over with: High school diploma (including GED) or higher: 84.0% (2008-2012 5-year est.); Bachelor's degree or higher: 13.2% (2008-2012 5-year est.); Master's degree or higher: 4.2% (2008-2012 5-year est.).

School District(s)

CCSD 168 (PK-08)
  2011-12 Enrollment: 1,730 . . . . (708) 758-1614

Housing: Homeownership rate: 68.5% (2008-2012 5-year est.); Median home value: $104,600 (2008-2012 5-year est.); Median contract rent: $956 per month (2008-2012 5-year est.); Median year structure built: 1971 (2008-2012 5-year est.).

Health Insurance: 54.7% Private; 34.9% Public; 16.8% None. (2008-2012 5-year est.)

Safety: Violent crime rate: 90.9 per 10,000 population; Property crime rate: 507.7 per 10,000 population (2012).

Transportation: Commute to work: 92.1% car, 5.7% public transportation, 0.0% walk, 2.2% work from home (2008-2012 5-year est.); Travel time to work: 12.4% less than 15 minutes, 34.4% 15 to 30 minutes, 24.5% 30 to 45 minutes, 14.9% 45 to 60 minutes, 13.9% 60 minutes or more (2008-2012 5-year est.)

Additional Information Contacts

Village of Sauk Village . . . . (708) 758-3330
  http://www.saukvillage.org

SCHAUMBURG (village). Aka Schaumburg Center. Covers a land area of 19.218 square miles and a water area of 0.113 square miles. Located at 42.03° N. Lat; 88.08° W. Long. Elevation is 794 feet.

Population: 68,586 (1990); 75,386 (2000); 74,227 (2010); Density: 3,864.9 persons per square mile (2008-2012 5-year est.); Race: 70.9% White, 4.1% Black/African American, 19.0% Asian, 0.1% American Indian/Alaska Native, 0.0% Native Hawaiian/Other Pacific Islander, 5.9% Some other race, 2.0% Two or more races, 9.0% Hispanic of any race (2008-2012 5-year est.); Average household size: 2.40 (2008-2012 5-year est.); Median age: 37.2 (2008-2012 5-year est.); Males per 100 females: 95.6 (2008-2012 5-year est.); Marriage status: 30.6% never married, 54.1% now married, 5.5% widowed, 9.8% divorced (2008-2012 5-year est.); Foreign born: 25.7% (2008-2012 5-year est.); Ancestry (includes multiple ancestries): 21.1% German, 14.6% Polish, 12.8% Irish, 11.1% Italian, 4.6% English (2008-2012 5-year est.).

Economy: Unemployment rate: 5.5% (April 2014); Total civilian labor force: 46,378 (April 2014); Single-family building permits issued: 1 (2013); Multi-family building permits issued: 31 (2013); Homeowner vacancy rate: 1.5%. Rental vacancy rate: 9.5%. (2008-2012 5-year est.); Employment by occupation: 21.6% management, business, and financial, 11.1% computer, engineering, and science, 9.7% education, legal, community service, arts, and media, 3.8% healthcare practitioners, 9.8% service, 28.3% sales and office, 5.6% natural resources, construction, and maintenance, 10.1% production, transportation, and material moving (2008-2012 5-year est.).

Income: Per capita income: $35,689 (2008-2012 5-year est.); Median household income: $70,060 (2008-2012 5-year est.); Average household income: $84,336 (2008-2012 5-year est.); Percent of households with income of $100,000 or more: 29.2% (2008-2012 5-year est.); Poverty rate: 6.4% (2008-2012 5-year est.).

Taxes: Total city taxes per capita: $962 (2011); City property taxes per capita: $370 (2011).

Education: Percent of population age 25 and over with: High school diploma (including GED) or higher: 94.7% (2008-2012 5-year est.);

Bachelor's degree or higher: 44.2% (2008-2012 5-year est.); Master's degree or higher: 15.1% (2008-2012 5-year est.).

School District(s)

Schaumburg CCSD 54 (PK-08)
2011-12 Enrollment: 14,083 . . . . (847) 357-5000
Township HSD 211 (09-12)
2011-12 Enrollment: 12,593 . . . . (847) 755-6600

Four-year College(s)

American InterContinental University-Online (Private, For-profit)
Fall 2012 Enrollment: 18,207 . . . . (877) 701-3800
2012-13 Tuition: In-state $14,043; Out-of-state $14,043
Argosy University-Schaumburg (Private, For-profit)
Fall 2012 Enrollment: 594 . . . . (847) 969-4900
2012-13 Tuition: In-state $12,685; Out-of-state $12,685
The Illinois Institute of Art-Schaumburg (Private, For-profit)
Fall 2012 Enrollment: 1,282 . . . . (847) 619-3450
2012-13 Tuition: In-state $17,688; Out-of-state $17,688
University of Phoenix-Chicago Campus (Private, For-profit)
Fall 2012 Enrollment: 1,090 . . . . (847) 413-1922
2012-13 Tuition: In-state $11,320; Out-of-state $11,320

Two-year College(s)

Prince Institute of Professional Studies (Private, For-profit)
Fall 2012 Enrollment: 33 . . . . (847) 592-6600
2012-13 Tuition: In-state $9,885; Out-of-state $9,885
Housing: Homeownership rate: 66.8% (2008-2012 5-year est.); Median home value: $252,300 (2008-2012 5-year est.); Median contract rent: $1,085 per month (2008-2012 5-year est.); Median year structure built: 1977 (2008-2012 5-year est.).
Health Insurance: 80.4% Private; 18.6% Public; 9.8% None. (2008-2012 5-year est.)
Safety: Violent crime rate: 9.1 per 10,000 population; Property crime rate: 333.4 per 10,000 population (2012).
Transportation: Commute to work: 91.5% car, 3.6% public transportation, 0.7% walk, 2.9% work from home (2008-2012 5-year est.); Travel time to work: 23.3% less than 15 minutes, 33.5% 15 to 30 minutes, 23.6% 30 to 45 minutes, 9.9% 45 to 60 minutes, 9.7% 60 minutes or more (2008-2012 5-year est.)
Airports: Schaumburg Municipal Helistop (general aviation); Schaumburg Regional Airport (general aviation)

Additional Information Contacts

Schaumburg Business Association . . . . (847) 413-1010
http://www.schaumburgbusiness.com
Village of Schaumburg . . . . (847) 895-4500
http://www.ci.schaumburg.il.us

SCHILLER PARK (village). Covers a land area of 2.769 square miles and a water area of 0 square miles. Located at 41.96° N. Lat; 87.87° W. Long. Elevation is 640 feet.

History: Named for Johann Christopher Friedrich von Schiller (1759-1805), a German poet. Incorporated 1914.
Population: 11,189 (1990); 11,850 (2000); 11,793 (2010); Density: 4,255.2 persons per square mile (2008-2012 5-year est.); Race: 79.6% White, 2.3% Black/African American, 7.1% Asian, 0.5% American Indian/Alaska Native, 0.0% Native Hawaiian/Other Pacific Islander, 10.5% Some other race, 1.7% Two or more races, 21.8% Hispanic of any race (2008-2012 5-year est.); Average household size: 2.60 (2008-2012 5-year est.); Median age: 34.2 (2008-2012 5-year est.); Males per 100 females: 114.0 (2008-2012 5-year est.); Marriage status: 29.8% never married, 54.2% now married, 6.4% widowed, 9.7% divorced (2008-2012 5-year est.); Foreign born: 44.2% (2008-2012 5-year est.); Ancestry (includes multiple ancestries): 27.8% Polish, 10.0% Italian, 6.0% Irish, 4.8% German, 4.0% Bulgarian (2008-2012 5-year est.).
Economy: Single-family building permits issued: 0 (2013); Multi-family building permits issued: 0 (2013); Homeowner vacancy rate: 4.9%. Rental vacancy rate: 3.9%. (2008-2012 5-year est.); Employment by occupation: 13.5% management, business, and financial, 2.9% computer, engineering, and science, 6.6% education, legal, community service, arts, and media, 1.9% healthcare practitioners, 21.8% service, 18.7% sales and office, 10.6% natural resources, construction, and maintenance, 23.9% production, transportation, and material moving (2008-2012 5-year est.).
Income: Per capita income: $22,611 (2008-2012 5-year est.); Median household income: $41,862 (2008-2012 5-year est.); Average household income: $56,056 (2008-2012 5-year est.); Percent of households with income of $100,000 or more: 13.4% (2008-2012 5-year est.); Poverty rate: 10.7% (2008-2012 5-year est.).

Taxes: Total city taxes per capita: $1,012 (2011); City property taxes per capita: $687 (2011).
Education: Percent of population age 25 and over with: High school diploma (including GED) or higher: 83.2% (2008-2012 5-year est.); Bachelor's degree or higher: 20.6% (2008-2012 5-year est.); Master's degree or higher: 5.5% (2008-2012 5-year est.).

School District(s)

Schiller Park SD 81 (PK-08)
2011-12 Enrollment: 1,330 . . . . (847) 671-1816
Housing: Homeownership rate: 61.4% (2008-2012 5-year est.); Median home value: $228,000 (2008-2012 5-year est.); Median contract rent: $789 per month (2008-2012 5-year est.); Median year structure built: 1961 (2008-2012 5-year est.).
Health Insurance: 59.3% Private; 24.1% Public; 23.5% None. (2008-2012 5-year est.)
Safety: Violent crime rate: 9.3 per 10,000 population; Property crime rate: 187.3 per 10,000 population (2012).
Transportation: Commute to work: 89.4% car, 3.6% public transportation, 1.0% walk, 3.4% work from home (2008-2012 5-year est.); Travel time to work: 16.2% less than 15 minutes, 34.4% 15 to 30 minutes, 30.0% 30 to 45 minutes, 8.2% 45 to 60 minutes, 11.2% 60 minutes or more (2008-2012 5-year est.)

Additional Information Contacts

Franklin Park/Schiller Park Chamber of Commerce . . . . . . (708) 865-9510
http://www.chamberbyohare.org
Village of Schiller Park . . . . (847) 678-2550
http://www.villageofschillerpark.com

SKOKIE (village). Aka Niles Center. Covers a land area of 10.063 square miles and a water area of 0 square miles. Located at 42.04° N. Lat; 87.74° W. Long. Elevation is 607 feet.

History: Named for the Potawatomi translation of "marsh". Hebrew Theological College (1922) was moved here from Chicago in 1958. National Jewish Theater. Incorporated 1888.
Population: 59,432 (1990); 63,348 (2000); 64,784 (2010); Density: 6,418.5 persons per square mile (2008-2012 5-year est.); Race: 64.1% White, 7.4% Black/African American, 24.8% Asian, 0.1% American Indian/Alaska Native, 0.0% Native Hawaiian/Other Pacific Islander, 3.6% Some other race, 2.0% Two or more races, 8.6% Hispanic of any race (2008-2012 5-year est.); Average household size: 2.75 (2008-2012 5-year est.); Median age: 43.7 (2008-2012 5-year est.); Males per 100 females: 92.5 (2008-2012 5-year est.); Marriage status: 28.0% never married, 56.4% now married, 7.2% widowed, 8.4% divorced (2008-2012 5-year est.); Foreign born: 41.1% (2008-2012 5-year est.); Ancestry (includes multiple ancestries): 8.8% German, 6.2% Russian, 5.8% Irish, 5.8% Polish, 5.6% Assyrian/Chaldean/Syriac (2008-2012 5-year est.).
Economy: Unemployment rate: 6.2% (April 2014); Total civilian labor force: 33,083 (April 2014); Single-family building permits issued: 3 (2013); Multi-family building permits issued: 0 (2013); Homeowner vacancy rate: 1.6%. Rental vacancy rate: 9.8%. (2008-2012 5-year est.); Employment by occupation: 16.9% management, business, and financial, 5.5% computer, engineering, and science, 14.2% education, legal, community service, arts, and media, 8.8% healthcare practitioners, 14.3% service, 25.7% sales and office, 5.1% natural resources, construction, and maintenance, 9.6% production, transportation, and material moving (2008-2012 5-year est.).
Income: Per capita income: $32,868 (2008-2012 5-year est.); Median household income: $67,030 (2008-2012 5-year est.); Average household income: $88,225 (2008-2012 5-year est.); Percent of households with income of $100,000 or more: 30.8% (2008-2012 5-year est.); Poverty rate: 9.5% (2008-2012 5-year est.).
Taxes: Total city taxes per capita: $859 (2011); City property taxes per capita: $487 (2011).
Education: Percent of population age 25 and over with: High school diploma (including GED) or higher: 88.9% (2008-2012 5-year est.); Bachelor's degree or higher: 45.8% (2008-2012 5-year est.); Master's degree or higher: 18.8% (2008-2012 5-year est.).

School District(s)

East Prairie SD 73 (PK-08)
2011-12 Enrollment: 557 . . . . (847) 673-1141
Evanston CCSD 65 (PK-08)
2011-12 Enrollment: 7,271 . . . . (847) 859-8010
Fairview SD 72 (PK-08)
2011-12 Enrollment: 656 . . . . (847) 929-1050
Niles Twp CHSD 219 (09-12)
2011-12 Enrollment: 4,810 . . . . (847) 626-3000

Skokie SD 68 (PK-08)
    2011-12 Enrollment: 1,773 . . . . (847) 676-9000
Skokie SD 69 (PK-08)
    2011-12 Enrollment: 1,721 . . . . (847) 675-7666
Skokie SD 73-5 (PK-08)
    2011-12 Enrollment: 1,092 . . . . (847) 324-0509

Four-year College(s)

Hebrew Theological College (Private, Not-for-profit, Jewish)
    Fall 2012 Enrollment: 457 . . . . (847) 982-2500
    2012-13 Tuition: In-state $18,030; Out-of-state $18,030
Knowledge Systems Institute (Private, Not-for-profit)
    Fall 2012 Enrollment: 126 . . . . (847) 679-3135

Two-year College(s)

Chicago ORT Technical Institute (Private, Not-for-profit)
    Fall 2012 Enrollment: 397 . . . . (847) 324-5588
Sanford-Brown College-Skokie (Private, For-profit)
    Fall 2012 Enrollment: 296 . . . . (847) 983-1200
    2012-13 Tuition: In-state $16,192; Out-of-state $16,192

Vocational/Technical School(s)

Computer Systems Institute (Private, For-profit)
    Fall 2012 Enrollment: 1,900 . . . . (847) 967-5030
    2012-13 Tuition: $13,950
Estelle Skin Care and Spa Institute (Private, For-profit)
    Fall 2012 Enrollment: 101 . . . . (847) 329-9174
    2012-13 Tuition: $9,875
European Massage Therapy School-Skokie (Private, For-profit)
    Fall 2012 Enrollment: 79 . . . . (847) 673-7595
Everest College-Skokie (Private, For-profit)
    Fall 2012 Enrollment: 473 . . . . (847) 470-0277
    2012-13 Tuition: $16,320

Housing: Homeownership rate: 73.7% (2008-2012 5-year est.); Median home value: $315,700 (2008-2012 5-year est.); Median contract rent: $968 per month (2008-2012 5-year est.); Median year structure built: 1958 (2008-2012 5-year est.).

Health Insurance: 68.7% Private; 28.7% Public; 14.8% None. (2008-2012 5-year est.)

Hospitals: Rush North Shore Medical Center (268 beds)

Safety: Violent crime rate: 20.6 per 10,000 population; Property crime rate: 242.3 per 10,000 population (2012).

Transportation: Commute to work: 84.1% car, 9.3% public transportation, 1.6% walk, 3.9% work from home (2008-2012 5-year est.); Travel time to work: 21.4% less than 15 minutes, 33.1% 15 to 30 minutes, 21.6% 30 to 45 minutes, 11.1% 45 to 60 minutes, 12.8% 60 minutes or more (2008-2012 5-year est.)

Additional Information Contacts

Skokie Chamber of Commerce . . . . (847) 673-0240
    http://www.skokiechamber.org
Village of Skokie . . . . (847) 673-0500
    http://www.skokie.com

SOUTH BARRINGTON (village). Covers a land area of 7.343 square miles and a water area of 0.279 square miles. Located at 42.09° N. Lat; 88.16° W. Long. Elevation is 853 feet.

History: The Village of South Barrington was incorporated in December of 1959 and lies in the southeastern portion of Barrington Township and a small portion of western Palatine Township.

Population: 2,937 (1990); 3,760 (2000); 4,565 (2010); Density: 645.2 persons per square mile (2008-2012 5-year est.); Race: 67.9% White, 0.9% Black/African American, 25.6% Asian, 0.0% American Indian/Alaska Native, 0.0% Native Hawaiian/Other Pacific Islander, 5.6% Some other race, 5.6% Two or more races, 4.6% Hispanic of any race (2008-2012 5-year est.); Average household size: 3.29 (2008-2012 5-year est.); Median age: 44.6 (2008-2012 5-year est.); Males per 100 females: 87.1 (2008-2012 5-year est.); Marriage status: 23.1% never married, 71.0% now married, 2.7% widowed, 3.1% divorced (2008-2012 5-year est.); Foreign born: 23.2% (2008-2012 5-year est.); Ancestry (includes multiple ancestries): 20.2% German, 12.1% Polish, 9.4% Irish, 7.7% Italian, 3.8% Greek (2008-2012 5-year est.).

Economy: Single-family building permits issued: 39 (2013); Multi-family building permits issued: 0 (2013); Homeowner vacancy rate: 0.0%. Rental vacancy rate: 0.0%. (2008-2012 5-year est.); Employment by occupation: 21.2% management, business, and financial, 8.0% computer, engineering, and science, 15.0% education, legal, community service, arts, and media, 17.0% healthcare practitioners, 5.6% service, 25.7% sales and office,

2.4% natural resources, construction, and maintenance, 5.1% production, transportation, and material moving (2008-2012 5-year est.).

Income: Per capita income: $67,543 (2008-2012 5-year est.); Median household income: $166,250 (2008-2012 5-year est.); Average household income: $218,048 (2008-2012 5-year est.); Percent of households with income of $100,000 or more: 78.0% (2008-2012 5-year est.); Poverty rate: 3.8% (2008-2012 5-year est.).

Education: Percent of population age 25 and over with: High school diploma (including GED) or higher: 98.5% (2008-2012 5-year est.); Bachelor's degree or higher: 77.6% (2008-2012 5-year est.); Master's degree or higher: 35.7% (2008-2012 5-year est.).

School District(s)

Barrington CUSD 220 (PK-12)
    2011-12 Enrollment: 9,088 . . . . (847) 381-6300

Housing: Homeownership rate: 100.0% (2008-2012 5-year est.); Median home value: $820,000 (2008-2012 5-year est.); Median contract rent: n/a per month (2008-2012 5-year est.); Median year structure built: 1987 (2008-2012 5-year est.).

Health Insurance: 94.0% Private; 16.9% Public; 2.4% None. (2008-2012 5-year est.)

Safety: Violent crime rate: 2.2 per 10,000 population; Property crime rate: 218.0 per 10,000 population (2012).

Transportation: Commute to work: 90.3% car, 0.5% public transportation, 1.7% walk, 6.9% work from home (2008-2012 5-year est.); Travel time to work: 21.2% less than 15 minutes, 33.0% 15 to 30 minutes, 25.9% 30 to 45 minutes, 9.5% 45 to 60 minutes, 10.5% 60 minutes or more (2008-2012 5-year est.)

SOUTH CHICAGO HEIGHTS (village). Covers a land area of 1.581 square miles and a water area of 0.016 square miles. Located at 41.48° N. Lat; 87.64° W. Long. Elevation is 715 feet.

History: Incorporated 1907.

Population: 3,597 (1990); 3,970 (2000); 4,139 (2010); Density: 2,608.0 persons per square mile (2008-2012 5-year est.); Race: 59.9% White, 17.3% Black/African American, 0.0% Asian, 0.7% American Indian/Alaska Native, 0.0% Native Hawaiian/Other Pacific Islander, 22.1% Some other race, 3.5% Two or more races, 36.5% Hispanic of any race (2008-2012 5-year est.); Average household size: 2.78 (2008-2012 5-year est.); Median age: 36.3 (2008-2012 5-year est.); Males per 100 females: 104.8 (2008-2012 5-year est.); Marriage status: 36.7% never married, 46.4% now married, 9.3% widowed, 7.6% divorced (2008-2012 5-year est.); Foreign born: 14.6% (2008-2012 5-year est.); Ancestry (includes multiple ancestries): 13.0% German, 12.9% Italian, 7.2% Irish, 6.9% Polish, 3.4% Swedish (2008-2012 5-year est.).

Economy: Single-family building permits issued: 0 (2013); Multi-family building permits issued: 0 (2013); Homeowner vacancy rate: 0.0%. Rental vacancy rate: 14.6%. (2008-2012 5-year est.); Employment by occupation: 6.0% management, business, and financial, 0.6% computer, engineering, and science, 4.8% education, legal, community service, arts, and media, 4.3% healthcare practitioners, 21.9% service, 33.3% sales and office, 12.2% natural resources, construction, and maintenance, 16.9% production, transportation, and material moving (2008-2012 5-year est.).

Income: Per capita income: $20,873 (2008-2012 5-year est.); Median household income: $48,958 (2008-2012 5-year est.); Average household income: $56,645 (2008-2012 5-year est.); Percent of households with income of $100,000 or more: 3.0% (2008-2012 5-year est.); Poverty rate: 16.5% (2008-2012 5-year est.).

Education: Percent of population age 25 and over with: High school diploma (including GED) or higher: 82.3% (2008-2012 5-year est.); Bachelor's degree or higher: 10.5% (2008-2012 5-year est.); Master's degree or higher: 4.3% (2008-2012 5-year est.).

School District(s)

Chicago Heights SD 170 (PK-08)
    2011-12 Enrollment: 3,232 . . . . (708) 756-4165
Steger SD 194 (PK-08)
    2011-12 Enrollment: 1,569 . . . . (708) 755-0022

Housing: Homeownership rate: 68.7% (2008-2012 5-year est.); Median home value: $115,400 (2008-2012 5-year est.); Median contract rent: $701 per month (2008-2012 5-year est.); Median year structure built: 1958 (2008-2012 5-year est.).

Health Insurance: 55.2% Private; 33.9% Public; 21.8% None. (2008-2012 5-year est.)

Safety: Violent crime rate: 24.0 per 10,000 population; Property crime rate: 389.4 per 10,000 population (2012).

Transportation: Commute to work: 93.0% car, 4.4% public transportation, 0.8% walk, 0.7% work from home (2008-2012 5-year est.); Travel time to work: 36.1% less than 15 minutes, 28.6% 15 to 30 minutes, 22.3% 30 to 45 minutes, 8.1% 45 to 60 minutes, 4.9% 60 minutes or more (2008-2012 5-year est.)

SOUTH HOLLAND (village). Covers a land area of 7.266 square miles and a water area of 0.016 square miles. Located at 41.60° N. Lat; 87.60° W. Long. Elevation is 600 feet.
History: Named for the province of South Holland, Netherlands, home of early settlers. South Holland was settled in 1840 by immigrants from the Netherlands. An early industry was the raising of onions.
Population: 22,105 (1990); 22,147 (2000); 22,030 (2010); Density: 3,026.9 persons per square mile (2008-2012 5-year est.); Race: 20.2% White, 77.6% Black/African American, 0.6% Asian, 0.1% American Indian/Alaska Native, 0.1% Native Hawaiian/Other Pacific Islander, 1.4% Some other race, 0.8% Two or more races, 3.7% Hispanic of any race (2008-2012 5-year est.); Average household size: 2.96 (2008-2012 5-year est.); Median age: 40.3 (2008-2012 5-year est.); Males per 100 females: 94.8 (2008-2012 5-year est.); Marriage status: 34.4% never married, 46.4% now married, 8.1% widowed, 11.1% divorced (2008-2012 5-year est.); Foreign born: 3.8% (2008-2012 5-year est.); Ancestry (includes multiple ancestries): 4.5% Dutch, 2.9% Polish, 2.8% German, 2.0% Irish, 2.0% Italian (2008-2012 5-year est.).
Economy: Single-family building permits issued: 0 (2013); Multi-family building permits issued: 0 (2013); Homeowner vacancy rate: 2.1%. Rental vacancy rate: 8.8%. (2008-2012 5-year est.); Employment by occupation: 12.8% management, business, and financial, 2.5% computer, engineering, and science, 13.4% education, legal, community service, arts, and media, 8.0% healthcare practitioners, 16.2% service, 26.5% sales and office, 7.6% natural resources, construction, and maintenance, 13.0% production, transportation, and material moving (2008-2012 5-year est.).
Income: Per capita income: $26,021 (2008-2012 5-year est.); Median household income: $64,285 (2008-2012 5-year est.); Average household income: $75,209 (2008-2012 5-year est.); Percent of households with income of $100,000 or more: 24.3% (2008-2012 5-year est.); Poverty rate: 9.1% (2008-2012 5-year est.).
Taxes: Total city taxes per capita: $902 (2011); City property taxes per capita: $706 (2011).
Education: Percent of population age 25 and over with: High school diploma (including GED) or higher: 90.9% (2008-2012 5-year est.); Bachelor's degree or higher: 27.9% (2008-2012 5-year est.); Master's degree or higher: 11.0% (2008-2012 5-year est.).
School District(s)
Dolton SD 149 (PK-08)
    2011-12 Enrollment: 3,135 . . . . (708) 868-7861
Exc Children Have Opportunities (KG-12)
    2011-12 Enrollment: n/a . . . . (708) 333-7880
South Holland SD 150 (PK-08)
    2011-12 Enrollment: 994. . . . . (708) 339-4240
South Holland SD 151 (PK-08)
    2011-12 Enrollment: 1,494 . . . . (708) 339-1516
Thornton Twp HSD 205 (09-12)
    2011-12 Enrollment: 5,283 . . . . (708) 225-4000
Two-year College(s)
South Suburban College (Public)
    Fall 2012 Enrollment: 6,211 . . . . (708) 596-2000
    2012-13 Tuition: In-state $9,689; Out-of-state $10,763
Housing: Homeownership rate: 89.4% (2008-2012 5-year est.); Median home value: $169,100 (2008-2012 5-year est.); Median contract rent: $1,204 per month (2008-2012 5-year est.); Median year structure built: 1966 (2008-2012 5-year est.).
Health Insurance: 70.9% Private; 29.1% Public; 13.6% None. (2008-2012 5-year est.)
Safety: Violent crime rate: 34.3 per 10,000 population; Property crime rate: 232.2 per 10,000 population (2012).
Transportation: Commute to work: 89.8% car, 5.9% public transportation, 1.0% walk, 2.7% work from home (2008-2012 5-year est.); Travel time to work: 16.3% less than 15 minutes, 22.9% 15 to 30 minutes, 27.4% 30 to 45 minutes, 16.8% 45 to 60 minutes, 16.5% 60 minutes or more (2008-2012 5-year est.)
Additional Information Contacts
South Holland Business Association . . . . (708) 596-0065
    http://www.shba.org

Village of South Holland . . . . (708) 210-2900
    http://www.southholland.org

STICKNEY (village). Covers a land area of 1.925 square miles and a water area of 0.036 square miles. Located at 41.82° N. Lat; 87.77° W. Long. Elevation is 604 feet.
History: Incorporated 1913.
Population: 5,678 (1990); 6,148 (2000); 6,786 (2010); Density: 3,496.4 persons per square mile (2008-2012 5-year est.); Race: 78.0% White, 2.6% Black/African American, 0.0% Asian, 2.2% American Indian/Alaska Native, 0.0% Native Hawaiian/Other Pacific Islander, 17.2% Some other race, 2.3% Two or more races, 46.7% Hispanic of any race (2008-2012 5-year est.); Average household size: 2.86 (2008-2012 5-year est.); Median age: 34.0 (2008-2012 5-year est.); Males per 100 females: 91.5 (2008-2012 5-year est.); Marriage status: 30.4% never married, 50.4% now married, 11.2% widowed, 8.0% divorced (2008-2012 5-year est.); Foreign born: 17.0% (2008-2012 5-year est.); Ancestry (includes multiple ancestries): 19.3% Polish, 15.6% Italian, 12.7% German, 11.9% Irish, 8.0% Czech (2008-2012 5-year est.).
Economy: Single-family building permits issued: 0 (2013); Multi-family building permits issued: 0 (2013); Homeowner vacancy rate: 8.2%. Rental vacancy rate: 11.1%. (2008-2012 5-year est.); Employment by occupation: 13.2% management, business, and financial, 3.8% computer, engineering, and science, 5.2% education, legal, community service, arts, and media, 4.4% healthcare practitioners, 20.6% service, 20.9% sales and office, 10.9% natural resources, construction, and maintenance, 21.1% production, transportation, and material moving (2008-2012 5-year est.).
Income: Per capita income: $22,697 (2008-2012 5-year est.); Median household income: $43,832 (2008-2012 5-year est.); Average household income: $64,224 (2008-2012 5-year est.); Percent of households with income of $100,000 or more: 17.6% (2008-2012 5-year est.); Poverty rate: 8.1% (2008-2012 5-year est.).
Education: Percent of population age 25 and over with: High school diploma (including GED) or higher: 79.3% (2008-2012 5-year est.); Bachelor's degree or higher: 9.2% (2008-2012 5-year est.); Master's degree or higher: 2.2% (2008-2012 5-year est.).
School District(s)
Lyons SD 103 (PK-08)
    2011-12 Enrollment: 2,486 . . . . (708) 783-4100
Housing: Homeownership rate: 76.8% (2008-2012 5-year est.); Median home value: $180,300 (2008-2012 5-year est.); Median contract rent: $780 per month (2008-2012 5-year est.); Median year structure built: 1956 (2008-2012 5-year est.).
Health Insurance: 55.4% Private; 32.2% Public; 22.6% None. (2008-2012 5-year est.)
Transportation: Commute to work: 86.8% car, 6.7% public transportation, 4.0% walk, 2.0% work from home (2008-2012 5-year est.); Travel time to work: 27.1% less than 15 minutes, 26.6% 15 to 30 minutes, 20.6% 30 to 45 minutes, 10.2% 45 to 60 minutes, 15.5% 60 minutes or more (2008-2012 5-year est.)
Additional Information Contacts
Village of Stickney . . . . (708) 749-4400
    http://www.villageofstickney.com

STONE PARK (village). Covers a land area of 0.344 square miles and a water area of 0 square miles. Located at 41.90° N. Lat; 87.88° W. Long. Elevation is 640 feet.
History: Incorporated 1939.
Population: 4,383 (1990); 5,127 (2000); 4,946 (2010); Density: 14,382.8 persons per square mile (2008-2012 5-year est.); Race: 47.8% White, 1.1% Black/African American, 1.6% Asian, 0.0% American Indian/Alaska Native, 0.0% Native Hawaiian/Other Pacific Islander, 49.5% Some other race, 3.1% Two or more races, 88.5% Hispanic of any race (2008-2012 5-year est.); Average household size: 3.86 (2008-2012 5-year est.); Median age: 29.2 (2008-2012 5-year est.); Males per 100 females: 99.0 (2008-2012 5-year est.); Marriage status: 33.0% never married, 55.5% now married, 4.6% widowed, 6.9% divorced (2008-2012 5-year est.); Foreign born: 46.5% (2008-2012 5-year est.); Ancestry (includes multiple ancestries): 1.9% Irish, 1.5% German, 1.5% Italian, 0.7% English, 0.6% American (2008-2012 5-year est.).
Economy: Single-family building permits issued: 0 (2013); Multi-family building permits issued: 0 (2013); Homeowner vacancy rate: 0.0%. Rental vacancy rate: 12.5%. (2008-2012 5-year est.); Employment by occupation: 7.1% management, business, and financial, 0.4% computer, engineering, and science, 2.3% education, legal, community service, arts, and media,

2.1% healthcare practitioners, 16.6% service, 23.5% sales and office, 12.5% natural resources, construction, and maintenance, 35.5% production, transportation, and material moving (2008-2012 5-year est.).
Income: Per capita income: $15,554 (2008-2012 5-year est.); Median household income: $44,886 (2008-2012 5-year est.); Average household income: $55,713 (2008-2012 5-year est.); Percent of households with income of $100,000 or more: 17.1% (2008-2012 5-year est.); Poverty rate: 17.9% (2008-2012 5-year est.).
Education: Percent of population age 25 and over with: High school diploma (including GED) or higher: 54.2% (2008-2012 5-year est.); Bachelor's degree or higher: 3.6% (2008-2012 5-year est.); Master's degree or higher: 0.4% (2008-2012 5-year est.).

School District(s)
Bellwood SD 88 (PK-08)
    2011-12 Enrollment: 2,879 . . . . (708) 344-9344
Housing: Homeownership rate: 60.6% (2008-2012 5-year est.); Median home value: $171,500 (2008-2012 5-year est.); Median contract rent: $766 per month (2008-2012 5-year est.); Median year structure built: 1960 (2008-2012 5-year est.).
Health Insurance: 43.2% Private; 33.9% Public; 26.9% None. (2008-2012 5-year est.)
Safety: Violent crime rate: 24.2 per 10,000 population; Property crime rate: 189.2 per 10,000 population (2012).
Transportation: Commute to work: 95.0% car, 3.0% public transportation, 0.4% walk, 1.0% work from home (2008-2012 5-year est.); Travel time to work: 22.8% less than 15 minutes, 39.2% 15 to 30 minutes, 20.5% 30 to 45 minutes, 9.6% 45 to 60 minutes, 7.9% 60 minutes or more (2008-2012 5-year est.).

STREAMWOOD (village). Covers a land area of 7.815 square miles and a water area of 0.034 square miles. Located at 42.02° N. Lat; 88.18° W. Long. Elevation is 807 feet.
Population: 30,987 (1990); 36,407 (2000); 39,858 (2010); Density: 5,143.9 persons per square mile (2008-2012 5-year est.); Race: 61.2% White, 4.3% Black/African American, 15.0% Asian, 0.2% American Indian/Alaska Native, 0.0% Native Hawaiian/Other Pacific Islander, 19.3% Some other race, 1.5% Two or more races, 28.7% Hispanic of any race (2008-2012 5-year est.); Average household size: 3.01 (2008-2012 5-year est.); Median age: 34.5 (2008-2012 5-year est.); Males per 100 females: 97.1 (2008-2012 5-year est.); Marriage status: 29.6% never married, 58.0% now married, 4.6% widowed, 7.8% divorced (2008-2012 5-year est.); Foreign born: 29.4% (2008-2012 5-year est.); Ancestry (includes multiple ancestries): 16.3% German, 13.2% Polish, 9.4% Irish, 8.2% Italian, 3.8% English (2008-2012 5-year est.).
Economy: Unemployment rate: 7.1% (April 2014); Total civilian labor force: 23,646 (April 2014); Single-family building permits issued: 14 (2013); Multi-family building permits issued: 0 (2013); Homeowner vacancy rate: 3.9%. Rental vacancy rate: 0.0%. (2008-2012 5-year est.); Employment by occupation: 13.3% management, business, and financial, 7.3% computer, engineering, and science, 6.8% education, legal, community service, arts, and media, 4.5% healthcare practitioners, 15.7% service, 31.4% sales and office, 7.2% natural resources, construction, and maintenance, 13.8% production, transportation, and material moving (2008-2012 5-year est.).
Income: Per capita income: $29,326 (2008-2012 5-year est.); Median household income: $71,306 (2008-2012 5-year est.); Average household income: $86,356 (2008-2012 5-year est.); Percent of households with income of $100,000 or more: 31.3% (2008-2012 5-year est.); Poverty rate: 5.5% (2008-2012 5-year est.).
Taxes: Total city taxes per capita: $409 (2011); City property taxes per capita: $251 (2011).
Education: Percent of population age 25 and over with: High school diploma (including GED) or higher: 86.1% (2008-2012 5-year est.); Bachelor's degree or higher: 32.3% (2008-2012 5-year est.); Master's degree or higher: 9.2% (2008-2012 5-year est.).

School District(s)
SD U-46 (PK-12)
    2011-12 Enrollment: 40,687 . . . . (847) 888-5000
Township HSD 211 (09-12)
    2011-12 Enrollment: 12,593 . . . . (847) 755-6600
Housing: Homeownership rate: 87.6% (2008-2012 5-year est.); Median home value: $205,500 (2008-2012 5-year est.); Median contract rent: $1,230 per month (2008-2012 5-year est.); Median year structure built: 1980 (2008-2012 5-year est.).
Health Insurance: 72.7% Private; 19.9% Public; 13.7% None. (2008-2012 5-year est.)

Safety: Violent crime rate: 8.5 per 10,000 population; Property crime rate: 175.5 per 10,000 population (2012).
Transportation: Commute to work: 91.2% car, 3.7% public transportation, 0.6% walk, 3.4% work from home (2008-2012 5-year est.); Travel time to work: 14.7% less than 15 minutes, 37.8% 15 to 30 minutes, 25.4% 30 to 45 minutes, 9.3% 45 to 60 minutes, 12.8% 60 minutes or more (2008-2012 5-year est.).
Additional Information Contacts
Streamwood Chamber of Commerce . . . . (630) 837-5200
    http://www.streamwoodchamber.com
Village of Streamwood . . . . (630) 736-3800
    http://www.streamwood.org

SUMMIT (village). Covers a land area of 2.119 square miles and a water area of 0.137 square miles. Located at 41.79° N. Lat; 87.81° W. Long. Elevation is 614 feet.
History: Summit developed around the Corn Products Company Plant, a corn refinery. It was named for its location at the crest of the watershed between the Great Lakes and the Mississippi drainage systems. Rain falling on the east side of town drains into the Atlantic Ocean; that falling on the west side into the Gulf of Mexico.
Population: 9,971 (1990); 10,637 (2000); 11,054 (2010); Density: 5,270.6 persons per square mile (2008-2012 5-year est.); Race: 70.6% White, 8.6% Black/African American, 3.2% Asian, 0.4% American Indian/Alaska Native, 0.0% Native Hawaiian/Other Pacific Islander, 17.2% Some other race, 2.7% Two or more races, 67.3% Hispanic of any race (2008-2012 5-year est.); Average household size: 3.47 (2008-2012 5-year est.); Median age: 29.6 (2008-2012 5-year est.); Males per 100 females: 96.0 (2008-2012 5-year est.); Marriage status: 43.3% never married, 43.3% now married, 4.3% widowed, 9.1% divorced (2008-2012 5-year est.); Foreign born: 35.3% (2008-2012 5-year est.); Ancestry (includes multiple ancestries): 7.9% Polish, 6.0% German, 5.3% Irish, 1.8% Italian, 1.4% English (2008-2012 5-year est.).
Economy: Single-family building permits issued: 0 (2013); Multi-family building permits issued: 0 (2013); Homeowner vacancy rate: 2.4%. Rental vacancy rate: 11.9%. (2008-2012 5-year est.); Employment by occupation: 6.9% management, business, and financial, 2.9% computer, engineering, and science, 4.5% education, legal, community service, arts, and media, 2.1% healthcare practitioners, 21.5% service, 21.4% sales and office, 7.9% natural resources, construction, and maintenance, 32.8% production, transportation, and material moving (2008-2012 5-year est.).
Income: Per capita income: $16,529 (2008-2012 5-year est.); Median household income: $49,070 (2008-2012 5-year est.); Average household income: $53,882 (2008-2012 5-year est.); Percent of households with income of $100,000 or more: 10.2% (2008-2012 5-year est.); Poverty rate: 19.5% (2008-2012 5-year est.).
Education: Percent of population age 25 and over with: High school diploma (including GED) or higher: 67.5% (2008-2012 5-year est.); Bachelor's degree or higher: 11.2% (2008-2012 5-year est.); Master's degree or higher: 3.3% (2008-2012 5-year est.).

School District(s)
Argo CHSD 217 (09-12)
    2011-12 Enrollment: 1,877 . . . . (708) 728-3200
Summit SD 104 (PK-08)
    2011-12 Enrollment: 1,832 . . . . (708) 458-0505
Housing: Homeownership rate: 55.1% (2008-2012 5-year est.); Median home value: $190,100 (2008-2012 5-year est.); Median contract rent: $690 per month (2008-2012 5-year est.); Median year structure built: 1950 (2008-2012 5-year est.).
Health Insurance: 44.5% Private; 32.6% Public; 29.7% None. (2008-2012 5-year est.)
Safety: Violent crime rate: 54.0 per 10,000 population; Property crime rate: 287.2 per 10,000 population (2012).
Transportation: Commute to work: 85.6% car, 5.5% public transportation, 5.4% walk, 2.4% work from home (2008-2012 5-year est.); Travel time to work: 24.5% less than 15 minutes, 37.6% 15 to 30 minutes, 19.6% 30 to 45 minutes, 9.4% 45 to 60 minutes, 8.9% 60 minutes or more (2008-2012 5-year est.); Amtrak: Train service available.
Additional Information Contacts
Argo-Summit Chamber of Commerce . . . . (708) 458-3033
Village of Summit . . . . (708) 563-4823
    http://thevillageofsummit.com

SUMMIT ARGO (unincorporated postal area)
Zip Code: 60501

Covers a land area of 4.836 square miles and a water area of 0.374 square miles. Located at 41.78° N. Lat; 87.82° W. Long. Population: 11,626 (2010); Density: 2,403.7 persons per square mile (2010); Race: 59.0% White, 9.0% Black/African American, 1.8% Asian, 0.8% American Indian/Alaska Native, 0.1% Native Hawaiian/Other Pacific Islander, 29.3% Some other race, 3.6% Two or more races, 61.8% Hispanic of any race (2010); Average household size: 3.30 (2010); Median age: 30.6 (2010); Males per 100 females: 102.6 (2010); Homeownership rate: 54.1% (2010)

THORNTON (village).
Covers a land area of 2.349 square miles and a water area of 0.026 square miles. Located at 41.57° N. Lat; 87.62° W. Long. Elevation is 597 feet.

History: Incorporated 1900.

Population: 2,778 (1990); 2,582 (2000); 2,338 (2010); Density: 1,157.2 persons per square mile (2008-2012 5-year est.); Race: 82.7% White, 12.9% Black/African American, 0.2% Asian, 0.7% American Indian/Alaska Native, 0.0% Native Hawaiian/Other Pacific Islander, 3.5% Some other race, 1.5% Two or more races, 11.3% Hispanic of any race (2008-2012 5-year est.); Average household size: 2.58 (2008-2012 5-year est.); Median age: 43.1 (2008-2012 5-year est.); Males per 100 females: 84.0 (2008-2012 5-year est.); Marriage status: 26.5% never married, 49.5% now married, 9.7% widowed, 14.3% divorced (2008-2012 5-year est.); Foreign born: 5.0% (2008-2012 5-year est.); Ancestry (includes multiple ancestries): 23.9% German, 18.1% Irish, 16.1% Polish, 13.6% Italian, 4.6% French (2008-2012 5-year est.).

Economy: Single-family building permits issued: 0 (2013); Multi-family building permits issued: 0 (2013); Homeowner vacancy rate: 4.2%. Rental vacancy rate: 11.2%. (2008-2012 5-year est.); Employment by occupation: 6.3% management, business, and financial, 0.8% computer, engineering, and science, 2.2% education, legal, community service, arts, and media, 8.2% healthcare practitioners, 22.0% service, 31.8% sales and office, 12.1% natural resources, construction, and maintenance, 16.6% production, transportation, and material moving (2008-2012 5-year est.).

Income: Per capita income: $23,631 (2008-2012 5-year est.); Median household income: $52,156 (2008-2012 5-year est.); Average household income: $58,661 (2008-2012 5-year est.); Percent of households with income of $100,000 or more: 17.7% (2008-2012 5-year est.); Poverty rate: 12.2% (2008-2012 5-year est.).

Taxes: Total city taxes per capita: $1,462 (2011); City property taxes per capita: $1,170 (2011).

Education: Percent of population age 25 and over with: High school diploma (including GED) or higher: 87.4% (2008-2012 5-year est.); Bachelor's degree or higher: 12.2% (2008-2012 5-year est.); Master's degree or higher: 3.7% (2008-2012 5-year est.).

School District(s)
Thornton SD 154 (PK-08)
   2011-12 Enrollment: 225. . . . . (708) 877-5160

Housing: Homeownership rate: 85.0% (2008-2012 5-year est.); Median home value: $131,100 (2008-2012 5-year est.); Median contract rent: $710 per month (2008-2012 5-year est.); Median year structure built: 1955 (2008-2012 5-year est.).

Health Insurance: 64.7% Private; 33.8% Public; 15.4% None. (2008-2012 5-year est.)

Safety: Violent crime rate: 21.3 per 10,000 population; Property crime rate: 221.4 per 10,000 population (2012).

Transportation: Commute to work: 91.6% car, 5.1% public transportation, 0.8% walk, 2.5% work from home (2008-2012 5-year est.); Travel time to work: 24.5% less than 15 minutes, 29.6% 15 to 30 minutes, 15.3% 30 to 45 minutes, 10.6% 45 to 60 minutes, 20.0% 60 minutes or more (2008-2012 5-year est.)

TINLEY PARK (village).
Covers a land area of 16.021 square miles and a water area of 0.019 square miles. Located at 41.57° N. Lat; 87.80° W. Long. Elevation is 699 feet.

Population: 37,121 (1990); 48,401 (2000); 56,703 (2010); Density: 3,516.6 persons per square mile (2008-2012 5-year est.); Race: 88.3% White, 3.2% Black/African American, 3.9% Asian, 0.0% American Indian/Alaska Native, 0.0% Native Hawaiian/Other Pacific Islander, 4.6% Some other race, 1.5% Two or more races, 8.4% Hispanic of any race (2008-2012 5-year est.); Average household size: 2.67 (2008-2012 5-year est.); Median age: 38.8 (2008-2012 5-year est.); Males per 100 females: 94.2 (2008-2012 5-year est.); Marriage status: 28.3% never married, 55.5% now married, 6.6% widowed, 9.6% divorced (2008-2012 5-year est.); Foreign born: 8.2% (2008-2012 5-year est.); Ancestry (includes multiple ancestries): 26.2% Irish, 22.0% German, 20.4% Polish, 12.4% Italian, 4.7% English (2008-2012 5-year est.).

Economy: Unemployment rate: 6.6% (April 2014); Total civilian labor force: 31,421 (April 2014); Single-family building permits issued: 23 (2013); Multi-family building permits issued: 0 (2013); Homeowner vacancy rate: 1.1%. Rental vacancy rate: 5.9%. (2008-2012 5-year est.); Employment by occupation: 14.7% management, business, and financial, 4.8% computer, engineering, and science, 10.1% education, legal, community service, arts, and media, 8.5% healthcare practitioners, 12.9% service, 28.2% sales and office, 8.2% natural resources, construction, and maintenance, 12.5% production, transportation, and material moving (2008-2012 5-year est.).

Income: Per capita income: $32,782 (2008-2012 5-year est.); Median household income: $77,989 (2008-2012 5-year est.); Average household income: $86,166 (2008-2012 5-year est.); Percent of households with income of $100,000 or more: 34.1% (2008-2012 5-year est.); Poverty rate: 5.8% (2008-2012 5-year est.).

Education: Percent of population age 25 and over with: High school diploma (including GED) or higher: 93.8% (2008-2012 5-year est.); Bachelor's degree or higher: 32.8% (2008-2012 5-year est.); Master's degree or higher: 9.9% (2008-2012 5-year est.).

School District(s)
Arbor Park SD 145 (PK-08)
   2011-12 Enrollment: 1,461 . . . . (708) 687-8040
Bremen CHSD 228 (09-12)
   2011-12 Enrollment: 5,491 . . . . (708) 389-1175
Kirby SD 140 (PK-08)
   2011-12 Enrollment: 3,735 . . . . (708) 532-6462
Summit Hill SD 161 (PK-08)
   2011-12 Enrollment: 3,527 . . . . (815) 469-9103
Tinley Park CCSD 146 (PK-08)
   2011-12 Enrollment: 2,408 . . . . (708) 614-4500

Two-year College(s)
Sanford-Brown College-Tinley Park (Private, For-profit)
   Fall 2012 Enrollment: 243. . . . . (708) 781-2035
   2012-13 Tuition: In-state $15,959; Out-of-state $15,959

Vocational/Technical School(s)
Regency Beauty Institute-Tinley Park (Private, For-profit)
   Fall 2012 Enrollment: 83. . . . . (800) 787-6456
   2012-13 Tuition: $16,425

Housing: Homeownership rate: 85.5% (2008-2012 5-year est.); Median home value: $240,800 (2008-2012 5-year est.); Median contract rent: $891 per month (2008-2012 5-year est.); Median year structure built: 1986 (2008-2012 5-year est.).

Health Insurance: 83.8% Private; 21.6% Public; 6.5% None. (2008-2012 5-year est.)

Hospitals: Tinley Park Mental Health Center (150 beds)

Safety: Violent crime rate: 7.5 per 10,000 population; Property crime rate: 147.2 per 10,000 population (2012).

Transportation: Commute to work: 86.8% car, 9.1% public transportation, 1.2% walk, 2.2% work from home (2008-2012 5-year est.); Travel time to work: 20.0% less than 15 minutes, 26.7% 15 to 30 minutes, 22.9% 30 to 45 minutes, 12.1% 45 to 60 minutes, 18.3% 60 minutes or more (2008-2012 5-year est.)

Additional Information Contacts
Tinley Park Chamber of Commerce . . . . (708) 532-5700
   http://www.tinleychamber.org
Village of Tinley Park. . . . . (708) 444-5000
   http://www.tinleypark.org

WESTCHESTER (village).
Covers a land area of 3.686 square miles and a water area of 0 square miles. Located at 41.85° N. Lat; 87.89° W. Long. Elevation is 636 feet.

Population: 17,301 (1990); 16,824 (2000); 16,718 (2010); Density: 4,526.2 persons per square mile (2008-2012 5-year est.); Race: 68.6% White, 18.7% Black/African American, 4.1% Asian, 0.1% American Indian/Alaska Native, 0.0% Native Hawaiian/Other Pacific Islander, 8.5% Some other race, 1.3% Two or more races, 13.9% Hispanic of any race (2008-2012 5-year est.); Average household size: 2.60 (2008-2012 5-year est.); Median age: 45.4 (2008-2012 5-year est.); Males per 100 females: 94.8 (2008-2012 5-year est.); Marriage status: 27.5% never married, 57.2% now married, 8.7% widowed, 6.6% divorced (2008-2012 5-year est.); Foreign born: 14.0% (2008-2012 5-year est.); Ancestry (includes multiple ancestries): 14.8% Irish, 14.5% German, 13.6% Polish, 13.6% Italian, 4.4% Czech (2008-2012 5-year est.).

Economy: Single-family building permits issued: 0 (2013); Multi-family building permits issued: 0 (2013); Homeowner vacancy rate: 1.6%. Rental vacancy rate: 0.0%. (2008-2012 5-year est.); Employment by occupation: 16.1% management, business, and financial, 4.8% computer, engineering, and science, 13.3% education, legal, community service, arts, and media, 6.4% healthcare practitioners, 13.4% service, 28.5% sales and office, 6.6% natural resources, construction, and maintenance, 10.9% production, transportation, and material moving (2008-2012 5-year est.).

Income: Per capita income: $30,883 (2008-2012 5-year est.); Median household income: $69,989 (2008-2012 5-year est.); Average household income: $78,197 (2008-2012 5-year est.); Percent of households with income of $100,000 or more: 28.9% (2008-2012 5-year est.); Poverty rate: 6.0% (2008-2012 5-year est.).

Education: Percent of population age 25 and over with: High school diploma (including GED) or higher: 89.1% (2008-2012 5-year est.); Bachelor's degree or higher: 33.5% (2008-2012 5-year est.); Master's degree or higher: 11.1% (2008-2012 5-year est.).

School District(s)
Westchester SD 92-5 (PK-08)
   2011-12 Enrollment: 1,261 . . . . (708) 450-2700

Housing: Homeownership rate: 91.1% (2008-2012 5-year est.); Median home value: $262,100 (2008-2012 5-year est.); Median contract rent: $1,265 per month (2008-2012 5-year est.); Median year structure built: 1957 (2008-2012 5-year est.).

Health Insurance: 81.2% Private; 29.3% Public; 7.7% None. (2008-2012 5-year est.)

Safety: Violent crime rate: 8.9 per 10,000 population; Property crime rate: 144.1 per 10,000 population (2012).

Transportation: Commute to work: 89.8% car, 5.8% public transportation, 1.1% walk, 1.7% work from home (2008-2012 5-year est.); Travel time to work: 20.5% less than 15 minutes, 35.0% 15 to 30 minutes, 23.2% 30 to 45 minutes, 9.9% 45 to 60 minutes, 11.4% 60 minutes or more (2008-2012 5-year est.)

Additional Information Contacts
Village of Westchester . . . . (708) 345-0020
   http://www.westchester-il.org
Westchester Chamber of Commerce . . . . (708) 240-8400
   http://www.westchesterchamber.org

WESTERN SPRINGS (village). Covers a land area of 2.792 square miles and a water area of 0 square miles. Located at 41.80° N. Lat; 87.90° W. Long. Elevation is 673 feet.

History: Western Springs was named for the mineral springs, believed to be medicinal when the community was settled by the Quakers in 1866.

Population: 11,984 (1990); 12,493 (2000); 12,975 (2010); Density: 4,603.6 persons per square mile (2008-2012 5-year est.); Race: 98.2% White, 0.2% Black/African American, 0.3% Asian, 0.0% American Indian/Alaska Native, 0.0% Native Hawaiian/Other Pacific Islander, 1.3% Some other race, 0.7% Two or more races, 4.1% Hispanic of any race (2008-2012 5-year est.); Average household size: 3.02 (2008-2012 5-year est.); Median age: 42.7 (2008-2012 5-year est.); Males per 100 females: 98.5 (2008-2012 5-year est.); Marriage status: 21.9% never married, 68.3% now married, 5.4% widowed, 4.5% divorced (2008-2012 5-year est.); Foreign born: 3.6% (2008-2012 5-year est.); Ancestry (includes multiple ancestries): 33.7% Irish, 26.1% German, 13.5% Italian, 11.7% English, 11.3% Polish (2008-2012 5-year est.).

Economy: Single-family building permits issued: 46 (2013); Multi-family building permits issued: 0 (2013); Homeowner vacancy rate: 2.3%. Rental vacancy rate: 0.0%. (2008-2012 5-year est.); Employment by occupation: 31.9% management, business, and financial, 3.7% computer, engineering, and science, 22.4% education, legal, community service, arts, and media, 7.2% healthcare practitioners, 4.9% service, 23.7% sales and office, 2.5% natural resources, construction, and maintenance, 3.6% production, transportation, and material moving (2008-2012 5-year est.).

Income: Per capita income: $59,292 (2008-2012 5-year est.); Median household income: $137,331 (2008-2012 5-year est.); Average household income: $177,578 (2008-2012 5-year est.); Percent of households with income of $100,000 or more: 65.6% (2008-2012 5-year est.); Poverty rate: 1.8% (2008-2012 5-year est.).

Taxes: Total city taxes per capita: $657 (2011); City property taxes per capita: $477 (2011).

Education: Percent of population age 25 and over with: High school diploma (including GED) or higher: 99.0% (2008-2012 5-year est.); Bachelor's degree or higher: 75.4% (2008-2012 5-year est.); Master's degree or higher: 35.0% (2008-2012 5-year est.).

School District(s)
Western Springs SD 101 (PK-08)
   2011-12 Enrollment: 1,497 . . . . (708) 246-3700

Housing: Homeownership rate: 96.6% (2008-2012 5-year est.); Median home value: $550,000 (2008-2012 5-year est.); Median contract rent: $1,554 per month (2008-2012 5-year est.); Median year structure built: 1957 (2008-2012 5-year est.).

Health Insurance: 92.9% Private; 16.8% Public; 2.8% None. (2008-2012 5-year est.)

Safety: Violent crime rate: 0.8 per 10,000 population; Property crime rate: 37.6 per 10,000 population (2012).

Transportation: Commute to work: 67.5% car, 19.8% public transportation, 1.5% walk, 9.3% work from home (2008-2012 5-year est.); Travel time to work: 23.9% less than 15 minutes, 20.6% 15 to 30 minutes, 25.7% 30 to 45 minutes, 19.5% 45 to 60 minutes, 10.4% 60 minutes or more (2008-2012 5-year est.)

Additional Information Contacts
Village of Western Springs . . . . (708) 246-1800
   http://www.wsprings.com
Western Springs Business Association . . . . (708) 784-3126
   http://www.westernspringsbusiness.com

WHEELING (village). Covers a land area of 8.701 square miles and a water area of 0.060 square miles. Located at 42.13° N. Lat; 87.92° W. Long. Elevation is 650 feet.

History: Named for Wheeling, West Virginia. The first building in Wheeling was a country store established in 1830 on the Chicago-Milwaukee stage route.

Population: 29,911 (1990); 34,496 (2000); 37,648 (2010); Density: 4,318.4 persons per square mile (2008-2012 5-year est.); Race: 74.3% White, 1.4% Black/African American, 14.1% Asian, 0.1% American Indian/Alaska Native, 0.0% Native Hawaiian/Other Pacific Islander, 10.1% Some other race, 1.1% Two or more races, 32.4% Hispanic of any race (2008-2012 5-year est.); Average household size: 2.60 (2008-2012 5-year est.); Median age: 35.8 (2008-2012 5-year est.); Males per 100 females: 94.4 (2008-2012 5-year est.); Marriage status: 27.8% never married, 56.6% now married, 6.6% widowed, 8.9% divorced (2008-2012 5-year est.); Foreign born: 42.0% (2008-2012 5-year est.); Ancestry (includes multiple ancestries): 12.2% German, 9.6% Polish, 7.4% Irish, 6.3% Russian, 4.9% Italian (2008-2012 5-year est.).

Economy: Unemployment rate: 6.1% (April 2014); Total civilian labor force: 22,725 (April 2014); Single-family building permits issued: 15 (2013); Multi-family building permits issued: 0 (2013); Homeowner vacancy rate: 2.5%. Rental vacancy rate: 4.6%. (2008-2012 5-year est.); Employment by occupation: 13.0% management, business, and financial, 9.1% computer, engineering, and science, 6.3% education, legal, community service, arts, and media, 2.5% healthcare practitioners, 18.8% service, 27.1% sales and office, 5.4% natural resources, construction, and maintenance, 17.9% production, transportation, and material moving (2008-2012 5-year est.).

Income: Per capita income: $27,362 (2008-2012 5-year est.); Median household income: $57,364 (2008-2012 5-year est.); Average household income: $69,237 (2008-2012 5-year est.); Percent of households with income of $100,000 or more: 22.2% (2008-2012 5-year est.); Poverty rate: 10.4% (2008-2012 5-year est.).

Taxes: Total city taxes per capita: $784 (2011); City property taxes per capita: $527 (2011).

Education: Percent of population age 25 and over with: High school diploma (including GED) or higher: 86.4% (2008-2012 5-year est.); Bachelor's degree or higher: 37.0% (2008-2012 5-year est.); Master's degree or higher: 11.0% (2008-2012 5-year est.).

School District(s)
Township HSD 214 (09-12)
   2011-12 Enrollment: 12,305 . . . . (847) 718-7600
Wheeling CCSD 21 (PK-08)
   2011-12 Enrollment: 6,866 . . . . (847) 537-8270

Two-year College(s)
SOLEX College (Private, For-profit)
   Fall 2012 Enrollment: 102 . . . . (847) 229-9595
Worsham College of Mortuary Science (Private, For-profit)
   Fall 2012 Enrollment: 140 . . . . (847) 808-8444

Vocational/Technical School(s)
SOLEX Medical Academy (Private, For-profit)
   Fall 2012 Enrollment: 27 . . . . (847) 229-9595
   2012-13 Tuition: $10,095

Housing: Homeownership rate: 65.1% (2008-2012 5-year est.); Median home value: $211,100 (2008-2012 5-year est.); Median contract rent: $927 per month (2008-2012 5-year est.); Median year structure built: 1977 (2008-2012 5-year est.).

Health Insurance: 65.7% Private; 25.1% Public; 17.4% None. (2008-2012 5-year est.)

Safety: Violent crime rate: 8.2 per 10,000 population; Property crime rate: 142.7 per 10,000 population (2012).

Transportation: Commute to work: 92.2% car, 2.4% public transportation, 1.0% walk, 3.0% work from home (2008-2012 5-year est.); Travel time to work: 23.8% less than 15 minutes, 37.4% 15 to 30 minutes, 25.3% 30 to 45 minutes, 6.7% 45 to 60 minutes, 6.8% 60 minutes or more (2008-2012 5-year est.)

Airports: Chicago Executive Airport (reliver airport)

Additional Information Contacts

Village of Wheeling . . . . (847) 459-2600
  http://vi.wheeling.il.us
Wheeling/Prospect Heights Area Chamber of Commerce & Industr . . (847) 541-0170
  http://www.wphchamber.com

WILLOW SPRINGS (village). Covers a land area of 4.015 square miles and a water area of 0.106 square miles. Located at 41.73° N. Lat; 87.88° W. Long. Elevation is 617 feet.

Population: 4,509 (1990); 5,027 (2000); 5,524 (2010); Density: 1,358.8 persons per square mile (2008-2012 5-year est.); Race: 94.3% White, 1.8% Black/African American, 2.0% Asian, 0.0% American Indian/Alaska Native, 0.0% Native Hawaiian/Other Pacific Islander, 1.9% Some other race, 1.0% Two or more races, 6.5% Hispanic of any race (2008-2012 5-year est.); Average household size: 2.33 (2008-2012 5-year est.); Median age: 44.7 (2008-2012 5-year est.); Males per 100 females: 94.1 (2008-2012 5-year est.); Marriage status: 24.7% never married, 56.7% now married, 9.1% widowed, 9.4% divorced (2008-2012 5-year est.); Foreign born: 14.4% (2008-2012 5-year est.); Ancestry (includes multiple ancestries): 22.3% Polish, 17.3% Irish, 15.9% German, 8.9% Italian, 6.1% Lithuanian (2008-2012 5-year est.).

Economy: Single-family building permits issued: 2 (2013); Multi-family building permits issued: 0 (2013); Homeowner vacancy rate: 0.0%. Rental vacancy rate: 0.0%. (2008-2012 5-year est.); Employment by occupation: 19.6% management, business, and financial, 3.8% computer, engineering, and science, 11.5% education, legal, community service, arts, and media, 5.0% healthcare practitioners, 12.1% service, 27.8% sales and office, 7.3% natural resources, construction, and maintenance, 12.9% production, transportation, and material moving (2008-2012 5-year est.).

Income: Per capita income: $37,521 (2008-2012 5-year est.); Median household income: $70,972 (2008-2012 5-year est.); Average household income: $85,798 (2008-2012 5-year est.); Percent of households with income of $100,000 or more: 31.6% (2008-2012 5-year est.); Poverty rate: 4.8% (2008-2012 5-year est.).

Education: Percent of population age 25 and over with: High school diploma (including GED) or higher: 93.8% (2008-2012 5-year est.); Bachelor's degree or higher: 32.4% (2008-2012 5-year est.); Master's degree or higher: 14.4% (2008-2012 5-year est.).

School District(s)

Willow Springs SD 108 (KG-08)
  2011-12 Enrollment: 291 . . . . (708) 839-6828

Housing: Homeownership rate: 84.7% (2008-2012 5-year est.); Median home value: $329,400 (2008-2012 5-year est.); Median contract rent: $772 per month (2008-2012 5-year est.); Median year structure built: 1980 (2008-2012 5-year est.).

Health Insurance: 83.6% Private; 22.2% Public; 7.8% None. (2008-2012 5-year est.)

Safety: Violent crime rate: 7.2 per 10,000 population; Property crime rate: 66.7 per 10,000 population (2012).

Transportation: Commute to work: 86.8% car, 5.2% public transportation, 0.4% walk, 6.3% work from home (2008-2012 5-year est.); Travel time to work: 23.6% less than 15 minutes, 29.1% 15 to 30 minutes, 21.8% 30 to 45 minutes, 15.0% 45 to 60 minutes, 10.6% 60 minutes or more (2008-2012 5-year est.)

Additional Information Contacts

Village of Willow Springs . . . . (708) 467-3700
  http://www.willowsprings-il.gov

WILMETTE (village). Covers a land area of 5.403 square miles and a water area of 0.009 square miles. Located at 42.08° N. Lat; 87.73° W. Long. Elevation is 636 feet.

History: Wilmette was named for Antoine Ouilmette, a French-Canadian who settled here when his wife received the land under a government treaty in 1829.

Population: 26,690 (1990); 27,651 (2000); 27,087 (2010); Density: 5,034.4 persons per square mile (2008-2012 5-year est.); Race: 84.6% White, 1.1% Black/African American, 12.4% Asian, 0.1% American Indian/Alaska Native, 0.0% Native Hawaiian/Other Pacific Islander, 1.8% Some other race, 1.5% Two or more races, 4.5% Hispanic of any race (2008-2012 5-year est.); Average household size: 2.84 (2008-2012 5-year est.); Median age: 43.5 (2008-2012 5-year est.); Males per 100 females: 102.0 (2008-2012 5-year est.); Marriage status: 23.5% never married, 64.0% now married, 6.3% widowed, 6.2% divorced (2008-2012 5-year est.); Foreign born: 16.9% (2008-2012 5-year est.); Ancestry (includes multiple ancestries): 23.1% German, 17.7% Irish, 10.5% English, 6.6% Polish, 6.4% Italian (2008-2012 5-year est.).

Economy: Unemployment rate: 5.1% (April 2014); Total civilian labor force: 13,095 (April 2014); Single-family building permits issued: 44 (2013); Multi-family building permits issued: 0 (2013); Homeowner vacancy rate: 1.1%. Rental vacancy rate: 6.5%. (2008-2012 5-year est.); Employment by occupation: 28.9% management, business, and financial, 6.7% computer, engineering, and science, 24.3% education, legal, community service, arts, and media, 8.5% healthcare practitioners, 6.5% service, 19.8% sales and office, 2.1% natural resources, construction, and maintenance, 3.2% production, transportation, and material moving (2008-2012 5-year est.).

Income: Per capita income: $68,612 (2008-2012 5-year est.); Median household income: $130,088 (2008-2012 5-year est.); Average household income: $194,261 (2008-2012 5-year est.); Percent of households with income of $100,000 or more: 60.6% (2008-2012 5-year est.); Poverty rate: 2.6% (2008-2012 5-year est.).

Taxes: Total city taxes per capita: $821 (2011); City property taxes per capita: $502 (2011).

Education: Percent of population age 25 and over with: High school diploma (including GED) or higher: 98.1% (2008-2012 5-year est.); Bachelor's degree or higher: 79.0% (2008-2012 5-year est.); Master's degree or higher: 44.1% (2008-2012 5-year est.).

School District(s)

Avoca SD 37 (PK-08)
  2011-12 Enrollment: 656 . . . . (847) 251-3587
Wilmette SD 39 (PK-08)
  2011-12 Enrollment: 3,679 . . . . (847) 512-6030

Housing: Homeownership rate: 84.4% (2008-2012 5-year est.); Median home value: $643,600 (2008-2012 5-year est.); Median contract rent: $1,422 per month (2008-2012 5-year est.); Median year structure built: 1953 (2008-2012 5-year est.).

Health Insurance: 90.5% Private; 17.8% Public; 4.1% None. (2008-2012 5-year est.)

Safety: Violent crime rate: 4.0 per 10,000 population; Property crime rate: 154.3 per 10,000 population (2012).

Transportation: Commute to work: 66.8% car, 19.2% public transportation, 3.4% walk, 9.5% work from home (2008-2012 5-year est.); Travel time to work: 21.9% less than 15 minutes, 24.3% 15 to 30 minutes, 22.3% 30 to 45 minutes, 14.1% 45 to 60 minutes, 17.4% 60 minutes or more (2008-2012 5-year est.)

Additional Information Contacts

Village of Wilmette . . . . (847) 251-2700
  http://www.wilmette.com
Wilmette Chamber of Commerce . . . . (847) 251-3800
  http://www.wilmettechamber.org

WINNETKA (village). Covers a land area of 3.810 square miles and a water area of 0.083 square miles. Located at 42.11° N. Lat; 87.74° W. Long. Elevation is 653 feet.

History: Named for a variation of the Algonquian translation of "beautiful". Winnetka was incorporated in 1869. The Winnetka public school system, organized in 1919 with Carleton Washburne as superintendent, gained recognition for innovative eucation.

Population: 12,174 (1990); 12,419 (2000); 12,187 (2010); Density: 3,204.5 persons per square mile (2008-2012 5-year est.); Race: 93.2% White, 0.1% Black/African American, 3.4% Asian, 0.3% American Indian/Alaska Native, 0.0% Native Hawaiian/Other Pacific Islander, 3.0% Some other race, 2.5% Two or more races, 3.5% Hispanic of any race (2008-2012 5-year est.); Average household size: 3.14 (2008-2012 5-year

est.); Median age: 40.5 (2008-2012 5-year est.); Males per 100 females: 94.5 (2008-2012 5-year est.); Marriage status: 23.7% never married, 68.8% now married, 3.3% widowed, 4.3% divorced (2008-2012 5-year est.); Foreign born: 5.6% (2008-2012 5-year est.); Ancestry (includes multiple ancestries): 27.4% German, 22.3% Irish, 15.2% English, 5.4% Italian, 4.8% Polish (2008-2012 5-year est.).

Economy: Single-family building permits issued: 30 (2013); Multi-family building permits issued: 0 (2013); Homeowner vacancy rate: 4.4%. Rental vacancy rate: 14.1%. (2008-2012 5-year est.); Employment by occupation: 34.8% management, business, and financial, 5.5% computer, engineering, and science, 22.6% education, legal, community service, arts, and media, 7.5% healthcare practitioners, 5.7% service, 19.9% sales and office, 2.1% natural resources, construction, and maintenance, 1.9% production, transportation, and material moving (2008-2012 5-year est.).

Income: Per capita income: $94,832 (2008-2012 5-year est.); Median household income: $203,995 (2008-2012 5-year est.); Average household income: $295,195 (2008-2012 5-year est.); Percent of households with income of $100,000 or more: 76.2% (2008-2012 5-year est.); Poverty rate: 2.1% (2008-2012 5-year est.).

Taxes: Total city taxes per capita: $1,283 (2011); City property taxes per capita: $1,006 (2011).

Education: Percent of population age 25 and over with: High school diploma (including GED) or higher: 99.2% (2008-2012 5-year est.); Bachelor's degree or higher: 88.4% (2008-2012 5-year est.); Master's degree or higher: 48.4% (2008-2012 5-year est.).

School District(s)
New Trier Twp HSD 203 (09-12)
    2011-12 Enrollment: 4,234 . . . . (847) 784-6109
Winnetka SD 36 (PK-08)
    2011-12 Enrollment: 1,810 . . . . (847) 446-9400

Housing: Homeownership rate: 91.2% (2008-2012 5-year est.); Median home value: $951,900 (2008-2012 5-year est.); Median contract rent: $970 per month (2008-2012 5-year est.); Median year structure built: Before 1940 (2008-2012 5-year est.).

Health Insurance: 92.3% Private; 15.3% Public; 2.3% None. (2008-2012 5-year est.)

Safety: Violent crime rate: 3.3 per 10,000 population; Property crime rate: 138.0 per 10,000 population (2012).

Transportation: Commute to work: 60.1% car, 25.7% public transportation, 2.2% walk, 9.5% work from home (2008-2012 5-year est.); Travel time to work: 22.3% less than 15 minutes, 17.7% 15 to 30 minutes, 22.5% 30 to 45 minutes, 21.6% 45 to 60 minutes, 15.9% 60 minutes or more (2008-2012 5-year est.)

Additional Information Contacts
Village of Winnetka . . . . (847) 501-6000
    http://www.villageofwinnetka.org
Winnetka-Northfield Chamber of Commerce . . . . (847) 446-4451
    http://www.winnetkachamber.com

WORTH (village).
Covers a land area of 2.369 square miles and a water area of 0.013 square miles. Located at 41.69° N. Lat; 87.79° W. Long. Elevation is 610 feet.

Population: 11,208 (1990); 11,047 (2000); 10,789 (2010); Density: 4,553.8 persons per square mile (2008-2012 5-year est.); Race: 91.3% White, 2.8% Black/African American, 1.3% Asian, 0.3% American Indian/Alaska Native, 0.0% Native Hawaiian/Other Pacific Islander, 4.3% Some other race, 1.4% Two or more races, 12.8% Hispanic of any race (2008-2012 5-year est.); Average household size: 2.49 (2008-2012 5-year est.); Median age: 37.3 (2008-2012 5-year est.); Males per 100 females: 94.5 (2008-2012 5-year est.); Marriage status: 30.3% never married, 52.9% now married, 5.8% widowed, 11.0% divorced (2008-2012 5-year est.); Foreign born: 16.4% (2008-2012 5-year est.); Ancestry (includes multiple ancestries): 25.2% Polish, 22.5% Irish, 14.2% German, 10.0% Italian, 4.3% American (2008-2012 5-year est.).

Economy: Single-family building permits issued: 0 (2013); Multi-family building permits issued: 0 (2013); Homeowner vacancy rate: 2.9%. Rental vacancy rate: 5.6%. (2008-2012 5-year est.); Employment by occupation: 10.5% management, business, and financial, 2.8% computer, engineering, and science, 6.8% education, legal, community service, arts, and media, 5.2% healthcare practitioners, 17.5% service, 27.0% sales and office, 13.8% natural resources, construction, and maintenance, 16.5% production, transportation, and material moving (2008-2012 5-year est.).

Income: Per capita income: $26,572 (2008-2012 5-year est.); Median household income: $55,669 (2008-2012 5-year est.); Average household income: $63,850 (2008-2012 5-year est.); Percent of households with

income of $100,000 or more: 17.2% (2008-2012 5-year est.); Poverty rate: 12.9% (2008-2012 5-year est.).

Education: Percent of population age 25 and over with: High school diploma (including GED) or higher: 88.5% (2008-2012 5-year est.); Bachelor's degree or higher: 15.5% (2008-2012 5-year est.); Master's degree or higher: 3.2% (2008-2012 5-year est.).

School District(s)
Region 07 South Cook Isc 4 (PK-12)
    2011-12 Enrollment: n/a . . . . (708) 754-6600
Worth SD 127 (PK-08)
    2011-12 Enrollment: 1,043 . . . . (708) 448-2800

Housing: Homeownership rate: 74.3% (2008-2012 5-year est.); Median home value: $188,000 (2008-2012 5-year est.); Median contract rent: $819 per month (2008-2012 5-year est.); Median year structure built: 1964 (2008-2012 5-year est.).

Health Insurance: 67.5% Private; 26.1% Public; 17.2% None. (2008-2012 5-year est.)

Safety: Violent crime rate: 4.6 per 10,000 population; Property crime rate: 111.6 per 10,000 population (2012).

Transportation: Commute to work: 88.8% car, 6.8% public transportation, 1.3% walk, 2.6% work from home (2008-2012 5-year est.); Travel time to work: 18.3% less than 15 minutes, 26.8% 15 to 30 minutes, 21.9% 30 to 45 minutes, 16.9% 45 to 60 minutes, 16.2% 60 minutes or more (2008-2012 5-year est.)

Additional Information Contacts
Chicago Ridge/Worth Chamber of Commerce . . . . (708) 923-2050
    http://www.crwchamber.org
Village of Worth . . . . (708) 448-1181
    http://www.villageofworth.com

Crawford County

Located in southeastern Illinois; bounded on the east by the Wabash River and the Indiana border; drained by the Embarrass River. Covers a land area of 443.629 square miles, a water area of 2.189 square miles, and is located in the Central Time Zone at 39.00° N. Lat., 87.76° W. Long. The county was founded in 1816. County seat is Robinson.

Weather Station: Palestine 2 W   Elevation: 470 feet

	Jan	Feb	Mar	Apr	May	Jun	Jul	Aug	Sep	Oct	Nov	Dec
High	39	44	55	67	77	86	88	87	81	69	55	42
Low	23	27	35	45	54	62	66	65	55	45	36	26
Precip	3.0	2.5	3.4	4.3	5.1	4.0	3.8	3.7	3.5	3.5	3.9	3.2
Snow	4.9	3.6	1.5	0.1	0.0	0.0	0.0	0.0	0.0	0.1	0.5	4.1

High and Low temperatures in degrees Fahrenheit; Precipitation and Snow in inches

Population: 19,464 (1990); 20,452 (2000); 19,817 (2010); Race: 93.1% White, 2.9% Black/African American, 0.5% Asian, 0.6% American Indian/Alaska Native, 0.0% Native Hawaiian/Other Pacific Islander, 2.9% Some other race, 2.5% Two or more races, 1.9% Hispanic of any race (2008-2012 5-year est.); Density: 44.2 persons per square mile (2008-2012 5-year est.); Average household size: 2.44 (2008-2012 5-year est.); Median age: 42.0 (2008-2012 5-year est.); Males per 100 females: 105.9 (2008-2012 5-year est.).

Religion: Six largest groups: 18.9% Baptist, 7.1% Methodist/Pietist, 2.8% Non-denominational Protestant, 2.7% Catholicism, 1.6% Presbyterian-Reformed, 1.4% Holiness (2010)

Economy: Unemployment rate: 7.0% (April 2014); Total civilian labor force: 8,894 (April 2014); Leading industries: 28.6% manufacturing; 14.9% health care and social assistance; 13.1% administration, support, waste management, remediation services (2012); Farms: 599 totaling 214,995 acres (2012); Companies that employ 500 or more persons: 2 (2012); Companies that employ 100 to 499 persons: 9 (2012); Companies that employ less than 100 persons: 424 (2012); Black-owned businesses: n/a (2007); Hispanic-owned businesses: n/a (2007); Asian-owned businesses: n/a (2007); Women-owned businesses: 421 (2007); Single-family building permits issued: 5 (2013); Multi-family building permits issued: 0 (2013).

Income: Per capita income: $24,535 (2008-2012 5-year est.); Median household income: $44,617 (2008-2012 5-year est.); Average household income: $60,008 (2008-2012 5-year est.); Percent of households with income of $100,000 or more: 15.7% (2008-2012 5-year est.); Poverty rate: 15.0% (2008-2012 5-year est.); Bankruptcy rate: 2.91% (2013).

Education: Percent of population age 25 and over with: High school diploma (including GED) or higher: 88.2% (2008-2012 5-year est.); Bachelor's degree or higher: 15.6% (2008-2012 5-year est.); Master's degree or higher: 5.4% (2008-2012 5-year est.).

Housing: Homeownership rate: 81.0% (2008-2012 5-year est.); Median home value: $74,700 (2008-2012 5-year est.); Median contract rent: $382 per month (2008-2012 5-year est.); Median year structure built: 1959 (2008-2012 5-year est.)

Health: Birth rate: 107.2 per 10,000 population (2013); Death rate: 122.0 per 10,000 population (2013); Age-adjusted cancer mortality rate: 165.7 deaths per 100,000 population (2011); Number of physicians: 11.6 per 10,000 population (2011); Hospital beds: 31.8 per 10,000 population (2010); Hospital admissions: 601.0 per 10,000 population (2010).

Elections: 2012 Presidential election results: 33.2% Obama, 64.9% Romney

National and State Parks: Crawford County State Fish and Wildlife Area

Additional Information Contacts

Crawford County Government. . . . . (618) 546-1212
   http://www.crawfordcountycentral.com

Crawford County Communities

ANNAPOLIS (CDP). Covers a land area of 0.031 square miles and a water area of 0 square miles. Located at 39.15° N. Lat; 87.82° W. Long. Elevation is 584 feet.

Population: n/a (1990); n/a (2000); 55 (2010); Density: 2,456.4 persons per square mile (2008-2012 5-year est.); Race: 100.0% White, 0.0% Black/African American, 0.0% Asian, 0.0% American Indian/Alaska Native, 0.0% Native Hawaiian/Other Pacific Islander, 0.0% Some other race, 0.0% Two or more races, 0.0% Hispanic of any race (2008-2012 5-year est.); Average household size: 3.04 (2008-2012 5-year est.); Median age: 25.8 (2008-2012 5-year est.); Males per 100 females: 85.4 (2008-2012 5-year est.); Marriage status: 9.8% never married, 54.9% now married, 7.8% widowed, 27.5% divorced (2008-2012 5-year est.); Foreign born: 0.0% (2008-2012 5-year est.); Ancestry (includes multiple ancestries): 32.9% American, 21.1% German, 19.7% Italian, 7.9% English, 7.9% Dutch (2008-2012 5-year est.).

Economy: Homeowner vacancy rate: 0.0%. Rental vacancy rate: 0.0%. (2008-2012 5-year est.); Employment by occupation: 0.0% management, business, and financial, 0.0% computer, engineering, and science, 0.0% education, legal, community service, arts, and media, 0.0% healthcare practitioners, 48.4% service, 19.4% sales and office, 0.0% natural resources, construction, and maintenance, 32.3% production, transportation, and material moving (2008-2012 5-year est.).

Income: Per capita income: $11,616 (2008-2012 5-year est.); Median household income: $47,917 (2008-2012 5-year est.); Average household income: $34,600 (2008-2012 5-year est.); Percent of households with income of $100,000 or more: n/a (2008-2012 5-year est.); Poverty rate: 27.6% (2008-2012 5-year est.).

Education: Percent of population age 25 and over with: High school diploma (including GED) or higher: 100.0% (2008-2012 5-year est.); Bachelor's degree or higher: 19.6% (2008-2012 5-year est.); Master's degree or higher: 0.0% (2008-2012 5-year est.).

Housing: Homeownership rate: 84.0% (2008-2012 5-year est.); Median home value: $27,500 (2008-2012 5-year est.); Median contract rent: n/a per month (2008-2012 5-year est.); Median year structure built: 1978 (2008-2012 5-year est.).

Health Insurance: 27.6% Private; 51.3% Public; 32.9% None. (2008-2012 5-year est.)

Transportation: Commute to work: 32.3% car, 0.0% public transportation, 48.4% walk, 0.0% work from home (2008-2012 5-year est.); Travel time to work: 67.7% less than 15 minutes, 32.3% 15 to 30 minutes, 0.0% 30 to 45 minutes, 0.0% 45 to 60 minutes, 0.0% 60 minutes or more (2008-2012 5-year est.)

FLAT ROCK (village). Covers a land area of 0.855 square miles and a water area of 0 square miles. Located at 38.90° N. Lat; 87.67° W. Long. Elevation is 502 feet.

Population: 421 (1990); 415 (2000); 331 (2010); Density: 496.9 persons per square mile (2008-2012 5-year est.); Race: 96.5% White, 0.5% Black/African American, 0.0% Asian, 0.0% American Indian/Alaska Native, 0.0% Native Hawaiian/Other Pacific Islander, 3.0% Some other race, 3.1% Two or more races, 0.0% Hispanic of any race (2008-2012 5-year est.); Average household size: 2.26 (2008-2012 5-year est.); Median age: 42.3 (2008-2012 5-year est.); Males per 100 females: 89.7 (2008-2012 5-year est.); Marriage status: 31.7% never married, 38.2% now married, 12.2% widowed, 17.9% divorced (2008-2012 5-year est.); Foreign born: 0.0% (2008-2012 5-year est.); Ancestry (includes multiple ancestries): 25.2%

German, 11.8% Irish, 9.2% English, 8.2% American, 5.4% Dutch (2008-2012 5-year est.).

Economy: Homeowner vacancy rate: 0.0%. Rental vacancy rate: 0.0%. (2008-2012 5-year est.); Employment by occupation: 4.7% management, business, and financial, 0.0% computer, engineering, and science, 4.2% education, legal, community service, arts, and media, 6.3% healthcare practitioners, 21.6% service, 27.4% sales and office, 13.7% natural resources, construction, and maintenance, 22.1% production, transportation, and material moving (2008-2012 5-year est.).

Income: Per capita income: $20,806 (2008-2012 5-year est.); Median household income: $33,333 (2008-2012 5-year est.); Average household income: $44,177 (2008-2012 5-year est.); Percent of households with income of $100,000 or more: 9.6% (2008-2012 5-year est.); Poverty rate: 20.9% (2008-2012 5-year est.).

Education: Percent of population age 25 and over with: High school diploma (including GED) or higher: 88.6% (2008-2012 5-year est.); Bachelor's degree or higher: 9.3% (2008-2012 5-year est.); Master's degree or higher: 0.7% (2008-2012 5-year est.).

Housing: Homeownership rate: 92.0% (2008-2012 5-year est.); Median home value: $48,900 (2008-2012 5-year est.); Median contract rent: $282 per month (2008-2012 5-year est.); Median year structure built: 1949 (2008-2012 5-year est.).

Health Insurance: 59.5% Private; 44.0% Public; 15.1% None. (2008-2012 5-year est.)

Transportation: Commute to work: 95.7% car, 0.0% public transportation, 4.3% walk, 0.0% work from home (2008-2012 5-year est.); Travel time to work: 33.5% less than 15 minutes, 55.1% 15 to 30 minutes, 5.9% 30 to 45 minutes, 1.6% 45 to 60 minutes, 3.8% 60 minutes or more (2008-2012 5-year est.)

HUTSONVILLE (village). Covers a land area of 0.623 square miles and a water area of 0 square miles. Located at 39.11° N. Lat; 87.66° W. Long. Elevation is 436 feet.

Population: 622 (1990); 568 (2000); 554 (2010); Density: 1,126.0 persons per square mile (2008-2012 5-year est.); Race: 94.4% White, 0.6% Black/African American, 0.1% Asian, 1.1% American Indian/Alaska Native, 0.0% Native Hawaiian/Other Pacific Islander, 3.8% Some other race, 3.7% Two or more races, 0.1% Hispanic of any race (2008-2012 5-year est.); Average household size: 2.79 (2008-2012 5-year est.); Median age: 38.2 (2008-2012 5-year est.); Males per 100 females: 117.3 (2008-2012 5-year est.); Marriage status: 35.7% never married, 41.9% now married, 3.3% widowed, 19.1% divorced (2008-2012 5-year est.); Foreign born: 0.1% (2008-2012 5-year est.); Ancestry (includes multiple ancestries): 22.9% German, 20.7% English, 12.5% American, 12.0% Irish, 3.6% Dutch (2008-2012 5-year est.).

Economy: Single-family building permits issued: 3 (2013); Multi-family building permits issued: 0 (2013); Homeowner vacancy rate: 0.0%. Rental vacancy rate: 0.0%. (2008-2012 5-year est.); Employment by occupation: 11.4% management, business, and financial, 0.0% computer, engineering, and science, 10.6% education, legal, community service, arts, and media, 5.5% healthcare practitioners, 21.6% service, 22.5% sales and office, 7.2% natural resources, construction, and maintenance, 21.2% production, transportation, and material moving (2008-2012 5-year est.).

Income: Per capita income: $17,291 (2008-2012 5-year est.); Median household income: $41,406 (2008-2012 5-year est.); Average household income: $49,322 (2008-2012 5-year est.); Percent of households with income of $100,000 or more: 14.9% (2008-2012 5-year est.); Poverty rate: 26.5% (2008-2012 5-year est.).

Education: Percent of population age 25 and over with: High school diploma (including GED) or higher: 91.3% (2008-2012 5-year est.); Bachelor's degree or higher: 16.9% (2008-2012 5-year est.); Master's degree or higher: 7.8% (2008-2012 5-year est.).

School District(s)

Hutsonville CUSD 1 (PK-12)
   2011-12 Enrollment: 364. . . . . (618) 563-4912

Housing: Homeownership rate: 72.9% (2008-2012 5-year est.); Median home value: $54,300 (2008-2012 5-year est.); Median contract rent: $284 per month (2008-2012 5-year est.); Median year structure built: 1941 (2008-2012 5-year est.).

Health Insurance: 59.8% Private; 55.0% Public; 2.0% None. (2008-2012 5-year est.)

Transportation: Commute to work: 84.1% car, 1.7% public transportation, 11.2% walk, 3.0% work from home (2008-2012 5-year est.); Travel time to work: 31.1% less than 15 minutes, 44.9% 15 to 30 minutes, 11.6% 30 to

45 minutes, 4.0% 45 to 60 minutes, 8.4% 60 minutes or more (2008-2012 5-year est.)

OBLONG (village). Covers a land area of 0.965 square miles and a water area of 0.008 square miles. Located at 39.00° N. Lat; 87.91° W. Long. Elevation is 512 feet.

History: Incorporated 1883.

Population: 1,616 (1990); 1,580 (2000); 1,466 (2010); Density: 1,537.3 persons per square mile (2008-2012 5-year est.); Race: 97.8% White, 0.0% Black/African American, 0.0% Asian, 0.1% American Indian/Alaska Native, 0.0% Native Hawaiian/Other Pacific Islander, 2.1% Some other race, 2.1% Two or more races, 0.3% Hispanic of any race (2008-2012 5-year est.); Average household size: 2.43 (2008-2012 5-year est.); Median age: 43.8 (2008-2012 5-year est.); Males per 100 females: 99.7 (2008-2012 5-year est.); Marriage status: 25.1% never married, 52.8% now married, 8.6% widowed, 13.5% divorced (2008-2012 5-year est.); Foreign born: 0.5% (2008-2012 5-year est.); Ancestry (includes multiple ancestries): 21.1% German, 10.8% American, 9.8% English, 8.0% Irish, 3.4% Scotch-Irish (2008-2012 5-year est.).

Economy: Homeowner vacancy rate: 0.4%. Rental vacancy rate: 14.1%. (2008-2012 5-year est.); Employment by occupation: 4.8% management, business, and financial, 3.1% computer, engineering, and science, 9.1% education, legal, community service, arts, and media, 9.7% healthcare practitioners, 18.4% service, 12.3% sales and office, 9.1% natural resources, construction, and maintenance, 33.5% production, transportation, and material moving (2008-2012 5-year est.).

Income: Per capita income: $21,179 (2008-2012 5-year est.); Median household income: $40,129 (2008-2012 5-year est.); Average household income: $50,427 (2008-2012 5-year est.); Percent of households with income of $100,000 or more: 11.3% (2008-2012 5-year est.); Poverty rate: 15.7% (2008-2012 5-year est.).

Education: Percent of population age 25 and over with: High school diploma (including GED) or higher: 86.5% (2008-2012 5-year est.); Bachelor's degree or higher: 12.0% (2008-2012 5-year est.); Master's degree or higher: 3.3% (2008-2012 5-year est.).

School District(s)

Oblong CUSD 4 (PK-12)
    2011-12 Enrollment: 627 . . . . (618) 592-3933

Housing: Homeownership rate: 80.4% (2008-2012 5-year est.); Median home value: $58,800 (2008-2012 5-year est.); Median contract rent: $313 per month (2008-2012 5-year est.); Median year structure built: 1953 (2008-2012 5-year est.).

Health Insurance: 66.9% Private; 44.7% Public; 9.3% None. (2008-2012 5-year est.)

Safety: Violent crime rate: 74.8 per 10,000 population; Property crime rate: 136.1 per 10,000 population (2012).

Transportation: Commute to work: 93.9% car, 0.3% public transportation, 1.9% walk, 2.0% work from home (2008-2012 5-year est.); Travel time to work: 31.7% less than 15 minutes, 47.9% 15 to 30 minutes, 12.7% 30 to 45 minutes, 3.5% 45 to 60 minutes, 4.2% 60 minutes or more (2008-2012 5-year est.)

Additional Information Contacts

Oblong Chamber of Commerce . . . . (618) 592-4355
    http://www.theonlyoblong.com

PALESTINE (village). Covers a land area of 0.788 square miles and a water area of 0 square miles. Located at 39.00° N. Lat; 87.61° W. Long. Elevation is 449 feet.

History: Palestine was the location in 1830 of one of the six land offices in Illinois, where settlers came to register their land claims.

Population: 1,619 (1990); 1,366 (2000); 1,369 (2010); Density: 1,936.1 persons per square mile (2008-2012 5-year est.); Race: 97.1% White, 0.0% Black/African American, 1.3% Asian, 0.1% American Indian/Alaska Native, 0.0% Native Hawaiian/Other Pacific Islander, 1.5% Some other race, 1.5% Two or more races, 0.5% Hispanic of any race (2008-2012 5-year est.); Average household size: 2.60 (2008-2012 5-year est.); Median age: 38.2 (2008-2012 5-year est.); Males per 100 females: 97.4 (2008-2012 5-year est.); Marriage status: 21.5% never married, 53.3% now married, 10.6% widowed, 14.6% divorced (2008-2012 5-year est.); Foreign born: 0.7% (2008-2012 5-year est.); Ancestry (includes multiple ancestries): 23.3% German, 19.7% American, 17.6% Irish, 8.5% English, 2.4% Dutch (2008-2012 5-year est.).

Economy: Homeowner vacancy rate: 0.0%. Rental vacancy rate: 0.0%. (2008-2012 5-year est.); Employment by occupation: 2.3% management, business, and financial, 1.2% computer, engineering, and science, 7.4%

education, legal, community service, arts, and media, 1.2% healthcare practitioners, 23.3% service, 24.3% sales and office, 11.5% natural resources, construction, and maintenance, 28.7% production, transportation, and material moving (2008-2012 5-year est.).

Income: Per capita income: $18,431 (2008-2012 5-year est.); Median household income: $37,313 (2008-2012 5-year est.); Average household income: $46,281 (2008-2012 5-year est.); Percent of households with income of $100,000 or more: 5.9% (2008-2012 5-year est.); Poverty rate: 16.0% (2008-2012 5-year est.).

Education: Percent of population age 25 and over with: High school diploma (including GED) or higher: 86.8% (2008-2012 5-year est.); Bachelor's degree or higher: 9.0% (2008-2012 5-year est.); Master's degree or higher: 4.1% (2008-2012 5-year est.).

School District(s)

Palestine CUSD 3 (PK-12)
    2011-12 Enrollment: 392 . . . . (618) 586-2713

Housing: Homeownership rate: 81.9% (2008-2012 5-year est.); Median home value: $50,100 (2008-2012 5-year est.); Median contract rent: $402 per month (2008-2012 5-year est.); Median year structure built: 1946 (2008-2012 5-year est.).

Health Insurance: 60.6% Private; 48.7% Public; 11.3% None. (2008-2012 5-year est.)

Safety: Violent crime rate: 36.4 per 10,000 population; Property crime rate: 87.4 per 10,000 population (2012).

Transportation: Commute to work: 90.7% car, 1.3% public transportation, 5.1% walk, 1.4% work from home (2008-2012 5-year est.); Travel time to work: 40.9% less than 15 minutes, 37.3% 15 to 30 minutes, 10.7% 30 to 45 minutes, 6.2% 45 to 60 minutes, 4.9% 60 minutes or more (2008-2012 5-year est.)

Additional Information Contacts

Palestine Chamber of Commerce . . . . (618) 586-2222
    http://www.pioneercity.com/chamberofcommerce

ROBINSON (city). County seat. Covers a land area of 4.736 square miles and a water area of 0.063 square miles. Located at 39.01° N. Lat; 87.73° W. Long. Elevation is 531 feet.

History: Lincoln Trail College here. Incorporated 1875.

Population: 6,740 (1990); 6,822 (2000); 7,713 (2010); Density: 1,616.5 persons per square mile (2008-2012 5-year est.); Race: 87.7% White, 6.7% Black/African American, 0.9% Asian, 0.2% American Indian/Alaska Native, 0.0% Native Hawaiian/Other Pacific Islander, 4.5% Some other race, 3.4% Two or more races, 4.4% Hispanic of any race (2008-2012 5-year est.); Average household size: 2.38 (2008-2012 5-year est.); Median age: 39.8 (2008-2012 5-year est.); Males per 100 females: 105.6 (2008-2012 5-year est.); Marriage status: 28.3% never married, 48.9% now married, 7.6% widowed, 15.3% divorced (2008-2012 5-year est.); Foreign born: 1.9% (2008-2012 5-year est.); Ancestry (includes multiple ancestries): 28.4% German, 11.7% American, 11.4% Irish, 8.8% English, 2.6% Dutch (2008-2012 5-year est.).

Economy: Single-family building permits issued: 2 (2013); Multi-family building permits issued: 0 (2013); Homeowner vacancy rate: 0.0%. Rental vacancy rate: 7.5%. (2008-2012 5-year est.); Employment by occupation: 6.8% management, business, and financial, 4.2% computer, engineering, and science, 6.0% education, legal, community service, arts, and media, 6.4% healthcare practitioners, 21.5% service, 26.0% sales and office, 7.9% natural resources, construction, and maintenance, 21.1% production, transportation, and material moving (2008-2012 5-year est.).

Income: Per capita income: $20,496 (2008-2012 5-year est.); Median household income: $38,720 (2008-2012 5-year est.); Average household income: $49,308 (2008-2012 5-year est.); Percent of households with income of $100,000 or more: 11.1% (2008-2012 5-year est.); Poverty rate: 20.9% (2008-2012 5-year est.).

Education: Percent of population age 25 and over with: High school diploma (including GED) or higher: 86.5% (2008-2012 5-year est.); Bachelor's degree or higher: 14.3% (2008-2012 5-year est.); Master's degree or higher: 5.5% (2008-2012 5-year est.).

School District(s)

Robinson CUSD 2 (PK-12)
    2011-12 Enrollment: 1,663 . . . . (618) 544-7511
Twin Rivers Career & Tech Ed Sys
    2011-12 Enrollment: n/a . . . . (618) 544-8664

Two-year College(s)

Illinois Eastern Community Colleges-Lincoln Trail College (Public)
    Fall 2012 Enrollment: 1,055 . . . . (618) 393-2982
    2012-13 Tuition: In-state $8,361; Out-of-state $10,412

Housing: Homeownership rate: 68.8% (2008-2012 5-year est.); Median home value: $71,500 (2008-2012 5-year est.); Median contract rent: $401 per month (2008-2012 5-year est.); Median year structure built: 1956 (2008-2012 5-year est.).
Health Insurance: 58.3% Private; 45.0% Public; 12.5% None. (2008-2012 5-year est.)
Hospitals: Crawford Memorial Hospital (93 beds)
Safety: Violent crime rate: 41.4 per 10,000 population; Property crime rate: 186.3 per 10,000 population (2012).
Transportation: Commute to work: 94.0% car, 0.3% public transportation, 1.2% walk, 2.3% work from home (2008-2012 5-year est.); Travel time to work: 72.0% less than 15 minutes, 11.3% 15 to 30 minutes, 9.5% 30 to 45 minutes, 2.5% 45 to 60 minutes, 4.7% 60 minutes or more (2008-2012 5-year est.)
Airports: Crawford County Airport (general aviation)
Additional Information Contacts
City of Robinson . . . . (618) 544-7616
   http://www.cityofrobinson.com
Robinson Chamber of Commerce . . . . (618) 546-1557
   http://www.robinsonchamber.org

STOY (village). Covers a land area of 0.896 square miles and a water area of 0 square miles. Located at 39.00° N. Lat; 87.83° W. Long. Elevation is 489 feet.
Population: 135 (1990); 119 (2000); 104 (2010); Density: 122.8 persons per square mile (2008-2012 5-year est.); Race: 100.0% White, 0.0% Black/African American, 0.0% Asian, 0.0% American Indian/Alaska Native, 0.0% Native Hawaiian/Other Pacific Islander, 0.0% Some other race, 0.0% Two or more races, 0.0% Hispanic of any race (2008-2012 5-year est.); Average household size: 1.83 (2008-2012 5-year est.); Median age: 50.5 (2008-2012 5-year est.); Males per 100 females: 64.2 (2008-2012 5-year est.); Marriage status: 43.2% never married, 45.3% now married, 5.3% widowed, 6.3% divorced (2008-2012 5-year est.); Foreign born: 0.0% (2008-2012 5-year est.); Ancestry (includes multiple ancestries): 55.5% German, 29.1% Dutch, 20.0% Irish, 7.3% English, 6.4% Scottish (2008-2012 5-year est.).
Economy: Homeowner vacancy rate: 0.0%. Rental vacancy rate: 0.0%. (2008-2012 5-year est.); Employment by occupation: 15.6% management, business, and financial, 0.0% computer, engineering, and science, 0.0% education, legal, community service, arts, and media, 0.0% healthcare practitioners, 31.1% service, 28.9% sales and office, 0.0% natural resources, construction, and maintenance, 24.4% production, transportation, and material moving (2008-2012 5-year est.).
Income: Per capita income: $28,679 (2008-2012 5-year est.); Median household income: $41,667 (2008-2012 5-year est.); Average household income: $49,680 (2008-2012 5-year est.); Percent of households with income of $100,000 or more: 5.0% (2008-2012 5-year est.); Poverty rate: 7.3% (2008-2012 5-year est.).
Education: Percent of population age 25 and over with: High school diploma (including GED) or higher: 98.9% (2008-2012 5-year est.); Bachelor's degree or higher: 40.0% (2008-2012 5-year est.); Master's degree or higher: 35.6% (2008-2012 5-year est.).
Housing: Homeownership rate: 100.0% (2008-2012 5-year est.); Median home value: $14,700 (2008-2012 5-year est.); Median contract rent: n/a per month (2008-2012 5-year est.); Median year structure built: 1948 (2008-2012 5-year est.).
Health Insurance: 87.3% Private; 12.7% Public; 6.4% None. (2008-2012 5-year est.)
Transportation: Commute to work: 88.9% car, 0.0% public transportation, 0.0% walk, 11.1% work from home (2008-2012 5-year est.); Travel time to work: 27.5% less than 15 minutes, 40.0% 15 to 30 minutes, 0.0% 30 to 45 minutes, 27.5% 45 to 60 minutes, 5.0% 60 minutes or more (2008-2012 5-year est.)

WEST YORK (CDP). Covers a land area of 0.133 square miles and a water area of 0 square miles. Located at 39.17° N. Lat; 87.67° W. Long. Elevation is 512 feet.
Population: n/a (1990); n/a (2000); 129 (2010); Density: 745.8 persons per square mile (2008-2012 5-year est.); Race: 100.0% White, 0.0% Black/African American, 0.0% Asian, 0.0% American Indian/Alaska Native, 0.0% Native Hawaiian/Other Pacific Islander, 0.0% Some other race, 0.0% Two or more races, 0.0% Hispanic of any race (2008-2012 5-year est.); Average household size: 2.83 (2008-2012 5-year est.); Median age: 34.7 (2008-2012 5-year est.); Males per 100 females: 39.4 (2008-2012 5-year est.); Marriage status: 15.5% never married, 76.1% now married, 8.5%

widowed, 0.0% divorced (2008-2012 5-year est.); Foreign born: 0.0% (2008-2012 5-year est.); Ancestry (includes multiple ancestries): 22.2% German, 16.2% Dutch, 6.1% English (2008-2012 5-year est.).
Economy: Homeowner vacancy rate: 0.0%. Rental vacancy rate: 0.0%. (2008-2012 5-year est.); Employment by occupation: 0.0% management, business, and financial, 0.0% computer, engineering, and science, 15.4% education, legal, community service, arts, and media, 0.0% healthcare practitioners, 15.4% service, 12.8% sales and office, 0.0% natural resources, construction, and maintenance, 56.4% production, transportation, and material moving (2008-2012 5-year est.).
Income: Per capita income: $14,267 (2008-2012 5-year est.); Median household income: $34,297 (2008-2012 5-year est.); Average household income: $42,260 (2008-2012 5-year est.); Percent of households with income of $100,000 or more: n/a (2008-2012 5-year est.); Poverty rate: 22.2% (2008-2012 5-year est.).
Education: Percent of population age 25 and over with: High school diploma (including GED) or higher: 62.0% (2008-2012 5-year est.); Bachelor's degree or higher: 8.5% (2008-2012 5-year est.); Master's degree or higher: 8.5% (2008-2012 5-year est.).
Housing: Homeownership rate: 100.0% (2008-2012 5-year est.); Median home value: $15,600 (2008-2012 5-year est.); Median contract rent: n/a per month (2008-2012 5-year est.); Median year structure built: 1988 (2008-2012 5-year est.).
Health Insurance: 77.8% Private; 65.7% Public; 22.2% None. (2008-2012 5-year est.)
Transportation: Commute to work: 100.0% car, 0.0% public transportation, 0.0% walk, 0.0% work from home (2008-2012 5-year est.); Travel time to work: 0.0% less than 15 minutes, 63.6% 15 to 30 minutes, 0.0% 30 to 45 minutes, 15.2% 45 to 60 minutes, 21.2% 60 minutes or more (2008-2012 5-year est.)

Cumberland County

Located in southeast central Illinois; drained by the Embarrass River. Covers a land area of 346.024 square miles, a water area of 0.979 square miles, and is located in the Central Time Zone at 39.27° N. Lat., 88.24° W. Long. The county was founded in 1843. County seat is Toledo.

Cumberland County is part of the Charleston-Mattoon, IL Micropolitan Statistical Area. The entire metro area includes: Coles County, IL; Cumberland County, IL

Population: 10,670 (1990); 11,253 (2000); 11,048 (2010); Race: 98.2% White, 0.5% Black/African American, 0.7% Asian, 0.1% American Indian/Alaska Native, 0.1% Native Hawaiian/Other Pacific Islander, 0.4% Some other race, 0.4% Two or more races, 0.6% Hispanic of any race (2008-2012 5-year est.); Density: 31.7 persons per square mile (2008-2012 5-year est.); Average household size: 2.63 (2008-2012 5-year est.); Median age: 40.6 (2008-2012 5-year est.); Males per 100 females: 100.2 (2008-2012 5-year est.).
Religion: Six largest groups: 13.9% Baptist, 5.4% Methodist/Pietist, 4.4% Catholicism, 1.8% Presbyterian-Reformed, 1.3% Holiness, 0.4% Non-denominational Protestant (2010)
Economy: Unemployment rate: 6.4% (April 2014); Total civilian labor force: 5,272 (April 2014); Leading industries: 14.6% health care and social assistance; 10.4% retail trade; 5.4% transportation & warehousing (2012); Farms: 733 totaling 170,149 acres (2012); Companies that employ 500 or more persons: 0 (2012); Companies that employ 100 to 499 persons: 2 (2012); Companies that employ less than 100 persons: 174 (2012); Black-owned businesses: n/a (2007); Hispanic-owned businesses: n/a (2007); Asian-owned businesses: n/a (2007); Women-owned businesses: n/a (2007); Single-family building permits issued: 1 (2013); Multi-family building permits issued: 0 (2013).
Income: Per capita income: $22,292 (2008-2012 5-year est.); Median household income: $44,430 (2008-2012 5-year est.); Average household income: $57,029 (2008-2012 5-year est.); Percent of households with income of $100,000 or more: 11.9% (2008-2012 5-year est.); Poverty rate: 13.4% (2008-2012 5-year est.); Bankruptcy rate: 3.38% (2013).
Education: Percent of population age 25 and over with: High school diploma (including GED) or higher: 89.1% (2008-2012 5-year est.); Bachelor's degree or higher: 12.3% (2008-2012 5-year est.); Master's degree or higher: 3.8% (2008-2012 5-year est.).
Housing: Homeownership rate: 82.7% (2008-2012 5-year est.); Median home value: $82,400 (2008-2012 5-year est.); Median contract rent: $358

per month (2008-2012 5-year est.); Median year structure built: 1969 (2008-2012 5-year est.)

Health: Birth rate: 109.7 per 10,000 population (2013); Death rate: 92.3 per 10,000 population (2013); Age-adjusted cancer mortality rate: 270.8 deaths per 100,000 population (2011); Number of physicians: 0.0 per 10,000 population (2011); Hospital beds: 0.0 per 10,000 population (2010); Hospital admissions: 0.0 per 10,000 population (2010).

Elections: 2012 Presidential election results: 31.0% Obama, 66.3% Romney

Additional Information Contacts

Cumberland County Government . . . . (217) 849-2631
    http://cumberlandco.org

Cumberland County Communities

GREENUP (village). Covers a land area of 1.747 square miles and a water area of 0.002 square miles. Located at 39.25° N. Lat; 88.16° W. Long. Elevation is 591 feet.

History: Greenup was named for William C. Greenup, the first clerk of the Illinois Territorial Legislature, who donated the townsite. The village was incorporated in 1836, and served for a time as the seat of Cumberland County.

Population: 1,616 (1990); 1,532 (2000); 1,513 (2010); Density: 928.2 persons per square mile (2008-2012 5-year est.); Race: 99.3% White, 0.2% Black/African American, 0.2% Asian, 0.0% American Indian/Alaska Native, 0.4% Native Hawaiian/Other Pacific Islander, 0.0% Some other race, 0.0% Two or more races, 0.0% Hispanic of any race (2008-2012 5-year est.); Average household size: 2.15 (2008-2012 5-year est.); Median age: 46.2 (2008-2012 5-year est.); Males per 100 females: 88.8 (2008-2012 5-year est.); Marriage status: 19.7% never married, 48.0% now married, 11.9% widowed, 20.5% divorced (2008-2012 5-year est.); Foreign born: 0.3% (2008-2012 5-year est.); Ancestry (includes multiple ancestries): 35.5% German, 14.2% English, 12.9% American, 11.9% Irish, 2.9% French (2008-2012 5-year est.).

Economy: Homeowner vacancy rate: 1.5%. Rental vacancy rate: 4.8%. (2008-2012 5-year est.); Employment by occupation: 6.4% management, business, and financial, 2.5% computer, engineering, and science, 15.6% education, legal, community service, arts, and media, 5.3% healthcare practitioners, 14.1% service, 30.5% sales and office, 8.4% natural resources, construction, and maintenance, 17.2% production, transportation, and material moving (2008-2012 5-year est.).

Income: Per capita income: $20,393 (2008-2012 5-year est.); Median household income: $33,649 (2008-2012 5-year est.); Average household income: $43,045 (2008-2012 5-year est.); Percent of households with income of $100,000 or more: 7.5% (2008-2012 5-year est.); Poverty rate: 14.7% (2008-2012 5-year est.).

Education: Percent of population age 25 and over with: High school diploma (including GED) or higher: 85.9% (2008-2012 5-year est.); Bachelor's degree or higher: 13.1% (2008-2012 5-year est.); Master's degree or higher: 3.7% (2008-2012 5-year est.).

Housing: Homeownership rate: 79.6% (2008-2012 5-year est.); Median home value: $66,700 (2008-2012 5-year est.); Median contract rent: $328 per month (2008-2012 5-year est.); Median year structure built: 1957 (2008-2012 5-year est.).

Health Insurance: 69.8% Private; 45.4% Public; 11.0% None. (2008-2012 5-year est.)

Safety: Violent crime rate: 111.8 per 10,000 population; Property crime rate: 203.8 per 10,000 population (2012).

Transportation: Commute to work: 88.5% car, 0.0% public transportation, 3.2% walk, 5.9% work from home (2008-2012 5-year est.); Travel time to work: 46.0% less than 15 minutes, 17.6% 15 to 30 minutes, 28.4% 30 to 45 minutes, 4.1% 45 to 60 minutes, 3.8% 60 minutes or more (2008-2012 5-year est.)

JEWETT (village). Covers a land area of 1.005 square miles and a water area of 0 square miles. Located at 39.21° N. Lat; 88.24° W. Long. Elevation is 584 feet.

History: The village of Jewett grew from the town of Pleasantville, which had been a stagecoach stop in the mid-1800's.

Population: 194 (1990); 232 (2000); 223 (2010); Density: 245.8 persons per square mile (2008-2012 5-year est.); Race: 96.8% White, 0.0% Black/African American, 0.0% Asian, 2.0% American Indian/Alaska Native, 0.0% Native Hawaiian/Other Pacific Islander, 1.2% Some other race, 0.0% Two or more races, 3.6% Hispanic of any race (2008-2012 5-year est.); Average household size: 2.63 (2008-2012 5-year est.); Median age: 36.8

(2008-2012 5-year est.); Males per 100 females: 80.3 (2008-2012 5-year est.); Marriage status: 26.3% never married, 52.5% now married, 4.5% widowed, 16.7% divorced (2008-2012 5-year est.); Foreign born: 0.0% (2008-2012 5-year est.); Ancestry (includes multiple ancestries): 26.3% German, 16.6% Irish, 15.4% American, 9.7% Dutch, 6.1% English (2008-2012 5-year est.).

Economy: Homeowner vacancy rate: 2.5%. Rental vacancy rate: 0.0%. (2008-2012 5-year est.); Employment by occupation: 2.7% management, business, and financial, 0.0% computer, engineering, and science, 0.9% education, legal, community service, arts, and media, 2.7% healthcare practitioners, 25.5% service, 23.6% sales and office, 16.4% natural resources, construction, and maintenance, 28.2% production, transportation, and material moving (2008-2012 5-year est.).

Income: Per capita income: $14,091 (2008-2012 5-year est.); Median household income: $28,750 (2008-2012 5-year est.); Average household income: $35,615 (2008-2012 5-year est.); Percent of households with income of $100,000 or more: 1.1% (2008-2012 5-year est.); Poverty rate: 32.8% (2008-2012 5-year est.).

Education: Percent of population age 25 and over with: High school diploma (including GED) or higher: 81.9% (2008-2012 5-year est.); Bachelor's degree or higher: 1.9% (2008-2012 5-year est.); Master's degree or higher: 1.3% (2008-2012 5-year est.).

Housing: Homeownership rate: 81.9% (2008-2012 5-year est.); Median home value: $51,500 (2008-2012 5-year est.); Median contract rent: $350 per month (2008-2012 5-year est.); Median year structure built: 1967 (2008-2012 5-year est.).

Health Insurance: 46.2% Private; 42.1% Public; 16.2% None. (2008-2012 5-year est.)

Transportation: Commute to work: 98.2% car, 0.0% public transportation, 0.0% walk, 1.8% work from home (2008-2012 5-year est.); Travel time to work: 13.1% less than 15 minutes, 45.8% 15 to 30 minutes, 25.2% 30 to 45 minutes, 11.2% 45 to 60 minutes, 4.7% 60 minutes or more (2008-2012 5-year est.)

NEOGA (city). Covers a land area of 1.429 square miles and a water area of 0 square miles. Located at 39.32° N. Lat; 88.45° W. Long. Elevation is 659 feet.

History: The name of Neoga is of Indian origin, meaning "place of the Deity."

Population: 1,678 (1990); 1,854 (2000); 1,636 (2010); Density: 1,291.3 persons per square mile (2008-2012 5-year est.); Race: 96.3% White, 1.5% Black/African American, 0.0% Asian, 0.2% American Indian/Alaska Native, 0.0% Native Hawaiian/Other Pacific Islander, 2.0% Some other race, 2.0% Two or more races, 1.1% Hispanic of any race (2008-2012 5-year est.); Average household size: 2.70 (2008-2012 5-year est.); Median age: 39.5 (2008-2012 5-year est.); Males per 100 females: 87.1 (2008-2012 5-year est.); Marriage status: 25.6% never married, 52.4% now married, 10.2% widowed, 11.8% divorced (2008-2012 5-year est.); Foreign born: 0.1% (2008-2012 5-year est.); Ancestry (includes multiple ancestries): 36.1% German, 15.7% Irish, 12.1% English, 9.2% American, 4.8% Dutch (2008-2012 5-year est.).

Economy: Single-family building permits issued: 1 (2013); Multi-family building permits issued: 0 (2013); Homeowner vacancy rate: 0.0%. Rental vacancy rate: 0.0%. (2008-2012 5-year est.); Employment by occupation: 13.4% management, business, and financial, 1.6% computer, engineering, and science, 12.6% education, legal, community service, arts, and media, 4.2% healthcare practitioners, 18.5% service, 16.9% sales and office, 5.3% natural resources, construction, and maintenance, 27.5% production, transportation, and material moving (2008-2012 5-year est.).

Income: Per capita income: $18,223 (2008-2012 5-year est.); Median household income: $36,000 (2008-2012 5-year est.); Average household income: $48,687 (2008-2012 5-year est.); Percent of households with income of $100,000 or more: 8.4% (2008-2012 5-year est.); Poverty rate: 15.0% (2008-2012 5-year est.).

Education: Percent of population age 25 and over with: High school diploma (including GED) or higher: 89.9% (2008-2012 5-year est.); Bachelor's degree or higher: 19.6% (2008-2012 5-year est.); Master's degree or higher: 5.9% (2008-2012 5-year est.).

School District(s)

Neoga CUSD 3 (PK-12)
    2011-12 Enrollment: 766 . . . . (217) 895-2201

Housing: Homeownership rate: 75.4% (2008-2012 5-year est.); Median home value: $83,100 (2008-2012 5-year est.); Median contract rent: $327 per month (2008-2012 5-year est.); Median year structure built: 1965 (2008-2012 5-year est.).

Health Insurance: 60.8% Private; 39.2% Public; 13.3% None. (2008-2012 5-year est.)
Safety: Violent crime rate: 18.3 per 10,000 population; Property crime rate: 115.6 per 10,000 population (2012).
Transportation: Commute to work: 95.2% car, 0.3% public transportation, 0.0% walk, 2.6% work from home (2008-2012 5-year est.); Travel time to work: 26.2% less than 15 minutes, 42.4% 15 to 30 minutes, 22.1% 30 to 45 minutes, 4.9% 45 to 60 minutes, 4.5% 60 minutes or more (2008-2012 5-year est.)
Additional Information Contacts
Neoga Area Chamber of Commerce . . . . (217) 895-3237

TOLEDO (village). County seat. Covers a land area of 0.908 square miles and a water area of 0 square miles. Located at 39.27° N. Lat; 88.24° W. Long. Elevation is 597 feet.

Population: 1,199 (1990); 1,166 (2000); 1,238 (2010); Density: 1,232.0 persons per square mile (2008-2012 5-year est.); Race: 97.8% White, 2.2% Black/African American, 0.0% Asian, 0.0% American Indian/Alaska Native, 0.0% Native Hawaiian/Other Pacific Islander, 0.0% Some other race, 0.0% Two or more races, 0.4% Hispanic of any race (2008-2012 5-year est.); Average household size: 2.28 (2008-2012 5-year est.); Median age: 36.6 (2008-2012 5-year est.); Males per 100 females: 104.2 (2008-2012 5-year est.); Marriage status: 28.3% never married, 42.2% now married, 8.7% widowed, 20.8% divorced (2008-2012 5-year est.); Foreign born: 1.3% (2008-2012 5-year est.); Ancestry (includes multiple ancestries): 28.2% German, 20.6% Irish, 9.0% English, 6.3% American, 3.1% Italian (2008-2012 5-year est.).
Economy: Homeowner vacancy rate: 3.0%. Rental vacancy rate: 0.0%. (2008-2012 5-year est.); Employment by occupation: 11.5% management, business, and financial, 2.5% computer, engineering, and science, 1.6% education, legal, community service, arts, and media, 5.1% healthcare practitioners, 18.8% service, 20.2% sales and office, 17.6% natural resources, construction, and maintenance, 22.7% production, transportation, and material moving (2008-2012 5-year est.).
Income: Per capita income: $18,672 (2008-2012 5-year est.); Median household income: $32,083 (2008-2012 5-year est.); Average household income: $42,649 (2008-2012 5-year est.); Percent of households with income of $100,000 or more: 9.1% (2008-2012 5-year est.); Poverty rate: 14.3% (2008-2012 5-year est.).
Education: Percent of population age 25 and over with: High school diploma (including GED) or higher: 88.3% (2008-2012 5-year est.); Bachelor's degree or higher: 8.2% (2008-2012 5-year est.); Master's degree or higher: 1.8% (2008-2012 5-year est.).
School District(s)
Cumberland CUSD 77 (PK-12)
    2011-12 Enrollment: 1,005 . . . . (217) 923-3132
Housing: Homeownership rate: 74.7% (2008-2012 5-year est.); Median home value: $61,200 (2008-2012 5-year est.); Median contract rent: $329 per month (2008-2012 5-year est.); Median year structure built: 1960 (2008-2012 5-year est.).
Health Insurance: 55.6% Private; 49.4% Public; 10.3% None. (2008-2012 5-year est.)
Transportation: Commute to work: 93.4% car, 0.0% public transportation, 2.6% walk, 2.6% work from home (2008-2012 5-year est.); Travel time to work: 40.2% less than 15 minutes, 22.4% 15 to 30 minutes, 28.4% 30 to 45 minutes, 7.7% 45 to 60 minutes, 1.3% 60 minutes or more (2008-2012 5-year est.)

De Witt County

Located in central Illinois; drained by Salt Creek. Covers a land area of 397.513 square miles, a water area of 7.571 square miles, and is located in the Central Time Zone at 40.18° N. Lat., 88.90° W. Long. The county was founded in 1839. County seat is Clinton.

De Witt County is part of the Bloomington, IL Metropolitan Statistical Area. The entire metro area includes: De Witt County, IL; McLean County, IL

Population: 16,516 (1990); 16,798 (2000); 16,561 (2010); Race: 97.2% White, 1.3% Black/African American, 0.1% Asian, 0.0% American Indian/Alaska Native, 0.0% Native Hawaiian/Other Pacific Islander, 1.4% Some other race, 0.6% Two or more races, 2.1% Hispanic of any race (2008-2012 5-year est.); Density: 41.5 persons per square mile (2008-2012 5-year est.); Average household size: 2.39 (2008-2012 5-year

est.); Median age: 42.0 (2008-2012 5-year est.); Males per 100 females: 99.4 (2008-2012 5-year est.).
Religion: Six largest groups: 17.9% Baptist, 8.4% Methodist/Pietist, 6.4% Catholicism, 1.9% Pentecostal, 1.3% Holiness, 1.3% Presbyterian-Reformed (2010)
Economy: Unemployment rate: 6.6% (April 2014); Total civilian labor force: 8,172 (April 2014); Leading industries: 14.8% retail trade; 12.8% health care and social assistance; 11.3% manufacturing (2012); Farms: 511 totaling 195,512 acres (2012); Companies that employ 500 or more persons: 1 (2012); Companies that employ 100 to 499 persons: 5 (2012); Companies that employ less than 100 persons: 380 (2012); Black-owned businesses: n/a (2007); Hispanic-owned businesses: n/a (2007); Asian-owned businesses: n/a (2007); Women-owned businesses: n/a (2007); Single-family building permits issued: 20 (2013); Multi-family building permits issued: 0 (2013).
Income: Per capita income: $27,222 (2008-2012 5-year est.); Median household income: $49,626 (2008-2012 5-year est.); Average household income: $65,007 (2008-2012 5-year est.); Percent of households with income of $100,000 or more: 16.7% (2008-2012 5-year est.); Poverty rate: 10.4% (2008-2012 5-year est.); Bankruptcy rate: 4.08% (2013).
Taxes: Total county taxes per capita: $221 (2011); County property taxes per capita: $221 (2011).
Education: Percent of population age 25 and over with: High school diploma (including GED) or higher: 91.4% (2008-2012 5-year est.); Bachelor's degree or higher: 17.1% (2008-2012 5-year est.); Master's degree or higher: 3.5% (2008-2012 5-year est.).
Housing: Homeownership rate: 77.5% (2008-2012 5-year est.); Median home value: $105,100 (2008-2012 5-year est.); Median contract rent: $434 per month (2008-2012 5-year est.); Median year structure built: 1959 (2008-2012 5-year est.).
Health: Birth rate: 119.4 per 10,000 population (2013); Death rate: 123.6 per 10,000 population (2013); Age-adjusted cancer mortality rate: 200.5 deaths per 100,000 population (2011); Number of physicians: 6.0 per 10,000 population (2011); Hospital beds: 15.1 per 10,000 population (2010); Hospital admissions: 207.7 per 10,000 population (2010).
Elections: 2012 Presidential election results: 35.4% Obama, 62.4% Romney
National and State Parks: Clinton Lake State Recreational Area; Weldon Springs State Park
Additional Information Contacts
De Witt County Government . . . . (217) 935-7780
    http://www.dewittcountyill.com

De Witt County Communities

CLINTON (city). County seat. Covers a land area of 3.381 square miles and a water area of <.001 square miles. Located at 40.15° N. Lat; 88.96° W. Long. Elevation is 732 feet.

History: Clinton was the site of Abraham's Lincoln speech in which he gave the oft-quoted lines of "you can fool all the people part of the time and part of the people all of the time, but you cannot fool all the people all the time."
Population: 7,437 (1990); 7,485 (2000); 7,225 (2010); Density: 2,072.5 persons per square mile (2008-2012 5-year est.); Race: 94.5% White, 2.8% Black/African American, 0.2% Asian, 0.1% American Indian/Alaska Native, 0.0% Native Hawaiian/Other Pacific Islander, 2.4% Some other race, 1.0% Two or more races, 4.6% Hispanic of any race (2008-2012 5-year est.); Average household size: 2.21 (2008-2012 5-year est.); Median age: 42.3 (2008-2012 5-year est.); Males per 100 females: 92.5 (2008-2012 5-year est.); Marriage status: 27.2% never married, 49.4% now married, 8.0% widowed, 15.4% divorced (2008-2012 5-year est.); Foreign born: 3.2% (2008-2012 5-year est.); Ancestry (includes multiple ancestries): 25.8% American, 18.5% German, 14.8% English, 13.0% Irish, 2.8% Dutch (2008-2012 5-year est.).
Economy: Single-family building permits issued: 3 (2013); Multi-family building permits issued: 0 (2013); Homeowner vacancy rate: 1.6%. Rental vacancy rate: 5.7%. (2008-2012 5-year est.); Employment by occupation: 10.6% management, business, and financial, 2.0% computer, engineering, and science, 6.0% education, legal, community service, arts, and media, 4.1% healthcare practitioners, 20.8% service, 27.4% sales and office, 11.3% natural resources, construction, and maintenance, 17.7% production, transportation, and material moving (2008-2012 5-year est.).
Income: Per capita income: $27,505 (2008-2012 5-year est.); Median household income: $41,719 (2008-2012 5-year est.); Average household income: $61,080 (2008-2012 5-year est.); Percent of households with

income of $100,000 or more: 10.4% (2008-2012 5-year est.); Poverty rate: 13.9% (2008-2012 5-year est.).
Education: Percent of population age 25 and over with: High school diploma (including GED) or higher: 88.0% (2008-2012 5-year est.); Bachelor's degree or higher: 14.4% (2008-2012 5-year est.); Master's degree or higher: 3.7% (2008-2012 5-year est.).

School District(s)
Clinton CUSD 15 (PK-12)
    2011-12 Enrollment: 1,970 .... (217) 935-8321
Housing: Homeownership rate: 67.7% (2008-2012 5-year est.); Median home value: $85,800 (2008-2012 5-year est.); Median contract rent: $425 per month (2008-2012 5-year est.); Median year structure built: 1954 (2008-2012 5-year est.).
Health Insurance: 69.2% Private; 39.2% Public; 10.0% None. (2008-2012 5-year est.)
Hospitals: Dr. John Warner Hospital (43 beds)
Transportation: Commute to work: 94.2% car, 0.1% public transportation, 3.2% walk, 1.6% work from home (2008-2012 5-year est.); Travel time to work: 49.6% less than 15 minutes, 16.2% 15 to 30 minutes, 25.5% 30 to 45 minutes, 6.2% 45 to 60 minutes, 2.4% 60 minutes or more (2008-2012 5-year est.)
Additional Information Contacts
City of Clinton .... (217) 935-9438
    http://www.clintonillinois.com
Clinton Area Chamber of Commerce .... (217) 935-3364
    http://www.clintonilchamber.com

DE WITT (village). Covers a land area of 0.263 square miles and a water area of 0 square miles. Located at 40.18° N. Lat; 88.79° W. Long. Elevation is 735 feet.
Population: 122 (1990); 188 (2000); 184 (2010); Density: 700.2 persons per square mile (2008-2012 5-year est.); Race: 99.5% White, 0.0% Black/African American, 0.0% Asian, 0.0% American Indian/Alaska Native, 0.0% Native Hawaiian/Other Pacific Islander, 0.5% Some other race, 0.5% Two or more races, 0.0% Hispanic of any race (2008-2012 5-year est.); Average household size: 2.39 (2008-2012 5-year est.); Median age: 41.7 (2008-2012 5-year est.); Males per 100 females: 97.8 (2008-2012 5-year est.); Marriage status: 30.4% never married, 48.7% now married, 8.9% widowed, 12.0% divorced (2008-2012 5-year est.); Foreign born: 0.0% (2008-2012 5-year est.); Ancestry (includes multiple ancestries): 37.0% American, 20.1% German, 8.7% Scottish, 6.5% Dutch, 6.0% English (2008-2012 5-year est.).
Economy: Homeowner vacancy rate: 8.1%. Rental vacancy rate: 0.0%. (2008-2012 5-year est.); Employment by occupation: 4.0% management, business, and financial, 6.7% computer, engineering, and science, 0.0% education, legal, community service, arts, and media, 0.0% healthcare practitioners, 16.0% service, 34.7% sales and office, 13.3% natural resources, construction, and maintenance, 25.3% production, transportation, and material moving (2008-2012 5-year est.).
Income: Per capita income: $21,458 (2008-2012 5-year est.); Median household income: $38,438 (2008-2012 5-year est.); Average household income: $51,486 (2008-2012 5-year est.); Percent of households with income of $100,000 or more: 5.2% (2008-2012 5-year est.); Poverty rate: 8.7% (2008-2012 5-year est.).
Education: Percent of population age 25 and over with: High school diploma (including GED) or higher: 86.5% (2008-2012 5-year est.); Bachelor's degree or higher: 9.5% (2008-2012 5-year est.); Master's degree or higher: 0.8% (2008-2012 5-year est.).
Housing: Homeownership rate: 74.0% (2008-2012 5-year est.); Median home value: $88,800 (2008-2012 5-year est.); Median contract rent: $425 per month (2008-2012 5-year est.); Median year structure built: 1949 (2008-2012 5-year est.).
Health Insurance: 47.3% Private; 45.7% Public; 27.2% None. (2008-2012 5-year est.)
Transportation: Commute to work: 90.1% car, 4.2% public transportation, 0.0% walk, 5.6% work from home (2008-2012 5-year est.); Travel time to work: 11.9% less than 15 minutes, 40.3% 15 to 30 minutes, 23.9% 30 to 45 minutes, 19.4% 45 to 60 minutes, 4.5% 60 minutes or more (2008-2012 5-year est.)

FARMER CITY (city). Covers a land area of 2.399 square miles and a water area of 0.049 square miles. Located at 40.25° N. Lat; 88.64° W. Long. Elevation is 725 feet.
History: Incorporated 1869.

Population: 2,114 (1990); 2,055 (2000); 2,037 (2010); Density: 908.3 persons per square mile (2008-2012 5-year est.); Race: 99.5% White, 0.5% Black/African American, 0.0% Asian, 0.0% American Indian/Alaska Native, 0.0% Native Hawaiian/Other Pacific Islander, 0.0% Some other race, 0.0% Two or more races, 0.0% Hispanic of any race (2008-2012 5-year est.); Average household size: 2.59 (2008-2012 5-year est.); Median age: 40.1 (2008-2012 5-year est.); Males per 100 females: 97.2 (2008-2012 5-year est.); Marriage status: 27.1% never married, 51.7% now married, 8.7% widowed, 12.5% divorced (2008-2012 5-year est.); Foreign born: 0.8% (2008-2012 5-year est.); Ancestry (includes multiple ancestries): 25.0% German, 24.0% American, 19.1% English, 16.7% Irish, 2.7% Lithuanian (2008-2012 5-year est.).
Economy: Homeowner vacancy rate: 2.9%. Rental vacancy rate: 0.0%. (2008-2012 5-year est.); Employment by occupation: 14.7% management, business, and financial, 1.9% computer, engineering, and science, 6.9% education, legal, community service, arts, and media, 7.0% healthcare practitioners, 19.5% service, 20.6% sales and office, 16.4% natural resources, construction, and maintenance, 13.0% production, transportation, and material moving (2008-2012 5-year est.).
Income: Per capita income: $23,778 (2008-2012 5-year est.); Median household income: $48,065 (2008-2012 5-year est.); Average household income: $58,486 (2008-2012 5-year est.); Percent of households with income of $100,000 or more: 12.2% (2008-2012 5-year est.); Poverty rate: 13.9% (2008-2012 5-year est.).
Education: Percent of population age 25 and over with: High school diploma (including GED) or higher: 91.1% (2008-2012 5-year est.); Bachelor's degree or higher: 18.4% (2008-2012 5-year est.); Master's degree or higher: 5.5% (2008-2012 5-year est.).

School District(s)
Blue Ridge CUSD 18 (PK-12)
    2011-12 Enrollment: 809........................ (309) 928-9141
Housing: Homeownership rate: 76.9% (2008-2012 5-year est.); Median home value: $105,400 (2008-2012 5-year est.); Median contract rent: $450 per month (2008-2012 5-year est.); Median year structure built: 1955 (2008-2012 5-year est.).
Health Insurance: 68.8% Private; 35.2% Public; 9.3% None. (2008-2012 5-year est.)
Transportation: Commute to work: 95.7% car, 0.4% public transportation, 1.6% walk, 2.2% work from home (2008-2012 5-year est.); Travel time to work: 38.2% less than 15 minutes, 22.0% 15 to 30 minutes, 24.7% 30 to 45 minutes, 9.2% 45 to 60 minutes, 5.8% 60 minutes or more (2008-2012 5-year est.)

KENNEY (village). Covers a land area of 0.301 square miles and a water area of 0 square miles. Located at 40.10° N. Lat; 89.09° W. Long. Elevation is 650 feet.
Population: 390 (1990); 374 (2000); 326 (2010); Density: 1,174.2 persons per square mile (2008-2012 5-year est.); Race: 98.6% White, 0.0% Black/African American, 0.0% Asian, 0.0% American Indian/Alaska Native, 0.0% Native Hawaiian/Other Pacific Islander, 1.4% Some other race, 1.4% Two or more races, 0.0% Hispanic of any race (2008-2012 5-year est.); Average household size: 2.29 (2008-2012 5-year est.); Median age: 40.0 (2008-2012 5-year est.); Males per 100 females: 90.8 (2008-2012 5-year est.); Marriage status: 24.3% never married, 49.3% now married, 11.4% widowed, 15.0% divorced (2008-2012 5-year est.); Foreign born: 0.0% (2008-2012 5-year est.); Ancestry (includes multiple ancestries): 48.2% American, 13.6% German, 7.6% Irish, 5.1% English, 5.1% Dutch (2008-2012 5-year est.).
Economy: Homeowner vacancy rate: 0.0%. Rental vacancy rate: 0.0%. (2008-2012 5-year est.); Employment by occupation: 6.7% management, business, and financial, 2.0% computer, engineering, and science, 8.0% education, legal, community service, arts, and media, 4.0% healthcare practitioners, 13.3% service, 27.3% sales and office, 16.7% natural resources, construction, and maintenance, 22.0% production, transportation, and material moving (2008-2012 5-year est.).
Income: Per capita income: $23,715 (2008-2012 5-year est.); Median household income: $46,667 (2008-2012 5-year est.); Average household income: $54,310 (2008-2012 5-year est.); Percent of households with income of $100,000 or more: 9.1% (2008-2012 5-year est.); Poverty rate: 11.8% (2008-2012 5-year est.).
Education: Percent of population age 25 and over with: High school diploma (including GED) or higher: 85.2% (2008-2012 5-year est.); Bachelor's degree or higher: 10.5% (2008-2012 5-year est.); Master's degree or higher: 1.3% (2008-2012 5-year est.).

Housing: Homeownership rate: 82.5% (2008-2012 5-year est.); Median home value: $66,600 (2008-2012 5-year est.); Median contract rent: $408 per month (2008-2012 5-year est.); Median year structure built: Before 1940 (2008-2012 5-year est.).
Health Insurance: 74.5% Private; 38.2% Public; 4.8% None. (2008-2012 5-year est.)
Transportation: Commute to work: 98.0% car, 0.0% public transportation, 0.0% walk, 0.0% work from home (2008-2012 5-year est.); Travel time to work: 37.3% less than 15 minutes, 32.0% 15 to 30 minutes, 22.7% 30 to 45 minutes, 5.3% 45 to 60 minutes, 2.7% 60 minutes or more (2008-2012 5-year est.)

LANE (unincorporated postal area)
Zip Code: 61750
Covers a land area of 1.192 square miles and a water area of 0 square miles. Located at 40.12° N. Lat; 88.85° W. Long. Elevation is 728 feet.
Population: 133 (2010); Density: 111.5 persons per square mile (2010); Race: 98.5% White, 0.0% Black/African American, 0.8% Asian, 0.0% American Indian/Alaska Native, 0.0% Native Hawaiian/Other Pacific Islander, 0.7% Some other race, 0.8% Two or more races, 0.0% Hispanic of any race (2010); Average household size: 2.38 (2010); Median age: 41.5 (2010); Males per 100 females: 114.5 (2010); Homeownership rate: 89.3% (2010)

WAPELLA (village). Covers a land area of 0.528 square miles and a water area of 0 square miles. Located at 40.22° N. Lat; 88.96° W. Long. Elevation is 745 feet.
Population: 608 (1990); 651 (2000); 558 (2010); Density: 927.4 persons per square mile (2008-2012 5-year est.); Race: 99.4% White, 0.0% Black/African American, 0.0% Asian, 0.0% American Indian/Alaska Native, 0.0% Native Hawaiian/Other Pacific Islander, 0.6% Some other race, 0.6% Two or more races, 0.0% Hispanic of any race (2008-2012 5-year est.); Average household size: 2.47 (2008-2012 5-year est.); Median age: 37.0 (2008-2012 5-year est.); Males per 100 females: 109.4 (2008-2012 5-year est.); Marriage status: 19.7% never married, 62.5% now married, 5.1% widowed, 12.8% divorced (2008-2012 5-year est.); Foreign born: 0.0% (2008-2012 5-year est.); Ancestry (includes multiple ancestries): 26.9% Irish, 23.9% German, 20.0% American, 10.0% English, 5.5% Italian (2008-2012 5-year est.).
Economy: Single-family building permits issued: 0 (2013); Multi-family building permits issued: 0 (2013); Homeowner vacancy rate: 1.6%. Rental vacancy rate: 0.0%. (2008-2012 5-year est.); Employment by occupation: 11.4% management, business, and financial, 0.7% computer, engineering, and science, 4.4% education, legal, community service, arts, and media, 1.8% healthcare practitioners, 26.7% service, 15.4% sales and office, 23.8% natural resources, construction, and maintenance, 15.8% production, transportation, and material moving (2008-2012 5-year est.).
Income: Per capita income: $25,186 (2008-2012 5-year est.); Median household income: $50,900 (2008-2012 5-year est.); Average household income: $65,008 (2008-2012 5-year est.); Percent of households with income of $100,000 or more: 22.7% (2008-2012 5-year est.); Poverty rate: 7.8% (2008-2012 5-year est.).
Education: Percent of population age 25 and over with: High school diploma (including GED) or higher: 95.1% (2008-2012 5-year est.); Bachelor's degree or higher: 7.0% (2008-2012 5-year est.); Master's degree or higher: 0.6% (2008-2012 5-year est.).
Housing: Homeownership rate: 92.9% (2008-2012 5-year est.); Median home value: $103,800 (2008-2012 5-year est.); Median contract rent: $419 per month (2008-2012 5-year est.); Median year structure built: 1965 (2008-2012 5-year est.).
Health Insurance: 85.9% Private; 29.6% Public; 6.5% None. (2008-2012 5-year est.)
Transportation: Commute to work: 100.0% car, 0.0% public transportation, 0.0% walk, 0.0% work from home (2008-2012 5-year est.); Travel time to work: 29.6% less than 15 minutes, 34.5% 15 to 30 minutes, 30.0% 30 to 45 minutes, 2.2% 45 to 60 minutes, 3.7% 60 minutes or more (2008-2012 5-year est.)

WAYNESVILLE (village). Covers a land area of 0.323 square miles and a water area of 0 square miles. Located at 40.24° N. Lat; 89.12° W. Long. Elevation is 735 feet.
Population: 440 (1990); 452 (2000); 434 (2010); Density: 1,720.7 persons per square mile (2008-2012 5-year est.); Race: 98.4% White, 0.0% Black/African American, 0.0% Asian, 0.0% American Indian/Alaska Native, 0.0% Native Hawaiian/Other Pacific Islander, 1.6% Some other race, 1.6%

Two or more races, 0.0% Hispanic of any race (2008-2012 5-year est.); Average household size: 2.62 (2008-2012 5-year est.); Median age: 40.7 (2008-2012 5-year est.); Males per 100 females: 105.9 (2008-2012 5-year est.); Marriage status: 23.8% never married, 63.7% now married, 5.9% widowed, 6.5% divorced (2008-2012 5-year est.); Foreign born: 0.9% (2008-2012 5-year est.); Ancestry (includes multiple ancestries): 36.9% American, 27.7% German, 15.5% English, 7.2% Irish, 2.2% Norwegian (2008-2012 5-year est.).
Economy: Homeowner vacancy rate: 0.9%. Rental vacancy rate: 0.0%. (2008-2012 5-year est.); Employment by occupation: 11.3% management, business, and financial, 1.0% computer, engineering, and science, 1.3% education, legal, community service, arts, and media, 1.0% healthcare practitioners, 17.2% service, 30.5% sales and office, 15.6% natural resources, construction, and maintenance, 22.2% production, transportation, and material moving (2008-2012 5-year est.).
Income: Per capita income: $23,252 (2008-2012 5-year est.); Median household income: $58,333 (2008-2012 5-year est.); Average household income: $59,169 (2008-2012 5-year est.); Percent of households with income of $100,000 or more: 17.4% (2008-2012 5-year est.); Poverty rate: 9.4% (2008-2012 5-year est.).
Education: Percent of population age 25 and over with: High school diploma (including GED) or higher: 88.0% (2008-2012 5-year est.); Bachelor's degree or higher: 14.5% (2008-2012 5-year est.); Master's degree or higher: 1.5% (2008-2012 5-year est.).
Housing: Homeownership rate: 98.6% (2008-2012 5-year est.); Median home value: $78,900 (2008-2012 5-year est.); Median contract rent: n/a per month (2008-2012 5-year est.); Median year structure built: 1960 (2008-2012 5-year est.).
Health Insurance: 77.3% Private; 38.1% Public; 3.6% None. (2008-2012 5-year est.)
Transportation: Commute to work: 92.3% car, 1.3% public transportation, 2.7% walk, 0.0% work from home (2008-2012 5-year est.); Travel time to work: 18.7% less than 15 minutes, 30.0% 15 to 30 minutes, 40.0% 30 to 45 minutes, 6.0% 45 to 60 minutes, 5.3% 60 minutes or more (2008-2012 5-year est.)

WELDON (village). Covers a land area of 0.271 square miles and a water area of 0 square miles. Located at 40.12° N. Lat; 88.75° W. Long. Elevation is 712 feet.
Population: 361 (1990); 440 (2000); 429 (2010); Density: 1,288.5 persons per square mile (2008-2012 5-year est.); Race: 98.0% White, 0.0% Black/African American, 0.0% Asian, 0.0% American Indian/Alaska Native, 0.0% Native Hawaiian/Other Pacific Islander, 2.0% Some other race, 1.1% Two or more races, 0.9% Hispanic of any race (2008-2012 5-year est.); Average household size: 2.25 (2008-2012 5-year est.); Median age: 40.8 (2008-2012 5-year est.); Males per 100 females: 100.6 (2008-2012 5-year est.); Marriage status: 22.4% never married, 53.7% now married, 9.6% widowed, 14.2% divorced (2008-2012 5-year est.); Foreign born: 0.0% (2008-2012 5-year est.); Ancestry (includes multiple ancestries): 26.9% American, 17.2% German, 10.3% English, 7.7% Irish, 7.2% Polish (2008-2012 5-year est.).
Economy: Homeowner vacancy rate: 7.8%. Rental vacancy rate: 12.5%. (2008-2012 5-year est.); Employment by occupation: 8.1% management, business, and financial, 1.4% computer, engineering, and science, 12.2% education, legal, community service, arts, and media, 0.7% healthcare practitioners, 13.5% service, 33.8% sales and office, 22.3% natural resources, construction, and maintenance, 8.1% production, transportation, and material moving (2008-2012 5-year est.).
Income: Per capita income: $23,348 (2008-2012 5-year est.); Median household income: $38,542 (2008-2012 5-year est.); Average household income: $51,265 (2008-2012 5-year est.); Percent of households with income of $100,000 or more: 10.3% (2008-2012 5-year est.); Poverty rate: 10.0% (2008-2012 5-year est.).
Education: Percent of population age 25 and over with: High school diploma (including GED) or higher: 92.1% (2008-2012 5-year est.); Bachelor's degree or higher: 15.5% (2008-2012 5-year est.); Master's degree or higher: 4.0% (2008-2012 5-year est.).
School District(s)
Deland-Weldon CUSD 57 (PK-12)
    2011-12 Enrollment: 207 . . . . (217) 736-2311
Housing: Homeownership rate: 81.9% (2008-2012 5-year est.); Median home value: $75,400 (2008-2012 5-year est.); Median contract rent: $244 per month (2008-2012 5-year est.); Median year structure built: 1946 (2008-2012 5-year est.).

Health Insurance: 64.5% Private; 41.0% Public; 11.7% None. (2008-2012 5-year est.)

Transportation: Commute to work: 97.2% car, 0.0% public transportation, 0.0% walk, 2.8% work from home (2008-2012 5-year est.); Travel time to work: 15.1% less than 15 minutes, 28.1% 15 to 30 minutes, 50.4% 30 to 45 minutes, 6.5% 45 to 60 minutes, 0.0% 60 minutes or more (2008-2012 5-year est.)

De Kalb County

Located in northern Illinois; drained by branches of the Kishwaukee River. Covers a land area of 631.307 square miles, a water area of 3.353 square miles, and is located in the Central Time Zone at 41.89° N. Lat., 88.77° W. Long. The county was founded in 1837. County seat is Sycamore.

De Kalb County is part of the Chicago-Naperville-Elgin, IL-IN-WI Metropolitan Statistical Area. The entire metro area includes: Chicago-Naperville-Arlington Heights, IL Metropolitan Division (Cook County, IL; DuPage County, IL; Grundy County, IL; Kendall County, IL; McHenry County, IL; Will County, IL); Elgin, IL Metropolitan Division (DeKalb County, IL; Kane County, IL); Gary, IN Metropolitan Division (Jasper County, IN; Lake County, IN; Newton County, IN; Porter County, IN); Lake County-Kenosha County, IL-WI Metropolitan Division (Lake County, IL; Kenosha County, WI)

Population: 77,932 (1990); 88,969 (2000); 105,160 (2010); Race: 84.1% White, 6.2% Black/African American, 2.4% Asian, 0.2% American Indian/Alaska Native, 0.0% Native Hawaiian/Other Pacific Islander, 7.1% Some other race, 2.2% Two or more races, 10.2% Hispanic of any race (2008-2012 5-year est.); Density: 165.7 persons per square mile (2008-2012 5-year est.); Average household size: 2.56 (2008-2012 5-year est.); Median age: 29.4 (2008-2012 5-year est.); Males per 100 females: 99.1 (2008-2012 5-year est.).

Religion: Six largest groups: 18.5% Catholicism, 7.4% Lutheran, 6.1% Methodist/Pietist, 3.1% Muslim Estimate, 2.6% Presbyterian-Reformed, 2.5% Baptist (2010)

Economy: Unemployment rate: 6.8% (April 2014); Total civilian labor force: 58,448 (April 2014); Leading industries: 18.5% health care and social assistance; 17.3% retail trade; 13.8% manufacturing (2012); Farms: 880 totaling 397,771 acres (2012); Companies that employ 500 or more persons: 2 (2012); Companies that employ 100 to 499 persons: 43 (2012); Companies that employ less than 100 persons: 1,930 (2012); Black-owned businesses: 163 (2007); Hispanic-owned businesses: 172 (2007); Asian-owned businesses: 161 (2007); Women-owned businesses: 2,445 (2007); Single-family building permits issued: 44 (2013); Multi-family building permits issued: 25 (2013).

Income: Per capita income: $24,063 (2008-2012 5-year est.); Median household income: $53,575 (2008-2012 5-year est.); Average household income: $64,535 (2008-2012 5-year est.); Percent of households with income of $100,000 or more: 19.8% (2008-2012 5-year est.); Poverty rate: 16.9% (2008-2012 5-year est.); Bankruptcy rate: 3.89% (2013).

Taxes: Total county taxes per capita: $219 (2011); County property taxes per capita: $206 (2011).

Education: Percent of population age 25 and over with: High school diploma (including GED) or higher: 91.1% (2008-2012 5-year est.); Bachelor's degree or higher: 29.0% (2008-2012 5-year est.); Master's degree or higher: 10.8% (2008-2012 5-year est.).

Housing: Homeownership rate: 61.6% (2008-2012 5-year est.); Median home value: $179,300 (2008-2012 5-year est.); Median contract rent: $689 per month (2008-2012 5-year est.); Median year structure built: 1975 (2008-2012 5-year est.)

Health: Birth rate: 115.5 per 10,000 population (2013); Death rate: 63.5 per 10,000 population (2013); Age-adjusted cancer mortality rate: 171.6 deaths per 100,000 population (2011); Number of physicians: 9.2 per 10,000 population (2011); Hospital beds: 17.9 per 10,000 population (2010); Hospital admissions: 686.8 per 10,000 population (2010).

Elections: 2012 Presidential election results: 51.6% Obama, 46.1% Romney

National and State Parks: Shabbona Lake State Recreational Area

Additional Information Contacts

De Kalb County Government . . . . (815) 895-7149
http://www.dekalbcounty.org

De Kalb County Communities

CLARE (unincorporated postal area)
Zip Code: 60111
Covers a land area of 20.397 square miles and a water area of 0.074 square miles. Located at 42.00° N. Lat; 88.80° W. Long. Population: 258 (2010); Density: 12.6 persons per square mile (2010); Race: 96.9% White, 2.7% Black/African American, 0.0% Asian, 0.4% American Indian/Alaska Native, 0.0% Native Hawaiian/Other Pacific Islander, 0.0% Some other race, 0.0% Two or more races, 4.3% Hispanic of any race (2010); Average household size: 2.48 (2010); Median age: 48.0 (2010); Males per 100 females: 106.4 (2010); Homeownership rate: 79.8% (2010)

CORTLAND (town). Covers a land area of 3.630 square miles and a water area of 0.008 square miles. Located at 41.94° N. Lat; 88.69° W. Long. Elevation is 902 feet.

Population: 963 (1990); 2,066 (2000); 4,270 (2010); Density: 1,179.1 persons per square mile (2008-2012 5-year est.); Race: 87.8% White, 3.3% Black/African American, 0.8% Asian, 0.0% American Indian/Alaska Native, 0.0% Native Hawaiian/Other Pacific Islander, 8.1% Some other race, 4.8% Two or more races, 12.9% Hispanic of any race (2008-2012 5-year est.); Average household size: 3.37 (2008-2012 5-year est.); Median age: 27.4 (2008-2012 5-year est.); Males per 100 females: 100.0 (2008-2012 5-year est.); Marriage status: 36.8% never married, 53.9% now married, 2.2% widowed, 7.1% divorced (2008-2012 5-year est.); Foreign born: 8.7% (2008-2012 5-year est.); Ancestry (includes multiple ancestries): 46.6% German, 21.4% Irish, 10.1% Polish, 8.6% Italian, 6.7% Swedish (2008-2012 5-year est.).

Economy: Single-family building permits issued: 0 (2013); Multi-family building permits issued: 0 (2013); Homeowner vacancy rate: 0.0%. Rental vacancy rate: 9.7%. (2008-2012 5-year est.); Employment by occupation: 11.5% management, business, and financial, 3.6% computer, engineering, and science, 9.4% education, legal, community service, arts, and media, 2.8% healthcare practitioners, 16.3% service, 29.8% sales and office, 9.5% natural resources, construction, and maintenance, 17.1% production, transportation, and material moving (2008-2012 5-year est.).

Income: Per capita income: $22,155 (2008-2012 5-year est.); Median household income: $70,764 (2008-2012 5-year est.); Average household income: $73,041 (2008-2012 5-year est.); Percent of households with income of $100,000 or more: 21.3% (2008-2012 5-year est.); Poverty rate: 10.6% (2008-2012 5-year est.).

Taxes: Total city taxes per capita: $284 (2011); City property taxes per capita: $207 (2011).

Education: Percent of population age 25 and over with: High school diploma (including GED) or higher: 91.4% (2008-2012 5-year est.); Bachelor's degree or higher: 23.2% (2008-2012 5-year est.); Master's degree or higher: 4.4% (2008-2012 5-year est.).

School District(s)
Dekalb CUSD 428 (PK-12)
    2011-12 Enrollment: 6,104 . . . . (815) 754-2350

Housing: Homeownership rate: 76.6% (2008-2012 5-year est.); Median home value: $164,400 (2008-2012 5-year est.); Median contract rent: $841 per month (2008-2012 5-year est.); Median year structure built: 2000 (2008-2012 5-year est.).

Health Insurance: 75.3% Private; 19.3% Public; 9.3% None. (2008-2012 5-year est.)

Safety: Violent crime rate: 7.1 per 10,000 population; Property crime rate: 79.9 per 10,000 population (2012).

Transportation: Commute to work: 89.4% car, 0.8% public transportation, 1.5% walk, 7.8% work from home (2008-2012 5-year est.); Travel time to work: 41.5% less than 15 minutes, 9.5% 15 to 30 minutes, 25.8% 30 to 45 minutes, 6.3% 45 to 60 minutes, 16.9% 60 minutes or more (2008-2012 5-year est.)

Additional Information Contacts
Town of Cortland . . . . (815) 756-9041
http://www.cortlandil.org

DEKALB (city). Covers a land area of 14.651 square miles and a water area of 0.162 square miles. Located at 41.93° N. Lat; 88.75° W. Long. Elevation is 879 feet.

History: De Kalb was named for Baron Johann De Kalb, a major general in the Revolutionary Army. In 1874 Joseph E. Glidden patented an improved barbed wire, and Jacob Haish patented a barbed wire

manufacturing process. The two patents overlapped and caused a long legal battle, but until 1938 De Kalb was known as the barbed wire capital of the world.

Population: 34,925 (1990); 39,018 (2000); 43,862 (2010); Density: 3,026.4 persons per square mile (2008-2012 5-year est.); Race: 73.7% White, 12.4% Black/African American, 4.0% Asian, 0.1% American Indian/Alaska Native, 0.1% Native Hawaiian/Other Pacific Islander, 9.7% Some other race, 2.9% Two or more races, 12.5% Hispanic of any race (2008-2012 5-year est.); Average household size: 2.43 (2008-2012 5-year est.); Median age: 23.5 (2008-2012 5-year est.); Males per 100 females: 100.0 (2008-2012 5-year est.); Marriage status: 57.8% never married, 31.3% now married, 3.9% widowed, 7.0% divorced (2008-2012 5-year est.); Foreign born: 9.1% (2008-2012 5-year est.); Ancestry (includes multiple ancestries): 23.5% German, 14.4% Irish, 7.2% English, 7.2% Polish, 6.3% Italian (2008-2012 5-year est.).

Economy: Unemployment rate: 6.8% (April 2014); Total civilian labor force: 23,644 (April 2014); Single-family building permits issued: 3 (2013); Multi-family building permits issued: 0 (2013); Homeowner vacancy rate: 3.1%. Rental vacancy rate: 3.7%. (2008-2012 5-year est.); Employment by occupation: 9.7% management, business, and financial, 3.0% computer, engineering, and science, 16.9% education, legal, community service, arts, and media, 4.0% healthcare practitioners, 21.5% service, 27.9% sales and office, 5.1% natural resources, construction, and maintenance, 11.8% production, transportation, and material moving (2008-2012 5-year est.).

Income: Per capita income: $19,464 (2008-2012 5-year est.); Median household income: $39,412 (2008-2012 5-year est.); Average household income: $53,355 (2008-2012 5-year est.); Percent of households with income of $100,000 or more: 14.5% (2008-2012 5-year est.); Poverty rate: 30.3% (2008-2012 5-year est.).

Taxes: Total city taxes per capita: $683 (2011); City property taxes per capita: $351 (2011).

Education: Percent of population age 25 and over with: High school diploma (including GED) or higher: 90.5% (2008-2012 5-year est.); Bachelor's degree or higher: 35.2% (2008-2012 5-year est.); Master's degree or higher: 14.3% (2008-2012 5-year est.).

School District(s)

Dekalb CUSD 428 (PK-12)
  2011-12 Enrollment: 6,104 . . . . (815) 754-2350
Dekalb CUSD 428 (PK-12)
  2011-12 Enrollment: 6,104 . . . . (815) 754-2350
Kishwaukee Educ Consortium
  2011-12 Enrollment: n/a . . . . (815) 825-2000

Four-year College(s)

Northern Illinois University (Public)
  Fall 2012 Enrollment: 21,869 . . . . (800) 892-3050
  2012-13 Tuition: In-state $13,066; Out-of-state $22,554

Housing: Homeownership rate: 44.3% (2008-2012 5-year est.); Median home value: $171,200 (2008-2012 5-year est.); Median contract rent: $676 per month (2008-2012 5-year est.); Median year structure built: 1974 (2008-2012 5-year est.).

Health Insurance: 75.5% Private; 21.7% Public; 9.9% None. (2008-2012 5-year est.)

Hospitals: Kishwaukee Community Hospital (172 beds)

Safety: Violent crime rate: 44.8 per 10,000 population; Property crime rate: 298.2 per 10,000 population (2012).

Transportation: Commute to work: 80.4% car, 4.9% public transportation, 8.5% walk, 4.2% work from home (2008-2012 5-year est.); Travel time to work: 52.4% less than 15 minutes, 22.8% 15 to 30 minutes, 9.8% 30 to 45 minutes, 6.4% 45 to 60 minutes, 8.5% 60 minutes or more (2008-2012 5-year est.)

Airports: DeKalb Taylor Municipal Airport (general aviation)

Additional Information Contacts

City of De Kalb . . . . (815) 748-2000
  http://www.cityofdekalb.com
De Kalb Chamber of Commerce . . . . (815) 756-6306
  http://www.dekalb.org

ESMOND (unincorporated postal area)

Zip Code: 60129
  Covers a land area of 17.101 square miles and a water area of 0 square miles. Located at 42.00° N. Lat; 88.97° W. Long. Population: 242 (2010); Density: 14.2 persons per square mile (2010); Race: 97.5% White, 0.0% Black/African American, 0.4% Asian, 0.0% American Indian/Alaska Native, 0.0% Native Hawaiian/Other Pacific Islander, 2.1% Some other race, 2.1% Two or more races, 1.2% Hispanic of any

race (2010); Average household size: 2.60 (2010); Median age: 43.3 (2010); Males per 100 females: 105.1 (2010); Homeownership rate: 74.2% (2010)

GENOA (city). Covers a land area of 2.601 square miles and a water area of 0.055 square miles. Located at 42.09° N. Lat; 88.69° W. Long. Elevation is 833 feet.

Population: 3,083 (1990); 4,169 (2000); 5,193 (2010); Density: 2,188.8 persons per square mile (2008-2012 5-year est.); Race: 93.4% White, 0.0% Black/African American, 2.6% Asian, 0.2% American Indian/Alaska Native, 0.0% Native Hawaiian/Other Pacific Islander, 3.8% Some other race, 0.4% Two or more races, 5.3% Hispanic of any race (2008-2012 5-year est.); Average household size: 2.80 (2008-2012 5-year est.); Median age: 32.4 (2008-2012 5-year est.); Males per 100 females: 96.6 (2008-2012 5-year est.); Marriage status: 30.7% never married, 57.0% now married, 5.1% widowed, 7.3% divorced (2008-2012 5-year est.); Foreign born: 6.2% (2008-2012 5-year est.); Ancestry (includes multiple ancestries): 38.4% German, 17.8% Irish, 10.6% Polish, 8.2% Italian, 6.4% English (2008-2012 5-year est.).

Economy: Single-family building permits issued: 3 (2013); Multi-family building permits issued: 0 (2013); Homeowner vacancy rate: 3.4%. Rental vacancy rate: 0.0%. (2008-2012 5-year est.); Employment by occupation: 15.5% management, business, and financial, 3.4% computer, engineering, and science, 8.4% education, legal, community service, arts, and media, 4.3% healthcare practitioners, 23.9% service, 20.3% sales and office, 8.6% natural resources, construction, and maintenance, 15.7% production, transportation, and material moving (2008-2012 5-year est.).

Income: Per capita income: $22,347 (2008-2012 5-year est.); Median household income: $54,773 (2008-2012 5-year est.); Average household income: $62,042 (2008-2012 5-year est.); Percent of households with income of $100,000 or more: 16.3% (2008-2012 5-year est.); Poverty rate: 7.8% (2008-2012 5-year est.).

Education: Percent of population age 25 and over with: High school diploma (including GED) or higher: 89.3% (2008-2012 5-year est.); Bachelor's degree or higher: 13.6% (2008-2012 5-year est.); Master's degree or higher: 4.3% (2008-2012 5-year est.).

School District(s)

Genoa Kingston CUSD 424 (PK-12)
  2011-12 Enrollment: 1,905 . . . . (815) 784-6222

Housing: Homeownership rate: 71.2% (2008-2012 5-year est.); Median home value: $171,800 (2008-2012 5-year est.); Median contract rent: $621 per month (2008-2012 5-year est.); Median year structure built: 1976 (2008-2012 5-year est.).

Health Insurance: 75.1% Private; 23.1% Public; 10.4% None. (2008-2012 5-year est.)

Safety: Violent crime rate: 15.5 per 10,000 population; Property crime rate: 112.1 per 10,000 population (2012).

Transportation: Commute to work: 95.8% car, 0.0% public transportation, 0.6% walk, 3.0% work from home (2008-2012 5-year est.); Travel time to work: 17.9% less than 15 minutes, 30.1% 15 to 30 minutes, 27.2% 30 to 45 minutes, 9.0% 45 to 60 minutes, 15.9% 60 minutes or more (2008-2012 5-year est.)

Additional Information Contacts

Genoa Area Chamber of Commerce . . . . (815) 784-2212
  http://genoaareachamber.com

HINCKLEY (village). Covers a land area of 0.841 square miles and a water area of 0.008 square miles. Located at 41.77° N. Lat; 88.64° W. Long. Elevation is 745 feet.

Population: 1,682 (1990); 1,994 (2000); 2,070 (2010); Density: 2,449.8 persons per square mile (2008-2012 5-year est.); Race: 98.3% White, 0.5% Black/African American, 0.4% Asian, 0.0% American Indian/Alaska Native, 0.2% Native Hawaiian/Other Pacific Islander, 0.6% Some other race, 0.5% Two or more races, 1.7% Hispanic of any race (2008-2012 5-year est.); Average household size: 2.54 (2008-2012 5-year est.); Median age: 39.5 (2008-2012 5-year est.); Males per 100 females: 95.0 (2008-2012 5-year est.); Marriage status: 25.1% never married, 60.1% now married, 5.7% widowed, 9.1% divorced (2008-2012 5-year est.); Foreign born: 1.3% (2008-2012 5-year est.); Ancestry (includes multiple ancestries): 39.1% German, 22.4% Irish, 11.5% English, 8.4% Norwegian, 6.2% Swedish (2008-2012 5-year est.).

Economy: Single-family building permits issued: 0 (2013); Multi-family building permits issued: 0 (2013); Homeowner vacancy rate: 0.0%. Rental vacancy rate: 0.0%. (2008-2012 5-year est.); Employment by occupation: 14.3% management, business, and financial, 3.8% computer, engineering,

and science, 10.0% education, legal, community service, arts, and media, 2.7% healthcare practitioners, 21.1% service, 28.1% sales and office, 12.2% natural resources, construction, and maintenance, 7.8% production, transportation, and material moving (2008-2012 5-year est.).
Income: Per capita income: $32,306 (2008-2012 5-year est.); Median household income: $67,969 (2008-2012 5-year est.); Average household income: $81,812 (2008-2012 5-year est.); Percent of households with income of $100,000 or more: 31.7% (2008-2012 5-year est.); Poverty rate: 6.3% (2008-2012 5-year est.).
Education: Percent of population age 25 and over with: High school diploma (including GED) or higher: 94.5% (2008-2012 5-year est.); Bachelor's degree or higher: 27.7% (2008-2012 5-year est.); Master's degree or higher: 8.0% (2008-2012 5-year est.).

School District(s)
Hinckley Big Rock CUSD 429 (PK-12)
    2011-12 Enrollment: 714 . . . . (815) 286-7575
Housing: Homeownership rate: 80.2% (2008-2012 5-year est.); Median home value: $193,700 (2008-2012 5-year est.); Median contract rent: $736 per month (2008-2012 5-year est.); Median year structure built: 1973 (2008-2012 5-year est.).
Health Insurance: 81.7% Private; 23.5% Public; 7.4% None. (2008-2012 5-year est.)
Transportation: Commute to work: 90.7% car, 0.0% public transportation, 1.6% walk, 4.2% work from home (2008-2012 5-year est.); Travel time to work: 19.1% less than 15 minutes, 30.3% 15 to 30 minutes, 28.4% 30 to 45 minutes, 9.1% 45 to 60 minutes, 13.0% 60 minutes or more (2008-2012 5-year est.)

KINGSTON (village). Covers a land area of 0.992 square miles and a water area of 0.025 square miles. Located at 42.10° N. Lat; 88.76° W. Long. Elevation is 794 feet.
Population: 562 (1990); 980 (2000); 1,164 (2010); Density: 1,079.7 persons per square mile (2008-2012 5-year est.); Race: 98.3% White, 0.3% Black/African American, 0.0% Asian, 0.0% American Indian/Alaska Native, 0.0% Native Hawaiian/Other Pacific Islander, 1.4% Some other race, 0.4% Two or more races, 4.8% Hispanic of any race (2008-2012 5-year est.); Average household size: 3.01 (2008-2012 5-year est.); Median age: 36.4 (2008-2012 5-year est.); Males per 100 females: 91.9 (2008-2012 5-year est.); Marriage status: 27.1% never married, 49.2% now married, 6.4% widowed, 17.3% divorced (2008-2012 5-year est.); Foreign born: 1.1% (2008-2012 5-year est.); Ancestry (includes multiple ancestries): 48.3% German, 23.7% Irish, 10.4% English, 8.5% Italian, 7.8% Polish (2008-2012 5-year est.).
Economy: Single-family building permits issued: 0 (2013); Multi-family building permits issued: 0 (2013); Homeowner vacancy rate: 0.0%. Rental vacancy rate: 0.0%. (2008-2012 5-year est.); Employment by occupation: 9.3% management, business, and financial, 0.8% computer, engineering, and science, 6.1% education, legal, community service, arts, and media, 5.3% healthcare practitioners, 16.9% service, 21.0% sales and office, 19.5% natural resources, construction, and maintenance, 21.0% production, transportation, and material moving (2008-2012 5-year est.).
Income: Per capita income: $26,183 (2008-2012 5-year est.); Median household income: $76,458 (2008-2012 5-year est.); Average household income: $77,059 (2008-2012 5-year est.); Percent of households with income of $100,000 or more: 26.2% (2008-2012 5-year est.); Poverty rate: 5.4% (2008-2012 5-year est.).
Education: Percent of population age 25 and over with: High school diploma (including GED) or higher: 91.8% (2008-2012 5-year est.); Bachelor's degree or higher: 11.9% (2008-2012 5-year est.); Master's degree or higher: 4.7% (2008-2012 5-year est.).

School District(s)
Genoa Kingston CUSD 424 (PK-12)
    2011-12 Enrollment: 1,905 . . . . (815) 784-6222
Housing: Homeownership rate: 86.0% (2008-2012 5-year est.); Median home value: $187,800 (2008-2012 5-year est.); Median contract rent: $781 per month (2008-2012 5-year est.); Median year structure built: 1991 (2008-2012 5-year est.).
Health Insurance: 77.5% Private; 15.4% Public; 14.8% None. (2008-2012 5-year est.)
Safety: Violent crime rate: 0.0 per 10,000 population; Property crime rate: 69.0 per 10,000 population (2012).
Transportation: Commute to work: 94.3% car, 0.7% public transportation, 1.1% walk, 3.5% work from home (2008-2012 5-year est.); Travel time to work: 17.2% less than 15 minutes, 29.1% 15 to 30 minutes, 20.1% 30 to

45 minutes, 10.6% 45 to 60 minutes, 22.9% 60 minutes or more (2008-2012 5-year est.)

KIRKLAND (village). Covers a land area of 1.215 square miles and a water area of 0.012 square miles. Located at 42.09° N. Lat; 88.85° W. Long. Elevation is 768 feet.
Population: 1,011 (1990); 1,166 (2000); 1,744 (2010); Density: 1,518.1 persons per square mile (2008-2012 5-year est.); Race: 96.7% White, 0.3% Black/African American, 0.0% Asian, 0.0% American Indian/Alaska Native, 0.0% Native Hawaiian/Other Pacific Islander, 3.0% Some other race, 2.9% Two or more races, 6.4% Hispanic of any race (2008-2012 5-year est.); Average household size: 2.95 (2008-2012 5-year est.); Median age: 31.4 (2008-2012 5-year est.); Males per 100 females: 96.7 (2008-2012 5-year est.); Marriage status: 31.6% never married, 54.6% now married, 4.8% widowed, 9.0% divorced (2008-2012 5-year est.); Foreign born: 4.6% (2008-2012 5-year est.); Ancestry (includes multiple ancestries): 39.8% German, 23.1% Irish, 11.6% English, 8.9% Polish, 7.5% Italian (2008-2012 5-year est.).
Economy: Single-family building permits issued: 0 (2013); Multi-family building permits issued: 0 (2013); Homeowner vacancy rate: 1.9%. Rental vacancy rate: 0.0%. (2008-2012 5-year est.); Employment by occupation: 9.6% management, business, and financial, 1.3% computer, engineering, and science, 6.6% education, legal, community service, arts, and media, 6.2% healthcare practitioners, 18.9% service, 21.6% sales and office, 11.7% natural resources, construction, and maintenance, 24.1% production, transportation, and material moving (2008-2012 5-year est.).
Income: Per capita income: $22,963 (2008-2012 5-year est.); Median household income: $57,604 (2008-2012 5-year est.); Average household income: $66,489 (2008-2012 5-year est.); Percent of households with income of $100,000 or more: 20.6% (2008-2012 5-year est.); Poverty rate: 9.1% (2008-2012 5-year est.).
Education: Percent of population age 25 and over with: High school diploma (including GED) or higher: 90.4% (2008-2012 5-year est.); Bachelor's degree or higher: 16.9% (2008-2012 5-year est.); Master's degree or higher: 6.1% (2008-2012 5-year est.).

School District(s)
Hiawatha CUSD 426 (PK-12)
    2011-12 Enrollment: 606 . . . . (815) 522-6676
Housing: Homeownership rate: 80.6% (2008-2012 5-year est.); Median home value: $151,700 (2008-2012 5-year est.); Median contract rent: $626 per month (2008-2012 5-year est.); Median year structure built: 1964 (2008-2012 5-year est.).
Health Insurance: 63.8% Private; 25.9% Public; 18.8% None. (2008-2012 5-year est.)
Transportation: Commute to work: 92.6% car, 0.0% public transportation, 2.0% walk, 4.3% work from home (2008-2012 5-year est.); Travel time to work: 18.8% less than 15 minutes, 20.1% 15 to 30 minutes, 27.4% 30 to 45 minutes, 14.2% 45 to 60 minutes, 19.5% 60 minutes or more (2008-2012 5-year est.)

MALTA (village). Covers a land area of 0.574 square miles and a water area of 0.034 square miles. Located at 41.93° N. Lat; 88.87° W. Long. Elevation is 909 feet.
Population: 865 (1990); 969 (2000); 1,164 (2010); Density: 1,750.3 persons per square mile (2008-2012 5-year est.); Race: 93.2% White, 1.3% Black/African American, 1.3% Asian, 0.0% American Indian/Alaska Native, 0.0% Native Hawaiian/Other Pacific Islander, 4.2% Some other race, 3.9% Two or more races, 5.0% Hispanic of any race (2008-2012 5-year est.); Average household size: 2.77 (2008-2012 5-year est.); Median age: 33.4 (2008-2012 5-year est.); Males per 100 females: 84.9 (2008-2012 5-year est.); Marriage status: 26.2% never married, 55.3% now married, 8.5% widowed, 10.0% divorced (2008-2012 5-year est.); Foreign born: 2.4% (2008-2012 5-year est.); Ancestry (includes multiple ancestries): 31.5% German, 19.9% Irish, 10.4% American, 8.7% English, 6.0% Norwegian (2008-2012 5-year est.).
Economy: Single-family building permits issued: 0 (2013); Multi-family building permits issued: 0 (2013); Homeowner vacancy rate: 10.2%. Rental vacancy rate: 0.0%. (2008-2012 5-year est.); Employment by occupation: 8.7% management, business, and financial, 3.8% computer, engineering, and science, 5.2% education, legal, community service, arts, and media, 2.8% healthcare practitioners, 25.7% service, 32.5% sales and office, 5.7% natural resources, construction, and maintenance, 15.6% production, transportation, and material moving (2008-2012 5-year est.).
Income: Per capita income: $20,525 (2008-2012 5-year est.); Median household income: $51,354 (2008-2012 5-year est.); Average household

income: $55,117 (2008-2012 5-year est.); Percent of households with income of $100,000 or more: 12.4% (2008-2012 5-year est.); Poverty rate: 11.6% (2008-2012 5-year est.).

Taxes: Total city taxes per capita: $194 (2011); City property taxes per capita: $113 (2011).

Education: Percent of population age 25 and over with: High school diploma (including GED) or higher: 87.8% (2008-2012 5-year est.); Bachelor's degree or higher: 19.3% (2008-2012 5-year est.); Master's degree or higher: 5.2% (2008-2012 5-year est.).

School District(s)

De Kalb Roe (07-12)
  2011-12 Enrollment: n/a . . . . (815) 217-0460
Dekalb CUSD 428 (PK-12)
  2011-12 Enrollment: 6,104 . . . . (815) 754-2350
Kec Area Voc Center (11-12)
  2011-12 Enrollment: n/a . . . . (815) 825-2000

Two-year College(s)

Kishwaukee College (Public)
  Fall 2012 Enrollment: 4,921 . . . . (815) 825-2086
  2012-13 Tuition: In-state $9,600; Out-of-state $12,960

Housing: Homeownership rate: 84.8% (2008-2012 5-year est.); Median home value: $149,100 (2008-2012 5-year est.); Median contract rent: $497 per month (2008-2012 5-year est.); Median year structure built: 1965 (2008-2012 5-year est.).

Health Insurance: 68.1% Private; 36.2% Public; 11.2% None. (2008-2012 5-year est.)

Safety: Violent crime rate: 0.0 per 10,000 population; Property crime rate: 86.3 per 10,000 population (2012).

Transportation: Commute to work: 99.3% car, 0.0% public transportation, 0.7% walk, 0.0% work from home (2008-2012 5-year est.); Travel time to work: 29.2% less than 15 minutes, 42.5% 15 to 30 minutes, 10.0% 30 to 45 minutes, 6.7% 45 to 60 minutes, 11.6% 60 minutes or more (2008-2012 5-year est.)

SANDWICH (city). Covers a land area of 4.690 square miles and a water area of 0.016 square miles. Located at 41.65° N. Lat; 88.62° W. Long. Elevation is 666 feet.

History: Sandwich was named for Sandwich, Massachusetts. Early industries were the manufacture of plows, reapers, windmills, and cornshellers.

Population: 5,567 (1990); 6,509 (2000); 7,421 (2010); Density: 1,612.7 persons per square mile (2008-2012 5-year est.); Race: 93.8% White, 0.4% Black/African American, 0.5% Asian, 0.1% American Indian/Alaska Native, 0.0% Native Hawaiian/Other Pacific Islander, 5.2% Some other race, 0.5% Two or more races, 10.7% Hispanic of any race (2008-2012 5-year est.); Average household size: 2.66 (2008-2012 5-year est.); Median age: 37.9 (2008-2012 5-year est.); Males per 100 females: 98.8 (2008-2012 5-year est.); Marriage status: 24.8% never married, 59.9% now married, 5.6% widowed, 9.6% divorced (2008-2012 5-year est.); Foreign born: 4.9% (2008-2012 5-year est.); Ancestry (includes multiple ancestries): 35.8% German, 17.0% Irish, 9.1% English, 8.3% Norwegian, 7.5% Italian (2008-2012 5-year est.).

Economy: Single-family building permits issued: 0 (2013); Multi-family building permits issued: 0 (2013); Homeowner vacancy rate: 1.8%. Rental vacancy rate: 10.5%. (2008-2012 5-year est.); Employment by occupation: 10.3% management, business, and financial, 1.3% computer, engineering, and science, 8.8% education, legal, community service, arts, and media, 3.9% healthcare practitioners, 16.6% service, 26.6% sales and office, 7.4% natural resources, construction, and maintenance, 25.1% production, transportation, and material moving (2008-2012 5-year est.).

Income: Per capita income: $26,552 (2008-2012 5-year est.); Median household income: $58,583 (2008-2012 5-year est.); Average household income: $71,635 (2008-2012 5-year est.); Percent of households with income of $100,000 or more: 26.5% (2008-2012 5-year est.); Poverty rate: 8.4% (2008-2012 5-year est.).

Education: Percent of population age 25 and over with: High school diploma (including GED) or higher: 90.9% (2008-2012 5-year est.); Bachelor's degree or higher: 18.4% (2008-2012 5-year est.); Master's degree or higher: 6.5% (2008-2012 5-year est.).

School District(s)

Indian Valley Area Voc Ctr (11-12)
  2011-12 Enrollment: n/a . . . . (815) 786-9873
Sandwich CUSD 430 (PK-12)
  2011-12 Enrollment: 2,364 . . . . (815) 786-2187

Housing: Homeownership rate: 72.8% (2008-2012 5-year est.); Median home value: $181,100 (2008-2012 5-year est.); Median contract rent: $680 per month (2008-2012 5-year est.); Median year structure built: 1972 (2008-2012 5-year est.).

Health Insurance: 73.5% Private; 25.0% Public; 12.3% None. (2008-2012 5-year est.)

Hospitals: Valley West Community Hospital (84 beds)

Transportation: Commute to work: 92.8% car, 0.4% public transportation, 2.9% walk, 2.8% work from home (2008-2012 5-year est.); Travel time to work: 27.0% less than 15 minutes, 21.7% 15 to 30 minutes, 26.5% 30 to 45 minutes, 15.6% 45 to 60 minutes, 9.3% 60 minutes or more (2008-2012 5-year est.)

Additional Information Contacts
City of Sandwich . . . . (815) 786-9321
  http://www.sandwich.il.us
Sandwich Chamber of Commerce . . . . (815) 312-4963
  http://www.sandwich-il.org

SHABBONA (village). Covers a land area of 0.828 square miles and a water area of <.001 square miles. Located at 41.77° N. Lat; 88.88° W. Long. Elevation is 899 feet.

Population: 897 (1990); 929 (2000); 925 (2010); Density: 1,067.8 persons per square mile (2008-2012 5-year est.); Race: 94.1% White, 1.0% Black/African American, 0.0% Asian, 0.0% American Indian/Alaska Native, 0.0% Native Hawaiian/Other Pacific Islander, 4.9% Some other race, 4.9% Two or more races, 2.6% Hispanic of any race (2008-2012 5-year est.); Average household size: 2.33 (2008-2012 5-year est.); Median age: 47.6 (2008-2012 5-year est.); Males per 100 females: 96.0 (2008-2012 5-year est.); Marriage status: 22.1% never married, 50.6% now married, 14.9% widowed, 12.4% divorced (2008-2012 5-year est.); Foreign born: 1.1% (2008-2012 5-year est.); Ancestry (includes multiple ancestries): 41.0% German, 14.9% English, 10.4% Irish, 9.0% Italian, 7.4% Norwegian (2008-2012 5-year est.).

Economy: Single-family building permits issued: 0 (2013); Multi-family building permits issued: 0 (2013); Homeowner vacancy rate: 4.8%. Rental vacancy rate: 20.3%. (2008-2012 5-year est.); Employment by occupation: 6.1% management, business, and financial, 3.3% computer, engineering, and science, 11.0% education, legal, community service, arts, and media, 1.0% healthcare practitioners, 22.0% service, 22.5% sales and office, 13.6% natural resources, construction, and maintenance, 20.5% production, transportation, and material moving (2008-2012 5-year est.).

Income: Per capita income: $24,162 (2008-2012 5-year est.); Median household income: $47,031 (2008-2012 5-year est.); Average household income: $58,145 (2008-2012 5-year est.); Percent of households with income of $100,000 or more: 13.5% (2008-2012 5-year est.); Poverty rate: 6.4% (2008-2012 5-year est.).

Education: Percent of population age 25 and over with: High school diploma (including GED) or higher: 85.4% (2008-2012 5-year est.); Bachelor's degree or higher: 17.5% (2008-2012 5-year est.); Master's degree or higher: 6.3% (2008-2012 5-year est.).

School District(s)

Indian Creek CUSD 425 (PK-12)
  2011-12 Enrollment: 782 . . . . (815) 824-2197

Housing: Homeownership rate: 67.2% (2008-2012 5-year est.); Median home value: $153,000 (2008-2012 5-year est.); Median contract rent: $675 per month (2008-2012 5-year est.); Median year structure built: 1957 (2008-2012 5-year est.).

Health Insurance: 65.7% Private; 33.2% Public; 14.2% None. (2008-2012 5-year est.)

Transportation: Commute to work: 90.4% car, 0.0% public transportation, 5.3% walk, 4.3% work from home (2008-2012 5-year est.); Travel time to work: 33.6% less than 15 minutes, 19.7% 15 to 30 minutes, 21.7% 30 to 45 minutes, 17.2% 45 to 60 minutes, 7.8% 60 minutes or more (2008-2012 5-year est.)

SOMONAUK (village). Covers a land area of 2.415 square miles and a water area of 0.005 square miles. Located at 41.63° N. Lat; 88.69° W. Long. Elevation is 686 feet.

Population: 1,263 (1990); 1,295 (2000); 1,893 (2010); Density: 911.4 persons per square mile (2008-2012 5-year est.); Race: 87.1% White, 2.4% Black/African American, 0.2% Asian, 0.7% American Indian/Alaska Native, 0.0% Native Hawaiian/Other Pacific Islander, 9.6% Some other race, 4.7% Two or more races, 9.9% Hispanic of any race (2008-2012 5-year est.); Average household size: 2.68 (2008-2012 5-year est.); Median age: 38.5 (2008-2012 5-year est.); Males per 100 females: 109.0

(2008-2012 5-year est.); Marriage status: 22.0% never married, 57.2% now married, 9.6% widowed, 11.1% divorced (2008-2012 5-year est.); Foreign born: 3.2% (2008-2012 5-year est.); Ancestry (includes multiple ancestries): 34.3% German, 13.2% Irish, 8.7% Norwegian, 7.9% Polish, 7.7% French (2008-2012 5-year est.).

Economy: Single-family building permits issued: 0 (2013); Multi-family building permits issued: 0 (2013); Homeowner vacancy rate: 0.0%. Rental vacancy rate: 0.0%. (2008-2012 5-year est.); Employment by occupation: 9.3% management, business, and financial, 2.4% computer, engineering, and science, 5.3% education, legal, community service, arts, and media, 5.5% healthcare practitioners, 16.9% service, 26.4% sales and office, 16.3% natural resources, construction, and maintenance, 18.0% production, transportation, and material moving (2008-2012 5-year est.).

Income: Per capita income: $25,961 (2008-2012 5-year est.); Median household income: $58,516 (2008-2012 5-year est.); Average household income: $69,358 (2008-2012 5-year est.); Percent of households with income of $100,000 or more: 20.9% (2008-2012 5-year est.); Poverty rate: 8.6% (2008-2012 5-year est.).

Education: Percent of population age 25 and over with: High school diploma (including GED) or higher: 91.0% (2008-2012 5-year est.); Bachelor's degree or higher: 13.7% (2008-2012 5-year est.); Master's degree or higher: 2.6% (2008-2012 5-year est.).

School District(s)

Somonauk CUSD 432 (PK-12)
 2011-12 Enrollment: 891 . . . . (815) 498-2314

Housing: Homeownership rate: 78.0% (2008-2012 5-year est.); Median home value: $176,000 (2008-2012 5-year est.); Median contract rent: $670 per month (2008-2012 5-year est.); Median year structure built: 1969 (2008-2012 5-year est.).

Health Insurance: 73.7% Private; 30.6% Public; 11.4% None. (2008-2012 5-year est.)

Transportation: Commute to work: 93.0% car, 0.0% public transportation, 4.0% walk, 3.0% work from home (2008-2012 5-year est.); Travel time to work: 28.9% less than 15 minutes, 17.3% 15 to 30 minutes, 21.6% 30 to 45 minutes, 19.7% 45 to 60 minutes, 12.5% 60 minutes or more (2008-2012 5-year est.)

SYCAMORE (city). County seat. Covers a land area of 9.730 square miles and a water area of 0.038 square miles. Located at 42.00° N. Lat; 88.68° W. Long. Elevation is 869 feet.

Population: 9,708 (1990); 12,020 (2000); 17,519 (2010); Density: 1,799.0 persons per square mile (2008-2012 5-year est.); Race: 88.3% White, 3.3% Black/African American, 1.6% Asian, 0.0% American Indian/Alaska Native, 0.0% Native Hawaiian/Other Pacific Islander, 6.8% Some other race, 1.0% Two or more races, 10.5% Hispanic of any race (2008-2012 5-year est.); Average household size: 2.48 (2008-2012 5-year est.); Median age: 34.8 (2008-2012 5-year est.); Males per 100 females: 93.9 (2008-2012 5-year est.); Marriage status: 31.5% never married, 52.3% now married, 4.6% widowed, 11.6% divorced (2008-2012 5-year est.); Foreign born: 7.0% (2008-2012 5-year est.); Ancestry (includes multiple ancestries): 34.0% German, 19.9% Irish, 9.5% English, 7.8% Polish, 7.4% Italian (2008-2012 5-year est.).

Economy: Single-family building permits issued: 28 (2013); Multi-family building permits issued: 25 (2013); Homeowner vacancy rate: 2.0%. Rental vacancy rate: 1.9%. (2008-2012 5-year est.); Employment by occupation: 16.1% management, business, and financial, 4.0% computer, engineering, and science, 14.0% education, legal, community service, arts, and media, 4.1% healthcare practitioners, 15.6% service, 24.9% sales and office, 8.0% natural resources, construction, and maintenance, 13.4% production, transportation, and material moving (2008-2012 5-year est.).

Income: Per capita income: $29,821 (2008-2012 5-year est.); Median household income: $61,320 (2008-2012 5-year est.); Average household income: $73,022 (2008-2012 5-year est.); Percent of households with income of $100,000 or more: 23.2% (2008-2012 5-year est.); Poverty rate: 7.6% (2008-2012 5-year est.).

Education: Percent of population age 25 and over with: High school diploma (including GED) or higher: 93.7% (2008-2012 5-year est.); Bachelor's degree or higher: 36.6% (2008-2012 5-year est.); Master's degree or higher: 13.2% (2008-2012 5-year est.).

School District(s)

Sycamore CUSD 427 (PK-12)
 2011-12 Enrollment: 3,840 . . . . (815) 899-8103

Vocational/Technical School(s)

Hair Professionals Career College Inc (Private, For-profit)
 Fall 2012 Enrollment: 53 . . . . (815) 756-3596
 2012-13 Tuition: $16,950

Housing: Homeownership rate: 66.7% (2008-2012 5-year est.); Median home value: $175,500 (2008-2012 5-year est.); Median contract rent: $768 per month (2008-2012 5-year est.); Median year structure built: 1984 (2008-2012 5-year est.).

Health Insurance: 79.7% Private; 18.8% Public; 10.2% None. (2008-2012 5-year est.)

Hospitals: Kindred Hospital - Sycamore (77 beds)

Safety: Violent crime rate: 7.4 per 10,000 population; Property crime rate: 145.0 per 10,000 population (2012).

Transportation: Commute to work: 92.3% car, 0.0% public transportation, 1.9% walk, 3.6% work from home (2008-2012 5-year est.); Travel time to work: 35.5% less than 15 minutes, 23.3% 15 to 30 minutes, 18.0% 30 to 45 minutes, 10.6% 45 to 60 minutes, 12.6% 60 minutes or more (2008-2012 5-year est.)

Additional Information Contacts

City of Sycamore . . . . (815) 895-4515
 http://www.cityofsycamore.com
Sycamore Chamber of Commerce . . . . (815) 895-3456
 http://www.sycamorechamber.com

WATERMAN (village). Covers a land area of 1.475 square miles and a water area of 0.002 square miles. Located at 41.77° N. Lat; 88.76° W. Long. Elevation is 823 feet.

Population: 1,074 (1990); 1,224 (2000); 1,506 (2010); Density: 1,017.4 persons per square mile (2008-2012 5-year est.); Race: 91.3% White, 3.9% Black/African American, 0.9% Asian, 0.0% American Indian/Alaska Native, 0.0% Native Hawaiian/Other Pacific Islander, 3.9% Some other race, 3.8% Two or more races, 4.3% Hispanic of any race (2008-2012 5-year est.); Average household size: 2.80 (2008-2012 5-year est.); Median age: 37.1 (2008-2012 5-year est.); Males per 100 females: 96.7 (2008-2012 5-year est.); Marriage status: 25.4% never married, 60.0% now married, 4.0% widowed, 10.6% divorced (2008-2012 5-year est.); Foreign born: 1.1% (2008-2012 5-year est.); Ancestry (includes multiple ancestries): 43.2% German, 12.0% English, 11.5% Irish, 6.9% Norwegian, 6.7% Dutch (2008-2012 5-year est.).

Economy: Single-family building permits issued: 0 (2013); Multi-family building permits issued: 0 (2013); Homeowner vacancy rate: 0.7%. Rental vacancy rate: 0.0%. (2008-2012 5-year est.); Employment by occupation: 14.0% management, business, and financial, 6.6% computer, engineering, and science, 8.8% education, legal, community service, arts, and media, 5.2% healthcare practitioners, 18.6% service, 22.3% sales and office, 10.7% natural resources, construction, and maintenance, 13.8% production, transportation, and material moving (2008-2012 5-year est.).

Income: Per capita income: $25,964 (2008-2012 5-year est.); Median household income: $65,556 (2008-2012 5-year est.); Average household income: $72,746 (2008-2012 5-year est.); Percent of households with income of $100,000 or more: 22.4% (2008-2012 5-year est.); Poverty rate: 8.4% (2008-2012 5-year est.).

Education: Percent of population age 25 and over with: High school diploma (including GED) or higher: 96.2% (2008-2012 5-year est.); Bachelor's degree or higher: 21.3% (2008-2012 5-year est.); Master's degree or higher: 6.5% (2008-2012 5-year est.).

School District(s)

Indian Creek CUSD 425 (PK-12)
 2011-12 Enrollment: 782 . . . . (815) 824-2197

Housing: Homeownership rate: 84.7% (2008-2012 5-year est.); Median home value: $177,900 (2008-2012 5-year est.); Median contract rent: $701 per month (2008-2012 5-year est.); Median year structure built: 1968 (2008-2012 5-year est.).

Health Insurance: 74.7% Private; 22.8% Public; 12.1% None. (2008-2012 5-year est.)

Transportation: Commute to work: 94.2% car, 0.5% public transportation, 2.9% walk, 2.0% work from home (2008-2012 5-year est.); Travel time to work: 26.9% less than 15 minutes, 27.6% 15 to 30 minutes, 27.2% 30 to 45 minutes, 11.4% 45 to 60 minutes, 6.9% 60 minutes or more (2008-2012 5-year est.)

Douglas County

Located in east central Illinois; drained by the Embarrass and Kaskaskia Rivers. Covers a land area of 416.665 square miles, a water area of 0.559

square miles, and is located in the Central Time Zone at 39.77° N. Lat., 88.22° W. Long. The county was founded in 1859. County seat is Tuscola.

Weather Station: Tuscola   Elevation: 652 feet

	Jan	Feb	Mar	Apr	May	Jun	Jul	Aug	Sep	Oct	Nov	Dec
High	35	40	52	65	76	85	87	86	80	67	53	40
Low	19	22	31	42	53	62	65	63	55	43	34	24
Precip	2.2	2.2	2.8	4.0	4.1	4.1	4.5	3.4	3.2	3.4	3.8	2.9
Snow	6.3	5.1	2.3	0.2	tr	0.0	0.0	0.0	0.0	tr	1.0	4.7

High and Low temperatures in degrees Fahrenheit; Precipitation and Snow in inches

Population: 19,464 (1990); 19,922 (2000); 19,980 (2010); Race: 95.8% White, 0.4% Black/African American, 0.8% Asian, 0.2% American Indian/Alaska Native, 0.0% Native Hawaiian/Other Pacific Islander, 2.8% Some other race, 1.1% Two or more races, 6.2% Hispanic of any race (2008-2012 5-year est.); Density: 47.7 persons per square mile (2008-2012 5-year est.); Average household size: 2.58 (2008-2012 5-year est.); Median age: 38.3 (2008-2012 5-year est.); Males per 100 females: 96.8 (2008-2012 5-year est.).
Religion: Six largest groups: 19.2% Baptist, 15.2% European Free-Church, 11.8% Methodist/Pietist, 10.5% Catholicism, 4.0% Presbyterian-Reformed, 1.9% Lutheran (2010)
Economy: Unemployment rate: 6.2% (April 2014); Total civilian labor force: 9,577 (April 2014); Leading industries: 36.0% manufacturing; 19.6% retail trade; 10.7% accommodation & food services (2012); Farms: 735 totaling 262,839 acres (2012); Companies that employ 500 or more persons: 0 (2012); Companies that employ 100 to 499 persons: 4 (2012); Companies that employ less than 100 persons: 579 (2012); Black-owned businesses: n/a (2007); Hispanic-owned businesses: n/a (2007); Asian-owned businesses: n/a (2007); Women-owned businesses: n/a (2007); Single-family building permits issued: 12 (2013); Multi-family building permits issued: 0 (2013).
Income: Per capita income: $23,870 (2008-2012 5-year est.); Median household income: $50,589 (2008-2012 5-year est.); Average household income: $61,226 (2008-2012 5-year est.); Percent of households with income of $100,000 or more: 15.6% (2008-2012 5-year est.); Poverty rate: 10.1% (2008-2012 5-year est.); Bankruptcy rate: 1.97% (2013).
Education: Percent of population age 25 and over with: High school diploma (including GED) or higher: 84.4% (2008-2012 5-year est.); Bachelor's degree or higher: 15.6% (2008-2012 5-year est.); Master's degree or higher: 4.3% (2008-2012 5-year est.).
Housing: Homeownership rate: 78.4% (2008-2012 5-year est.); Median home value: $98,800 (2008-2012 5-year est.); Median contract rent: $481 per month (2008-2012 5-year est.); Median year structure built: 1964 (2008-2012 5-year est.)
Health: Birth rate: 130.7 per 10,000 population (2013); Death rate: 85.0 per 10,000 population (2013); Age-adjusted cancer mortality rate: 174.0 deaths per 100,000 population (2011); Number of physicians: 4.5 per 10,000 population (2011); Hospital beds: 0.0 per 10,000 population (2010); Hospital admissions: 0.0 per 10,000 population (2010).
Elections: 2012 Presidential election results: 30.8% Obama, 67.6% Romney
National and State Parks: Walnut Point State Park
Additional Information Contacts
Douglas County Government . . . . (217) 253-2411
   http://www.douglascountyil.com

Douglas County Communities

ARCOLA (city). Covers a land area of 1.996 square miles and a water area of 0.021 square miles. Located at 39.68° N. Lat; 88.30° W. Long. Elevation is 679 feet.
History: Arcola was laid out in 1855 and named for a town in Italy. Broom corn was grown here, some for the local manufacture of brooms and some for export.
Population: 2,678 (1990); 2,652 (2000); 2,916 (2010); Density: 1,489.9 persons per square mile (2008-2012 5-year est.); Race: 87.9% White, 0.7% Black/African American, 0.3% Asian, 0.0% American Indian/Alaska Native, 0.0% Native Hawaiian/Other Pacific Islander, 11.1% Some other race, 2.2% Two or more races, 25.1% Hispanic of any race (2008-2012 5-year est.); Average household size: 2.43 (2008-2012 5-year est.); Median age: 37.0 (2008-2012 5-year est.); Males per 100 females: 81.8 (2008-2012 5-year est.); Marriage status: 18.6% never married, 60.6% now married, 11.0% widowed, 9.7% divorced (2008-2012 5-year est.); Foreign born: 15.5% (2008-2012 5-year est.); Ancestry (includes multiple

ancestries): 24.0% German, 15.4% Irish, 12.0% American, 10.1% English, 2.3% Scottish (2008-2012 5-year est.).
Economy: Single-family building permits issued: 1 (2013); Multi-family building permits issued: 0 (2013); Homeowner vacancy rate: 0.0%. Rental vacancy rate: 0.0%. (2008-2012 5-year est.); Employment by occupation: 12.1% management, business, and financial, 2.4% computer, engineering, and science, 3.1% education, legal, community service, arts, and media, 3.7% healthcare practitioners, 11.1% service, 30.6% sales and office, 12.5% natural resources, construction, and maintenance, 24.6% production, transportation, and material moving (2008-2012 5-year est.).
Income: Per capita income: $22,061 (2008-2012 5-year est.); Median household income: $43,617 (2008-2012 5-year est.); Average household income: $54,211 (2008-2012 5-year est.); Percent of households with income of $100,000 or more: 10.2% (2008-2012 5-year est.); Poverty rate: 15.0% (2008-2012 5-year est.).
Education: Percent of population age 25 and over with: High school diploma (including GED) or higher: 82.7% (2008-2012 5-year est.); Bachelor's degree or higher: 13.1% (2008-2012 5-year est.); Master's degree or higher: 3.8% (2008-2012 5-year est.).
School District(s)
Arcola CUSD 306 (PK-12)
   2011-12 Enrollment: 790 . . . . (217) 268-4963
Eastern Il Area of Spec Educ (PK-12)
   2011-12 Enrollment: n/a . . . . (217) 348-7700
Housing: Homeownership rate: 74.5% (2008-2012 5-year est.); Median home value: $80,400 (2008-2012 5-year est.); Median contract rent: $532 per month (2008-2012 5-year est.); Median year structure built: 1974 (2008-2012 5-year est.).
Health Insurance: 64.7% Private; 33.5% Public; 15.9% None. (2008-2012 5-year est.)
Safety: Violent crime rate: 13.8 per 10,000 population; Property crime rate: 117.4 per 10,000 population (2012).
Transportation: Commute to work: 90.5% car, 0.0% public transportation, 6.5% walk, 3.0% work from home (2008-2012 5-year est.); Travel time to work: 60.3% less than 15 minutes, 23.5% 15 to 30 minutes, 7.0% 30 to 45 minutes, 5.3% 45 to 60 minutes, 3.9% 60 minutes or more (2008-2012 5-year est.)
Additional Information Contacts
Arcola Chamber of Commerce . . . . (217) 268-4530
   http://www.arcolachamber.com
City of Arcola . . . . (217) 268-4966
   http://www.arcolaillinois.org

ARTHUR (village). Covers a land area of 1.318 square miles and a water area of 0 square miles. Located at 39.71° N. Lat; 88.47° W. Long. Elevation is 663 feet.
History: Arthur was settled in 1864 by a group of Amish colonists. The village was platted in 1873 by the Paris & Decatur Railroad Company. An early industry was the production of brooms.
Population: 2,112 (1990); 2,203 (2000); 2,288 (2010); Density: 1,825.7 persons per square mile (2008-2012 5-year est.); Race: 98.0% White, 0.2% Black/African American, 0.0% Asian, 0.7% American Indian/Alaska Native, 0.0% Native Hawaiian/Other Pacific Islander, 1.1% Some other race, 1.0% Two or more races, 3.1% Hispanic of any race (2008-2012 5-year est.); Average household size: 2.44 (2008-2012 5-year est.); Median age: 37.5 (2008-2012 5-year est.); Males per 100 females: 100.1 (2008-2012 5-year est.); Marriage status: 20.6% never married, 58.0% now married, 7.9% widowed, 13.5% divorced (2008-2012 5-year est.); Foreign born: 2.2% (2008-2012 5-year est.); Ancestry (includes multiple ancestries): 30.1% German, 15.1% American, 11.1% English, 7.9% Irish, 2.2% Scotch-Irish (2008-2012 5-year est.).
Economy: Single-family building permits issued: 2 (2013); Multi-family building permits issued: 0 (2013); Homeowner vacancy rate: 0.0%. Rental vacancy rate: 2.7%. (2008-2012 5-year est.); Employment by occupation: 10.3% management, business, and financial, 7.3% computer, engineering, and science, 6.4% education, legal, community service, arts, and media, 6.1% healthcare practitioners, 12.8% service, 22.7% sales and office, 11.0% natural resources, construction, and maintenance, 23.3% production, transportation, and material moving (2008-2012 5-year est.).
Income: Per capita income: $24,846 (2008-2012 5-year est.); Median household income: $47,813 (2008-2012 5-year est.); Average household income: $60,930 (2008-2012 5-year est.); Percent of households with income of $100,000 or more: 12.4% (2008-2012 5-year est.); Poverty rate: 5.8% (2008-2012 5-year est.).

Education: Percent of population age 25 and over with: High school diploma (including GED) or higher: 86.1% (2008-2012 5-year est.); Bachelor's degree or higher: 14.1% (2008-2012 5-year est.); Master's degree or higher: 3.5% (2008-2012 5-year est.).

School District(s)

Arthur CUSD 305 (PK-12)

   2011-12 Enrollment: 523 . . . . (217) 543-2511

Housing: Homeownership rate: 78.1% (2008-2012 5-year est.); Median home value: $92,900 (2008-2012 5-year est.); Median contract rent: $500 per month (2008-2012 5-year est.); Median year structure built: 1961 (2008-2012 5-year est.).

Health Insurance: 77.7% Private; 35.2% Public; 6.9% None. (2008-2012 5-year est.)

Safety: Violent crime rate: 22.0 per 10,000 population; Property crime rate: 175.7 per 10,000 population (2012).

Transportation: Commute to work: 88.7% car, 0.0% public transportation, 4.1% walk, 3.7% work from home (2008-2012 5-year est.); Travel time to work: 69.0% less than 15 minutes, 15.5% 15 to 30 minutes, 8.2% 30 to 45 minutes, 3.1% 45 to 60 minutes, 4.1% 60 minutes or more (2008-2012 5-year est.)

CAMARGO (village).

Covers a land area of 1.257 square miles and a water area of 0.013 square miles. Located at 39.80° N. Lat; 88.17° W. Long. Elevation is 663 feet.

Population: 372 (1990); 469 (2000); 445 (2010); Density: 399.3 persons per square mile (2008-2012 5-year est.); Race: 92.4% White, 0.0% Black/African American, 7.2% Asian, 0.0% American Indian/Alaska Native, 0.0% Native Hawaiian/Other Pacific Islander, 0.4% Some other race, 0.0% Two or more races, 1.0% Hispanic of any race (2008-2012 5-year est.); Average household size: 2.74 (2008-2012 5-year est.); Median age: 36.7 (2008-2012 5-year est.); Males per 100 females: 108.3 (2008-2012 5-year est.); Marriage status: 29.1% never married, 54.0% now married, 5.7% widowed, 11.1% divorced (2008-2012 5-year est.); Foreign born: 0.0% (2008-2012 5-year est.); Ancestry (includes multiple ancestries): 28.9% German, 17.7% Irish, 9.8% English, 9.0% American, 5.4% Dutch (2008-2012 5-year est.).

Economy: Single-family building permits issued: 0 (2013); Multi-family building permits issued: 0 (2013); Homeowner vacancy rate: 6.6%. Rental vacancy rate: 0.0%. (2008-2012 5-year est.); Employment by occupation: 10.0% management, business, and financial, 0.8% computer, engineering, and science, 1.9% education, legal, community service, arts, and media, 8.5% healthcare practitioners, 20.5% service, 32.4% sales and office, 7.7% natural resources, construction, and maintenance, 18.1% production, transportation, and material moving (2008-2012 5-year est.).

Income: Per capita income: $22,953 (2008-2012 5-year est.); Median household income: $53,125 (2008-2012 5-year est.); Average household income: $60,673 (2008-2012 5-year est.); Percent of households with income of $100,000 or more: 16.4% (2008-2012 5-year est.); Poverty rate: 5.6% (2008-2012 5-year est.).

Education: Percent of population age 25 and over with: High school diploma (including GED) or higher: 92.1% (2008-2012 5-year est.); Bachelor's degree or higher: 14.5% (2008-2012 5-year est.); Master's degree or higher: 2.1% (2008-2012 5-year est.).

Housing: Homeownership rate: 93.4% (2008-2012 5-year est.); Median home value: $92,500 (2008-2012 5-year est.); Median contract rent: $450 per month (2008-2012 5-year est.); Median year structure built: 1979 (2008-2012 5-year est.).

Health Insurance: 62.0% Private; 40.4% Public; 15.3% None. (2008-2012 5-year est.)

Transportation: Commute to work: 87.0% car, 0.0% public transportation, 6.1% walk, 5.3% work from home (2008-2012 5-year est.); Travel time to work: 23.1% less than 15 minutes, 21.4% 15 to 30 minutes, 42.3% 30 to 45 minutes, 12.8% 45 to 60 minutes, 0.4% 60 minutes or more (2008-2012 5-year est.)

GARRETT (village).

Covers a land area of 0.134 square miles and a water area of 0 square miles. Located at 39.80° N. Lat; 88.42° W. Long. Elevation is 669 feet.

Population: 169 (1990); 198 (2000); 162 (2010); Density: 1,276.9 persons per square mile (2008-2012 5-year est.); Race: 99.4% White, 0.0% Black/African American, 0.0% Asian, 0.0% American Indian/Alaska Native, 0.0% Native Hawaiian/Other Pacific Islander, 0.6% Some other race, 0.6% Two or more races, 2.9% Hispanic of any race (2008-2012 5-year est.); Average household size: 2.85 (2008-2012 5-year est.); Median age: 37.1 (2008-2012 5-year est.); Males per 100 females: 155.2 (2008-2012 5-year

est.); Marriage status: 23.3% never married, 45.0% now married, 7.5% widowed, 24.2% divorced (2008-2012 5-year est.); Foreign born: 0.0% (2008-2012 5-year est.); Ancestry (includes multiple ancestries): 34.5% German, 11.7% American, 9.4% Scottish, 8.8% Irish, 5.3% Italian (2008-2012 5-year est.).

Economy: Homeowner vacancy rate: 0.0%. Rental vacancy rate: 40.0%. (2008-2012 5-year est.); Employment by occupation: 4.0% management, business, and financial, 2.0% computer, engineering, and science, 0.0% education, legal, community service, arts, and media, 0.0% healthcare practitioners, 14.0% service, 18.0% sales and office, 28.0% natural resources, construction, and maintenance, 34.0% production, transportation, and material moving (2008-2012 5-year est.).

Income: Per capita income: $12,060 (2008-2012 5-year est.); Median household income: $24,167 (2008-2012 5-year est.); Average household income: $32,123 (2008-2012 5-year est.); Percent of households with income of $100,000 or more: 1.7% (2008-2012 5-year est.); Poverty rate: 49.7% (2008-2012 5-year est.).

Education: Percent of population age 25 and over with: High school diploma (including GED) or higher: 78.8% (2008-2012 5-year est.); Bachelor's degree or higher: 0.0% (2008-2012 5-year est.); Master's degree or higher: 0.0% (2008-2012 5-year est.).

Housing: Homeownership rate: 90.0% (2008-2012 5-year est.); Median home value: $49,200 (2008-2012 5-year est.); Median contract rent: $317 per month (2008-2012 5-year est.); Median year structure built: Before 1940 (2008-2012 5-year est.).

Health Insurance: 36.8% Private; 58.5% Public; 14.0% None. (2008-2012 5-year est.)

Transportation: Commute to work: 100.0% car, 0.0% public transportation, 0.0% walk, 0.0% work from home (2008-2012 5-year est.); Travel time to work: 40.8% less than 15 minutes, 32.7% 15 to 30 minutes, 14.3% 30 to 45 minutes, 12.2% 45 to 60 minutes, 0.0% 60 minutes or more (2008-2012 5-year est.)

HINDSBORO (village).

Covers a land area of 0.306 square miles and a water area of 0 square miles. Located at 39.68° N. Lat; 88.13° W. Long. Elevation is 650 feet.

Population: 346 (1990); 361 (2000); 313 (2010); Density: 1,051.0 persons per square mile (2008-2012 5-year est.); Race: 95.3% White, 1.2% Black/African American, 0.0% Asian, 0.0% American Indian/Alaska Native, 0.0% Native Hawaiian/Other Pacific Islander, 3.5% Some other race, 3.4% Two or more races, 2.5% Hispanic of any race (2008-2012 5-year est.); Average household size: 2.70 (2008-2012 5-year est.); Median age: 43.2 (2008-2012 5-year est.); Males per 100 females: 122.1 (2008-2012 5-year est.); Marriage status: 26.8% never married, 58.7% now married, 6.7% widowed, 7.8% divorced (2008-2012 5-year est.); Foreign born: 0.9% (2008-2012 5-year est.); Ancestry (includes multiple ancestries): 22.0% German, 20.5% American, 10.2% English, 4.7% Irish, 1.6% Canadian (2008-2012 5-year est.).

Economy: Single-family building permits issued: 0 (2013); Multi-family building permits issued: 0 (2013); Homeowner vacancy rate: 0.0%. Rental vacancy rate: 0.0%. (2008-2012 5-year est.); Employment by occupation: 3.5% management, business, and financial, 4.3% computer, engineering, and science, 4.3% education, legal, community service, arts, and media, 4.3% healthcare practitioners, 20.6% service, 22.7% sales and office, 11.3% natural resources, construction, and maintenance, 29.1% production, transportation, and material moving (2008-2012 5-year est.).

Income: Per capita income: $19,083 (2008-2012 5-year est.); Median household income: $37,000 (2008-2012 5-year est.); Average household income: $51,632 (2008-2012 5-year est.); Percent of households with income of $100,000 or more: 8.7% (2008-2012 5-year est.); Poverty rate: 16.5% (2008-2012 5-year est.).

Education: Percent of population age 25 and over with: High school diploma (including GED) or higher: 85.2% (2008-2012 5-year est.); Bachelor's degree or higher: 7.0% (2008-2012 5-year est.); Master's degree or higher: 0.9% (2008-2012 5-year est.).

Housing: Homeownership rate: 86.2% (2008-2012 5-year est.); Median home value: $62,000 (2008-2012 5-year est.); Median contract rent: $375 per month (2008-2012 5-year est.); Median year structure built: 1942 (2008-2012 5-year est.).

Health Insurance: 69.6% Private; 35.1% Public; 9.6% None. (2008-2012 5-year est.)

Transportation: Commute to work: 96.3% car, 1.5% public transportation, 0.0% walk, 2.2% work from home (2008-2012 5-year est.); Travel time to work: 31.8% less than 15 minutes, 40.2% 15 to 30 minutes, 9.8% 30 to 45

minutes, 7.6% 45 to 60 minutes, 10.6% 60 minutes or more (2008-2012 5-year est.)

MURDOCK (unincorporated postal area)
Zip Code: 61941

Covers a land area of 1.367 square miles and a water area of 0 square miles. Located at 39.80° N. Lat; 88.07° W. Long. Elevation is 640 feet. Population: 57 (2010); Density: 41.7 persons per square mile (2010); Race: 98.2% White, 1.8% Black/African American, 0.0% Asian, 0.0% American Indian/Alaska Native, 0.0% Native Hawaiian/Other Pacific Islander, 0.0% Some other race, 0.0% Two or more races, 0.0% Hispanic of any race (2010); Average household size: 1.97 (2010); Median age: 51.3 (2010); Males per 100 females: 119.2 (2010); Homeownership rate: 93.1% (2010)

NEWMAN (city). Covers a land area of 0.626 square miles and a water area of 0 square miles. Located at 39.80° N. Lat; 87.99° W. Long. Elevation is 653 feet.

History: Newman was founded in 1857 and named for B. Newman, son-in-law of the Methodist circuit-rider Peter Cartwright. Early industries included tile factories, and later a corn cannery and dairy products plant.
Population: 960 (1990); 956 (2000); 865 (2010); Density: 1,358.5 persons per square mile (2008-2012 5-year est.); Race: 98.5% White, 0.0% Black/African American, 0.0% Asian, 0.0% American Indian/Alaska Native, 0.0% Native Hawaiian/Other Pacific Islander, 1.5% Some other race, 0.9% Two or more races, 1.1% Hispanic of any race (2008-2012 5-year est.); Average household size: 2.31 (2008-2012 5-year est.); Median age: 42.6 (2008-2012 5-year est.); Males per 100 females: 83.2 (2008-2012 5-year est.); Marriage status: 21.7% never married, 52.2% now married, 10.6% widowed, 15.4% divorced (2008-2012 5-year est.); Foreign born: 0.4% (2008-2012 5-year est.); Ancestry (includes multiple ancestries): 21.4% German, 16.4% Irish, 13.1% American, 12.4% English, 3.5% Dutch (2008-2012 5-year est.).
Economy: Single-family building permits issued: 0 (2013); Multi-family building permits issued: 0 (2013); Homeowner vacancy rate: 0.0%. Rental vacancy rate: 10.7%. (2008-2012 5-year est.); Employment by occupation: 11.2% management, business, and financial, 1.0% computer, engineering, and science, 6.1% education, legal, community service, arts, and media, 11.4% healthcare practitioners, 17.3% service, 27.9% sales and office, 10.4% natural resources, construction, and maintenance, 14.7% production, transportation, and material moving (2008-2012 5-year est.).
Income: Per capita income: $21,518 (2008-2012 5-year est.); Median household income: $41,250 (2008-2012 5-year est.); Average household income: $49,305 (2008-2012 5-year est.); Percent of households with income of $100,000 or more: 4.6% (2008-2012 5-year est.); Poverty rate: 17.3% (2008-2012 5-year est.).
Education: Percent of population age 25 and over with: High school diploma (including GED) or higher: 90.5% (2008-2012 5-year est.); Bachelor's degree or higher: 11.6% (2008-2012 5-year est.); Master's degree or higher: 2.3% (2008-2012 5-year est.).
School District(s)
Shiloh CUSD 1 (PK-12)
    2011-12 Enrollment: 434 . . . . (217) 887-2364
Housing: Homeownership rate: 73.6% (2008-2012 5-year est.); Median home value: $63,900 (2008-2012 5-year est.); Median contract rent: $379 per month (2008-2012 5-year est.); Median year structure built: 1945 (2008-2012 5-year est.).
Health Insurance: 62.2% Private; 41.4% Public; 11.9% None. (2008-2012 5-year est.)
Transportation: Commute to work: 94.0% car, 0.0% public transportation, 4.4% walk, 0.8% work from home (2008-2012 5-year est.); Travel time to work: 27.4% less than 15 minutes, 20.1% 15 to 30 minutes, 15.9% 30 to 45 minutes, 23.0% 45 to 60 minutes, 13.6% 60 minutes or more (2008-2012 5-year est.)

TUSCOLA (city). County seat. Covers a land area of 2.742 square miles and a water area of 0.007 square miles. Located at 39.80° N. Lat; 88.27° W. Long. Elevation is 653 feet.

History: The extension of the Illinois Central Railroad across the prairies in 1855 opened the land to cultivation and resulted in the settling of Tuscola in 1857. The name is of Indian origin and means "a level plain."
Population: 4,155 (1990); 4,448 (2000); 4,480 (2010); Density: 1,561.0 persons per square mile (2008-2012 5-year est.); Race: 94.7% White, 1.2% Black/African American, 2.0% Asian, 0.0% American Indian/Alaska Native, 0.0% Native Hawaiian/Other Pacific Islander, 2.1% Some other

race, 1.0% Two or more races, 4.0% Hispanic of any race (2008-2012 5-year est.); Average household size: 2.31 (2008-2012 5-year est.); Median age: 40.3 (2008-2012 5-year est.); Males per 100 females: 106.3 (2008-2012 5-year est.); Marriage status: 19.3% never married, 55.1% now married, 11.1% widowed, 14.5% divorced (2008-2012 5-year est.); Foreign born: 4.7% (2008-2012 5-year est.); Ancestry (includes multiple ancestries): 27.8% German, 16.9% English, 12.6% Irish, 8.4% American, 4.2% Scottish (2008-2012 5-year est.).
Economy: Single-family building permits issued: 2 (2013); Multi-family building permits issued: 0 (2013); Homeowner vacancy rate: 2.8%. Rental vacancy rate: 8.7%. (2008-2012 5-year est.); Employment by occupation: 10.1% management, business, and financial, 2.9% computer, engineering, and science, 6.9% education, legal, community service, arts, and media, 7.5% healthcare practitioners, 15.6% service, 30.1% sales and office, 9.6% natural resources, construction, and maintenance, 17.4% production, transportation, and material moving (2008-2012 5-year est.).
Income: Per capita income: $25,328 (2008-2012 5-year est.); Median household income: $49,848 (2008-2012 5-year est.); Average household income: $57,790 (2008-2012 5-year est.); Percent of households with income of $100,000 or more: 11.3% (2008-2012 5-year est.); Poverty rate: 9.8% (2008-2012 5-year est.).
Education: Percent of population age 25 and over with: High school diploma (including GED) or higher: 90.7% (2008-2012 5-year est.); Bachelor's degree or higher: 16.2% (2008-2012 5-year est.); Master's degree or higher: 6.3% (2008-2012 5-year est.).
School District(s)
Tuscola CUSD 301 (PK-12)
    2011-12 Enrollment: 1,009 . . . . (217) 253-4241
Housing: Homeownership rate: 73.7% (2008-2012 5-year est.); Median home value: $95,900 (2008-2012 5-year est.); Median contract rent: $513 per month (2008-2012 5-year est.); Median year structure built: 1962 (2008-2012 5-year est.).
Health Insurance: 74.0% Private; 27.1% Public; 14.8% None. (2008-2012 5-year est.)
Safety: Violent crime rate: 56.2 per 10,000 population; Property crime rate: 155.1 per 10,000 population (2012).
Transportation: Commute to work: 96.3% car, 0.0% public transportation, 0.0% walk, 2.0% work from home (2008-2012 5-year est.); Travel time to work: 46.0% less than 15 minutes, 18.8% 15 to 30 minutes, 31.6% 30 to 45 minutes, 2.0% 45 to 60 minutes, 1.7% 60 minutes or more (2008-2012 5-year est.)
Airports: Tuscola Airport (general aviation)
Additional Information Contacts
Tuscola Chamber of Commerce . . . . (217) 253-5013
    http://tuscolacms7.surface51media.com/content/chamber-commerce

VILLA GROVE (city). Covers a land area of 1.500 square miles and a water area of 0.007 square miles. Located at 39.86° N. Lat; 88.16° W. Long. Elevation is 653 feet.

Population: 2,734 (1990); 2,553 (2000); 2,537 (2010); Density: 1,607.4 persons per square mile (2008-2012 5-year est.); Race: 97.0% White, 0.0% Black/African American, 1.2% Asian, 0.4% American Indian/Alaska Native, 0.0% Native Hawaiian/Other Pacific Islander, 1.4% Some other race, 0.4% Two or more races, 5.6% Hispanic of any race (2008-2012 5-year est.); Average household size: 2.30 (2008-2012 5-year est.); Median age: 39.8 (2008-2012 5-year est.); Males per 100 females: 93.8 (2008-2012 5-year est.); Marriage status: 19.3% never married, 56.7% now married, 8.2% widowed, 15.7% divorced (2008-2012 5-year est.); Foreign born: 4.5% (2008-2012 5-year est.); Ancestry (includes multiple ancestries): 29.4% German, 13.6% Irish, 11.8% American, 9.2% English, 7.0% Scottish (2008-2012 5-year est.).
Economy: Single-family building permits issued: 0 (2013); Multi-family building permits issued: 0 (2013); Homeowner vacancy rate: 0.0%. Rental vacancy rate: 5.3%. (2008-2012 5-year est.); Employment by occupation: 7.4% management, business, and financial, 1.4% computer, engineering, and science, 13.1% education, legal, community service, arts, and media, 5.9% healthcare practitioners, 13.1% service, 24.3% sales and office, 18.4% natural resources, construction, and maintenance, 16.5% production, transportation, and material moving (2008-2012 5-year est.).
Income: Per capita income: $22,861 (2008-2012 5-year est.); Median household income: $43,846 (2008-2012 5-year est.); Average household income: $52,406 (2008-2012 5-year est.); Percent of households with income of $100,000 or more: 12.7% (2008-2012 5-year est.); Poverty rate: 15.3% (2008-2012 5-year est.).

Education: Percent of population age 25 and over with: High school diploma (including GED) or higher: 94.1% (2008-2012 5-year est.); Bachelor's degree or higher: 20.9% (2008-2012 5-year est.); Master's degree or higher: 5.9% (2008-2012 5-year est.).

School District(s)
Villa Grove CUSD 302 (PK-12)
    2011-12 Enrollment: 646. . . . . (217) 832-2261

Housing: Homeownership rate: 76.0% (2008-2012 5-year est.); Median home value: $86,100 (2008-2012 5-year est.); Median contract rent: $480 per month (2008-2012 5-year est.); Median year structure built: 1957 (2008-2012 5-year est.).

Health Insurance: 71.0% Private; 31.4% Public; 13.1% None. (2008-2012 5-year est.)

Transportation: Commute to work: 94.1% car, 0.0% public transportation, 1.7% walk, 3.2% work from home (2008-2012 5-year est.); Travel time to work: 27.5% less than 15 minutes, 20.8% 15 to 30 minutes, 40.1% 30 to 45 minutes, 6.1% 45 to 60 minutes, 5.6% 60 minutes or more (2008-2012 5-year est.)

Du Page County

Located in northeastern Illinois; drained by the Du Page River. Covers a land area of 327.499 square miles, a water area of 8.913 square miles, and is located in the Central Time Zone at 41.85° N. Lat., 88.09° W. Long. The county was founded in 1939. County seat is Wheaton.

Du Page County is part of the Chicago-Naperville-Elgin, IL-IN-WI Metropolitan Statistical Area. The entire metro area includes: Chicago-Naperville-Arlington Heights, IL Metropolitan Division (Cook County, IL; DuPage County, IL; Grundy County, IL; Kendall County, IL; McHenry County, IL; Will County, IL); Elgin, IL Metropolitan Division (DeKalb County, IL; Kane County, IL); Gary, IN Metropolitan Division (Jasper County, IN; Lake County, IN; Newton County, IN; Porter County, IN); Lake County-Kenosha County, IL-WI Metropolitan Division (Lake County, IL; Kenosha County, WI)

Population: 781,666 (1990); 904,161 (2000); 916,924 (2010); Race: 80.4% White, 4.6% Black/African American, 10.2% Asian, 0.2% American Indian/Alaska Native, 0.0% Native Hawaiian/Other Pacific Islander, 4.6% Some other race, 2.0% Two or more races, 13.3% Hispanic of any race (2008-2012 5-year est.); Density: 2,831.8 persons per square mile (2008-2012 5-year est.); Average household size: 2.70 (2008-2012 5-year est.); Median age: 38.2 (2008-2012 5-year est.); Males per 100 females: 96.2 (2008-2012 5-year est.)

Religion: Six largest groups: 40.8% Catholicism, 6.5% Muslim Estimate, 5.5% Lutheran, 5.1% Non-denominational Protestant, 3.0% Methodist/Pietist, 2.8% Presbyterian-Reformed (2010)

Economy: Unemployment rate: 6.0% (April 2014); Total civilian labor force: 524,057 (April 2014); Leading industries: 11.3% administration, support, waste management, remediation services; 11.1% health care and social assistance; 10.4% retail trade (2012); Farms: 74 totaling 7,252 acres (2012); Companies that employ 500 or more persons: 102 (2012); Companies that employ 100 to 499 persons: 868 (2012); Companies that employ less than 100 persons: 32,113 (2012); Black-owned businesses: 2,379 (2007); Hispanic-owned businesses: 4,079 (2007); Asian-owned businesses: 8,523 (2007); Women-owned businesses: 26,506 (2007); Single-family building permits issued: 1,001 (2013); Multi-family building permits issued: 326 (2013).

Income: Per capita income: $38,398 (2008-2012 5-year est.); Median household income: $78,538 (2008-2012 5-year est.); Average household income: $103,422 (2008-2012 5-year est.); Percent of households with income of $100,000 or more: 37.6% (2008-2012 5-year est.); Poverty rate: 6.6% (2008-2012 5-year est.); Bankruptcy rate: 4.15% (2013).

Taxes: Total county taxes per capita: $172 (2011); County property taxes per capita: $132 (2011).

Education: Percent of population age 25 and over with: High school diploma (including GED) or higher: 91.9% (2008-2012 5-year est.); Bachelor's degree or higher: 45.9% (2008-2012 5-year est.); Master's degree or higher: 17.6% (2008-2012 5-year est.).

Housing: Homeownership rate: 75.0% (2008-2012 5-year est.); Median home value: $298,500 (2008-2012 5-year est.); Median contract rent: $970 per month (2008-2012 5-year est.); Median year structure built: 1977 (2008-2012 5-year est.)

Health: Birth rate: 114.8 per 10,000 population (2013); Death rate: 64.2 per 10,000 population (2013); Age-adjusted cancer mortality rate: 161.6

deaths per 100,000 population (2011); Number of physicians: 46.2 per 10,000 population (2011); Hospital beds: 24.9 per 10,000 population (2010); Hospital admissions: 1,268.1 per 10,000 population (2010).

Environment: Air Quality Index: 73.2% good, 26.8% moderate, 0.0% unhealthy for sensitive individuals, 0.0% unhealthy (percent of days in 2013)

Elections: 2012 Presidential election results: 49.7% Obama, 48.7% Romney

Additional Information Contacts
Du Page County Government . . . . (630) 407-5500
    http://www.co.dupage.il.us

Du Page County Communities

ADDISON (village). Covers a land area of 9.768 square miles and a water area of 0.210 square miles. Located at 41.93° N. Lat; 88.01° W. Long. Elevation is 689 feet.

History: Addison developed as a community of German Lutherans in the 1840's. It was named for the 18th-century essayist, Joseph Addison.

Population: 32,058 (1990); 35,914 (2000); 36,942 (2010); Density: 3,785.4 persons per square mile (2008-2012 5-year est.); Race: 81.6% White, 3.4% Black/African American, 6.6% Asian, 0.2% American Indian/Alaska Native, 0.0% Native Hawaiian/Other Pacific Islander, 8.2% Some other race, 1.0% Two or more races, 38.8% Hispanic of any race (2008-2012 5-year est.); Average household size: 3.08 (2008-2012 5-year est.); Median age: 34.3 (2008-2012 5-year est.); Males per 100 females: 95.9 (2008-2012 5-year est.); Marriage status: 31.5% never married, 55.6% now married, 6.0% widowed, 6.9% divorced (2008-2012 5-year est.); Foreign born: 34.5% (2008-2012 5-year est.); Ancestry (includes multiple ancestries): 13.4% Italian, 12.4% German, 12.4% Polish, 8.4% Irish, 2.5% Greek (2008-2012 5-year est.).

Economy: Unemployment rate: 8.1% (April 2014); Total civilian labor force: 19,987 (April 2014); Single-family building permits issued: 3 (2013); Multi-family building permits issued: 0 (2013); Homeowner vacancy rate: 1.9%. Rental vacancy rate: 4.5%. (2008-2012 5-year est.); Employment by occupation: 11.6% management, business, and financial, 3.2% computer, engineering, and science, 6.1% education, legal, community service, arts, and media, 4.9% healthcare practitioners, 15.1% service, 29.3% sales and office, 8.5% natural resources, construction, and maintenance, 21.3% production, transportation, and material moving (2008-2012 5-year est.).

Income: Per capita income: $24,666 (2008-2012 5-year est.); Median household income: $59,104 (2008-2012 5-year est.); Average household income: $73,917 (2008-2012 5-year est.); Percent of households with income of $100,000 or more: 25.0% (2008-2012 5-year est.); Poverty rate: 12.2% (2008-2012 5-year est.).

Taxes: Total city taxes per capita: $566 (2011); City property taxes per capita: $325 (2011).

Education: Percent of population age 25 and over with: High school diploma (including GED) or higher: 78.0% (2008-2012 5-year est.); Bachelor's degree or higher: 20.6% (2008-2012 5-year est.); Master's degree or higher: 5.0% (2008-2012 5-year est.).

School District(s)
Addison SD 4 (PK-08)
    2011-12 Enrollment: 4,296 . . . . (630) 458-2425
Dupage HSD 88 (09-12)
    2011-12 Enrollment: 4,077 . . . . (630) 530-3980
Dupage Roe (07-12)
    2011-12 Enrollment: n/a . . . . (630) 407-5800
Technology Center of Dupage (11-12)
    2011-12 Enrollment: n/a . . . . (630) 691-7591

Four-year College(s)
Chamberlain College of Nursing-Illinois (Private, For-profit)
    Fall 2012 Enrollment: 2,701 . . . . (630) 953-3680
    2012-13 Tuition: In-state $16,960; Out-of-state $16,960

Housing: Homeownership rate: 71.2% (2008-2012 5-year est.); Median home value: $262,500 (2008-2012 5-year est.); Median contract rent: $847 per month (2008-2012 5-year est.); Median year structure built: 1973 (2008-2012 5-year est.).

Health Insurance: 59.1% Private; 30.7% Public; 18.8% None. (2008-2012 5-year est.)

Safety: Violent crime rate: 19.9 per 10,000 population; Property crime rate: 194.0 per 10,000 population (2012).

Transportation: Commute to work: 93.1% car, 3.5% public transportation, 0.8% walk, 1.5% work from home (2008-2012 5-year est.); Travel time to work: 24.1% less than 15 minutes, 36.4% 15 to 30 minutes, 22.6% 30 to

45 minutes, 7.4% 45 to 60 minutes, 9.6% 60 minutes or more (2008-2012 5-year est.)

Additional Information Contacts
Addison Chamber of Commerce & Industry . . . . (630) 543-4300
   http://addisonchamber.org
Village of Addison . . . . (630) 543-4100
   http://www.addisonadvantage.org

BARTLETT (village). Covers a land area of 15.626 square miles and a water area of 0.236 square miles. Located at 41.96° N. Lat; 88.18° W. Long.

Population: 19,373 (1990); 36,706 (2000); 41,208 (2010); Density: 2,624.9 persons per square mile (2008-2012 5-year est.); Race: 79.2% White, 2.6% Black/African American, 13.1% Asian, 0.1% American Indian/Alaska Native, 0.0% Native Hawaiian/Other Pacific Islander, 5.0% Some other race, 1.5% Two or more races, 10.6% Hispanic of any race (2008-2012 5-year est.); Average household size: 2.96 (2008-2012 5-year est.); Median age: 36.7 (2008-2012 5-year est.); Males per 100 females: 98.2 (2008-2012 5-year est.); Marriage status: 26.4% never married, 64.3% now married, 3.6% widowed, 5.7% divorced (2008-2012 5-year est.); Foreign born: 17.3% (2008-2012 5-year est.); Ancestry (includes multiple ancestries): 27.5% German, 17.4% Italian, 15.7% Irish, 15.7% Polish, 4.4% English (2008-2012 5-year est.).

Economy: Unemployment rate: 6.1% (April 2014); Total civilian labor force: 23,706 (April 2014); Single-family building permits issued: 3 (2013); Multi-family building permits issued: 0 (2013); Homeowner vacancy rate: 1.3%. Rental vacancy rate: 0.0%. (2008-2012 5-year est.); Employment by occupation: 22.7% management, business, and financial, 6.8% computer, engineering, and science, 8.9% education, legal, community service, arts, and media, 5.4% healthcare practitioners, 10.7% service, 30.7% sales and office, 5.3% natural resources, construction, and maintenance, 9.3% production, transportation, and material moving (2008-2012 5-year est.).

Income: Per capita income: $36,403 (2008-2012 5-year est.); Median household income: $96,127 (2008-2012 5-year est.); Average household income: $106,173 (2008-2012 5-year est.); Percent of households with income of $100,000 or more: 47.0% (2008-2012 5-year est.); Poverty rate: 5.3% (2008-2012 5-year est.).

Education: Percent of population age 25 and over with: High school diploma (including GED) or higher: 93.2% (2008-2012 5-year est.); Bachelor's degree or higher: 42.9% (2008-2012 5-year est.); Master's degree or higher: 14.9% (2008-2012 5-year est.).

School District(s)
SD U-46 (PK-12)
   2011-12 Enrollment: 40,687 . . . . (847) 888-5000
SD U-46 (PK-12)
   2011-12 Enrollment: 40,687 . . . . (847) 888-5000

Housing: Homeownership rate: 88.2% (2008-2012 5-year est.); Median home value: $293,700 (2008-2012 5-year est.); Median contract rent: $1,030 per month (2008-2012 5-year est.); Median year structure built: 1991 (2008-2012 5-year est.).

Health Insurance: 84.8% Private; 16.2% Public; 6.1% None. (2008-2012 5-year est.)

Safety: Violent crime rate: 7.5 per 10,000 population; Property crime rate: 76.4 per 10,000 population (2012).

Transportation: Commute to work: 88.5% car, 4.3% public transportation, 0.7% walk, 5.7% work from home (2008-2012 5-year est.); Travel time to work: 14.4% less than 15 minutes, 28.4% 15 to 30 minutes, 29.8% 30 to 45 minutes, 13.1% 45 to 60 minutes, 14.3% 60 minutes or more (2008-2012 5-year est.)

Additional Information Contacts
Bartlett Chamber of Commerce. . . . . (630) 830-0324
   http://www.bartlettchamber.com
Village of Bartlett. . . . . (630) 837-0800
   http://www.village.bartlett.il.us

BENSENVILLE (village). Covers a land area of 5.567 square miles and a water area of 0.048 square miles. Located at 41.96° N. Lat; 87.94° W. Long. Elevation is 679 feet.

Population: 17,767 (1990); 20,703 (2000); 18,352 (2010); Density: 3,319.3 persons per square mile (2008-2012 5-year est.); Race: 83.4% White, 4.4% Black/African American, 3.9% Asian, 0.4% American Indian/Alaska Native, 0.0% Native Hawaiian/Other Pacific Islander, 7.9% Some other race, 0.9% Two or more races, 51.2% Hispanic of any race (2008-2012 5-year est.); Average household size: 2.88 (2008-2012 5-year est.); Median age: 34.0 (2008-2012 5-year est.); Males per 100 females:

96.5 (2008-2012 5-year est.); Marriage status: 34.9% never married, 48.9% now married, 6.7% widowed, 9.5% divorced (2008-2012 5-year est.); Foreign born: 34.6% (2008-2012 5-year est.); Ancestry (includes multiple ancestries): 11.7% German, 10.6% Polish, 8.4% Italian, 7.9% Irish, 3.0% English (2008-2012 5-year est.).

Economy: Single-family building permits issued: 1 (2013); Multi-family building permits issued: 0 (2013); Homeowner vacancy rate: 1.4%. Rental vacancy rate: 9.3%. (2008-2012 5-year est.); Employment by occupation: 11.9% management, business, and financial, 3.0% computer, engineering, and science, 5.7% education, legal, community service, arts, and media, 2.5% healthcare practitioners, 18.9% service, 22.6% sales and office, 10.2% natural resources, construction, and maintenance, 25.2% production, transportation, and material moving (2008-2012 5-year est.).

Income: Per capita income: $22,672 (2008-2012 5-year est.); Median household income: $58,043 (2008-2012 5-year est.); Average household income: $63,678 (2008-2012 5-year est.); Percent of households with income of $100,000 or more: 15.6% (2008-2012 5-year est.); Poverty rate: 16.7% (2008-2012 5-year est.).

Taxes: Total city taxes per capita: $806 (2011); City property taxes per capita: $465 (2011).

Education: Percent of population age 25 and over with: High school diploma (including GED) or higher: 76.6% (2008-2012 5-year est.); Bachelor's degree or higher: 16.6% (2008-2012 5-year est.); Master's degree or higher: 5.4% (2008-2012 5-year est.).

School District(s)
Bensenville SD 2 (PK-08)
   2011-12 Enrollment: 2,105 . . . . (630) 766-5940
Fenton CHSD 100 (09-12)
   2011-12 Enrollment: 1,579 . . . . (630) 860-6257
Vocational/Technical School(s)
Star Truck Driving School-Bensenville (Private, For-profit)
   Fall 2012 Enrollment: 73 . . . . (630) 236-7200
   2012-13 Tuition: $4,595

Housing: Homeownership rate: 54.7% (2008-2012 5-year est.); Median home value: $247,900 (2008-2012 5-year est.); Median contract rent: $819 per month (2008-2012 5-year est.); Median year structure built: 1968 (2008-2012 5-year est.).

Health Insurance: 56.7% Private; 26.0% Public; 24.2% None. (2008-2012 5-year est.)

Transportation: Commute to work: 87.1% car, 3.9% public transportation, 5.1% walk, 3.2% work from home (2008-2012 5-year est.); Travel time to work: 23.5% less than 15 minutes, 38.7% 15 to 30 minutes, 21.6% 30 to 45 minutes, 6.3% 45 to 60 minutes, 9.9% 60 minutes or more (2008-2012 5-year est.)

Additional Information Contacts
Bensenville Chamber of Commerce . . . . (630) 860-3800
   http://www.bensenvillechamber.com
Village of Bensenville . . . . (630) 766-8200
   http://www.bensenville.il.us

BLOOMINGDALE (village). Covers a land area of 6.783 square miles and a water area of 0.260 square miles. Located at 41.95° N. Lat; 88.09° W. Long. Elevation is 764 feet.

Population: 16,614 (1990); 21,675 (2000); 22,018 (2010); Density: 3,247.6 persons per square mile (2008-2012 5-year est.); Race: 82.9% White, 2.8% Black/African American, 11.7% Asian, 0.1% American Indian/Alaska Native, 0.0% Native Hawaiian/Other Pacific Islander, 2.5% Some other race, 1.5% Two or more races, 6.9% Hispanic of any race (2008-2012 5-year est.); Average household size: 2.39 (2008-2012 5-year est.); Median age: 43.1 (2008-2012 5-year est.); Males per 100 females: 98.1 (2008-2012 5-year est.); Marriage status: 25.5% never married, 56.6% now married, 6.8% widowed, 11.1% divorced (2008-2012 5-year est.); Foreign born: 19.3% (2008-2012 5-year est.); Ancestry (includes multiple ancestries): 24.0% Italian, 19.3% German, 15.6% Polish, 13.1% Irish, 4.5% English (2008-2012 5-year est.).

Economy: Single-family building permits issued: 2 (2013); Multi-family building permits issued: 0 (2013); Homeowner vacancy rate: 2.0%. Rental vacancy rate: 7.0%. (2008-2012 5-year est.); Employment by occupation: 21.3% management, business, and financial, 4.9% computer, engineering, and science, 8.3% education, legal, community service, arts, and media, 5.1% healthcare practitioners, 10.8% service, 33.3% sales and office, 7.7% natural resources, construction, and maintenance, 8.6% production, transportation, and material moving (2008-2012 5-year est.).

Income: Per capita income: $38,833 (2008-2012 5-year est.); Median household income: $71,075 (2008-2012 5-year est.); Average household

income: $93,920 (2008-2012 5-year est.); Percent of households with income of $100,000 or more: 31.9% (2008-2012 5-year est.); Poverty rate: 5.9% (2008-2012 5-year est.).

Education: Percent of population age 25 and over with: High school diploma (including GED) or higher: 92.6% (2008-2012 5-year est.); Bachelor's degree or higher: 35.2% (2008-2012 5-year est.); Master's degree or higher: 10.4% (2008-2012 5-year est.).

School District(s)

Bloomingdale SD 13 (PK-08)
    2011-12 Enrollment: 1,185 . . . . (630) 893-9590

CCSD 93 (PK-08)
    2011-12 Enrollment: 3,879 . . . . (630) 539-3000

Marquardt SD 15 (PK-08)
    2011-12 Enrollment: 2,732 . . . . (630) 469-7615

Vocational/Technical School(s)

Pivot Point Academy (Private, For-profit)
    Fall 2012 Enrollment: 201 . . . . (847) 985-5900
    2012-13 Tuition: $18,393

Housing: Homeownership rate: 74.3% (2008-2012 5-year est.); Median home value: $286,300 (2008-2012 5-year est.); Median contract rent: $1,112 per month (2008-2012 5-year est.); Median year structure built: 1982 (2008-2012 5-year est.).

Health Insurance: 79.2% Private; 22.4% Public; 9.1% None. (2008-2012 5-year est.)

Safety: Violent crime rate: 5.9 per 10,000 population; Property crime rate: 295.8 per 10,000 population (2012).

Transportation: Commute to work: 92.3% car, 2.6% public transportation, 0.9% walk, 4.0% work from home (2008-2012 5-year est.); Travel time to work: 20.9% less than 15 minutes, 33.7% 15 to 30 minutes, 26.8% 30 to 45 minutes, 11.4% 45 to 60 minutes, 7.2% 60 minutes or more (2008-2012 5-year est.)

Additional Information Contacts

Bloomingdale Chamber of Commerce . . . . (630) 980-9082
    http://www.bloomingdalechamber.com

Village of Bloomingdale. . . . . (630) 893-7000
    http://www.villageofbloomingdale.org

BURR RIDGE (village). Covers a land area of 6.996 square miles and a water area of 0.141 square miles. Located at 41.75° N. Lat; 87.92° W. Long. Elevation is 702 feet.

History: The International Harvester Company and the Burr Ridges Estates merged with Harvester, changing the community's name to Burr Ridge. The town name is derived from a group of bur oaks (scientists spell it with one r) on a ridge.

Population: 7,669 (1990); 10,408 (2000); 10,559 (2010); Density: 1,513.6 persons per square mile (2008-2012 5-year est.); Race: 80.1% White, 3.5% Black/African American, 15.5% Asian, 0.0% American Indian/Alaska Native, 0.0% Native Hawaiian/Other Pacific Islander, 0.9% Some other race, 0.8% Two or more races, 4.6% Hispanic of any race (2008-2012 5-year est.); Average household size: 2.73 (2008-2012 5-year est.); Median age: 47.9 (2008-2012 5-year est.); Males per 100 females: 96.8 (2008-2012 5-year est.); Marriage status: 22.4% never married, 61.5% now married, 9.9% widowed, 6.3% divorced (2008-2012 5-year est.); Foreign born: 18.4% (2008-2012 5-year est.); Ancestry (includes multiple ancestries): 17.4% Irish, 16.7% German, 11.2% Italian, 10.3% Polish, 6.4% English (2008-2012 5-year est.).

Economy: Single-family building permits issued: 12 (2013); Multi-family building permits issued: 0 (2013); Homeowner vacancy rate: 1.9%. Rental vacancy rate: 18.5%. (2008-2012 5-year est.); Employment by occupation: 29.8% management, business, and financial, 5.5% computer, engineering, and science, 12.4% education, legal, community service, arts, and media, 19.9% healthcare practitioners, 5.6% service, 20.4% sales and office, 2.5% natural resources, construction, and maintenance, 3.8% production, transportation, and material moving (2008-2012 5-year est.).

Income: Per capita income: $81,816 (2008-2012 5-year est.); Median household income: $133,188 (2008-2012 5-year est.); Average household income: $224,596 (2008-2012 5-year est.); Percent of households with income of $100,000 or more: 56.7% (2008-2012 5-year est.); Poverty rate: 4.3% (2008-2012 5-year est.).

Education: Percent of population age 25 and over with: High school diploma (including GED) or higher: 95.9% (2008-2012 5-year est.); Bachelor's degree or higher: 68.0% (2008-2012 5-year est.); Master's degree or higher: 33.7% (2008-2012 5-year est.).

School District(s)

CCSD 180 (PK-08)
    2011-12 Enrollment: 666 . . . . (630) 734-6600

Gower SD 62 (PK-08)
    2011-12 Enrollment: 852 . . . . (630) 986-5383

Hinsdale CCSD 181 (PK-08)
    2011-12 Enrollment: 3,982 . . . . (630) 887-1070

Pleasantdale SD 107 (PK-08)
    2011-12 Enrollment: 806 . . . . (708) 784-2013

Vocational/Technical School(s)

Everest College-Burr Ridge (Private, For-profit)
    Fall 2012 Enrollment: 364 . . . . (630) 920-1102
    2012-13 Tuition: $19,380

Housing: Homeownership rate: 93.3% (2008-2012 5-year est.); Median home value: $684,800 (2008-2012 5-year est.); Median contract rent: $1,380 per month (2008-2012 5-year est.); Median year structure built: 1986 (2008-2012 5-year est.).

Health Insurance: 87.6% Private; 20.2% Public; 2.6% None. (2008-2012 5-year est.)

Safety: Violent crime rate: 1.9 per 10,000 population; Property crime rate: 145.8 per 10,000 population (2012).

Transportation: Commute to work: 87.0% car, 4.1% public transportation, 0.8% walk, 7.1% work from home (2008-2012 5-year est.); Travel time to work: 17.3% less than 15 minutes, 27.7% 15 to 30 minutes, 25.7% 30 to 45 minutes, 17.4% 45 to 60 minutes, 11.9% 60 minutes or more (2008-2012 5-year est.)

Additional Information Contacts

Village of Burr Ridge . . . . (630) 654-8181
    http://www.burr-ridge.gov

Willowbrook/Burr Ridge Chamber of Commerce & Industry (630) 654-0909
    http://www.wbbrchamber.org

CAROL STREAM (village). Covers a land area of 9.094 square miles and a water area of 0.326 square miles. Located at 41.92° N. Lat; 88.13° W. Long. Elevation is 758 feet.

Population: 31,716 (1990); 40,438 (2000); 39,711 (2010); Density: 4,384.2 persons per square mile (2008-2012 5-year est.); Race: 76.7% White, 5.5% Black/African American, 13.8% Asian, 0.2% American Indian/Alaska Native, 0.0% Native Hawaiian/Other Pacific Islander, 3.8% Some other race, 1.4% Two or more races, 14.4% Hispanic of any race (2008-2012 5-year est.); Average household size: 2.70 (2008-2012 5-year est.); Median age: 36.4 (2008-2012 5-year est.); Males per 100 females: 96.3 (2008-2012 5-year est.); Marriage status: 29.8% never married, 57.9% now married, 4.3% widowed, 8.0% divorced (2008-2012 5-year est.); Foreign born: 19.9% (2008-2012 5-year est.); Ancestry (includes multiple ancestries): 23.0% German, 13.6% Irish, 13.4% Italian, 11.7% Polish, 5.9% English (2008-2012 5-year est.).

Economy: Unemployment rate: 6.2% (April 2014); Total civilian labor force: 23,014 (April 2014); Single-family building permits issued: 32 (2013); Multi-family building permits issued: 0 (2013); Homeowner vacancy rate: 0.6%. Rental vacancy rate: 6.0%. (2008-2012 5-year est.); Employment by occupation: 14.0% management, business, and financial, 5.8% computer, engineering, and science, 9.3% education, legal, community service, arts, and media, 5.1% healthcare practitioners, 15.8% service, 30.0% sales and office, 6.6% natural resources, construction, and maintenance, 13.5% production, transportation, and material moving (2008-2012 5-year est.).

Income: Per capita income: $30,577 (2008-2012 5-year est.); Median household income: $73,705 (2008-2012 5-year est.); Average household income: $81,427 (2008-2012 5-year est.); Percent of households with income of $100,000 or more: 32.7% (2008-2012 5-year est.); Poverty rate: 9.1% (2008-2012 5-year est.).

Taxes: Total city taxes per capita: $222 (2011); City property taxes per capita: $15 (2011).

Education: Percent of population age 25 and over with: High school diploma (including GED) or higher: 90.2% (2008-2012 5-year est.); Bachelor's degree or higher: 35.9% (2008-2012 5-year est.); Master's degree or higher: 11.0% (2008-2012 5-year est.).

School District(s)

Benjamin SD 25 (PK-08)
    2011-12 Enrollment: 748 . . . . (630) 876-7800

CCSD 93 (PK-08)
    2011-12 Enrollment: 3,879 . . . . (630) 539-3000

Glenbard Twp HSD 87 (09-12)
    2011-12 Enrollment: 8,891 . . . . (630) 469-9100

SD U-46 (PK-12)
   2011-12 Enrollment: 40,687 . . . . (847) 888-5000
Housing: Homeownership rate: 68.2% (2008-2012 5-year est.); Median home value: $248,100 (2008-2012 5-year est.); Median contract rent: $914 per month (2008-2012 5-year est.); Median year structure built: 1983 (2008-2012 5-year est.).
Health Insurance: 77.9% Private; 21.2% Public; 10.8% None. (2008-2012 5-year est.)
Safety: Violent crime rate: 9.0 per 10,000 population; Property crime rate: 120.0 per 10,000 population (2012).
Transportation: Commute to work: 91.6% car, 3.0% public transportation, 1.0% walk, 3.4% work from home (2008-2012 5-year est.); Travel time to work: 24.1% less than 15 minutes, 30.3% 15 to 30 minutes, 25.5% 30 to 45 minutes, 8.8% 45 to 60 minutes, 11.3% 60 minutes or more (2008-2012 5-year est.)
Additional Information Contacts
Carol Stream Chamber of Commerce . . . . (630) 665-3325
   http://www.carolstreamchamber.com
Village of Carol Stream . . . . (630) 665-7050
   http://www.carolstream.org

CLARENDON HILLS (village). Covers a land area of 1.803 square miles and a water area of 0.010 square miles. Located at 41.80° N. Lat; 87.96° W. Long. Elevation is 728 feet.

History: Incorporated in 1924. The villag motto is: To honor, commemorate and celebrate the volunteer community.
Population: 6,994 (1990); 7,610 (2000); 8,427 (2010); Density: 4,678.8 persons per square mile (2008-2012 5-year est.); Race: 85.7% White, 2.5% Black/African American, 8.2% Asian, 0.2% American Indian/Alaska Native, 0.0% Native Hawaiian/Other Pacific Islander, 3.4% Some other race, 1.1% Two or more races, 7.8% Hispanic of any race (2008-2012 5-year est.); Average household size: 2.68 (2008-2012 5-year est.); Median age: 39.6 (2008-2012 5-year est.); Males per 100 females: 86.1 (2008-2012 5-year est.); Marriage status: 25.3% never married, 62.8% now married, 5.3% widowed, 6.6% divorced (2008-2012 5-year est.); Foreign born: 11.6% (2008-2012 5-year est.); Ancestry (includes multiple ancestries): 21.2% German, 18.5% Irish, 12.5% Italian, 8.3% Polish, 6.0% English (2008-2012 5-year est.).
Economy: Single-family building permits issued: 18 (2013); Multi-family building permits issued: 0 (2013); Homeowner vacancy rate: 1.6%. Rental vacancy rate: 15.6%. (2008-2012 5-year est.); Employment by occupation: 28.3% management, business, and financial, 7.7% computer, engineering, and science, 16.4% education, legal, community service, arts, and media, 7.2% healthcare practitioners, 9.0% service, 27.1% sales and office, 1.5% natural resources, construction, and maintenance, 2.9% production, transportation, and material moving (2008-2012 5-year est.).
Income: Per capita income: $58,298 (2008-2012 5-year est.); Median household income: $105,278 (2008-2012 5-year est.); Average household income: $156,123 (2008-2012 5-year est.); Percent of households with income of $100,000 or more: 53.6% (2008-2012 5-year est.); Poverty rate: 3.7% (2008-2012 5-year est.).
Taxes: Total city taxes per capita: $574 (2011); City property taxes per capita: $397 (2011).
Education: Percent of population age 25 and over with: High school diploma (including GED) or higher: 96.9% (2008-2012 5-year est.); Bachelor's degree or higher: 71.0% (2008-2012 5-year est.); Master's degree or higher: 32.0% (2008-2012 5-year est.).
School District(s)
Hinsdale CCSD 181 (PK-08)
   2011-12 Enrollment: 3,982 . . . . (630) 887-1070
Maercker SD 60 (PK-08)
   2011-12 Enrollment: 1,341 . . . . (630) 515-4840
Housing: Homeownership rate: 77.7% (2008-2012 5-year est.); Median home value: $569,700 (2008-2012 5-year est.); Median contract rent: $842 per month (2008-2012 5-year est.); Median year structure built: 1971 (2008-2012 5-year est.).
Health Insurance: 88.8% Private; 16.3% Public; 4.7% None. (2008-2012 5-year est.)
Transportation: Commute to work: 69.3% car, 17.2% public transportation, 4.9% walk, 6.8% work from home (2008-2012 5-year est.); Travel time to work: 22.9% less than 15 minutes, 34.8% 15 to 30 minutes, 15.6% 30 to 45 minutes, 12.5% 45 to 60 minutes, 14.2% 60 minutes or more (2008-2012 5-year est.)
Additional Information Contacts

Clarendon Hills Chamber of Commerce . . . . (630) 323-8700
   http://www.clarendonhillschamber.com
Village of Clarendon Hills . . . . (630) 286-5400
   http://www.clarendonhills.us

DARIEN (city). Covers a land area of 6.178 square miles and a water area of 0.123 square miles. Located at 41.75° N. Lat; 87.98° W. Long. Elevation is 758 feet.

Population: 18,341 (1990); 22,860 (2000); 22,086 (2010); Density: 3,587.4 persons per square mile (2008-2012 5-year est.); Race: 83.1% White, 3.3% Black/African American, 11.5% Asian, 0.0% American Indian/Alaska Native, 0.0% Native Hawaiian/Other Pacific Islander, 2.1% Some other race, 1.2% Two or more races, 3.0% Hispanic of any race (2008-2012 5-year est.); Average household size: 2.49 (2008-2012 5-year est.); Median age: 46.1 (2008-2012 5-year est.); Males per 100 females: 96.7 (2008-2012 5-year est.); Marriage status: 23.8% never married, 58.7% now married, 7.3% widowed, 10.3% divorced (2008-2012 5-year est.); Foreign born: 19.1% (2008-2012 5-year est.); Ancestry (includes multiple ancestries): 21.4% German, 17.1% Polish, 15.0% Irish, 14.5% Italian, 5.1% Czeoh (2008-2012 5-year est.).
Economy: Single-family building permits issued: 5 (2013); Multi-family building permits issued: 0 (2013); Homeowner vacancy rate: 0.0%. Rental vacancy rate: 3.6%. (2008-2012 5-year est.); Employment by occupation: 20.4% management, business, and financial, 7.2% computer, engineering, and science, 11.9% education, legal, community service, arts, and media, 7.8% healthcare practitioners, 12.3% service, 27.5% sales and office, 5.6% natural resources, construction, and maintenance, 7.2% production, transportation, and material moving (2008-2012 5-year est.).
Income: Per capita income: $39,877 (2008-2012 5-year est.); Median household income: $74,206 (2008-2012 5-year est.); Average household income: $98,080 (2008-2012 5-year est.); Percent of households with income of $100,000 or more: 35.6% (2008-2012 5-year est.); Poverty rate: 6.4% (2008-2012 5-year est.).
Taxes: Total city taxes per capita: $249 (2011); City property taxes per capita: $103 (2011).
Education: Percent of population age 25 and over with: High school diploma (including GED) or higher: 94.2% (2008-2012 5-year est.); Bachelor's degree or higher: 47.1% (2008-2012 5-year est.); Master's degree or higher: 18.9% (2008-2012 5-year est.).
School District(s)
Cass SD 63 (PK-08)
   2011-12 Enrollment: 789 . . . . (630) 985-2000
Center Cass SD 66 (PK-08)
   2011-12 Enrollment: 1,086 . . . . (630) 783-5000
Darien SD 61 (PK-08)
   2011-12 Enrollment: 1,648 . . . . (630) 968-7505
Hinsdale Twp HSD 86 (09-12)
   2011-12 Enrollment: 4,531 . . . . (630) 655-6100
Lagrange Area Dept Spec Ed-Ladse
   2011-12 Enrollment: n/a . . . . (708) 354-5730
Vocational/Technical School(s)
Regency Beauty Institute-Darien (Private, For-profit)
   Fall 2012 Enrollment: 37 . . . . (800) 787-6456
   2012-13 Tuition: $16,425
Housing: Homeownership rate: 84.4% (2008-2012 5-year est.); Median home value: $314,900 (2008-2012 5-year est.); Median contract rent: $948 per month (2008-2012 5-year est.); Median year structure built: 1977 (2008-2012 5-year est.).
Health Insurance: 84.3% Private; 24.1% Public; 6.8% None. (2008-2012 5-year est.)
Safety: Violent crime rate: 5.8 per 10,000 population; Property crime rate: 139.8 per 10,000 population (2012).
Transportation: Commute to work: 89.1% car, 3.9% public transportation, 1.7% walk, 4.3% work from home (2008-2012 5-year est.); Travel time to work: 22.7% less than 15 minutes, 31.9% 15 to 30 minutes, 23.0% 30 to 45 minutes, 11.1% 45 to 60 minutes, 11.4% 60 minutes or more (2008-2012 5-year est.)
Additional Information Contacts
City of Darien. . . . . (630) 852-5000
   http://www.darien.il.us
Darien Chamber of Commerce . . . . (630) 968-0004
   http://www.darienchamber.com

DOWNERS GROVE (village). Covers a land area of 14.305 square miles and a water area of 0.147 square miles. Located at 41.80° N. Lat; 88.02° W. Long. Elevation is 741 feet.

History: Named for Pierce Downer, an eary settler. Downers Grove was settled in 1832 by Pierce Downer at the intersection of two trails. The town was incorporated in 1873.

Population: 46,858 (1990); 48,724 (2000); 47,833 (2010); Density: 3,398.8 persons per square mile (2008-2012 5-year est.); Race: 89.7% White, 2.9% Black/African American, 5.5% Asian, 0.1% American Indian/Alaska Native, 0.0% Native Hawaiian/Other Pacific Islander, 1.8% Some other race, 0.7% Two or more races, 4.6% Hispanic of any race (2008-2012 5-year est.); Average household size: 2.56 (2008-2012 5-year est.); Median age: 41.8 (2008-2012 5-year est.); Males per 100 females: 92.4 (2008-2012 5-year est.); Marriage status: 27.9% never married, 57.7% now married, 6.3% widowed, 8.1% divorced (2008-2012 5-year est.); Foreign born: 8.9% (2008-2012 5-year est.); Ancestry (includes multiple ancestries): 26.5% German, 20.7% Irish, 13.9% Italian, 13.7% Polish, 8.2% English (2008-2012 5-year est.).

Economy: Unemployment rate: 5.3% (April 2014); Total civilian labor force: 27,269 (April 2014); Single-family building permits issued: 74 (2013); Multi-family building permits issued: 0 (2013); Homeowner vacancy rate: 2.6%. Rental vacancy rate: 6.3%. (2008-2012 5-year est.); Employment by occupation: 23.1% management, business, and financial, 7.2% computer, engineering, and science, 14.5% education, legal, community service, arts, and media, 6.2% healthcare practitioners, 10.7% service, 28.1% sales and office, 4.7% natural resources, construction, and maintenance, 5.5% production, transportation, and material moving (2008-2012 5-year est.).

Income: Per capita income: $41,949 (2008-2012 5-year est.); Median household income: $82,181 (2008-2012 5-year est.); Average household income: $107,573 (2008-2012 5-year est.); Percent of households with income of $100,000 or more: 41.9% (2008-2012 5-year est.); Poverty rate: 4.3% (2008-2012 5-year est.).

Taxes: Total city taxes per capita: $721 (2011); City property taxes per capita: $433 (2011).

Education: Percent of population age 25 and over with: High school diploma (including GED) or higher: 96.1% (2008-2012 5-year est.); Bachelor's degree or higher: 52.3% (2008-2012 5-year est.); Master's degree or higher: 20.5% (2008-2012 5-year est.).

School District(s)

CHSD 99 (09-12)
    2011-12 Enrollment: 5,196 . . . . (630) 795-7100
Center Cass SD 66 (PK-08)
    2011-12 Enrollment: 1,086 . . . . (630) 783-5000
Downers Grove GSD 58 (PK-08)
    2011-12 Enrollment: 5,047 . . . . (630) 719-5800
Sch Assoc Sped Educ Dupage Sased (09-12)
    2011-12 Enrollment: n/a . . . . (630) 778-4500

Four-year College(s)

DeVry University's Keller Graduate School of Management-Illinois (Private, For-profit)
    Fall 2012 Enrollment: 9,345 . . . . (630) 515-3000
Midwestern University-Downers Grove (Private, Not-for-profit)
    Fall 2012 Enrollment: 2,554 . . . . (630) 969-4400

Vocational/Technical School(s)

Universal Spa Training Academy (Private, For-profit)
    Fall 2012 Enrollment: 55 . . . . (630) 968-6800
    2012-13 Tuition: $9,950
University of Aesthetics-Downers Grove (Private, For-profit)
    Fall 2012 Enrollment: 12 . . . . (773) 635-1000
    2012-13 Tuition: $10,785

Housing: Homeownership rate: 80.6% (2008-2012 5-year est.); Median home value: $340,700 (2008-2012 5-year est.); Median contract rent: $979 per month (2008-2012 5-year est.); Median year structure built: 1972 (2008-2012 5-year est.).

Health Insurance: 88.7% Private; 19.6% Public; 5.1% None. (2008-2012 5-year est.)

Hospitals: Advocate Good Samaritan Hospital (327 beds)

Safety: Violent crime rate: 6.0 per 10,000 population; Property crime rate: 206.3 per 10,000 population (2012).

Transportation: Commute to work: 79.6% car, 11.3% public transportation, 2.2% walk, 5.7% work from home (2008-2012 5-year est.); Travel time to work: 25.3% less than 15 minutes, 32.2% 15 to 30 minutes, 20.5% 30 to 45 minutes, 11.0% 45 to 60 minutes, 11.1% 60 minutes or more (2008-2012 5-year est.)

Additional Information Contacts

Downers Grove Area Chamber of Commerce . . . . (630) 968-4050
    http://www.downersgrove.org
Village of Downers Grove . . . . (630) 434-5500
    http://www.downers.us

ELMHURST (city). Covers a land area of 10.254 square miles and a water area of 0.056 square miles. Located at 41.90° N. Lat; 87.94° W. Long. Elevation is 686 feet.

History: Elmhurst was first known as Cottage Hill, named for the home built in 1843 by J.L. Hovey. The later name of Elmhurst referred to a double row of elm trees that grew along Cottage Hill Avenue. Poet Carl Sandburg lived in Elmhurst at one time.

Population: 42,029 (1990); 42,762 (2000); 44,121 (2010); Density: 4,328.7 persons per square mile (2008-2012 5-year est.); Race: 89.5% White, 1.7% Black/African American, 5.7% Asian, 0.0% American Indian/Alaska Native, 0.0% Native Hawaiian/Other Pacific Islander, 3.1% Some other race, 1.5% Two or more races, 6.1% Hispanic of any race (2008-2012 5-year est.); Average household size: 2.82 (2008-2012 5-year est.); Median age: 39.5 (2008-2012 5-year est.); Males per 100 females: 95.0 (2008-2012 5-year est.); Marriage status: 27.5% never married, 57.7% now married, 7.1% widowed, 7.8% divorced (2008-2012 5-year est.); Foreign born: 9.7% (2008-2012 5-year est.); Ancestry (includes multiple ancestries): 27.8% German, 25.7% Irish, 16.2% Italian, 10.7% Polish, 6.0% English (2008-2012 5-year est.).

Economy: Unemployment rate: 5.2% (April 2014); Total civilian labor force: 24,383 (April 2014); Single-family building permits issued: 118 (2013); Multi-family building permits issued: 0 (2013); Homeowner vacancy rate: 2.2%. Rental vacancy rate: 10.4%. (2008-2012 5-year est.); Employment by occupation: 22.1% management, business, and financial, 6.4% computer, engineering, and science, 14.3% education, legal, community service, arts, and media, 7.3% healthcare practitioners, 10.8% service, 27.4% sales and office, 5.7% natural resources, construction, and maintenance, 6.0% production, transportation, and material moving (2008-2012 5-year est.).

Income: Per capita income: $42,706 (2008-2012 5-year est.); Median household income: $94,424 (2008-2012 5-year est.); Average household income: $122,418 (2008-2012 5-year est.); Percent of households with income of $100,000 or more: 47.9% (2008-2012 5-year est.); Poverty rate: 3.4% (2008-2012 5-year est.).

Taxes: Total city taxes per capita: $788 (2011); City property taxes per capita: $460 (2011).

Education: Percent of population age 25 and over with: High school diploma (including GED) or higher: 94.9% (2008-2012 5-year est.); Bachelor's degree or higher: 56.1% (2008-2012 5-year est.); Master's degree or higher: 21.8% (2008-2012 5-year est.).

School District(s)

Elmhurst SD 205 (PK-12)
    2011-12 Enrollment: 8,340 . . . . (630) 834-4530
Salt Creek SD 48 (PK-08)
    2011-12 Enrollment: 484 . . . . (630) 279-8400

Four-year College(s)

Elmhurst College (Private, Not-for-profit, United Church of Christ)
    Fall 2012 Enrollment: 3,298 . . . . (630) 617-3500
    2012-13 Tuition: In-state $31,650; Out-of-state $31,650

Housing: Homeownership rate: 81.4% (2008-2012 5-year est.); Median home value: $377,200 (2008-2012 5-year est.); Median contract rent: $1,060 per month (2008-2012 5-year est.); Median year structure built: 1959 (2008-2012 5-year est.).

Health Insurance: 88.9% Private; 17.8% Public; 4.8% None. (2008-2012 5-year est.)

Hospitals: Elmhurst Memorial Hospital (427 beds)

Safety: Violent crime rate: 7.2 per 10,000 population; Property crime rate: 139.9 per 10,000 population (2012).

Transportation: Commute to work: 81.6% car, 9.6% public transportation, 2.1% walk, 5.7% work from home (2008-2012 5-year est.); Travel time to work: 26.3% less than 15 minutes, 29.5% 15 to 30 minutes, 23.5% 30 to 45 minutes, 9.1% 45 to 60 minutes, 11.6% 60 minutes or more (2008-2012 5-year est.)

Additional Information Contacts

City of Elmhurst . . . . (630) 530-3000
    http://www.elmhurst.org
Elmhurst Chamber of Commerce & Industry . . . . (630) 834-6060
    http://www.elmhurstchamber.org

EOLA (unincorporated postal area)

Zip Code: 60519

Covers a land area of 0.062 square miles and a water area of 0 square miles. Located at 41.77° N. Lat; 88.24° W. Long. Population: 88 (2010); Density: 1,418.3 persons per square mile (2010); Race: 100.0% White, 0.0% Black/African American, 0.0% Asian, 0.0% American Indian/Alaska Native, 0.0% Native Hawaiian/Other Pacific Islander, 0.0% Some other race, 0.0% Two or more races, 10.2% Hispanic of any race (2010); Average household size: 2.84 (2010); Median age: 35.5 (2010); Males per 100 females: 95.6 (2010); Homeownership rate: 71.0% (2010)

GLEN ELLYN (village). Covers a land area of 6.611 square miles and a water area of 0.163 square miles. Located at 41.87° N. Lat; 88.06° W. Long. Elevation is 741 feet.

History: Glen Ellyn was named when the town was platted by Thomas E. Hill for his wife Ellyn. When the Galena & Chicago Union Railroad was constructed south of town in 1849, the residents transplanted their town to the present site, platted in 1851.

Population: 24,944 (1990); 26,999 (2000); 27,450 (2010); Density: 4,160.1 persons per square mile (2008-2012 5-year est.); Race: 89.7% White, 3.4% Black/African American, 4.9% Asian, 0.2% American Indian/Alaska Native, 0.1% Native Hawaiian/Other Pacific Islander, 1.7% Some other race, 1.4% Two or more races, 4.3% Hispanic of any race (2008-2012 5-year est.); Average household size: 2.62 (2008-2012 5-year est.); Median age: 40.2 (2008-2012 5-year est.); Males per 100 females: 90.3 (2008-2012 5-year est.); Marriage status: 25.0% never married, 59.9% now married, 5.6% widowed, 9.5% divorced (2008-2012 5-year est.); Foreign born: 9.5% (2008-2012 5-year est.); Ancestry (includes multiple ancestries): 28.3% German, 24.3% Irish, 11.9% English, 11.6% Polish, 10.2% Italian (2008-2012 5-year est.).

Economy: Unemployment rate: 5.1% (April 2014); Total civilian labor force: 14,711 (April 2014); Single-family building permits issued: 29 (2013); Multi-family building permits issued: 0 (2013); Homeowner vacancy rate: 1.4%. Rental vacancy rate: 5.0%. (2008-2012 5-year est.); Employment by occupation: 28.8% management, business, and financial, 5.4% computer, engineering, and science, 15.3% education, legal, community service, arts, and media, 4.6% healthcare practitioners, 10.7% service, 24.9% sales and office, 3.6% natural resources, construction, and maintenance, 6.7% production, transportation, and material moving (2008-2012 5-year est.).

Income: Per capita income: $50,590 (2008-2012 5-year est.); Median household income: $90,640 (2008-2012 5-year est.); Average household income: $130,754 (2008-2012 5-year est.); Percent of households with income of $100,000 or more: 46.3% (2008-2012 5-year est.); Poverty rate: 6.8% (2008-2012 5-year est.).

Education: Percent of population age 25 and over with: High school diploma (including GED) or higher: 94.9% (2008-2012 5-year est.); Bachelor's degree or higher: 61.6% (2008-2012 5-year est.); Master's degree or higher: 24.7% (2008-2012 5-year est.).

School District(s)

CCSD 89 (PK-08)

    2011-12 Enrollment: 2,000 . . . . (630) 469-8900

Glen Ellyn SD 41 (PK-08)

    2011-12 Enrollment: 3,642 . . . . (630) 790-6400

Glenbard Twp HSD 87 (09-12)

    2011-12 Enrollment: 8,891 . . . . (630) 469-9100

Philip J Rock Center and School (04-12)

    2011-12 Enrollment: n/a . . . . (630) 790-2474

Two-year College(s)

College of DuPage (Public)

    Fall 2012 Enrollment: 26,156 . . . . (630) 942-2800

    2012-13 Tuition: In-state $10,336; Out-of-state $12,576

Housing: Homeownership rate: 75.6% (2008-2012 5-year est.); Median home value: $399,100 (2008-2012 5-year est.); Median contract rent: $854 per month (2008-2012 5-year est.); Median year structure built: 1969 (2008-2012 5-year est.).

Health Insurance: 86.5% Private; 19.2% Public; 5.9% None. (2008-2012 5-year est.)

Safety: Violent crime rate: 5.8 per 10,000 population; Property crime rate: 131.2 per 10,000 population (2012).

Transportation: Commute to work: 77.1% car, 10.9% public transportation, 3.1% walk, 8.1% work from home (2008-2012 5-year est.); Travel time to work: 26.5% less than 15 minutes, 31.9% 15 to 30 minutes, 19.7% 30 to 45 minutes, 8.4% 45 to 60 minutes, 13.4% 60 minutes or more (2008-2012 5-year est.)

Additional Information Contacts

Glen Ellyn Chamber of Commerce . . . . (630) 469-0907

    http://www.glenellynchamber.com

Village of Glen Ellyn . . . . (630) 469-5000

    http://www.glenellyn.org

GLENDALE HEIGHTS (village). Covers a land area of 5.372 square miles and a water area of 0.140 square miles. Located at 41.92° N. Lat; 88.08° W. Long. Elevation is 761 feet.

Population: 27,973 (1990); 31,765 (2000); 34,208 (2010); Density: 6,358.2 persons per square mile (2008-2012 5-year est.); Race: 62.5% White, 7.1% Black/African American, 23.0% Asian, 0.8% American Indian/Alaska Native, 0.1% Native Hawaiian/Other Pacific Islander, 6.5% Some other race, 2.8% Two or more races, 30.7% Hispanic of any race (2008-2012 5-year est.); Average household size: 3.06 (2008-2012 5-year est.); Median age: 31.6 (2008-2012 5-year est.); Males per 100 females: 104.3 (2008-2012 5-year est.); Marriage status: 34.1% never married, 53.4% now married, 3.2% widowed, 9.3% divorced (2008-2012 5-year est.); Foreign born: 34.4% (2008-2012 5-year est.); Ancestry (includes multiple ancestries): 12.5% German, 8.6% Polish, 6.6% Italian, 6.3% Irish, 2.5% English (2008-2012 5-year est.).

Economy: Unemployment rate: 7.3% (April 2014); Total civilian labor force: 20,406 (April 2014); Single-family building permits issued: 0 (2013); Multi-family building permits issued: 0 (2013); Homeowner vacancy rate: 1.2%. Rental vacancy rate: 8.3%. (2008-2012 5-year est.); Employment by occupation: 10.6% management, business, and financial, 5.9% computer, engineering, and science, 4.8% education, legal, community service, arts, and media, 4.9% healthcare practitioners, 16.4% service, 29.4% sales and office, 7.6% natural resources, construction, and maintenance, 20.4% production, transportation, and material moving (2008-2012 5-year est.).

Income: Per capita income: $24,159 (2008-2012 5-year est.); Median household income: $62,208 (2008-2012 5-year est.); Average household income: $71,440 (2008-2012 5-year est.); Percent of households with income of $100,000 or more: 21.0% (2008-2012 5-year est.); Poverty rate: 12.1% (2008-2012 5-year est.).

Education: Percent of population age 25 and over with: High school diploma (including GED) or higher: 82.1% (2008-2012 5-year est.); Bachelor's degree or higher: 28.8% (2008-2012 5-year est.); Master's degree or higher: 7.3% (2008-2012 5-year est.).

School District(s)

Coop Assoc for Spec Educ

    2011-12 Enrollment: n/a . . . . (630) 942-5600

Marquardt SD 15 (PK-08)

    2011-12 Enrollment: 2,732 . . . . (630) 469-7615

Queen Bee SD 16 (PK-08)

    2011-12 Enrollment: 1,955 . . . . (630) 260-6105

Two-year College(s)

Universal Technical Institute of Illinois Inc (Private, For-profit)

    Fall 2012 Enrollment: 1,450 . . . . (630) 529-2662

Vocational/Technical School(s)

Tricoci University of Beauty Culture-Glendale Heights (Private, For-profit)

    Fall 2012 Enrollment: 103 . . . . (630) 528-3336

    2012-13 Tuition: $18,050

Housing: Homeownership rate: 72.0% (2008-2012 5-year est.); Median home value: $198,900 (2008-2012 5-year est.); Median contract rent: $916 per month (2008-2012 5-year est.); Median year structure built: 1977 (2008-2012 5-year est.).

Health Insurance: 66.6% Private; 25.2% Public; 13.7% None. (2008-2012 5-year est.)

Hospitals: Adventist GlenOaks Hospital (186 beds)

Safety: Violent crime rate: 7.8 per 10,000 population; Property crime rate: 171.2 per 10,000 population (2012).

Transportation: Commute to work: 93.4% car, 1.6% public transportation, 1.3% walk, 2.5% work from home (2008-2012 5-year est.); Travel time to work: 24.5% less than 15 minutes, 34.3% 15 to 30 minutes, 25.4% 30 to 45 minutes, 6.2% 45 to 60 minutes, 9.5% 60 minutes or more (2008-2012 5-year est.)

Additional Information Contacts

Glendale Heights Chamber of Commerce . . . . (630) 909-5361

    http://www.glendaleheightschamber.com

Village of Glendale Heights . . . . (630) 260-6000

    http://www.glendaleheights.org

HINSDALE (village). Covers a land area of 4.603 square miles and a water area of 0.033 square miles. Located at 41.80° N. Lat; 87.93° W. Long. Elevation is 699 feet.

History: Hinsdale developed along the route of the Chicago, Burlington & Quincy Railroad, and was named for railroad director H.W. Hinsdale. In 1923 Hinsdale annexed nearby Fullersburg, which had been settled in 1835 by Jacob Fuller and his family.

Population: 16,029 (1990); 17,349 (2000); 16,816 (2010); Density: 3,605.1 persons per square mile (2008-2012 5-year est.); Race: 90.2% White, 0.8% Black/African American, 7.3% Asian, 0.1% American Indian/Alaska Native, 0.0% Native Hawaiian/Other Pacific Islander, 1.6% Some other race, 1.5% Two or more races, 6.0% Hispanic of any race (2008-2012 5-year est.); Average household size: 3.03 (2008-2012 5-year est.); Median age: 40.8 (2008-2012 5-year est.); Males per 100 females: 95.5 (2008-2012 5-year est.); Marriage status: 21.3% never married, 68.5% now married, 5.7% widowed, 4.5% divorced (2008-2012 5-year est.); Foreign born: 10.1% (2008-2012 5-year est.); Ancestry (includes multiple ancestries): 24.9% German, 21.2% Irish, 12.6% English, 10.1% Polish, 10.1% Italian (2008-2012 5-year est.).

Economy: Single-family building permits issued: 55 (2013); Multi-family building permits issued: 24 (2013); Homeowner vacancy rate: 6.6%. Rental vacancy rate: 3.1%. (2008-2012 5-year est.); Employment by occupation: 35.8% management, business, and financial, 4.0% computer, engineering, and science, 16.2% education, legal, community service, arts, and media, 10.9% healthcare practitioners, 7.1% service, 19.6% sales and office, 2.8% natural resources, construction, and maintenance, 3.6% production, transportation, and material moving (2008-2012 5-year est.).

Income: Per capita income: $78,902 (2008-2012 5-year est.); Median household income: $165,598 (2008-2012 5-year est.); Average household income: $241,451 (2008-2012 5-year est.); Percent of households with income of $100,000 or more: 63.9% (2008-2012 5-year est.); Poverty rate: 3.1% (2008-2012 5-year est.).

Education: Percent of population age 25 and over with: High school diploma (including GED) or higher: 97.9% (2008-2012 5-year est.); Bachelor's degree or higher: 75.3% (2008-2012 5-year est.); Master's degree or higher: 37.5% (2008-2012 5-year est.).

School District(s)

Hinsdale CCSD 181 (PK-08)
    2011-12 Enrollment: 3,982 . . . . (630) 887-1070
Hinsdale Twp HSD 86 (09-12)
    2011-12 Enrollment: 4,531 . . . . (630) 655-6100

Housing: Homeownership rate: 83.7% (2008-2012 5-year est.); Median home value: $828,600 (2008-2012 5-year est.); Median contract rent: $1,273 per month (2008-2012 5-year est.); Median year structure built: 1972 (2008-2012 5-year est.).

Health Insurance: 92.7% Private; 14.2% Public; 2.7% None. (2008-2012 5-year est.)

Hospitals: Hinsdale Hospital (426 beds)

Safety: Violent crime rate: 1.2 per 10,000 population; Property crime rate: 106.9 per 10,000 population (2012).

Transportation: Commute to work: 69.9% car, 17.1% public transportation, 1.8% walk, 9.1% work from home (2008-2012 5-year est.); Travel time to work: 24.0% less than 15 minutes, 24.1% 15 to 30 minutes, 23.4% 30 to 45 minutes, 15.2% 45 to 60 minutes, 13.2% 60 minutes or more (2008-2012 5-year est.)

Additional Information Contacts

Hinsdale Chamber of Commerce . . . . (630) 323-3952
    http://www.hinsdalechamber.com
Village of Hinsdale . . . . (630) 789-7000
    http://www.villageofhinsdale.org

ITASCA (village). Covers a land area of 4.951 square miles and a water area of 0.123 square miles. Located at 41.98° N. Lat; 88.02° W. Long. Elevation is 702 feet.

Population: 6,947 (1990); 8,302 (2000); 8,649 (2010); Density: 1,715.5 persons per square mile (2008-2012 5-year est.); Race: 77.7% White, 0.5% Black/African American, 11.9% Asian, 0.0% American Indian/Alaska Native, 0.0% Native Hawaiian/Other Pacific Islander, 9.9% Some other race, 6.0% Two or more races, 12.3% Hispanic of any race (2008-2012 5-year est.); Average household size: 2.65 (2008-2012 5-year est.); Median age: 41.2 (2008-2012 5-year est.); Males per 100 females: 97.9 (2008-2012 5-year est.); Marriage status: 23.7% never married, 60.1% now married, 5.6% widowed, 10.6% divorced (2008-2012 5-year est.); Foreign born: 24.9% (2008-2012 5-year est.); Ancestry (includes multiple

ancestries): 20.6% German, 18.1% Polish, 16.8% Irish, 15.2% Italian, 3.4% English (2008-2012 5-year est.).

Economy: Single-family building permits issued: 6 (2013); Multi-family building permits issued: 0 (2013); Homeowner vacancy rate: 3.6%. Rental vacancy rate: 3.0%. (2008-2012 5-year est.); Employment by occupation: 20.7% management, business, and financial, 7.5% computer, engineering, and science, 6.0% education, legal, community service, arts, and media, 6.3% healthcare practitioners, 14.8% service, 24.7% sales and office, 7.5% natural resources, construction, and maintenance, 12.7% production, transportation, and material moving (2008-2012 5-year est.).

Income: Per capita income: $34,112 (2008-2012 5-year est.); Median household income: $77,368 (2008-2012 5-year est.); Average household income: $89,390 (2008-2012 5-year est.); Percent of households with income of $100,000 or more: 34.0% (2008-2012 5-year est.); Poverty rate: 6.3% (2008-2012 5-year est.).

Taxes: Total city taxes per capita: $675 (2011); City property taxes per capita: $507 (2011).

Education: Percent of population age 25 and over with: High school diploma (including GED) or higher: 89.2% (2008-2012 5-year est.); Bachelor's degree or higher: 39.5% (2008-2012 5-year est.); Master's degree or higher: 12.0% (2008-2012 5-year est.).

School District(s)

Itasca SD 10 (PK-08)
    2011-12 Enrollment: 935 . . . . (630) 773-1232

Vocational/Technical School(s)

Environmental Technical Institute-Itasca (Private, For-profit)
    Fall 2012 Enrollment: 190 . . . . (630) 285-9100
    2012-13 Tuition: $13,710

Housing: Homeownership rate: 72.0% (2008-2012 5-year est.); Median home value: $314,800 (2008-2012 5-year est.); Median contract rent: $983 per month (2008-2012 5-year est.); Median year structure built: 1975 (2008-2012 5-year est.).

Health Insurance: 81.7% Private; 18.6% Public; 9.6% None. (2008-2012 5-year est.)

Safety: Violent crime rate: 2.3 per 10,000 population; Property crime rate: 104.4 per 10,000 population (2012).

Transportation: Commute to work: 87.7% car, 4.6% public transportation, 2.3% walk, 4.0% work from home (2008-2012 5-year est.); Travel time to work: 22.1% less than 15 minutes, 37.8% 15 to 30 minutes, 25.1% 30 to 45 minutes, 7.6% 45 to 60 minutes, 7.4% 60 minutes or more (2008-2012 5-year est.)

Additional Information Contacts

Village of Itasca . . . . (630) 773-0835
    http://www.itasca.com

LISLE (village). Covers a land area of 6.840 square miles and a water area of 0.181 square miles. Located at 41.79° N. Lat; 88.09° W. Long. Elevation is 673 feet.

History: Lisle was permanently settled in 1832 by James and Luther Hatch, after the Blackhawk War. The two brothers settled land near what is now Ogden Avenue and began a small farming community. This early beginning makes Lisle the oldest settlement in DuPage County.

Population: 19,512 (1990); 21,182 (2000); 22,390 (2010); Density: 3,282.5 persons per square mile (2008-2012 5-year est.); Race: 79.2% White, 4.6% Black/African American, 10.2% Asian, 0.0% American Indian/Alaska Native, 0.0% Native Hawaiian/Other Pacific Islander, 6.0% Some other race, 3.2% Two or more races, 6.9% Hispanic of any race (2008-2012 5-year est.); Average household size: 2.37 (2008-2012 5-year est.); Median age: 37.4 (2008-2012 5-year est.); Males per 100 females: 97.7 (2008-2012 5-year est.); Marriage status: 31.8% never married, 53.9% now married, 5.0% widowed, 9.3% divorced (2008-2012 5-year est.); Foreign born: 13.1% (2008-2012 5-year est.); Ancestry (includes multiple ancestries): 23.8% German, 18.9% Irish, 11.8% Polish, 10.9% Italian, 5.4% English (2008-2012 5-year est.).

Economy: Single-family building permits issued: 55 (2013); Multi-family building permits issued: 0 (2013); Homeowner vacancy rate: 2.3%. Rental vacancy rate: 8.8%. (2008-2012 5-year est.); Employment by occupation: 20.5% management, business, and financial, 10.9% computer, engineering, and science, 12.0% education, legal, community service, arts, and media, 5.9% healthcare practitioners, 12.8% service, 25.9% sales and office, 5.2% natural resources, construction, and maintenance, 6.8% production, transportation, and material moving (2008-2012 5-year est.).

Income: Per capita income: $42,096 (2008-2012 5-year est.); Median household income: $72,440 (2008-2012 5-year est.); Average household income: $101,560 (2008-2012 5-year est.); Percent of households with

income of $100,000 or more: 38.1% (2008-2012 5-year est.); Poverty rate: 7.5% (2008-2012 5-year est.).

Taxes: Total city taxes per capita: $473 (2011); City property taxes per capita: $180 (2011).

Education: Percent of population age 25 and over with: High school diploma (including GED) or higher: 95.0% (2008-2012 5-year est.); Bachelor's degree or higher: 54.3% (2008-2012 5-year est.); Master's degree or higher: 22.5% (2008-2012 5-year est.).

School District(s)

Lisle CUSD 202 (PK-12)
   2011-12 Enrollment: 1,618 . . . . (630) 493-8001
Naperville CUSD 203 (PK-12)
   2011-12 Enrollment: 17,768 . . . . (630) 420-6311

Four-year College(s)

Benedictine University (Private, Not-for-profit, Roman Catholic)
   Fall 2012 Enrollment: 6,508 . . . . (630) 829-6000
   2012-13 Tuition: In-state $24,137; Out-of-state $24,137

Vocational/Technical School(s)

Empire Beauty School-Lisle (Private, For-profit)
   Fall 2012 Enrollment: 192 . . . . (800) 920-4593
   2012-13 Tuition: $17,595

Housing: Homeownership rate: 62.8% (2008-2012 5-year est.); Median home value: $328,200 (2008-2012 5-year est.); Median contract rent: $949 per month (2008-2012 5-year est.); Median year structure built: 1979 (2008-2012 5-year est.).

Health Insurance: 80.7% Private; 19.8% Public; 11.0% None. (2008-2012 5-year est.)

Safety: Violent crime rate: 8.0 per 10,000 population; Property crime rate: 113.5 per 10,000 population (2012).

Transportation: Commute to work: 83.0% car, 7.9% public transportation, 2.8% walk, 5.4% work from home (2008-2012 5-year est.); Travel time to work: 23.2% less than 15 minutes, 33.5% 15 to 30 minutes, 21.2% 30 to 45 minutes, 9.4% 45 to 60 minutes, 12.7% 60 minutes or more (2008-2012 5-year est.)

Additional Information Contacts

Lisle Area Chamber of Commerce . . . . (630) 964-0052
   http://www.lislechamber.com
Lisle Convention & Visitors Bureau . . . . (630) 769-1000
   http://www.stayinlisle.com
Village of Lisle . . . . (630) 271-4100
   http://www.villageoflisle.org

LOMBARD (village). Covers a land area of 10.252 square miles and a water area of 0.199 square miles. Located at 41.87° N. Lat; 88.02° W. Long. Elevation is 719 feet.

History: Lombard was settled in 1834 by Winslow Churchill. The town was platted in 1868 by Joseph Lombard of Chicago, for whom it was named. Lombard has been known for its many varieties of lilacs, displayed in Lilacia Park, the gift of Colonel William Plum who collected lilacs from around the world.

Population: 39,408 (1990); 42,322 (2000); 43,165 (2010); Density: 4,211.8 persons per square mile (2008-2012 5-year est.); Race: 81.8% White, 5.1% Black/African American, 8.9% Asian, 0.1% American Indian/Alaska Native, 0.0% Native Hawaiian/Other Pacific Islander, 4.1% Some other race, 2.5% Two or more races, 7.9% Hispanic of any race (2008-2012 5-year est.); Average household size: 2.41 (2008-2012 5-year est.); Median age: 39.9 (2008-2012 5-year est.); Males per 100 females: 93.2 (2008-2012 5-year est.); Marriage status: 32.2% never married, 51.2% now married, 7.3% widowed, 9.4% divorced (2008-2012 5-year est.); Foreign born: 13.6% (2008-2012 5-year est.); Ancestry (includes multiple ancestries): 28.0% German, 19.6% Irish, 14.4% Italian, 12.8% Polish, 7.3% English (2008-2012 5-year est.).

Economy: Unemployment rate: 6.1% (April 2014); Total civilian labor force: 24,767 (April 2014); Single-family building permits issued: 37 (2013); Multi-family building permits issued: 4 (2013); Homeowner vacancy rate: 2.0%. Rental vacancy rate: 7.9%. (2008-2012 5-year est.); Employment by occupation: 17.5% management, business, and financial, 7.3% computer, engineering, and science, 10.7% education, legal, community service, arts, and media, 7.1% healthcare practitioners, 14.1% service, 28.8% sales and office, 6.7% natural resources, construction, and maintenance, 7.8% production, transportation, and material moving (2008-2012 5-year est.).

Income: Per capita income: $34,246 (2008-2012 5-year est.); Median household income: $71,721 (2008-2012 5-year est.); Average household income: $82,293 (2008-2012 5-year est.); Percent of households with

income of $100,000 or more: 31.4% (2008-2012 5-year est.); Poverty rate: 5.6% (2008-2012 5-year est.).

Taxes: Total city taxes per capita: $461 (2011); City property taxes per capita: $193 (2011).

Education: Percent of population age 25 and over with: High school diploma (including GED) or higher: 93.0% (2008-2012 5-year est.); Bachelor's degree or higher: 42.1% (2008-2012 5-year est.); Master's degree or higher: 13.9% (2008-2012 5-year est.).

School District(s)

Glenbard Twp HSD 87 (09-12)
   2011-12 Enrollment: 8,891 . . . . (630) 469-9100
Lombard SD 44 (PK-08)
   2011-12 Enrollment: 3,138 . . . . (630) 827-4400
SD 45 Dupage County (PK-08)
   2011-12 Enrollment: 3,315 . . . . (630) 516-7700
Sch Assoc Sped Educ Dupage Sased (09-12)
   2011-12 Enrollment: n/a . . . . (630) 778-4500

Four-year College(s)

National University of Health Sciences (Private, Not-for-profit)
   Fall 2012 Enrollment: 806 . . . . (630) 629-2000
Northern Baptist Theological Seminary (Private, Not-for-profit, American Baptist)
   Fall 2012 Enrollment: 204 . . . . (630) 620-2180

Vocational/Technical School(s)

Illinois Center for Broadcasting (Private, For-profit)
   Fall 2012 Enrollment: 222 . . . . (630) 916-1700
   2012-13 Tuition: $15,816

Housing: Homeownership rate: 71.5% (2008-2012 5-year est.); Median home value: $254,200 (2008-2012 5-year est.); Median contract rent: $1,055 per month (2008-2012 5-year est.); Median year structure built: 1969 (2008-2012 5-year est.).

Health Insurance: 82.3% Private; 21.3% Public; 9.1% None. (2008-2012 5-year est.)

Safety: Violent crime rate: 12.4 per 10,000 population; Property crime rate: 262.6 per 10,000 population (2012).

Transportation: Commute to work: 88.2% car, 5.2% public transportation, 1.9% walk, 3.1% work from home (2008-2012 5-year est.); Travel time to work: 25.1% less than 15 minutes, 34.1% 15 to 30 minutes, 21.3% 30 to 45 minutes, 10.3% 45 to 60 minutes, 9.1% 60 minutes or more (2008-2012 5-year est.)

Additional Information Contacts

Lombard Area Chamber of Commerce & Industry . . . . (630) 627-5040
   http://www.lombardchamber.com
Village of Lombard . . . . (630) 620-5700
   http://www.villageoflombard.org

MEDINAH (unincorporated postal area)

Zip Code: 60157
   Covers a land area of 1.484 square miles and a water area of 0.037 square miles. Located at 41.97° N. Lat; 88.05° W. Long. Population: 2,380 (2010); Density: 1,603.4 persons per square mile (2010); Race: 94.5% White, 0.4% Black/African American, 3.2% Asian, 0.2% American Indian/Alaska Native, 0.0% Native Hawaiian/Other Pacific Islander, 1.7% Some other race, 1.1% Two or more races, 5.3% Hispanic of any race (2010); Average household size: 2.85 (2010); Median age: 46.3 (2010); Males per 100 females: 100.0 (2010); Homeownership rate: 94.7% (2010)

NAPERVILLE (city). Covers a land area of 38.769 square miles and a water area of 0.553 square miles. Located at 41.75° N. Lat; 88.16° W. Long. Elevation is 709 feet.

History: Named for Captain Joseph Naper, founder. The first settlement at Naperville was Fort Payne, built in 1832. That same year, Joseph Naper built a saw mill and platted the town site. From 1839 to 1868 Naperville was the seat of DuPage County.

Population: 85,351 (1990); 128,358 (2000); 141,853 (2010); Density: 3,666.4 persons per square mile (2008-2012 5-year est.); Race: 76.2% White, 4.8% Black/African American, 15.5% Asian, 0.1% American Indian/Alaska Native, 0.1% Native Hawaiian/Other Pacific Islander, 3.3% Some other race, 2.0% Two or more races, 5.9% Hispanic of any race (2008-2012 5-year est.); Average household size: 2.86 (2008-2012 5-year est.); Median age: 38.0 (2008-2012 5-year est.); Males per 100 females: 95.2 (2008-2012 5-year est.); Marriage status: 26.2% never married, 63.1% now married, 3.6% widowed, 7.1% divorced (2008-2012 5-year est.); Foreign born: 16.9% (2008-2012 5-year est.); Ancestry (includes

multiple ancestries): 22.2% German, 16.6% Irish, 10.4% Italian, 10.0% Polish, 7.6% English (2008-2012 5-year est.).

Economy: Unemployment rate: 5.7% (April 2014); Total civilian labor force: 76,735 (April 2014); Single-family building permits issued: 297 (2013); Multi-family building permits issued: 298 (2013); Homeowner vacancy rate: 2.1%. Rental vacancy rate: 7.5%. (2008-2012 5-year est.); Employment by occupation: 25.3% management, business, and financial, 10.8% computer, engineering, and science, 13.5% education, legal, community service, arts, and media, 6.5% healthcare practitioners, 9.7% service, 26.9% sales and office, 2.4% natural resources, construction, and maintenance, 4.9% production, transportation, and material moving (2008-2012 5-year est.).

Income: Per capita income: $46,598 (2008-2012 5-year est.); Median household income: $108,252 (2008-2012 5-year est.); Average household income: $134,222 (2008-2012 5-year est.); Percent of households with income of $100,000 or more: 53.5% (2008-2012 5-year est.); Poverty rate: 3.8% (2008-2012 5-year est.).

Taxes: Total city taxes per capita: $566 (2011); City property taxes per capita: $367 (2011).

Education: Percent of population age 25 and over with: High school diploma (including GED) or higher: 96.5% (2008-2012 5-year est.); Bachelor's degree or higher: 66.1% (2008-2012 5-year est.); Master's degree or higher: 29.1% (2008-2012 5-year est.).

School District(s)
Indian Prairie CUSD 204 (PK-12)
    2011-12 Enrollment: 29,286 . . . . (630) 375-3000
Indian Prairie CUSD 204 (PK-12)
    2011-12 Enrollment: 29,286 . . . . (630) 375-3000
Naperville CUSD 203 (PK-12)
    2011-12 Enrollment: 17,768 . . . . (630) 420-6311
Naperville CUSD 203 (PK-12)
    2011-12 Enrollment: 17,768 . . . . (630) 420-6311
Sch Assoc Sped Educ Dupage Sased (09-12)
    2011-12 Enrollment: n/a . . . . (630) 778-4500

Four-year College(s)
North Central College (Private, Not-for-profit, United Methodist)
    Fall 2012 Enrollment: 3,042 . . . . (630) 637-5100
    2012-13 Tuition: In-state $31,071; Out-of-state $31,071

Housing: Homeownership rate: 77.0% (2008-2012 5-year est.); Median home value: $384,500 (2008-2012 5-year est.); Median contract rent: $1,111 per month (2008-2012 5-year est.); Median year structure built: 1987 (2008-2012 5-year est.).

Health Insurance: 89.0% Private; 13.1% Public; 5.4% None. (2008-2012 5-year est.)

Hospitals: Edward Hospital (179 beds)

Safety: Violent crime rate: 8.3 per 10,000 population; Property crime rate: 143.1 per 10,000 population (2012).

Transportation: Commute to work: 80.7% car, 9.3% public transportation, 1.3% walk, 7.6% work from home (2008-2012 5-year est.); Travel time to work: 20.5% less than 15 minutes, 29.4% 15 to 30 minutes, 19.2% 30 to 45 minutes, 11.2% 45 to 60 minutes, 19.6% 60 minutes or more (2008-2012 5-year est.); Amtrak: Train service available.

Additional Information Contacts
City of Naperville . . . . (630) 420-6111
    http://www.naperville.il.us
Naperville Area Chamber of Commerce . . . . (630) 355-4141
    http://www.naperville.net

OAK BROOK (village). Covers a land area of 7.949 square miles and a water area of 0.329 square miles. Located at 41.84° N. Lat; 87.95° W. Long. Elevation is 663 feet.

History: Oak Brook was incorporated as a Village in 1958, due in large part to the efforts of Paul Butler, a prominent civic leader and landowner whose father had first moved to the vicinity in 1898 and opened a dairy farm shortly thereafter.

Population: 9,178 (1990); 8,702 (2000); 7,883 (2010); Density: 994.5 persons per square mile (2008-2012 5-year est.); Race: 68.1% White, 2.4% Black/African American, 24.6% Asian, 0.0% American Indian/Alaska Native, 0.0% Native Hawaiian/Other Pacific Islander, 4.9% Some other race, 2.4% Two or more races, 5.1% Hispanic of any race (2008-2012 5-year est.); Average household size: 2.68 (2008-2012 5-year est.); Median age: 53.2 (2008-2012 5-year est.); Males per 100 females: 104.9 (2008-2012 5-year est.); Marriage status: 22.3% never married, 66.5% now married, 7.1% widowed, 4.1% divorced (2008-2012 5-year est.); Foreign born: 25.8% (2008-2012 5-year est.); Ancestry (includes multiple

ancestries): 17.9% Italian, 13.6% German, 9.7% Irish, 7.4% English, 5.6% Polish (2008-2012 5-year est.).

Economy: Single-family building permits issued: 19 (2013); Multi-family building permits issued: 0 (2013); Homeowner vacancy rate: 5.8%. Rental vacancy rate: 0.0%. (2008-2012 5-year est.); Employment by occupation: 34.3% management, business, and financial, 4.5% computer, engineering, and science, 3.9% education, legal, community service, arts, and media, 22.4% healthcare practitioners, 6.1% service, 24.6% sales and office, 1.8% natural resources, construction, and maintenance, 2.3% production, transportation, and material moving (2008-2012 5-year est.).

Income: Per capita income: $76,567 (2008-2012 5-year est.); Median household income: $131,458 (2008-2012 5-year est.); Average household income: $207,020 (2008-2012 5-year est.); Percent of households with income of $100,000 or more: 62.0% (2008-2012 5-year est.); Poverty rate: 2.8% (2008-2012 5-year est.).

Taxes: Total city taxes per capita: $1,334 (2011); City property taxes per capita: $41 (2011).

Education: Percent of population age 25 and over with: High school diploma (including GED) or higher: 94.8% (2008-2012 5-year est.); Bachelor's degree or higher: 59.4% (2008-2012 5-year est.); Master's degree or higher: 34.9% (2008-2012 5-year est.).

School District(s)
Butler SD 53 (PK-08)
    2011-12 Enrollment: 442 . . . . (630) 573-2887

Four-year College(s)
ITT Technical Institute-Oak Brook (Private, For-profit)
    Fall 2012 Enrollment: 405 . . . . (630) 472-7000
    2012-13 Tuition: In-state $18,048; Out-of-state $18,048

Vocational/Technical School(s)
G Skin & Beauty Institute (Private, For-profit)
    Fall 2012 Enrollment: 195 . . . . (815) 786-7266
    2012-13 Tuition: $16,466

Housing: Homeownership rate: 94.2% (2008-2012 5-year est.); Median home value: $813,800 (2008-2012 5-year est.); Median contract rent: $1,391 per month (2008-2012 5-year est.); Median year structure built: 1977 (2008-2012 5-year est.).

Health Insurance: 86.6% Private; 35.1% Public; 1.8% None. (2008-2012 5-year est.)

Safety: Violent crime rate: 3.8 per 10,000 population; Property crime rate: 758.1 per 10,000 population (2012).

Transportation: Commute to work: 90.8% car, 0.3% public transportation, 1.5% walk, 7.4% work from home (2008-2012 5-year est.); Travel time to work: 26.7% less than 15 minutes, 28.2% 15 to 30 minutes, 25.8% 30 to 45 minutes, 9.7% 45 to 60 minutes, 9.6% 60 minutes or more (2008-2012 5-year est.)

Additional Information Contacts
Greater Oak Brook Chamber of Commerce . . . . (630) 472-9377
    http://www.obchamber.com
Village of Oak Brook . . . . (630) 368-5000
    http://www.oak-brook.org

OAKBROOK TERRACE (city). Covers a land area of 1.246 square miles and a water area of 0.028 square miles. Located at 41.85° N. Lat; 87.97° W. Long. Elevation is 686 feet.

Population: 1,907 (1990); 2,300 (2000); 2,134 (2010); Density: 1,770.0 persons per square mile (2008-2012 5-year est.); Race: 82.9% White, 2.4% Black/African American, 11.4% Asian, 0.0% American Indian/Alaska Native, 0.0% Native Hawaiian/Other Pacific Islander, 3.3% Some other race, 2.5% Two or more races, 5.0% Hispanic of any race (2008-2012 5-year est.); Average household size: 1.96 (2008-2012 5-year est.); Median age: 40.9 (2008-2012 5-year est.); Males per 100 females: 102.7 (2008-2012 5-year est.); Marriage status: 32.9% never married, 43.5% now married, 8.1% widowed, 15.5% divorced (2008-2012 5-year est.); Foreign born: 17.1% (2008-2012 5-year est.); Ancestry (includes multiple ancestries): 25.4% German, 18.2% Irish, 14.3% Italian, 9.4% Polish, 6.3% English (2008-2012 5-year est.).

Economy: Single-family building permits issued: 11 (2013); Multi-family building permits issued: 0 (2013); Homeowner vacancy rate: 0.0%. Rental vacancy rate: 9.8%. (2008-2012 5-year est.); Employment by occupation: 18.1% management, business, and financial, 11.2% computer, engineering, and science, 12.3% education, legal, community service, arts, and media, 3.7% healthcare practitioners, 12.9% service, 30.0% sales and office, 5.8% natural resources, construction, and maintenance, 6.1% production, transportation, and material moving (2008-2012 5-year est.).

Income: Per capita income: $40,335 (2008-2012 5-year est.); Median household income: $62,454 (2008-2012 5-year est.); Average household income: $78,020 (2008-2012 5-year est.); Percent of households with income of $100,000 or more: 22.6% (2008-2012 5-year est.); Poverty rate: 9.9% (2008-2012 5-year est.).

Education: Percent of population age 25 and over with: High school diploma (including GED) or higher: 91.7% (2008-2012 5-year est.); Bachelor's degree or higher: 39.8% (2008-2012 5-year est.); Master's degree or higher: 16.8% (2008-2012 5-year est.).

School District(s)

Salt Creek SD 48 (PK-08)
   2011-12 Enrollment: 484. . . . . (630) 279-8400

Housing: Homeownership rate: 50.6% (2008-2012 5-year est.); Median home value: $306,900 (2008-2012 5-year est.); Median contract rent: $1,145 per month (2008-2012 5-year est.); Median year structure built: 1973 (2008-2012 5-year est.).

Health Insurance: 78.4% Private; 26.0% Public; 13.3% None. (2008-2012 5-year est.)

Safety: Violent crime rate: 23.3 per 10,000 population; Property crime rate: 539.5 per 10,000 population (2012).

Transportation: Commute to work: 92.0% car, 1.9% public transportation, 1.8% walk, 3.6% work from home (2008-2012 5-year est.); Travel time to work: 27.6% less than 15 minutes, 30.6% 15 to 30 minutes, 26.9% 30 to 45 minutes, 7.0% 45 to 60 minutes, 7.9% 60 minutes or more (2008-2012 5-year est.)

ROSELLE (village).

Covers a land area of 5.412 square miles and a water area of 0.073 square miles. Located at 41.98° N. Lat; 88.09° W. Long. Elevation is 771 feet.

Population: 20,819 (1990); 23,115 (2000); 22,763 (2010); Density: 4,215.8 persons per square mile (2008-2012 5-year est.); Race: 82.4% White, 5.7% Black/African American, 9.2% Asian, 0.5% American Indian/Alaska Native, 0.8% Native Hawaiian/Other Pacific Islander, 1.4% Some other race, 1.0% Two or more races, 8.5% Hispanic of any race (2008-2012 5-year est.); Average household size: 2.67 (2008-2012 5-year est.); Median age: 36.9 (2008-2012 5-year est.); Males per 100 females: 90.1 (2008-2012 5-year est.); Marriage status: 29.1% never married, 56.7% now married, 3.8% widowed, 10.4% divorced (2008-2012 5-year est.); Foreign born: 16.1% (2008-2012 5-year est.); Ancestry (includes multiple ancestries): 23.3% German, 17.0% Italian, 16.0% Polish, 15.5% Irish, 4.8% English (2008-2012 5-year est.).

Economy: Single-family building permits issued: 14 (2013); Multi-family building permits issued: 0 (2013); Homeowner vacancy rate: 2.9%. Rental vacancy rate: 4.2%. (2008-2012 5-year est.); Employment by occupation: 20.2% management, business, and financial, 6.3% computer, engineering, and science, 8.3% education, legal, community service, arts, and media, 6.4% healthcare practitioners, 12.5% service, 32.1% sales and office, 5.9% natural resources, construction, and maintenance, 8.2% production, transportation, and material moving (2008-2012 5-year est.).

Income: Per capita income: $35,432 (2008-2012 5-year est.); Median household income: $76,878 (2008-2012 5-year est.); Average household income: $93,716 (2008-2012 5-year est.); Percent of households with income of $100,000 or more: 36.2% (2008-2012 5-year est.); Poverty rate: 4.1% (2008-2012 5-year est.).

Education: Percent of population age 25 and over with: High school diploma (including GED) or higher: 95.2% (2008-2012 5-year est.); Bachelor's degree or higher: 39.0% (2008-2012 5-year est.); Master's degree or higher: 13.4% (2008-2012 5-year est.).

School District(s)

Keeneyville SD 20 (PK-08)
   2011-12 Enrollment: 1,620 . . . . (630) 894-4606
Lake Park CHSD 108 (09-12)
   2011-12 Enrollment: 2,825 . . . . (630) 529-4500
Medinah SD 11 (KG-08)
   2011-12 Enrollment: 637. . . . . (630) 893-3737
North Dupage Sp Ed Cooperative
   2011-12 Enrollment: n/a . . . . (630) 894-0490
Roselle SD 12 (KG-08)
   2011-12 Enrollment: 668. . . . . (630) 529-2091
Schaumburg CCSD 54 (PK-08)
   2011-12 Enrollment: 14,083 . . . . (847) 357-5000

Housing: Homeownership rate: 77.7% (2008-2012 5-year est.); Median home value: $268,500 (2008-2012 5-year est.); Median contract rent: $946 per month (2008-2012 5-year est.); Median year structure built: 1977 (2008-2012 5-year est.).

Health Insurance: 83.3% Private; 17.8% Public; 6.9% None. (2008-2012 5-year est.)

Safety: Violent crime rate: 5.2 per 10,000 population; Property crime rate: 133.5 per 10,000 population (2012).

Transportation: Commute to work: 89.0% car, 5.8% public transportation, 1.4% walk, 3.5% work from home (2008-2012 5-year est.); Travel time to work: 18.5% less than 15 minutes, 32.4% 15 to 30 minutes, 28.9% 30 to 45 minutes, 9.5% 45 to 60 minutes, 10.6% 60 minutes or more (2008-2012 5-year est.)

Additional Information Contacts

Roselle Chamber of Commerce & Industry . . . . (630) 894-3010
   http://www.rosellechamber.com
Village of Roselle . . . . (630) 980-2000
   http://www.roselle.il.us

VILLA PARK (village).

Covers a land area of 4.706 square miles and a water area of 0.049 square miles. Located at 41.89° N. Lat; 87.98° W. Long. Elevation is 702 feet.

Population: 22,253 (1990); 22,075 (2000); 21,904 (2010); Density: 4,720.2 persons per square mile (2008-2012 5-year est.); Race: 86.7% White, 3.6% Black/African American, 5.0% Asian, 0.1% American Indian/Alaska Native, 0.0% Native Hawaiian/Other Pacific Islander, 4.6% Some other race, 0.8% Two or more races, 20.6% Hispanic of any race (2008-2012 5-year est.); Average household size: 2.76 (2008-2012 5-year est.); Median age: 36.2 (2008-2012 5-year est.); Males per 100 females: 97.5 (2008-2012 5-year est.); Marriage status: 29.2% never married, 55.5% now married, 4.6% widowed, 10.6% divorced (2008-2012 5-year est.); Foreign born: 15.8% (2008-2012 5-year est.); Ancestry (includes multiple ancestries): 22.1% German, 18.9% Irish, 12.5% Polish, 11.1% Italian, 6.1% English (2008-2012 5-year est.).

Economy: Single-family building permits issued: 0 (2013); Multi-family building permits issued: 0 (2013); Homeowner vacancy rate: 2.0%. Rental vacancy rate: 12.4%. (2008-2012 5-year est.); Employment by occupation: 13.9% management, business, and financial, 5.9% computer, engineering, and science, 10.5% education, legal, community service, arts, and media, 3.4% healthcare practitioners, 16.1% service, 27.9% sales and office, 9.3% natural resources, construction, and maintenance, 12.9% production, transportation, and material moving (2008-2012 5-year est.).

Income: Per capita income: $28,691 (2008-2012 5-year est.); Median household income: $68,812 (2008-2012 5-year est.); Average household income: $77,536 (2008-2012 5-year est.); Percent of households with income of $100,000 or more: 28.6% (2008-2012 5-year est.); Poverty rate: 8.1% (2008-2012 5-year est.).

Education: Percent of population age 25 and over with: High school diploma (including GED) or higher: 88.7% (2008-2012 5-year est.); Bachelor's degree or higher: 31.7% (2008-2012 5-year est.); Master's degree or higher: 9.1% (2008-2012 5-year est.).

School District(s)

Dupage HSD 88 (09-12)
   2011-12 Enrollment: 4,077 . . . . (630) 530-3980
SD 45 Dupage County (PK-08)
   2011-12 Enrollment: 3,315 . . . . (630) 516-7700
Salt Creek SD 48 (PK-08)
   2011-12 Enrollment: 484. . . . . (630) 279-8400

Vocational/Technical School(s)

Cannella School of Hair Design-Villa Park (Private, For-profit)
   Fall 2012 Enrollment: 91. . . . . (630) 833-6118
   2012-13 Tuition: $10,190
Ms Roberts Academy of Beauty Culture-Villa Park (Private, For-profit)
   Fall 2012 Enrollment: 120 . . . . (630) 941-3880
   2012-13 Tuition: $15,200

Housing: Homeownership rate: 71.0% (2008-2012 5-year est.); Median home value: $254,100 (2008-2012 5-year est.); Median contract rent: $873 per month (2008-2012 5-year est.); Median year structure built: 1957 (2008-2012 5-year est.).

Health Insurance: 74.1% Private; 24.5% Public; 12.7% None. (2008-2012 5-year est.)

Safety: Violent crime rate: 18.1 per 10,000 population; Property crime rate: 205.7 per 10,000 population (2012).

Transportation: Commute to work: 90.6% car, 3.1% public transportation, 1.1% walk, 2.2% work from home (2008-2012 5-year est.); Travel time to work: 26.0% less than 15 minutes, 37.4% 15 to 30 minutes, 20.4% 30 to 45 minutes, 9.0% 45 to 60 minutes, 7.2% 60 minutes or more (2008-2012 5-year est.)

Additional Information Contacts

Villa Park Chamber of Commerce . . . . (630) 941-9133
 http://www.villaparkchamber.org
Village of Villa Park . . . . (630) 834-8500
 http://www.invillapark.com

WARRENVILLE (city). Covers a land area of 5.459 square miles and a water area of 0.158 square miles. Located at 41.82° N. Lat; 88.19° W. Long. Elevation is 696 feet.

History: Named for Daniel Warren (1780-1866), town founder. Warrenville was settled in the 1830's around a tannery and gristmill.

Population: 11,333 (1990); 13,363 (2000); 13,140 (2010); Density: 2,444.8 persons per square mile (2008-2012 5-year est.); Race: 87.2% White, 5.3% Black/African American, 3.0% Asian, 0.0% American Indian/Alaska Native, 0.1% Native Hawaiian/Other Pacific Islander, 4.4% Some other race, 2.8% Two or more races, 14.6% Hispanic of any race (2008-2012 5-year est.); Average household size: 2.79 (2008-2012 5-year est.); Median age: 36.9 (2008-2012 5-year est.); Males per 100 females: 102.3 (2008-2012 5-year est.); Marriage status: 33.7% never married, 51.1% now married, 4.0% widowed, 11.2% divorced (2008-2012 5-year est.); Foreign born: 10.5% (2008-2012 5-year est.); Ancestry (includes multiple ancestries): 27.8% German, 17.5% Irish, 8.6% Polish, 8.5% English, 7.1% Italian (2008-2012 5-year est.).

Economy: Single-family building permits issued: 5 (2013); Multi-family building permits issued: 0 (2013); Homeowner vacancy rate: 2.9%. Rental vacancy rate: 12.2%. (2008-2012 5-year est.); Employment by occupation: 18.4% management, business, and financial, 7.8% computer, engineering, and science, 9.9% education, legal, community service, arts, and media, 4.7% healthcare practitioners, 12.8% service, 27.9% sales and office, 9.3% natural resources, construction, and maintenance, 9.3% production, transportation, and material moving (2008-2012 5-year est.).

Income: Per capita income: $31,697 (2008-2012 5-year est.); Median household Income: $71,949 (2008-2012 5-year est.); Average household income: $86,322 (2008-2012 5-year est.); Percent of households with income of $100,000 or more: 28.2% (2008-2012 5-year est.); Poverty rate: 7.9% (2008-2012 5-year est.).

Education: Percent of population age 25 and over with: High school diploma (including GED) or higher: 93.3% (2008-2012 5-year est.); Bachelor's degree or higher: 38.6% (2008-2012 5-year est.); Master's degree or higher: 11.5% (2008-2012 5-year est.).

School District(s)
CUSD 200 (PK-12)
 2011-12 Enrollment: 13,423 . . . . (630) 682-2002
Idjj SD 428 (06-12)
 2011-12 Enrollment: 784 . . . . (309) 584-0506

Housing: Homeownership rate: 78.2% (2008-2012 5-year est.); Median home value: $221,500 (2008-2012 5-year est.); Median contract rent: $1,093 per month (2008-2012 5-year est.); Median year structure built: 1978 (2008-2012 5-year est.).

Health Insurance: 74.9% Private; 21.4% Public; 12.8% None. (2008-2012 5-year est.)

Safety: Violent crime rate: 3.8 per 10,000 population; Property crime rate: 117.1 per 10,000 population (2012).

Transportation: Commute to work: 89.6% car, 3.1% public transportation, 2.3% walk, 2.5% work from home (2008-2012 5-year est.); Travel time to work: 26.3% less than 15 minutes, 38.4% 15 to 30 minutes, 20.4% 30 to 45 minutes, 7.7% 45 to 60 minutes, 7.3% 60 minutes or more (2008-2012 5-year est.)

Additional Information Contacts
City of Warrenville . . . . (630) 393-9427
 http://www.warrenville.il.us
Western DuPage Chamber of Commerce . . . . (630) 231-3003
 http://www.westerndupagechamber.com

WAYNE (village). Covers a land area of 5.783 square miles and a water area of 0.088 square miles. Located at 41.95° N. Lat; 88.25° W. Long. Elevation is 758 feet.

Population: 1,541 (1990); 2,137 (2000); 2,431 (2010); Density: 477.3 persons per square mile (2008-2012 5-year est.); Race: 94.5% White, 1.0% Black/African American, 3.5% Asian, 0.0% American Indian/Alaska Native, 0.0% Native Hawaiian/Other Pacific Islander, 1.0% Some other race, 1.1% Two or more races, 0.0% Hispanic of any race (2008-2012 5-year est.); Average household size: 3.13 (2008-2012 5-year est.); Median age: 44.9 (2008-2012 5-year est.); Males per 100 females: 86.4 (2008-2012 5-year est.); Marriage status: 23.2% never married, 70.5% now married, 2.9% widowed, 3.4% divorced (2008-2012 5-year est.);

Foreign born: 5.0% (2008-2012 5-year est.); Ancestry (includes multiple ancestries): 39.4% German, 21.1% Irish, 17.7% Italian, 16.0% English, 11.5% Polish (2008-2012 5-year est.).

Economy: Single-family building permits issued: 0 (2013); Multi-family building permits issued: 0 (2013); Homeowner vacancy rate: 0.0%. Rental vacancy rate: 0.0%. (2008-2012 5-year est.); Employment by occupation: 28.3% management, business, and financial, 3.0% computer, engineering, and science, 12.2% education, legal, community service, arts, and media, 4.8% healthcare practitioners, 11.3% service, 31.8% sales and office, 4.5% natural resources, construction, and maintenance, 4.0% production, transportation, and material moving (2008-2012 5-year est.).

Income: Per capita income: $61,082 (2008-2012 5-year est.); Median household income: $151,875 (2008-2012 5-year est.); Average household income: $190,293 (2008-2012 5-year est.); Percent of households with income of $100,000 or more: 66.4% (2008-2012 5-year est.); Poverty rate: 1.2% (2008-2012 5-year est.).

Education: Percent of population age 25 and over with: High school diploma (including GED) or higher: 98.1% (2008-2012 5-year est.); Bachelor's degree or higher: 47.9% (2008-2012 5-year est.); Master's degree or higher: 17.6% (2008-2012 5-year est.).

School District(s)
SD U-46 (PK-12)
 2011-12 Enrollment: 40,687 . . . . (847) 888-5000

Housing: Homeownership rate: 99.0% (2008-2012 5-year est.); Median home value: $630,300 (2008-2012 5-year est.); Median contract rent: $2,000+ per month (2008-2012 5-year est.); Median year structure built: 1984 (2008-2012 5-year est.).

Health Insurance: 88.1% Private; 13.2% Public; 9.3% None. (2008-2012 5-year est.)

Safety: Violent crime rate: 0.0 per 10,000 population; Property crime rate: 61.2 per 10,000 population (2012).

Transportation: Commute to work: 90.0% car, 3.7% public transportation, 0.4% walk, 4.2% work from home (2008-2012 5-year est.); Travel time to work: 19.6% less than 15 minutes, 25.8% 15 to 30 minutes, 30.8% 30 to 45 minutes, 6.2% 45 to 60 minutes, 17.6% 60 minutes or more (2008-2012 5-year est.)

WEST CHICAGO (city). Covers a land area of 14.798 square miles and a water area of 0.341 square miles. Located at 41.91° N. Lat; 88.25° W. Long. Elevation is 784 feet.

Population: 14,796 (1990); 23,469 (2000); 27,086 (2010); Density: 1,829.9 persons per square mile (2008-2012 5-year est.); Race: 83.8% White, 2.7% Black/African American, 5.2% Asian, 0.0% American Indian/Alaska Native, 0.0% Native Hawaiian/Other Pacific Islander, 8.3% Some other race, 1.6% Two or more races, 48.4% Hispanic of any race (2008-2012 5-year est.); Average household size: 3.45 (2008-2012 5-year est.); Median age: 30.8 (2008-2012 5-year est.); Males per 100 females: 105.1 (2008-2012 5-year est.); Marriage status: 32.8% never married, 55.7% now married, 2.9% widowed, 8.6% divorced (2008-2012 5-year est.); Foreign born: 32.1% (2008-2012 5-year est.); Ancestry (includes multiple ancestries): 12.3% German, 8.8% Irish, 7.2% Polish, 6.6% Italian, 3.9% English (2008-2012 5-year est.).

Economy: Unemployment rate: 7.3% (April 2014); Total civilian labor force: 14,899 (April 2014); Single-family building permits issued: 5 (2013); Multi-family building permits issued: 0 (2013); Homeowner vacancy rate: 2.6%. Rental vacancy rate: 3.8%. (2008-2012 5-year est.); Employment by occupation: 13.1% management, business, and financial, 4.8% computer, engineering, and science, 6.8% education, legal, community service, arts, and media, 2.5% healthcare practitioners, 18.6% service, 24.4% sales and office, 7.1% natural resources, construction, and maintenance, 22.7% production, transportation, and material moving (2008-2012 5-year est.).

Income: Per capita income: $25,862 (2008-2012 5-year est.); Median household income: $65,111 (2008-2012 5-year est.); Average household income: $87,548 (2008-2012 5-year est.); Percent of households with income of $100,000 or more: 30.4% (2008-2012 5-year est.); Poverty rate: 15.1% (2008-2012 5-year est.).

Taxes: Total city taxes per capita: $321 (2011); City property taxes per capita: $177 (2011).

Education: Percent of population age 25 and over with: High school diploma (including GED) or higher: 74.0% (2008-2012 5-year est.); Bachelor's degree or higher: 25.4% (2008-2012 5-year est.); Master's degree or higher: 7.4% (2008-2012 5-year est.).

School District(s)
Benjamin SD 25 (PK-08)
 2011-12 Enrollment: 748 . . . . (630) 876-7800

CHSD 94 (09-12)
   2011-12 Enrollment: 2,153 . . . . (630) 876-6210
Saint Charles CUSD 303 (PK-12)
   2011-12 Enrollment: 13,672 . . . . (630) 513-3030
West Chicago ESD 33 (PK-08)
   2011-12 Enrollment: 4,406 . . . . (630) 293-6000
Housing: Homeownership rate: 66.7% (2008-2012 5-year est.); Median home value: $243,100 (2008-2012 5-year est.); Median contract rent: $806 per month (2008-2012 5-year est.); Median year structure built: 1981 (2008-2012 5-year est.).
Health Insurance: 59.1% Private; 28.5% Public; 17.9% None. (2008-2012 5-year est.)
Safety: Violent crime rate: 8.8 per 10,000 population; Property crime rate: 127.9 per 10,000 population (2012).
Transportation: Commute to work: 90.3% car, 3.0% public transportation, 1.6% walk, 3.0% work from home (2008-2012 5-year est.); Travel time to work: 28.7% less than 15 minutes, 34.1% 15 to 30 minutes, 17.9% 30 to 45 minutes, 10.6% 45 to 60 minutes, 8.6% 60 minutes or more (2008-2012 5-year est.)
Airports: DuPage Airport (reliver airport)
Additional Information Contacts
City of West Chicago. . . . . (630) 293-2200
   http://www.westchicago.org
West Chicago Chamber of Commerce & Industry . . . . (630) 231-3003
   http://www.wegochamber.org

WESTMONT (village).
Covers a land area of 5.030 square miles and a water area of 0.106 square miles. Located at 41.79° N. Lat; 87.97° W. Long. Elevation is 748 feet.
Population: 21,228 (1990); 24,554 (2000); 24,685 (2010); Density: 4,990.7 persons per square mile (2008-2012 5-year est.); Race: 70.8% White, 8.1% Black/African American, 13.1% Asian, 0.4% American Indian/Alaska Native, 0.0% Native Hawaiian/Other Pacific Islander, 7.6% Some other race, 2.2% Two or more races, 9.3% Hispanic of any race (2008-2012 5-year est.); Average household size: 2.28 (2008-2012 5-year est.); Median age: 40.5 (2008-2012 5-year est.); Males per 100 females: 86.8 (2008-2012 5-year est.); Marriage status: 28.9% never married, 52.1% now married, 8.7% widowed, 10.3% divorced (2008-2012 5-year est.); Foreign born: 22.8% (2008-2012 5-year est.); Ancestry (includes multiple ancestries): 19.0% German, 13.1% Irish, 12.5% Polish, 8.1% Italian, 4.8% English (2008-2012 5-year est.).
Economy: Unemployment rate: 6.5% (April 2014); Total civilian labor force: 13,507 (April 2014); Single-family building permits issued: 25 (2013); Multi-family building permits issued: 0 (2013); Homeowner vacancy rate: 2.7%. Rental vacancy rate: 7.3%. (2008-2012 5-year est.); Employment by occupation: 17.6% management, business, and financial, 9.5% computer, engineering, and science, 10.1% education, legal, community service, arts, and media, 6.6% healthcare practitioners, 16.5% service, 23.7% sales and office, 6.3% natural resources, construction, and maintenance, 9.7% production, transportation, and material moving (2008-2012 5-year est.).
Income: Per capita income: $35,294 (2008-2012 5-year est.); Median household income: $60,149 (2008-2012 5-year est.); Average household income: $80,364 (2008-2012 5-year est.); Percent of households with income of $100,000 or more: 25.6% (2008-2012 5-year est.); Poverty rate: 7.5% (2008-2012 5-year est.).
Education: Percent of population age 25 and over with: High school diploma (including GED) or higher: 92.4% (2008-2012 5-year est.); Bachelor's degree or higher: 41.9% (2008-2012 5-year est.); Master's degree or higher: 16.3% (2008-2012 5-year est.).
School District(s)
CUSD 201 (PK-12)
   2011-12 Enrollment: 1,498 . . . . (630) 468-8004
Maercker SD 60 (PK-08)
   2011-12 Enrollment: 1,341 . . . . (630) 515-4840
Sch Assoc Sped Educ Dupage Sased (09-12)
   2011-12 Enrollment: n/a . . . . (630) 778-4500
Housing: Homeownership rate: 51.9% (2008-2012 5-year est.); Median home value: $288,200 (2008-2012 5-year est.); Median contract rent: $892 per month (2008-2012 5-year est.); Median year structure built: 1977 (2008-2012 5-year est.).
Health Insurance: 73.5% Private; 24.9% Public; 13.5% None. (2008-2012 5-year est.)
Safety: Violent crime rate: 10.9 per 10,000 population; Property crime rate: 156.4 per 10,000 population (2012).

Transportation: Commute to work: 82.3% car, 9.0% public transportation, 2.3% walk, 5.0% work from home (2008-2012 5-year est.); Travel time to work: 23.1% less than 15 minutes, 31.7% 15 to 30 minutes, 20.6% 30 to 45 minutes, 11.7% 45 to 60 minutes, 12.9% 60 minutes or more (2008-2012 5-year est.)
Additional Information Contacts
Village of Westmont . . . . (630) 981-6200
   http://www.westmont.illinois.gov
Westmont Chamber of Commerce & Tourism Bureau . . . . (630) 960-5553
   http://www.westmontchamber.com

WHEATON (city).
County seat. Covers a land area of 11.252 square miles and a water area of 0.186 square miles. Located at 41.86° N. Lat; 88.11° W. Long. Elevation is 758 feet.
History: Named for the Wheaton family, early settlers. Wheaton was settled in 1838 by Warren and Jesse Wheaton, who were instrumental in bringing to the town the railroad, a college, and the county courthouse. In 1853, Warren Wheaton donated the land for the Illinois Institute, which seven years later became Wheaton College. In 1867 the seat of DuPage County was moved from Naperville to Wheaton, and the courthouse was built on land donated by Warren Wheaton.
Population: 51,464 (1990); 55,416 (2000); 52,894 (2010); Density: 4,724.0 persons per square mile (2008-2012 5-year est.); Race: 86.9% White, 3.4% Black/African American, 6.3% Asian, 0.1% American Indian/Alaska Native, 0.0% Native Hawaiian/Other Pacific Islander, 3.3% Some other race, 2.8% Two or more races, 4.9% Hispanic of any race (2008-2012 5-year est.); Average household size: 2.61 (2008-2012 5-year est.); Median age: 37.8 (2008-2012 5-year est.); Males per 100 females: 94.8 (2008-2012 5-year est.); Marriage status: 32.0% never married, 55.7% now married, 4.7% widowed, 7.7% divorced (2008-2012 5-year est.); Foreign born: 11.4% (2008-2012 5-year est.); Ancestry (includes multiple ancestries): 25.4% German, 17.3% Irish, 12.1% English, 11.0% Italian, 10.0% Polish (2008-2012 5-year est.).
Economy: Unemployment rate: 5.4% (April 2014); Total civilian labor force: 28,808 (April 2014); Single-family building permits issued: 49 (2013); Multi-family building permits issued: 0 (2013); Homeowner vacancy rate: 1.8%. Rental vacancy rate: 7.1%. (2008-2012 5-year est.); Employment by occupation: 21.3% management, business, and financial, 9.7% computer, engineering, and science, 18.6% education, legal, community service, arts, and media, 5.3% healthcare practitioners, 10.8% service, 24.4% sales and office, 3.9% natural resources, construction, and maintenance, 6.0% production, transportation, and material moving (2008-2012 5-year est.).
Income: Per capita income: $41,153 (2008-2012 5-year est.); Median household income: $86,074 (2008-2012 5-year est.); Average household income: $112,657 (2008-2012 5-year est.); Percent of households with income of $100,000 or more: 43.8% (2008-2012 5-year est.); Poverty rate: 6.4% (2008-2012 5-year est.).
Taxes: Total city taxes per capita: $598 (2011); City property taxes per capita: $423 (2011).
Education: Percent of population age 25 and over with: High school diploma (including GED) or higher: 95.3% (2008-2012 5-year est.); Bachelor's degree or higher: 61.0% (2008-2012 5-year est.); Master's degree or higher: 25.8% (2008-2012 5-year est.).
School District(s)
CCSD 89 (PK-08)
   2011-12 Enrollment: 2,000 . . . . (630) 469-8900
CUSD 200 (PK-12)
   2011-12 Enrollment: 13,423 . . . . (630) 682-2002
Dupage Roe (07-12)
   2011-12 Enrollment: n/a . . . . (630) 407-5800
Sch Assoc Sped Educ Dupage Sased (09-12)
   2011-12 Enrollment: n/a . . . . (630) 778-4500
Four-year College(s)
Wheaton College (Private, Not-for-profit, Undenominational)
   Fall 2012 Enrollment: 3,034 . . . . (630) 752-5000
   2012-13 Tuition: In-state $30,120; Out-of-state $30,120
Housing: Homeownership rate: 72.2% (2008-2012 5-year est.); Median home value: $344,900 (2008-2012 5-year est.); Median contract rent: $1,080 per month (2008-2012 5-year est.); Median year structure built: 1974 (2008-2012 5-year est.).
Health Insurance: 84.3% Private; 19.2% Public; 7.0% None. (2008-2012 5-year est.)
Hospitals: Marianjoy Rehabilitation Hospital (120 beds)
Safety: Violent crime rate: 2.3 per 10,000 population; Property crime rate: 108.9 per 10,000 population (2012).

Transportation: Commute to work: 79.2% car, 7.7% public transportation, 4.8% walk, 7.4% work from home (2008-2012 5-year est.); Travel time to work: 30.4% less than 15 minutes, 30.5% 15 to 30 minutes, 17.6% 30 to 45 minutes, 8.6% 45 to 60 minutes, 12.8% 60 minutes or more (2008-2012 5-year est.)

Additional Information Contacts
City of Wheaton . . . . (630) 260-2000
    http://www.wheaton.il.us
Wheaton Chamber of Commerce . . . . (630) 668-6464
    http://www.wheatonchamber.com

WILLOWBROOK (village). Covers a land area of 2.686 square miles and a water area of 0.062 square miles. Located at 41.76° N. Lat; 87.95° W. Long. Elevation is 732 feet.

Population: 8,598 (1990); 8,967 (2000); 8,540 (2010); Density: 3,192.1 persons per square mile (2008-2012 5-year est.); Race: 78.0% White, 4.3% Black/African American, 12.8% Asian, 0.5% American Indian/Alaska Native, 0.0% Native Hawaiian/Other Pacific Islander, 4.4% Some other race, 2.5% Two or more races, 5.4% Hispanic of any race (2008-2012 5-year est.); Average household size: 2.06 (2008-2012 5-year est.); Median age: 46.6 (2008-2012 5-year est.); Males per 100 females: 83.3 (2008-2012 5-year est.); Marriage status: 27.4% never married, 51.8% now married, 10.3% widowed, 10.5% divorced (2008-2012 5-year est.); Foreign born: 23.3% (2008-2012 5-year est.); Ancestry (includes multiple ancestries): 17.7% German, 17.5% Irish, 12.7% Polish, 9.9% Italian, 5.6% English (2008-2012 5-year est.).
Economy: Single-family building permits issued: 1 (2013); Multi-family building permits issued: 0 (2013); Homeowner vacancy rate: 4.6%. Rental vacancy rate: 8.1%. (2008-2012 5-year est.); Employment by occupation: 22.5% management, business, and financial, 11.0% computer, engineering, and science, 12.2% education, legal, community service, arts, and media, 6.8% healthcare practitioners, 10.6% service, 19.6% sales and office, 4.0% natural resources, construction, and maintenance, 13.3% production, transportation, and material moving (2008-2012 5-year est.).
Income: Per capita income: $43,786 (2008-2012 5-year est.); Median household income: $58,798 (2008-2012 5-year est.); Average household income: $89,618 (2008-2012 5-year est.); Percent of households with income of $100,000 or more: 30.7% (2008-2012 5-year est.); Poverty rate: 5.7% (2008-2012 5-year est.).
Education: Percent of population age 25 and over with: High school diploma (including GED) or higher: 93.1% (2008-2012 5-year est.); Bachelor's degree or higher: 45.0% (2008-2012 5-year est.); Master's degree or higher: 21.4% (2008-2012 5-year est.).
Housing: Homeownership rate: 71.2% (2008-2012 5-year est.); Median home value: $271,500 (2008-2012 5-year est.); Median contract rent: $1,055 per month (2008-2012 5-year est.); Median year structure built: 1978 (2008-2012 5-year est.).
Health Insurance: 79.3% Private; 29.3% Public; 9.8% None. (2008-2012 5-year est.)
Safety: Violent crime rate: 18.6 per 10,000 population; Property crime rate: 215.1 per 10,000 population (2012).
Transportation: Commute to work: 90.0% car, 7.2% public transportation, 0.3% walk, 2.1% work from home (2008-2012 5-year est.); Travel time to work: 16.4% less than 15 minutes, 37.4% 15 to 30 minutes, 26.7% 30 to 45 minutes, 10.4% 45 to 60 minutes, 9.1% 60 minutes or more (2008-2012 5-year est.)
Additional Information Contacts
Village of Willowbrook . . . . (630) 323-8215
    http://www.willowbrookil.org

WINFIELD (village). Covers a land area of 2.992 square miles and a water area of 0.040 square miles. Located at 41.88° N. Lat; 88.15° W. Long. Elevation is 771 feet.

Population: 7,096 (1990); 8,718 (2000); 9,080 (2010); Density: 3,064.6 persons per square mile (2008-2012 5-year est.); Race: 92.1% White, 0.8% Black/African American, 3.8% Asian, 0.0% American Indian/Alaska Native, 0.0% Native Hawaiian/Other Pacific Islander, 3.3% Some other race, 2.9% Two or more races, 6.6% Hispanic of any race (2008-2012 5-year est.); Average household size: 2.57 (2008-2012 5-year est.); Median age: 43.0 (2008-2012 5-year est.); Males per 100 females: 92.0 (2008-2012 5-year est.); Marriage status: 22.7% never married, 63.0% now married, 5.6% widowed, 8.7% divorced (2008-2012 5-year est.); Foreign born: 6.7% (2008-2012 5-year est.); Ancestry (includes multiple ancestries): 31.8% German, 18.0% Irish, 12.0% Italian, 11.1% Polish, 10.8% English (2008-2012 5-year est.).

Economy: Single-family building permits issued: 37 (2013); Multi-family building permits issued: 0 (2013); Homeowner vacancy rate: 3.3%. Rental vacancy rate: 0.0%. (2008-2012 5-year est.); Employment by occupation: 24.4% management, business, and financial, 7.9% computer, engineering, and science, 15.4% education, legal, community service, arts, and media, 10.0% healthcare practitioners, 9.0% service, 23.6% sales and office, 4.6% natural resources, construction, and maintenance, 5.1% production, transportation, and material moving (2008-2012 5-year est.).
Income: Per capita income: $43,641 (2008-2012 5-year est.); Median household income: $95,869 (2008-2012 5-year est.); Average household income: $112,833 (2008-2012 5-year est.); Percent of households with income of $100,000 or more: 46.1% (2008-2012 5-year est.); Poverty rate: 4.9% (2008-2012 5-year est.).
Taxes: Total city taxes per capita: $350 (2011); City property taxes per capita: $180 (2011).
Education: Percent of population age 25 and over with: High school diploma (including GED) or higher: 96.7% (2008-2012 5-year est.); Bachelor's degree or higher: 56.1% (2008-2012 5-year est.); Master's degree or higher: 23.2% (2008-2012 5-year est.).

School District(s)
CUSD 200 (PK-12)
    2011-12 Enrollment: 13,423 . . . . (630) 682-2002
Winfield SD 34 (PK-08)
    2011-12 Enrollment: 356 . . . . (630) 909-4900
Housing: Homeownership rate: 94.3% (2008-2012 5-year est.); Median home value: $300,500 (2008-2012 5-year est.); Median contract rent: $1,014 per month (2008-2012 5-year est.); Median year structure built: 1984 (2008-2012 5-year est.).
Health Insurance: 89.7% Private; 17.2% Public; 4.5% None. (2008-2012 5-year est.)
Hospitals: Behavioral Health Services of Central DuPage Hospital (32 beds); Central DuPage Hospital Behavioral Health Services (20 beds)
Safety: Violent crime rate: 0.0 per 10,000 population; Property crime rate: 59.0 per 10,000 population (2012).
Transportation: Commute to work: 90.6% car, 4.5% public transportation, 1.1% walk, 3.6% work from home (2008-2012 5-year est.); Travel time to work: 24.9% less than 15 minutes, 27.3% 15 to 30 minutes, 26.3% 30 to 45 minutes, 8.3% 45 to 60 minutes, 13.3% 60 minutes or more (2008-2012 5-year est.)
Additional Information Contacts
Village of Winfield . . . . (630) 933-7100
    http://www.villageofwinfield.com
Winfield Chamber of Commerce . . . . (630) 682-3712

WOOD DALE (city). Covers a land area of 4.722 square miles and a water area of 0.114 square miles. Located at 41.97° N. Lat; 87.98° W. Long. Elevation is 692 feet.

Population: 12,425 (1990); 13,535 (2000); 13,770 (2010); Density: 2,918.1 persons per square mile (2008-2012 5-year est.); Race: 89.3% White, 0.8% Black/African American, 3.6% Asian, 0.1% American Indian/Alaska Native, 0.0% Native Hawaiian/Other Pacific Islander, 6.2% Some other race, 2.7% Two or more races, 21.8% Hispanic of any race (2008-2012 5-year est.); Average household size: 2.67 (2008-2012 5-year est.); Median age: 41.8 (2008-2012 5-year est.); Males per 100 females: 93.7 (2008-2012 5-year est.); Marriage status: 25.9% never married, 54.3% now married, 8.0% widowed, 11.8% divorced (2008-2012 5-year est.); Foreign born: 25.5% (2008-2012 5-year est.); Ancestry (includes multiple ancestries): 22.1% Polish, 18.6% German, 15.5% Italian, 8.6% Irish, 3.4% English (2008-2012 5-year est.).
Economy: Single-family building permits issued: 3 (2013); Multi-family building permits issued: 0 (2013); Homeowner vacancy rate: 2.8%. Rental vacancy rate: 0.0%. (2008-2012 5-year est.); Employment by occupation: 16.5% management, business, and financial, 4.7% computer, engineering, and science, 5.0% education, legal, community service, arts, and media, 4.6% healthcare practitioners, 14.4% service, 28.6% sales and office, 9.0% natural resources, construction, and maintenance, 17.1% production, transportation, and material moving (2008-2012 5-year est.).
Income: Per capita income: $28,455 (2008-2012 5-year est.); Median household income: $62,345 (2008-2012 5-year est.); Average household income: $74,222 (2008-2012 5-year est.); Percent of households with income of $100,000 or more: 21.9% (2008-2012 5-year est.); Poverty rate: 9.1% (2008-2012 5-year est.).
Education: Percent of population age 25 and over with: High school diploma (including GED) or higher: 85.1% (2008-2012 5-year est.);

Bachelor's degree or higher: 21.3% (2008-2012 5-year est.); Master's degree or higher: 5.9% (2008-2012 5-year est.).

School District(s)

Wood Dale SD 7 (PK-08)

    2011-12 Enrollment: 1,178 . . . . (630) 595-9510

Housing: Homeownership rate: 80.3% (2008-2012 5-year est.); Median home value: $249,700 (2008-2012 5-year est.); Median contract rent: $1,044 per month (2008-2012 5-year est.); Median year structure built: 1975 (2008-2012 5-year est.).

Health Insurance: 68.1% Private; 31.7% Public; 13.9% None. (2008-2012 5-year est.)

Safety: Violent crime rate: 4.3 per 10,000 population; Property crime rate: 160.0 per 10,000 population (2012).

Transportation: Commute to work: 90.7% car, 3.9% public transportation, 1.9% walk, 2.7% work from home (2008-2012 5-year est.); Travel time to work: 23.0% less than 15 minutes, 36.5% 15 to 30 minutes, 23.1% 30 to 45 minutes, 11.2% 45 to 60 minutes, 6.2% 60 minutes or more (2008-2012 5-year est.)

Additional Information Contacts

City of Wood Dale . . . . (630) 766-4900

    http://www.wooddale.com

Wood Dale Chamber of Commerce . . . . (630) 595-0505

    http://www.wooddalechamber.com

WOODRIDGE (village).

Covers a land area of 9.422 square miles and a water area of 0.162 square miles. Located at 41.74° N. Lat; 88.04° W. Long. Elevation is 732 feet.

Population: 26,256 (1990); 30,934 (2000); 32,971 (2010); Density: 3,494.4 persons per square mile (2008-2012 5-year est.); Race: 69.5% White, 9.0% Black/African American, 12.9% Asian, 0.2% American Indian/Alaska Native, 0.0% Native Hawaiian/Other Pacific Islander, 8.4% Some other race, 3.0% Two or more races, 13.3% Hispanic of any race (2008-2012 5-year est.); Average household size: 2.59 (2008-2012 5-year est.); Median age: 36.6 (2008-2012 5-year est.); Males per 100 females: 98.5 (2008-2012 5-year est.); Marriage status: 31.9% never married, 56.2% now married, 2.9% widowed, 9.0% divorced (2008-2012 5-year est.); Foreign born: 20.4% (2008-2012 5-year est.); Ancestry (includes multiple ancestries): 19.8% German, 12.4% Irish, 11.7% Polish, 11.0% Italian, 5.2% English (2008-2012 5-year est.).

Economy: Unemployment rate: 6.7% (April 2014); Total civilian labor force: 19,748 (April 2014); Single-family building permits issued: 20 (2013); Multi-family building permits issued: 0 (2013); Homeowner vacancy rate: 4.1%. Rental vacancy rate: 7.4%. (2008-2012 5-year est.); Employment by occupation: 15.9% management, business, and financial, 9.8% computer, engineering, and science, 9.5% education, legal, community service, arts, and media, 6.8% healthcare practitioners, 14.2% service, 29.7% sales and office, 5.4% natural resources, construction, and maintenance, 8.7% production, transportation, and material moving (2008-2012 5-year est.).

Income: Per capita income: $35,929 (2008-2012 5-year est.); Median household income: $76,218 (2008-2012 5-year est.); Average household income: $92,026 (2008-2012 5-year est.); Percent of households with income of $100,000 or more: 33.5% (2008-2012 5-year est.); Poverty rate: 5.9% (2008-2012 5-year est.).

Taxes: Total city taxes per capita: $412 (2011); City property taxes per capita: $214 (2011).

Education: Percent of population age 25 and over with: High school diploma (including GED) or higher: 93.9% (2008-2012 5-year est.); Bachelor's degree or higher: 44.4% (2008-2012 5-year est.); Master's degree or higher: 15.6% (2008-2012 5-year est.).

School District(s)

Woodridge SD 68 (PK-08)

    2011-12 Enrollment: 2,990 . . . . (630) 985-7925

Four-year College(s)

Westwood College-Dupage (Private, For-profit)

    Fall 2012 Enrollment: 278 . . . . (630) 434-7655

    2012-13 Tuition: In-state $14,517; Out-of-state $14,517

Housing: Homeownership rate: 66.7% (2008-2012 5-year est.); Median home value: $267,500 (2008-2012 5-year est.); Median contract rent: $959 per month (2008-2012 5-year est.); Median year structure built: 1978 (2008-2012 5-year est.).

Health Insurance: 81.6% Private; 15.3% Public; 9.1% None. (2008-2012 5-year est.)

Safety: Violent crime rate: 11.4 per 10,000 population; Property crime rate: 157.5 per 10,000 population (2012).

Transportation: Commute to work: 86.7% car, 5.2% public transportation, 2.3% walk, 3.7% work from home (2008-2012 5-year est.); Travel time to work: 16.4% less than 15 minutes, 34.8% 15 to 30 minutes, 22.4% 30 to 45 minutes, 13.3% 45 to 60 minutes, 13.1% 60 minutes or more (2008-2012 5-year est.)

Additional Information Contacts

Downers Grove Area Chamber of Commerce & Industry . . (630) 968-4050

    http://chamber630.com

Village of Woodridge . . . . (630) 852-7000

    http://www.vil.woodridge.il.us

Edgar County

Located in eastern Illinois; bounded on the east by Indiana; drained by tributaries of the Wabash River. Covers a land area of 623.374 square miles, a water area of 0.622 square miles, and is located in the Central Time Zone at 39.68° N. Lat., 87.75° W. Long. The county was founded in 1823. County seat is Paris.

Weather Station: Paris Waterworks								Elevation: 680 feet			
	Jan	Feb	Mar	Apr	May	Jun	Jul	Aug	Sep	Oct	Nov	Dec
High	35	40	51	64	74	83	86	85	78	66	52	39
Low	19	23	32	42	53	63	66	64	56	45	35	24
Precip	2.4	2.3	2.9	4.1	4.4	4.4	4.4	4.1	3.2	3.4	3.7	3.0
Snow	8.4	5.7	2.9	0.2	0.0	0.0	0.0	0.0	0.0	0.1	0.8	5.4

High and Low temperatures in degrees Fahrenheit; Precipitation and Snow in inches

Population: 19,595 (1990); 19,704 (2000); 18,576 (2010); Race: 98.1% White, 0.4% Black/African American, 0.7% Asian, 0.0% American Indian/Alaska Native, 0.0% Native Hawaiian/Other Pacific Islander, 0.8% Some other race, 0.6% Two or more races, 1.1% Hispanic of any race (2008-2012 5-year est.); Density: 29.1 persons per square mile (2008-2012 5-year est.); Average household size: 2.31 (2008-2012 5-year est.); Median age: 43.0 (2008-2012 5-year est.); Males per 100 females: 94.2 (2008-2012 5-year est.).

Religion: Six largest groups: 18.1% Baptist, 8.0% Methodist/Pietist, 6.1% Catholicism, 3.4% Non-denominational Protestant, 1.8% Lutheran, 1.6% Presbyterian-Reformed (2010)

Economy: Unemployment rate: 6.7% (April 2014); Total civilian labor force: 9,426 (April 2014); Leading industries: 29.3% manufacturing; 15.2% health care and social assistance; 10.8% retail trade (2012); Farms: 673 totaling 351,684 acres (2012); Companies that employ 500 or more persons: 2 (2012); Companies that employ 100 to 499 persons: 9 (2012); Companies that employ less than 100 persons: 338 (2012); Black-owned businesses: n/a (2007); Hispanic-owned businesses: n/a (2007); Asian-owned businesses: n/a (2007); Women-owned businesses: n/a (2007); Single-family building permits issued: 2 (2013); Multi-family building permits issued: 0 (2013).

Income: Per capita income: $23,724 (2008-2012 5-year est.); Median household income: $42,730 (2008-2012 5-year est.); Average household income: $54,986 (2008-2012 5-year est.); Percent of households with income of $100,000 or more: 14.3% (2008-2012 5-year est.); Poverty rate: 15.7% (2008-2012 5-year est.); Bankruptcy rate: 2.70% (2013).

Education: Percent of population age 25 and over with: High school diploma (including GED) or higher: 87.3% (2008-2012 5-year est.); Bachelor's degree or higher: 16.0% (2008-2012 5-year est.); Master's degree or higher: 4.0% (2008-2012 5-year est.).

Housing: Homeownership rate: 75.1% (2008-2012 5-year est.); Median home value: $72,500 (2008-2012 5-year est.); Median contract rent: $393 per month (2008-2012 5-year est.); Median year structure built: 1955 (2008-2012 5-year est.)

Health: Birth rate: 97.4 per 10,000 population (2013); Death rate: 122.5 per 10,000 population (2013); Age-adjusted cancer mortality rate: 166.7 deaths per 100,000 population (2011); Number of physicians: 6.5 per 10,000 population (2011); Hospital beds: 13.5 per 10,000 population (2010); Hospital admissions: 293.9 per 10,000 population (2010).

Elections: 2012 Presidential election results: 32.8% Obama, 65.6% Romney

Additional Information Contacts

Edgar County Government . . . . (217) 466-7433

    http://www.edgarcountyillinois.com

Edgar County Communities

BROCTON (village). Covers a land area of 0.578 square miles and a water area of 0 square miles. Located at 39.72° N. Lat; 87.93° W. Long. Elevation is 663 feet.

Population: 322 (1990); 322 (2000); 322 (2010); Density: 740.1 persons per square mile (2008-2012 5-year est.); Race: 98.1% White, 0.0% Black/African American, 0.0% Asian, 0.5% American Indian/Alaska Native, 0.0% Native Hawaiian/Other Pacific Islander, 1.4% Some other race, 1.4% Two or more races, 1.6% Hispanic of any race (2008-2012 5-year est.); Average household size: 2.55 (2008-2012 5-year est.); Median age: 31.4 (2008-2012 5-year est.); Males per 100 females: 117.3 (2008-2012 5-year est.); Marriage status: 22.3% never married, 60.7% now married, 5.9% widowed, 11.1% divorced (2008-2012 5-year est.); Foreign born: 0.5% (2008-2012 5-year est.); Ancestry (includes multiple ancestries): 20.1% German, 18.5% Irish, 14.5% American, 6.5% English, 4.4% Italian (2008-2012 5-year est.).

Economy: Single-family building permits issued: 0 (2013); Multi-family building permits issued: 0 (2013); Homeowner vacancy rate: 0.0%. Rental vacancy rate: 0.0%. (2008-2012 5-year est.); Employment by occupation: 2.8% management, business, and financial, 2.8% computer, engineering, and science, 4.5% education, legal, community service, arts, and media, 3.4% healthcare practitioners, 22.9% service, 14.0% sales and office, 21.8% natural resources, construction, and maintenance, 27.9% production, transportation, and material moving (2008-2012 5-year est.).

Income: Per capita income: $15,838 (2008-2012 5-year est.); Median household income: $37,188 (2008-2012 5-year est.); Average household income: $40,265 (2008-2012 5-year est.); Percent of households with income of $100,000 or more: 0.6% (2008-2012 5-year est.); Poverty rate: 20.1% (2008-2012 5-year est.).

Education: Percent of population age 25 and over with: High school diploma (including GED) or higher: 74.5% (2008-2012 5-year est.); Bachelor's degree or higher: 3.7% (2008-2012 5-year est.); Master's degree or higher: 0.4% (2008-2012 5-year est.).

Housing: Homeownership rate: 81.0% (2008-2012 5-year est.); Median home value: $40,700 (2008-2012 5-year est.); Median contract rent: $334 per month (2008-2012 5-year est.); Median year structure built: 1941 (2008-2012 5-year est.).

Health Insurance: 50.7% Private; 42.5% Public; 21.0% None. (2008-2012 5-year est.)

Transportation: Commute to work: 96.6% car, 0.0% public transportation, 0.0% walk, 0.0% work from home (2008-2012 5-year est.); Travel time to work: 30.5% less than 15 minutes, 27.6% 15 to 30 minutes, 17.8% 30 to 45 minutes, 11.5% 45 to 60 minutes, 12.6% 60 minutes or more (2008-2012 5-year est.)

CHRISMAN (city). Covers a land area of 0.747 square miles and a water area of 0 square miles. Located at 39.80° N. Lat; 87.68° W. Long. Elevation is 650 feet.

History: Chrisman was platted in 1872 by Matthias Chrisman, and grew as a trading center and shipping point.

Population: 1,136 (1990); 1,318 (2000); 1,343 (2010); Density: 1,768.0 persons per square mile (2008-2012 5-year est.); Race: 98.0% White, 1.3% Black/African American, 0.2% Asian, 0.0% American Indian/Alaska Native, 0.0% Native Hawaiian/Other Pacific Islander, 0.5% Some other race, 0.6% Two or more races, 0.7% Hispanic of any race (2008-2012 5-year est.); Average household size: 2.26 (2008-2012 5-year est.); Median age: 45.4 (2008-2012 5-year est.); Males per 100 females: 94.1 (2008-2012 5-year est.); Marriage status: 17.6% never married, 54.2% now married, 12.4% widowed, 15.8% divorced (2008-2012 5-year est.); Foreign born: 0.4% (2008-2012 5-year est.); Ancestry (includes multiple ancestries): 24.6% German, 14.6% Irish, 13.9% English, 9.7% American, 6.3% French (2008-2012 5-year est.).

Economy: Single-family building permits issued: 0 (2013); Multi-family building permits issued: 0 (2013); Homeowner vacancy rate: 2.1%. Rental vacancy rate: 0.0%. (2008-2012 5-year est.); Employment by occupation: 7.4% management, business, and financial, 1.3% computer, engineering, and science, 11.5% education, legal, community service, arts, and media, 3.8% healthcare practitioners, 22.9% service, 22.2% sales and office, 8.6% natural resources, construction, and maintenance, 22.3% production, transportation, and material moving (2008-2012 5-year est.).

Income: Per capita income: $20,937 (2008-2012 5-year est.); Median household income: $37,417 (2008-2012 5-year est.); Average household income: $47,765 (2008-2012 5-year est.); Percent of households with

income of $100,000 or more: 12.2% (2008-2012 5-year est.); Poverty rate: 13.9% (2008-2012 5-year est.).

Education: Percent of population age 25 and over with: High school diploma (including GED) or higher: 85.7% (2008-2012 5-year est.); Bachelor's degree or higher: 11.0% (2008-2012 5-year est.); Master's degree or higher: 3.3% (2008-2012 5-year est.).

School District(s)
Edgar County CUD 6 (PK-12)
    2011-12 Enrollment: 369 . . . . (217) 269-2513

Housing: Homeownership rate: 75.2% (2008-2012 5-year est.); Median home value: $66,900 (2008-2012 5-year est.); Median contract rent: $350 per month (2008-2012 5-year est.); Median year structure built: 1948 (2008-2012 5-year est.).

Health Insurance: 73.9% Private; 38.5% Public; 8.2% None. (2008-2012 5-year est.)

Transportation: Commute to work: 95.8% car, 0.0% public transportation, 0.9% walk, 2.1% work from home (2008-2012 5-year est.); Travel time to work: 36.8% less than 15 minutes, 32.4% 15 to 30 minutes, 21.8% 30 to 45 minutes, 5.8% 45 to 60 minutes, 3.3% 60 minutes or more (2008-2012 5-year est.)

HUME (village). Covers a land area of 0.535 square miles and a water area of 0 square miles. Located at 39.80° N. Lat; 87.87° W. Long. Elevation is 663 feet.

Population: 406 (1990); 382 (2000); 380 (2010); Density: 796.0 persons per square mile (2008-2012 5-year est.); Race: 99.1% White, 0.0% Black/African American, 0.0% Asian, 0.9% American Indian/Alaska Native, 0.0% Native Hawaiian/Other Pacific Islander, 0.0% Some other race, 0.0% Two or more races, 0.0% Hispanic of any race (2008-2012 5-year est.); Average household size: 2.17 (2008-2012 5-year est.); Median age: 44.9 (2008-2012 5-year est.); Males per 100 females: 99.1 (2008-2012 5-year est.); Marriage status: 23.8% never married, 51.8% now married, 7.1% widowed, 17.3% divorced (2008-2012 5-year est.); Foreign born: 1.2% (2008-2012 5-year est.); Ancestry (includes multiple ancestries): 27.9% German, 20.7% Irish, 13.8% American, 9.4% English, 5.4% French (2008-2012 5-year est.).

Economy: Homeowner vacancy rate: 0.0%. Rental vacancy rate: 6.0%. (2008-2012 5-year est.); Employment by occupation: 11.0% management, business, and financial, 1.7% computer, engineering, and science, 0.0% education, legal, community service, arts, and media, 5.5% healthcare practitioners, 24.9% service, 26.0% sales and office, 15.5% natural resources, construction, and maintenance, 15.5% production, transportation, and material moving (2008-2012 5-year est.).

Income: Per capita income: $23,181 (2008-2012 5-year est.); Median household income: $31,250 (2008-2012 5-year est.); Average household income: $50,205 (2008-2012 5-year est.); Percent of households with income of $100,000 or more: 14.2% (2008-2012 5-year est.); Poverty rate: 13.6% (2008-2012 5-year est.).

Education: Percent of population age 25 and over with: High school diploma (including GED) or higher: 83.7% (2008-2012 5-year est.); Bachelor's degree or higher: 9.6% (2008-2012 5-year est.); Master's degree or higher: 3.0% (2008-2012 5-year est.).

School District(s)
Shiloh CUSD 1 (PK-12)
    2011-12 Enrollment: 434 . . . . (217) 887-2364

Housing: Homeownership rate: 76.0% (2008-2012 5-year est.); Median home value: $67,100 (2008-2012 5-year est.); Median contract rent: $341 per month (2008-2012 5-year est.); Median year structure built: Before 1940 (2008-2012 5-year est.).

Health Insurance: 63.8% Private; 40.8% Public; 17.4% None. (2008-2012 5-year est.)

Transportation: Commute to work: 91.5% car, 0.0% public transportation, 3.4% walk, 2.8% work from home (2008-2012 5-year est.); Travel time to work: 31.4% less than 15 minutes, 25.0% 15 to 30 minutes, 19.8% 30 to 45 minutes, 12.8% 45 to 60 minutes, 11.0% 60 minutes or more (2008-2012 5-year est.)

KANSAS (village). Covers a land area of 1.025 square miles and a water area of 0 square miles. Located at 39.55° N. Lat; 87.94° W. Long. Elevation is 712 feet.

Population: 887 (1990); 842 (2000); 787 (2010); Density: 811.5 persons per square mile (2008-2012 5-year est.); Race: 99.5% White, 0.0% Black/African American, 0.0% Asian, 0.0% American Indian/Alaska Native, 0.0% Native Hawaiian/Other Pacific Islander, 0.5% Some other race, 0.5% Two or more races, 0.0% Hispanic of any race (2008-2012 5-year est.);

Average household size: 2.36 (2008-2012 5-year est.); Median age: 42.6 (2008-2012 5-year est.); Males per 100 females: 84.1 (2008-2012 5-year est.); Marriage status: 17.9% never married, 63.0% now married, 6.4% widowed, 12.7% divorced (2008-2012 5-year est.); Foreign born: 0.4% (2008-2012 5-year est.); Ancestry (includes multiple ancestries): 23.7% German, 14.9% Irish, 12.5% American, 11.5% English, 3.4% Scottish (2008-2012 5-year est.).

Economy: Homeowner vacancy rate: 2.7%. Rental vacancy rate: 0.0%. (2008-2012 5-year est.); Employment by occupation: 9.0% management, business, and financial, 2.0% computer, engineering, and science, 7.3% education, legal, community service, arts, and media, 1.7% healthcare practitioners, 13.1% service, 32.4% sales and office, 11.1% natural resources, construction, and maintenance, 23.3% production, transportation, and material moving (2008-2012 5-year est.).

Income: Per capita income: $18,078 (2008-2012 5-year est.); Median household income: $34,063 (2008-2012 5-year est.); Average household income: $41,933 (2008-2012 5-year est.); Percent of households with income of $100,000 or more: 7.0% (2008-2012 5-year est.); Poverty rate: 16.7% (2008-2012 5-year est.).

Education: Percent of population age 25 and over with: High school diploma (including GED) or higher: 90.7% (2008-2012 5-year est.); Bachelor's degree or higher: 16.3% (2008-2012 5-year est.); Master's degree or higher: 6.1% (2008-2012 5-year est.).

School District(s)

Eastern II Area of Spec Educ (PK-12)
    2011-12 Enrollment: n/a . . . . (217) 348-7700
Kansas CUSD 3 (PK-12)
    2011-12 Enrollment: 250. . . . . (217) 948-5174

Housing: Homeownership rate: 70.5% (2008-2012 5-year est.); Median home value: $63,100 (2008-2012 5-year est.); Median contract rent: $277 per month (2008-2012 5-year est.); Median year structure built: 1943 (2008-2012 5-year est.).

Health Insurance: 55.4% Private; 51.1% Public; 10.8% None. (2008-2012 5-year est.)

Transportation: Commute to work: 91.4% car, 0.0% public transportation, 3.7% walk, 2.5% work from home (2008-2012 5-year est.); Travel time to work: 25.2% less than 15 minutes, 41.6% 15 to 30 minutes, 17.0% 30 to 45 minutes, 6.9% 45 to 60 minutes, 9.1% 60 minutes or more (2008-2012 5-year est.).

METCALF (village). Covers a land area of 0.686 square miles and a water area of 0 square miles. Located at 39.80° N. Lat; 87.81° W. Long. Elevation is 689 feet.

Population: 227 (1990); 213 (2000); 189 (2010); Density: 285.5 persons per square mile (2008-2012 5-year est.); Race: 100.0% White, 0.0% Black/African American, 0.0% Asian, 0.0% American Indian/Alaska Native, 0.0% Native Hawaiian/Other Pacific Islander, 0.0% Some other race, 0.0% Two or more races, 0.0% Hispanic of any race (2008-2012 5-year est.); Average household size: 2.31 (2008-2012 5-year est.); Median age: 42.8 (2008-2012 5-year est.); Males per 100 females: 90.3 (2008-2012 5-year est.); Marriage status: 18.7% never married, 52.4% now married, 9.6% widowed, 19.3% divorced (2008-2012 5-year est.); Foreign born: 1.0% (2008-2012 5-year est.); Ancestry (includes multiple ancestries): 28.6% American, 10.2% German, 10.2% Irish, 3.1% English, 2.6% French (2008-2012 5-year est.).

Economy: Homeowner vacancy rate: 0.0%. Rental vacancy rate: 0.0%. (2008-2012 5-year est.); Employment by occupation: 5.9% management, business, and financial, 0.0% computer, engineering, and science, 0.0% education, legal, community service, arts, and media, 0.0% healthcare practitioners, 11.8% service, 20.0% sales and office, 20.0% natural resources, construction, and maintenance, 42.4% production, transportation, and material moving (2008-2012 5-year est.).

Income: Per capita income: $17,623 (2008-2012 5-year est.); Median household income: $27,375 (2008-2012 5-year est.); Average household income: $39,108 (2008-2012 5-year est.); Percent of households with income of $100,000 or more: 9.4% (2008-2012 5-year est.); Poverty rate: 32.1% (2008-2012 5-year est.).

Education: Percent of population age 25 and over with: High school diploma (including GED) or higher: 76.6% (2008-2012 5-year est.); Bachelor's degree or higher: 0.0% (2008-2012 5-year est.); Master's degree or higher: 0.0% (2008-2012 5-year est.).

Housing: Homeownership rate: 94.1% (2008-2012 5-year est.); Median home value: $28,200 (2008-2012 5-year est.); Median contract rent: $363 per month (2008-2012 5-year est.); Median year structure built: Before 1940 (2008-2012 5-year est.).

Health Insurance: 56.1% Private; 59.2% Public; 6.1% None. (2008-2012 5-year est.)

Transportation: Commute to work: 92.7% car, 7.3% public transportation, 0.0% walk, 0.0% work from home (2008-2012 5-year est.); Travel time to work: 9.8% less than 15 minutes, 28.0% 15 to 30 minutes, 32.9% 30 to 45 minutes, 15.9% 45 to 60 minutes, 13.4% 60 minutes or more (2008-2012 5-year est.)

PARIS (city). County seat. Covers a land area of 5.506 square miles and a water area of 0.390 square miles. Located at 39.61° N. Lat; 87.69° W. Long. Elevation is 722 feet.

History: Paris was the site of several speeches by Abraham Lincoln. The town was platted in 1853 and grew as the seat of Edgar County.

Population: 8,987 (1990); 9,077 (2000); 8,837 (2010); Density: 1,615.6 persons per square mile (2008-2012 5-year est.); Race: 97.4% White, 0.5% Black/African American, 1.3% Asian, 0.0% American Indian/Alaska Native, 0.0% Native Hawaiian/Other Pacific Islander, 0.8% Some other race, 0.4% Two or more races, 1.6% Hispanic of any race (2008-2012 5-year est.); Average household size: 2.23 (2008-2012 5-year est.); Median age: 41.6 (2008-2012 5-year est.); Males per 100 females: 83.3 (2008-2012 5-year est.); Marriage status: 26.6% never married, 48.6% now married, 9.4% widowed, 15.4% divorced (2008-2012 5-year est.); Foreign born: 1.4% (2008-2012 5-year est.); Ancestry (includes multiple ancestries): 18.9% German, 14.1% American, 13.7% Irish, 9.2% English, 3.1% Scottish (2008-2012 5-year est.).

Economy: Single-family building permits issued: 2 (2013); Multi-family building permits issued: 0 (2013); Homeowner vacancy rate: 1.9%. Rental vacancy rate: 4.3%. (2008-2012 5-year est.); Employment by occupation: 4.5% management, business, and financial, 4.4% computer, engineering, and science, 8.9% education, legal, community service, arts, and media, 2.2% healthcare practitioners, 22.0% service, 22.4% sales and office, 11.2% natural resources, construction, and maintenance, 24.5% production, transportation, and material moving (2008-2012 5-year est.).

Income: Per capita income: $20,939 (2008-2012 5-year est.); Median household income: $38,227 (2008-2012 5-year est.); Average household income: $47,533 (2008-2012 5-year est.); Percent of households with income of $100,000 or more: 9.6% (2008-2012 5-year est.); Poverty rate: 20.8% (2008-2012 5-year est.).

Taxes: Total city taxes per capita: $336 (2011); City property taxes per capita: $161 (2011).

Education: Percent of population age 25 and over with: High school diploma (including GED) or higher: 84.4% (2008-2012 5-year est.); Bachelor's degree or higher: 14.0% (2008-2012 5-year est.); Master's degree or higher: 2.6% (2008-2012 5-year est.).

School District(s)

Clk/cls/cmbn/dglas/edgr/mltr/shlb
    2011-12 Enrollment: n/a . . . . (217) 348-0151
Paris CUSD 4 (PK-12)
    2011-12 Enrollment: 720. . . . . (217) 465-5391
Paris Cooperative High School (09-12)
    2011-12 Enrollment: n/a . . . . (217) 466-1175
Paris-Union SD 95 (PK-12)
    2011-12 Enrollment: 1,354 . . . . (217) 465-8448

Housing: Homeownership rate: 69.2% (2008-2012 5-year est.); Median home value: $64,200 (2008-2012 5-year est.); Median contract rent: $395 per month (2008-2012 5-year est.); Median year structure built: 1957 (2008-2012 5-year est.).

Health Insurance: 59.4% Private; 43.6% Public; 13.4% None. (2008-2012 5-year est.)

Hospitals: Paris Community Hospital (49 beds)

Transportation: Commute to work: 88.7% car, 0.2% public transportation, 4.9% walk, 5.5% work from home (2008-2012 5-year est.); Travel time to work: 59.5% less than 15 minutes, 15.0% 15 to 30 minutes, 11.3% 30 to 45 minutes, 4.7% 45 to 60 minutes, 9.4% 60 minutes or more (2008-2012 5-year est.)

Airports: Edgar County Airport (general aviation)

Additional Information Contacts

City of Paris . . . . (217) 465-7601
    http://parisillinois.org
Paris Area Chamber of Commerce & Tourism . . . . (217) 465-4179
    http://www.parisilchamber.com

REDMON (village). Covers a land area of 0.148 square miles and a water area of 0 square miles. Located at 39.64° N. Lat; 87.86° W. Long. Elevation is 689 feet.

Population: 201 (1990); 199 (2000); 173 (2010); Density: 1,310.9 persons per square mile (2008-2012 5-year est.); Race: 100.0% White, 0.0% Black/African American, 0.0% Asian, 0.0% American Indian/Alaska Native, 0.0% Native Hawaiian/Other Pacific Islander, 0.0% Some other race, 0.0% Two or more races, 0.0% Hispanic of any race (2008-2012 5-year est.); Average household size: 2.02 (2008-2012 5-year est.); Median age: 46.8 (2008-2012 5-year est.); Males per 100 females: 125.6 (2008-2012 5-year est.); Marriage status: 24.3% never married, 44.4% now married, 16.0% widowed, 15.4% divorced (2008-2012 5-year est.); Foreign born: 0.0% (2008-2012 5-year est.); Ancestry (includes multiple ancestries): 27.3% English, 18.6% German, 9.8% Irish, 7.7% American, 3.1% Dutch (2008-2012 5-year est.).

Economy: Homeowner vacancy rate: 0.0%. Rental vacancy rate: 13.3%. (2008-2012 5-year est.); Employment by occupation: 4.3% management, business, and financial, 3.2% computer, engineering, and science, 1.1% education, legal, community service, arts, and media, 4.3% healthcare practitioners, 26.6% service, 28.7% sales and office, 7.4% natural resources, construction, and maintenance, 24.5% production, transportation, and material moving (2008-2012 5-year est.).

Income: Per capita income: $18,959 (2008-2012 5-year est.); Median household income: $27,167 (2008-2012 5-year est.); Average household income: $37,617 (2008-2012 5-year est.); Percent of households with income of $100,000 or more: 1.0% (2008-2012 5-year est.); Poverty rate: 12.9% (2008-2012 5-year est.).

Education: Percent of population age 25 and over with: High school diploma (including GED) or higher: 86.4% (2008-2012 5-year est.); Bachelor's degree or higher: 1.4% (2008-2012 5-year est.); Master's degree or higher: 0.0% (2008-2012 5-year est.).

Housing: Homeownership rate: 59.4% (2008-2012 5-year est.); Median home value: $55,000 (2008-2012 5-year est.); Median contract rent: $400 per month (2008-2012 5-year est.); Median year structure built: Before 1940 (2008-2012 5-year est.).

Health Insurance: 50.0% Private; 56.7% Public; 12.4% None. (2008-2012 5-year est.)

Transportation: Commute to work: 97.9% car, 0.0% public transportation, 0.0% walk, 0.0% work from home (2008-2012 5-year est.); Travel time to work: 18.1% less than 15 minutes, 57.4% 15 to 30 minutes, 13.8% 30 to 45 minutes, 10.6% 45 to 60 minutes, 0.0% 60 minutes or more (2008-2012 5-year est.)

VERMILION (village). Covers a land area of 0.761 square miles and a water area of 0 square miles. Located at 39.58° N. Lat; 87.59° W. Long. Elevation is 692 feet.

History: Formerly Vermillion.

Population: 283 (1990); 239 (2000); 225 (2010); Density: 267.9 persons per square mile (2008-2012 5-year est.); Race: 100.0% White, 0.0% Black/African American, 0.0% Asian, 0.0% American Indian/Alaska Native, 0.0% Native Hawaiian/Other Pacific Islander, 0.0% Some other race, 0.0% Two or more races, 1.0% Hispanic of any race (2008-2012 5-year est.); Average household size: 2.46 (2008-2012 5-year est.); Median age: 53.0 (2008-2012 5-year est.); Males per 100 females: 74.4 (2008-2012 5-year est.); Marriage status: 21.5% never married, 48.8% now married, 20.3% widowed, 9.3% divorced (2008-2012 5-year est.); Foreign born: 0.0% (2008-2012 5-year est.); Ancestry (includes multiple ancestries): 19.6% Irish, 19.1% German, 6.4% American, 5.9% Italian, 5.4% English (2008-2012 5-year est.).

Economy: Single-family building permits issued: 0 (2013); Multi-family building permits issued: 0 (2013); Homeowner vacancy rate: 6.1%. Rental vacancy rate: 0.0%. (2008-2012 5-year est.); Employment by occupation: 1.5% management, business, and financial, 0.0% computer, engineering, and science, 3.0% education, legal, community service, arts, and media, 0.0% healthcare practitioners, 32.8% service, 22.4% sales and office, 3.0% natural resources, construction, and maintenance, 37.3% production, transportation, and material moving (2008-2012 5-year est.).

Income: Per capita income: $16,816 (2008-2012 5-year est.); Median household income: $35,694 (2008-2012 5-year est.); Average household income: $38,978 (2008-2012 5-year est.); Percent of households with income of $100,000 or more: 3.6% (2008-2012 5-year est.); Poverty rate: 24.5% (2008-2012 5-year est.).

Education: Percent of population age 25 and over with: High school diploma (including GED) or higher: 79.9% (2008-2012 5-year est.);

Bachelor's degree or higher: 5.3% (2008-2012 5-year est.); Master's degree or higher: 1.2% (2008-2012 5-year est.).

Housing: Homeownership rate: 86.7% (2008-2012 5-year est.); Median home value: $43,600 (2008-2012 5-year est.); Median contract rent: $339 per month (2008-2012 5-year est.); Median year structure built: Before 1940 (2008-2012 5-year est.).

Health Insurance: 51.0% Private; 63.7% Public; 7.8% None. (2008-2012 5-year est.)

Transportation: Commute to work: 100.0% car, 0.0% public transportation, 0.0% walk, 0.0% work from home (2008-2012 5-year est.); Travel time to work: 24.1% less than 15 minutes, 29.3% 15 to 30 minutes, 44.8% 30 to 45 minutes, 1.7% 45 to 60 minutes, 0.0% 60 minutes or more (2008-2012 5-year est.)

Edwards County

Located in southeastern Illinois; drained by the Little Wabash River. Covers a land area of 222.416 square miles, a water area of 0.305 square miles, and is located in the Central Time Zone at 38.42° N. Lat., 88.05° W. Long. The county was founded in 1814. County seat is Albion.

Weather Station: Albion   Elevation: 529 feet

	Jan	Feb	Mar	Apr	May	Jun	Jul	Aug	Sep	Oct	Nov	Dec
High	39	45	55	67	77	86	90	89	82	71	55	43
Low	24	27	35	46	56	65	68	67	59	47	37	26
Precip	2.6	2.5	4.0	4.9	5.4	3.7	3.6	3.2	2.8	3.7	4.1	3.0
Snow	2.0	2.4	1.0	0.0	0.0	0.0	0.0	0.0	0.0	0.1	tr	2.6

High and Low temperatures in degrees Fahrenheit; Precipitation and Snow in inches

Population: 7,440 (1990); 6,971 (2000); 6,721 (2010); Race: 97.5% White, 0.9% Black/African American, 0.3% Asian, 0.0% American Indian/Alaska Native, 0.0% Native Hawaiian/Other Pacific Islander, 1.3% Some other race, 1.2% Two or more races, 0.0% Hispanic of any race (2008-2012 5-year est.); Density: 30.2 persons per square mile (2008-2012 5-year est.); Average household size: 2.42 (2008-2012 5-year est.); Median age: 43.1 (2008-2012 5-year est.); Males per 100 females: 98.5 (2008-2012 5-year est.).

Religion: Six largest groups: 36.6% Baptist, 16.4% Methodist/Pietist, 7.4% Non-denominational Protestant, 1.5% Presbyterian-Reformed, 0.7% Holiness, 0.2% Episcopalianism/Anglicanism (2010)

Economy: Unemployment rate: 7.5% (April 2014); Total civilian labor force: 2,741 (April 2014); Leading industries: 9.4% retail trade; 9.4% wholesale trade; 5.7% health care and social assistance (2012); Farms: 365 totaling 106,737 acres (2012); Companies that employ 500 or more persons: 1 (2012); Companies that employ 100 to 499 persons: 0 (2012); Companies that employ less than 100 persons: 150 (2012); Black-owned businesses: n/a (2007); Hispanic-owned businesses: n/a (2007); Asian-owned businesses: n/a (2007); Women-owned businesses: 111 (2007); Single-family building permits issued: n/a (2013); Multi-family building permits issued: n/a (2013).

Income: Per capita income: $20,758 (2008-2012 5-year est.); Median household income: $39,238 (2008-2012 5-year est.); Average household income: $48,024 (2008-2012 5-year est.); Percent of households with income of $100,000 or more: 8.8% (2008-2012 5-year est.); Poverty rate: 11.1% (2008-2012 5-year est.); Bankruptcy rate: 1.65% (2013).

Education: Percent of population age 25 and over with: High school diploma (including GED) or higher: 88.4% (2008-2012 5-year est.); Bachelor's degree or higher: 11.4% (2008-2012 5-year est.); Master's degree or higher: 3.1% (2008-2012 5-year est.).

Housing: Homeownership rate: 79.7% (2008-2012 5-year est.); Median home value: $62,100 (2008-2012 5-year est.); Median contract rent: $312 per month (2008-2012 5-year est.); Median year structure built: 1961 (2008-2012 5-year est.)

Health: Birth rate: 122.9 per 10,000 population (2013); Death rate: 98.9 per 10,000 population (2013); Age-adjusted cancer mortality rate: 246.2 deaths per 100,000 population (2011); Number of physicians: 0.0 per 10,000 population (2011); Hospital beds: 0.0 per 10,000 population (2010); Hospital admissions: 0.0 per 10,000 population (2010).

Elections: 2012 Presidential election results: 23.4% Obama, 74.5% Romney

Additional Information Contacts

Edwards County Government . . . . (618) 445-2115

Edwards County Communities

ALBION (city). County seat. Covers a land area of 2.150 square miles and a water area of 0.046 square miles. Located at 38.38° N. Lat; 88.06° W. Long. Elevation is 522 feet.

History: In 1818 Morris Birkbeck and George Flower came from England to find a place that would provide a better life for the English working class. They settled on this section of prairie and led many English colonists here, who named the town Albion, remembering their former homeland.

Population: 2,116 (1990); 1,933 (2000); 1,988 (2010); Density: 989.4 persons per square mile (2008-2012 5-year est.); Race: 93.7% White, 2.1% Black/African American, 1.1% Asian, 0.0% American Indian/Alaska Native, 0.0% Native Hawaiian/Other Pacific Islander, 3.1% Some other race, 3.1% Two or more races, 0.0% Hispanic of any race (2008-2012 5-year est.); Average household size: 2.26 (2008-2012 5-year est.); Median age: 40.9 (2008-2012 5-year est.); Males per 100 females: 93.2 (2008-2012 5-year est.); Marriage status: 25.5% never married, 53.3% now married, 9.8% widowed, 11.4% divorced (2008-2012 5-year est.); Foreign born: 1.8% (2008-2012 5-year est.); Ancestry (includes multiple ancestries): 23.6% German, 21.1% English, 11.6% American, 10.7% Irish, 1.8% Scottish (2008-2012 5-year est.).

Economy: Homeowner vacancy rate: 0.0%. Rental vacancy rate: 19.8%. (2008-2012 5-year est.); Employment by occupation: 9.2% management, business, and financial, 1.0% computer, engineering, and science, 8.4% education, legal, community service, arts, and media, 3.2% healthcare practitioners, 19.5% service, 20.0% sales and office, 8.8% natural resources, construction, and maintenance, 29.9% production, transportation, and material moving (2008-2012 5-year est.).

Income: Per capita income: $18,898 (2008-2012 5-year est.); Median household income: $35,205 (2008-2012 5-year est.); Average household income: $41,131 (2008-2012 5-year est.); Percent of households with income of $100,000 or more: 4.5% (2008-2012 5-year est.); Poverty rate: 12.0% (2008-2012 5-year est.).

Taxes: Total city taxes per capita: $150 (2011); City property taxes per capita: $150 (2011).

Education: Percent of population age 25 and over with: High school diploma (including GED) or higher: 88.3% (2008-2012 5-year est.); Bachelor's degree or higher: 11.4% (2008-2012 5-year est.); Master's degree or higher: 3.3% (2008-2012 5-year est.).

School District(s)
Edwards County CUSD 1 (PK-12)
   2011-12 Enrollment: 967 . . . . (618) 445-2814

Housing: Homeownership rate: 72.1% (2008-2012 5-year est.); Median home value: $52,000 (2008-2012 5-year est.); Median contract rent: $286 per month (2008-2012 5-year est.); Median year structure built: 1959 (2008-2012 5-year est.).

Health Insurance: 74.3% Private; 40.0% Public; 7.9% None. (2008-2012 5-year est.)

Safety: Violent crime rate: 10.2 per 10,000 population; Property crime rate: 86.8 per 10,000 population (2012).

Transportation: Commute to work: 87.9% car, 0.4% public transportation, 6.8% walk, 3.0% work from home (2008-2012 5-year est.); Travel time to work: 54.9% less than 15 minutes, 23.6% 15 to 30 minutes, 12.2% 30 to 45 minutes, 7.0% 45 to 60 minutes, 2.3% 60 minutes or more (2008-2012 5-year est.)

Additional Information Contacts
Albion Area Chamber of Commerce . . . . (618) 445-2303
  http://www.albionchamber.com

BONE GAP (village). Covers a land area of 0.599 square miles and a water area of 0 square miles. Located at 38.44° N. Lat; 88.00° W. Long. Elevation is 482 feet.

Population: 271 (1990); 272 (2000); 246 (2010); Density: 350.7 persons per square mile (2008-2012 5-year est.); Race: 100.0% White, 0.0% Black/African American, 0.0% Asian, 0.0% American Indian/Alaska Native, 0.0% Native Hawaiian/Other Pacific Islander, 0.0% Some other race, 0.0% Two or more races, 0.0% Hispanic of any race (2008-2012 5-year est.); Average household size: 2.66 (2008-2012 5-year est.); Median age: 40.5 (2008-2012 5-year est.); Males per 100 females: 90.9 (2008-2012 5-year est.); Marriage status: 17.6% never married, 64.2% now married, 7.5% widowed, 10.7% divorced (2008-2012 5-year est.); Foreign born: 0.0% (2008-2012 5-year est.); Ancestry (includes multiple ancestries): 12.9% German, 7.1% English, 2.9% American, 2.4% Dutch, 1.0% Scottish (2008-2012 5-year est.).

Economy: Homeowner vacancy rate: 0.0%. Rental vacancy rate: 0.0%. (2008-2012 5-year est.); Employment by occupation: 0.0% management, business, and financial, 1.4% computer, engineering, and science, 6.8% education, legal, community service, arts, and media, 0.0% healthcare practitioners, 21.6% service, 18.9% sales and office, 12.2% natural resources, construction, and maintenance, 39.2% production, transportation, and material moving (2008-2012 5-year est.).

Income: Per capita income: $14,875 (2008-2012 5-year est.); Median household income: $32,188 (2008-2012 5-year est.); Average household income: $38,389 (2008-2012 5-year est.); Percent of households with income of $100,000 or more: 3.8% (2008-2012 5-year est.); Poverty rate: 12.4% (2008-2012 5-year est.).

Education: Percent of population age 25 and over with: High school diploma (including GED) or higher: 71.9% (2008-2012 5-year est.); Bachelor's degree or higher: 3.7% (2008-2012 5-year est.); Master's degree or higher: 0.0% (2008-2012 5-year est.).

Housing: Homeownership rate: 87.3% (2008-2012 5-year est.); Median home value: $48,600 (2008-2012 5-year est.); Median contract rent: $363 per month (2008-2012 5-year est.); Median year structure built: 1961 (2008-2012 5-year est.).

Health Insurance: 64.3% Private; 33.3% Public; 13.3% None. (2008-2012 5-year est.)

Transportation: Commute to work: 85.1% car, 0.0% public transportation, 6.8% walk, 8.1% work from home (2008-2012 5-year est.); Travel time to work: 39.7% less than 15 minutes, 27.9% 15 to 30 minutes, 32.4% 30 to 45 minutes, 0.0% 45 to 60 minutes, 0.0% 60 minutes or more (2008-2012 5-year est.)

BROWNS (village). Covers a land area of 0.292 square miles and a water area of 0 square miles. Located at 38.38° N. Lat; 87.98° W. Long. Elevation is 407 feet.

Population: 207 (1990); 175 (2000); 134 (2010); Density: 370.0 persons per square mile (2008-2012 5-year est.); Race: 95.4% White, 0.0% Black/African American, 0.0% Asian, 0.0% American Indian/Alaska Native, 0.0% Native Hawaiian/Other Pacific Islander, 4.6% Some other race, 4.6% Two or more races, 0.0% Hispanic of any race (2008-2012 5-year est.); Average household size: 2.04 (2008-2012 5-year est.); Median age: 51.5 (2008-2012 5-year est.); Males per 100 females: 120.4 (2008-2012 5-year est.); Marriage status: 19.6% never married, 63.9% now married, 9.3% widowed, 7.2% divorced (2008-2012 5-year est.); Foreign born: 0.0% (2008-2012 5-year est.); Ancestry (includes multiple ancestries): 24.1% American, 15.7% German, 14.8% English, 9.3% Irish, 5.6% Belgian (2008-2012 5-year est.).

Economy: Homeowner vacancy rate: 0.0%. Rental vacancy rate: 0.0%. (2008-2012 5-year est.); Employment by occupation: 4.2% management, business, and financial, 0.0% computer, engineering, and science, 0.0% education, legal, community service, arts, and media, 6.9% healthcare practitioners, 11.1% service, 33.3% sales and office, 12.5% natural resources, construction, and maintenance, 31.9% production, transportation, and material moving (2008-2012 5-year est.).

Income: Per capita income: $23,855 (2008-2012 5-year est.); Median household income: $43,646 (2008-2012 5-year est.); Average household income: $47,360 (2008-2012 5-year est.); Percent of households with income of $100,000 or more: 5.7% (2008-2012 5-year est.); Poverty rate: 7.4% (2008-2012 5-year est.).

Education: Percent of population age 25 and over with: High school diploma (including GED) or higher: 76.2% (2008-2012 5-year est.); Bachelor's degree or higher: 0.0% (2008-2012 5-year est.); Master's degree or higher: 0.0% (2008-2012 5-year est.).

Housing: Homeownership rate: 96.2% (2008-2012 5-year est.); Median home value: $45,000 (2008-2012 5-year est.); Median contract rent: <$101 per month (2008-2012 5-year est.); Median year structure built: 1961 (2008-2012 5-year est.).

Health Insurance: 72.2% Private; 24.1% Public; 14.8% None. (2008-2012 5-year est.)

Transportation: Commute to work: 100.0% car, 0.0% public transportation, 0.0% walk, 0.0% work from home (2008-2012 5-year est.); Travel time to work: 33.8% less than 15 minutes, 41.2% 15 to 30 minutes, 20.6% 30 to 45 minutes, 0.0% 45 to 60 minutes, 4.4% 60 minutes or more (2008-2012 5-year est.)

ELLERY (unincorporated postal area)
Zip Code: 62833
   Covers a land area of 46.218 square miles and a water area of 0.184 square miles. Located at 38.36° N. Lat; 88.16° W. Long. Population:

383 (2010); Density: 8.3 persons per square mile (2010); Race: 98.2% White, 0.0% Black/African American, 0.0% Asian, 0.0% American Indian/Alaska Native, 0.0% Native Hawaiian/Other Pacific Islander, 1.8% Some other race, 1.8% Two or more races, 2.3% Hispanic of any race (2010); Average household size: 2.41 (2010); Median age: 45.2 (2010); Males per 100 females: 110.4 (2010); Homeownership rate: 88.1% (2010)

WEST SALEM (village). Covers a land area of 1.562 square miles and a water area of <.001 square miles. Located at 38.52° N. Lat; 88.01° W. Long. Elevation is 525 feet.

History: West Salem was settled in 1838 by German Moravians from North Carolina.

Population: 1,042 (1990); 1,001 (2000); 897 (2010); Density: 595.8 persons per square mile (2008-2012 5-year est.); Race: 97.7% White, 1.9% Black/African American, 0.0% Asian, 0.0% American Indian/Alaska Native, 0.0% Native Hawaiian/Other Pacific Islander, 0.4% Some other race, 0.3% Two or more races, 0.0% Hispanic of any race (2008-2012 5-year est.); Average household size: 2.51 (2008-2012 5-year est.); Median age: 38.7 (2008-2012 5-year est.); Males per 100 females: 88.1 (2008-2012 5-year est.); Marriage status: 27.1% never married, 56.6% now married, 8.4% widowed, 7.9% divorced (2008-2012 5-year est.); Foreign born: 0.4% (2008-2012 5-year est.); Ancestry (includes multiple ancestries): 20.9% German, 18.8% English, 14.6% American, 8.5% Irish, 2.0% Scottish (2008-2012 5-year est.).

Economy: Homeowner vacancy rate: 7.0%. Rental vacancy rate: 0.0%. (2008-2012 5-year est.); Employment by occupation: 9.5% management, business, and financial, 0.9% computer, engineering, and science, 17.1% education, legal, community service, arts, and media, 0.9% healthcare practitioners, 8.7% service, 26.3% sales and office, 5.8% natural resources, construction, and maintenance, 30.9% production, transportation, and material moving (2008-2012 5-year est.).

Income: Per capita income: $18,502 (2008-2012 5-year est.); Median household income: $39,615 (2008-2012 5-year est.); Average household income: $46,003 (2008-2012 5-year est.); Percent of households with income of $100,000 or more: 6.7% (2008-2012 5-year est.); Poverty rate: 7.6% (2008-2012 5-year est.).

Education: Percent of population age 25 and over with: High school diploma (including GED) or higher: 88.4% (2008-2012 5-year est.); Bachelor's degree or higher: 17.5% (2008-2012 5-year est.); Master's degree or higher: 2.8% (2008-2012 5-year est.).

School District(s)

Edwards County CUSD 1 (PK-12)

    2011-12 Enrollment: 967 . . . . (618) 445-2814

Housing: Homeownership rate: 84.3% (2008-2012 5-year est.); Median home value: $48,000 (2008-2012 5-year est.); Median contract rent: $242 per month (2008-2012 5-year est.); Median year structure built: 1950 (2008-2012 5-year est.).

Health Insurance: 61.2% Private; 43.0% Public; 11.5% None. (2008-2012 5-year est.)

Transportation: Commute to work: 92.0% car, 1.2% public transportation, 1.8% walk, 3.9% work from home (2008-2012 5-year est.); Travel time to work: 23.8% less than 15 minutes, 44.4% 15 to 30 minutes, 19.8% 30 to 45 minutes, 0.6% 45 to 60 minutes, 11.4% 60 minutes or more (2008-2012 5-year est.)

Effingham County

Located in southeast central Illinois; drained by the Little Wabash River. Covers a land area of 478.777 square miles, a water area of 1.229 square miles, and is located in the Central Time Zone at 39.05° N. Lat., 88.59° W. Long. The county was founded in 1831. County seat is Effingham.

Effingham County is part of the Effingham, IL Micropolitan Statistical Area. The entire metro area includes: Effingham County, IL

Weather Station: Effingham										Elevation: 606 feet	
	Jan	Feb	Mar	Apr	May	Jun	Jul	Aug	Sep	Oct	Nov	Dec
High	36	41	52	64	74	84	87	86	79	67	54	40
Low	20	22	32	42	52	62	66	64	55	43	35	23
Precip	2.4	2.7	3.2	3.9	5.1	4.2	4.3	2.9	3.1	3.7	4.0	3.3
Snow	5.7	5.1	2.1	0.1	0.0	0.0	0.0	0.0	0.0	tr	1.0	3.8

High and Low temperatures in degrees Fahrenheit; Precipitation and Snow in inches

Population: 31,704 (1990); 34,264 (2000); 34,242 (2010); Race: 97.6% White, 0.3% Black/African American, 0.4% Asian, 0.1% American

Indian/Alaska Native, 0.0% Native Hawaiian/Other Pacific Islander, 1.6% Some other race, 0.8% Two or more races, 1.7% Hispanic of any race (2008-2012 5-year est.); Density: 71.7 persons per square mile (2008-2012 5-year est.); Average household size: 2.48 (2008-2012 5-year est.); Median age: 39.5 (2008-2012 5-year est.); Males per 100 females: 99.1 (2008-2012 5-year est.).

Religion: Six largest groups: 29.6% Catholicism, 18.0% Baptist, 10.7% Lutheran, 6.0% Methodist/Pietist, 2.1% Non-denominational Protestant, 0.8% Latter-day Saints (2010)

Economy: Unemployment rate: 5.6% (April 2014); Total civilian labor force: 17,701 (April 2014); Leading industries: 17.4% manufacturing; 16.6% retail trade; 15.1% health care and social assistance (2012); Farms: 1,302 totaling 287,023 acres (2012); Companies that employ 500 or more persons: 2 (2012); Companies that employ 100 to 499 persons: 25 (2012); Companies that employ less than 100 persons: 1,174 (2012); Black-owned businesses: n/a (2007); Hispanic-owned businesses: n/a (2007); Asian-owned businesses: n/a (2007); Women-owned businesses: n/a (2007); Single-family building permits issued: 22 (2013); Multi-family building permits issued: 13 (2013).

Income: Per capita income: $26,029 (2008-2012 5-year est.); Median household income: $51,009 (2008-2012 5-year est.); Average household income: $64,605 (2008-2012 5-year est.); Percent of households with income of $100,000 or more: 16.5% (2008-2012 5-year est.); Poverty rate: 9.7% (2008-2012 5-year est.); Bankruptcy rate: 2.76% (2013).

Taxes: Total county taxes per capita: $95 (2011); County property taxes per capita: $95 (2011).

Education: Percent of population age 25 and over with: High school diploma (including GED) or higher: 90.5% (2008-2012 5-year est.); Bachelor's degree or higher: 19.3% (2008-2012 5-year est.); Master's degree or higher: 5.7% (2008-2012 5-year est.).

Housing: Homeownership rate: 78.9% (2008-2012 5-year est.); Median home value: $112,800 (2008-2012 5-year est.); Median contract rent: $423 per month (2008-2012 5-year est.); Median year structure built: 1974 (2008-2012 5-year est.)

Health: Birth rate: 130.0 per 10,000 population (2013); Death rate: 93.6 per 10,000 population (2013); Age-adjusted cancer mortality rate: 203.3 deaths per 100,000 population (2011); Number of physicians: 23.6 per 10,000 population (2011); Hospital beds: 42.6 per 10,000 population (2010); Hospital admissions: 2,068.5 per 10,000 population (2010).

Environment: Air Quality Index: 93.9% good, 6.1% moderate, 0.0% unhealthy for sensitive individuals, 0.0% unhealthy (percent of days in 2013)

Elections: 2012 Presidential election results: 23.2% Obama, 75.3% Romney

Additional Information Contacts

Effingham County Government . . . . (217) 342-6535
    http://www.co.effingham.il.us
Effingham County Chamber of Commerce . . . . (217) 342-4147
    http://www.effinghamchamber.org

Effingham County Communities

ALTAMONT (city). Covers a land area of 1.407 square miles and a water area of 0 square miles. Located at 39.06° N. Lat; 88.75° W. Long. Elevation is 620 feet.

History: Altamont was organized in 1872 along the Pennsylvania and Baltimore & Ohio Railroads. Named for a nearby hill, Altamont developed as a wheat shipping center.

Population: 2,296 (1990); 2,283 (2000); 2,319 (2010); Density: 1,519.1 persons per square mile (2008-2012 5-year est.); Race: 97.5% White, 0.0% Black/African American, 0.6% Asian, 0.0% American Indian/Alaska Native, 0.0% Native Hawaiian/Other Pacific Islander, 1.9% Some other race, 1.9% Two or more races, 1.0% Hispanic of any race (2008-2012 5-year est.); Average household size: 2.43 (2008-2012 5-year est.); Median age: 41.8 (2008-2012 5-year est.); Males per 100 females: 101.6 (2008-2012 5-year est.); Marriage status: 27.0% never married, 55.6% now married, 10.5% widowed, 6.8% divorced (2008-2012 5-year est.); Foreign born: 2.5% (2008-2012 5-year est.); Ancestry (includes multiple ancestries): 37.2% German, 20.1% American, 8.3% Irish, 7.9% English, 2.7% Danish (2008-2012 5-year est.).

Economy: Single-family building permits issued: 1 (2013); Multi-family building permits issued: 0 (2013); Homeowner vacancy rate: 0.0%. Rental vacancy rate: 0.0%. (2008-2012 5-year est.); Employment by occupation: 12.2% management, business, and financial, 3.5% computer, engineering, and science, 10.1% education, legal, community service, arts, and media,

2.9% healthcare practitioners, 16.7% service, 25.5% sales and office, 9.4% natural resources, construction, and maintenance, 19.7% production, transportation, and material moving (2008-2012 5-year est.).
Income: Per capita income: $21,621 (2008-2012 5-year est.); Median household income: $48,527 (2008-2012 5-year est.); Average household income: $52,834 (2008-2012 5-year est.); Percent of households with income of $100,000 or more: 12.2% (2008-2012 5-year est.); Poverty rate: 10.3% (2008-2012 5-year est.).
Education: Percent of population age 25 and over with: High school diploma (including GED) or higher: 85.6% (2008-2012 5-year est.); Bachelor's degree or higher: 17.0% (2008-2012 5-year est.); Master's degree or higher: 4.0% (2008-2012 5-year est.).
School District(s)
Altamont CUSD 10 (PK-12)
   2011-12 Enrollment: 809 . . . . (618) 483-6195
Housing: Homeownership rate: 73.7% (2008-2012 5-year est.); Median home value: $81,000 (2008-2012 5-year est.); Median contract rent: $368 per month (2008-2012 5-year est.); Median year structure built: 1967 (2008-2012 5-year est.).
Health Insurance: 69.3% Private; 40.7% Public; 10.4% None. (2008-2012 5-year est.)
Safety: Violent crime rate: 12.9 per 10,000 population; Property crime rate: 133.4 per 10,000 population (2012).
Transportation: Commute to work: 93.0% car, 0.0% public transportation, 4.2% walk, 2.0% work from home (2008-2012 5-year est.); Travel time to work: 26.8% less than 15 minutes, 51.2% 15 to 30 minutes, 15.0% 30 to 45 minutes, 0.4% 45 to 60 minutes, 6.7% 60 minutes or more (2008-2012 5-year est.)
Additional Information Contacts
Altamont Chamber of Commerce . . . . (618) 483-5714
   http://www.altamontchamber.com
City of Altamont . . . . (618) 483-5212
   http://www.altamontil.net

BEECHER CITY (village).
Covers a land area of 0.902 square miles and a water area of 0 square miles. Located at 39.19° N. Lat; 88.79° W. Long. Elevation is 610 feet.
Population: 437 (1990); 493 (2000); 463 (2010); Density: 398.0 persons per square mile (2008-2012 5-year est.); Race: 100.0% White, 0.0% Black/African American, 0.0% Asian, 0.0% American Indian/Alaska Native, 0.0% Native Hawaiian/Other Pacific Islander, 0.0% Some other race, 0.0% Two or more races, 0.0% Hispanic of any race (2008-2012 5-year est.); Average household size: 2.44 (2008-2012 5-year est.); Median age: 34.5 (2008-2012 5-year est.); Males per 100 females: 81.3 (2008-2012 5-year est.); Marriage status: 23.7% never married, 47.4% now married, 13.0% widowed, 15.9% divorced (2008-2012 5-year est.); Foreign born: 0.0% (2008-2012 5-year est.); Ancestry (includes multiple ancestries): 18.9% German, 12.5% Irish, 12.0% American, 6.7% English, 3.6% Scottish (2008-2012 5-year est.).
Economy: Single-family building permits issued: 0 (2013); Multi-family building permits issued: 0 (2013); Homeowner vacancy rate: 5.7%. Rental vacancy rate: 26.2%. (2008-2012 5-year est.); Employment by occupation: 9.2% management, business, and financial, 0.0% computer, engineering, and science, 7.1% education, legal, community service, arts, and media, 1.4% healthcare practitioners, 22.0% service, 18.4% sales and office, 13.5% natural resources, construction, and maintenance, 28.4% production, transportation, and material moving (2008-2012 5-year est.).
Income: Per capita income: $15,701 (2008-2012 5-year est.); Median household income: $31,042 (2008-2012 5-year est.); Average household income: $38,856 (2008-2012 5-year est.); Percent of households with income of $100,000 or more: 4.8% (2008-2012 5-year est.); Poverty rate: 17.8% (2008-2012 5-year est.).
Education: Percent of population age 25 and over with: High school diploma (including GED) or higher: 81.4% (2008-2012 5-year est.); Bachelor's degree or higher: 6.2% (2008-2012 5-year est.); Master's degree or higher: 1.8% (2008-2012 5-year est.).
School District(s)
Beecher City CUSD 20 (PK-12)
   2011-12 Enrollment: 369 . . . . (618) 487-5100
Housing: Homeownership rate: 78.9% (2008-2012 5-year est.); Median home value: $53,600 (2008-2012 5-year est.); Median contract rent: $325 per month (2008-2012 5-year est.); Median year structure built: 1947 (2008-2012 5-year est.).
Health Insurance: 64.1% Private; 36.5% Public; 12.8% None. (2008-2012 5-year est.)

Transportation: Commute to work: 96.3% car, 0.0% public transportation, 1.5% walk, 2.2% work from home (2008-2012 5-year est.); Travel time to work: 9.8% less than 15 minutes, 63.6% 15 to 30 minutes, 24.2% 30 to 45 minutes, 1.5% 45 to 60 minutes, 0.8% 60 minutes or more (2008-2012 5-year est.)

DIETERICH (village).
Covers a land area of 1.160 square miles and a water area of 0 square miles. Located at 39.06° N. Lat; 88.38° W. Long. Elevation is 587 feet.
Population: 568 (1990); 591 (2000); 617 (2010); Density: 494.7 persons per square mile (2008-2012 5-year est.); Race: 98.8% White, 0.0% Black/African American, 0.0% Asian, 0.0% American Indian/Alaska Native, 0.0% Native Hawaiian/Other Pacific Islander, 1.2% Some other race, 1.2% Two or more races, 0.0% Hispanic of any race (2008-2012 5-year est.); Average household size: 2.57 (2008-2012 5-year est.); Median age: 45.4 (2008-2012 5-year est.); Males per 100 females: 97.9 (2008-2012 5-year est.); Marriage status: 19.4% never married, 66.0% now married, 5.8% widowed, 8.8% divorced (2008-2012 5-year est.); Foreign born: 0.0% (2008-2012 5-year est.); Ancestry (includes multiple ancestries): 46.5% German, 17.6% American, 14.1% Irish, 8.0% English, 5.6% French (2008-2012 5-year est.).
Economy: Homeowner vacancy rate: 0.0%. Rental vacancy rate: 0.0%. (2008-2012 5-year est.); Employment by occupation: 12.2% management, business, and financial, 0.4% computer, engineering, and science, 5.1% education, legal, community service, arts, and media, 4.7% healthcare practitioners, 18.4% service, 22.4% sales and office, 14.1% natural resources, construction, and maintenance, 22.7% production, transportation, and material moving (2008-2012 5-year est.).
Income: Per capita income: $22,895 (2008-2012 5-year est.); Median household income: $43,125 (2008-2012 5-year est.); Average household income: $57,349 (2008-2012 5-year est.); Percent of households with income of $100,000 or more: 14.3% (2008-2012 5-year est.); Poverty rate: 12.5% (2008-2012 5-year est.).
Education: Percent of population age 25 and over with: High school diploma (including GED) or higher: 81.3% (2008-2012 5-year est.); Bachelor's degree or higher: 15.1% (2008-2012 5-year est.); Master's degree or higher: 4.6% (2008-2012 5-year est.).
School District(s)
Dieterich CUSD 30 (PK-12)
   2011-12 Enrollment: 443 . . . . (217) 925-5249
Housing: Homeownership rate: 87.0% (2008-2012 5-year est.); Median home value: $86,900 (2008-2012 5-year est.); Median contract rent: $375 per month (2008-2012 5-year est.); Median year structure built: 1965 (2008-2012 5-year est.).
Health Insurance: 61.5% Private; 48.1% Public; 10.8% None. (2008-2012 5-year est.)
Transportation: Commute to work: 97.6% car, 0.0% public transportation, 0.4% walk, 0.8% work from home (2008-2012 5-year est.); Travel time to work: 29.7% less than 15 minutes, 52.8% 15 to 30 minutes, 10.6% 30 to 45 minutes, 2.4% 45 to 60 minutes, 4.5% 60 minutes or more (2008-2012 5-year est.)

EDGEWOOD (village).
Covers a land area of 1.001 square miles and a water area of 0.011 square miles. Located at 38.92° N. Lat; 88.66° W. Long. Elevation is 574 feet.
Population: 502 (1990); 527 (2000); 440 (2010); Density: 388.7 persons per square mile (2008-2012 5-year est.); Race: 95.6% White, 0.0% Black/African American, 3.6% Asian, 0.0% American Indian/Alaska Native, 0.0% Native Hawaiian/Other Pacific Islander, 0.8% Some other race, 0.0% Two or more races, 0.8% Hispanic of any race (2008-2012 5-year est.); Average household size: 2.15 (2008-2012 5-year est.); Median age: 49.5 (2008-2012 5-year est.); Males per 100 females: 82.6 (2008-2012 5-year est.); Marriage status: 26.0% never married, 56.0% now married, 7.1% widowed, 10.9% divorced (2008-2012 5-year est.); Foreign born: 0.8% (2008-2012 5-year est.); Ancestry (includes multiple ancestries): 18.3% German, 8.7% English, 7.2% Irish, 6.4% American, 2.3% Italian (2008-2012 5-year est.).
Economy: Homeowner vacancy rate: 0.0%. Rental vacancy rate: 0.0%. (2008-2012 5-year est.); Employment by occupation: 2.5% management, business, and financial, 0.0% computer, engineering, and science, 0.0% education, legal, community service, arts, and media, 0.0% healthcare practitioners, 27.6% service, 13.6% sales and office, 11.6% natural resources, construction, and maintenance, 44.7% production, transportation, and material moving (2008-2012 5-year est.).

Income: Per capita income: $20,130 (2008-2012 5-year est.); Median household income: $36,750 (2008-2012 5-year est.); Average household income: $42,657 (2008-2012 5-year est.); Percent of households with income of $100,000 or more: 4.4% (2008-2012 5-year est.); Poverty rate: 16.7% (2008-2012 5-year est.).

Education: Percent of population age 25 and over with: High school diploma (including GED) or higher: 74.6% (2008-2012 5-year est.); Bachelor's degree or higher: 1.0% (2008-2012 5-year est.); Master's degree or higher: 0.0% (2008-2012 5-year est.).

School District(s)
Effingham CUSD 40 (PK-12)
   2011-12 Enrollment: 2,760 . . . . (217) 540-1501

Housing: Homeownership rate: 80.7% (2008-2012 5-year est.); Median home value: $55,600 (2008-2012 5-year est.); Median contract rent: $363 per month (2008-2012 5-year est.); Median year structure built: 1957 (2008-2012 5-year est.).

Health Insurance: 59.1% Private; 41.6% Public; 15.9% None. (2008-2012 5-year est.)

Transportation: Commute to work: 96.5% car, 0.0% public transportation, 0.0% walk, 0.0% work from home (2008-2012 5-year est.); Travel time to work: 5.5% less than 15 minutes, 44.7% 15 to 30 minutes, 42.7% 30 to 45 minutes, 0.0% 45 to 60 minutes, 7.0% 60 minutes or more (2008-2012 5-year est.)

EFFINGHAM (city). County seat. Covers a land area of 9.864 square miles and a water area of 0.061 square miles. Located at 39.12° N. Lat; 88.55° W. Long. Elevation is 594 feet.

History: Effingham was settled by German immigrants, and was incorporated as a village in 1861.

Population: 11,851 (1990); 12,384 (2000); 12,328 (2010); Density: 1,246.6 persons per square mile (2008-2012 5-year est.); Race: 97.6% White, 0.6% Black/African American, 0.2% Asian, 0.2% American Indian/Alaska Native, 0.0% Native Hawaiian/Other Pacific Islander, 1.4% Some other race, 0.9% Two or more races, 2.4% Hispanic of any race (2008-2012 5-year est.); Average household size: 2.16 (2008-2012 5-year est.); Median age: 40.1 (2008-2012 5-year est.); Males per 100 females: 94.3 (2008-2012 5-year est.); Marriage status: 25.2% never married, 48.8% now married, 11.7% widowed, 14.3% divorced (2008-2012 5-year est.); Foreign born: 1.7% (2008-2012 5-year est.); Ancestry (includes multiple ancestries): 40.4% German, 12.7% Irish, 9.6% English, 7.3% American, 2.4% Scotch-Irish (2008-2012 5-year est.).

Economy: Single-family building permits issued: 14 (2013); Multi-family building permits issued: 13 (2013); Homeowner vacancy rate: 0.6%. Rental vacancy rate: 5.7%. (2008-2012 5-year est.); Employment by occupation: 11.1% management, business, and financial, 4.0% computer, engineering, and science, 9.4% education, legal, community service, arts, and media, 6.0% healthcare practitioners, 19.0% service, 26.8% sales and office, 6.7% natural resources, construction, and maintenance, 16.8% production, transportation, and material moving (2008-2012 5-year est.).

Income: Per capita income: $25,221 (2008-2012 5-year est.); Median household income: $42,421 (2008-2012 5-year est.); Average household income: $55,487 (2008-2012 5-year est.); Percent of households with income of $100,000 or more: 12.4% (2008-2012 5-year est.); Poverty rate: 12.2% (2008-2012 5-year est.).

Education: Percent of population age 25 and over with: High school diploma (including GED) or higher: 89.0% (2008-2012 5-year est.); Bachelor's degree or higher: 22.5% (2008-2012 5-year est.); Master's degree or higher: 6.3% (2008-2012 5-year est.).

School District(s)
Bond/effingham/fayette Roe (07-12)
   2011-12 Enrollment: n/a . . . . (618) 283-5011
Eastern II Area of Spec Educ (PK-12)
   2011-12 Enrollment: n/a . . . . (217) 348-7700
Effingham CUSD 40 (PK-12)
   2011-12 Enrollment: 2,760 . . . . (217) 540-1501

Housing: Homeownership rate: 64.9% (2008-2012 5-year est.); Median home value: $111,000 (2008-2012 5-year est.); Median contract rent: $436 per month (2008-2012 5-year est.); Median year structure built: 1972 (2008-2012 5-year est.).

Health Insurance: 71.8% Private; 33.8% Public; 8.4% None. (2008-2012 5-year est.)

Hospitals: St. Anthony's Memorial Hospital (146 beds)

Safety: Violent crime rate: 20.3 per 10,000 population; Property crime rate: 340.2 per 10,000 population (2012).

Transportation: Commute to work: 93.0% car, 0.5% public transportation, 1.2% walk, 2.9% work from home (2008-2012 5-year est.); Travel time to work: 68.2% less than 15 minutes, 17.6% 15 to 30 minutes, 8.3% 30 to 45 minutes, 3.2% 45 to 60 minutes, 2.7% 60 minutes or more (2008-2012 5-year est.); Amtrak: Train service available.

Airports: Effingham County Memorial Airport (general aviation)

Additional Information Contacts
City of Effingham . . . . (217) 342-5304
   http://www.effinghamil.com
Effingham County Chamber of Commerce . . . . (217) 342-4147
   http://www.effinghamchamber.org

MASON (town). Covers a land area of 1.287 square miles and a water area of 0.005 square miles. Located at 38.95° N. Lat; 88.63° W. Long. Elevation is 581 feet.

Population: 387 (1990); 396 (2000); 345 (2010); Density: 280.4 persons per square mile (2008-2012 5-year est.); Race: 98.6% White, 0.0% Black/African American, 1.4% Asian, 0.0% American Indian/Alaska Native, 0.0% Native Hawaiian/Other Pacific Islander, 0.0% Some other race, 0.0% Two or more races, 0.0% Hispanic of any race (2008-2012 5-year est.); Average household size: 2.64 (2008-2012 5-year est.); Median age: 36.5 (2008-2012 5-year est.); Males per 100 females: 80.5 (2008-2012 5-year est.); Marriage status: 29.8% never married, 41.5% now married, 9.6% widowed, 19.1% divorced (2008-2012 5-year est.); Foreign born: 0.8% (2008-2012 5-year est.); Ancestry (includes multiple ancestries): 24.9% German, 10.5% American, 8.3% English, 7.5% Irish, 2.2% Dutch (2008-2012 5-year est.).

Economy: Homeowner vacancy rate: 0.0%. Rental vacancy rate: 0.0%. (2008-2012 5-year est.); Employment by occupation: 5.1% management, business, and financial, 0.0% computer, engineering, and science, 1.9% education, legal, community service, arts, and media, 1.3% healthcare practitioners, 15.3% service, 24.2% sales and office, 12.7% natural resources, construction, and maintenance, 39.5% production, transportation, and material moving (2008-2012 5-year est.).

Income: Per capita income: $15,298 (2008-2012 5-year est.); Median household income: $37,083 (2008-2012 5-year est.); Average household income: $40,118 (2008-2012 5-year est.); Percent of households with income of $100,000 or more: 0.7% (2008-2012 5-year est.); Poverty rate: 17.7% (2008-2012 5-year est.).

Education: Percent of population age 25 and over with: High school diploma (including GED) or higher: 73.9% (2008-2012 5-year est.); Bachelor's degree or higher: 2.7% (2008-2012 5-year est.); Master's degree or higher: 1.4% (2008-2012 5-year est.).

Housing: Homeownership rate: 83.9% (2008-2012 5-year est.); Median home value: $54,400 (2008-2012 5-year est.); Median contract rent: $329 per month (2008-2012 5-year est.); Median year structure built: 1963 (2008-2012 5-year est.).

Health Insurance: 49.9% Private; 50.1% Public; 18.0% None. (2008-2012 5-year est.)

Transportation: Commute to work: 89.2% car, 0.0% public transportation, 0.7% walk, 8.1% work from home (2008-2012 5-year est.); Travel time to work: 8.8% less than 15 minutes, 54.4% 15 to 30 minutes, 24.3% 30 to 45 minutes, 3.7% 45 to 60 minutes, 8.8% 60 minutes or more (2008-2012 5-year est.)

MONTROSE (village). Covers a land area of 0.690 square miles and a water area of 0 square miles. Located at 39.17° N. Lat; 88.38° W. Long. Elevation is 600 feet.

Population: 306 (1990); 257 (2000); 201 (2010); Density: 302.7 persons per square mile (2008-2012 5-year est.); Race: 93.3% White, 0.0% Black/African American, 0.0% Asian, 0.0% American Indian/Alaska Native, 0.0% Native Hawaiian/Other Pacific Islander, 6.7% Some other race, 6.7% Two or more races, 2.9% Hispanic of any race (2008-2012 5-year est.); Average household size: 2.52 (2008-2012 5-year est.); Median age: 42.4 (2008-2012 5-year est.); Males per 100 females: 69.9 (2008-2012 5-year est.); Marriage status: 29.1% never married, 34.9% now married, 18.9% widowed, 17.1% divorced (2008-2012 5-year est.); Foreign born: 0.0% (2008-2012 5-year est.); Ancestry (includes multiple ancestries): 23.9% English, 16.3% German, 11.5% American, 6.2% Irish, 4.3% Dutch (2008-2012 5-year est.).

Economy: Single-family building permits issued: 0 (2013); Multi-family building permits issued: 0 (2013); Homeowner vacancy rate: 0.0%. Rental vacancy rate: 20.0%. (2008-2012 5-year est.); Employment by occupation: 7.4% management, business, and financial, 0.0% computer, engineering, and science, 4.3% education, legal, community service, arts, and media,

1.1% healthcare practitioners, 11.7% service, 20.2% sales and office, 21.3% natural resources, construction, and maintenance, 34.0% production, transportation, and material moving (2008-2012 5-year est.).
Income: Per capita income: $16,015 (2008-2012 5-year est.); Median household income: $31,250 (2008-2012 5-year est.); Average household income: $37,853 (2008-2012 5-year est.); Percent of households with income of $100,000 or more: 2.4% (2008-2012 5-year est.); Poverty rate: 12.4% (2008-2012 5-year est.).
Education: Percent of population age 25 and over with: High school diploma (including GED) or higher: 77.0% (2008-2012 5-year est.); Bachelor's degree or higher: 10.1% (2008-2012 5-year est.); Master's degree or higher: 2.0% (2008-2012 5-year est.).
Housing: Homeownership rate: 88.0% (2008-2012 5-year est.); Median home value: $55,600 (2008-2012 5-year est.); Median contract rent: $417 per month (2008-2012 5-year est.); Median year structure built: 1959 (2008-2012 5-year est.).
Health Insurance: 64.1% Private; 41.1% Public; 8.1% None. (2008-2012 5-year est.)
Transportation: Commute to work: 96.8% car, 1.1% public transportation, 2.2% walk, 0.0% work from home (2008-2012 5-year est.); Travel time to work: 20.4% less than 15 minutes, 50.5% 15 to 30 minutes, 23.7% 30 to 45 minutes, 3.2% 45 to 60 minutes, 2.2% 60 minutes or more (2008-2012 5-year est.)

SHUMWAY (village).
Covers a land area of 0.332 square miles and a water area of 0 square miles. Located at 39.18° N. Lat; 88.65° W. Long. Elevation is 656 feet.
Population: 243 (1990); 217 (2000); 202 (2010); Density: 451.9 persons per square mile (2008-2012 5-year est.); Race: 100.0% White, 0.0% Black/African American, 0.0% Asian, 0.0% American Indian/Alaska Native, 0.0% Native Hawaiian/Other Pacific Islander, 0.0% Some other race, 0.0% Two or more races, 0.0% Hispanic of any race (2008-2012 5-year est.); Average household size: 2.50 (2008-2012 5-year est.); Median age: 41.5 (2008-2012 5-year est.); Males per 100 females: 94.8 (2008-2012 5-year est.); Marriage status: 20.0% never married, 67.2% now married, 5.6% widowed, 7.2% divorced (2008-2012 5-year est.); Foreign born: 0.0% (2008-2012 5-year est.); Ancestry (includes multiple ancestries): 43.3% German, 12.7% Irish, 11.3% American, 2.7% French, 2.7% Polish (2008-2012 5-year est.).
Economy: Homeowner vacancy rate: 0.0%. Rental vacancy rate: 0.0%. (2008-2012 5-year est.); Employment by occupation: 12.3% management, business, and financial, 1.2% computer, engineering, and science, 4.9% education, legal, community service, arts, and media, 8.6% healthcare practitioners, 18.5% service, 21.0% sales and office, 7.4% natural resources, construction, and maintenance, 25.9% production, transportation, and material moving (2008-2012 5-year est.).
Income: Per capita income: $17,653 (2008-2012 5-year est.); Median household income: $40,000 (2008-2012 5-year est.); Average household income: $44,588 (2008-2012 5-year est.); Percent of households with income of $100,000 or more: 1.7% (2008-2012 5-year est.); Poverty rate: 14.0% (2008-2012 5-year est.).
Education: Percent of population age 25 and over with: High school diploma (including GED) or higher: 86.8% (2008-2012 5-year est.); Bachelor's degree or higher: 10.4% (2008-2012 5-year est.); Master's degree or higher: 3.8% (2008-2012 5-year est.).
Housing: Homeownership rate: 85.0% (2008-2012 5-year est.); Median home value: $48,500 (2008-2012 5-year est.); Median contract rent: $413 per month (2008-2012 5-year est.); Median year structure built: 1947 (2008-2012 5-year est.).
Health Insurance: 64.0% Private; 48.7% Public; 4.7% None. (2008-2012 5-year est.)
Transportation: Commute to work: 100.0% car, 0.0% public transportation, 0.0% walk, 0.0% work from home (2008-2012 5-year est.); Travel time to work: 30.4% less than 15 minutes, 40.5% 15 to 30 minutes, 24.1% 30 to 45 minutes, 2.5% 45 to 60 minutes, 2.5% 60 minutes or more (2008-2012 5-year est.)

TEUTOPOLIS (village).
Covers a land area of 1.629 square miles and a water area of 0 square miles. Located at 39.13° N. Lat; 88.48° W. Long. Elevation is 607 feet.
History: Teutopolis was established in 1839 by a group of German Catholics from Cincinnati, Ohio.
Population: 1,417 (1990); 1,559 (2000); 1,530 (2010); Density: 1,115.1 persons per square mile (2008-2012 5-year est.); Race: 98.7% White, 0.2% Black/African American, 0.0% Asian, 0.0% American Indian/Alaska

Native, 0.0% Native Hawaiian/Other Pacific Islander, 1.1% Some other race, 0.0% Two or more races, 0.6% Hispanic of any race (2008-2012 5-year est.); Average household size: 2.76 (2008-2012 5-year est.); Median age: 34.9 (2008-2012 5-year est.); Males per 100 females: 116.6 (2008-2012 5-year est.); Marriage status: 23.8% never married, 69.6% now married, 5.1% widowed, 1.5% divorced (2008-2012 5-year est.); Foreign born: 0.6% (2008-2012 5-year est.); Ancestry (includes multiple ancestries): 62.9% German, 6.9% American, 5.5% Irish, 3.9% English, 1.6% French (2008-2012 5-year est.).
Economy: Single-family building permits issued: 7 (2013); Multi-family building permits issued: 0 (2013); Homeowner vacancy rate: 0.0%. Rental vacancy rate: 0.0%. (2008-2012 5-year est.); Employment by occupation: 13.1% management, business, and financial, 4.2% computer, engineering, and science, 9.7% education, legal, community service, arts, and media, 4.1% healthcare practitioners, 17.1% service, 28.2% sales and office, 6.3% natural resources, construction, and maintenance, 17.2% production, transportation, and material moving (2008-2012 5-year est.).
Income: Per capita income: $30,138 (2008-2012 5-year est.); Median household income: $62,679 (2008-2012 5-year est.); Average household income: $82,172 (2008-2012 5-year est.); Percent of households with income of $100,000 or more: 20.3% (2008-2012 5-year est.); Poverty rate: 1.5% (2008-2012 5-year est.).
Education: Percent of population age 25 and over with: High school diploma (including GED) or higher: 93.9% (2008-2012 5-year est.); Bachelor's degree or higher: 28.0% (2008-2012 5-year est.); Master's degree or higher: 7.5% (2008-2012 5-year est.).
School District(s)
Teutopolis CUSD 50 (PK-12)
    2011-12 Enrollment: 1,118 . . . . (217) 857-3535
Housing: Homeownership rate: 85.2% (2008-2012 5-year est.); Median home value: $146,700 (2008-2012 5-year est.); Median contract rent: $453 per month (2008-2012 5-year est.); Median year structure built: 1969 (2008-2012 5-year est.).
Health Insurance: 86.6% Private; 22.8% Public; 1.8% None. (2008-2012 5-year est.)
Safety: Violent crime rate: 0.0 per 10,000 population; Property crime rate: 65.3 per 10,000 population (2012).
Transportation: Commute to work: 93.1% car, 0.3% public transportation, 1.3% walk, 3.5% work from home (2008-2012 5-year est.); Travel time to work: 58.1% less than 15 minutes, 28.8% 15 to 30 minutes, 6.8% 30 to 45 minutes, 1.2% 45 to 60 minutes, 5.2% 60 minutes or more (2008-2012 5-year est.)

WATSON (village).
Covers a land area of 1.119 square miles and a water area of 0 square miles. Located at 39.03° N. Lat; 88.57° W. Long. Elevation is 561 feet.
Population: 646 (1990); 729 (2000); 754 (2010); Density: 635.6 persons per square mile (2008-2012 5-year est.); Race: 97.5% White, 0.0% Black/African American, 1.4% Asian, 0.0% American Indian/Alaska Native, 0.0% Native Hawaiian/Other Pacific Islander, 1.1% Some other race, 1.1% Two or more races, 0.0% Hispanic of any race (2008-2012 5-year est.); Average household size: 2.90 (2008-2012 5-year est.); Median age: 32.5 (2008-2012 5-year est.); Males per 100 females: 104.9 (2008-2012 5-year est.); Marriage status: 24.1% never married, 59.9% now married, 3.2% widowed, 12.8% divorced (2008-2012 5-year est.); Foreign born: 0.8% (2008-2012 5-year est.); Ancestry (includes multiple ancestries): 32.5% German, 13.6% Irish, 11.3% English, 7.9% American, 7.0% Italian (2008-2012 5-year est.).
Economy: Homeowner vacancy rate: 3.0%. Rental vacancy rate: 31.0%. (2008-2012 5-year est.); Employment by occupation: 2.9% management, business, and financial, 4.6% computer, engineering, and science, 2.9% education, legal, community service, arts, and media, 2.3% healthcare practitioners, 20.6% service, 29.5% sales and office, 10.3% natural resources, construction, and maintenance, 26.9% production, transportation, and material moving (2008-2012 5-year est.).
Income: Per capita income: $16,172 (2008-2012 5-year est.); Median household income: $49,226 (2008-2012 5-year est.); Average household income: $45,693 (2008-2012 5-year est.); Percent of households with income of $100,000 or more: 1.6% (2008-2012 5-year est.); Poverty rate: 12.3% (2008-2012 5-year est.).
Education: Percent of population age 25 and over with: High school diploma (including GED) or higher: 93.0% (2008-2012 5-year est.); Bachelor's degree or higher: 13.3% (2008-2012 5-year est.); Master's degree or higher: 0.9% (2008-2012 5-year est.).

Housing: Homeownership rate: 91.8% (2008-2012 5-year est.); Median home value: $74,300 (2008-2012 5-year est.); Median contract rent: $345 per month (2008-2012 5-year est.); Median year structure built: 1977 (2008-2012 5-year est.).

Health Insurance: 71.4% Private; 27.4% Public; 12.5% None. (2008-2012 5-year est.)

Transportation: Commute to work: 99.4% car, 0.0% public transportation, 0.0% walk, 0.6% work from home (2008-2012 5-year est.); Travel time to work: 23.8% less than 15 minutes, 56.2% 15 to 30 minutes, 13.2% 30 to 45 minutes, 0.9% 45 to 60 minutes, 5.9% 60 minutes or more (2008-2012 5-year est.)

Fayette County

Located in south central Illinois; drained by the Kaskaskia River. Covers a land area of 716.482 square miles, a water area of 8.861 square miles, and is located in the Central Time Zone at 39.00° N. Lat., 89.02° W. Long. The county was founded in 1821. County seat is Vandalia.

Weather Station: Vandalia   Elevation: 540 feet

	Jan	Feb	Mar	Apr	May	Jun	Jul	Aug	Sep	Oct	Nov	Dec
High	37	42	52	65	75	84	87	87	80	67	54	41
Low	21	24	33	43	53	63	66	64	55	43	34	24
Precip	2.8	2.6	3.4	3.9	5.1	4.0	3.5	2.8	3.2	3.4	3.6	3.0
Snow	5.1	3.0	1.5	tr	0.0	0.0	0.0	0.0	0.0	tr	0.7	3.2

High and Low temperatures in degrees Fahrenheit; Precipitation and Snow in inches

Population: 20,893 (1990); 21,802 (2000); 22,140 (2010); Race: 93.8% White, 1.8% Black/African American, 1.2% Asian, 0.1% American Indian/Alaska Native, 0.1% Native Hawaiian/Other Pacific Islander, 3.0% Some other race, 2.6% Two or more races, 1.4% Hispanic of any race (2008-2012 5-year est.); Density: 30.7 persons per square mile (2008-2012 5-year est.); Average household size: 2.58 (2008-2012 5-year est.); Median age: 39.7 (2008-2012 5-year est.); Males per 100 females: 103.3 (2008-2012 5-year est.).

Religion: Six largest groups: 25.1% Baptist, 9.0% Lutheran, 4.9% Methodist/Pietist, 2.6% Catholicism, 1.5% Holiness, 1.3% Presbyterian-Reformed (2010)

Economy: Unemployment rate: 8.1% (April 2014); Total civilian labor force: 9,142 (April 2014); Leading industries: 19.6% retail trade; 19.5% health care and social assistance; 10.6% manufacturing (2012); Farms: 1,240 totaling 303,140 acres (2012); Companies that employ 500 or more persons: 0 (2012); Companies that employ 100 to 499 persons: 6 (2012); Companies that employ less than 100 persons: 484 (2012); Black-owned businesses: n/a (2007); Hispanic-owned businesses: n/a (2007); Asian-owned businesses: n/a (2007); Women-owned businesses: n/a (2007); Single-family building permits issued: 0 (2013); Multi-family building permits issued: 0 (2013).

Income: Per capita income: $22,194 (2008-2012 5-year est.); Median household income: $43,724 (2008-2012 5-year est.); Average household income: $56,109 (2008-2012 5-year est.); Percent of households with income of $100,000 or more: 12.9% (2008-2012 5-year est.); Poverty rate: 18.3% (2008-2012 5-year est.); Bankruptcy rate: 1.73% (2013).

Education: Percent of population age 25 and over with: High school diploma (including GED) or higher: 84.7% (2008-2012 5-year est.); Bachelor's degree or higher: 13.9% (2008-2012 5-year est.); Master's degree or higher: 5.5% (2008-2012 5-year est.).

Housing: Homeownership rate: 81.0% (2008-2012 5-year est.); Median home value: $79,600 (2008-2012 5-year est.); Median contract rent: $359 per month (2008-2012 5-year est.); Median year structure built: 1963 (2008-2012 5-year est.)

Health: Birth rate: 109.7 per 10,000 population (2013); Death rate: 90.7 per 10,000 population (2013); Age-adjusted cancer mortality rate: 163.8 deaths per 100,000 population (2011); Number of physicians: 3.2 per 10,000 population (2011); Hospital beds: 49.7 per 10,000 population (2010); Hospital admissions: 663.1 per 10,000 population (2010).

Elections: 2012 Presidential election results: 31.8% Obama, 66.4% Romney

National and State Parks: Carlyle Lake State Wildlife Management Area; Ramsey Lake State Park; Vandalia State House Historic Site

Additional Information Contacts

Fayette County Government . . . . (618) 283-5000
    http://209.175.254.253

Fayette County Communities

BINGHAM (village). Covers a land area of 0.274 square miles and a water area of 0 square miles. Located at 39.11° N. Lat; 89.21° W. Long. Elevation is 600 feet.

Population: 98 (1990); 117 (2000); 83 (2010); Density: 416.7 persons per square mile (2008-2012 5-year est.); Race: 100.0% White, 0.0% Black/African American, 0.0% Asian, 0.0% American Indian/Alaska Native, 0.0% Native Hawaiian/Other Pacific Islander, 0.0% Some other race, 0.0% Two or more races, 0.0% Hispanic of any race (2008-2012 5-year est.); Average household size: 3.17 (2008-2012 5-year est.); Median age: 29.7 (2008-2012 5-year est.); Males per 100 females: 171.4 (2008-2012 5-year est.); Marriage status: 28.4% never married, 55.7% now married, 2.3% widowed, 13.6% divorced (2008-2012 5-year est.); Foreign born: 0.0% (2008-2012 5-year est.); Ancestry (includes multiple ancestries): 15.8% German, 14.0% Irish, 6.1% Dutch, 0.9% Polish, 0.9% English (2008-2012 5-year est.).

Economy: Homeowner vacancy rate: 0.0%. Rental vacancy rate: 0.0%. (2008-2012 5-year est.); Employment by occupation: 20.6% management, business, and financial, 0.0% computer, engineering, and science, 0.0% education, legal, community service, arts, and media, 0.0% healthcare practitioners, 0.0% service, 20.6% sales and office, 20.6% natural resources, construction, and maintenance, 38.2% production, transportation, and material moving (2008-2012 5-year est.).

Income: Per capita income: $7,987 (2008-2012 5-year est.); Median household income: $21,250 (2008-2012 5-year est.); Average household income: $24,953 (2008-2012 5-year est.); Percent of households with income of $100,000 or more: n/a (2008-2012 5-year est.); Poverty rate: 53.5% (2008-2012 5-year est.).

Education: Percent of population age 25 and over with: High school diploma (including GED) or higher: 59.1% (2008-2012 5-year est.); Bachelor's degree or higher: 0.0% (2008-2012 5-year est.); Master's degree or higher: 0.0% (2008-2012 5-year est.).

Housing: Homeownership rate: 83.3% (2008-2012 5-year est.); Median home value: $55,000 (2008-2012 5-year est.); Median contract rent: $225 per month (2008-2012 5-year est.); Median year structure built: 1963 (2008-2012 5-year est.).

Health Insurance: 24.6% Private; 69.3% Public; 20.2% None. (2008-2012 5-year est.)

Transportation: Commute to work: 88.2% car, 0.0% public transportation, 0.0% walk, 0.0% work from home (2008-2012 5-year est.); Travel time to work: 38.2% less than 15 minutes, 11.8% 15 to 30 minutes, 0.0% 30 to 45 minutes, 50.0% 45 to 60 minutes, 0.0% 60 minutes or more (2008-2012 5-year est.)

BROWNSTOWN (village). Covers a land area of 0.774 square miles and a water area of 0 square miles. Located at 38.99° N. Lat; 88.96° W. Long. Elevation is 594 feet.

Population: 668 (1990); 705 (2000); 759 (2010); Density: 957.1 persons per square mile (2008-2012 5-year est.); Race: 89.9% White, 0.1% Black/African American, 0.0% Asian, 0.0% American Indian/Alaska Native, 0.0% Native Hawaiian/Other Pacific Islander, 10.0% Some other race, 8.1% Two or more races, 2.2% Hispanic of any race (2008-2012 5-year est.); Average household size: 2.45 (2008-2012 5-year est.); Median age: 39.3 (2008-2012 5-year est.); Males per 100 females: 83.4 (2008-2012 5-year est.); Marriage status: 21.4% never married, 50.3% now married, 11.8% widowed, 16.5% divorced (2008-2012 5-year est.); Foreign born: 0.0% (2008-2012 5-year est.); Ancestry (includes multiple ancestries): 18.1% German, 12.8% American, 10.5% Irish, 8.0% English, 4.3% French (2008-2012 5-year est.).

Economy: Homeowner vacancy rate: 0.0%. Rental vacancy rate: 0.0%. (2008-2012 5-year est.); Employment by occupation: 2.2% management, business, and financial, 1.4% computer, engineering, and science, 11.2% education, legal, community service, arts, and media, 9.4% healthcare practitioners, 25.2% service, 21.9% sales and office, 11.9% natural resources, construction, and maintenance, 16.9% production, transportation, and material moving (2008-2012 5-year est.).

Income: Per capita income: $18,720 (2008-2012 5-year est.); Median household income: $24,625 (2008-2012 5-year est.); Average household income: $41,721 (2008-2012 5-year est.); Percent of households with income of $100,000 or more: 3.7% (2008-2012 5-year est.); Poverty rate: 27.3% (2008-2012 5-year est.).

Education: Percent of population age 25 and over with: High school diploma (including GED) or higher: 81.4% (2008-2012 5-year est.);

Bachelor's degree or higher: 8.0% (2008-2012 5-year est.); Master's degree or higher: 2.6% (2008-2012 5-year est.).

School District(s)

Brownstown CUSD 201 (PK-12)

    2011-12 Enrollment: 399 . . . . (618) 427-3355

Housing: Homeownership rate: 73.4% (2008-2012 5-year est.); Median home value: $61,800 (2008-2012 5-year est.); Median contract rent: $306 per month (2008-2012 5-year est.); Median year structure built: 1958 (2008-2012 5-year est.).

Health Insurance: 38.2% Private; 59.0% Public; 17.7% None. (2008-2012 5-year est.)

Transportation: Commute to work: 86.3% car, 0.7% public transportation, 4.3% walk, 8.6% work from home (2008-2012 5-year est.); Travel time to work: 39.8% less than 15 minutes, 24.8% 15 to 30 minutes, 16.9% 30 to 45 minutes, 5.9% 45 to 60 minutes, 12.6% 60 minutes or more (2008-2012 5-year est.)

FARINA (village). Covers a land area of 1.457 square miles and a water area of 0.007 square miles. Located at 38.83° N. Lat; 88.78° W. Long. Elevation is 581 feet.

Population: 575 (1990); 558 (2000); 518 (2010); Density: 378.8 persons per square mile (2008-2012 5-year est.); Race: 98.2% White, 0.5% Black/African American, 0.0% Asian, 0.0% American Indian/Alaska Native, 0.0% Native Hawaiian/Other Pacific Islander, 1.3% Some other race, 0.5% Two or more races, 1.3% Hispanic of any race (2008-2012 5-year est.); Average household size: 2.67 (2008-2012 5-year est.); Median age: 36.0 (2008-2012 5-year est.); Males per 100 females: 109.1 (2008-2012 5-year est.); Marriage status: 24.7% never married, 60.6% now married, 5.9% widowed, 8.8% divorced (2008-2012 5-year est.); Foreign born: 1.3% (2008-2012 5-year est.); Ancestry (includes multiple ancestries): 27.9% American, 18.8% German, 10.9% Irish, 8.9% English, 1.8% Welsh (2008-2012 5-year est.).

Economy: Homeowner vacancy rate: 0.0%. Rental vacancy rate: 28.8%. (2008-2012 5-year est.); Employment by occupation: 0.0% management, business, and financial, 2.9% computer, engineering, and science, 0.8% education, legal, community service, arts, and media, 7.1% healthcare practitioners, 17.6% service, 24.8% sales and office, 10.1% natural resources, construction, and maintenance, 36.6% production, transportation, and material moving (2008-2012 5-year est.).

Income: Per capita income: $19,835 (2008-2012 5-year est.); Median household income: $34,792 (2008-2012 5-year est.); Average household income: $50,365 (2008-2012 5-year est.); Percent of households with income of $100,000 or more: 8.4% (2008-2012 5-year est.); Poverty rate: 22.5% (2008-2012 5-year est.).

Education: Percent of population age 25 and over with: High school diploma (including GED) or higher: 82.4% (2008-2012 5-year est.); Bachelor's degree or higher: 10.9% (2008-2012 5-year est.); Master's degree or higher: 2.3% (2008-2012 5-year est.).

School District(s)

South Central CUD 401 (PK-12)

    2011-12 Enrollment: 723 . . . . (618) 547-3414

Housing: Homeownership rate: 76.8% (2008-2012 5-year est.); Median home value: $57,300 (2008-2012 5-year est.); Median contract rent: $367 per month (2008-2012 5-year est.); Median year structure built: 1957 (2008-2012 5-year est.).

Health Insurance: 52.0% Private; 58.5% Public; 10.0% None. (2008-2012 5-year est.)

Transportation: Commute to work: 88.0% car, 1.7% public transportation, 0.9% walk, 7.3% work from home (2008-2012 5-year est.); Travel time to work: 28.1% less than 15 minutes, 28.6% 15 to 30 minutes, 28.6% 30 to 45 minutes, 2.3% 45 to 60 minutes, 12.4% 60 minutes or more (2008-2012 5-year est.).

RAMSEY (village). Covers a land area of 1.011 square miles and a water area of 0 square miles. Located at 39.14° N. Lat; 89.11° W. Long. Elevation is 610 feet.

Population: 963 (1990); 1,056 (2000); 1,037 (2010); Density: 1,098.9 persons per square mile (2008-2012 5-year est.); Race: 99.2% White, 0.0% Black/African American, 0.0% Asian, 0.0% American Indian/Alaska Native, 0.0% Native Hawaiian/Other Pacific Islander, 0.8% Some other race, 0.8% Two or more races, 0.0% Hispanic of any race (2008-2012 5-year est.); Average household size: 2.45 (2008-2012 5-year est.); Median age: 31.5 (2008-2012 5-year est.); Males per 100 females: 89.9 (2008-2012 5-year est.); Marriage status: 31.3% never married, 45.3% now married, 12.6% widowed, 10.9% divorced (2008-2012 5-year est.);

Foreign born: 0.0% (2008-2012 5-year est.); Ancestry (includes multiple ancestries): 26.1% German, 23.9% American, 18.5% Irish, 3.7% Italian, 3.4% English (2008-2012 5-year est.).

Economy: Homeowner vacancy rate: 0.9%. Rental vacancy rate: 3.1%. (2008-2012 5-year est.); Employment by occupation: 2.5% management, business, and financial, 8.7% computer, engineering, and science, 4.6% education, legal, community service, arts, and media, 1.4% healthcare practitioners, 28.1% service, 19.0% sales and office, 14.9% natural resources, construction, and maintenance, 20.8% production, transportation, and material moving (2008-2012 5-year est.).

Income: Per capita income: $16,248 (2008-2012 5-year est.); Median household income: $30,455 (2008-2012 5-year est.); Average household income: $38,133 (2008-2012 5-year est.); Percent of households with income of $100,000 or more: 3.7% (2008-2012 5-year est.); Poverty rate: 21.4% (2008-2012 5-year est.).

Education: Percent of population age 25 and over with: High school diploma (including GED) or higher: 80.3% (2008-2012 5-year est.); Bachelor's degree or higher: 4.2% (2008-2012 5-year est.); Master's degree or higher: 1.5% (2008-2012 5-year est.).

School District(s)

Ramsey CUSD 204 (PK-12)

    2011-12 Enrollment: 507 . . . . (618) 423-2335

Housing: Homeownership rate: 72.7% (2008-2012 5-year est.); Median home value: $58,000 (2008-2012 5-year est.); Median contract rent: $287 per month (2008-2012 5-year est.); Median year structure built: 1963 (2008-2012 5-year est.).

Health Insurance: 53.8% Private; 46.8% Public; 11.7% None. (2008-2012 5-year est.)

Safety: Violent crime rate: 29.0 per 10,000 population; Property crime rate: 193.1 per 10,000 population (2012).

Transportation: Commute to work: 96.7% car, 0.0% public transportation, 0.7% walk, 0.7% work from home (2008-2012 5-year est.); Travel time to work: 20.7% less than 15 minutes, 46.6% 15 to 30 minutes, 15.1% 30 to 45 minutes, 4.5% 45 to 60 minutes, 13.2% 60 minutes or more (2008-2012 5-year est.)

SAINT ELMO (city). Covers a land area of 0.953 square miles and a water area of 0.024 square miles. Located at 39.02° N. Lat; 88.85° W. Long. Elevation is 620 feet.

History: St. Elmo was settled in 1830 by a group of Kentucky Catholics, and developed as a railroad and brick manufacturing town. Later, oil was discovered and the economy boomed.

Population: 1,473 (1990); 1,456 (2000); 1,426 (2010); Density: 1,634.3 persons per square mile (2008-2012 5-year est.); Race: 98.9% White, 0.0% Black/African American, 0.0% Asian, 0.0% American Indian/Alaska Native, 0.0% Native Hawaiian/Other Pacific Islander, 1.1% Some other race, 1.1% Two or more races, 1.2% Hispanic of any race (2008-2012 5-year est.); Average household size: 2.45 (2008-2012 5-year est.); Median age: 37.9 (2008-2012 5-year est.); Males per 100 females: 94.0 (2008-2012 5-year est.); Marriage status: 22.4% never married, 57.9% now married, 9.2% widowed, 10.4% divorced (2008-2012 5-year est.); Foreign born: 0.6% (2008-2012 5-year est.); Ancestry (includes multiple ancestries): 17.8% German, 16.0% Irish, 15.0% American, 8.8% English, 3.2% Dutch (2008-2012 5-year est.).

Economy: Single-family building permits issued: 0 (2013); Multi-family building permits issued: 0 (2013); Homeowner vacancy rate: 4.3%. Rental vacancy rate: 5.4%. (2008-2012 5-year est.); Employment by occupation: 6.9% management, business, and financial, 0.7% computer, engineering, and science, 4.0% education, legal, community service, arts, and media, 1.6% healthcare practitioners, 29.0% service, 19.8% sales and office, 16.2% natural resources, construction, and maintenance, 21.7% production, transportation, and material moving (2008-2012 5-year est.).

Income: Per capita income: $16,336 (2008-2012 5-year est.); Median household income: $33,507 (2008-2012 5-year est.); Average household income: $38,416 (2008-2012 5-year est.); Percent of households with income of $100,000 or more: 2.4% (2008-2012 5-year est.); Poverty rate: 25.4% (2008-2012 5-year est.).

Education: Percent of population age 25 and over with: High school diploma (including GED) or higher: 81.9% (2008-2012 5-year est.); Bachelor's degree or higher: 7.4% (2008-2012 5-year est.); Master's degree or higher: 3.1% (2008-2012 5-year est.).

School District(s)

Saint Elmo CUSD 202 (PK-12)

    2011-12 Enrollment: 494 . . . . (618) 829-3264

Housing: Homeownership rate: 77.4% (2008-2012 5-year est.); Median home value: $59,200 (2008-2012 5-year est.); Median contract rent: $266 per month (2008-2012 5-year est.); Median year structure built: 1960 (2008-2012 5-year est.).

Health Insurance: 52.6% Private; 52.2% Public; 14.0% None. (2008-2012 5-year est.)

Transportation: Commute to work: 89.2% car, 1.2% public transportation, 3.5% walk, 4.8% work from home (2008-2012 5-year est.); Travel time to work: 26.4% less than 15 minutes, 37.6% 15 to 30 minutes, 27.5% 30 to 45 minutes, 5.5% 45 to 60 minutes, 3.1% 60 minutes or more (2008-2012 5-year est.)

SAINT PETER (village). Covers a land area of 0.521 square miles and a water area of 0 square miles. Located at 38.87° N. Lat; 88.85° W. Long. Elevation is 597 feet.

Population: 353 (1990); 386 (2000); 359 (2010); Density: 576.3 persons per square mile (2008-2012 5-year est.); Race: 100.0% White, 0.0% Black/African American, 0.0% Asian, 0.0% American Indian/Alaska Native, 0.0% Native Hawaiian/Other Pacific Islander, 0.0% Some other race, 0.0% Two or more races, 0.0% Hispanic of any race (2008-2012 5-year est.); Average household size: 2.16 (2008-2012 5-year est.); Median age: 43.2 (2008-2012 5-year est.); Males per 100 females: 85.2 (2008-2012 5-year est.); Marriage status: 32.8% never married, 40.1% now married, 13.5% widowed, 13.5% divorced (2008-2012 5-year est.); Foreign born: 0.0% (2008-2012 5-year est.); Ancestry (includes multiple ancestries): 40.0% German, 10.0% American, 4.7% English, 4.0% Irish, 1.7% French (2008-2012 5-year est.).

Economy: Homeowner vacancy rate: 0.0%. Rental vacancy rate: 0.0%. (2008-2012 5-year est.); Employment by occupation: 8.6% management, business, and financial, 0.0% computer, engineering, and science, 4.0% education, legal, community service, arts, and media, 3.4% healthcare practitioners, 18.3% service, 32.6% sales and office, 19.4% natural resources, construction, and maintenance, 13.7% production, transportation, and material moving (2008-2012 5-year est.).

Income: Per capita income: $22,334 (2008-2012 5-year est.); Median household income: $34,688 (2008-2012 5-year est.); Average household income: $44,723 (2008-2012 5-year est.); Percent of households with income of $100,000 or more: 9.4% (2008-2012 5-year est.); Poverty rate: 17.7% (2008-2012 5-year est.).

Education: Percent of population age 25 and over with: High school diploma (including GED) or higher: 90.7% (2008-2012 5-year est.); Bachelor's degree or higher: 10.7% (2008-2012 5-year est.); Master's degree or higher: 2.8% (2008-2012 5-year est.).

Housing: Homeownership rate: 92.1% (2008-2012 5-year est.); Median home value: $61,600 (2008-2012 5-year est.); Median contract rent: $192 per month (2008-2012 5-year est.); Median year structure built: 1954 (2008-2012 5-year est.).

Health Insurance: 75.0% Private; 41.0% Public; 8.3% None. (2008-2012 5-year est.)

Transportation: Commute to work: 89.5% car, 0.0% public transportation, 4.1% walk, 5.3% work from home (2008-2012 5-year est.); Travel time to work: 25.9% less than 15 minutes, 31.5% 15 to 30 minutes, 37.0% 30 to 45 minutes, 4.3% 45 to 60 minutes, 1.2% 60 minutes or more (2008-2012 5-year est.)

SHOBONIER (unincorporated postal area)

Zip Code: 62885

Covers a land area of 48.731 square miles and a water area of 0.043 square miles. Located at 38.85° N. Lat; 89.05° W. Long. Elevation is 515 feet. Population: 839 (2010); Density: 17.2 persons per square mile (2010); Race: 98.8% White, 0.2% Black/African American, 0.2% Asian, 0.0% American Indian/Alaska Native, 0.1% Native Hawaiian/Other Pacific Islander, 0.7% Some other race, 0.6% Two or more races, 0.2% Hispanic of any race (2010); Average household size: 2.63 (2010); Median age: 39.4 (2010); Males per 100 females: 99.8 (2010); Homeownership rate: 85.9% (2010)

VANDALIA (city). County seat. Covers a land area of 8.101 square miles and a water area of 0.016 square miles. Located at 38.97° N. Lat; 89.11° W. Long. Elevation is 518 feet.

History: Vandalia was laid out in 1819 at the direction of the Illinois State Legislature, and served until 1839 as the capital. Three capitol buildings were erected in Vandalia during its 20 years as the state capital.

Population: 6,114 (1990); 6,975 (2000); 7,042 (2010); Density: 752.5 persons per square mile (2008-2012 5-year est.); Race: 88.1% White, 6.4% Black/African American, 3.2% Asian, 0.0% American Indian/Alaska Native, 0.2% Native Hawaiian/Other Pacific Islander, 2.1% Some other race, 0.9% Two or more races, 4.0% Hispanic of any race (2008-2012 5-year est.); Average household size: 2.35 (2008-2012 5-year est.); Median age: 38.0 (2008-2012 5-year est.); Males per 100 females: 114.5 (2008-2012 5-year est.); Marriage status: 38.8% never married, 40.1% now married, 7.6% widowed, 13.5% divorced (2008-2012 5-year est.); Foreign born: 5.0% (2008-2012 5-year est.); Ancestry (includes multiple ancestries): 25.2% German, 12.8% American, 8.5% English, 7.8% Irish, 3.0% French (2008-2012 5-year est.).

Economy: Single-family building permits issued: 0 (2013); Multi-family building permits issued: 0 (2013); Homeowner vacancy rate: 2.3%. Rental vacancy rate: 15.2%. (2008-2012 5-year est.); Employment by occupation: 8.6% management, business, and financial, 1.5% computer, engineering, and science, 7.8% education, legal, community service, arts, and media, 9.9% healthcare practitioners, 25.8% service, 24.0% sales and office, 6.0% natural resources, construction, and maintenance, 16.5% production, transportation, and material moving (2008-2012 5-year est.).

Income: Per capita income: $22,815 (2008-2012 5-year est.); Median household income: $48,004 (2008-2012 5-year est.); Average household income: $56,524 (2008-2012 5-year est.); Percent of households with income of $100,000 or more: 13.1% (2008-2012 5-year est.); Poverty rate: 17.7% (2008-2012 5-year est.).

Education: Percent of population age 25 and over with: High school diploma (including GED) or higher: 84.3% (2008-2012 5-year est.); Bachelor's degree or higher: 19.7% (2008-2012 5-year est.); Master's degree or higher: 8.2% (2008-2012 5-year est.).

School District(s)

Bond/effingham/fayette Roe (07-12)

    2011-12 Enrollment: n/a . . . . (618) 283-5011

Okaw Area Vocational Center (11-12)

    2011-12 Enrollment: n/a . . . . (618) 283-5150

Vandalia CUSD 203 (PK-12)

    2011-12 Enrollment: 1,557 . . . . (618) 283-4525

Housing: Homeownership rate: 67.0% (2008-2012 5-year est.); Median home value: $76,500 (2008-2012 5-year est.); Median contract rent: $401 per month (2008-2012 5-year est.); Median year structure built: 1955 (2008-2012 5-year est.).

Health Insurance: 62.1% Private; 40.1% Public; 15.3% None. (2008-2012 5-year est.)

Hospitals: Fayette County Hospital (160 beds)

Safety: Violent crime rate: 44.0 per 10,000 population; Property crime rate: 298.2 per 10,000 population (2012).

Transportation: Commute to work: 89.9% car, 0.7% public transportation, 1.9% walk, 4.7% work from home (2008-2012 5-year est.); Travel time to work: 70.1% less than 15 minutes, 14.6% 15 to 30 minutes, 7.6% 30 to 45 minutes, 1.4% 45 to 60 minutes, 6.3% 60 minutes or more (2008-2012 5-year est.)

Airports: Vandalia Municipal Airport (general aviation)

Additional Information Contacts

City of Vandalia . . . . (618) 283-1152

    http://www.vandaliaillinois.com

Vandalia Chamber of Commerce . . . . (618) 283-2728

    http://www.vandaliachamber.org

Ford County

Located in east central Illinois; drained by the Mackinaw River. Covers a land area of 485.616 square miles, a water area of 0.626 square miles, and is located in the Central Time Zone at 40.59° N. Lat., 88.22° W. Long. The county was founded in 1859. County seat is Paxton.

Ford County is part of the Champaign-Urbana, IL Metropolitan Statistical Area. The entire metro area includes: Champaign County, IL; Ford County, IL; Piatt County, IL

Weather Station: Gibson City 1 E									Elevation: 750 feet		
	Jan	Feb	Mar	Apr	May	Jun	Jul	Aug	Sep	Oct	Nov	Dec
High	32	36	48	61	73	82	85	83	78	64	50	36
Low	16	19	29	39	50	60	63	61	52	40	31	20
Precip	1.6	1.7	2.6	3.4	4.2	3.9	3.8	3.9	2.7	3.0	3.3	2.4
Snow	5.6	6.0	1.7	0.8	0.0	0.0	0.0	0.0	0.0	0.1	1.1	5.2

High and Low temperatures in degrees Fahrenheit; Precipitation and Snow in inches

Weather Station: Piper City   Elevation: 669 feet

	Jan	Feb	Mar	Apr	May	Jun	Jul	Aug	Sep	Oct	Nov	Dec
High	33	38	49	63	74	83	86	84	78	65	51	37
Low	16	19	28	38	49	59	63	60	52	41	31	20
Precip	2.5	2.2	2.9	3.6	4.4	3.8	4.7	3.9	2.6	3.3	3.4	2.9
Snow	8.2	6.9	3.2	1.0	tr	0.0	0.0	0.0	0.0	0.2	1.4	6.6

High and Low temperatures in degrees Fahrenheit; Precipitation and Snow in inches

Population: 14,275 (1990); 14,241 (2000); 14,081 (2010); Race: 97.6% White, 0.5% Black/African American, 0.2% Asian, 0.2% American Indian/Alaska Native, 0.0% Native Hawaiian/Other Pacific Islander, 1.5% Some other race, 1.1% Two or more races, 2.3% Hispanic of any race (2008-2012 5-year est.); Density: 28.8 persons per square mile (2008-2012 5-year est.); Average household size: 2.42 (2008-2012 5-year est.); Median age: 42.5 (2008-2012 5-year est.); Males per 100 females: 94.4 (2008-2012 5-year est.).
Religion: Six largest groups: 12.9% Methodist/Pietist, 12.6% Catholicism, 9.9% Baptist, 8.7% Lutheran, 6.2% Non-denominational Protestant, 3.0% Presbyterian-Reformed (2010)
Economy: Unemployment rate: 6.3% (April 2014); Total civilian labor force: 6,583 (April 2014); Leading industries: 27.0% health care and social assistance; 14.0% manufacturing; 13.0% retail trade (2012); Farms: 546 totaling 308,181 acres (2012); Companies that employ 500 or more persons: 0 (2012); Companies that employ 100 to 499 persons: 6 (2012); Companies that employ less than 100 persons: 361 (2012); Black-owned businesses: n/a (2007); Hispanic-owned businesses: n/a (2007); Asian-owned businesses: n/a (2007); Women-owned businesses: 468 (2007); Single-family building permits issued: 15 (2013); Multi-family building permits issued: 50 (2013).
Income: Per capita income: $26,042 (2008-2012 5-year est.); Median household income: $50,203 (2008-2012 5-year est.); Average household income: $63,229 (2008-2012 5-year est.); Percent of households with income of $100,000 or more: 16.7% (2008-2012 5-year est.); Poverty rate: 9.9% (2008-2012 5-year est.); Bankruptcy rate: 2.14% (2013).
Taxes: Total county taxes per capita: $228 (2011); County property taxes per capita: $168 (2011).
Education: Percent of population age 25 and over with: High school diploma (including GED) or higher: 88.0% (2008-2012 5-year est.); Bachelor's degree or higher: 17.0% (2008-2012 5-year est.); Master's degree or higher: 3.9% (2008-2012 5-year est.).
Housing: Homeownership rate: 78.3% (2008-2012 5-year est.); Median home value: $91,500 (2008-2012 5-year est.); Median contract rent: $417 per month (2008-2012 5-year est.); Median year structure built: 1954 (2008-2012 5-year est.)
Health: Birth rate: 96.2 per 10,000 population (2013); Death rate: 139.5 per 10,000 population (2013); Age-adjusted cancer mortality rate: 138.0 deaths per 100,000 population (2011); Number of physicians: 8.6 per 10,000 population (2011); Hospital beds: 47.6 per 10,000 population (2010); Hospital admissions: 667.6 per 10,000 population (2010).
Elections: 2012 Presidential election results: 27.6% Obama, 70.4% Romney
Additional Information Contacts
Ford County Government . . . . (217) 379-9400
   http://www.fordcountycourthouse.com

Ford County Communities

CABERY (village). Covers a land area of 0.344 square miles and a water area of 0 square miles. Located at 41.00° N. Lat; 88.20° W. Long. Elevation is 699 feet.
Population: 268 (1990); 263 (2000); 266 (2010); Density: 951.9 persons per square mile (2008-2012 5-year est.); Race: 98.5% White, 0.0% Black/African American, 0.0% Asian, 0.0% American Indian/Alaska Native, 0.0% Native Hawaiian/Other Pacific Islander, 1.5% Some other race, 1.5% Two or more races, 0.0% Hispanic of any race (2008-2012 5-year est.); Average household size: 2.34 (2008-2012 5-year est.); Median age: 37.1 (2008-2012 5-year est.); Males per 100 females: 100.6 (2008-2012 5-year est.); Marriage status: 34.4% never married, 48.8% now married, 7.7% widowed, 9.1% divorced (2008-2012 5-year est.); Foreign born: 0.6% (2008-2012 5-year est.); Ancestry (includes multiple ancestries): 40.4% German, 12.2% American, 12.2% French, 11.3% Irish, 8.0% Italian (2008-2012 5-year est.).
Economy: Homeowner vacancy rate: 3.9%. Rental vacancy rate: 0.0%. (2008-2012 5-year est.); Employment by occupation: 6.9% management, business, and financial, 1.5% computer, engineering, and science, 8.5% education, legal, community service, arts, and media, 1.5% healthcare

practitioners, 16.2% service, 24.6% sales and office, 22.3% natural resources, construction, and maintenance, 18.5% production, transportation, and material moving (2008-2012 5-year est.).
Income: Per capita income: $16,197 (2008-2012 5-year est.); Median household income: $34,500 (2008-2012 5-year est.); Average household income: $38,798 (2008-2012 5-year est.); Percent of households with income of $100,000 or more: 4.3% (2008-2012 5-year est.); Poverty rate: 25.7% (2008-2012 5-year est.).
Education: Percent of population age 25 and over with: High school diploma (including GED) or higher: 83.7% (2008-2012 5-year est.); Bachelor's degree or higher: 7.1% (2008-2012 5-year est.); Master's degree or higher: 3.6% (2008-2012 5-year est.).
Housing: Homeownership rate: 70.0% (2008-2012 5-year est.); Median home value: $74,500 (2008-2012 5-year est.); Median contract rent: $456 per month (2008-2012 5-year est.); Median year structure built: 1943 (2008-2012 5-year est.).
Health Insurance: 53.2% Private; 29.1% Public; 33.3% None. (2008-2012 5-year est.)
Transportation: Commute to work: 98.4% car, 0.0% public transportation, 0.0% walk, 1.6% work from home (2008-2012 5-year est.); Travel time to work: 23.8% less than 15 minutes, 14.3% 15 to 30 minutes, 31.7% 30 to 45 minutes, 19.8% 45 to 60 minutes, 10.3% 60 minutes or more (2008-2012 5-year est.)

ELLIOTT (village). Covers a land area of 0.484 square miles and a water area of 0 square miles. Located at 40.47° N. Lat; 88.28° W. Long. Elevation is 781 feet.
Population: 309 (1990); 341 (2000); 295 (2010); Density: 572.4 persons per square mile (2008-2012 5-year est.); Race: 94.6% White, 0.0% Black/African American, 0.0% Asian, 0.0% American Indian/Alaska Native, 0.0% Native Hawaiian/Other Pacific Islander, 5.4% Some other race, 5.4% Two or more races, 11.6% Hispanic of any race (2008-2012 5-year est.); Average household size: 2.69 (2008-2012 5-year est.); Median age: 44.5 (2008-2012 5-year est.); Males per 100 females: 89.7 (2008-2012 5-year est.); Marriage status: 22.3% never married, 64.8% now married, 5.6% widowed, 7.3% divorced (2008-2012 5-year est.); Foreign born: 1.1% (2008-2012 5-year est.); Ancestry (includes multiple ancestries): 26.7% German, 26.0% American, 10.1% Italian, 6.5% English, 5.8% Irish (2008-2012 5-year est.).
Economy: Homeowner vacancy rate: 0.0%. Rental vacancy rate: 0.0%. (2008-2012 5-year est.); Employment by occupation: 14.0% management, business, and financial, 2.2% computer, engineering, and science, 2.2% education, legal, community service, arts, and media, 4.4% healthcare practitioners, 22.8% service, 27.9% sales and office, 7.4% natural resources, construction, and maintenance, 19.1% production, transportation, and material moving (2008-2012 5-year est.).
Income: Per capita income: $21,953 (2008-2012 5-year est.); Median household income: $50,875 (2008-2012 5-year est.); Average household income: $57,371 (2008-2012 5-year est.); Percent of households with income of $100,000 or more: 9.7% (2008-2012 5-year est.); Poverty rate: 2.9% (2008-2012 5-year est.).
Education: Percent of population age 25 and over with: High school diploma (including GED) or higher: 87.2% (2008-2012 5-year est.); Bachelor's degree or higher: 7.2% (2008-2012 5-year est.); Master's degree or higher: 1.5% (2008-2012 5-year est.).
Housing: Homeownership rate: 87.4% (2008-2012 5-year est.); Median home value: $83,300 (2008-2012 5-year est.); Median contract rent: $556 per month (2008-2012 5-year est.); Median year structure built: 1951 (2008-2012 5-year est.).
Health Insurance: 70.0% Private; 26.7% Public; 15.2% None. (2008-2012 5-year est.)
Transportation: Commute to work: 96.3% car, 0.0% public transportation, 0.0% walk, 3.7% work from home (2008-2012 5-year est.); Travel time to work: 51.9% less than 15 minutes, 20.9% 15 to 30 minutes, 17.1% 30 to 45 minutes, 7.0% 45 to 60 minutes, 3.1% 60 minutes or more (2008-2012 5-year est.)

GIBSON CITY (city). Covers a land area of 2.320 square miles and a water area of 0.029 square miles. Located at 40.47° N. Lat; 88.38° W. Long. Elevation is 748 feet.
Population: n/a (1990); n/a (2000); 3,407 (2010); Density: 1,493.7 persons per square mile (2008-2012 5-year est.); Race: 96.2% White, 0.0% Black/African American, 0.4% Asian, 0.5% American Indian/Alaska Native, 0.0% Native Hawaiian/Other Pacific Islander, 2.9% Some other race, 2.9% Two or more races, 0.0% Hispanic of any race (2008-2012

5-year est.); Average household size: 2.22 (2008-2012 5-year est.); Median age: 41.2 (2008-2012 5-year est.); Males per 100 females: 92.2 (2008-2012 5-year est.); Marriage status: 23.7% never married, 53.7% now married, 8.6% widowed, 14.0% divorced (2008-2012 5-year est.); Foreign born: 0.3% (2008-2012 5-year est.); Ancestry (includes multiple ancestries): 36.6% German, 19.1% Irish, 19.0% American, 8.8% English, 3.6% Swedish (2008-2012 5-year est.).
Economy: Single-family building permits issued: 2 (2013); Multi-family building permits issued: 50 (2013); Homeowner vacancy rate: 0.9%. Rental vacancy rate: 6.4%. (2008-2012 5-year est.); Employment by occupation: 13.5% management, business, and financial, 6.5% computer, engineering, and science, 9.5% education, legal, community service, arts, and media, 6.6% healthcare practitioners, 13.9% service, 28.7% sales and office, 10.4% natural resources, construction, and maintenance, 10.9% production, transportation, and material moving (2008-2012 5-year est.).
Income: Per capita income: $28,986 (2008-2012 5-year est.); Median household income: $41,483 (2008-2012 5-year est.); Average household income: $63,646 (2008-2012 5-year est.); Percent of households with income of $100,000 or more: 20.0% (2008-2012 5-year est.); Poverty rate: 9.4% (2008-2012 5-year est.).
Education: Percent of population age 25 and over with: High school diploma (including GED) or higher: 88.9% (2008-2012 5-year est.); Bachelor's degree or higher: 22.2% (2008-2012 5-year est.); Master's degree or higher: 3.8% (2008-2012 5-year est.).

School District(s)
Gibson City-Melvin-Sibley CUSD 5 (PK-12)
    2011-12 Enrollment: 1,062 . . . . (217) 784-8296
Housing: Homeownership rate: 68.7% (2008-2012 5-year est.); Median home value: $100,100 (2008-2012 5-year est.); Median contract rent: $385 per month (2008-2012 5-year est.); Median year structure built: 1954 (2008-2012 5-year est.).
Health Insurance: 75.3% Private; 33.9% Public; 8.4% None. (2008-2012 5-year est.)
Safety: Violent crime rate: 14.8 per 10,000 population; Property crime rate: 118.2 per 10,000 population (2012).
Transportation: Commute to work: 91.2% car, 0.0% public transportation, 5.3% walk, 2.1% work from home (2008-2012 5-year est.); Travel time to work: 53.2% less than 15 minutes, 8.5% 15 to 30 minutes, 25.8% 30 to 45 minutes, 7.6% 45 to 60 minutes, 4.9% 60 minutes or more (2008-2012 5-year est.)

KEMPTON (village). Covers a land area of 0.213 square miles and a water area of 0 square miles. Located at 40.94° N. Lat; 88.24° W. Long. Elevation is 735 feet.
Population: 219 (1990); 235 (2000); 231 (2010); Density: 860.5 persons per square mile (2008-2012 5-year est.); Race: 99.5% White, 0.0% Black/African American, 0.0% Asian, 0.0% American Indian/Alaska Native, 0.0% Native Hawaiian/Other Pacific Islander, 0.5% Some other race, 0.5% Two or more races, 3.8% Hispanic of any race (2008-2012 5-year est.); Average household size: 1.99 (2008-2012 5-year est.); Median age: 44.1 (2008-2012 5-year est.); Males per 100 females: 117.9 (2008-2012 5-year est.); Marriage status: 16.8% never married, 51.0% now married, 9.4% widowed, 22.8% divorced (2008-2012 5-year est.); Foreign born: 0.5% (2008-2012 5-year est.); Ancestry (includes multiple ancestries): 38.3% German, 21.3% English, 19.1% Irish, 9.8% Dutch, 7.1% American (2008-2012 5-year est.).
Economy: Homeowner vacancy rate: 0.0%. Rental vacancy rate: 0.0%. (2008-2012 5-year est.); Employment by occupation: 11.0% management, business, and financial, 0.0% computer, engineering, and science, 1.2% education, legal, community service, arts, and media, 0.0% healthcare practitioners, 15.9% service, 32.9% sales and office, 17.1% natural resources, construction, and maintenance, 22.0% production, transportation, and material moving (2008-2012 5-year est.).
Income: Per capita income: $31,308 (2008-2012 5-year est.); Median household income: $35,833 (2008-2012 5-year est.); Average household income: $72,979 (2008-2012 5-year est.); Percent of households with income of $100,000 or more: 10.9% (2008-2012 5-year est.); Poverty rate: 15.8% (2008-2012 5-year est.).
Education: Percent of population age 25 and over with: High school diploma (including GED) or higher: 86.8% (2008-2012 5-year est.); Bachelor's degree or higher: 6.2% (2008-2012 5-year est.); Master's degree or higher: 3.9% (2008-2012 5-year est.).

School District(s)
Tri Point CUSD 6-J (PK-12)
    2011-12 Enrollment: 483 . . . . (815) 253-6299

Housing: Homeownership rate: 71.7% (2008-2012 5-year est.); Median home value: $81,500 (2008-2012 5-year est.); Median contract rent: $338 per month (2008-2012 5-year est.); Median year structure built: Before 1940 (2008-2012 5-year est.).
Health Insurance: 56.3% Private; 39.3% Public; 19.7% None. (2008-2012 5-year est.)
Transportation: Commute to work: 86.6% car, 0.0% public transportation, 1.2% walk, 9.8% work from home (2008-2012 5-year est.); Travel time to work: 13.5% less than 15 minutes, 13.5% 15 to 30 minutes, 28.4% 30 to 45 minutes, 31.1% 45 to 60 minutes, 13.5% 60 minutes or more (2008-2012 5-year est.)

MELVIN (village). Covers a land area of 0.334 square miles and a water area of 0 square miles. Located at 40.57° N. Lat; 88.25° W. Long. Elevation is 814 feet.
Population: 466 (1990); 465 (2000); 452 (2010); Density: 1,791.8 persons per square mile (2008-2012 5-year est.); Race: 97.8% White, 2.2% Black/African American, 0.0% Asian, 0.0% American Indian/Alaska Native, 0.0% Native Hawaiian/Other Pacific Islander, 0.0% Some other race, 0.0% Two or more races, 5.0% Hispanic of any race (2008-2012 5-year est.); Average household size: 2.60 (2008-2012 5-year est.); Median age: 39.6 (2008-2012 5-year est.); Males per 100 females: 94.5 (2008-2012 5-year est.); Marriage status: 26.1% never married, 56.0% now married, 7.2% widowed, 10.7% divorced (2008-2012 5-year est.); Foreign born: 0.3% (2008-2012 5-year est.); Ancestry (includes multiple ancestries): 42.1% German, 15.4% American, 11.2% Irish, 10.5% English, 7.3% Polish (2008-2012 5-year est.).
Economy: Homeowner vacancy rate: 3.4%. Rental vacancy rate: 0.0%. (2008-2012 5-year est.); Employment by occupation: 10.0% management, business, and financial, 0.8% computer, engineering, and science, 10.5% education, legal, community service, arts, and media, 0.4% healthcare practitioners, 11.3% service, 28.0% sales and office, 18.0% natural resources, construction, and maintenance, 20.9% production, transportation, and material moving (2008-2012 5-year est.).
Income: Per capita income: $18,567 (2008-2012 5-year est.); Median household income: $44,231 (2008-2012 5-year est.); Average household income: $48,804 (2008-2012 5-year est.); Percent of households with income of $100,000 or more: 7.0% (2008-2012 5-year est.); Poverty rate: 11.1% (2008-2012 5-year est.).
Education: Percent of population age 25 and over with: High school diploma (including GED) or higher: 84.5% (2008-2012 5-year est.); Bachelor's degree or higher: 7.9% (2008-2012 5-year est.); Master's degree or higher: 2.8% (2008-2012 5-year est.).
Housing: Homeownership rate: 85.2% (2008-2012 5-year est.); Median home value: $66,800 (2008-2012 5-year est.); Median contract rent: $325 per month (2008-2012 5-year est.); Median year structure built: 1952 (2008-2012 5-year est.).
Health Insurance: 68.8% Private; 49.9% Public; 7.2% None. (2008-2012 5-year est.)
Transportation: Commute to work: 94.0% car, 0.0% public transportation, 4.3% walk, 0.9% work from home (2008-2012 5-year est.); Travel time to work: 30.5% less than 15 minutes, 27.0% 15 to 30 minutes, 14.2% 30 to 45 minutes, 12.4% 45 to 60 minutes, 15.9% 60 minutes or more (2008-2012 5-year est.)

PAXTON (city). County seat. Covers a land area of 2.297 square miles and a water area of 0 square miles. Located at 40.46° N. Lat; 88.10° W. Long. Elevation is 791 feet.
History: Paxton was settled in the 1850's by immigrants from Sweden.
Population: 4,289 (1990); 4,525 (2000); 4,473 (2010); Density: 1,912.1 persons per square mile (2008-2012 5-year est.); Race: 96.7% White, 1.2% Black/African American, 0.2% Asian, 0.1% American Indian/Alaska Native, 0.0% Native Hawaiian/Other Pacific Islander, 1.8% Some other race, 0.6% Two or more races, 3.5% Hispanic of any race (2008-2012 5-year est.); Average household size: 2.47 (2008-2012 5-year est.); Median age: 39.6 (2008-2012 5-year est.); Males per 100 females: 90.0 (2008-2012 5-year est.); Marriage status: 18.5% never married, 56.8% now married, 11.7% widowed, 12.9% divorced (2008-2012 5-year est.); Foreign born: 1.8% (2008-2012 5-year est.); Ancestry (includes multiple ancestries): 28.8% German, 21.2% American, 14.6% Irish, 7.7% English, 5.1% Swedish (2008-2012 5-year est.).
Economy: Single-family building permits issued: 4 (2013); Multi-family building permits issued: 0 (2013); Homeowner vacancy rate: 1.6%. Rental vacancy rate: 7.9%. (2008-2012 5-year est.); Employment by occupation: 8.0% management, business, and financial, 2.1% computer, engineering,

and science, 7.5% education, legal, community service, arts, and media, 6.5% healthcare practitioners, 20.2% service, 27.2% sales and office, 8.1% natural resources, construction, and maintenance, 20.4% production, transportation, and material moving (2008-2012 5-year est.).
Income: Per capita income: $24,615 (2008-2012 5-year est.); Median household income: $48,917 (2008-2012 5-year est.); Average household income: $61,211 (2008-2012 5-year est.); Percent of households with income of $100,000 or more: 13.6% (2008-2012 5-year est.); Poverty rate: 11.1% (2008-2012 5-year est.).
Taxes: Total city taxes per capita: $192 (2011); City property taxes per capita: $147 (2011).
Education: Percent of population age 25 and over with: High school diploma (including GED) or higher: 85.4% (2008-2012 5-year est.); Bachelor's degree or higher: 16.3% (2008-2012 5-year est.); Master's degree or higher: 4.1% (2008-2012 5-year est.).

School District(s)
Paxton-Buckley-Loda CUD 10 (PK-12)
    2011-12 Enrollment: 1,474 . . . . (217) 379-3314
Housing: Homeownership rate: 80.8% (2008-2012 5-year est.); Median home value: $89,500 (2008-2012 5-year est.); Median contract rent: $426 per month (2008-2012 5-year est.); Median year structure built: 1955 (2008-2012 5-year est.).
Health Insurance: 80.0% Private; 32.5% Public; 4.8% None. (2008-2012 5-year est.)
Safety: Violent crime rate: 9.0 per 10,000 population; Property crime rate: 126.0 per 10,000 population (2012).
Transportation: Commute to work: 97.1% car, 0.0% public transportation, 1.4% walk, 1.5% work from home (2008-2012 5-year est.); Travel time to work: 46.2% less than 15 minutes, 24.6% 15 to 30 minutes, 19.9% 30 to 45 minutes, 5.0% 45 to 60 minutes, 4.2% 60 minutes or more (2008-2012 5-year est.)
Additional Information Contacts
Paxton Area Chamber of Commerce . . . . (217) 379-4655
    http://www.paxtonchamber.org

PIPER CITY (village). Covers a land area of 0.547 square miles and a water area of 0 square miles. Located at 40.76° N. Lat; 88.19° W. Long. Elevation is 673 feet.
Population: 760 (1990); 781 (2000); 826 (2010); Density: 1,377.5 persons per square mile (2008-2012 5-year est.); Race: 99.3% White, 0.0% Black/African American, 0.0% Asian, 0.3% American Indian/Alaska Native, 0.0% Native Hawaiian/Other Pacific Islander, 0.4% Some other race, 0.0% Two or more races, 4.0% Hispanic of any race (2008-2012 5-year est.); Average household size: 2.59 (2008-2012 5-year est.); Median age: 45.6 (2008-2012 5-year est.); Males per 100 females: 96.4 (2008-2012 5-year est.); Marriage status: 21.5% never married, 54.1% now married, 15.6% widowed, 8.8% divorced (2008-2012 5-year est.); Foreign born: 0.4% (2008-2012 5-year est.); Ancestry (includes multiple ancestries): 39.9% German, 27.5% Irish, 11.9% American, 9.4% English, 5.3% Lithuanian (2008-2012 5-year est.).
Economy: Single-family building permits issued: 0 (2013); Multi-family building permits issued: 0 (2013); Homeowner vacancy rate: 3.3%. Rental vacancy rate: 0.0%. (2008-2012 5-year est.); Employment by occupation: 4.5% management, business, and financial, 1.6% computer, engineering, and science, 6.1% education, legal, community service, arts, and media, 2.3% healthcare practitioners, 21.9% service, 11.3% sales and office, 13.9% natural resources, construction, and maintenance, 38.4% production, transportation, and material moving (2008-2012 5-year est.).
Income: Per capita income: $17,934 (2008-2012 5-year est.); Median household income: $29,783 (2008-2012 5-year est.); Average household income: $44,532 (2008-2012 5-year est.); Percent of households with income of $100,000 or more: 6.7% (2008-2012 5-year est.); Poverty rate: 13.1% (2008-2012 5-year est.).
Education: Percent of population age 25 and over with: High school diploma (including GED) or higher: 77.6% (2008-2012 5-year est.); Bachelor's degree or higher: 6.3% (2008-2012 5-year est.); Master's degree or higher: 1.8% (2008-2012 5-year est.).

School District(s)
Tri Point CUSD 6-J (PK-12)
    2011-12 Enrollment: 483 . . . . (815) 253-6299
Housing: Homeownership rate: 87.7% (2008-2012 5-year est.); Median home value: $67,600 (2008-2012 5-year est.); Median contract rent: $490 per month (2008-2012 5-year est.); Median year structure built: 1948 (2008-2012 5-year est.).

Health Insurance: 57.4% Private; 42.2% Public; 17.4% None. (2008-2012 5-year est.)
Transportation: Commute to work: 87.3% car, 1.3% public transportation, 2.7% walk, 6.3% work from home (2008-2012 5-year est.); Travel time to work: 28.8% less than 15 minutes, 26.3% 15 to 30 minutes, 26.3% 30 to 45 minutes, 7.5% 45 to 60 minutes, 11.0% 60 minutes or more (2008-2012 5-year est.)

ROBERTS (village). Covers a land area of 0.492 square miles and a water area of 0 square miles. Located at 40.61° N. Lat; 88.18° W. Long. Elevation is 781 feet.
Population: 397 (1990); 387 (2000); 362 (2010); Density: 637.9 persons per square mile (2008-2012 5-year est.); Race: 99.7% White, 0.0% Black/African American, 0.0% Asian, 0.0% American Indian/Alaska Native, 0.0% Native Hawaiian/Other Pacific Islander, 0.3% Some other race, 0.3% Two or more races, 1.6% Hispanic of any race (2008-2012 5-year est.); Average household size: 2.04 (2008-2012 5-year est.); Median age: 47.5 (2008-2012 5-year est.); Males per 100 females: 96.3 (2008-2012 5-year est.); Marriage status: 19.1% never married, 52.6% now married, 13.2% widowed, 15.1% divorced (2008-2012 5-year est.); Foreign born: 0.3% (2008-2012 5-year est.); Ancestry (includes multiple ancestries): 43.0% German, 17.2% English, 15.3% American, 5.7% French, 5.4% Irish (2008-2012 5-year est.).
Economy: Homeowner vacancy rate: 3.5%. Rental vacancy rate: 18.2%. (2008-2012 5-year est.); Employment by occupation: 4.8% management, business, and financial, 1.6% computer, engineering, and science, 11.9% education, legal, community service, arts, and media, 2.4% healthcare practitioners, 17.5% service, 25.4% sales and office, 12.7% natural resources, construction, and maintenance, 23.8% production, transportation, and material moving (2008-2012 5-year est.).
Income: Per capita income: $20,043 (2008-2012 5-year est.); Median household income: $35,577 (2008-2012 5-year est.); Average household income: $40,868 (2008-2012 5-year est.); Percent of households with income of $100,000 or more: 1.9% (2008-2012 5-year est.); Poverty rate: 15.0% (2008-2012 5-year est.).
Education: Percent of population age 25 and over with: High school diploma (including GED) or higher: 87.1% (2008-2012 5-year est.); Bachelor's degree or higher: 12.1% (2008-2012 5-year est.); Master's degree or higher: 2.5% (2008-2012 5-year est.).
Housing: Homeownership rate: 88.3% (2008-2012 5-year est.); Median home value: $64,900 (2008-2012 5-year est.); Median contract rent: $296 per month (2008-2012 5-year est.); Median year structure built: 1954 (2008-2012 5-year est.).
Health Insurance: 63.4% Private; 40.8% Public; 14.0% None. (2008-2012 5-year est.)
Transportation: Commute to work: 94.1% car, 0.0% public transportation, 0.0% walk, 5.9% work from home (2008-2012 5-year est.); Travel time to work: 35.7% less than 15 minutes, 30.4% 15 to 30 minutes, 15.2% 30 to 45 minutes, 15.2% 45 to 60 minutes, 3.6% 60 minutes or more (2008-2012 5-year est.)

SIBLEY (village). Covers a land area of 0.511 square miles and a water area of 0.013 square miles. Located at 40.59° N. Lat; 88.38° W. Long. Elevation is 827 feet.
Population: 359 (1990); 329 (2000); 272 (2010); Density: 671.4 persons per square mile (2008-2012 5-year est.); Race: 96.5% White, 1.5% Black/African American, 2.0% Asian, 0.0% American Indian/Alaska Native, 0.0% Native Hawaiian/Other Pacific Islander, 0.0% Some other race, 0.0% Two or more races, 1.2% Hispanic of any race (2008-2012 5-year est.); Average household size: 2.21 (2008-2012 5-year est.); Median age: 41.5 (2008-2012 5-year est.); Males per 100 females: 97.1 (2008-2012 5-year est.); Marriage status: 19.0% never married, 63.1% now married, 6.1% widowed, 11.8% divorced (2008-2012 5-year est.); Foreign born: 2.3% (2008-2012 5-year est.); Ancestry (includes multiple ancestries): 35.6% German, 27.1% American, 12.5% Irish, 8.5% English, 3.8% Swedish (2008-2012 5-year est.).
Economy: Homeowner vacancy rate: 3.1%. Rental vacancy rate: 0.0%. (2008-2012 5-year est.); Employment by occupation: 9.3% management, business, and financial, 0.0% computer, engineering, and science, 6.4% education, legal, community service, arts, and media, 3.5% healthcare practitioners, 10.5% service, 30.8% sales and office, 9.9% natural resources, construction, and maintenance, 29.7% production, transportation, and material moving (2008-2012 5-year est.).
Income: Per capita income: $28,255 (2008-2012 5-year est.); Median household income: $44,750 (2008-2012 5-year est.); Average household

income: $63,092 (2008-2012 5-year est.); Percent of households with income of $100,000 or more: 12.9% (2008-2012 5-year est.); Poverty rate: 12.0% (2008-2012 5-year est.).

Education: Percent of population age 25 and over with: High school diploma (including GED) or higher: 89.6% (2008-2012 5-year est.); Bachelor's degree or higher: 6.1% (2008-2012 5-year est.); Master's degree or higher: 0.0% (2008-2012 5-year est.).

Housing: Homeownership rate: 80.0% (2008-2012 5-year est.); Median home value: $64,800 (2008-2012 5-year est.); Median contract rent: $445 per month (2008-2012 5-year est.); Median year structure built: Before 1940 (2008-2012 5-year est.).

Health Insurance: 82.8% Private; 31.2% Public; 6.1% None. (2008-2012 5-year est.)

Transportation: Commute to work: 98.8% car, 0.0% public transportation, 0.0% walk, 1.2% work from home (2008-2012 5-year est.); Travel time to work: 39.8% less than 15 minutes, 24.8% 15 to 30 minutes, 18.0% 30 to 45 minutes, 9.3% 45 to 60 minutes, 8.1% 60 minutes or more (2008-2012 5-year est.)

Franklin County

Located in southern Illinois; bounded on the northwest by the Little Muddy River; drained by the Big Muddy River. Covers a land area of 408.889 square miles, a water area of 22.555 square miles, and is located in the Central Time Zone at 37.99° N. Lat., 88.93° W. Long. The county was founded in 1818. County seat is Benton.

Population: 40,319 (1990); 39,018 (2000); 39,561 (2010); Race: 97.8% White, 0.2% Black/African American, 0.4% Asian, 0.1% American Indian/Alaska Native, 0.0% Native Hawaiian/Other Pacific Islander, 1.5% Some other race, 1.3% Two or more races, 1.3% Hispanic of any race (2008-2012 5-year est.); Density: 96.6 persons per square mile (2008-2012 5-year est.); Average household size: 2.43 (2008-2012 5-year est.); Median age: 41.8 (2008-2012 5-year est.); Males per 100 females: 97.2 (2008-2012 5-year est.).

Religion: Six largest groups: 37.5% Baptist, 7.7% Catholicism, 4.0% Pentecostal, 3.3% Methodist/Pietist, 1.0% Holiness, 0.8% Adventist (2010)

Economy: Unemployment rate: 9.4% (April 2014); Total civilian labor force: 16,673 (April 2014); Leading industries: 21.7% retail trade; 18.5% health care and social assistance; 11.7% manufacturing (2012); Farms: 711 totaling 181,349 acres (2012); Companies that employ 500 or more persons: 0 (2012); Companies that employ 100 to 499 persons: 8 (2012); Companies that employ less than 100 persons: 755 (2012); Black-owned businesses: n/a (2007); Hispanic-owned businesses: n/a (2007); Asian-owned businesses: n/a (2007); Women-owned businesses: 676 (2007); Single-family building permits issued: 7 (2013); Multi-family building permits issued: 0 (2013).

Income: Per capita income: $20,233 (2008-2012 5-year est.); Median household income: $37,158 (2008-2012 5-year est.); Average household income: $48,448 (2008-2012 5-year est.); Percent of households with income of $100,000 or more: 8.9% (2008-2012 5-year est.); Poverty rate: 18.8% (2008-2012 5-year est.); Bankruptcy rate: 5.58% (2013).

Taxes: Total county taxes per capita: $57 (2011); County property taxes per capita: $53 (2011).

Education: Percent of population age 25 and over with: High school diploma (including GED) or higher: 86.8% (2008-2012 5-year est.); Bachelor's degree or higher: 12.9% (2008-2012 5-year est.); Master's degree or higher: 4.3% (2008-2012 5-year est.).

Housing: Homeownership rate: 77.3% (2008-2012 5-year est.); Median home value: $63,900 (2008-2012 5-year est.); Median contract rent: $367 per month (2008-2012 5-year est.); Median year structure built: 1963 (2008-2012 5-year est.).

Health: Birth rate: 120.9 per 10,000 population (2013); Death rate: 129.1 per 10,000 population (2013); Age-adjusted cancer mortality rate: 238.6 deaths per 100,000 population (2011); Number of physicians: 5.3 per 10,000 population (2011); Hospital beds: 6.3 per 10,000 population (2010); Hospital admissions: 94.5 per 10,000 population (2010).

Elections: 2012 Presidential election results: 40.5% Obama, 57.3% Romney

National and State Parks: Wayne Fitzgerrell State Park

Additional Information Contacts

Franklin County Government . . . . (618) 438-3221
    http://franklincountyil.org

Franklin County Communities

BENTON (city). County seat. Covers a land area of 5.482 square miles and a water area of 0.180 square miles. Located at 38.01° N. Lat; 88.92° W. Long. Elevation is 472 feet.

History: Incorporated 1841.

Population: 7,216 (1990); 6,880 (2000); 7,087 (2010); Density: 1,328.7 persons per square mile (2008-2012 5-year est.); Race: 97.0% White, 0.5% Black/African American, 0.3% Asian, 0.1% American Indian/Alaska Native, 0.0% Native Hawaiian/Other Pacific Islander, 2.1% Some other race, 1.7% Two or more races, 2.8% Hispanic of any race (2008-2012 5-year est.); Average household size: 2.39 (2008-2012 5-year est.); Median age: 40.6 (2008-2012 5-year est.); Males per 100 females: 89.3 (2008-2012 5-year est.); Marriage status: 26.2% never married, 40.0% now married, 13.0% widowed, 20.7% divorced (2008-2012 5-year est.); Foreign born: 0.8% (2008-2012 5-year est.); Ancestry (includes multiple ancestries): 24.8% German, 16.8% English, 13.4% Irish, 11.7% American, 6.5% Italian (2008-2012 5-year est.).

Economy: Single-family building permits issued: 5 (2013); Multi-family building permits issued: 0 (2013); Homeowner vacancy rate: 0.8%. Rental vacancy rate: 6.3%. (2008-2012 5-year est.); Employment by occupation: 8.7% management, business, and financial, 1.0% computer, engineering, and science, 8.8% education, legal, community service, arts, and media, 6.1% healthcare practitioners, 25.7% service, 23.9% sales and office, 13.6% natural resources, construction, and maintenance, 12.1% production, transportation, and material moving (2008-2012 5-year est.).

Income: Per capita income: $19,254 (2008-2012 5-year est.); Median household income: $29,844 (2008-2012 5-year est.); Average household income: $45,825 (2008-2012 5-year est.); Percent of households with income of $100,000 or more: 10.5% (2008-2012 5-year est.); Poverty rate: 23.6% (2008-2012 5-year est.).

Education: Percent of population age 25 and over with: High school diploma (including GED) or higher: 83.1% (2008-2012 5-year est.); Bachelor's degree or higher: 14.9% (2008-2012 5-year est.); Master's degree or higher: 4.8% (2008-2012 5-year est.).

School District(s)

Benton CCSD 47 (PK-08)
    2011-12 Enrollment: 1,161 . . . . (618) 439-3136
Benton Cons HSD 103 (09-12)
    2011-12 Enrollment: 581 . . . . (618) 439-6415
Franklin/williamson Roe (PK-12)
    2011-12 Enrollment: n/a . . . . (618) 438-9711

Housing: Homeownership rate: 65.4% (2008-2012 5-year est.); Median home value: $61,900 (2008-2012 5-year est.); Median contract rent: $404 per month (2008-2012 5-year est.); Median year structure built: 1958 (2008-2012 5-year est.).

Health Insurance: 51.5% Private; 50.2% Public; 14.7% None. (2008-2012 5-year est.)

Hospitals: Franklin Hospital (25 beds)

Safety: Violent crime rate: 11.3 per 10,000 population; Property crime rate: 366.1 per 10,000 population (2012).

Transportation: Commute to work: 89.6% car, 0.7% public transportation, 5.0% walk, 3.6% work from home (2008-2012 5-year est.); Travel time to work: 48.2% less than 15 minutes, 23.7% 15 to 30 minutes, 18.0% 30 to 45 minutes, 5.3% 45 to 60 minutes, 4.8% 60 minutes or more (2008-2012 5-year est.)

Airports: Benton Municipal Airport (general aviation)

Additional Information Contacts

Benton - West City Chamber of Commerce . . . . (618) 438-2121
    http://www.bentonwestcitychamber.com
City of Benton . . . . (618) 439-6131
    http://bentonil.com

BUCKNER (village). Covers a land area of 0.872 square miles and a water area of 0.021 square miles. Located at 37.98° N. Lat; 89.02° W. Long. Elevation is 404 feet.

Population: 478 (1990); 479 (2000); 462 (2010); Density: 456.5 persons per square mile (2008-2012 5-year est.); Race: 100.0% White, 0.0% Black/African American, 0.0% Asian, 0.0% American Indian/Alaska Native, 0.0% Native Hawaiian/Other Pacific Islander, 0.0% Some other race, 0.0% Two or more races, 1.3% Hispanic of any race (2008-2012 5-year est.); Average household size: 2.11 (2008-2012 5-year est.); Median age: 49.8 (2008-2012 5-year est.); Males per 100 females: 88.6 (2008-2012 5-year est.); Marriage status: 9.4% never married, 66.8% now married, 12.9%

widowed, 11.0% divorced (2008-2012 5-year est.); Foreign born: 0.0% (2008-2012 5-year est.); Ancestry (includes multiple ancestries): 28.1% Italian, 19.3% Irish, 17.6% German, 11.8% English, 7.3% American (2008-2012 5-year est.).

Economy: Homeowner vacancy rate: 0.0%. Rental vacancy rate: 0.0%. (2008-2012 5-year est.); Employment by occupation: 11.1% management, business, and financial, 0.0% computer, engineering, and science, 8.3% education, legal, community service, arts, and media, 0.0% healthcare practitioners, 20.4% service, 23.1% sales and office, 8.3% natural resources, construction, and maintenance, 28.7% production, transportation, and material moving (2008-2012 5-year est.).

Income: Per capita income: $14,447 (2008-2012 5-year est.); Median household income: $29,063 (2008-2012 5-year est.); Average household income: $30,103 (2008-2012 5-year est.); Percent of households with income of $100,000 or more: n/a (2008-2012 5-year est.); Poverty rate: 29.1% (2008-2012 5-year est.).

Education: Percent of population age 25 and over with: High school diploma (including GED) or higher: 81.0% (2008-2012 5-year est.); Bachelor's degree or higher: 11.4% (2008-2012 5-year est.); Master's degree or higher: 1.0% (2008-2012 5-year est.).

Housing: Homeownership rate: 67.2% (2008-2012 5-year est.); Median home value: $48,300 (2008-2012 5-year est.); Median contract rent: $385 per month (2008-2012 5-year est.); Median year structure built: 1960 (2008-2012 5-year est.).

Health Insurance: 39.4% Private; 71.9% Public; 12.1% None. (2008-2012 5-year est.)

Transportation: Commute to work: 95.4% car, 0.0% public transportation, 0.0% walk, 4.6% work from home (2008-2012 5-year est.); Travel time to work: 17.5% less than 15 minutes, 40.8% 15 to 30 minutes, 31.1% 30 to 45 minutes, 10.7% 45 to 60 minutes, 0.0% 60 minutes or more (2008-2012 5-year est.)

CHRISTOPHER (city). Covers a land area of 1.579 square miles and a water area of 0.006 square miles. Located at 37.97° N. Lat; 89.05° W. Long. Elevation is 440 feet.

History: Incorporated 1903.

Population: 2,774 (1990); 2,836 (2000); 2,382 (2010); Density: 1,665.3 persons per square mile (2008-2012 5-year est.); Race: 100.0% White, 0.0% Black/African American, 0.0% Asian, 0.0% American Indian/Alaska Native, 0.0% Native Hawaiian/Other Pacific Islander, 0.0% Some other race, 0.0% Two or more races, 1.2% Hispanic of any race (2008-2012 5-year est.); Average household size: 2.27 (2008-2012 5-year est.); Median age: 39.1 (2008-2012 5-year est.); Males per 100 females: 93.9 (2008-2012 5-year est.); Marriage status: 24.8% never married, 48.8% now married, 7.3% widowed, 19.1% divorced (2008-2012 5-year est.); Foreign born: 0.0% (2008-2012 5-year est.); Ancestry (includes multiple ancestries): 18.7% German, 15.6% English, 14.7% American, 13.8% Irish, 8.0% Italian (2008-2012 5-year est.).

Economy: Single-family building permits issued: 1 (2013); Multi-family building permits issued: 0 (2013); Homeowner vacancy rate: 5.9%. Rental vacancy rate: 0.0%. (2008-2012 5-year est.); Employment by occupation: 5.8% management, business, and financial, 2.6% computer, engineering, and science, 5.2% education, legal, community service, arts, and media, 9.4% healthcare practitioners, 23.5% service, 27.8% sales and office, 8.5% natural resources, construction, and maintenance, 17.2% production, transportation, and material moving (2008-2012 5-year est.).

Income: Per capita income: $18,732 (2008-2012 5-year est.); Median household income: $32,300 (2008-2012 5-year est.); Average household income: $41,590 (2008-2012 5-year est.); Percent of households with income of $100,000 or more: 9.4% (2008-2012 5-year est.); Poverty rate: 25.7% (2008-2012 5-year est.).

Education: Percent of population age 25 and over with: High school diploma (including GED) or higher: 92.4% (2008-2012 5-year est.); Bachelor's degree or higher: 10.3% (2008-2012 5-year est.); Master's degree or higher: 2.8% (2008-2012 5-year est.).

School District(s)

Christopher USD 99 (PK-12)
  2011-12 Enrollment: 871 . . . . (618) 724-9461

Housing: Homeownership rate: 72.1% (2008-2012 5-year est.); Median home value: $49,100 (2008-2012 5-year est.); Median contract rent: $322 per month (2008-2012 5-year est.); Median year structure built: 1950 (2008-2012 5-year est.).

Health Insurance: 50.8% Private; 44.2% Public; 17.7% None. (2008-2012 5-year est.)

Transportation: Commute to work: 93.9% car, 0.0% public transportation, 4.4% walk, 0.9% work from home (2008-2012 5-year est.); Travel time to work: 21.6% less than 15 minutes, 38.8% 15 to 30 minutes, 24.4% 30 to 45 minutes, 13.0% 45 to 60 minutes, 2.2% 60 minutes or more (2008-2012 5-year est.)

COELLO (unincorporated postal area)
Zip Code: 62825
  Covers a land area of 0.313 square miles and a water area of <.001 square miles. Located at 37.99° N. Lat; 89.06° W. Long. Elevation is 469 feet. Population: 203 (2010); Density: 646.7 persons per square mile (2010); Race: 100.0% White, 0.0% Black/African American, 0.0% Asian, 0.0% American Indian/Alaska Native, 0.0% Native Hawaiian/Other Pacific Islander, 0.0% Some other race, 0.0% Two or more races, 1.0% Hispanic of any race (2010); Average household size: 2.39 (2010); Median age: 42.1 (2010); Males per 100 females: 107.1 (2010); Homeownership rate: 88.2% (2010)

EWING (village). Covers a land area of 1.009 square miles and a water area of 0.001 square miles. Located at 38.09° N. Lat; 88.85° W. Long. Elevation is 469 feet.

Population: 264 (1990); 310 (2000); 307 (2010); Density: 270.6 persons per square mile (2008-2012 5-year est.); Race: 100.0% White, 0.0% Black/African American, 0.0% Asian, 0.0% American Indian/Alaska Native, 0.0% Native Hawaiian/Other Pacific Islander, 0.0% Some other race, 0.0% Two or more races, 0.0% Hispanic of any race (2008-2012 5-year est.); Average household size: 2.42 (2008-2012 5-year est.); Median age: 41.1 (2008-2012 5-year est.); Males per 100 females: 111.6 (2008-2012 5-year est.); Marriage status: 18.9% never married, 57.6% now married, 9.7% widowed, 13.8% divorced (2008-2012 5-year est.); Foreign born: 0.0% (2008-2012 5-year est.); Ancestry (includes multiple ancestries): 22.0% German, 12.8% American, 12.1% Italian, 11.4% English, 10.3% Irish (2008-2012 5-year est.).

Economy: Homeowner vacancy rate: 0.0%. Rental vacancy rate: 0.0%. (2008-2012 5-year est.); Employment by occupation: 9.6% management, business, and financial, 8.5% computer, engineering, and science, 10.6% education, legal, community service, arts, and media, 3.2% healthcare practitioners, 13.8% service, 24.5% sales and office, 7.4% natural resources, construction, and maintenance, 22.3% production, transportation, and material moving (2008-2012 5-year est.).

Income: Per capita income: $18,948 (2008-2012 5-year est.); Median household income: $36,875 (2008-2012 5-year est.); Average household income: $44,399 (2008-2012 5-year est.); Percent of households with income of $100,000 or more: 5.3% (2008-2012 5-year est.); Poverty rate: 19.6% (2008-2012 5-year est.).

Education: Percent of population age 25 and over with: High school diploma (including GED) or higher: 82.5% (2008-2012 5-year est.); Bachelor's degree or higher: 7.9% (2008-2012 5-year est.); Master's degree or higher: 1.6% (2008-2012 5-year est.).

School District(s)

Ewing Northern CCSD 115 (PK-08)
  2011-12 Enrollment: 239 . . . . (618) 629-2181

Housing: Homeownership rate: 80.5% (2008-2012 5-year est.); Median home value: $50,300 (2008-2012 5-year est.); Median contract rent: $435 per month (2008-2012 5-year est.); Median year structure built: 1974 (2008-2012 5-year est.).

Health Insurance: 49.5% Private; 49.8% Public; 14.7% None. (2008-2012 5-year est.)

Transportation: Commute to work: 94.4% car, 0.0% public transportation, 1.1% walk, 4.4% work from home (2008-2012 5-year est.); Travel time to work: 34.9% less than 15 minutes, 31.4% 15 to 30 minutes, 18.6% 30 to 45 minutes, 9.3% 45 to 60 minutes, 5.8% 60 minutes or more (2008-2012 5-year est.)

HANAFORD (village). Aka Logan. Covers a land area of 1.007 square miles and a water area of 0.007 square miles. Located at 37.96° N. Lat; 88.83° W. Long. Elevation is 476 feet.

History: Also called Logan.

Population: 380 (1990); 55 (2000); 327 (2010); Density: 215.4 persons per square mile (2008-2012 5-year est.); Race: 100.0% White, 0.0% Black/African American, 0.0% Asian, 0.0% American Indian/Alaska Native, 0.0% Native Hawaiian/Other Pacific Islander, 0.0% Some other race, 0.0% Two or more races, 0.0% Hispanic of any race (2008-2012 5-year est.); Average household size: 2.24 (2008-2012 5-year est.); Median age: 51.4 (2008-2012 5-year est.); Males per 100 females: 123.7 (2008-2012 5-year

est.); Marriage status: 16.3% never married, 42.9% now married, 14.3% widowed, 26.5% divorced (2008-2012 5-year est.); Foreign born: 0.0% (2008-2012 5-year est.); Ancestry (includes multiple ancestries): 27.6% Irish, 22.1% German, 21.7% English, 8.8% Polish, 7.8% Dutch (2008-2012 5-year est.).

Economy: Homeowner vacancy rate: 0.0%. Rental vacancy rate: 33.3%. (2008-2012 5-year est.); Employment by occupation: 8.3% management, business, and financial, 0.0% computer, engineering, and science, 2.4% education, legal, community service, arts, and media, 0.0% healthcare practitioners, 10.7% service, 20.2% sales and office, 20.2% natural resources, construction, and maintenance, 38.1% production, transportation, and material moving (2008-2012 5-year est.).

Income: Per capita income: $23,970 (2008-2012 5-year est.); Median household income: $37,212 (2008-2012 5-year est.); Average household income: $51,293 (2008-2012 5-year est.); Percent of households with income of $100,000 or more: 4.1% (2008-2012 5-year est.); Poverty rate: 15.2% (2008-2012 5-year est.).

Education: Percent of population age 25 and over with: High school diploma (including GED) or higher: 85.2% (2008-2012 5-year est.); Bachelor's degree or higher: 2.3% (2008-2012 5-year est.); Master's degree or higher: 0.0% (2008-2012 5-year est.).

Housing: Homeownership rate: 89.7% (2008-2012 5-year est.); Median home value: $53,500 (2008-2012 5-year est.); Median contract rent: $386 per month (2008-2012 5-year est.); Median year structure built: 1976 (2008-2012 5-year est.).

Health Insurance: 55.8% Private; 43.8% Public; 12.4% None. (2008-2012 5-year est.)

Transportation: Commute to work: 97.6% car, 0.0% public transportation, 0.0% walk, 2.4% work from home (2008-2012 5-year est.); Travel time to work: 21.0% less than 15 minutes, 22.2% 15 to 30 minutes, 35.8% 30 to 45 minutes, 6.2% 45 to 60 minutes, 14.8% 60 minutes or more (2008-2012 5-year est.)

LOGAN (unincorporated postal area)
Zip Code: 62856

Covers a land area of 0.929 square miles and a water area of 0.006 square miles. Located at 37.95° N. Lat; 88.83° W. Long. Elevation is 476 feet. Population: 324 (2010); Density: 348.4 persons per square mile (2010); Race: 97.8% White, 0.0% Black/African American, 0.3% Asian, 0.0% American Indian/Alaska Native, 0.0% Native Hawaiian/Other Pacific Islander, 1.9% Some other race, 1.9% Two or more races, 0.0% Hispanic of any race (2010); Average household size: 2.23 (2010); Median age: 47.0 (2010); Males per 100 females: 95.2 (2010); Homeownership rate: 88.2% (2010)

MACEDONIA (village). Covers a land area of 0.266 square miles and a water area of 0.005 square miles. Located at 38.05° N. Lat; 88.70° W. Long. Elevation is 535 feet.
Population: 58 (1990); 51 (2000); 63 (2010); Density: 116.5 persons per square mile (2008-2012 5-year est.); Race: 100.0% White, 0.0% Black/African American, 0.0% Asian, 0.0% American Indian/Alaska Native, 0.0% Native Hawaiian/Other Pacific Islander, 0.0% Some other race, 0.0% Two or more races, 0.0% Hispanic of any race (2008-2012 5-year est.); Average household size: 2.21 (2008-2012 5-year est.); Median age: 51.6 (2008-2012 5-year est.); Males per 100 females: 181.8 (2008-2012 5-year est.); Marriage status: 25.8% never married, 67.7% now married, 0.0% widowed, 6.5% divorced (2008-2012 5-year est.); Foreign born: 12.9% (2008-2012 5-year est.); Ancestry (includes multiple ancestries): 54.8% Irish, 22.6% German, 12.9% Ukrainian, 6.5% Lithuanian, 3.2% Greek (2008-2012 5-year est.).

Economy: Homeowner vacancy rate: 0.0%. Rental vacancy rate: 0.0%. (2008-2012 5-year est.); Employment by occupation: 42.9% management, business, and financial, 0.0% computer, engineering, and science, 0.0% education, legal, community service, arts, and media, 0.0% healthcare practitioners, 0.0% service, 0.0% sales and office, 57.1% natural resources, construction, and maintenance, 0.0% production, transportation, and material moving (2008-2012 5-year est.).

Income: Per capita income: $18,406 (2008-2012 5-year est.); Median household income: $42,500 (2008-2012 5-year est.); Average household income: $41,014 (2008-2012 5-year est.); Percent of households with income of $100,000 or more: n/a (2008-2012 5-year est.); Poverty rate: 0.0% (2008-2012 5-year est.).

Education: Percent of population age 25 and over with: High school diploma (including GED) or higher: 84.0% (2008-2012 5-year est.);

Bachelor's degree or higher: 16.0% (2008-2012 5-year est.); Master's degree or higher: 16.0% (2008-2012 5-year est.).

Housing: Homeownership rate: 100.0% (2008-2012 5-year est.); Median home value: $45,000 (2008-2012 5-year est.); Median contract rent: n/a per month (2008-2012 5-year est.); Median year structure built: 1961 (2008-2012 5-year est.).

Health Insurance: 87.1% Private; 29.0% Public; 0.0% None. (2008-2012 5-year est.)

Transportation: Commute to work: 57.1% car, 0.0% public transportation, 0.0% walk, 42.9% work from home (2008-2012 5-year est.); Travel time to work: 0.0% less than 15 minutes, 0.0% 15 to 30 minutes, 0.0% 30 to 45 minutes, 100.0% 45 to 60 minutes, 0.0% 60 minutes or more (2008-2012 5-year est.)

MULKEYTOWN (CDP). Covers a land area of 0.275 square miles and a water area of <.001 square miles. Located at 37.97° N. Lat; 89.11° W. Long. Elevation is 446 feet.
Population: n/a (1990); n/a (2000); 175 (2010); Density: 367.1 persons per square mile (2008-2012 5-year est.); Race: 100.0% White, 0.0% Black/African American, 0.0% Asian, 0.0% American Indian/Alaska Native, 0.0% Native Hawaiian/Other Pacific Islander, 0.0% Some other race, 0.0% Two or more races, 0.0% Hispanic of any race (2008-2012 5-year est.); Average household size: 1.98 (2008-2012 5-year est.); Median age: 52.2 (2008-2012 5-year est.); Males per 100 females: 98.0 (2008-2012 5-year est.); Marriage status: 0.0% never married, 73.8% now married, 26.2% widowed, 0.0% divorced (2008-2012 5-year est.); Foreign born: 0.0% (2008-2012 5-year est.); Ancestry (includes multiple ancestries): 37.6% German, 25.7% French, 15.8% American, 10.9% Polish, 8.9% Italian (2008-2012 5-year est.).

Economy: Homeowner vacancy rate: 0.0%. Rental vacancy rate: 0.0%. (2008-2012 5-year est.); Employment by occupation: 0.0% management, business, and financial, 45.5% computer, engineering, and science, 27.3% education, legal, community service, arts, and media, 0.0% healthcare practitioners, 27.3% service, 0.0% sales and office, 0.0% natural resources, construction, and maintenance, 0.0% production, transportation, and material moving (2008-2012 5-year est.).

Income: Per capita income: $22,243 (2008-2012 5-year est.); Median household income: $36,094 (2008-2012 5-year est.); Average household income: $39,076 (2008-2012 5-year est.); Percent of households with income of $100,000 or more: n/a (2008-2012 5-year est.); Poverty rate: 17.8% (2008-2012 5-year est.).

Education: Percent of population age 25 and over with: High school diploma (including GED) or higher: 76.2% (2008-2012 5-year est.); Bachelor's degree or higher: 21.4% (2008-2012 5-year est.); Master's degree or higher: 10.7% (2008-2012 5-year est.).

School District(s)
Zeigler-Royalton CUSD 188 (PK-12)
    2011-12 Enrollment: 629 . . . . (618) 596-5841

Housing: Homeownership rate: 92.2% (2008-2012 5-year est.); Median home value: $65,000 (2008-2012 5-year est.); Median contract rent: n/a per month (2008-2012 5-year est.); Median year structure built: 1965 (2008-2012 5-year est.).

Health Insurance: 52.5% Private; 67.3% Public; 0.0% None. (2008-2012 5-year est.)

Transportation: Commute to work: 100.0% car, 0.0% public transportation, 0.0% walk, 0.0% work from home (2008-2012 5-year est.); Travel time to work: 72.7% less than 15 minutes, 0.0% 15 to 30 minutes, 27.3% 30 to 45 minutes, 0.0% 45 to 60 minutes, 0.0% 60 minutes or more (2008-2012 5-year est.)

NORTH CITY (village). Aka Coello. Covers a land area of 2.183 square miles and a water area of 0.056 square miles. Located at 37.99° N. Lat; 89.06° W. Long.
Population: 538 (1990); 630 (2000); 608 (2010); Density: 352.7 persons per square mile (2008-2012 5-year est.); Race: 99.0% White, 0.0% Black/African American, 0.0% Asian, 0.0% American Indian/Alaska Native, 0.0% Native Hawaiian/Other Pacific Islander, 1.0% Some other race, 1.0% Two or more races, 0.0% Hispanic of any race (2008-2012 5-year est.); Average household size: 2.68 (2008-2012 5-year est.); Median age: 40.3 (2008-2012 5-year est.); Males per 100 females: 123.2 (2008-2012 5-year est.); Marriage status: 15.4% never married, 72.2% now married, 4.7% widowed, 7.7% divorced (2008-2012 5-year est.); Foreign born: 2.9% (2008-2012 5-year est.); Ancestry (includes multiple ancestries): 23.0% German, 17.3% English, 15.5% American, 10.6% Irish, 10.3% Italian (2008-2012 5-year est.).

Economy: Single-family building permits issued: 0 (2013); Multi-family building permits issued: 0 (2013); Homeowner vacancy rate: 0.0%. Rental vacancy rate: 0.0%. (2008-2012 5-year est.); Employment by occupation: 6.1% management, business, and financial, 2.2% computer, engineering, and science, 13.1% education, legal, community service, arts, and media, 3.8% healthcare practitioners, 19.4% service, 20.1% sales and office, 7.0% natural resources, construction, and maintenance, 28.3% production, transportation, and material moving (2008-2012 5-year est.).
Income: Per capita income: $19,842 (2008-2012 5-year est.); Median household income: $52,250 (2008-2012 5-year est.); Average household income: $53,149 (2008-2012 5-year est.); Percent of households with income of $100,000 or more: 13.6% (2008-2012 5-year est.); Poverty rate: 15.1% (2008-2012 5-year est.).
Education: Percent of population age 25 and over with: High school diploma (including GED) or higher: 88.4% (2008-2012 5-year est.); Bachelor's degree or higher: 17.0% (2008-2012 5-year est.); Master's degree or higher: 5.4% (2008-2012 5-year est.).
Housing: Homeownership rate: 88.2% (2008-2012 5-year est.); Median home value: $62,500 (2008-2012 5-year est.); Median contract rent: $377 per month (2008-2012 5-year est.); Median year structure built: 1971 (2008-2012 5-year est.).
Health Insurance: 56.4% Private; 40.9% Public; 11.3% None. (2008-2012 5-year est.)
Transportation: Commute to work: 94.2% car, 0.0% public transportation, 1.0% walk, 2.9% work from home (2008-2012 5-year est.); Travel time to work: 23.2% less than 15 minutes, 40.4% 15 to 30 minutes, 17.9% 30 to 45 minutes, 12.3% 45 to 60 minutes, 6.3% 60 minutes or more (2008-2012 5-year est.)

ORIENT (city).
Covers a land area of 0.744 square miles and a water area of 0.008 square miles. Located at 37.92° N. Lat; 88.98° W. Long. Elevation is 482 feet.
Population: 428 (1990); 296 (2000); 358 (2010); Density: 458.4 persons per square mile (2008-2012 5-year est.); Race: 97.9% White, 0.0% Black/African American, 0.0% Asian, 0.0% American Indian/Alaska Native, 0.0% Native Hawaiian/Other Pacific Islander, 2.1% Some other race, 2.1% Two or more races, 0.0% Hispanic of any race (2008-2012 5-year est.); Average household size: 2.16 (2008-2012 5-year est.); Median age: 46.5 (2008-2012 5-year est.); Males per 100 females: 84.3 (2008-2012 5-year est.); Marriage status: 19.3% never married, 50.3% now married, 2.6% widowed, 27.8% divorced (2008-2012 5-year est.); Foreign born: 0.0% (2008-2012 5-year est.); Ancestry (includes multiple ancestries): 28.2% German, 24.9% English, 24.6% Irish, 5.9% Italian, 5.6% American (2008-2012 5-year est.).
Economy: Homeowner vacancy rate: 0.0%. Rental vacancy rate: 0.0%. (2008-2012 5-year est.); Employment by occupation: 11.3% management, business, and financial, 0.0% computer, engineering, and science, 1.6% education, legal, community service, arts, and media, 5.4% healthcare practitioners, 29.6% service, 24.2% sales and office, 4.8% natural resources, construction, and maintenance, 23.1% production, transportation, and material moving (2008-2012 5-year est.).
Income: Per capita income: $19,879 (2008-2012 5-year est.); Median household income: $33,472 (2008-2012 5-year est.); Average household income: $41,249 (2008-2012 5-year est.); Percent of households with income of $100,000 or more: 1.2% (2008-2012 5-year est.); Poverty rate: 18.0% (2008-2012 5-year est.).
Education: Percent of population age 25 and over with: High school diploma (including GED) or higher: 88.6% (2008-2012 5-year est.); Bachelor's degree or higher: 4.8% (2008-2012 5-year est.); Master's degree or higher: 0.7% (2008-2012 5-year est.).
Housing: Homeownership rate: 79.7% (2008-2012 5-year est.); Median home value: $32,600 (2008-2012 5-year est.); Median contract rent: $379 per month (2008-2012 5-year est.); Median year structure built: Before 1940 (2008-2012 5-year est.).
Health Insurance: 58.7% Private; 37.2% Public; 18.2% None. (2008-2012 5-year est.)
Transportation: Commute to work: 100.0% car, 0.0% public transportation, 0.0% walk, 0.0% work from home (2008-2012 5-year est.); Travel time to work: 24.2% less than 15 minutes, 54.3% 15 to 30 minutes, 9.7% 30 to 45 minutes, 5.9% 45 to 60 minutes, 5.9% 60 minutes or more (2008-2012 5-year est.)

ROYALTON (village).
Covers a land area of 1.115 square miles and a water area of 0.008 square miles. Located at 37.88° N. Lat; 89.11° W. Long. Elevation is 394 feet.
History: Incorporated 1907.
Population: 1,191 (1990); 1,130 (2000); 1,151 (2010); Density: 1,006.2 persons per square mile (2008-2012 5-year est.); Race: 99.5% White, 0.0% Black/African American, 0.2% Asian, 0.0% American Indian/Alaska Native, 0.0% Native Hawaiian/Other Pacific Islander, 0.3% Some other race, 0.0% Two or more races, 1.4% Hispanic of any race (2008-2012 5-year est.); Average household size: 2.57 (2008-2012 5-year est.); Median age: 37.8 (2008-2012 5-year est.); Males per 100 females: 108.6 (2008-2012 5-year est.); Marriage status: 26.5% never married, 54.0% now married, 6.0% widowed, 13.5% divorced (2008-2012 5-year est.); Foreign born: 1.3% (2008-2012 5-year est.); Ancestry (includes multiple ancestries): 18.1% English, 14.2% German, 12.9% Irish, 10.0% American, 7.8% Italian (2008-2012 5-year est.).
Economy: Single-family building permits issued: 2 (2013); Multi-family building permits issued: 0 (2013); Homeowner vacancy rate: 5.5%. Rental vacancy rate: 8.8%. (2008-2012 5-year est.); Employment by occupation: 6.3% management, business, and financial, 4.0% computer, engineering, and science, 4.0% education, legal, community service, arts, and media, 14.2% healthcare practitioners, 15.0% service, 18.3% sales and office, 17.0% natural resources, construction, and maintenance, 21.3% production, transportation, and material moving (2008-2012 5-year est.).
Income: Per capita income: $17,075 (2008-2012 5-year est.); Median household income: $36,250 (2008-2012 5-year est.); Average household income: $42,979 (2008-2012 5-year est.); Percent of households with income of $100,000 or more: 5.7% (2008-2012 5-year est.); Poverty rate: 22.5% (2008-2012 5-year est.).
Education: Percent of population age 25 and over with: High school diploma (including GED) or higher: 83.4% (2008-2012 5-year est.); Bachelor's degree or higher: 8.5% (2008-2012 5-year est.); Master's degree or higher: 1.0% (2008-2012 5-year est.).
Housing: Homeownership rate: 78.7% (2008-2012 5-year est.); Median home value: $48,300 (2008-2012 5-year est.); Median contract rent: $338 per month (2008-2012 5-year est.); Median year structure built: 1959 (2008-2012 5-year est.).
Health Insurance: 57.5% Private; 47.4% Public; 13.1% None. (2008-2012 5-year est.)
Transportation: Commute to work: 92.7% car, 0.0% public transportation, 0.5% walk, 3.9% work from home (2008-2012 5-year est.); Travel time to work: 14.8% less than 15 minutes, 41.3% 15 to 30 minutes, 28.4% 30 to 45 minutes, 7.9% 45 to 60 minutes, 7.7% 60 minutes or more (2008-2012 5-year est.)

SESSER (city).
Covers a land area of 1.015 square miles and a water area of <.001 square miles. Located at 38.09° N. Lat; 89.05° W. Long. Elevation is 479 feet.
History: Incorporated 1906.
Population: 2,087 (1990); 2,128 (2000); 1,931 (2010); Density: 2,052.6 persons per square mile (2008-2012 5-year est.); Race: 94.3% White, 0.0% Black/African American, 0.6% Asian, 1.5% American Indian/Alaska Native, 0.0% Native Hawaiian/Other Pacific Islander, 3.6% Some other race, 3.3% Two or more races, 0.7% Hispanic of any race (2008-2012 5-year est.); Average household size: 2.55 (2008-2012 5-year est.); Median age: 41.4 (2008-2012 5-year est.); Males per 100 females: 110.0 (2008-2012 5-year est.); Marriage status: 21.4% never married, 54.5% now married, 8.9% widowed, 15.2% divorced (2008-2012 5-year est.); Foreign born: 1.2% (2008-2012 5-year est.); Ancestry (includes multiple ancestries): 23.2% German, 20.0% Irish, 18.8% English, 10.3% American, 4.6% Italian (2008-2012 5-year est.).
Economy: Single-family building permits issued: 1 (2013); Multi-family building permits issued: 0 (2013); Homeowner vacancy rate: 3.4%. Rental vacancy rate: 0.0%. (2008-2012 5-year est.); Employment by occupation: 2.8% management, business, and financial, 0.0% computer, engineering, and science, 7.6% education, legal, community service, arts, and media, 6.6% healthcare practitioners, 20.4% service, 23.7% sales and office, 13.4% natural resources, construction, and maintenance, 25.4% production, transportation, and material moving (2008-2012 5-year est.).
Income: Per capita income: $18,466 (2008-2012 5-year est.); Median household income: $38,011 (2008-2012 5-year est.); Average household income: $46,546 (2008-2012 5-year est.); Percent of households with income of $100,000 or more: 8.2% (2008-2012 5-year est.); Poverty rate: 20.7% (2008-2012 5-year est.).

Education: Percent of population age 25 and over with: High school diploma (including GED) or higher: 89.8% (2008-2012 5-year est.); Bachelor's degree or higher: 14.0% (2008-2012 5-year est.); Master's degree or higher: 4.5% (2008-2012 5-year est.).

School District(s)
Sesser-Valier CUSD 196 (PK-12)
    2011-12 Enrollment: 759. . . . . (618) 625-5105
Housing: Homeownership rate: 83.6% (2008-2012 5-year est.); Median home value: $62,000 (2008-2012 5-year est.); Median contract rent: $357 per month (2008-2012 5-year est.); Median year structure built: 1954 (2008-2012 5-year est.).
Health Insurance: 57.5% Private; 49.8% Public; 13.3% None. (2008-2012 5-year est.)
Transportation: Commute to work: 94.4% car, 0.0% public transportation, 0.0% walk, 2.7% work from home (2008-2012 5-year est.); Travel time to work: 18.4% less than 15 minutes, 39.7% 15 to 30 minutes, 30.9% 30 to 45 minutes, 4.8% 45 to 60 minutes, 6.2% 60 minutes or more (2008-2012 5-year est.)

Additional Information Contacts
City of Sesser . . . . (618) 625-3611
    http://www.sesser.org
Sesser Area Chamber of Commerce . . . . (618) 625-5566
    http://sesserchamber.com

THOMPSONVILLE (village). Covers a land area of 2.031 square miles and a water area of 0.016 square miles. Located at 37.91° N. Lat; 88.77° W. Long. Elevation is 502 feet.
Population: 602 (1990); 571 (2000); 543 (2010); Density: 339.3 persons per square mile (2008-2012 5-year est.); Race: 98.1% White, 1.9% Black/African American, 0.0% Asian, 0.0% American Indian/Alaska Native, 0.0% Native Hawaiian/Other Pacific Islander, 0.0% Some other race, 0.0% Two or more races, 6.4% Hispanic of any race (2008-2012 5-year est.); Average household size: 2.93 (2008-2012 5-year est.); Median age: 33.8 (2008-2012 5-year est.); Males per 100 females: 100.9 (2008-2012 5-year est.); Marriage status: 18.3% never married, 63.2% now married, 5.3% widowed, 13.1% divorced (2008-2012 5-year est.); Foreign born: 3.0% (2008-2012 5-year est.); Ancestry (includes multiple ancestries): 27.3% German, 18.6% English, 13.8% Irish, 8.6% American, 3.8% Scotch-Irish (2008-2012 5-year est.).
Economy: Homeowner vacancy rate: 5.0%. Rental vacancy rate: 23.2%. (2008-2012 5-year est.); Employment by occupation: 3.4% management, business, and financial, 0.0% computer, engineering, and science, 8.0% education, legal, community service, arts, and media, 2.7% healthcare practitioners, 18.9% service, 40.2% sales and office, 9.5% natural resources, construction, and maintenance, 17.4% production, transportation, and material moving (2008-2012 5-year est.).
Income: Per capita income: $14,792 (2008-2012 5-year est.); Median household income: $39,821 (2008-2012 5-year est.); Average household income: $42,318 (2008-2012 5-year est.); Percent of households with income of $100,000 or more: 3.0% (2008-2012 5-year est.); Poverty rate: 14.9% (2008-2012 5-year est.).
Education: Percent of population age 25 and over with: High school diploma (including GED) or higher: 86.3% (2008-2012 5-year est.); Bachelor's degree or higher: 8.1% (2008-2012 5-year est.); Master's degree or higher: 1.6% (2008-2012 5-year est.).

School District(s)
Thompsonville CUSD 174 (PK-12)
    2011-12 Enrollment: 354. . . . . (618) 627-2446
Housing: Homeownership rate: 73.2% (2008-2012 5-year est.); Median home value: $54,500 (2008-2012 5-year est.); Median contract rent: $325 per month (2008-2012 5-year est.); Median year structure built: 1975 (2008-2012 5-year est.).
Health Insurance: 54.6% Private; 41.1% Public; 18.4% None. (2008-2012 5-year est.)
Transportation: Commute to work: 100.0% car, 0.0% public transportation, 0.0% walk, 0.0% work from home (2008-2012 5-year est.); Travel time to work: 29.3% less than 15 minutes, 34.9% 15 to 30 minutes, 21.7% 30 to 45 minutes, 7.6% 45 to 60 minutes, 6.4% 60 minutes or more (2008-2012 5-year est.)

VALIER (village). Covers a land area of 1.124 square miles and a water area of 0.008 square miles. Located at 38.02° N. Lat; 89.04° W. Long. Elevation is 459 feet.
Population: 708 (1990); 662 (2000); 669 (2010); Density: 536.5 persons per square mile (2008-2012 5-year est.); Race: 100.0% White, 0.0%

Black/African American, 0.0% Asian, 0.0% American Indian/Alaska Native, 0.0% Native Hawaiian/Other Pacific Islander, 0.0% Some other race, 0.0% Two or more races, 5.0% Hispanic of any race (2008-2012 5-year est.); Average household size: 2.33 (2008-2012 5-year est.); Median age: 44.7 (2008-2012 5-year est.); Males per 100 females: 114.6 (2008-2012 5-year est.); Marriage status: 9.0% never married, 77.2% now married, 2.2% widowed, 11.6% divorced (2008-2012 5-year est.); Foreign born: 1.3% (2008-2012 5-year est.); Ancestry (includes multiple ancestries): 26.4% Irish, 25.2% German, 13.1% English, 10.1% Dutch, 8.1% French (2008-2012 5-year est.).
Economy: Single-family building permits issued: 0 (2013); Multi-family building permits issued: 0 (2013); Homeowner vacancy rate: 1.2%. Rental vacancy rate: 40.7%. (2008-2012 5-year est.); Employment by occupation: 10.0% management, business, and financial, 0.0% computer, engineering, and science, 2.3% education, legal, community service, arts, and media, 3.2% healthcare practitioners, 31.7% service, 22.6% sales and office, 13.6% natural resources, construction, and maintenance, 16.7% production, transportation, and material moving (2008-2012 5-year est.).
Income: Per capita income: $17,126 (2008-2012 5-year est.); Median household income: $32,426 (2008-2012 5-year est.); Average household income: $39,210 (2008-2012 5-year est.); Percent of households with income of $100,000 or more: 2.3% (2008-2012 5-year est.); Poverty rate: 18.7% (2008-2012 5-year est.).
Education: Percent of population age 25 and over with: High school diploma (including GED) or higher: 84.4% (2008-2012 5-year est.); Bachelor's degree or higher: 7.9% (2008-2012 5-year est.); Master's degree or higher: 3.1% (2008-2012 5-year est.).
Housing: Homeownership rate: 93.8% (2008-2012 5-year est.); Median home value: $52,100 (2008-2012 5-year est.); Median contract rent: $375 per month (2008-2012 5-year est.); Median year structure built: 1946 (2008-2012 5-year est.).
Health Insurance: 63.3% Private; 40.0% Public; 13.4% None. (2008-2012 5-year est.)
Transportation: Commute to work: 89.1% car, 0.0% public transportation, 3.2% walk, 7.7% work from home (2008-2012 5-year est.); Travel time to work: 19.6% less than 15 minutes, 27.9% 15 to 30 minutes, 20.6% 30 to 45 minutes, 12.7% 45 to 60 minutes, 19.1% 60 minutes or more (2008-2012 5-year est.)

WEST CITY (village). Covers a land area of 1.608 square miles and a water area of 0.017 square miles. Located at 38.00° N. Lat; 88.95° W. Long. Elevation is 456 feet.
History: Incorporated 1911.
Population: 747 (1990); 716 (2000); 661 (2010); Density: 499.4 persons per square mile (2008-2012 5-year est.); Race: 99.4% White, 0.0% Black/African American, 0.0% Asian, 0.0% American Indian/Alaska Native, 0.0% Native Hawaiian/Other Pacific Islander, 0.6% Some other race, 0.6% Two or more races, 0.0% Hispanic of any race (2008-2012 5-year est.); Average household size: 2.19 (2008-2012 5-year est.); Median age: 39.4 (2008-2012 5-year est.); Males per 100 females: 103.3 (2008-2012 5-year est.); Marriage status: 21.3% never married, 45.8% now married, 12.1% widowed, 20.8% divorced (2008-2012 5-year est.); Foreign born: 1.5% (2008-2012 5-year est.); Ancestry (includes multiple ancestries): 25.2% German, 19.4% Irish, 15.4% English, 5.1% Polish, 3.9% Italian (2008-2012 5-year est.).
Economy: Single-family building permits issued: 0 (2013); Multi-family building permits issued: 0 (2013); Homeowner vacancy rate: 0.0%. Rental vacancy rate: 0.0%. (2008-2012 5-year est.); Employment by occupation: 3.9% management, business, and financial, 1.1% computer, engineering, and science, 6.7% education, legal, community service, arts, and media, 5.3% healthcare practitioners, 26.7% service, 18.0% sales and office, 12.6% natural resources, construction, and maintenance, 25.6% production, transportation, and material moving (2008-2012 5-year est.).
Income: Per capita income: $18,516 (2008-2012 5-year est.); Median household income: $35,714 (2008-2012 5-year est.); Average household income: $39,979 (2008-2012 5-year est.); Percent of households with income of $100,000 or more: 3.3% (2008-2012 5-year est.); Poverty rate: 16.6% (2008-2012 5-year est.).
Education: Percent of population age 25 and over with: High school diploma (including GED) or higher: 80.8% (2008-2012 5-year est.); Bachelor's degree or higher: 6.5% (2008-2012 5-year est.); Master's degree or higher: 3.7% (2008-2012 5-year est.).
Housing: Homeownership rate: 67.5% (2008-2012 5-year est.); Median home value: $41,300 (2008-2012 5-year est.); Median contract rent: $378

per month (2008-2012 5-year est.); Median year structure built: 1971 (2008-2012 5-year est.).
Health Insurance: 46.9% Private; 49.2% Public; 24.2% None. (2008-2012 5-year est.)
Safety: Violent crime rate: 165.9 per 10,000 population; Property crime rate: 859.7 per 10,000 population (2012).
Transportation: Commute to work: 93.3% car, 1.2% public transportation, 2.9% walk, 2.0% work from home (2008-2012 5-year est.); Travel time to work: 52.7% less than 15 minutes, 18.6% 15 to 30 minutes, 14.8% 30 to 45 minutes, 6.2% 45 to 60 minutes, 7.7% 60 minutes or more (2008-2012 5-year est.)

WEST FRANKFORT (city).
Covers a land area of 4.974 square miles and a water area of 0.041 square miles. Located at 37.90° N. Lat; 88.93° W. Long. Elevation is 400 feet.
History: Incorporated 1901; annexed Frankfort Heights in 1923.
Population: 8,526 (1990); 8,196 (2000); 8,182 (2010); Density: 1,687.4 persons per square mile (2008-2012 5-year est.); Race: 95.9% White, 0.1% Black/African American, 1.2% Asian, 0.0% American Indian/Alaska Native, 0.0% Native Hawaiian/Other Pacific Islander, 2.8% Some other race, 2.6% Two or more races, 0.7% Hispanic of any race (2008-2012 5-year est.); Average household size: 2.35 (2008-2012 5-year est.); Median age: 41.1 (2008-2012 5-year est.); Males per 100 females: 94.5 (2008-2012 5-year est.); Marriage status: 21.3% never married, 44.1% now married, 9.2% widowed, 25.4% divorced (2008-2012 5-year est.); Foreign born: 0.9% (2008-2012 5-year est.); Ancestry (includes multiple ancestries): 22.9% German, 18.3% Irish, 13.9% English, 7.4% Italian, 6.9% American (2008-2012 5-year est.).
Economy: Single-family building permits issued: 0 (2013); Multi-family building permits issued: 0 (2013); Homeowner vacancy rate: 4.2%. Rental vacancy rate: 7.4%. (2008-2012 5-year est.); Employment by occupation: 9.2% management, business, and financial, 4.2% computer, engineering, and science, 8.4% education, legal, community service, arts, and media, 2.7% healthcare practitioners, 18.6% service, 25.3% sales and office, 17.8% natural resources, construction, and maintenance, 13.9% production, transportation, and material moving (2008-2012 5-year est.).
Income: Per capita income: $18,569 (2008-2012 5-year est.); Median household income: $33,295 (2008-2012 5-year est.); Average household income: $43,447 (2008-2012 5-year est.); Percent of households with income of $100,000 or more: 6.1% (2008-2012 5-year est.); Poverty rate: 23.3% (2008-2012 5-year est.).
Education: Percent of population age 25 and over with: High school diploma (including GED) or higher: 83.4% (2008-2012 5-year est.); Bachelor's degree or higher: 11.2% (2008-2012 5-year est.); Master's degree or higher: 3.8% (2008-2012 5-year est.).

School District(s)
Frankfort CUSD 168 (PK-12)
   2011-12 Enrollment: 1,905 . . . . (618) 937-2421
Housing: Homeownership rate: 69.6% (2008-2012 5-year est.); Median home value: $57,200 (2008-2012 5-year est.); Median contract rent: $387 per month (2008-2012 5-year est.); Median year structure built: 1952 (2008-2012 5-year est.).
Health Insurance: 44.3% Private; 54.6% Public; 16.5% None. (2008-2012 5-year est.)
Safety: Violent crime rate: 30.5 per 10,000 population; Property crime rate: 145.2 per 10,000 population (2012).
Transportation: Commute to work: 92.6% car, 0.7% public transportation, 0.2% walk, 4.5% work from home (2008-2012 5-year est.); Travel time to work: 36.3% less than 15 minutes, 42.1% 15 to 30 minutes, 14.5% 30 to 45 minutes, 4.1% 45 to 60 minutes, 3.0% 60 minutes or more (2008-2012 5-year est.)
Additional Information Contacts
City of West Frankfort . . . . (618) 932-3262
   http://www.westfrankfort-il.com
West Frankfort Chamber of Commerce . . . . (618) 932-2181
   http://www.westfrankfort-il.com

WHITTINGTON (unincorporated postal area)
Zip Code: 62897
   Covers a land area of 12.465 square miles and a water area of 1.157 square miles. Located at 38.09° N. Lat; 88.89° W. Long. Elevation is 443 feet. Population: 398 (2010); Density: 31.9 persons per square mile (2010); Race: 99.2% White, 0.0% Black/African American, 0.0% Asian, 0.0% American Indian/Alaska Native, 0.0% Native Hawaiian/Other Pacific Islander, 0.8% Some other race, 0.8% Two or more races, 0.5%

Hispanic of any race (2010); Average household size: 2.41 (2010); Median age: 46.0 (2010); Males per 100 females: 103.1 (2010); Homeownership rate: 85.4% (2010)

ZEIGLER (city).
Covers a land area of 1.354 square miles and a water area of 0.007 square miles. Located at 37.91° N. Lat; 89.05° W. Long. Elevation is 410 feet.
Population: 1,746 (1990); 1,669 (2000); 1,801 (2010); Density: 1,373.9 persons per square mile (2008-2012 5-year est.); Race: 98.7% White, 0.2% Black/African American, 0.0% Asian, 0.0% American Indian/Alaska Native, 0.0% Native Hawaiian/Other Pacific Islander, 1.1% Some other race, 1.1% Two or more races, 1.6% Hispanic of any race (2008-2012 5-year est.); Average household size: 2.71 (2008-2012 5-year est.); Median age: 39.7 (2008-2012 5-year est.); Males per 100 females: 90.4 (2008-2012 5-year est.); Marriage status: 31.2% never married, 48.0% now married, 10.1% widowed, 10.7% divorced (2008-2012 5-year est.); Foreign born: 0.4% (2008-2012 5-year est.); Ancestry (includes multiple ancestries): 21.3% German, 16.0% English, 12.2% Irish, 7.9% Polish, 7.0% American (2008-2012 5-year est.).
Economy: Single-family building permits issued: 0 (2013); Multi-family building permits issued: 0 (2013); Homeowner vacancy rate: 6.3%. Rental vacancy rate: 15.9%. (2008-2012 5-year est.); Employment by occupation: 13.3% management, business, and financial, 0.3% computer, engineering, and science, 4.5% education, legal, community service, arts, and media, 3.2% healthcare practitioners, 27.8% service, 18.0% sales and office, 16.1% natural resources, construction, and maintenance, 16.9% production, transportation, and material moving (2008-2012 5-year est.).
Income: Per capita income: $15,487 (2008-2012 5-year est.); Median household income: $31,422 (2008-2012 5-year est.); Average household income: $41,847 (2008-2012 5-year est.); Percent of households with income of $100,000 or more: 3.2% (2008-2012 5-year est.); Poverty rate: 26.8% (2008-2012 5-year est.).
Education: Percent of population age 25 and over with: High school diploma (including GED) or higher: 84.3% (2008-2012 5-year est.); Bachelor's degree or higher: 11.1% (2008-2012 5-year est.); Master's degree or higher: 2.5% (2008-2012 5-year est.).
Housing: Homeownership rate: 77.2% (2008-2012 5-year est.); Median home value: $44,300 (2008-2012 5-year est.); Median contract rent: $346 per month (2008-2012 5-year est.); Median year structure built: 1948 (2008-2012 5-year est.).
Health Insurance: 46.3% Private; 56.6% Public; 14.1% None. (2008-2012 5-year est.)
Safety: Violent crime rate: 470.9 per 10,000 population; Property crime rate: 354.6 per 10,000 population (2012).
Transportation: Commute to work: 93.0% car, 0.5% public transportation, 1.1% walk, 4.6% work from home (2008-2012 5-year est.); Travel time to work: 21.7% less than 15 minutes, 39.9% 15 to 30 minutes, 23.1% 30 to 45 minutes, 4.6% 45 to 60 minutes, 10.6% 60 minutes or more (2008-2012 5-year est.)

Fulton County

Located in west central Illinois; bounded on the southeast by the Illinois River; drained by the Spoon River. Covers a land area of 865.595 square miles, a water area of 16.979 square miles, and is located in the Central Time Zone at 40.47° N. Lat., 90.21° W. Long. The county was founded in 1823. County seat is Lewistown.

Fulton County is part of the Canton, IL Micropolitan Statistical Area. The entire metro area includes: Fulton County, IL

Population: 38,080 (1990); 38,250 (2000); 37,069 (2010); Race: 94.6% White, 3.4% Black/African American, 0.1% Asian, 0.1% American Indian/Alaska Native, 0.1% Native Hawaiian/Other Pacific Islander, 1.7% Some other race, 1.3% Two or more races, 2.4% Hispanic of any race (2008-2012 5-year est.); Density: 42.4 persons per square mile (2008-2012 5-year est.); Average household size: 2.37 (2008-2012 5-year est.); Median age: 42.3 (2008-2012 5-year est.); Males per 100 females: 107.6 (2008-2012 5-year est.).
Religion: Six largest groups: 10.9% Methodist/Pietist, 9.6% Baptist, 3.9% Non-denominational Protestant, 3.3% Catholicism, 2.7% Holiness, 2.3% Presbyterian-Reformed (2010)
Economy: Unemployment rate: 8.4% (April 2014); Total civilian labor force: 16,835 (April 2014); Leading industries: 29.7% health care and social assistance; 19.9% retail trade; 11.1% accommodation & food

services (2012); Farms: 970 totaling 355,010 acres (2012); Companies that employ 500 or more persons: 1 (2012); Companies that employ 100 to 499 persons: 7 (2012); Companies that employ less than 100 persons: 662 (2012); Black-owned businesses: n/a (2007); Hispanic-owned businesses: n/a (2007); Asian-owned businesses: n/a (2007); Women-owned businesses: 731 (2007); Single-family building permits issued: 32 (2013); Multi-family building permits issued: 2 (2013).

Income: Per capita income: $21,396 (2008-2012 5-year est.); Median household income: $43,363 (2008-2012 5-year est.); Average household income: $52,669 (2008-2012 5-year est.); Percent of households with income of $100,000 or more: 11.4% (2008-2012 5-year est.); Poverty rate: 14.8% (2008-2012 5-year est.); Bankruptcy rate: 3.44% (2013).

Taxes: Total county taxes per capita: $120 (2011); County property taxes per capita: $120 (2011).

Education: Percent of population age 25 and over with: High school diploma (including GED) or higher: 85.1% (2008-2012 5-year est.); Bachelor's degree or higher: 14.4% (2008-2012 5-year est.); Master's degree or higher: 4.0% (2008-2012 5-year est.).

Housing: Homeownership rate: 74.4% (2008-2012 5-year est.); Median home value: $81,800 (2008-2012 5-year est.); Median contract rent: $440 per month (2008-2012 5-year est.); Median year structure built: 1954 (2008-2012 5-year est.).

Health: Birth rate: 94.1 per 10,000 population (2013); Death rate: 124.6 per 10,000 population (2013); Age-adjusted cancer mortality rate: 199.1 deaths per 100,000 population (2011); Number of physicians: 6.2 per 10,000 population (2011); Hospital beds: 26.7 per 10,000 population (2010); Hospital admissions: 682.0 per 10,000 population (2010).

Elections: 2012 Presidential election results: 54.3% Obama, 43.2% Romney

National and State Parks: Anderson Lake State Conservation Area; Dickson Mounds State Park; Rice Lake State Conservation Area

Additional Information Contacts

Fulton County Government . . . . (309) 547-3041
    http://www.fultonco.org

Fulton County Communities

ASTORIA (town). Aka formerly Vienna. Covers a land area of 0.586 square miles and a water area of 0 square miles. Located at 40.23° N. Lat; 90.36° W. Long. Elevation is 712 feet.

History: The villages of Washington, laid out in 1836, and Vienna, platted in 1837, were later combined and named Astoria, for John Jacob Astor who owned land in the area. Astoria was a station on the stagecoach line between Peoria and Quincy.

Population: 1,205 (1990); 1,193 (2000); 1,141 (2010); Density: 2,175.9 persons per square mile (2008-2012 5-year est.); Race: 97.0% White, 0.0% Black/African American, 1.0% Asian, 0.0% American Indian/Alaska Native, 0.2% Native Hawaiian/Other Pacific Islander, 1.8% Some other race, 1.3% Two or more races, 1.5% Hispanic of any race (2008-2012 5-year est.); Average household size: 2.42 (2008-2012 5-year est.); Median age: 40.1 (2008-2012 5-year est.); Males per 100 females: 109.2 (2008-2012 5-year est.); Marriage status: 24.9% never married, 49.4% now married, 10.6% widowed, 15.1% divorced (2008-2012 5-year est.); Foreign born: 0.0% (2008-2012 5-year est.); Ancestry (includes multiple ancestries): 21.6% German, 19.9% American, 11.4% English, 9.6% Dutch, 8.9% Irish (2008-2012 5-year est.).

Economy: Single-family building permits issued: 1 (2013); Multi-family building permits issued: 0 (2013); Homeowner vacancy rate: 1.9%. Rental vacancy rate: 0.0%. (2008-2012 5-year est.); Employment by occupation: 11.5% management, business, and financial, 2.3% computer, engineering, and science, 7.7% education, legal, community service, arts, and media, 6.6% healthcare practitioners, 21.7% service, 15.3% sales and office, 6.4% natural resources, construction, and maintenance, 28.5% production, transportation, and material moving (2008-2012 5-year est.).

Income: Per capita income: $20,062 (2008-2012 5-year est.); Median household income: $39,539 (2008-2012 5-year est.); Average household income: $46,187 (2008-2012 5-year est.); Percent of households with income of $100,000 or more: 4.6% (2008-2012 5-year est.); Poverty rate: 10.2% (2008-2012 5-year est.).

Education: Percent of population age 25 and over with: High school diploma (including GED) or higher: 85.6% (2008-2012 5-year est.); Bachelor's degree or higher: 11.4% (2008-2012 5-year est.); Master's degree or higher: 1.1% (2008-2012 5-year est.).

School District(s)

Astoria CUSD 1 (PK-12)
    2011-12 Enrollment: 402. . . . . (309) 329-2111

Housing: Homeownership rate: 82.2% (2008-2012 5-year est.); Median home value: $50,300 (2008-2012 5-year est.); Median contract rent: $332 per month (2008-2012 5-year est.); Median year structure built: 1947 (2008-2012 5-year est.).

Health Insurance: 65.4% Private; 41.5% Public; 8.7% None. (2008-2012 5-year est.)

Transportation: Commute to work: 94.7% car, 0.0% public transportation, 2.2% walk, 2.2% work from home (2008-2012 5-year est.); Travel time to work: 31.7% less than 15 minutes, 17.5% 15 to 30 minutes, 26.1% 30 to 45 minutes, 7.9% 45 to 60 minutes, 16.8% 60 minutes or more (2008-2012 5-year est.)

AVON (village). Covers a land area of 0.454 square miles and a water area of 0 square miles. Located at 40.66° N. Lat; 90.44° W. Long. Elevation is 640 feet.

Population: 957 (1990); 915 (2000); 799 (2010); Density: 1,515.9 persons per square mile (2008-2012 5-year est.); Race: 92.9% White, 0.0% Black/African American, 1.3% Asian, 0.9% American Indian/Alaska Native, 0.0% Native Hawaiian/Other Pacific Islander, 4.9% Some other race, 0.6% Two or more races, 4.8% Hispanic of any race (2008-2012 5-year est.); Average household size: 2.18 (2008-2012 5-year est.); Median age: 45.6 (2008-2012 5-year est.); Males per 100 females: 114.3 (2008-2012 5-year est.); Marriage status: 29.4% never married, 44.4% now married, 11.1% widowed, 15.1% divorced (2008-2012 5-year est.); Foreign born: 5.7% (2008-2012 5-year est.); Ancestry (includes multiple ancestries): 29.1% German, 23.4% English, 12.9% Irish, 12.6% American, 7.8% Dutch (2008-2012 5-year est.).

Economy: Single-family building permits issued: 0 (2013); Multi-family building permits issued: 0 (2013); Homeowner vacancy rate: 4.8%. Rental vacancy rate: 0.0%. (2008-2012 5-year est.); Employment by occupation: 11.9% management, business, and financial, 3.2% computer, engineering, and science, 3.2% education, legal, community service, arts, and media, 4.5% healthcare practitioners, 26.0% service, 11.9% sales and office, 8.7% natural resources, construction, and maintenance, 30.8% production, transportation, and material moving (2008-2012 5-year est.).

Income: Per capita income: $21,219 (2008-2012 5-year est.); Median household income: $35,357 (2008-2012 5-year est.); Average household income: $45,205 (2008-2012 5-year est.); Percent of households with income of $100,000 or more: 6.2% (2008-2012 5-year est.); Poverty rate: 18.0% (2008-2012 5-year est.).

Education: Percent of population age 25 and over with: High school diploma (including GED) or higher: 78.0% (2008-2012 5-year est.); Bachelor's degree or higher: 8.6% (2008-2012 5-year est.); Master's degree or higher: 4.0% (2008-2012 5-year est.).

School District(s)

Avon CUSD 176 (PK-12)
    2011-12 Enrollment: 227. . . . . (309) 465-3708

Housing: Homeownership rate: 71.1% (2008-2012 5-year est.); Median home value: $55,500 (2008-2012 5-year est.); Median contract rent: $386 per month (2008-2012 5-year est.); Median year structure built: 1956 (2008-2012 5-year est.).

Health Insurance: 45.2% Private; 51.4% Public; 23.3% None. (2008-2012 5-year est.)

Transportation: Commute to work: 88.1% car, 0.0% public transportation, 8.9% walk, 2.0% work from home (2008-2012 5-year est.); Travel time to work: 40.2% less than 15 minutes, 13.9% 15 to 30 minutes, 27.4% 30 to 45 minutes, 1.7% 45 to 60 minutes, 16.9% 60 minutes or more (2008-2012 5-year est.)

BANNER (village). Covers a land area of 1.290 square miles and a water area of 0 square miles. Located at 40.51° N. Lat; 89.92° W. Long. Elevation is 469 feet.

Population: 160 (1990); 149 (2000); 189 (2010); Density: 127.2 persons per square mile (2008-2012 5-year est.); Race: 100.0% White, 0.0% Black/African American, 0.0% Asian, 0.0% American Indian/Alaska Native, 0.0% Native Hawaiian/Other Pacific Islander, 0.0% Some other race, 0.0% Two or more races, 4.3% Hispanic of any race (2008-2012 5-year est.); Average household size: 2.00 (2008-2012 5-year est.); Median age: 41.3 (2008-2012 5-year est.); Males per 100 females: 107.6 (2008-2012 5-year est.); Marriage status: 18.5% never married, 53.8% now married, 19.2% widowed, 8.5% divorced (2008-2012 5-year est.); Foreign born: 0.0% (2008-2012 5-year est.); Ancestry (includes multiple ancestries): 39.0%

German, 16.5% Irish, 16.5% English, 7.9% American, 4.3% Italian (2008-2012 5-year est.).
Economy: Homeowner vacancy rate: 6.6%. Rental vacancy rate: 0.0%. (2008-2012 5-year est.); Employment by occupation: 4.7% management, business, and financial, 4.7% computer, engineering, and science, 3.1% education, legal, community service, arts, and media, 1.6% healthcare practitioners, 20.3% service, 20.3% sales and office, 28.1% natural resources, construction, and maintenance, 17.2% production, transportation, and material moving (2008-2012 5-year est.).
Income: Per capita income: $21,266 (2008-2012 5-year est.); Median household income: $31,923 (2008-2012 5-year est.); Average household income: $41,959 (2008-2012 5-year est.); Percent of households with income of $100,000 or more: 4.9% (2008-2012 5-year est.); Poverty rate: 11.6% (2008-2012 5-year est.).
Education: Percent of population age 25 and over with: High school diploma (including GED) or higher: 88.8% (2008-2012 5-year est.); Bachelor's degree or higher: 7.2% (2008-2012 5-year est.); Master's degree or higher: 1.6% (2008-2012 5-year est.).
Housing: Homeownership rate: 86.6% (2008-2012 5-year est.); Median home value: $100,600 (2008-2012 5-year est.); Median contract rent: $438 per month (2008-2012 5-year est.); Median year structure built: 1961 (2008-2012 5-year est.).
Health Insurance: 79.3% Private; 40.2% Public; 1.8% None. (2008-2012 5-year est.)
Transportation: Commute to work: 98.4% car, 0.0% public transportation, 0.0% walk, 1.6% work from home (2008-2012 5-year est.); Travel time to work: 11.1% less than 15 minutes, 27.0% 15 to 30 minutes, 34.9% 30 to 45 minutes, 12.7% 45 to 60 minutes, 14.3% 60 minutes or more (2008-2012 5-year est.).

BRYANT (village). Covers a land area of 0.235 square miles and a water area of 0 square miles. Located at 40.47° N. Lat; 90.09° W. Long. Elevation is 607 feet.
Population: 273 (1990); 255 (2000); 220 (2010); Density: 792.1 persons per square mile (2008-2012 5-year est.); Race: 94.6% White, 2.7% Black/African American, 0.0% Asian, 0.0% American Indian/Alaska Native, 0.0% Native Hawaiian/Other Pacific Islander, 2.7% Some other race, 2.7% Two or more races, 0.0% Hispanic of any race (2008-2012 5-year est.); Average household size: 2.19 (2008-2012 5-year est.); Median age: 47.4 (2008-2012 5-year est.); Males per 100 females: 111.4 (2008-2012 5-year est.); Marriage status: 19.7% never married, 52.0% now married, 5.9% widowed, 22.4% divorced (2008-2012 5-year est.); Foreign born: 2.7% (2008-2012 5-year est.); Ancestry (includes multiple ancestries): 26.3% German, 22.6% American, 14.0% Irish, 11.8% English, 3.8% Croatian (2008-2012 5-year est.).
Economy: Homeowner vacancy rate: 0.0%. Rental vacancy rate: 0.0%. (2008-2012 5-year est.); Employment by occupation: 14.5% management, business, and financial, 9.6% computer, engineering, and science, 2.4% education, legal, community service, arts, and media, 3.6% healthcare practitioners, 14.5% service, 16.9% sales and office, 18.1% natural resources, construction, and maintenance, 20.5% production, transportation, and material moving (2008-2012 5-year est.).
Income: Per capita income: $21,006 (2008-2012 5-year est.); Median household income: $38,542 (2008-2012 5-year est.); Average household income: $42,651 (2008-2012 5-year est.); Percent of households with income of $100,000 or more: 1.2% (2008-2012 5-year est.); Poverty rate: 23.1% (2008-2012 5-year est.).
Education: Percent of population age 25 and over with: High school diploma (including GED) or higher: 86.9% (2008-2012 5-year est.); Bachelor's degree or higher: 9.5% (2008-2012 5-year est.); Master's degree or higher: 7.3% (2008-2012 5-year est.).
Housing: Homeownership rate: 78.8% (2008-2012 5-year est.); Median home value: $67,700 (2008-2012 5-year est.); Median contract rent: $433 per month (2008-2012 5-year est.); Median year structure built: 1963 (2008-2012 5-year est.).
Health Insurance: 67.2% Private; 41.4% Public; 13.4% None. (2008-2012 5-year est.)
Transportation: Commute to work: 97.4% car, 0.0% public transportation, 0.0% walk, 2.6% work from home (2008-2012 5-year est.); Travel time to work: 28.9% less than 15 minutes, 31.6% 15 to 30 minutes, 15.8% 30 to 45 minutes, 14.5% 45 to 60 minutes, 9.2% 60 minutes or more (2008-2012 5-year est.).

CANTON (city). Covers a land area of 7.904 square miles and a water area of 0.163 square miles. Located at 40.56° N. Lat; 90.04° W. Long. Elevation is 646 feet.
History: Canton was founded in 1825 by Isaac Swan of New York. He selected the name for the town in the belief that the city of Canton in China was located directly opposite on the globe.
Population: 13,922 (1990); 15,288 (2000); 14,704 (2010); Density: 1,859.7 persons per square mile (2008-2012 5-year est.); Race: 90.6% White, 7.8% Black/African American, 0.1% Asian, 0.0% American Indian/Alaska Native, 0.1% Native Hawaiian/Other Pacific Islander, 1.4% Some other race, 1.4% Two or more races, 3.1% Hispanic of any race (2008-2012 5-year est.); Average household size: 2.28 (2008-2012 5-year est.); Median age: 37.7 (2008-2012 5-year est.); Males per 100 females: 121.5 (2008-2012 5-year est.); Marriage status: 35.3% never married, 43.0% now married, 6.8% widowed, 14.9% divorced (2008-2012 5-year est.); Foreign born: 3.2% (2008-2012 5-year est.); Ancestry (includes multiple ancestries): 21.7% German, 15.5% American, 13.8% English, 10.8% Irish, 3.3% Italian (2008-2012 5-year est.).
Economy: Single-family building permits issued: 2 (2013); Multi-family building permits issued: 2 (2013); Homeowner vacancy rate: 2.9%. Rental vacancy rate: 2.6%. (2008-2012 5-year est.); Employment by occupation: 10.1% management, business, and financial, 2.3% computer, engineering, and science, 9.2% education, legal, community service, arts, and media, 7.2% healthcare practitioners, 22.3% service, 26.6% sales and office, 5.5% natural resources, construction, and maintenance, 16.8% production, transportation, and material moving (2008-2012 5-year est.).
Income: Per capita income: $18,985 (2008-2012 5-year est.); Median household income: $39,387 (2008-2012 5-year est.); Average household income: $48,725 (2008-2012 5-year est.); Percent of households with income of $100,000 or more: 10.7% (2008-2012 5-year est.); Poverty rate: 21.9% (2008-2012 5-year est.).
Education: Percent of population age 25 and over with: High school diploma (including GED) or higher: 81.8% (2008-2012 5-year est.); Bachelor's degree or higher: 16.0% (2008-2012 5-year est.); Master's degree or higher: 5.0% (2008-2012 5-year est.).

School District(s)

Canton Union SD 66 (PK-12)
    2011-12 Enrollment: 2,636 . . . . (309) 647-9411
Fulton/schuyler Roe (06-12)
    2011-12 Enrollment: n/a . . . . (309) 518-8029

Two-year College(s)

Graham Hospital School of Nursing (Private, Not-for-profit)
    Fall 2012 Enrollment: 75 . . . . (309) 647-4086
    2012-13 Tuition: In-state $10,778; Out-of-state $10,778
Spoon River College (Public)
    Fall 2012 Enrollment: 1,883 . . . . (309) 647-4645
    2012-13 Tuition: In-state $7,470; Out-of-state $8,550

Vocational/Technical School(s)

Innovations Design Academy (Private, For-profit)
    Fall 2012 Enrollment: 26 . . . . (309) 647-4224
    2012-13 Tuition: $14,200

Housing: Homeownership rate: 60.6% (2008-2012 5-year est.); Median home value: $84,800 (2008-2012 5-year est.); Median contract rent: $473 per month (2008-2012 5-year est.); Median year structure built: 1952 (2008-2012 5-year est.).
Health Insurance: 62.2% Private; 43.0% Public; 10.2% None. (2008-2012 5-year est.)
Hospitals: Graham Hospital (124 beds)
Safety: Violent crime rate: 30.0 per 10,000 population; Property crime rate: 243.3 per 10,000 population (2012).
Transportation: Commute to work: 94.4% car, 0.1% public transportation, 2.5% walk, 1.2% work from home (2008-2012 5-year est.); Travel time to work: 48.2% less than 15 minutes, 11.5% 15 to 30 minutes, 13.5% 30 to 45 minutes, 18.0% 45 to 60 minutes, 8.7% 60 minutes or more (2008-2012 5-year est.)
Airports: Ingersoll Airport (general aviation)
Additional Information Contacts
Canton Area Chamber of Commerce . . . . (309) 647-2677
    http://www.cantonillinois.org
City of Canton . . . . (309) 647-0065
    http://www.cantonillinois.org

CUBA (city). Covers a land area of 0.543 square miles and a water area of 0 square miles. Located at 40.49° N. Lat; 90.19° W. Long. Elevation is 682 feet.

History: Incorporated 1853.

Population: 1,440 (1990); 1,418 (2000); 1,294 (2010); Density: 2,778.0 persons per square mile (2008-2012 5-year est.); Race: 90.9% White, 2.9% Black/African American, 0.3% Asian, 0.1% American Indian/Alaska Native, 0.0% Native Hawaiian/Other Pacific Islander, 5.8% Some other race, 0.8% Two or more races, 2.7% Hispanic of any race (2008-2012 5-year est.); Average household size: 2.55 (2008-2012 5-year est.); Median age: 40.5 (2008-2012 5-year est.); Males per 100 females: 97.8 (2008-2012 5-year est.); Marriage status: 29.7% never married, 43.8% now married, 11.1% widowed, 15.4% divorced (2008-2012 5-year est.); Foreign born: 2.1% (2008-2012 5-year est.); Ancestry (includes multiple ancestries): 22.1% American, 18.5% German, 13.2% Irish, 9.7% English, 4.4% Italian (2008-2012 5-year est.).

Economy: Single-family building permits issued: 0 (2013); Multi-family building permits issued: 0 (2013); Homeowner vacancy rate: 0.0%. Rental vacancy rate: 10.8%. (2008-2012 5-year est.); Employment by occupation: 6.0% management, business, and financial, 2.1% computer, engineering, and science, 5.0% education, legal, community service, arts, and media, 6.4% healthcare practitioners, 23.7% service, 23.4% sales and office, 15.1% natural resources, construction, and maintenance, 18.3% production, transportation, and material moving (2008-2012 5-year est.).

Income: Per capita income: $19,152 (2008-2012 5-year est.); Median household income: $41,667 (2008-2012 5-year est.); Average household income: $48,219 (2008-2012 5-year est.); Percent of households with income of $100,000 or more: 6.0% (2008-2012 5-year est.); Poverty rate: 14.0% (2008-2012 5-year est.).

Education: Percent of population age 25 and over with: High school diploma (including GED) or higher: 83.2% (2008-2012 5-year est.); Bachelor's degree or higher: 9.6% (2008-2012 5-year est.); Master's degree or higher: 2.8% (2008-2012 5-year est.).

School District(s)

CUSD 3 Fulton County (PK-12)

    2011-12 Enrollment: 504 . . . . (309) 785-5021

Housing: Homeownership rate: 71.2% (2008-2012 5-year est.); Median home value: $63,800 (2008-2012 5-year est.); Median contract rent: $441 per month (2008-2012 5-year est.); Median year structure built: 1952 (2008-2012 5-year est.).

Health Insurance: 58.5% Private; 41.8% Public; 14.1% None. (2008-2012 5-year est.)

Transportation: Commute to work: 92.0% car, 0.0% public transportation, 4.2% walk, 3.8% work from home (2008-2012 5-year est.); Travel time to work: 28.1% less than 15 minutes, 20.7% 15 to 30 minutes, 19.7% 30 to 45 minutes, 13.2% 45 to 60 minutes, 18.4% 60 minutes or more (2008-2012 5-year est.)

DUNFERMLINE (village). Covers a land area of 0.131 square miles and a water area of 0 square miles. Located at 40.49° N. Lat; 90.03° W. Long. Elevation is 633 feet.

Population: 259 (1990); 262 (2000); 300 (2010); Density: 1,688.7 persons per square mile (2008-2012 5-year est.); Race: 99.1% White, 0.0% Black/African American, 0.0% Asian, 0.0% American Indian/Alaska Native, 0.0% Native Hawaiian/Other Pacific Islander, 0.9% Some other race, 0.9% Two or more races, 5.0% Hispanic of any race (2008-2012 5-year est.); Average household size: 2.07 (2008-2012 5-year est.); Median age: 39.3 (2008-2012 5-year est.); Males per 100 females: 100.9 (2008-2012 5-year est.); Marriage status: 24.7% never married, 44.0% now married, 15.4% widowed, 15.9% divorced (2008-2012 5-year est.); Foreign born: 0.0% (2008-2012 5-year est.); Ancestry (includes multiple ancestries): 27.1% American, 11.8% German, 11.3% English, 9.0% Irish, 5.4% Polish (2008-2012 5-year est.).

Economy: Single-family building permits issued: 0 (2013); Multi-family building permits issued: 0 (2013); Homeowner vacancy rate: 0.0%. Rental vacancy rate: 0.0%. (2008-2012 5-year est.); Employment by occupation: 10.3% management, business, and financial, 0.0% computer, engineering, and science, 5.6% education, legal, community service, arts, and media, 8.7% healthcare practitioners, 27.0% service, 12.7% sales and office, 17.5% natural resources, construction, and maintenance, 18.3% production, transportation, and material moving (2008-2012 5-year est.).

Income: Per capita income: $24,384 (2008-2012 5-year est.); Median household income: $49,750 (2008-2012 5-year est.); Average household income: $49,860 (2008-2012 5-year est.); Percent of households with income of $100,000 or more: 3.7% (2008-2012 5-year est.); Poverty rate: 15.4% (2008-2012 5-year est.).

Education: Percent of population age 25 and over with: High school diploma (including GED) or higher: 80.9% (2008-2012 5-year est.); Bachelor's degree or higher: 15.4% (2008-2012 5-year est.); Master's degree or higher: 8.6% (2008-2012 5-year est.).

Housing: Homeownership rate: 90.7% (2008-2012 5-year est.); Median home value: $70,400 (2008-2012 5-year est.); Median contract rent: $525 per month (2008-2012 5-year est.); Median year structure built: 1958 (2008-2012 5-year est.).

Health Insurance: 75.6% Private; 22.2% Public; 18.1% None. (2008-2012 5-year est.)

Transportation: Commute to work: 95.2% car, 0.0% public transportation, 0.0% walk, 2.4% work from home (2008-2012 5-year est.); Travel time to work: 22.8% less than 15 minutes, 31.7% 15 to 30 minutes, 7.3% 30 to 45 minutes, 11.4% 45 to 60 minutes, 26.8% 60 minutes or more (2008-2012 5-year est.)

ELLISVILLE (village). Covers a land area of 0.271 square miles and a water area of 0 square miles. Located at 40.63° N. Lat; 90.31° W. Long. Elevation is 551 feet.

Population: 116 (1990); 87 (2000); 96 (2010); Density: 438.6 persons per square mile (2008-2012 5-year est.); Race: 98.3% White, 0.0% Black/African American, 0.0% Asian, 0.0% American Indian/Alaska Native, 0.0% Native Hawaiian/Other Pacific Islander, 1.7% Some other race, 1.7% Two or more races, 1.7% Hispanic of any race (2008-2012 5-year est.); Average household size: 2.90 (2008-2012 5-year est.); Median age: 32.4 (2008-2012 5-year est.); Males per 100 females: 80.3 (2008-2012 5-year est.); Marriage status: 32.6% never married, 55.8% now married, 2.3% widowed, 9.3% divorced (2008-2012 5-year est.); Foreign born: 5.9% (2008-2012 5-year est.); Ancestry (includes multiple ancestries): 24.4% Irish, 21.0% German, 20.2% American, 5.9% Croatian, 5.0% Swedish (2008-2012 5-year est.).

Economy: Homeowner vacancy rate: 0.0%. Rental vacancy rate: 0.0%. (2008-2012 5-year est.); Employment by occupation: 4.3% management, business, and financial, 0.0% computer, engineering, and science, 8.5% education, legal, community service, arts, and media, 6.4% healthcare practitioners, 38.3% service, 19.1% sales and office, 17.0% natural resources, construction, and maintenance, 6.4% production, transportation, and material moving (2008-2012 5-year est.).

Income: Per capita income: $13,347 (2008-2012 5-year est.); Median household income: $25,208 (2008-2012 5-year est.); Average household income: $37,773 (2008-2012 5-year est.); Percent of households with income of $100,000 or more: 4.9% (2008-2012 5-year est.); Poverty rate: 30.3% (2008-2012 5-year est.).

Education: Percent of population age 25 and over with: High school diploma (including GED) or higher: 72.4% (2008-2012 5-year est.); Bachelor's degree or higher: 2.6% (2008-2012 5-year est.); Master's degree or higher: 0.0% (2008-2012 5-year est.).

Housing: Homeownership rate: 85.4% (2008-2012 5-year est.); Median home value: $41,000 (2008-2012 5-year est.); Median contract rent: n/a per month (2008-2012 5-year est.); Median year structure built: Before 1940 (2008-2012 5-year est.).

Health Insurance: 58.0% Private; 49.6% Public; 6.7% None. (2008-2012 5-year est.)

Transportation: Commute to work: 87.2% car, 0.0% public transportation, 0.0% walk, 12.8% work from home (2008-2012 5-year est.); Travel time to work: 14.6% less than 15 minutes, 31.7% 15 to 30 minutes, 24.4% 30 to 45 minutes, 2.4% 45 to 60 minutes, 26.8% 60 minutes or more (2008-2012 5-year est.)

FAIRVIEW (village). Covers a land area of 4.214 square miles and a water area of 0.074 square miles. Located at 40.65° N. Lat; 90.18° W. Long. Elevation is 735 feet.

Population: 510 (1990); 493 (2000); 522 (2010); Density: 117.0 persons per square mile (2008-2012 5-year est.); Race: 99.6% White, 0.0% Black/African American, 0.0% Asian, 0.2% American Indian/Alaska Native, 0.0% Native Hawaiian/Other Pacific Islander, 0.2% Some other race, 0.2% Two or more races, 0.0% Hispanic of any race (2008-2012 5-year est.); Average household size: 2.59 (2008-2012 5-year est.); Median age: 36.5 (2008-2012 5-year est.); Males per 100 females: 93.3 (2008-2012 5-year est.); Marriage status: 22.0% never married, 65.1% now married, 9.4% widowed, 3.5% divorced (2008-2012 5-year est.); Foreign born: 0.0% (2008-2012 5-year est.); Ancestry (includes multiple ancestries): 41.6%

German, 15.4% Irish, 12.4% American, 12.0% English, 4.5% Dutch (2008-2012 5-year est.).
Economy: Single-family building permits issued: 0 (2013); Multi-family building permits issued: 0 (2013); Homeowner vacancy rate: 3.6%. Rental vacancy rate: 0.0%. (2008-2012 5-year est.); Employment by occupation: 10.6% management, business, and financial, 3.2% computer, engineering, and science, 18.1% education, legal, community service, arts, and media, 6.0% healthcare practitioners, 16.2% service, 17.1% sales and office, 13.4% natural resources, construction, and maintenance, 15.3% production, transportation, and material moving (2008-2012 5-year est.).
Income: Per capita income: $22,795 (2008-2012 5-year est.); Median household income: $53,125 (2008-2012 5-year est.); Average household income: $59,169 (2008-2012 5-year est.); Percent of households with income of $100,000 or more: 18.4% (2008-2012 5-year est.); Poverty rate: 5.7% (2008-2012 5-year est.).
Education: Percent of population age 25 and over with: High school diploma (including GED) or higher: 94.6% (2008-2012 5-year est.); Bachelor's degree or higher: 24.4% (2008-2012 5-year est.); Master's degree or higher: 10.4% (2008-2012 5-year est.).
Housing: Homeownership rate: 91.6% (2008-2012 5-year est.); Median home value: $78,200 (2008-2012 5-year est.); Median contract rent: $350 per month (2008-2012 5-year est.); Median year structure built: 1948 (2008-2012 5-year est.).
Health Insurance: 86.4% Private; 28.8% Public; 4.5% None. (2008-2012 5-year est.)
Transportation: Commute to work: 94.8% car, 0.9% public transportation, 0.9% walk, 1.9% work from home (2008-2012 5-year est.); Travel time to work: 30.1% less than 15 minutes, 25.8% 15 to 30 minutes, 13.4% 30 to 45 minutes, 23.9% 45 to 60 minutes, 6.7% 60 minutes or more (2008-2012 5-year est.)

FARMINGTON (city). Covers a land area of 1.445 square miles and a water area of 0 square miles. Located at 40.70° N. Lat; 90.00° W. Long. Elevation is 745 feet.
History: Farmington was laid out in 1834, and grew as a mining town. In 1856 Farmington was the scene of a "whiskey war" when a group of women marched on the saloons, breaking windows and smashing bottles.
Population: 2,535 (1990); 2,601 (2000); 2,448 (2010); Density: 1,576.7 persons per square mile (2008-2012 5-year est.); Race: 98.4% White, 0.3% Black/African American, 0.0% Asian, 0.0% American Indian/Alaska Native, 0.0% Native Hawaiian/Other Pacific Islander, 1.3% Some other race, 1.3% Two or more races, 4.7% Hispanic of any race (2008-2012 5-year est.); Average household size: 2.59 (2008-2012 5-year est.); Median age: 42.1 (2008-2012 5-year est.); Males per 100 females: 102.4 (2008-2012 5-year est.); Marriage status: 19.7% never married, 63.9% now married, 6.4% widowed, 10.0% divorced (2008-2012 5-year est.); Foreign born: 2.8% (2008-2012 5-year est.); Ancestry (includes multiple ancestries): 29.0% German, 17.2% American, 12.6% English, 9.3% Irish, 7.5% Italian (2008-2012 5-year est.).
Economy: Single-family building permits issued: 1 (2013); Multi-family building permits issued: 0 (2013); Homeowner vacancy rate: 0.0%. Rental vacancy rate: 21.0%. (2008-2012 5-year est.); Employment by occupation: 6.5% management, business, and financial, 5.4% computer, engineering, and science, 8.2% education, legal, community service, arts, and media, 8.1% healthcare practitioners, 12.4% service, 22.6% sales and office, 14.7% natural resources, construction, and maintenance, 22.0% production, transportation, and material moving (2008-2012 5-year est.).
Income: Per capita income: $20,218 (2008-2012 5-year est.); Median household income: $47,625 (2008-2012 5-year est.); Average household income: $51,440 (2008-2012 5-year est.); Percent of households with income of $100,000 or more: 9.5% (2008-2012 5-year est.); Poverty rate: 12.2% (2008-2012 5-year est.).
Education: Percent of population age 25 and over with: High school diploma (including GED) or higher: 91.0% (2008-2012 5-year est.); Bachelor's degree or higher: 10.8% (2008-2012 5-year est.); Master's degree or higher: 2.1% (2008-2012 5-year est.).

School District(s)
Farmington Central CUSD 265 (PK-12)
  2011-12 Enrollment: 1,478 . . . . (309) 245-1000
Housing: Homeownership rate: 87.2% (2008-2012 5-year est.); Median home value: $95,000 (2008-2012 5-year est.); Median contract rent: $433 per month (2008-2012 5-year est.); Median year structure built: 1943 (2008-2012 5-year est.).
Health Insurance: 64.2% Private; 36.0% Public; 12.2% None. (2008-2012 5-year est.)

Safety: Violent crime rate: 49.2 per 10,000 population; Property crime rate: 245.8 per 10,000 population (2012).
Transportation: Commute to work: 91.2% car, 0.0% public transportation, 1.7% walk, 3.3% work from home (2008-2012 5-year est.); Travel time to work: 33.9% less than 15 minutes, 18.4% 15 to 30 minutes, 32.8% 30 to 45 minutes, 13.1% 45 to 60 minutes, 1.8% 60 minutes or more (2008-2012 5-year est.)

FIATT (unincorporated postal area)
Zip Code: 61433
  Covers a land area of 1.060 square miles and a water area of 0.070 square miles. Located at 40.55° N. Lat; 90.16° W. Long. Elevation is 673 feet. Population: 74 (2010); Density: 69.8 persons per square mile (2010); Race: 100.0% White, 0.0% Black/African American, 0.0% Asian, 0.0% American Indian/Alaska Native, 0.0% Native Hawaiian/Other Pacific Islander, 0.0% Some other race, 0.0% Two or more races, 0.0% Hispanic of any race (2010); Average household size: 2.96 (2010); Median age: 30.0 (2010); Males per 100 females: 100.0 (2010); Homeownership rate: 76.0% (2010)

IPAVA (village). Covers a land area of 0.268 square miles and a water area of 0 square miles. Located at 40.35° N. Lat; 90.32° W. Long. Elevation is 659 feet.
History: Vestiges of Camp Ellis, a World War II prisoner-of-war camp, nearby.
Population: 483 (1990); 506 (2000); 470 (2010); Density: 2,022.1 persons per square mile (2008-2012 5-year est.); Race: 96.5% White, 0.0% Black/African American, 0.0% Asian, 0.2% American Indian/Alaska Native, 0.0% Native Hawaiian/Other Pacific Islander, 3.3% Some other race, 3.3% Two or more races, 1.5% Hispanic of any race (2008-2012 5-year est.); Average household size: 2.42 (2008-2012 5-year est.); Median age: 44.3 (2008-2012 5-year est.); Males per 100 females: 99.3 (2008-2012 5-year est.); Marriage status: 19.9% never married, 64.4% now married, 7.2% widowed, 8.5% divorced (2008-2012 5-year est.); Foreign born: 0.0% (2008-2012 5-year est.); Ancestry (includes multiple ancestries): 23.8% German, 19.0% American, 15.1% Irish, 10.3% English, 4.2% Dutch (2008-2012 5-year est.).
Economy: Single-family building permits issued: 0 (2013); Multi-family building permits issued: 0 (2013); Homeowner vacancy rate: 6.5%. Rental vacancy rate: 0.0%. (2008-2012 5-year est.); Employment by occupation: 21.5% management, business, and financial, 0.0% computer, engineering, and science, 7.4% education, legal, community service, arts, and media, 6.2% healthcare practitioners, 6.6% service, 15.3% sales and office, 28.5% natural resources, construction, and maintenance, 14.5% production, transportation, and material moving (2008-2012 5-year est.).
Income: Per capita income: $24,705 (2008-2012 5-year est.); Median household income: $52,727 (2008-2012 5-year est.); Average household income: $56,664 (2008-2012 5-year est.); Percent of households with income of $100,000 or more: 8.0% (2008-2012 5-year est.); Poverty rate: 14.0% (2008-2012 5-year est.).
Education: Percent of population age 25 and over with: High school diploma (including GED) or higher: 91.4% (2008-2012 5-year est.); Bachelor's degree or higher: 14.0% (2008-2012 5-year est.); Master's degree or higher: 1.0% (2008-2012 5-year est.).
Housing: Homeownership rate: 83.5% (2008-2012 5-year est.); Median home value: $69,100 (2008-2012 5-year est.); Median contract rent: $375 per month (2008-2012 5-year est.); Median year structure built: 1952 (2008-2012 5-year est.).
Health Insurance: 73.4% Private; 33.2% Public; 5.2% None. (2008-2012 5-year est.)
Transportation: Commute to work: 93.8% car, 0.0% public transportation, 2.1% walk, 4.2% work from home (2008-2012 5-year est.); Travel time to work: 23.0% less than 15 minutes, 24.8% 15 to 30 minutes, 31.3% 30 to 45 minutes, 3.5% 45 to 60 minutes, 17.4% 60 minutes or more (2008-2012 5-year est.)

LEWISTOWN (city). County seat. Covers a land area of 2.000 square miles and a water area of 0 square miles. Located at 40.40° N. Lat; 90.16° W. Long. Elevation is 591 feet.
History: Lewiston was founded in 1821 by Major Ossian M. Ross, who had received the land for his service in the War of 1812. The town was named for the Major's son, Lewis. In 1823 Ross organized Fulton County and had Lewiston named as the seat, with the courthouse built on land he donated.

Population: 2,572 (1990); 2,522 (2000); 2,384 (2010); Density: 1,148.1 persons per square mile (2008-2012 5-year est.); Race: 96.2% White, 1.4% Black/African American, 0.0% Asian, 0.1% American Indian/Alaska Native, 0.0% Native Hawaiian/Other Pacific Islander, 2.3% Some other race, 1.4% Two or more races, 3.8% Hispanic of any race (2008-2012 5-year est.); Average household size: 2.12 (2008-2012 5-year est.); Median age: 44.3 (2008-2012 5-year est.); Males per 100 females: 101.1 (2008-2012 5-year est.); Marriage status: 26.4% never married, 47.4% now married, 8.9% widowed, 17.2% divorced (2008-2012 5-year est.); Foreign born: 2.5% (2008-2012 5-year est.); Ancestry (includes multiple ancestries): 20.9% German, 19.2% American, 10.7% Irish, 7.4% English, 4.7% Polish (2008-2012 5-year est.).
Economy: Single-family building permits issued: 0 (2013); Multi-family building permits issued: 0 (2013); Homeowner vacancy rate: 0.0%. Rental vacancy rate: 18.4%. (2008-2012 5-year est.); Employment by occupation: 8.7% management, business, and financial, 1.3% computer, engineering, and science, 11.0% education, legal, community service, arts, and media, 6.3% healthcare practitioners, 26.2% service, 19.4% sales and office, 10.8% natural resources, construction, and maintenance, 16.2% production, transportation, and material moving (2008-2012 5-year est.).
Income: Per capita income: $21,101 (2008-2012 5-year est.); Median household income: $36,932 (2008-2012 5-year est.); Average household income: $46,210 (2008-2012 5-year est.); Percent of households with income of $100,000 or more: 6.7% (2008-2012 5-year est.); Poverty rate: 13.9% (2008-2012 5-year est.).
Education: Percent of population age 25 and over with: High school diploma (including GED) or higher: 85.3% (2008-2012 5-year est.); Bachelor's degree or higher: 12.8% (2008-2012 5-year est.); Master's degree or higher: 1.7% (2008-2012 5-year est.).

School District(s)

Lewistown CUSD 97 (PK-12)
    2011-12 Enrollment: 748. . . . . (309) 547-5826
West Central Il Spec Educ Coop
    2011-12 Enrollment: n/a . . . . (309) 837-3911
Housing: Homeownership rate: 71.2% (2008-2012 5-year est.); Median home value: $67,100 (2008-2012 5-year est.); Median contract rent: $426 per month (2008-2012 5-year est.); Median year structure built: 1954 (2008-2012 5-year est.).
Health Insurance: 69.3% Private; 42.7% Public; 8.5% None. (2008-2012 5-year est.)
Transportation: Commute to work: 92.6% car, 0.0% public transportation, 5.7% walk, 1.7% work from home (2008-2012 5-year est.); Travel time to work: 35.8% less than 15 minutes, 27.1% 15 to 30 minutes, 10.2% 30 to 45 minutes, 12.6% 45 to 60 minutes, 14.2% 60 minutes or more (2008-2012 5-year est.)
Additional Information Contacts
Lewistown Chamber of Commerce . . . . (309) 547-4306
    http://lewistownchamber.org

LIVERPOOL (village). Covers a land area of 0.084 square miles and a water area of 0.001 square miles. Located at 40.39° N. Lat; 90.00° W. Long. Elevation is 446 feet.
History: Liverpool, named for the town in England, began as a river town and shipping center. Commercial fishing developed later.
Population: 129 (1990); 119 (2000); 129 (2010); Density: 1,176.5 persons per square mile (2008-2012 5-year est.); Race: 100.0% White, 0.0% Black/African American, 0.0% Asian, 0.0% American Indian/Alaska Native, 0.0% Native Hawaiian/Other Pacific Islander, 0.0% Some other race, 0.0% Two or more races, 0.0% Hispanic of any race (2008-2012 5-year est.); Average household size: 2.68 (2008-2012 5-year est.); Median age: 30.8 (2008-2012 5-year est.); Males per 100 females: 102.0 (2008-2012 5-year est.); Marriage status: 33.8% never married, 46.5% now married, 0.0% widowed, 19.7% divorced (2008-2012 5-year est.); Foreign born: 0.0% (2008-2012 5-year est.); Ancestry (includes multiple ancestries): 37.4% English, 23.2% German, 7.1% Irish, 6.1% Italian, 3.0% Norwegian (2008-2012 5-year est.).
Economy: Homeowner vacancy rate: 0.0%. Rental vacancy rate: 11.5%. (2008-2012 5-year est.); Employment by occupation: 14.8% management, business, and financial, 0.0% computer, engineering, and science, 3.7% education, legal, community service, arts, and media, 11.1% healthcare practitioners, 22.2% service, 18.5% sales and office, 7.4% natural resources, construction, and maintenance, 22.2% production, transportation, and material moving (2008-2012 5-year est.).
Income: Per capita income: $14,605 (2008-2012 5-year est.); Median household income: $27,250 (2008-2012 5-year est.); Average household

income: $38,641 (2008-2012 5-year est.); Percent of households with income of $100,000 or more: 5.4% (2008-2012 5-year est.); Poverty rate: 34.3% (2008-2012 5-year est.).
Education: Percent of population age 25 and over with: High school diploma (including GED) or higher: 80.4% (2008-2012 5-year est.); Bachelor's degree or higher: 7.1% (2008-2012 5-year est.); Master's degree or higher: 0.0% (2008-2012 5-year est.).
Housing: Homeownership rate: 37.8% (2008-2012 5-year est.); Median home value: $53,300 (2008-2012 5-year est.); Median contract rent: $290 per month (2008-2012 5-year est.); Median year structure built: 1964 (2008-2012 5-year est.).
Health Insurance: 57.6% Private; 56.6% Public; 6.1% None. (2008-2012 5-year est.)
Transportation: Commute to work: 88.9% car, 0.0% public transportation, 7.4% walk, 3.7% work from home (2008-2012 5-year est.); Travel time to work: 15.4% less than 15 minutes, 26.9% 15 to 30 minutes, 34.6% 30 to 45 minutes, 11.5% 45 to 60 minutes, 11.5% 60 minutes or more (2008-2012 5-year est.)

LONDON MILLS (village). Covers a land area of 0.683 square miles and a water area of 0 square miles. Located at 40.71° N. Lat; 90.27° W. Long. Elevation is 541 feet.
Population: 485 (1990); 447 (2000); 392 (2010); Density: 632.3 persons per square mile (2008-2012 5-year est.); Race: 97.0% White, 0.7% Black/African American, 0.0% Asian, 0.0% American Indian/Alaska Native, 0.0% Native Hawaiian/Other Pacific Islander, 2.3% Some other race, 2.3% Two or more races, 3.0% Hispanic of any race (2008-2012 5-year est.); Average household size: 3.06 (2008-2012 5-year est.); Median age: 36.0 (2008-2012 5-year est.); Males per 100 females: 108.7 (2008-2012 5-year est.); Marriage status: 31.8% never married, 53.2% now married, 4.4% widowed, 10.6% divorced (2008-2012 5-year est.); Foreign born: 0.0% (2008-2012 5-year est.); Ancestry (includes multiple ancestries): 22.7% Irish, 19.2% German, 12.7% American, 7.9% English, 6.3% Swedish (2008-2012 5-year est.).
Economy: Homeowner vacancy rate: 0.0%. Rental vacancy rate: 0.0%. (2008-2012 5-year est.); Employment by occupation: 15.6% management, business, and financial, 1.2% computer, engineering, and science, 9.0% education, legal, community service, arts, and media, 3.6% healthcare practitioners, 22.2% service, 12.0% sales and office, 13.2% natural resources, construction, and maintenance, 23.4% production, transportation, and material moving (2008-2012 5-year est.).
Income: Per capita income: $19,119 (2008-2012 5-year est.); Median household income: $38,750 (2008-2012 5-year est.); Average household income: $52,548 (2008-2012 5-year est.); Percent of households with income of $100,000 or more: 12.1% (2008-2012 5-year est.); Poverty rate: 28.9% (2008-2012 5-year est.).
Education: Percent of population age 25 and over with: High school diploma (including GED) or higher: 86.9% (2008-2012 5-year est.); Bachelor's degree or higher: 20.9% (2008-2012 5-year est.); Master's degree or higher: 10.4% (2008-2012 5-year est.).

School District(s)

Spoon River Valley CUSD 4 (PK-12)
    2011-12 Enrollment: 437. . . . . (309) 778-2204
Housing: Homeownership rate: 85.1% (2008-2012 5-year est.); Median home value: $49,400 (2008-2012 5-year est.); Median contract rent: $513 per month (2008-2012 5-year est.); Median year structure built: Before 1940 (2008-2012 5-year est.).
Health Insurance: 73.1% Private; 37.0% Public; 5.3% None. (2008-2012 5-year est.)
Transportation: Commute to work: 98.8% car, 0.6% public transportation, 0.0% walk, 0.0% work from home (2008-2012 5-year est.); Travel time to work: 26.9% less than 15 minutes, 23.4% 15 to 30 minutes, 28.1% 30 to 45 minutes, 7.2% 45 to 60 minutes, 14.4% 60 minutes or more (2008-2012 5-year est.)

MARIETTA (village). Covers a land area of 0.273 square miles and a water area of 0 square miles. Located at 40.50° N. Lat; 90.39° W. Long. Elevation is 650 feet.
Population: 142 (1990); 150 (2000); 112 (2010); Density: 742.5 persons per square mile (2008-2012 5-year est.); Race: 97.0% White, 0.0% Black/African American, 0.0% Asian, 0.0% American Indian/Alaska Native, 0.0% Native Hawaiian/Other Pacific Islander, 3.0% Some other race, 0.0% Two or more races, 3.0% Hispanic of any race (2008-2012 5-year est.); Average household size: 2.57 (2008-2012 5-year est.); Median age: 42.8 (2008-2012 5-year est.); Males per 100 females: 86.2 (2008-2012 5-year

est.); Marriage status: 27.2% never married, 64.7% now married, 0.5% widowed, 7.6% divorced (2008-2012 5-year est.); Foreign born: 2.5% (2008-2012 5-year est.); Ancestry (includes multiple ancestries): 21.2% German, 14.3% American, 8.4% Turkish, 2.0% Swedish, 1.0% Scottish (2008-2012 5-year est.).

Economy: Homeowner vacancy rate: 8.2%. Rental vacancy rate: 0.0%. (2008-2012 5-year est.); Employment by occupation: 3.8% management, business, and financial, 0.0% computer, engineering, and science, 0.0% education, legal, community service, arts, and media, 3.8% healthcare practitioners, 6.3% service, 8.9% sales and office, 55.7% natural resources, construction, and maintenance, 21.5% production, transportation, and material moving (2008-2012 5-year est.).

Income: Per capita income: $19,478 (2008-2012 5-year est.); Median household income: $41,792 (2008-2012 5-year est.); Average household income: $52,467 (2008-2012 5-year est.); Percent of households with income of $100,000 or more: 7.6% (2008-2012 5-year est.); Poverty rate: 6.9% (2008-2012 5-year est.).

Education: Percent of population age 25 and over with: High school diploma (including GED) or higher: 95.0% (2008-2012 5-year est.); Bachelor's degree or higher: 7.2% (2008-2012 5-year est.); Master's degree or higher: 0.0% (2008-2012 5-year est.).

Housing: Homeownership rate: 98.7% (2008-2012 5-year est.); Median home value: $53,900 (2008-2012 5-year est.); Median contract rent: n/a per month (2008-2012 5-year est.); Median year structure built: 1946 (2008-2012 5-year est.).

Health Insurance: 86.7% Private; 22.7% Public; 7.4% None. (2008-2012 5-year est.)

Transportation: Commute to work: 98.7% car, 0.0% public transportation, 0.0% walk, 0.0% work from home (2008-2012 5-year est.); Travel time to work: 2.5% less than 15 minutes, 24.1% 15 to 30 minutes, 11.4% 30 to 45 minutes, 40.5% 45 to 60 minutes, 21.5% 60 minutes or more (2008-2012 5-year est.).

NORRIS (village). Covers a land area of 0.283 square miles and a water area of 0 square miles. Located at 40.63° N. Lat; 90.03° W. Long. Elevation is 728 feet.

Population: 212 (1990); 194 (2000); 213 (2010); Density: 918.1 persons per square mile (2008-2012 5-year est.); Race: 99.6% White, 0.0% Black/African American, 0.0% Asian, 0.4% American Indian/Alaska Native, 0.0% Native Hawaiian/Other Pacific Islander, 0.0% Some other race, 0.0% Two or more races, 0.0% Hispanic of any race (2008-2012 5-year est.); Average household size: 2.68 (2008-2012 5-year est.); Median age: 38.2 (2008-2012 5-year est.); Males per 100 females: 98.5 (2008-2012 5-year est.); Marriage status: 12.6% never married, 72.7% now married, 3.3% widowed, 11.5% divorced (2008-2012 5-year est.); Foreign born: 5.0% (2008-2012 5-year est.); Ancestry (includes multiple ancestries): 25.4% American, 16.2% Irish, 15.8% English, 14.2% Italian, 10.0% German (2008-2012 5-year est.).

Economy: Homeowner vacancy rate: 0.0%. Rental vacancy rate: 35.3%. (2008-2012 5-year est.); Employment by occupation: 8.7% management, business, and financial, 0.0% computer, engineering, and science, 15.0% education, legal, community service, arts, and media, 8.7% healthcare practitioners, 19.7% service, 14.2% sales and office, 15.0% natural resources, construction, and maintenance, 18.9% production, transportation, and material moving (2008-2012 5-year est.).

Income: Per capita income: $19,232 (2008-2012 5-year est.); Median household income: $33,472 (2008-2012 5-year est.); Average household income: $49,370 (2008-2012 5-year est.); Percent of households with income of $100,000 or more: 10.3% (2008-2012 5-year est.); Poverty rate: 2.7% (2008-2012 5-year est.).

Education: Percent of population age 25 and over with: High school diploma (including GED) or higher: 85.5% (2008-2012 5-year est.); Bachelor's degree or higher: 25.6% (2008-2012 5-year est.); Master's degree or higher: 5.2% (2008-2012 5-year est.).

Housing: Homeownership rate: 88.7% (2008-2012 5-year est.); Median home value: $64,000 (2008-2012 5-year est.); Median contract rent: $425 per month (2008-2012 5-year est.); Median year structure built: Before 1940 (2008-2012 5-year est.).

Health Insurance: 84.6% Private; 29.2% Public; 3.8% None. (2008-2012 5-year est.)

Transportation: Commute to work: 100.0% car, 0.0% public transportation, 0.0% walk, 0.0% work from home (2008-2012 5-year est.); Travel time to work: 44.3% less than 15 minutes, 23.5% 15 to 30 minutes, 15.7% 30 to 45 minutes, 8.7% 45 to 60 minutes, 7.8% 60 minutes or more (2008-2012 5-year est.)

SAINT DAVID (village). Covers a land area of 0.299 square miles and a water area of 0 square miles. Located at 40.49° N. Lat; 90.05° W. Long. Elevation is 627 feet.

Population: 603 (1990); 587 (2000); 589 (2010); Density: 1,444.4 persons per square mile (2008-2012 5-year est.); Race: 98.4% White, 0.0% Black/African American, 0.0% Asian, 0.2% American Indian/Alaska Native, 1.4% Native Hawaiian/Other Pacific Islander, 0.0% Some other race, 0.0% Two or more races, 0.0% Hispanic of any race (2008-2012 5-year est.); Average household size: 2.20 (2008-2012 5-year est.); Median age: 54.5 (2008-2012 5-year est.); Males per 100 females: 100.0 (2008-2012 5-year est.); Marriage status: 18.0% never married, 58.7% now married, 7.0% widowed, 16.2% divorced (2008-2012 5-year est.); Foreign born: 3.2% (2008-2012 5-year est.); Ancestry (includes multiple ancestries): 21.5% American, 21.1% German, 17.1% English, 12.0% Irish, 9.3% Italian (2008-2012 5-year est.).

Economy: Single-family building permits issued: 0 (2013); Multi-family building permits issued: 0 (2013); Homeowner vacancy rate: 0.0%. Rental vacancy rate: 14.3%. (2008-2012 5-year est.); Employment by occupation: 3.5% management, business, and financial, 3.5% computer, engineering, and science, 5.0% education, legal, community service, arts, and media, 5.4% healthcare practitioners, 33.2% service, 27.2% sales and office, 8.9% natural resources, construction, and maintenance, 13.4% production, transportation, and material moving (2008-2012 5-year est.).

Income: Per capita income: $21,365 (2008-2012 5-year est.); Median household income: $35,833 (2008-2012 5-year est.); Average household income: $45,520 (2008-2012 5-year est.); Percent of households with income of $100,000 or more: 9.2% (2008-2012 5-year est.); Poverty rate: 12.3% (2008-2012 5-year est.).

Education: Percent of population age 25 and over with: High school diploma (including GED) or higher: 88.3% (2008-2012 5-year est.); Bachelor's degree or higher: 7.6% (2008-2012 5-year est.); Master's degree or higher: 1.2% (2008-2012 5-year est.).

Housing: Homeownership rate: 87.8% (2008-2012 5-year est.); Median home value: $60,000 (2008-2012 5-year est.); Median contract rent: $325 per month (2008-2012 5-year est.); Median year structure built: 1943 (2008-2012 5-year est.).

Health Insurance: 67.6% Private; 50.7% Public; 5.6% None. (2008-2012 5-year est.)

Transportation: Commute to work: 95.0% car, 0.0% public transportation, 4.0% walk, 1.0% work from home (2008-2012 5-year est.); Travel time to work: 35.5% less than 15 minutes, 30.0% 15 to 30 minutes, 3.0% 30 to 45 minutes, 14.5% 45 to 60 minutes, 17.0% 60 minutes or more (2008-2012 5-year est.)

SMITHFIELD (village). Covers a land area of 0.465 square miles and a water area of 0 square miles. Located at 40.47° N. Lat; 90.29° W. Long. Elevation is 646 feet.

Population: 277 (1990); 214 (2000); 230 (2010); Density: 647.8 persons per square mile (2008-2012 5-year est.); Race: 99.7% White, 0.0% Black/African American, 0.0% Asian, 0.0% American Indian/Alaska Native, 0.0% Native Hawaiian/Other Pacific Islander, 0.3% Some other race, 0.3% Two or more races, 0.0% Hispanic of any race (2008-2012 5-year est.); Average household size: 2.87 (2008-2012 5-year est.); Median age: 33.9 (2008-2012 5-year est.); Males per 100 females: 115.0 (2008-2012 5-year est.); Marriage status: 8.6% never married, 76.9% now married, 10.4% widowed, 4.1% divorced (2008-2012 5-year est.); Foreign born: 10.6% (2008-2012 5-year est.); Ancestry (includes multiple ancestries): 26.2% American, 24.6% German, 21.9% Irish, 13.3% Ukrainian, 7.6% Italian (2008-2012 5-year est.).

Economy: Homeowner vacancy rate: 0.0%. Rental vacancy rate: 16.7%. (2008-2012 5-year est.); Employment by occupation: 2.9% management, business, and financial, 1.9% computer, engineering, and science, 3.8% education, legal, community service, arts, and media, 1.9% healthcare practitioners, 11.5% service, 24.0% sales and office, 14.4% natural resources, construction, and maintenance, 39.4% production, transportation, and material moving (2008-2012 5-year est.).

Income: Per capita income: $16,529 (2008-2012 5-year est.); Median household income: $44,750 (2008-2012 5-year est.); Average household income: $45,014 (2008-2012 5-year est.); Percent of households with income of $100,000 or more: 3.8% (2008-2012 5-year est.); Poverty rate: 9.0% (2008-2012 5-year est.).

Education: Percent of population age 25 and over with: High school diploma (including GED) or higher: 73.6% (2008-2012 5-year est.); Bachelor's degree or higher: 6.1% (2008-2012 5-year est.); Master's degree or higher: 1.0% (2008-2012 5-year est.).

Housing: Homeownership rate: 81.0% (2008-2012 5-year est.); Median home value: $55,000 (2008-2012 5-year est.); Median contract rent: $290 per month (2008-2012 5-year est.); Median year structure built: 1945 (2008-2012 5-year est.).

Health Insurance: 60.1% Private; 50.5% Public; 12.6% None. (2008-2012 5-year est.)

Transportation: Commute to work: 96.2% car, 0.0% public transportation, 1.9% walk, 0.0% work from home (2008-2012 5-year est.); Travel time to work: 6.7% less than 15 minutes, 43.3% 15 to 30 minutes, 12.5% 30 to 45 minutes, 11.5% 45 to 60 minutes, 26.0% 60 minutes or more (2008-2012 5-year est.)

TABLE GROVE (village). Covers a land area of 0.282 square miles and a water area of 0 square miles. Located at 40.37° N. Lat; 90.43° W. Long. Elevation is 725 feet.

Population: 408 (1990); 396 (2000); 416 (2010); Density: 1,554.8 persons per square mile (2008-2012 5-year est.); Race: 98.2% White, 0.5% Black/African American, 0.0% Asian, 0.2% American Indian/Alaska Native, 0.0% Native Hawaiian/Other Pacific Islander, 1.1% Some other race, 0.0% Two or more races, 2.1% Hispanic of any race (2008-2012 5-year est.); Average household size: 2.56 (2008-2012 5-year est.); Median age: 29.7 (2008-2012 5-year est.); Males per 100 females: 97.3 (2008-2012 5-year est.); Marriage status: 12.7% never married, 66.9% now married, 5.5% widowed, 14.9% divorced (2008-2012 5-year est.); Foreign born: 0.5% (2008-2012 5-year est.); Ancestry (includes multiple ancestries): 28.1% American, 23.1% German, 15.8% Irish, 9.4% English, 5.5% Dutch (2008-2012 5-year est.).

Economy: Single-family building permits issued: 0 (2013); Multi-family building permits issued: 0 (2013); Homeowner vacancy rate: 0.0%. Rental vacancy rate: 24.3%. (2008-2012 5-year est.); Employment by occupation: 12.4% management, business, and financial, 1.6% computer, engineering, and science, 2.6% education, legal, community service, arts, and media, 12.4% healthcare practitioners, 13.5% service, 21.2% sales and office, 20.7% natural resources, construction, and maintenance, 15.5% production, transportation, and material moving (2008-2012 5-year est.).

Income: Per capita income: $19,107 (2008-2012 5-year est.); Median household income: $39,125 (2008-2012 5-year est.); Average household income: $47,409 (2008-2012 5-year est.); Percent of households with income of $100,000 or more: 5.3% (2008-2012 5-year est.); Poverty rate: 8.2% (2008-2012 5-year est.).

Education: Percent of population age 25 and over with: High school diploma (including GED) or higher: 92.5% (2008-2012 5-year est.); Bachelor's degree or higher: 13.9% (2008-2012 5-year est.); Master's degree or higher: 3.2% (2008-2012 5-year est.).

School District(s)

V I T CUSD 2 (PK-12)
    2011-12 Enrollment: 370 . . . . (309) 758-5138

Housing: Homeownership rate: 83.6% (2008-2012 5-year est.); Median home value: $63,500 (2008-2012 5-year est.); Median contract rent: $358 per month (2008-2012 5-year est.); Median year structure built: 1943 (2008-2012 5-year est.).

Health Insurance: 79.9% Private; 33.3% Public; 3.0% None. (2008-2012 5-year est.)

Transportation: Commute to work: 88.8% car, 0.0% public transportation, 4.3% walk, 6.9% work from home (2008-2012 5-year est.); Travel time to work: 25.1% less than 15 minutes, 48.6% 15 to 30 minutes, 15.4% 30 to 45 minutes, 4.0% 45 to 60 minutes, 6.9% 60 minutes or more (2008-2012 5-year est.)

VERMONT (village). Covers a land area of 1.258 square miles and a water area of 0 square miles. Located at 40.30° N. Lat; 90.43° W. Long. Elevation is 692 feet.

Population: 806 (1990); 792 (2000); 667 (2010); Density: 594.5 persons per square mile (2008-2012 5-year est.); Race: 97.5% White, 2.1% Black/African American, 0.0% Asian, 0.1% American Indian/Alaska Native, 0.0% Native Hawaiian/Other Pacific Islander, 0.3% Some other race, 0.3% Two or more races, 0.0% Hispanic of any race (2008-2012 5-year est.); Average household size: 2.25 (2008-2012 5-year est.); Median age: 40.5 (2008-2012 5-year est.); Males per 100 females: 116.8 (2008-2012 5-year est.); Marriage status: 30.5% never married, 48.6% now married, 7.5% widowed, 13.4% divorced (2008-2012 5-year est.); Foreign born: 0.8% (2008-2012 5-year est.); Ancestry (includes multiple ancestries): 22.5% American, 19.8% German, 10.8% English, 7.8% Irish, 5.7% French (2008-2012 5-year est.).

Economy: Homeowner vacancy rate: 0.0%. Rental vacancy rate: 0.0%. (2008-2012 5-year est.); Employment by occupation: 10.8% management, business, and financial, 0.5% computer, engineering, and science, 10.0% education, legal, community service, arts, and media, 1.3% healthcare practitioners, 19.2% service, 19.0% sales and office, 8.7% natural resources, construction, and maintenance, 30.5% production, transportation, and material moving (2008-2012 5-year est.).

Income: Per capita income: $21,867 (2008-2012 5-year est.); Median household income: $47,875 (2008-2012 5-year est.); Average household income: $49,951 (2008-2012 5-year est.); Percent of households with income of $100,000 or more: 7.2% (2008-2012 5-year est.); Poverty rate: 10.4% (2008-2012 5-year est.).

Education: Percent of population age 25 and over with: High school diploma (including GED) or higher: 83.7% (2008-2012 5-year est.); Bachelor's degree or higher: 12.0% (2008-2012 5-year est.); Master's degree or higher: 2.0% (2008-2012 5-year est.).

Housing: Homeownership rate: 89.2% (2008-2012 5-year est.); Median home value: $47,600 (2008-2012 5-year est.); Median contract rent: $293 per month (2008-2012 5-year est.); Median year structure built: Before 1940 (2008-2012 5-year est.).

Health Insurance: 72.1% Private; 30.7% Public; 10.7% None. (2008-2012 5-year est.)

Transportation: Commute to work: 90.5% car, 0.0% public transportation, 4.6% walk, 2.3% work from home (2008-2012 5-year est.); Travel time to work: 32.2% less than 15 minutes, 25.1% 15 to 30 minutes, 31.7% 30 to 45 minutes, 3.2% 45 to 60 minutes, 7.9% 60 minutes or more (2008-2012 5-year est.)

Gallatin County

Located in southeastern Illinois, partly in the Ozarks; bounded on the northeast by the Wabash River and the Indiana border, and on the southeast by the Ohio River and the Kentucky border; includes part of Shawnee National Forest. Covers a land area of 323.071 square miles, a water area of 5.111 square miles, and is located in the Central Time Zone at 37.77° N. Lat., 88.23° W. Long. The county was founded in 1812. County seat is Shawneetown.

Population: 6,909 (1990); 6,445 (2000); 5,589 (2010); Race: 97.1% White, 0.4% Black/African American, 0.2% Asian, 0.4% American Indian/Alaska Native, 0.0% Native Hawaiian/Other Pacific Islander, 1.9% Some other race, 1.7% Two or more races, 0.4% Hispanic of any race (2008-2012 5-year est.); Density: 16.8 persons per square mile (2008-2012 5-year est.); Average household size: 2.35 (2008-2012 5-year est.); Median age: 45.0 (2008-2012 5-year est.); Males per 100 females: 94.5 (2008-2012 5-year est.).

Religion: Six largest groups: 22.3% Catholicism, 16.4% Baptist, 5.4% Non-denominational Protestant, 2.7% Methodist/Pietist, 2.6% Presbyterian-Reformed, 2.1% Pentecostal (2010)

Economy: Unemployment rate: 7.2% (April 2014); Total civilian labor force: 2,401 (April 2014); Leading industries: 29.9% transportation & warehousing; 12.1% health care and social assistance; 9.0% retail trade (2012); Farms: 203 totaling 186,250 acres (2012); Companies that employ 500 or more persons: 0 (2012); Companies that employ 100 to 499 persons: 1 (2012); Companies that employ less than 100 persons: 97 (2012); Black-owned businesses: n/a (2007); Hispanic-owned businesses: n/a (2007); Asian-owned businesses: n/a (2007); Women-owned businesses: n/a (2007); Single-family building permits issued: n/a (2013); Multi-family building permits issued: n/a (2013).

Income: Per capita income: $24,055 (2008-2012 5-year est.); Median household income: $38,934 (2008-2012 5-year est.); Average household income: $56,207 (2008-2012 5-year est.); Percent of households with income of $100,000 or more: 10.8% (2008-2012 5-year est.); Poverty rate: 17.5% (2008-2012 5-year est.); Bankruptcy rate: 2.58% (2013).

Education: Percent of population age 25 and over with: High school diploma (including GED) or higher: 78.9% (2008-2012 5-year est.); Bachelor's degree or higher: 9.8% (2008-2012 5-year est.); Master's degree or higher: 2.9% (2008-2012 5-year est.).

Housing: Homeownership rate: 79.1% (2008-2012 5-year est.); Median home value: $59,700 (2008-2012 5-year est.); Median contract rent: $213 per month (2008-2012 5-year est.); Median year structure built: 1969 (2008-2012 5-year est.)

Health: Birth rate: 86.8 per 10,000 population (2013); Death rate: 145.9 per 10,000 population (2013); Age-adjusted cancer mortality rate: Unreliable deaths per 100,000 population (2011); Number of physicians:

3.6 per 10,000 population (2011); Hospital beds: 0.0 per 10,000 population (2010); Hospital admissions: 0.0 per 10,000 population (2010).
Elections: 2012 Presidential election results: 40.0% Obama, 58.1% Romney
Additional Information Contacts
Gallatin County Government . . . . (618) 269-3025

Gallatin County Communities

EQUALITY (village). Covers a land area of 0.891 square miles and a water area of 0.016 square miles. Located at 37.74° N. Lat; 88.34° W. Long. Elevation is 410 feet.
History: Formerly county seat and site of salt works.
Population: 748 (1990); 721 (2000); 595 (2010); Density: 840.2 persons per square mile (2008-2012 5-year est.); Race: 98.3% White, 0.1% Black/African American, 0.0% Asian, 0.0% American Indian/Alaska Native, 0.0% Native Hawaiian/Other Pacific Islander, 1.6% Some other race, 1.6% Two or more races, 0.0% Hispanic of any race (2008-2012 5-year est.); Average household size: 2.26 (2008-2012 5-year est.); Median age: 42.2 (2008-2012 5-year est.); Males per 100 females: 114.0 (2008-2012 5-year est.); Marriage status: 24.5% never married, 51.7% now married, 5.9% widowed, 17.8% divorced (2008-2012 5-year est.); Foreign born: 0.0% (2008-2012 5-year est.); Ancestry (includes multiple ancestries): 23.2% German, 21.9% Irish, 13.8% English, 12.8% American, 6.3% French (2008-2012 5-year est.).
Economy: Homeowner vacancy rate: 1.6%. Rental vacancy rate: 0.0%. (2008-2012 5-year est.); Employment by occupation: 6.2% management, business, and financial, 0.0% computer, engineering, and science, 10.5% education, legal, community service, arts, and media, 4.2% healthcare practitioners, 29.4% service, 23.5% sales and office, 22.2% natural resources, construction, and maintenance, 3.9% production, transportation, and material moving (2008-2012 5-year est.).
Income: Per capita income: $22,759 (2008-2012 5-year est.); Median household income: $32,250 (2008-2012 5-year est.); Average household income: $52,867 (2008-2012 5-year est.); Percent of households with income of $100,000 or more: 6.6% (2008-2012 5-year est.); Poverty rate: 19.6% (2008-2012 5-year est.).
Education: Percent of population age 25 and over with: High school diploma (including GED) or higher: 73.2% (2008-2012 5-year est.); Bachelor's degree or higher: 12.4% (2008-2012 5-year est.); Master's degree or higher: 4.1% (2008-2012 5-year est.).
Housing: Homeownership rate: 74.0% (2008-2012 5-year est.); Median home value: $48,500 (2008-2012 5-year est.); Median contract rent: $259 per month (2008-2012 5-year est.); Median year structure built: 1965 (2008-2012 5-year est.).
Health Insurance: 46.6% Private; 51.4% Public; 20.4% None. (2008-2012 5-year est.)
Transportation: Commute to work: 94.0% car, 1.7% public transportation, 0.0% walk, 4.3% work from home (2008-2012 5-year est.); Travel time to work: 35.1% less than 15 minutes, 44.4% 15 to 30 minutes, 8.7% 30 to 45 minutes, 3.8% 45 to 60 minutes, 8.0% 60 minutes or more (2008-2012 5-year est.)

JUNCTION (village). Covers a land area of 0.878 square miles and a water area of 0.003 square miles. Located at 37.72° N. Lat; 88.24° W. Long. Elevation is 361 feet.
Population: 201 (1990); 139 (2000); 129 (2010); Density: 173.1 persons per square mile (2008-2012 5-year est.); Race: 100.0% White, 0.0% Black/African American, 0.0% Asian, 0.0% American Indian/Alaska Native, 0.0% Native Hawaiian/Other Pacific Islander, 0.0% Some other race, 0.0% Two or more races, 0.0% Hispanic of any race (2008-2012 5-year est.); Average household size: 2.87 (2008-2012 5-year est.); Median age: 41.8 (2008-2012 5-year est.); Males per 100 females: 90.0 (2008-2012 5-year est.); Marriage status: 23.5% never married, 64.4% now married, 3.0% widowed, 9.1% divorced (2008-2012 5-year est.); Foreign born: 0.0% (2008-2012 5-year est.); Ancestry (includes multiple ancestries): 19.1% American, 10.5% Irish, 5.9% Italian, 4.6% German, 4.6% Russian (2008-2012 5-year est.).
Economy: Homeowner vacancy rate: 0.0%. Rental vacancy rate: 0.0%. (2008-2012 5-year est.); Employment by occupation: 1.4% management, business, and financial, 2.8% computer, engineering, and science, 0.0% education, legal, community service, arts, and media, 13.9% healthcare practitioners, 22.2% service, 40.3% sales and office, 2.8% natural

resources, construction, and maintenance, 16.7% production, transportation, and material moving (2008-2012 5-year est.).
Income: Per capita income: $18,774 (2008-2012 5-year est.); Median household income: $43,125 (2008-2012 5-year est.); Average household income: $49,975 (2008-2012 5-year est.); Percent of households with income of $100,000 or more: 17.0% (2008-2012 5-year est.); Poverty rate: 2.0% (2008-2012 5-year est.).
Education: Percent of population age 25 and over with: High school diploma (including GED) or higher: 74.3% (2008-2012 5-year est.); Bachelor's degree or higher: 0.0% (2008-2012 5-year est.); Master's degree or higher: 0.0% (2008-2012 5-year est.).
School District(s)
Gallatin CUSD 7 (PK-12)
    2011-12 Enrollment: 777 . . . . (618) 272-3821
Housing: Homeownership rate: 94.3% (2008-2012 5-year est.); Median home value: $45,000 (2008-2012 5-year est.); Median contract rent: $188 per month (2008-2012 5-year est.); Median year structure built: 1977 (2008-2012 5-year est.).
Health Insurance: 66.4% Private; 39.5% Public; 11.8% None. (2008-2012 5-year est.)
Transportation: Commute to work: 96.8% car, 0.0% public transportation, 0.0% walk, 3.2% work from home (2008-2012 5-year est.); Travel time to work: 40.0% less than 15 minutes, 26.7% 15 to 30 minutes, 15.0% 30 to 45 minutes, 1.7% 45 to 60 minutes, 16.7% 60 minutes or more (2008-2012 5-year est.)

NEW HAVEN (village). Covers a land area of 1.228 square miles and a water area of 0.028 square miles. Located at 37.90° N. Lat; 88.13° W. Long. Elevation is 367 feet.
Population: 459 (1990); 477 (2000); 433 (2010); Density: 360.8 persons per square mile (2008-2012 5-year est.); Race: 97.5% White, 0.0% Black/African American, 0.0% Asian, 0.0% American Indian/Alaska Native, 0.0% Native Hawaiian/Other Pacific Islander, 2.5% Some other race, 2.5% Two or more races, 0.0% Hispanic of any race (2008-2012 5-year est.); Average household size: 2.50 (2008-2012 5-year est.); Median age: 46.6 (2008-2012 5-year est.); Males per 100 females: 99.5 (2008-2012 5-year est.); Marriage status: 28.2% never married, 52.3% now married, 8.9% widowed, 10.7% divorced (2008-2012 5-year est.); Foreign born: 0.2% (2008-2012 5-year est.); Ancestry (includes multiple ancestries): 22.1% Irish, 19.4% English, 19.0% German, 7.2% French, 6.3% Polish (2008-2012 5-year est.).
Economy: Homeowner vacancy rate: 1.9%. Rental vacancy rate: 0.0%. (2008-2012 5-year est.); Employment by occupation: 1.2% management, business, and financial, 0.0% computer, engineering, and science, 1.8% education, legal, community service, arts, and media, 8.2% healthcare practitioners, 32.7% service, 18.7% sales and office, 15.2% natural resources, construction, and maintenance, 22.2% production, transportation, and material moving (2008-2012 5-year est.).
Income: Per capita income: $17,389 (2008-2012 5-year est.); Median household income: $36,420 (2008-2012 5-year est.); Average household income: $41,678 (2008-2012 5-year est.); Percent of households with income of $100,000 or more: 8.5% (2008-2012 5-year est.); Poverty rate: 28.9% (2008-2012 5-year est.).
Education: Percent of population age 25 and over with: High school diploma (including GED) or higher: 65.7% (2008-2012 5-year est.); Bachelor's degree or higher: 3.1% (2008-2012 5-year est.); Master's degree or higher: 2.2% (2008-2012 5-year est.).
Housing: Homeownership rate: 80.8% (2008-2012 5-year est.); Median home value: $34,300 (2008-2012 5-year est.); Median contract rent: $154 per month (2008-2012 5-year est.); Median year structure built: 1973 (2008-2012 5-year est.).
Health Insurance: 52.4% Private; 48.8% Public; 11.3% None. (2008-2012 5-year est.)
Transportation: Commute to work: 87.3% car, 4.2% public transportation, 0.0% walk, 3.0% work from home (2008-2012 5-year est.); Travel time to work: 8.7% less than 15 minutes, 23.6% 15 to 30 minutes, 26.1% 30 to 45 minutes, 17.4% 45 to 60 minutes, 24.2% 60 minutes or more (2008-2012 5-year est.)

OLD SHAWNEETOWN (village). Covers a land area of 0.534 square miles and a water area of <.001 square miles. Located at 37.70° N. Lat; 88.14° W. Long. Elevation is 351 feet.
Population: 356 (1990); 278 (2000); 193 (2010); Density: 374.5 persons per square mile (2008-2012 5-year est.); Race: 100.0% White, 0.0% Black/African American, 0.0% Asian, 0.0% American Indian/Alaska Native,

0.0% Native Hawaiian/Other Pacific Islander, 0.0% Some other race, 0.0% Two or more races, 0.0% Hispanic of any race (2008-2012 5-year est.); Average household size: 2.86 (2008-2012 5-year est.); Median age: 32.9 (2008-2012 5-year est.); Males per 100 females: 106.2 (2008-2012 5-year est.); Marriage status: 38.5% never married, 47.8% now married, 6.2% widowed, 7.5% divorced (2008-2012 5-year est.); Foreign born: 0.0% (2008-2012 5-year est.); Ancestry (includes multiple ancestries): 23.0% German, 22.0% Irish, 18.0% English, 10.0% American, 2.5% French (2008-2012 5-year est.).

Economy: Homeowner vacancy rate: 1.7%. Rental vacancy rate: 0.0%. (2008-2012 5-year est.); Employment by occupation: 0.0% management, business, and financial, 2.7% computer, engineering, and science, 0.0% education, legal, community service, arts, and media, 2.7% healthcare practitioners, 33.8% service, 6.8% sales and office, 23.0% natural resources, construction, and maintenance, 31.1% production, transportation, and material moving (2008-2012 5-year est.).

Income: Per capita income: $11,367 (2008-2012 5-year est.); Median household income: $21,250 (2008-2012 5-year est.); Average household income: $33,184 (2008-2012 5-year est.); Percent of households with income of $100,000 or more: n/a (2008-2012 5-year est.); Poverty rate: 36.5% (2008-2012 5-year est.).

Education: Percent of population age 25 and over with: High school diploma (including GED) or higher: 63.6% (2008-2012 5-year est.); Bachelor's degree or higher: 2.1% (2008-2012 5-year est.); Master's degree or higher: 0.0% (2008-2012 5-year est.).

Housing: Homeownership rate: 82.9% (2008-2012 5-year est.); Median home value: $20,000 (2008-2012 5-year est.); Median contract rent: n/a per month (2008-2012 5-year est.); Median year structure built: 1970 (2008-2012 5-year est.).

Health Insurance: 37.0% Private; 50.0% Public; 23.0% None. (2008-2012 5-year est.)

Transportation: Commute to work: 79.7% car, 0.0% public transportation, 5.4% walk, 0.0% work from home (2008-2012 5-year est.); Travel time to work: 43.2% less than 15 minutes, 27.0% 15 to 30 minutes, 17.6% 30 to 45 minutes, 10.8% 45 to 60 minutes, 1.4% 60 minutes or more (2008-2012 5-year est.)

OMAHA (village).

Covers a land area of 0.817 square miles and a water area of 0.003 square miles. Located at 37.89° N. Lat; 88.31° W. Long. Elevation is 374 feet.

Population: 273 (1990); 263 (2000); 266 (2010); Density: 296.3 persons per square mile (2008-2012 5-year est.); Race: 98.8% White, 0.0% Black/African American, 0.0% Asian, 0.0% American Indian/Alaska Native, 0.0% Native Hawaiian/Other Pacific Islander, 1.2% Some other race, 1.2% Two or more races, 0.0% Hispanic of any race (2008-2012 5-year est.); Average household size: 2.07 (2008-2012 5-year est.); Median age: 49.5 (2008-2012 5-year est.); Males per 100 females: 89.1 (2008-2012 5-year est.); Marriage status: 23.6% never married, 58.6% now married, 9.5% widowed, 8.2% divorced (2008-2012 5-year est.); Foreign born: 0.0% (2008-2012 5-year est.); Ancestry (includes multiple ancestries): 24.8% Irish, 22.7% German, 17.8% American, 11.2% English, 8.3% French (2008-2012 5-year est.).

Economy: Homeowner vacancy rate: 12.6%. Rental vacancy rate: 0.0%. (2008-2012 5-year est.); Employment by occupation: 10.1% management, business, and financial, 0.8% computer, engineering, and science, 11.8% education, legal, community service, arts, and media, 6.7% healthcare practitioners, 25.2% service, 19.3% sales and office, 5.0% natural resources, construction, and maintenance, 21.0% production, transportation, and material moving (2008-2012 5-year est.).

Income: Per capita income: $21,991 (2008-2012 5-year est.); Median household income: $36,875 (2008-2012 5-year est.); Average household income: $42,485 (2008-2012 5-year est.); Percent of households with income of $100,000 or more: 6.0% (2008-2012 5-year est.); Poverty rate: 12.0% (2008-2012 5-year est.).

Education: Percent of population age 25 and over with: High school diploma (including GED) or higher: 84.1% (2008-2012 5-year est.); Bachelor's degree or higher: 11.3% (2008-2012 5-year est.); Master's degree or higher: 5.6% (2008-2012 5-year est.).

Housing: Homeownership rate: 82.9% (2008-2012 5-year est.); Median home value: $49,400 (2008-2012 5-year est.); Median contract rent: $221 per month (2008-2012 5-year est.); Median year structure built: 1960 (2008-2012 5-year est.).

Health Insurance: 53.3% Private; 44.2% Public; 16.7% None. (2008-2012 5-year est.)

Transportation: Commute to work: 88.3% car, 0.0% public transportation, 0.8% walk, 8.3% work from home (2008-2012 5-year est.); Travel time to work: 34.5% less than 15 minutes, 22.7% 15 to 30 minutes, 14.5% 30 to 45 minutes, 10.0% 45 to 60 minutes, 18.2% 60 minutes or more (2008-2012 5-year est.)

RIDGWAY (village).

Covers a land area of 0.911 square miles and a water area of <.001 square miles. Located at 37.80° N. Lat; 88.26° W. Long. Elevation is 371 feet.

History: Incorporated 1886.

Population: 1,103 (1990); 928 (2000); 869 (2010); Density: 897.3 persons per square mile (2008-2012 5-year est.); Race: 98.4% White, 1.0% Black/African American, 0.0% Asian, 0.6% American Indian/Alaska Native, 0.0% Native Hawaiian/Other Pacific Islander, 0.0% Some other race, 0.0% Two or more races, 0.0% Hispanic of any race (2008-2012 5-year est.); Average household size: 2.10 (2008-2012 5-year est.); Median age: 51.8 (2008-2012 5-year est.); Males per 100 females: 90.4 (2008-2012 5-year est.); Marriage status: 20.8% never married, 48.4% now married, 14.8% widowed, 15.9% divorced (2008-2012 5-year est.); Foreign born: 0.0% (2008-2012 5-year est.); Ancestry (includes multiple ancestries): 33.8% German, 33.2% Irish, 14.4% English, 7.3% American, 3.5% French (2008-2012 5-year est.).

Economy: Homeowner vacancy rate: 5.1%. Rental vacancy rate: 12.1%. (2008-2012 5-year est.); Employment by occupation: 3.3% management, business, and financial, 3.9% computer, engineering, and science, 8.9% education, legal, community service, arts, and media, 10.1% healthcare practitioners, 21.4% service, 23.8% sales and office, 16.4% natural resources, construction, and maintenance, 12.2% production, transportation, and material moving (2008-2012 5-year est.).

Income: Per capita income: $21,838 (2008-2012 5-year est.); Median household income: $33,125 (2008-2012 5-year est.); Average household income: $45,271 (2008-2012 5-year est.); Percent of households with income of $100,000 or more: 11.7% (2008-2012 5-year est.); Poverty rate: 18.8% (2008-2012 5-year est.).

Education: Percent of population age 25 and over with: High school diploma (including GED) or higher: 85.4% (2008-2012 5-year est.); Bachelor's degree or higher: 13.1% (2008-2012 5-year est.); Master's degree or higher: 5.3% (2008-2012 5-year est.).

Housing: Homeownership rate: 78.8% (2008-2012 5-year est.); Median home value: $56,900 (2008-2012 5-year est.); Median contract rent: $217 per month (2008-2012 5-year est.); Median year structure built: 1965 (2008-2012 5-year est.).

Health Insurance: 59.3% Private; 45.0% Public; 15.5% None. (2008-2012 5-year est.)

Transportation: Commute to work: 96.3% car, 0.0% public transportation, 3.7% walk, 0.0% work from home (2008-2012 5-year est.); Travel time to work: 34.9% less than 15 minutes, 32.1% 15 to 30 minutes, 15.7% 30 to 45 minutes, 10.2% 45 to 60 minutes, 7.1% 60 minutes or more (2008-2012 5-year est.)

SHAWNEETOWN (city).

Aka New Shawneetown. County seat. Covers a land area of 0.675 square miles and a water area of 0.009 square miles. Located at 37.72° N. Lat; 88.19° W. Long. Elevation is 400 feet.

History: Shawneetown, settled in the early 1800s, developed as a port on the Ohio River and as a financial center when Chicago was still a small village. Salt was an important export for the growing town, through which travelers and merchandise passed on the river. Shawneetown State Historical Site is here. Gallatin County Courthouse and most residents moved to (new) Shawneetown in late 1930s after disastrous Ohio River flood of 1937. The first state chartered bank opened here.

Population: 1,575 (1990); 1,410 (2000); 1,239 (2010); Density: 1,797.7 persons per square mile (2008-2012 5-year est.); Race: 95.6% White, 1.2% Black/African American, 1.0% Asian, 0.3% American Indian/Alaska Native, 0.0% Native Hawaiian/Other Pacific Islander, 1.9% Some other race, 0.9% Two or more races, 1.7% Hispanic of any race (2008-2012 5-year est.); Average household size: 2.26 (2008-2012 5-year est.); Median age: 40.9 (2008-2012 5-year est.); Males per 100 females: 90.7 (2008-2012 5-year est.); Marriage status: 18.4% never married, 53.1% now married, 11.8% widowed, 16.7% divorced (2008-2012 5-year est.); Foreign born: 1.1% (2008-2012 5-year est.); Ancestry (includes multiple ancestries): 25.3% German, 21.5% Irish, 8.7% Dutch, 8.2% English, 3.1% American (2008-2012 5-year est.).

Economy: Homeowner vacancy rate: 0.0%. Rental vacancy rate: 9.0%. (2008-2012 5-year est.); Employment by occupation: 3.2% management,

business, and financial, 0.5% computer, engineering, and science, 7.5% education, legal, community service, arts, and media, 10.5% healthcare practitioners, 23.8% service, 21.2% sales and office, 13.1% natural resources, construction, and maintenance, 20.2% production, transportation, and material moving (2008-2012 5-year est.).

Income: Per capita income: $16,005 (2008-2012 5-year est.); Median household income: $23,565 (2008-2012 5-year est.); Average household income: $35,288 (2008-2012 5-year est.); Percent of households with income of $100,000 or more: 2.1% (2008-2012 5-year est.); Poverty rate: 26.5% (2008-2012 5-year est.).

Education: Percent of population age 25 and over with: High school diploma (including GED) or higher: 73.8% (2008-2012 5-year est.); Bachelor's degree or higher: 4.0% (2008-2012 5-year est.); Master's degree or higher: 1.7% (2008-2012 5-year est.).

Housing: Homeownership rate: 73.4% (2008-2012 5-year est.); Median home value: $51,700 (2008-2012 5-year est.); Median contract rent: $191 per month (2008-2012 5-year est.); Median year structure built: 1965 (2008-2012 5-year est.).

Health Insurance: 47.6% Private; 53.6% Public; 13.2% None. (2008-2012 5-year est.)

Transportation: Commute to work: 95.9% car, 1.5% public transportation, 0.8% walk, 1.8% work from home (2008-2012 5-year est.); Travel time to work: 40.3% less than 15 minutes, 21.0% 15 to 30 minutes, 26.5% 30 to 45 minutes, 4.4% 45 to 60 minutes, 7.8% 60 minutes or more (2008-2012 5-year est.)

Greene County

Located in southwest central Illinois; bounded on the west by the Illinois River; drained by Macoupin and Apple Creeks. Covers a land area of 543.019 square miles, a water area of 3.253 square miles, and is located in the Central Time Zone at 39.36° N. Lat., 90.39° W. Long. The county was founded in 1821. County seat is Carrollton.

Weather Station: White Hall 1 E   Elevation: 580 feet

	Jan	Feb	Mar	Apr	May	Jun	Jul	Aug	Sep	Oct	Nov	Dec
High	36	41	52	64	74	83	86	85	79	67	53	39
Low	19	22	31	42	52	62	65	64	55	43	33	22
Precip	1.7	1.8	3.0	3.8	4.4	3.8	3.6	3.1	3.1	3.1	3.5	2.6
Snow	4.7	3.9	2.0	0.4	0.0	0.0	0.0	0.0	0.0	tr	0.5	3.6

High and Low temperatures in degrees Fahrenheit; Precipitation and Snow in inches

Population: 15,317 (1990); 14,761 (2000); 13,886 (2010); Race: 95.4% White, 1.3% Black/African American, 0.2% Asian, 0.0% American Indian/Alaska Native, 0.3% Native Hawaiian/Other Pacific Islander, 2.8% Some other race, 2.3% Two or more races, 0.9% Hispanic of any race (2008-2012 5-year est.); Density: 25.1 persons per square mile (2008-2012 5-year est.); Average household size: 2.32 (2008-2012 5-year est.); Median age: 41.3 (2008-2012 5-year est.); Males per 100 females: 102.3 (2008-2012 5-year est.).

Religion: Six largest groups: 30.6% Baptist, 12.7% Catholicism, 4.6% Methodist/Pietist, 1.9% Lutheran, 1.5% Non-denominational Protestant, 1.4% European Free-Church (2010)

Economy: Unemployment rate: 6.7% (April 2014); Total civilian labor force: 6,225 (April 2014); Leading industries: 21.3% retail trade; 21.2% health care and social assistance; 11.0% accommodation & food services (2012); Farms: 689 totaling 290,124 acres (2012); Companies that employ 500 or more persons: 0 (2012); Companies that employ 100 to 499 persons: 2 (2012); Companies that employ less than 100 persons: 263 (2012); Black-owned businesses: n/a (2007); Hispanic-owned businesses: n/a (2007); Asian-owned businesses: n/a (2007); Women-owned businesses: n/a (2007); Single-family building permits issued: 2 (2013); Multi-family building permits issued: 0 (2013).

Income: Per capita income: $22,466 (2008-2012 5-year est.); Median household income: $42,556 (2008-2012 5-year est.); Average household income: $53,257 (2008-2012 5-year est.); Percent of households with income of $100,000 or more: 10.1% (2008-2012 5-year est.); Poverty rate: 12.0% (2008-2012 5-year est.); Bankruptcy rate: 1.40% (2013).

Education: Percent of population age 25 and over with: High school diploma (including GED) or higher: 86.2% (2008-2012 5-year est.); Bachelor's degree or higher: 12.5% (2008-2012 5-year est.); Master's degree or higher: 4.3% (2008-2012 5-year est.).

Housing: Homeownership rate: 76.3% (2008-2012 5-year est.); Median home value: $73,300 (2008-2012 5-year est.); Median contract rent: $386 per month (2008-2012 5-year est.); Median year structure built: 1954 (2008-2012 5-year est.)

Health: Birth rate: 110.1 per 10,000 population (2013); Death rate: 116.7 per 10,000 population (2013); Age-adjusted cancer mortality rate: 154.1 deaths per 100,000 population (2011); Number of physicians: 5.8 per 10,000 population (2011); Hospital beds: 46.8 per 10,000 population (2010); Hospital admissions: 678.4 per 10,000 population (2010).

Elections: 2012 Presidential election results: 36.0% Obama, 61.4% Romney

Additional Information Contacts

Greene County Government . . . . (217) 942-5443

Greene County Communities

CARROLLTON (city). County seat. Covers a land area of 1.902 square miles and a water area of 0.002 square miles. Located at 39.29° N. Lat; 90.41° W. Long. Elevation is 620 feet.

History: Carrollton was settled in 1818 and developed as the seat of Green County.

Population: 2,507 (1990); 2,605 (2000); 2,484 (2010); Density: 1,354.2 persons per square mile (2008-2012 5-year est.); Race: 97.6% White, 0.4% Black/African American, 0.2% Asian, 0.0% American Indian/Alaska Native, 0.0% Native Hawaiian/Other Pacific Islander, 1.8% Some other race, 1.8% Two or more races, 0.1% Hispanic of any race (2008-2012 5-year est.); Average household size: 2.04 (2008-2012 5-year est.); Median age: 45.4 (2008-2012 5-year est.); Males per 100 females: 89.4 (2008-2012 5-year est.); Marriage status: 17.2% never married, 56.7% now married, 13.8% widowed, 12.2% divorced (2008-2012 5-year est.); Foreign born: 0.7% (2008-2012 5-year est.); Ancestry (includes multiple ancestries): 37.5% German, 14.7% Irish, 11.1% English, 8.5% American, 5.4% French (2008-2012 5-year est.).

Economy: Single-family building permits issued: 1 (2013); Multi-family building permits issued: 0 (2013); Homeowner vacancy rate: 2.7%. Rental vacancy rate: 4.2%. (2008-2012 5-year est.); Employment by occupation: 10.5% management, business, and financial, 0.9% computer, engineering, and science, 12.8% education, legal, community service, arts, and media, 8.2% healthcare practitioners, 19.3% service, 17.0% sales and office, 15.3% natural resources, construction, and maintenance, 16.0% production, transportation, and material moving (2008-2012 5-year est.).

Income: Per capita income: $25,109 (2008-2012 5-year est.); Median household income: $41,438 (2008-2012 5-year est.); Average household income: $51,487 (2008-2012 5-year est.); Percent of households with income of $100,000 or more: 6.9% (2008-2012 5-year est.); Poverty rate: 7.6% (2008-2012 5-year est.).

Education: Percent of population age 25 and over with: High school diploma (including GED) or higher: 89.0% (2008-2012 5-year est.); Bachelor's degree or higher: 19.2% (2008-2012 5-year est.); Master's degree or higher: 7.1% (2008-2012 5-year est.).

School District(s)

Carrollton CUSD 1 (PK-12)
    2011-12 Enrollment: 625 . . . . (217) 942-5314

Housing: Homeownership rate: 72.2% (2008-2012 5-year est.); Median home value: $83,700 (2008-2012 5-year est.); Median contract rent: $422 per month (2008-2012 5-year est.); Median year structure built: 1961 (2008-2012 5-year est.).

Health Insurance: 67.2% Private; 42.0% Public; 10.5% None. (2008-2012 5-year est.)

Hospitals: Thomas H. Boyd Memorial Hospital (65 beds)

Safety: Violent crime rate: 77.0 per 10,000 population; Property crime rate: 162.0 per 10,000 population (2012).

Transportation: Commute to work: 87.7% car, 0.0% public transportation, 3.5% walk, 6.7% work from home (2008-2012 5-year est.); Travel time to work: 51.9% less than 15 minutes, 19.8% 15 to 30 minutes, 7.8% 30 to 45 minutes, 6.4% 45 to 60 minutes, 14.1% 60 minutes or more (2008-2012 5-year est.)

ELDRED (village). Covers a land area of 0.134 square miles and a water area of 0 square miles. Located at 39.29° N. Lat; 90.55° W. Long. Elevation is 449 feet.

Population: 254 (1990); 211 (2000); 201 (2010); Density: 1,159.0 persons per square mile (2008-2012 5-year est.); Race: 95.5% White, 0.0% Black/African American, 0.0% Asian, 0.0% American Indian/Alaska Native, 0.0% Native Hawaiian/Other Pacific Islander, 4.5% Some other race, 4.5% Two or more races, 0.6% Hispanic of any race (2008-2012 5-year est.); Average household size: 1.74 (2008-2012 5-year est.); Median age: 51.5 (2008-2012 5-year est.); Males per 100 females: 80.2 (2008-2012 5-year

est.); Marriage status: 27.1% never married, 37.1% now married, 25.0% widowed, 10.7% divorced (2008-2012 5-year est.); Foreign born: 0.0% (2008-2012 5-year est.); Ancestry (includes multiple ancestries): 34.2% German, 23.2% English, 13.5% Scottish, 7.7% Dutch, 4.5% American (2008-2012 5-year est.).

Economy: Homeowner vacancy rate: 0.0%. Rental vacancy rate: 8.1%. (2008-2012 5-year est.); Employment by occupation: 9.4% management, business, and financial, 3.8% computer, engineering, and science, 13.2% education, legal, community service, arts, and media, 3.8% healthcare practitioners, 17.0% service, 20.8% sales and office, 13.2% natural resources, construction, and maintenance, 18.9% production, transportation, and material moving (2008-2012 5-year est.).

Income: Per capita income: $25,956 (2008-2012 5-year est.); Median household income: $37,344 (2008-2012 5-year est.); Average household income: $45,275 (2008-2012 5-year est.); Percent of households with income of $100,000 or more: 3.3% (2008-2012 5-year est.); Poverty rate: 19.4% (2008-2012 5-year est.).

Education: Percent of population age 25 and over with: High school diploma (including GED) or higher: 91.2% (2008-2012 5-year est.); Bachelor's degree or higher: 8.8% (2008-2012 5-year est.); Master's degree or higher: 5.6% (2008-2012 5-year est.).

Housing: Homeownership rate: 61.8% (2008-2012 5-year est.); Median home value: $30,900 (2008-2012 5-year est.); Median contract rent: $233 per month (2008-2012 5-year est.); Median year structure built: 1950 (2008-2012 5-year est.).

Health Insurance: 60.6% Private; 40.0% Public; 14.2% None. (2008-2012 5-year est.)

Transportation: Commute to work: 77.4% car, 0.0% public transportation, 7.5% walk, 15.1% work from home (2008-2012 5-year est.); Travel time to work: 17.8% less than 15 minutes, 20.0% 15 to 30 minutes, 15.6% 30 to 45 minutes, 24.4% 45 to 60 minutes, 22.2% 60 minutes or more (2008-2012 5-year est.)

GREENFIELD (city). Covers a land area of 1.718 square miles and a water area of 0.063 square miles. Located at 39.34° N. Lat; 90.21° W. Long. Elevation is 587 feet.

History: Incorporated 1837.

Population: 1,162 (1990); 1,179 (2000); 1,071 (2010); Density: 820.1 persons per square mile (2008-2012 5-year est.); Race: 99.3% White, 0.0% Black/African American, 0.0% Asian, 0.0% American Indian/Alaska Native, 0.0% Native Hawaiian/Other Pacific Islander, 0.7% Some other race, 0.7% Two or more races, 0.0% Hispanic of any race (2008-2012 5-year est.); Average household size: 2.28 (2008-2012 5-year est.); Median age: 35.1 (2008-2012 5-year est.); Males per 100 females: 87.9 (2008-2012 5-year est.); Marriage status: 23.1% never married, 49.1% now married, 12.6% widowed, 15.1% divorced (2008-2012 5-year est.); Foreign born: 0.3% (2008-2012 5-year est.); Ancestry (includes multiple ancestries): 35.1% German, 22.7% Irish, 13.0% American, 12.3% English, 2.3% Scottish (2008-2012 5-year est.).

Economy: Single-family building permits issued: 1 (2013); Multi-family building permits issued: 0 (2013); Homeowner vacancy rate: 3.1%. Rental vacancy rate: 0.0%. (2008-2012 5-year est.); Employment by occupation: 6.3% management, business, and financial, 0.9% computer, engineering, and science, 7.8% education, legal, community service, arts, and media, 8.8% healthcare practitioners, 16.6% service, 20.9% sales and office, 17.8% natural resources, construction, and maintenance, 20.8% production, transportation, and material moving (2008-2012 5-year est.).

Income: Per capita income: $22,153 (2008-2012 5-year est.); Median household income: $39,712 (2008-2012 5-year est.); Average household income: $50,231 (2008-2012 5-year est.); Percent of households with income of $100,000 or more: 6.1% (2008-2012 5-year est.); Poverty rate: 13.5% (2008-2012 5-year est.).

Education: Percent of population age 25 and over with: High school diploma (including GED) or higher: 88.3% (2008-2012 5-year est.); Bachelor's degree or higher: 9.9% (2008-2012 5-year est.); Master's degree or higher: 4.5% (2008-2012 5-year est.).

School District(s)

Greenfield CUSD 10 (PK-12)

2011-12 Enrollment: 497 . . . . (217) 368-2447

Housing: Homeownership rate: 76.0% (2008-2012 5-year est.); Median home value: $68,200 (2008-2012 5-year est.); Median contract rent: $417 per month (2008-2012 5-year est.); Median year structure built: 1957 (2008-2012 5-year est.).

Health Insurance: 62.9% Private; 38.3% Public; 10.1% None. (2008-2012 5-year est.)

Safety: Violent crime rate: 9.4 per 10,000 population; Property crime rate: 94.0 per 10,000 population (2012).

Transportation: Commute to work: 94.1% car, 0.0% public transportation, 4.0% walk, 1.5% work from home (2008-2012 5-year est.); Travel time to work: 34.7% less than 15 minutes, 12.0% 15 to 30 minutes, 37.2% 30 to 45 minutes, 6.1% 45 to 60 minutes, 10.0% 60 minutes or more (2008-2012 5-year est.)

HILLVIEW (village). Covers a land area of 0.816 square miles and a water area of 0 square miles. Located at 39.45° N. Lat; 90.54° W. Long. Elevation is 440 feet.

Population: 271 (1990); 179 (2000); 193 (2010); Density: 171.6 persons per square mile (2008-2012 5-year est.); Race: 100.0% White, 0.0% Black/African American, 0.0% Asian, 0.0% American Indian/Alaska Native, 0.0% Native Hawaiian/Other Pacific Islander, 0.0% Some other race, 0.0% Two or more races, 5.0% Hispanic of any race (2008-2012 5-year est.); Average household size: 2.80 (2008-2012 5-year est.); Median age: 36.7 (2008-2012 5-year est.); Males per 100 females: 118.8 (2008-2012 5-year est.); Marriage status: 36.1% never married, 51.3% now married, 0.0% widowed, 12.6% divorced (2008-2012 5-year est.); Foreign born: 0.0% (2008-2012 5-year est.); Ancestry (includes multiple ancestries): 35.0% German, 11.4% Irish, 6.4% American, 3.6% Dutch, 3.6% English (2008-2012 5-year est.).

Economy: Homeowner vacancy rate: 3.2%. Rental vacancy rate: 0.0%. (2008-2012 5-year est.); Employment by occupation: 0.0% management, business, and financial, 0.0% computer, engineering, and science, 0.0% education, legal, community service, arts, and media, 6.0% healthcare practitioners, 56.0% service, 24.0% sales and office, 0.0% natural resources, construction, and maintenance, 14.0% production, transportation, and material moving (2008-2012 5-year est.).

Income: Per capita income: $13,976 (2008-2012 5-year est.); Median household income: $41,250 (2008-2012 5-year est.); Average household income: $40,366 (2008-2012 5-year est.); Percent of households with income of $100,000 or more: n/a (2008-2012 5-year est.); Poverty rate: 41.0% (2008-2012 5-year est.).

Education: Percent of population age 25 and over with: High school diploma (including GED) or higher: 76.7% (2008-2012 5-year est.); Bachelor's degree or higher: 2.2% (2008-2012 5-year est.); Master's degree or higher: 0.0% (2008-2012 5-year est.).

Housing: Homeownership rate: 60.0% (2008-2012 5-year est.); Median home value: $37,500 (2008-2012 5-year est.); Median contract rent: n/a per month (2008-2012 5-year est.); Median year structure built: Before 1940 (2008-2012 5-year est.).

Health Insurance: 42.8% Private; 53.6% Public; 14.5% None. (2008-2012 5-year est.)

Transportation: Commute to work: 100.0% car, 0.0% public transportation, 0.0% walk, 0.0% work from home (2008-2012 5-year est.); Travel time to work: 15.4% less than 15 minutes, 26.9% 15 to 30 minutes, 50.0% 30 to 45 minutes, 3.8% 45 to 60 minutes, 3.8% 60 minutes or more (2008-2012 5-year est.)

KANE (village). Covers a land area of 0.544 square miles and a water area of 0 square miles. Located at 39.19° N. Lat; 90.35° W. Long. Elevation is 561 feet.

Population: 456 (1990); 459 (2000); 438 (2010); Density: 753.3 persons per square mile (2008-2012 5-year est.); Race: 91.5% White, 0.0% Black/African American, 0.0% Asian, 0.0% American Indian/Alaska Native, 0.0% Native Hawaiian/Other Pacific Islander, 8.5% Some other race, 8.5% Two or more races, 1.0% Hispanic of any race (2008-2012 5-year est.); Average household size: 2.43 (2008-2012 5-year est.); Median age: 36.0 (2008-2012 5-year est.); Males per 100 females: 96.2 (2008-2012 5-year est.); Marriage status: 32.9% never married, 43.1% now married, 5.7% widowed, 18.3% divorced (2008-2012 5-year est.); Foreign born: 0.0% (2008-2012 5-year est.); Ancestry (includes multiple ancestries): 27.8% German, 20.0% Irish, 12.9% Dutch, 7.6% English, 6.6% Italian (2008-2012 5-year est.).

Economy: Homeowner vacancy rate: 2.2%. Rental vacancy rate: 0.0%. (2008-2012 5-year est.); Employment by occupation: 5.2% management, business, and financial, 2.6% computer, engineering, and science, 4.7% education, legal, community service, arts, and media, 4.2% healthcare practitioners, 22.5% service, 16.8% sales and office, 18.3% natural resources, construction, and maintenance, 25.7% production, transportation, and material moving (2008-2012 5-year est.).

Income: Per capita income: $16,762 (2008-2012 5-year est.); Median household income: $34,375 (2008-2012 5-year est.); Average household

income: $43,156 (2008-2012 5-year est.); Percent of households with income of $100,000 or more: 4.7% (2008-2012 5-year est.); Poverty rate: 17.6% (2008-2012 5-year est.).

Education: Percent of population age 25 and over with: High school diploma (including GED) or higher: 82.5% (2008-2012 5-year est.); Bachelor's degree or higher: 7.5% (2008-2012 5-year est.); Master's degree or higher: 0.0% (2008-2012 5-year est.).

Housing: Homeownership rate: 79.9% (2008-2012 5-year est.); Median home value: $70,200 (2008-2012 5-year est.); Median contract rent: $305 per month (2008-2012 5-year est.); Median year structure built: 1941 (2008-2012 5-year est.).

Health Insurance: 53.9% Private; 33.7% Public; 20.7% None. (2008-2012 5-year est.)

Transportation: Commute to work: 96.2% car, 0.0% public transportation, 3.8% walk, 0.0% work from home (2008-2012 5-year est.); Travel time to work: 33.0% less than 15 minutes, 20.0% 15 to 30 minutes, 19.5% 30 to 45 minutes, 14.1% 45 to 60 minutes, 13.5% 60 minutes or more (2008-2012 5-year est.)

PATTERSON (unincorporated postal area)

Zip Code: 62078

Covers a land area of 0.445 square miles and a water area of 0 square miles. Located at 39.47° N. Lat; 90.48° W. Long. Elevation is 679 feet. Population: 119 (2010); Density: 267.0 persons per square mile (2010); Race: 100.0% White, 0.0% Black/African American, 0.0% Asian, 0.0% American Indian/Alaska Native, 0.0% Native Hawaiian/Other Pacific Islander, 0.0% Some other race, 0.0% Two or more races, 0.0% Hispanic of any race (2010); Average household size: 2.77 (2010); Median age: 35.8 (2010); Males per 100 females: 101.7 (2010); Homeownership rate: 79.1% (2010)

ROCKBRIDGE (village). Covers a land area of 0.737 square miles and a water area of 0 square miles. Located at 39.27° N. Lat; 90.21° W. Long. Elevation is 541 feet.

Population: 212 (1990); 189 (2000); 169 (2010); Density: 290.4 persons per square mile (2008-2012 5-year est.); Race: 87.4% White, 0.0% Black/African American, 0.0% Asian, 0.0% American Indian/Alaska Native, 0.0% Native Hawaiian/Other Pacific Islander, 12.6% Some other race, 8.4% Two or more races, 13.1% Hispanic of any race (2008-2012 5-year est.); Average household size: 2.43 (2008-2012 5-year est.); Median age: 47.3 (2008-2012 5-year est.); Males per 100 females: 76.9 (2008-2012 5-year est.); Marriage status: 17.4% never married, 62.9% now married, 3.9% widowed, 15.7% divorced (2008-2012 5-year est.); Foreign born: 0.0% (2008-2012 5-year est.); Ancestry (includes multiple ancestries): 32.7% German, 20.6% Irish, 12.6% Dutch, 6.1% Polish, 6.1% English (2008-2012 5-year est.).

Economy: Homeowner vacancy rate: 2.3%. Rental vacancy rate: 0.0%. (2008-2012 5-year est.); Employment by occupation: 13.3% management, business, and financial, 0.0% computer, engineering, and science, 13.3% education, legal, community service, arts, and media, 0.0% healthcare practitioners, 15.7% service, 28.9% sales and office, 3.6% natural resources, construction, and maintenance, 25.3% production, transportation, and material moving (2008-2012 5-year est.).

Income: Per capita income: $25,716 (2008-2012 5-year est.); Median household income: $45,000 (2008-2012 5-year est.); Average household income: $62,118 (2008-2012 5-year est.); Percent of households with income of $100,000 or more: 14.8% (2008-2012 5-year est.); Poverty rate: 1.9% (2008-2012 5-year est.).

Education: Percent of population age 25 and over with: High school diploma (including GED) or higher: 79.5% (2008-2012 5-year est.); Bachelor's degree or higher: 4.3% (2008-2012 5-year est.); Master's degree or higher: 0.0% (2008-2012 5-year est.).

Housing: Homeownership rate: 95.5% (2008-2012 5-year est.); Median home value: $55,700 (2008-2012 5-year est.); Median contract rent: n/a per month (2008-2012 5-year est.); Median year structure built: 1964 (2008-2012 5-year est.).

Health Insurance: 64.5% Private; 46.3% Public; 13.1% None. (2008-2012 5-year est.)

Transportation: Commute to work: 100.0% car, 0.0% public transportation, 0.0% walk, 0.0% work from home (2008-2012 5-year est.); Travel time to work: 17.3% less than 15 minutes, 18.5% 15 to 30 minutes, 30.9% 30 to 45 minutes, 19.8% 45 to 60 minutes, 13.6% 60 minutes or more (2008-2012 5-year est.)

ROODHOUSE (city). Covers a land area of 1.127 square miles and a water area of 0 square miles. Located at 39.48° N. Lat; 90.37° W. Long. Elevation is 656 feet.

History: Roodhouse was laid out by an early settler, John Roodhouse, and developed as a railroad center.

Population: 2,139 (1990); 2,214 (2000); 1,814 (2010); Density: 1,626.5 persons per square mile (2008-2012 5-year est.); Race: 94.7% White, 0.0% Black/African American, 0.0% Asian, 0.0% American Indian/Alaska Native, 2.1% Native Hawaiian/Other Pacific Islander, 3.2% Some other race, 2.5% Two or more races, 0.7% Hispanic of any race (2008-2012 5-year est.); Average household size: 2.10 (2008-2012 5-year est.); Median age: 41.9 (2008-2012 5-year est.); Males per 100 females: 106.7 (2008-2012 5-year est.); Marriage status: 21.0% never married, 52.9% now married, 7.4% widowed, 18.7% divorced (2008-2012 5-year est.); Foreign born: 0.0% (2008-2012 5-year est.); Ancestry (includes multiple ancestries): 23.2% German, 17.3% American, 12.5% Irish, 10.7% English, 4.9% French (2008-2012 5-year est.).

Economy: Homeowner vacancy rate: 2.0%. Rental vacancy rate: 0.0%. (2008-2012 5-year est.); Employment by occupation: 11.5% management, business, and financial, 2.0% computer, engineering, and science, 8.4% education, legal, community service, arts, and media, 3.4% healthcare practitioners, 21.2% service, 17.1% sales and office, 12.8% natural resources, construction, and maintenance, 23.6% production, transportation, and material moving (2008-2012 5-year est.).

Income: Per capita income: $20,283 (2008-2012 5-year est.); Median household income: $35,972 (2008-2012 5-year est.); Average household income: $42,955 (2008-2012 5-year est.); Percent of households with income of $100,000 or more: 5.1% (2008-2012 5-year est.); Poverty rate: 11.8% (2008-2012 5-year est.).

Education: Percent of population age 25 and over with: High school diploma (including GED) or higher: 83.4% (2008-2012 5-year est.); Bachelor's degree or higher: 12.4% (2008-2012 5-year est.); Master's degree or higher: 6.8% (2008-2012 5-year est.).

School District(s)

North Greene CUSD 3 (PK-12)

    2011-12 Enrollment: 944 . . . . (217) 374-2842

Housing: Homeownership rate: 77.9% (2008-2012 5-year est.); Median home value: $57,000 (2008-2012 5-year est.); Median contract rent: $417 per month (2008-2012 5-year est.); Median year structure built: 1951 (2008-2012 5-year est.).

Health Insurance: 75.9% Private; 37.6% Public; 6.4% None. (2008-2012 5-year est.)

Transportation: Commute to work: 90.2% car, 0.0% public transportation, 7.8% walk, 2.0% work from home (2008-2012 5-year est.); Travel time to work: 34.2% less than 15 minutes, 25.2% 15 to 30 minutes, 21.4% 30 to 45 minutes, 1.4% 45 to 60 minutes, 17.7% 60 minutes or more (2008-2012 5-year est.)

WHITE HALL (city). Aka Whitehall. Covers a land area of 2.577 square miles and a water area of 0.057 square miles. Located at 39.44° N. Lat; 90.40° W. Long. Elevation is 571 feet.

History: White Hall was founded in 1820 and developed around the manufacture of pottery from local clay.

Population: 2,814 (1990); 2,629 (2000); 2,520 (2010); Density: 1,012.5 persons per square mile (2008-2012 5-year est.); Race: 94.4% White, 0.9% Black/African American, 0.0% Asian, 0.0% American Indian/Alaska Native, 0.0% Native Hawaiian/Other Pacific Islander, 4.7% Some other race, 4.4% Two or more races, 0.3% Hispanic of any race (2008-2012 5-year est.); Average household size: 2.55 (2008-2012 5-year est.); Median age: 39.2 (2008-2012 5-year est.); Males per 100 females: 88.6 (2008-2012 5-year est.); Marriage status: 24.4% never married, 51.4% now married, 10.1% widowed, 14.1% divorced (2008-2012 5-year est.); Foreign born: 1.1% (2008-2012 5-year est.); Ancestry (includes multiple ancestries): 20.1% German, 16.0% American, 15.4% Irish, 14.0% English, 2.7% Polish (2008-2012 5-year est.).

Economy: Homeowner vacancy rate: 3.7%. Rental vacancy rate: 17.7%. (2008-2012 5-year est.); Employment by occupation: 3.0% management, business, and financial, 3.8% computer, engineering, and science, 6.5% education, legal, community service, arts, and media, 8.8% healthcare practitioners, 30.5% service, 16.6% sales and office, 9.6% natural resources, construction, and maintenance, 21.2% production, transportation, and material moving (2008-2012 5-year est.).

Income: Per capita income: $18,146 (2008-2012 5-year est.); Median household income: $31,837 (2008-2012 5-year est.); Average household income: $46,995 (2008-2012 5-year est.); Percent of households with

income of $100,000 or more: 10.3% (2008-2012 5-year est.); Poverty rate: 21.5% (2008-2012 5-year est.).
Education: Percent of population age 25 and over with: High school diploma (including GED) or higher: 80.6% (2008-2012 5-year est.); Bachelor's degree or higher: 9.0% (2008-2012 5-year est.); Master's degree or higher: 3.3% (2008-2012 5-year est.).

School District(s)

North Greene CUSD 3 (PK-12)
  2011-12 Enrollment: 944 . . . . (217) 374-2842
Housing: Homeownership rate: 75.6% (2008-2012 5-year est.); Median home value: $57,400 (2008-2012 5-year est.); Median contract rent: $398 per month (2008-2012 5-year est.); Median year structure built: 1948 (2008-2012 5-year est.).
Health Insurance: 56.7% Private; 53.0% Public; 6.7% None. (2008-2012 5-year est.)
Safety: Violent crime rate: 67.9 per 10,000 population; Property crime rate: 151.7 per 10,000 population (2012).
Transportation: Commute to work: 91.5% car, 0.0% public transportation, 4.6% walk, 2.9% work from home (2008-2012 5-year est.); Travel time to work: 47.5% less than 15 minutes, 10.7% 15 to 30 minutes, 22.3% 30 to 45 minutes, 2.8% 45 to 60 minutes, 16.8% 60 minutes or more (2008-2012 5-year est.)

WILMINGTON (village). Aka Patterson. Covers a land area of 0.786 square miles and a water area of 0 square miles. Located at 39.48° N. Lat; 90.49° W. Long.
Population: 129 (1990); 120 (2000); 142 (2010); Density: 197.1 persons per square mile (2008-2012 5-year est.); Race: 96.1% White, 0.0% Black/African American, 0.0% Asian, 0.0% American Indian/Alaska Native, 0.0% Native Hawaiian/Other Pacific Islander, 3.9% Some other race, 2.6% Two or more races, 1.3% Hispanic of any race (2008-2012 5-year est.); Average household size: 2.58 (2008-2012 5-year est.); Median age: 32.3 (2008-2012 5-year est.); Males per 100 females: 93.8 (2008-2012 5-year est.); Marriage status: 19.3% never married, 63.3% now married, 7.3% widowed, 10.1% divorced (2008-2012 5-year est.); Foreign born: 1.3% (2008-2012 5-year est.); Ancestry (includes multiple ancestries): 36.8% English, 31.0% German, 12.9% Irish, 5.8% Polish, 3.9% Dutch (2008-2012 5-year est.).
Economy: Homeowner vacancy rate: 0.0%. Rental vacancy rate: 0.0%. (2008-2012 5-year est.); Employment by occupation: 34.4% management, business, and financial, 0.0% computer, engineering, and science, 6.6% education, legal, community service, arts, and media, 6.6% healthcare practitioners, 16.4% service, 13.1% sales and office, 9.8% natural resources, construction, and maintenance, 13.1% production, transportation, and material moving (2008-2012 5-year est.).
Income: Per capita income: $16,735 (2008-2012 5-year est.); Median household income: $51,250 (2008-2012 5-year est.); Average household income: $44,662 (2008-2012 5-year est.); Percent of households with income of $100,000 or more: 5.0% (2008-2012 5-year est.); Poverty rate: 11.0% (2008-2012 5-year est.).
Education: Percent of population age 25 and over with: High school diploma (including GED) or higher: 67.4% (2008-2012 5-year est.); Bachelor's degree or higher: 5.4% (2008-2012 5-year est.); Master's degree or higher: 0.0% (2008-2012 5-year est.).
Housing: Homeownership rate: 86.7% (2008-2012 5-year est.); Median home value: $45,000 (2008-2012 5-year est.); Median contract rent: $300 per month (2008-2012 5-year est.); Median year structure built: 1955 (2008-2012 5-year est.).
Health Insurance: 74.8% Private; 38.7% Public; 11.0% None. (2008-2012 5-year est.)
Transportation: Commute to work: 71.9% car, 0.0% public transportation, 0.0% walk, 28.1% work from home (2008-2012 5-year est.); Travel time to work: 29.3% less than 15 minutes, 22.0% 15 to 30 minutes, 39.0% 30 to 45 minutes, 7.3% 45 to 60 minutes, 2.4% 60 minutes or more (2008-2012 5-year est.)

WRIGHTS (unincorporated postal area)
Zip Code: 62098
  Covers a land area of 3.261 square miles and a water area of 0 square miles. Located at 39.38° N. Lat; 90.30° W. Long. Elevation is 574 feet.
Population: 91 (2010); Density: 27.9 persons per square mile (2010); Race: 98.9% White, 0.0% Black/African American, 0.0% Asian, 0.0% American Indian/Alaska Native, 0.0% Native Hawaiian/Other Pacific Islander, 1.1% Some other race, 1.1% Two or more races, 2.2% Hispanic of any race (2010); Average household size: 2.76 (2010);

Median age: 32.3 (2010); Males per 100 females: 97.8 (2010); Homeownership rate: 87.9% (2010)

Grundy County

Located in northeastern Illinois; drained by the Illinois, Des Plaines, and Kankakee Rivers. Covers a land area of 418.043 square miles, a water area of 12.404 square miles, and is located in the Central Time Zone at 41.29° N. Lat., 88.40° W. Long. The county was founded in 1841. County seat is Morris.

Grundy County is part of the Chicago-Naperville-Elgin, IL-IN-WI Metropolitan Statistical Area. The entire metro area includes: Chicago-Naperville-Arlington Heights, IL Metropolitan Division (Cook County, IL; DuPage County, IL; Grundy County, IL; Kendall County, IL; McHenry County, IL; Will County, IL); Elgin, IL Metropolitan Division (DeKalb County, IL; Kane County, IL); Gary, IN Metropolitan Division (Jasper County, IN; Lake County, IN; Newton County, IN; Porter County, IN); Lake County-Kenosha County, IL-WI Metropolitan Division (Lake County, IL; Kenosha County, WI)

Population: 32,337 (1990); 37,535 (2000); 50,063 (2010); Race: 95.4% White, 1.1% Black/African American, 0.4% Asian, 0.1% American Indian/Alaska Native, 0.0% Native Hawaiian/Other Pacific Islander, 3.0% Some other race, 1.5% Two or more races, 8.2% Hispanic of any race (2008-2012 5-year est.); Density: 120.1 persons per square mile (2008-2012 5-year est.); Average household size: 2.76 (2008-2012 5-year est.); Median age: 36.4 (2008-2012 5-year est.); Males per 100 females: 99.8 (2008-2012 5-year est.).
Religion: Six largest groups: 21.4% Catholicism, 7.5% Baptist, 5.3% Methodist/Pietist, 2.4% Non-denominational Protestant, 1.9% Presbyterian-Reformed, 1.6% Lutheran (2010)
Economy: Unemployment rate: 8.2% (April 2014); Total civilian labor force: 27,296 (April 2014); Leading industries: 15.9% transportation & warehousing; 14.0% health care and social assistance; 12.6% retail trade (2012); Farms: 431 totaling 217,016 acres (2012); Companies that employ 500 or more persons: 4 (2012); Companies that employ 100 to 499 persons: 15 (2012); Companies that employ less than 100 persons: 1,086 (2012); Black-owned businesses: n/a (2007); Hispanic-owned businesses: 89 (2007); Asian-owned businesses: 46 (2007); Women-owned businesses: 1,223 (2007); Single-family building permits issued: 60 (2013); Multi-family building permits issued: 105 (2013).
Income: Per capita income: $28,075 (2008-2012 5-year est.); Median household income: $63,840 (2008-2012 5-year est.); Average household income: $75,309 (2008-2012 5-year est.); Percent of households with income of $100,000 or more: 26.2% (2008-2012 5-year est.); Poverty rate: 8.6% (2008-2012 5-year est.); Bankruptcy rate: 5.62% (2013).
Taxes: Total county taxes per capita: $294 (2011); County property taxes per capita: $260 (2011).
Education: Percent of population age 25 and over with: High school diploma (including GED) or higher: 91.1% (2008-2012 5-year est.); Bachelor's degree or higher: 19.1% (2008-2012 5-year est.); Master's degree or higher: 5.7% (2008-2012 5-year est.).
Housing: Homeownership rate: 76.1% (2008-2012 5-year est.); Median home value: $186,500 (2008-2012 5-year est.); Median contract rent: $728 per month (2008-2012 5-year est.); Median year structure built: 1982 (2008-2012 5-year est.)
Health: Birth rate: 127.4 per 10,000 population (2013); Death rate: 73.1 per 10,000 population (2013); Age-adjusted cancer mortality rate: 210.3 deaths per 100,000 population (2011); Number of physicians: 9.8 per 10,000 population (2011); Hospital beds: 17.2 per 10,000 population (2010); Hospital admissions: 879.7 per 10,000 population (2010).
Elections: 2012 Presidential election results: 44.5% Obama, 53.4% Romney
National and State Parks: Gebhard Woods State Park; Goose Lake Prairie State Park; Heidecke State Fish and Wildlife Area; Mazonia State Fish and Wildlife Area; William Stratton State Access Area
Additional Information Contacts
Grundy County Government . . . . (815) 941-3400
  http://www.grundyco.org
Grundy County Chamber of Commerce . . . . (815) 634-8662
  http://www.grundychamber.com
Grundy County Chamber of Commerce . . . . (815) 942-0113
  http://www.grundychamber.com

Grundy County Communities

BRACEVILLE (village). Covers a land area of 2.805 square miles and a water area of 0.064 square miles. Located at 41.22° N. Lat; 88.27° W. Long. Elevation is 577 feet.

History: Braceville boomed as a coal-mining town in the late 1800's, but declined when the mines closed.

Population: 587 (1990); 792 (2000); 793 (2010); Density: 302.3 persons per square mile (2008-2012 5-year est.); Race: 95.8% White, 0.0% Black/African American, 0.0% Asian, 0.6% American Indian/Alaska Native, 0.0% Native Hawaiian/Other Pacific Islander, 3.6% Some other race, 2.7% Two or more races, 3.1% Hispanic of any race (2008-2012 5-year est.); Average household size: 2.88 (2008-2012 5-year est.); Median age: 33.2 (2008-2012 5-year est.); Males per 100 females: 123.7 (2008-2012 5-year est.); Marriage status: 24.7% never married, 57.8% now married, 3.8% widowed, 13.8% divorced (2008-2012 5-year est.); Foreign born: 0.7% (2008-2012 5-year est.); Ancestry (includes multiple ancestries): 33.4% German, 18.9% Irish, 13.7% Italian, 11.3% English, 11.2% Polish (2008-2012 5-year est.).

Economy: Single-family building permits issued: 0 (2013); Multi-family building permits issued: 0 (2013); Homeowner vacancy rate: 2.6%. Rental vacancy rate: 0.0%. (2008-2012 5-year est.); Employment by occupation: 4.9% management, business, and financial, 2.9% computer, engineering, and science, 1.7% education, legal, community service, arts, and media, 1.2% healthcare practitioners, 20.0% service, 25.5% sales and office, 13.0% natural resources, construction, and maintenance, 30.7% production, transportation, and material moving (2008-2012 5-year est.).

Income: Per capita income: $21,189 (2008-2012 5-year est.); Median household income: $56,667 (2008-2012 5-year est.); Average household income: $59,327 (2008-2012 5-year est.); Percent of households with income of $100,000 or more: 10.5% (2008-2012 5-year est.); Poverty rate: 14.8% (2008-2012 5-year est.).

Education: Percent of population age 25 and over with: High school diploma (including GED) or higher: 85.6% (2008-2012 5-year est.); Bachelor's degree or higher: 4.6% (2008-2012 5-year est.); Master's degree or higher: 1.7% (2008-2012 5-year est.).

School District(s)

Braceville SD 75 (KG-08)
    2011-12 Enrollment: 194 . . . . (815) 237-8040

Housing: Homeownership rate: 85.7% (2008-2012 5-year est.); Median home value: $137,200 (2008-2012 5-year est.); Median contract rent: $686 per month (2008-2012 5-year est.); Median year structure built: 1962 (2008-2012 5-year est.).

Health Insurance: 69.1% Private; 27.6% Public; 10.4% None. (2008-2012 5-year est.)

Transportation: Commute to work: 97.9% car, 0.0% public transportation, 1.5% walk, 0.6% work from home (2008-2012 5-year est.); Travel time to work: 16.8% less than 15 minutes, 21.6% 15 to 30 minutes, 40.5% 30 to 45 minutes, 8.1% 45 to 60 minutes, 12.9% 60 minutes or more (2008-2012 5-year est.)

CARBON HILL (village). Covers a land area of 0.184 square miles and a water area of 0 square miles. Located at 41.30° N. Lat; 88.30° W. Long. Elevation is 561 feet.

Population: 362 (1990); 392 (2000); 345 (2010); Density: 2,641.1 persons per square mile (2008-2012 5-year est.); Race: 94.7% White, 0.0% Black/African American, 2.5% Asian, 0.0% American Indian/Alaska Native, 0.0% Native Hawaiian/Other Pacific Islander, 2.8% Some other race, 0.0% Two or more races, 12.8% Hispanic of any race (2008-2012 5-year est.); Average household size: 2.81 (2008-2012 5-year est.); Median age: 35.5 (2008-2012 5-year est.); Males per 100 females: 91.3 (2008-2012 5-year est.); Marriage status: 32.3% never married, 49.7% now married, 6.1% widowed, 11.9% divorced (2008-2012 5-year est.); Foreign born: 4.3% (2008-2012 5-year est.); Ancestry (includes multiple ancestries): 25.5% German, 18.9% Irish, 12.8% Italian, 9.9% Polish, 6.4% English (2008-2012 5-year est.).

Economy: Single-family building permits issued: 0 (2013); Multi-family building permits issued: 0 (2013); Homeowner vacancy rate: 0.0%. Rental vacancy rate: 0.0%. (2008-2012 5-year est.); Employment by occupation: 5.8% management, business, and financial, 3.6% computer, engineering, and science, 3.6% education, legal, community service, arts, and media, 3.1% healthcare practitioners, 36.0% service, 16.0% sales and office, 4.4% natural resources, construction, and maintenance, 27.6% production, transportation, and material moving (2008-2012 5-year est.).

Income: Per capita income: $22,069 (2008-2012 5-year est.); Median household income: $51,250 (2008-2012 5-year est.); Average household income: $57,049 (2008-2012 5-year est.); Percent of households with income of $100,000 or more: 10.9% (2008-2012 5-year est.); Poverty rate: 12.3% (2008-2012 5-year est.).

Education: Percent of population age 25 and over with: High school diploma (including GED) or higher: 82.8% (2008-2012 5-year est.); Bachelor's degree or higher: 9.2% (2008-2012 5-year est.); Master's degree or higher: 2.2% (2008-2012 5-year est.).

Housing: Homeownership rate: 78.0% (2008-2012 5-year est.); Median home value: $161,300 (2008-2012 5-year est.); Median contract rent: $586 per month (2008-2012 5-year est.); Median year structure built: 1965 (2008-2012 5-year est.).

Health Insurance: 69.5% Private; 29.2% Public; 11.9% None. (2008-2012 5-year est.)

Transportation: Commute to work: 98.6% car, 0.0% public transportation, 0.0% walk, 1.4% work from home (2008-2012 5-year est.); Travel time to work: 25.3% less than 15 minutes, 34.1% 15 to 30 minutes, 21.7% 30 to 45 minutes, 10.6% 45 to 60 minutes, 8.3% 60 minutes or more (2008-2012 5-year est.)

COAL CITY (village). Covers a land area of 4.904 square miles and a water area of 0.094 square miles. Located at 41.28° N. Lat; 88.28° W. Long. Elevation is 564 feet.

History: Coal City began when shaft mines were opened here in 1875. The shaft mines were followed by strip mining.

Population: 3,907 (1990); 4,797 (2000); 5,587 (2010); Density: 1,090.2 persons per square mile (2008-2012 5-year est.); Race: 97.0% White, 0.9% Black/African American, 0.0% Asian, 0.1% American Indian/Alaska Native, 0.0% Native Hawaiian/Other Pacific Islander, 2.0% Some other race, 2.0% Two or more races, 2.3% Hispanic of any race (2008-2012 5-year est.); Average household size: 2.69 (2008-2012 5-year est.); Median age: 36.4 (2008-2012 5-year est.); Males per 100 females: 95.0 (2008-2012 5-year est.); Marriage status: 32.2% never married, 49.1% now married, 8.0% widowed, 10.6% divorced (2008-2012 5-year est.); Foreign born: 0.7% (2008-2012 5-year est.); Ancestry (includes multiple ancestries): 26.1% German, 23.0% Irish, 16.7% Italian, 10.3% English, 9.2% Polish (2008-2012 5-year est.).

Economy: Single-family building permits issued: 2 (2013); Multi-family building permits issued: 0 (2013); Homeowner vacancy rate: 1.7%. Rental vacancy rate: 10.7%. (2008-2012 5-year est.); Employment by occupation: 7.9% management, business, and financial, 2.9% computer, engineering, and science, 8.4% education, legal, community service, arts, and media, 6.0% healthcare practitioners, 16.8% service, 24.1% sales and office, 13.5% natural resources, construction, and maintenance, 20.5% production, transportation, and material moving (2008-2012 5-year est.).

Income: Per capita income: $26,617 (2008-2012 5-year est.); Median household income: $57,269 (2008-2012 5-year est.); Average household income: $68,325 (2008-2012 5-year est.); Percent of households with income of $100,000 or more: 23.2% (2008-2012 5-year est.); Poverty rate: 7.0% (2008-2012 5-year est.).

Education: Percent of population age 25 and over with: High school diploma (including GED) or higher: 91.5% (2008-2012 5-year est.); Bachelor's degree or higher: 14.2% (2008-2012 5-year est.); Master's degree or higher: 4.0% (2008-2012 5-year est.).

School District(s)

Coal City CUSD 1 (PK-12)
    2011-12 Enrollment: 2,082 . . . . (815) 634-2287

Housing: Homeownership rate: 79.8% (2008-2012 5-year est.); Median home value: $165,700 (2008-2012 5-year est.); Median contract rent: $756 per month (2008-2012 5-year est.); Median year structure built: 1973 (2008-2012 5-year est.).

Health Insurance: 84.1% Private; 21.8% Public; 6.8% None. (2008-2012 5-year est.)

Safety: Violent crime rate: 3.6 per 10,000 population; Property crime rate: 234.0 per 10,000 population (2012).

Transportation: Commute to work: 93.8% car, 0.5% public transportation, 0.0% walk, 3.0% work from home (2008-2012 5-year est.); Travel time to work: 30.6% less than 15 minutes, 29.6% 15 to 30 minutes, 17.5% 30 to 45 minutes, 8.8% 45 to 60 minutes, 13.6% 60 minutes or more (2008-2012 5-year est.)

Additional Information Contacts
Grundy County Chamber of Commerce . . . . (815) 634-8662
    http://www.grundychamber.com

Village of Coal City . . . . (815) 634-8608
  http://coalcity-il.com

DIAMOND (village). Covers a land area of 1.888 square miles and a water area of 0 square miles. Located at 41.29° N. Lat; 88.25° W. Long. Elevation is 564 feet.
Population: 1,077 (1990); 1,393 (2000); 2,527 (2010); Density: 1,402.7 persons per square mile (2008-2012 5-year est.); Race: 93.5% White, 2.4% Black/African American, 0.8% Asian, 0.0% American Indian/Alaska Native, 0.0% Native Hawaiian/Other Pacific Islander, 3.3% Some other race, 3.2% Two or more races, 3.6% Hispanic of any race (2008-2012 5-year est.); Average household size: 2.75 (2008-2012 5-year est.); Median age: 33.5 (2008-2012 5-year est.); Males per 100 females: 89.0 (2008-2012 5-year est.); Marriage status: 31.2% never married, 50.3% now married, 6.0% widowed, 12.4% divorced (2008-2012 5-year est.); Foreign born: 1.9% (2008-2012 5-year est.); Ancestry (includes multiple ancestries): 36.6% German, 23.0% Irish, 14.8% Italian, 9.0% English, 5.3% French (2008-2012 5-year est.).
Economy: Single-family building permits issued: 2 (2013); Multi-family building permits issued: 0 (2013); Homeowner vacancy rate: 2.9%. Rental vacancy rate: 8.2%. (2008-2012 5-year est.); Employment by occupation: 5.8% management, business, and financial, 3.3% computer, engineering, and science, 4.0% education, legal, community service, arts, and media, 4.6% healthcare practitioners, 17.7% service, 27.9% sales and office, 14.1% natural resources, construction, and maintenance, 22.7% production, transportation, and material moving (2008-2012 5-year est.).
Income: Per capita income: $23,831 (2008-2012 5-year est.); Median household income: $59,853 (2008-2012 5-year est.); Average household income: $63,775 (2008-2012 5-year est.); Percent of households with income of $100,000 or more: 20.7% (2008-2012 5-year est.); Poverty rate: 14.0% (2008-2012 5-year est.).
Education: Percent of population age 25 and over with: High school diploma (including GED) or higher: 89.6% (2008-2012 5-year est.); Bachelor's degree or higher: 10.7% (2008-2012 5-year est.); Master's degree or higher: 2.3% (2008-2012 5-year est.).
Housing: Homeownership rate: 69.7% (2008-2012 5-year est.); Median home value: $187,200 (2008-2012 5-year est.); Median contract rent: $717 per month (2008-2012 5-year est.); Median year structure built: 1994 (2008-2012 5-year est.).
Health Insurance: 62.5% Private; 32.3% Public; 12.0% None. (2008-2012 5-year est.)
Safety: Violent crime rate: 0.0 per 10,000 population; Property crime rate: 189.6 per 10,000 population (2012).
Transportation: Commute to work: 95.0% car, 1.6% public transportation, 3.0% walk, 0.0% work from home (2008-2012 5-year est.); Travel time to work: 38.5% less than 15 minutes, 28.9% 15 to 30 minutes, 18.2% 30 to 45 minutes, 7.3% 45 to 60 minutes, 7.0% 60 minutes or more (2008-2012 5-year est.)

EAST BROOKLYN (village). Covers a land area of 0.054 square miles and a water area of <.001 square miles. Located at 41.17° N. Lat; 88.27° W. Long. Elevation is 584 feet.
Population: 80 (1990); 123 (2000); 106 (2010); Density: 1,694.5 persons per square mile (2008-2012 5-year est.); Race: 96.7% White, 0.0% Black/African American, 0.0% Asian, 3.3% American Indian/Alaska Native, 0.0% Native Hawaiian/Other Pacific Islander, 0.0% Some other race, 0.0% Two or more races, 6.5% Hispanic of any race (2008-2012 5-year est.); Average household size: 2.56 (2008-2012 5-year est.); Median age: 37.6 (2008-2012 5-year est.); Males per 100 females: 64.3 (2008-2012 5-year est.); Marriage status: 50.0% never married, 36.1% now married, 12.5% widowed, 1.4% divorced (2008-2012 5-year est.); Foreign born: 0.0% (2008-2012 5-year est.); Ancestry (includes multiple ancestries): 40.2% German, 29.3% Polish, 27.2% Italian, 13.0% Irish, 7.6% Danish (2008-2012 5-year est.).
Economy: Single-family building permits issued: 0 (2013); Multi-family building permits issued: 0 (2013); Homeowner vacancy rate: 0.0%. Rental vacancy rate: 0.0%. (2008-2012 5-year est.); Employment by occupation: 0.0% management, business, and financial, 32.1% computer, engineering, and science, 7.1% education, legal, community service, arts, and media, 7.1% healthcare practitioners, 3.6% service, 21.4% sales and office, 10.7% natural resources, construction, and maintenance, 17.9% production, transportation, and material moving (2008-2012 5-year est.).
Income: Per capita income: $19,846 (2008-2012 5-year est.); Median household income: $46,250 (2008-2012 5-year est.); Average household income: $49,819 (2008-2012 5-year est.); Percent of households with income of $100,000 or more: 5.6% (2008-2012 5-year est.); Poverty rate: 21.7% (2008-2012 5-year est.).
Education: Percent of population age 25 and over with: High school diploma (including GED) or higher: 94.8% (2008-2012 5-year est.); Bachelor's degree or higher: 10.3% (2008-2012 5-year est.); Master's degree or higher: 6.9% (2008-2012 5-year est.).
Housing: Homeownership rate: 63.9% (2008-2012 5-year est.); Median home value: $156,300 (2008-2012 5-year est.); Median contract rent: $836 per month (2008-2012 5-year est.); Median year structure built: 1954 (2008-2012 5-year est.).
Health Insurance: 53.3% Private; 44.6% Public; 21.7% None. (2008-2012 5-year est.)
Transportation: Commute to work: 78.6% car, 0.0% public transportation, 0.0% walk, 21.4% work from home (2008-2012 5-year est.); Travel time to work: 13.6% less than 15 minutes, 27.3% 15 to 30 minutes, 54.5% 30 to 45 minutes, 4.5% 45 to 60 minutes, 0.0% 60 minutes or more (2008-2012 5-year est.)

GARDNER (village). Covers a land area of 2.916 square miles and a water area of 0.028 square miles. Located at 41.19° N. Lat; 88.31° W. Long. Elevation is 587 feet.
Population: 1,237 (1990); 1,406 (2000); 1,463 (2010); Density: 460.6 persons per square mile (2008-2012 5-year est.); Race: 96.4% White, 0.3% Black/African American, 0.2% Asian, 0.0% American Indian/Alaska Native, 0.0% Native Hawaiian/Other Pacific Islander, 3.1% Some other race, 2.0% Two or more races, 5.9% Hispanic of any race (2008-2012 5-year est.); Average household size: 2.69 (2008-2012 5-year est.); Median age: 35.7 (2008-2012 5-year est.); Males per 100 females: 121.6 (2008-2012 5-year est.); Marriage status: 26.8% never married, 55.5% now married, 4.5% widowed, 13.2% divorced (2008-2012 5-year est.); Foreign born: 2.2% (2008-2012 5-year est.); Ancestry (includes multiple ancestries): 25.3% German, 20.0% Irish, 15.3% Italian, 13.3% English, 8.6% Norwegian (2008-2012 5-year est.).
Economy: Single-family building permits issued: 0 (2013); Multi-family building permits issued: 0 (2013); Homeowner vacancy rate: 0.0%. Rental vacancy rate: 23.1%. (2008-2012 5-year est.); Employment by occupation: 7.4% management, business, and financial, 0.0% computer, engineering, and science, 5.8% education, legal, community service, arts, and media, 5.1% healthcare practitioners, 13.4% service, 20.2% sales and office, 16.2% natural resources, construction, and maintenance, 31.9% production, transportation, and material moving (2008-2012 5-year est.).
Income: Per capita income: $28,095 (2008-2012 5-year est.); Median household income: $66,806 (2008-2012 5-year est.); Average household income: $73,162 (2008-2012 5-year est.); Percent of households with income of $100,000 or more: 21.6% (2008-2012 5-year est.); Poverty rate: 10.5% (2008-2012 5-year est.).
Education: Percent of population age 25 and over with: High school diploma (including GED) or higher: 92.0% (2008-2012 5-year est.); Bachelor's degree or higher: 10.6% (2008-2012 5-year est.); Master's degree or higher: 0.6% (2008-2012 5-year est.).
School District(s)
Gardner CCSD 72c (PK-08)
    2011-12 Enrollment: 211 . . . . (815) 237-2313
Gardner S Wilmington Twp HSD 73 (09-12)
    2011-12 Enrollment: 197 . . . . (815) 237-2176
Housing: Homeownership rate: 77.4% (2008-2012 5-year est.); Median home value: $140,800 (2008-2012 5-year est.); Median contract rent: $602 per month (2008-2012 5-year est.); Median year structure built: 1961 (2008-2012 5-year est.).
Health Insurance: 75.8% Private; 30.8% Public; 7.2% None. (2008-2012 5-year est.)
Transportation: Commute to work: 93.9% car, 0.0% public transportation, 1.7% walk, 2.0% work from home (2008-2012 5-year est.); Travel time to work: 23.7% less than 15 minutes, 21.3% 15 to 30 minutes, 31.0% 30 to 45 minutes, 14.9% 45 to 60 minutes, 9.2% 60 minutes or more (2008-2012 5-year est.)

KINSMAN (village). Covers a land area of 0.066 square miles and a water area of 0 square miles. Located at 41.19° N. Lat; 88.57° W. Long. Elevation is 659 feet.
Population: 112 (1990); 109 (2000); 99 (2010); Density: 1,915.9 persons per square mile (2008-2012 5-year est.); Race: 100.0% White, 0.0% Black/African American, 0.0% Asian, 0.0% American Indian/Alaska Native, 0.0% Native Hawaiian/Other Pacific Islander, 0.0% Some other race, 0.0% Two or more races, 5.5% Hispanic of any race (2008-2012 5-year est.);

Average household size: 3.34 (2008-2012 5-year est.); Median age: 38.6 (2008-2012 5-year est.); Males per 100 females: 78.9 (2008-2012 5-year est.); Marriage status: 16.5% never married, 60.4% now married, 6.6% widowed, 16.5% divorced (2008-2012 5-year est.); Foreign born: 0.0% (2008-2012 5-year est.); Ancestry (includes multiple ancestries): 28.3% German, 23.6% Irish, 12.6% English, 9.4% Norwegian, 7.1% Polish (2008-2012 5-year est.).

Economy: Single-family building permits issued: 0 (2013); Multi-family building permits issued: 0 (2013); Homeowner vacancy rate: 0.0%. Rental vacancy rate: 0.0%. (2008-2012 5-year est.); Employment by occupation: 18.9% management, business, and financial, 0.0% computer, engineering, and science, 0.0% education, legal, community service, arts, and media, 0.0% healthcare practitioners, 18.9% service, 18.9% sales and office, 43.2% natural resources, construction, and maintenance, 0.0% production, transportation, and material moving (2008-2012 5-year est.).

Income: Per capita income: $15,691 (2008-2012 5-year est.); Median household income: $51,250 (2008-2012 5-year est.); Average household income: $49,324 (2008-2012 5-year est.); Percent of households with income of $100,000 or more: 5.3% (2008-2012 5-year est.); Poverty rate: 26.8% (2008-2012 5-year est.).

Education: Percent of population age 25 and over with: High school diploma (including GED) or higher: 92.9% (2008-2012 5-year est.); Bachelor's degree or higher: 0.0% (2008-2012 5-year est.); Master's degree or higher: 0.0% (2008-2012 5-year est.).

Housing: Homeownership rate: 84.2% (2008-2012 5-year est.); Median home value: $76,700 (2008-2012 5-year est.); Median contract rent: n/a per month (2008-2012 5-year est.); Median year structure built: Before 1940 (2008-2012 5-year est.).

Health Insurance: 75.6% Private; 37.0% Public; 5.5% None. (2008-2012 5-year est.)

Transportation: Commute to work: 97.1% car, 0.0% public transportation, 0.0% walk, 2.9% work from home (2008-2012 5-year est.); Travel time to work: 0.0% less than 15 minutes, 64.7% 15 to 30 minutes, 23.5% 30 to 45 minutes, 5.9% 45 to 60 minutes, 5.9% 60 minutes or more (2008-2012 5-year est.)

MAZON (village). Covers a land area of 0.590 square miles and a water area of 0.006 square miles. Located at 41.24° N. Lat; 88.42° W. Long. Elevation is 587 feet.

History: Near the Mazon River, a classic source of fossils from a middle Pennsylvanian formation.

Population: 764 (1990); 904 (2000); 1,015 (2010); Density: 1,713.5 persons per square mile (2008-2012 5-year est.); Race: 92.0% White, 0.0% Black/African American, 0.6% Asian, 0.0% American Indian/Alaska Native, 0.0% Native Hawaiian/Other Pacific Islander, 7.4% Some other race, 7.2% Two or more races, 1.5% Hispanic of any race (2008-2012 5-year est.); Average household size: 2.58 (2008-2012 5-year est.); Median age: 35.7 (2008-2012 5-year est.); Males per 100 females: 107.2 (2008-2012 5-year est.); Marriage status: 16.9% never married, 63.1% now married, 6.8% widowed, 13.2% divorced (2008-2012 5-year est.); Foreign born: 5.4% (2008-2012 5-year est.); Ancestry (includes multiple ancestries): 27.5% German, 23.2% Irish, 19.6% Italian, 11.3% English, 6.0% Norwegian (2008-2012 5-year est.).

Economy: Single-family building permits issued: 0 (2013); Multi-family building permits issued: 0 (2013); Homeowner vacancy rate: 7.0%. Rental vacancy rate: 14.0%. (2008-2012 5-year est.); Employment by occupation: 19.3% management, business, and financial, 2.4% computer, engineering, and science, 4.3% education, legal, community service, arts, and media, 5.2% healthcare practitioners, 19.7% service, 15.9% sales and office, 12.2% natural resources, construction, and maintenance, 21.0% production, transportation, and material moving (2008-2012 5-year est.).

Income: Per capita income: $27,533 (2008-2012 5-year est.); Median household income: $66,300 (2008-2012 5-year est.); Average household income: $69,067 (2008-2012 5-year est.); Percent of households with income of $100,000 or more: 23.4% (2008-2012 5-year est.); Poverty rate: 8.1% (2008-2012 5-year est.).

Education: Percent of population age 25 and over with: High school diploma (including GED) or higher: 86.7% (2008-2012 5-year est.); Bachelor's degree or higher: 9.2% (2008-2012 5-year est.); Master's degree or higher: 2.9% (2008-2012 5-year est.).

School District(s)

Mazon-Verona-Kinsman ESD 2c (PK-08)

    2011-12 Enrollment: 332 . . . . (815) 448-2200

Housing: Homeownership rate: 75.0% (2008-2012 5-year est.); Median home value: $156,200 (2008-2012 5-year est.); Median contract rent: $617

per month (2008-2012 5-year est.); Median year structure built: 1971 (2008-2012 5-year est.).

Health Insurance: 76.9% Private; 22.3% Public; 11.8% None. (2008-2012 5-year est.)

Transportation: Commute to work: 97.4% car, 0.0% public transportation, 0.0% walk, 2.6% work from home (2008-2012 5-year est.); Travel time to work: 15.8% less than 15 minutes, 44.1% 15 to 30 minutes, 18.9% 30 to 45 minutes, 11.8% 45 to 60 minutes, 9.4% 60 minutes or more (2008-2012 5-year est.)

MINOOKA (village). Covers a land area of 9.453 square miles and a water area of 0.076 square miles. Located at 41.45° N. Lat; 88.28° W. Long. Elevation is 610 feet.

Population: 2,561 (1990); 3,971 (2000); 10,924 (2010); Density: 1,115.9 persons per square mile (2008-2012 5-year est.); Race: 93.1% White, 1.4% Black/African American, 1.4% Asian, 0.1% American Indian/Alaska Native, 0.0% Native Hawaiian/Other Pacific Islander, 4.0% Some other race, 3.6% Two or more races, 14.1% Hispanic of any race (2008-2012 5-year est.); Average household size: 3.11 (2008-2012 5-year est.); Median age: 32.2 (2008-2012 5-year est.); Males per 100 females: 92.4 (2008-2012 5-year est.); Marriage status: 27.5% never married, 60.9% now married, 1.7% widowed, 9.9% divorced (2008-2012 5-year est.); Foreign born: 3.7% (2008-2012 5-year est.); Ancestry (includes multiple ancestries): 30.3% German, 20.7% Irish, 15.6% Polish, 14.5% Italian, 9.1% English (2008-2012 5-year est.).

Economy: Single-family building permits issued: 32 (2013); Multi-family building permits issued: 0 (2013); Homeowner vacancy rate: 0.8%. Rental vacancy rate: 0.0%. (2008-2012 5-year est.); Employment by occupation: 16.9% management, business, and financial, 5.1% computer, engineering, and science, 11.4% education, legal, community service, arts, and media, 6.3% healthcare practitioners, 14.1% service, 29.1% sales and office, 9.5% natural resources, construction, and maintenance, 7.7% production, transportation, and material moving (2008-2012 5-year est.).

Income: Per capita income: $31,974 (2008-2012 5-year est.); Median household income: $88,486 (2008-2012 5-year est.); Average household income: $97,719 (2008-2012 5-year est.); Percent of households with income of $100,000 or more: 42.1% (2008-2012 5-year est.); Poverty rate: 5.0% (2008-2012 5-year est.).

Education: Percent of population age 25 and over with: High school diploma (including GED) or higher: 95.4% (2008-2012 5-year est.); Bachelor's degree or higher: 28.9% (2008-2012 5-year est.); Master's degree or higher: 9.8% (2008-2012 5-year est.).

School District(s)

Grundy/kendall Roe (08-12)

    2011-12 Enrollment: n/a . . . . (815) 941-3247

Minooka CCSD 201 (PK-08)

    2011-12 Enrollment: 3,963 . . . . (815) 467-6121

Minooka CHSD 111 (09-12)

    2011-12 Enrollment: 2,543 . . . . (815) 467-2557

Housing: Homeownership rate: 89.6% (2008-2012 5-year est.); Median home value: $216,400 (2008-2012 5-year est.); Median contract rent: $1,056 per month (2008-2012 5-year est.); Median year structure built: 2002 (2008-2012 5-year est.).

Health Insurance: 80.9% Private; 19.2% Public; 7.5% None. (2008-2012 5-year est.)

Safety: Violent crime rate: 3.6 per 10,000 population; Property crime rate: 133.2 per 10,000 population (2012).

Transportation: Commute to work: 92.6% car, 1.7% public transportation, 0.5% walk, 5.2% work from home (2008-2012 5-year est.); Travel time to work: 19.3% less than 15 minutes, 33.9% 15 to 30 minutes, 17.9% 30 to 45 minutes, 11.3% 45 to 60 minutes, 17.6% 60 minutes or more (2008-2012 5-year est.)

Additional Information Contacts

Channahon Minooka Chamber of Commerce . . . . (815) 521-9999

    http://www.grundychamber.com/cm_chamber/index.html

Village of Minooka . . . . (815) 467-2151

    http://www.minooka.com

MORRIS (city). County seat. Covers a land area of 9.443 square miles and a water area of 0.364 square miles. Located at 41.37° N. Lat; 88.43° W. Long. Elevation is 515 feet.

History: Morris was platted in 1842 and named for Isaac N. Morris, an Illinois & Michigan Canal commissioner, who negotiated to have the village named as the county seat. Morris grew as a shipping and paper manufacturing center.

Population: 10,270 (1990); 11,928 (2000); 13,636 (2010); Density: 1,471.6 persons per square mile (2008-2012 5-year est.); Race: 94.6% White, 2.0% Black/African American, 0.6% Asian, 0.0% American Indian/Alaska Native, 0.0% Native Hawaiian/Other Pacific Islander, 2.8% Some other race, 1.1% Two or more races, 10.6% Hispanic of any race (2008-2012 5-year est.); Average household size: 2.59 (2008-2012 5-year est.); Median age: 38.1 (2008-2012 5-year est.); Males per 100 females: 102.2 (2008-2012 5-year est.); Marriage status: 29.9% never married, 52.3% now married, 6.6% widowed, 11.2% divorced (2008-2012 5-year est.); Foreign born: 5.5% (2008-2012 5-year est.); Ancestry (includes multiple ancestries): 29.4% German, 19.2% Irish, 12.4% Norwegian, 9.1% Italian, 7.3% Polish (2008-2012 5-year est.).
Economy: Single-family building permits issued: 14 (2013); Multi-family building permits issued: 105 (2013); Homeowner vacancy rate: 5.1%. Rental vacancy rate: 11.0%. (2008-2012 5-year est.); Employment by occupation: 10.0% management, business, and financial, 5.2% computer, engineering, and science, 9.6% education, legal, community service, arts, and media, 4.9% healthcare practitioners, 17.8% service, 24.9% sales and office, 10.4% natural resources, construction, and maintenance, 17.2% production, transportation, and material moving (2008-2012 5-year est.).
Income: Per capita income: $27,714 (2008-2012 5-year est.); Median household income: $57,417 (2008-2012 5-year est.); Average household income: $70,546 (2008-2012 5-year est.); Percent of households with income of $100,000 or more: 21.2% (2008-2012 5-year est.); Poverty rate: 9.4% (2008-2012 5-year est.).
Education: Percent of population age 25 and over with: High school diploma (including GED) or higher: 90.2% (2008-2012 5-year est.); Bachelor's degree or higher: 21.8% (2008-2012 5-year est.); Master's degree or higher: 8.0% (2008-2012 5-year est.).

School District(s)
Grundy Area Vocational Center (11-12)
   2011-12 Enrollment: n/a . . . . (815) 942-4390
Grundy/kendall Roe (08-12)
   2011-12 Enrollment: n/a . . . . (815) 941-3247
Morris CHSD 101 (09-12)
   2011-12 Enrollment: 994 . . . . (815) 941-5326
Morris SD 54 (PK-08)
   2011-12 Enrollment: 1,195 . . . . (815) 942-0056
Nettle Creek CCSD 24c (PK-08)
   2011-12 Enrollment: 92 . . . . (815) 942-0511
Saratoga CCSD 60c (PK-08)
   2011-12 Enrollment: 797 . . . . (815) 942-2128
Housing: Homeownership rate: 60.1% (2008-2012 5-year est.); Median home value: $194,000 (2008-2012 5-year est.); Median contract rent: $706 per month (2008-2012 5-year est.); Median year structure built: 1978 (2008-2012 5-year est.).
Health Insurance: 76.3% Private; 26.4% Public; 8.6% None. (2008-2012 5-year est.)
Hospitals: Morris Hospital (82 beds)
Safety: Violent crime rate: 16.8 per 10,000 population; Property crime rate: 369.7 per 10,000 population (2012).
Transportation: Commute to work: 93.5% car, 0.2% public transportation, 2.9% walk, 2.0% work from home (2008-2012 5-year est.); Travel time to work: 44.7% less than 15 minutes, 17.7% 15 to 30 minutes, 19.5% 30 to 45 minutes, 5.8% 45 to 60 minutes, 12.3% 60 minutes or more (2008-2012 5-year est.)
Airports: Morris Municipal Airport (general aviation)
Additional Information Contacts
City of Morris . . . . (815) 942-0103
   http://www.morrisil.org
Grundy County Chamber of Commerce . . . . (815) 942-0113
   http://www.grundychamber.com

SOUTH WILMINGTON (village). Covers a land area of 0.561

square miles and a water area of 0 square miles. Located at 41.17° N. Lat; 88.28° W. Long. Elevation is 587 feet.
Population: 698 (1990); 621 (2000); 681 (2010); Density: 1,100.1 persons per square mile (2008-2012 5-year est.); Race: 99.4% White, 0.0% Black/African American, 0.0% Asian, 0.0% American Indian/Alaska Native, 0.0% Native Hawaiian/Other Pacific Islander, 0.6% Some other race, 0.6% Two or more races, 1.6% Hispanic of any race (2008-2012 5-year est.); Average household size: 2.42 (2008-2012 5-year est.); Median age: 32.1 (2008-2012 5-year est.); Males per 100 females: 102.3 (2008-2012 5-year est.); Marriage status: 34.4% never married, 46.2% now married, 7.2% widowed, 12.2% divorced (2008-2012 5-year est.); Foreign born: 0.6%

(2008-2012 5-year est.); Ancestry (includes multiple ancestries): 26.1% German, 25.8% Italian, 12.5% Irish, 12.5% English, 6.5% Norwegian (2008-2012 5-year est.).
Economy: Single-family building permits issued: 0 (2013); Multi-family building permits issued: 0 (2013); Homeowner vacancy rate: 2.3%. Rental vacancy rate: 18.9%. (2008-2012 5-year est.); Employment by occupation: 8.4% management, business, and financial, 2.8% computer, engineering, and science, 4.0% education, legal, community service, arts, and media, 5.0% healthcare practitioners, 18.0% service, 24.8% sales and office, 20.5% natural resources, construction, and maintenance, 16.5% production, transportation, and material moving (2008-2012 5-year est.).
Income: Per capita income: $28,872 (2008-2012 5-year est.); Median household income: $62,321 (2008-2012 5-year est.); Average household income: $66,691 (2008-2012 5-year est.); Percent of households with income of $100,000 or more: 18.1% (2008-2012 5-year est.); Poverty rate: 6.2% (2008-2012 5-year est.).
Education: Percent of population age 25 and over with: High school diploma (including GED) or higher: 91.4% (2008-2012 5-year est.); Bachelor's degree or higher: 12.0% (2008-2012 5-year est.); Master's degree or higher: 1.4% (2008-2012 5-year est.).

School District(s)
South Wilmington CCSD 74 (PK-08)
   2011-12 Enrollment: 98 . . . . (815) 237-2281
Housing: Homeownership rate: 83.1% (2008-2012 5-year est.); Median home value: $123,800 (2008-2012 5-year est.); Median contract rent: $625 per month (2008-2012 5-year est.); Median year structure built: 1955 (2008-2012 5-year est.).
Health Insurance: 72.3% Private; 21.7% Public; 15.2% None. (2008-2012 5-year est.)
Transportation: Commute to work: 91.7% car, 4.8% public transportation, 2.2% walk, 1.3% work from home (2008-2012 5-year est.); Travel time to work: 11.6% less than 15 minutes, 19.6% 15 to 30 minutes, 42.1% 30 to 45 minutes, 14.1% 45 to 60 minutes, 12.5% 60 minutes or more (2008-2012 5-year est.)

VERONA (village). Covers a land area of 0.161 square miles and a

water area of 0 square miles. Located at 41.22° N. Lat; 88.50° W. Long. Elevation is 630 feet.
Population: 242 (1990); 257 (2000); 215 (2010); Density: 1,220.7 persons per square mile (2008-2012 5-year est.); Race: 94.4% White, 0.0% Black/African American, 0.0% Asian, 0.0% American Indian/Alaska Native, 0.0% Native Hawaiian/Other Pacific Islander, 5.6% Some other race, 0.0% Two or more races, 15.3% Hispanic of any race (2008-2012 5-year est.); Average household size: 2.84 (2008-2012 5-year est.); Median age: 37.6 (2008-2012 5-year est.); Males per 100 females: 110.8 (2008-2012 5-year est.); Marriage status: 25.3% never married, 63.3% now married, 4.4% widowed, 7.0% divorced (2008-2012 5-year est.); Foreign born: 3.1% (2008-2012 5-year est.); Ancestry (includes multiple ancestries): 38.3% German, 15.3% Irish, 12.2% Swedish, 10.7% Italian, 10.2% Norwegian (2008-2012 5-year est.).
Economy: Single-family building permits issued: 0 (2013); Multi-family building permits issued: 0 (2013); Homeowner vacancy rate: 0.0%. Rental vacancy rate: 0.0%. (2008-2012 5-year est.); Employment by occupation: 2.1% management, business, and financial, 3.1% computer, engineering, and science, 2.1% education, legal, community service, arts, and media, 5.2% healthcare practitioners, 17.5% service, 37.1% sales and office, 27.8% natural resources, construction, and maintenance, 5.2% production, transportation, and material moving (2008-2012 5-year est.).
Income: Per capita income: $26,721 (2008-2012 5-year est.); Median household income: $66,250 (2008-2012 5-year est.); Average household income: $72,197 (2008-2012 5-year est.); Percent of households with income of $100,000 or more: 26.1% (2008-2012 5-year est.); Poverty rate: 7.1% (2008-2012 5-year est.).
Education: Percent of population age 25 and over with: High school diploma (including GED) or higher: 94.2% (2008-2012 5-year est.); Bachelor's degree or higher: 5.8% (2008-2012 5-year est.); Master's degree or higher: 1.4% (2008-2012 5-year est.).
Housing: Homeownership rate: 91.3% (2008-2012 5-year est.); Median home value: $125,800 (2008-2012 5-year est.); Median contract rent: n/a per month (2008-2012 5-year est.); Median year structure built: 1945 (2008-2012 5-year est.).
Health Insurance: 77.0% Private; 31.1% Public; 7.7% None. (2008-2012 5-year est.)
Transportation: Commute to work: 100.0% car, 0.0% public transportation, 0.0% walk, 0.0% work from home (2008-2012 5-year est.);

Travel time to work: 2.1% less than 15 minutes, 32.0% 15 to 30 minutes, 33.0% 30 to 45 minutes, 10.3% 45 to 60 minutes, 22.7% 60 minutes or more (2008-2012 5-year est.)

Hamilton County

Located in southeastern Illinois; drained by the North Fork of the Saline River. Covers a land area of 434.665 square miles, a water area of 1.226 square miles, and is located in the Central Time Zone at 38.09° N. Lat., 88.54° W. Long. The county was founded in 1821. County seat is McLeansboro.

Population: 8,499 (1990); 8,621 (2000); 8,457 (2010); Race: 98.6% White, 0.4% Black/African American, 0.0% Asian, 0.3% American Indian/Alaska Native, 0.0% Native Hawaiian/Other Pacific Islander, 0.7% Some other race, 0.4% Two or more races, 1.3% Hispanic of any race (2008-2012 5-year est.); Density: 19.3 persons per square mile (2008-2012 5-year est.); Average household size: 2.37 (2008-2012 5-year est.); Median age: 43.3 (2008-2012 5-year est.); Males per 100 females: 96.1 (2008-2012 5-year est.).

Religion: Six largest groups: 31.7% Baptist, 13.7% Catholicism, 4.4% Pentecostal, 3.1% Methodist/Pietist, 1.4% European Free-Church, 0.6% Presbyterian-Reformed (2010)

Economy: Unemployment rate: 6.8% (April 2014); Total civilian labor force: 4,225 (April 2014); Leading industries: 33.5% health care and social assistance; 11.9% retail trade; 9.0% other services (except public administration) (2012); Farms: 695 totaling 223,319 acres (2012); Companies that employ 500 or more persons: 0 (2012); Companies that employ 100 to 499 persons: 1 (2012); Companies that employ less than 100 persons: 199 (2012); Black-owned businesses: n/a (2007); Hispanic-owned businesses: n/a (2007); Asian-owned businesses: n/a (2007); Women-owned businesses: n/a (2007); Single-family building permits issued: 0 (2013); Multi-family building permits issued: 0 (2013).

Income: Per capita income: $21,510 (2008-2012 5-year est.); Median household income: $37,904 (2008-2012 5-year est.); Average household income: $52,175 (2008-2012 5-year est.); Percent of households with income of $100,000 or more: 13.5% (2008-2012 5-year est.); Poverty rate: 12.9% (2008-2012 5-year est.); Bankruptcy rate: 1.80% (2013).

Education: Percent of population age 25 and over with: High school diploma (including GED) or higher: 83.1% (2008-2012 5-year est.); Bachelor's degree or higher: 14.6% (2008-2012 5-year est.); Master's degree or higher: 6.4% (2008-2012 5-year est.).

Housing: Homeownership rate: 79.7% (2008-2012 5-year est.); Median home value: $75,100 (2008-2012 5-year est.); Median contract rent: $294 per month (2008-2012 5-year est.); Median year structure built: 1965 (2008-2012 5-year est.)

Health: Birth rate: 108.7 per 10,000 population (2013); Death rate: 127.9 per 10,000 population (2013); Age-adjusted cancer mortality rate: 279.7 deaths per 100,000 population (2011); Number of physicians: 4.8 per 10,000 population (2011); Hospital beds: 100.5 per 10,000 population (2010); Hospital admissions: 1,197.8 per 10,000 population (2010).

Environment: Air Quality Index: 84.0% good, 16.0% moderate, 0.0% unhealthy for sensitive individuals, 0.0% unhealthy (percent of days in 2013)

Elections: 2012 Presidential election results: 32.2% Obama, 65.2% Romney

National and State Parks: Hamilton County State Conservation Area

Additional Information Contacts

Hamilton County Government . . . . (618) 643-2721

Hamilton County Chamber of Commerce
http://hamcochamber.org

Hamilton County Communities

BELLE PRAIRIE CITY (town). Aka Belle Prairie. Covers a land area of 0.448 square miles and a water area of 0 square miles. Located at 38.22° N. Lat; 88.56° W. Long. Elevation is 476 feet.

Population: 64 (1990); 60 (2000); 54 (2010); Density: 250.0 persons per square mile (2008-2012 5-year est.); Race: 100.0% White, 0.0% Black/African American, 0.0% Asian, 0.0% American Indian/Alaska Native, 0.0% Native Hawaiian/Other Pacific Islander, 0.0% Some other race, 0.0% Two or more races, 0.0% Hispanic of any race (2008-2012 5-year est.); Average household size: 2.80 (2008-2012 5-year est.); Median age: 44.5 (2008-2012 5-year est.); Males per 100 females: 111.3 (2008-2012 5-year est.); Marriage status: 16.9% never married, 80.9% now married, 1.1%

widowed, 1.1% divorced (2008-2012 5-year est.); Foreign born: 0.0% (2008-2012 5-year est.); Ancestry (includes multiple ancestries): 65.2% German, 16.1% Irish, 9.8% American, 8.9% English, 0.9% Polish (2008-2012 5-year est.).

Economy: Homeowner vacancy rate: 0.0%. Rental vacancy rate: 0.0%. (2008-2012 5-year est.); Employment by occupation: 30.6% management, business, and financial, 0.0% computer, engineering, and science, 1.4% education, legal, community service, arts, and media, 0.0% healthcare practitioners, 18.1% service, 16.7% sales and office, 12.5% natural resources, construction, and maintenance, 20.8% production, transportation, and material moving (2008-2012 5-year est.).

Income: Per capita income: $29,014 (2008-2012 5-year est.); Median household income: $86,389 (2008-2012 5-year est.); Average household income: $81,148 (2008-2012 5-year est.); Percent of households with income of $100,000 or more: 40.0% (2008-2012 5-year est.); Poverty rate: 2.7% (2008-2012 5-year est.).

Education: Percent of population age 25 and over with: High school diploma (including GED) or higher: 81.0% (2008-2012 5-year est.); Bachelor's degree or higher: 4.8% (2008-2012 5-year est.); Master's degree or higher: 0.0% (2008-2012 5-year est.).

Housing: Homeownership rate: 100.0% (2008-2012 5-year est.); Median home value: $166,200 (2008-2012 5-year est.); Median contract rent: n/a per month (2008-2012 5-year est.); Median year structure built: 1986 (2008-2012 5-year est.).

Health Insurance: 93.8% Private; 5.4% Public; 5.4% None. (2008-2012 5-year est.)

Transportation: Commute to work: 93.0% car, 0.0% public transportation, 0.0% walk, 7.0% work from home (2008-2012 5-year est.); Travel time to work: 16.7% less than 15 minutes, 13.6% 15 to 30 minutes, 56.1% 30 to 45 minutes, 0.0% 45 to 60 minutes, 13.6% 60 minutes or more (2008-2012 5-year est.)

BROUGHTON (village). Covers a land area of 1.992 square miles and a water area of 0.005 square miles. Located at 37.93° N. Lat; 88.46° W. Long. Elevation is 377 feet.

Population: 218 (1990); 193 (2000); 194 (2010); Density: 147.6 persons per square mile (2008-2012 5-year est.); Race: 97.6% White, 0.0% Black/African American, 0.0% Asian, 0.0% American Indian/Alaska Native, 0.0% Native Hawaiian/Other Pacific Islander, 2.4% Some other race, 2.4% Two or more races, 0.0% Hispanic of any race (2008-2012 5-year est.); Average household size: 2.80 (2008-2012 5-year est.); Median age: 34.5 (2008-2012 5-year est.); Males per 100 females: 82.6 (2008-2012 5-year est.); Marriage status: 31.6% never married, 33.5% now married, 13.4% widowed, 21.5% divorced (2008-2012 5-year est.); Foreign born: 0.0% (2008-2012 5-year est.); Ancestry (includes multiple ancestries): 26.9% Italian, 20.7% Irish, 15.6% Dutch, 11.6% German, 9.9% Scottish (2008-2012 5-year est.).

Economy: Homeowner vacancy rate: 2.0%. Rental vacancy rate: 0.0%. (2008-2012 5-year est.); Employment by occupation: 9.4% management, business, and financial, 0.0% computer, engineering, and science, 0.0% education, legal, community service, arts, and media, 0.0% healthcare practitioners, 43.8% service, 31.3% sales and office, 15.6% natural resources, construction, and maintenance, 0.0% production, transportation, and material moving (2008-2012 5-year est.).

Income: Per capita income: $13,351 (2008-2012 5-year est.); Median household income: $34,911 (2008-2012 5-year est.); Average household income: $42,803 (2008-2012 5-year est.); Percent of households with income of $100,000 or more: 2.9% (2008-2012 5-year est.); Poverty rate: 37.3% (2008-2012 5-year est.).

Education: Percent of population age 25 and over with: High school diploma (including GED) or higher: 75.1% (2008-2012 5-year est.); Bachelor's degree or higher: 4.0% (2008-2012 5-year est.); Master's degree or higher: 1.2% (2008-2012 5-year est.).

Housing: Homeownership rate: 91.4% (2008-2012 5-year est.); Median home value: $23,500 (2008-2012 5-year est.); Median contract rent: n/a per month (2008-2012 5-year est.); Median year structure built: 1946 (2008-2012 5-year est.).

Health Insurance: 25.5% Private; 81.3% Public; 7.1% None. (2008-2012 5-year est.)

Transportation: Commute to work: 90.0% car, 0.0% public transportation, 0.0% walk, 10.0% work from home (2008-2012 5-year est.); Travel time to work: 0.0% less than 15 minutes, 72.2% 15 to 30 minutes, 16.7% 30 to 45 minutes, 0.0% 45 to 60 minutes, 11.1% 60 minutes or more (2008-2012 5-year est.)

DAHLGREN (village). Covers a land area of 0.996 square miles and a water area of 0 square miles. Located at 38.20° N. Lat; 88.68° W. Long. Elevation is 515 feet.

Population: 512 (1990); 514 (2000); 525 (2010); Density: 435.6 persons per square mile (2008-2012 5-year est.); Race: 99.8% White, 0.0% Black/African American, 0.0% Asian, 0.0% American Indian/Alaska Native, 0.0% Native Hawaiian/Other Pacific Islander, 0.2% Some other race, 0.2% Two or more races, 0.2% Hispanic of any race (2008-2012 5-year est.); Average household size: 2.21 (2008-2012 5-year est.); Median age: 48.4 (2008-2012 5-year est.); Males per 100 females: 90.4 (2008-2012 5-year est.); Marriage status: 12.2% never married, 67.1% now married, 11.3% widowed, 9.3% divorced (2008-2012 5-year est.); Foreign born: 0.0% (2008-2012 5-year est.); Ancestry (includes multiple ancestries): 33.6% German, 32.0% Irish, 10.8% English, 6.9% Dutch, 6.9% Polish (2008-2012 5-year est.).

Economy: Homeowner vacancy rate: 3.0%. Rental vacancy rate: 20.0%. (2008-2012 5-year est.); Employment by occupation: 5.7% management, business, and financial, 0.6% computer, engineering, and science, 12.7% education, legal, community service, arts, and media, 6.3% healthcare practitioners, 17.1% service, 14.6% sales and office, 13.3% natural resources, construction, and maintenance, 29.7% production, transportation, and material moving (2008-2012 5-year est.).

Income: Per capita income: $17,763 (2008-2012 5-year est.); Median household income: $30,781 (2008-2012 5-year est.); Average household income: $39,763 (2008-2012 5-year est.); Percent of households with income of $100,000 or more: 5.1% (2008-2012 5-year est.); Poverty rate: 12.3% (2008-2012 5-year est.).

Education: Percent of population age 25 and over with: High school diploma (including GED) or higher: 89.1% (2008-2012 5-year est.); Bachelor's degree or higher: 10.0% (2008-2012 5-year est.); Master's degree or higher: 2.7% (2008-2012 5-year est.).

School District(s)

Hamilton County CUSD 10 (PK-12)
    2011-12 Enrollment: 1,264 . . . . (618) 643-2328
Housing: Homeownership rate: 79.5% (2008-2012 5-year est.); Median home value: $47,500 (2008-2012 5-year est.); Median contract rent: $293 per month (2008-2012 5-year est.); Median year structure built: 1951 (2008-2012 5-year est.).

Health Insurance: 74.0% Private; 35.5% Public; 11.6% None. (2008-2012 5-year est.)

Transportation: Commute to work: 99.4% car, 0.0% public transportation, 0.0% walk, 0.0% work from home (2008-2012 5-year est.); Travel time to work: 12.7% less than 15 minutes, 41.1% 15 to 30 minutes, 32.3% 30 to 45 minutes, 1.3% 45 to 60 minutes, 12.7% 60 minutes or more (2008-2012 5-year est.)

DALE (unincorporated postal area)

Zip Code: 62829

    Covers a land area of 1.711 square miles and a water area of <.001 square miles. Located at 37.97° N. Lat; 88.48° W. Long. Elevation is 400 feet. Population: 72 (2010); Density: 42.1 persons per square mile (2010); Race: 100.0% White, 0.0% Black/African American, 0.0% Asian, 0.0% American Indian/Alaska Native, 0.0% Native Hawaiian/Other Pacific Islander, 0.0% Some other race, 0.0% Two or more races, 0.0% Hispanic of any race (2010); Average household size: 2.48 (2010); Median age: 46.7 (2010); Males per 100 females: 125.0 (2010); Homeownership rate: 82.8% (2010)

MCLEANSBORO (city). County seat. Covers a land area of 2.613 square miles and a water area of 0.131 square miles. Located at 38.09° N. Lat; 88.54° W. Long. Elevation is 502 feet.

History: Incorporated 1840.

Population: 2,677 (1990); 2,945 (2000); 2,883 (2010); Density: 994.4 persons per square mile (2008-2012 5-year est.); Race: 97.0% White, 1.2% Black/African American, 0.0% Asian, 1.0% American Indian/Alaska Native, 0.0% Native Hawaiian/Other Pacific Islander, 0.8% Some other race, 0.8% Two or more races, 1.4% Hispanic of any race (2008-2012 5-year est.); Average household size: 2.14 (2008-2012 5-year est.); Median age: 43.2 (2008-2012 5-year est.); Males per 100 females: 88.3 (2008-2012 5-year est.); Marriage status: 22.8% never married, 48.3% now married, 15.2% widowed, 13.7% divorced (2008-2012 5-year est.); Foreign born: 0.4% (2008-2012 5-year est.); Ancestry (includes multiple ancestries): 29.7% German, 19.2% Irish, 14.2% American, 9.5% English, 5.0% Dutch (2008-2012 5-year est.).

Economy: Single-family building permits issued: 0 (2013); Multi-family building permits issued: 0 (2013); Homeowner vacancy rate: 0.0%. Rental vacancy rate: 11.8%. (2008-2012 5-year est.); Employment by occupation: 6.9% management, business, and financial, 2.7% computer, engineering, and science, 3.0% education, legal, community service, arts, and media, 5.0% healthcare practitioners, 15.9% service, 29.6% sales and office, 4.8% natural resources, construction, and maintenance, 32.0% production, transportation, and material moving (2008-2012 5-year est.).

Income: Per capita income: $17,891 (2008-2012 5-year est.); Median household income: $25,709 (2008-2012 5-year est.); Average household income: $39,331 (2008-2012 5-year est.); Percent of households with income of $100,000 or more: 10.4% (2008-2012 5-year est.); Poverty rate: 19.8% (2008-2012 5-year est.).

Education: Percent of population age 25 and over with: High school diploma (including GED) or higher: 79.0% (2008-2012 5-year est.); Bachelor's degree or higher: 13.2% (2008-2012 5-year est.); Master's degree or higher: 5.2% (2008-2012 5-year est.).

School District(s)

Hamilton County CUSD 10 (PK-12)
    2011-12 Enrollment: 1,264 . . . . (618) 643-2328
Housing: Homeownership rate: 61.0% (2008-2012 5-year est.); Median home value: $51,700 (2008-2012 5-year est.); Median contract rent: $330 per month (2008-2012 5-year est.); Median year structure built: 1963 (2008-2012 5-year est.).

Health Insurance: 59.4% Private; 51.1% Public; 12.8% None. (2008-2012 5-year est.)

Hospitals: Hamilton Memorial Hospital

Transportation: Commute to work: 95.9% car, 0.5% public transportation, 1.3% walk, 2.4% work from home (2008-2012 5-year est.); Travel time to work: 43.0% less than 15 minutes, 17.8% 15 to 30 minutes, 23.1% 30 to 45 minutes, 9.3% 45 to 60 minutes, 6.8% 60 minutes or more (2008-2012 5-year est.)

Additional Information Contacts

Hamilton County Chamber of Commerce . . . .
    http://hamcochamber.org

Hancock County

Located in western Illinois; bounded on the west by Lake Keokuk (on the Mississippi River) and the Iowa and Missouri borders; drained by the La Moine River and Bear Creek. Covers a land area of 793.726 square miles, a water area of 20.670 square miles, and is located in the Central Time Zone at 40.41° N. Lat., 91.17° W. Long. The county was founded in 1825. County seat is Carthage.

Hancock County is part of the Fort Madison-Keokuk, IA-IL-MO Micropolitan Statistical Area. The entire metro area includes: Hancock County, IL; Lee County, IA; Clark County, MO

Weather Station: La Harpe   Elevation: 700 feet

	Jan	Feb	Mar	Apr	May	Jun	Jul	Aug	Sep	Oct	Nov	Dec
High	34	39	50	63	74	83	87	85	78	65	51	37
Low	15	18	28	39	50	60	63	61	52	40	30	18
Precip	1.5	1.7	2.7	3.8	4.6	4.7	4.4	3.7	3.9	3.0	2.9	2.4
Snow	6.0	3.7	2.7	0.8	0.0	0.0	0.0	0.0	0.0	tr	0.9	5.0

High and Low temperatures in degrees Fahrenheit; Precipitation and Snow in inches

Population: 21,373 (1990); 20,121 (2000); 19,104 (2010); Race: 97.8% White, 0.3% Black/African American, 0.3% Asian, 0.4% American Indian/Alaska Native, 0.0% Native Hawaiian/Other Pacific Islander, 1.2% Some other race, 1.1% Two or more races, 1.0% Hispanic of any race (2008-2012 5-year est.); Density: 23.8 persons per square mile (2008-2012 5-year est.); Average household size: 2.33 (2008-2012 5-year est.); Median age: 44.7 (2008-2012 5-year est.); Males per 100 females: 97.2 (2008-2012 5-year est.).

Religion: Six largest groups: 9.7% Methodist/Pietist, 9.4% Baptist, 8.0% Catholicism, 7.5% Lutheran, 7.4% Presbyterian-Reformed, 5.1% Latter-day Saints (2010)

Economy: Unemployment rate: 7.2% (April 2014); Total civilian labor force: 8,120 (April 2014); Leading industries: 18.9% health care and social assistance; 15.4% retail trade; 9.2% wholesale trade (2012); Farms: 1,090 totaling 386,262 acres (2012); Companies that employ 500 or more persons: 0 (2012); Companies that employ 100 to 499 persons: 1 (2012); Companies that employ less than 100 persons: 392 (2012); Black-owned businesses: n/a (2007); Hispanic-owned businesses: n/a (2007); Asian-owned businesses: n/a (2007); Women-owned businesses: 640

(2007); Single-family building permits issued: 5 (2013); Multi-family building permits issued: 0 (2013).

Income: Per capita income: $23,088 (2008-2012 5-year est.); Median household income: $42,494 (2008-2012 5-year est.); Average household income: $53,493 (2008-2012 5-year est.); Percent of households with income of $100,000 or more: 11.3% (2008-2012 5-year est.); Poverty rate: 13.9% (2008-2012 5-year est.); Bankruptcy rate: 2.06% (2013).

Taxes: Total county taxes per capita: $207 (2011); County property taxes per capita: $175 (2011).

Education: Percent of population age 25 and over with: High school diploma (including GED) or higher: 91.1% (2008-2012 5-year est.); Bachelor's degree or higher: 18.4% (2008-2012 5-year est.); Master's degree or higher: 5.2% (2008-2012 5-year est.).

Housing: Homeownership rate: 78.3% (2008-2012 5-year est.); Median home value: $80,100 (2008-2012 5-year est.); Median contract rent: $364 per month (2008-2012 5-year est.); Median year structure built: 1956 (2008-2012 5-year est.)

Health: Birth rate: 97.2 per 10,000 population (2013); Death rate: 102.6 per 10,000 population (2013); Age-adjusted cancer mortality rate: 137.8 deaths per 100,000 population (2011); Number of physicians: 5.8 per 10,000 population (2011); Hospital beds: 9.4 per 10,000 population (2010); Hospital admissions: 348.6 per 10,000 population (2010).

Elections: 2012 Presidential election results: 39.4% Obama, 58.5% Romney

National and State Parks: Montebello State Park; Nauvoo State Park

Additional Information Contacts

Hancock County Government . . . . (217) 357-3911
    http://www.hancockcountycourthouse.org

Hancock County Communities

AUGUSTA (village). Covers a land area of 0.715 square miles and a water area of 0 square miles. Located at 40.23° N. Lat; 90.95° W. Long. Elevation is 663 feet.

Population: 614 (1990); 657 (2000); 587 (2010); Density: 1,066.9 persons per square mile (2008-2012 5-year est.); Race: 99.7% White, 0.0% Black/African American, 0.0% Asian, 0.3% American Indian/Alaska Native, 0.0% Native Hawaiian/Other Pacific Islander, 0.0% Some other race, 0.0% Two or more races, 0.0% Hispanic of any race (2008-2012 5-year est.); Average household size: 2.22 (2008-2012 5-year est.); Median age: 45.4 (2008-2012 5-year est.); Males per 100 females: 110.2 (2008-2012 5-year est.); Marriage status: 24.8% never married, 51.4% now married, 9.5% widowed, 14.3% divorced (2008-2012 5-year est.); Foreign born: 1.2% (2008-2012 5-year est.); Ancestry (includes multiple ancestries): 22.9% German, 17.2% American, 15.2% English, 8.3% Irish, 2.8% Swedish (2008-2012 5-year est.).

Economy: Homeowner vacancy rate: 0.0%. Rental vacancy rate: 0.0%. (2008-2012 5-year est.); Employment by occupation: 12.4% management, business, and financial, 0.8% computer, engineering, and science, 3.9% education, legal, community service, arts, and media, 5.0% healthcare practitioners, 24.0% service, 18.5% sales and office, 21.3% natural resources, construction, and maintenance, 14.1% production, transportation, and material moving (2008-2012 5-year est.).

Income: Per capita income: $20,547 (2008-2012 5-year est.); Median household income: $39,107 (2008-2012 5-year est.); Average household income: $45,278 (2008-2012 5-year est.); Percent of households with income of $100,000 or more: 6.1% (2008-2012 5-year est.); Poverty rate: 11.9% (2008-2012 5-year est.).

Education: Percent of population age 25 and over with: High school diploma (including GED) or higher: 88.9% (2008-2012 5-year est.); Bachelor's degree or higher: 11.6% (2008-2012 5-year est.); Master's degree or higher: 4.2% (2008-2012 5-year est.).

School District(s)

Southeastern CUSD 337 (PK-12)

    2011-12 Enrollment: 559 . . . . (217) 392-2172

Housing: Homeownership rate: 72.1% (2008-2012 5-year est.); Median home value: $60,000 (2008-2012 5-year est.); Median contract rent: $443 per month (2008-2012 5-year est.); Median year structure built: Before 1940 (2008-2012 5-year est.).

Health Insurance: 60.7% Private; 41.3% Public; 13.0% None. (2008-2012 5-year est.)

Transportation: Commute to work: 93.1% car, 0.0% public transportation, 5.8% walk, 1.1% work from home (2008-2012 5-year est.); Travel time to work: 34.6% less than 15 minutes, 16.5% 15 to 30 minutes, 29.6% 30 to

45 minutes, 5.0% 45 to 60 minutes, 14.2% 60 minutes or more (2008-2012 5-year est.)

BASCO (village). Covers a land area of 0.222 square miles and a water area of 0 square miles. Located at 40.33° N. Lat; 91.20° W. Long. Elevation is 630 feet.

Population: 99 (1990); 107 (2000); 98 (2010); Density: 589.4 persons per square mile (2008-2012 5-year est.); Race: 99.2% White, 0.0% Black/African American, 0.0% Asian, 0.0% American Indian/Alaska Native, 0.0% Native Hawaiian/Other Pacific Islander, 0.8% Some other race, 0.8% Two or more races, 0.0% Hispanic of any race (2008-2012 5-year est.); Average household size: 1.75 (2008-2012 5-year est.); Median age: 46.8 (2008-2012 5-year est.); Males per 100 females: 89.9 (2008-2012 5-year est.); Marriage status: 20.9% never married, 50.9% now married, 14.5% widowed, 13.6% divorced (2008-2012 5-year est.); Foreign born: 0.0% (2008-2012 5-year est.); Ancestry (includes multiple ancestries): 32.8% German, 32.8% American, 13.0% Irish, 6.1% English, 4.6% Swedish (2008-2012 5-year est.).

Economy: Homeowner vacancy rate: 0.0%. Rental vacancy rate: 0.0%. (2008-2012 5-year est.); Employment by occupation: 0.0% management, business, and financial, 0.0% computer, engineering, and science, 3.8% education, legal, community service, arts, and media, 3.8% healthcare practitioners, 25.3% service, 11.4% sales and office, 27.8% natural resources, construction, and maintenance, 27.8% production, transportation, and material moving (2008-2012 5-year est.).

Income: Per capita income: $22,835 (2008-2012 5-year est.); Median household income: $36,250 (2008-2012 5-year est.); Average household income: $41,056 (2008-2012 5-year est.); Percent of households with income of $100,000 or more: 6.7% (2008-2012 5-year est.); Poverty rate: 9.8% (2008-2012 5-year est.).

Education: Percent of population age 25 and over with: High school diploma (including GED) or higher: 76.6% (2008-2012 5-year est.); Bachelor's degree or higher: 0.0% (2008-2012 5-year est.); Master's degree or higher: 0.0% (2008-2012 5-year est.).

Housing: Homeownership rate: 88.0% (2008-2012 5-year est.); Median home value: $35,000 (2008-2012 5-year est.); Median contract rent: n/a per month (2008-2012 5-year est.); Median year structure built: Before 1940 (2008-2012 5-year est.).

Health Insurance: 73.3% Private; 32.8% Public; 8.4% None. (2008-2012 5-year est.)

Transportation: Commute to work: 100.0% car, 0.0% public transportation, 0.0% walk, 0.0% work from home (2008-2012 5-year est.); Travel time to work: 8.1% less than 15 minutes, 70.3% 15 to 30 minutes, 12.2% 30 to 45 minutes, 9.5% 45 to 60 minutes, 0.0% 60 minutes or more (2008-2012 5-year est.)

BENTLEY (town). Aka Bently. Covers a land area of 0.143 square miles and a water area of 0.001 square miles. Located at 40.34° N. Lat; 91.11° W. Long. Elevation is 676 feet.

Population: 36 (1990); 43 (2000); 35 (2010); Density: 272.5 persons per square mile (2008-2012 5-year est.); Race: 84.6% White, 0.0% Black/African American, 0.0% Asian, 0.0% American Indian/Alaska Native, 0.0% Native Hawaiian/Other Pacific Islander, 15.4% Some other race, 15.4% Two or more races, 0.0% Hispanic of any race (2008-2012 5-year est.); Average household size: 1.63 (2008-2012 5-year est.); Median age: 49.2 (2008-2012 5-year est.); Males per 100 females: 44.4 (2008-2012 5-year est.); Marriage status: 20.5% never married, 43.6% now married, 10.3% widowed, 25.6% divorced (2008-2012 5-year est.); Foreign born: 0.0% (2008-2012 5-year est.); Ancestry (includes multiple ancestries): 25.6% American, 20.5% European, 15.4% German, 12.8% Hungarian, 12.8% French (2008-2012 5-year est.).

Economy: Homeowner vacancy rate: 0.0%. Rental vacancy rate: 0.0%. (2008-2012 5-year est.); Employment by occupation: 16.7% management, business, and financial, 3.3% computer, engineering, and science, 10.0% education, legal, community service, arts, and media, 0.0% healthcare practitioners, 20.0% service, 23.3% sales and office, 3.3% natural resources, construction, and maintenance, 23.3% production, transportation, and material moving (2008-2012 5-year est.).

Income: Per capita income: $19,985 (2008-2012 5-year est.); Median household income: $27,500 (2008-2012 5-year est.); Average household income: $30,288 (2008-2012 5-year est.); Percent of households with income of $100,000 or more: n/a (2008-2012 5-year est.); Poverty rate: 5.1% (2008-2012 5-year est.).

Education: Percent of population age 25 and over with: High school diploma (including GED) or higher: 67.6% (2008-2012 5-year est.);

Bachelor's degree or higher: 20.6% (2008-2012 5-year est.); Master's degree or higher: 0.0% (2008-2012 5-year est.).
Housing: Homeownership rate: 62.5% (2008-2012 5-year est.); Median home value: $39,500 (2008-2012 5-year est.); Median contract rent: n/a per month (2008-2012 5-year est.); Median year structure built: Before 1940 (2008-2012 5-year est.).
Health Insurance: 66.7% Private; 12.8% Public; 25.6% None. (2008-2012 5-year est.)
Transportation: Commute to work: 93.3% car, 0.0% public transportation, 0.0% walk, 6.7% work from home (2008-2012 5-year est.); Travel time to work: 17.9% less than 15 minutes, 14.3% 15 to 30 minutes, 32.1% 30 to 45 minutes, 35.7% 45 to 60 minutes, 0.0% 60 minutes or more (2008-2012 5-year est.)

BOWEN (village). Covers a land area of 0.428 square miles and a water area of 0 square miles. Located at 40.23° N. Lat; 91.06° W. Long. Elevation is 689 feet.
Population: 462 (1990); 535 (2000); 494 (2010); Density: 1,392.7 persons per square mile (2008-2012 5-year est.); Race: 98.8% White, 0.3% Black/African American, 0.0% Asian, 0.0% American Indian/Alaska Native, 0.0% Native Hawaiian/Other Pacific Islander, 0.9% Some other race, 0.8% Two or more races, 0.0% Hispanic of any race (2008-2012 5-year est.); Average household size: 2.61 (2008-2012 5-year est.); Median age: 35.3 (2008-2012 5-year est.); Males per 100 females: 98.0 (2008-2012 5-year est.); Marriage status: 27.1% never married, 61.1% now married, 2.2% widowed, 9.6% divorced (2008-2012 5-year est.); Foreign born: 0.5% (2008-2012 5-year est.); Ancestry (includes multiple ancestries): 33.6% German, 15.1% American, 12.1% English, 9.9% Irish, 4.5% Italian (2008-2012 5-year est.).
Economy: Homeowner vacancy rate: 0.0%. Rental vacancy rate: 21.7%. (2008-2012 5-year est.); Employment by occupation: 11.7% management, business, and financial, 1.9% computer, engineering, and science, 8.3% education, legal, community service, arts, and media, 4.5% healthcare practitioners, 13.5% service, 27.8% sales and office, 5.3% natural resources, construction, and maintenance, 27.1% production, transportation, and material moving (2008-2012 5-year est.).
Income: Per capita income: $18,581 (2008-2012 5-year est.); Median household income: $42,188 (2008-2012 5-year est.); Average household income: $47,763 (2008-2012 5-year est.); Percent of households with income of $100,000 or more: 10.1% (2008-2012 5-year est.); Poverty rate: 14.2% (2008-2012 5-year est.).
Education: Percent of population age 25 and over with: High school diploma (including GED) or higher: 92.1% (2008-2012 5-year est.); Bachelor's degree or higher: 17.0% (2008-2012 5-year est.); Master's degree or higher: 8.9% (2008-2012 5-year est.).
School District(s)
Southeastern CUSD 337 (PK-12)
　　2011-12 Enrollment: 559. . . . . (217) 392-2172
Housing: Homeownership rate: 84.2% (2008-2012 5-year est.); Median home value: $57,500 (2008-2012 5-year est.); Median contract rent: $1,261 per month (2008-2012 5-year est.); Median year structure built: 1951 (2008-2012 5-year est.).
Health Insurance: 59.1% Private; 48.2% Public; 7.7% None. (2008-2012 5-year est.)
Transportation: Commute to work: 91.2% car, 0.0% public transportation, 4.6% walk, 2.3% work from home (2008-2012 5-year est.); Travel time to work: 34.0% less than 15 minutes, 17.2% 15 to 30 minutes, 20.7% 30 to 45 minutes, 19.5% 45 to 60 minutes, 8.6% 60 minutes or more (2008-2012 5-year est.)

CARTHAGE (city). County seat. Covers a land area of 2.436 square miles and a water area of 0 square miles. Located at 40.41° N. Lat; 91.13° W. Long. Elevation is 669 feet.
History: Incorporated 1837. In 1844, Joseph Smith, Mormon leader, and his brother were killed in the city jail by a mob; the old jail is now property of the Mormon Church.
Population: 2,657 (1990); 2,725 (2000); 2,605 (2010); Density: 1,074.7 persons per square mile (2008-2012 5-year est.); Race: 99.0% White, 0.2% Black/African American, 0.0% Asian, 0.2% American Indian/Alaska Native, 0.0% Native Hawaiian/Other Pacific Islander, 0.6% Some other race, 0.6% Two or more races, 0.0% Hispanic of any race (2008-2012 5-year est.); Average household size: 2.20 (2008-2012 5-year est.); Median age: 44.8 (2008-2012 5-year est.); Males per 100 females: 88.6 (2008-2012 5-year est.); Marriage status: 25.7% never married, 49.7% now married, 8.9% widowed, 15.8% divorced (2008-2012 5-year est.);

Foreign born: 0.0% (2008-2012 5-year est.); Ancestry (includes multiple ancestries): 31.7% German, 15.8% English, 15.2% American, 11.0% Irish, 4.8% Swedish (2008-2012 5-year est.).
Economy: Single-family building permits issued: 4 (2013); Multi-family building permits issued: 0 (2013); Homeowner vacancy rate: 5.2%. Rental vacancy rate: 0.0%. (2008-2012 5-year est.); Employment by occupation: 9.9% management, business, and financial, 2.1% computer, engineering, and science, 6.9% education, legal, community service, arts, and media, 6.1% healthcare practitioners, 20.2% service, 26.5% sales and office, 12.8% natural resources, construction, and maintenance, 15.5% production, transportation, and material moving (2008-2012 5-year est.).
Income: Per capita income: $22,654 (2008-2012 5-year est.); Median household income: $46,731 (2008-2012 5-year est.); Average household income: $50,121 (2008-2012 5-year est.); Percent of households with income of $100,000 or more: 7.0% (2008-2012 5-year est.); Poverty rate: 13.0% (2008-2012 5-year est.).
Education: Percent of population age 25 and over with: High school diploma (including GED) or higher: 93.5% (2008-2012 5-year est.); Bachelor's degree or higher: 21.8% (2008-2012 5-year est.); Master's degree or higher: 6.7% (2008-2012 5-year est.).
School District(s)
Carthage ESD 317 (PK-08)
　　2011-12 Enrollment: 438. . . . . (217) 357-3922
Hancock/mcdonough Roe (07-12)
　　2011-12 Enrollment: n/a . . . . (309) 837-4821
Illini West HSD 307 (09-12)
　　2011-12 Enrollment: 396. . . . . (217) 357-9607
Housing: Homeownership rate: 62.5% (2008-2012 5-year est.); Median home value: $86,900 (2008-2012 5-year est.); Median contract rent: $382 per month (2008-2012 5-year est.); Median year structure built: 1948 (2008-2012 5-year est.).
Health Insurance: 66.2% Private; 42.8% Public; 10.0% None. (2008-2012 5-year est.)
Hospitals: Memorial Hospital (67 beds)
Safety: Violent crime rate: 0.0 per 10,000 population; Property crime rate: 188.8 per 10,000 population (2012).
Transportation: Commute to work: 93.2% car, 0.0% public transportation, 1.4% walk, 4.1% work from home (2008-2012 5-year est.); Travel time to work: 44.3% less than 15 minutes, 25.4% 15 to 30 minutes, 16.9% 30 to 45 minutes, 10.2% 45 to 60 minutes, 3.2% 60 minutes or more (2008-2012 5-year est.)
Additional Information Contacts
Carthage Area Chamber of Commerce. . . . . (217) 357-3024
　　http://www.carthage-il.com
City of Carthage . . . . (217) 357-3119
　　http://www.carthage-il.com

DALLAS CITY (city). Covers a land area of 2.374 square miles and a water area of 0.902 square miles. Located at 40.64° N. Lat; 91.16° W. Long. Elevation is 545 feet.
Population: 1,037 (1990); 1,055 (2000); 945 (2010); Density: 488.6 persons per square mile (2008-2012 5-year est.); Race: 98.2% White, 0.5% Black/African American, 0.8% Asian, 0.0% American Indian/Alaska Native, 0.0% Native Hawaiian/Other Pacific Islander, 0.5% Some other race, 0.5% Two or more races, 0.0% Hispanic of any race (2008-2012 5-year est.); Average household size: 2.24 (2008-2012 5-year est.); Median age: 38.2 (2008-2012 5-year est.); Males per 100 females: 66.2 (2008-2012 5-year est.); Marriage status: 21.7% never married, 49.9% now married, 8.6% widowed, 19.8% divorced (2008-2012 5-year est.); Foreign born: 0.8% (2008-2012 5-year est.); Ancestry (includes multiple ancestries): 42.0% German, 16.4% Irish, 6.8% American, 5.9% Swedish, 5.8% English (2008-2012 5-year est.).
Economy: Homeowner vacancy rate: 2.5%. Rental vacancy rate: 0.0%. (2008-2012 5-year est.); Employment by occupation: 6.9% management, business, and financial, 2.1% computer, engineering, and science, 14.8% education, legal, community service, arts, and media, 1.1% healthcare practitioners, 19.0% service, 20.1% sales and office, 6.3% natural resources, construction, and maintenance, 29.8% production, transportation, and material moving (2008-2012 5-year est.).
Income: Per capita income: $20,726 (2008-2012 5-year est.); Median household income: $37,596 (2008-2012 5-year est.); Average household income: $47,437 (2008-2012 5-year est.); Percent of households with income of $100,000 or more: 5.2% (2008-2012 5-year est.); Poverty rate: 13.8% (2008-2012 5-year est.).

Education: Percent of population age 25 and over with: High school diploma (including GED) or higher: 90.5% (2008-2012 5-year est.); Bachelor's degree or higher: 20.4% (2008-2012 5-year est.); Master's degree or higher: 5.5% (2008-2012 5-year est.).

School District(s)

Dallas ESD 327 (PK-08)

    2011-12 Enrollment: 226. . . . . (217) 852-3204

Housing: Homeownership rate: 72.8% (2008-2012 5-year est.); Median home value: $72,600 (2008-2012 5-year est.); Median contract rent: $360 per month (2008-2012 5-year est.); Median year structure built: 1954 (2008-2012 5-year est.).

Health Insurance: 72.8% Private; 41.0% Public; 8.6% None. (2008-2012 5-year est.)

Transportation: Commute to work: 87.1% car, 3.1% public transportation, 3.6% walk, 4.4% work from home (2008-2012 5-year est.); Travel time to work: 17.6% less than 15 minutes, 45.2% 15 to 30 minutes, 26.9% 30 to 45 minutes, 3.8% 45 to 60 minutes, 6.5% 60 minutes or more (2008-2012 5-year est.).

ELVASTON (village). Covers a land area of 0.799 square miles and a water area of <.001 square miles. Located at 40.40° N. Lat; 91.25° W. Long. Elevation is 659 feet.

Population: 198 (1990); 152 (2000); 165 (2010); Density: 152.8 persons per square mile (2008-2012 5-year est.); Race: 99.2% White, 0.0% Black/African American, 0.0% Asian, 0.0% American Indian/Alaska Native, 0.0% Native Hawaiian/Other Pacific Islander, 0.8% Some other race, 0.8% Two or more races, 5.7% Hispanic of any race (2008-2012 5-year est.); Average household size: 2.22 (2008-2012 5-year est.); Median age: 44.5 (2008-2012 5-year est.); Males per 100 females: 100.0 (2008-2012 5-year est.); Marriage status: 28.0% never married, 49.5% now married, 8.6% widowed, 14.0% divorced (2008-2012 5-year est.); Foreign born: 0.0% (2008-2012 5-year est.); Ancestry (includes multiple ancestries): 33.6% German, 25.4% Irish, 15.6% English, 8.2% American, 4.9% French (2008-2012 5-year est.).

Economy: Homeowner vacancy rate: 0.0%. Rental vacancy rate: 0.0%. (2008-2012 5-year est.); Employment by occupation: 0.0% management, business, and financial, 0.0% computer, engineering, and science, 0.0% education, legal, community service, arts, and media, 6.5% healthcare practitioners, 23.9% service, 15.2% sales and office, 21.7% natural resources, construction, and maintenance, 32.6% production, transportation, and material moving (2008-2012 5-year est.).

Income: Per capita income: $18,727 (2008-2012 5-year est.); Median household income: $33,125 (2008-2012 5-year est.); Average household income: $41,233 (2008-2012 5-year est.); Percent of households with income of $100,000 or more: 7.2% (2008-2012 5-year est.); Poverty rate: 25.4% (2008-2012 5-year est.).

Education: Percent of population age 25 and over with: High school diploma (including GED) or higher: 91.4% (2008-2012 5-year est.); Bachelor's degree or higher: 3.7% (2008-2012 5-year est.); Master's degree or higher: 0.0% (2008-2012 5-year est.).

Housing: Homeownership rate: 92.7% (2008-2012 5-year est.); Median home value: $60,400 (2008-2012 5-year est.); Median contract rent: n/a per month (2008-2012 5-year est.); Median year structure built: Before 1940 (2008-2012 5-year est.).

Health Insurance: 70.8% Private; 64.2% Public; 9.2% None. (2008-2012 5-year est.)

Transportation: Commute to work: 95.7% car, 0.0% public transportation, 4.3% walk, 0.0% work from home (2008-2012 5-year est.); Travel time to work: 29.8% less than 15 minutes, 31.9% 15 to 30 minutes, 29.8% 30 to 45 minutes, 4.3% 45 to 60 minutes, 4.3% 60 minutes or more (2008-2012 5-year est.).

FERRIS (village). Covers a land area of 1.967 square miles and a water area of 0 square miles. Located at 40.47° N. Lat; 91.17° W. Long. Elevation is 682 feet.

Population: 177 (1990); 168 (2000); 156 (2010); Density: 102.7 persons per square mile (2008-2012 5-year est.); Race: 100.0% White, 0.0% Black/African American, 0.0% Asian, 0.0% American Indian/Alaska Native, 0.0% Native Hawaiian/Other Pacific Islander, 0.0% Some other race, 0.0% Two or more races, 10.9% Hispanic of any race (2008-2012 5-year est.); Average household size: 2.73 (2008-2012 5-year est.); Median age: 38.6 (2008-2012 5-year est.); Males per 100 females: 122.0 (2008-2012 5-year est.); Marriage status: 31.3% never married, 63.2% now married, 3.1% widowed, 2.5% divorced (2008-2012 5-year est.); Foreign born: 2.5% (2008-2012 5-year est.); Ancestry (includes multiple ancestries): 21.8%

German, 14.9% Irish, 12.4% American, 7.9% Greek, 6.4% Norwegian (2008-2012 5-year est.).

Economy: Homeowner vacancy rate: 0.0%. Rental vacancy rate: 0.0%. (2008-2012 5-year est.); Employment by occupation: 19.8% management, business, and financial, 0.0% computer, engineering, and science, 13.2% education, legal, community service, arts, and media, 0.0% healthcare practitioners, 12.1% service, 23.1% sales and office, 19.8% natural resources, construction, and maintenance, 12.1% production, transportation, and material moving (2008-2012 5-year est.).

Income: Per capita income: $20,682 (2008-2012 5-year est.); Median household income: $45,000 (2008-2012 5-year est.); Average household income: $56,634 (2008-2012 5-year est.); Percent of households with income of $100,000 or more: 12.2% (2008-2012 5-year est.); Poverty rate: 3.5% (2008-2012 5-year est.).

Education: Percent of population age 25 and over with: High school diploma (including GED) or higher: 89.7% (2008-2012 5-year est.); Bachelor's degree or higher: 16.2% (2008-2012 5-year est.); Master's degree or higher: 0.0% (2008-2012 5-year est.).

Housing: Homeownership rate: 85.1% (2008-2012 5-year est.); Median home value: $56,900 (2008-2012 5-year est.); Median contract rent: n/a per month (2008-2012 5-year est.); Median year structure built: Before 1940 (2008-2012 5-year est.).

Health Insurance: 68.8% Private; 33.2% Public; 5.9% None. (2008-2012 5-year est.)

Transportation: Commute to work: 100.0% car, 0.0% public transportation, 0.0% walk, 0.0% work from home (2008-2012 5-year est.); Travel time to work: 40.9% less than 15 minutes, 18.2% 15 to 30 minutes, 25.0% 30 to 45 minutes, 9.1% 45 to 60 minutes, 6.8% 60 minutes or more (2008-2012 5-year est.)

HAMILTON (city). Covers a land area of 3.560 square miles and a water area of 1.794 square miles. Located at 40.39° N. Lat; 91.36° W. Long. Elevation is 643 feet.

History: Incorporated 1859.

Population: 3,281 (1990); 3,029 (2000); 2,951 (2010); Density: 794.5 persons per square mile (2008-2012 5-year est.); Race: 97.1% White, 0.3% Black/African American, 0.3% Asian, 0.0% American Indian/Alaska Native, 0.0% Native Hawaiian/Other Pacific Islander, 2.3% Some other race, 1.5% Two or more races, 1.2% Hispanic of any race (2008-2012 5-year est.); Average household size: 2.39 (2008-2012 5-year est.); Median age: 44.9 (2008-2012 5-year est.); Males per 100 females: 94.4 (2008-2012 5-year est.); Marriage status: 19.8% never married, 54.1% now married, 7.1% widowed, 19.0% divorced (2008-2012 5-year est.); Foreign born: 1.1% (2008-2012 5-year est.); Ancestry (includes multiple ancestries): 34.2% German, 16.0% Irish, 11.4% English, 8.4% American, 6.1% Scottish (2008-2012 5-year est.).

Economy: Single-family building permits issued: 0 (2013); Multi-family building permits issued: 0 (2013); Homeowner vacancy rate: 3.0%. Rental vacancy rate: 0.0%. (2008-2012 5-year est.); Employment by occupation: 7.4% management, business, and financial, 2.4% computer, engineering, and science, 11.8% education, legal, community service, arts, and media, 6.2% healthcare practitioners, 17.7% service, 23.6% sales and office, 7.0% natural resources, construction, and maintenance, 24.0% production, transportation, and material moving (2008-2012 5-year est.).

Income: Per capita income: $23,706 (2008-2012 5-year est.); Median household income: $48,514 (2008-2012 5-year est.); Average household income: $56,715 (2008-2012 5-year est.); Percent of households with income of $100,000 or more: 9.8% (2008-2012 5-year est.); Poverty rate: 7.8% (2008-2012 5-year est.).

Education: Percent of population age 25 and over with: High school diploma (including GED) or higher: 91.7% (2008-2012 5-year est.); Bachelor's degree or higher: 18.2% (2008-2012 5-year est.); Master's degree or higher: 6.2% (2008-2012 5-year est.).

School District(s)

Hamilton CCSD 328 (PK-12)

    2011-12 Enrollment: 590. . . . . (866) 332-3880

Housing: Homeownership rate: 83.2% (2008-2012 5-year est.); Median home value: $84,500 (2008-2012 5-year est.); Median contract rent: $400 per month (2008-2012 5-year est.); Median year structure built: 1968 (2008-2012 5-year est.).

Health Insurance: 79.2% Private; 30.8% Public; 4.7% None. (2008-2012 5-year est.)

Transportation: Commute to work: 94.5% car, 0.1% public transportation, 0.8% walk, 4.6% work from home (2008-2012 5-year est.); Travel time to work: 40.3% less than 15 minutes, 41.8% 15 to 30 minutes, 7.2% 30 to 45

minutes, 2.2% 45 to 60 minutes, 8.4% 60 minutes or more (2008-2012 5-year est.)

LA HARPE (city). Covers a land area of 1.360 square miles and a water area of 0 square miles. Located at 40.58° N. Lat; 90.97° W. Long. Elevation is 699 feet.

History: Incorporated 1859.

Population: 1,407 (1990); 1,385 (2000); 1,235 (2010); Density: 955.3 persons per square mile (2008-2012 5-year est.); Race: 98.5% White, 0.0% Black/African American, 0.9% Asian, 0.0% American Indian/Alaska Native, 0.0% Native Hawaiian/Other Pacific Islander, 0.6% Some other race, 0.6% Two or more races, 0.9% Hispanic of any race (2008-2012 5-year est.); Average household size: 2.17 (2008-2012 5-year est.); Median age: 48.4 (2008-2012 5-year est.); Males per 100 females: 88.8 (2008-2012 5-year est.); Marriage status: 20.5% never married, 55.4% now married, 12.0% widowed, 12.1% divorced (2008-2012 5-year est.); Foreign born: 0.0% (2008-2012 5-year est.); Ancestry (includes multiple ancestries): 22.9% German, 15.0% American, 14.6% English, 7.9% Irish, 5.5% Swedish (2008-2012 5-year est.).

Economy: Homeowner vacancy rate: 1.0%. Rental vacancy rate: 11.3%. (2008-2012 5-year est.); Employment by occupation: 7.2% management, business, and financial, 0.5% computer, engineering, and science, 14.5% education, legal, community service, arts, and media, 4.8% healthcare practitioners, 18.3% service, 21.7% sales and office, 10.2% natural resources, construction, and maintenance, 22.9% production, transportation, and material moving (2008-2012 5-year est.).

Income: Per capita income: $21,794 (2008-2012 5-year est.); Median household income: $36,222 (2008-2012 5-year est.); Average household income: $47,416 (2008-2012 5-year est.); Percent of households with income of $100,000 or more: 6.9% (2008-2012 5-year est.); Poverty rate: 7.0% (2008-2012 5-year est.).

Education: Percent of population age 25 and over with: High school diploma (including GED) or higher: 93.4% (2008-2012 5-year est.); Bachelor's degree or higher: 18.7% (2008-2012 5-year est.); Master's degree or higher: 5.7% (2008-2012 5-year est.).

School District(s)

La Harpe CSD 347 (PK-08)

    2011-12 Enrollment: 225. . . . . (217) 659-7739

Housing: Homeownership rate: 83.8% (2008-2012 5-year est.); Median home value: $66,000 (2008-2012 5-year est.); Median contract rent: $275 per month (2008-2012 5-year est.); Median year structure built: 1962 (2008-2012 5-year est.).

Health Insurance: 67.4% Private; 39.1% Public; 14.4% None. (2008-2012 5-year est.)

Transportation: Commute to work: 85.4% car, 0.0% public transportation, 4.5% walk, 8.2% work from home (2008-2012 5-year est.); Travel time to work: 40.0% less than 15 minutes, 14.7% 15 to 30 minutes, 28.3% 30 to 45 minutes, 12.5% 45 to 60 minutes, 4.5% 60 minutes or more (2008-2012 5-year est.)

NAUVOO (city). Covers a land area of 3.386 square miles and a water area of 1.441 square miles. Located at 40.54° N. Lat; 91.38° W. Long. Elevation is 650 feet.

History: Joseph Smith built the city of Nauvoo in 1839 as the headquarters for the Mormon church, on the site of a small settlement called Commerce. The charter for Nauvoo gave it a measure of autonomy such as maintaining its own militia and courts. Internal discord and outside opposition troubled the church, and in 1845 the Nauvoo charter was repealed and Brigham Young soon led the members westward. In 1849 the deserted city became the scene of the Icarian colony attempt at a Utopian communistic society, which crumbled in 1856. The resettlement of Nauvoo, mostly by German immigrants, began in the 1860's. Joseph Smith and his brother Hyrum were buried in Nauvoo.

Population: 1,108 (1990); 1,063 (2000); 1,149 (2010); Density: 351.1 persons per square mile (2008-2012 5-year est.); Race: 93.9% White, 2.7% Black/African American, 1.7% Asian, 0.0% American Indian/Alaska Native, 0.0% Native Hawaiian/Other Pacific Islander, 1.7% Some other race, 1.8% Two or more races, 0.8% Hispanic of any race (2008-2012 5-year est.); Average household size: 2.24 (2008-2012 5-year est.); Median age: 52.2 (2008-2012 5-year est.); Males per 100 females: 84.6 (2008-2012 5-year est.); Marriage status: 23.3% never married, 63.4% now married, 6.4% widowed, 6.8% divorced (2008-2012 5-year est.); Foreign born: 5.2% (2008-2012 5-year est.); Ancestry (includes multiple ancestries): 30.3% German, 23.0% English, 9.2% American, 7.5% Irish, 3.8% French (2008-2012 5-year est.).

Economy: Single-family building permits issued: 0 (2013); Multi-family building permits issued: 0 (2013); Homeowner vacancy rate: 2.5%. Rental vacancy rate: 0.0%. (2008-2012 5-year est.); Employment by occupation: 16.2% management, business, and financial, 7.1% computer, engineering, and science, 8.8% education, legal, community service, arts, and media, 5.1% healthcare practitioners, 21.0% service, 17.4% sales and office, 3.8% natural resources, construction, and maintenance, 20.7% production, transportation, and material moving (2008-2012 5-year est.).

Income: Per capita income: $25,752 (2008-2012 5-year est.); Median household income: $39,563 (2008-2012 5-year est.); Average household income: $60,164 (2008-2012 5-year est.); Percent of households with income of $100,000 or more: 16.5% (2008-2012 5-year est.); Poverty rate: 13.7% (2008-2012 5-year est.).

Education: Percent of population age 25 and over with: High school diploma (including GED) or higher: 91.9% (2008-2012 5-year est.); Bachelor's degree or higher: 26.6% (2008-2012 5-year est.); Master's degree or higher: 8.7% (2008-2012 5-year est.).

School District(s)

Nauvoo-Colusa CUSD 325 (PK-08)

    2011-12 Enrollment: 289. . . . . (217) 453-6639

Housing: Homeownership rate: 61.4% (2008-2012 5-year est.); Median home value: $130,100 (2008-2012 5-year est.); Median contract rent: $473 per month (2008-2012 5-year est.); Median year structure built: 1972 (2008-2012 5-year est.).

Health Insurance: 73.1% Private; 39.4% Public; 9.4% None. (2008-2012 5-year est.)

Transportation: Commute to work: 83.5% car, 0.0% public transportation, 6.7% walk, 8.8% work from home (2008-2012 5-year est.); Travel time to work: 61.2% less than 15 minutes, 22.4% 15 to 30 minutes, 14.7% 30 to 45 minutes, 1.1% 45 to 60 minutes, 0.6% 60 minutes or more (2008-2012 5-year est.)

Additional Information Contacts

Nauvoo Chamber of Commerce . . . . (217) 453-6648

    http://www.nauvoochamber.org

NIOTA (unincorporated postal area)

Zip Code: 62358

    Covers a land area of 43.107 square miles and a water area of 1.121 square miles. Located at 40.58° N. Lat; 91.25° W. Long. Elevation is 522 feet. Population: 752 (2010); Density: 17.4 persons per square mile (2010); Race: 98.0% White, 0.4% Black/African American, 0.4% Asian, 0.3% American Indian/Alaska Native, 0.0% Native Hawaiian/Other Pacific Islander, 0.9% Some other race, 0.1% Two or more races, 1.6% Hispanic of any race (2010); Average household size: 2.43 (2010); Median age: 43.5 (2010); Males per 100 females: 106.6 (2010); Homeownership rate: 84.1% (2010)

PLYMOUTH (village). Covers a land area of 0.561 square miles and a water area of 0 square miles. Located at 40.29° N. Lat; 90.92° W. Long. Elevation is 650 feet.

Population: 521 (1990); 562 (2000); 505 (2010); Density: 816.4 persons per square mile (2008-2012 5-year est.); Race: 98.5% White, 0.0% Black/African American, 0.0% Asian, 0.2% American Indian/Alaska Native, 0.0% Native Hawaiian/Other Pacific Islander, 1.3% Some other race, 1.3% Two or more races, 0.0% Hispanic of any race (2008-2012 5-year est.); Average household size: 2.18 (2008-2012 5-year est.); Median age: 50.8 (2008-2012 5-year est.); Males per 100 females: 113.0 (2008-2012 5-year est.); Marriage status: 24.7% never married, 51.7% now married, 8.2% widowed, 15.4% divorced (2008-2012 5-year est.); Foreign born: 1.7% (2008-2012 5-year est.); Ancestry (includes multiple ancestries): 27.3% German, 21.0% American, 18.1% English, 8.7% Irish, 3.5% Lebanese (2008-2012 5-year est.).

Economy: Homeowner vacancy rate: 0.0%. Rental vacancy rate: 0.0%. (2008-2012 5-year est.); Employment by occupation: 7.8% management, business, and financial, 0.0% computer, engineering, and science, 4.4% education, legal, community service, arts, and media, 1.5% healthcare practitioners, 18.0% service, 30.7% sales and office, 11.2% natural resources, construction, and maintenance, 26.3% production, transportation, and material moving (2008-2012 5-year est.).

Income: Per capita income: $18,477 (2008-2012 5-year est.); Median household income: $28,056 (2008-2012 5-year est.); Average household income: $38,869 (2008-2012 5-year est.); Percent of households with income of $100,000 or more: 3.8% (2008-2012 5-year est.); Poverty rate: 26.0% (2008-2012 5-year est.).

Education: Percent of population age 25 and over with: High school diploma (including GED) or higher: 79.1% (2008-2012 5-year est.); Bachelor's degree or higher: 12.5% (2008-2012 5-year est.); Master's degree or higher: 1.7% (2008-2012 5-year est.).

Housing: Homeownership rate: 80.0% (2008-2012 5-year est.); Median home value: $43,900 (2008-2012 5-year est.); Median contract rent: $270 per month (2008-2012 5-year est.); Median year structure built: 1942 (2008-2012 5-year est.).

Health Insurance: 67.0% Private; 50.9% Public; 13.3% None. (2008-2012 5-year est.)

Transportation: Commute to work: 93.7% car, 4.9% public transportation, 0.0% walk, 1.5% work from home (2008-2012 5-year est.); Travel time to work: 22.8% less than 15 minutes, 27.2% 15 to 30 minutes, 36.6% 30 to 45 minutes, 6.9% 45 to 60 minutes, 6.4% 60 minutes or more (2008-2012 5-year est.)

PONTOOSUC (village).
Covers a land area of 1.406 square miles and a water area of 0.667 square miles. Located at 40.63° N. Lat; 91.21° W. Long. Elevation is 525 feet.

Population: 264 (1990); 171 (2000); 146 (2010); Density: 73.3 persons per square mile (2008-2012 5-year est.); Race: 100.0% White, 0.0% Black/African American, 0.0% Asian, 0.0% American Indian/Alaska Native, 0.0% Native Hawaiian/Other Pacific Islander, 0.0% Some other race, 0.0% Two or more races, 0.0% Hispanic of any race (2008-2012 5-year est.); Average household size: 2.29 (2008-2012 5-year est.); Median age: 44.4 (2008-2012 5-year est.); Males per 100 females: 171.1 (2008-2012 5-year est.); Marriage status: 21.4% never married, 63.1% now married, 3.6% widowed, 11.9% divorced (2008-2012 5-year est.); Foreign born: 0.0% (2008-2012 5-year est.); Ancestry (includes multiple ancestries): 29.1% German, 10.7% Irish, 10.7% English, 6.8% Swedish, 5.8% American (2008-2012 5-year est.).

Economy: Homeowner vacancy rate: 0.0%. Rental vacancy rate: 0.0%. (2008-2012 5-year est.); Employment by occupation: 12.8% management, business, and financial, 2.6% computer, engineering, and science, 2.6% education, legal, community service, arts, and media, 7.7% healthcare practitioners, 23.1% service, 12.8% sales and office, 15.4% natural resources, construction, and maintenance, 23.1% production, transportation, and material moving (2008-2012 5-year est.).

Income: Per capita income: $19,718 (2008-2012 5-year est.); Median household income: $31,875 (2008-2012 5-year est.); Average household income: $43,224 (2008-2012 5-year est.); Percent of households with income of $100,000 or more: 13.3% (2008-2012 5-year est.); Poverty rate: 24.3% (2008-2012 5-year est.).

Education: Percent of population age 25 and over with: High school diploma (including GED) or higher: 89.7% (2008-2012 5-year est.); Bachelor's degree or higher: 1.3% (2008-2012 5-year est.); Master's degree or higher: 0.0% (2008-2012 5-year est.).

Housing: Homeownership rate: 88.9% (2008-2012 5-year est.); Median home value: $62,900 (2008-2012 5-year est.); Median contract rent: $213 per month (2008-2012 5-year est.); Median year structure built: 1958 (2008-2012 5-year est.).

Health Insurance: 62.1% Private; 39.8% Public; 16.5% None. (2008-2012 5-year est.)

Transportation: Commute to work: 76.9% car, 0.0% public transportation, 0.0% walk, 23.1% work from home (2008-2012 5-year est.); Travel time to work: 3.3% less than 15 minutes, 56.7% 15 to 30 minutes, 33.3% 30 to 45 minutes, 6.7% 45 to 60 minutes, 0.0% 60 minutes or more (2008-2012 5-year est.)

SUTTER (unincorporated postal area)
Zip Code: 62373

Covers a land area of 35.935 square miles and a water area of 0.140 square miles. Located at 40.24° N. Lat; 91.33° W. Long. Elevation is 656 feet. Population: 300 (2010); Density: 8.3 persons per square mile (2010); Race: 99.7% White, 0.3% Black/African American, 0.0% Asian, 0.0% American Indian/Alaska Native, 0.0% Native Hawaiian/Other Pacific Islander, 0.0% Some other race, 0.0% Two or more races, 0.0% Hispanic of any race (2010); Average household size: 2.65 (2010); Median age: 46.1 (2010); Males per 100 females: 94.8 (2010); Homeownership rate: 91.1% (2010)

WARSAW (city).
Covers a land area of 6.520 square miles and a water area of 0.949 square miles. Located at 40.35° N. Lat; 91.43° W. Long. Elevation is 577 feet.

History: Laid out 1834, incorporated 1837. Two forts were established here in 1814.

Population: 1,882 (1990); 1,793 (2000); 1,607 (2010); Density: 242.5 persons per square mile (2008-2012 5-year est.); Race: 97.4% White, 0.0% Black/African American, 0.0% Asian, 0.4% American Indian/Alaska Native, 0.1% Native Hawaiian/Other Pacific Islander, 2.1% Some other race, 1.8% Two or more races, 1.6% Hispanic of any race (2008-2012 5-year est.); Average household size: 2.26 (2008-2012 5-year est.); Median age: 44.1 (2008-2012 5-year est.); Males per 100 females: 87.5 (2008-2012 5-year est.); Marriage status: 23.1% never married, 52.8% now married, 6.7% widowed, 17.4% divorced (2008-2012 5-year est.); Foreign born: 0.7% (2008-2012 5-year est.); Ancestry (includes multiple ancestries): 39.8% German, 14.5% Irish, 13.2% American, 8.4% English, 4.2% Dutch (2008-2012 5-year est.).

Economy: Single-family building permits issued: 1 (2013); Multi-family building permits issued: 0 (2013); Homeowner vacancy rate: 0.5%. Rental vacancy rate: 8.8%. (2008-2012 5-year est.); Employment by occupation: 8.3% management, business, and financial, 3.4% computer, engineering, and science, 7.2% education, legal, community service, arts, and media, 4.8% healthcare practitioners, 18.2% service, 29.5% sales and office, 5.6% natural resources, construction, and maintenance, 23.1% production, transportation, and material moving (2008-2012 5-year est.).

Income: Per capita income: $22,360 (2008-2012 5-year est.); Median household income: $43,250 (2008-2012 5-year est.); Average household income: $49,546 (2008-2012 5-year est.); Percent of households with income of $100,000 or more: 8.3% (2008-2012 5-year est.); Poverty rate: 14.1% (2008-2012 5-year est.).

Education: Percent of population age 25 and over with: High school diploma (including GED) or higher: 90.2% (2008-2012 5-year est.); Bachelor's degree or higher: 13.0% (2008-2012 5-year est.); Master's degree or higher: 3.6% (2008-2012 5-year est.).

School District(s)
Warsaw CUSD 316 (PK-12)
    2011-12 Enrollment: 462. . . . . (217) 256-4282

Housing: Homeownership rate: 83.7% (2008-2012 5-year est.); Median home value: $72,800 (2008-2012 5-year est.); Median contract rent: $339 per month (2008-2012 5-year est.); Median year structure built: 1950 (2008-2012 5-year est.).

Health Insurance: 67.1% Private; 36.1% Public; 11.8% None. (2008-2012 5-year est.)

Safety: Violent crime rate: 0.0 per 10,000 population; Property crime rate: 199.8 per 10,000 population (2012).

Transportation: Commute to work: 92.6% car, 0.0% public transportation, 2.6% walk, 3.1% work from home (2008-2012 5-year est.); Travel time to work: 33.2% less than 15 minutes, 37.9% 15 to 30 minutes, 10.1% 30 to 45 minutes, 13.4% 45 to 60 minutes, 5.5% 60 minutes or more (2008-2012 5-year est.)

WEST POINT (village).
Covers a land area of 0.168 square miles and a water area of 0 square miles. Located at 40.26° N. Lat; 91.18° W. Long. Elevation is 669 feet.

Population: 214 (1990); 195 (2000); 178 (2010); Density: 1,316.4 persons per square mile (2008-2012 5-year est.); Race: 100.0% White, 0.0% Black/African American, 0.0% Asian, 0.0% American Indian/Alaska Native, 0.0% Native Hawaiian/Other Pacific Islander, 0.0% Some other race, 0.0% Two or more races, 0.0% Hispanic of any race (2008-2012 5-year est.); Average household size: 2.63 (2008-2012 5-year est.); Median age: 43.5 (2008-2012 5-year est.); Males per 100 females: 95.6 (2008-2012 5-year est.); Marriage status: 26.9% never married, 54.3% now married, 2.9% widowed, 16.0% divorced (2008-2012 5-year est.); Foreign born: 0.0% (2008-2012 5-year est.); Ancestry (includes multiple ancestries): 31.2% German, 19.9% Irish, 19.9% American, 7.7% English, 2.3% Welsh (2008-2012 5-year est.).

Economy: Homeowner vacancy rate: 3.7%. Rental vacancy rate: 0.0%. (2008-2012 5-year est.); Employment by occupation: 7.8% management, business, and financial, 0.0% computer, engineering, and science, 5.2% education, legal, community service, arts, and media, 2.6% healthcare practitioners, 31.2% service, 13.0% sales and office, 7.8% natural resources, construction, and maintenance, 32.5% production, transportation, and material moving (2008-2012 5-year est.).

Income: Per capita income: $15,248 (2008-2012 5-year est.); Median household income: $33,438 (2008-2012 5-year est.); Average household

income: $38,413 (2008-2012 5-year est.); Percent of households with income of $100,000 or more: 3.6% (2008-2012 5-year est.); Poverty rate: 28.5% (2008-2012 5-year est.).

Education: Percent of population age 25 and over with: High school diploma (including GED) or higher: 74.8% (2008-2012 5-year est.); Bachelor's degree or higher: 16.3% (2008-2012 5-year est.); Master's degree or higher: 3.4% (2008-2012 5-year est.).

Housing: Homeownership rate: 92.9% (2008-2012 5-year est.); Median home value: $34,400 (2008-2012 5-year est.); Median contract rent: n/a per month (2008-2012 5-year est.); Median year structure built: Before 1940 (2008-2012 5-year est.).

Health Insurance: 49.8% Private; 43.0% Public; 18.1% None. (2008-2012 5-year est.)

Transportation: Commute to work: 92.2% car, 0.0% public transportation, 7.8% walk, 0.0% work from home (2008-2012 5-year est.); Travel time to work: 18.2% less than 15 minutes, 31.2% 15 to 30 minutes, 37.7% 30 to 45 minutes, 6.5% 45 to 60 minutes, 6.5% 60 minutes or more (2008-2012 5-year est.)

Hardin County

Located in southeastern Illinois; bounded on the south and east by the Ohio River and the Kentucky border; drained by Big Creek; includes part of Shawnee National Forest. Covers a land area of 177.528 square miles, a water area of 4.051 square miles, and is located in the Central Time Zone at 37.52° N. Lat., 88.27° W. Long. The county was founded in 1839. County seat is Elizabethtown.

Weather Station: Rosiclare 5 NW | | | | | | | | | Elevation: 399 feet

	Jan	Feb	Mar	Apr	May	Jun	Jul	Aug	Sep	Oct	Nov	Dec
High	43	48	58	69	77	84	88	88	81	70	58	46
Low	23	26	34	43	52	61	65	64	55	43	35	26
Precip	3.6	3.8	4.6	4.6	5.5	4.4	4.3	3.2	3.5	3.8	4.2	4.5
Snow	2.4	2.2	0.5	tr	0.0	0.0	0.0	0.0	0.0	0.2	tr	1.2

High and Low temperatures in degrees Fahrenheit; Precipitation and Snow in inches

Population: 5,189 (1990); 4,800 (2000); 4,320 (2010); Race: 95.9% White, 0.8% Black/African American, 1.1% Asian, 0.2% American Indian/Alaska Native, 0.0% Native Hawaiian/Other Pacific Islander, 2.0% Some other race, 2.0% Two or more races, 0.5% Hispanic of any race (2008-2012 5-year est.); Density: 24.0 persons per square mile (2008-2012 5-year est.); Average household size: 2.21 (2008-2012 5-year est.); Median age: 45.9 (2008-2012 5-year est.); Males per 100 females: 117.3 (2008-2012 5-year est.).

Religion: Four largest groups: 23.8% Baptist, 3.5% Catholicism, 1.2% Methodist/Pietist, 0.0% Other Groups (2010)

Economy: Unemployment rate: 8.4% (April 2014); Total civilian labor force: 1,570 (April 2014); Leading industries: 45.3% health care and social assistance; 7.1% retail trade; 3.9% accommodation & food services (2012); Farms: 150 totaling 33,205 acres (2012); Companies that employ 500 or more persons: 0 (2012); Companies that employ 100 to 499 persons: 2 (2012); Companies that employ less than 100 persons: 63 (2012); Black-owned businesses: n/a (2007); Hispanic-owned businesses: n/a (2007); Asian-owned businesses: n/a (2007); Women-owned businesses: n/a (2007); Single-family building permits issued: 0 (2013); Multi-family building permits issued: 0 (2013).

Income: Per capita income: $22,457 (2008-2012 5-year est.); Median household income: $35,632 (2008-2012 5-year est.); Average household income: $49,752 (2008-2012 5-year est.); Percent of households with income of $100,000 or more: 9.2% (2008-2012 5-year est.); Poverty rate: 20.8% (2008-2012 5-year est.); Bankruptcy rate: 2.11% (2013).

Education: Percent of population age 25 and over with: High school diploma (including GED) or higher: 81.7% (2008-2012 5-year est.); Bachelor's degree or higher: 12.3% (2008-2012 5-year est.); Master's degree or higher: 4.1% (2008-2012 5-year est.).

Housing: Homeownership rate: 79.5% (2008-2012 5-year est.); Median home value: $72,400 (2008-2012 5-year est.); Median contract rent: $213 per month (2008-2012 5-year est.); Median year structure built: 1967 (2008-2012 5-year est.)

Health: Birth rate: 95.7 per 10,000 population (2013); Death rate: 138.7 per 10,000 population (2013); Age-adjusted cancer mortality rate: Unreliable deaths per 100,000 population (2011); Number of physicians: 7.0 per 10,000 population (2011); Hospital beds: 57.9 per 10,000 population (2010); Hospital admissions: 1,567.1 per 10,000 population (2010).

Elections: 2012 Presidential election results: 31.8% Obama, 65.9% Romney

National and State Parks: Cave-In-Rock State Park

Additional Information Contacts

Hardin County Government. . . . . (618) 287-2251
   http://www.hardincountyil.org

Hardin County Communities

CAVE-IN-ROCK (village). Covers a land area of 0.374 square miles and a water area of 0.052 square miles. Located at 37.47° N. Lat; 88.17° W. Long. Elevation is 371 feet.

History: Cave-in-Rock was named for a natural cave above the water line in the Ohio River bluff, a landmark for boatmen. The cave served as a pirate's den for a number of thieves beginning with Samuel Mason, who in 1797 lured victims there by promises of liquor and entertainment, and then robbed them.

Population: 381 (1990); 346 (2000); 318 (2010); Density: 671.9 persons per square mile (2008-2012 5-year est.); Race: 98.8% White, 1.2% Black/African American, 0.0% Asian, 0.0% American Indian/Alaska Native, 0.0% Native Hawaiian/Other Pacific Islander, 0.0% Some other race, 0.0% Two or more races, 0.4% Hispanic of any race (2008-2012 5-year est.); Average household size: 2.22 (2008-2012 5-year est.); Median age: 46.3 (2008-2012 5-year est.); Males per 100 females: 90.2 (2008-2012 5-year est.); Marriage status: 25.9% never married, 38.6% now married, 15.0% widowed, 20.5% divorced (2008-2012 5-year est.); Foreign born: 0.0% (2008-2012 5-year est.); Ancestry (includes multiple ancestries): 27.1% German, 23.5% Irish, 18.7% American, 12.7% English, 4.8% Scotch-Irish (2008-2012 5-year est.).

Economy: Single-family building permits issued: 0 (2013); Multi-family building permits issued: 0 (2013); Homeowner vacancy rate: 5.6%. Rental vacancy rate: 8.0%. (2008-2012 5-year est.); Employment by occupation: 5.1% management, business, and financial, 0.0% computer, engineering, and science, 0.0% education, legal, community service, arts, and media, 10.3% healthcare practitioners, 25.6% service, 30.8% sales and office, 12.8% natural resources, construction, and maintenance, 15.4% production, transportation, and material moving (2008-2012 5-year est.).

Income: Per capita income: $11,561 (2008-2012 5-year est.); Median household income: $16,442 (2008-2012 5-year est.); Average household income: $24,386 (2008-2012 5-year est.); Percent of households with income of $100,000 or more: 1.8% (2008-2012 5-year est.); Poverty rate: 42.6% (2008-2012 5-year est.).

Education: Percent of population age 25 and over with: High school diploma (including GED) or higher: 65.4% (2008-2012 5-year est.); Bachelor's degree or higher: 4.8% (2008-2012 5-year est.); Master's degree or higher: 1.6% (2008-2012 5-year est.).

Housing: Homeownership rate: 59.3% (2008-2012 5-year est.); Median home value: $46,300 (2008-2012 5-year est.); Median contract rent: $263 per month (2008-2012 5-year est.); Median year structure built: 1955 (2008-2012 5-year est.).

Health Insurance: 34.7% Private; 72.9% Public; 10.4% None. (2008-2012 5-year est.)

Transportation: Commute to work: 100.0% car, 0.0% public transportation, 0.0% walk, 0.0% work from home (2008-2012 5-year est.); Travel time to work: 23.1% less than 15 minutes, 30.8% 15 to 30 minutes, 25.6% 30 to 45 minutes, 12.8% 45 to 60 minutes, 7.7% 60 minutes or more (2008-2012 5-year est.)

ELIZABETHTOWN (village). County seat. Covers a land area of 0.705 square miles and a water area of 0.005 square miles. Located at 37.45° N. Lat; 88.30° W. Long. Elevation is 364 feet.

Population: 427 (1990); 348 (2000); 299 (2010); Density: 528.8 persons per square mile (2008-2012 5-year est.); Race: 100.0% White, 0.0% Black/African American, 0.0% Asian, 0.0% American Indian/Alaska Native, 0.0% Native Hawaiian/Other Pacific Islander, 0.0% Some other race, 0.0% Two or more races, 0.0% Hispanic of any race (2008-2012 5-year est.); Average household size: 1.93 (2008-2012 5-year est.); Median age: 38.9 (2008-2012 5-year est.); Males per 100 females: 93.3 (2008-2012 5-year est.); Marriage status: 18.6% never married, 50.0% now married, 6.4% widowed, 25.0% divorced (2008-2012 5-year est.); Foreign born: 0.0% (2008-2012 5-year est.); Ancestry (includes multiple ancestries): 27.9% Irish, 23.9% German, 12.6% English, 5.1% Welsh, 4.8% American (2008-2012 5-year est.).

Economy: Single-family building permits issued: 0 (2013); Multi-family building permits issued: 0 (2013); Homeowner vacancy rate: 4.1%. Rental

vacancy rate: 4.9%. (2008-2012 5-year est.); Employment by occupation: 7.3% management, business, and financial, 0.0% computer, engineering, and science, 12.8% education, legal, community service, arts, and media, 4.9% healthcare practitioners, 32.9% service, 7.3% sales and office, 19.5% natural resources, construction, and maintenance, 15.2% production, transportation, and material moving (2008-2012 5-year est.).
Income: Per capita income: $18,617 (2008-2012 5-year est.); Median household income: $25,313 (2008-2012 5-year est.); Average household income: $35,028 (2008-2012 5-year est.); Percent of households with income of $100,000 or more: 5.2% (2008-2012 5-year est.); Poverty rate: 29.3% (2008-2012 5-year est.).
Education: Percent of population age 25 and over with: High school diploma (including GED) or higher: 87.7% (2008-2012 5-year est.); Bachelor's degree or higher: 11.2% (2008-2012 5-year est.); Master's degree or higher: 4.3% (2008-2012 5-year est.).

School District(s)
Hardin County CUSD 1 (PK-12)
  2011-12 Enrollment: 637 . . . . (618) 287-2411
Housing: Homeownership rate: 60.1% (2008-2012 5-year est.); Median home value: $66,500 (2008-2012 5-year est.); Median contract rent: $178 per month (2008-2012 5-year est.); Median year structure built: 1972 (2008-2012 5-year est.).
Health Insurance: 48.0% Private; 47.5% Public; 19.6% None. (2008-2012 5-year est.)
Transportation: Commute to work: 84.6% car, 5.8% public transportation, 1.9% walk, 3.2% work from home (2008-2012 5-year est.); Travel time to work: 59.6% less than 15 minutes, 21.9% 15 to 30 minutes, 6.0% 30 to 45 minutes, 6.6% 45 to 60 minutes, 6.0% 60 minutes or more (2008-2012 5-year est.)

ROSICLARE (city). Covers a land area of 1.938 square miles and a water area of 0.181 square miles. Located at 37.42° N. Lat; 88.35° W. Long. Elevation is 354 feet.
History: Incorporated as village 1874, as city 1932.
Population: 1,378 (1990); 1,213 (2000); 1,160 (2010); Density: 568.6 persons per square mile (2008-2012 5-year est.); Race: 93.6% White, 1.0% Black/African American, 3.6% Asian, 0.0% American Indian/Alaska Native, 0.0% Native Hawaiian/Other Pacific Islander, 1.8% Some other race, 1.8% Two or more races, 1.4% Hispanic of any race (2008-2012 5-year est.); Average household size: 2.23 (2008-2012 5-year est.); Median age: 36.8 (2008-2012 5-year est.); Males per 100 females: 104.1 (2008-2012 5-year est.); Marriage status: 28.3% never married, 44.5% now married, 8.5% widowed, 18.7% divorced (2008-2012 5-year est.); Foreign born: 3.6% (2008-2012 5-year est.); Ancestry (includes multiple ancestries): 26.0% Irish, 25.1% German, 13.5% English, 4.3% Scottish, 4.3% Dutch (2008-2012 5-year est.).
Economy: Single-family building permits issued: 0 (2013); Multi-family building permits issued: 0 (2013); Homeowner vacancy rate: 4.3%. Rental vacancy rate: 5.8%. (2008-2012 5-year est.); Employment by occupation: 5.7% management, business, and financial, 5.4% computer, engineering, and science, 1.1% education, legal, community service, arts, and media, 4.0% healthcare practitioners, 25.1% service, 19.9% sales and office, 13.5% natural resources, construction, and maintenance, 25.3% production, transportation, and material moving (2008-2012 5-year est.).
Income: Per capita income: $16,783 (2008-2012 5-year est.); Median household income: $22,950 (2008-2012 5-year est.); Average household income: $37,062 (2008-2012 5-year est.); Percent of households with income of $100,000 or more: 8.6% (2008-2012 5-year est.); Poverty rate: 37.6% (2008-2012 5-year est.).
Education: Percent of population age 25 and over with: High school diploma (including GED) or higher: 76.5% (2008-2012 5-year est.); Bachelor's degree or higher: 4.3% (2008-2012 5-year est.); Master's degree or higher: 3.6% (2008-2012 5-year est.).
Housing: Homeownership rate: 66.3% (2008-2012 5-year est.); Median home value: $45,300 (2008-2012 5-year est.); Median contract rent: $211 per month (2008-2012 5-year est.); Median year structure built: 1953 (2008-2012 5-year est.).
Health Insurance: 42.4% Private; 57.5% Public; 15.2% None. (2008-2012 5-year est.)
Hospitals: Hardin County General Hospital (48 beds)
Transportation: Commute to work: 88.1% car, 0.6% public transportation, 5.8% walk, 2.8% work from home (2008-2012 5-year est.); Travel time to work: 65.7% less than 15 minutes, 13.1% 15 to 30 minutes, 11.1% 30 to 45 minutes, 6.0% 45 to 60 minutes, 4.0% 60 minutes or more (2008-2012 5-year est.)

Henderson County

Located in western Illinois; bounded on the west by the Mississippi River and the Iowa border; drained by Henderson Creek. Covers a land area of 378.872 square miles, a water area of 16.348 square miles, and is located in the Central Time Zone at 40.82° N. Lat., 90.94° W. Long. The county was founded in 1841. County seat is Oquawka.

Henderson County is part of the Burlington, IA-IL Micropolitan Statistical Area. The entire metro area includes: Henderson County, IL; Des Moines County, IA

Population: 8,096 (1990); 8,213 (2000); 7,331 (2010); Race: 96.7% White, 0.3% Black/African American, 0.3% Asian, 0.1% American Indian/Alaska Native, 0.2% Native Hawaiian/Other Pacific Islander, 2.4% Some other race, 1.0% Two or more races, 1.1% Hispanic of any race (2008-2012 5-year est.); Density: 18.6 persons per square mile (2008-2012 5-year est.); Average household size: 2.24 (2008-2012 5-year est.); Median age: 47.6 (2008-2012 5-year est.); Males per 100 females: 97.1 (2008-2012 5-year est.).
Religion: Six largest groups: 11.1% Methodist/Pietist, 8.5% Baptist, 4.3% Presbyterian-Reformed, 2.6% Catholicism, 2.5% Lutheran, 2.0% Holiness (2010)
Economy: Unemployment rate: 6.8% (April 2014); Total civilian labor force: 3,790 (April 2014); Leading industries: 15.5% wholesale trade; 15.3% retail trade; 6.7% transportation & warehousing (2012); Farms: 396 totaling 171,574 acres (2012); Companies that employ 500 or more persons: 0 (2012); Companies that employ 100 to 499 persons: 0 (2012); Companies that employ less than 100 persons: 117 (2012); Black-owned businesses: n/a (2007); Hispanic-owned businesses: n/a (2007); Asian-owned businesses: n/a (2007); Women-owned businesses: n/a (2007); Single-family building permits issued: 11 (2013); Multi-family building permits issued: 0 (2013).
Income: Per capita income: $24,684 (2008-2012 5-year est.); Median household income: $49,612 (2008-2012 5-year est.); Average household income: $57,170 (2008-2012 5-year est.); Percent of households with income of $100,000 or more: 15.3% (2008-2012 5-year est.); Poverty rate: 10.4% (2008-2012 5-year est.); Bankruptcy rate: 1.85% (2013).
Education: Percent of population age 25 and over with: High school diploma (including GED) or higher: 87.6% (2008-2012 5-year est.); Bachelor's degree or higher: 15.3% (2008-2012 5-year est.); Master's degree or higher: 3.8% (2008-2012 5-year est.).
Housing: Homeownership rate: 80.6% (2008-2012 5-year est.); Median home value: $84,400 (2008-2012 5-year est.); Median contract rent: $363 per month (2008-2012 5-year est.); Median year structure built: 1965 (2008-2012 5-year est.)
Health: Birth rate: 95.9 per 10,000 population (2013); Death rate: 117.3 per 10,000 population (2013); Age-adjusted cancer mortality rate: Unreliable deaths per 100,000 population (2011); Number of physicians: 4.2 per 10,000 population (2011); Hospital beds: 0.0 per 10,000 population (2010); Hospital admissions: 0.0 per 10,000 population (2010).
Elections: 2012 Presidential election results: 55.5% Obama, 43.2% Romney
National and State Parks: Big River State Forest; Delabar State Park; Oquawka State Wildlife Refuge
Additional Information Contacts
Henderson County Government . . . . (309) 867-2911

Henderson County Communities

BIGGSVILLE (village). Covers a land area of 0.337 square miles and a water area of 0 square miles. Located at 40.85° N. Lat; 90.86° W. Long. Elevation is 686 feet.
Population: 349 (1990); 343 (2000); 304 (2010); Density: 1,028.9 persons per square mile (2008-2012 5-year est.); Race: 99.4% White, 0.0% Black/African American, 0.0% Asian, 0.0% American Indian/Alaska Native, 0.0% Native Hawaiian/Other Pacific Islander, 0.6% Some other race, 0.6% Two or more races, 0.0% Hispanic of any race (2008-2012 5-year est.); Average household size: 2.13 (2008-2012 5-year est.); Median age: 38.3 (2008-2012 5-year est.); Males per 100 females: 85.6 (2008-2012 5-year est.); Marriage status: 15.8% never married, 54.2% now married, 14.7% widowed, 15.4% divorced (2008-2012 5-year est.); Foreign born: 0.0% (2008-2012 5-year est.); Ancestry (includes multiple ancestries): 20.7%

German, 12.1% Irish, 9.2% American, 8.1% English, 3.7% Scottish (2008-2012 5-year est.).
Economy: Single-family building permits issued: 0 (2013); Multi-family building permits issued: 0 (2013); Homeowner vacancy rate: 0.0%. Rental vacancy rate: 15.0%. (2008-2012 5-year est.); Employment by occupation: 10.8% management, business, and financial, 0.0% computer, engineering, and science, 9.6% education, legal, community service, arts, and media, 9.0% healthcare practitioners, 6.0% service, 21.6% sales and office, 22.2% natural resources, construction, and maintenance, 21.0% production, transportation, and material moving (2008-2012 5-year est.).
Income: Per capita income: $23,515 (2008-2012 5-year est.); Median household income: $44,792 (2008-2012 5-year est.); Average household income: $51,549 (2008-2012 5-year est.); Percent of households with income of $100,000 or more: 6.7% (2008-2012 5-year est.); Poverty rate: 2.3% (2008-2012 5-year est.).
Education: Percent of population age 25 and over with: High school diploma (including GED) or higher: 91.5% (2008-2012 5-year est.); Bachelor's degree or higher: 13.9% (2008-2012 5-year est.); Master's degree or higher: 5.8% (2008-2012 5-year est.).

School District(s)

West Central CUSD 235 (PK-12)
  2011-12 Enrollment: 980. . . . . (309) 627-2371
Housing: Homeownership rate: 89.6% (2008-2012 5-year est.); Median home value: $62,900 (2008-2012 5-year est.); Median contract rent: $414 per month (2008-2012 5-year est.); Median year structure built: 1948 (2008-2012 5-year est.).
Health Insurance: 73.8% Private; 44.7% Public; 10.4% None. (2008-2012 5-year est.)
Transportation: Commute to work: 85.0% car, 0.0% public transportation, 9.0% walk, 6.0% work from home (2008-2012 5-year est.); Travel time to work: 29.9% less than 15 minutes, 47.8% 15 to 30 minutes, 10.2% 30 to 45 minutes, 3.2% 45 to 60 minutes, 8.9% 60 minutes or more (2008-2012 5-year est.)

CARMAN (unincorporated postal area)

Zip Code: 61425
  Covers a land area of 30.983 square miles and a water area of 1.388 square miles. Located at 40.75° N. Lat; 91.04° W. Long. Elevation is 535 feet. Population: 483 (2010); Density: 15.6 persons per square mile (2010); Race: 99.0% White, 0.6% Black/African American, 0.0% Asian, 0.0% American Indian/Alaska Native, 0.0% Native Hawaiian/Other Pacific Islander, 0.4% Some other race, 0.4% Two or more races, 0.0% Hispanic of any race (2010); Average household size: 2.14 (2010); Median age: 51.4 (2010); Males per 100 females: 100.4 (2010); Homeownership rate: 90.3% (2010)

GLADSTONE (village). Covers a land area of 0.392 square miles and a water area of 0 square miles. Located at 40.86° N. Lat; 90.96° W. Long. Elevation is 551 feet.

History: Gladstone was platted in 1856 and settled by Irish, Swedish, and German immigrants. The town developed around the quarrying of limestone on nearby Henderson Creek.
Population: 270 (1990); 284 (2000); 281 (2010); Density: 806.5 persons per square mile (2008-2012 5-year est.); Race: 99.7% White, 0.0% Black/African American, 0.0% Asian, 0.3% American Indian/Alaska Native, 0.0% Native Hawaiian/Other Pacific Islander, 0.0% Some other race, 0.0% Two or more races, 0.0% Hispanic of any race (2008-2012 5-year est.); Average household size: 2.23 (2008-2012 5-year est.); Median age: 41.5 (2008-2012 5-year est.); Males per 100 females: 69.0 (2008-2012 5-year est.); Marriage status: 18.4% never married, 51.3% now married, 11.1% widowed, 19.2% divorced (2008-2012 5-year est.); Foreign born: 0.0% (2008-2012 5-year est.); Ancestry (includes multiple ancestries): 31.0% German, 16.1% Irish, 7.9% American, 7.0% Swedish, 6.3% English (2008-2012 5-year est.).
Economy: Single-family building permits issued: 1 (2013); Multi-family building permits issued: 0 (2013); Homeowner vacancy rate: 0.0%. Rental vacancy rate: 0.0%. (2008-2012 5-year est.); Employment by occupation: 5.0% management, business, and financial, 0.0% computer, engineering, and science, 2.5% education, legal, community service, arts, and media, 5.0% healthcare practitioners, 24.2% service, 26.7% sales and office, 9.9% natural resources, construction, and maintenance, 26.7% production, transportation, and material moving (2008-2012 5-year est.).
Income: Per capita income: $22,086 (2008-2012 5-year est.); Median household income: $48,750 (2008-2012 5-year est.); Average household income: $49,756 (2008-2012 5-year est.); Percent of households with

income of $100,000 or more: 5.6% (2008-2012 5-year est.); Poverty rate: 2.2% (2008-2012 5-year est.).
Education: Percent of population age 25 and over with: High school diploma (including GED) or higher: 93.6% (2008-2012 5-year est.); Bachelor's degree or higher: 6.8% (2008-2012 5-year est.); Master's degree or higher: 0.9% (2008-2012 5-year est.).
Housing: Homeownership rate: 90.8% (2008-2012 5-year est.); Median home value: $54,800 (2008-2012 5-year est.); Median contract rent: $235 per month (2008-2012 5-year est.); Median year structure built: 1962 (2008-2012 5-year est.).
Health Insurance: 69.6% Private; 34.8% Public; 8.9% None. (2008-2012 5-year est.)
Transportation: Commute to work: 98.8% car, 0.0% public transportation, 0.0% walk, 1.2% work from home (2008-2012 5-year est.); Travel time to work: 14.5% less than 15 minutes, 48.4% 15 to 30 minutes, 16.4% 30 to 45 minutes, 13.2% 45 to 60 minutes, 7.5% 60 minutes or more (2008-2012 5-year est.)

GULF PORT (village). Aka Gulfport. Covers a land area of 1.496 square miles and a water area of 0.924 square miles. Located at 40.80° N. Lat; 91.08° W. Long. Elevation is 518 feet.

Population: 209 (1990); 207 (2000); 54 (2010); Density: 12.7 persons per square mile (2008-2012 5-year est.); Race: 100.0% White, 0.0% Black/African American, 0.0% Asian, 0.0% American Indian/Alaska Native, 0.0% Native Hawaiian/Other Pacific Islander, 0.0% Some other race, 0.0% Two or more races, 0.0% Hispanic of any race (2008-2012 5-year est.); Average household size: 1.58 (2008-2012 5-year est.); Median age: 55.3 (2008-2012 5-year est.); Males per 100 females: 137.5 (2008-2012 5-year est.); Marriage status: 26.3% never married, 52.6% now married, 15.8% widowed, 5.3% divorced (2008-2012 5-year est.); Foreign born: 5.3% (2008-2012 5-year est.); Ancestry (includes multiple ancestries): 42.1% German, 36.8% American, 15.8% Irish, 10.5% English (2008-2012 5-year est.).
Economy: Single-family building permits issued: 0 (2013); Multi-family building permits issued: 0 (2013); Homeowner vacancy rate: 0.0%. Rental vacancy rate: 0.0%. (2008-2012 5-year est.); Employment by occupation: 37.5% management, business, and financial, 0.0% computer, engineering, and science, 0.0% education, legal, community service, arts, and media, 0.0% healthcare practitioners, 0.0% service, 25.0% sales and office, 12.5% natural resources, construction, and maintenance, 25.0% production, transportation, and material moving (2008-2012 5-year est.).
Income: Per capita income: $18,653 (2008-2012 5-year est.); Median household income: $35,833 (2008-2012 5-year est.); Average household income: $31,742 (2008-2012 5-year est.); Percent of households with income of $100,000 or more: n/a (2008-2012 5-year est.); Poverty rate: 10.5% (2008-2012 5-year est.).
Education: Percent of population age 25 and over with: High school diploma (including GED) or higher: 76.5% (2008-2012 5-year est.); Bachelor's degree or higher: 0.0% (2008-2012 5-year est.); Master's degree or higher: 0.0% (2008-2012 5-year est.).
Housing: Homeownership rate: 100.0% (2008-2012 5-year est.); Median home value: $106,300 (2008-2012 5-year est.); Median contract rent: n/a per month (2008-2012 5-year est.); Median year structure built: 1968 (2008-2012 5-year est.).
Health Insurance: 63.2% Private; 47.4% Public; 10.5% None. (2008-2012 5-year est.)
Transportation: Commute to work: 100.0% car, 0.0% public transportation, 0.0% walk, 0.0% work from home (2008-2012 5-year est.); Travel time to work: 87.5% less than 15 minutes, 0.0% 15 to 30 minutes, 0.0% 30 to 45 minutes, 0.0% 45 to 60 minutes, 12.5% 60 minutes or more (2008-2012 5-year est.)

LOMAX (village). Covers a land area of 1.042 square miles and a water area of 0 square miles. Located at 40.68° N. Lat; 91.08° W. Long. Elevation is 548 feet.

Population: 473 (1990); 477 (2000); 454 (2010); Density: 354.2 persons per square mile (2008-2012 5-year est.); Race: 96.7% White, 0.0% Black/African American, 0.0% Asian, 0.0% American Indian/Alaska Native, 0.0% Native Hawaiian/Other Pacific Islander, 3.3% Some other race, 0.5% Two or more races, 2.2% Hispanic of any race (2008-2012 5-year est.); Average household size: 2.04 (2008-2012 5-year est.); Median age: 52.7 (2008-2012 5-year est.); Males per 100 females: 87.3 (2008-2012 5-year est.); Marriage status: 17.5% never married, 65.3% now married, 9.1% widowed, 8.1% divorced (2008-2012 5-year est.); Foreign born: 4.3% (2008-2012 5-year est.); Ancestry (includes multiple ancestries): 26.8%

German, 19.8% Irish, 11.4% English, 4.6% Iranian, 4.6% Greek (2008-2012 5-year est.).

Economy: Single-family building permits issued: 0 (2013); Multi-family building permits issued: 0 (2013); Homeowner vacancy rate: 0.0%. Rental vacancy rate: 9.4%. (2008-2012 5-year est.); Employment by occupation: 7.5% management, business, and financial, 3.4% computer, engineering, and science, 12.3% education, legal, community service, arts, and media, 2.7% healthcare practitioners, 14.4% service, 12.3% sales and office, 14.4% natural resources, construction, and maintenance, 32.9% production, transportation, and material moving (2008-2012 5-year est.).

Income: Per capita income: $21,722 (2008-2012 5-year est.); Median household income: $38,750 (2008-2012 5-year est.); Average household income: $44,540 (2008-2012 5-year est.); Percent of households with income of $100,000 or more: 6.2% (2008-2012 5-year est.); Poverty rate: 15.4% (2008-2012 5-year est.).

Education: Percent of population age 25 and over with: High school diploma (including GED) or higher: 79.9% (2008-2012 5-year est.); Bachelor's degree or higher: 12.0% (2008-2012 5-year est.); Master's degree or higher: 5.5% (2008-2012 5-year est.).

Housing: Homeownership rate: 73.5% (2008-2012 5-year est.); Median home value: $58,800 (2008-2012 5-year est.); Median contract rent: $319 per month (2008-2012 5-year est.); Median year structure built: 1942 (2008-2012 5-year est.).

Health Insurance: 62.9% Private; 39.0% Public; 16.5% None. (2008-2012 5-year est.)

Transportation: Commute to work: 100.0% car, 0.0% public transportation, 0.0% walk, 0.0% work from home (2008-2012 5-year est.); Travel time to work: 18.3% less than 15 minutes, 38.7% 15 to 30 minutes, 40.1% 30 to 45 minutes, 2.8% 45 to 60 minutes, 0.0% 60 minutes or more (2008-2012 5-year est.)

MEDIA (village). Covers a land area of 1.698 square miles and a water area of 0 square miles. Located at 40.77° N. Lat; 90.83° W. Long. Elevation is 709 feet.

Population: 146 (1990); 130 (2000); 107 (2010); Density: 64.8 persons per square mile (2008-2012 5-year est.); Race: 100.0% White, 0.0% Black/African American, 0.0% Asian, 0.0% American Indian/Alaska Native, 0.0% Native Hawaiian/Other Pacific Islander, 0.0% Some other race, 0.0% Two or more races, 0.0% Hispanic of any race (2008-2012 5-year est.); Average household size: 2.04 (2008-2012 5-year est.); Median age: 52.0 (2008-2012 5-year est.); Males per 100 females: 54.9 (2008-2012 5-year est.); Marriage status: 18.5% never married, 44.6% now married, 21.7% widowed, 15.2% divorced (2008-2012 5-year est.); Foreign born: 0.0% (2008-2012 5-year est.); Ancestry (includes multiple ancestries): 27.3% German, 23.6% Irish, 11.8% Swedish, 11.8% English, 9.1% American (2008-2012 5-year est.).

Economy: Single-family building permits issued: 0 (2013); Multi-family building permits issued: 0 (2013); Homeowner vacancy rate: 0.0%. Rental vacancy rate: 0.0%. (2008-2012 5-year est.); Employment by occupation: 16.1% management, business, and financial, 0.0% computer, engineering, and science, 1.8% education, legal, community service, arts, and media, 0.0% healthcare practitioners, 5.4% service, 33.9% sales and office, 23.2% natural resources, construction, and maintenance, 19.6% production, transportation, and material moving (2008-2012 5-year est.).

Income: Per capita income: $22,723 (2008-2012 5-year est.); Median household income: $33,750 (2008-2012 5-year est.); Average household income: $46,450 (2008-2012 5-year est.); Percent of households with income of $100,000 or more: 1.9% (2008-2012 5-year est.); Poverty rate: 16.4% (2008-2012 5-year est.).

Education: Percent of population age 25 and over with: High school diploma (including GED) or higher: 86.8% (2008-2012 5-year est.); Bachelor's degree or higher: 3.9% (2008-2012 5-year est.); Master's degree or higher: 0.0% (2008-2012 5-year est.).

School District(s)
West Central CUSD 235 (PK-12)
    2011-12 Enrollment: 980. . . . . (309) 627-2371
Housing: Homeownership rate: 79.6% (2008-2012 5-year est.); Median home value: $59,500 (2008-2012 5-year est.); Median contract rent: $321 per month (2008-2012 5-year est.); Median year structure built: Before 1940 (2008-2012 5-year est.).

Health Insurance: 63.6% Private; 38.2% Public; 12.7% None. (2008-2012 5-year est.)

Transportation: Commute to work: 91.1% car, 0.0% public transportation, 0.0% walk, 8.9% work from home (2008-2012 5-year est.); Travel time to work: 17.6% less than 15 minutes, 33.3% 15 to 30 minutes, 23.5% 30 to

45 minutes, 13.7% 45 to 60 minutes, 11.8% 60 minutes or more (2008-2012 5-year est.)

OQUAWKA (village). County seat. Covers a land area of 1.468 square miles and a water area of 0.389 square miles. Located at 40.94° N. Lat; 90.95° W. Long. Elevation is 554 feet.

History: Oquawka began as a trading post built in 1827 by the Phelps brothers. The name is of Indian origin, a variation of Ozaukee meaning "yellow banks." An early industry was the manufacture of pearl button blanks from mussel shells.

Population: 1,442 (1990); 1,539 (2000); 1,371 (2010); Density: 818.0 persons per square mile (2008-2012 5-year est.); Race: 97.9% White, 0.9% Black/African American, 0.2% Asian, 0.0% American Indian/Alaska Native, 0.0% Native Hawaiian/Other Pacific Islander, 1.0% Some other race, 0.3% Two or more races, 2.1% Hispanic of any race (2008-2012 5-year est.); Average household size: 2.09 (2008-2012 5-year est.); Median age: 48.3 (2008-2012 5-year est.); Males per 100 females: 107.1 (2008-2012 5-year est.); Marriage status: 17.6% never married, 53.4% now married, 10.5% widowed, 18.5% divorced (2008-2012 5-year est.); Foreign born: 0.7% (2008-2012 5-year est.); Ancestry (includes multiple ancestries): 16.3% German, 12.5% Irish, 8.5% English, 6.8% Swedish, 4.2% Dutch (2008-2012 5-year est.).

Economy: Single-family building permits issued: 1 (2013); Multi-family building permits issued: 0 (2013); Homeowner vacancy rate: 1.8%. Rental vacancy rate: 0.0%. (2008-2012 5-year est.); Employment by occupation: 5.2% management, business, and financial, 0.9% computer, engineering, and science, 4.1% education, legal, community service, arts, and media, 5.6% healthcare practitioners, 21.2% service, 17.7% sales and office, 11.4% natural resources, construction, and maintenance, 33.9% production, transportation, and material moving (2008-2012 5-year est.).

Income: Per capita income: $19,915 (2008-2012 5-year est.); Median household income: $32,885 (2008-2012 5-year est.); Average household income: $43,157 (2008-2012 5-year est.); Percent of households with income of $100,000 or more: 10.5% (2008-2012 5-year est.); Poverty rate: 13.7% (2008-2012 5-year est.).

Education: Percent of population age 25 and over with: High school diploma (including GED) or higher: 70.9% (2008-2012 5-year est.); Bachelor's degree or higher: 5.2% (2008-2012 5-year est.); Master's degree or higher: 1.7% (2008-2012 5-year est.).

Housing: Homeownership rate: 79.0% (2008-2012 5-year est.); Median home value: $52,700 (2008-2012 5-year est.); Median contract rent: $347 per month (2008-2012 5-year est.); Median year structure built: 1969 (2008-2012 5-year est.).

Health Insurance: 66.2% Private; 37.1% Public; 11.0% None. (2008-2012 5-year est.)

Safety: Violent crime rate: 52.0 per 10,000 population; Property crime rate: 215.5 per 10,000 population (2012).

Transportation: Commute to work: 96.3% car, 0.0% public transportation, 0.9% walk, 1.5% work from home (2008-2012 5-year est.); Travel time to work: 27.2% less than 15 minutes, 51.8% 15 to 30 minutes, 13.5% 30 to 45 minutes, 3.1% 45 to 60 minutes, 4.4% 60 minutes or more (2008-2012 5-year est.)

RARITAN (village). Covers a land area of 0.098 square miles and a water area of 0 square miles. Located at 40.70° N. Lat; 90.83° W. Long. Elevation is 761 feet.

Population: 146 (1990); 140 (2000); 138 (2010); Density: 1,280.4 persons per square mile (2008-2012 5-year est.); Race: 97.6% White, 0.0% Black/African American, 0.0% Asian, 0.0% American Indian/Alaska Native, 0.0% Native Hawaiian/Other Pacific Islander, 2.4% Some other race, 2.4% Two or more races, 0.0% Hispanic of any race (2008-2012 5-year est.); Average household size: 1.95 (2008-2012 5-year est.); Median age: 50.9 (2008-2012 5-year est.); Males per 100 females: 111.9 (2008-2012 5-year est.); Marriage status: 28.2% never married, 41.0% now married, 6.8% widowed, 23.9% divorced (2008-2012 5-year est.); Foreign born: 6.4% (2008-2012 5-year est.); Ancestry (includes multiple ancestries): 19.2% German, 16.0% Irish, 11.2% Polish, 10.4% American, 8.0% Dutch (2008-2012 5-year est.).

Economy: Single-family building permits issued: 0 (2013); Multi-family building permits issued: 0 (2013); Homeowner vacancy rate: 12.5%. Rental vacancy rate: 0.0%. (2008-2012 5-year est.); Employment by occupation: 11.0% management, business, and financial, 0.0% computer, engineering, and science, 0.0% education, legal, community service, arts, and media, 3.3% healthcare practitioners, 25.3% service, 36.3% sales and office,

14.3% natural resources, construction, and maintenance, 9.9% production, transportation, and material moving (2008-2012 5-year est.).
Income: Per capita income: $28,802 (2008-2012 5-year est.); Median household income: $56,250 (2008-2012 5-year est.); Average household income: $67,275 (2008-2012 5-year est.); Percent of households with income of $100,000 or more: 25.0% (2008-2012 5-year est.); Poverty rate: 8.0% (2008-2012 5-year est.).
Education: Percent of population age 25 and over with: High school diploma (including GED) or higher: 94.8% (2008-2012 5-year est.); Bachelor's degree or higher: 14.4% (2008-2012 5-year est.); Master's degree or higher: 0.0% (2008-2012 5-year est.).
Housing: Homeownership rate: 65.6% (2008-2012 5-year est.); Median home value: $51,800 (2008-2012 5-year est.); Median contract rent: $1,175 per month (2008-2012 5-year est.); Median year structure built: Before 1940 (2008-2012 5-year est.).
Health Insurance: 73.6% Private; 35.2% Public; 11.2% None. (2008-2012 5-year est.)
Transportation: Commute to work: 74.7% car, 0.0% public transportation, 12.1% walk, 9.9% work from home (2008-2012 5-year est.); Travel time to work: 31.7% less than 15 minutes, 40.2% 15 to 30 minutes, 24.4% 30 to 45 minutes, 0.0% 45 to 60 minutes, 3.7% 60 minutes or more (2008-2012 5-year est.)

STRONGHURST (village). Covers a land area of 0.887 square miles and a water area of 0 square miles. Located at 40.75° N. Lat; 90.91° W. Long. Elevation is 676 feet.
Population: 799 (1990); 896 (2000); 883 (2010); Density: 1,177.8 persons per square mile (2008-2012 5-year est.); Race: 96.5% White, 1.0% Black/African American, 0.0% Asian, 0.5% American Indian/Alaska Native, 0.0% Native Hawaiian/Other Pacific Islander, 2.0% Some other race, 2.1% Two or more races, 0.3% Hispanic of any race (2008-2012 5-year est.); Average household size: 2.39 (2008-2012 5-year est.); Median age: 38.9 (2008-2012 5-year est.); Males per 100 females: 77.7 (2008-2012 5-year est.); Marriage status: 23.3% never married, 58.4% now married, 5.8% widowed, 12.6% divorced (2008-2012 5-year est.); Foreign born: 2.3% (2008-2012 5-year est.); Ancestry (includes multiple ancestries): 26.1% German, 11.0% English, 10.6% Irish, 6.6% Swedish, 2.6% American (2008-2012 5-year est.).
Economy: Single-family building permits issued: 0 (2013); Multi-family building permits issued: 0 (2013); Homeowner vacancy rate: 6.6%. Rental vacancy rate: 5.6%. (2008-2012 5-year est.); Employment by occupation: 7.1% management, business, and financial, 0.4% computer, engineering, and science, 9.2% education, legal, community service, arts, and media, 4.2% healthcare practitioners, 23.1% service, 22.1% sales and office, 12.5% natural resources, construction, and maintenance, 21.3% production, transportation, and material moving (2008-2012 5-year est.).
Income: Per capita income: $21,129 (2008-2012 5-year est.); Median household income: $46,563 (2008-2012 5-year est.); Average household income: $51,094 (2008-2012 5-year est.); Percent of households with income of $100,000 or more: 6.5% (2008-2012 5-year est.); Poverty rate: 15.9% (2008-2012 5-year est.).
Education: Percent of population age 25 and over with: High school diploma (including GED) or higher: 90.9% (2008-2012 5-year est.); Bachelor's degree or higher: 9.2% (2008-2012 5-year est.); Master's degree or higher: 2.6% (2008-2012 5-year est.).

School District(s)
West Central CUSD 235 (PK-12)
    2011-12 Enrollment: 980......................... (309) 627-2371
Housing: Homeownership rate: 60.0% (2008-2012 5-year est.); Median home value: $86,400 (2008-2012 5-year est.); Median contract rent: $365 per month (2008-2012 5-year est.); Median year structure built: 1960 (2008-2012 5-year est.).
Health Insurance: 62.5% Private; 40.0% Public; 7.9% None. (2008-2012 5-year est.)
Safety: Violent crime rate: 0.0 per 10,000 population; Property crime rate: 23.1 per 10,000 population (2012).
Transportation: Commute to work: 92.5% car, 0.0% public transportation, 4.7% walk, 2.0% work from home (2008-2012 5-year est.); Travel time to work: 47.4% less than 15 minutes, 28.4% 15 to 30 minutes, 15.8% 30 to 45 minutes, 4.6% 45 to 60 minutes, 3.8% 60 minutes or more (2008-2012 5-year est.)

Henry County

Located in northwestern Illinois; bounded on the northwest by the Rock River; drained by the Green and Edwards Rivers. Covers a land area of 822.985 square miles, a water area of 2.658 square miles, and is located in the Central Time Zone at 41.35° N. Lat., 90.13° W. Long. The county was founded in 1825. County seat is Cambridge.

Henry County is part of the Davenport-Moline-Rock Island, IA-IL Metropolitan Statistical Area. The entire metro area includes: Henry County, IL; Mercer County, IL; Rock Island County, IL; Scott County, IA

Weather Station: Galva   Elevation: 810 feet

	Jan	Feb	Mar	Apr	May	Jun	Jul	Aug	Sep	Oct	Nov	Dec
High	31	35	47	61	72	81	85	83	76	63	48	34
Low	14	18	28	39	50	60	64	62	52	41	30	18
Precip	1.5	1.6	2.6	3.8	4.0	4.3	3.9	4.4	3.5	2.9	2.8	2.1
Snow	5.6	5.0	2.4	1.2	0.0	0.0	0.0	0.0	0.0	0.3	1.0	5.4

High and Low temperatures in degrees Fahrenheit; Precipitation and Snow in inches

Weather Station: Geneseo   Elevation: 639 feet

	Jan	Feb	Mar	Apr	May	Jun	Jul	Aug	Sep	Oct	Nov	Dec
High	31	35	48	62	73	82	85	83	76	63	48	34
Low	15	19	29	40	51	61	65	63	54	43	31	19
Precip	1.5	1.7	2.6	3.6	4.1	4.0	4.0	4.6	3.3	3.4	2.8	2.2
Snow	7.7	5.5	2.7	1.1	0.0	0.0	0.0	0.0	0.0	0.1	0.9	7.4

High and Low temperatures in degrees Fahrenheit; Precipitation and Snow in inches

Weather Station: Kewanee 1 E   Elevation: 779 feet

	Jan	Feb	Mar	Apr	May	Jun	Jul	Aug	Sep	Oct	Nov	Dec
High	30	34	47	61	71	81	84	82	76	63	48	34
Low	13	16	27	38	49	59	63	61	51	40	30	18
Precip	1.7	1.8	2.5	3.5	4.2	4.3	3.8	4.4	3.3	2.7	2.8	2.2
Snow	7.4	6.4	2.7	1.0	tr	0.0	0.0	0.0	0.0	0.3	0.8	6.8

High and Low temperatures in degrees Fahrenheit; Precipitation and Snow in inches

Population: 51,159 (1990); 51,020 (2000); 50,486 (2010); Race: 94.4% White, 1.6% Black/African American, 0.3% Asian, 0.2% American Indian/Alaska Native, 0.0% Native Hawaiian/Other Pacific Islander, 3.5% Some other race, 1.5% Two or more races, 4.9% Hispanic of any race (2008-2012 5-year est.); Density: 61.0 persons per square mile (2008-2012 5-year est.); Average household size: 2.42 (2008-2012 5-year est.); Median age: 41.9 (2008-2012 5-year est.); Males per 100 females: 98.2 (2008-2012 5-year est.).
Religion: Six largest groups: 12.7% Catholicism, 11.0% Methodist/Pietist, 10.9% Lutheran, 4.5% Baptist, 2.5% Presbyterian-Reformed, 1.1% Pentecostal (2010)
Economy: Unemployment rate: 6.1% (April 2014); Total civilian labor force: 26,377 (April 2014); Leading industries: 29.5% manufacturing; 13.7% retail trade; 11.9% health care and social assistance (2012); Farms: 1,373 totaling 479,294 acres (2012); Companies that employ 500 or more persons: 1 (2012); Companies that employ 100 to 499 persons: 14 (2012); Companies that employ less than 100 persons: 1,056 (2012); Black-owned businesses: n/a (2007); Hispanic-owned businesses: n/a (2007); Asian-owned businesses: n/a (2007); Women-owned businesses: n/a (2007); Single-family building permits issued: 51 (2013); Multi-family building permits issued: 8 (2013).
Income: Per capita income: $26,644 (2008-2012 5-year est.); Median household income: $52,284 (2008-2012 5-year est.); Average household income: $64,738 (2008-2012 5-year est.); Percent of households with income of $100,000 or more: 18.0% (2008-2012 5-year est.); Poverty rate: 10.1% (2008-2012 5-year est.); Bankruptcy rate: 2.29% (2013).
Taxes: Total county taxes per capita: $141 (2011); County property taxes per capita: $137 (2011).
Education: Percent of population age 25 and over with: High school diploma (including GED) or higher: 88.5% (2008-2012 5-year est.); Bachelor's degree or higher: 19.8% (2008-2012 5-year est.); Master's degree or higher: 6.8% (2008-2012 5-year est.).
Housing: Homeownership rate: 78.6% (2008-2012 5-year est.); Median home value: $108,800 (2008-2012 5-year est.); Median contract rent: $458 per month (2008-2012 5-year est.); Median year structure built: 1957 (2008-2012 5-year est.).
Health: Birth rate: 107.7 per 10,000 population (2013); Death rate: 104.3 per 10,000 population (2013); Age-adjusted cancer mortality rate: 173.6 deaths per 100,000 population (2011); Number of physicians: 5.2 per 10,000 population (2011); Hospital beds: 20.6 per 10,000 population (2010); Hospital admissions: 430.0 per 10,000 population (2010).

Elections: 2012 Presidential election results: 50.7% Obama, 47.6% Romney
National and State Parks: Johnson Sauk Trail State Park
Additional Information Contacts
Henry County Government . . . . (309) 937-3578
http://www.co.henry.il.us

Henry County Communities

ALPHA (village). Covers a land area of 0.321 square miles and a water area of 0 square miles. Located at 41.19° N. Lat; 90.38° W. Long. Elevation is 801 feet.
Population: 753 (1990); 726 (2000); 671 (2010); Density: 1,730.1 persons per square mile (2008-2012 5-year est.); Race: 99.3% White, 0.0% Black/African American, 0.0% Asian, 0.0% American Indian/Alaska Native, 0.0% Native Hawaiian/Other Pacific Islander, 0.7% Some other race, 0.4% Two or more races, 1.3% Hispanic of any race (2008-2012 5-year est.); Average household size: 1.98 (2008-2012 5-year est.); Median age: 52.9 (2008-2012 5-year est.); Males per 100 females: 87.2 (2008-2012 5-year est.); Marriage status: 16.1% never married, 60.7% now married, 11.8% widowed, 11.4% divorced (2008-2012 5-year est.); Foreign born: 1.1% (2008-2012 5-year est.); Ancestry (includes multiple ancestries): 28.8% German, 25.9% Swedish, 16.5% Irish, 12.6% English, 5.2% American (2008-2012 5-year est.).
Economy: Single-family building permits issued: 0 (2013); Multi-family building permits issued: 0 (2013); Homeowner vacancy rate: 1.7%. Rental vacancy rate: 0.0%. (2008-2012 5-year est.); Employment by occupation: 10.9% management, business, and financial, 1.9% computer, engineering, and science, 9.4% education, legal, community service, arts, and media, 4.1% healthcare practitioners, 22.1% service, 21.0% sales and office, 17.2% natural resources, construction, and maintenance, 13.5% production, transportation, and material moving (2008-2012 5-year est.).
Income: Per capita income: $27,772 (2008-2012 5-year est.); Median household income: $48,625 (2008-2012 5-year est.); Average household income: $55,651 (2008-2012 5-year est.); Percent of households with income of $100,000 or more: 11.8% (2008-2012 5-year est.); Poverty rate: 1.6% (2008-2012 5-year est.).
Education: Percent of population age 25 and over with: High school diploma (including GED) or higher: 95.8% (2008-2012 5-year est.); Bachelor's degree or higher: 19.7% (2008-2012 5-year est.); Master's degree or higher: 5.1% (2008-2012 5-year est.).
School District(s)
Alwood CUSD 225 (PK-12)
    2011-12 Enrollment: 439 . . . . (309) 334-2719
Housing: Homeownership rate: 79.0% (2008-2012 5-year est.); Median home value: $92,200 (2008-2012 5-year est.); Median contract rent: $430 per month (2008-2012 5-year est.); Median year structure built: 1954 (2008-2012 5-year est.).
Health Insurance: 82.6% Private; 32.9% Public; 5.6% None. (2008-2012 5-year est.)
Transportation: Commute to work: 87.6% car, 0.0% public transportation, 3.1% walk, 6.9% work from home (2008-2012 5-year est.); Travel time to work: 37.8% less than 15 minutes, 31.1% 15 to 30 minutes, 15.4% 30 to 45 minutes, 13.3% 45 to 60 minutes, 2.5% 60 minutes or more (2008-2012 5-year est.)

ANDOVER (village). Covers a land area of 0.993 square miles and a water area of 0 square miles. Located at 41.29° N. Lat; 90.29° W. Long. Elevation is 774 feet.
Population: 579 (1990); 594 (2000); 578 (2010); Density: 657.9 persons per square mile (2008-2012 5-year est.); Race: 99.2% White, 0.0% Black/African American, 0.0% Asian, 0.0% American Indian/Alaska Native, 0.0% Native Hawaiian/Other Pacific Islander, 0.8% Some other race, 0.0% Two or more races, 3.8% Hispanic of any race (2008-2012 5-year est.); Average household size: 2.71 (2008-2012 5-year est.); Median age: 44.6 (2008-2012 5-year est.); Males per 100 females: 78.4 (2008-2012 5-year est.); Marriage status: 20.3% never married, 58.6% now married, 9.2% widowed, 11.9% divorced (2008-2012 5-year est.); Foreign born: 1.8% (2008-2012 5-year est.); Ancestry (includes multiple ancestries): 32.9% German, 23.4% Swedish, 18.7% Irish, 7.0% English, 4.6% Welsh (2008-2012 5-year est.).
Economy: Single-family building permits issued: 1 (2013); Multi-family building permits issued: 0 (2013); Homeowner vacancy rate: 0.0%. Rental vacancy rate: 0.0%. (2008-2012 5-year est.); Employment by occupation: 4.3% management, business, and financial, 1.1% computer, engineering,

and science, 7.2% education, legal, community service, arts, and media, 6.9% healthcare practitioners, 28.9% service, 23.8% sales and office, 9.7% natural resources, construction, and maintenance, 18.1% production, transportation, and material moving (2008-2012 5-year est.).
Income: Per capita income: $22,639 (2008-2012 5-year est.); Median household income: $60,875 (2008-2012 5-year est.); Average household income: $61,481 (2008-2012 5-year est.); Percent of households with income of $100,000 or more: 14.9% (2008-2012 5-year est.); Poverty rate: 7.7% (2008-2012 5-year est.).
Education: Percent of population age 25 and over with: High school diploma (including GED) or higher: 85.1% (2008-2012 5-year est.); Bachelor's degree or higher: 6.2% (2008-2012 5-year est.); Master's degree or higher: 5.5% (2008-2012 5-year est.).
Housing: Homeownership rate: 90.0% (2008-2012 5-year est.); Median home value: $111,900 (2008-2012 5-year est.); Median contract rent: $450 per month (2008-2012 5-year est.); Median year structure built: 1971 (2008-2012 5-year est.).
Health Insurance: 81.3% Private; 37.4% Public; 2.0% None. (2008-2012 5-year est.)
Transportation: Commute to work: 96.4% car, 0.0% public transportation, 0.0% walk, 0.0% work from home (2008-2012 5-year est.); Travel time to work: 21.7% less than 15 minutes, 18.4% 15 to 30 minutes, 54.2% 30 to 45 minutes, 5.8% 45 to 60 minutes, 0.0% 60 minutes or more (2008-2012 5-year est.)

ANNAWAN (town). Covers a land area of 1.976 square miles and a water area of 0 square miles. Located at 41.39° N. Lat; 89.89° W. Long. Elevation is 630 feet.
History: Annawan developed as the center of a stock farming and coal mining region.
Population: 802 (1990); 868 (2000); 878 (2010); Density: 469.6 persons per square mile (2008-2012 5-year est.); Race: 92.8% White, 4.3% Black/African American, 0.4% Asian, 0.3% American Indian/Alaska Native, 0.0% Native Hawaiian/Other Pacific Islander, 2.2% Some other race, 1.4% Two or more races, 3.8% Hispanic of any race (2008-2012 5-year est.); Average household size: 2.44 (2008-2012 5-year est.); Median age: 38.3 (2008-2012 5-year est.); Males per 100 females: 89.8 (2008-2012 5-year est.); Marriage status: 24.7% never married, 57.4% now married, 6.3% widowed, 11.6% divorced (2008-2012 5-year est.); Foreign born: 1.9% (2008-2012 5-year est.); Ancestry (includes multiple ancestries): 30.7% German, 21.1% Belgian, 10.7% Irish, 9.1% Swedish, 8.0% English (2008-2012 5-year est.).
Economy: Single-family building permits issued: 1 (2013); Multi-family building permits issued: 0 (2013); Homeowner vacancy rate: 2.8%. Rental vacancy rate: 6.3%. (2008-2012 5-year est.); Employment by occupation: 15.1% management, business, and financial, 3.1% computer, engineering, and science, 12.2% education, legal, community service, arts, and media, 5.6% healthcare practitioners, 10.9% service, 29.0% sales and office, 10.0% natural resources, construction, and maintenance, 14.0% production, transportation, and material moving (2008-2012 5-year est.).
Income: Per capita income: $27,974 (2008-2012 5-year est.); Median household income: $56,094 (2008-2012 5-year est.); Average household income: $66,540 (2008-2012 5-year est.); Percent of households with income of $100,000 or more: 26.4% (2008-2012 5-year est.); Poverty rate: 8.9% (2008-2012 5-year est.).
Education: Percent of population age 25 and over with: High school diploma (including GED) or higher: 94.3% (2008-2012 5-year est.); Bachelor's degree or higher: 25.9% (2008-2012 5-year est.); Master's degree or higher: 6.7% (2008-2012 5-year est.).
School District(s)
Annawan CUSD 226 (PK-12)
    2011-12 Enrollment: 393 . . . . (309) 935-6781
Housing: Homeownership rate: 72.4% (2008-2012 5-year est.); Median home value: $102,100 (2008-2012 5-year est.); Median contract rent: $440 per month (2008-2012 5-year est.); Median year structure built: 1955 (2008-2012 5-year est.).
Health Insurance: 81.7% Private; 28.4% Public; 5.8% None. (2008-2012 5-year est.)
Transportation: Commute to work: 93.4% car, 0.0% public transportation, 4.3% walk, 2.3% work from home (2008-2012 5-year est.); Travel time to work: 35.0% less than 15 minutes, 35.7% 15 to 30 minutes, 12.1% 30 to 45 minutes, 13.2% 45 to 60 minutes, 3.9% 60 minutes or more (2008-2012 5-year est.)

ATKINSON

ATKINSON (town). Covers a land area of 1.576 square miles and a water area of 0.016 square miles. Located at 41.41° N. Lat; 90.00° W. Long. Elevation is 659 feet.

Population: 950 (1990); 1,001 (2000); 972 (2010); Density: 734.2 persons per square mile (2008-2012 5-year est.); Race: 98.6% White, 0.0% Black/African American, 0.0% Asian, 0.7% American Indian/Alaska Native, 0.0% Native Hawaiian/Other Pacific Islander, 0.7% Some other race, 0.7% Two or more races, 0.6% Hispanic of any race (2008-2012 5-year est.); Average household size: 2.33 (2008-2012 5-year est.); Median age: 42.0 (2008-2012 5-year est.); Males per 100 females: 116.7 (2008-2012 5-year est.); Marriage status: 18.4% never married, 62.9% now married, 6.3% widowed, 12.3% divorced (2008-2012 5-year est.); Foreign born: 0.0% (2008-2012 5-year est.); Ancestry (includes multiple ancestries): 25.7% German, 24.8% Belgian, 15.0% Swedish, 6.0% English, 5.6% American (2008-2012 5-year est.).

Economy: Single-family building permits issued: 0 (2013); Multi-family building permits issued: 0 (2013); Homeowner vacancy rate: 0.0%. Rental vacancy rate: 7.4%. (2008-2012 5-year est.); Employment by occupation: 10.1% management, business, and financial, 0.6% computer, engineering, and science, 4.6% education, legal, community service, arts, and media, 4.0% healthcare practitioners, 21.6% service, 29.3% sales and office, 16.9% natural resources, construction, and maintenance, 12.9% production, transportation, and material moving (2008-2012 5-year est.).

Income: Per capita income: $26,677 (2008-2012 5-year est.); Median household income: $54,821 (2008-2012 5-year est.); Average household income: $63,732 (2008-2012 5-year est.); Percent of households with income of $100,000 or more: 20.3% (2008-2012 5-year est.); Poverty rate: 10.9% (2008-2012 5-year est.).

Education: Percent of population age 25 and over with: High school diploma (including GED) or higher: 92.0% (2008-2012 5-year est.); Bachelor's degree or higher: 10.3% (2008-2012 5-year est.); Master's degree or higher: 1.6% (2008-2012 5-year est.).

School District(s)

Henry-Stark County Spec Ed Dist

   2011-12 Enrollment: n/a . . . . (309) 852-5696

Housing: Homeownership rate: 78.7% (2008-2012 5-year est.); Median home value: $93,100 (2008-2012 5-year est.); Median contract rent: $407 per month (2008-2012 5-year est.); Median year structure built: 1958 (2008-2012 5-year est.).

Health Insurance: 79.4% Private; 24.1% Public; 9.8% None. (2008-2012 5-year est.)

Transportation: Commute to work: 94.9% car, 0.0% public transportation, 1.7% walk, 2.5% work from home (2008-2012 5-year est.); Travel time to work: 42.2% less than 15 minutes, 25.1% 15 to 30 minutes, 23.0% 30 to 45 minutes, 5.4% 45 to 60 minutes, 4.3% 60 minutes or more (2008-2012 5-year est.)

BISHOP HILL

BISHOP HILL (village). Covers a land area of 0.535 square miles and a water area of 0 square miles. Located at 41.20° N. Lat; 90.12° W. Long. Elevation is 784 feet.

History: Bishop Hill was settled in 1846 by a group of Swedish emigrants led by Erik Jansson, who envisioned a communistic society based on religion. Jansson's leadership lasted only a few years, and by 1861 the communal property had been divided among individuals.

Population: 131 (1990); 125 (2000); 128 (2010); Density: 239.4 persons per square mile (2008-2012 5-year est.); Race: 100.0% White, 0.0% Black/African American, 0.0% Asian, 0.0% American Indian/Alaska Native, 0.0% Native Hawaiian/Other Pacific Islander, 0.0% Some other race, 0.0% Two or more races, 0.0% Hispanic of any race (2008-2012 5-year est.); Average household size: 2.06 (2008-2012 5-year est.); Median age: 55.3 (2008-2012 5-year est.); Males per 100 females: 103.2 (2008-2012 5-year est.); Marriage status: 24.6% never married, 63.1% now married, 6.6% widowed, 5.7% divorced (2008-2012 5-year est.); Foreign born: 4.7% (2008-2012 5-year est.); Ancestry (includes multiple ancestries): 25.8% Swedish, 15.6% German, 11.7% Italian, 9.4% Polish, 9.4% English (2008-2012 5-year est.).

Economy: Single-family building permits issued: 0 (2013); Multi-family building permits issued: 0 (2013); Homeowner vacancy rate: 0.0%. Rental vacancy rate: 0.0%. (2008-2012 5-year est.); Employment by occupation: 21.5% management, business, and financial, 6.2% computer, engineering, and science, 13.8% education, legal, community service, arts, and media, 0.0% healthcare practitioners, 0.0% service, 33.8% sales and office, 9.2% natural resources, construction, and maintenance, 15.4% production, transportation, and material moving (2008-2012 5-year est.).

Income: Per capita income: $39,980 (2008-2012 5-year est.); Median household income: $63,929 (2008-2012 5-year est.); Average household income: $82,915 (2008-2012 5-year est.); Percent of households with income of $100,000 or more: 11.3% (2008-2012 5-year est.); Poverty rate: 1.6% (2008-2012 5-year est.).

Education: Percent of population age 25 and over with: High school diploma (including GED) or higher: 97.1% (2008-2012 5-year est.); Bachelor's degree or higher: 28.6% (2008-2012 5-year est.); Master's degree or higher: 11.4% (2008-2012 5-year est.).

Housing: Homeownership rate: 96.8% (2008-2012 5-year est.); Median home value: $96,000 (2008-2012 5-year est.); Median contract rent: n/a per month (2008-2012 5-year est.); Median year structure built: Before 1940 (2008-2012 5-year est.).

Health Insurance: 89.8% Private; 28.1% Public; 5.5% None. (2008-2012 5-year est.)

Transportation: Commute to work: 61.5% car, 0.0% public transportation, 12.3% walk, 26.2% work from home (2008-2012 5-year est.); Travel time to work: 29.2% less than 15 minutes, 27.1% 15 to 30 minutes, 16.7% 30 to 45 minutes, 12.5% 45 to 60 minutes, 14.6% 60 minutes or more (2008-2012 5-year est.)

CAMBRIDGE

CAMBRIDGE (village). County seat. Covers a land area of 2.143 square miles and a water area of 0.014 square miles. Located at 41.29° N. Lat; 90.19° W. Long. Elevation is 810 feet.

History: Incorporated 1861.

Population: 2,124 (1990); 2,180 (2000); 2,160 (2010); Density: 1,081.9 persons per square mile (2008-2012 5-year est.); Race: 92.9% White, 3.7% Black/African American, 0.8% Asian, 0.1% American Indian/Alaska Native, 0.0% Native Hawaiian/Other Pacific Islander, 2.5% Some other race, 0.7% Two or more races, 3.6% Hispanic of any race (2008-2012 5-year est.); Average household size: 2.40 (2008-2012 5-year est.); Median age: 35.5 (2008-2012 5-year est.); Males per 100 females: 96.9 (2008-2012 5-year est.); Marriage status: 27.4% never married, 56.9% now married, 6.3% widowed, 9.3% divorced (2008-2012 5-year est.); Foreign born: 2.1% (2008-2012 5-year est.); Ancestry (includes multiple ancestries): 26.3% German, 18.5% Irish, 15.8% Swedish, 9.0% English, 6.4% Belgian (2008-2012 5-year est.).

Economy: Single-family building permits issued: 1 (2013); Multi-family building permits issued: 0 (2013); Homeowner vacancy rate: 2.8%. Rental vacancy rate: 12.6%. (2008-2012 5-year est.); Employment by occupation: 15.4% management, business, and financial, 3.8% computer, engineering, and science, 11.8% education, legal, community service, arts, and media, 5.0% healthcare practitioners, 20.9% service, 17.2% sales and office, 6.5% natural resources, construction, and maintenance, 19.3% production, transportation, and material moving (2008-2012 5-year est.).

Income: Per capita income: $24,737 (2008-2012 5-year est.); Median household income: $52,016 (2008-2012 5-year est.); Average household income: $59,678 (2008-2012 5-year est.); Percent of households with income of $100,000 or more: 14.9% (2008-2012 5-year est.); Poverty rate: 11.1% (2008-2012 5-year est.).

Education: Percent of population age 25 and over with: High school diploma (including GED) or higher: 90.1% (2008-2012 5-year est.); Bachelor's degree or higher: 20.3% (2008-2012 5-year est.); Master's degree or higher: 7.5% (2008-2012 5-year est.).

School District(s)

Cambridge CUSD 227 (PK-12)

   2011-12 Enrollment: 537 . . . . (309) 937-2144

Housing: Homeownership rate: 83.5% (2008-2012 5-year est.); Median home value: $94,100 (2008-2012 5-year est.); Median contract rent: $400 per month (2008-2012 5-year est.); Median year structure built: 1957 (2008-2012 5-year est.).

Health Insurance: 78.5% Private; 32.2% Public; 6.5% None. (2008-2012 5-year est.)

Safety: Violent crime rate: 4.6 per 10,000 population; Property crime rate: 60.4 per 10,000 population (2012).

Transportation: Commute to work: 96.1% car, 0.0% public transportation, 2.0% walk, 0.4% work from home (2008-2012 5-year est.); Travel time to work: 33.2% less than 15 minutes, 30.1% 15 to 30 minutes, 23.5% 30 to 45 minutes, 10.8% 45 to 60 minutes, 2.4% 60 minutes or more (2008-2012 5-year est.)

Additional Information Contacts

Village of Cambridge . . . . (309) 937-2570

   http://www.cambridgeil.org

CLEVELAND (village).
Covers a land area of 0.358 square miles and a water area of 0.006 square miles. Located at 41.50° N. Lat; 90.32° W. Long. Elevation is 571 feet.

Population: 283 (1990); 253 (2000); 188 (2010); Density: 566.7 persons per square mile (2008-2012 5-year est.); Race: 73.4% White, 25.1% Black/African American, 0.0% Asian, 1.0% American Indian/Alaska Native, 0.0% Native Hawaiian/Other Pacific Islander, 0.5% Some other race, 0.5% Two or more races, 3.0% Hispanic of any race (2008-2012 5-year est.); Average household size: 2.86 (2008-2012 5-year est.); Median age: 36.8 (2008-2012 5-year est.); Males per 100 females: 88.0 (2008-2012 5-year est.); Marriage status: 12.0% never married, 66.9% now married, 9.0% widowed, 12.0% divorced (2008-2012 5-year est.); Foreign born: 2.5% (2008-2012 5-year est.); Ancestry (includes multiple ancestries): 21.2% German, 12.8% Swedish, 9.9% Belgian, 8.9% Irish, 7.9% English (2008-2012 5-year est.).

Economy: Single-family building permits issued: 0 (2013); Multi-family building permits issued: 0 (2013); Homeowner vacancy rate: 0.0%. Rental vacancy rate: 0.0%. (2008-2012 5-year est.); Employment by occupation: 8.5% management, business, and financial, 0.0% computer, engineering, and science, 0.0% education, legal, community service, arts, and media, 2.1% healthcare practitioners, 20.2% service, 29.8% sales and office, 24.5% natural resources, construction, and maintenance, 14.9% production, transportation, and material moving (2008-2012 5-year est.).

Income: Per capita income: $23,714 (2008-2012 5-year est.); Median household income: $47,188 (2008-2012 5-year est.); Average household income: $68,255 (2008-2012 5-year est.); Percent of households with income of $100,000 or more: 14.1% (2008-2012 5-year est.); Poverty rate: 27.6% (2008-2012 5-year est.).

Education: Percent of population age 25 and over with: High school diploma (including GED) or higher: 77.5% (2008-2012 5-year est.); Bachelor's degree or higher: 1.7% (2008-2012 5-year est.); Master's degree or higher: 0.8% (2008-2012 5-year est.).

Housing: Homeownership rate: 95.8% (2008-2012 5-year est.); Median home value: $78,200 (2008-2012 5-year est.); Median contract rent: n/a per month (2008-2012 5-year est.); Median year structure built: 1963 (2008-2012 5-year est.).

Health Insurance: 60.1% Private; 37.4% Public; 12.8% None. (2008-2012 5-year est.)

Transportation: Commute to work: 96.8% car, 0.0% public transportation, 0.0% walk, 3.2% work from home (2008-2012 5-year est.); Travel time to work: 8.9% less than 15 minutes, 66.7% 15 to 30 minutes, 17.8% 30 to 45 minutes, 6.7% 45 to 60 minutes, 0.0% 60 minutes or more (2008-2012 5-year est.)

COLONA (city).
Covers a land area of 4.019 square miles and a water area of 0.106 square miles. Located at 41.48° N. Lat; 90.34° W. Long. Elevation is 604 feet.

Population: 2,237 (1990); 5,173 (2000); 5,099 (2010); Density: 1,247.2 persons per square mile (2008-2012 5-year est.); Race: 92.5% White, 1.4% Black/African American, 0.0% Asian, 0.0% American Indian/Alaska Native, 0.0% Native Hawaiian/Other Pacific Islander, 6.1% Some other race, 2.1% Two or more races, 7.4% Hispanic of any race (2008-2012 5-year est.); Average household size: 2.49 (2008-2012 5-year est.); Median age: 37.4 (2008-2012 5-year est.); Males per 100 females: 95.5 (2008-2012 5-year est.); Marriage status: 25.6% never married, 58.1% now married, 5.8% widowed, 10.5% divorced (2008-2012 5-year est.); Foreign born: 1.8% (2008-2012 5-year est.); Ancestry (includes multiple ancestries): 24.4% German, 17.0% Irish, 8.6% American, 5.8% English, 4.0% Norwegian (2008-2012 5-year est.).

Economy: Single-family building permits issued: 23 (2013); Multi-family building permits issued: 2 (2013); Homeowner vacancy rate: 2.7%. Rental vacancy rate: 0.0%. (2008-2012 5-year est.); Employment by occupation: 11.9% management, business, and financial, 1.8% computer, engineering, and science, 4.3% education, legal, community service, arts, and media, 5.5% healthcare practitioners, 12.1% service, 19.8% sales and office, 21.7% natural resources, construction, and maintenance, 22.8% production, transportation, and material moving (2008-2012 5-year est.).

Income: Per capita income: $22,322 (2008-2012 5-year est.); Median household income: $48,348 (2008-2012 5-year est.); Average household income: $56,403 (2008-2012 5-year est.); Percent of households with income of $100,000 or more: 9.1% (2008-2012 5-year est.); Poverty rate: 13.4% (2008-2012 5-year est.).

Education: Percent of population age 25 and over with: High school diploma (including GED) or higher: 83.1% (2008-2012 5-year est.);

Bachelor's degree or higher: 7.4% (2008-2012 5-year est.); Master's degree or higher: 2.2% (2008-2012 5-year est.).

School District(s)
Colona SD 190 (PK-08)
    2011-12 Enrollment: 462 . . . . (309) 792-1232

Housing: Homeownership rate: 83.0% (2008-2012 5-year est.); Median home value: $97,800 (2008-2012 5-year est.); Median contract rent: $517 per month (2008-2012 5-year est.); Median year structure built: 1966 (2008-2012 5-year est.).

Health Insurance: 76.8% Private; 29.4% Public; 4.1% None. (2008-2012 5-year est.)

Transportation: Commute to work: 99.4% car, 0.0% public transportation, 0.0% walk, 0.6% work from home (2008-2012 5-year est.); Travel time to work: 22.3% less than 15 minutes, 41.2% 15 to 30 minutes, 28.4% 30 to 45 minutes, 4.5% 45 to 60 minutes, 3.6% 60 minutes or more (2008-2012 5-year est.)

Additional Information Contacts
City of Colona . . . . (309) 792-0571
    http://www.colonail.com

GALVA (city).
Covers a land area of 2.856 square miles and a water area of 0 square miles. Located at 41.17° N. Lat; 90.04° W. Long. Elevation is 850 feet.

History: Galva was founded in 1854 by a group of Swedish settlers, who named it for their home in Sweden, Gefle. These first residents had been members of the religious colony at Bishop Hill.

Population: 2,742 (1990); 2,758 (2000); 2,589 (2010); Density: 912.5 persons per square mile (2008-2012 5-year est.); Race: 98.0% White, 0.0% Black/African American, 1.3% Asian, 0.0% American Indian/Alaska Native, 0.0% Native Hawaiian/Other Pacific Islander, 0.7% Some other race, 0.7% Two or more races, 2.7% Hispanic of any race (2008-2012 5-year est.); Average household size: 2.21 (2008-2012 5-year est.); Median age: 45.0 (2008-2012 5-year est.); Males per 100 females: 112.4 (2008-2012 5-year est.); Marriage status: 23.8% never married, 55.4% now married, 11.8% widowed, 9.0% divorced (2008-2012 5-year est.); Foreign born: 2.6% (2008-2012 5-year est.); Ancestry (includes multiple ancestries): 26.1% German, 24.5% Swedish, 14.2% English, 10.4% Irish, 5.8% American (2008-2012 5-year est.).

Economy: Single-family building permits issued: 1 (2013); Multi-family building permits issued: 0 (2013); Homeowner vacancy rate: 3.0%. Rental vacancy rate: 18.8%. (2008-2012 5-year est.); Employment by occupation: 10.3% management, business, and financial, 3.9% computer, engineering, and science, 8.5% education, legal, community service, arts, and media, 6.3% healthcare practitioners, 20.9% service, 21.6% sales and office, 15.6% natural resources, construction, and maintenance, 13.0% production, transportation, and material moving (2008-2012 5-year est.).

Income: Per capita income: $25,579 (2008-2012 5-year est.); Median household income: $41,750 (2008-2012 5-year est.); Average household income: $56,090 (2008-2012 5-year est.); Percent of households with income of $100,000 or more: 11.5% (2008-2012 5-year est.); Poverty rate: 8.9% (2008-2012 5-year est.).

Education: Percent of population age 25 and over with: High school diploma (including GED) or higher: 90.1% (2008-2012 5-year est.); Bachelor's degree or higher: 15.9% (2008-2012 5-year est.); Master's degree or higher: 5.3% (2008-2012 5-year est.).

School District(s)
Galva CUSD 224 (PK-12)
    2011-12 Enrollment: 597 . . . . (309) 932-2108

Housing: Homeownership rate: 73.7% (2008-2012 5-year est.); Median home value: $74,500 (2008-2012 5-year est.); Median contract rent: $396 per month (2008-2012 5-year est.); Median year structure built: 1953 (2008-2012 5-year est.).

Health Insurance: 72.9% Private; 42.4% Public; 9.1% None. (2008-2012 5-year est.)

Transportation: Commute to work: 94.3% car, 0.0% public transportation, 2.2% walk, 1.2% work from home (2008-2012 5-year est.); Travel time to work: 44.2% less than 15 minutes, 32.3% 15 to 30 minutes, 14.4% 30 to 45 minutes, 3.7% 45 to 60 minutes, 5.5% 60 minutes or more (2008-2012 5-year est.)

GENESEO (city). Covers a land area of 4.386 square miles and a water area of 0.008 square miles. Located at 41.45° N. Lat; 90.15° W. Long. Elevation is 650 feet.

History: Geneseo was settled in 1836 by people from New York, and named for Geneseo in that state. Early industries were a corn and pea cannery, and a bandage factory.

Population: 5,990 (1990); 6,480 (2000); 6,586 (2010); Density: 1,505.6 persons per square mile (2008-2012 5-year est.); Race: 95.4% White, 0.1% Black/African American, 0.2% Asian, 0.0% American Indian/Alaska Native, 0.0% Native Hawaiian/Other Pacific Islander, 4.3% Some other race, 3.8% Two or more races, 2.3% Hispanic of any race (2008-2012 5-year est.); Average household size: 2.47 (2008-2012 5-year est.); Median age: 40.8 (2008-2012 5-year est.); Males per 100 females: 88.6 (2008-2012 5-year est.); Marriage status: 20.7% never married, 60.0% now married, 9.7% widowed, 9.6% divorced (2008-2012 5-year est.); Foreign born: 0.7% (2008-2012 5-year est.); Ancestry (includes multiple ancestries): 31.1% German, 19.6% Irish, 11.3% Swedish, 10.8% English, 8.7% Italian (2008-2012 5-year est.).

Economy: Single-family building permits issued: 2 (2013); Multi-family building permits issued: 6 (2013); Homeowner vacancy rate: 0.0%. Rental vacancy rate: 0.0%. (2008-2012 5-year est.); Employment by occupation: 13.6% management, business, and financial, 3.4% computer, engineering, and science, 8.3% education, legal, community service, arts, and media, 5.7% healthcare practitioners, 23.3% service, 28.5% sales and office, 5.6% natural resources, construction, and maintenance, 11.8% production, transportation, and material moving (2008-2012 5-year est.).

Income: Per capita income: $27,702 (2008-2012 5-year est.); Median household income: $54,583 (2008-2012 5-year est.); Average household income: $68,839 (2008-2012 5-year est.); Percent of households with income of $100,000 or more: 21.6% (2008-2012 5-year est.); Poverty rate: 5.2% (2008-2012 5-year est.).

Education: Percent of population age 25 and over with: High school diploma (including GED) or higher: 93.9% (2008-2012 5-year est.); Bachelor's degree or higher: 26.3% (2008-2012 5-year est.); Master's degree or higher: 9.4% (2008-2012 5-year est.).

School District(s)

Bureau/henry/stark Roe (06-12)
    2011-12 Enrollment: n/a . . . . (309) 936-7890
Geneseo CUSD 228 (PK-12)
    2011-12 Enrollment: 2,646 . . . . (309) 945-0450
Rock Island Roe
    2011-12 Enrollment: n/a . . . . (309) 736-1111

Housing: Homeownership rate: 75.9% (2008-2012 5-year est.); Median home value: $135,500 (2008-2012 5-year est.); Median contract rent: $578 per month (2008-2012 5-year est.); Median year structure built: 1959 (2008-2012 5-year est.).

Health Insurance: 83.2% Private; 28.7% Public; 7.7% None. (2008-2012 5-year est.)

Hospitals: Hammond-Henry Hospital (105 beds)

Safety: Violent crime rate: 6.1 per 10,000 population; Property crime rate: 146.1 per 10,000 population (2012).

Transportation: Commute to work: 94.8% car, 0.0% public transportation, 2.9% walk, 1.7% work from home (2008-2012 5-year est.); Travel time to work: 58.8% less than 15 minutes, 17.2% 15 to 30 minutes, 14.5% 30 to 45 minutes, 3.7% 45 to 60 minutes, 5.8% 60 minutes or more (2008-2012 5-year est.)

Additional Information Contacts

City of Geneseo. . . . . (309) 944-6419
    http://www.cityofgeneseo.com
Geneseo Chamber of Commerce . . . . (309) 944-2686
    http://www.geneseo.org

HOOPPOLE (village). Covers a land area of 0.343 square miles and a water area of 0 square miles. Located at 41.52° N. Lat; 89.91° W. Long. Elevation is 623 feet.

History: In a grove of hickory trees near Hooppole, coopers cut bands to use in the crafting of their barrels, and from this the town was named.

Population: 196 (1990); 162 (2000); 204 (2010); Density: 894.7 persons per square mile (2008-2012 5-year est.); Race: 95.1% White, 0.0% Black/African American, 0.0% Asian, 4.6% American Indian/Alaska Native, 0.0% Native Hawaiian/Other Pacific Islander, 0.3% Some other race, 0.3% Two or more races, 0.0% Hispanic of any race (2008-2012 5-year est.); Average household size: 2.82 (2008-2012 5-year est.); Median age: 44.1 (2008-2012 5-year est.); Males per 100 females: 86.1 (2008-2012 5-year est.); Marriage status: 18.9% never married, 62.2% now married, 6.3%

widowed, 12.6% divorced (2008-2012 5-year est.); Foreign born: 0.0% (2008-2012 5-year est.); Ancestry (includes multiple ancestries): 26.1% German, 15.6% Swedish, 8.8% Irish, 4.9% Norwegian, 4.6% Belgian (2008-2012 5-year est.).

Economy: Single-family building permits issued: 0 (2013); Multi-family building permits issued: 0 (2013); Homeowner vacancy rate: 0.0%. Rental vacancy rate: 0.0%. (2008-2012 5-year est.); Employment by occupation: 18.7% management, business, and financial, 3.3% computer, engineering, and science, 8.9% education, legal, community service, arts, and media, 1.6% healthcare practitioners, 20.3% service, 13.8% sales and office, 18.7% natural resources, construction, and maintenance, 14.6% production, transportation, and material moving (2008-2012 5-year est.).

Income: Per capita income: $17,235 (2008-2012 5-year est.); Median household income: $43,523 (2008-2012 5-year est.); Average household income: $48,499 (2008-2012 5-year est.); Percent of households with income of $100,000 or more: 2.8% (2008-2012 5-year est.); Poverty rate: 20.9% (2008-2012 5-year est.).

Education: Percent of population age 25 and over with: High school diploma (including GED) or higher: 90.3% (2008-2012 5-year est.); Bachelor's degree or higher: 11.6% (2008-2012 5-year est.); Master's degree or higher: 1.9% (2008-2012 5-year est.).

Housing: Homeownership rate: 94.5% (2008-2012 5-year est.); Median home value: $67,200 (2008-2012 5-year est.); Median contract rent: $338 per month (2008-2012 5-year est.); Median year structure built: Before 1940 (2008-2012 5-year est.).

Health Insurance: 67.8% Private; 45.6% Public; 8.8% None. (2008-2012 5-year est.)

Transportation: Commute to work: 94.1% car, 0.0% public transportation, 2.5% walk, 1.7% work from home (2008-2012 5-year est.); Travel time to work: 6.8% less than 15 minutes, 42.7% 15 to 30 minutes, 14.5% 30 to 45 minutes, 29.1% 45 to 60 minutes, 6.8% 60 minutes or more (2008-2012 5-year est.)

KEWANEE (city). Covers a land area of 6.711 square miles and a water area of 0.012 square miles. Located at 41.24° N. Lat; 89.93° W. Long. Elevation is 850 feet.

History: Kewanee was established in 1836 by the Connecticut Association to promote Protestantism in Illinois. The town was first called Wethersfield after the town in Connecticut. When the railroad line was laid a mile north, a settlement developed around the depot. By 1857 the new settlement, named Kewanee, had surpassed the older Wethersfield, which was incorporated with Kewanee in 1924.

Population: 12,969 (1990); 12,944 (2000); 12,916 (2010); Density: 1,922.6 persons per square mile (2008-2012 5-year est.); Race: 88.3% White, 3.8% Black/African American, 0.2% Asian, 0.3% American Indian/Alaska Native, 0.0% Native Hawaiian/Other Pacific Islander, 7.4% Some other race, 1.7% Two or more races, 12.0% Hispanic of any race (2008-2012 5-year est.); Average household size: 2.36 (2008-2012 5-year est.); Median age: 38.5 (2008-2012 5-year est.); Males per 100 females: 101.7 (2008-2012 5-year est.); Marriage status: 29.2% never married, 45.5% now married, 9.9% widowed, 15.4% divorced (2008-2012 5-year est.); Foreign born: 5.7% (2008-2012 5-year est.); Ancestry (includes multiple ancestries): 24.6% German, 12.4% Irish, 9.5% English, 7.3% Swedish, 6.7% Belgian (2008-2012 5-year est.).

Economy: Single-family building permits issued: 2 (2013); Multi-family building permits issued: 0 (2013); Homeowner vacancy rate: 2.2%. Rental vacancy rate: 3.8%. (2008-2012 5-year est.); Employment by occupation: 6.9% management, business, and financial, 3.7% computer, engineering, and science, 7.1% education, legal, community service, arts, and media, 4.2% healthcare practitioners, 20.8% service, 23.6% sales and office, 10.9% natural resources, construction, and maintenance, 22.7% production, transportation, and material moving (2008-2012 5-year est.).

Income: Per capita income: $21,124 (2008-2012 5-year est.); Median household income: $37,813 (2008-2012 5-year est.); Average household income: $50,597 (2008-2012 5-year est.); Percent of households with income of $100,000 or more: 9.6% (2008-2012 5-year est.); Poverty rate: 18.0% (2008-2012 5-year est.).

Education: Percent of population age 25 and over with: High school diploma (including GED) or higher: 79.1% (2008-2012 5-year est.); Bachelor's degree or higher: 14.7% (2008-2012 5-year est.); Master's degree or higher: 5.0% (2008-2012 5-year est.).

School District(s)

Idjj SD 428 (06-12)
    2011-12 Enrollment: 784 . . . . (309) 584-0506

Kewanee CUSD 229 (PK-12)
   2011-12 Enrollment: 1,904 . . . . (309) 853-3341
Wethersfield CUSD 230 (PK-12)
   2011-12 Enrollment: 684 . . . . (309) 853-4860
Housing: Homeownership rate: 68.8% (2008-2012 5-year est.); Median home value: $62,600 (2008-2012 5-year est.); Median contract rent: $431 per month (2008-2012 5-year est.); Median year structure built: 1945 (2008-2012 5-year est.).
Health Insurance: 58.3% Private; 43.4% Public; 15.4% None. (2008-2012 5-year est.)
Hospitals: Kewanee Hospital (82 beds)
Safety: Violent crime rate: 31.8 per 10,000 population; Property crime rate: 381.9 per 10,000 population (2012).
Transportation: Commute to work: 96.0% car, 0.4% public transportation, 0.9% walk, 1.4% work from home (2008-2012 5-year est.); Travel time to work: 54.6% less than 15 minutes, 19.6% 15 to 30 minutes, 11.1% 30 to 45 minutes, 6.8% 45 to 60 minutes, 7.9% 60 minutes or more (2008-2012 5-year est.); Amtrak: Train service available.
Airports: Kewanee Municipal Airport (general aviation)
Additional Information Contacts
City of Kewanee . . . . (309) 852-2611
   http://cityofkewanee.com
Kewanee Chamber of Commerce . . . . (309) 852-2175
   http://www.kewanee-il.com

LYNN CENTER (unincorporated postal area)
Zip Code: 61262

Covers a land area of 43.031 square miles and a water area of 0.035 square miles. Located at 41.27° N. Lat; 90.34° W. Long. Elevation is 758 feet. Population: 1,188 (2010); Density: 27.6 persons per square mile (2010); Race: 98.5% White, 0.4% Black/African American, 0.3% Asian, 0.1% American Indian/Alaska Native, 0.0% Native Hawaiian/Other Pacific Islander, 0.7% Some other race, 0.5% Two or more races, 2.4% Hispanic of any race (2010); Average household size: 2.51 (2010); Median age: 45.6 (2010); Males per 100 females: 104.5 (2010); Homeownership rate: 87.5% (2010)

OPHEIM (unincorporated postal area)
Zip Code: 61468

Covers a land area of 1.948 square miles and a water area of 0 square miles. Located at 41.25° N. Lat; 90.38° W. Long. Population: 104 (2010); Density: 53.4 persons per square mile (2010); Race: 98.1% White, 1.0% Black/African American, 0.0% Asian, 0.0% American Indian/Alaska Native, 0.0% Native Hawaiian/Other Pacific Islander, 0.9% Some other race, 1.0% Two or more races, 2.9% Hispanic of any race (2010); Average household size: 2.89 (2010); Median age: 36.8 (2010); Males per 100 females: 116.7 (2010); Homeownership rate: 91.6% (2010)

ORION (village). Covers a land area of 0.913 square miles and a water area of 0 square miles. Located at 41.35° N. Lat; 90.38° W. Long. Elevation is 774 feet.
Population: 1,821 (1990); 1,713 (2000); 1,861 (2010); Density: 2,118.5 persons per square mile (2008-2012 5-year est.); Race: 97.1% White, 0.0% Black/African American, 0.2% Asian, 0.0% American Indian/Alaska Native, 0.0% Native Hawaiian/Other Pacific Islander, 2.7% Some other race, 2.5% Two or more races, 1.8% Hispanic of any race (2008-2012 5-year est.); Average household size: 2.49 (2008-2012 5-year est.); Median age: 40.8 (2008-2012 5-year est.); Males per 100 females: 95.2 (2008-2012 5-year est.); Marriage status: 17.6% never married, 68.2% now married, 5.0% widowed, 9.2% divorced (2008-2012 5-year est.); Foreign born: 0.7% (2008-2012 5-year est.); Ancestry (includes multiple ancestries): 32.5% German, 18.0% Swedish, 16.9% Irish, 8.2% English, 8.1% Belgian (2008-2012 5-year est.).
Economy: Single-family building permits issued: 1 (2013); Multi-family building permits issued: 0 (2013); Homeowner vacancy rate: 2.2%. Rental vacancy rate: 0.0%. (2008-2012 5-year est.); Employment by occupation: 15.4% management, business, and financial, 2.9% computer, engineering, and science, 9.6% education, legal, community service, arts, and media, 2.9% healthcare practitioners, 11.8% service, 27.3% sales and office, 7.8% natural resources, construction, and maintenance, 22.5% production, transportation, and material moving (2008-2012 5-year est.).
Income: Per capita income: $30,115 (2008-2012 5-year est.); Median household income: $65,700 (2008-2012 5-year est.); Average household income: $74,706 (2008-2012 5-year est.); Percent of households with

income of $100,000 or more: 24.6% (2008-2012 5-year est.); Poverty rate: 2.8% (2008-2012 5-year est.).
Education: Percent of population age 25 and over with: High school diploma (including GED) or higher: 93.7% (2008-2012 5-year est.); Bachelor's degree or higher: 24.2% (2008-2012 5-year est.); Master's degree or higher: 6.8% (2008-2012 5-year est.).
         School District(s)
Orion CUSD 223 (PK-12)
   2011-12 Enrollment: 1,066 . . . . (309) 526-3388
Housing: Homeownership rate: 85.3% (2008-2012 5-year est.); Median home value: $131,600 (2008-2012 5-year est.); Median contract rent: $496 per month (2008-2012 5-year est.); Median year structure built: 1963 (2008-2012 5-year est.).
Health Insurance: 86.3% Private; 23.9% Public; 5.1% None. (2008-2012 5-year est.)
Safety: Violent crime rate: 0.0 per 10,000 population; Property crime rate: 59.3 per 10,000 population (2012).
Transportation: Commute to work: 97.0% car, 0.0% public transportation, 0.0% walk, 2.5% work from home (2008-2012 5-year est.); Travel time to work: 21.6% less than 15 minutes, 47.7% 15 to 30 minutes, 25.0% 30 to 45 minutes, 2.0% 45 to 60 minutes, 3.8% 60 minutes or more (2008-2012 5-year est.)

OSCO (unincorporated postal area)
Zip Code: 61274

Covers a land area of 24.445 square miles and a water area of 0 square miles. Located at 41.36° N. Lat; 90.27° W. Long. Elevation is 771 feet. Population: 351 (2010); Density: 14.4 persons per square mile (2010); Race: 97.4% White, 0.9% Black/African American, 0.3% Asian, 0.0% American Indian/Alaska Native, 0.0% Native Hawaiian/Other Pacific Islander, 1.4% Some other race, 1.4% Two or more races, 1.7% Hispanic of any race (2010); Average household size: 2.56 (2010); Median age: 42.6 (2010); Males per 100 females: 123.6 (2010); Homeownership rate: 70.1% (2010)

WOODHULL (village). Covers a land area of 0.825 square miles and a water area of 0 square miles. Located at 41.18° N. Lat; 90.32° W. Long. Elevation is 810 feet.
Population: 808 (1990); 809 (2000); 811 (2010); Density: 1,029.4 persons per square mile (2008-2012 5-year est.); Race: 96.3% White, 0.2% Black/African American, 0.0% Asian, 0.2% American Indian/Alaska Native, 0.0% Native Hawaiian/Other Pacific Islander, 3.3% Some other race, 1.8% Two or more races, 3.8% Hispanic of any race (2008-2012 5-year est.); Average household size: 2.48 (2008-2012 5-year est.); Median age: 42.4 (2008-2012 5-year est.); Males per 100 females: 94.3 (2008-2012 5-year est.); Marriage status: 20.7% never married, 63.3% now married, 5.4% widowed, 10.6% divorced (2008-2012 5-year est.); Foreign born: 1.4% (2008-2012 5-year est.); Ancestry (includes multiple ancestries): 27.3% Swedish, 23.7% German, 19.3% Irish, 13.3% English, 8.8% American (2008-2012 5-year est.).
Economy: Single-family building permits issued: 0 (2013); Multi-family building permits issued: 0 (2013); Homeowner vacancy rate: 0.0%. Rental vacancy rate: 0.0%. (2008-2012 5-year est.); Employment by occupation: 9.1% management, business, and financial, 1.5% computer, engineering, and science, 11.3% education, legal, community service, arts, and media, 4.2% healthcare practitioners, 14.6% service, 25.4% sales and office, 11.3% natural resources, construction, and maintenance, 22.6% production, transportation, and material moving (2008-2012 5-year est.).
Income: Per capita income: $26,238 (2008-2012 5-year est.); Median household income: $54,141 (2008-2012 5-year est.); Average household income: $62,721 (2008-2012 5-year est.); Percent of households with income of $100,000 or more: 16.2% (2008-2012 5-year est.); Poverty rate: 15.5% (2008-2012 5-year est.).
Education: Percent of population age 25 and over with: High school diploma (including GED) or higher: 91.2% (2008-2012 5-year est.); Bachelor's degree or higher: 15.4% (2008-2012 5-year est.); Master's degree or higher: 4.1% (2008-2012 5-year est.).
         School District(s)
Alwood CUSD 225 (PK-12)
   2011-12 Enrollment: 439 . . . . (309) 334-2719
Housing: Homeownership rate: 81.2% (2008-2012 5-year est.); Median home value: $89,000 (2008-2012 5-year est.); Median contract rent: $414 per month (2008-2012 5-year est.); Median year structure built: 1950 (2008-2012 5-year est.).

Health Insurance: 77.0% Private; 32.7% Public; 6.1% None. (2008-2012 5-year est.)

Safety: Violent crime rate: 0.0 per 10,000 population; Property crime rate: 49.4 per 10,000 population (2012).

Transportation: Commute to work: 93.6% car, 0.0% public transportation, 2.7% walk, 1.4% work from home (2008-2012 5-year est.); Travel time to work: 39.0% less than 15 minutes, 24.4% 15 to 30 minutes, 17.6% 30 to 45 minutes, 12.3% 45 to 60 minutes, 6.7% 60 minutes or more (2008-2012 5-year est.)

Iroquois County

Located in eastern Illinois; bounded on the east by Indiana; drained by the Iroquois River and Sugar Creek. Covers a land area of 1,117.316 square miles, a water area of 1.611 square miles, and is located in the Central Time Zone at 40.75° N. Lat., 87.83° W. Long. The county was founded in 1833. County seat is Watseka.

Weather Station: Watseka 2 NW   Elevation: 620 feet

	Jan	Feb	Mar	Apr	May	Jun	Jul	Aug	Sep	Oct	Nov	Dec
High	32	37	48	61	72	82	84	83	78	64	50	36
Low	16	19	28	38	49	59	63	60	52	40	32	20
Precip	1.8	1.7	2.9	3.8	4.0	4.2	4.4	3.5	3.3	3.3	3.2	2.5
Snow	5.8	5.0	1.9	0.8	0.0	0.0	0.0	0.0	0.0	tr	0.7	5.2

High and Low temperatures in degrees Fahrenheit; Precipitation and Snow in inches

Population: 30,787 (1990); 31,334 (2000); 29,718 (2010); Race: 96.1% White, 1.1% Black/African American, 0.5% Asian, 0.2% American Indian/Alaska Native, 0.0% Native Hawaiian/Other Pacific Islander, 2.1% Some other race, 0.9% Two or more races, 5.5% Hispanic of any race (2008-2012 5-year est.); Density: 26.2 persons per square mile (2008-2012 5-year est.); Average household size: 2.43 (2008-2012 5-year est.); Median age: 43.2 (2008-2012 5-year est.); Males per 100 females: 96.4 (2008-2012 5-year est.).

Religion: Six largest groups: 17.6% Lutheran, 13.1% Catholicism, 10.1% Methodist/Pietist, 5.8% Baptist, 2.4% Presbyterian-Reformed, 1.3% Non-denominational Protestant (2010)

Economy: Unemployment rate: 6.5% (April 2014); Total civilian labor force: 15,598 (April 2014); Leading industries: 25.7% health care and social assistance; 16.2% retail trade; 11.2% wholesale trade (2012); Farms: 1,470 totaling 669,280 acres (2012); Companies that employ 500 or more persons: 0 (2012); Companies that employ 100 to 499 persons: 8 (2012); Companies that employ less than 100 persons: 710 (2012); Black-owned businesses: n/a (2007); Hispanic-owned businesses: n/a (2007); Asian-owned businesses: n/a (2007); Women-owned businesses: 646 (2007); Single-family building permits issued: 25 (2013); Multi-family building permits issued: 3 (2013).

Income: Per capita income: $24,884 (2008-2012 5-year est.); Median household income: $47,908 (2008-2012 5-year est.); Average household income: $61,741 (2008-2012 5-year est.); Percent of households with income of $100,000 or more: 14.8% (2008-2012 5-year est.); Poverty rate: 11.7% (2008-2012 5-year est.); Bankruptcy rate: 3.15% (2013).

Taxes: Total county taxes per capita: $141 (2011); County property taxes per capita: $132 (2011).

Education: Percent of population age 25 and over with: High school diploma (including GED) or higher: 87.7% (2008-2012 5-year est.); Bachelor's degree or higher: 14.1% (2008-2012 5-year est.); Master's degree or higher: 4.2% (2008-2012 5-year est.).

Housing: Homeownership rate: 75.8% (2008-2012 5-year est.); Median home value: $99,400 (2008-2012 5-year est.); Median contract rent: $477 per month (2008-2012 5-year est.); Median year structure built: 1957 (2008-2012 5-year est.)

Health: Birth rate: 106.3 per 10,000 population (2013); Death rate: 113.2 per 10,000 population (2013); Age-adjusted cancer mortality rate: 195.0 deaths per 100,000 population (2011); Number of physicians: 7.1 per 10,000 population (2011); Hospital beds: 30.3 per 10,000 population (2010); Hospital admissions: 710.3 per 10,000 population (2010).

Elections: 2012 Presidential election results: 26.7% Obama, 71.4% Romney

National and State Parks: Iroquois County State Conservation Area

Additional Information Contacts

Iroquois County Government . . . . (815) 432-6960
    http://www.co.iroquois.il.us

Iroquois County Communities

ASHKUM (village). Covers a land area of 0.805 square miles and a water area of 0 square miles. Located at 40.88° N. Lat; 87.95° W. Long. Elevation is 669 feet.

Population: 650 (1990); 724 (2000); 761 (2010); Density: 818.8 persons per square mile (2008-2012 5-year est.); Race: 97.9% White, 0.5% Black/African American, 0.0% Asian, 0.0% American Indian/Alaska Native, 0.0% Native Hawaiian/Other Pacific Islander, 1.6% Some other race, 1.7% Two or more races, 0.5% Hispanic of any race (2008-2012 5-year est.); Average household size: 2.62 (2008-2012 5-year est.); Median age: 31.6 (2008-2012 5-year est.); Males per 100 females: 98.5 (2008-2012 5-year est.); Marriage status: 24.0% never married, 56.5% now married, 6.5% widowed, 13.1% divorced (2008-2012 5-year est.); Foreign born: 0.0% (2008-2012 5-year est.); Ancestry (includes multiple ancestries): 39.5% German, 22.2% Irish, 16.1% French, 12.9% American, 7.0% English (2008-2012 5-year est.).

Economy: Single-family building permits issued: 2 (2013); Multi-family building permits issued: 0 (2013); Homeowner vacancy rate: 5.0%. Rental vacancy rate: 2.4%. (2008-2012 5-year est.); Employment by occupation: 9.7% management, business, and financial, 2.8% computer, engineering, and science, 6.6% education, legal, community service, arts, and media, 4.4% healthcare practitioners, 10.7% service, 39.2% sales and office, 11.0% natural resources, construction, and maintenance, 15.7% production, transportation, and material moving (2008-2012 5-year est.).

Income: Per capita income: $25,128 (2008-2012 5-year est.); Median household income: $48,929 (2008-2012 5-year est.); Average household income: $64,113 (2008-2012 5-year est.); Percent of households with income of $100,000 or more: 8.4% (2008-2012 5-year est.); Poverty rate: 8.1% (2008-2012 5-year est.).

Education: Percent of population age 25 and over with: High school diploma (including GED) or higher: 90.8% (2008-2012 5-year est.); Bachelor's degree or higher: 12.6% (2008-2012 5-year est.); Master's degree or higher: 2.1% (2008-2012 5-year est.).

School District(s)

Central CUSD 4 (PK-12)
    2011-12 Enrollment: 1,129 . . . . (815) 694-2231

Housing: Homeownership rate: 67.9% (2008-2012 5-year est.); Median home value: $124,600 (2008-2012 5-year est.); Median contract rent: $541 per month (2008-2012 5-year est.); Median year structure built: 1955 (2008-2012 5-year est.).

Health Insurance: 83.3% Private; 25.2% Public; 6.4% None. (2008-2012 5-year est.)

Transportation: Commute to work: 90.7% car, 0.0% public transportation, 2.9% walk, 4.8% work from home (2008-2012 5-year est.); Travel time to work: 35.7% less than 15 minutes, 35.4% 15 to 30 minutes, 20.5% 30 to 45 minutes, 6.7% 45 to 60 minutes, 1.7% 60 minutes or more (2008-2012 5-year est.)

BEAVERVILLE (village). Covers a land area of 0.262 square miles and a water area of 0.005 square miles. Located at 40.95° N. Lat; 87.65° W. Long. Elevation is 676 feet.

Population: 278 (1990); 391 (2000); 362 (2010); Density: 1,395.2 persons per square mile (2008-2012 5-year est.); Race: 93.4% White, 0.0% Black/African American, 0.5% Asian, 1.1% American Indian/Alaska Native, 0.0% Native Hawaiian/Other Pacific Islander, 5.0% Some other race, 3.0% Two or more races, 6.8% Hispanic of any race (2008-2012 5-year est.); Average household size: 2.49 (2008-2012 5-year est.); Median age: 34.0 (2008-2012 5-year est.); Males per 100 females: 101.1 (2008-2012 5-year est.); Marriage status: 21.7% never married, 55.4% now married, 8.9% widowed, 14.0% divorced (2008-2012 5-year est.); Foreign born: 1.1% (2008-2012 5-year est.); Ancestry (includes multiple ancestries): 24.0% German, 19.7% French, 17.8% Irish, 13.9% American, 7.7% French Canadian (2008-2012 5-year est.).

Economy: Single-family building permits issued: 1 (2013); Multi-family building permits issued: 0 (2013); Homeowner vacancy rate: 1.6%. Rental vacancy rate: 0.0%. (2008-2012 5-year est.); Employment by occupation: 7.1% management, business, and financial, 0.8% computer, engineering, and science, 3.1% education, legal, community service, arts, and media, 1.6% healthcare practitioners, 18.1% service, 29.1% sales and office, 18.9% natural resources, construction, and maintenance, 21.3% production, transportation, and material moving (2008-2012 5-year est.).

Income: Per capita income: $18,975 (2008-2012 5-year est.); Median household income: $37,625 (2008-2012 5-year est.); Average household

income: $47,403 (2008-2012 5-year est.); Percent of households with income of $100,000 or more: 8.8% (2008-2012 5-year est.); Poverty rate: 23.5% (2008-2012 5-year est.).

Education: Percent of population age 25 and over with: High school diploma (including GED) or higher: 81.0% (2008-2012 5-year est.); Bachelor's degree or higher: 9.0% (2008-2012 5-year est.); Master's degree or higher: 2.7% (2008-2012 5-year est.).

Housing: Homeownership rate: 81.6% (2008-2012 5-year est.); Median home value: $82,700 (2008-2012 5-year est.); Median contract rent: $479 per month (2008-2012 5-year est.); Median year structure built: 1953 (2008-2012 5-year est.).

Health Insurance: 53.0% Private; 54.6% Public; 8.5% None. (2008-2012 5-year est.)

Transportation: Commute to work: 94.5% car, 0.0% public transportation, 1.6% walk, 3.1% work from home (2008-2012 5-year est.); Travel time to work: 20.3% less than 15 minutes, 32.5% 15 to 30 minutes, 31.7% 30 to 45 minutes, 11.4% 45 to 60 minutes, 4.1% 60 minutes or more (2008-2012 5-year est.)

BUCKLEY (village). Covers a land area of 0.337 square miles and a water area of 0.006 square miles. Located at 40.60° N. Lat; 88.04° W. Long. Elevation is 702 feet.

Population: 557 (1990); 593 (2000); 600 (2010); Density: 1,715.9 persons per square mile (2008-2012 5-year est.); Race: 98.8% White, 0.0% Black/African American, 0.0% Asian, 0.0% American Indian/Alaska Native, 0.0% Native Hawaiian/Other Pacific Islander, 1.2% Some other race, 0.0% Two or more races, 9.7% Hispanic of any race (2008-2012 5-year est.); Average household size: 2.41 (2008-2012 5-year est.); Median age: 45.0 (2008-2012 5-year est.); Males per 100 females: 83.2 (2008-2012 5-year est.); Marriage status: 28.2% never married, 57.3% now married, 9.1% widowed, 5.4% divorced (2008-2012 5-year est.); Foreign born: 2.1% (2008-2012 5-year est.); Ancestry (includes multiple ancestries): 50.3% German, 16.8% American, 5.9% Irish, 5.9% English, 3.6% Italian (2008-2012 5-year est.).

Economy: Single-family building permits issued: 0 (2013); Multi-family building permits issued: 0 (2013); Homeowner vacancy rate: 4.5%. Rental vacancy rate: 0.0%. (2008-2012 5-year est.); Employment by occupation: 10.0% management, business, and financial, 3.9% computer, engineering, and science, 6.8% education, legal, community service, arts, and media, 5.7% healthcare practitioners, 12.5% service, 34.5% sales and office, 10.3% natural resources, construction, and maintenance, 16.4% production, transportation, and material moving (2008-2012 5-year est.).

Income: Per capita income: $23,833 (2008-2012 5-year est.); Median household income: $49,773 (2008-2012 5-year est.); Average household income: $56,231 (2008-2012 5-year est.); Percent of households with income of $100,000 or more: 9.2% (2008-2012 5-year est.); Poverty rate: 9.5% (2008-2012 5-year est.).

Education: Percent of population age 25 and over with: High school diploma (including GED) or higher: 95.7% (2008-2012 5-year est.); Bachelor's degree or higher: 7.1% (2008-2012 5-year est.); Master's degree or higher: 1.5% (2008-2012 5-year est.).

Housing: Homeownership rate: 79.6% (2008-2012 5-year est.); Median home value: $83,700 (2008-2012 5-year est.); Median contract rent: $428 per month (2008-2012 5-year est.); Median year structure built: 1944 (2008-2012 5-year est.).

Health Insurance: 72.5% Private; 31.8% Public; 9.7% None. (2008-2012 5-year est.)

Transportation: Commute to work: 94.3% car, 0.0% public transportation, 5.7% walk, 0.0% work from home (2008-2012 5-year est.); Travel time to work: 31.0% less than 15 minutes, 20.3% 15 to 30 minutes, 21.4% 30 to 45 minutes, 14.9% 45 to 60 minutes, 12.5% 60 minutes or more (2008-2012 5-year est.)

CHEBANSE (village). Covers a land area of 1.186 square miles and a water area of 0 square miles. Located at 41.01° N. Lat; 87.91° W. Long.

History: Chebanse developed as an agricultural community, settled by many people of German descent.

Population: 1,082 (1990); 1,148 (2000); 1,062 (2010); Density: 1,017.7 persons per square mile (2008-2012 5-year est.); Race: 96.3% White, 0.0% Black/African American, 0.8% Asian, 0.4% American Indian/Alaska Native, 0.0% Native Hawaiian/Other Pacific Islander, 2.5% Some other race, 2.5% Two or more races, 0.0% Hispanic of any race (2008-2012 5-year est.); Average household size: 2.76 (2008-2012 5-year est.); Median age: 33.4 (2008-2012 5-year est.); Males per 100 females: 100.2 (2008-2012 5-year est.); Marriage status: 32.4% never married, 52.1%

now married, 4.8% widowed, 10.7% divorced (2008-2012 5-year est.); Foreign born: 1.4% (2008-2012 5-year est.); Ancestry (includes multiple ancestries): 37.0% German, 21.1% French, 18.5% Irish, 13.7% Polish, 12.9% American (2008-2012 5-year est.).

Economy: Single-family building permits issued: 0 (2013); Multi-family building permits issued: 0 (2013); Homeowner vacancy rate: 0.9%. Rental vacancy rate: 8.1%. (2008-2012 5-year est.); Employment by occupation: 9.8% management, business, and financial, 2.7% computer, engineering, and science, 5.1% education, legal, community service, arts, and media, 5.1% healthcare practitioners, 18.1% service, 23.1% sales and office, 19.8% natural resources, construction, and maintenance, 16.2% production, transportation, and material moving (2008-2012 5-year est.).

Income: Per capita income: $26,388 (2008-2012 5-year est.); Median household income: $59,783 (2008-2012 5-year est.); Average household income: $71,285 (2008-2012 5-year est.); Percent of households with income of $100,000 or more: 20.0% (2008-2012 5-year est.); Poverty rate: 6.0% (2008-2012 5-year est.).

Education: Percent of population age 25 and over with: High school diploma (including GED) or higher: 92.4% (2008-2012 5-year est.); Bachelor's degree or higher: 12.5% (2008-2012 5-year est.); Master's degree or higher: 2.9% (2008-2012 5-year est.).

School District(s)

Central CUSD 4 (PK-12)
    2011-12 Enrollment: 1,129 . . . . (815) 694-2231

Housing: Homeownership rate: 71.5% (2008-2012 5-year est.); Median home value: $133,600 (2008-2012 5-year est.); Median contract rent: $641 per month (2008-2012 5-year est.); Median year structure built: 1953 (2008-2012 5-year est.).

Health Insurance: 70.1% Private; 28.3% Public; 13.9% None. (2008-2012 5-year est.)

Safety: Violent crime rate: 0.0 per 10,000 population; Property crime rate: 19.0 per 10,000 population (2012).

Transportation: Commute to work: 91.9% car, 1.9% public transportation, 0.8% walk, 5.5% work from home (2008-2012 5-year est.); Travel time to work: 25.3% less than 15 minutes, 51.8% 15 to 30 minutes, 9.8% 30 to 45 minutes, 2.5% 45 to 60 minutes, 10.6% 60 minutes or more (2008-2012 5-year est.)

CISSNA PARK (village). Covers a land area of 0.700 square miles and a water area of 0 square miles. Located at 40.57° N. Lat; 87.89° W. Long. Elevation is 666 feet.

History: Cissna Park developed as the center of a community of members of the Apostolic Church, known as New Amish, led by Samuel Frolich of Switzerland.

Population: 805 (1990); 811 (2000); 846 (2010); Density: 1,260.7 persons per square mile (2008-2012 5-year est.); Race: 100.0% White, 0.0% Black/African American, 0.0% Asian, 0.0% American Indian/Alaska Native, 0.0% Native Hawaiian/Other Pacific Islander, 0.0% Some other race, 0.0% Two or more races, 0.0% Hispanic of any race (2008-2012 5-year est.); Average household size: 2.16 (2008-2012 5-year est.); Median age: 48.3 (2008-2012 5-year est.); Males per 100 females: 85.3 (2008-2012 5-year est.); Marriage status: 20.4% never married, 56.6% now married, 15.4% widowed, 7.7% divorced (2008-2012 5-year est.); Foreign born: 0.5% (2008-2012 5-year est.); Ancestry (includes multiple ancestries): 60.2% German, 15.9% American, 12.5% Irish, 6.3% Swedish, 5.1% English (2008-2012 5-year est.).

Economy: Single-family building permits issued: 0 (2013); Multi-family building permits issued: 0 (2013); Homeowner vacancy rate: 0.0%. Rental vacancy rate: 0.0%. (2008-2012 5-year est.); Employment by occupation: 11.9% management, business, and financial, 0.0% computer, engineering, and science, 14.8% education, legal, community service, arts, and media, 5.9% healthcare practitioners, 15.0% service, 25.5% sales and office, 15.9% natural resources, construction, and maintenance, 11.0% production, transportation, and material moving (2008-2012 5-year est.).

Income: Per capita income: $23,344 (2008-2012 5-year est.); Median household income: $42,875 (2008-2012 5-year est.); Average household income: $50,592 (2008-2012 5-year est.); Percent of households with income of $100,000 or more: 12.9% (2008-2012 5-year est.); Poverty rate: 9.1% (2008-2012 5-year est.).

Education: Percent of population age 25 and over with: High school diploma (including GED) or higher: 94.6% (2008-2012 5-year est.); Bachelor's degree or higher: 13.3% (2008-2012 5-year est.); Master's degree or higher: 4.8% (2008-2012 5-year est.).

Cissna Park CUSD 6 (KG-12)
2011-12 Enrollment: 306 . . . . (815) 457-2171
Housing: Homeownership rate: 73.7% (2008-2012 5-year est.); Median home value: $90,400 (2008-2012 5-year est.); Median contract rent: $280 per month (2008-2012 5-year est.); Median year structure built: 1960 (2008-2012 5-year est.).
Health Insurance: 77.3% Private; 39.3% Public; 9.0% None. (2008-2012 5-year est.)
Transportation: Commute to work: 84.2% car, 1.9% public transportation, 9.6% walk, 4.3% work from home (2008-2012 5-year est.); Travel time to work: 50.1% less than 15 minutes, 22.3% 15 to 30 minutes, 15.0% 30 to 45 minutes, 5.8% 45 to 60 minutes, 6.8% 60 minutes or more (2008-2012 5-year est.)

CLAYTONVILLE (unincorporated postal area)
Zip Code: 60926
Covers a land area of 2.764 square miles and a water area of 0 square miles. Located at 40.56° N. Lat; 87.82° W. Long. Elevation is 659 feet. Population: 67 (2010); Density: 24.2 persons per square mile (2010); Race: 91.0% White, 0.0% Black/African American, 0.0% Asian, 0.0% American Indian/Alaska Native, 0.0% Native Hawaiian/Other Pacific Islander, 9.0% Some other race, 0.0% Two or more races, 9.0% Hispanic of any race (2010); Average household size: 2.31 (2010); Median age: 34.5 (2010); Males per 100 females: 103.0 (2010); Homeownership rate: 86.2% (2010)

CLIFTON (village). Covers a land area of 0.881 square miles and a water area of 0 square miles. Located at 40.93° N. Lat; 87.93° W. Long. Elevation is 669 feet.
Population: 1,347 (1990); 1,317 (2000); 1,468 (2010); Density: 1,684.1 persons per square mile (2008-2012 5-year est.); Race: 98.2% White, 0.0% Black/African American, 0.3% Asian, 0.0% American Indian/Alaska Native, 0.0% Native Hawaiian/Other Pacific Islander, 1.5% Some other race, 1.5% Two or more races, 0.0% Hispanic of any race (2008-2012 5-year est.); Average household size: 2.56 (2008-2012 5-year est.); Median age: 33.0 (2008-2012 5-year est.); Males per 100 females: 87.5 (2008-2012 5-year est.); Marriage status: 25.3% never married, 58.6% now married, 6.0% widowed, 10.2% divorced (2008-2012 5-year est.); Foreign born: 1.8% (2008-2012 5-year est.); Ancestry (includes multiple ancestries): 33.5% German, 22.6% Irish, 17.5% American, 13.0% French, 8.1% English (2008-2012 5-year est.).
Economy: Single-family building permits issued: 1 (2013); Multi-family building permits issued: 0 (2013); Homeowner vacancy rate: 0.0%. Rental vacancy rate: 0.0%. (2008-2012 5-year est.); Employment by occupation: 12.8% management, business, and financial, 2.4% computer, engineering, and science, 9.6% education, legal, community service, arts, and media, 8.3% healthcare practitioners, 16.5% service, 19.1% sales and office, 15.6% natural resources, construction, and maintenance, 15.5% production, transportation, and material moving (2008-2012 5-year est.).
Income: Per capita income: $26,227 (2008-2012 5-year est.); Median household income: $60,345 (2008-2012 5-year est.); Average household income: $67,717 (2008-2012 5-year est.); Percent of households with income of $100,000 or more: 16.9% (2008-2012 5-year est.); Poverty rate: 4.2% (2008-2012 5-year est.).
Education: Percent of population age 25 and over with: High school diploma (including GED) or higher: 95.4% (2008-2012 5-year est.); Bachelor's degree or higher: 14.5% (2008-2012 5-year est.); Master's degree or higher: 4.5% (2008-2012 5-year est.).
Central CUSD 4 (PK-12)
2011-12 Enrollment: 1,129 . . . . (815) 694-2231
Housing: Homeownership rate: 70.6% (2008-2012 5-year est.); Median home value: $136,500 (2008-2012 5-year est.); Median contract rent: $548 per month (2008-2012 5-year est.); Median year structure built: 1960 (2008-2012 5-year est.).
Health Insurance: 82.3% Private; 25.0% Public; 7.8% None. (2008-2012 5-year est.)
Transportation: Commute to work: 92.1% car, 0.0% public transportation, 4.4% walk, 2.2% work from home (2008-2012 5-year est.); Travel time to work: 28.7% less than 15 minutes, 45.4% 15 to 30 minutes, 19.6% 30 to 45 minutes, 2.2% 45 to 60 minutes, 4.1% 60 minutes or more (2008-2012 5-year est.)

CRESCENT CITY (village). Aka Crescent. Covers a land area of 0.504 square miles and a water area of 0 square miles. Located at 40.77° N. Lat; 87.86° W. Long. Elevation is 640 feet.
Population: 541 (1990); 631 (2000); 615 (2010); Density: 1,152.4 persons per square mile (2008-2012 5-year est.); Race: 98.5% White, 0.0% Black/African American, 1.5% Asian, 0.0% American Indian/Alaska Native, 0.0% Native Hawaiian/Other Pacific Islander, 0.0% Some other race, 0.0% Two or more races, 1.4% Hispanic of any race (2008-2012 5-year est.); Average household size: 2.31 (2008-2012 5-year est.); Median age: 43.3 (2008-2012 5-year est.); Males per 100 females: 86.8 (2008-2012 5-year est.); Marriage status: 22.2% never married, 59.4% now married, 8.3% widowed, 10.1% divorced (2008-2012 5-year est.); Foreign born: 0.5% (2008-2012 5-year est.); Ancestry (includes multiple ancestries): 52.3% German, 17.0% Irish, 13.4% American, 8.8% English, 6.0% French (2008-2012 5-year est.).
Economy: Single-family building permits issued: 0 (2013); Multi-family building permits issued: 0 (2013); Homeowner vacancy rate: 0.0%. Rental vacancy rate: 0.0%. (2008-2012 5-year est.); Employment by occupation: 7.4% management, business, and financial, 2.5% computer, engineering, and science, 13.2% education, legal, community service, arts, and media, 8.3% healthcare practitioners, 15.4% service, 20.6% sales and office, 20.9% natural resources, construction, and maintenance, 11.7% production, transportation, and material moving (2008-2012 5-year est.).
Income: Per capita income: $25,077 (2008-2012 5-year est.); Median household income: $47,500 (2008-2012 5-year est.); Average household income: $57,890 (2008-2012 5-year est.); Percent of households with income of $100,000 or more: 13.5% (2008-2012 5-year est.); Poverty rate: 10.4% (2008-2012 5-year est.).
Education: Percent of population age 25 and over with: High school diploma (including GED) or higher: 93.0% (2008-2012 5-year est.); Bachelor's degree or higher: 19.2% (2008-2012 5-year est.); Master's degree or higher: 5.1% (2008-2012 5-year est.).
Crescent Iroquois CUSD 249 (KG-08)
2011-12 Enrollment: 92 . . . . (815) 683-2141
Housing: Homeownership rate: 91.7% (2008-2012 5-year est.); Median home value: $95,300 (2008-2012 5-year est.); Median contract rent: $373 per month (2008-2012 5-year est.); Median year structure built: 1959 (2008-2012 5-year est.).
Health Insurance: 82.1% Private; 29.6% Public; 5.5% None. (2008-2012 5-year est.)
Transportation: Commute to work: 95.7% car, 0.0% public transportation, 0.0% walk, 3.7% work from home (2008-2012 5-year est.); Travel time to work: 38.3% less than 15 minutes, 33.9% 15 to 30 minutes, 17.6% 30 to 45 minutes, 4.2% 45 to 60 minutes, 6.1% 60 minutes or more (2008-2012 5-year est.)

DANFORTH (village). Covers a land area of 0.467 square miles and a water area of 0 square miles. Located at 40.82° N. Lat; 87.98° W. Long. Elevation is 653 feet.
History: Danforth was settled by immigrants from the Netherlands, on land purchased in the 1850's by A.H. and George Danforth. The swampy land was ditched and drained by the Dutch, who built windmills and established farms.
Population: 457 (1990); 587 (2000); 604 (2010); Density: 1,288.2 persons per square mile (2008-2012 5-year est.); Race: 97.0% White, 0.0% Black/African American, 1.0% Asian, 0.0% American Indian/Alaska Native, 0.0% Native Hawaiian/Other Pacific Islander, 2.0% Some other race, 0.0% Two or more races, 7.7% Hispanic of any race (2008-2012 5-year est.); Average household size: 2.06 (2008-2012 5-year est.); Median age: 52.0 (2008-2012 5-year est.); Males per 100 females: 65.1 (2008-2012 5-year est.); Marriage status: 21.5% never married, 36.1% now married, 30.7% widowed, 11.6% divorced (2008-2012 5-year est.); Foreign born: 1.2% (2008-2012 5-year est.); Ancestry (includes multiple ancestries): 32.4% German, 10.8% Irish, 10.5% French, 8.2% American, 5.3% Italian (2008-2012 5-year est.).
Economy: Single-family building permits issued: 0 (2013); Multi-family building permits issued: 0 (2013); Homeowner vacancy rate: 7.8%. Rental vacancy rate: 0.0%. (2008-2012 5-year est.); Employment by occupation: 8.4% management, business, and financial, 2.3% computer, engineering, and science, 10.3% education, legal, community service, arts, and media, 9.8% healthcare practitioners, 15.4% service, 18.7% sales and office, 21.0% natural resources, construction, and maintenance, 14.0% production, transportation, and material moving (2008-2012 5-year est.).

Income: Per capita income: $19,355 (2008-2012 5-year est.); Median household income: $36,136 (2008-2012 5-year est.); Average household income: $45,869 (2008-2012 5-year est.); Percent of households with income of $100,000 or more: 4.6% (2008-2012 5-year est.); Poverty rate: 16.1% (2008-2012 5-year est.).

Education: Percent of population age 25 and over with: High school diploma (including GED) or higher: 82.9% (2008-2012 5-year est.); Bachelor's degree or higher: 8.2% (2008-2012 5-year est.); Master's degree or higher: 3.9% (2008-2012 5-year est.).

School District(s)

Iroquois West CUSD 10 (PK-12)

    2011-12 Enrollment: 1,008 . . . . (815) 265-4642

Housing: Homeownership rate: 65.7% (2008-2012 5-year est.); Median home value: $95,600 (2008-2012 5-year est.); Median contract rent: $542 per month (2008-2012 5-year est.); Median year structure built: Before 1940 (2008-2012 5-year est.).

Health Insurance: 72.4% Private; 35.1% Public; 10.3% None. (2008-2012 5-year est.)

Transportation: Commute to work: 92.8% car, 0.0% public transportation, 2.4% walk, 4.8% work from home (2008-2012 5-year est.); Travel time to work: 30.8% less than 15 minutes, 36.4% 15 to 30 minutes, 18.2% 30 to 45 minutes, 9.1% 45 to 60 minutes, 5.6% 60 minutes or more (2008-2012 5-year est.)

DONOVAN (village). Covers a land area of 0.311 square miles and a water area of 0 square miles. Located at 40.89° N. Lat; 87.61° W. Long. Elevation is 673 feet.

History: Donovan was settled by Swedish immigrants after the railroad was built here, and named for the operator of the Buckhorn Tavern.

Population: 361 (1990); 351 (2000); 304 (2010); Density: 1,142.9 persons per square mile (2008-2012 5-year est.); Race: 95.5% White, 2.8% Black/African American, 0.0% Asian, 1.7% American Indian/Alaska Native, 0.0% Native Hawaiian/Other Pacific Islander, 0.0% Some other race, 0.0% Two or more races, 3.9% Hispanic of any race (2008-2012 5-year est.); Average household size: 2.55 (2008-2012 5-year est.); Median age: 34.8 (2008-2012 5-year est.); Males per 100 females: 74.0 (2008-2012 5-year est.); Marriage status: 26.6% never married, 46.4% now married, 11.5% widowed, 15.5% divorced (2008-2012 5-year est.); Foreign born: 2.0% (2008-2012 5-year est.); Ancestry (includes multiple ancestries): 26.5% German, 20.0% American, 16.9% French, 16.9% Irish, 6.2% Italian (2008-2012 5-year est.).

Economy: Single-family building permits issued: 0 (2013); Multi-family building permits issued: 0 (2013); Homeowner vacancy rate: 0.0%. Rental vacancy rate: 17.4%. (2008-2012 5-year est.); Employment by occupation: 9.6% management, business, and financial, 3.0% computer, engineering, and science, 4.2% education, legal, community service, arts, and media, 7.8% healthcare practitioners, 22.2% service, 21.6% sales and office, 10.8% natural resources, construction, and maintenance, 21.0% production, transportation, and material moving (2008-2012 5-year est.).

Income: Per capita income: $19,912 (2008-2012 5-year est.); Median household income: $41,563 (2008-2012 5-year est.); Average household income: $50,255 (2008-2012 5-year est.); Percent of households with income of $100,000 or more: 11.4% (2008-2012 5-year est.); Poverty rate: 12.7% (2008-2012 5-year est.).

Education: Percent of population age 25 and over with: High school diploma (including GED) or higher: 95.9% (2008-2012 5-year est.); Bachelor's degree or higher: 11.4% (2008-2012 5-year est.); Master's degree or higher: 5.9% (2008-2012 5-year est.).

School District(s)

Donovan CUSD 3 (PK-12)

    2011-12 Enrollment: 401 . . . . (815) 486-7397

Housing: Homeownership rate: 72.7% (2008-2012 5-year est.); Median home value: $78,800 (2008-2012 5-year est.); Median contract rent: $406 per month (2008-2012 5-year est.); Median year structure built: 1941 (2008-2012 5-year est.).

Health Insurance: 51.8% Private; 41.1% Public; 16.9% None. (2008-2012 5-year est.)

Transportation: Commute to work: 85.5% car, 0.0% public transportation, 9.1% walk, 3.0% work from home (2008-2012 5-year est.); Travel time to work: 25.6% less than 15 minutes, 31.9% 15 to 30 minutes, 21.9% 30 to 45 minutes, 11.9% 45 to 60 minutes, 8.8% 60 minutes or more (2008-2012 5-year est.)

GILMAN (city). Covers a land area of 2.226 square miles and a water area of 0.020 square miles. Located at 40.77° N. Lat; 87.98° W. Long. Elevation is 650 feet.

History: Incorporated 1867.

Population: 1,816 (1990); 1,793 (2000); 1,814 (2010); Density: 835.3 persons per square mile (2008-2012 5-year est.); Race: 91.0% White, 0.4% Black/African American, 0.3% Asian, 0.3% American Indian/Alaska Native, 0.0% Native Hawaiian/Other Pacific Islander, 8.0% Some other race, 0.8% Two or more races, 22.9% Hispanic of any race (2008-2012 5-year est.); Average household size: 2.48 (2008-2012 5-year est.); Median age: 38.2 (2008-2012 5-year est.); Males per 100 females: 80.5 (2008-2012 5-year est.); Marriage status: 21.0% never married, 52.8% now married, 10.0% widowed, 16.2% divorced (2008-2012 5-year est.); Foreign born: 10.8% (2008-2012 5-year est.); Ancestry (includes multiple ancestries): 27.8% German, 13.1% Irish, 9.3% American, 8.6% English, 3.8% French (2008-2012 5-year est.).

Economy: Single-family building permits issued: 2 (2013); Multi-family building permits issued: 0 (2013); Homeowner vacancy rate: 0.0%. Rental vacancy rate: 5.5%. (2008-2012 5-year est.); Employment by occupation: 6.4% management, business, and financial, 0.8% computer, engineering, and science, 9.6% education, legal, community service, arts, and media, 6.6% healthcare practitioners, 27.4% service, 14.5% sales and office, 14.4% natural resources, construction, and maintenance, 20.3% production, transportation, and material moving (2008-2012 5-year est.).

Income: Per capita income: $18,634 (2008-2012 5-year est.); Median household income: $40,781 (2008-2012 5-year est.); Average household income: $48,401 (2008-2012 5-year est.); Percent of households with income of $100,000 or more: 7.3% (2008-2012 5-year est.); Poverty rate: 16.5% (2008-2012 5-year est.).

Education: Percent of population age 25 and over with: High school diploma (including GED) or higher: 74.9% (2008-2012 5-year est.); Bachelor's degree or higher: 7.5% (2008-2012 5-year est.); Master's degree or higher: 3.9% (2008-2012 5-year est.).

School District(s)

Iroquois West CUSD 10 (PK-12)

    2011-12 Enrollment: 1,008 . . . . (815) 265-4642

Housing: Homeownership rate: 62.3% (2008-2012 5-year est.); Median home value: $89,200 (2008-2012 5-year est.); Median contract rent: $473 per month (2008-2012 5-year est.); Median year structure built: 1956 (2008-2012 5-year est.).

Health Insurance: 57.6% Private; 45.4% Public; 12.7% None. (2008-2012 5-year est.)

Transportation: Commute to work: 91.5% car, 0.0% public transportation, 0.4% walk, 4.7% work from home (2008-2012 5-year est.); Travel time to work: 46.3% less than 15 minutes, 20.0% 15 to 30 minutes, 14.2% 30 to 45 minutes, 6.0% 45 to 60 minutes, 13.6% 60 minutes or more (2008-2012 5-year est.); Amtrak: Train service available.

Additional Information Contacts

Gilman Chamber of Commerce . . . . (815) 265-4818

IROQUOIS (village). Covers a land area of 0.599 square miles and a water area of 0 square miles. Located at 40.83° N. Lat; 87.58° W. Long. Elevation is 659 feet.

History: Iroquois was the name given by the Big Four Railroad in 1871 to its station on the Iroquois River. In 1875 the town of Concord, on the other side of the river, was incorporated under the Iroquois name.

Population: 199 (1990); 207 (2000); 154 (2010); Density: 289.0 persons per square mile (2008-2012 5-year est.); Race: 93.6% White, 0.0% Black/African American, 0.0% Asian, 0.0% American Indian/Alaska Native, 0.0% Native Hawaiian/Other Pacific Islander, 6.4% Some other race, 6.4% Two or more races, 0.0% Hispanic of any race (2008-2012 5-year est.); Average household size: 2.40 (2008-2012 5-year est.); Median age: 45.5 (2008-2012 5-year est.); Males per 100 females: 127.6 (2008-2012 5-year est.); Marriage status: 23.5% never married, 58.1% now married, 13.2% widowed, 5.1% divorced (2008-2012 5-year est.); Foreign born: 0.0% (2008-2012 5-year est.); Ancestry (includes multiple ancestries): 46.2% German, 33.5% Irish, 10.4% American, 6.9% English, 3.5% French (2008-2012 5-year est.).

Economy: Single-family building permits issued: 0 (2013); Multi-family building permits issued: 0 (2013); Homeowner vacancy rate: 0.0%. Rental vacancy rate: 0.0%. (2008-2012 5-year est.); Employment by occupation: 14.5% management, business, and financial, 0.0% computer, engineering, and science, 3.6% education, legal, community service, arts, and media, 0.0% healthcare practitioners, 24.1% service, 18.1% sales and office,

10.8% natural resources, construction, and maintenance, 28.9% production, transportation, and material moving (2008-2012 5-year est.).
Income: Per capita income: $22,998 (2008-2012 5-year est.); Median household income: $50,000 (2008-2012 5-year est.); Average household income: $58,656 (2008-2012 5-year est.); Percent of households with income of $100,000 or more: 9.8% (2008-2012 5-year est.); Poverty rate: 4.6% (2008-2012 5-year est.).
Education: Percent of population age 25 and over with: High school diploma (including GED) or higher: 85.1% (2008-2012 5-year est.); Bachelor's degree or higher: 15.7% (2008-2012 5-year est.); Master's degree or higher: 7.4% (2008-2012 5-year est.).
Housing: Homeownership rate: 94.4% (2008-2012 5-year est.); Median home value: $67,100 (2008-2012 5-year est.); Median contract rent: $425 per month (2008-2012 5-year est.); Median year structure built: 1951 (2008-2012 5-year est.).
Health Insurance: 85.0% Private; 23.7% Public; 9.8% None. (2008-2012 5-year est.)
Transportation: Commute to work: 95.1% car, 0.0% public transportation, 3.7% walk, 0.0% work from home (2008-2012 5-year est.); Travel time to work: 42.7% less than 15 minutes, 42.7% 15 to 30 minutes, 2.4% 30 to 45 minutes, 3.7% 45 to 60 minutes, 8.5% 60 minutes or more (2008-2012 5-year est.)

LODA (village). Covers a land area of 1.447 square miles and a water area of 0.008 square miles. Located at 40.52° N. Lat; 88.08° W. Long. Elevation is 778 feet.
Population: 390 (1990); 419 (2000); 407 (2010); Density: 308.3 persons per square mile (2008-2012 5-year est.); Race: 96.2% White, 0.4% Black/African American, 0.0% Asian, 0.0% American Indian/Alaska Native, 0.0% Native Hawaiian/Other Pacific Islander, 3.4% Some other race, 3.4% Two or more races, 2.2% Hispanic of any race (2008-2012 5-year est.); Average household size: 2.70 (2008-2012 5-year est.); Median age: 40.2 (2008-2012 5-year est.); Males per 100 females: 94.8 (2008-2012 5-year est.); Marriage status: 19.9% never married, 62.0% now married, 4.3% widowed, 13.8% divorced (2008-2012 5-year est.); Foreign born: 2.0% (2008-2012 5-year est.); Ancestry (includes multiple ancestries): 37.4% American, 28.3% German, 9.9% English, 8.3% Irish, 4.9% Polish (2008-2012 5-year est.).
Economy: Single-family building permits issued: 2 (2013); Multi-family building permits issued: 0 (2013); Homeowner vacancy rate: 0.0%. Rental vacancy rate: 22.4%. (2008-2012 5-year est.); Employment by occupation: 17.0% management, business, and financial, 0.5% computer, engineering, and science, 9.9% education, legal, community service, arts, and media, 7.1% healthcare practitioners, 14.6% service, 17.9% sales and office, 10.8% natural resources, construction, and maintenance, 22.2% production, transportation, and material moving (2008-2012 5-year est.).
Income: Per capita income: $23,715 (2008-2012 5-year est.); Median household income: $54,531 (2008-2012 5-year est.); Average household income: $66,291 (2008-2012 5-year est.); Percent of households with income of $100,000 or more: 13.3% (2008-2012 5-year est.); Poverty rate: 16.4% (2008-2012 5-year est.).
Education: Percent of population age 25 and over with: High school diploma (including GED) or higher: 82.2% (2008-2012 5-year est.); Bachelor's degree or higher: 6.3% (2008-2012 5-year est.); Master's degree or higher: 1.0% (2008-2012 5-year est.).
Housing: Homeownership rate: 77.0% (2008-2012 5-year est.); Median home value: $81,500 (2008-2012 5-year est.); Median contract rent: $630 per month (2008-2012 5-year est.); Median year structure built: Before 1940 (2008-2012 5-year est.).
Health Insurance: 52.0% Private; 49.1% Public; 16.1% None. (2008-2012 5-year est.)
Transportation: Commute to work: 88.4% car, 0.0% public transportation, 4.8% walk, 6.8% work from home (2008-2012 5-year est.); Travel time to work: 30.6% less than 15 minutes, 21.2% 15 to 30 minutes, 23.3% 30 to 45 minutes, 13.0% 45 to 60 minutes, 11.9% 60 minutes or more (2008-2012 5-year est.)

MARTINTON (village). Covers a land area of 0.276 square miles and a water area of 0 square miles. Located at 40.92° N. Lat; 87.73° W. Long. Elevation is 627 feet.
History: Martinton was founded in 1871 as a station on the Chicago & Eastern Illinois Railway, and named for Porter Martin, an early resident.
Population: 299 (1990); 375 (2000); 381 (2010); Density: 1,124.1 persons per square mile (2008-2012 5-year est.); Race: 97.7% White, 0.0% Black/African American, 1.9% Asian, 0.0% American Indian/Alaska Native,

0.0% Native Hawaiian/Other Pacific Islander, 0.4% Some other race, 0.0% Two or more races, 1.6% Hispanic of any race (2008-2012 5-year est.); Average household size: 2.70 (2008-2012 5-year est.); Median age: 36.2 (2008-2012 5-year est.); Males per 100 females: 100.0 (2008-2012 5-year est.); Marriage status: 24.7% never married, 60.2% now married, 3.5% widowed, 11.7% divorced (2008-2012 5-year est.); Foreign born: 2.3% (2008-2012 5-year est.); Ancestry (includes multiple ancestries): 38.1% German, 26.8% French, 20.6% Irish, 16.1% American, 7.4% Italian (2008-2012 5-year est.).
Economy: Single-family building permits issued: 1 (2013); Multi-family building permits issued: 0 (2013); Homeowner vacancy rate: 0.0%. Rental vacancy rate: 15.6%. (2008-2012 5-year est.); Employment by occupation: 15.4% management, business, and financial, 1.3% computer, engineering, and science, 9.0% education, legal, community service, arts, and media, 4.5% healthcare practitioners, 10.9% service, 16.7% sales and office, 17.9% natural resources, construction, and maintenance, 24.4% production, transportation, and material moving (2008-2012 5-year est.).
Income: Per capita income: $23,294 (2008-2012 5-year est.); Median household income: $61,094 (2008-2012 5-year est.); Average household income: $63,118 (2008-2012 5-year est.); Percent of households with income of $100,000 or more: 7.8% (2008-2012 5-year est.); Poverty rate: 1.9% (2008-2012 5-year est.).
Education: Percent of population age 25 and over with: High school diploma (including GED) or higher: 94.4% (2008-2012 5-year est.); Bachelor's degree or higher: 9.7% (2008-2012 5-year est.); Master's degree or higher: 6.2% (2008-2012 5-year est.).
Housing: Homeownership rate: 76.5% (2008-2012 5-year est.); Median home value: $88,000 (2008-2012 5-year est.); Median contract rent: $531 per month (2008-2012 5-year est.); Median year structure built: Before 1940 (2008-2012 5-year est.).
Health Insurance: 79.4% Private; 25.5% Public; 7.1% None. (2008-2012 5-year est.)
Transportation: Commute to work: 93.5% car, 0.0% public transportation, 5.8% walk, 0.0% work from home (2008-2012 5-year est.); Travel time to work: 9.7% less than 15 minutes, 37.7% 15 to 30 minutes, 39.6% 30 to 45 minutes, 8.4% 45 to 60 minutes, 4.5% 60 minutes or more (2008-2012 5-year est.)

MILFORD (village). Covers a land area of 0.644 square miles and a water area of 0 square miles. Located at 40.63° N. Lat; 87.70° W. Long. Elevation is 669 feet.
History: Milford, incorporated as a village in 1874, was first laid out in 1836 by William Pickerel who operated a mill near a ford on Sugar Creek.
Population: 1,512 (1990); 1,369 (2000); 1,306 (2010); Density: 1,807.2 persons per square mile (2008-2012 5-year est.); Race: 99.8% White, 0.0% Black/African American, 0.0% Asian, 0.0% American Indian/Alaska Native, 0.0% Native Hawaiian/Other Pacific Islander, 0.2% Some other race, 0.2% Two or more races, 4.0% Hispanic of any race (2008-2012 5-year est.); Average household size: 2.11 (2008-2012 5-year est.); Median age: 46.9 (2008-2012 5-year est.); Males per 100 females: 90.8 (2008-2012 5-year est.); Marriage status: 21.1% never married, 54.6% now married, 11.8% widowed, 12.4% divorced (2008-2012 5-year est.); Foreign born: 1.2% (2008-2012 5-year est.); Ancestry (includes multiple ancestries): 36.2% German, 15.6% American, 13.1% English, 7.3% Irish, 6.9% French (2008-2012 5-year est.).
Economy: Single-family building permits issued: 0 (2013); Multi-family building permits issued: 0 (2013); Homeowner vacancy rate: 10.2%. Rental vacancy rate: 13.9%. (2008-2012 5-year est.); Employment by occupation: 16.6% management, business, and financial, 1.9% computer, engineering, and science, 7.2% education, legal, community service, arts, and media, 2.6% healthcare practitioners, 19.5% service, 13.9% sales and office, 10.1% natural resources, construction, and maintenance, 28.3% production, transportation, and material moving (2008-2012 5-year est.).
Income: Per capita income: $24,063 (2008-2012 5-year est.); Median household income: $35,694 (2008-2012 5-year est.); Average household income: $51,675 (2008-2012 5-year est.); Percent of households with income of $100,000 or more: 10.7% (2008-2012 5-year est.); Poverty rate: 13.9% (2008-2012 5-year est.).
Education: Percent of population age 25 and over with: High school diploma (including GED) or higher: 84.1% (2008-2012 5-year est.); Bachelor's degree or higher: 15.5% (2008-2012 5-year est.); Master's degree or higher: 4.8% (2008-2012 5-year est.).

School District(s)
Iroquois Special Education (KG-12)
　2011-12 Enrollment: n/a . . . . (815) 683-2662

Milford CCSD 280 (PK-08)
    2011-12 Enrollment: 470........................ (815) 889-5176
Milford Twp HSD 233 (09-12)
    2011-12 Enrollment: 194........................ (815) 889-5176
Housing: Homeownership rate: 73.0% (2008-2012 5-year est.); Median home value: $67,600 (2008-2012 5-year est.); Median contract rent: $420 per month (2008-2012 5-year est.); Median year structure built: 1953 (2008-2012 5-year est.).
Health Insurance: 61.9% Private; 41.2% Public; 13.5% None. (2008-2012 5-year est.)
Transportation: Commute to work: 93.8% car, 0.0% public transportation, 1.9% walk, 4.3% work from home (2008-2012 5-year est.); Travel time to work: 38.0% less than 15 minutes, 35.1% 15 to 30 minutes, 5.8% 30 to 45 minutes, 11.1% 45 to 60 minutes, 10.0% 60 minutes or more (2008-2012 5-year est.)

ONARGA (village). Covers a land area of 1.328 square miles and a water area of 0 square miles. Located at 40.71° N. Lat; 88.01° W. Long. Elevation is 669 feet.
History: Benjamin Hardy, the composer of the song "Darling Nellie Gray," lived in Onarga.
Population: 1,281 (1990); 1,438 (2000); 1,368 (2010); Density: 1,037.4 persons per square mile (2008-2012 5-year est.); Race: 87.3% White, 2.4% Black/African American, 0.0% Asian, 0.5% American Indian/Alaska Native, 0.0% Native Hawaiian/Other Pacific Islander, 9.8% Some other race, 2.5% Two or more races, 40.0% Hispanic of any race (2008-2012 5-year est.); Average household size: 2.75 (2008-2012 5-year est.); Median age: 38.1 (2008-2012 5-year est.); Males per 100 females: 117.0 (2008-2012 5-year est.); Marriage status: 34.3% never married, 50.8% now married, 6.2% widowed, 8.8% divorced (2008-2012 5-year est.); Foreign born: 19.2% (2008-2012 5-year est.); Ancestry (includes multiple ancestries): 20.7% German, 10.3% English, 9.7% Irish, 7.6% American, 2.8% French (2008-2012 5-year est.).
Economy: Single-family building permits issued: 4 (2013); Multi-family building permits issued: 0 (2013); Homeowner vacancy rate: 2.2%. Rental vacancy rate: 0.0%. (2008-2012 5-year est.); Employment by occupation: 5.4% management, business, and financial, 0.6% computer, engineering, and science, 6.9% education, legal, community service, arts, and media, 1.6% healthcare practitioners, 15.8% service, 21.4% sales and office, 15.5% natural resources, construction, and maintenance, 32.9% production, transportation, and material moving (2008-2012 5-year est.).
Income: Per capita income: $18,266 (2008-2012 5-year est.); Median household income: $44,762 (2008-2012 5-year est.); Average household income: $52,620 (2008-2012 5-year est.); Percent of households with income of $100,000 or more: 10.2% (2008-2012 5-year est.); Poverty rate: 16.9% (2008-2012 5-year est.).
Education: Percent of population age 25 and over with: High school diploma (including GED) or higher: 70.9% (2008-2012 5-year est.); Bachelor's degree or higher: 10.6% (2008-2012 5-year est.); Master's degree or higher: 3.1% (2008-2012 5-year est.).
School District(s)
Iroquois West CUSD 10 (PK-12)
    2011-12 Enrollment: 1,008 .... (815) 265-4642
Housing: Homeownership rate: 75.6% (2008-2012 5-year est.); Median home value: $85,400 (2008-2012 5-year est.); Median contract rent: $505 per month (2008-2012 5-year est.); Median year structure built: 1941 (2008-2012 5-year est.).
Health Insurance: 55.2% Private; 37.6% Public; 17.0% None. (2008-2012 5-year est.)
Transportation: Commute to work: 90.1% car, 0.0% public transportation, 3.6% walk, 5.2% work from home (2008-2012 5-year est.); Travel time to work: 54.3% less than 15 minutes, 17.2% 15 to 30 minutes, 12.8% 30 to 45 minutes, 11.7% 45 to 60 minutes, 4.0% 60 minutes or more (2008-2012 5-year est.)
Additional Information Contacts
Onarga Chamber of Commerce................................
    http://onargachamber.com

PAPINEAU (village). Covers a land area of 0.226 square miles and a water area of 0 square miles. Located at 40.97° N. Lat; 87.72° W. Long. Elevation is 630 feet.
Population: 142 (1990); 196 (2000); 171 (2010); Density: 1,027.6 persons per square mile (2008-2012 5-year est.); Race: 94.0% White, 0.0% Black/African American, 0.4% Asian, 0.0% American Indian/Alaska Native, 0.0% Native Hawaiian/Other Pacific Islander, 5.6% Some other race, 5.6%

Two or more races, 0.0% Hispanic of any race (2008-2012 5-year est.); Average household size: 3.57 (2008-2012 5-year est.); Median age: 40.3 (2008-2012 5-year est.); Males per 100 females: 91.7 (2008-2012 5-year est.); Marriage status: 35.2% never married, 64.3% now married, 0.0% widowed, 0.5% divorced (2008-2012 5-year est.); Foreign born: 0.4% (2008-2012 5-year est.); Ancestry (includes multiple ancestries): 48.3% American, 17.7% French, 17.2% German, 9.1% Dutch, 6.9% Irish (2008-2012 5-year est.).
Economy: Single-family building permits issued: 0 (2013); Multi-family building permits issued: 0 (2013); Homeowner vacancy rate: 0.0%. Rental vacancy rate: 0.0%. (2008-2012 5-year est.); Employment by occupation: 14.4% management, business, and financial, 0.0% computer, engineering, and science, 1.6% education, legal, community service, arts, and media, 17.6% healthcare practitioners, 3.2% service, 28.0% sales and office, 8.8% natural resources, construction, and maintenance, 26.4% production, transportation, and material moving (2008-2012 5-year est.).
Income: Per capita income: $20,797 (2008-2012 5-year est.); Median household income: $78,906 (2008-2012 5-year est.); Average household income: $76,762 (2008-2012 5-year est.); Percent of households with income of $100,000 or more: 38.5% (2008-2012 5-year est.); Poverty rate: 15.5% (2008-2012 5-year est.).
Education: Percent of population age 25 and over with: High school diploma (including GED) or higher: 87.3% (2008-2012 5-year est.); Bachelor's degree or higher: 3.0% (2008-2012 5-year est.); Master's degree or higher: 0.7% (2008-2012 5-year est.).
Housing: Homeownership rate: 87.7% (2008-2012 5-year est.); Median home value: $94,500 (2008-2012 5-year est.); Median contract rent: $425 per month (2008-2012 5-year est.); Median year structure built: 1953 (2008-2012 5-year est.).
Health Insurance: 71.6% Private; 23.3% Public; 10.8% None. (2008-2012 5-year est.)
Transportation: Commute to work: 76.8% car, 0.0% public transportation, 0.0% walk, 22.4% work from home (2008-2012 5-year est.); Travel time to work: 9.3% less than 15 minutes, 13.4% 15 to 30 minutes, 41.2% 30 to 45 minutes, 24.7% 45 to 60 minutes, 11.3% 60 minutes or more (2008-2012 5-year est.)

SHELDON (village). Covers a land area of 0.750 square miles and a water area of 0 square miles. Located at 40.77° N. Lat; 87.57° W. Long. Elevation is 682 feet.
History: Sheldon was established in 1860 by the Toledo, Peoria & Western Railroad as a switching point, and named for a railroad director. The town was a grain shipping center.
Population: 1,109 (1990); 1,232 (2000); 1,070 (2010); Density: 1,320.7 persons per square mile (2008-2012 5-year est.); Race: 97.2% White, 1.9% Black/African American, 0.1% Asian, 0.8% American Indian/Alaska Native, 0.0% Native Hawaiian/Other Pacific Islander, 0.0% Some other race, 0.0% Two or more races, 5.5% Hispanic of any race (2008-2012 5-year est.); Average household size: 2.60 (2008-2012 5-year est.); Median age: 37.7 (2008-2012 5-year est.); Males per 100 females: 117.3 (2008-2012 5-year est.); Marriage status: 28.2% never married, 48.2% now married, 8.4% widowed, 15.3% divorced (2008-2012 5-year est.); Foreign born: 1.6% (2008-2012 5-year est.); Ancestry (includes multiple ancestries): 24.5% German, 16.0% Irish, 15.8% American, 10.8% English, 4.2% French (2008-2012 5-year est.).
Economy: Single-family building permits issued: 0 (2013); Multi-family building permits issued: 0 (2013); Homeowner vacancy rate: 3.1%. Rental vacancy rate: 6.7%. (2008-2012 5-year est.); Employment by occupation: 3.6% management, business, and financial, 1.3% computer, engineering, and science, 5.8% education, legal, community service, arts, and media, 8.3% healthcare practitioners, 22.2% service, 13.0% sales and office, 15.2% natural resources, construction, and maintenance, 30.5% production, transportation, and material moving (2008-2012 5-year est.).
Income: Per capita income: $18,117 (2008-2012 5-year est.); Median household income: $42,500 (2008-2012 5-year est.); Average household income: $48,301 (2008-2012 5-year est.); Percent of households with income of $100,000 or more: 3.5% (2008-2012 5-year est.); Poverty rate: 18.3% (2008-2012 5-year est.).
Education: Percent of population age 25 and over with: High school diploma (including GED) or higher: 86.4% (2008-2012 5-year est.); Bachelor's degree or higher: 9.0% (2008-2012 5-year est.); Master's degree or higher: 3.4% (2008-2012 5-year est.).
School District(s)
Milford CCSD 280 (PK-08)
    2011-12 Enrollment: 470........................ (815) 889-5176

Housing: Homeownership rate: 73.9% (2008-2012 5-year est.); Median home value: $61,300 (2008-2012 5-year est.); Median contract rent: $463 per month (2008-2012 5-year est.); Median year structure built: 1943 (2008-2012 5-year est.).
Health Insurance: 62.3% Private; 36.4% Public; 10.5% None. (2008-2012 5-year est.)
Transportation: Commute to work: 97.3% car, 1.6% public transportation, 0.4% walk, 0.7% work from home (2008-2012 5-year est.); Travel time to work: 35.7% less than 15 minutes, 43.3% 15 to 30 minutes, 6.3% 30 to 45 minutes, 5.9% 45 to 60 minutes, 8.8% 60 minutes or more (2008-2012 5-year est.)

THAWVILLE (village). Covers a land area of 0.328 square miles and a water area of 0 square miles. Located at 40.67° N. Lat; 88.11° W. Long. Elevation is 689 feet.
Population: 241 (1990); 258 (2000); 241 (2010); Density: 505.7 persons per square mile (2008-2012 5-year est.); Race: 93.4% White, 0.0% Black/African American, 0.0% Asian, 0.0% American Indian/Alaska Native, 0.0% Native Hawaiian/Other Pacific Islander, 6.6% Some other race, 6.6% Two or more races, 7.8% Hispanic of any race (2008-2012 5-year est.); Average household size: 2.31 (2008-2012 5-year est.); Median age: 49.0 (2008-2012 5-year est.); Males per 100 females: 82.4 (2008-2012 5-year est.); Marriage status: 13.2% never married, 66.7% now married, 6.2% widowed, 14.0% divorced (2008-2012 5-year est.); Foreign born: 0.0% (2008-2012 5-year est.); Ancestry (includes multiple ancestries): 44.6% German, 10.8% English, 10.2% American, 9.0% French, 9.0% Irish (2008-2012 5-year est.).
Economy: Single-family building permits issued: 0 (2013); Multi-family building permits issued: 3 (2013); Homeowner vacancy rate: 4.8%. Rental vacancy rate: 0.0%. (2008-2012 5-year est.); Employment by occupation: 26.4% management, business, and financial, 0.0% computer, engineering, and science, 2.8% education, legal, community service, arts, and media, 5.6% healthcare practitioners, 27.8% service, 18.1% sales and office, 5.6% natural resources, construction, and maintenance, 13.9% production, transportation, and material moving (2008-2012 5-year est.).
Income: Per capita income: $19,284 (2008-2012 5-year est.); Median household income: $38,636 (2008-2012 5-year est.); Average household income: $44,463 (2008-2012 5-year est.); Percent of households with income of $100,000 or more: 5.6% (2008-2012 5-year est.); Poverty rate: 21.1% (2008-2012 5-year est.).
Education: Percent of population age 25 and over with: High school diploma (including GED) or higher: 82.5% (2008-2012 5-year est.); Bachelor's degree or higher: 8.8% (2008-2012 5-year est.); Master's degree or higher: 4.4% (2008-2012 5-year est.).

School District(s)
Iroquois West CUSD 10 (PK-12)
    2011-12 Enrollment: 1,008 . . . . (815) 265-4642
Housing: Homeownership rate: 83.3% (2008-2012 5-year est.); Median home value: $59,100 (2008-2012 5-year est.); Median contract rent: $600 per month (2008-2012 5-year est.); Median year structure built: 1953 (2008-2012 5-year est.).
Health Insurance: 67.5% Private; 41.6% Public; 7.2% None. (2008-2012 5-year est.)
Transportation: Commute to work: 79.7% car, 0.0% public transportation, 2.9% walk, 17.4% work from home (2008-2012 5-year est.); Travel time to work: 29.8% less than 15 minutes, 26.3% 15 to 30 minutes, 15.8% 30 to 45 minutes, 12.3% 45 to 60 minutes, 15.8% 60 minutes or more (2008-2012 5-year est.)

WATSEKA (city). County seat. Covers a land area of 3.051 square miles and a water area of 0 square miles. Located at 40.77° N. Lat; 87.73° W. Long. Elevation is 633 feet.
History: Watseka was first called South Middleport when it was laid out in 1860. The name was changed in 1865 to honor the Potawatomi wife (Watch-e-kee) of Gurdon Hubbard of the American Fur Company. Watseka developed as the seat of Iroquois County.
Population: 5,424 (1990); 5,670 (2000); 5,255 (2010); Density: 1,845.2 persons per square mile (2008-2012 5-year est.); Race: 97.5% White, 0.5% Black/African American, 1.4% Asian, 0.0% American Indian/Alaska Native, 0.0% Native Hawaiian/Other Pacific Islander, 0.6% Some other race, 0.3% Two or more races, 2.8% Hispanic of any race (2008-2012 5-year est.); Average household size: 2.12 (2008-2012 5-year est.); Median age: 45.8 (2008-2012 5-year est.); Males per 100 females: 86.1 (2008-2012 5-year est.); Marriage status: 26.3% never married, 46.7% now married, 13.4% widowed, 13.6% divorced (2008-2012 5-year est.);

Foreign born: 4.8% (2008-2012 5-year est.); Ancestry (includes multiple ancestries): 29.7% German, 16.4% Irish, 14.3% American, 11.3% English, 8.5% French (2008-2012 5-year est.).
Economy: Single-family building permits issued: 0 (2013); Multi-family building permits issued: 0 (2013); Homeowner vacancy rate: 2.8%. Rental vacancy rate: 4.2%. (2008-2012 5-year est.); Employment by occupation: 7.4% management, business, and financial, 0.2% computer, engineering, and science, 6.6% education, legal, community service, arts, and media, 3.7% healthcare practitioners, 25.0% service, 27.5% sales and office, 9.6% natural resources, construction, and maintenance, 20.0% production, transportation, and material moving (2008-2012 5-year est.).
Income: Per capita income: $20,861 (2008-2012 5-year est.); Median household income: $34,690 (2008-2012 5-year est.); Average household income: $45,381 (2008-2012 5-year est.); Percent of households with income of $100,000 or more: 7.7% (2008-2012 5-year est.); Poverty rate: 14.7% (2008-2012 5-year est.).
Education: Percent of population age 25 and over with: High school diploma (including GED) or higher: 82.8% (2008-2012 5-year est.); Bachelor's degree or higher: 10.3% (2008-2012 5-year est.); Master's degree or higher: 2.4% (2008-2012 5-year est.).

School District(s)
Iroquois Area Reg Del System
    2011-12 Enrollment: n/a . . . . (815) 432-5471
Iroquois County CUSD 9 (PK-12)
    2011-12 Enrollment: 1,200 . . . . (815) 432-4931
Housing: Homeownership rate: 67.8% (2008-2012 5-year est.); Median home value: $81,700 (2008-2012 5-year est.); Median contract rent: $480 per month (2008-2012 5-year est.); Median year structure built: 1958 (2008-2012 5-year est.).
Health Insurance: 70.3% Private; 42.7% Public; 10.3% None. (2008-2012 5-year est.)
Hospitals: Iroquois Memorial Hospital & Resident Home (94 beds)
Safety: Violent crime rate: 11.5 per 10,000 population; Property crime rate: 305.1 per 10,000 population (2012).
Transportation: Commute to work: 89.7% car, 0.0% public transportation, 3.6% walk, 3.5% work from home (2008-2012 5-year est.); Travel time to work: 64.7% less than 15 minutes, 7.4% 15 to 30 minutes, 12.7% 30 to 45 minutes, 5.2% 45 to 60 minutes, 10.1% 60 minutes or more (2008-2012 5-year est.)
Additional Information Contacts
City of Watseka . . . . (815) 432-2711
    http://www.watsekacity.org
Watseka Area Chamber of Commerce . . . . (815) 432-2416
    http://www.watsekachamber.org

WELLINGTON (village). Covers a land area of 0.276 square miles and a water area of 0 square miles. Located at 40.54° N. Lat; 87.68° W. Long. Elevation is 699 feet.
Population: 294 (1990); 264 (2000); 242 (2010); Density: 779.9 persons per square mile (2008-2012 5-year est.); Race: 90.2% White, 0.0% Black/African American, 0.0% Asian, 3.7% American Indian/Alaska Native, 0.0% Native Hawaiian/Other Pacific Islander, 6.1% Some other race, 6.0% Two or more races, 11.2% Hispanic of any race (2008-2012 5-year est.); Average household size: 2.01 (2008-2012 5-year est.); Median age: 47.6 (2008-2012 5-year est.); Males per 100 females: 83.8 (2008-2012 5-year est.); Marriage status: 17.9% never married, 61.8% now married, 5.8% widowed, 14.5% divorced (2008-2012 5-year est.); Foreign born: 0.0% (2008-2012 5-year est.); Ancestry (includes multiple ancestries): 33.0% German, 18.6% American, 17.7% English, 11.2% Irish, 4.2% Swedish (2008-2012 5-year est.).
Economy: Single-family building permits issued: 0 (2013); Multi-family building permits issued: 0 (2013); Homeowner vacancy rate: 0.0%. Rental vacancy rate: 0.0%. (2008-2012 5-year est.); Employment by occupation: 7.0% management, business, and financial, 0.0% computer, engineering, and science, 5.0% education, legal, community service, arts, and media, 2.0% healthcare practitioners, 13.0% service, 31.0% sales and office, 15.0% natural resources, construction, and maintenance, 27.0% production, transportation, and material moving (2008-2012 5-year est.).
Income: Per capita income: $21,859 (2008-2012 5-year est.); Median household income: $40,208 (2008-2012 5-year est.); Average household income: $45,578 (2008-2012 5-year est.); Percent of households with income of $100,000 or more: 4.7% (2008-2012 5-year est.); Poverty rate: 16.0% (2008-2012 5-year est.).
Education: Percent of population age 25 and over with: High school diploma (including GED) or higher: 92.5% (2008-2012 5-year est.);

Bachelor's degree or higher: 3.8% (2008-2012 5-year est.); Master's degree or higher: 0.0% (2008-2012 5-year est.).
Housing: Homeownership rate: 75.7% (2008-2012 5-year est.); Median home value: $65,900 (2008-2012 5-year est.); Median contract rent: $2,000+ per month (2008-2012 5-year est.); Median year structure built: 1941 (2008-2012 5-year est.).
Health Insurance: 51.2% Private; 52.1% Public; 13.0% None. (2008-2012 5-year est.)
Transportation: Commute to work: 81.9% car, 0.0% public transportation, 6.4% walk, 3.2% work from home (2008-2012 5-year est.); Travel time to work: 47.3% less than 15 minutes, 20.9% 15 to 30 minutes, 20.9% 30 to 45 minutes, 0.0% 45 to 60 minutes, 11.0% 60 minutes or more (2008-2012 5-year est.)

WOODLAND (village). Covers a land area of 0.456 square miles and a water area of 0 square miles. Located at 40.71° N. Lat; 87.73° W. Long. Elevation is 633 feet.
Population: 313 (1990); 319 (2000); 324 (2010); Density: 610.3 persons per square mile (2008-2012 5-year est.); Race: 100.0% White, 0.0% Black/African American, 0.0% Asian, 0.0% American Indian/Alaska Native, 0.0% Native Hawaiian/Other Pacific Islander, 0.0% Some other race, 0.0% Two or more races, 0.0% Hispanic of any race (2008-2012 5-year est.); Average household size: 2.32 (2008-2012 5-year est.); Median age: 31.3 (2008-2012 5-year est.); Males per 100 females: 139.7 (2008-2012 5-year est.); Marriage status: 28.8% never married, 44.2% now married, 10.2% widowed, 16.7% divorced (2008-2012 5-year est.); Foreign born: 0.0% (2008-2012 5-year est.); Ancestry (includes multiple ancestries): 44.6% German, 21.2% Irish, 20.5% American, 15.1% English, 6.5% French (2008-2012 5-year est.).
Economy: Single-family building permits issued: 0 (2013); Multi-family building permits issued: 0 (2013); Homeowner vacancy rate: 0.0%. Rental vacancy rate: 8.8%. (2008-2012 5-year est.); Employment by occupation: 1.5% management, business, and financial, 0.0% computer, engineering, and science, 0.0% education, legal, community service, arts, and media, 3.7% healthcare practitioners, 26.1% service, 24.6% sales and office, 10.4% natural resources, construction, and maintenance, 33.6% production, transportation, and material moving (2008-2012 5-year est.).
Income: Per capita income: $16,301 (2008-2012 5-year est.); Median household income: $39,063 (2008-2012 5-year est.); Average household income: $37,793 (2008-2012 5-year est.); Percent of households with income of $100,000 or more: n/a (2008-2012 5-year est.); Poverty rate: 19.6% (2008-2012 5-year est.).
Education: Percent of population age 25 and over with: High school diploma (including GED) or higher: 80.0% (2008-2012 5-year est.); Bachelor's degree or higher: 0.0% (2008-2012 5-year est.); Master's degree or higher: 0.0% (2008-2012 5-year est.).

School District(s)
Iroquois County CUSD 9 (PK-12)
    2011-12 Enrollment: 1,200 . . . . (815) 432-4931
Housing: Homeownership rate: 74.2% (2008-2012 5-year est.); Median home value: $56,500 (2008-2012 5-year est.); Median contract rent: $375 per month (2008-2012 5-year est.); Median year structure built: 1955 (2008-2012 5-year est.).
Health Insurance: 57.2% Private; 50.7% Public; 7.9% None. (2008-2012 5-year est.)
Transportation: Commute to work: 98.5% car, 0.0% public transportation, 1.5% walk, 0.0% work from home (2008-2012 5-year est.); Travel time to work: 58.0% less than 15 minutes, 24.4% 15 to 30 minutes, 9.2% 30 to 45 minutes, 4.6% 45 to 60 minutes, 3.8% 60 minutes or more (2008-2012 5-year est.)

Jackson County

Located in southwestern Illinois; bounded on the southwest by the Mississippi River and the Missouri border; drained by the Big Muddy and Little Muddy Rivers; includes part of Shawnee National Forest. Covers a land area of 584.081 square miles, a water area of 18.298 square miles, and is located in the Central Time Zone at 37.79° N. Lat., 89.38° W. Long. The county was founded in 1816. County seat is Murphysboro.

Jackson County is part of the Carbondale-Marion, IL Metropolitan Statistical Area. The entire metro area includes: Jackson County, IL; Williamson County, IL

Weather Station: Carbondale Sewage Plant									Elevation: 390 feet		
	Jan	Feb	Mar	Apr	May	Jun	Jul	Aug	Sep	Oct	Nov	Dec
High	41	46	56	67	76	85	88	88	81	69	57	45
Low	23	26	34	44	54	63	67	64	55	43	35	26
Precip	3.2	3.1	4.3	4.5	5.5	4.6	3.7	3.1	3.1	3.7	4.4	4.1
Snow	2.9	3.6	1.1	tr	0.0	0.0	0.0	0.0	0.0	0.1	0.3	2.7

High and Low temperatures in degrees Fahrenheit; Precipitation and Snow in inches

Population: 61,067 (1990); 59,612 (2000); 60,218 (2010); Race: 78.2% White, 14.4% Black/African American, 3.3% Asian, 0.4% American Indian/Alaska Native, 0.0% Native Hawaiian/Other Pacific Islander, 3.7% Some other race, 2.9% Two or more races, 4.0% Hispanic of any race (2008-2012 5-year est.); Density: 102.9 persons per square mile (2008-2012 5-year est.); Average household size: 2.31 (2008-2012 5-year est.); Median age: 29.1 (2008-2012 5-year est.); Males per 100 females: 102.3 (2008-2012 5-year est.).
Religion: Six largest groups: 16.9% Baptist, 7.0% Catholicism, 6.1% Lutheran, 5.5% Muslim Estimate, 3.8% Methodist/Pietist, 3.4% Non-denominational Protestant (2010)
Economy: Unemployment rate: 5.6% (April 2014); Total civilian labor force: 30,797 (April 2014); Leading industries: 22.4% retail trade; 20.4% health care and social assistance; 17.4% accommodation & food services (2012); Farms: 783 totaling 214,197 acres (2012); Companies that employ 500 or more persons: 1 (2012); Companies that employ 100 to 499 persons: 20 (2012); Companies that employ less than 100 persons: 1,310 (2012); Black-owned businesses: n/a (2007); Hispanic-owned businesses: n/a (2007); Asian-owned businesses: 173 (2007); Women-owned businesses: 1,190 (2007); Single-family building permits issued: 8 (2013); Multi-family building permits issued: 34 (2013).
Income: Per capita income: $19,943 (2008-2012 5-year est.); Median household income: $32,819 (2008-2012 5-year est.); Average household income: $48,341 (2008-2012 5-year est.); Percent of households with income of $100,000 or more: 12.6% (2008-2012 5-year est.); Poverty rate: 29.5% (2008-2012 5-year est.); Bankruptcy rate: 3.08% (2013).
Taxes: Total county taxes per capita: $188 (2011); County property taxes per capita: $145 (2011).
Education: Percent of population age 25 and over with: High school diploma (including GED) or higher: 90.6% (2008-2012 5-year est.); Bachelor's degree or higher: 36.0% (2008-2012 5-year est.); Master's degree or higher: 17.4% (2008-2012 5-year est.).
Housing: Homeownership rate: 53.6% (2008-2012 5-year est.); Median home value: $96,900 (2008-2012 5-year est.); Median contract rent: $520 per month (2008-2012 5-year est.); Median year structure built: 1974 (2008-2012 5-year est.)
Health: Birth rate: 108.8 per 10,000 population (2013); Death rate: 71.2 per 10,000 population (2013); Age-adjusted cancer mortality rate: 168.3 deaths per 100,000 population (2011); Number of physicians: 29.7 per 10,000 population (2011); Hospital beds: 29.6 per 10,000 population (2010); Hospital admissions: 1,717.4 per 10,000 population (2010).
Elections: 2012 Presidential election results: 53.4% Obama, 43.1% Romney
National and State Parks: Giant City State Park; Lake Murphysboro State Park
Additional Information Contacts
Jackson County Government . . . . (618) 687-7360
    http://www.jacksoncounty-il.gov

Jackson County Communities

AVA (city). Covers a land area of 1.057 square miles and a water area of 0.009 square miles. Located at 37.89° N. Lat; 89.50° W. Long. Elevation is 604 feet.
Population: 674 (1990); 662 (2000); 654 (2010); Density: 651.8 persons per square mile (2008-2012 5-year est.); Race: 98.0% White, 0.0% Black/African American, 0.0% Asian, 0.0% American Indian/Alaska Native, 0.0% Native Hawaiian/Other Pacific Islander, 2.0% Some other race, 2.0% Two or more races, 0.0% Hispanic of any race (2008-2012 5-year est.); Average household size: 2.33 (2008-2012 5-year est.); Median age: 43.3 (2008-2012 5-year est.); Males per 100 females: 80.4 (2008-2012 5-year est.); Marriage status: 19.0% never married, 55.4% now married, 11.8% widowed, 13.8% divorced (2008-2012 5-year est.); Foreign born: 1.0% (2008-2012 5-year est.); Ancestry (includes multiple ancestries): 38.6% German, 19.2% Irish, 17.3% English, 7.7% French, 6.0% American (2008-2012 5-year est.).
Economy: Homeowner vacancy rate: 1.5%. Rental vacancy rate: 0.0%. (2008-2012 5-year est.); Employment by occupation: 12.3% management,

business, and financial, 2.2% computer, engineering, and science, 6.8% education, legal, community service, arts, and media, 8.3% healthcare practitioners, 16.0% service, 26.8% sales and office, 11.4% natural resources, construction, and maintenance, 16.3% production, transportation, and material moving (2008-2012 5-year est.).

Income: Per capita income: $24,922 (2008-2012 5-year est.); Median household income: $42,500 (2008-2012 5-year est.); Average household income: $56,260 (2008-2012 5-year est.); Percent of households with income of $100,000 or more: 12.9% (2008-2012 5-year est.); Poverty rate: 10.6% (2008-2012 5-year est.).

Education: Percent of population age 25 and over with: High school diploma (including GED) or higher: 88.4% (2008-2012 5-year est.); Bachelor's degree or higher: 12.0% (2008-2012 5-year est.); Master's degree or higher: 4.1% (2008-2012 5-year est.).

Housing: Homeownership rate: 67.2% (2008-2012 5-year est.); Median home value: $61,500 (2008-2012 5-year est.); Median contract rent: $332 per month (2008-2012 5-year est.); Median year structure built: 1971 (2008-2012 5-year est.).

Health Insurance: 61.4% Private; 41.5% Public; 11.6% None. (2008-2012 5-year est.)

Transportation: Commute to work: 90.1% car, 0.0% public transportation, 4.8% walk, 5.1% work from home (2008-2012 5-year est.); Travel time to work: 27.6% less than 15 minutes, 37.4% 15 to 30 minutes, 19.2% 30 to 45 minutes, 14.1% 45 to 60 minutes, 1.7% 60 minutes or more (2008-2012 5-year est.)

CAMPBELL HILL (village). Covers a land area of 0.416 square miles and a water area of 0.001 square miles. Located at 37.93° N. Lat; 89.55° W. Long. Elevation is 561 feet.

Population: 351 (1990); 333 (2000); 336 (2010); Density: 675.1 persons per square mile (2008-2012 5-year est.); Race: 100.0% White, 0.0% Black/African American, 0.0% Asian, 0.0% American Indian/Alaska Native, 0.0% Native Hawaiian/Other Pacific Islander, 0.0% Some other race, 0.0% Two or more races, 0.0% Hispanic of any race (2008-2012 5-year est.); Average household size: 2.20 (2008-2012 5-year est.); Median age: 42.4 (2008-2012 5-year est.); Males per 100 females: 128.5 (2008-2012 5-year est.); Marriage status: 17.7% never married, 66.5% now married, 4.4% widowed, 11.3% divorced (2008-2012 5-year est.); Foreign born: 0.0% (2008-2012 5-year est.); Ancestry (includes multiple ancestries): 55.5% German, 11.4% Irish, 7.8% English, 6.8% American, 4.3% Polish (2008-2012 5-year est.).

Economy: Single-family building permits issued: 0 (2013); Multi-family building permits issued: 0 (2013); Homeowner vacancy rate: 0.0%. Rental vacancy rate: 0.0%. (2008-2012 5-year est.); Employment by occupation: 4.0% management, business, and financial, 0.6% computer, engineering, and science, 9.7% education, legal, community service, arts, and media, 1.7% healthcare practitioners, 16.5% service, 15.9% sales and office, 9.1% natural resources, construction, and maintenance, 42.6% production, transportation, and material moving (2008-2012 5-year est.).

Income: Per capita income: $25,272 (2008-2012 5-year est.); Median household income: $40,000 (2008-2012 5-year est.); Average household income: $51,920 (2008-2012 5-year est.); Percent of households with income of $100,000 or more: 10.2% (2008-2012 5-year est.); Poverty rate: 7.5% (2008-2012 5-year est.).

Education: Percent of population age 25 and over with: High school diploma (including GED) or higher: 80.3% (2008-2012 5-year est.); Bachelor's degree or higher: 9.9% (2008-2012 5-year est.); Master's degree or higher: 1.4% (2008-2012 5-year est.).

School District(s)
Trico CUSD 176 (PK-12)
   2011-12 Enrollment: 1,014 . . . . (618) 426-1111

Housing: Homeownership rate: 82.0% (2008-2012 5-year est.); Median home value: $68,400 (2008-2012 5-year est.); Median contract rent: $388 per month (2008-2012 5-year est.); Median year structure built: 1950 (2008-2012 5-year est.).

Health Insurance: 69.0% Private; 34.5% Public; 8.9% None. (2008-2012 5-year est.)

Transportation: Commute to work: 92.9% car, 0.0% public transportation, 5.9% walk, 0.0% work from home (2008-2012 5-year est.); Travel time to work: 38.2% less than 15 minutes, 32.9% 15 to 30 minutes, 11.2% 30 to 45 minutes, 15.3% 45 to 60 minutes, 2.4% 60 minutes or more (2008-2012 5-year est.)

CARBONDALE (city). Covers a land area of 17.085 square miles and a water area of 0.429 square miles. Located at 37.72° N. Lat; 89.22° W. Long. Elevation is 413 feet.

History: Carbondale developed as a coal mining center and a division point on the Illinois Central Railroad. In 1874 the Southern Illinois State Normal University was founded here.

Population: 27,033 (1990); 20,681 (2000); 25,902 (2010); Density: 1,519.5 persons per square mile (2008-2012 5-year est.); Race: 62.9% White, 25.7% Black/African American, 5.9% Asian, 0.4% American Indian/Alaska Native, 0.1% Native Hawaiian/Other Pacific Islander, 5.0% Some other race, 3.7% Two or more races, 5.8% Hispanic of any race (2008-2012 5-year est.); Average household size: 2.18 (2008-2012 5-year est.); Median age: 23.3 (2008-2012 5-year est.); Males per 100 females: 106.3 (2008-2012 5-year est.); Marriage status: 69.6% never married, 20.3% now married, 3.3% widowed, 6.8% divorced (2008-2012 5-year est.); Foreign born: 10.0% (2008-2012 5-year est.); Ancestry (includes multiple ancestries): 18.6% German, 9.5% Irish, 7.8% English, 3.6% Italian, 3.2% Polish (2008-2012 5-year est.).

Economy: Unemployment rate: 5.4% (April 2014); Total civilian labor force: 13,532 (April 2014); Single-family building permits issued: 7 (2013); Multi-family building permits issued: 34 (2013); Homeowner vacancy rate: 5.0%. Rental vacancy rate: 14.0%. (2008-2012 5-year est.); Employment by occupation: 7.4% management, business, and financial, 4.0% computer, engineering, and science, 27.1% education, legal, community service, arts, and media, 3.7% healthcare practitioners, 26.4% service, 24.2% sales and office, 1.8% natural resources, construction, and maintenance, 5.3% production, transportation, and material moving (2008-2012 5-year est.).

Income: Per capita income: $14,779 (2008-2012 5-year est.); Median household income: $17,743 (2008-2012 5-year est.); Average household income: $36,495 (2008-2012 5-year est.); Percent of households with income of $100,000 or more: 9.5% (2008-2012 5-year est.); Poverty rate: 48.0% (2008-2012 5-year est.).

Taxes: Total city taxes per capita: $478 (2011); City property taxes per capita: $37 (2011).

Education: Percent of population age 25 and over with: High school diploma (including GED) or higher: 92.9% (2008-2012 5-year est.); Bachelor's degree or higher: 52.1% (2008-2012 5-year est.); Master's degree or higher: 27.1% (2008-2012 5-year est.).

School District(s)
Carbondale CHSD 165 (09-12)
   2011-12 Enrollment: 1,109 . . . . (618) 457-4722
Carbondale ESD 95 (PK-08)
   2011-12 Enrollment: 1,411 . . . . (618) 457-3591
Giant City CCSD 130 (PK-08)
   2011-12 Enrollment: 280 . . . . (618) 457-5391
Unity Point CCSD 140 (PK-08)
   2011-12 Enrollment: 697 . . . . (618) 529-4151

Four-year College(s)
Southern Illinois University Carbondale (Public)
   Fall 2012 Enrollment: 18,197 . . . . (618) 453-2121
   2012-13 Tuition: In-state $11,528; Out-of-state $23,781

Housing: Homeownership rate: 28.6% (2008-2012 5-year est.); Median home value: $115,000 (2008-2012 5-year est.); Median contract rent: $564 per month (2008-2012 5-year est.); Median year structure built: 1975 (2008-2012 5-year est.).

Health Insurance: 74.7% Private; 23.1% Public; 8.7% None. (2008-2012 5-year est.)

Hospitals: Memorial Hospital Carbondale (150 beds)

Safety: Violent crime rate: 100.1 per 10,000 population; Property crime rate: 420.5 per 10,000 population (2012).

Transportation: Commute to work: 76.2% car, 1.2% public transportation, 15.1% walk, 2.7% work from home (2008-2012 5-year est.); Travel time to work: 72.1% less than 15 minutes, 19.4% 15 to 30 minutes, 6.2% 30 to 45 minutes, 1.3% 45 to 60 minutes, 1.0% 60 minutes or more (2008-2012 5-year est.); Amtrak: Train service available.

Airports: Southern Illinois Airport (general aviation)

Additional Information Contacts
Carbondale Chamber of Commerce . . . . (618) 549-2146
   http://www.carbondalechamber.com
City of Carbondale. . . . . (618) 549-5302
   http://explorecarbondale.com

DE SOTO

DE SOTO (village). Covers a land area of 0.912 square miles and a water area of 0.012 square miles. Located at 37.82° N. Lat; 89.23° W. Long. Elevation is 400 feet.

Population: 1,500 (1990); 1,653 (2000); 1,590 (2010); Density: 1,620.1 persons per square mile (2008-2012 5-year est.); Race: 90.9% White, 1.3% Black/African American, 4.6% Asian, 0.0% American Indian/Alaska Native, 0.0% Native Hawaiian/Other Pacific Islander, 3.2% Some other race, 3.2% Two or more races, 0.9% Hispanic of any race (2008-2012 5-year est.); Average household size: 2.46 (2008-2012 5-year est.); Median age: 36.3 (2008-2012 5-year est.); Males per 100 females: 96.5 (2008-2012 5-year est.); Marriage status: 28.1% never married, 48.2% now married, 7.4% widowed, 16.3% divorced (2008-2012 5-year est.); Foreign born: 4.3% (2008-2012 5-year est.); Ancestry (includes multiple ancestries): 25.0% German, 17.9% Irish, 13.5% English, 6.2% French, 6.1% American (2008-2012 5-year est.).

Economy: Single-family building permits issued: 0 (2013); Multi-family building permits issued: 0 (2013); Homeowner vacancy rate: 0.0%. Rental vacancy rate: 8.4%. (2008-2012 5-year est.); Employment by occupation: 8.7% management, business, and financial, 2.5% computer, engineering, and science, 11.5% education, legal, community service, arts, and media, 4.3% healthcare practitioners, 23.5% service, 27.1% sales and office, 10.5% natural resources, construction, and maintenance, 12.0% production, transportation, and material moving (2008-2012 5-year est.).

Income: Per capita income: $18,754 (2008-2012 5-year est.); Median household income: $36,719 (2008-2012 5-year est.); Average household income: $44,804 (2008-2012 5-year est.); Percent of households with income of $100,000 or more: 6.7% (2008-2012 5-year est.); Poverty rate: 22.2% (2008-2012 5-year est.).

Education: Percent of population age 25 and over with: High school diploma (including GED) or higher: 88.1% (2008-2012 5-year est.); Bachelor's degree or higher: 22.3% (2008-2012 5-year est.); Master's degree or higher: 9.5% (2008-2012 5-year est.).

School District(s)

Desoto CSD 86 (PK-08)

    2011-12 Enrollment: 274 . . . . (618) 867-2317

Housing: Homeownership rate: 66.3% (2008-2012 5-year est.); Median home value: $78,700 (2008-2012 5-year est.); Median contract rent: $425 per month (2008-2012 5-year est.); Median year structure built: 1973 (2008-2012 5-year est.).

Health Insurance: 61.3% Private; 37.2% Public; 16.0% None. (2008-2012 5-year est.)

Safety: Violent crime rate: 12.5 per 10,000 population; Property crime rate: 62.7 per 10,000 population (2012).

Transportation: Commute to work: 96.2% car, 1.7% public transportation, 1.2% walk, 0.9% work from home (2008-2012 5-year est.); Travel time to work: 24.9% less than 15 minutes, 48.1% 15 to 30 minutes, 14.8% 30 to 45 minutes, 8.8% 45 to 60 minutes, 3.4% 60 minutes or more (2008-2012 5-year est.).

DOWELL

DOWELL (village). Covers a land area of 0.390 square miles and a water area of 0.001 square miles. Located at 37.94° N. Lat; 89.24° W. Long. Elevation is 400 feet.

History: Dowell grew around the Kathleen Coal Company Mine in 1916, and was named for George Dowell, legal advisor for the Progressive Miners of America.

Population: 465 (1990); 441 (2000); 408 (2010); Density: 751.1 persons per square mile (2008-2012 5-year est.); Race: 99.7% White, 0.0% Black/African American, 0.0% Asian, 0.0% American Indian/Alaska Native, 0.0% Native Hawaiian/Other Pacific Islander, 0.3% Some other race, 0.3% Two or more races, 0.0% Hispanic of any race (2008-2012 5-year est.); Average household size: 2.24 (2008-2012 5-year est.); Median age: 43.9 (2008-2012 5-year est.); Males per 100 females: 80.9 (2008-2012 5-year est.); Marriage status: 23.0% never married, 55.6% now married, 9.1% widowed, 12.3% divorced (2008-2012 5-year est.); Foreign born: 0.0% (2008-2012 5-year est.); Ancestry (includes multiple ancestries): 33.8% English, 27.0% German, 21.5% Irish, 12.6% Dutch, 8.2% Hungarian (2008-2012 5-year est.).

Economy: Single-family building permits issued: 0 (2013); Multi-family building permits issued: 0 (2013); Homeowner vacancy rate: 0.0%. Rental vacancy rate: 0.0%. (2008-2012 5-year est.); Employment by occupation: 11.2% management, business, and financial, 0.0% computer, engineering, and science, 2.8% education, legal, community service, arts, and media, 23.1% healthcare practitioners, 30.8% service, 13.3% sales and office, 4.2% natural resources, construction, and maintenance, 14.7% production, transportation, and material moving (2008-2012 5-year est.).

Income: Per capita income: $17,633 (2008-2012 5-year est.); Median household income: $31,563 (2008-2012 5-year est.); Average household income: $38,696 (2008-2012 5-year est.); Percent of households with income of $100,000 or more: 2.3% (2008-2012 5-year est.); Poverty rate: 22.0% (2008-2012 5-year est.).

Education: Percent of population age 25 and over with: High school diploma (including GED) or higher: 87.0% (2008-2012 5-year est.); Bachelor's degree or higher: 2.3% (2008-2012 5-year est.); Master's degree or higher: 0.0% (2008-2012 5-year est.).

Housing: Homeownership rate: 93.1% (2008-2012 5-year est.); Median home value: $51,300 (2008-2012 5-year est.); Median contract rent: $365 per month (2008-2012 5-year est.); Median year structure built: Before 1940 (2008-2012 5-year est.).

Health Insurance: 58.0% Private; 41.0% Public; 17.4% None. (2008-2012 5-year est.)

Transportation: Commute to work: 100.0% car, 0.0% public transportation, 0.0% walk, 0.0% work from home (2008-2012 5-year est.); Travel time to work: 28.7% less than 15 minutes, 27.3% 15 to 30 minutes, 37.1% 30 to 45 minutes, 7.0% 45 to 60 minutes, 0.0% 60 minutes or more (2008-2012 5-year est.)

ELKVILLE

ELKVILLE (village). Covers a land area of 0.763 square miles and a water area of 0.005 square miles. Located at 37.91° N. Lat; 89.24° W. Long. Elevation is 400 feet.

Population: 958 (1990); 1,001 (2000); 928 (2010); Density: 1,333.4 persons per square mile (2008-2012 5-year est.); Race: 95.6% White, 2.6% Black/African American, 0.0% Asian, 0.0% American Indian/Alaska Native, 0.0% Native Hawaiian/Other Pacific Islander, 1.8% Some other race, 1.9% Two or more races, 5.2% Hispanic of any race (2008-2012 5-year est.); Average household size: 2.77 (2008-2012 5-year est.); Median age: 36.1 (2008-2012 5-year est.); Males per 100 females: 148.9 (2008-2012 5-year est.); Marriage status: 28.7% never married, 51.9% now married, 4.5% widowed, 14.9% divorced (2008-2012 5-year est.); Foreign born: 2.9% (2008-2012 5-year est.); Ancestry (includes multiple ancestries): 29.7% German, 16.8% English, 8.3% Irish, 5.7% Scottish, 5.0% American (2008-2012 5-year est.).

Economy: Single-family building permits issued: 0 (2013); Multi-family building permits issued: 0 (2013); Homeowner vacancy rate: 0.0%. Rental vacancy rate: 16.4%. (2008-2012 5-year est.); Employment by occupation: 13.3% management, business, and financial, 0.6% computer, engineering, and science, 4.1% education, legal, community service, arts, and media, 1.3% healthcare practitioners, 18.0% service, 27.9% sales and office, 11.6% natural resources, construction, and maintenance, 23.2% production, transportation, and material moving (2008-2012 5-year est.).

Income: Per capita income: $19,012 (2008-2012 5-year est.); Median household income: $35,833 (2008-2012 5-year est.); Average household income: $48,218 (2008-2012 5-year est.); Percent of households with income of $100,000 or more: 9.6% (2008-2012 5-year est.); Poverty rate: 21.1% (2008-2012 5-year est.).

Education: Percent of population age 25 and over with: High school diploma (including GED) or higher: 87.6% (2008-2012 5-year est.); Bachelor's degree or higher: 10.3% (2008-2012 5-year est.); Master's degree or higher: 2.5% (2008-2012 5-year est.).

School District(s)

Elverado CUSD 196 (PK-12)

    2011-12 Enrollment: 508 . . . . (618) 568-1321

Housing: Homeownership rate: 68.2% (2008-2012 5-year est.); Median home value: $64,500 (2008-2012 5-year est.); Median contract rent: $363 per month (2008-2012 5-year est.); Median year structure built: 1970 (2008-2012 5-year est.).

Health Insurance: 48.1% Private; 38.4% Public; 21.6% None. (2008-2012 5-year est.)

Transportation: Commute to work: 96.1% car, 0.7% public transportation, 0.7% walk, 0.0% work from home (2008-2012 5-year est.); Travel time to work: 18.1% less than 15 minutes, 35.8% 15 to 30 minutes, 36.1% 30 to 45 minutes, 5.9% 45 to 60 minutes, 4.1% 60 minutes or more (2008-2012 5-year est.)

GORHAM

GORHAM (village). Covers a land area of 1.219 square miles and a water area of 0.011 square miles. Located at 37.72° N. Lat; 89.48° W. Long. Elevation is 361 feet.

Population: 290 (1990); 256 (2000); 236 (2010); Density: 247.7 persons per square mile (2008-2012 5-year est.); Race: 98.3% White, 0.0% Black/African American, 0.0% Asian, 0.0% American Indian/Alaska Native, 0.0% Native Hawaiian/Other Pacific Islander, 1.7% Some other race, 1.7%

Two or more races, 0.0% Hispanic of any race (2008-2012 5-year est.); Average household size: 2.85 (2008-2012 5-year est.); Median age: 30.7 (2008-2012 5-year est.); Males per 100 females: 88.8 (2008-2012 5-year est.); Marriage status: 25.2% never married, 51.4% now married, 7.1% widowed, 16.2% divorced (2008-2012 5-year est.); Foreign born: 0.0% (2008-2012 5-year est.); Ancestry (includes multiple ancestries): 23.5% German, 11.6% English, 7.9% American, 2.6% French, 2.0% Scottish (2008-2012 5-year est.).

Economy: Homeowner vacancy rate: 0.0%. Rental vacancy rate: 0.0%. (2008-2012 5-year est.); Employment by occupation: 10.0% management, business, and financial, 7.5% computer, engineering, and science, 0.0% education, legal, community service, arts, and media, 3.8% healthcare practitioners, 11.3% service, 22.5% sales and office, 10.0% natural resources, construction, and maintenance, 35.0% production, transportation, and material moving (2008-2012 5-year est.).

Income: Per capita income: $10,955 (2008-2012 5-year est.); Median household income: $27,115 (2008-2012 5-year est.); Average household income: $31,083 (2008-2012 5-year est.); Percent of households with income of $100,000 or more: n/a (2008-2012 5-year est.); Poverty rate: 42.2% (2008-2012 5-year est.).

Education: Percent of population age 25 and over with: High school diploma (including GED) or higher: 67.8% (2008-2012 5-year est.); Bachelor's degree or higher: 0.0% (2008-2012 5-year est.); Master's degree or higher: 0.0% (2008-2012 5-year est.).

Housing: Homeownership rate: 74.5% (2008-2012 5-year est.); Median home value: $30,400 (2008-2012 5-year est.); Median contract rent: $280 per month (2008-2012 5-year est.); Median year structure built: 1951 (2008-2012 5-year est.).

Health Insurance: 38.4% Private; 60.9% Public; 11.6% None. (2008-2012 5-year est.)

Transportation: Commute to work: 90.9% car, 0.0% public transportation, 0.0% walk, 5.2% work from home (2008-2012 5-year est.); Travel time to work: 19.2% less than 15 minutes, 12.3% 15 to 30 minutes, 57.5% 30 to 45 minutes, 9.6% 45 to 60 minutes, 1.4% 60 minutes or more (2008-2012 5-year est.)

GRAND TOWER (city).
Covers a land area of 1.248 square miles and a water area of 0.003 square miles. Located at 37.64° N. Lat; 89.51° W. Long. Elevation is 361 feet.

History: Grand Tower was named for the 60-foot-high Tower Rock in the middle of the Mississippi River.

Population: 775 (1990); 624 (2000); 605 (2010); Density: 389.3 persons per square mile (2008-2012 5-year est.); Race: 97.7% White, 0.6% Black/African American, 0.2% Asian, 0.0% American Indian/Alaska Native, 0.0% Native Hawaiian/Other Pacific Islander, 1.5% Some other race, 1.4% Two or more races, 0.0% Hispanic of any race (2008-2012 5-year est.); Average household size: 2.45 (2008-2012 5-year est.); Median age: 44.3 (2008-2012 5-year est.); Males per 100 females: 103.3 (2008-2012 5-year est.); Marriage status: 21.7% never married, 53.4% now married, 7.7% widowed, 17.1% divorced (2008-2012 5-year est.); Foreign born: 0.2% (2008-2012 5-year est.); Ancestry (includes multiple ancestries): 24.3% German, 16.5% Irish, 15.4% English, 5.6% American, 3.7% Scotch-Irish (2008-2012 5-year est.).

Economy: Single-family building permits issued: 0 (2013); Multi-family building permits issued: 0 (2013); Homeowner vacancy rate: 0.0%. Rental vacancy rate: 20.0%. (2008-2012 5-year est.); Employment by occupation: 0.0% management, business, and financial, 0.0% computer, engineering, and science, 4.2% education, legal, community service, arts, and media, 4.2% healthcare practitioners, 23.3% service, 15.0% sales and office, 19.2% natural resources, construction, and maintenance, 34.2% production, transportation, and material moving (2008-2012 5-year est.).

Income: Per capita income: $14,176 (2008-2012 5-year est.); Median household income: $29,643 (2008-2012 5-year est.); Average household income: $33,928 (2008-2012 5-year est.); Percent of households with income of $100,000 or more: 1.5% (2008-2012 5-year est.); Poverty rate: 30.9% (2008-2012 5-year est.).

Education: Percent of population age 25 and over with: High school diploma (including GED) or higher: 64.3% (2008-2012 5-year est.); Bachelor's degree or higher: 3.0% (2008-2012 5-year est.); Master's degree or higher: 0.0% (2008-2012 5-year est.).

School District(s)

Shawnee CUSD 84 (KG-12)
 2011-12 Enrollment: 413 . . . . (618) 833-5709

Housing: Homeownership rate: 71.2% (2008-2012 5-year est.); Median home value: $37,500 (2008-2012 5-year est.); Median contract rent: $292

per month (2008-2012 5-year est.); Median year structure built: 1966 (2008-2012 5-year est.).

Health Insurance: 40.9% Private; 56.0% Public; 14.8% None. (2008-2012 5-year est.)

Transportation: Commute to work: 93.2% car, 0.0% public transportation, 1.7% walk, 0.0% work from home (2008-2012 5-year est.); Travel time to work: 32.5% less than 15 minutes, 23.9% 15 to 30 minutes, 13.7% 30 to 45 minutes, 9.4% 45 to 60 minutes, 20.5% 60 minutes or more (2008-2012 5-year est.)

HARRISON (CDP).
Covers a land area of 2.056 square miles and a water area of 0.037 square miles. Located at 37.80° N. Lat; 89.34° W. Long. Elevation is 407 feet.

Population: n/a (1990); n/a (2000); 970 (2010); Density: 492.2 persons per square mile (2008-2012 5-year est.); Race: 97.3% White, 0.0% Black/African American, 0.0% Asian, 1.2% American Indian/Alaska Native, 0.0% Native Hawaiian/Other Pacific Islander, 1.5% Some other race, 0.0% Two or more races, 1.5% Hispanic of any race (2008-2012 5-year est.); Average household size: 2.94 (2008-2012 5-year est.); Median age: 29.4 (2008-2012 5-year est.); Males per 100 females: 68.4 (2008-2012 5-year est.); Marriage status: 25.3% never married, 44.0% now married, 9.8% widowed, 20.9% divorced (2008-2012 5-year est.); Foreign born: 0.7% (2008-2012 5-year est.); Ancestry (includes multiple ancestries): 28.0% Irish, 24.0% American, 16.0% German, 8.4% English, 6.9% Italian (2008-2012 5-year est.).

Economy: Homeowner vacancy rate: 0.0%. Rental vacancy rate: 0.0%. (2008-2012 5-year est.); Employment by occupation: 12.4% management, business, and financial, 0.0% computer, engineering, and science, 11.3% education, legal, community service, arts, and media, 10.0% healthcare practitioners, 28.3% service, 22.0% sales and office, 10.0% natural resources, construction, and maintenance, 5.9% production, transportation, and material moving (2008-2012 5-year est.).

Income: Per capita income: $20,532 (2008-2012 5-year est.); Median household income: $46,100 (2008-2012 5-year est.); Average household income: $60,640 (2008-2012 5-year est.); Percent of households with income of $100,000 or more: 7.9% (2008-2012 5-year est.); Poverty rate: 14.7% (2008-2012 5-year est.).

Education: Percent of population age 25 and over with: High school diploma (including GED) or higher: 96.6% (2008-2012 5-year est.); Bachelor's degree or higher: 13.7% (2008-2012 5-year est.); Master's degree or higher: 9.6% (2008-2012 5-year est.).

Housing: Homeownership rate: 64.8% (2008-2012 5-year est.); Median home value: $96,600 (2008-2012 5-year est.); Median contract rent: $594 per month (2008-2012 5-year est.); Median year structure built: 1961 (2008-2012 5-year est.).

Health Insurance: 61.8% Private; 41.5% Public; 20.7% None. (2008-2012 5-year est.)

Transportation: Commute to work: 95.3% car, 0.0% public transportation, 0.0% walk, 2.4% work from home (2008-2012 5-year est.); Travel time to work: 48.9% less than 15 minutes, 35.1% 15 to 30 minutes, 6.8% 30 to 45 minutes, 0.0% 45 to 60 minutes, 9.2% 60 minutes or more (2008-2012 5-year est.)

JACOB (unincorporated postal area)
Zip Code: 62950

Covers a land area of 30.085 square miles and a water area of 1.066 square miles. Located at 37.74° N. Lat; 89.56° W. Long. Elevation is 361 feet. Population: 193 (2010); Density: 6.4 persons per square mile (2010); Race: 99.5% White, 0.0% Black/African American, 0.0% Asian, 0.5% American Indian/Alaska Native, 0.0% Native Hawaiian/Other Pacific Islander, 0.0% Some other race, 0.0% Two or more races, 1.0% Hispanic of any race (2010); Average household size: 2.30 (2010); Median age: 44.3 (2010); Males per 100 females: 107.5 (2010); Homeownership rate: 82.1% (2010)

MAKANDA (village).
Covers a land area of 5.286 square miles and a water area of 0.051 square miles. Located at 37.62° N. Lat; 89.24° W. Long. Elevation is 446 feet.

Population: 404 (1990); 419 (2000); 561 (2010); Density: 93.6 persons per square mile (2008-2012 5-year est.); Race: 79.0% White, 8.1% Black/African American, 12.5% Asian, 0.0% American Indian/Alaska Native, 0.0% Native Hawaiian/Other Pacific Islander, 0.4% Some other race, 0.0% Two or more races, 1.2% Hispanic of any race (2008-2012 5-year est.); Average household size: 2.20 (2008-2012 5-year est.); Median age: 49.2 (2008-2012 5-year est.); Males per 100 females: 116.2

(2008-2012 5-year est.); Marriage status: 33.1% never married, 54.4% now married, 3.3% widowed, 9.1% divorced (2008-2012 5-year est.); Foreign born: 5.5% (2008-2012 5-year est.); Ancestry (includes multiple ancestries): 13.7% German, 12.3% Irish, 10.3% English, 6.1% Swedish, 5.1% Dutch (2008-2012 5-year est.).

Economy: Homeowner vacancy rate: 4.4%. Rental vacancy rate: 40.8%. (2008-2012 5-year est.); Employment by occupation: 13.3% management, business, and financial, 0.7% computer, engineering, and science, 24.8% education, legal, community service, arts, and media, 15.8% healthcare practitioners, 13.7% service, 16.5% sales and office, 10.4% natural resources, construction, and maintenance, 4.7% production, transportation, and material moving (2008-2012 5-year est.).

Income: Per capita income: $52,718 (2008-2012 5-year est.); Median household income: $58,125 (2008-2012 5-year est.); Average household income: $115,329 (2008-2012 5-year est.); Percent of households with income of $100,000 or more: 33.4% (2008-2012 5-year est.); Poverty rate: 1.8% (2008-2012 5-year est.).

Education: Percent of population age 25 and over with: High school diploma (including GED) or higher: 100.0% (2008-2012 5-year est.); Bachelor's degree or higher: 54.1% (2008-2012 5-year est.); Master's degree or higher: 28.0% (2008-2012 5-year est.).

Housing: Homeownership rate: 87.1% (2008-2012 5-year est.); Median home value: $163,300 (2008-2012 5-year est.); Median contract rent: $603 per month (2008-2012 5-year est.); Median year structure built: 1989 (2008-2012 5-year est.).

Health Insurance: 85.7% Private; 14.3% Public; 10.7% None. (2008-2012 5-year est.)

Transportation: Commute to work: 97.4% car, 0.0% public transportation, 0.0% walk, 1.8% work from home (2008-2012 5-year est.); Travel time to work: 24.1% less than 15 minutes, 60.5% 15 to 30 minutes, 9.8% 30 to 45 minutes, 3.8% 45 to 60 minutes, 1.9% 60 minutes or more (2008-2012 5-year est.)

MURPHYSBORO (city). County seat. Covers a land area of 5.152 square miles and a water area of 0.085 square miles. Located at 37.77° N. Lat; 89.33° W. Long. Elevation is 420 feet.

History: A memorial to John A. Logan is in the city. Incorporated 1867.

Population: 9,176 (1990); 13,295 (2000); 7,970 (2010); Density: 1,585.0 persons per square mile (2008-2012 5-year est.); Race: 84.4% White, 11.7% Black/African American, 0.3% Asian, 0.1% American Indian/Alaska Native, 0.0% Native Hawaiian/Other Pacific Islander, 3.5% Some other race, 3.3% Two or more races, 1.3% Hispanic of any race (2008-2012 5-year est.); Average household size: 2.16 (2008-2012 5-year est.); Median age: 40.5 (2008-2012 5-year est.); Males per 100 females: 88.3 (2008-2012 5-year est.); Marriage status: 36.7% never married, 36.7% now married, 11.0% widowed, 15.7% divorced (2008-2012 5-year est.); Foreign born: 0.7% (2008-2012 5-year est.); Ancestry (includes multiple ancestries): 24.8% German, 10.8% Irish, 10.4% American, 7.0% English, 6.8% Italian (2008-2012 5-year est.).

Economy: Single-family building permits issued: 1 (2013); Multi-family building permits issued: 0 (2013); Homeowner vacancy rate: 4.2%. Rental vacancy rate: 12.6%. (2008-2012 5-year est.); Employment by occupation: 6.9% management, business, and financial, 1.1% computer, engineering, and science, 14.0% education, legal, community service, arts, and media, 7.4% healthcare practitioners, 24.6% service, 19.9% sales and office, 9.7% natural resources, construction, and maintenance, 16.5% production, transportation, and material moving (2008-2012 5-year est.).

Income: Per capita income: $19,269 (2008-2012 5-year est.); Median household income: $29,936 (2008-2012 5-year est.); Average household income: $41,468 (2008-2012 5-year est.); Percent of households with income of $100,000 or more: 6.7% (2008-2012 5-year est.); Poverty rate: 26.3% (2008-2012 5-year est.).

Education: Percent of population age 25 and over with: High school diploma (including GED) or higher: 85.4% (2008-2012 5-year est.); Bachelor's degree or higher: 21.7% (2008-2012 5-year est.); Master's degree or higher: 9.0% (2008-2012 5-year est.).

School District(s)

Idjj SD 428 (06-12)
    2011-12 Enrollment: 784 . . . . (309) 584-0506
Jackson/perry Roe (06-09)
    2011-12 Enrollment: n/a . . . . (618) 687-7290
Murphysboro CUSD 186 (PK-12)
    2011-12 Enrollment: 2,133 . . . . (618) 684-3781
Tri-County Sp Ed Jnt Agreement
    2011-12 Enrollment: n/a . . . . (618) 684-2109

Housing: Homeownership rate: 58.4% (2008-2012 5-year est.); Median home value: $69,800 (2008-2012 5-year est.); Median contract rent: $412 per month (2008-2012 5-year est.); Median year structure built: 1957 (2008-2012 5-year est.).

Health Insurance: 63.9% Private; 46.7% Public; 8.4% None. (2008-2012 5-year est.)

Hospitals: St. Joseph Memorial Hospital (59 beds)

Safety: Violent crime rate: 60.0 per 10,000 population; Property crime rate: 570.4 per 10,000 population (2012).

Transportation: Commute to work: 94.8% car, 0.0% public transportation, 3.3% walk, 0.5% work from home (2008-2012 5-year est.); Travel time to work: 41.1% less than 15 minutes, 35.7% 15 to 30 minutes, 14.4% 30 to 45 minutes, 6.0% 45 to 60 minutes, 2.8% 60 minutes or more (2008-2012 5-year est.)

Airports: Southern Illinois Airport (general aviation)

Additional Information Contacts

City of Murphysboro . . . . (618) 684-4961
    http://www.murphysboro-il.gov
Murphysboro Chamber of Commerce . . . . (618) 684-6421
    http://murphysborochamber.com

POMONA (unincorporated postal area)
Zip Code: 62975

Covers a land area of 23.165 square miles and a water area of 0.352 square miles. Located at 37.63° N. Lat; 89.38° W. Long. Elevation is 407 feet. Population: 279 (2010); Density: 12.0 persons per square mile (2010); Race: 99.3% White, 0.0% Black/African American, 0.0% Asian, 0.4% American Indian/Alaska Native, 0.0% Native Hawaiian/Other Pacific Islander, 0.3% Some other race, 0.4% Two or more races, 0.4% Hispanic of any race (2010); Average household size: 2.38 (2010); Median age: 48.1 (2010); Males per 100 females: 102.2 (2010); Homeownership rate: 94.9% (2010)

VERGENNES (village). Covers a land area of 0.352 square miles and a water area of 0.002 square miles. Located at 37.90° N. Lat; 89.34° W. Long. Elevation is 397 feet.

Population: 314 (1990); 491 (2000); 298 (2010); Density: 1,125.1 persons per square mile (2008-2012 5-year est.); Race: 98.0% White, 0.0% Black/African American, 0.0% Asian, 0.0% American Indian/Alaska Native, 0.0% Native Hawaiian/Other Pacific Islander, 2.0% Some other race, 0.0% Two or more races, 4.0% Hispanic of any race (2008-2012 5-year est.); Average household size: 2.96 (2008-2012 5-year est.); Median age: 36.2 (2008-2012 5-year est.); Males per 100 females: 101.0 (2008-2012 5-year est.); Marriage status: 19.6% never married, 60.7% now married, 9.5% widowed, 10.2% divorced (2008-2012 5-year est.); Foreign born: 4.0% (2008-2012 5-year est.); Ancestry (includes multiple ancestries): 21.2% German, 11.1% English, 7.3% American, 4.3% Irish, 3.5% Italian (2008-2012 5-year est.).

Economy: Homeowner vacancy rate: 0.0%. Rental vacancy rate: 0.0%. (2008-2012 5-year est.); Employment by occupation: 2.0% management, business, and financial, 4.1% computer, engineering, and science, 3.4% education, legal, community service, arts, and media, 7.4% healthcare practitioners, 18.9% service, 35.8% sales and office, 14.2% natural resources, construction, and maintenance, 14.2% production, transportation, and material moving (2008-2012 5-year est.).

Income: Per capita income: $17,252 (2008-2012 5-year est.); Median household income: $44,643 (2008-2012 5-year est.); Average household income: $50,127 (2008-2012 5-year est.); Percent of households with income of $100,000 or more: 12.7% (2008-2012 5-year est.); Poverty rate: 17.9% (2008-2012 5-year est.).

Education: Percent of population age 25 and over with: High school diploma (including GED) or higher: 85.6% (2008-2012 5-year est.); Bachelor's degree or higher: 7.6% (2008-2012 5-year est.); Master's degree or higher: 0.0% (2008-2012 5-year est.).

School District(s)

Elverado CUSD 196 (PK-12)
    2011-12 Enrollment: 508 . . . . (618) 568-1321

Housing: Homeownership rate: 83.6% (2008-2012 5-year est.); Median home value: $56,200 (2008-2012 5-year est.); Median contract rent: $410 per month (2008-2012 5-year est.); Median year structure built: 1974 (2008-2012 5-year est.).

Health Insurance: 61.9% Private; 39.6% Public; 8.8% None. (2008-2012 5-year est.)

Transportation: Commute to work: 96.6% car, 0.0% public transportation, 2.0% walk, 0.0% work from home (2008-2012 5-year est.); Travel time to

work: 18.9% less than 15 minutes, 31.1% 15 to 30 minutes, 33.8% 30 to 45 minutes, 13.5% 45 to 60 minutes, 2.7% 60 minutes or more (2008-2012 5-year est.)

Jasper County

Located in southeast central Illinois; drained by the Embarrass River. Covers a land area of 494.510 square miles, a water area of 3.610 square miles, and is located in the Central Time Zone at 39.00° N. Lat., 88.15° W. Long. The county was founded in 1831. County seat is Newton.

Weather Station: Newton 6 SSE   Elevation: 509 feet

	Jan	Feb	Mar	Apr	May	Jun	Jul	Aug	Sep	Oct	Nov	Dec
High	36	42	51	63	74	83	87	85	79	67	53	40
Low	20	24	32	42	52	62	66	62	54	43	34	24
Precip	2.3	2.4	3.6	4.0	4.9	4.0	4.2	2.9	3.2	3.2	4.0	3.0
Snow	4.3	3.0	2.0	0.1	tr	0.0	0.0	0.0	0.0	0.2	0.8	3.7

High and Low temperatures in degrees Fahrenheit; Precipitation and Snow in inches

Population: 10,609 (1990); 10,117 (2000); 9,698 (2010); Race: 98.1% White, 0.1% Black/African American, 0.2% Asian, 0.1% American Indian/Alaska Native, 0.0% Native Hawaiian/Other Pacific Islander, 1.5% Some other race, 0.8% Two or more races, 0.9% Hispanic of any race (2008-2012 5-year est.); Density: 19.5 persons per square mile (2008-2012 5-year est.); Average household size: 2.43 (2008-2012 5-year est.); Median age: 42.7 (2008-2012 5-year est.); Males per 100 females: 100.1 (2008-2012 5-year est.).
Religion: Six largest groups: 24.1% Catholicism, 16.5% Baptist, 4.7% Methodist/Pietist, 2.4% Lutheran, 2.2% Non-denominational Protestant, 1.5% Presbyterian-Reformed (2010)
Economy: Unemployment rate: 6.4% (April 2014); Total civilian labor force: 4,483 (April 2014); Leading industries: 17.3% manufacturing; 15.9% retail trade; 8.6% accommodation & food services (2012); Farms: 910 totaling 250,766 acres (2012); Companies that employ 500 or more persons: 0 (2012); Companies that employ 100 to 499 persons: 2 (2012); Companies that employ less than 100 persons: 207 (2012); Black-owned businesses: n/a (2007); Hispanic-owned businesses: n/a (2007); Asian-owned businesses: n/a (2007); Women-owned businesses: 224 (2007); Single-family building permits issued: 0 (2013); Multi-family building permits issued: 0 (2013).
Income: Per capita income: $23,859 (2008-2012 5-year est.); Median household income: $48,703 (2008-2012 5-year est.); Average household income: $57,812 (2008-2012 5-year est.); Percent of households with income of $100,000 or more: 13.2% (2008-2012 5-year est.); Poverty rate: 7.5% (2008-2012 5-year est.); Bankruptcy rate: 2.08% (2013).
Education: Percent of population age 25 and over with: High school diploma (including GED) or higher: 91.2% (2008-2012 5-year est.); Bachelor's degree or higher: 15.5% (2008-2012 5-year est.); Master's degree or higher: 6.2% (2008-2012 5-year est.).
Housing: Homeownership rate: 83.7% (2008-2012 5-year est.); Median home value: $82,800 (2008-2012 5-year est.); Median contract rent: $337 per month (2008-2012 5-year est.); Median year structure built: 1971 (2008-2012 5-year est.)
Health: Birth rate: 112.6 per 10,000 population (2013); Death rate: 86.5 per 10,000 population (2013); Age-adjusted cancer mortality rate: 152.3 deaths per 100,000 population (2011); Number of physicians: 2.1 per 10,000 population (2011); Hospital beds: 0.0 per 10,000 population (2010); Hospital admissions: 0.0 per 10,000 population (2010).
Elections: 2012 Presidential election results: 28.5% Obama, 69.7% Romney
National and State Parks: Newton Lake State Fish and Wildlife Area; Sam Parr State Park
Additional Information Contacts
Jasper County Government . . . . (618) 783-3409
   http://jaspercountyillinois.org
Jasper County Chamber of Commerce . . . . (618) 783-3399
   http://www.newtonillinois.com

Jasper County Communities

HIDALGO (village). Covers a land area of 0.344 square miles and a water area of 0 square miles. Located at 39.16° N. Lat; 88.15° W. Long. Elevation is 587 feet.
Population: 122 (1990); 123 (2000); 106 (2010); Density: 395.9 persons per square mile (2008-2012 5-year est.); Race: 98.5% White, 0.0%

Black/African American, 0.7% Asian, 0.0% American Indian/Alaska Native, 0.0% Native Hawaiian/Other Pacific Islander, 0.8% Some other race, 0.7% Two or more races, 0.7% Hispanic of any race (2008-2012 5-year est.); Average household size: 2.06 (2008-2012 5-year est.); Median age: 37.5 (2008-2012 5-year est.); Males per 100 females: 86.3 (2008-2012 5-year est.); Marriage status: 26.3% never married, 52.6% now married, 10.5% widowed, 10.5% divorced (2008-2012 5-year est.); Foreign born: 0.0% (2008-2012 5-year est.); Ancestry (includes multiple ancestries): 23.5% German, 22.1% American, 8.1% English, 5.1% Irish, 2.9% Welsh (2008-2012 5-year est.).
Economy: Homeowner vacancy rate: 0.0%. Rental vacancy rate: 0.0%. (2008-2012 5-year est.); Employment by occupation: 3.3% management, business, and financial, 0.0% computer, engineering, and science, 3.3% education, legal, community service, arts, and media, 18.3% healthcare practitioners, 8.3% service, 26.7% sales and office, 5.0% natural resources, construction, and maintenance, 35.0% production, transportation, and material moving (2008-2012 5-year est.).
Income: Per capita income: $24,377 (2008-2012 5-year est.); Median household income: $46,250 (2008-2012 5-year est.); Average household income: $49,061 (2008-2012 5-year est.); Percent of households with income of $100,000 or more: 6.1% (2008-2012 5-year est.); Poverty rate: 5.9% (2008-2012 5-year est.).
Education: Percent of population age 25 and over with: High school diploma (including GED) or higher: 82.6% (2008-2012 5-year est.); Bachelor's degree or higher: 4.7% (2008-2012 5-year est.); Master's degree or higher: 0.0% (2008-2012 5-year est.).
Housing: Homeownership rate: 93.9% (2008-2012 5-year est.); Median home value: $51,400 (2008-2012 5-year est.); Median contract rent: n/a per month (2008-2012 5-year est.); Median year structure built: 1941 (2008-2012 5-year est.).
Health Insurance: 76.5% Private; 33.1% Public; 4.4% None. (2008-2012 5-year est.)
Transportation: Commute to work: 94.4% car, 0.0% public transportation, 0.0% walk, 5.6% work from home (2008-2012 5-year est.); Travel time to work: 31.4% less than 15 minutes, 15.7% 15 to 30 minutes, 19.6% 30 to 45 minutes, 11.8% 45 to 60 minutes, 21.6% 60 minutes or more (2008-2012 5-year est.)

NEWTON (city). County seat. Covers a land area of 1.846 square miles and a water area of 0 square miles. Located at 38.99° N. Lat; 88.16° W. Long. Elevation is 535 feet.
History: Settled 1828, incorporated 1831.
Population: 3,154 (1990); 3,069 (2000); 2,849 (2010); Density: 1,536.0 persons per square mile (2008-2012 5-year est.); Race: 99.2% White, 0.2% Black/African American, 0.0% Asian, 0.0% American Indian/Alaska Native, 0.0% Native Hawaiian/Other Pacific Islander, 0.6% Some other race, 0.3% Two or more races, 0.6% Hispanic of any race (2008-2012 5-year est.); Average household size: 2.17 (2008-2012 5-year est.); Median age: 43.4 (2008-2012 5-year est.); Males per 100 females: 100.2 (2008-2012 5-year est.); Marriage status: 27.4% never married, 54.6% now married, 6.0% widowed, 12.0% divorced (2008-2012 5-year est.); Foreign born: 0.5% (2008-2012 5-year est.); Ancestry (includes multiple ancestries): 28.6% German, 10.7% English, 9.2% American, 7.8% Irish, 5.2% Italian (2008-2012 5-year est.).
Economy: Single-family building permits issued: 3 (2013); Multi-family building permits issued: 0 (2013); Homeowner vacancy rate: 2.6%. Rental vacancy rate: 16.4%. (2008-2012 5-year est.); Employment by occupation: 8.2% management, business, and financial, 1.0% computer, engineering, and science, 8.5% education, legal, community service, arts, and media, 4.3% healthcare practitioners, 11.2% service, 33.1% sales and office, 9.7% natural resources, construction, and maintenance, 24.0% production, transportation, and material moving (2008-2012 5-year est.).
Income: Per capita income: $22,351 (2008-2012 5-year est.); Median household income: $38,403 (2008-2012 5-year est.); Average household income: $49,642 (2008-2012 5-year est.); Percent of households with income of $100,000 or more: 8.9% (2008-2012 5-year est.); Poverty rate: 12.1% (2008-2012 5-year est.).
Education: Percent of population age 25 and over with: High school diploma (including GED) or higher: 90.9% (2008-2012 5-year est.); Bachelor's degree or higher: 16.9% (2008-2012 5-year est.); Master's degree or higher: 7.5% (2008-2012 5-year est.).
School District(s)
Jasper County CUD 1 (KG-12)
   2011-12 Enrollment: 1,435 . . . . (618) 783-8459

Housing: Homeownership rate: 66.1% (2008-2012 5-year est.); Median home value: $74,200 (2008-2012 5-year est.); Median contract rent: $346 per month (2008-2012 5-year est.); Median year structure built: 1970 (2008-2012 5-year est.).
Health Insurance: 59.2% Private; 49.9% Public; 14.3% None. (2008-2012 5-year est.)
Safety: Violent crime rate: 77.0 per 10,000 population; Property crime rate: 126.1 per 10,000 population (2012).
Transportation: Commute to work: 91.4% car, 0.0% public transportation, 1.1% walk, 5.2% work from home (2008-2012 5-year est.); Travel time to work: 54.2% less than 15 minutes, 10.3% 15 to 30 minutes, 25.6% 30 to 45 minutes, 5.9% 45 to 60 minutes, 4.0% 60 minutes or more (2008-2012 5-year est.)

Additional Information Contacts
Jasper County Chamber of Commerce . . . . (618) 783-3399
   http://www.newtonillinois.com

ROSE HILL (village). Covers a land area of 0.634 square miles and a water area of 0 square miles. Located at 39.10° N. Lat; 88.15° W. Long. Elevation is 564 feet.

Population: 78 (1990); 79 (2000); 80 (2010); Density: 143.5 persons per square mile (2008-2012 5-year est.); Race: 100.0% White, 0.0% Black/African American, 0.0% Asian, 0.0% American Indian/Alaska Native, 0.0% Native Hawaiian/Other Pacific Islander, 0.0% Some other race, 0.0% Two or more races, 0.0% Hispanic of any race (2008-2012 5-year est.); Average household size: 1.82 (2008-2012 5-year est.); Median age: 53.4 (2008-2012 5-year est.); Males per 100 females: 102.2 (2008-2012 5-year est.); Marriage status: 18.8% never married, 57.6% now married, 4.7% widowed, 18.8% divorced (2008-2012 5-year est.); Foreign born: 0.0% (2008-2012 5-year est.); Ancestry (includes multiple ancestries): 42.9% German, 25.3% Irish, 7.7% Italian, 6.6% American, 4.4% English (2008-2012 5-year est.).
Economy: Homeowner vacancy rate: 0.0%. Rental vacancy rate: 0.0%. (2008-2012 5-year est.); Employment by occupation: 16.0% management, business, and financial, 0.0% computer, engineering, and science, 0.0% education, legal, community service, arts, and media, 28.0% healthcare practitioners, 12.0% service, 24.0% sales and office, 0.0% natural resources, construction, and maintenance, 20.0% production, transportation, and material moving (2008-2012 5-year est.).
Income: Per capita income: $23,360 (2008-2012 5-year est.); Median household income: $26,875 (2008-2012 5-year est.); Average household income: $43,212 (2008-2012 5-year est.); Percent of households with income of $100,000 or more: 12.0% (2008-2012 5-year est.); Poverty rate: 13.2% (2008-2012 5-year est.).
Education: Percent of population age 25 and over with: High school diploma (including GED) or higher: 96.2% (2008-2012 5-year est.); Bachelor's degree or higher: 1.3% (2008-2012 5-year est.); Master's degree or higher: 0.0% (2008-2012 5-year est.).
Housing: Homeownership rate: 62.0% (2008-2012 5-year est.); Median home value: $34,400 (2008-2012 5-year est.); Median contract rent: $233 per month (2008-2012 5-year est.); Median year structure built: 1956 (2008-2012 5-year est.).
Health Insurance: 47.3% Private; 50.5% Public; 8.8% None. (2008-2012 5-year est.)
Transportation: Commute to work: 87.5% car, 0.0% public transportation, 0.0% walk, 12.5% work from home (2008-2012 5-year est.); Travel time to work: 9.5% less than 15 minutes, 38.1% 15 to 30 minutes, 19.0% 30 to 45 minutes, 33.3% 45 to 60 minutes, 0.0% 60 minutes or more (2008-2012 5-year est.)

SAINTE MARIE (village). Aka Saint Marie. Covers a land area of 1.109 square miles and a water area of 0 square miles. Located at 38.93° N. Lat; 88.03° W. Long. Elevation is 486 feet.

Population: 281 (1990); 261 (2000); 244 (2010); Density: 231.8 persons per square mile (2008-2012 5-year est.); Race: 97.7% White, 0.0% Black/African American, 0.8% Asian, 1.6% American Indian/Alaska Native, 0.0% Native Hawaiian/Other Pacific Islander, 0.0% Some other race, 0.0% Two or more races, 0.0% Hispanic of any race (2008-2012 5-year est.); Average household size: 2.22 (2008-2012 5-year est.); Median age: 46.9 (2008-2012 5-year est.); Males per 100 females: 97.7 (2008-2012 5-year est.); Marriage status: 19.1% never married, 59.1% now married, 5.5% widowed, 16.4% divorced (2008-2012 5-year est.); Foreign born: 0.8% (2008-2012 5-year est.); Ancestry (includes multiple ancestries): 44.7% German, 18.7% Irish, 9.7% American, 8.6% French, 6.2% Scottish (2008-2012 5-year est.).

Economy: Single-family building permits issued: 0 (2013); Multi-family building permits issued: 0 (2013); Homeowner vacancy rate: 0.0%. Rental vacancy rate: 0.0%. (2008-2012 5-year est.); Employment by occupation: 0.9% management, business, and financial, 6.6% computer, engineering, and science, 1.9% education, legal, community service, arts, and media, 6.6% healthcare practitioners, 15.1% service, 26.4% sales and office, 13.2% natural resources, construction, and maintenance, 29.2% production, transportation, and material moving (2008-2012 5-year est.).
Income: Per capita income: $23,739 (2008-2012 5-year est.); Median household income: $46,250 (2008-2012 5-year est.); Average household income: $50,928 (2008-2012 5-year est.); Percent of households with income of $100,000 or more: 6.9% (2008-2012 5-year est.); Poverty rate: 6.6% (2008-2012 5-year est.).
Education: Percent of population age 25 and over with: High school diploma (including GED) or higher: 91.2% (2008-2012 5-year est.); Bachelor's degree or higher: 16.5% (2008-2012 5-year est.); Master's degree or higher: 0.5% (2008-2012 5-year est.).

School District(s)
Jasper County CUD 1 (KG-12)
   2011-12 Enrollment: 1,435 . . . . (618) 783-8459
Housing: Homeownership rate: 82.8% (2008-2012 5-year est.); Median home value: $69,200 (2008-2012 5-year est.); Median contract rent: $175 per month (2008-2012 5-year est.); Median year structure built: 1961 (2008-2012 5-year est.).
Health Insurance: 77.0% Private; 43.2% Public; 4.3% None. (2008-2012 5-year est.)
Transportation: Commute to work: 86.8% car, 0.0% public transportation, 9.4% walk, 3.8% work from home (2008-2012 5-year est.); Travel time to work: 39.2% less than 15 minutes, 43.1% 15 to 30 minutes, 4.9% 30 to 45 minutes, 5.9% 45 to 60 minutes, 6.9% 60 minutes or more (2008-2012 5-year est.)

WEST LIBERTY (unincorporated postal area)
Zip Code: 62475
   Covers a land area of 30.241 square miles and a water area of 0.056 square miles. Located at 38.88° N. Lat; 88.04° W. Long. Elevation is 482 feet. Population: 387 (2010); Density: 12.8 persons per square mile (2010); Race: 99.2% White, 0.0% Black/African American, 0.0% Asian, 0.3% American Indian/Alaska Native, 0.0% Native Hawaiian/Other Pacific Islander, 0.5% Some other race, 0.5% Two or more races, 0.8% Hispanic of any race (2010); Average household size: 2.53 (2010); Median age: 44.9 (2010); Males per 100 females: 101.6 (2010); Homeownership rate: 88.9% (2010)

WHEELER (village). Covers a land area of 0.576 square miles and a water area of 0 square miles. Located at 39.04° N. Lat; 88.32° W. Long. Elevation is 561 feet.

Population: 161 (1990); 119 (2000); 147 (2010); Density: 213.6 persons per square mile (2008-2012 5-year est.); Race: 100.0% White, 0.0% Black/African American, 0.0% Asian, 0.0% American Indian/Alaska Native, 0.0% Native Hawaiian/Other Pacific Islander, 0.0% Some other race, 0.0% Two or more races, 0.0% Hispanic of any race (2008-2012 5-year est.); Average household size: 2.51 (2008-2012 5-year est.); Median age: 43.4 (2008-2012 5-year est.); Males per 100 females: 78.3 (2008-2012 5-year est.); Marriage status: 22.0% never married, 46.2% now married, 8.8% widowed, 23.1% divorced (2008-2012 5-year est.); Foreign born: 0.0% (2008-2012 5-year est.); Ancestry (includes multiple ancestries): 26.0% German, 8.1% English, 8.1% American, 7.3% Irish, 4.9% Dutch (2008-2012 5-year est.).
Economy: Homeowner vacancy rate: 0.0%. Rental vacancy rate: 0.0%. (2008-2012 5-year est.); Employment by occupation: 0.0% management, business, and financial, 0.0% computer, engineering, and science, 1.6% education, legal, community service, arts, and media, 0.0% healthcare practitioners, 54.1% service, 8.2% sales and office, 4.9% natural resources, construction, and maintenance, 31.1% production, transportation, and material moving (2008-2012 5-year est.).
Income: Per capita income: $12,099 (2008-2012 5-year est.); Median household income: $29,750 (2008-2012 5-year est.); Average household income: $30,363 (2008-2012 5-year est.); Percent of households with income of $100,000 or more: n/a (2008-2012 5-year est.); Poverty rate: 45.5% (2008-2012 5-year est.).
Education: Percent of population age 25 and over with: High school diploma (including GED) or higher: 81.2% (2008-2012 5-year est.); Bachelor's degree or higher: 1.2% (2008-2012 5-year est.); Master's degree or higher: 0.0% (2008-2012 5-year est.).

Housing: Homeownership rate: 71.4% (2008-2012 5-year est.); Median home value: $37,900 (2008-2012 5-year est.); Median contract rent: n/a per month (2008-2012 5-year est.); Median year structure built: 1945 (2008-2012 5-year est.).

Health Insurance: 47.2% Private; 43.9% Public; 17.9% None. (2008-2012 5-year est.)

Transportation: Commute to work: 81.0% car, 0.0% public transportation, 0.0% walk, 19.0% work from home (2008-2012 5-year est.); Travel time to work: 29.8% less than 15 minutes, 38.3% 15 to 30 minutes, 31.9% 30 to 45 minutes, 0.0% 45 to 60 minutes, 0.0% 60 minutes or more (2008-2012 5-year est.)

WILLOW HILL (village). Covers a land area of 1.039 square miles and a water area of 0 square miles. Located at 39.00° N. Lat; 88.02° W. Long. Elevation is 502 feet.

Population: 268 (1990); 250 (2000); 230 (2010); Density: 205.9 persons per square mile (2008-2012 5-year est.); Race: 100.0% White, 0.0% Black/African American, 0.0% Asian, 0.0% American Indian/Alaska Native, 0.0% Native Hawaiian/Other Pacific Islander, 0.0% Some other race, 0.0% Two or more races, 0.0% Hispanic of any race (2008-2012 5-year est.); Average household size: 2.49 (2008-2012 5-year est.); Median age: 36.3 (2008-2012 5-year est.); Males per 100 females: 84.5 (2008-2012 5-year est.); Marriage status: 23.0% never married, 51.3% now married, 5.9% widowed, 19.7% divorced (2008-2012 5-year est.); Foreign born: 0.0% (2008-2012 5-year est.); Ancestry (includes multiple ancestries): 26.6% German, 10.3% Irish, 10.3% English, 7.9% Norwegian, 5.6% Italian (2008-2012 5-year est.).

Economy: Single-family building permits issued: 0 (2013); Multi-family building permits issued: 0 (2013); Homeowner vacancy rate: 0.0%. Rental vacancy rate: 0.0%. (2008-2012 5-year est.); Employment by occupation: 21.2% management, business, and financial, 0.0% computer, engineering, and science, 15.3% education, legal, community service, arts, and media, 2.4% healthcare practitioners, 16.5% service, 5.9% sales and office, 4.7% natural resources, construction, and maintenance, 34.1% production, transportation, and material moving (2008-2012 5-year est.).

Income: Per capita income: $16,387 (2008-2012 5-year est.); Median household income: $28,125 (2008-2012 5-year est.); Average household income: $41,123 (2008-2012 5-year est.); Percent of households with income of $100,000 or more: 5.8% (2008-2012 5-year est.); Poverty rate: 32.0% (2008-2012 5-year est.).

Education: Percent of population age 25 and over with: High school diploma (including GED) or higher: 87.5% (2008-2012 5-year est.); Bachelor's degree or higher: 9.7% (2008-2012 5-year est.); Master's degree or higher: 0.0% (2008-2012 5-year est.).

School District(s)

Clay/cwford/jsper/lwrnce/rhland (PK-12)

   2011-12 Enrollment: n/a . . . . (618) 392-4631

Housing: Homeownership rate: 81.4% (2008-2012 5-year est.); Median home value: $38,800 (2008-2012 5-year est.); Median contract rent: $317 per month (2008-2012 5-year est.); Median year structure built: 1943 (2008-2012 5-year est.).

Health Insurance: 37.4% Private; 61.7% Public; 12.1% None. (2008-2012 5-year est.)

Transportation: Commute to work: 94.2% car, 0.0% public transportation, 5.8% walk, 0.0% work from home (2008-2012 5-year est.); Travel time to work: 23.2% less than 15 minutes, 49.3% 15 to 30 minutes, 11.6% 30 to 45 minutes, 10.1% 45 to 60 minutes, 5.8% 60 minutes or more (2008-2012 5-year est.)

YALE (village). Covers a land area of 0.575 square miles and a water area of 0 square miles. Located at 39.12° N. Lat; 88.02° W. Long. Elevation is 558 feet.

Population: 94 (1990); 97 (2000); 86 (2010); Density: 123.4 persons per square mile (2008-2012 5-year est.); Race: 91.5% White, 0.0% Black/African American, 8.5% Asian, 0.0% American Indian/Alaska Native, 0.0% Native Hawaiian/Other Pacific Islander, 0.0% Some other race, 0.0% Two or more races, 1.4% Hispanic of any race (2008-2012 5-year est.); Average household size: 2.63 (2008-2012 5-year est.); Median age: 37.5 (2008-2012 5-year est.); Males per 100 females: 77.5 (2008-2012 5-year est.); Marriage status: 20.6% never married, 57.1% now married, 15.9% widowed, 6.3% divorced (2008-2012 5-year est.); Foreign born: 4.2% (2008-2012 5-year est.); Ancestry (includes multiple ancestries): 21.1% American, 15.5% German, 2.8% Russian, 1.4% Scotch-Irish, 1.4% Dutch (2008-2012 5-year est.).

Economy: Homeowner vacancy rate: 0.0%. Rental vacancy rate: 0.0%. (2008-2012 5-year est.); Employment by occupation: 8.1% management, business, and financial, 0.0% computer, engineering, and science, 0.0% education, legal, community service, arts, and media, 0.0% healthcare practitioners, 27.0% service, 32.4% sales and office, 10.8% natural resources, construction, and maintenance, 21.6% production, transportation, and material moving (2008-2012 5-year est.).

Income: Per capita income: $35,790 (2008-2012 5-year est.); Median household income: $49,583 (2008-2012 5-year est.); Average household income: $92,544 (2008-2012 5-year est.); Percent of households with income of $100,000 or more: 14.8% (2008-2012 5-year est.); Poverty rate: 0.0% (2008-2012 5-year est.).

Education: Percent of population age 25 and over with: High school diploma (including GED) or higher: 89.8% (2008-2012 5-year est.); Bachelor's degree or higher: 8.2% (2008-2012 5-year est.); Master's degree or higher: 0.0% (2008-2012 5-year est.).

Housing: Homeownership rate: 88.9% (2008-2012 5-year est.); Median home value: $55,000 (2008-2012 5-year est.); Median contract rent: n/a per month (2008-2012 5-year est.); Median year structure built: Before 1940 (2008-2012 5-year est.).

Health Insurance: 67.6% Private; 22.5% Public; 14.1% None. (2008-2012 5-year est.)

Transportation: Commute to work: 69.4% car, 0.0% public transportation, 22.2% walk, 0.0% work from home (2008-2012 5-year est.); Travel time to work: 44.4% less than 15 minutes, 25.0% 15 to 30 minutes, 13.9% 30 to 45 minutes, 2.8% 45 to 60 minutes, 13.9% 60 minutes or more (2008-2012 5-year est.)

Jefferson County

Located in southern Illinois; drained by the Big Muddy River. Covers a land area of 571.169 square miles, a water area of 12.615 square miles, and is located in the Central Time Zone at 38.30° N. Lat., 88.92° W. Long. The county was founded in 1819. County seat is Mount Vernon.

Jefferson County is part of the Mount Vernon, IL Micropolitan Statistical Area. The entire metro area includes: Jefferson County, IL

Weather Station: Mt Vernon Mt Vernon-Outland A										Elevation: 465 feet	
	Jan	Feb	Mar	Apr	May	Jun	Jul	Aug	Sep	Oct	Nov	Dec
High	39	43	53	65	74	83	87	86	79	67	54	42
Low	21	24	33	44	53	63	67	64	56	44	35	24
Precip	2.3	2.8	3.9	4.3	5.1	3.8	3.7	3.0	3.2	3.7	4.1	3.2
Snow	3.8	4.7	1.3	0.2	0.0	0.0	0.0	0.0	0.0	0.2	0.3	3.3

High and Low temperatures in degrees Fahrenheit; Precipitation and Snow in inches

Population: 37,020 (1990); 40,045 (2000); 38,827 (2010); Race: 88.1% White, 8.0% Black/African American, 0.8% Asian, 0.2% American Indian/Alaska Native, 0.0% Native Hawaiian/Other Pacific Islander, 2.9% Some other race, 2.3% Two or more races, 2.1% Hispanic of any race (2008-2012 5-year est.); Density: 67.7 persons per square mile (2008-2012 5-year est.); Average household size: 2.43 (2008-2012 5-year est.); Median age: 40.5 (2008-2012 5-year est.); Males per 100 females: 106.0 (2008-2012 5-year est.).

Religion: Six largest groups: 35.8% Baptist, 7.0% Non-denominational Protestant, 4.5% Methodist/Pietist, 3.6% Catholicism, 1.7% Pentecostal, 1.0% Lutheran (2010)

Economy: Unemployment rate: 6.3% (April 2014); Total civilian labor force: 19,941 (April 2014); Leading industries: 20.2% health care and social assistance; 18.5% manufacturing; 13.8% retail trade (2012); Farms: 1,063 totaling 213,901 acres (2012); Companies that employ 500 or more persons: 3 (2012); Companies that employ 100 to 499 persons: 14 (2012); Companies that employ less than 100 persons: 963 (2012); Black-owned businesses: 83 (2007); Hispanic-owned businesses: n/a (2007); Asian-owned businesses: n/a (2007); Women-owned businesses: 528 (2007); Single-family building permits issued: 6 (2013); Multi-family building permits issued: 6 (2013).

Income: Per capita income: $22,201 (2008-2012 5-year est.); Median household income: $42,272 (2008-2012 5-year est.); Average household income: $55,555 (2008-2012 5-year est.); Percent of households with income of $100,000 or more: 12.9% (2008-2012 5-year est.); Poverty rate: 16.4% (2008-2012 5-year est.); Bankruptcy rate: 3.10% (2013).

Taxes: Total county taxes per capita: $118 (2011); County property taxes per capita: $62 (2011).

Education: Percent of population age 25 and over with: High school diploma (including GED) or higher: 86.9% (2008-2012 5-year est.);

Bachelor's degree or higher: 15.9% (2008-2012 5-year est.); Master's degree or higher: 5.9% (2008-2012 5-year est.).

Housing: Homeownership rate: 73.2% (2008-2012 5-year est.); Median home value: $86,000 (2008-2012 5-year est.); Median contract rent: $411 per month (2008-2012 5-year est.); Median year structure built: 1974 (2008-2012 5-year est.)

Health: Birth rate: 113.6 per 10,000 population (2013); Death rate: 110.2 per 10,000 population (2013); Age-adjusted cancer mortality rate: 210.7 deaths per 100,000 population (2011); Number of physicians: 25.0 per 10,000 population (2011); Hospital beds: 49.2 per 10,000 population (2010); Hospital admissions: 2,363.6 per 10,000 population (2010).

Elections: 2012 Presidential election results: 37.3% Obama, 60.1% Romney

National and State Parks: Mount Vernon State Game Farm; Rend Lake State Waterfowl Management Area

Additional Information Contacts

Jefferson County Government . . . . (618) 244-8020
  http://www.jeffersoncountyillinois.com
Jefferson County Chamber of Commerce . . . . (618) 242-5725
  http://southernillinois.com

Jefferson County Communities

BELLE RIVE (village). Covers a land area of 0.874 square miles and a water area of 0 square miles. Located at 38.23° N. Lat; 88.74° W. Long. Elevation is 479 feet.

Population: 396 (1990); 371 (2000); 361 (2010); Density: 472.3 persons per square mile (2008-2012 5-year est.); Race: 96.9% White, 0.0% Black/African American, 1.5% Asian, 0.0% American Indian/Alaska Native, 0.0% Native Hawaiian/Other Pacific Islander, 1.6% Some other race, 1.7% Two or more races, 2.7% Hispanic of any race (2008-2012 5-year est.); Average household size: 2.57 (2008-2012 5-year est.); Median age: 40.9 (2008-2012 5-year est.); Males per 100 females: 91.2 (2008-2012 5-year est.); Marriage status: 21.2% never married, 64.8% now married, 4.8% widowed, 9.1% divorced (2008-2012 5-year est.); Foreign born: 1.7% (2008-2012 5-year est.); Ancestry (includes multiple ancestries): 18.4% English, 17.7% German, 12.3% American, 11.4% Irish, 8.5% Italian (2008-2012 5-year est.).

Economy: Homeowner vacancy rate: 0.0%. Rental vacancy rate: 0.0%. (2008-2012 5-year est.); Employment by occupation: 8.0% management, business, and financial, 1.1% computer, engineering, and science, 18.3% education, legal, community service, arts, and media, 6.9% healthcare practitioners, 21.1% service, 16.0% sales and office, 6.9% natural resources, construction, and maintenance, 21.7% production, transportation, and material moving (2008-2012 5-year est.).

Income: Per capita income: $18,725 (2008-2012 5-year est.); Median household income: $45,938 (2008-2012 5-year est.); Average household income: $48,412 (2008-2012 5-year est.); Percent of households with income of $100,000 or more: 2.4% (2008-2012 5-year est.); Poverty rate: 17.7% (2008-2012 5-year est.).

Education: Percent of population age 25 and over with: High school diploma (including GED) or higher: 90.7% (2008-2012 5-year est.); Bachelor's degree or higher: 12.1% (2008-2012 5-year est.); Master's degree or higher: 6.0% (2008-2012 5-year est.).

School District(s)

Opdyke-Belle-Rive CCSD 5 (KG-08)
  2011-12 Enrollment: 181 . . . . (618) 756-2492

Housing: Homeownership rate: 83.9% (2008-2012 5-year est.); Median home value: $63,500 (2008-2012 5-year est.); Median contract rent: $425 per month (2008-2012 5-year est.); Median year structure built: 1977 (2008-2012 5-year est.).

Health Insurance: 62.7% Private; 50.8% Public; 8.2% None. (2008-2012 5-year est.)

Transportation: Commute to work: 93.1% car, 0.0% public transportation, 0.0% walk, 3.4% work from home (2008-2012 5-year est.); Travel time to work: 12.5% less than 15 minutes, 65.5% 15 to 30 minutes, 14.9% 30 to 45 minutes, 0.0% 45 to 60 minutes, 7.1% 60 minutes or more (2008-2012 5-year est.)

BLUFORD (village). Covers a land area of 1.452 square miles and a water area of 0.008 square miles. Located at 38.33° N. Lat; 88.74° W. Long. Elevation is 522 feet.

Population: 747 (1990); 785 (2000); 688 (2010); Density: 451.0 persons per square mile (2008-2012 5-year est.); Race: 99.5% White, 0.0% Black/African American, 0.0% Asian, 0.0% American Indian/Alaska Native,

0.0% Native Hawaiian/Other Pacific Islander, 0.5% Some other race, 0.5% Two or more races, 0.0% Hispanic of any race (2008-2012 5-year est.); Average household size: 2.62 (2008-2012 5-year est.); Median age: 40.0 (2008-2012 5-year est.); Males per 100 females: 118.3 (2008-2012 5-year est.); Marriage status: 26.0% never married, 56.3% now married, 6.7% widowed, 11.0% divorced (2008-2012 5-year est.); Foreign born: 0.0% (2008-2012 5-year est.); Ancestry (includes multiple ancestries): 26.3% English, 22.1% German, 11.6% Irish, 10.2% American, 4.4% French (2008-2012 5-year est.).

Economy: Single-family building permits issued: 0 (2013); Multi-family building permits issued: 0 (2013); Homeowner vacancy rate: 6.3%. Rental vacancy rate: 0.0%. (2008-2012 5-year est.); Employment by occupation: 7.7% management, business, and financial, 0.0% computer, engineering, and science, 3.9% education, legal, community service, arts, and media, 3.5% healthcare practitioners, 12.3% service, 24.9% sales and office, 18.2% natural resources, construction, and maintenance, 29.5% production, transportation, and material moving (2008-2012 5-year est.).

Income: Per capita income: $18,708 (2008-2012 5-year est.); Median household income: $46,667 (2008-2012 5-year est.); Average household income: $47,405 (2008-2012 5-year est.); Percent of households with income of $100,000 or more: 4.0% (2008-2012 5-year est.); Poverty rate: 12.9% (2008-2012 5-year est.).

Education: Percent of population age 25 and over with: High school diploma (including GED) or higher: 87.0% (2008-2012 5-year est.); Bachelor's degree or higher: 8.5% (2008-2012 5-year est.); Master's degree or higher: 1.1% (2008-2012 5-year est.).

School District(s)

Bluford CCSD 114 (PK-08)
  2011-12 Enrollment: 307 . . . . (618) 732-8242
Farrington CCSD 99 (KG-08)
  2011-12 Enrollment: 63 . . . . (618) 755-4414
Webber Twp HSD 204 (09-12)
  2011-12 Enrollment: 132 . . . . (618) 732-6121

Housing: Homeownership rate: 86.0% (2008-2012 5-year est.); Median home value: $54,100 (2008-2012 5-year est.); Median contract rent: $420 per month (2008-2012 5-year est.); Median year structure built: 1976 (2008-2012 5-year est.).

Health Insurance: 61.1% Private; 47.2% Public; 9.5% None. (2008-2012 5-year est.)

Transportation: Commute to work: 97.7% car, 0.0% public transportation, 1.5% walk, 0.8% work from home (2008-2012 5-year est.); Travel time to work: 7.6% less than 15 minutes, 60.5% 15 to 30 minutes, 12.2% 30 to 45 minutes, 8.4% 45 to 60 minutes, 11.4% 60 minutes or more (2008-2012 5-year est.)

BONNIE (village). Covers a land area of 1.232 square miles and a water area of <.001 square miles. Located at 38.20° N. Lat; 88.91° W. Long. Elevation is 427 feet.

Population: 411 (1990); 424 (2000); 397 (2010); Density: 363.5 persons per square mile (2008-2012 5-year est.); Race: 100.0% White, 0.0% Black/African American, 0.0% Asian, 0.0% American Indian/Alaska Native, 0.0% Native Hawaiian/Other Pacific Islander, 0.0% Some other race, 0.0% Two or more races, 1.1% Hispanic of any race (2008-2012 5-year est.); Average household size: 1.99 (2008-2012 5-year est.); Median age: 47.6 (2008-2012 5-year est.); Males per 100 females: 106.5 (2008-2012 5-year est.); Marriage status: 20.0% never married, 56.9% now married, 9.4% widowed, 13.8% divorced (2008-2012 5-year est.); Foreign born: 0.0% (2008-2012 5-year est.); Ancestry (includes multiple ancestries): 31.0% German, 27.7% Irish, 15.4% American, 15.0% English, 6.3% French (2008-2012 5-year est.).

Economy: Single-family building permits issued: 0 (2013); Multi-family building permits issued: 0 (2013); Homeowner vacancy rate: 1.1%. Rental vacancy rate: 13.7%. (2008-2012 5-year est.); Employment by occupation: 5.3% management, business, and financial, 0.8% computer, engineering, and science, 4.0% education, legal, community service, arts, and media, 10.5% healthcare practitioners, 15.0% service, 17.4% sales and office, 4.5% natural resources, construction, and maintenance, 42.5% production, transportation, and material moving (2008-2012 5-year est.).

Income: Per capita income: $23,843 (2008-2012 5-year est.); Median household income: $47,188 (2008-2012 5-year est.); Average household income: $46,257 (2008-2012 5-year est.); Percent of households with income of $100,000 or more: 4.9% (2008-2012 5-year est.); Poverty rate: 5.1% (2008-2012 5-year est.).

Education: Percent of population age 25 and over with: High school diploma (including GED) or higher: 84.4% (2008-2012 5-year est.);

Bachelor's degree or higher: 10.3% (2008-2012 5-year est.); Master's degree or higher: 0.6% (2008-2012 5-year est.).
Housing: Homeownership rate: 80.4% (2008-2012 5-year est.); Median home value: $54,000 (2008-2012 5-year est.); Median contract rent: $383 per month (2008-2012 5-year est.); Median year structure built: 1972 (2008-2012 5-year est.).
Health Insurance: 63.2% Private; 37.3% Public; 18.3% None. (2008-2012 5-year est.)
Transportation: Commute to work: 98.3% car, 0.0% public transportation, 1.7% walk, 0.0% work from home (2008-2012 5-year est.); Travel time to work: 24.4% less than 15 minutes, 65.1% 15 to 30 minutes, 4.2% 30 to 45 minutes, 4.2% 45 to 60 minutes, 2.1% 60 minutes or more (2008-2012 5-year est.)

DIX (village). Aka Rome. Covers a land area of 2.092 square miles and a water area of 0.010 square miles. Located at 38.44° N. Lat; 88.95° W. Long. Elevation is 600 feet.
Population: 456 (1990); 494 (2000); 461 (2010); Density: 250.5 persons per square mile (2008-2012 5-year est.); Race: 100.0% White, 0.0% Black/African American, 0.0% Asian, 0.0% American Indian/Alaska Native, 0.0% Native Hawaiian/Other Pacific Islander, 0.0% Some other race, 0.0% Two or more races, 1.9% Hispanic of any race (2008-2012 5-year est.); Average household size: 1.75 (2008-2012 5-year est.); Median age: 50.1 (2008-2012 5-year est.); Males per 100 females: 94.1 (2008-2012 5-year est.); Marriage status: 25.7% never married, 29.6% now married, 17.4% widowed, 27.3% divorced (2008-2012 5-year est.); Foreign born: 0.8% (2008-2012 5-year est.); Ancestry (includes multiple ancestries): 15.5% German, 14.5% American, 12.6% Irish, 11.3% English, 4.4% French (2008-2012 5-year est.).
Economy: Homeowner vacancy rate: 0.0%. Rental vacancy rate: 14.1%. (2008-2012 5-year est.); Employment by occupation: 2.5% management, business, and financial, 5.0% computer, engineering, and science, 11.8% education, legal, community service, arts, and media, 4.3% healthcare practitioners, 26.7% service, 10.6% sales and office, 21.7% natural resources, construction, and maintenance, 17.4% production, transportation, and material moving (2008-2012 5-year est.).
Income: Per capita income: $16,147 (2008-2012 5-year est.); Median household income: $17,059 (2008-2012 5-year est.); Average household income: $27,646 (2008-2012 5-year est.); Percent of households with income of $100,000 or more: 1.7% (2008-2012 5-year est.); Poverty rate: 34.7% (2008-2012 5-year est.).
Education: Percent of population age 25 and over with: High school diploma (including GED) or higher: 77.8% (2008-2012 5-year est.); Bachelor's degree or higher: 13.8% (2008-2012 5-year est.); Master's degree or higher: 6.0% (2008-2012 5-year est.).
School District(s)
Rome CCSD 2 (PK-08)
   2011-12 Enrollment: 338. . . . . (618) 266-7214
Housing: Homeownership rate: 31.0% (2008-2012 5-year est.); Median home value: $83,800 (2008-2012 5-year est.); Median contract rent: $217 per month (2008-2012 5-year est.); Median year structure built: 1979 (2008-2012 5-year est.).
Health Insurance: 45.2% Private; 70.0% Public; 7.3% None. (2008-2012 5-year est.)
Transportation: Commute to work: 94.2% car, 0.0% public transportation, 1.3% walk, 4.5% work from home (2008-2012 5-year est.); Travel time to work: 15.4% less than 15 minutes, 78.5% 15 to 30 minutes, 3.4% 30 to 45 minutes, 0.0% 45 to 60 minutes, 2.7% 60 minutes or more (2008-2012 5-year est.)

INA (village). Covers a land area of 2.454 square miles and a water area of 0 square miles. Located at 38.15° N. Lat; 88.90° W. Long. Elevation is 430 feet.
Population: 489 (1990); 2,455 (2000); 2,338 (2010); Density: 937.1 persons per square mile (2008-2012 5-year est.); Race: 59.3% White, 33.4% Black/African American, 0.0% Asian, 2.0% American Indian/Alaska Native, 0.0% Native Hawaiian/Other Pacific Islander, 5.3% Some other race, 4.9% Two or more races, 8.7% Hispanic of any race (2008-2012 5-year est.); Average household size: 2.41 (2008-2012 5-year est.); Median age: 38.1 (2008-2012 5-year est.); Males per 100 females: 614.3 (2008-2012 5-year est.); Marriage status: 51.6% never married, 24.1% now married, 2.9% widowed, 21.4% divorced (2008-2012 5-year est.); Foreign born: 4.0% (2008-2012 5-year est.); Ancestry (includes multiple ancestries): 17.2% German, 16.0% Irish, 7.8% English, 4.3% American, 3.7% Dutch (2008-2012 5-year est.).

Economy: Single-family building permits issued: 0 (2013); Multi-family building permits issued: 0 (2013); Homeowner vacancy rate: 0.0%. Rental vacancy rate: 0.0%. (2008-2012 5-year est.); Employment by occupation: 4.6% management, business, and financial, 0.0% computer, engineering, and science, 4.6% education, legal, community service, arts, and media, 3.5% healthcare practitioners, 19.1% service, 32.3% sales and office, 23.1% natural resources, construction, and maintenance, 12.9% production, transportation, and material moving (2008-2012 5-year est.).
Income: Per capita income: $6,603 (2008-2012 5-year est.); Median household income: $33,173 (2008-2012 5-year est.); Average household income: $44,462 (2008-2012 5-year est.); Percent of households with income of $100,000 or more: 11.1% (2008-2012 5-year est.); Poverty rate: 14.9% (2008-2012 5-year est.).
Education: Percent of population age 25 and over with: High school diploma (including GED) or higher: 64.7% (2008-2012 5-year est.); Bachelor's degree or higher: 4.0% (2008-2012 5-year est.); Master's degree or higher: 1.5% (2008-2012 5-year est.).
School District(s)
Ina CCSD 8 (PK-08)
   2011-12 Enrollment: 101. . . . . (618) 437-5361
Two-year College(s)
Rend Lake College (Public)
   Fall 2012 Enrollment: 3,699 . . . . (618) 437-5321
   2012-13 Tuition: In-state $4,320; Out-of-state $4,545
Housing: Homeownership rate: 65.7% (2008-2012 5-year est.); Median home value: $64,000 (2008-2012 5-year est.); Median contract rent: $283 per month (2008-2012 5-year est.); Median year structure built: 1972 (2008-2012 5-year est.).
Health Insurance: 54.2% Private; 37.6% Public; 17.5% None. (2008-2012 5-year est.)
Transportation: Commute to work: 95.3% car, 0.0% public transportation, 3.3% walk, 1.4% work from home (2008-2012 5-year est.); Travel time to work: 18.3% less than 15 minutes, 54.2% 15 to 30 minutes, 11.5% 30 to 45 minutes, 8.7% 45 to 60 minutes, 7.3% 60 minutes or more (2008-2012 5-year est.)

MOUNT VERNON (city). County seat. Covers a land area of 13.072 square miles and a water area of 0.081 square miles. Located at 38.32° N. Lat; 88.91° W. Long. Elevation is 512 feet.
History: Mount Vernon was settled by people from the southern states. It grew slowly as the seat of Jefferson County after 1819.
Population: 16,988 (1990); 16,269 (2000); 15,277 (2010); Density: 1,151.4 persons per square mile (2008-2012 5-year est.); Race: 80.2% White, 14.3% Black/African American, 1.6% Asian, 0.0% American Indian/Alaska Native, 0.0% Native Hawaiian/Other Pacific Islander, 3.9% Some other race, 3.1% Two or more races, 2.4% Hispanic of any race (2008-2012 5-year est.); Average household size: 2.26 (2008-2012 5-year est.); Median age: 37.2 (2008-2012 5-year est.); Males per 100 females: 94.1 (2008-2012 5-year est.); Marriage status: 30.6% never married, 43.8% now married, 11.4% widowed, 14.2% divorced (2008-2012 5-year est.); Foreign born: 2.3% (2008-2012 5-year est.); Ancestry (includes multiple ancestries): 25.2% German, 15.6% English, 13.1% Irish, 10.9% American, 3.1% French (2008-2012 5-year est.).
Economy: Single-family building permits issued: 6 (2013); Multi-family building permits issued: 6 (2013); Homeowner vacancy rate: 3.4%. Rental vacancy rate: 6.6%. (2008-2012 5-year est.); Employment by occupation: 8.4% management, business, and financial, 2.2% computer, engineering, and science, 10.7% education, legal, community service, arts, and media, 4.5% healthcare practitioners, 25.9% service, 24.7% sales and office, 7.6% natural resources, construction, and maintenance, 16.0% production, transportation, and material moving (2008-2012 5-year est.).
Income: Per capita income: $21,283 (2008-2012 5-year est.); Median household income: $32,539 (2008-2012 5-year est.); Average household income: $48,075 (2008-2012 5-year est.); Percent of households with income of $100,000 or more: 11.5% (2008-2012 5-year est.); Poverty rate: 23.7% (2008-2012 5-year est.).
Taxes: Total city taxes per capita: $450 (2011); City property taxes per capita: $64 (2011).
Education: Percent of population age 25 and over with: High school diploma (including GED) or higher: 86.4% (2008-2012 5-year est.); Bachelor's degree or higher: 18.8% (2008-2012 5-year est.); Master's degree or higher: 7.4% (2008-2012 5-year est.).
School District(s)
Bethel SD 82 (PK-08)
   2011-12 Enrollment: 165. . . . . (618) 244-8095

Dodds CCSD 7 (KG-08)
  2011-12 Enrollment: 116 . . . . (618) 244-8070
Franklin-Jefferson County Sp Ed Dist
  2011-12 Enrollment: n/a . . . . (618) 439-7231
Hamilton/jefferson Roe (06-12)
  2011-12 Enrollment: n/a . . . . (618) 244-8040
Mcclellan CCSD 12 (KG-08)
  2011-12 Enrollment: 48 . . . . (618) 244-8072
Mount Vernon SD 80 (PK-08)
  2011-12 Enrollment: 1,739 . . . . (618) 244-8080
Mt Vernon Area Voc Center (11-12)
  2011-12 Enrollment: n/a . . . . (618) 246-5602
Mt Vernon Twp HSD 201 (09-12)
  2011-12 Enrollment: 1,308 . . . . (618) 246-5908
Summersville SD 79 (PK-08)
  2011-12 Enrollment: 279 . . . . (618) 244-8079

Housing: Homeownership rate: 57.2% (2008-2012 5-year est.); Median home value: $76,200 (2008-2012 5-year est.); Median contract rent: $433 per month (2008-2012 5-year est.); Median year structure built: 1963 (2008-2012 5-year est.).
Health Insurance: 50.0% Private; 49.9% Public; 15.1% None. (2008-2012 5-year est.)
Hospitals: Crossroads Community Hospital (55 beds); Good Samaritan Regional Health Center (175 beds)
Safety: Violent crime rate: 124.6 per 10,000 population; Property crime rate: 587.8 per 10,000 population (2012).
Transportation: Commute to work: 89.0% car, 1.2% public transportation, 2.4% walk, 3.5% work from home (2008-2012 5-year est.); Travel time to work: 64.5% less than 15 minutes, 22.2% 15 to 30 minutes, 7.5% 30 to 45 minutes, 2.0% 45 to 60 minutes, 3.8% 60 minutes or more (2008-2012 5-year est.)
Airports: Mount Vernon Airport (general aviation)
Additional Information Contacts
City of Mount Vernon . . . . (618) 242-5000
  http://www.mtvernon.com
Jefferson County Chamber of Commerce . . . . (618) 242-5725
  http://southernillinois.com

NASON (city). Covers a land area of 0.906 square miles and a water area of 0 square miles. Located at 38.18° N. Lat; 88.97° W. Long. Elevation is 436 feet.
Population: 235 (1990); 234 (2000); 236 (2010); Density: 210.8 persons per square mile (2008-2012 5-year est.); Race: 99.0% White, 0.0% Black/African American, 1.0% Asian, 0.0% American Indian/Alaska Native, 0.0% Native Hawaiian/Other Pacific Islander, 0.0% Some other race, 0.0% Two or more races, 0.0% Hispanic of any race (2008-2012 5-year est.); Average household size: 2.15 (2008-2012 5-year est.); Median age: 44.7 (2008-2012 5-year est.); Males per 100 females: 141.8 (2008-2012 5-year est.); Marriage status: 19.5% never married, 59.2% now married, 8.0% widowed, 13.2% divorced (2008-2012 5-year est.); Foreign born: 1.0% (2008-2012 5-year est.); Ancestry (includes multiple ancestries): 21.5% Irish, 15.7% American, 15.7% German, 14.1% English, 6.3% Croatian (2008-2012 5-year est.).
Economy: Homeowner vacancy rate: 0.0%. Rental vacancy rate: 0.0%. (2008-2012 5-year est.); Employment by occupation: 7.2% management, business, and financial, 0.0% computer, engineering, and science, 4.8% education, legal, community service, arts, and media, 3.6% healthcare practitioners, 0.0% service, 48.2% sales and office, 9.6% natural resources, construction, and maintenance, 26.5% production, transportation, and material moving (2008-2012 5-year est.).
Income: Per capita income: $19,577 (2008-2012 5-year est.); Median household income: $42,656 (2008-2012 5-year est.); Average household income: $41,194 (2008-2012 5-year est.); Percent of households with income of $100,000 or more: 3.4% (2008-2012 5-year est.); Poverty rate: 12.6% (2008-2012 5-year est.).
Education: Percent of population age 25 and over with: High school diploma (including GED) or higher: 80.5% (2008-2012 5-year est.); Bachelor's degree or higher: 1.3% (2008-2012 5-year est.); Master's degree or higher: 0.0% (2008-2012 5-year est.).
Housing: Homeownership rate: 96.6% (2008-2012 5-year est.); Median home value: $50,000 (2008-2012 5-year est.); Median contract rent: n/a per month (2008-2012 5-year est.); Median year structure built: 1979 (2008-2012 5-year est.).
Health Insurance: 68.1% Private; 44.0% Public; 13.1% None. (2008-2012 5-year est.)

Transportation: Commute to work: 87.7% car, 0.0% public transportation, 0.0% walk, 3.7% work from home (2008-2012 5-year est.); Travel time to work: 12.8% less than 15 minutes, 78.2% 15 to 30 minutes, 0.0% 30 to 45 minutes, 3.8% 45 to 60 minutes, 5.1% 60 minutes or more (2008-2012 5-year est.)

OPDYKE (CDP). Covers a land area of 0.524 square miles and a water area of 0 square miles. Located at 38.26° N. Lat; 88.79° W. Long. Elevation is 515 feet.
Population: n/a (1990); n/a (2000); 254 (2010); Density: 681.3 persons per square mile (2008-2012 5-year est.); Race: 100.0% White, 0.0% Black/African American, 0.0% Asian, 0.0% American Indian/Alaska Native, 0.0% Native Hawaiian/Other Pacific Islander, 0.0% Some other race, 0.0% Two or more races, 2.2% Hispanic of any race (2008-2012 5-year est.); Average household size: 3.28 (2008-2012 5-year est.); Median age: 37.7 (2008-2012 5-year est.); Males per 100 females: 72.5 (2008-2012 5-year est.); Marriage status: 18.5% never married, 62.2% now married, 2.0% widowed, 17.3% divorced (2008-2012 5-year est.); Foreign born: 1.1% (2008-2012 5-year est.); Ancestry (includes multiple ancestries): 46.8% German, 25.2% Irish, 8.7% English, 7.3% Dutch, 5.6% French (2008-2012 5-year est.).
Economy: Homeowner vacancy rate: 0.0%. Rental vacancy rate: 0.0%. (2008-2012 5-year est.); Employment by occupation: 9.4% management, business, and financial, 10.2% computer, engineering, and science, 2.4% education, legal, community service, arts, and media, 3.1% healthcare practitioners, 13.4% service, 29.1% sales and office, 7.9% natural resources, construction, and maintenance, 24.4% production, transportation, and material moving (2008-2012 5-year est.).
Income: Per capita income: $17,129 (2008-2012 5-year est.); Median household income: $40,417 (2008-2012 5-year est.); Average household income: $55,287 (2008-2012 5-year est.); Percent of households with income of $100,000 or more: 12.0% (2008-2012 5-year est.); Poverty rate: 39.5% (2008-2012 5-year est.).
Education: Percent of population age 25 and over with: High school diploma (including GED) or higher: 81.4% (2008-2012 5-year est.); Bachelor's degree or higher: 11.9% (2008-2012 5-year est.); Master's degree or higher: 3.0% (2008-2012 5-year est.).
School District(s)
Opdyke-Belle-Rive CCSD 5 (KG-08)
  2011-12 Enrollment: 181 . . . . (618) 756-2492
Housing: Homeownership rate: 92.7% (2008-2012 5-year est.); Median home value: $73,800 (2008-2012 5-year est.); Median contract rent: $300 per month (2008-2012 5-year est.); Median year structure built: 1974 (2008-2012 5-year est.).
Health Insurance: 44.8% Private; 49.3% Public; 12.6% None. (2008-2012 5-year est.)
Transportation: Commute to work: 96.9% car, 0.0% public transportation, 0.0% walk, 0.0% work from home (2008-2012 5-year est.); Travel time to work: 39.4% less than 15 minutes, 26.0% 15 to 30 minutes, 22.0% 30 to 45 minutes, 12.6% 45 to 60 minutes, 0.0% 60 minutes or more (2008-2012 5-year est.)

SCHELLER (unincorporated postal area)
Zip Code: 62883
  Covers a land area of 40.394 square miles and a water area of 0.085 square miles. Located at 38.16° N. Lat; 89.12° W. Long. Elevation is 509 feet. Population: 591 (2010); Density: 14.6 persons per square mile (2010); Race: 99.2% White, 0.3% Black/African American, 0.0% Asian, 0.2% American Indian/Alaska Native, 0.0% Native Hawaiian/Other Pacific Islander, 0.3% Some other race, 0.3% Two or more races, 0.2% Hispanic of any race (2010); Average household size: 2.59 (2010); Median age: 42.5 (2010); Males per 100 females: 107.4 (2010); Homeownership rate: 90.8% (2010)

TEXICO (unincorporated postal area)
Zip Code: 62889
  Covers a land area of 30.303 square miles and a water area of 0.045 square miles. Located at 38.45° N. Lat; 88.82° W. Long. Elevation is 512 feet. Population: 851 (2010); Density: 28.1 persons per square mile (2010); Race: 96.5% White, 0.8% Black/African American, 0.5% Asian, 0.2% American Indian/Alaska Native, 0.0% Native Hawaiian/Other Pacific Islander, 2.0% Some other race, 1.4% Two or more races, 0.7% Hispanic of any race (2010); Average household size: 2.55 (2010); Median age: 43.4 (2010); Males per 100 females: 105.6 (2010); Homeownership rate: 87.7% (2010)

WALTONVILLE (village). Covers a land area of 1.183 square miles and a water area of 0.021 square miles. Located at 38.22° N. Lat; 89.03° W. Long. Elevation is 463 feet.
Population: 396 (1990); 422 (2000); 434 (2010); Density: 355.0 persons per square mile (2008-2012 5-year est.); Race: 100.0% White, 0.0% Black/African American, 0.0% Asian, 0.0% American Indian/Alaska Native, 0.0% Native Hawaiian/Other Pacific Islander, 0.0% Some other race, 0.0% Two or more races, 0.2% Hispanic of any race (2008-2012 5-year est.); Average household size: 2.50 (2008-2012 5-year est.); Median age: 36.6 (2008-2012 5-year est.); Males per 100 females: 99.1 (2008-2012 5-year est.); Marriage status: 27.7% never married, 51.5% now married, 6.6% widowed, 14.2% divorced (2008-2012 5-year est.); Foreign born: 0.0% (2008-2012 5-year est.); Ancestry (includes multiple ancestries): 18.8% German, 16.2% Irish, 13.6% American, 12.4% English, 9.0% Polish (2008-2012 5-year est.).
Economy: Homeowner vacancy rate: 0.0%. Rental vacancy rate: 0.0%. (2008-2012 5-year est.); Employment by occupation: 6.0% management, business, and financial, 0.0% computer, engineering, and science, 3.5% education, legal, community service, arts, and media, 6.0% healthcare practitioners, 21.5% service, 28.5% sales and office, 12.0% natural resources, construction, and maintenance, 22.5% production, transportation, and material moving (2008-2012 5-year est.).
Income: Per capita income: $19,545 (2008-2012 5-year est.); Median household income: $41,000 (2008-2012 5-year est.); Average household income: $48,606 (2008-2012 5-year est.); Percent of households with income of $100,000 or more: 7.7% (2008-2012 5-year est.); Poverty rate: 14.6% (2008-2012 5-year est.).
Education: Percent of population age 25 and over with: High school diploma (including GED) or higher: 83.0% (2008-2012 5-year est.); Bachelor's degree or higher: 6.4% (2008-2012 5-year est.); Master's degree or higher: 1.5% (2008-2012 5-year est.).
School District(s)
Waltonville CUSD 1 (PK-12)
   2011-12 Enrollment: 378. . . . . (618) 279-7211
Housing: Homeownership rate: 73.2% (2008-2012 5-year est.); Median home value: $70,300 (2008-2012 5-year est.); Median contract rent: $288 per month (2008-2012 5-year est.); Median year structure built: 1971 (2008-2012 5-year est.).
Health Insurance: 66.0% Private; 41.2% Public; 10.5% None. (2008-2012 5-year est.)
Transportation: Commute to work: 94.8% car, 1.0% public transportation, 0.0% walk, 2.6% work from home (2008-2012 5-year est.); Travel time to work: 10.1% less than 15 minutes, 58.2% 15 to 30 minutes, 12.7% 30 to 45 minutes, 9.5% 45 to 60 minutes, 9.5% 60 minutes or more (2008-2012 5-year est.)

WOODLAWN (village). Covers a land area of 0.862 square miles and a water area of 0 square miles. Located at 38.33° N. Lat; 89.03° W. Long. Elevation is 492 feet.
Population: 582 (1990); 630 (2000); 698 (2010); Density: 834.2 persons per square mile (2008-2012 5-year est.); Race: 97.2% White, 0.3% Black/African American, 0.3% Asian, 0.0% American Indian/Alaska Native, 0.0% Native Hawaiian/Other Pacific Islander, 2.2% Some other race, 1.8% Two or more races, 2.2% Hispanic of any race (2008-2012 5-year est.); Average household size: 2.46 (2008-2012 5-year est.); Median age: 41.5 (2008-2012 5-year est.); Males per 100 females: 100.8 (2008-2012 5-year est.); Marriage status: 16.3% never married, 63.6% now married, 5.8% widowed, 14.3% divorced (2008-2012 5-year est.); Foreign born: 0.3% (2008-2012 5-year est.); Ancestry (includes multiple ancestries): 23.5% German, 16.0% Irish, 9.5% English, 9.2% Polish, 8.2% American (2008-2012 5-year est.).
Economy: Homeowner vacancy rate: 3.0%. Rental vacancy rate: 0.0%. (2008-2012 5-year est.); Employment by occupation: 10.1% management, business, and financial, 0.0% computer, engineering, and science, 24.2% education, legal, community service, arts, and media, 3.9% healthcare practitioners, 16.0% service, 21.9% sales and office, 5.9% natural resources, construction, and maintenance, 18.0% production, transportation, and material moving (2008-2012 5-year est.).
Income: Per capita income: $21,684 (2008-2012 5-year est.); Median household income: $42,083 (2008-2012 5-year est.); Average household income: $52,976 (2008-2012 5-year est.); Percent of households with income of $100,000 or more: 13.3% (2008-2012 5-year est.); Poverty rate: 18.5% (2008-2012 5-year est.).
Education: Percent of population age 25 and over with: High school diploma (including GED) or higher: 87.6% (2008-2012 5-year est.);

Bachelor's degree or higher: 22.3% (2008-2012 5-year est.); Master's degree or higher: 14.1% (2008-2012 5-year est.).
School District(s)
Woodlawn CCSD 4 (PK-08)
   2011-12 Enrollment: 357. . . . . (618) 735-2661
Woodlawn CHSD 205 (09-12)
   2011-12 Enrollment: 190. . . . . (618) 735-2631
Housing: Homeownership rate: 77.4% (2008-2012 5-year est.); Median home value: $82,700 (2008-2012 5-year est.); Median contract rent: $269 per month (2008-2012 5-year est.); Median year structure built: 1981 (2008-2012 5-year est.).
Health Insurance: 61.5% Private; 55.8% Public; 6.1% None. (2008-2012 5-year est.)
Transportation: Commute to work: 95.4% car, 0.0% public transportation, 1.4% walk, 3.2% work from home (2008-2012 5-year est.); Travel time to work: 31.5% less than 15 minutes, 48.9% 15 to 30 minutes, 9.4% 30 to 45 minutes, 5.1% 45 to 60 minutes, 5.1% 60 minutes or more (2008-2012 5-year est.)

Jersey County

Located in western Illinois; bounded on the south by the Mississippi River and the Missouri border, and on the west by the Illinois River. Covers a land area of 369.271 square miles, a water area of 7.857 square miles, and is located in the Central Time Zone at 39.08° N. Lat., 90.36° W. Long. The county was founded in 1839. County seat is Jerseyville.

Jersey County is part of the St. Louis, MO-IL Metropolitan Statistical Area. The entire metro area includes: Bond County, IL; Calhoun County, IL; Clinton County, IL; Jersey County, IL; Macoupin County, IL; Madison County, IL; Monroe County, IL; Saint Clair County, IL; Franklin County, MO; Jefferson County, MO; Lincoln County, MO; Saint Charles County, MO; Saint Louis County, MO; Warren County, MO; Saint Louis city, MO

Weather Station: Jerseyville 2 SW										Elevation: 629 feet		
	Jan	Feb	Mar	Apr	May	Jun	Jul	Aug	Sep	Oct	Nov	Dec
High	37	42	53	65	74	83	87	86	79	67	54	40
Low	19	23	32	42	53	62	66	63	54	43	34	23
Precip	2.2	2.2	3.3	3.9	4.6	3.7	3.5	3.2	3.3	3.4	4.0	2.9
Snow	4.0	3.4	2.0	0.2	0.0	0.0	0.0	0.0	0.0	tr	0.8	3.1

High and Low temperatures in degrees Fahrenheit; Precipitation and Snow in inches

Population: 20,539 (1990); 21,668 (2000); 22,985 (2010); Race: 97.8% White, 0.7% Black/African American, 0.3% Asian, 0.1% American Indian/Alaska Native, 0.0% Native Hawaiian/Other Pacific Islander, 1.1% Some other race, 1.1% Two or more races, 1.0% Hispanic of any race (2008-2012 5-year est.); Density: 61.6 persons per square mile (2008-2012 5-year est.); Average household size: 2.52 (2008-2012 5-year est.); Median age: 41.3 (2008-2012 5-year est.); Males per 100 females: 96.2 (2008-2012 5-year est.).
Religion: Six largest groups: 30.3% Catholicism, 11.8% Baptist, 4.5% Methodist/Pietist, 3.2% Presbyterian-Reformed, 1.7% Pentecostal, 1.6% Non-denominational Protestant (2010)
Economy: Unemployment rate: 6.2% (April 2014); Total civilian labor force: 11,596 (April 2014); Leading industries: 23.5% health care and social assistance; 19.8% retail trade; 12.8% accommodation & food services (2012); Farms: 509 totaling 155,483 acres (2012); Companies that employ 500 or more persons: 1 (2012); Companies that employ 100 to 499 persons: 5 (2012); Companies that employ less than 100 persons: 428 (2012); Black-owned businesses: n/a (2007); Hispanic-owned businesses: n/a (2007); Asian-owned businesses: n/a (2007); Women-owned businesses: 697 (2007); Single-family building permits issued: 27 (2013); Multi-family building permits issued: 0 (2013).
Income: Per capita income: $25,682 (2008-2012 5-year est.); Median household income: $53,692 (2008-2012 5-year est.); Average household income: $65,827 (2008-2012 5-year est.); Percent of households with income of $100,000 or more: 17.7% (2008-2012 5-year est.); Poverty rate: 8.0% (2008-2012 5-year est.); Bankruptcy rate: 2.37% (2013).
Education: Percent of population age 25 and over with: High school diploma (including GED) or higher: 88.2% (2008-2012 5-year est.); Bachelor's degree or higher: 15.8% (2008-2012 5-year est.); Master's degree or higher: 6.5% (2008-2012 5-year est.).
Housing: Homeownership rate: 79.1% (2008-2012 5-year est.); Median home value: $118,900 (2008-2012 5-year est.); Median contract rent: $474 per month (2008-2012 5-year est.); Median year structure built: 1972 (2008-2012 5-year est.)

Health: Birth rate: 93.6 per 10,000 population (2013); Death rate: 83.9 per 10,000 population (2013); Age-adjusted cancer mortality rate: 181.3 deaths per 100,000 population (2011); Number of physicians: 9.6 per 10,000 population (2011); Hospital beds: 28.3 per 10,000 population (2010); Hospital admissions: 606.9 per 10,000 population (2010).

Environment: Air Quality Index: 84.2% good, 15.0% moderate, 0.8% unhealthy for sensitive individuals, 0.0% unhealthy (percent of days in 2013)

Elections: 2012 Presidential election results: 36.8% Obama, 60.7% Romney

National and State Parks: Pere Marquette State Park; Stump Lake State Fish And Waterfowl Manageme; The Glades State Fish And Waterfowl Manageme

Additional Information Contacts

Jersey County Government. . . . . (618) 498-5571
   http://jerseycountyclerk-il.us

Jersey County Business Association . . . . (618) 639-5222
   http://www.jerseycounty.org

Jersey County Communities

DOW (unincorporated postal area)

Zip Code: 62022

Covers a land area of 18.756 square miles and a water area of 0.011 square miles. Located at 39.00° N. Lat; 90.32° W. Long. Elevation is 673 feet. Population: 1,138 (2010); Density: 60.7 persons per square mile (2010); Race: 97.5% White, 0.2% Black/African American, 0.3% Asian, 0.2% American Indian/Alaska Native, 0.0% Native Hawaiian/Other Pacific Islander, 1.8% Some other race, 1.8% Two or more races, 0.4% Hispanic of any race (2010); Average household size: 2.65 (2010); Median age: 43.3 (2010); Males per 100 females: 105.8 (2010); Homeownership rate: 88.6% (2010)

ELSAH (village).

Covers a land area of 1.093 square miles and a water area of 0 square miles. Located at 38.95° N. Lat; 90.36° W. Long. Elevation is 433 feet.

History: The first settler in Elsah was Addision Greene in 1847, who chopped wood for the steamboats that came along the Mississippi River. The settlement of Jersey Landing developed and was purchased in 1853 by General James Semple, who changed its name to Elsah and built a distillery and two grist mills.

Population: 851 (1990); 635 (2000); 673 (2010); Density: 617.4 persons per square mile (2008-2012 5-year est.); Race: 95.0% White, 4.0% Black/African American, 0.3% Asian, 0.0% American Indian/Alaska Native, 0.0% Native Hawaiian/Other Pacific Islander, 0.7% Some other race, 0.7% Two or more races, 1.2% Hispanic of any race (2008-2012 5-year est.); Average household size: 1.81 (2008-2012 5-year est.); Median age: 20.8 (2008-2012 5-year est.); Males per 100 females: 72.2 (2008-2012 5-year est.); Marriage status: 83.2% never married, 9.3% now married, 1.8% widowed, 5.7% divorced (2008-2012 5-year est.); Foreign born: 7.9% (2008-2012 5-year est.); Ancestry (includes multiple ancestries): 41.3% German, 19.9% Irish, 15.1% English, 7.4% Scottish, 7.1% French (2008-2012 5-year est.).

Economy: Homeowner vacancy rate: 0.0%. Rental vacancy rate: 9.1%. (2008-2012 5-year est.); Employment by occupation: 9.4% management, business, and financial, 1.8% computer, engineering, and science, 15.8% education, legal, community service, arts, and media, 0.6% healthcare practitioners, 31.0% service, 37.7% sales and office, 2.0% natural resources, construction, and maintenance, 1.8% production, transportation, and material moving (2008-2012 5-year est.).

Income: Per capita income: $21,624 (2008-2012 5-year est.); Median household income: $60,104 (2008-2012 5-year est.); Average household income: $66,598 (2008-2012 5-year est.); Percent of households with income of $100,000 or more: 22.5% (2008-2012 5-year est.); Poverty rate: 13.0% (2008-2012 5-year est.).

Education: Percent of population age 25 and over with: High school diploma (including GED) or higher: 95.5% (2008-2012 5-year est.); Bachelor's degree or higher: 56.1% (2008-2012 5-year est.); Master's degree or higher: 24.2% (2008-2012 5-year est.).

Four-year College(s)

Principia College (Private, Not-for-profit)

  Fall 2012 Enrollment: 491 . . . . (618) 374-2131
  2012-13 Tuition: In-state $25,960; Out-of-state $25,960

Housing: Homeownership rate: 55.1% (2008-2012 5-year est.); Median home value: $172,300 (2008-2012 5-year est.); Median contract rent: $785

per month (2008-2012 5-year est.); Median year structure built: Before 1940 (2008-2012 5-year est.).

Health Insurance: 87.0% Private; 7.6% Public; 9.8% None. (2008-2012 5-year est.)

Transportation: Commute to work: 30.7% car, 2.3% public transportation, 63.2% walk, 2.9% work from home (2008-2012 5-year est.); Travel time to work: 72.9% less than 15 minutes, 15.1% 15 to 30 minutes, 3.6% 30 to 45 minutes, 2.4% 45 to 60 minutes, 6.0% 60 minutes or more (2008-2012 5-year est.)

FIDELITY (village).

Covers a land area of 0.110 square miles and a water area of 0 square miles. Located at 39.15° N. Lat; 90.16° W. Long. Elevation is 636 feet.

Population: 66 (1990); 105 (2000); 114 (2010); Density: 1,322.4 persons per square mile (2008-2012 5-year est.); Race: 100.0% White, 0.0% Black/African American, 0.0% Asian, 0.0% American Indian/Alaska Native, 0.0% Native Hawaiian/Other Pacific Islander, 0.0% Some other race, 0.0% Two or more races, 0.0% Hispanic of any race (2008-2012 5-year est.); Average household size: 3.15 (2008-2012 5-year est.); Median age: 26.5 (2008-2012 5-year est.); Males per 100 females: 66.7 (2008-2012 5-year est.); Marriage status: 35.6% never married, 47.5% now married, 0.0% widowed, 16.8% divorced (2008-2012 5-year est.); Foreign born: 0.0% (2008-2012 5-year est.); Ancestry (includes multiple ancestries): 28.3% German, 16.6% English, 8.3% Irish, 2.8% American, 1.4% French (2008-2012 5-year est.).

Economy: Homeowner vacancy rate: 13.3%. Rental vacancy rate: 0.0%. (2008-2012 5-year est.); Employment by occupation: 9.5% management, business, and financial, 0.0% computer, engineering, and science, 0.0% education, legal, community service, arts, and media, 9.5% healthcare practitioners, 45.2% service, 19.0% sales and office, 16.7% natural resources, construction, and maintenance, 0.0% production, transportation, and material moving (2008-2012 5-year est.).

Income: Per capita income: $9,824 (2008-2012 5-year est.); Median household income: $30,833 (2008-2012 5-year est.); Average household income: $32,093 (2008-2012 5-year est.); Percent of households with income of $100,000 or more: n/a (2008-2012 5-year est.); Poverty rate: 33.8% (2008-2012 5-year est.).

Education: Percent of population age 25 and over with: High school diploma (including GED) or higher: 63.2% (2008-2012 5-year est.); Bachelor's degree or higher: 3.9% (2008-2012 5-year est.); Master's degree or higher: 3.9% (2008-2012 5-year est.).

Housing: Homeownership rate: 56.5% (2008-2012 5-year est.); Median home value: $32,000 (2008-2012 5-year est.); Median contract rent: $446 per month (2008-2012 5-year est.); Median year structure built: 1986 (2008-2012 5-year est.).

Health Insurance: 19.3% Private; 52.4% Public; 31.7% None. (2008-2012 5-year est.)

Transportation: Commute to work: 97.6% car, 0.0% public transportation, 0.0% walk, 2.4% work from home (2008-2012 5-year est.); Travel time to work: 22.0% less than 15 minutes, 46.3% 15 to 30 minutes, 31.7% 30 to 45 minutes, 0.0% 45 to 60 minutes, 0.0% 60 minutes or more (2008-2012 5-year est.)

FIELDON (village).

Covers a land area of 0.200 square miles and a water area of 0 square miles. Located at 39.11° N. Lat; 90.50° W. Long. Elevation is 692 feet.

Population: 277 (1990); 271 (2000); 239 (2010); Density: 1,328.1 persons per square mile (2008-2012 5-year est.); Race: 98.5% White, 0.0% Black/African American, 0.0% Asian, 0.0% American Indian/Alaska Native, 0.0% Native Hawaiian/Other Pacific Islander, 1.5% Some other race, 1.5% Two or more races, 0.0% Hispanic of any race (2008-2012 5-year est.); Average household size: 2.22 (2008-2012 5-year est.); Median age: 42.5 (2008-2012 5-year est.); Males per 100 females: 101.5 (2008-2012 5-year est.); Marriage status: 23.4% never married, 51.9% now married, 11.3% widowed, 13.4% divorced (2008-2012 5-year est.); Foreign born: 1.5% (2008-2012 5-year est.); Ancestry (includes multiple ancestries): 44.7% German, 21.4% Irish, 10.5% French, 9.8% English, 9.4% American (2008-2012 5-year est.).

Economy: Single-family building permits issued: 0 (2013); Multi-family building permits issued: 0 (2013); Homeowner vacancy rate: 6.6%. Rental vacancy rate: 0.0%. (2008-2012 5-year est.); Employment by occupation: 2.1% management, business, and financial, 1.4% computer, engineering, and science, 4.3% education, legal, community service, arts, and media, 6.4% healthcare practitioners, 30.7% service, 13.6% sales and office,

10.7% natural resources, construction, and maintenance, 30.7% production, transportation, and material moving (2008-2012 5-year est.).
Income: Per capita income: $24,829 (2008-2012 5-year est.); Median household income: $45,000 (2008-2012 5-year est.); Average household income: $55,186 (2008-2012 5-year est.); Percent of households with income of $100,000 or more: 12.6% (2008-2012 5-year est.); Poverty rate: 4.6% (2008-2012 5-year est.).
Education: Percent of population age 25 and over with: High school diploma (including GED) or higher: 89.4% (2008-2012 5-year est.); Bachelor's degree or higher: 3.7% (2008-2012 5-year est.); Master's degree or higher: 1.6% (2008-2012 5-year est.).

School District(s)
Jersey CUSD 100 (PK-12)
    2011-12 Enrollment: 2,764 . . . . (618) 498-5561
Housing: Homeownership rate: 82.5% (2008-2012 5-year est.); Median home value: $78,900 (2008-2012 5-year est.); Median contract rent: $405 per month (2008-2012 5-year est.); Median year structure built: 1960 (2008-2012 5-year est.).
Health Insurance: 69.2% Private; 28.2% Public; 18.0% None. (2008-2012 5-year est.)
Transportation: Commute to work: 97.1% car, 0.0% public transportation, 0.0% walk, 1.4% work from home (2008-2012 5-year est.); Travel time to work: 8.8% less than 15 minutes, 33.1% 15 to 30 minutes, 30.1% 30 to 45 minutes, 13.2% 45 to 60 minutes, 14.7% 60 minutes or more (2008-2012 5-year est.)

GRAFTON (city). Covers a land area of 3.700 square miles and a water area of 0 square miles. Located at 38.98° N. Lat; 90.43° W. Long. Elevation is 449 feet.
History: City suffered greatly during a devastating flood (1993). Incorporated 1837.
Population: 918 (1990); 609 (2000); 674 (2010); Density: 201.9 persons per square mile (2008-2012 5-year est.); Race: 93.3% White, 6.2% Black/African American, 0.5% Asian, 0.0% American Indian/Alaska Native, 0.0% Native Hawaiian/Other Pacific Islander, 0.0% Some other race, 0.0% Two or more races, 0.3% Hispanic of any race (2008-2012 5-year est.); Average household size: 2.37 (2008-2012 5-year est.); Median age: 48.6 (2008-2012 5-year est.); Males per 100 females: 85.8 (2008-2012 5-year est.); Marriage status: 20.2% never married, 60.0% now married, 6.1% widowed, 13.7% divorced (2008-2012 5-year est.); Foreign born: 1.2% (2008-2012 5-year est.); Ancestry (includes multiple ancestries): 27.4% German, 20.6% English, 19.0% Irish, 10.2% American, 5.4% French (2008-2012 5-year est.).
Economy: Single-family building permits issued: 4 (2013); Multi-family building permits issued: 0 (2013); Homeowner vacancy rate: 6.2%. Rental vacancy rate: 12.7%. (2008-2012 5-year est.); Employment by occupation: 15.6% management, business, and financial, 9.2% computer, engineering, and science, 16.0% education, legal, community service, arts, and media, 7.3% healthcare practitioners, 15.6% service, 8.0% sales and office, 14.9% natural resources, construction, and maintenance, 13.4% production, transportation, and material moving (2008-2012 5-year est.).
Income: Per capita income: $49,711 (2008-2012 5-year est.); Median household income: $53,365 (2008-2012 5-year est.); Average household income: $117,159 (2008-2012 5-year est.); Percent of households with income of $100,000 or more: 27.0% (2008-2012 5-year est.); Poverty rate: 16.1% (2008-2012 5-year est.).
Education: Percent of population age 25 and over with: High school diploma (including GED) or higher: 88.7% (2008-2012 5-year est.); Bachelor's degree or higher: 28.7% (2008-2012 5-year est.); Master's degree or higher: 17.6% (2008-2012 5-year est.).

School District(s)
Idjj SD 428 (06-12)
    2011-12 Enrollment: 784. . . . . (309) 584-0506
Jersey CUSD 100 (PK-12)
    2011-12 Enrollment: 2,764 . . . . (618) 498-5561
Housing: Homeownership rate: 66.9% (2008-2012 5-year est.); Median home value: $177,800 (2008-2012 5-year est.); Median contract rent: $401 per month (2008-2012 5-year est.); Median year structure built: 1986 (2008-2012 5-year est.).
Health Insurance: 70.9% Private; 33.8% Public; 11.1% None. (2008-2012 5-year est.)
Safety: Violent crime rate: 0.0 per 10,000 population; Property crime rate: 238.1 per 10,000 population (2012).
Transportation: Commute to work: 90.5% car, 0.0% public transportation, 1.5% walk, 3.8% work from home (2008-2012 5-year est.); Travel time to

work: 25.0% less than 15 minutes, 19.4% 15 to 30 minutes, 36.5% 30 to 45 minutes, 3.6% 45 to 60 minutes, 15.5% 60 minutes or more (2008-2012 5-year est.)

JERSEYVILLE (city). County seat. Covers a land area of 5.081 square miles and a water area of 0 square miles. Located at 39.12° N. Lat; 90.33° W. Long. Elevation is 659 feet.
History: Plotted 1834, incorporated 1855.
Population: 7,382 (1990); 7,984 (2000); 8,465 (2010); Density: 1,738.4 persons per square mile (2008-2012 5-year est.); Race: 99.4% White, 0.2% Black/African American, 0.1% Asian, 0.0% American Indian/Alaska Native, 0.0% Native Hawaiian/Other Pacific Islander, 0.3% Some other race, 0.2% Two or more races, 1.9% Hispanic of any race (2008-2012 5-year est.); Average household size: 2.41 (2008-2012 5-year est.); Median age: 40.4 (2008-2012 5-year est.); Males per 100 females: 102.6 (2008-2012 5-year est.); Marriage status: 24.9% never married, 54.6% now married, 8.8% widowed, 11.6% divorced (2008-2012 5-year est.); Foreign born: 1.0% (2008-2012 5-year est.); Ancestry (includes multiple ancestries): 35.1% German, 16.4% Irish, 9.7% English, 7.9% American, 3.5% French (2008-2012 5-year est.).
Economy: Single-family building permits issued: 11 (2013); Multi-family building permits issued: 0 (2013); Homeowner vacancy rate: 1.2%. Rental vacancy rate: 11.7%. (2008-2012 5-year est.); Employment by occupation: 10.4% management, business, and financial, 2.2% computer, engineering, and science, 8.8% education, legal, community service, arts, and media, 8.9% healthcare practitioners, 18.3% service, 28.8% sales and office, 9.9% natural resources, construction, and maintenance, 12.6% production, transportation, and material moving (2008-2012 5-year est.).
Income: Per capita income: $23,613 (2008-2012 5-year est.); Median household income: $49,565 (2008-2012 5-year est.); Average household income: $57,577 (2008-2012 5-year est.); Percent of households with income of $100,000 or more: 13.6% (2008-2012 5-year est.); Poverty rate: 8.7% (2008-2012 5-year est.).
Education: Percent of population age 25 and over with: High school diploma (including GED) or higher: 89.4% (2008-2012 5-year est.); Bachelor's degree or higher: 16.5% (2008-2012 5-year est.); Master's degree or higher: 7.8% (2008-2012 5-year est.).

School District(s)
Calhoun/greene/jersy/macoupin Roe (07-12)
    2011-12 Enrollment: n/a . . . . (217) 854-4016
Jersey CUSD 100 (PK-12)
    2011-12 Enrollment: 2,764 . . . . (618) 498-5561
Housing: Homeownership rate: 69.7% (2008-2012 5-year est.); Median home value: $106,100 (2008-2012 5-year est.); Median contract rent: $485 per month (2008-2012 5-year est.); Median year structure built: 1962 (2008-2012 5-year est.).
Health Insurance: 75.5% Private; 29.4% Public; 9.4% None. (2008-2012 5-year est.)
Hospitals: Jersey Community Hospital (67 beds)
Safety: Violent crime rate: 35.5 per 10,000 population; Property crime rate: 349.5 per 10,000 population (2012).
Transportation: Commute to work: 96.1% car, 0.1% public transportation, 1.0% walk, 2.5% work from home (2008-2012 5-year est.); Travel time to work: 42.3% less than 15 minutes, 16.0% 15 to 30 minutes, 16.4% 30 to 45 minutes, 12.1% 45 to 60 minutes, 13.2% 60 minutes or more (2008-2012 5-year est.)
Additional Information Contacts
City of Jerseyville . . . . (618) 498-3312
    http://www.jerseyville-il.us
Jersey County Business Association . . . . (618) 639-5222
    http://www.jerseycounty.org

OTTERVILLE (town). Covers a land area of 1.011 square miles and a water area of 0 square miles. Located at 39.05° N. Lat; 90.40° W. Long. Elevation is 627 feet.
Population: 115 (1990); 120 (2000); 126 (2010); Density: 93.0 persons per square mile (2008-2012 5-year est.); Race: 100.0% White, 0.0% Black/African American, 0.0% Asian, 0.0% American Indian/Alaska Native, 0.0% Native Hawaiian/Other Pacific Islander, 0.0% Some other race, 0.0% Two or more races, 0.0% Hispanic of any race (2008-2012 5-year est.); Average household size: 2.61 (2008-2012 5-year est.); Median age: 46.8 (2008-2012 5-year est.); Males per 100 females: 67.9 (2008-2012 5-year est.); Marriage status: 24.7% never married, 41.2% now married, 12.9% widowed, 21.2% divorced (2008-2012 5-year est.); Foreign born: 0.0% (2008-2012 5-year est.); Ancestry (includes multiple ancestries): 31.9%

German, 16.0% English, 16.0% Irish, 8.5% American, 2.1% Finnish (2008-2012 5-year est.).

Economy: Homeowner vacancy rate: 0.0%. Rental vacancy rate: 0.0%. (2008-2012 5-year est.); Employment by occupation: 26.7% management, business, and financial, 10.0% computer, engineering, and science, 3.3% education, legal, community service, arts, and media, 0.0% healthcare practitioners, 6.7% service, 16.7% sales and office, 20.0% natural resources, construction, and maintenance, 16.7% production, transportation, and material moving (2008-2012 5-year est.).

Income: Per capita income: $18,596 (2008-2012 5-year est.); Median household income: $36,250 (2008-2012 5-year est.); Average household income: $47,058 (2008-2012 5-year est.); Percent of households with income of $100,000 or more: 8.3% (2008-2012 5-year est.); Poverty rate: 11.7% (2008-2012 5-year est.).

Education: Percent of population age 25 and over with: High school diploma (including GED) or higher: 80.3% (2008-2012 5-year est.); Bachelor's degree or higher: 4.2% (2008-2012 5-year est.); Master's degree or higher: 0.0% (2008-2012 5-year est.).

Housing: Homeownership rate: 88.9% (2008-2012 5-year est.); Median home value: $62,000 (2008-2012 5-year est.); Median contract rent: $338 per month (2008-2012 5-year est.); Median year structure built: 1969 (2008-2012 5-year est.).

Health Insurance: 45.7% Private; 47.9% Public; 19.1% None. (2008-2012 5-year est.)

Transportation: Commute to work: 91.7% car, 0.0% public transportation, 0.0% walk, 8.3% work from home (2008-2012 5-year est.); Travel time to work: 31.8% less than 15 minutes, 27.3% 15 to 30 minutes, 27.3% 30 to 45 minutes, 13.6% 45 to 60 minutes, 0.0% 60 minutes or more (2008-2012 5-year est.)

Jo Daviess County

Located in northwestern Illinois; bounded on the north by Wisconsin, and on the west by the Mississippi River and the Iowa border; drained by the Apple, Plum, and Galena Rivers; includes Charles Mound, highest point in the state (1,241 ft). Covers a land area of 601.087 square miles, a water area of 17.641 square miles, and is located in the Central Time Zone at 42.36° N. Lat., 90.21° W. Long. The county was founded in 1827. County seat is Galena.

Weather Station: Elizabeth 5 S   Elevation: 680 feet

	Jan	Feb	Mar	Apr	May	Jun	Jul	Aug	Sep	Oct	Nov	Dec
High	29	33	46	59	70	80	83	81	74	62	47	32
Low	10	14	25	35	45	56	59	57	48	37	27	14
Precip	1.2	na	2.4	3.4	3.9	4.9	3.4	4.6	3.5	2.7	2.8	1.8
Snow	9.0	na	2.4	1.0	tr	0.0	0.0	0.0	0.0	0.1	1.5	8.7

High and Low temperatures in degrees Fahrenheit; Precipitation and Snow in inches

Weather Station: Stockton 3 NNE   Elevation: 970 feet

	Jan	Feb	Mar	Apr	May	Jun	Jul	Aug	Sep	Oct	Nov	Dec
High	27	32	44	58	70	79	82	80	73	61	45	31
Low	11	15	26	37	48	58	61	59	50	39	29	16
Precip	1.1	1.4	2.2	3.5	3.8	5.0	3.5	4.8	3.8	2.9	2.6	1.7
Snow	9.2	7.1	4.4	1.6	0.1	0.0	0.0	0.0	0.0	0.3	1.8	9.3

High and Low temperatures in degrees Fahrenheit; Precipitation and Snow in inches

Population: 21,821 (1990); 22,289 (2000); 22,678 (2010); Race: 97.0% White, 0.5% Black/African American, 0.4% Asian, 0.3% American Indian/Alaska Native, 0.0% Native Hawaiian/Other Pacific Islander, 1.8% Some other race, 0.7% Two or more races, 2.8% Hispanic of any race (2008-2012 5-year est.); Density: 37.5 persons per square mile (2008-2012 5-year est.); Average household size: 2.31 (2008-2012 5-year est.); Median age: 47.2 (2008-2012 5-year est.); Males per 100 females: 100.7 (2008-2012 5-year est.).

Religion: Six largest groups: 34.6% Catholicism, 9.5% Methodist/Pietist, 9.1% Lutheran, 1.8% Presbyterian-Reformed, 0.6% Episcopalianism/Anglicanism, 0.4% Non-denominational Protestant (2010)

Economy: Unemployment rate: 6.3% (April 2014); Total civilian labor force: 12,056 (April 2014); Leading industries: 23.4% accommodation & food services; 15.3% manufacturing; 12.6% retail trade (2012); Farms: 935 totaling 271,793 acres (2012); Companies that employ 500 or more persons: 0 (2012); Companies that employ 100 to 499 persons: 14 (2012); Companies that employ less than 100 persons: 716 (2012); Black-owned businesses: n/a (2007); Hispanic-owned businesses: n/a (2007); Asian-owned businesses: n/a (2007); Women-owned businesses: 610

(2007); Single-family building permits issued: 39 (2013); Multi-family building permits issued: 0 (2013).

Income: Per capita income: $28,529 (2008-2012 5-year est.); Median household income: $52,164 (2008-2012 5-year est.); Average household income: $66,813 (2008-2012 5-year est.); Percent of households with income of $100,000 or more: 16.1% (2008-2012 5-year est.); Poverty rate: 10.1% (2008-2012 5-year est.); Bankruptcy rate: 1.68% (2013).

Education: Percent of population age 25 and over with: High school diploma (including GED) or higher: 90.9% (2008-2012 5-year est.); Bachelor's degree or higher: 22.8% (2008-2012 5-year est.); Master's degree or higher: 8.6% (2008-2012 5-year est.).

Housing: Homeownership rate: 78.9% (2008-2012 5-year est.); Median home value: $141,200 (2008-2012 5-year est.); Median contract rent: $449 per month (2008-2012 5-year est.); Median year structure built: 1971 (2008-2012 5-year est.).

Health: Birth rate: 85.7 per 10,000 population (2013); Death rate: 107.1 per 10,000 population (2013); Age-adjusted cancer mortality rate: 171.4 deaths per 100,000 population (2011); Number of physicians: 6.2 per 10,000 population (2011); Hospital beds: 36.2 per 10,000 population (2010); Hospital admissions: 373.5 per 10,000 population (2010).

Environment: Air Quality Index: 96.0% good, 4.0% moderate, 0.0% unhealthy for sensitive individuals, 0.0% unhealthy (percent of days in 2013)

Elections: 2012 Presidential election results: 49.6% Obama, 48.5% Romney

National and State Parks: Apple River Canyon State Park

Additional Information Contacts

Jo Daviess County Government . . . . (815) 777-0161
http://www.jodaviess.org

Jo Daviess County Communities

APPLE CANYON LAKE (CDP). Covers a land area of 3.714 square miles and a water area of 0.656 square miles. Located at 42.43° N. Lat; 90.16° W. Long.

Population: n/a (1990); n/a (2000); 558 (2010); Density: 120.3 persons per square mile (2008-2012 5-year est.); Race: 100.0% White, 0.0% Black/African American, 0.0% Asian, 0.0% American Indian/Alaska Native, 0.0% Native Hawaiian/Other Pacific Islander, 0.0% Some other race, 0.0% Two or more races, 0.0% Hispanic of any race (2008-2012 5-year est.); Average household size: 2.02 (2008-2012 5-year est.); Median age: 64.4 (2008-2012 5-year est.); Males per 100 females: 97.8 (2008-2012 5-year est.); Marriage status: 2.3% never married, 88.5% now married, 3.5% widowed, 5.6% divorced (2008-2012 5-year est.); Foreign born: 0.0% (2008-2012 5-year est.); Ancestry (includes multiple ancestries): 44.7% German, 21.9% American, 16.3% Irish, 15.2% English, 7.4% Italian (2008-2012 5-year est.).

Economy: Homeowner vacancy rate: 0.0%. Rental vacancy rate: 0.0%. (2008-2012 5-year est.); Employment by occupation: 0.0% management, business, and financial, 32.0% computer, engineering, and science, 14.7% education, legal, community service, arts, and media, 0.0% healthcare practitioners, 0.0% service, 21.3% sales and office, 4.0% natural resources, construction, and maintenance, 28.0% production, transportation, and material moving (2008-2012 5-year est.).

Income: Per capita income: $31,402 (2008-2012 5-year est.); Median household income: $56,250 (2008-2012 5-year est.); Average household income: $63,510 (2008-2012 5-year est.); Percent of households with income of $100,000 or more: 17.6% (2008-2012 5-year est.); Poverty rate: 3.1% (2008-2012 5-year est.).

Education: Percent of population age 25 and over with: High school diploma (including GED) or higher: 93.9% (2008-2012 5-year est.); Bachelor's degree or higher: 36.8% (2008-2012 5-year est.); Master's degree or higher: 14.8% (2008-2012 5-year est.).

Housing: Homeownership rate: 100.0% (2008-2012 5-year est.); Median home value: $212,800 (2008-2012 5-year est.); Median contract rent: n/a per month (2008-2012 5-year est.); Median year structure built: 1988 (2008-2012 5-year est.).

Health Insurance: 89.5% Private; 56.8% Public; 1.3% None. (2008-2012 5-year est.)

Transportation: Commute to work: 80.0% car, 0.0% public transportation, 4.0% walk, 16.0% work from home (2008-2012 5-year est.); Travel time to work: 4.8% less than 15 minutes, 11.1% 15 to 30 minutes, 41.3% 30 to 45 minutes, 25.4% 45 to 60 minutes, 17.5% 60 minutes or more (2008-2012 5-year est.)

APPLE RIVER (village). Covers a land area of 0.793 square miles and a water area of 0 square miles. Located at 42.50° N. Lat; 90.09° W. Long. Elevation is 1,010 feet.

Population: 414 (1990); 379 (2000); 366 (2010); Density: 504.7 persons per square mile (2008-2012 5-year est.); Race: 96.3% White, 0.0% Black/African American, 0.0% Asian, 2.3% American Indian/Alaska Native, 0.0% Native Hawaiian/Other Pacific Islander, 1.4% Some other race, 1.5% Two or more races, 0.8% Hispanic of any race (2008-2012 5-year est.); Average household size: 2.19 (2008-2012 5-year est.); Median age: 42.0 (2008-2012 5-year est.); Males per 100 females: 115.1 (2008-2012 5-year est.); Marriage status: 19.6% never married, 58.2% now married, 3.2% widowed, 19.0% divorced (2008-2012 5-year est.); Foreign born: 1.3% (2008-2012 5-year est.); Ancestry (includes multiple ancestries): 38.3% German, 22.8% Irish, 15.3% American, 12.8% English, 6.8% Norwegian (2008-2012 5-year est.).

Economy: Homeowner vacancy rate: 0.0%. Rental vacancy rate: 22.8%. (2008-2012 5-year est.); Employment by occupation: 5.2% management, business, and financial, 1.2% computer, engineering, and science, 4.0% education, legal, community service, arts, and media, 4.6% healthcare practitioners, 20.2% service, 25.4% sales and office, 21.4% natural resources, construction, and maintenance, 17.9% production, transportation, and material moving (2008-2012 5-year est.).

Income: Per capita income: $17,929 (2008-2012 5-year est.); Median household income: $34,018 (2008-2012 5-year est.); Average household income: $40,561 (2008-2012 5-year est.); Percent of households with income of $100,000 or more: 2.7% (2008-2012 5-year est.); Poverty rate: 15.1% (2008-2012 5-year est.).

Education: Percent of population age 25 and over with: High school diploma (including GED) or higher: 85.0% (2008-2012 5-year est.); Bachelor's degree or higher: 9.1% (2008-2012 5-year est.); Master's degree or higher: 2.4% (2008-2012 5-year est.).

Housing: Homeownership rate: 76.0% (2008-2012 5-year est.); Median home value: $70,700 (2008-2012 5-year est.); Median contract rent: $392 per month (2008-2012 5-year est.); Median year structure built: Before 1940 (2008-2012 5-year est.).

Health Insurance: 57.9% Private; 38.8% Public; 16.8% None. (2008-2012 5-year est.)

Transportation: Commute to work: 95.9% car, 0.6% public transportation, 2.3% walk, 1.2% work from home (2008-2012 5-year est.); Travel time to work: 19.4% less than 15 minutes, 27.6% 15 to 30 minutes, 23.5% 30 to 45 minutes, 16.5% 45 to 60 minutes, 12.9% 60 minutes or more (2008-2012 5-year est.)

EAST DUBUQUE (city). Covers a land area of 2.810 square miles and a water area of 0.081 square miles. Located at 42.49° N. Lat; 90.63° W. Long. Elevation is 610 feet.

History: Incorporated 1857.

Population: 1,914 (1990); 1,995 (2000); 1,704 (2010); Density: 702.1 persons per square mile (2008-2012 5-year est.); Race: 96.4% White, 1.7% Black/African American, 0.3% Asian, 0.0% American Indian/Alaska Native, 0.0% Native Hawaiian/Other Pacific Islander, 1.6% Some other race, 1.7% Two or more races, 1.3% Hispanic of any race (2008-2012 5-year est.); Average household size: 2.24 (2008-2012 5-year est.); Median age: 40.8 (2008-2012 5-year est.); Males per 100 females: 87.4 (2008-2012 5-year est.); Marriage status: 22.4% never married, 58.1% now married, 7.1% widowed, 12.3% divorced (2008-2012 5-year est.); Foreign born: 1.7% (2008-2012 5-year est.); Ancestry (includes multiple ancestries): 43.7% German, 27.4% Irish, 10.8% American, 5.3% French, 3.3% Dutch (2008-2012 5-year est.).

Economy: Single-family building permits issued: 1 (2013); Multi-family building permits issued: 0 (2013); Homeowner vacancy rate: 4.5%. Rental vacancy rate: 7.2%. (2008-2012 5-year est.); Employment by occupation: 14.2% management, business, and financial, 1.8% computer, engineering, and science, 7.3% education, legal, community service, arts, and media, 1.1% healthcare practitioners, 17.8% service, 32.1% sales and office, 5.3% natural resources, construction, and maintenance, 20.4% production, transportation, and material moving (2008-2012 5-year est.).

Income: Per capita income: $23,732 (2008-2012 5-year est.); Median household income: $41,071 (2008-2012 5-year est.); Average household income: $54,010 (2008-2012 5-year est.); Percent of households with income of $100,000 or more: 11.3% (2008-2012 5-year est.); Poverty rate: 10.9% (2008-2012 5-year est.).

Taxes: Total city taxes per capita: $325 (2011); City property taxes per capita: $238 (2011).

Education: Percent of population age 25 and over with: High school diploma (including GED) or higher: 91.3% (2008-2012 5-year est.); Bachelor's degree or higher: 17.1% (2008-2012 5-year est.); Master's degree or higher: 3.8% (2008-2012 5-year est.).

School District(s)

East Dubuque USD 119 (PK-12)

2011-12 Enrollment: 677 . . . . (815) 747-2111

Housing: Homeownership rate: 69.4% (2008-2012 5-year est.); Median home value: $129,900 (2008-2012 5-year est.); Median contract rent: $435 per month (2008-2012 5-year est.); Median year structure built: 1951 (2008-2012 5-year est.).

Health Insurance: 70.9% Private; 37.3% Public; 8.6% None. (2008-2012 5-year est.)

Safety: Violent crime rate: 52.7 per 10,000 population; Property crime rate: 158.2 per 10,000 population (2012).

Transportation: Commute to work: 97.8% car, 0.0% public transportation, 0.6% walk, 0.8% work from home (2008-2012 5-year est.); Travel time to work: 44.3% less than 15 minutes, 40.3% 15 to 30 minutes, 10.8% 30 to 45 minutes, 0.7% 45 to 60 minutes, 3.8% 60 minutes or more (2008-2012 5-year est.)

ELIZABETH (village). Covers a land area of 0.775 square miles and a water area of 0 square miles. Located at 42.32° N. Lat; 90.22° W. Long. Elevation is 801 feet.

History: Elizabeth was built on the site of the Apple River Fort, established during the Black Hawk War.

Population: 641 (1990); 682 (2000); 761 (2010); Density: 1,153.4 persons per square mile (2008-2012 5-year est.); Race: 100.0% White, 0.0% Black/African American, 0.0% Asian, 0.0% American Indian/Alaska Native, 0.0% Native Hawaiian/Other Pacific Islander, 0.0% Some other race, 0.0% Two or more races, 0.0% Hispanic of any race (2008-2012 5-year est.); Average household size: 2.45 (2008-2012 5-year est.); Median age: 40.8 (2008-2012 5-year est.); Males per 100 females: 108.4 (2008-2012 5-year est.); Marriage status: 19.7% never married, 58.7% now married, 9.7% widowed, 11.9% divorced (2008-2012 5-year est.); Foreign born: 2.6% (2008-2012 5-year est.); Ancestry (includes multiple ancestries): 41.9% German, 22.0% Irish, 10.3% American, 7.0% English, 4.3% French (2008-2012 5-year est.).

Economy: Homeowner vacancy rate: 0.0%. Rental vacancy rate: 0.0%. (2008-2012 5-year est.); Employment by occupation: 10.4% management, business, and financial, 2.5% computer, engineering, and science, 12.2% education, legal, community service, arts, and media, 3.7% healthcare practitioners, 30.1% service, 13.7% sales and office, 16.2% natural resources, construction, and maintenance, 11.2% production, transportation, and material moving (2008-2012 5-year est.).

Income: Per capita income: $18,990 (2008-2012 5-year est.); Median household income: $33,828 (2008-2012 5-year est.); Average household income: $46,981 (2008-2012 5-year est.); Percent of households with income of $100,000 or more: 11.7% (2008-2012 5-year est.); Poverty rate: 23.3% (2008-2012 5-year est.).

Education: Percent of population age 25 and over with: High school diploma (including GED) or higher: 91.5% (2008-2012 5-year est.); Bachelor's degree or higher: 17.6% (2008-2012 5-year est.); Master's degree or higher: 7.6% (2008-2012 5-year est.).

School District(s)

Carroll/jo Daviess/stephenson Roe (PK-12)

2011-12 Enrollment: n/a . . . . (815) 947-3810

Jo Daviess-Carroll Area Voc Ctr (11-12)

2011-12 Enrollment: n/a . . . . (815) 858-2203

Housing: Homeownership rate: 68.5% (2008-2012 5-year est.); Median home value: $93,900 (2008-2012 5-year est.); Median contract rent: $417 per month (2008-2012 5-year est.); Median year structure built: Before 1940 (2008-2012 5-year est.).

Health Insurance: 64.3% Private; 42.8% Public; 8.9% None. (2008-2012 5-year est.)

Safety: Violent crime rate: 26.3 per 10,000 population; Property crime rate: 26.3 per 10,000 population (2012).

Transportation: Commute to work: 87.2% car, 0.8% public transportation, 10.8% walk, 1.3% work from home (2008-2012 5-year est.); Travel time to work: 48.1% less than 15 minutes, 36.4% 15 to 30 minutes, 5.2% 30 to 45 minutes, 5.2% 45 to 60 minutes, 5.2% 60 minutes or more (2008-2012 5-year est.)

GALENA (city). County seat. Covers a land area of 4.162 square miles and a water area of 0.007 square miles. Located at 42.42° N. Lat; 90.43° W. Long. Elevation is 633 feet.

History: The lead deposits in the Galena area interested French explorers in the 1700's. The town of Galena was laid out in 1826 and named for the mineral galena, the principal ore of lead. By this time the government was controlling the mineral lands and issuing leases. Smelter operations were responsible for Galena's early growth, and traffic on the old Fever River made it a trading center until the middle of the 1800's, when the lead veins were exhausted and the river silted in. Ulysses S. Grant was a resident of Galena when he was chosen to lead the Federal troops in the Civil War.

Population: 3,647 (1990); 3,460 (2000); 3,429 (2010); Density: 833.4 persons per square mile (2008-2012 5-year est.); Race: 92.0% White, 0.7% Black/African American, 0.7% Asian, 0.0% American Indian/Alaska Native, 0.0% Native Hawaiian/Other Pacific Islander, 6.6% Some other race, 0.7% Two or more races, 11.6% Hispanic of any race (2008-2012 5-year est.); Average household size: 2.12 (2008-2012 5-year est.); Median age: 46.7 (2008-2012 5-year est.); Males per 100 females: 99.4 (2008-2012 5-year est.); Marriage status: 30.4% never married, 44.0% now married, 9.8% widowed, 15.9% divorced (2008-2012 5-year est.); Foreign born: 10.4% (2008-2012 5-year est.); Ancestry (includes multiple ancestries): 41.7% German, 17.7% Irish, 10.3% English, 9.6% American, 7.2% Polish (2008-2012 5-year est.).

Economy: Single-family building permits issued: 1 (2013); Multi-family building permits issued: 0 (2013); Homeowner vacancy rate: 5.4%. Rental vacancy rate: 2.3%. (2008-2012 5-year est.); Employment by occupation: 11.9% management, business, and financial, 1.6% computer, engineering, and science, 8.0% education, legal, community service, arts, and media, 1.9% healthcare practitioners, 21.3% service, 33.9% sales and office, 11.0% natural resources, construction, and maintenance, 10.2% production, transportation, and material moving (2008-2012 5-year est.).

Income: Per capita income: $25,158 (2008-2012 5-year est.); Median household income: $47,974 (2008-2012 5-year est.); Average household income: $55,926 (2008-2012 5-year est.); Percent of households with income of $100,000 or more: 12.1% (2008-2012 5-year est.); Poverty rate: 12.4% (2008-2012 5-year est.).

Education: Percent of population age 25 and over with: High school diploma (including GED) or higher: 85.5% (2008-2012 5-year est.); Bachelor's degree or higher: 23.6% (2008-2012 5-year est.); Master's degree or higher: 9.2% (2008-2012 5-year est.).

School District(s)

Galena USD 120 (PK-12)

    2011-12 Enrollment: 828 . . . . (815) 777-3086

Housing: Homeownership rate: 66.6% (2008-2012 5-year est.); Median home value: $156,500 (2008-2012 5-year est.); Median contract rent: $575 per month (2008-2012 5-year est.); Median year structure built: Before 1940 (2008-2012 5-year est.).

Health Insurance: 67.5% Private; 35.6% Public; 14.2% None. (2008-2012 5-year est.)

Hospitals: Galena-Stauss Hospital & Healthcare Center

Safety: Violent crime rate: 5.8 per 10,000 population; Property crime rate: 98.9 per 10,000 population (2012).

Transportation: Commute to work: 83.7% car, 2.5% public transportation, 7.9% walk, 5.8% work from home (2008-2012 5-year est.); Travel time to work: 55.3% less than 15 minutes, 31.9% 15 to 30 minutes, 9.3% 30 to 45 minutes, 1.6% 45 to 60 minutes, 1.9% 60 minutes or more (2008-2012 5-year est.)

Additional Information Contacts

Galena Area Chamber of Commerce . . . . (815) 777-9050
    http://www.galenachamber.com

HANOVER (village). Covers a land area of 1.053 square miles and a water area of 0 square miles. Located at 42.25° N. Lat; 90.27° W. Long. Elevation is 627 feet.

History: Hanover's early development depended on mining. When this declined, the town built a dam across the Apple River and established a grist mill. When a woolen mill was added in 1864, the town became a textile center.

Population: 908 (1990); 836 (2000); 844 (2010); Density: 778.5 persons per square mile (2008-2012 5-year est.); Race: 97.3% White, 0.9% Black/African American, 0.0% Asian, 0.2% American Indian/Alaska Native, 0.0% Native Hawaiian/Other Pacific Islander, 1.6% Some other race, 1.6% Two or more races, 0.4% Hispanic of any race (2008-2012 5-year est.); Average household size: 1.92 (2008-2012 5-year est.); Median age: 53.6 (2008-2012 5-year est.); Males per 100 females: 122.2 (2008-2012 5-year

est.); Marriage status: 25.2% never married, 53.9% now married, 8.3% widowed, 12.6% divorced (2008-2012 5-year est.); Foreign born: 0.2% (2008-2012 5-year est.); Ancestry (includes multiple ancestries): 37.7% German, 20.4% English, 19.6% Irish, 7.6% French, 6.0% American (2008-2012 5-year est.).

Economy: Single-family building permits issued: 0 (2013); Multi-family building permits issued: 0 (2013); Homeowner vacancy rate: 7.7%. Rental vacancy rate: 5.0%. (2008-2012 5-year est.); Employment by occupation: 6.0% management, business, and financial, 3.9% computer, engineering, and science, 3.5% education, legal, community service, arts, and media, 2.8% healthcare practitioners, 26.7% service, 23.4% sales and office, 11.4% natural resources, construction, and maintenance, 22.3% production, transportation, and material moving (2008-2012 5-year est.).

Income: Per capita income: $25,434 (2008-2012 5-year est.); Median household income: $41,900 (2008-2012 5-year est.); Average household income: $50,101 (2008-2012 5-year est.); Percent of households with income of $100,000 or more: 5.6% (2008-2012 5-year est.); Poverty rate: 16.3% (2008-2012 5-year est.).

Education: Percent of population age 25 and over with: High school diploma (including GED) or higher: 93.1% (2008-2012 5-year est.); Bachelor's degree or higher: 19.7% (2008-2012 5-year est.); Master's degree or higher: 5.1% (2008-2012 5-year est.).

School District(s)

Northwest Sp Ed Cooperative

    2011-12 Enrollment: n/a . . . . (815) 232-0332
River Ridge CUSD 210 (PK-12)

    2011-12 Enrollment: 520 . . . . (815) 858-9005

Housing: Homeownership rate: 73.0% (2008-2012 5-year est.); Median home value: $80,100 (2008-2012 5-year est.); Median contract rent: $322 per month (2008-2012 5-year est.); Median year structure built: 1950 (2008-2012 5-year est.).

Health Insurance: 73.3% Private; 37.3% Public; 11.7% None. (2008-2012 5-year est.)

Safety: Violent crime rate: 35.5 per 10,000 population; Property crime rate: 106.5 per 10,000 population (2012).

Transportation: Commute to work: 84.8% car, 0.0% public transportation, 10.8% walk, 3.0% work from home (2008-2012 5-year est.); Travel time to work: 38.2% less than 15 minutes, 38.2% 15 to 30 minutes, 9.2% 30 to 45 minutes, 3.6% 45 to 60 minutes, 10.9% 60 minutes or more (2008-2012 5-year est.)

Additional Information Contacts

Hanover Chamber of Commerce . . . . (815) 591-3800
    http://hanover-il.com

MENOMINEE (village). Covers a land area of 1.821 square miles and a water area of 0 square miles. Located at 42.47° N. Lat; 90.54° W. Long. Elevation is 761 feet.

Population: 187 (1990); 237 (2000); 248 (2010); Density: 109.8 persons per square mile (2008-2012 5-year est.); Race: 98.5% White, 0.0% Black/African American, 0.0% Asian, 1.5% American Indian/Alaska Native, 0.0% Native Hawaiian/Other Pacific Islander, 0.0% Some other race, 0.0% Two or more races, 0.0% Hispanic of any race (2008-2012 5-year est.); Average household size: 2.78 (2008-2012 5-year est.); Median age: 39.5 (2008-2012 5-year est.); Males per 100 females: 132.6 (2008-2012 5-year est.); Marriage status: 19.3% never married, 77.9% now married, 2.1% widowed, 0.7% divorced (2008-2012 5-year est.); Foreign born: 0.0% (2008-2012 5-year est.); Ancestry (includes multiple ancestries): 69.5% German, 33.0% Irish, 9.0% English, 5.5% American, 4.0% Polish (2008-2012 5-year est.).

Economy: Homeowner vacancy rate: 0.0%. Rental vacancy rate: 0.0%. (2008-2012 5-year est.); Employment by occupation: 5.1% management, business, and financial, 7.7% computer, engineering, and science, 12.0% education, legal, community service, arts, and media, 6.8% healthcare practitioners, 17.9% service, 17.1% sales and office, 19.7% natural resources, construction, and maintenance, 13.7% production, transportation, and material moving (2008-2012 5-year est.).

Income: Per capita income: $25,993 (2008-2012 5-year est.); Median household income: $71,250 (2008-2012 5-year est.); Average household income: $71,035 (2008-2012 5-year est.); Percent of households with income of $100,000 or more: 22.3% (2008-2012 5-year est.); Poverty rate: 4.0% (2008-2012 5-year est.).

Education: Percent of population age 25 and over with: High school diploma (including GED) or higher: 90.2% (2008-2012 5-year est.); Bachelor's degree or higher: 27.0% (2008-2012 5-year est.); Master's degree or higher: 10.7% (2008-2012 5-year est.).

Housing: Homeownership rate: 80.6% (2008-2012 5-year est.); Median home value: $158,300 (2008-2012 5-year est.); Median contract rent: $380 per month (2008-2012 5-year est.); Median year structure built: 1970 (2008-2012 5-year est.).
Health Insurance: 89.0% Private; 11.5% Public; 5.0% None. (2008-2012 5-year est.)
Transportation: Commute to work: 92.9% car, 0.0% public transportation, 0.0% walk, 7.1% work from home (2008-2012 5-year est.); Travel time to work: 30.8% less than 15 minutes, 55.8% 15 to 30 minutes, 5.8% 30 to 45 minutes, 6.7% 45 to 60 minutes, 1.0% 60 minutes or more (2008-2012 5-year est.)

NORA (village). Covers a land area of 0.908 square miles and a water area of 0 square miles. Located at 42.46° N. Lat; 89.95° W. Long. Elevation is 1,014 feet.
Population: 162 (1990); 118 (2000); 121 (2010); Density: 95.8 persons per square mile (2008-2012 5-year est.); Race: 100.0% White, 0.0% Black/African American, 0.0% Asian, 0.0% American Indian/Alaska Native, 0.0% Native Hawaiian/Other Pacific Islander, 0.0% Some other race, 0.0% Two or more races, 0.0% Hispanic of any race (2008-2012 5-year est.); Average household size: 1.98 (2008-2012 5-year est.); Median age: 39.3 (2008-2012 5-year est.); Males per 100 females: 93.3 (2008-2012 5-year est.); Marriage status: 35.9% never married, 44.9% now married, 9.0% widowed, 10.3% divorced (2008-2012 5-year est.); Foreign born: 0.0% (2008-2012 5-year est.); Ancestry (includes multiple ancestries): 47.1% German, 18.4% Norwegian, 17.2% Irish, 13.8% Swedish, 8.0% Czech (2008-2012 5-year est.).
Economy: Homeowner vacancy rate: 0.0%. Rental vacancy rate: 0.0%. (2008-2012 5-year est.); Employment by occupation: 0.0% management, business, and financial, 0.0% computer, engineering, and science, 6.5% education, legal, community service, arts, and media, 6.5% healthcare practitioners, 30.4% service, 15.2% sales and office, 21.7% natural resources, construction, and maintenance, 19.6% production, transportation, and material moving (2008-2012 5-year est.).
Income: Per capita income: $21,225 (2008-2012 5-year est.); Median household income: $40,000 (2008-2012 5-year est.); Average household income: $42,970 (2008-2012 5-year est.); Percent of households with income of $100,000 or more: 11.4% (2008-2012 5-year est.); Poverty rate: 19.5% (2008-2012 5-year est.).
Education: Percent of population age 25 and over with: High school diploma (including GED) or higher: 88.3% (2008-2012 5-year est.); Bachelor's degree or higher: 3.3% (2008-2012 5-year est.); Master's degree or higher: 0.0% (2008-2012 5-year est.).
Housing: Homeownership rate: 68.2% (2008-2012 5-year est.); Median home value: $60,000 (2008-2012 5-year est.); Median contract rent: $565 per month (2008-2012 5-year est.); Median year structure built: 1980 (2008-2012 5-year est.).
Health Insurance: 66.7% Private; 23.0% Public; 16.1% None. (2008-2012 5-year est.)
Transportation: Commute to work: 100.0% car, 0.0% public transportation, 0.0% walk, 0.0% work from home (2008-2012 5-year est.); Travel time to work: 20.0% less than 15 minutes, 28.9% 15 to 30 minutes, 44.4% 30 to 45 minutes, 6.7% 45 to 60 minutes, 0.0% 60 minutes or more (2008-2012 5-year est.)

SCALES MOUND (village). Covers a land area of 0.228 square miles and a water area of 0 square miles. Located at 42.48° N. Lat; 90.25° W. Long. Elevation is 955 feet.
Population: 388 (1990); 401 (2000); 376 (2010); Density: 1,852.2 persons per square mile (2008-2012 5-year est.); Race: 98.1% White, 0.0% Black/African American, 0.5% Asian, 0.0% American Indian/Alaska Native, 0.0% Native Hawaiian/Other Pacific Islander, 1.4% Some other race, 1.4% Two or more races, 3.1% Hispanic of any race (2008-2012 5-year est.); Average household size: 2.64 (2008-2012 5-year est.); Median age: 36.3 (2008-2012 5-year est.); Males per 100 females: 88.0 (2008-2012 5-year est.); Marriage status: 28.5% never married, 56.7% now married, 7.1% widowed, 7.7% divorced (2008-2012 5-year est.); Foreign born: 1.4% (2008-2012 5-year est.); Ancestry (includes multiple ancestries): 59.8% German, 11.8% English, 11.6% Irish, 5.0% American, 2.6% Italian (2008-2012 5-year est.).
Economy: Single-family building permits issued: 0 (2013); Multi-family building permits issued: 0 (2013); Homeowner vacancy rate: 6.9%. Rental vacancy rate: 0.0%. (2008-2012 5-year est.); Employment by occupation: 9.9% management, business, and financial, 0.4% computer, engineering, and science, 7.2% education, legal, community service, arts, and media,

0.9% healthcare practitioners, 30.9% service, 20.2% sales and office, 16.1% natural resources, construction, and maintenance, 14.3% production, transportation, and material moving (2008-2012 5-year est.).
Income: Per capita income: $20,691 (2008-2012 5-year est.); Median household income: $43,750 (2008-2012 5-year est.); Average household income: $56,160 (2008-2012 5-year est.); Percent of households with income of $100,000 or more: 14.4% (2008-2012 5-year est.); Poverty rate: 17.1% (2008-2012 5-year est.).
Education: Percent of population age 25 and over with: High school diploma (including GED) or higher: 96.5% (2008-2012 5-year est.); Bachelor's degree or higher: 14.3% (2008-2012 5-year est.); Master's degree or higher: 5.0% (2008-2012 5-year est.).
School District(s)
Scales Mound CUSD 211 (PK-12)
    2011-12 Enrollment: 255. . . . . (815) 845-2215
Housing: Homeownership rate: 75.6% (2008-2012 5-year est.); Median home value: $99,700 (2008-2012 5-year est.); Median contract rent: $465 per month (2008-2012 5-year est.); Median year structure built: Before 1940 (2008-2012 5-year est.).
Health Insurance: 78.7% Private; 34.5% Public; 7.3% None. (2008-2012 5-year est.)
Transportation: Commute to work: 88.7% car, 0.0% public transportation, 8.1% walk, 3.2% work from home (2008-2012 5-year est.); Travel time to work: 30.4% less than 15 minutes, 51.4% 15 to 30 minutes, 10.3% 30 to 45 minutes, 0.9% 45 to 60 minutes, 7.0% 60 minutes or more (2008-2012 5-year est.)

STOCKTON (village). Aka Plum River. Covers a land area of 1.596 square miles and a water area of 0 square miles. Located at 42.35° N. Lat; 90.00° W. Long. Elevation is 994 feet.
History: Stockton was named by Alanson Parker, an early settler, who saw the prospects of this becoming a stock raising center, which it did near the end of the 1800's. Before the cattle came, Stockton was the home of lead smelters.
Population: 1,871 (1990); 1,926 (2000); 1,862 (2010); Density: 1,204.3 persons per square mile (2008-2012 5-year est.); Race: 99.0% White, 0.2% Black/African American, 0.4% Asian, 0.0% American Indian/Alaska Native, 0.0% Native Hawaiian/Other Pacific Islander, 0.4% Some other race, 0.5% Two or more races, 0.8% Hispanic of any race (2008-2012 5-year est.); Average household size: 2.08 (2008-2012 5-year est.); Median age: 44.4 (2008-2012 5-year est.); Males per 100 females: 97.3 (2008-2012 5-year est.); Marriage status: 25.4% never married, 48.4% now married, 8.6% widowed, 17.6% divorced (2008-2012 5-year est.); Foreign born: 1.2% (2008-2012 5-year est.); Ancestry (includes multiple ancestries): 47.9% German, 15.8% Irish, 10.8% American, 5.3% English, 4.7% Dutch (2008-2012 5-year est.).
Economy: Single-family building permits issued: 0 (2013); Multi-family building permits issued: 0 (2013); Homeowner vacancy rate: 6.9%. Rental vacancy rate: 0.0%. (2008-2012 5-year est.); Employment by occupation: 6.4% management, business, and financial, 3.4% computer, engineering, and science, 9.5% education, legal, community service, arts, and media, 4.5% healthcare practitioners, 17.8% service, 21.2% sales and office, 11.1% natural resources, construction, and maintenance, 26.0% production, transportation, and material moving (2008-2012 5-year est.).
Income: Per capita income: $21,036 (2008-2012 5-year est.); Median household income: $37,113 (2008-2012 5-year est.); Average household income: $44,603 (2008-2012 5-year est.); Percent of households with income of $100,000 or more: 3.4% (2008-2012 5-year est.); Poverty rate: 15.1% (2008-2012 5-year est.).
Education: Percent of population age 25 and over with: High school diploma (including GED) or higher: 88.9% (2008-2012 5-year est.); Bachelor's degree or higher: 15.7% (2008-2012 5-year est.); Master's degree or higher: 2.0% (2008-2012 5-year est.).
School District(s)
Stockton CUSD 206 (PK-12)
    2011-12 Enrollment: 608. . . . . (815) 947-3391
Housing: Homeownership rate: 68.7% (2008-2012 5-year est.); Median home value: $88,600 (2008-2012 5-year est.); Median contract rent: $398 per month (2008-2012 5-year est.); Median year structure built: 1948 (2008-2012 5-year est.).
Health Insurance: 70.0% Private; 43.5% Public; 6.7% None. (2008-2012 5-year est.)
Safety: Violent crime rate: 48.3 per 10,000 population; Property crime rate: 123.3 per 10,000 population (2012).

Transportation: Commute to work: 88.3% car, 0.2% public transportation, 3.8% walk, 6.9% work from home (2008-2012 5-year est.); Travel time to work: 52.3% less than 15 minutes, 13.9% 15 to 30 minutes, 18.4% 30 to 45 minutes, 3.0% 45 to 60 minutes, 12.4% 60 minutes or more (2008-2012 5-year est.)

Additional Information Contacts
Stockton Chamber of Commerce . . . . (815) 947-2878
  http://www.stocktonil.com

THE GALENA TERRITORY (CDP).

Covers a land area of 11.384 square miles and a water area of 0.344 square miles. Located at 42.39° N. Lat; 90.33° W. Long.

Population: n/a (1990); n/a (2000); 1,058 (2010); Density: 86.0 persons per square mile (2008-2012 5-year est.); Race: 96.2% White, 2.8% Black/African American, 0.0% Asian, 0.0% American Indian/Alaska Native, 0.0% Native Hawaiian/Other Pacific Islander, 1.0% Some other race, 1.0% Two or more races, 1.6% Hispanic of any race (2008-2012 5-year est.); Average household size: 2.16 (2008-2012 5-year est.); Median age: 64.8 (2008-2012 5-year est.); Males per 100 females: 86.8 (2008-2012 5-year est.); Marriage status: 8.4% never married, 80.9% now married, 3.9% widowed, 6.7% divorced (2008-2012 5-year est.); Foreign born: 4.3% (2008-2012 5-year est.); Ancestry (includes multiple ancestries): 36.3% German, 15.8% Irish, 10.9% English, 9.5% Polish, 6.7% Italian (2008-2012 5-year est.).

Economy: Homeowner vacancy rate: 0.0%. Rental vacancy rate: 50.0%. (2008-2012 5-year est.); Employment by occupation: 27.9% management, business, and financial, 7.4% computer, engineering, and science, 18.5% education, legal, community service, arts, and media, 0.0% healthcare practitioners, 13.8% service, 30.2% sales and office, 2.3% natural resources, construction, and maintenance, 0.0% production, transportation, and material moving (2008-2012 5-year est.).

Income: Per capita income: $60,505 (2008-2012 5-year est.); Median household income: $81,188 (2008-2012 5-year est.); Average household income: $131,909 (2008-2012 5-year est.); Percent of households with income of $100,000 or more: 40.2% (2008-2012 5-year est.); Poverty rate: 1.8% (2008-2012 5-year est.).

Education: Percent of population age 25 and over with: High school diploma (including GED) or higher: 95.6% (2008-2012 5-year est.); Bachelor's degree or higher: 54.3% (2008-2012 5-year est.); Master's degree or higher: 29.9% (2008-2012 5-year est.).

Housing: Homeownership rate: 98.7% (2008-2012 5-year est.); Median home value: $281,200 (2008-2012 5-year est.); Median contract rent: n/a per month (2008-2012 5-year est.); Median year structure built: 1991 (2008-2012 5-year est.).

Health Insurance: 74.1% Private; 56.6% Public; 1.8% None. (2008-2012 5-year est.)

Transportation: Commute to work: 67.8% car, 0.0% public transportation, 4.4% walk, 27.9% work from home (2008-2012 5-year est.); Travel time to work: 28.8% less than 15 minutes, 35.3% 15 to 30 minutes, 11.2% 30 to 45 minutes, 14.9% 45 to 60 minutes, 9.8% 60 minutes or more (2008-2012 5-year est.)

WARREN (village).

Covers a land area of 0.967 square miles and a water area of 0 square miles. Located at 42.49° N. Lat; 89.99° W. Long. Elevation is 981 feet.

History: Warren began in 1850 with the name of Courtland, but was renamed in 1853 to honor the son of Alexander Burnett, who had founded the town in 1843. Warren was located at the crossing of the Old Sucker Trail with the Chicago-Galena Stagecoach Road, and later became a station on the railroad line between Galena and Chicago.

Population: 1,550 (1990); 1,496 (2000); 1,428 (2010); Density: 1,621.5 persons per square mile (2008-2012 5-year est.); Race: 98.2% White, 0.3% Black/African American, 0.0% Asian, 0.4% American Indian/Alaska Native, 0.4% Native Hawaiian/Other Pacific Islander, 0.7% Some other race, 0.6% Two or more races, 0.5% Hispanic of any race (2008-2012 5-year est.); Average household size: 2.39 (2008-2012 5-year est.); Median age: 43.5 (2008-2012 5-year est.); Males per 100 females: 103.9 (2008-2012 5-year est.); Marriage status: 23.3% never married, 57.2% now married, 8.5% widowed, 10.9% divorced (2008-2012 5-year est.); Foreign born: 0.5% (2008-2012 5-year est.); Ancestry (includes multiple ancestries): 36.2% German, 18.6% Irish, 15.2% English, 12.4% American, 7.7% Norwegian (2008-2012 5-year est.).

Economy: Single-family building permits issued: 0 (2013); Multi-family building permits issued: 0 (2013); Homeowner vacancy rate: 4.3%. Rental vacancy rate: 6.5%. (2008-2012 5-year est.); Employment by occupation:

13.8% management, business, and financial, 1.5% computer, engineering, and science, 6.5% education, legal, community service, arts, and media, 5.2% healthcare practitioners, 19.2% service, 16.8% sales and office, 16.6% natural resources, construction, and maintenance, 20.4% production, transportation, and material moving (2008-2012 5-year est.).

Income: Per capita income: $22,525 (2008-2012 5-year est.); Median household income: $49,960 (2008-2012 5-year est.); Average household income: $53,815 (2008-2012 5-year est.); Percent of households with income of $100,000 or more: 12.5% (2008-2012 5-year est.); Poverty rate: 9.4% (2008-2012 5-year est.).

Education: Percent of population age 25 and over with: High school diploma (including GED) or higher: 88.9% (2008-2012 5-year est.); Bachelor's degree or higher: 15.6% (2008-2012 5-year est.); Master's degree or higher: 5.9% (2008-2012 5-year est.).

School District(s)

Warren CUSD 205 (PK-12)
  2011-12 Enrollment: 453 . . . . (815) 745-2653

Housing: Homeownership rate: 84.8% (2008-2012 5-year est.); Median home value: $87,600 (2008-2012 5-year est.); Median contract rent: $368 per month (2008-2012 5-year est.); Median year structure built: 1942 (2008-2012 5-year est.).

Health Insurance: 75.9% Private; 29.9% Public; 10.3% None. (2008-2012 5-year est.)

Transportation: Commute to work: 93.0% car, 0.1% public transportation, 3.4% walk, 2.7% work from home (2008-2012 5-year est.); Travel time to work: 34.0% less than 15 minutes, 19.8% 15 to 30 minutes, 29.2% 30 to 45 minutes, 7.0% 45 to 60 minutes, 10.0% 60 minutes or more (2008-2012 5-year est.)

Johnson County

Located in southern Illinois, in the Ozarks; drained by the Cache River; includes part of Shawnee National Forest. Covers a land area of 343.915 square miles, a water area of 4.949 square miles, and is located in the Central Time Zone at 37.46° N. Lat., 88.88° W. Long. The county was founded in 1812. County seat is Vienna.

Population: 11,347 (1990); 12,878 (2000); 12,582 (2010); Race: 89.0% White, 9.5% Black/African American, 0.2% Asian, 0.0% American Indian/Alaska Native, 0.0% Native Hawaiian/Other Pacific Islander, 1.3% Some other race, 1.1% Two or more races, 2.1% Hispanic of any race (2008-2012 5-year est.); Density: 37.2 persons per square mile (2008-2012 5-year est.); Average household size: 2.47 (2008-2012 5-year est.); Median age: 42.0 (2008-2012 5-year est.); Males per 100 females: 132.1 (2008-2012 5-year est.).

Religion: Six largest groups: 26.5% Baptist, 5.2% Methodist/Pietist, 1.3% Catholicism, 1.2% Presbyterian-Reformed, 1.0% European Free-Church, 0.8% Pentecostal (2010)

Economy: Unemployment rate: 7.9% (April 2014); Total civilian labor force: 5,107 (April 2014); Leading industries: 17.4% retail trade; 14.9% accommodation & food services; 14.9% health care and social assistance (2012); Farms: 558 totaling 89,715 acres (2012); Companies that employ 500 or more persons: 0 (2012); Companies that employ 100 to 499 persons: 1 (2012); Companies that employ less than 100 persons: 170 (2012); Black-owned businesses: n/a (2007); Hispanic-owned businesses: n/a (2007); Asian-owned businesses: n/a (2007); Women-owned businesses: 269 (2007); Single-family building permits issued: 0 (2013); Multi-family building permits issued: 0 (2013).

Income: Per capita income: $18,560 (2008-2012 5-year est.); Median household income: $42,027 (2008-2012 5-year est.); Average household income: $52,968 (2008-2012 5-year est.); Percent of households with income of $100,000 or more: 11.7% (2008-2012 5-year est.); Poverty rate: 11.3% (2008-2012 5-year est.); Bankruptcy rate: 4.54% (2013).

Education: Percent of population age 25 and over with: High school diploma (including GED) or higher: 81.7% (2008-2012 5-year est.); Bachelor's degree or higher: 14.9% (2008-2012 5-year est.); Master's degree or higher: 3.7% (2008-2012 5-year est.).

Housing: Homeownership rate: 82.9% (2008-2012 5-year est.); Median home value: $92,500 (2008-2012 5-year est.); Median contract rent: $368 per month (2008-2012 5-year est.); Median year structure built: 1979 (2008-2012 5-year est.).

Health: Birth rate: 89.1 per 10,000 population (2013); Death rate: 96.2 per 10,000 population (2013); Age-adjusted cancer mortality rate: 152.3 deaths per 100,000 population (2011); Number of physicians: 2.4 per 10,000 population (2011); Hospital beds: 0.0 per 10,000 population (2010); Hospital admissions: 0.0 per 10,000 population (2010).

Elections: 2012 Presidential election results: 27.7% Obama, 69.9% Romney
National and State Parks: Cache River State Natural Area; Ferne Clyffe State Park
Additional Information Contacts
Johnson County Government . . . . (618) 658-3611
   http://www.johnsoncountyil.com

Johnson County Communities

BELKNAP (village). Covers a land area of 1.057 square miles and a water area of 0.002 square miles. Located at 37.32° N. Lat; 88.94° W. Long. Elevation is 404 feet.
Population: 125 (1990); 133 (2000); 104 (2010); Density: 99.3 persons per square mile (2008-2012 5-year est.); Race: 97.1% White, 2.9% Black/African American, 0.0% Asian, 0.0% American Indian/Alaska Native, 0.0% Native Hawaiian/Other Pacific Islander, 0.0% Some other race, 0.0% Two or more races, 0.0% Hispanic of any race (2008-2012 5-year est.); Average household size: 3.09 (2008-2012 5-year est.); Median age: 27.5 (2008-2012 5-year est.); Males per 100 females: 133.3 (2008-2012 5-year est.); Marriage status: 18.8% never married, 63.8% now married, 13.0% widowed, 4.3% divorced (2008-2012 5-year est.); Foreign born: 0.0% (2008-2012 5-year est.); Ancestry (includes multiple ancestries): 21.9% English, 18.1% German, 14.3% American, 7.6% Scotch-Irish, 6.7% Irish (2008-2012 5-year est.).
Economy: Homeowner vacancy rate: 0.0%. Rental vacancy rate: 0.0%. (2008-2012 5-year est.); Employment by occupation: 2.9% management, business, and financial, 0.0% computer, engineering, and science, 11.4% education, legal, community service, arts, and media, 0.0% healthcare practitioners, 14.3% service, 22.9% sales and office, 20.0% natural resources, construction, and maintenance, 28.6% production, transportation, and material moving (2008-2012 5-year est.).
Income: Per capita income: $13,458 (2008-2012 5-year est.); Median household income: $28,750 (2008-2012 5-year est.); Average household income: $37,132 (2008-2012 5-year est.); Percent of households with income of $100,000 or more: n/a (2008-2012 5-year est.); Poverty rate: 28.4% (2008-2012 5-year est.).
Education: Percent of population age 25 and over with: High school diploma (including GED) or higher: 71.9% (2008-2012 5-year est.); Bachelor's degree or higher: 0.0% (2008-2012 5-year est.); Master's degree or higher: 0.0% (2008-2012 5-year est.).
Housing: Homeownership rate: 94.1% (2008-2012 5-year est.); Median home value: $45,000 (2008-2012 5-year est.); Median contract rent: n/a per month (2008-2012 5-year est.); Median year structure built: 1953 (2008-2012 5-year est.).
Health Insurance: 55.2% Private; 50.5% Public; 3.8% None. (2008-2012 5-year est.)
Transportation: Commute to work: 91.4% car, 0.0% public transportation, 0.0% walk, 8.6% work from home (2008-2012 5-year est.); Travel time to work: 9.4% less than 15 minutes, 6.3% 15 to 30 minutes, 46.9% 30 to 45 minutes, 18.8% 45 to 60 minutes, 18.8% 60 minutes or more (2008-2012 5-year est.).

BUNCOMBE (village). Covers a land area of 1.187 square miles and a water area of 0.013 square miles. Located at 37.47° N. Lat; 88.97° W. Long. Elevation is 518 feet.
Population: 208 (1990); 186 (2000); 203 (2010); Density: 179.4 persons per square mile (2008-2012 5-year est.); Race: 100.0% White, 0.0% Black/African American, 0.0% Asian, 0.0% American Indian/Alaska Native, 0.0% Native Hawaiian/Other Pacific Islander, 0.0% Some other race, 0.0% Two or more races, 0.5% Hispanic of any race (2008-2012 5-year est.); Average household size: 2.63 (2008-2012 5-year est.); Median age: 34.7 (2008-2012 5-year est.); Males per 100 females: 102.9 (2008-2012 5-year est.); Marriage status: 20.3% never married, 59.5% now married, 10.8% widowed, 9.5% divorced (2008-2012 5-year est.); Foreign born: 0.0% (2008-2012 5-year est.); Ancestry (includes multiple ancestries): 10.3% Irish, 7.0% American, 6.1% English, 5.6% German, 4.7% Polish (2008-2012 5-year est.).
Economy: Homeowner vacancy rate: 0.0%. Rental vacancy rate: 19.2%. (2008-2012 5-year est.); Employment by occupation: 0.0% management, business, and financial, 8.1% computer, engineering, and science, 6.5% education, legal, community service, arts, and media, 4.8% healthcare practitioners, 38.7% service, 16.1% sales and office, 11.3% natural resources, construction, and maintenance, 14.5% production, transportation, and material moving (2008-2012 5-year est.).

Income: Per capita income: $14,754 (2008-2012 5-year est.); Median household income: $29,250 (2008-2012 5-year est.); Average household income: $40,519 (2008-2012 5-year est.); Percent of households with income of $100,000 or more: 12.3% (2008-2012 5-year est.); Poverty rate: 12.2% (2008-2012 5-year est.).
Education: Percent of population age 25 and over with: High school diploma (including GED) or higher: 66.7% (2008-2012 5-year est.); Bachelor's degree or higher: 14.0% (2008-2012 5-year est.); Master's degree or higher: 3.1% (2008-2012 5-year est.).
School District(s)
Buncombe CSD 43 (KG-08)
   2011-12 Enrollment: 80 . . . . (618) 658-8830
Lick Creek CCSD 16 (PK-08)
   2011-12 Enrollment: 135 . . . . (618) 833-2545
Housing: Homeownership rate: 74.1% (2008-2012 5-year est.); Median home value: $51,100 (2008-2012 5-year est.); Median contract rent: $425 per month (2008-2012 5-year est.); Median year structure built: 1950 (2008-2012 5-year est.).
Health Insurance: 58.2% Private; 49.3% Public; 8.9% None. (2008-2012 5-year est.)
Transportation: Commute to work: 90.3% car, 0.0% public transportation, 9.7% walk, 0.0% work from home (2008-2012 5-year est.); Travel time to work: 24.2% less than 15 minutes, 22.6% 15 to 30 minutes, 37.1% 30 to 45 minutes, 8.1% 45 to 60 minutes, 8.1% 60 minutes or more (2008-2012 5-year est.).

CYPRESS (village). Aka Whitehill. Covers a land area of 0.753 square miles and a water area of 0.003 square miles. Located at 37.37° N. Lat; 89.02° W. Long. Elevation is 390 feet.
Population: 275 (1990); 271 (2000); 234 (2010); Density: 466.3 persons per square mile (2008-2012 5-year est.); Race: 94.9% White, 2.0% Black/African American, 0.0% Asian, 0.0% American Indian/Alaska Native, 0.0% Native Hawaiian/Other Pacific Islander, 3.1% Some other race, 3.1% Two or more races, 1.7% Hispanic of any race (2008-2012 5-year est.); Average household size: 3.08 (2008-2012 5-year est.); Median age: 43.4 (2008-2012 5-year est.); Males per 100 females: 112.7 (2008-2012 5-year est.); Marriage status: 22.8% never married, 49.0% now married, 6.5% widowed, 21.7% divorced (2008-2012 5-year est.); Foreign born: 0.0% (2008-2012 5-year est.); Ancestry (includes multiple ancestries): 18.5% Irish, 18.2% German, 8.8% Dutch, 8.5% French, 6.6% Polish (2008-2012 5-year est.).
Economy: Homeowner vacancy rate: 0.0%. Rental vacancy rate: 18.2%. (2008-2012 5-year est.); Employment by occupation: 3.0% management, business, and financial, 0.0% computer, engineering, and science, 0.0% education, legal, community service, arts, and media, 5.2% healthcare practitioners, 23.1% service, 14.9% sales and office, 12.7% natural resources, construction, and maintenance, 41.0% production, transportation, and material moving (2008-2012 5-year est.).
Income: Per capita income: $15,298 (2008-2012 5-year est.); Median household income: $29,583 (2008-2012 5-year est.); Average household income: $42,711 (2008-2012 5-year est.); Percent of households with income of $100,000 or more: 7.9% (2008-2012 5-year est.); Poverty rate: 16.8% (2008-2012 5-year est.).
Education: Percent of population age 25 and over with: High school diploma (including GED) or higher: 73.1% (2008-2012 5-year est.); Bachelor's degree or higher: 0.9% (2008-2012 5-year est.); Master's degree or higher: 0.9% (2008-2012 5-year est.).
School District(s)
Cypress SD 64 (PK-08)
   2011-12 Enrollment: 142 . . . . (618) 657-2525
Housing: Homeownership rate: 84.2% (2008-2012 5-year est.); Median home value: $62,300 (2008-2012 5-year est.); Median contract rent: $439 per month (2008-2012 5-year est.); Median year structure built: 1953 (2008-2012 5-year est.).
Health Insurance: 38.2% Private; 41.9% Public; 29.3% None. (2008-2012 5-year est.)
Transportation: Commute to work: 93.9% car, 0.0% public transportation, 3.8% walk, 2.3% work from home (2008-2012 5-year est.); Travel time to work: 25.8% less than 15 minutes, 31.3% 15 to 30 minutes, 25.0% 30 to 45 minutes, 7.0% 45 to 60 minutes, 10.9% 60 minutes or more (2008-2012 5-year est.).

GOREVILLE (village). Covers a land area of 1.662 square miles and a water area of 0.019 square miles. Located at 37.55° N. Lat; 88.97° W. Long. Elevation is 735 feet.
Population: 872 (1990); 938 (2000); 1,049 (2010); Density: 735.3 persons per square mile (2008-2012 5-year est.); Race: 99.8% White, 0.0% Black/African American, 0.0% Asian, 0.2% American Indian/Alaska Native, 0.0% Native Hawaiian/Other Pacific Islander, 0.0% Some other race, 0.0% Two or more races, 0.0% Hispanic of any race (2008-2012 5-year est.); Average household size: 2.60 (2008-2012 5-year est.); Median age: 38.6 (2008-2012 5-year est.); Males per 100 females: 70.9 (2008-2012 5-year est.); Marriage status: 20.6% never married, 56.6% now married, 9.7% widowed, 13.1% divorced (2008-2012 5-year est.); Foreign born: 1.1% (2008-2012 5-year est.); Ancestry (includes multiple ancestries): 16.4% English, 14.6% German, 14.3% American, 9.6% Irish, 5.6% Polish (2008-2012 5-year est.).
Economy: Single-family building permits issued: 0 (2013); Multi-family building permits issued: 0 (2013); Homeowner vacancy rate: 0.0%. Rental vacancy rate: 0.0%. (2008-2012 5-year est.); Employment by occupation: 11.8% management, business, and financial, 0.6% computer, engineering, and science, 14.7% education, legal, community service, arts, and media, 7.4% healthcare practitioners, 26.5% service, 16.5% sales and office, 12.2% natural resources, construction, and maintenance, 10.4% production, transportation, and material moving (2008-2012 5-year est.).
Income: Per capita income: $20,019 (2008-2012 5-year est.); Median household income: $38,646 (2008-2012 5-year est.); Average household income: $49,642 (2008-2012 5-year est.); Percent of households with income of $100,000 or more: 11.9% (2008-2012 5-year est.); Poverty rate: 15.4% (2008-2012 5-year est.).
Education: Percent of population age 25 and over with: High school diploma (including GED) or higher: 87.3% (2008-2012 5-year est.); Bachelor's degree or higher: 20.2% (2008-2012 5-year est.); Master's degree or higher: 5.3% (2008-2012 5-year est.).

School District(s)

Five County Reg Voc Center (11-12)
    2011-12 Enrollment: n/a . . . . (618) 747-2703
Goreville CUD 1 (PK-12)
    2011-12 Enrollment: 634 . . . . (618) 995-9831
Housing: Homeownership rate: 68.7% (2008-2012 5-year est.); Median home value: $94,300 (2008-2012 5-year est.); Median contract rent: $415 per month (2008-2012 5-year est.); Median year structure built: 1979 (2008-2012 5-year est.).
Health Insurance: 63.7% Private; 36.9% Public; 13.0% None. (2008-2012 5-year est.)
Transportation: Commute to work: 97.4% car, 0.4% public transportation, 1.1% walk, 1.1% work from home (2008-2012 5-year est.); Travel time to work: 21.6% less than 15 minutes, 40.2% 15 to 30 minutes, 21.2% 30 to 45 minutes, 11.0% 45 to 60 minutes, 6.0% 60 minutes or more (2008-2012 5-year est.).

GRANTSBURG (unincorporated postal area)
Zip Code: 62943
    Covers a land area of 38.156 square miles and a water area of 0.355 square miles. Located at 37.35° N. Lat; 88.75° W. Long. Elevation is 377 feet. Population: 715 (2010); Density: 18.7 persons per square mile (2010); Race: 98.3% White, 0.0% Black/African American, 0.1% Asian, 0.1% American Indian/Alaska Native, 0.0% Native Hawaiian/Other Pacific Islander, 1.5% Some other race, 1.4% Two or more races, 0.6% Hispanic of any race (2010); Average household size: 2.46 (2010); Median age: 43.8 (2010); Males per 100 females: 110.3 (2010); Homeownership rate: 90.7% (2010)

NEW BURNSIDE (village). Covers a land area of 1.045 square miles and a water area of 0.008 square miles. Located at 37.58° N. Lat; 88.77° W. Long. Elevation is 541 feet.
History: New Burnside was founded in 1872 and named for Major General Ambrose E. Burnside, president of the Big Four Railroad. Fruit growing was an important industry.
Population: 259 (1990); 242 (2000); 211 (2010); Density: 140.7 persons per square mile (2008-2012 5-year est.); Race: 99.3% White, 0.0% Black/African American, 0.7% Asian, 0.0% American Indian/Alaska Native, 0.0% Native Hawaiian/Other Pacific Islander, 0.0% Some other race, 0.0% Two or more races, 1.4% Hispanic of any race (2008-2012 5-year est.); Average household size: 2.67 (2008-2012 5-year est.); Median age: 36.8 (2008-2012 5-year est.); Males per 100 females: 86.1 (2008-2012 5-year est.); Marriage status: 23.5% never married, 45.2% now married, 8.7%

widowed, 22.6% divorced (2008-2012 5-year est.); Foreign born: 0.7% (2008-2012 5-year est.); Ancestry (includes multiple ancestries): 19.0% German, 16.3% American, 15.0% English, 6.8% Norwegian, 6.1% Irish (2008-2012 5-year est.).
Economy: Homeowner vacancy rate: 0.0%. Rental vacancy rate: 0.0%. (2008-2012 5-year est.); Employment by occupation: 36.4% management, business, and financial, 0.0% computer, engineering, and science, 9.1% education, legal, community service, arts, and media, 0.0% healthcare practitioners, 9.1% service, 27.3% sales and office, 18.2% natural resources, construction, and maintenance, 0.0% production, transportation, and material moving (2008-2012 5-year est.).
Income: Per capita income: $14,544 (2008-2012 5-year est.); Median household income: $24,205 (2008-2012 5-year est.); Average household income: $38,571 (2008-2012 5-year est.); Percent of households with income of $100,000 or more: 3.6% (2008-2012 5-year est.); Poverty rate: 25.2% (2008-2012 5-year est.).
Education: Percent of population age 25 and over with: High school diploma (including GED) or higher: 82.2% (2008-2012 5-year est.); Bachelor's degree or higher: 7.8% (2008-2012 5-year est.); Master's degree or higher: 0.0% (2008-2012 5-year est.).
Housing: Homeownership rate: 92.7% (2008-2012 5-year est.); Median home value: $37,500 (2008-2012 5-year est.); Median contract rent: $217 per month (2008-2012 5-year est.); Median year structure built: 1963 (2008-2012 5-year est.).
Health Insurance: 53.1% Private; 68.7% Public; 4.1% None. (2008-2012 5-year est.)
Transportation: Commute to work: 90.9% car, 0.0% public transportation, 9.1% walk, 0.0% work from home (2008-2012 5-year est.); Travel time to work: 9.1% less than 15 minutes, 18.2% 15 to 30 minutes, 63.6% 30 to 45 minutes, 9.1% 45 to 60 minutes, 0.0% 60 minutes or more (2008-2012 5-year est.).

OZARK (unincorporated postal area)
Zip Code: 62972
    Covers a land area of 66.658 square miles and a water area of 1.296 square miles. Located at 37.54° N. Lat; 88.79° W. Long. Elevation is 689 feet. Population: 1,205 (2010); Density: 18.1 persons per square mile (2010); Race: 97.9% White, 0.1% Black/African American, 0.1% Asian, 0.2% American Indian/Alaska Native, 0.0% Native Hawaiian/Other Pacific Islander, 1.7% Some other race, 0.8% Two or more races, 1.9% Hispanic of any race (2010); Average household size: 2.44 (2010); Median age: 46.5 (2010); Males per 100 females: 112.1 (2010); Homeownership rate: 91.5% (2010)

SIMPSON (village). Covers a land area of 0.525 square miles and a water area of <.001 square miles. Located at 37.47° N. Lat; 88.76° W. Long. Elevation is 390 feet.
Population: 61 (1990); 54 (2000); 60 (2010); Density: 196.1 persons per square mile (2008-2012 5-year est.); Race: 100.0% White, 0.0% Black/African American, 0.0% Asian, 0.0% American Indian/Alaska Native, 0.0% Native Hawaiian/Other Pacific Islander, 0.0% Some other race, 0.0% Two or more races, 0.0% Hispanic of any race (2008-2012 5-year est.); Average household size: 3.68 (2008-2012 5-year est.); Median age: 21.5 (2008-2012 5-year est.); Males per 100 females: 110.2 (2008-2012 5-year est.); Marriage status: 19.7% never married, 62.3% now married, 11.5% widowed, 6.6% divorced (2008-2012 5-year est.); Foreign born: 0.0% (2008-2012 5-year est.); Ancestry (includes multiple ancestries): 18.4% Italian, 11.7% English, 2.9% German, 2.9% American (2008-2012 5-year est.).
Economy: Homeowner vacancy rate: 0.0%. Rental vacancy rate: 0.0%. (2008-2012 5-year est.); Employment by occupation: 39.1% management, business, and financial, 0.0% computer, engineering, and science, 0.0% education, legal, community service, arts, and media, 0.0% healthcare practitioners, 8.7% service, 0.0% sales and office, 13.0% natural resources, construction, and maintenance, 39.1% production, transportation, and material moving (2008-2012 5-year est.).
Income: Per capita income: $8,520 (2008-2012 5-year est.); Median household income: $19,688 (2008-2012 5-year est.); Average household income: $30,046 (2008-2012 5-year est.); Percent of households with income of $100,000 or more: n/a (2008-2012 5-year est.); Poverty rate: 36.9% (2008-2012 5-year est.).
Education: Percent of population age 25 and over with: High school diploma (including GED) or higher: 68.8% (2008-2012 5-year est.); Bachelor's degree or higher: 10.4% (2008-2012 5-year est.); Master's degree or higher: 0.0% (2008-2012 5-year est.).

Housing: Homeownership rate: 92.9% (2008-2012 5-year est.); Median home value: $58,000 (2008-2012 5-year est.); Median contract rent: n/a per month (2008-2012 5-year est.); Median year structure built: 1973 (2008-2012 5-year est.).
Health Insurance: 9.7% Private; 80.6% Public; 16.5% None. (2008-2012 5-year est.)
Transportation: Commute to work: 100.0% car, 0.0% public transportation, 0.0% walk, 0.0% work from home (2008-2012 5-year est.); Travel time to work: 17.4% less than 15 minutes, 0.0% 15 to 30 minutes, 39.1% 30 to 45 minutes, 8.7% 45 to 60 minutes, 34.8% 60 minutes or more (2008-2012 5-year est.)

VIENNA (city). County seat. Covers a land area of 2.845 square miles and a water area of 0.037 square miles. Located at 37.41° N. Lat; 88.89° W. Long. Elevation is 404 feet.
History: Incorporated 1837.
Population: 1,446 (1990); 1,234 (2000); 1,434 (2010); Density: 466.4 persons per square mile (2008-2012 5-year est.); Race: 96.0% White, 1.9% Black/African American, 0.1% Asian, 0.0% American Indian/Alaska Native, 0.0% Native Hawaiian/Other Pacific Islander, 2.0% Some other race, 2.0% Two or more races, 0.0% Hispanic of any race (2008-2012 5-year est.); Average household size: 2.05 (2008-2012 5-year est.); Median age: 43.7 (2008-2012 5-year est.); Males per 100 females: 76.7 (2008-2012 5-year est.); Marriage status: 23.7% never married, 37.2% now married, 19.0% widowed, 20.1% divorced (2008-2012 5-year est.); Foreign born: 0.5% (2008-2012 5-year est.); Ancestry (includes multiple ancestries): 23.3% German, 15.9% English, 15.4% Irish, 6.9% American, 6.0% Scotch-Irish (2008-2012 5-year est.).
Economy: Homeowner vacancy rate: 0.0%. Rental vacancy rate: 0.0%. (2008-2012 5-year est.); Employment by occupation: 9.0% management, business, and financial, 0.6% computer, engineering, and science, 8.8% education, legal, community service, arts, and media, 19.5% healthcare practitioners, 18.8% service, 25.9% sales and office, 8.4% natural resources, construction, and maintenance, 9.0% production, transportation, and material moving (2008-2012 5-year est.).
Income: Per capita income: $17,363 (2008-2012 5-year est.); Median household income: $25,560 (2008-2012 5-year est.); Average household income: $34,617 (2008-2012 5-year est.); Percent of households with income of $100,000 or more: 3.5% (2008-2012 5-year est.); Poverty rate: 22.5% (2008-2012 5-year est.).
Education: Percent of population age 25 and over with: High school diploma (including GED) or higher: 80.5% (2008-2012 5-year est.); Bachelor's degree or higher: 18.0% (2008-2012 5-year est.); Master's degree or higher: 3.9% (2008-2012 5-year est.).

School District(s)

Five County Reg Voc System
    2011-12 Enrollment: n/a . . . . (618) 747-2703
Vienna HSD 133 (09-12)
    2011-12 Enrollment: 334 . . . . (618) 658-4461
Vienna SD 55 (PK-08)
    2011-12 Enrollment: 426 . . . . (618) 658-8638

Housing: Homeownership rate: 48.2% (2008-2012 5-year est.); Median home value: $70,000 (2008-2012 5-year est.); Median contract rent: $318 per month (2008-2012 5-year est.); Median year structure built: 1968 (2008-2012 5-year est.).
Health Insurance: 55.3% Private; 52.3% Public; 9.7% None. (2008-2012 5-year est.)
Safety: Violent crime rate: 27.7 per 10,000 population; Property crime rate: 291.1 per 10,000 population (2012).
Transportation: Commute to work: 88.3% car, 1.8% public transportation, 7.6% walk, 1.1% work from home (2008-2012 5-year est.); Travel time to work: 50.6% less than 15 minutes, 17.4% 15 to 30 minutes, 21.6% 30 to 45 minutes, 6.0% 45 to 60 minutes, 4.4% 60 minutes or more (2008-2012 5-year est.)

Kane County

Located in northeastern Illinois; drained by the Fox River and Mill Creek. Covers a land area of 520.058 square miles, a water area of 4.143 square miles, and is located in the Central Time Zone at 41.94° N. Lat., 88.43° W. Long. The county was founded in 1836. County seat is Geneva.

Kane County is part of the Chicago-Naperville-Elgin, IL-IN-WI Metropolitan Statistical Area. The entire metro area includes:
Chicago-Naperville-Arlington Heights, IL Metropolitan Division (Cook

County, IL; DuPage County, IL; Grundy County, IL; Kendall County, IL; McHenry County, IL; Will County, IL); Elgin, IL Metropolitan Division (DeKalb County, IL; Kane County, IL); Gary, IN Metropolitan Division (Jasper County, IN; Lake County, IN; Newton County, IN; Porter County, IN); Lake County-Kenosha County, IL-WI Metropolitan Division (Lake County, IL; Kenosha County, WI)

Weather Station: Aurora

	Jan	Feb	Mar	Apr	May	Jun	Jul	Aug	Sep	Oct	Nov	Dec
High	31	36	48	61	72	81	85	83	76	63	49	35
Low	14	18	28	38	48	58	63	61	53	41	31	19
Precip	1.6	1.7	2.3	3.7	3.9	4.0	4.2	4.3	3.6	3.0	3.3	2.3
Snow	9.6	6.8	2.8	0.6	0.0	0.0	0.0	0.0	0.0	tr	0.9	7.7

High and Low temperatures in degrees Fahrenheit; Precipitation and Snow in inches

Weather Station: Elgin   Elevation: 763 feet

	Jan	Feb	Mar	Apr	May	Jun	Jul	Aug	Sep	Oct	Nov	Dec
High	29	34	45	58	70	79	83	82	75	62	47	33
Low	13	17	26	37	48	57	63	61	52	40	30	18
Precip	1.5	1.5	2.1	3.7	4.2	3.8	3.7	5.1	3.5	3.0	3.1	2.1
Snow	9.4	6.8	3.6	0.5	0.0	0.0	0.0	0.0	0.0	tr	0.8	8.1

High and Low temperatures in degrees Fahrenheit; Precipitation and Snow in inches

Population: 317,471 (1990); 404,119 (2000); 515,269 (2010); Race: 73.5% White, 5.4% Black/African American, 3.4% Asian, 0.3% American Indian/Alaska Native, 0.0% Native Hawaiian/Other Pacific Islander, 17.4% Some other race, 2.1% Two or more races, 30.5% Hispanic of any race (2008-2012 5-year est.); Density: 1,002.4 persons per square mile (2008-2012 5-year est.); Average household size: 2.99 (2008-2012 5-year est.); Median age: 34.7 (2008-2012 5-year est.); Males per 100 females: 99.5 (2008-2012 5-year est.).
Religion: Six largest groups: 30.2% Catholicism, 5.0% Lutheran, 3.3% Non-denominational Protestant, 2.6% Muslim Estimate, 2.5% Methodist/Pietist, 2.4% Baptist (2010)
Economy: Unemployment rate: 7.4% (April 2014); Total civilian labor force: 276,136 (April 2014); Leading industries: 17.0% manufacturing; 13.0% administration, support, waste management, remediation services; 12.8% retail trade (2012); Farms: 590 totaling 168,541 acres (2012); Companies that employ 500 or more persons: 27 (2012); Companies that employ 100 to 499 persons: 278 (2012); Companies that employ less than 100 persons: 12,027 (2012); Black-owned businesses: 1,583 (2007); Hispanic-owned businesses: 2,935 (2007); Asian-owned businesses: 1,718 (2007); Women-owned businesses: 11,533 (2007); Single-family building permits issued: 1,068 (2013); Multi-family building permits issued: 143 (2013).
Income: Per capita income: $29,730 (2008-2012 5-year est.); Median household income: $68,674 (2008-2012 5-year est.); Average household income: $87,965 (2008-2012 5-year est.); Percent of households with income of $100,000 or more: 31.9% (2008-2012 5-year est.); Poverty rate: 11.0% (2008-2012 5-year est.); Bankruptcy rate: 4.73% (2013).
Taxes: Total county taxes per capita: $190 (2011); County property taxes per capita: $166 (2011).
Education: Percent of population age 25 and over with: High school diploma (including GED) or higher: 83.1% (2008-2012 5-year est.); Bachelor's degree or higher: 31.9% (2008-2012 5-year est.); Master's degree or higher: 11.3% (2008-2012 5-year est.).
Housing: Homeownership rate: 75.9% (2008-2012 5-year est.); Median home value: $233,800 (2008-2012 5-year est.); Median contract rent: $847 per month (2008-2012 5-year est.); Median year structure built: 1979 (2008-2012 5-year est.).
Health: Birth rate: 129.7 per 10,000 population (2013); Death rate: 57.8 per 10,000 population (2013); Age-adjusted cancer mortality rate: 166.5 deaths per 100,000 population (2011); Number of physicians: 14.1 per 10,000 population (2011); Hospital beds: 21.9 per 10,000 population (2010); Hospital admissions: 745.4 per 10,000 population (2010).
Environment: Air Quality Index: 89.6% good, 10.4% moderate, 0.0% unhealthy for sensitive individuals, 0.0% unhealthy (percent of days in 2013)
Elections: 2012 Presidential election results: 49.6% Obama, 48.7% Romney
Additional Information Contacts
Kane County Government . . . . (630) 232-3400
    http://www.countyofkane.org
Northern Kane County Chamber of Commerce . . . . (847) 426-8565
    http://www.nkcchamber.com

Kane County Communities

AURORA (city). Covers a land area of 44.936 square miles and a water area of 0.859 square miles. Located at 41.76° N. Lat; 88.29° W. Long. Elevation is 679 feet.

History: Named for the Iroquoian translation of "constant dawn". Joseph McCarty of Elmira, New York, came to Illinois in 1834 and chose the site on the Fox River as superior to Chicago as a place to settle. The community of Aurora was platted in 1836 and a post office was soon established. Development along both sides of the river resulted in separate towns of East Aurora and West Aurora until 1857, when the two were joined in incorporation. Meanwhile, the Chicago, Burlington & Quincy Railroad had arrived with its tracks and shops, and with it a period of growth. Aurora, in 1881, was one of the first towns in the U.S. to have electric street lights.

Population: 99,581 (1990); 142,990 (2000); 197,899 (2010); Density: 4,374.4 persons per square mile (2008-2012 5-year est.); Race: 55.5% White, 9.4% Black/African American, 6.9% Asian, 0.3% American Indian/Alaska Native, 0.0% Native Hawaiian/Other Pacific Islander, 27.9% Some other race, 3.3% Two or more races, 41.5% Hispanic of any race (2008-2012 5-year est.); Average household size: 3.13 (2008-2012 5-year est.); Median age: 31.0 (2008-2012 5-year est.); Males per 100 females: 99.7 (2008-2012 5-year est.); Marriage status: 34.0% never married, 53.7% now married, 3.7% widowed, 8.7% divorced (2008-2012 5-year est.); Foreign born: 25.4% (2008-2012 5-year est.); Ancestry (includes multiple ancestries): 14.8% German, 9.3% Irish, 4.9% Polish, 4.7% English, 4.5% Italian (2008-2012 5-year est.).

Economy: Unemployment rate: 7.4% (April 2014); Total civilian labor force: 106,605 (April 2014); Single-family building permits issued: 154 (2013); Multi-family building permits issued: 0 (2013); Homeowner vacancy rate: 3.1%. Rental vacancy rate: 6.9%. (2008-2012 5-year est.); Employment by occupation: 13.8% management, business, and financial, 6.0% computer, engineering, and science, 8.6% education, legal, community service, arts, and media, 3.8% healthcare practitioners, 16.3% service, 25.4% sales and office, 6.5% natural resources, construction, and maintenance, 19.6% production, transportation, and material moving (2008-2012 5-year est.).

Income: Per capita income: $26,091 (2008-2012 5-year est.); Median household income: $62,589 (2008-2012 5-year est.); Average household income: $80,228 (2008-2012 5-year est.); Percent of households with income of $100,000 or more: 26.9% (2008-2012 5-year est.); Poverty rate: 13.6% (2008-2012 5-year est.).

Taxes: Total city taxes per capita: $795 (2011); City property taxes per capita: $550 (2011).

Education: Percent of population age 25 and over with: High school diploma (including GED) or higher: 77.3% (2008-2012 5-year est.); Bachelor's degree or higher: 30.9% (2008-2012 5-year est.); Master's degree or higher: 11.5% (2008-2012 5-year est.).

School District(s)

Aurora East USD 131 (PK-12)
    2011-12 Enrollment: 14,502 . . . . (630) 299-5554
Aurora West USD 129 (PK-12)
    2011-12 Enrollment: 12,467 . . . . (630) 301-5000
Il Mathematics & Science Academy (10-12)
    2011-12 Enrollment: 642. . . . . (630) 907-5038
Indian Prairie CUSD 204 (PK-12)
    2011-12 Enrollment: 29,286 . . . . (630) 375-3000
Kane Roe (08-12)
    2011-12 Enrollment: n/a . . . . (630) 232-5955
Oswego CUSD 308 (PK-12)
    2011-12 Enrollment: 17,150 . . . . (630) 636-3080

Four-year College(s)

Aurora University (Private, Not-for-profit)
    Fall 2012 Enrollment: 4,702 . . . . (630) 892-6431
    2012-13 Tuition: In-state $20,100; Out-of-state $20,100

Vocational/Technical School(s)

Regency Beauty Institute-Aurora (Private, For-profit)
    Fall 2012 Enrollment: 112. . . . . (800) 787-6456
    2012-13 Tuition: $16,425

Housing: Homeownership rate: 69.0% (2008-2012 5-year est.); Median home value: $194,300 (2008-2012 5-year est.); Median contract rent: $848 per month (2008-2012 5-year est.); Median year structure built: 1980 (2008-2012 5-year est.).

Health Insurance: 63.2% Private; 25.5% Public; 16.9% None. (2008-2012 5-year est.)

Hospitals: Provena Mercy Medical Center (356 beds); Rush-Copley Medical Center (183 beds)

Safety: Violent crime rate: 28.2 per 10,000 population; Property crime rate: 178.5 per 10,000 population (2012).

Transportation: Commute to work: 87.6% car, 5.0% public transportation, 1.1% walk, 3.7% work from home (2008-2012 5-year est.); Travel time to work: 22.9% less than 15 minutes, 35.5% 15 to 30 minutes, 20.0% 30 to 45 minutes, 8.7% 45 to 60 minutes, 12.9% 60 minutes or more (2008-2012 5-year est.)

Airports: Aurora Municipal Airport (reliver airport)

Additional Information Contacts

Aurora Hispanic Chamber of Commerce . . . . (630) 264-2422
    http://www.ahcc-il.com
Aurora Regional Chamber of Commerce . . . . (630) 256-3180
    http://www.aurorachamber.com
City of Aurora . . . . (630) 256-4636
    http://www.aurora-il.org

BATAVIA (city). Covers a land area of 9.637 square miles and a water area of 0.067 square miles. Located at 41.85° N. Lat; 88.31° W. Long. Elevation is 715 feet.

History: Batavia was settled in 1832 by people from New York, who chose the site for its water power, fertile soil, and surface limestone. They named the new town for their home in New York. Early Batavia had the nickname of Quarry City.

Population: 17,076 (1990); 23,866 (2000); 26,045 (2010); Density: 2,666.0 persons per square mile (2008-2012 5-year est.); Race: 90.4% White, 3.6% Black/African American, 1.6% Asian, 0.1% American Indian/Alaska Native, 0.0% Native Hawaiian/Other Pacific Islander, 4.3% Some other race, 1.4% Two or more races, 6.4% Hispanic of any race (2008-2012 5-year est.); Average household size: 2.77 (2008-2012 5-year est.); Median age: 39.7 (2008-2012 5-year est.); Males per 100 females: 91.4 (2008-2012 5-year est.); Marriage status: 25.7% never married, 61.4% now married, 5.1% widowed, 7.8% divorced (2008-2012 5-year est.); Foreign born: 4.9% (2008-2012 5-year est.); Ancestry (includes multiple ancestries): 32.5% German, 18.4% Irish, 13.1% Polish, 11.6% English, 11.6% Italian (2008-2012 5-year est.).

Economy: Unemployment rate: 6.4% (April 2014); Total civilian labor force: 14,412 (April 2014); Single-family building permits issued: 7 (2013); Multi-family building permits issued: 0 (2013); Homeowner vacancy rate: 1.3%. Rental vacancy rate: 6.8%. (2008-2012 5-year est.); Employment by occupation: 24.6% management, business, and financial, 7.2% computer, engineering, and science, 13.5% education, legal, community service, arts, and media, 5.7% healthcare practitioners, 11.6% service, 24.7% sales and office, 4.2% natural resources, construction, and maintenance, 8.3% production, transportation, and material moving (2008-2012 5-year est.).

Income: Per capita income: $38,565 (2008-2012 5-year est.); Median household income: $90,060 (2008-2012 5-year est.); Average household income: $106,739 (2008-2012 5-year est.); Percent of households with income of $100,000 or more: 44.1% (2008-2012 5-year est.); Poverty rate: 7.1% (2008-2012 5-year est.).

Taxes: Total city taxes per capita: $471 (2011); City property taxes per capita: $265 (2011).

Education: Percent of population age 25 and over with: High school diploma (including GED) or higher: 95.3% (2008-2012 5-year est.); Bachelor's degree or higher: 49.8% (2008-2012 5-year est.); Master's degree or higher: 20.6% (2008-2012 5-year est.).

School District(s)

Batavia USD 101 (PK-12)
    2011-12 Enrollment: 6,307 . . . . (630) 937-8834

Housing: Homeownership rate: 77.0% (2008-2012 5-year est.); Median home value: $286,600 (2008-2012 5-year est.); Median contract rent: $900 per month (2008-2012 5-year est.); Median year structure built: 1984 (2008-2012 5-year est.).

Health Insurance: 83.2% Private; 19.4% Public; 6.9% None. (2008-2012 5-year est.)

Safety: Violent crime rate: 12.5 per 10,000 population; Property crime rate: 182.1 per 10,000 population (2012).

Transportation: Commute to work: 84.6% car, 3.2% public transportation, 1.2% walk, 7.8% work from home (2008-2012 5-year est.); Travel time to work: 29.8% less than 15 minutes, 29.8% 15 to 30 minutes, 22.0% 30 to 45 minutes, 8.1% 45 to 60 minutes, 10.4% 60 minutes or more (2008-2012 5-year est.)

Additional Information Contacts
Batavia Chamber of Commerce .... (630) 879-7134
   http://www.bataviachamber.org
City of Batavia................................. (630) 454-2000
   http://www.cityofbatavia.net

BIG ROCK (village). Covers a land area of 4.328 square miles and a water area of 0 square miles. Located at 41.77° N. Lat; 88.53° W. Long. Elevation is 709 feet.

History: Incorporated July 26, 2001.

Population: n/a (1990); n/a (2000); 1,126 (2010); Density: 239.9 persons per square mile (2008-2012 5-year est.); Race: 96.4% White, 1.3% Black/African American, 0.0% Asian, 0.0% American Indian/Alaska Native, 0.0% Native Hawaiian/Other Pacific Islander, 2.3% Some other race, 2.2% Two or more races, 8.7% Hispanic of any race (2008-2012 5-year est.); Average household size: 2.63 (2008-2012 5-year est.); Median age: 43.3 (2008-2012 5-year est.); Males per 100 females: 88.7 (2008-2012 5-year est.); Marriage status: 28.5% never married, 61.5% now married, 4.1% widowed, 5.9% divorced (2008-2012 5-year est.); Foreign born: 1.9% (2008-2012 5-year est.); Ancestry (includes multiple ancestries): 39.5% German, 20.1% Irish, 9.2% English, 7.2% Swedish, 6.2% Italian (2008-2012 5-year est.).

Economy: Homeowner vacancy rate: 0.5%. Rental vacancy rate: 0.0%. (2008-2012 5-year est.); Employment by occupation: 14.3% management, business, and financial, 3.1% computer, engineering, and science, 9.6% education, legal, community service, arts, and media, 3.8% healthcare practitioners, 11.4% service, 18.7% sales and office, 17.4% natural resources, construction, and maintenance, 21.6% production, transportation, and material moving (2008-2012 5-year est.).

Income: Per capita income: $31,937 (2008-2012 5-year est.); Median household income: $63,750 (2008-2012 5-year est.); Average household income: $82,764 (2008-2012 5-year est.); Percent of households with income of $100,000 or more: 28.1% (2008-2012 5-year est.); Poverty rate: 8.0% (2008-2012 5-year est.).

Education: Percent of population age 25 and over with: High school diploma (including GED) or higher: 91.9% (2008-2012 5-year est.); Bachelor's degree or higher: 20.1% (2008-2012 5-year est.); Master's degree or higher: 4.5% (2008-2012 5-year est.).

School District(s)
Hinckley Big Rock CUSD 429 (PK-12)
   2011-12 Enrollment: 714........................ (815) 286-7575

Housing: Homeownership rate: 89.4% (2008-2012 5-year est.); Median home value: $226,100 (2008-2012 5-year est.); Median contract rent: $961 per month (2008-2012 5-year est.); Median year structure built: 1971 (2008-2012 5-year est.).

Health Insurance: 82.4% Private; 23.8% Public; 5.3% None. (2008-2012 5-year est.)

Transportation: Commute to work: 94.5% car, 0.6% public transportation, 2.4% walk, 0.6% work from home (2008-2012 5-year est.); Travel time to work: 28.7% less than 15 minutes, 25.1% 15 to 30 minutes, 26.8% 30 to 45 minutes, 9.5% 45 to 60 minutes, 9.8% 60 minutes or more (2008-2012 5-year est.)

BURLINGTON (village). Covers a land area of 7.148 square miles and a water area of 0 square miles. Located at 42.05° N. Lat; 88.57° W. Long. Elevation is 925 feet.

Population: 400 (1990); 452 (2000); 618 (2010); Density: 76.5 persons per square mile (2008-2012 5-year est.); Race: 95.4% White, 0.0% Black/African American, 0.0% Asian, 0.7% American Indian/Alaska Native, 0.0% Native Hawaiian/Other Pacific Islander, 3.9% Some other race, 0.0% Two or more races, 4.8% Hispanic of any race (2008-2012 5-year est.); Average household size: 2.54 (2008-2012 5-year est.); Median age: 41.1 (2008-2012 5-year est.); Males per 100 females: 98.2 (2008-2012 5-year est.); Marriage status: 23.7% never married, 66.1% now married, 0.7% widowed, 9.6% divorced (2008-2012 5-year est.); Foreign born: 5.7% (2008-2012 5-year est.); Ancestry (includes multiple ancestries): 42.8% German, 27.6% Irish, 10.4% Polish, 6.2% American, 5.1% Dutch (2008-2012 5-year est.).

Economy: Homeowner vacancy rate: 0.0%. Rental vacancy rate: 14.3%. (2008-2012 5-year est.); Employment by occupation: 10.7% management, business, and financial, 1.7% computer, engineering, and science, 14.5% education, legal, community service, arts, and media, 6.9% healthcare practitioners, 28.6% service, 11.7% sales and office, 16.2% natural resources, construction, and maintenance, 9.7% production, transportation, and material moving (2008-2012 5-year est.).

Income: Per capita income: $27,854 (2008-2012 5-year est.); Median household income: $60,231 (2008-2012 5-year est.); Average household income: $71,834 (2008-2012 5-year est.); Percent of households with income of $100,000 or more: 20.5% (2008-2012 5-year est.); Poverty rate: 6.9% (2008-2012 5-year est.).

Education: Percent of population age 25 and over with: High school diploma (including GED) or higher: 93.2% (2008-2012 5-year est.); Bachelor's degree or higher: 15.0% (2008-2012 5-year est.); Master's degree or higher: 8.7% (2008-2012 5-year est.).

School District(s)
Central CUSD 301 (PK-12)
   2011-12 Enrollment: 3,470 .... (847) 464-6005

Housing: Homeownership rate: 80.9% (2008-2012 5-year est.); Median home value: $208,000 (2008-2012 5-year est.); Median contract rent: $675 per month (2008-2012 5-year est.); Median year structure built: 1948 (2008-2012 5-year est.).

Health Insurance: 82.4% Private; 30.9% Public; 2.4% None. (2008-2012 5-year est.)

Transportation: Commute to work: 85.6% car, 0.4% public transportation, 10.4% walk, 3.6% work from home (2008-2012 5-year est.); Travel time to work: 24.6% less than 15 minutes, 36.6% 15 to 30 minutes, 18.3% 30 to 45 minutes, 13.1% 45 to 60 minutes, 7.5% 60 minutes or more (2008-2012 5-year est.)

CAMPTON HILLS (village). Covers a land area of 16.908 square miles and a water area of 0.082 square miles. Located at 41.95° N. Lat; 88.42° W. Long.

History: Incorporated May 14, 2007.

Population: n/a (1990); n/a (2000); 11,131 (2010); Density: 649.7 persons per square mile (2008-2012 5-year est.); Race: 96.8% White, 0.3% Black/African American, 1.5% Asian, 0.4% American Indian/Alaska Native, 0.0% Native Hawaiian/Other Pacific Islander, 1.0% Some other race, 1.0% Two or more races, 3.0% Hispanic of any race (2008-2012 5-year est.); Average household size: 3.18 (2008-2012 5-year est.); Median age: 43.0 (2008-2012 5-year est.); Males per 100 females: 100.1 (2008-2012 5-year est.); Marriage status: 24.3% never married, 68.8% now married, 3.6% widowed, 3.4% divorced (2008-2012 5-year est.); Foreign born: 5.1% (2008-2012 5-year est.); Ancestry (includes multiple ancestries): 27.0% German, 20.2% Irish, 15.8% Polish, 11.5% Italian, 8.4% English (2008-2012 5-year est.).

Economy: Single-family building permits issued: 2 (2013); Multi-family building permits issued: 0 (2013); Homeowner vacancy rate: 0.7%. Rental vacancy rate: 0.0%. (2008-2012 5-year est.); Employment by occupation: 28.6% management, business, and financial, 7.3% computer, engineering, and science, 9.1% education, legal, community service, arts, and media, 4.8% healthcare practitioners, 11.9% service, 26.7% sales and office, 5.6% natural resources, construction, and maintenance, 6.0% production, transportation, and material moving (2008-2012 5-year est.).

Income: Per capita income: $47,398 (2008-2012 5-year est.); Median household income: $128,633 (2008-2012 5-year est.); Average household income: $149,313 (2008-2012 5-year est.); Percent of households with income of $100,000 or more: 62.1% (2008-2012 5-year est.); Poverty rate: 3.7% (2008-2012 5-year est.).

Education: Percent of population age 25 and over with: High school diploma (including GED) or higher: 98.1% (2008-2012 5-year est.); Bachelor's degree or higher: 55.1% (2008-2012 5-year est.); Master's degree or higher: 18.2% (2008-2012 5-year est.).

Housing: Homeownership rate: 94.2% (2008-2012 5-year est.); Median home value: $445,700 (2008-2012 5-year est.); Median contract rent: $869 per month (2008-2012 5-year est.); Median year structure built: 1990 (2008-2012 5-year est.).

Health Insurance: 92.3% Private; 10.8% Public; 3.8% None. (2008-2012 5-year est.)

Safety: Violent crime rate: 5.3 per 10,000 population; Property crime rate: 39.1 per 10,000 population (2012).

Transportation: Commute to work: 80.5% car, 2.4% public transportation, 0.2% walk, 15.7% work from home (2008-2012 5-year est.); Travel time to work: 17.9% less than 15 minutes, 27.6% 15 to 30 minutes, 17.4% 30 to 45 minutes, 19.0% 45 to 60 minutes, 18.2% 60 minutes or more (2008-2012 5-year est.)

Additional Information Contacts
Village of Campton Hills .... (630) 584-5700
   http://www.villageofcamptonhills.org

CARPENTERSVILLE (village). Covers a land area of 7.904 square miles and a water area of 0.197 square miles. Located at 42.12° N. Lat; 88.29° W. Long. Elevation is 889 feet.

History: Named for D. G. Carpenter, an early settler. Carpentersville was settled in 1834 by Angelo Carpenter of Massachusetts and his father and uncle. Carpenter built several mills and a store, and in 1851 he platted the town. An early industry was the Illinois Iron and Bolt Company.

Population: 23,049 (1990); 30,586 (2000); 37,691 (2010); Density: 4,777.4 persons per square mile (2008-2012 5-year est.); Race: 67.5% White, 7.9% Black/African American, 3.9% Asian, 0.3% American Indian/Alaska Native, 0.0% Native Hawaiian/Other Pacific Islander, 20.4% Some other race, 2.5% Two or more races, 48.9% Hispanic of any race (2008-2012 5-year est.); Average household size: 3.41 (2008-2012 5-year est.); Median age: 29.8 (2008-2012 5-year est.); Males per 100 females: 104.0 (2008-2012 5-year est.); Marriage status: 35.8% never married, 51.3% now married, 4.1% widowed, 8.8% divorced (2008-2012 5-year est.); Foreign born: 28.5% (2008-2012 5-year est.); Ancestry (includes multiple ancestries): 15.2% German, 6.8% Polish, 6.7% Irish, 6.2% Italian, 2.9% English (2008-2012 5-year est.).

Economy: Unemployment rate: 9.9% (April 2014); Total civilian labor force: 18,900 (April 2014); Single-family building permits issued: 39 (2013); Multi-family building permits issued: 0 (2013); Homeowner vacancy rate: 1.9%. Rental vacancy rate: 7.5%. (2008-2012 5-year est.); Employment by occupation: 11.0% management, business, and financial, 6.9% computer, engineering, and science, 5.2% education, legal, community service, arts, and media, 3.0% healthcare practitioners, 17.4% service, 23.2% sales and office, 8.8% natural resources, construction, and maintenance, 24.5% production, transportation, and material moving (2008-2012 5-year est.).

Income: Per capita income: $20,850 (2008-2012 5-year est.); Median household income: $55,000 (2008-2012 5-year est.); Average household income: $69,166 (2008-2012 5-year est.); Percent of households with income of $100,000 or more: 22.4% (2008-2012 5-year est.); Poverty rate: 16.5% (2008-2012 5-year est.).

Education: Percent of population age 25 and over with: High school diploma (including GED) or higher: 73.7% (2008-2012 5-year est.); Bachelor's degree or higher: 20.7% (2008-2012 5-year est.); Master's degree or higher: 6.2% (2008-2012 5-year est.).

School District(s)

Barrington CUSD 220 (PK-12)
    2011-12 Enrollment: 9,088 . . . . (847) 381-6300
CUSD 300 (PK-12)
    2011-12 Enrollment: 20,810 . . . . (847) 551-8308
Kane Roe (08-12)
    2011-12 Enrollment: n/a . . . . (630) 232-5955

Housing: Homeownership rate: 74.3% (2008-2012 5-year est.); Median home value: $172,700 (2008-2012 5-year est.); Median contract rent: $811 per month (2008-2012 5-year est.); Median year structure built: 1979 (2008-2012 5-year est.).

Health Insurance: 54.9% Private; 30.7% Public; 19.0% None. (2008-2012 5-year est.)

Safety: Violent crime rate: 8.1 per 10,000 population; Property crime rate: 140.0 per 10,000 population (2012).

Transportation: Commute to work: 93.6% car, 1.2% public transportation, 0.8% walk, 2.5% work from home (2008-2012 5-year est.); Travel time to work: 14.7% less than 15 minutes, 32.3% 15 to 30 minutes, 31.9% 30 to 45 minutes, 12.1% 45 to 60 minutes, 9.0% 60 minutes or more (2008-2012 5-year est.)

Additional Information Contacts

Northern Kane County Chamber of Commerce . . . . (847) 426-8565
    http://www.nkcchamber.com
Village of Carpentersville. . . . . (847) 426-3439
    http://vil.carpentersville.il.us

DUNDEE (unincorporated postal area)

Zip Code: 60118

Covers a land area of 20.194 square miles and a water area of 0.632 square miles. Located at 42.10° N. Lat; 88.30° W. Long. Population: 15,851 (2010); Density: 784.9 persons per square mile (2010); Race: 90.0% White, 1.8% Black/African American, 4.3% Asian, 0.1% American Indian/Alaska Native, 0.0% Native Hawaiian/Other Pacific Islander, 3.8% Some other race, 1.7% Two or more races, 8.6% Hispanic of any race (2010); Average household size: 2.59 (2010); Median age: 42.3 (2010); Males per 100 females: 99.5 (2010); Homeownership rate: 78.3% (2010)

EAST DUNDEE (village). Covers a land area of 2.732 square miles and a water area of 0.239 square miles. Located at 42.10° N. Lat; 88.25° W. Long. Elevation is 768 feet.

History: East Dundee was settled mainly by German immigrants who left their home country during the 1848 Revolution.

Population: 2,721 (1990); 2,955 (2000); 2,860 (2010); Density: 1,056.4 persons per square mile (2008-2012 5-year est.); Race: 94.7% White, 2.8% Black/African American, 1.6% Asian, 0.0% American Indian/Alaska Native, 0.0% Native Hawaiian/Other Pacific Islander, 0.9% Some other race, 0.9% Two or more races, 11.2% Hispanic of any race (2008-2012 5-year est.); Average household size: 2.29 (2008-2012 5-year est.); Median age: 43.8 (2008-2012 5-year est.); Males per 100 females: 86.1 (2008-2012 5-year est.); Marriage status: 26.9% never married, 53.2% now married, 10.0% widowed, 10.0% divorced (2008-2012 5-year est.); Foreign born: 8.1% (2008-2012 5-year est.); Ancestry (includes multiple ancestries): 32.3% German, 21.4% Irish, 10.3% English, 8.2% Polish, 8.2% American (2008-2012 5-year est.).

Economy: Single-family building permits issued: 0 (2013); Multi-family building permits issued: 0 (2013); Homeowner vacancy rate: 3.1%. Rental vacancy rate: 0.0%. (2008-2012 5-year est.); Employment by occupation: 18.8% management, business, and financial, 2.7% computer, engineering, and science, 13.6% education, legal, community service, arts, and media, 1.8% healthcare practitioners, 7.9% service, 30.0% sales and office, 13.4% natural resources, construction, and maintenance, 11.9% production, transportation, and material moving (2008-2012 5-year est.).

Income: Per capita income: $34,419 (2008-2012 5-year est.); Median household income: $68,576 (2008-2012 5-year est.); Average household income: $77,292 (2008-2012 5-year est.); Percent of households with income of $100,000 or more: 29.7% (2008-2012 5-year est.); Poverty rate: 6.5% (2008-2012 5-year est.).

Education: Percent of population age 25 and over with: High school diploma (including GED) or higher: 95.5% (2008-2012 5-year est.); Bachelor's degree or higher: 30.5% (2008-2012 5-year est.); Master's degree or higher: 11.4% (2008-2012 5-year est.).

Housing: Homeownership rate: 82.4% (2008-2012 5-year est.); Median home value: $191,900 (2008-2012 5-year est.); Median contract rent: $894 per month (2008-2012 5-year est.); Median year structure built: 1967 (2008-2012 5-year est.).

Health Insurance: 84.2% Private; 26.3% Public; 7.0% None. (2008-2012 5-year est.)

Safety: Violent crime rate: 3.5 per 10,000 population; Property crime rate: 207.8 per 10,000 population (2012).

Transportation: Commute to work: 90.9% car, 1.1% public transportation, 2.3% walk, 3.1% work from home (2008-2012 5-year est.); Travel time to work: 14.6% less than 15 minutes, 34.4% 15 to 30 minutes, 23.5% 30 to 45 minutes, 13.1% 45 to 60 minutes, 14.4% 60 minutes or more (2008-2012 5-year est.)

Additional Information Contacts

Northern Kane County Chamber of Commerce . . . . (847) 426-8565
    http://www.nkcchamber.com

ELBURN (village). Covers a land area of 3.127 square miles and a water area of 0 square miles. Located at 41.87° N. Lat; 88.45° W. Long. Elevation is 853 feet.

History: Elburn began in 1854 when the Galena & Chicago Union Railroad line was laid, and developed as a farming center. It is said that when Lincoln visited Elburn in 1858, he was greeted by a group calling itself the Lincoln True Hearts, pledging support.

Population: 1,275 (1990); 2,756 (2000); 5,602 (2010); Density: 1,789.3 persons per square mile (2008-2012 5-year est.); Race: 92.8% White, 0.0% Black/African American, 2.8% Asian, 0.0% American Indian/Alaska Native, 0.0% Native Hawaiian/Other Pacific Islander, 4.4% Some other race, 0.8% Two or more races, 8.0% Hispanic of any race (2008-2012 5-year est.); Average household size: 3.18 (2008-2012 5-year est.); Median age: 34.1 (2008-2012 5-year est.); Males per 100 females: 102.9 (2008-2012 5-year est.); Marriage status: 25.0% never married, 62.5% now married, 3.2% widowed, 9.3% divorced (2008-2012 5-year est.); Foreign born: 5.8% (2008-2012 5-year est.); Ancestry (includes multiple ancestries): 50.1% German, 27.9% Irish, 10.0% Polish, 9.9% Italian, 7.4% English (2008-2012 5-year est.).

Economy: Single-family building permits issued: 8 (2013); Multi-family building permits issued: 0 (2013); Homeowner vacancy rate: 1.4%. Rental vacancy rate: 11.8%. (2008-2012 5-year est.); Employment by occupation: 17.9% management, business, and financial, 1.5% computer, engineering, and science, 7.7% education, legal, community service, arts, and media,

4.1% healthcare practitioners, 13.9% service, 31.0% sales and office, 14.5% natural resources, construction, and maintenance, 9.4% production, transportation, and material moving (2008-2012 5-year est.).
Income: Per capita income: $29,713 (2008-2012 5-year est.); Median household income: $81,758 (2008-2012 5-year est.); Average household income: $91,987 (2008-2012 5-year est.); Percent of households with income of $100,000 or more: 42.6% (2008-2012 5-year est.); Poverty rate: 5.7% (2008-2012 5-year est.).
Education: Percent of population age 25 and over with: High school diploma (including GED) or higher: 96.4% (2008-2012 5-year est.); Bachelor's degree or higher: 32.6% (2008-2012 5-year est.); Master's degree or higher: 8.2% (2008-2012 5-year est.).

School District(s)
Kaneland CUSD 302 (PK-12)
  2011-12 Enrollment: 4,835 . . . . (630) 365-5111
Housing: Homeownership rate: 85.6% (2008-2012 5-year est.); Median home value: $243,200 (2008-2012 5-year est.); Median contract rent: $853 per month (2008-2012 5-year est.); Median year structure built: 1997 (2008-2012 5-year est.).
Health Insurance: 83.8% Private; 13.1% Public; 8.5% None. (2008-2012 5-year est.)
Safety: Violent crime rate: 5.3 per 10,000 population; Property crime rate: 67.1 per 10,000 population (2012).
Transportation: Commute to work: 91.9% car, 3.1% public transportation, 1.7% walk, 2.9% work from home (2008-2012 5-year est.); Travel time to work: 15.1% less than 15 minutes, 33.0% 15 to 30 minutes, 23.2% 30 to 45 minutes, 8.3% 45 to 60 minutes, 20.5% 60 minutes or more (2008-2012 5-year est.)

ELGIN (city). Covers a land area of 37.163 square miles and a water area of 0.544 square miles. Located at 42.04° N. Lat; 88.32° W. Long. Elevation is 745 feet.
History: Named for a Scottish hymn, "Elgin," by James T. Gifford. Elgin was settled in 1835 by James and Hezekiah Gifford from New York, who dammed the river and built a sawmill and a gristmill. It was incorporated as a village in 1847 and as a town in 1854. An early industry here was the production of condensed milk, a process developed by Gail Borden. The Elgin watch industry, which made the name of Elgin known around the world, began in 1866, followed by the Elgin Watchmakers College which opened in the 1920's.
Population: 77,010 (1990); 94,487 (2000); 108,188 (2010); Density: 2,946.8 persons per square mile (2008-2012 5-year est.); Race: 66.1% White, 6.7% Black/African American, 5.3% Asian, 0.4% American Indian/Alaska Native, 0.0% Native Hawaiian/Other Pacific Islander, 21.5% Some other race, 2.5% Two or more races, 45.0% Hispanic of any race (2008-2012 5-year est.); Average household size: 3.05 (2008-2012 5-year est.); Median age: 32.5 (2008-2012 5-year est.); Males per 100 females: 98.4 (2008-2012 5-year est.); Marriage status: 32.5% never married, 52.6% now married, 5.7% widowed, 9.2% divorced (2008-2012 5-year est.); Foreign born: 26.2% (2008-2012 5-year est.); Ancestry (includes multiple ancestries): 17.0% German, 7.8% Irish, 5.4% English, 5.4% Polish, 5.3% Italian (2008-2012 5-year est.).
Economy: Unemployment rate: 9.0% (April 2014); Total civilian labor force: 59,470 (April 2014); Single-family building permits issued: 343 (2013); Multi-family building permits issued: 0 (2013); Homeowner vacancy rate: 3.3%. Rental vacancy rate: 5.6%. (2008-2012 5-year est.); Employment by occupation: 11.1% management, business, and financial, 4.4% computer, engineering, and science, 8.2% education, legal, community service, arts, and media, 3.3% healthcare practitioners, 17.9% service, 24.3% sales and office, 9.4% natural resources, construction, and maintenance, 21.3% production, transportation, and material moving (2008-2012 5-year est.).
Income: Per capita income: $23,601 (2008-2012 5-year est.); Median household income: $58,487 (2008-2012 5-year est.); Average household income: $70,870 (2008-2012 5-year est.); Percent of households with income of $100,000 or more: 22.3% (2008-2012 5-year est.); Poverty rate: 13.0% (2008-2012 5-year est.).
Taxes: Total city taxes per capita: $602 (2011); City property taxes per capita: $522 (2011).
Education: Percent of population age 25 and over with: High school diploma (including GED) or higher: 77.2% (2008-2012 5-year est.); Bachelor's degree or higher: 23.6% (2008-2012 5-year est.); Master's degree or higher: 7.6% (2008-2012 5-year est.).

School District(s)
Central CUSD 301 (PK-12)
  2011-12 Enrollment: 3,470 . . . . (847) 464-6005
Kane Roe (08-12)
  2011-12 Enrollment: n/a . . . . (630) 232-5955
SD U-46 (PK-12)
  2011-12 Enrollment: 40,687 . . . . (847) 888-5000
SD U-46 (PK-12)
  2011-12 Enrollment: 40,687 . . . . (847) 888-5000

Four-year College(s)
Judson University (Private, Not-for-profit, Baptist)
  Fall 2012 Enrollment: 1,098 . . . . (847) 628-2500
  2012-13 Tuition: In-state $27,000; Out-of-state $27,000

Two-year College(s)
Elgin Community College (Public)
  Fall 2012 Enrollment: 11,554 . . . . (847) 697-1000
  2012-13 Tuition: In-state $8,698; Out-of-state $11,362

Vocational/Technical School(s)
Cannella School of Hair Design-Elgin (Private, For-profit)
  Fall 2012 Enrollment: 87 . . . . (847) 742-6611
  2012-13 Tuition: $12,190
J Renee Career Facilitation (Private, For-profit)
  Fall 2012 Enrollment: 76 . . . . (815) 444-7751
  2012-13 Tuition: $22,215
Regency Beauty Institute-Elgin (Private, For-profit)
  Fall 2012 Enrollment: 70 . . . . (800) 787-6456
  2012-13 Tuition: $16,425
The Salon Professional Academy of Elgin (Private, For-profit)
  Fall 2012 Enrollment: 27 . . . . (847) 376-0740
  2012-13 Tuition: $14,818
Housing: Homeownership rate: 70.8% (2008-2012 5-year est.); Median home value: $190,700 (2008-2012 5-year est.); Median contract rent: $818 per month (2008-2012 5-year est.); Median year structure built: 1974 (2008-2012 5-year est.).
Health Insurance: 62.0% Private; 27.9% Public; 17.3% None. (2008-2012 5-year est.)
Hospitals: Provena Saint Joseph Hospital (260 beds); Sherman Hospital (353 beds)
Safety: Violent crime rate: 23.5 per 10,000 population; Property crime rate: 181.6 per 10,000 population (2012).
Transportation: Commute to work: 91.6% car, 2.6% public transportation, 2.1% walk, 2.5% work from home (2008-2012 5-year est.); Travel time to work: 24.1% less than 15 minutes, 31.6% 15 to 30 minutes, 23.6% 30 to 45 minutes, 9.9% 45 to 60 minutes, 10.8% 60 minutes or more (2008-2012 5-year est.)
Additional Information Contacts
City of Elgin . . . . (847) 931-6100
  http://www.cityofelgin.org
Elgin Area Chamber of Commerce . . . . (847) 741-5660
  http://www.elginchamber.com

GENEVA (city). County seat. Covers a land area of 9.745 square miles and a water area of 0.244 square miles. Located at 41.88° N. Lat; 88.33° W. Long. Elevation is 712 feet.
History: Named for Geneva, New York. Geneva was settled about 1832 by soldiers returning from the Black Hawk War and by pioneers heading west.
Population: 12,617 (1990); 19,515 (2000); 21,495 (2010); Density: 2,215.2 persons per square mile (2008-2012 5-year est.); Race: 92.7% White, 1.3% Black/African American, 1.5% Asian, 0.3% American Indian/Alaska Native, 0.1% Native Hawaiian/Other Pacific Islander, 4.1% Some other race, 0.4% Two or more races, 6.1% Hispanic of any race (2008-2012 5-year est.); Average household size: 2.73 (2008-2012 5-year est.); Median age: 41.5 (2008-2012 5-year est.); Males per 100 females: 102.5 (2008-2012 5-year est.); Marriage status: 25.6% never married, 61.7% now married, 4.1% widowed, 8.6% divorced (2008-2012 5-year est.); Foreign born: 5.0% (2008-2012 5-year est.); Ancestry (includes multiple ancestries): 35.4% German, 21.3% Irish, 13.1% Italian, 9.4% English, 7.8% Polish (2008-2012 5-year est.).
Economy: Single-family building permits issued: 12 (2013); Multi-family building permits issued: 0 (2013); Homeowner vacancy rate: 2.9%. Rental vacancy rate: 9.2%. (2008-2012 5-year est.); Employment by occupation: 24.7% management, business, and financial, 5.8% computer, engineering, and science, 13.8% education, legal, community service, arts, and media, 4.7% healthcare practitioners, 11.2% service, 27.7% sales and office,

5.8% natural resources, construction, and maintenance, 6.3% production, transportation, and material moving (2008-2012 5-year est.).

Income: Per capita income: $43,922 (2008-2012 5-year est.); Median household income: $93,385 (2008-2012 5-year est.); Average household income: $119,783 (2008-2012 5-year est.); Percent of households with income of $100,000 or more: 47.1% (2008-2012 5-year est.); Poverty rate: 2.9% (2008-2012 5-year est.).

Taxes: Total city taxes per capita: $393 (2011); City property taxes per capita: $276 (2011).

Education: Percent of population age 25 and over with: High school diploma (including GED) or higher: 95.7% (2008-2012 5-year est.); Bachelor's degree or higher: 57.4% (2008-2012 5-year est.); Master's degree or higher: 19.5% (2008-2012 5-year est.).

School District(s)

Geneva CUSD 304 (PK-12)
   2011-12 Enrollment: 5,959 . . . . (630) 463-3000

Housing: Homeownership rate: 82.2% (2008-2012 5-year est.); Median home value: $323,700 (2008-2012 5-year est.); Median contract rent: <$101 per month (2008-2012 5-year est.); Median year structure built: 1985 (2008-2012 5-year est.).

Health Insurance: 88.9% Private; 16.2% Public; 6.4% None. (2008-2012 5-year est.)

Hospitals: Delnor-Community Health System (118 beds)

Safety: Violent crime rate: 0.9 per 10,000 population; Property crime rate: 122.5 per 10,000 population (2012).

Transportation: Commute to work: 85.1% car, 4.2% public transportation, 1.6% walk, 8.0% work from home (2008-2012 5-year est.); Travel time to work: 34.4% less than 15 minutes, 24.0% 15 to 30 minutes, 19.0% 30 to 45 minutes, 9.6% 45 to 60 minutes, 13.0% 60 minutes or more (2008-2012 5-year est.)

Additional Information Contacts

City of Geneva. . . . . (630) 232-7494
   http://www.geneva.il.us
Geneva Chamber of Commerce . . . . (630) 232-6060
   http://www.genevachamber.com

GILBERTS (village).
Covers a land area of 5.547 square miles and a water area of 0.008 square miles. Located at 42.11° N. Lat; 88.37° W. Long. Elevation is 899 feet.

Population: 987 (1990); 1,279 (2000); 6,879 (2010); Density: 1,223.3 persons per square mile (2008-2012 5-year est.); Race: 74.2% White, 0.8% Black/African American, 10.2% Asian, 1.0% American Indian/Alaska Native, 0.0% Native Hawaiian/Other Pacific Islander, 13.8% Some other race, 5.6% Two or more races, 16.4% Hispanic of any race (2008-2012 5-year est.); Average household size: 3.23 (2008-2012 5-year est.); Median age: 32.6 (2008-2012 5-year est.); Males per 100 females: 98.4 (2008-2012 5-year est.); Marriage status: 29.4% never married, 63.0% now married, 1.9% widowed, 5.7% divorced (2008-2012 5-year est.); Foreign born: 18.5% (2008-2012 5-year est.); Ancestry (includes multiple ancestries): 23.2% Polish, 16.5% Irish, 14.9% German, 7.3% Italian, 3.7% Portuguese (2008-2012 5-year est.).

Economy: Single-family building permits issued: 38 (2013); Multi-family building permits issued: 0 (2013); Homeowner vacancy rate: 0.0%. Rental vacancy rate: 0.0%. (2008-2012 5-year est.); Employment by occupation: 18.8% management, business, and financial, 15.9% computer, engineering, and science, 8.0% education, legal, community service, arts, and media, 6.9% healthcare practitioners, 7.8% service, 31.6% sales and office, 6.1% natural resources, construction, and maintenance, 4.9% production, transportation, and material moving (2008-2012 5-year est.).

Income: Per capita income: $36,716 (2008-2012 5-year est.); Median household income: $107,930 (2008-2012 5-year est.); Average household income: $112,169 (2008-2012 5-year est.); Percent of households with income of $100,000 or more: 55.6% (2008-2012 5-year est.); Poverty rate: 0.8% (2008-2012 5-year est.).

Education: Percent of population age 25 and over with: High school diploma (including GED) or higher: 96.4% (2008-2012 5-year est.); Bachelor's degree or higher: 44.9% (2008-2012 5-year est.); Master's degree or higher: 14.3% (2008-2012 5-year est.).

School District(s)

CUSD 300 (PK-12)
   2011-12 Enrollment: 20,810 . . . . (847) 551-8308

Housing: Homeownership rate: 95.7% (2008-2012 5-year est.); Median home value: $280,400 (2008-2012 5-year est.); Median contract rent: $1,063 per month (2008-2012 5-year est.); Median year structure built: 2004 (2008-2012 5-year est.).

Health Insurance: 92.2% Private; 10.3% Public; 4.6% None. (2008-2012 5-year est.)

Safety: Violent crime rate: 4.3 per 10,000 population; Property crime rate: 43.2 per 10,000 population (2012).

Transportation: Commute to work: 85.2% car, 4.0% public transportation, 0.0% walk, 9.8% work from home (2008-2012 5-year est.); Travel time to work: 19.7% less than 15 minutes, 18.2% 15 to 30 minutes, 21.7% 30 to 45 minutes, 21.8% 45 to 60 minutes, 18.6% 60 minutes or more (2008-2012 5-year est.)

Additional Information Contacts

Northern Kane County Chamber of Commerce . . . . (847) 426-8565
   http://www.nkcchamber.com

HAMPSHIRE (village).
Covers a land area of 8.950 square miles and a water area of 0 square miles. Located at 42.12° N. Lat; 88.51° W. Long. Elevation is 899 feet.

Population: 1,843 (1990); 2,900 (2000); 5,563 (2010); Density: 689.8 persons per square mile (2008-2012 5-year est.); Race: 86.1% White, 0.3% Black/African American, 0.1% Asian, 0.0% American Indian/Alaska Native, 0.0% Native Hawaiian/Other Pacific Islander, 13.5% Some other race, 0.6% Two or more races, 20.9% Hispanic of any race (2008-2012 5-year est.); Average household size: 3.07 (2008-2012 5-year est.); Median age: 34.1 (2008-2012 5-year est.); Males per 100 females: 83.8 (2008-2012 5-year est.); Marriage status: 21.8% never married, 66.9% now married, 2.2% widowed, 9.1% divorced (2008-2012 5-year est.); Foreign born: 11.1% (2008-2012 5-year est.); Ancestry (includes multiple ancestries): 29.5% German, 24.4% Irish, 15.9% Italian, 12.2% Polish, 5.2% American (2008-2012 5-year est.).

Economy: Single-family building permits issued: 82 (2013); Multi-family building permits issued: 2 (2013); Homeowner vacancy rate: 0.0%. Rental vacancy rate: 0.0%. (2008-2012 5-year est.); Employment by occupation: 11.0% management, business, and financial, 4.0% computer, engineering, and science, 7.7% education, legal, community service, arts, and media, 0.9% healthcare practitioners, 19.6% service, 33.8% sales and office, 9.0% natural resources, construction, and maintenance, 14.0% production, transportation, and material moving (2008-2012 5-year est.).

Income: Per capita income: $27,515 (2008-2012 5-year est.); Median household income: $73,283 (2008-2012 5-year est.); Average household income: $82,233 (2008-2012 5-year est.); Percent of households with income of $100,000 or more: 33.8% (2008-2012 5-year est.); Poverty rate: 1.4% (2008-2012 5-year est.).

Education: Percent of population age 25 and over with: High school diploma (including GED) or higher: 84.4% (2008-2012 5-year est.); Bachelor's degree or higher: 20.6% (2008-2012 5-year est.); Master's degree or higher: 8.1% (2008-2012 5-year est.).

School District(s)

CUSD 300 (PK-12)
   2011-12 Enrollment: 20,810 . . . . (847) 551-8308

Housing: Homeownership rate: 78.3% (2008-2012 5-year est.); Median home value: $222,300 (2008-2012 5-year est.); Median contract rent: $1,078 per month (2008-2012 5-year est.); Median year structure built: 1999 (2008-2012 5-year est.).

Health Insurance: 83.9% Private; 16.7% Public; 7.0% None. (2008-2012 5-year est.)

Safety: Violent crime rate: 17.8 per 10,000 population; Property crime rate: 137.0 per 10,000 population (2012).

Transportation: Commute to work: 89.1% car, 3.9% public transportation, 1.3% walk, 5.7% work from home (2008-2012 5-year est.); Travel time to work: 16.0% less than 15 minutes, 27.4% 15 to 30 minutes, 23.9% 30 to 45 minutes, 11.6% 45 to 60 minutes, 21.1% 60 minutes or more (2008-2012 5-year est.)

Additional Information Contacts

Hampshire Area Chamber of Commerce . . . . (847) 683-1122
   http://www.hampshirechamber.org

KANEVILLE (village).
Covers a land area of 0.314 square miles and a water area of 0 square miles. Located at 41.83° N. Lat; 88.52° W. Long. Elevation is 791 feet.

History: Incorporated November 2006.

Population: n/a (1990); n/a (2000); 484 (2010); Density: 1,457.5 persons per square mile (2008-2012 5-year est.); Race: 99.1% White, 0.0% Black/African American, 0.0% Asian, 0.0% American Indian/Alaska Native, 0.0% Native Hawaiian/Other Pacific Islander, 0.9% Some other race, 0.9% Two or more races, 5.9% Hispanic of any race (2008-2012 5-year est.); Average household size: 2.58 (2008-2012 5-year est.); Median age: 43.8

(2008-2012 5-year est.); Males per 100 females: 117.6 (2008-2012 5-year est.); Marriage status: 33.6% never married, 51.9% now married, 6.3% widowed, 8.2% divorced (2008-2012 5-year est.); Foreign born: 0.0% (2008-2012 5-year est.); Ancestry (includes multiple ancestries): 33.5% German, 14.2% Italian, 12.3% Irish, 9.2% Swedish, 8.1% American (2008-2012 5-year est.).

Economy: Homeowner vacancy rate: 2.5%. Rental vacancy rate: 0.0%. (2008-2012 5-year est.); Employment by occupation: 19.9% management, business, and financial, 8.5% computer, engineering, and science, 8.1% education, legal, community service, arts, and media, 3.7% healthcare practitioners, 9.8% service, 18.3% sales and office, 20.3% natural resources, construction, and maintenance, 11.4% production, transportation, and material moving (2008-2012 5-year est.).

Income: Per capita income: $34,333 (2008-2012 5-year est.); Median household income: $84,375 (2008-2012 5-year est.); Average household income: $85,355 (2008-2012 5-year est.); Percent of households with income of $100,000 or more: 35.6% (2008-2012 5-year est.); Poverty rate: 5.8% (2008-2012 5-year est.).

Education: Percent of population age 25 and over with: High school diploma (including GED) or higher: 94.4% (2008-2012 5-year est.); Bachelor's degree or higher: 27.0% (2008-2012 5-year est.); Master's degree or higher: 4.1% (2008-2012 5-year est.).

Housing: Homeownership rate: 88.7% (2008-2012 5-year est.); Median home value: $233,600 (2008-2012 5-year est.); Median contract rent: $725 per month (2008-2012 5-year est.); Median year structure built: 1972 (2008-2012 5-year est.).

Health Insurance: 83.6% Private; 23.2% Public; 3.9% None. (2008-2012 5-year est.)

Transportation: Commute to work: 87.1% car, 0.0% public transportation, 3.4% walk, 9.5% work from home (2008-2012 5-year est.); Travel time to work: 13.3% less than 15 minutes, 44.8% 15 to 30 minutes, 28.6% 30 to 45 minutes, 6.7% 45 to 60 minutes, 6.7% 60 minutes or more (2008-2012 5-year est.)

LILY LAKE (village). Covers a land area of 2.744 square miles and a water area of <.001 square miles. Located at 41.95° N. Lat; 88.47° W. Long. Elevation is 961 feet.

Population: n/a (1990); 825 (2000); 993 (2010); Density: 373.2 persons per square mile (2008-2012 5-year est.); Race: 96.4% White, 1.1% Black/African American, 0.0% Asian, 0.0% American Indian/Alaska Native, 0.0% Native Hawaiian/Other Pacific Islander, 2.5% Some other race, 1.0% Two or more races, 4.0% Hispanic of any race (2008-2012 5-year est.); Average household size: 3.18 (2008-2012 5-year est.); Median age: 42.1 (2008-2012 5-year est.); Males per 100 females: 108.1 (2008-2012 5-year est.); Marriage status: 20.5% never married, 67.0% now married, 3.3% widowed, 9.2% divorced (2008-2012 5-year est.); Foreign born: 4.6% (2008-2012 5-year est.); Ancestry (includes multiple ancestries): 29.7% German, 21.6% Irish, 13.0% Polish, 12.1% American, 8.9% Italian (2008-2012 5-year est.).

Economy: Single-family building permits issued: 6 (2013); Multi-family building permits issued: 0 (2013); Homeowner vacancy rate: 0.7%. Rental vacancy rate: 0.0%. (2008-2012 5-year est.); Employment by occupation: 21.1% management, business, and financial, 6.8% computer, engineering, and science, 10.5% education, legal, community service, arts, and media, 2.7% healthcare practitioners, 10.9% service, 25.9% sales and office, 12.7% natural resources, construction, and maintenance, 9.4% production, transportation, and material moving (2008-2012 5-year est.).

Income: Per capita income: $34,453 (2008-2012 5-year est.); Median household income: $100,192 (2008-2012 5-year est.); Average household income: $108,557 (2008-2012 5-year est.); Percent of households with income of $100,000 or more: 50.3% (2008-2012 5-year est.); Poverty rate: 2.9% (2008-2012 5-year est.).

Education: Percent of population age 25 and over with: High school diploma (including GED) or higher: 91.5% (2008-2012 5-year est.); Bachelor's degree or higher: 23.8% (2008-2012 5-year est.); Master's degree or higher: 8.2% (2008-2012 5-year est.).

Housing: Homeownership rate: 91.9% (2008-2012 5-year est.); Median home value: $287,500 (2008-2012 5-year est.); Median contract rent: $1,292 per month (2008-2012 5-year est.); Median year structure built: 1982 (2008-2012 5-year est.).

Health Insurance: 91.9% Private; 18.4% Public; 2.7% None. (2008-2012 5-year est.)

Transportation: Commute to work: 91.6% car, 0.0% public transportation, 0.0% walk, 7.2% work from home (2008-2012 5-year est.); Travel time to work: 13.0% less than 15 minutes, 32.7% 15 to 30 minutes, 20.1% 30 to

45 minutes, 11.3% 45 to 60 minutes, 22.9% 60 minutes or more (2008-2012 5-year est.)

MAPLE PARK (village). Covers a land area of 2.353 square miles and a water area of 0.003 square miles. Located at 41.92° N. Lat; 88.62° W. Long. Elevation is 863 feet.

Population: 641 (1990); 765 (2000); 1,310 (2010); Density: 526.9 persons per square mile (2008-2012 5-year est.); Race: 96.0% White, 0.0% Black/African American, 1.9% Asian, 0.0% American Indian/Alaska Native, 0.0% Native Hawaiian/Other Pacific Islander, 2.1% Some other race, 2.2% Two or more races, 3.7% Hispanic of any race (2008-2012 5-year est.); Average household size: 2.71 (2008-2012 5-year est.); Median age: 32.4 (2008-2012 5-year est.); Males per 100 females: 101.6 (2008-2012 5-year est.); Marriage status: 19.6% never married, 64.9% now married, 2.4% widowed, 13.2% divorced (2008-2012 5-year est.); Foreign born: 4.0% (2008-2012 5-year est.); Ancestry (includes multiple ancestries): 36.7% German, 17.2% Irish, 14.5% Polish, 11.1% English, 9.8% Italian (2008-2012 5-year est.).

Economy: Single-family building permits issued: 0 (2013); Multi-family building permits issued: 0 (2013); Homeowner vacancy rate: 0.0%. Rental vacancy rate: 0.0%. (2008-2012 5-year est.); Employment by occupation: 13.5% management, business, and financial, 7.0% computer, engineering, and science, 6.4% education, legal, community service, arts, and media, 8.2% healthcare practitioners, 8.1% service, 32.6% sales and office, 13.8% natural resources, construction, and maintenance, 10.5% production, transportation, and material moving (2008-2012 5-year est.).

Income: Per capita income: $26,698 (2008-2012 5-year est.); Median household income: $63,409 (2008-2012 5-year est.); Average household income: $71,650 (2008-2012 5-year est.); Percent of households with income of $100,000 or more: 25.6% (2008-2012 5-year est.); Poverty rate: 6.4% (2008-2012 5-year est.).

Education: Percent of population age 25 and over with: High school diploma (including GED) or higher: 94.4% (2008-2012 5-year est.); Bachelor's degree or higher: 23.9% (2008-2012 5-year est.); Master's degree or higher: 4.6% (2008-2012 5-year est.).

School District(s)

Central CUSD 301 (PK-12)
    2011-12 Enrollment: 3,470 . . . . (847) 464-6005
Fox Valley Career Center (11-12)
    2011-12 Enrollment: n/a . . . . (630) 365-5113
Kaneland CUSD 302 (PK-12)
    2011-12 Enrollment: 4,835 . . . . (630) 365-5111

Housing: Homeownership rate: 80.3% (2008-2012 5-year est.); Median home value: $194,000 (2008-2012 5-year est.); Median contract rent: $1,020 per month (2008-2012 5-year est.); Median year structure built: 1995 (2008-2012 5-year est.).

Health Insurance: 81.5% Private; 21.0% Public; 5.1% None. (2008-2012 5-year est.)

Safety: Violent crime rate: 15.2 per 10,000 population; Property crime rate: 53.2 per 10,000 population (2012).

Transportation: Commute to work: 93.8% car, 1.5% public transportation, 0.8% walk, 3.5% work from home (2008-2012 5-year est.); Travel time to work: 10.6% less than 15 minutes, 32.5% 15 to 30 minutes, 19.9% 30 to 45 minutes, 19.9% 45 to 60 minutes, 17.0% 60 minutes or more (2008-2012 5-year est.)

MOOSEHEART (unincorporated postal area)
Zip Code: 60539
    Covers a land area of 0.749 square miles and a water area of 0.018 square miles. Located at 41.82° N. Lat; 88.33° W. Long. Elevation is 722 feet. Population: 341 (2010); Density: 454.9 persons per square mile (2010); Race: 71.0% White, 20.8% Black/African American, 1.5% Asian, 1.2% American Indian/Alaska Native, 0.0% Native Hawaiian/Other Pacific Islander, 5.5% Some other race, 3.8% Two or more races, 15.2% Hispanic of any race (2010); Average household size: 4.67 (2010); Median age: 15.9 (2010); Males per 100 females: 97.1 (2010); Homeownership rate: 0.0% (2010)

NORTH AURORA (village). Covers a land area of 7.177 square miles and a water area of 0.216 square miles. Located at 41.81° N. Lat; 88.34° W. Long. Elevation is 679 feet.

Population: 5,940 (1990); 10,585 (2000); 16,760 (2010); Density: 2,261.6 persons per square mile (2008-2012 5-year est.); Race: 78.2% White, 6.0% Black/African American, 6.0% Asian, 0.1% American Indian/Alaska Native, 0.0% Native Hawaiian/Other Pacific Islander, 9.7% Some other

race, 2.2% Two or more races, 13.0% Hispanic of any race (2008-2012 5-year est.); Average household size: 2.80 (2008-2012 5-year est.); Median age: 35.6 (2008-2012 5-year est.); Males per 100 females: 90.0 (2008-2012 5-year est.); Marriage status: 25.4% never married, 61.2% now married, 3.9% widowed, 9.6% divorced (2008-2012 5-year est.); Foreign born: 11.8% (2008-2012 5-year est.); Ancestry (includes multiple ancestries): 26.8% German, 13.2% Irish, 8.5% Polish, 7.5% Italian, 7.0% English (2008-2012 5-year est.).

Economy: Single-family building permits issued: 31 (2013); Multi-family building permits issued: 56 (2013); Homeowner vacancy rate: 1.0%. Rental vacancy rate: 7.2%. (2008-2012 5-year est.); Employment by occupation: 20.0% management, business, and financial, 4.8% computer, engineering, and science, 11.7% education, legal, community service, arts, and media, 5.4% healthcare practitioners, 13.8% service, 29.5% sales and office, 5.3% natural resources, construction, and maintenance, 9.5% production, transportation, and material moving (2008-2012 5-year est.).

Income: Per capita income: $33,026 (2008-2012 5-year est.); Median household income: $79,136 (2008-2012 5-year est.); Average household income: $91,743 (2008-2012 5-year est.); Percent of households with income of $100,000 or more: 37.7% (2008-2012 5-year est.); Poverty rate: 6.9% (2008-2012 5-year est.).

Education: Percent of population age 25 and over with: High school diploma (including GED) or higher: 91.8% (2008-2012 5-year est.); Bachelor's degree or higher: 41.0% (2008-2012 5-year est.); Master's degree or higher: 13.5% (2008-2012 5-year est.).

School District(s)
Aurora West USD 129 (PK-12)
　　2011-12 Enrollment: 12,467 . . . . (630) 301-5000

Vocational/Technical School(s)
Everest College-North Aurora (Private, For-profit)
　　Fall 2012 Enrollment: 323 . . . . (630) 896-2140
　　2012-13 Tuition: $16,320

Housing: Homeownership rate: 79.5% (2008-2012 5-year est.); Median home value: $258,200 (2008-2012 5-year est.); Median contract rent: $893 per month (2008-2012 5-year est.); Median year structure built: 1994 (2008-2012 5-year est.).

Health Insurance: 80.5% Private; 18.6% Public; 7.7% None. (2008-2012 5-year est.)

Safety: Violent crime rate: 18.3 per 10,000 population; Property crime rate: 164.2 per 10,000 population (2012).

Transportation: Commute to work: 90.4% car, 2.7% public transportation, 0.9% walk, 4.0% work from home (2008-2012 5-year est.); Travel time to work: 27.0% less than 15 minutes, 33.6% 15 to 30 minutes, 19.1% 30 to 45 minutes, 9.9% 45 to 60 minutes, 10.5% 60 minutes or more (2008-2012 5-year est.)

Additional Information Contacts
Aurora Regional Chamber of Commerce . . . . (630) 256-3180
　　http://www.aurorachamber.com/community_naurora.asp
Village of North Aurora . . . . (630) 897-8228
　　http://www.vil.north-aurora.il.us

PINGREE GROVE (village).
Covers a land area of 3.671 square miles and a water area of 0 square miles. Located at 42.09° N. Lat; 88.44° W. Long. Elevation is 912 feet.

Population: 138 (1990); 124 (2000); 4,532 (2010); Density: 1,205.4 persons per square mile (2008-2012 5-year est.); Race: 73.4% White, 0.2% Black/African American, 2.2% Asian, 0.0% American Indian/Alaska Native, 0.0% Native Hawaiian/Other Pacific Islander, 24.2% Some other race, 1.6% Two or more races, 35.3% Hispanic of any race (2008-2012 5-year est.); Average household size: 3.69 (2008-2012 5-year est.); Median age: 28.6 (2008-2012 5-year est.); Males per 100 females: 91.2 (2008-2012 5-year est.); Marriage status: 21.7% never married, 50.8% now married, 9.8% widowed, 17.6% divorced (2008-2012 5-year est.); Foreign born: 17.0% (2008-2012 5-year est.); Ancestry (includes multiple ancestries): 25.2% Polish, 17.7% German, 11.6% English, 10.6% Irish, 5.8% Swedish (2008-2012 5-year est.).

Economy: Single-family building permits issued: 147 (2013); Multi-family building permits issued: 2 (2013); Homeowner vacancy rate: 2.8%. Rental vacancy rate: 0.0%. (2008-2012 5-year est.); Employment by occupation: 11.7% management, business, and financial, 5.1% computer, engineering, and science, 15.6% education, legal, community service, arts, and media, 3.9% healthcare practitioners, 4.0% service, 32.9% sales and office, 2.6% natural resources, construction, and maintenance, 24.3% production, transportation, and material moving (2008-2012 5-year est.).

Income: Per capita income: $23,480 (2008-2012 5-year est.); Median household income: $74,837 (2008-2012 5-year est.); Average household income: $85,390 (2008-2012 5-year est.); Percent of households with income of $100,000 or more: 25.8% (2008-2012 5-year est.); Poverty rate: 26.1% (2008-2012 5-year est.).

Education: Percent of population age 25 and over with: High school diploma (including GED) or higher: 89.4% (2008-2012 5-year est.); Bachelor's degree or higher: 26.5% (2008-2012 5-year est.); Master's degree or higher: 7.4% (2008-2012 5-year est.).

School District(s)
CUSD 300 (PK-12)
　　2011-12 Enrollment: 20,810 . . . . (847) 551-8308

Housing: Homeownership rate: 83.9% (2008-2012 5-year est.); Median home value: $199,500 (2008-2012 5-year est.); Median contract rent: $1,708 per month (2008-2012 5-year est.); Median year structure built: n/a (2008-2012 5-year est.).

Health Insurance: 72.0% Private; 26.9% Public; 4.6% None. (2008-2012 5-year est.)

Safety: Violent crime rate: 8.7 per 10,000 population; Property crime rate: 48.1 per 10,000 population (2012).

Transportation: Commute to work: 97.9% car, 0.6% public transportation, 0.0% walk, 1.1% work from home (2008-2012 5-year est.); Travel time to work: 3.5% less than 15 minutes, 14.6% 15 to 30 minutes, 27.8% 30 to 45 minutes, 33.5% 45 to 60 minutes, 20.6% 60 minutes or more (2008-2012 5-year est.)

PRESTBURY (CDP).
Covers a land area of 0.635 square miles and a water area of 0.027 square miles. Located at 41.79° N. Lat; 88.42° W. Long.

Population: n/a (1990); n/a (2000); 1,722 (2010); Density: 2,868.6 persons per square mile (2008-2012 5-year est.); Race: 95.2% White, 0.0% Black/African American, 4.8% Asian, 0.0% American Indian/Alaska Native, 0.0% Native Hawaiian/Other Pacific Islander, 0.0% Some other race, 0.0% Two or more races, 6.3% Hispanic of any race (2008-2012 5-year est.); Average household size: 2.74 (2008-2012 5-year est.); Median age: 50.7 (2008-2012 5-year est.); Males per 100 females: 98.7 (2008-2012 5-year est.); Marriage status: 8.0% never married, 78.6% now married, 2.0% widowed, 11.4% divorced (2008-2012 5-year est.); Foreign born: 9.1% (2008-2012 5-year est.); Ancestry (Includes multiple ancestries): 37.7% German, 15.1% Irish, 14.9% Polish, 13.7% English, 8.1% French (2008-2012 5-year est.).

Economy: Homeowner vacancy rate: 0.0%. Rental vacancy rate: 0.0%. (2008-2012 5-year est.); Employment by occupation: 26.2% management, business, and financial, 8.1% computer, engineering, and science, 20.2% education, legal, community service, arts, and media, 3.6% healthcare practitioners, 6.8% service, 28.7% sales and office, 0.0% natural resources, construction, and maintenance, 6.5% production, transportation, and material moving (2008-2012 5-year est.).

Income: Per capita income: $44,130 (2008-2012 5-year est.); Median household income: $117,167 (2008-2012 5-year est.); Average household income: $120,872 (2008-2012 5-year est.); Percent of households with income of $100,000 or more: 56.2% (2008-2012 5-year est.); Poverty rate: 2.1% (2008-2012 5-year est.).

Education: Percent of population age 25 and over with: High school diploma (including GED) or higher: 98.0% (2008-2012 5-year est.); Bachelor's degree or higher: 60.0% (2008-2012 5-year est.); Master's degree or higher: 24.2% (2008-2012 5-year est.).

Housing: Homeownership rate: 100.0% (2008-2012 5-year est.); Median home value: $331,500 (2008-2012 5-year est.); Median contract rent: n/a per month (2008-2012 5-year est.); Median year structure built: 1987 (2008-2012 5-year est.).

Health Insurance: 84.6% Private; 28.6% Public; 5.3% None. (2008-2012 5-year est.)

Transportation: Commute to work: 94.7% car, 0.0% public transportation, 0.0% walk, 5.3% work from home (2008-2012 5-year est.); Travel time to work: 8.1% less than 15 minutes, 44.2% 15 to 30 minutes, 19.1% 30 to 45 minutes, 14.9% 45 to 60 minutes, 13.8% 60 minutes or more (2008-2012 5-year est.)

SAINT CHARLES (city).
Covers a land area of 14.605 square miles and a water area of 0.324 square miles. Located at 41.92° N. Lat; 88.31° W. Long. Elevation is 732 feet.

History: Named for Saint Charles Borromeo (1538-1584), an Italian cardinal. The community of St. Charles developed around a mill in the

mid-1800's, and became a residential area for people moving out from Chicago.

Population: 22,501 (1990); 27,896 (2000); 32,974 (2010); Density: 2,262.6 persons per square mile (2008-2012 5-year est.); Race: 92.0% White, 1.5% Black/African American, 2.4% Asian, 0.1% American Indian/Alaska Native, 0.1% Native Hawaiian/Other Pacific Islander, 3.9% Some other race, 1.1% Two or more races, 9.7% Hispanic of any race (2008-2012 5-year est.); Average household size: 2.62 (2008-2012 5-year est.); Median age: 39.6 (2008-2012 5-year est.); Males per 100 females: 101.5 (2008-2012 5-year est.); Marriage status: 25.7% never married, 59.7% now married, 5.1% widowed, 9.5% divorced (2008-2012 5-year est.); Foreign born: 10.0% (2008-2012 5-year est.); Ancestry (includes multiple ancestries): 31.4% German, 18.9% Irish, 12.4% Italian, 10.4% English, 10.3% Polish (2008-2012 5-year est.).

Economy: Unemployment rate: 5.7% (April 2014); Total civilian labor force: 19,304 (April 2014); Single-family building permits issued: 37 (2013); Multi-family building permits issued: 0 (2013); Homeowner vacancy rate: 1.4%. Rental vacancy rate: 6.1%. (2008-2012 5-year est.); Employment by occupation: 21.9% management, business, and financial, 6.3% computer, engineering, and science, 14.3% education, legal, community service, arts, and media, 4.8% healthcare practitioners, 13.1% service, 27.7% sales and office, 4.4% natural resources, construction, and maintenance, 7.6% production, transportation, and material moving (2008-2012 5-year est.).

Income: Per capita income: $41,627 (2008-2012 5-year est.); Median household income: $80,310 (2008-2012 5-year est.); Average household income: $109,303 (2008-2012 5-year est.); Percent of households with income of $100,000 or more: 41.3% (2008-2012 5-year est.); Poverty rate: 4.1% (2008-2012 5-year est.).

Taxes: Total city taxes per capita: $791 (2011); City property taxes per capita: $422 (2011).

Education: Percent of population age 25 and over with: High school diploma (including GED) or higher: 94.3% (2008-2012 5-year est.); Bachelor's degree or higher: 48.1% (2008-2012 5-year est.); Master's degree or higher: 17.7% (2008-2012 5-year est.).

School District(s)

Idjj SD 428 (06-12)
    2011-12 Enrollment: 784 . . . . (309) 584-0506
Kane Roe (08-12)
    2011-12 Enrollment: n/a . . . . (630) 232-5955
Mid-Valley Special Ed Coop
    2011-12 Enrollment: n/a . . . . (630) 513-4400
Saint Charles CUSD 303 (PK-12)
    2011-12 Enrollment: 13,672 . . . . (630) 513-3030
Saint Charles CUSD 303 (PK-12)
    2011-12 Enrollment: 13,672 . . . . (630) 513-3030

Housing: Homeownership rate: 73.1% (2008-2012 5-year est.); Median home value: $289,000 (2008-2012 5-year est.); Median contract rent: $975 per month (2008-2012 5-year est.); Median year structure built: 1983 (2008-2012 5-year est.).

Health Insurance: 86.4% Private; 18.4% Public; 6.8% None. (2008-2012 5-year est.)

Safety: Violent crime rate: 5.4 per 10,000 population; Property crime rate: 150.7 per 10,000 population (2012).

Transportation: Commute to work: 86.3% car, 3.8% public transportation, 2.3% walk, 7.2% work from home (2008-2012 5-year est.); Travel time to work: 30.1% less than 15 minutes, 24.9% 15 to 30 minutes, 20.1% 30 to 45 minutes, 12.2% 45 to 60 minutes, 12.7% 60 minutes or more (2008-2012 5-year est.)

Additional Information Contacts

City of Saint Charles . . . . (630) 377-4400
   http://www.stcharlesil.gov
St. Charles Chamber of Commerce . . . . (630) 584-8384
   http://www.stcharleschamber.com

SLEEPY HOLLOW (village). Covers a land area of 2.000 square miles and a water area of 0.026 square miles. Located at 42.09° N. Lat; 88.31° W. Long. Elevation is 738 feet.

History: Various streets in the village are named after characters in Washington Irving's The Legend of Sleepy Hollow, including Headless Horseman Drive and Ichabod Crane Drive. Although it shares its name with Washington Irving's famous short story "The Legend of Sleepy Hollow", Sleepy Hollow, Illinois is not the original town about which Irving wrote. That distinction belongs to the town of Sleepy Hollow, New York, formerly known as North Tarrytown.

Population: 3,241 (1990); 3,553 (2000); 3,304 (2010); Density: 1,673.9 persons per square mile (2008-2012 5-year est.); Race: 93.5% White, 1.3% Black/African American, 3.2% Asian, 0.0% American Indian/Alaska Native, 0.0% Native Hawaiian/Other Pacific Islander, 2.0% Some other race, 2.0% Two or more races, 5.8% Hispanic of any race (2008-2012 5-year est.); Average household size: 2.95 (2008-2012 5-year est.); Median age: 42.3 (2008-2012 5-year est.); Males per 100 females: 89.6 (2008-2012 5-year est.); Marriage status: 21.9% never married, 66.7% now married, 3.5% widowed, 7.9% divorced (2008-2012 5-year est.); Foreign born: 8.6% (2008-2012 5-year est.); Ancestry (includes multiple ancestries): 36.3% German, 20.3% Irish, 16.2% Polish, 15.3% Italian, 7.1% English (2008-2012 5-year est.).

Economy: Single-family building permits issued: 0 (2013); Multi-family building permits issued: 0 (2013); Homeowner vacancy rate: 2.6%. Rental vacancy rate: 11.4%. (2008-2012 5-year est.); Employment by occupation: 21.1% management, business, and financial, 6.7% computer, engineering, and science, 5.9% education, legal, community service, arts, and media, 6.4% healthcare practitioners, 11.0% service, 37.9% sales and office, 3.8% natural resources, construction, and maintenance, 7.2% production, transportation, and material moving (2008-2012 5-year est.).

Income: Per capita income: $37,411 (2008-2012 5-year est.); Median household income: $90,031 (2008-2012 5-year est.); Average household income: $109,813 (2008-2012 5-year est.); Percent of households with income of $100,000 or more: 44.2% (2008-2012 5-year est.); Poverty rate: 5.3% (2008-2012 5-year est.).

Education: Percent of population age 25 and over with: High school diploma (including GED) or higher: 98.0% (2008-2012 5-year est.); Bachelor's degree or higher: 38.8% (2008-2012 5-year est.); Master's degree or higher: 13.0% (2008-2012 5-year est.).

School District(s)

CUSD 300 (PK-12)
    2011-12 Enrollment: 20,810 . . . . (847) 551-8308

Housing: Homeownership rate: 91.1% (2008-2012 5-year est.); Median home value: $324,600 (2008-2012 5-year est.); Median contract rent: $896 per month (2008-2012 5-year est.); Median year structure built: 1979 (2008-2012 5-year est.).

Health Insurance: 85.2% Private; 17.7% Public; 7.8% None. (2008-2012 5-year est.)

Safety: Violent crime rate: 6.0 per 10,000 population; Property crime rate: 95.8 per 10,000 population (2012).

Transportation: Commute to work: 91.4% car, 2.2% public transportation, 0.5% walk, 5.1% work from home (2008-2012 5-year est.); Travel time to work: 24.5% less than 15 minutes, 22.8% 15 to 30 minutes, 28.3% 30 to 45 minutes, 12.3% 45 to 60 minutes, 12.0% 60 minutes or more (2008-2012 5-year est.)

Additional Information Contacts

Northern Kane County Chamber of Commerce . . . . (847) 426-8565
   http://www.nkcchamber.com

SOUTH ELGIN (village). Covers a land area of 6.988 square miles and a water area of 0.167 square miles. Located at 41.99° N. Lat; 88.31° W. Long. Elevation is 709 feet.

Population: 7,474 (1990); 16,100 (2000); 21,985 (2010); Density: 3,130.0 persons per square mile (2008-2012 5-year est.); Race: 85.7% White, 3.4% Black/African American, 7.6% Asian, 0.3% American Indian/Alaska Native, 0.0% Native Hawaiian/Other Pacific Islander, 3.0% Some other race, 0.8% Two or more races, 13.2% Hispanic of any race (2008-2012 5-year est.); Average household size: 3.08 (2008-2012 5-year est.); Median age: 34.1 (2008-2012 5-year est.); Males per 100 females: 105.3 (2008-2012 5-year est.); Marriage status: 28.5% never married, 58.2% now married, 4.5% widowed, 8.7% divorced (2008-2012 5-year est.); Foreign born: 11.0% (2008-2012 5-year est.); Ancestry (includes multiple ancestries): 32.5% German, 15.4% Irish, 13.6% Polish, 11.4% Italian, 6.8% English (2008-2012 5-year est.).

Economy: Single-family building permits issued: 3 (2013); Multi-family building permits issued: 0 (2013); Homeowner vacancy rate: 1.1%. Rental vacancy rate: 3.7%. (2008-2012 5-year est.); Employment by occupation: 18.7% management, business, and financial, 6.1% computer, engineering, and science, 10.2% education, legal, community service, arts, and media, 2.7% healthcare practitioners, 11.3% service, 29.1% sales and office, 9.6% natural resources, construction, and maintenance, 12.2% production, transportation, and material moving (2008-2012 5-year est.).

Income: Per capita income: $30,961 (2008-2012 5-year est.); Median household income: $84,061 (2008-2012 5-year est.); Average household income: $94,695 (2008-2012 5-year est.); Percent of households with

income of $100,000 or more: 37.7% (2008-2012 5-year est.); Poverty rate: 3.7% (2008-2012 5-year est.).

Education: Percent of population age 25 and over with: High school diploma (including GED) or higher: 92.4% (2008-2012 5-year est.); Bachelor's degree or higher: 33.7% (2008-2012 5-year est.); Master's degree or higher: 10.6% (2008-2012 5-year est.).

School District(s)

SD U-46 (PK-12)

    2011-12 Enrollment: 40,687 . . . . (847) 888-5000

Saint Charles CUSD 303 (PK-12)

    2011-12 Enrollment: 13,672 . . . . (630) 513-3030

Housing: Homeownership rate: 90.4% (2008-2012 5-year est.); Median home value: $218,600 (2008-2012 5-year est.); Median contract rent: $998 per month (2008-2012 5-year est.); Median year structure built: 1994 (2008-2012 5-year est.).

Health Insurance: 86.2% Private; 11.9% Public; 7.0% None. (2008-2012 5-year est.)

Safety: Violent crime rate: 16.2 per 10,000 population; Property crime rate: 144.5 per 10,000 population (2012).

Transportation: Commute to work: 90.8% car, 2.2% public transportation, 0.7% walk, 6.0% work from home (2008-2012 5-year est.); Travel time to work: 20.8% less than 15 minutes, 25.3% 15 to 30 minutes, 24.1% 30 to 45 minutes, 12.1% 45 to 60 minutes, 17.8% 60 minutes or more (2008-2012 5-year est.)

Additional Information Contacts

Elgin Area Chamber of Commerce . . . . (847) 741-5660

    http://www.elginchamber.com

Village of South Elgin . . . . (847) 742-5780

    http://www.southelgin.com

SUGAR GROVE (village). Covers a land area of 10.467 square miles and a water area of 0.015 square miles. Located at 41.77° N. Lat; 88.45° W. Long. Elevation is 719 feet.

Population: 2,005 (1990); 3,909 (2000); 8,997 (2010); Density: 843.7 persons per square mile (2008-2012 5-year est.); Race: 89.9% White, 0.3% Black/African American, 2.5% Asian, 0.3% American Indian/Alaska Native, 0.0% Native Hawaiian/Other Pacific Islander, 7.0% Some other race, 1.8% Two or more races, 7.7% Hispanic of any race (2008-2012 5-year est.); Average household size: 2.81 (2008-2012 5-year est.); Median age: 39.4 (2008-2012 5-year est.); Males per 100 females: 100.0 (2008-2012 5-year est.); Marriage status: 20.0% never married, 66.9% now married, 2.2% widowed, 10.9% divorced (2008-2012 5-year est.); Foreign born: 4.6% (2008-2012 5-year est.); Ancestry (includes multiple ancestries): 40.3% German, 16.1% Irish, 10.3% English, 10.3% Polish, 7.1% Italian (2008-2012 5-year est.).

Economy: Single-family building permits issued: 27 (2013); Multi-family building permits issued: 0 (2013); Homeowner vacancy rate: 5.2%. Rental vacancy rate: 0.0%. (2008-2012 5-year est.); Employment by occupation: 21.4% management, business, and financial, 5.0% computer, engineering, and science, 9.7% education, legal, community service, arts, and media, 7.4% healthcare practitioners, 12.0% service, 26.6% sales and office, 8.0% natural resources, construction, and maintenance, 9.8% production, transportation, and material moving (2008-2012 5-year est.).

Income: Per capita income: $44,406 (2008-2012 5-year est.); Median household income: $108,021 (2008-2012 5-year est.); Average household income: $122,763 (2008-2012 5-year est.); Percent of households with income of $100,000 or more: 56.6% (2008-2012 5-year est.); Poverty rate: 1.1% (2008-2012 5-year est.).

Education: Percent of population age 25 and over with: High school diploma (including GED) or higher: 96.2% (2008-2012 5-year est.); Bachelor's degree or higher: 40.9% (2008-2012 5-year est.); Master's degree or higher: 11.2% (2008-2012 5-year est.).

School District(s)

Kaneland CUSD 302 (PK-12)

    2011-12 Enrollment: 4,835 . . . . (630) 365-5111

Two-year College(s)

Waubonsee Community College (Public)

    Fall 2012 Enrollment: 11,146 . . . . (630) 466-7900

    2012-13 Tuition: In-state $6,727; Out-of-state $7,288

Housing: Homeownership rate: 91.2% (2008-2012 5-year est.); Median home value: $283,700 (2008-2012 5-year est.); Median contract rent: $1,088 per month (2008-2012 5-year est.); Median year structure built: 2001 (2008-2012 5-year est.).

Health Insurance: 91.2% Private; 13.3% Public; 3.9% None. (2008-2012 5-year est.)

Safety: Violent crime rate: 3.3 per 10,000 population; Property crime rate: 57.2 per 10,000 population (2012).

Transportation: Commute to work: 92.9% car, 1.5% public transportation, 0.3% walk, 3.1% work from home (2008-2012 5-year est.); Travel time to work: 14.7% less than 15 minutes, 29.1% 15 to 30 minutes, 20.2% 30 to 45 minutes, 17.2% 45 to 60 minutes, 18.7% 60 minutes or more (2008-2012 5-year est.)

Additional Information Contacts

Sugar Grove Chamber of Commerce & Industry. . . . . (630) 466-7895

    http://www.sugargrovechamber.org

Village of Sugar Grove . . . . (630) 466-4507

    http://www.sugar-grove.il.us

VIRGIL (village). Covers a land area of 2.109 square miles and a water area of 0 square miles. Located at 41.96° N. Lat; 88.53° W. Long. Elevation is 869 feet.

Population: n/a (1990); 266 (2000); 329 (2010); Density: 177.8 persons per square mile (2008-2012 5-year est.); Race: 95.5% White, 0.0% Black/African American, 4.5% Asian, 0.0% American Indian/Alaska Native, 0.0% Native Hawaiian/Other Pacific Islander, 0.0% Some other race, 0.0% Two or more races, 0.0% Hispanic of any race (2008-2012 5-year est.); Average household size: 3.27 (2008-2012 5-year est.); Median age: 38.9 (2008-2012 5-year est.); Males per 100 females: 119.3 (2008-2012 5-year est.); Marriage status: 30.6% never married, 65.7% now married, 1.9% widowed, 1.9% divorced (2008-2012 5-year est.); Foreign born: 3.2% (2008-2012 5-year est.); Ancestry (includes multiple ancestries): 44.5% German, 17.3% Swedish, 14.1% Polish, 10.9% Italian, 10.9% American (2008-2012 5-year est.).

Economy: Homeowner vacancy rate: 0.0%. Rental vacancy rate: 38.5%. (2008-2012 5-year est.); Employment by occupation: 13.6% management, business, and financial, 1.0% computer, engineering, and science, 5.6% education, legal, community service, arts, and media, 0.0% healthcare practitioners, 13.6% service, 29.3% sales and office, 11.1% natural resources, construction, and maintenance, 25.8% production, transportation, and material moving (2008-2012 5-year est.).

Income: Per capita income: $24,889 (2008-2012 5-year est.); Median household income: $85,417 (2008-2012 5-year est.); Average household income: $79,643 (2008-2012 5-year est.); Percent of households with income of $100,000 or more: 19.5% (2008-2012 5-year est.); Poverty rate: 5.9% (2008-2012 5-year est.).

Education: Percent of population age 25 and over with: High school diploma (including GED) or higher: 91.7% (2008-2012 5-year est.); Bachelor's degree or higher: 18.4% (2008-2012 5-year est.); Master's degree or higher: 4.4% (2008-2012 5-year est.).

Housing: Homeownership rate: 92.9% (2008-2012 5-year est.); Median home value: $232,100 (2008-2012 5-year est.); Median contract rent: $1,250 per month (2008-2012 5-year est.); Median year structure built: 1973 (2008-2012 5-year est.).

Health Insurance: 76.5% Private; 10.4% Public; 18.1% None. (2008-2012 5-year est.)

Transportation: Commute to work: 98.5% car, 0.0% public transportation, 0.0% walk, 1.5% work from home (2008-2012 5-year est.); Travel time to work: 14.9% less than 15 minutes, 40.0% 15 to 30 minutes, 31.3% 30 to 45 minutes, 4.1% 45 to 60 minutes, 9.7% 60 minutes or more (2008-2012 5-year est.)

WEST DUNDEE (village). Aka Dundee. Covers a land area of 3.714 square miles and a water area of 0.101 square miles. Located at 42.11° N. Lat; 88.34° W. Long. Elevation is 761 feet.

History: West Dundee was settled by Scots and English in the 1830's, and named for Dundee, Scotland. Allan Pinkerton (1819-1884) operated a coopers trade in West Dundee, but found a second career as a detective when his evidence resulted in the capture of some counterfeiters.

Population: 3,728 (1990); 5,428 (2000); 7,331 (2010); Density: 1,967.2 persons per square mile (2008-2012 5-year est.); Race: 84.2% White, 4.2% Black/African American, 10.4% Asian, 0.0% American Indian/Alaska Native, 0.0% Native Hawaiian/Other Pacific Islander, 1.2% Some other race, 1.3% Two or more races, 4.8% Hispanic of any race (2008-2012 5-year est.); Average household size: 2.55 (2008-2012 5-year est.); Median age: 40.5 (2008-2012 5-year est.); Males per 100 females: 100.2 (2008-2012 5-year est.); Marriage status: 25.1% never married, 63.4% now married, 2.8% widowed, 8.7% divorced (2008-2012 5-year est.); Foreign born: 13.3% (2008-2012 5-year est.); Ancestry (includes multiple ancestries): 34.4% German, 22.9% Irish, 12.0% Polish, 9.3% Italian, 8.9% English (2008-2012 5-year est.).

Economy: Single-family building permits issued: 5 (2013); Multi-family building permits issued: 0 (2013); Homeowner vacancy rate: 1.8%. Rental vacancy rate: 3.2%. (2008-2012 5-year est.); Employment by occupation: 19.3% management, business, and financial, 6.6% computer, engineering, and science, 15.0% education, legal, community service, arts, and media, 4.8% healthcare practitioners, 12.9% service, 28.1% sales and office, 2.7% natural resources, construction, and maintenance, 10.7% production, transportation, and material moving (2008-2012 5-year est.).
Income: Per capita income: $36,181 (2008-2012 5-year est.); Median household income: $76,786 (2008-2012 5-year est.); Average household income: $90,764 (2008-2012 5-year est.); Percent of households with income of $100,000 or more: 35.7% (2008-2012 5-year est.); Poverty rate: 7.4% (2008-2012 5-year est.).
Education: Percent of population age 25 and over with: High school diploma (including GED) or higher: 93.9% (2008-2012 5-year est.); Bachelor's degree or higher: 47.2% (2008-2012 5-year est.); Master's degree or higher: 16.2% (2008-2012 5-year est.).

School District(s)

CUSD 300 (PK-12)
   2011-12 Enrollment: 20,810 . . . . (847) 551-8308

Two-year College(s)

Hair Professionals Academy of Cosmetology (Private, For-profit)
   Fall 2012 Enrollment: 196 . . . . (847) 836-5900
Housing: Homeownership rate: 69.0% (2008-2012 5-year est.); Median home value: $276,100 (2008-2012 5-year est.); Median contract rent: $1,062 per month (2008-2012 5-year est.); Median year structure built: 1983 (2008-2012 5-year est.).
Health Insurance: 85.8% Private; 15.9% Public; 7.8% None. (2008-2012 5-year est.)
Safety: Violent crime rate: 5.4 per 10,000 population; Property crime rate: 337.6 per 10,000 population (2012).
Transportation: Commute to work: 85.6% car, 2.3% public transportation, 5.2% walk, 6.1% work from home (2008-2012 5-year est.); Travel time to work: 29.3% less than 15 minutes, 24.4% 15 to 30 minutes, 23.7% 30 to 45 minutes, 12.3% 45 to 60 minutes, 10.4% 60 minutes or more (2008-2012 5-year est.)
Additional Information Contacts
Northern Kane County Chamber of Commerce . . . . (847) 426-8565
   http://www.nkcchamber.com
Village of West Dundee. . . . . (847) 551-3800
   http://www.wdundee.org

Kankakee County

Located in northeastern Illinois; bounded on the east by Indiana; drained by the Kankakee and Iroquois Rivers. Covers a land area of 676.556 square miles, a water area of 4.808 square miles, and is located in the Central Time Zone at 41.14° N. Lat., 87.86° W. Long. The county was founded in 1853. County seat is Kankakee.

Kankakee County is part of the Kankakee, IL Metropolitan Statistical Area. The entire metro area includes: Kankakee County, IL

Weather Station: Kankakee Metro Wastwater										Elevation: 640 feet	
	Jan	Feb	Mar	Apr	May	Jun	Jul	Aug	Sep	Oct	Nov	Dec
High	33	37	48	61	73	82	85	83	78	65	51	37
Low	15	18	28	38	49	59	63	61	52	41	32	20
Precip	1.9	1.8	2.6	3.5	4.8	3.9	4.7	3.3	3.0	3.1	3.5	2.5
Snow	7.7	6.5	2.8	0.9	tr	0.0	0.0	0.0	0.0	tr	0.7	5.5

High and Low temperatures in degrees Fahrenheit; Precipitation and Snow in inches

Population: 96,255 (1990); 103,833 (2000); 113,449 (2010); Race: 79.3% White, 14.9% Black/African American, 1.1% Asian, 0.1% American Indian/Alaska Native, 0.0% Native Hawaiian/Other Pacific Islander, 4.6% Some other race, 2.2% Two or more races, 8.9% Hispanic of any race (2008-2012 5-year est.); Density: 166.8 persons per square mile (2008-2012 5-year est.); Average household size: 2.64 (2008-2012 5-year est.); Median age: 36.7 (2008-2012 5-year est.); Males per 100 females: 96.5 (2008-2012 5-year est.).
Religion: Six largest groups: 24.5% Catholicism, 5.3% Baptist, 4.7% Holiness, 4.1% Methodist/Pietist, 4.1% Lutheran, 2.5% Non-denominational Protestant (2010)
Economy: Unemployment rate: 8.7% (April 2014); Total civilian labor force: 54,760 (April 2014); Leading industries: 20.0% health care and social assistance; 15.1% retail trade; 13.7% manufacturing (2012); Farms: 818 totaling 342,637 acres (2012); Companies that employ 500 or more

persons: 7 (2012); Companies that employ 100 to 499 persons: 49 (2012); Companies that employ less than 100 persons: 2,314 (2012); Black-owned businesses: n/a (2007); Hispanic-owned businesses: n/a (2007); Asian-owned businesses: n/a (2007); Women-owned businesses: 2,356 (2007); Single-family building permits issued: 112 (2013); Multi-family building permits issued: 0 (2013).
Income: Per capita income: $23,535 (2008-2012 5-year est.); Median household income: $49,994 (2008-2012 5-year est.); Average household income: $62,452 (2008-2012 5-year est.); Percent of households with income of $100,000 or more: 18.0% (2008-2012 5-year est.); Poverty rate: 16.1% (2008-2012 5-year est.); Bankruptcy rate: 3.80% (2013).
Taxes: Total county taxes per capita: $144 (2011); County property taxes per capita: $140 (2011).
Education: Percent of population age 25 and over with: High school diploma (including GED) or higher: 85.6% (2008-2012 5-year est.); Bachelor's degree or higher: 16.9% (2008-2012 5-year est.); Master's degree or higher: 6.4% (2008-2012 5-year est.).
Housing: Homeownership rate: 69.2% (2008-2012 5-year est.); Median home value: $149,200 (2008-2012 5-year est.); Median contract rent: $625 per month (2008-2012 5-year est.); Median year structure built: 1971 (2008-2012 5-year est.)
Health: Birth rate: 119.1 per 10,000 population (2013); Death rate: 97.2 per 10,000 population (2013); Age-adjusted cancer mortality rate: 188.5 deaths per 100,000 population (2011); Number of physicians: 14.7 per 10,000 population (2011); Hospital beds: 41.3 per 10,000 population (2010); Hospital admissions: 1,683.5 per 10,000 population (2010).
Elections: 2012 Presidential election results: 47.5% Obama, 50.9% Romney
Additional Information Contacts
Kankakee County Government . . . . (815) 937-2990
   http://www.co.kankakee.il.us
Kankakee County Chamber of Commerce . . . . (815) 351-9068
   http://www.kankakeecountychamber.com

Kankakee County Communities

AROMA PARK (village). Covers a land area of 1.857 square miles and a water area of 0.261 square miles. Located at 41.07° N. Lat; 87.81° W. Long. Elevation is 617 feet.
Population: 690 (1990); 821 (2000); 743 (2010); Density: 314.4 persons per square mile (2008-2012 5-year est.); Race: 94.5% White, 2.7% Black/African American, 0.0% Asian, 0.0% American Indian/Alaska Native, 0.0% Native Hawaiian/Other Pacific Islander, 2.8% Some other race, 0.0% Two or more races, 8.6% Hispanic of any race (2008-2012 5-year est.); Average household size: 2.57 (2008-2012 5-year est.); Median age: 43.1 (2008-2012 5-year est.); Males per 100 females: 102.1 (2008-2012 5-year est.); Marriage status: 26.9% never married, 56.5% now married, 10.9% widowed, 5.7% divorced (2008-2012 5-year est.); Foreign born: 0.7% (2008-2012 5-year est.); Ancestry (includes multiple ancestries): 29.3% German, 15.6% French, 15.1% Irish, 11.0% English, 9.4% Dutch (2008-2012 5-year est.).
Economy: Single-family building permits issued: 0 (2013); Multi-family building permits issued: 0 (2013); Homeowner vacancy rate: 5.0%. Rental vacancy rate: 0.0%. (2008-2012 5-year est.); Employment by occupation: 9.7% management, business, and financial, 2.2% computer, engineering, and science, 11.2% education, legal, community service, arts, and media, 7.1% healthcare practitioners, 17.2% service, 19.4% sales and office, 10.4% natural resources, construction, and maintenance, 22.8% production, transportation, and material moving (2008-2012 5-year est.).
Income: Per capita income: $23,309 (2008-2012 5-year est.); Median household income: $46,607 (2008-2012 5-year est.); Average household income: $57,908 (2008-2012 5-year est.); Percent of households with income of $100,000 or more: 10.2% (2008-2012 5-year est.); Poverty rate: 7.8% (2008-2012 5-year est.).
Education: Percent of population age 25 and over with: High school diploma (including GED) or higher: 86.0% (2008-2012 5-year est.); Bachelor's degree or higher: 13.3% (2008-2012 5-year est.); Master's degree or higher: 7.1% (2008-2012 5-year est.).

School District(s)

Kankakee SD 111 (PK-12)
   2011-12 Enrollment: 5,670 . . . . (815) 933-0700
Housing: Homeownership rate: 92.0% (2008-2012 5-year est.); Median home value: $100,800 (2008-2012 5-year est.); Median contract rent: $440 per month (2008-2012 5-year est.); Median year structure built: 1955 (2008-2012 5-year est.).

Health Insurance: 62.0% Private; 39.4% Public; 13.1% None. (2008-2012 5-year est.)

Transportation: Commute to work: 96.2% car, 0.0% public transportation, 1.5% walk, 2.3% work from home (2008-2012 5-year est.); Travel time to work: 17.0% less than 15 minutes, 44.4% 15 to 30 minutes, 12.4% 30 to 45 minutes, 16.6% 45 to 60 minutes, 9.7% 60 minutes or more (2008-2012 5-year est.)

Additional Information Contacts

Kankakee County Chamber of Commerce . . . . (815) 351-9068
  http://www.kankakeecountychamber.com

BONFIELD (village). Covers a land area of 0.492 square miles and a water area of 0 square miles. Located at 41.15° N. Lat; 88.05° W. Long. Elevation is 630 feet.

Population: 299 (1990); 364 (2000); 382 (2010); Density: 563.3 persons per square mile (2008-2012 5-year est.); Race: 98.2% White, 0.7% Black/African American, 0.0% Asian, 0.0% American Indian/Alaska Native, 0.0% Native Hawaiian/Other Pacific Islander, 1.1% Some other race, 1.1% Two or more races, 0.7% Hispanic of any race (2008-2012 5-year est.); Average household size: 2.43 (2008-2012 5-year est.); Median age: 48.3 (2008-2012 5-year est.); Males per 100 females: 89.7 (2008-2012 5-year est.); Marriage status: 21.4% never married, 60.9% now married, 7.6% widowed, 10.1% divorced (2008-2012 5-year est.); Foreign born: 0.0% (2008-2012 5-year est.); Ancestry (includes multiple ancestries): 53.4% German, 14.4% American, 12.3% Irish, 10.5% French, 6.5% English (2008-2012 5-year est.).

Economy: Single-family building permits issued: 0 (2013); Multi-family building permits issued: 0 (2013); Homeowner vacancy rate: 0.0%. Rental vacancy rate: 0.0%. (2008-2012 5-year est.); Employment by occupation: 4.4% management, business, and financial, 2.9% computer, engineering, and science, 5.8% education, legal, community service, arts, and media, 12.4% healthcare practitioners, 13.1% service, 32.1% sales and office, 18.2% natural resources, construction, and maintenance, 10.9% production, transportation, and material moving (2008-2012 5-year est.).

Income: Per capita income: $28,801 (2008-2012 5-year est.); Median household income: $63,333 (2008-2012 5-year est.); Average household income: $71,865 (2008-2012 5-year est.); Percent of households with income of $100,000 or more: 16.7% (2008-2012 5-year est.); Poverty rate: 3.6% (2008-2012 5-year est.).

Education: Percent of population age 25 and over with: High school diploma (including GED) or higher: 92.6% (2008-2012 5-year est.); Bachelor's degree or higher: 7.9% (2008-2012 5-year est.); Master's degree or higher: 3.2% (2008-2012 5-year est.).

School District(s)

Herscher CUSD 2 (PK-12)
  2011-12 Enrollment: 1,980 . . . . (815) 426-2162

Housing: Homeownership rate: 90.4% (2008-2012 5-year est.); Median home value: $160,200 (2008-2012 5-year est.); Median contract rent: $542 per month (2008-2012 5-year est.); Median year structure built: 1970 (2008-2012 5-year est.).

Health Insurance: 82.7% Private; 28.5% Public; 6.9% None. (2008-2012 5-year est.)

Transportation: Commute to work: 88.5% car, 0.0% public transportation, 2.5% walk, 1.6% work from home (2008-2012 5-year est.); Travel time to work: 19.2% less than 15 minutes, 48.3% 15 to 30 minutes, 12.5% 30 to 45 minutes, 10.0% 45 to 60 minutes, 10.0% 60 minutes or more (2008-2012 5-year est.)

BOURBONNAIS (village). Covers a land area of 9.306 square miles and a water area of 0 square miles. Located at 41.18° N. Lat; 87.88° W. Long. Elevation is 650 feet.

History: Fur trader Noel La Vasseur established a trading post here in 1832, which drew French-Canadian settlers to the community named for Francois Bourbonnais. Bourbonnais was the first settlement on the Kankakee River.

Population: 13,934 (1990); 15,256 (2000); 18,631 (2010); Density: 1,996.8 persons per square mile (2008-2012 5-year est.); Race: 82.4% White, 12.0% Black/African American, 2.3% Asian, 0.3% American Indian/Alaska Native, 0.1% Native Hawaiian/Other Pacific Islander, 2.9% Some other race, 2.2% Two or more races, 3.9% Hispanic of any race (2008-2012 5-year est.); Average household size: 2.67 (2008-2012 5-year est.); Median age: 33.1 (2008-2012 5-year est.); Males per 100 females: 94.0 (2008-2012 5-year est.); Marriage status: 36.6% never married, 48.0% now married, 6.1% widowed, 9.3% divorced (2008-2012 5-year est.); Foreign born: 2.6% (2008-2012 5-year est.); Ancestry (includes

multiple ancestries): 28.8% German, 14.0% Irish, 9.5% French, 8.6% Polish, 8.4% English (2008-2012 5-year est.).

Economy: Single-family building permits issued: 50 (2013); Multi-family building permits issued: 0 (2013); Homeowner vacancy rate: 3.1%. Rental vacancy rate: 6.2%. (2008-2012 5-year est.); Employment by occupation: 13.1% management, business, and financial, 3.7% computer, engineering, and science, 13.8% education, legal, community service, arts, and media, 5.6% healthcare practitioners, 15.9% service, 26.7% sales and office, 8.4% natural resources, construction, and maintenance, 13.0% production, transportation, and material moving (2008-2012 5-year est.).

Income: Per capita income: $25,891 (2008-2012 5-year est.); Median household income: $62,027 (2008-2012 5-year est.); Average household income: $74,322 (2008-2012 5-year est.); Percent of households with income of $100,000 or more: 26.2% (2008-2012 5-year est.); Poverty rate: 12.5% (2008-2012 5-year est.).

Education: Percent of population age 25 and over with: High school diploma (including GED) or higher: 91.9% (2008-2012 5-year est.); Bachelor's degree or higher: 25.8% (2008-2012 5-year est.); Master's degree or higher: 10.2% (2008-2012 5-year est.).

School District(s)

Bourbonnais SD 53 (PK-08)
  2011-12 Enrollment: 2,555 . . . . (815) 929-5100
Kankakee Area Career Center (11-12)
  2011-12 Enrollment: n/a . . . . (815) 939-4971
Saint George CCSD 258 (PK-08)
  2011-12 Enrollment: 518 . . . . (815) 802-3102

Four-year College(s)

Olivet Nazarene University (Private, Not-for-profit, Church of the Nazarene)
  Fall 2012 Enrollment: 4,511 . . . . (815) 939-5011
  2012-13 Tuition: In-state $28,090; Out-of-state $28,090

Two-year College(s)

Paul Mitchell the school-Bradley Campus (Private, For-profit)
  Fall 2012 Enrollment: 365 . . . . (815) 932-5049

Housing: Homeownership rate: 65.9% (2008-2012 5-year est.); Median home value: $181,100 (2008-2012 5-year est.); Median contract rent: $740 per month (2008-2012 5-year est.); Median year structure built: 1979 (2008-2012 5-year est.).

Health Insurance: 76.3% Private; 24.2% Public; 10.5% None. (2008-2012 5-year est.)

Transportation: Commute to work: 89.7% car, 2.1% public transportation, 4.0% walk, 3.0% work from home (2008-2012 5-year est.); Travel time to work: 49.1% less than 15 minutes, 30.9% 15 to 30 minutes, 7.6% 30 to 45 minutes, 4.5% 45 to 60 minutes, 7.8% 60 minutes or more (2008-2012 5-year est.)

Additional Information Contacts

Kankakee County Chamber of Commerce . . . . (815) 351-9068
  http://www.kankakeecountychamber.com
Village of Bourbonnais . . . . (815) 937-3570
  http://www.villageofbourbonnais.com

BRADLEY (village). Covers a land area of 7.245 square miles and a water area of 0 square miles. Located at 41.16° N. Lat; 87.85° W. Long. Elevation is 636 feet.

History: Bradley was known as North Kankakee when it was organized in 1892, but soon was renamed for resident and factory-owner David Bradley.

Population: 10,792 (1990); 12,784 (2000); 15,895 (2010); Density: 2,177.8 persons per square mile (2008-2012 5-year est.); Race: 93.2% White, 4.0% Black/African American, 1.6% Asian, 0.1% American Indian/Alaska Native, 0.0% Native Hawaiian/Other Pacific Islander, 1.1% Some other race, 0.7% Two or more races, 6.5% Hispanic of any race (2008-2012 5-year est.); Average household size: 2.52 (2008-2012 5-year est.); Median age: 35.1 (2008-2012 5-year est.); Males per 100 females: 93.1 (2008-2012 5-year est.); Marriage status: 34.6% never married, 47.6% now married, 6.5% widowed, 11.4% divorced (2008-2012 5-year est.); Foreign born: 3.7% (2008-2012 5-year est.); Ancestry (includes multiple ancestries): 27.5% German, 15.7% Irish, 13.6% French, 8.0% English, 7.8% Polish (2008-2012 5-year est.).

Economy: Single-family building permits issued: 21 (2013); Multi-family building permits issued: 0 (2013); Homeowner vacancy rate: 1.1%. Rental vacancy rate: 5.5%. (2008-2012 5-year est.); Employment by occupation: 7.4% management, business, and financial, 2.6% computer, engineering, and science, 8.0% education, legal, community service, arts, and media, 5.5% healthcare practitioners, 22.9% service, 26.7% sales and office,

8.7% natural resources, construction, and maintenance, 18.3% production, transportation, and material moving (2008-2012 5-year est.).
Income: Per capita income: $26,154 (2008-2012 5-year est.); Median household income: $51,460 (2008-2012 5-year est.); Average household income: $64,854 (2008-2012 5-year est.); Percent of households with income of $100,000 or more: 19.7% (2008-2012 5-year est.); Poverty rate: 8.5% (2008-2012 5-year est.).
Education: Percent of population age 25 and over with: High school diploma (including GED) or higher: 90.9% (2008-2012 5-year est.); Bachelor's degree or higher: 16.6% (2008-2012 5-year est.); Master's degree or higher: 5.0% (2008-2012 5-year est.).

School District(s)
Bradley Bourbonnais CHSD 307 (09-12)
    2011-12 Enrollment: 2,109 . . . . (815) 937-3701
Bradley SD 61 (PK-08)
    2011-12 Enrollment: 1,661 . . . . (815) 933-3371
Housing: Homeownership rate: 66.3% (2008-2012 5-year est.); Median home value: $136,800 (2008-2012 5-year est.); Median contract rent: $739 per month (2008-2012 5-year est.); Median year structure built: 1973 (2008-2012 5-year est.).
Health Insurance: 73.4% Private; 28.0% Public; 9.9% None. (2008-2012 5-year est.)
Safety: Violent crime rate: 33.9 per 10,000 population; Property crime rate: 468.0 per 10,000 population (2012).
Transportation: Commute to work: 92.7% car, 1.3% public transportation, 1.2% walk, 3.0% work from home (2008-2012 5-year est.); Travel time to work: 48.7% less than 15 minutes, 24.6% 15 to 30 minutes, 8.4% 30 to 45 minutes, 8.5% 45 to 60 minutes, 9.7% 60 minutes or more (2008-2012 5-year est.)
Additional Information Contacts
Kankakee County Chamber of Commerce . . . . (815) 351-9068
  http://www.kankakeecountychamber.com
Village of Bradley . . . . (815) 932-2125
  http://www.bradleyil.org

BUCKINGHAM (village). Covers a land area of 0.252 square miles and a water area of 0 square miles. Located at 41.05° N. Lat; 88.17° W. Long. Elevation is 656 feet.
Population: 340 (1990); 237 (2000); 300 (2010); Density: 1,258.9 persons per square mile (2008-2012 5-year est.); Race: 96.5% White, 0.0% Black/African American, 0.0% Asian, 0.0% American Indian/Alaska Native, 0.0% Native Hawaiian/Other Pacific Islander, 3.5% Some other race, 3.5% Two or more races, 0.0% Hispanic of any race (2008-2012 5-year est.); Average household size: 3.37 (2008-2012 5-year est.); Median age: 29.9 (2008-2012 5-year est.); Males per 100 females: 98.1 (2008-2012 5-year est.); Marriage status: 41.5% never married, 39.4% now married, 7.7% widowed, 11.4% divorced (2008-2012 5-year est.); Foreign born: 0.0% (2008-2012 5-year est.); Ancestry (includes multiple ancestries): 29.3% German, 19.6% Italian, 13.2% Irish, 12.0% French, 10.4% Polish (2008-2012 5-year est.).
Economy: Single-family building permits issued: 0 (2013); Multi-family building permits issued: 0 (2013); Homeowner vacancy rate: 5.6%. Rental vacancy rate: 0.0%. (2008-2012 5-year est.); Employment by occupation: 4.7% management, business, and financial, 0.0% computer, engineering, and science, 3.1% education, legal, community service, arts, and media, 5.5% healthcare practitioners, 24.4% service, 29.1% sales and office, 16.5% natural resources, construction, and maintenance, 16.5% production, transportation, and material moving (2008-2012 5-year est.).
Income: Per capita income: $19,310 (2008-2012 5-year est.); Median household income: $51,875 (2008-2012 5-year est.); Average household income: $59,540 (2008-2012 5-year est.); Percent of households with income of $100,000 or more: 7.5% (2008-2012 5-year est.); Poverty rate: 16.7% (2008-2012 5-year est.).
Education: Percent of population age 25 and over with: High school diploma (including GED) or higher: 84.8% (2008-2012 5-year est.); Bachelor's degree or higher: 7.0% (2008-2012 5-year est.); Master's degree or higher: 0.0% (2008-2012 5-year est.).
Housing: Homeownership rate: 72.3% (2008-2012 5-year est.); Median home value: $92,500 (2008-2012 5-year est.); Median contract rent: $614 per month (2008-2012 5-year est.); Median year structure built: 1969 (2008-2012 5-year est.).
Health Insurance: 42.0% Private; 34.4% Public; 27.1% None. (2008-2012 5-year est.)
Transportation: Commute to work: 100.0% car, 0.0% public transportation, 0.0% walk, 0.0% work from home (2008-2012 5-year est.);

Travel time to work: 10.2% less than 15 minutes, 55.9% 15 to 30 minutes, 25.2% 30 to 45 minutes, 8.7% 45 to 60 minutes, 0.0% 60 minutes or more (2008-2012 5-year est.)

ESSEX (village). Covers a land area of 2.478 square miles and a water area of 0.026 square miles. Located at 41.18° N. Lat; 88.19° W. Long. Elevation is 591 feet.
Population: 482 (1990); 554 (2000); 802 (2010); Density: 331.7 persons per square mile (2008-2012 5-year est.); Race: 99.3% White, 0.0% Black/African American, 0.0% Asian, 0.0% American Indian/Alaska Native, 0.0% Native Hawaiian/Other Pacific Islander, 0.7% Some other race, 0.7% Two or more races, 4.3% Hispanic of any race (2008-2012 5-year est.); Average household size: 3.25 (2008-2012 5-year est.); Median age: 35.5 (2008-2012 5-year est.); Males per 100 females: 115.7 (2008-2012 5-year est.); Marriage status: 22.5% never married, 66.3% now married, 4.9% widowed, 6.4% divorced (2008-2012 5-year est.); Foreign born: 0.0% (2008-2012 5-year est.); Ancestry (includes multiple ancestries): 40.8% German, 22.3% Irish, 13.9% Polish, 12.7% Italian, 6.2% English (2008-2012 5-year est.).
Economy: Single-family building permits issued: 0 (2013); Multi-family building permits issued: 0 (2013); Homeowner vacancy rate: 4.9%. Rental vacancy rate: 0.0%. (2008-2012 5-year est.); Employment by occupation: 7.2% management, business, and financial, 0.5% computer, engineering, and science, 14.2% education, legal, community service, arts, and media, 3.6% healthcare practitioners, 16.0% service, 26.4% sales and office, 18.3% natural resources, construction, and maintenance, 13.7% production, transportation, and material moving (2008-2012 5-year est.).
Income: Per capita income: $25,277 (2008-2012 5-year est.); Median household income: $77,031 (2008-2012 5-year est.); Average household income: $78,978 (2008-2012 5-year est.); Percent of households with income of $100,000 or more: 36.0% (2008-2012 5-year est.); Poverty rate: 2.9% (2008-2012 5-year est.).
Education: Percent of population age 25 and over with: High school diploma (including GED) or higher: 91.5% (2008-2012 5-year est.); Bachelor's degree or higher: 15.6% (2008-2012 5-year est.); Master's degree or higher: 2.8% (2008-2012 5-year est.).
Housing: Homeownership rate: 92.1% (2008-2012 5-year est.); Median home value: $197,500 (2008-2012 5-year est.); Median contract rent: $625 per month (2008-2012 5-year est.); Median year structure built: 1996 (2008-2012 5-year est.).
Health Insurance: 83.5% Private; 14.8% Public; 8.6% None. (2008-2012 5-year est.)
Transportation: Commute to work: 93.0% car, 0.0% public transportation, 0.0% walk, 3.9% work from home (2008-2012 5-year est.); Travel time to work: 16.1% less than 15 minutes, 25.0% 15 to 30 minutes, 39.5% 30 to 45 minutes, 4.6% 45 to 60 minutes, 14.8% 60 minutes or more (2008-2012 5-year est.)

GRANT PARK (village). Covers a land area of 3.414 square miles and a water area of 0.026 square miles. Located at 41.24° N. Lat; 87.64° W. Long. Elevation is 699 feet.
Population: 1,024 (1990); 1,358 (2000); 1,331 (2010); Density: 443.4 persons per square mile (2008-2012 5-year est.); Race: 97.2% White, 0.3% Black/African American, 0.4% Asian, 0.9% American Indian/Alaska Native, 0.0% Native Hawaiian/Other Pacific Islander, 1.2% Some other race, 1.1% Two or more races, 3.0% Hispanic of any race (2008-2012 5-year est.); Average household size: 2.69 (2008-2012 5-year est.); Median age: 40.5 (2008-2012 5-year est.); Males per 100 females: 88.3 (2008-2012 5-year est.); Marriage status: 21.9% never married, 61.8% now married, 6.1% widowed, 10.2% divorced (2008-2012 5-year est.); Foreign born: 0.9% (2008-2012 5-year est.); Ancestry (includes multiple ancestries): 43.0% German, 17.1% Irish, 16.2% Italian, 13.1% Polish, 6.0% Swedish (2008-2012 5-year est.).
Economy: Single-family building permits issued: 0 (2013); Multi-family building permits issued: 0 (2013); Homeowner vacancy rate: 0.0%. Rental vacancy rate: 0.0%. (2008-2012 5-year est.); Employment by occupation: 7.5% management, business, and financial, 3.5% computer, engineering, and science, 4.0% education, legal, community service, arts, and media, 6.3% healthcare practitioners, 23.8% service, 18.6% sales and office, 17.0% natural resources, construction, and maintenance, 19.3% production, transportation, and material moving (2008-2012 5-year est.).
Income: Per capita income: $25,192 (2008-2012 5-year est.); Median household income: $54,559 (2008-2012 5-year est.); Average household income: $65,710 (2008-2012 5-year est.); Percent of households with

income of $100,000 or more: 20.3% (2008-2012 5-year est.); Poverty rate: 7.9% (2008-2012 5-year est.).

Education: Percent of population age 25 and over with: High school diploma (including GED) or higher: 90.1% (2008-2012 5-year est.); Bachelor's degree or higher: 12.9% (2008-2012 5-year est.); Master's degree or higher: 5.6% (2008-2012 5-year est.).

School District(s)

Grant Park CUSD 6 (PK-12)

    2011-12 Enrollment: 570. . . . . (815) 465-6013

Housing: Homeownership rate: 68.9% (2008-2012 5-year est.); Median home value: $185,100 (2008-2012 5-year est.); Median contract rent: $593 per month (2008-2012 5-year est.); Median year structure built: 1961 (2008-2012 5-year est.).

Health Insurance: 68.2% Private; 25.4% Public; 18.0% None. (2008-2012 5-year est.)

Safety: Violent crime rate: 0.0 per 10,000 population; Property crime rate: 104.9 per 10,000 population (2012).

Transportation: Commute to work: 93.3% car, 0.3% public transportation, 4.3% walk, 1.8% work from home (2008-2012 5-year est.); Travel time to work: 25.7% less than 15 minutes, 19.1% 15 to 30 minutes, 28.6% 30 to 45 minutes, 12.9% 45 to 60 minutes, 13.7% 60 minutes or more (2008-2012 5-year est.).

Additional Information Contacts

Grant Park Chamber of Commerce. . . . . (815) 465-6531
http://grantparkchamber.org

HERSCHER (village). Covers a land area of 1.810 square miles and a water area of 0 square miles. Located at 41.05° N. Lat; 88.10° W. Long. Elevation is 659 feet.

Population: 1,278 (1990); 1,523 (2000); 1,591 (2010); Density: 941.3 persons per square mile (2008-2012 5-year est.); Race: 97.8% White, 0.0% Black/African American, 0.6% Asian, 0.2% American Indian/Alaska Native, 0.0% Native Hawaiian/Other Pacific Islander, 1.4% Some other race, 0.4% Two or more races, 2.3% Hispanic of any race (2008-2012 5-year est.); Average household size: 2.81 (2008-2012 5-year est.); Median age: 37.2 (2008-2012 5-year est.); Males per 100 females: 96.5 (2008-2012 5-year est.); Marriage status: 23.7% never married, 53.3% now married, 10.9% widowed, 12.1% divorced (2008-2012 5-year est.); Foreign born: 1.8% (2008-2012 5-year est.); Ancestry (includes multiple ancestries): 40.7% German, 19.5% Irish, 15.3% French, 8.2% Polish, 6.6% Italian (2008-2012 5-year est.).

Economy: Single-family building permits issued: 1 (2013); Multi-family building permits issued: 0 (2013); Homeowner vacancy rate: 0.8%. Rental vacancy rate: 5.8%. (2008-2012 5-year est.); Employment by occupation: 16.0% management, business, and financial, 2.3% computer, engineering, and science, 7.0% education, legal, community service, arts, and media, 9.1% healthcare practitioners, 14.8% service, 16.8% sales and office, 16.2% natural resources, construction, and maintenance, 17.9% production, transportation, and material moving (2008-2012 5-year est.).

Income: Per capita income: $28,136 (2008-2012 5-year est.); Median household income: $65,417 (2008-2012 5-year est.); Average household income: $77,220 (2008-2012 5-year est.); Percent of households with income of $100,000 or more: 31.3% (2008-2012 5-year est.); Poverty rate: 8.7% (2008-2012 5-year est.).

Education: Percent of population age 25 and over with: High school diploma (including GED) or higher: 88.7% (2008-2012 5-year est.); Bachelor's degree or higher: 20.4% (2008-2012 5-year est.); Master's degree or higher: 6.4% (2008-2012 5-year est.).

School District(s)

Herscher CUSD 2 (PK-12)

    2011-12 Enrollment: 1,980 . . . . (815) 426-2162

Housing: Homeownership rate: 78.5% (2008-2012 5-year est.); Median home value: $147,300 (2008-2012 5-year est.); Median contract rent: $571 per month (2008-2012 5-year est.); Median year structure built: 1972 (2008-2012 5-year est.).

Health Insurance: 74.9% Private; 35.8% Public; 4.6% None. (2008-2012 5-year est.)

Safety: Violent crime rate: 6.3 per 10,000 population; Property crime rate: 75.2 per 10,000 population (2012).

Transportation: Commute to work: 85.4% car, 1.6% public transportation, 6.9% walk, 4.3% work from home (2008-2012 5-year est.); Travel time to work: 23.2% less than 15 minutes, 36.4% 15 to 30 minutes, 24.4% 30 to 45 minutes, 5.3% 45 to 60 minutes, 10.6% 60 minutes or more (2008-2012 5-year est.).

Additional Information Contacts

Herscher Chamber of Commerce . . . . (815) 426-2131
http://www.herscher.net

HOPKINS PARK (village). Aka Pembroke. Covers a land area of 3.747 square miles and a water area of 0 square miles. Located at 41.07° N. Lat; 87.61° W. Long. Elevation is 679 feet.

Population: 601 (1990); 711 (2000); 603 (2010); Density: 150.5 persons per square mile (2008-2012 5-year est.); Race: 8.9% White, 89.7% Black/African American, 0.0% Asian, 0.2% American Indian/Alaska Native, 0.0% Native Hawaiian/Other Pacific Islander, 1.2% Some other race, 1.2% Two or more races, 0.0% Hispanic of any race (2008-2012 5-year est.); Average household size: 2.19 (2008-2012 5-year est.); Median age: 36.5 (2008-2012 5-year est.); Males per 100 females: 86.1 (2008-2012 5-year est.); Marriage status: 44.8% never married, 16.0% now married, 21.3% widowed, 17.9% divorced (2008-2012 5-year est.); Foreign born: 0.0% (2008-2012 5-year est.); Ancestry (includes multiple ancestries): 1.4% German, 1.2% Polish, 1.1% Dutch, 0.5% Irish, 0.4% Scottish (2008-2012 5-year est.).

Economy: Single-family building permits issued: 0 (2013); Multi-family building permits issued: 0 (2013); Homeowner vacancy rate: 0.0%. Rental vacancy rate: 5.2%. (2008-2012 5-year est.); Employment by occupation: 13.1% management, business, and financial, 0.0% computer, engineering, and science, 3.3% education, legal, community service, arts, and media, 8.5% healthcare practitioners, 53.6% service, 12.4% sales and office, 2.6% natural resources, construction, and maintenance, 6.5% production, transportation, and material moving (2008-2012 5-year est.).

Income: Per capita income: $10,852 (2008-2012 5-year est.); Median household income: $16,667 (2008-2012 5-year est.); Average household income: $22,422 (2008-2012 5-year est.); Percent of households with income of $100,000 or more: n/a (2008-2012 5-year est.); Poverty rate: 30.7% (2008-2012 5-year est.).

Education: Percent of population age 25 and over with: High school diploma (including GED) or higher: 73.6% (2008-2012 5-year est.); Bachelor's degree or higher: 6.6% (2008-2012 5-year est.); Master's degree or higher: 0.6% (2008-2012 5-year est.).

Housing: Homeownership rate: 36.4% (2008-2012 5-year est.); Median home value: $66,700 (2008-2012 5-year est.); Median contract rent: $492 per month (2008-2012 5-year est.); Median year structure built: 1993 (2008-2012 5-year est.).

Health Insurance: 38.5% Private; 55.1% Public; 18.6% None. (2008-2012 5-year est.)

Transportation: Commute to work: 93.5% car, 0.0% public transportation, 0.0% walk, 6.5% work from home (2008-2012 5-year est.); Travel time to work: 8.4% less than 15 minutes, 27.3% 15 to 30 minutes, 59.4% 30 to 45 minutes, 1.4% 45 to 60 minutes, 3.5% 60 minutes or more (2008-2012 5-year est.)

IRWIN (village). Covers a land area of 0.039 square miles and a water area of 0 square miles. Located at 41.05° N. Lat; 87.98° W. Long. Elevation is 659 feet.

Population: 50 (1990); 92 (2000); 74 (2010); Density: 2,258.0 persons per square mile (2008-2012 5-year est.); Race: 100.0% White, 0.0% Black/African American, 0.0% Asian, 0.0% American Indian/Alaska Native, 0.0% Native Hawaiian/Other Pacific Islander, 0.0% Some other race, 0.0% Two or more races, 0.0% Hispanic of any race (2008-2012 5-year est.); Average household size: 2.84 (2008-2012 5-year est.); Median age: 32.3 (2008-2012 5-year est.); Males per 100 females: 60.0 (2008-2012 5-year est.); Marriage status: 42.9% never married, 31.4% now married, 7.1% widowed, 18.6% divorced (2008-2012 5-year est.); Foreign born: 0.0% (2008-2012 5-year est.); Ancestry (includes multiple ancestries): 19.3% Irish, 14.8% German, 10.2% French, 8.0% Norwegian, 8.0% Polish (2008-2012 5-year est.).

Economy: Single-family building permits issued: 0 (2013); Multi-family building permits issued: 0 (2013); Homeowner vacancy rate: 0.0%. Rental vacancy rate: 0.0%. (2008-2012 5-year est.); Employment by occupation: 12.9% management, business, and financial, 0.0% computer, engineering, and science, 9.7% education, legal, community service, arts, and media, 16.1% healthcare practitioners, 38.7% service, 6.5% sales and office, 12.9% natural resources, construction, and maintenance, 3.2% production, transportation, and material moving (2008-2012 5-year est.).

Income: Per capita income: $15,041 (2008-2012 5-year est.); Median household income: $41,750 (2008-2012 5-year est.); Average household income: $43,381 (2008-2012 5-year est.); Percent of households with income of $100,000 or more: 9.7% (2008-2012 5-year est.); Poverty rate: 37.5% (2008-2012 5-year est.).

Education: Percent of population age 25 and over with: High school diploma (including GED) or higher: 94.2% (2008-2012 5-year est.); Bachelor's degree or higher: 13.5% (2008-2012 5-year est.); Master's degree or higher: 3.8% (2008-2012 5-year est.).
Housing: Homeownership rate: 74.2% (2008-2012 5-year est.); Median home value: $131,900 (2008-2012 5-year est.); Median contract rent: $843 per month (2008-2012 5-year est.); Median year structure built: 1965 (2008-2012 5-year est.).
Health Insurance: 40.9% Private; 19.3% Public; 51.1% None. (2008-2012 5-year est.)
Transportation: Commute to work: 90.3% car, 0.0% public transportation, 9.7% walk, 0.0% work from home (2008-2012 5-year est.); Travel time to work: 22.6% less than 15 minutes, 41.9% 15 to 30 minutes, 19.4% 30 to 45 minutes, 0.0% 45 to 60 minutes, 16.1% 60 minutes or more (2008-2012 5-year est.)

KANKAKEE (city). County seat. Covers a land area of 14.137 square miles and a water area of 0.480 square miles. Located at 41.10° N. Lat; 87.87° W. Long. Elevation is 656 feet.

History: Kankakee developed around the Illinois Central Railroad depot, and was incorporated in 1855.
Population: 27,575 (1990); 27,491 (2000); 27,537 (2010); Density: 1,949.5 persons per square mile (2008-2012 5-year est.); Race: 52.2% White, 38.9% Black/African American, 0.1% Asian, 0.0% American Indian/Alaska Native, 0.0% Native Hawaiian/Other Pacific Islander, 8.8% Some other race, 3.4% Two or more races, 18.8% Hispanic of any race (2008-2012 5-year est.); Average household size: 2.71 (2008-2012 5-year est.); Median age: 32.3 (2008-2012 5-year est.); Males per 100 females: 101.6 (2008-2012 5-year est.); Marriage status: 43.2% never married, 37.4% now married, 6.7% widowed, 12.6% divorced (2008-2012 5-year est.); Foreign born: 9.5% (2008-2012 5-year est.); Ancestry (includes multiple ancestries): 13.3% German, 7.5% Irish, 6.8% French, 4.0% English, 2.7% Italian (2008-2012 5-year est.).
Economy: Unemployment rate: 11.2% (April 2014); Total civilian labor force: 11,511 (April 2014); Single-family building permits issued: 1 (2013); Multi-family building permits issued: 0 (2013); Homeowner vacancy rate: 3.8%. Rental vacancy rate: 7.8%. (2008-2012 5-year est.); Employment by occupation: 6.9% management, business, and financial, 1.9% computer, engineering, and science, 7.9% education, legal, community service, arts, and media, 5.8% healthcare practitioners, 26.9% service, 19.2% sales and office, 7.0% natural resources, construction, and maintenance, 24.4% production, transportation, and material moving (2008-2012 5-year est.).
Income: Per capita income: $15,482 (2008-2012 5-year est.); Median household income: $32,064 (2008-2012 5-year est.); Average household income: $41,637 (2008-2012 5-year est.); Percent of households with income of $100,000 or more: 7.5% (2008-2012 5-year est.); Poverty rate: 32.3% (2008-2012 5-year est.).
Taxes: Total city taxes per capita: $777 (2011); City property taxes per capita: $612 (2011).
Education: Percent of population age 25 and over with: High school diploma (including GED) or higher: 75.8% (2008-2012 5-year est.); Bachelor's degree or higher: 11.1% (2008-2012 5-year est.); Master's degree or higher: 3.2% (2008-2012 5-year est.).

School District(s)

Herscher CUSD 2 (PK-12)
    2011-12 Enrollment: 1,980 . . . . (815) 426-2162
Iroquois/kankakee Roe (06-12)
    2011-12 Enrollment: n/a . . . . (815) 937-2950
Kankakee Area Spec Educ Coop (04-12)
    2011-12 Enrollment: n/a . . . . (815) 939-3651
Kankakee SD 111 (PK-12)
    2011-12 Enrollment: 5,670 . . . . (815) 933-0700

Two-year College(s)

Kankakee Community College (Public)
    Fall 2012 Enrollment: 3,913 . . . . (815) 802-8500
    2012-13 Tuition: In-state $5,050; Out-of-state $14,533
Housing: Homeownership rate: 50.0% (2008-2012 5-year est.); Median home value: $102,200 (2008-2012 5-year est.); Median contract rent: $554 per month (2008-2012 5-year est.); Median year structure built: 1956 (2008-2012 5-year est.).
Health Insurance: 43.7% Private; 47.8% Public; 17.8% None. (2008-2012 5-year est.)
Hospitals: Riverside Medical Center (336 beds); St. Mary's Hospital of Kankakee (210 beds)

Safety: Violent crime rate: 85.8 per 10,000 population; Property crime rate: 435.0 per 10,000 population (2012).
Transportation: Commute to work: 88.1% car, 3.2% public transportation, 2.6% walk, 4.1% work from home (2008-2012 5-year est.); Travel time to work: 46.8% less than 15 minutes, 29.9% 15 to 30 minutes, 11.9% 30 to 45 minutes, 3.6% 45 to 60 minutes, 7.8% 60 minutes or more (2008-2012 5-year est.); Amtrak: Train service available.
Airports: Greater Kankakee Airport (general aviation)
Additional Information Contacts
City of Kankakee . . . . (815) 933-0480
   http://www.citykankakee-il.gov
Kankakee Regional Chamber of Commerce . . . . (815) 933-7721

LIMESTONE (village). Covers a land area of 2.183 square miles and a water area of 0 square miles. Located at 41.11° N. Lat; 87.95° W. Long.

History: Incorporated 2006.
Population: n/a (1990); n/a (2000); 1,598 (2010); Density: 746.8 persons per square mile (2008-2012 5-year est.); Race: 95.1% White, 3.2% Black/African American, 0.6% Asian, 0.0% American Indian/Alaska Native, 0.0% Native Hawaiian/Other Pacific Islander, 1.1% Some other race, 1.2% Two or more races, 0.9% Hispanic of any race (2008-2012 5-year est.); Average household size: 2.80 (2008-2012 5-year est.); Median age: 44.2 (2008-2012 5-year est.); Males per 100 females: 112.8 (2008-2012 5-year est.); Marriage status: 22.4% never married, 60.1% now married, 4.1% widowed, 13.4% divorced (2008-2012 5-year est.); Foreign born: 0.6% (2008-2012 5-year est.); Ancestry (includes multiple ancestries): 33.2% German, 17.5% French, 15.1% Irish, 11.8% English, 8.6% American (2008-2012 5-year est.).
Economy: Single-family building permits issued: 0 (2013); Multi-family building permits issued: 0 (2013); Homeowner vacancy rate: 0.0%. Rental vacancy rate: 0.0%. (2008-2012 5-year est.); Employment by occupation: 14.0% management, business, and financial, 3.7% computer, engineering, and science, 6.6% education, legal, community service, arts, and media, 9.8% healthcare practitioners, 17.3% service, 23.5% sales and office, 10.7% natural resources, construction, and maintenance, 14.4% production, transportation, and material moving (2008-2012 5-year est.).
Income: Per capita income: $29,928 (2008-2012 5-year est.); Median household income: $69,405 (2008-2012 5-year est.); Average household income: $81,207 (2008-2012 5-year est.); Percent of households with income of $100,000 or more: 30.3% (2008-2012 5-year est.); Poverty rate: 2.5% (2008-2012 5-year est.).
Education: Percent of population age 25 and over with: High school diploma (including GED) or higher: 88.6% (2008-2012 5-year est.); Bachelor's degree or higher: 19.3% (2008-2012 5-year est.); Master's degree or higher: 7.2% (2008-2012 5-year est.).
Housing: Homeownership rate: 88.5% (2008-2012 5-year est.); Median home value: $152,800 (2008-2012 5-year est.); Median contract rent: $756 per month (2008-2012 5-year est.); Median year structure built: 1966 (2008-2012 5-year est.).
Health Insurance: 87.5% Private; 23.9% Public; 5.2% None. (2008-2012 5-year est.)
Transportation: Commute to work: 93.2% car, 1.7% public transportation, 1.9% walk, 2.8% work from home (2008-2012 5-year est.); Travel time to work: 20.4% less than 15 minutes, 40.8% 15 to 30 minutes, 15.8% 30 to 45 minutes, 7.9% 45 to 60 minutes, 15.1% 60 minutes or more (2008-2012 5-year est.)

MANTENO (village). Covers a land area of 4.978 square miles and a water area of 0.034 square miles. Located at 41.25° N. Lat; 87.84° W. Long. Elevation is 686 feet.

History: Incorporated 1878.
Population: 3,488 (1990); 6,414 (2000); 9,204 (2010); Density: 1,858.7 persons per square mile (2008-2012 5-year est.); Race: 92.4% White, 2.6% Black/African American, 0.1% Asian, 0.0% American Indian/Alaska Native, 0.0% Native Hawaiian/Other Pacific Islander, 4.9% Some other race, 1.7% Two or more races, 7.7% Hispanic of any race (2008-2012 5-year est.); Average household size: 2.56 (2008-2012 5-year est.); Median age: 37.8 (2008-2012 5-year est.); Males per 100 females: 92.0 (2008-2012 5-year est.); Marriage status: 26.1% never married, 52.8% now married, 7.0% widowed, 14.1% divorced (2008-2012 5-year est.); Foreign born: 2.2% (2008-2012 5-year est.); Ancestry (includes multiple ancestries): 31.8% German, 24.3% Irish, 14.9% Italian, 14.8% Polish, 6.9% English (2008-2012 5-year est.).
Economy: Single-family building permits issued: 15 (2013); Multi-family building permits issued: 0 (2013); Homeowner vacancy rate: 1.2%. Rental

vacancy rate: 6.6%. (2008-2012 5-year est.); Employment by occupation: 14.9% management, business, and financial, 2.1% computer, engineering, and science, 12.3% education, legal, community service, arts, and media, 6.7% healthcare practitioners, 12.9% service, 25.6% sales and office, 10.0% natural resources, construction, and maintenance, 15.5% production, transportation, and material moving (2008-2012 5-year est.).
Income: Per capita income: $27,944 (2008-2012 5-year est.); Median household income: $65,482 (2008-2012 5-year est.); Average household income: $71,219 (2008-2012 5-year est.); Percent of households with income of $100,000 or more: 19.2% (2008-2012 5-year est.); Poverty rate: 6.8% (2008-2012 5-year est.).
Taxes: Total city taxes per capita: $382 (2011); City property taxes per capita: $294 (2011).
Education: Percent of population age 25 and over with: High school diploma (including GED) or higher: 90.6% (2008-2012 5-year est.); Bachelor's degree or higher: 24.4% (2008-2012 5-year est.); Master's degree or higher: 9.9% (2008-2012 5-year est.).

School District(s)
Manteno CUSD 5 (PK-12)
   2011-12 Enrollment: 2,305 . . . . (815) 928-7000
Housing: Homeownership rate: 74.5% (2008-2012 5-year est.); Median home value: $194,400 (2008-2012 5-year est.); Median contract rent: $722 per month (2008-2012 5-year est.); Median year structure built: 1995 (2008-2012 5-year est.).
Health Insurance: 80.1% Private; 25.0% Public; 9.3% None. (2008-2012 5-year est.)
Transportation: Commute to work: 87.6% car, 4.3% public transportation, 3.9% walk, 3.6% work from home (2008-2012 5-year est.); Travel time to work: 30.9% less than 15 minutes, 30.8% 15 to 30 minutes, 13.4% 30 to 45 minutes, 11.2% 45 to 60 minutes, 13.6% 60 minutes or more (2008-2012 5-year est.)
Additional Information Contacts
Manteno Chamber of Commerce . . . . (815) 468-6226
   http://www.mantenochamber.com
Village of Manteno . . . . (815) 929-4800
   http://manteno.govoffice.com

MOMENCE (city). Covers a land area of 1.531 square miles and a water area of 0.097 square miles. Located at 41.16° N. Lat; 87.66° W. Long. Elevation is 627 feet.
History: Momence, named for Isadore Momence, was laid out in 1844 on the Kankakee River. This was a camping place for travelers on the Hubbard Trail, who forded the Kankakee here.
Population: 2,968 (1990); 3,171 (2000); 3,310 (2010); Density: 2,258.7 persons per square mile (2008-2012 5-year est.); Race: 87.2% White, 3.2% Black/African American, 0.0% Asian, 0.0% American Indian/Alaska Native, 0.0% Native Hawaiian/Other Pacific Islander, 9.6% Some other race, 2.6% Two or more races, 18.4% Hispanic of any race (2008-2012 5-year est.); Average household size: 2.79 (2008-2012 5-year est.); Median age: 38.3 (2008-2012 5-year est.); Males per 100 females: 93.9 (2008-2012 5-year est.); Marriage status: 35.9% never married, 44.9% now married, 8.0% widowed, 11.2% divorced (2008-2012 5-year est.); Foreign born: 8.3% (2008-2012 5-year est.); Ancestry (includes multiple ancestries): 20.6% German, 17.6% Irish, 6.5% Italian, 6.2% English, 6.2% Dutch (2008-2012 5-year est.).
Economy: Single-family building permits issued: 3 (2013); Multi-family building permits issued: 0 (2013); Homeowner vacancy rate: 3.7%. Rental vacancy rate: 6.1%. (2008-2012 5-year est.); Employment by occupation: 8.9% management, business, and financial, 1.3% computer, engineering, and science, 14.7% education, legal, community service, arts, and media, 0.9% healthcare practitioners, 14.2% service, 30.8% sales and office, 11.3% natural resources, construction, and maintenance, 18.0% production, transportation, and material moving (2008-2012 5-year est.).
Income: Per capita income: $19,511 (2008-2012 5-year est.); Median household income: $44,570 (2008-2012 5-year est.); Average household income: $53,911 (2008-2012 5-year est.); Percent of households with income of $100,000 or more: 12.4% (2008-2012 5-year est.); Poverty rate: 25.5% (2008-2012 5-year est.).
Education: Percent of population age 25 and over with: High school diploma (including GED) or higher: 73.1% (2008-2012 5-year est.); Bachelor's degree or higher: 11.0% (2008-2012 5-year est.); Master's degree or higher: 5.8% (2008-2012 5-year est.).

School District(s)
Momence CUSD 1 (PK-12)
   2011-12 Enrollment: 1,290 . . . . (815) 472-3500

Housing: Homeownership rate: 67.9% (2008-2012 5-year est.); Median home value: $134,900 (2008-2012 5-year est.); Median contract rent: $579 per month (2008-2012 5-year est.); Median year structure built: 1944 (2008-2012 5-year est.).
Health Insurance: 56.6% Private; 37.6% Public; 16.0% None. (2008-2012 5-year est.)
Safety: Violent crime rate: 12.0 per 10,000 population; Property crime rate: 177.7 per 10,000 population (2012).
Transportation: Commute to work: 88.2% car, 1.3% public transportation, 7.2% walk, 3.2% work from home (2008-2012 5-year est.); Travel time to work: 55.3% less than 15 minutes, 27.6% 15 to 30 minutes, 5.3% 30 to 45 minutes, 4.8% 45 to 60 minutes, 7.0% 60 minutes or more (2008-2012 5-year est.)
Additional Information Contacts
Momence Chamber of Commerce . . . . (815) 472-4620
   http://www.momence.org

REDDICK (village). Covers a land area of 0.247 square miles and a water area of 0 square miles. Located at 41.10° N. Lat; 88.25° W. Long.
Population: 208 (1990); 219 (2000); 163 (2010); Density: 1,187.5 persons per square mile (2008-2012 5-year est.); Race: 100.0% White, 0.0% Black/African American, 0.0% Asian, 0.0% American Indian/Alaska Native, 0.0% Native Hawaiian/Other Pacific Islander, 0.0% Some other race, 0.0% Two or more races, 0.0% Hispanic of any race (2008-2012 5-year est.); Average household size: 2.57 (2008-2012 5-year est.); Median age: 40.2 (2008-2012 5-year est.); Males per 100 females: 115.4 (2008-2012 5-year est.); Marriage status: 33.2% never married, 54.7% now married, 9.0% widowed, 3.1% divorced (2008-2012 5-year est.); Foreign born: 1.4% (2008-2012 5-year est.); Ancestry (includes multiple ancestries): 43.3% German, 37.2% Irish, 11.6% Italian, 5.1% Dutch, 4.4% Hungarian (2008-2012 5-year est.).
Economy: Homeowner vacancy rate: 4.5%. Rental vacancy rate: 0.0%. (2008-2012 5-year est.); Employment by occupation: 10.3% management, business, and financial, 0.0% computer, engineering, and science, 3.7% education, legal, community service, arts, and media, 5.1% healthcare practitioners, 17.6% service, 36.0% sales and office, 15.4% natural resources, construction, and maintenance, 11.8% production, transportation, and material moving (2008-2012 5-year est.).
Income: Per capita income: $26,981 (2008-2012 5-year est.); Median household income: $61,250 (2008-2012 5-year est.); Average household income: $68,232 (2008-2012 5-year est.); Percent of households with income of $100,000 or more: 23.6% (2008-2012 5-year est.); Poverty rate: 0.0% (2008-2012 5-year est.).
Education: Percent of population age 25 and over with: High school diploma (including GED) or higher: 95.8% (2008-2012 5-year est.); Bachelor's degree or higher: 16.3% (2008-2012 5-year est.); Master's degree or higher: 2.6% (2008-2012 5-year est.).

School District(s)
Herscher CUSD 2 (PK-12)
   2011-12 Enrollment: 1,980 . . . . (815) 426-2162
Housing: Homeownership rate: 93.9% (2008-2012 5-year est.); Median home value: $116,800 (2008-2012 5-year est.); Median contract rent: $938 per month (2008-2012 5-year est.); Median year structure built: Before 1940 (2008-2012 5-year est.).
Health Insurance: 87.0% Private; 16.4% Public; 9.6% None. (2008-2012 5-year est.)
Transportation: Commute to work: 93.6% car, 0.0% public transportation, 0.0% walk, 1.8% work from home (2008-2012 5-year est.); Travel time to work: 5.6% less than 15 minutes, 17.6% 15 to 30 minutes, 60.2% 30 to 45 minutes, 4.6% 45 to 60 minutes, 12.0% 60 minutes or more (2008-2012 5-year est.)

SAINT ANNE (village). Covers a land area of 0.773 square miles and a water area of 0.023 square miles. Located at 41.02° N. Lat; 87.72° W. Long. Elevation is 666 feet.
History: In 1852 Father Charles Chiniquy and many of his French-Canadian parishioners immigrated here from Bourbonnais and founded the town of St. Anne.
Population: 1,153 (1990); 1,212 (2000); 1,257 (2010); Density: 1,770.1 persons per square mile (2008-2012 5-year est.); Race: 92.8% White, 1.3% Black/African American, 0.4% Asian, 0.3% American Indian/Alaska Native, 0.0% Native Hawaiian/Other Pacific Islander, 5.2% Some other race, 1.5% Two or more races, 15.7% Hispanic of any race (2008-2012 5-year est.); Average household size: 2.45 (2008-2012 5-year est.); Median age: 34.6 (2008-2012 5-year est.); Males per 100 females: 102.8

(2008-2012 5-year est.); Marriage status: 24.0% never married, 54.7% now married, 8.4% widowed, 12.9% divorced (2008-2012 5-year est.); Foreign born: 7.4% (2008-2012 5-year est.); Ancestry (includes multiple ancestries): 26.2% German, 20.1% French, 13.6% Irish, 9.1% Polish, 4.2% English (2008-2012 5-year est.).

Economy: Single-family building permits issued: 0 (2013); Multi-family building permits issued: 0 (2013); Homeowner vacancy rate: 0.0%. Rental vacancy rate: 3.3%. (2008-2012 5-year est.); Employment by occupation: 8.0% management, business, and financial, 0.0% computer, engineering, and science, 8.5% education, legal, community service, arts, and media, 2.6% healthcare practitioners, 11.6% service, 37.7% sales and office, 13.4% natural resources, construction, and maintenance, 18.1% production, transportation, and material moving (2008-2012 5-year est.).

Income: Per capita income: $18,965 (2008-2012 5-year est.); Median household income: $41,667 (2008-2012 5-year est.); Average household income: $45,981 (2008-2012 5-year est.); Percent of households with income of $100,000 or more: 4.7% (2008-2012 5-year est.); Poverty rate: 14.8% (2008-2012 5-year est.).

Education: Percent of population age 25 and over with: High school diploma (including GED) or higher: 80.5% (2008-2012 5-year est.); Bachelor's degree or higher: 9.0% (2008-2012 5-year est.); Master's degree or higher: 2.1% (2008-2012 5-year est.).

School District(s)
Saint Anne CCSD 256 (PK-08)
   2011-12 Enrollment: 370 . . . . (815) 427-8190
Saint Anne CHSD 302 (09-12)
   2011-12 Enrollment: 263 . . . . (815) 422-5022

Housing: Homeownership rate: 63.4% (2008-2012 5-year est.); Median home value: $97,300 (2008-2012 5-year est.); Median contract rent: $478 per month (2008-2012 5-year est.); Median year structure built: 1947 (2008-2012 5-year est.).

Health Insurance: 64.8% Private; 37.8% Public; 12.0% None. (2008-2012 5-year est.)

Safety: Violent crime rate: 15.8 per 10,000 population; Property crime rate: 253.4 per 10,000 population (2012).

Transportation: Commute to work: 95.3% car, 0.0% public transportation, 1.3% walk, 3.3% work from home (2008-2012 5-year est.); Travel time to work: 24.6% less than 15 minutes, 35.6% 15 to 30 minutes, 31.8% 30 to 45 minutes, 2.4% 45 to 60 minutes, 5.5% 60 minutes or more (2008-2012 5-year est.)

SAMMONS POINT (village).
Covers a land area of 1.818 square miles and a water area of 0 square miles. Located at 41.03° N. Lat; 87.86° W. Long.

History: Initially incorporated as a village on March 21, 2006, it was disincorporated on August 8, 2007, and incorporated again on February 5, 2008.

Population: n/a (1990); n/a (2000); 279 (2010); Density: 161.8 persons per square mile (2008-2012 5-year est.); Race: 94.2% White, 4.4% Black/African American, 0.0% Asian, 0.0% American Indian/Alaska Native, 0.0% Native Hawaiian/Other Pacific Islander, 1.4% Some other race, 1.4% Two or more races, 5.1% Hispanic of any race (2008-2012 5-year est.); Average household size: 2.53 (2008-2012 5-year est.); Median age: 57.1 (2008-2012 5-year est.); Males per 100 females: 93.4 (2008-2012 5-year est.); Marriage status: 22.4% never married, 58.1% now married, 4.4% widowed, 15.1% divorced (2008-2012 5-year est.); Foreign born: 0.0% (2008-2012 5-year est.); Ancestry (includes multiple ancestries): 29.3% German, 21.1% American, 10.2% French, 7.5% Irish, 6.1% Polish (2008-2012 5-year est.).

Economy: Single-family building permits issued: 0 (2013); Multi-family building permits issued: 0 (2013); Homeowner vacancy rate: 0.0%. Rental vacancy rate: 0.0%. (2008-2012 5-year est.); Employment by occupation: 7.7% management, business, and financial, 2.6% computer, engineering, and science, 1.3% education, legal, community service, arts, and media, 5.1% healthcare practitioners, 7.7% service, 32.1% sales and office, 10.3% natural resources, construction, and maintenance, 33.3% production, transportation, and material moving (2008-2012 5-year est.).

Income: Per capita income: $20,260 (2008-2012 5-year est.); Median household income: $24,929 (2008-2012 5-year est.); Average household income: $48,533 (2008-2012 5-year est.); Percent of households with income of $100,000 or more: 11.2% (2008-2012 5-year est.); Poverty rate: 12.6% (2008-2012 5-year est.).

Education: Percent of population age 25 and over with: High school diploma (including GED) or higher: 86.8% (2008-2012 5-year est.);

Bachelor's degree or higher: 32.9% (2008-2012 5-year est.); Master's degree or higher: 2.9% (2008-2012 5-year est.).

Housing: Homeownership rate: 83.6% (2008-2012 5-year est.); Median home value: $128,000 (2008-2012 5-year est.); Median contract rent: $670 per month (2008-2012 5-year est.); Median year structure built: 1974 (2008-2012 5-year est.).

Health Insurance: 72.8% Private; 49.3% Public; 16.0% None. (2008-2012 5-year est.)

Transportation: Commute to work: 93.6% car, 0.0% public transportation, 5.1% walk, 1.3% work from home (2008-2012 5-year est.); Travel time to work: 61.0% less than 15 minutes, 19.5% 15 to 30 minutes, 18.2% 30 to 45 minutes, 1.3% 45 to 60 minutes, 0.0% 60 minutes or more (2008-2012 5-year est.)

SUN RIVER TERRACE (village).
Covers a land area of 0.563 square miles and a water area of 0.001 square miles. Located at 41.12° N. Lat; 87.73° W. Long. Elevation is 614 feet.

Population: 532 (1990); 383 (2000); 528 (2010); Density: 708.3 persons per square mile (2008-2012 5-year est.); Race: 5.0% White, 91.0% Black/African American, 0.0% Asian, 0.0% American Indian/Alaska Native, 0.0% Native Hawaiian/Other Pacific Islander, 4.0% Some other race, 2.5% Two or more races, 4.0% Hispanic of any race (2008-2012 5-year est.); Average household size: 2.66 (2008-2012 5-year est.); Median age: 40.5 (2008-2012 5-year est.); Males per 100 females: 68.4 (2008-2012 5-year est.); Marriage status: 35.6% never married, 35.9% now married, 10.1% widowed, 18.3% divorced (2008-2012 5-year est.); Foreign born: 1.8% (2008-2012 5-year est.); Ancestry (includes multiple ancestries): 1.3% African, 0.8% German, 0.5% Arab, 0.5% American (2008-2012 5-year est.).

Economy: Single-family building permits issued: 0 (2013); Multi-family building permits issued: 0 (2013); Homeowner vacancy rate: 0.0%. Rental vacancy rate: 13.4%. (2008-2012 5-year est.); Employment by occupation: 6.9% management, business, and financial, 0.0% computer, engineering, and science, 23.1% education, legal, community service, arts, and media, 2.3% healthcare practitioners, 30.0% service, 16.9% sales and office, 10.8% natural resources, construction, and maintenance, 10.0% production, transportation, and material moving (2008-2012 5-year est.).

Income: Per capita income: $14,266 (2008-2012 5-year est.); Median household income: $24,063 (2008-2012 5-year est.); Average household income: $36,965 (2008-2012 5-year est.); Percent of households with income of $100,000 or more: 4.7% (2008-2012 5-year est.); Poverty rate: 20.3% (2008-2012 5-year est.).

Education: Percent of population age 25 and over with: High school diploma (including GED) or higher: 81.3% (2008-2012 5-year est.); Bachelor's degree or higher: 6.1% (2008-2012 5-year est.); Master's degree or higher: 2.0% (2008-2012 5-year est.).

Housing: Homeownership rate: 61.3% (2008-2012 5-year est.); Median home value: $104,400 (2008-2012 5-year est.); Median contract rent: $517 per month (2008-2012 5-year est.); Median year structure built: 1969 (2008-2012 5-year est.).

Health Insurance: 53.4% Private; 56.1% Public; 7.5% None. (2008-2012 5-year est.)

Transportation: Commute to work: 93.1% car, 6.9% public transportation, 0.0% walk, 0.0% work from home (2008-2012 5-year est.); Travel time to work: 19.2% less than 15 minutes, 48.5% 15 to 30 minutes, 20.8% 30 to 45 minutes, 11.5% 45 to 60 minutes, 0.0% 60 minutes or more (2008-2012 5-year est.)

UNION HILL (village).
Covers a land area of 0.045 square miles and a water area of 0 square miles. Located at 41.11° N. Lat; 88.15° W. Long. Elevation is 617 feet.

Population: 37 (1990); 66 (2000); 58 (2010); Density: 1,110.9 persons per square mile (2008-2012 5-year est.); Race: 100.0% White, 0.0% Black/African American, 0.0% Asian, 0.0% American Indian/Alaska Native, 0.0% Native Hawaiian/Other Pacific Islander, 0.0% Some other race, 0.0% Two or more races, 0.0% Hispanic of any race (2008-2012 5-year est.); Average household size: 2.94 (2008-2012 5-year est.); Median age: 31.0 (2008-2012 5-year est.); Males per 100 females: 117.4 (2008-2012 5-year est.); Marriage status: 6.7% never married, 76.7% now married, 0.0% widowed, 16.7% divorced (2008-2012 5-year est.); Foreign born: 0.0% (2008-2012 5-year est.); Ancestry (includes multiple ancestries): 54.0% German, 36.0% French, 10.0% European, 10.0% English, 6.0% Dutch (2008-2012 5-year est.).

Economy: Single-family building permits issued: 0 (2013); Multi-family building permits issued: 0 (2013); Homeowner vacancy rate: 0.0%. Rental

vacancy rate: 0.0%. (2008-2012 5-year est.); Employment by occupation: 13.6% management, business, and financial, 0.0% computer, engineering, and science, 22.7% education, legal, community service, arts, and media, 0.0% healthcare practitioners, 13.6% service, 27.3% sales and office, 0.0% natural resources, construction, and maintenance, 22.7% production, transportation, and material moving (2008-2012 5-year est.).
Income: Per capita income: $32,684 (2008-2012 5-year est.); Median household income: $79,250 (2008-2012 5-year est.); Average household income: $85,571 (2008-2012 5-year est.); Percent of households with income of $100,000 or more: 41.2% (2008-2012 5-year est.); Poverty rate: 0.0% (2008-2012 5-year est.).
Education: Percent of population age 25 and over with: High school diploma (including GED) or higher: 100.0% (2008-2012 5-year est.); Bachelor's degree or higher: 20.0% (2008-2012 5-year est.); Master's degree or higher: 16.7% (2008-2012 5-year est.).
Housing: Homeownership rate: 100.0% (2008-2012 5-year est.); Median home value: $117,500 (2008-2012 5-year est.); Median contract rent: n/a per month (2008-2012 5-year est.); Median year structure built: Before 1940 (2008-2012 5-year est.).
Health Insurance: 96.0% Private; 68.0% Public; 0.0% None. (2008-2012 5-year est.)
Transportation: Commute to work: 100.0% car, 0.0% public transportation, 0.0% walk, 0.0% work from home (2008-2012 5-year est.); Travel time to work: 4.5% less than 15 minutes, 13.6% 15 to 30 minutes, 36.4% 30 to 45 minutes, 31.8% 45 to 60 minutes, 13.6% 60 minutes or more (2008-2012 5-year est.)

Kendall County

Located in northeastern Illinois; drained by the Fox River. Covers a land area of 320.335 square miles, a water area of 1.985 square miles, and is located in the Central Time Zone at 41.59° N. Lat., 88.43° W. Long. The county was founded in 1841. County seat is Yorkville.

Kendall County is part of the Chicago-Naperville-Elgin, IL-IN-WI Metropolitan Statistical Area. The entire metro area includes: Chicago-Naperville-Arlington Heights, IL Metropolitan Division (Cook County, IL; DuPage County, IL; Grundy County, IL; Kendall County, IL; McHenry County, IL; Will County, IL); Elgin, IL Metropolitan Division (DeKalb County, IL; Kane County, IL); Gary, IN Metropolitan Division (Jasper County, IN; Lake County, IN; Newton County, IN; Porter County, IN); Lake County-Kenosha County, IL-WI Metropolitan Division (Lake County, IL; Kenosha County, WI)

Population: 39,413 (1990); 54,544 (2000); 114,736 (2010); Race: 84.5% White, 5.4% Black/African American, 3.1% Asian, 0.3% American Indian/Alaska Native, 0.0% Native Hawaiian/Other Pacific Islander, 6.7% Some other race, 2.8% Two or more races, 15.8% Hispanic of any race (2008-2012 5-year est.); Density: 368.7 persons per square mile (2008-2012 5-year est.); Average household size: 3.01 (2008-2012 5-year est.); Median age: 33.0 (2008-2012 5-year est.); Males per 100 females: 99.1 (2008-2012 5-year est.).
Religion: Six largest groups: 22.7% Catholicism, 3.0% Lutheran, 2.2% Methodist/Pietist, 1.6% Presbyterian-Reformed, 1.5% Pentecostal, 1.1% Baptist (2010)
Economy: Unemployment rate: 6.9% (April 2014); Total civilian labor force: 67,593 (April 2014); Leading industries: 22.7% retail trade; 13.3% accommodation & food services; 10.4% manufacturing (2012); Farms: 364 totaling 129,741 acres (2012); Companies that employ 500 or more persons: 2 (2012); Companies that employ 100 to 499 persons: 31 (2012); Companies that employ less than 100 persons: 1,944 (2012); Black-owned businesses: 256 (2007); Hispanic-owned businesses: 774 (2007); Asian-owned businesses: n/a (2007); Women-owned businesses: 2,722 (2007); Single-family building permits issued: 320 (2013); Multi-family building permits issued: 0 (2013).
Income: Per capita income: $31,856 (2008-2012 5-year est.); Median household income: $83,835 (2008-2012 5-year est.); Average household income: $95,465 (2008-2012 5-year est.); Percent of households with income of $100,000 or more: 38.9% (2008-2012 5-year est.); Poverty rate: 3.9% (2008-2012 5-year est.); Bankruptcy rate: 5.54% (2013).
Taxes: Total county taxes per capita: $235 (2011); County property taxes per capita: $231 (2011).
Education: Percent of population age 25 and over with: High school diploma (including GED) or higher: 92.6% (2008-2012 5-year est.);

Bachelor's degree or higher: 34.2% (2008-2012 5-year est.); Master's degree or higher: 11.8% (2008-2012 5-year est.).
Housing: Homeownership rate: 85.2% (2008-2012 5-year est.); Median home value: $229,400 (2008-2012 5-year est.); Median contract rent: $1,022 per month (2008-2012 5-year est.); Median year structure built: 2000 (2008-2012 5-year est.)
Health: Birth rate: 141.0 per 10,000 population (2013); Death rate: 38.7 per 10,000 population (2013); Age-adjusted cancer mortality rate: 166.1 deaths per 100,000 population (2011); Number of physicians: 6.1 per 10,000 population (2011); Hospital beds: 0.0 per 10,000 population (2010); Hospital admissions: 0.0 per 10,000 population (2010).
Elections: 2012 Presidential election results: 47.1% Obama, 51.2% Romney
National and State Parks: Silver Springs State Park
Additional Information Contacts
Kendall County Government . . . . (630) 553-4104
  http://www.co.kendall.il.us

Kendall County Communities

BOULDER HILL (CDP). Covers a land area of 1.436 square miles and a water area of 0.009 square miles. Located at 41.71° N. Lat; 88.34° W. Long. Elevation is 669 feet.
Population: 8,894 (1990); 8,169 (2000); 8,108 (2010); Density: 5,942.6 persons per square mile (2008-2012 5-year est.); Race: 84.3% White, 4.7% Black/African American, 2.3% Asian, 0.5% American Indian/Alaska Native, 0.0% Native Hawaiian/Other Pacific Islander, 8.2% Some other race, 2.3% Two or more races, 23.6% Hispanic of any race (2008-2012 5-year est.); Average household size: 3.01 (2008-2012 5-year est.); Median age: 33.0 (2008-2012 5-year est.); Males per 100 females: 86.3 (2008-2012 5-year est.); Marriage status: 27.7% never married, 57.8% now married, 4.0% widowed, 10.5% divorced (2008-2012 5-year est.); Foreign born: 8.5% (2008-2012 5-year est.); Ancestry (includes multiple ancestries): 28.2% German, 15.8% Irish, 9.7% English, 7.3% Polish, 5.3% American (2008-2012 5-year est.).
Economy: Homeowner vacancy rate: 0.3%. Rental vacancy rate: 0.0%. (2008-2012 5-year est.); Employment by occupation: 11.9% management, business, and financial, 4.8% computer, engineering, and science, 4.4% education, legal, community service, arts, and media, 2.1% healthcare practitioners, 17.2% service, 31.3% sales and office, 13.3% natural resources, construction, and maintenance, 15.0% production, transportation, and material moving (2008-2012 5-year est.).
Income: Per capita income: $23,633 (2008-2012 5-year est.); Median household income: $67,069 (2008-2012 5-year est.); Average household income: $70,980 (2008-2012 5-year est.); Percent of households with income of $100,000 or more: 20.2% (2008-2012 5-year est.); Poverty rate: 13.6% (2008-2012 5-year est.).
Education: Percent of population age 25 and over with: High school diploma (including GED) or higher: 86.5% (2008-2012 5-year est.); Bachelor's degree or higher: 15.0% (2008-2012 5-year est.); Master's degree or higher: 4.5% (2008-2012 5-year est.).
Housing: Homeownership rate: 83.3% (2008-2012 5-year est.); Median home value: $170,000 (2008-2012 5-year est.); Median contract rent: $946 per month (2008-2012 5-year est.); Median year structure built: 1971 (2008-2012 5-year est.).
Health Insurance: 73.6% Private; 24.0% Public; 12.3% None. (2008-2012 5-year est.)
Transportation: Commute to work: 96.3% car, 0.8% public transportation, 0.4% walk, 2.1% work from home (2008-2012 5-year est.); Travel time to work: 30.0% less than 15 minutes, 28.6% 15 to 30 minutes, 21.1% 30 to 45 minutes, 8.6% 45 to 60 minutes, 11.7% 60 minutes or more (2008-2012 5-year est.)

BRISTOL (unincorporated postal area)
Zip Code: 60512
  Covers a land area of 7.937 square miles and a water area of 0 square miles. Located at 41.70° N. Lat; 88.43° W. Long. Elevation is 640 feet. Population: 1,111 (2010); Density: 140.0 persons per square mile (2010); Race: 92.5% White, 0.6% Black/African American, 0.9% Asian, 0.2% American Indian/Alaska Native, 0.1% Native Hawaiian/Other Pacific Islander, 5.7% Some other race, 1.2% Two or more races, 9.2% Hispanic of any race (2010); Average household size: 2.74 (2010); Median age: 46.7 (2010); Males per 100 females: 109.6 (2010); Homeownership rate: 91.8% (2010)

LISBON (village). Covers a land area of 1.740 square miles and a water area of 0 square miles. Located at 41.48° N. Lat; 88.46° W. Long. Elevation is 669 feet.
Population: 216 (1990); 248 (2000); 285 (2010); Density: 181.6 persons per square mile (2008-2012 5-year est.); Race: 98.4% White, 0.0% Black/African American, 0.0% Asian, 0.0% American Indian/Alaska Native, 0.0% Native Hawaiian/Other Pacific Islander, 1.6% Some other race, 1.6% Two or more races, 9.8% Hispanic of any race (2008-2012 5-year est.); Average household size: 2.87 (2008-2012 5-year est.); Median age: 30.9 (2008-2012 5-year est.); Males per 100 females: 82.7 (2008-2012 5-year est.); Marriage status: 38.3% never married, 44.8% now married, 10.1% widowed, 6.9% divorced (2008-2012 5-year est.); Foreign born: 5.1% (2008-2012 5-year est.); Ancestry (includes multiple ancestries): 34.5% Norwegian, 23.7% German, 11.4% Irish, 10.1% Italian, 6.6% Greek (2008-2012 5-year est.).
Economy: Single-family building permits issued: 0 (2013); Multi-family building permits issued: 0 (2013); Homeowner vacancy rate: 0.0%. Rental vacancy rate: 5.9%. (2008-2012 5-year est.); Employment by occupation: 5.6% management, business, and financial, 3.2% computer, engineering, and science, 3.2% education, legal, community service, arts, and media, 6.3% healthcare practitioners, 12.7% service, 34.1% sales and office, 13.5% natural resources, construction, and maintenance, 21.4% production, transportation, and material moving (2008-2012 5-year est.).
Income: Per capita income: $24,311 (2008-2012 5-year est.); Median household income: $63,250 (2008-2012 5-year est.); Average household income: $67,238 (2008-2012 5-year est.); Percent of households with income of $100,000 or more: 17.2% (2008-2012 5-year est.); Poverty rate: 15.1% (2008-2012 5-year est.).
Education: Percent of population age 25 and over with: High school diploma (including GED) or higher: 88.1% (2008-2012 5-year est.); Bachelor's degree or higher: 11.9% (2008-2012 5-year est.); Master's degree or higher: 4.0% (2008-2012 5-year est.).
Housing: Homeownership rate: 70.9% (2008-2012 5-year est.); Median home value: $169,700 (2008-2012 5-year est.); Median contract rent: $417 per month (2008-2012 5-year est.); Median year structure built: 1948 (2008-2012 5-year est.).
Health Insurance: 62.3% Private; 30.7% Public; 18.4% None. (2008-2012 5-year est.)
Transportation: Commute to work: 96.0% car, 0.0% public transportation, 1.6% walk, 2.4% work from home (2008-2012 5-year est.); Travel time to work: 28.5% less than 15 minutes, 18.7% 15 to 30 minutes, 28.5% 30 to 45 minutes, 18.7% 45 to 60 minutes, 5.7% 60 minutes or more (2008-2012 5-year est.)

MILLBROOK (village). Covers a land area of 2.079 square miles and a water area of 0 square miles. Located at 41.60° N. Lat; 88.54° W. Long. Elevation is 627 feet.
History: Incorporated November 5, 2002.
Population: n/a (1990); n/a (2000); 335 (2010); Density: 130.3 persons per square mile (2008-2012 5-year est.); Race: 96.7% White, 0.0% Black/African American, 0.0% Asian, 0.0% American Indian/Alaska Native, 0.0% Native Hawaiian/Other Pacific Islander, 3.3% Some other race, 1.8% Two or more races, 10.3% Hispanic of any race (2008-2012 5-year est.); Average household size: 2.49 (2008-2012 5-year est.); Median age: 49.4 (2008-2012 5-year est.); Males per 100 females: 80.7 (2008-2012 5-year est.); Marriage status: 19.4% never married, 69.8% now married, 1.2% widowed, 9.5% divorced (2008-2012 5-year est.); Foreign born: 4.1% (2008-2012 5-year est.); Ancestry (includes multiple ancestries): 42.4% German, 11.4% Irish, 10.7% Polish, 9.2% Norwegian, 7.4% English (2008-2012 5-year est.).
Economy: Homeowner vacancy rate: 0.0%. Rental vacancy rate: 0.0%. (2008-2012 5-year est.); Employment by occupation: 10.1% management, business, and financial, 4.5% computer, engineering, and science, 9.5% education, legal, community service, arts, and media, 4.5% healthcare practitioners, 13.4% service, 27.4% sales and office, 11.7% natural resources, construction, and maintenance, 19.0% production, transportation, and material moving (2008-2012 5-year est.).
Income: Per capita income: $42,237 (2008-2012 5-year est.); Median household income: $98,750 (2008-2012 5-year est.); Average household income: $103,863 (2008-2012 5-year est.); Percent of households with income of $100,000 or more: 48.6% (2008-2012 5-year est.); Poverty rate: 1.8% (2008-2012 5-year est.).
Education: Percent of population age 25 and over with: High school diploma (including GED) or higher: 99.0% (2008-2012 5-year est.);

Bachelor's degree or higher: 29.9% (2008-2012 5-year est.); Master's degree or higher: 3.4% (2008-2012 5-year est.).
School District(s)
Newark CCSD 66 (PK-08)
   2011-12 Enrollment: 229. . . . . (815) 695-5143
Housing: Homeownership rate: 94.5% (2008-2012 5-year est.); Median home value: $279,200 (2008-2012 5-year est.); Median contract rent: $625 per month (2008-2012 5-year est.); Median year structure built: 1986 (2008-2012 5-year est.).
Health Insurance: 91.5% Private; 15.1% Public; 1.8% None. (2008-2012 5-year est.)
Transportation: Commute to work: 88.3% car, 1.7% public transportation, 3.4% walk, 6.7% work from home (2008-2012 5-year est.); Travel time to work: 22.8% less than 15 minutes, 25.7% 15 to 30 minutes, 17.4% 30 to 45 minutes, 9.6% 45 to 60 minutes, 24.6% 60 minutes or more (2008-2012 5-year est.)

MONTGOMERY (village). Covers a land area of 9.341 square miles and a water area of 0.172 square miles. Located at 41.72° N. Lat; 88.36° W. Long. Elevation is 640 feet.
Population: 4,267 (1990); 5,471 (2000); 18,438 (2010); Density: 1,940.2 persons per square mile (2008-2012 5-year est.); Race: 72.4% White, 8.1% Black/African American, 4.6% Asian, 0.1% American Indian/Alaska Native, 0.0% Native Hawaiian/Other Pacific Islander, 14.8% Some other race, 1.6% Two or more races, 31.7% Hispanic of any race (2008-2012 5-year est.); Average household size: 3.02 (2008-2012 5-year est.); Median age: 32.3 (2008-2012 5-year est.); Males per 100 females: 100.8 (2008-2012 5-year est.); Marriage status: 26.8% never married, 57.4% now married, 5.5% widowed, 10.3% divorced (2008-2012 5-year est.); Foreign born: 15.6% (2008-2012 5-year est.); Ancestry (includes multiple ancestries): 21.0% German, 10.5% Irish, 6.9% Polish, 6.1% Italian, 5.8% English (2008-2012 5-year est.).
Economy: Single-family building permits issued: 25 (2013); Multi-family building permits issued: 0 (2013); Homeowner vacancy rate: 0.6%. Rental vacancy rate: 4.1%. (2008-2012 5-year est.); Employment by occupation: 17.6% management, business, and financial, 6.3% computer, engineering, and science, 7.7% education, legal, community service, arts, and media, 4.2% healthcare practitioners, 12.7% service, 29.1% sales and office, 9.9% natural resources, construction, and maintenance, 12.4% production, transportation, and material moving (2008-2012 5-year est.).
Income: Per capita income: $25,913 (2008-2012 5-year est.); Median household income: $73,406 (2008-2012 5-year est.); Average household income: $77,195 (2008-2012 5-year est.); Percent of households with income of $100,000 or more: 27.1% (2008-2012 5-year est.); Poverty rate: 7.3% (2008-2012 5-year est.).
Education: Percent of population age 25 and over with: High school diploma (including GED) or higher: 86.5% (2008-2012 5-year est.); Bachelor's degree or higher: 28.9% (2008-2012 5-year est.); Master's degree or higher: 6.3% (2008-2012 5-year est.).
School District(s)
Aurora West USD 129 (PK-12)
   2011-12 Enrollment: 12,467 . . . . (630) 301-5000
Kaneland CUSD 302 (PK-12)
   2011-12 Enrollment: 4,835 . . . . (630) 365-5111
Oswego CUSD 308 (PK-12)
   2011-12 Enrollment: 17,150 . . . . (630) 636-3080
Housing: Homeownership rate: 84.1% (2008-2012 5-year est.); Median home value: $193,900 (2008-2012 5-year est.); Median contract rent: <$101 per month (2008-2012 5-year est.); Median year structure built: 2002 (2008-2012 5-year est.).
Health Insurance: 80.8% Private; 20.6% Public; 5.8% None. (2008-2012 5-year est.)
Safety: Violent crime rate: 9.6 per 10,000 population; Property crime rate: 195.8 per 10,000 population (2012).
Transportation: Commute to work: 92.8% car, 3.7% public transportation, 0.0% walk, 3.1% work from home (2008-2012 5-year est.); Travel time to work: 15.8% less than 15 minutes, 30.4% 15 to 30 minutes, 26.9% 30 to 45 minutes, 13.0% 45 to 60 minutes, 14.0% 60 minutes or more (2008-2012 5-year est.)

NEWARK (village). Covers a land area of 1.116 square miles and a water area of <.001 square miles. Located at 41.54° N. Lat; 88.58° W. Long. Elevation is 673 feet.
Population: 840 (1990); 887 (2000); 992 (2010); Density: 834.8 persons per square mile (2008-2012 5-year est.); Race: 97.0% White, 0.0%

Black/African American, 0.2% Asian, 0.0% American Indian/Alaska Native, 0.0% Native Hawaiian/Other Pacific Islander, 2.8% Some other race, 0.5% Two or more races, 11.2% Hispanic of any race (2008-2012 5-year est.); Average household size: 2.57 (2008-2012 5-year est.); Median age: 39.0 (2008-2012 5-year est.); Males per 100 females: 93.0 (2008-2012 5-year est.); Marriage status: 17.7% never married, 70.8% now married, 6.6% widowed, 4.8% divorced (2008-2012 5-year est.); Foreign born: 2.3% (2008-2012 5-year est.); Ancestry (includes multiple ancestries): 29.1% German, 18.3% Norwegian, 18.0% Irish, 11.7% English, 8.2% Polish (2008-2012 5-year est.).

Economy: Single-family building permits issued: 0 (2013); Multi-family building permits issued: 0 (2013); Homeowner vacancy rate: 0.0%. Rental vacancy rate: 0.0%. (2008-2012 5-year est.); Employment by occupation: 10.3% management, business, and financial, 1.4% computer, engineering, and science, 7.7% education, legal, community service, arts, and media, 5.1% healthcare practitioners, 17.6% service, 28.7% sales and office, 13.7% natural resources, construction, and maintenance, 15.4% production, transportation, and material moving (2008-2012 5-year est.).

Income: Per capita income: $28,996 (2008-2012 5-year est.); Median household income: $67,750 (2008-2012 5-year est.); Average household income: $73,025 (2008-2012 5-year est.); Percent of households with income of $100,000 or more: 21.3% (2008-2012 5-year est.); Poverty rate: 3.7% (2008-2012 5-year est.).

Education: Percent of population age 25 and over with: High school diploma (including GED) or higher: 91.5% (2008-2012 5-year est.); Bachelor's degree or higher: 19.0% (2008-2012 5-year est.); Master's degree or higher: 5.9% (2008-2012 5-year est.).

School District(s)

Lisbon CCSD 90 (KG-08)

   2011-12 Enrollment: 127 . . . . (815) 736-6324

Newark CCSD 66 (PK-08)

   2011-12 Enrollment: 229 . . . . (815) 695-5143

Newark CHSD 18 (09-12)

   2011-12 Enrollment: 187 . . . . (815) 695-5164

Housing: Homeownership rate: 73.6% (2008-2012 5-year est.); Median home value: $213,900 (2008-2012 5-year est.); Median contract rent: $663 per month (2008-2012 5-year est.); Median year structure built: 1966 (2008-2012 5-year est.).

Health Insurance: 75.6% Private; 26.1% Public; 12.6% None. (2008-2012 5-year est.)

Transportation: Commute to work: 81.6% car, 2.0% public transportation, 5.0% walk, 8.2% work from home (2008-2012 5-year est.); Travel time to work: 20.1% less than 15 minutes, 32.3% 15 to 30 minutes, 18.3% 30 to 45 minutes, 10.5% 45 to 60 minutes, 18.8% 60 minutes or more (2008-2012 5-year est.)

OSWEGO (village). Covers a land area of 15.528 square miles and a water area of 0.106 square miles. Located at 41.68° N. Lat; 88.34° W. Long. Elevation is 640 feet.

Population: 3,876 (1990); 13,326 (2000); 30,355 (2010); Density: 1,951.5 persons per square mile (2008-2012 5-year est.); Race: 86.7% White, 5.7% Black/African American, 3.2% Asian, 0.1% American Indian/Alaska Native, 0.0% Native Hawaiian/Other Pacific Islander, 4.3% Some other race, 3.4% Two or more races, 10.3% Hispanic of any race (2008-2012 5-year est.); Average household size: 3.09 (2008-2012 5-year est.); Median age: 33.7 (2008-2012 5-year est.); Males per 100 females: 99.0 (2008-2012 5-year est.); Marriage status: 22.6% never married, 67.8% now married, 3.6% widowed, 6.1% divorced (2008-2012 5-year est.); Foreign born: 6.2% (2008-2012 5-year est.); Ancestry (includes multiple ancestries): 28.5% German, 20.3% Irish, 12.2% Italian, 9.7% Polish, 8.3% English (2008-2012 5-year est.).

Economy: Unemployment rate: 6.8% (April 2014); Total civilian labor force: 17,646 (April 2014); Single-family building permits issued: 226 (2013); Multi-family building permits issued: 0 (2013); Homeowner vacancy rate: 0.6%. Rental vacancy rate: 8.8%. (2008-2012 5-year est.); Employment by occupation: 19.7% management, business, and financial, 7.4% computer, engineering, and science, 14.2% education, legal, community service, arts, and media, 7.2% healthcare practitioners, 9.7% service, 26.1% sales and office, 6.0% natural resources, construction, and maintenance, 9.8% production, transportation, and material moving (2008-2012 5-year est.).

Income: Per capita income: $34,046 (2008-2012 5-year est.); Median household income: $96,819 (2008-2012 5-year est.); Average household income: $105,031 (2008-2012 5-year est.); Percent of households with

income of $100,000 or more: 47.3% (2008-2012 5-year est.); Poverty rate: 3.8% (2008-2012 5-year est.).

Taxes: Total city taxes per capita: $184 (2011); City property taxes per capita: $50 (2011).

Education: Percent of population age 25 and over with: High school diploma (including GED) or higher: 96.0% (2008-2012 5-year est.); Bachelor's degree or higher: 44.7% (2008-2012 5-year est.); Master's degree or higher: 16.0% (2008-2012 5-year est.).

School District(s)

Grundy/kendall Roe (08-12)

   2011-12 Enrollment: n/a . . . . (815) 941-3247

Kendall County Spec Educ Coop (PK-12)

   2011-12 Enrollment: n/a . . . . (630) 553-5833

Oswego CUSD 308 (PK-12)

   2011-12 Enrollment: 17,150 . . . . (630) 636-3080

Vocational/Technical School(s)

Hair Professionals School of Cosmetology (Private, For-profit)

   Fall 2012 Enrollment: 76 . . . . (630) 554-2266

   2012-13 Tuition: $17,450

Housing: Homeownership rate: 87.4% (2008-2012 5-year est.); Median home value: $244,900 (2008-2012 5-year est.); Median contract rent: $1,368 per month (2008-2012 5-year est.); Median year structure built: 2001 (2008-2012 5-year est.).

Health Insurance: 89.3% Private; 11.2% Public; 5.4% None. (2008-2012 5-year est.)

Safety: Violent crime rate: 5.2 per 10,000 population; Property crime rate: 162.6 per 10,000 population (2012).

Transportation: Commute to work: 90.6% car, 4.2% public transportation, 0.4% walk, 4.0% work from home (2008-2012 5-year est.); Travel time to work: 22.9% less than 15 minutes, 27.4% 15 to 30 minutes, 21.4% 30 to 45 minutes, 10.9% 45 to 60 minutes, 17.4% 60 minutes or more (2008-2012 5-year est.)

Additional Information Contacts

Oswego Chamber of Commerce . . . . (630) 554-3505

   http://www.oswegochamber.org

Village of Oswego . . . . (630) 554-3618

   http://www.oswegoil.org

PLANO (city). Covers a land area of 7.458 square miles and a water area of 0.043 square miles. Located at 41.67° N. Lat; 88.53° W. Long. Elevation is 650 feet.

History: Plano was settled by a group of Norwegian Quakers led by Kleng Peerson in 1835.

Population: 5,104 (1990); 5,633 (2000); 10,856 (2010); Density: 1,421.6 persons per square mile (2008-2012 5-year est.); Race: 74.1% White, 5.5% Black/African American, 0.1% Asian, 2.3% American Indian/Alaska Native, 0.0% Native Hawaiian/Other Pacific Islander, 18.0% Some other race, 2.7% Two or more races, 34.1% Hispanic of any race (2008-2012 5-year est.); Average household size: 2.90 (2008-2012 5-year est.); Median age: 29.5 (2008-2012 5-year est.); Males per 100 females: 98.8 (2008-2012 5-year est.); Marriage status: 25.9% never married, 61.6% now married, 3.9% widowed, 8.5% divorced (2008-2012 5-year est.); Foreign born: 17.1% (2008-2012 5-year est.); Ancestry (includes multiple ancestries): 19.1% German, 18.0% Irish, 9.6% Italian, 7.1% Polish, 6.1% English (2008-2012 5-year est.).

Economy: Single-family building permits issued: 0 (2013); Multi-family building permits issued: 0 (2013); Homeowner vacancy rate: 2.1%. Rental vacancy rate: 5.8%. (2008-2012 5-year est.); Employment by occupation: 11.7% management, business, and financial, 2.4% computer, engineering, and science, 12.8% education, legal, community service, arts, and media, 4.3% healthcare practitioners, 11.1% service, 25.2% sales and office, 10.8% natural resources, construction, and maintenance, 21.8% production, transportation, and material moving (2008-2012 5-year est.).

Income: Per capita income: $25,568 (2008-2012 5-year est.); Median household income: $62,563 (2008-2012 5-year est.); Average household income: $72,719 (2008-2012 5-year est.); Percent of households with income of $100,000 or more: 25.7% (2008-2012 5-year est.); Poverty rate: 6.5% (2008-2012 5-year est.).

Education: Percent of population age 25 and over with: High school diploma (including GED) or higher: 81.0% (2008-2012 5-year est.); Bachelor's degree or higher: 21.6% (2008-2012 5-year est.); Master's degree or higher: 8.1% (2008-2012 5-year est.).

School District(s)

Grundy/kendall Roe (08-12)

   2011-12 Enrollment: n/a . . . . (815) 941-3247

Plano CUSD 88 (PK-12)

2011-12 Enrollment: 2,320 . . . . (630) 552-8978

Housing: Homeownership rate: 80.2% (2008-2012 5-year est.); Median home value: $167,500 (2008-2012 5-year est.); Median contract rent: $814 per month (2008-2012 5-year est.); Median year structure built: 1993 (2008-2012 5-year est.).

Health Insurance: 76.7% Private; 22.1% Public; 10.7% None. (2008-2012 5-year est.)

Safety: Violent crime rate: 4.5 per 10,000 population; Property crime rate: 123.2 per 10,000 population (2012).

Transportation: Commute to work: 94.4% car, 0.8% public transportation, 0.0% walk, 3.2% work from home (2008-2012 5-year est.); Travel time to work: 20.8% less than 15 minutes, 24.3% 15 to 30 minutes, 21.3% 30 to 45 minutes, 14.8% 45 to 60 minutes, 18.8% 60 minutes or more (2008-2012 5-year est.); Amtrak: Train service available.

Additional Information Contacts

City of Plano . . . . (630) 552-8275
   http://www.cityofplanoil.com
Plano Area Chamber of Commerce . . . . (630) 552-7272
   http://www.planocommerce.org

PLATTVILLE (village). Covers a land area of 2.273 square miles and a water area of 0 square miles. Located at 41.53° N. Lat; 88.39° W. Long. Elevation is 594 feet.

History: Incorporated March 2006.

Population: n/a (1990); n/a (2000); 242 (2010); Density: 102.5 persons per square mile (2008-2012 5-year est.); Race: 93.6% White, 0.0% Black/African American, 0.0% Asian, 0.0% American Indian/Alaska Native, 0.0% Native Hawaiian/Other Pacific Islander, 6.4% Some other race, 1.7% Two or more races, 5.6% Hispanic of any race (2008-2012 5-year est.); Average household size: 2.59 (2008-2012 5-year est.); Median age: 50.9 (2008-2012 5-year est.); Males per 100 females: 115.7 (2008-2012 5-year est.); Marriage status: 29.8% never married, 52.7% now married, 9.3% widowed, 8.3% divorced (2008-2012 5-year est.); Foreign born: 0.0% (2008-2012 5-year est.); Ancestry (includes multiple ancestries): 36.5% German, 26.2% Irish, 20.6% English, 7.3% Norwegian, 6.4% Italian (2008-2012 5-year est.).

Economy: Homeowner vacancy rate: 0.0%. Rental vacancy rate: 0.0%. (2008-2012 5-year est.); Employment by occupation: 12.0% management, business, and financial, 2.6% computer, engineering, and science, 0.0% education, legal, community service, arts, and media, 12.8% healthcare practitioners, 4.3% service, 33.3% sales and office, 12.0% natural resources, construction, and maintenance, 23.1% production, transportation, and material moving (2008-2012 5-year est.).

Income: Per capita income: $28,408 (2008-2012 5-year est.); Median household income: $66,667 (2008-2012 5-year est.); Average household income: $70,352 (2008-2012 5-year est.); Percent of households with income of $100,000 or more: 26.7% (2008-2012 5-year est.); Poverty rate: 9.9% (2008-2012 5-year est.).

Education: Percent of population age 25 and over with: High school diploma (including GED) or higher: 81.2% (2008-2012 5-year est.); Bachelor's degree or higher: 19.3% (2008-2012 5-year est.); Master's degree or higher: 4.4% (2008-2012 5-year est.).

Housing: Homeownership rate: 76.7% (2008-2012 5-year est.); Median home value: $217,900 (2008-2012 5-year est.); Median contract rent: $925 per month (2008-2012 5-year est.); Median year structure built: 1972 (2008-2012 5-year est.).

Health Insurance: 76.4% Private; 37.3% Public; 3.4% None. (2008-2012 5-year est.)

Transportation: Commute to work: 99.1% car, 0.0% public transportation, 0.0% walk, 0.9% work from home (2008-2012 5-year est.); Travel time to work: 0.0% less than 15 minutes, 40.5% 15 to 30 minutes, 39.7% 30 to 45 minutes, 3.4% 45 to 60 minutes, 16.4% 60 minutes or more (2008-2012 5-year est.)

YORKVILLE (city). County seat. Covers a land area of 19.966 square miles and a water area of 0.088 square miles. Located at 41.66° N. Lat; 88.44° W. Long. Elevation is 607 feet.

Population: 3,925 (1990); 6,189 (2000); 16,921 (2010); Density: 854.2 persons per square mile (2008-2012 5-year est.); Race: 88.0% White, 7.0% Black/African American, 1.6% Asian, 0.0% American Indian/Alaska Native, 0.0% Native Hawaiian/Other Pacific Islander, 3.4% Some other race, 2.4% Two or more races, 8.8% Hispanic of any race (2008-2012 5-year est.); Average household size: 2.81 (2008-2012 5-year est.); Median age: 32.9 (2008-2012 5-year est.); Males per 100 females: 110.1

(2008-2012 5-year est.); Marriage status: 28.3% never married, 60.6% now married, 3.3% widowed, 7.8% divorced (2008-2012 5-year est.); Foreign born: 5.8% (2008-2012 5-year est.); Ancestry (includes multiple ancestries): 25.7% German, 14.8% Irish, 14.0% Italian, 9.3% Polish, 8.9% English (2008-2012 5-year est.).

Economy: Single-family building permits issued: 81 (2013); Multi-family building permits issued: 0 (2013); Homeowner vacancy rate: 2.8%. Rental vacancy rate: 7.3%. (2008-2012 5-year est.); Employment by occupation: 14.7% management, business, and financial, 6.4% computer, engineering, and science, 11.5% education, legal, community service, arts, and media, 6.5% healthcare practitioners, 15.1% service, 26.9% sales and office, 10.0% natural resources, construction, and maintenance, 9.0% production, transportation, and material moving (2008-2012 5-year est.).

Income: Per capita income: $33,551 (2008-2012 5-year est.); Median household income: $80,570 (2008-2012 5-year est.); Average household income: $94,643 (2008-2012 5-year est.); Percent of households with income of $100,000 or more: 37.6% (2008-2012 5-year est.); Poverty rate: 1.7% (2008-2012 5-year est.).

Taxes: Total city taxes per capita: $572 (2011); City property taxes per capita: $282 (2011).

Education: Percent of population age 25 and over with: High school diploma (including GED) or higher: 93.3% (2008-2012 5-year est.); Bachelor's degree or higher: 30.5% (2008-2012 5-year est.); Master's degree or higher: 11.5% (2008-2012 5-year est.).

School District(s)

Grundy/kendall Roe (08-12)

2011-12 Enrollment: n/a . . . . (815) 941-3247
Yorkville CUSD 115 (PK-12)

2011-12 Enrollment: 5,470 . . . . (630) 553-4382

Housing: Homeownership rate: 75.3% (2008-2012 5-year est.); Median home value: $243,100 (2008-2012 5-year est.); Median contract rent: $977 per month (2008-2012 5-year est.); Median year structure built: 2002 (2008-2012 5-year est.).

Health Insurance: 78.3% Private; 18.6% Public; 9.7% None. (2008-2012 5-year est.)

Safety: Violent crime rate: 12.8 per 10,000 population; Property crime rate: 149.9 per 10,000 population (2012).

Transportation: Commute to work: 91.0% car, 0.9% public transportation, 1.3% walk, 5.5% work from home (2008-2012 5-year est.); Travel time to work: 21.8% less than 15 minutes, 27.2% 15 to 30 minutes, 20.8% 30 to 45 minutes, 15.5% 45 to 60 minutes, 14.8% 60 minutes or more (2008-2012 5-year est.)

Additional Information Contacts

United City of Yorkville . . . . (630) 553-4350
   http://www.yorkville.il.us
Yorkville Area Chamber of Commerce . . . . (630) 553-6853
   http://www.yorkvillechamber.org

Knox County

Located in northwest central Illinois; drained by the Spoon River and Pope and Henderson Creeks. Covers a land area of 716.395 square miles, a water area of 3.417 square miles, and is located in the Central Time Zone at 40.93° N. Lat., 90.21° W. Long. The county was founded in 1825. County seat is Galesburg.

Knox County is part of the Galesburg, IL Micropolitan Statistical Area. The entire metro area includes: Knox County, IL

Weather Station: Galesburg   Elevation: 770 feet

	Jan	Feb	Mar	Apr	May	Jun	Jul	Aug	Sep	Oct	Nov	Dec
High	31	36	49	62	73	81	85	83	76	63	49	34
Low	16	20	30	41	52	61	66	64	55	43	32	20
Precip	1.5	1.6	2.7	3.7	4.3	4.0	4.3	4.2	3.5	2.7	2.9	2.4
Snow	7.4	5.2	2.0	1.3	tr	0.0	0.0	0.0	0.0	tr	0.8	6.0

High and Low temperatures in degrees Fahrenheit; Precipitation and Snow in inches

Population: 56,393 (1990); 55,836 (2000); 52,919 (2010); Race: 88.1% White, 7.9% Black/African American, 0.8% Asian, 0.2% American Indian/Alaska Native, 0.0% Native Hawaiian/Other Pacific Islander, 3.0% Some other race, 1.5% Two or more races, 4.9% Hispanic of any race (2008-2012 5-year est.); Density: 72.9 persons per square mile (2008-2012 5-year est.); Average household size: 2.22 (2008-2012 5-year est.); Median age: 41.8 (2008-2012 5-year est.); Males per 100 females: 100.9 (2008-2012 5-year est.).

Religion: Six largest groups: 7.2% Methodist/Pietist, 6.3% Catholicism, 6.1% Baptist, 5.2% Lutheran, 2.7% Presbyterian-Reformed, 2.5% Non-denominational Protestant (2010)

Economy: Unemployment rate: 6.5% (April 2014); Total civilian labor force: 23,968 (April 2014); Leading industries: 23.0% health care and social assistance; 22.7% retail trade; 11.2% accommodation & food services (2012); Farms: 856 totaling 347,597 acres (2012); Companies that employ 500 or more persons: 2 (2012); Companies that employ 100 to 499 persons: 23 (2012); Companies that employ less than 100 persons: 1,062 (2012); Black-owned businesses: n/a (2007); Hispanic-owned businesses: n/a (2007); Asian-owned businesses: n/a (2007); Women-owned businesses: 1,066 (2007); Single-family building permits issued: 6 (2013); Multi-family building permits issued: 2 (2013).

Income: Per capita income: $21,653 (2008-2012 5-year est.); Median household income: $40,419 (2008-2012 5-year est.); Average household income: $51,190 (2008-2012 5-year est.); Percent of households with income of $100,000 or more: 10.1% (2008-2012 5-year est.); Poverty rate: 16.0% (2008-2012 5-year est.); Bankruptcy rate: 2.99% (2013).

Taxes: Total county taxes per capita: $171 (2011); County property taxes per capita: $150 (2011).

Education: Percent of population age 25 and over with: High school diploma (including GED) or higher: 85.9% (2008-2012 5-year est.); Bachelor's degree or higher: 16.9% (2008-2012 5-year est.); Master's degree or higher: 6.1% (2008-2012 5-year est.).

Housing: Homeownership rate: 67.0% (2008-2012 5-year est.); Median home value: $80,400 (2008-2012 5-year est.); Median contract rent: $417 per month (2008-2012 5-year est.); Median year structure built: 1954 (2008-2012 5-year est.)

Health: Birth rate: 101.4 per 10,000 population (2013); Death rate: 110.6 per 10,000 population (2013); Age-adjusted cancer mortality rate: 155.9 deaths per 100,000 population (2011); Number of physicians: 16.7 per 10,000 population (2011); Hospital beds: 49.7 per 10,000 population (2010); Hospital admissions: 1,659.7 per 10,000 population (2010).

Elections: 2012 Presidential election results: 57.7% Obama, 40.6% Romney

National and State Parks: Snakeden Hollow State Fish and Wildlife Area

Additional Information Contacts

Knox County Government . . . . (309) 343-3121
    http://www.co.knox.il.us

Knox County Communities

ABINGDON (city). Covers a land area of 1.458 square miles and a water area of 0 square miles. Located at 40.80° N. Lat; 90.40° W. Long. Elevation is 751 feet.

History: Incorporated 1857.

Population: 3,597 (1990); 3,612 (2000); 3,319 (2010); Density: 2,102.2 persons per square mile (2008-2012 5-year est.); Race: 91.4% White, 3.0% Black/African American, 0.0% Asian, 0.7% American Indian/Alaska Native, 0.0% Native Hawaiian/Other Pacific Islander, 4.9% Some other race, 4.9% Two or more races, 0.8% Hispanic of any race (2008-2012 5-year est.); Average household size: 2.24 (2008-2012 5-year est.); Median age: 41.3 (2008-2012 5-year est.); Males per 100 females: 101.8 (2008-2012 5-year est.); Marriage status: 22.6% never married, 47.1% now married, 14.1% widowed, 16.2% divorced (2008-2012 5-year est.); Foreign born: 0.2% (2008-2012 5-year est.); Ancestry (includes multiple ancestries): 23.1% German, 16.7% Irish, 11.1% Swedish, 9.3% American, 8.5% English (2008-2012 5-year est.).

Economy: Single-family building permits issued: 0 (2013); Multi-family building permits issued: 0 (2013); Homeowner vacancy rate: 3.6%. Rental vacancy rate: 0.0%. (2008-2012 5-year est.); Employment by occupation: 7.6% management, business, and financial, 1.7% computer, engineering, and science, 4.8% education, legal, community service, arts, and media, 4.7% healthcare practitioners, 12.9% service, 35.1% sales and office, 7.9% natural resources, construction, and maintenance, 25.4% production, transportation, and material moving (2008-2012 5-year est.).

Income: Per capita income: $20,209 (2008-2012 5-year est.); Median household income: $39,758 (2008-2012 5-year est.); Average household income: $45,415 (2008-2012 5-year est.); Percent of households with income of $100,000 or more: 2.2% (2008-2012 5-year est.); Poverty rate: 16.7% (2008-2012 5-year est.).

Taxes: Total city taxes per capita: $96 (2011); City property taxes per capita: $78 (2011).

Education: Percent of population age 25 and over with: High school diploma (including GED) or higher: 84.9% (2008-2012 5-year est.);

Bachelor's degree or higher: 8.0% (2008-2012 5-year est.); Master's degree or higher: 2.5% (2008-2012 5-year est.).

School District(s)

Abingdon CUSD 217 (PK-12)
    2011-12 Enrollment: 761 . . . . (309) 462-2301

Housing: Homeownership rate: 63.9% (2008-2012 5-year est.); Median home value: $62,900 (2008-2012 5-year est.); Median contract rent: $392 per month (2008-2012 5-year est.); Median year structure built: 1957 (2008-2012 5-year est.).

Health Insurance: 63.6% Private; 43.9% Public; 9.1% None. (2008-2012 5-year est.)

Transportation: Commute to work: 98.1% car, 0.0% public transportation, 1.3% walk, 0.0% work from home (2008-2012 5-year est.); Travel time to work: 38.7% less than 15 minutes, 39.9% 15 to 30 minutes, 7.7% 30 to 45 minutes, 1.3% 45 to 60 minutes, 12.5% 60 minutes or more (2008-2012 5-year est.)

ALTONA (village). Covers a land area of 0.997 square miles and a water area of 0 square miles. Located at 41.12° N. Lat; 90.16° W. Long. Elevation is 761 foot.

Population: 559 (1990); 570 (2000); 531 (2010); Density: 464.5 persons per square mile (2008-2012 5-year est.); Race: 97.8% White, 0.0% Black/African American, 0.6% Asian, 0.0% American Indian/Alaska Native, 0.0% Native Hawaiian/Other Pacific Islander, 1.6% Some other race, 0.6% Two or more races, 1.5% Hispanic of any race (2008-2012 5-year est.); Average household size: 2.33 (2008-2012 5-year est.); Median age: 43.6 (2008-2012 5-year est.); Males per 100 females: 99.6 (2008-2012 5-year est.); Marriage status: 34.8% never married, 51.7% now married, 6.6% widowed, 6.9% divorced (2008-2012 5-year est.); Foreign born: 0.6% (2008-2012 5-year est.); Ancestry (includes multiple ancestries): 23.3% German, 16.2% Swedish, 11.9% English, 9.9% Irish, 8.4% American (2008-2012 5-year est.).

Economy: Homeowner vacancy rate: 0.0%. Rental vacancy rate: 0.0%. (2008-2012 5-year est.); Employment by occupation: 3.3% management, business, and financial, 1.9% computer, engineering, and science, 7.4% education, legal, community service, arts, and media, 7.0% healthcare practitioners, 14.1% service, 30.7% sales and office, 9.6% natural resources, construction, and maintenance, 25.9% production, transportation, and material moving (2008-2012 5-year est.).

Income: Per capita income: $19,918 (2008-2012 5-year est.); Median household income: $42,625 (2008-2012 5-year est.); Average household income: $46,394 (2008-2012 5-year est.); Percent of households with income of $100,000 or more: 7.0% (2008-2012 5-year est.); Poverty rate: 11.9% (2008-2012 5-year est.).

Education: Percent of population age 25 and over with: High school diploma (including GED) or higher: 90.3% (2008-2012 5-year est.); Bachelor's degree or higher: 12.1% (2008-2012 5-year est.); Master's degree or higher: 2.5% (2008-2012 5-year est.).

School District(s)

R O W V A CUSD 208 (PK-12)
    2011-12 Enrollment: 702 . . . . (309) 483-3711

Housing: Homeownership rate: 85.9% (2008-2012 5-year est.); Median home value: $58,300 (2008-2012 5-year est.); Median contract rent: $329 per month (2008-2012 5-year est.); Median year structure built: 1945 (2008-2012 5-year est.).

Health Insurance: 76.9% Private; 28.5% Public; 6.5% None. (2008-2012 5-year est.)

Transportation: Commute to work: 93.6% car, 0.0% public transportation, 2.6% walk, 3.0% work from home (2008-2012 5-year est.); Travel time to work: 15.1% less than 15 minutes, 59.3% 15 to 30 minutes, 20.9% 30 to 45 minutes, 2.3% 45 to 60 minutes, 2.3% 60 minutes or more (2008-2012 5-year est.)

DAHINDA (unincorporated postal area)
Zip Code: 61428
    Covers a land area of 32.884 square miles and a water area of 0.914 square miles. Located at 40.94° N. Lat; 90.10° W. Long. Elevation is 584 feet. Population: 986 (2010); Density: 30.0 persons per square mile (2010); Race: 97.1% White, 0.9% Black/African American, 0.4% Asian, 0.1% American Indian/Alaska Native, 0.0% Native Hawaiian/Other Pacific Islander, 1.5% Some other race, 1.3% Two or more races, 1.3% Hispanic of any race (2010); Average household size: 2.20 (2010); Median age: 53.8 (2010); Males per 100 females: 101.2 (2010); Homeownership rate: 93.6% (2010)

EAST GALESBURG (village). Covers a land area of 1.438 square miles and a water area of 0.051 square miles. Located at 40.94° N. Lat; 90.31° W. Long. Elevation is 774 feet.

Population: 813 (1990); 839 (2000); 812 (2010); Density: 559.9 persons per square mile (2008-2012 5-year est.); Race: 96.5% White, 2.6% Black/African American, 0.0% Asian, 0.0% American Indian/Alaska Native, 0.0% Native Hawaiian/Other Pacific Islander, 0.9% Some other race, 0.0% Two or more races, 0.9% Hispanic of any race (2008-2012 5-year est.); Average household size: 2.33 (2008-2012 5-year est.); Median age: 48.1 (2008-2012 5-year est.); Males per 100 females: 104.8 (2008-2012 5-year est.); Marriage status: 21.6% never married, 61.5% now married, 4.5% widowed, 12.3% divorced (2008-2012 5-year est.); Foreign born: 0.0% (2008-2012 5-year est.); Ancestry (includes multiple ancestries): 26.5% German, 16.0% Swedish, 14.9% Irish, 13.9% English, 9.8% American (2008-2012 5-year est.).

Economy: Single-family building permits issued: 2 (2013); Multi-family building permits issued: 0 (2013); Homeowner vacancy rate: 2.0%. Rental vacancy rate: 0.0%. (2008-2012 5-year est.); Employment by occupation: 11.8% management, business, and financial, 1.7% computer, engineering, and science, 7.5% education, legal, community service, arts, and media, 6.0% healthcare practitioners, 14.7% service, 22.2% sales and office, 9.9% natural resources, construction, and maintenance, 26.1% production, transportation, and material moving (2008-2012 5-year est.).

Income: Per capita income: $27,105 (2008-2012 5-year est.); Median household income: $49,875 (2008-2012 5-year est.); Average household income: $64,586 (2008-2012 5-year est.); Percent of households with income of $100,000 or more: 11.3% (2008-2012 5-year est.); Poverty rate: 6.6% (2008-2012 5-year est.).

Education: Percent of population age 25 and over with: High school diploma (including GED) or higher: 84.5% (2008-2012 5-year est.); Bachelor's degree or higher: 12.2% (2008-2012 5-year est.); Master's degree or higher: 6.6% (2008-2012 5-year est.).

Housing: Homeownership rate: 69.3% (2008-2012 5-year est.); Median home value: $96,900 (2008-2012 5-year est.); Median contract rent: $525 per month (2008-2012 5-year est.); Median year structure built: 1969 (2008-2012 5-year est.).

Health Insurance: 73.2% Private; 33.7% Public; 11.3% None. (2008-2012 5-year est.)

Transportation: Commute to work: 99.5% car, 0.0% public transportation, 0.0% walk, 0.0% work from home (2008-2012 5-year est.); Travel time to work: 32.4% less than 15 minutes, 48.9% 15 to 30 minutes, 6.6% 30 to 45 minutes, 4.9% 45 to 60 minutes, 7.1% 60 minutes or more (2008-2012 5-year est.)

GALESBURG (city). County seat. Covers a land area of 17.750 square miles and a water area of 0.178 square miles. Located at 40.95° N. Lat; 90.38° W. Long. Elevation is 771 feet.

History: Galesburg was settled in 1836 on a site selected by an advance guard sent by Reverend George Washington Gale, a Presbyterian minister from New York who planned a town where morality and industry would rule. Among the early residents was the Ferris family, one of whom invented the ferris wheel, first shown at the Columbian Exposition in Chicago in 1893. Formerly Randall.

Population: 33,530 (1990); 33,706 (2000); 32,195 (2010); Density: 1,805.0 persons per square mile (2008-2012 5-year est.); Race: 82.6% White, 12.5% Black/African American, 1.1% Asian, 0.1% American Indian/Alaska Native, 0.0% Native Hawaiian/Other Pacific Islander, 3.7% Some other race, 1.3% Two or more races, 7.5% Hispanic of any race (2008-2012 5-year est.); Average household size: 2.12 (2008-2012 5-year est.); Median age: 39.8 (2008-2012 5-year est.); Males per 100 females: 101.1 (2008-2012 5-year est.); Marriage status: 37.4% never married, 39.4% now married, 8.2% widowed, 15.0% divorced (2008-2012 5-year est.); Foreign born: 3.8% (2008-2012 5-year est.); Ancestry (includes multiple ancestries): 19.1% German, 12.7% Irish, 9.1% English, 9.0% Swedish, 6.7% American (2008-2012 5-year est.).

Economy: Unemployment rate: 6.8% (April 2014); Total civilian labor force: 13,895 (April 2014); Single-family building permits issued: 4 (2013); Multi-family building permits issued: 2 (2013); Homeowner vacancy rate: 3.1%. Rental vacancy rate: 3.5%. (2008-2012 5-year est.); Employment by occupation: 8.0% management, business, and financial, 1.4% computer, engineering, and science, 11.5% education, legal, community service, arts, and media, 7.3% healthcare practitioners, 21.8% service, 26.3% sales and office, 7.1% natural resources, construction, and maintenance, 16.5% production, transportation, and material moving (2008-2012 5-year est.).

Income: Per capita income: $19,339 (2008-2012 5-year est.); Median household income: $33,109 (2008-2012 5-year est.); Average household income: $45,150 (2008-2012 5-year est.); Percent of households with income of $100,000 or more: 8.1% (2008-2012 5-year est.); Poverty rate: 21.1% (2008-2012 5-year est.).

Education: Percent of population age 25 and over with: High school diploma (including GED) or higher: 82.8% (2008-2012 5-year est.); Bachelor's degree or higher: 16.1% (2008-2012 5-year est.); Master's degree or higher: 7.2% (2008-2012 5-year est.).

School District(s)

Galesburg Area Voc Ctr (11-12)
  2011-12 Enrollment: n/a . . . . (309) 343-3733
Galesburg CUSD 205 (PK-12)
  2011-12 Enrollment: 4,592 . . . . (309) 343-1151
Knox Roe (07-12)
  2011-12 Enrollment: n/a . . . . (309) 345-3828

Four-year College(s)

Knox College (Private, Not-for-profit)
  Fall 2012 Enrollment: 1,394 . . . . (309) 341-7000
  2012-13 Tuition: In-state $36,492; Out-of-state $36,492

Two-year College(s)

Carl Sandburg College (Public)
  Fall 2012 Enrollment: 2,460 . . . . (309) 344-2518
  2012-13 Tuition: In-state $5,398; Out-of-state $6,518

Housing: Homeownership rate: 58.7% (2008-2012 5-year est.); Median home value: $73,900 (2008-2012 5-year est.); Median contract rent: $419 per month (2008-2012 5-year est.); Median year structure built: 1951 (2008-2012 5-year est.).

Health Insurance: 59.2% Private; 45.5% Public; 12.2% None. (2008-2012 5-year est.)

Hospitals: Galesburg Cottage Hospital (170 beds); OSF St Mary Medical Center (156 beds)

Safety: Violent crime rate: 38.2 per 10,000 population; Property crime rate: 340.9 per 10,000 population (2012).

Transportation: Commute to work: 88.2% car, 0.8% public transportation, 5.8% walk, 2.6% work from home (2008-2012 5-year est.); Travel time to work: 63.6% less than 15 minutes, 22.4% 15 to 30 minutes, 3.7% 30 to 45 minutes, 6.0% 45 to 60 minutes, 4.3% 60 minutes or more (2008-2012 5-year est.); Amtrak: Train service available.

Airports: Galesburg Municipal Airport (general aviation)

Additional Information Contacts

City of Galesburg. . . . . (309) 343-4181
  http://www.ci.galesburg.il.us
Galesburg Area Chamber of Commerce . . . . (309) 343-1194
  http://www.galesburg.org

GILSON (CDP). Covers a land area of 0.233 square miles and a water area of 0 square miles. Located at 40.86° N. Lat; 90.20° W. Long. Elevation is 679 feet.

Population: n/a (1990); n/a (2000); 190 (2010); Density: 660.5 persons per square mile (2008-2012 5-year est.); Race: 100.0% White, 0.0% Black/African American, 0.0% Asian, 0.0% American Indian/Alaska Native, 0.0% Native Hawaiian/Other Pacific Islander, 0.0% Some other race, 0.0% Two or more races, 0.0% Hispanic of any race (2008-2012 5-year est.); Average household size: 2.11 (2008-2012 5-year est.); Median age: 58.1 (2008-2012 5-year est.); Males per 100 females: 102.6 (2008-2012 5-year est.); Marriage status: 19.7% never married, 45.1% now married, 0.0% widowed, 35.2% divorced (2008-2012 5-year est.); Foreign born: 0.0% (2008-2012 5-year est.); Ancestry (includes multiple ancestries): 40.9% German, 29.9% Swedish, 11.7% English, 5.8% Croatian, 5.2% American (2008-2012 5-year est.).

Economy: Homeowner vacancy rate: 0.0%. Rental vacancy rate: 0.0%. (2008-2012 5-year est.); Employment by occupation: 0.0% management, business, and financial, 0.0% computer, engineering, and science, 0.0% education, legal, community service, arts, and media, 0.0% healthcare practitioners, 15.1% service, 53.4% sales and office, 12.3% natural resources, construction, and maintenance, 19.2% production, transportation, and material moving (2008-2012 5-year est.).

Income: Per capita income: $18,323 (2008-2012 5-year est.); Median household income: $28,472 (2008-2012 5-year est.); Average household income: $37,290 (2008-2012 5-year est.); Percent of households with income of $100,000 or more: 15.1% (2008-2012 5-year est.); Poverty rate: 11.0% (2008-2012 5-year est.).

Education: Percent of population age 25 and over with: High school diploma (including GED) or higher: 88.7% (2008-2012 5-year est.);

Bachelor's degree or higher: 0.0% (2008-2012 5-year est.); Master's degree or higher: 0.0% (2008-2012 5-year est.).
Housing: Homeownership rate: 63.0% (2008-2012 5-year est.); Median home value: $38,300 (2008-2012 5-year est.); Median contract rent: n/a per month (2008-2012 5-year est.); Median year structure built: 1968 (2008-2012 5-year est.).
Health Insurance: 58.4% Private; 27.3% Public; 35.7% None. (2008-2012 5-year est.)
Transportation: Commute to work: 100.0% car, 0.0% public transportation, 0.0% walk, 0.0% work from home (2008-2012 5-year est.); Travel time to work: 15.1% less than 15 minutes, 27.4% 15 to 30 minutes, 38.4% 30 to 45 minutes, 19.2% 45 to 60 minutes, 0.0% 60 minutes or more (2008-2012 5-year est.)

HENDERSON (village). Aka Soperville. Covers a land area of 0.276 square miles and a water area of 0 square miles. Located at 41.02° N. Lat; 90.35° W. Long. Elevation is 817 feet.
Population: 290 (1990); 319 (2000); 255 (2010); Density: 1,210.7 persons per square mile (2008-2012 5-year est.); Race: 90.1% White, 0.0% Black/African American, 0.9% Asian, 0.0% American Indian/Alaska Native, 0.0% Native Hawaiian/Other Pacific Islander, 9.0% Some other race, 6.9% Two or more races, 2.1% Hispanic of any race (2008-2012 5-year est.); Average household size: 2.49 (2008-2012 5-year est.); Median age: 44.3 (2008-2012 5-year est.); Males per 100 females: 98.8 (2008-2012 5-year est.); Marriage status: 16.6% never married, 64.0% now married, 5.5% widowed, 13.8% divorced (2008-2012 5-year est.); Foreign born: 3.0% (2008-2012 5-year est.); Ancestry (includes multiple ancestries): 24.3% English, 16.2% German, 15.6% Irish, 13.8% Swedish, 13.5% American (2008-2012 5-year est.).
Economy: Homeowner vacancy rate: 0.0%. Rental vacancy rate: 0.0%. (2008-2012 5-year est.); Employment by occupation: 5.1% management, business, and financial, 0.0% computer, engineering, and science, 8.9% education, legal, community service, arts, and media, 22.3% healthcare practitioners, 12.7% service, 26.1% sales and office, 3.2% natural resources, construction, and maintenance, 21.7% production, transportation, and material moving (2008-2012 5-year est.).
Income: Per capita income: $20,773 (2008-2012 5-year est.); Median household income: $53,571 (2008-2012 5-year est.); Average household income: $50,987 (2008-2012 5-year est.); Percent of households with income of $100,000 or more: 5.2% (2008-2012 5-year est.); Poverty rate: 7.5% (2008-2012 5-year est.).
Education: Percent of population age 25 and over with: High school diploma (including GED) or higher: 87.3% (2008-2012 5-year est.); Bachelor's degree or higher: 10.5% (2008-2012 5-year est.); Master's degree or higher: 4.4% (2008-2012 5-year est.).
Housing: Homeownership rate: 82.1% (2008-2012 5-year est.); Median home value: $67,500 (2008-2012 5-year est.); Median contract rent: $429 per month (2008-2012 5-year est.); Median year structure built: 1966 (2008-2012 5-year est.).
Health Insurance: 72.5% Private; 35.9% Public; 9.9% None. (2008-2012 5-year est.)
Transportation: Commute to work: 94.5% car, 0.0% public transportation, 1.4% walk, 4.1% work from home (2008-2012 5-year est.); Travel time to work: 30.0% less than 15 minutes, 47.1% 15 to 30 minutes, 2.9% 30 to 45 minutes, 11.4% 45 to 60 minutes, 8.6% 60 minutes or more (2008-2012 5-year est.)

KNOXVILLE (city). Covers a land area of 2.321 square miles and a water area of 0 square miles. Located at 40.91° N. Lat; 90.29° W. Long. Elevation is 781 feet.
History: Incorporated 1832. Formerly the county seat.
Population: 3,243 (1990); 3,183 (2000); 2,911 (2010); Density: 1,255.6 persons per square mile (2008-2012 5-year est.); Race: 98.7% White, 0.0% Black/African American, 0.0% Asian, 1.3% American Indian/Alaska Native, 0.0% Native Hawaiian/Other Pacific Islander, 0.0% Some other race, 0.0% Two or more races, 0.3% Hispanic of any race (2008-2012 5-year est.); Average household size: 2.39 (2008-2012 5-year est.); Median age: 42.6 (2008-2012 5-year est.); Males per 100 females: 77.4 (2008-2012 5-year est.); Marriage status: 19.3% never married, 60.2% now married, 12.3% widowed, 8.2% divorced (2008-2012 5-year est.); Foreign born: 0.2% (2008-2012 5-year est.); Ancestry (includes multiple ancestries): 20.7% German, 20.1% Irish, 14.1% English, 10.9% Swedish, 5.0% American (2008-2012 5-year est.).
Economy: Single-family building permits issued: 0 (2013); Multi-family building permits issued: 0 (2013); Homeowner vacancy rate: 0.0%. Rental

vacancy rate: 8.0%. (2008-2012 5-year est.); Employment by occupation: 15.2% management, business, and financial, 4.9% computer, engineering, and science, 9.5% education, legal, community service, arts, and media, 8.9% healthcare practitioners, 11.5% service, 24.5% sales and office, 8.7% natural resources, construction, and maintenance, 16.8% production, transportation, and material moving (2008-2012 5-year est.).
Income: Per capita income: $23,425 (2008-2012 5-year est.); Median household income: $50,598 (2008-2012 5-year est.); Average household income: $57,001 (2008-2012 5-year est.); Percent of households with income of $100,000 or more: 16.4% (2008-2012 5-year est.); Poverty rate: 3.7% (2008-2012 5-year est.).
Education: Percent of population age 25 and over with: High school diploma (including GED) or higher: 90.6% (2008-2012 5-year est.); Bachelor's degree or higher: 17.9% (2008-2012 5-year est.); Master's degree or higher: 3.6% (2008-2012 5-year est.).
School District(s)
Knoxville CUSD 202 (PK-12)
   2011-12 Enrollment: 1,147 . . . . (309) 289-2328
Housing: Homeownership rate: 76.8% (2008-2012 5-year est.); Median home value: $101,300 (2008-2012 5-year est.); Median contract rent: $461 per month (2008-2012 5-year est.); Median year structure built: 1967 (2008-2012 5-year est.).
Health Insurance: 76.0% Private; 28.9% Public; 8.2% None. (2008-2012 5-year est.)
Safety: Violent crime rate: 24.0 per 10,000 population; Property crime rate: 151.2 per 10,000 population (2012).
Transportation: Commute to work: 96.0% car, 0.0% public transportation, 0.6% walk, 2.8% work from home (2008-2012 5-year est.); Travel time to work: 38.0% less than 15 minutes, 39.3% 15 to 30 minutes, 6.8% 30 to 45 minutes, 8.6% 45 to 60 minutes, 7.3% 60 minutes or more (2008-2012 5-year est.)

MAQUON (village). Covers a land area of 0.159 square miles and a water area of 0 square miles. Located at 40.80° N. Lat; 90.16° W. Long. Elevation is 633 feet.
Population: 331 (1990); 318 (2000); 284 (2010); Density: 2,411.2 persons per square mile (2008-2012 5-year est.); Race: 100.0% White, 0.0% Black/African American, 0.0% Asian, 0.0% American Indian/Alaska Native, 0.0% Native Hawaiian/Other Pacific Islander, 0.0% Some other race, 0.0% Two or more races, 0.0% Hispanic of any race (2008-2012 5-year est.); Average household size: 2.57 (2008-2012 5-year est.); Median age: 41.9 (2008-2012 5-year est.); Males per 100 females: 91.5 (2008-2012 5-year est.); Marriage status: 24.3% never married, 58.3% now married, 4.7% widowed, 12.8% divorced (2008-2012 5-year est.); Foreign born: 0.0% (2008-2012 5-year est.); Ancestry (includes multiple ancestries): 17.2% German, 16.7% American, 13.6% Irish, 11.0% Swedish, 7.3% Italian (2008-2012 5-year est.).
Economy: Single-family building permits issued: 0 (2013); Multi-family building permits issued: 0 (2013); Homeowner vacancy rate: 2.8%. Rental vacancy rate: 0.0%. (2008-2012 5-year est.); Employment by occupation: 13.7% management, business, and financial, 0.0% computer, engineering, and science, 11.2% education, legal, community service, arts, and media, 1.0% healthcare practitioners, 24.4% service, 20.3% sales and office, 11.7% natural resources, construction, and maintenance, 17.8% production, transportation, and material moving (2008-2012 5-year est.).
Income: Per capita income: $21,122 (2008-2012 5-year est.); Median household income: $52,083 (2008-2012 5-year est.); Average household income: $54,370 (2008-2012 5-year est.); Percent of households with income of $100,000 or more: 2.7% (2008-2012 5-year est.); Poverty rate: 5.8% (2008-2012 5-year est.).
Education: Percent of population age 25 and over with: High school diploma (including GED) or higher: 91.6% (2008-2012 5-year est.); Bachelor's degree or higher: 14.9% (2008-2012 5-year est.); Master's degree or higher: 0.8% (2008-2012 5-year est.).
Housing: Homeownership rate: 89.3% (2008-2012 5-year est.); Median home value: $56,300 (2008-2012 5-year est.); Median contract rent: $400 per month (2008-2012 5-year est.); Median year structure built: Before 1940 (2008-2012 5-year est.).
Health Insurance: 76.8% Private; 23.0% Public; 13.1% None. (2008-2012 5-year est.)
Transportation: Commute to work: 97.9% car, 0.0% public transportation, 1.1% walk, 1.1% work from home (2008-2012 5-year est.); Travel time to work: 16.2% less than 15 minutes, 26.5% 15 to 30 minutes, 14.6% 30 to 45 minutes, 29.7% 45 to 60 minutes, 13.0% 60 minutes or more (2008-2012 5-year est.)

OAK RUN (CDP). Covers a land area of 3.536 square miles and a water area of 0.874 square miles. Located at 40.96° N. Lat; 90.13° W. Long. Elevation is 738 feet.
Population: n/a (1990); n/a (2000); 547 (2010); Density: 117.9 persons per square mile (2008-2012 5-year est.); Race: 97.1% White, 0.0% Black/African American, 2.9% Asian, 0.0% American Indian/Alaska Native, 0.0% Native Hawaiian/Other Pacific Islander, 0.0% Some other race, 0.0% Two or more races, 0.0% Hispanic of any race (2008-2012 5-year est.); Average household size: 1.78 (2008-2012 5-year est.); Median age: 58.2 (2008-2012 5-year est.); Males per 100 females: 118.3 (2008-2012 5-year est.); Marriage status: 17.5% never married, 65.7% now married, 7.0% widowed, 9.8% divorced (2008-2012 5-year est.); Foreign born: 4.8% (2008-2012 5-year est.); Ancestry (includes multiple ancestries): 39.8% German, 21.3% Irish, 13.7% English, 9.6% Dutch, 5.0% Swedish (2008-2012 5-year est.).
Economy: Homeowner vacancy rate: 12.7%. Rental vacancy rate: 0.0%. (2008-2012 5-year est.); Employment by occupation: 22.7% management, business, and financial, 7.3% computer, engineering, and science, 7.3% education, legal, community service, arts, and media, 16.6% healthcare practitioners, 10.1% service, 19.0% sales and office, 11.7% natural resources, construction, and maintenance, 5.3% production, transportation, and material moving (2008-2012 5-year est.).
Income: Per capita income: $51,953 (2008-2012 5-year est.); Median household income: $66,250 (2008-2012 5-year est.); Average household income: $91,681 (2008-2012 5-year est.); Percent of households with income of $100,000 or more: 29.9% (2008-2012 5-year est.); Poverty rate: 5.3% (2008-2012 5-year est.).
Education: Percent of population age 25 and over with: High school diploma (including GED) or higher: 98.2% (2008-2012 5-year est.); Bachelor's degree or higher: 36.8% (2008-2012 5-year est.); Master's degree or higher: 14.6% (2008-2012 5-year est.).
Housing: Homeownership rate: 100.0% (2008-2012 5-year est.); Median home value: $207,600 (2008-2012 5-year est.); Median contract rent: n/a per month (2008-2012 5-year est.); Median year structure built: 1996 (2008-2012 5-year est.).
Health Insurance: 89.4% Private; 35.7% Public; 5.3% None. (2008-2012 5-year est.)
Transportation: Commute to work: 87.3% car, 0.0% public transportation, 0.0% walk, 8.6% work from home (2008-2012 5-year est.); Travel time to work: 13.9% less than 15 minutes, 41.3% 15 to 30 minutes, 18.8% 30 to 45 minutes, 20.2% 45 to 60 minutes, 5.8% 60 minutes or more (2008-2012 5-year est.)

ONEIDA (city). Covers a land area of 0.762 square miles and a water area of 0 square miles. Located at 41.07° N. Lat; 90.22° W. Long. Elevation is 814 feet.
Population: 723 (1990); 752 (2000); 700 (2010); Density: 1,026.2 persons per square mile (2008-2012 5-year est.); Race: 99.2% White, 0.0% Black/African American, 0.0% Asian, 0.0% American Indian/Alaska Native, 0.0% Native Hawaiian/Other Pacific Islander, 0.8% Some other race, 0.4% Two or more races, 1.9% Hispanic of any race (2008-2012 5-year est.); Average household size: 2.54 (2008-2012 5-year est.); Median age: 39.6 (2008-2012 5-year est.); Males per 100 females: 99.0 (2008-2012 5-year est.); Marriage status: 29.8% never married, 50.6% now married, 6.9% widowed, 12.7% divorced (2008-2012 5-year est.); Foreign born: 0.0% (2008-2012 5-year est.); Ancestry (includes multiple ancestries): 24.4% Irish, 19.9% German, 19.1% Swedish, 13.8% American, 6.8% English (2008-2012 5-year est.).
Economy: Homeowner vacancy rate: 0.7%. Rental vacancy rate: 9.8%. (2008-2012 5-year est.); Employment by occupation: 6.2% management, business, and financial, 0.8% computer, engineering, and science, 11.6% education, legal, community service, arts, and media, 4.3% healthcare practitioners, 13.2% service, 22.0% sales and office, 19.6% natural resources, construction, and maintenance, 22.3% production, transportation, and material moving (2008-2012 5-year est.).
Income: Per capita income: $23,790 (2008-2012 5-year est.); Median household income: $54,444 (2008-2012 5-year est.); Average household income: $59,946 (2008-2012 5-year est.); Percent of households with income of $100,000 or more: 11.9% (2008-2012 5-year est.); Poverty rate: 2.2% (2008-2012 5-year est.).
Education: Percent of population age 25 and over with: High school diploma (including GED) or higher: 94.8% (2008-2012 5-year est.); Bachelor's degree or higher: 16.5% (2008-2012 5-year est.); Master's degree or higher: 6.2% (2008-2012 5-year est.).

R O W V A CUSD 208 (PK-12)
    2011-12 Enrollment: 702. . . . . (309) 483-3711
Housing: Homeownership rate: 85.1% (2008-2012 5-year est.); Median home value: $77,700 (2008-2012 5-year est.); Median contract rent: $332 per month (2008-2012 5-year est.); Median year structure built: 1959 (2008-2012 5-year est.).
Health Insurance: 69.2% Private; 36.6% Public; 8.1% None. (2008-2012 5-year est.)
Transportation: Commute to work: 93.2% car, 0.0% public transportation, 3.2% walk, 2.4% work from home (2008-2012 5-year est.); Travel time to work: 28.5% less than 15 minutes, 44.3% 15 to 30 minutes, 10.5% 30 to 45 minutes, 9.7% 45 to 60 minutes, 6.9% 60 minutes or more (2008-2012 5-year est.)

RIO (village). Covers a land area of 0.270 square miles and a water area of 0 square miles. Located at 41.11° N. Lat; 90.40° W. Long. Elevation is 778 feet.
Population: 260 (1990); 240 (2000); 220 (2010); Density: 777.7 persons per square mile (2008-2012 5-year est.); Race: 99.0% White, 0.0% Black/African American, 0.0% Asian, 0.0% American Indian/Alaska Native, 0.0% Native Hawaiian/Other Pacific Islander, 1.0% Some other race, 1.0% Two or more races, 0.0% Hispanic of any race (2008-2012 5-year est.); Average household size: 2.31 (2008-2012 5-year est.); Median age: 42.5 (2008-2012 5-year est.); Males per 100 females: 116.5 (2008-2012 5-year est.); Marriage status: 13.9% never married, 72.1% now married, 6.7% widowed, 7.3% divorced (2008-2012 5-year est.); Foreign born: 0.0% (2008-2012 5-year est.); Ancestry (includes multiple ancestries): 21.0% German, 15.7% Swedish, 13.8% Irish, 12.4% English, 7.6% French (2008-2012 5-year est.).
Economy: Homeowner vacancy rate: 0.0%. Rental vacancy rate: 0.0%. (2008-2012 5-year est.); Employment by occupation: 15.5% management, business, and financial, 2.1% computer, engineering, and science, 5.2% education, legal, community service, arts, and media, 4.1% healthcare practitioners, 15.5% service, 17.5% sales and office, 13.4% natural resources, construction, and maintenance, 26.8% production, transportation, and material moving (2008-2012 5-year est.).
Income: Per capita income: $23,718 (2008-2012 5-year est.); Median household income: $57,321 (2008-2012 5-year est.); Average household income: $55,497 (2008-2012 5-year est.); Percent of households with income of $100,000 or more: 4.4% (2008-2012 5-year est.); Poverty rate: 0.5% (2008-2012 5-year est.).
Education: Percent of population age 25 and over with: High school diploma (including GED) or higher: 87.7% (2008-2012 5-year est.); Bachelor's degree or higher: 8.9% (2008-2012 5-year est.); Master's degree or higher: 0.7% (2008-2012 5-year est.).
Housing: Homeownership rate: 83.5% (2008-2012 5-year est.); Median home value: $72,500 (2008-2012 5-year est.); Median contract rent: $380 per month (2008-2012 5-year est.); Median year structure built: 1957 (2008-2012 5-year est.).
Health Insurance: 87.6% Private; 26.2% Public; 4.3% None. (2008-2012 5-year est.)
Transportation: Commute to work: 87.6% car, 0.0% public transportation, 12.4% walk, 0.0% work from home (2008-2012 5-year est.); Travel time to work: 24.7% less than 15 minutes, 49.5% 15 to 30 minutes, 4.1% 30 to 45 minutes, 9.3% 45 to 60 minutes, 12.4% 60 minutes or more (2008-2012 5-year est.)

SAINT AUGUSTINE (village). Covers a land area of 0.631 square miles and a water area of 0 square miles. Located at 40.72° N. Lat; 90.41° W. Long. Elevation is 643 feet.
Population: 151 (1990); 152 (2000); 120 (2010); Density: 187.1 persons per square mile (2008-2012 5-year est.); Race: 100.0% White, 0.0% Black/African American, 0.0% Asian, 0.0% American Indian/Alaska Native, 0.0% Native Hawaiian/Other Pacific Islander, 0.0% Some other race, 0.0% Two or more races, 0.0% Hispanic of any race (2008-2012 5-year est.); Average household size: 1.97 (2008-2012 5-year est.); Median age: 52.0 (2008-2012 5-year est.); Males per 100 females: 122.6 (2008-2012 5-year est.); Marriage status: 12.5% never married, 70.5% now married, 7.1% widowed, 9.8% divorced (2008-2012 5-year est.); Foreign born: 0.0% (2008-2012 5-year est.); Ancestry (includes multiple ancestries): 19.5% American, 16.1% Irish, 15.3% German, 15.3% Swedish, 7.6% French Canadian (2008-2012 5-year est.).
Economy: Single-family building permits issued: 0 (2013); Multi-family building permits issued: 0 (2013); Homeowner vacancy rate: 3.7%. Rental

vacancy rate: 0.0%. (2008-2012 5-year est.); Employment by occupation: 22.4% management, business, and financial, 0.0% computer, engineering, and science, 0.0% education, legal, community service, arts, and media, 0.0% healthcare practitioners, 27.6% service, 22.4% sales and office, 1.7% natural resources, construction, and maintenance, 25.9% production, transportation, and material moving (2008-2012 5-year est.).

Income: Per capita income: $20,347 (2008-2012 5-year est.); Median household income: $38,333 (2008-2012 5-year est.); Average household income: $40,683 (2008-2012 5-year est.); Percent of households with income of $100,000 or more: 3.3% (2008-2012 5-year est.); Poverty rate: 9.3% (2008-2012 5-year est.).

Education: Percent of population age 25 and over with: High school diploma (including GED) or higher: 66.7% (2008-2012 5-year est.); Bachelor's degree or higher: 6.9% (2008-2012 5-year est.); Master's degree or higher: 0.0% (2008-2012 5-year est.).

Housing: Homeownership rate: 86.7% (2008-2012 5-year est.); Median home value: $48,500 (2008-2012 5-year est.); Median contract rent: n/a per month (2008-2012 5-year est.); Median year structure built: 1971 (2008-2012 5-year est.).

Health Insurance: 55.9% Private; 45.8% Public; 28.0% None. (2008-2012 5-year est.)

Transportation: Commute to work: 94.8% car, 0.0% public transportation, 5.2% walk, 0.0% work from home (2008-2012 5-year est.); Travel time to work: 48.3% less than 15 minutes, 25.9% 15 to 30 minutes, 19.0% 30 to 45 minutes, 0.0% 45 to 60 minutes, 6.9% 60 minutes or more (2008-2012 5-year est.)

VICTORIA (village). Covers a land area of 0.661 square miles and a water area of 0 square miles. Located at 41.03° N. Lat; 90.10° W. Long. Elevation is 833 feet.

Population: 299 (1990); 323 (2000); 316 (2010); Density: 494.4 persons per square mile (2008-2012 5-year est.); Race: 100.0% White, 0.0% Black/African American, 0.0% Asian, 0.0% American Indian/Alaska Native, 0.0% Native Hawaiian/Other Pacific Islander, 0.0% Some other race, 0.0% Two or more races, 0.0% Hispanic of any race (2008-2012 5-year est.); Average household size: 2.62 (2008-2012 5-year est.); Median age: 46.9 (2008-2012 5-year est.); Males per 100 females: 112.3 (2008-2012 5-year est.); Marriage status: 23.7% never married, 64.2% now married, 5.7% widowed, 6.5% divorced (2008-2012 5-year est.); Foreign born: 0.0% (2008-2012 5-year est.); Ancestry (includes multiple ancestries): 27.2% German, 22.6% Swedish, 13.1% Irish, 13.1% American, 10.1% English (2008-2012 5-year est.).

Economy: Single-family building permits issued: 0 (2013); Multi-family building permits issued: 0 (2013); Homeowner vacancy rate: 0.0%. Rental vacancy rate: 0.0%. (2008-2012 5-year est.); Employment by occupation: 12.4% management, business, and financial, 0.0% computer, engineering, and science, 6.8% education, legal, community service, arts, and media, 6.2% healthcare practitioners, 17.4% service, 26.1% sales and office, 17.4% natural resources, construction, and maintenance, 13.7% production, transportation, and material moving (2008-2012 5-year est.).

Income: Per capita income: $21,108 (2008-2012 5-year est.); Median household income: $44,861 (2008-2012 5-year est.); Average household income: $53,792 (2008-2012 5-year est.); Percent of households with income of $100,000 or more: 8.8% (2008-2012 5-year est.); Poverty rate: 5.5% (2008-2012 5-year est.).

Education: Percent of population age 25 and over with: High school diploma (including GED) or higher: 89.7% (2008-2012 5-year est.); Bachelor's degree or higher: 8.5% (2008-2012 5-year est.); Master's degree or higher: 0.0% (2008-2012 5-year est.).

Housing: Homeownership rate: 89.6% (2008-2012 5-year est.); Median home value: $54,200 (2008-2012 5-year est.); Median contract rent: $338 per month (2008-2012 5-year est.); Median year structure built: Before 1940 (2008-2012 5-year est.).

Health Insurance: 80.4% Private; 26.6% Public; 13.1% None. (2008-2012 5-year est.)

Transportation: Commute to work: 87.4% car, 0.0% public transportation, 6.9% walk, 5.7% work from home (2008-2012 5-year est.); Travel time to work: 22.0% less than 15 minutes, 44.0% 15 to 30 minutes, 21.3% 30 to 45 minutes, 6.0% 45 to 60 minutes, 6.7% 60 minutes or more (2008-2012 5-year est.)

WATAGA (village). Covers a land area of 0.863 square miles and a water area of 0 square miles. Located at 41.03° N. Lat; 90.28° W. Long. Elevation is 830 feet.

Population: 879 (1990); 857 (2000); 843 (2010); Density: 1,084.0 persons per square mile (2008-2012 5-year est.); Race: 96.5% White, 0.0% Black/African American, 0.0% Asian, 0.4% American Indian/Alaska Native, 0.0% Native Hawaiian/Other Pacific Islander, 3.1% Some other race, 2.9% Two or more races, 3.9% Hispanic of any race (2008-2012 5-year est.); Average household size: 2.34 (2008-2012 5-year est.); Median age: 35.4 (2008-2012 5-year est.); Males per 100 females: 112.0 (2008-2012 5-year est.); Marriage status: 27.7% never married, 55.7% now married, 3.8% widowed, 12.9% divorced (2008-2012 5-year est.); Foreign born: 0.3% (2008-2012 5-year est.); Ancestry (includes multiple ancestries): 19.8% German, 14.7% Irish, 11.3% American, 9.3% Swedish, 4.4% English (2008-2012 5-year est.).

Economy: Single-family building permits issued: 0 (2013); Multi-family building permits issued: 0 (2013); Homeowner vacancy rate: 0.0%. Rental vacancy rate: 9.2%. (2008-2012 5-year est.); Employment by occupation: 5.5% management, business, and financial, 1.3% computer, engineering, and science, 4.6% education, legal, community service, arts, and media, 7.5% healthcare practitioners, 21.7% service, 21.5% sales and office, 16.4% natural resources, construction, and maintenance, 21.5% production, transportation, and material moving (2008-2012 5-year est.).

Income: Per capita income: $20,350 (2008-2012 5-year est.); Median household income: $37,679 (2008-2012 5-year est.); Average household income: $47,340 (2008-2012 5-year est.); Percent of households with income of $100,000 or more: 7.1% (2008-2012 5-year est.); Poverty rate: 23.9% (2008-2012 5-year est.).

Education: Percent of population age 25 and over with: High school diploma (including GED) or higher: 88.0% (2008-2012 5-year est.); Bachelor's degree or higher: 12.4% (2008-2012 5-year est.); Master's degree or higher: 2.4% (2008-2012 5-year est.).

Housing: Homeownership rate: 65.2% (2008-2012 5-year est.); Median home value: $73,300 (2008-2012 5-year est.); Median contract rent: $383 per month (2008-2012 5-year est.); Median year structure built: 1971 (2008-2012 5-year est.).

Health Insurance: 62.6% Private; 33.8% Public; 14.5% None. (2008-2012 5-year est.)

Transportation: Commute to work: 93.4% car, 0.0% public transportation, 4.2% walk, 1.8% work from home (2008-2012 5-year est.); Travel time to work: 34.2% less than 15 minutes, 42.8% 15 to 30 minutes, 9.7% 30 to 45 minutes, 7.0% 45 to 60 minutes, 6.3% 60 minutes or more (2008-2012 5-year est.)

WILLIAMSFIELD (village). Covers a land area of 1.270 square miles and a water area of 0 square miles. Located at 40.93° N. Lat; 90.02° W. Long. Elevation is 705 feet.

Population: 571 (1990); 620 (2000); 578 (2010); Density: 478.7 persons per square mile (2008-2012 5-year est.); Race: 96.9% White, 1.0% Black/African American, 0.0% Asian, 0.0% American Indian/Alaska Native, 0.0% Native Hawaiian/Other Pacific Islander, 2.1% Some other race, 2.0% Two or more races, 0.7% Hispanic of any race (2008-2012 5-year est.); Average household size: 2.32 (2008-2012 5-year est.); Median age: 45.9 (2008-2012 5-year est.); Males per 100 females: 87.7 (2008-2012 5-year est.); Marriage status: 26.3% never married, 57.1% now married, 10.6% widowed, 10.0% divorced (2008-2012 5-year est.); Foreign born: 0.0% (2008-2012 5-year est.); Ancestry (includes multiple ancestries): 18.4% German, 16.6% American, 10.0% Swedish, 10.0% English, 6.4% Irish (2008-2012 5-year est.).

Economy: Homeowner vacancy rate: 0.0%. Rental vacancy rate: 5.7%. (2008-2012 5-year est.); Employment by occupation: 7.8% management, business, and financial, 0.8% computer, engineering, and science, 11.0% education, legal, community service, arts, and media, 8.6% healthcare practitioners, 18.8% service, 19.6% sales and office, 11.0% natural resources, construction, and maintenance, 22.4% production, transportation, and material moving (2008-2012 5-year est.).

Income: Per capita income: $22,647 (2008-2012 5-year est.); Median household income: $46,071 (2008-2012 5-year est.); Average household income: $52,491 (2008-2012 5-year est.); Percent of households with income of $100,000 or more: 10.9% (2008-2012 5-year est.); Poverty rate: 9.3% (2008-2012 5-year est.).

Education: Percent of population age 25 and over with: High school diploma (including GED) or higher: 87.2% (2008-2012 5-year est.); Bachelor's degree or higher: 13.7% (2008-2012 5-year est.); Master's degree or higher: 4.8% (2008-2012 5-year est.).

School District(s)
Williamsfield CUSD 210 (PK-12)

2011-12 Enrollment: 300. . . . . (309) 639-2219

Housing: Homeownership rate: 80.5% (2008-2012 5-year est.); Median home value: $75,600 (2008-2012 5-year est.); Median contract rent: $433 per month (2008-2012 5-year est.); Median year structure built: 1952 (2008-2012 5-year est.).

Health Insurance: 74.0% Private; 39.5% Public; 10.6% None. (2008-2012 5-year est.)

Transportation: Commute to work: 90.7% car, 0.0% public transportation, 4.0% walk, 4.0% work from home (2008-2012 5-year est.); Travel time to work: 33.2% less than 15 minutes, 21.0% 15 to 30 minutes, 32.4% 30 to 45 minutes, 11.8% 45 to 60 minutes, 1.7% 60 minutes or more (2008-2012 5-year est.)

YATES CITY (village).

YATES CITY (village). Covers a land area of 0.518 square miles and a water area of 0 square miles. Located at 40.78° N. Lat; 90.01° W. Long. Elevation is 669 feet.

Population: 760 (1990); 725 (2000); 693 (2010); Density: 1,710.9 persons per square mile (2008-2012 5-year est.); Race: 95.8% White, 0.0% Black/African American, 0.0% Asian, 0.0% American Indian/Alaska Native, 0.0% Native Hawaiian/Other Pacific Islander, 4.2% Some other race, 0.6% Two or more races, 0.3% Hispanic of any race (2008-2012 5-year est.); Average household size: 2.78 (2008-2012 5-year est.); Median age: 37.2 (2008-2012 5-year est.); Males per 100 females: 84.8 (2008-2012 5-year est.); Marriage status: 29.4% never married, 55.0% now married, 5.8% widowed, 9.8% divorced (2008-2012 5-year est.); Foreign born: 0.3% (2008-2012 5-year est.); Ancestry (includes multiple ancestries): 30.0% German, 16.8% English, 13.5% Irish, 8.0% American, 6.5% French (2008-2012 5-year est.).

Economy: Homeowner vacancy rate: 0.0%. Rental vacancy rate: 3.2%. (2008-2012 5-year est.); Employment by occupation: 8.6% management, business, and financial, 2.7% computer, engineering, and science, 4.3% education, legal, community service, arts, and media, 7.8% healthcare practitioners, 20.1% service, 25.9% sales and office, 24.1% natural resources, construction, and maintenance, 6.7% production, transportation, and material moving (2008-2012 5-year est.).

Income: Per capita income: $19,437 (2008-2012 5-year est.); Median household income: $51,058 (2008-2012 5-year est.); Average household income: $54,262 (2008-2012 5-year est.); Percent of households with income of $100,000 or more: 12.6% (2008-2012 5-year est.); Poverty rate: 15.3% (2008-2012 5-year est.).

Education: Percent of population age 25 and over with: High school diploma (including GED) or higher: 93.0% (2008-2012 5-year est.); Bachelor's degree or higher: 12.4% (2008-2012 5-year est.); Master's degree or higher: 1.8% (2008-2012 5-year est.).

Housing: Homeownership rate: 80.9% (2008-2012 5-year est.); Median home value: $85,100 (2008-2012 5-year est.); Median contract rent: $409 per month (2008-2012 5-year est.); Median year structure built: 1954 (2008-2012 5-year est.).

Health Insurance: 70.8% Private; 36.3% Public; 9.3% None. (2008-2012 5-year est.)

Transportation: Commute to work: 94.9% car, 0.0% public transportation, 0.5% walk, 4.5% work from home (2008-2012 5-year est.); Travel time to work: 21.2% less than 15 minutes, 17.8% 15 to 30 minutes, 45.1% 30 to 45 minutes, 13.6% 45 to 60 minutes, 2.2% 60 minutes or more (2008-2012 5-year est.)

La Salle County

Located in northern Illinois; drained by the Illinois, Fox, Vermilion, and Little Vermilion Rivers. Covers a land area of 1,135.124 square miles, a water area of 13.012 square miles, and is located in the Central Time Zone at 41.34° N. Lat., 88.89° W. Long. The county was founded in 1831. County seat is Ottawa.

La Salle County is part of the Ottawa-Peru, IL Micropolitan Statistical Area. The entire metro area includes: Bureau County, IL; LaSalle County, IL; Putnam County, IL

Population: 106,913 (1990); 111,509 (2000); 113,924 (2010); Race: 93.9% White, 1.8% Black/African American, 0.6% Asian, 0.2% American Indian/Alaska Native, 0.0% Native Hawaiian/Other Pacific Islander, 3.5% Some other race, 1.8% Two or more races, 8.0% Hispanic of any race (2008-2012 5-year est.); Density: 99.5 persons per square mile

(2008-2012 5-year est.); Average household size: 2.49 (2008-2012 5-year est.); Median age: 41.1 (2008-2012 5-year est.); Males per 100 females: 99.6 (2008-2012 5-year est.).

Religion: Six largest groups: 26.7% Catholicism, 5.8% Lutheran, 4.9% Methodist/Pietist, 2.4% Baptist, 1.9% Presbyterian-Reformed, 1.8% Holiness (2010)

Economy: Unemployment rate: 8.7% (April 2014); Total civilian labor force: 55,657 (April 2014); Leading industries: 15.8% retail trade; 15.3% health care and social assistance; 11.9% manufacturing (2012); Farms: 1,583 totaling 602,279 acres (2012); Companies that employ 500 or more persons: 6 (2012); Companies that employ 100 to 499 persons: 60 (2012); Companies that employ less than 100 persons: 2,683 (2012); Black-owned businesses: n/a (2007); Hispanic-owned businesses: n/a (2007); Asian-owned businesses: 276 (2007); Women-owned businesses: 2,291 (2007); Single-family building permits issued: 73 (2013); Multi-family building permits issued: 0 (2013).

Income: Per capita income: $25,641 (2008-2012 5-year est.); Median household income: $52,356 (2008-2012 5-year est.); Average household income: $63,584 (2008-2012 5-year est.); Percent of households with income of $100,000 or more: 17.5% (2008-2012 5-year est.); Poverty rate: 11.2% (2008-2012 5-year est.); Bankruptcy rate: 4.48% (2013).

Taxes: Total county taxes per capita: $273 (2011); County property taxes per capita: $217 (2011).

Education: Percent of population age 25 and over with: High school diploma (including GED) or higher: 88.2% (2008-2012 5-year est.); Bachelor's degree or higher: 15.7% (2008-2012 5-year est.); Master's degree or higher: 4.8% (2008-2012 5-year est.).

Housing: Homeownership rate: 76.5% (2008-2012 5-year est.); Median home value: $126,900 (2008-2012 5-year est.); Median contract rent: $504 per month (2008-2012 5-year est.); Median year structure built: 1958 (2008-2012 5-year est.).

Health: Birth rate: 106.3 per 10,000 population (2013); Death rate: 107.9 per 10,000 population (2013); Age-adjusted cancer mortality rate: 208.7 deaths per 100,000 population (2011); Number of physicians: 10.3 per 10,000 population (2011); Hospital beds: 25.8 per 10,000 population (2010); Hospital admissions: 984.3 per 10,000 population (2010).

Environment: Air Quality Index: 100.0% good, 0.0% moderate, 0.0% unhealthy for sensitive individuals, 0.0% unhealthy (percent of days in 2013)

Elections: 2012 Presidential election results: 48.8% Obama, 49.2% Romney

National and State Parks: Buffalo Rock State Park; Illini State Park; La Salle Lake State Fish and Wildlife Area; Marseilles State Fish and Wildlife Area; Matthiessen State Park; Norwegian Settlers State Memorial; Starved Rock State Park

Additional Information Contacts

La Salle County Government . . . . (815) 434-8200
http://www.lasallecounty.org

La Salle County Communities

CEDAR POINT (village).

CEDAR POINT (village). Covers a land area of 1.021 square miles and a water area of 0 square miles. Located at 41.27° N. Lat; 89.13° W. Long. Elevation is 659 feet.

Population: 275 (1990); 262 (2000); 277 (2010); Density: 249.8 persons per square mile (2008-2012 5-year est.); Race: 93.3% White, 1.6% Black/African American, 0.0% Asian, 5.1% American Indian/Alaska Native, 0.0% Native Hawaiian/Other Pacific Islander, 0.0% Some other race, 0.0% Two or more races, 7.1% Hispanic of any race (2008-2012 5-year est.); Average household size: 2.77 (2008-2012 5-year est.); Median age: 33.9 (2008-2012 5-year est.); Males per 100 females: 84.8 (2008-2012 5-year est.); Marriage status: 27.4% never married, 48.4% now married, 7.5% widowed, 16.7% divorced (2008-2012 5-year est.); Foreign born: 4.7% (2008-2012 5-year est.); Ancestry (includes multiple ancestries): 23.1% German, 20.4% Italian, 14.5% Irish, 12.5% Polish, 11.0% American (2008-2012 5-year est.).

Economy: Single-family building permits issued: 0 (2013); Multi-family building permits issued: 0 (2013); Homeowner vacancy rate: 3.5%. Rental vacancy rate: 33.3%. (2008-2012 5-year est.); Employment by occupation: 13.1% management, business, and financial, 1.6% computer, engineering, and science, 1.6% education, legal, community service, arts, and media, 1.6% healthcare practitioners, 18.0% service, 30.3% sales and office, 12.3% natural resources, construction, and maintenance, 21.3% production, transportation, and material moving (2008-2012 5-year est.).

Income: Per capita income: $19,856 (2008-2012 5-year est.); Median household income: $51,429 (2008-2012 5-year est.); Average household income: $52,911 (2008-2012 5-year est.); Percent of households with income of $100,000 or more: 7.6% (2008-2012 5-year est.); Poverty rate: 7.1% (2008-2012 5-year est.).

Education: Percent of population age 25 and over with: High school diploma (including GED) or higher: 99.4% (2008-2012 5-year est.); Bachelor's degree or higher: 9.9% (2008-2012 5-year est.); Master's degree or higher: 1.7% (2008-2012 5-year est.).

Housing: Homeownership rate: 89.1% (2008-2012 5-year est.); Median home value: $92,500 (2008-2012 5-year est.); Median contract rent: $425 per month (2008-2012 5-year est.); Median year structure built: 1951 (2008-2012 5-year est.).

Health Insurance: 76.1% Private; 29.0% Public; 7.5% None. (2008-2012 5-year est.)

Transportation: Commute to work: 91.8% car, 0.0% public transportation, 0.0% walk, 4.1% work from home (2008-2012 5-year est.); Travel time to work: 32.5% less than 15 minutes, 50.4% 15 to 30 minutes, 12.8% 30 to 45 minutes, 0.0% 45 to 60 minutes, 4.3% 60 minutes or more (2008-2012 5-year est.)

DANA (village). Covers a land area of 0.220 square miles and a water area of 0 square miles. Located at 40.96° N. Lat; 88.95° W. Long. Elevation is 669 feet.

Population: 165 (1990); 171 (2000); 159 (2010); Density: 939.1 persons per square mile (2008-2012 5-year est.); Race: 87.9% White, 0.0% Black/African American, 0.0% Asian, 0.0% American Indian/Alaska Native, 0.0% Native Hawaiian/Other Pacific Islander, 12.1% Some other race, 11.6% Two or more races, 0.5% Hispanic of any race (2008-2012 5-year est.); Average household size: 2.33 (2008-2012 5-year est.); Median age: 34.6 (2008-2012 5-year est.); Males per 100 females: 78.4 (2008-2012 5-year est.); Marriage status: 16.1% never married, 56.8% now married, 14.8% widowed, 12.3% divorced (2008-2012 5-year est.); Foreign born: 0.0% (2008-2012 5-year est.); Ancestry (includes multiple ancestries): 41.1% German, 22.7% English, 22.2% Norwegian, 11.6% Polish, 8.2% Irish (2008-2012 5-year est.).

Economy: Homeowner vacancy rate: 0.0%. Rental vacancy rate: 0.0%. (2008-2012 5-year est.); Employment by occupation: 3.4% management, business, and financial, 0.0% computer, engineering, and science, 0.0% education, legal, community service, arts, and media, 0.0% healthcare practitioners, 33.0% service, 9.1% sales and office, 15.9% natural resources, construction, and maintenance, 38.6% production, transportation, and material moving (2008-2012 5-year est.).

Income: Per capita income: $20,900 (2008-2012 5-year est.); Median household income: $38,750 (2008-2012 5-year est.); Average household income: $49,172 (2008-2012 5-year est.); Percent of households with income of $100,000 or more: 6.7% (2008-2012 5-year est.); Poverty rate: 11.6% (2008-2012 5-year est.).

Education: Percent of population age 25 and over with: High school diploma (including GED) or higher: 76.4% (2008-2012 5-year est.); Bachelor's degree or higher: 8.6% (2008-2012 5-year est.); Master's degree or higher: 2.1% (2008-2012 5-year est.).

Housing: Homeownership rate: 88.8% (2008-2012 5-year est.); Median home value: $74,100 (2008-2012 5-year est.); Median contract rent: n/a per month (2008-2012 5-year est.); Median year structure built: Before 1940 (2008-2012 5-year est.).

Health Insurance: 60.4% Private; 41.1% Public; 16.4% None. (2008-2012 5-year est.)

Transportation: Commute to work: 94.3% car, 0.0% public transportation, 0.0% walk, 5.7% work from home (2008-2012 5-year est.); Travel time to work: 10.8% less than 15 minutes, 15.7% 15 to 30 minutes, 31.3% 30 to 45 minutes, 21.7% 45 to 60 minutes, 20.5% 60 minutes or more (2008-2012 5-year est.)

DAYTON (CDP). Covers a land area of 2.249 square miles and a water area of 0.045 square miles. Located at 41.39° N. Lat; 88.80° W. Long. Elevation is 564 feet.

Population: n/a (1990); n/a (2000); 537 (2010); Density: 240.6 persons per square mile (2008-2012 5-year est.); Race: 93.5% White, 0.7% Black/African American, 1.1% Asian, 0.9% American Indian/Alaska Native, 0.0% Native Hawaiian/Other Pacific Islander, 3.8% Some other race, 3.0% Two or more races, 3.9% Hispanic of any race (2008-2012 5-year est.); Average household size: 2.65 (2008-2012 5-year est.); Median age: 42.2 (2008-2012 5-year est.); Males per 100 females: 117.3 (2008-2012 5-year est.); Marriage status: 20.3% never married, 62.1% now married, 2.5%

widowed, 15.1% divorced (2008-2012 5-year est.); Foreign born: 0.0% (2008-2012 5-year est.); Ancestry (includes multiple ancestries): 42.7% German, 28.1% Irish, 10.9% American, 10.2% Italian, 8.3% Polish (2008-2012 5-year est.).

Economy: Homeowner vacancy rate: 0.0%. Rental vacancy rate: 0.0%. (2008-2012 5-year est.); Employment by occupation: 6.1% management, business, and financial, 9.6% computer, engineering, and science, 6.8% education, legal, community service, arts, and media, 7.5% healthcare practitioners, 6.5% service, 19.5% sales and office, 12.6% natural resources, construction, and maintenance, 31.4% production, transportation, and material moving (2008-2012 5-year est.).

Income: Per capita income: $31,392 (2008-2012 5-year est.); Median household income: $72,000 (2008-2012 5-year est.); Average household income: $83,054 (2008-2012 5-year est.); Percent of households with income of $100,000 or more: 19.6% (2008-2012 5-year est.); Poverty rate: 8.9% (2008-2012 5-year est.).

Education: Percent of population age 25 and over with: High school diploma (including GED) or higher: 94.1% (2008-2012 5-year est.); Bachelor's degree or higher: 13.1% (2008-2012 5-year est.); Master's degree or higher: 9.8% (2008-2012 5-year est.).

Housing: Homeownership rate: 78.9% (2008-2012 5-year est.); Median home value: $167,100 (2008-2012 5-year est.); Median contract rent: $442 per month (2008-2012 5-year est.); Median year structure built: 1979 (2008-2012 5-year est.).

Health Insurance: 82.6% Private; 26.1% Public; 5.5% None. (2008-2012 5-year est.)

Transportation: Commute to work: 100.0% car, 0.0% public transportation, 0.0% walk, 0.0% work from home (2008-2012 5-year est.); Travel time to work: 40.6% less than 15 minutes, 44.0% 15 to 30 minutes, 7.2% 30 to 45 minutes, 2.7% 45 to 60 minutes, 5.5% 60 minutes or more (2008-2012 5-year est.)

EARLVILLE (city). Covers a land area of 1.203 square miles and a water area of 0 square miles. Located at 41.59° N. Lat; 88.92° W. Long. Elevation is 705 feet.

History: Founded c.1854, Incorporated 1869.

Population: 1,435 (1990); 1,778 (2000); 1,701 (2010); Density: 1,498.6 persons per square mile (2008-2012 5-year est.); Race: 98.1% White, 0.0% Black/African American, 0.0% Asian, 0.0% American Indian/Alaska Native, 0.0% Native Hawaiian/Other Pacific Islander, 1.9% Some other race, 1.8% Two or more races, 8.4% Hispanic of any race (2008-2012 5-year est.); Average household size: 2.52 (2008-2012 5-year est.); Median age: 33.4 (2008-2012 5-year est.); Males per 100 females: 121.2 (2008-2012 5-year est.); Marriage status: 27.2% never married, 50.7% now married, 6.5% widowed, 15.6% divorced (2008-2012 5-year est.); Foreign born: 1.2% (2008-2012 5-year est.); Ancestry (includes multiple ancestries): 31.7% German, 19.1% Irish, 13.2% English, 9.0% Norwegian, 6.5% Polish (2008-2012 5-year est.).

Economy: Single-family building permits issued: 0 (2013); Multi-family building permits issued: 0 (2013); Homeowner vacancy rate: 6.8%. Rental vacancy rate: 5.5%. (2008-2012 5-year est.); Employment by occupation: 5.9% management, business, and financial, 3.4% computer, engineering, and science, 6.7% education, legal, community service, arts, and media, 1.5% healthcare practitioners, 20.1% service, 21.8% sales and office, 12.3% natural resources, construction, and maintenance, 28.2% production, transportation, and material moving (2008-2012 5-year est.).

Income: Per capita income: $21,063 (2008-2012 5-year est.); Median household income: $51,964 (2008-2012 5-year est.); Average household income: $53,371 (2008-2012 5-year est.); Percent of households with income of $100,000 or more: 8.1% (2008-2012 5-year est.); Poverty rate: 13.3% (2008-2012 5-year est.).

Education: Percent of population age 25 and over with: High school diploma (including GED) or higher: 81.4% (2008-2012 5-year est.); Bachelor's degree or higher: 12.8% (2008-2012 5-year est.); Master's degree or higher: 3.7% (2008-2012 5-year est.).

School District(s)

Earlville CUSD 9 (PK-12)
　　2011-12 Enrollment: 448. . . . . (815) 246-8361
Serena CUSD 2 (KG-12)
　　2011-12 Enrollment: 820. . . . . (815) 496-2850

Housing: Homeownership rate: 66.2% (2008-2012 5-year est.); Median home value: $126,100 (2008-2012 5-year est.); Median contract rent: $635 per month (2008-2012 5-year est.); Median year structure built: 1958 (2008-2012 5-year est.).

Health Insurance: 64.4% Private; 30.0% Public; 15.5% None. (2008-2012 5-year est.)
Safety: Violent crime rate: 5.9 per 10,000 population; Property crime rate: 294.8 per 10,000 population (2012).
Transportation: Commute to work: 95.5% car, 0.5% public transportation, 1.5% walk, 1.8% work from home (2008-2012 5-year est.); Travel time to work: 10.8% less than 15 minutes, 25.2% 15 to 30 minutes, 34.0% 30 to 45 minutes, 16.5% 45 to 60 minutes, 13.4% 60 minutes or more (2008-2012 5-year est.)

GRAND RIDGE (village). Covers a land area of 0.462 square miles and a water area of 0 square miles. Located at 41.24° N. Lat; 88.83° W. Long. Elevation is 643 feet.
Population: 560 (1990); 546 (2000); 560 (2010); Density: 1,180.6 persons per square mile (2008-2012 5-year est.); Race: 94.7% White, 0.0% Black/African American, 0.6% Asian, 0.0% American Indian/Alaska Native, 0.0% Native Hawaiian/Other Pacific Islander, 4.7% Some other race, 4.8% Two or more races, 8.6% Hispanic of any race (2008-2012 5-year est.); Average household size: 2.85 (2008-2012 5-year est.); Median age: 35.1 (2008-2012 5-year est.); Males per 100 females: 96.8 (2008-2012 5-year est.); Marriage status: 30.0% never married, 53.5% now married, 9.4% widowed, 7.1% divorced (2008-2012 5-year est.); Foreign born: 2.0% (2008-2012 5-year est.); Ancestry (includes multiple ancestries): 38.2% Irish, 32.1% German, 7.7% English, 6.6% Czech, 5.3% Italian (2008-2012 5-year est.).
Economy: Single-family building permits issued: 0 (2013); Multi-family building permits issued: 0 (2013); Homeowner vacancy rate: 0.0%. Rental vacancy rate: 0.0%. (2008-2012 5-year est.); Employment by occupation: 8.4% management, business, and financial, 0.0% computer, engineering, and science, 12.0% education, legal, community service, arts, and media, 9.1% healthcare practitioners, 17.9% service, 29.2% sales and office, 10.6% natural resources, construction, and maintenance, 12.8% production, transportation, and material moving (2008-2012 5-year est.).
Income: Per capita income: $23,912 (2008-2012 5-year est.); Median household income: $64,375 (2008-2012 5-year est.); Average household income: $65,918 (2008-2012 5-year est.); Percent of households with income of $100,000 or more: 16.2% (2008-2012 5-year est.); Poverty rate: 9.4% (2008-2012 5-year est.).
Education: Percent of population age 25 and over with: High school diploma (including GED) or higher: 93.5% (2008-2012 5-year est.); Bachelor's degree or higher: 19.1% (2008-2012 5-year est.); Master's degree or higher: 3.5% (2008-2012 5-year est.).

School District(s)
Grand Ridge CCSD 95 (PK-08)
   2011-12 Enrollment: 329 . . . . (815) 249-6225
Housing: Homeownership rate: 90.6% (2008-2012 5-year est.); Median home value: $106,800 (2008-2012 5-year est.); Median contract rent: $525 per month (2008-2012 5-year est.); Median year structure built: Before 1940 (2008-2012 5-year est.).
Health Insurance: 81.1% Private; 30.3% Public; 5.9% None. (2008-2012 5-year est.)
Transportation: Commute to work: 98.1% car, 0.0% public transportation, 0.7% walk, 1.1% work from home (2008-2012 5-year est.); Travel time to work: 23.4% less than 15 minutes, 54.7% 15 to 30 minutes, 11.7% 30 to 45 minutes, 4.2% 45 to 60 minutes, 6.0% 60 minutes or more (2008-2012 5-year est.)

KANGLEY (village). Covers a land area of 0.261 square miles and a water area of 0 square miles. Located at 41.15° N. Lat; 88.87° W. Long. Elevation is 627 feet.
Population: 250 (1990); 287 (2000); 251 (2010); Density: 1,387.6 persons per square mile (2008-2012 5-year est.); Race: 98.6% White, 0.0% Black/African American, 0.0% Asian, 0.0% American Indian/Alaska Native, 0.0% Native Hawaiian/Other Pacific Islander, 1.4% Some other race, 0.3% Two or more races, 14.1% Hispanic of any race (2008-2012 5-year est.); Average household size: 2.97 (2008-2012 5-year est.); Median age: 36.4 (2008-2012 5-year est.); Males per 100 females: 135.1 (2008-2012 5-year est.); Marriage status: 29.7% never married, 58.3% now married, 3.5% widowed, 8.5% divorced (2008-2012 5-year est.); Foreign born: 1.1% (2008-2012 5-year est.); Ancestry (includes multiple ancestries): 27.9% German, 23.8% Irish, 13.5% English, 10.2% Slovak, 5.2% Polish (2008-2012 5-year est.).
Economy: Single-family building permits issued: 0 (2013); Multi-family building permits issued: 0 (2013); Homeowner vacancy rate: 0.0%. Rental vacancy rate: 0.0%. (2008-2012 5-year est.); Employment by occupation:

5.6% management, business, and financial, 1.9% computer, engineering, and science, 4.3% education, legal, community service, arts, and media, 3.7% healthcare practitioners, 22.2% service, 15.4% sales and office, 12.3% natural resources, construction, and maintenance, 34.6% production, transportation, and material moving (2008-2012 5-year est.).
Income: Per capita income: $19,400 (2008-2012 5-year est.); Median household income: $61,250 (2008-2012 5-year est.); Average household income: $56,465 (2008-2012 5-year est.); Percent of households with income of $100,000 or more: 9.8% (2008-2012 5-year est.); Poverty rate: 3.9% (2008-2012 5-year est.).
Education: Percent of population age 25 and over with: High school diploma (including GED) or higher: 82.7% (2008-2012 5-year est.); Bachelor's degree or higher: 5.5% (2008-2012 5-year est.); Master's degree or higher: 0.9% (2008-2012 5-year est.).
Housing: Homeownership rate: 83.6% (2008-2012 5-year est.); Median home value: $76,900 (2008-2012 5-year est.); Median contract rent: $516 per month (2008-2012 5-year est.); Median year structure built: Before 1940 (2008-2012 5-year est.).
Health Insurance: 80.4% Private; 28.7% Public; 7.2% None. (2008-2012 5-year est.)
Transportation: Commute to work: 97.5% car, 0.0% public transportation, 0.0% walk, 2.5% work from home (2008-2012 5-year est.); Travel time to work: 42.3% less than 15 minutes, 22.4% 15 to 30 minutes, 21.2% 30 to 45 minutes, 10.9% 45 to 60 minutes, 3.2% 60 minutes or more (2008-2012 5-year est.)

LAKE HOLIDAY (CDP). Covers a land area of 3.201 square miles and a water area of 0.483 square miles. Located at 41.62° N. Lat; 88.67° W. Long.
Population: n/a (1990); n/a (2000); 4,761 (2010); Density: 1,445.9 persons per square mile (2008-2012 5-year est.); Race: 98.0% White, 0.0% Black/African American, 0.0% Asian, 0.0% American Indian/Alaska Native, 0.0% Native Hawaiian/Other Pacific Islander, 2.0% Some other race, 1.7% Two or more races, 5.7% Hispanic of any race (2008-2012 5-year est.); Average household size: 2.84 (2008-2012 5-year est.); Median age: 35.9 (2008-2012 5-year est.); Males per 100 females: 91.8 (2008-2012 5-year est.); Marriage status: 24.4% never married, 62.5% now married, 4.6% widowed, 8.6% divorced (2008-2012 5-year est.); Foreign born: 2.5% (2008-2012 5-year est.); Ancestry (includes multiple ancestries): 39.7% German, 19.0% Irish, 11.5% Italian, 8.6% Polish, 8.0% English (2008-2012 5-year est.).
Economy: Homeowner vacancy rate: 9.1%. Rental vacancy rate: 0.0%. (2008-2012 5-year est.); Employment by occupation: 15.8% management, business, and financial, 6.0% computer, engineering, and science, 12.2% education, legal, community service, arts, and media, 3.0% healthcare practitioners, 7.0% service, 30.5% sales and office, 13.3% natural resources, construction, and maintenance, 12.3% production, transportation, and material moving (2008-2012 5-year est.).
Income: Per capita income: $31,323 (2008-2012 5-year est.); Median household income: $80,486 (2008-2012 5-year est.); Average household income: $90,337 (2008-2012 5-year est.); Percent of households with income of $100,000 or more: 27.4% (2008-2012 5-year est.); Poverty rate: 3.7% (2008-2012 5-year est.).
Education: Percent of population age 25 and over with: High school diploma (including GED) or higher: 93.1% (2008-2012 5-year est.); Bachelor's degree or higher: 25.6% (2008-2012 5-year est.); Master's degree or higher: 7.1% (2008-2012 5-year est.).
Housing: Homeownership rate: 93.0% (2008-2012 5-year est.); Median home value: $208,800 (2008-2012 5-year est.); Median contract rent: $1,023 per month (2008-2012 5-year est.); Median year structure built: 1991 (2008-2012 5-year est.).
Health Insurance: 89.0% Private; 13.4% Public; 7.7% None. (2008-2012 5-year est.)
Transportation: Commute to work: 92.1% car, 0.7% public transportation, 1.5% walk, 5.8% work from home (2008-2012 5-year est.); Travel time to work: 21.5% less than 15 minutes, 14.5% 15 to 30 minutes, 30.6% 30 to 45 minutes, 13.4% 45 to 60 minutes, 20.0% 60 minutes or more (2008-2012 5-year est.)

LASALLE (city). Aka La Salle-Peru. Covers a land area of 11.759 square miles and a water area of 0.093 square miles. Located at 41.36° N. Lat; 89.06° W. Long. Elevation is 571 feet.
History: La Salle was organized in 1827, and prospered with the opening of the Illinois & Michigan Canal in 1848. When the railroads replaced canal traffic, mining became an important industry for La Salle. The Matthiessen

& Hegeler Zinc Company plant was established here in 1858. The town was named for La Salle, the French explorer of North America, who crossed this area in 1679.

Population: 9,717 (1990); 9,796 (2000); 9,609 (2010); Density: 814.2 persons per square mile (2008-2012 5-year est.); Race: 93.5% White, 0.5% Black/African American, 0.4% Asian, 0.4% American Indian/Alaska Native, 0.0% Native Hawaiian/Other Pacific Islander, 5.2% Some other race, 2.9% Two or more races, 9.8% Hispanic of any race (2008-2012 5-year est.); Average household size: 2.33 (2008-2012 5-year est.); Median age: 40.0 (2008-2012 5-year est.); Males per 100 females: 112.3 (2008-2012 5-year est.); Marriage status: 31.5% never married, 46.7% now married, 7.8% widowed, 14.0% divorced (2008-2012 5-year est.); Foreign born: 4.3% (2008-2012 5-year est.); Ancestry (includes multiple ancestries): 36.0% German, 16.9% Irish, 16.0% Polish, 13.6% Italian, 5.3% English (2008-2012 5-year est.).

Economy: Single-family building permits issued: 2 (2013); Multi-family building permits issued: 0 (2013); Homeowner vacancy rate: 2.0%. Rental vacancy rate: 1.4%. (2008-2012 5-year est.); Employment by occupation: 9.0% management, business, and financial, 1.3% computer, engineering, and science, 7.2% education, legal, community service, arts, and media, 3.6% healthcare practitioners, 19.8% service, 28.1% sales and office, 8.0% natural resources, construction, and maintenance, 23.1% production, transportation, and material moving (2008-2012 5-year est.).

Income: Per capita income: $24,127 (2008-2012 5-year est.); Median household income: $45,175 (2008-2012 5-year est.); Average household income: $55,616 (2008-2012 5-year est.); Percent of households with income of $100,000 or more: 12.1% (2008-2012 5-year est.); Poverty rate: 16.4% (2008-2012 5-year est.).

Education: Percent of population age 25 and over with: High school diploma (including GED) or higher: 85.5% (2008-2012 5-year est.); Bachelor's degree or higher: 15.4% (2008-2012 5-year est.); Master's degree or higher: 2.4% (2008-2012 5-year est.).

School District(s)

Dimmick CCSD 175 (KG-08)
  2011-12 Enrollment: 112 . . . . (815) 223-2933
La Salle ESD 122 (PK-08)
  2011-12 Enrollment: 992 . . . . (815) 223-0786
La Salle-Peru Area Career Ctr (11-12)
  2011-12 Enrollment: n/a . . . . (815) 223-2454
La Salle-Peru Twp HSD 120 (09-12)
  2011-12 Enrollment: 1,249 . . . . (815) 223-2373

Vocational/Technical School(s)

Educators of Beauty-La Salle (Private, For-profit)
  Fall 2012 Enrollment: 31 . . . . (815) 223-7326
  2012-13 Tuition: $17,175

Housing: Homeownership rate: 66.2% (2008-2012 5-year est.); Median home value: $96,400 (2008-2012 5-year est.); Median contract rent: $419 per month (2008-2012 5-year est.); Median year structure built: Before 1940 (2008-2012 5-year est.).

Health Insurance: 65.3% Private; 33.9% Public; 12.7% None. (2008-2012 5-year est.)

Safety: Violent crime rate: 6.3 per 10,000 population; Property crime rate: 199.4 per 10,000 population (2012).

Transportation: Commute to work: 92.1% car, 0.8% public transportation, 4.1% walk, 1.8% work from home (2008-2012 5-year est.); Travel time to work: 58.6% less than 15 minutes, 29.3% 15 to 30 minutes, 6.3% 30 to 45 minutes, 1.5% 45 to 60 minutes, 4.3% 60 minutes or more (2008-2012 5-year est.)

Airports: Illinois Valley Regional Airport (general aviation)

Additional Information Contacts

City of La Salle . . . . (815) 223-4586
  http://www.lasalle-il.gov
Illinois Valley Area Chamber of Commerce . . . . (815) 223-0227
  http://www.ivaced.org

LELAND (village). Covers a land area of 0.534 square miles and a water area of 0 square miles. Located at 41.62° N. Lat; 88.80° W. Long. Elevation is 696 feet.

Population: 862 (1990); 970 (2000); 977 (2010); Density: 1,744.4 persons per square mile (2008-2012 5-year est.); Race: 99.0% White, 0.1% Black/African American, 0.5% Asian, 0.0% American Indian/Alaska Native, 0.0% Native Hawaiian/Other Pacific Islander, 0.4% Some other race, 0.0% Two or more races, 7.4% Hispanic of any race (2008-2012 5-year est.); Average household size: 2.80 (2008-2012 5-year est.); Median age: 36.2 (2008-2012 5-year est.); Males per 100 females: 95.8 (2008-2012 5-year

est.); Marriage status: 22.3% never married, 64.4% now married, 6.6% widowed, 6.8% divorced (2008-2012 5-year est.); Foreign born: 2.1% (2008-2012 5-year est.); Ancestry (includes multiple ancestries): 41.2% German, 15.7% Norwegian, 13.4% Irish, 12.3% English, 6.1% Polish (2008-2012 5-year est.).

Economy: Single-family building permits issued: 0 (2013); Multi-family building permits issued: 0 (2013); Homeowner vacancy rate: 1.8%. Rental vacancy rate: 42.2%. (2008-2012 5-year est.); Employment by occupation: 6.8% management, business, and financial, 1.9% computer, engineering, and science, 9.8% education, legal, community service, arts, and media, 4.0% healthcare practitioners, 15.7% service, 25.3% sales and office, 19.2% natural resources, construction, and maintenance, 17.3% production, transportation, and material moving (2008-2012 5-year est.).

Income: Per capita income: $21,752 (2008-2012 5-year est.); Median household income: $52,054 (2008-2012 5-year est.); Average household income: $60,432 (2008-2012 5-year est.); Percent of households with income of $100,000 or more: 12.0% (2008-2012 5-year est.); Poverty rate: 7.8% (2008-2012 5-year est.).

Education: Percent of population age 25 and over with: High school diploma (including GED) or higher: 92.4% (2008-2012 5-year est.); Bachelor's degree or higher: 19.4% (2008-2012 5-year est.); Master's degree or higher: 5.3% (2008-2012 5-year est.).

School District(s)

Leland CUSD 1 (PK-12)
  2011-12 Enrollment: 292 . . . . (815) 495-3821

Housing: Homeownership rate: 81.1% (2008-2012 5-year est.); Median home value: $144,100 (2008-2012 5-year est.); Median contract rent: $666 per month (2008-2012 5-year est.); Median year structure built: 1963 (2008-2012 5-year est.).

Health Insurance: 69.5% Private; 27.3% Public; 13.8% None. (2008-2012 5-year est.)

Safety: Violent crime rate: 61.7 per 10,000 population; Property crime rate: 113.1 per 10,000 population (2012).

Transportation: Commute to work: 90.6% car, 0.0% public transportation, 3.7% walk, 5.2% work from home (2008-2012 5-year est.); Travel time to work: 14.1% less than 15 minutes, 32.0% 15 to 30 minutes, 22.7% 30 to 45 minutes, 14.1% 45 to 60 minutes, 17.2% 60 minutes or more (2008-2012 5-year est.)

LEONORE (village). Covers a land area of 0.089 square miles and a water area of 0 square miles. Located at 41.19° N. Lat; 88.98° W. Long. Elevation is 679 feet.

Population: 134 (1990); 110 (2000); 130 (2010); Density: 890.7 persons per square mile (2008-2012 5-year est.); Race: 100.0% White, 0.0% Black/African American, 0.0% Asian, 0.0% American Indian/Alaska Native, 0.0% Native Hawaiian/Other Pacific Islander, 0.0% Some other race, 0.0% Two or more races, 0.0% Hispanic of any race (2008-2012 5-year est.); Average household size: 2.08 (2008-2012 5-year est.); Median age: 47.8 (2008-2012 5-year est.); Males per 100 females: 88.1 (2008-2012 5-year est.); Marriage status: 17.5% never married, 47.6% now married, 9.5% widowed, 25.4% divorced (2008-2012 5-year est.); Foreign born: 2.5% (2008-2012 5-year est.); Ancestry (includes multiple ancestries): 57.0% German, 25.3% English, 19.0% Irish, 17.7% Swedish, 13.9% Italian (2008-2012 5-year est.).

Economy: Single-family building permits issued: 0 (2013); Multi-family building permits issued: 0 (2013); Homeowner vacancy rate: 0.0%. Rental vacancy rate: 0.0%. (2008-2012 5-year est.); Employment by occupation: 19.4% management, business, and financial, 0.0% computer, engineering, and science, 5.6% education, legal, community service, arts, and media, 0.0% healthcare practitioners, 16.7% service, 11.1% sales and office, 5.6% natural resources, construction, and maintenance, 41.7% production, transportation, and material moving (2008-2012 5-year est.).

Income: Per capita income: $26,481 (2008-2012 5-year est.); Median household income: $48,125 (2008-2012 5-year est.); Average household income: $54,953 (2008-2012 5-year est.); Percent of households with income of $100,000 or more: 21.1% (2008-2012 5-year est.); Poverty rate: 11.7% (2008-2012 5-year est.).

Education: Percent of population age 25 and over with: High school diploma (including GED) or higher: 87.7% (2008-2012 5-year est.); Bachelor's degree or higher: 10.5% (2008-2012 5-year est.); Master's degree or higher: 0.0% (2008-2012 5-year est.).

Housing: Homeownership rate: 100.0% (2008-2012 5-year est.); Median home value: $87,500 (2008-2012 5-year est.); Median contract rent: n/a per month (2008-2012 5-year est.); Median year structure built: Before 1940 (2008-2012 5-year est.).

Health Insurance: 60.8% Private; 40.5% Public; 5.1% None. (2008-2012 5-year est.)
Transportation: Commute to work: 88.9% car, 0.0% public transportation, 5.6% walk, 5.6% work from home (2008-2012 5-year est.); Travel time to work: 26.5% less than 15 minutes, 47.1% 15 to 30 minutes, 11.8% 30 to 45 minutes, 0.0% 45 to 60 minutes, 14.7% 60 minutes or more (2008-2012 5-year est.)

LOSTANT (village). Covers a land area of 0.393 square miles and a water area of 0 square miles. Located at 41.14° N. Lat; 89.06° W. Long. Elevation is 696 feet.
Population: 510 (1990); 486 (2000); 498 (2010); Density: 975.1 persons per square mile (2008-2012 5-year est.); Race: 93.5% White, 0.5% Black/African American, 0.5% Asian, 0.8% American Indian/Alaska Native, 0.0% Native Hawaiian/Other Pacific Islander, 4.7% Some other race, 0.0% Two or more races, 12.0% Hispanic of any race (2008-2012 5-year est.); Average household size: 2.47 (2008-2012 5-year est.); Median age: 39.5 (2008-2012 5-year est.); Males per 100 females: 107.0 (2008-2012 5-year est.); Marriage status: 23.8% never married, 53.9% now married, 12.4% widowed, 9.9% divorced (2008-2012 5-year est.); Foreign born: 3.1% (2008-2012 5-year est.); Ancestry (includes multiple ancestries): 31.1% German, 13.6% Polish, 11.5% Irish, 9.9% American, 8.4% European (2008-2012 5-year est.).
Economy: Single-family building permits issued: 0 (2013); Multi-family building permits issued: 0 (2013); Homeowner vacancy rate: 0.0%. Rental vacancy rate: 0.0%. (2008-2012 5-year est.); Employment by occupation: 10.6% management, business, and financial, 0.5% computer, engineering, and science, 7.0% education, legal, community service, arts, and media, 2.5% healthcare practitioners, 16.1% service, 26.1% sales and office, 8.0% natural resources, construction, and maintenance, 29.1% production, transportation, and material moving (2008-2012 5-year est.).
Income: Per capita income: $27,919 (2008-2012 5-year est.); Median household income: $46,806 (2008-2012 5-year est.); Average household income: $61,152 (2008-2012 5-year est.); Percent of households with income of $100,000 or more: 18.0% (2008-2012 5-year est.); Poverty rate: 9.1% (2008-2012 5-year est.).
Education: Percent of population age 25 and over with: High school diploma (including GED) or higher: 88.6% (2008-2012 5-year est.); Bachelor's degree or higher: 12.2% (2008-2012 5-year est.); Master's degree or higher: 5.2% (2008-2012 5-year est.).
School District(s)
Lostant CUSD 425 (KG-08)
    2011-12 Enrollment: 96. . . . . (815) 368-3392
Housing: Homeownership rate: 87.1% (2008-2012 5-year est.); Median home value: $93,200 (2008-2012 5-year est.); Median contract rent: $633 per month (2008-2012 5-year est.); Median year structure built: 1951 (2008-2012 5-year est.).
Health Insurance: 66.1% Private; 41.8% Public; 14.1% None. (2008-2012 5-year est.)
Transportation: Commute to work: 79.4% car, 0.0% public transportation, 19.6% walk, 0.0% work from home (2008-2012 5-year est.); Travel time to work: 38.1% less than 15 minutes, 37.6% 15 to 30 minutes, 20.6% 30 to 45 minutes, 2.1% 45 to 60 minutes, 1.6% 60 minutes or more (2008-2012 5-year est.)

MARSEILLES (city). Covers a land area of 8.722 square miles and a water area of 0.486 square miles. Located at 41.28° N. Lat; 88.68° W. Long. Elevation is 518 feet.
History: Marseilles developed along a stretch of rapids on the Illinois River, providing water power for its early industries which included a paper mill.
Population: 4,811 (1990); 4,655 (2000); 5,094 (2010); Density: 575.8 persons per square mile (2008-2012 5-year est.); Race: 97.3% White, 0.0% Black/African American, 1.2% Asian, 0.0% American Indian/Alaska Native, 0.0% Native Hawaiian/Other Pacific Islander, 1.5% Some other race, 0.8% Two or more races, 4.9% Hispanic of any race (2008-2012 5-year est.); Average household size: 2.32 (2008-2012 5-year est.); Median age: 42.2 (2008-2012 5-year est.); Males per 100 females: 99.0 (2008-2012 5-year est.); Marriage status: 23.7% never married, 44.3% now married, 13.5% widowed, 18.6% divorced (2008-2012 5-year est.); Foreign born: 2.5% (2008-2012 5-year est.); Ancestry (includes multiple ancestries): 27.8% German, 26.2% Irish, 11.0% Italian, 7.8% English, 7.4% Polish (2008-2012 5-year est.).
Economy: Single-family building permits issued: 7 (2013); Multi-family building permits issued: 0 (2013); Homeowner vacancy rate: 3.2%. Rental

vacancy rate: 0.0%. (2008-2012 5-year est.); Employment by occupation: 5.6% management, business, and financial, 0.5% computer, engineering, and science, 3.3% education, legal, community service, arts, and media, 3.6% healthcare practitioners, 25.2% service, 17.8% sales and office, 20.8% natural resources, construction, and maintenance, 23.4% production, transportation, and material moving (2008-2012 5-year est.).
Income: Per capita income: $21,343 (2008-2012 5-year est.); Median household income: $38,667 (2008-2012 5-year est.); Average household income: $49,022 (2008-2012 5-year est.); Percent of households with income of $100,000 or more: 9.9% (2008-2012 5-year est.); Poverty rate: 15.8% (2008-2012 5-year est.).
Education: Percent of population age 25 and over with: High school diploma (including GED) or higher: 83.4% (2008-2012 5-year est.); Bachelor's degree or higher: 8.0% (2008-2012 5-year est.); Master's degree or higher: 2.9% (2008-2012 5-year est.).
School District(s)
Marseilles ESD 150 (PK-08)
    2011-12 Enrollment: 633. . . . . (815) 795-2162
Miller Twp CCSD 210 (KG-08)
    2011-12 Enrollment: 230. . . . . (815) 357-8151
Housing: Homeownership rate: 80.2% (2008-2012 5-year est.); Median home value: $99,500 (2008-2012 5-year est.); Median contract rent: $472 per month (2008-2012 5-year est.); Median year structure built: 1953 (2008-2012 5-year est.).
Health Insurance: 72.4% Private; 35.4% Public; 10.8% None. (2008-2012 5-year est.)
Safety: Violent crime rate: 9.8 per 10,000 population; Property crime rate: 84.3 per 10,000 population (2012).
Transportation: Commute to work: 96.2% car, 0.0% public transportation, 0.7% walk, 1.9% work from home (2008-2012 5-year est.); Travel time to work: 30.0% less than 15 minutes, 38.6% 15 to 30 minutes, 16.8% 30 to 45 minutes, 7.6% 45 to 60 minutes, 7.0% 60 minutes or more (2008-2012 5-year est.)
Additional Information Contacts
Illinois River Area Chamber of Commerce . . . . (815) 795-2323
    http://iracc.org

MENDOTA (city). Covers a land area of 4.995 square miles and a water area of 0.096 square miles. Located at 41.56° N. Lat; 89.10° W. Long. Elevation is 741 feet.
History: Mendota developed as a trading and processing center for the produce of an agricultural area.
Population: 7,018 (1990); 7,272 (2000); 7,372 (2010); Density: 1,428.9 persons per square mile (2008-2012 5-year est.); Race: 87.4% White, 0.6% Black/African American, 0.1% Asian, 0.0% American Indian/Alaska Native, 0.0% Native Hawaiian/Other Pacific Islander, 11.9% Some other race, 0.7% Two or more races, 29.5% Hispanic of any race (2008-2012 5-year est.); Average household size: 2.58 (2008-2012 5-year est.); Median age: 37.4 (2008-2012 5-year est.); Males per 100 females: 88.5 (2008-2012 5-year est.); Marriage status: 27.1% never married, 53.4% now married, 9.1% widowed, 10.4% divorced (2008-2012 5-year est.); Foreign born: 12.2% (2008-2012 5-year est.); Ancestry (includes multiple ancestries): 33.8% German, 13.9% Irish, 7.2% English, 4.6% American, 3.7% Norwegian (2008-2012 5-year est.).
Economy: Single-family building permits issued: 0 (2013); Multi-family building permits issued: 0 (2013); Homeowner vacancy rate: 4.2%. Rental vacancy rate: 2.9%. (2008-2012 5-year est.); Employment by occupation: 6.4% management, business, and financial, 0.9% computer, engineering, and science, 6.3% education, legal, community service, arts, and media, 5.8% healthcare practitioners, 18.4% service, 20.4% sales and office, 15.3% natural resources, construction, and maintenance, 26.4% production, transportation, and material moving (2008-2012 5-year est.).
Income: Per capita income: $21,995 (2008-2012 5-year est.); Median household income: $43,534 (2008-2012 5-year est.); Average household income: $55,927 (2008-2012 5-year est.); Percent of households with income of $100,000 or more: 10.5% (2008-2012 5-year est.); Poverty rate: 12.3% (2008-2012 5-year est.).
Taxes: Total city taxes per capita: $548 (2011); City property taxes per capita: $490 (2011).
Education: Percent of population age 25 and over with: High school diploma (including GED) or higher: 79.6% (2008-2012 5-year est.); Bachelor's degree or higher: 14.3% (2008-2012 5-year est.); Master's degree or higher: 5.1% (2008-2012 5-year est.).

School District(s)

Mendota CCSD 289 (PK-08)
  2011-12 Enrollment: 1,314 . . . . (815) 539-7631
Mendota Twp HSD 280 (09-12)
  2011-12 Enrollment: 627 . . . . (815) 539-7446
Housing: Homeownership rate: 72.3% (2008-2012 5-year est.); Median home value: $113,500 (2008-2012 5-year est.); Median contract rent: $483 per month (2008-2012 5-year est.); Median year structure built: 1956 (2008-2012 5-year est.).
Health Insurance: 62.6% Private; 40.4% Public; 13.2% None. (2008-2012 5-year est.)
Hospitals: Mendota Community Hospital (32 beds)
Safety: Violent crime rate: 17.7 per 10,000 population; Property crime rate: 213.6 per 10,000 population (2012).
Transportation: Commute to work: 93.7% car, 0.0% public transportation, 2.0% walk, 2.7% work from home (2008-2012 5-year est.); Travel time to work: 55.9% less than 15 minutes, 16.6% 15 to 30 minutes, 16.7% 30 to 45 minutes, 3.4% 45 to 60 minutes, 7.4% 60 minutes or more (2008-2012 5-year est.); Amtrak: Train service available.
Additional Information Contacts
City of Mendota . . . . (815) 539-7459
  http://www.mendota.il.us
Mendota Area Chamber of Commerce . . . . (815) 539-6507
  http://www.mendotachamber.com

MILLINGTON (village). Covers a land area of 0.687 square miles and a water area of 0.055 square miles. Located at 41.56° N. Lat; 88.60° W. Long.
Population: 470 (1990); 458 (2000); 665 (2010); Density: 1,118.1 persons per square mile (2008-2012 5-year est.); Race: 100.0% White, 0.0% Black/African American, 0.0% Asian, 0.0% American Indian/Alaska Native, 0.0% Native Hawaiian/Other Pacific Islander, 0.0% Some other race, 0.0% Two or more races, 0.9% Hispanic of any race (2008-2012 5-year est.); Average household size: 3.52 (2008-2012 5-year est.); Median age: 30.1 (2008-2012 5-year est.); Males per 100 females: 124.6 (2008-2012 5-year est.); Marriage status: 33.1% never married, 55.2% now married, 3.5% widowed, 8.1% divorced (2008-2012 5-year est.); Foreign born: 0.4% (2008-2012 5-year est.); Ancestry (includes multiple ancestries): 44.3% German, 17.8% Irish, 12.0% Polish, 11.8% English, 6.1% Scotch-Irish (2008-2012 5-year est.).
Economy: Single-family building permits issued: 1 (2013); Multi-family building permits issued: 0 (2013); Homeowner vacancy rate: 0.0%. Rental vacancy rate: 0.0%. (2008-2012 5-year est.); Employment by occupation: 14.9% management, business, and financial, 5.6% computer, engineering, and science, 3.1% education, legal, community service, arts, and media, 1.9% healthcare practitioners, 12.1% service, 27.2% sales and office, 24.8% natural resources, construction, and maintenance, 10.5% production, transportation, and material moving (2008-2012 5-year est.).
Income: Per capita income: $18,739 (2008-2012 5-year est.); Median household income: $62,000 (2008-2012 5-year est.); Average household income: $65,050 (2008-2012 5-year est.); Percent of households with income of $100,000 or more: 16.0% (2008-2012 5-year est.); Poverty rate: 17.5% (2008-2012 5-year est.).
Education: Percent of population age 25 and over with: High school diploma (including GED) or higher: 80.5% (2008-2012 5-year est.); Bachelor's degree or higher: 8.5% (2008-2012 5-year est.); Master's degree or higher: 0.9% (2008-2012 5-year est.).
Housing: Homeownership rate: 89.0% (2008-2012 5-year est.); Median home value: $170,600 (2008-2012 5-year est.); Median contract rent: $729 per month (2008-2012 5-year est.); Median year structure built: 1972 (2008-2012 5-year est.).
Health Insurance: 71.6% Private; 27.1% Public; 7.0% None. (2008-2012 5-year est.)
Transportation: Commute to work: 97.8% car, 0.0% public transportation, 0.9% walk, 1.2% work from home (2008-2012 5-year est.); Travel time to work: 9.8% less than 15 minutes, 28.1% 15 to 30 minutes, 32.2% 30 to 45 minutes, 10.4% 45 to 60 minutes, 19.6% 60 minutes or more (2008-2012 5-year est.).

NAPLATE (village). Covers a land area of 0.113 square miles and a water area of 0 square miles. Located at 41.33° N. Lat; 88.88° W. Long. Elevation is 463 feet.
Population: 609 (1990); 523 (2000); 496 (2010); Density: 4,358.9 persons per square mile (2008-2012 5-year est.); Race: 98.0% White, 1.2% Black/African American, 0.0% Asian, 0.0% American Indian/Alaska Native,

0.0% Native Hawaiian/Other Pacific Islander, 0.8% Some other race, 0.8% Two or more races, 3.1% Hispanic of any race (2008-2012 5-year est.); Average household size: 2.16 (2008-2012 5-year est.); Median age: 40.3 (2008-2012 5-year est.); Males per 100 females: 86.0 (2008-2012 5-year est.); Marriage status: 37.1% never married, 37.1% now married, 6.8% widowed, 18.9% divorced (2008-2012 5-year est.); Foreign born: 0.4% (2008-2012 5-year est.); Ancestry (includes multiple ancestries): 32.6% Irish, 32.6% German, 27.3% Italian, 8.1% Polish, 6.7% American (2008-2012 5-year est.).
Economy: Homeowner vacancy rate: 0.0%. Rental vacancy rate: 0.0%. (2008-2012 5-year est.); Employment by occupation: 5.0% management, business, and financial, 0.8% computer, engineering, and science, 1.7% education, legal, community service, arts, and media, 5.4% healthcare practitioners, 29.8% service, 31.0% sales and office, 5.8% natural resources, construction, and maintenance, 20.7% production, transportation, and material moving (2008-2012 5-year est.).
Income: Per capita income: $19,812 (2008-2012 5-year est.); Median household income: $33,224 (2008-2012 5-year est.); Average household income: $42,018 (2008-2012 5-year est.); Percent of households with income of $100,000 or more: 5.7% (2008-2012 5-year est.); Poverty rate: 19.6% (2008-2012 5-year est.).
Education: Percent of population age 25 and over with: High school diploma (including GED) or higher: 94.4% (2008-2012 5-year est.); Bachelor's degree or higher: 12.5% (2008-2012 5-year est.); Master's degree or higher: 0.9% (2008-2012 5-year est.).
Housing: Homeownership rate: 62.6% (2008-2012 5-year est.); Median home value: $95,600 (2008-2012 5-year est.); Median contract rent: $477 per month (2008-2012 5-year est.); Median year structure built: 1944 (2008-2012 5-year est.).
Health Insurance: 69.9% Private; 40.3% Public; 6.9% None. (2008-2012 5-year est.)
Transportation: Commute to work: 90.9% car, 0.0% public transportation, 6.6% walk, 0.0% work from home (2008-2012 5-year est.); Travel time to work: 37.6% less than 15 minutes, 40.9% 15 to 30 minutes, 8.7% 30 to 45 minutes, 5.8% 45 to 60 minutes, 7.0% 60 minutes or more (2008-2012 5-year est.)

NORTH UTICA (village). Aka Utica. Covers a land area of 3.455 square miles and a water area of 0.011 square miles. Located at 41.36° N. Lat; 89.01° W. Long.
Population: 848 (1990); 977 (2000); 1,352 (2010); Density: 343.3 persons per square mile (2008-2012 5-year est.); Race: 93.8% White, 0.0% Black/African American, 1.6% Asian, 0.0% American Indian/Alaska Native, 0.0% Native Hawaiian/Other Pacific Islander, 4.6% Some other race, 3.0% Two or more races, 3.5% Hispanic of any race (2008-2012 5-year est.); Average household size: 2.42 (2008-2012 5-year est.); Median age: 43.6 (2008-2012 5-year est.); Males per 100 females: 86.2 (2008-2012 5-year est.); Marriage status: 20.4% never married, 65.5% now married, 6.1% widowed, 8.0% divorced (2008-2012 5-year est.); Foreign born: 5.4% (2008-2012 5-year est.); Ancestry (includes multiple ancestries): 38.5% German, 15.8% Polish, 10.6% Irish, 10.2% English, 9.4% Italian (2008-2012 5-year est.).
Economy: Single-family building permits issued: 1 (2013); Multi-family building permits issued: 0 (2013); Homeowner vacancy rate: 1.9%. Rental vacancy rate: 9.4%. (2008-2012 5-year est.); Employment by occupation: 10.0% management, business, and financial, 5.9% computer, engineering, and science, 6.2% education, legal, community service, arts, and media, 6.8% healthcare practitioners, 19.9% service, 21.7% sales and office, 13.9% natural resources, construction, and maintenance, 15.7% production, transportation, and material moving (2008-2012 5-year est.).
Income: Per capita income: $27,998 (2008-2012 5-year est.); Median household income: $55,952 (2008-2012 5-year est.); Average household income: $67,728 (2008-2012 5-year est.); Percent of households with income of $100,000 or more: 22.8% (2008-2012 5-year est.); Poverty rate: 5.0% (2008-2012 5-year est.).
Education: Percent of population age 25 and over with: High school diploma (including GED) or higher: 93.1% (2008-2012 5-year est.); Bachelor's degree or higher: 16.1% (2008-2012 5-year est.); Master's degree or higher: 3.9% (2008-2012 5-year est.).
Housing: Homeownership rate: 84.3% (2008-2012 5-year est.); Median home value: $158,700 (2008-2012 5-year est.); Median contract rent: $593 per month (2008-2012 5-year est.); Median year structure built: 1976 (2008-2012 5-year est.).
Health Insurance: 83.1% Private; 29.1% Public; 5.0% None. (2008-2012 5-year est.)

Transportation: Commute to work: 93.0% car, 0.0% public transportation, 1.6% walk, 4.5% work from home (2008-2012 5-year est.); Travel time to work: 36.3% less than 15 minutes, 36.2% 15 to 30 minutes, 10.9% 30 to 45 minutes, 7.5% 45 to 60 minutes, 9.2% 60 minutes or more (2008-2012 5-year est.)

OGLESBY (city). Covers a land area of 4.114 square miles and a water area of 0 square miles. Located at 41.30° N. Lat; 89.07° W. Long. Elevation is 630 feet.
History: Oglesby developed as an industrial town, producing cement from the nearby limestone deposits. The town was named for Governor Richard J. Oglesby.
Population: 3,619 (1990); 3,647 (2000); 3,791 (2010); Density: 886.0 persons per square mile (2008-2012 5-year est.); Race: 99.3% White, 0.4% Black/African American, 0.0% Asian, 0.1% American Indian/Alaska Native, 0.0% Native Hawaiian/Other Pacific Islander, 0.2% Some other race, 0.2% Two or more races, 1.8% Hispanic of any race (2008-2012 5-year est.); Average household size: 2.29 (2008-2012 5-year est.); Median age: 40.5 (2008-2012 5-year est.); Males per 100 females: 90.7 (2008-2012 5-year est.); Marriage status: 17.8% never married, 63.9% now married, 9.4% widowed, 8.8% divorced (2008-2012 5-year est.); Foreign born: 1.1% (2008-2012 5-year est.); Ancestry (includes multiple ancestries): 30.0% German, 20.8% Polish, 20.2% Italian, 12.6% Irish, 10.7% English (2008-2012 5-year est.).
Economy: Single-family building permits issued: 1 (2013); Multi-family building permits issued: 0 (2013); Homeowner vacancy rate: 0.0%. Rental vacancy rate: 20.2%. (2008-2012 5-year est.); Employment by occupation: 8.7% management, business, and financial, 1.0% computer, engineering, and science, 10.3% education, legal, community service, arts, and media, 8.6% healthcare practitioners, 11.5% service, 22.6% sales and office, 15.7% natural resources, construction, and maintenance, 21.7% production, transportation, and material moving (2008-2012 5-year est.).
Income: Per capita income: $25,680 (2008-2012 5-year est.); Median household income: $58,495 (2008-2012 5-year est.); Average household income: $58,369 (2008-2012 5-year est.); Percent of households with income of $100,000 or more: 12.2% (2008-2012 5-year est.); Poverty rate: 6.7% (2008-2012 5-year est.).
Taxes: Total city taxes per capita: $907 (2011); City property taxes per capita: $834 (2011).
Education: Percent of population age 25 and over with: High school diploma (including GED) or higher: 89.6% (2008-2012 5-year est.); Bachelor's degree or higher: 15.0% (2008-2012 5-year est.); Master's degree or higher: 7.3% (2008-2012 5-year est.).

School District(s)
Oglesby ESD 125 (PK-08)
    2011-12 Enrollment: 627......................... (815) 883-9297
Two-year College(s)
Illinois Valley Community College (Public)
    Fall 2012 Enrollment: 3,944 .... (815) 224-2720
    2012-13 Tuition: In-state $8,698; Out-of-state $9,471
Housing: Homeownership rate: 82.4% (2008-2012 5-year est.); Median home value: $109,300 (2008-2012 5-year est.); Median contract rent: $507 per month (2008-2012 5-year est.); Median year structure built: 1951 (2008-2012 5-year est.).
Health Insurance: 82.1% Private; 29.9% Public; 6.8% None. (2008-2012 5-year est.)
Safety: Violent crime rate: 15.9 per 10,000 population; Property crime rate: 246.1 per 10,000 population (2012).
Transportation: Commute to work: 94.0% car, 0.0% public transportation, 0.1% walk, 3.1% work from home (2008-2012 5-year est.); Travel time to work: 49.9% less than 15 minutes, 29.3% 15 to 30 minutes, 11.7% 30 to 45 minutes, 2.0% 45 to 60 minutes, 7.1% 60 minutes or more (2008-2012 5-year est.)

OTTAWA (city). County seat. Covers a land area of 12.001 square miles and a water area of 0.799 square miles. Located at 41.35° N. Lat; 88.83° W. Long. Elevation is 482 feet.
History: Ottawa was laid out in 1830 by the Illinois & Michigan Canal commissioners. A settlement soon grew as the town was on the travel route between Chicago and the Illinois Valley. In 1858 Abraham Lincoln and Stephen Douglas held their first, highly-publicized debate in Ottawa.
Population: 17,451 (1990); 18,307 (2000); 18,768 (2010); Density: 1,604.6 persons per square mile (2008-2012 5-year est.); Race: 91.7% White, 3.5% Black/African American, 1.1% Asian, 0.2% American Indian/Alaska Native, 0.0% Native Hawaiian/Other Pacific Islander, 3.5%

Some other race, 2.7% Two or more races, 7.5% Hispanic of any race (2008-2012 5-year est.); Average household size: 2.39 (2008-2012 5-year est.); Median age: 41.0 (2008-2012 5-year est.); Males per 100 females: 107.5 (2008-2012 5-year est.); Marriage status: 29.5% never married, 49.0% now married, 8.3% widowed, 13.2% divorced (2008-2012 5-year est.); Foreign born: 3.4% (2008-2012 5-year est.); Ancestry (includes multiple ancestries): 29.8% German, 23.6% Irish, 10.2% English, 9.8% Italian, 7.2% Norwegian (2008-2012 5-year est.).
Economy: Single-family building permits issued: 27 (2013); Multi-family building permits issued: 0 (2013); Homeowner vacancy rate: 2.2%. Rental vacancy rate: 4.1%. (2008-2012 5-year est.); Employment by occupation: 10.0% management, business, and financial, 3.9% computer, engineering, and science, 7.4% education, legal, community service, arts, and media, 6.0% healthcare practitioners, 20.7% service, 26.7% sales and office, 9.5% natural resources, construction, and maintenance, 15.8% production, transportation, and material moving (2008-2012 5-year est.).
Income: Per capita income: $25,414 (2008-2012 5-year est.); Median household income: $47,480 (2008-2012 5-year est.); Average household income: $59,968 (2008-2012 5-year est.); Percent of households with income of $100,000 or more: 17.3% (2008-2012 5-year est.); Poverty rate: 13.0% (2008-2012 5-year est.).
Education: Percent of population age 25 and over with: High school diploma (including GED) or higher: 89.3% (2008-2012 5-year est.); Bachelor's degree or higher: 18.8% (2008-2012 5-year est.); Master's degree or higher: 6.8% (2008-2012 5-year est.).

School District(s)
Deer Park CCSD 82 (PK-08)
    2011-12 Enrollment: 109................... (815) 434-6930
La Salle Roe (06-12)
    2011-12 Enrollment: n/a .... (815) 434-0780
Ottawa ESD 141 (PK-08)
    2011-12 Enrollment: 2,082 .... (815) 433-1133
Ottawa Twp HSD 140 (09-12)
    2011-12 Enrollment: 1,440 .... (815) 433-1323
Rutland CCSD 230 (KG-08)
    2011-12 Enrollment: 70.................... (815) 433-2949
Wallace CCSD 195 (KG-08)
    2011-12 Enrollment: 323................... (815) 433-2986
Housing: Homeownership rate: 66.6% (2008-2012 5-year est.); Median home value: $132,900 (2008-2012 5-year est.); Median contract rent: $548 per month (2008-2012 5-year est.); Median year structure built: 1958 (2008-2012 5-year est.).
Health Insurance: 68.8% Private; 35.4% Public; 12.1% None. (2008-2012 5-year est.)
Hospitals: Community Hospital of Ottawa (124 beds)
Safety: Violent crime rate: 13.4 per 10,000 population; Property crime rate: 228.8 per 10,000 population (2012).
Transportation: Commute to work: 92.8% car, 0.2% public transportation, 3.3% walk, 1.7% work from home (2008-2012 5-year est.); Travel time to work: 48.1% less than 15 minutes, 26.6% 15 to 30 minutes, 10.4% 30 to 45 minutes, 6.9% 45 to 60 minutes, 8.1% 60 minutes or more (2008-2012 5-year est.)
Additional Information Contacts
City of Ottawa .... (815) 433-0161
    http://www.cityofottawa.org
Ottawa Area Chamber of Commerce & Industry .... (815) 433-0084
    http://www.ottawachamberillinois.com

PERU (city). Covers a land area of 8.965 square miles and a water area of 0.108 square miles. Located at 41.35° N. Lat; 89.13° W. Long. Elevation is 600 feet.
History: Peru's name is of Indian origin, meaning "plenty of everything." The town was founded in 1835 on the Illinois River, and became the terminus of the Illinois & Michigan Canal. River traffic influenced the development of Peru's early industries, which included the Peru Wheel Company and the Star Union Products Company.
Population: 9,302 (1990); 9,835 (2000); 10,295 (2010); Density: 1,136.6 persons per square mile (2008-2012 5-year est.); Race: 94.4% White, 1.1% Black/African American, 1.9% Asian, 0.1% American Indian/Alaska Native, 0.0% Native Hawaiian/Other Pacific Islander, 2.5% Some other race, 1.3% Two or more races, 5.6% Hispanic of any race (2008-2012 5-year est.); Average household size: 2.32 (2008-2012 5-year est.); Median age: 44.4 (2008-2012 5-year est.); Males per 100 females: 94.3 (2008-2012 5-year est.); Marriage status: 28.1% never married, 53.1% now married, 9.2% widowed, 9.6% divorced (2008-2012 5-year est.);

Foreign born: 3.0% (2008-2012 5-year est.); Ancestry (includes multiple ancestries): 31.1% German, 19.8% Polish, 18.1% Italian, 14.4% Irish, 7.6% English (2008-2012 5-year est.).
Economy: Single-family building permits issued: 6 (2013); Multi-family building permits issued: 0 (2013); Homeowner vacancy rate: 2.2%. Rental vacancy rate: 8.8%. (2008-2012 5-year est.); Employment by occupation: 12.6% management, business, and financial, 1.7% computer, engineering, and science, 7.5% education, legal, community service, arts, and media, 5.3% healthcare practitioners, 22.6% service, 27.2% sales and office, 6.6% natural resources, construction, and maintenance, 16.7% production, transportation, and material moving (2008-2012 5-year est.).
Income: Per capita income: $28,921 (2008-2012 5-year est.); Median household income: $51,694 (2008-2012 5-year est.); Average household income: $67,331 (2008-2012 5-year est.); Percent of households with income of $100,000 or more: 19.7% (2008-2012 5-year est.); Poverty rate: 9.8% (2008-2012 5-year est.).
Education: Percent of population age 25 and over with: High school diploma (including GED) or higher: 92.9% (2008-2012 5-year est.); Bachelor's degree or higher: 20.7% (2008-2012 5-year est.); Master's degree or higher: 6.9% (2008-2012 5-year est.).

School District(s)
La Salle Roe (06-12)
  2011-12 Enrollment: n/a . . . . (815) 434-0780
Lasalle Putnam Alliance (04-12)
  2011-12 Enrollment: n/a . . . . (815) 433-6433
Peru ESD 124 (PK-08)
  2011-12 Enrollment: 1,029 . . . . (815) 223-0486
Housing: Homeownership rate: 75.6% (2008-2012 5-year est.); Median home value: $122,600 (2008-2012 5-year est.); Median contract rent: $505 per month (2008-2012 5-year est.); Median year structure built: 1955 (2008-2012 5-year est.).
Health Insurance: 76.3% Private; 31.6% Public; 11.1% None. (2008-2012 5-year est.)
Hospitals: Illinois Valley Community Hospital
Safety: Violent crime rate: 9.7 per 10,000 population; Property crime rate: 223.2 per 10,000 population (2012).
Transportation: Commute to work: 93.7% car, 0.0% public transportation, 2.9% walk, 2.4% work from home (2008-2012 5-year est.); Travel time to work: 63.4% less than 15 minutes, 22.2% 15 to 30 minutes, 7.9% 30 to 45 minutes, 1.2% 45 to 60 minutes, 5.2% 60 minutes or more (2008-2012 5-year est.)
Airports: Illinois Valley Regional Airport (general aviation)
Additional Information Contacts
City of Peru . . . . (815) 223-0061
  http://www.peru.il.us

RANSOM (village). Covers a land area of 0.999 square miles and a water area of 0 square miles. Located at 41.16° N. Lat; 88.65° W. Long. Elevation is 705 feet.
Population: 438 (1990); 409 (2000); 384 (2010); Density: 374.2 persons per square mile (2008-2012 5-year est.); Race: 96.3% White, 0.0% Black/African American, 0.0% Asian, 0.8% American Indian/Alaska Native, 0.0% Native Hawaiian/Other Pacific Islander, 2.9% Some other race, 2.9% Two or more races, 0.8% Hispanic of any race (2008-2012 5-year est.); Average household size: 2.71 (2008-2012 5-year est.); Median age: 34.7 (2008-2012 5-year est.); Males per 100 females: 101.1 (2008-2012 5-year est.); Marriage status: 30.5% never married, 51.5% now married, 5.6% widowed, 12.5% divorced (2008-2012 5-year est.); Foreign born: 0.0% (2008-2012 5-year est.); Ancestry (includes multiple ancestries): 35.6% German, 25.9% Irish, 11.2% English, 9.4% Polish, 5.9% Slovak (2008-2012 5-year est.).
Economy: Single-family building permits issued: 0 (2013); Multi-family building permits issued: 0 (2013); Homeowner vacancy rate: 1.7%. Rental vacancy rate: 0.0%. (2008-2012 5-year est.); Employment by occupation: 5.1% management, business, and financial, 1.7% computer, engineering, and science, 6.9% education, legal, community service, arts, and media, 6.3% healthcare practitioners, 21.7% service, 19.4% sales and office, 11.4% natural resources, construction, and maintenance, 27.4% production, transportation, and material moving (2008-2012 5-year est.).
Income: Per capita income: $23,107 (2008-2012 5-year est.); Median household income: $50,000 (2008-2012 5-year est.); Average household income: $61,714 (2008-2012 5-year est.); Percent of households with income of $100,000 or more: 22.4% (2008-2012 5-year est.); Poverty rate: 13.0% (2008-2012 5-year est.).

Education: Percent of population age 25 and over with: High school diploma (including GED) or higher: 91.1% (2008-2012 5-year est.); Bachelor's degree or higher: 5.7% (2008-2012 5-year est.); Master's degree or higher: 2.4% (2008-2012 5-year est.).

School District(s)
Allen-Otter Creek CCSD 65 (KG-08)
  2011-12 Enrollment: 107 . . . . (815) 586-4611
Housing: Homeownership rate: 85.5% (2008-2012 5-year est.); Median home value: $85,300 (2008-2012 5-year est.); Median contract rent: $535 per month (2008-2012 5-year est.); Median year structure built: 1946 (2008-2012 5-year est.).
Health Insurance: 84.2% Private; 22.2% Public; 4.8% None. (2008-2012 5-year est.)
Transportation: Commute to work: 88.7% car, 1.2% public transportation, 7.7% walk, 0.0% work from home (2008-2012 5-year est.); Travel time to work: 28.0% less than 15 minutes, 32.7% 15 to 30 minutes, 20.2% 30 to 45 minutes, 9.5% 45 to 60 minutes, 9.5% 60 minutes or more (2008-2012 5-year est.)

RUTLAND (village). Covers a land area of 0.694 square miles and a water area of 0 square miles. Located at 40.98° N. Lat; 89.04° W. Long. Elevation is 702 feet.
Population: 391 (1990); 354 (2000); 318 (2010); Density: 435.2 persons per square mile (2008-2012 5-year est.); Race: 100.0% White, 0.0% Black/African American, 0.0% Asian, 0.0% American Indian/Alaska Native, 0.0% Native Hawaiian/Other Pacific Islander, 0.0% Some other race, 0.0% Two or more races, 0.0% Hispanic of any race (2008-2012 5-year est.); Average household size: 2.10 (2008-2012 5-year est.); Median age: 44.7 (2008-2012 5-year est.); Males per 100 females: 117.3 (2008-2012 5-year est.); Marriage status: 26.4% never married, 58.5% now married, 10.5% widowed, 4.7% divorced (2008-2012 5-year est.); Foreign born: 0.0% (2008-2012 5-year est.); Ancestry (includes multiple ancestries): 33.8% German, 12.9% Irish, 6.0% Polish, 5.6% French, 5.0% American (2008-2012 5-year est.).
Economy: Homeowner vacancy rate: 0.0%. Rental vacancy rate: 0.0%. (2008-2012 5-year est.); Employment by occupation: 5.9% management, business, and financial, 2.0% computer, engineering, and science, 1.3% education, legal, community service, arts, and media, 0.0% healthcare practitioners, 24.3% service, 15.8% sales and office, 17.8% natural resources, construction, and maintenance, 32.9% production, transportation, and material moving (2008-2012 5-year est.).
Income: Per capita income: $23,372 (2008-2012 5-year est.); Median household income: $44,375 (2008-2012 5-year est.); Average household income: $49,843 (2008-2012 5-year est.); Percent of households with income of $100,000 or more: 9.0% (2008-2012 5-year est.); Poverty rate: 8.9% (2008-2012 5-year est.).
Education: Percent of population age 25 and over with: High school diploma (including GED) or higher: 85.0% (2008-2012 5-year est.); Bachelor's degree or higher: 3.4% (2008-2012 5-year est.); Master's degree or higher: 0.0% (2008-2012 5-year est.).
Housing: Homeownership rate: 90.3% (2008-2012 5-year est.); Median home value: $60,600 (2008-2012 5-year est.); Median contract rent: $375 per month (2008-2012 5-year est.); Median year structure built: 1957 (2008-2012 5-year est.).
Health Insurance: 64.2% Private; 31.8% Public; 20.2% None. (2008-2012 5-year est.)
Transportation: Commute to work: 100.0% car, 0.0% public transportation, 0.0% walk, 0.0% work from home (2008-2012 5-year est.); Travel time to work: 43.4% less than 15 minutes, 25.7% 15 to 30 minutes, 11.8% 30 to 45 minutes, 7.9% 45 to 60 minutes, 11.2% 60 minutes or more (2008-2012 5-year est.)

SENECA (village). Aka Crotty. Covers a land area of 6.635 square miles and a water area of 0.428 square miles. Located at 41.29° N. Lat; 88.63° W. Long. Elevation is 509 feet.
History: Seneca was built along the Illinois & Michigan Canal, and developed as a sawmill town.
Population: 1,878 (1990); 2,053 (2000); 2,371 (2010); Density: 373.2 persons per square mile (2008-2012 5-year est.); Race: 98.8% White, 0.0% Black/African American, 0.0% Asian, 0.1% American Indian/Alaska Native, 0.0% Native Hawaiian/Other Pacific Islander, 1.1% Some other race, 0.5% Two or more races, 8.3% Hispanic of any race (2008-2012 5-year est.); Average household size: 2.84 (2008-2012 5-year est.); Median age: 31.2 (2008-2012 5-year est.); Males per 100 females: 116.1 (2008-2012 5-year est.); Marriage status: 32.9% never married, 45.8%

now married, 3.3% widowed, 18.0% divorced (2008-2012 5-year est.); Foreign born: 0.2% (2008-2012 5-year est.); Ancestry (includes multiple ancestries): 27.5% German, 27.1% Irish, 14.1% Norwegian, 7.4% English, 7.4% Polish (2008-2012 5-year est.).

Economy: Single-family building permits issued: 2 (2013); Multi-family building permits issued: 0 (2013); Homeowner vacancy rate: 0.0%. Rental vacancy rate: 0.0%. (2008-2012 5-year est.); Employment by occupation: 15.8% management, business, and financial, 2.2% computer, engineering, and science, 9.2% education, legal, community service, arts, and media, 3.0% healthcare practitioners, 17.7% service, 22.9% sales and office, 9.8% natural resources, construction, and maintenance, 19.4% production, transportation, and material moving (2008-2012 5-year est.).

Income: Per capita income: $24,782 (2008-2012 5-year est.); Median household income: $61,311 (2008-2012 5-year est.); Average household income: $68,958 (2008-2012 5-year est.); Percent of households with income of $100,000 or more: 15.6% (2008-2012 5-year est.); Poverty rate: 11.0% (2008-2012 5-year est.).

Education: Percent of population age 25 and over with: High school diploma (including GED) or higher: 92.1% (2008-2012 5-year est.); Bachelor's degree or higher: 16.8% (2008-2012 5-year est.); Master's degree or higher: 4.8% (2008-2012 5-year est.).

School District(s)

Seneca CCSD 170 (PK-08)

    2011-12 Enrollment: 532 . . . . (815) 357-8744

Seneca Twp HSD 160 (09-12)

    2011-12 Enrollment: 452 . . . . (815) 357-5000

Housing: Homeownership rate: 78.5% (2008-2012 5-year est.); Median home value: $162,800 (2008-2012 5-year est.); Median contract rent: $523 per month (2008-2012 5-year est.); Median year structure built: 1968 (2008-2012 5-year est.).

Health Insurance: 70.4% Private; 27.8% Public; 12.3% None. (2008-2012 5-year est.)

Safety: Violent crime rate: 59.2 per 10,000 population; Property crime rate: 270.7 per 10,000 population (2012).

Transportation: Commute to work: 96.7% car, 0.0% public transportation, 0.5% walk, 1.0% work from home (2008-2012 5-year est.); Travel time to work: 31.4% less than 15 minutes, 33.5% 15 to 30 minutes, 17.9% 30 to 45 minutes, 8.8% 45 to 60 minutes, 8.4% 60 minutes or more (2008-2012 5-year est.)

SERENA (unincorporated postal area)

Zip Code: 60549

Covers a land area of 23.770 square miles and a water area of 0.244 square miles. Located at 41.50° N. Lat; 88.73° W. Long. Elevation is 633 feet. Population: 643 (2010); Density: 27.0 persons per square mile (2010); Race: 98.0% White, 0.6% Black/African American, 0.0% Asian, 0.2% American Indian/Alaska Native, 0.0% Native Hawaiian/Other Pacific Islander, 1.2% Some other race, 1.1% Two or more races, 3.6% Hispanic of any race (2010); Average household size: 2.69 (2010); Median age: 42.5 (2010); Males per 100 females: 99.1 (2010); Homeownership rate: 81.1% (2010)

SHERIDAN (village).

Covers a land area of 1.994 square miles and a water area of 0.037 square miles. Located at 41.53° N. Lat; 88.68° W. Long. Elevation is 594 feet.

Population: 1,288 (1990); 2,411 (2000); 2,137 (2010); Density: 763.4 persons per square mile (2008-2012 5-year est.); Race: 62.9% White, 31.3% Black/African American, 0.7% Asian, 2.2% American Indian/Alaska Native, 0.0% Native Hawaiian/Other Pacific Islander, 2.9% Some other race, 2.6% Two or more races, 12.6% Hispanic of any race (2008-2012 5-year est.); Average household size: 2.54 (2008-2012 5-year est.); Median age: 36.4 (2008-2012 5-year est.); Males per 100 females: 278.6 (2008-2012 5-year est.); Marriage status: 52.9% never married, 28.5% now married, 3.1% widowed, 15.6% divorced (2008-2012 5-year est.); Foreign born: 1.6% (2008-2012 5-year est.); Ancestry (includes multiple ancestries): 22.1% German, 11.8% Irish, 8.9% Italian, 6.7% English, 5.0% Norwegian (2008-2012 5-year est.).

Economy: Single-family building permits issued: 0 (2013); Multi-family building permits issued: 0 (2013); Homeowner vacancy rate: 0.0%. Rental vacancy rate: 0.0%. (2008-2012 5-year est.); Employment by occupation: 4.1% management, business, and financial, 5.0% computer, engineering, and science, 5.9% education, legal, community service, arts, and media, 3.2% healthcare practitioners, 17.7% service, 31.6% sales and office, 15.9% natural resources, construction, and maintenance, 16.6% production, transportation, and material moving (2008-2012 5-year est.).

Income: Per capita income: $14,843 (2008-2012 5-year est.); Median household income: $57,750 (2008-2012 5-year est.); Average household income: $66,599 (2008-2012 5-year est.); Percent of households with income of $100,000 or more: 15.2% (2008-2012 5-year est.); Poverty rate: 9.0% (2008-2012 5-year est.).

Education: Percent of population age 25 and over with: High school diploma (including GED) or higher: 64.9% (2008-2012 5-year est.); Bachelor's degree or higher: 5.9% (2008-2012 5-year est.); Master's degree or higher: 3.5% (2008-2012 5-year est.).

School District(s)

Serena CUSD 2 (KG-12)

    2011-12 Enrollment: 820 . . . . (815) 496-2850

Housing: Homeownership rate: 74.0% (2008-2012 5-year est.); Median home value: $135,100 (2008-2012 5-year est.); Median contract rent: $688 per month (2008-2012 5-year est.); Median year structure built: 1946 (2008-2012 5-year est.).

Health Insurance: 82.5% Private; 20.1% Public; 7.5% None. (2008-2012 5-year est.)

Transportation: Commute to work: 89.0% car, 1.6% public transportation, 3.7% walk, 1.6% work from home (2008-2012 5-year est.); Travel time to work: 28.5% less than 15 minutes, 22.9% 15 to 30 minutes, 28.7% 30 to 45 minutes, 10.5% 45 to 60 minutes, 9.3% 60 minutes or more (2008-2012 5-year est.)

STREATOR (city).

Covers a land area of 6.066 square miles and a water area of 0.012 square miles. Located at 41.12° N. Lat; 88.83° W. Long. Elevation is 620 feet.

History: Coal mining began in Streator in 1872, and the name of the town was changed from Unionville to Streator to honor the president of the coal company. Streator was sited near deposits of shale, clay, and sand which led to the manufacturing of glass.

Population: 14,121 (1990); 14,190 (2000); 13,710 (2010); Density: 2,154.1 persons per square mile (2008-2012 5-year est.); Race: 92.7% White, 1.1% Black/African American, 0.4% Asian, 0.1% American Indian/Alaska Native, 0.0% Native Hawaiian/Other Pacific Islander, 5.7% Some other race, 2.5% Two or more races, 13.6% Hispanic of any race (2008-2012 5-year est.); Average household size: 2.45 (2008-2012 5-year est.); Median age: 38.6 (2008-2012 5-year est.); Males per 100 females: 87.7 (2008-2012 5-year est.); Marriage status: 32.0% never married, 47.6% now married, 9.6% widowed, 10.8% divorced (2008-2012 5-year est.); Foreign born: 7.5% (2008-2012 5-year est.); Ancestry (includes multiple ancestries): 28.9% German, 18.3% Irish, 12.3% Slovak, 6.6% English, 6.5% Italian (2008-2012 5-year est.).

Economy: Single-family building permits issued: 1 (2013); Multi-family building permits issued: 0 (2013); Homeowner vacancy rate: 3.9%. Rental vacancy rate: 7.7%. (2008-2012 5-year est.); Employment by occupation: 7.4% management, business, and financial, 3.3% computer, engineering, and science, 8.3% education, legal, community service, arts, and media, 2.2% healthcare practitioners, 25.0% service, 23.0% sales and office, 8.4% natural resources, construction, and maintenance, 22.4% production, transportation, and material moving (2008-2012 5-year est.).

Income: Per capita income: $20,631 (2008-2012 5-year est.); Median household income: $40,634 (2008-2012 5-year est.); Average household income: $49,117 (2008-2012 5-year est.); Percent of households with income of $100,000 or more: 9.4% (2008-2012 5-year est.); Poverty rate: 15.6% (2008-2012 5-year est.).

Education: Percent of population age 25 and over with: High school diploma (including GED) or higher: 84.9% (2008-2012 5-year est.); Bachelor's degree or higher: 10.1% (2008-2012 5-year est.); Master's degree or higher: 3.1% (2008-2012 5-year est.).

School District(s)

Streator ESD 44 (PK-08)

    2011-12 Enrollment: 1,997 . . . . (815) 672-2926

Streator Twp HSD 40 (09-12)

    2011-12 Enrollment: 889 . . . . (815) 672-0545

Woodland CUSD 5 (PK-12)

    2011-12 Enrollment: 493 . . . . (815) 672-5974

Housing: Homeownership rate: 72.6% (2008-2012 5-year est.); Median home value: $80,100 (2008-2012 5-year est.); Median contract rent: $462 per month (2008-2012 5-year est.); Median year structure built: 1949 (2008-2012 5-year est.).

Health Insurance: 62.8% Private; 37.0% Public; 13.6% None. (2008-2012 5-year est.)

Hospitals: St. Mary's Hospital (251 beds)

Safety: Violent crime rate: 5.9 per 10,000 population; Property crime rate: 314.7 per 10,000 population (2012).
Transportation: Commute to work: 93.5% car, 0.2% public transportation, 3.7% walk, 1.1% work from home (2008-2012 5-year est.); Travel time to work: 55.8% less than 15 minutes, 17.4% 15 to 30 minutes, 15.9% 30 to 45 minutes, 5.5% 45 to 60 minutes, 5.4% 60 minutes or more (2008-2012 5-year est.)
Additional Information Contacts
City of Streator . . . . (815) 672-2517
   http://www.ci.streator.il.us/cms
Streator Area Chamber of Commerce & Industry . . . . (815) 672-2921
   http://www.streatorchamber.com

TONICA (village).
Covers a land area of 1.363 square miles and a water area of 0 square miles. Located at 41.22° N. Lat; 89.07° W. Long. Elevation is 659 feet.
Population: 715 (1990); 685 (2000); 768 (2010); Density: 623.5 persons per square mile (2008-2012 5-year est.); Race: 98.5% White, 0.0% Black/African American, 0.0% Asian, 0.1% American Indian/Alaska Native, 0.0% Native Hawaiian/Other Pacific Islander, 1.4% Some other race, 0.9% Two or more races, 4.4% Hispanic of any race (2008-2012 5-year est.); Average household size: 2.76 (2008-2012 5-year est.); Median age: 37.8 (2008-2012 5-year est.); Males per 100 females: 92.7 (2008-2012 5-year est.); Marriage status: 20.7% never married, 61.1% now married, 7.9% widowed, 10.3% divorced (2008-2012 5-year est.); Foreign born: 1.5% (2008-2012 5-year est.); Ancestry (includes multiple ancestries): 38.9% German, 20.6% English, 17.1% Irish, 16.6% Italian, 11.9% Polish (2008-2012 5-year est.).
Economy: Single-family building permits issued: 0 (2013); Multi-family building permits issued: 0 (2013); Homeowner vacancy rate: 0.0%. Rental vacancy rate: 0.0%. (2008-2012 5-year est.); Employment by occupation: 13.0% management, business, and financial, 2.8% computer, engineering, and science, 7.8% education, legal, community service, arts, and media, 7.0% healthcare practitioners, 12.8% service, 25.0% sales and office, 13.5% natural resources, construction, and maintenance, 18.3% production, transportation, and material moving (2008-2012 5-year est.).
Income: Per capita income: $22,828 (2008-2012 5-year est.); Median household income: $48,333 (2008-2012 5-year est.); Average household income: $62,068 (2008-2012 5-year est.); Percent of households with income of $100,000 or more: 14.2% (2008-2012 5-year est.); Poverty rate: 2.7% (2008-2012 5-year est.).
Education: Percent of population age 25 and over with: High school diploma (including GED) or higher: 92.2% (2008-2012 5-year est.); Bachelor's degree or higher: 16.8% (2008-2012 5-year est.); Master's degree or higher: 4.6% (2008-2012 5-year est.).
School District(s)
Tonica CCSD 79 (PK-08)
   2011-12 Enrollment: 218 . . . . (815) 442-3420
Housing: Homeownership rate: 87.0% (2008-2012 5-year est.); Median home value: $109,900 (2008-2012 5-year est.); Median contract rent: $500 per month (2008-2012 5-year est.); Median year structure built: 1953 (2008-2012 5-year est.).
Health Insurance: 78.4% Private; 31.4% Public; 6.8% None. (2008-2012 5-year est.)
Safety: Violent crime rate: 13.1 per 10,000 population; Property crime rate: 65.4 per 10,000 population (2012).
Transportation: Commute to work: 91.5% car, 0.0% public transportation, 1.3% walk, 5.4% work from home (2008-2012 5-year est.); Travel time to work: 27.0% less than 15 minutes, 46.3% 15 to 30 minutes, 16.3% 30 to 45 minutes, 5.4% 45 to 60 minutes, 4.9% 60 minutes or more (2008-2012 5-year est.)

TROY GROVE (village).
Covers a land area of 0.687 square miles and a water area of 0 square miles. Located at 41.47° N. Lat; 89.08° W. Long. Elevation is 673 feet.
History: Troy Grove is the birthplace and boyhood home of James Butler "Wild Bill" Hickok (1837-1876), who toured with Buffalo Bill Cody in 1872-1873.
Population: 259 (1990); 305 (2000); 250 (2010); Density: 297.0 persons per square mile (2008-2012 5-year est.); Race: 92.2% White, 0.0% Black/African American, 1.5% Asian, 0.0% American Indian/Alaska Native, 0.0% Native Hawaiian/Other Pacific Islander, 6.3% Some other race, 1.5% Two or more races, 9.3% Hispanic of any race (2008-2012 5-year est.); Average household size: 2.22 (2008-2012 5-year est.); Median age: 39.6 (2008-2012 5-year est.); Males per 100 females: 106.1 (2008-2012 5-year

est.); Marriage status: 27.7% never married, 57.2% now married, 4.2% widowed, 10.8% divorced (2008-2012 5-year est.); Foreign born: 2.5% (2008-2012 5-year est.); Ancestry (includes multiple ancestries): 49.5% German, 21.6% Irish, 6.4% Swedish, 5.9% American, 4.9% Norwegian (2008-2012 5-year est.).
Economy: Homeowner vacancy rate: 0.0%. Rental vacancy rate: 0.0%. (2008-2012 5-year est.); Employment by occupation: 5.8% management, business, and financial, 1.7% computer, engineering, and science, 2.5% education, legal, community service, arts, and media, 8.3% healthcare practitioners, 17.4% service, 18.2% sales and office, 28.1% natural resources, construction, and maintenance, 18.2% production, transportation, and material moving (2008-2012 5-year est.).
Income: Per capita income: $28,404 (2008-2012 5-year est.); Median household income: $57,083 (2008-2012 5-year est.); Average household income: $66,157 (2008-2012 5-year est.); Percent of households with income of $100,000 or more: 15.2% (2008-2012 5-year est.); Poverty rate: 8.9% (2008-2012 5-year est.).
Education: Percent of population age 25 and over with: High school diploma (including GED) or higher: 90.8% (2008-2012 5-year est.); Bachelor's degree or higher: 12.2% (2008-2012 5-year est.); Master's degree or higher: 0.0% (2008-2012 5-year est.).
Housing: Homeownership rate: 84.8% (2008-2012 5-year est.); Median home value: $143,800 (2008-2012 5-year est.); Median contract rent: $463 per month (2008-2012 5-year est.); Median year structure built: 1951 (2008-2012 5-year est.).
Health Insurance: 85.8% Private; 11.3% Public; 4.4% None. (2008-2012 5-year est.)
Transportation: Commute to work: 93.3% car, 0.0% public transportation, 5.9% walk, 0.8% work from home (2008-2012 5-year est.); Travel time to work: 51.7% less than 15 minutes, 18.6% 15 to 30 minutes, 6.8% 30 to 45 minutes, 0.8% 45 to 60 minutes, 22.0% 60 minutes or more (2008-2012 5-year est.)

UTICA (unincorporated postal area)
Zip Code: 61373
   Covers a land area of 48.514 square miles and a water area of 0.445 square miles. Located at 41.40° N. Lat; 88.99° W. Long. Elevation is 476 feet. Population: 2,031 (2010); Density: 41.9 persons per square mile (2010); Race: 97.8% White, 0.2% Black/African American, 0.2% Asian, 0.1% American Indian/Alaska Native, 0.0% Native Hawaiian/Other Pacific Islander, 1.7% Some other race, 0.9% Two or more races, 3.0% Hispanic of any race (2010); Average household size: 2.48 (2010); Median age: 43.9 (2010); Males per 100 females: 94.0 (2010); Homeownership rate: 85.5% (2010)

WEDRON (unincorporated postal area)
Zip Code: 60557
   Covers a land area of 0.672 square miles and a water area of 0.088 square miles. Located at 41.44° N. Lat; 88.76° W. Long. Elevation is 538 feet. Population: 155 (2010); Density: 230.6 persons per square mile (2010); Race: 99.4% White, 0.0% Black/African American, 0.0% Asian, 0.0% American Indian/Alaska Native, 0.0% Native Hawaiian/Other Pacific Islander, 0.6% Some other race, 0.6% Two or more races, 1.9% Hispanic of any race (2010); Average household size: 2.67 (2010); Median age: 44.7 (2010); Males per 100 females: 134.8 (2010); Homeownership rate: 60.3% (2010)

Lake County

Located in northeastern Illinois; bounded on the east by Lake Michigan, and on the north by Wisconsin; drained by the Fox and Des Plaines Rivers; includes many lakes. Covers a land area of 443.670 square miles, a water area of 924.809 square miles, and is located in the Central Time Zone at 42.33° N. Lat., 87.44° W. Long. The county was founded in 1839. County seat is Waukegan.

Lake County is part of the Chicago-Naperville-Elgin, IL-IN-WI Metropolitan Statistical Area. The entire metro area includes:
Chicago-Naperville-Arlington Heights, IL Metropolitan Division (Cook County, IL; DuPage County, IL; Grundy County, IL; Kendall County, IL; McHenry County, IL; Will County, IL); Elgin, IL Metropolitan Division (DeKalb County, IL; Kane County, IL); Gary, IN Metropolitan Division (Jasper County, IN; Lake County, IN; Newton County, IN; Porter County, IN); Lake County-Kenosha County, IL-WI Metropolitan Division (Lake County, IL; Kenosha County, WI)

Weather Station: Antioch   Elevation: 750 feet

	Jan	Feb	Mar	Apr	May	Jun	Jul	Aug	Sep	Oct	Nov	Dec
High	30	33	44	57	68	78	82	81	74	61	47	34
Low	13	16	26	37	46	56	62	61	53	41	30	19
Precip	1.6	1.5	1.9	3.2	4.1	4.1	3.8	4.3	3.6	2.9	2.9	2.1
Snow	11.1	9.1	5.6	1.5	tr	0.0	0.0	0.0	0.0	0.1	1.7	10.1

High and Low temperatures in degrees Fahrenheit; Precipitation and Snow in inches

Population: 516,418 (1990); 644,356 (2000); 703,462 (2010); Race: 77.8% White, 6.8% Black/African American, 6.3% Asian, 0.2% American Indian/Alaska Native, 0.0% Native Hawaiian/Other Pacific Islander, 8.9% Some other race, 2.4% Two or more races, 19.9% Hispanic of any race (2008-2012 5-year est.); Density: 1,580.5 persons per square mile (2008-2012 5-year est.); Average household size: 2.84 (2008-2012 5-year est.); Median age: 36.7 (2008-2012 5-year est.); Males per 100 females: 99.7 (2008-2012 5-year est.).
Religion: Six largest groups: 30.0% Catholicism, 7.8% Non-denominational Protestant, 3.2% Lutheran, 2.6% Judaism, 2.3% Baptist, 1.6% Presbyterian-Reformed (2010)
Economy: Unemployment rate: 6.8% (April 2014); Total civilian labor force: 363,749 (April 2014); Leading industries: 13.6% manufacturing; 12.1% retail trade; 11.1% wholesale trade (2012); Farms: 349 totaling 30,039 acres (2012); Companies that employ 500 or more persons: 66 (2012); Companies that employ 100 to 499 persons: 400 (2012); Companies that employ less than 100 persons: 19,178 (2012); Black-owned businesses: 2,622 (2007); Hispanic-owned businesses: 3,648 (2007); Asian-owned businesses: 3,994 (2007); Women-owned businesses: 19,571 (2007); Single-family building permits issued: 635 (2013); Multi-family building permits issued: 104 (2013).
Income: Per capita income: $38,248 (2008-2012 5-year est.); Median household income: $79,085 (2008-2012 5-year est.); Average household income: $109,243 (2008-2012 5-year est.); Percent of households with income of $100,000 or more: 38.7% (2008-2012 5-year est.); Poverty rate: 8.7% (2008-2012 5-year est.); Bankruptcy rate: 4.16% (2013).
Taxes: Total county taxes per capita: $292 (2011); County property taxes per capita: $285 (2011).
Education: Percent of population age 25 and over with: High school diploma (including GED) or higher: 88.7% (2008-2012 5-year est.); Bachelor's degree or higher: 41.8% (2008-2012 5-year est.); Master's degree or higher: 16.7% (2008-2012 5-year est.).
Housing: Homeownership rate: 76.8% (2008-2012 5-year est.); Median home value: $267,700 (2008-2012 5-year est.); Median contract rent: $878 per month (2008-2012 5-year est.); Median year structure built: 1980 (2008-2012 5-year est.)
Health: Birth rate: 111.6 per 10,000 population (2013); Death rate: 60.1 per 10,000 population (2013); Age-adjusted cancer mortality rate: 158.7 deaths per 100,000 population (2011); Number of physicians: 34.6 per 10,000 population (2011); Hospital beds: 19.2 per 10,000 population (2010); Hospital admissions: 886.2 per 10,000 population (2010).
Environment: Air Quality Index: 93.8% good, 5.7% moderate, 0.6% unhealthy for sensitive individuals, 0.0% unhealthy (percent of days in 2013)
Elections: 2012 Presidential election results: 53.4% Obama, 45.3% Romney
National and State Parks: Chain O'Lakes State Park; Illinois Beach State Park; Volo Bog State Nature Preserve
Additional Information Contacts
Lake County Government . . . . (847) 377-2000
    http://www.lakecountyil.gov
Lake County Chamber of Commerce . . . . (847) 249-3800
    http://www.lakecountychamber.com

Lake County Communities

ANTIOCH (village). Covers a land area of 8.213 square miles and a water area of 0.385 square miles. Located at 42.47° N. Lat; 88.07° W. Long. Elevation is 784 feet.
History: Settled 1836, incorporated 1857.
Population: 6,105 (1990); 8,788 (2000); 14,430 (2010); Density: 1,727.2 persons per square mile (2008-2012 5-year est.); Race: 90.5% White, 2.5% Black/African American, 4.5% Asian, 0.0% American Indian/Alaska Native, 0.0% Native Hawaiian/Other Pacific Islander, 2.5% Some other race, 1.4% Two or more races, 7.0% Hispanic of any race (2008-2012 5-year est.); Average household size: 2.84 (2008-2012 5-year est.); Median age: 36.2 (2008-2012 5-year est.); Males per 100 females: 120.6

(2008-2012 5-year est.); Marriage status: 24.1% never married, 63.1% now married, 4.3% widowed, 8.5% divorced (2008-2012 5-year est.); Foreign born: 7.5% (2008-2012 5-year est.); Ancestry (includes multiple ancestries): 37.6% German, 20.8% Irish, 13.4% Polish, 8.1% Italian, 7.9% English (2008-2012 5-year est.).
Economy: Single-family building permits issued: 0 (2013); Multi-family building permits issued: 0 (2013); Homeowner vacancy rate: 3.5%. Rental vacancy rate: 5.8%. (2008-2012 5-year est.); Employment by occupation: 19.6% management, business, and financial, 7.2% computer, engineering, and science, 11.7% education, legal, community service, arts, and media, 4.5% healthcare practitioners, 12.9% service, 21.4% sales and office, 10.6% natural resources, construction, and maintenance, 12.1% production, transportation, and material moving (2008-2012 5-year est.).
Income: Per capita income: $32,162 (2008-2012 5-year est.); Median household income: $88,504 (2008-2012 5-year est.); Average household income: $90,715 (2008-2012 5-year est.); Percent of households with income of $100,000 or more: 40.7% (2008-2012 5-year est.); Poverty rate: 8.2% (2008-2012 5-year est.).
Education: Percent of population age 25 and over with: High school diploma (including GED) or higher: 94.4% (2008-2012 5-year est.); Bachelor's degree or higher: 32.6% (2008-2012 5-year est.); Master's degree or higher: 11.7% (2008-2012 5-year est.).

School District(s)
Antioch CCSD 34 (PK-08)
    2011-12 Enrollment: 3,088 . . . . (847) 838-8400
CHSD 117 (09-12)
    2011-12 Enrollment: 2,821 . . . . (847) 838-7679
Emmons SD 33 (KG-08)
    2011-12 Enrollment: 326 . . . . (847) 395-1105
Grass Lake SD 36 (PK-08)
    2011-12 Enrollment: 188 . . . . (847) 395-1550
Housing: Homeownership rate: 76.3% (2008-2012 5-year est.); Median home value: $231,800 (2008-2012 5-year est.); Median contract rent: $807 per month (2008-2012 5-year est.); Median year structure built: 1991 (2008-2012 5-year est.).
Health Insurance: 82.1% Private; 18.0% Public; 8.9% None. (2008-2012 5-year est.)
Safety: Violent crime rate: 10.3 per 10,000 population; Property crime rate: 146.3 per 10,000 population (2012).
Transportation: Commute to work: 90.3% car, 1.9% public transportation, 0.4% walk, 5.9% work from home (2008-2012 5-year est.); Travel time to work: 16.0% less than 15 minutes, 20.7% 15 to 30 minutes, 25.4% 30 to 45 minutes, 15.5% 45 to 60 minutes, 22.4% 60 minutes or more (2008-2012 5-year est.)
Additional Information Contacts
Antioch Chamber of Commerce . . . . (847) 395-2233
    http://www.antiochchamber.org
Village of Antioch . . . . (847) 395-1000
    http://www.antioch.il.gov

BANNOCKBURN (village). Covers a land area of 2.018 square miles and a water area of 0.023 square miles. Located at 42.19° N. Lat; 87.87° W. Long. Elevation is 686 feet.
Population: 1,388 (1990); 1,429 (2000); 1,583 (2010); Density: 721.6 persons per square mile (2008-2012 5-year est.); Race: 85.7% White, 5.8% Black/African American, 6.9% Asian, 0.0% American Indian/Alaska Native, 0.0% Native Hawaiian/Other Pacific Islander, 1.6% Some other race, 1.0% Two or more races, 4.3% Hispanic of any race (2008-2012 5-year est.); Average household size: 2.65 (2008-2012 5-year est.); Median age: 22.2 (2008-2012 5-year est.); Males per 100 females: 97.0 (2008-2012 5-year est.); Marriage status: 61.5% never married, 35.3% now married, 2.0% widowed, 1.1% divorced (2008-2012 5-year est.); Foreign born: 10.5% (2008-2012 5-year est.); Ancestry (includes multiple ancestries): 22.8% German, 11.3% Irish, 9.4% English, 7.0% Italian, 6.4% Polish (2008-2012 5-year est.).
Economy: Single-family building permits issued: 0 (2013); Multi-family building permits issued: 0 (2013); Homeowner vacancy rate: 0.9%. Rental vacancy rate: 0.0%. (2008-2012 5-year est.); Employment by occupation: 22.2% management, business, and financial, 0.9% computer, engineering, and science, 13.6% education, legal, community service, arts, and media, 5.8% healthcare practitioners, 18.9% service, 30.4% sales and office, 6.5% natural resources, construction, and maintenance, 1.6% production, transportation, and material moving (2008-2012 5-year est.).
Income: Per capita income: $61,587 (2008-2012 5-year est.); Median household income: $166,563 (2008-2012 5-year est.); Average household

income: $316,711 (2008-2012 5-year est.); Percent of households with income of $100,000 or more: 65.9% (2008-2012 5-year est.); Poverty rate: 9.6% (2008-2012 5-year est.).

Education: Percent of population age 25 and over with: High school diploma (including GED) or higher: 99.0% (2008-2012 5-year est.); Bachelor's degree or higher: 80.1% (2008-2012 5-year est.); Master's degree or higher: 35.9% (2008-2012 5-year est.).

School District(s)

Bannockburn SD 106 (KG-08)

   2011-12 Enrollment: 177 . . . . (847) 945-5900

Housing: Homeownership rate: 80.4% (2008-2012 5-year est.); Median home value: 1 million+ (2008-2012 5-year est.); Median contract rent: $897 per month (2008-2012 5-year est.); Median year structure built: 1964 (2008-2012 5-year est.).

Health Insurance: 89.5% Private; 14.2% Public; 4.0% None. (2008-2012 5-year est.)

Safety: Violent crime rate: 6.3 per 10,000 population; Property crime rate: 245.7 per 10,000 population (2012).

Transportation: Commute to work: 52.7% car, 1.7% public transportation, 29.1% walk, 15.8% work from home (2008-2012 5-year est.); Travel time to work: 47.7% less than 15 minutes, 24.1% 15 to 30 minutes, 16.7% 30 to 45 minutes, 4.5% 45 to 60 minutes, 7.0% 60 minutes or more (2008-2012 5-year est.)

Additional Information Contacts

DBR Chamber of Commerce . . . . (847) 945-4660
   http://www.dbrchamber.com

BEACH PARK (village). Covers a land area of 7.101 square miles and a water area of 0 square miles. Located at 42.44° N. Lat; 87.88° W. Long. Elevation is 699 feet.

Population: 9,513 (1990); 10,072 (2000); 13,638 (2010); Density: 1,898.6 persons per square mile (2008-2012 5-year est.); Race: 72.0% White, 11.5% Black/African American, 5.0% Asian, 0.9% American Indian/Alaska Native, 0.0% Native Hawaiian/Other Pacific Islander, 10.6% Some other race, 1.6% Two or more races, 24.8% Hispanic of any race (2008-2012 5-year est.); Average household size: 2.93 (2008-2012 5-year est.); Median age: 37.4 (2008-2012 5-year est.); Males per 100 females: 103.0 (2008-2012 5-year est.); Marriage status: 27.3% never married, 55.6% now married, 6.5% widowed, 10.6% divorced (2008-2012 5-year est.); Foreign born: 16.3% (2008-2012 5-year est.); Ancestry (includes multiple ancestries): 21.5% German, 13.4% Irish, 7.5% English, 6.4% Polish, 4.1% Italian (2008-2012 5-year est.).

Economy: Single-family building permits issued: 35 (2013); Multi-family building permits issued: 0 (2013); Homeowner vacancy rate: 0.0%. Rental vacancy rate: 2.3%. (2008-2012 5-year est.); Employment by occupation: 12.0% management, business, and financial, 3.9% computer, engineering, and science, 8.4% education, legal, community service, arts, and media, 5.0% healthcare practitioners, 17.1% service, 28.8% sales and office, 9.5% natural resources, construction, and maintenance, 15.3% production, transportation, and material moving (2008-2012 5-year est.).

Income: Per capita income: $26,955 (2008-2012 5-year est.); Median household income: $68,967 (2008-2012 5-year est.); Average household income: $77,636 (2008-2012 5-year est.); Percent of households with income of $100,000 or more: 30.0% (2008-2012 5-year est.); Poverty rate: 6.1% (2008-2012 5-year est.).

Taxes: Total city taxes per capita: $53 (2011); City property taxes per capita: $11 (2011).

Education: Percent of population age 25 and over with: High school diploma (including GED) or higher: 89.2% (2008-2012 5-year est.); Bachelor's degree or higher: 20.8% (2008-2012 5-year est.); Master's degree or higher: 7.8% (2008-2012 5-year est.).

School District(s)

Beach Park CCSD 3 (PK-08)

   2011-12 Enrollment: 2,448 . . . . (847) 599-5005

Housing: Homeownership rate: 87.0% (2008-2012 5-year est.); Median home value: $177,400 (2008-2012 5-year est.); Median contract rent: $758 per month (2008-2012 5-year est.); Median year structure built: 1983 (2008-2012 5-year est.).

Health Insurance: 73.1% Private; 23.9% Public; 11.7% None. (2008-2012 5-year est.)

Transportation: Commute to work: 91.6% car, 1.8% public transportation, 0.2% walk, 3.4% work from home (2008-2012 5-year est.); Travel time to work: 17.0% less than 15 minutes, 38.3% 15 to 30 minutes, 23.8% 30 to 45 minutes, 8.1% 45 to 60 minutes, 12.7% 60 minutes or more (2008-2012 5-year est.)

Additional Information Contacts

Village of Beach Park . . . . (847) 746-1770
   http://www.villageofbeachpark.com

BUFFALO GROVE (village). Covers a land area of 9.500 square miles and a water area of 0.029 square miles. Located at 42.17° N. Lat; 87.96° W. Long. Elevation is 679 feet.

Population: 36,427 (1990); 42,909 (2000); 41,496 (2010); Density: 4,385.8 persons per square mile (2008-2012 5-year est.); Race: 80.6% White, 1.2% Black/African American, 15.6% Asian, 0.1% American Indian/Alaska Native, 0.0% Native Hawaiian/Other Pacific Islander, 2.5% Some other race, 1.5% Two or more races, 5.5% Hispanic of any race (2008-2012 5-year est.); Average household size: 2.55 (2008-2012 5-year est.); Median age: 42.1 (2008-2012 5-year est.); Males per 100 females: 91.9 (2008-2012 5-year est.); Marriage status: 22.6% never married, 64.0% now married, 4.9% widowed, 8.6% divorced (2008-2012 5-year est.); Foreign born: 26.8% (2008-2012 5-year est.); Ancestry (includes multiple ancestries): 14.4% Russian, 13.5% German, 10.1% Polish, 7.6% Irish, 6.9% American (2008-2012 5-year est.).

Economy: Unemployment rate: 5.4% (April 2014); Total civilian labor force: 23,497 (April 2014); Single-family building permits issued: 6 (2013); Multi-family building permits issued: 0 (2013); Homeowner vacancy rate: 1.1%. Rental vacancy rate: 1.9%. (2008-2012 5-year est.); Employment by occupation: 25.8% management, business, and financial, 11.7% computer, engineering, and science, 14.5% education, legal, community service, arts, and media, 5.8% healthcare practitioners, 9.5% service, 24.0% sales and office, 3.2% natural resources, construction, and maintenance, 5.4% production, transportation, and material moving (2008-2012 5-year est.).

Income: Per capita income: $45,057 (2008-2012 5-year est.); Median household income: $93,567 (2008-2012 5-year est.); Average household income: $113,459 (2008-2012 5-year est.); Percent of households with income of $100,000 or more: 45.4% (2008-2012 5-year est.); Poverty rate: 3.9% (2008-2012 5-year est.).

Taxes: Total city taxes per capita: $501 (2011); City property taxes per capita: $317 (2011).

Education: Percent of population age 25 and over with: High school diploma (including GED) or higher: 96.3% (2008-2012 5-year est.); Bachelor's degree or higher: 60.9% (2008-2012 5-year est.); Master's degree or higher: 25.0% (2008-2012 5-year est.).

School District(s)

Aptakisic-Tripp CCSD 102 (PK-08)

   2011-12 Enrollment: 2,053 . . . . (847) 353-5650

Kildeer Countryside CCSD 96 (PK-08)

   2011-12 Enrollment: 3,134 . . . . (847) 459-4260

Township HSD 214 (09-12)

   2011-12 Enrollment: 12,305 . . . . (847) 718-7600

Wheeling CCSD 21 (PK-08)

   2011-12 Enrollment: 6,866 . . . . (847) 537-8270

Housing: Homeownership rate: 81.9% (2008-2012 5-year est.); Median home value: $314,400 (2008-2012 5-year est.); Median contract rent: $1,177 per month (2008-2012 5-year est.); Median year structure built: 1982 (2008-2012 5-year est.).

Health Insurance: 86.8% Private; 16.4% Public; 5.5% None. (2008-2012 5-year est.)

Safety: Violent crime rate: 1.2 per 10,000 population; Property crime rate: 89.2 per 10,000 population (2012).

Transportation: Commute to work: 88.8% car, 4.4% public transportation, 0.5% walk, 5.0% work from home (2008-2012 5-year est.); Travel time to work: 18.7% less than 15 minutes, 33.9% 15 to 30 minutes, 27.1% 30 to 45 minutes, 9.1% 45 to 60 minutes, 11.3% 60 minutes or more (2008-2012 5-year est.)

Additional Information Contacts

Buffalo Grove Area Chamber of Commerce . . . . (847) 541-7799
   http://bgacc.org

Village of Buffalo Grove . . . . (847) 459-2518
   http://www.vbg.org

CHANNEL LAKE (CDP). Covers a land area of 1.804 square miles and a water area of 0.598 square miles. Located at 42.48° N. Lat; 88.15° W. Long. Elevation is 745 feet.

Population: 1,660 (1990); 1,785 (2000); 1,664 (2010); Density: 947.3 persons per square mile (2008-2012 5-year est.); Race: 98.5% White, 0.0% Black/African American, 0.0% Asian, 0.0% American Indian/Alaska Native, 0.0% Native Hawaiian/Other Pacific Islander, 1.5% Some other race, 1.5% Two or more races, 1.2% Hispanic of any race (2008-2012

5-year est.); Average household size: 2.30 (2008-2012 5-year est.); Median age: 47.2 (2008-2012 5-year est.); Males per 100 females: 125.5 (2008-2012 5-year est.); Marriage status: 30.8% never married, 48.3% now married, 4.1% widowed, 16.8% divorced (2008-2012 5-year est.); Foreign born: 2.7% (2008-2012 5-year est.); Ancestry (includes multiple ancestries): 34.7% German, 20.2% Irish, 13.2% Polish, 12.0% English, 6.8% Czech (2008-2012 5-year est.).

Economy: Homeowner vacancy rate: 17.6%. Rental vacancy rate: 0.0%. (2008-2012 5-year est.); Employment by occupation: 12.5% management, business, and financial, 5.5% computer, engineering, and science, 8.0% education, legal, community service, arts, and media, 5.1% healthcare practitioners, 13.0% service, 31.8% sales and office, 8.3% natural resources, construction, and maintenance, 15.8% production, transportation, and material moving (2008-2012 5-year est.).

Income: Per capita income: $34,915 (2008-2012 5-year est.); Median household income: $54,811 (2008-2012 5-year est.); Average household income: $78,944 (2008-2012 5-year est.); Percent of households with income of $100,000 or more: 18.2% (2008-2012 5-year est.); Poverty rate: 7.7% (2008-2012 5-year est.).

Education: Percent of population age 25 and over with: High school diploma (including GED) or higher: 94.8% (2008-2012 5-year est.); Bachelor's degree or higher: 18.6% (2008-2012 5-year est.); Master's degree or higher: 3.5% (2008-2012 5-year est.).

Housing: Homeownership rate: 85.1% (2008-2012 5-year est.); Median home value: $172,400 (2008-2012 5-year est.); Median contract rent: $635 per month (2008-2012 5-year est.); Median year structure built: 1956 (2008-2012 5-year est.).

Health Insurance: 82.9% Private; 24.1% Public; 8.5% None. (2008-2012 5-year est.)

Transportation: Commute to work: 85.8% car, 3.7% public transportation, 0.0% walk, 9.2% work from home (2008-2012 5-year est.); Travel time to work: 11.8% less than 15 minutes, 29.7% 15 to 30 minutes, 19.0% 30 to 45 minutes, 7.3% 45 to 60 minutes, 32.3% 60 minutes or more (2008-2012 5-year est.)

DEER PARK (village).

Covers a land area of 3.714 square miles and a water area of 0.115 square miles. Located at 42.17° N. Lat; 88.09° W. Long. Elevation is 850 feet.

History: The Village of Deer Park was incorporated November 13, 1957. The village is located in both Lake & Cook Counties, east of the Village of Barrington, south of the Village of Lake Zurich, and it is 37 miles northwest of Chicago.

Population: 2,887 (1990); 3,102 (2000); 3,200 (2010); Density: 866.9 persons per square mile (2008-2012 5-year est.); Race: 94.0% White, 0.0% Black/African American, 5.7% Asian, 0.0% American Indian/Alaska Native, 0.0% Native Hawaiian/Other Pacific Islander, 0.3% Some other race, 0.1% Two or more races, 2.9% Hispanic of any race (2008-2012 5-year est.); Average household size: 2.93 (2008-2012 5-year est.); Median age: 47.9 (2008-2012 5-year est.); Males per 100 females: 103.5 (2008-2012 5-year est.); Marriage status: 22.2% never married, 72.1% now married, 2.7% widowed, 3.0% divorced (2008-2012 5-year est.); Foreign born: 13.7% (2008-2012 5-year est.); Ancestry (includes multiple ancestries): 29.8% German, 17.5% Polish, 13.3% Italian, 13.0% Irish, 6.7% English (2008-2012 5-year est.).

Economy: Single-family building permits issued: 5 (2013); Multi-family building permits issued: 0 (2013); Homeowner vacancy rate: 3.4%. Rental vacancy rate: 0.0%. (2008-2012 5-year est.); Employment by occupation: 31.7% management, business, and financial, 7.7% computer, engineering, and science, 16.6% education, legal, community service, arts, and media, 2.8% healthcare practitioners, 8.5% service, 26.9% sales and office, 3.1% natural resources, construction, and maintenance, 2.6% production, transportation, and material moving (2008-2012 5-year est.).

Income: Per capita income: $61,838 (2008-2012 5-year est.); Median household income: $144,881 (2008-2012 5-year est.); Average household income: $180,201 (2008-2012 5-year est.); Percent of households with income of $100,000 or more: 66.4% (2008-2012 5-year est.); Poverty rate: 1.4% (2008-2012 5-year est.).

Education: Percent of population age 25 and over with: High school diploma (including GED) or higher: 96.5% (2008-2012 5-year est.); Bachelor's degree or higher: 66.2% (2008-2012 5-year est.); Master's degree or higher: 30.4% (2008-2012 5-year est.).

Housing: Homeownership rate: 97.8% (2008-2012 5-year est.); Median home value: $579,600 (2008-2012 5-year est.); Median contract rent: $1,625 per month (2008-2012 5-year est.); Median year structure built: 1984 (2008-2012 5-year est.).

Health Insurance: 93.2% Private; 15.5% Public; 2.8% None. (2008-2012 5-year est.)

Transportation: Commute to work: 78.8% car, 7.6% public transportation, 0.3% walk, 11.5% work from home (2008-2012 5-year est.); Travel time to work: 19.4% less than 15 minutes, 31.2% 15 to 30 minutes, 24.9% 30 to 45 minutes, 8.2% 45 to 60 minutes, 16.3% 60 minutes or more (2008-2012 5-year est.)

DEERFIELD (village).

Covers a land area of 5.582 square miles and a water area of 0.040 square miles. Located at 42.17° N. Lat; 87.85° W. Long. Elevation is 686 feet.

History: Named for the abundance of deer in the area. Incorporated 1903.

Population: 17,327 (1990); 18,420 (2000); 18,225 (2010); Density: 3,305.6 persons per square mile (2008-2012 5-year est.); Race: 93.8% White, 0.5% Black/African American, 4.1% Asian, 0.0% American Indian/Alaska Native, 0.0% Native Hawaiian/Other Pacific Islander, 1.6% Some other race, 1.4% Two or more races, 5.2% Hispanic of any race (2008-2012 5-year est.); Average household size: 2.79 (2008-2012 5-year est.); Median age: 42.6 (2008-2012 5-year est.); Males per 100 females: 93.5 (2008-2012 5-year est.); Marriage status: 19.8% never married, 67.2% now married, 5.7% widowed, 7.3% divorced (2008-2012 5-year est.); Foreign born: 8.3% (2008-2012 5-year est.); Ancestry (includes multiple ancestries): 17.4% Russian, 15.9% German, 12.1% Polish, 9.8% American, 7.4% Irish (2008-2012 5-year est.).

Economy: Single-family building permits issued: 35 (2013); Multi-family building permits issued: 0 (2013); Homeowner vacancy rate: 0.8%. Rental vacancy rate: 2.1%. (2008-2012 5-year est.); Employment by occupation: 28.0% management, business, and financial, 6.8% computer, engineering, and science, 23.4% education, legal, community service, arts, and media, 5.6% healthcare practitioners, 9.4% service, 22.9% sales and office, 1.8% natural resources, construction, and maintenance, 2.1% production, transportation, and material moving (2008-2012 5-year est.).

Income: Per capita income: $62,405 (2008-2012 5-year est.); Median household income: $129,187 (2008-2012 5-year est.); Average household income: $174,156 (2008-2012 5-year est.); Percent of households with income of $100,000 or more: 61.7% (2008-2012 5-year est.); Poverty rate: 2.7% (2008-2012 5-year est.).

Taxes: Total city taxes per capita: $730 (2011); City property taxes per capita: $301 (2011).

Education: Percent of population age 25 and over with: High school diploma (including GED) or higher: 98.7% (2008-2012 5-year est.); Bachelor's degree or higher: 74.6% (2008-2012 5-year est.); Master's degree or higher: 38.2% (2008-2012 5-year est.).

School District(s)

Deerfield SD 109 (PK-08)
    2011-12 Enrollment: 3,124 . . . . (847) 945-1844
Twp HSD 113 (09-12)
    2011-12 Enrollment: 3,693 . . . . (224) 765-1001

Four-year College(s)

Trinity International University-Illinois (Private, Not-for-profit, Evangelical Free Church of America)
    Fall 2012 Enrollment: 2,287 . . . . (847) 945-8800
    2012-13 Tuition: In-state $25,840; Out-of-state $25,840

Housing: Homeownership rate: 88.3% (2008-2012 5-year est.); Median home value: $520,300 (2008-2012 5-year est.); Median contract rent: $1,521 per month (2008-2012 5-year est.); Median year structure built: 1967 (2008-2012 5-year est.).

Health Insurance: 92.7% Private; 16.2% Public; 3.1% None. (2008-2012 5-year est.)

Safety: Violent crime rate: 1.6 per 10,000 population; Property crime rate: 115.3 per 10,000 population (2012).

Transportation: Commute to work: 76.0% car, 10.7% public transportation, 1.7% walk, 9.8% work from home (2008-2012 5-year est.); Travel time to work: 29.7% less than 15 minutes, 27.3% 15 to 30 minutes, 17.5% 30 to 45 minutes, 10.1% 45 to 60 minutes, 15.3% 60 minutes or more (2008-2012 5-year est.)

Additional Information Contacts

DBR Chamber of Commerce . . . . (847) 945-4660
    http://www.dbrchamber.com
Village of Deerfield . . . . (847) 945-5000
    http://www.deerfield.il.us

FOREST LAKE (CDP).
Covers a land area of 0.455 square miles and a water area of 0.061 square miles. Located at 42.21° N. Lat; 88.05° W. Long. Elevation is 814 feet.

Population: 1,371 (1990); 1,530 (2000); 1,659 (2010); Density: 3,935.0 persons per square mile (2008-2012 5-year est.); Race: 95.5% White, 0.0% Black/African American, 4.5% Asian, 0.0% American Indian/Alaska Native, 0.0% Native Hawaiian/Other Pacific Islander, 0.0% Some other race, 0.0% Two or more races, 12.6% Hispanic of any race (2008-2012 5-year est.); Average household size: 2.72 (2008-2012 5-year est.); Median age: 46.3 (2008-2012 5-year est.); Males per 100 females: 95.0 (2008-2012 5-year est.); Marriage status: 20.4% never married, 64.3% now married, 3.3% widowed, 12.0% divorced (2008-2012 5-year est.); Foreign born: 12.9% (2008-2012 5-year est.); Ancestry (includes multiple ancestries): 37.6% German, 17.9% Irish, 12.7% Italian, 11.7% Polish, 5.9% English (2008-2012 5-year est.).

Economy: Homeowner vacancy rate: 0.0%. Rental vacancy rate: 0.0%. (2008-2012 5-year est.); Employment by occupation: 19.7% management, business, and financial, 9.1% computer, engineering, and science, 12.8% education, legal, community service, arts, and media, 4.6% healthcare practitioners, 11.5% service, 29.3% sales and office, 1.4% natural resources, construction, and maintenance, 11.6% production, transportation, and material moving (2008-2012 5-year est.).

Income: Per capita income: $33,100 (2008-2012 5-year est.); Median household income: $63,241 (2008-2012 5-year est.); Average household income: $90,182 (2008-2012 5-year est.); Percent of households with income of $100,000 or more: 35.4% (2008-2012 5-year est.); Poverty rate: 8.1% (2008-2012 5-year est.).

Education: Percent of population age 25 and over with: High school diploma (including GED) or higher: 90.4% (2008-2012 5-year est.); Bachelor's degree or higher: 54.8% (2008-2012 5-year est.); Master's degree or higher: 19.7% (2008-2012 5-year est.).

Housing: Homeownership rate: 85.4% (2008-2012 5-year est.); Median home value: $313,800 (2008-2012 5-year est.); Median contract rent: $2,000+ per month (2008-2012 5-year est.); Median year structure built: 1967 (2008-2012 5-year est.).

Health Insurance: 82.3% Private; 17.0% Public; 6.4% None. (2008-2012 5-year est.)

Transportation: Commute to work: 85.6% car, 0.0% public transportation, 0.0% walk, 11.4% work from home (2008-2012 5-year est.); Travel time to work: 18.6% less than 15 minutes, 32.4% 15 to 30 minutes, 25.2% 30 to 45 minutes, 13.0% 45 to 60 minutes, 10.8% 60 minutes or more (2008-2012 5-year est.)

FOX LAKE (village).
Covers a land area of 8.115 square miles and a water area of 1.822 square miles. Located at 42.43° N. Lat; 88.18° W. Long. Elevation is 748 feet.

History: Fox Lake developed as a resort community for vacationers who enjoyed the numerous lakes in the area.

Population: 7,478 (1990); 9,178 (2000); 10,579 (2010); Density: 1,326.9 persons per square mile (2008-2012 5-year est.); Race: 93.2% White, 1.5% Black/African American, 3.7% Asian, 0.3% American Indian/Alaska Native, 0.0% Native Hawaiian/Other Pacific Islander, 1.3% Some other race, 0.7% Two or more races, 10.4% Hispanic of any race (2008-2012 5-year est.); Average household size: 2.41 (2008-2012 5-year est.); Median age: 39.7 (2008-2012 5-year est.); Males per 100 females: 93.6 (2008-2012 5-year est.); Marriage status: 28.3% never married, 49.1% now married, 6.9% widowed, 15.7% divorced (2008-2012 5-year est.); Foreign born: 8.6% (2008-2012 5-year est.); Ancestry (includes multiple ancestries): 30.7% German, 22.4% Polish, 19.3% Irish, 11.6% Italian, 4.4% English (2008-2012 5-year est.).

Economy: Single-family building permits issued: 2 (2013); Multi-family building permits issued: 0 (2013); Homeowner vacancy rate: 0.9%. Rental vacancy rate: 0.0%. (2008-2012 5-year est.); Employment by occupation: 13.5% management, business, and financial, 3.7% computer, engineering, and science, 8.1% education, legal, community service, arts, and media, 3.9% healthcare practitioners, 13.6% service, 33.4% sales and office, 11.0% natural resources, construction, and maintenance, 12.8% production, transportation, and material moving (2008-2012 5-year est.).

Income: Per capita income: $28,403 (2008-2012 5-year est.); Median household income: $54,920 (2008-2012 5-year est.); Average household income: $67,770 (2008-2012 5-year est.); Percent of households with income of $100,000 or more: 21.9% (2008-2012 5-year est.); Poverty rate: 11.4% (2008-2012 5-year est.).

Education: Percent of population age 25 and over with: High school diploma (including GED) or higher: 90.7% (2008-2012 5-year est.);

Bachelor's degree or higher: 17.0% (2008-2012 5-year est.); Master's degree or higher: 4.1% (2008-2012 5-year est.).

School District(s)
Fox Lake Gsd 114 (PK-08)
    2011-12 Enrollment: 828 . . . . (847) 973-4027
Grant CHSD 124 (09-12)
    2011-12 Enrollment: 1,874 . . . . (847) 587-2561

Housing: Homeownership rate: 71.3% (2008-2012 5-year est.); Median home value: $181,700 (2008-2012 5-year est.); Median contract rent: $747 per month (2008-2012 5-year est.); Median year structure built: 1978 (2008-2012 5-year est.).

Health Insurance: 68.0% Private; 33.2% Public; 11.7% None. (2008-2012 5-year est.)

Safety: Violent crime rate: 24.5 per 10,000 population; Property crime rate: 263.5 per 10,000 population (2012).

Transportation: Commute to work: 91.7% car, 2.7% public transportation, 1.0% walk, 4.5% work from home (2008-2012 5-year est.); Travel time to work: 11.8% less than 15 minutes, 26.1% 15 to 30 minutes, 25.2% 30 to 45 minutes, 13.9% 45 to 60 minutes, 22.9% 60 minutes or more (2008-2012 5-year est.)

Additional Information Contacts
Fox Lake Area Chamber of Commerce & Industry . . . . (847) 587-7474
    http://www.discoverfoxlake.com
Village of Fox Lake . . . . (847) 587-2151
    http://www.foxlake.org

FOX LAKE HILLS (CDP).
Covers a land area of 1.273 square miles and a water area of 0.540 square miles. Located at 42.41° N. Lat; 88.13° W. Long. Elevation is 751 feet.

Population: 2,681 (1990); 2,561 (2000); 2,591 (2010); Density: 1,843.0 persons per square mile (2008-2012 5-year est.); Race: 94.8% White, 3.8% Black/African American, 0.0% Asian, 0.0% American Indian/Alaska Native, 0.0% Native Hawaiian/Other Pacific Islander, 1.4% Some other race, 1.3% Two or more races, 5.7% Hispanic of any race (2008-2012 5-year est.); Average household size: 2.75 (2008-2012 5-year est.); Median age: 35.2 (2008-2012 5-year est.); Males per 100 females: 101.3 (2008-2012 5-year est.); Marriage status: 28.8% never married, 52.7% now married, 3.7% widowed, 14.7% divorced (2008-2012 5-year est.); Foreign born: 3.9% (2008-2012 5-year est.); Ancestry (includes multiple ancestries): 37.2% German, 27.0% Polish, 10.1% Irish, 15.1% Italian, 7.6% American (2008-2012 5-year est.).

Economy: Homeowner vacancy rate: 3.5%. Rental vacancy rate: 0.0%. (2008-2012 5-year est.); Employment by occupation: 6.4% management, business, and financial, 4.6% computer, engineering, and science, 4.0% education, legal, community service, arts, and media, 3.3% healthcare practitioners, 13.7% service, 42.8% sales and office, 13.3% natural resources, construction, and maintenance, 11.9% production, transportation, and material moving (2008-2012 5-year est.).

Income: Per capita income: $28,742 (2008-2012 5-year est.); Median household income: $66,023 (2008-2012 5-year est.); Average household income: $78,975 (2008-2012 5-year est.); Percent of households with income of $100,000 or more: 33.8% (2008-2012 5-year est.); Poverty rate: 17.3% (2008-2012 5-year est.).

Education: Percent of population age 25 and over with: High school diploma (including GED) or higher: 94.4% (2008-2012 5-year est.); Bachelor's degree or higher: 13.8% (2008-2012 5-year est.); Master's degree or higher: 6.9% (2008-2012 5-year est.).

Housing: Homeownership rate: 83.3% (2008-2012 5-year est.); Median home value: $197,900 (2008-2012 5-year est.); Median contract rent: $1,340 per month (2008-2012 5-year est.); Median year structure built: 1971 (2008-2012 5-year est.).

Health Insurance: 76.9% Private; 25.0% Public; 11.4% None. (2008-2012 5-year est.)

Transportation: Commute to work: 86.8% car, 3.4% public transportation, 0.0% walk, 9.8% work from home (2008-2012 5-year est.); Travel time to work: 19.8% less than 15 minutes, 17.5% 15 to 30 minutes, 22.9% 30 to 45 minutes, 14.3% 45 to 60 minutes, 25.5% 60 minutes or more (2008-2012 5-year est.)

GAGES LAKE (CDP).
Covers a land area of 2.992 square miles and a water area of 0.208 square miles. Located at 42.35° N. Lat; 87.98° W. Long. Elevation is 768 feet.

Population: 8,349 (1990); 10,415 (2000); 10,198 (2010); Density: 3,254.4 persons per square mile (2008-2012 5-year est.); Race: 81.9% White, 4.6% Black/African American, 5.3% Asian, 0.9% American Indian/Alaska

Native, 0.0% Native Hawaiian/Other Pacific Islander, 7.3% Some other race, 4.4% Two or more races, 12.0% Hispanic of any race (2008-2012 5-year est.); Average household size: 2.60 (2008-2012 5-year est.); Median age: 41.2 (2008-2012 5-year est.); Males per 100 females: 108.1 (2008-2012 5-year est.); Marriage status: 24.7% never married, 61.0% now married, 4.3% widowed, 10.0% divorced (2008-2012 5-year est.); Foreign born: 14.0% (2008-2012 5-year est.); Ancestry (includes multiple ancestries): 26.1% German, 14.2% Irish, 9.9% Polish, 7.5% English, 6.9% Italian (2008-2012 5-year est.).

Economy: Homeowner vacancy rate: 0.1%. Rental vacancy rate: 4.3%. (2008-2012 5-year est.); Employment by occupation: 24.2% management, business, and financial, 8.0% computer, engineering, and science, 11.5% education, legal, community service, arts, and media, 2.6% healthcare practitioners, 8.6% service, 26.1% sales and office, 7.7% natural resources, construction, and maintenance, 11.2% production, transportation, and material moving (2008-2012 5-year est.).

Income: Per capita income: $39,008 (2008-2012 5-year est.); Median household income: $80,851 (2008-2012 5-year est.); Average household income: $101,581 (2008-2012 5-year est.); Percent of households with income of $100,000 or more: 39.9% (2008-2012 5-year est.); Poverty rate: 3.1% (2008-2012 5-year est.).

Education: Percent of population age 25 and over with: High school diploma (including GED) or higher: 93.3% (2008-2012 5-year est.); Bachelor's degree or higher: 40.9% (2008-2012 5-year est.); Master's degree or higher: 17.4% (2008-2012 5-year est.).

School District(s)

Spec Educ Dist Lake County/sedol
    2011-12 Enrollment: n/a . . . . (847) 548-8470
Woodland CCSD 50 (PK-08)
    2011-12 Enrollment: 6,522 . . . . (847) 596-5601

Housing: Homeownership rate: 82.7% (2008-2012 5-year est.); Median home value: $219,500 (2008-2012 5-year est.); Median contract rent: $1,086 per month (2008-2012 5-year est.); Median year structure built: 1981 (2008-2012 5-year est.).

Health Insurance: 82.3% Private; 18.8% Public; 7.4% None. (2008-2012 5-year est.)

Transportation: Commute to work: 91.3% car, 3.8% public transportation, 0.2% walk, 4.5% work from home (2008-2012 5-year est.); Travel time to work: 20.6% less than 15 minutes, 32.7% 15 to 30 minutes, 22.4% 30 to 45 minutes, 11.7% 45 to 60 minutes, 12.6% 60 minutes or more (2008-2012 5-year est.)

GRANDWOOD PARK (CDP). Covers a land area of 1.549 square miles and a water area of 0.022 square miles. Located at 42.39° N. Lat; 87.99° W. Long. Elevation is 745 feet.

Population: 2,470 (1990); 4,521 (2000); 5,202 (2010); Density: 3,410.0 persons per square mile (2008-2012 5-year est.); Race: 73.6% White, 4.7% Black/African American, 12.9% Asian, 0.0% American Indian/Alaska Native, 0.2% Native Hawaiian/Other Pacific Islander, 8.6% Some other race, 1.6% Two or more races, 14.7% Hispanic of any race (2008-2012 5-year est.); Average household size: 3.17 (2008-2012 5-year est.); Median age: 36.2 (2008-2012 5-year est.); Males per 100 females: 111.5 (2008-2012 5-year est.); Marriage status: 26.4% never married, 61.1% now married, 4.2% widowed, 8.3% divorced (2008-2012 5-year est.); Foreign born: 21.8% (2008-2012 5-year est.); Ancestry (includes multiple ancestries): 21.6% German, 15.5% Irish, 11.8% Polish, 6.5% Italian, 6.1% English (2008-2012 5-year est.).

Economy: Homeowner vacancy rate: 2.1%. Rental vacancy rate: 15.4%. (2008-2012 5-year est.); Employment by occupation: 17.8% management, business, and financial, 8.8% computer, engineering, and science, 10.2% education, legal, community service, arts, and media, 6.4% healthcare practitioners, 11.4% service, 25.9% sales and office, 9.9% natural resources, construction, and maintenance, 9.6% production, transportation, and material moving (2008-2012 5-year est.).

Income: Per capita income: $38,486 (2008-2012 5-year est.); Median household income: $101,763 (2008-2012 5-year est.); Average household income: $120,013 (2008-2012 5-year est.); Percent of households with income of $100,000 or more: 51.7% (2008-2012 5-year est.); Poverty rate: 4.9% (2008-2012 5-year est.).

Education: Percent of population age 25 and over with: High school diploma (including GED) or higher: 90.4% (2008-2012 5-year est.); Bachelor's degree or higher: 47.6% (2008-2012 5-year est.); Master's degree or higher: 16.4% (2008-2012 5-year est.).

Housing: Homeownership rate: 85.8% (2008-2012 5-year est.); Median home value: $260,900 (2008-2012 5-year est.); Median contract rent:

$1,110 per month (2008-2012 5-year est.); Median year structure built: 1990 (2008-2012 5-year est.).

Health Insurance: 79.6% Private; 15.0% Public; 11.2% None. (2008-2012 5-year est.)

Transportation: Commute to work: 85.1% car, 1.8% public transportation, 6.6% walk, 6.1% work from home (2008-2012 5-year est.); Travel time to work: 21.0% less than 15 minutes, 27.8% 15 to 30 minutes, 30.1% 30 to 45 minutes, 9.3% 45 to 60 minutes, 11.8% 60 minutes or more (2008-2012 5-year est.)

GRAYSLAKE (village). Aka Grays Lake. Covers a land area of 9.868 square miles and a water area of 0.208 square miles. Located at 42.34° N. Lat; 88.03° W. Long. Elevation is 784 feet.

History: Named for William Gray, an early settler. College of Lake County here. Incorporated 1895.

Population: 7,388 (1990); 18,506 (2000); 20,957 (2010); Density: 2,122.3 persons per square mile (2008-2012 5-year est.); Race: 85.1% White, 3.5% Black/African American, 6.7% Asian, 0.6% American Indian/Alaska Native, 0.0% Native Hawaiian/Other Pacific Islander, 4.1% Some other race, 2.9% Two or more races, 7.2% Hispanic of any race (2008-2012 5-year est.); Average household size: 2.77 (2008-2012 5-year est.); Median age: 36.0 (2008-2012 5-year est.); Males per 100 females: 94.1 (2008-2012 5-year est.); Marriage status: 26.4% never married, 60.0% now married, 3.3% widowed, 10.3% divorced (2008-2012 5-year est.); Foreign born: 11.2% (2008-2012 5-year est.); Ancestry (includes multiple ancestries): 29.8% German, 16.6% Irish, 13.6% Polish, 9.3% Italian, 7.2% English (2008-2012 5-year est.).

Economy: Single-family building permits issued: 2 (2013); Multi-family building permits issued: 0 (2013); Homeowner vacancy rate: 1.0%. Rental vacancy rate: 9.6%. (2008-2012 5-year est.); Employment by occupation: 19.9% management, business, and financial, 8.1% computer, engineering, and science, 11.2% education, legal, community service, arts, and media, 6.9% healthcare practitioners, 15.1% service, 27.9% sales and office, 4.6% natural resources, construction, and maintenance, 6.4% production, transportation, and material moving (2008-2012 5-year est.).

Income: Per capita income: $38,519 (2008-2012 5-year est.); Median household income: $95,559 (2008-2012 5-year est.); Average household income: $106,240 (2008-2012 5-year est.); Percent of households with income of $100,000 or more: 47.0% (2008-2012 5-year est.); Poverty rate: 3.6% (2008-2012 5-year est.).

Education: Percent of population age 25 and over with: High school diploma (including GED) or higher: 94.9% (2008-2012 5-year est.); Bachelor's degree or higher: 53.5% (2008-2012 5-year est.); Master's degree or higher: 19.5% (2008-2012 5-year est.).

School District(s)

Grayslake CCSD 46 (PK-08)
    2011-12 Enrollment: 4,125 . . . . (847) 223-3650
Grayslake CHSD 127 (09-12)
    2011-12 Enrollment: 2,968 . . . . (847) 986-3400
Lake County High Schools Tech Campus (11-12)
    2011-12 Enrollment: n/a . . . . (847) 543-6001
Lake Roe (06-12)
    2011-12 Enrollment: n/a . . . . (847) 543-7833
Prairie Crossing Charter School (KG-08)
    2011-12 Enrollment: 391 . . . . (847) 543-9722

Two-year College(s)

College of Lake County (Public)
    Fall 2012 Enrollment: 17,577 . . . . (847) 543-2000
    2012-13 Tuition: In-state $7,252; Out-of-state $9,590

Housing: Homeownership rate: 78.4% (2008-2012 5-year est.); Median home value: $240,800 (2008-2012 5-year est.); Median contract rent: $843 per month (2008-2012 5-year est.); Median year structure built: 1993 (2008-2012 5-year est.).

Health Insurance: 89.4% Private; 12.3% Public; 5.1% None. (2008-2012 5-year est.)

Safety: Violent crime rate: 15.2 per 10,000 population; Property crime rate: 194.8 per 10,000 population (2012).

Transportation: Commute to work: 88.3% car, 4.7% public transportation, 1.0% walk, 5.3% work from home (2008-2012 5-year est.); Travel time to work: 17.8% less than 15 minutes, 27.1% 15 to 30 minutes, 23.1% 30 to 45 minutes, 13.9% 45 to 60 minutes, 18.1% 60 minutes or more (2008-2012 5-year est.)

Airports: Campbell Airport (general aviation)
Additional Information Contacts

Grayslake Area Chamber of Commerce & Industry ...... (847) 223-6888
http://www.grayslakechamber.com
Village of Grayslake .... (847) 223-8515
http://www.villageofgrayslake.com

GREAT LAKES (unincorporated postal area)
Zip Code: 60088
Covers a land area of 2.324 square miles and a water area of 1.024 square miles. Located at 42.30° N. Lat; 87.84° W. Long. Elevation is 659 feet. Population: 15,761 (2010); Density: 6,780.4 persons per square mile (2010); Race: 67.2% White, 18.2% Black/African American, 4.5% Asian, 0.8% American Indian/Alaska Native, 0.2% Native Hawaiian/Other Pacific Islander, 9.1% Some other race, 5.1% Two or more races, 13.5% Hispanic of any race (2010); Average household size: 3.32 (2010); Median age: 21.3 (2010); Males per 100 females: 252.4 (2010); Homeownership rate: 0.6% (2010)

GREEN OAKS (village). Aka Oak Grove. Covers a land area of 4.022 square miles and a water area of 0.103 square miles. Located at 42.30° N. Lat; 87.91° W. Long. Elevation is 689 feet.
History: One of the earliest settlers was Thomas Madden, who bought some land about three miles east of the river in the year 1844; when the "Village Of Oak Grove" changed its name and founded Green Oaks in 1960, all 150 residents attended the celebration dinner.
Population: 2,101 (1990); 3,572 (2000); 3,866 (2010); Density: 957.8 persons per square mile (2008-2012 5-year est.); Race: 81.4% White, 0.9% Black/African American, 13.3% Asian, 0.0% American Indian/Alaska Native, 0.0% Native Hawaiian/Other Pacific Islander, 4.4% Some other race, 3.2% Two or more races, 4.2% Hispanic of any race (2008-2012 5-year est.); Average household size: 3.21 (2008-2012 5-year est.); Median age: 42.6 (2008-2012 5-year est.); Males per 100 females: 96.3 (2008-2012 5-year est.); Marriage status: 22.3% never married, 72.3% now married, 3.1% widowed, 2.3% divorced (2008-2012 5-year est.); Foreign born: 15.1% (2008-2012 5-year est.); Ancestry (includes multiple ancestries): 23.8% German, 16.0% Irish, 12.7% English, 9.9% Polish, 8.9% American (2008-2012 5-year est.).
Economy: Single-family building permits issued: 1 (2013); Multi-family building permits issued: 0 (2013); Homeowner vacancy rate: 0.0%. Rental vacancy rate: 0.0%. (2008-2012 5-year est.); Employment by occupation: 32.7% management, business, and financial, 7.5% computer, engineering, and science, 15.1% education, legal, community service, arts, and media, 5.5% healthcare practitioners, 9.6% service, 22.9% sales and office, 2.7% natural resources, construction, and maintenance, 4.0% production, transportation, and material moving (2008-2012 5-year est.).
Income: Per capita income: $63,770 (2008-2012 5-year est.); Median household income: $154,737 (2008-2012 5-year est.); Average household income: $207,858 (2008-2012 5-year est.); Percent of households with income of $100,000 or more: 64.7% (2008-2012 5-year est.); Poverty rate: 6.6% (2008-2012 5-year est.).
Education: Percent of population age 25 and over with: High school diploma (including GED) or higher: 95.2% (2008-2012 5-year est.); Bachelor's degree or higher: 67.2% (2008-2012 5-year est.); Master's degree or higher: 32.9% (2008-2012 5-year est.).
Housing: Homeownership rate: 96.7% (2008-2012 5-year est.); Median home value: $600,500 (2008-2012 5-year est.); Median contract rent: $2,000+ per month (2008-2012 5-year est.); Median year structure built: 1987 (2008-2012 5-year est.).
Health Insurance: 91.5% Private; 10.4% Public; 5.0% None. (2008-2012 5-year est.)
Transportation: Commute to work: 83.5% car, 3.5% public transportation, 0.0% walk, 9.7% work from home (2008-2012 5-year est.); Travel time to work: 22.7% less than 15 minutes, 40.5% 15 to 30 minutes, 18.2% 30 to 45 minutes, 10.4% 45 to 60 minutes, 8.2% 60 minutes or more (2008-2012 5-year est.)
Additional Information Contacts
GLMV Chamber of Commerce .... (847) 680-0750
http://www.glmvchamber.org

GURNEE (village). Covers a land area of 13.497 square miles and a water area of 0.076 square miles. Located at 42.37° N. Lat; 87.94° W. Long. Elevation is 679 feet.
Population: 13,701 (1990); 28,834 (2000); 31,295 (2010); Density: 2,313.2 persons per square mile (2008-2012 5-year est.); Race: 72.9% White, 9.2% Black/African American, 12.3% Asian, 0.0% American Indian/Alaska Native, 0.0% Native Hawaiian/Other Pacific Islander, 5.6% Some other race, 2.8% Two or more races, 10.6% Hispanic of any race (2008-2012 5-year est.); Average household size: 2.74 (2008-2012 5-year est.); Median age: 39.0 (2008-2012 5-year est.); Males per 100 females: 88.0 (2008-2012 5-year est.); Marriage status: 27.9% never married, 56.4% now married, 5.2% widowed, 10.4% divorced (2008-2012 5-year est.); Foreign born: 15.8% (2008-2012 5-year est.); Ancestry (includes multiple ancestries): 21.3% German, 15.1% Irish, 10.1% Polish, 8.6% Italian, 7.7% English (2008-2012 5-year est.).
Economy: Unemployment rate: 5.4% (April 2014); Total civilian labor force: 17,215 (April 2014); Single-family building permits issued: 4 (2013); Multi-family building permits issued: 0 (2013); Homeowner vacancy rate: 1.2%. Rental vacancy rate: 1.3%. (2008-2012 5-year est.); Employment by occupation: 21.1% management, business, and financial, 10.1% computer, engineering, and science, 10.3% education, legal, community service, arts, and media, 6.1% healthcare practitioners, 12.4% service, 27.4% sales and office, 4.8% natural resources, construction, and maintenance, 7.8% production, transportation, and material moving (2008-2012 5-year est.).
Income: Per capita income: $37,231 (2008-2012 5-year est.); Median household income: $83,750 (2008-2012 5-year est.); Average household income: $101,120 (2008-2012 5-year est.); Percent of households with income of $100,000 or more: 41.7% (2008-2012 5-year est.); Poverty rate: 4.1% (2008-2012 5-year est.).
Education: Percent of population age 25 and over with: High school diploma (including GED) or higher: 94.5% (2008-2012 5-year est.); Bachelor's degree or higher: 47.0% (2008-2012 5-year est.); Master's degree or higher: 16.2% (2008-2012 5-year est.).

School District(s)
Gurnee SD 56 (PK-08)
   2011-12 Enrollment: 2,122 .... (847) 336-0800
Warren Twp HSD 121 (09-12)
   2011-12 Enrollment: 4,522 .... (847) 548-7144
Woodland CCSD 50 (PK-08)
   2011-12 Enrollment: 6,522 .... (847) 596-5601
Housing: Homeownership rate: 74.6% (2008-2012 5-year est.); Median home value: $273,400 (2008-2012 5-year est.); Median contract rent: $966 per month (2008-2012 5-year est.); Median year structure built: 1990 (2008-2012 5-year est.).
Health Insurance: 81.6% Private; 18.3% Public; 7.4% None. (2008-2012 5-year est.)
Safety: Violent crime rate: 8.6 per 10,000 population; Property crime rate: 459.9 per 10,000 population (2012).
Transportation: Commute to work: 88.5% car, 3.7% public transportation, 0.4% walk, 6.5% work from home (2008-2012 5-year est.); Travel time to work: 19.6% less than 15 minutes, 35.8% 15 to 30 minutes, 22.9% 30 to 45 minutes, 10.0% 45 to 60 minutes, 11.7% 60 minutes or more (2008-2012 5-year est.)
Additional Information Contacts
Lake County Chamber of Commerce .... (847) 249-3800
http://www.lakecountychamber.com
Village of Gurnee .... (847) 599-7500
http://www.gurnee.il.us

HAINESVILLE (village). Covers a land area of 1.778 square miles and a water area of 0.034 square miles. Located at 42.34° N. Lat; 88.07° W. Long. Elevation is 801 feet.
Population: 134 (1990); 2,129 (2000); 3,597 (2010); Density: 1,979.6 persons per square mile (2008-2012 5-year est.); Race: 84.2% White, 1.5% Black/African American, 11.1% Asian, 0.0% American Indian/Alaska Native, 0.0% Native Hawaiian/Other Pacific Islander, 3.2% Some other race, 0.4% Two or more races, 13.6% Hispanic of any race (2008-2012 5-year est.); Average household size: 3.03 (2008-2012 5-year est.); Median age: 34.3 (2008-2012 5-year est.); Males per 100 females: 116.4 (2008-2012 5-year est.); Marriage status: 23.3% never married, 65.5% now married, 3.1% widowed, 8.1% divorced (2008-2012 5-year est.); Foreign born: 22.3% (2008-2012 5-year est.); Ancestry (includes multiple ancestries): 20.5% German, 13.4% Polish, 11.5% Irish, 9.5% Italian, 5.3% Russian (2008-2012 5-year est.).
Economy: Single-family building permits issued: 0 (2013); Multi-family building permits issued: 0 (2013); Homeowner vacancy rate: 7.5%. Rental vacancy rate: 17.5%. (2008-2012 5-year est.); Employment by occupation: 26.0% management, business, and financial, 8.3% computer, engineering, and science, 8.8% education, legal, community service, arts, and media, 3.4% healthcare practitioners, 13.9% service, 28.6% sales and office, 2.6% natural resources, construction, and maintenance, 8.5% production, transportation, and material moving (2008-2012 5-year est.).

Income: Per capita income: $33,051 (2008-2012 5-year est.); Median household income: $82,401 (2008-2012 5-year est.); Average household income: $98,326 (2008-2012 5-year est.); Percent of households with income of $100,000 or more: 44.1% (2008-2012 5-year est.); Poverty rate: 5.5% (2008-2012 5-year est.).

Education: Percent of population age 25 and over with: High school diploma (including GED) or higher: 90.3% (2008-2012 5-year est.); Bachelor's degree or higher: 52.6% (2008-2012 5-year est.); Master's degree or higher: 20.0% (2008-2012 5-year est.).

School District(s)
Grayslake CCSD 46 (PK-08)
   2011-12 Enrollment: 4,125 . . . . (847) 223-3650

Housing: Homeownership rate: 84.9% (2008-2012 5-year est.); Median home value: $174,200 (2008-2012 5-year est.); Median contract rent: $1,280 per month (2008-2012 5-year est.); Median year structure built: 1998 (2008-2012 5-year est.).

Health Insurance: 74.8% Private; 19.0% Public; 11.6% None. (2008-2012 5-year est.)

Transportation: Commute to work: 90.9% car, 3.5% public transportation, 0.0% walk, 4.7% work from home (2008-2012 5-year est.); Travel time to work: 10.3% less than 15 minutes, 25.2% 15 to 30 minutes, 31.3% 30 to 45 minutes, 15.6% 45 to 60 minutes, 17.6% 60 minutes or more (2008-2012 5-year est.)

HAWTHORN WOODS (village).
Covers a land area of 7.706 square miles and a water area of 0.216 square miles. Located at 42.24° N. Lat; 88.07° W. Long. Elevation is 801 feet.

History: The village is located approximately 40 miles northwest of downtown Chicago. It was officially incorporated in 1958.

Population: 4,423 (1990); 6,002 (2000); 7,663 (2010); Density: 966.9 persons per square mile (2008-2012 5-year est.); Race: 88.1% White, 3.4% Black/African American, 6.9% Asian, 0.0% American Indian/Alaska Native, 0.0% Native Hawaiian/Other Pacific Islander, 1.6% Some other race, 1.5% Two or more races, 7.0% Hispanic of any race (2008-2012 5-year est.); Average household size: 2.94 (2008-2012 5-year est.); Median age: 42.9 (2008-2012 5-year est.); Males per 100 females: 100.5 (2008-2012 5-year est.); Marriage status: 20.2% never married, 73.2% now married, 2.3% widowed, 4.3% divorced (2008-2012 5-year est.); Foreign born: 15.4% (2008-2012 5-year est.); Ancestry (includes multiple ancestries): 27.9% German, 13.8% Irish, 10.2% Italian, 9.0% Polish, 7.9% American (2008-2012 5-year est.).

Economy: Single-family building permits issued: 19 (2013); Multi-family building permits issued: 0 (2013); Homeowner vacancy rate: 1.5%. Rental vacancy rate: 0.0%. (2008-2012 5-year est.); Employment by occupation: 37.1% management, business, and financial, 11.2% computer, engineering, and science, 9.8% education, legal, community service, arts, and media, 7.0% healthcare practitioners, 8.1% service, 21.6% sales and office, 2.5% natural resources, construction, and maintenance, 2.7% production, transportation, and material moving (2008-2012 5-year est.).

Income: Per capita income: $62,396 (2008-2012 5-year est.); Median household income: $157,792 (2008-2012 5-year est.); Average household income: $183,053 (2008-2012 5-year est.); Percent of households with income of $100,000 or more: 77.7% (2008-2012 5-year est.); Poverty rate: 3.6% (2008-2012 5-year est.).

Education: Percent of population age 25 and over with: High school diploma (including GED) or higher: 95.8% (2008-2012 5-year est.); Bachelor's degree or higher: 66.8% (2008-2012 5-year est.); Master's degree or higher: 25.8% (2008-2012 5-year est.).

School District(s)
Lake Zurich CUSD 95 (PK-12)
   2011-12 Enrollment: 5,958 . . . . (847) 438-2831

Housing: Homeownership rate: 98.5% (2008-2012 5-year est.); Median home value: $492,000 (2008-2012 5-year est.); Median contract rent: $2,000+ per month (2008-2012 5-year est.); Median year structure built: 1989 (2008-2012 5-year est.).

Health Insurance: 93.1% Private; 13.4% Public; 2.5% None. (2008-2012 5-year est.)

Safety: Violent crime rate: 0.0 per 10,000 population; Property crime rate: 64.9 per 10,000 population (2012).

Transportation: Commute to work: 84.8% car, 2.7% public transportation, 0.4% walk, 9.5% work from home (2008-2012 5-year est.); Travel time to work: 16.9% less than 15 minutes, 20.7% 15 to 30 minutes, 34.9% 30 to 45 minutes, 20.5% 45 to 60 minutes, 7.0% 60 minutes or more (2008-2012 5-year est.)

Additional Information Contacts

Village of Hawthorn Woods . . . . (847) 438-5500
   http://www.vhw.org

HIGHLAND PARK (city).
Covers a land area of 12.199 square miles and a water area of 0.033 square miles. Located at 42.18° N. Lat; 87.81° W. Long. Elevation is 696 feet.

History: Named for its train station, by the railroad company. The Green Bay House tavern was opened in 1834 on the Chicago-Milwaukee post road, where the city of Highland Park later developed. The name was given by the railroad company to their station here, and the town was incorporated under that name in 1867.

Population: 30,575 (1990); 31,365 (2000); 29,763 (2010); Density: 2,451.8 persons per square mile (2008-2012 5-year est.); Race: 93.8% White, 2.2% Black/African American, 2.0% Asian, 0.0% American Indian/Alaska Native, 0.0% Native Hawaiian/Other Pacific Islander, 2.0% Some other race, 1.4% Two or more races, 5.1% Hispanic of any race (2008-2012 5-year est.); Average household size: 2.55 (2008-2012 5-year est.); Median age: 45.4 (2008-2012 5-year est.); Males per 100 females: 93.3 (2008-2012 5-year est.); Marriage status: 19.9% never married, 64.8% now married, 6.6% widowed, 8.8% divorced (2008-2012 5-year est.); Foreign born: 11.4% (2008-2012 5-year est.); Ancestry (includes multiple ancestries): 18.3% German, 18.2% Russian, 9.8% American, 9.4% Polish, 8.0% Irish (2008-2012 5-year est.).

Economy: Unemployment rate: 4.6% (April 2014); Total civilian labor force: 15,575 (April 2014); Single-family building permits issued: 18 (2013); Multi-family building permits issued: 0 (2013); Homeowner vacancy rate: 3.5%. Rental vacancy rate: 10.0%. (2008-2012 5-year est.); Employment by occupation: 25.7% management, business, and financial, 4.7% computer, engineering, and science, 19.6% education, legal, community service, arts, and media, 6.7% healthcare practitioners, 10.2% service, 26.1% sales and office, 3.1% natural resources, construction, and maintenance, 4.0% production, transportation, and material moving (2008-2012 5-year est.).

Income: Per capita income: $67,267 (2008-2012 5-year est.); Median household income: $115,321 (2008-2012 5-year est.); Average household income: $171,884 (2008-2012 5-year est.); Percent of households with income of $100,000 or more: 56.0% (2008-2012 5-year est.); Poverty rate: 5.7% (2008-2012 5-year est.).

Taxes: Total city taxes per capita: $904 (2011); City property taxes per capita: $479 (2011).

Education: Percent of population age 25 and over with: High school diploma (including GED) or higher: 96.6% (2008-2012 5-year est.); Bachelor's degree or higher: 68.0% (2008-2012 5-year est.); Master's degree or higher: 33.3% (2008-2012 5-year est.).

School District(s)
North Shore SD 112 (PK-08)
   2011-12 Enrollment: 4,475 . . . . (847) 681-6700
Northern Suburban Spec Ed Dist (KG-12)
   2011-12 Enrollment: n/a . . . . (847) 831-5100
Twp HSD 113 (09-12)
   2011-12 Enrollment: 3,693 . . . . (224) 765-1001

Housing: Homeownership rate: 82.8% (2008-2012 5-year est.); Median home value: $521,700 (2008-2012 5-year est.); Median contract rent: $1,249 per month (2008-2012 5-year est.); Median year structure built: 1963 (2008-2012 5-year est.).

Health Insurance: 87.1% Private; 23.8% Public; 5.8% None. (2008-2012 5-year est.)

Hospitals: Highland Park Hospital (239 beds)

Safety: Violent crime rate: 12.0 per 10,000 population; Property crime rate: 121.1 per 10,000 population (2012).

Transportation: Commute to work: 74.9% car, 10.1% public transportation, 1.8% walk, 11.3% work from home (2008-2012 5-year est.); Travel time to work: 23.6% less than 15 minutes, 33.5% 15 to 30 minutes, 19.3% 30 to 45 minutes, 8.3% 45 to 60 minutes, 15.4% 60 minutes or more (2008-2012 5-year est.)

Additional Information Contacts

City of Highland Park. . . . . (847) 432-0800
   http://www.cityhpil.com
Highland Park Chamber of Commerce . . . . (847) 432-0284
   http://www.chamberhp.com

HIGHWOOD (city).
Covers a land area of 0.714 square miles and a water area of 0 square miles. Located at 42.21° N. Lat; 87.81° W. Long. Elevation is 676 feet.

History: Fort Sheridan decommissioned in 1990s. Incorporated 1886.

Population: 5,331 (1990); 4,143 (2000); 5,405 (2010); Density: 7,555.4 persons per square mile (2008-2012 5-year est.); Race: 68.0% White, 3.7% Black/African American, 1.5% Asian, 0.0% American Indian/Alaska Native, 0.0% Native Hawaiian/Other Pacific Islander, 26.8% Some other race, 2.7% Two or more races, 50.9% Hispanic of any race (2008-2012 5-year est.); Average household size: 2.89 (2008-2012 5-year est.); Median age: 34.0 (2008-2012 5-year est.); Males per 100 females: 91.8 (2008-2012 5-year est.); Marriage status: 35.7% never married, 50.5% now married, 5.2% widowed, 8.6% divorced (2008-2012 5-year est.); Foreign born: 37.2% (2008-2012 5-year est.); Ancestry (includes multiple ancestries): 12.6% Italian, 5.6% German, 5.3% American, 2.5% Russian, 2.3% Irish (2008-2012 5-year est.).

Economy: Single-family building permits issued: 0 (2013); Multi-family building permits issued: 0 (2013); Homeowner vacancy rate: 1.3%. Rental vacancy rate: 4.3%. (2008-2012 5-year est.); Employment by occupation: 17.4% management, business, and financial, 1.9% computer, engineering, and science, 11.6% education, legal, community service, arts, and media, 1.8% healthcare practitioners, 37.8% service, 20.4% sales and office, 4.5% natural resources, construction, and maintenance, 4.7% production, transportation, and material moving (2008-2012 5-year est.).

Income: Per capita income: $28,799 (2008-2012 5-year est.); Median household income: $58,721 (2008-2012 5-year est.); Average household income: $82,270 (2008-2012 5-year est.); Percent of households with income of $100,000 or more: 21.6% (2008-2012 5-year est.); Poverty rate: 13.1% (2008-2012 5-year est.).

Education: Percent of population age 25 and over with: High school diploma (including GED) or higher: 77.4% (2008-2012 5-year est.); Bachelor's degree or higher: 25.8% (2008-2012 5-year est.); Master's degree or higher: 11.8% (2008-2012 5-year est.).

School District(s)

North Shore SD 112 (PK-08)

   2011-12 Enrollment: 4,475 . . . . (847) 681-6700

Housing: Homeownership rate: 49.7% (2008-2012 5-year est.); Median home value: $361,400 (2008-2012 5-year est.); Median contract rent: $1,132 per month (2008-2012 5-year est.); Median year structure built: 1961 (2008-2012 5-year est.).

Health Insurance: 54.8% Private; 31.3% Public; 26.4% None. (2008-2012 5-year est.)

Safety: Violent crime rate: 12.9 per 10,000 population; Property crime rate: 105.0 per 10,000 population (2012).

Transportation: Commute to work: 68.5% car, 13.8% public transportation, 5.7% walk, 9.7% work from home (2008-2012 5-year est.); Travel time to work: 27.8% less than 15 minutes, 36.5% 15 to 30 minutes, 22.4% 30 to 45 minutes, 4.7% 45 to 60 minutes, 8.5% 60 minutes or more (2008-2012 5-year est.)

Additional Information Contacts

Highwood Chamber of Commerce . . . . (847) 433-2100
   http://www.highwoodchamberofcommerce.com

INDIAN CREEK (village). Covers a land area of 0.257 square miles and a water area of 0 square miles. Located at 42.23° N. Lat; 87.98° W. Long. Elevation is 741 feet.

Population: 247 (1990); 194 (2000); 462 (2010); Density: 2,046.9 persons per square mile (2008-2012 5-year est.); Race: 67.5% White, 1.5% Black/African American, 30.2% Asian, 0.0% American Indian/Alaska Native, 0.0% Native Hawaiian/Other Pacific Islander, 0.8% Some other race, 0.2% Two or more races, 14.8% Hispanic of any race (2008-2012 5-year est.); Average household size: 2.95 (2008-2012 5-year est.); Median age: 38.7 (2008-2012 5-year est.); Males per 100 females: 97.7 (2008-2012 5-year est.); Marriage status: 15.9% never married, 75.6% now married, 6.2% widowed, 2.3% divorced (2008-2012 5-year est.); Foreign born: 34.4% (2008-2012 5-year est.); Ancestry (includes multiple ancestries): 12.7% German, 11.6% Polish, 10.1% Russian, 9.7% Irish, 8.9% American (2008-2012 5-year est.).

Economy: Single-family building permits issued: 0 (2013); Multi-family building permits issued: 0 (2013); Homeowner vacancy rate: 2.0%. Rental vacancy rate: 0.0%. (2008-2012 5-year est.); Employment by occupation: 21.8% management, business, and financial, 13.7% computer, engineering, and science, 12.6% education, legal, community service, arts, and media, 3.9% healthcare practitioners, 7.0% service, 34.0% sales and office, 3.5% natural resources, construction, and maintenance, 3.5% production, transportation, and material moving (2008-2012 5-year est.).

Income: Per capita income: $40,820 (2008-2012 5-year est.); Median household income: $118,173 (2008-2012 5-year est.); Average household income: $121,566 (2008-2012 5-year est.); Percent of households with income of $100,000 or more: 56.6% (2008-2012 5-year est.); Poverty rate: 1.3% (2008-2012 5-year est.).

Education: Percent of population age 25 and over with: High school diploma (including GED) or higher: 95.0% (2008-2012 5-year est.); Bachelor's degree or higher: 70.2% (2008-2012 5-year est.); Master's degree or higher: 27.3% (2008-2012 5-year est.).

Housing: Homeownership rate: 82.3% (2008-2012 5-year est.); Median home value: $408,000 (2008-2012 5-year est.); Median contract rent: $2,000+ per month (2008-2012 5-year est.); Median year structure built: 2002 (2008-2012 5-year est.).

Health Insurance: 91.1% Private; 9.9% Public; 5.5% None. (2008-2012 5-year est.)

Transportation: Commute to work: 81.4% car, 3.9% public transportation, 1.4% walk, 6.3% work from home (2008-2012 5-year est.); Travel time to work: 13.9% less than 15 minutes, 37.8% 15 to 30 minutes, 27.0% 30 to 45 minutes, 10.9% 45 to 60 minutes, 10.5% 60 minutes or more (2008-2012 5-year est.)

INGLESIDE (unincorporated postal area)

Zip Code: 60041

   Covers a land area of 9.609 square miles and a water area of 1.523 square miles. Located at 42.36° N. Lat; 88.15° W. Long. Elevation is 764 feet. Population: 9,250 (2010); Density: 962.6 persons per square mile (2010); Race: 90.8% White, 1.1% Black/African American, 1.0% Asian, 0.4% American Indian/Alaska Native, 0.1% Native Hawaiian/Other Pacific Islander, 6.6% Some other race, 2.5% Two or more races, 11.6% Hispanic of any race (2010); Average household size: 2.67 (2010); Median age: 39.7 (2010); Males per 100 females: 104.9 (2010); Homeownership rate: 78.2% (2010)

KILDEER (village). Covers a land area of 4.378 square miles and a water area of 0.213 square miles. Located at 42.19° N. Lat; 88.05° W. Long. Elevation is 778 feet.

History: A referendum for establishing the Village of Kildeer was held on March 22, 1958 and area residents voted to incorporate the new village with a population of 153, making it the 32nd municipality in Lake County. The polling place for this election was the home of Dorothea Huszagh. Brickman's immediate response was to file suit to have the referendum overturned.

Population: 2,257 (1990); 3,460 (2000); 3,968 (2010); Density: 902.6 persons per square mile (2008-2012 5-year est.); Race: 90.6% White, 1.1% Black/African American, 6.4% Asian, 0.0% American Indian/Alaska Native, 0.0% Native Hawaiian/Other Pacific Islander, 1.9% Some other race, 1.8% Two or more races, 5.2% Hispanic of any race (2008-2012 5-year est.); Average household size: 3.12 (2008-2012 5-year est.); Median age: 44.8 (2008-2012 5-year est.); Males per 100 females: 90.3 (2008-2012 5-year est.); Marriage status: 23.0% never married, 67.1% now married, 4.3% widowed, 5.6% divorced (2008-2012 5-year est.); Foreign born: 8.8% (2008-2012 5-year est.); Ancestry (includes multiple ancestries): 21.0% German, 16.1% American, 15.9% Irish, 14.1% Polish, 12.4% Italian (2008-2012 5-year est.).

Economy: Single-family building permits issued: 10 (2013); Multi-family building permits issued: 0 (2013); Homeowner vacancy rate: 1.9%. Rental vacancy rate: 0.0%. (2008-2012 5-year est.); Employment by occupation: 43.2% management, business, and financial, 7.0% computer, engineering, and science, 7.2% education, legal, community service, arts, and media, 9.3% healthcare practitioners, 7.0% service, 22.0% sales and office, 2.2% natural resources, construction, and maintenance, 2.1% production, transportation, and material moving (2008-2012 5-year est.).

Income: Per capita income: $60,651 (2008-2012 5-year est.); Median household income: $159,609 (2008-2012 5-year est.); Average household income: $187,754 (2008-2012 5-year est.); Percent of households with income of $100,000 or more: 72.6% (2008-2012 5-year est.); Poverty rate: 5.1% (2008-2012 5-year est.).

Education: Percent of population age 25 and over with: High school diploma (including GED) or higher: 99.1% (2008-2012 5-year est.); Bachelor's degree or higher: 66.9% (2008-2012 5-year est.); Master's degree or higher: 25.7% (2008-2012 5-year est.).

Housing: Homeownership rate: 95.9% (2008-2012 5-year est.); Median home value: $664,400 (2008-2012 5-year est.); Median contract rent: $934 per month (2008-2012 5-year est.); Median year structure built: 1985 (2008-2012 5-year est.).

Health Insurance: 96.3% Private; 9.4% Public; 1.0% None. (2008-2012 5-year est.)

Safety: Violent crime rate: 0.0 per 10,000 population; Property crime rate: 80.3 per 10,000 population (2012).
Transportation: Commute to work: 89.4% car, 3.6% public transportation, 0.0% walk, 6.6% work from home (2008-2012 5-year est.); Travel time to work: 11.6% less than 15 minutes, 28.7% 15 to 30 minutes, 35.9% 30 to 45 minutes, 12.9% 45 to 60 minutes, 10.8% 60 minutes or more (2008-2012 5-year est.)

KNOLLWOOD (CDP). Covers a land area of 0.665 square miles and a water area of 0 square miles. Located at 42.28° N. Lat; 87.88° W. Long. Elevation is 702 feet.
Population: n/a (1990); n/a (2000); 1,747 (2010); Density: 2,021.6 persons per square mile (2008-2012 5-year est.); Race: 85.2% White, 4.8% Black/African American, 2.3% Asian, 0.0% American Indian/Alaska Native, 0.0% Native Hawaiian/Other Pacific Islander, 7.7% Some other race, 4.5% Two or more races, 14.1% Hispanic of any race (2008-2012 5-year est.); Average household size: 2.32 (2008-2012 5-year est.); Median age: 41.3 (2008-2012 5-year est.); Males per 100 females: 107.2 (2008-2012 5-year est.); Marriage status: 25.3% never married, 59.5% now married, 5.0% widowed, 10.2% divorced (2008-2012 5-year est.); Foreign born: 13.6% (2008-2012 5-year est.); Ancestry (includes multiple ancestries): 14.9% German, 14.4% Irish, 10.9% English, 7.9% Polish, 7.9% American (2008-2012 5-year est.).
Economy: Homeowner vacancy rate: 12.2%. Rental vacancy rate: 28.3%. (2008-2012 5-year est.); Employment by occupation: 19.7% management, business, and financial, 2.0% computer, engineering, and science, 19.5% education, legal, community service, arts, and media, 9.1% healthcare practitioners, 5.9% service, 22.0% sales and office, 4.7% natural resources, construction, and maintenance, 17.1% production, transportation, and material moving (2008-2012 5-year est.).
Income: Per capita income: $39,876 (2008-2012 5-year est.); Median household income: $76,696 (2008-2012 5-year est.); Average household income: $89,996 (2008-2012 5-year est.); Percent of households with income of $100,000 or more: 43.8% (2008-2012 5-year est.); Poverty rate: 7.5% (2008-2012 5-year est.).
Education: Percent of population age 25 and over with: High school diploma (including GED) or higher: 87.6% (2008-2012 5-year est.); Bachelor's degree or higher: 45.0% (2008-2012 5-year est.); Master's degree or higher: 15.3% (2008-2012 5-year est.).
Housing: Homeownership rate: 81.1% (2008-2012 5-year est.); Median home value: $361,800 (2008-2012 5-year est.); Median contract rent: $824 per month (2008-2012 5-year est.); Median year structure built: 1974 (2008-2012 5-year est.).
Health Insurance: 69.6% Private; 23.1% Public; 12.8% None. (2008-2012 5-year est.)
Transportation: Commute to work: 86.4% car, 3.7% public transportation, 0.0% walk, 9.9% work from home (2008-2012 5-year est.); Travel time to work: 43.5% less than 15 minutes, 30.9% 15 to 30 minutes, 12.7% 30 to 45 minutes, 4.5% 45 to 60 minutes, 8.4% 60 minutes or more (2008-2012 5-year est.)

LAKE BARRINGTON (village). Covers a land area of 5.862 square miles and a water area of 0.307 square miles. Located at 42.21° N. Lat; 88.17° W. Long. Elevation is 804 feet.
History: Established in 1959, borrowing its name from the town of Great Barrington, Massachusetts.
Population: 3,855 (1990); 4,757 (2000); 4,973 (2010); Density: 830.8 persons per square mile (2008-2012 5-year est.); Race: 93.7% White, 1.0% Black/African American, 4.8% Asian, 0.0% American Indian/Alaska Native, 0.0% Native Hawaiian/Other Pacific Islander, 0.5% Some other race, 0.5% Two or more races, 0.6% Hispanic of any race (2008-2012 5-year est.); Average household size: 2.17 (2008-2012 5-year est.); Median age: 54.8 (2008-2012 5-year est.); Males per 100 females: 79.8 (2008-2012 5-year est.); Marriage status: 17.0% never married, 66.9% now married, 7.9% widowed, 8.2% divorced (2008-2012 5-year est.); Foreign born: 8.6% (2008-2012 5-year est.); Ancestry (includes multiple ancestries): 35.7% German, 17.8% Irish, 11.9% Italian, 10.3% Polish, 9.6% English (2008-2012 5-year est.).
Economy: Single-family building permits issued: 3 (2013); Multi-family building permits issued: 0 (2013); Homeowner vacancy rate: 0.4%. Rental vacancy rate: 0.0%. (2008-2012 5-year est.); Employment by occupation: 36.3% management, business, and financial, 5.2% computer, engineering, and science, 15.0% education, legal, community service, arts, and media, 7.0% healthcare practitioners, 6.8% service, 24.7% sales and office, 2.4%

natural resources, construction, and maintenance, 2.6% production, transportation, and material moving (2008-2012 5-year est.).
Income: Per capita income: $67,424 (2008-2012 5-year est.); Median household income: $93,013 (2008-2012 5-year est.); Average household income: $145,955 (2008-2012 5-year est.); Percent of households with income of $100,000 or more: 47.2% (2008-2012 5-year est.); Poverty rate: 2.4% (2008-2012 5-year est.).
Taxes: Total city taxes per capita: $319 (2011); City property taxes per capita: $244 (2011).
Education: Percent of population age 25 and over with: High school diploma (including GED) or higher: 98.1% (2008-2012 5-year est.); Bachelor's degree or higher: 65.3% (2008-2012 5-year est.); Master's degree or higher: 28.8% (2008-2012 5-year est.).
Housing: Homeownership rate: 87.2% (2008-2012 5-year est.); Median home value: $409,700 (2008-2012 5-year est.); Median contract rent: $1,258 per month (2008-2012 5-year est.); Median year structure built: 1984 (2008-2012 5-year est.).
Health Insurance: 88.7% Private; 32.0% Public; 0.6% None. (2008-2012 5-year est.)
Transportation: Commute to work: 77.6% car, 5.7% public transportation, 0.7% walk, 14.7% work from home (2008-2012 5-year est.); Travel time to work: 16.3% less than 15 minutes, 26.2% 15 to 30 minutes, 25.7% 30 to 45 minutes, 16.9% 45 to 60 minutes, 15.0% 60 minutes or more (2008-2012 5-year est.)

LAKE BLUFF (village). Covers a land area of 4.054 square miles and a water area of 0.007 square miles. Located at 42.28° N. Lat; 87.85° W. Long. Elevation is 659 feet.
History: Lake Bluff began in 1874 as a Methodist camp-meeting ground.
Population: 5,513 (1990); 6,056 (2000); 5,722 (2010); Density: 1,532.8 persons per square mile (2008-2012 5-year est.); Race: 89.8% White, 1.4% Black/African American, 7.4% Asian, 0.0% American Indian/Alaska Native, 0.0% Native Hawaiian/Other Pacific Islander, 1.4% Some other race, 1.5% Two or more races, 1.0% Hispanic of any race (2008-2012 5-year est.); Average household size: 2.96 (2008-2012 5-year est.); Median age: 43.1 (2008-2012 5-year est.); Males per 100 females: 92.1 (2008-2012 5-year est.); Marriage status: 19.5% never married, 69.7% now married, 3.8% widowed, 7.1% divorced (2008-2012 5-year est.); Foreign born: 8.8% (2008-2012 5-year est.); Ancestry (includes multiple ancestries): 26.1% German, 21.5% Irish, 20.5% English, 9.4% Italian, 6.6% Polish (2008-2012 5-year est.).
Economy: Single-family building permits issued: 6 (2013); Multi-family building permits issued: 0 (2013); Homeowner vacancy rate: 2.8%. Rental vacancy rate: 0.0%. (2008-2012 5-year est.); Employment by occupation: 29.1% management, business, and financial, 8.7% computer, engineering, and science, 19.8% education, legal, community service, arts, and media, 6.0% healthcare practitioners, 7.8% service, 21.3% sales and office, 2.9% natural resources, construction, and maintenance, 4.5% production, transportation, and material moving (2008-2012 5-year est.).
Income: Per capita income: $63,752 (2008-2012 5-year est.); Median household income: $146,500 (2008-2012 5-year est.); Average household income: $187,744 (2008-2012 5-year est.); Percent of households with income of $100,000 or more: 65.6% (2008-2012 5-year est.); Poverty rate: 4.8% (2008-2012 5-year est.).
Education: Percent of population age 25 and over with: High school diploma (including GED) or higher: 100.0% (2008-2012 5-year est.); Bachelor's degree or higher: 79.1% (2008-2012 5-year est.); Master's degree or higher: 37.0% (2008-2012 5-year est.).

School District(s)
Lake Bluff ESD 65 (KG-08)
    2011-12 Enrollment: 906 . . . . (847) 234-9400
Housing: Homeownership rate: 87.5% (2008-2012 5-year est.); Median home value: $647,600 (2008-2012 5-year est.); Median contract rent: $1,206 per month (2008-2012 5-year est.); Median year structure built: 1970 (2008-2012 5-year est.).
Health Insurance: 92.7% Private; 17.4% Public; 3.0% None. (2008-2012 5-year est.)
Safety: Violent crime rate: 0.0 per 10,000 population; Property crime rate: 109.6 per 10,000 population (2012).
Transportation: Commute to work: 72.4% car, 11.7% public transportation, 1.7% walk, 12.2% work from home (2008-2012 5-year est.); Travel time to work: 35.9% less than 15 minutes, 26.1% 15 to 30 minutes, 10.4% 30 to 45 minutes, 13.1% 45 to 60 minutes, 14.5% 60 minutes or more (2008-2012 5-year est.)
Additional Information Contacts

Village of Lake Bluff . . . . (847) 234-0774
    http://www.lakebluff.org

LAKE CATHERINE (CDP).

Covers a land area of 0.932 square miles and a water area of 0.544 square miles. Located at 42.49° N. Lat; 88.12° W. Long. Elevation is 748 feet.

Population: 1,515 (1990); 1,490 (2000); 1,379 (2010); Density: 1,344.2 persons per square mile (2008-2012 5-year est.); Race: 89.7% White, 3.0% Black/African American, 0.0% Asian, 0.0% American Indian/Alaska Native, 0.0% Native Hawaiian/Other Pacific Islander, 7.3% Some other race, 7.3% Two or more races, 0.6% Hispanic of any race (2008-2012 5-year est.); Average household size: 2.48 (2008-2012 5-year est.); Median age: 42.6 (2008-2012 5-year est.); Males per 100 females: 94.3 (2008-2012 5-year est.); Marriage status: 30.0% never married, 53.3% now married, 6.1% widowed, 10.6% divorced (2008-2012 5-year est.); Foreign born: 6.3% (2008-2012 5-year est.); Ancestry (includes multiple ancestries): 32.3% German, 29.6% Irish, 12.9% Polish, 8.4% American, 6.5% Italian (2008-2012 5-year est.).
Economy: Homeowner vacancy rate: 2.7%. Rental vacancy rate: 0.0%. (2008-2012 5-year est.); Employment by occupation: 16.4% management, business, and financial, 0.0% computer, engineering, and science, 4.8% education, legal, community service, arts, and media, 2.4% healthcare practitioners, 19.6% service, 19.6% sales and office, 21.4% natural resources, construction, and maintenance, 15.8% production, transportation, and material moving (2008-2012 5-year est.).
Income: Per capita income: $26,821 (2008-2012 5-year est.); Median household income: $42,028 (2008-2012 5-year est.); Average household income: $65,092 (2008-2012 5-year est.); Percent of households with income of $100,000 or more: 32.8% (2008-2012 5-year est.); Poverty rate: 11.5% (2008-2012 5-year est.).
Education: Percent of population age 25 and over with: High school diploma (including GED) or higher: 94.1% (2008-2012 5-year est.); Bachelor's degree or higher: 28.5% (2008-2012 5-year est.); Master's degree or higher: 6.0% (2008-2012 5-year est.).
Housing: Homeownership rate: 79.4% (2008-2012 5-year est.); Median home value: $184,000 (2008-2012 5-year est.); Median contract rent: $771 per month (2008-2012 5-year est.); Median year structure built: 1954 (2008-2012 5-year est.).
Health Insurance: 74.3% Private; 37.2% Public; 7.7% None. (2008-2012 5-year est.)
Transportation: Commute to work: 93.2% car, 0.0% public transportation, 0.0% walk, 1.7% work from home (2008-2012 5-year est.); Travel time to work: 21.6% less than 15 minutes, 26.3% 15 to 30 minutes, 14.1% 30 to 45 minutes, 14.3% 45 to 60 minutes, 23.6% 60 minutes or more (2008-2012 5-year est.)

LAKE FOREST (city).

Covers a land area of 17.178 square miles and a water area of 0.066 square miles. Located at 42.24° N. Lat; 87.86° W. Long. Elevation is 689 feet.
History: Named for Lake Michigan and for the forests in the area. Lake Forest was laid out in 1856 by David Hotchkiss, a St. Louis landscape architect, for a company of Chicago businessmen who had purchased land here. The town grew around Lake Forest College, opened in 1857.
Population: 17,836 (1990); 20,059 (2000); 19,375 (2010); Density: 1,110.1 persons per square mile (2008-2012 5-year est.); Race: 91.0% White, 1.0% Black/African American, 5.8% Asian, 0.1% American Indian/Alaska Native, 0.0% Native Hawaiian/Other Pacific Islander, 2.1% Some other race, 1.1% Two or more races, 2.8% Hispanic of any race (2008-2012 5-year est.); Average household size: 2.72 (2008-2012 5-year est.); Median age: 46.3 (2008-2012 5-year est.); Males per 100 females: 91.4 (2008-2012 5-year est.); Marriage status: 24.2% never married, 64.6% now married, 5.7% widowed, 5.5% divorced (2008-2012 5-year est.); Foreign born: 9.8% (2008-2012 5-year est.); Ancestry (includes multiple ancestries): 26.8% German, 17.9% Irish, 13.7% English, 9.8% Italian, 6.7% American (2008-2012 5-year est.).
Economy: Single-family building permits issued: 12 (2013); Multi-family building permits issued: 0 (2013); Homeowner vacancy rate: 4.7%. Rental vacancy rate: 9.6%. (2008-2012 5-year est.); Employment by occupation: 34.5% management, business, and financial, 4.4% computer, engineering, and science, 15.4% education, legal, community service, arts, and media, 7.1% healthcare practitioners, 7.8% service, 25.5% sales and office, 2.2% natural resources, construction, and maintenance, 3.2% production, transportation, and material moving (2008-2012 5-year est.).
Income: Per capita income: $84,139 (2008-2012 5-year est.); Median household income: $136,583 (2008-2012 5-year est.); Average household

income: $242,776 (2008-2012 5-year est.); Percent of households with income of $100,000 or more: 65.0% (2008-2012 5-year est.); Poverty rate: 4.5% (2008-2012 5-year est.).
Taxes: Total city taxes per capita: $1,688 (2011); City property taxes per capita: $1,329 (2011).
Education: Percent of population age 25 and over with: High school diploma (including GED) or higher: 97.8% (2008-2012 5-year est.); Bachelor's degree or higher: 75.1% (2008-2012 5-year est.); Master's degree or higher: 36.6% (2008-2012 5-year est.).

School District(s)
Lake Forest CHSD 115 (09-12)
    2011-12 Enrollment: 1,725 . . . . (847) 235-9657
Lake Forest SD 67 (KG-08)
    2011-12 Enrollment: 2,039 . . . . (847) 235-9657
Rondout SD 72 (KG-08)
    2011-12 Enrollment: 161 . . . . (847) 362-2021
Spec Educ Dist Lake County/sedol
    2011-12 Enrollment: n/a . . . . (847) 548-8470

Four-year College(s)
Lake Forest College (Private, Not-for-profit)
    Fall 2012 Enrollment: 1,562 . . . . (847) 234-3100
    2012-13 Tuition: In-state $38,300; Out-of-state $38,300
Lake Forest Graduate School of Management (Private, Not-for-profit)
    Fall 2012 Enrollment: 667 . . . . (847) 234-5005
Housing: Homeownership rate: 89.2% (2008-2012 5-year est.); Median home value: $866,200 (2008-2012 5-year est.); Median contract rent: $1,209 per month (2008-2012 5-year est.); Median year structure built: 1973 (2008-2012 5-year est.).
Health Insurance: 89.5% Private; 21.0% Public; 3.7% None. (2008-2012 5-year est.)
Hospitals: Lake Forest Hospital (261 beds)
Safety: Violent crime rate: 7.2 per 10,000 population; Property crime rate: 21.1 per 10,000 population (2012).
Transportation: Commute to work: 72.0% car, 9.6% public transportation, 5.8% walk, 11.2% work from home (2008-2012 5-year est.); Travel time to work: 28.2% less than 15 minutes, 29.0% 15 to 30 minutes, 16.5% 30 to 45 minutes, 9.4% 45 to 60 minutes, 16.8% 60 minutes or more (2008-2012 5-year est.)
Additional Information Contacts
City of Lake Forest . . . . (847) 234-2600
    http://www.cityoflakeforest.com
Lake Forest/Lake Bluff Chamber of Commerce . . . . (847) 234-4282
    http://www.lflbchamber.com

LAKE VILLA (village).

Covers a land area of 6.186 square miles and a water area of 0.804 square miles. Located at 42.42° N. Lat; 88.08° W. Long. Elevation is 791 feet.
History: Lake Villa grew around a railroad station and the resort trade. It was the site of the Allendale Farm School, an experimental community founded in 1897 as a home for neglected boys.
Population: 2,857 (1990); 5,864 (2000); 8,741 (2010); Density: 1,426.9 persons per square mile (2008-2012 5-year est.); Race: 88.8% White, 3.7% Black/African American, 5.3% Asian, 0.0% American Indian/Alaska Native, 0.1% Native Hawaiian/Other Pacific Islander, 2.1% Some other race, 1.1% Two or more races, 10.2% Hispanic of any race (2008-2012 5-year est.); Average household size: 2.86 (2008-2012 5-year est.); Median age: 35.2 (2008-2012 5-year est.); Males per 100 females: 98.4 (2008-2012 5-year est.); Marriage status: 24.9% never married, 61.7% now married, 5.4% widowed, 8.0% divorced (2008-2012 5-year est.); Foreign born: 8.0% (2008-2012 5-year est.); Ancestry (includes multiple ancestries): 31.8% German, 18.9% Irish, 14.6% Polish, 7.6% English, 6.7% Italian (2008-2012 5-year est.).
Economy: Single-family building permits issued: 24 (2013); Multi-family building permits issued: 0 (2013); Homeowner vacancy rate: 0.8%. Rental vacancy rate: 15.1%. (2008-2012 5-year est.); Employment by occupation: 22.5% management, business, and financial, 6.6% computer, engineering, and science, 9.1% education, legal, community service, arts, and media, 5.8% healthcare practitioners, 13.6% service, 27.5% sales and office, 7.0% natural resources, construction, and maintenance, 7.8% production, transportation, and material moving (2008-2012 5-year est.).
Income: Per capita income: $35,284 (2008-2012 5-year est.); Median household income: $89,313 (2008-2012 5-year est.); Average household income: $101,096 (2008-2012 5-year est.); Percent of households with income of $100,000 or more: 44.3% (2008-2012 5-year est.); Poverty rate: 2.9% (2008-2012 5-year est.).

Education: Percent of population age 25 and over with: High school diploma (including GED) or higher: 95.8% (2008-2012 5-year est.); Bachelor's degree or higher: 43.8% (2008-2012 5-year est.); Master's degree or higher: 12.6% (2008-2012 5-year est.).

School District(s)

CHSD 117 (09-12)
   2011-12 Enrollment: 2,821 . . . . (847) 838-7679
Lake Villa CCSD 41 (PK-08)
   2011-12 Enrollment: 3,108 . . . . (847) 245-8001

Housing: Homeownership rate: 76.1% (2008-2012 5-year est.); Median home value: $255,600 (2008-2012 5-year est.); Median contract rent: $863 per month (2008-2012 5-year est.); Median year structure built: 1994 (2008-2012 5-year est.).

Health Insurance: 85.0% Private; 12.8% Public; 7.4% None. (2008-2012 5-year est.)

Safety: Violent crime rate: 11.4 per 10,000 population; Property crime rate: 105.9 per 10,000 population (2012).

Transportation: Commute to work: 91.4% car, 2.6% public transportation, 0.2% walk, 5.3% work from home (2008-2012 5-year est.); Travel time to work: 16.1% less than 15 minutes, 25.5% 15 to 30 minutes, 26.0% 30 to 45 minutes, 15.6% 45 to 60 minutes, 16.7% 60 minutes or more (2008-2012 5-year est.)

Additional Information Contacts

Lindenhurst/Lake Villa Chamber of Commerce . . . . (847) 356-8446
   http://llvchamber.com
Village of Lake Villa . . . . (847) 356-6100
   http://www.lake-villa.org

LAKE ZURICH (village). Covers a land area of 6.765 square miles and a water area of 0.417 square miles. Located at 42.19° N. Lat; 88.09° W. Long. Elevation is 876 feet.

Population: 14,947 (1990); 18,104 (2000); 19,631 (2010); Density: 2,908.8 persons per square mile (2008-2012 5-year est.); Race: 89.3% White, 0.2% Black/African American, 7.7% Asian, 0.1% American Indian/Alaska Native, 0.0% Native Hawaiian/Other Pacific Islander, 2.7% Some other race, 1.7% Two or more races, 7.7% Hispanic of any race (2008-2012 5-year est.); Average household size: 3.07 (2008-2012 5-year est.); Median age: 37.4 (2008-2012 5-year est.); Males per 100 females: 96.5 (2008-2012 5-year est.); Marriage status: 25.6% never married, 63.7% now married, 3.7% widowed, 7.0% divorced (2008-2012 5-year est.); Foreign born: 16.5% (2008-2012 5-year est.); Ancestry (includes multiple ancestries): 26.6% German, 16.6% Polish, 16.3% Irish, 12.0% Italian, 7.8% English (2008-2012 5-year est.).

Economy: Single-family building permits issued: 23 (2013); Multi-family building permits issued: 0 (2013); Homeowner vacancy rate: 1.1%. Rental vacancy rate: 9.0%. (2008-2012 5-year est.); Employment by occupation: 21.4% management, business, and financial, 10.9% computer, engineering, and science, 11.3% education, legal, community service, arts, and media, 5.0% healthcare practitioners, 12.4% service, 25.2% sales and office, 5.1% natural resources, construction, and maintenance, 8.8% production, transportation, and material moving (2008-2012 5-year est.).

Income: Per capita income: $39,128 (2008-2012 5-year est.); Median household income: $109,299 (2008-2012 5-year est.); Average household income: $119,469 (2008-2012 5-year est.); Percent of households with income of $100,000 or more: 55.6% (2008-2012 5-year est.); Poverty rate: 4.7% (2008-2012 5-year est.).

Education: Percent of population age 25 and over with: High school diploma (including GED) or higher: 93.2% (2008-2012 5-year est.); Bachelor's degree or higher: 53.0% (2008-2012 5-year est.); Master's degree or higher: 18.9% (2008-2012 5-year est.).

School District(s)

Lake Zurich CUSD 95 (PK-12)
   2011-12 Enrollment: 5,958 . . . . (847) 438-2831

Housing: Homeownership rate: 89.5% (2008-2012 5-year est.); Median home value: $335,400 (2008-2012 5-year est.); Median contract rent: $969 per month (2008-2012 5-year est.); Median year structure built: 1983 (2008-2012 5-year est.).

Health Insurance: 85.9% Private; 12.7% Public; 7.1% None. (2008-2012 5-year est.)

Safety: Violent crime rate: 4.1 per 10,000 population; Property crime rate: 143.0 per 10,000 population (2012).

Transportation: Commute to work: 88.7% car, 3.3% public transportation, 0.8% walk, 5.3% work from home (2008-2012 5-year est.); Travel time to work: 18.6% less than 15 minutes, 26.5% 15 to 30 minutes, 30.1% 30 to 45 minutes, 12.9% 45 to 60 minutes, 11.9% 60 minutes or more (2008-2012 5-year est.)

Additional Information Contacts

Lake Zurich Area Chamber of Commerce . . . . (847) 438-5572
   http://www.lzacc.com
Village of Lake Zurich . . . . (847) 438-5141
   http://lakezurich.org

LAKEMOOR (village). Covers a land area of 5.008 square miles and a water area of 0.243 square miles. Located at 42.34° N. Lat; 88.20° W. Long. Elevation is 761 feet.

Population: 1,322 (1990); 2,788 (2000); 6,017 (2010); Density: 1,281.0 persons per square mile (2008-2012 5-year est.); Race: 86.3% White, 0.3% Black/African American, 3.9% Asian, 0.6% American Indian/Alaska Native, 0.0% Native Hawaiian/Other Pacific Islander, 8.9% Some other race, 0.4% Two or more races, 18.0% Hispanic of any race (2008-2012 5-year est.); Average household size: 2.84 (2008-2012 5-year est.); Median age: 31.4 (2008-2012 5-year est.); Males per 100 females: 92.2 (2008-2012 5-year est.); Marriage status: 35.7% never married, 53.9% now married, 1.7% widowed, 8.8% divorced (2008-2012 5-year est.); Foreign born: 12.9% (2008-2012 5-year est.); Ancestry (includes multiple ancestries): 33.3% German, 18.1% Polish, 17.3% Irish, 13.8% Italian, 6.8% Norwegian (2008-2012 5-year est.).

Economy: Single-family building permits issued: 0 (2013); Multi-family building permits issued: 0 (2013); Homeowner vacancy rate: 4.9%. Rental vacancy rate: 8.8%. (2008-2012 5-year est.); Employment by occupation: 16.0% management, business, and financial, 4.5% computer, engineering, and science, 4.6% education, legal, community service, arts, and media, 4.1% healthcare practitioners, 16.9% service, 26.3% sales and office, 10.1% natural resources, construction, and maintenance, 17.5% production, transportation, and material moving (2008-2012 5-year est.).

Income: Per capita income: $31,717 (2008-2012 5-year est.); Median household income: $76,514 (2008-2012 5-year est.); Average household income: $88,735 (2008-2012 5-year est.); Percent of households with income of $100,000 or more: 29.7% (2008-2012 5-year est.); Poverty rate: 7.8% (2008-2012 5-year est.).

Education: Percent of population age 25 and over with: High school diploma (including GED) or higher: 92.0% (2008-2012 5-year est.); Bachelor's degree or higher: 26.6% (2008-2012 5-year est.); Master's degree or higher: 5.4% (2008-2012 5-year est.).

Housing: Homeownership rate: 68.6% (2008-2012 5-year est.); Median home value: $196,500 (2008-2012 5-year est.); Median contract rent: $991 per month (2008-2012 5-year est.); Median year structure built: 1998 (2008-2012 5-year est.).

Health Insurance: 79.5% Private; 13.0% Public; 11.2% None. (2008-2012 5-year est.)

Transportation: Commute to work: 94.4% car, 1.4% public transportation, 0.0% walk, 2.5% work from home (2008-2012 5-year est.); Travel time to work: 13.8% less than 15 minutes, 30.7% 15 to 30 minutes, 20.5% 30 to 45 minutes, 13.2% 45 to 60 minutes, 21.8% 60 minutes or more (2008-2012 5-year est.)

LIBERTYVILLE (village). Covers a land area of 8.814 square miles and a water area of 0.338 square miles. Located at 42.29° N. Lat; 87.96° W. Long. Elevation is 699 feet.

History: Named for the community's patriotism. Daniel Webster (1782-1852) was one of the first purchasers of land in Independence Grove, which changed its name to Libertyville in 1837 when the post office was established. Settlers and vacationists were attracted by the mineral springs in the area.

Population: 19,174 (1990); 20,742 (2000); 20,315 (2010); Density: 2,313.2 persons per square mile (2008-2012 5-year est.); Race: 92.0% White, 1.3% Black/African American, 5.2% Asian, 0.3% American Indian/Alaska Native, 0.0% Native Hawaiian/Other Pacific Islander, 1.2% Some other race, 1.0% Two or more races, 4.1% Hispanic of any race (2008-2012 5-year est.); Average household size: 2.62 (2008-2012 5-year est.); Median age: 44.2 (2008-2012 5-year est.); Males per 100 females: 89.4 (2008-2012 5-year est.); Marriage status: 23.9% never married, 59.4% now married, 7.5% widowed, 9.3% divorced (2008-2012 5-year est.); Foreign born: 9.5% (2008-2012 5-year est.); Ancestry (includes multiple ancestries): 27.8% German, 17.2% Irish, 11.3% Italian, 10.5% English, 10.2% Polish (2008-2012 5-year est.).

Economy: Single-family building permits issued: 33 (2013); Multi-family building permits issued: 0 (2013); Homeowner vacancy rate: 2.4%. Rental vacancy rate: 6.8%. (2008-2012 5-year est.); Employment by occupation:

25.5% management, business, and financial, 10.7% computer, engineering, and science, 12.6% education, legal, community service, arts, and media, 6.9% healthcare practitioners, 8.9% service, 27.8% sales and office, 3.3% natural resources, construction, and maintenance, 4.4% production, transportation, and material moving (2008-2012 5-year est.).
Income: Per capita income: $50,179 (2008-2012 5-year est.); Median household income: $102,523 (2008-2012 5-year est.); Average household income: $133,021 (2008-2012 5-year est.); Percent of households with income of $100,000 or more: 51.7% (2008-2012 5-year est.); Poverty rate: 4.0% (2008-2012 5-year est.).
Education: Percent of population age 25 and over with: High school diploma (including GED) or higher: 95.4% (2008-2012 5-year est.); Bachelor's degree or higher: 60.8% (2008-2012 5-year est.); Master's degree or higher: 25.0% (2008-2012 5-year est.).

School District(s)
CHSD 128 (09-12)
    2011-12 Enrollment: 3,404 . . . . (847) 247-4510
Libertyville SD 70 (PK-08)
    2011-12 Enrollment: 2,534 . . . . (847) 362-9695
Oak Grove SD 68 (PK-08)
    2011-12 Enrollment: 881 . . . . (847) 996-1400

Vocational/Technical School(s)
Tricoci University of Beauty Culture-Libertyville (Private, For-profit)
    Fall 2012 Enrollment: 157 . . . . (630) 528-3336
    2012-13 Tuition: $18,050

Housing: Homeownership rate: 77.7% (2008-2012 5-year est.); Median home value: $419,800 (2008-2012 5-year est.); Median contract rent: $936 per month (2008-2012 5-year est.); Median year structure built: 1975 (2008-2012 5-year est.).
Health Insurance: 88.3% Private; 18.9% Public; 4.2% None. (2008-2012 5-year est.)
Hospitals: Condell Medical Center (305 beds)
Safety: Violent crime rate: 2.5 per 10,000 population; Property crime rate: 153.4 per 10,000 population (2012).
Transportation: Commute to work: 82.8% car, 5.4% public transportation, 2.0% walk, 7.8% work from home (2008-2012 5-year est.); Travel time to work: 31.0% less than 15 minutes, 35.4% 15 to 30 minutes, 14.7% 30 to 45 minutes, 7.6% 45 to 60 minutes, 11.3% 60 minutes or more (2008-2012 5-year est.)
Additional Information Contacts
GLMV Chamber of Commerce . . . . (847) 680-0750
    http://www.glmvchamber.org
Village of Libertyville . . . . (847) 362-2430
    http://www.libertyville.com/index.htm

LINCOLNSHIRE (village). Covers a land area of 4.578 square miles and a water area of 0.094 square miles. Located at 42.20° N. Lat; 87.92° W. Long. Elevation is 659 feet.
History: Lincolnshire was incorporated on August 5, 1957, from the unincorporated Half Day area when land was purchased to build a residential subdivision. The community underwent an aggressive era of expansion from 1983 to the 1990s.
Population: 4,931 (1990); 6,108 (2000); 7,275 (2010); Density: 1,578.8 persons per square mile (2008-2012 5-year est.); Race: 92.6% White, 0.0% Black/African American, 5.2% Asian, 0.2% American Indian/Alaska Native, 0.0% Native Hawaiian/Other Pacific Islander, 2.0% Some other race, 2.0% Two or more races, 2.2% Hispanic of any race (2008-2012 5-year est.); Average household size: 2.33 (2008-2012 5-year est.); Median age: 52.2 (2008-2012 5-year est.); Males per 100 females: 92.0 (2008-2012 5-year est.); Marriage status: 17.6% never married, 61.8% now married, 13.1% widowed, 7.5% divorced (2008-2012 5-year est.); Foreign born: 11.6% (2008-2012 5-year est.); Ancestry (includes multiple ancestries): 22.8% German, 13.3% Irish, 13.3% Polish, 10.1% American, 9.0% Russian (2008-2012 5-year est.).
Economy: Single-family building permits issued: 9 (2013); Multi-family building permits issued: 0 (2013); Homeowner vacancy rate: 5.9%. Rental vacancy rate: 4.6%. (2008-2012 5-year est.); Employment by occupation: 33.1% management, business, and financial, 6.3% computer, engineering, and science, 14.5% education, legal, community service, arts, and media, 7.4% healthcare practitioners, 7.3% service, 28.3% sales and office, 1.1% natural resources, construction, and maintenance, 2.1% production, transportation, and material moving (2008-2012 5-year est.).
Income: Per capita income: $68,133 (2008-2012 5-year est.); Median household income: $109,783 (2008-2012 5-year est.); Average household income: $160,758 (2008-2012 5-year est.); Percent of households with

income of $100,000 or more: 53.2% (2008-2012 5-year est.); Poverty rate: 3.7% (2008-2012 5-year est.).
Education: Percent of population age 25 and over with: High school diploma (including GED) or higher: 96.3% (2008-2012 5-year est.); Bachelor's degree or higher: 68.5% (2008-2012 5-year est.); Master's degree or higher: 36.5% (2008-2012 5-year est.).

School District(s)
Adlai E Stevenson HSD 125 (09-12)
    2011-12 Enrollment: 4,118 . . . . (847) 415-4000
Lincolnshire-Prairieview SD 103 (PK-08)
    2011-12 Enrollment: 1,633 . . . . (847) 295-4030

Housing: Homeownership rate: 82.2% (2008-2012 5-year est.); Median home value: $533,100 (2008-2012 5-year est.); Median contract rent: $2,000+ per month (2008-2012 5-year est.); Median year structure built: 1988 (2008-2012 5-year est.).
Health Insurance: 89.1% Private; 30.5% Public; 2.9% None. (2008-2012 5-year est.)
Safety: Violent crime rate: 2.7 per 10,000 population; Property crime rate: 113.6 per 10,000 population (2012).
Transportation: Commute to work: 78.9% car, 8.8% public transportation, 0.7% walk, 11.6% work from home (2008-2012 5-year est.); Travel time to work: 20.1% less than 15 minutes, 36.5% 15 to 30 minutes, 21.9% 30 to 45 minutes, 6.4% 45 to 60 minutes, 15.1% 60 minutes or more (2008-2012 5-year est.)
Additional Information Contacts
Greater Lincolnshire Chamber of Commerce . . . . (847) 793-2409
Village of Lincolnshire . . . . (847) 883-8600
    http://www.village.lincolnshire.il.us

LINDENHURST (village). Covers a land area of 4.442 square miles and a water area of 0.334 square miles. Located at 42.42° N. Lat; 88.03° W. Long. Elevation is 797 feet.
Population: 8,038 (1990); 12,539 (2000); 14,462 (2010); Density: 3,244.9 persons per square mile (2008-2012 5-year est.); Race: 89.2% White, 2.1% Black/African American, 4.3% Asian, 0.0% American Indian/Alaska Native, 0.0% Native Hawaiian/Other Pacific Islander, 4.4% Some other race, 2.6% Two or more races, 7.8% Hispanic of any race (2008-2012 5-year est.); Average household size: 2.91 (2008-2012 5-year est.); Median age: 36.7 (2008-2012 5-year est.); Males per 100 females: 94.5 (2008-2012 5-year est.); Marriage status: 22.7% never married, 63.7% now married, 5.2% widowed, 8.4% divorced (2008-2012 5-year est.); Foreign born: 8.0% (2008-2012 5-year est.); Ancestry (includes multiple ancestries): 28.9% German, 20.7% Irish, 11.6% Polish, 9.9% English, 9.2% Italian (2008-2012 5-year est.).
Economy: Single-family building permits issued: 17 (2013); Multi-family building permits issued: 0 (2013); Homeowner vacancy rate: 2.7%. Rental vacancy rate: 1.5%. (2008-2012 5-year est.); Employment by occupation: 22.5% management, business, and financial, 7.7% computer, engineering, and science, 12.8% education, legal, community service, arts, and media, 4.2% healthcare practitioners, 11.8% service, 25.3% sales and office, 7.8% natural resources, construction, and maintenance, 7.8% production, transportation, and material moving (2008-2012 5-year est.).
Income: Per capita income: $36,182 (2008-2012 5-year est.); Median household income: $96,796 (2008-2012 5-year est.); Average household income: $104,394 (2008-2012 5-year est.); Percent of households with income of $100,000 or more: 47.4% (2008-2012 5-year est.); Poverty rate: 3.3% (2008-2012 5-year est.).
Education: Percent of population age 25 and over with: High school diploma (including GED) or higher: 94.8% (2008-2012 5-year est.); Bachelor's degree or higher: 43.4% (2008-2012 5-year est.); Master's degree or higher: 14.4% (2008-2012 5-year est.).

School District(s)
Lake Villa CCSD 41 (PK-08)
    2011-12 Enrollment: 3,108 . . . . (847) 245-8001
Millburn CCSD 24 (PK-08)
    2011-12 Enrollment: 1,541 . . . . (847) 356-8331

Housing: Homeownership rate: 90.8% (2008-2012 5-year est.); Median home value: $228,200 (2008-2012 5-year est.); Median contract rent: $1,174 per month (2008-2012 5-year est.); Median year structure built: 1990 (2008-2012 5-year est.).
Health Insurance: 88.5% Private; 13.6% Public; 6.4% None. (2008-2012 5-year est.)
Safety: Violent crime rate: 4.1 per 10,000 population; Property crime rate: 60.6 per 10,000 population (2012).

Transportation: Commute to work: 93.5% car, 2.1% public transportation, 0.3% walk, 3.5% work from home (2008-2012 5-year est.); Travel time to work: 13.1% less than 15 minutes, 26.4% 15 to 30 minutes, 30.4% 30 to 45 minutes, 13.6% 45 to 60 minutes, 16.6% 60 minutes or more (2008-2012 5-year est.)

Additional Information Contacts

Lindenhurst/Lake Villa Chamber of Commerce . . . . (847) 356-8446
  http://www.llvchamber.com
Village of Lindenhurst . . . . (847) 356-8252
  http://lindenhurstil.org

LONG GROVE (village). Aka Longgrove. Covers a land area of 12.476 square miles and a water area of 0.235 square miles. Located at 42.19° N. Lat; 88.01° W. Long. Elevation is 732 feet.

History: The village now has very strict building ordinances to preserve its "country atmosphere." There are no sidewalks, street lights or curbs throughout the villages many communities. The village was incorporated in 1956.

Population: 4,740 (1990); 6,735 (2000); 8,043 (2010); Density: 643.7 persons per square mile (2008-2012 5-year est.); Race: 80.5% White, 3.3% Black/African American, 12.2% Asian, 0.1% American Indian/Alaska Native, 0.2% Native Hawaiian/Other Pacific Islander, 3.7% Some other race, 2.9% Two or more races, 2.8% Hispanic of any race (2008-2012 5-year est.); Average household size: 3.25 (2008-2012 5-year est.); Median age: 44.3 (2008-2012 5-year est.); Males per 100 females: 96.7 (2008-2012 5-year est.); Marriage status: 22.8% never married, 69.5% now married, 4.2% widowed, 3.5% divorced (2008-2012 5-year est.); Foreign born: 19.3% (2008-2012 5-year est.); Ancestry (includes multiple ancestries): 19.6% German, 10.0% Polish, 9.4% Italian, 9.4% Irish, 8.5% American (2008-2012 5-year est.).

Economy: Single-family building permits issued: 30 (2013); Multi-family building permits issued: 0 (2013); Homeowner vacancy rate: 1.9%. Rental vacancy rate: 0.0%. (2008-2012 5-year est.); Employment by occupation: 35.7% management, business, and financial, 11.2% computer, engineering, and science, 8.3% education, legal, community service, arts, and media, 7.3% healthcare practitioners, 6.8% service, 25.4% sales and office, 1.8% natural resources, construction, and maintenance, 3.5% production, transportation, and material moving (2008-2012 5-year est.).

Income: Per capita income: $71,313 (2008-2012 5-year est.); Median household income: $191,522 (2008-2012 5-year est.); Average household income: $239,158 (2008-2012 5-year est.); Percent of households with income of $100,000 or more: 75.3% (2008-2012 5-year est.); Poverty rate: 1.8% (2008-2012 5-year est.).

Education: Percent of population age 25 and over with: High school diploma (including GED) or higher: 97.4% (2008-2012 5-year est.); Bachelor's degree or higher: 66.9% (2008-2012 5-year est.); Master's degree or higher: 33.7% (2008-2012 5-year est.).

School District(s)

Kildeer Countryside CCSD 96 (PK-08)
  2011-12 Enrollment: 3,134 . . . . (847) 459-4260

Housing: Homeownership rate: 98.1% (2008-2012 5-year est.); Median home value: $715,300 (2008-2012 5-year est.); Median contract rent: $2,000+ per month (2008-2012 5-year est.); Median year structure built: 1991 (2008-2012 5-year est.).

Health Insurance: 93.8% Private; 11.0% Public; 3.3% None. (2008-2012 5-year est.)

Transportation: Commute to work: 80.2% car, 6.0% public transportation, 0.2% walk, 11.5% work from home (2008-2012 5-year est.); Travel time to work: 12.9% less than 15 minutes, 29.8% 15 to 30 minutes, 29.4% 30 to 45 minutes, 9.6% 45 to 60 minutes, 18.4% 60 minutes or more (2008-2012 5-year est.)

Additional Information Contacts

Village of Long Grove . . . . (847) 634-9440
  http://www.longgrove.net

LONG LAKE (CDP). Covers a land area of 1.030 square miles and a water area of 0.601 square miles. Located at 42.37° N. Lat; 88.13° W. Long. Elevation is 751 feet.

Population: 2,888 (1990); 3,356 (2000); 3,515 (2010); Density: 3,389.8 persons per square mile (2008-2012 5-year est.); Race: 92.7% White, 0.6% Black/African American, 1.2% Asian, 1.5% American Indian/Alaska Native, 0.0% Native Hawaiian/Other Pacific Islander, 4.0% Some other race, 2.6% Two or more races, 23.3% Hispanic of any race (2008-2012 5-year est.); Average household size: 2.84 (2008-2012 5-year est.); Median age: 39.8 (2008-2012 5-year est.); Males per 100 females: 135.2

(2008-2012 5-year est.); Marriage status: 29.7% never married, 53.8% now married, 5.9% widowed, 10.6% divorced (2008-2012 5-year est.); Foreign born: 14.1% (2008-2012 5-year est.); Ancestry (includes multiple ancestries): 33.4% German, 10.7% Polish, 10.3% Irish, 7.1% Italian, 4.7% English (2008-2012 5-year est.).

Economy: Homeowner vacancy rate: 0.0%. Rental vacancy rate: 20.7%. (2008-2012 5-year est.); Employment by occupation: 8.8% management, business, and financial, 3.0% computer, engineering, and science, 3.1% education, legal, community service, arts, and media, 1.7% healthcare practitioners, 17.4% service, 35.8% sales and office, 14.9% natural resources, construction, and maintenance, 15.4% production, transportation, and material moving (2008-2012 5-year est.).

Income: Per capita income: $23,464 (2008-2012 5-year est.); Median household income: $56,917 (2008-2012 5-year est.); Average household income: $65,340 (2008-2012 5-year est.); Percent of households with income of $100,000 or more: 15.2% (2008-2012 5-year est.); Poverty rate: 10.2% (2008-2012 5-year est.).

Education: Percent of population age 25 and over with: High school diploma (including GED) or higher: 84.1% (2008-2012 5-year est.); Bachelor's degree or higher: 15.7% (2008-2012 5-year est.); Master's degree or higher: 5.3% (2008-2012 5-year est.).

Housing: Homeownership rate: 78.5% (2008-2012 5-year est.); Median home value: $158,700 (2008-2012 5-year est.); Median contract rent: $1,025 per month (2008-2012 5-year est.); Median year structure built: 1949 (2008-2012 5-year est.).

Health Insurance: 61.9% Private; 26.6% Public; 21.0% None. (2008-2012 5-year est.)

Transportation: Commute to work: 86.4% car, 8.4% public transportation, 0.0% walk, 2.9% work from home (2008-2012 5-year est.); Travel time to work: 15.0% less than 15 minutes, 18.5% 15 to 30 minutes, 33.4% 30 to 45 minutes, 14.5% 45 to 60 minutes, 18.5% 60 minutes or more (2008-2012 5-year est.)

METTAWA (village). Covers a land area of 5.314 square miles and a water area of 0.080 square miles. Located at 42.24° N. Lat; 87.92° W. Long. Elevation is 682 feet.

Population: 348 (1990); 367 (2000); 547 (2010); Density: 94.5 persons per square mile (2008-2012 5-year est.); Race: 89.0% White, 0.0% Black/African American, 5.4% Asian, 0.0% American Indian/Alaska Native, 0.0% Native Hawaiian/Other Pacific Islander, 5.6% Some other race, 4.6% Two or more races, 5.2% Hispanic of any race (2008-2012 5-year est.); Average household size: 2.66 (2008-2012 5-year est.); Median age: 47.1 (2008-2012 5-year est.); Males per 100 females: 95.3 (2008-2012 5-year est.); Marriage status: 11.6% never married, 75.5% now married, 6.6% widowed, 6.3% divorced (2008-2012 5-year est.); Foreign born: 14.7% (2008-2012 5-year est.); Ancestry (includes multiple ancestries): 26.1% Irish, 21.3% German, 11.4% English, 7.8% American, 7.6% Italian (2008-2012 5-year est.).

Economy: Single-family building permits issued: 1 (2013); Multi-family building permits issued: 0 (2013); Homeowner vacancy rate: 7.2%. Rental vacancy rate: 0.0%. (2008-2012 5-year est.); Employment by occupation: 29.4% management, business, and financial, 9.5% computer, engineering, and science, 10.4% education, legal, community service, arts, and media, 5.7% healthcare practitioners, 15.2% service, 25.6% sales and office, 0.9% natural resources, construction, and maintenance, 3.3% production, transportation, and material moving (2008-2012 5-year est.).

Income: Per capita income: $74,207 (2008-2012 5-year est.); Median household income: $138,229 (2008-2012 5-year est.); Average household income: $195,178 (2008-2012 5-year est.); Percent of households with income of $100,000 or more: 59.8% (2008-2012 5-year est.); Poverty rate: 5.0% (2008-2012 5-year est.).

Education: Percent of population age 25 and over with: High school diploma (including GED) or higher: 97.2% (2008-2012 5-year est.); Bachelor's degree or higher: 65.4% (2008-2012 5-year est.); Master's degree or higher: 16.8% (2008-2012 5-year est.).

Housing: Homeownership rate: 92.1% (2008-2012 5-year est.); Median home value: $825,600 (2008-2012 5-year est.); Median contract rent: $981 per month (2008-2012 5-year est.); Median year structure built: 1986 (2008-2012 5-year est.).

Health Insurance: 87.6% Private; 23.1% Public; 2.0% None. (2008-2012 5-year est.)

Transportation: Commute to work: 77.9% car, 4.8% public transportation, 1.4% walk, 15.9% work from home (2008-2012 5-year est.); Travel time to work: 23.4% less than 15 minutes, 31.4% 15 to 30 minutes, 21.1% 30 to

45 minutes, 8.6% 45 to 60 minutes, 15.4% 60 minutes or more (2008-2012 5-year est.)

MUNDELEIN (village). Covers a land area of 9.565 square miles and a water area of 0.399 square miles. Located at 42.27° N. Lat; 88.01° W. Long. Elevation is 735 feet.

History: Named for Cardinal George William Mundelein (1872-1939), Archbishop of Chicago. The community here developed around the Sheldon School of Business Administration and was called Area, a reflection of the school's motto of "Ability, Reliability, Endurance, and Action." When this school was replaced by a Catholic seminary, the town name was changed to Mundelein for George Cardinal Mundelein, Archbishop of Chicago.

Population: 21,215 (1990); 30,935 (2000); 31,064 (2010); Density: 3,293.9 persons per square mile (2008-2012 5-year est.); Race: 82.8% White, 1.3% Black/African American, 8.1% Asian, 0.2% American Indian/Alaska Native, 0.0% Native Hawaiian/Other Pacific Islander, 7.6% Some other race, 1.0% Two or more races, 30.8% Hispanic of any race (2008-2012 5-year est.); Average household size: 2.93 (2008-2012 5-year est.); Median age: 36.6 (2008-2012 5-year est.); Males per 100 females: 107.3 (2008-2012 5-year est.); Marriage status: 29.1% never married, 59.8% now married, 4.0% widowed, 7.2% divorced (2008-2012 5-year est.); Foreign born: 29.3% (2008-2012 5-year est.); Ancestry (includes multiple ancestries): 19.2% German, 9.6% Polish, 9.5% Irish, 7.0% American, 5.6% Italian (2008-2012 5-year est.).

Economy: Unemployment rate: 7.3% (April 2014); Total civilian labor force: 16,777 (April 2014); Single-family building permits issued: 84 (2013); Multi-family building permits issued: 0 (2013); Homeowner vacancy rate: 1.2%. Rental vacancy rate: 9.4%. (2008-2012 5-year est.); Employment by occupation: 15.2% management, business, and financial, 8.2% computer, engineering, and science, 10.3% education, legal, community service, arts, and media, 2.7% healthcare practitioners, 16.6% service, 27.3% sales and office, 6.8% natural resources, construction, and maintenance, 13.0% production, transportation, and material moving (2008-2012 5-year est.).

Income: Per capita income: $35,422 (2008-2012 5-year est.); Median household income: $80,082 (2008-2012 5-year est.); Average household income: $102,584 (2008-2012 5-year est.); Percent of households with income of $100,000 or more: 39.2% (2008-2012 5-year est.); Poverty rate: 5.4% (2008-2012 5-year est.).

Education: Percent of population age 25 and over with: High school diploma (including GED) or higher: 85.6% (2008-2012 5-year est.); Bachelor's degree or higher: 40.5% (2008-2012 5-year est.); Master's degree or higher: 14.5% (2008-2012 5-year est.).

School District(s)

Diamond Lake SD 76 (PK-08)
    2011-12 Enrollment: 1,116 . . . . (847) 566-9221
Fremont SD 79 (PK-08)
    2011-12 Enrollment: 2,206 . . . . (847) 566-0169
Mundelein Cons HSD 120 (09-12)
    2011-12 Enrollment: 2,251 . . . . (847) 949-2200
Mundelein ESD 75 (PK-08)
    2011-12 Enrollment: 1,720 . . . . (847) 949-2700
Spec Educ Dist Lake County/sedol
    2011-12 Enrollment: n/a . . . . (847) 548-8470

Four-year College(s)

University of Saint Mary of the Lake (Private, Not-for-profit, Roman Catholic)
    Fall 2012 Enrollment: 215 . . . . (847) 566-6401

Housing: Homeownership rate: 79.5% (2008-2012 5-year est.); Median home value: $241,600 (2008-2012 5-year est.); Median contract rent: $986 per month (2008-2012 5-year est.); Median year structure built: 1982 (2008-2012 5-year est.).

Health Insurance: 72.3% Private; 19.6% Public; 15.7% None. (2008-2012 5-year est.)

Safety: Violent crime rate: 8.3 per 10,000 population; Property crime rate: 108.0 per 10,000 population (2012).

Transportation: Commute to work: 89.3% car, 2.8% public transportation, 0.8% walk, 5.0% work from home (2008-2012 5-year est.); Travel time to work: 26.3% less than 15 minutes, 26.8% 15 to 30 minutes, 23.1% 30 to 45 minutes, 11.6% 45 to 60 minutes, 12.2% 60 minutes or more (2008-2012 5-year est.)

Additional Information Contacts

GLMV Chamber of Commerce . . . . (847) 680-0750
    http://www.glmvchamber.org

Village of Mundelein . . . . (847) 949-3200
    http://www.mundelein-il.org

NORTH BARRINGTON (village). Covers a land area of 4.638 square miles and a water area of 0.256 square miles. Located at 42.21° N. Lat; 88.13° W. Long. Elevation is 791 feet.

History: The first settlers arrived in the 1830s and in 1854 the Chicago & Northwestern Railroad built its first station in the Village of Barrington. Subsequent generations have been attracted to the area by its appealing natural resources, and its accessibility to the metropolitan area, which provides a unique opportunity for countryside living with a proximity to urban development.

Population: 1,787 (1990); 2,918 (2000); 3,047 (2010); Density: 714.3 persons per square mile (2008-2012 5-year est.); Race: 93.6% White, 0.0% Black/African American, 3.4% Asian, 0.1% American Indian/Alaska Native, 0.0% Native Hawaiian/Other Pacific Islander, 2.9% Some other race, 0.9% Two or more races, 3.7% Hispanic of any race (2008-2012 5-year est.); Average household size: 2.94 (2008-2012 5-year est.); Median age: 46.4 (2008-2012 5-year est.); Males per 100 females: 81.9 (2008-2012 5-year est.); Marriage status: 19.9% never married, 70.9% now married, 2.7% widowed, 6.4% divorced (2008-2012 5-year est.); Foreign born: 8.0% (2008-2012 5-year est.); Ancestry (includes multiple ancestries): 20.0% German, 18.9% Irish, 13.8% English, 12.1% Italian, 11.1% Polish (2008-2012 5-year est.).

Economy: Single-family building permits issued: 1 (2013); Multi-family building permits issued: 0 (2013); Homeowner vacancy rate: 2.6%. Rental vacancy rate: 0.0%. (2008-2012 5-year est.); Employment by occupation: 38.8% management, business, and financial, 4.7% computer, engineering, and science, 11.1% education, legal, community service, arts, and media, 10.6% healthcare practitioners, 5.3% service, 24.6% sales and office, 3.2% natural resources, construction, and maintenance, 1.6% production, transportation, and material moving (2008-2012 5-year est.).

Income: Per capita income: $83,921 (2008-2012 5-year est.); Median household income: $152,917 (2008-2012 5-year est.); Average household income: $243,875 (2008-2012 5-year est.); Percent of households with income of $100,000 or more: 68.1% (2008-2012 5-year est.); Poverty rate: 2.7% (2008-2012 5-year est.).

Education: Percent of population age 25 and over with: High school diploma (including GED) or higher: 97.9% (2008-2012 5-year est.); Bachelor's degree or higher: 70.2% (2008-2012 5-year est.); Master's degree or higher: 26.1% (2008-2012 5-year est.).

Housing: Homeownership rate: 96.6% (2008-2012 5-year est.); Median home value: $764,000 (2008-2012 5-year est.); Median contract rent: $1,150 per month (2008-2012 5-year est.); Median year structure built: 1984 (2008-2012 5-year est.).

Health Insurance: 89.6% Private; 16.5% Public; 5.0% None. (2008-2012 5-year est.)

Transportation: Commute to work: 78.1% car, 9.3% public transportation, 1.0% walk, 8.1% work from home (2008-2012 5-year est.); Travel time to work: 18.8% less than 15 minutes, 20.3% 15 to 30 minutes, 27.6% 30 to 45 minutes, 13.7% 45 to 60 minutes, 19.7% 60 minutes or more (2008-2012 5-year est.)

NORTH CHICAGO (city). Covers a land area of 7.899 square miles and a water area of 0.015 square miles. Located at 42.32° N. Lat; 87.86° W. Long. Elevation is 659 feet.

History: Named for its location north of Chicago. A sit-down strike at a steel plant here in 1937 led to a U.S. Supreme Court decision (1939) ruling sit-down strikes illegal. Incorporated 1895.

Population: 34,978 (1990); 35,918 (2000); 32,574 (2010); Density: 4,010.3 persons per square mile (2008-2012 5-year est.); Race: 44.9% White, 31.5% Black/African American, 4.1% Asian, 0.5% American Indian/Alaska Native, 0.0% Native Hawaiian/Other Pacific Islander, 19.0% Some other race, 4.8% Two or more races, 28.0% Hispanic of any race (2008-2012 5-year est.); Average household size: 3.02 (2008-2012 5-year est.); Median age: 24.1 (2008-2012 5-year est.); Males per 100 females: 157.8 (2008-2012 5-year est.); Marriage status: 58.1% never married, 32.0% now married, 3.0% widowed, 7.0% divorced (2008-2012 5-year est.); Foreign born: 18.0% (2008-2012 5-year est.); Ancestry (includes multiple ancestries): 9.0% German, 8.9% Irish, 3.9% Italian, 2.8% Polish, 2.6% English (2008-2012 5-year est.).

Economy: Unemployment rate: 10.1% (April 2014); Total civilian labor force: 8,345 (April 2014); Single-family building permits issued: 0 (2013); Multi-family building permits issued: 0 (2013); Homeowner vacancy rate: 2.5%. Rental vacancy rate: 5.8%. (2008-2012 5-year est.); Employment by

occupation: 8.6% management, business, and financial, 4.3% computer, engineering, and science, 8.9% education, legal, community service, arts, and media, 3.6% healthcare practitioners, 24.4% service, 22.0% sales and office, 8.4% natural resources, construction, and maintenance, 19.7% production, transportation, and material moving (2008-2012 5-year est.).
Income: Per capita income: $18,012 (2008-2012 5-year est.); Median household income: $45,684 (2008-2012 5-year est.); Average household income: $55,008 (2008-2012 5-year est.); Percent of households with income of $100,000 or more: 12.9% (2008-2012 5-year est.); Poverty rate: 23.5% (2008-2012 5-year est.).
Taxes: Total city taxes per capita: $328 (2011); City property taxes per capita: $203 (2011).
Education: Percent of population age 25 and over with: High school diploma (including GED) or higher: 78.4% (2008-2012 5-year est.); Bachelor's degree or higher: 19.3% (2008-2012 5-year est.); Master's degree or higher: 5.0% (2008-2012 5-year est.).

School District(s)
North Chicago SD 187 (PK-12)
   2011-12 Enrollment: 3,837 . . . . (847) 689-8150

Four-year College(s)
Rosalind Franklin University of Medicine and Science (Private, Not-for-profit)
   Fall 2012 Enrollment: 2,084 . . . . (847) 578-3000
Housing: Homeownership rate: 37.0% (2008-2012 5-year est.); Median home value: $135,700 (2008-2012 5-year est.); Median contract rent: $860 per month (2008-2012 5-year est.); Median year structure built: 1971 (2008-2012 5-year est.).
Health Insurance: 46.6% Private; 38.6% Public; 21.7% None. (2008-2012 5-year est.)
Hospitals: North Chicago VA Medical Center
Safety: Violent crime rate: 24.5 per 10,000 population; Property crime rate: 58.4 per 10,000 population (2012).
Transportation: Commute to work: 48.1% car, 2.5% public transportation, 32.2% walk, 15.8% work from home (2008-2012 5-year est.); Travel time to work: 55.4% less than 15 minutes, 25.6% 15 to 30 minutes, 10.2% 30 to 45 minutes, 4.4% 45 to 60 minutes, 4.4% 60 minutes or more (2008-2012 5-year est.)
Additional Information Contacts
City of North Chicago . . . . (847) 596-8600
   http://www.northchicago.org
North Chicago Chamber of Commerce . . . . (847) 785-1912
   http://www.northchicagochamber.org

OLD MILL CREEK (village). Aka Mill Creek. Covers a land area of 10.631 square miles and a water area of 0.174 square miles. Located at 42.43° N. Lat; 87.98° W. Long. Elevation is 705 feet.
Population: 73 (1990); 251 (2000); 178 (2010); Density: 13.5 persons per square mile (2008-2012 5-year est.); Race: 94.4% White, 0.0% Black/African American, 0.0% Asian, 0.0% American Indian/Alaska Native, 0.0% Native Hawaiian/Other Pacific Islander, 5.6% Some other race, 3.5% Two or more races, 9.7% Hispanic of any race (2008-2012 5-year est.); Average household size: 1.64 (2008-2012 5-year est.); Median age: 48.7 (2008-2012 5-year est.); Males per 100 females: 171.7 (2008-2012 5-year est.); Marriage status: 29.6% never married, 32.0% now married, 8.0% widowed, 30.4% divorced (2008-2012 5-year est.); Foreign born: 11.1% (2008-2012 5-year est.); Ancestry (includes multiple ancestries): 28.5% German, 14.6% Irish, 9.0% European, 9.0% Norwegian, 7.6% Dutch (2008-2012 5-year est.).
Economy: Single-family building permits issued: 0 (2013); Multi-family building permits issued: 0 (2013); Homeowner vacancy rate: 0.0%. Rental vacancy rate: 0.0%. (2008-2012 5-year est.); Employment by occupation: 15.2% management, business, and financial, 4.5% computer, engineering, and science, 12.1% education, legal, community service, arts, and media, 0.0% healthcare practitioners, 27.3% service, 25.8% sales and office, 10.6% natural resources, construction, and maintenance, 4.5% production, transportation, and material moving (2008-2012 5-year est.).
Income: Per capita income: $66,546 (2008-2012 5-year est.); Median household income: $72,857 (2008-2012 5-year est.); Average household income: $106,861 (2008-2012 5-year est.); Percent of households with income of $100,000 or more: 36.3% (2008-2012 5-year est.); Poverty rate: 13.9% (2008-2012 5-year est.).
Education: Percent of population age 25 and over with: High school diploma (including GED) or higher: 97.5% (2008-2012 5-year est.); Bachelor's degree or higher: 45.4% (2008-2012 5-year est.); Master's degree or higher: 27.7% (2008-2012 5-year est.).

School District(s)
Millburn CCSD 24 (PK-08)
   2011-12 Enrollment: 1,541 . . . . (847) 356-8331
Housing: Homeownership rate: 53.4% (2008-2012 5-year est.); Median home value: $875,000 (2008-2012 5-year est.); Median contract rent: $850 per month (2008-2012 5-year est.); Median year structure built: Before 1940 (2008-2012 5-year est.).
Health Insurance: 78.5% Private; 20.1% Public; 17.4% None. (2008-2012 5-year est.)
Transportation: Commute to work: 74.2% car, 0.0% public transportation, 4.5% walk, 21.2% work from home (2008-2012 5-year est.); Travel time to work: 28.8% less than 15 minutes, 46.2% 15 to 30 minutes, 15.4% 30 to 45 minutes, 3.8% 45 to 60 minutes, 5.8% 60 minutes or more (2008-2012 5-year est.)

PARK CITY (city). Covers a land area of 1.185 square miles and a water area of 0.002 square miles. Located at 42.35° N. Lat; 87.89° W. Long. Elevation is 699 feet.
Population: 4,677 (1990); 6,637 (2000); 7,570 (2010); Density: 6,227.8 persons per square mile (2008-2012 5-year est.); Race: 51.2% White, 9.2% Black/African American, 7.8% Asian, 1.0% American Indian/Alaska Native, 0.0% Native Hawaiian/Other Pacific Islander, 30.8% Some other race, 7.8% Two or more races, 59.0% Hispanic of any race (2008-2012 5-year est.); Average household size: 2.86 (2008-2012 5-year est.); Median age: 29.4 (2008-2012 5-year est.); Males per 100 females: 86.0 (2008-2012 5-year est.); Marriage status: 30.9% never married, 53.6% now married, 3.6% widowed, 11.9% divorced (2008-2012 5-year est.); Foreign born: 37.7% (2008-2012 5-year est.); Ancestry (includes multiple ancestries): 7.7% German, 3.3% Irish, 2.3% Polish, 2.0% Italian, 2.0% American (2008-2012 5-year est.).
Economy: Single-family building permits issued: 0 (2013); Multi-family building permits issued: 0 (2013); Homeowner vacancy rate: 0.0%. Rental vacancy rate: 0.0%. (2008-2012 5-year est.); Employment by occupation: 8.4% management, business, and financial, 3.4% computer, engineering, and science, 1.9% education, legal, community service, arts, and media, 3.0% healthcare practitioners, 26.0% service, 18.1% sales and office, 10.6% natural resources, construction, and maintenance, 28.6% production, transportation, and material moving (2008-2012 5-year est.).
Income: Per capita income: $17,123 (2008-2012 5-year est.); Median household income: $41,901 (2008-2012 5-year est.); Average household income: $48,235 (2008-2012 5-year est.); Percent of households with income of $100,000 or more: 6.6% (2008-2012 5-year est.); Poverty rate: 16.1% (2008-2012 5-year est.).
Education: Percent of population age 25 and over with: High school diploma (including GED) or higher: 66.7% (2008-2012 5-year est.); Bachelor's degree or higher: 10.0% (2008-2012 5-year est.); Master's degree or higher: 3.4% (2008-2012 5-year est.).
Housing: Homeownership rate: 47.8% (2008-2012 5-year est.); Median home value: $25,900 (2008-2012 5-year est.); Median contract rent: $686 per month (2008-2012 5-year est.); Median year structure built: 1985 (2008-2012 5-year est.).
Health Insurance: 40.6% Private; 36.7% Public; 27.8% None. (2008-2012 5-year est.)
Transportation: Commute to work: 93.2% car, 1.7% public transportation, 2.2% walk, 2.8% work from home (2008-2012 5-year est.); Travel time to work: 34.6% less than 15 minutes, 27.4% 15 to 30 minutes, 27.8% 30 to 45 minutes, 4.4% 45 to 60 minutes, 5.8% 60 minutes or more (2008-2012 5-year est.)

RIVERWOODS (village). Covers a land area of 3.966 square miles and a water area of 0.046 square miles. Located at 42.17° N. Lat; 87.89° W. Long. Elevation is 656 feet.
History: Riverwoods was established on the banks of the Des Plaines River in 1949 by local steel magnate Edward L. Ryerson. Orphans of the Storm, an animal shelter founded in 1928 by famous dancer Irene Castle ia also a notable addition to this area.
Population: 2,868 (1990); 3,843 (2000); 3,660 (2010); Density: 971.9 persons per square mile (2008-2012 5-year est.); Race: 90.5% White, 0.2% Black/African American, 5.6% Asian, 1.4% American Indian/Alaska Native, 0.0% Native Hawaiian/Other Pacific Islander, 2.3% Some other race, 1.8% Two or more races, 1.8% Hispanic of any race (2008-2012 5-year est.); Average household size: 3.07 (2008-2012 5-year est.); Median age: 45.7 (2008-2012 5-year est.); Males per 100 females: 95.0 (2008-2012 5-year est.); Marriage status: 14.7% never married, 78.9% now married, 3.9% widowed, 2.6% divorced (2008-2012 5-year est.);

Foreign born: 10.6% (2008-2012 5-year est.); Ancestry (includes multiple ancestries): 14.9% Russian, 13.9% German, 13.3% Polish, 9.2% Irish, 8.0% American (2008-2012 5-year est.).

Economy: Single-family building permits issued: 2 (2013); Multi-family building permits issued: 0 (2013); Homeowner vacancy rate: 0.0%. Rental vacancy rate: 0.0%. (2008-2012 5-year est.); Employment by occupation: 34.1% management, business, and financial, 4.1% computer, engineering, and science, 21.1% education, legal, community service, arts, and media, 6.2% healthcare practitioners, 3.7% service, 25.3% sales and office, 2.3% natural resources, construction, and maintenance, 3.1% production, transportation, and material moving (2008-2012 5-year est.).

Income: Per capita income: $72,637 (2008-2012 5-year est.); Median household income: $166,579 (2008-2012 5-year est.); Average household income: $224,968 (2008-2012 5-year est.); Percent of households with income of $100,000 or more: 74.4% (2008-2012 5-year est.); Poverty rate: 1.5% (2008-2012 5-year est.).

Education: Percent of population age 25 and over with: High school diploma (including GED) or higher: 98.3% (2008-2012 5-year est.); Bachelor's degree or higher: 68.1% (2008-2012 5-year est.); Master's degree or higher: 34.3% (2008-2012 5-year est.).

Housing: Homeownership rate: 99.4% (2008-2012 5-year est.); Median home value: $758,500 (2008-2012 5-year est.); Median contract rent: $2,000+ per month (2008-2012 5-year est.); Median year structure built: 1978 (2008-2012 5-year est.).

Health Insurance: 90.3% Private; 17.0% Public; 3.3% None. (2008-2012 5-year est.)

Safety: Violent crime rate: 2.7 per 10,000 population; Property crime rate: 62.6 per 10,000 population (2012).

Transportation: Commute to work: 72.1% car, 8.0% public transportation, 0.3% walk, 18.5% work from home (2008-2012 5-year est.); Travel time to work: 26.8% less than 15 minutes, 37.0% 15 to 30 minutes, 16.5% 30 to 45 minutes, 6.4% 45 to 60 minutes, 13.3% 60 minutes or more (2008-2012 5-year est.)

Additional Information Contacts
DBR Chamber of Commerce . . . . (847) 945-4660
   http://www.dbrchamber.com

ROUND LAKE (village). Covers a land area of 5.466 square miles and a water area of 0.165 square miles. Located at 42.34° N. Lat; 88.10° W. Long. Elevation is 797 feet.

Population: 3,550 (1990); 5,842 (2000); 18,289 (2010); Density: 3,251.5 persons per square mile (2008-2012 5-year est.); Race: 72.5% White, 7.0% Black/African American, 10.4% Asian, 0.0% American Indian/Alaska Native, 0.0% Native Hawaiian/Other Pacific Islander, 10.1% Some other race, 4.5% Two or more races, 23.8% Hispanic of any race (2008-2012 5-year est.); Average household size: 3.10 (2008-2012 5-year est.); Median age: 31.7 (2008-2012 5-year est.); Males per 100 females: 95.8 (2008-2012 5-year est.); Marriage status: 26.3% never married, 63.0% now married, 2.9% widowed, 7.8% divorced (2008-2012 5-year est.); Foreign born: 24.1% (2008-2012 5-year est.); Ancestry (includes multiple ancestries): 17.9% German, 11.7% Irish, 9.0% Polish, 6.4% Italian, 4.9% English (2008-2012 5-year est.).

Economy: Single-family building permits issued: 30 (2013); Multi-family building permits issued: 0 (2013); Homeowner vacancy rate: 1.8%. Rental vacancy rate: 10.2%. (2008-2012 5-year est.); Employment by occupation: 18.9% management, business, and financial, 8.6% computer, engineering, and science, 10.6% education, legal, community service, arts, and media, 4.9% healthcare practitioners, 16.2% service, 22.6% sales and office, 6.0% natural resources, construction, and maintenance, 12.1% production, transportation, and material moving (2008-2012 5-year est.).

Income: Per capita income: $29,945 (2008-2012 5-year est.); Median household income: $80,954 (2008-2012 5-year est.); Average household income: $92,144 (2008-2012 5-year est.); Percent of households with income of $100,000 or more: 38.4% (2008-2012 5-year est.); Poverty rate: 8.1% (2008-2012 5-year est.).

Education: Percent of population age 25 and over with: High school diploma (including GED) or higher: 85.8% (2008-2012 5-year est.); Bachelor's degree or higher: 38.3% (2008-2012 5-year est.); Master's degree or higher: 11.8% (2008-2012 5-year est.).

School District(s)
Grayslake CCSD 46 (PK-08)
   2011-12 Enrollment: 4,125 . . . . (847) 223-3650
Round Lake CUSD 116 (PK-12)
   2011-12 Enrollment: 7,217 . . . . (847) 270-9001

Housing: Homeownership rate: 80.3% (2008-2012 5-year est.); Median home value: $203,100 (2008-2012 5-year est.); Median contract rent: $944 per month (2008-2012 5-year est.); Median year structure built: 2002 (2008-2012 5-year est.).

Health Insurance: 68.8% Private; 22.6% Public; 13.3% None. (2008-2012 5-year est.)

Safety: Violent crime rate: 15.2 per 10,000 population; Property crime rate: 100.1 per 10,000 population (2012).

Transportation: Commute to work: 90.9% car, 3.3% public transportation, 1.0% walk, 3.4% work from home (2008-2012 5-year est.); Travel time to work: 12.5% less than 15 minutes, 23.1% 15 to 30 minutes, 21.7% 30 to 45 minutes, 20.2% 45 to 60 minutes, 22.4% 60 minutes or more (2008-2012 5-year est.)

Additional Information Contacts
Round Lake Area Chamber of Commerce & Industry . . . . . (847) 546-2002
   http://www.rlchamber.org
Village of Round Lake . . . . (847) 546-5400
   http://www.eroundlake.com

ROUND LAKE BEACH (village). Covers a land area of 5.063 square miles and a water area of 0.154 square miles. Located at 42.38° N. Lat; 88.08° W. Long. Elevation is 764 feet.

History: Named for a small round lake close to the city. Incorporated 1937.

Population: 16,434 (1990); 25,859 (2000); 28,175 (2010); Density: 5,556.9 persons per square mile (2008-2012 5-year est.); Race: 85.0% White, 3.4% Black/African American, 2.7% Asian, 0.6% American Indian/Alaska Native, 0.0% Native Hawaiian/Other Pacific Islander, 8.3% Some other race, 2.5% Two or more races, 51.1% Hispanic of any race (2008-2012 5-year est.); Average household size: 3.45 (2008-2012 5-year est.); Median age: 29.4 (2008-2012 5-year est.); Males per 100 females: 96.2 (2008-2012 5-year est.); Marriage status: 32.9% never married, 55.0% now married, 4.1% widowed, 8.0% divorced (2008-2012 5-year est.); Foreign born: 29.9% (2008-2012 5-year est.); Ancestry (includes multiple ancestries): 14.4% German, 9.2% Irish, 8.8% Polish, 3.6% Italian, 3.3% English (2008-2012 5-year est.).

Economy: Unemployment rate: 10.4% (April 2014); Total civilian labor force: 14,992 (April 2014); Single-family building permits issued: 0 (2013); Multi-family building permits issued: 0 (2013); Homeowner vacancy rate: 3.0%. Rental vacancy rate: 8.3%. (2008-2012 5-year est.); Employment by occupation: 8.5% management, business, and financial, 4.0% computer, engineering, and science, 6.0% education, legal, community service, arts, and media, 2.9% healthcare practitioners, 21.9% service, 26.7% sales and office, 9.5% natural resources, construction, and maintenance, 20.6% production, transportation, and material moving (2008-2012 5-year est.).

Income: Per capita income: $20,266 (2008-2012 5-year est.); Median household income: $60,864 (2008-2012 5-year est.); Average household income: $68,382 (2008-2012 5-year est.); Percent of households with income of $100,000 or more: 19.7% (2008-2012 5-year est.); Poverty rate: 16.9% (2008-2012 5-year est.).

Taxes: Total city taxes per capita: $375 (2011); City property taxes per capita: $303 (2011).

Education: Percent of population age 25 and over with: High school diploma (including GED) or higher: 72.8% (2008-2012 5-year est.); Bachelor's degree or higher: 15.4% (2008-2012 5-year est.); Master's degree or higher: 5.7% (2008-2012 5-year est.).

School District(s)
Grayslake CCSD 46 (PK-08)
   2011-12 Enrollment: 4,125 . . . . (847) 223-3650
Round Lake CUSD 116 (PK-12)
   2011-12 Enrollment: 7,217 . . . . (847) 270-9001

Housing: Homeownership rate: 81.7% (2008-2012 5-year est.); Median home value: $155,000 (2008-2012 5-year est.); Median contract rent: $862 per month (2008-2012 5-year est.); Median year structure built: 1985 (2008-2012 5-year est.).

Health Insurance: 57.4% Private; 26.4% Public; 19.8% None. (2008-2012 5-year est.)

Safety: Violent crime rate: 12.4 per 10,000 population; Property crime rate: 267.8 per 10,000 population (2012).

Transportation: Commute to work: 93.7% car, 2.5% public transportation, 1.7% walk, 1.8% work from home (2008-2012 5-year est.); Travel time to work: 16.4% less than 15 minutes, 30.6% 15 to 30 minutes, 26.4% 30 to 45 minutes, 12.5% 45 to 60 minutes, 14.1% 60 minutes or more (2008-2012 5-year est.)

Additional Information Contacts

Round Lake Area Chamber of Commerce & Industry . . . . . (847) 546-2002
http://www.rlchamber.org
Village of Round Lake Beach . . . . (847) 546-2351
http://www.villageofroundlakebeach.com

ROUND LAKE HEIGHTS (village). Aka Indian Hills. Covers a land area of 0.565 square miles and a water area of 0.037 square miles. Located at 42.38° N. Lat; 88.11° W. Long. Elevation is 784 feet.

Population: 1,251 (1990); 1,347 (2000); 2,676 (2010); Density: 4,985.0 persons per square mile (2008-2012 5-year est.); Race: 79.9% White, 3.3% Black/African American, 8.0% Asian, 0.6% American Indian/Alaska Native, 0.0% Native Hawaiian/Other Pacific Islander, 8.2% Some other race, 2.0% Two or more races, 35.8% Hispanic of any race (2008-2012 5-year est.); Average household size: 3.37 (2008-2012 5-year est.); Median age: 32.4 (2008-2012 5-year est.); Males per 100 females: 102.2 (2008-2012 5-year est.); Marriage status: 28.0% never married, 59.8% now married, 5.1% widowed, 7.1% divorced (2008-2012 5-year est.); Foreign born: 23.4% (2008-2012 5-year est.); Ancestry (includes multiple ancestries): 19.0% German, 13.0% Polish, 12.0% Irish, 6.1% Italian, 3.8% English (2008-2012 5-year est.).
Economy: Single-family building permits issued: 0 (2013); Multi-family building permits issued: 0 (2013); Homeowner vacancy rate: 1.6%. Rental vacancy rate: 6.8%. (2008-2012 5-year est.); Employment by occupation: 15.0% management, business, and financial, 6.4% computer, engineering, and science, 5.4% education, legal, community service, arts, and media, 2.9% healthcare practitioners, 17.5% service, 27.1% sales and office, 9.2% natural resources, construction, and maintenance, 16.4% production, transportation, and material moving (2008-2012 5-year est.).
Income: Per capita income: $22,339 (2008-2012 5-year est.); Median household income: $64,038 (2008-2012 5-year est.); Average household income: $73,244 (2008-2012 5-year est.); Percent of households with income of $100,000 or more: 26.2% (2008-2012 5-year est.); Poverty rate: 7.7% (2008-2012 5-year est.).
Education: Percent of population age 25 and over with: High school diploma (including GED) or higher: 77.0% (2008-2012 5-year est.); Bachelor's degree or higher: 20.4% (2008-2012 5-year est.); Master's degree or higher: 7.3% (2008-2012 5-year est.).
School District(s)
Round Lake CUSD 116 (PK-12)
    2011-12 Enrollment: 7,217 . . . . (847) 270-9001
Housing: Homeownership rate: 85.2% (2008-2012 5-year est.); Median home value: $165,300 (2008-2012 5-year est.); Median contract rent: $843 per month (2008-2012 5-year est.); Median year structure built: 1993 (2008-2012 5-year est.).
Health Insurance: 62.9% Private; 25.6% Public; 16.6% None. (2008-2012 5-year est.)
Transportation: Commute to work: 92.2% car, 3.4% public transportation, 0.0% walk, 4.5% work from home (2008-2012 5-year est.); Travel time to work: 11.3% less than 15 minutes, 23.9% 15 to 30 minutes, 26.9% 30 to 45 minutes, 21.1% 45 to 60 minutes, 16.8% 60 minutes or more (2008-2012 5-year est.)
Additional Information Contacts
Round Lake Area Chamber of Commerce & Industry . . . . . (847) 546-2002
http://www.rlchamber.org

ROUND LAKE PARK (village). Covers a land area of 2.078 square miles and a water area of 0.200 square miles. Located at 42.35° N. Lat; 88.08° W. Long. Elevation is 791 feet.

History: Incorporated 1947.
Population: 4,045 (1990); 6,038 (2000); 7,505 (2010); Density: 3,552.8 persons per square mile (2008-2012 5-year est.); Race: 86.1% White, 2.5% Black/African American, 1.1% Asian, 1.2% American Indian/Alaska Native, 0.0% Native Hawaiian/Other Pacific Islander, 9.1% Some other race, 3.4% Two or more races, 46.6% Hispanic of any race (2008-2012 5-year est.); Average household size: 2.71 (2008-2012 5-year est.); Median age: 40.4 (2008-2012 5-year est.); Males per 100 females: 111.8 (2008-2012 5-year est.); Marriage status: 22.8% never married, 57.6% now married, 8.7% widowed, 10.9% divorced (2008-2012 5-year est.); Foreign born: 27.7% (2008-2012 5-year est.); Ancestry (includes multiple ancestries): 20.8% German, 14.4% Irish, 6.5% Polish, 6.1% Italian, 4.5% English (2008-2012 5-year est.).
Economy: Single-family building permits issued: 3 (2013); Multi-family building permits issued: 0 (2013); Homeowner vacancy rate: 5.0%. Rental vacancy rate: 0.0%. (2008-2012 5-year est.); Employment by occupation: 7.7% management, business, and financial, 2.2% computer, engineering,

and science, 0.9% education, legal, community service, arts, and media, 1.9% healthcare practitioners, 28.7% service, 29.8% sales and office, 11.8% natural resources, construction, and maintenance, 17.1% production, transportation, and material moving (2008-2012 5-year est.).
Income: Per capita income: $19,323 (2008-2012 5-year est.); Median household income: $43,085 (2008-2012 5-year est.); Average household income: $51,089 (2008-2012 5-year est.); Percent of households with income of $100,000 or more: 8.7% (2008-2012 5-year est.); Poverty rate: 18.2% (2008-2012 5-year est.).
Education: Percent of population age 25 and over with: High school diploma (including GED) or higher: 73.0% (2008-2012 5-year est.); Bachelor's degree or higher: 13.3% (2008-2012 5-year est.); Master's degree or higher: 4.4% (2008-2012 5-year est.).
School District(s)
Round Lake CUSD 116 (PK-12)
    2011-12 Enrollment: 7,217 . . . . (847) 270-9001
Housing: Homeownership rate: 86.8% (2008-2012 5-year est.); Median home value: $154,200 (2008-2012 5-year est.); Median contract rent: $960 per month (2008-2012 5-year est.); Median year structure built: 1991 (2008-2012 5-year est.).
Health Insurance: 49.8% Private; 48.2% Public; 23.5% None. (2008-2012 5-year est.)
Safety: Violent crime rate: 0.0 per 10,000 population; Property crime rate: 10.6 per 10,000 population (2012).
Transportation: Commute to work: 91.6% car, 3.4% public transportation, 2.2% walk, 2.8% work from home (2008-2012 5-year est.); Travel time to work: 19.9% less than 15 minutes, 30.2% 15 to 30 minutes, 17.5% 30 to 45 minutes, 18.6% 45 to 60 minutes, 13.9% 60 minutes or more (2008-2012 5-year est.)
Additional Information Contacts
Round Lake Area Chamber of Commerce & Industry . . . . . (847) 546-2002
http://www.rlchamber.org
Village of Round Lake Park. . . . . (847) 546-2790
http://www.roundlakepark.us

THIRD LAKE (village). Covers a land area of 0.590 square miles and a water area of 0.263 square miles. Located at 42.37° N. Lat; 88.01° W. Long. Elevation is 771 feet.

Population: 1,248 (1990); 1,355 (2000); 1,182 (2010); Density: 2,456.2 persons per square mile (2008-2012 5-year est.); Race: 94.2% White, 0.5% Black/African American, 0.8% Asian, 0.0% American Indian/Alaska Native, 0.0% Native Hawaiian/Other Pacific Islander, 4.5% Some other race, 3.0% Two or more races, 6.8% Hispanic of any race (2008-2012 5-year est.); Average household size: 3.08 (2008-2012 5-year est.); Median age: 39.5 (2008-2012 5-year est.); Males per 100 females: 107.4 (2008-2012 5-year est.); Marriage status: 24.5% never married, 70.7% now married, 1.0% widowed, 3.7% divorced (2008-2012 5-year est.); Foreign born: 4.9% (2008-2012 5-year est.); Ancestry (includes multiple ancestries): 37.4% German, 24.1% Irish, 14.8% Italian, 12.4% Polish, 11.0% English (2008-2012 5-year est.).
Economy: Single-family building permits issued: 0 (2013); Multi-family building permits issued: 0 (2013); Homeowner vacancy rate: 0.0%. Rental vacancy rate: 9.4%. (2008-2012 5-year est.); Employment by occupation: 26.3% management, business, and financial, 9.3% computer, engineering, and science, 14.0% education, legal, community service, arts, and media, 6.2% healthcare practitioners, 8.2% service, 25.1% sales and office, 6.1% natural resources, construction, and maintenance, 4.8% production, transportation, and material moving (2008-2012 5-year est.).
Income: Per capita income: $45,922 (2008-2012 5-year est.); Median household income: $119,500 (2008-2012 5-year est.); Average household income: $143,408 (2008-2012 5-year est.); Percent of households with income of $100,000 or more: 63.0% (2008-2012 5-year est.); Poverty rate: 6.4% (2008-2012 5-year est.).
Education: Percent of population age 25 and over with: High school diploma (including GED) or higher: 98.7% (2008-2012 5-year est.); Bachelor's degree or higher: 59.2% (2008-2012 5-year est.); Master's degree or higher: 25.4% (2008-2012 5-year est.).
Housing: Homeownership rate: 93.8% (2008-2012 5-year est.); Median home value: $288,000 (2008-2012 5-year est.); Median contract rent: $1,563 per month (2008-2012 5-year est.); Median year structure built: 1985 (2008-2012 5-year est.).
Health Insurance: 90.5% Private; 9.9% Public; 4.6% None. (2008-2012 5-year est.)
Transportation: Commute to work: 88.7% car, 3.6% public transportation, 0.6% walk, 6.3% work from home (2008-2012 5-year est.); Travel time to

work: 18.8% less than 15 minutes, 35.4% 15 to 30 minutes, 21.3% 30 to 45 minutes, 10.9% 45 to 60 minutes, 13.6% 60 minutes or more (2008-2012 5-year est.)

TOWER LAKES (village).
Covers a land area of 0.909 square miles and a water area of 0.125 square miles. Located at 42.23° N. Lat; 88.16° W. Long. Elevation is 781 feet.

Population: 1,333 (1990); 1,310 (2000); 1,283 (2010); Density: 1,573.0 persons per square mile (2008-2012 5-year est.); Race: 96.6% White, 0.0% Black/African American, 1.2% Asian, 0.0% American Indian/Alaska Native, 0.0% Native Hawaiian/Other Pacific Islander, 2.2% Some other race, 1.2% Two or more races, 2.0% Hispanic of any race (2008-2012 5-year est.); Average household size: 3.00 (2008-2012 5-year est.); Median age: 44.5 (2008-2012 5-year est.); Males per 100 females: 103.1 (2008-2012 5-year est.); Marriage status: 19.6% never married, 74.4% now married, 3.3% widowed, 2.8% divorced (2008-2012 5-year est.); Foreign born: 7.7% (2008-2012 5-year est.); Ancestry (includes multiple ancestries): 31.9% German, 28.2% Irish, 12.0% English, 10.6% American, 7.2% Polish (2008-2012 5-year est.).

Economy: Single-family building permits issued: 0 (2013); Multi-family building permits issued: 0 (2013); Homeowner vacancy rate: 0.0%. Rental vacancy rate: 0.0%. (2008-2012 5-year est.); Employment by occupation: 33.4% management, business, and financial, 8.7% computer, engineering, and science, 11.6% education, legal, community service, arts, and media, 4.0% healthcare practitioners, 5.7% service, 32.0% sales and office, 3.3% natural resources, construction, and maintenance, 1.2% production, transportation, and material moving (2008-2012 5-year est.).

Income: Per capita income: $63,297 (2008-2012 5-year est.); Median household income: $148,125 (2008-2012 5-year est.); Average household income: $192,990 (2008-2012 5-year est.); Percent of households with income of $100,000 or more: 72.1% (2008-2012 5-year est.); Poverty rate: 0.4% (2008-2012 5-year est.).

Education: Percent of population age 25 and over with: High school diploma (including GED) or higher: 100.0% (2008-2012 5-year est.); Bachelor's degree or higher: 66.7% (2008-2012 5-year est.); Master's degree or higher: 29.9% (2008-2012 5-year est.).

Housing: Homeownership rate: 98.5% (2008-2012 5-year est.); Median home value: $517,600 (2008-2012 5-year est.); Median contract rent: n/a per month (2008-2012 5-year est.); Median year structure built: 1968 (2008-2012 5-year est.).

Health Insurance: 95.7% Private; 14.1% Public; 1.5% None. (2008-2012 5-year est.)

Safety: Violent crime rate: 0.0 per 10,000 population; Property crime rate: 54.3 per 10,000 population (2012).

Transportation: Commute to work: 79.3% car, 8.5% public transportation, 0.6% walk, 11.5% work from home (2008-2012 5-year est.); Travel time to work: 15.3% less than 15 minutes, 20.9% 15 to 30 minutes, 25.4% 30 to 45 minutes, 10.9% 45 to 60 minutes, 27.5% 60 minutes or more (2008-2012 5-year est.)

VENETIAN VILLAGE (CDP).
Covers a land area of 1.835 square miles and a water area of 0.610 square miles. Located at 42.41° N. Lat; 88.05° W. Long. Elevation is 797 feet.

Population: 3,133 (1990); 3,082 (2000); 2,826 (2010); Density: 1,473.4 persons per square mile (2008-2012 5-year est.); Race: 95.9% White, 1.4% Black/African American, 0.3% Asian, 0.3% American Indian/Alaska Native, 0.0% Native Hawaiian/Other Pacific Islander, 2.1% Some other race, 0.9% Two or more races, 1.6% Hispanic of any race (2008-2012 5-year est.); Average household size: 2.37 (2008-2012 5-year est.); Median age: 40.6 (2008-2012 5-year est.); Males per 100 females: 102.0 (2008-2012 5-year est.); Marriage status: 19.6% never married, 61.1% now married, 3.8% widowed, 15.5% divorced (2008-2012 5-year est.); Foreign born: 4.8% (2008-2012 5-year est.); Ancestry (includes multiple ancestries): 35.7% German, 23.7% Irish, 16.2% Polish, 12.7% Italian, 11.2% English (2008-2012 5-year est.).

Economy: Homeowner vacancy rate: 0.0%. Rental vacancy rate: 0.0%. (2008-2012 5-year est.); Employment by occupation: 17.6% management, business, and financial, 6.3% computer, engineering, and science, 11.1% education, legal, community service, arts, and media, 1.6% healthcare practitioners, 10.6% service, 24.5% sales and office, 17.4% natural resources, construction, and maintenance, 10.8% production, transportation, and material moving (2008-2012 5-year est.).

Income: Per capita income: $32,026 (2008-2012 5-year est.); Median household income: $65,078 (2008-2012 5-year est.); Average household income: $75,176 (2008-2012 5-year est.); Percent of households with

income of $100,000 or more: 22.5% (2008-2012 5-year est.); Poverty rate: 1.8% (2008-2012 5-year est.).

Education: Percent of population age 25 and over with: High school diploma (including GED) or higher: 90.5% (2008-2012 5-year est.); Bachelor's degree or higher: 21.2% (2008-2012 5-year est.); Master's degree or higher: 8.4% (2008-2012 5-year est.).

Housing: Homeownership rate: 96.8% (2008-2012 5-year est.); Median home value: $173,300 (2008-2012 5-year est.); Median contract rent: $953 per month (2008-2012 5-year est.); Median year structure built: 1964 (2008-2012 5-year est.).

Health Insurance: 87.9% Private; 19.2% Public; 5.5% None. (2008-2012 5-year est.)

Transportation: Commute to work: 92.6% car, 1.3% public transportation, 1.3% walk, 4.2% work from home (2008-2012 5-year est.); Travel time to work: 13.2% less than 15 minutes, 16.7% 15 to 30 minutes, 41.8% 30 to 45 minutes, 7.7% 45 to 60 minutes, 20.7% 60 minutes or more (2008-2012 5-year est.)

VERNON HILLS (village).
Covers a land area of 7.708 square miles and a water area of 0.207 square miles. Located at 42.23° N. Lat; 87.96° W. Long. Elevation is 735 feet.

Population: 15,319 (1990); 20,120 (2000); 25,113 (2010); Density: 3,262.3 persons per square mile (2008-2012 5-year est.); Race: 76.3% White, 0.8% Black/African American, 17.8% Asian, 0.0% American Indian/Alaska Native, 0.0% Native Hawaiian/Other Pacific Islander, 5.1% Some other race, 2.9% Two or more races, 11.4% Hispanic of any race (2008-2012 5-year est.); Average household size: 2.68 (2008-2012 5-year est.); Median age: 37.9 (2008-2012 5-year est.); Males per 100 females: 96.7 (2008-2012 5-year est.); Marriage status: 26.0% never married, 61.6% now married, 4.6% widowed, 7.8% divorced (2008-2012 5-year est.); Foreign born: 27.9% (2008-2012 5-year est.); Ancestry (includes multiple ancestries): 16.0% German, 10.3% Irish, 9.3% Russian, 8.4% Polish, 6.5% American (2008-2012 5-year est.).

Economy: Unemployment rate: 4.7% (April 2014); Total civilian labor force: 15,147 (April 2014); Single-family building permits issued: 26 (2013); Multi-family building permits issued: 96 (2013); Homeowner vacancy rate: 4.8%. Rental vacancy rate: 3.1%. (2008-2012 5-year est.); Employment by occupation: 23.2% management, business, and financial, 11.9% computer, engineering, and science, 11.0% education, legal, community service, arts, and media, 6.0% healthcare practitioners, 9.7% service, 27.3% sales and office, 2.9% natural resources, construction, and maintenance, 8.1% production, transportation, and material moving (2008-2012 5-year est.).

Income: Per capita income: $42,544 (2008-2012 5-year est.); Median household income: $90,161 (2008-2012 5-year est.); Average household income: $113,335 (2008-2012 5-year est.); Percent of households with income of $100,000 or more: 43.6% (2008-2012 5-year est.); Poverty rate: 2.9% (2008-2012 5-year est.).

Education: Percent of population age 25 and over with: High school diploma (including GED) or higher: 94.5% (2008-2012 5-year est.); Bachelor's degree or higher: 57.7% (2008-2012 5-year est.); Master's degree or higher: 24.2% (2008-2012 5-year est.).

School District(s)

CHSD 128 (09-12)
   2011-12 Enrollment: 3,404 . . . . (847) 247-4510
Hawthorn CCSD 73 (PK-08)
   2011-12 Enrollment: 3,968 . . . . (847) 990-4244
Spec Educ Dist Lake County/sedol
   2011-12 Enrollment: n/a . . . . (847) 548-8470

Housing: Homeownership rate: 76.0% (2008-2012 5-year est.); Median home value: $325,100 (2008-2012 5-year est.); Median contract rent: $1,235 per month (2008-2012 5-year est.); Median year structure built: 1985 (2008-2012 5-year est.).

Health Insurance: 83.6% Private; 15.4% Public; 7.4% None. (2008-2012 5-year est.)

Safety: Violent crime rate: 7.1 per 10,000 population; Property crime rate: 228.4 per 10,000 population (2012).

Transportation: Commute to work: 87.3% car, 4.0% public transportation, 0.3% walk, 6.6% work from home (2008-2012 5-year est.); Travel time to work: 24.4% less than 15 minutes, 32.1% 15 to 30 minutes, 25.8% 30 to 45 minutes, 8.3% 45 to 60 minutes, 9.3% 60 minutes or more (2008-2012 5-year est.)

Additional Information Contacts
GLMV Chamber of Commerce . . . . (847) 680-0750
   http://www.glmvchamber.org

Village of Vernon Hills . . . . (847) 367-3700
   http://www.vernonhills.org

VOLO (village). Covers a land area of 3.923 square miles and a water area of 0.078 square miles. Located at 42.33° N. Lat; 88.16° W. Long. Elevation is 794 feet.

Population: n/a (1990); 180 (2000); 2,929 (2010); Density: 763.7 persons per square mile (2008-2012 5-year est.); Race: 90.6% White, 2.7% Black/African American, 4.0% Asian, 0.0% American Indian/Alaska Native, 0.0% Native Hawaiian/Other Pacific Islander, 2.7% Some other race, 1.9% Two or more races, 11.4% Hispanic of any race (2008-2012 5-year est.); Average household size: 2.51 (2008-2012 5-year est.); Median age: 30.2 (2008-2012 5-year est.); Males per 100 females: 96.7 (2008-2012 5-year est.); Marriage status: 19.1% never married, 67.2% now married, 1.7% widowed, 12.1% divorced (2008-2012 5-year est.); Foreign born: 13.5% (2008-2012 5-year est.); Ancestry (includes multiple ancestries): 26.7% German, 16.6% Irish, 16.0% Polish, 14.6% Italian, 5.8% English (2008-2012 5-year est.).

Economy: Single-family building permits issued: 96 (2013); Multi-family building permits issued: 0 (2013); Homeowner vacancy rate: 4.0%. Rental vacancy rate: 0.0%. (2008-2012 5-year est.); Employment by occupation: 15.5% management, business, and financial, 9.5% computer, engineering, and science, 12.0% education, legal, community service, arts, and media, 3.3% healthcare practitioners, 12.4% service, 34.2% sales and office, 7.4% natural resources, construction, and maintenance, 5.7% production, transportation, and material moving (2008-2012 5-year est.).

Income: Per capita income: $36,467 (2008-2012 5-year est.); Median household income: $85,868 (2008-2012 5-year est.); Average household income: $90,731 (2008-2012 5-year est.); Percent of households with income of $100,000 or more: 34.5% (2008-2012 5-year est.); Poverty rate: 3.0% (2008-2012 5-year est.).

Taxes: Total city taxes per capita: $6,747 (2011); City property taxes per capita: $2,415 (2011).

Education: Percent of population age 25 and over with: High school diploma (including GED) or higher: 96.0% (2008-2012 5-year est.); Bachelor's degree or higher: 46.5% (2008-2012 5-year est.); Master's degree or higher: 14.4% (2008-2012 5-year est.).

Housing: Homeownership rate: 85.8% (2008-2012 5-year est.); Median home value: $203,800 (2008-2012 5-year est.); Median contract rent: $1,143 per month (2008-2012 5-year est.); Median year structure built: n/a (2008-2012 5-year est.).

Health Insurance: 88.6% Private; 12.4% Public; 4.7% None. (2008-2012 5-year est.)

Transportation: Commute to work: 90.0% car, 2.3% public transportation, 1.3% walk, 5.6% work from home (2008-2012 5-year est.); Travel time to work: 9.6% less than 15 minutes, 22.2% 15 to 30 minutes, 26.2% 30 to 45 minutes, 23.9% 45 to 60 minutes, 18.1% 60 minutes or more (2008-2012 5-year est.)

WADSWORTH (village). Covers a land area of 9.576 square miles and a water area of 0.091 square miles. Located at 42.43° N. Lat; 87.90° W. Long. Elevation is 705 feet.

Population: 1,826 (1990); 3,083 (2000); 3,815 (2010); Density: 395.0 persons per square mile (2008-2012 5-year est.); Race: 95.8% White, 1.6% Black/African American, 1.0% Asian, 0.0% American Indian/Alaska Native, 0.0% Native Hawaiian/Other Pacific Islander, 1.6% Some other race, 1.2% Two or more races, 6.5% Hispanic of any race (2008-2012 5-year est.); Average household size: 3.06 (2008-2012 5-year est.); Median age: 44.9 (2008-2012 5-year est.); Males per 100 females: 112.3 (2008-2012 5-year est.); Marriage status: 27.5% never married, 64.3% now married, 3.2% widowed, 5.0% divorced (2008-2012 5-year est.); Foreign born: 8.0% (2008-2012 5-year est.); Ancestry (includes multiple ancestries): 31.2% German, 17.2% Irish, 14.8% English, 14.5% Polish, 6.5% Swedish (2008-2012 5-year est.).

Economy: Single-family building permits issued: 2 (2013); Multi-family building permits issued: 0 (2013); Homeowner vacancy rate: 0.0%. Rental vacancy rate: 0.0%. (2008-2012 5-year est.); Employment by occupation: 19.6% management, business, and financial, 7.1% computer, engineering, and science, 15.4% education, legal, community service, arts, and media, 6.0% healthcare practitioners, 11.1% service, 29.3% sales and office, 8.1% natural resources, construction, and maintenance, 3.4% production, transportation, and material moving (2008-2012 5-year est.).

Income: Per capita income: $40,255 (2008-2012 5-year est.); Median household income: $94,625 (2008-2012 5-year est.); Average household income: $121,638 (2008-2012 5-year est.); Percent of households with income of $100,000 or more: 48.3% (2008-2012 5-year est.); Poverty rate: 2.6% (2008-2012 5-year est.).

Education: Percent of population age 25 and over with: High school diploma (including GED) or higher: 91.9% (2008-2012 5-year est.); Bachelor's degree or higher: 35.3% (2008-2012 5-year est.); Master's degree or higher: 16.8% (2008-2012 5-year est.).

School District(s)
Beach Park CCSD 3 (PK-08)
   2011-12 Enrollment: 2,448 . . . . (847) 599-5005

Housing: Homeownership rate: 94.0% (2008-2012 5-year est.); Median home value: $353,200 (2008-2012 5-year est.); Median contract rent: $1,278 per month (2008-2012 5-year est.); Median year structure built: 1985 (2008-2012 5-year est.).

Health Insurance: 80.0% Private; 24.7% Public; 11.7% None. (2008-2012 5-year est.)

Transportation: Commute to work: 90.3% car, 2.6% public transportation, 0.0% walk, 5.9% work from home (2008-2012 5-year est.); Travel time to work: 18.7% less than 15 minutes, 39.6% 15 to 30 minutes, 20.8% 30 to 45 minutes, 8.1% 45 to 60 minutes, 12.8% 60 minutes or more (2008-2012 5-year est.)

WAUCONDA (village). Covers a land area of 5.049 square miles and a water area of 0.682 square miles. Located at 42.28° N. Lat; 88.14° W. Long. Elevation is 804 feet.

History: Wauconda was settled in 1836 by Justus Bangs. The name he gave the village probably came from a favorite book of his, and was Indian in origin.

Population: 6,294 (1990); 9,448 (2000); 13,603 (2010); Density: 2,567.0 persons per square mile (2008-2012 5-year est.); Race: 89.2% White, 0.7% Black/African American, 3.7% Asian, 0.0% American Indian/Alaska Native, 1.5% Native Hawaiian/Other Pacific Islander, 4.9% Some other race, 2.2% Two or more races, 19.5% Hispanic of any race (2008-2012 5-year est.); Average household size: 2.68 (2008-2012 5-year est.); Median age: 35.5 (2008-2012 5-year est.); Males per 100 females: 97.5 (2008-2012 5-year est.); Marriage status: 30.4% never married, 51.0% now married, 6.0% widowed, 12.5% divorced (2008-2012 5-year est.); Foreign born: 15.9% (2008-2012 5-year est.); Ancestry (includes multiple ancestries): 25.7% German, 15.5% Irish, 11.5% Italian, 9.5% Polish, 7.5% American (2008-2012 5-year est.).

Economy: Single-family building permits issued: 17 (2013); Multi-family building permits issued: 0 (2013); Homeowner vacancy rate: 2.7%. Rental vacancy rate: 5.0%. (2008-2012 5-year est.); Employment by occupation: 21.9% management, business, and financial, 3.4% computer, engineering, and science, 9.5% education, legal, community service, arts, and media, 3.7% healthcare practitioners, 17.3% service, 25.0% sales and office, 8.9% natural resources, construction, and maintenance, 10.2% production, transportation, and material moving (2008-2012 5-year est.).

Income: Per capita income: $33,876 (2008-2012 5-year est.); Median household income: $74,552 (2008-2012 5-year est.); Average household income: $90,492 (2008-2012 5-year est.); Percent of households with income of $100,000 or more: 34.0% (2008-2012 5-year est.); Poverty rate: 4.9% (2008-2012 5-year est.).

Education: Percent of population age 25 and over with: High school diploma (including GED) or higher: 87.8% (2008-2012 5-year est.); Bachelor's degree or higher: 32.9% (2008-2012 5-year est.); Master's degree or higher: 10.2% (2008-2012 5-year est.).

School District(s)
Wauconda CUSD 118 (PK-12)
   2011-12 Enrollment: 4,492 . . . . (847) 526-7690

Housing: Homeownership rate: 75.6% (2008-2012 5-year est.); Median home value: $223,500 (2008-2012 5-year est.); Median contract rent: $857 per month (2008-2012 5-year est.); Median year structure built: 1988 (2008-2012 5-year est.).

Health Insurance: 74.1% Private; 20.7% Public; 13.6% None. (2008-2012 5-year est.)

Safety: Violent crime rate: 7.3 per 10,000 population; Property crime rate: 114.2 per 10,000 population (2012).

Transportation: Commute to work: 89.4% car, 1.7% public transportation, 1.7% walk, 4.1% work from home (2008-2012 5-year est.); Travel time to work: 21.0% less than 15 minutes, 28.9% 15 to 30 minutes, 24.5% 30 to 45 minutes, 12.4% 45 to 60 minutes, 13.2% 60 minutes or more (2008-2012 5-year est.)

Additional Information Contacts
Village of Wauconda . . . . (847) 526-9600
   http://www.wauconda-il.gov

Wauconda Area Chamber of Commerce . . . . (847) 526-5580
  http://www.waucondaareachamber.org

WAUKEGAN (city). County seat. Covers a land area of 23.673 square miles and a water area of 0.209 square miles. Located at 42.37° N. Lat; 87.87° W. Long. Elevation is 653 feet.

History: Named for the Indian translation of "sheltering place". Waukegan began with the founding of Little Fort by the French in the 1700's, the present name being of Indian origin meaning "fort or trading post." Settlers came to Little Fort in 1835, and in 1846 it was designated as a U.S. port of entry. Waukegan was incorporated as a village in 1849, and as a city in 1859.

Population: 69,392 (1990); 87,901 (2000); 89,078 (2010); Density: 3,758.7 persons per square mile (2008-2012 5-year est.); Race: 50.8% White, 16.8% Black/African American, 4.0% Asian, 0.2% American Indian/Alaska Native, 0.0% Native Hawaiian/Other Pacific Islander, 28.2% Some other race, 3.1% Two or more races, 53.1% Hispanic of any race (2008-2012 5-year est.); Average household size: 3.03 (2008-2012 5-year est.); Median age: 30.7 (2008-2012 5-year est.); Males per 100 females: 100.2 (2008-2012 5-year est.); Marriage status: 37.4% never married, 48.7% now married, 4.8% widowed, 9.1% divorced (2008-2012 5-year est.); Foreign born: 31.3% (2008-2012 5-year est.); Ancestry (includes multiple ancestries): 7.9% German, 5.2% Irish, 2.7% Polish, 2.7% Italian, 2.6% English (2008-2012 5-year est.).

Economy: Unemployment rate: 9.6% (April 2014); Total civilian labor force: 42,772 (April 2014); Single-family building permits issued: 29 (2013); Multi-family building permits issued: 8 (2013); Homeowner vacancy rate: 4.1%. Rental vacancy rate: 9.1%. (2008-2012 5-year est.); Employment by occupation: 9.7% management, business, and financial, 4.0% computer, engineering, and science, 5.7% education, legal, community service, arts, and media, 2.6% healthcare practitioners, 22.8% service, 22.8% sales and office, 8.2% natural resources, construction, and maintenance, 24.2% production, transportation, and material moving (2008-2012 5-year est.).

Income: Per capita income: $20,324 (2008-2012 5-year est.); Median household income: $46,256 (2008-2012 5-year est.); Average household income: $61,035 (2008-2012 5-year est.); Percent of households with income of $100,000 or more: 16.1% (2008-2012 5-year est.); Poverty rate: 18.8% (2008-2012 5-year est.).

Taxes: Total city taxes per capita: $485 (2011); City property taxes per capita: $289 (2011).

Education: Percent of population age 25 and over with: High school diploma (including GED) or higher: 70.3% (2008-2012 5-year est.); Bachelor's degree or higher: 17.3% (2008-2012 5-year est.); Master's degree or higher: 5.6% (2008-2012 5-year est.).

School District(s)
Waukegan CUSD 60 (PK-12)
  2011-12 Enrollment: 16,597 . . . . (847) 336-3100
Vocational/Technical School(s)
State Career College (Private, For-profit)
  Fall 2012 Enrollment: 59 . . . . (847) 693-3838
  2012-13 Tuition: $10,100

Housing: Homeownership rate: 54.9% (2008-2012 5-year est.); Median home value: $152,600 (2008-2012 5-year est.); Median contract rent: $739 per month (2008-2012 5-year est.); Median year structure built: 1963 (2008-2012 5-year est.).

Health Insurance: 51.6% Private; 33.5% Public; 21.4% None. (2008-2012 5-year est.)

Hospitals: Vista Health - Saint Therese Medical Center (388 beds); Vista Medical Center East (299 beds)

Safety: Violent crime rate: 46.9 per 10,000 population; Property crime rate: 300.4 per 10,000 population (2012).

Transportation: Commute to work: 90.3% car, 3.8% public transportation, 1.4% walk, 3.3% work from home (2008-2012 5-year est.); Travel time to work: 23.7% less than 15 minutes, 37.5% 15 to 30 minutes, 24.0% 30 to 45 minutes, 7.0% 45 to 60 minutes, 7.8% 60 minutes or more (2008-2012 5-year est.)

Airports: Waukegan Regional Airport (reliver airport)

Additional Information Contacts
City of Waukegan . . . . (847) 599-2500
  http://www.waukeganweb.net
City of Waukegan Chamber of Commerce . . . . (847) 623-6800
  http://www.waukeganchamber.org

WINTHROP HARBOR (village). Covers a land area of 4.668 square miles and a water area of 0.091 square miles. Located at 42.48° N. Lat; 87.83° W. Long. Elevation is 636 feet.

History: The Winthrop Harbor and Dock Company purchased land here in 1892, but plans to develop the harbor and town were abandoned. The community that grew here depended on dairying.

Population: 6,240 (1990); 6,670 (2000); 6,742 (2010); Density: 1,446.5 persons per square mile (2008-2012 5-year est.); Race: 93.9% White, 1.1% Black/African American, 1.8% Asian, 0.0% American Indian/Alaska Native, 0.0% Native Hawaiian/Other Pacific Islander, 3.2% Some other race, 2.2% Two or more races, 8.5% Hispanic of any race (2008-2012 5-year est.); Average household size: 2.64 (2008-2012 5-year est.); Median age: 43.6 (2008-2012 5-year est.); Males per 100 females: 102.9 (2008-2012 5-year est.); Marriage status: 23.1% never married, 63.7% now married, 3.3% widowed, 9.9% divorced (2008-2012 5-year est.); Foreign born: 3.8% (2008-2012 5-year est.); Ancestry (includes multiple ancestries): 29.2% German, 16.5% Irish, 11.0% English, 10.4% Polish, 7.7% Italian (2008-2012 5-year est.).

Economy: Single-family building permits issued: 0 (2013); Multi-family building permits issued: 0 (2013); Homeowner vacancy rate: 1.6%. Rental vacancy rate: 17.2%. (2008-2012 5-year est.); Employment by occupation: 13.7% management, business, and financial, 6.6% computer, engineering, and science, 7.3% education, legal, community service, arts, and media, 3.7% healthcare practitioners, 16.8% service, 28.5% sales and office, 7.7% natural resources, construction, and maintenance, 15.7% production, transportation, and material moving (2008-2012 5-year est.).

Income: Per capita income: $30,326 (2008-2012 5-year est.); Median household income: $71,890 (2008-2012 5-year est.); Average household income: $79,241 (2008-2012 5-year est.); Percent of households with income of $100,000 or more: 32.5% (2008-2012 5-year est.); Poverty rate: 6.3% (2008-2012 5-year est.).

Education: Percent of population age 25 and over with: High school diploma (including GED) or higher: 92.8% (2008-2012 5-year est.); Bachelor's degree or higher: 20.4% (2008-2012 5-year est.); Master's degree or higher: 7.0% (2008-2012 5-year est.).

School District(s)
Winthrop Harbor SD 1 (KG-08)
  2011-12 Enrollment: 590 . . . . (847) 731-3085

Housing: Homeownership rate: 84.2% (2008-2012 5-year est.); Median home value: $201,500 (2008-2012 5-year est.); Median contract rent: $888 per month (2008-2012 5-year est.); Median year structure built: 1975 (2008-2012 5-year est.).

Health Insurance: 80.2% Private; 27.2% Public; 7.1% None. (2008-2012 5-year est.)

Safety: Violent crime rate: 22.1 per 10,000 population; Property crime rate: 147.6 per 10,000 population (2012).

Transportation: Commute to work: 94.9% car, 0.7% public transportation, 1.2% walk, 2.7% work from home (2008-2012 5-year est.); Travel time to work: 27.7% less than 15 minutes, 32.7% 15 to 30 minutes, 21.1% 30 to 45 minutes, 13.0% 45 to 60 minutes, 5.5% 60 minutes or more (2008-2012 5-year est.)

Additional Information Contacts
Village of Winthrop Harbor . . . . (847) 872-3846
  http://www.whpd.org/village
Winthrop Harbor Chamber of Commerce . . . .
  http://www.cocwh.com

ZION (city). Covers a land area of 9.808 square miles and a water area of 0.003 square miles. Located at 42.46° N. Lat; 87.85° W. Long. Elevation is 650 feet.

History: Named for Mount Zion in Palestine. Zion began as the dream of John Alexander Dowie (1847-1907), the Scottish founder of the Christian Catholic Apostolic Church, who planned Zion as a city where the tenets of the church would govern. In 1899 Dowie's followers began to settle here. Dowie was succeeded by Wilbur Glenn Voliva, who attempted to industrialize Zion, but the church owned all industries and commercial establishments. In 1939, after several bankruptcies, titles were transferred to individuals.

Population: 19,775 (1990); 22,866 (2000); 24,413 (2010); Density: 2,487.8 persons per square mile (2008-2012 5-year est.); Race: 48.9% White, 33.2% Black/African American, 2.3% Asian, 0.3% American Indian/Alaska Native, 0.1% Native Hawaiian/Other Pacific Islander, 15.2% Some other race, 5.3% Two or more races, 22.5% Hispanic of any race (2008-2012 5-year est.); Average household size: 2.96 (2008-2012 5-year est.); Median age: 30.8 (2008-2012 5-year est.); Males per 100 females:

91.9 (2008-2012 5-year est.); Marriage status: 36.1% never married, 47.0% now married, 4.5% widowed, 12.4% divorced (2008-2012 5-year est.); Foreign born: 12.1% (2008-2012 5-year est.); Ancestry (includes multiple ancestries): 12.3% German, 10.9% Irish, 4.1% American, 3.5% English, 3.1% Polish (2008-2012 5-year est.).

Economy: Unemployment rate: 9.4% (April 2014); Total civilian labor force: 11,538 (April 2014); Single-family building permits issued: 0 (2013); Multi-family building permits issued: 0 (2013); Homeowner vacancy rate: 7.0%. Rental vacancy rate: 11.2%. (2008-2012 5-year est.); Employment by occupation: 8.8% management, business, and financial, 3.2% computer, engineering, and science, 8.2% education, legal, community service, arts, and media, 4.5% healthcare practitioners, 18.6% service, 29.3% sales and office, 8.3% natural resources, construction, and maintenance, 18.9% production, transportation, and material moving (2008-2012 5-year est.).

Income: Per capita income: $20,512 (2008-2012 5-year est.); Median household income: $50,807 (2008-2012 5-year est.); Average household income: $60,099 (2008-2012 5-year est.); Percent of households with income of $100,000 or more: 16.9% (2008-2012 5-year est.); Poverty rate: 15.1% (2008-2012 5-year est.).

Taxes: Total city taxes per capita: $483 (2011); City property taxes per capita: $254 (2011).

Education: Percent of population age 25 and over with: High school diploma (including GED) or higher: 82.7% (2008-2012 5-year est.); Bachelor's degree or higher: 14.2% (2008-2012 5-year est.); Master's degree or higher: 4.9% (2008-2012 5-year est.).

School District(s)

Lake Roe (06-12)
   2011-12 Enrollment: n/a . . . . (847) 543-7833
Zion ESD 6 (PK-08)
   2011-12 Enrollment: 2,766 . . . . (847) 872-5455
Zion-Benton Twp HSD 126 (09-12)
   2011-12 Enrollment: 2,810 . . . . (847) 731-9792

Housing: Homeownership rate: 56.6% (2008-2012 5-year est.); Median home value: $157,500 (2008-2012 5-year est.); Median contract rent: $739 per month (2008-2012 5-year est.); Median year structure built: 1973 (2008-2012 5-year est.).

Health Insurance: 60.1% Private; 35.1% Public; 13.8% None. (2008-2012 5-year est.)

Hospitals: Midwestern Regional Medical Center (95 beds)

Safety: Violent crime rate: 59.1 per 10,000 population; Property crime rate: 422.9 per 10,000 population (2012).

Transportation: Commute to work: 91.8% car, 2.5% public transportation, 0.8% walk, 3.6% work from home (2008-2012 5-year est.); Travel time to work: 19.1% less than 15 minutes, 37.4% 15 to 30 minutes, 23.4% 30 to 45 minutes, 11.2% 45 to 60 minutes, 8.9% 60 minutes or more (2008-2012 5-year est.)

Additional Information Contacts
City of Zion . . . . (847) 746-4000
   http://www.cityofzion.com
Zion Area Chamber of Commerce . . . . (847) 872-5405
   http://www.zionchamber.com

Lawrence County

Located in southeastern Illinois; bounded on the east by the Wabash River and the Indiana border; drained by the Embarrass River. Covers a land area of 372.178 square miles, a water area of 1.961 square miles, and is located in the Central Time Zone at 38.72° N. Lat., 87.73° W. Long. The county was founded in 1821. County seat is Lawrenceville.

Population: 15,972 (1990); 15,452 (2000); 16,833 (2010); Race: 74.6% White, 21.8% Black/African American, 0.1% Asian, 0.2% American Indian/Alaska Native, 0.3% Native Hawaiian/Other Pacific Islander, 3.0% Some other race, 1.5% Two or more races, 5.0% Hispanic of any race (2008-2012 5-year est.); Density: 44.6 persons per square mile (2008-2012 5-year est.); Average household size: 1.80 (2008-2012 5-year est.); Median age: 40.8 (2008-2012 5-year est.); Males per 100 females: 167.1 (2008-2012 5-year est.).

Religion: Six largest groups: 13.9% Methodist/Pietist, 13.4% Baptist, 3.6% Catholicism, 2.7% Non-denominational Protestant, 2.6% Holiness, 2.1% Pentecostal (2010)

Economy: Unemployment rate: 6.4% (April 2014); Total civilian labor force: 7,241 (April 2014); Leading industries: 18.1% health care and social assistance; 15.1% manufacturing; 12.3% retail trade (2012); Farms: 379 totaling 184,111 acres (2012); Companies that employ 500 or more

persons: 0 (2012); Companies that employ 100 to 499 persons: 9 (2012); Companies that employ less than 100 persons: 274 (2012); Black-owned businesses: n/a (2007); Hispanic-owned businesses: n/a (2007); Asian-owned businesses: n/a (2007); Women-owned businesses: n/a (2007); Single-family building permits issued: 41 (2013); Multi-family building permits issued: 0 (2013).

Income: Per capita income: $18,576 (2008-2012 5-year est.); Median household income: $39,324 (2008-2012 5-year est.); Average household income: $51,119 (2008-2012 5-year est.); Percent of households with income of $100,000 or more: 11.3% (2008-2012 5-year est.); Poverty rate: 13.6% (2008-2012 5-year est.); Bankruptcy rate: 2.35% (2013).

Education: Percent of population age 25 and over with: High school diploma (including GED) or higher: 77.7% (2008-2012 5-year est.); Bachelor's degree or higher: 9.5% (2008-2012 5-year est.); Master's degree or higher: 2.3% (2008-2012 5-year est.).

Housing: Homeownership rate: 73.4% (2008-2012 5-year est.); Median home value: $65,200 (2008-2012 5-year est.); Median contract rent: $348 per month (2008-2012 5-year est.); Median year structure built: 1956 (2008-2012 5-year est.)

Health: Birth rate: 96.0 per 10,000 population (2013); Death rate: 123.8 per 10,000 population (2013); Age-adjusted cancer mortality rate: 205.3 deaths per 100,000 population (2011); Number of physicians: 6.6 per 10,000 population (2011); Hospital beds: 14.9 per 10,000 population (2010); Hospital admissions: 537.6 per 10,000 population (2010).

Elections: 2012 Presidential election results: 33.6% Obama, 64.4% Romney

National and State Parks: Lincoln Trail State Memorial; Red Hills State Park

Additional Information Contacts
Lawrence County Government . . . . (618) 943-2346
   http://www.lawrencecountyillinois.com
Lawrence County Chamber of Commerce . . . . (618) 943-3516
   http://www.lawrencecountychamberofcommerce.com/

Lawrence County Communities

BRIDGEPORT (city). Covers a land area of 1.049 square miles and a water area of 0.025 square miles. Located at 38.71° N. Lat; 87.76° W. Long. Elevation is 446 feet.

History: Bridgeport was the center of an early oil boom, when a company built a pumping station and supply yards here.

Population: 2,118 (1990); 2,168 (2000); 1,886 (2010); Density: 1,273.0 persons per square mile (2008-2012 5-year est.); Race: 98.0% White, 1.8% Black/African American, 0.2% Asian, 0.0% American Indian/Alaska Native, 0.0% Native Hawaiian/Other Pacific Islander, 0.0% Some other race, 0.0% Two or more races, 0.4% Hispanic of any race (2008-2012 5-year est.); Average household size: 1.78 (2008-2012 5-year est.); Median age: 45.5 (2008-2012 5-year est.); Males per 100 females: 78.5 (2008-2012 5-year est.); Marriage status: 10.0% never married, 64.8% now married, 12.5% widowed, 12.6% divorced (2008-2012 5-year est.); Foreign born: 1.3% (2008-2012 5-year est.); Ancestry (includes multiple ancestries): 13.2% German, 13.2% American, 11.2% English, 8.6% Irish, 4.5% French (2008-2012 5-year est.).

Economy: Homeowner vacancy rate: 3.1%. Rental vacancy rate: 5.6%. (2008-2012 5-year est.); Employment by occupation: 4.4% management, business, and financial, 0.0% computer, engineering, and science, 4.9% education, legal, community service, arts, and media, 2.6% healthcare practitioners, 24.7% service, 23.8% sales and office, 10.7% natural resources, construction, and maintenance, 28.9% production, transportation, and material moving (2008-2012 5-year est.).

Income: Per capita income: $20,832 (2008-2012 5-year est.); Median household income: $31,359 (2008-2012 5-year est.); Average household income: $38,885 (2008-2012 5-year est.); Percent of households with income of $100,000 or more: 6.0% (2008-2012 5-year est.); Poverty rate: 21.4% (2008-2012 5-year est.).

Education: Percent of population age 25 and over with: High school diploma (including GED) or higher: 88.7% (2008-2012 5-year est.); Bachelor's degree or higher: 9.0% (2008-2012 5-year est.); Master's degree or higher: 2.3% (2008-2012 5-year est.).

School District(s)

Red Hill CUSD 10 (PK-12)
   2011-12 Enrollment: 1,104 . . . . (618) 945-2061

Housing: Homeownership rate: 70.5% (2008-2012 5-year est.); Median home value: $49,100 (2008-2012 5-year est.); Median contract rent: $317

per month (2008-2012 5-year est.); Median year structure built: 1962 (2008-2012 5-year est.).

Health Insurance: 62.0% Private; 48.4% Public; 14.9% None. (2008-2012 5-year est.)

Transportation: Commute to work: 97.3% car, 0.0% public transportation, 1.0% walk, 0.9% work from home (2008-2012 5-year est.); Travel time to work: 49.5% less than 15 minutes, 33.1% 15 to 30 minutes, 12.7% 30 to 45 minutes, 2.4% 45 to 60 minutes, 2.3% 60 minutes or more (2008-2012 5-year est.)

LAWRENCEVILLE (city). County seat. Covers a land area of 2.195 square miles and a water area of 0 square miles. Located at 38.73° N. Lat; 87.69° W. Long. Elevation is 469 feet.

History: The first settler here was Captain Toussaint Dubois, veteran of the American Revolution, who came about 1780 and planted an orchard. Jessie K. Dubois, the captain's son, was a friend of Abraham Lincoln and one of the pall bearers at his funeral. Lawrenceville was organized in 1821 and named for Captain James Lawrence, commander of the "Chesapeake" in the War of 1812, who said, "Don't give up the ship." Lawrenceville developed as an oil town in the early 1900's, and as the seat of Lawrence County.

Population: 4,897 (1990); 4,745 (2000); 4,348 (2010); Density: 2,148.4 persons per square mile (2008-2012 5-year est.); Race: 82.1% White, 14.8% Black/African American, 0.2% Asian, 0.3% American Indian/Alaska Native, 0.0% Native Hawaiian/Other Pacific Islander, 2.6% Some other race, 0.4% Two or more races, 4.3% Hispanic of any race (2008-2012 5-year est.); Average household size: 1.62 (2008-2012 5-year est.); Median age: 42.4 (2008-2012 5-year est.); Males per 100 females: 117.3 (2008-2012 5-year est.); Marriage status: 26.6% never married, 46.7% now married, 13.7% widowed, 13.0% divorced (2008-2012 5-year est.); Foreign born: 2.5% (2008-2012 5-year est.); Ancestry (includes multiple ancestries): 15.5% German, 11.1% Irish, 9.9% English, 9.3% American, 2.4% French (2008-2012 5-year est.).

Economy: Single-family building permits issued: 41 (2013); Multi-family building permits issued: 0 (2013); Homeowner vacancy rate: 6.5%. Rental vacancy rate: 1.4%. (2008-2012 5-year est.); Employment by occupation: 8.9% management, business, and financial, 1.8% computer, engineering, and science, 7.8% education, legal, community service, arts, and media, 7.1% healthcare practitioners, 27.0% service, 19.0% sales and office, 7.5% natural resources, construction, and maintenance, 20.9% production, transportation, and material moving (2008-2012 5-year est.).

Income: Per capita income: $19,042 (2008-2012 5-year est.); Median household income: $30,242 (2008-2012 5-year est.); Average household income: $40,665 (2008-2012 5-year est.); Percent of households with income of $100,000 or more: 4.7% (2008-2012 5-year est.); Poverty rate: 17.4% (2008-2012 5-year est.).

Education: Percent of population age 25 and over with: High school diploma (including GED) or higher: 76.8% (2008-2012 5-year est.); Bachelor's degree or higher: 9.7% (2008-2012 5-year est.); Master's degree or higher: 2.8% (2008-2012 5-year est.).

School District(s)

Lawrence County CUD 20 (PK-12)

   2011-12 Enrollment: 1,237 . . . . (618) 943-2326

Housing: Homeownership rate: 58.5% (2008-2012 5-year est.); Median home value: $56,700 (2008-2012 5-year est.); Median contract rent: $341 per month (2008-2012 5-year est.); Median year structure built: 1950 (2008-2012 5-year est.).

Health Insurance: 64.5% Private; 45.7% Public; 13.2% None. (2008-2012 5-year est.)

Hospitals: Lawrence County Memorial Hospital (25 beds)

Safety: Violent crime rate: 16.2 per 10,000 population; Property crime rate: 219.8 per 10,000 population (2012).

Transportation: Commute to work: 94.9% car, 0.0% public transportation, 1.1% walk, 1.3% work from home (2008-2012 5-year est.); Travel time to work: 56.4% less than 15 minutes, 36.1% 15 to 30 minutes, 3.5% 30 to 45 minutes, 2.4% 45 to 60 minutes, 1.6% 60 minutes or more (2008-2012 5-year est.)

Airports: Lawrenceville-Vincennes International Airport (general aviation)

Additional Information Contacts

City of Lawrenceville . . . . (618) 943-2116

   http://lawrencecity.com

Lawrence County Chamber of Commerce . . . . (618) 943-3516

   http://www.lawrencecountychamberofcommerce.com/

RUSSELLVILLE (village). Covers a land area of 0.466 square miles and a water area of 0 square miles. Located at 38.82° N. Lat; 87.53° W. Long. Elevation is 427 feet.

History: Russellville grew around a ferry that crossed the Wabash River here.

Population: 133 (1990); 119 (2000); 94 (2010); Density: 109.5 persons per square mile (2008-2012 5-year est.); Race: 100.0% White, 0.0% Black/African American, 0.0% Asian, 0.0% American Indian/Alaska Native, 0.0% Native Hawaiian/Other Pacific Islander, 0.0% Some other race, 0.0% Two or more races, 0.0% Hispanic of any race (2008-2012 5-year est.); Average household size: 1.65 (2008-2012 5-year est.); Median age: 54.3 (2008-2012 5-year est.); Males per 100 females: 59.4 (2008-2012 5-year est.); Marriage status: 12.5% never married, 41.7% now married, 20.8% widowed, 25.0% divorced (2008-2012 5-year est.); Foreign born: 0.0% (2008-2012 5-year est.); Ancestry (includes multiple ancestries): 17.6% French, 11.8% English, 5.9% German, 5.9% American, 3.9% Swiss (2008-2012 5-year est.).

Economy: Homeowner vacancy rate: 10.7%. Rental vacancy rate: 40.0%. (2008-2012 5-year est.); Employment by occupation: 0.0% management, business, and financial, 0.0% computer, engineering, and science, 30.4% education, legal, community service, arts, and media, 0.0% healthcare practitioners, 13.0% service, 17.4% sales and office, 4.3% natural resources, construction, and maintenance, 34.8% production, transportation, and material moving (2008-2012 5-year est.).

Income: Per capita income: $24,337 (2008-2012 5-year est.); Median household income: $41,563 (2008-2012 5-year est.); Average household income: $40,771 (2008-2012 5-year est.); Percent of households with income of $100,000 or more: 6.5% (2008-2012 5-year est.); Poverty rate: 13.7% (2008-2012 5-year est.).

Education: Percent of population age 25 and over with: High school diploma (including GED) or higher: 84.8% (2008-2012 5-year est.); Bachelor's degree or higher: 23.9% (2008-2012 5-year est.); Master's degree or higher: 4.3% (2008-2012 5-year est.).

Housing: Homeownership rate: 80.6% (2008-2012 5-year est.); Median home value: $33,800 (2008-2012 5-year est.); Median contract rent: $313 per month (2008-2012 5-year est.); Median year structure built: 1973 (2008-2012 5-year est.).

Health Insurance: 64.7% Private; 37.3% Public; 15.7% None. (2008-2012 5-year est.)

Transportation: Commute to work: 95.7% car, 0.0% public transportation, 4.3% walk, 0.0% work from home (2008-2012 5-year est.); Travel time to work: 4.3% less than 15 minutes, 78.3% 15 to 30 minutes, 8.7% 30 to 45 minutes, 0.0% 45 to 60 minutes, 8.7% 60 minutes or more (2008-2012 5-year est.)

SAINT FRANCISVILLE (city). Covers a land area of 0.746 square miles and a water area of 0.034 square miles. Located at 38.59° N. Lat; 87.65° W. Long. Elevation is 466 feet.

Population: 851 (1990); 759 (2000); 697 (2010); Density: 876.6 persons per square mile (2008-2012 5-year est.); Race: 100.0% White, 0.0% Black/African American, 0.0% Asian, 0.0% American Indian/Alaska Native, 0.0% Native Hawaiian/Other Pacific Islander, 0.0% Some other race, 0.0% Two or more races, 0.0% Hispanic of any race (2008-2012 5-year est.); Average household size: 1.90 (2008-2012 5-year est.); Median age: 42.7 (2008-2012 5-year est.); Males per 100 females: 109.6 (2008-2012 5-year est.); Marriage status: 14.1% never married, 63.8% now married, 13.1% widowed, 9.0% divorced (2008-2012 5-year est.); Foreign born: 0.0% (2008-2012 5-year est.); Ancestry (includes multiple ancestries): 12.1% German, 4.4% French, 3.4% Irish, 2.6% Italian, 1.8% American (2008-2012 5-year est.).

Economy: Homeowner vacancy rate: 0.0%. Rental vacancy rate: 1.0%. (2008-2012 5-year est.); Employment by occupation: 14.0% management, business, and financial, 5.0% computer, engineering, and science, 3.3% education, legal, community service, arts, and media, 8.0% healthcare practitioners, 10.0% service, 16.4% sales and office, 12.4% natural resources, construction, and maintenance, 30.8% production, transportation, and material moving (2008-2012 5-year est.).

Income: Per capita income: $24,149 (2008-2012 5-year est.); Median household income: $35,417 (2008-2012 5-year est.); Average household income: $48,429 (2008-2012 5-year est.); Percent of households with income of $100,000 or more: 10.2% (2008-2012 5-year est.); Poverty rate: 15.7% (2008-2012 5-year est.).

Education: Percent of population age 25 and over with: High school diploma (including GED) or higher: 86.1% (2008-2012 5-year est.);

Bachelor's degree or higher: 8.9% (2008-2012 5-year est.); Master's degree or higher: 1.9% (2008-2012 5-year est.).
Housing: Homeownership rate: 71.6% (2008-2012 5-year est.); Median home value: $47,500 (2008-2012 5-year est.); Median contract rent: $340 per month (2008-2012 5-year est.); Median year structure built: 1942 (2008-2012 5-year est.).
Health Insurance: 62.8% Private; 37.8% Public; 13.8% None. (2008-2012 5-year est.)
Transportation: Commute to work: 100.0% car, 0.0% public transportation, 0.0% walk, 0.0% work from home (2008-2012 5-year est.); Travel time to work: 17.9% less than 15 minutes, 55.7% 15 to 30 minutes, 16.8% 30 to 45 minutes, 1.4% 45 to 60 minutes, 8.2% 60 minutes or more (2008-2012 5-year est.)

SUMNER (city). Covers a land area of 1.365 square miles and a water area of 0 square miles. Located at 38.72° N. Lat; 87.87° W. Long. Elevation is 449 feet.
History: Incorporated 1887.
Population: 1,083 (1990); 1,022 (2000); 3,174 (2010); Density: 3,716.3 persons per square mile (2008-2012 5-year est.); Race: 35.5% White, 57.1% Black/African American, 0.1% Asian, 0.3% American Indian/Alaska Native, 0.5% Native Hawaiian/Other Pacific Islander, 6.5% Some other race, 4.1% Two or more races, 11.6% Hispanic of any race (2008-2012 5-year est.); Average household size: 1.63 (2008-2012 5-year est.); Median age: 33.2 (2008-2012 5-year est.); Males per 100 females: ***.* (2008-2012 5-year est.); Marriage status: 64.5% never married, 23.0% now married, 3.0% widowed, 9.4% divorced (2008-2012 5-year est.); Foreign born: 4.8% (2008-2012 5-year est.); Ancestry (includes multiple ancestries): 8.9% German, 4.6% Irish, 3.7% American, 2.2% English, 1.8% Dutch (2008-2012 5-year est.).
Economy: Homeowner vacancy rate: 0.0%. Rental vacancy rate: 9.4%. (2008-2012 5-year est.); Employment by occupation: 4.6% management, business, and financial, 0.8% computer, engineering, and science, 4.3% education, legal, community service, arts, and media, 9.7% healthcare practitioners, 22.2% service, 24.9% sales and office, 7.8% natural resources, construction, and maintenance, 25.7% production, transportation, and material moving (2008-2012 5-year est.).
Income: Per capita income: $4,355 (2008-2012 5-year est.); Median household income: $31,932 (2008-2012 5-year est.); Average household income: $40,238 (2008-2012 5-year est.); Percent of households with income of $100,000 or more: 2.7% (2008-2012 5-year est.); Poverty rate: 16.0% (2008-2012 5-year est.).
Education: Percent of population age 25 and over with: High school diploma (including GED) or higher: 60.8% (2008-2012 5-year est.); Bachelor's degree or higher: 2.4% (2008-2012 5-year est.); Master's degree or higher: 0.1% (2008-2012 5-year est.).
School District(s)
Red Hill CUSD 10 (PK-12)
   2011-12 Enrollment: 1,104 . . . . (618) 945-2061
Housing: Homeownership rate: 71.3% (2008-2012 5-year est.); Median home value: $36,400 (2008-2012 5-year est.); Median contract rent: $292 per month (2008-2012 5-year est.); Median year structure built: 1951 (2008-2012 5-year est.).
Health Insurance: 60.6% Private; 38.4% Public; 17.3% None. (2008-2012 5-year est.)
Transportation: Commute to work: 92.9% car, 4.4% public transportation, 1.2% walk, 1.5% work from home (2008-2012 5-year est.); Travel time to work: 39.7% less than 15 minutes, 29.6% 15 to 30 minutes, 14.6% 30 to 45 minutes, 11.3% 45 to 60 minutes, 4.8% 60 minutes or more (2008-2012 5-year est.)

Lee County

Located in northern Illinois; drained by the Rock, Green, and Kyte Rivers. Covers a land area of 724.896 square miles, a water area of 4.057 square miles, and is located in the Central Time Zone at 41.75° N. Lat., 89.30° W. Long. The county was founded in 1839. County seat is Dixon.

Lee County is part of the Dixon, IL Micropolitan Statistical Area. The entire metro area includes: Lee County, IL

Weather Station: Dixon 1 NW   Elevation: 700 feet

	Jan	Feb	Mar	Apr	May	Jun	Jul	Aug	Sep	Oct	Nov	Dec
High	29	34	46	60	71	80	83	81	75	62	48	33
Low	12	16	27	38	49	58	62	61	51	39	29	17
Precip	1.5	1.6	2.4	3.5	4.3	4.7	4.1	4.6	3.5	2.9	2.7	2.1
Snow	10.3	6.9	3.7	0.8	0.0	0.0	0.0	0.0	0.0	0.1	1.3	8.5

High and Low temperatures in degrees Fahrenheit; Precipitation and Snow in inches

Weather Station: Paw Paw 2 NW   Elevation: 950 feet

	Jan	Feb	Mar	Apr	May	Jun	Jul	Aug	Sep	Oct	Nov	Dec
High	28	32	44	58	70	79	82	80	74	61	46	32
Low	12	16	25	36	47	58	61	59	51	39	29	16
Precip	1.3	1.4	2.1	3.1	4.5	4.0	4.1	4.3	3.6	2.8	3.0	2.0
Snow	8.8	6.5	3.9	0.8	tr	0.0	0.0	0.0	0.0	0.2	1.2	8.5

High and Low temperatures in degrees Fahrenheit; Precipitation and Snow in inches

Population: 34,392 (1990); 36,062 (2000); 36,031 (2010); Race: 92.0% White, 4.5% Black/African American, 0.6% Asian, 0.1% American Indian/Alaska Native, 0.0% Native Hawaiian/Other Pacific Islander, 2.8% Some other race, 1.8% Two or more races, 5.0% Hispanic of any race (2008-2012 5-year est.); Density: 48.5 persons per square mile (2008-2012 5-year est.); Average household size: 2.45 (2008-2012 5-year est.); Median age: 41.6 (2008-2012 5-year est.); Males per 100 females: 108.6 (2008-2012 5-year est.).
Religion: Six largest groups: 23.3% Catholicism, 10.8% Lutheran, 7.2% Methodist/Pietist, 4.2% Baptist, 1.5% Non-denominational Protestant, 1.3% European Free-Church (2010)
Economy: Unemployment rate: 7.1% (April 2014); Total civilian labor force: 17,208 (April 2014); Leading industries: 26.9% manufacturing; 20.2% health care and social assistance; 12.8% retail trade (2012); Farms: 835 totaling 369,047 acres (2012); Companies that employ 500 or more persons: 2 (2012); Companies that employ 100 to 499 persons: 18 (2012); Companies that employ less than 100 persons: 690 (2012); Black-owned businesses: n/a (2007); Hispanic-owned businesses: n/a (2007); Asian-owned businesses: n/a (2007); Women-owned businesses: 644 (2007); Single-family building permits issued: 25 (2013); Multi-family building permits issued: 4 (2013).
Income: Per capita income: $25,484 (2008-2012 5-year est.); Median household income: $50,342 (2008-2012 5-year est.); Average household income: $64,006 (2008-2012 5-year est.); Percent of households with income of $100,000 or more: 15.5% (2008-2012 5-year est.); Poverty rate: 10.0% (2008-2012 5-year est.); Bankruptcy rate: 3.31% (2013).
Education: Percent of population age 25 and over with: High school diploma (including GED) or higher: 86.2% (2008-2012 5-year est.); Bachelor's degree or higher: 14.9% (2008-2012 5-year est.); Master's degree or higher: 4.3% (2008-2012 5-year est.).
Housing: Homeownership rate: 74.5% (2008-2012 5-year est.); Median home value: $113,000 (2008-2012 5-year est.); Median contract rent: $482 per month (2008-2012 5-year est.); Median year structure built: 1956 (2008-2012 5-year est.)
Health: Birth rate: 103.3 per 10,000 population (2013); Death rate: 106.7 per 10,000 population (2013); Age-adjusted cancer mortality rate: 186.0 deaths per 100,000 population (2011); Number of physicians: 17.7 per 10,000 population (2011); Hospital beds: 22.2 per 10,000 population (2010); Hospital admissions: 1,269.2 per 10,000 population (2010).
Elections: 2012 Presidential election results: 45.4% Obama, 52.7% Romney
National and State Parks: Franklin Creek State Park; Green River State Wildlife Management Area; Hennepin Canal Parkway State Park
Additional Information Contacts
Lee County Government . . . . (815) 288-3309
  http://www.leecountyil.com

Lee County Communities

AMBOY (city). Covers a land area of 6.294 square miles and a water area of 0 square miles. Located at 41.73° N. Lat; 89.37° W. Long. Elevation is 745 feet.
History: In Amboy in 1854, Scotch-Irish immigrants Samuel Carson and John T. Pirie opened a small grocery store which later became the firm of Carson Pirie Scott & Company.
Population: 2,377 (1990); 2,561 (2000); 2,500 (2010); Density: 401.5 persons per square mile (2008-2012 5-year est.); Race: 99.4% White, 0.1% Black/African American, 0.3% Asian, 0.0% American Indian/Alaska Native, 0.0% Native Hawaiian/Other Pacific Islander, 0.2% Some other race, 0.2% Two or more races, 7.0% Hispanic of any race (2008-2012

5-year est.); Average household size: 2.42 (2008-2012 5-year est.); Median age: 42.0 (2008-2012 5-year est.); Males per 100 females: 96.8 (2008-2012 5-year est.); Marriage status: 26.9% never married, 43.9% now married, 13.6% widowed, 15.6% divorced (2008-2012 5-year est.); Foreign born: 1.2% (2008-2012 5-year est.); Ancestry (includes multiple ancestries): 35.4% German, 22.8% Irish, 11.7% American, 8.8% English, 6.8% Italian (2008-2012 5-year est.).

Economy: Single-family building permits issued: 0 (2013); Multi-family building permits issued: 0 (2013); Homeowner vacancy rate: 0.0%. Rental vacancy rate: 10.7%. (2008-2012 5-year est.); Employment by occupation: 6.0% management, business, and financial, 3.2% computer, engineering, and science, 6.4% education, legal, community service, arts, and media, 4.6% healthcare practitioners, 25.3% service, 17.7% sales and office, 13.1% natural resources, construction, and maintenance, 23.8% production, transportation, and material moving (2008-2012 5-year est.).

Income: Per capita income: $22,443 (2008-2012 5-year est.); Median household income: $43,378 (2008-2012 5-year est.); Average household income: $54,531 (2008-2012 5-year est.); Percent of households with income of $100,000 or more: 13.4% (2008-2012 5-year est.); Poverty rate: 11.8% (2008-2012 5-year est.).

Education: Percent of population age 25 and over with: High school diploma (including GED) or higher: 80.4% (2008-2012 5-year est.); Bachelor's degree or higher: 11.9% (2008-2012 5-year est.); Master's degree or higher: 4.9% (2008-2012 5-year est.).

School District(s)
Amboy CUSD 272 (PK-12)
   2011-12 Enrollment: 816 . . . . (815) 857-2164
Housing: Homeownership rate: 71.5% (2008-2012 5-year est.); Median home value: $93,600 (2008-2012 5-year est.); Median contract rent: $466 per month (2008-2012 5-year est.); Median year structure built: 1957 (2008-2012 5-year est.).
Health Insurance: 66.9% Private; 32.3% Public; 13.1% None. (2008-2012 5-year est.)
Safety: Violent crime rate: 32.5 per 10,000 population; Property crime rate: 154.5 per 10,000 population (2012).
Transportation: Commute to work: 87.0% car, 5.6% public transportation, 2.7% walk, 1.7% work from home (2008-2012 5-year est.); Travel time to work: 37.3% less than 15 minutes, 38.4% 15 to 30 minutes, 9.8% 30 to 45 minutes, 4.3% 45 to 60 minutes, 10.2% 60 minutes or more (2008-2012 5-year est.)

ASHTON (village). Covers a land area of 0.656 square miles and a water area of 0 square miles. Located at 41.87° N. Lat; 89.22° W. Long. Elevation is 823 feet.
Population: 1,042 (1990); 1,142 (2000); 972 (2010); Density: 1,536.2 persons per square mile (2008-2012 5-year est.); Race: 96.3% White, 0.3% Black/African American, 0.0% Asian, 0.0% American Indian/Alaska Native, 0.0% Native Hawaiian/Other Pacific Islander, 3.4% Some other race, 3.4% Two or more races, 2.0% Hispanic of any race (2008-2012 5-year est.); Average household size: 2.28 (2008-2012 5-year est.); Median age: 41.7 (2008-2012 5-year est.); Males per 100 females: 101.4 (2008-2012 5-year est.); Marriage status: 34.9% never married, 43.5% now married, 8.3% widowed, 13.3% divorced (2008-2012 5-year est.); Foreign born: 0.6% (2008-2012 5-year est.); Ancestry (includes multiple ancestries): 35.1% German, 17.9% Irish, 9.0% English, 7.1% American, 5.2% Swedish (2008-2012 5-year est.).
Economy: Single-family building permits issued: 0 (2013); Multi-family building permits issued: 0 (2013); Homeowner vacancy rate: 0.0%. Rental vacancy rate: 0.0%. (2008-2012 5-year est.); Employment by occupation: 9.5% management, business, and financial, 1.5% computer, engineering, and science, 7.7% education, legal, community service, arts, and media, 1.4% healthcare practitioners, 15.0% service, 19.6% sales and office, 9.5% natural resources, construction, and maintenance, 35.8% production, transportation, and material moving (2008-2012 5-year est.).
Income: Per capita income: $23,516 (2008-2012 5-year est.); Median household income: $45,192 (2008-2012 5-year est.); Average household income: $53,836 (2008-2012 5-year est.); Percent of households with income of $100,000 or more: 13.4% (2008-2012 5-year est.); Poverty rate: 7.9% (2008-2012 5-year est.).
Education: Percent of population age 25 and over with: High school diploma (including GED) or higher: 84.9% (2008-2012 5-year est.); Bachelor's degree or higher: 10.8% (2008-2012 5-year est.); Master's degree or higher: 2.7% (2008-2012 5-year est.).

School District(s)
Ashton-Franklin Center CUSD 275 (PK-12)
   2011-12 Enrollment: 564 . . . . (815) 453-7461
Housing: Homeownership rate: 68.2% (2008-2012 5-year est.); Median home value: $94,800 (2008-2012 5-year est.); Median contract rent: $398 per month (2008-2012 5-year est.); Median year structure built: Before 1940 (2008-2012 5-year est.).
Health Insurance: 73.5% Private; 33.5% Public; 10.0% None. (2008-2012 5-year est.)
Transportation: Commute to work: 86.7% car, 2.8% public transportation, 7.5% walk, 3.1% work from home (2008-2012 5-year est.); Travel time to work: 44.9% less than 15 minutes, 28.6% 15 to 30 minutes, 17.5% 30 to 45 minutes, 5.5% 45 to 60 minutes, 3.4% 60 minutes or more (2008-2012 5-year est.)

COMPTON (village). Covers a land area of 0.165 square miles and a water area of 0 square miles. Located at 41.69° N. Lat; 89.09° W. Long. Elevation is 968 feet.
Population: 343 (1990); 347 (2000); 303 (2010); Density: 1,940.6 persons per square mile (2008-2012 5-year est.); Race: 98.1% White, 0.0% Black/African American, 0.0% Asian, 0.0% American Indian/Alaska Native, 0.0% Native Hawaiian/Other Pacific Islander, 1.9% Some other race, 0.6% Two or more races, 4.1% Hispanic of any race (2008-2012 5-year est.); Average household size: 2.67 (2008-2012 5-year est.); Median age: 32.8 (2008-2012 5-year est.); Males per 100 females: 127.0 (2008-2012 5-year est.); Marriage status: 29.1% never married, 53.4% now married, 2.0% widowed, 15.4% divorced (2008-2012 5-year est.); Foreign born: 4.1% (2008-2012 5-year est.); Ancestry (includes multiple ancestries): 24.7% German, 23.4% Irish, 9.1% American, 5.6% Norwegian, 5.3% English (2008-2012 5-year est.).
Economy: Homeowner vacancy rate: 8.5%. Rental vacancy rate: 14.8%. (2008-2012 5-year est.); Employment by occupation: 4.8% management, business, and financial, 1.4% computer, engineering, and science, 8.2% education, legal, community service, arts, and media, 2.7% healthcare practitioners, 21.8% service, 15.6% sales and office, 10.9% natural resources, construction, and maintenance, 34.7% production, transportation, and material moving (2008-2012 5-year est.).
Income: Per capita income: $21,755 (2008-2012 5-year est.); Median household income: $50,000 (2008-2012 5-year est.); Average household income: $58,006 (2008-2012 5-year est.); Percent of households with income of $100,000 or more: 10.0% (2008-2012 5-year est.); Poverty rate: 13.1% (2008-2012 5-year est.).
Education: Percent of population age 25 and over with: High school diploma (including GED) or higher: 87.3% (2008-2012 5-year est.); Bachelor's degree or higher: 14.7% (2008-2012 5-year est.); Master's degree or higher: 2.5% (2008-2012 5-year est.).
Housing: Homeownership rate: 80.8% (2008-2012 5-year est.); Median home value: $94,400 (2008-2012 5-year est.); Median contract rent: $619 per month (2008-2012 5-year est.); Median year structure built: Before 1940 (2008-2012 5-year est.).
Health Insurance: 72.5% Private; 22.8% Public; 12.8% None. (2008-2012 5-year est.)
Transportation: Commute to work: 97.9% car, 0.0% public transportation, 1.4% walk, 0.7% work from home (2008-2012 5-year est.); Travel time to work: 11.7% less than 15 minutes, 42.8% 15 to 30 minutes, 22.8% 30 to 45 minutes, 15.9% 45 to 60 minutes, 6.9% 60 minutes or more (2008-2012 5-year est.)

DIXON (city). County seat. Covers a land area of 7.431 square miles and a water area of 0.432 square miles. Located at 41.84° N. Lat; 89.48° W. Long. Elevation is 682 feet.
History: Dixon was settled in 1830 by John Dixon, who operated a trading post and tavern. Industry soon came to Dixon because of the water power available from the Rock River.
Population: 15,144 (1990); 15,941 (2000); 15,733 (2010); Density: 2,063.3 persons per square mile (2008-2012 5-year est.); Race: 85.1% White, 10.0% Black/African American, 0.8% Asian, 0.3% American Indian/Alaska Native, 0.0% Native Hawaiian/Other Pacific Islander, 3.8% Some other race, 2.4% Two or more races, 7.4% Hispanic of any race (2008-2012 5-year est.); Average household size: 2.28 (2008-2012 5-year est.); Median age: 39.4 (2008-2012 5-year est.); Males per 100 females: 121.8 (2008-2012 5-year est.); Marriage status: 34.5% never married, 43.9% now married, 9.2% widowed, 12.4% divorced (2008-2012 5-year est.); Foreign born: 2.5% (2008-2012 5-year est.); Ancestry (includes

multiple ancestries): 30.4% German, 18.7% Irish, 8.6% English, 6.8% American, 5.2% Dutch (2008-2012 5-year est.).
Economy: Single-family building permits issued: 11 (2013); Multi-family building permits issued: 4 (2013); Homeowner vacancy rate: 0.9%. Rental vacancy rate: 5.6%. (2008-2012 5-year est.); Employment by occupation: 9.0% management, business, and financial, 3.9% computer, engineering, and science, 6.3% education, legal, community service, arts, and media, 6.9% healthcare practitioners, 22.2% service, 21.9% sales and office, 6.5% natural resources, construction, and maintenance, 23.3% production, transportation, and material moving (2008-2012 5-year est.).
Income: Per capita income: $21,254 (2008-2012 5-year est.); Median household income: $39,924 (2008-2012 5-year est.); Average household income: $52,025 (2008-2012 5-year est.); Percent of households with income of $100,000 or more: 9.6% (2008-2012 5-year est.); Poverty rate: 11.5% (2008-2012 5-year est.).
Education: Percent of population age 25 and over with: High school diploma (including GED) or higher: 82.3% (2008-2012 5-year est.); Bachelor's degree or higher: 13.6% (2008-2012 5-year est.); Master's degree or higher: 2.9% (2008-2012 5-year est.).

School District(s)
Dixon USD 170 (PK-12)
    2011-12 Enrollment: 2,767 . . . . (815) 284-7722

Two-year College(s)
Sauk Valley Community College (Public)
    Fall 2012 Enrollment: 2,230 . . . . (815) 288-5511
    2012-13 Tuition: In-state $8,406; Out-of-state $8,666
Housing: Homeownership rate: 65.9% (2008-2012 5-year est.); Median home value: $93,500 (2008-2012 5-year est.); Median contract rent: $474 per month (2008-2012 5-year est.); Median year structure built: 1953 (2008-2012 5-year est.).
Health Insurance: 67.6% Private; 35.7% Public; 11.9% None. (2008-2012 5-year est.)
Hospitals: Katherine Shaw Bethea Hospital
Safety: Violent crime rate: 11.0 per 10,000 population; Property crime rate: 239.7 per 10,000 population (2012).
Transportation: Commute to work: 92.5% car, 1.7% public transportation, 1.6% walk, 3.1% work from home (2008-2012 5-year est.); Travel time to work: 56.5% less than 15 minutes, 24.3% 15 to 30 minutes, 8.7% 30 to 45 minutes, 4.4% 45 to 60 minutes, 6.1% 60 minutes or more (2008-2012 5-year est.)
Airports: Dixon Municipal Airport (general aviation)
Additional Information Contacts
City of Dixon . . . . (815) 288-1485
    http://discoverdixon.org
Dixon Area Chamber of Commerce & Industry . . . . (815) 284-3361
    http://www.dixonillinoischamber.com

ELDENA (unincorporated postal area)
Zip Code: 61324
    Covers a land area of 0.194 square miles and a water area of 0 square miles. Located at 41.76° N. Lat; 89.41° W. Long. Elevation is 801 feet.
    Population: 109 (2010); Density: 560.2 persons per square mile (2010); Race: 99.1% White, 0.0% Black/African American, 0.0% Asian, 0.0% American Indian/Alaska Native, 0.0% Native Hawaiian/Other Pacific Islander, 0.9% Some other race, 0.9% Two or more races, 3.7% Hispanic of any race (2010); Average household size: 2.79 (2010); Median age: 45.9 (2010); Males per 100 females: 113.7 (2010); Homeownership rate: 87.2% (2010)

FRANKLIN GROVE (village). Covers a land area of 0.485 square miles and a water area of 0 square miles. Located at 41.84° N. Lat; 89.30° W. Long. Elevation is 804 feet.
Population: 968 (1990); 1,052 (2000); 1,021 (2010); Density: 2,416.8 persons per square mile (2008-2012 5-year est.); Race: 96.9% White, 0.8% Black/African American, 0.0% Asian, 0.0% American Indian/Alaska Native, 0.0% Native Hawaiian/Other Pacific Islander, 2.3% Some other race, 0.0% Two or more races, 1.1% Hispanic of any race (2008-2012 5-year est.); Average household size: 2.97 (2008-2012 5-year est.); Median age: 38.7 (2008-2012 5-year est.); Males per 100 females: 94.2 (2008-2012 5-year est.); Marriage status: 19.1% never married, 60.9% now married, 12.9% widowed, 7.1% divorced (2008-2012 5-year est.); Foreign born: 1.7% (2008-2012 5-year est.); Ancestry (includes multiple ancestries): 32.5% German, 22.9% Irish, 17.3% American, 10.1% English, 5.2% Swedish (2008-2012 5-year est.).

Economy: Single-family building permits issued: 0 (2013); Multi-family building permits issued: 0 (2013); Homeowner vacancy rate: 4.2%. Rental vacancy rate: 15.9%. (2008-2012 5-year est.); Employment by occupation: 11.0% management, business, and financial, 3.7% computer, engineering, and science, 3.7% education, legal, community service, arts, and media, 4.5% healthcare practitioners, 19.1% service, 19.6% sales and office, 16.8% natural resources, construction, and maintenance, 21.7% production, transportation, and material moving (2008-2012 5-year est.).
Income: Per capita income: $19,327 (2008-2012 5-year est.); Median household income: $46,136 (2008-2012 5-year est.); Average household income: $56,015 (2008-2012 5-year est.); Percent of households with income of $100,000 or more: 10.4% (2008-2012 5-year est.); Poverty rate: 7.2% (2008-2012 5-year est.).
Education: Percent of population age 25 and over with: High school diploma (including GED) or higher: 83.4% (2008-2012 5-year est.); Bachelor's degree or higher: 7.7% (2008-2012 5-year est.); Master's degree or higher: 1.3% (2008-2012 5-year est.).

School District(s)
Ashton-Franklin Center CUSD 275 (PK-12)
    2011-12 Enrollment: 564 . . . . (815) 453-7461
Housing: Homeownership rate: 70.4% (2008-2012 5-year est.); Median home value: $92,100 (2008-2012 5-year est.); Median contract rent: $516 per month (2008-2012 5-year est.); Median year structure built: Before 1940 (2008-2012 5-year est.).
Health Insurance: 62.2% Private; 30.9% Public; 16.6% None. (2008-2012 5-year est.)
Safety: Violent crime rate: 0.0 per 10,000 population; Property crime rate: 89.6 per 10,000 population (2012).
Transportation: Commute to work: 92.9% car, 0.4% public transportation, 4.0% walk, 1.1% work from home (2008-2012 5-year est.); Travel time to work: 30.2% less than 15 minutes, 36.6% 15 to 30 minutes, 11.1% 30 to 45 minutes, 8.8% 45 to 60 minutes, 13.3% 60 minutes or more (2008-2012 5-year est.)

HARMON (village). Covers a land area of 0.146 square miles and a water area of 0 square miles. Located at 41.72° N. Lat; 89.56° W. Long. Elevation is 676 feet.
Population: 186 (1990); 149 (2000); 120 (2010); Density: 1,077.0 persons per square mile (2008-2012 5-year est.); Race: 99.4% White, 0.0% Black/African American, 0.0% Asian, 0.0% American Indian/Alaska Native, 0.0% Native Hawaiian/Other Pacific Islander, 0.6% Some other race, 0.6% Two or more races, 1.3% Hispanic of any race (2008-2012 5-year est.); Average household size: 2.38 (2008-2012 5-year est.); Median age: 41.6 (2008-2012 5-year est.); Males per 100 females: 115.1 (2008-2012 5-year est.); Marriage status: 38.1% never married, 47.8% now married, 6.0% widowed, 8.2% divorced (2008-2012 5-year est.); Foreign born: 0.0% (2008-2012 5-year est.); Ancestry (includes multiple ancestries): 42.7% German, 19.7% Irish, 12.1% English, 4.5% American, 1.9% Polish (2008-2012 5-year est.).
Economy: Homeowner vacancy rate: 0.0%. Rental vacancy rate: 0.0%. (2008-2012 5-year est.); Employment by occupation: 26.6% management, business, and financial, 0.0% computer, engineering, and science, 1.3% education, legal, community service, arts, and media, 2.5% healthcare practitioners, 21.5% service, 13.9% sales and office, 12.7% natural resources, construction, and maintenance, 21.5% production, transportation, and material moving (2008-2012 5-year est.).
Income: Per capita income: $22,275 (2008-2012 5-year est.); Median household income: $43,750 (2008-2012 5-year est.); Average household income: $49,553 (2008-2012 5-year est.); Percent of households with income of $100,000 or more: 12.1% (2008-2012 5-year est.); Poverty rate: 6.4% (2008-2012 5-year est.).
Education: Percent of population age 25 and over with: High school diploma (including GED) or higher: 90.3% (2008-2012 5-year est.); Bachelor's degree or higher: 3.5% (2008-2012 5-year est.); Master's degree or higher: 0.9% (2008-2012 5-year est.).
Housing: Homeownership rate: 77.3% (2008-2012 5-year est.); Median home value: $81,200 (2008-2012 5-year est.); Median contract rent: $423 per month (2008-2012 5-year est.); Median year structure built: 1941 (2008-2012 5-year est.).
Health Insurance: 73.9% Private; 25.5% Public; 17.8% None. (2008-2012 5-year est.)
Transportation: Commute to work: 86.1% car, 0.0% public transportation, 7.6% walk, 6.3% work from home (2008-2012 5-year est.); Travel time to work: 18.9% less than 15 minutes, 64.9% 15 to 30 minutes, 9.5% 30 to 45

minutes, 6.8% 45 to 60 minutes, 0.0% 60 minutes or more (2008-2012 5-year est.)

LEE (village).
Covers a land area of 0.162 square miles and a water area of 0 square miles. Located at 41.79° N. Lat; 88.94° W. Long. Elevation is 938 feet.

Population: 319 (1990); 313 (2000); 337 (2010); Density: 2,191.8 persons per square mile (2008-2012 5-year est.); Race: 99.2% White, 0.0% Black/African American, 0.0% Asian, 0.3% American Indian/Alaska Native, 0.0% Native Hawaiian/Other Pacific Islander, 0.5% Some other race, 0.6% Two or more races, 1.7% Hispanic of any race (2008-2012 5-year est.); Average household size: 2.76 (2008-2012 5-year est.); Median age: 38.0 (2008-2012 5-year est.); Males per 100 females: 82.6 (2008-2012 5-year est.); Marriage status: 34.0% never married, 44.0% now married, 4.5% widowed, 17.5% divorced (2008-2012 5-year est.); Foreign born: 1.1% (2008-2012 5-year est.); Ancestry (includes multiple ancestries): 35.7% German, 33.7% Irish, 19.7% English, 11.0% Norwegian, 5.1% Czech (2008-2012 5-year est.).

Economy: Single-family building permits issued: 1 (2013); Multi-family building permits issued: 0 (2013); Homeowner vacancy rate: 0.0%. Rental vacancy rate: 13.5%. (2008-2012 5-year est.); Employment by occupation: 3.0% management, business, and financial, 6.7% computer, engineering, and science, 15.2% education, legal, community service, arts, and media, 0.0% healthcare practitioners, 10.4% service, 23.2% sales and office, 14.0% natural resources, construction, and maintenance, 27.4% production, transportation, and material moving (2008-2012 5-year est.).

Income: Per capita income: $23,378 (2008-2012 5-year est.); Median household income: $45,250 (2008-2012 5-year est.); Average household income: $63,729 (2008-2012 5-year est.); Percent of households with income of $100,000 or more: 13.2% (2008-2012 5-year est.); Poverty rate: 19.7% (2008-2012 5-year est.).

Education: Percent of population age 25 and over with: High school diploma (including GED) or higher: 89.9% (2008-2012 5-year est.); Bachelor's degree or higher: 14.7% (2008-2012 5-year est.); Master's degree or higher: 7.8% (2008-2012 5-year est.).

Housing: Homeownership rate: 65.1% (2008-2012 5-year est.); Median home value: $125,000 (2008-2012 5-year est.); Median contract rent: $547 per month (2008-2012 5-year est.); Median year structure built: 1966 (2008-2012 5-year est.).

Health Insurance: 63.2% Private; 30.3% Public; 20.8% None. (2008-2012 5-year est.)

Transportation: Commute to work: 95.6% car, 0.0% public transportation, 0.0% walk, 4.4% work from home (2008-2012 5-year est.); Travel time to work: 17.8% less than 15 minutes, 35.5% 15 to 30 minutes, 26.3% 30 to 45 minutes, 9.9% 45 to 60 minutes, 10.5% 60 minutes or more (2008-2012 5-year est.)

LEE CENTER (unincorporated postal area)
Zip Code: 61331

Covers a land area of 0.027 square miles and a water area of 0 square miles. Located at 41.74° N. Lat; 89.27° W. Long. Elevation is 794 feet. Population: 55 (2010); Density: 1,990.8 persons per square mile (2010); Race: 98.2% White, 0.0% Black/African American, 0.0% Asian, 0.0% American Indian/Alaska Native, 0.0% Native Hawaiian/Other Pacific Islander, 1.8% Some other race, 1.8% Two or more races, 0.0% Hispanic of any race (2010); Average household size: 2.29 (2010); Median age: 30.8 (2010); Males per 100 females: 96.4 (2010); Homeownership rate: 66.7% (2010)

NACHUSA (unincorporated postal area)
Zip Code: 61057

Covers a land area of 1.694 square miles and a water area of 0 square miles. Located at 41.82° N. Lat; 89.38° W. Long. Elevation is 791 feet. Population: 168 (2010); Density: 99.1 persons per square mile (2010); Race: 94.0% White, 1.2% Black/African American, 0.0% Asian, 0.0% American Indian/Alaska Native, 0.0% Native Hawaiian/Other Pacific Islander, 4.8% Some other race, 4.2% Two or more races, 8.3% Hispanic of any race (2010); Average household size: 2.77 (2010); Median age: 28.2 (2010); Males per 100 females: 110.0 (2010); Homeownership rate: 83.0% (2010)

NELSON (village).
Covers a land area of 0.244 square miles and a water area of 0.004 square miles. Located at 41.80° N. Lat; 89.61° W. Long. Elevation is 653 feet.

Population: 200 (1990); 163 (2000); 170 (2010); Density: 1,156.8 persons per square mile (2008-2012 5-year est.); Race: 97.2% White, 0.0% Black/African American, 0.0% Asian, 0.0% American Indian/Alaska Native, 0.0% Native Hawaiian/Other Pacific Islander, 2.8% Some other race, 2.1% Two or more races, 7.8% Hispanic of any race (2008-2012 5-year est.); Average household size: 3.53 (2008-2012 5-year est.); Median age: 28.7 (2008-2012 5-year est.); Males per 100 females: 113.6 (2008-2012 5-year est.); Marriage status: 43.1% never married, 38.1% now married, 7.9% widowed, 10.9% divorced (2008-2012 5-year est.); Foreign born: 0.4% (2008-2012 5-year est.); Ancestry (includes multiple ancestries): 54.6% German, 22.3% American, 13.8% Irish, 12.4% Dutch, 4.6% English (2008-2012 5-year est.).

Economy: Homeowner vacancy rate: 0.0%. Rental vacancy rate: 0.0%. (2008-2012 5-year est.); Employment by occupation: 4.7% management, business, and financial, 0.0% computer, engineering, and science, 1.6% education, legal, community service, arts, and media, 0.0% healthcare practitioners, 14.1% service, 34.4% sales and office, 7.0% natural resources, construction, and maintenance, 38.3% production, transportation, and material moving (2008-2012 5-year est.).

Income: Per capita income: $16,684 (2008-2012 5-year est.); Median household income: $43,750 (2008-2012 5-year est.); Average household income: $56,450 (2008-2012 5-year est.); Percent of households with income of $100,000 or more: 17.5% (2008-2012 5-year est.); Poverty rate: 7.8% (2008-2012 5-year est.).

Education: Percent of population age 25 and over with: High school diploma (including GED) or higher: 80.5% (2008-2012 5-year est.); Bachelor's degree or higher: 6.0% (2008-2012 5-year est.); Master's degree or higher: 0.0% (2008-2012 5-year est.).

School District(s)
Nelson Public SD No 8 (PK-08)

    2011-12 Enrollment: 40 . . . . (815) 251-4412

Housing: Homeownership rate: 86.3% (2008-2012 5-year est.); Median home value: $63,400 (2008-2012 5-year est.); Median contract rent: $456 per month (2008-2012 5-year est.); Median year structure built: Before 1940 (2008-2012 5-year est.).

Health Insurance: 52.1% Private; 50.4% Public; 7.8% None. (2008-2012 5-year est.)

Transportation: Commute to work: 99.2% car, 0.0% public transportation, 0.0% walk, 0.8% work from home (2008-2012 5-year est.); Travel time to work: 19.5% less than 15 minutes, 62.6% 15 to 30 minutes, 14.6% 30 to 45 minutes, 3.3% 45 to 60 minutes, 0.0% 60 minutes or more (2008-2012 5-year est.)

PAW PAW (village).
Aka Pawpaw. Covers a land area of 0.586 square miles and a water area of 0 square miles. Located at 41.69° N. Lat; 88.98° W. Long. Elevation is 945 feet.

Population: 791 (1990); 852 (2000); 870 (2010); Density: 1,641.6 persons per square mile (2008-2012 5-year est.); Race: 97.5% White, 1.2% Black/African American, 0.0% Asian, 0.0% American Indian/Alaska Native, 0.0% Native Hawaiian/Other Pacific Islander, 1.3% Some other race, 1.0% Two or more races, 2.5% Hispanic of any race (2008-2012 5-year est.); Average household size: 2.61 (2008-2012 5-year est.); Median age: 38.2 (2008-2012 5-year est.); Males per 100 females: 83.2 (2008-2012 5-year est.); Marriage status: 30.2% never married, 50.1% now married, 5.1% widowed, 14.6% divorced (2008-2012 5-year est.); Foreign born: 0.0% (2008-2012 5-year est.); Ancestry (includes multiple ancestries): 43.6% German, 14.0% Irish, 8.6% English, 7.1% Italian, 7.0% Scottish (2008-2012 5-year est.).

Economy: Single-family building permits issued: 0 (2013); Multi-family building permits issued: 0 (2013); Homeowner vacancy rate: 2.3%. Rental vacancy rate: 15.8%. (2008-2012 5-year est.); Employment by occupation: 9.3% management, business, and financial, 4.4% computer, engineering, and science, 7.8% education, legal, community service, arts, and media, 3.1% healthcare practitioners, 20.8% service, 23.1% sales and office, 11.3% natural resources, construction, and maintenance, 20.2% production, transportation, and material moving (2008-2012 5-year est.).

Income: Per capita income: $25,466 (2008-2012 5-year est.); Median household income: $58,594 (2008-2012 5-year est.); Average household income: $64,094 (2008-2012 5-year est.); Percent of households with income of $100,000 or more: 10.8% (2008-2012 5-year est.); Poverty rate: 18.5% (2008-2012 5-year est.).

Education: Percent of population age 25 and over with: High school diploma (including GED) or higher: 91.4% (2008-2012 5-year est.); Bachelor's degree or higher: 14.5% (2008-2012 5-year est.); Master's degree or higher: 3.0% (2008-2012 5-year est.).

School District(s)

Paw Paw CUSD 271 (PK-12)
    2011-12 Enrollment: 270 . . . . (815) 627-2841
Housing: Homeownership rate: 78.3% (2008-2012 5-year est.); Median home value: $127,500 (2008-2012 5-year est.); Median contract rent: $560 per month (2008-2012 5-year est.); Median year structure built: Before 1940 (2008-2012 5-year est.).
Health Insurance: 67.0% Private; 33.1% Public; 13.6% None. (2008-2012 5-year est.)
Transportation: Commute to work: 93.3% car, 0.0% public transportation, 2.3% walk, 4.4% work from home (2008-2012 5-year est.); Travel time to work: 17.8% less than 15 minutes, 24.1% 15 to 30 minutes, 21.9% 30 to 45 minutes, 14.2% 45 to 60 minutes, 21.9% 60 minutes or more (2008-2012 5-year est.)

STEWARD (village). Covers a land area of 0.205 square miles and a water area of 0 square miles. Located at 41.85° N. Lat; 89.02° W. Long. Elevation is 820 feet.
Population: 282 (1990); 271 (2000); 256 (2010); Density: 1,436.5 persons per square mile (2008-2012 5-year est.); Race: 100.0% White, 0.0% Black/African American, 0.0% Asian, 0.0% American Indian/Alaska Native, 0.0% Native Hawaiian/Other Pacific Islander, 0.0% Some other race, 0.0% Two or more races, 5.8% Hispanic of any race (2008-2012 5-year est.); Average household size: 3.06 (2008-2012 5-year est.); Median age: 34.1 (2008-2012 5-year est.); Males per 100 females: 114.6 (2008-2012 5-year est.); Marriage status: 26.9% never married, 64.9% now married, 4.8% widowed, 3.4% divorced (2008-2012 5-year est.); Foreign born: 0.7% (2008-2012 5-year est.); Ancestry (includes multiple ancestries): 42.5% German, 18.0% Irish, 9.5% American, 7.8% English, 7.5% Norwegian (2008-2012 5-year est.).
Economy: Homeowner vacancy rate: 0.0%. Rental vacancy rate: 0.0%. (2008-2012 5-year est.); Employment by occupation: 16.5% management, business, and financial, 3.1% computer, engineering, and science, 11.0% education, legal, community service, arts, and media, 7.9% healthcare practitioners, 11.0% service, 19.7% sales and office, 7.9% natural resources, construction, and maintenance, 22.8% production, transportation, and material moving (2008-2012 5-year est.).
Income: Per capita income: $19,936 (2008-2012 5-year est.); Median household income: $63,000 (2008-2012 5-year est.); Average household income: $61,461 (2008-2012 5-year est.); Percent of households with income of $100,000 or more: 19.8% (2008-2012 5-year est.); Poverty rate: 20.4% (2008-2012 5-year est.).
Education: Percent of population age 25 and over with: High school diploma (including GED) or higher: 85.8% (2008-2012 5-year est.); Bachelor's degree or higher: 16.5% (2008-2012 5-year est.); Master's degree or higher: 1.7% (2008-2012 5-year est.).

School District(s)

Steward ESD 220 (KG-08)
    2011-12 Enrollment: 67 . . . . (815) 396-2413
Housing: Homeownership rate: 81.3% (2008-2012 5-year est.); Median home value: $115,900 (2008-2012 5-year est.); Median contract rent: $241 per month (2008-2012 5-year est.); Median year structure built: Before 1940 (2008-2012 5-year est.).
Health Insurance: 77.2% Private; 33.7% Public; 4.1% None. (2008-2012 5-year est.)
Transportation: Commute to work: 97.6% car, 0.0% public transportation, 0.0% walk, 0.8% work from home (2008-2012 5-year est.); Travel time to work: 16.9% less than 15 minutes, 35.5% 15 to 30 minutes, 28.2% 30 to 45 minutes, 8.1% 45 to 60 minutes, 11.3% 60 minutes or more (2008-2012 5-year est.)

SUBLETTE (village). Covers a land area of 0.347 square miles and a water area of 0 square miles. Located at 41.64° N. Lat; 89.23° W. Long. Elevation is 919 feet.
Population: 394 (1990); 456 (2000); 449 (2010); Density: 1,132.3 persons per square mile (2008-2012 5-year est.); Race: 100.0% White, 0.0% Black/African American, 0.0% Asian, 0.0% American Indian/Alaska Native, 0.0% Native Hawaiian/Other Pacific Islander, 0.0% Some other race, 0.0% Two or more races, 2.8% Hispanic of any race (2008-2012 5-year est.); Average household size: 1.98 (2008-2012 5-year est.); Median age: 49.2 (2008-2012 5-year est.); Males per 100 females: 85.4 (2008-2012 5-year

est.); Marriage status: 25.4% never married, 54.1% now married, 11.1% widowed, 9.4% divorced (2008-2012 5-year est.); Foreign born: 1.0% (2008-2012 5-year est.); Ancestry (includes multiple ancestries): 51.7% German, 14.8% Irish, 10.2% Polish, 9.7% American, 8.4% French (2008-2012 5-year est.).
Economy: Homeowner vacancy rate: 0.0%. Rental vacancy rate: 0.0%. (2008-2012 5-year est.); Employment by occupation: 15.9% management, business, and financial, 0.5% computer, engineering, and science, 9.8% education, legal, community service, arts, and media, 0.9% healthcare practitioners, 17.8% service, 31.3% sales and office, 12.6% natural resources, construction, and maintenance, 11.2% production, transportation, and material moving (2008-2012 5-year est.).
Income: Per capita income: $29,127 (2008-2012 5-year est.); Median household income: $48,333 (2008-2012 5-year est.); Average household income: $57,775 (2008-2012 5-year est.); Percent of households with income of $100,000 or more: 18.7% (2008-2012 5-year est.); Poverty rate: 3.8% (2008-2012 5-year est.).
Education: Percent of population age 25 and over with: High school diploma (including GED) or higher: 89.4% (2008-2012 5-year est.); Bachelor's degree or higher: 9.6% (2008-2012 5-year est.); Master's degree or higher: 4.6% (2008-2012 5-year est.).
Housing: Homeownership rate: 73.7% (2008-2012 5-year est.); Median home value: $112,500 (2008-2012 5-year est.); Median contract rent: $329 per month (2008-2012 5-year est.); Median year structure built: 1967 (2008-2012 5-year est.).
Health Insurance: 77.1% Private; 40.7% Public; 7.6% None. (2008-2012 5-year est.)
Transportation: Commute to work: 88.8% car, 0.0% public transportation, 3.7% walk, 5.6% work from home (2008-2012 5-year est.); Travel time to work: 52.0% less than 15 minutes, 23.3% 15 to 30 minutes, 13.9% 30 to 45 minutes, 5.0% 45 to 60 minutes, 5.9% 60 minutes or more (2008-2012 5-year est.)

WEST BROOKLYN (village). Covers a land area of 0.107 square miles and a water area of 0 square miles. Located at 41.69° N. Lat; 89.15° W. Long. Elevation is 945 feet.
Population: 164 (1990); 174 (2000); 142 (2010); Density: 1,339.3 persons per square mile (2008-2012 5-year est.); Race: 100.0% White, 0.0% Black/African American, 0.0% Asian, 0.0% American Indian/Alaska Native, 0.0% Native Hawaiian/Other Pacific Islander, 0.0% Some other race, 0.0% Two or more races, 4.9% Hispanic of any race (2008-2012 5-year est.); Average household size: 2.17 (2008-2012 5-year est.); Median age: 48.8 (2008-2012 5-year est.); Males per 100 females: 138.3 (2008-2012 5-year est.); Marriage status: 26.0% never married, 58.0% now married, 0.8% widowed, 15.3% divorced (2008-2012 5-year est.); Foreign born: 1.4% (2008-2012 5-year est.); Ancestry (includes multiple ancestries): 27.3% German, 17.5% Irish, 12.6% French, 7.0% Scotch-Irish, 7.0% American (2008-2012 5-year est.).
Economy: Homeowner vacancy rate: 6.5%. Rental vacancy rate: 0.0%. (2008-2012 5-year est.); Employment by occupation: 7.9% management, business, and financial, 1.1% computer, engineering, and science, 0.0% education, legal, community service, arts, and media, 2.2% healthcare practitioners, 19.1% service, 19.1% sales and office, 37.1% natural resources, construction, and maintenance, 13.5% production, transportation, and material moving (2008-2012 5-year est.).
Income: Per capita income: $27,592 (2008-2012 5-year est.); Median household income: $58,750 (2008-2012 5-year est.); Average household income: $57,848 (2008-2012 5-year est.); Percent of households with income of $100,000 or more: 10.6% (2008-2012 5-year est.); Poverty rate: 2.9% (2008-2012 5-year est.).
Education: Percent of population age 25 and over with: High school diploma (including GED) or higher: 81.0% (2008-2012 5-year est.); Bachelor's degree or higher: 2.9% (2008-2012 5-year est.); Master's degree or higher: 0.0% (2008-2012 5-year est.).
Housing: Homeownership rate: 87.9% (2008-2012 5-year est.); Median home value: $101,500 (2008-2012 5-year est.); Median contract rent: $650 per month (2008-2012 5-year est.); Median year structure built: Before 1940 (2008-2012 5-year est.).
Health Insurance: 69.9% Private; 31.5% Public; 9.1% None. (2008-2012 5-year est.)
Transportation: Commute to work: 91.9% car, 0.0% public transportation, 5.8% walk, 2.3% work from home (2008-2012 5-year est.); Travel time to work: 29.8% less than 15 minutes, 29.8% 15 to 30 minutes, 7.1% 30 to 45 minutes, 3.6% 45 to 60 minutes, 29.8% 60 minutes or more (2008-2012 5-year est.)

Livingston County

Located in east central Illinois; drained by the Vermilion River. Covers a land area of 1,044.285 square miles, a water area of 1.642 square miles, and is located in the Central Time Zone at 40.89° N. Lat., 88.55° W. Long. The county was founded in 1837. County seat is Pontiac.

Livingston County is part of the Pontiac, IL Micropolitan Statistical Area. The entire metro area includes: Livingston County, IL

Weather Station: Pontiac — Elevation: 649 feet

	Jan	Feb	Mar	Apr	May	Jun	Jul	Aug	Sep	Oct	Nov	Dec
High	32	36	48	62	73	81	84	82	77	64	50	36
Low	16	20	29	40	50	61	64	63	54	42	32	20
Precip	1.9	1.6	2.8	3.3	3.9	3.6	4.1	3.7	3.0	3.0	3.2	2.5
Snow	8.0	6.8	2.8	0.8	0.0	0.0	0.0	0.0	0.0	tr	0.8	5.8

High and Low temperatures in degrees Fahrenheit; Precipitation and Snow in inches

Population: 39,301 (1990); 39,678 (2000); 38,950 (2010); Race: 90.9% White, 6.0% Black/African American, 0.6% Asian, 0.0% American Indian/Alaska Native, 0.0% Native Hawaiian/Other Pacific Islander, 2.5% Some other race, 1.1% Two or more races, 4.0% Hispanic of any race (2008-2012 5-year est.); Density: 36.9 persons per square mile (2008-2012 5-year est.); Average household size: 2.38 (2008-2012 5-year est.); Median age: 40.2 (2008-2012 5-year est.); Males per 100 females: 99.6 (2008-2012 5-year est.).
Religion: Six largest groups: 11.7% Catholicism, 11.6% Lutheran, 9.3% Methodist/Pietist, 6.1% Baptist, 4.0% European Free-Church, 2.3% Presbyterian-Reformed (2010)
Economy: Unemployment rate: 6.6% (April 2014); Total civilian labor force: 17,584 (April 2014); Leading industries: 27.6% manufacturing; 17.5% health care and social assistance; 14.0% retail trade (2012); Farms: 1,349 totaling 656,275 acres (2012); Companies that employ 500 or more persons: 2 (2012); Companies that employ 100 to 499 persons: 20 (2012); Companies that employ less than 100 persons: 881 (2012); Black-owned businesses: n/a (2007); Hispanic-owned businesses: n/a (2007); Asian-owned businesses: 64 (2007); Women-owned businesses: 683 (2007); Single-family building permits issued: 28 (2013); Multi-family building permits issued: 4 (2013).
Income: Per capita income: $23,512 (2008-2012 5-year est.); Median household income: $54,339 (2008-2012 5-year est.); Average household income: $62,728 (2008-2012 5-year est.); Percent of households with income of $100,000 or more: 14.7% (2008-2012 5-year est.); Poverty rate: 10.8% (2008-2012 5-year est.); Bankruptcy rate: 3.08% (2013).
Taxes: Total county taxes per capita: $182 (2011); County property taxes per capita: $180 (2011).
Education: Percent of population age 25 and over with: High school diploma (including GED) or higher: 84.9% (2008-2012 5-year est.); Bachelor's degree or higher: 13.8% (2008-2012 5-year est.); Master's degree or higher: 4.7% (2008-2012 5-year est.).
Housing: Homeownership rate: 74.3% (2008-2012 5-year est.); Median home value: $108,300 (2008-2012 5-year est.); Median contract rent: $476 per month (2008-2012 5-year est.); Median year structure built: 1958 (2008-2012 5-year est.)
Health: Birth rate: 108.7 per 10,000 population (2013); Death rate: 92.7 per 10,000 population (2013); Age-adjusted cancer mortality rate: 188.5 deaths per 100,000 population (2011); Number of physicians: 9.0 per 10,000 population (2011); Hospital beds: 10.8 per 10,000 population (2010); Hospital admissions: 414.1 per 10,000 population (2010).
Elections: 2012 Presidential election results: 33.4% Obama, 64.9% Romney
Additional Information Contacts
Livingston County Government . . . . (815) 844-2006
http://www.livingstoncounty-il.org

Livingston County Communities

ANCONA (unincorporated postal area)
Zip Code: 61311
Covers a land area of 15.579 square miles and a water area of 0 square miles. Located at 41.03° N. Lat; 88.86° W. Long. Elevation is 620 feet. Population: 232 (2010); Density: 14.9 persons per square mile (2010); Race: 97.4% White, 0.9% Black/African American, 0.9% Asian, 0.0% American Indian/Alaska Native, 0.0% Native Hawaiian/Other Pacific Islander, 0.8% Some other race, 0.9% Two or more races, 1.3% Hispanic of any race (2010); Average household size: 2.39 (2010); Median age: 51.0 (2010); Males per 100 females: 107.1 (2010); Homeownership rate: 89.6% (2010)

BLACKSTONE (unincorporated postal area)
Zip Code: 61313
Covers a land area of 42.017 square miles and a water area of 0 square miles. Located at 41.07° N. Lat; 88.66° W. Long. Elevation is 738 feet. Population: 282 (2010); Density: 6.7 persons per square mile (2010); Race: 96.5% White, 0.0% Black/African American, 0.0% Asian, 0.0% American Indian/Alaska Native, 0.0% Native Hawaiian/Other Pacific Islander, 3.5% Some other race, 1.4% Two or more races, 5.0% Hispanic of any race (2010); Average household size: 2.52 (2010); Median age: 47.0 (2010); Males per 100 females: 107.4 (2010); Homeownership rate: 83.0% (2010)

CAMPUS (village). Covers a land area of 0.092 square miles and a water area of 0 square miles. Located at 41.02° N. Lat; 88.31° W. Long. Elevation is 656 feet.
Population: 137 (1990); 145 (2000); 166 (2010); Density: 1,441.7 persons per square mile (2008-2012 5-year est.); Race: 99.2% White, 0.0% Black/African American, 0.0% Asian, 0.0% American Indian/Alaska Native, 0.0% Native Hawaiian/Other Pacific Islander, 0.8% Some other race, 0.8% Two or more races, 0.0% Hispanic of any race (2008-2012 5-year est.); Average household size: 2.71 (2008-2012 5-year est.); Median age: 28.8 (2008-2012 5-year est.); Males per 100 females: 72.7 (2008-2012 5-year est.); Marriage status: 45.4% never married, 45.4% now married, 6.5% widowed, 2.8% divorced (2008-2012 5-year est.); Foreign born: 2.3% (2008-2012 5-year est.); Ancestry (includes multiple ancestries): 48.9% Irish, 39.1% German, 15.8% Dutch, 3.8% American, 3.8% Polish (2008-2012 5-year est.).
Economy: Homeowner vacancy rate: 0.0%. Rental vacancy rate: 0.0%. (2008-2012 5-year est.); Employment by occupation: 1.6% management, business, and financial, 0.0% computer, engineering, and science, 3.3% education, legal, community service, arts, and media, 0.0% healthcare practitioners, 41.0% service, 16.4% sales and office, 9.8% natural resources, construction, and maintenance, 27.9% production, transportation, and material moving (2008-2012 5-year est.).
Income: Per capita income: $20,129 (2008-2012 5-year est.); Median household income: $47,321 (2008-2012 5-year est.); Average household income: $54,918 (2008-2012 5-year est.); Percent of households with income of $100,000 or more: 16.3% (2008-2012 5-year est.); Poverty rate: 24.1% (2008-2012 5-year est.).
Education: Percent of population age 25 and over with: High school diploma (including GED) or higher: 96.2% (2008-2012 5-year est.); Bachelor's degree or higher: 6.4% (2008-2012 5-year est.); Master's degree or higher: 1.3% (2008-2012 5-year est.).
Housing: Homeownership rate: 75.5% (2008-2012 5-year est.); Median home value: $101,000 (2008-2012 5-year est.); Median contract rent: $428 per month (2008-2012 5-year est.); Median year structure built: Before 1940 (2008-2012 5-year est.).
Health Insurance: 53.4% Private; 35.3% Public; 26.3% None. (2008-2012 5-year est.)
Transportation: Commute to work: 95.1% car, 0.0% public transportation, 4.9% walk, 0.0% work from home (2008-2012 5-year est.); Travel time to work: 21.3% less than 15 minutes, 24.6% 15 to 30 minutes, 44.3% 30 to 45 minutes, 4.9% 45 to 60 minutes, 4.9% 60 minutes or more (2008-2012 5-year est.)

CHATSWORTH (town). Covers a land area of 2.713 square miles and a water area of <.001 square miles. Located at 40.71° N. Lat; 88.30° W. Long. Elevation is 735 feet.
History: Chatsworth was laid out in 1858, and devloped as a farming community and manufacturer of tiles and bricks from local clay.
Population: 1,186 (1990); 1,265 (2000); 1,205 (2010); Density: 447.5 persons per square mile (2008-2012 5-year est.); Race: 96.0% White, 0.0% Black/African American, 1.3% Asian, 0.0% American Indian/Alaska Native, 0.0% Native Hawaiian/Other Pacific Islander, 2.7% Some other race, 0.7% Two or more races, 4.9% Hispanic of any race (2008-2012 5-year est.); Average household size: 2.43 (2008-2012 5-year est.); Median age: 38.0 (2008-2012 5-year est.); Males per 100 females: 90.3 (2008-2012 5-year est.); Marriage status: 25.8% never married, 48.9% now married, 11.1% widowed, 14.3% divorced (2008-2012 5-year est.); Foreign born: 1.6% (2008-2012 5-year est.); Ancestry (includes multiple ancestries): 32.9% German, 13.9% Irish, 11.1% American, 6.8% Italian, 6.3% English (2008-2012 5-year est.).

Economy: Single-family building permits issued: 0 (2013); Multi-family building permits issued: 0 (2013); Homeowner vacancy rate: 1.4%. Rental vacancy rate: 4.8%. (2008-2012 5-year est.); Employment by occupation: 8.2% management, business, and financial, 2.3% computer, engineering, and science, 6.1% education, legal, community service, arts, and media, 2.1% healthcare practitioners, 19.2% service, 25.1% sales and office, 11.2% natural resources, construction, and maintenance, 25.8% production, transportation, and material moving (2008-2012 5-year est.).
Income: Per capita income: $17,313 (2008-2012 5-year est.); Median household income: $31,618 (2008-2012 5-year est.); Average household income: $42,040 (2008-2012 5-year est.); Percent of households with income of $100,000 or more: 5.2% (2008-2012 5-year est.); Poverty rate: 25.5% (2008-2012 5-year est.).
Education: Percent of population age 25 and over with: High school diploma (including GED) or higher: 79.7% (2008-2012 5-year est.); Bachelor's degree or higher: 7.7% (2008-2012 5-year est.); Master's degree or higher: 2.5% (2008-2012 5-year est.).

School District(s)
Prairie Central CUSD 8 (PK-12)
    2011-12 Enrollment: 2,159 . . . . (815) 692-2504
Housing: Homeownership rate: 68.0% (2008-2012 5-year est.); Median home value: $69,400 (2008-2012 5-year est.); Median contract rent: $368 per month (2008-2012 5-year est.); Median year structure built: 1957 (2008-2012 5-year est.).
Health Insurance: 53.1% Private; 52.6% Public; 8.0% None. (2008-2012 5-year est.)
Transportation: Commute to work: 89.8% car, 1.7% public transportation, 4.5% walk, 0.0% work from home (2008-2012 5-year est.); Travel time to work: 44.8% less than 15 minutes, 22.3% 15 to 30 minutes, 17.1% 30 to 45 minutes, 6.4% 45 to 60 minutes, 9.5% 60 minutes or more (2008-2012 5-year est.)

CORNELL (village). Covers a land area of 0.641 square miles and a water area of 0 square miles. Located at 40.99° N. Lat; 88.73° W. Long. Elevation is 630 feet.
Population: 556 (1990); 511 (2000); 467 (2010); Density: 689.5 persons per square mile (2008-2012 5-year est.); Race: 92.8% White, 0.0% Black/African American, 0.0% Asian, 0.0% American Indian/Alaska Native, 0.0% Native Hawaiian/Other Pacific Islander, 7.2% Some other race, 7.2% Two or more races, 0.2% Hispanic of any race (2008-2012 5-year est.); Average household size: 2.39 (2008-2012 5-year est.); Median age: 33.1 (2008-2012 5-year est.); Males per 100 females: 119.9 (2008-2012 5-year est.); Marriage status: 22.6% never married, 53.0% now married, 5.8% widowed, 18.6% divorced (2008-2012 5-year est.); Foreign born: 0.0% (2008-2012 5-year est.); Ancestry (includes multiple ancestries): 36.4% German, 17.9% Irish, 16.7% American, 12.0% English, 5.7% Finnish (2008-2012 5-year est.).
Economy: Single-family building permits issued: 2 (2013); Multi-family building permits issued: 0 (2013); Homeowner vacancy rate: 2.8%. Rental vacancy rate: 0.0%. (2008-2012 5-year est.); Employment by occupation: 3.5% management, business, and financial, 7.0% computer, engineering, and science, 7.9% education, legal, community service, arts, and media, 2.6% healthcare practitioners, 18.1% service, 26.9% sales and office, 11.0% natural resources, construction, and maintenance, 22.9% production, transportation, and material moving (2008-2012 5-year est.).
Income: Per capita income: $21,634 (2008-2012 5-year est.); Median household income: $49,625 (2008-2012 5-year est.); Average household income: $51,910 (2008-2012 5-year est.); Percent of households with income of $100,000 or more: 9.8% (2008-2012 5-year est.); Poverty rate: 18.6% (2008-2012 5-year est.).
Education: Percent of population age 25 and over with: High school diploma (including GED) or higher: 94.2% (2008-2012 5-year est.); Bachelor's degree or higher: 21.2% (2008-2012 5-year est.); Master's degree or higher: 6.5% (2008-2012 5-year est.).

School District(s)
Cornell CCSD 426 (PK-08)
    2011-12 Enrollment: 104 . . . . (815) 358-2214
Housing: Homeownership rate: 71.4% (2008-2012 5-year est.); Median home value: $79,200 (2008-2012 5-year est.); Median contract rent: $450 per month (2008-2012 5-year est.); Median year structure built: 1958 (2008-2012 5-year est.).
Health Insurance: 66.5% Private; 39.4% Public; 6.6% None. (2008-2012 5-year est.)
Transportation: Commute to work: 95.4% car, 4.6% public transportation, 0.0% walk, 0.0% work from home (2008-2012 5-year est.); Travel time to work: 12.0% less than 15 minutes, 56.5% 15 to 30 minutes, 8.8% 30 to 45 minutes, 5.1% 45 to 60 minutes, 17.6% 60 minutes or more (2008-2012 5-year est.)

CULLOM (village). Covers a land area of 0.333 square miles and a water area of 0 square miles. Located at 40.88° N. Lat; 88.27° W. Long. Elevation is 682 feet.
Population: 568 (1990); 563 (2000); 555 (2010); Density: 1,618.0 persons per square mile (2008-2012 5-year est.); Race: 98.0% White, 0.6% Black/African American, 0.0% Asian, 0.0% American Indian/Alaska Native, 0.0% Native Hawaiian/Other Pacific Islander, 1.4% Some other race, 0.4% Two or more races, 2.2% Hispanic of any race (2008-2012 5-year est.); Average household size: 2.13 (2008-2012 5-year est.); Median age: 45.5 (2008-2012 5-year est.); Males per 100 females: 90.1 (2008-2012 5-year est.); Marriage status: 24.3% never married, 52.9% now married, 8.6% widowed, 14.3% divorced (2008-2012 5-year est.); Foreign born: 1.9% (2008-2012 5-year est.); Ancestry (includes multiple ancestries): 34.6% German, 19.1% American, 14.7% English, 7.4% Irish, 5.0% Polish (2008-2012 5-year est.).
Economy: Single-family building permits issued: 0 (2013); Multi-family building permits issued: 0 (2013); Homeowner vacancy rate: 3.8%. Rental vacancy rate: 0.0%. (2008-2012 5-year est.); Employment by occupation: 1.6% management, business, and financial, 1.6% computer, engineering, and science, 14.1% education, legal, community service, arts, and media, 4.7% healthcare practitioners, 21.2% service, 25.5% sales and office, 12.2% natural resources, construction, and maintenance, 19.2% production, transportation, and material moving (2008-2012 5-year est.).
Income: Per capita income: $22,988 (2008-2012 5-year est.); Median household income: $43,929 (2008-2012 5-year est.); Average household income: $49,062 (2008-2012 5-year est.); Percent of households with income of $100,000 or more: 6.4% (2008-2012 5-year est.); Poverty rate: 8.0% (2008-2012 5-year est.).
Education: Percent of population age 25 and over with: High school diploma (including GED) or higher: 91.0% (2008-2012 5-year est.); Bachelor's degree or higher: 20.4% (2008-2012 5-year est.); Master's degree or higher: 5.6% (2008-2012 5-year est.).

School District(s)
Tri Point CUSD 6-J (PK-12)
    2011-12 Enrollment: 483 . . . . (815) 253-6299
Housing: Homeownership rate: 78.2% (2008-2012 5-year est.); Median home value: $84,000 (2008-2012 5-year est.); Median contract rent: $447 per month (2008-2012 5-year est.); Median year structure built: 1953 (2008-2012 5-year est.).
Health Insurance: 72.7% Private; 43.7% Public; 6.9% None. (2008-2012 5-year est.)
Transportation: Commute to work: 78.3% car, 0.0% public transportation, 12.3% walk, 5.5% work from home (2008-2012 5-year est.); Travel time to work: 31.4% less than 15 minutes, 22.6% 15 to 30 minutes, 18.4% 30 to 45 minutes, 7.9% 45 to 60 minutes, 19.7% 60 minutes or more (2008-2012 5-year est.)

DWIGHT (village). Covers a land area of 3.217 square miles and a water area of 0.010 square miles. Located at 41.10° N. Lat; 88.42° W. Long. Elevation is 630 feet.
History: In Dwight, Dr. Leslie Keeley, a Civil War surgeon, established the Keeley Institute for the treatment of alcoholism and drug addiction, and achieved much success and acclaim.
Population: 4,230 (1990); 4,363 (2000); 4,260 (2010); Density: 1,275.3 persons per square mile (2008-2012 5-year est.); Race: 95.6% White, 0.8% Black/African American, 0.0% Asian, 0.0% American Indian/Alaska Native, 0.0% Native Hawaiian/Other Pacific Islander, 3.6% Some other race, 1.9% Two or more races, 3.1% Hispanic of any race (2008-2012 5-year est.); Average household size: 2.42 (2008-2012 5-year est.); Median age: 42.5 (2008-2012 5-year est.); Males per 100 females: 92.1 (2008-2012 5-year est.); Marriage status: 26.3% never married, 55.1% now married, 7.8% widowed, 10.8% divorced (2008-2012 5-year est.); Foreign born: 1.2% (2008-2012 5-year est.); Ancestry (includes multiple ancestries): 36.0% German, 19.5% Irish, 14.1% English, 10.7% American, 10.1% Italian (2008-2012 5-year est.).
Economy: Single-family building permits issued: 0 (2013); Multi-family building permits issued: 0 (2013); Homeowner vacancy rate: 0.0%. Rental vacancy rate: 7.3%. (2008-2012 5-year est.); Employment by occupation: 8.5% management, business, and financial, 3.4% computer, engineering, and science, 11.5% education, legal, community service, arts, and media, 5.9% healthcare practitioners, 19.5% service, 12.1% sales and office,

11.2% natural resources, construction, and maintenance, 28.0% production, transportation, and material moving (2008-2012 5-year est.).
Income: Per capita income: $25,167 (2008-2012 5-year est.); Median household income: $49,857 (2008-2012 5-year est.); Average household income: $62,176 (2008-2012 5-year est.); Percent of households with income of $100,000 or more: 19.6% (2008-2012 5-year est.); Poverty rate: 14.2% (2008-2012 5-year est.).
Education: Percent of population age 25 and over with: High school diploma (including GED) or higher: 87.9% (2008-2012 5-year est.); Bachelor's degree or higher: 13.7% (2008-2012 5-year est.); Master's degree or higher: 5.7% (2008-2012 5-year est.).

School District(s)
Dwight Common SD 232 (PK-08)
    2011-12 Enrollment: 606 . . . . (815) 584-6216
Dwight Twp HSD 230 (09-12)
    2011-12 Enrollment: 299 . . . . (815) 584-6216
Housing: Homeownership rate: 62.1% (2008-2012 5-year est.); Median home value: $126,000 (2008-2012 5-year est.); Median contract rent: $534 per month (2008-2012 5-year est.); Median year structure built: 1964 (2008-2012 5-year est.).
Health Insurance: 68.1% Private; 35.1% Public; 11.2% None. (2008-2012 5-year est.)
Safety: Violent crime rate: 4.7 per 10,000 population; Property crime rate: 129.3 per 10,000 population (2012).
Transportation: Commute to work: 94.9% car, 0.3% public transportation, 1.8% walk, 2.7% work from home (2008-2012 5-year est.); Travel time to work: 47.3% less than 15 minutes, 16.3% 15 to 30 minutes, 19.2% 30 to 45 minutes, 6.2% 45 to 60 minutes, 10.8% 60 minutes or more (2008-2012 5-year est.); Amtrak: Train service available.
Additional Information Contacts
Dwight Area Chamber of Commerce . . . . (815) 584-2091
Village of Dwight . . . . (815) 584-3077
    http://www.dwightillinois.org

EMINGTON (village). Covers a land area of 0.114 square miles and a water area of 0 square miles. Located at 40.97° N. Lat; 88.36° W. Long. Elevation is 715 feet.
Population: 135 (1990); 120 (2000); 117 (2010); Density: 1,054.6 persons per square mile (2008-2012 5-year est.); Race: 100.0% White, 0.0% Black/African American, 0.0% Asian, 0.0% American Indian/Alaska Native, 0.0% Native Hawaiian/Other Pacific Islander, 0.0% Some other race, 0.0% Two or more races, 0.0% Hispanic of any race (2008-2012 5-year est.); Average household size: 2.55 (2008-2012 5-year est.); Median age: 27.2 (2008-2012 5-year est.); Males per 100 females: 130.8 (2008-2012 5-year est.); Marriage status: 30.3% never married, 50.0% now married, 7.9% widowed, 11.8% divorced (2008-2012 5-year est.); Foreign born: 0.0% (2008-2012 5-year est.); Ancestry (includes multiple ancestries): 37.5% German, 21.7% Italian, 18.3% Polish, 13.3% Irish, 6.7% American (2008-2012 5-year est.).
Economy: Single-family building permits issued: 0 (2013); Multi-family building permits issued: 0 (2013); Homeowner vacancy rate: 0.0%. Rental vacancy rate: 0.0%. (2008-2012 5-year est.); Employment by occupation: 5.3% management, business, and financial, 0.0% computer, engineering, and science, 3.5% education, legal, community service, arts, and media, 3.5% healthcare practitioners, 21.1% service, 17.5% sales and office, 19.3% natural resources, construction, and maintenance, 29.8% production, transportation, and material moving (2008-2012 5-year est.).
Income: Per capita income: $17,287 (2008-2012 5-year est.); Median household income: $35,625 (2008-2012 5-year est.); Average household income: $41,406 (2008-2012 5-year est.); Percent of households with income of $100,000 or more: 6.4% (2008-2012 5-year est.); Poverty rate: 6.7% (2008-2012 5-year est.).
Education: Percent of population age 25 and over with: High school diploma (including GED) or higher: 88.7% (2008-2012 5-year est.); Bachelor's degree or higher: 5.6% (2008-2012 5-year est.); Master's degree or higher: 0.0% (2008-2012 5-year est.).
Housing: Homeownership rate: 83.0% (2008-2012 5-year est.); Median home value: $78,900 (2008-2012 5-year est.); Median contract rent: $413 per month (2008-2012 5-year est.); Median year structure built: Before 1940 (2008-2012 5-year est.).
Health Insurance: 76.7% Private; 26.7% Public; 8.3% None. (2008-2012 5-year est.)
Transportation: Commute to work: 100.0% car, 0.0% public transportation, 0.0% walk, 0.0% work from home (2008-2012 5-year est.); Travel time to work: 18.9% less than 15 minutes, 43.4% 15 to 30 minutes,

11.3% 30 to 45 minutes, 15.1% 45 to 60 minutes, 11.3% 60 minutes or more (2008-2012 5-year est.)

FAIRBURY (city). Covers a land area of 1.798 square miles and a water area of 0 square miles. Located at 40.75° N. Lat; 88.52° W. Long. Elevation is 682 feet.
History: Incorporated 1890.
Population: 3,643 (1990); 3,968 (2000); 3,757 (2010); Density: 2,131.6 persons per square mile (2008-2012 5-year est.); Race: 96.3% White, 0.5% Black/African American, 1.3% Asian, 0.0% American Indian/Alaska Native, 0.0% Native Hawaiian/Other Pacific Islander, 1.9% Some other race, 1.3% Two or more races, 3.2% Hispanic of any race (2008-2012 5-year est.); Average household size: 2.44 (2008-2012 5-year est.); Median age: 38.7 (2008-2012 5-year est.); Males per 100 females: 96.0 (2008-2012 5-year est.); Marriage status: 18.4% never married, 63.6% now married, 6.8% widowed, 11.2% divorced (2008-2012 5-year est.); Foreign born: 1.4% (2008-2012 5-year est.); Ancestry (includes multiple ancestries): 44.4% German, 18.6% Irish, 12.1% English, 10.2% American, 7.0% Swiss (2008-2012 5-year est.).
Economy: Single-family building permits issued: 3 (2013); Multi-family building permits issued: 0 (2013); Homeowner vacancy rate: 0.9%. Rental vacancy rate: 10.7%. (2008-2012 5-year est.); Employment by occupation: 3.8% management, business, and financial, 0.8% computer, engineering, and science, 13.2% education, legal, community service, arts, and media, 7.3% healthcare practitioners, 14.7% service, 27.7% sales and office, 13.5% natural resources, construction, and maintenance, 19.0% production, transportation, and material moving (2008-2012 5-year est.).
Income: Per capita income: $25,769 (2008-2012 5-year est.); Median household income: $57,371 (2008-2012 5-year est.); Average household income: $64,653 (2008-2012 5-year est.); Percent of households with income of $100,000 or more: 13.6% (2008-2012 5-year est.); Poverty rate: 8.6% (2008-2012 5-year est.).
Education: Percent of population age 25 and over with: High school diploma (including GED) or higher: 87.4% (2008-2012 5-year est.); Bachelor's degree or higher: 20.1% (2008-2012 5-year est.); Master's degree or higher: 7.9% (2008-2012 5-year est.).

School District(s)
Prairie Central CUSD 8 (PK-12)
    2011-12 Enrollment: 2,159 . . . . (815) 692-2504
Housing: Homeownership rate: 76.0% (2008-2012 5-year est.); Median home value: $113,400 (2008-2012 5-year est.); Median contract rent: $496 per month (2008-2012 5-year est.); Median year structure built: 1962 (2008-2012 5-year est.).
Health Insurance: 77.6% Private; 38.1% Public; 3.4% None. (2008-2012 5-year est.)
Safety: Violent crime rate: 8.0 per 10,000 population; Property crime rate: 221.3 per 10,000 population (2012).
Transportation: Commute to work: 93.7% car, 0.0% public transportation, 2.2% walk, 3.9% work from home (2008-2012 5-year est.); Travel time to work: 52.5% less than 15 minutes, 18.5% 15 to 30 minutes, 8.1% 30 to 45 minutes, 13.5% 45 to 60 minutes, 7.3% 60 minutes or more (2008-2012 5-year est.)

FLANAGAN (village). Covers a land area of 0.535 square miles and a water area of 0 square miles. Located at 40.88° N. Lat; 88.86° W. Long. Elevation is 673 feet.
Population: 987 (1990); 1,083 (2000); 1,110 (2010); Density: 1,855.4 persons per square mile (2008-2012 5-year est.); Race: 98.5% White, 0.0% Black/African American, 0.7% Asian, 0.0% American Indian/Alaska Native, 0.0% Native Hawaiian/Other Pacific Islander, 0.8% Some other race, 0.8% Two or more races, 2.4% Hispanic of any race (2008-2012 5-year est.); Average household size: 2.12 (2008-2012 5-year est.); Median age: 50.7 (2008-2012 5-year est.); Males per 100 females: 72.8 (2008-2012 5-year est.); Marriage status: 18.6% never married, 54.8% now married, 13.9% widowed, 12.7% divorced (2008-2012 5-year est.); Foreign born: 0.7% (2008-2012 5-year est.); Ancestry (includes multiple ancestries): 44.1% German, 16.2% Irish, 13.0% English, 12.9% American, 5.0% Dutch (2008-2012 5-year est.).
Economy: Single-family building permits issued: 5 (2013); Multi-family building permits issued: 0 (2013); Homeowner vacancy rate: 4.0%. Rental vacancy rate: 16.0%. (2008-2012 5-year est.); Employment by occupation: 10.6% management, business, and financial, 1.3% computer, engineering, and science, 12.3% education, legal, community service, arts, and media, 3.2% healthcare practitioners, 22.6% service, 25.4% sales and office,

7.3% natural resources, construction, and maintenance, 17.2% production, transportation, and material moving (2008-2012 5-year est.).
Income: Per capita income: $29,142 (2008-2012 5-year est.); Median household income: $54,667 (2008-2012 5-year est.); Average household income: $62,999 (2008-2012 5-year est.); Percent of households with income of $100,000 or more: 11.6% (2008-2012 5-year est.); Poverty rate: 9.3% (2008-2012 5-year est.).
Education: Percent of population age 25 and over with: High school diploma (including GED) or higher: 89.1% (2008-2012 5-year est.); Bachelor's degree or higher: 19.6% (2008-2012 5-year est.); Master's degree or higher: 5.5% (2008-2012 5-year est.).

School District(s)

Flanagan-Cornell Dist 74 (PK-12)
    2011-12 Enrollment: 334 . . . . (815) 796-2233
Housing: Homeownership rate: 79.0% (2008-2012 5-year est.); Median home value: $94,300 (2008-2012 5-year est.); Median contract rent: $543 per month (2008-2012 5-year est.); Median year structure built: 1957 (2008-2012 5-year est.).
Health Insurance: 82.8% Private; 37.2% Public; 4.2% None. (2008-2012 5-year est.)
Transportation: Commute to work: 96.0% car, 0.0% public transportation, 2.6% walk, 0.7% work from home (2008-2012 5-year est.); Travel time to work: 32.2% less than 15 minutes, 44.1% 15 to 30 minutes, 8.6% 30 to 45 minutes, 6.2% 45 to 60 minutes, 8.9% 60 minutes or more (2008-2012 5-year est.)

FORREST (village). Covers a land area of 0.677 square miles and a water area of 0 square miles. Located at 40.75° N. Lat; 88.41° W. Long. Elevation is 686 feet.
History: Forrest was settled in 1836, but grew in the 1860's when German-Amish immigrants arrived.
Population: 1,124 (1990); 1,225 (2000); 1,220 (2010); Density: 1,674.3 persons per square mile (2008-2012 5-year est.); Race: 98.5% White, 0.0% Black/African American, 0.0% Asian, 0.4% American Indian/Alaska Native, 0.0% Native Hawaiian/Other Pacific Islander, 1.1% Some other race, 0.5% Two or more races, 5.3% Hispanic of any race (2008-2012 5-year est.); Average household size: 2.46 (2008-2012 5-year est.); Median age: 35.8 (2008-2012 5-year est.); Males per 100 females: 91.1 (2008-2012 5-year est.); Marriage status: 27.5% never married, 55.6% now married, 6.5% widowed, 10.4% divorced (2008-2012 5-year est.); Foreign born: 4.6% (2008-2012 5-year est.); Ancestry (includes multiple ancestries): 44.0% German, 19.1% American, 15.8% Irish, 6.4% English, 3.5% Italian (2008-2012 5-year est.).
Economy: Single-family building permits issued: 3 (2013); Multi-family building permits issued: 0 (2013); Homeowner vacancy rate: 0.0%. Rental vacancy rate: 7.9%. (2008-2012 5-year est.); Employment by occupation: 8.1% management, business, and financial, 1.7% computer, engineering, and science, 8.7% education, legal, community service, arts, and media, 2.1% healthcare practitioners, 7.3% service, 29.9% sales and office, 18.7% natural resources, construction, and maintenance, 23.5% production, transportation, and material moving (2008-2012 5-year est.).
Income: Per capita income: $21,218 (2008-2012 5-year est.); Median household income: $48,438 (2008-2012 5-year est.); Average household income: $52,580 (2008-2012 5-year est.); Percent of households with income of $100,000 or more: 8.0% (2008-2012 5-year est.); Poverty rate: 18.3% (2008-2012 5-year est.).
Education: Percent of population age 25 and over with: High school diploma (including GED) or higher: 83.5% (2008-2012 5-year est.); Bachelor's degree or higher: 9.8% (2008-2012 5-year est.); Master's degree or higher: 1.6% (2008-2012 5-year est.).

School District(s)

Prairie Central CUSD 8 (PK-12)
    2011-12 Enrollment: 2,159 . . . . (815) 692-2504
Housing: Homeownership rate: 74.8% (2008-2012 5-year est.); Median home value: $87,300 (2008-2012 5-year est.); Median contract rent: $462 per month (2008-2012 5-year est.); Median year structure built: 1953 (2008-2012 5-year est.).
Health Insurance: 65.4% Private; 40.5% Public; 10.2% None. (2008-2012 5-year est.)
Transportation: Commute to work: 90.3% car, 0.0% public transportation, 4.8% walk, 3.1% work from home (2008-2012 5-year est.); Travel time to work: 55.5% less than 15 minutes, 21.2% 15 to 30 minutes, 11.2% 30 to 45 minutes, 5.2% 45 to 60 minutes, 7.0% 60 minutes or more (2008-2012 5-year est.)

GRAYMONT (unincorporated postal area)
Zip Code: 61743
    Covers a land area of 15.115 square miles and a water area of 0 square miles. Located at 40.87° N. Lat; 88.78° W. Long. Elevation is 653 feet. Population: 212 (2010); Density: 14.0 persons per square mile (2010); Race: 97.6% White, 0.0% Black/African American, 0.0% Asian, 0.0% American Indian/Alaska Native, 0.0% Native Hawaiian/Other Pacific Islander, 2.4% Some other race, 2.4% Two or more races, 0.9% Hispanic of any race (2010); Average household size: 2.47 (2010); Median age: 44.5 (2010); Males per 100 females: 94.5 (2010); Homeownership rate: 83.7% (2010)

LONG POINT (village). Covers a land area of 0.185 square miles and a water area of 0 square miles. Located at 41.01° N. Lat; 88.89° W. Long. Elevation is 640 feet.
Population: 208 (1990); 247 (2000); 226 (2010); Density: 1,280.8 persons per square mile (2008-2012 5-year est.); Race: 98.3% White, 0.0% Black/African American, 0.8% Asian, 0.0% American Indian/Alaska Native, 0.0% Native Hawaiian/Other Pacific Islander, 0.9% Some other race, 0.8% Two or more races, 3.8% Hispanic of any race (2008-2012 5-year est.); Average household size: 2.76 (2008-2012 5-year est.); Median age: 31.8 (2008-2012 5-year est.); Males per 100 females: 76.9 (2008-2012 5-year est.); Marriage status: 22.5% never married, 58.0% now married, 8.9% widowed, 10.7% divorced (2008-2012 5-year est.); Foreign born: 0.8% (2008-2012 5-year est.); Ancestry (includes multiple ancestries): 40.1% German, 38.4% Irish, 29.5% Polish, 11.0% English, 10.5% American (2008-2012 5-year est.).
Economy: Homeowner vacancy rate: 2.6%. Rental vacancy rate: 0.0%. (2008-2012 5-year est.); Employment by occupation: 15.1% management, business, and financial, 3.2% computer, engineering, and science, 4.3% education, legal, community service, arts, and media, 3.2% healthcare practitioners, 9.7% service, 22.6% sales and office, 11.8% natural resources, construction, and maintenance, 30.1% production, transportation, and material moving (2008-2012 5-year est.).
Income: Per capita income: $20,842 (2008-2012 5-year est.); Median household income: $50,577 (2008-2012 5-year est.); Average household income: $57,984 (2008-2012 5-year est.); Percent of households with income of $100,000 or more: 16.3% (2008-2012 5-year est.); Poverty rate: 1.3% (2008-2012 5-year est.).
Education: Percent of population age 25 and over with: High school diploma (including GED) or higher: 92.1% (2008-2012 5-year est.); Bachelor's degree or higher: 11.4% (2008-2012 5-year est.); Master's degree or higher: 5.0% (2008-2012 5-year est.).
Housing: Homeownership rate: 86.0% (2008-2012 5-year est.); Median home value: $80,000 (2008-2012 5-year est.); Median contract rent: $332 per month (2008-2012 5-year est.); Median year structure built: Before 1940 (2008-2012 5-year est.).
Health Insurance: 55.3% Private; 56.1% Public; 6.3% None. (2008-2012 5-year est.)
Transportation: Commute to work: 93.5% car, 0.0% public transportation, 1.1% walk, 5.4% work from home (2008-2012 5-year est.); Travel time to work: 21.6% less than 15 minutes, 48.9% 15 to 30 minutes, 15.9% 30 to 45 minutes, 11.4% 45 to 60 minutes, 2.3% 60 minutes or more (2008-2012 5-year est.)

ODELL (village). Covers a land area of 1.115 square miles and a water area of 0.016 square miles. Located at 41.00° N. Lat; 88.52° W. Long. Elevation is 719 feet.
Population: 1,030 (1990); 1,014 (2000); 1,046 (2010); Density: 961.6 persons per square mile (2008-2012 5-year est.); Race: 98.5% White, 0.0% Black/African American, 0.0% Asian, 0.0% American Indian/Alaska Native, 0.0% Native Hawaiian/Other Pacific Islander, 1.5% Some other race, 1.5% Two or more races, 3.8% Hispanic of any race (2008-2012 5-year est.); Average household size: 2.61 (2008-2012 5-year est.); Median age: 36.0 (2008-2012 5-year est.); Males per 100 females: 107.4 (2008-2012 5-year est.); Marriage status: 33.1% never married, 49.8% now married, 5.3% widowed, 11.7% divorced (2008-2012 5-year est.); Foreign born: 1.0% (2008-2012 5-year est.); Ancestry (includes multiple ancestries): 44.4% German, 18.7% Irish, 11.0% American, 8.8% English, 4.9% French (2008-2012 5-year est.).
Economy: Single-family building permits issued: 1 (2013); Multi-family building permits issued: 0 (2013); Homeowner vacancy rate: 0.9%. Rental vacancy rate: 0.0%. (2008-2012 5-year est.); Employment by occupation: 10.6% management, business, and financial, 1.9% computer, engineering, and science, 7.5% education, legal, community service, arts, and media,

7.7% healthcare practitioners, 19.3% service, 16.4% sales and office, 13.9% natural resources, construction, and maintenance, 22.4% production, transportation, and material moving (2008-2012 5-year est.).
Income: Per capita income: $29,326 (2008-2012 5-year est.); Median household income: $53,359 (2008-2012 5-year est.); Average household income: $73,441 (2008-2012 5-year est.); Percent of households with income of $100,000 or more: 18.3% (2008-2012 5-year est.); Poverty rate: 11.9% (2008-2012 5-year est.).
Education: Percent of population age 25 and over with: High school diploma (including GED) or higher: 88.9% (2008-2012 5-year est.); Bachelor's degree or higher: 13.9% (2008-2012 5-year est.); Master's degree or higher: 6.0% (2008-2012 5-year est.).

School District(s)
Odell CCSD 435 (PK-08)
  2011-12 Enrollment: 172...................... (815) 998-2272
Housing: Homeownership rate: 80.3% (2008-2012 5-year est.); Median home value: $102,900 (2008-2012 5-year est.); Median contract rent: $558 per month (2008-2012 5-year est.); Median year structure built: 1941 (2008-2012 5-year est.).
Health Insurance: 65.3% Private; 42.2% Public; 9.2% None. (2008-2012 5-year est.)
Transportation: Commute to work: 92.3% car, 0.0% public transportation, 5.6% walk, 1.8% work from home (2008-2012 5-year est.); Travel time to work: 41.4% less than 15 minutes, 37.6% 15 to 30 minutes, 3.4% 30 to 45 minutes, 5.5% 45 to 60 minutes, 12.1% 60 minutes or more (2008-2012 5-year est.)

PONTIAC (city).
County seat. Covers a land area of 7.735 square miles and a water area of 0.140 square miles. Located at 40.88° N. Lat; 88.65° W. Long. Elevation is 646 feet.
History: Pontiac was founded in 1837 and named for the Ottawa Chief Pontiac. Jesse W. Fell was a leader in the development of Pontiac, and chose the name for the town. Pontiac developed as the seat of Livingston County.
Population: 11,428 (1990); 11,864 (2000); 11,931 (2010); Density: 1,578.6 persons per square mile (2008-2012 5-year est.); Race: 84.7% White, 11.4% Black/African American, 0.2% Asian, 0.0% American Indian/Alaska Native, 0.1% Native Hawaiian/Other Pacific Islander, 3.6% Some other race, 1.2% Two or more races, 5.8% Hispanic of any race (2008-2012 5-year est.); Average household size: 2.22 (2008-2012 5-year est.); Median age: 39.3 (2008-2012 5-year est.); Males per 100 females: 132.3 (2008-2012 5-year est.); Marriage status: 34.9% never married, 41.8% now married, 7.7% widowed, 15.6% divorced (2008-2012 5-year est.); Foreign born: 2.2% (2008-2012 5-year est.); Ancestry (includes multiple ancestries): 27.4% German, 16.8% Irish, 10.7% American, 7.6% English, 5.3% Italian (2008-2012 5-year est.).
Economy: Single-family building permits issued: 0 (2013); Multi-family building permits issued: 4 (2013); Homeowner vacancy rate: 2.2%. Rental vacancy rate: 6.8%. (2008-2012 5-year est.); Employment by occupation: 6.8% management, business, and financial, 1.2% computer, engineering, and science, 7.1% education, legal, community service, arts, and media, 6.2% healthcare practitioners, 24.6% service, 22.5% sales and office, 9.0% natural resources, construction, and maintenance, 22.6% production, transportation, and material moving (2008-2012 5-year est.).
Income: Per capita income: $21,086 (2008-2012 5-year est.); Median household income: $46,382 (2008-2012 5-year est.); Average household income: $57,139 (2008-2012 5-year est.); Percent of households with income of $100,000 or more: 12.2% (2008-2012 5-year est.); Poverty rate: 12.4% (2008-2012 5-year est.).
Education: Percent of population age 25 and over with: High school diploma (including GED) or higher: 83.0% (2008-2012 5-year est.); Bachelor's degree or higher: 11.7% (2008-2012 5-year est.); Master's degree or higher: 3.7% (2008-2012 5-year est.).

School District(s)
Livingston Area Career Cntr (11-12)
  2011-12 Enrollment: n/a .... (815) 842-2557
Livingston County Spec Services Unit
  2011-12 Enrollment: n/a .... (815) 844-7115
Pontiac CCSD 429 (PK-08)
  2011-12 Enrollment: 1,310 .... (815) 844-5632
Pontiac Twp HSD 90 (09-12)
  2011-12 Enrollment: 814........................ (815) 844-6113

Vocational/Technical School(s)
Unity Cosmetology College (Private, For-profit)
  Fall 2012 Enrollment: 50 .... (815) 844-3100
  2012-13 Tuition: $16,500
Housing: Homeownership rate: 67.7% (2008-2012 5-year est.); Median home value: $97,900 (2008-2012 5-year est.); Median contract rent: $481 per month (2008-2012 5-year est.); Median year structure built: 1961 (2008-2012 5-year est.).
Health Insurance: 70.3% Private; 33.7% Public; 9.0% None. (2008-2012 5-year est.)
Hospitals: St. James OSF (89 beds)
Transportation: Commute to work: 94.3% car, 0.1% public transportation, 2.3% walk, 1.9% work from home (2008-2012 5-year est.); Travel time to work: 72.1% less than 15 minutes, 11.3% 15 to 30 minutes, 7.0% 30 to 45 minutes, 5.9% 45 to 60 minutes, 3.8% 60 minutes or more (2008-2012 5-year est.); Amtrak: Train service available.
Airports: Pontiac Municipal Airport (general aviation)
Additional Information Contacts
City of Pontiac...................................... (815) 844-3396
  http://pontiac.org
Pontiac Area Chamber of Commerce .... (815) 844-5131
  http://www.pontiacchamber.org

SAUNEMIN (village).
Covers a land area of 0.253 square miles and a water area of 0 square miles. Located at 40.89° N. Lat; 88.41° W. Long. Elevation is 689 feet.
Population: 399 (1990); 456 (2000); 420 (2010); Density: 1,289.6 persons per square mile (2008-2012 5-year est.); Race: 99.4% White, 0.0% Black/African American, 0.0% Asian, 0.0% American Indian/Alaska Native, 0.0% Native Hawaiian/Other Pacific Islander, 0.6% Some other race, 0.6% Two or more races, 3.1% Hispanic of any race (2008-2012 5-year est.); Average household size: 2.74 (2008-2012 5-year est.); Median age: 40.8 (2008-2012 5-year est.); Males per 100 females: 132.9 (2008-2012 5-year est.); Marriage status: 25.9% never married, 57.3% now married, 5.9% widowed, 11.0% divorced (2008-2012 5-year est.); Foreign born: 0.0% (2008-2012 5-year est.); Ancestry (includes multiple ancestries): 38.0% German, 29.8% Irish, 9.5% English, 8.6% Italian, 8.6% French (2008-2012 5-year est.).
Economy: Homeowner vacancy rate: 4.2%. Rental vacancy rate: 0.0%. (2008-2012 5-year est.); Employment by occupation: 2.2% management, business, and financial, 1.5% computer, engineering, and science, 3.0% education, legal, community service, arts, and media, 5.2% healthcare practitioners, 24.4% service, 29.6% sales and office, 7.4% natural resources, construction, and maintenance, 26.7% production, transportation, and material moving (2008-2012 5-year est.).
Income: Per capita income: $20,410 (2008-2012 5-year est.); Median household income: $49,306 (2008-2012 5-year est.); Average household income: $55,824 (2008-2012 5-year est.); Percent of households with income of $100,000 or more: 10.1% (2008-2012 5-year est.); Poverty rate: 17.1% (2008-2012 5-year est.).
Education: Percent of population age 25 and over with: High school diploma (including GED) or higher: 91.0% (2008-2012 5-year est.); Bachelor's degree or higher: 7.1% (2008-2012 5-year est.); Master's degree or higher: 1.4% (2008-2012 5-year est.).

School District(s)
Saunemin CCSD 438 (PK-08)
  2011-12 Enrollment: 137........................ (815) 832-4421
Housing: Homeownership rate: 95.0% (2008-2012 5-year est.); Median home value: $77,500 (2008-2012 5-year est.); Median contract rent: $500 per month (2008-2012 5-year est.); Median year structure built: 1951 (2008-2012 5-year est.).
Health Insurance: 77.6% Private; 32.2% Public; 8.6% None. (2008-2012 5-year est.)
Transportation: Commute to work: 98.5% car, 0.0% public transportation, 0.7% walk, 0.7% work from home (2008-2012 5-year est.); Travel time to work: 3.7% less than 15 minutes, 75.4% 15 to 30 minutes, 11.9% 30 to 45 minutes, 1.5% 45 to 60 minutes, 7.5% 60 minutes or more (2008-2012 5-year est.)

STRAWN (village).
Covers a land area of 0.515 square miles and a water area of 0 square miles. Located at 40.65° N. Lat; 88.40° W. Long. Elevation is 771 feet.
Population: 132 (1990); 104 (2000); 100 (2010); Density: 248.3 persons per square mile (2008-2012 5-year est.); Race: 96.1% White, 0.0% Black/African American, 0.0% Asian, 0.0% American Indian/Alaska Native,

0.0% Native Hawaiian/Other Pacific Islander, 3.9% Some other race, 1.6% Two or more races, 0.0% Hispanic of any race (2008-2012 5-year est.); Average household size: 2.72 (2008-2012 5-year est.); Median age: 33.3 (2008-2012 5-year est.); Males per 100 females: 85.5 (2008-2012 5-year est.); Marriage status: 31.8% never married, 51.1% now married, 6.8% widowed, 10.2% divorced (2008-2012 5-year est.); Foreign born: 0.0% (2008-2012 5-year est.); Ancestry (includes multiple ancestries): 34.4% Irish, 29.7% American, 21.9% German, 12.5% English, 8.6% Dutch (2008-2012 5-year est.).

Economy: Homeowner vacancy rate: 0.0%. Rental vacancy rate: 0.0%. (2008-2012 5-year est.); Employment by occupation: 5.2% management, business, and financial, 15.5% computer, engineering, and science, 0.0% education, legal, community service, arts, and media, 0.0% healthcare practitioners, 19.0% service, 22.4% sales and office, 6.9% natural resources, construction, and maintenance, 31.0% production, transportation, and material moving (2008-2012 5-year est.).

Income: Per capita income: $19,087 (2008-2012 5-year est.); Median household income: $48,125 (2008-2012 5-year est.); Average household income: $51,868 (2008-2012 5-year est.); Percent of households with income of $100,000 or more: 12.8% (2008-2012 5-year est.); Poverty rate: 5.5% (2008-2012 5-year est.).

Education: Percent of population age 25 and over with: High school diploma (including GED) or higher: 86.1% (2008-2012 5-year est.); Bachelor's degree or higher: 4.2% (2008-2012 5-year est.); Master's degree or higher: 0.0% (2008-2012 5-year est.).

Housing: Homeownership rate: 87.2% (2008-2012 5-year est.); Median home value: $57,500 (2008-2012 5-year est.); Median contract rent: $375 per month (2008-2012 5-year est.); Median year structure built: 1946 (2008-2012 5-year est.).

Health Insurance: 82.8% Private; 28.1% Public; 3.1% None. (2008-2012 5-year est.)

Transportation: Commute to work: 94.7% car, 0.0% public transportation, 0.0% walk, 5.3% work from home (2008-2012 5-year est.); Travel time to work: 31.5% less than 15 minutes, 33.3% 15 to 30 minutes, 13.0% 30 to 45 minutes, 11.1% 45 to 60 minutes, 11.1% 60 minutes or more (2008-2012 5-year est.)

Logan County

Located in central Illinois; drained by Salt and Kickapoo Creeks. Covers a land area of 618.059 square miles, a water area of 0.868 square miles, and is located in the Central Time Zone at 40.13° N. Lat., 89.37° W. Long. The county was founded in 1839. County seat is Lincoln.

Logan County is part of the Lincoln, IL Micropolitan Statistical Area. The entire metro area includes: Logan County, IL

Weather Station: Lincoln										Elevation: 583 feet	
	Jan	Feb	Mar	Apr	May	Jun	Jul	Aug	Sep	Oct	Nov	Dec
High	34	39	51	64	75	83	86	84	79	66	52	38
Low	17	21	30	40	51	61	64	62	53	41	32	21
Precip	2.0	1.6	2.7	3.7	4.1	3.9	5.0	3.9	3.0	3.3	3.3	2.6
Snow	6.1	4.9	1.8	0.5	0.0	0.0	0.0	0.0	0.0	tr	0.7	5.4

High and Low temperatures in degrees Fahrenheit; Precipitation and Snow in inches

Population: 30,798 (1990); 31,183 (2000); 30,305 (2010); Race: 83.9% White, 11.9% Black/African American, 1.3% Asian, 0.1% American Indian/Alaska Native, 0.0% Native Hawaiian/Other Pacific Islander, 2.8% Some other race, 1.2% Two or more races, 3.0% Hispanic of any race (2008-2012 5-year est.); Density: 48.6 persons per square mile (2008-2012 5-year est.); Average household size: 2.14 (2008-2012 5-year est.); Median age: 39.4 (2008-2012 5-year est.); Males per 100 females: 105.0 (2008-2012 5-year est.).

Religion: Six largest groups: 13.9% Baptist, 11.5% Lutheran, 7.5% Catholicism, 6.3% Methodist/Pietist, 3.2% Non-denominational Protestant, 2.7% Presbyterian-Reformed (2010)

Economy: Unemployment rate: 6.6% (April 2014); Total civilian labor force: 12,697 (April 2014); Leading industries: 19.5% health care and social assistance; 14.3% retail trade; 12.8% manufacturing (2012); Farms: 779 totaling 363,272 acres (2012); Companies that employ 500 or more persons: 0 (2012); Companies that employ 100 to 499 persons: 11 (2012); Companies that employ less than 100 persons: 601 (2012); Black-owned businesses: n/a (2007); Hispanic-owned businesses: n/a (2007); Asian-owned businesses: n/a (2007); Women-owned businesses: 434 (2007); Single-family building permits issued: 12 (2013); Multi-family building permits issued: 0 (2013).

Income: Per capita income: $21,255 (2008-2012 5-year est.); Median household income: $46,647 (2008-2012 5-year est.); Average household income: $58,910 (2008-2012 5-year est.); Percent of households with income of $100,000 or more: 15.3% (2008-2012 5-year est.); Poverty rate: 13.2% (2008-2012 5-year est.); Bankruptcy rate: 3.60% (2013).

Taxes: Total county taxes per capita: $114 (2011); County property taxes per capita: $108 (2011).

Education: Percent of population age 25 and over with: High school diploma (including GED) or higher: 84.9% (2008-2012 5-year est.); Bachelor's degree or higher: 17.3% (2008-2012 5-year est.); Master's degree or higher: 4.8% (2008-2012 5-year est.).

Housing: Homeownership rate: 70.2% (2008-2012 5-year est.); Median home value: $97,000 (2008-2012 5-year est.); Median contract rent: $411 per month (2008-2012 5-year est.); Median year structure built: 1960 (2008-2012 5-year est.)

Health: Birth rate: 97.8 per 10,000 population (2013); Death rate: 101.5 per 10,000 population (2013); Age-adjusted cancer mortality rate: 160.7 deaths per 100,000 population (2011); Number of physicians: 5.6 per 10,000 population (2011); Hospital beds: 8.2 per 10,000 population (2010); Hospital admissions: 323.0 per 10,000 population (2010).

Elections: 2012 Presidential election results: 33.0% Obama, 65.1% Romney

National and State Parks: Railsplitter State Park

Additional Information Contacts
Logan County Government . . . . (217) 732-4148
  http://www.co.logan.il.us
Lincoln/Logan County Chamber of Commerce . . . . (217) 735-2385
  http://www.lincolnillinois.com

Logan County Communities

ATLANTA (city). Covers a land area of 1.264 square miles and a water area of 0.008 square miles. Located at 40.26° N. Lat; 89.23° W. Long. Elevation is 709 feet.

History: Atlanta came into existence when the Chicago & Mississippi Railroad placed its tracks a mile away from the village of Newcastle, and the village moved to the railroad. The railroad station had been named Zenia, but town and railroad adopted the name of Atlanta in 1855.

Population: 1,616 (1990); 1,649 (2000); 1,692 (2010); Density: 976.6 persons per square mile (2008-2012 5-year est.); Race: 96.9% White, 0.6% Black/African American, 0.5% Asian, 0.0% American Indian/Alaska Native, 0.0% Native Hawaiian/Other Pacific Islander, 2.0% Some other race, 1.7% Two or more races, 0.4% Hispanic of any race (2008-2012 5-year est.); Average household size: 2.05 (2008-2012 5-year est.); Median age: 46.0 (2008-2012 5-year est.); Males per 100 females: 89.3 (2008-2012 5-year est.); Marriage status: 17.7% never married, 67.5% now married, 4.7% widowed, 10.2% divorced (2008-2012 5-year est.); Foreign born: 0.6% (2008-2012 5-year est.); Ancestry (includes multiple ancestries): 29.1% American, 24.1% German, 13.5% English, 9.6% Irish, 3.6% Dutch (2008-2012 5-year est.).

Economy: Single-family building permits issued: 0 (2013); Multi-family building permits issued: 0 (2013); Homeowner vacancy rate: 7.1%. Rental vacancy rate: 0.0%. (2008-2012 5-year est.); Employment by occupation: 13.5% management, business, and financial, 2.1% computer, engineering, and science, 9.8% education, legal, community service, arts, and media, 2.4% healthcare practitioners, 24.3% service, 27.8% sales and office, 8.0% natural resources, construction, and maintenance, 12.1% production, transportation, and material moving (2008-2012 5-year est.).

Income: Per capita income: $25,740 (2008-2012 5-year est.); Median household income: $46,944 (2008-2012 5-year est.); Average household income: $56,057 (2008-2012 5-year est.); Percent of households with income of $100,000 or more: 13.4% (2008-2012 5-year est.); Poverty rate: 7.9% (2008-2012 5-year est.).

Education: Percent of population age 25 and over with: High school diploma (including GED) or higher: 90.5% (2008-2012 5-year est.); Bachelor's degree or higher: 16.1% (2008-2012 5-year est.); Master's degree or higher: 1.3% (2008-2012 5-year est.).

School District(s)
Olympia CUSD 16 (PK-12)
  2011-12 Enrollment: 1,940 . . . . (309) 379-6011
Housing: Homeownership rate: 75.1% (2008-2012 5-year est.); Median home value: $95,300 (2008-2012 5-year est.); Median contract rent: $471 per month (2008-2012 5-year est.); Median year structure built: 1966 (2008-2012 5-year est.).

Health Insurance: 70.1% Private; 40.3% Public; 6.8% None. (2008-2012 5-year est.)

Transportation: Commute to work: 93.7% car, 0.2% public transportation, 3.9% walk, 1.5% work from home (2008-2012 5-year est.); Travel time to work: 23.1% less than 15 minutes, 33.4% 15 to 30 minutes, 35.7% 30 to 45 minutes, 5.1% 45 to 60 minutes, 2.6% 60 minutes or more (2008-2012 5-year est.)

BEASON (CDP). Covers a land area of 0.625 square miles and a water area of 0 square miles. Located at 40.14° N. Lat; 89.20° W. Long. Elevation is 640 feet.

Population: n/a (1990); n/a (2000); 189 (2010); Density: 219.3 persons per square mile (2008-2012 5-year est.); Race: 100.0% White, 0.0% Black/African American, 0.0% Asian, 0.0% American Indian/Alaska Native, 0.0% Native Hawaiian/Other Pacific Islander, 0.0% Some other race, 0.0% Two or more races, 0.0% Hispanic of any race (2008-2012 5-year est.); Average household size: 1.85 (2008-2012 5-year est.); Median age: 19.5 (2008-2012 5-year est.); Males per 100 females: 71.3 (2008-2012 5-year est.); Marriage status: 61.0% never married, 18.7% now married, 1.6% widowed, 18.7% divorced (2008-2012 5-year est.); Foreign born: 0.0% (2008-2012 5-year est.); Ancestry (includes multiple ancestries): 40.1% American, 8.8% German, 2.2% Welsh (2008-2012 5-year est.).

Economy: Homeowner vacancy rate: 0.0%. Rental vacancy rate: 0.0%. (2008-2012 5-year est.); Employment by occupation: 0.0% management, business, and financial, 0.0% computer, engineering, and science, 0.0% education, legal, community service, arts, and media, 4.8% healthcare practitioners, 17.7% service, 56.5% sales and office, 3.2% natural resources, construction, and maintenance, 17.7% production, transportation, and material moving (2008-2012 5-year est.).

Income: Per capita income: $14,178 (2008-2012 5-year est.); Median household income: $24,207 (2008-2012 5-year est.); Average household income: $33,007 (2008-2012 5-year est.); Percent of households with income of $100,000 or more: 4.1% (2008-2012 5-year est.); Poverty rate: 49.6% (2008-2012 5-year est.).

Education: Percent of population age 25 and over with: High school diploma (including GED) or higher: 100.0% (2008-2012 5-year est.); Bachelor's degree or higher: 6.1% (2008-2012 5-year est.); Master's degree or higher: 0.0% (2008-2012 5-year est.).

Housing: Homeownership rate: 47.3% (2008-2012 5-year est.); Median home value: $62,100 (2008-2012 5-year est.); Median contract rent: n/a per month (2008-2012 5-year est.); Median year structure built: 1962 (2008-2012 5-year est.).

Health Insurance: 27.7% Private; 24.8% Public; 59.1% None. (2008-2012 5-year est.)

Transportation: Commute to work: 100.0% car, 0.0% public transportation, 0.0% walk, 0.0% work from home (2008-2012 5-year est.); Travel time to work: 6.5% less than 15 minutes, 77.4% 15 to 30 minutes, 6.5% 30 to 45 minutes, 9.7% 45 to 60 minutes, 0.0% 60 minutes or more (2008-2012 5-year est.)

BROADWELL (village). Covers a land area of 0.181 square miles and a water area of 0 square miles. Located at 40.07° N. Lat; 89.44° W. Long. Elevation is 591 feet.

Population: 146 (1990); 169 (2000); 145 (2010); Density: 385.7 persons per square mile (2008-2012 5-year est.); Race: 97.1% White, 0.0% Black/African American, 0.0% Asian, 0.0% American Indian/Alaska Native, 0.0% Native Hawaiian/Other Pacific Islander, 2.9% Some other race, 2.9% Two or more races, 0.0% Hispanic of any race (2008-2012 5-year est.); Average household size: 1.79 (2008-2012 5-year est.); Median age: 53.5 (2008-2012 5-year est.); Males per 100 females: 94.4 (2008-2012 5-year est.); Marriage status: 18.2% never married, 72.7% now married, 4.5% widowed, 4.5% divorced (2008-2012 5-year est.); Foreign born: 0.0% (2008-2012 5-year est.); Ancestry (includes multiple ancestries): 28.6% American, 28.6% German, 8.6% Dutch, 8.6% English, 4.3% Irish (2008-2012 5-year est.).

Economy: Single-family building permits issued: 0 (2013); Multi-family building permits issued: 0 (2013); Homeowner vacancy rate: 0.0%. Rental vacancy rate: 0.0%. (2008-2012 5-year est.); Employment by occupation: 7.7% management, business, and financial, 15.4% computer, engineering, and science, 2.6% education, legal, community service, arts, and media, 7.7% healthcare practitioners, 17.9% service, 33.3% sales and office, 7.7% natural resources, construction, and maintenance, 7.7% production, transportation, and material moving (2008-2012 5-year est.).

Income: Per capita income: $24,773 (2008-2012 5-year est.); Median household income: $39,688 (2008-2012 5-year est.); Average household

income: $49,977 (2008-2012 5-year est.); Percent of households with income of $100,000 or more: 15.4% (2008-2012 5-year est.); Poverty rate: 4.3% (2008-2012 5-year est.).

Education: Percent of population age 25 and over with: High school diploma (including GED) or higher: 81.0% (2008-2012 5-year est.); Bachelor's degree or higher: 19.0% (2008-2012 5-year est.); Master's degree or higher: 3.4% (2008-2012 5-year est.).

Housing: Homeownership rate: 71.8% (2008-2012 5-year est.); Median home value: $77,500 (2008-2012 5-year est.); Median contract rent: $381 per month (2008-2012 5-year est.); Median year structure built: Before 1940 (2008-2012 5-year est.).

Health Insurance: 84.3% Private; 44.3% Public; 4.3% None. (2008-2012 5-year est.)

Transportation: Commute to work: 92.3% car, 0.0% public transportation, 0.0% walk, 7.7% work from home (2008-2012 5-year est.); Travel time to work: 38.9% less than 15 minutes, 50.0% 15 to 30 minutes, 11.1% 30 to 45 minutes, 0.0% 45 to 60 minutes, 0.0% 60 minutes or more (2008-2012 5-year est.)

CHESTNUT (CDP). Covers a land area of 0.110 square miles and a water area of 0 square miles. Located at 40.05° N. Lat; 89.19° W. Long. Elevation is 617 feet.

Population: n/a (1990); n/a (2000); 246 (2010); Density: 1,412.8 persons per square mile (2008-2012 5-year est.); Race: 60.6% White, 0.0% Black/African American, 39.4% Asian, 0.0% American Indian/Alaska Native, 0.0% Native Hawaiian/Other Pacific Islander, 0.0% Some other race, 0.0% Two or more races, 0.0% Hispanic of any race (2008-2012 5-year est.); Average household size: 2.87 (2008-2012 5-year est.); Median age: 27.9 (2008-2012 5-year est.); Males per 100 females: 112.3 (2008-2012 5-year est.); Marriage status: 0.0% never married, 51.1% now married, 0.0% widowed, 48.9% divorced (2008-2012 5-year est.); Foreign born: 23.2% (2008-2012 5-year est.); Ancestry (includes multiple ancestries): 18.1% German, 7.7% American, 3.9% English (2008-2012 5-year est.).

Economy: Homeowner vacancy rate: 0.0%. Rental vacancy rate: 0.0%. (2008-2012 5-year est.); Employment by occupation: 30.3% management, business, and financial, 0.0% computer, engineering, and science, 0.0% education, legal, community service, arts, and media, 0.0% healthcare practitioners, 27.3% service, 33.3% sales and office, 0.0% natural resources, construction, and maintenance, 9.1% production, transportation, and material moving (2008-2012 5-year est.).

Income: Per capita income: $16,939 (2008-2012 5-year est.); Median household income: $33,250 (2008-2012 5-year est.); Average household income: $47,015 (2008-2012 5-year est.); Percent of households with income of $100,000 or more: n/a (2008-2012 5-year est.); Poverty rate: 36.8% (2008-2012 5-year est.).

Education: Percent of population age 25 and over with: High school diploma (including GED) or higher: 89.4% (2008-2012 5-year est.); Bachelor's degree or higher: 38.3% (2008-2012 5-year est.); Master's degree or higher: 14.9% (2008-2012 5-year est.).

Housing: Homeownership rate: 55.6% (2008-2012 5-year est.); Median home value: $98,300 (2008-2012 5-year est.); Median contract rent: $367 per month (2008-2012 5-year est.); Median year structure built: 1943 (2008-2012 5-year est.).

Health Insurance: 57.4% Private; 51.0% Public; 1.9% None. (2008-2012 5-year est.)

Transportation: Commute to work: 78.8% car, 0.0% public transportation, 0.0% walk, 21.2% work from home (2008-2012 5-year est.); Travel time to work: 0.0% less than 15 minutes, 57.7% 15 to 30 minutes, 42.3% 30 to 45 minutes, 0.0% 45 to 60 minutes, 0.0% 60 minutes or more (2008-2012 5-year est.)

CORNLAND (CDP). Covers a land area of 0.095 square miles and a water area of 0 square miles. Located at 39.94° N. Lat; 89.40° W. Long. Elevation is 604 feet.

Population: n/a (1990); n/a (2000); 93 (2010); Density: 611.7 persons per square mile (2008-2012 5-year est.); Race: 100.0% White, 0.0% Black/African American, 0.0% Asian, 0.0% American Indian/Alaska Native, 0.0% Native Hawaiian/Other Pacific Islander, 0.0% Some other race, 0.0% Two or more races, 0.0% Hispanic of any race (2008-2012 5-year est.); Average household size: 3.22 (2008-2012 5-year est.); Median age: 45.8 (2008-2012 5-year est.); Males per 100 females: 87.1 (2008-2012 5-year est.); Marriage status: 2.4% never married, 97.6% now married, 0.0% widowed, 0.0% divorced (2008-2012 5-year est.); Foreign born: 0.0%

(2008-2012 5-year est.); Ancestry (includes multiple ancestries): 27.6% American, 12.1% Irish, 12.1% German (2008-2012 5-year est.).

Economy: Homeowner vacancy rate: 0.0%. Rental vacancy rate: 0.0%. (2008-2012 5-year est.); Employment by occupation: 35.0% management, business, and financial, 25.0% computer, engineering, and science, 0.0% education, legal, community service, arts, and media, 40.0% healthcare practitioners, 0.0% service, 0.0% sales and office, 0.0% natural resources, construction, and maintenance, 0.0% production, transportation, and material moving (2008-2012 5-year est.).

Income: Per capita income: $20,593 (2008-2012 5-year est.); Median household income: $56,071 (2008-2012 5-year est.); Average household income: $58,417 (2008-2012 5-year est.); Percent of households with income of $100,000 or more: 27.8% (2008-2012 5-year est.); Poverty rate: 0.0% (2008-2012 5-year est.).

Education: Percent of population age 25 and over with: High school diploma (including GED) or higher: 83.3% (2008-2012 5-year est.); Bachelor's degree or higher: 11.9% (2008-2012 5-year est.); Master's degree or higher: 0.0% (2008-2012 5-year est.).

Housing: Homeownership rate: 100.0% (2008-2012 5-year est.); Median home value: $26,700 (2008-2012 5-year est.); Median contract rent: n/a per month (2008-2012 5-year est.); Median year structure built: 1956 (2008-2012 5-year est.).

Health Insurance: 98.3% Private; 15.5% Public; 1.7% None. (2008-2012 5-year est.)

Transportation: Commute to work: 100.0% car, 0.0% public transportation, 0.0% walk, 0.0% work from home (2008-2012 5-year est.); Travel time to work: 35.0% less than 15 minutes, 0.0% 15 to 30 minutes, 65.0% 30 to 45 minutes, 0.0% 45 to 60 minutes, 0.0% 60 minutes or more (2008-2012 5-year est.)

ELKHART (village). Aka Elk Hart City. Covers a land area of 1.453 square miles and a water area of 0.009 square miles. Located at 40.01° N. Lat; 89.48° W. Long. Elevation is 594 feet.

History: Elkhart was the home of Richard J. Oglesby (1824-1899), a man of many occupations (farmer, carpenter, ropemaker, lawyer, miner, soldier) who served three times as the governor of Illinois, and as a U.S. senator.

Population: 475 (1990); 443 (2000); 405 (2010); Density: 200.3 persons per square mile (2008-2012 5-year est.); Race: 95.5% White, 0.7% Black/African American, 0.0% Asian, 0.0% American Indian/Alaska Native, 0.0% Native Hawaiian/Other Pacific Islander, 3.8% Some other race, 3.8% Two or more races, 0.3% Hispanic of any race (2008-2012 5-year est.); Average household size: 2.12 (2008-2012 5-year est.); Median age: 37.5 (2008-2012 5-year est.); Males per 100 females: 79.6 (2008-2012 5-year est.); Marriage status: 26.9% never married, 58.3% now married, 7.4% widowed, 7.4% divorced (2008-2012 5-year est.); Foreign born: 1.0% (2008-2012 5-year est.); Ancestry (includes multiple ancestries): 25.4% American, 19.9% German, 13.1% Irish, 10.0% English, 3.1% Swedish (2008-2012 5-year est.).

Economy: Single-family building permits issued: 0 (2013); Multi-family building permits issued: 0 (2013); Homeowner vacancy rate: 0.0%. Rental vacancy rate: 0.0%. (2008-2012 5-year est.); Employment by occupation: 8.2% management, business, and financial, 3.2% computer, engineering, and science, 10.8% education, legal, community service, arts, and media, 13.3% healthcare practitioners, 17.7% service, 24.1% sales and office, 15.2% natural resources, construction, and maintenance, 7.6% production, transportation, and material moving (2008-2012 5-year est.).

Income: Per capita income: $26,829 (2008-2012 5-year est.); Median household income: $62,000 (2008-2012 5-year est.); Average household income: $69,668 (2008-2012 5-year est.); Percent of households with income of $100,000 or more: 19.1% (2008-2012 5-year est.); Poverty rate: 6.9% (2008-2012 5-year est.).

Education: Percent of population age 25 and over with: High school diploma (including GED) or higher: 91.0% (2008-2012 5-year est.); Bachelor's degree or higher: 19.2% (2008-2012 5-year est.); Master's degree or higher: 4.0% (2008-2012 5-year est.).

Housing: Homeownership rate: 85.3% (2008-2012 5-year est.); Median home value: $100,000 (2008-2012 5-year est.); Median contract rent: $419 per month (2008-2012 5-year est.); Median year structure built: 1952 (2008-2012 5-year est.).

Health Insurance: 76.4% Private; 34.7% Public; 3.5% None. (2008-2012 5-year est.)

Transportation: Commute to work: 87.6% car, 0.0% public transportation, 0.6% walk, 6.2% work from home (2008-2012 5-year est.); Travel time to work: 16.6% less than 15 minutes, 43.7% 15 to 30 minutes, 26.5% 30 to

45 minutes, 4.0% 45 to 60 minutes, 9.3% 60 minutes or more (2008-2012 5-year est.)

EMDEN (village). Covers a land area of 0.234 square miles and a water area of 0 square miles. Located at 40.30° N. Lat; 89.49° W. Long. Elevation is 591 feet.

Population: 459 (1990); 515 (2000); 485 (2010); Density: 1,395.2 persons per square mile (2008-2012 5-year est.); Race: 96.9% White, 0.0% Black/African American, 0.0% Asian, 0.3% American Indian/Alaska Native, 0.0% Native Hawaiian/Other Pacific Islander, 2.8% Some other race, 2.8% Two or more races, 0.0% Hispanic of any race (2008-2012 5-year est.); Average household size: 2.02 (2008-2012 5-year est.); Median age: 46.5 (2008-2012 5-year est.); Males per 100 females: 95.8 (2008-2012 5-year est.); Marriage status: 20.7% never married, 60.5% now married, 11.7% widowed, 7.1% divorced (2008-2012 5-year est.); Foreign born: 0.6% (2008-2012 5-year est.); Ancestry (includes multiple ancestries): 55.7% German, 14.4% American, 12.2% English, 8.9% Irish, 2.4% Italian (2008-2012 5-year est.).

Economy: Single-family building permits issued: 1 (2013); Multi-family building permits issued: 0 (2013); Homeowner vacancy rate: 1.6%. Rental vacancy rate: 22.2%. (2008-2012 5-year est.); Employment by occupation: 14.2% management, business, and financial, 0.7% computer, engineering, and science, 6.8% education, legal, community service, arts, and media, 6.1% healthcare practitioners, 11.5% service, 35.1% sales and office, 9.5% natural resources, construction, and maintenance, 16.2% production, transportation, and material moving (2008-2012 5-year est.).

Income: Per capita income: $24,203 (2008-2012 5-year est.); Median household income: $50,455 (2008-2012 5-year est.); Average household income: $53,472 (2008-2012 5-year est.); Percent of households with income of $100,000 or more: 4.9% (2008-2012 5-year est.); Poverty rate: 9.2% (2008-2012 5-year est.).

Education: Percent of population age 25 and over with: High school diploma (including GED) or higher: 92.8% (2008-2012 5-year est.); Bachelor's degree or higher: 17.7% (2008-2012 5-year est.); Master's degree or higher: 3.0% (2008-2012 5-year est.).

School District(s)

Hartsburg Emden CUSD 21 (KG-12)

    2011-12 Enrollment: 222 . . . . (217) 642-5244

Housing: Homeownership rate: 78.4% (2008-2012 5-year est.); Median home value: $75,300 (2008-2012 5-year est.); Median contract rent: $458 per month (2008-2012 5-year est.); Median year structure built: 1955 (2008-2012 5-year est.).

Health Insurance: 72.5% Private; 42.8% Public; 11.6% None. (2008-2012 5-year est.)

Transportation: Commute to work: 91.5% car, 0.0% public transportation, 4.3% walk, 3.5% work from home (2008-2012 5-year est.); Travel time to work: 27.9% less than 15 minutes, 47.8% 15 to 30 minutes, 15.4% 30 to 45 minutes, 5.1% 45 to 60 minutes, 3.7% 60 minutes or more (2008-2012 5-year est.)

HARTSBURG (village). Covers a land area of 0.138 square miles and a water area of 0 square miles. Located at 40.25° N. Lat; 89.44° W. Long. Elevation is 604 feet.

Population: 306 (1990); 358 (2000); 314 (2010); Density: 1,735.5 persons per square mile (2008-2012 5-year est.); Race: 99.2% White, 0.0% Black/African American, 0.0% Asian, 0.0% American Indian/Alaska Native, 0.0% Native Hawaiian/Other Pacific Islander, 0.8% Some other race, 0.8% Two or more races, 1.3% Hispanic of any race (2008-2012 5-year est.); Average household size: 2.45 (2008-2012 5-year est.); Median age: 42.5 (2008-2012 5-year est.); Males per 100 females: 67.8 (2008-2012 5-year est.); Marriage status: 24.2% never married, 48.0% now married, 14.6% widowed, 13.1% divorced (2008-2012 5-year est.); Foreign born: 0.8% (2008-2012 5-year est.); Ancestry (includes multiple ancestries): 53.3% German, 10.8% American, 7.1% Irish, 5.4% English, 5.0% European (2008-2012 5-year est.).

Economy: Single-family building permits issued: 0 (2013); Multi-family building permits issued: 0 (2013); Homeowner vacancy rate: 6.3%. Rental vacancy rate: 33.3%. (2008-2012 5-year est.); Employment by occupation: 9.9% management, business, and financial, 2.5% computer, engineering, and science, 5.0% education, legal, community service, arts, and media, 8.3% healthcare practitioners, 24.8% service, 18.2% sales and office, 12.4% natural resources, construction, and maintenance, 19.0% production, transportation, and material moving (2008-2012 5-year est.).

Income: Per capita income: $22,064 (2008-2012 5-year est.); Median household income: $41,250 (2008-2012 5-year est.); Average household

income: $55,321 (2008-2012 5-year est.); Percent of households with income of $100,000 or more: 10.1% (2008-2012 5-year est.); Poverty rate: 5.8% (2008-2012 5-year est.).

Education: Percent of population age 25 and over with: High school diploma (including GED) or higher: 94.4% (2008-2012 5-year est.); Bachelor's degree or higher: 16.0% (2008-2012 5-year est.); Master's degree or higher: 4.3% (2008-2012 5-year est.).

School District(s)

Hartsburg Emden CUSD 21 (KG-12)

   2011-12 Enrollment: 222. . . . . (217) 642-5244

Housing: Homeownership rate: 91.8% (2008-2012 5-year est.); Median home value: $76,900 (2008-2012 5-year est.); Median contract rent: $425 per month (2008-2012 5-year est.); Median year structure built: 1943 (2008-2012 5-year est.).

Health Insurance: 86.7% Private; 35.0% Public; 6.7% None. (2008-2012 5-year est.)

Transportation: Commute to work: 92.4% car, 0.0% public transportation, 1.7% walk, 1.7% work from home (2008-2012 5-year est.); Travel time to work: 39.7% less than 15 minutes, 40.5% 15 to 30 minutes, 10.3% 30 to 45 minutes, 8.6% 45 to 60 minutes, 0.9% 60 minutes or more (2008-2012 5-year est.)

LAKE FORK (unincorporated postal area)

Zip Code: 62541

Covers a land area of 0.410 square miles and a water area of 0 square miles. Located at 39.96° N. Lat; 89.35° W. Long. Elevation is 600 feet. Population: 57 (2010); Density: 138.8 persons per square mile (2010); Race: 89.5% White, 1.8% Black/African American, 1.8% Asian, 1.8% American Indian/Alaska Native, 0.0% Native Hawaiian/Other Pacific Islander, 5.1% Some other race, 3.5% Two or more races, 8.8% Hispanic of any race (2010); Average household size: 2.19 (2010); Median age: 50.5 (2010); Males per 100 females: 119.2 (2010); Homeownership rate: 92.3% (2010)

LATHAM (village). Covers a land area of 0.278 square miles and a water area of 0 square miles. Located at 39.97° N. Lat; 89.16° W. Long. Elevation is 614 feet.

Population: 482 (1990); 371 (2000); 380 (2010); Density: 1,088.1 persons per square mile (2008-2012 5-year est.); Race: 97.4% White, 0.0% Black/African American, 0.0% Asian, 0.0% American Indian/Alaska Native, 0.0% Native Hawaiian/Other Pacific Islander, 2.6% Some other race, 0.0% Two or more races, 2.6% Hispanic of any race (2008-2012 5-year est.); Average household size: 2.16 (2008-2012 5-year est.); Median age: 41.3 (2008-2012 5-year est.); Males per 100 females: 94.2 (2008-2012 5-year est.); Marriage status: 12.9% never married, 59.2% now married, 12.9% widowed, 15.0% divorced (2008-2012 5-year est.); Foreign born: 2.6% (2008-2012 5-year est.); Ancestry (includes multiple ancestries): 33.0% German, 20.1% American, 11.6% English, 10.2% Irish, 4.3% Dutch (2008-2012 5-year est.).

Economy: Single-family building permits issued: 0 (2013); Multi-family building permits issued: 0 (2013); Homeowner vacancy rate: 0.0%. Rental vacancy rate: 0.0%. (2008-2012 5-year est.); Employment by occupation: 10.4% management, business, and financial, 0.7% computer, engineering, and science, 9.7% education, legal, community service, arts, and media, 1.5% healthcare practitioners, 12.7% service, 21.6% sales and office, 17.9% natural resources, construction, and maintenance, 25.4% production, transportation, and material moving (2008-2012 5-year est.).

Income: Per capita income: $21,377 (2008-2012 5-year est.); Median household income: $43,125 (2008-2012 5-year est.); Average household income: $47,743 (2008-2012 5-year est.); Percent of households with income of $100,000 or more: 6.4% (2008-2012 5-year est.); Poverty rate: 12.5% (2008-2012 5-year est.).

Education: Percent of population age 25 and over with: High school diploma (including GED) or higher: 91.1% (2008-2012 5-year est.); Bachelor's degree or higher: 15.5% (2008-2012 5-year est.); Master's degree or higher: 1.9% (2008-2012 5-year est.).

Housing: Homeownership rate: 75.0% (2008-2012 5-year est.); Median home value: $82,100 (2008-2012 5-year est.); Median contract rent: $417 per month (2008-2012 5-year est.); Median year structure built: 1944 (2008-2012 5-year est.).

Health Insurance: 77.2% Private; 31.4% Public; 11.2% None. (2008-2012 5-year est.)

Transportation: Commute to work: 97.0% car, 0.0% public transportation, 2.3% walk, 0.8% work from home (2008-2012 5-year est.); Travel time to work: 22.0% less than 15 minutes, 45.5% 15 to 30 minutes, 24.2% 30 to

45 minutes, 8.3% 45 to 60 minutes, 0.0% 60 minutes or more (2008-2012 5-year est.)

LAWNDALE (unincorporated postal area)

Zip Code: 61751

Covers a land area of 1.661 square miles and a water area of 0 square miles. Located at 40.21° N. Lat; 89.29° W. Long. Elevation is 600 feet. Population: 124 (2010); Density: 74.6 persons per square mile (2010); Race: 100.0% White, 0.0% Black/African American, 0.0% Asian, 0.0% American Indian/Alaska Native, 0.0% Native Hawaiian/Other Pacific Islander, 0.0% Some other race, 0.0% Two or more races, 0.0% Hispanic of any race (2010); Average household size: 2.53 (2010); Median age: 44.0 (2010); Males per 100 females: 110.2 (2010); Homeownership rate: 79.6% (2010)

LINCOLN (city). County seat. Covers a land area of 6.401 square miles and a water area of 0 square miles. Located at 40.15° N. Lat; 89.37° W. Long. Elevation is 581 feet.

History: Lincoln was settled in 1853 on land owned by promoter Colonel Latham, who hired Springfield lawyer Abraham Lincoln to draw up the documents for the town lots and decided to name the town Lincoln. The seat of Logan County was changed from Mount Pulaski to Lincoln, which is the only town named for Lincoln with his knowledge and consent.

Population: 15,418 (1990); 15,369 (2000); 14,504 (2010); Density: 2,227.6 persons per square mile (2008-2012 5-year est.); Race: 92.6% White, 3.9% Black/African American, 1.9% Asian, 0.0% American Indian/Alaska Native, 0.1% Native Hawaiian/Other Pacific Islander, 1.5% Some other race, 1.4% Two or more races, 1.1% Hispanic of any race (2008-2012 5-year est.); Average household size: 2.00 (2008-2012 5-year est.); Median age: 41.6 (2008-2012 5-year est.); Males per 100 females: 77.7 (2008-2012 5-year est.); Marriage status: 28.1% never married, 49.2% now married, 9.5% widowed, 13.3% divorced (2008-2012 5-year est.); Foreign born: 1.9% (2008-2012 5-year est.); Ancestry (includes multiple ancestries): 29.2% German, 18.0% American, 14.4% Irish, 11.9% English, 3.1% Italian (2008-2012 5-year est.).

Economy: Single-family building permits issued: 1 (2013); Multi-family building permits issued: 0 (2013); Homeowner vacancy rate: 2.7%. Rental vacancy rate: 4.3%. (2008-2012 5-year est.); Employment by occupation: 12.5% management, business, and financial, 1.4% computer, engineering, and science, 11.5% education, legal, community service, arts, and media, 3.7% healthcare practitioners, 26.6% service, 25.9% sales and office, 5.9% natural resources, construction, and maintenance, 12.4% production, transportation, and material moving (2008-2012 5-year est.).

Income: Per capita income: $23,493 (2008-2012 5-year est.); Median household income: $38,677 (2008-2012 5-year est.); Average household income: $51,209 (2008-2012 5-year est.); Percent of households with income of $100,000 or more: 11.3% (2008-2012 5-year est.); Poverty rate: 17.0% (2008-2012 5-year est.).

Education: Percent of population age 25 and over with: High school diploma (including GED) or higher: 87.1% (2008-2012 5-year est.); Bachelor's degree or higher: 20.7% (2008-2012 5-year est.); Master's degree or higher: 5.7% (2008-2012 5-year est.).

School District(s)

Chester-East Lincoln CCSD 61 (PK-08)

   2011-12 Enrollment: 281. . . . . (217) 732-4136

Lincoln CHSD 404 (09-12)

   2011-12 Enrollment: 838. . . . . (217) 732-4131

Lincoln ESD 27 (PK-08)

   2011-12 Enrollment: 1,298 . . . . (217) 732-2522

Lincolnland Technical Ed Ctr (11-12)

   2011-12 Enrollment: n/a . . . . (217) 732-4131

West Lincoln-Broadwell ESD 92 (KG-08)

   2011-12 Enrollment: 164. . . . . (217) 732-2630

Four-year College(s)

Lincoln Christian University (Private, Not-for-profit, Christian Churches and Churches of Christ)

   Fall 2012 Enrollment: 1,066 . . . . (217) 732-3168

   2012-13 Tuition: In-state $15,300; Out-of-state $15,300

Lincoln College (Private, Not-for-profit)

   Fall 2012 Enrollment: 1,232 . . . . (217) 732-3155

   2012-13 Tuition: In-state $17,500; Out-of-state $17,500

Housing: Homeownership rate: 63.5% (2008-2012 5-year est.); Median home value: $92,000 (2008-2012 5-year est.); Median contract rent: $404 per month (2008-2012 5-year est.); Median year structure built: 1961 (2008-2012 5-year est.).

Health Insurance: 71.9% Private; 38.8% Public; 8.9% None. (2008-2012 5-year est.)
Hospitals: Abraham Lincoln Memorial Hospital (66 beds)
Safety: Violent crime rate: 40.2 per 10,000 population; Property crime rate: 289.1 per 10,000 population (2012).
Transportation: Commute to work: 91.7% car, 1.0% public transportation, 4.2% walk, 1.0% work from home (2008-2012 5-year est.); Travel time to work: 62.4% less than 15 minutes, 11.1% 15 to 30 minutes, 14.4% 30 to 45 minutes, 9.2% 45 to 60 minutes, 2.8% 60 minutes or more (2008-2012 5-year est.); Amtrak: Train service available.
Airports: Logan County Airport (general aviation)
Additional Information Contacts
City of Lincoln . . . . (217) 735-2815
　http://www.lincolnil.gov
Lincoln/Logan County Chamber of Commerce . . . . (217) 735-2385
　http://www.lincolnillinois.com

MIDDLETOWN (village). Covers a land area of 0.240 square miles and a water area of 0 square miles. Located at 40.10° N. Lat; 89.59° W. Long. Elevation is 584 feet.
Population: 436 (1990); 434 (2000); 324 (2010); Density: 1,183.4 persons per square mile (2008-2012 5-year est.); Race: 97.2% White, 1.8% Black/African American, 0.0% Asian, 0.0% American Indian/Alaska Native, 0.0% Native Hawaiian/Other Pacific Islander, 1.0% Some other race, 1.1% Two or more races, 0.4% Hispanic of any race (2008-2012 5-year est.); Average household size: 2.10 (2008-2012 5-year est.); Median age: 40.0 (2008-2012 5-year est.); Males per 100 females: 65.1 (2008-2012 5-year est.); Marriage status: 22.0% never married, 48.4% now married, 14.8% widowed, 14.8% divorced (2008-2012 5-year est.); Foreign born: 0.0% (2008-2012 5-year est.); Ancestry (includes multiple ancestries): 36.3% American, 20.4% German, 8.1% Irish, 7.0% Italian, 6.7% English (2008-2012 5-year est.).
Economy: Single-family building permits issued: 0 (2013); Multi-family building permits issued: 0 (2013); Homeowner vacancy rate: 9.9%. Rental vacancy rate: 0.0%. (2008-2012 5-year est.); Employment by occupation: 7.0% management, business, and financial, 0.0% computer, engineering, and science, 4.4% education, legal, community service, arts, and media, 5.3% healthcare practitioners, 15.8% service, 29.8% sales and office, 7.0% natural resources, construction, and maintenance, 30.7% production, transportation, and material moving (2008-2012 5-year est.).
Income: Per capita income: $19,531 (2008-2012 5-year est.); Median household income: $39,464 (2008-2012 5-year est.); Average household income: $45,453 (2008-2012 5-year est.); Percent of households with income of $100,000 or more: 4.5% (2008-2012 5-year est.); Poverty rate: 19.1% (2008-2012 5-year est.).
Education: Percent of population age 25 and over with: High school diploma (including GED) or higher: 75.1% (2008-2012 5-year est.); Bachelor's degree or higher: 8.0% (2008-2012 5-year est.); Master's degree or higher: 2.0% (2008-2012 5-year est.).
School District(s)
New Holland-Middletown Ed 88 (KG-08)
　2011-12 Enrollment: 103 . . . . (217) 445-2421
Housing: Homeownership rate: 80.7% (2008-2012 5-year est.); Median home value: $56,900 (2008-2012 5-year est.); Median contract rent: $404 per month (2008-2012 5-year est.); Median year structure built: Before 1940 (2008-2012 5-year est.).
Health Insurance: 59.5% Private; 51.8% Public; 9.2% None. (2008-2012 5-year est.)
Transportation: Commute to work: 99.1% car, 0.0% public transportation, 0.0% walk, 0.0% work from home (2008-2012 5-year est.); Travel time to work: 9.6% less than 15 minutes, 56.1% 15 to 30 minutes, 21.1% 30 to 45 minutes, 7.9% 45 to 60 minutes, 5.3% 60 minutes or more (2008-2012 5-year est.)

MOUNT PULASKI (city). Covers a land area of 1.132 square miles and a water area of 0 square miles. Located at 40.01° N. Lat; 89.28° W. Long. Elevation is 663 feet.
History: Mount Pulaski served as the seat of Logan County from 1847 to 1853.
Population: 1,610 (1990); 1,701 (2000); 1,566 (2010); Density: 1,107.2 persons per square mile (2008-2012 5-year est.); Race: 99.6% White, 0.0% Black/African American, 0.0% Asian, 0.2% American Indian/Alaska Native, 0.0% Native Hawaiian/Other Pacific Islander, 0.2% Some other race, 0.2% Two or more races, 0.2% Hispanic of any race (2008-2012 5-year est.); Average household size: 2.18 (2008-2012 5-year est.);

Median age: 45.8 (2008-2012 5-year est.); Males per 100 females: 81.3 (2008-2012 5-year est.); Marriage status: 19.2% never married, 57.3% now married, 12.7% widowed, 10.8% divorced (2008-2012 5-year est.); Foreign born: 2.1% (2008-2012 5-year est.); Ancestry (includes multiple ancestries): 35.4% German, 17.6% Irish, 16.6% American, 9.7% English, 1.8% New Zealander (2008-2012 5-year est.).
Economy: Single-family building permits issued: 0 (2013); Multi-family building permits issued: 0 (2013); Homeowner vacancy rate: 0.7%. Rental vacancy rate: 8.3%. (2008-2012 5-year est.); Employment by occupation: 9.1% management, business, and financial, 2.0% computer, engineering, and science, 11.5% education, legal, community service, arts, and media, 6.2% healthcare practitioners, 17.1% service, 29.5% sales and office, 8.5% natural resources, construction, and maintenance, 16.2% production, transportation, and material moving (2008-2012 5-year est.).
Income: Per capita income: $25,849 (2008-2012 5-year est.); Median household income: $48,125 (2008-2012 5-year est.); Average household income: $61,470 (2008-2012 5-year est.); Percent of households with income of $100,000 or more: 16.4% (2008-2012 5-year est.); Poverty rate: 8.2% (2008-2012 5-year est.).
Education: Percent of population age 25 and over with: High school diploma (including GED) or higher: 88.6% (2008-2012 5-year est.); Bachelor's degree or higher: 17.8% (2008-2012 5-year est.); Master's degree or higher: 5.2% (2008-2012 5-year est.).
School District(s)
Mt Pulaski CUSD 23 (PK-12)
　2011-12 Enrollment: 504 . . . . (217) 792-7222
Housing: Homeownership rate: 79.7% (2008-2012 5-year est.); Median home value: $93,700 (2008-2012 5-year est.); Median contract rent: $374 per month (2008-2012 5-year est.); Median year structure built: 1951 (2008-2012 5-year est.).
Health Insurance: 70.5% Private; 34.8% Public; 13.1% None. (2008-2012 5-year est.)
Safety: Violent crime rate: 12.9 per 10,000 population; Property crime rate: 32.1 per 10,000 population (2012).
Transportation: Commute to work: 92.0% car, 0.2% public transportation, 3.9% walk, 2.8% work from home (2008-2012 5-year est.); Travel time to work: 34.7% less than 15 minutes, 24.0% 15 to 30 minutes, 20.8% 30 to 45 minutes, 12.8% 45 to 60 minutes, 7.8% 60 minutes or more (2008-2012 5-year est.)

NEW HOLLAND (village). Covers a land area of 0.285 square miles and a water area of 0 square miles. Located at 40.18° N. Lat; 89.58° W. Long. Elevation is 554 feet.
Population: 330 (1990); 318 (2000); 269 (2010); Density: 698.2 persons per square mile (2008-2012 5-year est.); Race: 98.0% White, 0.0% Black/African American, 0.0% Asian, 2.0% American Indian/Alaska Native, 0.0% Native Hawaiian/Other Pacific Islander, 0.0% Some other race, 0.0% Two or more races, 0.0% Hispanic of any race (2008-2012 5-year est.); Average household size: 2.19 (2008-2012 5-year est.); Median age: 44.2 (2008-2012 5-year est.); Males per 100 females: 86.0 (2008-2012 5-year est.); Marriage status: 9.5% never married, 63.3% now married, 10.1% widowed, 17.1% divorced (2008-2012 5-year est.); Foreign born: 0.0% (2008-2012 5-year est.); Ancestry (includes multiple ancestries): 30.7% German, 24.6% American, 14.1% English, 11.6% Irish, 7.5% Dutch (2008-2012 5-year est.).
Economy: Homeowner vacancy rate: 7.2%. Rental vacancy rate: 6.7%. (2008-2012 5-year est.); Employment by occupation: 4.7% management, business, and financial, 0.9% computer, engineering, and science, 11.3% education, legal, community service, arts, and media, 9.4% healthcare practitioners, 10.4% service, 38.7% sales and office, 12.3% natural resources, construction, and maintenance, 12.3% production, transportation, and material moving (2008-2012 5-year est.).
Income: Per capita income: $26,477 (2008-2012 5-year est.); Median household income: $47,083 (2008-2012 5-year est.); Average household income: $57,333 (2008-2012 5-year est.); Percent of households with income of $100,000 or more: 8.8% (2008-2012 5-year est.); Poverty rate: 9.2% (2008-2012 5-year est.).
Education: Percent of population age 25 and over with: High school diploma (including GED) or higher: 95.2% (2008-2012 5-year est.); Bachelor's degree or higher: 19.9% (2008-2012 5-year est.); Master's degree or higher: 8.2% (2008-2012 5-year est.).
Housing: Homeownership rate: 84.6% (2008-2012 5-year est.); Median home value: $84,700 (2008-2012 5-year est.); Median contract rent: $625 per month (2008-2012 5-year est.); Median year structure built: Before 1940 (2008-2012 5-year est.).

Health Insurance: 84.9% Private; 31.7% Public; 8.5% None. (2008-2012 5-year est.)

Transportation: Commute to work: 87.7% car, 0.0% public transportation, 8.5% walk, 0.9% work from home (2008-2012 5-year est.); Travel time to work: 34.3% less than 15 minutes, 28.6% 15 to 30 minutes, 14.3% 30 to 45 minutes, 17.1% 45 to 60 minutes, 5.7% 60 minutes or more (2008-2012 5-year est.)

Macon County

Located in central Illinois; drained by the Sangamon River. Covers a land area of 580.689 square miles, a water area of 5.176 square miles, and is located in the Central Time Zone at 39.86° N. Lat., 88.96° W. Long. The county was founded in 1829. County seat is Decatur.

Macon County is part of the Decatur, IL Metropolitan Statistical Area. The entire metro area includes: Macon County, IL

Weather Station: Decatur   Elevation: 620 feet

	Jan	Feb	Mar	Apr	May	Jun	Jul	Aug	Sep	Oct	Nov	Dec
High	36	41	53	66	76	85	88	86	80	67	53	40
Low	19	23	32	42	52	61	65	64	56	44	35	24
Precip	2.2	2.0	2.7	3.7	4.6	4.0	3.8	3.7	3.1	3.4	3.4	2.7
Snow	6.0	4.3	1.9	0.2	tr	0.0	0.0	0.0	0.0	tr	0.7	5.0

High and Low temperatures in degrees Fahrenheit; Precipitation and Snow in inches

Population: 117,206 (1990); 114,706 (2000); 110,768 (2010); Race: 79.6% White, 15.9% Black/African American, 1.1% Asian, 0.1% American Indian/Alaska Native, 0.0% Native Hawaiian/Other Pacific Islander, 3.3% Some other race, 2.8% Two or more races, 1.9% Hispanic of any race (2008-2012 5-year est.); Density: 189.4 persons per square mile (2008-2012 5-year est.); Average household size: 2.38 (2008-2012 5-year est.); Median age: 40.4 (2008-2012 5-year est.); Males per 100 females: 92.2 (2008-2012 5-year est.).

Religion: Six largest groups: 10.3% Catholicism, 8.5% Baptist, 5.6% Lutheran, 5.3% Methodist/Pietist, 5.2% Non-denominational Protestant, 3.9% Presbyterian-Reformed (2010)

Economy: Unemployment rate: 9.1% (April 2014); Total civilian labor force: 51,497 (April 2014); Leading industries: 16.8% manufacturing; 16.7% health care and social assistance; 11.9% retail trade (2012); Farms: 674 totaling 336,576 acres (2012); Companies that employ 500 or more persons: 10 (2012); Companies that employ 100 to 499 persons: 65 (2012); Companies that employ less than 100 persons: 2,370 (2012); Black-owned businesses: n/a (2007); Hispanic-owned businesses: 56 (2007); Asian-owned businesses: 181 (2007); Women-owned businesses: 2,544 (2007); Single-family building permits issued: 67 (2013); Multi-family building permits issued: 12 (2013).

Income: Per capita income: $25,948 (2008-2012 5-year est.); Median household income: $46,165 (2008-2012 5-year est.); Average household income: $62,100 (2008-2012 5-year est.); Percent of households with income of $100,000 or more: 15.8% (2008-2012 5-year est.); Poverty rate: 16.2% (2008-2012 5-year est.); Bankruptcy rate: 4.39% (2013).

Taxes: Total county taxes per capita: $179 (2011); County property taxes per capita: $177 (2011).

Education: Percent of population age 25 and over with: High school diploma (including GED) or higher: 87.5% (2008-2012 5-year est.); Bachelor's degree or higher: 21.9% (2008-2012 5-year est.); Master's degree or higher: 7.6% (2008-2012 5-year est.).

Housing: Homeownership rate: 69.5% (2008-2012 5-year est.); Median home value: $92,500 (2008-2012 5-year est.); Median contract rent: $488 per month (2008-2012 5-year est.); Median year structure built: 1962 (2008-2012 5-year est.)

Health: Birth rate: 117.6 per 10,000 population (2013); Death rate: 104.1 per 10,000 population (2013); Age-adjusted cancer mortality rate: 190.5 deaths per 100,000 population (2011); Number of physicians: 23.5 per 10,000 population (2011); Hospital beds: 40.3 per 10,000 population (2010); Hospital admissions: 1,701.9 per 10,000 population (2010).

Environment: Air Quality Index: 80.3% good, 19.7% moderate, 0.0% unhealthy for sensitive individuals, 0.0% unhealthy (percent of days in 2013)

Elections: 2012 Presidential election results: 46.5% Obama, 51.8% Romney

National and State Parks: Lincoln Trail Homestead State Park; Spitler Woods State Park

Additional Information Contacts

Macon County Government . . . . (217) 424-1305
http://www.co.macon.il.us

Macon County Communities

ARGENTA (village). Covers a land area of 0.656 square miles and a water area of 0 square miles. Located at 39.99° N. Lat; 88.82° W. Long. Elevation is 686 feet.

Population: 940 (1990); 921 (2000); 947 (2010); Density: 1,451.0 persons per square mile (2008-2012 5-year est.); Race: 97.8% White, 0.2% Black/African American, 0.4% Asian, 0.3% American Indian/Alaska Native, 0.0% Native Hawaiian/Other Pacific Islander, 1.3% Some other race, 1.3% Two or more races, 0.7% Hispanic of any race (2008-2012 5-year est.); Average household size: 2.35 (2008-2012 5-year est.); Median age: 41.7 (2008-2012 5-year est.); Males per 100 females: 90.0 (2008-2012 5-year est.); Marriage status: 27.3% never married, 53.4% now married, 8.0% widowed, 11.3% divorced (2008-2012 5-year est.); Foreign born: 1.5% (2008-2012 5-year est.); Ancestry (includes multiple ancestries): 30.0% American, 25.2% German, 11.0% Irish, 6.5% English, 4.0% French (2008-2012 5-year est.).

Economy: Single-family building permits issued: 0 (2013); Multi-family building permits issued: 0 (2013); Homeowner vacancy rate: 3.1%. Rental vacancy rate: 0.0%. (2008-2012 5-year est.); Employment by occupation: 6.4% management, business, and financial, 2.1% computer, engineering, and science, 13.2% education, legal, community service, arts, and media, 6.4% healthcare practitioners, 8.7% service, 32.6% sales and office, 18.9% natural resources, construction, and maintenance, 11.7% production, transportation, and material moving (2008-2012 5-year est.).

Income: Per capita income: $30,108 (2008-2012 5-year est.); Median household income: $55,096 (2008-2012 5-year est.); Average household income: $70,581 (2008-2012 5-year est.); Percent of households with income of $100,000 or more: 24.9% (2008-2012 5-year est.); Poverty rate: 5.1% (2008-2012 5-year est.).

Education: Percent of population age 25 and over with: High school diploma (including GED) or higher: 91.7% (2008-2012 5-year est.); Bachelor's degree or higher: 17.7% (2008-2012 5-year est.); Master's degree or higher: 5.6% (2008-2012 5-year est.).

School District(s)

Argenta-Oreana CUSD 1 (PK-12)
    2011-12 Enrollment: 1,067 . . . . (217) 795-2313

Housing: Homeownership rate: 75.6% (2008-2012 5-year est.); Median home value: $92,100 (2008-2012 5-year est.); Median contract rent: $420 per month (2008-2012 5-year est.); Median year structure built: 1954 (2008-2012 5-year est.).

Health Insurance: 74.9% Private; 29.1% Public; 8.1% None. (2008-2012 5-year est.)

Transportation: Commute to work: 92.2% car, 0.0% public transportation, 0.4% walk, 1.3% work from home (2008-2012 5-year est.); Travel time to work: 20.4% less than 15 minutes, 49.7% 15 to 30 minutes, 18.6% 30 to 45 minutes, 4.8% 45 to 60 minutes, 6.6% 60 minutes or more (2008-2012 5-year est.)

BLUE MOUND (village). Covers a land area of 0.592 square miles and a water area of 0 square miles. Located at 39.70° N. Lat; 89.12° W. Long. Elevation is 623 feet.

Population: 1,161 (1990); 1,129 (2000); 1,158 (2010); Density: 2,263.6 persons per square mile (2008-2012 5-year est.); Race: 99.0% White, 0.0% Black/African American, 0.0% Asian, 0.0% American Indian/Alaska Native, 0.0% Native Hawaiian/Other Pacific Islander, 1.0% Some other race, 1.0% Two or more races, 1.3% Hispanic of any race (2008-2012 5-year est.); Average household size: 2.53 (2008-2012 5-year est.); Median age: 38.0 (2008-2012 5-year est.); Males per 100 females: 91.8 (2008-2012 5-year est.); Marriage status: 15.8% never married, 61.3% now married, 7.7% widowed, 15.2% divorced (2008-2012 5-year est.); Foreign born: 0.4% (2008-2012 5-year est.); Ancestry (includes multiple ancestries): 32.6% American, 24.0% German, 11.6% Irish, 8.4% English, 4.0% Italian (2008-2012 5-year est.).

Economy: Single-family building permits issued: 0 (2013); Multi-family building permits issued: 0 (2013); Homeowner vacancy rate: 1.9%. Rental vacancy rate: 5.6%. (2008-2012 5-year est.); Employment by occupation: 7.1% management, business, and financial, 1.7% computer, engineering, and science, 3.2% education, legal, community service, arts, and media, 4.5% healthcare practitioners, 16.5% service, 24.7% sales and office, 14.6% natural resources, construction, and maintenance, 27.7% production, transportation, and material moving (2008-2012 5-year est.).

Income: Per capita income: $21,023 (2008-2012 5-year est.); Median household income: $47,596 (2008-2012 5-year est.); Average household income: $52,870 (2008-2012 5-year est.); Percent of households with income of $100,000 or more: 9.8% (2008-2012 5-year est.); Poverty rate: 9.0% (2008-2012 5-year est.).

Education: Percent of population age 25 and over with: High school diploma (including GED) or higher: 83.4% (2008-2012 5-year est.); Bachelor's degree or higher: 8.5% (2008-2012 5-year est.); Master's degree or higher: 4.1% (2008-2012 5-year est.).

School District(s)

Meridian CUSD 15 (PK-12)

　2011-12 Enrollment: 1,126 . . . . (217) 764-5269

Housing: Homeownership rate: 77.7% (2008-2012 5-year est.); Median home value: $77,600 (2008-2012 5-year est.); Median contract rent: $458 per month (2008-2012 5-year est.); Median year structure built: 1957 (2008-2012 5-year est.).

Health Insurance: 64.5% Private; 36.3% Public; 13.4% None. (2008-2012 5-year est.)

Safety: Violent crime rate: 34.5 per 10,000 population; Property crime rate: 250.4 per 10,000 population (2012).

Transportation: Commute to work: 96.1% car, 0.0% public transportation, 1.4% walk, 1.2% work from home (2008-2012 5-year est.); Travel time to work: 13.8% less than 15 minutes, 47.0% 15 to 30 minutes, 33.2% 30 to 45 minutes, 2.1% 45 to 60 minutes, 3.9% 60 minutes or more (2008-2012 5-year est.).

BOODY (CDP). Covers a land area of 1.016 square miles and a water area of 0 square miles. Located at 39.77° N. Lat; 89.05° W. Long. Elevation is 682 feet.

Population: n/a (1990); n/a (2000); 276 (2010); Density: 215.6 persons per square mile (2008-2012 5-year est.); Race: 100.0% White, 0.0% Black/African American, 0.0% Asian, 0.0% American Indian/Alaska Native, 0.0% Native Hawaiian/Other Pacific Islander, 0.0% Some other race, 0.0% Two or more races, 0.0% Hispanic of any race (2008-2012 5-year est.); Average household size: 2.92 (2008-2012 5-year est.); Median age: 37.2 (2008-2012 5-year est.); Males per 100 females: 92.1 (2008-2012 5-year est.); Marriage status: 7.9% never married, 41.1% now married, 8.6% widowed, 42.4% divorced (2008-2012 5-year est.); Foreign born: 0.0% (2008-2012 5-year est.); Ancestry (includes multiple ancestries): 51.1% American, 21.5% English, 16.0% Irish, 15.5% German, 4.6% Dutch (2008-2012 5-year est.).

Economy: Homeowner vacancy rate: 0.0%. Rental vacancy rate: 0.0%. (2008-2012 5-year est.); Employment by occupation: 6.4% management, business, and financial, 4.0% computer, engineering, and science, 0.0% education, legal, community service, arts, and media, 0.0% healthcare practitioners, 9.6% service, 32.0% sales and office, 48.0% natural resources, construction, and maintenance, 0.0% production, transportation, and material moving (2008-2012 5-year est.).

Income: Per capita income: $24,585 (2008-2012 5-year est.); Median household income: $78,558 (2008-2012 5-year est.); Average household income: $71,132 (2008-2012 5-year est.); Percent of households with income of $100,000 or more: n/a (2008-2012 5-year est.); Poverty rate: 0.0% (2008-2012 5-year est.).

Education: Percent of population age 25 and over with: High school diploma (including GED) or higher: 91.4% (2008-2012 5-year est.); Bachelor's degree or higher: 5.8% (2008-2012 5-year est.); Master's degree or higher: 0.0% (2008-2012 5-year est.).

Housing: Homeownership rate: 93.3% (2008-2012 5-year est.); Median home value: $103,000 (2008-2012 5-year est.); Median contract rent: n/a per month (2008-2012 5-year est.); Median year structure built: 1985 (2008-2012 5-year est.).

Health Insurance: 60.7% Private; 19.6% Public; 22.4% None. (2008-2012 5-year est.)

Transportation: Commute to work: 100.0% car, 0.0% public transportation, 0.0% walk, 0.0% work from home (2008-2012 5-year est.); Travel time to work: 19.2% less than 15 minutes, 67.2% 15 to 30 minutes, 0.0% 30 to 45 minutes, 9.6% 45 to 60 minutes, 4.0% 60 minutes or more (2008-2012 5-year est.).

DECATUR (city). County seat. Covers a land area of 42.224 square miles and a water area of 4.690 square miles. Located at 39.86° N. Lat; 88.93° W. Long. Elevation is 673 feet.

History: Decatur was named and designated the seat of Macon County in 1829, though there was no settlement here at the time. In 1830 Abraham Lincoln and his family settled nearby, and in 1836 Richard J. Oglesby, who was to become a senator, three times governor of the state, and a friend of Lincoln's. First an agricultural center, manufacturing began in Decatur with the arrival of the railroad in 1854. Coal was discovered under the city in 1874.

Population: 83,885 (1990); 81,860 (2000); 76,122 (2010); Density: 1,802.1 persons per square mile (2008-2012 5-year est.); Race: 72.3% White, 22.8% Black/African American, 1.1% Asian, 0.1% American Indian/Alaska Native, 0.0% Native Hawaiian/Other Pacific Islander, 3.7% Some other race, 3.5% Two or more races, 2.1% Hispanic of any race (2008-2012 5-year est.); Average household size: 2.31 (2008-2012 5-year est.); Median age: 38.8 (2008-2012 5-year est.); Males per 100 females: 89.1 (2008-2012 5-year est.); Marriage status: 32.9% never married, 44.4% now married, 7.9% widowed, 14.9% divorced (2008-2012 5-year est.); Foreign born: 2.0% (2008-2012 5-year est.); Ancestry (includes multiple ancestries): 19.2% German, 16.3% American, 11.9% Irish, 9.3% English, 2.1% Polish (2008-2012 5-year est.).

Economy: Unemployment rate: 10.2% (April 2014); Total civilian labor force: 33,910 (April 2014); Single-family building permits issued: 13 (2013); Multi-family building permits issued: 0 (2013); Homeowner vacancy rate: 3.5%. Rental vacancy rate: 8.8%. (2008-2012 5-year est.); Employment by occupation: 10.0% management, business, and financial, 4.9% computer, engineering, and science, 9.2% education, legal, community service, arts, and media, 4.8% healthcare practitioners, 21.5% service, 25.0% sales and office, 8.2% natural resources, construction, and maintenance, 16.4% production, transportation, and material moving (2008-2012 5-year est.).

Income: Per capita income: $23,056 (2008-2012 5-year est.); Median household income: $39,635 (2008-2012 5-year est.); Average household income: $53,890 (2008-2012 5-year est.); Percent of households with income of $100,000 or more: 11.3% (2008-2012 5-year est.); Poverty rate: 21.4% (2008-2012 5-year est.).

Taxes: Total city taxes per capita: $431 (2011); City property taxes per capita: $174 (2011).

Education: Percent of population age 25 and over with: High school diploma (including GED) or higher: 85.4% (2008-2012 5-year est.); Bachelor's degree or higher: 20.0% (2008-2012 5-year est.); Master's degree or higher: 7.1% (2008-2012 5-year est.).

School District(s)

Decatur SD 61 (PK-12)

　2011-12 Enrollment: 9,007 . . . . (217) 424-3011

Heartland Region

　2011-12 Enrollment: n/a . . . . (217) 875-7211

Heartland Technical Academy (11-12)

　2011-12 Enrollment: n/a . . . . (217) 875-7211

Macon/piatt Roe (07-12)

　2011-12 Enrollment: n/a . . . . (217) 872-3721

Four-year College(s)

Millikin University (Private, Not-for-profit, Presbyterian Church (USA))

　Fall 2012 Enrollment: 2,347 . . . . (217) 424-6211

　2012-13 Tuition: In-state $28,612; Out-of-state $28,612

Two-year College(s)

Mr John's School of Cosmetology Esthetics & Nails-Decatur (Private, For-profit)

　Fall 2012 Enrollment: 77 . . . . (217) 423-8173

Richland Community College (Public)

　Fall 2012 Enrollment: 3,272 . . . . (217) 875-7200

　2012-13 Tuition: In-state $6,552; Out-of-state $11,052

Vocational/Technical School(s)

Shear Learning Academy of Cosmetology (Private, For-profit)

　Fall 2012 Enrollment: 24 . . . . (217) 425-9117

　2012-13 Tuition: $14,350

Housing: Homeownership rate: 62.6% (2008-2012 5-year est.); Median home value: $80,100 (2008-2012 5-year est.); Median contract rent: $487 per month (2008-2012 5-year est.); Median year structure built: 1958 (2008-2012 5-year est.).

Health Insurance: 59.5% Private; 41.4% Public; 14.0% None. (2008-2012 5-year est.)

Hospitals: Decatur Memorial Hospital (314 beds); St. Mary's Hospital (371 beds)

Safety: Violent crime rate: 46.2 per 10,000 population; Property crime rate: 321.6 per 10,000 population (2012).

Transportation: Commute to work: 92.4% car, 1.7% public transportation, 2.5% walk, 1.5% work from home (2008-2012 5-year est.); Travel time to work: 51.8% less than 15 minutes, 35.4% 15 to 30 minutes, 5.9% 30 to 45 minutes, 3.5% 45 to 60 minutes, 3.4% 60 minutes or more (2008-2012 5-year est.).

Airports: Decatur Airport (general aviation)
Additional Information Contacts
City of Decatur. . . . . (217) 424-2700
  http://www.decaturil.gov
Greater Decatur Chamber of Commerce . . . . (217) 422-2200
  http://www.decaturchamber.com

ELWIN (unincorporated postal area)
Zip Code: 62532
Covers a land area of 2.078 square miles and a water area of 0 square miles. Located at 39.76° N. Lat; 88.98° W. Long. Elevation is 712 feet.
Population: 105 (2010); Density: 50.5 persons per square mile (2010); Race: 100.0% White, 0.0% Black/African American, 0.0% Asian, 0.0% American Indian/Alaska Native, 0.0% Native Hawaiian/Other Pacific Islander, 0.0% Some other race, 0.0% Two or more races, 0.0% Hispanic of any race (2010); Average household size: 2.56 (2010); Median age: 44.9 (2010); Males per 100 females: 90.9 (2010); Homeownership rate: 97.6% (2010)

FORSYTH (village). Covers a land area of 3.167 square miles and a water area of 0 square miles. Located at 39.93° N. Lat; 88.96° W. Long. Elevation is 679 feet.
Population: 1,275 (1990); 2,434 (2000); 3,490 (2010); Density: 1,195.2 persons per square mile (2008-2012 5-year est.); Race: 85.9% White, 2.0% Black/African American, 7.9% Asian, 0.0% American Indian/Alaska Native, 0.0% Native Hawaiian/Other Pacific Islander, 4.2% Some other race, 0.2% Two or more races, 4.4% Hispanic of any race (2008-2012 5-year est.); Average household size: 2.73 (2008-2012 5-year est.); Median age: 42.5 (2008-2012 5-year est.); Males per 100 females: 101.4 (2008-2012 5-year est.); Marriage status: 20.9% never married, 69.4% now married, 5.7% widowed, 3.9% divorced (2008-2012 5-year est.); Foreign born: 8.4% (2008-2012 5-year est.); Ancestry (includes multiple ancestries): 21.2% German, 16.9% Irish, 12.0% English, 11.5% American, 3.3% Dutch (2008-2012 5-year est.).
Economy: Single-family building permits issued: 9 (2013); Multi-family building permits issued: 12 (2013); Homeowner vacancy rate: 0.6%. Rental vacancy rate: 0.0%. (2008-2012 5-year est.); Employment by occupation: 20.2% management, business, and financial, 13.1% computer, engineering, and science, 13.9% education, legal, community service, arts, and media, 12.5% healthcare practitioners, 7.1% service, 15.0% sales and office, 7.6% natural resources, construction, and maintenance, 10.4% production, transportation, and material moving (2008-2012 5-year est.).
Income: Per capita income: $45,920 (2008-2012 5-year est.); Median household income: $101,389 (2008-2012 5-year est.); Average household income: $124,631 (2008-2012 5-year est.); Percent of households with income of $100,000 or more: 50.7% (2008-2012 5-year est.); Poverty rate: 6.9% (2008-2012 5-year est.).
Education: Percent of population age 25 and over with: High school diploma (including GED) or higher: 96.0% (2008-2012 5-year est.); Bachelor's degree or higher: 52.1% (2008-2012 5-year est.); Master's degree or higher: 22.8% (2008-2012 5-year est.).
School District(s)
Maroa Forsyth CUSD 2 (PK-12)
  2011-12 Enrollment: 1,166 . . . . (217) 794-3488
Housing: Homeownership rate: 90.6% (2008-2012 5-year est.); Median home value: $229,300 (2008-2012 5-year est.); Median contract rent: $513 per month (2008-2012 5-year est.); Median year structure built: 1993 (2008-2012 5-year est.).
Health Insurance: 92.5% Private; 20.1% Public; 3.0% None. (2008-2012 5-year est.)
Transportation: Commute to work: 93.1% car, 0.0% public transportation, 0.0% walk, 5.2% work from home (2008-2012 5-year est.); Travel time to work: 45.4% less than 15 minutes, 40.2% 15 to 30 minutes, 2.7% 30 to 45 minutes, 6.3% 45 to 60 minutes, 5.4% 60 minutes or more (2008-2012 5-year est.)

HARRISTOWN (village). Covers a land area of 1.851 square miles and a water area of 0 square miles. Located at 39.84° N. Lat; 89.06° W. Long. Elevation is 689 feet.
Population: 1,319 (1990); 1,338 (2000); 1,367 (2010); Density: 832.1 persons per square mile (2008-2012 5-year est.); Race: 99.2% White, 0.0% Black/African American, 0.3% Asian, 0.0% American Indian/Alaska Native, 0.0% Native Hawaiian/Other Pacific Islander, 0.5% Some other race, 0.5% Two or more races, 0.3% Hispanic of any race (2008-2012 5-year est.); Average household size: 2.64 (2008-2012 5-year est.);

Median age: 42.4 (2008-2012 5-year est.); Males per 100 females: 90.1 (2008-2012 5-year est.); Marriage status: 20.2% never married, 60.7% now married, 5.7% widowed, 13.4% divorced (2008-2012 5-year est.); Foreign born: 1.2% (2008-2012 5-year est.); Ancestry (includes multiple ancestries): 28.3% German, 18.2% Irish, 15.5% American, 12.6% English, 2.4% Scotch-Irish (2008-2012 5-year est.).
Economy: Single-family building permits issued: 1 (2013); Multi-family building permits issued: 0 (2013); Homeowner vacancy rate: 0.0%. Rental vacancy rate: 13.5%. (2008-2012 5-year est.); Employment by occupation: 9.2% management, business, and financial, 1.0% computer, engineering, and science, 11.5% education, legal, community service, arts, and media, 5.1% healthcare practitioners, 11.4% service, 28.7% sales and office, 12.6% natural resources, construction, and maintenance, 20.7% production, transportation, and material moving (2008-2012 5-year est.).
Income: Per capita income: $25,047 (2008-2012 5-year est.); Median household income: $57,813 (2008-2012 5-year est.); Average household income: $63,973 (2008-2012 5-year est.); Percent of households with income of $100,000 or more: 12.6% (2008-2012 5-year est.); Poverty rate: 10.5% (2008-2012 5-year est.).
Education: Percent of population age 25 and over with: High school diploma (including GED) or higher: 92.1% (2008-2012 5-year est.); Bachelor's degree or higher: 14.9% (2008-2012 5-year est.); Master's degree or higher: 4.2% (2008-2012 5-year est.).
School District(s)
Sangamon Valley CUSD 9 (PK-12)
  2011-12 Enrollment: 782 . . . . (217) 668-2338
Housing: Homeownership rate: 90.2% (2008-2012 5-year est.); Median home value: $88,700 (2008-2012 5-year est.); Median contract rent: $397 per month (2008-2012 5-year est.); Median year structure built: 1961 (2008-2012 5-year est.).
Health Insurance: 69.4% Private; 30.5% Public; 11.0% None. (2008-2012 5-year est.)
Transportation: Commute to work: 93.1% car, 0.0% public transportation, 1.1% walk, 5.5% work from home (2008-2012 5-year est.); Travel time to work: 25.4% less than 15 minutes, 57.6% 15 to 30 minutes, 7.8% 30 to 45 minutes, 6.0% 45 to 60 minutes, 3.3% 60 minutes or more (2008-2012 5-year est.)

LONG CREEK (village). Covers a land area of 2.828 square miles and a water area of 0 square miles. Located at 39.81° N. Lat; 88.85° W. Long. Elevation is 669 feet.
Population: 1,250 (1990); 1,364 (2000); 1,328 (2010); Density: 471.0 persons per square mile (2008-2012 5-year est.); Race: 99.1% White, 0.0% Black/African American, 0.2% Asian, 0.0% American Indian/Alaska Native, 0.0% Native Hawaiian/Other Pacific Islander, 0.7% Some other race, 0.7% Two or more races, 1.5% Hispanic of any race (2008-2012 5-year est.); Average household size: 2.80 (2008-2012 5-year est.); Median age: 41.2 (2008-2012 5-year est.); Males per 100 females: 107.8 (2008-2012 5-year est.); Marriage status: 23.4% never married, 62.4% now married, 6.6% widowed, 7.7% divorced (2008-2012 5-year est.); Foreign born: 0.2% (2008-2012 5-year est.); Ancestry (includes multiple ancestries): 25.2% German, 20.5% American, 15.0% Irish, 12.7% English, 3.5% Italian (2008-2012 5-year est.).
Economy: Single-family building permits issued: 4 (2013); Multi-family building permits issued: 0 (2013); Homeowner vacancy rate: 0.0%. Rental vacancy rate: 0.0%. (2008-2012 5-year est.); Employment by occupation: 10.2% management, business, and financial, 4.1% computer, engineering, and science, 7.2% education, legal, community service, arts, and media, 9.5% healthcare practitioners, 21.5% service, 21.9% sales and office, 14.0% natural resources, construction, and maintenance, 11.5% production, transportation, and material moving (2008-2012 5-year est.).
Income: Per capita income: $32,330 (2008-2012 5-year est.); Median household income: $76,667 (2008-2012 5-year est.); Average household income: $87,332 (2008-2012 5-year est.); Percent of households with income of $100,000 or more: 30.5% (2008-2012 5-year est.); Poverty rate: 4.5% (2008-2012 5-year est.).
Education: Percent of population age 25 and over with: High school diploma (including GED) or higher: 92.8% (2008-2012 5-year est.); Bachelor's degree or higher: 19.6% (2008-2012 5-year est.); Master's degree or higher: 6.5% (2008-2012 5-year est.).
Housing: Homeownership rate: 93.9% (2008-2012 5-year est.); Median home value: $122,500 (2008-2012 5-year est.); Median contract rent: $745 per month (2008-2012 5-year est.); Median year structure built: 1973 (2008-2012 5-year est.).

Health Insurance: 87.2% Private; 26.8% Public; 3.2% None. (2008-2012 5-year est.)
Transportation: Commute to work: 96.8% car, 0.0% public transportation, 1.2% walk, 1.0% work from home (2008-2012 5-year est.); Travel time to work: 29.4% less than 15 minutes, 56.9% 15 to 30 minutes, 8.8% 30 to 45 minutes, 1.9% 45 to 60 minutes, 3.0% 60 minutes or more (2008-2012 5-year est.)

MACON (city). Covers a land area of 1.426 square miles and a water area of 0 square miles. Located at 39.71° N. Lat; 89.00° W. Long. Elevation is 715 feet.
Population: 1,282 (1990); 1,213 (2000); 1,138 (2010); Density: 856.3 persons per square mile (2008-2012 5-year est.); Race: 99.7% White, 0.0% Black/African American, 0.0% Asian, 0.0% American Indian/Alaska Native, 0.0% Native Hawaiian/Other Pacific Islander, 0.3% Some other race, 0.3% Two or more races, 0.4% Hispanic of any race (2008-2012 5-year est.); Average household size: 2.36 (2008-2012 5-year est.); Median age: 39.7 (2008-2012 5-year est.); Males per 100 females: 83.1 (2008-2012 5-year est.); Marriage status: 24.2% never married, 54.0% now married, 8.1% widowed, 13.7% divorced (2008-2012 5-year est.); Foreign born: 0.2% (2008-2012 5-year est.); Ancestry (includes multiple ancestries): 28.2% German, 23.3% American, 13.2% English, 11.8% Irish, 3.4% Dutch (2008-2012 5-year est.).
Economy: Single-family building permits issued: 2 (2013); Multi-family building permits issued: 0 (2013); Homeowner vacancy rate: 5.6%. Rental vacancy rate: 0.0%. (2008-2012 5-year est.); Employment by occupation: 9.4% management, business, and financial, 4.2% computer, engineering, and science, 7.5% education, legal, community service, arts, and media, 4.2% healthcare practitioners, 11.1% service, 35.3% sales and office, 14.2% natural resources, construction, and maintenance, 14.0% production, transportation, and material moving (2008-2012 5-year est.).
Income: Per capita income: $25,311 (2008-2012 5-year est.); Median household income: $53,214 (2008-2012 5-year est.); Average household income: $60,273 (2008-2012 5-year est.); Percent of households with income of $100,000 or more: 18.7% (2008-2012 5-year est.); Poverty rate: 9.5% (2008-2012 5-year est.).
Education: Percent of population age 25 and over with: High school diploma (including GED) or higher: 91.2% (2008-2012 5-year est.); Bachelor's degree or higher: 19.0% (2008-2012 5-year est.); Master's degree or higher: 4.5% (2008-2012 5-year est.).
School District(s)
Meridian CUSD 15 (PK-12)
    2011-12 Enrollment: 1,126 . . . . (217) 764-5269
Housing: Homeownership rate: 79.3% (2008-2012 5-year est.); Median home value: $84,600 (2008-2012 5-year est.); Median contract rent: $418 per month (2008-2012 5-year est.); Median year structure built: 1956 (2008-2012 5-year est.).
Health Insurance: 76.2% Private; 36.1% Public; 5.5% None. (2008-2012 5-year est.)
Transportation: Commute to work: 94.2% car, 0.0% public transportation, 1.7% walk, 3.2% work from home (2008-2012 5-year est.); Travel time to work: 21.3% less than 15 minutes, 51.7% 15 to 30 minutes, 16.6% 30 to 45 minutes, 5.2% 45 to 60 minutes, 5.1% 60 minutes or more (2008-2012 5-year est.)

MAROA (city). Covers a land area of 1.778 square miles and a water area of 0 square miles. Located at 40.04° N. Lat; 88.96° W. Long. Elevation is 725 feet.
Population: 1,602 (1990); 1,654 (2000); 1,801 (2010); Density: 1,102.2 persons per square mile (2008-2012 5-year est.); Race: 94.2% White, 0.8% Black/African American, 2.0% Asian, 0.0% American Indian/Alaska Native, 0.0% Native Hawaiian/Other Pacific Islander, 3.0% Some other race, 2.9% Two or more races, 2.0% Hispanic of any race (2008-2012 5-year est.); Average household size: 2.63 (2008-2012 5-year est.); Median age: 37.0 (2008-2012 5-year est.); Males per 100 females: 92.0 (2008-2012 5-year est.); Marriage status: 29.0% never married, 54.3% now married, 5.3% widowed, 11.4% divorced (2008-2012 5-year est.); Foreign born: 1.2% (2008-2012 5-year est.); Ancestry (includes multiple ancestries): 24.4% German, 20.0% American, 13.1% Irish, 9.8% English, 5.2% French (2008-2012 5-year est.).
Economy: Single-family building permits issued: 2 (2013); Multi-family building permits issued: 0 (2013); Homeowner vacancy rate: 2.1%. Rental vacancy rate: 3.2%. (2008-2012 5-year est.); Employment by occupation: 11.6% management, business, and financial, 2.8% computer, engineering, and science, 8.7% education, legal, community service, arts, and media,

6.5% healthcare practitioners, 16.0% service, 18.3% sales and office, 15.7% natural resources, construction, and maintenance, 20.3% production, transportation, and material moving (2008-2012 5-year est.).
Income: Per capita income: $23,017 (2008-2012 5-year est.); Median household income: $53,083 (2008-2012 5-year est.); Average household income: $59,279 (2008-2012 5-year est.); Percent of households with income of $100,000 or more: 12.3% (2008-2012 5-year est.); Poverty rate: 6.1% (2008-2012 5-year est.).
Education: Percent of population age 25 and over with: High school diploma (including GED) or higher: 83.3% (2008-2012 5-year est.); Bachelor's degree or higher: 15.7% (2008-2012 5-year est.); Master's degree or higher: 2.9% (2008-2012 5-year est.).
School District(s)
Maroa Forsyth CUSD 2 (PK-12)
    2011-12 Enrollment: 1,166 . . . . (217) 794-3488
Housing: Homeownership rate: 76.8% (2008-2012 5-year est.); Median home value: $85,400 (2008-2012 5-year est.); Median contract rent: $454 per month (2008-2012 5-year est.); Median year structure built: 1967 (2008-2012 5-year est.).
Health Insurance: 71.7% Private; 32.1% Public; 13.6% None. (2008-2012 5-year est.)
Safety: Violent crime rate: 11.1 per 10,000 population; Property crime rate: 66.6 per 10,000 population (2012).
Transportation: Commute to work: 97.0% car, 0.0% public transportation, 1.7% walk, 1.0% work from home (2008-2012 5-year est.); Travel time to work: 25.2% less than 15 minutes, 52.3% 15 to 30 minutes, 14.2% 30 to 45 minutes, 4.0% 45 to 60 minutes, 4.3% 60 minutes or more (2008-2012 5-year est.)

MOUNT ZION (village). Covers a land area of 4.198 square miles and a water area of 0.003 square miles. Located at 39.78° N. Lat; 88.89° W. Long. Elevation is 696 feet.
Population: 4,522 (1990); 4,845 (2000); 5,833 (2010); Density: 1,358.4 persons per square mile (2008-2012 5-year est.); Race: 95.3% White, 2.7% Black/African American, 0.0% Asian, 0.0% American Indian/Alaska Native, 0.0% Native Hawaiian/Other Pacific Islander, 2.0% Some other race, 0.5% Two or more races, 2.9% Hispanic of any race (2008-2012 5-year est.); Average household size: 2.62 (2008-2012 5-year est.); Median age: 37.0 (2008-2012 5-year est.); Males per 100 females: 103.2 (2008-2012 5-year est.); Marriage status: 22.3% never married, 64.7% now married, 6.0% widowed, 7.1% divorced (2008-2012 5-year est.); Foreign born: 2.9% (2008-2012 5-year est.); Ancestry (includes multiple ancestries): 28.6% American, 22.2% German, 9.2% Irish, 8.9% English, 4.5% Italian (2008-2012 5-year est.).
Economy: Single-family building permits issued: 16 (2013); Multi-family building permits issued: 0 (2013); Homeowner vacancy rate: 0.0%. Rental vacancy rate: 0.0%. (2008-2012 5-year est.); Employment by occupation: 16.8% management, business, and financial, 7.7% computer, engineering, and science, 9.4% education, legal, community service, arts, and media, 9.7% healthcare practitioners, 12.7% service, 24.7% sales and office, 7.2% natural resources, construction, and maintenance, 11.9% production, transportation, and material moving (2008-2012 5-year est.).
Income: Per capita income: $31,699 (2008-2012 5-year est.); Median household income: $62,958 (2008-2012 5-year est.); Average household income: $82,610 (2008-2012 5-year est.); Percent of households with income of $100,000 or more: 24.7% (2008-2012 5-year est.); Poverty rate: 6.6% (2008-2012 5-year est.).
Education: Percent of population age 25 and over with: High school diploma (including GED) or higher: 93.9% (2008-2012 5-year est.); Bachelor's degree or higher: 33.8% (2008-2012 5-year est.); Master's degree or higher: 10.9% (2008-2012 5-year est.).
School District(s)
Mt Zion CUSD 3 (PK-12)
    2011-12 Enrollment: 2,503 . . . . (217) 864-2366
Housing: Homeownership rate: 78.0% (2008-2012 5-year est.); Median home value: $134,000 (2008-2012 5-year est.); Median contract rent: $605 per month (2008-2012 5-year est.); Median year structure built: 1976 (2008-2012 5-year est.).
Health Insurance: 82.7% Private; 18.2% Public; 11.0% None. (2008-2012 5-year est.)
Safety: Violent crime rate: 10.3 per 10,000 population; Property crime rate: 72.0 per 10,000 population (2012).
Transportation: Commute to work: 90.4% car, 0.0% public transportation, 6.6% walk, 1.4% work from home (2008-2012 5-year est.); Travel time to work: 30.1% less than 15 minutes, 55.7% 15 to 30 minutes, 9.0% 30 to 45

minutes, 0.5% 45 to 60 minutes, 4.7% 60 minutes or more (2008-2012 5-year est.)

Additional Information Contacts
Mount Zion Chamber of Commerce . . . . (217) 864-2526
  http://www.mtzionchamber.org

NIANTIC (village). Covers a land area of 1.069 square miles and a water area of 0 square miles. Located at 39.85° N. Lat; 89.16° W. Long. Elevation is 604 feet.

Population: 647 (1990); 738 (2000); 707 (2010); Density: 709.2 persons per square mile (2008-2012 5-year est.); Race: 98.9% White, 0.0% Black/African American, 0.0% Asian, 0.0% American Indian/Alaska Native, 0.0% Native Hawaiian/Other Pacific Islander, 1.1% Some other race, 1.1% Two or more races, 0.0% Hispanic of any race (2008-2012 5-year est.); Average household size: 2.37 (2008-2012 5-year est.); Median age: 38.4 (2008-2012 5-year est.); Males per 100 females: 89.0 (2008-2012 5-year est.); Marriage status: 21.9% never married, 53.6% now married, 8.4% widowed, 16.1% divorced (2008-2012 5-year est.); Foreign born: 1.1% (2008-2012 5-year est.); Ancestry (includes multiple ancestries): 25.2% American, 21.8% German, 17.2% Irish, 12.8% English, 4.1% Polish (2008-2012 5-year est.).

Economy: Single-family building permits issued: 0 (2013); Multi-family building permits issued: 0 (2013); Homeowner vacancy rate: 4.8%. Rental vacancy rate: 0.0%. (2008-2012 5-year est.); Employment by occupation: 22.2% management, business, and financial, 1.6% computer, engineering, and science, 4.9% education, legal, community service, arts, and media, 11.4% healthcare practitioners, 10.8% service, 18.4% sales and office, 11.9% natural resources, construction, and maintenance, 18.9% production, transportation, and material moving (2008-2012 5-year est.).

Income: Per capita income: $23,649 (2008-2012 5-year est.); Median household income: $53,333 (2008-2012 5-year est.); Average household income: $54,643 (2008-2012 5-year est.); Percent of households with income of $100,000 or more: 8.4% (2008-2012 5-year est.); Poverty rate: 4.4% (2008-2012 5-year est.).

Education: Percent of population age 25 and over with: High school diploma (including GED) or higher: 89.6% (2008-2012 5-year est.); Bachelor's degree or higher: 20.8% (2008-2012 5-year est.); Master's degree or higher: 8.0% (2008-2012 5-year est.).

School District(s)
Sangamon Valley CUSD 9 (PK-12)
  2011-12 Enrollment: 782 . . . . (217) 668-2338

Housing: Homeownership rate: 90.9% (2008-2012 5-year est.); Median home value: $97,000 (2008-2012 5-year est.); Median contract rent: $463 per month (2008-2012 5-year est.); Median year structure built: 1959 (2008-2012 5-year est.).

Health Insurance: 77.7% Private; 23.4% Public; 8.7% None. (2008-2012 5-year est.)

Transportation: Commute to work: 98.3% car, 0.0% public transportation, 0.0% walk, 0.9% work from home (2008-2012 5-year est.); Travel time to work: 19.8% less than 15 minutes, 43.9% 15 to 30 minutes, 32.6% 30 to 45 minutes, 1.2% 45 to 60 minutes, 2.6% 60 minutes or more (2008-2012 5-year est.)

OREANA (village). Covers a land area of 0.498 square miles and a water area of 0 square miles. Located at 39.94° N. Lat; 88.87° W. Long. Elevation is 689 feet.

Population: 847 (1990); 892 (2000); 875 (2010); Density: 2,169.9 persons per square mile (2008-2012 5-year est.); Race: 96.6% White, 0.7% Black/African American, 0.8% Asian, 0.0% American Indian/Alaska Native, 0.0% Native Hawaiian/Other Pacific Islander, 1.9% Some other race, 1.4% Two or more races, 0.3% Hispanic of any race (2008-2012 5-year est.); Average household size: 2.76 (2008-2012 5-year est.); Median age: 33.8 (2008-2012 5-year est.); Males per 100 females: 87.5 (2008-2012 5-year est.); Marriage status: 19.9% never married, 65.6% now married, 5.1% widowed, 9.4% divorced (2008-2012 5-year est.); Foreign born: 0.6% (2008-2012 5-year est.); Ancestry (includes multiple ancestries): 26.2% German, 21.9% American, 12.1% Irish, 10.1% English, 4.9% Scottish (2008-2012 5-year est.).

Economy: Single-family building permits issued: 0 (2013); Multi-family building permits issued: 0 (2013); Homeowner vacancy rate: 0.0%. Rental vacancy rate: 12.2%. (2008-2012 5-year est.); Employment by occupation: 5.8% management, business, and financial, 3.0% computer, engineering, and science, 9.0% education, legal, community service, arts, and media, 9.4% healthcare practitioners, 14.6% service, 23.2% sales and office,

21.0% natural resources, construction, and maintenance, 13.8% production, transportation, and material moving (2008-2012 5-year est.).

Income: Per capita income: $23,715 (2008-2012 5-year est.); Median household income: $59,375 (2008-2012 5-year est.); Average household income: $63,860 (2008-2012 5-year est.); Percent of households with income of $100,000 or more: 9.7% (2008-2012 5-year est.); Poverty rate: 4.9% (2008-2012 5-year est.).

Education: Percent of population age 25 and over with: High school diploma (including GED) or higher: 92.0% (2008-2012 5-year est.); Bachelor's degree or higher: 18.4% (2008-2012 5-year est.); Master's degree or higher: 3.9% (2008-2012 5-year est.).

School District(s)
Argenta-Oreana CUSD 1 (PK-12)
  2011-12 Enrollment: 1,067 . . . . (217) 795-2313

Housing: Homeownership rate: 89.0% (2008-2012 5-year est.); Median home value: $98,000 (2008-2012 5-year est.); Median contract rent: $525 per month (2008-2012 5-year est.); Median year structure built: 1963 (2008-2012 5-year est.).

Health Insurance: 79.2% Private; 29.4% Public; 5.1% None. (2008-2012 5-year est.)

Transportation: Commute to work: 95.8% car, 0.0% public transportation, 1.2% walk, 3.0% work from home (2008-2012 5-year est.); Travel time to work: 34.9% less than 15 minutes, 44.1% 15 to 30 minutes, 11.9% 30 to 45 minutes, 2.5% 45 to 60 minutes, 6.7% 60 minutes or more (2008-2012 5-year est.)

WARRENSBURG (village). Covers a land area of 0.689 square miles and a water area of 0 square miles. Located at 39.93° N. Lat; 89.06° W. Long. Elevation is 705 feet.

Population: 1,274 (1990); 1,289 (2000); 1,210 (2010); Density: 1,577.2 persons per square mile (2008-2012 5-year est.); Race: 94.9% White, 1.7% Black/African American, 0.0% Asian, 0.0% American Indian/Alaska Native, 0.0% Native Hawaiian/Other Pacific Islander, 3.4% Some other race, 1.2% Two or more races, 1.7% Hispanic of any race (2008-2012 5-year est.); Average household size: 2.40 (2008-2012 5-year est.); Median age: 40.3 (2008-2012 5-year est.); Males per 100 females: 115.7 (2008-2012 5-year est.); Marriage status: 25.0% never married, 55.9% now married, 3.0% widowed, 16.1% divorced (2008-2012 5-year est.); Foreign born: 0.0% (2008-2012 5-year est.); Ancestry (includes multiple ancestries): 25.9% German, 23.0% American, 19.3% Irish, 8.8% English, 4.1% Dutch (2008-2012 5-year est.).

Economy: Single-family building permits issued: 0 (2013); Multi-family building permits issued: 0 (2013); Homeowner vacancy rate: 0.9%. Rental vacancy rate: 7.7%. (2008-2012 5-year est.); Employment by occupation: 7.5% management, business, and financial, 1.9% computer, engineering, and science, 10.6% education, legal, community service, arts, and media, 8.4% healthcare practitioners, 16.3% service, 20.4% sales and office, 12.7% natural resources, construction, and maintenance, 22.1% production, transportation, and material moving (2008-2012 5-year est.).

Income: Per capita income: $29,614 (2008-2012 5-year est.); Median household income: $54,833 (2008-2012 5-year est.); Average household income: $68,907 (2008-2012 5-year est.); Percent of households with income of $100,000 or more: 15.2% (2008-2012 5-year est.); Poverty rate: 7.5% (2008-2012 5-year est.).

Education: Percent of population age 25 and over with: High school diploma (including GED) or higher: 93.7% (2008-2012 5-year est.); Bachelor's degree or higher: 23.3% (2008-2012 5-year est.); Master's degree or higher: 3.4% (2008-2012 5-year est.).

School District(s)
Warrensburg-Latham CUSD 11 (PK-12)
  2011-12 Enrollment: 1,052 . . . . (217) 672-3514

Housing: Homeownership rate: 75.7% (2008-2012 5-year est.); Median home value: $101,900 (2008-2012 5-year est.); Median contract rent: $391 per month (2008-2012 5-year est.); Median year structure built: 1972 (2008-2012 5-year est.).

Health Insurance: 78.7% Private; 21.8% Public; 11.9% None. (2008-2012 5-year est.)

Safety: Violent crime rate: 41.3 per 10,000 population; Property crime rate: 107.4 per 10,000 population (2012).

Transportation: Commute to work: 96.2% car, 0.3% public transportation, 0.3% walk, 1.4% work from home (2008-2012 5-year est.); Travel time to work: 29.0% less than 15 minutes, 55.1% 15 to 30 minutes, 10.8% 30 to 45 minutes, 2.6% 45 to 60 minutes, 2.4% 60 minutes or more (2008-2012 5-year est.)

Macoupin County

Located in southwest central Illinois; drained by Macoupin, Cahokia, and Otter Creeks. Covers a land area of 862.906 square miles, a water area of 4.744 square miles, and is located in the Central Time Zone at 39.27° N. Lat., 89.93° W. Long. The county was founded in 1829. County seat is Carlinville.

Macoupin County is part of the St. Louis, MO-IL Metropolitan Statistical Area. The entire metro area includes: Bond County, IL; Calhoun County, IL; Clinton County, IL; Jersey County, IL; Macoupin County, IL; Madison County, IL; Monroe County, IL; Saint Clair County, IL; Franklin County, MO; Jefferson County, MO; Lincoln County, MO; Saint Charles County, MO; Saint Louis County, MO; Warren County, MO; Saint Louis city, MO

Weather Station: Carlinville   Elevation: 629 feet

	Jan	Feb	Mar	Apr	May	Jun	Jul	Aug	Sep	Oct	Nov	Dec
High	36	42	53	65	75	84	87	86	79	67	53	40
Low	21	25	33	43	53	63	66	64	56	45	35	25
Precip	2.1	2.1	3.1	4.0	4.0	3.5	3.6	3.2	3.2	3.2	3.7	2.8
Snow	5.9	4.4	2.7	0.4	tr	0.0	0.0	0.0	0.0	tr	0.9	3.4

High and Low temperatures in degrees Fahrenheit; Precipitation and Snow in inches

Weather Station: Virden   Elevation: 674 feet

	Jan	Feb	Mar	Apr	May	Jun	Jul	Aug	Sep	Oct	Nov	Dec
High	37	41	53	66	76	84	87	86	80	68	53	40
Low	21	25	33	44	54	63	67	65	57	46	36	24
Precip	1.9	2.1	2.8	3.5	4.2	3.8	3.5	2.7	2.9	3.1	3.5	2.5
Snow	5.1	5.6	3.0	0.4	0.0	0.0	0.0	0.0	0.0	tr	0.8	4.6

High and Low temperatures in degrees Fahrenheit; Precipitation and Snow in inches

Population: 47,679 (1990); 49,019 (2000); 47,765 (2010); Race: 97.5% White, 0.6% Black/African American, 0.3% Asian, 0.1% American Indian/Alaska Native, 0.0% Native Hawaiian/Other Pacific Islander, 1.5% Some other race, 1.3% Two or more races, 0.9% Hispanic of any race (2008-2012 5-year est.); Density: 54.7 persons per square mile (2008-2012 5-year est.); Average household size: 2.41 (2008-2012 5-year est.); Median age: 41.9 (2008-2012 5-year est.); Males per 100 females: 96.4 (2008-2012 5-year est.).

Religion: Six largest groups: 16.1% Catholicism, 15.7% Baptist, 8.8% Lutheran, 5.9% Methodist/Pietist, 3.0% Presbyterian-Reformed, 2.1% Pentecostal (2010)

Economy: Unemployment rate: 6.8% (April 2014); Total civilian labor force: 23,457 (April 2014); Leading industries: 20.5% health care and social assistance; 15.1% retail trade; 8.1% accommodation & food services (2012); Farms: 1,190 totaling 438,592 acres (2012); Companies that employ 500 or more persons: 0 (2012); Companies that employ 100 to 499 persons: 13 (2012); Companies that employ less than 100 persons: 906 (2012); Black-owned businesses: n/a (2007); Hispanic-owned businesses: n/a (2007); Asian-owned businesses: n/a (2007); Women-owned businesses: 1,366 (2007); Single-family building permits issued: 50 (2013); Multi-family building permits issued: 2 (2013).

Income: Per capita income: $24,267 (2008-2012 5-year est.); Median household income: $48,788 (2008-2012 5-year est.); Average household income: $59,021 (2008-2012 5-year est.); Percent of households with income of $100,000 or more: 14.8% (2008-2012 5-year est.); Poverty rate: 12.1% (2008-2012 5-year est.); Bankruptcy rate: 2.45% (2013).

Taxes: Total county taxes per capita: $120 (2011); County property taxes per capita: $118 (2011).

Education: Percent of population age 25 and over with: High school diploma (including GED) or higher: 88.6% (2008-2012 5-year est.); Bachelor's degree or higher: 15.7% (2008-2012 5-year est.); Master's degree or higher: 5.1% (2008-2012 5-year est.).

Housing: Homeownership rate: 77.1% (2008-2012 5-year est.); Median home value: $93,600 (2008-2012 5-year est.); Median contract rent: $413 per month (2008-2012 5-year est.); Median year structure built: 1962 (2008-2012 5-year est.)

Health: Birth rate: 90.2 per 10,000 population (2013); Death rate: 119.2 per 10,000 population (2013); Age-adjusted cancer mortality rate: 189.8 deaths per 100,000 population (2011); Number of physicians: 4.6 per 10,000 population (2011); Hospital beds: 10.5 per 10,000 population (2010); Hospital admissions: 206.0 per 10,000 population (2010).

Environment: Air Quality Index: 96.4% good, 3.6% moderate, 0.0% unhealthy for sensitive individuals, 0.0% unhealthy (percent of days in 2013)

Elections: 2012 Presidential election results: 45.1% Obama, 52.1% Romney

National and State Parks: Beaver Dam State Park
Additional Information Contacts
Macoupin County Government . . . . (217) 854-3214
   http://www.macoupincountyil.gov

Macoupin County Communities

BENLD (city). Covers a land area of 1.060 square miles and a water area of 0 square miles. Located at 39.09° N. Lat; 89.80° W. Long. Elevation is 633 feet.

History: Incorporated 1904; reincorporated 1930 as city.

Population: 1,604 (1990); 1,541 (2000); 1,556 (2010); Density: 1,625.4 persons per square mile (2008-2012 5-year est.); Race: 96.4% White, 0.0% Black/African American, 1.7% Asian, 0.0% American Indian/Alaska Native, 0.0% Native Hawaiian/Other Pacific Islander, 1.9% Some other race, 1.5% Two or more races, 2.5% Hispanic of any race (2008-2012 5-year est.); Average household size: 2.36 (2008-2012 5-year est.); Median age: 38.7 (2008-2012 5-year est.); Males per 100 females: 109.9 (2008-2012 5-year est.); Marriage status: 29.9% never married, 47.8% now married, 8.6% widowed, 13.8% divorced (2008-2012 5-year est.); Foreign born: 1.7% (2008-2012 5-year est.); Ancestry (includes multiple ancestries): 23.7% German, 17.1% Irish, 13.2% Italian, 11.0% French, 9.4% English (2008-2012 5-year est.).

Economy: Single-family building permits issued: 0 (2013); Multi-family building permits issued: 0 (2013); Homeowner vacancy rate: 2.0%. Rental vacancy rate: 0.0%. (2008-2012 5-year est.); Employment by occupation: 8.7% management, business, and financial, 2.8% computer, engineering, and science, 4.6% education, legal, community service, arts, and media, 3.9% healthcare practitioners, 26.5% service, 27.4% sales and office, 10.3% natural resources, construction, and maintenance, 15.8% production, transportation, and material moving (2008-2012 5-year est.).

Income: Per capita income: $20,225 (2008-2012 5-year est.); Median household income: $41,484 (2008-2012 5-year est.); Average household income: $47,008 (2008-2012 5-year est.); Percent of households with income of $100,000 or more: 8.7% (2008-2012 5-year est.); Poverty rate: 20.3% (2008-2012 5-year est.).

Education: Percent of population age 25 and over with: High school diploma (including GED) or higher: 89.0% (2008-2012 5-year est.); Bachelor's degree or higher: 11.3% (2008-2012 5-year est.); Master's degree or higher: 2.6% (2008-2012 5-year est.).

Housing: Homeownership rate: 74.3% (2008-2012 5-year est.); Median home value: $65,800 (2008-2012 5-year est.); Median contract rent: $463 per month (2008-2012 5-year est.); Median year structure built: Before 1940 (2008-2012 5-year est.).

Health Insurance: 63.5% Private; 40.0% Public; 12.5% None. (2008-2012 5-year est.)

Safety: Violent crime rate: 6.4 per 10,000 population; Property crime rate: 25.7 per 10,000 population (2012).

Transportation: Commute to work: 93.3% car, 0.5% public transportation, 3.0% walk, 3.1% work from home (2008-2012 5-year est.); Travel time to work: 31.7% less than 15 minutes, 25.7% 15 to 30 minutes, 13.5% 30 to 45 minutes, 10.0% 45 to 60 minutes, 19.1% 60 minutes or more (2008-2012 5-year est.)

BRIGHTON (village). Covers a land area of 1.874 square miles and a water area of 0.039 square miles. Located at 39.04° N. Lat; 90.14° W. Long. Elevation is 663 feet.

Population: 2,270 (1990); 2,196 (2000); 2,254 (2010); Density: 1,112.0 persons per square mile (2008-2012 5-year est.); Race: 97.3% White, 0.2% Black/African American, 0.0% Asian, 0.4% American Indian/Alaska Native, 0.0% Native Hawaiian/Other Pacific Islander, 2.1% Some other race, 2.0% Two or more races, 0.8% Hispanic of any race (2008-2012 5-year est.); Average household size: 2.57 (2008-2012 5-year est.); Median age: 37.3 (2008-2012 5-year est.); Males per 100 females: 103.9 (2008-2012 5-year est.); Marriage status: 27.8% never married, 52.6% now married, 8.9% widowed, 10.7% divorced (2008-2012 5-year est.); Foreign born: 1.3% (2008-2012 5-year est.); Ancestry (includes multiple ancestries): 38.4% German, 15.3% Irish, 10.5% American, 10.1% English, 6.6% French (2008-2012 5-year est.).

Economy: Single-family building permits issued: 5 (2013); Multi-family building permits issued: 0 (2013); Homeowner vacancy rate: 3.5%. Rental vacancy rate: 0.0%. (2008-2012 5-year est.); Employment by occupation: 12.9% management, business, and financial, 3.8% computer, engineering, and science, 4.7% education, legal, community service, arts, and media, 7.2% healthcare practitioners, 15.9% service, 23.8% sales and office,

12.3% natural resources, construction, and maintenance, 19.4% production, transportation, and material moving (2008-2012 5-year est.).
Income: Per capita income: $23,583 (2008-2012 5-year est.); Median household income: $55,944 (2008-2012 5-year est.); Average household income: $60,752 (2008-2012 5-year est.); Percent of households with income of $100,000 or more: 13.3% (2008-2012 5-year est.); Poverty rate: 11.7% (2008-2012 5-year est.).
Education: Percent of population age 25 and over with: High school diploma (including GED) or higher: 88.3% (2008-2012 5-year est.); Bachelor's degree or higher: 11.1% (2008-2012 5-year est.); Master's degree or higher: 4.0% (2008-2012 5-year est.).

School District(s)
Southwestern CUSD 9 (PK-12)
    2011-12 Enrollment: 1,663 . . . . (618) 729-3221
Housing: Homeownership rate: 83.6% (2008-2012 5-year est.); Median home value: $106,800 (2008-2012 5-year est.); Median contract rent: $403 per month (2008-2012 5-year est.); Median year structure built: 1969 (2008-2012 5-year est.).
Health Insurance: 75.3% Private; 28.5% Public; 11.3% None. (2008-2012 5-year est.)
Safety: Violent crime rate: 0.0 per 10,000 population; Property crime rate: 40.0 per 10,000 population (2012).
Transportation: Commute to work: 94.6% car, 2.4% public transportation, 0.6% walk, 1.7% work from home (2008-2012 5-year est.); Travel time to work: 19.2% less than 15 minutes, 41.8% 15 to 30 minutes, 22.3% 30 to 45 minutes, 11.6% 45 to 60 minutes, 5.0% 60 minutes or more (2008-2012 5-year est.)

BUNKER HILL (city). Covers a land area of 1.261 square miles and a water area of 0.025 square miles. Located at 39.04° N. Lat; 89.95° W. Long. Elevation is 663 feet.
History: Incorporated 1857.
Population: 1,722 (1990); 1,801 (2000); 1,774 (2010); Density: 1,363.1 persons per square mile (2008-2012 5-year est.); Race: 98.3% White, 0.0% Black/African American, 0.0% Asian, 0.0% American Indian/Alaska Native, 0.0% Native Hawaiian/Other Pacific Islander, 1.7% Some other race, 1.7% Two or more races, 3.3% Hispanic of any race (2008-2012 5-year est.); Average household size: 2.27 (2008-2012 5-year est.); Median age: 41.6 (2008-2012 5-year est.); Males per 100 females: 89.7 (2008-2012 5-year est.); Marriage status: 24.1% never married, 49.6% now married, 9.3% widowed, 17.0% divorced (2008-2012 5-year est.); Foreign born: 0.8% (2008-2012 5-year est.); Ancestry (includes multiple ancestries): 42.0% German, 13.8% Irish, 13.3% English, 8.6% American, 5.2% Dutch (2008-2012 5-year est.).
Economy: Homeowner vacancy rate: 1.7%. Rental vacancy rate: 11.7%. (2008-2012 5-year est.); Employment by occupation: 5.9% management, business, and financial, 3.8% computer, engineering, and science, 11.1% education, legal, community service, arts, and media, 3.4% healthcare practitioners, 16.2% service, 21.6% sales and office, 17.6% natural resources, construction, and maintenance, 20.4% production, transportation, and material moving (2008-2012 5-year est.).
Income: Per capita income: $22,871 (2008-2012 5-year est.); Median household income: $44,375 (2008-2012 5-year est.); Average household income: $52,533 (2008-2012 5-year est.); Percent of households with income of $100,000 or more: 9.7% (2008-2012 5-year est.); Poverty rate: 15.1% (2008-2012 5-year est.).
Education: Percent of population age 25 and over with: High school diploma (including GED) or higher: 84.9% (2008-2012 5-year est.); Bachelor's degree or higher: 14.1% (2008-2012 5-year est.); Master's degree or higher: 4.5% (2008-2012 5-year est.).

School District(s)
Bunker Hill CUSD 8 (PK-12)
    2011-12 Enrollment: 706 . . . . (618) 585-3116
Housing: Homeownership rate: 70.3% (2008-2012 5-year est.); Median home value: $91,400 (2008-2012 5-year est.); Median contract rent: $488 per month (2008-2012 5-year est.); Median year structure built: 1963 (2008-2012 5-year est.).
Health Insurance: 65.6% Private; 35.5% Public; 16.4% None. (2008-2012 5-year est.)
Transportation: Commute to work: 96.4% car, 0.0% public transportation, 0.4% walk, 2.7% work from home (2008-2012 5-year est.); Travel time to work: 16.8% less than 15 minutes, 35.3% 15 to 30 minutes, 29.0% 30 to 45 minutes, 14.9% 45 to 60 minutes, 4.0% 60 minutes or more (2008-2012 5-year est.)

CARLINVILLE (city). County seat. Covers a land area of 2.995 square miles and a water area of 0 square miles. Located at 39.28° N. Lat; 89.88° W. Long. Elevation is 620 feet.
History: Carlinville was the site of the "million-dollar courthouse" of Macoupin County, completed in 1870 at a cost of $1,380,500, and opposed by the taxpayers. Built of limestone, the courthouse was designed as two rectangles crossing at the center under a dome that rose 191 feet.
Population: 5,416 (1990); 5,685 (2000); 5,917 (2010); Density: 1,936.2 persons per square mile (2008-2012 5-year est.); Race: 97.7% White, 0.5% Black/African American, 0.2% Asian, 0.0% American Indian/Alaska Native, 0.0% Native Hawaiian/Other Pacific Islander, 1.6% Some other race, 1.6% Two or more races, 0.7% Hispanic of any race (2008-2012 5-year est.); Average household size: 2.23 (2008-2012 5-year est.); Median age: 40.4 (2008-2012 5-year est.); Males per 100 females: 102.0 (2008-2012 5-year est.); Marriage status: 29.2% never married, 46.1% now married, 8.8% widowed, 15.8% divorced (2008-2012 5-year est.); Foreign born: 0.1% (2008-2012 5-year est.); Ancestry (includes multiple ancestries): 32.9% German, 19.5% English, 17.3% Irish, 11.9% American, 3.8% Scottish (2008-2012 5-year est.).
Economy: Single-family building permits issued: 2 (2013); Multi-family building permits issued: 0 (2013); Homeowner vacancy rate: 4.1%. Rental vacancy rate: 8.0%. (2008-2012 5-year est.); Employment by occupation: 13.6% management, business, and financial, 4.5% computer, engineering, and science, 13.4% education, legal, community service, arts, and media, 1.5% healthcare practitioners, 18.4% service, 25.1% sales and office, 5.9% natural resources, construction, and maintenance, 17.6% production, transportation, and material moving (2008-2012 5-year est.).
Income: Per capita income: $23,354 (2008-2012 5-year est.); Median household income: $43,247 (2008-2012 5-year est.); Average household income: $55,654 (2008-2012 5-year est.); Percent of households with income of $100,000 or more: 14.0% (2008-2012 5-year est.); Poverty rate: 13.5% (2008-2012 5-year est.).
Education: Percent of population age 25 and over with: High school diploma (including GED) or higher: 83.5% (2008-2012 5-year est.); Bachelor's degree or higher: 20.2% (2008-2012 5-year est.); Master's degree or higher: 8.0% (2008-2012 5-year est.).

School District(s)
Calhoun/greene/jersy/macoupin Roe (07-12)
    2011-12 Enrollment: n/a . . . . (217) 854-4016
Carlinville CUSD 1 (PK-12)
    2011-12 Enrollment: 1,436 . . . . (217) 854-9823
Four-year College(s)
Blackburn College (Private, Not-for-profit, Presbyterian Church (USA))
    Fall 2012 Enrollment: 541 . . . . (217) 854-3231
    2012-13 Tuition: In-state $17,502; Out-of-state $17,502
Housing: Homeownership rate: 64.0% (2008-2012 5-year est.); Median home value: $86,000 (2008-2012 5-year est.); Median contract rent: $432 per month (2008-2012 5-year est.); Median year structure built: 1954 (2008-2012 5-year est.).
Health Insurance: 69.5% Private; 40.1% Public; 7.7% None. (2008-2012 5-year est.)
Hospitals: Carlinville Area Hospital (33 beds)
Safety: Violent crime rate: 35.5 per 10,000 population; Property crime rate: 268.9 per 10,000 population (2012).
Transportation: Commute to work: 87.5% car, 0.0% public transportation, 8.5% walk, 2.9% work from home (2008-2012 5-year est.); Travel time to work: 66.6% less than 15 minutes, 15.6% 15 to 30 minutes, 3.6% 30 to 45 minutes, 6.5% 45 to 60 minutes, 7.7% 60 minutes or more (2008-2012 5-year est.); Amtrak: Train service available.
Additional Information Contacts
Carlinville Community Chamber of Commerce . . . . (217) 854-2141
    http://carlinvillechamber.com
City of Carlinville . . . . (217) 854-4076
    http://www.cityofcarlinville.com

CHESTERFIELD (village). Covers a land area of 0.541 square miles and a water area of 0 square miles. Located at 39.26° N. Lat; 90.07° W. Long. Elevation is 587 feet.
Population: 230 (1990); 223 (2000); 188 (2010); Density: 310.7 persons per square mile (2008-2012 5-year est.); Race: 100.0% White, 0.0% Black/African American, 0.0% Asian, 0.0% American Indian/Alaska Native, 0.0% Native Hawaiian/Other Pacific Islander, 0.0% Some other race, 0.0% Two or more races, 0.0% Hispanic of any race (2008-2012 5-year est.); Average household size: 2.37 (2008-2012 5-year est.); Median age: 35.5 (2008-2012 5-year est.); Males per 100 females: 107.4 (2008-2012 5-year

est.); Marriage status: 11.8% never married, 60.3% now married, 11.8% widowed, 16.2% divorced (2008-2012 5-year est.); Foreign born: 0.0% (2008-2012 5-year est.); Ancestry (includes multiple ancestries): 30.4% German, 22.6% Irish, 11.9% English, 10.1% American, 9.5% Dutch (2008-2012 5-year est.).

Economy: Homeowner vacancy rate: 0.0%. Rental vacancy rate: 0.0%. (2008-2012 5-year est.); Employment by occupation: 10.9% management, business, and financial, 0.0% computer, engineering, and science, 3.1% education, legal, community service, arts, and media, 1.6% healthcare practitioners, 20.3% service, 12.5% sales and office, 10.9% natural resources, construction, and maintenance, 40.6% production, transportation, and material moving (2008-2012 5-year est.).

Income: Per capita income: $18,234 (2008-2012 5-year est.); Median household income: $44,063 (2008-2012 5-year est.); Average household income: $43,254 (2008-2012 5-year est.); Percent of households with income of $100,000 or more: 5.6% (2008-2012 5-year est.); Poverty rate: 20.8% (2008-2012 5-year est.).

Education: Percent of population age 25 and over with: High school diploma (including GED) or higher: 76.2% (2008-2012 5-year est.); Bachelor's degree or higher: 5.7% (2008-2012 5-year est.); Master's degree or higher: 2.5% (2008-2012 5-year est.).

Housing: Homeownership rate: 94.4% (2008-2012 5-year est.); Median home value: $55,000 (2008-2012 5-year est.); Median contract rent: $350 per month (2008-2012 5-year est.); Median year structure built: Before 1940 (2008-2012 5-year est.).

Health Insurance: 54.8% Private; 27.4% Public; 20.2% None. (2008-2012 5-year est.)

Transportation: Commute to work: 93.8% car, 0.0% public transportation, 0.0% walk, 6.3% work from home (2008-2012 5-year est.); Travel time to work: 3.3% less than 15 minutes, 40.0% 15 to 30 minutes, 8.3% 30 to 45 minutes, 21.7% 45 to 60 minutes, 26.7% 60 minutes or more (2008-2012 5-year est.)

DORCHESTER (village). Covers a land area of 0.719 square miles and a water area of 0 square miles. Located at 39.09° N. Lat; 89.89° W. Long. Elevation is 656 feet.

Population: 145 (1990); 142 (2000); 151 (2010); Density: 203.0 persons per square mile (2008-2012 5-year est.); Race: 94.5% White, 0.0% Black/African American, 2.1% Asian, 0.0% American Indian/Alaska Native, 0.0% Native Hawaiian/Other Pacific Islander, 3.4% Some other race, 3.4% Two or more races, 0.0% Hispanic of any race (2008-2012 5-year est.); Average household size: 2.65 (2008-2012 5-year est.); Median age: 50.3 (2008-2012 5-year est.); Males per 100 females: 82.5 (2008-2012 5-year est.); Marriage status: 18.8% never married, 63.2% now married, 4.3% widowed, 13.7% divorced (2008-2012 5-year est.); Foreign born: 2.1% (2008-2012 5-year est.); Ancestry (includes multiple ancestries): 50.0% German, 24.7% English, 6.2% Scottish, 6.2% Irish, 4.8% Scotch-Irish (2008-2012 5-year est.).

Economy: Single-family building permits issued: 0 (2013); Multi-family building permits issued: 0 (2013); Homeowner vacancy rate: 0.0%. Rental vacancy rate: 58.3%. (2008-2012 5-year est.); Employment by occupation: 0.0% management, business, and financial, 0.0% computer, engineering, and science, 6.3% education, legal, community service, arts, and media, 8.3% healthcare practitioners, 14.6% service, 35.4% sales and office, 22.9% natural resources, construction, and maintenance, 12.5% production, transportation, and material moving (2008-2012 5-year est.).

Income: Per capita income: $16,395 (2008-2012 5-year est.); Median household income: $37,321 (2008-2012 5-year est.); Average household income: $43,755 (2008-2012 5-year est.); Percent of households with income of $100,000 or more: 3.6% (2008-2012 5-year est.); Poverty rate: 24.5% (2008-2012 5-year est.).

Education: Percent of population age 25 and over with: High school diploma (including GED) or higher: 86.5% (2008-2012 5-year est.); Bachelor's degree or higher: 8.7% (2008-2012 5-year est.); Master's degree or higher: 0.0% (2008-2012 5-year est.).

Housing: Homeownership rate: 90.9% (2008-2012 5-year est.); Median home value: $71,400 (2008-2012 5-year est.); Median contract rent: $292 per month (2008-2012 5-year est.); Median year structure built: 1948 (2008-2012 5-year est.).

Health Insurance: 57.5% Private; 44.5% Public; 17.1% None. (2008-2012 5-year est.)

Transportation: Commute to work: 95.8% car, 0.0% public transportation, 0.0% walk, 4.2% work from home (2008-2012 5-year est.); Travel time to work: 10.9% less than 15 minutes, 30.4% 15 to 30 minutes, 28.3% 30 to

45 minutes, 10.9% 45 to 60 minutes, 19.6% 60 minutes or more (2008-2012 5-year est.)

EAGARVILLE (village). Aka Eagerville. Covers a land area of 0.909 square miles and a water area of 0.019 square miles. Located at 39.11° N. Lat; 89.78° W. Long. Elevation is 643 feet.

Population: 127 (1990); 128 (2000); 127 (2010); Density: 71.5 persons per square mile (2008-2012 5-year est.); Race: 93.8% White, 0.0% Black/African American, 3.1% Asian, 0.0% American Indian/Alaska Native, 0.0% Native Hawaiian/Other Pacific Islander, 3.1% Some other race, 3.1% Two or more races, 0.0% Hispanic of any race (2008-2012 5-year est.); Average household size: 1.81 (2008-2012 5-year est.); Median age: 51.5 (2008-2012 5-year est.); Males per 100 females: 109.7 (2008-2012 5-year est.); Marriage status: 9.1% never married, 52.7% now married, 1.8% widowed, 36.4% divorced (2008-2012 5-year est.); Foreign born: 3.1% (2008-2012 5-year est.); Ancestry (includes multiple ancestries): 29.2% German, 13.8% French, 9.2% English, 7.7% Dutch, 6.2% Italian (2008-2012 5-year est.).

Economy: Homeowner vacancy rate: 16.3%. Rental vacancy rate: 0.0%. (2008-2012 5-year est.); Employment by occupation: 0.0% management, business, and financial, 3.1% computer, engineering, and science, 12.5% education, legal, community service, arts, and media, 3.1% healthcare practitioners, 34.4% service, 34.4% sales and office, 12.5% natural resources, construction, and maintenance, 0.0% production, transportation, and material moving (2008-2012 5-year est.).

Income: Per capita income: $32,457 (2008-2012 5-year est.); Median household income: $75,417 (2008-2012 5-year est.); Average household income: $57,553 (2008-2012 5-year est.); Percent of households with income of $100,000 or more: 2.8% (2008-2012 5-year est.); Poverty rate: 15.4% (2008-2012 5-year est.).

Education: Percent of population age 25 and over with: High school diploma (including GED) or higher: 92.5% (2008-2012 5-year est.); Bachelor's degree or higher: 11.3% (2008-2012 5-year est.); Master's degree or higher: 0.0% (2008-2012 5-year est.).

Housing: Homeownership rate: 100.0% (2008-2012 5-year est.); Median home value: $92,000 (2008-2012 5-year est.); Median contract rent: n/a per month (2008-2012 5-year est.); Median year structure built: 1981 (2008-2012 5-year est.).

Health Insurance: 70.8% Private; 36.9% Public; 13.8% None. (2008-2012 5-year est.)

Transportation: Commute to work: 100.0% car, 0.0% public transportation, 0.0% walk, 0.0% work from home (2008-2012 5-year est.); Travel time to work: 9.4% less than 15 minutes, 40.6% 15 to 30 minutes, 6.3% 30 to 45 minutes, 0.0% 45 to 60 minutes, 43.8% 60 minutes or more (2008-2012 5-year est.)

EAST GILLESPIE (village). Covers a land area of 0.319 square miles and a water area of 0 square miles. Located at 39.14° N. Lat; 89.81° W. Long. Elevation is 659 feet.

Population: 205 (1990); 234 (2000); 270 (2010); Density: 640.1 persons per square mile (2008-2012 5-year est.); Race: 98.5% White, 0.0% Black/African American, 1.0% Asian, 0.0% American Indian/Alaska Native, 0.0% Native Hawaiian/Other Pacific Islander, 0.5% Some other race, 0.5% Two or more races, 0.0% Hispanic of any race (2008-2012 5-year est.); Average household size: 2.40 (2008-2012 5-year est.); Median age: 45.0 (2008-2012 5-year est.); Males per 100 females: 108.2 (2008-2012 5-year est.); Marriage status: 19.0% never married, 61.9% now married, 10.1% widowed, 8.9% divorced (2008-2012 5-year est.); Foreign born: 1.0% (2008-2012 5-year est.); Ancestry (includes multiple ancestries): 31.4% German, 21.1% Scottish, 19.6% Italian, 15.7% English, 8.3% Irish (2008-2012 5-year est.).

Economy: Single-family building permits issued: 0 (2013); Multi-family building permits issued: 0 (2013); Homeowner vacancy rate: 3.8%. Rental vacancy rate: 33.3%. (2008-2012 5-year est.); Employment by occupation: 12.9% management, business, and financial, 4.0% computer, engineering, and science, 7.9% education, legal, community service, arts, and media, 5.0% healthcare practitioners, 13.9% service, 18.8% sales and office, 12.9% natural resources, construction, and maintenance, 24.8% production, transportation, and material moving (2008-2012 5-year est.).

Income: Per capita income: $27,808 (2008-2012 5-year est.); Median household income: $58,250 (2008-2012 5-year est.); Average household income: $65,180 (2008-2012 5-year est.); Percent of households with income of $100,000 or more: 22.4% (2008-2012 5-year est.); Poverty rate: 4.9% (2008-2012 5-year est.).

Education: Percent of population age 25 and over with: High school diploma (including GED) or higher: 90.8% (2008-2012 5-year est.); Bachelor's degree or higher: 21.7% (2008-2012 5-year est.); Master's degree or higher: 3.9% (2008-2012 5-year est.).
Housing: Homeownership rate: 88.2% (2008-2012 5-year est.); Median home value: $109,700 (2008-2012 5-year est.); Median contract rent: $475 per month (2008-2012 5-year est.); Median year structure built: 1971 (2008-2012 5-year est.).
Health Insurance: 75.0% Private; 33.8% Public; 8.8% None. (2008-2012 5-year est.)
Transportation: Commute to work: 88.2% car, 3.2% public transportation, 0.0% walk, 4.3% work from home (2008-2012 5-year est.); Travel time to work: 22.5% less than 15 minutes, 28.1% 15 to 30 minutes, 18.0% 30 to 45 minutes, 11.2% 45 to 60 minutes, 20.2% 60 minutes or more (2008-2012 5-year est.)

GILLESPIE (city). Covers a land area of 1.455 square miles and a water area of <.001 square miles. Located at 39.13° N. Lat; 89.82° W. Long. Elevation is 659 feet.
Population: 3,645 (1990); 3,412 (2000); 3,319 (2010); Density: 2,274.1 persons per square mile (2008-2012 5-year est.); Race: 98.6% White, 0.0% Black/African American, 0.0% Asian, 0.0% American Indian/Alaska Native, 0.0% Native Hawaiian/Other Pacific Islander, 1.4% Some other race, 1.4% Two or more races, 0.9% Hispanic of any race (2008-2012 5-year est.); Average household size: 2.38 (2008-2012 5-year est.); Median age: 35.9 (2008-2012 5-year est.); Males per 100 females: 123.5 (2008-2012 5-year est.); Marriage status: 24.5% never married, 50.5% now married, 7.0% widowed, 17.9% divorced (2008-2012 5-year est.); Foreign born: 1.3% (2008-2012 5-year est.); Ancestry (includes multiple ancestries): 32.4% German, 19.3% Irish, 14.3% Italian, 8.4% English, 5.1% American (2008-2012 5-year est.).
Economy: Single-family building permits issued: 2 (2013); Multi-family building permits issued: 0 (2013); Homeowner vacancy rate: 2.4%. Rental vacancy rate: 7.5%. (2008-2012 5-year est.); Employment by occupation: 11.6% management, business, and financial, 1.3% computer, engineering, and science, 9.1% education, legal, community service, arts, and media, 4.2% healthcare practitioners, 25.6% service, 21.0% sales and office, 10.5% natural resources, construction, and maintenance, 16.7% production, transportation, and material moving (2008-2012 5-year est.).
Income: Per capita income: $21,915 (2008-2012 5-year est.); Median household income: $40,256 (2008-2012 5-year est.); Average household income: $51,932 (2008-2012 5-year est.); Percent of households with income of $100,000 or more: 13.1% (2008-2012 5-year est.); Poverty rate: 19.5% (2008-2012 5-year est.).
Education: Percent of population age 25 and over with: High school diploma (including GED) or higher: 91.5% (2008-2012 5-year est.); Bachelor's degree or higher: 15.3% (2008-2012 5-year est.); Master's degree or higher: 5.1% (2008-2012 5-year est.).
School District(s)
Gillespie CUSD 7 (PK-12)
   2011-12 Enrollment: 1,340 . . . . (217) 839-2464
Housing: Homeownership rate: 76.9% (2008-2012 5-year est.); Median home value: $79,100 (2008-2012 5-year est.); Median contract rent: $406 per month (2008-2012 5-year est.); Median year structure built: 1949 (2008-2012 5-year est.).
Health Insurance: 63.5% Private; 36.7% Public; 12.5% None. (2008-2012 5-year est.)
Safety: Violent crime rate: 18.1 per 10,000 population; Property crime rate: 196.1 per 10,000 population (2012).
Transportation: Commute to work: 95.3% car, 0.0% public transportation, 3.3% walk, 1.4% work from home (2008-2012 5-year est.); Travel time to work: 30.5% less than 15 minutes, 29.6% 15 to 30 minutes, 10.2% 30 to 45 minutes, 12.0% 45 to 60 minutes, 17.6% 60 minutes or more (2008-2012 5-year est.)
Additional Information Contacts
Coal Country Chamber of Commerce . . . . (217) 839-4888
   http://coalcountrychamber.com

GIRARD (city). Covers a land area of 0.935 square miles and a water area of 0 square miles. Located at 39.45° N. Lat; 89.78° W. Long. Elevation is 669 feet.
History: Incorporated 1855.
Population: 2,164 (1990); 2,245 (2000); 2,103 (2010); Density: 2,410.3 persons per square mile (2008-2012 5-year est.); Race: 98.7% White, 0.5% Black/African American, 0.4% Asian, 0.0% American Indian/Alaska

Native, 0.0% Native Hawaiian/Other Pacific Islander, 0.4% Some other race, 0.4% Two or more races, 0.6% Hispanic of any race (2008-2012 5-year est.); Average household size: 2.55 (2008-2012 5-year est.); Median age: 35.0 (2008-2012 5-year est.); Males per 100 females: 98.3 (2008-2012 5-year est.); Marriage status: 22.2% never married, 53.7% now married, 10.6% widowed, 13.5% divorced (2008-2012 5-year est.); Foreign born: 2.1% (2008-2012 5-year est.); Ancestry (includes multiple ancestries): 28.0% German, 18.9% Irish, 12.5% English, 8.6% American, 6.7% Swedish (2008-2012 5-year est.).
Economy: Homeowner vacancy rate: 1.3%. Rental vacancy rate: 5.6%. (2008-2012 5-year est.); Employment by occupation: 5.4% management, business, and financial, 2.7% computer, engineering, and science, 2.5% education, legal, community service, arts, and media, 4.6% healthcare practitioners, 16.8% service, 30.1% sales and office, 13.9% natural resources, construction, and maintenance, 24.0% production, transportation, and material moving (2008-2012 5-year est.).
Income: Per capita income: $21,206 (2008-2012 5-year est.); Median household income: $45,676 (2008-2012 5-year est.); Average household income: $53,685 (2008-2012 5-year est.); Percent of households with income of $100,000 or more: 8.6% (2008-2012 5-year est.); Poverty rate: 16.7% (2008-2012 5-year est.).
Education: Percent of population age 25 and over with: High school diploma (including GED) or higher: 91.5% (2008-2012 5-year est.); Bachelor's degree or higher: 7.7% (2008-2012 5-year est.); Master's degree or higher: 1.5% (2008-2012 5-year est.).
School District(s)
North Mac CUSD 34 (PK-12)
   2011-12 Enrollment: 1,643 . . . . (217) 627-2915
Housing: Homeownership rate: 62.0% (2008-2012 5-year est.); Median home value: $74,000 (2008-2012 5-year est.); Median contract rent: $426 per month (2008-2012 5-year est.); Median year structure built: 1966 (2008-2012 5-year est.).
Health Insurance: 57.9% Private; 30.6% Public; 23.5% None. (2008-2012 5-year est.)
Safety: Violent crime rate: 100.0 per 10,000 population; Property crime rate: 47.6 per 10,000 population (2012).
Transportation: Commute to work: 92.7% car, 0.0% public transportation, 2.5% walk, 3.1% work from home (2008-2012 5-year est.); Travel time to work: 26.2% less than 15 minutes, 19.4% 15 to 30 minutes, 28.0% 30 to 45 minutes, 18.6% 45 to 60 minutes, 7.9% 60 minutes or more (2008-2012 5-year est.)

HETTICK (village). Covers a land area of 0.365 square miles and a water area of 0 square miles. Located at 39.36° N. Lat; 90.04° W. Long. Elevation is 597 feet.
Population: 211 (1990); 182 (2000); 181 (2010); Density: 1,001.9 persons per square mile (2008-2012 5-year est.); Race: 98.1% White, 0.0% Black/African American, 0.0% Asian, 0.0% American Indian/Alaska Native, 0.0% Native Hawaiian/Other Pacific Islander, 1.9% Some other race, 1.9% Two or more races, 0.0% Hispanic of any race (2008-2012 5-year est.); Average household size: 2.82 (2008-2012 5-year est.); Median age: 30.9 (2008-2012 5-year est.); Males per 100 females: 149.0 (2008-2012 5-year est.); Marriage status: 18.6% never married, 44.1% now married, 18.3% widowed, 19.0% divorced (2008-2012 5-year est.); Foreign born: 0.0% (2008-2012 5-year est.); Ancestry (includes multiple ancestries): 26.8% German, 14.5% Irish, 13.1% English, 7.1% American, 0.5% Polish (2008-2012 5-year est.).
Economy: Homeowner vacancy rate: 0.0%. Rental vacancy rate: 0.0%. (2008-2012 5-year est.); Employment by occupation: 7.1% management, business, and financial, 0.0% computer, engineering, and science, 1.8% education, legal, community service, arts, and media, 11.3% healthcare practitioners, 16.1% service, 32.1% sales and office, 15.5% natural resources, construction, and maintenance, 16.1% production, transportation, and material moving (2008-2012 5-year est.).
Income: Per capita income: $19,371 (2008-2012 5-year est.); Median household income: $43,929 (2008-2012 5-year est.); Average household income: $53,646 (2008-2012 5-year est.); Percent of households with income of $100,000 or more: 10.7% (2008-2012 5-year est.); Poverty rate: 32.8% (2008-2012 5-year est.).
Education: Percent of population age 25 and over with: High school diploma (including GED) or higher: 83.3% (2008-2012 5-year est.); Bachelor's degree or higher: 5.8% (2008-2012 5-year est.); Master's degree or higher: 0.4% (2008-2012 5-year est.).
Housing: Homeownership rate: 73.1% (2008-2012 5-year est.); Median home value: $69,500 (2008-2012 5-year est.); Median contract rent: $229

per month (2008-2012 5-year est.); Median year structure built: Before 1940 (2008-2012 5-year est.).

Health Insurance: 31.1% Private; 54.6% Public; 20.2% None. (2008-2012 5-year est.)

Transportation: Commute to work: 86.8% car, 0.0% public transportation, 8.4% walk, 4.2% work from home (2008-2012 5-year est.); Travel time to work: 36.3% less than 15 minutes, 37.5% 15 to 30 minutes, 20.6% 30 to 45 minutes, 2.5% 45 to 60 minutes, 3.1% 60 minutes or more (2008-2012 5-year est.).

LAKE KA-HO (village). Covers a land area of 0.270 square miles and a water area of 0.053 square miles. Located at 39.10° N. Lat; 89.75° W. Long. Elevation is 653 feet.

History: Incorporated 2000.

Population: n/a (1990); n/a (2000); 237 (2010); Density: 887.6 persons per square mile (2008-2012 5-year est.); Race: 85.0% White, 0.0% Black/African American, 0.0% Asian, 0.0% American Indian/Alaska Native, 0.0% Native Hawaiian/Other Pacific Islander, 15.0% Some other race, 15.0% Two or more races, 2.5% Hispanic of any race (2008-2012 5-year est.); Average household size: 2.26 (2008-2012 5-year est.); Median age: 43.5 (2008-2012 5-year est.); Males per 100 females: 105.1 (2008-2012 5-year est.); Marriage status: 9.4% never married, 52.5% now married, 8.8% widowed, 29.3% divorced (2008-2012 5-year est.); Foreign born: 0.0% (2008-2012 5-year est.); Ancestry (includes multiple ancestries): 27.9% German, 25.4% Irish, 11.3% American, 8.3% English, 6.7% French (2008-2012 5-year est.).

Economy: Single-family building permits issued: 0 (2013); Multi-family building permits issued: 0 (2013); Homeowner vacancy rate: 9.3%. Rental vacancy rate: 0.0%. (2008-2012 5-year est.); Employment by occupation: 2.2% management, business, and financial, 0.0% computer, engineering, and science, 5.6% education, legal, community service, arts, and media, 0.0% healthcare practitioners, 14.4% service, 26.7% sales and office, 11.1% natural resources, construction, and maintenance, 40.0% production, transportation, and material moving (2008-2012 5-year est.).

Income: Per capita income: $20,330 (2008-2012 5-year est.); Median household income: $34,615 (2008-2012 5-year est.); Average household income: $44,789 (2008-2012 5-year est.); Percent of households with income of $100,000 or more: 7.5% (2008-2012 5-year est.); Poverty rate: 4.7% (2008-2012 5-year est.).

Education: Percent of population age 25 and over with: High school diploma (including GED) or higher: 88.4% (2008-2012 5-year est.); Bachelor's degree or higher: 2.9% (2008-2012 5-year est.); Master's degree or higher: 1.2% (2008-2012 5-year est.).

Housing: Homeownership rate: 91.5% (2008-2012 5-year est.); Median home value: $54,200 (2008-2012 5-year est.); Median contract rent: $513 per month (2008-2012 5-year est.); Median year structure built: 1983 (2008-2012 5-year est.).

Health Insurance: 62.4% Private; 50.9% Public; 12.4% None. (2008-2012 5-year est.)

Transportation: Commute to work: 95.3% car, 0.0% public transportation, 0.0% walk, 0.0% work from home (2008-2012 5-year est.); Travel time to work: 15.3% less than 15 minutes, 32.9% 15 to 30 minutes, 8.2% 30 to 45 minutes, 15.3% 45 to 60 minutes, 28.2% 60 minutes or more (2008-2012 5-year est.).

MEDORA (village). Covers a land area of 0.379 square miles and a water area of 0 square miles. Located at 39.18° N. Lat; 90.14° W. Long. Elevation is 610 feet.

Population: 420 (1990); 501 (2000); 419 (2010); Density: 973.3 persons per square mile (2008-2012 5-year est.); Race: 95.4% White, 0.0% Black/African American, 1.4% Asian, 0.0% American Indian/Alaska Native, 0.0% Native Hawaiian/Other Pacific Islander, 3.2% Some other race, 3.3% Two or more races, 0.0% Hispanic of any race (2008-2012 5-year est.); Average household size: 2.32 (2008-2012 5-year est.); Median age: 45.8 (2008-2012 5-year est.); Males per 100 females: 95.2 (2008-2012 5-year est.); Marriage status: 22.3% never married, 58.9% now married, 7.3% widowed, 11.5% divorced (2008-2012 5-year est.); Foreign born: 1.4% (2008-2012 5-year est.); Ancestry (includes multiple ancestries): 36.3% German, 34.1% Irish, 13.3% English, 8.1% American, 4.3% Polish (2008-2012 5-year est.).

Economy: Homeowner vacancy rate: 2.4%. Rental vacancy rate: 10.0%. (2008-2012 5-year est.); Employment by occupation: 5.6% management, business, and financial, 3.1% computer, engineering, and science, 5.0% education, legal, community service, arts, and media, 0.6% healthcare practitioners, 9.3% service, 30.4% sales and office, 16.1% natural

resources, construction, and maintenance, 29.8% production, transportation, and material moving (2008-2012 5-year est.).

Income: Per capita income: $21,317 (2008-2012 5-year est.); Median household income: $39,375 (2008-2012 5-year est.); Average household income: $49,305 (2008-2012 5-year est.); Percent of households with income of $100,000 or more: 12.6% (2008-2012 5-year est.); Poverty rate: 13.6% (2008-2012 5-year est.).

Education: Percent of population age 25 and over with: High school diploma (including GED) or higher: 87.2% (2008-2012 5-year est.); Bachelor's degree or higher: 12.1% (2008-2012 5-year est.); Master's degree or higher: 5.2% (2008-2012 5-year est.).

School District(s)

Southwestern CUSD 9 (PK-12)
    2011-12 Enrollment: 1,663 . . . . (618) 729-3221

Housing: Homeownership rate: 77.4% (2008-2012 5-year est.); Median home value: $65,000 (2008-2012 5-year est.); Median contract rent: $388 per month (2008-2012 5-year est.); Median year structure built: 1947 (2008-2012 5-year est.).

Health Insurance: 75.3% Private; 35.5% Public; 12.5% None. (2008-2012 5-year est.)

Transportation: Commute to work: 93.4% car, 0.0% public transportation, 6.6% walk, 0.0% work from home (2008-2012 5-year est.); Travel time to work: 16.4% less than 15 minutes, 21.7% 15 to 30 minutes, 28.3% 30 to 45 minutes, 18.4% 45 to 60 minutes, 15.1% 60 minutes or more (2008-2012 5-year est.).

MODESTO (village). Covers a land area of 0.559 square miles and a water area of 0 square miles. Located at 39.48° N. Lat; 89.98° W. Long. Elevation is 679 feet.

Population: 240 (1990); 252 (2000); 189 (2010); Density: 471.9 persons per square mile (2008-2012 5-year est.); Race: 99.6% White, 0.0% Black/African American, 0.0% Asian, 0.4% American Indian/Alaska Native, 0.0% Native Hawaiian/Other Pacific Islander, 0.0% Some other race, 0.0% Two or more races, 1.1% Hispanic of any race (2008-2012 5-year est.); Average household size: 3.00 (2008-2012 5-year est.); Median age: 32.6 (2008-2012 5-year est.); Males per 100 females: 70.3 (2008-2012 5-year est.); Marriage status: 32.6% never married, 49.7% now married, 5.1% widowed, 12.6% divorced (2008-2012 5-year est.); Foreign born: 0.0% (2008-2012 5-year est.); Ancestry (includes multiple ancestries): 42.8% American, 24.6% German, 12.9% Irish, 8.7% English, 2.3% Norwegian (2008-2012 5-year est.).

Economy: Homeowner vacancy rate: 0.0%. Rental vacancy rate: 0.0%. (2008-2012 5-year est.); Employment by occupation: 5.8% management, business, and financial, 2.3% computer, engineering, and science, 2.3% education, legal, community service, arts, and media, 3.5% healthcare practitioners, 15.1% service, 32.6% sales and office, 27.9% natural resources, construction, and maintenance, 10.5% production, transportation, and material moving (2008-2012 5-year est.).

Income: Per capita income: $15,277 (2008-2012 5-year est.); Median household income: $41,667 (2008-2012 5-year est.); Average household income: $46,640 (2008-2012 5-year est.); Percent of households with income of $100,000 or more: 5.7% (2008-2012 5-year est.); Poverty rate: 14.8% (2008-2012 5-year est.).

Education: Percent of population age 25 and over with: High school diploma (including GED) or higher: 90.1% (2008-2012 5-year est.); Bachelor's degree or higher: 8.7% (2008-2012 5-year est.); Master's degree or higher: 1.9% (2008-2012 5-year est.).

Housing: Homeownership rate: 81.8% (2008-2012 5-year est.); Median home value: $58,900 (2008-2012 5-year est.); Median contract rent: $369 per month (2008-2012 5-year est.); Median year structure built: 1950 (2008-2012 5-year est.).

Health Insurance: 58.7% Private; 50.4% Public; 9.1% None. (2008-2012 5-year est.)

Transportation: Commute to work: 90.2% car, 0.0% public transportation, 7.3% walk, 2.4% work from home (2008-2012 5-year est.); Travel time to work: 22.5% less than 15 minutes, 35.0% 15 to 30 minutes, 26.3% 30 to 45 minutes, 15.0% 45 to 60 minutes, 1.3% 60 minutes or more (2008-2012 5-year est.).

MOUNT CLARE (village). Covers a land area of 1.512 square miles and a water area of 0.039 square miles. Located at 39.10° N. Lat; 89.83° W. Long. Elevation is 643 feet.

Population: 297 (1990); 433 (2000); 278 (2010); Density: 207.0 persons per square mile (2008-2012 5-year est.); Race: 98.7% White, 0.0% Black/African American, 0.0% Asian, 0.3% American Indian/Alaska Native,

0.0% Native Hawaiian/Other Pacific Islander, 1.0% Some other race, 1.0% Two or more races, 0.0% Hispanic of any race (2008-2012 5-year est.); Average household size: 2.47 (2008-2012 5-year est.); Median age: 48.5 (2008-2012 5-year est.); Males per 100 females: 79.9 (2008-2012 5-year est.); Marriage status: 26.6% never married, 40.6% now married, 19.9% widowed, 12.9% divorced (2008-2012 5-year est.); Foreign born: 0.0% (2008-2012 5-year est.); Ancestry (includes multiple ancestries): 35.1% German, 17.3% Irish, 13.4% American, 12.8% Italian, 12.1% French (2008-2012 5-year est.).

Economy: Homeowner vacancy rate: 10.8%. Rental vacancy rate: 23.1%. (2008-2012 5-year est.); Employment by occupation: 1.8% management, business, and financial, 1.8% computer, engineering, and science, 9.8% education, legal, community service, arts, and media, 7.1% healthcare practitioners, 31.3% service, 27.7% sales and office, 10.7% natural resources, construction, and maintenance, 9.8% production, transportation, and material moving (2008-2012 5-year est.).

Income: Per capita income: $18,134 (2008-2012 5-year est.); Median household income: $33,750 (2008-2012 5-year est.); Average household income: $45,768 (2008-2012 5-year est.); Percent of households with income of $100,000 or more: 7.2% (2008-2012 5-year est.); Poverty rate: 19.6% (2008-2012 5-year est.).

Education: Percent of population age 25 and over with: High school diploma (including GED) or higher: 80.3% (2008-2012 5-year est.); Bachelor's degree or higher: 11.3% (2008-2012 5-year est.); Master's degree or higher: 4.2% (2008-2012 5-year est.).

Housing: Homeownership rate: 82.0% (2008-2012 5-year est.); Median home value: $76,400 (2008-2012 5-year est.); Median contract rent: $414 per month (2008-2012 5-year est.); Median year structure built: 1943 (2008-2012 5-year est.).

Health Insurance: 54.4% Private; 52.2% Public; 10.9% None. (2008-2012 5-year est.)

Transportation: Commute to work: 94.4% car, 0.0% public transportation, 3.7% walk, 1.9% work from home (2008-2012 5-year est.); Travel time to work: 28.3% less than 15 minutes, 41.5% 15 to 30 minutes, 9.4% 30 to 45 minutes, 11.3% 45 to 60 minutes, 9.4% 60 minutes or more (2008-2012 5-year est.)

MOUNT OLIVE (city). Covers a land area of 1.153 square miles and a water area of 0.003 square miles. Located at 39.07° N. Lat; 89.73° W. Long. Elevation is 686 feet.

History: Mount Olive, an early coal-mining town, was connected with two labor organizers. Alexander Bradley (1866-1918) was a leader in union organization. "Mother" Jones (1830-1930), born Mary Harris in Ireland, was buried in Mount Olive.

Population: 2,126 (1990); 2,150 (2000); 2,099 (2010); Density: 1,864.4 persons per square mile (2008-2012 5-year est.); Race: 98.5% White, 0.0% Black/African American, 0.0% Asian, 0.0% American Indian/Alaska Native, 0.0% Native Hawaiian/Other Pacific Islander, 1.5% Some other race, 1.5% Two or more races, 0.0% Hispanic of any race (2008-2012 5-year est.); Average household size: 2.29 (2008-2012 5-year est.); Median age: 39.9 (2008-2012 5-year est.); Males per 100 females: 89.4 (2008-2012 5-year est.); Marriage status: 23.4% never married, 56.0% now married, 5.3% widowed, 15.3% divorced (2008-2012 5-year est.); Foreign born: 1.8% (2008-2012 5-year est.); Ancestry (includes multiple ancestries): 37.8% German, 13.8% Irish, 9.2% American, 7.2% Italian, 6.2% English (2008-2012 5-year est.).

Economy: Single-family building permits issued: 1 (2013); Multi-family building permits issued: 0 (2013); Homeowner vacancy rate: 1.9%. Rental vacancy rate: 0.0%. (2008-2012 5-year est.); Employment by occupation: 11.3% management, business, and financial, 2.2% computer, engineering, and science, 6.4% education, legal, community service, arts, and media, 5.3% healthcare practitioners, 23.7% service, 21.6% sales and office, 12.8% natural resources, construction, and maintenance, 16.7% production, transportation, and material moving (2008-2012 5-year est.).

Income: Per capita income: $22,792 (2008-2012 5-year est.); Median household income: $45,250 (2008-2012 5-year est.); Average household income: $51,942 (2008-2012 5-year est.); Percent of households with income of $100,000 or more: 10.7% (2008-2012 5-year est.); Poverty rate: 14.7% (2008-2012 5-year est.).

Education: Percent of population age 25 and over with: High school diploma (including GED) or higher: 89.0% (2008-2012 5-year est.); Bachelor's degree or higher: 11.2% (2008-2012 5-year est.); Master's degree or higher: 3.6% (2008-2012 5-year est.).

School District(s)
Mount Olive CUSD 5 (PK-12)
    2011-12 Enrollment: 540. . . . . (217) 999-7831
Housing: Homeownership rate: 79.5% (2008-2012 5-year est.); Median home value: $74,600 (2008-2012 5-year est.); Median contract rent: $428 per month (2008-2012 5-year est.); Median year structure built: 1944 (2008-2012 5-year est.).

Health Insurance: 73.1% Private; 33.8% Public; 8.5% None. (2008-2012 5-year est.)

Safety: Violent crime rate: 9.5 per 10,000 population; Property crime rate: 76.1 per 10,000 population (2012).

Transportation: Commute to work: 94.2% car, 0.0% public transportation, 0.7% walk, 4.5% work from home (2008-2012 5-year est.); Travel time to work: 36.0% less than 15 minutes, 20.4% 15 to 30 minutes, 13.0% 30 to 45 minutes, 15.4% 45 to 60 minutes, 15.1% 60 minutes or more (2008-2012 5-year est.)

NILWOOD (town). Covers a land area of 0.465 square miles and a water area of 0 square miles. Located at 39.40° N. Lat; 89.81° W. Long. Elevation is 669 feet.

Population: 238 (1990); 284 (2000); 239 (2010); Density: 453.4 persons per square mile (2008-2012 5-year est.); Race: 98.1% White, 0.0% Black/African American, 0.0% Asian, 0.0% American Indian/Alaska Native, 0.0% Native Hawaiian/Other Pacific Islander, 1.9% Some other race, 1.9% Two or more races, 0.0% Hispanic of any race (2008-2012 5-year est.); Average household size: 2.51 (2008-2012 5-year est.); Median age: 42.6 (2008-2012 5-year est.); Males per 100 females: 81.9 (2008-2012 5-year est.); Marriage status: 22.8% never married, 48.0% now married, 8.2% widowed, 21.1% divorced (2008-2012 5-year est.); Foreign born: 0.0% (2008-2012 5-year est.); Ancestry (includes multiple ancestries): 25.6% German, 15.6% English, 15.2% American, 4.3% Scottish, 4.3% Irish (2008-2012 5-year est.).

Economy: Homeowner vacancy rate: 14.8%. Rental vacancy rate: 0.0%. (2008-2012 5-year est.); Employment by occupation: 5.6% management, business, and financial, 4.2% computer, engineering, and science, 2.8% education, legal, community service, arts, and media, 1.4% healthcare practitioners, 29.2% service, 31.9% sales and office, 13.9% natural resources, construction, and maintenance, 11.1% production, transportation, and material moving (2008-2012 5-year est.).

Income: Per capita income: $19,524 (2008-2012 5-year est.); Median household income: $44,375 (2008-2012 5-year est.); Average household income: $47,115 (2008-2012 5-year est.); Percent of households with income of $100,000 or more: 6.0% (2008-2012 5-year est.); Poverty rate: 16.6% (2008-2012 5-year est.).

Education: Percent of population age 25 and over with: High school diploma (including GED) or higher: 88.2% (2008-2012 5-year est.); Bachelor's degree or higher: 11.8% (2008-2012 5-year est.); Master's degree or higher: 1.3% (2008-2012 5-year est.).

Housing: Homeownership rate: 89.3% (2008-2012 5-year est.); Median home value: $49,700 (2008-2012 5-year est.); Median contract rent: $244 per month (2008-2012 5-year est.); Median year structure built: 1962 (2008-2012 5-year est.).

Health Insurance: 68.2% Private; 41.2% Public; 10.0% None. (2008-2012 5-year est.)

Transportation: Commute to work: 84.7% car, 0.0% public transportation, 4.2% walk, 11.1% work from home (2008-2012 5-year est.); Travel time to work: 29.7% less than 15 minutes, 37.5% 15 to 30 minutes, 10.9% 30 to 45 minutes, 21.9% 45 to 60 minutes, 0.0% 60 minutes or more (2008-2012 5-year est.)

PALMYRA (village). Covers a land area of 0.999 square miles and a water area of 0 square miles. Located at 39.43° N. Lat; 90.00° W. Long. Elevation is 673 feet.

Population: 722 (1990); 733 (2000); 698 (2010); Density: 689.7 persons per square mile (2008-2012 5-year est.); Race: 96.7% White, 0.0% Black/African American, 0.0% Asian, 0.0% American Indian/Alaska Native, 0.7% Native Hawaiian/Other Pacific Islander, 2.6% Some other race, 2.3% Two or more races, 0.4% Hispanic of any race (2008-2012 5-year est.); Average household size: 2.39 (2008-2012 5-year est.); Median age: 38.9 (2008-2012 5-year est.); Males per 100 females: 79.9 (2008-2012 5-year est.); Marriage status: 26.5% never married, 47.8% now married, 11.5% widowed, 14.2% divorced (2008-2012 5-year est.); Foreign born: 0.0% (2008-2012 5-year est.); Ancestry (includes multiple ancestries): 23.1% German, 19.0% American, 14.5% English, 9.4% Irish, 3.3% Dutch (2008-2012 5-year est.).

Economy: Homeowner vacancy rate: 0.0%. Rental vacancy rate: 0.0%. (2008-2012 5-year est.); Employment by occupation: 8.0% management, business, and financial, 1.1% computer, engineering, and science, 3.1% education, legal, community service, arts, and media, 1.9% healthcare practitioners, 27.2% service, 24.1% sales and office, 8.8% natural resources, construction, and maintenance, 25.7% production, transportation, and material moving (2008-2012 5-year est.).

Income: Per capita income: $15,935 (2008-2012 5-year est.); Median household income: $24,632 (2008-2012 5-year est.); Average household income: $37,486 (2008-2012 5-year est.); Percent of households with income of $100,000 or more: 4.1% (2008-2012 5-year est.); Poverty rate: 22.2% (2008-2012 5-year est.).

Education: Percent of population age 25 and over with: High school diploma (including GED) or higher: 76.1% (2008-2012 5-year est.); Bachelor's degree or higher: 7.7% (2008-2012 5-year est.); Master's degree or higher: 1.1% (2008-2012 5-year est.).

School District(s)
Northwestern CUSD 2 (PK-12)
　　2011-12 Enrollment: 357. . . . . (217) 436-2210

Housing: Homeownership rate: 54.5% (2008-2012 5-year est.); Median home value: $72,100 (2008-2012 5-year est.); Median contract rent: $246 per month (2008-2012 5-year est.); Median year structure built: 1949 (2008-2012 5-year est.).

Health Insurance: 48.2% Private; 53.3% Public; 15.5% None. (2008-2012 5-year est.)

Transportation: Commute to work: 93.0% car, 0.8% public transportation, 3.1% walk, 0.8% work from home (2008-2012 5-year est.); Travel time to work: 15.7% less than 15 minutes, 30.7% 15 to 30 minutes, 18.1% 30 to 45 minutes, 13.0% 45 to 60 minutes, 22.4% 60 minutes or more (2008-2012 5-year est.)

PIASA (unincorporated postal area)
Zip Code: 62079
　　Covers a land area of 9.483 square miles and a water area of 0.046 square miles. Located at 39.11° N. Lat; 90.14° W. Long. Elevation is 594 feet. Population: 256 (2010); Density: 27.0 persons per square mile (2010); Race: 98.4% White, 1.6% Black/African American, 0.0% Asian, 0.0% American Indian/Alaska Native, 0.0% Native Hawaiian/Other Pacific Islander, 0.0% Some other race, 0.0% Two or more races, 0.0% Hispanic of any race (2010); Average household size: 2.51 (2010); Median age: 45.2 (2010); Males per 100 females: 93.9 (2010); Homeownership rate: 90.2% (2010)

ROYAL LAKES (village). Aka Royal Lake. Covers a land area of 0.466 square miles and a water area of 0.046 square miles. Located at 39.11° N. Lat; 89.96° W. Long.
Population: 272 (1990); 190 (2000); 197 (2010); Density: 483.0 persons per square mile (2008-2012 5-year est.); Race: 16.9% White, 68.4% Black/African American, 0.9% Asian, 0.0% American Indian/Alaska Native, 0.0% Native Hawaiian/Other Pacific Islander, 13.8% Some other race, 13.8% Two or more races, 0.9% Hispanic of any race (2008-2012 5-year est.); Average household size: 2.56 (2008-2012 5-year est.); Median age: 36.5 (2008-2012 5-year est.); Males per 100 females: 90.7 (2008-2012 5-year est.); Marriage status: 28.7% never married, 57.5% now married, 7.2% widowed, 6.6% divorced (2008-2012 5-year est.); Foreign born: 16.0% (2008-2012 5-year est.); Ancestry (includes multiple ancestries): 31.1% African, 5.8% Irish, 4.4% American, 3.6% English, 2.7% German (2008-2012 5-year est.).

Economy: Single-family building permits issued: 0 (2013); Multi-family building permits issued: 0 (2013); Homeowner vacancy rate: 13.2%. Rental vacancy rate: 0.0%. (2008-2012 5-year est.); Employment by occupation: 5.0% management, business, and financial, 1.3% computer, engineering, and science, 0.0% education, legal, community service, arts, and media, 2.5% healthcare practitioners, 32.5% service, 11.3% sales and office, 7.5% natural resources, construction, and maintenance, 40.0% production, transportation, and material moving (2008-2012 5-year est.).

Income: Per capita income: $14,583 (2008-2012 5-year est.); Median household income: $28,864 (2008-2012 5-year est.); Average household income: $35,836 (2008-2012 5-year est.); Percent of households with income of $100,000 or more: 5.7% (2008-2012 5-year est.); Poverty rate: 17.5% (2008-2012 5-year est.).

Education: Percent of population age 25 and over with: High school diploma (including GED) or higher: 86.5% (2008-2012 5-year est.); Bachelor's degree or higher: 5.8% (2008-2012 5-year est.); Master's degree or higher: 1.9% (2008-2012 5-year est.).

Housing: Homeownership rate: 67.0% (2008-2012 5-year est.); Median home value: $64,600 (2008-2012 5-year est.); Median contract rent: $333 per month (2008-2012 5-year est.); Median year structure built: 1977 (2008-2012 5-year est.).

Health Insurance: 58.2% Private; 44.9% Public; 8.4% None. (2008-2012 5-year est.)

Transportation: Commute to work: 81.3% car, 13.3% public transportation, 5.3% walk, 0.0% work from home (2008-2012 5-year est.); Travel time to work: 29.3% less than 15 minutes, 5.3% 15 to 30 minutes, 49.3% 30 to 45 minutes, 9.3% 45 to 60 minutes, 6.7% 60 minutes or more (2008-2012 5-year est.)

SAWYERVILLE (village). Covers a land area of 0.988 square miles and a water area of 0.014 square miles. Located at 39.08° N. Lat; 89.80° W. Long. Elevation is 630 feet.
Population: 312 (1990); 295 (2000); 279 (2010); Density: 254.2 persons per square mile (2008-2012 5-year est.); Race: 97.6% White, 0.0% Black/African American, 0.0% Asian, 0.0% American Indian/Alaska Native, 0.0% Native Hawaiian/Other Pacific Islander, 2.4% Some other race, 2.4% Two or more races, 0.0% Hispanic of any race (2008-2012 5-year est.); Average household size: 2.61 (2008-2012 5-year est.); Median age: 39.3 (2008-2012 5-year est.); Males per 100 females: 99.2 (2008-2012 5-year est.); Marriage status: 17.4% never married, 70.1% now married, 4.9% widowed, 7.6% divorced (2008-2012 5-year est.); Foreign born: 0.0% (2008-2012 5-year est.); Ancestry (includes multiple ancestries): 30.7% German, 23.5% Italian, 13.5% French, 8.8% Scottish, 8.8% American (2008-2012 5-year est.).

Economy: Homeowner vacancy rate: 0.0%. Rental vacancy rate: 0.0%. (2008-2012 5-year est.); Employment by occupation: 33.7% management, business, and financial, 0.0% computer, engineering, and science, 3.4% education, legal, community service, arts, and media, 2.2% healthcare practitioners, 14.6% service, 13.5% sales and office, 18.0% natural resources, construction, and maintenance, 14.6% production, transportation, and material moving (2008-2012 5-year est.).

Income: Per capita income: $19,075 (2008-2012 5-year est.); Median household income: $40,000 (2008-2012 5-year est.); Average household income: $48,747 (2008-2012 5-year est.); Percent of households with income of $100,000 or more: 1.0% (2008-2012 5-year est.); Poverty rate: 35.5% (2008-2012 5-year est.).

Education: Percent of population age 25 and over with: High school diploma (including GED) or higher: 83.7% (2008-2012 5-year est.); Bachelor's degree or higher: 13.4% (2008-2012 5-year est.); Master's degree or higher: 4.7% (2008-2012 5-year est.).

Housing: Homeownership rate: 69.8% (2008-2012 5-year est.); Median home value: $117,000 (2008-2012 5-year est.); Median contract rent: $440 per month (2008-2012 5-year est.); Median year structure built: 1954 (2008-2012 5-year est.).

Health Insurance: 58.6% Private; 55.8% Public; 4.8% None. (2008-2012 5-year est.)

Transportation: Commute to work: 100.0% car, 0.0% public transportation, 0.0% walk, 0.0% work from home (2008-2012 5-year est.); Travel time to work: 25.0% less than 15 minutes, 23.8% 15 to 30 minutes, 21.4% 30 to 45 minutes, 27.4% 45 to 60 minutes, 2.4% 60 minutes or more (2008-2012 5-year est.)

SCOTTVILLE (village). Aka Scottsville. Covers a land area of 0.997 square miles and a water area of 0 square miles. Located at 39.48° N. Lat; 90.10° W. Long. Elevation is 659 feet.
Population: 165 (1990); 140 (2000); 116 (2010); Density: 130.4 persons per square mile (2008-2012 5-year est.); Race: 100.0% White, 0.0% Black/African American, 0.0% Asian, 0.0% American Indian/Alaska Native, 0.0% Native Hawaiian/Other Pacific Islander, 0.0% Some other race, 0.0% Two or more races, 0.0% Hispanic of any race (2008-2012 5-year est.); Average household size: 2.89 (2008-2012 5-year est.); Median age: 37.4 (2008-2012 5-year est.); Males per 100 females: 124.1 (2008-2012 5-year est.); Marriage status: 27.1% never married, 67.8% now married, 0.8% widowed, 4.2% divorced (2008-2012 5-year est.); Foreign born: 0.0% (2008-2012 5-year est.); Ancestry (includes multiple ancestries): 40.0% German, 9.2% Irish, 9.2% American, 6.9% French, 5.4% English (2008-2012 5-year est.).

Economy: Homeowner vacancy rate: 0.0%. Rental vacancy rate: 0.0%. (2008-2012 5-year est.); Employment by occupation: 9.3% management, business, and financial, 9.3% computer, engineering, and science, 8.0% education, legal, community service, arts, and media, 9.3% healthcare practitioners, 18.7% service, 8.0% sales and office, 12.0% natural

resources, construction, and maintenance, 25.3% production, transportation, and material moving (2008-2012 5-year est.).
Income: Per capita income: $26,577 (2008-2012 5-year est.); Median household income: $61,250 (2008-2012 5-year est.); Average household income: $74,933 (2008-2012 5-year est.); Percent of households with income of $100,000 or more: 33.3% (2008-2012 5-year est.); Poverty rate: 30.8% (2008-2012 5-year est.).
Education: Percent of population age 25 and over with: High school diploma (including GED) or higher: 81.9% (2008-2012 5-year est.); Bachelor's degree or higher: 26.5% (2008-2012 5-year est.); Master's degree or higher: 12.0% (2008-2012 5-year est.).
Housing: Homeownership rate: 91.1% (2008-2012 5-year est.); Median home value: $58,600 (2008-2012 5-year est.); Median contract rent: n/a per month (2008-2012 5-year est.); Median year structure built: 1974 (2008-2012 5-year est.).
Health Insurance: 61.5% Private; 44.6% Public; 4.6% None. (2008-2012 5-year est.)
Transportation: Commute to work: 98.4% car, 0.0% public transportation, 0.0% walk, 1.6% work from home (2008-2012 5-year est.); Travel time to work: 4.9% less than 15 minutes, 44.3% 15 to 30 minutes, 32.8% 30 to 45 minutes, 0.0% 45 to 60 minutes, 18.0% 60 minutes or more (2008-2012 5-year est.)

SHIPMAN (town). Covers a land area of 1.315 square miles and a water area of 0.013 square miles. Located at 39.12° N. Lat; 90.05° W. Long. Elevation is 636 feet.
Population: 624 (1990); 655 (2000); 624 (2010); Density: 620.4 persons per square mile (2008-2012 5-year est.); Race: 96.1% White, 0.0% Black/African American, 0.0% Asian, 0.1% American Indian/Alaska Native, 0.0% Native Hawaiian/Other Pacific Islander, 3.8% Some other race, 0.2% Two or more races, 5.3% Hispanic of any race (2008-2012 5-year est.); Average household size: 2.94 (2008-2012 5-year est.); Median age: 30.3 (2008-2012 5-year est.); Males per 100 females: 110.3 (2008-2012 5-year est.); Marriage status: 16.7% never married, 64.8% now married, 5.5% widowed, 13.0% divorced (2008-2012 5-year est.); Foreign born: 4.3% (2008-2012 5-year est.); Ancestry (includes multiple ancestries): 35.8% German, 12.3% Scotch-Irish, 12.1% English, 8.8% Irish, 6.7% American (2008-2012 5-year est.).
Economy: Homeowner vacancy rate: 0.0%. Rental vacancy rate: 6.7%. (2008-2012 5-year est.); Employment by occupation: 18.3% management, business, and financial, 0.0% computer, engineering, and science, 7.1% education, legal, community service, arts, and media, 7.1% healthcare practitioners, 15.6% service, 18.6% sales and office, 11.9% natural resources, construction, and maintenance, 21.4% production, transportation, and material moving (2008-2012 5-year est.).
Income: Per capita income: $21,376 (2008-2012 5-year est.); Median household income: $45,625 (2008-2012 5-year est.); Average household income: $61,836 (2008-2012 5-year est.); Percent of households with income of $100,000 or more: 12.6% (2008-2012 5-year est.); Poverty rate: 21.7% (2008-2012 5-year est.).
Education: Percent of population age 25 and over with: High school diploma (including GED) or higher: 89.0% (2008-2012 5-year est.); Bachelor's degree or higher: 6.5% (2008-2012 5-year est.); Master's degree or higher: 3.5% (2008-2012 5-year est.).
School District(s)
Southwestern CUSD 9 (PK-12)
    2011-12 Enrollment: 1,663 . . . . (618) 729-3221
Housing: Homeownership rate: 70.1% (2008-2012 5-year est.); Median home value: $68,700 (2008-2012 5-year est.); Median contract rent: $370 per month (2008-2012 5-year est.); Median year structure built: 1962 (2008-2012 5-year est.).
Health Insurance: 73.8% Private; 30.4% Public; 8.0% None. (2008-2012 5-year est.)
Transportation: Commute to work: 94.1% car, 0.0% public transportation, 1.7% walk, 4.2% work from home (2008-2012 5-year est.); Travel time to work: 19.0% less than 15 minutes, 23.7% 15 to 30 minutes, 42.7% 30 to 45 minutes, 8.0% 45 to 60 minutes, 6.6% 60 minutes or more (2008-2012 5-year est.)

STANDARD CITY (village). Aka South Standard. Covers a land area of 0.636 square miles and a water area of 0.003 square miles. Located at 39.35° N. Lat; 89.78° W. Long. Elevation is 640 feet.
Population: 128 (1990); 138 (2000); 152 (2010); Density: 306.5 persons per square mile (2008-2012 5-year est.); Race: 99.5% White, 0.0% Black/African American, 0.0% Asian, 0.0% American Indian/Alaska Native,

0.0% Native Hawaiian/Other Pacific Islander, 0.5% Some other race, 0.5% Two or more races, 0.0% Hispanic of any race (2008-2012 5-year est.); Average household size: 2.60 (2008-2012 5-year est.); Median age: 36.6 (2008-2012 5-year est.); Males per 100 females: 103.1 (2008-2012 5-year est.); Marriage status: 16.9% never married, 50.7% now married, 2.7% widowed, 29.7% divorced (2008-2012 5-year est.); Foreign born: 0.0% (2008-2012 5-year est.); Ancestry (includes multiple ancestries): 42.6% German, 19.0% Italian, 15.9% English, 13.8% American, 13.3% Irish (2008-2012 5-year est.).
Economy: Homeowner vacancy rate: 0.0%. Rental vacancy rate: 0.0%. (2008-2012 5-year est.); Employment by occupation: 7.5% management, business, and financial, 0.0% computer, engineering, and science, 7.5% education, legal, community service, arts, and media, 5.4% healthcare practitioners, 4.3% service, 45.2% sales and office, 23.7% natural resources, construction, and maintenance, 6.5% production, transportation, and material moving (2008-2012 5-year est.).
Income: Per capita income: $16,526 (2008-2012 5-year est.); Median household income: $32,188 (2008-2012 5-year est.); Average household income: $41,819 (2008-2012 5-year est.); Percent of households with income of $100,000 or more: n/a (2008-2012 5-year est.); Poverty rate: 20.5% (2008-2012 5-year est.).
Education: Percent of population age 25 and over with: High school diploma (including GED) or higher: 94.0% (2008-2012 5-year est.); Bachelor's degree or higher: 8.2% (2008-2012 5-year est.); Master's degree or higher: 4.5% (2008-2012 5-year est.).
Housing: Homeownership rate: 74.7% (2008-2012 5-year est.); Median home value: $58,900 (2008-2012 5-year est.); Median contract rent: $479 per month (2008-2012 5-year est.); Median year structure built: 1966 (2008-2012 5-year est.).
Health Insurance: 70.8% Private; 23.6% Public; 9.2% None. (2008-2012 5-year est.)
Transportation: Commute to work: 95.7% car, 0.0% public transportation, 0.0% walk, 4.3% work from home (2008-2012 5-year est.); Travel time to work: 9.0% less than 15 minutes, 28.1% 15 to 30 minutes, 29.2% 30 to 45 minutes, 18.0% 45 to 60 minutes, 15.7% 60 minutes or more (2008-2012 5-year est.)

STAUNTON (city). Covers a land area of 3.062 square miles and a water area of 0.028 square miles. Located at 39.01° N. Lat; 89.79° W. Long. Elevation is 620 feet.
History: Staunton was settled in 1817 by John Wood of Virginia, and a village was laid out in 1835. Staunton was named for one of its founders, and operated as a trading point for settlers. Later, coal mining was an important industry.
Population: 4,806 (1990); 5,030 (2000); 5,139 (2010); Density: 1,629.4 persons per square mile (2008-2012 5-year est.); Race: 99.2% White, 0.0% Black/African American, 0.3% Asian, 0.0% American Indian/Alaska Native, 0.0% Native Hawaiian/Other Pacific Islander, 0.5% Some other race, 0.5% Two or more races, 0.8% Hispanic of any race (2008-2012 5-year est.); Average household size: 2.12 (2008-2012 5-year est.); Median age: 44.9 (2008-2012 5-year est.); Males per 100 females: 77.2 (2008-2012 5-year est.); Marriage status: 23.7% never married, 54.5% now married, 12.0% widowed, 9.9% divorced (2008-2012 5-year est.); Foreign born: 0.4% (2008-2012 5-year est.); Ancestry (includes multiple ancestries): 45.2% German, 20.1% Italian, 15.7% Irish, 7.0% English, 6.1% American (2008-2012 5-year est.).
Economy: Single-family building permits issued: 2 (2013); Multi-family building permits issued: 2 (2013); Homeowner vacancy rate: 6.1%. Rental vacancy rate: 5.1%. (2008-2012 5-year est.); Employment by occupation: 13.0% management, business, and financial, 0.7% computer, engineering, and science, 6.5% education, legal, community service, arts, and media, 3.0% healthcare practitioners, 15.0% service, 28.8% sales and office, 11.4% natural resources, construction, and maintenance, 21.5% production, transportation, and material moving (2008-2012 5-year est.).
Income: Per capita income: $26,142 (2008-2012 5-year est.); Median household income: $45,633 (2008-2012 5-year est.); Average household income: $55,562 (2008-2012 5-year est.); Percent of households with income of $100,000 or more: 10.5% (2008-2012 5-year est.); Poverty rate: 12.6% (2008-2012 5-year est.).
Education: Percent of population age 25 and over with: High school diploma (including GED) or higher: 90.1% (2008-2012 5-year est.); Bachelor's degree or higher: 19.2% (2008-2012 5-year est.); Master's degree or higher: 8.0% (2008-2012 5-year est.).

School District(s)

Staunton CUSD 6 (PK-12)

2011-12 Enrollment: 1,310 . . . . (618) 635-2962

Housing: Homeownership rate: 73.5% (2008-2012 5-year est.); Median home value: $102,800 (2008-2012 5-year est.); Median contract rent: $416 per month (2008-2012 5-year est.); Median year structure built: 1958 (2008-2012 5-year est.).

Health Insurance: 70.8% Private; 41.0% Public; 7.5% None. (2008-2012 5-year est.)

Hospitals: Community Memorial Hospital (49 beds)

Transportation: Commute to work: 96.3% car, 0.0% public transportation, 2.2% walk, 0.8% work from home (2008-2012 5-year est.); Travel time to work: 35.5% less than 15 minutes, 13.4% 15 to 30 minutes, 31.1% 30 to 45 minutes, 13.5% 45 to 60 minutes, 6.5% 60 minutes or more (2008-2012 5-year est.)

Additional Information Contacts

City of Staunton. . . . . (618) 635-2233

   http://www.stauntonil.com

Staunton Chamber of Commerce . . . . (618) 635-8356

   http://www.stauntonil.com/chamber/welcome.aspx

VIRDEN (city).
Covers a land area of 1.827 square miles and a water area of 0 square miles. Located at 39.51° N. Lat; 89.77° W. Long. Elevation is 686 feet.

History: Virden was a coal mining town and the location of the Virden riot in 1898 when mine operators refused to pay the rates established by the Illinois Coal Operators Association.

Population: 3,635 (1990); 3,488 (2000); 3,425 (2010); Density: 1,973.3 persons per square mile (2008-2012 5-year est.); Race: 98.5% White, 0.4% Black/African American, 0.0% Asian, 0.3% American Indian/Alaska Native, 0.0% Native Hawaiian/Other Pacific Islander, 0.8% Some other race, 0.9% Two or more races, 0.0% Hispanic of any race (2008-2012 5-year est.); Average household size: 2.42 (2008-2012 5-year est.); Median age: 36.5 (2008-2012 5-year est.); Males per 100 females: 87.7 (2008-2012 5-year est.); Marriage status: 27.8% never married, 43.9% now married, 9.1% widowed, 19.1% divorced (2008-2012 5-year est.); Foreign born: 0.3% (2008-2012 5-year est.); Ancestry (includes multiple ancestries): 27.5% German, 17.1% Irish, 11.4% English, 10.5% American, 4.9% Italian (2008-2012 5-year est.).

Economy: Homeowner vacancy rate: 2.5%. Rental vacancy rate: 6.0%. (2008-2012 5-year est.); Employment by occupation: 8.9% management, business, and financial, 2.1% computer, engineering, and science, 3.6% education, legal, community service, arts, and media, 7.0% healthcare practitioners, 16.4% service, 28.2% sales and office, 17.2% natural resources, construction, and maintenance, 16.6% production, transportation, and material moving (2008-2012 5-year est.).

Income: Per capita income: $20,315 (2008-2012 5-year est.); Median household income: $41,653 (2008-2012 5-year est.); Average household income: $49,283 (2008-2012 5-year est.); Percent of households with income of $100,000 or more: 10.0% (2008-2012 5-year est.); Poverty rate: 14.2% (2008-2012 5-year est.).

Education: Percent of population age 25 and over with: High school diploma (including GED) or higher: 84.4% (2008-2012 5-year est.); Bachelor's degree or higher: 10.4% (2008-2012 5-year est.); Master's degree or higher: 2.7% (2008-2012 5-year est.).

School District(s)

North Mac CUSD 34 (PK-12)

2011-12 Enrollment: 1,643 . . . . (217) 627-2915

Housing: Homeownership rate: 67.8% (2008-2012 5-year est.); Median home value: $73,700 (2008-2012 5-year est.); Median contract rent: $465 per month (2008-2012 5-year est.); Median year structure built: 1953 (2008-2012 5-year est.).

Health Insurance: 62.2% Private; 35.6% Public; 14.3% None. (2008-2012 5-year est.)

Safety: Violent crime rate: 31.6 per 10,000 population; Property crime rate: 180.9 per 10,000 population (2012).

Transportation: Commute to work: 94.0% car, 0.0% public transportation, 3.1% walk, 0.7% work from home (2008-2012 5-year est.); Travel time to work: 30.8% less than 15 minutes, 20.8% 15 to 30 minutes, 29.4% 30 to 45 minutes, 15.3% 45 to 60 minutes, 3.7% 60 minutes or more (2008-2012 5-year est.)

Additional Information Contacts

Virden Area Chamber of Commerce . . . . (217) 965-4747

   http://virdenchamber.com

WHITE CITY (village).
Covers a land area of 1.212 square miles and a water area of 0.004 square miles. Located at 39.07° N. Lat; 89.77° W. Long. Elevation is 653 feet.

Population: 229 (1990); 221 (2000); 232 (2010); Density: 181.5 persons per square mile (2008-2012 5-year est.); Race: 99.5% White, 0.0% Black/African American, 0.0% Asian, 0.0% American Indian/Alaska Native, 0.0% Native Hawaiian/Other Pacific Islander, 0.5% Some other race, 0.5% Two or more races, 0.9% Hispanic of any race (2008-2012 5-year est.); Average household size: 2.32 (2008-2012 5-year est.); Median age: 43.0 (2008-2012 5-year est.); Males per 100 females: 100.0 (2008-2012 5-year est.); Marriage status: 20.6% never married, 65.0% now married, 4.4% widowed, 10.0% divorced (2008-2012 5-year est.); Foreign born: 0.0% (2008-2012 5-year est.); Ancestry (includes multiple ancestries): 52.7% German, 28.6% Irish, 9.5% English, 9.5% French, 6.8% Dutch (2008-2012 5-year est.).

Economy: Single-family building permits issued: 0 (2013); Multi-family building permits issued: 0 (2013); Homeowner vacancy rate: 0.0%. Rental vacancy rate: 0.0%. (2008-2012 5-year est.); Employment by occupation: 3.3% management, business, and financial, 2.2% computer, engineering, and science, 12.1% education, legal, community service, arts, and media, 3.3% healthcare practitioners, 13.2% service, 29.7% sales and office, 22.0% natural resources, construction, and maintenance, 14.3% production, transportation, and material moving (2008-2012 5-year est.).

Income: Per capita income: $18,822 (2008-2012 5-year est.); Median household income: $32,292 (2008-2012 5-year est.); Average household income: $43,656 (2008-2012 5-year est.); Percent of households with income of $100,000 or more: 7.4% (2008-2012 5-year est.); Poverty rate: 10.9% (2008-2012 5-year est.).

Education: Percent of population age 25 and over with: High school diploma (including GED) or higher: 92.4% (2008-2012 5-year est.); Bachelor's degree or higher: 7.6% (2008-2012 5-year est.); Master's degree or higher: 0.0% (2008-2012 5-year est.).

Housing: Homeownership rate: 86.3% (2008-2012 5-year est.); Median home value: $75,800 (2008-2012 5-year est.); Median contract rent: $296 per month (2008-2012 5-year est.); Median year structure built: 1971 (2008-2012 5-year est.).

Health Insurance: 61.4% Private; 44.5% Public; 6.4% None. (2008-2012 5-year est.)

Transportation: Commute to work: 100.0% car, 0.0% public transportation, 0.0% walk, 0.0% work from home (2008-2012 5-year est.); Travel time to work: 16.5% less than 15 minutes, 39.6% 15 to 30 minutes, 28.6% 30 to 45 minutes, 13.2% 45 to 60 minutes, 2.2% 60 minutes or more (2008-2012 5-year est.)

WILSONVILLE (village).
Covers a land area of 0.956 square miles and a water area of 0.026 square miles. Located at 39.07° N. Lat; 89.86° W. Long. Elevation is 643 feet.

Population: 609 (1990); 604 (2000); 586 (2010); Density: 540.0 persons per square mile (2008-2012 5-year est.); Race: 93.2% White, 0.0% Black/African American, 0.0% Asian, 0.0% American Indian/Alaska Native, 0.0% Native Hawaiian/Other Pacific Islander, 6.8% Some other race, 6.8% Two or more races, 0.0% Hispanic of any race (2008-2012 5-year est.); Average household size: 2.54 (2008-2012 5-year est.); Median age: 42.1 (2008-2012 5-year est.); Males per 100 females: 95.5 (2008-2012 5-year est.); Marriage status: 34.2% never married, 42.5% now married, 11.3% widowed, 12.0% divorced (2008-2012 5-year est.); Foreign born: 0.8% (2008-2012 5-year est.); Ancestry (includes multiple ancestries): 39.0% German, 24.2% Irish, 15.9% English, 15.3% Italian, 3.5% American (2008-2012 5-year est.).

Economy: Homeowner vacancy rate: 8.9%. Rental vacancy rate: 25.0%. (2008-2012 5-year est.); Employment by occupation: 9.9% management, business, and financial, 4.4% computer, engineering, and science, 7.1% education, legal, community service, arts, and media, 5.5% healthcare practitioners, 32.4% service, 8.2% sales and office, 17.6% natural resources, construction, and maintenance, 14.8% production, transportation, and material moving (2008-2012 5-year est.).

Income: Per capita income: $18,546 (2008-2012 5-year est.); Median household income: $33,125 (2008-2012 5-year est.); Average household income: $47,026 (2008-2012 5-year est.); Percent of households with income of $100,000 or more: 4.9% (2008-2012 5-year est.); Poverty rate: 21.1% (2008-2012 5-year est.).

Education: Percent of population age 25 and over with: High school diploma (including GED) or higher: 75.7% (2008-2012 5-year est.); Bachelor's degree or higher: 8.0% (2008-2012 5-year est.); Master's degree or higher: 0.0% (2008-2012 5-year est.).

Housing: Homeownership rate: 85.2% (2008-2012 5-year est.); Median home value: $53,500 (2008-2012 5-year est.); Median contract rent: $394 per month (2008-2012 5-year est.); Median year structure built: 1955 (2008-2012 5-year est.).
Health Insurance: 37.8% Private; 46.9% Public; 24.8% None. (2008-2012 5-year est.)
Transportation: Commute to work: 100.0% car, 0.0% public transportation, 0.0% walk, 0.0% work from home (2008-2012 5-year est.); Travel time to work: 13.7% less than 15 minutes, 22.4% 15 to 30 minutes, 16.8% 30 to 45 minutes, 20.5% 45 to 60 minutes, 26.7% 60 minutes or more (2008-2012 5-year est.)

Madison County

Located in southwestern Illinois; bounded on the west by the Mississippi River and the Missouri border; drained by Cahokia and Silver Creeks. Covers a land area of 715.582 square miles, a water area of 24.980 square miles, and is located in the Central Time Zone at 38.83° N. Lat., 89.90° W. Long. The county was founded in 1812. County seat is Edwardsville.

Madison County is part of the St. Louis, MO-IL Metropolitan Statistical Area. The entire metro area includes: Bond County, IL; Calhoun County, IL; Clinton County, IL; Jersey County, IL; Macoupin County, IL; Madison County, IL; Monroe County, IL; Saint Clair County, IL; Franklin County, MO; Jefferson County, MO; Lincoln County, MO; Saint Charles County, MO; Saint Louis County, MO; Warren County, MO; Saint Louis city, MO

Weather Station: Alton Melvin Price L&D									Elevation: 430 feet		
	Jan	Feb	Mar	Apr	May	Jun	Jul	Aug	Sep	Oct	Nov	Dec
High	38	42	53	65	75	84	88	87	80	67	54	42
Low	22	25	35	45	56	65	69	68	60	47	37	26
Precip	2.4	2.3	3.2	4.2	5.1	3.6	3.8	3.3	3.1	3.2	3.8	2.9
Snow	1.4	1.8	0.8	0.2	0.0	0.0	0.0	0.0	0.0	tr	0.1	0.5

High and Low temperatures in degrees Fahrenheit; Precipitation and Snow in inches

Population: 249,238 (1990); 258,941 (2000); 269,282 (2010); Race: 88.6% White, 7.9% Black/African American, 0.9% Asian, 0.2% American Indian/Alaska Native, 0.0% Native Hawaiian/Other Pacific Islander, 2.4% Some other race, 1.9% Two or more races, 2.7% Hispanic of any race (2008-2012 5-year est.); Density: 374.4 persons per square mile (2008-2012 5-year est.); Average household size: 2.45 (2008-2012 5-year est.); Median age: 38.4 (2008-2012 5-year est.); Males per 100 females: 95.5 (2008-2012 5-year est.).
Religion: Six largest groups: 13.8% Catholicism, 12.3% Baptist, 5.6% Lutheran, 4.6% Presbyterian-Reformed, 3.4% Methodist/Pietist, 3.3% Non-denominational Protestant (2010)
Economy: Unemployment rate: 6.0% (April 2014); Total civilian labor force: 135,980 (April 2014); Leading industries: 16.8% health care and social assistance; 15.1% retail trade; 15.0% manufacturing (2012); Farms: 1,110 totaling 307,135 acres (2012); Companies that employ 500 or more persons: 9 (2012); Companies that employ 100 to 499 persons: 110 (2012); Companies that employ less than 100 persons: 5,799 (2012); Black-owned businesses: 569 (2007); Hispanic-owned businesses: 526 (2007); Asian-owned businesses: n/a (2007); Women-owned businesses: 5,762 (2007); Single-family building permits issued: 385 (2013); Multi-family building permits issued: 140 (2013).
Income: Per capita income: $26,797 (2008-2012 5-year est.); Median household income: $52,756 (2008-2012 5-year est.); Average household income: $66,093 (2008-2012 5-year est.); Percent of households with income of $100,000 or more: 19.7% (2008-2012 5-year est.); Poverty rate: 13.8% (2008-2012 5-year est.); Bankruptcy rate: 3.85% (2013).
Taxes: Total county taxes per capita: $117 (2011); County property taxes per capita: $116 (2011).
Education: Percent of population age 25 and over with: High school diploma (including GED) or higher: 90.6% (2008-2012 5-year est.); Bachelor's degree or higher: 23.5% (2008-2012 5-year est.); Master's degree or higher: 8.3% (2008-2012 5-year est.).
Housing: Homeownership rate: 73.7% (2008-2012 5-year est.); Median home value: $124,900 (2008-2012 5-year est.); Median contract rent: $567 per month (2008-2012 5-year est.); Median year structure built: 1966 (2008-2012 5-year est.)
Health: Birth rate: 118.2 per 10,000 population (2013); Death rate: 99.5 per 10,000 population (2013); Age-adjusted cancer mortality rate: 190.1 deaths per 100,000 population (2011); Number of physicians: 12.2 per

10,000 population (2011); Hospital beds: 42.0 per 10,000 population (2010); Hospital admissions: 1,082.4 per 10,000 population (2010).
Environment: Air Quality Index: 43.8% good, 54.8% moderate, 1.4% unhealthy for sensitive individuals, 0.0% unhealthy (percent of days in 2013)
Elections: 2012 Presidential election results: 48.1% Obama, 49.5% Romney
National and State Parks: Horseshoe Lake State Park; Lovejoy State Memorial
Additional Information Contacts
Madison County Government . . . . (618) 692-6290
http://www.co.madison.il.us
Southwestern Madison County Chamber of Commerce . . . (618) 876-6400
http://www.chamberswmadisoncounty.com

Madison County Communities

ALHAMBRA (village). Covers a land area of 0.757 square miles and a water area of 0.008 square miles. Located at 38.89° N. Lat; 89.74° W. Long. Elevation is 564 feet.
Population: 709 (1990); 630 (2000); 681 (2010); Density: 875.9 persons per square mile (2008-2012 5-year est.); Race: 100.0% White, 0.0% Black/African American, 0.0% Asian, 0.0% American Indian/Alaska Native, 0.0% Native Hawaiian/Other Pacific Islander, 0.0% Some other race, 0.0% Two or more races, 0.0% Hispanic of any race (2008-2012 5-year est.); Average household size: 2.17 (2008-2012 5-year est.); Median age: 47.0 (2008-2012 5-year est.); Males per 100 females: 76.3 (2008-2012 5-year est.); Marriage status: 26.7% never married, 42.2% now married, 21.8% widowed, 9.3% divorced (2008-2012 5-year est.); Foreign born: 0.0% (2008-2012 5-year est.); Ancestry (includes multiple ancestries): 54.8% German, 15.7% Irish, 8.6% English, 3.9% French, 3.5% Polish (2008-2012 5-year est.).
Economy: Single-family building permits issued: 0 (2013); Multi-family building permits issued: 0 (2013); Homeowner vacancy rate: 0.0%. Rental vacancy rate: 10.3%. (2008-2012 5-year est.); Employment by occupation: 8.1% management, business, and financial, 1.6% computer, engineering, and science, 6.5% education, legal, community service, arts, and media, 5.5% healthcare practitioners, 17.4% service, 25.8% sales and office, 18.7% natural resources, construction, and maintenance, 16.5% production, transportation, and material moving (2008-2012 5-year est.).
Income: Per capita income: $24,535 (2008-2012 5-year est.); Median household income: $39,688 (2008-2012 5-year est.); Average household income: $54,925 (2008-2012 5-year est.); Percent of households with income of $100,000 or more: 22.9% (2008-2012 5-year est.); Poverty rate: 15.2% (2008-2012 5-year est.).
Education: Percent of population age 25 and over with: High school diploma (including GED) or higher: 85.1% (2008-2012 5-year est.); Bachelor's degree or higher: 11.2% (2008-2012 5-year est.); Master's degree or higher: 1.9% (2008-2012 5-year est.).
School District(s)
Highland CUSD 5 (PK-12)
2011-12 Enrollment: 3,080 . . . . (618) 654-2106
Housing: Homeownership rate: 71.9% (2008-2012 5-year est.); Median home value: $106,300 (2008-2012 5-year est.); Median contract rent: $442 per month (2008-2012 5-year est.); Median year structure built: 1962 (2008-2012 5-year est.).
Health Insurance: 76.3% Private; 31.8% Public; 5.5% None. (2008-2012 5-year est.)
Transportation: Commute to work: 94.5% car, 0.0% public transportation, 1.7% walk, 3.8% work from home (2008-2012 5-year est.); Travel time to work: 8.5% less than 15 minutes, 44.5% 15 to 30 minutes, 28.8% 30 to 45 minutes, 8.5% 45 to 60 minutes, 9.6% 60 minutes or more (2008-2012 5-year est.)

ALTON (city). Covers a land area of 15.470 square miles and a water area of 1.266 square miles. Located at 38.90° N. Lat; 90.15° W. Long. Elevation is 499 feet.
History: Alton's first known settler arrived about 1783, but significant settlement began between 1816 and 1818, when three towns were founded at this advantageous river location. One of these, planned by Colonel Rufus Easton and named for one of his sons, Alton, absorbed the other towns and was incorporated as a city in 1837. Alton was the site of the Lincoln-Shields duel in 1842, and the last Lincoln-Douglas debate in 1858.

Population: 32,905 (1990); 30,496 (2000); 27,865 (2010); Density: 1,801.4 persons per square mile (2008-2012 5-year est.); Race: 71.0% White, 24.1% Black/African American, 0.6% Asian, 0.6% American Indian/Alaska Native, 0.0% Native Hawaiian/Other Pacific Islander, 3.7% Some other race, 3.4% Two or more races, 2.0% Hispanic of any race (2008-2012 5-year est.); Average household size: 2.39 (2008-2012 5-year est.); Median age: 33.9 (2008-2012 5-year est.); Males per 100 females: 91.2 (2008-2012 5-year est.); Marriage status: 34.8% never married, 42.5% now married, 6.7% widowed, 16.0% divorced (2008-2012 5-year est.); Foreign born: 1.5% (2008-2012 5-year est.); Ancestry (includes multiple ancestries): 24.9% German, 12.3% Irish, 9.5% English, 4.8% American, 4.3% Italian (2008-2012 5-year est.).
Economy: Unemployment rate: 8.0% (April 2014); Total civilian labor force: 12,720 (April 2014); Single-family building permits issued: 1 (2013); Multi-family building permits issued: 12 (2013); Homeowner vacancy rate: 2.6%. Rental vacancy rate: 5.3%. (2008-2012 5-year est.); Employment by occupation: 8.8% management, business, and financial, 3.8% computer, engineering, and science, 12.8% education, legal, community service, arts, and media, 5.0% healthcare practitioners, 22.4% service, 23.1% sales and office, 8.6% natural resources, construction, and maintenance, 15.6% production, transportation, and material moving (2008-2012 5-year est.).
Income: Per capita income: $19,217 (2008-2012 5-year est.); Median household income: $35,776 (2008-2012 5-year est.); Average household income: $45,833 (2008-2012 5-year est.); Percent of households with income of $100,000 or more: 7.2% (2008-2012 5-year est.); Poverty rate: 23.5% (2008-2012 5-year est.).
Taxes: Total city taxes per capita: $353 (2011); City property taxes per capita: $138 (2011).
Education: Percent of population age 25 and over with: High school diploma (including GED) or higher: 88.4% (2008-2012 5-year est.); Bachelor's degree or higher: 18.3% (2008-2012 5-year est.); Master's degree or higher: 6.8% (2008-2012 5-year est.).
School District(s)
Alton CUSD 11 (PK-12)
   2011-12 Enrollment: 6,408 . . . . (618) 474-2600
Vocational/Technical School(s)
CALC Institute of Technology (Private, For-profit)
   Fall 2012 Enrollment: 182 . . . . (618) 474-0616
   2012-13 Tuition: $11,071
Housing: Homeownership rate: 62.4% (2008-2012 5-year est.); Median home value: $85,000 (2008-2012 5-year est.); Median contract rent: $516 per month (2008-2012 5-year est.); Median year structure built: 1948 (2008-2012 5-year est.).
Health Insurance: 60.4% Private; 42.8% Public; 11.7% None. (2008-2012 5-year est.)
Hospitals: Alton Memorial Hospital (222 beds); Saint Anthony's Health Center (192 beds)
Safety: Violent crime rate: 45.0 per 10,000 population; Property crime rate: 442.5 per 10,000 population (2012).
Transportation: Commute to work: 93.7% car, 1.5% public transportation, 1.4% walk, 2.1% work from home (2008-2012 5-year est.); Travel time to work: 34.5% less than 15 minutes, 33.9% 15 to 30 minutes, 19.1% 30 to 45 minutes, 8.0% 45 to 60 minutes, 4.6% 60 minutes or more (2008-2012 5-year est.); Amtrak: Train service available.
Airports: St. Louis Regional Airport (reliver airport)
Additional Information Contacts
City of Alton . . . . (618) 463-3500
   http://www.alton-il.com
RiverBend Growth Association . . . . (618) 467-2280
   http://www.growthassociation.com

BETHALTO (village). Covers a land area of 7.518 square miles and a water area of 0.080 square miles. Located at 38.90° N. Lat; 90.05° W. Long. Elevation is 525 feet.
History: Incorporated 1869.
Population: 9,507 (1990); 9,454 (2000); 9,521 (2010); Density: 1,264.5 persons per square mile (2008-2012 5-year est.); Race: 96.3% White, 1.0% Black/African American, 0.8% Asian, 0.0% American Indian/Alaska Native, 0.2% Native Hawaiian/Other Pacific Islander, 1.7% Some other race, 1.7% Two or more races, 1.1% Hispanic of any race (2008-2012 5-year est.); Average household size: 2.41 (2008-2012 5-year est.); Median age: 37.5 (2008-2012 5-year est.); Males per 100 females: 93.5 (2008-2012 5-year est.); Marriage status: 26.2% never married, 54.6% now married, 8.8% widowed, 10.3% divorced (2008-2012 5-year est.); Foreign born: 0.6% (2008-2012 5-year est.); Ancestry (includes multiple

ancestries): 34.1% German, 12.8% Irish, 12.6% English, 8.7% American, 7.6% Italian (2008-2012 5-year est.).
Economy: Single-family building permits issued: 9 (2013); Multi-family building permits issued: 0 (2013); Homeowner vacancy rate: 1.6%. Rental vacancy rate: 3.2%. (2008-2012 5-year est.); Employment by occupation: 11.7% management, business, and financial, 7.6% computer, engineering, and science, 6.9% education, legal, community service, arts, and media, 6.2% healthcare practitioners, 14.9% service, 29.2% sales and office, 8.5% natural resources, construction, and maintenance, 15.0% production, transportation, and material moving (2008-2012 5-year est.).
Income: Per capita income: $28,747 (2008-2012 5-year est.); Median household income: $57,500 (2008-2012 5-year est.); Average household income: $69,358 (2008-2012 5-year est.); Percent of households with income of $100,000 or more: 23.7% (2008-2012 5-year est.); Poverty rate: 13.5% (2008-2012 5-year est.).
Education: Percent of population age 25 and over with: High school diploma (including GED) or higher: 91.0% (2008-2012 5-year est.); Bachelor's degree or higher: 21.8% (2008-2012 5-year est.); Master's degree or higher: 6.1% (2008-2012 5-year est.).
School District(s)
Bethalto CUSD 8 (PK-12)
   2011-12 Enrollment: 2,603 . . . . (618) 377-7200
Housing: Homeownership rate: 69.5% (2008-2012 5-year est.); Median home value: $125,100 (2008-2012 5-year est.); Median contract rent: $572 per month (2008-2012 5-year est.); Median year structure built: 1972 (2008-2012 5-year est.).
Health Insurance: 72.2% Private; 34.2% Public; 5.5% None. (2008-2012 5-year est.)
Safety: Violent crime rate: 62.1 per 10,000 population; Property crime rate: 193.8 per 10,000 population (2012).
Transportation: Commute to work: 95.4% car, 0.2% public transportation, 1.0% walk, 3.0% work from home (2008-2012 5-year est.); Travel time to work: 23.5% less than 15 minutes, 43.5% 15 to 30 minutes, 18.8% 30 to 45 minutes, 8.8% 45 to 60 minutes, 5.4% 60 minutes or more (2008-2012 5-year est.)
Additional Information Contacts
Village of Bethalto . . . . (618) 377-8051
   http://www.bethalto.com

COLLINSVILLE (city). Covers a land area of 14.680 square miles and a water area of 0.194 square miles. Located at 38.68° N. Lat; 90.01° W. Long. Elevation is 561 feet.
History: Named for William Collins and his family, founders of the town. Collinsville was settled in 1817 by William Collins and his brothers from Connecticut. Between the five brothers they operated a store, blacksmith shop, shoe shop, wagon shop, sawmill, tannery, distillery, and a church. Collinsville was incorporated as a village in 1856, and as a city in 1859. The arrival of the railroad in 1869 led to mining of a coal seam and building of an ore-smelting furnace.
Population: 22,446 (1990); 24,707 (2000); 25,579 (2010); Density: 1,728.2 persons per square mile (2008-2012 5-year est.); Race: 83.5% White, 13.1% Black/African American, 0.4% Asian, 0.1% American Indian/Alaska Native, 0.0% Native Hawaiian/Other Pacific Islander, 2.9% Some other race, 2.5% Two or more races, 3.7% Hispanic of any race (2008-2012 5-year est.); Average household size: 2.27 (2008-2012 5-year est.); Median age: 37.0 (2008-2012 5-year est.); Males per 100 females: 96.8 (2008-2012 5-year est.); Marriage status: 34.2% never married, 45.7% now married, 6.1% widowed, 14.0% divorced (2008-2012 5-year est.); Foreign born: 1.9% (2008-2012 5-year est.); Ancestry (includes multiple ancestries): 27.1% German, 13.2% Irish, 9.9% English, 8.6% Italian, 5.2% American (2008-2012 5-year est.).
Economy: Unemployment rate: 5.9% (April 2014); Total civilian labor force: 13,687 (April 2014); Single-family building permits issued: 5 (2013); Multi-family building permits issued: 0 (2013); Homeowner vacancy rate: 2.5%. Rental vacancy rate: 4.8%. (2008-2012 5-year est.); Employment by occupation: 11.9% management, business, and financial, 6.6% computer, engineering, and science, 9.5% education, legal, community service, arts, and media, 4.5% healthcare practitioners, 17.4% service, 27.8% sales and office, 9.5% natural resources, construction, and maintenance, 12.8% production, transportation, and material moving (2008-2012 5-year est.).
Income: Per capita income: $26,957 (2008-2012 5-year est.); Median household income: $47,229 (2008-2012 5-year est.); Average household income: $60,347 (2008-2012 5-year est.); Percent of households with income of $100,000 or more: 15.6% (2008-2012 5-year est.); Poverty rate: 16.6% (2008-2012 5-year est.).

Taxes: Total city taxes per capita: $251 (2011); City property taxes per capita: $164 (2011).
Education: Percent of population age 25 and over with: High school diploma (including GED) or higher: 91.6% (2008-2012 5-year est.); Bachelor's degree or higher: 23.8% (2008-2012 5-year est.); Master's degree or higher: 7.3% (2008-2012 5-year est.).

School District(s)
Collinsville Area Career Ctr (11-12)
   2011-12 Enrollment: n/a . . . . (618) 346-6320
Collinsville CUSD 10 (PK-12)
   2011-12 Enrollment: 6,645 . . . . (618) 346-6350
Collinsville CUSD 10 (PK-12)
   2011-12 Enrollment: 6,645 . . . . (618) 346-6350

Two-year College(s)
Sanford-Brown College-Collinsville (Private, For-profit)
   Fall 2012 Enrollment: 282 . . . . (618) 344-5600
Housing: Homeownership rate: 61.7% (2008-2012 5-year est.); Median home value: $119,800 (2008-2012 5-year est.); Median contract rent: $605 per month (2008-2012 5-year est.); Median year structure built: 1966 (2008-2012 5-year est.).
Health Insurance: 69.4% Private; 30.3% Public; 11.7% None. (2008-2012 5-year est.)
Safety: Violent crime rate: 16.1 per 10,000 population; Property crime rate: 297.0 per 10,000 population (2012).
Transportation: Commute to work: 93.1% car, 2.4% public transportation, 0.4% walk, 2.5% work from home (2008-2012 5-year est.); Travel time to work: 24.5% less than 15 minutes, 36.5% 15 to 30 minutes, 28.0% 30 to 45 minutes, 7.4% 45 to 60 minutes, 3.6% 60 minutes or more (2008-2012 5-year est.)
Additional Information Contacts
City of Collinsville . . . . (618) 346-5200
   http://www2.collinsvilleil.org
Collinsville Chamber of Commerce . . . . (618) 344-2884
   http://www.discovercollinsville.com

COTTAGE HILLS (unincorporated postal area)
Zip Code: 62018
   Covers a land area of 3.172 square miles and a water area of 0.024 square miles. Located at 38.90° N. Lat; 90.08° W. Long. Elevation is 512 feet. Population: 3,604 (2010); Density: 1,136.0 persons per square mile (2010); Race: 93.2% White, 3.7% Black/African American, 0.1% Asian, 0.4% American Indian/Alaska Native, 0.2% Native Hawaiian/Other Pacific Islander, 2.4% Some other race, 1.9% Two or more races, 1.7% Hispanic of any race (2010); Average household size: 2.67 (2010); Median age: 36.8 (2010); Males per 100 females: 101.2 (2010); Homeownership rate: 71.4% (2010)

DORSEY (unincorporated postal area)
Zip Code: 62021
   Covers a land area of 20.033 square miles and a water area of 0.278 square miles. Located at 38.98° N. Lat; 89.97° W. Long. Elevation is 587 feet. Population: 936 (2010); Density: 46.7 persons per square mile (2010); Race: 98.2% White, 0.1% Black/African American, 0.3% Asian, 0.1% American Indian/Alaska Native, 0.0% Native Hawaiian/Other Pacific Islander, 1.3% Some other race, 1.1% Two or more races, 0.9% Hispanic of any race (2010); Average household size: 2.43 (2010); Median age: 48.8 (2010); Males per 100 females: 104.8 (2010); Homeownership rate: 90.4% (2010)

EAST ALTON (village). Covers a land area of 5.328 square miles and a water area of 0.234 square miles. Located at 38.88° N. Lat; 90.11° W. Long. Elevation is 436 feet.
History: In 1893 the Western Cartridge Company established a powder mill in East Alton and began the manufacture of ammunition.
Population: 7,063 (1990); 6,830 (2000); 6,301 (2010); Density: 1,184.1 persons per square mile (2008-2012 5-year est.); Race: 96.4% White, 0.3% Black/African American, 0.6% Asian, 0.0% American Indian/Alaska Native, 0.0% Native Hawaiian/Other Pacific Islander, 2.7% Some other race, 2.6% Two or more races, 1.0% Hispanic of any race (2008-2012 5-year est.); Average household size: 2.29 (2008-2012 5-year est.); Median age: 41.9 (2008-2012 5-year est.); Males per 100 females: 96.7 (2008-2012 5-year est.); Marriage status: 26.4% never married, 43.5% now married, 8.6% widowed, 21.6% divorced (2008-2012 5-year est.); Foreign born: 0.5% (2008-2012 5-year est.); Ancestry (includes multiple

ancestries): 35.2% German, 16.6% Irish, 11.0% American, 7.8% English, 5.9% Italian (2008-2012 5-year est.).
Economy: Single-family building permits issued: 47 (2013); Multi-family building permits issued: 0 (2013); Homeowner vacancy rate: 5.8%. Rental vacancy rate: 3.7%. (2008-2012 5-year est.); Employment by occupation: 5.4% management, business, and financial, 0.9% computer, engineering, and science, 5.3% education, legal, community service, arts, and media, 4.0% healthcare practitioners, 22.0% service, 24.8% sales and office, 14.0% natural resources, construction, and maintenance, 23.7% production, transportation, and material moving (2008-2012 5-year est.).
Income: Per capita income: $22,120 (2008-2012 5-year est.); Median household income: $36,418 (2008-2012 5-year est.); Average household income: $49,841 (2008-2012 5-year est.); Percent of households with income of $100,000 or more: 12.2% (2008-2012 5-year est.); Poverty rate: 23.0% (2008-2012 5-year est.).
Education: Percent of population age 25 and over with: High school diploma (including GED) or higher: 87.3% (2008-2012 5-year est.); Bachelor's degree or higher: 7.2% (2008-2012 5-year est.); Master's degree or higher: 2.1% (2008-2012 5-year est.).

School District(s)
East Alton SD 13 (PK-08)
   2011-12 Enrollment: 855 . . . . (618) 433-2051
Housing: Homeownership rate: 64.1% (2008-2012 5-year est.); Median home value: $74,400 (2008-2012 5-year est.); Median contract rent: $422 per month (2008-2012 5-year est.); Median year structure built: 1952 (2008-2012 5-year est.).
Health Insurance: 57.4% Private; 47.8% Public; 10.1% None. (2008-2012 5-year est.)
Safety: Violent crime rate: 23.9 per 10,000 population; Property crime rate: 448.7 per 10,000 population (2012).
Transportation: Commute to work: 93.8% car, 3.3% public transportation, 0.6% walk, 0.9% work from home (2008-2012 5-year est.); Travel time to work: 33.4% less than 15 minutes, 30.2% 15 to 30 minutes, 22.3% 30 to 45 minutes, 11.0% 45 to 60 minutes, 3.0% 60 minutes or more (2008-2012 5-year est.)
Additional Information Contacts
Village of East Alton . . . . (618) 259-7714
   http://www.eastaltonvillage.org

EDWARDSVILLE (city). County seat. Covers a land area of 19.564 square miles and a water area of 0.605 square miles. Located at 38.79° N. Lat; 89.99° W. Long. Elevation is 541 feet.
History: Edwardsville was settled by James Gillham of Kentucky in 1800. Some of his friends followed and a town was platted in 1813, named for Ninian Edwards, governor of Illinois Territory from 1809-1818. Edwardsville was incorporated in 1837.
Population: 14,579 (1990); 21,491 (2000); 24,293 (2010); Density: 1,231.5 persons per square mile (2008-2012 5-year est.); Race: 87.3% White, 8.0% Black/African American, 2.4% Asian, 0.1% American Indian/Alaska Native, 0.0% Native Hawaiian/Other Pacific Islander, 2.2% Some other race, 1.9% Two or more races, 2.1% Hispanic of any race (2008-2012 5-year est.); Average household size: 2.52 (2008-2012 5-year est.); Median age: 31.2 (2008-2012 5-year est.); Males per 100 females: 99.5 (2008-2012 5-year est.); Marriage status: 40.2% never married, 47.8% now married, 3.1% widowed, 8.9% divorced (2008-2012 5-year est.); Foreign born: 4.1% (2008-2012 5-year est.); Ancestry (includes multiple ancestries): 34.8% German, 13.4% Irish, 12.2% English, 6.4% Italian, 6.1% American (2008-2012 5-year est.).
Economy: Single-family building permits issued: 47 (2013); Multi-family building permits issued: 72 (2013); Homeowner vacancy rate: 2.5%. Rental vacancy rate: 0.0%. (2008-2012 5-year est.); Employment by occupation: 18.2% management, business, and financial, 7.8% computer, engineering, and science, 13.3% education, legal, community service, arts, and media, 7.3% healthcare practitioners, 16.7% service, 24.1% sales and office, 5.6% natural resources, construction, and maintenance, 6.9% production, transportation, and material moving (2008-2012 5-year est.).
Income: Per capita income: $33,023 (2008-2012 5-year est.); Median household income: $73,759 (2008-2012 5-year est.); Average household income: $91,595 (2008-2012 5-year est.); Percent of households with income of $100,000 or more: 34.5% (2008-2012 5-year est.); Poverty rate: 11.6% (2008-2012 5-year est.).
Education: Percent of population age 25 and over with: High school diploma (including GED) or higher: 95.9% (2008-2012 5-year est.); Bachelor's degree or higher: 50.4% (2008-2012 5-year est.); Master's degree or higher: 19.6% (2008-2012 5-year est.).

School District(s)

Edwardsville CUSD 7 (PK-12)
    2011-12 Enrollment: 7,480 . . . . (618) 656-1182

Four-year College(s)

Southern Illinois University Edwardsville (Public)
    Fall 2012 Enrollment: 14,055 . . . . (618) 650-2000
    2012-13 Tuition: In-state $9,251; Out-of-state $19,673

Vocational/Technical School(s)

Alvareitas College of Cosmetology-Edwardsville (Private, For-profit)
    Fall 2012 Enrollment: 54 . . . . (618) 656-2593
    2012-13 Tuition: $12,600

Housing: Homeownership rate: 69.9% (2008-2012 5-year est.); Median home value: $196,300 (2008-2012 5-year est.); Median contract rent: $705 per month (2008-2012 5-year est.); Median year structure built: 1976 (2008-2012 5-year est.).

Health Insurance: 87.5% Private; 15.0% Public; 7.2% None. (2008-2012 5-year est.)

Safety: Violent crime rate: 8.3 per 10,000 population; Property crime rate: 180.8 per 10,000 population (2012).

Transportation: Commute to work: 90.3% car, 2.1% public transportation, 3.1% walk, 3.1% work from home (2008-2012 5-year est.); Travel time to work: 37.9% less than 15 minutes, 25.4% 15 to 30 minutes, 24.5% 30 to 45 minutes, 8.3% 45 to 60 minutes, 3.8% 60 minutes or more (2008-2012 5-year est.).

Additional Information Contacts

City of Edwardsville . . . . (618) 692-7500
    http://www.cityofedwardsville.com
Edwardsville/Glen Carbon Chamber of Commerce . . . . . . (618) 656-7600
    http://www.edglenchamber.com

GLEN CARBON (village). Covers a land area of 10.036 square miles and a water area of 0.148 square miles. Located at 38.76° N. Lat; 89.98° W. Long. Elevation is 466 feet.

History: Incorporated 1892.

Population: 7,731 (1990); 10,425 (2000); 12,934 (2010); Density: 1,308.1 persons per square mile (2008-2012 5-year est.); Race: 83.6% White, 11.2% Black/African American, 2.3% Asian, 0.0% American Indian/Alaska Native, 0.0% Native Hawaiian/Other Pacific Islander, 2.9% Some other race, 2.2% Two or more races, 4.5% Hispanic of any race (2008-2012 5-year est.); Average household size: 2.63 (2008-2012 5-year est.); Median age: 33.4 (2008-2012 5-year est.); Males per 100 females: 91.4 (2008-2012 5-year est.); Marriage status: 31.8% never married, 52.1% now married, 7.7% widowed, 8.3% divorced (2008-2012 5-year est.); Foreign born: 6.3% (2008-2012 5-year est.); Ancestry (includes multiple ancestries): 29.0% German, 12.1% English, 11.8% Irish, 6.0% American, 5.7% Polish (2008-2012 5-year est.).

Economy: Single-family building permits issued: 42 (2013); Multi-family building permits issued: 0 (2013); Homeowner vacancy rate: 2.9%. Rental vacancy rate: 9.3%. (2008-2012 5-year est.); Employment by occupation: 17.8% management, business, and financial, 4.5% computer, engineering, and science, 13.4% education, legal, community service, arts, and media, 9.5% healthcare practitioners, 18.2% service, 24.0% sales and office, 5.2% natural resources, construction, and maintenance, 7.5% production, transportation, and material moving (2008-2012 5-year est.).

Income: Per capita income: $30,697 (2008-2012 5-year est.); Median household income: $66,296 (2008-2012 5-year est.); Average household income: $80,913 (2008-2012 5-year est.); Percent of households with income of $100,000 or more: 30.6% (2008-2012 5-year est.); Poverty rate: 10.5% (2008-2012 5-year est.).

Education: Percent of population age 25 and over with: High school diploma (including GED) or higher: 94.1% (2008-2012 5-year est.); Bachelor's degree or higher: 45.6% (2008-2012 5-year est.); Master's degree or higher: 17.9% (2008-2012 5-year est.).

School District(s)

Edwardsville CUSD 7 (PK-12)
    2011-12 Enrollment: 7,480 . . . . (618) 656-1182

Housing: Homeownership rate: 67.4% (2008-2012 5-year est.); Median home value: $201,800 (2008-2012 5-year est.); Median contract rent: $723 per month (2008-2012 5-year est.); Median year structure built: 1989 (2008-2012 5-year est.).

Health Insurance: 79.6% Private; 21.9% Public; 8.5% None. (2008-2012 5-year est.)

Safety: Violent crime rate: 6.2 per 10,000 population; Property crime rate: 56.6 per 10,000 population (2012).

Transportation: Commute to work: 95.6% car, 0.8% public transportation, 0.6% walk, 2.7% work from home (2008-2012 5-year est.); Travel time to work: 26.2% less than 15 minutes, 36.1% 15 to 30 minutes, 26.1% 30 to 45 minutes, 8.5% 45 to 60 minutes, 3.1% 60 minutes or more (2008-2012 5-year est.)

Additional Information Contacts

Edwardsville/Glen Carbon Chamber of Commerce . . . . . . (618) 656-7600
    http://www.edglenchamber.com
Village of Glen Carbon . . . . (618) 288-1200
    http://www.glen-carbon.il.us

GODFREY (village). Covers a land area of 34.639 square miles and a water area of 1.998 square miles. Located at 38.95° N. Lat; 90.22° W. Long. Elevation is 610 feet.

History: Godfrey grew around the Monticello College and Preparatory School for Girls, founded in 1835 by a retired Cape Cod sea captain, Benjamin Godfrey.

Population: 5,436 (1990); 16,286 (2000); 17,982 (2010); Density: 517.9 persons per square mile (2008-2012 5-year est.); Race: 95.1% White, 2.9% Black/African American, 0.3% Asian, 0.2% American Indian/Alaska Native, 0.0% Native Hawaiian/Other Pacific Islander, 1.5% Some other race, 1.3% Two or more races, 1.5% Hispanic of any race (2008-2012 5-year est.); Average household size: 2.31 (2008-2012 5-year est.); Median age: 45.7 (2008-2012 5-year est.); Males per 100 females: 90.4 (2008-2012 5-year est.); Marriage status: 25.3% never married, 57.0% now married, 8.8% widowed, 8.9% divorced (2008-2012 5-year est.); Foreign born: 1.6% (2008-2012 5-year est.); Ancestry (includes multiple ancestries): 38.9% German, 13.7% English, 13.4% Irish, 9.5% American, 4.0% French (2008-2012 5-year est.).

Economy: Single-family building permits issued: 6 (2013); Multi-family building permits issued: 12 (2013); Homeowner vacancy rate: 0.7%. Rental vacancy rate: 0.0%. (2008-2012 5-year est.); Employment by occupation: 14.3% management, business, and financial, 4.4% computer, engineering, and science, 8.2% education, legal, community service, arts, and media, 8.3% healthcare practitioners, 14.5% service, 26.1% sales and office, 9.6% natural resources, construction, and maintenance, 14.5% production, transportation, and material moving (2008-2012 5-year est.).

Income: Per capita income: $29,140 (2008-2012 5-year est.); Median household income: $52,705 (2008-2012 5-year est.); Average household income: $67,759 (2008-2012 5-year est.); Percent of households with income of $100,000 or more: 20.5% (2008-2012 5-year est.); Poverty rate: 11.8% (2008-2012 5-year est.).

Education: Percent of population age 25 and over with: High school diploma (including GED) or higher: 91.6% (2008-2012 5-year est.); Bachelor's degree or higher: 24.9% (2008-2012 5-year est.); Master's degree or higher: 8.9% (2008-2012 5-year est.).

School District(s)

Alton CUSD 11 (PK-12)
    2011-12 Enrollment: 6,408 . . . . (618) 474-2600

Two-year College(s)

Lewis and Clark Community College (Public)
    Fall 2012 Enrollment: 8,483 . . . . (618) 468-7000
    2012-13 Tuition: In-state $8,624; Out-of-state $11,340

Vocational/Technical School(s)

Alvareitas College of Cosmetology-Godfrey (Private, For-profit)
    Fall 2012 Enrollment: 41 . . . . (618) 466-8952
    2012-13 Tuition: $12,600

Housing: Homeownership rate: 82.0% (2008-2012 5-year est.); Median home value: $141,700 (2008-2012 5-year est.); Median contract rent: $591 per month (2008-2012 5-year est.); Median year structure built: 1970 (2008-2012 5-year est.).

Health Insurance: 79.4% Private; 32.3% Public; 6.4% None. (2008-2012 5-year est.)

Safety: Violent crime rate: 12.2 per 10,000 population; Property crime rate: 151.4 per 10,000 population (2012).

Transportation: Commute to work: 91.0% car, 1.7% public transportation, 2.1% walk, 4.5% work from home (2008-2012 5-year est.); Travel time to work: 33.3% less than 15 minutes, 32.3% 15 to 30 minutes, 18.3% 30 to 45 minutes, 11.4% 45 to 60 minutes, 4.7% 60 minutes or more (2008-2012 5-year est.)

Additional Information Contacts

RiverBend Growth Association . . . . (618) 467-2280
    http://www.growthassociation.com
Village of Godfrey . . . . (618) 466-3324
    http://www.godfreyil.org

GRANITE CITY (city). Covers a land area of 19.289 square miles and a water area of 1.413 square miles. Located at 38.73° N. Lat; 90.13° W. Long. Elevation is 423 feet.

History: Farmers settled here in the early 1800's, but Granite City began when William F. Niedringhaus purchased land here for his National Enameling and Stamping Company plant. The American Steel Foundry followed, and in 1896 Granite City was incorporated, named for the granite ware produced there.

Population: 32,862 (1990); 31,301 (2000); 29,849 (2010); Density: 1,551.0 persons per square mile (2008-2012 5-year est.); Race: 90.7% White, 5.1% Black/African American, 0.4% Asian, 0.3% American Indian/Alaska Native, 0.0% Native Hawaiian/Other Pacific Islander, 3.5% Some other race, 2.6% Two or more races, 4.5% Hispanic of any race (2008-2012 5-year est.); Average household size: 2.42 (2008-2012 5-year est.); Median age: 37.7 (2008-2012 5-year est.); Males per 100 females: 96.2 (2008-2012 5-year est.); Marriage status: 27.0% never married, 48.3% now married, 8.8% widowed, 15.9% divorced (2008-2012 5-year est.); Foreign born: 2.1% (2008-2012 5-year est.); Ancestry (includes multiple ancestries): 20.4% German, 19.1% Irish, 10.7% English, 9.6% American, 4.9% Italian (2008-2012 5-year est.).

Economy: Unemployment rate: 7.0% (April 2014); Total civilian labor force: 14,213 (April 2014); Single-family building permits issued: 12 (2013); Multi-family building permits issued: 0 (2013); Homeowner vacancy rate: 2.4%. Rental vacancy rate: 5.4%. (2008-2012 5-year est.); Employment by occupation: 10.0% management, business, and financial, 2.2% computer, engineering, and science, 8.2% education, legal, community service, arts, and media, 5.1% healthcare practitioners, 21.0% service, 25.5% sales and office, 8.0% natural resources, construction, and maintenance, 20.1% production, transportation, and material moving (2008-2012 5-year est.).

Income: Per capita income: $20,798 (2008-2012 5-year est.); Median household income: $41,799 (2008-2012 5-year est.); Average household income: $50,138 (2008-2012 5-year est.); Percent of households with income of $100,000 or more: 10.0% (2008-2012 5-year est.); Poverty rate: 18.8% (2008-2012 5-year est.).

Education: Percent of population age 25 and over with: High school diploma (including GED) or higher: 85.8% (2008-2012 5-year est.); Bachelor's degree or higher: 11.9% (2008-2012 5-year est.); Master's degree or higher: 3.4% (2008-2012 5-year est.).

School District(s)

Granite City CUSD 9 (PK-12)
   2011-12 Enrollment: 6,873 . . . . (618) 451-5800

Housing: Homeownership rate: 71.0% (2008-2012 5-year est.); Median home value: $83,600 (2008-2012 5-year est.); Median contract rent: $466 per month (2008-2012 5-year est.); Median year structure built: 1954 (2008-2012 5-year est.).

Health Insurance: 60.1% Private; 40.4% Public; 13.4% None. (2008-2012 5-year est.)

Hospitals: Gateway Regional Medical Center (393 beds)

Safety: Violent crime rate: 57.8 per 10,000 population; Property crime rate: 282.1 per 10,000 population (2012).

Transportation: Commute to work: 93.4% car, 1.7% public transportation, 0.7% walk, 3.1% work from home (2008-2012 5-year est.); Travel time to work: 31.4% less than 15 minutes, 35.6% 15 to 30 minutes, 24.2% 30 to 45 minutes, 5.9% 45 to 60 minutes, 2.9% 60 minutes or more (2008-2012 5-year est.).

Additional Information Contacts

City of Granite City . . . . (618) 452-6200
   http://www.granitecity.illinois.gov
Southwestern Madison County Chamber of Commerce . . . (618) 876-6400
   http://www.chamberswmadisoncounty.com

GRANTFORK (village). Covers a land area of 0.296 square miles and a water area of 0.008 square miles. Located at 38.83° N. Lat; 89.67° W. Long. Elevation is 535 feet.

Population: 273 (1990); 254 (2000); 337 (2010); Density: 1,144.7 persons per square mile (2008-2012 5-year est.); Race: 99.4% White, 0.0% Black/African American, 0.0% Asian, 0.0% American Indian/Alaska Native, 0.0% Native Hawaiian/Other Pacific Islander, 0.6% Some other race, 0.6% Two or more races, 1.5% Hispanic of any race (2008-2012 5-year est.); Average household size: 2.53 (2008-2012 5-year est.); Median age: 37.1 (2008-2012 5-year est.); Males per 100 females: 110.6 (2008-2012 5-year est.); Marriage status: 28.7% never married, 56.3% now married, 6.1% widowed, 9.0% divorced (2008-2012 5-year est.); Foreign born: 1.5% (2008-2012 5-year est.); Ancestry (includes multiple ancestries): 38.9% German, 16.2% Irish, 8.0% American, 5.6% Dutch, 4.7% English (2008-2012 5-year est.).

Economy: Single-family building permits issued: 0 (2013); Multi-family building permits issued: 0 (2013); Homeowner vacancy rate: 0.0%. Rental vacancy rate: 0.0%. (2008-2012 5-year est.); Employment by occupation: 13.9% management, business, and financial, 0.0% computer, engineering, and science, 6.6% education, legal, community service, arts, and media, 7.9% healthcare practitioners, 30.5% service, 16.6% sales and office, 16.6% natural resources, construction, and maintenance, 7.9% production, transportation, and material moving (2008-2012 5-year est.).

Income: Per capita income: $22,368 (2008-2012 5-year est.); Median household income: $46,875 (2008-2012 5-year est.); Average household income: $57,728 (2008-2012 5-year est.); Percent of households with income of $100,000 or more: 14.2% (2008-2012 5-year est.); Poverty rate: 8.0% (2008-2012 5-year est.).

Education: Percent of population age 25 and over with: High school diploma (including GED) or higher: 89.7% (2008-2012 5-year est.); Bachelor's degree or higher: 10.7% (2008-2012 5-year est.); Master's degree or higher: 0.4% (2008-2012 5-year est.).

Housing: Homeownership rate: 97.0% (2008-2012 5-year est.); Median home value: $113,900 (2008-2012 5-year est.); Median contract rent: $567 per month (2008-2012 5-year est.); Median year structure built: 1985 (2008-2012 5-year est.).

Health Insurance: 71.1% Private; 34.2% Public; 7.4% None. (2008-2012 5-year est.)

Safety: Violent crime rate: 0.0 per 10,000 population; Property crime rate: 0.0 per 10,000 population (2012).

Transportation: Commute to work: 86.6% car, 1.3% public transportation, 1.3% walk, 9.4% work from home (2008-2012 5-year est.); Travel time to work: 18.5% less than 15 minutes, 39.3% 15 to 30 minutes, 25.9% 30 to 45 minutes, 11.1% 45 to 60 minutes, 5.2% 60 minutes or more (2008-2012 5-year est.).

HAMEL (village). Covers a land area of 1.155 square miles and a water area of 0.010 square miles. Located at 38.89° N. Lat; 89.84° W. Long. Elevation is 545 feet.

Population: 530 (1990); 570 (2000); 816 (2010); Density: 593.1 persons per square mile (2008-2012 5-year est.); Race: 96.1% White, 0.7% Black/African American, 0.0% Asian, 0.0% American Indian/Alaska Native, 0.0% Native Hawaiian/Other Pacific Islander, 3.2% Some other race, 3.2% Two or more races, 0.0% Hispanic of any race (2008-2012 5-year est.); Average household size: 2.41 (2008-2012 5-year est.); Median age: 37.5 (2008-2012 5-year est.); Males per 100 females: 79.8 (2008-2012 5-year est.); Marriage status: 13.4% never married, 71.8% now married, 4.3% widowed, 10.5% divorced (2008-2012 5-year est.); Foreign born: 1.9% (2008-2012 5-year est.); Ancestry (includes multiple ancestries): 58.0% German, 12.1% Irish, 7.9% English, 6.1% French, 5.7% American (2008-2012 5-year est.).

Economy: Homeowner vacancy rate: 3.6%. Rental vacancy rate: 0.0%. (2008-2012 5-year est.); Employment by occupation: 9.3% management, business, and financial, 9.5% computer, engineering, and science, 11.4% education, legal, community service, arts, and media, 5.8% healthcare practitioners, 24.4% service, 27.1% sales and office, 6.9% natural resources, construction, and maintenance, 5.6% production, transportation, and material moving (2008-2012 5-year est.).

Income: Per capita income: $33,178 (2008-2012 5-year est.); Median household income: $76,250 (2008-2012 5-year est.); Average household income: $79,914 (2008-2012 5-year est.); Percent of households with income of $100,000 or more: 32.4% (2008-2012 5-year est.); Poverty rate: 5.0% (2008-2012 5-year est.).

Education: Percent of population age 25 and over with: High school diploma (including GED) or higher: 96.7% (2008-2012 5-year est.); Bachelor's degree or higher: 38.6% (2008-2012 5-year est.); Master's degree or higher: 11.0% (2008-2012 5-year est.).

School District(s)

Edwardsville CUSD 7 (PK-12)
   2011-12 Enrollment: 7,480 . . . . (618) 656-1182

Housing: Homeownership rate: 83.1% (2008-2012 5-year est.); Median home value: $158,600 (2008-2012 5-year est.); Median contract rent: $633 per month (2008-2012 5-year est.); Median year structure built: 1977 (2008-2012 5-year est.).

Health Insurance: 87.9% Private; 26.7% Public; 3.2% None. (2008-2012 5-year est.)

Transportation: Commute to work: 93.6% car, 0.5% public transportation, 0.0% walk, 4.5% work from home (2008-2012 5-year est.); Travel time to

work: 10.9% less than 15 minutes, 50.6% 15 to 30 minutes, 31.6% 30 to 45 minutes, 5.9% 45 to 60 minutes, 1.1% 60 minutes or more (2008-2012 5-year est.)

HARTFORD (village). Covers a land area of 4.664 square miles and a water area of 0.220 square miles. Located at 38.81° N. Lat; 90.09° W. Long. Elevation is 430 feet.

History: In 1915 the International Shoe Company established a tannery in Hartford, and the town developed around it.

Population: 1,676 (1990); 1,545 (2000); 1,429 (2010); Density: 330.4 persons per square mile (2008-2012 5-year est.); Race: 98.8% White, 0.0% Black/African American, 0.6% Asian, 0.4% American Indian/Alaska Native, 0.0% Native Hawaiian/Other Pacific Islander, 0.2% Some other race, 0.2% Two or more races, 0.1% Hispanic of any race (2008-2012 5-year est.); Average household size: 2.37 (2008-2012 5-year est.); Median age: 44.7 (2008-2012 5-year est.); Males per 100 females: 89.1 (2008-2012 5-year est.); Marriage status: 18.4% never married, 56.0% now married, 9.3% widowed, 16.3% divorced (2008-2012 5-year est.); Foreign born: 0.6% (2008-2012 5-year est.); Ancestry (includes multiple ancestries): 25.8% German, 13.7% Irish, 10.3% American, 9.8% English, 6.2% Dutch (2008-2012 5-year est.).

Economy: Single-family building permits issued: 2 (2013); Multi-family building permits issued: 0 (2013); Homeowner vacancy rate: 2.2%. Rental vacancy rate: 6.3%. (2008-2012 5-year est.); Employment by occupation: 9.4% management, business, and financial, 1.9% computer, engineering, and science, 6.0% education, legal, community service, arts, and media, 2.9% healthcare practitioners, 18.3% service, 19.2% sales and office, 17.8% natural resources, construction, and maintenance, 24.6% production, transportation, and material moving (2008-2012 5-year est.).

Income: Per capita income: $21,799 (2008-2012 5-year est.); Median household income: $44,408 (2008-2012 5-year est.); Average household income: $51,094 (2008-2012 5-year est.); Percent of households with income of $100,000 or more: 8.9% (2008-2012 5-year est.); Poverty rate: 8.2% (2008-2012 5-year est.).

Education: Percent of population age 25 and over with: High school diploma (including GED) or higher: 85.2% (2008-2012 5-year est.); Bachelor's degree or higher: 6.4% (2008-2012 5-year est.); Master's degree or higher: 1.1% (2008-2012 5-year est.).

School District(s)
Wood River-Hartford ESD 15 (PK-08)
    2011-12 Enrollment: 791 . . . . (618) 254-0607

Housing: Homeownership rate: 81.8% (2008-2012 5-year est.); Median home value: $67,600 (2008-2012 5-year est.); Median contract rent: $490 per month (2008-2012 5-year est.); Median year structure built: 1950 (2008-2012 5-year est.).

Health Insurance: 70.9% Private; 41.3% Public; 10.1% None. (2008-2012 5-year est.)

Safety: Violent crime rate: 14.0 per 10,000 population; Property crime rate: 203.7 per 10,000 population (2012).

Transportation: Commute to work: 90.6% car, 1.0% public transportation, 3.9% walk, 3.1% work from home (2008-2012 5-year est.); Travel time to work: 33.4% less than 15 minutes, 35.9% 15 to 30 minutes, 21.8% 30 to 45 minutes, 5.9% 45 to 60 minutes, 3.0% 60 minutes or more (2008-2012 5-year est.)

HIGHLAND (city). Covers a land area of 6.550 square miles and a water area of 1.041 square miles. Located at 38.77° N. Lat; 89.68° W. Long. Elevation is 525 feet.

History: Highland was settled about 1804 by families from Kentucky and North Carolina. In 1831 a group of Swiss colonists led by Dr. Caspar Koepfli located in Highland, and the community became a dairy producer. A leading firm here in the early 1900's was the Wicks Organ Company.

Population: 7,525 (1990); 8,438 (2000); 9,919 (2010); Density: 1,440.3 persons per square mile (2008-2012 5-year est.); Race: 94.5% White, 0.2% Black/African American, 1.5% Asian, 0.0% American Indian/Alaska Native, 0.0% Native Hawaiian/Other Pacific Islander, 3.8% Some other race, 0.8% Two or more races, 1.1% Hispanic of any race (2008-2012 5-year est.); Average household size: 2.34 (2008-2012 5-year est.); Median age: 37.6 (2008-2012 5-year est.); Males per 100 females: 86.0 (2008-2012 5-year est.); Marriage status: 22.8% never married, 57.3% now married, 7.7% widowed, 12.3% divorced (2008-2012 5-year est.); Foreign born: 2.2% (2008-2012 5-year est.); Ancestry (includes multiple ancestries): 45.1% German, 11.2% Irish, 9.4% American, 6.9% English, 5.4% Italian (2008-2012 5-year est.).

Economy: Single-family building permits issued: 20 (2013); Multi-family building permits issued: 28 (2013); Homeowner vacancy rate: 0.9%. Rental vacancy rate: 13.1%. (2008-2012 5-year est.); Employment by occupation: 15.8% management, business, and financial, 4.1% computer, engineering, and science, 8.7% education, legal, community service, arts, and media, 6.5% healthcare practitioners, 18.8% service, 25.2% sales and office, 10.4% natural resources, construction, and maintenance, 10.5% production, transportation, and material moving (2008-2012 5-year est.).

Income: Per capita income: $28,009 (2008-2012 5-year est.); Median household income: $54,024 (2008-2012 5-year est.); Average household income: $65,793 (2008-2012 5-year est.); Percent of households with income of $100,000 or more: 19.8% (2008-2012 5-year est.); Poverty rate: 5.4% (2008-2012 5-year est.).

Education: Percent of population age 25 and over with: High school diploma (including GED) or higher: 93.9% (2008-2012 5-year est.); Bachelor's degree or higher: 26.5% (2008-2012 5-year est.); Master's degree or higher: 9.1% (2008-2012 5-year est.).

School District(s)
Highland CUSD 5 (PK-12)
    2011-12 Enrollment: 3,080 . . . . (618) 654-2106

Housing: Homeownership rate: 70.1% (2008-2012 5-year est.); Median home value: $155,400 (2008-2012 5-year est.); Median contract rent: $593 per month (2008-2012 5-year est.); Median year structure built: 1973 (2008-2012 5-year est.).

Health Insurance: 81.0% Private; 23.7% Public; 7.5% None. (2008-2012 5-year est.)

Hospitals: St. Joseph's Hospital (106 beds)

Safety: Violent crime rate: 9.1 per 10,000 population; Property crime rate: 127.3 per 10,000 population (2012).

Transportation: Commute to work: 88.4% car, 2.7% public transportation, 0.9% walk, 5.7% work from home (2008-2012 5-year est.); Travel time to work: 43.7% less than 15 minutes, 23.0% 15 to 30 minutes, 17.4% 30 to 45 minutes, 8.2% 45 to 60 minutes, 7.7% 60 minutes or more (2008-2012 5-year est.)

Additional Information Contacts
City of Highland . . . . (618) 654-9891
    http://www.highlandil.gov
Highland Chamber of Commerce . . . . (618) 654-3721
    http://www.highlandillinois.com

HOLIDAY SHORES (CDP). Covers a land area of 1.623 square miles and a water area of 0.467 square miles. Located at 38.92° N. Lat; 89.94° W. Long. Elevation is 518 feet.

Population: n/a (1990); n/a (2000); 2,882 (2010); Density: 1,800.2 persons per square mile (2008-2012 5-year est.); Race: 93.1% White, 3.2% Black/African American, 0.6% Asian, 0.0% American Indian/Alaska Native, 0.0% Native Hawaiian/Other Pacific Islander, 3.1% Some other race, 2.6% Two or more races, 0.0% Hispanic of any race (2008-2012 5-year est.); Average household size: 2.72 (2008-2012 5-year est.); Median age: 37.7 (2008-2012 5-year est.); Males per 100 females: 105.8 (2008-2012 5-year est.); Marriage status: 18.5% never married, 67.7% now married, 4.2% widowed, 9.7% divorced (2008-2012 5-year est.); Foreign born: 1.9% (2008-2012 5-year est.); Ancestry (includes multiple ancestries): 34.4% German, 17.0% English, 10.5% Irish, 9.4% Italian, 8.7% American (2008-2012 5-year est.).

Economy: Homeowner vacancy rate: 0.0%. Rental vacancy rate: 0.0%. (2008-2012 5-year est.); Employment by occupation: 23.1% management, business, and financial, 6.7% computer, engineering, and science, 13.1% education, legal, community service, arts, and media, 6.7% healthcare practitioners, 9.2% service, 25.7% sales and office, 10.3% natural resources, construction, and maintenance, 5.1% production, transportation, and material moving (2008-2012 5-year est.).

Income: Per capita income: $36,805 (2008-2012 5-year est.); Median household income: $86,400 (2008-2012 5-year est.); Average household income: $98,867 (2008-2012 5-year est.); Percent of households with income of $100,000 or more: 40.6% (2008-2012 5-year est.); Poverty rate: 1.1% (2008-2012 5-year est.).

Education: Percent of population age 25 and over with: High school diploma (including GED) or higher: 97.9% (2008-2012 5-year est.); Bachelor's degree or higher: 38.6% (2008-2012 5-year est.); Master's degree or higher: 12.5% (2008-2012 5-year est.).

Housing: Homeownership rate: 95.7% (2008-2012 5-year est.); Median home value: $184,900 (2008-2012 5-year est.); Median contract rent: n/a per month (2008-2012 5-year est.); Median year structure built: 1988 (2008-2012 5-year est.).

Health Insurance: 85.8% Private; 16.1% Public; 7.4% None. (2008-2012 5-year est.)
Transportation: Commute to work: 91.1% car, 0.8% public transportation, 0.0% walk, 6.2% work from home (2008-2012 5-year est.); Travel time to work: 10.8% less than 15 minutes, 30.5% 15 to 30 minutes, 24.6% 30 to 45 minutes, 15.0% 45 to 60 minutes, 19.1% 60 minutes or more (2008-2012 5-year est.)

LIVINGSTON (village). Covers a land area of 1.054 square miles and a water area of 0.013 square miles. Located at 38.97° N. Lat; 89.76° W. Long. Elevation is 591 feet.
History: Incorporated 1905.
Population: 928 (1990); 825 (2000); 858 (2010); Density: 726.6 persons per square mile (2008-2012 5-year est.); Race: 97.0% White, 1.0% Black/African American, 0.3% Asian, 0.0% American Indian/Alaska Native, 0.0% Native Hawaiian/Other Pacific Islander, 1.7% Some other race, 1.7% Two or more races, 1.2% Hispanic of any race (2008-2012 5-year est.); Average household size: 2.21 (2008-2012 5-year est.); Median age: 44.3 (2008-2012 5-year est.); Males per 100 females: 102.6 (2008-2012 5-year est.); Marriage status: 27.5% never married, 52.2% now married, 7.5% widowed, 12.7% divorced (2008-2012 5-year est.); Foreign born: 0.3% (2008-2012 5-year est.); Ancestry (includes multiple ancestries): 29.6% German, 14.4% Irish, 12.5% Italian, 8.1% English, 6.4% American (2008-2012 5-year est.).
Economy: Single-family building permits issued: 0 (2013); Multi-family building permits issued: 0 (2013); Homeowner vacancy rate: 0.0%. Rental vacancy rate: 19.8%. (2008-2012 5-year est.); Employment by occupation: 7.6% management, business, and financial, 2.5% computer, engineering, and science, 2.7% education, legal, community service, arts, and media, 6.5% healthcare practitioners, 24.8% service, 23.4% sales and office, 14.4% natural resources, construction, and maintenance, 18.0% production, transportation, and material moving (2008-2012 5-year est.).
Income: Per capita income: $22,645 (2008-2012 5-year est.); Median household income: $42,383 (2008-2012 5-year est.); Average household income: $50,599 (2008-2012 5-year est.); Percent of households with income of $100,000 or more: 11.0% (2008-2012 5-year est.); Poverty rate: 15.1% (2008-2012 5-year est.).
Education: Percent of population age 25 and over with: High school diploma (including GED) or higher: 94.5% (2008-2012 5-year est.); Bachelor's degree or higher: 6.2% (2008-2012 5-year est.); Master's degree or higher: 0.9% (2008-2012 5-year est.).
School District(s)
Staunton CUSD 6 (PK-12)
    2011-12 Enrollment: 1,310 . . . . (618) 635-2962
Housing: Homeownership rate: 79.3% (2008-2012 5-year est.); Median home value: $84,000 (2008-2012 5-year est.); Median contract rent: $450 per month (2008-2012 5-year est.); Median year structure built: 1954 (2008-2012 5-year est.).
Health Insurance: 63.2% Private; 43.7% Public; 10.1% None. (2008-2012 5-year est.)
Transportation: Commute to work: 98.0% car, 0.0% public transportation, 0.6% walk, 1.4% work from home (2008-2012 5-year est.); Travel time to work: 11.6% less than 15 minutes, 23.5% 15 to 30 minutes, 42.0% 30 to 45 minutes, 15.9% 45 to 60 minutes, 7.0% 60 minutes or more (2008-2012 5-year est.)

MADISON (city). Covers a land area of 14.554 square miles and a water area of 2.631 square miles. Located at 38.68° N. Lat; 90.11° W. Long. Elevation is 413 feet.
History: The Madison Land Syndicate was formed in 1887 by a group of St. Louis businessmen who promoted the construction of Merchants Bridge over the Mississippi River. An American Car and Foundry plant was built near the new bridge, and the town of Madison was incorporated in 1891 by the Land Syndicate.
Population: 4,629 (1990); 4,545 (2000); 3,891 (2010); Density: 291.9 persons per square mile (2008-2012 5-year est.); Race: 47.4% White, 46.0% Black/African American, 0.0% Asian, 0.0% American Indian/Alaska Native, 0.0% Native Hawaiian/Other Pacific Islander, 6.6% Some other race, 5.9% Two or more races, 4.1% Hispanic of any race (2008-2012 5-year est.); Average household size: 2.27 (2008-2012 5-year est.); Median age: 36.7 (2008-2012 5-year est.); Males per 100 females: 85.3 (2008-2012 5-year est.); Marriage status: 46.7% never married, 28.0% now married, 8.4% widowed, 16.8% divorced (2008-2012 5-year est.); Foreign born: 4.3% (2008-2012 5-year est.); Ancestry (includes multiple

ancestries): 13.4% European, 10.1% German, 8.4% Irish, 3.3% American, 2.8% Polish (2008-2012 5-year est.).
Economy: Single-family building permits issued: 0 (2013); Multi-family building permits issued: 0 (2013); Homeowner vacancy rate: 4.1%. Rental vacancy rate: 0.0%. (2008-2012 5-year est.); Employment by occupation: 5.0% management, business, and financial, 0.7% computer, engineering, and science, 3.4% education, legal, community service, arts, and media, 1.3% healthcare practitioners, 35.3% service, 17.8% sales and office, 11.0% natural resources, construction, and maintenance, 25.5% production, transportation, and material moving (2008-2012 5-year est.).
Income: Per capita income: $18,053 (2008-2012 5-year est.); Median household income: $22,056 (2008-2012 5-year est.); Average household income: $40,740 (2008-2012 5-year est.); Percent of households with income of $100,000 or more: 5.3% (2008-2012 5-year est.); Poverty rate: 37.4% (2008-2012 5-year est.).
Education: Percent of population age 25 and over with: High school diploma (including GED) or higher: 72.4% (2008-2012 5-year est.); Bachelor's degree or higher: 6.7% (2008-2012 5-year est.); Master's degree or higher: 3.3% (2008-2012 5-year est.).
School District(s)
Madison CUSD 12 (PK-12)
    2011-12 Enrollment: 792 . . . . (618) 877-1712
Housing: Homeownership rate: 58.1% (2008-2012 5-year est.); Median home value: $50,900 (2008-2012 5-year est.); Median contract rent: $529 per month (2008-2012 5-year est.); Median year structure built: 1950 (2008-2012 5-year est.).
Health Insurance: 33.2% Private; 51.1% Public; 22.9% None. (2008-2012 5-year est.)
Transportation: Commute to work: 85.6% car, 6.9% public transportation, 0.9% walk, 5.5% work from home (2008-2012 5-year est.); Travel time to work: 37.2% less than 15 minutes, 38.0% 15 to 30 minutes, 12.1% 30 to 45 minutes, 7.8% 45 to 60 minutes, 4.9% 60 minutes or more (2008-2012 5-year est.)

MARINE (village). Covers a land area of 0.689 square miles and a water area of 0.020 square miles. Located at 38.79° N. Lat; 89.78° W. Long. Elevation is 522 feet.
Population: 972 (1990); 910 (2000); 960 (2010); Density: 1,692.3 persons per square mile (2008-2012 5-year est.); Race: 99.1% White, 0.0% Black/African American, 0.0% Asian, 0.0% American Indian/Alaska Native, 0.0% Native Hawaiian/Other Pacific Islander, 0.9% Some other race, 0.9% Two or more races, 0.0% Hispanic of any race (2008-2012 5-year est.); Average household size: 2.55 (2008-2012 5-year est.); Median age: 36.3 (2008-2012 5-year est.); Males per 100 females: 109.7 (2008-2012 5-year est.); Marriage status: 31.7% never married, 53.8% now married, 4.7% widowed, 9.8% divorced (2008-2012 5-year est.); Foreign born: 0.0% (2008-2012 5-year est.); Ancestry (includes multiple ancestries): 49.8% German, 14.8% Irish, 6.5% American, 6.3% English, 5.1% Polish (2008-2012 5-year est.).
Economy: Single-family building permits issued: 1 (2013); Multi-family building permits issued: 0 (2013); Homeowner vacancy rate: 3.6%. Rental vacancy rate: 0.0%. (2008-2012 5-year est.); Employment by occupation: 12.0% management, business, and financial, 2.8% computer, engineering, and science, 11.9% education, legal, community service, arts, and media, 1.2% healthcare practitioners, 20.2% service, 24.7% sales and office, 12.2% natural resources, construction, and maintenance, 15.1% production, transportation, and material moving (2008-2012 5-year est.).
Income: Per capita income: $28,133 (2008-2012 5-year est.); Median household income: $54,911 (2008-2012 5-year est.); Average household income: $71,174 (2008-2012 5-year est.); Percent of households with income of $100,000 or more: 18.4% (2008-2012 5-year est.); Poverty rate: 5.0% (2008-2012 5-year est.).
Education: Percent of population age 25 and over with: High school diploma (including GED) or higher: 91.2% (2008-2012 5-year est.); Bachelor's degree or higher: 18.5% (2008-2012 5-year est.); Master's degree or higher: 4.5% (2008-2012 5-year est.).
School District(s)
Triad CUSD 2 (PK-12)
    2011-12 Enrollment: 3,652 . . . . (618) 667-8851
Housing: Homeownership rate: 81.4% (2008-2012 5-year est.); Median home value: $127,900 (2008-2012 5-year est.); Median contract rent: $597 per month (2008-2012 5-year est.); Median year structure built: 1957 (2008-2012 5-year est.).
Health Insurance: 74.4% Private; 26.4% Public; 10.3% None. (2008-2012 5-year est.)

Safety: Violent crime rate: 20.9 per 10,000 population; Property crime rate: 52.2 per 10,000 population (2012).
Transportation: Commute to work: 96.0% car, 0.8% public transportation, 0.8% walk, 1.8% work from home (2008-2012 5-year est.); Travel time to work: 18.6% less than 15 minutes, 39.2% 15 to 30 minutes, 31.1% 30 to 45 minutes, 7.2% 45 to 60 minutes, 3.9% 60 minutes or more (2008-2012 5-year est.)

MARYVILLE (village).

MARYVILLE (village). Covers a land area of 5.340 square miles and a water area of 0.078 square miles. Located at 38.73° N. Lat; 89.97° W. Long. Elevation is 577 feet.
Population: 2,576 (1990); 4,651 (2000); 7,487 (2010); Density: 1,400.9 persons per square mile (2008-2012 5-year est.); Race: 95.7% White, 2.0% Black/African American, 0.5% Asian, 0.0% American Indian/Alaska Native, 0.0% Native Hawaiian/Other Pacific Islander, 1.8% Some other race, 0.7% Two or more races, 4.5% Hispanic of any race (2008-2012 5-year est.); Average household size: 2.40 (2008-2012 5-year est.); Median age: 42.3 (2008-2012 5-year est.); Males per 100 females: 97.0 (2008-2012 5-year est.); Marriage status: 23.2% never married, 60.8% now married, 9.1% widowed, 7.0% divorced (2008-2012 5-year est.); Foreign born: 1.1% (2008-2012 5-year est.); Ancestry (includes multiple ancestries): 36.4% German, 15.7% Irish, 11.4% Italian, 7.6% English, 6.9% American (2008-2012 5-year est.).
Economy: Single-family building permits issued: 33 (2013); Multi-family building permits issued: 12 (2013); Homeowner vacancy rate: 0.0%. Rental vacancy rate: 0.0%. (2008-2012 5-year est.); Employment by occupation: 16.6% management, business, and financial, 8.7% computer, engineering, and science, 14.9% education, legal, community service, arts, and media, 5.4% healthcare practitioners, 11.8% service, 27.8% sales and office, 4.5% natural resources, construction, and maintenance, 10.4% production, transportation, and material moving (2008-2012 5-year est.).
Income: Per capita income: $34,987 (2008-2012 5-year est.); Median household income: $76,580 (2008-2012 5-year est.); Average household income: $84,753 (2008-2012 5-year est.); Percent of households with income of $100,000 or more: 35.5% (2008-2012 5-year est.); Poverty rate: 5.0% (2008-2012 5-year est.).
Education: Percent of population age 25 and over with: High school diploma (including GED) or higher: 94.6% (2008-2012 5-year est.); Bachelor's degree or higher: 37.4% (2008-2012 5-year est.); Master's degree or higher: 15.1% (2008-2012 5-year est.).

School District(s)

Collinsville CUSD 10 (PK-12)
    2011-12 Enrollment: 6,645 . . . . (618) 346-6350
Housing: Homeownership rate: 81.6% (2008-2012 5-year est.); Median home value: $197,800 (2008-2012 5-year est.); Median contract rent: $633 per month (2008-2012 5-year est.); Median year structure built: 1994 (2008-2012 5-year est.).
Health Insurance: 89.3% Private; 20.5% Public; 2.9% None. (2008-2012 5-year est.)
Hospitals: Anderson Hospital (130 beds)
Safety: Violent crime rate: 16.1 per 10,000 population; Property crime rate: 50.9 per 10,000 population (2012).
Transportation: Commute to work: 94.6% car, 0.0% public transportation, 1.2% walk, 3.4% work from home (2008-2012 5-year est.); Travel time to work: 26.1% less than 15 minutes, 36.4% 15 to 30 minutes, 29.5% 30 to 45 minutes, 5.8% 45 to 60 minutes, 2.3% 60 minutes or more (2008-2012 5-year est.)
Additional Information Contacts
Village of Maryville . . . . (618) 345-7028
    http://www.vil.maryville.il.us

MITCHELL (CDP).

MITCHELL (CDP). Covers a land area of 0.588 square miles and a water area of 0 square miles. Located at 38.76° N. Lat; 90.08° W. Long. Elevation is 427 feet.
Population: n/a (1990); n/a (2000); 1,356 (2010); Density: 2,246.0 persons per square mile (2008-2012 5-year est.); Race: 97.3% White, 1.7% Black/African American, 1.1% Asian, 0.0% American Indian/Alaska Native, 0.0% Native Hawaiian/Other Pacific Islander, 0.0% Some other race, 0.0% Two or more races, 0.0% Hispanic of any race (2008-2012 5-year est.); Average household size: 2.40 (2008-2012 5-year est.); Median age: 46.1 (2008-2012 5-year est.); Males per 100 females: 85.8 (2008-2012 5-year est.); Marriage status: 24.5% never married, 53.3% now married, 11.1% widowed, 11.1% divorced (2008-2012 5-year est.); Foreign born: 1.1% (2008-2012 5-year est.); Ancestry (includes multiple

ancestries): 20.2% American, 10.1% German, 8.9% English, 5.3% Dutch, 5.2% Scotch-Irish (2008-2012 5-year est.).
Economy: Homeowner vacancy rate: 0.0%. Rental vacancy rate: 0.0%. (2008-2012 5-year est.); Employment by occupation: 7.1% management, business, and financial, 1.2% computer, engineering, and science, 3.9% education, legal, community service, arts, and media, 15.3% healthcare practitioners, 13.5% service, 24.6% sales and office, 13.5% natural resources, construction, and maintenance, 20.9% production, transportation, and material moving (2008-2012 5-year est.).
Income: Per capita income: $25,755 (2008-2012 5-year est.); Median household income: $56,808 (2008-2012 5-year est.); Average household income: $61,231 (2008-2012 5-year est.); Percent of households with income of $100,000 or more: 8.4% (2008-2012 5-year est.); Poverty rate: 2.6% (2008-2012 5-year est.).
Education: Percent of population age 25 and over with: High school diploma (including GED) or higher: 94.5% (2008-2012 5-year est.); Bachelor's degree or higher: 13.3% (2008-2012 5-year est.); Master's degree or higher: 2.0% (2008-2012 5-year est.).
Housing: Homeownership rate: 93.1% (2008-2012 5-year est.); Median home value: $94,700 (2008-2012 5-year est.); Median contract rent: n/a per month (2008-2012 5-year est.); Median year structure built: 1962 (2008-2012 5-year est.).
Health Insurance: 79.8% Private; 30.4% Public; 10.9% None. (2008-2012 5-year est.)
Transportation: Commute to work: 87.3% car, 0.0% public transportation, 0.0% walk, 12.7% work from home (2008-2012 5-year est.); Travel time to work: 23.9% less than 15 minutes, 46.8% 15 to 30 minutes, 19.2% 30 to 45 minutes, 10.1% 45 to 60 minutes, 0.0% 60 minutes or more (2008-2012 5-year est.)

MORO (unincorporated postal area)

Zip Code: 62067
    Covers a land area of 18.419 square miles and a water area of 0.164 square miles. Located at 38.92° N. Lat; 89.98° W. Long. Elevation is 531 feet. Population: 2,401 (2010); Density: 130.4 persons per square mile (2010); Race: 97.8% White, 0.5% Black/African American, 0.7% Asian, 0.0% American Indian/Alaska Native, 0.0% Native Hawaiian/Other Pacific Islander, 1.0% Some other race, 0.6% Two or more races, 1.2% Hispanic of any race (2010); Average household size: 2.49 (2010); Median age: 42.6 (2010); Males per 100 females: 95.7 (2010); Homeownership rate: 86.0% (2010)

NEW DOUGLAS (village).

NEW DOUGLAS (village). Covers a land area of 1.065 square miles and a water area of 0.002 square miles. Located at 38.97° N. Lat; 89.66° W. Long. Elevation is 620 feet.
Population: 387 (1990); 369 (2000); 319 (2010); Density: 354.1 persons per square mile (2008-2012 5-year est.); Race: 95.8% White, 0.8% Black/African American, 0.0% Asian, 0.0% American Indian/Alaska Native, 0.0% Native Hawaiian/Other Pacific Islander, 3.4% Some other race, 3.4% Two or more races, 0.0% Hispanic of any race (2008-2012 5-year est.); Average household size: 2.79 (2008-2012 5-year est.); Median age: 40.2 (2008-2012 5-year est.); Males per 100 females: 99.5 (2008-2012 5-year est.); Marriage status: 23.3% never married, 58.9% now married, 4.8% widowed, 13.0% divorced (2008-2012 5-year est.); Foreign born: 2.1% (2008-2012 5-year est.); Ancestry (includes multiple ancestries): 39.3% German, 19.6% Irish, 13.8% English, 11.1% Polish, 10.9% French (2008-2012 5-year est.).
Economy: Single-family building permits issued: 0 (2013); Multi-family building permits issued: 0 (2013); Homeowner vacancy rate: 0.0%. Rental vacancy rate: 6.0%. (2008-2012 5-year est.); Employment by occupation: 3.8% management, business, and financial, 2.7% computer, engineering, and science, 9.2% education, legal, community service, arts, and media, 1.1% healthcare practitioners, 21.2% service, 27.2% sales and office, 21.7% natural resources, construction, and maintenance, 13.0% production, transportation, and material moving (2008-2012 5-year est.).
Income: Per capita income: $23,467 (2008-2012 5-year est.); Median household income: $49,306 (2008-2012 5-year est.); Average household income: $62,104 (2008-2012 5-year est.); Percent of households with income of $100,000 or more: 16.3% (2008-2012 5-year est.); Poverty rate: 17.8% (2008-2012 5-year est.).
Education: Percent of population age 25 and over with: High school diploma (including GED) or higher: 84.3% (2008-2012 5-year est.); Bachelor's degree or higher: 7.1% (2008-2012 5-year est.); Master's degree or higher: 2.8% (2008-2012 5-year est.).

School District(s)

Highland CUSD 5 (PK-12)

    2011-12 Enrollment: 3,080 . . . . (618) 654-2106

Housing: Homeownership rate: 65.2% (2008-2012 5-year est.); Median home value: $88,000 (2008-2012 5-year est.); Median contract rent: $467 per month (2008-2012 5-year est.); Median year structure built: 1953 (2008-2012 5-year est.).

Health Insurance: 56.0% Private; 37.9% Public; 16.7% None. (2008-2012 5-year est.)

Transportation: Commute to work: 96.3% car, 0.0% public transportation, 0.6% walk, 1.9% work from home (2008-2012 5-year est.); Travel time to work: 12.0% less than 15 minutes, 32.9% 15 to 30 minutes, 19.6% 30 to 45 minutes, 25.9% 45 to 60 minutes, 9.5% 60 minutes or more (2008-2012 5-year est.).

PONTOON BEACH (village). Covers a land area of 10.016 square miles and a water area of 2.544 square miles. Located at 38.71° N. Lat; 90.08° W. Long. Elevation is 417 feet.

Population: 4,013 (1990); 5,620 (2000); 5,836 (2010); Density: 578.1 persons per square mile (2008-2012 5-year est.); Race: 85.0% White, 9.6% Black/African American, 2.2% Asian, 0.0% American Indian/Alaska Native, 0.0% Native Hawaiian/Other Pacific Islander, 3.2% Some other race, 1.7% Two or more races, 4.9% Hispanic of any race (2008-2012 5-year est.); Average household size: 2.60 (2008-2012 5-year est.); Median age: 38.4 (2008-2012 5-year est.); Males per 100 females: 93.0 (2008-2012 5-year est.); Marriage status: 32.2% never married, 51.3% now married, 5.2% widowed, 11.3% divorced (2008-2012 5-year est.); Foreign born: 6.4% (2008-2012 5-year est.); Ancestry (includes multiple ancestries): 22.5% German, 14.6% Irish, 8.8% English, 7.5% American, 4.1% Dutch (2008-2012 5-year est.).

Economy: Single-family building permits issued: 3 (2013); Multi-family building permits issued: 0 (2013); Homeowner vacancy rate: 0.0%. Rental vacancy rate: 17.6%. (2008-2012 5-year est.); Employment by occupation: 9.3% management, business, and financial, 3.7% computer, engineering, and science, 7.5% education, legal, community service, arts, and media, 4.8% healthcare practitioners, 21.0% service, 21.5% sales and office, 9.4% natural resources, construction, and maintenance, 22.8% production, transportation, and material moving (2008-2012 5-year est.).

Income: Per capita income: $25,046 (2008-2012 5-year est.); Median household income: $53,159 (2008-2012 5-year est.); Average household income: $63,854 (2008-2012 5-year est.); Percent of households with income of $100,000 or more: 19.7% (2008-2012 5-year est.); Poverty rate: 19.3% (2008-2012 5-year est.).

Education: Percent of population age 25 and over with: High school diploma (including GED) or higher: 85.6% (2008-2012 5-year est.); Bachelor's degree or higher: 16.2% (2008-2012 5-year est.); Master's degree or higher: 3.9% (2008-2012 5-year est.).

Housing: Homeownership rate: 77.1% (2008-2012 5-year est.); Median home value: $90,700 (2008-2012 5-year est.); Median contract rent: $589 per month (2008-2012 5-year est.); Median year structure built: 1976 (2008-2012 5-year est.).

Health Insurance: 63.1% Private; 29.3% Public; 16.2% None. (2008-2012 5-year est.)

Safety: Violent crime rate: 5.2 per 10,000 population; Property crime rate: 194.1 per 10,000 population (2012).

Transportation: Commute to work: 96.0% car, 0.9% public transportation, 1.3% walk, 0.2% work from home (2008-2012 5-year est.); Travel time to work: 22.0% less than 15 minutes, 44.9% 15 to 30 minutes, 26.3% 30 to 45 minutes, 3.7% 45 to 60 minutes, 3.1% 60 minutes or more (2008-2012 5-year est.).

Additional Information Contacts

Village of Pontoon Beach . . . . (618) 931-6100

    http://pontoon-beach.org

ROSEWOOD HEIGHTS (CDP). Covers a land area of 1.655 square miles and a water area of 0.003 square miles. Located at 38.89° N. Lat; 90.07° W. Long. Elevation is 548 feet.

Population: 4,821 (1990); 4,262 (2000); 4,038 (2010); Density: 2,452.3 persons per square mile (2008-2012 5-year est.); Race: 99.3% White, 0.4% Black/African American, 0.3% Asian, 0.0% American Indian/Alaska Native, 0.0% Native Hawaiian/Other Pacific Islander, 0.0% Some other race, 0.0% Two or more races, 0.0% Hispanic of any race (2008-2012 5-year est.); Average household size: 2.49 (2008-2012 5-year est.); Median age: 41.9 (2008-2012 5-year est.); Males per 100 females: 104.6 (2008-2012 5-year est.); Marriage status: 23.2% never married, 61.5%

now married, 3.4% widowed, 11.9% divorced (2008-2012 5-year est.); Foreign born: 0.7% (2008-2012 5-year est.); Ancestry (includes multiple ancestries): 28.4% German, 21.4% Irish, 10.8% American, 9.3% English, 6.9% French (2008-2012 5-year est.).

Economy: Homeowner vacancy rate: 0.0%. Rental vacancy rate: 12.8%. (2008-2012 5-year est.); Employment by occupation: 14.7% management, business, and financial, 0.8% computer, engineering, and science, 6.5% education, legal, community service, arts, and media, 4.4% healthcare practitioners, 12.0% service, 30.2% sales and office, 7.6% natural resources, construction, and maintenance, 23.9% production, transportation, and material moving (2008-2012 5-year est.).

Income: Per capita income: $25,754 (2008-2012 5-year est.); Median household income: $55,797 (2008-2012 5-year est.); Average household income: $63,865 (2008-2012 5-year est.); Percent of households with income of $100,000 or more: 19.4% (2008-2012 5-year est.); Poverty rate: 11.1% (2008-2012 5-year est.).

Education: Percent of population age 25 and over with: High school diploma (including GED) or higher: 92.5% (2008-2012 5-year est.); Bachelor's degree or higher: 11.1% (2008-2012 5-year est.); Master's degree or higher: 3.7% (2008-2012 5-year est.).

Housing: Homeownership rate: 86.9% (2008-2012 5-year est.); Median home value: $112,600 (2008-2012 5-year est.); Median contract rent: $586 per month (2008-2012 5-year est.); Median year structure built: 1959 (2008-2012 5-year est.).

Health Insurance: 78.0% Private; 31.5% Public; 7.6% None. (2008-2012 5-year est.)

Transportation: Commute to work: 96.4% car, 0.0% public transportation, 0.0% walk, 2.9% work from home (2008-2012 5-year est.); Travel time to work: 36.1% less than 15 minutes, 31.8% 15 to 30 minutes, 24.1% 30 to 45 minutes, 6.4% 45 to 60 minutes, 1.6% 60 minutes or more (2008-2012 5-year est.).

ROXANA (village). Covers a land area of 7.230 square miles and a water area of 0.132 square miles. Located at 38.82° N. Lat; 90.05° W. Long. Elevation is 446 feet.

History: Incorporated 1921.

Population: 1,562 (1990); 1,547 (2000); 1,542 (2010); Density: 217.4 persons per square mile (2008-2012 5-year est.); Race: 96.2% White, 1.5% Black/African American, 0.1% Asian, 0.0% American Indian/Alaska Native, 0.0% Native Hawaiian/Other Pacific Islander, 2.2% Some other race, 2.2% Two or more races, 3.1% Hispanic of any race (2008-2012 5-year est.); Average household size: 2.54 (2008-2012 5-year est.); Median age: 35.9 (2008-2012 5-year est.); Males per 100 females: 95.3 (2008-2012 5-year est.); Marriage status: 26.7% never married, 53.6% now married, 6.0% widowed, 13.7% divorced (2008-2012 5-year est.); Foreign born: 2.9% (2008-2012 5-year est.); Ancestry (includes multiple ancestries): 27.6% German, 19.1% Irish, 9.4% American, 7.3% English, 5.9% Polish (2008-2012 5-year est.).

Economy: Single-family building permits issued: 0 (2013); Multi-family building permits issued: 0 (2013); Homeowner vacancy rate: 0.0%. Rental vacancy rate: 5.4%. (2008-2012 5-year est.); Employment by occupation: 10.7% management, business, and financial, 3.0% computer, engineering, and science, 7.2% education, legal, community service, arts, and media, 4.5% healthcare practitioners, 23.2% service, 21.5% sales and office, 9.9% natural resources, construction, and maintenance, 20.1% production, transportation, and material moving (2008-2012 5-year est.).

Income: Per capita income: $21,304 (2008-2012 5-year est.); Median household income: $47,619 (2008-2012 5-year est.); Average household income: $53,482 (2008-2012 5-year est.); Percent of households with income of $100,000 or more: 11.5% (2008-2012 5-year est.); Poverty rate: 17.2% (2008-2012 5-year est.).

Education: Percent of population age 25 and over with: High school diploma (including GED) or higher: 90.9% (2008-2012 5-year est.); Bachelor's degree or higher: 11.9% (2008-2012 5-year est.); Master's degree or higher: 2.9% (2008-2012 5-year est.).

School District(s)

Roxana CUSD 1 (PK-12)

    2011-12 Enrollment: 1,891 . . . . (618) 254-7541

Housing: Homeownership rate: 68.9% (2008-2012 5-year est.); Median home value: $81,100 (2008-2012 5-year est.); Median contract rent: $549 per month (2008-2012 5-year est.); Median year structure built: 1948 (2008-2012 5-year est.).

Health Insurance: 67.2% Private; 36.5% Public; 12.4% None. (2008-2012 5-year est.)

Safety: Violent crime rate: 45.5 per 10,000 population; Property crime rate: 298.9 per 10,000 population (2012).
Transportation: Commute to work: 95.4% car, 2.9% public transportation, 0.0% walk, 1.2% work from home (2008-2012 5-year est.); Travel time to work: 34.0% less than 15 minutes, 39.4% 15 to 30 minutes, 15.4% 30 to 45 minutes, 7.5% 45 to 60 minutes, 3.8% 60 minutes or more (2008-2012 5-year est.)

SAINT JACOB (village). Covers a land area of 0.763 square miles and a water area of 0.006 square miles. Located at 38.72° N. Lat; 89.77° W. Long. Elevation is 512 feet.

History: St. Jacob was built near the site of Fort Chilton, established in 1812.
Population: 752 (1990); 801 (2000); 1,098 (2010); Density: 1,850.5 persons per square mile (2008-2012 5-year est.); Race: 96.4% White, 0.0% Black/African American, 1.2% Asian, 0.0% American Indian/Alaska Native, 0.0% Native Hawaiian/Other Pacific Islander, 2.4% Some other race, 2.4% Two or more races, 1.0% Hispanic of any race (2008-2012 5-year est.); Average household size: 2.61 (2008-2012 5-year est.); Median age: 35.9 (2008-2012 5-year est.); Males per 100 females: 91.8 (2008-2012 5-year est.); Marriage status: 23.1% never married, 66.4% now married, 5.1% widowed, 5.4% divorced (2008-2012 5-year est.); Foreign born: 1.6% (2008-2012 5-year est.); Ancestry (includes multiple ancestries): 44.8% German, 14.6% Irish, 12.7% English, 5.5% American, 4.5% Polish (2008-2012 5-year est.).
Economy: Single-family building permits issued: 8 (2013); Multi-family building permits issued: 0 (2013); Homeowner vacancy rate: 2.2%. Rental vacancy rate: 0.0%. (2008-2012 5-year est.); Employment by occupation: 13.9% management, business, and financial, 5.2% computer, engineering, and science, 10.2% education, legal, community service, arts, and media, 7.1% healthcare practitioners, 15.1% service, 17.9% sales and office, 17.2% natural resources, construction, and maintenance, 13.4% production, transportation, and material moving (2008-2012 5-year est.).
Income: Per capita income: $31,100 (2008-2012 5-year est.); Median household income: $77,500 (2008-2012 5-year est.); Average household income: $81,019 (2008-2012 5-year est.); Percent of households with income of $100,000 or more: 27.9% (2008-2012 5-year est.); Poverty rate: 4.3% (2008-2012 5-year est.).
Education: Percent of population age 25 and over with: High school diploma (including GED) or higher: 95.4% (2008-2012 5-year est.); Bachelor's degree or higher: 27.3% (2008-2012 5-year est.); Master's degree or higher: 6.8% (2008-2012 5-year est.).
School District(s)
Triad CUSD 2 (PK-12)
   2011-12 Enrollment: 3,652 . . . . (618) 667-8851
Triad CUSD 2 (PK-12)
   2011-12 Enrollment: 3,652 . . . . (618) 667-8851
Housing: Homeownership rate: 87.6% (2008-2012 5-year est.); Median home value: $155,900 (2008-2012 5-year est.); Median contract rent: $498 per month (2008-2012 5-year est.); Median year structure built: 1977 (2008-2012 5-year est.).
Health Insurance: 85.7% Private; 20.3% Public; 5.5% None. (2008-2012 5-year est.)
Transportation: Commute to work: 95.1% car, 0.8% public transportation, 1.1% walk, 1.6% work from home (2008-2012 5-year est.); Travel time to work: 11.1% less than 15 minutes, 28.2% 15 to 30 minutes, 50.6% 30 to 45 minutes, 7.2% 45 to 60 minutes, 2.8% 60 minutes or more (2008-2012 5-year est.)
Airports: St. Louis Metro-East Airport (general aviation)

SOUTH ROXANA (village). Covers a land area of 1.525 square miles and a water area of 0.071 square miles. Located at 38.82° N. Lat; 90.07° W. Long. Elevation is 440 feet.

Population: 1,961 (1990); 1,888 (2000); 2,053 (2010); Density: 1,469.2 persons per square mile (2008-2012 5-year est.); Race: 98.4% White, 1.3% Black/African American, 0.0% Asian, 0.0% American Indian/Alaska Native, 0.0% Native Hawaiian/Other Pacific Islander, 0.3% Some other race, 0.3% Two or more races, 0.2% Hispanic of any race (2008-2012 5-year est.); Average household size: 2.54 (2008-2012 5-year est.); Median age: 33.2 (2008-2012 5-year est.); Males per 100 females: 96.3 (2008-2012 5-year est.); Marriage status: 33.8% never married, 42.6% now married, 5.0% widowed, 18.6% divorced (2008-2012 5-year est.); Foreign born: 0.2% (2008-2012 5-year est.); Ancestry (includes multiple ancestries): 30.6% German, 17.8% Irish, 10.5% English, 9.1% American, 5.0% French (2008-2012 5-year est.).

Economy: Single-family building permits issued: 3 (2013); Multi-family building permits issued: 0 (2013); Homeowner vacancy rate: 1.7%. Rental vacancy rate: 12.4%. (2008-2012 5-year est.); Employment by occupation: 7.8% management, business, and financial, 0.6% computer, engineering, and science, 4.7% education, legal, community service, arts, and media, 4.6% healthcare practitioners, 18.7% service, 19.9% sales and office, 12.6% natural resources, construction, and maintenance, 31.0% production, transportation, and material moving (2008-2012 5-year est.).
Income: Per capita income: $20,153 (2008-2012 5-year est.); Median household income: $47,798 (2008-2012 5-year est.); Average household income: $50,212 (2008-2012 5-year est.); Percent of households with income of $100,000 or more: 7.8% (2008-2012 5-year est.); Poverty rate: 15.6% (2008-2012 5-year est.).
Education: Percent of population age 25 and over with: High school diploma (including GED) or higher: 85.1% (2008-2012 5-year est.); Bachelor's degree or higher: 6.4% (2008-2012 5-year est.); Master's degree or higher: 1.8% (2008-2012 5-year est.).
School District(s)
Roxana CUSD 1 (PK-12)
   2011-12 Enrollment: 1,891 . . . . (618) 254-7541
Housing: Homeownership rate: 64.6% (2008-2012 5-year est.); Median home value: $67,700 (2008-2012 5-year est.); Median contract rent: $539 per month (2008-2012 5-year est.); Median year structure built: 1958 (2008-2012 5-year est.).
Health Insurance: 59.7% Private; 36.9% Public; 15.0% None. (2008-2012 5-year est.)
Transportation: Commute to work: 96.2% car, 0.4% public transportation, 2.6% walk, 0.8% work from home (2008-2012 5-year est.); Travel time to work: 24.8% less than 15 minutes, 40.0% 15 to 30 minutes, 24.1% 30 to 45 minutes, 8.9% 45 to 60 minutes, 2.3% 60 minutes or more (2008-2012 5-year est.)

TROY (city). Covers a land area of 5.291 square miles and a water area of 0.059 square miles. Located at 38.73° N. Lat; 89.89° W. Long. Elevation is 561 feet.

History: Troy began as the community of Columbia, with a grist mill and tavern built by John G. Jarvis about 1814. When the property was purchased in 1819 by land speculators, it was renamed Troy, for the New York town. In 1857 Mechanicsburg, which had been platted in 1836, merged with Troy, and in 1891 Brookside did the same. Troy was incorporated as a city in 1892.
Population: 6,046 (1990); 8,524 (2000); 9,888 (2010); Density: 1,882.4 persons per square mile (2008-2012 5-year est.); Race: 85.7% White, 9.7% Black/African American, 1.0% Asian, 0.5% American Indian/Alaska Native, 0.0% Native Hawaiian/Other Pacific Islander, 3.1% Some other race, 2.1% Two or more races, 6.5% Hispanic of any race (2008-2012 5-year est.); Average household size: 2.65 (2008-2012 5-year est.); Median age: 35.4 (2008-2012 5-year est.); Males per 100 females: 125.4 (2008-2012 5-year est.); Marriage status: 31.6% never married, 54.4% now married, 3.5% widowed, 10.4% divorced (2008-2012 5-year est.); Foreign born: 2.6% (2008-2012 5-year est.); Ancestry (includes multiple ancestries): 31.6% German, 13.5% Irish, 8.1% English, 6.9% American, 6.0% Italian (2008-2012 5-year est.).
Economy: Single-family building permits issued: 27 (2013); Multi-family building permits issued: 4 (2013); Homeowner vacancy rate: 0.0%. Rental vacancy rate: 4.5%. (2008-2012 5-year est.); Employment by occupation: 15.7% management, business, and financial, 7.2% computer, engineering, and science, 6.8% education, legal, community service, arts, and media, 3.8% healthcare practitioners, 18.1% service, 24.8% sales and office, 11.8% natural resources, construction, and maintenance, 11.8% production, transportation, and material moving (2008-2012 5-year est.).
Income: Per capita income: $28,140 (2008-2012 5-year est.); Median household income: $68,297 (2008-2012 5-year est.); Average household income: $81,890 (2008-2012 5-year est.); Percent of households with income of $100,000 or more: 30.3% (2008-2012 5-year est.); Poverty rate: 9.5% (2008-2012 5-year est.).
Education: Percent of population age 25 and over with: High school diploma (including GED) or higher: 91.3% (2008-2012 5-year est.); Bachelor's degree or higher: 22.4% (2008-2012 5-year est.); Master's degree or higher: 6.3% (2008-2012 5-year est.).
School District(s)
Madison Roe (06-12)
   2011-12 Enrollment: n/a . . . . (618) 692-6200
Triad CUSD 2 (PK-12)
   2011-12 Enrollment: 3,652 . . . . (618) 667-8851

Housing: Homeownership rate: 71.4% (2008-2012 5-year est.); Median home value: $170,300 (2008-2012 5-year est.); Median contract rent: $581 per month (2008-2012 5-year est.); Median year structure built: 1987 (2008-2012 5-year est.).
Health Insurance: 77.1% Private; 25.1% Public; 7.6% None. (2008-2012 5-year est.)
Transportation: Commute to work: 95.3% car, 1.0% public transportation, 0.6% walk, 2.6% work from home (2008-2012 5-year est.); Travel time to work: 22.3% less than 15 minutes, 35.8% 15 to 30 minutes, 31.2% 30 to 45 minutes, 8.4% 45 to 60 minutes, 2.3% 60 minutes or more (2008-2012 5-year est.)

Additional Information Contacts
City of Troy . . . . (618) 667-9924
   http://www.troyil.us
Troy/Maryville/St. Jacob Marine Area Chamber of Commerce . . . . . . (618) 667-8769
   http://www.troycoc.com

VENICE (city). Covers a land area of 1.819 square miles and a water area of <.001 square miles. Located at 38.67° N. Lat; 90.17° W. Long. Elevation is 410 feet.
History: Before the construction of levees, Venice experienced frequent flooding of its streets, which led to its being named after the Italian city of waterways. A ferry landing was established here in 1804. The town was platted in 1841 and incorporated in 1873.
Population: 3,571 (1990); 2,528 (2000); 1,890 (2010); Density: 883.9 persons per square mile (2008-2012 5-year est.); Race: 2.4% White, 96.1% Black/African American, 0.1% Asian, 0.0% American Indian/Alaska Native, 0.0% Native Hawaiian/Other Pacific Islander, 1.4% Some other race, 1.4% Two or more races, 0.2% Hispanic of any race (2008-2012 5-year est.); Average household size: 2.29 (2008-2012 5-year est.); Median age: 41.0 (2008-2012 5-year est.); Males per 100 females: 63.9 (2008-2012 5-year est.); Marriage status: 48.3% never married, 27.9% now married, 9.3% widowed, 14.5% divorced (2008-2012 5-year est.); Foreign born: 0.1% (2008-2012 5-year est.); Ancestry (includes multiple ancestries): 1.0% African, 0.7% American, 0.6% German, 0.2% Belizean, 0.2% Irish (2008-2012 5-year est.).
Economy: Single-family building permits issued: 0 (2013); Multi-family building permits issued: 0 (2013); Homeowner vacancy rate: 10.6%. Rental vacancy rate: 0.0%. (2008-2012 5-year est.); Employment by occupation: 2.7% management, business, and financial, 7.4% computer, engineering, and science, 6.4% education, legal, community service, arts, and media, 1.6% healthcare practitioners, 35.3% service, 23.9% sales and office, 7.0% natural resources, construction, and maintenance, 15.7% production, transportation, and material moving (2008-2012 5-year est.).
Income: Per capita income: $14,608 (2008-2012 5-year est.); Median household income: $21,908 (2008-2012 5-year est.); Average household income: $32,201 (2008-2012 5-year est.); Percent of households with income of $100,000 or more: 4.1% (2008-2012 5-year est.); Poverty rate: 42.2% (2008-2012 5-year est.).
Education: Percent of population age 25 and over with: High school diploma (including GED) or higher: 76.8% (2008-2012 5-year est.); Bachelor's degree or higher: 11.3% (2008-2012 5-year est.); Master's degree or higher: 4.3% (2008-2012 5-year est.).

School District(s)
Venice CUSD 3 (KG-08)
   2011-12 Enrollment: 109 . . . . (618) 274-7953
Housing: Homeownership rate: 48.9% (2008-2012 5-year est.); Median home value: $34,300 (2008-2012 5-year est.); Median contract rent: $363 per month (2008-2012 5-year est.); Median year structure built: 1951 (2008-2012 5-year est.).
Health Insurance: 33.2% Private; 59.8% Public; 15.4% None. (2008-2012 5-year est.)
Transportation: Commute to work: 84.6% car, 10.8% public transportation, 0.6% walk, 4.1% work from home (2008-2012 5-year est.); Travel time to work: 27.8% less than 15 minutes, 36.7% 15 to 30 minutes, 27.8% 30 to 45 minutes, 5.7% 45 to 60 minutes, 2.1% 60 minutes or more (2008-2012 5-year est.)

WILLIAMSON (village). Covers a land area of 1.506 square miles and a water area of 0.046 square miles. Located at 38.99° N. Lat; 89.76° W. Long. Elevation is 604 feet.
Population: 278 (1990); 251 (2000); 230 (2010); Density: 162.0 persons per square mile (2008-2012 5-year est.); Race: 98.4% White, 0.8% Black/African American, 0.0% Asian, 0.0% American Indian/Alaska Native,

0.0% Native Hawaiian/Other Pacific Islander, 0.8% Some other race, 0.8% Two or more races, 0.0% Hispanic of any race (2008-2012 5-year est.); Average household size: 2.54 (2008-2012 5-year est.); Median age: 42.0 (2008-2012 5-year est.); Males per 100 females: 83.5 (2008-2012 5-year est.); Marriage status: 29.2% never married, 54.5% now married, 6.4% widowed, 9.9% divorced (2008-2012 5-year est.); Foreign born: 0.0% (2008-2012 5-year est.); Ancestry (includes multiple ancestries): 25.8% German, 16.0% English, 13.9% Italian, 7.8% American, 7.4% Irish (2008-2012 5-year est.).
Economy: Single-family building permits issued: 0 (2013); Multi-family building permits issued: 0 (2013); Homeowner vacancy rate: 2.5%. Rental vacancy rate: 0.0%. (2008-2012 5-year est.); Employment by occupation: 4.1% management, business, and financial, 4.1% computer, engineering, and science, 0.0% education, legal, community service, arts, and media, 0.0% healthcare practitioners, 18.6% service, 32.0% sales and office, 5.2% natural resources, construction, and maintenance, 36.1% production, transportation, and material moving (2008-2012 5-year est.).
Income: Per capita income: $18,177 (2008-2012 5-year est.); Median household income: $33,750 (2008-2012 5-year est.); Average household income: $43,651 (2008-2012 5-year est.); Percent of households with income of $100,000 or more: 9.4% (2008-2012 5-year est.); Poverty rate: 16.4% (2008-2012 5-year est.).
Education: Percent of population age 25 and over with: High school diploma (including GED) or higher: 85.6% (2008-2012 5-year est.); Bachelor's degree or higher: 0.6% (2008-2012 5-year est.); Master's degree or higher: 0.0% (2008-2012 5-year est.).
Housing: Homeownership rate: 79.2% (2008-2012 5-year est.); Median home value: $66,200 (2008-2012 5-year est.); Median contract rent: $418 per month (2008-2012 5-year est.); Median year structure built: 1948 (2008-2012 5-year est.).
Health Insurance: 63.1% Private; 42.2% Public; 11.5% None. (2008-2012 5-year est.)
Transportation: Commute to work: 96.8% car, 0.0% public transportation, 2.1% walk, 1.1% work from home (2008-2012 5-year est.); Travel time to work: 27.7% less than 15 minutes, 30.9% 15 to 30 minutes, 19.1% 30 to 45 minutes, 14.9% 45 to 60 minutes, 7.4% 60 minutes or more (2008-2012 5-year est.)

WOOD RIVER (city). Covers a land area of 6.979 square miles and a water area of 0.174 square miles. Located at 38.86° N. Lat; 90.08° W. Long. Elevation is 436 feet.
History: Named for a small stream that used to be in the city. Wood River was selected by the Standard Oil Company in 1907 as the site of its refinery because of the rail and river transportation available here.
Population: 11,490 (1990); 11,296 (2000); 10,657 (2010); Density: 1,525.0 persons per square mile (2008-2012 5-year est.); Race: 95.5% White, 0.8% Black/African American, 1.6% Asian, 0.0% American Indian/Alaska Native, 0.0% Native Hawaiian/Other Pacific Islander, 2.1% Some other race, 1.7% Two or more races, 2.2% Hispanic of any race (2008-2012 5-year est.); Average household size: 2.31 (2008-2012 5-year est.); Median age: 39.4 (2008-2012 5-year est.); Males per 100 females: 83.2 (2008-2012 5-year est.); Marriage status: 26.0% never married, 46.4% now married, 10.3% widowed, 17.3% divorced (2008-2012 5-year est.); Foreign born: 2.2% (2008-2012 5-year est.); Ancestry (includes multiple ancestries): 32.5% German, 18.9% Irish, 12.6% English, 8.7% American, 6.3% Italian (2008-2012 5-year est.).
Economy: Single-family building permits issued: 3 (2013); Multi-family building permits issued: 0 (2013); Homeowner vacancy rate: 2.0%. Rental vacancy rate: 10.9%. (2008-2012 5-year est.); Employment by occupation: 9.3% management, business, and financial, 3.9% computer, engineering, and science, 7.1% education, legal, community service, arts, and media, 5.5% healthcare practitioners, 22.8% service, 26.3% sales and office, 7.8% natural resources, construction, and maintenance, 17.2% production, transportation, and material moving (2008-2012 5-year est.).
Income: Per capita income: $22,461 (2008-2012 5-year est.); Median household income: $47,953 (2008-2012 5-year est.); Average household income: $51,557 (2008-2012 5-year est.); Percent of households with income of $100,000 or more: 9.0% (2008-2012 5-year est.); Poverty rate: 13.2% (2008-2012 5-year est.).
Education: Percent of population age 25 and over with: High school diploma (including GED) or higher: 88.6% (2008-2012 5-year est.); Bachelor's degree or higher: 13.0% (2008-2012 5-year est.); Master's degree or higher: 3.5% (2008-2012 5-year est.).

School District(s)

East Alton-Wood River CHSD 14 (09-12)
   2011-12 Enrollment: 595 . . . . (618) 254-3151
Wood River-Hartford ESD 15 (PK-08)
   2011-12 Enrollment: 791 . . . . (618) 254-0607
Housing: Homeownership rate: 74.7% (2008-2012 5-year est.); Median home value: $88,200 (2008-2012 5-year est.); Median contract rent: $535 per month (2008-2012 5-year est.); Median year structure built: 1953 (2008-2012 5-year est.).
Health Insurance: 65.4% Private; 36.7% Public; 14.2% None. (2008-2012 5-year est.)
Safety: Violent crime rate: 27.3 per 10,000 population; Property crime rate: 417.7 per 10,000 population (2012).
Transportation: Commute to work: 93.4% car, 0.9% public transportation, 0.8% walk, 2.9% work from home (2008-2012 5-year est.); Travel time to work: 29.5% less than 15 minutes, 40.3% 15 to 30 minutes, 21.6% 30 to 45 minutes, 5.4% 45 to 60 minutes, 3.2% 60 minutes or more (2008-2012 5-year est.)

Additional Information Contacts
City of Wood River . . . . (618) 251-3100
   http://www.woodriver.org
River Bend Growth Association . . . . (618) 467-2280
   http://www.woodriver.org/business/GrowthAssociation.htm

WORDEN (village). Covers a land area of 0.706 square miles and a water area of 0.012 square miles. Located at 38.93° N. Lat; 89.84° W. Long. Elevation is 568 feet.
History: Incorporated 1877.
Population: 896 (1990); 905 (2000); 1,044 (2010); Density: 1,552.7 persons per square mile (2008-2012 5-year est.); Race: 100.0% White, 0.0% Black/African American, 0.0% Asian, 0.0% American Indian/Alaska Native, 0.0% Native Hawaiian/Other Pacific Islander, 0.0% Some other race, 0.0% Two or more races, 1.9% Hispanic of any race (2008-2012 5-year est.); Average household size: 2.54 (2008-2012 5-year est.); Median age: 35.7 (2008-2012 5-year est.); Males per 100 females: 87.0 (2008-2012 5-year est.); Marriage status: 20.1% never married, 64.5% now married, 6.3% widowed, 9.1% divorced (2008-2012 5-year est.); Foreign born: 0.5% (2008-2012 5-year est.); Ancestry (includes multiple ancestries): 36.0% German, 17.7% Irish, 9.4% American, 8.6% English, 3.2% Scotch-Irish (2008-2012 5-year est.).
Economy: Single-family building permits issued: 2 (2013); Multi-family building permits issued: 0 (2013); Homeowner vacancy rate: 1.6%. Rental vacancy rate: 8.6%. (2008-2012 5-year est.); Employment by occupation: 7.6% management, business, and financial, 7.2% computer, engineering, and science, 7.9% education, legal, community service, arts, and media, 5.8% healthcare practitioners, 14.9% service, 19.4% sales and office, 16.9% natural resources, construction, and maintenance, 20.2% production, transportation, and material moving (2008-2012 5-year est.).
Income: Per capita income: $23,148 (2008-2012 5-year est.); Median household income: $53,125 (2008-2012 5-year est.); Average household income: $58,518 (2008-2012 5-year est.); Percent of households with income of $100,000 or more: 17.9% (2008-2012 5-year est.); Poverty rate: 16.8% (2008-2012 5-year est.).
Education: Percent of population age 25 and over with: High school diploma (including GED) or higher: 86.5% (2008-2012 5-year est.); Bachelor's degree or higher: 12.1% (2008-2012 5-year est.); Master's degree or higher: 2.6% (2008-2012 5-year est.).

School District(s)

Edwardsville CUSD 7 (PK-12)
   2011-12 Enrollment: 7,480 . . . . (618) 656-1182
Housing: Homeownership rate: 82.8% (2008-2012 5-year est.); Median home value: $106,400 (2008-2012 5-year est.); Median contract rent: $420 per month (2008-2012 5-year est.); Median year structure built: 1959 (2008-2012 5-year est.).
Health Insurance: 66.3% Private; 30.9% Public; 13.5% None. (2008-2012 5-year est.)
Transportation: Commute to work: 92.7% car, 0.0% public transportation, 1.9% walk, 5.4% work from home (2008-2012 5-year est.); Travel time to work: 9.5% less than 15 minutes, 38.3% 15 to 30 minutes, 32.8% 30 to 45 minutes, 13.4% 45 to 60 minutes, 5.9% 60 minutes or more (2008-2012 5-year est.)

Marion County

Located in south central Illinois; drained by Skillet Fork, Crooked Creek, and a headstream of Kaskaskia River. Covers a land area of 572.363 square miles, a water area of 3.673 square miles, and is located in the Central Time Zone at 38.65° N. Lat., 88.92° W. Long. The county was founded in 1823. County seat is Salem.

Marion County is part of the Centralia, IL Micropolitan Statistical Area. The entire metro area includes: Marion County, IL

Weather Station: Salem Leckrone Arpt　　　　　　　**Elevation: 569 feet**

	Jan	Feb	Mar	Apr	May	Jun	Jul	Aug	Sep	Oct	Nov	Dec
High	39	44	55	67	76	85	88	87	80	69	55	42
Low	22	25	34	44	54	63	67	65	57	45	36	25
Precip	2.8	2.6	3.8	3.7	5.0	4.1	3.9	3.4	3.1	3.8	4.1	3.2
Snow	4.4	3.9	1.0	0.1	0.0	0.0	0.0	0.0	0.0	0.1	0.3	3.2

High and Low temperatures in degrees Fahrenheit; Precipitation and Snow in inches

Population: 41,561 (1990); 41,691 (2000); 39,437 (2010); Race: 93.3% White, 3.3% Black/African American, 0.6% Asian, 0.1% American Indian/Alaska Native, 0.0% Native Hawaiian/Other Pacific Islander, 2.7% Some other race, 2.5% Two or more races, 1.4% Hispanic of any race (2008-2012 5-year est.); Density: 67.9 persons per square mile (2008-2012 5-year est.); Average household size: 2.42 (2008-2012 5-year est.); Median age: 41.4 (2008-2012 5-year est.); Males per 100 females: 95.0 (2008-2012 5-year est.).
Religion: Six largest groups: 25.4% Baptist, 8.4% Muslim Estimate, 6.4% Catholicism, 5.6% Methodist/Pietist, 5.3% Lutheran, 3.8% Non-denominational Protestant (2010)
Economy: Unemployment rate: 8.4% (April 2014); Total civilian labor force: 16,890 (April 2014); Leading industries: 26.8% health care and social assistance; 22.7% manufacturing; 12.5% retail trade (2012); Farms: 1,152 totaling 266,828 acres (2012); Companies that employ 500 or more persons: 2 (2012); Companies that employ 100 to 499 persons: 17 (2012); Companies that employ less than 100 persons: 933 (2012); Black-owned businesses: n/a (2007); Hispanic-owned businesses: n/a (2007); Asian-owned businesses: n/a (2007); Women-owned businesses: n/a (2007); Single-family building permits issued: 1 (2013); Multi-family building permits issued: 0 (2013).
Income: Per capita income: $21,696 (2008-2012 5-year est.); Median household income: $41,723 (2008-2012 5-year est.); Average household income: $52,412 (2008-2012 5-year est.); Percent of households with income of $100,000 or more: 11.2% (2008-2012 5-year est.); Poverty rate: 16.1% (2008-2012 5-year est.); Bankruptcy rate: 3.57% (2013).
Taxes: Total county taxes per capita: $106 (2011); County property taxes per capita: $85 (2011).
Education: Percent of population age 25 and over with: High school diploma (including GED) or higher: 85.8% (2008-2012 5-year est.); Bachelor's degree or higher: 13.7% (2008-2012 5-year est.); Master's degree or higher: 4.3% (2008-2012 5-year est.).
Housing: Homeownership rate: 74.6% (2008-2012 5-year est.); Median home value: $71,800 (2008-2012 5-year est.); Median contract rent: $413 per month (2008-2012 5-year est.); Median year structure built: 1970 (2008-2012 5-year est.)
Health: Birth rate: 128.4 per 10,000 population (2013); Death rate: 103.6 per 10,000 population (2013); Age-adjusted cancer mortality rate: 250.5 deaths per 100,000 population (2011); Number of physicians: 15.9 per 10,000 population (2011); Hospital beds: 34.7 per 10,000 population (2010); Hospital admissions: 2,108.2 per 10,000 population (2010).
Elections: 2012 Presidential election results: 39.5% Obama, 58.7% Romney
National and State Parks: Stephen A Forbes State Park
Additional Information Contacts
Marion County Government . . . . (618) 548-3400

Marion County Communities

ALMA (village). Covers a land area of 1.079 square miles and a water area of 0 square miles. Located at 38.72° N. Lat; 88.91° W. Long. Elevation is 623 feet.
Population: 388 (1990); 386 (2000); 320 (2010); Density: 270.6 persons per square mile (2008-2012 5-year est.); Race: 99.7% White, 0.0% Black/African American, 0.0% Asian, 0.0% American Indian/Alaska Native, 0.0% Native Hawaiian/Other Pacific Islander, 0.3% Some other race, 0.3%

Two or more races, 0.0% Hispanic of any race (2008-2012 5-year est.); Average household size: 2.21 (2008-2012 5-year est.); Median age: 41.6 (2008-2012 5-year est.); Males per 100 females: 80.2 (2008-2012 5-year est.); Marriage status: 19.3% never married, 48.0% now married, 10.3% widowed, 22.4% divorced (2008-2012 5-year est.); Foreign born: 0.0% (2008-2012 5-year est.); Ancestry (includes multiple ancestries): 26.4% German, 13.0% Irish, 10.6% American, 5.8% English, 2.4% Scotch-Irish (2008-2012 5-year est.).

Economy: Homeowner vacancy rate: 6.1%. Rental vacancy rate: 6.5%. (2008-2012 5-year est.); Employment by occupation: 4.0% management, business, and financial, 2.0% computer, engineering, and science, 1.0% education, legal, community service, arts, and media, 10.1% healthcare practitioners, 29.3% service, 20.2% sales and office, 8.1% natural resources, construction, and maintenance, 25.3% production, transportation, and material moving (2008-2012 5-year est.).

Income: Per capita income: $13,641 (2008-2012 5-year est.); Median household income: $21,250 (2008-2012 5-year est.); Average household income: $28,709 (2008-2012 5-year est.); Percent of households with income of $100,000 or more: 0.8% (2008-2012 5-year est.); Poverty rate: 27.7% (2008-2012 5-year est.).

Education: Percent of population age 25 and over with: High school diploma (including GED) or higher: 76.8% (2008-2012 5-year est.); Bachelor's degree or higher: 7.4% (2008-2012 5-year est.); Master's degree or higher: 0.0% (2008-2012 5-year est.).

Housing: Homeownership rate: 70.5% (2008-2012 5-year est.); Median home value: $62,800 (2008-2012 5-year est.); Median contract rent: $283 per month (2008-2012 5-year est.); Median year structure built: 1964 (2008-2012 5-year est.).

Health Insurance: 37.0% Private; 60.6% Public; 20.5% None. (2008-2012 5-year est.)

Transportation: Commute to work: 81.8% car, 0.0% public transportation, 6.1% walk, 7.1% work from home (2008-2012 5-year est.); Travel time to work: 26.1% less than 15 minutes, 47.8% 15 to 30 minutes, 12.0% 30 to 45 minutes, 6.5% 45 to 60 minutes, 7.6% 60 minutes or more (2008-2012 5-year est.)

CENTRAL CITY (village). Covers a land area of 0.583 square miles and a water area of 0 square miles. Located at 38.55° N. Lat; 89.13° W. Long. Elevation is 486 feet.

History: Central City was settled by German immigrants, and incorporated in 1857.

Population: 1,390 (1990); 1,371 (2000); 1,172 (2010); Density: 2,048.3 persons per square mile (2008-2012 5-year est.); Race: 93.2% White, 1.3% Black/African American, 0.0% Asian, 0.0% American Indian/Alaska Native, 0.0% Native Hawaiian/Other Pacific Islander, 5.5% Some other race, 4.9% Two or more races, 3.3% Hispanic of any race (2008-2012 5-year est.); Average household size: 2.42 (2008-2012 5-year est.); Median age: 34.2 (2008-2012 5-year est.); Males per 100 females: 86.3 (2008-2012 5-year est.); Marriage status: 27.1% never married, 50.3% now married, 10.6% widowed, 12.0% divorced (2008-2012 5-year est.); Foreign born: 0.8% (2008-2012 5-year est.); Ancestry (includes multiple ancestries): 28.6% German, 19.7% Irish, 15.1% English, 8.5% American, 3.9% French (2008-2012 5-year est.).

Economy: Single-family building permits issued: 0 (2013); Multi-family building permits issued: 0 (2013); Homeowner vacancy rate: 0.8%. Rental vacancy rate: 4.7%. (2008-2012 5-year est.); Employment by occupation: 3.6% management, business, and financial, 1.3% computer, engineering, and science, 8.3% education, legal, community service, arts, and media, 7.2% healthcare practitioners, 27.9% service, 25.1% sales and office, 4.9% natural resources, construction, and maintenance, 21.7% production, transportation, and material moving (2008-2012 5-year est.).

Income: Per capita income: $16,946 (2008-2012 5-year est.); Median household income: $29,511 (2008-2012 5-year est.); Average household income: $39,569 (2008-2012 5-year est.); Percent of households with income of $100,000 or more: 4.9% (2008-2012 5-year est.); Poverty rate: 21.3% (2008-2012 5-year est.).

Education: Percent of population age 25 and over with: High school diploma (including GED) or higher: 83.9% (2008-2012 5-year est.); Bachelor's degree or higher: 4.9% (2008-2012 5-year est.); Master's degree or higher: 0.4% (2008-2012 5-year est.).

Housing: Homeownership rate: 71.4% (2008-2012 5-year est.); Median home value: $39,000 (2008-2012 5-year est.); Median contract rent: $423 per month (2008-2012 5-year est.); Median year structure built: 1963 (2008-2012 5-year est.).

Health Insurance: 53.6% Private; 51.6% Public; 13.9% None. (2008-2012 5-year est.)

Safety: Violent crime rate: 17.1 per 10,000 population; Property crime rate: 299.4 per 10,000 population (2012).

Transportation: Commute to work: 95.0% car, 0.6% public transportation, 0.0% walk, 2.5% work from home (2008-2012 5-year est.); Travel time to work: 61.8% less than 15 minutes, 20.7% 15 to 30 minutes, 5.6% 30 to 45 minutes, 5.4% 45 to 60 minutes, 6.6% 60 minutes or more (2008-2012 5-year est.)

CENTRALIA (city). Covers a land area of 8.193 square miles and a water area of 1.033 square miles. Located at 38.52° N. Lat; 89.12° W. Long. Elevation is 492 feet.

History: Centralia was laid out by the Illinois Central Railroad in 1853, and named for the company. Many early residents were of German descent. Since Centralia was located in a fruit-producing area, the railroad company was interested in refrigerated cars for shipping the fruit, and in 1868 the first such train began operation between Centralia and Chicago.

Population: 14,274 (1990); 14,136 (2000); 13,032 (2010); Density: 1,589.1 persons per square mile (2008-2012 5-year est.); Race: 84.7% White, 9.1% Black/African American, 0.5% Asian, 0.2% American Indian/Alaska Native, 0.0% Native Hawaiian/Other Pacific Islander, 5.5% Some other race, 4.8% Two or more races, 2.9% Hispanic of any race (2008-2012 5-year est.); Average household size: 2.26 (2008-2012 5-year est.); Median age: 42.7 (2008-2012 5-year est.); Males per 100 females: 87.9 (2008-2012 5-year est.); Marriage status: 27.2% never married, 45.0% now married, 10.7% widowed, 17.2% divorced (2008-2012 5-year est.); Foreign born: 1.2% (2008-2012 5-year est.); Ancestry (includes multiple ancestries): 25.1% German, 17.0% Irish, 12.0% English, 9.9% American, 2.9% Polish (2008-2012 5-year est.).

Economy: Single-family building permits issued: 0 (2013); Multi-family building permits issued: 0 (2013); Homeowner vacancy rate: 2.0%. Rental vacancy rate: 3.9%. (2008-2012 5-year est.); Employment by occupation: 10.0% management, business, and financial, 2.6% computer, engineering, and science, 10.4% education, legal, community service, arts, and media, 5.6% healthcare practitioners, 21.4% service, 23.5% sales and office, 7.6% natural resources, construction, and maintenance, 19.0% production, transportation, and material moving (2008-2012 5-year est.).

Income: Per capita income: $21,115 (2008-2012 5-year est.); Median household income: $35,000 (2008-2012 5-year est.); Average household income: $47,722 (2008-2012 5-year est.); Percent of households with income of $100,000 or more: 8.3% (2008-2012 5-year est.); Poverty rate: 18.9% (2008-2012 5-year est.).

Taxes: Total city taxes per capita: $228 (2011); City property taxes per capita: $151 (2011).

Education: Percent of population age 25 and over with: High school diploma (including GED) or higher: 85.3% (2008-2012 5-year est.); Bachelor's degree or higher: 14.1% (2008-2012 5-year est.); Master's degree or higher: 5.2% (2008-2012 5-year est.).

School District(s)

Central City SD 133 (PK-08)
    2011-12 Enrollment: 257 . . . . (618) 532-9521
Centralia HSD 200 (09-12)
    2011-12 Enrollment: 1,013 . . . . (618) 532-7391
Centralia SD 135 (PK-08)
    2011-12 Enrollment: 1,358 . . . . (618) 532-1907
Centralia SD 135 (PK-08)
    2011-12 Enrollment: 1,358 . . . . (618) 532-1907
Clinton/marion/washington Roe (PK-12)
    2011-12 Enrollment: n/a . . . . (618) 594-2432
Clinton/marion/washington Roe (PK-12)
    2011-12 Enrollment: n/a . . . . (618) 594-2432
Grand Prairie CCSD 6 (KG-08)
    2011-12 Enrollment: 72 . . . . (618) 249-6289
Kaskaskia Spec Educ District
    2011-12 Enrollment: n/a . . . . (618) 532-4721
North Wamac SD 186 (KG-08)
    2011-12 Enrollment: 121 . . . . (618) 532-1826
Raccoon CSD 1 (PK-08)
    2011-12 Enrollment: 241 . . . . (618) 532-7329
Willow Grove SD 46 (PK-08)
    2011-12 Enrollment: 191 . . . . (618) 532-3313

Two-year College(s)

Kaskaskia College (Public)

Fall 2012 Enrollment: 5,104 . . . . (618) 545-3000

2012-13 Tuition: In-state $6,112; Out-of-state $12,864

Housing: Homeownership rate: 66.9% (2008-2012 5-year est.); Median home value: $65,100 (2008-2012 5-year est.); Median contract rent: $413 per month (2008-2012 5-year est.); Median year structure built: 1961 (2008-2012 5-year est.).

Health Insurance: 60.8% Private; 50.1% Public; 10.7% None. (2008-2012 5-year est.)

Hospitals: St. Mary's Good Samaritan (276 beds)

Transportation: Commute to work: 90.7% car, 0.5% public transportation, 2.9% walk, 2.7% work from home (2008-2012 5-year est.); Travel time to work: 51.2% less than 15 minutes, 20.6% 15 to 30 minutes, 16.5% 30 to 45 minutes, 3.1% 45 to 60 minutes, 8.6% 60 minutes or more (2008-2012 5-year est.); Amtrak: Train service available.

Airports: Centralia Municipal Airport (general aviation)

Additional Information Contacts

City of Centralia. . . . . (618) 533-7623
http://cityofcentralia.org

The Greater Centralia Chamber of Commerce . . . . (618) 532-6789
http://www.centraliail.com

IUKA (village). Covers a land area of 0.791 square miles and a water area of 0.002 square miles. Located at 38.62° N. Lat; 88.79° W. Long. Elevation is 518 feet.

Population: 388 (1990); 598 (2000); 489 (2010); Density: 647.6 persons per square mile (2008-2012 5-year est.); Race: 97.3% White, 0.0% Black/African American, 1.8% Asian, 0.0% American Indian/Alaska Native, 0.0% Native Hawaiian/Other Pacific Islander, 0.9% Some other race, 1.0% Two or more races, 0.6% Hispanic of any race (2008-2012 5-year est.); Average household size: 2.51 (2008-2012 5-year est.); Median age: 41.0 (2008-2012 5-year est.); Males per 100 females: 82.9 (2008-2012 5-year est.); Marriage status: 23.2% never married, 51.7% now married, 7.5% widowed, 17.5% divorced (2008-2012 5-year est.); Foreign born: 0.2% (2008-2012 5-year est.); Ancestry (includes multiple ancestries): 19.7% English, 18.6% German, 17.8% Irish, 2.9% Dutch, 2.0% Swedish (2008-2012 5-year est.).

Economy: Homeowner vacancy rate: 4.4%. Rental vacancy rate: 0.0%. (2008-2012 5-year est.); Employment by occupation: 3.6% management, business, and financial, 1.5% computer, engineering, and science, 2.5% education, legal, community service, arts, and media, 4.1% healthcare practitioners, 27.9% service, 15.7% sales and office, 22.3% natural resources, construction, and maintenance, 22.3% production, transportation, and material moving (2008-2012 5-year est.).

Income: Per capita income: $18,461 (2008-2012 5-year est.); Median household income: $37,500 (2008-2012 5-year est.); Average household income: $46,645 (2008-2012 5-year est.); Percent of households with income of $100,000 or more: 7.9% (2008-2012 5-year est.); Poverty rate: 16.8% (2008-2012 5-year est.).

Education: Percent of population age 25 and over with: High school diploma (including GED) or higher: 78.6% (2008-2012 5-year est.); Bachelor's degree or higher: 5.5% (2008-2012 5-year est.); Master's degree or higher: 1.7% (2008-2012 5-year est.).

School District(s)

Iuka CCSD 7 (PK-08)

2011-12 Enrollment: 249. . . . . (618) 323-6233

Housing: Homeownership rate: 85.3% (2008-2012 5-year est.); Median home value: $50,000 (2008-2012 5-year est.); Median contract rent: $325 per month (2008-2012 5-year est.); Median year structure built: 1973 (2008-2012 5-year est.).

Health Insurance: 44.9% Private; 56.1% Public; 11.1% None. (2008-2012 5-year est.)

Transportation: Commute to work: 88.1% car, 0.0% public transportation, 5.7% walk, 4.7% work from home (2008-2012 5-year est.); Travel time to work: 20.1% less than 15 minutes, 55.4% 15 to 30 minutes, 11.4% 30 to 45 minutes, 7.6% 45 to 60 minutes, 5.4% 60 minutes or more (2008-2012 5-year est.)

JUNCTION CITY (village). Aka Glenridge. Covers a land area of 0.676 square miles and a water area of 0.018 square miles. Located at 38.58° N. Lat; 89.13° W. Long. Elevation is 492 feet.

Population: 539 (1990); 559 (2000); 482 (2010); Density: 749.5 persons per square mile (2008-2012 5-year est.); Race: 98.2% White, 0.8% Black/African American, 1.0% Asian, 0.0% American Indian/Alaska Native,

0.0% Native Hawaiian/Other Pacific Islander, 0.0% Some other race, 0.0% Two or more races, 0.0% Hispanic of any race (2008-2012 5-year est.); Average household size: 2.65 (2008-2012 5-year est.); Median age: 36.6 (2008-2012 5-year est.); Males per 100 females: 111.3 (2008-2012 5-year est.); Marriage status: 30.1% never married, 53.5% now married, 5.9% widowed, 10.5% divorced (2008-2012 5-year est.); Foreign born: 1.0% (2008-2012 5-year est.); Ancestry (includes multiple ancestries): 21.7% German, 21.1% Irish, 17.6% American, 4.7% Polish, 3.6% English (2008-2012 5-year est.).

Economy: Homeowner vacancy rate: 0.0%. Rental vacancy rate: 0.0%. (2008-2012 5-year est.); Employment by occupation: 0.0% management, business, and financial, 0.0% computer, engineering, and science, 3.7% education, legal, community service, arts, and media, 3.7% healthcare practitioners, 25.9% service, 11.6% sales and office, 13.9% natural resources, construction, and maintenance, 41.2% production, transportation, and material moving (2008-2012 5-year est.).

Income: Per capita income: $17,072 (2008-2012 5-year est.); Median household income: $43,403 (2008-2012 5-year est.); Average household income: $43,561 (2008-2012 5-year est.); Percent of households with income of $100,000 or more: 2.1% (2008-2012 5-year est.); Poverty rate: 30.1% (2008-2012 5-year est.).

Education: Percent of population age 25 and over with: High school diploma (including GED) or higher: 73.2% (2008-2012 5-year est.); Bachelor's degree or higher: 2.5% (2008-2012 5-year est.); Master's degree or higher: 1.6% (2008-2012 5-year est.).

Housing: Homeownership rate: 86.4% (2008-2012 5-year est.); Median home value: $29,200 (2008-2012 5-year est.); Median contract rent: $285 per month (2008-2012 5-year est.); Median year structure built: 1977 (2008-2012 5-year est.).

Health Insurance: 44.8% Private; 47.1% Public; 13.2% None. (2008-2012 5-year est.)

Transportation: Commute to work: 90.3% car, 0.0% public transportation, 3.7% walk, 1.4% work from home (2008-2012 5-year est.); Travel time to work: 19.7% less than 15 minutes, 54.9% 15 to 30 minutes, 12.7% 30 to 45 minutes, 6.6% 45 to 60 minutes, 6.1% 60 minutes or more (2008-2012 5-year est.)

KELL (village). Covers a land area of 1.008 square miles and a water area of 0.002 square miles. Located at 38.49° N. Lat; 88.90° W. Long. Elevation is 610 feet.

Population: 213 (1990); 231 (2000); 219 (2010); Density: 214.2 persons per square mile (2008-2012 5-year est.); Race: 98.1% White, 0.0% Black/African American, 0.0% Asian, 0.0% American Indian/Alaska Native, 0.0% Native Hawaiian/Other Pacific Islander, 1.9% Some other race, 1.9% Two or more races, 5.6% Hispanic of any race (2008-2012 5-year est.); Average household size: 2.88 (2008-2012 5-year est.); Median age: 40.5 (2008-2012 5-year est.); Males per 100 females: 83.1 (2008-2012 5-year est.); Marriage status: 24.7% never married, 63.8% now married, 3.4% widowed, 8.0% divorced (2008-2012 5-year est.); Foreign born: 0.9% (2008-2012 5-year est.); Ancestry (includes multiple ancestries): 17.6% Irish, 12.5% English, 11.1% German, 9.3% American, 2.3% Polish (2008-2012 5-year est.).

Economy: Homeowner vacancy rate: 0.0%. Rental vacancy rate: 0.0%. (2008-2012 5-year est.); Employment by occupation: 6.3% management, business, and financial, 0.0% computer, engineering, and science, 2.1% education, legal, community service, arts, and media, 10.5% healthcare practitioners, 26.3% service, 30.5% sales and office, 8.4% natural resources, construction, and maintenance, 15.8% production, transportation, and material moving (2008-2012 5-year est.).

Income: Per capita income: $14,830 (2008-2012 5-year est.); Median household income: $39,063 (2008-2012 5-year est.); Average household income: $42,576 (2008-2012 5-year est.); Percent of households with income of $100,000 or more: 2.7% (2008-2012 5-year est.); Poverty rate: 18.4% (2008-2012 5-year est.).

Education: Percent of population age 25 and over with: High school diploma (including GED) or higher: 85.8% (2008-2012 5-year est.); Bachelor's degree or higher: 3.0% (2008-2012 5-year est.); Master's degree or higher: 0.0% (2008-2012 5-year est.).

School District(s)

Kell CSD 2 (PK-08)

2011-12 Enrollment: 110. . . . . (618) 822-6234

Housing: Homeownership rate: 93.3% (2008-2012 5-year est.); Median home value: $54,300 (2008-2012 5-year est.); Median contract rent: $392 per month (2008-2012 5-year est.); Median year structure built: 1957 (2008-2012 5-year est.).

Health Insurance: 42.1% Private; 57.4% Public; 10.6% None. (2008-2012 5-year est.)
Transportation: Commute to work: 85.3% car, 0.0% public transportation, 3.2% walk, 3.2% work from home (2008-2012 5-year est.); Travel time to work: 14.1% less than 15 minutes, 60.9% 15 to 30 minutes, 22.8% 30 to 45 minutes, 0.0% 45 to 60 minutes, 2.2% 60 minutes or more (2008-2012 5-year est.)

KINMUNDY (city). Covers a land area of 1.048 square miles and a water area of 0.270 square miles. Located at 38.77° N. Lat; 88.85° W. Long. Elevation is 604 feet.
Population: 879 (1990); 892 (2000); 796 (2010); Density: 766.0 persons per square mile (2008-2012 5-year est.); Race: 97.8% White, 0.0% Black/African American, 0.0% Asian, 0.0% American Indian/Alaska Native, 0.0% Native Hawaiian/Other Pacific Islander, 2.2% Some other race, 2.2% Two or more races, 1.1% Hispanic of any race (2008-2012 5-year est.); Average household size: 2.18 (2008-2012 5-year est.); Median age: 39.3 (2008-2012 5-year est.); Males per 100 females: 82.5 (2008-2012 5-year est.); Marriage status: 18.6% never married, 49.0% now married, 11.0% widowed, 21.4% divorced (2008-2012 5-year est.); Foreign born: 0.9% (2008-2012 5-year est.); Ancestry (includes multiple ancestries): 23.5% German, 20.9% English, 18.3% Irish, 11.0% American, 3.0% Dutch (2008-2012 5-year est.).
Economy: Homeowner vacancy rate: 0.0%. Rental vacancy rate: 12.0%. (2008-2012 5-year est.); Employment by occupation: 4.1% management, business, and financial, 0.0% computer, engineering, and science, 8.2% education, legal, community service, arts, and media, 6.9% healthcare practitioners, 14.1% service, 16.9% sales and office, 13.5% natural resources, construction, and maintenance, 36.4% production, transportation, and material moving (2008-2012 5-year est.).
Income: Per capita income: $17,042 (2008-2012 5-year est.); Median household income: $32,727 (2008-2012 5-year est.); Average household income: $36,233 (2008-2012 5-year est.); Percent of households with income of $100,000 or more: 2.7% (2008-2012 5-year est.); Poverty rate: 17.2% (2008-2012 5-year est.).
Education: Percent of population age 25 and over with: High school diploma (including GED) or higher: 87.8% (2008-2012 5-year est.); Bachelor's degree or higher: 7.3% (2008-2012 5-year est.); Master's degree or higher: 2.1% (2008-2012 5-year est.).
School District(s)
South Central CUD 401 (PK-12)
    2011-12 Enrollment: 723. . . . . (618) 547-3414
Housing: Homeownership rate: 82.1% (2008-2012 5-year est.); Median home value: $55,300 (2008-2012 5-year est.); Median contract rent: $330 per month (2008-2012 5-year est.); Median year structure built: 1972 (2008-2012 5-year est.).
Health Insurance: 53.3% Private; 43.2% Public; 18.3% None. (2008-2012 5-year est.)
Transportation: Commute to work: 90.6% car, 0.0% public transportation, 2.3% walk, 7.2% work from home (2008-2012 5-year est.); Travel time to work: 31.9% less than 15 minutes, 35.8% 15 to 30 minutes, 18.2% 30 to 45 minutes, 8.1% 45 to 60 minutes, 6.0% 60 minutes or more (2008-2012 5-year est.)

ODIN (village). Covers a land area of 1.004 square miles and a water area of 0 square miles. Located at 38.62° N. Lat; 89.05° W. Long. Elevation is 528 feet.
History: Odin developed as a mining and agricultural center along the Illinois Central Railroad.
Population: 1,150 (1990); 1,122 (2000); 1,076 (2010); Density: 1,109.0 persons per square mile (2008-2012 5-year est.); Race: 95.5% White, 0.0% Black/African American, 0.0% Asian, 0.0% American Indian/Alaska Native, 0.0% Native Hawaiian/Other Pacific Islander, 4.5% Some other race, 4.5% Two or more races, 0.1% Hispanic of any race (2008-2012 5-year est.); Average household size: 2.51 (2008-2012 5-year est.); Median age: 39.6 (2008-2012 5-year est.); Males per 100 females: 92.7 (2008-2012 5-year est.); Marriage status: 23.6% never married, 46.8% now married, 11.4% widowed, 18.2% divorced (2008-2012 5-year est.); Foreign born: 0.0% (2008-2012 5-year est.); Ancestry (includes multiple ancestries): 27.6% German, 11.0% Irish, 8.7% English, 8.6% Italian, 8.4% American (2008-2012 5-year est.).
Economy: Single-family building permits issued: 0 (2013); Multi-family building permits issued: 0 (2013); Homeowner vacancy rate: 0.0%. Rental vacancy rate: 8.3%. (2008-2012 5-year est.); Employment by occupation: 4.8% management, business, and financial, 0.9% computer, engineering,

and science, 6.9% education, legal, community service, arts, and media, 11.7% healthcare practitioners, 30.0% service, 12.6% sales and office, 4.3% natural resources, construction, and maintenance, 28.8% production, transportation, and material moving (2008-2012 5-year est.).
Income: Per capita income: $19,942 (2008-2012 5-year est.); Median household income: $40,870 (2008-2012 5-year est.); Average household income: $50,587 (2008-2012 5-year est.); Percent of households with income of $100,000 or more: 9.3% (2008-2012 5-year est.); Poverty rate: 13.5% (2008-2012 5-year est.).
Education: Percent of population age 25 and over with: High school diploma (including GED) or higher: 81.6% (2008-2012 5-year est.); Bachelor's degree or higher: 3.8% (2008-2012 5-year est.); Master's degree or higher: 1.2% (2008-2012 5-year est.).
School District(s)
Odin PSD 722 (PK-12)
    2011-12 Enrollment: 305. . . . . (618) 775-8266
Housing: Homeownership rate: 76.3% (2008-2012 5-year est.); Median home value: $48,300 (2008-2012 5-year est.); Median contract rent: $381 per month (2008-2012 5-year est.); Median year structure built: 1968 (2008-2012 5-year est.).
Health Insurance: 59.9% Private; 44.6% Public; 11.7% None. (2008-2012 5-year est.)
Transportation: Commute to work: 94.4% car, 0.0% public transportation, 4.9% walk, 0.7% work from home (2008-2012 5-year est.); Travel time to work: 30.8% less than 15 minutes, 47.7% 15 to 30 minutes, 8.5% 30 to 45 minutes, 12.7% 45 to 60 minutes, 0.5% 60 minutes or more (2008-2012 5-year est.)

PATOKA (village). Covers a land area of 1.110 square miles and a water area of 0 square miles. Located at 38.75° N. Lat; 89.10° W. Long. Elevation is 505 feet.
History: Patoka was named for an Indian chief. Oil was discovered in Patoka in 1937, bringing new growth to the town.
Population: 656 (1990); 633 (2000); 584 (2010); Density: 578.6 persons per square mile (2008-2012 5-year est.); Race: 99.4% White, 0.0% Black/African American, 0.0% Asian, 0.0% American Indian/Alaska Native, 0.0% Native Hawaiian/Other Pacific Islander, 0.6% Some other race, 0.6% Two or more races, 1.2% Hispanic of any race (2008-2012 5-year est.); Average household size: 2.57 (2008-2012 5-year est.); Median age: 45.4 (2008-2012 5-year est.); Males per 100 females: 97.6 (2008-2012 5-year est.); Marriage status: 17.5% never married, 58.8% now married, 8.9% widowed, 14.9% divorced (2008-2012 5-year est.); Foreign born: 0.0% (2008-2012 5-year est.); Ancestry (includes multiple ancestries): 18.4% German, 18.1% English, 14.0% Irish, 12.9% American, 4.2% French (2008-2012 5-year est.).
Economy: Homeowner vacancy rate: 3.1%. Rental vacancy rate: 0.0%. (2008-2012 5-year est.); Employment by occupation: 1.2% management, business, and financial, 0.0% computer, engineering, and science, 4.1% education, legal, community service, arts, and media, 11.5% healthcare practitioners, 25.9% service, 11.9% sales and office, 14.4% natural resources, construction, and maintenance, 30.9% production, transportation, and material moving (2008-2012 5-year est.).
Income: Per capita income: $18,277 (2008-2012 5-year est.); Median household income: $37,614 (2008-2012 5-year est.); Average household income: $45,708 (2008-2012 5-year est.); Percent of households with income of $100,000 or more: 9.6% (2008-2012 5-year est.); Poverty rate: 16.9% (2008-2012 5-year est.).
Education: Percent of population age 25 and over with: High school diploma (including GED) or higher: 77.1% (2008-2012 5-year est.); Bachelor's degree or higher: 3.8% (2008-2012 5-year est.); Master's degree or higher: 0.8% (2008-2012 5-year est.).
School District(s)
Patoka CUSD 100 (PK-12)
    2011-12 Enrollment: 259. . . . . (618) 432-5440
Housing: Homeownership rate: 74.8% (2008-2012 5-year est.); Median home value: $43,100 (2008-2012 5-year est.); Median contract rent: $338 per month (2008-2012 5-year est.); Median year structure built: 1961 (2008-2012 5-year est.).
Health Insurance: 50.5% Private; 51.4% Public; 14.0% None. (2008-2012 5-year est.)
Transportation: Commute to work: 96.1% car, 0.0% public transportation, 2.6% walk, 1.3% work from home (2008-2012 5-year est.); Travel time to work: 13.7% less than 15 minutes, 48.0% 15 to 30 minutes, 23.3% 30 to 45 minutes, 2.2% 45 to 60 minutes, 12.8% 60 minutes or more (2008-2012 5-year est.)

SALEM (city). County seat. Covers a land area of 6.941 square miles and a water area of 0.157 square miles. Located at 38.63° N. Lat; 88.96° W. Long. Elevation is 538 feet.

History: Salem was laid out in 1813 on the St. Louis-Vincennes stagecoach route, and incorporated in 1837. William Jennings Bryan (1860-1925) was born and grew up in Salem. Oil was discovered in Salem in 1939.

Population: 7,470 (1990); 7,909 (2000); 7,485 (2010); Density: 1,067.1 persons per square mile (2008-2012 5-year est.); Race: 95.8% White, 1.0% Black/African American, 0.9% Asian, 0.0% American Indian/Alaska Native, 0.0% Native Hawaiian/Other Pacific Islander, 2.3% Some other race, 1.9% Two or more races, 1.1% Hispanic of any race (2008-2012 5-year est.); Average household size: 2.31 (2008-2012 5-year est.); Median age: 38.8 (2008-2012 5-year est.); Males per 100 females: 91.8 (2008-2012 5-year est.); Marriage status: 26.0% never married, 51.9% now married, 9.7% widowed, 12.4% divorced (2008-2012 5-year est.); Foreign born: 1.2% (2008-2012 5-year est.); Ancestry (includes multiple ancestries): 25.4% German, 18.5% Irish, 13.6% English, 11.1% American, 3.7% Dutch (2008-2012 5-year est.).

Economy: Single-family building permits issued: 1 (2013); Multi-family building permits issued: 0 (2013); Homeowner vacancy rate: 2.4%. Rental vacancy rate: 3.4%. (2008-2012 5-year est.); Employment by occupation: 9.1% management, business, and financial, 1.8% computer, engineering, and science, 11.2% education, legal, community service, arts, and media, 8.6% healthcare practitioners, 20.5% service, 21.1% sales and office, 5.5% natural resources, construction, and maintenance, 22.3% production, transportation, and material moving (2008-2012 5-year est.).

Income: Per capita income: $21,266 (2008-2012 5-year est.); Median household income: $36,559 (2008-2012 5-year est.); Average household income: $49,699 (2008-2012 5-year est.); Percent of households with income of $100,000 or more: 10.1% (2008-2012 5-year est.); Poverty rate: 20.5% (2008-2012 5-year est.).

Education: Percent of population age 25 and over with: High school diploma (including GED) or higher: 86.6% (2008-2012 5-year est.); Bachelor's degree or higher: 19.8% (2008-2012 5-year est.); Master's degree or higher: 6.6% (2008-2012 5-year est.).

School District(s)
Clinton/marion/washington Roe (PK-12)
    2011-12 Enrollment: n/a . . . . (618) 594-2432
Marion/clinton/wash County Ctes
    2011-12 Enrollment: n/a . . . . (618) 548-6385
Salem CHSD 600 (09-12)
    2011-12 Enrollment: 769 . . . . (618) 548-0727
Salem SD 111 (PK-08)
    2011-12 Enrollment: 1,016 . . . . (618) 548-7702
Selmaville CCSD 10 (KG-08)
    2011-12 Enrollment: 215 . . . . (618) 548-2416

Housing: Homeownership rate: 63.4% (2008-2012 5-year est.); Median home value: $72,200 (2008-2012 5-year est.); Median contract rent: $410 per month (2008-2012 5-year est.); Median year structure built: 1970 (2008-2012 5-year est.).

Health Insurance: 63.3% Private; 43.9% Public; 9.1% None. (2008-2012 5-year est.)

Hospitals: Salem Township Hospital (46 beds)

Safety: Violent crime rate: 10.7 per 10,000 population; Property crime rate: 456.8 per 10,000 population (2012).

Transportation: Commute to work: 88.3% car, 0.9% public transportation, 3.6% walk, 5.4% work from home (2008-2012 5-year est.); Travel time to work: 56.1% less than 15 minutes, 20.8% 15 to 30 minutes, 12.6% 30 to 45 minutes, 4.4% 45 to 60 minutes, 6.1% 60 minutes or more (2008-2012 5-year est.)

Airports: Salem-Leckrone Airport (general aviation)

Additional Information Contacts
City of Salem . . . . (618) 548-2222
    http://www.salemil.us
Greater Salem Chamber of Commerce . . . . (618) 548-3010
    http://www.salemilchamber.com

SANDOVAL (village). Covers a land area of 1.002 square miles and a water area of 0 square miles. Located at 38.61° N. Lat; 89.12° W. Long. Elevation is 509 feet.

History: Incorporated 1859.

Population: 1,535 (1990); 1,434 (2000); 1,274 (2010); Density: 1,101.9 persons per square mile (2008-2012 5-year est.); Race: 92.4% White, 0.3% Black/African American, 0.5% Asian, 0.7% American Indian/Alaska Native, 0.3% Native Hawaiian/Other Pacific Islander, 5.8% Some other race, 5.8% Two or more races, 2.5% Hispanic of any race (2008-2012 5-year est.); Average household size: 2.45 (2008-2012 5-year est.); Median age: 34.8 (2008-2012 5-year est.); Males per 100 females: 79.2 (2008-2012 5-year est.); Marriage status: 22.9% never married, 54.2% now married, 8.3% widowed, 14.6% divorced (2008-2012 5-year est.); Foreign born: 1.0% (2008-2012 5-year est.); Ancestry (includes multiple ancestries): 34.1% German, 16.0% Irish, 12.7% English, 4.2% Italian, 4.2% American (2008-2012 5-year est.).

Economy: Single-family building permits issued: 0 (2013); Multi-family building permits issued: 0 (2013); Homeowner vacancy rate: 6.3%. Rental vacancy rate: 0.0%. (2008-2012 5-year est.); Employment by occupation: 7.6% management, business, and financial, 3.9% computer, engineering, and science, 7.6% education, legal, community service, arts, and media, 5.6% healthcare practitioners, 26.2% service, 26.2% sales and office, 5.1% natural resources, construction, and maintenance, 17.6% production, transportation, and material moving (2008-2012 5-year est.).

Income: Per capita income: $15,996 (2008-2012 5-year est.); Median household income: $26,667 (2008-2012 5-year est.); Average household income: $38,328 (2008-2012 5-year est.); Percent of households with income of $100,000 or more: 6.3% (2008-2012 5-year est.); Poverty rate: 27.4% (2008-2012 5-year est.).

Education: Percent of population age 25 and over with: High school diploma (including GED) or higher: 76.5% (2008-2012 5-year est.); Bachelor's degree or higher: 8.1% (2008-2012 5-year est.); Master's degree or higher: 1.6% (2008-2012 5-year est.).

School District(s)
Sandoval CUSD 501 (PK-12)
    2011-12 Enrollment: 532 . . . . (618) 247-3233

Housing: Homeownership rate: 59.1% (2008-2012 5-year est.); Median home value: $59,200 (2008-2012 5-year est.); Median contract rent: $201 per month (2008-2012 5-year est.); Median year structure built: 1971 (2008-2012 5-year est.).

Health Insurance: 39.3% Private; 56.1% Public; 14.7% None. (2008-2012 5-year est.)

Transportation: Commute to work: 93.4% car, 0.0% public transportation, 3.5% walk, 0.5% work from home (2008-2012 5-year est.); Travel time to work: 37.6% less than 15 minutes, 42.6% 15 to 30 minutes, 6.9% 30 to 45 minutes, 2.3% 45 to 60 minutes, 10.7% 60 minutes or more (2008-2012 5-year est.)

VERNON (village). Covers a land area of 0.912 square miles and a water area of 0 square miles. Located at 38.80° N. Lat; 89.09° W. Long. Elevation is 515 feet.

History: Vernon developed as the center of a peach and pear growing area.

Population: 207 (1990); 178 (2000); 129 (2010); Density: 137.0 persons per square mile (2008-2012 5-year est.); Race: 91.2% White, 0.0% Black/African American, 0.0% Asian, 0.8% American Indian/Alaska Native, 0.0% Native Hawaiian/Other Pacific Islander, 8.0% Some other race, 6.4% Two or more races, 12.0% Hispanic of any race (2008-2012 5-year est.); Average household size: 2.23 (2008-2012 5-year est.); Median age: 48.9 (2008-2012 5-year est.); Males per 100 females: 73.6 (2008-2012 5-year est.); Marriage status: 18.4% never married, 64.3% now married, 9.2% widowed, 8.2% divorced (2008-2012 5-year est.); Foreign born: 1.6% (2008-2012 5-year est.); Ancestry (includes multiple ancestries): 20.0% German, 16.8% Irish, 12.0% American, 11.2% Dutch, 10.4% English (2008-2012 5-year est.).

Economy: Homeowner vacancy rate: 12.5%. Rental vacancy rate: 0.0%. (2008-2012 5-year est.); Employment by occupation: 8.3% management, business, and financial, 0.0% computer, engineering, and science, 0.0% education, legal, community service, arts, and media, 0.0% healthcare practitioners, 36.1% service, 16.7% sales and office, 19.4% natural resources, construction, and maintenance, 19.4% production, transportation, and material moving (2008-2012 5-year est.).

Income: Per capita income: $15,650 (2008-2012 5-year est.); Median household income: $23,750 (2008-2012 5-year est.); Average household income: $32,752 (2008-2012 5-year est.); Percent of households with income of $100,000 or more: 5.4% (2008-2012 5-year est.); Poverty rate: 28.8% (2008-2012 5-year est.).

Education: Percent of population age 25 and over with: High school diploma (including GED) or higher: 72.3% (2008-2012 5-year est.); Bachelor's degree or higher: 0.0% (2008-2012 5-year est.); Master's degree or higher: 0.0% (2008-2012 5-year est.).

Housing: Homeownership rate: 87.5% (2008-2012 5-year est.); Median home value: $40,700 (2008-2012 5-year est.); Median contract rent: $763 per month (2008-2012 5-year est.); Median year structure built: 1961 (2008-2012 5-year est.).
Health Insurance: 59.2% Private; 63.2% Public; 9.6% None. (2008-2012 5-year est.)
Transportation: Commute to work: 86.1% car, 0.0% public transportation, 8.3% walk, 5.6% work from home (2008-2012 5-year est.); Travel time to work: 50.0% less than 15 minutes, 44.1% 15 to 30 minutes, 0.0% 30 to 45 minutes, 2.9% 45 to 60 minutes, 2.9% 60 minutes or more (2008-2012 5-year est.)

WALNUT HILL (village).
Covers a land area of 0.371 square miles and a water area of <.001 square miles. Located at 38.48° N. Lat; 89.04° W. Long. Elevation is 568 feet.
Population: 133 (1990); 109 (2000); 108 (2010); Density: 180.8 persons per square mile (2008-2012 5-year est.); Race: 100.0% White, 0.0% Black/African American, 0.0% Asian, 0.0% American Indian/Alaska Native, 0.0% Native Hawaiian/Other Pacific Islander, 0.0% Some other race, 0.0% Two or more races, 0.0% Hispanic of any race (2008-2012 5-year est.); Average household size: 2.16 (2008-2012 5-year est.); Median age: 37.7 (2008-2012 5-year est.); Males per 100 females: 86.1 (2008-2012 5-year est.); Marriage status: 14.3% never married, 36.7% now married, 10.2% widowed, 38.8% divorced (2008-2012 5-year est.); Foreign born: 0.0% (2008-2012 5-year est.); Ancestry (includes multiple ancestries): 40.3% German, 6.0% English, 4.5% Irish, 3.0% American, 1.5% Scotch-Irish (2008-2012 5-year est.).
Economy: Homeowner vacancy rate: 0.0%. Rental vacancy rate: 0.0%. (2008-2012 5-year est.); Employment by occupation: 6.7% management, business, and financial, 0.0% computer, engineering, and science, 23.3% education, legal, community service, arts, and media, 6.7% healthcare practitioners, 6.7% service, 10.0% sales and office, 3.3% natural resources, construction, and maintenance, 43.3% production, transportation, and material moving (2008-2012 5-year est.).
Income: Per capita income: $14,210 (2008-2012 5-year est.); Median household income: $25,625 (2008-2012 5-year est.); Average household income: $29,287 (2008-2012 5-year est.); Percent of households with income of $100,000 or more: n/a (2008-2012 5-year est.); Poverty rate: 25.4% (2008-2012 5-year est.).
Education: Percent of population age 25 and over with: High school diploma (including GED) or higher: 68.8% (2008-2012 5-year est.); Bachelor's degree or higher: 18.8% (2008-2012 5-year est.); Master's degree or higher: 0.0% (2008-2012 5-year est.).
Housing: Homeownership rate: 61.3% (2008-2012 5-year est.); Median home value: $19,200 (2008-2012 5-year est.); Median contract rent: $469 per month (2008-2012 5-year est.); Median year structure built: 1978 (2008-2012 5-year est.).
Health Insurance: 70.1% Private; 22.4% Public; 14.9% None. (2008-2012 5-year est.)
Transportation: Commute to work: 100.0% car, 0.0% public transportation, 0.0% walk, 0.0% work from home (2008-2012 5-year est.); Travel time to work: 53.3% less than 15 minutes, 43.3% 15 to 30 minutes, 3.3% 30 to 45 minutes, 0.0% 45 to 60 minutes, 0.0% 60 minutes or more (2008-2012 5-year est.)

Marshall County

Located in north central Illinois; drained by the Illinois River and Sandy Creek. Covers a land area of 386.789 square miles, a water area of 11.725 square miles, and is located in the Central Time Zone at 41.03° N. Lat., 89.34° W. Long. The county was founded in 1839. County seat is Lacon.

Marshall County is part of the Peoria, IL Metropolitan Statistical Area. The entire metro area includes: Marshall County, IL; Peoria County, IL; Stark County, IL; Tazewell County, IL; Woodford County, IL

Weather Station: Lacon 1 N											Elevation: 459 feet	
	Jan	Feb	Mar	Apr	May	Jun	Jul	Aug	Sep	Oct	Nov	Dec
High	34	38	51	64	75	84	87	86	79	66	52	38
Low	18	21	31	41	51	60	65	63	54	43	33	22
Precip	1.9	1.8	3.1	3.9	4.4	3.8	3.8	3.7	3.2	3.2	3.2	2.3
Snow	6.5	5.0	2.9	0.8	tr	0.0	0.0	0.0	0.0	tr	0.8	6.1

High and Low temperatures in degrees Fahrenheit; Precipitation and Snow in inches

Population: 12,846 (1990); 13,180 (2000); 12,640 (2010); Race: 96.7% White, 0.4% Black/African American, 0.6% Asian, 0.1% American Indian/Alaska Native, 0.0% Native Hawaiian/Other Pacific Islander, 2.2% Some other race, 0.7% Two or more races, 2.6% Hispanic of any race (2008-2012 5-year est.); Density: 31.8 persons per square mile (2008-2012 5-year est.); Average household size: 2.41 (2008-2012 5-year est.); Median age: 44.9 (2008-2012 5-year est.); Males per 100 females: 98.2 (2008-2012 5-year est.).
Religion: Six largest groups: 18.1% Catholicism, 12.4% Lutheran, 9.0% Baptist, 5.2% Presbyterian-Reformed, 4.8% Methodist/Pietist, 2.0% Non-denominational Protestant (2010)
Economy: Unemployment rate: 6.6% (April 2014); Total civilian labor force: 6,535 (April 2014); Leading industries: 31.5% manufacturing; 16.6% health care and social assistance; 13.1% retail trade (2012); Farms: 440 totaling 209,094 acres (2012); Companies that employ 500 or more persons: 0 (2012); Companies that employ 100 to 499 persons: 4 (2012); Companies that employ less than 100 persons: 275 (2012); Black-owned businesses: n/a (2007); Hispanic-owned businesses: n/a (2007); Asian-owned businesses: n/a (2007); Women-owned businesses: n/a (2007); Single-family building permits issued: 6 (2013); Multi-family building permits issued: 0 (2013).
Income: Per capita income: $25,985 (2008-2012 5-year est.); Median household income: $52,565 (2008-2012 5-year est.); Average household income: $62,372 (2008-2012 5-year est.); Percent of households with income of $100,000 or more: 16.2% (2008-2012 5-year est.); Poverty rate: 10.2% (2008-2012 5-year est.); Bankruptcy rate: 4.06% (2013).
Education: Percent of population age 25 and over with: High school diploma (including GED) or higher: 91.0% (2008-2012 5-year est.); Bachelor's degree or higher: 16.5% (2008-2012 5-year est.); Master's degree or higher: 3.9% (2008-2012 5-year est.).
Housing: Homeownership rate: 81.7% (2008-2012 5-year est.); Median home value: $103,500 (2008-2012 5-year est.); Median contract rent: $426 per month (2008-2012 5-year est.); Median year structure built: 1960 (2008-2012 5-year est.)
Health: Birth rate: 89.7 per 10,000 population (2013); Death rate: 111.9 per 10,000 population (2013); Age-adjusted cancer mortality rate: 120.6 deaths per 100,000 population (2011); Number of physicians: 2.4 per 10,000 population (2011); Hospital beds: 0.0 per 10,000 population (2010); Hospital admissions: 0.0 per 10,000 population (2010).
Elections: 2012 Presidential election results: 42.0% Obama, 56.3% Romney
National and State Parks: Cameron National Wildlife Refuge; Marshall County State Conservation Areas; Sparland State Conservation Area
Additional Information Contacts
Marshall County Government . . . . (309) 246-6325
   http://www.marshallcountyillinois.com

Marshall County Communities

CAMP GROVE (unincorporated postal area)
Zip Code: 61424
   Covers a land area of 0.730 square miles and a water area of 0 square miles. Located at 41.07° N. Lat; 89.63° W. Long. Elevation is 840 feet. Population: 100 (2010); Density: 136.9 persons per square mile (2010); Race: 97.0% White, 3.0% Black/African American, 0.0% Asian, 0.0% American Indian/Alaska Native, 0.0% Native Hawaiian/Other Pacific Islander, 0.0% Some other race, 0.0% Two or more races, 1.0% Hispanic of any race (2010); Average household size: 2.44 (2010); Median age: 34.3 (2010); Males per 100 females: 108.3 (2010); Homeownership rate: 73.1% (2010)

HENRY (city).
Covers a land area of 1.324 square miles and a water area of 0.072 square miles. Located at 41.11° N. Lat; 89.36° W. Long. Elevation is 492 feet.
History: Founded in early 1840s; incorporated 1854.
Population: 2,591 (1990); 2,540 (2000); 2,464 (2010); Density: 1,910.0 persons per square mile (2008-2012 5-year est.); Race: 97.5% White, 0.2% Black/African American, 0.9% Asian, 0.0% American Indian/Alaska Native, 0.0% Native Hawaiian/Other Pacific Islander, 1.4% Some other race, 1.3% Two or more races, 0.8% Hispanic of any race (2008-2012 5-year est.); Average household size: 2.31 (2008-2012 5-year est.); Median age: 43.4 (2008-2012 5-year est.); Males per 100 females: 88.4 (2008-2012 5-year est.); Marriage status: 25.3% never married, 50.4% now married, 11.4% widowed, 12.9% divorced (2008-2012 5-year est.); Foreign born: 1.2% (2008-2012 5-year est.); Ancestry (includes multiple

ancestries): 39.7% German, 16.8% Irish, 15.0% English, 7.9% American, 5.4% Italian (2008-2012 5-year est.).
Economy: Single-family building permits issued: 2 (2013); Multi-family building permits issued: 0 (2013); Homeowner vacancy rate: 6.3%. Rental vacancy rate: 0.0%. (2008-2012 5-year est.); Employment by occupation: 6.5% management, business, and financial, 3.4% computer, engineering, and science, 9.0% education, legal, community service, arts, and media, 4.5% healthcare practitioners, 26.2% service, 19.8% sales and office, 12.1% natural resources, construction, and maintenance, 18.5% production, transportation, and material moving (2008-2012 5-year est.).
Income: Per capita income: $24,281 (2008-2012 5-year est.); Median household income: $44,569 (2008-2012 5-year est.); Average household income: $56,888 (2008-2012 5-year est.); Percent of households with income of $100,000 or more: 11.3% (2008-2012 5-year est.); Poverty rate: 10.9% (2008-2012 5-year est.).
Education: Percent of population age 25 and over with: High school diploma (including GED) or higher: 88.4% (2008-2012 5-year est.); Bachelor's degree or higher: 16.5% (2008-2012 5-year est.); Master's degree or higher: 2.9% (2008-2012 5-year est.).

School District(s)
Henry-Senachwine CUSD 5 (PK-12)
   2011-12 Enrollment: 627 . . . . (309) 364-3614
Housing: Homeownership rate: 77.2% (2008-2012 5-year est.); Median home value: $84,500 (2008-2012 5-year est.); Median contract rent: $410 per month (2008-2012 5-year est.); Median year structure built: 1951 (2008-2012 5-year est.).
Health Insurance: 75.4% Private; 34.8% Public; 8.7% None. (2008-2012 5-year est.)
Transportation: Commute to work: 94.6% car, 0.0% public transportation, 0.5% walk, 3.8% work from home (2008-2012 5-year est.); Travel time to work: 43.3% less than 15 minutes, 21.3% 15 to 30 minutes, 14.8% 30 to 45 minutes, 12.5% 45 to 60 minutes, 8.1% 60 minutes or more (2008-2012 5-year est.).
Additional Information Contacts
Henry Area Chamber of Commerce . . . . (309) 364-3261
   http://www.henrychamber.org

HOPEWELL (village).
Covers a land area of 1.135 square miles and a water area of 0 square miles. Located at 40.98° N. Lat; 89.46° W. Long. Elevation is 633 feet.
Population: 343 (1990); 396 (2000); 410 (2010); Density: 377.0 persons per square mile (2008-2012 5-year est.); Race: 99.3% White, 0.7% Black/African American, 0.0% Asian, 0.0% American Indian/Alaska Native, 0.0% Native Hawaiian/Other Pacific Islander, 0.0% Some other race, 0.0% Two or more races, 2.1% Hispanic of any race (2008-2012 5-year est.); Average household size: 2.73 (2008-2012 5-year est.); Median age: 44.2 (2008-2012 5-year est.); Males per 100 females: 103.8 (2008-2012 5-year est.); Marriage status: 17.1% never married, 74.0% now married, 1.7% widowed, 7.2% divorced (2008-2012 5-year est.); Foreign born: 1.4% (2008-2012 5-year est.); Ancestry (includes multiple ancestries): 38.3% German, 16.1% Irish, 10.3% Italian, 8.6% Polish, 8.4% American (2008-2012 5-year est.).
Economy: Single-family building permits issued: 1 (2013); Multi-family building permits issued: 0 (2013); Homeowner vacancy rate: 0.0%. Rental vacancy rate: 0.0%. (2008-2012 5-year est.); Employment by occupation: 16.6% management, business, and financial, 13.5% computer, engineering, and science, 9.4% education, legal, community service, arts, and media, 7.2% healthcare practitioners, 7.2% service, 24.7% sales and office, 8.1% natural resources, construction, and maintenance, 13.5% production, transportation, and material moving (2008-2012 5-year est.).
Income: Per capita income: $35,390 (2008-2012 5-year est.); Median household income: $83,750 (2008-2012 5-year est.); Average household income: $94,196 (2008-2012 5-year est.); Percent of households with income of $100,000 or more: 40.7% (2008-2012 5-year est.); Poverty rate: 3.5% (2008-2012 5-year est.).
Education: Percent of population age 25 and over with: High school diploma (including GED) or higher: 96.5% (2008-2012 5-year est.); Bachelor's degree or higher: 34.9% (2008-2012 5-year est.); Master's degree or higher: 10.5% (2008-2012 5-year est.).
Housing: Homeownership rate: 97.5% (2008-2012 5-year est.); Median home value: $166,700 (2008-2012 5-year est.); Median contract rent: $833 per month (2008-2012 5-year est.); Median year structure built: 1978 (2008-2012 5-year est.).
Health Insurance: 87.9% Private; 17.1% Public; 5.4% None. (2008-2012 5-year est.)

Transportation: Commute to work: 97.2% car, 0.0% public transportation, 0.0% walk, 0.9% work from home (2008-2012 5-year est.); Travel time to work: 9.8% less than 15 minutes, 40.7% 15 to 30 minutes, 39.7% 30 to 45 minutes, 5.1% 45 to 60 minutes, 4.7% 60 minutes or more (2008-2012 5-year est.)

LA ROSE (village).
Covers a land area of 0.255 square miles and a water area of 0 square miles. Located at 40.98° N. Lat; 89.23° W. Long. Elevation is 682 feet.
Population: 130 (1990); 159 (2000); 144 (2010); Density: 478.6 persons per square mile (2008-2012 5-year est.); Race: 100.0% White, 0.0% Black/African American, 0.0% Asian, 0.0% American Indian/Alaska Native, 0.0% Native Hawaiian/Other Pacific Islander, 0.0% Some other race, 0.0% Two or more races, 0.0% Hispanic of any race (2008-2012 5-year est.); Average household size: 2.18 (2008-2012 5-year est.); Median age: 45.3 (2008-2012 5-year est.); Males per 100 females: 79.4 (2008-2012 5-year est.); Marriage status: 27.1% never married, 53.3% now married, 9.3% widowed, 10.3% divorced (2008-2012 5-year est.); Foreign born: 0.0% (2008-2012 5-year est.); Ancestry (includes multiple ancestries): 38.5% German, 29.5% Irish, 16.4% English, 5.7% American, 4.9% Dutch (2008-2012 5-year est.).
Economy: Homeowner vacancy rate: 0.0%. Rental vacancy rate: 0.0%. (2008-2012 5-year est.); Employment by occupation: 12.1% management, business, and financial, 0.0% computer, engineering, and science, 0.0% education, legal, community service, arts, and media, 1.5% healthcare practitioners, 30.3% service, 12.1% sales and office, 6.1% natural resources, construction, and maintenance, 37.9% production, transportation, and material moving (2008-2012 5-year est.).
Income: Per capita income: $25,693 (2008-2012 5-year est.); Median household income: $54,000 (2008-2012 5-year est.); Average household income: $57,591 (2008-2012 5-year est.); Percent of households with income of $100,000 or more: 7.2% (2008-2012 5-year est.); Poverty rate: 16.4% (2008-2012 5-year est.).
Education: Percent of population age 25 and over with: High school diploma (including GED) or higher: 96.8% (2008-2012 5-year est.); Bachelor's degree or higher: 10.6% (2008-2012 5-year est.); Master's degree or higher: 10.6% (2008-2012 5-year est.).
Housing: Homeownership rate: 98.2% (2008-2012 5-year est.); Median home value: $69,000 (2008-2012 5-year est.); Median contract rent: n/a per month (2008-2012 5-year est.); Median year structure built: Before 1940 (2008-2012 5-year est.).
Health Insurance: 77.0% Private; 29.5% Public; 12.3% None. (2008-2012 5-year est.)
Transportation: Commute to work: 97.0% car, 0.0% public transportation, 1.5% walk, 1.5% work from home (2008-2012 5-year est.); Travel time to work: 29.2% less than 15 minutes, 30.8% 15 to 30 minutes, 24.6% 30 to 45 minutes, 10.8% 45 to 60 minutes, 4.6% 60 minutes or more (2008-2012 5-year est.)

LACON (city).
County seat. Covers a land area of 1.596 square miles and a water area of 0.041 square miles. Located at 41.02° N. Lat; 89.41° W. Long. Elevation is 476 feet.
History: Laid out as Columbia in 1826; incorporated 1839.
Population: 1,986 (1990); 1,979 (2000); 1,937 (2010); Density: 1,227.0 persons per square mile (2008-2012 5-year est.); Race: 99.4% White, 0.4% Black/African American, 0.0% Asian, 0.0% American Indian/Alaska Native, 0.0% Native Hawaiian/Other Pacific Islander, 0.2% Some other race, 0.2% Two or more races, 1.6% Hispanic of any race (2008-2012 5-year est.); Average household size: 2.34 (2008-2012 5-year est.); Median age: 47.8 (2008-2012 5-year est.); Males per 100 females: 96.8 (2008-2012 5-year est.); Marriage status: 24.6% never married, 55.9% now married, 10.6% widowed, 8.8% divorced (2008-2012 5-year est.); Foreign born: 1.7% (2008-2012 5-year est.); Ancestry (includes multiple ancestries): 32.0% German, 29.2% Irish, 18.0% English, 8.2% American, 5.2% Polish (2008-2012 5-year est.).
Economy: Single-family building permits issued: 0 (2013); Multi-family building permits issued: 0 (2013); Homeowner vacancy rate: 2.8%. Rental vacancy rate: 9.0%. (2008-2012 5-year est.); Employment by occupation: 9.2% management, business, and financial, 2.6% computer, engineering, and science, 5.8% education, legal, community service, arts, and media, 7.6% healthcare practitioners, 18.3% service, 27.7% sales and office, 11.2% natural resources, construction, and maintenance, 17.5% production, transportation, and material moving (2008-2012 5-year est.).
Income: Per capita income: $24,993 (2008-2012 5-year est.); Median household income: $53,063 (2008-2012 5-year est.); Average household

income: $58,101 (2008-2012 5-year est.); Percent of households with income of $100,000 or more: 18.2% (2008-2012 5-year est.); Poverty rate: 10.0% (2008-2012 5-year est.).

Education: Percent of population age 25 and over with: High school diploma (including GED) or higher: 91.2% (2008-2012 5-year est.); Bachelor's degree or higher: 14.3% (2008-2012 5-year est.); Master's degree or higher: 3.6% (2008-2012 5-year est.).

School District(s)

Midland CUSD 7 (PK-12)
  2011-12 Enrollment: 797......................... (309) 463-2364

Housing: Homeownership rate: 79.6% (2008-2012 5-year est.); Median home value: $95,400 (2008-2012 5-year est.); Median contract rent: $443 per month (2008-2012 5-year est.); Median year structure built: 1951 (2008-2012 5-year est.).

Health Insurance: 78.8% Private; 34.5% Public; 8.2% None. (2008-2012 5-year est.)

Safety: Violent crime rate: 15.6 per 10,000 population; Property crime rate: 98.9 per 10,000 population (2012).

Transportation: Commute to work: 89.7% car, 0.0% public transportation, 8.9% walk, 0.7% work from home (2008-2012 5-year est.); Travel time to work: 44.1% less than 15 minutes, 17.3% 15 to 30 minutes, 18.0% 30 to 45 minutes, 8.6% 45 to 60 minutes, 12.0% 60 minutes or more (2008-2012 5-year est.)

Airports: Marshall County Airport (general aviation)

Additional Information Contacts

Lacon Chamber of Commerce .... (309) 246-5222
  http://www.laconchamber.com

SPARLAND (village). Covers a land area of 0.572 square miles and a water area of 0 square miles. Located at 41.03° N. Lat; 89.44° W. Long. Elevation is 472 feet.

Population: 412 (1990); 504 (2000); 406 (2010); Density: 795.1 persons per square mile (2008-2012 5-year est.); Race: 94.7% White, 0.0% Black/African American, 0.0% Asian, 0.0% American Indian/Alaska Native, 0.0% Native Hawaiian/Other Pacific Islander, 5.3% Some other race, 0.7% Two or more races, 5.1% Hispanic of any race (2008-2012 5-year est.); Average household size: 2.81 (2008-2012 5-year est.); Median age: 41.1 (2008-2012 5-year est.); Males per 100 females: 92.8 (2008-2012 5-year est.); Marriage status: 25.9% never married, 60.0% now married, 6.5% widowed, 7.6% divorced (2008-2012 5-year est.); Foreign born: 0.0% (2008-2012 5-year est.); Ancestry (includes multiple ancestries): 40.7% German, 25.7% Irish, 9.7% English, 5.7% American, 4.2% French (2008-2012 5-year est.).

Economy: Homeowner vacancy rate: 0.0%. Rental vacancy rate: 0.0%. (2008-2012 5-year est.); Employment by occupation: 4.9% management, business, and financial, 1.6% computer, engineering, and science, 8.2% education, legal, community service, arts, and media, 3.3% healthcare practitioners, 27.3% service, 25.1% sales and office, 6.6% natural resources, construction, and maintenance, 23.0% production, transportation, and material moving (2008-2012 5-year est.).

Income: Per capita income: $18,011 (2008-2012 5-year est.); Median household income: $45,000 (2008-2012 5-year est.); Average household income: $49,749 (2008-2012 5-year est.); Percent of households with income of $100,000 or more: 5.6% (2008-2012 5-year est.); Poverty rate: 18.3% (2008-2012 5-year est.).

Education: Percent of population age 25 and over with: High school diploma (including GED) or higher: 76.5% (2008-2012 5-year est.); Bachelor's degree or higher: 1.3% (2008-2012 5-year est.); Master's degree or higher: 0.6% (2008-2012 5-year est.).

School District(s)

Midland CUSD 7 (PK-12)
  2011-12 Enrollment: 797......................... (309) 463-2364

Housing: Homeownership rate: 86.4% (2008-2012 5-year est.); Median home value: $78,900 (2008-2012 5-year est.); Median contract rent: $660 per month (2008-2012 5-year est.); Median year structure built: 1949 (2008-2012 5-year est.).

Health Insurance: 63.9% Private; 36.5% Public; 15.3% None. (2008-2012 5-year est.)

Transportation: Commute to work: 98.3% car, 0.0% public transportation, 0.0% walk, 0.6% work from home (2008-2012 5-year est.); Travel time to work: 25.0% less than 15 minutes, 29.0% 15 to 30 minutes, 26.1% 30 to 45 minutes, 14.8% 45 to 60 minutes, 5.1% 60 minutes or more (2008-2012 5-year est.)

TOLUCA (city). Covers a land area of 1.062 square miles and a water area of 0 square miles. Located at 41.00° N. Lat; 89.13° W. Long. Elevation is 692 feet.

History: Incorporated 1894.

Population: 1,315 (1990); 1,339 (2000); 1,414 (2010); Density: 1,286.1 persons per square mile (2008-2012 5-year est.); Race: 86.7% White, 2.0% Black/African American, 0.0% Asian, 0.4% American Indian/Alaska Native, 0.0% Native Hawaiian/Other Pacific Islander, 10.9% Some other race, 1.0% Two or more races, 14.1% Hispanic of any race (2008-2012 5-year est.); Average household size: 2.19 (2008-2012 5-year est.); Median age: 45.6 (2008-2012 5-year est.); Males per 100 females: 85.3 (2008-2012 5-year est.); Marriage status: 22.8% never married, 50.4% now married, 13.5% widowed, 13.4% divorced (2008-2012 5-year est.); Foreign born: 7.0% (2008-2012 5-year est.); Ancestry (includes multiple ancestries): 42.5% German, 14.3% Italian, 10.1% Irish, 8.3% English, 6.2% Polish (2008-2012 5-year est.).

Economy: Single-family building permits issued: 0 (2013); Multi-family building permits issued: 0 (2013); Homeowner vacancy rate: 2.2%. Rental vacancy rate: 0.0%. (2008-2012 5-year est.); Employment by occupation: 13.6% management, business, and financial, 2.0% computer, engineering, and science, 3.8% education, legal, community service, arts, and media, 3.2% healthcare practitioners, 19.8% service, 18.6% sales and office, 9.5% natural resources, construction, and maintenance, 29.6% production, transportation, and material moving (2008-2012 5-year est.).

Income: Per capita income: $28,245 (2008-2012 5-year est.); Median household income: $42,014 (2008-2012 5-year est.); Average household income: $62,044 (2008-2012 5-year est.); Percent of households with income of $100,000 or more: 11.1% (2008-2012 5-year est.); Poverty rate: 11.4% (2008-2012 5-year est.).

Education: Percent of population age 25 and over with: High school diploma (including GED) or higher: 86.5% (2008-2012 5-year est.); Bachelor's degree or higher: 15.5% (2008-2012 5-year est.); Master's degree or higher: 4.1% (2008-2012 5-year est.).

School District(s)

Fieldcrest CUSD 6 (PK-12)
  2011-12 Enrollment: 1,226 .... (309) 432-2177

Housing: Homeownership rate: 76.2% (2008-2012 5-year est.); Median home value: $88,200 (2008-2012 5-year est.); Median contract rent: $410 per month (2008-2012 5-year est.); Median year structure built: 1949 (2000-2012 5-year est.).

Health Insurance: 69.4% Private; 31.6% Public; 14.2% None. (2008-2012 5-year est.)

Transportation: Commute to work: 86.0% car, 0.0% public transportation, 9.4% walk, 3.3% work from home (2008-2012 5-year est.); Travel time to work: 46.2% less than 15 minutes, 17.4% 15 to 30 minutes, 13.4% 30 to 45 minutes, 12.0% 45 to 60 minutes, 10.9% 60 minutes or more (2008-2012 5-year est.)

VARNA (village). Covers a land area of 0.297 square miles and a water area of 0 square miles. Located at 41.04° N. Lat; 89.22° W. Long. Elevation is 728 feet.

Population: 405 (1990); 436 (2000); 384 (2010); Density: 1,243.5 persons per square mile (2008-2012 5-year est.); Race: 96.7% White, 0.3% Black/African American, 0.8% Asian, 0.5% American Indian/Alaska Native, 0.0% Native Hawaiian/Other Pacific Islander, 1.7% Some other race, 1.6% Two or more races, 0.5% Hispanic of any race (2008-2012 5-year est.); Average household size: 2.54 (2008-2012 5-year est.); Median age: 38.9 (2008-2012 5-year est.); Males per 100 females: 99.5 (2008-2012 5-year est.); Marriage status: 14.9% never married, 69.1% now married, 8.9% widowed, 7.1% divorced (2008-2012 5-year est.); Foreign born: 0.8% (2008-2012 5-year est.); Ancestry (includes multiple ancestries): 55.3% German, 23.3% Irish, 13.3% English, 12.7% Swedish, 11.4% Italian (2008-2012 5-year est.).

Economy: Homeowner vacancy rate: 0.0%. Rental vacancy rate: 0.0%. (2008-2012 5-year est.); Employment by occupation: 9.4% management, business, and financial, 10.1% computer, engineering, and science, 6.9% education, legal, community service, arts, and media, 10.7% healthcare practitioners, 13.2% service, 18.9% sales and office, 10.1% natural resources, construction, and maintenance, 20.8% production, transportation, and material moving (2008-2012 5-year est.).

Income: Per capita income: $23,770 (2008-2012 5-year est.); Median household income: $57,969 (2008-2012 5-year est.); Average household income: $60,979 (2008-2012 5-year est.); Percent of households with income of $100,000 or more: 13.1% (2008-2012 5-year est.); Poverty rate: 4.6% (2008-2012 5-year est.).

Education: Percent of population age 25 and over with: High school diploma (including GED) or higher: 96.1% (2008-2012 5-year est.); Bachelor's degree or higher: 11.0% (2008-2012 5-year est.); Master's degree or higher: 2.4% (2008-2012 5-year est.).

School District(s)

Midland CUSD 7 (PK-12)

  2011-12 Enrollment: 797 . . . . (309) 463-2364

Housing: Homeownership rate: 97.9% (2008-2012 5-year est.); Median home value: $86,500 (2008-2012 5-year est.); Median contract rent: n/a per month (2008-2012 5-year est.); Median year structure built: Before 1940 (2008-2012 5-year est.).

Health Insurance: 78.3% Private; 28.3% Public; 8.4% None. (2008-2012 5-year est.)

Transportation: Commute to work: 91.9% car, 0.0% public transportation, 1.3% walk, 3.8% work from home (2008-2012 5-year est.); Travel time to work: 24.7% less than 15 minutes, 17.5% 15 to 30 minutes, 27.9% 30 to 45 minutes, 17.5% 45 to 60 minutes, 12.3% 60 minutes or more (2008-2012 5-year est.)

WENONA (city). Covers a land area of 0.740 square miles and a water area of 0 square miles. Located at 41.05° N. Lat; 89.05° W. Long. Elevation is 699 feet.

History: Wenona's early economy was based on soy beans and corn.

Population: 950 (1990); 1,065 (2000); 1,056 (2010); Density: 1,476.3 persons per square mile (2008-2012 5-year est.); Race: 96.2% White, 0.0% Black/African American, 0.0% Asian, 0.2% American Indian/Alaska Native, 0.0% Native Hawaiian/Other Pacific Islander, 3.6% Some other race, 1.6% Two or more races, 3.8% Hispanic of any race (2008-2012 5-year est.); Average household size: 2.34 (2008-2012 5-year est.); Median age: 41.1 (2008-2012 5-year est.); Males per 100 females: 102.8 (2008-2012 5-year est.); Marriage status: 30.3% never married, 48.4% now married, 8.6% widowed, 12.7% divorced (2008-2012 5-year est.); Foreign born: 1.3% (2008-2012 5-year est.); Ancestry (includes multiple ancestries): 32.6% German, 13.2% Irish, 8.6% English, 8.0% Polish, 7.4% Italian (2008-2012 5-year est.).

Economy: Single-family building permits issued: 0 (2013); Multi-family building permits issued: 0 (2013); Homeowner vacancy rate: 1.8%. Rental vacancy rate: 13.3%. (2008-2012 5-year est.); Employment by occupation: 10.4% management, business, and financial, 0.0% computer, engineering, and science, 4.7% education, legal, community service, arts, and media, 6.1% healthcare practitioners, 25.0% service, 14.0% sales and office, 14.6% natural resources, construction, and maintenance, 25.2% production, transportation, and material moving (2008-2012 5-year est.).

Income: Per capita income: $22,933 (2008-2012 5-year est.); Median household income: $41,000 (2008-2012 5-year est.); Average household income: $51,763 (2008-2012 5-year est.); Percent of households with income of $100,000 or more: 11.0% (2008-2012 5-year est.); Poverty rate: 13.2% (2008-2012 5-year est.).

Education: Percent of population age 25 and over with: High school diploma (including GED) or higher: 83.4% (2008-2012 5-year est.); Bachelor's degree or higher: 14.8% (2008-2012 5-year est.); Master's degree or higher: 4.5% (2008-2012 5-year est.).

School District(s)

Fieldcrest CUSD 6 (PK-12)

  2011-12 Enrollment: 1,226 . . . . (309) 432-2177

Housing: Homeownership rate: 80.5% (2008-2012 5-year est.); Median home value: $85,400 (2008-2012 5-year est.); Median contract rent: $455 per month (2008-2012 5-year est.); Median year structure built: 1949 (2008-2012 5-year est.).

Health Insurance: 69.3% Private; 35.6% Public; 11.3% None. (2008-2012 5-year est.)

Transportation: Commute to work: 96.2% car, 1.0% public transportation, 1.6% walk, 0.6% work from home (2008-2012 5-year est.); Travel time to work: 49.7% less than 15 minutes, 24.1% 15 to 30 minutes, 12.9% 30 to 45 minutes, 7.0% 45 to 60 minutes, 6.4% 60 minutes or more (2008-2012 5-year est.)

Mason County

Located in central Illinois; bounded on the west by the Illinois River, and on the south by the Sangamon River and Salt Creek. Covers a land area of 539.238 square miles, a water area of 24.226 square miles, and is located in the Central Time Zone at 40.24° N. Lat., 89.91° W. Long. The county was founded in 1841. County seat is Havana.

Weather Station: Havana 4 NNE   Elevation: 459 feet

	Jan	Feb	Mar	Apr	May	Jun	Jul	Aug	Sep	Oct	Nov	Dec
High	34	39	51	64	74	84	88	86	80	67	52	38
Low	16	20	30	40	51	61	65	62	52	41	31	20
Precip	2.1	2.1	2.8	3.6	4.5	4.2	3.9	3.8	3.2	3.0	3.2	2.8
Snow	9.3	7.5	3.1	1.1	tr	0.0	0.0	0.0	0.0	tr	1.0	7.5

High and Low temperatures in degrees Fahrenheit; Precipitation and Snow in inches

Weather Station: Mason City 1 W   Elevation: 584 feet

	Jan	Feb	Mar	Apr	May	Jun	Jul	Aug	Sep	Oct	Nov	Dec
High	34	40	52	65	75	84	86	85	79	67	51	38
Low	18	22	31	42	52	62	65	63	55	44	33	22
Precip	1.7	1.6	2.3	3.5	4.0	4.0	4.4	3.5	3.1	2.9	3.2	2.3
Snow	4.4	3.8	1.7	0.5	0.0	0.0	0.0	0.0	0.0	tr	0.4	4.2

High and Low temperatures in degrees Fahrenheit; Precipitation and Snow in inches

Population: 16,269 (1990); 16,038 (2000); 14,666 (2010); Race: 98.2% White, 0.9% Black/African American, 0.3% Asian, 0.1% American Indian/Alaska Native, 0.1% Native Hawaiian/Other Pacific Islander, 0.4% Some other race, 0.3% Two or more races, 0.8% Hispanic of any race (2008-2012 5-year est.); Density: 26.7 persons per square mile (2008-2012 5-year est.); Average household size: 2.25 (2008-2012 5-year est.); Median age: 44.3 (2008-2012 5-year est.); Males per 100 females: 96.6 (2008-2012 5-year est.).

Religion: Six largest groups: 12.8% Baptist, 10.0% Lutheran, 9.4% Methodist/Pietist, 4.7% Catholicism, 2.1% Pentecostal, 2.1% Holiness (2010)

Economy: Unemployment rate: 8.4% (April 2014); Total civilian labor force: 6,947 (April 2014); Leading industries: 17.7% retail trade; 12.7% wholesale trade; 11.0% transportation & warehousing (2012); Farms: 490 totaling 289,841 acres (2012); Companies that employ 500 or more persons: 0 (2012); Companies that employ 100 to 499 persons: 2 (2012); Companies that employ less than 100 persons: 304 (2012); Black-owned businesses: n/a (2007); Hispanic-owned businesses: n/a (2007); Asian-owned businesses: n/a (2007); Women-owned businesses: 197 (2007); Single-family building permits issued: 7 (2013); Multi-family building permits issued: 0 (2013).

Income: Per capita income: $23,967 (2008-2012 5-year est.); Median household income: $42,394 (2008-2012 5-year est.); Average household income: $55,433 (2008-2012 5-year est.); Percent of households with income of $100,000 or more: 13.5% (2008-2012 5-year est.); Poverty rate: 17.0% (2008-2012 5-year est.); Bankruptcy rate: 3.35% (2013).

Taxes: Total county taxes per capita: $241 (2011); County property taxes per capita: $194 (2011).

Education: Percent of population age 25 and over with: High school diploma (including GED) or higher: 84.9% (2008-2012 5-year est.); Bachelor's degree or higher: 14.9% (2008-2012 5-year est.); Master's degree or higher: 5.4% (2008-2012 5-year est.).

Housing: Homeownership rate: 79.7% (2008-2012 5-year est.); Median home value: $81,600 (2008-2012 5-year est.); Median contract rent: $403 per month (2008-2012 5-year est.); Median year structure built: 1959 (2008-2012 5-year est.)

Health: Birth rate: 102.5 per 10,000 population (2013); Death rate: 126.3 per 10,000 population (2013); Age-adjusted cancer mortality rate: 204.6 deaths per 100,000 population (2011); Number of physicians: 6.2 per 10,000 population (2011); Hospital beds: 13.6 per 10,000 population (2010); Hospital admissions: 298.6 per 10,000 population (2010).

Elections: 2012 Presidential election results: 45.7% Obama, 52.1% Romney

National and State Parks: Chautauqua National Wildlife Refuge; Chautauqua National Migratory Waterfowl Refuge; Mason County State Wildlife Refuge and Recreation; Sand Ridge State Forest

Additional Information Contacts

Mason County Government . . . . (309) 543-6661

  http://www.masoncountyil.org

Mason County Communities

BATH (village). Covers a land area of 0.365 square miles and a water area of <.001 square miles. Located at 40.19° N. Lat; 90.14° W. Long. Elevation is 463 feet.

History: Bath was surveyed in 1836 by Abraham Lincoln, who was then the Deputy Surveyor of Sangamon County. Bath served as the county seat from 1843 to 1851.

Population: 388 (1990); 310 (2000); 333 (2010); Density: 949.1 persons per square mile (2008-2012 5-year est.); Race: 100.0% White, 0.0%

Black/African American, 0.0% Asian, 0.0% American Indian/Alaska Native, 0.0% Native Hawaiian/Other Pacific Islander, 0.0% Some other race, 0.0% Two or more races, 0.0% Hispanic of any race (2008-2012 5-year est.); Average household size: 2.31 (2008-2012 5-year est.); Median age: 44.2 (2008-2012 5-year est.); Males per 100 females: 61.7 (2008-2012 5-year est.); Marriage status: 26.8% never married, 40.4% now married, 13.9% widowed, 18.8% divorced (2008-2012 5-year est.); Foreign born: 0.0% (2008-2012 5-year est.); Ancestry (includes multiple ancestries): 24.6% American, 22.8% German, 13.0% Irish, 9.5% English, 3.2% French (2008-2012 5-year est.).

Economy: Single-family building permits issued: 0 (2013); Multi-family building permits issued: 0 (2013); Homeowner vacancy rate: 0.0%. Rental vacancy rate: 0.0%. (2008-2012 5-year est.); Employment by occupation: 4.3% management, business, and financial, 0.0% computer, engineering, and science, 3.5% education, legal, community service, arts, and media, 15.7% healthcare practitioners, 17.4% service, 15.7% sales and office, 13.9% natural resources, construction, and maintenance, 29.6% production, transportation, and material moving (2008-2012 5-year est.).

Income: Per capita income: $17,155 (2008-2012 5-year est.); Median household income: $23,571 (2008-2012 5-year est.); Average household income: $40,280 (2008-2012 5-year est.); Percent of households with income of $100,000 or more: 10.7% (2008-2012 5-year est.); Poverty rate: 24.2% (2008-2012 5-year est.).

Education: Percent of population age 25 and over with: High school diploma (including GED) or higher: 70.2% (2008-2012 5-year est.); Bachelor's degree or higher: 7.9% (2008-2012 5-year est.); Master's degree or higher: 0.9% (2008-2012 5-year est.).

Housing: Homeownership rate: 81.3% (2008-2012 5-year est.); Median home value: $51,900 (2008-2012 5-year est.); Median contract rent: $439 per month (2008-2012 5-year est.); Median year structure built: 1965 (2008-2012 5-year est.).

Health Insurance: 50.3% Private; 44.2% Public; 28.9% None. (2008-2012 5-year est.)

Transportation: Commute to work: 91.2% car, 0.0% public transportation, 0.0% walk, 1.8% work from home (2008-2012 5-year est.); Travel time to work: 22.5% less than 15 minutes, 30.6% 15 to 30 minutes, 15.3% 30 to 45 minutes, 19.8% 45 to 60 minutes, 11.7% 60 minutes or more (2008-2012 5-year est.)

EASTON (village). Covers a land area of 0.240 square miles and a water area of 0 square miles. Located at 40.23° N. Lat; 89.84° W. Long. Elevation is 512 feet.

Population: 351 (1990); 373 (2000); 321 (2010); Density: 1,483.4 persons per square mile (2008-2012 5-year est.); Race: 100.0% White, 0.0% Black/African American, 0.0% Asian, 0.0% American Indian/Alaska Native, 0.0% Native Hawaiian/Other Pacific Islander, 0.0% Some other race, 0.0% Two or more races, 0.0% Hispanic of any race (2008-2012 5-year est.); Average household size: 2.54 (2008-2012 5-year est.); Median age: 40.2 (2008-2012 5-year est.); Males per 100 females: 89.4 (2008-2012 5-year est.); Marriage status: 24.2% never married, 59.9% now married, 7.6% widowed, 8.3% divorced (2008-2012 5-year est.); Foreign born: 0.0% (2008-2012 5-year est.); Ancestry (includes multiple ancestries): 34.0% German, 16.6% American, 12.9% English, 5.6% Irish, 3.7% French (2008-2012 5-year est.).

Economy: Single-family building permits issued: 0 (2013); Multi-family building permits issued: 0 (2013); Homeowner vacancy rate: 0.0%. Rental vacancy rate: 0.0%. (2008-2012 5-year est.); Employment by occupation: 10.4% management, business, and financial, 3.7% computer, engineering, and science, 2.2% education, legal, community service, arts, and media, 6.7% healthcare practitioners, 17.0% service, 14.1% sales and office, 17.0% natural resources, construction, and maintenance, 28.9% production, transportation, and material moving (2008-2012 5-year est.).

Income: Per capita income: $18,763 (2008-2012 5-year est.); Median household income: $41,563 (2008-2012 5-year est.); Average household income: $50,027 (2008-2012 5-year est.); Percent of households with income of $100,000 or more: 9.2% (2008-2012 5-year est.); Poverty rate: 17.1% (2008-2012 5-year est.).

Education: Percent of population age 25 and over with: High school diploma (including GED) or higher: 79.8% (2008-2012 5-year est.); Bachelor's degree or higher: 12.4% (2008-2012 5-year est.); Master's degree or higher: 5.0% (2008-2012 5-year est.).

Housing: Homeownership rate: 80.7% (2008-2012 5-year est.); Median home value: $60,200 (2008-2012 5-year est.); Median contract rent: $397 per month (2008-2012 5-year est.); Median year structure built: Before 1940 (2008-2012 5-year est.).

Health Insurance: 40.7% Private; 45.5% Public; 27.5% None. (2008-2012 5-year est.)

Safety: Violent crime rate: 0.0 per 10,000 population; Property crime rate: 31.6 per 10,000 population (2012).

Transportation: Commute to work: 96.2% car, 0.0% public transportation, 1.5% walk, 2.3% work from home (2008-2012 5-year est.); Travel time to work: 38.0% less than 15 minutes, 21.7% 15 to 30 minutes, 8.5% 30 to 45 minutes, 10.9% 45 to 60 minutes, 20.9% 60 minutes or more (2008-2012 5-year est.)

FOREST CITY (village). Covers a land area of 0.523 square miles and a water area of 0 square miles. Located at 40.37° N. Lat; 89.83° W. Long. Elevation is 492 feet.

Population: 321 (1990); 287 (2000); 246 (2010); Density: 545.3 persons per square mile (2008-2012 5-year est.); Race: 100.0% White, 0.0% Black/African American, 0.0% Asian, 0.0% American Indian/Alaska Native, 0.0% Native Hawaiian/Other Pacific Islander, 0.0% Some other race, 0.0% Two or more races, 0.0% Hispanic of any race (2008-2012 5-year est.); Average household size: 2.39 (2008-2012 5-year est.); Median age: 51.3 (2008-2012 5-year est.); Males per 100 females: 91.3 (2008-2012 5-year est.); Marriage status: 15.4% never married, 66.0% now married, 10.0% widowed, 8.7% divorced (2008-2012 5-year est.); Foreign born: 0.0% (2008-2012 5-year est.); Ancestry (includes multiple ancestries): 49.8% German, 16.1% American, 13.7% English, 12.3% Irish, 9.5% Dutch (2008-2012 5-year est.).

Economy: Homeowner vacancy rate: 1.0%. Rental vacancy rate: 0.0%. (2008-2012 5-year est.); Employment by occupation: 11.9% management, business, and financial, 0.0% computer, engineering, and science, 11.9% education, legal, community service, arts, and media, 11.0% healthcare practitioners, 9.2% service, 15.6% sales and office, 31.2% natural resources, construction, and maintenance, 9.2% production, transportation, and material moving (2008-2012 5-year est.).

Income: Per capita income: $24,974 (2008-2012 5-year est.); Median household income: $40,208 (2008-2012 5-year est.); Average household income: $63,535 (2008-2012 5-year est.); Percent of households with income of $100,000 or more: 10.9% (2008-2012 5-year est.); Poverty rate: 7.0% (2008-2012 5-year est.).

Education: Percent of population age 25 and over with: High school diploma (including GED) or higher: 79.4% (2008-2012 5-year est.); Bachelor's degree or higher: 6.2% (2008-2012 5-year est.); Master's degree or higher: 0.0% (2008-2012 5-year est.).

Housing: Homeownership rate: 87.4% (2008-2012 5-year est.); Median home value: $70,000 (2008-2012 5-year est.); Median contract rent: $707 per month (2008-2012 5-year est.); Median year structure built: 1966 (2008-2012 5-year est.).

Health Insurance: 78.9% Private; 53.7% Public; 5.3% None. (2008-2012 5-year est.)

Transportation: Commute to work: 97.1% car, 0.0% public transportation, 1.9% walk, 0.0% work from home (2008-2012 5-year est.); Travel time to work: 41.3% less than 15 minutes, 31.7% 15 to 30 minutes, 12.5% 30 to 45 minutes, 7.7% 45 to 60 minutes, 6.7% 60 minutes or more (2008-2012 5-year est.)

GOOFY RIDGE (CDP). Covers a land area of 1.349 square miles and a water area of 0 square miles. Located at 40.39° N. Lat; 89.94° W. Long. Elevation is 482 feet.

Population: n/a (1990); n/a (2000); 350 (2010); Density: 197.2 persons per square mile (2008-2012 5-year est.); Race: 100.0% White, 0.0% Black/African American, 0.0% Asian, 0.0% American Indian/Alaska Native, 0.0% Native Hawaiian/Other Pacific Islander, 0.0% Some other race, 0.0% Two or more races, 0.0% Hispanic of any race (2008-2012 5-year est.); Average household size: 2.00 (2008-2012 5-year est.); Median age: 40.9 (2008-2012 5-year est.); Males per 100 females: 116.3 (2008-2012 5-year est.); Marriage status: 49.6% never married, 45.2% now married, 3.1% widowed, 2.2% divorced (2008-2012 5-year est.); Foreign born: 0.0% (2008-2012 5-year est.); Ancestry (includes multiple ancestries): 15.8% English, 11.3% German, 9.0% American, 4.5% Irish, 2.6% Dutch (2008-2012 5-year est.).

Economy: Homeowner vacancy rate: 0.0%. Rental vacancy rate: 0.0%. (2008-2012 5-year est.); Employment by occupation: 0.0% management, business, and financial, 0.0% computer, engineering, and science, 0.0% education, legal, community service, arts, and media, 0.0% healthcare practitioners, 15.3% service, 0.0% sales and office, 0.0% natural resources, construction, and maintenance, 84.7% production, transportation, and material moving (2008-2012 5-year est.).

Income: Per capita income: $10,720 (2008-2012 5-year est.); Median household income: $15,750 (2008-2012 5-year est.); Average household income: $21,442 (2008-2012 5-year est.); Percent of households with income of $100,000 or more: n/a (2008-2012 5-year est.); Poverty rate: 33.1% (2008-2012 5-year est.).

Education: Percent of population age 25 and over with: High school diploma (including GED) or higher: 76.2% (2008-2012 5-year est.); Bachelor's degree or higher: 0.0% (2008-2012 5-year est.); Master's degree or higher: 0.0% (2008-2012 5-year est.).

Housing: Homeownership rate: 73.7% (2008-2012 5-year est.); Median home value: $29,700 (2008-2012 5-year est.); Median contract rent: $414 per month (2008-2012 5-year est.); Median year structure built: 1965 (2008-2012 5-year est.).

Health Insurance: 13.2% Private; 59.4% Public; 32.0% None. (2008-2012 5-year est.)

Transportation: Commute to work: 100.0% car, 0.0% public transportation, 0.0% walk, 0.0% work from home (2008-2012 5-year est.); Travel time to work: 0.0% less than 15 minutes, 0.0% 15 to 30 minutes, 35.5% 30 to 45 minutes, 0.0% 45 to 60 minutes, 64.5% 60 minutes or more (2008-2012 5-year est.)

HAVANA (city). County seat. Covers a land area of 2.741 square miles and a water area of 0.165 square miles. Located at 40.30° N. Lat; 90.06° W. Long. Elevation is 476 feet.

History: Havana grew up around the ferry across the Spoon River, established in 1824 by Major Ossian M. Ross. Havana shared in the prosperity brought by steamboat travel on the Illinois River, shipping grain and produce to market. Commercial fishing was important here in the early 1900's.

Population: 3,610 (1990); 3,577 (2000); 3,301 (2010); Density: 1,196.9 persons per square mile (2008-2012 5-year est.); Race: 96.2% White, 3.5% Black/African American, 0.0% Asian, 0.0% American Indian/Alaska Native, 0.0% Native Hawaiian/Other Pacific Islander, 0.3% Some other race, 0.3% Two or more races, 1.3% Hispanic of any race (2008-2012 5-year est.); Average household size: 2.16 (2008-2012 5-year est.); Median age: 44.7 (2008-2012 5-year est.); Males per 100 females: 74.9 (2008-2012 5-year est.); Marriage status: 22.7% never married, 51.0% now married, 13.2% widowed, 13.2% divorced (2008-2012 5-year est.); Foreign born: 1.5% (2008-2012 5-year est.); Ancestry (includes multiple ancestries): 29.7% German, 17.5% American, 8.2% Irish, 6.2% English, 3.0% Polish (2008-2012 5-year est.).

Economy: Single-family building permits issued: 1 (2013); Multi-family building permits issued: 0 (2013); Homeowner vacancy rate: 0.0%. Rental vacancy rate: 0.0%. (2008-2012 5-year est.); Employment by occupation: 5.8% management, business, and financial, 1.0% computer, engineering, and science, 9.9% education, legal, community service, arts, and media, 9.1% healthcare practitioners, 28.3% service, 22.6% sales and office, 8.9% natural resources, construction, and maintenance, 14.4% production, transportation, and material moving (2008-2012 5-year est.).

Income: Per capita income: $19,503 (2008-2012 5-year est.); Median household income: $30,723 (2008-2012 5-year est.); Average household income: $44,462 (2008-2012 5-year est.); Percent of households with income of $100,000 or more: 8.1% (2008-2012 5-year est.); Poverty rate: 23.3% (2008-2012 5-year est.).

Education: Percent of population age 25 and over with: High school diploma (including GED) or higher: 83.8% (2008-2012 5-year est.); Bachelor's degree or higher: 12.5% (2008-2012 5-year est.); Master's degree or higher: 5.8% (2008-2012 5-year est.).

School District(s)

Havana CUSD 126 (PK-12)

    2011-12 Enrollment: 1,153 . . . . (309) 543-3384

Housing: Homeownership rate: 69.6% (2008-2012 5-year est.); Median home value: $76,600 (2008-2012 5-year est.); Median contract rent: $339 per month (2008-2012 5-year est.); Median year structure built: 1946 (2008-2012 5-year est.).

Health Insurance: 56.6% Private; 46.3% Public; 14.6% None. (2008-2012 5-year est.)

Hospitals: Mason District Hospital (48 beds)

Safety: Violent crime rate: 88.9 per 10,000 population; Property crime rate: 232.9 per 10,000 population (2012).

Transportation: Commute to work: 83.8% car, 0.8% public transportation, 9.1% walk, 5.4% work from home (2008-2012 5-year est.); Travel time to work: 71.5% less than 15 minutes, 7.6% 15 to 30 minutes, 8.4% 30 to 45 minutes, 8.4% 45 to 60 minutes, 4.1% 60 minutes or more (2008-2012 5-year est.)

Airports: Havana Regional Airport (general aviation)

Additional Information Contacts

Havana Area Chamber of Commerce . . . . (309) 543-3528

    http://www.scenichavana.com

KILBOURNE (village). Covers a land area of 0.889 square miles and a water area of 0 square miles. Located at 40.15° N. Lat; 90.01° W. Long. Elevation is 495 feet.

Population: 350 (1990); 375 (2000); 302 (2010); Density: 259.7 persons per square mile (2008-2012 5-year est.); Race: 100.0% White, 0.0% Black/African American, 0.0% Asian, 0.0% American Indian/Alaska Native, 0.0% Native Hawaiian/Other Pacific Islander, 0.0% Some other race, 0.0% Two or more races, 0.0% Hispanic of any race (2008-2012 5-year est.); Average household size: 2.03 (2008-2012 5-year est.); Median age: 48.7 (2008-2012 5-year est.); Males per 100 females: 100.9 (2008-2012 5-year est.); Marriage status: 12.1% never married, 55.8% now married, 14.1% widowed, 18.1% divorced (2008-2012 5-year est.); Foreign born: 0.9% (2008-2012 5-year est.); Ancestry (includes multiple ancestries): 38.1% American, 16.9% German, 5.6% Irish, 3.0% Dutch, 3.0% English (2008-2012 5-year est.).

Economy: Homeowner vacancy rate: 0.0%. Rental vacancy rate: 0.0%. (2008-2012 5-year est.); Employment by occupation: 3.1% management, business, and financial, 2.1% computer, engineering, and science, 0.0% education, legal, community service, arts, and media, 5.2% healthcare practitioners, 21.6% service, 15.5% sales and office, 25.8% natural resources, construction, and maintenance, 26.8% production, transportation, and material moving (2008-2012 5-year est.).

Income: Per capita income: $21,238 (2008-2012 5-year est.); Median household income: $42,727 (2008-2012 5-year est.); Average household income: $45,171 (2008-2012 5-year est.); Percent of households with income of $100,000 or more: 3.5% (2008-2012 5-year est.); Poverty rate: 14.3% (2008-2012 5-year est.).

Education: Percent of population age 25 and over with: High school diploma (including GED) or higher: 80.4% (2008-2012 5-year est.); Bachelor's degree or higher: 2.8% (2008-2012 5-year est.); Master's degree or higher: 0.0% (2008-2012 5-year est.).

Housing: Homeownership rate: 87.7% (2008-2012 5-year est.); Median home value: $47,000 (2008-2012 5-year est.); Median contract rent: $363 per month (2008-2012 5-year est.); Median year structure built: 1950 (2008-2012 5-year est.).

Health Insurance: 66.2% Private; 35.5% Public; 15.2% None. (2008-2012 5-year est.)

Transportation: Commute to work: 94.2% car, 0.0% public transportation, 0.0% walk, 2.3% work from home (2008-2012 5-year est.); Travel time to work: 17.9% less than 15 minutes, 48.8% 15 to 30 minutes, 3.6% 30 to 45 minutes, 16.7% 45 to 60 minutes, 13.1% 60 minutes or more (2008-2012 5-year est.)

MANITO (village). Covers a land area of 1.441 square miles and a water area of 0 square miles. Located at 40.42° N. Lat; 89.78° W. Long. Elevation is 495 feet.

Population: 1,711 (1990); 1,733 (2000); 1,642 (2010); Density: 1,342.0 persons per square mile (2008-2012 5-year est.); Race: 98.9% White, 0.0% Black/African American, 0.4% Asian, 0.0% American Indian/Alaska Native, 0.0% Native Hawaiian/Other Pacific Islander, 0.7% Some other race, 0.8% Two or more races, 1.0% Hispanic of any race (2008-2012 5-year est.); Average household size: 2.39 (2008-2012 5-year est.); Median age: 39.6 (2008-2012 5-year est.); Males per 100 females: 102.1 (2008-2012 5-year est.); Marriage status: 28.4% never married, 55.4% now married, 6.5% widowed, 9.7% divorced (2008-2012 5-year est.); Foreign born: 0.4% (2008-2012 5-year est.); Ancestry (includes multiple ancestries): 33.7% German, 14.8% American, 10.3% Irish, 9.7% English, 3.2% French (2008-2012 5-year est.).

Economy: Single-family building permits issued: 0 (2013); Multi-family building permits issued: 0 (2013); Homeowner vacancy rate: 0.0%. Rental vacancy rate: 0.0%. (2008-2012 5-year est.); Employment by occupation: 12.8% management, business, and financial, 4.0% computer, engineering, and science, 7.6% education, legal, community service, arts, and media, 7.8% healthcare practitioners, 16.0% service, 21.6% sales and office, 8.3% natural resources, construction, and maintenance, 21.9% production, transportation, and material moving (2008-2012 5-year est.).

Income: Per capita income: $23,079 (2008-2012 5-year est.); Median household income: $48,571 (2008-2012 5-year est.); Average household income: $55,682 (2008-2012 5-year est.); Percent of households with

income of $100,000 or more: 11.1% (2008-2012 5-year est.); Poverty rate: 10.7% (2008-2012 5-year est.).

Education: Percent of population age 25 and over with: High school diploma (including GED) or higher: 89.6% (2008-2012 5-year est.); Bachelor's degree or higher: 14.9% (2008-2012 5-year est.); Master's degree or higher: 4.6% (2008-2012 5-year est.).

School District(s)

Midwest Central CUSD 191 (PK-12)

    2011-12 Enrollment: 1,108 . . . . (309) 968-6868

Spring Lake CCSD 606 (PK-08)

    2011-12 Enrollment: 74 . . . . (309) 545-2241

Housing: Homeownership rate: 76.7% (2008-2012 5-year est.); Median home value: $109,900 (2008-2012 5-year est.); Median contract rent: $416 per month (2008-2012 5-year est.); Median year structure built: 1967 (2008-2012 5-year est.).

Health Insurance: 75.1% Private; 33.8% Public; 9.5% None. (2008-2012 5-year est.)

Transportation: Commute to work: 95.2% car, 0.0% public transportation, 3.6% walk, 0.9% work from home (2008-2012 5-year est.); Travel time to work: 27.9% less than 15 minutes, 25.2% 15 to 30 minutes, 17.7% 30 to 45 minutes, 21.8% 45 to 60 minutes, 7.4% 60 minutes or more (2008-2012 5-year est.)

MASON CITY (city). Covers a land area of 1.014 square miles and a water area of 0 square miles. Located at 40.20° N. Lat; 89.70° W. Long. Elevation is 581 feet.

History: Incorporated 1869.

Population: 2,323 (1990); 2,558 (2000); 2,343 (2010); Density: 2,282.2 persons per square mile (2008-2012 5-year est.); Race: 97.0% White, 0.5% Black/African American, 1.4% Asian, 0.9% American Indian/Alaska Native, 0.0% Native Hawaiian/Other Pacific Islander, 0.2% Some other race, 0.3% Two or more races, 0.9% Hispanic of any race (2008-2012 5-year est.); Average household size: 2.12 (2008-2012 5-year est.); Median age: 46.2 (2008-2012 5-year est.); Males per 100 females: 105.8 (2008-2012 5-year est.); Marriage status: 23.4% never married, 50.3% now married, 9.2% widowed, 17.2% divorced (2008-2012 5-year est.); Foreign born: 2.4% (2008-2012 5-year est.); Ancestry (includes multiple ancestries): 26.9% German, 12.8% American, 10.2% English, 8.2% Irish, 3.2% Polish (2008-2012 5-year est.).

Economy: Single-family building permits issued: 0 (2013); Multi-family building permits issued: 0 (2013); Homeowner vacancy rate: 0.0%. Rental vacancy rate: 4.1%. (2008-2012 5-year est.); Employment by occupation: 8.6% management, business, and financial, 0.9% computer, engineering, and science, 6.2% education, legal, community service, arts, and media, 1.8% healthcare practitioners, 28.4% service, 20.6% sales and office, 7.2% natural resources, construction, and maintenance, 26.4% production, transportation, and material moving (2008-2012 5-year est.).

Income: Per capita income: $22,732 (2008-2012 5-year est.); Median household income: $34,923 (2008-2012 5-year est.); Average household income: $48,400 (2008-2012 5-year est.); Percent of households with income of $100,000 or more: 7.2% (2008-2012 5-year est.); Poverty rate: 25.3% (2008-2012 5-year est.).

Education: Percent of population age 25 and over with: High school diploma (including GED) or higher: 82.8% (2008-2012 5-year est.); Bachelor's degree or higher: 9.3% (2008-2012 5-year est.); Master's degree or higher: 2.6% (2008-2012 5-year est.).

School District(s)

Illini Central CUSD 189 (PK-12)

    2011-12 Enrollment: 846 . . . . (217) 482-5180

Housing: Homeownership rate: 68.9% (2008-2012 5-year est.); Median home value: $73,300 (2008-2012 5-year est.); Median contract rent: $395 per month (2008-2012 5-year est.); Median year structure built: 1955 (2008-2012 5-year est.).

Health Insurance: 64.0% Private; 45.8% Public; 10.1% None. (2008-2012 5-year est.)

Transportation: Commute to work: 88.2% car, 0.0% public transportation, 4.8% walk, 0.6% work from home (2008-2012 5-year est.); Travel time to work: 44.9% less than 15 minutes, 17.2% 15 to 30 minutes, 22.9% 30 to 45 minutes, 8.6% 45 to 60 minutes, 6.4% 60 minutes or more (2008-2012 5-year est.)

SAN JOSE (village). Covers a land area of 0.500 square miles and a water area of 0 square miles. Located at 40.31° N. Lat; 89.60° W. Long. **Population:** 519 (1990); 696 (2000); 642 (2010); Density: 1,284.9 persons per square mile (2008-2012 5-year est.); Race: 98.3% White, 1.4%

Black/African American, 0.0% Asian, 0.0% American Indian/Alaska Native, 0.0% Native Hawaiian/Other Pacific Islander, 0.3% Some other race, 0.0% Two or more races, 1.1% Hispanic of any race (2008-2012 5-year est.); Average household size: 2.75 (2008-2012 5-year est.); Median age: 35.9 (2008-2012 5-year est.); Males per 100 females: 102.2 (2008-2012 5-year est.); Marriage status: 25.0% never married, 60.9% now married, 4.3% widowed, 9.8% divorced (2008-2012 5-year est.); Foreign born: 0.0% (2008-2012 5-year est.); Ancestry (includes multiple ancestries): 32.5% German, 20.8% American, 18.0% Irish, 8.1% English, 4.7% Dutch (2008-2012 5-year est.).

Economy: Single-family building permits issued: 1 (2013); Multi-family building permits issued: 0 (2013); Homeowner vacancy rate: 1.5%. Rental vacancy rate: 0.0%. (2008-2012 5-year est.); Employment by occupation: 8.6% management, business, and financial, 2.8% computer, engineering, and science, 10.0% education, legal, community service, arts, and media, 2.8% healthcare practitioners, 15.2% service, 20.3% sales and office, 14.8% natural resources, construction, and maintenance, 25.5% production, transportation, and material moving (2008-2012 5-year est.).

Income: Per capita income: $20,344 (2008-2012 5-year est.); Median household income: $53,056 (2008-2012 5-year est.); Average household income: $57,183 (2008-2012 5-year est.); Percent of households with income of $100,000 or more: 6.8% (2008-2012 5-year est.); Poverty rate: 12.5% (2008-2012 5-year est.).

Education: Percent of population age 25 and over with: High school diploma (including GED) or higher: 87.8% (2008-2012 5-year est.); Bachelor's degree or higher: 10.9% (2008-2012 5-year est.); Master's degree or higher: 4.6% (2008-2012 5-year est.).

Housing: Homeownership rate: 84.2% (2008-2012 5-year est.); Median home value: $69,800 (2008-2012 5-year est.); Median contract rent: $471 per month (2008-2012 5-year est.); Median year structure built: 1953 (2008-2012 5-year est.).

Health Insurance: 69.8% Private; 33.6% Public; 10.9% None. (2008-2012 5-year est.)

Transportation: Commute to work: 93.8% car, 0.0% public transportation, 1.0% walk, 2.4% work from home (2008-2012 5-year est.); Travel time to work: 20.4% less than 15 minutes, 31.3% 15 to 30 minutes, 30.6% 30 to 45 minutes, 8.5% 45 to 60 minutes, 9.2% 60 minutes or more (2008-2012 5-year est.)

TOPEKA (village). Covers a land area of 0.137 square miles and a water area of 0 square miles. Located at 40.33° N. Lat; 89.93° W. Long. Elevation is 472 feet.

Population: 93 (1990); 90 (2000); 76 (2010); Density: 299.7 persons per square mile (2008-2012 5-year est.); Race: 90.2% White, 0.0% Black/African American, 0.0% Asian, 0.0% American Indian/Alaska Native, 0.0% Native Hawaiian/Other Pacific Islander, 9.8% Some other race, 9.8% Two or more races, 17.1% Hispanic of any race (2008-2012 5-year est.); Average household size: 2.28 (2008-2012 5-year est.); Median age: 44.5 (2008-2012 5-year est.); Males per 100 females: 173.3 (2008-2012 5-year est.); Marriage status: 30.6% never married, 58.3% now married, 0.0% widowed, 11.1% divorced (2008-2012 5-year est.); Foreign born: 0.0% (2008-2012 5-year est.); Ancestry (includes multiple ancestries): 26.8% Irish, 17.1% German, 14.6% English, 12.2% French, 4.9% American (2008-2012 5-year est.).

Economy: Homeowner vacancy rate: 0.0%. Rental vacancy rate: 0.0%. (2008-2012 5-year est.); Employment by occupation: 0.0% management, business, and financial, 0.0% computer, engineering, and science, 18.2% education, legal, community service, arts, and media, 27.3% healthcare practitioners, 18.2% service, 9.1% sales and office, 0.0% natural resources, construction, and maintenance, 27.3% production, transportation, and material moving (2008-2012 5-year est.).

Income: Per capita income: $17,780 (2008-2012 5-year est.); Median household income: $32,500 (2008-2012 5-year est.); Average household income: $44,583 (2008-2012 5-year est.); Percent of households with income of $100,000 or more: 11.1% (2008-2012 5-year est.); Poverty rate: 56.1% (2008-2012 5-year est.).

Education: Percent of population age 25 and over with: High school diploma (including GED) or higher: 67.7% (2008-2012 5-year est.); Bachelor's degree or higher: 6.5% (2008-2012 5-year est.); Master's degree or higher: 0.0% (2008-2012 5-year est.).

Housing: Homeownership rate: 88.9% (2008-2012 5-year est.); Median home value: $47,500 (2008-2012 5-year est.); Median contract rent: n/a per month (2008-2012 5-year est.); Median year structure built: 1971 (2008-2012 5-year est.).

Health Insurance: 29.3% Private; 63.4% Public; 22.0% None. (2008-2012 5-year est.)

Transportation: Commute to work: 100.0% car, 0.0% public transportation, 0.0% walk, 0.0% work from home (2008-2012 5-year est.); Travel time to work: 18.2% less than 15 minutes, 9.1% 15 to 30 minutes, 45.5% 30 to 45 minutes, 27.3% 45 to 60 minutes, 0.0% 60 minutes or more (2008-2012 5-year est.)

Massac County

Located in southern Illinois; bounded on the south and east by the Ohio River and the Kentucky border, and on the northwest by the Cache River; includes part of Shawnee National Forest. Covers a land area of 237.218 square miles, a water area of 4.596 square miles, and is located in the Central Time Zone at 37.22° N. Lat., 88.71° W. Long. The county was founded in 1843. County seat is Metropolis.

Massac County is part of the Paducah, KY-IL Micropolitan Statistical Area. The entire metro area includes: Massac County, IL; Ballard County, KY; Livingston County, KY; McCracken County, KY

Weather Station: Brookport Dam 52									Elevation: 330 feet		
	Jan	Feb	Mar	Apr	May	Jun	Jul	Aug	Sep	Oct	Nov	Dec
High	44	48	58	69	77	86	89	89	82	70	58	46
Low	26	30	37	47	56	64	69	67	59	47	38	29
Precip	3.5	3.9	4.1	4.6	5.0	4.1	4.2	2.8	3.5	4.0	4.2	4.6
Snow	2.1	2.4	0.6	tr	0.0	0.0	0.0	0.0	0.0	0.0	0.0	1.7

High and Low temperatures in degrees Fahrenheit; Precipitation and Snow in inches

Population: 14,752 (1990); 15,161 (2000); 15,429 (2010); Race: 90.9% White, 5.3% Black/African American, 0.4% Asian, 0.1% American Indian/Alaska Native, 0.0% Native Hawaiian/Other Pacific Islander, 3.3% Some other race, 3.1% Two or more races, 1.1% Hispanic of any race (2008-2012 5-year est.); Density: 64.0 persons per square mile (2008-2012 5-year est.); Average household size: 2.45 (2008-2012 5-year est.); Median age: 42.3 (2008-2012 5-year est.); Males per 100 females: 90.1 (2008-2012 5-year est.).

Religion: Six largest groups: 45.2% Baptist, 6.5% Methodist/Pietist, 4.0% Non-denominational Protestant, 3.0% Presbyterian-Reformed, 2.7% Lutheran, 2.4% Pentecostal (2010)

Economy: Unemployment rate: 6.4% (April 2014); Total civilian labor force: 7,116 (April 2014); Leading industries: 20.8% health care and social assistance; 9.1% retail trade; 5.5% transportation & warehousing (2012); Farms: 412 totaling 102,249 acres (2012); Companies that employ 500 or more persons: 1 (2012); Companies that employ 100 to 499 persons: 4 (2012); Companies that employ less than 100 persons: 228 (2012); Black-owned businesses: n/a (2007); Hispanic-owned businesses: n/a (2007); Asian-owned businesses: n/a (2007); Women-owned businesses: 330 (2007); Single-family building permits issued: 2 (2013); Multi-family building permits issued: 0 (2013).

Income: Per capita income: $21,466 (2008-2012 5-year est.); Median household income: $42,190 (2008-2012 5-year est.); Average household income: $51,982 (2008-2012 5-year est.); Percent of households with income of $100,000 or more: 10.6% (2008-2012 5-year est.); Poverty rate: 16.0% (2008-2012 5-year est.); Bankruptcy rate: 3.09% (2013).

Education: Percent of population age 25 and over with: High school diploma (including GED) or higher: 84.9% (2008-2012 5-year est.); Bachelor's degree or higher: 16.7% (2008-2012 5-year est.); Master's degree or higher: 4.1% (2008-2012 5-year est.).

Housing: Homeownership rate: 78.4% (2008-2012 5-year est.); Median home value: $82,700 (2008-2012 5-year est.); Median contract rent: $366 per month (2008-2012 5-year est.); Median year structure built: 1971 (2008-2012 5-year est.)

Health: Birth rate: 113.4 per 10,000 population (2013); Death rate: 111.5 per 10,000 population (2013); Age-adjusted cancer mortality rate: 154.8 deaths per 100,000 population (2011); Number of physicians: 3.3 per 10,000 population (2011); Hospital beds: 16.2 per 10,000 population (2010); Hospital admissions: 617.0 per 10,000 population (2010).

Elections: 2012 Presidential election results: 32.2% Obama, 65.9% Romney

National and State Parks: Fort Massac State Park; Mermet Lake State Conservation Area

Additional Information Contacts

Massac County Government . . . . (618) 524-5213

Massac County Communities

BROOKPORT (city). Covers a land area of 0.653 square miles and a water area of 0.006 square miles. Located at 37.13° N. Lat; 88.63° W. Long. Elevation is 338 feet.

History: Brookport developed as an agricultural trading center on the Ohio River. The flooding of the river in 1937 damaged much of Brookport.

Population: 1,070 (1990); 1,054 (2000); 984 (2010); Density: 1,411.0 persons per square mile (2008-2012 5-year est.); Race: 89.5% White, 8.2% Black/African American, 0.0% Asian, 0.0% American Indian/Alaska Native, 0.0% Native Hawaiian/Other Pacific Islander, 2.3% Some other race, 1.3% Two or more races, 0.9% Hispanic of any race (2008-2012 5-year est.); Average household size: 2.25 (2008-2012 5-year est.); Median age: 45.9 (2008-2012 5-year est.); Males per 100 females: 90.9 (2008-2012 5-year est.); Marriage status: 22.5% never married, 44.3% now married, 11.4% widowed, 21.8% divorced (2008-2012 5-year est.); Foreign born: 0.0% (2008-2012 5-year est.); Ancestry (includes multiple ancestries): 15.6% German, 10.4% English, 10.4% Irish, 8.9% American, 4.7% Italian (2008-2012 5-year est.).

Economy: Single-family building permits issued: 0 (2013); Multi-family building permits issued: 0 (2013); Homeowner vacancy rate: 0.0%. Rental vacancy rate: 3.8%. (2008-2012 5-year est.); Employment by occupation: 5.5% management, business, and financial, 0.8% computer, engineering, and science, 7.1% education, legal, community service, arts, and media, 9.2% healthcare practitioners, 27.7% service, 20.7% sales and office, 21.5% natural resources, construction, and maintenance, 7.6% production, transportation, and material moving (2008-2012 5-year est.).

Income: Per capita income: $17,513 (2008-2012 5-year est.); Median household income: $35,125 (2008-2012 5-year est.); Average household income: $38,281 (2008-2012 5-year est.); Percent of households with income of $100,000 or more: 2.2% (2008-2012 5-year est.); Poverty rate: 19.6% (2008-2012 5-year est.).

Education: Percent of population age 25 and over with: High school diploma (including GED) or higher: 77.3% (2008-2012 5-year est.); Bachelor's degree or higher: 6.4% (2008-2012 5-year est.); Master's degree or higher: 1.7% (2008-2012 5-year est.).

School District(s)

Massac Ud 1 (PK-12)

    2011-12 Enrollment: 2,135 . . . . (618) 524-9376

Housing: Homeownership rate: 75.1% (2008-2012 5-year est.); Median home value: $56,800 (2008-2012 5-year est.); Median contract rent: $361 per month (2008-2012 5-year est.); Median year structure built: 1964 (2008-2012 5-year est.).

Health Insurance: 47.4% Private; 48.2% Public; 16.1% None. (2008-2012 5-year est.)

Transportation: Commute to work: 96.8% car, 0.0% public transportation, 0.9% walk, 2.4% work from home (2008-2012 5-year est.); Travel time to work: 33.7% less than 15 minutes, 46.1% 15 to 30 minutes, 16.0% 30 to 45 minutes, 4.2% 45 to 60 minutes, 0.0% 60 minutes or more (2008-2012 5-year est.)

JOPPA (village). Covers a land area of 0.486 square miles and a water area of 0.018 square miles. Located at 37.21° N. Lat; 88.85° W. Long. Elevation is 354 feet.

Population: 492 (1990); 409 (2000); 360 (2010); Density: 640.2 persons per square mile (2008-2012 5-year est.); Race: 70.1% White, 16.4% Black/African American, 1.3% Asian, 1.3% American Indian/Alaska Native, 0.0% Native Hawaiian/Other Pacific Islander, 10.9% Some other race, 10.9% Two or more races, 0.0% Hispanic of any race (2008-2012 5-year est.); Average household size: 2.83 (2008-2012 5-year est.); Median age: 35.2 (2008-2012 5-year est.); Males per 100 females: 94.4 (2008-2012 5-year est.); Marriage status: 28.7% never married, 43.5% now married, 12.6% widowed, 15.2% divorced (2008-2012 5-year est.); Foreign born: 1.3% (2008-2012 5-year est.); Ancestry (includes multiple ancestries): 12.9% German, 10.6% Irish, 8.7% American, 7.4% English, 2.6% European (2008-2012 5-year est.).

Economy: Homeowner vacancy rate: 0.0%. Rental vacancy rate: 8.9%. (2008-2012 5-year est.); Employment by occupation: 8.8% management, business, and financial, 0.9% computer, engineering, and science, 7.0% education, legal, community service, arts, and media, 1.8% healthcare practitioners, 40.4% service, 28.9% sales and office, 1.8% natural resources, construction, and maintenance, 10.5% production, transportation, and material moving (2008-2012 5-year est.).

Income: Per capita income: $12,798 (2008-2012 5-year est.); Median household income: $31,000 (2008-2012 5-year est.); Average household income: $34,901 (2008-2012 5-year est.); Percent of households with income of $100,000 or more: n/a (2008-2012 5-year est.); Poverty rate: 47.6% (2008-2012 5-year est.).

Education: Percent of population age 25 and over with: High school diploma (including GED) or higher: 84.4% (2008-2012 5-year est.); Bachelor's degree or higher: 14.5% (2008-2012 5-year est.); Master's degree or higher: 0.0% (2008-2012 5-year est.).

School District(s)

Joppa-Maple Grove Ud 38 (PK-12)

    2011-12 Enrollment: 279. . . . . (618) 543-9023

Housing: Homeownership rate: 62.7% (2008-2012 5-year est.); Median home value: $44,100 (2008-2012 5-year est.); Median contract rent: $248 per month (2008-2012 5-year est.); Median year structure built: 1956 (2008-2012 5-year est.).

Health Insurance: 31.2% Private; 54.7% Public; 31.8% None. (2008-2012 5-year est.)

Transportation: Commute to work: 90.8% car, 0.0% public transportation, 2.8% walk, 1.8% work from home (2008-2012 5-year est.); Travel time to work: 21.5% less than 15 minutes, 41.1% 15 to 30 minutes, 29.9% 30 to 45 minutes, 3.7% 45 to 60 minutes, 3.7% 60 minutes or more (2008-2012 5-year est.)

METROPOLIS (city). County seat. Covers a land area of 5.868 square miles and a water area of 0.112 square miles. Located at 37.15° N. Lat; 88.69° W. Long. Elevation is 361 feet.

History: The first settlement in Metropolis was in 1796. This was platted in 1836 as the City of Massac. Metropolis City was platted in 1839 by William A. McBane and James H.G. Wilcox, who dreamed that their community would be a metropolis. Metropolis City was incorporated in 1845, and in 1892 the two communities united.

Population: 6,734 (1990); 6,482 (2000); 6,537 (2010); Density: 1,114.0 persons per square mile (2008-2012 5-year est.); Race: 91.4% White, 5.2% Black/African American, 0.6% Asian, 0.2% American Indian/Alaska Native, 0.0% Native Hawaiian/Other Pacific Islander, 2.6% Some other race, 2.0% Two or more races, 2.4% Hispanic of any race (2008-2012 5-year est.); Average household size: 2.27 (2008-2012 5-year est.); Median age: 39.8 (2008-2012 5-year est.); Males per 100 females: 78.7 (2008-2012 5-year est.); Marriage status: 21.5% never married, 48.9% now married, 12.4% widowed, 17.3% divorced (2008-2012 5-year est.); Foreign born: 0.9% (2008-2012 5-year est.); Ancestry (includes multiple ancestries): 21.6% German, 11.8% Irish, 5.7% English, 5.0% American, 3.5% Italian (2008-2012 5-year est.).

Economy: Single-family building permits issued: 2 (2013); Multi-family building permits issued: 0 (2013); Homeowner vacancy rate: 3.5%. Rental vacancy rate: 9.1%. (2008-2012 5-year est.); Employment by occupation: 8.2% management, business, and financial, 3.4% computer, engineering, and science, 8.1% education, legal, community service, arts, and media, 5.3% healthcare practitioners, 26.1% service, 22.3% sales and office, 8.7% natural resources, construction, and maintenance, 17.9% production, transportation, and material moving (2008-2012 5-year est.).

Income: Per capita income: $18,221 (2008-2012 5-year est.); Median household income: $34,167 (2008-2012 5-year est.); Average household income: $41,830 (2008-2012 5-year est.); Percent of households with income of $100,000 or more: 5.6% (2008-2012 5-year est.); Poverty rate: 19.6% (2008-2012 5-year est.).

Education: Percent of population age 25 and over with: High school diploma (including GED) or higher: 82.0% (2008-2012 5-year est.); Bachelor's degree or higher: 16.7% (2008-2012 5-year est.); Master's degree or higher: 4.2% (2008-2012 5-year est.).

School District(s)

Alxndr/john/masc/pulski/unon Roe (06-12)

    2011-12 Enrollment: n/a . . . . (618) 634-2292

Five County Reg Voc System

    2011-12 Enrollment: n/a . . . . (618) 747-2703

Joppa-Maple Grove Ud 38 (PK-12)

    2011-12 Enrollment: 279. . . . . (618) 543-9023

Massac Ud 1 (PK-12)

    2011-12 Enrollment: 2,135 . . . . (618) 524-9376

Housing: Homeownership rate: 64.5% (2008-2012 5-year est.); Median home value: $74,900 (2008-2012 5-year est.); Median contract rent: $345 per month (2008-2012 5-year est.); Median year structure built: 1958 (2008-2012 5-year est.).

Health Insurance: 57.9% Private; 46.7% Public; 13.7% None. (2008-2012 5-year est.)

Hospitals: Massac Memorial Hospital (57 beds)

Safety: Violent crime rate: 83.9 per 10,000 population; Property crime rate: 399.6 per 10,000 population (2012).

Transportation: Commute to work: 91.3% car, 0.7% public transportation, 3.2% walk, 1.0% work from home (2008-2012 5-year est.); Travel time to work: 47.8% less than 15 minutes, 38.0% 15 to 30 minutes, 6.2% 30 to 45 minutes, 4.0% 45 to 60 minutes, 3.9% 60 minutes or more (2008-2012 5-year est.)

Airports: Metropolis Municipal Airport (general aviation)

Additional Information Contacts

City of Metropolis. . . . . (618) 524-2711

    http://www.cityofmetropolis.com

Metropolis Chamber of Commerce . . . . (618) 524-2714

    http://www.metropolischamber.com

McDonough County

Located in western Illinois; drained by the La Moine River. Covers a land area of 589.407 square miles, a water area of 0.777 square miles, and is located in the Central Time Zone at 40.46° N. Lat., 90.68° W. Long. The county was founded in 1826. County seat is Macomb.

McDonough County is part of the Macomb, IL Micropolitan Statistical Area. The entire metro area includes: McDonough County, IL

Population: 35,244 (1990); 32,913 (2000); 32,612 (2010); Race: 90.8% White, 5.1% Black/African American, 2.3% Asian, 0.2% American Indian/Alaska Native, 0.0% Native Hawaiian/Other Pacific Islander, 1.6% Some other race, 1.2% Two or more races, 2.6% Hispanic of any race (2008-2012 5-year est.); Density: 55.3 persons per square mile (2008-2012 5-year est.); Average household size: 2.11 (2008-2012 5-year est.); Median age: 29.4 (2008-2012 5-year est.); Males per 100 females: 98.7 (2008-2012 5-year est.).

Religion: Six largest groups: 10.2% Baptist, 5.9% Methodist/Pietist, 5.1% Muslim Estimate, 4.4% Catholicism, 2.9% Pentecostal, 2.3% Presbyterian-Reformed (2010)

Economy: Unemployment rate: 5.8% (April 2014); Total civilian labor force: 15,929 (April 2014); Leading industries: 19.5% health care and social assistance; 17.3% accommodation & food services; 16.7% retail trade (2012); Farms: 740 totaling 292,044 acres (2012); Companies that employ 500 or more persons: 2 (2012); Companies that employ 100 to 499 persons: 10 (2012); Companies that employ less than 100 persons: 680 (2012); Black-owned businesses: n/a (2007); Hispanic-owned businesses: n/a (2007); Asian-owned businesses: n/a (2007); Women-owned businesses: n/a (2007); Single-family building permits issued: 9 (2013); Multi-family building permits issued: 0 (2013).

Income: Per capita income: $19,897 (2008-2012 5-year est.); Median household income: $35,812 (2008-2012 5-year est.); Average household income: $48,989 (2008-2012 5-year est.); Percent of households with income of $100,000 or more: 10.5% (2008-2012 5-year est.); Poverty rate: 22.3% (2008-2012 5-year est.); Bankruptcy rate: 1.85% (2013).

Education: Percent of population age 25 and over with: High school diploma (including GED) or higher: 91.4% (2008-2012 5-year est.); Bachelor's degree or higher: 32.9% (2008-2012 5-year est.); Master's degree or higher: 15.3% (2008-2012 5-year est.).

Housing: Homeownership rate: 61.0% (2008-2012 5-year est.); Median home value: $86,500 (2008-2012 5-year est.); Median contract rent: $512 per month (2008-2012 5-year est.); Median year structure built: 1965 (2008-2012 5-year est.)

Health: Birth rate: 96.1 per 10,000 population (2013); Death rate: 87.2 per 10,000 population (2013); Age-adjusted cancer mortality rate: 172.1 deaths per 100,000 population (2011); Number of physicians: 12.0 per 10,000 population (2011); Hospital beds: 27.0 per 10,000 population (2010); Hospital admissions: 752.5 per 10,000 population (2010).

Elections: 2012 Presidential election results: 47.9% Obama, 49.4% Romney

National and State Parks: Argyle Lake State Park

Additional Information Contacts

McDonough County Government . . . . (309) 833-2474

McDonough County Communities

ADAIR (CDP). Covers a land area of 0.430 square miles and a water area of 0 square miles. Located at 40.42° N. Lat; 90.50° W. Long. Elevation is 646 feet.

Population: n/a (1990); n/a (2000); 210 (2010); Density: 493.4 persons per square mile (2008-2012 5-year est.); Race: 100.0% White, 0.0% Black/African American, 0.0% Asian, 0.0% American Indian/Alaska Native, 0.0% Native Hawaiian/Other Pacific Islander, 0.0% Some other race, 0.0% Two or more races, 0.0% Hispanic of any race (2008-2012 5-year est.); Average household size: 2.38 (2008-2012 5-year est.); Median age: 39.7 (2008-2012 5-year est.); Males per 100 females: 73.8 (2008-2012 5-year est.); Marriage status: 19.2% never married, 76.9% now married, 3.8% widowed, 0.0% divorced (2008-2012 5-year est.); Foreign born: 0.0% (2008-2012 5-year est.); Ancestry (includes multiple ancestries): 46.2% Irish, 28.8% German, 12.7% Dutch, 6.6% English (2008-2012 5-year est.).

Economy: Homeowner vacancy rate: 0.0%. Rental vacancy rate: 0.0%. (2008-2012 5-year est.); Employment by occupation: 7.9% management, business, and financial, 0.0% computer, engineering, and science, 0.0% education, legal, community service, arts, and media, 0.0% healthcare practitioners, 32.9% service, 6.6% sales and office, 21.1% natural resources, construction, and maintenance, 31.6% production, transportation, and material moving (2008-2012 5-year est.).

Income: Per capita income: $16,009 (2008-2012 5-year est.); Median household income: $31,801 (2008-2012 5-year est.); Average household income: $39,627 (2008-2012 5-year est.); Percent of households with income of $100,000 or more: n/a (2008-2012 5-year est.); Poverty rate: 0.0% (2008-2012 5-year est.).

Education: Percent of population age 25 and over with: High school diploma (including GED) or higher: 73.2% (2008-2012 5-year est.); Bachelor's degree or higher: 4.6% (2008-2012 5-year est.); Master's degree or higher: 0.0% (2008-2012 5-year est.).

Housing: Homeownership rate: 71.9% (2008-2012 5-year est.); Median home value: $43,300 (2008-2012 5-year est.); Median contract rent: $367 per month (2008-2012 5-year est.); Median year structure built: 1974 (2008-2012 5-year est.).

Health Insurance: 50.5% Private; 71.7% Public; 10.8% None. (2008-2012 5-year est.)

Transportation: Commute to work: 100.0% car, 0.0% public transportation, 0.0% walk, 0.0% work from home (2008-2012 5-year est.); Travel time to work: 67.2% less than 15 minutes, 32.8% 15 to 30 minutes, 0.0% 30 to 45 minutes, 0.0% 45 to 60 minutes, 0.0% 60 minutes or more (2008-2012 5-year est.).

BARDOLPH (village). Covers a land area of 0.594 square miles and a water area of 0 square miles. Located at 40.50° N. Lat; 90.56° W. Long. Elevation is 673 feet.

Population: 301 (1990); 253 (2000); 251 (2010); Density: 380.2 persons per square mile (2008-2012 5-year est.); Race: 100.0% White, 0.0% Black/African American, 0.0% Asian, 0.0% American Indian/Alaska Native, 0.0% Native Hawaiian/Other Pacific Islander, 0.0% Some other race, 0.0% Two or more races, 7.1% Hispanic of any race (2008-2012 5-year est.); Average household size: 2.48 (2008-2012 5-year est.); Median age: 32.6 (2008-2012 5-year est.); Males per 100 females: 88.3 (2008-2012 5-year est.); Marriage status: 36.8% never married, 37.4% now married, 5.2% widowed, 20.6% divorced (2008-2012 5-year est.); Foreign born: 0.0% (2008-2012 5-year est.); Ancestry (includes multiple ancestries): 20.8% German, 19.5% English, 15.5% Irish, 6.2% American, 2.7% French (2008-2012 5-year est.).

Economy: Homeowner vacancy rate: 0.0%. Rental vacancy rate: 0.0%. (2008-2012 5-year est.); Employment by occupation: 3.1% management, business, and financial, 0.0% computer, engineering, and science, 1.0% education, legal, community service, arts, and media, 3.1% healthcare practitioners, 56.7% service, 18.6% sales and office, 1.0% natural resources, construction, and maintenance, 16.5% production, transportation, and material moving (2008-2012 5-year est.).

Income: Per capita income: $13,173 (2008-2012 5-year est.); Median household income: $28,393 (2008-2012 5-year est.); Average household income: $33,749 (2008-2012 5-year est.); Percent of households with income of $100,000 or more: n/a (2008-2012 5-year est.); Poverty rate: 28.2% (2008-2012 5-year est.).

Education: Percent of population age 25 and over with: High school diploma (including GED) or higher: 82.0% (2008-2012 5-year est.);

Bachelor's degree or higher: 16.5% (2008-2012 5-year est.); Master's degree or higher: 0.8% (2008-2012 5-year est.).

Housing: Homeownership rate: 75.8% (2008-2012 5-year est.); Median home value: $47,300 (2008-2012 5-year est.); Median contract rent: $271 per month (2008-2012 5-year est.); Median year structure built: 1964 (2008-2012 5-year est.).

Health Insurance: 31.4% Private; 68.6% Public; 8.0% None. (2008-2012 5-year est.)

Transportation: Commute to work: 96.8% car, 0.0% public transportation, 3.2% walk, 0.0% work from home (2008-2012 5-year est.); Travel time to work: 33.3% less than 15 minutes, 50.5% 15 to 30 minutes, 8.6% 30 to 45 minutes, 2.2% 45 to 60 minutes, 5.4% 60 minutes or more (2008-2012 5-year est.)

BLANDINSVILLE (village). Covers a land area of 0.880 square miles and a water area of 0 square miles. Located at 40.55° N. Lat; 90.87° W. Long. Elevation is 728 feet.

Population: 762 (1990); 777 (2000); 651 (2010); Density: 758.7 persons per square mile (2008-2012 5-year est.); Race: 100.0% White, 0.0% Black/African American, 0.0% Asian, 0.0% American Indian/Alaska Native, 0.0% Native Hawaiian/Other Pacific Islander, 0.0% Some other race, 0.0% Two or more races, 0.0% Hispanic of any race (2008-2012 5-year est.); Average household size: 1.91 (2008-2012 5-year est.); Median age: 52.0 (2008-2012 5-year est.); Males per 100 females: 97.6 (2008-2012 5-year est.); Marriage status: 14.3% never married, 60.0% now married, 10.3% widowed, 15.4% divorced (2008-2012 5-year est.); Foreign born: 0.4% (2008-2012 5-year est.); Ancestry (includes multiple ancestries): 21.3% Irish, 21.0% German, 13.8% American, 12.1% English, 3.3% Swedish (2008-2012 5-year est.).

Economy: Homeowner vacancy rate: 3.2%. Rental vacancy rate: 12.5%. (2008-2012 5-year est.); Employment by occupation: 7.8% management, business, and financial, 0.9% computer, engineering, and science, 7.5% education, legal, community service, arts, and media, 4.5% healthcare practitioners, 19.7% service, 24.2% sales and office, 11.3% natural resources, construction, and maintenance, 24.2% production, transportation, and material moving (2008-2012 5-year est.).

Income: Per capita income: $23,629 (2008-2012 5-year est.); Median household income: $40,694 (2008-2012 5-year est.); Average household income: $46,701 (2008-2012 5-year est.); Percent of households with income of $100,000 or more: 6.9% (2008-2012 5-year est.); Poverty rate: 14.7% (2008-2012 5-year est.).

Education: Percent of population age 25 and over with: High school diploma (including GED) or higher: 93.8% (2008-2012 5-year est.); Bachelor's degree or higher: 14.8% (2008-2012 5-year est.); Master's degree or higher: 2.5% (2008-2012 5-year est.).

Housing: Homeownership rate: 86.0% (2008-2012 5-year est.); Median home value: $63,800 (2008-2012 5-year est.); Median contract rent: $287 per month (2008-2012 5-year est.); Median year structure built: 1943 (2008-2012 5-year est.).

Health Insurance: 69.2% Private; 39.5% Public; 12.7% None. (2008-2012 5-year est.)

Safety: Violent crime rate: 0.0 per 10,000 population; Property crime rate: 30.8 per 10,000 population (2012).

Transportation: Commute to work: 95.4% car, 0.6% public transportation, 3.3% walk, 0.6% work from home (2008-2012 5-year est.); Travel time to work: 28.4% less than 15 minutes, 44.3% 15 to 30 minutes, 13.1% 30 to 45 minutes, 4.6% 45 to 60 minutes, 9.5% 60 minutes or more (2008-2012 5-year est.)

BUSHNELL (city). Covers a land area of 2.126 square miles and a water area of 0.008 square miles. Located at 40.55° N. Lat; 90.50° W. Long. Elevation is 653 feet.

History: Incorporated 1865.

Population: 3,288 (1990); 3,221 (2000); 3,117 (2010); Density: 1,448.2 persons per square mile (2008-2012 5-year est.); Race: 94.7% White, 1.5% Black/African American, 0.0% Asian, 0.0% American Indian/Alaska Native, 0.0% Native Hawaiian/Other Pacific Islander, 3.8% Some other race, 0.9% Two or more races, 1.4% Hispanic of any race (2008-2012 5-year est.); Average household size: 2.13 (2008-2012 5-year est.); Median age: 41.4 (2008-2012 5-year est.); Males per 100 females: 97.8 (2008-2012 5-year est.); Marriage status: 23.9% never married, 52.8% now married, 12.9% widowed, 10.4% divorced (2008-2012 5-year est.); Foreign born: 0.2% (2008-2012 5-year est.); Ancestry (includes multiple ancestries): 23.7% American, 23.0% German, 14.3% Irish, 11.6% English, 2.8% Polish (2008-2012 5-year est.).

Economy: Homeowner vacancy rate: 0.0%. Rental vacancy rate: 0.0%. (2008-2012 5-year est.); Employment by occupation: 10.6% management, business, and financial, 3.4% computer, engineering, and science, 9.2% education, legal, community service, arts, and media, 3.8% healthcare practitioners, 13.6% service, 15.9% sales and office, 6.8% natural resources, construction, and maintenance, 36.7% production, transportation, and material moving (2008-2012 5-year est.).
Income: Per capita income: $20,812 (2008-2012 5-year est.); Median household income: $33,871 (2008-2012 5-year est.); Average household income: $44,733 (2008-2012 5-year est.); Percent of households with income of $100,000 or more: 8.0% (2008-2012 5-year est.); Poverty rate: 16.4% (2008-2012 5-year est.).
Education: Percent of population age 25 and over with: High school diploma (including GED) or higher: 86.5% (2008-2012 5-year est.); Bachelor's degree or higher: 12.7% (2008-2012 5-year est.); Master's degree or higher: 3.2% (2008-2012 5-year est.).

School District(s)
Bushnell Prairie City CUSD 170 (PK-12)
   2011-12 Enrollment: 810 . . . . (309) 772-9461
Housing: Homeownership rate: 78.7% (2008-2012 5-year est.); Median home value: $62,200 (2008-2012 5-year est.); Median contract rent: $334 per month (2008-2012 5-year est.); Median year structure built: 1955 (2008-2012 5-year est.).
Health Insurance: 62.3% Private; 40.3% Public; 13.5% None. (2008-2012 5-year est.)
Transportation: Commute to work: 92.7% car, 0.0% public transportation, 2.4% walk, 1.8% work from home (2008-2012 5-year est.); Travel time to work: 43.9% less than 15 minutes, 33.2% 15 to 30 minutes, 12.4% 30 to 45 minutes, 5.1% 45 to 60 minutes, 5.4% 60 minutes or more (2008-2012 5-year est.)

COLCHESTER (city). Covers a land area of 0.998 square miles and a water area of 0 square miles. Located at 40.43° N. Lat; 90.79° W. Long. Elevation is 692 feet.
History: Incorporated 1867.
Population: 1,645 (1990); 1,493 (2000); 1,401 (2010); Density: 1,276.5 persons per square mile (2008-2012 5-year est.); Race: 94.8% White, 1.7% Black/African American, 0.0% Asian, 0.2% American Indian/Alaska Native, 0.4% Native Hawaiian/Other Pacific Islander, 2.9% Some other race, 2.9% Two or more races, 0.0% Hispanic of any race (2008-2012 5-year est.); Average household size: 2.13 (2008-2012 5-year est.); Median age: 43.3 (2008-2012 5-year est.); Males per 100 females: 81.5 (2008-2012 5-year est.); Marriage status: 24.4% never married, 52.9% now married, 9.3% widowed, 13.4% divorced (2008-2012 5-year est.); Foreign born: 0.8% (2008-2012 5-year est.); Ancestry (includes multiple ancestries): 22.7% German, 19.0% Irish, 12.6% English, 6.0% American, 3.6% Swedish (2008-2012 5-year est.).
Economy: Homeowner vacancy rate: 2.2%. Rental vacancy rate: 0.0%. (2008-2012 5-year est.); Employment by occupation: 7.3% management, business, and financial, 0.0% computer, engineering, and science, 6.2% education, legal, community service, arts, and media, 4.5% healthcare practitioners, 26.7% service, 27.1% sales and office, 8.4% natural resources, construction, and maintenance, 20.0% production, transportation, and material moving (2008-2012 5-year est.).
Income: Per capita income: $20,228 (2008-2012 5-year est.); Median household income: $37,979 (2008-2012 5-year est.); Average household income: $42,667 (2008-2012 5-year est.); Percent of households with income of $100,000 or more: 3.4% (2008-2012 5-year est.); Poverty rate: 11.2% (2008-2012 5-year est.).
Education: Percent of population age 25 and over with: High school diploma (including GED) or higher: 87.6% (2008-2012 5-year est.); Bachelor's degree or higher: 17.4% (2008-2012 5-year est.); Master's degree or higher: 3.8% (2008-2012 5-year est.).

School District(s)
West Prairie CUSD 103 (PK-12)
   2011-12 Enrollment: 658 . . . . (309) 776-3180
Housing: Homeownership rate: 76.3% (2008-2012 5-year est.); Median home value: $61,400 (2008-2012 5-year est.); Median contract rent: $382 per month (2008-2012 5-year est.); Median year structure built: 1953 (2008-2012 5-year est.).
Health Insurance: 60.4% Private; 43.7% Public; 15.4% None. (2008-2012 5-year est.)
Safety: Violent crime rate: 7.2 per 10,000 population; Property crime rate: 78.7 per 10,000 population (2012).

Transportation: Commute to work: 85.9% car, 0.0% public transportation, 4.0% walk, 2.5% work from home (2008-2012 5-year est.); Travel time to work: 38.3% less than 15 minutes, 54.5% 15 to 30 minutes, 1.2% 30 to 45 minutes, 0.8% 45 to 60 minutes, 5.3% 60 minutes or more (2008-2012 5-year est.)

GEORGETOWN (CDP). Covers a land area of 0.144 square miles and a water area of 0 square miles. Located at 40.46° N. Lat; 90.72° W. Long.
Population: n/a (1990); n/a (2000); 404 (2010); Density: 2,690.4 persons per square mile (2008-2012 5-year est.); Race: 97.2% White, 1.8% Black/African American, 0.0% Asian, 1.0% American Indian/Alaska Native, 0.0% Native Hawaiian/Other Pacific Islander, 0.0% Some other race, 0.0% Two or more races, 1.5% Hispanic of any race (2008-2012 5-year est.); Average household size: 2.02 (2008-2012 5-year est.); Median age: 42.1 (2008-2012 5-year est.); Males per 100 females: 75.6 (2008-2012 5-year est.); Marriage status: 9.9% never married, 56.0% now married, 10.2% widowed, 23.9% divorced (2008-2012 5-year est.); Foreign born: 1.5% (2008-2012 5-year est.); Ancestry (includes multiple ancestries): 28.1% German, 18.3% English, 14.7% American, 11.3% Scottish, 8.8% Italian (2008-2012 5-year est.).
Economy: Homeowner vacancy rate: 0.0%. Rental vacancy rate: 0.0%. (2008-2012 5-year est.); Employment by occupation: 16.1% management, business, and financial, 0.0% computer, engineering, and science, 36.6% education, legal, community service, arts, and media, 5.9% healthcare practitioners, 18.5% service, 17.1% sales and office, 0.0% natural resources, construction, and maintenance, 5.9% production, transportation, and material moving (2008-2012 5-year est.).
Income: Per capita income: $33,905 (2008-2012 5-year est.); Median household income: $67,321 (2008-2012 5-year est.); Average household income: $67,080 (2008-2012 5-year est.); Percent of households with income of $100,000 or more: 17.7% (2008-2012 5-year est.); Poverty rate: 0.0% (2008-2012 5-year est.).
Education: Percent of population age 25 and over with: High school diploma (including GED) or higher: 100.0% (2008-2012 5-year est.); Bachelor's degree or higher: 61.9% (2008-2012 5-year est.); Master's degree or higher: 40.7% (2008-2012 5-year est.).
Housing: Homeownership rate: 88.0% (2008-2012 5-year est.); Median home value: $92,400 (2008-2012 5-year est.); Median contract rent: $821 per month (2008-2012 5-year est.); Median year structure built: 1975 (2008-2012 5-year est.).
Health Insurance: 92.5% Private; 22.7% Public; 2.1% None. (2008-2012 5-year est.)
Transportation: Commute to work: 97.4% car, 0.0% public transportation, 0.0% walk, 0.0% work from home (2008-2012 5-year est.); Travel time to work: 87.4% less than 15 minutes, 12.6% 15 to 30 minutes, 0.0% 30 to 45 minutes, 0.0% 45 to 60 minutes, 0.0% 60 minutes or more (2008-2012 5-year est.)

GOOD HOPE (village). Covers a land area of 0.292 square miles and a water area of 0 square miles. Located at 40.56° N. Lat; 90.68° W. Long. Elevation is 709 feet.
History: When Good Hope was platted in 1866, it was called Sheridan by its founder, J.E. Morris. The town of Milan was laid out next to Sheridan the following year. Since both were served by the post office which was called Good Hope, that is the name that survived.
Population: 416 (1990); 415 (2000); 396 (2010); Density: 1,436.3 persons per square mile (2008-2012 5-year est.); Race: 94.3% White, 0.7% Black/African American, 0.0% Asian, 0.0% American Indian/Alaska Native, 0.0% Native Hawaiian/Other Pacific Islander, 5.0% Some other race, 2.9% Two or more races, 3.6% Hispanic of any race (2008-2012 5-year est.); Average household size: 2.19 (2008-2012 5-year est.); Median age: 48.2 (2008-2012 5-year est.); Males per 100 females: 98.6 (2008-2012 5-year est.); Marriage status: 21.9% never married, 56.7% now married, 9.3% widowed, 12.1% divorced (2008-2012 5-year est.); Foreign born: 2.9% (2008-2012 5-year est.); Ancestry (includes multiple ancestries): 23.2% German, 14.3% American, 13.4% English, 11.5% Irish, 2.9% European (2008-2012 5-year est.).
Economy: Homeowner vacancy rate: 0.0%. Rental vacancy rate: 0.0%. (2008-2012 5-year est.); Employment by occupation: 7.2% management, business, and financial, 5.3% computer, engineering, and science, 7.7% education, legal, community service, arts, and media, 10.1% healthcare practitioners, 13.0% service, 27.1% sales and office, 9.7% natural resources, construction, and maintenance, 19.8% production, transportation, and material moving (2008-2012 5-year est.).

Income: Per capita income: $25,331 (2008-2012 5-year est.); Median household income: $46,369 (2008-2012 5-year est.); Average household income: $55,986 (2008-2012 5-year est.); Percent of households with income of $100,000 or more: 8.3% (2008-2012 5-year est.); Poverty rate: 8.4% (2008-2012 5-year est.).

Education: Percent of population age 25 and over with: High school diploma (including GED) or higher: 95.6% (2008-2012 5-year est.); Bachelor's degree or higher: 26.3% (2008-2012 5-year est.); Master's degree or higher: 8.2% (2008-2012 5-year est.).

School District(s)
West Prairie CUSD 103 (PK-12)
   2011-12 Enrollment: 658 . . . . (309) 776-3180

Housing: Homeownership rate: 79.6% (2008-2012 5-year est.); Median home value: $71,300 (2008-2012 5-year est.); Median contract rent: $406 per month (2008-2012 5-year est.); Median year structure built: 1953 (2008-2012 5-year est.).

Health Insurance: 72.8% Private; 39.4% Public; 4.1% None. (2008-2012 5-year est.)

Transportation: Commute to work: 93.6% car, 0.0% public transportation, 2.0% walk, 4.4% work from home (2008-2012 5-year est.); Travel time to work: 40.0% less than 15 minutes, 42.1% 15 to 30 minutes, 5.6% 30 to 45 minutes, 5.1% 45 to 60 minutes, 7.2% 60 minutes or more (2008-2012 5-year est.)

INDUSTRY (village). Covers a land area of 0.459 square miles and a water area of <.001 square miles. Located at 40.33° N. Lat; 90.61° W. Long. Elevation is 659 feet.

History: The first settler in Industry was William Carter who came in 1826. The village was organized in the 1840's.

Population: 571 (1990); 540 (2000); 478 (2010); Density: 1,034.8 persons per square mile (2008-2012 5-year est.); Race: 96.2% White, 0.6% Black/African American, 0.0% Asian, 0.4% American Indian/Alaska Native, 0.0% Native Hawaiian/Other Pacific Islander, 2.8% Some other race, 2.7% Two or more races, 1.9% Hispanic of any race (2008-2012 5-year est.); Average household size: 2.23 (2008-2012 5-year est.); Median age: 41.6 (2008-2012 5-year est.); Males per 100 females: 86.3 (2008-2012 5-year est.); Marriage status: 18.9% never married, 66.5% now married, 7.0% widowed, 7.6% divorced (2008-2012 5-year est.); Foreign born: 4.8% (2008-2012 5-year est.); Ancestry (includes multiple ancestries): 21.5% German, 19.2% American, 15.8% Irish, 8.0% English, 5.1% Italian (2008-2012 5-year est.).

Economy: Homeowner vacancy rate: 0.0%. Rental vacancy rate: 0.0%. (2008-2012 5-year est.); Employment by occupation: 2.4% management, business, and financial, 0.0% computer, engineering, and science, 7.1% education, legal, community service, arts, and media, 5.2% healthcare practitioners, 25.2% service, 30.0% sales and office, 7.6% natural resources, construction, and maintenance, 22.4% production, transportation, and material moving (2008-2012 5-year est.).

Income: Per capita income: $19,994 (2008-2012 5-year est.); Median household income: $41,875 (2008-2012 5-year est.); Average household income: $46,432 (2008-2012 5-year est.); Percent of households with income of $100,000 or more: 4.7% (2008-2012 5-year est.); Poverty rate: 14.3% (2008-2012 5-year est.).

Education: Percent of population age 25 and over with: High school diploma (including GED) or higher: 91.9% (2008-2012 5-year est.); Bachelor's degree or higher: 19.5% (2008-2012 5-year est.); Master's degree or higher: 3.9% (2008-2012 5-year est.).

Housing: Homeownership rate: 87.8% (2008-2012 5-year est.); Median home value: $68,400 (2008-2012 5-year est.); Median contract rent: $385 per month (2008-2012 5-year est.); Median year structure built: 1954 (2008-2012 5-year est.).

Health Insurance: 65.1% Private; 45.7% Public; 6.8% None. (2008-2012 5-year est.)

Transportation: Commute to work: 82.2% car, 1.0% public transportation, 8.7% walk, 5.3% work from home (2008-2012 5-year est.); Travel time to work: 33.0% less than 15 minutes, 39.6% 15 to 30 minutes, 11.7% 30 to 45 minutes, 2.0% 45 to 60 minutes, 13.7% 60 minutes or more (2008-2012 5-year est.)

MACOMB (city). County seat. Covers a land area of 10.694 square miles and a water area of 0.431 square miles. Located at 40.47° N. Lat; 90.68° W. Long. Elevation is 705 feet.

History: Macomb was settled in 1830, incorporated as a village in 1841, and as a city in 1856. Many of the early settlers were from New England,

and they named the town for Alexander Macomb, Commander-in-Chief of the U.S. Army from 1828 to 1841.

Population: 19,952 (1990); 18,558 (2000); 19,288 (2010); Density: 1,801.0 persons per square mile (2008-2012 5-year est.); Race: 87.0% White, 7.9% Black/African American, 3.5% Asian, 0.3% American Indian/Alaska Native, 0.0% Native Hawaiian/Other Pacific Islander, 1.3% Some other race, 1.2% Two or more races, 3.8% Hispanic of any race (2008-2012 5-year est.); Average household size: 1.96 (2008-2012 5-year est.); Median age: 23.2 (2008-2012 5-year est.); Males per 100 females: 102.1 (2008-2012 5-year est.); Marriage status: 60.9% never married, 26.9% now married, 4.3% widowed, 7.9% divorced (2008-2012 5-year est.); Foreign born: 4.9% (2008-2012 5-year est.); Ancestry (includes multiple ancestries): 24.3% German, 15.6% Irish, 11.3% American, 9.7% English, 6.4% Italian (2008-2012 5-year est.).

Economy: Single-family building permits issued: 9 (2013); Multi-family building permits issued: 0 (2013); Homeowner vacancy rate: 1.1%. Rental vacancy rate: 3.8%. (2008-2012 5-year est.); Employment by occupation: 9.0% management, business, and financial, 3.9% computer, engineering, and science, 17.7% education, legal, community service, arts, and media, 3.8% healthcare practitioners, 24.4% service, 25.7% sales and office, 5.6% natural resources, construction, and maintenance, 9.9% production, transportation, and material moving (2008-2012 5-year est.).

Income: Per capita income: $17,350 (2008-2012 5-year est.); Median household income: $26,966 (2008-2012 5-year est.); Average household income: $44,412 (2008-2012 5-year est.); Percent of households with income of $100,000 or more: 11.0% (2008-2012 5-year est.); Poverty rate: 33.3% (2008-2012 5-year est.).

Education: Percent of population age 25 and over with: High school diploma (including GED) or higher: 92.7% (2008-2012 5-year est.); Bachelor's degree or higher: 43.9% (2008-2012 5-year est.); Master's degree or higher: 22.0% (2008-2012 5-year est.).

School District(s)
Hancock/mcdonough Roe (07-12)
   2011-12 Enrollment: n/a . . . . (309) 837-4821
Macomb CUSD 185 (PK-12)
   2011-12 Enrollment: 1,997 . . . . (309) 833-4161
West Central II Spec Educ Coop
   2011-12 Enrollment: n/a . . . . (309) 837-3911
Western Area Career System 265
   2011-12 Enrollment: n/a . . . . (309) 837-4821

Four-year College(s)
Western Illinois University (Public)
   Fall 2012 Enrollment: 12,205 . . . . (309) 295-1414
   2012-13 Tuition: In-state $11,182; Out-of-state $15,188

Housing: Homeownership rate: 44.0% (2008-2012 5-year est.); Median home value: $96,000 (2008-2012 5-year est.); Median contract rent: $549 per month (2008-2012 5-year est.); Median year structure built: 1968 (2008-2012 5-year est.).

Health Insurance: 78.2% Private; 23.8% Public; 9.0% None. (2008-2012 5-year est.)

Hospitals: McDonough District Hospital (113 beds)

Safety: Violent crime rate: 24.9 per 10,000 population; Property crime rate: 216.7 per 10,000 population (2012).

Transportation: Commute to work: 80.4% car, 1.9% public transportation, 12.4% walk, 3.1% work from home (2008-2012 5-year est.); Travel time to work: 77.9% less than 15 minutes, 13.3% 15 to 30 minutes, 4.3% 30 to 45 minutes, 2.2% 45 to 60 minutes, 2.3% 60 minutes or more (2008-2012 5-year est.); Amtrak: Train service available.

Airports: Macomb Municipal Airport (general aviation)

Additional Information Contacts
City of Macomb . . . . (309) 833-2558
   http://www.cityofmacomb.com
Macomb Area Chamber of Commerce & Downtown Development Corp
   (309) 837-4855
   http://www.macombareachamber.com
Macomb Convention & Visitors Bureau . . . . (309) 833-1315
   http://www.makeitmacomb.com

PRAIRIE CITY (village). Covers a land area of 1.017 square miles and a water area of 0 square miles. Located at 40.62° N. Lat; 90.46° W. Long. Elevation is 669 feet.

Population: 497 (1990); 461 (2000); 379 (2010); Density: 532.8 persons per square mile (2008-2012 5-year est.); Race: 97.6% White, 1.7% Black/African American, 0.7% Asian, 0.0% American Indian/Alaska Native, 0.0% Native Hawaiian/Other Pacific Islander, 0.0% Some other race, 0.0%

Two or more races, 0.0% Hispanic of any race (2008-2012 5-year est.); Average household size: 2.76 (2008-2012 5-year est.); Median age: 38.9 (2008-2012 5-year est.); Males per 100 females: 100.7 (2008-2012 5-year est.); Marriage status: 24.5% never married, 57.0% now married, 11.7% widowed, 6.8% divorced (2008-2012 5-year est.); Foreign born: 1.7% (2008-2012 5-year est.); Ancestry (includes multiple ancestries): 22.3% German, 12.0% Irish, 11.6% American, 7.0% English, 7.0% Italian (2008-2012 5-year est.).

Economy: Homeowner vacancy rate: 0.0%. Rental vacancy rate: 10.0%. (2008-2012 5-year est.); Employment by occupation: 8.3% management, business, and financial, 2.8% computer, engineering, and science, 2.8% education, legal, community service, arts, and media, 5.0% healthcare practitioners, 42.2% service, 11.9% sales and office, 10.1% natural resources, construction, and maintenance, 17.0% production, transportation, and material moving (2008-2012 5-year est.).

Income: Per capita income: $16,299 (2008-2012 5-year est.); Median household income: $33,889 (2008-2012 5-year est.); Average household income: $44,847 (2008-2012 5-year est.); Percent of households with income of $100,000 or more: 3.8% (2008-2012 5-year est.); Poverty rate: 15.8% (2008-2012 5-year est.).

Education: Percent of population age 25 and over with: High school diploma (including GED) or higher: 84.8% (2008-2012 5-year est.); Bachelor's degree or higher: 8.9% (2008-2012 5-year est.); Master's degree or higher: 2.4% (2008-2012 5-year est.).

Housing: Homeownership rate: 85.5% (2008-2012 5-year est.); Median home value: $46,000 (2008-2012 5-year est.); Median contract rent: $475 per month (2008-2012 5-year est.); Median year structure built: 1954 (2008-2012 5-year est.).

Health Insurance: 49.7% Private; 47.4% Public; 14.2% None. (2008-2012 5-year est.)

Transportation: Commute to work: 96.7% car, 0.0% public transportation, 0.5% walk, 1.4% work from home (2008-2012 5-year est.); Travel time to work: 38.1% less than 15 minutes, 36.2% 15 to 30 minutes, 19.0% 30 to 45 minutes, 4.8% 45 to 60 minutes, 1.9% 60 minutes or more (2008-2012 5-year est.)

SCIOTA (village). Covers a land area of 0.321 square miles and a water area of 0 square miles. Located at 40.56° N. Lat; 90.75° W. Long. Elevation is 758 feet.

Population: 68 (1990); 58 (2000); 61 (2010); Density: 258.4 persons per square mile (2008-2012 5-year est.); Race: 100.0% White, 0.0% Black/African American, 0.0% Asian, 0.0% American Indian/Alaska Native, 0.0% Native Hawaiian/Other Pacific Islander, 0.0% Some other race, 0.0% Two or more races, 0.0% Hispanic of any race (2008-2012 5-year est.); Average household size: 2.77 (2008-2012 5-year est.); Median age: 35.6 (2008-2012 5-year est.); Males per 100 females: 107.5 (2008-2012 5-year est.); Marriage status: 2.0% never married, 74.5% now married, 3.9% widowed, 19.6% divorced (2008-2012 5-year est.); Foreign born: 0.0% (2008-2012 5-year est.); Ancestry (includes multiple ancestries): 26.5% English, 18.1% German, 12.0% Irish, 8.4% American, 6.0% European (2008-2012 5-year est.).

Economy: Homeowner vacancy rate: 0.0%. Rental vacancy rate: 0.0%. (2008-2012 5-year est.); Employment by occupation: 11.1% management, business, and financial, 0.0% computer, engineering, and science, 13.3% education, legal, community service, arts, and media, 4.4% healthcare practitioners, 8.9% service, 31.1% sales and office, 2.2% natural resources, construction, and maintenance, 28.9% production, transportation, and material moving (2008-2012 5-year est.).

Income: Per capita income: $20,331 (2008-2012 5-year est.); Median household income: $49,000 (2008-2012 5-year est.); Average household income: $57,227 (2008-2012 5-year est.); Percent of households with income of $100,000 or more: 6.7% (2008-2012 5-year est.); Poverty rate: 0.0% (2008-2012 5-year est.).

Education: Percent of population age 25 and over with: High school diploma (including GED) or higher: 100.0% (2008-2012 5-year est.); Bachelor's degree or higher: 3.9% (2008-2012 5-year est.); Master's degree or higher: 0.0% (2008-2012 5-year est.).

School District(s)

West Prairie CUSD 103 (PK-12)

    2011-12 Enrollment: 658. . . . . (309) 776-3180

Housing: Homeownership rate: 60.0% (2008-2012 5-year est.); Median home value: $50,000 (2008-2012 5-year est.); Median contract rent: $388 per month (2008-2012 5-year est.); Median year structure built: 1941 (2008-2012 5-year est.).

Health Insurance: 88.0% Private; 55.4% Public; 2.4% None. (2008-2012 5-year est.)

Transportation: Commute to work: 73.8% car, 0.0% public transportation, 19.0% walk, 7.1% work from home (2008-2012 5-year est.); Travel time to work: 20.5% less than 15 minutes, 66.7% 15 to 30 minutes, 0.0% 30 to 45 minutes, 0.0% 45 to 60 minutes, 12.8% 60 minutes or more (2008-2012 5-year est.)

TENNESSEE (village). Covers a land area of 0.432 square miles and a water area of 0 square miles. Located at 40.41° N. Lat; 90.84° W. Long. Elevation is 686 feet.

Population: 127 (1990); 144 (2000); 115 (2010); Density: 397.7 persons per square mile (2008-2012 5-year est.); Race: 100.0% White, 0.0% Black/African American, 0.0% Asian, 0.0% American Indian/Alaska Native, 0.0% Native Hawaiian/Other Pacific Islander, 0.0% Some other race, 0.0% Two or more races, 0.0% Hispanic of any race (2008-2012 5-year est.); Average household size: 2.73 (2008-2012 5-year est.); Median age: 34.6 (2008-2012 5-year est.); Males per 100 females: 81.1 (2008-2012 5-year est.); Marriage status: 32.3% never married, 37.6% now married, 6.8% widowed, 23.3% divorced (2008-2012 5-year est.); Foreign born: 2.9% (2008-2012 5-year est.); Ancestry (includes multiple ancestries): 16.3% Irish, 15.1% German, 11.6% English, 9.3% American, 4.7% Scottish (2008-2012 5-year est.).

Economy: Homeowner vacancy rate: 0.0%. Rental vacancy rate: 0.0%. (2008-2012 5-year est.); Employment by occupation: 13.5% management, business, and financial, 0.0% computer, engineering, and science, 2.7% education, legal, community service, arts, and media, 9.5% healthcare practitioners, 23.0% service, 20.3% sales and office, 29.7% natural resources, construction, and maintenance, 1.4% production, transportation, and material moving (2008-2012 5-year est.).

Income: Per capita income: $14,175 (2008-2012 5-year est.); Median household income: $36,250 (2008-2012 5-year est.); Average household income: $41,798 (2008-2012 5-year est.); Percent of households with income of $100,000 or more: n/a (2008-2012 5-year est.); Poverty rate: 30.2% (2008-2012 5-year est.).

Education: Percent of population age 25 and over with: High school diploma (including GED) or higher: 81.9% (2008-2012 5-year est.); Bachelor's degree or higher: 16.4% (2008-2012 5-year est.); Master's degree or higher: 4.3% (2008-2012 5-year est.).

Housing: Homeownership rate: 85.7% (2008-2012 5-year est.); Median home value: $59,100 (2008-2012 5-year est.); Median contract rent: n/a per month (2008-2012 5-year est.); Median year structure built: 1955 (2008-2012 5-year est.).

Health Insurance: 32.6% Private; 46.5% Public; 33.7% None. (2008-2012 5-year est.)

Transportation: Commute to work: 93.2% car, 0.0% public transportation, 0.0% walk, 4.1% work from home (2008-2012 5-year est.); Travel time to work: 23.9% less than 15 minutes, 42.3% 15 to 30 minutes, 25.4% 30 to 45 minutes, 0.0% 45 to 60 minutes, 8.5% 60 minutes or more (2008-2012 5-year est.)

McHenry County

Located in northeastern Illinois; bounded on the north by Wisconsin; drained by the Fox and Kishwaukee Rivers; includes many lakes. Covers a land area of 603.171 square miles, a water area of 7.642 square miles, and is located in the Central Time Zone at 42.32° N. Lat., 88.45° W. Long. The county was founded in 1836. County seat is Woodstock.

McHenry County is part of the Chicago-Naperville-Elgin, IL-IN-WI Metropolitan Statistical Area. The entire metro area includes: Chicago-Naperville-Arlington Heights, IL Metropolitan Division (Cook County, IL; DuPage County, IL; Grundy County, IL; Kendall County, IL; McHenry County, IL; Will County, IL); Elgin, IL Metropolitan Division (DeKalb County, IL; Kane County, IL); Gary, IN Metropolitan Division (Jasper County, IN; Lake County, IN; Newton County, IN; Porter County, IN); Lake County-Kenosha County, IL-WI Metropolitan Division (Lake County, IL; Kenosha County, WI)

Weather Station: Marengo									Elevation: 819 feet			
	Jan	Feb	Mar	Apr	May	Jun	Jul	Aug	Sep	Oct	Nov	Dec
High	29	33	45	59	71	81	84	82	76	62	47	33
Low	12	14	25	36	46	56	61	59	50	38	28	17
Precip	1.3	1.3	2.0	3.2	4.0	4.0	3.7	4.8	3.0	2.9	2.6	1.9
Snow	9.3	8.0	3.3	1.1	0.1	0.0	0.0	0.0	0.0	0.1	1.7	7.6

High and Low temperatures in degrees Fahrenheit; Precipitation and Snow in inches

Population: 183,241 (1990); 260,077 (2000); 308,760 (2010); Race: 90.7% White, 1.1% Black/African American, 2.6% Asian, 0.2% American Indian/Alaska Native, 0.0% Native Hawaiian/Other Pacific Islander, 5.4% Some other race, 1.6% Two or more races, 11.4% Hispanic of any race (2008-2012 5-year est.); Density: 510.2 persons per square mile (2008-2012 5-year est.); Average household size: 2.81 (2008-2012 5-year est.); Median age: 38.0 (2008-2012 5-year est.); Males per 100 females: 99.5 (2008-2012 5-year est.).

Religion: Six largest groups: 35.1% Catholicism, 7.6% Lutheran, 2.4% Methodist/Pietist, 2.1% Muslim Estimate, 1.8% Presbyterian-Reformed, 1.8% Non-denominational Protestant (2010)

Economy: Unemployment rate: 6.9% (April 2014); Total civilian labor force: 173,434 (April 2014); Leading industries: 17.9% retail trade; 17.8% manufacturing; 12.4% health care and social assistance (2012); Farms: 911 totaling 234,211 acres (2012); Companies that employ 500 or more persons: 10 (2012); Companies that employ 100 to 499 persons: 112 (2012); Companies that employ less than 100 persons: 7,580 (2012); Black-owned businesses: 196 (2007); Hispanic-owned businesses: 845 (2007); Asian-owned businesses: 946 (2007); Women-owned businesses: 8,533 (2007); Single-family building permits issued: 358 (2013); Multi-family building permits issued: 80 (2013).

Income: Per capita income: $32,408 (2008-2012 5-year est.); Median household income: $77,325 (2008-2012 5-year est.); Average household income: $90,540 (2008-2012 5-year est.); Percent of households with income of $100,000 or more: 34.3% (2008-2012 5-year est.); Poverty rate: 7.5% (2008-2012 5-year est.); Bankruptcy rate: 4.58% (2013).

Taxes: Total county taxes per capita: $312 (2011); County property taxes per capita: $280 (2011).

Education: Percent of population age 25 and over with: High school diploma (including GED) or higher: 92.2% (2008-2012 5-year est.); Bachelor's degree or higher: 32.5% (2008-2012 5-year est.); Master's degree or higher: 10.3% (2008-2012 5-year est.).

Housing: Homeownership rate: 82.9% (2008-2012 5-year est.); Median home value: $233,400 (2008-2012 5-year est.); Median contract rent: $890 per month (2008-2012 5-year est.); Median year structure built: 1986 (2008-2012 5-year est.)

Health: Birth rate: 106.8 per 10,000 population (2013); Death rate: 58.6 per 10,000 population (2013); Age-adjusted cancer mortality rate: 187.5 deaths per 100,000 population (2011); Number of physicians: 12.8 per 10,000 population (2011); Hospital beds: 11.6 per 10,000 population (2010); Hospital admissions: 651.3 per 10,000 population (2010).

Environment: Air Quality Index: 77.5% good, 22.3% moderate, 0.3% unhealthy for sensitive individuals, 0.0% unhealthy (percent of days in 2013)

Elections: 2012 Presidential election results: 44.7% Obama, 53.5% Romney

National and State Parks: Moraine Hills State Park

Additional Information Contacts
McHenry County Government . . . . (815) 334-4000
    http://www.co.mchenry.il.us

McHenry County Communities

ALGONQUIN (village). Covers a land area of 12.226 square miles and a water area of 0.180 square miles. Located at 42.16° N. Lat; 88.32° W. Long. Elevation is 741 feet.

Population: 11,663 (1990); 23,276 (2000); 30,046 (2010); Density: 2,447.6 persons per square mile (2008-2012 5-year est.); Race: 84.9% White, 2.7% Black/African American, 8.3% Asian, 0.1% American Indian/Alaska Native, 0.0% Native Hawaiian/Other Pacific Islander, 4.0% Some other race, 1.1% Two or more races, 8.6% Hispanic of any race (2008-2012 5-year est.); Average household size: 2.88 (2008-2012 5-year est.); Median age: 38.8 (2008-2012 5-year est.); Males per 100 females: 100.3 (2008-2012 5-year est.); Marriage status: 23.8% never married, 65.6% now married, 3.9% widowed, 6.6% divorced (2008-2012 5-year est.); Foreign born: 12.6% (2008-2012 5-year est.); Ancestry (includes multiple ancestries): 28.3% German, 17.1% Polish, 14.6% Irish, 13.2% Italian, 6.8% English (2008-2012 5-year est.).

Economy: Unemployment rate: 6.3% (April 2014); Total civilian labor force: 16,558 (April 2014); Single-family building permits issued: 4 (2013); Multi-family building permits issued: 0 (2013); Homeowner vacancy rate: 0.8%. Rental vacancy rate: 5.1%. (2008-2012 5-year est.); Employment by occupation: 20.5% management, business, and financial, 9.5% computer,

engineering, and science, 9.8% education, legal, community service, arts, and media, 6.1% healthcare practitioners, 10.9% service, 29.2% sales and office, 5.7% natural resources, construction, and maintenance, 8.3% production, transportation, and material moving (2008-2012 5-year est.).

Income: Per capita income: $39,368 (2008-2012 5-year est.); Median household income: $100,269 (2008-2012 5-year est.); Average household income: $112,325 (2008-2012 5-year est.); Percent of households with income of $100,000 or more: 50.2% (2008-2012 5-year est.); Poverty rate: 3.0% (2008-2012 5-year est.).

Taxes: Total city taxes per capita: $399 (2011); City property taxes per capita: $197 (2011).

Education: Percent of population age 25 and over with: High school diploma (including GED) or higher: 95.5% (2008-2012 5-year est.); Bachelor's degree or higher: 46.9% (2008-2012 5-year est.); Master's degree or higher: 16.9% (2008-2012 5-year est.).

School District(s)
CSD 158 (PK-12)
    2011-12 Enrollment: 9,285 . . . . (847) 659-6158
CUSD 300 (PK-12)
    2011-12 Enrollment: 20,810 . . . . (847) 551-8308
CUSD 300 (PK-12)
    2011-12 Enrollment: 20,810 . . . . (847) 551-8308

Housing: Homeownership rate: 88.3% (2008-2012 5-year est.); Median home value: $264,000 (2008-2012 5-year est.); Median contract rent: $1,312 per month (2008-2012 5-year est.); Median year structure built: 1992 (2008-2012 5-year est.).

Health Insurance: 86.9% Private; 14.0% Public; 6.2% None. (2008-2012 5-year est.)

Safety: Violent crime rate: 9.6 per 10,000 population; Property crime rate: 166.5 per 10,000 population (2012).

Transportation: Commute to work: 87.9% car, 3.4% public transportation, 0.4% walk, 7.0% work from home (2008-2012 5-year est.); Travel time to work: 16.7% less than 15 minutes, 22.9% 15 to 30 minutes, 23.2% 30 to 45 minutes, 15.7% 45 to 60 minutes, 21.5% 60 minutes or more (2008-2012 5-year est.)

Additional Information Contacts
Algonquin/Lake in the Hills Chamber of Commerce . . . . . . (847) 658-5300
    http://www.alchamber.com
Village of Algonquin . . . . (847) 658-2700
    http://www.algonquin.org

BULL VALLEY (village). Covers a land area of 8.747 square miles and a water area of 0.011 square miles. Located at 42.32° N. Lat; 88.36° W. Long. Elevation is 922 feet.

Population: 574 (1990); 726 (2000); 1,077 (2010); Density: 114.7 persons per square mile (2008-2012 5-year est.); Race: 95.9% White, 0.0% Black/African American, 0.3% Asian, 0.0% American Indian/Alaska Native, 0.0% Native Hawaiian/Other Pacific Islander, 3.8% Some other race, 1.6% Two or more races, 4.0% Hispanic of any race (2008-2012 5-year est.); Average household size: 2.46 (2008-2012 5-year est.); Median age: 52.2 (2008-2012 5-year est.); Males per 100 females: 113.4 (2008-2012 5-year est.); Marriage status: 15.8% never married, 74.8% now married, 1.5% widowed, 7.9% divorced (2008-2012 5-year est.); Foreign born: 8.2% (2008-2012 5-year est.); Ancestry (includes multiple ancestries): 37.7% German, 14.9% Polish, 14.9% Irish, 13.1% Italian, 11.3% English (2008-2012 5-year est.).

Economy: Single-family building permits issued: 0 (2013); Multi-family building permits issued: 0 (2013); Homeowner vacancy rate: 5.8%. Rental vacancy rate: 38.0%. (2008-2012 5-year est.); Employment by occupation: 25.1% management, business, and financial, 11.3% computer, engineering, and science, 13.3% education, legal, community service, arts, and media, 6.5% healthcare practitioners, 9.1% service, 23.0% sales and office, 7.1% natural resources, construction, and maintenance, 4.6% production, transportation, and material moving (2008-2012 5-year est.).

Income: Per capita income: $59,329 (2008-2012 5-year est.); Median household income: $119,861 (2008-2012 5-year est.); Average household income: $145,714 (2008-2012 5-year est.); Percent of households with income of $100,000 or more: 56.1% (2008-2012 5-year est.); Poverty rate: 3.6% (2008-2012 5-year est.).

Education: Percent of population age 25 and over with: High school diploma (including GED) or higher: 98.1% (2008-2012 5-year est.); Bachelor's degree or higher: 58.1% (2008-2012 5-year est.); Master's degree or higher: 26.2% (2008-2012 5-year est.).

Housing: Homeownership rate: 92.4% (2008-2012 5-year est.); Median home value: $470,700 (2008-2012 5-year est.); Median contract rent:

$2,000+ per month (2008-2012 5-year est.); Median year structure built: 1981 (2008-2012 5-year est.).

Health Insurance: 85.3% Private; 23.3% Public; 8.1% None. (2008-2012 5-year est.)

Transportation: Commute to work: 86.5% car, 2.9% public transportation, 0.0% walk, 10.7% work from home (2008-2012 5-year est.); Travel time to work: 21.8% less than 15 minutes, 27.5% 15 to 30 minutes, 15.6% 30 to 45 minutes, 8.5% 45 to 60 minutes, 26.6% 60 minutes or more (2008-2012 5-year est.)

CARY (village).
Covers a land area of 6.269 square miles and a water area of 0.088 square miles. Located at 42.21° N. Lat; 88.25° W. Long. Elevation is 823 feet.

Population: 10,043 (1990); 15,531 (2000); 18,271 (2010); Density: 2,903.5 persons per square mile (2008-2012 5-year est.); Race: 92.0% White, 0.5% Black/African American, 1.6% Asian, 0.0% American Indian/Alaska Native, 0.0% Native Hawaiian/Other Pacific Islander, 5.9% Some other race, 0.8% Two or more races, 9.6% Hispanic of any race (2008-2012 5-year est.); Average household size: 3.09 (2008-2012 5-year est.); Median age: 36.7 (2008-2012 5-year est.); Males per 100 females: 99.0 (2008-2012 5-year est.); Marriage status: 26.1% never married, 63.7% now married, 3.0% widowed, 7.2% divorced (2008-2012 5-year est.); Foreign born: 8.8% (2008-2012 5-year est.); Ancestry (includes multiple ancestries): 34.9% German, 21.8% Irish, 14.4% Polish, 11.2% Italian, 7.3% English (2008-2012 5-year est.).

Economy: Single-family building permits issued: 9 (2013); Multi-family building permits issued: 0 (2013); Homeowner vacancy rate: 1.8%. Rental vacancy rate: 8.5%. (2008-2012 5-year est.); Employment by occupation: 23.4% management, business, and financial, 8.9% computer, engineering, and science, 12.8% education, legal, community service, arts, and media, 4.2% healthcare practitioners, 13.5% service, 24.8% sales and office, 3.8% natural resources, construction, and maintenance, 8.5% production, transportation, and material moving (2008-2012 5-year est.).

Income: Per capita income: $35,450 (2008-2012 5-year est.); Median household income: $101,051 (2008-2012 5-year est.); Average household income: $108,999 (2008-2012 5-year est.); Percent of households with income of $100,000 or more: 51.4% (2008-2012 5-year est.); Poverty rate: 6.2% (2008-2012 5-year est.).

Taxes: Total city taxes per capita: $216 (2011); City property taxes per capita: $137 (2011).

Education: Percent of population age 25 and over with: High school diploma (including GED) or higher: 94.9% (2008-2012 5-year est.); Bachelor's degree or higher: 50.6% (2008-2012 5-year est.); Master's degree or higher: 16.9% (2008-2012 5-year est.).

School District(s)
CHSD 155 (09-12)
    2011-12 Enrollment: 7,009 . . . . (815) 455-8500
Cary CCSD 26 (PK-08)
    2011-12 Enrollment: 2,796 . . . . (847) 639-7788

Housing: Homeownership rate: 90.0% (2008-2012 5-year est.); Median home value: $253,700 (2008-2012 5-year est.); Median contract rent: $922 per month (2008-2012 5-year est.); Median year structure built: 1989 (2008-2012 5-year est.).

Health Insurance: 85.8% Private; 12.7% Public; 7.9% None. (2008-2012 5-year est.)

Safety: Violent crime rate: 4.4 per 10,000 population; Property crime rate: 118.1 per 10,000 population (2012).

Transportation: Commute to work: 86.0% car, 5.7% public transportation, 1.3% walk, 6.5% work from home (2008-2012 5-year est.); Travel time to work: 18.5% less than 15 minutes, 22.6% 15 to 30 minutes, 24.1% 30 to 45 minutes, 14.2% 45 to 60 minutes, 20.6% 60 minutes or more (2008-2012 5-year est.)

Additional Information Contacts
Cary Grove Area Chamber of Commerce . . . . (847) 639-2800
  http://www.carygrovechamber.com
Village of Cary . . . . (847) 639-0003
  http://www.caryillinois.com

CHEMUNG (CDP).
Covers a land area of 0.280 square miles and a water area of 0 square miles. Located at 42.42° N. Lat; 88.66° W. Long. Elevation is 896 feet.

Population: n/a (1990); n/a (2000); 308 (2010); Density: 761.4 persons per square mile (2008-2012 5-year est.); Race: 100.0% White, 0.0% Black/African American, 0.0% Asian, 0.0% American Indian/Alaska Native, 0.0% Native Hawaiian/Other Pacific Islander, 0.0% Some other race, 0.0%

Two or more races, 0.0% Hispanic of any race (2008-2012 5-year est.); Average household size: 2.03 (2008-2012 5-year est.); Median age: 40.2 (2008-2012 5-year est.); Males per 100 females: 88.5 (2008-2012 5-year est.); Marriage status: 30.8% never married, 63.7% now married, 5.5% widowed, 0.0% divorced (2008-2012 5-year est.); Foreign born: 0.0% (2008-2012 5-year est.); Ancestry (includes multiple ancestries): 43.7% Norwegian, 38.0% German, 24.4% Swedish, 17.8% Irish, 16.9% Danish (2008-2012 5-year est.).

Economy: Homeowner vacancy rate: 0.0%. Rental vacancy rate: 0.0%. (2008-2012 5-year est.); Employment by occupation: 0.0% management, business, and financial, 0.0% computer, engineering, and science, 0.0% education, legal, community service, arts, and media, 0.0% healthcare practitioners, 0.0% service, 60.6% sales and office, 7.9% natural resources, construction, and maintenance, 31.5% production, transportation, and material moving (2008-2012 5-year est.).

Income: Per capita income: $25,040 (2008-2012 5-year est.); Median household income: $31,406 (2008-2012 5-year est.); Average household income: $50,269 (2008-2012 5-year est.); Percent of households with income of $100,000 or more: n/a (2008-2012 5-year est.); Poverty rate: 4.7% (2008-2012 5-year est.).

Education: Percent of population age 25 and over with: High school diploma (including GED) or higher: 100.0% (2008-2012 5-year est.); Bachelor's degree or higher: 0.0% (2008-2012 5-year est.); Master's degree or higher: 0.0% (2008-2012 5-year est.).

Housing: Homeownership rate: 100.0% (2008-2012 5-year est.); Median home value: $163,800 (2008-2012 5-year est.); Median contract rent: n/a per month (2008-2012 5-year est.); Median year structure built: Before 1940 (2008-2012 5-year est.).

Health Insurance: 77.5% Private; 15.0% Public; 7.5% None. (2008-2012 5-year est.)

Transportation: Commute to work: 100.0% car, 0.0% public transportation, 0.0% walk, 0.0% work from home (2008-2012 5-year est.); Travel time to work: 52.0% less than 15 minutes, 16.5% 15 to 30 minutes, 4.7% 30 to 45 minutes, 18.9% 45 to 60 minutes, 7.9% 60 minutes or more (2008-2012 5-year est.)

CRYSTAL LAKE (city).
Covers a land area of 18.352 square miles and a water area of 0.607 square miles. Located at 42.23° N. Lat; 88.34° W. Long. Elevation is 915 feet.

History: Named for the small lake around which the town developed. Crystal Lake was settled in 1825 when the Erie Canal opened, and grew when the Chicago & North Western Railroad arrived.

Population: 24,512 (1990); 38,000 (2000); 40,743 (2010); Density: 2,226.8 persons per square mile (2008-2012 5-year est.); Race: 90.2% White, 2.0% Black/African American, 2.2% Asian, 0.0% American Indian/Alaska Native, 0.0% Native Hawaiian/Other Pacific Islander, 5.6% Some other race, 1.5% Two or more races, 12.0% Hispanic of any race (2008-2012 5-year est.); Average household size: 2.86 (2008-2012 5-year est.); Median age: 35.2 (2008-2012 5-year est.); Males per 100 females: 98.2 (2008-2012 5-year est.); Marriage status: 29.4% never married, 55.6% now married, 5.2% widowed, 9.8% divorced (2008-2012 5-year est.); Foreign born: 11.3% (2008-2012 5-year est.); Ancestry (includes multiple ancestries): 29.9% German, 19.0% Irish, 14.4% Polish, 11.9% Italian, 7.5% English (2008-2012 5-year est.).

Economy: Unemployment rate: 6.3% (April 2014); Total civilian labor force: 21,482 (April 2014); Single-family building permits issued: 24 (2013); Multi-family building permits issued: 68 (2013); Homeowner vacancy rate: 2.8%. Rental vacancy rate: 7.9%. (2008-2012 5-year est.); Employment by occupation: 16.9% management, business, and financial, 7.2% computer, engineering, and science, 12.2% education, legal, community service, arts, and media, 3.9% healthcare practitioners, 16.0% service, 28.6% sales and office, 4.3% natural resources, construction, and maintenance, 10.9% production, transportation, and material moving (2008-2012 5-year est.).

Income: Per capita income: $31,172 (2008-2012 5-year est.); Median household income: $78,311 (2008-2012 5-year est.); Average household income: $88,510 (2008-2012 5-year est.); Percent of households with income of $100,000 or more: 34.4% (2008-2012 5-year est.); Poverty rate: 6.2% (2008-2012 5-year est.).

Education: Percent of population age 25 and over with: High school diploma (including GED) or higher: 92.6% (2008-2012 5-year est.); Bachelor's degree or higher: 40.0% (2008-2012 5-year est.); Master's degree or higher: 13.2% (2008-2012 5-year est.).

School District(s)
CHSD 155 (09-12)
    2011-12 Enrollment: 7,009 . . . . (815) 455-8500

Crystal Lake CCSD 47 (PK-08)
  2011-12 Enrollment: 8,214 . . . . (815) 459-6070
Prairie Grove CSD 46 (PK-08)
  2011-12 Enrollment: 915. . . . . (815) 459-3023

Two-year College(s)

McHenry County College (Public)
  Fall 2012 Enrollment: 7,194 . . . . (815) 455-3700
  2012-13 Tuition: In-state $8,309; Out-of-state $10,079

Vocational/Technical School(s)

Cosmetology & Spa Institute (Private, For-profit)
  Fall 2012 Enrollment: 146 . . . . (815) 455-5900
  2012-13 Tuition: $14,000
First Institute Inc (Private, For-profit)
  Fall 2012 Enrollment: 235 . . . . (815) 459-3500
  2012-13 Tuition: $13,600
Regency Beauty Institute-Crystal Lake (Private, For-profit)
  Fall 2012 Enrollment: 58 . . . . (800) 787-6456
  2012-13 Tuition: $16,425

Housing: Homeownership rate: 77.1% (2008-2012 5-year est.); Median home value: $223,600 (2008-2012 5-year est.); Median contract rent: $981 per month (2008-2012 5-year est.); Median year structure built: 1983 (2008-2012 5-year est.).

Health Insurance: 79.6% Private; 20.5% Public; 9.9% None. (2008-2012 5-year est.)

Safety: Violent crime rate: 15.2 per 10,000 population; Property crime rate: 197.1 per 10,000 population (2012).

Transportation: Commute to work: 88.1% car, 3.9% public transportation, 1.4% walk, 5.9% work from home (2008-2012 5-year est.); Travel time to work: 28.4% less than 15 minutes, 27.5% 15 to 30 minutes, 13.9% 30 to 45 minutes, 11.2% 45 to 60 minutes, 19.0% 60 minutes or more (2008-2012 5-year est.)

Additional Information Contacts
City of Crystal Lake . . . . (815) 459-2020
  http://www.crystallake.org
Crystal Lake Chamber of Commerce . . . . (815) 459-1300
  http://www.clchamber.com

FOX RIVER GROVE (village).

Covers a land area of 1.779 square miles and a water area of 0 square miles. Located at 42.20° N. Lat; 88.21° W. Long. Elevation is 817 feet.

History: Fox River Grove developed as a summer resort town.

Population: 3,551 (1990); 4,862 (2000); 4,854 (2010); Density: 2,658.3 persons per square mile (2008-2012 5-year est.); Race: 96.9% White, 0.1% Black/African American, 0.6% Asian, 0.0% American Indian/Alaska Native, 0.0% Native Hawaiian/Other Pacific Islander, 2.4% Some other race, 0.6% Two or more races, 4.5% Hispanic of any race (2008-2012 5-year est.); Average household size: 2.96 (2008-2012 5-year est.); Median age: 40.8 (2008-2012 5-year est.); Males per 100 females: 96.9 (2008-2012 5-year est.); Marriage status: 31.0% never married, 53.8% now married, 4.9% widowed, 10.3% divorced (2008-2012 5-year est.); Foreign born: 6.6% (2008-2012 5-year est.); Ancestry (includes multiple ancestries): 33.5% German, 17.2% Irish, 11.1% Italian, 10.9% Polish, 8.4% American (2008-2012 5-year est.).

Economy: Single-family building permits issued: 1 (2013); Multi-family building permits issued: 0 (2013); Homeowner vacancy rate: 4.1%. Rental vacancy rate: 0.0%. (2008-2012 5-year est.); Employment by occupation: 16.2% management, business, and financial, 8.2% computer, engineering, and science, 9.3% education, legal, community service, arts, and media, 6.1% healthcare practitioners, 15.4% service, 30.0% sales and office, 5.1% natural resources, construction, and maintenance, 9.6% production, transportation, and material moving (2008-2012 5-year est.).

Income: Per capita income: $36,501 (2008-2012 5-year est.); Median household income: $90,701 (2008-2012 5-year est.); Average household income: $106,762 (2008-2012 5-year est.); Percent of households with income of $100,000 or more: 45.7% (2008-2012 5-year est.); Poverty rate: 4.4% (2008-2012 5-year est.).

Education: Percent of population age 25 and over with: High school diploma (including GED) or higher: 94.1% (2008-2012 5-year est.); Bachelor's degree or higher: 40.5% (2008-2012 5-year est.); Master's degree or higher: 10.8% (2008-2012 5-year est.).

School District(s)

Fox River Grove CSD 3 (PK-08)
  2011-12 Enrollment: 507 . . . . (847) 516-5100

Housing: Homeownership rate: 89.0% (2008-2012 5-year est.); Median home value: $260,100 (2008-2012 5-year est.); Median contract rent: $840 per month (2008-2012 5-year est.); Median year structure built: 1974 (2008-2012 5-year est.).

Health Insurance: 82.9% Private; 19.6% Public; 7.4% None. (2008-2012 5-year est.)

Safety: Violent crime rate: 4.2 per 10,000 population; Property crime rate: 208.5 per 10,000 population (2012).

Transportation: Commute to work: 90.6% car, 3.6% public transportation, 2.8% walk, 1.6% work from home (2008-2012 5-year est.); Travel time to work: 27.0% less than 15 minutes, 23.5% 15 to 30 minutes, 21.0% 30 to 45 minutes, 16.0% 45 to 60 minutes, 12.4% 60 minutes or more (2008-2012 5-year est.)

Additional Information Contacts
Cary Grove Area Chamber of Commerce . . . . (847) 639-2800
  http://www.carygrovechamber.com
Village of Fox River Grove . . . . (847) 639-3170
  http://www.foxrivergrove.org

GREENWOOD (village).

Covers a land area of 1.857 square miles and a water area of 0 square miles. Located at 42.39° N. Lat; 88.39° W. Long. Elevation is 856 feet.

Population: n/a (1990); 244 (2000); 255 (2010); Density: 149.7 persons per square mile (2008-2012 5-year est.); Race: 96.4% White, 0.0% Black/African American, 0.7% Asian, 0.0% American Indian/Alaska Native, 0.0% Native Hawaiian/Other Pacific Islander, 2.9% Some other race, 0.0% Two or more races, 5.8% Hispanic of any race (2008-2012 5-year est.); Average household size: 2.87 (2008-2012 5-year est.); Median age: 35.7 (2008-2012 5-year est.); Males per 100 females: 122.4 (2008-2012 5-year est.); Marriage status: 25.8% never married, 62.2% now married, 2.3% widowed, 9.7% divorced (2008-2012 5-year est.); Foreign born: 3.2% (2008-2012 5-year est.); Ancestry (includes multiple ancestries): 55.0% German, 23.7% Irish, 8.3% English, 8.3% Norwegian, 6.8% Swedish (2008-2012 5-year est.).

Economy: Homeowner vacancy rate: 5.2%. Rental vacancy rate: 0.0%. (2008-2012 5-year est.); Employment by occupation: 9.6% management, business, and financial, 3.5% computer, engineering, and science, 2.6% education, legal, community service, arts, and media, 7.0% healthcare practitioners, 12.3% service, 25.4% sales and office, 22.8% natural resources, construction, and maintenance, 16.7% production, transportation, and material moving (2008-2012 5-year est.).

Income: Per capita income: $25,952 (2008-2012 5-year est.); Median household income: $65,625 (2008-2012 5-year est.); Average household income: $75,272 (2008-2012 5-year est.); Percent of households with income of $100,000 or more: 28.9% (2008-2012 5-year est.); Poverty rate: 16.9% (2008-2012 5-year est.).

Education: Percent of population age 25 and over with: High school diploma (including GED) or higher: 90.6% (2008-2012 5-year est.); Bachelor's degree or higher: 20.0% (2008-2012 5-year est.); Master's degree or higher: 8.9% (2008-2012 5-year est.).

Housing: Homeownership rate: 75.3% (2008-2012 5-year est.); Median home value: $241,700 (2008-2012 5-year est.); Median contract rent: $1,271 per month (2008-2012 5-year est.); Median year structure built: 1944 (2008-2012 5-year est.).

Health Insurance: 79.9% Private; 16.9% Public; 11.9% None. (2008-2012 5-year est.)

Transportation: Commute to work: 92.0% car, 0.0% public transportation, 2.7% walk, 3.5% work from home (2008-2012 5-year est.); Travel time to work: 8.3% less than 15 minutes, 46.8% 15 to 30 minutes, 19.3% 30 to 45 minutes, 0.0% 45 to 60 minutes, 25.7% 60 minutes or more (2008-2012 5-year est.)

Airports: Galt Field (general aviation)

HARVARD (city).

Covers a land area of 8.576 square miles and a water area of 0 square miles. Located at 42.43° N. Lat; 88.62° W. Long. Elevation is 958 feet.

History: Incorporated 1867.

Population: 5,975 (1990); 7,996 (2000); 9,447 (2010); Density: 1,069.4 persons per square mile (2008-2012 5-year est.); Race: 73.0% White, 0.1% Black/African American, 1.8% Asian, 0.0% American Indian/Alaska Native, 0.0% Native Hawaiian/Other Pacific Islander, 25.1% Some other race, 2.0% Two or more races, 46.1% Hispanic of any race (2008-2012 5-year est.); Average household size: 3.11 (2008-2012 5-year est.); Median age: 27.8 (2008-2012 5-year est.); Males per 100 females: 97.4 (2008-2012 5-year est.); Marriage status: 30.1% never married, 52.0% now married, 5.6% widowed, 12.4% divorced (2008-2012 5-year est.); Foreign born: 27.8% (2008-2012 5-year est.); Ancestry (includes multiple

ancestries): 18.9% German, 13.4% Irish, 7.3% Polish, 5.2% English, 3.8% American (2008-2012 5-year est.).

Economy: Single-family building permits issued: 1 (2013); Multi-family building permits issued: 0 (2013); Homeowner vacancy rate: 0.0%. Rental vacancy rate: 11.6%. (2008-2012 5-year est.); Employment by occupation: 6.0% management, business, and financial, 3.5% computer, engineering, and science, 6.1% education, legal, community service, arts, and media, 3.0% healthcare practitioners, 18.1% service, 17.6% sales and office, 13.8% natural resources, construction, and maintenance, 31.8% production, transportation, and material moving (2008-2012 5-year est.).

Income: Per capita income: $16,118 (2008-2012 5-year est.); Median household income: $37,646 (2008-2012 5-year est.); Average household income: $49,391 (2008-2012 5-year est.); Percent of households with income of $100,000 or more: 8.0% (2008-2012 5-year est.); Poverty rate: 31.6% (2008-2012 5-year est.).

Education: Percent of population age 25 and over with: High school diploma (including GED) or higher: 74.7% (2008-2012 5-year est.); Bachelor's degree or higher: 9.5% (2008-2012 5-year est.); Master's degree or higher: 2.5% (2008-2012 5-year est.).

School District(s)

Harvard CUSD 50 (PK-12)
    2011-12 Enrollment: 2,438 . . . . (815) 943-4022

Housing: Homeownership rate: 60.8% (2008-2012 5-year est.); Median home value: $134,400 (2008-2012 5-year est.); Median contract rent: $790 per month (2008-2012 5-year est.); Median year structure built: 1970 (2008-2012 5-year est.).

Health Insurance: 52.8% Private; 38.2% Public; 17.3% None. (2008-2012 5-year est.)

Hospitals: Mercy Harvard Hospital (46 beds)

Safety: Violent crime rate: 12.7 per 10,000 population; Property crime rate: 139.6 per 10,000 population (2012).

Transportation: Commute to work: 91.0% car, 2.9% public transportation, 2.9% walk, 1.5% work from home (2008-2012 5-year est.); Travel time to work: 20.1% less than 15 minutes, 22.4% 15 to 30 minutes, 27.0% 30 to 45 minutes, 15.4% 45 to 60 minutes, 15.1% 60 minutes or more (2008-2012 5-year est.)

Airports: Dacy Airport (general aviation)

Additional Information Contacts

City of Harvard . . . . (815) 943-6468
    http://www.cityofharvard.org
Harvard Chamber of Commerce & Industry . . . . (815) 943-4404
    http://www.harvcc.net

HEBRON (village).
Covers a land area of 1.955 square miles and a water area of 0 square miles. Located at 42.47° N. Lat; 88.43° W. Long. Elevation is 928 feet.

Population: 809 (1990); 1,038 (2000); 1,216 (2010); Density: 553.5 persons per square mile (2008-2012 5-year est.); Race: 96.8% White, 0.7% Black/African American, 1.4% Asian, 0.0% American Indian/Alaska Native, 0.0% Native Hawaiian/Other Pacific Islander, 1.1% Some other race, 0.5% Two or more races, 5.7% Hispanic of any race (2008-2012 5-year est.); Average household size: 2.54 (2008-2012 5-year est.); Median age: 41.1 (2008-2012 5-year est.); Males per 100 females: 94.3 (2008-2012 5-year est.); Marriage status: 33.0% never married, 43.4% now married, 5.9% widowed, 17.7% divorced (2008-2012 5-year est.); Foreign born: 4.6% (2008-2012 5-year est.); Ancestry (includes multiple ancestries): 39.1% German, 16.3% Irish, 10.5% English, 9.8% Italian, 8.9% Polish (2008-2012 5-year est.).

Economy: Single-family building permits issued: 4 (2013); Multi-family building permits issued: 0 (2013); Homeowner vacancy rate: 5.3%. Rental vacancy rate: 13.2%. (2008-2012 5-year est.); Employment by occupation: 9.0% management, business, and financial, 2.3% computer, engineering, and science, 6.5% education, legal, community service, arts, and media, 2.7% healthcare practitioners, 14.1% service, 23.1% sales and office, 12.1% natural resources, construction, and maintenance, 30.1% production, transportation, and material moving (2008-2012 5-year est.).

Income: Per capita income: $26,420 (2008-2012 5-year est.); Median household income: $49,063 (2008-2012 5-year est.); Average household income: $65,492 (2008-2012 5-year est.); Percent of households with income of $100,000 or more: 15.0% (2008-2012 5-year est.); Poverty rate: 13.1% (2008-2012 5-year est.).

Education: Percent of population age 25 and over with: High school diploma (including GED) or higher: 85.5% (2008-2012 5-year est.); Bachelor's degree or higher: 13.4% (2008-2012 5-year est.); Master's degree or higher: 1.9% (2008-2012 5-year est.).

School District(s)

Alden Hebron SD 19 (PK-12)
    2011-12 Enrollment: 450 . . . . (815) 648-2886

Housing: Homeownership rate: 76.2% (2008-2012 5-year est.); Median home value: $153,500 (2008-2012 5-year est.); Median contract rent: $708 per month (2008-2012 5-year est.); Median year structure built: 1958 (2008-2012 5-year est.).

Health Insurance: 67.6% Private; 23.3% Public; 16.8% None. (2008-2012 5-year est.)

Transportation: Commute to work: 88.4% car, 3.1% public transportation, 4.4% walk, 2.4% work from home (2008-2012 5-year est.); Travel time to work: 25.8% less than 15 minutes, 22.9% 15 to 30 minutes, 21.6% 30 to 45 minutes, 10.9% 45 to 60 minutes, 18.8% 60 minutes or more (2008-2012 5-year est.)

HOLIDAY HILLS (village).
Covers a land area of 0.951 square miles and a water area of 0.040 square miles. Located at 42.30° N. Lat; 88.23° W. Long. Elevation is 741 feet.

Population: 807 (1990); 831 (2000); 610 (2010); Density: 721.2 persons per square mile (2008-2012 5-year est.); Race: 98.5% White, 0.0% Black/African American, 0.0% Asian, 1.0% American Indian/Alaska Native, 0.0% Native Hawaiian/Other Pacific Islander, 0.5% Some other race, 0.4% Two or more races, 3.6% Hispanic of any race (2008-2012 5-year est.); Average household size: 2.49 (2008-2012 5-year est.); Median age: 45.7 (2008-2012 5-year est.); Males per 100 females: 101.8 (2008-2012 5-year est.); Marriage status: 28.0% never married, 57.4% now married, 5.7% widowed, 8.8% divorced (2008-2012 5-year est.); Foreign born: 4.5% (2008-2012 5-year est.); Ancestry (Includes multiple ancestries): 37.6% German, 17.9% Irish, 16.3% Polish, 12.0% English, 8.2% American (2008-2012 5-year est.).

Economy: Single-family building permits issued: 0 (2013); Multi-family building permits issued: 0 (2013); Homeowner vacancy rate: 0.0%. Rental vacancy rate: 0.0%. (2008-2012 5-year est.); Employment by occupation: 13.2% management, business, and financial, 1.9% computer, engineering, and science, 7.1% education, legal, community service, arts, and media, 2.2% healthcare practitioners, 18.1% service, 20.6% sales and office, 13.2% natural resources, construction, and maintenance, 15.7% production, transportation, and material moving (2008-2012 5-year est.).

Income: Per capita income: $26,640 (2008-2012 5-year est.); Median household income: $55,000 (2008-2012 5-year est.); Average household income: $64,769 (2008-2012 5-year est.); Percent of households with income of $100,000 or more: 21.4% (2008-2012 5-year est.); Poverty rate: 15.3% (2008-2012 5-year est.).

Education: Percent of population age 25 and over with: High school diploma (including GED) or higher: 91.4% (2008-2012 5-year est.); Bachelor's degree or higher: 14.6% (2008-2012 5-year est.); Master's degree or higher: 3.2% (2008-2012 5-year est.).

Housing: Homeownership rate: 92.8% (2008-2012 5-year est.); Median home value: $166,700 (2008-2012 5-year est.); Median contract rent: $1,083 per month (2008-2012 5-year est.); Median year structure built: 1965 (2008-2012 5-year est.).

Health Insurance: 70.4% Private; 22.4% Public; 19.5% None. (2008-2012 5-year est.)

Transportation: Commute to work: 94.6% car, 1.1% public transportation, 0.0% walk, 4.3% work from home (2008-2012 5-year est.); Travel time to work: 15.7% less than 15 minutes, 30.3% 15 to 30 minutes, 16.3% 30 to 45 minutes, 11.3% 45 to 60 minutes, 26.4% 60 minutes or more (2008-2012 5-year est.)

HUNTLEY (village).
Covers a land area of 14.069 square miles and a water area of 0.032 square miles. Located at 42.16° N. Lat; 88.44° W. Long. Elevation is 889 feet.

Population: 2,453 (1990); 5,730 (2000); 24,291 (2010); Density: 1,698.5 persons per square mile (2008-2012 5-year est.); Race: 88.6% White, 1.6% Black/African American, 6.3% Asian, 0.2% American Indian/Alaska Native, 0.0% Native Hawaiian/Other Pacific Islander, 3.3% Some other race, 2.7% Two or more races, 6.3% Hispanic of any race (2008-2012 5-year est.); Average household size: 2.43 (2008-2012 5-year est.); Median age: 44.1 (2008-2012 5-year est.); Males per 100 females: 88.8 (2008-2012 5-year est.); Marriage status: 14.3% never married, 70.5% now married, 7.6% widowed, 7.6% divorced (2008-2012 5-year est.); Foreign born: 8.4% (2008-2012 5-year est.); Ancestry (includes multiple ancestries): 29.6% German, 17.4% Polish, 16.0% Irish, 14.8% Italian, 7.2% English (2008-2012 5-year est.).

Economy: Single-family building permits issued: 176 (2013); Multi-family building permits issued: 0 (2013); Homeowner vacancy rate: 0.1%. Rental vacancy rate: 26.2%. (2008-2012 5-year est.); Employment by occupation: 23.4% management, business, and financial, 5.0% computer, engineering, and science, 8.7% education, legal, community service, arts, and media, 5.4% healthcare practitioners, 10.5% service, 28.7% sales and office, 7.3% natural resources, construction, and maintenance, 11.0% production, transportation, and material moving (2008-2012 5-year est.).
Income: Per capita income: $35,289 (2008-2012 5-year est.); Median household income: $70,524 (2008-2012 5-year est.); Average household income: $85,295 (2008-2012 5-year est.); Percent of households with income of $100,000 or more: 31.3% (2008-2012 5-year est.); Poverty rate: 3.4% (2008-2012 5-year est.).
Taxes: Total city taxes per capita: $398 (2011); City property taxes per capita: $270 (2011).
Education: Percent of population age 25 and over with: High school diploma (including GED) or higher: 96.1% (2008-2012 5-year est.); Bachelor's degree or higher: 32.5% (2008-2012 5-year est.); Master's degree or higher: 10.1% (2008-2012 5-year est.).

School District(s)
CSD 158 (PK-12)
    2011-12 Enrollment: 9,285 . . . . (847) 659-6158
Housing: Homeownership rate: 93.5% (2008-2012 5-year est.); Median home value: $237,800 (2008-2012 5-year est.); Median contract rent: $1,295 per month (2008-2012 5-year est.); Median year structure built: 2003 (2008-2012 5-year est.).
Health Insurance: 87.5% Private; 33.1% Public; 4.0% None. (2008-2012 5-year est.)
Safety: Violent crime rate: 2.5 per 10,000 population; Property crime rate: 87.8 per 10,000 population (2012).
Transportation: Commute to work: 92.8% car, 1.8% public transportation, 0.0% walk, 4.8% work from home (2008-2012 5-year est.); Travel time to work: 15.9% less than 15 minutes, 22.6% 15 to 30 minutes, 20.0% 30 to 45 minutes, 20.7% 45 to 60 minutes, 20.8% 60 minutes or more (2008-2012 5-year est.)
Additional Information Contacts
Huntley Area Chamber of Commerce . . . . (847) 669-0166
    http://www.huntleychamber.org
Village of Huntley . . . . (847) 515-5200
    http://www.huntley.il.us

ISLAND LAKE (village). Covers a land area of 3.388 square miles and a water area of 0.207 square miles. Located at 42.28° N. Lat; 88.20° W. Long.
Population: 4,449 (1990); 8,153 (2000); 8,080 (2010); Density: 2,394.8 persons per square mile (2008-2012 5-year est.); Race: 90.6% White, 0.3% Black/African American, 1.9% Asian, 0.0% American Indian/Alaska Native, 0.0% Native Hawaiian/Other Pacific Islander, 7.2% Some other race, 3.0% Two or more races, 18.5% Hispanic of any race (2008-2012 5-year est.); Average household size: 2.86 (2008-2012 5-year est.); Median age: 34.8 (2008-2012 5-year est.); Males per 100 females: 88.4 (2008-2012 5-year est.); Marriage status: 27.0% never married, 56.0% now married, 4.7% widowed, 12.3% divorced (2008-2012 5-year est.); Foreign born: 11.9% (2008-2012 5-year est.); Ancestry (includes multiple ancestries): 29.4% German, 18.0% Irish, 11.8% Polish, 9.3% Italian, 7.4% English (2008-2012 5-year est.).
Economy: Single-family building permits issued: 14 (2013); Multi-family building permits issued: 0 (2013); Homeowner vacancy rate: 1.6%. Rental vacancy rate: 0.0%. (2008-2012 5-year est.); Employment by occupation: 15.8% management, business, and financial, 5.1% computer, engineering, and science, 5.7% education, legal, community service, arts, and media, 2.1% healthcare practitioners, 14.1% service, 27.5% sales and office, 13.4% natural resources, construction, and maintenance, 16.1% production, transportation, and material moving (2008-2012 5-year est.).
Income: Per capita income: $26,019 (2008-2012 5-year est.); Median household income: $67,432 (2008-2012 5-year est.); Average household income: $73,935 (2008-2012 5-year est.); Percent of households with income of $100,000 or more: 24.4% (2008-2012 5-year est.); Poverty rate: 9.6% (2008-2012 5-year est.).
Education: Percent of population age 25 and over with: High school diploma (including GED) or higher: 90.4% (2008-2012 5-year est.); Bachelor's degree or higher: 21.0% (2008-2012 5-year est.); Master's degree or higher: 6.3% (2008-2012 5-year est.).

School District(s)
Wauconda CUSD 118 (PK-12)
    2011-12 Enrollment: 4,492 . . . . (847) 526-7690
Wauconda CUSD 118 (PK-12)
    2011-12 Enrollment: 4,492 . . . . (847) 526-7690
Housing: Homeownership rate: 84.3% (2008-2012 5-year est.); Median home value: $190,000 (2008-2012 5-year est.); Median contract rent: $1,035 per month (2008-2012 5-year est.); Median year structure built: 1988 (2008-2012 5-year est.).
Health Insurance: 75.8% Private; 19.7% Public; 11.4% None. (2008-2012 5-year est.)
Safety: Violent crime rate: 8.6 per 10,000 population; Property crime rate: 232.1 per 10,000 population (2012).
Transportation: Commute to work: 93.9% car, 1.8% public transportation, 0.4% walk, 2.8% work from home (2008-2012 5-year est.); Travel time to work: 18.1% less than 15 minutes, 24.8% 15 to 30 minutes, 25.5% 30 to 45 minutes, 16.7% 45 to 60 minutes, 15.0% 60 minutes or more (2008-2012 5-year est.)
Additional Information Contacts
Island Lake Area Chamber of Commerce . . . . (847) 604-4522
    http://www.islandlakechamber.org
Village of Island Lake . . . . (847) 526-8764
    http://www.villageofislandlake.com

JOHNSBURG (village). Aka Sunnyside. Covers a land area of 7.079 square miles and a water area of 0.594 square miles. Located at 42.38° N. Lat; 88.25° W. Long. Elevation is 751 feet.
Population: n/a (1990); 5,391 (2000); 6,337 (2010); Density: 893.5 persons per square mile (2008-2012 5-year est.); Race: 97.3% White, 1.2% Black/African American, 0.1% Asian, 0.8% American Indian/Alaska Native, 0.0% Native Hawaiian/Other Pacific Islander, 0.6% Some other race, 0.6% Two or more races, 3.1% Hispanic of any race (2008-2012 5-year est.); Average household size: 2.87 (2008-2012 5-year est.); Median age: 40.8 (2008-2012 5-year est.); Males per 100 females: 103.6 (2008-2012 5-year est.); Marriage status: 24.1% never married, 62.4% now married, 3.0% widowed, 10.5% divorced (2008-2012 5-year est.); Foreign born: 1.6% (2008-2012 5-year est.); Ancestry (includes multiple ancestries): 35.7% German, 21.2% Irish, 12.8% Polish, 9.0% Italian, 7.7% English (2008-2012 5-year est.).
Economy: Single-family building permits issued: 7 (2013); Multi-family building permits issued: 0 (2013); Homeowner vacancy rate: 2.7%. Rental vacancy rate: 11.8%. (2008-2012 5-year est.); Employment by occupation: 19.3% management, business, and financial, 5.2% computer, engineering, and science, 9.9% education, legal, community service, arts, and media, 5.2% healthcare practitioners, 13.5% service, 29.5% sales and office, 6.8% natural resources, construction, and maintenance, 10.6% production, transportation, and material moving (2008-2012 5-year est.).
Income: Per capita income: $34,296 (2008-2012 5-year est.); Median household income: $78,963 (2008-2012 5-year est.); Average household income: $97,835 (2008-2012 5-year est.); Percent of households with income of $100,000 or more: 37.3% (2008-2012 5-year est.); Poverty rate: 5.9% (2008-2012 5-year est.).
Education: Percent of population age 25 and over with: High school diploma (including GED) or higher: 96.4% (2008-2012 5-year est.); Bachelor's degree or higher: 27.6% (2008-2012 5-year est.); Master's degree or higher: 10.9% (2008-2012 5-year est.).

School District(s)
Johnsburg CUSD 12 (PK-12)
    2011-12 Enrollment: 2,334 . . . . (815) 385-6916
Housing: Homeownership rate: 87.1% (2008-2012 5-year est.); Median home value: $291,100 (2008-2012 5-year est.); Median contract rent: $1,159 per month (2008-2012 5-year est.); Median year structure built: 1986 (2008-2012 5-year est.).
Health Insurance: 85.8% Private; 20.0% Public; 5.3% None. (2008-2012 5-year est.)
Transportation: Commute to work: 90.2% car, 0.2% public transportation, 1.5% walk, 5.3% work from home (2008-2012 5-year est.); Travel time to work: 32.9% less than 15 minutes, 19.8% 15 to 30 minutes, 22.3% 30 to 45 minutes, 12.3% 45 to 60 minutes, 12.7% 60 minutes or more (2008-2012 5-year est.)
Additional Information Contacts
Village of Johnsburg . . . . (815) 385-6023
    http://www.johnsburg.org

LAKE IN THE HILLS (village). Covers a land area of 10.377 square miles and a water area of 0.234 square miles. Located at 42.18° N. Lat; 88.32° W. Long. Elevation is 866 feet.
Population: 5,866 (1990); 23,152 (2000); 28,965 (2010); Density: 2,784.4 persons per square mile (2008-2012 5-year est.); Race: 90.0% White, 1.4% Black/African American, 4.5% Asian, 0.2% American Indian/Alaska Native, 0.0% Native Hawaiian/Other Pacific Islander, 3.9% Some other race, 2.1% Two or more races, 9.0% Hispanic of any race (2008-2012 5-year est.); Average household size: 2.95 (2008-2012 5-year est.); Median age: 36.3 (2008-2012 5-year est.); Males per 100 females: 102.9 (2008-2012 5-year est.); Marriage status: 23.2% never married, 62.2% now married, 3.3% widowed, 11.3% divorced (2008-2012 5-year est.); Foreign born: 10.9% (2008-2012 5-year est.); Ancestry (includes multiple ancestries): 28.5% German, 19.0% Irish, 17.5% Polish, 14.1% Italian, 5.5% English (2008-2012 5-year est.).
Economy: Unemployment rate: 7.0% (April 2014); Total civilian labor force: 16,801 (April 2014); Single-family building permits issued: 18 (2013); Multi-family building permits issued: 0 (2013); Homeowner vacancy rate: 1.5%. Rental vacancy rate: 5.8%. (2008-2012 5-year est.); Employment by occupation: 19.1% management, business, and financial, 5.3% computer, engineering, and science, 7.6% education, legal, community service, arts, and media, 4.5% healthcare practitioners, 11.5% service, 29.2% sales and office, 9.1% natural resources, construction, and maintenance, 13.7% production, transportation, and material moving (2008-2012 5-year est.).
Income: Per capita income: $32,560 (2008-2012 5-year est.); Median household income: $85,429 (2008-2012 5-year est.); Average household income: $95,017 (2008-2012 5-year est.); Percent of households with income of $100,000 or more: 38.2% (2008-2012 5-year est.); Poverty rate: 5.6% (2008-2012 5-year est.).
Education: Percent of population age 25 and over with: High school diploma (including GED) or higher: 94.6% (2008-2012 5-year est.); Bachelor's degree or higher: 30.6% (2008-2012 5-year est.); Master's degree or higher: 8.3% (2008-2012 5-year est.).

School District(s)
CSD 158 (PK-12)
   2011-12 Enrollment: 9,285 . . . . (847) 659-6158
CUSD 300 (PK-12)
   2011-12 Enrollment: 20,810 . . . . (847) 551-8308
Housing: Homeownership rate: 91.0% (2008-2012 5-year est.); Median home value: $223,300 (2008-2012 5-year est.); Median contract rent: $1,126 per month (2008-2012 5-year est.); Median year structure built: 1995 (2008-2012 5-year est.).
Health Insurance: 83.3% Private; 13.8% Public; 8.8% None. (2008-2012 5-year est.)
Transportation: Commute to work: 92.5% car, 1.7% public transportation, 0.3% walk, 4.8% work from home (2008-2012 5-year est.); Travel time to work: 17.2% less than 15 minutes, 25.7% 15 to 30 minutes, 18.8% 30 to 45 minutes, 18.1% 45 to 60 minutes, 20.3% 60 minutes or more (2008-2012 5-year est.)
Airports: Lake in the Hills Airport (reliver airport)
Additional Information Contacts
Algonquin/Lake in the Hills Chamber of Commerce . . . . . . (847) 658-5300
   http://www.alchamber.com
Village of Lake in the Hills . . . . (847) 960-7400
   http://www.lith.org

LAKEWOOD (village). Covers a land area of 3.666 square miles and a water area of 0.304 square miles. Located at 42.22° N. Lat; 88.39° W. Long. Elevation is 889 feet.
History: The Village of Lakewood was incorporated on July 10, 1933. In 1993 the Village Board developed a vision statement which has become the basis for making decisions to preserve this way of life. The statement reads, "Lakewood will remain a friendly community providing families with quality living in a natural setting", adopted as our mission statement.
Population: 1,609 (1990); 2,337 (2000); 3,811 (2010); Density: 1,141.2 persons per square mile (2008-2012 5-year est.); Race: 92.2% White, 3.1% Black/African American, 3.0% Asian, 0.0% American Indian/Alaska Native, 0.0% Native Hawaiian/Other Pacific Islander, 1.7% Some other race, 1.6% Two or more races, 2.8% Hispanic of any race (2008-2012 5-year est.); Average household size: 3.05 (2008-2012 5-year est.); Median age: 43.5 (2008-2012 5-year est.); Males per 100 females: 100.4 (2008-2012 5-year est.); Marriage status: 20.9% never married, 68.5% now married, 5.4% widowed, 5.2% divorced (2008-2012 5-year est.); Foreign born: 5.1% (2008-2012 5-year est.); Ancestry (includes multiple

ancestries): 34.1% German, 20.1% Irish, 18.1% Polish, 10.7% English, 5.6% Swedish (2008-2012 5-year est.).
Economy: Single-family building permits issued: 3 (2013); Multi-family building permits issued: 0 (2013); Homeowner vacancy rate: 0.0%. Rental vacancy rate: 0.0%. (2008-2012 5-year est.); Employment by occupation: 35.9% management, business, and financial, 3.0% computer, engineering, and science, 10.5% education, legal, community service, arts, and media, 4.9% healthcare practitioners, 5.8% service, 31.0% sales and office, 2.2% natural resources, construction, and maintenance, 6.7% production, transportation, and material moving (2008-2012 5-year est.).
Income: Per capita income: $54,678 (2008-2012 5-year est.); Median household income: $124,778 (2008-2012 5-year est.); Average household income: $166,560 (2008-2012 5-year est.); Percent of households with income of $100,000 or more: 67.0% (2008-2012 5-year est.); Poverty rate: 1.8% (2008-2012 5-year est.).
Education: Percent of population age 25 and over with: High school diploma (including GED) or higher: 99.6% (2008-2012 5-year est.); Bachelor's degree or higher: 64.1% (2008-2012 5-year est.); Master's degree or higher: 20.7% (2008-2012 5-year est.).
Housing: Homeownership rate: 98.3% (2008-2012 5-year est.); Median home value: $433,100 (2008-2012 5-year est.); Median contract rent: $2,000+ per month (2008-2012 5-year est.); Median year structure built: 1994 (2008-2012 5-year est.).
Health Insurance: 96.0% Private; 16.0% Public; 2.2% None. (2008-2012 5-year est.)
Safety: Violent crime rate: 0.0 per 10,000 population; Property crime rate: 80.4 per 10,000 population (2012).
Transportation: Commute to work: 87.1% car, 2.5% public transportation, 2.4% walk, 8.0% work from home (2008-2012 5-year est.); Travel time to work: 22.7% less than 15 minutes, 29.1% 15 to 30 minutes, 18.4% 30 to 45 minutes, 10.4% 45 to 60 minutes, 19.4% 60 minutes or more (2008-2012 5-year est.)

MARENGO (city). Covers a land area of 5.010 square miles and a water area of 0 square miles. Located at 42.25° N. Lat; 88.61° W. Long. Elevation is 833 feet.
History: Marengo was the birthplace of Egbert Van Alstyne who composed the songs "In the Shade of the Old Apple Tree," and "Pony Boy." An early industry here was the McGill Metal Products Plant, a manufacturer of mousetraps.
Population: 4,768 (1990); 6,355 (2000); 7,648 (2010); Density: 1,531.9 persons per square mile (2008-2012 5-year est.); Race: 90.7% White, 1.2% Black/African American, 0.9% Asian, 0.2% American Indian/Alaska Native, 0.0% Native Hawaiian/Other Pacific Islander, 7.0% Some other race, 3.6% Two or more races, 15.4% Hispanic of any race (2008-2012 5-year est.); Average household size: 2.76 (2008-2012 5-year est.); Median age: 35.3 (2008-2012 5-year est.); Males per 100 females: 94.3 (2008-2012 5-year est.); Marriage status: 23.2% never married, 59.3% now married, 5.8% widowed, 11.7% divorced (2008-2012 5-year est.); Foreign born: 9.4% (2008-2012 5-year est.); Ancestry (includes multiple ancestries): 36.4% German, 16.7% Irish, 11.1% Polish, 10.1% Italian, 6.9% English (2008-2012 5-year est.).
Economy: Single-family building permits issued: 0 (2013); Multi-family building permits issued: 0 (2013); Homeowner vacancy rate: 0.0%. Rental vacancy rate: 0.0%. (2008-2012 5-year est.); Employment by occupation: 11.9% management, business, and financial, 3.2% computer, engineering, and science, 13.5% education, legal, community service, arts, and media, 3.2% healthcare practitioners, 21.2% service, 26.5% sales and office, 7.7% natural resources, construction, and maintenance, 12.8% production, transportation, and material moving (2008-2012 5-year est.).
Income: Per capita income: $24,842 (2008-2012 5-year est.); Median household income: $58,766 (2008-2012 5-year est.); Average household income: $67,944 (2008-2012 5-year est.); Percent of households with income of $100,000 or more: 18.7% (2008-2012 5-year est.); Poverty rate: 11.3% (2008-2012 5-year est.).
Education: Percent of population age 25 and over with: High school diploma (including GED) or higher: 88.8% (2008-2012 5-year est.); Bachelor's degree or higher: 21.6% (2008-2012 5-year est.); Master's degree or higher: 6.8% (2008-2012 5-year est.).

School District(s)
Marengo CHSD 154 (09-12)
   2011-12 Enrollment: 820 . . . . (815) 568-6511
Marengo-Union E Cons D 165 (PK-08)
   2011-12 Enrollment: 1,083 . . . . (815) 568-8323

Riley CCSD 18 (KG-08)
　2011-12 Enrollment: 300 . . . . (815) 568-8637
Housing: Homeownership rate: 71.2% (2008-2012 5-year est.); Median home value: $184,800 (2008-2012 5-year est.); Median contract rent: $684 per month (2008-2012 5-year est.); Median year structure built: 1972 (2008-2012 5-year est.).
Health Insurance: 72.3% Private; 31.1% Public; 9.5% None. (2008-2012 5-year est.)
Transportation: Commute to work: 90.1% car, 0.3% public transportation, 4.1% walk, 3.2% work from home (2008-2012 5-year est.); Travel time to work: 30.4% less than 15 minutes, 22.8% 15 to 30 minutes, 20.9% 30 to 45 minutes, 9.9% 45 to 60 minutes, 16.1% 60 minutes or more (2008-2012 5-year est.)
Additional Information Contacts
City of Marengo. . . . . (815) 568-6937
　http://www.cityofmarengo.com
Marengo Union Chamber of Commerce . . . . (815) 568-6680
　http://www.marengo-union.com

MCCULLOM LAKE (village). Covers a land area of 0.374 square miles and a water area of 0 square miles. Located at 42.37° N. Lat; 88.30° W. Long. Elevation is 787 feet.
Population: 1,033 (1990); 1,038 (2000); 1,049 (2010); Density: 2,816.5 persons per square mile (2008-2012 5-year est.); Race: 96.4% White, 0.0% Black/African American, 0.0% Asian, 0.0% American Indian/Alaska Native, 0.0% Native Hawaiian/Other Pacific Islander, 3.6% Some other race, 1.3% Two or more races, 6.5% Hispanic of any race (2008-2012 5-year est.); Average household size: 2.68 (2008-2012 5-year est.); Median age: 39.4 (2008-2012 5-year est.); Males per 100 females: 95.5 (2008-2012 5-year est.); Marriage status: 35.3% never married, 51.5% now married, 3.7% widowed, 9.5% divorced (2008-2012 5-year est.); Foreign born: 4.8% (2008-2012 5-year est.); Ancestry (includes multiple ancestries): 34.2% German, 21.0% Irish, 15.7% Polish, 8.1% English, 8.0% Italian (2008-2012 5-year est.).
Economy: Single-family building permits issued: 0 (2013); Multi-family building permits issued: 0 (2013); Homeowner vacancy rate: 5.0%. Rental vacancy rate: 0.0%. (2008-2012 5-year est.); Employment by occupation: 9.7% management, business, and financial, 2.2% computer, engineering, and science, 2.6% education, legal, community service, arts, and media, 1.7% healthcare practitioners, 21.6% service, 37.4% sales and office, 11.7% natural resources, construction, and maintenance, 13.0% production, transportation, and material moving (2008-2012 5-year est.).
Income: Per capita income: $24,256 (2008-2012 5-year est.); Median household income: $55,435 (2008-2012 5-year est.); Average household income: $63,233 (2008-2012 5-year est.); Percent of households with income of $100,000 or more: 16.2% (2008-2012 5-year est.); Poverty rate: 11.4% (2008-2012 5-year est.).
Education: Percent of population age 25 and over with: High school diploma (including GED) or higher: 83.6% (2008-2012 5-year est.); Bachelor's degree or higher: 9.5% (2008-2012 5-year est.); Master's degree or higher: 0.7% (2008-2012 5-year est.).
Housing: Homeownership rate: 70.8% (2008-2012 5-year est.); Median home value: $151,900 (2008-2012 5-year est.); Median contract rent: $823 per month (2008-2012 5-year est.); Median year structure built: 1954 (2008-2012 5-year est.).
Health Insurance: 65.4% Private; 28.1% Public; 14.5% None. (2008-2012 5-year est.)
Transportation: Commute to work: 93.8% car, 0.6% public transportation, 1.1% walk, 4.5% work from home (2008-2012 5-year est.); Travel time to work: 23.3% less than 15 minutes, 35.4% 15 to 30 minutes, 12.5% 30 to 45 minutes, 11.1% 45 to 60 minutes, 17.8% 60 minutes or more (2008-2012 5-year est.)

MCHENRY (city). Covers a land area of 14.741 square miles and a water area of 0.435 square miles. Located at 42.34° N. Lat; 88.29° W. Long. Elevation is 797 feet.
History: Named for William McHenry (1774-1839), who fought in the Black Hawk War of 1832. McHenry began in 1836 when Dr. Christy C. Wheeler became the first postmaster and storekeeper. McHenry was located on the Chicago Pike route and entertained many travelers. Later the economy depended on butter, cheese, and pickle production.
Population: 16,177 (1990); 21,501 (2000); 26,992 (2010); Density: 1,822.2 persons per square mile (2008-2012 5-year est.); Race: 90.3% White, 0.2% Black/African American, 1.9% Asian, 0.2% American Indian/Alaska Native, 0.0% Native Hawaiian/Other Pacific Islander, 7.4%

Some other race, 2.5% Two or more races, 11.0% Hispanic of any race (2008-2012 5-year est.); Average household size: 2.69 (2008-2012 5-year est.); Median age: 37.7 (2008-2012 5-year est.); Males per 100 females: 99.1 (2008-2012 5-year est.); Marriage status: 28.4% never married, 56.5% now married, 6.7% widowed, 8.4% divorced (2008-2012 5-year est.); Foreign born: 8.3% (2008-2012 5-year est.); Ancestry (includes multiple ancestries): 38.1% German, 18.7% Irish, 15.9% Polish, 8.4% Italian, 6.9% English (2008-2012 5-year est.).
Economy: Unemployment rate: 7.2% (April 2014); Total civilian labor force: 15,072 (April 2014); Single-family building permits issued: 7 (2013); Multi-family building permits issued: 12 (2013); Homeowner vacancy rate: 3.9%. Rental vacancy rate: 8.8%. (2008-2012 5-year est.); Employment by occupation: 11.6% management, business, and financial, 4.8% computer, engineering, and science, 10.0% education, legal, community service, arts, and media, 4.4% healthcare practitioners, 18.9% service, 28.6% sales and office, 8.7% natural resources, construction, and maintenance, 13.0% production, transportation, and material moving (2008-2012 5-year est.).
Income: Per capita income: $30,302 (2008-2012 5-year est.); Median household income: $67,740 (2008-2012 5-year est.); Average household income: $80,610 (2008-2012 5-year est.); Percent of households with income of $100,000 or more: 26.8% (2008-2012 5-year est.); Poverty rate: 8.7% (2008-2012 5-year est.).
Education: Percent of population age 25 and over with: High school diploma (including GED) or higher: 91.1% (2008-2012 5-year est.); Bachelor's degree or higher: 25.1% (2008-2012 5-year est.); Master's degree or higher: 6.2% (2008-2012 5-year est.).
School District(s)
Mchenry CCSD 15 (PK-08)
　2011-12 Enrollment: 4,845 . . . . (815) 385-7210
Mchenry CHSD 156 (09-12)
　2011-12 Enrollment: 2,537 . . . . (815) 385-7900
Housing: Homeownership rate: 77.5% (2008-2012 5-year est.); Median home value: $205,200 (2008-2012 5-year est.); Median contract rent: $900 per month (2008-2012 5-year est.); Median year structure built: 1984 (2008-2012 5-year est.).
Health Insurance: 75.8% Private; 22.9% Public; 11.3% None. (2008-2012 5-year est.)
Hospitals: Centegra Northern Illinois Medical Center (196 beds)
Safety: Violent crime rate: 13.0 per 10,000 population; Property crime rate: 154.3 per 10,000 population (2012).
Transportation: Commute to work: 91.7% car, 2.0% public transportation, 1.7% walk, 3.8% work from home (2008-2012 5-year est.); Travel time to work: 28.7% less than 15 minutes, 30.8% 15 to 30 minutes, 15.6% 30 to 45 minutes, 10.4% 45 to 60 minutes, 14.5% 60 minutes or more (2008-2012 5-year est.)
Additional Information Contacts
City of McHenry. . . . . (815) 363-2100
　http://www.ci.mchenry.il.us
McHenry Area Chamber of Commerce . . . . (815) 385-4300
　http://www.mchenrychamber.com

OAKWOOD HILLS (village). Covers a land area of 1.178 square miles and a water area of 0.082 square miles. Located at 42.25° N. Lat; 88.24° W. Long. Elevation is 827 feet.
Population: 1,498 (1990); 2,194 (2000); 2,083 (2010); Density: 1,923.3 persons per square mile (2008-2012 5-year est.); Race: 94.8% White, 0.0% Black/African American, 2.1% Asian, 0.0% American Indian/Alaska Native, 0.0% Native Hawaiian/Other Pacific Islander, 3.1% Some other race, 2.1% Two or more races, 6.8% Hispanic of any race (2008-2012 5-year est.); Average household size: 2.69 (2008-2012 5-year est.); Median age: 42.4 (2008-2012 5-year est.); Males per 100 females: 105.4 (2008-2012 5-year est.); Marriage status: 26.3% never married, 57.2% now married, 3.9% widowed, 12.6% divorced (2008-2012 5-year est.); Foreign born: 5.7% (2008-2012 5-year est.); Ancestry (includes multiple ancestries): 42.9% German, 18.9% Irish, 17.5% Polish, 13.2% Italian, 7.3% Swedish (2008-2012 5-year est.).
Economy: Single-family building permits issued: 0 (2013); Multi-family building permits issued: 0 (2013); Homeowner vacancy rate: 0.0%. Rental vacancy rate: 0.0%. (2008-2012 5-year est.); Employment by occupation: 16.8% management, business, and financial, 6.8% computer, engineering, and science, 9.3% education, legal, community service, arts, and media, 4.6% healthcare practitioners, 14.5% service, 29.3% sales and office, 7.7% natural resources, construction, and maintenance, 10.9% production, transportation, and material moving (2008-2012 5-year est.).

Income: Per capita income: $38,302 (2008-2012 5-year est.); Median household income: $84,728 (2008-2012 5-year est.); Average household income: $102,692 (2008-2012 5-year est.); Percent of households with income of $100,000 or more: 39.9% (2008-2012 5-year est.); Poverty rate: 4.3% (2008-2012 5-year est.).

Education: Percent of population age 25 and over with: High school diploma (including GED) or higher: 95.6% (2008-2012 5-year est.); Bachelor's degree or higher: 37.4% (2008-2012 5-year est.); Master's degree or higher: 12.2% (2008-2012 5-year est.).

Housing: Homeownership rate: 93.0% (2008-2012 5-year est.); Median home value: $230,800 (2008-2012 5-year est.); Median contract rent: $863 per month (2008-2012 5-year est.); Median year structure built: 1978 (2008-2012 5-year est.).

Health Insurance: 82.5% Private; 14.3% Public; 11.8% None. (2008-2012 5-year est.)

Safety: Violent crime rate: 33.6 per 10,000 population; Property crime rate: 67.1 per 10,000 population (2012).

Transportation: Commute to work: 90.0% car, 2.2% public transportation, 0.8% walk, 5.2% work from home (2008-2012 5-year est.); Travel time to work: 23.1% less than 15 minutes, 27.3% 15 to 30 minutes, 21.4% 30 to 45 minutes, 14.2% 45 to 60 minutes, 14.0% 60 minutes or more (2008-2012 5-year est.)

PISTAKEE HIGHLANDS (CDP). Aka Pistakee. Covers a land area of 1.319 square miles and a water area of 0.283 square miles. Located at 42.40° N. Lat; 88.21° W. Long. Elevation is 758 feet.

Population: 3,848 (1990); 3,812 (2000); 3,454 (2010); Density: 2,391.5 persons per square mile (2008-2012 5-year est.); Race: 99.8% White, 0.0% Black/African American, 0.0% Asian, 0.0% American Indian/Alaska Native, 0.0% Native Hawaiian/Other Pacific Islander, 0.2% Some other race, 0.2% Two or more races, 2.7% Hispanic of any race (2008-2012 5-year est.); Average household size: 2.55 (2008-2012 5-year est.); Median age: 41.5 (2008-2012 5-year est.); Males per 100 females: 95.4 (2008-2012 5-year est.); Marriage status: 28.6% never married, 55.1% now married, 5.2% widowed, 11.2% divorced (2008-2012 5-year est.); Foreign born: 0.8% (2008-2012 5-year est.); Ancestry (includes multiple ancestries): 36.1% German, 20.0% Irish, 15.5% Polish, 11.3% Italian, 9.3% English (2008-2012 5-year est.).

Economy: Homeowner vacancy rate: 0.0%. Rental vacancy rate: 0.0%. (2008-2012 5-year est.); Employment by occupation: 17.4% management, business, and financial, 3.5% computer, engineering, and science, 4.4% education, legal, community service, arts, and media, 1.3% healthcare practitioners, 6.1% service, 37.4% sales and office, 15.8% natural resources, construction, and maintenance, 14.1% production, transportation, and material moving (2008-2012 5-year est.).

Income: Per capita income: $28,208 (2008-2012 5-year est.); Median household income: $56,950 (2008-2012 5-year est.); Average household income: $70,803 (2008-2012 5-year est.); Percent of households with income of $100,000 or more: 21.2% (2008-2012 5-year est.); Poverty rate: 6.3% (2008-2012 5-year est.).

Education: Percent of population age 25 and over with: High school diploma (including GED) or higher: 90.3% (2008-2012 5-year est.); Bachelor's degree or higher: 14.4% (2008-2012 5-year est.); Master's degree or higher: 3.2% (2008-2012 5-year est.).

Housing: Homeownership rate: 88.5% (2008-2012 5-year est.); Median home value: $167,700 (2008-2012 5-year est.); Median contract rent: $980 per month (2008-2012 5-year est.); Median year structure built: 1965 (2008-2012 5-year est.).

Health Insurance: 79.2% Private; 23.6% Public; 10.2% None. (2008-2012 5-year est.)

Transportation: Commute to work: 96.4% car, 0.0% public transportation, 0.6% walk, 1.3% work from home (2008-2012 5-year est.); Travel time to work: 23.4% less than 15 minutes, 24.9% 15 to 30 minutes, 19.2% 30 to 45 minutes, 14.5% 45 to 60 minutes, 18.0% 60 minutes or more (2008-2012 5-year est.)

PORT BARRINGTON (village). Covers a land area of 1.150 square miles and a water area of 0.136 square miles. Located at 42.24° N. Lat; 88.20° W. Long. Elevation is 738 feet.

Population: n/a (1990); n/a (2000); 1,517 (2010); Density: 1,399.5 persons per square mile (2008-2012 5-year est.); Race: 89.3% White, 1.2% Black/African American, 7.3% Asian, 0.0% American Indian/Alaska Native, 0.0% Native Hawaiian/Other Pacific Islander, 2.2% Some other race, 1.2% Two or more races, 5.6% Hispanic of any race (2008-2012 5-year est.); Average household size: 2.78 (2008-2012 5-year est.);

Median age: 41.2 (2008-2012 5-year est.); Males per 100 females: 103.8 (2008-2012 5-year est.); Marriage status: 19.6% never married, 69.1% now married, 3.2% widowed, 8.0% divorced (2008-2012 5-year est.); Foreign born: 13.2% (2008-2012 5-year est.); Ancestry (includes multiple ancestries): 29.2% German, 19.0% Italian, 17.2% Irish, 16.6% Polish, 6.1% Swedish (2008-2012 5-year est.).

Economy: Single-family building permits issued: 2 (2013); Multi-family building permits issued: 0 (2013); Homeowner vacancy rate: 1.2%. Rental vacancy rate: 0.0%. (2008-2012 5-year est.); Employment by occupation: 24.6% management, business, and financial, 7.4% computer, engineering, and science, 7.9% education, legal, community service, arts, and media, 4.4% healthcare practitioners, 10.0% service, 32.6% sales and office, 7.3% natural resources, construction, and maintenance, 5.8% production, transportation, and material moving (2008-2012 5-year est.).

Income: Per capita income: $46,279 (2008-2012 5-year est.); Median household income: $107,404 (2008-2012 5-year est.); Average household income: $129,397 (2008-2012 5-year est.); Percent of households with income of $100,000 or more: 54.3% (2008-2012 5-year est.); Poverty rate: 3.8% (2008-2012 5-year est.).

Education: Percent of population age 25 and over with: High school diploma (including GED) or higher: 95.4% (2008-2012 5-year est.); Bachelor's degree or higher: 49.5% (2008-2012 5-year est.); Master's degree or higher: 15.4% (2008-2012 5-year est.).

Housing: Homeownership rate: 98.8% (2008-2012 5-year est.); Median home value: $301,700 (2008-2012 5-year est.); Median contract rent: $2,000+ per month (2008-2012 5-year est.); Median year structure built: 1998 (2008-2012 5-year est.).

Health Insurance: 90.2% Private; 14.7% Public; 4.5% None. (2008-2012 5-year est.)

Transportation: Commute to work: 84.2% car, 6.7% public transportation, 0.0% walk, 9.0% work from home (2008-2012 5-year est.); Travel time to work: 9.9% less than 15 minutes, 26.6% 15 to 30 minutes, 25.9% 30 to 45 minutes, 15.4% 45 to 60 minutes, 22.2% 60 minutes or more (2008-2012 5-year est.)

PRAIRIE GROVE (village). Covers a land area of 5.710 square miles and a water area of 0.004 square miles. Located at 42.27° N. Lat; 88.27° W. Long. Elevation is 758 feet.

Population: 654 (1990); 960 (2000); 1,904 (2010); Density: 313.0 persons per square mile (2008-2012 5-year est.); Race: 92.6% White, 1.8% Black/African American, 2.8% Asian, 0.0% American Indian/Alaska Native, 0.0% Native Hawaiian/Other Pacific Islander, 2.8% Some other race, 1.7% Two or more races, 3.6% Hispanic of any race (2008-2012 5-year est.); Average household size: 2.92 (2008-2012 5-year est.); Median age: 42.4 (2008-2012 5-year est.); Males per 100 females: 97.7 (2008-2012 5-year est.); Marriage status: 23.4% never married, 64.0% now married, 3.3% widowed, 9.2% divorced (2008-2012 5-year est.); Foreign born: 7.2% (2008-2012 5-year est.); Ancestry (includes multiple ancestries): 36.6% German, 19.7% Irish, 13.3% English, 12.0% Italian, 11.1% Polish (2008-2012 5-year est.).

Economy: Single-family building permits issued: 1 (2013); Multi-family building permits issued: 0 (2013); Homeowner vacancy rate: 1.3%. Rental vacancy rate: 20.0%. (2008-2012 5-year est.); Employment by occupation: 25.1% management, business, and financial, 9.1% computer, engineering, and science, 12.0% education, legal, community service, arts, and media, 6.3% healthcare practitioners, 6.3% service, 28.1% sales and office, 8.8% natural resources, construction, and maintenance, 4.5% production, transportation, and material moving (2008-2012 5-year est.).

Income: Per capita income: $53,251 (2008-2012 5-year est.); Median household income: $121,635 (2008-2012 5-year est.); Average household income: $156,236 (2008-2012 5-year est.); Percent of households with income of $100,000 or more: 60.4% (2008-2012 5-year est.); Poverty rate: 2.7% (2008-2012 5-year est.).

Education: Percent of population age 25 and over with: High school diploma (including GED) or higher: 98.0% (2008-2012 5-year est.); Bachelor's degree or higher: 54.8% (2008-2012 5-year est.); Master's degree or higher: 20.7% (2008-2012 5-year est.).

Housing: Homeownership rate: 93.5% (2008-2012 5-year est.); Median home value: $409,400 (2008-2012 5-year est.); Median contract rent: $1,156 per month (2008-2012 5-year est.); Median year structure built: 1995 (2008-2012 5-year est.).

Health Insurance: 94.1% Private; 9.6% Public; 3.2% None. (2008-2012 5-year est.)

Transportation: Commute to work: 86.5% car, 5.0% public transportation, 1.5% walk, 6.3% work from home (2008-2012 5-year est.); Travel time to

work: 21.7% less than 15 minutes, 25.3% 15 to 30 minutes, 15.9% 30 to 45 minutes, 14.6% 45 to 60 minutes, 22.5% 60 minutes or more (2008-2012 5-year est.)

RICHMOND (village). Covers a land area of 4.224 square miles and a water area of 0 square miles. Located at 42.46° N. Lat; 88.31° W. Long. Elevation is 820 feet.

History: Richmond was settled in 1837, and developed around a grist mill.

Population: 1,016 (1990); 1,091 (2000); 1,874 (2010); Density: 495.3 persons per square mile (2008-2012 5-year est.); Race: 99.4% White, 0.0% Black/African American, 0.6% Asian, 0.0% American Indian/Alaska Native, 0.0% Native Hawaiian/Other Pacific Islander, 0.0% Some other race, 0.0% Two or more races, 6.5% Hispanic of any race (2008-2012 5-year est.); Average household size: 2.00 (2008-2012 5-year est.); Median age: 39.1 (2008-2012 5-year est.); Males per 100 females: 97.0 (2008-2012 5-year est.); Marriage status: 32.1% never married, 48.7% now married, 4.1% widowed, 15.1% divorced (2008-2012 5-year est.); Foreign born: 3.3% (2008-2012 5-year est.); Ancestry (includes multiple ancestries): 40.4% German, 18.4% Irish, 10.7% Italian, 8.7% Polish, 7.4% English (2008-2012 5-year est.).

Economy: Single-family building permits issued: 5 (2013); Multi-family building permits issued: 0 (2013); Homeowner vacancy rate: 0.0%. Rental vacancy rate: 3.1%. (2008-2012 5-year est.); Employment by occupation: 16.1% management, business, and financial, 10.7% computer, engineering, and science, 11.6% education, legal, community service, arts, and media, 3.6% healthcare practitioners, 15.2% service, 22.9% sales and office, 7.7% natural resources, construction, and maintenance, 12.1% production, transportation, and material moving (2008-2012 5-year est.).

Income: Per capita income: $33,543 (2008-2012 5-year est.); Median household income: $52,500 (2008-2012 5-year est.); Average household income: $66,705 (2008-2012 5-year est.); Percent of households with income of $100,000 or more: 20.3% (2008-2012 5-year est.); Poverty rate: 6.3% (2008-2012 5-year est.).

Education: Percent of population age 25 and over with: High school diploma (including GED) or higher: 93.8% (2008-2012 5-year est.); Bachelor's degree or higher: 25.0% (2008-2012 5-year est.); Master's degree or higher: 9.1% (2008-2012 5-year est.).

School District(s)

Nippersink SD 2 (PK-08)
    2011-12 Enrollment: 1,400 . . . . (815) 678-4242
Richmond-Burton CHSD 157 (09-12)
    2011-12 Enrollment: 788. . . . . (815) 678-4525

Housing: Homeownership rate: 52.3% (2008-2012 5-year est.); Median home value: $190,000 (2008-2012 5-year est.); Median contract rent: $752 per month (2008-2012 5-year est.); Median year structure built: 1997 (2008-2012 5-year est.).

Health Insurance: 80.8% Private; 17.8% Public; 10.8% None. (2008-2012 5-year est.)

Safety: Violent crime rate: 0.0 per 10,000 population; Property crime rate: 191.8 per 10,000 population (2012).

Transportation: Commute to work: 93.6% car, 0.0% public transportation, 2.5% walk, 3.9% work from home (2008-2012 5-year est.); Travel time to work: 21.3% less than 15 minutes, 18.5% 15 to 30 minutes, 23.7% 30 to 45 minutes, 16.4% 45 to 60 minutes, 20.1% 60 minutes or more (2008-2012 5-year est.)

Additional Information Contacts

Richmond/Spring Grove Chamber of Commerce . . . . (815) 678-7742
    http://www.rsgchamber.com

RINGWOOD (village). Covers a land area of 3.856 square miles and a water area of 0 square miles. Located at 42.40° N. Lat; 88.30° W. Long. Elevation is 856 feet.

Population: n/a (1990); 471 (2000); 836 (2010); Density: 216.1 persons per square mile (2008-2012 5-year est.); Race: 96.8% White, 1.0% Black/African American, 0.6% Asian, 0.0% American Indian/Alaska Native, 0.0% Native Hawaiian/Other Pacific Islander, 1.6% Some other race, 1.3% Two or more races, 2.8% Hispanic of any race (2008-2012 5-year est.); Average household size: 2.80 (2008-2012 5-year est.); Median age: 42.8 (2008-2012 5-year est.); Males per 100 females: 107.7 (2008-2012 5-year est.); Marriage status: 21.4% never married, 64.3% now married, 2.1% widowed, 12.2% divorced (2008-2012 5-year est.); Foreign born: 3.1% (2008-2012 5-year est.); Ancestry (includes multiple ancestries): 42.0% German, 21.2% Irish, 17.6% Italian, 15.7% Polish, 7.1% English (2008-2012 5-year est.).

Economy: Homeowner vacancy rate: 0.0%. Rental vacancy rate: 0.0%. (2008-2012 5-year est.); Employment by occupation: 19.7% management, business, and financial, 5.3% computer, engineering, and science, 10.1% education, legal, community service, arts, and media, 3.4% healthcare practitioners, 14.4% service, 22.8% sales and office, 16.3% natural resources, construction, and maintenance, 7.9% production, transportation, and material moving (2008-2012 5-year est.).

Income: Per capita income: $34,554 (2008-2012 5-year est.); Median household income: $84,750 (2008-2012 5-year est.); Average household income: $98,136 (2008-2012 5-year est.); Percent of households with income of $100,000 or more: 35.4% (2008-2012 5-year est.); Poverty rate: 8.6% (2008-2012 5-year est.).

Education: Percent of population age 25 and over with: High school diploma (including GED) or higher: 97.1% (2008-2012 5-year est.); Bachelor's degree or higher: 24.6% (2008-2012 5-year est.); Master's degree or higher: 5.7% (2008-2012 5-year est.).

School District(s)

Johnsburg CUSD 12 (PK-12)
    2011-12 Enrollment: 2,334 . . . . (815) 385-6916

Housing: Homeownership rate: 85.2% (2008-2012 5-year est.); Median home value: $301,900 (2008-2012 5-year est.); Median contract rent: $888 per month (2008-2012 5-year est.); Median year structure built: 1984 (2008-2012 5-year est.).

Health Insurance: 83.7% Private; 15.7% Public; 5.6% None. (2008-2012 5-year est.)

Transportation: Commute to work: 93.5% car, 1.2% public transportation, 1.2% walk, 3.1% work from home (2008-2012 5-year est.); Travel time to work: 26.2% less than 15 minutes, 22.7% 15 to 30 minutes, 25.7% 30 to 45 minutes, 11.5% 45 to 60 minutes, 14.0% 60 minutes or more (2008-2012 5-year est.)

SPRING GROVE (village). Covers a land area of 8.683 square miles and a water area of 0.031 square miles. Located at 42.45° N. Lat; 88.24° W. Long. Elevation is 764 feet.

Population: 1,066 (1990); 3,880 (2000); 5,778 (2010); Density: 627.9 persons per square mile (2008-2012 5-year est.); Race: 93.2% White, 2.5% Black/African American, 2.7% Asian, 0.0% American Indian/Alaska Native, 0.0% Native Hawaiian/Other Pacific Islander, 1.6% Some other race, 0.7% Two or more races, 3.6% Hispanic of any race (2008-2012 5-year est.); Average household size: 3.11 (2008-2012 5-year est.); Median age: 41.8 (2008-2012 5-year est.); Males per 100 females: 102.7 (2008-2012 5-year est.); Marriage status: 23.4% never married, 67.1% now married, 2.2% widowed, 7.2% divorced (2008-2012 5-year est.); Foreign born: 3.6% (2008-2012 5-year est.); Ancestry (includes multiple ancestries): 36.3% German, 23.4% Irish, 22.2% Polish, 16.9% Italian, 8.8% English (2008-2012 5-year est.).

Economy: Single-family building permits issued: 6 (2013); Multi-family building permits issued: 0 (2013); Homeowner vacancy rate: 0.0%. Rental vacancy rate: 0.0%. (2008-2012 5-year est.); Employment by occupation: 22.2% management, business, and financial, 7.5% computer, engineering, and science, 9.0% education, legal, community service, arts, and media, 5.6% healthcare practitioners, 16.7% service, 22.4% sales and office, 5.6% natural resources, construction, and maintenance, 11.1% production, transportation, and material moving (2008-2012 5-year est.).

Income: Per capita income: $33,795 (2008-2012 5-year est.); Median household income: $100,231 (2008-2012 5-year est.); Average household income: $105,214 (2008-2012 5-year est.); Percent of households with income of $100,000 or more: 50.6% (2008-2012 5-year est.); Poverty rate: 3.4% (2008-2012 5-year est.).

Education: Percent of population age 25 and over with: High school diploma (including GED) or higher: 94.2% (2008-2012 5-year est.); Bachelor's degree or higher: 31.8% (2008-2012 5-year est.); Master's degree or higher: 10.2% (2008-2012 5-year est.).

School District(s)

Fox Lake Gsd 114 (PK-08)
    2011-12 Enrollment: 828. . . . . (847) 973-4027
Nippersink SD 2 (PK-08)
    2011-12 Enrollment: 1,400 . . . . (815) 678-4242

Housing: Homeownership rate: 94.1% (2008-2012 5-year est.); Median home value: $321,800 (2008-2012 5-year est.); Median contract rent: $1,578 per month (2008-2012 5-year est.); Median year structure built: 1996 (2008-2012 5-year est.).

Health Insurance: 93.3% Private; 14.6% Public; 3.9% None. (2008-2012 5-year est.)

Safety: Violent crime rate: 1.7 per 10,000 population; Property crime rate: 88.2 per 10,000 population (2012).
Transportation: Commute to work: 88.1% car, 2.9% public transportation, 0.0% walk, 7.9% work from home (2008-2012 5-year est.); Travel time to work: 19.1% less than 15 minutes, 29.3% 15 to 30 minutes, 20.9% 30 to 45 minutes, 13.9% 45 to 60 minutes, 16.8% 60 minutes or more (2008-2012 5-year est.)
Additional Information Contacts
Village of Spring Grove . . . . (815) 675-2121
   http://www.springgrovevillage.com

TROUT VALLEY (village). Covers a land area of 0.431 square miles and a water area of 0.002 square miles. Located at 42.20° N. Lat; 88.25° W. Long. Elevation is 794 feet.
Population: n/a (1990); 599 (2000); 537 (2010); Density: 1,355.3 persons per square mile (2008-2012 5-year est.); Race: 96.2% White, 0.3% Black/African American, 1.0% Asian, 0.3% American Indian/Alaska Native, 0.0% Native Hawaiian/Other Pacific Islander, 2.2% Some other race, 1.7% Two or more races, 3.3% Hispanic of any race (2008-2012 5-year est.); Average household size: 2.83 (2008-2012 5-year est.); Median age: 46.3 (2008-2012 5-year est.); Males per 100 females: 81.4 (2008-2012 5-year est.); Marriage status: 24.6% never married, 59.3% now married, 7.7% widowed, 8.3% divorced (2008-2012 5-year est.); Foreign born: 3.8% (2008-2012 5-year est.); Ancestry (includes multiple ancestries): 33.0% German, 32.9% Irish, 12.3% English, 9.8% Polish, 9.2% Italian (2008-2012 5-year est.).
Economy: Homeowner vacancy rate: 3.4%. Rental vacancy rate: 0.0%. (2008-2012 5-year est.); Employment by occupation: 27.2% management, business, and financial, 4.8% computer, engineering, and science, 10.0% education, legal, community service, arts, and media, 5.9% healthcare practitioners, 7.9% service, 39.7% sales and office, 2.1% natural resources, construction, and maintenance, 2.4% production, transportation, and material moving (2008-2012 5-year est.).
Income: Per capita income: $55,786 (2008-2012 5-year est.); Median household income: $123,750 (2008-2012 5-year est.); Average household income: $153,044 (2008-2012 5-year est.); Percent of households with income of $100,000 or more: 61.6% (2008-2012 5-year est.); Poverty rate: 3.3% (2008-2012 5-year est.).
Education: Percent of population age 25 and over with: High school diploma (including GED) or higher: 98.3% (2008-2012 5-year est.); Bachelor's degree or higher: 53.6% (2008-2012 5-year est.); Master's degree or higher: 18.2% (2008-2012 5-year est.).
Housing: Homeownership rate: 95.6% (2008-2012 5-year est.); Median home value: $417,600 (2008-2012 5-year est.); Median contract rent: n/a per month (2008-2012 5-year est.); Median year structure built: 1966 (2008-2012 5-year est.).
Health Insurance: 91.8% Private; 13.9% Public; 5.7% None. (2008-2012 5-year est.)
Transportation: Commute to work: 76.1% car, 9.2% public transportation, 1.1% walk, 10.6% work from home (2008-2012 5-year est.); Travel time to work: 18.9% less than 15 minutes, 22.4% 15 to 30 minutes, 24.4% 30 to 45 minutes, 15.0% 45 to 60 minutes, 19.3% 60 minutes or more (2008-2012 5-year est.)

UNION (village). Covers a land area of 0.830 square miles and a water area of 0 square miles. Located at 42.23° N. Lat; 88.54° W. Long. Elevation is 840 feet.
History: Illinois Railroad Museum here.
Population: 542 (1990); 576 (2000); 580 (2010); Density: 865.8 persons per square mile (2008-2012 5-year est.); Race: 99.4% White, 0.0% Black/African American, 0.0% Asian, 0.0% American Indian/Alaska Native, 0.0% Native Hawaiian/Other Pacific Islander, 0.6% Some other race, 0.0% Two or more races, 3.9% Hispanic of any race (2008-2012 5-year est.); Average household size: 3.09 (2008-2012 5-year est.); Median age: 33.5 (2008-2012 5-year est.); Males per 100 females: 109.6 (2008-2012 5-year est.); Marriage status: 33.1% never married, 54.9% now married, 4.9% widowed, 7.2% divorced (2008-2012 5-year est.); Foreign born: 0.4% (2008-2012 5-year est.); Ancestry (includes multiple ancestries): 62.9% German, 19.6% Italian, 12.1% Irish, 6.7% Polish, 6.5% English (2008-2012 5-year est.).
Economy: Single-family building permits issued: 0 (2013); Multi-family building permits issued: 0 (2013); Homeowner vacancy rate: 0.0%. Rental vacancy rate: 20.8%. (2008-2012 5-year est.); Employment by occupation: 13.3% management, business, and financial, 6.1% computer, engineering, and science, 14.7% education, legal, community service, arts, and media,

0.0% healthcare practitioners, 23.7% service, 23.7% sales and office, 9.8% natural resources, construction, and maintenance, 8.7% production, transportation, and material moving (2008-2012 5-year est.).
Income: Per capita income: $21,317 (2008-2012 5-year est.); Median household income: $55,938 (2008-2012 5-year est.); Average household income: $64,801 (2008-2012 5-year est.); Percent of households with income of $100,000 or more: 17.6% (2008-2012 5-year est.); Poverty rate: 21.4% (2008-2012 5-year est.).
Education: Percent of population age 25 and over with: High school diploma (including GED) or higher: 96.7% (2008-2012 5-year est.); Bachelor's degree or higher: 20.5% (2008-2012 5-year est.); Master's degree or higher: 6.2% (2008-2012 5-year est.).
School District(s)
Mchenry Roe (08-12)
   2011-12 Enrollment: n/a . . . . (847) 665-0595
Spec Ed Dist of Mchenry Co-Sedom
   2011-12 Enrollment: n/a . . . . (815) 338-3622
Housing: Homeownership rate: 91.8% (2008-2012 5-year est.); Median home value: $179,100 (2008-2012 5-year est.); Median contract rent: $636 per month (2008-2012 5-year est.); Median year structure built: 1951 (2008-2012 5-year est.).
Health Insurance: 73.4% Private; 26.0% Public; 9.3% None. (2008-2012 5-year est.)
Transportation: Commute to work: 93.9% car, 0.0% public transportation, 1.2% walk, 4.9% work from home (2008-2012 5-year est.); Travel time to work: 25.4% less than 15 minutes, 26.9% 15 to 30 minutes, 16.5% 30 to 45 minutes, 19.3% 45 to 60 minutes, 11.9% 60 minutes or more (2008-2012 5-year est.)

WONDER LAKE (village). Aka Wonder Center. Covers a land area of 4.781 square miles and a water area of 1.145 square miles. Located at 42.38° N. Lat; 88.35° W. Long. Elevation is 837 feet.
Population: 1,024 (1990); 1,345 (2000); 4,026 (2010); Density: 768.0 persons per square mile (2008-2012 5-year est.); Race: 91.7% White, 0.0% Black/African American, 0.2% Asian, 0.0% American Indian/Alaska Native, 0.0% Native Hawaiian/Other Pacific Islander, 8.1% Some other race, 5.4% Two or more races, 10.8% Hispanic of any race (2008-2012 5-year est.); Average household size: 2.74 (2008-2012 5-year est.); Median age: 38.5 (2008-2012 5-year est.); Males per 100 females: 109.1 (2008-2012 5-year est.); Marriage status: 26.8% never married, 56.7% now married, 4.3% widowed, 12.2% divorced (2008-2012 5-year est.); Foreign born: 4.5% (2008-2012 5-year est.); Ancestry (includes multiple ancestries): 28.1% German, 16.0% Polish, 15.8% Irish, 9.6% Italian, 8.3% Swedish (2008-2012 5-year est.).
Economy: Single-family building permits issued: 0 (2013); Multi-family building permits issued: 0 (2013); Homeowner vacancy rate: 5.6%. Rental vacancy rate: 0.0%. (2008-2012 5-year est.); Employment by occupation: 13.8% management, business, and financial, 3.6% computer, engineering, and science, 11.0% education, legal, community service, arts, and media, 4.0% healthcare practitioners, 8.1% service, 32.7% sales and office, 16.3% natural resources, construction, and maintenance, 10.5% production, transportation, and material moving (2008-2012 5-year est.).
Income: Per capita income: $29,800 (2008-2012 5-year est.); Median household income: $80,461 (2008-2012 5-year est.); Average household income: $80,409 (2008-2012 5-year est.); Percent of households with income of $100,000 or more: 28.1% (2008-2012 5-year est.); Poverty rate: 6.8% (2008-2012 5-year est.).
Education: Percent of population age 25 and over with: High school diploma (including GED) or higher: 92.8% (2008-2012 5-year est.); Bachelor's degree or higher: 26.3% (2008-2012 5-year est.); Master's degree or higher: 8.4% (2008-2012 5-year est.).
School District(s)
Harrison SD 36 (PK-08)
   2011-12 Enrollment: 473 . . . . (815) 653-2311
Housing: Homeownership rate: 87.9% (2008-2012 5-year est.); Median home value: $188,400 (2008-2012 5-year est.); Median contract rent: $945 per month (2008-2012 5-year est.); Median year structure built: 1973 (2008-2012 5-year est.).
Health Insurance: 82.0% Private; 16.6% Public; 9.6% None. (2008-2012 5-year est.)
Transportation: Commute to work: 94.6% car, 1.4% public transportation, 0.7% walk, 3.3% work from home (2008-2012 5-year est.); Travel time to work: 11.7% less than 15 minutes, 33.6% 15 to 30 minutes, 20.2% 30 to 45 minutes, 13.0% 45 to 60 minutes, 21.6% 60 minutes or more (2008-2012 5-year est.)

Airports: Galt Field (general aviation)

WOODSTOCK (city). County seat. Covers a land area of 13.551 square miles and a water area of 0 square miles. Located at 42.31° N. Lat; 88.44° W. Long. Elevation is 945 feet.

History: Woodstock was settled in the 1830's and 1840's by people from Vermont, who named it for the Vermont town. After 1844, Woodstock grew as the seat of McHenry County.

Population: 14,353 (1990); 20,151 (2000); 24,770 (2010); Density: 1,828.7 persons per square mile (2008-2012 5-year est.); Race: 86.4% White, 1.5% Black/African American, 2.3% Asian, 0.5% American Indian/Alaska Native, 0.0% Native Hawaiian/Other Pacific Islander, 9.3% Some other race, 1.8% Two or more races, 22.3% Hispanic of any race (2008-2012 5-year est.); Average household size: 2.62 (2008-2012 5-year est.); Median age: 35.4 (2008-2012 5-year est.); Males per 100 females: 92.9 (2008-2012 5-year est.); Marriage status: 28.5% never married, 53.0% now married, 5.8% widowed, 12.7% divorced (2008-2012 5-year est.); Foreign born: 15.2% (2008-2012 5-year est.); Ancestry (includes multiple ancestries): 27.9% German, 16.5% Irish, 9.9% Polish, 6.9% English, 6.6% Italian (2008-2012 5-year est.).

Economy: Single-family building permits issued: 48 (2013); Multi-family building permits issued: 0 (2013); Homeowner vacancy rate: 4.6%. Rental vacancy rate: 8.0%. (2008-2012 5-year est.); Employment by occupation: 12.8% management, business, and financial, 4.2% computer, engineering, and science, 12.3% education, legal, community service, arts, and media, 5.4% healthcare practitioners, 15.7% service, 24.5% sales and office, 8.3% natural resources, construction, and maintenance, 16.8% production, transportation, and material moving (2008-2012 5-year est.).

Income: Per capita income: $26,168 (2008-2012 5-year est.); Median household income: $56,479 (2008-2012 5-year est.); Average household income: $68,238 (2008-2012 5-year est.); Percent of households with income of $100,000 or more: 21.4% (2008-2012 5-year est.); Poverty rate: 13.3% (2008-2012 5-year est.).

Taxes: Total city taxes per capita: $468 (2011); City property taxes per capita: $419 (2011).

Education: Percent of population age 25 and over with: High school diploma (including GED) or higher: 87.3% (2008-2012 5-year est.); Bachelor's degree or higher: 30.1% (2008-2012 5-year est.); Master's degree or higher: 10.1% (2008-2012 5-year est.).

School District(s)

Mchenry County Coop for Employ Educ
    2011-12 Enrollment: n/a . . . . (815) 334-0183
Spec Ed Dist of Mchenry Co-Sedom
    2011-12 Enrollment: n/a . . . . (815) 338-3622
Woodstock CUSD 200 (PK-12)
    2011-12 Enrollment: 6,408 . . . . (815) 337-5406

Housing: Homeownership rate: 68.1% (2008-2012 5-year est.); Median home value: $190,300 (2008-2012 5-year est.); Median contract rent: $816 per month (2008-2012 5-year est.); Median year structure built: 1985 (2008-2012 5-year est.).

Health Insurance: 72.7% Private; 25.1% Public; 11.1% None. (2008-2012 5-year est.)

Hospitals: Centegra Memorial Medical Center (154 beds)

Safety: Violent crime rate: 14.9 per 10,000 population; Property crime rate: 153.6 per 10,000 population (2012).

Transportation: Commute to work: 90.1% car, 2.9% public transportation, 1.9% walk, 3.7% work from home (2008-2012 5-year est.); Travel time to work: 32.2% less than 15 minutes, 33.0% 15 to 30 minutes, 12.0% 30 to 45 minutes, 6.4% 45 to 60 minutes, 16.4% 60 minutes or more (2008-2012 5-year est.)

Additional Information Contacts

City of Woodstock . . . . (815) 338-4300
    http://www.woodstock-il.com
Woodstock Chamber of Commerce & Industry . . . . (815) 338-2436
    http://www.woodstockilchamber.com

McLean County

Located in central Illinois; drained by the Sangamon and Mackinaw Rivers; includes Lake Bloomington. Covers a land area of 1,183.378 square miles, a water area of 2.892 square miles, and is located in the Central Time Zone at 40.49° N. Lat., 88.84° W. Long. The county was founded in 1830. County seat is Bloomington.

McLean County is part of the Bloomington, IL Metropolitan Statistical Area. The entire metro area includes: De Witt County, IL; McLean County, IL

Weather Station: Chenoa   Elevation: 711 feet

	Jan	Feb	Mar	Apr	May	Jun	Jul	Aug	Sep	Oct	Nov	Dec
High	33	38	50	64	75	83	85	84	78	65	51	37
Low	17	20	30	40	51	61	64	62	54	43	33	21
Precip	1.7	1.3	2.9	3.3	4.0	3.8	3.5	3.2	2.9	3.1	2.9	2.2
Snow	5.0	5.5	1.8	0.9	tr	0.0	0.0	0.0	0.0	0.1	1.0	4.2

High and Low temperatures in degrees Fahrenheit; Precipitation and Snow in inches

Weather Station: Normal   Elevation: 785 feet

	Jan	Feb	Mar	Apr	May	Jun	Jul	Aug	Sep	Oct	Nov	Dec
High	34	39	50	63	74	83	86	84	78	66	51	37
Low	17	21	29	40	51	61	65	63	54	43	32	21
Precip	2.1	1.9	2.8	3.7	4.4	4.0	4.1	4.0	3.0	3.3	3.2	2.5
Snow	6.1	5.3	1.8	0.8	tr	0.0	0.0	0.0	0.0	0.1	0.7	4.9

High and Low temperatures in degrees Fahrenheit; Precipitation and Snow in inches

Population: 129,180 (1990); 150,433 (2000); 169,572 (2010); Race: 84.8% White, 7.2% Black/African American, 4.3% Asian, 0.2% American Indian/Alaska Native, 0.0% Native Hawaiian/Other Pacific Islander, 3.5% Some other race, 2.4% Two or more races, 4.4% Hispanic of any race (2008-2012 5-year est.); Density: 145.6 persons per square mile (2008-2012 5-year est.); Average household size: 2.52 (2008-2012 5-year est.); Median age: 32.2 (2008-2012 5-year est.); Males per 100 females: 94.3 (2008-2012 5-year est.).

Religion: Six largest groups: 9.0% Catholicism, 8.5% Baptist, 7.2% Non-denominational Protestant, 6.4% Methodist/Pietist, 6.0% Lutheran, 3.9% Muslim Estimate (2010)

Economy: Unemployment rate: 5.5% (April 2014); Total civilian labor force: 87,651 (April 2014); Leading industries: 29.6% finance & insurance; 12.3% retail trade; 10.9% health care and social assistance (2012); Farms: 1,489 totaling 692,291 acres (2012); Companies that employ 500 or more persons: 11 (2012); Companies that employ 100 to 499 persons: 74 (2012); Companies that employ less than 100 persons: 3,629 (2012); Black-owned businesses: 682 (2007); Hispanic-owned businesses: 176 (2007); Asian-owned businesses: 501 (2007); Women-owned businesses: 3,787 (2007); Single-family building permits issued: 393 (2013); Multi-family building permits issued: 281 (2013).

Income: Per capita income: $29,960 (2008-2012 5-year est.); Median household income: $61,049 (2008-2012 5-year est.); Average household income: $77,524 (2008-2012 5-year est.); Percent of households with income of $100,000 or more: 26.1% (2008-2012 5-year est.); Poverty rate: 14.0% (2008-2012 5-year est.); Bankruptcy rate: 2.32% (2013).

Taxes: Total county taxes per capita: $215 (2011); County property taxes per capita: $166 (2011).

Education: Percent of population age 25 and over with: High school diploma (including GED) or higher: 94.2% (2008-2012 5-year est.); Bachelor's degree or higher: 41.8% (2008-2012 5-year est.); Master's degree or higher: 12.7% (2008-2012 5-year est.).

Housing: Homeownership rate: 67.2% (2008-2012 5-year est.); Median home value: $156,600 (2008-2012 5-year est.); Median contract rent: $602 per month (2008-2012 5-year est.); Median year structure built: 1977 (2008-2012 5-year est.)

Health: Birth rate: 119.0 per 10,000 population (2013); Death rate: 62.6 per 10,000 population (2013); Age-adjusted cancer mortality rate: 162.7 deaths per 100,000 population (2011); Number of physicians: 20.7 per 10,000 population (2011); Hospital beds: 20.9 per 10,000 population (2010); Hospital admissions: 1,006.7 per 10,000 population (2010).

Environment: Air Quality Index: 85.4% good, 14.6% moderate, 0.0% unhealthy for sensitive individuals, 0.0% unhealthy (percent of days in 2013)

Elections: 2012 Presidential election results: 43.4% Obama, 54.5% Romney

National and State Parks: Moraine View State Park

Additional Information Contacts

McLean County Government . . . . (309) 888-5190
    http://www.mcleancountyil.gov
McLean County Chamber of Commerce . . . . (309) 829-6344
    http://www.mcleancochamber.org

McLean County Communities

ANCHOR (village). Covers a land area of 0.191 square miles and a water area of 0 square miles. Located at 40.57° N. Lat; 88.54° W. Long. Elevation is 778 feet.

Population: 178 (1990); 175 (2000); 146 (2010); Density: 565.2 persons per square mile (2008-2012 5-year est.); Race: 95.4% White, 1.9% Black/African American, 0.0% Asian, 0.0% American Indian/Alaska Native, 0.0% Native Hawaiian/Other Pacific Islander, 2.7% Some other race, 2.8% Two or more races, 0.0% Hispanic of any race (2008-2012 5-year est.); Average household size: 2.16 (2008-2012 5-year est.); Median age: 44.5 (2008-2012 5-year est.); Males per 100 females: 100.0 (2008-2012 5-year est.); Marriage status: 25.3% never married, 46.0% now married, 5.7% widowed, 23.0% divorced (2008-2012 5-year est.); Foreign born: 0.0% (2008-2012 5-year est.); Ancestry (includes multiple ancestries): 42.6% German, 19.4% Irish, 10.2% American, 8.3% English, 5.6% Italian (2008-2012 5-year est.).

Economy: Single-family building permits issued: 0 (2013); Multi-family building permits issued: 0 (2013); Homeowner vacancy rate: 15.6%. Rental vacancy rate: 0.0%. (2008-2012 5-year est.); Employment by occupation: 18.4% management, business, and financial, 2.0% computer, engineering, and science, 0.0% education, legal, community service, arts, and media, 0.0% healthcare practitioners, 18.4% service, 30.6% sales and office, 16.3% natural resources, construction, and maintenance, 14.3% production, transportation, and material moving (2008-2012 5-year est.).

Income: Per capita income: $17,698 (2008-2012 5-year est.); Median household income: $44,500 (2008-2012 5-year est.); Average household income: $38,460 (2008-2012 5-year est.); Percent of households with income of $100,000 or more: n/a (2008-2012 5-year est.); Poverty rate: 22.2% (2008-2012 5-year est.).

Education: Percent of population age 25 and over with: High school diploma (including GED) or higher: 78.4% (2008-2012 5-year est.); Bachelor's degree or higher: 0.0% (2008-2012 5-year est.); Master's degree or higher: 0.0% (2008-2012 5-year est.).

Housing: Homeownership rate: 76.0% (2008-2012 5-year est.); Median home value: $80,000 (2008-2012 5-year est.); Median contract rent: n/a per month (2008-2012 5-year est.); Median year structure built: 1959 (2008-2012 5-year est.).

Health Insurance: 48.1% Private; 58.3% Public; 15.7% None. (2008-2012 5-year est.)

Transportation: Commute to work: 95.9% car, 0.0% public transportation, 0.0% walk, 4.1% work from home (2008-2012 5-year est.); Travel time to work: 14.9% less than 15 minutes, 19.1% 15 to 30 minutes, 27.7% 30 to 45 minutes, 23.4% 45 to 60 minutes, 14.9% 60 minutes or more (2008-2012 5-year est.)

ARROWSMITH (village). Covers a land area of 0.201 square miles and a water area of 0 square miles. Located at 40.45° N. Lat; 88.63° W. Long. Elevation is 883 feet.

Population: 313 (1990); 298 (2000); 294 (2010); Density: 1,945.7 persons per square mile (2008-2012 5-year est.); Race: 96.4% White, 0.3% Black/African American, 1.5% Asian, 0.0% American Indian/Alaska Native, 0.0% Native Hawaiian/Other Pacific Islander, 1.8% Some other race, 1.8% Two or more races, 1.0% Hispanic of any race (2008-2012 5-year est.); Average household size: 2.85 (2008-2012 5-year est.); Median age: 32.9 (2008-2012 5-year est.); Males per 100 females: 86.2 (2008-2012 5-year est.); Marriage status: 16.4% never married, 75.3% now married, 4.5% widowed, 3.8% divorced (2008-2012 5-year est.); Foreign born: 2.6% (2008-2012 5-year est.); Ancestry (includes multiple ancestries): 22.3% German, 22.0% American, 15.9% Irish, 6.9% Norwegian, 5.4% English (2008-2012 5-year est.).

Economy: Single-family building permits issued: 0 (2013); Multi-family building permits issued: 0 (2013); Homeowner vacancy rate: 0.0%. Rental vacancy rate: 0.0%. (2008-2012 5-year est.); Employment by occupation: 18.9% management, business, and financial, 2.4% computer, engineering, and science, 0.0% education, legal, community service, arts, and media, 6.1% healthcare practitioners, 13.4% service, 32.3% sales and office, 18.3% natural resources, construction, and maintenance, 8.5% production, transportation, and material moving (2008-2012 5-year est.).

Income: Per capita income: $17,797 (2008-2012 5-year est.); Median household income: $48,750 (2008-2012 5-year est.); Average household income: $49,653 (2008-2012 5-year est.); Percent of households with income of $100,000 or more: 5.1% (2008-2012 5-year est.); Poverty rate: 6.6% (2008-2012 5-year est.).

Education: Percent of population age 25 and over with: High school diploma (including GED) or higher: 89.6% (2008-2012 5-year est.); Bachelor's degree or higher: 17.3% (2008-2012 5-year est.); Master's degree or higher: 5.2% (2008-2012 5-year est.).

Housing: Homeownership rate: 82.5% (2008-2012 5-year est.); Median home value: $92,700 (2008-2012 5-year est.); Median contract rent: $547 per month (2008-2012 5-year est.); Median year structure built: 1959 (2008-2012 5-year est.).

Health Insurance: 62.9% Private; 36.6% Public; 13.0% None. (2008-2012 5-year est.)

Transportation: Commute to work: 85.8% car, 0.0% public transportation, 9.9% walk, 4.3% work from home (2008-2012 5-year est.); Travel time to work: 19.4% less than 15 minutes, 39.4% 15 to 30 minutes, 23.2% 30 to 45 minutes, 11.6% 45 to 60 minutes, 6.5% 60 minutes or more (2008-2012 5-year est.)

BELLFLOWER (village). Covers a land area of 0.367 square miles and a water area of 0 square miles. Located at 40.34° N. Lat; 88.53° W. Long. Elevation is 784 feet.

Population: 405 (1990); 408 (2000); 357 (2010); Density: 891.7 persons per square mile (2008-2012 5-year est.); Race: 100.0% White, 0.0% Black/African American, 0.0% Asian, 0.0% American Indian/Alaska Native, 0.0% Native Hawaiian/Other Pacific Islander, 0.0% Some other race, 0.0% Two or more races, 0.0% Hispanic of any race (2008-2012 5-year est.); Average household size: 2.92 (2008-2012 5-year est.); Median age: 33.7 (2008-2012 5-year est.); Males per 100 females: 92.4 (2008-2012 5-year est.); Marriage status: 39.8% never married, 49.0% now married, 4.2% widowed, 6.9% divorced (2008-2012 5-year est.); Foreign born: 0.3% (2008-2012 5-year est.); Ancestry (includes multiple ancestries): 34.9% American, 30.0% German, 14.7% English, 10.1% Irish, 7.3% Italian (2008-2012 5-year est.).

Economy: Single-family building permits issued: 0 (2013); Multi-family building permits issued: 0 (2013); Homeowner vacancy rate: 0.0%. Rental vacancy rate: 0.0%. (2008-2012 5-year est.); Employment by occupation: 12.9% management, business, and financial, 3.9% computer, engineering, and science, 6.7% education, legal, community service, arts, and media, 3.4% healthcare practitioners, 13.5% service, 25.8% sales and office, 14.6% natural resources, construction, and maintenance, 19.1% production, transportation, and material moving (2008-2012 5-year est.).

Income: Per capita income: $23,122 (2008-2012 5-year est.); Median household income: $57,813 (2008-2012 5-year est.); Average household income: $64,529 (2008-2012 5-year est.); Percent of households with income of $100,000 or more: 17.0% (2008-2012 5-year est.); Poverty rate: 13.7% (2008-2012 5-year est.).

Education: Percent of population age 25 and over with: High school diploma (including GED) or higher: 90.0% (2008-2012 5-year est.); Bachelor's degree or higher: 14.5% (2008-2012 5-year est.); Master's degree or higher: 3.5% (2008-2012 5-year est.).

Housing: Homeownership rate: 97.3% (2008-2012 5-year est.); Median home value: $77,900 (2008-2012 5-year est.); Median contract rent: $338 per month (2008-2012 5-year est.); Median year structure built: 1947 (2008-2012 5-year est.).

Health Insurance: 59.9% Private; 33.9% Public; 15.3% None. (2008-2012 5-year est.)

Transportation: Commute to work: 93.8% car, 0.0% public transportation, 1.1% walk, 5.1% work from home (2008-2012 5-year est.); Travel time to work: 10.8% less than 15 minutes, 20.4% 15 to 30 minutes, 54.5% 30 to 45 minutes, 13.8% 45 to 60 minutes, 0.6% 60 minutes or more (2008-2012 5-year est.)

BLOOMINGTON (city). County seat. Covers a land area of 27.217 square miles and a water area of 0.009 square miles. Located at 40.48° N. Lat; 88.97° W. Long. Elevation is 797 feet.

History: Bloomington was laid out in 1831 on land belonging to James Allin, adjoining the settlement called Blooming Grove. Allin also donated land for the county courthouse. Bloomington's growth was given impetus by the founding in 1853 of Illinois Wesleyan University, and the arrival in 1854 of both the Illinois Central and the Chicago & Mississippi Railroads. Adlai Stevenson (1835-1914) practiced law in Bloomington before serving in Congress and as vice-president, and returned to Bloomington in 1900.

Population: 51,972 (1990); 64,808 (2000); 76,610 (2010); Density: 2,811.7 persons per square mile (2008-2012 5-year est.); Race: 78.9% White, 10.0% Black/African American, 7.0% Asian, 0.2% American Indian/Alaska Native, 0.0% Native Hawaiian/Other Pacific Islander, 3.9% Some other race, 2.6% Two or more races, 5.2% Hispanic of any race

(2008-2012 5-year est.); Average household size: 2.43 (2008-2012 5-year est.); Median age: 33.9 (2008-2012 5-year est.); Males per 100 females: 94.9 (2008-2012 5-year est.); Marriage status: 33.9% never married, 49.3% now married, 4.9% widowed, 11.9% divorced (2008-2012 5-year est.); Foreign born: 8.5% (2008-2012 5-year est.); Ancestry (includes multiple ancestries): 26.8% German, 14.3% Irish, 10.2% English, 9.5% American, 3.4% Italian (2008-2012 5-year est.).

Economy: Unemployment rate: 5.6% (April 2014); Total civilian labor force: 40,759 (April 2014); Single-family building permits issued: 197 (2013); Multi-family building permits issued: 172 (2013); Homeowner vacancy rate: 3.5%. Rental vacancy rate: 10.7%. (2008-2012 5-year est.); Employment by occupation: 17.3% management, business, and financial, 11.5% computer, engineering, and science, 11.4% education, legal, community service, arts, and media, 4.5% healthcare practitioners, 15.7% service, 25.9% sales and office, 5.3% natural resources, construction, and maintenance, 8.3% production, transportation, and material moving (2008-2012 5-year est.).

Income: Per capita income: $32,593 (2008-2012 5-year est.); Median household income: $59,956 (2008-2012 5-year est.); Average household income: $79,875 (2008-2012 5-year est.); Percent of households with income of $100,000 or more: 26.2% (2008-2012 5-year est.); Poverty rate: 11.2% (2008-2012 5-year est.).

Taxes: Total city taxes per capita: $759 (2011); City property taxes per capita: $352 (2011).

Education: Percent of population age 25 and over with: High school diploma (including GED) or higher: 93.8% (2008-2012 5-year est.); Bachelor's degree or higher: 45.4% (2008-2012 5-year est.); Master's degree or higher: 14.1% (2008-2012 5-year est.).

School District(s)
Bloomington Area Career Center (11-12)
    2011-12 Enrollment: n/a . . . . (309) 829-8671
Bloomington SD 87 (PK-12)
    2011-12 Enrollment: 5,586 . . . . (309) 827-6031
De Witt/livingston/mclean Roe (07-12)
    2011-12 Enrollment: n/a . . . . (309) 888-5120
Mclean County USD 5 (PK-12)
    2011-12 Enrollment: 13,309 . . . . (309) 888-6970

Four-year College(s)
Illinois Wesleyan University (Private, Not-for-profit)
    Fall 2012 Enrollment: 2,013 . . . . (309) 556-1000
    2012-13 Tuition: In-state $37,954; Out-of-state $37,954

Vocational/Technical School(s)
Hairmasters Institute of Cosmetology (Private, For-profit)
    Fall 2012 Enrollment: 118 . . . . (309) 828-1884
    2012-13 Tuition: $13,500

Housing: Homeownership rate: 63.9% (2008-2012 5-year est.); Median home value: $159,800 (2008-2012 5-year est.); Median contract rent: $603 per month (2008-2012 5-year est.); Median year structure built: 1979 (2008-2012 5-year est.).

Health Insurance: 77.3% Private; 24.8% Public; 8.8% None. (2008-2012 5-year est.)

Hospitals: BroMenn Regional Medical Center (224 beds); St. Joseph Medical Center (182 beds)

Safety: Violent crime rate: 48.2 per 10,000 population; Property crime rate: 233.1 per 10,000 population (2012).

Transportation: Commute to work: 90.5% car, 1.9% public transportation, 3.1% walk, 2.9% work from home (2008-2012 5-year est.); Travel time to work: 54.8% less than 15 minutes, 34.1% 15 to 30 minutes, 4.5% 30 to 45 minutes, 3.5% 45 to 60 minutes, 3.1% 60 minutes or more (2008-2012 5-year est.); Amtrak: Train service available.

Airports: Central Illinois Regional Airport at Bloomington-Normal (primary service/non-hub)

Additional Information Contacts
Bloomington-Normal Area Convention & Visitors Bureau . . (309) 665-0033
    http://www.bloomingtonnormalcvb.org
City of Bloomington . . . . (309) 434-2210
    http://www.cityblm.org
McLean County Chamber of Commerce . . . . (309) 829-6344
    http://www.mcleancochamber.org

CARLOCK (village). Covers a land area of 0.412 square miles and a water area of 0 square miles. Located at 40.58° N. Lat; 89.13° W. Long. Elevation is 771 feet.

Population: 418 (1990); 456 (2000); 552 (2010); Density: 1,824.4 persons per square mile (2008-2012 5-year est.); Race: 90.2% White, 9.3%

Black/African American, 0.3% Asian, 0.0% American Indian/Alaska Native, 0.0% Native Hawaiian/Other Pacific Islander, 0.2% Some other race, 0.3% Two or more races, 0.4% Hispanic of any race (2008-2012 5-year est.); Average household size: 2.89 (2008-2012 5-year est.); Median age: 33.1 (2008-2012 5-year est.); Males per 100 females: 113.6 (2008-2012 5-year est.); Marriage status: 35.5% never married, 52.0% now married, 2.2% widowed, 10.3% divorced (2008-2012 5-year est.); Foreign born: 0.3% (2008-2012 5-year est.); Ancestry (includes multiple ancestries): 29.4% German, 15.6% American, 11.8% Irish, 5.5% English, 4.9% French (2008-2012 5-year est.).

Economy: Single-family building permits issued: 0 (2013); Multi-family building permits issued: 0 (2013); Homeowner vacancy rate: 0.0%. Rental vacancy rate: 0.0%. (2008-2012 5-year est.); Employment by occupation: 8.6% management, business, and financial, 5.0% computer, engineering, and science, 11.4% education, legal, community service, arts, and media, 1.9% healthcare practitioners, 10.7% service, 28.3% sales and office, 10.7% natural resources, construction, and maintenance, 23.3% production, transportation, and material moving (2008-2012 5-year est.).

Income: Per capita income: $27,054 (2008-2012 5-year est.); Median household income: $65,000 (2008-2012 5-year est.); Average household income: $76,537 (2008-2012 5-year est.); Percent of households with income of $100,000 or more: 27.0% (2008-2012 5-year est.); Poverty rate: 4.7% (2008-2012 5-year est.).

Education: Percent of population age 25 and over with: High school diploma (including GED) or higher: 93.8% (2008-2012 5-year est.); Bachelor's degree or higher: 31.2% (2008-2012 5-year est.); Master's degree or higher: 16.6% (2008-2012 5-year est.).

School District(s)
Mclean County USD 5 (PK-12)
    2011-12 Enrollment: 13,309 . . . . (309) 888-6970

Housing: Homeownership rate: 86.2% (2008-2012 5-year est.); Median home value: $119,000 (2008-2012 5-year est.); Median contract rent: $560 per month (2008-2012 5-year est.); Median year structure built: 1957 (2008-2012 5-year est.).

Health Insurance: 81.5% Private; 23.1% Public; 9.0% None. (2008-2012 5-year est.)

Transportation: Commute to work: 91.9% car, 0.0% public transportation, 0.0% walk, 2.7% work from home (2008-2012 5-year est.); Travel time to work: 12.4% less than 15 minutes, 58.9% 15 to 30 minutes, 23.9% 30 to 45 minutes, 2.0% 45 to 60 minutes, 2.8% 60 minutes or more (2008-2012 5-year est.)

CHENOA (city). Covers a land area of 2.426 square miles and a water area of 0.045 square miles. Located at 40.74° N. Lat; 88.73° W. Long. Elevation is 719 feet.

History: Chenoa was laid out in 1856 by Matthew T. Scott, and grew up around the junction of the Peoria & Oquawka and the Chicago & Mississippi Railroads. Chenoa is of Indian origin and means "white dove."

Population: 1,732 (1990); 1,845 (2000); 1,785 (2010); Density: 767.1 persons per square mile (2008-2012 5-year est.); Race: 95.6% White, 0.7% Black/African American, 0.9% Asian, 0.0% American Indian/Alaska Native, 0.0% Native Hawaiian/Other Pacific Islander, 2.8% Some other race, 0.4% Two or more races, 4.7% Hispanic of any race (2008-2012 5-year est.); Average household size: 2.55 (2008-2012 5-year est.); Median age: 36.6 (2008-2012 5-year est.); Males per 100 females: 81.4 (2008-2012 5-year est.); Marriage status: 23.6% never married, 56.0% now married, 6.1% widowed, 14.4% divorced (2008-2012 5-year est.); Foreign born: 2.9% (2008-2012 5-year est.); Ancestry (includes multiple ancestries): 35.8% German, 16.8% Irish, 13.7% American, 10.1% English, 4.1% Dutch (2008-2012 5-year est.).

Economy: Single-family building permits issued: 1 (2013); Multi-family building permits issued: 0 (2013); Homeowner vacancy rate: 5.3%. Rental vacancy rate: 0.0%. (2008-2012 5-year est.); Employment by occupation: 15.2% management, business, and financial, 0.2% computer, engineering, and science, 8.5% education, legal, community service, arts, and media, 3.2% healthcare practitioners, 24.1% service, 21.5% sales and office, 6.8% natural resources, construction, and maintenance, 20.5% production, transportation, and material moving (2008-2012 5-year est.).

Income: Per capita income: $23,328 (2008-2012 5-year est.); Median household income: $51,920 (2008-2012 5-year est.); Average household income: $57,782 (2008-2012 5-year est.); Percent of households with income of $100,000 or more: 11.7% (2008-2012 5-year est.); Poverty rate: 9.9% (2008-2012 5-year est.).

Education: Percent of population age 25 and over with: High school diploma (including GED) or higher: 86.8% (2008-2012 5-year est.);

Bachelor's degree or higher: 20.6% (2008-2012 5-year est.); Master's degree or higher: 7.1% (2008-2012 5-year est.).

School District(s)

Prairie Central CUSD 8 (PK-12)

    2011-12 Enrollment: 2,159 . . . . (815) 692-2504

Housing: Homeownership rate: 75.4% (2008-2012 5-year est.); Median home value: $91,700 (2008-2012 5-year est.); Median contract rent: $535 per month (2008-2012 5-year est.); Median year structure built: 1953 (2008-2012 5-year est.).

Health Insurance: 66.9% Private; 30.5% Public; 14.3% None. (2008-2012 5-year est.)

Safety: Violent crime rate: 3.1 per 10,000 population; Property crime rate: 123.5 per 10,000 population (2012).

Transportation: Commute to work: 93.2% car, 0.0% public transportation, 2.8% walk, 1.6% work from home (2008-2012 5-year est.); Travel time to work: 26.7% less than 15 minutes, 23.8% 15 to 30 minutes, 33.3% 30 to 45 minutes, 8.3% 45 to 60 minutes, 7.9% 60 minutes or more (2008-2012 5-year est.)

COLFAX (village). Covers a land area of 0.549 square miles and a water area of 0 square miles. Located at 40.57° N. Lat; 88.62° W. Long. Elevation is 755 feet.

History: Site of defunct coal mine.

Population: 854 (1990); 989 (2000); 1,061 (2010); Density: 1,889.1 persons per square mile (2008-2012 5-year est.); Race: 96.3% White, 0.2% Black/African American, 0.0% Asian, 0.0% American Indian/Alaska Native, 0.0% Native Hawaiian/Other Pacific Islander, 3.5% Some other race, 2.4% Two or more races, 1.3% Hispanic of any race (2008-2012 5-year est.); Average household size: 2.52 (2008-2012 5-year est.); Median age: 39.8 (2008-2012 5-year est.); Males per 100 females: 106.4 (2008-2012 5-year est.); Marriage status: 26.5% never married, 52.2% now married, 10.0% widowed, 11.2% divorced (2008-2012 5-year est.); Foreign born: 0.6% (2008-2012 5-year est.); Ancestry (includes multiple ancestries): 43.2% German, 15.1% Irish, 12.6% American, 12.5% English, 3.2% Swedish (2008-2012 5-year est.).

Economy: Single-family building permits issued: 0 (2013); Multi-family building permits issued: 0 (2013); Homeowner vacancy rate: 0.0%. Rental vacancy rate: 0.0%. (2008-2012 5-year est.); Employment by occupation: 11.6% management, business, and financial, 4.9% computer, engineering, and science, 6.1% education, legal, community service, arts, and media, 2.9% healthcare practitioners, 18.7% service, 20.0% sales and office, 14.7% natural resources, construction, and maintenance, 21.2% production, transportation, and material moving (2008-2012 5-year est.).

Income: Per capita income: $24,096 (2008-2012 5-year est.); Median household income: $52,250 (2008-2012 5-year est.); Average household income: $61,375 (2008-2012 5-year est.); Percent of households with income of $100,000 or more: 16.1% (2008-2012 5-year est.); Poverty rate: 11.6% (2008-2012 5-year est.).

Education: Percent of population age 25 and over with: High school diploma (including GED) or higher: 92.6% (2008-2012 5-year est.); Bachelor's degree or higher: 17.8% (2008-2012 5-year est.); Master's degree or higher: 1.0% (2008-2012 5-year est.).

School District(s)

Ridgeview CUSD 19 (PK-12)

    2011-12 Enrollment: 633. . . . . (309) 723-5111

Housing: Homeownership rate: 83.1% (2008-2012 5-year est.); Median home value: $91,200 (2008-2012 5-year est.); Median contract rent: $408 per month (2008-2012 5-year est.); Median year structure built: 1952 (2008-2012 5-year est.).

Health Insurance: 69.5% Private; 34.8% Public; 11.8% None. (2008-2012 5-year est.)

Safety: Violent crime rate: 0.0 per 10,000 population; Property crime rate: 300.2 per 10,000 population (2012).

Transportation: Commute to work: 95.5% car, 0.0% public transportation, 0.4% walk, 4.1% work from home (2008-2012 5-year est.); Travel time to work: 17.5% less than 15 minutes, 18.1% 15 to 30 minutes, 49.9% 30 to 45 minutes, 8.5% 45 to 60 minutes, 6.0% 60 minutes or more (2008-2012 5-year est.)

COOKSVILLE (village). Covers a land area of 0.239 square miles and a water area of 0 square miles. Located at 40.54° N. Lat; 88.71° W. Long. Elevation is 768 feet.

Population: 211 (1990); 213 (2000); 182 (2010); Density: 660.9 persons per square mile (2008-2012 5-year est.); Race: 100.0% White, 0.0% Black/African American, 0.0% Asian, 0.0% American Indian/Alaska Native,

0.0% Native Hawaiian/Other Pacific Islander, 0.0% Some other race, 0.0% Two or more races, 0.0% Hispanic of any race (2008-2012 5-year est.); Average household size: 1.98 (2008-2012 5-year est.); Median age: 44.7 (2008-2012 5-year est.); Males per 100 females: 143.1 (2008-2012 5-year est.); Marriage status: 22.5% never married, 52.9% now married, 9.4% widowed, 15.2% divorced (2008-2012 5-year est.); Foreign born: 0.0% (2008-2012 5-year est.); Ancestry (includes multiple ancestries): 63.3% German, 20.9% Irish, 15.8% English, 7.0% French, 5.7% Czech (2008-2012 5-year est.).

Economy: Single-family building permits issued: 0 (2013); Multi-family building permits issued: 0 (2013); Homeowner vacancy rate: 0.0%. Rental vacancy rate: 0.0%. (2008-2012 5-year est.); Employment by occupation: 11.1% management, business, and financial, 2.2% computer, engineering, and science, 4.4% education, legal, community service, arts, and media, 5.6% healthcare practitioners, 20.0% service, 17.8% sales and office, 21.1% natural resources, construction, and maintenance, 17.8% production, transportation, and material moving (2008-2012 5-year est.).

Income: Per capita income: $28,859 (2008-2012 5-year est.); Median household income: $46,000 (2008-2012 5-year est.); Average household income: $56,708 (2008-2012 5-year est.); Percent of households with income of $100,000 or more: 13.8% (2008-2012 5-year est.); Poverty rate: 9.7% (2008-2012 5-year est.).

Education: Percent of population age 25 and over with: High school diploma (including GED) or higher: 94.4% (2008-2012 5-year est.); Bachelor's degree or higher: 4.0% (2008-2012 5-year est.); Master's degree or higher: 2.4% (2008-2012 5-year est.).

Housing: Homeownership rate: 87.5% (2008-2012 5-year est.); Median home value: $77,700 (2008-2012 5-year est.); Median contract rent: $438 per month (2008-2012 5-year est.); Median year structure built: Before 1940 (2008-2012 5-year est.).

Health Insurance: 79.7% Private; 32.3% Public; 6.3% None. (2008-2012 5-year est.)

Transportation: Commute to work: 89.8% car, 0.0% public transportation, 6.8% walk, 1.1% work from home (2008-2012 5-year est.); Travel time to work: 25.3% less than 15 minutes, 55.2% 15 to 30 minutes, 11.5% 30 to 45 minutes, 0.0% 45 to 60 minutes, 8.0% 60 minutes or more (2008-2012 5-year est.)

CROPSEY (unincorporated postal area)

Zip Code: 61731

    Covers a land area of 22.246 square miles and a water area of 0 square miles. Located at 40.61° N. Lat; 88.48° W. Long. Elevation is 801 feet. Population: 280 (2010); Density: 12.6 persons per square mile (2010); Race: 96.4% White, 0.4% Black/African American, 0.0% Asian, 0.4% American Indian/Alaska Native, 0.0% Native Hawaiian/Other Pacific Islander, 2.8% Some other race, 2.9% Two or more races, 3.2% Hispanic of any race (2010); Average household size: 3.01 (2010); Median age: 37.6 (2010); Males per 100 females: 105.9 (2010); Homeownership rate: 83.8% (2010)

DANVERS (village). Covers a land area of 0.855 square miles and a water area of 0 square miles. Located at 40.53° N. Lat; 89.18° W. Long. Elevation is 814 feet.

Population: 981 (1990); 1,183 (2000); 1,154 (2010); Density: 1,199.3 persons per square mile (2008-2012 5-year est.); Race: 95.4% White, 0.0% Black/African American, 0.0% Asian, 0.0% American Indian/Alaska Native, 0.0% Native Hawaiian/Other Pacific Islander, 4.6% Some other race, 4.6% Two or more races, 3.7% Hispanic of any race (2008-2012 5-year est.); Average household size: 2.40 (2008-2012 5-year est.); Median age: 41.5 (2008-2012 5-year est.); Males per 100 females: 96.9 (2008-2012 5-year est.); Marriage status: 20.3% never married, 66.4% now married, 4.9% widowed, 8.4% divorced (2008-2012 5-year est.); Foreign born: 0.9% (2008-2012 5-year est.); Ancestry (includes multiple ancestries): 44.0% German, 19.1% Irish, 6.6% American, 6.4% English, 4.9% Polish (2008-2012 5-year est.).

Economy: Single-family building permits issued: 0 (2013); Multi-family building permits issued: 0 (2013); Homeowner vacancy rate: 3.8%. Rental vacancy rate: 0.0%. (2008-2012 5-year est.); Employment by occupation: 12.3% management, business, and financial, 7.9% computer, engineering, and science, 10.4% education, legal, community service, arts, and media, 6.0% healthcare practitioners, 14.8% service, 27.1% sales and office, 6.2% natural resources, construction, and maintenance, 15.5% production, transportation, and material moving (2008-2012 5-year est.).

Income: Per capita income: $31,170 (2008-2012 5-year est.); Median household income: $63,333 (2008-2012 5-year est.); Average household

income: $74,009 (2008-2012 5-year est.); Percent of households with income of $100,000 or more: 25.5% (2008-2012 5-year est.); Poverty rate: 2.1% (2008-2012 5-year est.).

Education: Percent of population age 25 and over with: High school diploma (including GED) or higher: 93.6% (2008-2012 5-year est.); Bachelor's degree or higher: 30.3% (2008-2012 5-year est.); Master's degree or higher: 8.9% (2008-2012 5-year est.).

School District(s)

Olympia CUSD 16 (PK-12)

   2011-12 Enrollment: 1,940 . . . . (309) 379-6011

Housing: Homeownership rate: 87.9% (2008-2012 5-year est.); Median home value: $120,000 (2008-2012 5-year est.); Median contract rent: $463 per month (2008-2012 5-year est.); Median year structure built: 1955 (2008-2012 5-year est.).

Health Insurance: 85.3% Private; 25.3% Public; 6.6% None. (2008-2012 5-year est.)

Transportation: Commute to work: 93.0% car, 1.4% public transportation, 1.4% walk, 3.6% work from home (2008-2012 5-year est.); Travel time to work: 9.2% less than 15 minutes, 56.4% 15 to 30 minutes, 25.9% 30 to 45 minutes, 4.4% 45 to 60 minutes, 4.1% 60 minutes or more (2008-2012 5-year est.)

DOWNS (village). Covers a land area of 2.613 square miles and a water area of 0 square miles. Located at 40.40° N. Lat; 88.89° W. Long. Elevation is 804 feet.

Population: 620 (1990); 776 (2000); 1,005 (2010); Density: 340.2 persons per square mile (2008-2012 5-year est.); Race: 99.4% White, 0.0% Black/African American, 0.4% Asian, 0.0% American Indian/Alaska Native, 0.0% Native Hawaiian/Other Pacific Islander, 0.2% Some other race, 0.1% Two or more races, 0.0% Hispanic of any race (2008-2012 5-year est.); Average household size: 2.54 (2008-2012 5-year est.); Median age: 36.9 (2008-2012 5-year est.); Males per 100 females: 102.5 (2008-2012 5-year est.); Marriage status: 22.5% never married, 62.3% now married, 4.6% widowed, 10.5% divorced (2008-2012 5-year est.); Foreign born: 0.4% (2008-2012 5-year est.); Ancestry (includes multiple ancestries): 33.7% German, 15.4% American, 15.2% Irish, 10.9% English, 4.8% Swedish (2008-2012 5-year est.).

Economy: Single-family building permits issued: 0 (2013); Multi-family building permits issued: 0 (2013); Homeowner vacancy rate: 0.0%. Rental vacancy rate: 0.0%. (2008-2012 5-year est.); Employment by occupation: 8.6% management, business, and financial, 8.2% computer, engineering, and science, 11.1% education, legal, community service, arts, and media, 5.2% healthcare practitioners, 16.1% service, 29.1% sales and office, 14.0% natural resources, construction, and maintenance, 7.7% production, transportation, and material moving (2008-2012 5-year est.).

Income: Per capita income: $30,927 (2008-2012 5-year est.); Median household income: $65,556 (2008-2012 5-year est.); Average household income: $76,758 (2008-2012 5-year est.); Percent of households with income of $100,000 or more: 27.2% (2008-2012 5-year est.); Poverty rate: 3.8% (2008-2012 5-year est.).

Education: Percent of population age 25 and over with: High school diploma (including GED) or higher: 94.6% (2008-2012 5-year est.); Bachelor's degree or higher: 30.7% (2008-2012 5-year est.); Master's degree or higher: 7.1% (2008-2012 5-year est.).

School District(s)

Tri Valley CUSD 3 (PK-12)

   2011-12 Enrollment: 1,032 . . . . (309) 378-2351

Housing: Homeownership rate: 82.3% (2008-2012 5-year est.); Median home value: $155,600 (2008-2012 5-year est.); Median contract rent: $563 per month (2008-2012 5-year est.); Median year structure built: 1965 (2008-2012 5-year est.).

Health Insurance: 90.7% Private; 15.5% Public; 5.7% None. (2008-2012 5-year est.)

Transportation: Commute to work: 93.1% car, 0.0% public transportation, 0.8% walk, 3.8% work from home (2008-2012 5-year est.); Travel time to work: 35.0% less than 15 minutes, 51.1% 15 to 30 minutes, 6.1% 30 to 45 minutes, 2.0% 45 to 60 minutes, 5.9% 60 minutes or more (2008-2012 5-year est.)

ELLSWORTH (village). Covers a land area of 0.228 square miles and a water area of 0 square miles. Located at 40.45° N. Lat; 88.72° W. Long. Elevation is 866 feet.

Population: 224 (1990); 271 (2000); 195 (2010); Density: 1,001.3 persons per square mile (2008-2012 5-year est.); Race: 99.1% White, 0.0% Black/African American, 0.0% Asian, 0.9% American Indian/Alaska Native,

0.0% Native Hawaiian/Other Pacific Islander, 0.0% Some other race, 0.0% Two or more races, 0.0% Hispanic of any race (2008-2012 5-year est.); Average household size: 2.96 (2008-2012 5-year est.); Median age: 39.3 (2008-2012 5-year est.); Males per 100 females: 96.6 (2008-2012 5-year est.); Marriage status: 38.3% never married, 53.1% now married, 6.6% widowed, 2.0% divorced (2008-2012 5-year est.); Foreign born: 0.0% (2008-2012 5-year est.); Ancestry (includes multiple ancestries): 41.2% German, 21.9% Irish, 14.9% American, 5.7% English, 5.3% Polish (2008-2012 5-year est.).

Economy: Single-family building permits issued: 0 (2013); Multi-family building permits issued: 0 (2013); Homeowner vacancy rate: 0.0%. Rental vacancy rate: 0.0%. (2008-2012 5-year est.); Employment by occupation: 13.2% management, business, and financial, 5.3% computer, engineering, and science, 3.5% education, legal, community service, arts, and media, 3.5% healthcare practitioners, 16.7% service, 23.7% sales and office, 17.5% natural resources, construction, and maintenance, 16.7% production, transportation, and material moving (2008-2012 5-year est.).

Income: Per capita income: $22,276 (2008-2012 5-year est.); Median household income: $51,406 (2008-2012 5-year est.); Average household income: $63,470 (2008-2012 5-year est.); Percent of households with income of $100,000 or more: 18.2% (2008-2012 5-year est.); Poverty rate: 6.1% (2008-2012 5-year est.).

Education: Percent of population age 25 and over with: High school diploma (including GED) or higher: 97.1% (2008-2012 5-year est.); Bachelor's degree or higher: 10.1% (2008-2012 5-year est.); Master's degree or higher: 1.4% (2008-2012 5-year est.).

Housing: Homeownership rate: 79.2% (2008-2012 5-year est.); Median home value: $102,000 (2008-2012 5-year est.); Median contract rent: $394 per month (2008-2012 5-year est.); Median year structure built: Before 1940 (2008-2012 5-year est.).

Health Insurance: 66.7% Private; 27.2% Public; 16.2% None. (2008-2012 5-year est.)

Transportation: Commute to work: 95.5% car, 0.0% public transportation, 0.0% walk, 4.5% work from home (2008-2012 5-year est.); Travel time to work: 3.8% less than 15 minutes, 58.1% 15 to 30 minutes, 25.7% 30 to 45 minutes, 2.9% 45 to 60 minutes, 9.5% 60 minutes or more (2008-2012 5-year est.)

GRIDLEY (village). Covers a land area of 1.234 square miles and a water area of 0 square miles. Located at 40.74° N. Lat; 88.88° W. Long. Elevation is 755 feet.

History: Gridley was named for Asahel Gridley (1810-1881), a New Yorker who came to Illinois in 1831 and served in the Civil War as a brigadier general.

Population: 1,304 (1990); 1,411 (2000); 1,432 (2010); Density: 1,150.2 persons per square mile (2008-2012 5-year est.); Race: 98.1% White, 0.0% Black/African American, 0.8% Asian, 0.4% American Indian/Alaska Native, 0.0% Native Hawaiian/Other Pacific Islander, 0.7% Some other race, 0.4% Two or more races, 0.8% Hispanic of any race (2008-2012 5-year est.); Average household size: 2.67 (2008-2012 5-year est.); Median age: 39.3 (2008-2012 5-year est.); Males per 100 females: 91.5 (2008-2012 5-year est.); Marriage status: 21.5% never married, 59.4% now married, 8.2% widowed, 10.8% divorced (2008-2012 5-year est.); Foreign born: 2.3% (2008-2012 5-year est.); Ancestry (includes multiple ancestries): 43.1% German, 19.6% American, 14.0% English, 11.1% Irish, 3.8% French (2008-2012 5-year est.).

Economy: Single-family building permits issued: 0 (2013); Multi-family building permits issued: 0 (2013); Homeowner vacancy rate: 0.0%. Rental vacancy rate: 0.0%. (2008-2012 5-year est.); Employment by occupation: 11.1% management, business, and financial, 2.5% computer, engineering, and science, 10.0% education, legal, community service, arts, and media, 3.2% healthcare practitioners, 20.3% service, 22.5% sales and office, 10.5% natural resources, construction, and maintenance, 19.8% production, transportation, and material moving (2008-2012 5-year est.).

Income: Per capita income: $25,326 (2008-2012 5-year est.); Median household income: $62,321 (2008-2012 5-year est.); Average household income: $65,786 (2008-2012 5-year est.); Percent of households with income of $100,000 or more: 18.4% (2008-2012 5-year est.); Poverty rate: 3.5% (2008-2012 5-year est.).

Education: Percent of population age 25 and over with: High school diploma (including GED) or higher: 92.0% (2008-2012 5-year est.); Bachelor's degree or higher: 17.5% (2008-2012 5-year est.); Master's degree or higher: 3.6% (2008-2012 5-year est.).

School District(s)

El Paso-Gridley CUSD 11 (PK-12)

2011-12 Enrollment: 1,278 . . . . (309) 527-4410

Housing: Homeownership rate: 81.0% (2008-2012 5-year est.); Median home value: $113,000 (2008-2012 5-year est.); Median contract rent: $490 per month (2008-2012 5-year est.); Median year structure built: 1967 (2008-2012 5-year est.).

Health Insurance: 82.7% Private; 28.0% Public; 4.9% None. (2008-2012 5-year est.)

Transportation: Commute to work: 92.0% car, 0.0% public transportation, 3.1% walk, 4.4% work from home (2008-2012 5-year est.); Travel time to work: 32.6% less than 15 minutes, 19.9% 15 to 30 minutes, 38.4% 30 to 45 minutes, 6.2% 45 to 60 minutes, 2.9% 60 minutes or more (2008-2012 5-year est.).

HEYWORTH (village).
Covers a land area of 1.885 square miles and a water area of 0 square miles. Located at 40.32° N. Lat; 88.98° W. Long. Elevation is 755 feet.

Population: 1,627 (1990); 2,431 (2000); 2,841 (2010); Density: 1,543.4 persons per square mile (2008-2012 5-year est.); Race: 93.9% White, 0.6% Black/African American, 0.5% Asian, 0.0% American Indian/Alaska Native, 0.0% Native Hawaiian/Other Pacific Islander, 5.0% Some other race, 5.0% Two or more races, 0.9% Hispanic of any race (2008-2012 5-year est.); Average household size: 2.82 (2008-2012 5-year est.); Median age: 34.8 (2008-2012 5-year est.); Males per 100 females: 104.3 (2008-2012 5-year est.); Marriage status: 26.3% never married, 59.2% now married, 4.5% widowed, 10.0% divorced (2008-2012 5-year est.); Foreign born: 1.1% (2008-2012 5-year est.); Ancestry (includes multiple ancestries): 35.2% German, 20.5% American, 11.4% English, 8.7% Irish, 3.8% Swedish (2008-2012 5-year est.).

Economy: Single-family building permits issued: 9 (2013); Multi-family building permits issued: 0 (2013); Homeowner vacancy rate: 2.7%. Rental vacancy rate: 10.4%. (2008-2012 5-year est.); Employment by occupation: 19.6% management, business, and financial, 6.2% computer, engineering, and science, 10.9% education, legal, community service, arts, and media, 6.5% healthcare practitioners, 7.5% service, 31.5% sales and office, 8.2% natural resources, construction, and maintenance, 9.6% production, transportation, and material moving (2008-2012 5-year est.).

Income: Per capita income: $28,031 (2008-2012 5-year est.); Median household income: $74,271 (2008-2012 5-year est.); Average household income: $77,516 (2008-2012 5-year est.); Percent of households with income of $100,000 or more: 31.3% (2008-2012 5-year est.); Poverty rate: 9.1% (2008-2012 5-year est.).

Education: Percent of population age 25 and over with: High school diploma (including GED) or higher: 89.8% (2008-2012 5-year est.); Bachelor's degree or higher: 25.2% (2008-2012 5-year est.); Master's degree or higher: 5.8% (2008-2012 5-year est.).

School District(s)

Heyworth CUSD 4 (PK-12)

2011-12 Enrollment: 970 . . . . (309) 473-3727

Housing: Homeownership rate: 80.8% (2008-2012 5-year est.); Median home value: $146,800 (2008-2012 5-year est.); Median contract rent: $472 per month (2008-2012 5-year est.); Median year structure built: 1978 (2008-2012 5-year est.).

Health Insurance: 76.1% Private; 22.9% Public; 9.4% None. (2008-2012 5-year est.)

Safety: Violent crime rate: 42.0 per 10,000 population; Property crime rate: 115.4 per 10,000 population (2012).

Transportation: Commute to work: 95.8% car, 0.0% public transportation, 1.4% walk, 2.1% work from home (2008-2012 5-year est.); Travel time to work: 18.0% less than 15 minutes, 54.9% 15 to 30 minutes, 15.2% 30 to 45 minutes, 6.1% 45 to 60 minutes, 5.8% 60 minutes or more (2008-2012 5-year est.).

HUDSON (village).
Covers a land area of 0.832 square miles and a water area of 0 square miles. Located at 40.61° N. Lat; 88.99° W. Long. Elevation is 768 feet.

History: Hudson was settled in 1836 by a group of New Yorkers called the Hudson Colony.

Population: 1,006 (1990); 1,510 (2000); 1,838 (2010); Density: 2,336.1 persons per square mile (2008-2012 5-year est.); Race: 97.8% White, 0.2% Black/African American, 0.2% Asian, 0.1% American Indian/Alaska Native, 0.0% Native Hawaiian/Other Pacific Islander, 1.7% Some other race, 1.8% Two or more races, 1.0% Hispanic of any race (2008-2012 5-year est.); Average household size: 3.10 (2008-2012 5-year est.);

Median age: 36.4 (2008-2012 5-year est.); Males per 100 females: 107.0 (2008-2012 5-year est.); Marriage status: 23.2% never married, 68.8% now married, 2.5% widowed, 5.5% divorced (2008-2012 5-year est.); Foreign born: 0.8% (2008-2012 5-year est.); Ancestry (includes multiple ancestries): 35.4% German, 19.5% Irish, 13.9% American, 11.6% English, 4.1% Polish (2008-2012 5-year est.).

Economy: Single-family building permits issued: 4 (2013); Multi-family building permits issued: 0 (2013); Homeowner vacancy rate: 0.0%. Rental vacancy rate: 0.0%. (2008-2012 5-year est.); Employment by occupation: 15.0% management, business, and financial, 7.0% computer, engineering, and science, 12.4% education, legal, community service, arts, and media, 4.2% healthcare practitioners, 12.3% service, 27.3% sales and office, 13.6% natural resources, construction, and maintenance, 8.2% production, transportation, and material moving (2008-2012 5-year est.).

Income: Per capita income: $29,467 (2008-2012 5-year est.); Median household income: $87,273 (2008-2012 5-year est.); Average household income: $89,518 (2008-2012 5-year est.); Percent of households with income of $100,000 or more: 38.5% (2008-2012 5-year est.); Poverty rate: 5.2% (2008-2012 5-year est.).

Education: Percent of population age 25 and over with: High school diploma (including GED) or higher: 97.1% (2008-2012 5-year est.); Bachelor's degree or higher: 38.9% (2008-2012 5-year est.); Master's degree or higher: 11.9% (2008-2012 5-year est.).

School District(s)

Mclean County USD 5 (PK-12)

2011-12 Enrollment: 13,309 . . . . (309) 888-6970

Housing: Homeownership rate: 92.5% (2008-2012 5-year est.); Median home value: $173,300 (2008-2012 5-year est.); Median contract rent: $438 per month (2008-2012 5-year est.); Median year structure built: 1987 (2008-2012 5-year est.).

Health Insurance: 88.7% Private; 11.3% Public; 7.5% None. (2008-2012 5-year est.)

Safety: Violent crime rate: 10.8 per 10,000 population; Property crime rate: 32.4 per 10,000 population (2012).

Transportation: Commute to work: 95.4% car, 0.0% public transportation, 0.9% walk, 1.9% work from home (2008-2012 5-year est.); Travel time to work: 15.6% less than 15 minutes, 66.7% 15 to 30 minutes, 11.9% 30 to 45 minutes, 3.0% 45 to 60 minutes, 2.7% 60 minutes or more (2008-2012 5-year est.).

LE ROY (city).
Aka Leroy. Covers a land area of 2.322 square miles and a water area of 0.016 square miles. Located at 40.34° N. Lat; 88.76° W. Long. Elevation is 791 feet.

History: Incorporated 1857.

Population: 2,777 (1990); 3,332 (2000); 3,560 (2010); Density: 1,587.0 persons per square mile (2008-2012 5-year est.); Race: 98.5% White, 0.0% Black/African American, 0.1% Asian, 0.7% American Indian/Alaska Native, 0.0% Native Hawaiian/Other Pacific Islander, 0.7% Some other race, 0.1% Two or more races, 1.5% Hispanic of any race (2008-2012 5-year est.); Average household size: 2.55 (2008-2012 5-year est.); Median age: 36.7 (2008-2012 5-year est.); Males per 100 females: 96.6 (2008-2012 5-year est.); Marriage status: 24.5% never married, 56.8% now married, 7.3% widowed, 11.4% divorced (2008-2012 5-year est.); Foreign born: 0.3% (2008-2012 5-year est.); Ancestry (includes multiple ancestries): 29.7% German, 17.3% Irish, 17.0% American, 12.2% English, 3.3% Italian (2008-2012 5-year est.).

Economy: Single-family building permits issued: 11 (2013); Multi-family building permits issued: 0 (2013); Homeowner vacancy rate: 2.8%. Rental vacancy rate: 7.9%. (2008-2012 5-year est.); Employment by occupation: 17.1% management, business, and financial, 5.4% computer, engineering, and science, 5.6% education, legal, community service, arts, and media, 7.1% healthcare practitioners, 19.4% service, 26.4% sales and office, 8.2% natural resources, construction, and maintenance, 10.8% production, transportation, and material moving (2008-2012 5-year est.).

Income: Per capita income: $24,713 (2008-2012 5-year est.); Median household income: $59,219 (2008-2012 5-year est.); Average household income: $63,170 (2008-2012 5-year est.); Percent of households with income of $100,000 or more: 17.5% (2008-2012 5-year est.); Poverty rate: 6.5% (2008-2012 5-year est.).

Education: Percent of population age 25 and over with: High school diploma (including GED) or higher: 93.8% (2008-2012 5-year est.); Bachelor's degree or higher: 25.0% (2008-2012 5-year est.); Master's degree or higher: 2.9% (2008-2012 5-year est.).

School District(s)
Leroy CUSD 2 (PK-12)
    2011-12 Enrollment: 831 . . . . (309) 962-4211
Housing: Homeownership rate: 84.2% (2008-2012 5-year est.); Median home value: $136,200 (2008-2012 5-year est.); Median contract rent: $474 per month (2008-2012 5-year est.); Median year structure built: 1973 (2008-2012 5-year est.).
Health Insurance: 82.4% Private; 29.1% Public; 4.0% None. (2008-2012 5-year est.)
Transportation: Commute to work: 92.6% car, 0.0% public transportation, 4.6% walk, 2.4% work from home (2008-2012 5-year est.); Travel time to work: 32.1% less than 15 minutes, 37.1% 15 to 30 minutes, 26.8% 30 to 45 minutes, 2.8% 45 to 60 minutes, 1.2% 60 minutes or more (2008-2012 5-year est.)

LEXINGTON (city). Covers a land area of 1.330 square miles and a water area of 0 square miles. Located at 40.64° N. Lat; 88.78° W. Long. Elevation is 751 feet.
History: Lexington was settled in 1828 and named for the battlefield in Massachusetts. The town developed along the Chicago & Mississippi Railroad as a produce center.
Population: 1,809 (1990); 1,912 (2000); 2,060 (2010); Density: 1,525.6 persons per square mile (2008-2012 5-year est.); Race: 98.8% White, 0.0% Black/African American, 0.4% Asian, 0.0% American Indian/Alaska Native, 0.0% Native Hawaiian/Other Pacific Islander, 0.8% Some other race, 0.8% Two or more races, 2.5% Hispanic of any race (2008-2012 5-year est.); Average household size: 2.38 (2008-2012 5-year est.); Median age: 40.4 (2008-2012 5-year est.); Males per 100 females: 82.3 (2008-2012 5-year est.); Marriage status: 23.3% never married, 59.2% now married, 9.0% widowed, 8.5% divorced (2008-2012 5-year est.); Foreign born: 0.8% (2008-2012 5-year est.); Ancestry (includes multiple ancestries): 40.8% German, 17.3% Irish, 12.9% English, 12.3% American, 3.5% Swedish (2008-2012 5-year est.).
Economy: Single-family building permits issued: 4 (2013); Multi-family building permits issued: 0 (2013); Homeowner vacancy rate: 1.1%. Rental vacancy rate: 6.6%. (2008-2012 5-year est.); Employment by occupation: 15.0% management, business, and financial, 3.1% computer, engineering, and science, 10.0% education, legal, community service, arts, and media, 4.9% healthcare practitioners, 12.5% service, 28.5% sales and office, 14.1% natural resources, construction, and maintenance, 12.0% production, transportation, and material moving (2008-2012 5-year est.).
Income: Per capita income: $29,708 (2008-2012 5-year est.); Median household income: $61,929 (2008-2012 5-year est.); Average household income: $69,495 (2008-2012 5-year est.); Percent of households with income of $100,000 or more: 19.2% (2008-2012 5-year est.); Poverty rate: 6.8% (2008-2012 5-year est.).
Education: Percent of population age 25 and over with: High school diploma (including GED) or higher: 96.2% (2008-2012 5-year est.); Bachelor's degree or higher: 30.9% (2008-2012 5-year est.); Master's degree or higher: 8.5% (2008-2012 5-year est.).

School District(s)
Lexington CUSD 7 (PK-12)
    2011-12 Enrollment: 523 . . . . (309) 365-4141
Housing: Homeownership rate: 83.5% (2008-2012 5-year est.); Median home value: $124,000 (2008-2012 5-year est.); Median contract rent: $493 per month (2008-2012 5-year est.); Median year structure built: 1965 (2008-2012 5-year est.).
Health Insurance: 81.4% Private; 30.1% Public; 7.0% None. (2008-2012 5-year est.)
Transportation: Commute to work: 90.6% car, 0.5% public transportation, 3.3% walk, 3.2% work from home (2008-2012 5-year est.); Travel time to work: 22.4% less than 15 minutes, 45.1% 15 to 30 minutes, 27.7% 30 to 45 minutes, 2.0% 45 to 60 minutes, 2.8% 60 minutes or more (2008-2012 5-year est.)

MCLEAN (village). Covers a land area of 0.434 square miles and a water area of 0 square miles. Located at 40.32° N. Lat; 89.17° W. Long. Elevation is 709 feet.
Population: 797 (1990); 808 (2000); 830 (2010); Density: 1,887.4 persons per square mile (2008-2012 5-year est.); Race: 98.7% White, 0.0% Black/African American, 0.7% Asian, 0.0% American Indian/Alaska Native, 0.0% Native Hawaiian/Other Pacific Islander, 0.6% Some other race, 0.0% Two or more races, 1.6% Hispanic of any race (2008-2012 5-year est.); Average household size: 2.30 (2008-2012 5-year est.); Median age: 45.0 (2008-2012 5-year est.); Males per 100 females: 78.0 (2008-2012 5-year

est.); Marriage status: 21.1% never married, 61.0% now married, 9.4% widowed, 8.5% divorced (2008-2012 5-year est.); Foreign born: 2.1% (2008-2012 5-year est.); Ancestry (includes multiple ancestries): 27.5% German, 22.3% American, 13.1% Irish, 10.7% English, 5.1% Polish (2008-2012 5-year est.).
Economy: Single-family building permits issued: 0 (2013); Multi-family building permits issued: 0 (2013); Homeowner vacancy rate: 2.7%. Rental vacancy rate: 7.0%. (2008-2012 5-year est.); Employment by occupation: 12.0% management, business, and financial, 5.8% computer, engineering, and science, 9.7% education, legal, community service, arts, and media, 2.1% healthcare practitioners, 13.6% service, 28.9% sales and office, 13.2% natural resources, construction, and maintenance, 14.8% production, transportation, and material moving (2008-2012 5-year est.).
Income: Per capita income: $29,067 (2008-2012 5-year est.); Median household income: $51,786 (2008-2012 5-year est.); Average household income: $65,775 (2008-2012 5-year est.); Percent of households with income of $100,000 or more: 19.4% (2008-2012 5-year est.); Poverty rate: 6.2% (2008-2012 5-year est.).
Education: Percent of population age 25 and over with: High school diploma (including GED) or higher: 93.1% (2008-2012 5-year est.); Bachelor's degree or higher: 12.2% (2008-2012 5-year est.); Master's degree or higher: 1.7% (2008-2012 5-year est.).
Housing: Homeownership rate: 90.7% (2008-2012 5-year est.); Median home value: $109,400 (2008-2012 5-year est.); Median contract rent: $550 per month (2008-2012 5-year est.); Median year structure built: 1958 (2008-2012 5-year est.).
Health Insurance: 76.9% Private; 37.4% Public; 8.4% None. (2008-2012 5-year est.)
Safety: Violent crime rate: 0.0 per 10,000 population; Property crime rate: 60.0 per 10,000 population (2012).
Transportation: Commute to work: 97.9% car, 0.0% public transportation, 0.0% walk, 0.9% work from home (2008-2012 5-year est.); Travel time to work: 13.4% less than 15 minutes, 53.1% 15 to 30 minutes, 25.4% 30 to 45 minutes, 1.9% 45 to 60 minutes, 6.3% 60 minutes or more (2008-2012 5-year est.)

NORMAL (town). Covers a land area of 18.348 square miles and a water area of 0.062 square miles. Located at 40.52° N. Lat; 88.99° W. Long. Elevation is 801 feet.
History: Normal began as North Bloomington, but soon changed its name to Normal when the Illinois State Normal University was founded here in 1857.
Population: 40,023 (1990); 45,386 (2000); 52,497 (2010); Density: 2,887.8 persons per square mile (2008-2012 5-year est.); Race: 84.2% White, 8.1% Black/African American, 3.3% Asian, 0.2% American Indian/Alaska Native, 0.0% Native Hawaiian/Other Pacific Islander, 4.2% Some other race, 2.8% Two or more races, 5.0% Hispanic of any race (2008-2012 5-year est.); Average household size: 2.57 (2008-2012 5-year est.); Median age: 23.7 (2008-2012 5-year est.); Males per 100 females: 90.6 (2008-2012 5-year est.); Marriage status: 54.0% never married, 36.0% now married, 3.0% widowed, 7.1% divorced (2008-2012 5-year est.); Foreign born: 4.5% (2008-2012 5-year est.); Ancestry (includes multiple ancestries): 27.8% German, 15.9% Irish, 9.8% English, 9.6% American, 5.1% Italian (2008-2012 5-year est.).
Economy: Unemployment rate: 5.5% (April 2014); Total civilian labor force: 26,744 (April 2014); Single-family building permits issued: 117 (2013); Multi-family building permits issued: 109 (2013); Homeowner vacancy rate: 2.2%. Rental vacancy rate: 6.1%. (2008-2012 5-year est.); Employment by occupation: 14.4% management, business, and financial, 6.5% computer, engineering, and science, 15.4% education, legal, community service, arts, and media, 3.4% healthcare practitioners, 21.4% service, 28.2% sales and office, 3.4% natural resources, construction, and maintenance, 7.4% production, transportation, and material moving (2008-2012 5-year est.).
Income: Per capita income: $23,708 (2008-2012 5-year est.); Median household income: $51,994 (2008-2012 5-year est.); Average household income: $66,020 (2008-2012 5-year est.); Percent of households with income of $100,000 or more: 22.0% (2008-2012 5-year est.); Poverty rate: 24.8% (2008-2012 5-year est.).
Taxes: Total city taxes per capita: $570 (2011); City property taxes per capita: $203 (2011).
Education: Percent of population age 25 and over with: High school diploma (including GED) or higher: 95.2% (2008-2012 5-year est.); Bachelor's degree or higher: 47.1% (2008-2012 5-year est.); Master's degree or higher: 15.7% (2008-2012 5-year est.).

School District(s)

Isu Laboratory Schools (PK-12)
    2011-12 Enrollment: 994. . . . . (309) 438-8542
Mclean County USD 5 (PK-12)
    2011-12 Enrollment: 13,309 . . . . (309) 888-6970

Four-year College(s)

Illinois State University (Public)
    Fall 2012 Enrollment: 20,628 . . . . (309) 438-2111
    2012-13 Tuition: In-state $12,726; Out-of-state $20,016

Two-year College(s)

Heartland Community College (Public)
    Fall 2012 Enrollment: 5,456 . . . . (309) 268-8000
    2012-13 Tuition: In-state $7,890; Out-of-state $11,700

Vocational/Technical School(s)

Paul Mitchell the School-Normal (Private, For-profit)
    Fall 2012 Enrollment: 113. . . . . (309) 862-3400
    2012-13 Tuition: $16,925

Housing: Homeownership rate: 56.8% (2008-2012 5-year est.); Median home value: $159,500 (2008-2012 5-year est.); Median contract rent: $632 per month (2008-2012 5-year est.); Median year structure built: 1981 (2008-2012 5-year est.).

Health Insurance: 82.7% Private; 19.6% Public; 6.4% None. (2008-2012 5-year est.)

Hospitals: Bromenn Healthcare

Safety: Violent crime rate: 21.6 per 10,000 population; Property crime rate: 247.4 per 10,000 population (2012).

Transportation: Commute to work: 81.6% car, 2.2% public transportation, 10.6% walk, 3.6% work from home (2008-2012 5-year est.); Travel time to work: 53.1% less than 15 minutes, 34.8% 15 to 30 minutes, 5.7% 30 to 45 minutes, 3.4% 45 to 60 minutes, 3.0% 60 minutes or more (2008-2012 5-year est.); Amtrak: Train service available.

Airports: Central Illinois Regional Airport at Bloomington-Normal (primary service/non-hub)

Additional Information Contacts

Town of Normal. . . . . (309) 454-2444
    http://www.normal.org

SAYBROOK (village). Covers a land area of 0.783 square miles and a water area of 0.029 square miles. Located at 40.43° N. Lat; 88.53° W. Long. Elevation is 801 feet.

Population: 767 (1990); 764 (2000); 693 (2010); Density: 969.1 persons per square mile (2008-2012 5-year est.); Race: 96.4% White, 0.7% Black/African American, 0.0% Asian, 0.0% American Indian/Alaska Native, 0.0% Native Hawaiian/Other Pacific Islander, 2.9% Some other race, 0.7% Two or more races, 2.1% Hispanic of any race (2008-2012 5-year est.); Average household size: 2.77 (2008-2012 5-year est.); Median age: 37.0 (2008-2012 5-year est.); Males per 100 females: 101.3 (2008-2012 5-year est.); Marriage status: 24.3% never married, 57.5% now married, 8.1% widowed, 10.1% divorced (2008-2012 5-year est.); Foreign born: 0.4% (2008-2012 5-year est.); Ancestry (includes multiple ancestries): 24.9% German, 19.9% American, 15.2% Irish, 6.3% English, 6.1% Scottish (2008-2012 5-year est.).

Economy: Single-family building permits issued: 1 (2013); Multi-family building permits issued: 0 (2013); Homeowner vacancy rate: 6.8%. Rental vacancy rate: 14.1%. (2008-2012 5-year est.); Employment by occupation: 11.5% management, business, and financial, 3.0% computer, engineering, and science, 3.0% education, legal, community service, arts, and media, 2.0% healthcare practitioners, 19.8% service, 22.5% sales and office, 13.8% natural resources, construction, and maintenance, 24.5% production, transportation, and material moving (2008-2012 5-year est.).

Income: Per capita income: $24,992 (2008-2012 5-year est.); Median household income: $55,833 (2008-2012 5-year est.); Average household income: $67,458 (2008-2012 5-year est.); Percent of households with income of $100,000 or more: 18.3% (2008-2012 5-year est.); Poverty rate: 7.2% (2008-2012 5-year est.).

Education: Percent of population age 25 and over with: High school diploma (including GED) or higher: 90.1% (2008-2012 5-year est.); Bachelor's degree or higher: 8.1% (2008-2012 5-year est.); Master's degree or higher: 3.2% (2008-2012 5-year est.).

Housing: Homeownership rate: 75.5% (2008-2012 5-year est.); Median home value: $86,800 (2008-2012 5-year est.); Median contract rent: $365 per month (2008-2012 5-year est.); Median year structure built: 1959 (2008-2012 5-year est.).

Health Insurance: 69.7% Private; 34.5% Public; 12.0% None. (2008-2012 5-year est.)

Transportation: Commute to work: 86.5% car, 0.0% public transportation, 4.5% walk, 8.5% work from home (2008-2012 5-year est.); Travel time to work: 31.7% less than 15 minutes, 22.4% 15 to 30 minutes, 27.0% 30 to 45 minutes, 14.8% 45 to 60 minutes, 4.1% 60 minutes or more (2008-2012 5-year est.)

SHIRLEY (unincorporated postal area)

Zip Code: 61772

Covers a land area of 27.862 square miles and a water area of 0 square miles. Located at 40.38° N. Lat; 89.06° W. Long. Elevation is 764 feet. Population: 351 (2010); Density: 12.6 persons per square mile (2010); Race: 93.2% White, 4.6% Black/African American, 0.3% Asian, 0.6% American Indian/Alaska Native, 0.0% Native Hawaiian/Other Pacific Islander, 1.3% Some other race, 0.9% Two or more races, 2.8% Hispanic of any race (2010); Average household size: 2.47 (2010); Median age: 45.3 (2010); Males per 100 females: 106.5 (2010); Homeownership rate: 79.6% (2010)

STANFORD (village). Covers a land area of 0.662 square miles and a water area of 0 square miles. Located at 40.43° N. Lat; 89.22° W. Long. Elevation is 679 feet.

Population: 620 (1990); 670 (2000); 596 (2010); Density: 1,183.4 persons per square mile (2008-2012 5-year est.); Race: 94.8% White, 0.0% Black/African American, 0.0% Asian, 0.1% American Indian/Alaska Native, 0.0% Native Hawaiian/Other Pacific Islander, 5.1% Some other race, 5.1% Two or more races, 0.1% Hispanic of any race (2008-2012 5-year est.); Average household size: 3.08 (2008-2012 5-year est.); Median age: 28.8 (2008-2012 5-year est.); Males per 100 females: 110.5 (2008-2012 5-year est.); Marriage status: 28.8% never married, 54.0% now married, 5.9% widowed, 11.3% divorced (2008-2012 5-year est.); Foreign born: 0.0% (2008-2012 5-year est.); Ancestry (includes multiple ancestries): 24.1% American, 22.9% German, 16.5% Irish, 13.8% English, 2.3% Swedish (2008-2012 5-year est.).

Economy: Single-family building permits issued: 0 (2013); Multi-family building permits issued: 0 (2013); Homeowner vacancy rate: 2.8%. Rental vacancy rate: 15.2%. (2008-2012 5-year est.); Employment by occupation: 12.3% management, business, and financial, 3.5% computer, engineering, and science, 5.0% education, legal, community service, arts, and media, 2.9% healthcare practitioners, 15.8% service, 28.1% sales and office, 9.9% natural resources, construction, and maintenance, 32.5% production, transportation, and material moving (2008-2012 5-year est.).

Income: Per capita income: $20,156 (2008-2012 5-year est.); Median household income: $56,875 (2008-2012 5-year est.); Average household income: $59,445 (2008-2012 5-year est.); Percent of households with income of $100,000 or more: 13.4% (2008-2012 5-year est.); Poverty rate: 21.7% (2008-2012 5-year est.).

Education: Percent of population age 25 and over with: High school diploma (including GED) or higher: 93.6% (2008-2012 5-year est.); Bachelor's degree or higher: 7.3% (2008-2012 5-year est.); Master's degree or higher: 0.4% (2008-2012 5-year est.).

School District(s)

Olympia CUSD 16 (PK-12)
    2011-12 Enrollment: 1,940 . . . . (309) 379-6011

Housing: Homeownership rate: 78.0% (2008-2012 5-year est.); Median home value: $93,800 (2008-2012 5-year est.); Median contract rent: $483 per month (2008-2012 5-year est.); Median year structure built: 1951 (2008-2012 5-year est.).

Health Insurance: 56.1% Private; 35.9% Public; 15.5% None. (2008-2012 5-year est.)

Transportation: Commute to work: 96.4% car, 1.2% public transportation, 1.2% walk, 0.6% work from home (2008-2012 5-year est.); Travel time to work: 8.6% less than 15 minutes, 53.9% 15 to 30 minutes, 31.5% 30 to 45 minutes, 0.6% 45 to 60 minutes, 5.4% 60 minutes or more (2008-2012 5-year est.)

TOWANDA (village). Covers a land area of 0.750 square miles and a water area of 0 square miles. Located at 40.56° N. Lat; 88.90° W. Long. Elevation is 781 feet.

History: The first settler in Towanda was John Smith, who built a home in 1826 at Smith's Grove. The town of Towanda was laid out in 1854 when the railroad reached the community. The name is of Indian origin and means "where we bury our dead."

Population: 856 (1990); 493 (2000); 480 (2010); Density: 781.7 persons per square mile (2008-2012 5-year est.); Race: 97.6% White, 0.0% Black/African American, 0.9% Asian, 0.0% American Indian/Alaska Native,

0.0% Native Hawaiian/Other Pacific Islander, 1.5% Some other race, 1.5% Two or more races, 2.6% Hispanic of any race (2008-2012 5-year est.); Average household size: 2.78 (2008-2012 5-year est.); Median age: 40.7 (2008-2012 5-year est.); Males per 100 females: 94.0 (2008-2012 5-year est.); Marriage status: 19.7% never married, 65.5% now married, 4.7% widowed, 10.1% divorced (2008-2012 5-year est.); Foreign born: 0.0% (2008-2012 5-year est.); Ancestry (includes multiple ancestries): 30.5% German, 18.4% American, 15.5% Irish, 13.3% English, 6.3% Italian (2008-2012 5-year est.).

Economy: Single-family building permits issued: 0 (2013); Multi-family building permits issued: 0 (2013); Homeowner vacancy rate: 0.0%. Rental vacancy rate: 0.0%. (2008-2012 5-year est.); Employment by occupation: 10.4% management, business, and financial, 0.7% computer, engineering, and science, 8.2% education, legal, community service, arts, and media, 4.3% healthcare practitioners, 9.3% service, 33.0% sales and office, 19.4% natural resources, construction, and maintenance, 14.7% production, transportation, and material moving (2008-2012 5-year est.).

Income: Per capita income: $24,550 (2008-2012 5-year est.); Median household income: $64,250 (2008-2012 5-year est.); Average household income: $66,474 (2008-2012 5-year est.); Percent of households with income of $100,000 or more: 18.5% (2008-2012 5-year est.); Poverty rate: 5.8% (2008-2012 5-year est.).

Education: Percent of population age 25 and over with: High school diploma (including GED) or higher: 91.6% (2008-2012 5-year est.); Bachelor's degree or higher: 16.4% (2008-2012 5-year est.); Master's degree or higher: 2.5% (2008-2012 5-year est.).

School District(s)

Mclean County USD 5 (PK-12)

   2011-12 Enrollment: 13,309 . . . . (309) 888-6970

Housing: Homeownership rate: 83.4% (2008-2012 5-year est.); Median home value: $112,800 (2008-2012 5-year est.); Median contract rent: $461 per month (2008-2012 5-year est.); Median year structure built: 1956 (2008-2012 5-year est.).

Health Insurance: 72.5% Private; 37.0% Public; 6.5% None. (2008-2012 5-year est.)

Transportation: Commute to work: 94.9% car, 0.0% public transportation, 0.7% walk, 4.3% work from home (2008-2012 5-year est.); Travel time to work: 28.7% less than 15 minutes, 54.3% 15 to 30 minutes, 7.5% 30 to 45 minutes, 0.0% 45 to 60 minutes, 9.4% 60 minutes or more (2008-2012 5-year est.)

TWIN GROVE (CDP). Covers a land area of 3.971 square miles and a water area of 0.003 square miles. Located at 40.48° N. Lat; 89.10° W. Long. Elevation is 820 feet.

Population: n/a (1990); n/a (2000); 1,564 (2010); Density: 378.8 persons per square mile (2008-2012 5-year est.); Race: 96.0% White, 1.1% Black/African American, 0.6% Asian, 1.6% American Indian/Alaska Native, 0.0% Native Hawaiian/Other Pacific Islander, 0.7% Some other race, 0.7% Two or more races, 0.7% Hispanic of any race (2008-2012 5-year est.); Average household size: 2.61 (2008-2012 5-year est.); Median age: 42.5 (2008-2012 5-year est.); Males per 100 females: 113.3 (2008-2012 5-year est.); Marriage status: 20.2% never married, 75.7% now married, 0.9% widowed, 3.1% divorced (2008-2012 5-year est.); Foreign born: 1.0% (2008-2012 5-year est.); Ancestry (includes multiple ancestries): 35.2% German, 21.5% Irish, 9.1% American, 7.0% English, 3.9% Swedish (2008-2012 5-year est.).

Economy: Homeowner vacancy rate: 0.0%. Rental vacancy rate: 0.0%. (2008-2012 5-year est.); Employment by occupation: 27.2% management, business, and financial, 8.4% computer, engineering, and science, 11.8% education, legal, community service, arts, and media, 6.7% healthcare practitioners, 11.6% service, 20.4% sales and office, 6.8% natural resources, construction, and maintenance, 7.2% production, transportation, and material moving (2008-2012 5-year est.).

Income: Per capita income: $61,271 (2008-2012 5-year est.); Median household income: $102,411 (2008-2012 5-year est.); Average household income: $158,823 (2008-2012 5-year est.); Percent of households with income of $100,000 or more: 52.3% (2008-2012 5-year est.); Poverty rate: 4.4% (2008-2012 5-year est.).

Education: Percent of population age 25 and over with: High school diploma (including GED) or higher: 99.3% (2008-2012 5-year est.); Bachelor's degree or higher: 53.6% (2008-2012 5-year est.); Master's degree or higher: 16.7% (2008-2012 5-year est.).

Housing: Homeownership rate: 95.5% (2008-2012 5-year est.); Median home value: $249,400 (2008-2012 5-year est.); Median contract rent: n/a

per month (2008-2012 5-year est.); Median year structure built: 1990 (2008-2012 5-year est.).

Health Insurance: 90.6% Private; 20.3% Public; 2.1% None. (2008-2012 5-year est.)

Transportation: Commute to work: 98.6% car, 0.0% public transportation, 0.0% walk, 0.0% work from home (2008-2012 5-year est.); Travel time to work: 30.8% less than 15 minutes, 55.1% 15 to 30 minutes, 7.6% 30 to 45 minutes, 3.9% 45 to 60 minutes, 2.6% 60 minutes or more (2008-2012 5-year est.)

Menard County

Located in central Illinois; drained by the Sangamon River and Salt Creek. Covers a land area of 314.437 square miles, a water area of 1.020 square miles, and is located in the Central Time Zone at 40.02° N. Lat., 89.79° W. Long. The county was founded in 1839. County seat is Petersburg.

Menard County is part of the Springfield, IL Metropolitan Statistical Area. The entire metro area includes: Menard County, IL; Sangamon County, IL

Population: 11,164 (1990); 12,486 (2000); 12,705 (2010); Race: 97.4% White, 0.9% Black/African American, 0.4% Asian, 0.0% American Indian/Alaska Native, 0.0% Native Hawaiian/Other Pacific Islander, 1.3% Some other race, 1.3% Two or more races, 1.0% Hispanic of any race (2008-2012 5-year est.); Density: 40.4 persons per square mile (2008-2012 5-year est.); Average household size: 2.48 (2008-2012 5-year est.); Median age: 43.0 (2008-2012 5-year est.); Males per 100 females: 95.2 (2008-2012 5-year est.).

Religion: Six largest groups: 21.3% Baptist, 7.9% Methodist/Pietist, 7.5% Catholicism, 4.1% Presbyterian-Reformed, 4.0% Lutheran, 0.5% Pentecostal (2010)

Economy: Unemployment rate: 5.8% (April 2014); Total civilian labor force: 6,815 (April 2014); Leading industries: 23.4% retail trade; 14.2% accommodation & food services; 9.8% other services (except public administration) (2012); Farms: 369 totaling 157,755 acres (2012); Companies that employ 500 or more persons: 0 (2012); Companies that employ 100 to 499 persons: 0 (2012); Companies that employ less than 100 persons: 213 (2012); Black-owned businesses: n/a (2007); Hispanic-owned businesses: n/a (2007); Asian-owned businesses: n/a (2007); Women-owned businesses: n/a (2007); Single-family building permits issued: 12 (2013); Multi-family building permits issued: 0 (2013).

Income: Per capita income: $27,577 (2008-2012 5-year est.); Median household income: $59,428 (2008-2012 5-year est.); Average household income: $68,042 (2008-2012 5-year est.); Percent of households with income of $100,000 or more: 22.4% (2008-2012 5-year est.); Poverty rate: 9.3% (2008-2012 5-year est.); Bankruptcy rate: 1.97% (2013).

Education: Percent of population age 25 and over with: High school diploma (including GED) or higher: 91.8% (2008-2012 5-year est.); Bachelor's degree or higher: 21.0% (2008-2012 5-year est.); Master's degree or higher: 6.4% (2008-2012 5-year est.).

Housing: Homeownership rate: 80.8% (2008-2012 5-year est.); Median home value: $116,800 (2008-2012 5-year est.); Median contract rent: $407 per month (2008-2012 5-year est.); Median year structure built: 1973 (2008-2012 5-year est.)

Health: Birth rate: 92.0 per 10,000 population (2013); Death rate: 102.3 per 10,000 population (2013); Age-adjusted cancer mortality rate: 147.7 deaths per 100,000 population (2011); Number of physicians: 4.7 per 10,000 population (2011); Hospital beds: 0.0 per 10,000 population (2010); Hospital admissions: 0.0 per 10,000 population (2010).

Elections: 2012 Presidential election results: 34.1% Obama, 64.2% Romney

National and State Parks: Lincolns New Salem State Park

Additional Information Contacts

Menard County Government . . . . (217) 632-2415
  http://menardcountyil.com

Menard County Communities

ATHENS (city). Covers a land area of 1.683 square miles and a water area of 0 square miles. Located at 39.96° N. Lat; 89.72° W. Long. Elevation is 600 feet.

History: Incorporated 1892.

Population: 1,404 (1990); 1,726 (2000); 1,988 (2010); Density: 1,233.6 persons per square mile (2008-2012 5-year est.); Race: 94.3% White, 1.6% Black/African American, 0.0% Asian, 0.0% American Indian/Alaska

Native, 0.0% Native Hawaiian/Other Pacific Islander, 4.1% Some other race, 4.1% Two or more races, 2.3% Hispanic of any race (2008-2012 5-year est.); Average household size: 2.64 (2008-2012 5-year est.); Median age: 33.8 (2008-2012 5-year est.); Males per 100 females: 82.7 (2008-2012 5-year est.); Marriage status: 20.2% never married, 59.7% now married, 7.9% widowed, 12.2% divorced (2008-2012 5-year est.); Foreign born: 0.6% (2008-2012 5-year est.); Ancestry (includes multiple ancestries): 31.2% German, 15.8% American, 12.3% English, 11.8% Irish, 6.5% Italian (2008-2012 5-year est.).

Economy: Single-family building permits issued: 2 (2013); Multi-family building permits issued: 0 (2013); Homeowner vacancy rate: 0.0%. Rental vacancy rate: 0.0%. (2008-2012 5-year est.); Employment by occupation: 11.7% management, business, and financial, 8.9% computer, engineering, and science, 8.6% education, legal, community service, arts, and media, 5.8% healthcare practitioners, 13.7% service, 30.1% sales and office, 12.0% natural resources, construction, and maintenance, 9.1% production, transportation, and material moving (2008-2012 5-year est.).

Income: Per capita income: $23,717 (2008-2012 5-year est.); Median household income: $60,050 (2008-2012 5-year est.); Average household income: $62,354 (2008-2012 5-year est.); Percent of households with income of $100,000 or more: 19.6% (2008-2012 5-year est.); Poverty rate: 7.5% (2008-2012 5-year est.).

Education: Percent of population age 25 and over with: High school diploma (including GED) or higher: 92.6% (2008-2012 5-year est.); Bachelor's degree or higher: 18.5% (2008-2012 5-year est.); Master's degree or higher: 4.5% (2008-2012 5-year est.).

School District(s)
Athens CUSD 213 (PK-12)
   2011-12 Enrollment: 1,128 . . . . (217) 636-8761
Logan/mason/menard Roe (06-12)
   2011-12 Enrollment: n/a . . . . (217) 732-8388

Housing: Homeownership rate: 79.9% (2008-2012 5-year est.); Median home value: $100,500 (2008-2012 5-year est.); Median contract rent: $387 per month (2008-2012 5-year est.); Median year structure built: 1973 (2008-2012 5-year est.).
Health Insurance: 76.7% Private; 29.7% Public; 6.3% None. (2008-2012 5-year est.)
Transportation: Commute to work: 94.9% car, 0.0% public transportation, 1.2% walk, 3.8% work from home (2008-2012 5-year est.); Travel time to work: 10.6% less than 15 minutes, 32.9% 15 to 30 minutes, 47.5% 30 to 45 minutes, 4.9% 45 to 60 minutes, 4.1% 60 minutes or more (2008-2012 5-year est.)

GREENVIEW (village).
Covers a land area of 0.851 square miles and a water area of 0 square miles. Located at 40.08° N. Lat; 89.74° W. Long. Elevation is 541 feet.

Population: 848 (1990); 862 (2000); 778 (2010); Density: 905.1 persons per square mile (2008-2012 5-year est.); Race: 99.0% White, 0.0% Black/African American, 0.0% Asian, 0.0% American Indian/Alaska Native, 0.0% Native Hawaiian/Other Pacific Islander, 1.0% Some other race, 1.0% Two or more races, 0.4% Hispanic of any race (2008-2012 5-year est.); Average household size: 2.37 (2008-2012 5-year est.); Median age: 43.0 (2008-2012 5-year est.); Males per 100 females: 94.0 (2008-2012 5-year est.); Marriage status: 20.9% never married, 50.5% now married, 8.5% widowed, 20.1% divorced (2008-2012 5-year est.); Foreign born: 0.3% (2008-2012 5-year est.); Ancestry (includes multiple ancestries): 38.4% German, 23.9% American, 14.5% Irish, 9.0% English, 7.5% Dutch (2008-2012 5-year est.).
Economy: Single-family building permits issued: 0 (2013); Multi-family building permits issued: 0 (2013); Homeowner vacancy rate: 0.0%. Rental vacancy rate: 0.0%. (2008-2012 5-year est.); Employment by occupation: 8.9% management, business, and financial, 2.7% computer, engineering, and science, 1.1% education, legal, community service, arts, and media, 7.8% healthcare practitioners, 22.0% service, 32.8% sales and office, 10.0% natural resources, construction, and maintenance, 14.9% production, transportation, and material moving (2008-2012 5-year est.).
Income: Per capita income: $24,899 (2008-2012 5-year est.); Median household income: $48,173 (2008-2012 5-year est.); Average household income: $56,621 (2008-2012 5-year est.); Percent of households with income of $100,000 or more: 14.1% (2008-2012 5-year est.); Poverty rate: 3.1% (2008-2012 5-year est.).
Education: Percent of population age 25 and over with: High school diploma (including GED) or higher: 88.4% (2008-2012 5-year est.); Bachelor's degree or higher: 11.6% (2008-2012 5-year est.); Master's degree or higher: 4.2% (2008-2012 5-year est.).

School District(s)
Greenview CUSD 200 (PK-12)
   2011-12 Enrollment: 257 . . . . (217) 968-2295

Housing: Homeownership rate: 83.4% (2008-2012 5-year est.); Median home value: $77,200 (2008-2012 5-year est.); Median contract rent: $479 per month (2008-2012 5-year est.); Median year structure built: 1956 (2008-2012 5-year est.).
Health Insurance: 64.5% Private; 32.3% Public; 16.9% None. (2008-2012 5-year est.)
Transportation: Commute to work: 89.7% car, 0.0% public transportation, 6.4% walk, 3.9% work from home (2008-2012 5-year est.); Travel time to work: 23.6% less than 15 minutes, 15.0% 15 to 30 minutes, 49.3% 30 to 45 minutes, 7.4% 45 to 60 minutes, 4.8% 60 minutes or more (2008-2012 5-year est.)

LAKE PETERSBURG (CDP).
Covers a land area of 1.763 square miles and a water area of 0.275 square miles. Located at 39.98° N. Lat; 89.87° W. Long.

Population: n/a (1990); n/a (2000); 719 (2010); Density: 441.3 persons per square mile (2008-2012 5-year est.); Race: 97.0% White, 0.0% Black/African American, 3.0% Asian, 0.0% American Indian/Alaska Native, 0.0% Native Hawaiian/Other Pacific Islander, 0.0% Some other race, 0.0% Two or more races, 0.4% Hispanic of any race (2008-2012 5-year est.); Average household size: 2.08 (2008-2012 5-year est.); Median age: 55.9 (2008-2012 5-year est.); Males per 100 females: 77.6 (2008-2012 5-year est.); Marriage status: 10.5% never married, 67.6% now married, 11.8% widowed, 10.0% divorced (2008-2012 5-year est.); Foreign born: 1.3% (2008-2012 5-year est.); Ancestry (includes multiple ancestries): 37.1% German, 21.5% English, 15.9% Irish, 5.8% Italian, 4.1% Dutch (2008-2012 5-year est.).
Economy: Homeowner vacancy rate: 0.0%. Rental vacancy rate: 0.0%. (2008-2012 5-year est.); Employment by occupation: 23.1% management, business, and financial, 2.5% computer, engineering, and science, 20.0% education, legal, community service, arts, and media, 9.7% healthcare practitioners, 7.5% service, 22.5% sales and office, 5.8% natural resources, construction, and maintenance, 8.9% production, transportation, and material moving (2008-2012 5-year est.).
Income: Per capita income: $40,611 (2008-2012 5-year est.); Median household income: $76,071 (2008-2012 5-year est.); Average household income: $82,576 (2008-2012 5-year est.); Percent of households with income of $100,000 or more: 36.1% (2008-2012 5-year est.); Poverty rate: 7.2% (2008-2012 5-year est.).
Education: Percent of population age 25 and over with: High school diploma (including GED) or higher: 96.1% (2008-2012 5-year est.); Bachelor's degree or higher: 49.8% (2008-2012 5-year est.); Master's degree or higher: 23.3% (2008-2012 5-year est.).
Housing: Homeownership rate: 97.3% (2008-2012 5-year est.); Median home value: $211,000 (2008-2012 5-year est.); Median contract rent: n/a per month (2008-2012 5-year est.); Median year structure built: 1974 (2008-2012 5-year est.).
Health Insurance: 91.0% Private; 36.8% Public; 1.3% None. (2008-2012 5-year est.)
Transportation: Commute to work: 94.4% car, 0.0% public transportation, 0.0% walk, 5.6% work from home (2008-2012 5-year est.); Travel time to work: 38.8% less than 15 minutes, 5.6% 15 to 30 minutes, 40.0% 30 to 45 minutes, 9.4% 45 to 60 minutes, 6.2% 60 minutes or more (2008-2012 5-year est.)

OAKFORD (village).
Covers a land area of 0.249 square miles and a water area of 0 square miles. Located at 40.10° N. Lat; 89.97° W. Long. Elevation is 495 feet.

Population: 246 (1990); 309 (2000); 286 (2010); Density: 1,253.8 persons per square mile (2008-2012 5-year est.); Race: 98.7% White, 0.0% Black/African American, 0.0% Asian, 1.3% American Indian/Alaska Native, 0.0% Native Hawaiian/Other Pacific Islander, 0.0% Some other race, 0.0% Two or more races, 2.6% Hispanic of any race (2008-2012 5-year est.); Average household size: 2.20 (2008-2012 5-year est.); Median age: 41.6 (2008-2012 5-year est.); Males per 100 females: 61.7 (2008-2012 5-year est.); Marriage status: 21.0% never married, 41.5% now married, 24.2% widowed, 13.3% divorced (2008-2012 5-year est.); Foreign born: 0.0% (2008-2012 5-year est.); Ancestry (includes multiple ancestries): 39.4% American, 21.5% German, 20.5% English, 18.9% Irish, 6.7% Dutch (2008-2012 5-year est.).
Economy: Homeowner vacancy rate: 5.3%. Rental vacancy rate: 0.0%. (2008-2012 5-year est.); Employment by occupation: 1.4% management,

business, and financial, 0.0% computer, engineering, and science, 6.4% education, legal, community service, arts, and media, 20.0% healthcare practitioners, 27.1% service, 12.1% sales and office, 12.1% natural resources, construction, and maintenance, 20.7% production, transportation, and material moving (2008-2012 5-year est.).
Income: Per capita income: $23,994 (2008-2012 5-year est.); Median household income: $57,500 (2008-2012 5-year est.); Average household income: $52,541 (2008-2012 5-year est.); Percent of households with income of $100,000 or more: 9.9% (2008-2012 5-year est.); Poverty rate: 12.5% (2008-2012 5-year est.).
Education: Percent of population age 25 and over with: High school diploma (including GED) or higher: 93.3% (2008-2012 5-year est.); Bachelor's degree or higher: 3.1% (2008-2012 5-year est.); Master's degree or higher: 1.8% (2008-2012 5-year est.).
Housing: Homeownership rate: 75.4% (2008-2012 5-year est.); Median home value: $54,200 (2008-2012 5-year est.); Median contract rent: $361 per month (2008-2012 5-year est.); Median year structure built: 1953 (2008-2012 5-year est.).
Health Insurance: 53.2% Private; 37.8% Public; 15.1% None. (2008-2012 5-year est.)
Transportation: Commute to work: 100.0% car, 0.0% public transportation, 0.0% walk, 0.0% work from home (2008-2012 5-year est.); Travel time to work: 29.6% less than 15 minutes, 34.1% 15 to 30 minutes, 6.7% 30 to 45 minutes, 14.1% 45 to 60 minutes, 15.6% 60 minutes or more (2008-2012 5-year est.)

PETERSBURG (city). County seat. Covers a land area of 1.457 square miles and a water area of 0 square miles. Located at 40.01° N. Lat; 89.85° W. Long. Elevation is 512 feet.

History: Founded c.1836, incorporated 1841. Ann Rutledge's grave is here. Lincoln's New Salem (State Historic Site) is South.
Population: 2,261 (1990); 2,299 (2000); 2,260 (2010); Density: 1,532.8 persons per square mile (2008-2012 5-year est.); Race: 95.9% White, 1.3% Black/African American, 0.4% Asian, 0.0% American Indian/Alaska Native, 0.0% Native Hawaiian/Other Pacific Islander, 2.4% Some other race, 2.3% Two or more races, 1.3% Hispanic of any race (2008-2012 5-year est.); Average household size: 2.19 (2008-2012 5-year est.); Median age: 43.5 (2008-2012 5-year est.); Males per 100 females: 93.1 (2008-2012 5-year est.); Marriage status: 19.2% never married, 54.9% now married, 10.7% widowed, 15.2% divorced (2008-2012 5-year est.); Foreign born: 0.9% (2008-2012 5-year est.); Ancestry (includes multiple ancestries): 29.5% German, 28.2% American, 12.7% English, 11.7% Irish, 3.0% Scottish (2008-2012 5-year est.).
Economy: Single-family building permits issued: 0 (2013); Multi-family building permits issued: 0 (2013); Homeowner vacancy rate: 2.5%. Rental vacancy rate: 8.5%. (2008-2012 5-year est.); Employment by occupation: 11.3% management, business, and financial, 4.9% computer, engineering, and science, 7.9% education, legal, community service, arts, and media, 5.6% healthcare practitioners, 22.4% service, 32.4% sales and office, 5.8% natural resources, construction, and maintenance, 9.6% production, transportation, and material moving (2008-2012 5-year est.).
Income: Per capita income: $23,323 (2008-2012 5-year est.); Median household income: $41,591 (2008-2012 5-year est.); Average household income: $52,152 (2008-2012 5-year est.); Percent of households with income of $100,000 or more: 15.0% (2008-2012 5-year est.); Poverty rate: 16.9% (2008-2012 5-year est.).
Education: Percent of population age 25 and over with: High school diploma (including GED) or higher: 90.8% (2008-2012 5-year est.); Bachelor's degree or higher: 17.5% (2008-2012 5-year est.); Master's degree or higher: 5.4% (2008-2012 5-year est.).
School District(s)
Porta CUSD 202 (PK-12)
    2011-12 Enrollment: 1,199 . . . . (217) 632-3803
Housing: Homeownership rate: 59.6% (2008-2012 5-year est.); Median home value: $96,400 (2008-2012 5-year est.); Median contract rent: $376 per month (2008-2012 5-year est.); Median year structure built: 1956 (2008-2012 5-year est.).
Health Insurance: 63.7% Private; 44.4% Public; 7.9% None. (2008-2012 5-year est.)
Transportation: Commute to work: 87.9% car, 0.0% public transportation, 2.1% walk, 8.3% work from home (2008-2012 5-year est.); Travel time to work: 42.8% less than 15 minutes, 7.5% 15 to 30 minutes, 35.7% 30 to 45 minutes, 12.0% 45 to 60 minutes, 2.0% 60 minutes or more (2008-2012 5-year est.)
Additional Information Contacts

Petersburg Chamber of Commerce . . . . (217) 415-4378
    http://www.petersburgilchamber.com

TALLULA (village). Covers a land area of 0.531 square miles and a water area of 0 square miles. Located at 39.95° N. Lat; 89.94° W. Long. Elevation is 623 feet.

Population: 598 (1990); 638 (2000); 488 (2010); Density: 1,121.5 persons per square mile (2008-2012 5-year est.); Race: 92.8% White, 3.9% Black/African American, 0.0% Asian, 0.0% American Indian/Alaska Native, 0.0% Native Hawaiian/Other Pacific Islander, 3.3% Some other race, 3.4% Two or more races, 3.9% Hispanic of any race (2008-2012 5-year est.); Average household size: 3.03 (2008-2012 5-year est.); Median age: 40.0 (2008-2012 5-year est.); Males per 100 females: 125.8 (2008-2012 5-year est.); Marriage status: 30.9% never married, 51.7% now married, 6.1% widowed, 11.2% divorced (2008-2012 5-year est.); Foreign born: 0.0% (2008-2012 5-year est.); Ancestry (includes multiple ancestries): 36.1% American, 17.6% German, 11.4% Irish, 7.4% English, 6.0% Dutch (2008-2012 5-year est.).
Economy: Homeowner vacancy rate: 0.0%. Rental vacancy rate: 0.0%. (2008-2012 5-year est.); Employment by occupation: 14.8% management, business, and financial, 2.7% computer, engineering, and science, 6.8% education, legal, community service, arts, and media, 6.8% healthcare practitioners, 26.9% service, 22.0% sales and office, 9.1% natural resources, construction, and maintenance, 11.0% production, transportation, and material moving (2008-2012 5-year est.).
Income: Per capita income: $19,036 (2008-2012 5-year est.); Median household income: $56,250 (2008-2012 5-year est.); Average household income: $54,417 (2008-2012 5-year est.); Percent of households with income of $100,000 or more: 5.1% (2008-2012 5-year est.); Poverty rate: 15.9% (2008-2012 5-year est.).
Education: Percent of population age 25 and over with: High school diploma (including GED) or higher: 82.0% (2008-2012 5-year est.); Bachelor's degree or higher: 9.0% (2008-2012 5-year est.); Master's degree or higher: 2.9% (2008-2012 5-year est.).
Housing: Homeownership rate: 83.2% (2008-2012 5-year est.); Median home value: $70,800 (2008-2012 5-year est.); Median contract rent: $511 per month (2008-2012 5-year est.); Median year structure built: 1950 (2008-2012 5-year est.).
Health Insurance: 61.2% Private; 44.1% Public; 10.6% None. (2008-2012 5-year est.)
Transportation: Commute to work: 93.4% car, 0.0% public transportation, 1.9% walk, 4.6% work from home (2008-2012 5-year est.); Travel time to work: 24.3% less than 15 minutes, 20.6% 15 to 30 minutes, 42.5% 30 to 45 minutes, 7.3% 45 to 60 minutes, 5.3% 60 minutes or more (2008-2012 5-year est.)

Mercer County

Located in northwestern Illinois; bounded on the west by the Mississippi River and the Iowa border; drained by the Edwards River. Covers a land area of 561.202 square miles, a water area of 7.492 square miles, and is located in the Central Time Zone at 41.20° N. Lat., 90.74° W. Long. The county was founded in 1825. County seat is Aledo.

Mercer County is part of the Davenport-Moline-Rock Island, IA-IL Metropolitan Statistical Area. The entire metro area includes: Henry County, IL; Mercer County, IL; Rock Island County, IL; Scott County, IA

Weather Station: Aledo   Elevation: 720 feet

	Jan	Feb	Mar	Apr	May	Jun	Jul	Aug	Sep	Oct	Nov	Dec
High	31	36	48	62	72	81	85	83	76	63	49	34
Low	15	18	28	39	50	60	63	62	53	42	31	18
Precip	1.4	1.5	2.4	3.7	4.3	4.5	4.0	4.5	3.3	3.0	2.3	2.0
Snow	6.8	4.5	2.7	0.8	tr	0.0	0.0	0.0	0.0	0.1	0.6	5.2

High and Low temperatures in degrees Fahrenheit; Precipitation and Snow in inches

Population: 17,290 (1990); 16,957 (2000); 16,434 (2010); Race: 97.8% White, 0.5% Black/African American, 0.3% Asian, 0.1% American Indian/Alaska Native, 0.0% Native Hawaiian/Other Pacific Islander, 1.3% Some other race, 0.5% Two or more races, 1.8% Hispanic of any race (2008-2012 5-year est.); Density: 28.9 persons per square mile (2008-2012 5-year est.); Average household size: 2.40 (2008-2012 5-year est.); Median age: 43.7 (2008-2012 5-year est.); Males per 100 females: 97.6 (2008-2012 5-year est.).

Religion: Six largest groups: 10.8% Lutheran, 9.3% Catholicism, 8.3% Baptist, 7.9% Methodist/Pietist, 6.9% Presbyterian-Reformed, 1.3% Non-denominational Protestant (2010)

Economy: Unemployment rate: 6.6% (April 2014); Total civilian labor force: 8,292 (April 2014); Leading industries: 27.1% manufacturing; 14.6% health care and social assistance; 14.5% retail trade (2012); Farms: 715 totaling 251,998 acres (2012); Companies that employ 500 or more persons: 0 (2012); Companies that employ 100 to 499 persons: 2 (2012); Companies that employ less than 100 persons: 274 (2012); Black-owned businesses: n/a (2007); Hispanic-owned businesses: n/a (2007); Asian-owned businesses: n/a (2007); Women-owned businesses: 445 (2007); Single-family building permits issued: 14 (2013); Multi-family building permits issued: 0 (2013).

Income: Per capita income: $26,468 (2008-2012 5-year est.); Median household income: $52,700 (2008-2012 5-year est.); Average household income: $63,572 (2008-2012 5-year est.); Percent of households with income of $100,000 or more: 16.1% (2008-2012 5-year est.); Poverty rate: 10.4% (2008-2012 5-year est.); Bankruptcy rate: 2.84% (2013).

Education: Percent of population age 25 and over with: High school diploma (including GED) or higher: 89.1% (2008-2012 5-year est.); Bachelor's degree or higher: 14.1% (2008-2012 5-year est.); Master's degree or higher: 4.8% (2008-2012 5-year est.).

Housing: Homeownership rate: 80.3% (2008-2012 5-year est.); Median home value: $95,100 (2008-2012 5-year est.); Median contract rent: $386 per month (2008-2012 5-year est.); Median year structure built: 1955 (2008-2012 5-year est.)

Health: Birth rate: 93.3 per 10,000 population (2013); Death rate: 106.3 per 10,000 population (2013); Age-adjusted cancer mortality rate: 171.0 deaths per 100,000 population (2011); Number of physicians: 4.3 per 10,000 population (2011); Hospital beds: 13.4 per 10,000 population (2010); Hospital admissions: 178.3 per 10,000 population (2010).

Elections: 2012 Presidential election results: 52.8% Obama, 45.4% Romney

National and State Parks: Mark Twain National Wildlife Refuge

Additional Information Contacts

Mercer County Government . . . . (309) 582-2138
  http://mercercountyil.org

Mercer County Communities

ALEDO (city). County seat. Covers a land area of 2.377 square miles and a water area of 0.012 square miles. Located at 41.20° N. Lat; 90.74° W. Long. Elevation is 735 feet.

History: Aledo developed as a trading center, and as the seat of Mercer County.

Population: 3,681 (1990); 3,613 (2000); 3,640 (2010); Density: 1,603.4 persons per square mile (2008-2012 5-year est.); Race: 95.8% White, 1.6% Black/African American, 0.3% Asian, 0.1% American Indian/Alaska Native, 0.0% Native Hawaiian/Other Pacific Islander, 2.2% Some other race, 0.1% Two or more races, 3.1% Hispanic of any race (2008-2012 5-year est.); Average household size: 2.34 (2008-2012 5-year est.); Median age: 35.3 (2008-2012 5-year est.); Males per 100 females: 91.0 (2008-2012 5-year est.); Marriage status: 27.7% never married, 51.2% now married, 10.9% widowed, 10.2% divorced (2008-2012 5-year est.); Foreign born: 0.5% (2008-2012 5-year est.); Ancestry (includes multiple ancestries): 21.4% German, 19.2% Irish, 13.6% English, 7.7% Swedish, 4.3% American (2008-2012 5-year est.).

Economy: Single-family building permits issued: 0 (2013); Multi-family building permits issued: 0 (2013); Homeowner vacancy rate: 0.0%. Rental vacancy rate: 0.0%. (2008-2012 5-year est.); Employment by occupation: 5.8% management, business, and financial, 2.3% computer, engineering, and science, 14.4% education, legal, community service, arts, and media, 7.5% healthcare practitioners, 15.7% service, 27.5% sales and office, 8.0% natural resources, construction, and maintenance, 18.7% production, transportation, and material moving (2008-2012 5-year est.).

Income: Per capita income: $20,850 (2008-2012 5-year est.); Median household income: $39,709 (2008-2012 5-year est.); Average household income: $49,478 (2008-2012 5-year est.); Percent of households with income of $100,000 or more: 9.8% (2008-2012 5-year est.); Poverty rate: 21.8% (2008-2012 5-year est.).

Education: Percent of population age 25 and over with: High school diploma (including GED) or higher: 87.1% (2008-2012 5-year est.); Bachelor's degree or higher: 14.7% (2008-2012 5-year est.); Master's degree or higher: 5.1% (2008-2012 5-year est.).

School District(s)

Mercer County SD 404 (PK-12)
    2011-12 Enrollment: 1,330 . . . . (309) 582-2238

Housing: Homeownership rate: 63.7% (2008-2012 5-year est.); Median home value: $96,000 (2008-2012 5-year est.); Median contract rent: $391 per month (2008-2012 5-year est.); Median year structure built: 1946 (2008-2012 5-year est.).

Health Insurance: 68.3% Private; 39.5% Public; 9.3% None. (2008-2012 5-year est.)

Transportation: Commute to work: 86.9% car, 0.0% public transportation, 4.4% walk, 7.0% work from home (2008-2012 5-year est.); Travel time to work: 56.6% less than 15 minutes, 5.5% 15 to 30 minutes, 13.2% 30 to 45 minutes, 15.9% 45 to 60 minutes, 8.8% 60 minutes or more (2008-2012 5-year est.)

Airports: Mercer County Airport (general aviation)

Additional Information Contacts

City of Aledo . . . . (309) 582-7241
  http://aledoil.org

JOY (village). Covers a land area of 0.428 square miles and a water area of 0 square miles. Located at 41.20° N. Lat; 90.88° W. Long. Elevation is 686 feet.

Population: 452 (1990); 373 (2000); 417 (2010); Density: 1,098.7 persons per square mile (2008-2012 5-year est.); Race: 100.0% White, 0.0% Black/African American, 0.0% Asian, 0.0% American Indian/Alaska Native, 0.0% Native Hawaiian/Other Pacific Islander, 0.0% Some other race, 0.0% Two or more races, 1.1% Hispanic of any race (2008-2012 5-year est.); Average household size: 2.41 (2008-2012 5-year est.); Median age: 37.3 (2008-2012 5-year est.); Males per 100 females: 97.5 (2008-2012 5-year est.); Marriage status: 21.3% never married, 63.6% now married, 4.0% widowed, 11.2% divorced (2008-2012 5-year est.); Foreign born: 0.4% (2008-2012 5-year est.); Ancestry (includes multiple ancestries): 17.7% German, 8.7% American, 7.0% Irish, 6.8% Swedish, 6.0% English (2008-2012 5-year est.).

Economy: Single-family building permits issued: 0 (2013); Multi-family building permits issued: 0 (2013); Homeowner vacancy rate: 6.3%. Rental vacancy rate: 0.0%. (2008-2012 5-year est.); Employment by occupation: 6.0% management, business, and financial, 0.5% computer, engineering, and science, 0.5% education, legal, community service, arts, and media, 8.7% healthcare practitioners, 21.6% service, 16.1% sales and office, 25.7% natural resources, construction, and maintenance, 21.1% production, transportation, and material moving (2008-2012 5-year est.).

Income: Per capita income: $22,907 (2008-2012 5-year est.); Median household income: $48,958 (2008-2012 5-year est.); Average household income: $54,914 (2008-2012 5-year est.); Percent of households with income of $100,000 or more: 8.7% (2008-2012 5-year est.); Poverty rate: 7.0% (2008-2012 5-year est.).

Education: Percent of population age 25 and over with: High school diploma (including GED) or higher: 89.2% (2008-2012 5-year est.); Bachelor's degree or higher: 3.3% (2008-2012 5-year est.); Master's degree or higher: 0.6% (2008-2012 5-year est.).

School District(s)

Mercer County SD 404 (PK-12)
    2011-12 Enrollment: 1,330 . . . . (309) 582-2238

Housing: Homeownership rate: 76.9% (2008-2012 5-year est.); Median home value: $58,000 (2008-2012 5-year est.); Median contract rent: $346 per month (2008-2012 5-year est.); Median year structure built: Before 1940 (2008-2012 5-year est.).

Health Insurance: 64.0% Private; 40.4% Public; 6.8% None. (2008-2012 5-year est.)

Transportation: Commute to work: 94.5% car, 0.0% public transportation, 0.9% walk, 4.6% work from home (2008-2012 5-year est.); Travel time to work: 36.2% less than 15 minutes, 28.5% 15 to 30 minutes, 10.6% 30 to 45 minutes, 5.3% 45 to 60 minutes, 19.3% 60 minutes or more (2008-2012 5-year est.)

KEITHSBURG (city). Covers a land area of 2.558 square miles and a water area of 0.621 square miles. Located at 41.10° N. Lat; 90.94° W. Long. Elevation is 545 feet.

History: Incorporated 1857.

Population: 747 (1990); 714 (2000); 609 (2010); Density: 212.6 persons per square mile (2008-2012 5-year est.); Race: 98.5% White, 0.0% Black/African American, 0.0% Asian, 0.0% American Indian/Alaska Native, 0.0% Native Hawaiian/Other Pacific Islander, 1.5% Some other race, 1.5% Two or more races, 0.4% Hispanic of any race (2008-2012 5-year est.);

Average household size: 1.96 (2008-2012 5-year est.); Median age: 52.3 (2008-2012 5-year est.); Males per 100 females: 102.2 (2008-2012 5-year est.); Marriage status: 18.1% never married, 60.0% now married, 11.5% widowed, 10.4% divorced (2008-2012 5-year est.); Foreign born: 0.0% (2008-2012 5-year est.); Ancestry (includes multiple ancestries): 21.0% German, 17.3% Irish, 14.3% American, 11.0% English, 5.1% Polish (2008-2012 5-year est.).

Economy: Single-family building permits issued: 1 (2013); Multi-family building permits issued: 0 (2013); Homeowner vacancy rate: 3.2%. Rental vacancy rate: 0.0%. (2008-2012 5-year est.); Employment by occupation: 5.6% management, business, and financial, 0.0% computer, engineering, and science, 6.0% education, legal, community service, arts, and media, 4.7% healthcare practitioners, 11.2% service, 15.9% sales and office, 13.3% natural resources, construction, and maintenance, 43.3% production, transportation, and material moving (2008-2012 5-year est.).

Income: Per capita income: $26,694 (2008-2012 5-year est.); Median household income: $37,857 (2008-2012 5-year est.); Average household income: $52,351 (2008-2012 5-year est.); Percent of households with income of $100,000 or more: 8.3% (2008-2012 5-year est.); Poverty rate: 14.0% (2008-2012 5-year est.).

Education: Percent of population age 25 and over with: High school diploma (including GED) or higher: 74.9% (2008-2012 5-year est.); Bachelor's degree or higher: 3.7% (2008-2012 5-year est.); Master's degree or higher: 0.7% (2008-2012 5-year est.).

Housing: Homeownership rate: 86.3% (2008-2012 5-year est.); Median home value: $54,300 (2008-2012 5-year est.); Median contract rent: $348 per month (2008-2012 5-year est.); Median year structure built: 1971 (2008-2012 5-year est.).

Health Insurance: 67.3% Private; 41.7% Public; 10.8% None. (2008-2012 5-year est.)

Transportation: Commute to work: 95.6% car, 0.0% public transportation, 3.5% walk, 0.0% work from home (2008-2012 5-year est.); Travel time to work: 16.2% less than 15 minutes, 28.4% 15 to 30 minutes, 27.5% 30 to 45 minutes, 18.3% 45 to 60 minutes, 9.6% 60 minutes or more (2008-2012 5-year est.)

MATHERVILLE (village). Covers a land area of 0.391 square miles and a water area of 0.008 square miles. Located at 41.26° N. Lat; 90.61° W. Long. Elevation is 748 feet.

Population: 708 (1990); 772 (2000); 723 (2010); Density: 2,104.8 persons per square mile (2008-2012 5-year est.); Race: 96.0% White, 0.0% Black/African American, 0.0% Asian, 0.0% American Indian/Alaska Native, 0.0% Native Hawaiian/Other Pacific Islander, 4.0% Some other race, 2.4% Two or more races, 3.5% Hispanic of any race (2008-2012 5-year est.); Average household size: 2.33 (2008-2012 5-year est.); Median age: 41.4 (2008-2012 5-year est.); Males per 100 females: 90.1 (2008-2012 5-year est.); Marriage status: 15.9% never married, 63.1% now married, 4.0% widowed, 17.1% divorced (2008-2012 5-year est.); Foreign born: 0.0% (2008-2012 5-year est.); Ancestry (includes multiple ancestries): 19.8% German, 14.0% Irish, 10.3% English, 8.7% Swedish, 7.3% Dutch (2008-2012 5-year est.).

Economy: Single-family building permits issued: 0 (2013); Multi-family building permits issued: 0 (2013); Homeowner vacancy rate: 0.0%. Rental vacancy rate: 10.3%. (2008-2012 5-year est.); Employment by occupation: 7.0% management, business, and financial, 4.6% computer, engineering, and science, 3.9% education, legal, community service, arts, and media, 4.4% healthcare practitioners, 23.5% service, 25.7% sales and office, 8.7% natural resources, construction, and maintenance, 22.2% production, transportation, and material moving (2008-2012 5-year est.).

Income: Per capita income: $25,652 (2008-2012 5-year est.); Median household income: $52,917 (2008-2012 5-year est.); Average household income: $58,749 (2008-2012 5-year est.); Percent of households with income of $100,000 or more: 12.4% (2008-2012 5-year est.); Poverty rate: 9.2% (2008-2012 5-year est.).

Education: Percent of population age 25 and over with: High school diploma (including GED) or higher: 91.4% (2008-2012 5-year est.); Bachelor's degree or higher: 3.2% (2008-2012 5-year est.); Master's degree or higher: 1.1% (2008-2012 5-year est.).

School District(s)

Sherrard CUSD 200 (PK-12)
    2011-12 Enrollment: 1,595 . . . . (309) 593-4075

Housing: Homeownership rate: 77.9% (2008-2012 5-year est.); Median home value: $93,800 (2008-2012 5-year est.); Median contract rent: $525 per month (2008-2012 5-year est.); Median year structure built: 1961 (2008-2012 5-year est.).

Health Insurance: 72.3% Private; 30.3% Public; 7.7% None. (2008-2012 5-year est.)

Transportation: Commute to work: 100.0% car, 0.0% public transportation, 0.0% walk, 0.0% work from home (2008-2012 5-year est.); Travel time to work: 12.3% less than 15 minutes, 32.4% 15 to 30 minutes, 42.1% 30 to 45 minutes, 9.6% 45 to 60 minutes, 3.6% 60 minutes or more (2008-2012 5-year est.)

NEW BOSTON (city). Covers a land area of 0.933 square miles and a water area of 0.463 square miles. Located at 41.17° N. Lat; 91.00° W. Long. Elevation is 568 feet.

Population: 620 (1990); 632 (2000); 683 (2010); Density: 903.5 persons per square mile (2008-2012 5-year est.); Race: 98.6% White, 0.0% Black/African American, 1.2% Asian, 0.2% American Indian/Alaska Native, 0.0% Native Hawaiian/Other Pacific Islander, 0.0% Some other race, 0.0% Two or more races, 0.9% Hispanic of any race (2008-2012 5-year est.); Average household size: 2.45 (2008-2012 5-year est.); Median age: 48.2 (2008-2012 5-year est.); Males per 100 females: 94.2 (2008-2012 5-year est.); Marriage status: 26.5% never married, 52.7% now married, 3.4% widowed, 17.4% divorced (2008-2012 5-year est.); Foreign born: 1.1% (2008-2012 5-year est.); Ancestry (includes multiple ancestries): 20.5% German, 12.2% Irish, 8.9% English, 8.2% American, 5.8% Swedish (2008-2012 5-year est.).

Economy: Homeowner vacancy rate: 0.0%. Rental vacancy rate: 0.0%. (2008-2012 5-year est.); Employment by occupation: 3.7% management, business, and financial, 1.5% computer, engineering, and science, 3.2% education, legal, community service, arts, and media, 5.4% healthcare practitioners, 13.8% service, 20.6% sales and office, 16.0% natural resources, construction, and maintenance, 35.9% production, transportation, and material moving (2008-2012 5-year est.).

Income: Per capita income: $21,183 (2008-2012 5-year est.); Median household income: $43,393 (2008-2012 5-year est.); Average household income: $50,415 (2008-2012 5-year est.); Percent of households with income of $100,000 or more: 11.0% (2008-2012 5-year est.); Poverty rate: 16.8% (2008-2012 5-year est.).

Education: Percent of population age 25 and over with: High school diploma (including GED) or higher: 84.8% (2008-2012 5-year est.); Bachelor's degree or higher: 6.9% (2008-2012 5-year est.); Master's degree or higher: 1.3% (2008-2012 5-year est.).

School District(s)

Mercer County SD 404 (PK-12)
    2011-12 Enrollment: 1,330 . . . . (309) 582-2238

Housing: Homeownership rate: 83.4% (2008-2012 5-year est.); Median home value: $65,600 (2008-2012 5-year est.); Median contract rent: $348 per month (2008-2012 5-year est.); Median year structure built: 1960 (2008-2012 5-year est.).

Health Insurance: 54.8% Private; 41.9% Public; 19.5% None. (2008-2012 5-year est.)

Transportation: Commute to work: 96.0% car, 0.0% public transportation, 0.0% walk, 0.8% work from home (2008-2012 5-year est.); Travel time to work: 10.4% less than 15 minutes, 34.9% 15 to 30 minutes, 40.3% 30 to 45 minutes, 3.8% 45 to 60 minutes, 10.6% 60 minutes or more (2008-2012 5-year est.)

NEW WINDSOR (unincorporated postal area)

Zip Code: 61465

    Covers a land area of 41.790 square miles and a water area of 0.014 square miles. Located at 41.21° N. Lat; 90.47° W. Long. Elevation is 804 feet. Population: 1,213 (2010); Density: 29.0 persons per square mile (2010); Race: 97.6% White, 0.0% Black/African American, 1.1% Asian, 0.0% American Indian/Alaska Native, 0.0% Native Hawaiian/Other Pacific Islander, 1.3% Some other race, 0.8% Two or more races, 2.6% Hispanic of any race (2010); Average household size: 2.43 (2010); Median age: 42.6 (2010); Males per 100 females: 101.5 (2010); Homeownership rate: 81.6% (2010)

NORTH HENDERSON (village). Covers a land area of 0.226 square miles and a water area of 0 square miles. Located at 41.09° N. Lat; 90.47° W. Long. Elevation is 774 feet.

Population: 184 (1990); 187 (2000); 187 (2010); Density: 923.6 persons per square mile (2008-2012 5-year est.); Race: 99.5% White, 0.0% Black/African American, 0.0% Asian, 0.0% American Indian/Alaska Native, 0.0% Native Hawaiian/Other Pacific Islander, 0.5% Some other race, 0.5% Two or more races, 0.0% Hispanic of any race (2008-2012 5-year est.); Average household size: 2.65 (2008-2012 5-year est.); Median age: 41.1

(2008-2012 5-year est.); Males per 100 females: 137.5 (2008-2012 5-year est.); Marriage status: 26.3% never married, 54.4% now married, 2.3% widowed, 17.0% divorced (2008-2012 5-year est.); Foreign born: 0.0% (2008-2012 5-year est.); Ancestry (includes multiple ancestries): 27.8% German, 18.2% Irish, 15.3% Swedish, 9.1% English, 6.2% American (2008-2012 5-year est.).

Economy: Homeowner vacancy rate: 0.0%. Rental vacancy rate: 0.0%. (2008-2012 5-year est.); Employment by occupation: 5.0% management, business, and financial, 7.9% computer, engineering, and science, 9.9% education, legal, community service, arts, and media, 7.9% healthcare practitioners, 9.9% service, 20.8% sales and office, 13.9% natural resources, construction, and maintenance, 24.8% production, transportation, and material moving (2008-2012 5-year est.).

Income: Per capita income: $20,170 (2008-2012 5-year est.); Median household income: $49,219 (2008-2012 5-year est.); Average household income: $53,877 (2008-2012 5-year est.); Percent of households with income of $100,000 or more: 12.6% (2008-2012 5-year est.); Poverty rate: 7.7% (2008-2012 5-year est.).

Education: Percent of population age 25 and over with: High school diploma (including GED) or higher: 95.4% (2008-2012 5-year est.); Bachelor's degree or higher: 9.2% (2008-2012 5-year est.); Master's degree or higher: 3.8% (2008-2012 5-year est.).

Housing: Homeownership rate: 91.1% (2008-2012 5-year est.); Median home value: $60,000 (2008-2012 5-year est.); Median contract rent: n/a per month (2008-2012 5-year est.); Median year structure built: Before 1940 (2008-2012 5-year est.).

Health Insurance: 74.6% Private; 31.6% Public; 11.5% None. (2008-2012 5-year est.)

Transportation: Commute to work: 93.1% car, 0.0% public transportation, 0.0% walk, 4.0% work from home (2008-2012 5-year est.); Travel time to work: 9.3% less than 15 minutes, 72.2% 15 to 30 minutes, 13.4% 30 to 45 minutes, 0.0% 45 to 60 minutes, 5.2% 60 minutes or more (2008-2012 5-year est.)

PREEMPTION (unincorporated postal area)

Zip Code: 61276

Covers a land area of 2.336 square miles and a water area of 0 square miles. Located at 41.30° N. Lat; 90.58° W. Long. Elevation is 810 feet. Population: 138 (2010); Density: 59.1 persons per square mile (2010); Race: 100.0% White, 0.0% Black/African American, 0.0% Asian, 0.0% American Indian/Alaska Native, 0.0% Native Hawaiian/Other Pacific Islander, 0.0% Some other race, 0.0% Two or more races, 5.1% Hispanic of any race (2010); Average household size: 2.82 (2010); Median age: 37.3 (2010); Males per 100 females: 97.1 (2010); Homeownership rate: 89.8% (2010)

SEATON (village). Covers a land area of 1.579 square miles and a water area of 0 square miles. Located at 41.10° N. Lat; 90.80° W. Long. Elevation is 614 feet.

Population: 221 (1990); 242 (2000); 222 (2010); Density: 187.5 persons per square mile (2008-2012 5-year est.); Race: 99.7% White, 0.0% Black/African American, 0.0% Asian, 0.0% American Indian/Alaska Native, 0.0% Native Hawaiian/Other Pacific Islander, 0.3% Some other race, 0.0% Two or more races, 0.3% Hispanic of any race (2008-2012 5-year est.); Average household size: 2.37 (2008-2012 5-year est.); Median age: 44.6 (2008-2012 5-year est.); Males per 100 females: 96.0 (2008-2012 5-year est.); Marriage status: 21.0% never married, 62.1% now married, 7.0% widowed, 9.9% divorced (2008-2012 5-year est.); Foreign born: 0.0% (2008-2012 5-year est.); Ancestry (includes multiple ancestries): 24.0% German, 17.9% Swedish, 15.5% English, 15.5% Irish, 3.4% American (2008-2012 5-year est.).

Economy: Single-family building permits issued: 0 (2013); Multi-family building permits issued: 0 (2013); Homeowner vacancy rate: 0.0%. Rental vacancy rate: 0.0%. (2008-2012 5-year est.); Employment by occupation: 17.1% management, business, and financial, 2.1% computer, engineering, and science, 5.5% education, legal, community service, arts, and media, 2.7% healthcare practitioners, 18.5% service, 22.6% sales and office, 10.3% natural resources, construction, and maintenance, 21.2% production, transportation, and material moving (2008-2012 5-year est.).

Income: Per capita income: $22,989 (2008-2012 5-year est.); Median household income: $48,281 (2008-2012 5-year est.); Average household income: $52,750 (2008-2012 5-year est.); Percent of households with income of $100,000 or more: 6.4% (2008-2012 5-year est.); Poverty rate: 9.5% (2008-2012 5-year est.).

Education: Percent of population age 25 and over with: High school diploma (including GED) or higher: 86.1% (2008-2012 5-year est.); Bachelor's degree or higher: 11.0% (2008-2012 5-year est.); Master's degree or higher: 2.9% (2008-2012 5-year est.).

Housing: Homeownership rate: 96.8% (2008-2012 5-year est.); Median home value: $56,100 (2008-2012 5-year est.); Median contract rent: $1,225 per month (2008-2012 5-year est.); Median year structure built: Before 1940 (2008-2012 5-year est.).

Health Insurance: 74.3% Private; 34.5% Public; 9.1% None. (2008-2012 5-year est.)

Transportation: Commute to work: 91.1% car, 0.0% public transportation, 3.4% walk, 1.4% work from home (2008-2012 5-year est.); Travel time to work: 33.3% less than 15 minutes, 43.8% 15 to 30 minutes, 4.9% 30 to 45 minutes, 10.4% 45 to 60 minutes, 7.6% 60 minutes or more (2008-2012 5-year est.)

SHERRARD (village). Covers a land area of 0.926 square miles and a water area of 0.232 square miles. Located at 41.31° N. Lat; 90.50° W. Long. Elevation is 801 feet.

Population: 697 (1990); 694 (2000); 640 (2010); Density: 900.4 persons per square mile (2008-2012 5-year est.); Race: 98.0% White, 0.0% Black/African American, 0.4% Asian, 0.7% American Indian/Alaska Native, 0.0% Native Hawaiian/Other Pacific Islander, 0.9% Some other race, 0.8% Two or more races, 3.4% Hispanic of any race (2008-2012 5-year est.); Average household size: 2.50 (2008-2012 5-year est.); Median age: 39.2 (2008-2012 5-year est.); Males per 100 females: 101.9 (2008-2012 5-year est.); Marriage status: 20.2% never married, 67.3% now married, 5.2% widowed, 7.3% divorced (2008-2012 5-year est.); Foreign born: 0.0% (2008-2012 5-year est.); Ancestry (includes multiple ancestries): 29.9% German, 21.1% Irish, 16.2% Swedish, 11.9% English, 7.1% Belgian (2008-2012 5-year est.).

Economy: Single-family building permits issued: 0 (2013); Multi-family building permits issued: 0 (2013); Homeowner vacancy rate: 0.0%. Rental vacancy rate: 8.9%. (2008-2012 5-year est.); Employment by occupation: 15.7% management, business, and financial, 1.9% computer, engineering, and science, 2.6% education, legal, community service, arts, and media, 6.8% healthcare practitioners, 14.7% service, 17.8% sales and office, 21.3% natural resources, construction, and maintenance, 19.4% production, transportation, and material moving (2008-2012 5-year est.).

Income: Per capita income: $24,872 (2008-2012 5-year est.); Median household income: $58,125 (2008-2012 5-year est.); Average household income: $61,890 (2008-2012 5-year est.); Percent of households with income of $100,000 or more: 12.3% (2008-2012 5-year est.); Poverty rate: 1.8% (2008-2012 5-year est.).

Taxes: Total city taxes per capita: $305 (2011); City property taxes per capita: $268 (2011).

Education: Percent of population age 25 and over with: High school diploma (including GED) or higher: 96.9% (2008-2012 5-year est.); Bachelor's degree or higher: 13.5% (2008-2012 5-year est.); Master's degree or higher: 2.8% (2008-2012 5-year est.).

School District(s)

Sherrard CUSD 200 (PK-12)
    2011-12 Enrollment: 1,595 . . . . (309) 593-4075
Sherrard CUSD 200 (PK-12)
    2011-12 Enrollment: 1,595 . . . . (309) 593-4075

Housing: Homeownership rate: 87.7% (2008-2012 5-year est.); Median home value: $107,400 (2008-2012 5-year est.); Median contract rent: $584 per month (2008-2012 5-year est.); Median year structure built: 1956 (2008-2012 5-year est.).

Health Insurance: 89.9% Private; 21.8% Public; 4.7% None. (2008-2012 5-year est.)

Transportation: Commute to work: 92.5% car, 0.0% public transportation, 3.1% walk, 4.3% work from home (2008-2012 5-year est.); Travel time to work: 14.6% less than 15 minutes, 32.3% 15 to 30 minutes, 46.2% 30 to 45 minutes, 5.6% 45 to 60 minutes, 1.3% 60 minutes or more (2008-2012 5-year est.)

VIOLA (village). Covers a land area of 0.838 square miles and a water area of 0.015 square miles. Located at 41.21° N. Lat; 90.59° W. Long. Elevation is 791 feet.

History: Viola developed as a coal mining town.

Population: 964 (1990); 956 (2000); 955 (2010); Density: 1,229.3 persons per square mile (2008-2012 5-year est.); Race: 99.4% White, 0.0% Black/African American, 0.0% Asian, 0.0% American Indian/Alaska Native, 0.0% Native Hawaiian/Other Pacific Islander, 0.6% Some other race, 0.4%

Two or more races, 4.8% Hispanic of any race (2008-2012 5-year est.); Average household size: 2.31 (2008-2012 5-year est.); Median age: 45.0 (2008-2012 5-year est.); Males per 100 females: 104.0 (2008-2012 5-year est.); Marriage status: 16.8% never married, 67.1% now married, 8.4% widowed, 7.7% divorced (2008-2012 5-year est.); Foreign born: 1.6% (2008-2012 5-year est.); Ancestry (includes multiple ancestries): 30.3% German, 14.4% Irish, 12.7% English, 7.0% Swedish, 6.4% American (2008-2012 5-year est.).

Economy: Single-family building permits issued: 1 (2013); Multi-family building permits issued: 0 (2013); Homeowner vacancy rate: 0.0%. Rental vacancy rate: 0.0%. (2008-2012 5-year est.); Employment by occupation: 17.2% management, business, and financial, 0.7% computer, engineering, and science, 8.9% education, legal, community service, arts, and media, 3.9% healthcare practitioners, 12.6% service, 23.0% sales and office, 15.9% natural resources, construction, and maintenance, 17.8% production, transportation, and material moving (2008-2012 5-year est.).

Income: Per capita income: $25,269 (2008-2012 5-year est.); Median household income: $51,750 (2008-2012 5-year est.); Average household income: $57,958 (2008-2012 5-year est.); Percent of households with income of $100,000 or more: 8.7% (2008-2012 5-year est.); Poverty rate: 6.6% (2008-2012 5-year est.).

Education: Percent of population age 25 and over with: High school diploma (including GED) or higher: 90.8% (2008-2012 5-year est.); Bachelor's degree or higher: 11.4% (2008-2012 5-year est.); Master's degree or higher: 3.2% (2008-2012 5-year est.).

School District(s)
Sherrard CUSD 200 (PK-12)
    2011-12 Enrollment: 1,595 . . . . (309) 593-4075

Housing: Homeownership rate: 85.9% (2008-2012 5-year est.); Median home value: $86,900 (2008-2012 5-year est.); Median contract rent: $358 per month (2008-2012 5-year est.); Median year structure built: 1952 (2008-2012 5-year est.).

Health Insurance: 86.6% Private; 32.6% Public; 5.5% None. (2008-2012 5-year est.)

Transportation: Commute to work: 95.0% car, 0.0% public transportation, 2.6% walk, 0.7% work from home (2008-2012 5-year est.); Travel time to work: 20.3% less than 15 minutes, 30.0% 15 to 30 minutes, 30.9% 30 to 45 minutes, 15.9% 45 to 60 minutes, 2.9% 60 minutes or more (2008-2012 5-year est.)

Additional Information Contacts
Aledo Area Chamber of Commerce . . . . (309) 582-5373
    http://aledochamber.org

WINDSOR (village). Aka New Windsor. Covers a land area of 0.438 square miles and a water area of 0 square miles. Located at 41.20° N. Lat; 90.44° W. Long.

Population: 774 (1990); 720 (2000); 748 (2010); Density: 1,884.6 persons per square mile (2008-2012 5-year est.); Race: 97.7% White, 0.0% Black/African American, 1.0% Asian, 0.0% American Indian/Alaska Native, 0.0% Native Hawaiian/Other Pacific Islander, 1.3% Some other race, 0.2% Two or more races, 1.8% Hispanic of any race (2008-2012 5-year est.); Average household size: 2.43 (2008-2012 5-year est.); Median age: 41.4 (2008-2012 5-year est.); Males per 100 females: 99.3 (2008-2012 5-year est.); Marriage status: 20.4% never married, 65.2% now married, 5.1% widowed, 9.3% divorced (2008-2012 5-year est.); Foreign born: 2.3% (2008-2012 5-year est.); Ancestry (includes multiple ancestries): 29.2% German, 18.5% Irish, 16.1% Swedish, 14.8% English, 9.3% American (2008-2012 5-year est.).

Economy: Single-family building permits issued: 0 (2013); Multi-family building permits issued: 0 (2013); Homeowner vacancy rate: 0.0%. Rental vacancy rate: 0.0%. (2008-2012 5-year est.); Employment by occupation: 5.8% management, business, and financial, 2.8% computer, engineering, and science, 16.8% education, legal, community service, arts, and media, 4.8% healthcare practitioners, 8.8% service, 25.0% sales and office, 15.5% natural resources, construction, and maintenance, 20.8% production, transportation, and material moving (2008-2012 5-year est.).

Income: Per capita income: $27,673 (2008-2012 5-year est.); Median household income: $56,000 (2008-2012 5-year est.); Average household income: $67,156 (2008-2012 5-year est.); Percent of households with income of $100,000 or more: 19.4% (2008-2012 5-year est.); Poverty rate: 5.9% (2008-2012 5-year est.).

Education: Percent of population age 25 and over with: High school diploma (including GED) or higher: 86.3% (2008-2012 5-year est.); Bachelor's degree or higher: 18.6% (2008-2012 5-year est.); Master's degree or higher: 11.7% (2008-2012 5-year est.).

Housing: Homeownership rate: 77.1% (2008-2012 5-year est.); Median home value: $83,300 (2008-2012 5-year est.); Median contract rent: $320 per month (2008-2012 5-year est.); Median year structure built: 1956 (2008-2012 5-year est.).

Health Insurance: 78.2% Private; 29.6% Public; 9.1% None. (2008-2012 5-year est.)

Transportation: Commute to work: 93.4% car, 0.0% public transportation, 1.3% walk, 3.6% work from home (2008-2012 5-year est.); Travel time to work: 12.4% less than 15 minutes, 30.3% 15 to 30 minutes, 40.6% 30 to 45 minutes, 10.8% 45 to 60 minutes, 5.8% 60 minutes or more (2008-2012 5-year est.)

Monroe County

Located in southwestern Illinois; bounded on the west by the Mississippi River and the Missouri border; drained by the Kaskaskia River. Covers a land area of 385.011 square miles, a water area of 13.025 square miles, and is located in the Central Time Zone at 38.28° N. Lat., 90.18° W. Long. The county was founded in 1816. County seat is Waterloo.

Monroe County is part of the St. Louis, MO-IL Metropolitan Statistical Area. The entire metro area includes: Bond County, IL; Calhoun County, IL; Clinton County, IL; Jersey County, IL; Macoupin County, IL; Madison County, IL; Monroe County, IL; Saint Clair County, IL; Franklin County, MO; Jefferson County, MO; Lincoln County, MO; Saint Charles County, MO; Saint Louis County, MO; Warren County, MO; Saint Louis city, MO

Population: 22,422 (1990); 27,619 (2000); 32,957 (2010); Race: 98.2% White, 0.2% Black/African American, 0.5% Asian, 0.1% American Indian/Alaska Native, 0.1% Native Hawaiian/Other Pacific Islander, 0.9% Some other race, 0.9% Two or more races, 1.4% Hispanic of any race (2008-2012 5-year est.); Density: 86.5 persons per square mile (2008-2012 5-year est.); Average household size: 2.63 (2008-2012 5-year est.); Median age: 40.5 (2008-2012 5-year est.); Males per 100 females: 97.4 (2008-2012 5-year est.).

Religion: Six largest groups: 28.0% Catholicism, 12.3% Presbyterian-Reformed, 9.1% Baptist, 7.9% Lutheran, 5.4% Non-denominational Protestant, 0.7% Latter-day Saints (2010)

Economy: Unemployment rate: 4.8% (April 2014); Total civilian labor force: 18,447 (April 2014); Leading industries: 18.0% retail trade; 14.5% accommodation & food services; 12.3% health care and social assistance (2012); Farms: 563 totaling 193,201 acres (2012); Companies that employ 500 or more persons: 0 (2012); Companies that employ 100 to 499 persons: 8 (2012); Companies that employ less than 100 persons: 780 (2012); Black-owned businesses: n/a (2007); Hispanic-owned businesses: n/a (2007); Asian-owned businesses: n/a (2007); Women-owned businesses: 912 (2007); Single-family building permits issued: 121 (2013); Multi-family building permits issued: 0 (2013).

Income: Per capita income: $32,334 (2008-2012 5-year est.); Median household income: $71,033 (2008-2012 5-year est.); Average household income: $85,239 (2008-2012 5-year est.); Percent of households with income of $100,000 or more: 31.1% (2008-2012 5-year est.); Poverty rate: 4.9% (2008-2012 5-year est.); Bankruptcy rate: 2.42% (2013).

Taxes: Total county taxes per capita: $254 (2011); County property taxes per capita: $254 (2011).

Education: Percent of population age 25 and over with: High school diploma (including GED) or higher: 92.9% (2008-2012 5-year est.); Bachelor's degree or higher: 25.5% (2008-2012 5-year est.); Master's degree or higher: 8.0% (2008-2012 5-year est.).

Housing: Homeownership rate: 82.0% (2008-2012 5-year est.); Median home value: $198,300 (2008-2012 5-year est.); Median contract rent: $641 per month (2008-2012 5-year est.); Median year structure built: 1986 (2008-2012 5-year est.).

Health: Birth rate: 88.7 per 10,000 population (2013); Death rate: 83.0 per 10,000 population (2013); Age-adjusted cancer mortality rate: 192.5 deaths per 100,000 population (2011); Number of physicians: 6.3 per 10,000 population (2011); Hospital beds: 0.0 per 10,000 population (2010); Hospital admissions: 0.0 per 10,000 population (2010).

Elections: 2012 Presidential election results: 35.6% Obama, 62.5% Romney

National and State Parks: Illinois Caverns State Natural Area

Additional Information Contacts
Monroe County Government. . . . . (618) 939-8681
    http://www.monroecountyil.org

Monroe County Communities

COLUMBIA (city). Covers a land area of 10.412 square miles and a water area of 0.066 square miles. Located at 38.46° N. Lat; 90.22° W. Long. Elevation is 502 feet.

History: Columbia was established as a stop on the Kaskaskia-Cahokia trail. Many early residents were of German descent. The quarrying of Keokuk limestone began here in 1840.

Population: 5,524 (1990); 7,922 (2000); 9,707 (2010); Density: 930.4 persons per square mile (2008-2012 5-year est.); Race: 96.9% White, 0.7% Black/African American, 0.9% Asian, 0.2% American Indian/Alaska Native, 0.0% Native Hawaiian/Other Pacific Islander, 1.3% Some other race, 1.3% Two or more races, 2.9% Hispanic of any race (2008-2012 5-year est.); Average household size: 2.49 (2008-2012 5-year est.); Median age: 39.6 (2008-2012 5-year est.); Males per 100 females: 92.4 (2008-2012 5-year est.); Marriage status: 24.3% never married, 57.0% now married, 6.9% widowed, 11.8% divorced (2008-2012 5-year est.); Foreign born: 0.5% (2008-2012 5-year est.); Ancestry (includes multiple ancestries): 49.5% German, 18.3% Irish, 12.4% English, 7.1% American, 5.8% Italian (2008-2012 5-year est.).

Economy: Single-family building permits issued: 61 (2013); Multi-family building permits issued: 0 (2013); Homeowner vacancy rate: 0.0%. Rental vacancy rate: 8.1%. (2008-2012 5-year est.); Employment by occupation: 18.5% management, business, and financial, 6.8% computer, engineering, and science, 10.7% education, legal, community service, arts, and media, 6.7% healthcare practitioners, 16.9% service, 26.6% sales and office, 5.3% natural resources, construction, and maintenance, 8.5% production, transportation, and material moving (2008-2012 5-year est.).

Income: Per capita income: $32,462 (2008-2012 5-year est.); Median household income: $62,234 (2008-2012 5-year est.); Average household income: $82,240 (2008-2012 5-year est.); Percent of households with income of $100,000 or more: 30.3% (2008-2012 5-year est.); Poverty rate: 4.1% (2008-2012 5-year est.).

Education: Percent of population age 25 and over with: High school diploma (including GED) or higher: 94.3% (2008-2012 5-year est.); Bachelor's degree or higher: 32.6% (2008-2012 5-year est.); Master's degree or higher: 8.7% (2008-2012 5-year est.).

School District(s)
Columbia CUSD 4 (PK-12)
    2011-12 Enrollment: 2,060 . . . . (618) 281-4772

Housing: Homeownership rate: 80.1% (2008-2012 5-year est.); Median home value: $198,400 (2008-2012 5-year est.); Median contract rent: $651 per month (2008-2012 5-year est.); Median year structure built: 1985 (2008-2012 5-year est.).

Health Insurance: 85.1% Private; 25.1% Public; 3.5% None. (2008-2012 5-year est.)

Safety: Violent crime rate: 10.2 per 10,000 population; Property crime rate: 93.7 per 10,000 population (2012).

Transportation: Commute to work: 94.4% car, 0.3% public transportation, 2.0% walk, 3.1% work from home (2008-2012 5-year est.); Travel time to work: 21.0% less than 15 minutes, 34.2% 15 to 30 minutes, 32.6% 30 to 45 minutes, 8.3% 45 to 60 minutes, 3.9% 60 minutes or more (2008-2012 5-year est.)

Additional Information Contacts
City of Columbia . . . . (618) 281-7144
    http://www.columbiaillinois.com

FULTS (village). Covers a land area of 0.066 square miles and a water area of 0 square miles. Located at 38.16° N. Lat; 90.21° W. Long. Elevation is 394 feet.

History: Heavily damaged in floods of 1993.

Population: 45 (1990); 28 (2000); 26 (2010); Density: 561.3 persons per square mile (2008-2012 5-year est.); Race: 100.0% White, 0.0% Black/African American, 0.0% Asian, 0.0% American Indian/Alaska Native, 0.0% Native Hawaiian/Other Pacific Islander, 0.0% Some other race, 0.0% Two or more races, 0.0% Hispanic of any race (2008-2012 5-year est.); Average household size: 3.08 (2008-2012 5-year est.); Median age: 51.8 (2008-2012 5-year est.); Males per 100 females: 68.2 (2008-2012 5-year est.); Marriage status: 33.3% never married, 63.9% now married, 2.8% widowed, 0.0% divorced (2008-2012 5-year est.); Foreign born: 0.0% (2008-2012 5-year est.); Ancestry (includes multiple ancestries): 81.1% German, 8.1% Irish, 8.1% French, 5.4% Polish, 2.7% Italian (2008-2012 5-year est.).

Economy: Homeowner vacancy rate: 0.0%. Rental vacancy rate: 0.0%. (2008-2012 5-year est.); Employment by occupation: 18.2% management, business, and financial, 0.0% computer, engineering, and science, 0.0% education, legal, community service, arts, and media, 0.0% healthcare practitioners, 13.6% service, 63.6% sales and office, 0.0% natural resources, construction, and maintenance, 4.5% production, transportation, and material moving (2008-2012 5-year est.).

Income: Per capita income: $31,389 (2008-2012 5-year est.); Median household income: $86,875 (2008-2012 5-year est.); Average household income: $91,167 (2008-2012 5-year est.); Percent of households with income of $100,000 or more: 33.3% (2008-2012 5-year est.); Poverty rate: 0.0% (2008-2012 5-year est.).

Education: Percent of population age 25 and over with: High school diploma (including GED) or higher: 89.7% (2008-2012 5-year est.); Bachelor's degree or higher: 24.1% (2008-2012 5-year est.); Master's degree or higher: 0.0% (2008-2012 5-year est.).

Housing: Homeownership rate: 100.0% (2008-2012 5-year est.); Median home value: $98,000 (2008-2012 5-year est.); Median contract rent: n/a per month (2008-2012 5-year est.); Median year structure built: 1950 (2008-2012 5-year est.).

Health Insurance: 97.3% Private; 2.7% Public; 0.0% None. (2008-2012 5-year est.)

Transportation: Commute to work: 100.0% car, 0.0% public transportation, 0.0% walk, 0.0% work from home (2008-2012 5-year est.); Travel time to work: 22.7% less than 15 minutes, 45.5% 15 to 30 minutes, 0.0% 30 to 45 minutes, 0.0% 45 to 60 minutes, 31.8% 60 minutes or more (2008-2012 5-year est.)

HECKER (village). Covers a land area of 0.240 square miles and a water area of 0 square miles. Located at 38.30° N. Lat; 89.99° W. Long. Elevation is 472 feet.

Population: 534 (1990); 475 (2000); 481 (2010); Density: 1,979.1 persons per square mile (2008-2012 5-year est.); Race: 93.5% White, 0.0% Black/African American, 0.0% Asian, 0.0% American Indian/Alaska Native, 0.0% Native Hawaiian/Other Pacific Islander, 6.5% Some other race, 5.7% Two or more races, 4.6% Hispanic of any race (2008-2012 5-year est.); Average household size: 2.60 (2008-2012 5-year est.); Median age: 33.3 (2008-2012 5-year est.); Males per 100 females: 96.3 (2008-2012 5-year est.); Marriage status: 19.5% never married, 73.7% now married, 4.1% widowed, 2.7% divorced (2008-2012 5-year est.); Foreign born: 0.8% (2008-2012 5-year est.); Ancestry (includes multiple ancestries): 55.6% German, 22.7% Irish, 14.7% French, 10.1% English, 6.7% Italian (2008-2012 5-year est.).

Economy: Single-family building permits issued: 2 (2013); Multi-family building permits issued: 0 (2013); Homeowner vacancy rate: 0.0%. Rental vacancy rate: 20.7%. (2008-2012 5-year est.); Employment by occupation: 11.5% management, business, and financial, 10.1% computer, engineering, and science, 2.4% education, legal, community service, arts, and media, 0.0% healthcare practitioners, 8.2% service, 32.2% sales and office, 11.5% natural resources, construction, and maintenance, 24.0% production, transportation, and material moving (2008-2012 5-year est.).

Income: Per capita income: $25,799 (2008-2012 5-year est.); Median household income: $56,953 (2008-2012 5-year est.); Average household income: $69,546 (2008-2012 5-year est.); Percent of households with income of $100,000 or more: 21.3% (2008-2012 5-year est.); Poverty rate: 9.7% (2008-2012 5-year est.).

Education: Percent of population age 25 and over with: High school diploma (including GED) or higher: 89.1% (2008-2012 5-year est.); Bachelor's degree or higher: 13.1% (2008-2012 5-year est.); Master's degree or higher: 0.6% (2008-2012 5-year est.).

Housing: Homeownership rate: 74.9% (2008-2012 5-year est.); Median home value: $124,400 (2008-2012 5-year est.); Median contract rent: $431 per month (2008-2012 5-year est.); Median year structure built: 1972 (2008-2012 5-year est.).

Health Insurance: 84.8% Private; 27.8% Public; 4.8% None. (2008-2012 5-year est.)

Transportation: Commute to work: 90.3% car, 3.9% public transportation, 1.0% walk, 4.8% work from home (2008-2012 5-year est.); Travel time to work: 21.3% less than 15 minutes, 36.0% 15 to 30 minutes, 20.8% 30 to 45 minutes, 9.6% 45 to 60 minutes, 12.2% 60 minutes or more (2008-2012 5-year est.)

MAEYSTOWN (village). Covers a land area of 0.297 square miles and a water area of 0.002 square miles. Located at 38.23° N. Lat; 90.23° W. Long. Elevation is 469 feet.

Population: 116 (1990); 148 (2000); 157 (2010); Density: 596.7 persons per square mile (2008-2012 5-year est.); Race: 100.0% White, 0.0% Black/African American, 0.0% Asian, 0.0% American Indian/Alaska Native, 0.0% Native Hawaiian/Other Pacific Islander, 0.0% Some other race, 0.0% Two or more races, 1.7% Hispanic of any race (2008-2012 5-year est.); Average household size: 2.53 (2008-2012 5-year est.); Median age: 35.1 (2008-2012 5-year est.); Males per 100 females: 73.5 (2008-2012 5-year est.); Marriage status: 7.7% never married, 75.4% now married, 13.1% widowed, 3.8% divorced (2008-2012 5-year est.); Foreign born: 0.0% (2008-2012 5-year est.); Ancestry (includes multiple ancestries): 68.4% German, 18.6% Irish, 16.9% English, 10.2% Swiss, 2.8% Welsh (2008-2012 5-year est.).

Economy: Homeowner vacancy rate: 0.0%. Rental vacancy rate: 33.3%. (2008-2012 5-year est.); Employment by occupation: 11.8% management, business, and financial, 11.8% computer, engineering, and science, 13.7% education, legal, community service, arts, and media, 2.0% healthcare practitioners, 7.8% service, 25.5% sales and office, 15.7% natural resources, construction, and maintenance, 11.8% production, transportation, and material moving (2008-2012 5-year est.).

Income: Per capita income: $34,544 (2008-2012 5-year est.); Median household income: $70,000 (2008-2012 5-year est.); Average household income: $87,293 (2008-2012 5-year est.); Percent of households with income of $100,000 or more: 20.0% (2008-2012 5-year est.); Poverty rate: 0.0% (2008-2012 5-year est.).

Education: Percent of population age 25 and over with: High school diploma (including GED) or higher: 90.9% (2008-2012 5-year est.); Bachelor's degree or higher: 25.6% (2008-2012 5-year est.); Master's degree or higher: 8.3% (2008-2012 5-year est.).

Housing: Homeownership rate: 88.6% (2008-2012 5-year est.); Median home value: $157,500 (2008-2012 5-year est.); Median contract rent: $450 per month (2008-2012 5-year est.); Median year structure built: 1970 (2008-2012 5-year est.).

Health Insurance: 68.9% Private; 43.5% Public; 4.5% None. (2008-2012 5-year est.)

Transportation: Commute to work: 90.2% car, 0.0% public transportation, 2.0% walk, 7.8% work from home (2008-2012 5-year est.); Travel time to work: 19.1% less than 15 minutes, 40.4% 15 to 30 minutes, 4.3% 30 to 45 minutes, 19.1% 45 to 60 minutes, 17.0% 60 minutes or more (2008-2012 5-year est.)

RENAULT (unincorporated postal area)

Zip Code: 62279

Covers a land area of 0.133 square miles and a water area of 0.001 square miles. Located at 38.15° N. Lat; 90.13° W. Long. Elevation is 682 feet. Population: 69 (2010); Density: 518.2 persons per square mile (2010); Race: 94.2% White, 0.0% Black/African American, 0.0% Asian, 0.0% American Indian/Alaska Native, 0.0% Native Hawaiian/Other Pacific Islander, 5.8% Some other race, 5.8% Two or more races, 0.0% Hispanic of any race (2010); Average household size: 2.30 (2010); Median age: 41.2 (2010); Males per 100 females: 86.5 (2010); Homeownership rate: 73.4% (2010)

VALMEYER (village). Aka Maeys. Covers a land area of 3.579 square miles and a water area of 0.054 square miles. Located at 38.31° N. Lat; 90.30° W. Long. Elevation is 735 feet.

History: Town established by Swiss farmers at the end of the 19th century on rich Mississippi bottom land. Town flooded twice in September and October of 1993, with 90% of the homes beyond repair. A new town was constructed two miles east of the old Valmeyer on 500 acres of former dairy lands.

Population: 897 (1990); 608 (2000); 1,263 (2010); Density: 458.5 persons per square mile (2008-2012 5-year est.); Race: 98.5% White, 0.1% Black/African American, 0.4% Asian, 0.0% American Indian/Alaska Native, 0.0% Native Hawaiian/Other Pacific Islander, 1.0% Some other race, 1.0% Two or more races, 1.0% Hispanic of any race (2008-2012 5-year est.); Average household size: 3.03 (2008-2012 5-year est.); Median age: 32.6 (2008-2012 5-year est.); Males per 100 females: 97.7 (2008-2012 5-year est.); Marriage status: 18.5% never married, 71.2% now married, 4.5% widowed, 5.8% divorced (2008-2012 5-year est.); Foreign born: 0.4% (2008-2012 5-year est.); Ancestry (includes multiple ancestries): 45.3% German, 17.0% Irish, 6.5% American, 5.9% Italian, 4.6% French (2008-2012 5-year est.).

Economy: Single-family building permits issued: 2 (2013); Multi-family building permits issued: 0 (2013); Homeowner vacancy rate: 0.0%. Rental vacancy rate: 0.0%. (2008-2012 5-year est.); Employment by occupation: 14.6% management, business, and financial, 4.9% computer, engineering, and science, 6.1% education, legal, community service, arts, and media, 5.8% healthcare practitioners, 17.4% service, 23.7% sales and office, 10.0% natural resources, construction, and maintenance, 17.4% production, transportation, and material moving (2008-2012 5-year est.).

Income: Per capita income: $24,014 (2008-2012 5-year est.); Median household income: $70,865 (2008-2012 5-year est.); Average household income: $75,312 (2008-2012 5-year est.); Percent of households with income of $100,000 or more: 21.1% (2008-2012 5-year est.); Poverty rate: 5.1% (2008-2012 5-year est.).

Education: Percent of population age 25 and over with: High school diploma (including GED) or higher: 95.5% (2008-2012 5-year est.); Bachelor's degree or higher: 16.8% (2008-2012 5-year est.); Master's degree or higher: 5.3% (2008-2012 5-year est.).

School District(s)

Valmeyer CUSD 3 (PK-12)

    2011-12 Enrollment: 511 . . . . (618) 935-2100

Housing: Homeownership rate: 81.5% (2008-2012 5-year est.); Median home value: $173,500 (2008-2012 5-year est.); Median contract rent: $800 per month (2008-2012 5-year est.); Median year structure built: 2000 (2008-2012 5-year est.).

Health Insurance: 80.9% Private; 25.1% Public; 3.8% None. (2008-2012 5-year est.)

Safety: Violent crime rate: 0.0 per 10,000 population; Property crime rate: 78.4 per 10,000 population (2012).

Transportation: Commute to work: 93.4% car, 0.0% public transportation, 1.3% walk, 3.2% work from home (2008-2012 5-year est.); Travel time to work: 19.7% less than 15 minutes, 27.1% 15 to 30 minutes, 21.5% 30 to 45 minutes, 19.2% 45 to 60 minutes, 12.5% 60 minutes or more (2008-2012 5-year est.)

WATERLOO (city). County seat. Covers a land area of 7.523 square miles and a water area of 0.140 square miles. Located at 38.34° N. Lat; 90.15° W. Long. Elevation is 709 feet.

History: Waterloo was established on the trail from Fort Chartres to Cahokia, and developed as the seat of Monroe County. For a time it had a reputation as a place for quick marriages.

Population: 5,072 (1990); 7,614 (2000); 9,811 (2010); Density: 1,306.1 persons per square mile (2008-2012 5-year est.); Race: 99.1% White, 0.1% Black/African American, 0.6% Asian, 0.0% American Indian/Alaska Native, 0.0% Native Hawaiian/Other Pacific Islander, 0.2% Some other race, 0.1% Two or more races, 1.0% Hispanic of any race (2008-2012 5-year est.); Average household size: 2.49 (2008-2012 5-year est.); Median age: 40.6 (2008-2012 5-year est.); Males per 100 females: 92.9 (2008-2012 5-year est.); Marriage status: 23.8% never married, 61.6% now married, 6.1% widowed, 8.5% divorced (2008-2012 5-year est.); Foreign born: 1.5% (2008-2012 5-year est.); Ancestry (includes multiple ancestries): 50.0% German, 17.2% Irish, 10.8% English, 8.9% American, 7.4% French (2008-2012 5-year est.).

Economy: Single-family building permits issued: 24 (2013); Multi-family building permits issued: 0 (2013); Homeowner vacancy rate: 5.2%. Rental vacancy rate: 4.6%. (2008-2012 5-year est.); Employment by occupation: 15.0% management, business, and financial, 2.7% computer, engineering, and science, 5.8% education, legal, community service, arts, and media, 5.5% healthcare practitioners, 17.3% service, 31.0% sales and office, 8.9% natural resources, construction, and maintenance, 13.6% production, transportation, and material moving (2008-2012 5-year est.).

Income: Per capita income: $33,897 (2008-2012 5-year est.); Median household income: $71,714 (2008-2012 5-year est.); Average household income: $83,764 (2008-2012 5-year est.); Percent of households with income of $100,000 or more: 28.5% (2008-2012 5-year est.); Poverty rate: 3.0% (2008-2012 5-year est.).

Education: Percent of population age 25 and over with: High school diploma (including GED) or higher: 93.4% (2008-2012 5-year est.); Bachelor's degree or higher: 24.2% (2008-2012 5-year est.); Master's degree or higher: 8.3% (2008-2012 5-year est.).

School District(s)

Waterloo CUSD 5 (PK-12)

    2011-12 Enrollment: 2,741 . . . . (618) 939-3453

Housing: Homeownership rate: 77.6% (2008-2012 5-year est.); Median home value: $184,900 (2008-2012 5-year est.); Median contract rent: $644

per month (2008-2012 5-year est.); Median year structure built: 1987 (2008-2012 5-year est.).
Health Insurance: 83.4% Private; 22.4% Public; 8.2% None. (2008-2012 5-year est.)
Safety: Violent crime rate: 0.0 per 10,000 population; Property crime rate: 59.5 per 10,000 population (2012).
Transportation: Commute to work: 94.9% car, 1.5% public transportation, 1.1% walk, 2.5% work from home (2008-2012 5-year est.); Travel time to work: 24.4% less than 15 minutes, 17.6% 15 to 30 minutes, 36.4% 30 to 45 minutes, 15.1% 45 to 60 minutes, 6.5% 60 minutes or more (2008-2012 5-year est.)
Additional Information Contacts
City of Waterloo . . . . (618) 939-8600
　　http://www.waterloo.il.us
Waterloo Chamber of Commerce . . . . (618) 939-5300
　　http://www.enjoywaterloo.com

Montgomery County

Located in south central Illinois; drained by Shoal and Macoupin Creeks. Covers a land area of 703.686 square miles, a water area of 5.990 square miles, and is located in the Central Time Zone at 39.23° N. Lat., 89.48° W. Long. The county was founded in 1821. County seat is Hillsboro.

Weather Station: Hillsboro　　　　　　　　　　Elevation: 629 feet

	Jan	Feb	Mar	Apr	May	Jun	Jul	Aug	Sep	Oct	Nov	Dec
High	39	44	55	68	77	86	90	88	82	69	55	42
Low	22	25	34	44	54	63	67	65	56	46	36	25
Precip	2.3	2.1	3.0	4.0	5.0	3.8	3.6	3.1	3.3	3.5	3.9	2.9
Snow	5.1	3.8	1.7	0.2	tr	0.0	0.0	0.0	0.0	tr	0.5	3.6

High and Low temperatures in degrees Fahrenheit; Precipitation and Snow in inches

Population: 30,728 (1990); 30,652 (2000); 30,104 (2010); Race: 91.2% White, 7.4% Black/African American, 0.5% Asian, 0.1% American Indian/Alaska Native, 0.0% Native Hawaiian/Other Pacific Islander, 0.8% Some other race, 0.6% Two or more races, 1.5% Hispanic of any race (2008-2012 5-year est.); Density: 42.2 persons per square mile (2008-2012 5-year est.); Average household size: 2.18 (2008-2012 5-year est.); Median age: 41.8 (2008-2012 5-year est.); Males per 100 females: 111.4 (2008-2012 5-year est.).
Religion: Six largest groups: 17.9% Baptist, 10.9% Lutheran, 6.8% Catholicism, 4.1% Methodist/Pietist, 2.1% Non-denominational Protestant, 1.8% Presbyterian-Reformed (2010)
Economy: Unemployment rate: 8.9% (April 2014); Total civilian labor force: 12,154 (April 2014); Leading industries: 20.6% retail trade; 17.5% health care and social assistance; 12.0% accommodation & food services (2012); Farms: 1,021 totaling 382,388 acres (2012); Companies that employ 500 or more persons: 0 (2012); Companies that employ 100 to 499 persons: 8 (2012); Companies that employ less than 100 persons: 699 (2012); Black-owned businesses: n/a (2007); Hispanic-owned businesses: n/a (2007); Asian-owned businesses: n/a (2007); Women-owned businesses: 794 (2007); Single-family building permits issued: 16 (2013); Multi-family building permits issued: 7 (2013).
Income: Per capita income: $21,550 (2008-2012 5-year est.); Median household income: $42,261 (2008-2012 5-year est.); Average household income: $57,420 (2008-2012 5-year est.); Percent of households with income of $100,000 or more: 12.7% (2008-2012 5-year est.); Poverty rate: 14.2% (2008-2012 5-year est.); Bankruptcy rate: 3.21% (2013).
Taxes: Total county taxes per capita: $128 (2011); County property taxes per capita: $119 (2011).
Education: Percent of population age 25 and over with: High school diploma (including GED) or higher: 84.9% (2008-2012 5-year est.); Bachelor's degree or higher: 12.4% (2008-2012 5-year est.); Master's degree or higher: 4.4% (2008-2012 5-year est.).
Housing: Homeownership rate: 74.7% (2008-2012 5-year est.); Median home value: $81,100 (2008-2012 5-year est.); Median contract rent: $410 per month (2008-2012 5-year est.); Median year structure built: 1959 (2008-2012 5-year est.)
Health: Birth rate: 102.2 per 10,000 population (2013); Death rate: 125.4 per 10,000 population (2013); Age-adjusted cancer mortality rate: 220.9 deaths per 100,000 population (2011); Number of physicians: 6.7 per 10,000 population (2011); Hospital beds: 20.3 per 10,000 population (2010); Hospital admissions: 720.5 per 10,000 population (2010).
Elections: 2012 Presidential election results: 41.7% Obama, 55.9% Romney

National and State Parks: Coffeen Lake State Fish and Wildlife Area
Additional Information Contacts
Montgomery County Government . . . . (217) 532-9530
　　http://www.montgomeryco.com

Montgomery County Communities

BUTLER (village). Covers a land area of 0.577 square miles and a water area of 0 square miles. Located at 39.20° N. Lat; 89.53° W. Long. Elevation is 630 feet.
Population: 156 (1990); 197 (2000); 180 (2010); Density: 227.2 persons per square mile (2008-2012 5-year est.); Race: 98.5% White, 0.0% Black/African American, 0.0% Asian, 0.0% American Indian/Alaska Native, 0.0% Native Hawaiian/Other Pacific Islander, 1.5% Some other race, 1.5% Two or more races, 0.8% Hispanic of any race (2008-2012 5-year est.); Average household size: 2.08 (2008-2012 5-year est.); Median age: 39.9 (2008-2012 5-year est.); Males per 100 females: 72.4 (2008-2012 5-year est.); Marriage status: 30.6% never married, 55.6% now married, 5.6% widowed, 8.3% divorced (2008-2012 5-year est.); Foreign born: 0.0% (2008-2012 5-year est.); Ancestry (includes multiple ancestries): 14.5% German, 7.6% American, 6.9% Irish, 5.3% Slovak, 5.3% Dutch (2008-2012 5-year est.).
Economy: Homeowner vacancy rate: 0.0%. Rental vacancy rate: 0.0%. (2008-2012 5-year est.); Employment by occupation: 3.5% management, business, and financial, 0.0% computer, engineering, and science, 3.5% education, legal, community service, arts, and media, 8.8% healthcare practitioners, 22.8% service, 28.1% sales and office, 19.3% natural resources, construction, and maintenance, 14.0% production, transportation, and material moving (2008-2012 5-year est.).
Income: Per capita income: $18,471 (2008-2012 5-year est.); Median household income: $28,594 (2008-2012 5-year est.); Average household income: $48,410 (2008-2012 5-year est.); Percent of households with income of $100,000 or more: 7.9% (2008-2012 5-year est.); Poverty rate: 25.2% (2008-2012 5-year est.).
Education: Percent of population age 25 and over with: High school diploma (including GED) or higher: 87.9% (2008-2012 5-year est.); Bachelor's degree or higher: 4.4% (2008-2012 5-year est.); Master's degree or higher: 0.0% (2008-2012 5-year est.).
Housing: Homeownership rate: 76.2% (2008-2012 5-year est.); Median home value: $56,700 (2008-2012 5-year est.); Median contract rent: $335 per month (2008-2012 5-year est.); Median year structure built: 1965 (2008-2012 5-year est.).
Health Insurance: 62.6% Private; 43.5% Public; 10.7% None. (2008-2012 5-year est.)
Transportation: Commute to work: 96.4% car, 0.0% public transportation, 0.0% walk, 3.6% work from home (2008-2012 5-year est.); Travel time to work: 9.4% less than 15 minutes, 45.3% 15 to 30 minutes, 1.9% 30 to 45 minutes, 32.1% 45 to 60 minutes, 11.3% 60 minutes or more (2008-2012 5-year est.)

COALTON (village). Covers a land area of 0.533 square miles and a water area of 0 square miles. Located at 39.28° N. Lat; 89.30° W. Long. Elevation is 676 feet.
Population: 359 (1990); 307 (2000); 304 (2010); Density: 518.0 persons per square mile (2008-2012 5-year est.); Race: 100.0% White, 0.0% Black/African American, 0.0% Asian, 0.0% American Indian/Alaska Native, 0.0% Native Hawaiian/Other Pacific Islander, 0.0% Some other race, 0.0% Two or more races, 0.7% Hispanic of any race (2008-2012 5-year est.); Average household size: 2.01 (2008-2012 5-year est.); Median age: 49.2 (2008-2012 5-year est.); Males per 100 females: 79.2 (2008-2012 5-year est.); Marriage status: 20.7% never married, 58.9% now married, 10.0% widowed, 10.4% divorced (2008-2012 5-year est.); Foreign born: 0.0% (2008-2012 5-year est.); Ancestry (includes multiple ancestries): 29.7% German, 12.3% Irish, 10.5% English, 7.2% American, 6.2% Polish (2008-2012 5-year est.).
Economy: Homeowner vacancy rate: 0.0%. Rental vacancy rate: 0.0%. (2008-2012 5-year est.); Employment by occupation: 5.0% management, business, and financial, 0.0% computer, engineering, and science, 14.3% education, legal, community service, arts, and media, 4.3% healthcare practitioners, 36.4% service, 19.3% sales and office, 15.0% natural resources, construction, and maintenance, 5.7% production, transportation, and material moving (2008-2012 5-year est.).
Income: Per capita income: $21,487 (2008-2012 5-year est.); Median household income: $28,125 (2008-2012 5-year est.); Average household income: $45,498 (2008-2012 5-year est.); Percent of households with

income of $100,000 or more: 9.5% (2008-2012 5-year est.); Poverty rate: 20.8% (2008-2012 5-year est.).

Education: Percent of population age 25 and over with: High school diploma (including GED) or higher: 88.5% (2008-2012 5-year est.); Bachelor's degree or higher: 12.4% (2008-2012 5-year est.); Master's degree or higher: 1.8% (2008-2012 5-year est.).

Housing: Homeownership rate: 88.3% (2008-2012 5-year est.); Median home value: $59,800 (2008-2012 5-year est.); Median contract rent: $375 per month (2008-2012 5-year est.); Median year structure built: 1969 (2008-2012 5-year est.).

Health Insurance: 73.9% Private; 34.8% Public; 9.4% None. (2008-2012 5-year est.)

Transportation: Commute to work: 97.8% car, 0.0% public transportation, 2.2% walk, 0.0% work from home (2008-2012 5-year est.); Travel time to work: 53.2% less than 15 minutes, 21.6% 15 to 30 minutes, 9.4% 30 to 45 minutes, 7.9% 45 to 60 minutes, 7.9% 60 minutes or more (2008-2012 5-year est.)

COFFEEN (city). Covers a land area of 1.191 square miles and a water area of 0 square miles. Located at 39.09° N. Lat; 89.39° W. Long. Elevation is 630 feet.

Population: 736 (1990); 709 (2000); 685 (2010); Density: 386.1 persons per square mile (2008-2012 5-year est.); Race: 98.9% White, 0.0% Black/African American, 0.4% Asian, 0.0% American Indian/Alaska Native, 0.0% Native Hawaiian/Other Pacific Islander, 0.7% Some other race, 0.7% Two or more races, 0.2% Hispanic of any race (2008-2012 5-year est.); Average household size: 1.84 (2008-2012 5-year est.); Median age: 47.9 (2008-2012 5-year est.); Males per 100 females: 68.5 (2008-2012 5-year est.); Marriage status: 22.5% never married, 40.5% now married, 14.2% widowed, 22.8% divorced (2008-2012 5-year est.); Foreign born: 0.4% (2008-2012 5-year est.); Ancestry (includes multiple ancestries): 20.2% German, 12.8% Irish, 9.6% English, 6.7% American, 2.8% Dutch (2008-2012 5-year est.).

Economy: Homeowner vacancy rate: 0.0%. Rental vacancy rate: 6.9%. (2008-2012 5-year est.); Employment by occupation: 8.3% management, business, and financial, 1.6% computer, engineering, and science, 6.3% education, legal, community service, arts, and media, 7.3% healthcare practitioners, 31.3% service, 26.0% sales and office, 4.7% natural resources, construction, and maintenance, 14.6% production, transportation, and material moving (2008-2012 5-year est.).

Income: Per capita income: $19,947 (2008-2012 5-year est.); Median household income: $27,262 (2008-2012 5-year est.); Average household income: $36,832 (2008-2012 5-year est.); Percent of households with income of $100,000 or more: 5.2% (2008-2012 5-year est.); Poverty rate: 23.3% (2008-2012 5-year est.).

Education: Percent of population age 25 and over with: High school diploma (including GED) or higher: 83.5% (2008-2012 5-year est.); Bachelor's degree or higher: 2.8% (2008-2012 5-year est.); Master's degree or higher: 0.0% (2008-2012 5-year est.).

School District(s)

Hillsboro CUSD 3 (PK-12)
    2011-12 Enrollment: 1,926 . . . . (217) 532-2942

Housing: Homeownership rate: 67.6% (2008-2012 5-year est.); Median home value: $59,100 (2008-2012 5-year est.); Median contract rent: $182 per month (2008-2012 5-year est.); Median year structure built: 1949 (2008-2012 5-year est.).

Health Insurance: 53.5% Private; 49.3% Public; 18.3% None. (2008-2012 5-year est.)

Transportation: Commute to work: 92.1% car, 0.0% public transportation, 1.6% walk, 6.3% work from home (2008-2012 5-year est.); Travel time to work: 40.2% less than 15 minutes, 41.3% 15 to 30 minutes, 7.3% 30 to 45 minutes, 1.7% 45 to 60 minutes, 9.5% 60 minutes or more (2008-2012 5-year est.)

DONNELLSON (village). Covers a land area of 0.325 square miles and a water area of 0 square miles. Located at 39.03° N. Lat; 89.47° W. Long. Elevation is 614 feet.

Population: 167 (1990); 243 (2000); 210 (2010); Density: 698.1 persons per square mile (2008-2012 5-year est.); Race: 100.0% White, 0.0% Black/African American, 0.0% Asian, 0.0% American Indian/Alaska Native, 0.0% Native Hawaiian/Other Pacific Islander, 0.0% Some other race, 0.0% Two or more races, 0.0% Hispanic of any race (2008-2012 5-year est.); Average household size: 2.34 (2008-2012 5-year est.); Median age: 33.5 (2008-2012 5-year est.); Males per 100 females: 89.2 (2008-2012 5-year est.); Marriage status: 26.9% never married, 36.3% now married, 7.5%

widowed, 29.4% divorced (2008-2012 5-year est.); Foreign born: 2.6% (2008-2012 5-year est.); Ancestry (includes multiple ancestries): 14.1% English, 11.0% German, 8.8% Irish, 2.6% Scotch-Irish, 1.8% French (2008-2012 5-year est.).

Economy: Homeowner vacancy rate: 9.8%. Rental vacancy rate: 0.0%. (2008-2012 5-year est.); Employment by occupation: 8.4% management, business, and financial, 0.0% computer, engineering, and science, 3.6% education, legal, community service, arts, and media, 0.0% healthcare practitioners, 20.5% service, 26.5% sales and office, 9.6% natural resources, construction, and maintenance, 31.3% production, transportation, and material moving (2008-2012 5-year est.).

Income: Per capita income: $17,807 (2008-2012 5-year est.); Median household income: $43,021 (2008-2012 5-year est.); Average household income: $42,300 (2008-2012 5-year est.); Percent of households with income of $100,000 or more: 3.1% (2008-2012 5-year est.); Poverty rate: 25.2% (2008-2012 5-year est.).

Education: Percent of population age 25 and over with: High school diploma (including GED) or higher: 79.6% (2008-2012 5-year est.); Bachelor's degree or higher: 6.1% (2008-2012 5-year est.); Master's degree or higher: 4.8% (2008-2012 5-year est.).

Housing: Homeownership rate: 76.3% (2008-2012 5-year est.); Median home value: $52,500 (2008-2012 5-year est.); Median contract rent: $350 per month (2008-2012 5-year est.); Median year structure built: 1966 (2008-2012 5-year est.).

Health Insurance: 51.5% Private; 59.0% Public; 7.9% None. (2008-2012 5-year est.)

Transportation: Commute to work: 92.5% car, 0.0% public transportation, 0.0% walk, 7.5% work from home (2008-2012 5-year est.); Travel time to work: 18.9% less than 15 minutes, 56.8% 15 to 30 minutes, 13.5% 30 to 45 minutes, 2.7% 45 to 60 minutes, 8.1% 60 minutes or more (2008-2012 5-year est.)

FARMERSVILLE (village). Covers a land area of 0.903 square miles and a water area of 0.008 square miles. Located at 39.44° N. Lat; 89.65° W. Long. Elevation is 643 feet.

Population: 698 (1990); 768 (2000); 724 (2010); Density: 701.7 persons per square mile (2008-2012 5-year est.); Race: 99.4% White, 0.0% Black/African American, 0.3% Asian, 0.0% American Indian/Alaska Native, 0.0% Native Hawaiian/Other Pacific Islander, 0.3% Some other race, 0.3% Two or more races, 0.3% Hispanic of any race (2008-2012 5-year est.); Average household size: 1.96 (2008-2012 5-year est.); Median age: 45.4 (2008-2012 5-year est.); Males per 100 females: 77.6 (2008-2012 5-year est.); Marriage status: 20.5% never married, 57.9% now married, 7.2% widowed, 14.4% divorced (2008-2012 5-year est.); Foreign born: 1.4% (2008-2012 5-year est.); Ancestry (includes multiple ancestries): 21.0% German, 10.3% American, 9.6% Irish, 7.7% English, 2.4% Dutch (2008-2012 5-year est.).

Economy: Homeowner vacancy rate: 5.5%. Rental vacancy rate: 0.0%. (2008-2012 5-year est.); Employment by occupation: 9.2% management, business, and financial, 4.3% computer, engineering, and science, 6.9% education, legal, community service, arts, and media, 4.0% healthcare practitioners, 14.5% service, 37.0% sales and office, 7.2% natural resources, construction, and maintenance, 16.8% production, transportation, and material moving (2008-2012 5-year est.).

Income: Per capita income: $29,983 (2008-2012 5-year est.); Median household income: $47,431 (2008-2012 5-year est.); Average household income: $72,866 (2008-2012 5-year est.); Percent of households with income of $100,000 or more: 13.9% (2008-2012 5-year est.); Poverty rate: 18.4% (2008-2012 5-year est.).

Education: Percent of population age 25 and over with: High school diploma (including GED) or higher: 89.7% (2008-2012 5-year est.); Bachelor's degree or higher: 11.4% (2008-2012 5-year est.); Master's degree or higher: 1.9% (2008-2012 5-year est.).

School District(s)

Panhandle CUSD 2 (PK-12)
    2011-12 Enrollment: 514 . . . . (217) 229-4215

Housing: Homeownership rate: 80.2% (2008-2012 5-year est.); Median home value: $87,000 (2008-2012 5-year est.); Median contract rent: $400 per month (2008-2012 5-year est.); Median year structure built: 1974 (2008-2012 5-year est.).

Health Insurance: 70.0% Private; 35.5% Public; 9.1% None. (2008-2012 5-year est.)

Transportation: Commute to work: 88.4% car, 1.2% public transportation, 1.4% walk, 6.6% work from home (2008-2012 5-year est.); Travel time to work: 28.5% less than 15 minutes, 31.6% 15 to 30 minutes, 23.2% 30 to

45 minutes, 8.4% 45 to 60 minutes, 8.4% 60 minutes or more (2008-2012 5-year est.)

FILLMORE (village). Covers a land area of 1.011 square miles and a water area of 0 square miles. Located at 39.12° N. Lat; 89.28° W. Long. Elevation is 633 feet.
Population: 326 (1990); 362 (2000); 330 (2010); Density: 424.4 persons per square mile (2008-2012 5-year est.); Race: 98.8% White, 0.2% Black/African American, 0.9% Asian, 0.0% American Indian/Alaska Native, 0.0% Native Hawaiian/Other Pacific Islander, 0.1% Some other race, 0.0% Two or more races, 0.0% Hispanic of any race (2008-2012 5-year est.); Average household size: 3.04 (2008-2012 5-year est.); Median age: 22.8 (2008-2012 5-year est.); Males per 100 females: 123.4 (2008-2012 5-year est.); Marriage status: 33.7% never married, 54.5% now married, 6.5% widowed, 5.4% divorced (2008-2012 5-year est.); Foreign born: 2.1% (2008-2012 5-year est.); Ancestry (includes multiple ancestries): 11.4% American, 8.6% German, 3.5% English, 3.0% Irish, 2.3% Italian (2008-2012 5-year est.).
Economy: Homeowner vacancy rate: 5.7%. Rental vacancy rate: 0.0%. (2008-2012 5-year est.); Employment by occupation: 10.0% management, business, and financial, 4.6% computer, engineering, and science, 6.2% education, legal, community service, arts, and media, 7.7% healthcare practitioners, 20.8% service, 23.8% sales and office, 6.9% natural resources, construction, and maintenance, 20.0% production, transportation, and material moving (2008-2012 5-year est.).
Income: Per capita income: $12,643 (2008-2012 5-year est.); Median household income: $32,386 (2008-2012 5-year est.); Average household income: $43,930 (2008-2012 5-year est.); Percent of households with income of $100,000 or more: 9.9% (2008-2012 5-year est.); Poverty rate: 16.3% (2008-2012 5-year est.).
Education: Percent of population age 25 and over with: High school diploma (including GED) or higher: 85.4% (2008-2012 5-year est.); Bachelor's degree or higher: 6.3% (2008-2012 5-year est.); Master's degree or higher: 2.4% (2008-2012 5-year est.).
Housing: Homeownership rate: 82.3% (2008-2012 5-year est.); Median home value: $46,000 (2008-2012 5-year est.); Median contract rent: $288 per month (2008-2012 5-year est.); Median year structure built: 1959 (2008-2012 5-year est.).
Health Insurance: 58.4% Private; 46.6% Public; 7.8% None. (2008-2012 5-year est.)
Transportation: Commute to work: 98.5% car, 0.0% public transportation, 0.0% walk, 0.0% work from home (2008-2012 5-year est.); Travel time to work: 12.8% less than 15 minutes, 48.1% 15 to 30 minutes, 27.1% 30 to 45 minutes, 2.3% 45 to 60 minutes, 9.8% 60 minutes or more (2008-2012 5-year est.)

HARVEL (village). Covers a land area of 0.723 square miles and a water area of 0 square miles. Located at 39.36° N. Lat; 89.53° W. Long. Elevation is 636 feet.
Population: 213 (1990); 235 (2000); 223 (2010); Density: 268.4 persons per square mile (2008-2012 5-year est.); Race: 100.0% White, 0.0% Black/African American, 0.0% Asian, 0.0% American Indian/Alaska Native, 0.0% Native Hawaiian/Other Pacific Islander, 0.0% Some other race, 0.0% Two or more races, 0.0% Hispanic of any race (2008-2012 5-year est.); Average household size: 2.16 (2008-2012 5-year est.); Median age: 37.5 (2008-2012 5-year est.); Males per 100 females: 120.5 (2008-2012 5-year est.); Marriage status: 26.5% never married, 51.5% now married, 15.4% widowed, 6.6% divorced (2008-2012 5-year est.); Foreign born: 0.0% (2008-2012 5-year est.); Ancestry (includes multiple ancestries): 11.3% German, 3.6% French, 3.1% Dutch, 2.6% English, 2.1% American (2008-2012 5-year est.).
Economy: Homeowner vacancy rate: 4.2%. Rental vacancy rate: 0.0%. (2008-2012 5-year est.); Employment by occupation: 2.5% management, business, and financial, 1.3% computer, engineering, and science, 6.3% education, legal, community service, arts, and media, 2.5% healthcare practitioners, 30.4% service, 17.7% sales and office, 25.3% natural resources, construction, and maintenance, 13.9% production, transportation, and material moving (2008-2012 5-year est.).
Income: Per capita income: $17,595 (2008-2012 5-year est.); Median household income: $22,188 (2008-2012 5-year est.); Average household income: $39,097 (2008-2012 5-year est.); Percent of households with income of $100,000 or more: 4.4% (2008-2012 5-year est.); Poverty rate: 34.5% (2008-2012 5-year est.).
Education: Percent of population age 25 and over with: High school diploma (including GED) or higher: 86.2% (2008-2012 5-year est.);

Bachelor's degree or higher: 7.3% (2008-2012 5-year est.); Master's degree or higher: 3.3% (2008-2012 5-year est.).
Housing: Homeownership rate: 71.1% (2008-2012 5-year est.); Median home value: $72,000 (2008-2012 5-year est.); Median contract rent: $433 per month (2008-2012 5-year est.); Median year structure built: 1942 (2008-2012 5-year est.).
Health Insurance: 58.2% Private; 57.2% Public; 5.7% None. (2008-2012 5-year est.)
Transportation: Commute to work: 92.4% car, 6.3% public transportation, 0.0% walk, 0.0% work from home (2008-2012 5-year est.); Travel time to work: 46.8% less than 15 minutes, 2.5% 15 to 30 minutes, 27.8% 30 to 45 minutes, 11.4% 45 to 60 minutes, 11.4% 60 minutes or more (2008-2012 5-year est.)

HILLSBORO (city). County seat. Covers a land area of 6.552 square miles and a water area of 1.772 square miles. Located at 39.17° N. Lat; 89.47° W. Long. Elevation is 633 feet.
History: Incorporated 1855.
Population: 4,400 (1990); 4,359 (2000); 6,207 (2010); Density: 1,123.9 persons per square mile (2008-2012 5-year est.); Race: 73.8% White, 23.4% Black/African American, 0.8% Asian, 0.0% American Indian/Alaska Native, 0.0% Native Hawaiian/Other Pacific Islander, 2.0% Some other race, 1.3% Two or more races, 4.2% Hispanic of any race (2008-2012 5-year est.); Average household size: 2.12 (2008-2012 5-year est.); Median age: 39.2 (2008-2012 5-year est.); Males per 100 females: 233.8 (2008-2012 5-year est.); Marriage status: 40.1% never married, 38.1% now married, 6.1% widowed, 15.7% divorced (2008-2012 5-year est.); Foreign born: 2.2% (2008-2012 5-year est.); Ancestry (includes multiple ancestries): 16.3% German, 10.1% Irish, 8.5% American, 7.8% English, 3.3% Italian (2008-2012 5-year est.).
Economy: Homeowner vacancy rate: 3.5%. Rental vacancy rate: 0.0%. (2008-2012 5-year est.); Employment by occupation: 8.0% management, business, and financial, 1.4% computer, engineering, and science, 6.0% education, legal, community service, arts, and media, 13.6% healthcare practitioners, 34.3% service, 16.1% sales and office, 12.0% natural resources, construction, and maintenance, 8.5% production, transportation, and material moving (2008-2012 5-year est.).
Income: Per capita income: $16,329 (2008-2012 5-year est.); Median household income: $42,210 (2008-2012 5-year est.); Average household income: $62,420 (2008-2012 5-year est.); Percent of households with income of $100,000 or more: 14.3% (2008-2012 5-year est.); Poverty rate: 5.9% (2008-2012 5-year est.).
Education: Percent of population age 25 and over with: High school diploma (including GED) or higher: 80.5% (2008-2012 5-year est.); Bachelor's degree or higher: 7.6% (2008-2012 5-year est.); Master's degree or higher: 3.7% (2008-2012 5-year est.).

School District(s)
Hillsboro CUSD 3 (PK-12)
    2011-12 Enrollment: 1,926 . . . . (217) 532-2942
Housing: Homeownership rate: 66.2% (2008-2012 5-year est.); Median home value: $80,700 (2008-2012 5-year est.); Median contract rent: $495 per month (2008-2012 5-year est.); Median year structure built: 1955 (2008-2012 5-year est.).
Health Insurance: 70.5% Private; 34.1% Public; 9.5% None. (2008-2012 5-year est.)
Hospitals: Hillsboro Area Hospital (100 beds)
Safety: Violent crime rate: 9.7 per 10,000 population; Property crime rate: 123.2 per 10,000 population (2012).
Transportation: Commute to work: 86.8% car, 0.0% public transportation, 4.8% walk, 7.4% work from home (2008-2012 5-year est.); Travel time to work: 59.7% less than 15 minutes, 26.2% 15 to 30 minutes, 2.8% 30 to 45 minutes, 5.9% 45 to 60 minutes, 5.3% 60 minutes or more (2008-2012 5-year est.)
Additional Information Contacts
Hillsboro Chamber of Commerce . . . . (217) 532-3711
    http://www.hillsborochamber.net

IRVING (village). Covers a land area of 0.840 square miles and a water area of 0 square miles. Located at 39.21° N. Lat; 89.41° W. Long. Elevation is 656 feet.
Population: 516 (1990); 2,484 (2000); 495 (2010); Density: 395.0 persons per square mile (2008-2012 5-year est.); Race: 98.8% White, 1.2% Black/African American, 0.0% Asian, 0.0% American Indian/Alaska Native, 0.0% Native Hawaiian/Other Pacific Islander, 0.0% Some other race, 0.0% Two or more races, 0.0% Hispanic of any race (2008-2012 5-year est.);

Average household size: 2.11 (2008-2012 5-year est.); Median age: 40.5 (2008-2012 5-year est.); Males per 100 females: 101.2 (2008-2012 5-year est.); Marriage status: 24.9% never married, 47.2% now married, 12.8% widowed, 15.1% divorced (2008-2012 5-year est.); Foreign born: 0.0% (2008-2012 5-year est.); Ancestry (includes multiple ancestries): 19.9% German, 9.9% Irish, 9.3% English, 3.3% American, 1.8% Russian (2008-2012 5-year est.).

Economy: Homeowner vacancy rate: 0.0%. Rental vacancy rate: 0.0%. (2008-2012 5-year est.); Employment by occupation: 8.8% management, business, and financial, 1.5% computer, engineering, and science, 5.9% education, legal, community service, arts, and media, 5.1% healthcare practitioners, 12.5% service, 14.7% sales and office, 10.3% natural resources, construction, and maintenance, 41.2% production, transportation, and material moving (2008-2012 5-year est.).

Income: Per capita income: $15,426 (2008-2012 5-year est.); Median household income: $38,750 (2008-2012 5-year est.); Average household income: $41,004 (2008-2012 5-year est.); Percent of households with income of $100,000 or more: 7.2% (2008-2012 5-year est.); Poverty rate: 18.4% (2008-2012 5-year est.).

Education: Percent of population age 25 and over with: High school diploma (including GED) or higher: 83.0% (2008-2012 5-year est.); Bachelor's degree or higher: 7.8% (2008-2012 5-year est.); Master's degree or higher: 1.9% (2008-2012 5-year est.).

Housing: Homeownership rate: 85.0% (2008-2012 5-year est.); Median home value: $60,000 (2008-2012 5-year est.); Median contract rent: $271 per month (2008-2012 5-year est.); Median year structure built: 1948 (2008-2012 5-year est.).

Health Insurance: 39.8% Private; 49.7% Public; 19.9% None. (2008-2012 5-year est.)

Safety: Violent crime rate: 0.0 per 10,000 population; Property crime rate: 224.0 per 10,000 population (2012).

Transportation: Commute to work: 100.0% car, 0.0% public transportation, 0.0% walk, 0.0% work from home (2008-2012 5-year est.); Travel time to work: 36.1% less than 15 minutes, 37.6% 15 to 30 minutes, 9.0% 30 to 45 minutes, 9.8% 45 to 60 minutes, 7.5% 60 minutes or more (2008-2012 5-year est.)

LITCHFIELD (city). Covers a land area of 6.448 square miles and a water area of 0.375 square miles. Located at 39.18° N. Lat; 89.64° W. Long. Elevation is 689 feet.

History: Litchfield was incorporated in 1859 and developed around a coal field. An early employer was the International Stove Company.

Population: 6,883 (1990); 6,815 (2000); 6,939 (2010); Density: 1,099.0 persons per square mile (2008-2012 5-year est.); Race: 98.3% White, 1.0% Black/African American, 0.3% Asian, 0.1% American Indian/Alaska Native, 0.0% Native Hawaiian/Other Pacific Islander, 0.3% Some other race, 0.0% Two or more races, 0.4% Hispanic of any race (2008-2012 5-year est.); Average household size: 2.11 (2008-2012 5-year est.); Median age: 41.6 (2008-2012 5-year est.); Males per 100 females: 71.9 (2008-2012 5-year est.); Marriage status: 19.1% never married, 58.8% now married, 8.2% widowed, 14.0% divorced (2008-2012 5-year est.); Foreign born: 0.8% (2008-2012 5-year est.); Ancestry (includes multiple ancestries): 29.0% German, 8.9% American, 8.8% English, 8.5% Irish, 5.4% Italian (2008-2012 5-year est.).

Economy: Homeowner vacancy rate: 3.3%. Rental vacancy rate: 0.0%. (2008-2012 5-year est.); Employment by occupation: 10.8% management, business, and financial, 2.5% computer, engineering, and science, 10.5% education, legal, community service, arts, and media, 5.8% healthcare practitioners, 24.6% service, 22.0% sales and office, 10.5% natural resources, construction, and maintenance, 13.2% production, transportation, and material moving (2008-2012 5-year est.).

Income: Per capita income: $19,676 (2008-2012 5-year est.); Median household income: $34,141 (2008-2012 5-year est.); Average household income: $45,994 (2008-2012 5-year est.); Percent of households with income of $100,000 or more: 8.0% (2008-2012 5-year est.); Poverty rate: 21.3% (2008-2012 5-year est.).

Taxes: Total city taxes per capita: $312 (2011); City property taxes per capita: $274 (2011).

Education: Percent of population age 25 and over with: High school diploma (including GED) or higher: 83.7% (2008-2012 5-year est.); Bachelor's degree or higher: 14.8% (2008-2012 5-year est.); Master's degree or higher: 5.1% (2008-2012 5-year est.).

School District(s)

Litchfield CUSD 12 (PK-12)
    2011-12 Enrollment: 1,528 . . . . (217) 324-2157

Vocational/Technical School(s)

Tri-County Beauty Academy (Private, For-profit)
    Fall 2012 Enrollment: 19 . . . . (217) 324-9062
    2012-13 Tuition: $12,150

Housing: Homeownership rate: 64.6% (2008-2012 5-year est.); Median home value: $78,500 (2008-2012 5-year est.); Median contract rent: $388 per month (2008-2012 5-year est.); Median year structure built: 1957 (2008-2012 5-year est.).

Health Insurance: 66.7% Private; 48.1% Public; 4.8% None. (2008-2012 5-year est.)

Hospitals: St. Francis Hospital (25 beds)

Safety: Violent crime rate: 16.0 per 10,000 population; Property crime rate: 318.3 per 10,000 population (2012).

Transportation: Commute to work: 93.8% car, 0.4% public transportation, 1.1% walk, 3.4% work from home (2008-2012 5-year est.); Travel time to work: 58.8% less than 15 minutes, 12.8% 15 to 30 minutes, 8.2% 30 to 45 minutes, 11.7% 45 to 60 minutes, 8.4% 60 minutes or more (2008-2012 5-year est.)

Airports: Litchfield Municipal Airport (general aviation)

Additional Information Contacts

City of Litchfield . . . . (217) 324-2022
    http://www.cityoflitchfieldil.com
Litchfield Chamber of Commerce . . . . (217) 324-2533
    http://www.litchfieldchamber.com

NOKOMIS (city). Covers a land area of 1.304 square miles and a water area of 0 square miles. Located at 39.30° N. Lat; 89.29° W. Long. Elevation is 673 feet.

History: Incorporated 1867.

Population: 2,534 (1990); 2,389 (2000); 2,256 (2010); Density: 1,799.9 persons per square mile (2008-2012 5-year est.); Race: 99.2% White, 0.1% Black/African American, 0.4% Asian, 0.0% American Indian/Alaska Native, 0.0% Native Hawaiian/Other Pacific Islander, 0.3% Some other race, 0.2% Two or more races, 0.6% Hispanic of any race (2008-2012 5-year est.); Average household size: 2.10 (2008-2012 5-year est.); Median age: 42.9 (2008-2012 5-year est.); Males per 100 females: 89.9 (2008-2012 5-year est.); Marriage status: 15.7% never married, 58.7% now married, 10.2% widowed, 15.4% divorced (2008-2012 5-year est.); Foreign born: 0.9% (2008-2012 5-year est.); Ancestry (includes multiple ancestries): 30.1% German, 11.4% Irish, 7.2% English, 7.1% American, 4.9% French (2008-2012 5-year est.).

Economy: Homeowner vacancy rate: 2.2%. Rental vacancy rate: 5.6%. (2008-2012 5-year est.); Employment by occupation: 12.8% management, business, and financial, 3.4% computer, engineering, and science, 8.0% education, legal, community service, arts, and media, 2.6% healthcare practitioners, 15.6% service, 30.3% sales and office, 9.5% natural resources, construction, and maintenance, 17.8% production, transportation, and material moving (2008-2012 5-year est.).

Income: Per capita income: $22,749 (2008-2012 5-year est.); Median household income: $37,667 (2008-2012 5-year est.); Average household income: $52,956 (2008-2012 5-year est.); Percent of households with income of $100,000 or more: 13.5% (2008-2012 5-year est.); Poverty rate: 7.8% (2008-2012 5-year est.).

Education: Percent of population age 25 and over with: High school diploma (including GED) or higher: 88.0% (2008-2012 5-year est.); Bachelor's degree or higher: 11.5% (2008-2012 5-year est.); Master's degree or higher: 5.4% (2008-2012 5-year est.).

School District(s)

Christian/montgomery Roe (PK-12)
    2011-12 Enrollment: n/a . . . . (217) 824-4730
Nokomis CUSD 22 (PK-12)
    2011-12 Enrollment: 676 . . . . (217) 563-7311

Housing: Homeownership rate: 71.7% (2008-2012 5-year est.); Median home value: $61,000 (2008-2012 5-year est.); Median contract rent: $402 per month (2008-2012 5-year est.); Median year structure built: 1951 (2008-2012 5-year est.).

Health Insurance: 74.2% Private; 40.4% Public; 6.3% None. (2008-2012 5-year est.)

Safety: Violent crime rate: 58.1 per 10,000 population; Property crime rate: 317.2 per 10,000 population (2012).

Transportation: Commute to work: 92.9% car, 0.4% public transportation, 4.3% walk, 1.7% work from home (2008-2012 5-year est.); Travel time to work: 44.7% less than 15 minutes, 22.5% 15 to 30 minutes, 12.7% 30 to 45 minutes, 5.3% 45 to 60 minutes, 14.9% 60 minutes or more (2008-2012 5-year est.)

Additional Information Contacts
Nokomis Chamber of Commerce. . . . .
  http://nokomischamberofcommerce.com

OHLMAN (village). Covers a land area of 0.385 square miles and a water area of 0 square miles. Located at 39.34° N. Lat; 89.22° W. Long. Elevation is 689 feet.

History: As of the 2000 Census, the village had a total population of 0. A recount in 2004 issued a revised population of 148.
Population: 82 (1990); n/a (2000); 135 (2010); Density: 252.0 persons per square mile (2008-2012 5-year est.); Race: 95.9% White, 1.0% Black/African American, 0.0% Asian, 3.1% American Indian/Alaska Native, 0.0% Native Hawaiian/Other Pacific Islander, 0.0% Some other race, 0.0% Two or more races, 0.0% Hispanic of any race (2008-2012 5-year est.); Average household size: 2.02 (2008-2012 5-year est.); Median age: 58.4 (2008-2012 5-year est.); Males per 100 females: 90.2 (2008-2012 5-year est.); Marriage status: 18.2% never married, 54.5% now married, 15.6% widowed, 11.7% divorced (2008-2012 5-year est.); Foreign born: 0.0% (2008-2012 5-year est.); Ancestry (includes multiple ancestries): 34.0% German, 14.4% Irish, 14.4% American, 9.3% English, 3.1% Pennsylvania German (2008-2012 5-year est.).
Economy: Homeowner vacancy rate: 12.0%. Rental vacancy rate: 0.0%. (2008-2012 5-year est.); Employment by occupation: 0.0% management, business, and financial, 4.3% computer, engineering, and science, 0.0% education, legal, community service, arts, and media, 0.0% healthcare practitioners, 43.5% service, 21.7% sales and office, 0.0% natural resources, construction, and maintenance, 30.4% production, transportation, and material moving (2008-2012 5-year est.).
Income: Per capita income: $19,372 (2008-2012 5-year est.); Median household income: $36,250 (2008-2012 5-year est.); Average household income: $40,225 (2008-2012 5-year est.); Percent of households with income of $100,000 or more: 4.2% (2008-2012 5-year est.); Poverty rate: 17.5% (2008-2012 5-year est.).
Education: Percent of population age 25 and over with: High school diploma (including GED) or higher: 84.0% (2008-2012 5-year est.); Bachelor's degree or higher: 16.0% (2008-2012 5-year est.); Master's degree or higher: 0.0% (2008-2012 5-year est.).
Housing: Homeownership rate: 91.7% (2008-2012 5-year est.); Median home value: $50,000 (2008-2012 5-year est.); Median contract rent: <$101 per month (2008-2012 5-year est.); Median year structure built: Before 1940 (2008-2012 5-year est.).
Health Insurance: 66.0% Private; 51.5% Public; 11.3% None. (2008-2012 5-year est.)
Transportation: Commute to work: 100.0% car, 0.0% public transportation, 0.0% walk, 0.0% work from home (2008-2012 5-year est.); Travel time to work: 60.9% less than 15 minutes, 21.7% 15 to 30 minutes, 8.7% 30 to 45 minutes, 0.0% 45 to 60 minutes, 8.7% 60 minutes or more (2008-2012 5-year est.)

PANAMA (village). Covers a land area of 0.359 square miles and a water area of <.001 square miles. Located at 39.03° N. Lat; 89.52° W. Long.

Population: 294 (1990); 323 (2000); 343 (2010); Density: 500.8 persons per square mile (2008-2012 5-year est.); Race: 100.0% White, 0.0% Black/African American, 0.0% Asian, 0.0% American Indian/Alaska Native, 0.0% Native Hawaiian/Other Pacific Islander, 0.0% Some other race, 0.0% Two or more races, 8.9% Hispanic of any race (2008-2012 5-year est.); Average household size: 1.73 (2008-2012 5-year est.); Median age: 47.9 (2008-2012 5-year est.); Males per 100 females: 68.2 (2008-2012 5-year est.); Marriage status: 22.4% never married, 36.1% now married, 21.1% widowed, 20.4% divorced (2008-2012 5-year est.); Foreign born: 0.0% (2008-2012 5-year est.); Ancestry (includes multiple ancestries): 15.0% German, 7.2% Irish, 6.1% English, 5.0% Italian, 2.2% American (2008-2012 5-year est.).
Economy: Homeowner vacancy rate: 5.9%. Rental vacancy rate: 0.0%. (2008-2012 5-year est.); Employment by occupation: 6.1% management, business, and financial, 0.0% computer, engineering, and science, 6.1% education, legal, community service, arts, and media, 0.0% healthcare practitioners, 22.4% service, 14.3% sales and office, 16.3% natural resources, construction, and maintenance, 34.7% production, transportation, and material moving (2008-2012 5-year est.).
Income: Per capita income: $16,609 (2008-2012 5-year est.); Median household income: $24,375 (2008-2012 5-year est.); Average household income: $32,955 (2008-2012 5-year est.); Percent of households with

income of $100,000 or more: 4.8% (2008-2012 5-year est.); Poverty rate: 18.3% (2008-2012 5-year est.).
Education: Percent of population age 25 and over with: High school diploma (including GED) or higher: 78.9% (2008-2012 5-year est.); Bachelor's degree or higher: 0.0% (2008-2012 5-year est.); Master's degree or higher: 0.0% (2008-2012 5-year est.).
Housing: Homeownership rate: 76.9% (2008-2012 5-year est.); Median home value: $55,900 (2008-2012 5-year est.); Median contract rent: $431 per month (2008-2012 5-year est.); Median year structure built: Before 1940 (2008-2012 5-year est.).
Health Insurance: 67.8% Private; 47.2% Public; 14.4% None. (2008-2012 5-year est.)
Transportation: Commute to work: 93.9% car, 0.0% public transportation, 0.0% walk, 6.1% work from home (2008-2012 5-year est.); Travel time to work: 13.0% less than 15 minutes, 43.5% 15 to 30 minutes, 21.7% 30 to 45 minutes, 4.3% 45 to 60 minutes, 17.4% 60 minutes or more (2008-2012 5-year est.)

RAYMOND (village). Covers a land area of 1.321 square miles and a water area of 0 square miles. Located at 39.32° N. Lat; 89.58° W. Long. Elevation is 643 feet.

Population: 820 (1990); 927 (2000); 1,006 (2010); Density: 685.1 persons per square mile (2008-2012 5-year est.); Race: 98.6% White, 0.1% Black/African American, 1.2% Asian, 0.0% American Indian/Alaska Native, 0.0% Native Hawaiian/Other Pacific Islander, 0.1% Some other race, 0.1% Two or more races, 0.3% Hispanic of any race (2008-2012 5-year est.); Average household size: 2.37 (2008-2012 5-year est.); Median age: 40.0 (2008-2012 5-year est.); Males per 100 females: 85.8 (2008-2012 5-year est.); Marriage status: 22.8% never married, 61.9% now married, 9.1% widowed, 6.3% divorced (2008-2012 5-year est.); Foreign born: 1.4% (2008-2012 5-year est.); Ancestry (includes multiple ancestries): 25.9% German, 14.4% English, 9.9% Irish, 3.9% American, 3.6% Italian (2008-2012 5-year est.).
Economy: Homeowner vacancy rate: 0.0%. Rental vacancy rate: 6.8%. (2008-2012 5-year est.); Employment by occupation: 9.7% management, business, and financial, 3.3% computer, engineering, and science, 8.9% education, legal, community service, arts, and media, 6.7% healthcare practitioners, 19.2% service, 20.6% sales and office, 17.8% natural resources, construction, and maintenance, 13.9% production, transportation, and material moving (2008-2012 5-year est.).
Income: Per capita income: $20,167 (2008-2012 5-year est.); Median household income: $45,536 (2008-2012 5-year est.); Average household income: $52,620 (2008-2012 5-year est.); Percent of households with income of $100,000 or more: 12.3% (2008-2012 5-year est.); Poverty rate: 18.7% (2008-2012 5-year est.).
Education: Percent of population age 25 and over with: High school diploma (including GED) or higher: 88.0% (2008-2012 5-year est.); Bachelor's degree or higher: 10.9% (2008-2012 5-year est.); Master's degree or higher: 5.0% (2008-2012 5-year est.).
School District(s)
Panhandle CUSD 2 (PK-12)
    2011-12 Enrollment: 514. . . . . (217) 229-4215
Housing: Homeownership rate: 85.6% (2008-2012 5-year est.); Median home value: $76,700 (2008-2012 5-year est.); Median contract rent: $414 per month (2008-2012 5-year est.); Median year structure built: 1960 (2008-2012 5-year est.).
Health Insurance: 67.0% Private; 40.0% Public; 7.4% None. (2008-2012 5-year est.)
Safety: Violent crime rate: 30.2 per 10,000 population; Property crime rate: 20.1 per 10,000 population (2012).
Transportation: Commute to work: 90.8% car, 0.0% public transportation, 0.3% walk, 6.5% work from home (2008-2012 5-year est.); Travel time to work: 32.9% less than 15 minutes, 28.8% 15 to 30 minutes, 15.6% 30 to 45 minutes, 13.3% 45 to 60 minutes, 9.5% 60 minutes or more (2008-2012 5-year est.)

SCHRAM CITY (village). Covers a land area of 0.733 square miles and a water area of 0 square miles. Located at 39.16° N. Lat; 89.46° W. Long. Elevation is 607 feet.

Population: 692 (1990); 653 (2000); 586 (2010); Density: 581.5 persons per square mile (2008-2012 5-year est.); Race: 100.0% White, 0.0% Black/African American, 0.0% Asian, 0.0% American Indian/Alaska Native, 0.0% Native Hawaiian/Other Pacific Islander, 0.0% Some other race, 0.0% Two or more races, 0.9% Hispanic of any race (2008-2012 5-year est.); Average household size: 1.94 (2008-2012 5-year est.); Median age: 50.5

(2008-2012 5-year est.); Males per 100 females: 86.0 (2008-2012 5-year est.); Marriage status: 15.0% never married, 66.9% now married, 11.7% widowed, 6.4% divorced (2008-2012 5-year est.); Foreign born: 0.9% (2008-2012 5-year est.); Ancestry (includes multiple ancestries): 27.0% German, 12.9% Irish, 9.4% English, 9.2% Italian, 4.2% American (2008-2012 5-year est.).

Economy: Homeowner vacancy rate: 3.6%. Rental vacancy rate: 0.0%. (2008-2012 5-year est.); Employment by occupation: 9.5% management, business, and financial, 6.1% computer, engineering, and science, 6.7% education, legal, community service, arts, and media, 9.5% healthcare practitioners, 20.1% service, 23.5% sales and office, 8.9% natural resources, construction, and maintenance, 15.6% production, transportation, and material moving (2008-2012 5-year est.).

Income: Per capita income: $22,754 (2008-2012 5-year est.); Median household income: $42,000 (2008-2012 5-year est.); Average household income: $46,470 (2008-2012 5-year est.); Percent of households with income of $100,000 or more: 5.9% (2008-2012 5-year est.); Poverty rate: 13.8% (2008-2012 5-year est.).

Education: Percent of population age 25 and over with: High school diploma (including GED) or higher: 80.7% (2008-2012 5-year est.); Bachelor's degree or higher: 6.4% (2008-2012 5-year est.); Master's degree or higher: 2.1% (2008-2012 5-year est.).

Housing: Homeownership rate: 78.6% (2008-2012 5-year est.); Median home value: $71,400 (2008-2012 5-year est.); Median contract rent: $481 per month (2008-2012 5-year est.); Median year structure built: 1956 (2008-2012 5-year est.).

Health Insurance: 70.2% Private; 54.9% Public; 5.6% None. (2008-2012 5-year est.)

Transportation: Commute to work: 92.1% car, 1.7% public transportation, 0.6% walk, 4.0% work from home (2008-2012 5-year est.); Travel time to work: 51.8% less than 15 minutes, 25.3% 15 to 30 minutes, 4.1% 30 to 45 minutes, 2.4% 45 to 60 minutes, 16.5% 60 minutes or more (2008-2012 5-year est.).

TAYLOR SPRINGS (village). Covers a land area of 1.004 square miles and a water area of 0.033 square miles. Located at 39.13° N. Lat; 89.50° W. Long. Elevation is 627 feet.

Population: 670 (1990); 583 (2000); 690 (2010); Density: 591.4 persons per square mile (2008-2012 5-year est.); Race: 98.0% White, 0.0% Black/African American, 2.0% Asian, 0.0% American Indian/Alaska Native, 0.0% Native Hawaiian/Other Pacific Islander, 0.0% Some other race, 0.0% Two or more races, 0.3% Hispanic of any race (2008-2012 5-year est.); Average household size: 2.10 (2008-2012 5-year est.); Median age: 49.4 (2008-2012 5-year est.); Males per 100 females: 68.8 (2008-2012 5-year est.); Marriage status: 14.7% never married, 45.5% now married, 23.3% widowed, 16.5% divorced (2008-2012 5-year est.); Foreign born: 0.7% (2008-2012 5-year est.); Ancestry (includes multiple ancestries): 12.6% American, 12.3% German, 9.3% Irish, 6.4% English, 3.5% Italian (2008-2012 5-year est.).

Economy: Homeowner vacancy rate: 0.0%. Rental vacancy rate: 15.0%. (2008-2012 5-year est.); Employment by occupation: 8.3% management, business, and financial, 8.3% computer, engineering, and science, 2.9% education, legal, community service, arts, and media, 12.7% healthcare practitioners, 20.0% service, 23.9% sales and office, 10.7% natural resources, construction, and maintenance, 13.2% production, transportation, and material moving (2008-2012 5-year est.).

Income: Per capita income: $19,261 (2008-2012 5-year est.); Median household income: $35,875 (2008-2012 5-year est.); Average household income: $47,711 (2008-2012 5-year est.); Percent of households with income of $100,000 or more: 11.4% (2008-2012 5-year est.); Poverty rate: 16.8% (2008-2012 5-year est.).

Education: Percent of population age 25 and over with: High school diploma (including GED) or higher: 86.4% (2008-2012 5-year est.); Bachelor's degree or higher: 9.2% (2008-2012 5-year est.); Master's degree or higher: 2.2% (2008-2012 5-year est.).

Housing: Homeownership rate: 78.5% (2008-2012 5-year est.); Median home value: $70,300 (2008-2012 5-year est.); Median contract rent: $415 per month (2008-2012 5-year est.); Median year structure built: 1947 (2008-2012 5-year est.).

Health Insurance: 62.6% Private; 51.1% Public; 5.6% None. (2008-2012 5-year est.)

Transportation: Commute to work: 89.7% car, 0.0% public transportation, 0.5% walk, 9.3% work from home (2008-2012 5-year est.); Travel time to work: 64.2% less than 15 minutes, 19.3% 15 to 30 minutes, 5.1% 30 to 45

minutes, 3.4% 45 to 60 minutes, 8.0% 60 minutes or more (2008-2012 5-year est.)

WAGGONER (village). Covers a land area of 0.263 square miles and a water area of 0 square miles. Located at 39.38° N. Lat; 89.65° W. Long. Elevation is 640 feet.

Population: 221 (1990); 245 (2000); 266 (2010); Density: 637.9 persons per square mile (2008-2012 5-year est.); Race: 97.0% White, 0.0% Black/African American, 0.0% Asian, 0.0% American Indian/Alaska Native, 0.0% Native Hawaiian/Other Pacific Islander, 3.0% Some other race, 0.0% Two or more races, 3.0% Hispanic of any race (2008-2012 5-year est.); Average household size: 2.58 (2008-2012 5-year est.); Median age: 30.7 (2008-2012 5-year est.); Males per 100 females: 88.8 (2008-2012 5-year est.); Marriage status: 34.9% never married, 42.1% now married, 6.3% widowed, 16.7% divorced (2008-2012 5-year est.); Foreign born: 0.0% (2008-2012 5-year est.); Ancestry (includes multiple ancestries): 28.0% German, 20.8% Irish, 11.9% American, 6.5% English, 4.8% Polish (2008-2012 5-year est.).

Economy: Homeowner vacancy rate: 0.0%. Rental vacancy rate: 0.0%. (2008-2012 5-year est.); Employment by occupation: 7.2% management, business, and financial, 0.0% computer, engineering, and science, 5.8% education, legal, community service, arts, and media, 1.4% healthcare practitioners, 7.2% service, 26.1% sales and office, 17.4% natural resources, construction, and maintenance, 34.8% production, transportation, and material moving (2008-2012 5-year est.).

Income: Per capita income: $14,546 (2008-2012 5-year est.); Median household income: $31,607 (2008-2012 5-year est.); Average household income: $38,575 (2008-2012 5-year est.); Percent of households with income of $100,000 or more: 1.5% (2008-2012 5-year est.); Poverty rate: 35.7% (2008-2012 5-year est.).

Education: Percent of population age 25 and over with: High school diploma (including GED) or higher: 76.5% (2008-2012 5-year est.); Bachelor's degree or higher: 2.0% (2008-2012 5-year est.); Master's degree or higher: 0.0% (2008-2012 5-year est.).

Housing: Homeownership rate: 80.0% (2008-2012 5-year est.); Median home value: $43,000 (2008-2012 5-year est.); Median contract rent: $361 per month (2008-2012 5-year est.); Median year structure built: 1962 (2008-2012 5-year est.).

Health Insurance: 45.2% Private; 47.0% Public; 16.1% None. (2008-2012 5-year est.)

Transportation: Commute to work: 98.5% car, 0.0% public transportation, 0.0% walk, 1.5% work from home (2008-2012 5-year est.); Travel time to work: 15.2% less than 15 minutes, 33.3% 15 to 30 minutes, 43.9% 30 to 45 minutes, 3.0% 45 to 60 minutes, 4.5% 60 minutes or more (2008-2012 5-year est.)

WALSHVILLE (village). Covers a land area of 0.254 square miles and a water area of 0 square miles. Located at 39.07° N. Lat; 89.62° W. Long. Elevation is 617 feet.

Population: 44 (1990); 89 (2000); 64 (2010); Density: 208.9 persons per square mile (2008-2012 5-year est.); Race: 100.0% White, 0.0% Black/African American, 0.0% Asian, 0.0% American Indian/Alaska Native, 0.0% Native Hawaiian/Other Pacific Islander, 0.0% Some other race, 0.0% Two or more races, 0.0% Hispanic of any race (2008-2012 5-year est.); Average household size: 2.41 (2008-2012 5-year est.); Median age: 24.8 (2008-2012 5-year est.); Males per 100 females: 82.8 (2008-2012 5-year est.); Marriage status: 64.3% never married, 28.6% now married, 0.0% widowed, 7.1% divorced (2008-2012 5-year est.); Foreign born: 0.0% (2008-2012 5-year est.); Ancestry (includes multiple ancestries): 43.4% American, 17.0% German, 11.3% Slovak, 9.4% Scottish, 5.7% Norwegian (2008-2012 5-year est.).

Economy: Homeowner vacancy rate: 24.0%. Rental vacancy rate: 0.0%. (2008-2012 5-year est.); Employment by occupation: 0.0% management, business, and financial, 0.0% computer, engineering, and science, 0.0% education, legal, community service, arts, and media, 3.3% healthcare practitioners, 40.0% service, 10.0% sales and office, 36.7% natural resources, construction, and maintenance, 10.0% production, transportation, and material moving (2008-2012 5-year est.).

Income: Per capita income: $13,149 (2008-2012 5-year est.); Median household income: $39,063 (2008-2012 5-year est.); Average household income: $42,068 (2008-2012 5-year est.); Percent of households with income of $100,000 or more: n/a (2008-2012 5-year est.); Poverty rate: 52.8% (2008-2012 5-year est.).

Education: Percent of population age 25 and over with: High school diploma (including GED) or higher: 68.0% (2008-2012 5-year est.);

Bachelor's degree or higher: 4.0% (2008-2012 5-year est.); Master's degree or higher: 0.0% (2008-2012 5-year est.).
Housing: Homeownership rate: 86.4% (2008-2012 5-year est.); Median home value: $37,800 (2008-2012 5-year est.); Median contract rent: n/a per month (2008-2012 5-year est.); Median year structure built: 1990 (2008-2012 5-year est.).
Health Insurance: 17.0% Private; 60.4% Public; 32.1% None. (2008-2012 5-year est.)
Transportation: Commute to work: 100.0% car, 0.0% public transportation, 0.0% walk, 0.0% work from home (2008-2012 5-year est.); Travel time to work: 14.3% less than 15 minutes, 35.7% 15 to 30 minutes, 32.1% 30 to 45 minutes, 7.1% 45 to 60 minutes, 10.7% 60 minutes or more (2008-2012 5-year est.)

WENONAH (village). Covers a land area of 1.512 square miles and a water area of 0 square miles. Located at 39.32° N. Lat; 89.29° W. Long. Elevation is 673 feet.
Population: 40 (1990); 44 (2000); 37 (2010); Density: 14.6 persons per square mile (2008-2012 5-year est.); Race: 95.5% White, 0.0% Black/African American, 0.0% Asian, 0.0% American Indian/Alaska Native, 0.0% Native Hawaiian/Other Pacific Islander, 4.5% Some other race, 4.5% Two or more races, 0.0% Hispanic of any race (2008-2012 5-year est.); Average household size: 3.14 (2008-2012 5-year est.); Median age: 48.5 (2008-2012 5-year est.); Males per 100 females: 46.7 (2008-2012 5-year est.); Marriage status: 14.3% never married, 78.6% now married, 0.0% widowed, 7.1% divorced (2008-2012 5-year est.); Foreign born: 0.0% (2008-2012 5-year est.); Ancestry (includes multiple ancestries): 31.8% Italian, 9.1% German, 9.1% Irish (2008-2012 5-year est.).
Economy: Homeowner vacancy rate: 0.0%. Rental vacancy rate: 0.0%. (2008-2012 5-year est.); Employment by occupation: 0.0% management, business, and financial, 0.0% computer, engineering, and science, 0.0% education, legal, community service, arts, and media, 0.0% healthcare practitioners, 0.0% service, 100.0% sales and office, 0.0% natural resources, construction, and maintenance, 0.0% production, transportation, and material moving (2008-2012 5-year est.).
Income: Per capita income: $12,273 (2008-2012 5-year est.); Median household income: $48,125 (2008-2012 5-year est.); Average household income: $39,643 (2008-2012 5-year est.); Percent of households with income of $100,000 or more: n/a (2008-2012 5-year est.); Poverty rate: 0.0% (2008-2012 5-year est.).
Education: Percent of population age 25 and over with: High school diploma (including GED) or higher: 75.0% (2008-2012 5-year est.); Bachelor's degree or higher: 16.7% (2008-2012 5-year est.); Master's degree or higher: 0.0% (2008-2012 5-year est.).
Housing: Homeownership rate: 100.0% (2008-2012 5-year est.); Median home value: $97,500 (2008-2012 5-year est.); Median contract rent: n/a per month (2008-2012 5-year est.); Median year structure built: Before 1940 (2008-2012 5-year est.).
Health Insurance: 59.1% Private; 63.6% Public; 0.0% None. (2008-2012 5-year est.)
Transportation: Commute to work: 100.0% car, 0.0% public transportation, 0.0% walk, 0.0% work from home (2008-2012 5-year est.); Travel time to work: 100.0% less than 15 minutes, 0.0% 15 to 30 minutes, 0.0% 30 to 45 minutes, 0.0% 45 to 60 minutes, 0.0% 60 minutes or more (2008-2012 5-year est.)

WITT (city). Covers a land area of 1.400 square miles and a water area of 0 square miles. Located at 39.25° N. Lat; 89.35° W. Long. Elevation is 663 feet.
Population: 866 (1990); 991 (2000); 903 (2010); Density: 558.5 persons per square mile (2008-2012 5-year est.); Race: 99.9% White, 0.0% Black/African American, 0.0% Asian, 0.0% American Indian/Alaska Native, 0.0% Native Hawaiian/Other Pacific Islander, 0.1% Some other race, 0.1% Two or more races, 0.1% Hispanic of any race (2008-2012 5-year est.); Average household size: 2.04 (2008-2012 5-year est.); Median age: 42.0 (2008-2012 5-year est.); Males per 100 females: 84.4 (2008-2012 5-year est.); Marriage status: 27.2% never married, 49.1% now married, 9.9% widowed, 13.8% divorced (2008-2012 5-year est.); Foreign born: 0.0% (2008-2012 5-year est.); Ancestry (includes multiple ancestries): 21.9% German, 10.9% American, 10.5% English, 7.7% Irish, 5.0% Italian (2008-2012 5-year est.).
Economy: Homeowner vacancy rate: 5.2%. Rental vacancy rate: 8.1%. (2008-2012 5-year est.); Employment by occupation: 10.3% management, business, and financial, 0.7% computer, engineering, and science, 3.3% education, legal, community service, arts, and media, 5.6% healthcare

practitioners, 22.3% service, 26.9% sales and office, 17.3% natural resources, construction, and maintenance, 13.6% production, transportation, and material moving (2008-2012 5-year est.).
Income: Per capita income: $18,787 (2008-2012 5-year est.); Median household income: $31,875 (2008-2012 5-year est.); Average household income: $42,691 (2008-2012 5-year est.); Percent of households with income of $100,000 or more: 6.0% (2008-2012 5-year est.); Poverty rate: 18.8% (2008-2012 5-year est.).
Education: Percent of population age 25 and over with: High school diploma (including GED) or higher: 85.1% (2008-2012 5-year est.); Bachelor's degree or higher: 8.7% (2008-2012 5-year est.); Master's degree or higher: 1.5% (2008-2012 5-year est.).
Housing: Homeownership rate: 76.3% (2008-2012 5-year est.); Median home value: $60,600 (2008-2012 5-year est.); Median contract rent: $288 per month (2008-2012 5-year est.); Median year structure built: 1952 (2008-2012 5-year est.).
Health Insurance: 53.8% Private; 47.1% Public; 16.9% None. (2008-2012 5-year est.)
Safety: Violent crime rate: 0.0 per 10,000 population; Property crime rate: 33.5 per 10,000 population (2012).
Transportation: Commute to work: 100.0% car, 0.0% public transportation, 0.0% walk, 0.0% work from home (2008-2012 5-year est.); Travel time to work: 29.9% less than 15 minutes, 30.9% 15 to 30 minutes, 21.8% 30 to 45 minutes, 8.1% 45 to 60 minutes, 9.4% 60 minutes or more (2008-2012 5-year est.)

Morgan County

Located in west central Illinois; bounded on the west by the Illinois River; includes part of Lake Meredosia. Covers a land area of 568.791 square miles, a water area of 3.506 square miles, and is located in the Central Time Zone at 39.72° N. Lat., 90.20° W. Long. The county was founded in 1823. County seat is Jacksonville.

Morgan County is part of the Jacksonville, IL Micropolitan Statistical Area. The entire metro area includes: Morgan County, IL; Scott County, IL

Weather Station: Jacksonville 2 E										Elevation: 609 feet		
	Jan	Feb	Mar	Apr	May	Jun	Jul	Aug	Sep	Oct	Nov	Dec
High	36	40	52	64	74	83	86	85	79	67	53	39
Low	18	20	29	39	50	59	63	61	52	41	32	21
Precip	1.6	1.7	2.8	3.9	4.7	4.3	3.8	3.5	3.6	3.0	3.6	2.5
Snow	6.0	5.0	2.6	0.4	0.0	0.0	0.0	0.0	0.0	tr	0.6	5.6

High and Low temperatures in degrees Fahrenheit; Precipitation and Snow in inches

Population: 36,397 (1990); 36,616 (2000); 35,547 (2010); Race: 91.7% White, 6.3% Black/African American, 0.2% Asian, 0.1% American Indian/Alaska Native, 0.0% Native Hawaiian/Other Pacific Islander, 1.7% Some other race, 1.6% Two or more races, 2.0% Hispanic of any race (2008-2012 5-year est.); Density: 62.1 persons per square mile (2008-2012 5-year est.); Average household size: 2.33 (2008-2012 5-year est.); Median age: 40.9 (2008-2012 5-year est.); Males per 100 females: 100.7 (2008-2012 5-year est.).
Religion: Six largest groups: 15.2% Baptist, 12.6% Catholicism, 6.1% Methodist/Pietist, 6.1% Lutheran, 2.6% Non-denominational Protestant, 2.2% Presbyterian-Reformed (2010)
Economy: Unemployment rate: 6.4% (April 2014); Total civilian labor force: 16,374 (April 2014); Leading industries: 19.0% health care and social assistance; 15.3% retail trade; 14.3% manufacturing (2012); Farms: 757 totaling 309,158 acres (2012); Companies that employ 500 or more persons: 3 (2012); Companies that employ 100 to 499 persons: 15 (2012); Companies that employ less than 100 persons: 857 (2012); Black-owned businesses: n/a (2007); Hispanic-owned businesses: n/a (2007); Asian-owned businesses: n/a (2007); Women-owned businesses: 708 (2007); Single-family building permits issued: 2 (2013); Multi-family building permits issued: 2 (2013).
Income: Per capita income: $24,082 (2008-2012 5-year est.); Median household income: $46,763 (2008-2012 5-year est.); Average household income: $59,397 (2008-2012 5-year est.); Percent of households with income of $100,000 or more: 14.9% (2008-2012 5-year est.); Poverty rate: 13.9% (2008-2012 5-year est.); Bankruptcy rate: 2.35% (2013).
Education: Percent of population age 25 and over with: High school diploma (including GED) or higher: 88.1% (2008-2012 5-year est.); Bachelor's degree or higher: 20.8% (2008-2012 5-year est.); Master's degree or higher: 7.4% (2008-2012 5-year est.).

Housing: Homeownership rate: 70.9% (2008-2012 5-year est.); Median home value: $91,600 (2008-2012 5-year est.); Median contract rent: $440 per month (2008-2012 5-year est.); Median year structure built: 1961 (2008-2012 5-year est.)

Health: Birth rate: 102.7 per 10,000 population (2013); Death rate: 101.5 per 10,000 population (2013); Age-adjusted cancer mortality rate: 226.0 deaths per 100,000 population (2011); Number of physicians: 12.6 per 10,000 population (2011); Hospital beds: 31.5 per 10,000 population (2010); Hospital admissions: 1,053.8 per 10,000 population (2010).

Elections: 2012 Presidential election results: 41.2% Obama, 56.6% Romney

Additional Information Contacts

Morgan County Government . . . . (217) 243-8581
   http://www.morgancounty-il.com

Morgan County Communities

ALEXANDER (unincorporated postal area)

Zip Code: 62601

Covers a land area of 44.798 square miles and a water area of <.001 square miles. Located at 39.74° N. Lat; 90.03° W. Long. Elevation is 659 feet. Population: 434 (2010); Density: 9.7 persons per square mile (2010); Race: 98.6% White, 0.7% Black/African American, 0.0% Asian, 0.2% American Indian/Alaska Native, 0.0% Native Hawaiian/Other Pacific Islander, 0.5% Some other race, 0.5% Two or more races, 0.5% Hispanic of any race (2010); Average household size: 2.40 (2010); Median age: 47.8 (2010); Males per 100 females: 108.7 (2010); Homeownership rate: 85.6% (2010)

CHAPIN (village). Covers a land area of 0.974 square miles and a water area of 0 square miles. Located at 39.77° N. Lat; 90.40° W. Long. Elevation is 620 feet.

Population: 632 (1990); 592 (2000); 512 (2010); Density: 629.1 persons per square mile (2008-2012 5-year est.); Race: 100.0% White, 0.0% Black/African American, 0.0% Asian, 0.0% American Indian/Alaska Native, 0.0% Native Hawaiian/Other Pacific Islander, 0.0% Some other race, 0.0% Two or more races, 0.0% Hispanic of any race (2008-2012 5-year est.); Average household size: 2.47 (2008-2012 5-year est.); Median age: 38.7 (2008-2012 5-year est.); Males per 100 females: 76.7 (2008-2012 5-year est.); Marriage status: 14.1% never married, 65.4% now married, 9.1% widowed, 11.4% divorced (2008-2012 5-year est.); Foreign born: 0.0% (2008-2012 5-year est.); Ancestry (includes multiple ancestries): 31.3% German, 27.4% American, 16.6% English, 10.6% Irish, 3.8% Dutch (2008-2012 5-year est.).

Economy: Homeowner vacancy rate: 3.0%. Rental vacancy rate: 0.0%. (2008-2012 5-year est.); Employment by occupation: 19.1% management, business, and financial, 1.1% computer, engineering, and science, 12.7% education, legal, community service, arts, and media, 3.5% healthcare practitioners, 22.3% service, 22.3% sales and office, 7.1% natural resources, construction, and maintenance, 12.0% production, transportation, and material moving (2008-2012 5-year est.).

Income: Per capita income: $20,673 (2008-2012 5-year est.); Median household income: $44,722 (2008-2012 5-year est.); Average household income: $51,095 (2008-2012 5-year est.); Percent of households with income of $100,000 or more: 4.8% (2008-2012 5-year est.); Poverty rate: 8.0% (2008-2012 5-year est.).

Education: Percent of population age 25 and over with: High school diploma (including GED) or higher: 86.0% (2008-2012 5-year est.); Bachelor's degree or higher: 14.7% (2008-2012 5-year est.); Master's degree or higher: 6.2% (2008-2012 5-year est.).

Housing: Homeownership rate: 92.3% (2008-2012 5-year est.); Median home value: $59,900 (2008-2012 5-year est.); Median contract rent: $277 per month (2008-2012 5-year est.); Median year structure built: 1952 (2008-2012 5-year est.).

Health Insurance: 57.0% Private; 55.7% Public; 9.3% None. (2008-2012 5-year est.)

Transportation: Commute to work: 95.6% car, 0.0% public transportation, 1.5% walk, 2.9% work from home (2008-2012 5-year est.); Travel time to work: 18.9% less than 15 minutes, 53.2% 15 to 30 minutes, 9.8% 30 to 45 minutes, 13.2% 45 to 60 minutes, 4.9% 60 minutes or more (2008-2012 5-year est.)

CONCORD (village). Covers a land area of 0.271 square miles and a water area of 0 square miles. Located at 39.82° N. Lat; 90.37° W. Long. Elevation is 594 feet.

Population: 172 (1990); 176 (2000); 167 (2010); Density: 571.3 persons per square mile (2008-2012 5-year est.); Race: 100.0% White, 0.0% Black/African American, 0.0% Asian, 0.0% American Indian/Alaska Native, 0.0% Native Hawaiian/Other Pacific Islander, 0.0% Some other race, 0.0% Two or more races, 0.0% Hispanic of any race (2008-2012 5-year est.); Average household size: 2.01 (2008-2012 5-year est.); Median age: 35.7 (2008-2012 5-year est.); Males per 100 females: 124.6 (2008-2012 5-year est.); Marriage status: 36.1% never married, 44.4% now married, 2.3% widowed, 17.3% divorced (2008-2012 5-year est.); Foreign born: 0.0% (2008-2012 5-year est.); Ancestry (includes multiple ancestries): 33.5% German, 23.9% English, 16.8% American, 14.8% Irish, 7.7% Polish (2008-2012 5-year est.).

Economy: Homeowner vacancy rate: 0.0%. Rental vacancy rate: 0.0%. (2008-2012 5-year est.); Employment by occupation: 23.1% management, business, and financial, 7.7% computer, engineering, and science, 3.3% education, legal, community service, arts, and media, 4.4% healthcare practitioners, 27.5% service, 6.6% sales and office, 11.0% natural resources, construction, and maintenance, 16.5% production, transportation, and material moving (2008-2012 5-year est.).

Income: Per capita income: $27,750 (2008-2012 5-year est.); Median household income: $49,063 (2008-2012 5-year est.); Average household income: $56,577 (2008-2012 5-year est.); Percent of households with income of $100,000 or more: 5.2% (2008-2012 5-year est.); Poverty rate: 0.0% (2008-2012 5-year est.).

Education: Percent of population age 25 and over with: High school diploma (including GED) or higher: 83.9% (2008-2012 5-year est.); Bachelor's degree or higher: 28.6% (2008-2012 5-year est.); Master's degree or higher: 0.0% (2008-2012 5-year est.).

School District(s)

Triopia CUSD 27 (PK-12)
   2011-12 Enrollment: 382 . . . . (217) 457-2283

Housing: Homeownership rate: 93.5% (2008-2012 5-year est.); Median home value: $70,000 (2008-2012 5-year est.); Median contract rent: n/a per month (2008-2012 5-year est.); Median year structure built: Before 1940 (2008-2012 5-year est.).

Health Insurance: 83.2% Private; 14.8% Public; 12.3% None. (2008-2012 5-year est.)

Transportation: Commute to work: 91.9% car, 0.0% public transportation, 0.0% walk, 8.1% work from home (2008-2012 5-year est.); Travel time to work: 6.3% less than 15 minutes, 77.2% 15 to 30 minutes, 10.1% 30 to 45 minutes, 3.8% 45 to 60 minutes, 2.5% 60 minutes or more (2008-2012 5-year est.)

FRANKLIN (village). Covers a land area of 0.744 square miles and a water area of 0 square miles. Located at 39.62° N. Lat; 90.05° W. Long. Elevation is 682 feet.

Population: 634 (1990); 586 (2000); 610 (2010); Density: 893.1 persons per square mile (2008-2012 5-year est.); Race: 97.9% White, 0.8% Black/African American, 0.0% Asian, 0.0% American Indian/Alaska Native, 0.0% Native Hawaiian/Other Pacific Islander, 1.3% Some other race, 1.4% Two or more races, 0.0% Hispanic of any race (2008-2012 5-year est.); Average household size: 2.70 (2008-2012 5-year est.); Median age: 38.3 (2008-2012 5-year est.); Males per 100 females: 97.6 (2008-2012 5-year est.); Marriage status: 19.7% never married, 66.5% now married, 2.3% widowed, 11.5% divorced (2008-2012 5-year est.); Foreign born: 0.5% (2008-2012 5-year est.); Ancestry (includes multiple ancestries): 29.5% American, 21.4% German, 16.1% English, 15.8% Irish, 2.7% Swedish (2008-2012 5-year est.).

Economy: Homeowner vacancy rate: 8.4%. Rental vacancy rate: 0.0%. (2008-2012 5-year est.); Employment by occupation: 4.3% management, business, and financial, 2.8% computer, engineering, and science, 10.6% education, legal, community service, arts, and media, 2.5% healthcare practitioners, 17.4% service, 27.3% sales and office, 19.3% natural resources, construction, and maintenance, 15.8% production, transportation, and material moving (2008-2012 5-year est.).

Income: Per capita income: $24,785 (2008-2012 5-year est.); Median household income: $43,667 (2008-2012 5-year est.); Average household income: $66,152 (2008-2012 5-year est.); Percent of households with income of $100,000 or more: 14.2% (2008-2012 5-year est.); Poverty rate: 15.0% (2008-2012 5-year est.).

Education: Percent of population age 25 and over with: High school diploma (including GED) or higher: 89.4% (2008-2012 5-year est.);

Bachelor's degree or higher: 15.4% (2008-2012 5-year est.); Master's degree or higher: 6.8% (2008-2012 5-year est.).

School District(s)
Franklin CUSD 1 (PK-12)
    2011-12 Enrollment: 318........................ (217) 478-3011
Housing: Homeownership rate: 75.6% (2008-2012 5-year est.); Median home value: $88,300 (2008-2012 5-year est.); Median contract rent: $440 per month (2008-2012 5-year est.); Median year structure built: 1955 (2008-2012 5-year est.).
Health Insurance: 66.1% Private; 33.3% Public; 10.7% None. (2008-2012 5-year est.)
Transportation: Commute to work: 93.6% car, 0.0% public transportation, 2.6% walk, 3.8% work from home (2008-2012 5-year est.); Travel time to work: 18.6% less than 15 minutes, 31.2% 15 to 30 minutes, 34.9% 30 to 45 minutes, 5.6% 45 to 60 minutes, 9.6% 60 minutes or more (2008-2012 5-year est.).

JACKSONVILLE (city). County seat. Covers a land area of 10.474 square miles and a water area of 0.193 square miles. Located at 39.73° N. Lat; 90.23° W. Long. Elevation is 610 feet.

History: Jacksonville was founded in 1825, and named for Andrew Jackson. The first settlers were southerners, but they were followed by people from New England. Abolitionist sentiment was strong, and Jacksonville served as a station on the Underground Railroad. Both William Jennings Bryan (1883) and Stephen A. Douglas (1834) began their law practices in Jacksonville, and Abraham Lincoln was a frequent speaker here.
Population: 19,324 (1990); 18,940 (2000); 19,446 (2010); Density: 1,852.3 persons per square mile (2008-2012 5-year est.); Race: 87.7% White, 9.8% Black/African American, 0.3% Asian, 0.0% American Indian/Alaska Native, 0.0% Native Hawaiian/Other Pacific Islander, 2.2% Some other race, 2.0% Two or more races, 3.0% Hispanic of any race (2008-2012 5-year est.); Average household size: 2.31 (2008-2012 5-year est.); Median age: 37.3 (2008-2012 5-year est.); Males per 100 females: 97.9 (2008-2012 5-year est.); Marriage status: 35.5% never married, 42.3% now married, 7.2% widowed, 15.0% divorced (2008-2012 5-year est.); Foreign born: 2.1% (2008-2012 5-year est.); Ancestry (includes multiple ancestries): 25.3% German, 22.3% American, 11.7% Irish, 10.6% English, 2.0% Italian (2008-2012 5-year est.).
Economy: Single-family building permits issued: 2 (2013); Multi-family building permits issued: 2 (2013); Homeowner vacancy rate: 1.1%. Rental vacancy rate: 1.9%. (2008-2012 5-year est.); Employment by occupation: 8.5% management, business, and financial, 1.8% computer, engineering, and science, 14.3% education, legal, community service, arts, and media, 3.7% healthcare practitioners, 27.6% service, 22.4% sales and office, 8.0% natural resources, construction, and maintenance, 13.6% production, transportation, and material moving (2008-2012 5-year est.).
Income: Per capita income: $21,467 (2008-2012 5-year est.); Median household income: $41,228 (2008-2012 5-year est.); Average household income: $53,937 (2008-2012 5-year est.); Percent of households with income of $100,000 or more: 13.0% (2008-2012 5-year est.); Poverty rate: 18.1% (2008-2012 5-year est.).
Education: Percent of population age 25 and over with: High school diploma (including GED) or higher: 86.2% (2008-2012 5-year est.); Bachelor's degree or higher: 21.9% (2008-2012 5-year est.); Master's degree or higher: 8.0% (2008-2012 5-year est.).

School District(s)
Brown/cass/morgan/scott Roe (06-12)
    2011-12 Enrollment: n/a........................ (217) 243-1804
Dept of Human Services (PK-12)
    2011-12 Enrollment: n/a........................ (217) 524-1379
Four Rivers Spec Educ Dist (03-12)
    2011-12 Enrollment: n/a........................ (217) 245-7174
Jacksonville SD 117 (PK-12)
    2011-12 Enrollment: 3,658 .... (217) 243-9411

Four-year College(s)
Illinois College (Private, Not-for-profit, Presbyterian Church (USA))
    Fall 2012 Enrollment: 987........................ (217) 245-3000
    2012-13 Tuition: In-state $26,500; Out-of-state $26,500
MacMurray College (Private, Not-for-profit, United Methodist)
    Fall 2012 Enrollment: 575........................ (217) 479-7000
    2012-13 Tuition: In-state $21,400; Out-of-state $21,400

Vocational/Technical School(s)
Mr John's School of Cosmetology Esthetics & Nails-Jacksonville (Private, For-profit)

    Fall 2012 Enrollment: 34........................ (217) 243-1744
    2012-13 Tuition: $15,095
Housing: Homeownership rate: 59.3% (2008-2012 5-year est.); Median home value: $90,700 (2008-2012 5-year est.); Median contract rent: $457 per month (2008-2012 5-year est.); Median year structure built: 1958 (2008-2012 5-year est.).
Health Insurance: 64.3% Private; 39.5% Public; 9.3% None. (2008-2012 5-year est.)
Hospitals: Passavant Area Hospital (99 beds)
Safety: Violent crime rate: 29.3 per 10,000 population; Property crime rate: 190.7 per 10,000 population (2012).
Transportation: Commute to work: 89.4% car, 0.5% public transportation, 5.3% walk, 2.4% work from home (2008-2012 5-year est.); Travel time to work: 69.9% less than 15 minutes, 12.8% 15 to 30 minutes, 7.6% 30 to 45 minutes, 6.1% 45 to 60 minutes, 3.6% 60 minutes or more (2008-2012 5-year est.).
Airports: Jacksonville Municipal Airport (general aviation)
Additional Information Contacts
City of Jacksonville .... (217) 479-4600
    http://www.jacksonvilleil.com
Jacksonville Area Chamber of Commerce .... (217) 245-2174
    http://www.jacksonvilleareachamber.org

LYNNVILLE (village). Covers a land area of 0.079 square miles and a water area of 0 square miles. Located at 39.69° N. Lat; 90.35° W. Long. Elevation is 620 feet.

Population: 125 (1990); 137 (2000); 117 (2010); Density: 1,471.5 persons per square mile (2008-2012 5-year est.); Race: 95.7% White, 0.0% Black/African American, 0.0% Asian, 0.0% American Indian/Alaska Native, 0.0% Native Hawaiian/Other Pacific Islander, 4.3% Some other race, 4.3% Two or more races, 0.0% Hispanic of any race (2008-2012 5-year est.); Average household size: 2.47 (2008-2012 5-year est.); Median age: 21.8 (2008-2012 5-year est.); Males per 100 females: 58.9 (2008-2012 5-year est.); Marriage status: 40.0% never married, 27.5% now married, 8.8% widowed, 23.8% divorced (2008-2012 5-year est.); Foreign born: 0.0% (2008-2012 5-year est.); Ancestry (includes multiple ancestries): 42.2% German, 37.1% Irish, 35.3% American, 0.9% Swiss, 0.9% Dutch (2008-2012 5-year est.).
Economy: Homeowner vacancy rate: 0.0%. Rental vacancy rate: 0.0%. (2008-2012 5-year est.); Employment by occupation: 1.8% management, business, and financial, 0.0% computer, engineering, and science, 0.0% education, legal, community service, arts, and media, 8.8% healthcare practitioners, 45.6% service, 10.5% sales and office, 3.5% natural resources, construction, and maintenance, 29.8% production, transportation, and material moving (2008-2012 5-year est.).
Income: Per capita income: $18,162 (2008-2012 5-year est.); Median household income: $40,750 (2008-2012 5-year est.); Average household income: $45,715 (2008-2012 5-year est.); Percent of households with income of $100,000 or more: 8.5% (2008-2012 5-year est.); Poverty rate: 1.7% (2008-2012 5-year est.).
Education: Percent of population age 25 and over with: High school diploma (including GED) or higher: 90.9% (2008-2012 5-year est.); Bachelor's degree or higher: 5.5% (2008-2012 5-year est.); Master's degree or higher: 0.0% (2008-2012 5-year est.).
Housing: Homeownership rate: 87.2% (2008-2012 5-year est.); Median home value: $57,200 (2008-2012 5-year est.); Median contract rent: $330 per month (2008-2012 5-year est.); Median year structure built: 1976 (2008-2012 5-year est.).
Health Insurance: 84.5% Private; 13.8% Public; 8.6% None. (2008-2012 5-year est.)
Transportation: Commute to work: 100.0% car, 0.0% public transportation, 0.0% walk, 0.0% work from home (2008-2012 5-year est.); Travel time to work: 12.3% less than 15 minutes, 42.1% 15 to 30 minutes, 21.1% 30 to 45 minutes, 17.5% 45 to 60 minutes, 7.0% 60 minutes or more (2008-2012 5-year est.).

MEREDOSIA (village). Covers a land area of 0.833 square miles and a water area of 0.037 square miles. Located at 39.83° N. Lat; 90.56° W. Long. Elevation is 446 feet.

History: The name of Meredosia is from the French "marais d'osier" meaning "swamp of the basket reeds." The town was located at the mouth of Meredosia Lake. The railroad connecting with the Illinois & Michigan Canal was constructed here in 1838, but the Canal continued to hold supremacy over the railroad until 1878.

Population: 1,134 (1990); 1,041 (2000); 1,044 (2010); Density: 1,210.3 persons per square mile (2008-2012 5-year est.); Race: 98.0% White, 0.5% Black/African American, 0.0% Asian, 0.4% American Indian/Alaska Native, 0.0% Native Hawaiian/Other Pacific Islander, 1.1% Some other race, 1.1% Two or more races, 0.4% Hispanic of any race (2008-2012 5-year est.); Average household size: 2.19 (2008-2012 5-year est.); Median age: 46.6 (2008-2012 5-year est.); Males per 100 females: 81.9 (2008-2012 5-year est.); Marriage status: 19.4% never married, 55.6% now married, 11.7% widowed, 13.3% divorced (2008-2012 5-year est.); Foreign born: 0.2% (2008-2012 5-year est.); Ancestry (includes multiple ancestries): 29.3% American, 28.7% German, 17.5% Irish, 11.5% English, 3.7% Dutch (2008-2012 5-year est.).
Economy: Single-family building permits issued: 0 (2013); Multi-family building permits issued: 0 (2013); Homeowner vacancy rate: 0.0%. Rental vacancy rate: 0.0%. (2008-2012 5-year est.); Employment by occupation: 9.2% management, business, and financial, 0.0% computer, engineering, and science, 13.7% education, legal, community service, arts, and media, 4.3% healthcare practitioners, 13.5% service, 22.5% sales and office, 11.8% natural resources, construction, and maintenance, 25.1% production, transportation, and material moving (2008-2012 5-year est.).
Income: Per capita income: $20,383 (2008-2012 5-year est.); Median household income: $32,305 (2008-2012 5-year est.); Average household income: $44,554 (2008-2012 5-year est.); Percent of households with income of $100,000 or more: 4.3% (2008-2012 5-year est.); Poverty rate: 12.5% (2008-2012 5-year est.).
Education: Percent of population age 25 and over with: High school diploma (including GED) or higher: 84.5% (2008-2012 5-year est.); Bachelor's degree or higher: 8.0% (2008-2012 5-year est.); Master's degree or higher: 1.4% (2008-2012 5-year est.).

School District(s)

Meredosia-Chambersburg CUSD 11 (PK-12)
    2011-12 Enrollment: 262 . . . . (217) 584-1744
Housing: Homeownership rate: 73.3% (2008-2012 5-year est.); Median home value: $63,500 (2008-2012 5-year est.); Median contract rent: $319 per month (2008-2012 5-year est.); Median year structure built: 1959 (2008-2012 5-year est.).
Health Insurance: 67.4% Private; 43.4% Public; 15.5% None. (2008-2012 5-year est.)
Safety: Violent crime rate: 19.1 per 10,000 population; Property crime rate: 220.1 per 10,000 population (2012).
Transportation: Commute to work: 91.6% car, 0.0% public transportation, 1.0% walk, 5.5% work from home (2008-2012 5-year est.); Travel time to work: 44.7% less than 15 minutes, 27.8% 15 to 30 minutes, 21.0% 30 to 45 minutes, 1.5% 45 to 60 minutes, 5.1% 60 minutes or more (2008-2012 5-year est.).

MURRAYVILLE (village). Covers a land area of 0.490 square miles and a water area of 0 square miles. Located at 39.58° N. Lat; 90.25° W. Long. Elevation is 692 feet.

Population: 673 (1990); 644 (2000); 587 (2010); Density: 1,216.2 persons per square mile (2008-2012 5-year est.); Race: 100.0% White, 0.0% Black/African American, 0.0% Asian, 0.0% American Indian/Alaska Native, 0.0% Native Hawaiian/Other Pacific Islander, 0.0% Some other race, 0.0% Two or more races, 0.0% Hispanic of any race (2008-2012 5-year est.); Average household size: 2.42 (2008-2012 5-year est.); Median age: 38.8 (2008-2012 5-year est.); Males per 100 females: 79.5 (2008-2012 5-year est.); Marriage status: 20.3% never married, 63.2% now married, 5.7% widowed, 10.8% divorced (2008-2012 5-year est.); Foreign born: 0.0% (2008-2012 5-year est.); Ancestry (includes multiple ancestries): 33.2% American, 14.8% German, 13.3% Irish, 11.9% English, 5.4% Dutch (2008-2012 5-year est.).
Economy: Homeowner vacancy rate: 0.0%. Rental vacancy rate: 0.0%. (2008-2012 5-year est.); Employment by occupation: 8.0% management, business, and financial, 0.0% computer, engineering, and science, 5.1% education, legal, community service, arts, and media, 2.2% healthcare practitioners, 23.4% service, 32.4% sales and office, 11.9% natural resources, construction, and maintenance, 17.0% production, transportation, and material moving (2008-2012 5-year est.).
Income: Per capita income: $22,221 (2008-2012 5-year est.); Median household income: $43,125 (2008-2012 5-year est.); Average household income: $52,510 (2008-2012 5-year est.); Percent of households with income of $100,000 or more: 13.0% (2008-2012 5-year est.); Poverty rate: 12.2% (2008-2012 5-year est.).
Education: Percent of population age 25 and over with: High school diploma (including GED) or higher: 95.0% (2008-2012 5-year est.);

Bachelor's degree or higher: 7.2% (2008-2012 5-year est.); Master's degree or higher: 1.2% (2008-2012 5-year est.).

School District(s)

Jacksonville SD 117 (PK-12)
    2011-12 Enrollment: 3,658 . . . . (217) 243-9411
Housing: Homeownership rate: 74.4% (2008-2012 5-year est.); Median home value: $66,200 (2008-2012 5-year est.); Median contract rent: $338 per month (2008-2012 5-year est.); Median year structure built: 1963 (2008-2012 5-year est.).
Health Insurance: 80.5% Private; 26.2% Public; 6.4% None. (2008-2012 5-year est.)
Transportation: Commute to work: 89.2% car, 0.0% public transportation, 0.7% walk, 4.9% work from home (2008-2012 5-year est.); Travel time to work: 14.8% less than 15 minutes, 64.1% 15 to 30 minutes, 5.9% 30 to 45 minutes, 8.3% 45 to 60 minutes, 6.9% 60 minutes or more (2008-2012 5-year est.).

SOUTH JACKSONVILLE (village). Covers a land area of 2.290 square miles and a water area of 0.058 square miles. Located at 39.70° N. Lat; 90.22° W. Long. Elevation is 620 feet.

Population: 3,187 (1990); 3,475 (2000); 3,331 (2010); Density: 1,454.1 persons per square mile (2008-2012 5-year est.); Race: 89.3% White, 9.6% Black/African American, 0.0% Asian, 0.5% American Indian/Alaska Native, 0.0% Native Hawaiian/Other Pacific Islander, 0.6% Some other race, 0.7% Two or more races, 2.7% Hispanic of any race (2008-2012 5-year est.); Average household size: 2.10 (2008-2012 5-year est.); Median age: 40.6 (2008-2012 5-year est.); Males per 100 females: 118.4 (2008-2012 5-year est.); Marriage status: 27.9% never married, 51.8% now married, 6.0% widowed, 14.4% divorced (2008-2012 5-year est.); Foreign born: 1.1% (2008-2012 5-year est.); Ancestry (includes multiple ancestries): 34.4% German, 17.9% English, 15.7% American, 15.1% Irish, 3.0% French (2008-2012 5-year est.).
Economy: Single-family building permits issued: 0 (2013); Multi-family building permits issued: 0 (2013); Homeowner vacancy rate: 0.0%. Rental vacancy rate: 0.0%. (2008-2012 5-year est.); Employment by occupation: 16.0% management, business, and financial, 2.6% computer, engineering, and science, 12.8% education, legal, community service, arts, and media, 11.8% healthcare practitioners, 9.5% service, 25.9% sales and office, 7.7% natural resources, construction, and maintenance, 13.7% production, transportation, and material moving (2008-2012 5-year est.).
Income: Per capita income: $26,929 (2008-2012 5-year est.); Median household income: $54,392 (2008-2012 5-year est.); Average household income: $63,988 (2008-2012 5-year est.); Percent of households with income of $100,000 or more: 14.5% (2008-2012 5-year est.); Poverty rate: 9.5% (2008-2012 5-year est.).
Education: Percent of population age 25 and over with: High school diploma (including GED) or higher: 87.9% (2008-2012 5-year est.); Bachelor's degree or higher: 22.2% (2008-2012 5-year est.); Master's degree or higher: 8.5% (2008-2012 5-year est.).
Housing: Homeownership rate: 75.4% (2008-2012 5-year est.); Median home value: $93,400 (2008-2012 5-year est.); Median contract rent: $336 per month (2008-2012 5-year est.); Median year structure built: 1967 (2008-2012 5-year est.).
Health Insurance: 85.2% Private; 28.1% Public; 4.3% None. (2008-2012 5-year est.)
Transportation: Commute to work: 98.3% car, 0.0% public transportation, 0.0% walk, 1.0% work from home (2008-2012 5-year est.); Travel time to work: 75.9% less than 15 minutes, 9.9% 15 to 30 minutes, 5.6% 30 to 45 minutes, 7.4% 45 to 60 minutes, 1.1% 60 minutes or more (2008-2012 5-year est.).

WAVERLY (city). Covers a land area of 1.033 square miles and a water area of 0 square miles. Located at 39.59° N. Lat; 89.95° W. Long. Elevation is 682 feet.

History: Incorporated 1867.
Population: 1,402 (1990); 1,346 (2000); 1,307 (2010); Density: 1,402.7 persons per square mile (2008-2012 5-year est.); Race: 96.9% White, 0.0% Black/African American, 0.0% Asian, 0.0% American Indian/Alaska Native, 0.0% Native Hawaiian/Other Pacific Islander, 3.1% Some other race, 3.1% Two or more races, 0.6% Hispanic of any race (2008-2012 5-year est.); Average household size: 2.37 (2008-2012 5-year est.); Median age: 38.2 (2008-2012 5-year est.); Males per 100 females: 98.2 (2008-2012 5-year est.); Marriage status: 23.4% never married, 57.3% now married, 10.4% widowed, 9.0% divorced (2008-2012 5-year est.); Foreign born: 0.4% (2008-2012 5-year est.); Ancestry (includes multiple

ancestries): 30.9% American, 26.3% German, 11.1% English, 11.0% Irish, 2.9% French (2008-2012 5-year est.).

Economy: Single-family building permits issued: 0 (2013); Multi-family building permits issued: 0 (2013); Homeowner vacancy rate: 0.0%. Rental vacancy rate: 0.0%. (2008-2012 5-year est.); Employment by occupation: 10.3% management, business, and financial, 0.7% computer, engineering, and science, 10.6% education, legal, community service, arts, and media, 2.2% healthcare practitioners, 21.9% service, 33.3% sales and office, 4.8% natural resources, construction, and maintenance, 16.2% production, transportation, and material moving (2008-2012 5-year est.).

Income: Per capita income: $19,310 (2008-2012 5-year est.); Median household income: $42,024 (2008-2012 5-year est.); Average household income: $45,533 (2008-2012 5-year est.); Percent of households with income of $100,000 or more: 3.1% (2008-2012 5-year est.); Poverty rate: 14.4% (2008-2012 5-year est.).

Education: Percent of population age 25 and over with: High school diploma (including GED) or higher: 88.8% (2008-2012 5-year est.); Bachelor's degree or higher: 16.0% (2008-2012 5-year est.); Master's degree or higher: 5.9% (2008-2012 5-year est.).

School District(s)
Waverly CUSD 6 (PK-12)
   2011-12 Enrollment: 395. . . . . (217) 435-8121

Housing: Homeownership rate: 78.9% (2008-2012 5-year est.); Median home value: $73,900 (2008-2012 5-year est.); Median contract rent: $434 per month (2008-2012 5-year est.); Median year structure built: 1941 (2008-2012 5-year est.).

Health Insurance: 63.7% Private; 43.6% Public; 12.2% None. (2008-2012 5-year est.)

Safety: Violent crime rate: 15.3 per 10,000 population; Property crime rate: 68.8 per 10,000 population (2012).

Transportation: Commute to work: 93.3% car, 0.0% public transportation, 5.1% walk, 0.9% work from home (2008-2012 5-year est.); Travel time to work: 27.8% less than 15 minutes, 18.3% 15 to 30 minutes, 31.2% 30 to 45 minutes, 17.9% 45 to 60 minutes, 4.8% 60 minutes or more (2008-2012 5-year est.)

WOODSON (village). Covers a land area of 0.391 square miles and a water area of 0 square miles. Located at 39.63° N. Lat; 90.23° W. Long. Elevation is 679 feet.

Population: 472 (1990); 559 (2000); 512 (2010); Density: 1,101.1 persons per square mile (2008-2012 5-year est.); Race: 99.5% White, 0.0% Black/African American, 0.0% Asian, 0.0% American Indian/Alaska Native, 0.0% Native Hawaiian/Other Pacific Islander, 0.5% Some other race, 0.5% Two or more races, 3.1% Hispanic of any race (2008-2012 5-year est.); Average household size: 2.37 (2008-2012 5-year est.); Median age: 44.8 (2008-2012 5-year est.); Males per 100 females: 73.5 (2008-2012 5-year est.); Marriage status: 14.3% never married, 72.4% now married, 5.1% widowed, 8.1% divorced (2008-2012 5-year est.); Foreign born: 0.0% (2008-2012 5-year est.); Ancestry (includes multiple ancestries): 34.1% American, 29.2% German, 16.5% Irish, 11.8% English, 5.7% Scottish (2008-2012 5-year est.).

Economy: Homeowner vacancy rate: 0.0%. Rental vacancy rate: 0.0%. (2008-2012 5-year est.); Employment by occupation: 14.8% management, business, and financial, 3.3% computer, engineering, and science, 6.9% education, legal, community service, arts, and media, 2.0% healthcare practitioners, 19.7% service, 26.0% sales and office, 1.3% natural resources, construction, and maintenance, 26.0% production, transportation, and material moving (2008-2012 5-year est.).

Income: Per capita income: $27,458 (2008-2012 5-year est.); Median household income: $59,500 (2008-2012 5-year est.); Average household income: $64,409 (2008-2012 5-year est.); Percent of households with income of $100,000 or more: 17.9% (2008-2012 5-year est.); Poverty rate: 8.9% (2008-2012 5-year est.).

Education: Percent of population age 25 and over with: High school diploma (including GED) or higher: 88.7% (2008-2012 5-year est.); Bachelor's degree or higher: 8.3% (2008-2012 5-year est.); Master's degree or higher: 5.0% (2008-2012 5-year est.).

Housing: Homeownership rate: 89.8% (2008-2012 5-year est.); Median home value: $96,400 (2008-2012 5-year est.); Median contract rent: $544 per month (2008-2012 5-year est.); Median year structure built: 1977 (2008-2012 5-year est.).

Health Insurance: 71.3% Private; 33.9% Public; 4.6% None. (2008-2012 5-year est.)

Transportation: Commute to work: 95.2% car, 0.0% public transportation, 1.0% walk, 3.7% work from home (2008-2012 5-year est.); Travel time to work: 24.0% less than 15 minutes, 57.6% 15 to 30 minutes, 11.0% 30 to 45 minutes, 2.8% 45 to 60 minutes, 4.6% 60 minutes or more (2008-2012 5-year est.)

Moultrie County

Located in central Illinois; drained by the Kaskaskia River. Covers a land area of 335.943 square miles, a water area of 8.534 square miles, and is located in the Central Time Zone at 39.64° N. Lat., 88.63° W. Long. The county was founded in 1843. County seat is Sullivan.

Population: 13,930 (1990); 14,287 (2000); 14,846 (2010); Race: 98.4% White, 0.4% Black/African American, 0.3% Asian, 0.0% American Indian/Alaska Native, 0.1% Native Hawaiian/Other Pacific Islander, 0.8% Some other race, 0.4% Two or more races, 0.9% Hispanic of any race (2008-2012 5-year est.); Density: 44.5 persons per square mile (2008-2012 5-year est.); Average household size: 2.56 (2008-2012 5-year est.); Median age: 41.0 (2008-2012 5-year est.); Males per 100 females: 95.4 (2008-2012 5-year est.).

Religion: Six largest groups: 19.1% Baptist, 10.0% European Free-Church, 8.8% Non-denominational Protestant, 5.7% Methodist/Pietist, 2.8% Lutheran, 2.7% Catholicism (2010)

Economy: Unemployment rate: 5.4% (April 2014); Total civilian labor force: 7,422 (April 2014); Leading industries: 16.1% health care and social assistance; 8.2% retail trade; 6.0% construction (2012); Farms: 553 totaling 204,987 acres (2012); Companies that employ 500 or more persons: 1 (2012); Companies that employ 100 to 499 persons: 5 (2012); Companies that employ less than 100 persons: 308 (2012); Black-owned businesses: n/a (2007); Hispanic-owned businesses: n/a (2007); Asian-owned businesses: n/a (2007); Women-owned businesses: n/a (2007); Single-family building permits issued: 26 (2013); Multi-family building permits issued: 12 (2013).

Income: Per capita income: $23,985 (2008-2012 5-year est.); Median household income: $50,005 (2008-2012 5-year est.); Average household income: $61,196 (2008-2012 5-year est.); Percent of households with income of $100,000 or more: 14.5% (2008-2012 5-year est.); Poverty rate: 10.7% (2008-2012 5-year est.); Bankruptcy rate: 2.88% (2013).

Taxes: Total county taxes per capita: $159 (2011); County property taxes per capita: $159 (2011).

Education: Percent of population age 25 and over with: High school diploma (including GED) or higher: 83.6% (2008-2012 5-year est.); Bachelor's degree or higher: 13.8% (2008-2012 5-year est.); Master's degree or higher: 5.0% (2008-2012 5-year est.).

Housing: Homeownership rate: 80.1% (2008-2012 5-year est.); Median home value: $94,100 (2008-2012 5-year est.); Median contract rent: $463 per month (2008-2012 5-year est.); Median year structure built: 1963 (2008-2012 5-year est.)

Health: Birth rate: 111.6 per 10,000 population (2013); Death rate: 100.2 per 10,000 population (2013); Age-adjusted cancer mortality rate: 211.6 deaths per 100,000 population (2011); Number of physicians: 4.0 per 10,000 population (2011); Hospital beds: 0.0 per 10,000 population (2010); Hospital admissions: 0.0 per 10,000 population (2010).

Elections: 2012 Presidential election results: 35.4% Obama, 62.5% Romney

National and State Parks: Kaskaskia River State Fish and Wildlife Management; West Okaw River State Fish and Wildlife Management

Additional Information Contacts
Moultrie County Government . . . . (217) 728-4389
   http://moultriecountyil.com

Moultrie County Communities

ALLENVILLE (village). Covers a land area of 0.581 square miles and a water area of 0 square miles. Located at 39.56° N. Lat; 88.54° W. Long. Elevation is 650 feet.

Population: 166 (1990); 154 (2000); 148 (2010); Density: 223.9 persons per square mile (2008-2012 5-year est.); Race: 100.0% White, 0.0% Black/African American, 0.0% Asian, 0.0% American Indian/Alaska Native, 0.0% Native Hawaiian/Other Pacific Islander, 0.0% Some other race, 0.0% Two or more races, 0.0% Hispanic of any race (2008-2012 5-year est.); Average household size: 1.94 (2008-2012 5-year est.); Median age: 57.4 (2008-2012 5-year est.); Males per 100 females: 132.1 (2008-2012 5-year est.); Marriage status: 13.0% never married, 76.4% now married, 2.4% widowed, 8.1% divorced (2008-2012 5-year est.); Foreign born: 0.0% (2008-2012 5-year est.); Ancestry (includes multiple ancestries): 36.2%

American, 13.1% German, 9.2% Irish, 5.4% English, 2.3% Scotch-Irish (2008-2012 5-year est.).

Economy: Single-family building permits issued: 0 (2013); Multi-family building permits issued: 0 (2013); Homeowner vacancy rate: 0.0%. Rental vacancy rate: 0.0%. (2008-2012 5-year est.); Employment by occupation: 2.0% management, business, and financial, 2.0% computer, engineering, and science, 4.0% education, legal, community service, arts, and media, 4.0% healthcare practitioners, 10.0% service, 16.0% sales and office, 20.0% natural resources, construction, and maintenance, 42.0% production, transportation, and material moving (2008-2012 5-year est.).

Income: Per capita income: $21,682 (2008-2012 5-year est.); Median household income: $33,125 (2008-2012 5-year est.); Average household income: $41,799 (2008-2012 5-year est.); Percent of households with income of $100,000 or more: 4.5% (2008-2012 5-year est.); Poverty rate: 2.3% (2008-2012 5-year est.).

Education: Percent of population age 25 and over with: High school diploma (including GED) or higher: 74.4% (2008-2012 5-year est.); Bachelor's degree or higher: 5.1% (2008-2012 5-year est.); Master's degree or higher: 5.1% (2008-2012 5-year est.).

Housing: Homeownership rate: 95.5% (2008-2012 5-year est.); Median home value: $75,000 (2008-2012 5-year est.); Median contract rent: n/a per month (2008-2012 5-year est.); Median year structure built: 1973 (2008-2012 5-year est.).

Health Insurance: 60.8% Private; 59.2% Public; 7.7% None. (2008-2012 5-year est.)

Transportation: Commute to work: 100.0% car, 0.0% public transportation, 0.0% walk, 0.0% work from home (2008-2012 5-year est.); Travel time to work: 36.0% less than 15 minutes, 30.0% 15 to 30 minutes, 10.0% 30 to 45 minutes, 10.0% 45 to 60 minutes, 14.0% 60 minutes or more (2008-2012 5-year est.)

BETHANY (village). Covers a land area of 0.966 square miles and a water area of 0.002 square miles. Located at 39.64° N. Lat; 88.74° W. Long. Elevation is 650 feet.

Population: 1,369 (1990); 1,287 (2000); 1,352 (2010); Density: 1,427.0 persons per square mile (2008-2012 5-year est.); Race: 99.3% White, 0.0% Black/African American, 0.0% Asian, 0.0% American Indian/Alaska Native, 0.0% Native Hawaiian/Other Pacific Islander, 0.7% Some other race, 0.7% Two or more races, 1.7% Hispanic of any race (2008-2012 5-year est.); Average household size: 2.39 (2008-2012 5-year est.); Median age: 37.9 (2008-2012 5-year est.); Males per 100 females: 83.9 (2008-2012 5-year est.); Marriage status: 16.1% never married, 58.8% now married, 7.9% widowed, 17.2% divorced (2008-2012 5-year est.); Foreign born: 0.3% (2008-2012 5-year est.); Ancestry (includes multiple ancestries): 19.5% German, 10.2% American, 10.2% Irish, 8.3% English, 3.1% Scottish (2008-2012 5-year est.).

Economy: Single-family building permits issued: 0 (2013); Multi-family building permits issued: 0 (2013); Homeowner vacancy rate: 3.2%. Rental vacancy rate: 3.1%. (2008-2012 5-year est.); Employment by occupation: 7.8% management, business, and financial, 2.0% computer, engineering, and science, 9.8% education, legal, community service, arts, and media, 5.0% healthcare practitioners, 18.2% service, 24.2% sales and office, 8.7% natural resources, construction, and maintenance, 24.3% production, transportation, and material moving (2008-2012 5-year est.).

Income: Per capita income: $22,896 (2008-2012 5-year est.); Median household income: $42,765 (2008-2012 5-year est.); Average household income: $53,890 (2008-2012 5-year est.); Percent of households with income of $100,000 or more: 9.2% (2008-2012 5-year est.); Poverty rate: 10.5% (2008-2012 5-year est.).

Education: Percent of population age 25 and over with: High school diploma (including GED) or higher: 92.0% (2008-2012 5-year est.); Bachelor's degree or higher: 9.6% (2008-2012 5-year est.); Master's degree or higher: 3.3% (2008-2012 5-year est.).

School District(s)
Okaw Valley CUSD 302 (PK-12)
    2011-12 Enrollment: 557 . . . . (217) 665-3232

Housing: Homeownership rate: 78.5% (2008-2012 5-year est.); Median home value: $75,800 (2008-2012 5-year est.); Median contract rent: $366 per month (2008-2012 5-year est.); Median year structure built: 1960 (2008-2012 5-year est.).

Health Insurance: 68.0% Private; 35.3% Public; 10.0% None. (2008-2012 5-year est.)

Transportation: Commute to work: 95.0% car, 0.0% public transportation, 2.7% walk, 0.9% work from home (2008-2012 5-year est.); Travel time to work: 26.2% less than 15 minutes, 24.8% 15 to 30 minutes, 35.0% 30 to 45 minutes, 9.4% 45 to 60 minutes, 4.6% 60 minutes or more (2008-2012 5-year est.)

DALTON CITY (village). Covers a land area of 0.607 square miles and a water area of 0.003 square miles. Located at 39.72° N. Lat; 88.81° W. Long. Elevation is 689 feet.

Population: 573 (1990); 581 (2000); 544 (2010); Density: 757.4 persons per square mile (2008-2012 5-year est.); Race: 97.4% White, 0.0% Black/African American, 2.6% Asian, 0.0% American Indian/Alaska Native, 0.0% Native Hawaiian/Other Pacific Islander, 0.0% Some other race, 0.0% Two or more races, 6.3% Hispanic of any race (2008-2012 5-year est.); Average household size: 2.69 (2008-2012 5-year est.); Median age: 37.1 (2008-2012 5-year est.); Males per 100 females: 109.1 (2008-2012 5-year est.); Marriage status: 17.0% never married, 67.8% now married, 0.9% widowed, 14.4% divorced (2008-2012 5-year est.); Foreign born: 5.7% (2008-2012 5-year est.); Ancestry (includes multiple ancestries): 22.6% German, 17.0% American, 12.6% English, 11.5% Irish, 5.2% Swiss (2008-2012 5-year est.).

Economy: Single-family building permits issued: 0 (2013); Multi-family building permits issued: 0 (2013); Homeowner vacancy rate: 0.0%. Rental vacancy rate: 0.0%. (2008-2012 5-year est.); Employment by occupation: 7.4% management, business, and financial, 3.3% computer, engineering, and science, 1.2% education, legal, community service, arts, and media, 3.3% healthcare practitioners, 29.3% service, 15.7% sales and office, 13.2% natural resources, construction, and maintenance, 26.4% production, transportation, and material moving (2008-2012 5-year est.).

Income: Per capita income: $23,441 (2008-2012 5-year est.); Median household income: $56,875 (2008-2012 5-year est.); Average household income: $62,695 (2008-2012 5-year est.); Percent of households with income of $100,000 or more: 15.2% (2008-2012 5-year est.); Poverty rate: 3.1% (2008-2012 5-year est.).

Education: Percent of population age 25 and over with: High school diploma (including GED) or higher: 91.0% (2008-2012 5-year est.); Bachelor's degree or higher: 7.4% (2008-2012 5-year est.); Master's degree or higher: 1.7% (2008-2012 5-year est.).

Housing: Homeownership rate: 77.8% (2008-2012 5-year est.); Median home value: $88,200 (2008-2012 5-year est.); Median contract rent: $434 per month (2008-2012 5-year est.); Median year structure built: 1960 (2008-2012 5-year est.).

Health Insurance: 68.9% Private; 22.0% Public; 18.5% None. (2008-2012 5-year est.)

Transportation: Commute to work: 99.6% car, 0.0% public transportation, 0.4% walk, 0.0% work from home (2008-2012 5-year est.); Travel time to work: 20.7% less than 15 minutes, 42.6% 15 to 30 minutes, 26.4% 30 to 45 minutes, 2.9% 45 to 60 minutes, 7.4% 60 minutes or more (2008-2012 5-year est.)

GAYS (village). Covers a land area of 0.407 square miles and a water area of 0 square miles. Located at 39.46° N. Lat; 88.50° W. Long. Elevation is 755 feet.

Population: 237 (1990); 259 (2000); 281 (2010); Density: 754.8 persons per square mile (2008-2012 5-year est.); Race: 99.0% White, 0.0% Black/African American, 0.0% Asian, 0.0% American Indian/Alaska Native, 0.0% Native Hawaiian/Other Pacific Islander, 1.0% Some other race, 0.0% Two or more races, 0.0% Hispanic of any race (2008-2012 5-year est.); Average household size: 2.56 (2008-2012 5-year est.); Median age: 43.5 (2008-2012 5-year est.); Males per 100 females: 73.4 (2008-2012 5-year est.); Marriage status: 30.9% never married, 51.6% now married, 5.8% widowed, 11.6% divorced (2008-2012 5-year est.); Foreign born: 0.0% (2008-2012 5-year est.); Ancestry (includes multiple ancestries): 24.4% German, 8.8% Irish, 8.5% American, 4.9% English, 4.2% French (2008-2012 5-year est.).

Economy: Single-family building permits issued: 0 (2013); Multi-family building permits issued: 0 (2013); Homeowner vacancy rate: 0.0%. Rental vacancy rate: 0.0%. (2008-2012 5-year est.); Employment by occupation: 9.5% management, business, and financial, 1.4% computer, engineering, and science, 8.8% education, legal, community service, arts, and media, 6.1% healthcare practitioners, 11.5% service, 27.0% sales and office, 11.5% natural resources, construction, and maintenance, 24.3% production, transportation, and material moving (2008-2012 5-year est.).

Income: Per capita income: $20,710 (2008-2012 5-year est.); Median household income: $48,571 (2008-2012 5-year est.); Average household income: $54,656 (2008-2012 5-year est.); Percent of households with income of $100,000 or more: 5.8% (2008-2012 5-year est.); Poverty rate: 4.2% (2008-2012 5-year est.).

Education: Percent of population age 25 and over with: High school diploma (including GED) or higher: 91.5% (2008-2012 5-year est.); Bachelor's degree or higher: 12.6% (2008-2012 5-year est.); Master's degree or higher: 4.0% (2008-2012 5-year est.).
Housing: Homeownership rate: 85.0% (2008-2012 5-year est.); Median home value: $68,100 (2008-2012 5-year est.); Median contract rent: $500 per month (2008-2012 5-year est.); Median year structure built: 1957 (2008-2012 5-year est.).
Health Insurance: 59.0% Private; 29.6% Public; 24.1% None. (2008-2012 5-year est.)
Transportation: Commute to work: 100.0% car, 0.0% public transportation, 0.0% walk, 0.0% work from home (2008-2012 5-year est.); Travel time to work: 13.2% less than 15 minutes, 59.7% 15 to 30 minutes, 27.1% 30 to 45 minutes, 0.0% 45 to 60 minutes, 0.0% 60 minutes or more (2008-2012 5-year est.)

LOVINGTON (village). Covers a land area of 0.807 square miles and a water area of 0 square miles. Located at 39.71° N. Lat; 88.63° W. Long. Elevation is 679 feet.
History: Incorporated 1873.
Population: 1,143 (1990); 1,222 (2000); 1,130 (2010); Density: 1,441.8 persons per square mile (2008-2012 5-year est.); Race: 98.8% White, 0.3% Black/African American, 0.0% Asian, 0.2% American Indian/Alaska Native, 0.0% Native Hawaiian/Other Pacific Islander, 0.7% Some other race, 0.8% Two or more races, 0.0% Hispanic of any race (2008-2012 5-year est.); Average household size: 2.34 (2008-2012 5-year est.); Median age: 35.3 (2008-2012 5-year est.); Males per 100 females: 98.5 (2008-2012 5-year est.); Marriage status: 31.0% never married, 48.5% now married, 7.1% widowed, 13.4% divorced (2008-2012 5-year est.); Foreign born: 0.5% (2008-2012 5-year est.); Ancestry (includes multiple ancestries): 22.0% German, 10.4% English, 8.1% Irish, 7.2% American, 2.1% Polish (2008-2012 5-year est.).
Economy: Single-family building permits issued: 0 (2013); Multi-family building permits issued: 0 (2013); Homeowner vacancy rate: 6.0%. Rental vacancy rate: 6.5%. (2008-2012 5-year est.); Employment by occupation: 17.2% management, business, and financial, 0.4% computer, engineering, and science, 8.1% education, legal, community service, arts, and media, 3.8% healthcare practitioners, 18.7% service, 15.8% sales and office, 9.7% natural resources, construction, and maintenance, 26.4% production, transportation, and material moving (2008-2012 5-year est.)
Income: Per capita income: $20,911 (2008-2012 5-year est.); Median household income: $41,932 (2008-2012 5-year est.); Average household income: $49,227 (2008-2012 5-year est.); Percent of households with income of $100,000 or more: 7.3% (2008-2012 5-year est.); Poverty rate: 11.8% (2008-2012 5-year est.).
Education: Percent of population age 25 and over with: High school diploma (including GED) or higher: 89.0% (2008-2012 5-year est.); Bachelor's degree or higher: 8.6% (2008-2012 5-year est.); Master's degree or higher: 6.3% (2008-2012 5-year est.).
School District(s)
Lovington CUSD 303 (PK-12)
    2011-12 Enrollment: 312 . . . . (217) 873-4310
Housing: Homeownership rate: 69.9% (2008-2012 5-year est.); Median home value: $70,100 (2008-2012 5-year est.); Median contract rent: $428 per month (2008-2012 5-year est.); Median year structure built: 1952 (2008-2012 5-year est.).
Health Insurance: 62.4% Private; 34.2% Public; 11.7% None. (2008-2012 5-year est.)
Safety: Violent crime rate: 17.7 per 10,000 population; Property crime rate: 141.7 per 10,000 population (2012).
Transportation: Commute to work: 96.1% car, 0.0% public transportation, 2.1% walk, 1.9% work from home (2008-2012 5-year est.); Travel time to work: 29.7% less than 15 minutes, 37.3% 15 to 30 minutes, 22.5% 30 to 45 minutes, 3.8% 45 to 60 minutes, 6.7% 60 minutes or more (2008-2012 5-year est.)

SULLIVAN (city). County seat. Covers a land area of 2.672 square miles and a water area of 0.004 square miles. Located at 39.60° N. Lat; 88.61° W. Long. Elevation is 673 feet.
History: Incorporated 1869.
Population: 4,354 (1990); 4,326 (2000); 4,440 (2010); Density: 1,669.8 persons per square mile (2008-2012 5-year est.); Race: 97.4% White, 1.1% Black/African American, 0.8% Asian, 0.0% American Indian/Alaska Native, 0.5% Native Hawaiian/Other Pacific Islander, 0.2% Some other race, 0.2% Two or more races, 0.0% Hispanic of any race (2008-2012

5-year est.); Average household size: 2.25 (2008-2012 5-year est.); Median age: 42.0 (2008-2012 5-year est.); Males per 100 females: 87.2 (2008-2012 5-year est.); Marriage status: 21.6% never married, 52.3% now married, 11.7% widowed, 14.5% divorced (2008-2012 5-year est.); Foreign born: 1.6% (2008-2012 5-year est.); Ancestry (includes multiple ancestries): 14.6% American, 13.4% German, 11.7% Irish, 9.7% English, 2.1% Scotch-Irish (2008-2012 5-year est.).
Economy: Single-family building permits issued: 7 (2013); Multi-family building permits issued: 10 (2013); Homeowner vacancy rate: 4.9%. Rental vacancy rate: 6.0%. (2008-2012 5-year est.); Employment by occupation: 8.4% management, business, and financial, 3.1% computer, engineering, and science, 8.3% education, legal, community service, arts, and media, 7.0% healthcare practitioners, 20.5% service, 20.7% sales and office, 7.9% natural resources, construction, and maintenance, 24.1% production, transportation, and material moving (2008-2012 5-year est.).
Income: Per capita income: $23,329 (2008-2012 5-year est.); Median household income: $41,169 (2008-2012 5-year est.); Average household income: $52,734 (2008-2012 5-year est.); Percent of households with income of $100,000 or more: 11.5% (2008-2012 5-year est.); Poverty rate: 15.3% (2008-2012 5-year est.).
Education: Percent of population age 25 and over with: High school diploma (including GED) or higher: 87.9% (2008-2012 5-year est.); Bachelor's degree or higher: 18.0% (2008-2012 5-year est.); Master's degree or higher: 7.6% (2008-2012 5-year est.).
School District(s)
Eastern Il Area of Spec Educ (PK-12)
    2011-12 Enrollment: n/a . . . . (217) 348-7700
Sullivan CUSD 300 (PK-12)
    2011-12 Enrollment: 1,213 . . . . (217) 728-8341
Housing: Homeownership rate: 72.7% (2008-2012 5-year est.); Median home value: $86,900 (2008-2012 5-year est.); Median contract rent: $467 per month (2008-2012 5-year est.); Median year structure built: 1957 (2008-2012 5-year est.).
Health Insurance: 73.7% Private; 36.9% Public; 7.8% None. (2008-2012 5-year est.)
Transportation: Commute to work: 89.0% car, 0.0% public transportation, 5.1% walk, 2.3% work from home (2008-2012 5-year est.); Travel time to work: 50.7% less than 15 minutes, 21.1% 15 to 30 minutes, 19.4% 30 to 45 minutes, 3.6% 45 to 60 minutes, 5.3% 60 minutes or more (2008-2012 5-year est.)
Additional Information Contacts
Sullivan Chamber & Economic Development . . . . (217) 728-4223
    http://www.sullivan-chamber.com

Ogle County

Located in northern Illinois; drained by the Rock, Leaf, and Kyte Rivers. Covers a land area of 758.574 square miles, a water area of 4.411 square miles, and is located in the Central Time Zone at 42.04° N. Lat., 89.32° W. Long. The county was founded in 1836. County seat is Oregon.

Ogle County is part of the Rochelle, IL Micropolitan Statistical Area. The entire metro area includes: Ogle County, IL

Weather Station: Rochelle									Elevation: 774 feet		
	Jan	Feb	Mar	Apr	May	Jun	Jul	Aug	Sep	Oct	Nov	Dec
High	29	33	45	59	71	80	83	82	75	62	47	33
Low	12	16	26	37	48	58	61	60	51	39	29	16
Precip	1.4	1.5	1.9	3.2	4.0	4.1	3.5	4.3	3.3	2.9	2.5	1.9
Snow	6.1	4.4	2.5	0.6	0.0	0.0	0.0	0.0	0.0	tr	0.6	6.0

High and Low temperatures in degrees Fahrenheit; Precipitation and Snow in inches

Population: 45,957 (1990); 51,032 (2000); 53,497 (2010); Race: 96.3% White, 0.9% Black/African American, 0.6% Asian, 0.0% American Indian/Alaska Native, 0.0% Native Hawaiian/Other Pacific Islander, 2.2% Some other races, 1.3% Two or more races, 8.9% Hispanic of any race (2008-2012 5-year est.); Density: 69.7 persons per square mile (2008-2012 5-year est.); Average household size: 2.54 (2008-2012 5-year est.); Median age: 40.9 (2008-2012 5-year est.); Males per 100 females: 98.9 (2008-2012 5-year est.).
Religion: Six largest groups: 14.3% Catholicism, 7.8% Lutheran, 6.5% Methodist/Pietist, 5.9% Presbyterian-Reformed, 1.6% Pentecostal, 1.6% Non-denominational Protestant (2010)
Economy: Unemployment rate: 8.3% (April 2014); Total civilian labor force: 25,017 (April 2014); Leading industries: 24.8% manufacturing; 11.7% health care and social assistance; 11.2% retail trade (2012); Farms:

1,148 totaling 376,422 acres (2012); Companies that employ 500 or more persons: 3 (2012); Companies that employ 100 to 499 persons: 16 (2012); Companies that employ less than 100 persons: 1,046 (2012); Black-owned businesses: n/a (2007); Hispanic-owned businesses: n/a (2007); Asian-owned businesses: n/a (2007); Women-owned businesses: n/a (2007); Single-family building permits issued: 24 (2013); Multi-family building permits issued: 0 (2013).

Income: Per capita income: $26,331 (2008-2012 5-year est.); Median household income: $55,590 (2008-2012 5-year est.); Average household income: $66,194 (2008-2012 5-year est.); Percent of households with income of $100,000 or more: 19.5% (2008-2012 5-year est.); Poverty rate: 10.0% (2008-2012 5-year est.); Bankruptcy rate: 3.80% (2013).

Taxes: Total county taxes per capita: $214 (2011); County property taxes per capita: $208 (2011).

Education: Percent of population age 25 and over with: High school diploma (including GED) or higher: 88.4% (2008-2012 5-year est.); Bachelor's degree or higher: 18.9% (2008-2012 5-year est.); Master's degree or higher: 6.8% (2008-2012 5-year est.).

Housing: Homeownership rate: 74.8% (2008-2012 5-year est.); Median home value: $151,400 (2008-2012 5-year est.); Median contract rent: $512 per month (2008-2012 5-year est.); Median year structure built: 1969 (2008-2012 5-year est.)

Health: Birth rate: 104.6 per 10,000 population (2013); Death rate: 86.5 per 10,000 population (2013); Age-adjusted cancer mortality rate: 184.3 deaths per 100,000 population (2011); Number of physicians: 7.1 per 10,000 population (2011); Hospital beds: 4.7 per 10,000 population (2010); Hospital admissions: 123.6 per 10,000 population (2010).

Elections: 2012 Presidential election results: 40.7% Obama, 57.4% Romney

National and State Parks: Lowden State Park; White Pines Forest State Park

Additional Information Contacts
Ogle County Government . . . . (815) 732-1110
  http://www.oglecounty.org

Ogle County Communities

ADELINE (village). Covers a land area of 0.264 square miles and a water area of 0 square miles. Located at 42.14° N. Lat; 89.49° W. Long. Elevation is 797 feet.

Population: 141 (1990); 139 (2000); 85 (2010); Density: 409.7 persons per square mile (2008-2012 5-year est.); Race: 95.4% White, 0.0% Black/African American, 0.0% Asian, 0.0% American Indian/Alaska Native, 0.0% Native Hawaiian/Other Pacific Islander, 4.6% Some other race, 4.6% Two or more races, 0.0% Hispanic of any race (2008-2012 5-year est.); Average household size: 2.77 (2008-2012 5-year est.); Median age: 35.3 (2008-2012 5-year est.); Males per 100 females: 96.4 (2008-2012 5-year est.); Marriage status: 36.2% never married, 45.7% now married, 6.4% widowed, 11.7% divorced (2008-2012 5-year est.); Foreign born: 0.0% (2008-2012 5-year est.); Ancestry (includes multiple ancestries): 20.4% English, 17.6% American, 17.6% Irish, 17.6% German, 8.3% Swedish (2008-2012 5-year est.).

Economy: Homeowner vacancy rate: 0.0%. Rental vacancy rate: 0.0%. (2008-2012 5-year est.); Employment by occupation: 0.0% management, business, and financial, 0.0% computer, engineering, and science, 0.0% education, legal, community service, arts, and media, 3.6% healthcare practitioners, 7.3% service, 9.1% sales and office, 23.6% natural resources, construction, and maintenance, 56.4% production, transportation, and material moving (2008-2012 5-year est.).

Income: Per capita income: $22,056 (2008-2012 5-year est.); Median household income: $48,438 (2008-2012 5-year est.); Average household income: $55,036 (2008-2012 5-year est.); Percent of households with income of $100,000 or more: 15.4% (2008-2012 5-year est.); Poverty rate: 12.7% (2008-2012 5-year est.).

Education: Percent of population age 25 and over with: High school diploma (including GED) or higher: 93.1% (2008-2012 5-year est.); Bachelor's degree or higher: 6.9% (2008-2012 5-year est.); Master's degree or higher: 0.0% (2008-2012 5-year est.).

Housing: Homeownership rate: 87.2% (2008-2012 5-year est.); Median home value: $87,500 (2008-2012 5-year est.); Median contract rent: $242 per month (2008-2012 5-year est.); Median year structure built: Before 1940 (2008-2012 5-year est.).

Health Insurance: 69.4% Private; 27.8% Public; 15.7% None. (2008-2012 5-year est.)

Transportation: Commute to work: 96.4% car, 0.0% public transportation, 3.6% walk, 0.0% work from home (2008-2012 5-year est.); Travel time to work: 7.3% less than 15 minutes, 65.5% 15 to 30 minutes, 5.5% 30 to 45 minutes, 18.2% 45 to 60 minutes, 3.6% 60 minutes or more (2008-2012 5-year est.)

BAILEYVILLE (unincorporated postal area)
Zip Code: 61007
  Covers a land area of 26.756 square miles and a water area of 0 square miles. Located at 42.19° N. Lat; 89.58° W. Long. Elevation is 925 feet. Population: 534 (2010); Density: 20.0 persons per square mile (2010); Race: 98.5% White, 0.2% Black/African American, 0.4% Asian, 0.2% American Indian/Alaska Native, 0.0% Native Hawaiian/Other Pacific Islander, 0.7% Some other race, 0.4% Two or more races, 0.6% Hispanic of any race (2010); Average household size: 2.58 (2010); Median age: 44.5 (2010); Males per 100 females: 113.6 (2010); Homeownership rate: 83.6% (2010)

BYRON (city). Covers a land area of 3.571 square miles and a water area of 0.002 square miles. Located at 42.13° N. Lat; 89.26° W. Long. Elevation is 728 feet.

History: Byron was founded in 1835 by settlers from New England, and named for the English poet Lord Byron. Many houses in Byron were stations on the Underground Railroad, offering escape for slaves from the south.

Population: 2,284 (1990); 2,917 (2000); 3,753 (2010); Density: 1,038.6 persons per square mile (2008-2012 5-year est.); Race: 95.1% White, 4.2% Black/African American, 0.1% Asian, 0.0% American Indian/Alaska Native, 0.0% Native Hawaiian/Other Pacific Islander, 0.6% Some other race, 0.6% Two or more races, 3.0% Hispanic of any race (2008-2012 5-year est.); Average household size: 2.75 (2008-2012 5-year est.); Median age: 31.3 (2008-2012 5-year est.); Males per 100 females: 89.6 (2008-2012 5-year est.); Marriage status: 26.2% never married, 53.2% now married, 6.9% widowed, 13.7% divorced (2008-2012 5-year est.); Foreign born: 0.4% (2008-2012 5-year est.); Ancestry (includes multiple ancestries): 38.0% German, 20.3% Irish, 8.5% Italian, 8.4% English, 7.5% American (2008-2012 5-year est.).

Economy: Single-family building permits issued: 2 (2013); Multi-family building permits issued: 0 (2013); Homeowner vacancy rate: 0.0%. Rental vacancy rate: 0.0%. (2008-2012 5-year est.); Employment by occupation: 8.7% management, business, and financial, 6.8% computer, engineering, and science, 15.9% education, legal, community service, arts, and media, 4.9% healthcare practitioners, 14.1% service, 32.2% sales and office, 2.8% natural resources, construction, and maintenance, 14.5% production, transportation, and material moving (2008-2012 5-year est.).

Income: Per capita income: $24,442 (2008-2012 5-year est.); Median household income: $53,355 (2008-2012 5-year est.); Average household income: $66,857 (2008-2012 5-year est.); Percent of households with income of $100,000 or more: 20.6% (2008-2012 5-year est.); Poverty rate: 8.8% (2008-2012 5-year est.).

Taxes: Total city taxes per capita: $852 (2011); City property taxes per capita: $803 (2011).

Education: Percent of population age 25 and over with: High school diploma (including GED) or higher: 93.8% (2008-2012 5-year est.); Bachelor's degree or higher: 23.8% (2008-2012 5-year est.); Master's degree or higher: 10.7% (2008-2012 5-year est.).

School District(s)
Byron CUSD 226 (PK-12)
  2011-12 Enrollment: 1,562 . . . . (815) 234-5491

Housing: Homeownership rate: 70.8% (2008-2012 5-year est.); Median home value: $150,900 (2008-2012 5-year est.); Median contract rent: $483 per month (2008-2012 5-year est.); Median year structure built: 1984 (2008-2012 5-year est.).

Health Insurance: 82.8% Private; 20.9% Public; 6.6% None. (2008-2012 5-year est.)

Safety: Violent crime rate: 0.0 per 10,000 population; Property crime rate: 144.9 per 10,000 population (2012).

Transportation: Commute to work: 96.6% car, 0.0% public transportation, 0.0% walk, 1.3% work from home (2008-2012 5-year est.); Travel time to work: 22.0% less than 15 minutes, 40.0% 15 to 30 minutes, 25.7% 30 to 45 minutes, 3.9% 45 to 60 minutes, 8.3% 60 minutes or more (2008-2012 5-year est.)

Additional Information Contacts
Byron Area Chamber of Commerce . . . . (815) 234-5500
  http://byronchamber01.businesscatalyst.com

City of Byron . . . . (815) 234-8709
http://www.cityofbyron.com

CHANA (unincorporated postal area)
Zip Code: 61015
Covers a land area of 40.974 square miles and a water area of 0.052 square miles. Located at 41.99° N. Lat; 89.19° W. Long. Elevation is 781 feet. Population: 946 (2010); Density: 23.1 persons per square mile (2010); Race: 97.3% White, 0.8% Black/African American, 0.0% Asian, 0.1% American Indian/Alaska Native, 0.0% Native Hawaiian/Other Pacific Islander, 1.8% Some other race, 1.0% Two or more races, 2.4% Hispanic of any race (2010); Average household size: 2.52 (2010); Median age: 46.9 (2010); Males per 100 females: 105.7 (2010); Homeownership rate: 85.9% (2010)

CRESTON (village). Covers a land area of 1.142 square miles and a water area of 0 square miles. Located at 41.93° N. Lat; 88.97° W. Long. Elevation is 906 feet.
Population: 535 (1990); 543 (2000); 662 (2010); Density: 608.5 persons per square mile (2008-2012 5-year est.); Race: 100.0% White, 0.0% Black/African American, 0.0% Asian, 0.0% American Indian/Alaska Native, 0.0% Native Hawaiian/Other Pacific Islander, 0.0% Some other race, 0.0% Two or more races, 10.8% Hispanic of any race (2008-2012 5-year est.); Average household size: 3.06 (2008-2012 5-year est.); Median age: 28.4 (2008-2012 5-year est.); Males per 100 females: 79.1 (2008-2012 5-year est.); Marriage status: 30.1% never married, 55.7% now married, 4.9% widowed, 9.3% divorced (2008-2012 5-year est.); Foreign born: 6.2% (2008-2012 5-year est.); Ancestry (includes multiple ancestries): 35.4% German, 25.2% Irish, 19.1% English, 13.4% Norwegian, 10.2% American (2008-2012 5-year est.).
Economy: Single-family building permits issued: 1 (2013); Multi-family building permits issued: 0 (2013); Homeowner vacancy rate: 4.2%. Rental vacancy rate: 0.0%. (2008-2012 5-year est.); Employment by occupation: 11.0% management, business, and financial, 2.8% computer, engineering, and science, 11.2% education, legal, community service, arts, and media, 3.9% healthcare practitioners, 28.9% service, 17.1% sales and office, 8.7% natural resources, construction, and maintenance, 16.3% production, transportation, and material moving (2008-2012 5-year est.).
Income: Per capita income: $22,595 (2008-2012 5-year est.); Median household income: $52,321 (2008-2012 5-year est.); Average household income: $68,883 (2008-2012 5-year est.); Percent of households with income of $100,000 or more: 24.2% (2008-2012 5-year est.); Poverty rate: 5.3% (2008-2012 5-year est.).
Education: Percent of population age 25 and over with: High school diploma (including GED) or higher: 88.4% (2008-2012 5-year est.); Bachelor's degree or higher: 15.1% (2008-2012 5-year est.); Master's degree or higher: 5.9% (2008-2012 5-year est.).

School District(s)
Creston CCSD 161 (KG-08)
2011-12 Enrollment: 124 . . . . (815) 384-3920
Housing: Homeownership rate: 70.9% (2008-2012 5-year est.); Median home value: $141,900 (2008-2012 5-year est.); Median contract rent: $638 per month (2008-2012 5-year est.); Median year structure built: 1956 (2008-2012 5-year est.).
Health Insurance: 79.3% Private; 18.4% Public; 9.5% None. (2008-2012 5-year est.)
Transportation: Commute to work: 87.6% car, 1.7% public transportation, 3.7% walk, 6.2% work from home (2008-2012 5-year est.); Travel time to work: 35.6% less than 15 minutes, 35.0% 15 to 30 minutes, 20.1% 30 to 45 minutes, 2.4% 45 to 60 minutes, 6.9% 60 minutes or more (2008-2012 5-year est.)

DAVIS JUNCTION (village). Covers a land area of 4.238 square miles and a water area of 0 square miles. Located at 42.11° N. Lat; 89.09° W. Long. Elevation is 791 feet.
Population: 246 (1990); 491 (2000); 2,373 (2010); Density: 642.6 persons per square mile (2008-2012 5-year est.); Race: 95.7% White, 1.1% Black/African American, 1.1% Asian, 0.0% American Indian/Alaska Native, 0.0% Native Hawaiian/Other Pacific Islander, 2.1% Some other race, 0.9% Two or more races, 19.6% Hispanic of any race (2008-2012 5-year est.); Average household size: 3.23 (2008-2012 5-year est.); Median age: 30.4 (2008-2012 5-year est.); Males per 100 females: 104.0 (2008-2012 5-year est.); Marriage status: 21.6% never married, 69.9% now married, 1.7% widowed, 6.8% divorced (2008-2012 5-year est.); Foreign born: 12.3% (2008-2012 5-year est.); Ancestry (includes multiple ancestries): 34.4%

German, 12.8% Irish, 9.4% Swedish, 8.4% English, 4.4% Polish (2008-2012 5-year est.).
Economy: Single-family building permits issued: 1 (2013); Multi-family building permits issued: 0 (2013); Homeowner vacancy rate: 1.0%. Rental vacancy rate: 0.0%. (2008-2012 5-year est.); Employment by occupation: 12.1% management, business, and financial, 4.4% computer, engineering, and science, 8.0% education, legal, community service, arts, and media, 2.8% healthcare practitioners, 11.0% service, 24.6% sales and office, 19.1% natural resources, construction, and maintenance, 18.0% production, transportation, and material moving (2008-2012 5-year est.).
Income: Per capita income: $21,042 (2008-2012 5-year est.); Median household income: $66,017 (2008-2012 5-year est.); Average household income: $68,148 (2008-2012 5-year est.); Percent of households with income of $100,000 or more: 17.1% (2008-2012 5-year est.); Poverty rate: 4.6% (2008-2012 5-year est.).
Taxes: Total city taxes per capita: $76 (2011); City property taxes per capita: $27 (2011).
Education: Percent of population age 25 and over with: High school diploma (including GED) or higher: 85.3% (2008-2012 5-year est.); Bachelor's degree or higher: 20.0% (2008-2012 5-year est.); Master's degree or higher: 4.2% (2008-2012 5-year est.).
Housing: Homeownership rate: 88.4% (2008-2012 5-year est.); Median home value: $147,900 (2008-2012 5-year est.); Median contract rent: $335 per month (2008-2012 5-year est.); Median year structure built: 2000 (2008-2012 5-year est.).
Health Insurance: 79.6% Private; 20.3% Public; 7.5% None. (2008-2012 5-year est.)
Transportation: Commute to work: 98.6% car, 0.0% public transportation, 0.7% walk, 0.7% work from home (2008-2012 5-year est.); Travel time to work: 12.2% less than 15 minutes, 38.8% 15 to 30 minutes, 27.5% 30 to 45 minutes, 8.3% 45 to 60 minutes, 13.1% 60 minutes or more (2008-2012 5-year est.)

FORRESTON (village). Covers a land area of 0.903 square miles and a water area of 0 square miles. Located at 42.13° N. Lat; 89.58° W. Long. Elevation is 938 feet.
History: The first sauerkraut festival was held in Forreston in 1913.
Population: 1,361 (1990); 1,469 (2000); 1,446 (2010); Density: 1,751.2 persons per square mile (2008-2012 5-year est.); Race: 96.7% White, 0.0% Black/African American, 0.1% Asian, 0.0% American Indian/Alaska Native, 0.0% Native Hawaiian/Other Pacific Islander, 3.2% Some other race, 1.9% Two or more races, 3.4% Hispanic of any race (2008-2012 5-year est.); Average household size: 2.68 (2008-2012 5-year est.); Median age: 38.8 (2008-2012 5-year est.); Males per 100 females: 99.0 (2008-2012 5-year est.); Marriage status: 28.0% never married, 50.2% now married, 5.0% widowed, 16.9% divorced (2008-2012 5-year est.); Foreign born: 1.4% (2008-2012 5-year est.); Ancestry (includes multiple ancestries): 46.5% German, 16.3% Irish, 14.0% American, 4.2% English, 3.2% Dutch (2008-2012 5-year est.).
Economy: Single-family building permits issued: 0 (2013); Multi-family building permits issued: 0 (2013); Homeowner vacancy rate: 2.2%. Rental vacancy rate: 12.5%. (2008-2012 5-year est.); Employment by occupation: 10.3% management, business, and financial, 1.7% computer, engineering, and science, 4.9% education, legal, community service, arts, and media, 2.0% healthcare practitioners, 24.6% service, 22.8% sales and office, 10.0% natural resources, construction, and maintenance, 23.5% production, transportation, and material moving (2008-2012 5-year est.).
Income: Per capita income: $20,070 (2008-2012 5-year est.); Median household income: $42,460 (2008-2012 5-year est.); Average household income: $52,786 (2008-2012 5-year est.); Percent of households with income of $100,000 or more: 14.1% (2008-2012 5-year est.); Poverty rate: 14.4% (2008-2012 5-year est.).
Education: Percent of population age 25 and over with: High school diploma (including GED) or higher: 89.2% (2008-2012 5-year est.); Bachelor's degree or higher: 14.5% (2008-2012 5-year est.); Master's degree or higher: 3.0% (2008-2012 5-year est.).

School District(s)
Forrestville Valley CUSD 221 (PK-12)
2011-12 Enrollment: 865 . . . . (815) 938-2036
Housing: Homeownership rate: 73.9% (2008-2012 5-year est.); Median home value: $99,700 (2008-2012 5-year est.); Median contract rent: $475 per month (2008-2012 5-year est.); Median year structure built: 1954 (2008-2012 5-year est.).
Health Insurance: 61.1% Private; 36.1% Public; 11.9% None. (2008-2012 5-year est.)

Transportation: Commute to work: 90.4% car, 0.0% public transportation, 3.7% walk, 5.9% work from home (2008-2012 5-year est.); Travel time to work: 30.8% less than 15 minutes, 35.3% 15 to 30 minutes, 15.5% 30 to 45 minutes, 12.1% 45 to 60 minutes, 6.3% 60 minutes or more (2008-2012 5-year est.)

GRAND DETOUR (CDP).
Covers a land area of 1.170 square miles and a water area of 0.244 square miles. Located at 41.90° N. Lat; 89.41° W. Long. Elevation is 656 feet.
Population: n/a (1990); n/a (2000); 429 (2010); Density: 400.9 persons per square mile (2008-2012 5-year est.); Race: 100.0% White, 0.0% Black/African American, 0.0% Asian, 0.0% American Indian/Alaska Native, 0.0% Native Hawaiian/Other Pacific Islander, 0.0% Some other race, 0.0% Two or more races, 14.5% Hispanic of any race (2008-2012 5-year est.); Average household size: 2.00 (2008-2012 5-year est.); Median age: 50.9 (2008-2012 5-year est.); Males per 100 females: 128.8 (2008-2012 5-year est.); Marriage status: 35.8% never married, 41.5% now married, 0.0% widowed, 22.8% divorced (2008-2012 5-year est.); Foreign born: 0.0% (2008-2012 5-year est.); Ancestry (includes multiple ancestries): 31.1% Irish, 30.1% German, 16.6% English, 8.1% American, 5.1% Italian (2008-2012 5-year est.).
Economy: Homeowner vacancy rate: 0.0%. Rental vacancy rate: 0.0%. (2008-2012 5-year est.); Employment by occupation: 10.3% management, business, and financial, 0.0% computer, engineering, and science, 3.0% education, legal, community service, arts, and media, 7.3% healthcare practitioners, 11.9% service, 37.7% sales and office, 2.6% natural resources, construction, and maintenance, 27.2% production, transportation, and material moving (2008-2012 5-year est.).
Income: Per capita income: $27,127 (2008-2012 5-year est.); Median household income: $41,375 (2008-2012 5-year est.); Average household income: $54,373 (2008-2012 5-year est.); Percent of households with income of $100,000 or more: 18.3% (2008-2012 5-year est.); Poverty rate: 18.5% (2008-2012 5-year est.).
Education: Percent of population age 25 and over with: High school diploma (including GED) or higher: 93.4% (2008-2012 5-year est.); Bachelor's degree or higher: 18.3% (2008-2012 5-year est.); Master's degree or higher: 10.7% (2008-2012 5-year est.).
Housing: Homeownership rate: 70.2% (2008-2012 5-year est.); Median home value: $153,400 (2008-2012 5-year est.); Median contract rent: $411 per month (2008-2012 5-year est.); Median year structure built: 1955 (2008-2012 5-year est.).
Health Insurance: 56.3% Private; 22.2% Public; 26.7% None. (2008-2012 5-year est.)
Transportation: Commute to work: 80.2% car, 0.0% public transportation, 15.4% walk, 4.4% work from home (2008-2012 5-year est.); Travel time to work: 42.1% less than 15 minutes, 34.6% 15 to 30 minutes, 3.2% 30 to 45 minutes, 10.4% 45 to 60 minutes, 9.6% 60 minutes or more (2008-2012 5-year est.)

HILLCREST (village).
Covers a land area of 3.161 square miles and a water area of 0 square miles. Located at 41.97° N. Lat; 89.06° W. Long. Elevation is 830 feet.
Population: 828 (1990); 1,158 (2000); 1,326 (2010); Density: 402.8 persons per square mile (2008-2012 5-year est.); Race: 85.7% White, 0.5% Black/African American, 0.0% Asian, 1.3% American Indian/Alaska Native, 0.0% Native Hawaiian/Other Pacific Islander, 12.5% Some other race, 3.7% Two or more races, 27.3% Hispanic of any race (2008-2012 5-year est.); Average household size: 3.00 (2008-2012 5-year est.); Median age: 39.8 (2008-2012 5-year est.); Males per 100 females: 97.7 (2008-2012 5-year est.); Marriage status: 25.2% never married, 62.1% now married, 1.6% widowed, 11.2% divorced (2008-2012 5-year est.); Foreign born: 14.4% (2008-2012 5-year est.); Ancestry (includes multiple ancestries): 24.5% German, 11.2% Irish, 7.7% American, 6.8% English, 3.2% Swedish (2008-2012 5-year est.).
Economy: Single-family building permits issued: 0 (2013); Multi-family building permits issued: 0 (2013); Homeowner vacancy rate: 0.0%. Rental vacancy rate: 28.9%. (2008-2012 5-year est.); Employment by occupation: 6.4% management, business, and financial, 3.6% computer, engineering, and science, 6.2% education, legal, community service, arts, and media, 4.6% healthcare practitioners, 15.8% service, 19.3% sales and office, 17.4% natural resources, construction, and maintenance, 26.6% production, transportation, and material moving (2008-2012 5-year est.).
Income: Per capita income: $23,782 (2008-2012 5-year est.); Median household income: $63,261 (2008-2012 5-year est.); Average household income: $68,888 (2008-2012 5-year est.); Percent of households with income of $100,000 or more: 14.9% (2008-2012 5-year est.); Poverty rate: 5.1% (2008-2012 5-year est.).
Education: Percent of population age 25 and over with: High school diploma (including GED) or higher: 80.9% (2008-2012 5-year est.); Bachelor's degree or higher: 14.0% (2008-2012 5-year est.); Master's degree or higher: 2.8% (2008-2012 5-year est.).
Housing: Homeownership rate: 93.6% (2008-2012 5-year est.); Median home value: $140,400 (2008-2012 5-year est.); Median contract rent: $575 per month (2008-2012 5-year est.); Median year structure built: 1978 (2008-2012 5-year est.).
Health Insurance: 83.3% Private; 21.5% Public; 6.4% None. (2008-2012 5-year est.)
Transportation: Commute to work: 97.3% car, 0.0% public transportation, 0.3% walk, 1.7% work from home (2008-2012 5-year est.); Travel time to work: 47.4% less than 15 minutes, 26.0% 15 to 30 minutes, 15.3% 30 to 45 minutes, 5.9% 45 to 60 minutes, 5.4% 60 minutes or more (2008-2012 5-year est.)

HOLCOMB (unincorporated postal area)
Zip Code: 61043
Covers a land area of 1.885 square miles and a water area of 0 square miles. Located at 42.05° N. Lat; 89.10° W. Long. Elevation is 840 feet.
Population: 131 (2010); Density: 69.5 persons per square mile (2010); Race: 93.9% White, 3.8% Black/African American, 0.0% Asian, 0.8% American Indian/Alaska Native, 0.0% Native Hawaiian/Other Pacific Islander, 1.5% Some other race, 1.5% Two or more races, 2.3% Hispanic of any race (2010); Average household size: 2.62 (2010); Median age: 42.2 (2010); Males per 100 females: 125.9 (2010); Homeownership rate: 80.0% (2010)

LEAF RIVER (village).
Covers a land area of 0.833 square miles and a water area of 0 square miles. Located at 42.12° N. Lat; 89.40° W. Long. Elevation is 725 feet.
Population: 546 (1990); 555 (2000); 443 (2010); Density: 482.4 persons per square mile (2008-2012 5-year est.); Race: 100.0% White, 0.0% Black/African American, 0.0% Asian, 0.0% American Indian/Alaska Native, 0.0% Native Hawaiian/Other Pacific Islander, 0.0% Some other race, 0.0% Two or more races, 0.0% Hispanic of any race (2008-2012 5-year est.); Average household size: 1.88 (2008-2012 5-year est.); Median age: 48.3 (2008-2012 5-year est.); Males per 100 females: 100.0 (2008-2012 5-year est.); Marriage status: 30.7% never married, 44.4% now married, 10.9% widowed, 14.0% divorced (2008-2012 5-year est.); Foreign born: 0.0% (2008-2012 5-year est.); Ancestry (includes multiple ancestries): 43.0% German, 10.0% Irish, 9.7% Italian, 9.2% American, 8.0% Hungarian (2008-2012 5-year est.).
Economy: Single-family building permits issued: 0 (2013); Multi-family building permits issued: 0 (2013); Homeowner vacancy rate: 0.6%. Rental vacancy rate: 0.0%. (2008-2012 5-year est.); Employment by occupation: 3.1% management, business, and financial, 1.5% computer, engineering, and science, 7.7% education, legal, community service, arts, and media, 6.2% healthcare practitioners, 9.3% service, 24.2% sales and office, 11.3% natural resources, construction, and maintenance, 36.6% production, transportation, and material moving (2008-2012 5-year est.).
Income: Per capita income: $23,602 (2008-2012 5-year est.); Median household income: $42,273 (2008-2012 5-year est.); Average household income: $43,766 (2008-2012 5-year est.); Percent of households with income of $100,000 or more: 4.2% (2008-2012 5-year est.); Poverty rate: 13.2% (2008-2012 5-year est.).
Education: Percent of population age 25 and over with: High school diploma (including GED) or higher: 88.0% (2008-2012 5-year est.); Bachelor's degree or higher: 5.2% (2008-2012 5-year est.); Master's degree or higher: 0.0% (2008-2012 5-year est.).
Housing: Homeownership rate: 76.6% (2008-2012 5-year est.); Median home value: $90,000 (2008-2012 5-year est.); Median contract rent: $517 per month (2008-2012 5-year est.); Median year structure built: Before 1940 (2008-2012 5-year est.).
Health Insurance: 59.0% Private; 43.5% Public; 12.9% None. (2008-2012 5-year est.)
Transportation: Commute to work: 100.0% car, 0.0% public transportation, 0.0% walk, 0.0% work from home (2008-2012 5-year est.); Travel time to work: 47.6% less than 15 minutes, 29.6% 15 to 30 minutes, 14.3% 30 to 45 minutes, 6.3% 45 to 60 minutes, 2.1% 60 minutes or more (2008-2012 5-year est.)

LINDENWOOD (unincorporated postal area)

Zip Code: 61049

Covers a land area of 20.400 square miles and a water area of 0.020 square miles. Located at 42.04° N. Lat; 89.00° W. Long. Elevation is 771 feet. Population: 585 (2010); Density: 28.7 persons per square mile (2010); Race: 96.4% White, 0.7% Black/African American, 0.3% Asian, 0.2% American Indian/Alaska Native, 0.0% Native Hawaiian/Other Pacific Islander, 2.4% Some other race, 1.4% Two or more races, 4.3% Hispanic of any race (2010); Average household size: 2.84 (2010); Median age: 40.0 (2010); Males per 100 females: 109.7 (2010); Homeownership rate: 85.0% (2010)

LOST NATION (CDP).

Covers a land area of 2.441 square miles and a water area of 0.111 square miles. Located at 41.91° N. Lat; 89.37° W. Long. Elevation is 705 feet.

Population: n/a (1990); n/a (2000); 708 (2010); Density: 299.1 persons per square mile (2008-2012 5-year est.); Race: 100.0% White, 0.0% Black/African American, 0.0% Asian, 0.0% American Indian/Alaska Native, 0.0% Native Hawaiian/Other Pacific Islander, 0.0% Some other race, 0.0% Two or more races, 0.0% Hispanic of any race (2008-2012 5-year est.); Average household size: 2.47 (2008-2012 5-year est.); Median age: 53.2 (2008-2012 5-year est.); Males per 100 females: 102.2 (2008-2012 5-year est.); Marriage status: 16.8% never married, 78.6% now married, 1.3% widowed, 3.3% divorced (2008-2012 5-year est.); Foreign born: 4.1% (2008-2012 5-year est.); Ancestry (includes multiple ancestries): 32.1% German, 31.2% English, 15.6% Irish, 9.6% British, 7.7% Polish (2008-2012 5-year est.).

Economy: Homeowner vacancy rate: 0.0%. Rental vacancy rate: 0.0%. (2008-2012 5-year est.); Employment by occupation: 10.3% management, business, and financial, 3.5% computer, engineering, and science, 4.5% education, legal, community service, arts, and media, 8.7% healthcare practitioners, 27.6% service, 23.1% sales and office, 0.0% natural resources, construction, and maintenance, 22.4% production, transportation, and material moving (2008-2012 5-year est.).

Income: Per capita income: $32,948 (2008-2012 5-year est.); Median household income: $54,886 (2008-2012 5-year est.); Average household income: $81,155 (2008-2012 5-year est.); Percent of households with income of $100,000 or more: 42.6% (2008-2012 5-year est.); Poverty rate: 6.2% (2008-2012 5-year est.).

Education: Percent of population age 25 and over with: High school diploma (including GED) or higher: 98.4% (2008-2012 5-year est.); Bachelor's degree or higher: 23.4% (2008-2012 5-year est.); Master's degree or higher: 9.1% (2008-2012 5-year est.).

Housing: Homeownership rate: 100.0% (2008-2012 5-year est.); Median home value: $191,500 (2008-2012 5-year est.); Median contract rent: n/a per month (2008-2012 5-year est.); Median year structure built: 1991 (2008-2012 5-year est.).

Health Insurance: 97.1% Private; 39.0% Public; 0.0% None. (2008-2012 5-year est.)

Transportation: Commute to work: 92.4% car, 0.0% public transportation, 0.0% walk, 7.6% work from home (2008-2012 5-year est.); Travel time to work: 0.0% less than 15 minutes, 64.6% 15 to 30 minutes, 23.2% 30 to 45 minutes, 5.4% 45 to 60 minutes, 6.8% 60 minutes or more (2008-2012 5-year est.)

MONROE CENTER (village).

Covers a land area of 1.207 square miles and a water area of 0 square miles. Located at 42.10° N. Lat; 88.99° W. Long. Elevation is 853 feet.

Population: n/a (1990); n/a (2000); 471 (2010); Density: 388.6 persons per square mile (2008-2012 5-year est.); Race: 99.8% White, 0.0% Black/African American, 0.2% Asian, 0.0% American Indian/Alaska Native, 0.0% Native Hawaiian/Other Pacific Islander, 0.0% Some other race, 0.0% Two or more races, 2.8% Hispanic of any race (2008-2012 5-year est.); Average household size: 3.07 (2008-2012 5-year est.); Median age: 34.5 (2008-2012 5-year est.); Males per 100 females: 122.3 (2008-2012 5-year est.); Marriage status: 29.4% never married, 62.1% now married, 2.4% widowed, 6.2% divorced (2008-2012 5-year est.); Foreign born: 0.6% (2008-2012 5-year est.); Ancestry (includes multiple ancestries): 23.0% German, 14.1% Irish, 12.4% American, 10.4% English, 8.3% Norwegian (2008-2012 5-year est.).

Economy: Single-family building permits issued: 0 (2013); Multi-family building permits issued: 0 (2013); Homeowner vacancy rate: 5.5%. Rental vacancy rate: 27.3%. (2008-2012 5-year est.); Employment by occupation: 6.9% management, business, and financial, 2.4% computer, engineering, and science, 3.7% education, legal, community service, arts, and media,

2.0% healthcare practitioners, 17.5% service, 26.8% sales and office, 22.4% natural resources, construction, and maintenance, 18.3% production, transportation, and material moving (2008-2012 5-year est.).

Income: Per capita income: $23,506 (2008-2012 5-year est.); Median household income: $68,875 (2008-2012 5-year est.); Average household income: $69,343 (2008-2012 5-year est.); Percent of households with income of $100,000 or more: 18.3% (2008-2012 5-year est.); Poverty rate: 2.6% (2008-2012 5-year est.).

Education: Percent of population age 25 and over with: High school diploma (including GED) or higher: 88.8% (2008-2012 5-year est.); Bachelor's degree or higher: 18.1% (2008-2012 5-year est.); Master's degree or higher: 4.3% (2008-2012 5-year est.).

School District(s)

Meridian CUSD 223 (PK-12)

2011-12 Enrollment: 1,980 . . . . (815) 645-2606

Housing: Homeownership rate: 89.5% (2008-2012 5-year est.); Median home value: $137,500 (2008-2012 5-year est.); Median contract rent: $481 per month (2008-2012 5-year est.); Median year structure built: 1954 (2008-2012 5-year est.).

Health Insurance: 92.3% Private; 13.9% Public; 4.7% None. (2008-2012 5-year est.)

Transportation: Commute to work: 98.8% car, 0.0% public transportation, 1.2% walk, 0.0% work from home (2008-2012 5-year est.); Travel time to work: 4.5% less than 15 minutes, 52.9% 15 to 30 minutes, 24.0% 30 to 45 minutes, 8.7% 45 to 60 minutes, 9.9% 60 minutes or more (2008-2012 5-year est.)

MOUNT MORRIS (village).

Covers a land area of 1.501 square miles and a water area of 0 square miles. Located at 42.05° N. Lat; 89.43° W. Long. Elevation is 909 feet.

History: Mount Morris was settled in 1838 by a group from Maryland. The railroad bypassed Mount Morris, but the town continued to grow. An early industry was the Kable Brothers printing company founded in 1898.

Population: 2,919 (1990); 3,013 (2000); 2,998 (2010); Density: 2,038.3 persons per square mile (2008-2012 5-year est.); Race: 94.3% White, 0.2% Black/African American, 0.3% Asian, 0.0% American Indian/Alaska Native, 0.0% Native Hawaiian/Other Pacific Islander, 5.2% Some other race, 2.6% Two or more races, 7.1% Hispanic of any race (2008-2012 5-year est.); Average household size: 2.33 (2008-2012 5-year est.); Median age: 42.1 (2008-2012 5-year est.); Males per 100 females: 92.0 (2008-2012 5-year est.); Marriage status: 23.1% never married, 54.1% now married, 12.1% widowed, 10.7% divorced (2008-2012 5-year est.); Foreign born: 3.0% (2008-2012 5-year est.); Ancestry (includes multiple ancestries): 37.2% German, 19.4% Irish, 7.5% American, 6.3% English, 5.5% Italian (2008-2012 5-year est.).

Economy: Single-family building permits issued: 0 (2013); Multi-family building permits issued: 0 (2013); Homeowner vacancy rate: 7.8%. Rental vacancy rate: 0.0%. (2008-2012 5-year est.); Employment by occupation: 7.1% management, business, and financial, 3.6% computer, engineering, and science, 15.6% education, legal, community service, arts, and media, 5.1% healthcare practitioners, 19.4% service, 22.6% sales and office, 6.3% natural resources, construction, and maintenance, 20.4% production, transportation, and material moving (2008-2012 5-year est.).

Income: Per capita income: $23,966 (2008-2012 5-year est.); Median household income: $48,594 (2008-2012 5-year est.); Average household income: $55,980 (2008-2012 5-year est.); Percent of households with income of $100,000 or more: 10.1% (2008-2012 5-year est.); Poverty rate: 20.8% (2008-2012 5-year est.).

Education: Percent of population age 25 and over with: High school diploma (including GED) or higher: 85.6% (2008-2012 5-year est.); Bachelor's degree or higher: 20.4% (2008-2012 5-year est.); Master's degree or higher: 7.6% (2008-2012 5-year est.).

School District(s)

Oregon CUSD 220 (PK-12)

2011-12 Enrollment: 1,559 . . . . (815) 732-2186

Housing: Homeownership rate: 62.9% (2008-2012 5-year est.); Median home value: $122,900 (2008-2012 5-year est.); Median contract rent: $433 per month (2008-2012 5-year est.); Median year structure built: 1953 (2008-2012 5-year est.).

Health Insurance: 69.6% Private; 36.3% Public; 9.5% None. (2008-2012 5-year est.)

Safety: Violent crime rate: 10.1 per 10,000 population; Property crime rate: 114.2 per 10,000 population (2012).

Transportation: Commute to work: 97.9% car, 0.0% public transportation, 1.6% walk, 0.5% work from home (2008-2012 5-year est.); Travel time to

work: 41.4% less than 15 minutes, 30.8% 15 to 30 minutes, 20.1% 30 to 45 minutes, 4.3% 45 to 60 minutes, 3.4% 60 minutes or more (2008-2012 5-year est.)

OREGON (city). County seat. Covers a land area of 1.964 square miles and a water area of 0.068 square miles. Located at 42.01° N. Lat; 89.34° W. Long. Elevation is 709 feet.

History: Oregon developed as a trading center and industrial town, and as the seat of Ogle County. It was also known as an artistic community, with the Eagle's Nest Art Colony established nearby in 1898.

Population: 3,891 (1990); 4,060 (2000); 3,721 (2010); Density: 1,869.1 persons per square mile (2008-2012 5-year est.); Race: 97.4% White, 1.2% Black/African American, 0.0% Asian, 0.0% American Indian/Alaska Native, 0.0% Native Hawaiian/Other Pacific Islander, 1.4% Some other race, 1.4% Two or more races, 0.7% Hispanic of any race (2008-2012 5-year est.); Average household size: 2.22 (2008-2012 5-year est.); Median age: 45.3 (2008-2012 5-year est.); Males per 100 females: 97.5 (2008-2012 5-year est.); Marriage status: 28.2% never married, 50.5% now married, 7.8% widowed, 13.5% divorced (2008-2012 5-year est.); Foreign born: 4.9% (2008-2012 5-year est.); Ancestry (includes multiple ancestries): 39.9% German, 9.8% Irish, 8.7% English, 7.4% Italian, 5.7% American (2008-2012 5-year est.).

Economy: Single-family building permits issued: 2 (2013); Multi-family building permits issued: 0 (2013); Homeowner vacancy rate: 3.5%. Rental vacancy rate: 19.5%. (2008-2012 5-year est.); Employment by occupation: 11.5% management, business, and financial, 2.5% computer, engineering, and science, 7.4% education, legal, community service, arts, and media, 4.2% healthcare practitioners, 21.5% service, 23.5% sales and office, 8.0% natural resources, construction, and maintenance, 21.4% production, transportation, and material moving (2008-2012 5-year est.).

Income: Per capita income: $25,510 (2008-2012 5-year est.); Median household income: $47,808 (2008-2012 5-year est.); Average household income: $56,265 (2008-2012 5-year est.); Percent of households with income of $100,000 or more: 14.4% (2008-2012 5-year est.); Poverty rate: 12.8% (2008-2012 5-year est.).

Education: Percent of population age 25 and over with: High school diploma (including GED) or higher: 89.4% (2008-2012 5-year est.); Bachelor's degree or higher: 17.2% (2008-2012 5-year est.); Master's degree or higher: 5.9% (2008-2012 5-year est.).

School District(s)

Oregon CUSD 220 (PK-12)
   2011-12 Enrollment: 1,559 . . . . (815) 732-2186

Housing: Homeownership rate: 57.6% (2008-2012 5-year est.); Median home value: $119,300 (2008-2012 5-year est.); Median contract rent: $479 per month (2008-2012 5-year est.); Median year structure built: 1949 (2008-2012 5-year est.).

Health Insurance: 74.2% Private; 33.6% Public; 14.1% None. (2008-2012 5-year est.)

Transportation: Commute to work: 91.5% car, 0.4% public transportation, 4.8% walk, 2.1% work from home (2008-2012 5-year est.); Travel time to work: 48.8% less than 15 minutes, 18.9% 15 to 30 minutes, 12.5% 30 to 45 minutes, 10.1% 45 to 60 minutes, 9.7% 60 minutes or more (2008-2012 5-year est.)

Additional Information Contacts

Oregon Area Chamber of Commerce . . . . (815) 732-2100
   http://www.oregonil.com

POLO (city). Covers a land area of 1.355 square miles and a water area of 0 square miles. Located at 41.98° N. Lat; 89.58° W. Long. Elevation is 863 feet.

History: The city of Polo was named for Venetian traveler Marco Polo, and developed as a trading center for a stock raising area.

Population: 2,514 (1990); 2,477 (2000); 2,355 (2010); Density: 1,778.6 persons per square mile (2008-2012 5-year est.); Race: 99.1% White, 0.0% Black/African American, 0.0% Asian, 0.0% American Indian/Alaska Native, 0.0% Native Hawaiian/Other Pacific Islander, 0.9% Some other race, 0.9% Two or more races, 6.6% Hispanic of any race (2008-2012 5-year est.); Average household size: 2.47 (2008-2012 5-year est.); Median age: 39.0 (2008-2012 5-year est.); Males per 100 females: 110.7 (2008-2012 5-year est.); Marriage status: 27.5% never married, 46.4% now married, 12.4% widowed, 13.7% divorced (2008-2012 5-year est.); Foreign born: 1.2% (2008-2012 5-year est.); Ancestry (includes multiple ancestries): 33.1% German, 14.6% Irish, 12.2% American, 8.7% English, 4.0% Swedish (2008-2012 5-year est.).

Economy: Single-family building permits issued: 0 (2013); Multi-family building permits issued: 0 (2013); Homeowner vacancy rate: 1.0%. Rental vacancy rate: 5.2%. (2008-2012 5-year est.); Employment by occupation: 15.6% management, business, and financial, 2.3% computer, engineering, and science, 5.5% education, legal, community service, arts, and media, 8.3% healthcare practitioners, 19.4% service, 18.1% sales and office, 15.2% natural resources, construction, and maintenance, 15.5% production, transportation, and material moving (2008-2012 5-year est.).

Income: Per capita income: $28,430 (2008-2012 5-year est.); Median household income: $49,519 (2008-2012 5-year est.); Average household income: $69,368 (2008-2012 5-year est.); Percent of households with income of $100,000 or more: 17.4% (2008-2012 5-year est.); Poverty rate: 10.5% (2008-2012 5-year est.).

Education: Percent of population age 25 and over with: High school diploma (including GED) or higher: 93.6% (2008-2012 5-year est.); Bachelor's degree or higher: 13.7% (2008-2012 5-year est.); Master's degree or higher: 3.7% (2008-2012 5-year est.).

School District(s)

Polo CUSD 222 (PK-12)
   2011-12 Enrollment: 674 . . . . (815) 946-3815

Housing: Homeownership rate: 75.1% (2008-2012 5-year est.); Median home value: $90,800 (2008-2012 5-year est.); Median contract rent: $548 per month (2008-2012 5-year est.); Median year structure built: Before 1940 (2008-2012 5-year est.).

Health Insurance: 78.2% Private; 35.8% Public; 6.1% None. (2008-2012 5-year est.)

Safety: Violent crime rate: 12.8 per 10,000 population; Property crime rate: 158.1 per 10,000 population (2012).

Transportation: Commute to work: 86.7% car, 0.0% public transportation, 8.4% walk, 3.3% work from home (2008-2012 5-year est.); Travel time to work: 28.0% less than 15 minutes, 41.4% 15 to 30 minutes, 21.9% 30 to 45 minutes, 2.4% 45 to 60 minutes, 6.2% 60 minutes or more (2008-2012 5-year est.)

Additional Information Contacts

Polo Chamber of Commerce . . . . (815) 946-3131
   http://www.poloil.org/ChamberCommerce.html

ROCHELLE (city). Covers a land area of 12.900 square miles and a water area of 0.019 square miles. Located at 41.92° N. Lat; 89.06° W. Long. Elevation is 823 feet.

History: Rochelle developed as an agricultural center and the home of the Del Monte cannery. Charles Butterfield, composer of "When You and I Were Young, Maggie," and Francis Rose, who wrote "Just Before the Battle, Mother," both lived in Rochelle.

Population: 8,769 (1990); 9,424 (2000); 9,574 (2010); Density: 742.5 persons per square mile (2008-2012 5-year est.); Race: 93.4% White, 2.2% Black/African American, 1.5% Asian, 0.0% American Indian/Alaska Native, 0.0% Native Hawaiian/Other Pacific Islander, 2.9% Some other race, 1.8% Two or more races, 23.6% Hispanic of any race (2008-2012 5-year est.); Average household size: 2.40 (2008-2012 5-year est.); Median age: 36.9 (2008-2012 5-year est.); Males per 100 females: 92.4 (2008-2012 5-year est.); Marriage status: 32.3% never married, 45.4% now married, 7.7% widowed, 14.6% divorced (2008-2012 5-year est.); Foreign born: 10.3% (2008-2012 5-year est.); Ancestry (includes multiple ancestries): 30.7% German, 12.8% Irish, 9.8% American, 8.0% English, 4.5% Italian (2008-2012 5-year est.).

Economy: Single-family building permits issued: 3 (2013); Multi-family building permits issued: 0 (2013); Homeowner vacancy rate: 2.1%. Rental vacancy rate: 7.3%. (2008-2012 5-year est.); Employment by occupation: 12.3% management, business, and financial, 2.5% computer, engineering, and science, 6.8% education, legal, community service, arts, and media, 2.4% healthcare practitioners, 12.1% service, 26.0% sales and office, 11.1% natural resources, construction, and maintenance, 26.8% production, transportation, and material moving (2008-2012 5-year est.).

Income: Per capita income: $22,947 (2008-2012 5-year est.); Median household income: $46,250 (2008-2012 5-year est.); Average household income: $54,034 (2008-2012 5-year est.); Percent of households with income of $100,000 or more: 12.9% (2008-2012 5-year est.); Poverty rate: 18.1% (2008-2012 5-year est.).

Taxes: Total city taxes per capita: $313 (2011); City property taxes per capita: $141 (2011).

Education: Percent of population age 25 and over with: High school diploma (including GED) or higher: 80.1% (2008-2012 5-year est.); Bachelor's degree or higher: 15.3% (2008-2012 5-year est.); Master's degree or higher: 5.2% (2008-2012 5-year est.).

School District(s)

Rochelle CCSD 231 (PK-08)
    2011-12 Enrollment: 1,749 . . . . (815) 562-6363
Rochelle Twp HSD 212 (09-12)
    2011-12 Enrollment: 942. . . . . (815) 562-4161
Housing: Homeownership rate: 57.3% (2008-2012 5-year est.); Median home value: $132,400 (2008-2012 5-year est.); Median contract rent: $531 per month (2008-2012 5-year est.); Median year structure built: 1967 (2008-2012 5-year est.).
Health Insurance: 63.3% Private; 40.8% Public; 13.3% None. (2008-2012 5-year est.)
Hospitals: Rochelle Community Hospital (42 beds)
Transportation: Commute to work: 87.9% car, 0.3% public transportation, 6.1% walk, 4.4% work from home (2008-2012 5-year est.); Travel time to work: 56.4% less than 15 minutes, 13.8% 15 to 30 minutes, 19.0% 30 to 45 minutes, 6.7% 45 to 60 minutes, 4.1% 60 minutes or more (2008-2012 5-year est.)
Airports: Rochelle Municipal Airport (general aviation)
Additional Information Contacts
City of Rochelle . . . . (815) 562-6161
    http://www.cityofrochelle.net
Rochelle Area Chamber of Commerce . . . . (815) 562-4189
    http://www.rochellechamber.org

STILLMAN VALLEY (village). Covers a land area of 0.543 square miles and a water area of 0 square miles. Located at 42.10° N. Lat; 89.18° W. Long. Elevation is 712 feet.
History: The Battle of Stillman's Run took place here in 1832, where a monument was placed to mark the dead.
Population: 848 (1990); 1,048 (2000); 1,120 (2010); Density: 1,875.3 persons per square mile (2008-2012 5-year est.); Race: 96.8% White, 0.0% Black/African American, 2.8% Asian, 0.0% American Indian/Alaska Native, 0.0% Native Hawaiian/Other Pacific Islander, 0.4% Some other race, 0.4% Two or more races, 0.0% Hispanic of any race (2008-2012 5-year est.); Average household size: 2.44 (2008-2012 5-year est.); Median age: 36.2 (2008-2012 5-year est.); Males per 100 females: 76.7 (2008-2012 5-year est.); Marriage status: 21.6% never married, 60.0% now married, 7.0% widowed, 11.4% divorced (2008-2012 5-year est.); Foreign born: 1.1% (2008-2012 5-year est.); Ancestry (includes multiple ancestries): 46.0% German, 19.4% Swedish, 13.3% Irish, 9.2% English, 8.1% American (2008-2012 5-year est.).
Economy: Single-family building permits issued: 0 (2013); Multi-family building permits issued: 0 (2013); Homeowner vacancy rate: 0.0%. Rental vacancy rate: 6.2%. (2008-2012 5-year est.); Employment by occupation: 10.3% management, business, and financial, 1.3% computer, engineering, and science, 5.9% education, legal, community service, arts, and media, 6.9% healthcare practitioners, 21.6% service, 23.3% sales and office, 9.4% natural resources, construction, and maintenance, 21.2% production, transportation, and material moving (2008-2012 5-year est.).
Income: Per capita income: $22,233 (2008-2012 5-year est.); Median household income: $42,232 (2008-2012 5-year est.); Average household income: $53,711 (2008-2012 5-year est.); Percent of households with income of $100,000 or more: 10.1% (2008-2012 5-year est.); Poverty rate: 8.8% (2008-2012 5-year est.).
Education: Percent of population age 25 and over with: High school diploma (including GED) or higher: 91.8% (2008-2012 5-year est.); Bachelor's degree or higher: 11.4% (2008-2012 5-year est.); Master's degree or higher: 2.9% (2008-2012 5-year est.).

School District(s)

Meridian CUSD 223 (PK-12)
    2011-12 Enrollment: 1,980 . . . . (815) 645-2606
Housing: Homeownership rate: 70.7% (2008-2012 5-year est.); Median home value: $133,200 (2008-2012 5-year est.); Median contract rent: $625 per month (2008-2012 5-year est.); Median year structure built: 1963 (2008-2012 5-year est.).
Health Insurance: 75.3% Private; 20.8% Public; 15.7% None. (2008-2012 5-year est.)
Transportation: Commute to work: 93.5% car, 0.0% public transportation, 1.8% walk, 4.1% work from home (2008-2012 5-year est.); Travel time to work: 26.1% less than 15 minutes, 35.9% 15 to 30 minutes, 31.0% 30 to 45 minutes, 6.2% 45 to 60 minutes, 0.8% 60 minutes or more (2008-2012 5-year est.)

WOOSUNG (unincorporated postal area)
Zip Code: 61091

Covers a land area of 0.812 square miles and a water area of 0 square miles. Located at 41.90° N. Lat; 89.52° W. Long. Elevation is 827 feet. Population: 63 (2010); Density: 77.5 persons per square mile (2010); Race: 93.7% White, 0.0% Black/African American, 0.0% Asian, 0.0% American Indian/Alaska Native, 0.0% Native Hawaiian/Other Pacific Islander, 6.3% Some other race, 6.3% Two or more races, 7.9% Hispanic of any race (2010); Average household size: 2.52 (2010); Median age: 47.8 (2010); Males per 100 females: 117.2 (2010); Homeownership rate: 52.0% (2010)

Peoria County

Located in central Illinois; bounded on the east and south by the Illinois River and Lake Peoria; drained by the Spoon River and Kickapoo Creek. Covers a land area of 619.209 square miles, a water area of 11.390 square miles, and is located in the Central Time Zone at 40.79° N. Lat., 89.77° W. Long. The county was founded in 1825. County seat is Peoria.

Peoria County is part of the Peoria, IL Metropolitan Statistical Area. The entire metro area includes: Marshall County, IL; Peoria County, IL; Stark County, IL; Tazewell County, IL; Woodford County, IL

Weather Station: Peoria Greater Peoria Arpt   Elevation: 651 feet

	Jan	Feb	Mar	Apr	May	Jun	Jul	Aug	Sep	Oct	Nov	Dec
High	33	38	50	63	73	82	86	84	77	64	50	36
Low	17	21	31	41	52	61	66	64	55	43	33	21
Precip	1.7	1.8	2.8	3.6	4.1	3.6	3.7	3.4	3.1	2.9	3.1	2.4
Snow	6.8	5.9	2.9	0.9	tr	tr	tr	0.0	tr	tr	1.3	6.5

High and Low temperatures in degrees Fahrenheit; Precipitation and Snow in inches

Weather Station: Princeville   Elevation: 734 feet

	Jan	Feb	Mar	Apr	May	Jun	Jul	Aug	Sep	Oct	Nov	Dec
High	32	37	49	63	73	82	85	83	77	65	50	36
Low	13	17	26	37	48	57	61	59	50	39	29	17
Precip	2.1	1.9	2.9	3.6	4.5	3.7	3.9	3.9	3.4	2.8	3.0	2.4
Snow	6.1	5.9	2.3	0.4	tr	0.0	0.0	0.0	0.0	tr	1.0	5.9

High and Low temperatures in degrees Fahrenheit; Precipitation and Snow in inches

Population: 182,827 (1990); 183,433 (2000); 186,494 (2010); Race: 75.3% White, 17.7% Black/African American, 3.2% Asian, 0.3% American Indian/Alaska Native, 0.0% Native Hawaiian/Other Pacific Islander, 3.5% Some other race, 2.5% Two or more races, 3.8% Hispanic of any race (2008-2012 5-year est.); Density: 302.4 persons per square mile (2008-2012 5-year est.); Average household size: 2.38 (2008-2012 5-year est.); Median age: 36.7 (2008-2012 5-year est.); Males per 100 females: 94.0 (2008-2012 5-year est.).
Religion: Six largest groups: 14.0% Catholicism, 10.6% Muslim Estimate, 5.6% Lutheran, 5.6% Baptist, 5.1% Non-denominational Protestant, 4.2% Methodist/Pietist (2010)
Economy: Unemployment rate: 7.6% (April 2014); Total civilian labor force: 93,585 (April 2014); Leading industries: 20.3% health care and social assistance; 9.8% retail trade; 8.4% administration, support, waste management, remediation services (2012); Farms: 917 totaling 250,263 acres (2012); Companies that employ 500 or more persons: 19 (2012); Companies that employ 100 to 499 persons: 111 (2012); Companies that employ less than 100 persons: 4,457 (2012); Black-owned businesses: n/a (2007); Hispanic-owned businesses: 161 (2007); Asian-owned businesses: 375 (2007); Women-owned businesses: 3,994 (2007); Single-family building permits issued: 221 (2013); Multi-family building permits issued: 6 (2013).
Income: Per capita income: $28,979 (2008-2012 5-year est.); Median household income: $50,925 (2008-2012 5-year est.); Average household income: $69,721 (2008-2012 5-year est.); Percent of households with income of $100,000 or more: 19.5% (2008-2012 5-year est.); Poverty rate: 16.8% (2008-2012 5-year est.); Bankruptcy rate: 3.68% (2013).
Taxes: Total county taxes per capita: $189 (2011); County property taxes per capita: $130 (2011).
Education: Percent of population age 25 and over with: High school diploma (including GED) or higher: 89.7% (2008-2012 5-year est.); Bachelor's degree or higher: 28.8% (2008-2012 5-year est.); Master's degree or higher: 10.9% (2008-2012 5-year est.).
Housing: Homeownership rate: 66.9% (2008-2012 5-year est.); Median home value: $124,000 (2008-2012 5-year est.); Median contract rent: $545 per month (2008-2012 5-year est.); Median year structure built: 1962 (2008-2012 5-year est.)

Health: Birth rate: 138.8 per 10,000 population (2013); Death rate: 91.4 per 10,000 population (2013); Age-adjusted cancer mortality rate: 201.9 deaths per 100,000 population (2011); Number of physicians: 52.3 per 10,000 population (2011); Hospital beds: 58.2 per 10,000 population (2010); Hospital admissions: 2,776.1 per 10,000 population (2010).
Environment: Air Quality Index: 70.4% good, 29.6% moderate, 0.0% unhealthy for sensitive individuals, 0.0% unhealthy (percent of days in 2013)
Elections: 2012 Presidential election results: 51.3% Obama, 46.9% Romney
National and State Parks: Jubilee College State Park; Spring Branch State Conservation Area; Spring Lake State Park
Additional Information Contacts
Peoria County Government . . . . (309) 672-6056
  http://www.peoriacounty.org

Peoria County Communities

BARTONVILLE (village). Covers a land area of 8.187 square miles and a water area of 0.425 square miles. Located at 40.64° N. Lat; 89.66° W. Long. Elevation is 505 feet.
History: Bartonville developed as a coal mining community, with factories that manufactured steel wire and fence.
Population: 5,643 (1990); 6,310 (2000); 6,471 (2010); Density: 787.6 persons per square mile (2008-2012 5-year est.); Race: 95.6% White, 2.9% Black/African American, 0.4% Asian, 0.2% American Indian/Alaska Native, 0.0% Native Hawaiian/Other Pacific Islander, 0.9% Some other race, 0.9% Two or more races, 1.6% Hispanic of any race (2008-2012 5-year est.); Average household size: 2.41 (2008-2012 5-year est.); Median age: 38.7 (2008-2012 5-year est.); Males per 100 females: 105.2 (2008-2012 5-year est.); Marriage status: 31.0% never married, 47.7% now married, 7.2% widowed, 14.1% divorced (2008-2012 5-year est.); Foreign born: 0.6% (2008-2012 5-year est.); Ancestry (includes multiple ancestries): 35.1% German, 13.5% American, 12.7% Irish, 11.4% English, 3.6% Italian (2008-2012 5-year est.).
Economy: Single-family building permits issued: 4 (2013); Multi-family building permits issued: 0 (2013); Homeowner vacancy rate: 2.2%. Rental vacancy rate: 2.0%. (2008-2012 5-year est.); Employment by occupation: 7.4% management, business, and financial, 1.7% computer, engineering, and science, 7.1% education, legal, community service, arts, and media, 5.2% healthcare practitioners, 12.5% service, 33.9% sales and office, 9.8% natural resources, construction, and maintenance, 22.4% production, transportation, and material moving (2008-2012 5-year est.).
Income: Per capita income: $25,828 (2008-2012 5-year est.); Median household income: $50,442 (2008-2012 5-year est.); Average household income: $61,683 (2008-2012 5-year est.); Percent of households with income of $100,000 or more: 16.4% (2008-2012 5-year est.); Poverty rate: 10.4% (2008-2012 5-year est.).
Education: Percent of population age 25 and over with: High school diploma (including GED) or higher: 91.0% (2008-2012 5-year est.); Bachelor's degree or higher: 12.8% (2008-2012 5-year est.); Master's degree or higher: 3.6% (2008-2012 5-year est.).

School District(s)
Bartonville SD 66 (PK-08)
  2011-12 Enrollment: 272 . . . . (309) 697-3253
Monroe SD 70 (KG-08)
  2011-12 Enrollment: 291 . . . . (309) 697-3120
Housing: Homeownership rate: 76.3% (2008-2012 5-year est.); Median home value: $107,100 (2008-2012 5-year est.); Median contract rent: $520 per month (2008-2012 5-year est.); Median year structure built: 1956 (2008-2012 5-year est.).
Health Insurance: 76.3% Private; 32.3% Public; 7.9% None. (2008-2012 5-year est.)
Safety: Violent crime rate: 38.5 per 10,000 population; Property crime rate: 313.0 per 10,000 population (2012).
Transportation: Commute to work: 95.3% car, 0.0% public transportation, 1.4% walk, 1.1% work from home (2008-2012 5-year est.); Travel time to work: 26.8% less than 15 minutes, 56.5% 15 to 30 minutes, 13.0% 30 to 45 minutes, 0.4% 45 to 60 minutes, 3.2% 60 minutes or more (2008-2012 5-year est.)

BELLEVUE (village). Covers a land area of 2.080 square miles and a water area of 0 square miles. Located at 40.69° N. Lat; 89.67° W. Long. Elevation is 676 feet.
History: Incorporated 1941.

Population: 1,491 (1990); 1,887 (2000); 1,978 (2010); Density: 1,013.9 persons per square mile (2008-2012 5-year est.); Race: 92.9% White, 0.2% Black/African American, 1.5% Asian, 0.0% American Indian/Alaska Native, 0.0% Native Hawaiian/Other Pacific Islander, 5.4% Some other race, 5.1% Two or more races, 2.5% Hispanic of any race (2008-2012 5-year est.); Average household size: 2.56 (2008-2012 5-year est.); Median age: 38.8 (2008-2012 5-year est.); Males per 100 females: 97.8 (2008-2012 5-year est.); Marriage status: 29.3% never married, 51.6% now married, 5.7% widowed, 13.3% divorced (2008-2012 5-year est.); Foreign born: 0.9% (2008-2012 5-year est.); Ancestry (includes multiple ancestries): 32.0% German, 19.2% Irish, 9.8% English, 7.3% Italian, 6.9% American (2008-2012 5-year est.).
Economy: Single-family building permits issued: 4 (2013); Multi-family building permits issued: 0 (2013); Homeowner vacancy rate: 1.0%. Rental vacancy rate: 0.0%. (2008-2012 5-year est.); Employment by occupation: 5.7% management, business, and financial, 4.3% computer, engineering, and science, 9.3% education, legal, community service, arts, and media, 4.4% healthcare practitioners, 17.3% service, 31.0% sales and office, 8.8% natural resources, construction, and maintenance, 19.2% production, transportation, and material moving (2008-2012 5-year est.).
Income: Per capita income: $25,423 (2008-2012 5-year est.); Median household income: $51,107 (2008-2012 5-year est.); Average household income: $63,291 (2008-2012 5-year est.); Percent of households with income of $100,000 or more: 14.7% (2008-2012 5-year est.); Poverty rate: 12.4% (2008-2012 5-year est.).
Education: Percent of population age 25 and over with: High school diploma (including GED) or higher: 84.4% (2008-2012 5-year est.); Bachelor's degree or higher: 13.2% (2008-2012 5-year est.); Master's degree or higher: 4.8% (2008-2012 5-year est.).
Housing: Homeownership rate: 84.8% (2008-2012 5-year est.); Median home value: $84,100 (2008-2012 5-year est.); Median contract rent: $513 per month (2008-2012 5-year est.); Median year structure built: 1967 (2008-2012 5-year est.).
Health Insurance: 65.2% Private; 37.3% Public; 10.8% None. (2008-2012 5-year est.)
Transportation: Commute to work: 93.7% car, 0.9% public transportation, 2.6% walk, 0.5% work from home (2008-2012 5-year est.); Travel time to work: 35.1% less than 15 minutes, 49.2% 15 to 30 minutes, 7.4% 30 to 45 minutes, 0.5% 45 to 60 minutes, 7.8% 60 minutes or more (2008-2012 5-year est.)

BRIMFIELD (village). Covers a land area of 0.779 square miles and a water area of 0.005 square miles. Located at 40.84° N. Lat; 89.88° W. Long. Elevation is 702 feet.
Population: 797 (1990); 933 (2000); 868 (2010); Density: 1,168.4 persons per square mile (2008-2012 5-year est.); Race: 96.4% White, 0.0% Black/African American, 0.0% Asian, 0.0% American Indian/Alaska Native, 0.0% Native Hawaiian/Other Pacific Islander, 3.6% Some other race, 2.1% Two or more races, 1.5% Hispanic of any race (2008-2012 5-year est.); Average household size: 2.76 (2008-2012 5-year est.); Median age: 33.4 (2008-2012 5-year est.); Males per 100 females: 120.3 (2008-2012 5-year est.); Marriage status: 24.2% never married, 57.9% now married, 7.2% widowed, 10.6% divorced (2008-2012 5-year est.); Foreign born: 0.2% (2008-2012 5-year est.); Ancestry (includes multiple ancestries): 35.4% German, 17.9% Irish, 11.6% English, 10.8% American, 7.3% Polish (2008-2012 5-year est.).
Economy: Single-family building permits issued: 0 (2013); Multi-family building permits issued: 0 (2013); Homeowner vacancy rate: 2.6%. Rental vacancy rate: 0.0%. (2008-2012 5-year est.); Employment by occupation: 9.2% management, business, and financial, 5.3% computer, engineering, and science, 15.3% education, legal, community service, arts, and media, 3.3% healthcare practitioners, 18.8% service, 20.4% sales and office, 12.0% natural resources, construction, and maintenance, 15.8% production, transportation, and material moving (2008-2012 5-year est.).
Income: Per capita income: $19,793 (2008-2012 5-year est.); Median household income: $51,000 (2008-2012 5-year est.); Average household income: $54,138 (2008-2012 5-year est.); Percent of households with income of $100,000 or more: 12.7% (2008-2012 5-year est.); Poverty rate: 17.9% (2008-2012 5-year est.).
Education: Percent of population age 25 and over with: High school diploma (including GED) or higher: 90.2% (2008-2012 5-year est.); Bachelor's degree or higher: 22.3% (2008-2012 5-year est.); Master's degree or higher: 6.3% (2008-2012 5-year est.).

School District(s)

Brimfield CUSD 309 (PK-12)

2011-12 Enrollment: 759 . . . . (309) 446-3378

Housing: Homeownership rate: 76.7% (2008-2012 5-year est.); Median home value: $111,600 (2008-2012 5-year est.); Median contract rent: $445 per month (2008-2012 5-year est.); Median year structure built: 1963 (2008-2012 5-year est.).

Health Insurance: 66.2% Private; 40.2% Public; 6.6% None. (2008-2012 5-year est.)

Transportation: Commute to work: 94.6% car, 0.0% public transportation, 4.3% walk, 1.0% work from home (2008-2012 5-year est.); Travel time to work: 25.8% less than 15 minutes, 40.8% 15 to 30 minutes, 28.9% 30 to 45 minutes, 2.6% 45 to 60 minutes, 1.8% 60 minutes or more (2008-2012 5-year est.).

CHILLICOTHE (city). Covers a land area of 5.131 square miles and a water area of 0.285 square miles. Located at 40.92° N. Lat; 89.50° W. Long. Elevation is 499 feet.

History: Incorporated 1861.

Population: 5,959 (1990); 5,996 (2000); 6,097 (2010); Density: 1,196.5 persons per square mile (2008-2012 5-year est.); Race: 94.9% White, 0.2% Black/African American, 1.2% Asian, 0.3% American Indian/Alaska Native, 0.0% Native Hawaiian/Other Pacific Islander, 3.4% Some other race, 2.1% Two or more races, 4.2% Hispanic of any race (2008-2012 5-year est.); Average household size: 2.46 (2008-2012 5-year est.); Median age: 40.1 (2008-2012 5-year est.); Males per 100 females: 91.7 (2008-2012 5-year est.); Marriage status: 24.6% never married, 55.4% now married, 5.8% widowed, 14.2% divorced (2008-2012 5-year est.); Foreign born: 2.3% (2008-2012 5-year est.); Ancestry (includes multiple ancestries): 39.4% German, 22.5% Irish, 13.8% English, 8.2% American, 4.8% French (2008-2012 5-year est.).

Economy: Single-family building permits issued: 8 (2013); Multi-family building permits issued: 0 (2013); Homeowner vacancy rate: 2.6%. Rental vacancy rate: 0.0%. (2008-2012 5-year est.); Employment by occupation: 8.6% management, business, and financial, 5.2% computer, engineering, and science, 10.8% education, legal, community service, arts, and media, 6.0% healthcare practitioners, 18.5% service, 23.0% sales and office, 11.8% natural resources, construction, and maintenance, 16.2% production, transportation, and material moving (2008-2012 5-year est.).

Income: Per capita income: $23,862 (2008-2012 5-year est.); Median household income: $50,337 (2008-2012 5-year est.); Average household income: $58,533 (2008-2012 5-year est.); Percent of households with income of $100,000 or more: 10.9% (2008-2012 5-year est.); Poverty rate: 9.9% (2008-2012 5-year est.).

Education: Percent of population age 25 and over with: High school diploma (including GED) or higher: 91.6% (2008-2012 5-year est.); Bachelor's degree or higher: 19.3% (2008-2012 5-year est.); Master's degree or higher: 5.0% (2008-2012 5-year est.).

School District(s)

Il Valley Central USD 321 (PK-12)

2011-12 Enrollment: 2,189 . . . . (309) 274-5418

Housing: Homeownership rate: 72.9% (2008-2012 5-year est.); Median home value: $108,400 (2008-2012 5-year est.); Median contract rent: $430 per month (2008-2012 5-year est.); Median year structure built: 1958 (2008-2012 5-year est.).

Health Insurance: 77.6% Private; 23.5% Public; 11.7% None. (2008-2012 5-year est.)

Safety: Violent crime rate: 34.4 per 10,000 population; Property crime rate: 206.2 per 10,000 population (2012).

Transportation: Commute to work: 92.7% car, 1.1% public transportation, 2.8% walk, 1.7% work from home (2008-2012 5-year est.); Travel time to work: 41.7% less than 15 minutes, 35.3% 15 to 30 minutes, 16.7% 30 to 45 minutes, 4.2% 45 to 60 minutes, 2.1% 60 minutes or more (2008-2012 5-year est.).

Additional Information Contacts

Chillicothe Chamber of Commerce . . . . (309) 274-4556
  http://www.chillicothechamber.com
City of Chillicothe . . . . (309) 274-2020
  http://www.cityofchillicotheil.com

DUNLAP (village). Covers a land area of 0.544 square miles and a water area of 0 square miles. Located at 40.86° N. Lat; 89.68° W. Long. Elevation is 735 feet.

Population: 851 (1990); 926 (2000); 1,386 (2010); Density: 2,920.1 persons per square mile (2008-2012 5-year est.); Race: 96.2% White,

0.4% Black/African American, 2.3% Asian, 0.2% American Indian/Alaska Native, 0.0% Native Hawaiian/Other Pacific Islander, 0.9% Some other race, 0.5% Two or more races, 1.3% Hispanic of any race (2008-2012 5-year est.); Average household size: 3.08 (2008-2012 5-year est.); Median age: 33.6 (2008-2012 5-year est.); Males per 100 females: 106.5 (2008-2012 5-year est.); Marriage status: 21.3% never married, 66.6% now married, 4.2% widowed, 7.9% divorced (2008-2012 5-year est.); Foreign born: 3.0% (2008-2012 5-year est.); Ancestry (includes multiple ancestries): 34.6% German, 20.7% Irish, 15.8% English, 8.8% American, 5.4% Swedish (2008-2012 5-year est.).

Economy: Homeowner vacancy rate: 2.6%. Rental vacancy rate: 10.9%. (2008-2012 5-year est.); Employment by occupation: 24.9% management, business, and financial, 6.7% computer, engineering, and science, 9.6% education, legal, community service, arts, and media, 10.3% healthcare practitioners, 6.6% service, 25.5% sales and office, 6.7% natural resources, construction, and maintenance, 9.5% production, transportation, and material moving (2008-2012 5-year est.).

Income: Per capita income: $35,478 (2008-2012 5-year est.); Median household income: $84,766 (2008-2012 5-year est.); Average household income: $108,352 (2008-2012 5-year est.); Percent of households with income of $100,000 or more: 44.7% (2008-2012 5-year est.); Poverty rate: 1.1% (2008-2012 5-year est.).

Education: Percent of population age 25 and over with: High school diploma (including GED) or higher: 95.3% (2008-2012 5-year est.); Bachelor's degree or higher: 48.7% (2008-2012 5-year est.); Master's degree or higher: 17.9% (2008-2012 5-year est.).

School District(s)

Dunlap CUSD 323 (PK-12)

2011-12 Enrollment: 3,785 . . . . (309) 691-3955

Housing: Homeownership rate: 79.4% (2008-2012 5-year est.); Median home value: $188,800 (2008-2012 5-year est.); Median contract rent: $529 per month (2008-2012 5-year est.); Median year structure built: 1970 (2008-2012 5-year est.).

Health Insurance: 85.7% Private; 13.2% Public; 6.3% None. (2008-2012 5-year est.)

Hospitals: Greenview Regional Hospital (211 beds)

Transportation: Commute to work: 95.2% car, 0.4% public transportation, 2.2% walk, 2.2% work from home (2008-2012 5-year est.); Travel time to work: 27.1% less than 15 minutes, 56.4% 15 to 30 minutes, 14.2% 30 to 45 minutes, 1.0% 45 to 60 minutes, 1.2% 60 minutes or more (2000-2012 5-year est.)

EDELSTEIN (unincorporated postal area)

Zip Code: 61526

Covers a land area of 31.921 square miles and a water area of 0.008 square miles. Located at 40.92° N. Lat; 89.61° W. Long. Elevation is 814 feet. Population: 1,088 (2010); Density: 34.1 persons per square mile (2010); Race: 97.5% White, 0.3% Black/African American, 0.4% Asian, 0.0% American Indian/Alaska Native, 0.0% Native Hawaiian/Other Pacific Islander, 1.8% Some other race, 1.7% Two or more races, 0.8% Hispanic of any race (2010); Average household size: 2.73 (2010); Median age: 43.7 (2010); Males per 100 females: 101.9 (2010); Homeownership rate: 91.9% (2010)

EDWARDS (unincorporated postal area)

Zip Code: 61528

Covers a land area of 18.289 square miles and a water area of 0 square miles. Located at 40.77° N. Lat; 89.72° W. Long. Elevation is 525 feet. Population: 2,668 (2010); Density: 145.9 persons per square mile (2010); Race: 88.7% White, 1.6% Black/African American, 8.0% Asian, 0.1% American Indian/Alaska Native, 0.0% Native Hawaiian/Other Pacific Islander, 1.6% Some other race, 1.0% Two or more races, 1.3% Hispanic of any race (2010); Average household size: 2.84 (2010); Median age: 37.1 (2010); Males per 100 females: 104.4 (2010); Homeownership rate: 93.2% (2010)

ELMWOOD (city). Covers a land area of 1.425 square miles and a water area of 0 square miles. Located at 40.78° N. Lat; 89.97° W. Long. Elevation is 643 feet.

History: Incorporated 1867. Lorado Taft born here; his statue *Pioneers of the Prairies* (1928) is in city park.

Population: 1,841 (1990); 1,945 (2000); 2,097 (2010); Density: 1,622.6 persons per square mile (2008-2012 5-year est.); Race: 97.2% White, 0.6% Black/African American, 0.1% Asian, 0.0% American Indian/Alaska Native, 0.0% Native Hawaiian/Other Pacific Islander, 2.1% Some other

race, 1.8% Two or more races, 3.5% Hispanic of any race (2008-2012 5-year est.); Average household size: 2.64 (2008-2012 5-year est.); Median age: 34.9 (2008-2012 5-year est.); Males per 100 females: 97.5 (2008-2012 5-year est.); Marriage status: 20.1% never married, 63.6% now married, 6.5% widowed, 9.8% divorced (2008-2012 5-year est.); Foreign born: 0.6% (2008-2012 5-year est.); Ancestry (includes multiple ancestries): 33.5% German, 14.7% Irish, 13.7% English, 10.5% American, 7.9% Polish (2008-2012 5-year est.).

Economy: Homeowner vacancy rate: 3.4%. Rental vacancy rate: 6.1%. (2008-2012 5-year est.); Employment by occupation: 8.5% management, business, and financial, 5.2% computer, engineering, and science, 9.2% education, legal, community service, arts, and media, 4.8% healthcare practitioners, 22.5% service, 31.8% sales and office, 8.5% natural resources, construction, and maintenance, 9.5% production, transportation, and material moving (2008-2012 5-year est.).

Income: Per capita income: $23,910 (2008-2012 5-year est.); Median household income: $62,583 (2008-2012 5-year est.); Average household income: $63,478 (2008-2012 5-year est.); Percent of households with income of $100,000 or more: 13.3% (2008-2012 5-year est.); Poverty rate: 3.2% (2008-2012 5-year est.).

Education: Percent of population age 25 and over with: High school diploma (including GED) or higher: 96.2% (2008-2012 5-year est.); Bachelor's degree or higher: 25.4% (2008-2012 5-year est.); Master's degree or higher: 2.3% (2008-2012 5-year est.).

School District(s)

Elmwood CUSD 322 (PK-12)
  2011-12 Enrollment: 683 . . . . (309) 742-8464

Housing: Homeownership rate: 83.5% (2008-2012 5-year est.); Median home value: $112,100 (2008-2012 5-year est.); Median contract rent: $552 per month (2008-2012 5-year est.); Median year structure built: 1953 (2008-2012 5-year est.).

Health Insurance: 79.9% Private; 32.5% Public; 4.6% None. (2008-2012 5-year est.)

Safety: Violent crime rate: 38.0 per 10,000 population; Property crime rate: 342.4 per 10,000 population (2012).

Transportation: Commute to work: 92.4% car, 0.0% public transportation, 2.3% walk, 2.9% work from home (2008-2012 5-year est.); Travel time to work: 29.5% less than 15 minutes, 14.4% 15 to 30 minutes, 43.4% 30 to 45 minutes, 9.0% 45 to 60 minutes, 3.7% 60 minutes or more (2008-2012 5-year est.).

GLASFORD (village). Covers a land area of 0.899 square miles and a water area of 0 square miles. Located at 40.57° N. Lat; 89.81° W. Long. Elevation is 614 feet.

Population: 1,115 (1990); 1,076 (2000); 1,022 (2010); Density: 1,130.0 persons per square mile (2008-2012 5-year est.); Race: 98.6% White, 0.0% Black/African American, 0.0% Asian, 0.7% American Indian/Alaska Native, 0.0% Native Hawaiian/Other Pacific Islander, 0.7% Some other race, 0.7% Two or more races, 0.7% Hispanic of any race (2008-2012 5-year est.); Average household size: 2.30 (2008-2012 5-year est.); Median age: 38.1 (2008-2012 5-year est.); Males per 100 females: 76.1 (2008-2012 5-year est.); Marriage status: 25.6% never married, 51.9% now married, 6.4% widowed, 16.1% divorced (2008-2012 5-year est.); Foreign born: 0.6% (2008-2012 5-year est.); Ancestry (includes multiple ancestries): 31.9% German, 15.6% American, 12.3% English, 7.3% Irish, 3.6% Italian (2008-2012 5-year est.).

Economy: Single-family building permits issued: 0 (2013); Multi-family building permits issued: 0 (2013); Homeowner vacancy rate: 2.6%. Rental vacancy rate: 0.0%. (2008-2012 5-year est.); Employment by occupation: 9.7% management, business, and financial, 3.1% computer, engineering, and science, 7.0% education, legal, community service, arts, and media, 5.0% healthcare practitioners, 16.1% service, 26.2% sales and office, 11.2% natural resources, construction, and maintenance, 21.7% production, transportation, and material moving (2008-2012 5-year est.).

Income: Per capita income: $22,151 (2008-2012 5-year est.); Median household income: $44,250 (2008-2012 5-year est.); Average household income: $50,237 (2008-2012 5-year est.); Percent of households with income of $100,000 or more: 11.8% (2008-2012 5-year est.); Poverty rate: 13.4% (2008-2012 5-year est.).

Education: Percent of population age 25 and over with: High school diploma (including GED) or higher: 92.3% (2008-2012 5-year est.); Bachelor's degree or higher: 12.7% (2008-2012 5-year est.); Master's degree or higher: 3.5% (2008-2012 5-year est.).

School District(s)

Illini Bluffs CUSD 327 (PK-12)
  2011-12 Enrollment: 959 . . . . (309) 389-2231

Housing: Homeownership rate: 76.5% (2008-2012 5-year est.); Median home value: $85,300 (2008-2012 5-year est.); Median contract rent: $391 per month (2008-2012 5-year est.); Median year structure built: 1958 (2008-2012 5-year est.).

Health Insurance: 71.2% Private; 28.9% Public; 15.6% None. (2008-2012 5-year est.)

Safety: Violent crime rate: 58.6 per 10,000 population; Property crime rate: 0.0 per 10,000 population (2012).

Transportation: Commute to work: 93.7% car, 0.0% public transportation, 1.8% walk, 0.6% work from home (2008-2012 5-year est.); Travel time to work: 13.5% less than 15 minutes, 32.9% 15 to 30 minutes, 46.3% 30 to 45 minutes, 4.1% 45 to 60 minutes, 3.3% 60 minutes or more (2008-2012 5-year est.)

HANNA CITY (village). Aka Hanna. Covers a land area of 0.478 square miles and a water area of 0 square miles. Located at 40.69° N. Lat; 89.79° W. Long. Elevation is 728 feet.

Population: 1,205 (1990); 1,013 (2000); 1,225 (2010); Density: 2,861.1 persons per square mile (2008-2012 5-year est.); Race: 98.2% White, 1.1% Black/African American, 0.0% Asian, 0.0% American Indian/Alaska Native, 0.0% Native Hawaiian/Other Pacific Islander, 0.7% Some other race, 0.6% Two or more races, 2.8% Hispanic of any race (2008-2012 5-year est.); Average household size: 2.57 (2008-2012 5-year est.); Median age: 36.2 (2008-2012 5-year est.); Males per 100 females: 86.6 (2008-2012 5-year est.); Marriage status: 28.8% never married, 55.3% now married, 7.3% widowed, 8.6% divorced (2008-2012 5-year est.); Foreign born: 1.2% (2008-2012 5-year est.); Ancestry (includes multiple ancestries): 35.2% German, 12.3% English, 12.1% Irish, 6.8% American, 5.6% French (2008-2012 5-year est.).

Economy: Homeowner vacancy rate: 3.5%. Rental vacancy rate: 14.4%. (2008-2012 5-year est.); Employment by occupation: 13.4% management, business, and financial, 6.5% computer, engineering, and science, 6.5% education, legal, community service, arts, and media, 4.9% healthcare practitioners, 12.2% service, 25.0% sales and office, 11.2% natural resources, construction, and maintenance, 20.3% production, transportation, and material moving (2008-2012 5-year est.).

Income: Per capita income: $24,775 (2008-2012 5-year est.); Median household income: $60,515 (2008-2012 5-year est.); Average household income: $63,390 (2008-2012 5-year est.); Percent of households with income of $100,000 or more: 14.3% (2008-2012 5-year est.); Poverty rate: 4.2% (2008-2012 5-year est.).

Education: Percent of population age 25 and over with: High school diploma (including GED) or higher: 93.8% (2008-2012 5-year est.); Bachelor's degree or higher: 12.6% (2008-2012 5-year est.); Master's degree or higher: 2.5% (2008-2012 5-year est.).

School District(s)

Peoria Roe (06-12)
  2011-12 Enrollment: n/a . . . . (309) 672-6906

Housing: Homeownership rate: 78.7% (2008-2012 5-year est.); Median home value: $108,600 (2008-2012 5-year est.); Median contract rent: $493 per month (2008-2012 5-year est.); Median year structure built: 1964 (2008-2012 5-year est.).

Health Insurance: 74.5% Private; 32.7% Public; 7.6% None. (2008-2012 5-year est.)

Transportation: Commute to work: 96.4% car, 0.0% public transportation, 1.2% walk, 0.6% work from home (2008-2012 5-year est.); Travel time to work: 14.0% less than 15 minutes, 60.6% 15 to 30 minutes, 14.6% 30 to 45 minutes, 6.3% 45 to 60 minutes, 4.6% 60 minutes or more (2008-2012 5-year est.)

KINGSTON MINES (village). Covers a land area of 1.376 square miles and a water area of 0.148 square miles. Located at 40.56° N. Lat; 89.77° W. Long. Elevation is 463 feet.

Population: 293 (1990); 259 (2000); 302 (2010); Density: 167.9 persons per square mile (2008-2012 5-year est.); Race: 94.8% White, 0.9% Black/African American, 0.0% Asian, 0.0% American Indian/Alaska Native, 0.0% Native Hawaiian/Other Pacific Islander, 4.3% Some other race, 4.3% Two or more races, 1.7% Hispanic of any race (2008-2012 5-year est.); Average household size: 2.57 (2008-2012 5-year est.); Median age: 40.7 (2008-2012 5-year est.); Males per 100 females: 100.9 (2008-2012 5-year est.); Marriage status: 25.7% never married, 50.3% now married, 9.3% widowed, 14.8% divorced (2008-2012 5-year est.); Foreign born: 4.8%

(2008-2012 5-year est.); Ancestry (includes multiple ancestries): 29.0% German, 16.5% Irish, 12.1% American, 11.3% Dutch, 5.2% English (2008-2012 5-year est.).

Economy: Single-family building permits issued: 0 (2013); Multi-family building permits issued: 0 (2013); Homeowner vacancy rate: 0.0%. Rental vacancy rate: 35.3%. (2008-2012 5-year est.); Employment by occupation: 9.4% management, business, and financial, 3.1% computer, engineering, and science, 6.3% education, legal, community service, arts, and media, 4.2% healthcare practitioners, 22.9% service, 7.3% sales and office, 19.8% natural resources, construction, and maintenance, 27.1% production, transportation, and material moving (2008-2012 5-year est.).

Income: Per capita income: $22,466 (2008-2012 5-year est.); Median household income: $51,250 (2008-2012 5-year est.); Average household income: $57,433 (2008-2012 5-year est.); Percent of households with income of $100,000 or more: 15.5% (2008-2012 5-year est.); Poverty rate: 8.3% (2008-2012 5-year est.).

Education: Percent of population age 25 and over with: High school diploma (including GED) or higher: 78.7% (2008-2012 5-year est.); Bachelor's degree or higher: 2.6% (2008-2012 5-year est.); Master's degree or higher: 2.6% (2008-2012 5-year est.).

Housing: Homeownership rate: 87.8% (2008-2012 5-year est.); Median home value: $78,300 (2008-2012 5-year est.); Median contract rent: $375 per month (2008-2012 5-year est.); Median year structure built: 1947 (2008-2012 5-year est.).

Health Insurance: 62.3% Private; 31.6% Public; 22.9% None. (2008-2012 5-year est.)

Transportation: Commute to work: 100.0% car, 0.0% public transportation, 0.0% walk, 0.0% work from home (2008-2012 5-year est.); Travel time to work: 18.1% less than 15 minutes, 28.7% 15 to 30 minutes, 46.8% 30 to 45 minutes, 2.1% 45 to 60 minutes, 4.3% 60 minutes or more (2008-2012 5-year est.).

LAKE CAMELOT (CDP). Covers a land area of 1.735 square miles and a water area of 0.139 square miles. Located at 40.63° N. Lat; 89.75° W. Long.

Population: n/a (1990); n/a (2000); 1,686 (2010); Density: 940.2 persons per square mile (2008-2012 5-year est.); Race: 99.0% White, 0.0% Black/African American, 1.0% Asian, 0.0% American Indian/Alaska Native, 0.0% Native Hawaiian/Other Pacific Islander, 0.0% Some other race, 0.0% Two or more races, 0.0% Hispanic of any race (2008-2012 5-year est.); Average household size: 2.77 (2008-2012 5-year est.); Median age: 38.4 (2008-2012 5-year est.); Males per 100 females: 76.9 (2008-2012 5-year est.); Marriage status: 14.7% never married, 78.8% now married, 1.3% widowed, 5.3% divorced (2008-2012 5-year est.); Foreign born: 3.5% (2008-2012 5-year est.); Ancestry (includes multiple ancestries): 33.0% German, 15.1% English, 13.1% Irish, 5.9% Italian, 5.2% American (2008-2012 5-year est.).

Economy: Homeowner vacancy rate: 0.0%. Rental vacancy rate: 0.0%. (2008-2012 5-year est.); Employment by occupation: 24.7% management, business, and financial, 9.5% computer, engineering, and science, 15.1% education, legal, community service, arts, and media, 6.8% healthcare practitioners, 0.7% service, 17.6% sales and office, 9.6% natural resources, construction, and maintenance, 16.0% production, transportation, and material moving (2008-2012 5-year est.).

Income: Per capita income: $34,201 (2008-2012 5-year est.); Median household income: $87,098 (2008-2012 5-year est.); Average household income: $94,002 (2008-2012 5-year est.); Percent of households with income of $100,000 or more: 43.0% (2008-2012 5-year est.); Poverty rate: 1.0% (2008-2012 5-year est.).

Education: Percent of population age 25 and over with: High school diploma (including GED) or higher: 96.0% (2008-2012 5-year est.); Bachelor's degree or higher: 39.5% (2008-2012 5-year est.); Master's degree or higher: 20.1% (2008-2012 5-year est.).

Housing: Homeownership rate: 96.6% (2008-2012 5-year est.); Median home value: $180,500 (2008-2012 5-year est.); Median contract rent: n/a per month (2008-2012 5-year est.); Median year structure built: 1991 (2008-2012 5-year est.).

Health Insurance: 96.1% Private; 10.2% Public; 1.5% None. (2008-2012 5-year est.)

Transportation: Commute to work: 96.1% car, 0.9% public transportation, 1.6% walk, 0.9% work from home (2008-2012 5-year est.); Travel time to work: 8.8% less than 15 minutes, 47.2% 15 to 30 minutes, 39.0% 30 to 45 minutes, 2.9% 45 to 60 minutes, 2.0% 60 minutes or more (2008-2012 5-year est.)

LAURA (unincorporated postal area)
Zip Code: 61451

Covers a land area of 23.011 square miles and a water area of 0.105 square miles. Located at 40.93° N. Lat; 89.93° W. Long. Elevation is 728 feet. Population: 393 (2010); Density: 17.1 persons per square mile (2010); Race: 98.0% White, 0.0% Black/African American, 0.3% Asian, 0.3% American Indian/Alaska Native, 0.0% Native Hawaiian/Other Pacific Islander, 1.4% Some other race, 0.3% Two or more races, 3.1% Hispanic of any race (2010); Average household size: 2.66 (2010); Median age: 41.6 (2010); Males per 100 females: 106.8 (2010); Homeownership rate: 85.2% (2010)

MAPLETON (village). Covers a land area of 0.908 square miles and a water area of 0 square miles. Located at 40.57° N. Lat; 89.72° W. Long. Elevation is 469 feet.

Population: 216 (1990); 227 (2000); 270 (2010); Density: 313.9 persons per square mile (2008-2012 5-year est.); Race: 98.9% White, 0.0% Black/African American, 0.0% Asian, 0.0% American Indian/Alaska Native, 0.0% Native Hawaiian/Other Pacific Islander, 1.1% Some other race, 0.0% Two or more races, 2.1% Hispanic of any race (2008-2012 5-year est.); Average household size: 2.54 (2008-2012 5-year est.); Median age: 38.4 (2008-2012 5-year est.); Males per 100 females: 92.6 (2008-2012 5-year est.); Marriage status: 30.4% never married, 51.7% now married, 3.9% widowed, 13.9% divorced (2008-2012 5-year est.); Foreign born: 1.1% (2008-2012 5-year est.); Ancestry (includes multiple ancestries): 36.5% German, 16.5% English, 8.4% American, 7.7% Irish, 4.2% European (2008-2012 5-year est.).

Economy: Single-family building permits issued: 3 (2013); Multi-family building permits issued: 0 (2013); Homeowner vacancy rate: 0.0%. Rental vacancy rate: 0.0%. (2008-2012 5-year est.); Employment by occupation: 6.1% management, business, and financial, 4.3% computer, engineering, and science, 10.4% education, legal, community service, arts, and media, 7.0% healthcare practitioners, 15.7% service, 18.3% sales and office, 6.1% natural resources, construction, and maintenance, 32.2% production, transportation, and material moving (2008-2012 5-year est.).

Income: Per capita income: $20,474 (2008-2012 5-year est.); Median household income: $41,667 (2008-2012 5-year est.); Average household income: $52,428 (2008-2012 5-year est.); Percent of households with income of $100,000 or more: 12.5% (2008-2012 5-year est.); Poverty rate: 8.1% (2008-2012 5-year est.).

Education: Percent of population age 25 and over with: High school diploma (including GED) or higher: 92.8% (2008-2012 5-year est.); Bachelor's degree or higher: 8.8% (2008-2012 5-year est.); Master's degree or higher: 3.1% (2008-2012 5-year est.).

Housing: Homeownership rate: 81.3% (2008-2012 5-year est.); Median home value: $88,100 (2008-2012 5-year est.); Median contract rent: $525 per month (2008-2012 5-year est.); Median year structure built: 1962 (2008-2012 5-year est.).

Health Insurance: 79.3% Private; 33.7% Public; 7.4% None. (2008-2012 5-year est.)

Transportation: Commute to work: 92.9% car, 0.0% public transportation, 0.9% walk, 0.0% work from home (2008-2012 5-year est.); Travel time to work: 17.0% less than 15 minutes, 41.1% 15 to 30 minutes, 35.7% 30 to 45 minutes, 1.8% 45 to 60 minutes, 4.5% 60 minutes or more (2008-2012 5-year est.)

MOSSVILLE (unincorporated postal area)
Zip Code: 61552

Covers a land area of 0.532 square miles and a water area of 0 square miles. Located at 40.81° N. Lat; 89.56° W. Long. Elevation is 469 feet. Population: 239 (2010); Density: 448.8 persons per square mile (2010); Race: 95.0% White, 1.7% Black/African American, 2.9% Asian, 0.0% American Indian/Alaska Native, 0.0% Native Hawaiian/Other Pacific Islander, 0.4% Some other race, 0.4% Two or more races, 5.4% Hispanic of any race (2010); Average household size: 2.63 (2010); Median age: 37.6 (2010); Males per 100 females: 91.2 (2010); Homeownership rate: 85.7% (2010)

NORWOOD (village). Aka Norwood Park. Covers a land area of 0.288 square miles and a water area of 0 square miles. Located at 40.71° N. Lat; 89.70° W. Long. Elevation is 696 feet.

Population: 495 (1990); 473 (2000); 478 (2010); Density: 1,411.6 persons per square mile (2008-2012 5-year est.); Race: 94.6% White, 1.0% Black/African American, 0.7% Asian, 0.0% American Indian/Alaska Native, 0.0% Native Hawaiian/Other Pacific Islander, 3.7% Some other race, 3.7%

Two or more races, 1.2% Hispanic of any race (2008-2012 5-year est.); Average household size: 2.25 (2008-2012 5-year est.); Median age: 51.1 (2008-2012 5-year est.); Males per 100 females: 91.1 (2008-2012 5-year est.); Marriage status: 16.8% never married, 67.2% now married, 7.1% widowed, 8.8% divorced (2008-2012 5-year est.); Foreign born: 0.7% (2008-2012 5-year est.); Ancestry (includes multiple ancestries): 22.1% American, 21.1% German, 10.6% English, 8.1% Irish, 5.2% French (2008-2012 5-year est.).

Economy: Homeowner vacancy rate: 0.0%. Rental vacancy rate: 0.0%. (2008-2012 5-year est.); Employment by occupation: 6.0% management, business, and financial, 2.0% computer, engineering, and science, 5.0% education, legal, community service, arts, and media, 10.1% healthcare practitioners, 15.1% service, 29.6% sales and office, 6.5% natural resources, construction, and maintenance, 25.6% production, transportation, and material moving (2008-2012 5-year est.).

Income: Per capita income: $23,964 (2008-2012 5-year est.); Median household income: $45,083 (2008-2012 5-year est.); Average household income: $52,749 (2008-2012 5-year est.); Percent of households with income of $100,000 or more: 11.0% (2008-2012 5-year est.); Poverty rate: 7.5% (2008-2012 5-year est.).

Education: Percent of population age 25 and over with: High school diploma (including GED) or higher: 84.3% (2008-2012 5-year est.); Bachelor's degree or higher: 8.2% (2008-2012 5-year est.); Master's degree or higher: 3.1% (2008-2012 5-year est.).

Housing: Homeownership rate: 97.2% (2008-2012 5-year est.); Median home value: $85,000 (2008-2012 5-year est.); Median contract rent: $567 per month (2008-2012 5-year est.); Median year structure built: 1956 (2008-2012 5-year est.).

Health Insurance: 74.4% Private; 40.5% Public; 4.7% None. (2008-2012 5-year est.)

Safety: Violent crime rate: 0.0 per 10,000 population; Property crime rate: 0.0 per 10,000 population (2012).

Transportation: Commute to work: 96.3% car, 1.1% public transportation, 0.0% walk, 1.1% work from home (2008-2012 5-year est.); Travel time to work: 17.6% less than 15 minutes, 59.9% 15 to 30 minutes, 15.5% 30 to 45 minutes, 3.7% 45 to 60 minutes, 3.2% 60 minutes or more (2008-2012 5-year est.)

PEORIA (city). County seat. Covers a land area of 48.007 square miles and a water area of 2.220 square miles. Located at 40.75° N. Lat; 89.62° W. Long. Elevation is 502 feet.

History: Peoria began with the establishment by the French of Fort Pimiteoui on Lake Peoria in 1691. This trading post thrived for over a century, and the village which grew around it was at times called Au Pe, Le Pe, Opa, Au Pay, and Piorias. The American Fort Clark was erected here in 1813 and settlers from New England moved in. When Peoria County was created in 1825, the French-Indian name of Peoria was given to the community at Fort Clark, which became the county seat. Peoria was incorporated as a town in 1835, and received a city charter in 1845. In a speech in Peoria in 1854, following a talk by Stephen Douglas that lasted all afternoon, Abraham Lincoln first publicly denounced slavery.

Population: 113,504 (1990); 112,936 (2000); 115,007 (2010); Density: 2,390.3 persons per square mile (2008-2012 5-year est.); Race: 63.9% White, 26.6% Black/African American, 4.6% Asian, 0.4% American Indian/Alaska Native, 0.0% Native Hawaiian/Other Pacific Islander, 4.5% Some other race, 3.1% Two or more races, 5.0% Hispanic of any race (2008-2012 5-year est.); Average household size: 2.33 (2008-2012 5-year est.); Median age: 33.7 (2008-2012 5-year est.); Males per 100 females: 91.7 (2008-2012 5-year est.); Marriage status: 40.2% never married, 42.2% now married, 6.2% widowed, 11.4% divorced (2008-2012 5-year est.); Foreign born: 6.5% (2008-2012 5-year est.); Ancestry (includes multiple ancestries): 22.6% German, 12.2% Irish, 8.1% English, 4.2% American, 3.7% Italian (2008-2012 5-year est.).

Economy: Unemployment rate: 7.8% (April 2014); Total civilian labor force: 55,077 (April 2014); Single-family building permits issued: 147 (2013); Multi-family building permits issued: 6 (2013); Homeowner vacancy rate: 2.9%. Rental vacancy rate: 7.7%. (2008-2012 5-year est.); Employment by occupation: 13.7% management, business, and financial, 7.8% computer, engineering, and science, 11.2% education, legal, community service, arts, and media, 7.5% healthcare practitioners, 19.7% service, 24.6% sales and office, 4.4% natural resources, construction, and maintenance, 11.2% production, transportation, and material moving (2008-2012 5-year est.).

Income: Per capita income: $28,752 (2008-2012 5-year est.); Median household income: $45,772 (2008-2012 5-year est.); Average household

income: $68,130 (2008-2012 5-year est.); Percent of households with income of $100,000 or more: 18.5% (2008-2012 5-year est.); Poverty rate: 22.2% (2008-2012 5-year est.).

Taxes: Total city taxes per capita: $670 (2011); City property taxes per capita: $303 (2011).

Education: Percent of population age 25 and over with: High school diploma (including GED) or higher: 88.9% (2008-2012 5-year est.); Bachelor's degree or higher: 32.7% (2008-2012 5-year est.); Master's degree or higher: 13.0% (2008-2012 5-year est.).

School District(s)

Dunlap CUSD 323 (PK-12)
  2011-12 Enrollment: 3,785 . . . . (309) 691-3955
Hollis CSD 328 (KG-08)
  2011-12 Enrollment: 164. . . . . (309) 697-1325
Limestone CHSD 310 (09-12)
  2011-12 Enrollment: 1,181 . . . . (309) 697-6271
Limestone Walters CCSD 316 (KG-08)
  2011-12 Enrollment: 187. . . . . (309) 697-3035
Norwood ESD 63 (PK-08)
  2011-12 Enrollment: 469. . . . . (309) 676-3523
Oak Grove SD 68 (PK-08)
  2011-12 Enrollment: 393. . . . . (309) 697-3367
Peoria Educ Reg for Empl Traing
  2011-12 Enrollment: n/a . . . . (309) 693-7373
Peoria Roe (06-12)
  2011-12 Enrollment: n/a . . . . (309) 672-6906
Peoria SD 150 (PK-12)
  2011-12 Enrollment: 14,057 . . . . (309) 672-6768
Pleasant Hill SD 69 (PK-08)
  2011-12 Enrollment: 246. . . . . (309) 637-6829
Pleasant Valley SD 62 (PK-08)
  2011-12 Enrollment: 517. . . . . (309) 673-6750
Spec Educ Assoc of Peoria County
  2011-12 Enrollment: n/a . . . . (309) 697-0880

Four-year College(s)

Bradley University (Private, Not-for-profit)
  Fall 2012 Enrollment: 5,451 . . . . (309) 676-7611
  2012-13 Tuition: In-state $28,284; Out-of-state $28,284
Methodist College (Private, Not-for-profit)
  Fall 2012 Enrollment: 528 . . . . (309) 672-5513
  2012-13 Tuition: In-state $16,448; Out-of-state $16,448
Midstate College (Private, For-profit)
  Fall 2012 Enrollment: 592 . . . . (309) 692-4092
  2012-13 Tuition: In-state $15,225; Out-of-state $15,225
Saint Francis Medical Center College of Nursing (Private, Not-for-profit, Roman Catholic)
  Fall 2012 Enrollment: 627 . . . . (309) 655-2201

Vocational/Technical School(s)

Regency Beauty Institute-Peoria (Private, For-profit)
  Fall 2012 Enrollment: 71. . . . . (800) 787-6456
  2012-13 Tuition: $16,425
Tricoci University of Beauty Culture-Peoria (Private, For-profit)
  Fall 2012 Enrollment: 110 . . . . (630) 528-3336
  2012-13 Tuition: $18,050

Housing: Homeownership rate: 58.4% (2008-2012 5-year est.); Median home value: $124,400 (2008-2012 5-year est.); Median contract rent: $555 per month (2008-2012 5-year est.); Median year structure built: 1962 (2008-2012 5-year est.).

Health Insurance: 64.7% Private; 35.8% Public; 12.0% None. (2008-2012 5-year est.)

Hospitals: Methodist Medical Center of Illinois (330 beds); Proctor Hospital (175 beds); Saint Francis Medical Center (731 beds)

Safety: Violent crime rate: 79.7 per 10,000 population; Property crime rate: 435.6 per 10,000 population (2012).

Transportation: Commute to work: 89.7% car, 2.9% public transportation, 2.7% walk, 3.0% work from home (2008-2012 5-year est.); Travel time to work: 40.3% less than 15 minutes, 48.3% 15 to 30 minutes, 6.4% 30 to 45 minutes, 2.5% 45 to 60 minutes, 2.5% 60 minutes or more (2008-2012 5-year est.); Amtrak: Train service available.

Airports: General Downing - Peoria International Airport (primary service/non-hub); Mount Hawley Auxiliary Airport (general aviation)

Additional Information Contacts

City of Peoria. . . . . (309) 494-8565
  http://www.peoriagov.org

Peoria Area Chamber of Commerce . . . . (309) 495-5900
  http://www.peoriachamber.org

PEORIA HEIGHTS (village). Covers a land area of 2.654 square miles and a water area of 4.319 square miles. Located at 40.78° N. Lat; 89.54° W. Long. Elevation is 784 feet.

History: Incorporated 1898.

Population: 6,930 (1990); 6,635 (2000); 6,156 (2010); Density: 2,341.9 persons per square mile (2008-2012 5-year est.); Race: 92.5% White, 4.4% Black/African American, 0.4% Asian, 0.0% American Indian/Alaska Native, 0.0% Native Hawaiian/Other Pacific Islander, 2.7% Some other race, 2.3% Two or more races, 2.6% Hispanic of any race (2008-2012 5-year est.); Average household size: 2.05 (2008-2012 5-year est.); Median age: 41.3 (2008-2012 5-year est.); Males per 100 females: 97.5 (2008-2012 5-year est.); Marriage status: 34.3% never married, 38.1% now married, 7.4% widowed, 20.1% divorced (2008-2012 5-year est.); Foreign born: 2.6% (2008-2012 5-year est.); Ancestry (includes multiple ancestries): 33.8% German, 17.8% Irish, 9.3% English, 7.2% American, 5.7% French (2008-2012 5-year est.).

Economy: Single-family building permits issued: 0 (2013); Multi-family building permits issued: 0 (2013); Homeowner vacancy rate: 5.8%. Rental vacancy rate: 9.4%. (2008-2012 5-year est.); Employment by occupation: 13.9% management, business, and financial, 3.2% computer, engineering, and science, 9.8% education, legal, community service, arts, and media, 5.0% healthcare practitioners, 18.3% service, 31.6% sales and office, 9.1% natural resources, construction, and maintenance, 9.1% production, transportation, and material moving (2008-2012 5-year est.).

Income: Per capita income: $31,320 (2008-2012 5-year est.); Median household income: $43,073 (2008-2012 5-year est.); Average household income: $63,793 (2008-2012 5-year est.); Percent of households with income of $100,000 or more: 11.9% (2008-2012 5-year est.); Poverty rate: 12.8% (2008-2012 5-year est.).

Education: Percent of population age 25 and over with: High school diploma (including GED) or higher: 89.5% (2008-2012 5-year est.); Bachelor's degree or higher: 20.2% (2008-2012 5-year est.); Master's degree or higher: 7.9% (2008-2012 5-year est.).

School District(s)

Peoria Heights CUSD 325 (PK-12)
  2011-12 Enrollment: 831 . . . . (309) 686-8800

Housing: Homeownership rate: 65.9% (2008-2012 5-year est.); Median home value: $85,000 (2008-2012 5-year est.); Median contract rent: $520 per month (2008-2012 5-year est.); Median year structure built: 1954 (2008-2012 5-year est.).

Health Insurance: 70.4% Private; 27.8% Public; 12.4% None. (2008-2012 5-year est.)

Safety: Violent crime rate: 29.2 per 10,000 population; Property crime rate: 337.1 per 10,000 population (2012).

Transportation: Commute to work: 91.8% car, 2.5% public transportation, 1.8% walk, 2.0% work from home (2008-2012 5-year est.); Travel time to work: 41.4% less than 15 minutes, 47.0% 15 to 30 minutes, 5.6% 30 to 45 minutes, 1.1% 45 to 60 minutes, 4.9% 60 minutes or more (2008-2012 5-year est.)

Additional Information Contacts

Peoria Heights Chamber of Commerce . . . . (309) 685-4812
  http://peoriaheightschamber.com
Village of Peoria Heights . . . . (309) 686-2375
  http://www.peoriaheights.org

PRINCEVILLE (village). Covers a land area of 1.657 square miles and a water area of 0 square miles. Located at 40.93° N. Lat; 89.75° W. Long. Elevation is 738 feet.

Population: 1,421 (1990); 1,621 (2000); 1,738 (2010); Density: 1,264.9 persons per square mile (2008-2012 5-year est.); Race: 93.2% White, 2.4% Black/African American, 0.0% Asian, 0.0% American Indian/Alaska Native, 0.2% Native Hawaiian/Other Pacific Islander, 4.2% Some other race, 2.6% Two or more races, 7.1% Hispanic of any race (2008-2012 5-year est.); Average household size: 2.66 (2008-2012 5-year est.); Median age: 35.0 (2008-2012 5-year est.); Males per 100 females: 88.7 (2008-2012 5-year est.); Marriage status: 24.8% never married, 53.5% now married, 10.3% widowed, 11.5% divorced (2008-2012 5-year est.); Foreign born: 0.8% (2008-2012 5-year est.); Ancestry (includes multiple ancestries): 42.8% German, 16.0% Irish, 8.2% English, 6.2% American, 3.6% Swedish (2008-2012 5-year est.).

Economy: Single-family building permits issued: 2 (2013); Multi-family building permits issued: 0 (2013); Homeowner vacancy rate: 0.0%. Rental vacancy rate: 8.6%. (2008-2012 5-year est.); Employment by occupation: 14.3% management, business, and financial, 3.9% computer, engineering, and science, 7.3% education, legal, community service, arts, and media, 7.9% healthcare practitioners, 15.7% service, 22.5% sales and office, 10.6% natural resources, construction, and maintenance, 17.8% production, transportation, and material moving (2008-2012 5-year est.).

Income: Per capita income: $24,000 (2008-2012 5-year est.); Median household income: $49,600 (2008-2012 5-year est.); Average household income: $62,833 (2008-2012 5-year est.); Percent of households with income of $100,000 or more: 15.2% (2008-2012 5-year est.); Poverty rate: 11.5% (2008-2012 5-year est.).

Education: Percent of population age 25 and over with: High school diploma (including GED) or higher: 88.8% (2008-2012 5-year est.); Bachelor's degree or higher: 16.2% (2008-2012 5-year est.); Master's degree or higher: 6.5% (2008-2012 5-year est.).

School District(s)

Princeville CUSD 326 (PK-12)
  2011-12 Enrollment: 784 . . . . (309) 385-2213

Housing: Homeownership rate: 74.4% (2008-2012 5-year est.); Median home value: $114,900 (2008-2012 5-year est.); Median contract rent: $488 per month (2008-2012 5-year est.); Median year structure built: 1956 (2008-2012 5-year est.).

Health Insurance: 67.4% Private; 35.1% Public; 10.3% None. (2008-2012 5-year est.)

Transportation: Commute to work: 92.3% car, 0.1% public transportation, 2.7% walk, 3.7% work from home (2008-2012 5-year est.); Travel time to work: 32.3% less than 15 minutes, 33.5% 15 to 30 minutes, 27.6% 30 to 45 minutes, 3.4% 45 to 60 minutes, 3.2% 60 minutes or more (2008-2012 5-year est.)

ROME (CDP). Covers a land area of 1.889 square miles and a water area of 0.611 square miles. Located at 40.87° N. Lat; 89.51° W. Long. Elevation is 463 feet.

Population: 1,902 (1990); 1,776 (2000); 1,738 (2010); Density: 854.5 persons per square mile (2008-2012 5-year est.); Race: 99.6% White, 0.4% Black/African American, 0.0% Asian, 0.0% American Indian/Alaska Native, 0.0% Native Hawaiian/Other Pacific Islander, 0.0% Some other race, 0.1% Two or more races, 0.6% Hispanic of any race (2008-2012 5-year est.); Average household size: 2.56 (2008-2012 5-year est.); Median age: 39.3 (2008-2012 5-year est.); Males per 100 females: 105.3 (2008-2012 5-year est.); Marriage status: 32.7% never married, 47.8% now married, 8.2% widowed, 11.4% divorced (2008-2012 5-year est.); Foreign born: 1.5% (2008-2012 5-year est.); Ancestry (includes multiple ancestries): 26.3% German, 23.0% Irish, 12.3% English, 7.2% American, 3.4% Scottish (2008-2012 5-year est.).

Economy: Homeowner vacancy rate: 0.0%. Rental vacancy rate: 0.0%. (2008-2012 5-year est.); Employment by occupation: 9.7% management, business, and financial, 3.0% computer, engineering, and science, 6.8% education, legal, community service, arts, and media, 6.2% healthcare practitioners, 13.0% service, 21.6% sales and office, 13.3% natural resources, construction, and maintenance, 26.4% production, transportation, and material moving (2008-2012 5-year est.).

Income: Per capita income: $26,720 (2008-2012 5-year est.); Median household income: $63,409 (2008-2012 5-year est.); Average household income: $67,009 (2008-2012 5-year est.); Percent of households with income of $100,000 or more: 15.8% (2008-2012 5-year est.); Poverty rate: 5.4% (2008-2012 5-year est.).

Education: Percent of population age 25 and over with: High school diploma (including GED) or higher: 92.4% (2008-2012 5-year est.); Bachelor's degree or higher: 13.3% (2008-2012 5-year est.); Master's degree or higher: 4.4% (2008-2012 5-year est.).

Housing: Homeownership rate: 84.3% (2008-2012 5-year est.); Median home value: $102,500 (2008-2012 5-year est.); Median contract rent: $456 per month (2008-2012 5-year est.); Median year structure built: 1962 (2008-2012 5-year est.).

Health Insurance: 65.4% Private; 43.1% Public; 8.2% None. (2008-2012 5-year est.)

Transportation: Commute to work: 90.8% car, 0.1% public transportation, 0.0% walk, 5.1% work from home (2008-2012 5-year est.); Travel time to work: 24.5% less than 15 minutes, 48.5% 15 to 30 minutes, 17.3% 30 to 45 minutes, 4.9% 45 to 60 minutes, 4.8% 60 minutes or more (2008-2012 5-year est.)

TRIVOLI (unincorporated postal area)
Zip Code: 61569

Covers a land area of 39.413 square miles and a water area of 0.336 square miles. Located at 40.68° N. Lat; 89.90° W. Long. Elevation is 751 feet. Population: 1,220 (2010); Density: 31.0 persons per square mile (2010); Race: 97.9% White, 0.2% Black/African American, 0.2% Asian, 0.1% American Indian/Alaska Native, 0.0% Native Hawaiian/Other Pacific Islander, 1.6% Some other race, 1.4% Two or more races, 1.1% Hispanic of any race (2010); Average household size: 2.44 (2010); Median age: 46.2 (2010); Males per 100 females: 102.0 (2010); Homeownership rate: 89.2% (2010)

WEST PEORIA (city). Covers a land area of 1.268 square miles and a water area of 0 square miles. Located at 40.70° N. Lat; 89.63° W. Long. Elevation is 594 feet.

History: Bradley University to East.

Population: 5,314 (1990); 4,762 (2000); 4,458 (2010); Density: 3,539.2 persons per square mile (2008-2012 5-year est.); Race: 81.4% White, 10.4% Black/African American, 2.5% Asian, 0.2% American Indian/Alaska Native, 0.2% Native Hawaiian/Other Pacific Islander, 5.3% Some other race, 5.2% Two or more races, 2.7% Hispanic of any race (2008-2012 5-year est.); Average household size: 2.28 (2008-2012 5-year est.); Median age: 36.4 (2008-2012 5-year est.); Males per 100 females: 82.7 (2008-2012 5-year est.); Marriage status: 29.7% never married, 48.1% now married, 8.9% widowed, 13.2% divorced (2008-2012 5-year est.); Foreign born: 2.7% (2008-2012 5-year est.); Ancestry (includes multiple ancestries): 28.9% German, 24.8% Irish, 9.6% English, 6.9% French, 6.6% American (2008-2012 5-year est.).

Economy: Single-family building permits issued: 0 (2013); Multi-family building permits issued: 0 (2013); Homeowner vacancy rate: 0.7%. Rental vacancy rate: 6.1%. (2008-2012 5-year est.); Employment by occupation: 8.7% management, business, and financial, 5.1% computer, engineering, and science, 12.1% education, legal, community service, arts, and media, 6.2% healthcare practitioners, 18.3% service, 26.5% sales and office, 8.7% natural resources, construction, and maintenance, 14.4% production, transportation, and material moving (2008-2012 5-year est.).

Income: Per capita income: $27,146 (2008-2012 5-year est.); Median household income: $48,327 (2008-2012 5-year est.); Average household income: $62,358 (2008-2012 5-year est.); Percent of households with income of $100,000 or more: 15.8% (2008-2012 5-year est.); Poverty rate: 13.5% (2008-2012 5-year est.).

Education: Percent of population age 25 and over with: High school diploma (including GED) or higher: 90.1% (2008-2012 5-year est.); Bachelor's degree or higher: 35.7% (2008-2012 5-year est.); Master's degree or higher: 16.1% (2008-2012 5-year est.).

School District(s)

Peoria SD 150 (PK-12)
    2011-12 Enrollment: 14,057 . . . . (309) 672-6768

Housing: Homeownership rate: 74.8% (2008-2012 5-year est.); Median home value: $100,500 (2008-2012 5-year est.); Median contract rent: $469 per month (2008-2012 5-year est.); Median year structure built: 1947 (2008-2012 5-year est.).

Health Insurance: 67.3% Private; 35.1% Public; 8.1% None. (2008-2012 5-year est.)

Transportation: Commute to work: 90.7% car, 0.2% public transportation, 4.0% walk, 1.9% work from home (2008-2012 5-year est.); Travel time to work: 36.8% less than 15 minutes, 46.5% 15 to 30 minutes, 11.3% 30 to 45 minutes, 2.0% 45 to 60 minutes, 3.4% 60 minutes or more (2008-2012 5-year est.)

Perry County

Located in southwestern Illinois; bounded partly on the east by the Little Muddy River; drained by Beaucoup and Galum Creeks. Covers a land area of 441.761 square miles, a water area of 5.192 square miles, and is located in the Central Time Zone at 38.08° N. Lat., 89.37° W. Long. The county was founded in 1827. County seat is Pinckneyville.

Weather Station: Du Quoin 4 SE									Elevation: 419 feet		
	Jan	Feb	Mar	Apr	May	Jun	Jul	Aug	Sep	Oct	Nov	Dec
High	41	46	56	68	77	85	88	88	81	69	56	44
Low	24	28	36	46	55	64	68	65	56	46	36	27
Precip	2.8	2.7	4.2	4.2	5.6	4.5	3.8	3.1	3.5	3.9	4.2	3.5
Snow	3.2	3.4	1.0	0.2	0.0	0.0	0.0	0.0	0.0	0.2	0.6	2.9

High and Low temperatures in degrees Fahrenheit; Precipitation and Snow in inches

Population: 21,412 (1990); 23,094 (2000); 22,350 (2010); Race: 88.3% White, 8.9% Black/African American, 0.5% Asian, 0.4% American Indian/Alaska Native, 0.0% Native Hawaiian/Other Pacific Islander, 1.9% Some other race, 1.2% Two or more races, 2.7% Hispanic of any race (2008-2012 5-year est.); Density: 50.0 persons per square mile (2008-2012 5-year est.); Average household size: 2.47 (2008-2012 5-year est.); Median age: 39.7 (2008-2012 5-year est.); Males per 100 females: 119.4 (2008-2012 5-year est.).

Religion: Six largest groups: 29.6% Baptist, 13.6% Catholicism, 5.0% Methodist/Pietist, 4.0% Presbyterian-Reformed, 3.4% Non-denominational Protestant, 1.2% Lutheran (2010)

Economy: Unemployment rate: 8.5% (April 2014); Total civilian labor force: 9,112 (April 2014); Leading industries: 19.8% health care and social assistance; 16.4% retail trade; 10.5% accommodation & food services (2012); Farms: 560 totaling 180,635 acres (2012); Companies that employ 500 or more persons: 0 (2012); Companies that employ 100 to 499 persons: 8 (2012); Companies that employ less than 100 persons: 420 (2012); Black-owned businesses: n/a (2007); Hispanic-owned businesses: n/a (2007); Asian-owned businesses: n/a (2007); Women-owned businesses: 286 (2007); Single-family building permits issued: 35 (2013); Multi-family building permits issued: 0 (2013).

Income: Per capita income: $19,151 (2008-2012 5-year est.); Median household income: $42,013 (2008-2012 5-year est.); Average household income: $50,432 (2008-2012 5-year est.); Percent of households with income of $100,000 or more: 10.6% (2008-2012 5-year est.); Poverty rate: 17.1% (2008-2012 5-year est.); Bankruptcy rate: 4.04% (2013).

Education: Percent of population age 25 and over with: High school diploma (including GED) or higher: 84.2% (2008-2012 5-year est.); Bachelor's degree or higher: 14.6% (2008-2012 5-year est.); Master's degree or higher: 4.3% (2008-2012 5-year est.).

Housing: Homeownership rate: 78.6% (2008-2012 5-year est.); Median home value: $77,200 (2008-2012 5-year est.); Median contract rent: $367 per month (2008-2012 5-year est.); Median year structure built: 1967 (2008-2012 5-year est.)

Health: Birth rate: 98.2 per 10,000 population (2013); Death rate: 100.1 per 10,000 population (2013); Age-adjusted cancer mortality rate: 171.0 deaths per 100,000 population (2011); Number of physicians: 6.3 per 10,000 population (2011); Hospital beds: 22.4 per 10,000 population (2010); Hospital admissions: 502.5 per 10,000 population (2010).

Elections: 2012 Presidential election results: 40.0% Obama, 57.7% Romney

National and State Parks: Pyramid State Park

Additional Information Contacts

Perry County Government. . . . . (618) 357-5116
    http://www.perrycountyil.org

Perry County Communities

CUTLER (village). Covers a land area of 0.469 square miles and a water area of 0 square miles. Located at 38.03° N. Lat; 89.57° W. Long. Elevation is 499 feet.

Population: 523 (1990); 543 (2000); 441 (2010); Density: 1,074.1 persons per square mile (2008-2012 5-year est.); Race: 99.2% White, 0.0% Black/African American, 0.0% Asian, 0.8% American Indian/Alaska Native, 0.0% Native Hawaiian/Other Pacific Islander, 0.0% Some other race, 0.0% Two or more races, 2.6% Hispanic of any race (2008-2012 5-year est.); Average household size: 2.78 (2008-2012 5-year est.); Median age: 42.8 (2008-2012 5-year est.); Males per 100 females: 115.4 (2008-2012 5-year est.); Marriage status: 34.6% never married, 48.6% now married, 3.7% widowed, 13.1% divorced (2008-2012 5-year est.); Foreign born: 2.6% (2008-2012 5-year est.); Ancestry (includes multiple ancestries): 33.7% German, 15.9% Irish, 9.1% Italian, 5.6% English, 5.2% American (2008-2012 5-year est.).

Economy: Homeowner vacancy rate: 0.0%. Rental vacancy rate: 25.8%. (2008-2012 5-year est.); Employment by occupation: 2.9% management, business, and financial, 0.8% computer, engineering, and science, 3.7% education, legal, community service, arts, and media, 2.0% healthcare practitioners, 13.5% service, 18.0% sales and office, 20.0% natural resources, construction, and maintenance, 39.2% production, transportation, and material moving (2008-2012 5-year est.).

Income: Per capita income: $19,359 (2008-2012 5-year est.); Median household income: $40,417 (2008-2012 5-year est.); Average household income: $49,657 (2008-2012 5-year est.); Percent of households with income of $100,000 or more: 11.1% (2008-2012 5-year est.); Poverty rate: 17.5% (2008-2012 5-year est.).

Education: Percent of population age 25 and over with: High school diploma (including GED) or higher: 69.0% (2008-2012 5-year est.); Bachelor's degree or higher: 5.0% (2008-2012 5-year est.); Master's degree or higher: 0.6% (2008-2012 5-year est.).

Housing: Homeownership rate: 72.9% (2008-2012 5-year est.); Median home value: $46,000 (2008-2012 5-year est.); Median contract rent: $283 per month (2008-2012 5-year est.); Median year structure built: 1964 (2008-2012 5-year est.).

Health Insurance: 52.2% Private; 33.7% Public; 19.8% None. (2008-2012 5-year est.)

Transportation: Commute to work: 91.9% car, 0.0% public transportation, 3.4% walk, 1.3% work from home (2008-2012 5-year est.); Travel time to work: 41.2% less than 15 minutes, 31.3% 15 to 30 minutes, 14.2% 30 to 45 minutes, 3.9% 45 to 60 minutes, 9.4% 60 minutes or more (2008-2012 5-year est.)

DU QUOIN (city). Covers a land area of 6.979 square miles and a water area of 0.081 square miles. Located at 38.00° N. Lat; 89.23° W. Long. Elevation is 459 feet.

History: Du Quoin developed as a coal mining town. It was named for Jean Baptiste Du Quoigne, chief of the Kaskaskia tribe.

Population: 6,697 (1990); 6,448 (2000); 6,109 (2010); Density: 872.5 persons per square mile (2008-2012 5-year est.); Race: 86.1% White, 10.5% Black/African American, 0.9% Asian, 0.2% American Indian/Alaska Native, 0.0% Native Hawaiian/Other Pacific Islander, 2.3% Some other race, 1.8% Two or more races, 2.7% Hispanic of any race (2008-2012 5-year est.); Average household size: 2.38 (2008-2012 5-year est.); Median age: 38.5 (2008-2012 5-year est.); Males per 100 females: 96.9 (2008-2012 5-year est.); Marriage status: 25.3% never married, 45.2% now married, 13.3% widowed, 16.3% divorced (2008-2012 5-year est.); Foreign born: 2.1% (2008-2012 5-year est.); Ancestry (includes multiple ancestries): 27.7% German, 14.8% Irish, 10.5% American, 8.7% English, 5.2% Italian (2008-2012 5-year est.).

Economy: Homeowner vacancy rate: 0.0%. Rental vacancy rate: 4.7%. (2008-2012 5-year est.); Employment by occupation: 10.5% management, business, and financial, 0.2% computer, engineering, and science, 13.2% education, legal, community service, arts, and media, 5.0% healthcare practitioners, 25.4% service, 18.6% sales and office, 9.4% natural resources, construction, and maintenance, 17.7% production, transportation, and material moving (2008-2012 5-year est.).

Income: Per capita income: $18,255 (2008-2012 5-year est.); Median household income: $33,374 (2008-2012 5-year est.); Average household income: $42,732 (2008-2012 5-year est.); Percent of households with income of $100,000 or more: 7.4% (2008-2012 5-year est.); Poverty rate: 24.2% (2008-2012 5-year est.).

Education: Percent of population age 25 and over with: High school diploma (including GED) or higher: 83.6% (2008-2012 5-year est.); Bachelor's degree or higher: 15.1% (2008-2012 5-year est.); Master's degree or higher: 4.3% (2008-2012 5-year est.).

School District(s)

Duquoin CUSD 300 (PK-12)
   2011-12 Enrollment: 1,556 . . . . (618) 542-3856
Tri-County Sp Ed Jnt Agreement
   2011-12 Enrollment: n/a . . . . (618) 684-2109

Housing: Homeownership rate: 66.7% (2008-2012 5-year est.); Median home value: $59,300 (2008-2012 5-year est.); Median contract rent: $377 per month (2008-2012 5-year est.); Median year structure built: 1959 (2008-2012 5-year est.).

Health Insurance: 55.1% Private; 52.3% Public; 10.3% None. (2008-2012 5-year est.)

Hospitals: Marshall Browning Hospital (25 beds)

Safety: Violent crime rate: 16.4 per 10,000 population; Property crime rate: 167.6 per 10,000 population (2012).

Transportation: Commute to work: 94.0% car, 2.5% public transportation, 1.1% walk, 1.7% work from home (2008-2012 5-year est.); Travel time to work: 41.2% less than 15 minutes, 13.2% 15 to 30 minutes, 23.2% 30 to 45 minutes, 18.6% 45 to 60 minutes, 3.8% 60 minutes or more (2008-2012 5-year est.); Amtrak: Train service available.

Airports: Pinckneyville-DuQuoin Airport (general aviation)

Additional Information Contacts
City of Du Quoin . . . . (618) 542-3841
   http://www.duquoin.org
Du Quoin Chamber of Commerce . . . . (618) 542-9570
   http://duquoin.org/chamber-of-commerce

PINCKNEYVILLE (city). County seat. Covers a land area of 4.038 square miles and a water area of 0.275 square miles. Located at 38.09° N. Lat; 89.40° W. Long. Elevation is 433 feet.

History: Pyramid State Park to South, created from reclaimed coal strip mines. Incorporated 1861.

Population: 3,372 (1990); 5,464 (2000); 5,648 (2010); Density: 1,394.4 persons per square mile (2008-2012 5-year est.); Race: 72.9% White, 21.9% Black/African American, 1.0% Asian, 0.3% American Indian/Alaska Native, 0.0% Native Hawaiian/Other Pacific Islander, 3.9% Some other race, 1.9% Two or more races, 6.1% Hispanic of any race (2008-2012 5-year est.); Average household size: 2.44 (2008-2012 5-year est.); Median age: 35.9 (2008-2012 5-year est.); Males per 100 females: 189.2 (2008-2012 5-year est.); Marriage status: 45.4% never married, 35.5% now married, 10.1% widowed, 9.0% divorced (2008-2012 5-year est.); Foreign born: 2.6% (2008-2012 5-year est.); Ancestry (includes multiple ancestries): 28.3% German, 15.1% Irish, 8.6% American, 4.9% English, 4.7% Polish (2008-2012 5-year est.).

Economy: Homeowner vacancy rate: 0.0%. Rental vacancy rate: 23.6%. (2008-2012 5-year est.); Employment by occupation: 6.5% management, business, and financial, 1.7% computer, engineering, and science, 17.5% education, legal, community service, arts, and media, 5.7% healthcare practitioners, 28.4% service, 14.5% sales and office, 11.6% natural resources, construction, and maintenance, 14.2% production, transportation, and material moving (2008-2012 5-year est.).

Income: Per capita income: $14,085 (2008-2012 5-year est.); Median household income: $44,022 (2008-2012 5-year est.); Average household income: $51,833 (2008-2012 5-year est.); Percent of households with income of $100,000 or more: 13.8% (2008-2012 5-year est.); Poverty rate: 15.8% (2008-2012 5-year est.).

Education: Percent of population age 25 and over with: High school diploma (including GED) or higher: 75.4% (2008-2012 5-year est.); Bachelor's degree or higher: 17.0% (2008-2012 5-year est.); Master's degree or higher: 7.6% (2008-2012 5-year est.).

School District(s)

CCSD 204 (PK-08)
   2011-12 Enrollment: 159 . . . . (618) 357-2419
Pinckneyville CHSD 101 (09-12)
   2011-12 Enrollment: 443 . . . . (618) 357-5013
Pinckneyville SD 50 (PK-08)
   2011-12 Enrollment: 574 . . . . (618) 357-5161

Housing: Homeownership rate: 76.4% (2008-2012 5-year est.); Median home value: $74,300 (2008-2012 5-year est.); Median contract rent: $338 per month (2008-2012 5-year est.); Median year structure built: 1956 (2008-2012 5-year est.).

Health Insurance: 72.5% Private; 34.4% Public; 9.7% None. (2008-2012 5-year est.)

Hospitals: Pinckneyville Community Hospital (85 beds)

Safety: Violent crime rate: 17.7 per 10,000 population; Property crime rate: 40.8 per 10,000 population (2012).

Transportation: Commute to work: 95.7% car, 0.0% public transportation, 2.3% walk, 2.0% work from home (2008-2012 5-year est.); Travel time to work: 38.9% less than 15 minutes, 28.5% 15 to 30 minutes, 20.5% 30 to 45 minutes, 5.5% 45 to 60 minutes, 6.6% 60 minutes or more (2008-2012 5-year est.)

Airports: Pinckneyville-DuQuoin Airport (general aviation)

Additional Information Contacts
City of Pinckneyville . . . . (618) 357-6916
   http://www.ci.pinckneyville.il.us
Pinckneyville Chamber of Commerce . . . . (618) 357-3243
   http://www.pinckneyville.com

SAINT JOHNS (village). Covers a land area of 0.727 square miles and a water area of 0.037 square miles. Located at 38.03° N. Lat; 89.24° W. Long. Elevation is 463 feet.

Population: 262 (1990); 218 (2000); 219 (2010); Density: 225.7 persons per square mile (2008-2012 5-year est.); Race: 95.1% White, 0.0% Black/African American, 0.0% Asian, 1.8% American Indian/Alaska Native, 0.0% Native Hawaiian/Other Pacific Islander, 3.1% Some other race, 3.0% Two or more races, 0.0% Hispanic of any race (2008-2012 5-year est.); Average household size: 2.16 (2008-2012 5-year est.); Median age: 46.2 (2008-2012 5-year est.); Males per 100 females: 110.3 (2008-2012 5-year est.); Marriage status: 21.3% never married, 46.0% now married, 9.3% widowed, 23.3% divorced (2008-2012 5-year est.); Foreign born: 0.0% (2008-2012 5-year est.); Ancestry (includes multiple ancestries): 23.8%

English, 17.7% German, 17.1% Irish, 9.8% Italian, 9.8% American (2008-2012 5-year est.).
Economy: Homeowner vacancy rate: 0.0%. Rental vacancy rate: 0.0%. (2008-2012 5-year est.); Employment by occupation: 11.4% management, business, and financial, 1.4% computer, engineering, and science, 5.7% education, legal, community service, arts, and media, 8.6% healthcare practitioners, 24.3% service, 20.0% sales and office, 11.4% natural resources, construction, and maintenance, 17.1% production, transportation, and material moving (2008-2012 5-year est.).
Income: Per capita income: $42,290 (2008-2012 5-year est.); Median household income: $47,857 (2008-2012 5-year est.); Average household income: $89,176 (2008-2012 5-year est.); Percent of households with income of $100,000 or more: 3.9% (2008-2012 5-year est.); Poverty rate: 17.1% (2008-2012 5-year est.).
Education: Percent of population age 25 and over with: High school diploma (including GED) or higher: 86.0% (2008-2012 5-year est.); Bachelor's degree or higher: 3.9% (2008-2012 5-year est.); Master's degree or higher: 3.1% (2008-2012 5-year est.).
Housing: Homeownership rate: 76.3% (2008-2012 5-year est.); Median home value: $31,300 (2008-2012 5-year est.); Median contract rent: $285 per month (2008-2012 5-year est.); Median year structure built: 1976 (2008-2012 5-year est.).
Health Insurance: 59.8% Private; 43.3% Public; 21.3% None. (2008-2012 5-year est.)
Transportation: Commute to work: 98.5% car, 0.0% public transportation, 1.5% walk, 0.0% work from home (2008-2012 5-year est.); Travel time to work: 38.8% less than 15 minutes, 20.9% 15 to 30 minutes, 14.9% 30 to 45 minutes, 9.0% 45 to 60 minutes, 16.4% 60 minutes or more (2008-2012 5-year est.).

TAMAROA (village). Covers a land area of 0.958 square miles and a water area of 0 square miles. Located at 38.14° N. Lat; 89.23° W. Long. Elevation is 509 feet.
History: Tamaroa was named for the Tamaroa Indians that lived in this area.
Population: 780 (1990); 740 (2000); 638 (2010); Density: 790.9 persons per square mile (2008-2012 5-year est.); Race: 98.5% White, 0.0% Black/African American, 0.0% Asian, 0.9% American Indian/Alaska Native, 0.0% Native Hawaiian/Other Pacific Islander, 0.6% Some other race, 0.5% Two or more races, 0.0% Hispanic of any race (2008-2012 5-year est.); Average household size: 2.62 (2008-2012 5-year est.); Median age: 34.8 (2008-2012 5-year est.); Males per 100 females: 100.5 (2008-2012 5-year est.); Marriage status: 32.0% never married, 45.7% now married, 5.0% widowed, 17.4% divorced (2008-2012 5-year est.); Foreign born: 0.0% (2008-2012 5-year est.); Ancestry (includes multiple ancestries): 21.0% German, 13.5% Irish, 10.7% English, 10.7% Polish, 6.1% French (2008-2012 5-year est.).
Economy: Homeowner vacancy rate: 8.2%. Rental vacancy rate: 16.9%. (2008-2012 5-year est.); Employment by occupation: 1.4% management, business, and financial, 4.0% computer, engineering, and science, 6.2% education, legal, community service, arts, and media, 6.5% healthcare practitioners, 18.5% service, 13.8% sales and office, 16.7% natural resources, construction, and maintenance, 33.0% production, transportation, and material moving (2008-2012 5-year est.).
Income: Per capita income: $15,047 (2008-2012 5-year est.); Median household income: $36,771 (2008-2012 5-year est.); Average household income: $38,106 (2008-2012 5-year est.); Percent of households with income of $100,000 or more: 4.5% (2008-2012 5-year est.); Poverty rate: 26.1% (2008-2012 5-year est.).
Education: Percent of population age 25 and over with: High school diploma (including GED) or higher: 81.4% (2008-2012 5-year est.); Bachelor's degree or higher: 8.7% (2008-2012 5-year est.); Master's degree or higher: 0.0% (2008-2012 5-year est.).

School District(s)
Tamaroa SD 5 (PK-08)
    2011-12 Enrollment: 110. . . . . (618) 496-5513
Housing: Homeownership rate: 81.3% (2008-2012 5-year est.); Median home value: $54,200 (2008-2012 5-year est.); Median contract rent: $259 per month (2008-2012 5-year est.); Median year structure built: 1959 (2008-2012 5-year est.).
Health Insurance: 55.9% Private; 48.4% Public; 9.6% None. (2008-2012 5-year est.)
Transportation: Commute to work: 97.0% car, 0.0% public transportation, 1.5% walk, 1.5% work from home (2008-2012 5-year est.); Travel time to work: 16.6% less than 15 minutes, 30.1% 15 to 30 minutes, 24.3% 30 to

45 minutes, 22.8% 45 to 60 minutes, 6.2% 60 minutes or more (2008-2012 5-year est.)

WILLISVILLE (village). Covers a land area of 0.390 square miles and a water area of 0 square miles. Located at 37.98° N. Lat; 89.59° W. Long. Elevation is 495 feet.
Population: 577 (1990); 694 (2000); 633 (2010); Density: 1,279.3 persons per square mile (2008-2012 5-year est.); Race: 100.0% White, 0.0% Black/African American, 0.0% Asian, 0.0% American Indian/Alaska Native, 0.0% Native Hawaiian/Other Pacific Islander, 0.0% Some other race, 0.0% Two or more races, 0.0% Hispanic of any race (2008-2012 5-year est.); Average household size: 2.43 (2008-2012 5-year est.); Median age: 34.4 (2008-2012 5-year est.); Males per 100 females: 80.1 (2008-2012 5-year est.); Marriage status: 21.3% never married, 52.4% now married, 9.8% widowed, 16.5% divorced (2008-2012 5-year est.); Foreign born: 0.0% (2008-2012 5-year est.); Ancestry (includes multiple ancestries): 42.1% German, 17.6% French, 12.4% Irish, 8.4% American, 5.4% English (2008-2012 5-year est.).
Economy: Homeowner vacancy rate: 0.0%. Rental vacancy rate: 21.3%. (2008-2012 5-year est.); Employment by occupation: 5.9% management, business, and financial, 0.0% computer, engineering, and science, 5.4% education, legal, community service, arts, and media, 2.9% healthcare practitioners, 28.8% service, 8.8% sales and office, 15.1% natural resources, construction, and maintenance, 33.2% production, transportation, and material moving (2008-2012 5-year est.).
Income: Per capita income: $14,347 (2008-2012 5-year est.); Median household income: $28,618 (2008-2012 5-year est.); Average household income: $34,617 (2008-2012 5-year est.); Percent of households with income of $100,000 or more: 1.0% (2008-2012 5-year est.); Poverty rate: 18.0% (2008-2012 5-year est.).
Education: Percent of population age 25 and over with: High school diploma (including GED) or higher: 76.6% (2008-2012 5-year est.); Bachelor's degree or higher: 6.6% (2008-2012 5-year est.); Master's degree or higher: 3.2% (2008-2012 5-year est.).
Housing: Homeownership rate: 82.0% (2008-2012 5-year est.); Median home value: $35,800 (2008-2012 5-year est.); Median contract rent: $393 per month (2008-2012 5-year est.); Median year structure built: 1964 (2008-2012 5-year est.).
Health Insurance: 43.5% Private; 57.7% Public; 12.8% None. (2008-2012 5-year est.)
Safety: Violent crime rate: 15.9 per 10,000 population; Property crime rate: 95.2 per 10,000 population (2012).
Transportation: Commute to work: 98.5% car, 0.0% public transportation, 0.0% walk, 0.5% work from home (2008-2012 5-year est.); Travel time to work: 21.2% less than 15 minutes, 39.4% 15 to 30 minutes, 16.3% 30 to 45 minutes, 4.4% 45 to 60 minutes, 18.7% 60 minutes or more (2008-2012 5-year est.)

Piatt County

Located in central Illinois; drained by the Sangamon River. Covers a land area of 439.202 square miles, a water area of 0.260 square miles, and is located in the Central Time Zone at 40.01° N. Lat., 88.59° W. Long. The county was founded in 1841. County seat is Monticello.

Piatt County is part of the Champaign-Urbana, IL Metropolitan Statistical Area. The entire metro area includes: Champaign County, IL; Ford County, IL; Piatt County, IL

Population: 15,548 (1990); 16,365 (2000); 16,729 (2010); Race: 98.1% White, 0.5% Black/African American, 0.2% Asian, 0.0% American Indian/Alaska Native, 0.0% Native Hawaiian/Other Pacific Islander, 1.2% Some other race, 1.1% Two or more races, 1.0% Hispanic of any race (2008-2012 5-year est.); Density: 37.6 persons per square mile (2008-2012 5-year est.); Average household size: 2.57 (2008-2012 5-year est.); Median age: 42.8 (2008-2012 5-year est.); Males per 100 females: 97.6 (2008-2012 5-year est.).
Religion: Six largest groups: 14.6% Methodist/Pietist, 9.1% Baptist, 4.5% Catholicism, 3.8% Presbyterian-Reformed, 2.6% Lutheran, 1.7% European Free-Church (2010)
Economy: Unemployment rate: 6.0% (April 2014); Total civilian labor force: 8,309 (April 2014); Leading industries: 18.6% retail trade; 18.0% health care and social assistance; 12.8% wholesale trade (2012); Farms: 426 totaling 259,048 acres (2012); Companies that employ 500 or more persons: 0 (2012); Companies that employ 100 to 499 persons: 2 (2012);

Companies that employ less than 100 persons: 334 (2012); Black-owned businesses: n/a (2007); Hispanic-owned businesses: n/a (2007); Asian-owned businesses: n/a (2007); Women-owned businesses: n/a (2007); Single-family building permits issued: 24 (2013); Multi-family building permits issued: 0 (2013).

Income: Per capita income: $28,930 (2008-2012 5-year est.); Median household income: $62,125 (2008-2012 5-year est.); Average household income: $73,825 (2008-2012 5-year est.); Percent of households with income of $100,000 or more: 21.8% (2008-2012 5-year est.); Poverty rate: 6.3% (2008-2012 5-year est.); Bankruptcy rate: 3.09% (2013).

Education: Percent of population age 25 and over with: High school diploma (including GED) or higher: 92.7% (2008-2012 5-year est.); Bachelor's degree or higher: 24.8% (2008-2012 5-year est.); Master's degree or higher: 8.7% (2008-2012 5-year est.).

Housing: Homeownership rate: 83.5% (2008-2012 5-year est.); Median home value: $120,800 (2008-2012 5-year est.); Median contract rent: $508 per month (2008-2012 5-year est.); Median year structure built: 1965 (2008-2012 5-year est.)

Health: Birth rate: 99.2 per 10,000 population (2013); Death rate: 99.8 per 10,000 population (2013); Age-adjusted cancer mortality rate: 175.4 deaths per 100,000 population (2011); Number of physicians: 6.0 per 10,000 population (2011); Hospital beds: 9.6 per 10,000 population (2010); Hospital admissions: 190.1 per 10,000 population (2010).

Elections: 2012 Presidential election results: 35.4% Obama, 62.2% Romney

Additional Information Contacts

Piatt County Government . . . . (217) 762-9487
  http://www.piattcounty.org

Piatt County Communities

ATWOOD (village). Covers a land area of 0.625 square miles and a water area of 0 square miles. Located at 39.80° N. Lat; 88.46° W. Long.
Population: 1,253 (1990); 1,290 (2000); 1,224 (2010); Density: 1,827.5 persons per square mile (2008-2012 5-year est.); Race: 97.7% White, 0.0% Black/African American, 0.0% Asian, 0.5% American Indian/Alaska Native, 0.0% Native Hawaiian/Other Pacific Islander, 1.8% Some other race, 1.7% Two or more races, 0.4% Hispanic of any race (2008-2012 5-year est.); Average household size: 2.27 (2008-2012 5-year est.); Median age: 46.2 (2008-2012 5-year est.); Males per 100 females: 87.1 (2008-2012 5-year est.); Marriage status: 19.5% never married, 60.3% now married, 9.6% widowed, 10.6% divorced (2008-2012 5-year est.); Foreign born: 0.3% (2008-2012 5-year est.); Ancestry (includes multiple ancestries): 29.7% German, 20.2% American, 11.3% Irish, 10.9% English, 3.1% Dutch (2008-2012 5-year est.).
Economy: Single-family building permits issued: 2 (2013); Multi-family building permits issued: 0 (2013); Homeowner vacancy rate: 4.1%. Rental vacancy rate: 11.4%. (2008-2012 5-year est.); Employment by occupation: 10.3% management, business, and financial, 0.0% computer, engineering, and science, 4.7% education, legal, community service, arts, and media, 6.0% healthcare practitioners, 16.6% service, 27.5% sales and office, 18.6% natural resources, construction, and maintenance, 16.3% production, transportation, and material moving (2008-2012 5-year est.).
Income: Per capita income: $23,835 (2008-2012 5-year est.); Median household income: $51,705 (2008-2012 5-year est.); Average household income: $53,489 (2008-2012 5-year est.); Percent of households with income of $100,000 or more: 7.9% (2008-2012 5-year est.); Poverty rate: 4.3% (2008-2012 5-year est.).
Education: Percent of population age 25 and over with: High school diploma (including GED) or higher: 91.8% (2008-2012 5-year est.); Bachelor's degree or higher: 10.0% (2008-2012 5-year est.); Master's degree or higher: 1.9% (2008-2012 5-year est.).
School District(s)
Atwood Hammond CUSD 39 (PK-12)
  2011-12 Enrollment: 430. . . . . (217) 578-3111
Atwood Hammond CUSD 39 (PK-12)
  2011-12 Enrollment: 430. . . . . (217) 578-3111
Housing: Homeownership rate: 84.5% (2008-2012 5-year est.); Median home value: $82,300 (2008-2012 5-year est.); Median contract rent: $493 per month (2008-2012 5-year est.); Median year structure built: 1955 (2008-2012 5-year est.).
Health Insurance: 68.2% Private; 37.6% Public; 11.5% None. (2008-2012 5-year est.)
Safety: Violent crime rate: 16.4 per 10,000 population; Property crime rate: 114.8 per 10,000 population (2012).

Transportation: Commute to work: 94.7% car, 0.0% public transportation, 0.4% walk, 1.7% work from home (2008-2012 5-year est.); Travel time to work: 39.2% less than 15 minutes, 36.9% 15 to 30 minutes, 15.1% 30 to 45 minutes, 6.3% 45 to 60 minutes, 2.4% 60 minutes or more (2008-2012 5-year est.)

BEMENT (village). Covers a land area of 0.808 square miles and a water area of 0 square miles. Located at 39.92° N. Lat; 88.57° W. Long. Elevation is 689 feet.
History: Incorporated 1874. Bryant Cottage State Historical Site.
Population: 1,668 (1990); 1,784 (2000); 1,730 (2010); Density: 2,357.6 persons per square mile (2008-2012 5-year est.); Race: 95.9% White, 0.6% Black/African American, 0.5% Asian, 0.0% American Indian/Alaska Native, 0.0% Native Hawaiian/Other Pacific Islander, 3.0% Some other race, 2.9% Two or more races, 2.2% Hispanic of any race (2008-2012 5-year est.); Average household size: 2.76 (2008-2012 5-year est.); Median age: 38.3 (2008-2012 5-year est.); Males per 100 females: 91.6 (2008-2012 5-year est.); Marriage status: 27.6% never married, 51.9% now married, 8.6% widowed, 11.9% divorced (2008-2012 5-year est.); Foreign born: 2.0% (2008-2012 5-year est.); Ancestry (includes multiple ancestries): 24.4% German, 22.6% American, 13.7% Irish, 7.6% English, 4.3% French (2008-2012 5-year est.).
Economy: Single-family building permits issued: 0 (2013); Multi-family building permits issued: 0 (2013); Homeowner vacancy rate: 0.0%. Rental vacancy rate: 14.8%. (2008-2012 5-year est.); Employment by occupation: 8.0% management, business, and financial, 1.3% computer, engineering, and science, 4.7% education, legal, community service, arts, and media, 2.8% healthcare practitioners, 30.1% service, 20.3% sales and office, 12.5% natural resources, construction, and maintenance, 20.4% production, transportation, and material moving (2008-2012 5-year est.).
Income: Per capita income: $21,661 (2008-2012 5-year est.); Median household income: $48,854 (2008-2012 5-year est.); Average household income: $57,758 (2008-2012 5-year est.); Percent of households with income of $100,000 or more: 12.1% (2008-2012 5-year est.); Poverty rate: 12.1% (2008-2012 5-year est.).
Education: Percent of population age 25 and over with: High school diploma (including GED) or higher: 87.1% (2008-2012 5-year est.); Bachelor's degree or higher: 11.7% (2008-2012 5-year est.); Master's degree or higher: 2.1% (2008-2012 5-year est.).
School District(s)
Bement CUSD 5 (PK-12)
  2011-12 Enrollment: 375. . . . . (217) 678-4200
Housing: Homeownership rate: 83.8% (2008-2012 5-year est.); Median home value: $80,600 (2008-2012 5-year est.); Median contract rent: $391 per month (2008-2012 5-year est.); Median year structure built: 1958 (2008-2012 5-year est.).
Health Insurance: 62.1% Private; 33.1% Public; 15.7% None. (2008-2012 5-year est.)
Transportation: Commute to work: 91.8% car, 0.3% public transportation, 3.5% walk, 2.9% work from home (2008-2012 5-year est.); Travel time to work: 42.7% less than 15 minutes, 17.2% 15 to 30 minutes, 29.1% 30 to 45 minutes, 7.6% 45 to 60 minutes, 3.3% 60 minutes or more (2008-2012 5-year est.)

CERRO GORDO (village). Covers a land area of 0.769 square miles and a water area of 0 square miles. Located at 39.89° N. Lat; 88.73° W. Long. Elevation is 745 feet.
History: Incorporated 1873.
Population: 1,436 (1990); 1,436 (2000); 1,403 (2010); Density: 1,721.8 persons per square mile (2008-2012 5-year est.); Race: 98.9% White, 0.0% Black/African American, 0.0% Asian, 0.0% American Indian/Alaska Native, 0.0% Native Hawaiian/Other Pacific Islander, 1.1% Some other race, 1.0% Two or more races, 0.2% Hispanic of any race (2008-2012 5-year est.); Average household size: 2.66 (2008-2012 5-year est.); Median age: 42.1 (2008-2012 5-year est.); Males per 100 females: 96.7 (2008-2012 5-year est.); Marriage status: 22.5% never married, 63.5% now married, 8.3% widowed, 5.7% divorced (2008-2012 5-year est.); Foreign born: 0.0% (2008-2012 5-year est.); Ancestry (includes multiple ancestries): 27.1% German, 25.8% American, 12.3% Irish, 11.7% English, 2.3% Scottish (2008-2012 5-year est.).
Economy: Single-family building permits issued: 1 (2013); Multi-family building permits issued: 0 (2013); Homeowner vacancy rate: 0.0%. Rental vacancy rate: 24.6%. (2008-2012 5-year est.); Employment by occupation: 11.1% management, business, and financial, 0.6% computer, engineering, and science, 6.7% education, legal, community service, arts, and media,

4.4% healthcare practitioners, 19.4% service, 21.6% sales and office, 14.8% natural resources, construction, and maintenance, 21.3% production, transportation, and material moving (2008-2012 5-year est.).

Income: Per capita income: $22,860 (2008-2012 5-year est.); Median household income: $57,632 (2008-2012 5-year est.); Average household income: $60,053 (2008-2012 5-year est.); Percent of households with income of $100,000 or more: 10.0% (2008-2012 5-year est.); Poverty rate: 4.7% (2008-2012 5-year est.).

Education: Percent of population age 25 and over with: High school diploma (including GED) or higher: 93.4% (2008-2012 5-year est.); Bachelor's degree or higher: 12.9% (2008-2012 5-year est.); Master's degree or higher: 3.6% (2008-2012 5-year est.).

School District(s)

Cerro Gordo CUSD 100 (PK-12)

2011-12 Enrollment: 582. . . . . (217) 763-5221

Housing: Homeownership rate: 79.7% (2008-2012 5-year est.); Median home value: $91,000 (2008-2012 5-year est.); Median contract rent: $551 per month (2008-2012 5-year est.); Median year structure built: 1956 (2008-2012 5-year est.).

Health Insurance: 81.2% Private; 28.8% Public; 7.1% None. (2008-2012 5-year est.)

Transportation: Commute to work: 96.9% car, 0.0% public transportation, 1.9% walk, 1.2% work from home (2008-2012 5-year est.); Travel time to work: 14.6% less than 15 minutes, 62.3% 15 to 30 minutes, 19.3% 30 to 45 minutes, 3.3% 45 to 60 minutes, 0.5% 60 minutes or more (2008-2012 5-year est.).

CISCO (village). Covers a land area of 0.366 square miles and a water area of 0 square miles. Located at 40.01° N. Lat; 88.72° W. Long. Elevation is 689 feet.

Population: 282 (1990); 264 (2000); 261 (2010); Density: 772.9 persons per square mile (2008-2012 5-year est.); Race: 97.9% White, 2.1% Black/African American, 0.0% Asian, 0.0% American Indian/Alaska Native, 0.0% Native Hawaiian/Other Pacific Islander, 0.0% Some other race, 0.0% Two or more races, 1.4% Hispanic of any race (2008-2012 5-year est.); Average household size: 2.89 (2008-2012 5-year est.); Median age: 34.1 (2008-2012 5-year est.); Males per 100 females: 122.8 (2008-2012 5-year est.); Marriage status: 14.7% never married, 67.0% now married, 6.8% widowed, 11.5% divorced (2008-2012 5-year est.); Foreign born: 0.0% (2008-2012 5-year est.); Ancestry (includes multiple ancestries): 36.4% American, 19.1% English, 13.8% Irish, 11.7% German, 3.9% Norwegian (2008-2012 5-year est.).

Economy: Single-family building permits issued: 0 (2013); Multi-family building permits issued: 0 (2013); Homeowner vacancy rate: 0.0%. Rental vacancy rate: 0.0%. (2008-2012 5-year est.); Employment by occupation: 10.7% management, business, and financial, 2.7% computer, engineering, and science, 1.8% education, legal, community service, arts, and media, 6.3% healthcare practitioners, 9.8% service, 21.4% sales and office, 18.8% natural resources, construction, and maintenance, 28.6% production, transportation, and material moving (2008-2012 5-year est.).

Income: Per capita income: $21,006 (2008-2012 5-year est.); Median household income: $56,875 (2008-2012 5-year est.); Average household income: $60,605 (2008-2012 5-year est.); Percent of households with income of $100,000 or more: 5.1% (2008-2012 5-year est.); Poverty rate: 2.1% (2008-2012 5-year est.).

Education: Percent of population age 25 and over with: High school diploma (including GED) or higher: 93.8% (2008-2012 5-year est.); Bachelor's degree or higher: 16.5% (2008-2012 5-year est.); Master's degree or higher: 0.6% (2008-2012 5-year est.).

Housing: Homeownership rate: 85.7% (2008-2012 5-year est.); Median home value: $80,000 (2008-2012 5-year est.); Median contract rent: $675 per month (2008-2012 5-year est.); Median year structure built: 1955 (2008-2012 5-year est.).

Health Insurance: 83.0% Private; 29.3% Public; 5.7% None. (2008-2012 5-year est.)

Transportation: Commute to work: 94.5% car, 0.0% public transportation, 1.8% walk, 1.8% work from home (2008-2012 5-year est.); Travel time to work: 29.6% less than 15 minutes, 33.3% 15 to 30 minutes, 32.4% 30 to 45 minutes, 4.6% 45 to 60 minutes, 0.0% 60 minutes or more (2008-2012 5-year est.).

DE LAND (village). Aka Deland. Covers a land area of 0.411 square miles and a water area of 0 square miles. Located at 40.12° N. Lat; 88.64° W. Long. Elevation is 702 feet.

Population: 458 (1990); 475 (2000); 446 (2010); Density: 1,237.1 persons per square mile (2008-2012 5-year est.); Race: 96.1% White, 0.0% Black/African American, 0.0% Asian, 0.0% American Indian/Alaska Native, 0.0% Native Hawaiian/Other Pacific Islander, 3.9% Some other race, 3.9% Two or more races, 1.8% Hispanic of any race (2008-2012 5-year est.); Average household size: 2.75 (2008-2012 5-year est.); Median age: 40.8 (2008-2012 5-year est.); Males per 100 females: 124.8 (2008-2012 5-year est.); Marriage status: 28.0% never married, 54.0% now married, 9.1% widowed, 8.9% divorced (2008-2012 5-year est.); Foreign born: 0.4% (2008-2012 5-year est.); Ancestry (includes multiple ancestries): 36.8% American, 26.0% German, 9.4% English, 9.3% Irish, 4.3% Belgian (2008-2012 5-year est.).

Economy: Single-family building permits issued: 0 (2013); Multi-family building permits issued: 0 (2013); Homeowner vacancy rate: 10.2%. Rental vacancy rate: 0.0%. (2008-2012 5-year est.); Employment by occupation: 7.3% management, business, and financial, 6.0% computer, engineering, and science, 5.6% education, legal, community service, arts, and media, 8.2% healthcare practitioners, 21.9% service, 14.2% sales and office, 12.4% natural resources, construction, and maintenance, 24.5% production, transportation, and material moving (2008-2012 5-year est.).

Income: Per capita income: $21,330 (2008-2012 5-year est.); Median household income: $48,750 (2008-2012 5-year est.); Average household income: $56,251 (2008-2012 5-year est.); Percent of households with income of $100,000 or more: 16.7% (2008-2012 5-year est.); Poverty rate: 6.8% (2008-2012 5-year est.).

Education: Percent of population age 25 and over with: High school diploma (including GED) or higher: 91.9% (2008-2012 5-year est.); Bachelor's degree or higher: 8.7% (2008-2012 5-year est.); Master's degree or higher: 3.3% (2008-2012 5-year est.).

School District(s)

Deland-Weldon CUSD 57 (PK-12)

2011-12 Enrollment: 207. . . . . (217) 736-2311

Housing: Homeownership rate: 85.9% (2008-2012 5-year est.); Median home value: $85,900 (2008-2012 5-year est.); Median contract rent: $425 per month (2008-2012 5-year est.); Median year structure built: Before 1940 (2008-2012 5-year est.).

Health Insurance: 76.8% Private; 19.5% Public; 13.0% None. (2008-2012 5-year est.)

Transportation: Commute to work: 94.6% car, 4.5% public transportation, 0.9% walk, 0.0% work from home (2008-2012 5-year est.); Travel time to work: 22.6% less than 15 minutes, 32.6% 15 to 30 minutes, 34.8% 30 to 45 minutes, 9.5% 45 to 60 minutes, 0.5% 60 minutes or more (2008-2012 5-year est.).

HAMMOND (village). Covers a land area of 0.756 square miles and a water area of <.001 square miles. Located at 39.80° N. Lat; 88.59° W. Long. Elevation is 673 feet.

Population: 527 (1990); 518 (2000); 509 (2010); Density: 516.2 persons per square mile (2008-2012 5-year est.); Race: 99.0% White, 0.0% Black/African American, 0.0% Asian, 0.0% American Indian/Alaska Native, 0.0% Native Hawaiian/Other Pacific Islander, 1.0% Some other race, 0.0% Two or more races, 1.0% Hispanic of any race (2008-2012 5-year est.); Average household size: 1.92 (2008-2012 5-year est.); Median age: 49.5 (2008-2012 5-year est.); Males per 100 females: 108.6 (2008-2012 5-year est.); Marriage status: 14.9% never married, 56.4% now married, 8.4% widowed, 20.3% divorced (2008-2012 5-year est.); Foreign born: 0.0% (2008-2012 5-year est.); Ancestry (includes multiple ancestries): 22.3% German, 19.5% American, 14.1% English, 9.0% Irish, 4.9% Italian (2008-2012 5-year est.).

Economy: Single-family building permits issued: 0 (2013); Multi-family building permits issued: 0 (2013); Homeowner vacancy rate: 0.0%. Rental vacancy rate: 0.0%. (2008-2012 5-year est.); Employment by occupation: 10.2% management, business, and financial, 0.0% computer, engineering, and science, 2.4% education, legal, community service, arts, and media, 2.4% healthcare practitioners, 19.8% service, 19.2% sales and office, 12.0% natural resources, construction, and maintenance, 34.1% production, transportation, and material moving (2008-2012 5-year est.).

Income: Per capita income: $22,428 (2008-2012 5-year est.); Median household income: $37,656 (2008-2012 5-year est.); Average household income: $45,189 (2008-2012 5-year est.); Percent of households with income of $100,000 or more: 4.4% (2008-2012 5-year est.); Poverty rate: 6.2% (2008-2012 5-year est.).

Education: Percent of population age 25 and over with: High school diploma (including GED) or higher: 87.0% (2008-2012 5-year est.); Bachelor's degree or higher: 2.0% (2008-2012 5-year est.); Master's degree or higher: 0.0% (2008-2012 5-year est.).
Housing: Homeownership rate: 70.9% (2008-2012 5-year est.); Median home value: $73,000 (2008-2012 5-year est.); Median contract rent: $294 per month (2008-2012 5-year est.); Median year structure built: 1960 (2008-2012 5-year est.).
Health Insurance: 71.0% Private; 44.6% Public; 8.7% None. (2008-2012 5-year est.)
Transportation: Commute to work: 93.4% car, 0.0% public transportation, 1.8% walk, 0.0% work from home (2008-2012 5-year est.); Travel time to work: 24.0% less than 15 minutes, 35.3% 15 to 30 minutes, 26.3% 30 to 45 minutes, 11.4% 45 to 60 minutes, 3.0% 60 minutes or more (2008-2012 5-year est.)

LAPLACE (CDP). Covers a land area of 0.709 square miles and a water area of 0 square miles. Located at 39.80° N. Lat; 88.72° W. Long. Elevation is 702 feet.
Population: n/a (1990); n/a (2000); 259 (2010); Density: 214.3 persons per square mile (2008-2012 5-year est.); Race: 78.3% White, 21.7% Black/African American, 0.0% Asian, 0.0% American Indian/Alaska Native, 0.0% Native Hawaiian/Other Pacific Islander, 0.0% Some other race, 0.0% Two or more races, 5.9% Hispanic of any race (2008-2012 5-year est.); Average household size: 2.62 (2008-2012 5-year est.); Median age: 54.1 (2008-2012 5-year est.); Males per 100 females: 85.4 (2008-2012 5-year est.); Marriage status: 16.3% never married, 73.0% now married, 5.7% widowed, 5.0% divorced (2008-2012 5-year est.); Foreign born: 5.9% (2008-2012 5-year est.); Ancestry (includes multiple ancestries): 28.3% German, 21.7% Dutch, 10.5% English, 5.9% Irish, 5.9% British (2008-2012 5-year est.).
Economy: Homeowner vacancy rate: 0.0%. Rental vacancy rate: 0.0%. (2008-2012 5-year est.); Employment by occupation: 13.0% management, business, and financial, 0.0% computer, engineering, and science, 6.5% education, legal, community service, arts, and media, 26.1% healthcare practitioners, 7.6% service, 8.7% sales and office, 0.0% natural resources, construction, and maintenance, 38.0% production, transportation, and material moving (2008-2012 5-year est.).
Income: Per capita income: $41,363 (2008-2012 5-year est.); Median household income: $78,889 (2008-2012 5-year est.); Average household income: $90,924 (2008-2012 5-year est.); Percent of households with income of $100,000 or more: 43.1% (2008-2012 5-year est.); Poverty rate: 0.0% (2008-2012 5-year est.).
Education: Percent of population age 25 and over with: High school diploma (including GED) or higher: 92.2% (2008-2012 5-year est.); Bachelor's degree or higher: 11.7% (2008-2012 5-year est.); Master's degree or higher: 0.0% (2008-2012 5-year est.).
Housing: Homeownership rate: 84.5% (2008-2012 5-year est.); Median home value: $145,800 (2008-2012 5-year est.); Median contract rent: n/a per month (2008-2012 5-year est.); Median year structure built: 1971 (2008-2012 5-year est.).
Health Insurance: 86.8% Private; 21.1% Public; 8.6% None. (2008-2012 5-year est.)
Transportation: Commute to work: 88.1% car, 0.0% public transportation, 11.9% walk, 0.0% work from home (2008-2012 5-year est.); Travel time to work: 40.5% less than 15 minutes, 33.3% 15 to 30 minutes, 3.6% 30 to 45 minutes, 15.5% 45 to 60 minutes, 7.1% 60 minutes or more (2008-2012 5-year est.)

MANSFIELD (village). Covers a land area of 0.528 square miles and a water area of 0.025 square miles. Located at 40.21° N. Lat; 88.51° W. Long. Elevation is 728 feet.
Population: 929 (1990); 949 (2000); 906 (2010); Density: 2,007.1 persons per square mile (2008-2012 5-year est.); Race: 97.2% White, 0.0% Black/African American, 2.3% Asian, 0.0% American Indian/Alaska Native, 0.0% Native Hawaiian/Other Pacific Islander, 0.5% Some other race, 0.6% Two or more races, 0.3% Hispanic of any race (2008-2012 5-year est.); Average household size: 2.41 (2008-2012 5-year est.); Median age: 48.5 (2008-2012 5-year est.); Males per 100 females: 88.4 (2008-2012 5-year est.); Marriage status: 20.7% never married, 58.9% now married, 10.4% widowed, 10.0% divorced (2008-2012 5-year est.); Foreign born: 2.5% (2008-2012 5-year est.); Ancestry (includes multiple ancestries): 25.0% American, 21.7% German, 12.6% Irish, 10.9% English, 3.6% French (2008-2012 5-year est.).

Economy: Single-family building permits issued: 0 (2013); Multi-family building permits issued: 0 (2013); Homeowner vacancy rate: 0.0%. Rental vacancy rate: 6.3%. (2008-2012 5-year est.); Employment by occupation: 13.7% management, business, and financial, 3.7% computer, engineering, and science, 8.4% education, legal, community service, arts, and media, 4.1% healthcare practitioners, 17.6% service, 21.7% sales and office, 11.1% natural resources, construction, and maintenance, 19.7% production, transportation, and material moving (2008-2012 5-year est.).
Income: Per capita income: $23,921 (2008-2012 5-year est.); Median household income: $47,321 (2008-2012 5-year est.); Average household income: $55,964 (2008-2012 5-year est.); Percent of households with income of $100,000 or more: 14.4% (2008-2012 5-year est.); Poverty rate: 15.2% (2008-2012 5-year est.).
Education: Percent of population age 25 and over with: High school diploma (including GED) or higher: 90.6% (2008-2012 5-year est.); Bachelor's degree or higher: 13.2% (2008-2012 5-year est.); Master's degree or higher: 2.4% (2008-2012 5-year est.).

School District(s)
Blue Ridge CUSD 18 (PK-12)
    2011-12 Enrollment: 809. . . . . (309) 928-9141
Housing: Homeownership rate: 79.7% (2008-2012 5-year est.); Median home value: $107,600 (2008-2012 5-year est.); Median contract rent: $525 per month (2008-2012 5-year est.); Median year structure built: 1962 (2008-2012 5-year est.).
Health Insurance: 70.0% Private; 41.6% Public; 8.5% None. (2008-2012 5-year est.)
Transportation: Commute to work: 92.5% car, 0.0% public transportation, 2.1% walk, 2.9% work from home (2008-2012 5-year est.); Travel time to work: 23.9% less than 15 minutes, 45.6% 15 to 30 minutes, 26.0% 30 to 45 minutes, 3.0% 45 to 60 minutes, 1.5% 60 minutes or more (2008-2012 5-year est.)

MILMINE (unincorporated postal area)
Zip Code: 61855
    Covers a land area of 10.193 square miles and a water area of 0 square miles. Located at 39.92° N. Lat; 88.66° W. Long. Elevation is 712 feet.
Population: 96 (2010); Density: 9.4 persons per square mile (2010); Race: 97.9% White, 0.0% Black/African American, 0.0% Asian, 0.0% American Indian/Alaska Native, 0.0% Native Hawaiian/Other Pacific Islander, 2.1% Some other race, 2.1% Two or more races, 0.0% Hispanic of any race (2010); Average household size: 2.18 (2010); Median age: 47.0 (2010); Males per 100 females: 123.3 (2010); Homeownership rate: 77.3% (2010)

MONTICELLO (city). County seat. Covers a land area of 3.802 square miles and a water area of 0.029 square miles. Located at 40.03° N. Lat; 88.57° W. Long. Elevation is 659 feet.
History: Incorporated 1841.
Population: 4,549 (1990); 5,138 (2000); 5,548 (2010); Density: 1,393.1 persons per square mile (2008-2012 5-year est.); Race: 98.4% White, 0.6% Black/African American, 0.0% Asian, 0.0% American Indian/Alaska Native, 0.0% Native Hawaiian/Other Pacific Islander, 1.0% Some other race, 1.0% Two or more races, 1.2% Hispanic of any race (2008-2012 5-year est.); Average household size: 2.39 (2008-2012 5-year est.); Median age: 42.5 (2008-2012 5-year est.); Males per 100 females: 95.1 (2008-2012 5-year est.); Marriage status: 23.2% never married, 60.7% now married, 8.1% widowed, 8.0% divorced (2008-2012 5-year est.); Foreign born: 2.0% (2008-2012 5-year est.); Ancestry (includes multiple ancestries): 27.6% German, 16.6% Irish, 14.8% English, 13.1% American, 4.4% Polish (2008-2012 5-year est.).
Economy: Single-family building permits issued: 10 (2013); Multi-family building permits issued: 0 (2013); Homeowner vacancy rate: 2.8%. Rental vacancy rate: 16.4%. (2008-2012 5-year est.); Employment by occupation: 10.8% management, business, and financial, 4.5% computer, engineering, and science, 19.3% education, legal, community service, arts, and media, 5.2% healthcare practitioners, 14.2% service, 23.2% sales and office, 7.2% natural resources, construction, and maintenance, 15.5% production, transportation, and material moving (2008-2012 5-year est.).
Income: Per capita income: $33,889 (2008-2012 5-year est.); Median household income: $64,269 (2008-2012 5-year est.); Average household income: $82,161 (2008-2012 5-year est.); Percent of households with income of $100,000 or more: 24.2% (2008-2012 5-year est.); Poverty rate: 3.2% (2008-2012 5-year est.).
Education: Percent of population age 25 and over with: High school diploma (including GED) or higher: 93.3% (2008-2012 5-year est.);

Bachelor's degree or higher: 35.3% (2008-2012 5-year est.); Master's degree or higher: 15.4% (2008-2012 5-year est.).

School District(s)
Monticello CUSD 25 (PK-12)
   2011-12 Enrollment: 1,694 . . . . (217) 762-8511
Housing: Homeownership rate: 81.4% (2008-2012 5-year est.); Median home value: $151,200 (2008-2012 5-year est.); Median contract rent: $531 per month (2008-2012 5-year est.); Median year structure built: 1969 (2008-2012 5-year est.).
Health Insurance: 83.4% Private; 28.5% Public; 5.6% None. (2008-2012 5-year est.)
Hospitals: John & Mary Kirby Hospital (17 beds)
Safety: Violent crime rate: 12.7 per 10,000 population; Property crime rate: 59.6 per 10,000 population (2012).
Transportation: Commute to work: 93.0% car, 0.0% public transportation, 2.9% walk, 4.1% work from home (2008-2012 5-year est.); Travel time to work: 40.7% less than 15 minutes, 20.2% 15 to 30 minutes, 34.3% 30 to 45 minutes, 0.6% 45 to 60 minutes, 4.3% 60 minutes or more (2008-2012 5-year est.)
Airports: Piatt County Airport (general aviation)
Additional Information Contacts
City of Monticello. . . . . (217) 762-2583
   http://www.cityofmonticello.net
Monticello Chamber of Commerce . . . . (217) 762-7921
   http://www.monticellochamber.org

WHITE HEATH (CDP). Covers a land area of 0.347 square miles and a water area of 0 square miles. Located at 40.09° N. Lat; 88.51° W. Long. Elevation is 722 feet.
Population: n/a (1990); n/a (2000); 290 (2010); Density: 678.1 persons per square mile (2008-2012 5-year est.); Race: 100.0% White, 0.0% Black/African American, 0.0% Asian, 0.0% American Indian/Alaska Native, 0.0% Native Hawaiian/Other Pacific Islander, 0.0% Some other race, 0.0% Two or more races, 6.8% Hispanic of any race (2008-2012 5-year est.); Average household size: 2.08 (2008-2012 5-year est.); Median age: 43.1 (2008-2012 5-year est.); Males per 100 females: 95.8 (2008-2012 5-year est.); Marriage status: 34.5% never married, 43.8% now married, 6.8% widowed, 14.9% divorced (2008-2012 5-year est.); Foreign born: 0.0% (2008-2012 5-year est.); Ancestry (includes multiple ancestries): 29.4% German, 22.1% American, 16.2% Irish, 12.8% French, 12.3% Italian (2008-2012 5-year est.).
Economy: Homeowner vacancy rate: 0.0%. Rental vacancy rate: 16.1%. (2008-2012 5-year est.); Employment by occupation: 15.1% management, business, and financial, 0.0% computer, engineering, and science, 4.8% education, legal, community service, arts, and media, 0.0% healthcare practitioners, 18.1% service, 16.9% sales and office, 28.3% natural resources, construction, and maintenance, 16.9% production, transportation, and material moving (2008-2012 5-year est.).
Income: Per capita income: $28,940 (2008-2012 5-year est.); Median household income: $35,139 (2008-2012 5-year est.); Average household income: $61,026 (2008-2012 5-year est.); Percent of households with income of $100,000 or more: 19.5% (2008-2012 5-year est.); Poverty rate: 9.8% (2008-2012 5-year est.).
Education: Percent of population age 25 and over with: High school diploma (including GED) or higher: 81.1% (2008-2012 5-year est.); Bachelor's degree or higher: 8.3% (2008-2012 5-year est.); Master's degree or higher: 0.0% (2008-2012 5-year est.).

School District(s)
Monticello CUSD 25 (PK-12)
   2011-12 Enrollment: 1,694 . . . . (217) 762-8511
Housing: Homeownership rate: 58.4% (2008-2012 5-year est.); Median home value: $102,900 (2008-2012 5-year est.); Median contract rent: $561 per month (2008-2012 5-year est.); Median year structure built: 1975 (2008-2012 5-year est.).
Health Insurance: 59.1% Private; 28.1% Public; 22.1% None. (2008-2012 5-year est.)
Transportation: Commute to work: 88.6% car, 0.0% public transportation, 0.0% walk, 6.0% work from home (2008-2012 5-year est.); Travel time to work: 5.8% less than 15 minutes, 58.3% 15 to 30 minutes, 35.9% 30 to 45 minutes, 0.0% 45 to 60 minutes, 0.0% 60 minutes or more (2008-2012 5-year est.)

Pike County

Located in western Illinois; bounded on the west and southwest by the Mississippi River and the Missouri border, and on the east by the Illinois River. Covers a land area of 831.381 square miles, a water area of 17.503 square miles, and is located in the Central Time Zone at 39.63° N. Lat., 90.89° W. Long. The county was founded in 1821. County seat is Pittsfield.
Population: 17,577 (1990); 17,384 (2000); 16,430 (2010); Race: 96.9% White, 1.4% Black/African American, 0.3% Asian, 0.3% American Indian/Alaska Native, 0.0% Native Hawaiian/Other Pacific Islander, 1.1% Some other race, 0.9% Two or more races, 1.1% Hispanic of any race (2008-2012 5-year est.); Density: 19.6 persons per square mile (2008-2012 5-year est.); Average household size: 2.40 (2008-2012 5-year est.); Median age: 42.0 (2008-2012 5-year est.); Males per 100 females: 99.0 (2008-2012 5-year est.).
Religion: Six largest groups: 15.6% Baptist, 9.5% Methodist/Pietist, 3.9% Pentecostal, 3.2% Holiness, 2.9% Non-denominational Protestant, 2.2% Catholicism (2010)
Economy: Unemployment rate: 5.5% (April 2014); Total civilian labor force: 8,312 (April 2014); Leading industries: 18.7% retail trade; 18.1% health care and social assistance; 11.1% accommodation & food services (2012); Farms: 970 totaling 411,446 acres (2012); Companies that employ 500 or more persons: 0 (2012); Companies that employ 100 to 499 persons: 4 (2012); Companies that employ less than 100 persons: 369 (2012); Black-owned businesses: n/a (2007); Hispanic-owned businesses: n/a (2007); Asian-owned businesses: n/a (2007); Women-owned businesses: n/a (2007); Single-family building permits issued: 14 (2013); Multi-family building permits issued: 15 (2013).
Income: Per capita income: $20,637 (2008-2012 5-year est.); Median household income: $40,445 (2008-2012 5-year est.); Average household income: $50,304 (2008-2012 5-year est.); Percent of households with income of $100,000 or more: 10.1% (2008-2012 5-year est.); Poverty rate: 16.7% (2008-2012 5-year est.); Bankruptcy rate: 1.90% (2013).
Education: Percent of population age 25 and over with: High school diploma (including GED) or higher: 85.1% (2008-2012 5-year est.); Bachelor's degree or higher: 12.9% (2008-2012 5-year est.); Master's degree or higher: 3.8% (2008-2012 5-year est.).
Housing: Homeownership rate: 77.8% (2008-2012 5-year est.); Median home value: $76,500 (2008-2012 5-year est.); Median contract rent: $325 per month (2008-2012 5-year est.); Median year structure built: 1959 (2008-2012 5-year est.)
Health: Birth rate: 101.5 per 10,000 population (2013); Death rate: 110.8 per 10,000 population (2013); Age-adjusted cancer mortality rate: 175.4 deaths per 100,000 population (2011); Number of physicians: 8.5 per 10,000 population (2011); Hospital beds: 10.3 per 10,000 population (2010); Hospital admissions: 421.8 per 10,000 population (2010).
Elections: 2012 Presidential election results: 31.3% Obama, 66.7% Romney
Additional Information Contacts
Pike County Government . . . . (217) 285-6812
   http://www.pikeil.org
Pike County Chamber of Commerce. . . . . (217) 285-2971
   http://www.pikeil.org

Pike County Communities

BARRY (city). Covers a land area of 1.414 square miles and a water area of 0 square miles. Located at 39.70° N. Lat; 91.04° W. Long. Elevation is 712 feet.
History: Barry developed as a trading center for a dairying and agricultural area.
Population: 1,391 (1990); 1,368 (2000); 1,318 (2010); Density: 988.0 persons per square mile (2008-2012 5-year est.); Race: 98.3% White, 0.0% Black/African American, 0.1% Asian, 0.0% American Indian/Alaska Native, 0.0% Native Hawaiian/Other Pacific Islander, 1.6% Some other race, 0.6% Two or more races, 1.7% Hispanic of any race (2008-2012 5-year est.); Average household size: 2.29 (2008-2012 5-year est.); Median age: 39.7 (2008-2012 5-year est.); Males per 100 females: 90.3 (2008-2012 5-year est.); Marriage status: 26.4% never married, 45.2% now married, 15.3% widowed, 13.1% divorced (2008-2012 5-year est.); Foreign born: 1.1% (2008-2012 5-year est.); Ancestry (includes multiple ancestries): 21.6% German, 16.0% American, 15.6% English, 10.6% Irish, 6.6% Italian (2008-2012 5-year est.).
Economy: Single-family building permits issued: 0 (2013); Multi-family building permits issued: 0 (2013); Homeowner vacancy rate: 0.4%. Rental

vacancy rate: 6.5%. (2008-2012 5-year est.); Employment by occupation: 3.2% management, business, and financial, 4.3% computer, engineering, and science, 5.7% education, legal, community service, arts, and media, 4.7% healthcare practitioners, 20.7% service, 23.5% sales and office, 14.0% natural resources, construction, and maintenance, 23.9% production, transportation, and material moving (2008-2012 5-year est.).

Income: Per capita income: $19,860 (2008-2012 5-year est.); Median household income: $32,083 (2008-2012 5-year est.); Average household income: $46,246 (2008-2012 5-year est.); Percent of households with income of $100,000 or more: 7.4% (2008-2012 5-year est.); Poverty rate: 14.8% (2008-2012 5-year est.).

Education: Percent of population age 25 and over with: High school diploma (including GED) or higher: 85.5% (2008-2012 5-year est.); Bachelor's degree or higher: 8.5% (2008-2012 5-year est.); Master's degree or higher: 1.9% (2008-2012 5-year est.).

School District(s)

Western CUSD 12 (PK-12)

    2011-12 Enrollment: 661. . . . . (217) 335-2323

Housing: Homeownership rate: 77.5% (2008-2012 5-year est.); Median home value: $53,700 (2008-2012 5-year est.); Median contract rent: $340 per month (2008-2012 5-year est.); Median year structure built: 1952 (2008-2012 5-year est.).

Health Insurance: 59.5% Private; 40.8% Public; 13.6% None. (2008-2012 5-year est.)

Safety: Violent crime rate: 15.2 per 10,000 population; Property crime rate: 22.8 per 10,000 population (2012).

Transportation: Commute to work: 85.1% car, 0.0% public transportation, 7.4% walk, 4.1% work from home (2008-2012 5-year est.); Travel time to work: 32.7% less than 15 minutes, 18.9% 15 to 30 minutes, 31.3% 30 to 45 minutes, 10.4% 45 to 60 minutes, 6.8% 60 minutes or more (2008-2012 5-year est.)

BAYLIS (village). Covers a land area of 0.468 square miles and a water area of 0 square miles. Located at 39.73° N. Lat; 90.91° W. Long. Elevation is 863 feet.

Population: 257 (1990); 265 (2000); 205 (2010); Density: 266.9 persons per square mile (2008-2012 5-year est.); Race: 100.0% White, 0.0% Black/African American, 0.0% Asian, 0.0% American Indian/Alaska Native, 0.0% Native Hawaiian/Other Pacific Islander, 0.0% Some other race, 0.0% Two or more races, 3.2% Hispanic of any race (2008-2012 5-year est.); Average household size: 1.98 (2008-2012 5-year est.); Median age: 52.3 (2008-2012 5-year est.); Males per 100 females: 52.4 (2008-2012 5-year est.); Marriage status: 12.3% never married, 57.0% now married, 7.9% widowed, 22.8% divorced (2008-2012 5-year est.); Foreign born: 3.2% (2008-2012 5-year est.); Ancestry (includes multiple ancestries): 25.6% American, 16.8% German, 8.0% French, 8.0% Irish, 7.2% English (2008-2012 5-year est.).

Economy: Homeowner vacancy rate: 12.2%. Rental vacancy rate: 0.0%. (2008-2012 5-year est.); Employment by occupation: 4.2% management, business, and financial, 0.0% computer, engineering, and science, 0.0% education, legal, community service, arts, and media, 8.3% healthcare practitioners, 58.3% service, 16.7% sales and office, 0.0% natural resources, construction, and maintenance, 12.5% production, transportation, and material moving (2008-2012 5-year est.).

Income: Per capita income: $18,135 (2008-2012 5-year est.); Median household income: $26,125 (2008-2012 5-year est.); Average household income: $33,903 (2008-2012 5-year est.); Percent of households with income of $100,000 or more: 6.4% (2008-2012 5-year est.); Poverty rate: 8.8% (2008-2012 5-year est.).

Education: Percent of population age 25 and over with: High school diploma (including GED) or higher: 64.8% (2008-2012 5-year est.); Bachelor's degree or higher: 4.8% (2008-2012 5-year est.); Master's degree or higher: 1.0% (2008-2012 5-year est.).

Housing: Homeownership rate: 68.3% (2008-2012 5-year est.); Median home value: $31,300 (2008-2012 5-year est.); Median contract rent: $353 per month (2008-2012 5-year est.); Median year structure built: Before 1940 (2008-2012 5-year est.).

Health Insurance: 48.8% Private; 55.2% Public; 10.4% None. (2008-2012 5-year est.)

Transportation: Commute to work: 91.5% car, 8.5% public transportation, 0.0% walk, 0.0% work from home (2008-2012 5-year est.); Travel time to work: 2.1% less than 15 minutes, 57.4% 15 to 30 minutes, 10.6% 30 to 45 minutes, 29.8% 45 to 60 minutes, 0.0% 60 minutes or more (2008-2012 5-year est.)

CHAMBERSBURG (unincorporated postal area)

Zip Code: 62323

Covers a land area of 41.646 square miles and a water area of 0.539 square miles. Located at 39.79° N. Lat; 90.68° W. Long. Elevation is 466 feet. Population: 290 (2010); Density: 7.0 persons per square mile (2010); Race: 100.0% White, 0.0% Black/African American, 0.0% Asian, 0.0% American Indian/Alaska Native, 0.0% Native Hawaiian/Other Pacific Islander, 0.0% Some other race, 0.0% Two or more races, 0.0% Hispanic of any race (2010); Average household size: 2.50 (2010); Median age: 41.0 (2010); Males per 100 females: 107.1 (2010); Homeownership rate: 81.9% (2010)

DETROIT (village). Covers a land area of 0.244 square miles and a water area of 0 square miles. Located at 39.62° N. Lat; 90.68° W. Long. Elevation is 640 feet.

Population: 126 (1990); 93 (2000); 83 (2010); Density: 512.7 persons per square mile (2008-2012 5-year est.); Race: 100.0% White, 0.0% Black/African American, 0.0% Asian, 0.0% American Indian/Alaska Native, 0.0% Native Hawaiian/Other Pacific Islander, 0.0% Some other race, 0.0% Two or more races, 0.0% Hispanic of any race (2008-2012 5-year est.); Average household size: 2.50 (2008-2012 5-year est.); Median age: 41.3 (2008-2012 5-year est.); Males per 100 females: 150.0 (2008-2012 5-year est.); Marriage status: 25.8% never married, 53.3% now married, 0.8% widowed, 20.0% divorced (2008-2012 5-year est.); Foreign born: 0.0% (2008-2012 5-year est.); Ancestry (includes multiple ancestries): 32.8% German, 20.8% American, 9.6% Irish, 3.2% French, 2.4% Canadian (2008-2012 5-year est.).

Economy: Homeowner vacancy rate: 0.0%. Rental vacancy rate: 0.0%. (2008-2012 5-year est.); Employment by occupation: 13.5% management, business, and financial, 0.0% computer, engineering, and science, 0.0% education, legal, community service, arts, and media, 0.0% healthcare practitioners, 28.1% service, 15.6% sales and office, 20.8% natural resources, construction, and maintenance, 21.9% production, transportation, and material moving (2008-2012 5-year est.).

Income: Per capita income: $28,088 (2008-2012 5-year est.); Median household income: $81,154 (2008-2012 5-year est.); Average household income: $70,524 (2008-2012 5-year est.); Percent of households with income of $100,000 or more: 8.0% (2008-2012 5-year est.); Poverty rate: 2.4% (2008-2012 5-year est.).

Education: Percent of population age 25 and over with: High school diploma (including GED) or higher: 90.0% (2008-2012 5-year est.); Bachelor's degree or higher: 0.0% (2008-2012 5-year est.); Master's degree or higher: 0.0% (2008-2012 5-year est.).

Housing: Homeownership rate: 88.0% (2008-2012 5-year est.); Median home value: $87,800 (2008-2012 5-year est.); Median contract rent: n/a per month (2008-2012 5-year est.); Median year structure built: Before 1940 (2008-2012 5-year est.).

Health Insurance: 70.4% Private; 15.2% Public; 22.4% None. (2008-2012 5-year est.)

Transportation: Commute to work: 83.7% car, 0.0% public transportation, 9.3% walk, 7.0% work from home (2008-2012 5-year est.); Travel time to work: 32.5% less than 15 minutes, 17.5% 15 to 30 minutes, 41.3% 30 to 45 minutes, 3.8% 45 to 60 minutes, 5.0% 60 minutes or more (2008-2012 5-year est.)

EL DARA (village). Covers a land area of 0.966 square miles and a water area of 0 square miles. Located at 39.62° N. Lat; 90.99° W. Long. Elevation is 735 feet.

Population: 94 (1990); 89 (2000); 78 (2010); Density: 172.8 persons per square mile (2008-2012 5-year est.); Race: 100.0% White, 0.0% Black/African American, 0.0% Asian, 0.0% American Indian/Alaska Native, 0.0% Native Hawaiian/Other Pacific Islander, 0.0% Some other race, 0.0% Two or more races, 0.0% Hispanic of any race (2008-2012 5-year est.); Average household size: 2.83 (2008-2012 5-year est.); Median age: 57.3 (2008-2012 5-year est.); Males per 100 females: 92.0 (2008-2012 5-year est.); Marriage status: 25.2% never married, 73.6% now married, 0.0% widowed, 1.2% divorced (2008-2012 5-year est.); Foreign born: 0.0% (2008-2012 5-year est.); Ancestry (includes multiple ancestries): 44.9% Irish, 6.0% English, 1.8% German, 1.8% French, 1.8% American (2008-2012 5-year est.).

Economy: Homeowner vacancy rate: 0.0%. Rental vacancy rate: 0.0%. (2008-2012 5-year est.); Employment by occupation: 2.2% management, business, and financial, 0.0% computer, engineering, and science, 3.6% education, legal, community service, arts, and media, 0.0% healthcare practitioners, 32.4% service, 57.6% sales and office, 0.0% natural

resources, construction, and maintenance, 4.3% production, transportation, and material moving (2008-2012 5-year est.).
Income: Per capita income: $25,790 (2008-2012 5-year est.); Median household income: $66,066 (2008-2012 5-year est.); Average household income: $71,100 (2008-2012 5-year est.); Percent of households with income of $100,000 or more: 10.2% (2008-2012 5-year est.); Poverty rate: 0.0% (2008-2012 5-year est.).
Education: Percent of population age 25 and over with: High school diploma (including GED) or higher: 98.3% (2008-2012 5-year est.); Bachelor's degree or higher: 7.8% (2008-2012 5-year est.); Master's degree or higher: 2.6% (2008-2012 5-year est.).
Housing: Homeownership rate: 100.0% (2008-2012 5-year est.); Median home value: $34,300 (2008-2012 5-year est.); Median contract rent: n/a per month (2008-2012 5-year est.); Median year structure built: 1944 (2008-2012 5-year est.).
Health Insurance: 39.5% Private; 49.1% Public; 13.8% None. (2008-2012 5-year est.)
Transportation: Commute to work: 100.0% car, 0.0% public transportation, 0.0% walk, 0.0% work from home (2008-2012 5-year est.); Travel time to work: 27.3% less than 15 minutes, 32.4% 15 to 30 minutes, 35.3% 30 to 45 minutes, 5.0% 45 to 60 minutes, 0.0% 60 minutes or more (2008-2012 5-year est.)

FLORENCE (village). Covers a land area of 0.208 square miles and a water area of 0 square miles. Located at 39.63° N. Lat; 90.61° W. Long. Elevation is 453 feet.
Population: 45 (1990); 71 (2000); 38 (2010); Density: 134.3 persons per square mile (2008-2012 5-year est.); Race: 100.0% White, 0.0% Black/African American, 0.0% Asian, 0.0% American Indian/Alaska Native, 0.0% Native Hawaiian/Other Pacific Islander, 0.0% Some other race, 0.0% Two or more races, 0.0% Hispanic of any race (2008-2012 5-year est.); Average household size: 1.87 (2008-2012 5-year est.); Median age: 63.5 (2008-2012 5-year est.); Males per 100 females: 115.4 (2008-2012 5-year est.); Marriage status: 32.1% never married, 17.9% now married, 32.1% widowed, 17.9% divorced (2008-2012 5-year est.); Foreign born: 0.0% (2008-2012 5-year est.); Ancestry (includes multiple ancestries): 17.9% Italian, 17.9% Polish, 17.9% American, 17.9% Irish, 10.7% Lithuanian (2008-2012 5-year est.).
Economy: Homeowner vacancy rate: 0.0%. Rental vacancy rate: 0.0%. (2008-2012 5-year est.); Employment by occupation: 0.0% management, business, and financial, 0.0% computer, engineering, and science, 0.0% education, legal, community service, arts, and media, 0.0% healthcare practitioners, 11.1% service, 0.0% sales and office, 22.2% natural resources, construction, and maintenance, 66.7% production, transportation, and material moving (2008-2012 5-year est.).
Income: Per capita income: $18,046 (2008-2012 5-year est.); Median household income: $40,250 (2008-2012 5-year est.); Average household income: $32,093 (2008-2012 5-year est.); Percent of households with income of $100,000 or more: n/a (2008-2012 5-year est.); Poverty rate: 25.0% (2008-2012 5-year est.).
Education: Percent of population age 25 and over with: High school diploma (including GED) or higher: 53.6% (2008-2012 5-year est.); Bachelor's degree or higher: 0.0% (2008-2012 5-year est.); Master's degree or higher: 0.0% (2008-2012 5-year est.).
Housing: Homeownership rate: 80.0% (2008-2012 5-year est.); Median home value: $85,000 (2008-2012 5-year est.); Median contract rent: n/a per month (2008-2012 5-year est.); Median year structure built: 1953 (2008-2012 5-year est.).
Health Insurance: 53.6% Private; 57.1% Public; 21.4% None. (2008-2012 5-year est.)
Transportation: Commute to work: 66.7% car, 0.0% public transportation, 33.3% walk, 0.0% work from home (2008-2012 5-year est.); Travel time to work: 33.3% less than 15 minutes, 33.3% 15 to 30 minutes, 0.0% 30 to 45 minutes, 33.3% 45 to 60 minutes, 0.0% 60 minutes or more (2008-2012 5-year est.)

GRIGGSVILLE (city). Covers a land area of 1.077 square miles and a water area of 0 square miles. Located at 39.71° N. Lat; 90.73° W. Long. Elevation is 705 feet.
History: Incorporated 1878.
Population: 1,218 (1990); 1,258 (2000); 1,226 (2010); Density: 1,109.9 persons per square mile (2008-2012 5-year est.); Race: 92.2% White, 5.6% Black/African American, 0.0% Asian, 1.3% American Indian/Alaska Native, 0.0% Native Hawaiian/Other Pacific Islander, 0.9% Some other race, 0.3% Two or more races, 4.3% Hispanic of any race (2008-2012

5-year est.); Average household size: 2.47 (2008-2012 5-year est.); Median age: 43.7 (2008-2012 5-year est.); Males per 100 females: 80.5 (2008-2012 5-year est.); Marriage status: 23.5% never married, 54.1% now married, 8.6% widowed, 13.8% divorced (2008-2012 5-year est.); Foreign born: 0.5% (2008-2012 5-year est.); Ancestry (includes multiple ancestries): 24.4% German, 17.0% American, 13.2% English, 11.9% Irish, 3.0% Scotch-Irish (2008-2012 5-year est.).
Economy: Single-family building permits issued: 0 (2013); Multi-family building permits issued: 0 (2013); Homeowner vacancy rate: 6.6%. Rental vacancy rate: 11.8%. (2008-2012 5-year est.); Employment by occupation: 12.8% management, business, and financial, 2.9% computer, engineering, and science, 7.8% education, legal, community service, arts, and media, 4.1% healthcare practitioners, 18.5% service, 23.9% sales and office, 12.8% natural resources, construction, and maintenance, 17.3% production, transportation, and material moving (2008-2012 5-year est.).
Income: Per capita income: $17,782 (2008-2012 5-year est.); Median household income: $34,592 (2008-2012 5-year est.); Average household income: $42,732 (2008-2012 5-year est.); Percent of households with income of $100,000 or more: 7.9% (2008-2012 5-year est.); Poverty rate: 31.6% (2008-2012 5-year est.).
Education: Percent of population age 25 and over with: High school diploma (including GED) or higher: 85.9% (2008-2012 5-year est.); Bachelor's degree or higher: 9.3% (2008-2012 5-year est.); Master's degree or higher: 3.8% (2008-2012 5-year est.).
School District(s)
Griggsville-Perry CUSD 4 (PK-12)
    2011-12 Enrollment: 421 . . . . (217) 833-2352
Housing: Homeownership rate: 76.7% (2008-2012 5-year est.); Median home value: $72,300 (2008-2012 5-year est.); Median contract rent: $302 per month (2008-2012 5-year est.); Median year structure built: 1951 (2008-2012 5-year est.).
Health Insurance: 61.1% Private; 51.2% Public; 6.7% None. (2008-2012 5-year est.)
Transportation: Commute to work: 97.5% car, 0.0% public transportation, 1.9% walk, 0.6% work from home (2008-2012 5-year est.); Travel time to work: 39.5% less than 15 minutes, 30.6% 15 to 30 minutes, 13.0% 30 to 45 minutes, 10.8% 45 to 60 minutes, 6.2% 60 minutes or more (2008-2012 5-year est.)

HULL (village). Aka Hulls. Covers a land area of 1.844 square miles and a water area of 0.011 square miles. Located at 39.71° N. Lat; 91.20° W. Long. Elevation is 469 feet.
Population: 514 (1990); 474 (2000); 461 (2010); Density: 230.4 persons per square mile (2008-2012 5-year est.); Race: 97.4% White, 0.7% Black/African American, 0.5% Asian, 0.0% American Indian/Alaska Native, 0.0% Native Hawaiian/Other Pacific Islander, 1.4% Some other race, 1.4% Two or more races, 3.8% Hispanic of any race (2008-2012 5-year est.); Average household size: 2.49 (2008-2012 5-year est.); Median age: 38.2 (2008-2012 5-year est.); Males per 100 females: 80.1 (2008-2012 5-year est.); Marriage status: 24.6% never married, 49.2% now married, 10.0% widowed, 16.1% divorced (2008-2012 5-year est.); Foreign born: 2.1% (2008-2012 5-year est.); Ancestry (includes multiple ancestries): 22.1% German, 17.4% Irish, 11.1% English, 9.6% American, 4.0% Scotch-Irish (2008-2012 5-year est.).
Economy: Single-family building permits issued: 0 (2013); Multi-family building permits issued: 0 (2013); Homeowner vacancy rate: 2.5%. Rental vacancy rate: 0.0%. (2008-2012 5-year est.); Employment by occupation: 9.2% management, business, and financial, 0.0% computer, engineering, and science, 7.0% education, legal, community service, arts, and media, 2.7% healthcare practitioners, 15.1% service, 27.6% sales and office, 11.9% natural resources, construction, and maintenance, 26.5% production, transportation, and material moving (2008-2012 5-year est.).
Income: Per capita income: $17,022 (2008-2012 5-year est.); Median household income: $35,139 (2008-2012 5-year est.); Average household income: $42,629 (2008-2012 5-year est.); Percent of households with income of $100,000 or more: 3.0% (2008-2012 5-year est.); Poverty rate: 28.1% (2008-2012 5-year est.).
Education: Percent of population age 25 and over with: High school diploma (including GED) or higher: 87.8% (2008-2012 5-year est.); Bachelor's degree or higher: 8.9% (2008-2012 5-year est.); Master's degree or higher: 2.6% (2008-2012 5-year est.).
School District(s)
Western CUSD 12 (PK-12)
    2011-12 Enrollment: 661 . . . . (217) 335-2323

Housing: Homeownership rate: 68.4% (2008-2012 5-year est.); Median home value: $49,200 (2008-2012 5-year est.); Median contract rent: $425 per month (2008-2012 5-year est.); Median year structure built: 1952 (2008-2012 5-year est.).
Health Insurance: 47.5% Private; 50.1% Public; 14.8% None. (2008-2012 5-year est.)
Transportation: Commute to work: 97.2% car, 0.0% public transportation, 1.1% walk, 1.7% work from home (2008-2012 5-year est.); Travel time to work: 13.0% less than 15 minutes, 44.1% 15 to 30 minutes, 39.0% 30 to 45 minutes, 3.4% 45 to 60 minutes, 0.6% 60 minutes or more (2008-2012 5-year est.)

KINDERHOOK (village).
Covers a land area of 0.881 square miles and a water area of 0 square miles. Located at 39.70° N. Lat; 91.15° W. Long. Elevation is 486 feet.
Population: 257 (1990); 249 (2000); 216 (2010); Density: 223.7 persons per square mile (2008-2012 5-year est.); Race: 100.0% White, 0.0% Black/African American, 0.0% Asian, 0.0% American Indian/Alaska Native, 0.0% Native Hawaiian/Other Pacific Islander, 0.0% Some other race, 0.0% Two or more races, 0.0% Hispanic of any race (2008-2012 5-year est.); Average household size: 2.21 (2008-2012 5-year est.); Median age: 34.7 (2008-2012 5-year est.); Males per 100 females: 71.3 (2008-2012 5-year est.); Marriage status: 21.0% never married, 63.1% now married, 7.0% widowed, 8.9% divorced (2008-2012 5-year est.); Foreign born: 0.0% (2008-2012 5-year est.); Ancestry (includes multiple ancestries): 27.9% German, 10.2% Irish, 8.1% English, 7.6% Italian, 7.6% Dutch (2008-2012 5-year est.).
Economy: Homeowner vacancy rate: 0.0%. Rental vacancy rate: 0.0%. (2008-2012 5-year est.); Employment by occupation: 4.0% management, business, and financial, 0.0% computer, engineering, and science, 1.0% education, legal, community service, arts, and media, 7.0% healthcare practitioners, 24.0% service, 15.0% sales and office, 17.0% natural resources, construction, and maintenance, 32.0% production, transportation, and material moving (2008-2012 5-year est.).
Income: Per capita income: $21,234 (2008-2012 5-year est.); Median household income: $41,477 (2008-2012 5-year est.); Average household income: $46,157 (2008-2012 5-year est.); Percent of households with income of $100,000 or more: 4.5% (2008-2012 5-year est.); Poverty rate: 9.6% (2008-2012 5-year est.).
Education: Percent of population age 25 and over with: High school diploma (including GED) or higher: 92.0% (2008-2012 5-year est.); Bachelor's degree or higher: 8.0% (2008-2012 5-year est.); Master's degree or higher: 2.2% (2008-2012 5-year est.).

School District(s)
Western CUSD 12 (PK-12)
    2011-12 Enrollment: 661 . . . . (217) 335-2323
Housing: Homeownership rate: 96.6% (2008-2012 5-year est.); Median home value: $65,000 (2008-2012 5-year est.); Median contract rent: n/a per month (2008-2012 5-year est.); Median year structure built: 1963 (2008-2012 5-year est.).
Health Insurance: 64.0% Private; 52.3% Public; 8.1% None. (2008-2012 5-year est.)
Transportation: Commute to work: 96.0% car, 2.0% public transportation, 2.0% walk, 0.0% work from home (2008-2012 5-year est.); Travel time to work: 26.0% less than 15 minutes, 28.0% 15 to 30 minutes, 35.0% 30 to 45 minutes, 3.0% 45 to 60 minutes, 8.0% 60 minutes or more (2008-2012 5-year est.)

MILTON (village).
Covers a land area of 0.378 square miles and a water area of 0 square miles. Located at 39.56° N. Lat; 90.65° W. Long. Elevation is 666 feet.
Population: 270 (1990); 274 (2000); 271 (2010); Density: 1,124.6 persons per square mile (2008-2012 5-year est.); Race: 98.8% White, 0.0% Black/African American, 0.0% Asian, 0.0% American Indian/Alaska Native, 0.0% Native Hawaiian/Other Pacific Islander, 1.2% Some other race, 0.0% Two or more races, 1.2% Hispanic of any race (2008-2012 5-year est.); Average household size: 3.63 (2008-2012 5-year est.); Median age: 25.7 (2008-2012 5-year est.); Males per 100 females: 111.4 (2008-2012 5-year est.); Marriage status: 13.6% never married, 77.0% now married, 5.7% widowed, 3.8% divorced (2008-2012 5-year est.); Foreign born: 0.0% (2008-2012 5-year est.); Ancestry (includes multiple ancestries): 24.9% German, 12.2% Irish, 11.5% American, 8.2% English, 3.8% French (2008-2012 5-year est.).
Economy: Homeowner vacancy rate: 9.9%. Rental vacancy rate: 0.0%. (2008-2012 5-year est.); Employment by occupation: 12.5% management,

business, and financial, 0.0% computer, engineering, and science, 1.5% education, legal, community service, arts, and media, 3.7% healthcare practitioners, 17.6% service, 18.4% sales and office, 22.8% natural resources, construction, and maintenance, 23.5% production, transportation, and material moving (2008-2012 5-year est.).
Income: Per capita income: $14,716 (2008-2012 5-year est.); Median household income: $42,150 (2008-2012 5-year est.); Average household income: $52,669 (2008-2012 5-year est.); Percent of households with income of $100,000 or more: 20.0% (2008-2012 5-year est.); Poverty rate: 39.1% (2008-2012 5-year est.).
Education: Percent of population age 25 and over with: High school diploma (including GED) or higher: 77.5% (2008-2012 5-year est.); Bachelor's degree or higher: 5.0% (2008-2012 5-year est.); Master's degree or higher: 0.9% (2008-2012 5-year est.).
Housing: Homeownership rate: 84.3% (2008-2012 5-year est.); Median home value: $61,300 (2008-2012 5-year est.); Median contract rent: $369 per month (2008-2012 5-year est.); Median year structure built: 1971 (2008-2012 5-year est.).
Health Insurance: 45.3% Private; 54.9% Public; 3.6% None. (2008-2012 5-year est.)
Transportation: Commute to work: 86.3% car, 0.0% public transportation, 12.2% walk, 1.4% work from home (2008-2012 5-year est.); Travel time to work: 21.2% less than 15 minutes, 43.1% 15 to 30 minutes, 22.6% 30 to 45 minutes, 13.1% 45 to 60 minutes, 0.0% 60 minutes or more (2008-2012 5-year est.)

NEBO (village).
Covers a land area of 0.434 square miles and a water area of 0.007 square miles. Located at 39.44° N. Lat; 90.79° W. Long. Elevation is 482 feet.
Population: 402 (1990); 408 (2000); 340 (2010); Density: 1,146.1 persons per square mile (2008-2012 5-year est.); Race: 99.0% White, 0.0% Black/African American, 0.0% Asian, 0.0% American Indian/Alaska Native, 0.0% Native Hawaiian/Other Pacific Islander, 1.0% Some other race, 1.0% Two or more races, 1.2% Hispanic of any race (2008-2012 5-year est.); Average household size: 2.67 (2008-2012 5-year est.); Median age: 26.4 (2008-2012 5-year est.); Males per 100 females: 140.1 (2008-2012 5-year est.); Marriage status: 33.5% never married, 47.1% now married, 8.8% widowed, 10.6% divorced (2008-2012 5-year est.); Foreign born: 0.0% (2008-2012 5-year est.); Ancestry (includes multiple ancestries): 12.3% German, 11.1% American, 6.6% Irish, 5.8% Scottish, 4.4% English (2008-2012 5-year est.).
Economy: Homeowner vacancy rate: 0.0%. Rental vacancy rate: 0.0%. (2008-2012 5-year est.); Employment by occupation: 0.0% management, business, and financial, 0.0% computer, engineering, and science, 0.0% education, legal, community service, arts, and media, 10.1% healthcare practitioners, 25.2% service, 19.4% sales and office, 20.1% natural resources, construction, and maintenance, 25.2% production, transportation, and material moving (2008-2012 5-year est.).
Income: Per capita income: $10,560 (2008-2012 5-year est.); Median household income: $23,636 (2008-2012 5-year est.); Average household income: $28,084 (2008-2012 5-year est.); Percent of households with income of $100,000 or more: 1.6% (2008-2012 5-year est.); Poverty rate: 41.9% (2008-2012 5-year est.).
Education: Percent of population age 25 and over with: High school diploma (including GED) or higher: 57.4% (2008-2012 5-year est.); Bachelor's degree or higher: 0.7% (2008-2012 5-year est.); Master's degree or higher: 0.0% (2008-2012 5-year est.).
Housing: Homeownership rate: 90.9% (2008-2012 5-year est.); Median home value: $34,200 (2008-2012 5-year est.); Median contract rent: $261 per month (2008-2012 5-year est.); Median year structure built: 1966 (2008-2012 5-year est.).
Health Insurance: 31.2% Private; 69.4% Public; 11.9% None. (2008-2012 5-year est.)
Transportation: Commute to work: 94.1% car, 5.9% public transportation, 0.0% walk, 0.0% work from home (2008-2012 5-year est.); Travel time to work: 11.9% less than 15 minutes, 31.1% 15 to 30 minutes, 20.7% 30 to 45 minutes, 20.7% 45 to 60 minutes, 15.6% 60 minutes or more (2008-2012 5-year est.)

NEW CANTON (town).
Covers a land area of 0.765 square miles and a water area of 0 square miles. Located at 39.64° N. Lat; 91.10° W. Long. Elevation is 476 feet.
Population: 405 (1990); 417 (2000); 359 (2010); Density: 475.9 persons per square mile (2008-2012 5-year est.); Race: 98.4% White, 0.0% Black/African American, 0.0% Asian, 0.0% American Indian/Alaska Native,

0.0% Native Hawaiian/Other Pacific Islander, 1.6% Some other race, 1.6% Two or more races, 0.0% Hispanic of any race (2008-2012 5-year est.); Average household size: 2.33 (2008-2012 5-year est.); Median age: 40.1 (2008-2012 5-year est.); Males per 100 females: 111.6 (2008-2012 5-year est.); Marriage status: 24.0% never married, 46.7% now married, 7.0% widowed, 22.3% divorced (2008-2012 5-year est.); Foreign born: 0.0% (2008-2012 5-year est.); Ancestry (includes multiple ancestries): 25.3% German, 11.8% Irish, 9.9% English, 5.5% American, 4.4% Scottish (2008-2012 5-year est.).

Economy: Homeowner vacancy rate: 2.6%. Rental vacancy rate: 0.0%. (2008-2012 5-year est.); Employment by occupation: 0.7% management, business, and financial, 0.0% computer, engineering, and science, 2.8% education, legal, community service, arts, and media, 12.8% healthcare practitioners, 12.8% service, 29.8% sales and office, 7.8% natural resources, construction, and maintenance, 33.3% production, transportation, and material moving (2008-2012 5-year est.).

Income: Per capita income: $16,120 (2008-2012 5-year est.); Median household income: $32,321 (2008-2012 5-year est.); Average household income: $36,477 (2008-2012 5-year est.); Percent of households with income of $100,000 or more: n/a (2008-2012 5-year est.); Poverty rate: 18.2% (2008-2012 5-year est.).

Education: Percent of population age 25 and over with: High school diploma (including GED) or higher: 84.7% (2008-2012 5-year est.); Bachelor's degree or higher: 1.1% (2008-2012 5-year est.); Master's degree or higher: 0.8% (2008-2012 5-year est.).

Housing: Homeownership rate: 71.8% (2008-2012 5-year est.); Median home value: $42,900 (2008-2012 5-year est.); Median contract rent: $275 per month (2008-2012 5-year est.); Median year structure built: 1966 (2008-2012 5-year est.).

Health Insurance: 57.4% Private; 41.5% Public; 16.8% None. (2008-2012 5-year est.)

Transportation: Commute to work: 90.4% car, 0.0% public transportation, 0.0% walk, 5.2% work from home (2008-2012 5-year est.); Travel time to work: 8.6% less than 15 minutes, 26.6% 15 to 30 minutes, 35.2% 30 to 45 minutes, 23.4% 45 to 60 minutes, 6.3% 60 minutes or more (2008-2012 5-year est.)

NEW SALEM (village). Covers a land area of 1.046 square miles and a water area of 0 square miles. Located at 39.71° N. Lat; 90.85° W. Long. Elevation is 784 feet.

Population: 147 (1990); 136 (2000); 137 (2010); Density: 135.7 persons per square mile (2008-2012 5-year est.); Race: 89.4% White, 10.6% Black/African American, 0.0% Asian, 0.0% American Indian/Alaska Native, 0.0% Native Hawaiian/Other Pacific Islander, 0.0% Some other race, 0.0% Two or more races, 3.5% Hispanic of any race (2008-2012 5-year est.); Average household size: 2.78 (2008-2012 5-year est.); Median age: 26.8 (2008-2012 5-year est.); Males per 100 females: 71.1 (2008-2012 5-year est.); Marriage status: 43.3% never married, 47.4% now married, 3.1% widowed, 6.2% divorced (2008-2012 5-year est.); Foreign born: 0.0% (2008-2012 5-year est.); Ancestry (includes multiple ancestries): 21.8% Irish, 21.8% German, 15.5% American, 14.8% English, 4.2% Italian (2008-2012 5-year est.).

Economy: Homeowner vacancy rate: 16.3%. Rental vacancy rate: 0.0%. (2008-2012 5-year est.); Employment by occupation: 3.9% management, business, and financial, 0.0% computer, engineering, and science, 0.0% education, legal, community service, arts, and media, 5.9% healthcare practitioners, 27.5% service, 17.6% sales and office, 19.6% natural resources, construction, and maintenance, 25.5% production, transportation, and material moving (2008-2012 5-year est.).

Income: Per capita income: $10,835 (2008-2012 5-year est.); Median household income: $30,000 (2008-2012 5-year est.); Average household income: $32,732 (2008-2012 5-year est.); Percent of households with income of $100,000 or more: 4.0% (2008-2012 5-year est.); Poverty rate: 40.9% (2008-2012 5-year est.).

Education: Percent of population age 25 and over with: High school diploma (including GED) or higher: 84.4% (2008-2012 5-year est.); Bachelor's degree or higher: 6.5% (2008-2012 5-year est.); Master's degree or higher: 0.0% (2008-2012 5-year est.).

Housing: Homeownership rate: 72.0% (2008-2012 5-year est.); Median home value: $40,000 (2008-2012 5-year est.); Median contract rent: $367 per month (2008-2012 5-year est.); Median year structure built: Before 1940 (2008-2012 5-year est.).

Health Insurance: 27.5% Private; 62.0% Public; 18.3% None. (2008-2012 5-year est.)

Transportation: Commute to work: 96.1% car, 3.9% public transportation, 0.0% walk, 0.0% work from home (2008-2012 5-year est.); Travel time to work: 19.6% less than 15 minutes, 62.7% 15 to 30 minutes, 9.8% 30 to 45 minutes, 0.0% 45 to 60 minutes, 7.8% 60 minutes or more (2008-2012 5-year est.)

PEARL (village). Covers a land area of 1.509 square miles and a water area of 0.084 square miles. Located at 39.46° N. Lat; 90.62° W. Long. Elevation is 459 feet.

Population: 177 (1990); 187 (2000); 138 (2010); Density: 118.0 persons per square mile (2008-2012 5-year est.); Race: 80.3% White, 0.0% Black/African American, 0.0% Asian, 12.4% American Indian/Alaska Native, 0.0% Native Hawaiian/Other Pacific Islander, 7.3% Some other race, 7.3% Two or more races, 0.0% Hispanic of any race (2008-2012 5-year est.); Average household size: 2.78 (2008-2012 5-year est.); Median age: 30.7 (2008-2012 5-year est.); Males per 100 females: 122.5 (2008-2012 5-year est.); Marriage status: 21.0% never married, 55.5% now married, 3.4% widowed, 20.2% divorced (2008-2012 5-year est.); Foreign born: 0.0% (2008-2012 5-year est.); Ancestry (includes multiple ancestries): 16.9% German, 15.7% Scottish, 11.8% Irish, 11.2% Arab, 8.4% English (2008-2012 5-year est.).

Economy: Homeowner vacancy rate: 3.3%. Rental vacancy rate: 0.0%. (2008-2012 5-year est.); Employment by occupation: 0.0% management, business, and financial, 0.0% computer, engineering, and science, 0.0% education, legal, community service, arts, and media, 8.1% healthcare practitioners, 29.7% service, 5.4% sales and office, 32.4% natural resources, construction, and maintenance, 24.3% production, transportation, and material moving (2008-2012 5-year est.).

Income: Per capita income: $9,903 (2008-2012 5-year est.); Median household income: $25,000 (2008-2012 5-year est.); Average household income: $29,639 (2008-2012 5-year est.); Percent of households with income of $100,000 or more: n/a (2008-2012 5-year est.); Poverty rate: 40.0% (2008-2012 5-year est.).

Education: Percent of population age 25 and over with: High school diploma (including GED) or higher: 71.3% (2008-2012 5-year est.); Bachelor's degree or higher: 3.7% (2008-2012 5-year est.); Master's degree or higher: 0.0% (2008-2012 5-year est.).

Housing: Homeownership rate: 90.6% (2008-2012 5-year est.); Median home value: $55,000 (2008-2012 5-year est.); Median contract rent: n/a per month (2008-2012 5-year est.); Median year structure built: 1943 (2008-2012 5-year est.).

Health Insurance: 10.1% Private; 70.2% Public; 23.0% None. (2008-2012 5-year est.)

Transportation: Commute to work: 89.2% car, 0.0% public transportation, 0.0% walk, 10.8% work from home (2008-2012 5-year est.); Travel time to work: 12.1% less than 15 minutes, 24.2% 15 to 30 minutes, 0.0% 30 to 45 minutes, 18.2% 45 to 60 minutes, 45.5% 60 minutes or more (2008-2012 5-year est.)

PERRY (village). Covers a land area of 0.382 square miles and a water area of 0 square miles. Located at 39.78° N. Lat; 90.75° W. Long. Elevation is 591 feet.

Population: 491 (1990); 437 (2000); 397 (2010); Density: 1,069.9 persons per square mile (2008-2012 5-year est.); Race: 96.6% White, 0.0% Black/African American, 0.0% Asian, 0.7% American Indian/Alaska Native, 0.0% Native Hawaiian/Other Pacific Islander, 2.7% Some other race, 2.7% Two or more races, 0.0% Hispanic of any race (2008-2012 5-year est.); Average household size: 2.12 (2008-2012 5-year est.); Median age: 50.9 (2008-2012 5-year est.); Males per 100 females: 77.1 (2008-2012 5-year est.); Marriage status: 16.5% never married, 54.0% now married, 13.1% widowed, 16.5% divorced (2008-2012 5-year est.); Foreign born: 1.0% (2008-2012 5-year est.); Ancestry (includes multiple ancestries): 28.6% English, 27.9% German, 6.4% American, 5.9% Irish, 2.2% Swedish (2008-2012 5-year est.).

Economy: Single-family building permits issued: 0 (2013); Multi-family building permits issued: 0 (2013); Homeowner vacancy rate: 0.0%. Rental vacancy rate: 6.8% (2008-2012 5-year est.); Employment by occupation: 5.3% management, business, and financial, 2.9% computer, engineering, and science, 8.2% education, legal, community service, arts, and media, 6.5% healthcare practitioners, 11.2% service, 28.2% sales and office, 31.2% natural resources, construction, and maintenance, 6.5% production, transportation, and material moving (2008-2012 5-year est.).

Income: Per capita income: $18,550 (2008-2012 5-year est.); Median household income: $31,797 (2008-2012 5-year est.); Average household income: $39,131 (2008-2012 5-year est.); Percent of households with

income of $100,000 or more: 2.1% (2008-2012 5-year est.); Poverty rate: 40.0% (2008-2012 5-year est.).
Education: Percent of population age 25 and over with: High school diploma (including GED) or higher: 87.8% (2008-2012 5-year est.); Bachelor's degree or higher: 10.8% (2008-2012 5-year est.); Master's degree or higher: 4.0% (2008-2012 5-year est.).

School District(s)
Griggsville-Perry CUSD 4 (PK-12)
    2011-12 Enrollment: 421 . . . . (217) 833-2352
Housing: Homeownership rate: 74.1% (2008-2012 5-year est.); Median home value: $44,500 (2008-2012 5-year est.); Median contract rent: $275 per month (2008-2012 5-year est.); Median year structure built: 1964 (2008-2012 5-year est.).
Health Insurance: 55.7% Private; 60.4% Public; 10.8% None. (2008-2012 5-year est.)
Transportation: Commute to work: 89.9% car, 0.0% public transportation, 4.2% walk, 1.2% work from home (2008-2012 5-year est.); Travel time to work: 25.9% less than 15 minutes, 30.1% 15 to 30 minutes, 22.9% 30 to 45 minutes, 10.8% 45 to 60 minutes, 10.2% 60 minutes or more (2008-2012 5-year est.)

PITTSFIELD (city). County seat. Covers a land area of 4.584 square miles and a water area of 0.388 square miles. Located at 39.61° N. Lat; 90.82° W. Long. Elevation is 732 feet.
History: Pittsfield was founded in 1833 by settlers from Pittsfield, Massachusetts. The town developed as the seat of Pike County, and as a pork-packing center, using barrels made of white oak that grew around the town. John Hay (1838-1905), Secretary of State under Presidents McKinley and Theodore Roosevelt, was a resident of Pittsfield for several years.
Population: 4,231 (1990); 4,211 (2000); 4,576 (2010); Density: 1,037.1 persons per square mile (2008-2012 5-year est.); Race: 95.4% White, 2.9% Black/African American, 1.0% Asian, 0.3% American Indian/Alaska Native, 0.0% Native Hawaiian/Other Pacific Islander, 0.4% Some other race, 0.3% Two or more races, 1.3% Hispanic of any race (2008-2012 5-year est.); Average household size: 2.31 (2008-2012 5-year est.); Median age: 40.2 (2008-2012 5-year est.); Males per 100 females: 100.2 (2008-2012 5-year est.); Marriage status: 30.0% never married, 47.7% now married, 9.7% widowed, 12.6% divorced (2008-2012 5-year est.); Foreign born: 0.8% (2008-2012 5-year est.); Ancestry (includes multiple ancestries): 24.9% German, 20.3% American, 12.4% English, 11.9% Irish, 2.9% Italian (2008-2012 5-year est.).
Economy: Single-family building permits issued: 3 (2013); Multi-family building permits issued: 15 (2013); Homeowner vacancy rate: 0.7%. Rental vacancy rate: 0.0%. (2008-2012 5-year est.); Employment by occupation: 10.7% management, business, and financial, 2.4% computer, engineering, and science, 6.6% education, legal, community service, arts, and media, 2.2% healthcare practitioners, 28.1% service, 26.6% sales and office, 9.9% natural resources, construction, and maintenance, 13.5% production, transportation, and material moving (2008-2012 5-year est.).
Income: Per capita income: $20,213 (2008-2012 5-year est.); Median household income: $39,063 (2008-2012 5-year est.); Average household income: $49,591 (2008-2012 5-year est.); Percent of households with income of $100,000 or more: 11.7% (2008-2012 5-year est.); Poverty rate: 15.5% (2008-2012 5-year est.).
Taxes: Total city taxes per capita: $135 (2011); City property taxes per capita: $132 (2011).
Education: Percent of population age 25 and over with: High school diploma (including GED) or higher: 86.4% (2008-2012 5-year est.); Bachelor's degree or higher: 19.8% (2008-2012 5-year est.); Master's degree or higher: 5.7% (2008-2012 5-year est.).

School District(s)
Adams/pike Roe (PK-12)
    2011-12 Enrollment: n/a . . . . (217) 277-2080
Pikeland CUSD 10 (PK-12)
    2011-12 Enrollment: 1,317 . . . . (217) 285-2147
Housing: Homeownership rate: 65.1% (2008-2012 5-year est.); Median home value: $89,300 (2008-2012 5-year est.); Median contract rent: $325 per month (2008-2012 5-year est.); Median year structure built: 1966 (2008-2012 5-year est.).
Health Insurance: 64.7% Private; 37.2% Public; 13.3% None. (2008-2012 5-year est.)
Hospitals: Illinois Community Hospital (37 beds)
Safety: Violent crime rate: 0.0 per 10,000 population; Property crime rate: 2.2 per 10,000 population (2012).

Transportation: Commute to work: 87.9% car, 0.0% public transportation, 1.7% walk, 7.1% work from home (2008-2012 5-year est.); Travel time to work: 68.9% less than 15 minutes, 17.1% 15 to 30 minutes, 5.8% 30 to 45 minutes, 2.8% 45 to 60 minutes, 5.4% 60 minutes or more (2008-2012 5-year est.)
Airports: Pittsfield Penstone Municipal Airport (general aviation)
Additional Information Contacts
Pike County Chamber of Commerce . . . . (217) 285-2971
    http://www.pikeil.org

PLEASANT HILL (village). Covers a land area of 0.785 square miles and a water area of 0.025 square miles. Located at 39.44° N. Lat; 90.87° W. Long. Elevation is 469 feet.
Population: 1,030 (1990); 1,047 (2000); 966 (2010); Density: 1,690.6 persons per square mile (2008-2012 5-year est.); Race: 99.4% White, 0.6% Black/African American, 0.0% Asian, 0.0% American Indian/Alaska Native, 0.0% Native Hawaiian/Other Pacific Islander, 0.0% Some other race, 0.0% Two or more races, 0.0% Hispanic of any race (2008-2012 5-year est.); Average household size: 2.54 (2008-2012 5-year est.); Median age: 35.6 (2008-2012 5-year est.); Males per 100 females: 107.3 (2008-2012 5-year est.); Marriage status: 19.0% never married, 63.0% now married, 6.8% widowed, 11.1% divorced (2008-2012 5-year est.); Foreign born: 0.0% (2008-2012 5-year est.); Ancestry (includes multiple ancestries): 23.0% German, 17.4% American, 9.9% Irish, 9.0% English, 5.3% Scottish (2008-2012 5-year est.).
Economy: Homeowner vacancy rate: 2.2%. Rental vacancy rate: 0.0%. (2008-2012 5-year est.); Employment by occupation: 4.6% management, business, and financial, 1.7% computer, engineering, and science, 1.9% education, legal, community service, arts, and media, 3.4% healthcare practitioners, 28.8% service, 22.5% sales and office, 18.5% natural resources, construction, and maintenance, 18.5% production, transportation, and material moving (2008-2012 5-year est.).
Income: Per capita income: $19,318 (2008-2012 5-year est.); Median household income: $42,750 (2008-2012 5-year est.); Average household income: $48,905 (2008-2012 5-year est.); Percent of households with income of $100,000 or more: 8.0% (2008-2012 5-year est.); Poverty rate: 20.4% (2008-2012 5-year est.).
Education: Percent of population age 25 and over with: High school diploma (including GED) or higher: 87.5% (2008-2012 5-year est.); Bachelor's degree or higher: 6.3% (2008-2012 5-year est.); Master's degree or higher: 1.2% (2008-2012 5-year est.).

School District(s)
Pleasant Hill CUSD 3 (PK-12)
    2011-12 Enrollment: 321 . . . . (217) 734-2311
Housing: Homeownership rate: 78.1% (2008-2012 5-year est.); Median home value: $68,200 (2008-2012 5-year est.); Median contract rent: $375 per month (2008-2012 5-year est.); Median year structure built: 1961 (2008-2012 5-year est.).
Health Insurance: 58.7% Private; 40.8% Public; 11.3% None. (2008-2012 5-year est.)
Safety: Violent crime rate: 0.0 per 10,000 population; Property crime rate: 186.5 per 10,000 population (2012).
Transportation: Commute to work: 95.9% car, 0.0% public transportation, 1.4% walk, 1.6% work from home (2008-2012 5-year est.); Travel time to work: 19.3% less than 15 minutes, 31.9% 15 to 30 minutes, 25.7% 30 to 45 minutes, 7.6% 45 to 60 minutes, 15.5% 60 minutes or more (2008-2012 5-year est.)

ROCKPORT (unincorporated postal area)
Zip Code: 62370
    Covers a land area of 62.980 square miles and a water area of 3.439 square miles. Located at 39.51° N. Lat; 91.00° W. Long. Elevation is 489 feet. Population: 520 (2010); Density: 8.3 persons per square mile (2010); Race: 99.4% White, 0.0% Black/African American, 0.0% Asian, 0.0% American Indian/Alaska Native, 0.0% Native Hawaiian/Other Pacific Islander, 0.6% Some other race, 0.4% Two or more races, 0.6% Hispanic of any race (2010); Average household size: 2.37 (2010); Median age: 45.4 (2010); Males per 100 females: 103.1 (2010); Homeownership rate: 83.1% (2010)

TIME (village). Covers a land area of 0.438 square miles and a water area of 0 square miles. Located at 39.56° N. Lat; 90.72° W. Long. Elevation is 692 feet.
Population: 36 (1990); 29 (2000); 23 (2010); Density: 48.0 persons per square mile (2008-2012 5-year est.); Race: 100.0% White, 0.0%

Black/African American, 0.0% Asian, 0.0% American Indian/Alaska Native, 0.0% Native Hawaiian/Other Pacific Islander, 0.0% Some other race, 0.0% Two or more races, 0.0% Hispanic of any race (2008-2012 5-year est.); Average household size: 2.63 (2008-2012 5-year est.); Median age: 64.3 (2008-2012 5-year est.); Males per 100 females: 425.0 (2008-2012 5-year est.); Marriage status: 0.0% never married, 19.0% now married, 42.9% widowed, 38.1% divorced (2008-2012 5-year est.); Foreign born: 42.9% (2008-2012 5-year est.); Ancestry (includes multiple ancestries): 38.1% German, 19.0% English, 9.5% Scotch-Irish (2008-2012 5-year est.).

Economy: Homeowner vacancy rate: 0.0%. Rental vacancy rate: 0.0%. (2008-2012 5-year est.); Employment by occupation: 0.0% management, business, and financial, 0.0% computer, engineering, and science, 0.0% education, legal, community service, arts, and media, 0.0% healthcare practitioners, 0.0% service, 100.0% sales and office, 0.0% natural resources, construction, and maintenance, 0.0% production, transportation, and material moving (2008-2012 5-year est.).

Income: Per capita income: $15,295 (2008-2012 5-year est.); Median household income: $36,250 (2008-2012 5-year est.); Average household income: $37,588 (2008-2012 5-year est.); Percent of households with income of $100,000 or more: n/a (2008-2012 5-year est.); Poverty rate: 28.6% (2008-2012 5-year est.).

Education: Percent of population age 25 and over with: High school diploma (including GED) or higher: 76.2% (2008-2012 5-year est.); Bachelor's degree or higher: 0.0% (2008-2012 5-year est.); Master's degree or higher: 0.0% (2008-2012 5-year est.).

Housing: Homeownership rate: 100.0% (2008-2012 5-year est.); Median home value: $22,500 (2008-2012 5-year est.); Median contract rent: n/a per month (2008-2012 5-year est.); Median year structure built: 1975 (2008-2012 5-year est.).

Health Insurance: 38.1% Private; 61.9% Public; 19.0% None. (2008-2012 5-year est.)

Transportation: Commute to work: 100.0% car, 0.0% public transportation, 0.0% walk, 0.0% work from home (2008-2012 5-year est.); Travel time to work: 0.0% less than 15 minutes, 100.0% 15 to 30 minutes, 0.0% 30 to 45 minutes, 0.0% 45 to 60 minutes, 0.0% 60 minutes or more (2008-2012 5-year est.)

Pope County

Located in southeastern Illinois, partly in the Ozarks; bounded on the east by the Ohio River and the Kentucky border; drained by tributaries of the Ohio River; includes part of Shawnee National Forest. Covers a land area of 368.770 square miles, a water area of 5.532 square miles, and is located in the Central Time Zone at 37.42° N. Lat., 88.54° W. Long. The county was founded in 1816. County seat is Golconda.

Weather Station: Dixon Springs Agr Center — Elevation: 540 feet

	Jan	Feb	Mar	Apr	May	Jun	Jul	Aug	Sep	Oct	Nov	Dec
High	44	50	59	70	78	86	89	89	83	72	59	47
Low	26	30	38	47	56	64	68	66	58	47	39	30
Precip	3.6	3.5	4.5	4.6	5.5	4.1	4.2	3.3	3.6	3.7	4.4	4.5
Snow	2.5	3.1	0.7	tr	0.0	0.0	0.0	0.0	0.0	0.2	tr	1.1

High and Low temperatures in degrees Fahrenheit; Precipitation and Snow in inches

Weather Station: Smithland Lock & Dam — Elevation: 356 feet

	Jan	Feb	Mar	Apr	May	Jun	Jul	Aug	Sep	Oct	Nov	Dec
High	42	47	57	68	77	85	89	88	81	70	58	46
Low	25	28	36	45	55	64	68	67	59	47	37	28
Precip	3.4	3.8	4.2	4.5	5.1	4.2	4.3	2.7	3.6	3.9	4.1	4.6
Snow	1.6	1.5	0.4	tr	0.0	0.0	0.0	0.0	0.0	tr	tr	1.6

High and Low temperatures in degrees Fahrenheit; Precipitation and Snow in inches

Population: 4,373 (1990); 4,413 (2000); 4,470 (2010); Race: 93.6% White, 4.7% Black/African American, 0.3% Asian, 0.0% American Indian/Alaska Native, 0.0% Native Hawaiian/Other Pacific Islander, 1.4% Some other race, 1.5% Two or more races, 2.4% Hispanic of any race (2008-2012 5-year est.); Density: 11.6 persons per square mile (2008-2012 5-year est.); Average household size: 2.27 (2008-2012 5-year est.); Median age: 47.9 (2008-2012 5-year est.); Males per 100 females: 98.3 (2008-2012 5-year est.).

Religion: Six largest groups: 19.8% Baptist, 3.2% Pentecostal, 1.7% Lutheran, 1.4% Methodist/Pietist, 0.8% Presbyterian-Reformed, 0.0% Other Groups (2010)

Economy: Unemployment rate: 8.2% (April 2014); Total civilian labor force: 1,783 (April 2014); Leading industries: 40.9% health care and social assistance; 21.3% retail trade; 10.7% other services (except public

administration) (2012); Farms: 349 totaling 77,997 acres (2012); Companies that employ 500 or more persons: 0 (2012); Companies that employ 100 to 499 persons: 0 (2012); Companies that employ less than 100 persons: 57 (2012); Black-owned businesses: n/a (2007); Hispanic-owned businesses: n/a (2007); Asian-owned businesses: n/a (2007); Women-owned businesses: n/a (2007); Single-family building permits issued: 0 (2013); Multi-family building permits issued: 0 (2013).

Income: Per capita income: $20,885 (2008-2012 5-year est.); Median household income: $39,854 (2008-2012 5-year est.); Average household income: $48,880 (2008-2012 5-year est.); Percent of households with income of $100,000 or more: 8.4% (2008-2012 5-year est.); Poverty rate: 14.7% (2008-2012 5-year est.); Bankruptcy rate: 1.41% (2013).

Education: Percent of population age 25 and over with: High school diploma (including GED) or higher: 87.8% (2008-2012 5-year est.); Bachelor's degree or higher: 13.0% (2008-2012 5-year est.); Master's degree or higher: 5.3% (2008-2012 5-year est.).

Housing: Homeownership rate: 80.1% (2008-2012 5-year est.); Median home value: $93,000 (2008-2012 5-year est.); Median contract rent: $315 per month (2008-2012 5-year est.); Median year structure built: 1972 (2008-2012 5-year est.)

Health: Birth rate: 69.6 per 10,000 population (2013); Death rate: 46.4 per 10,000 population (2013); Age-adjusted cancer mortality rate: Unreliable deaths per 100,000 population (2011); Number of physicians: 2.3 per 10,000 population (2011); Hospital beds: 0.0 per 10,000 population (2010); Hospital admissions: 0.0 per 10,000 population (2010).

Elections: 2012 Presidential election results: 29.2% Obama, 68.1% Romney

National and State Parks: Dixon Springs State Park; Dog Island State Wetlands; Millstone Bluff National Register Site; Shawnee National Forest

Additional Information Contacts
Pope County Government . . . . (618) 683-4466

Pope County Communities

EDDYVILLE (village). Covers a land area of 0.293 square miles and a water area of <.001 square miles. Located at 37.50° N. Lat; 88.59° W. Long. Elevation is 699 feet.

Population: 151 (1990); 153 (2000); 101 (2010); Density: 355.0 persons per square mile (2008-2012 5-year est.); Race: 100.0% White, 0.0% Black/African American, 0.0% Asian, 0.0% American Indian/Alaska Native, 0.0% Native Hawaiian/Other Pacific Islander, 0.0% Some other race, 0.0% Two or more races, 0.0% Hispanic of any race (2008-2012 5-year est.); Average household size: 2.36 (2008-2012 5-year est.); Median age: 32.8 (2008-2012 5-year est.); Males per 100 females: 79.3 (2008-2012 5-year est.); Marriage status: 27.2% never married, 42.0% now married, 14.8% widowed, 16.0% divorced (2008-2012 5-year est.); Foreign born: 0.0% (2008-2012 5-year est.); Ancestry (includes multiple ancestries): 34.6% German, 24.0% Irish, 20.2% English, 20.2% French Canadian, 10.6% Dutch (2008-2012 5-year est.).

Economy: Homeowner vacancy rate: 0.0%. Rental vacancy rate: 34.8%. (2008-2012 5-year est.); Employment by occupation: 13.0% management, business, and financial, 0.0% computer, engineering, and science, 8.7% education, legal, community service, arts, and media, 0.0% healthcare practitioners, 58.7% service, 0.0% sales and office, 19.6% natural resources, construction, and maintenance, 0.0% production, transportation, and material moving (2008-2012 5-year est.).

Income: Per capita income: $10,209 (2008-2012 5-year est.); Median household income: $17,500 (2008-2012 5-year est.); Average household income: $23,825 (2008-2012 5-year est.); Percent of households with income of $100,000 or more: n/a (2008-2012 5-year est.); Poverty rate: 60.6% (2008-2012 5-year est.).

Education: Percent of population age 25 and over with: High school diploma (including GED) or higher: 73.1% (2008-2012 5-year est.); Bachelor's degree or higher: 0.0% (2008-2012 5-year est.); Master's degree or higher: 0.0% (2008-2012 5-year est.).

Housing: Homeownership rate: 65.9% (2008-2012 5-year est.); Median home value: $60,600 (2008-2012 5-year est.); Median contract rent: $154 per month (2008-2012 5-year est.); Median year structure built: 1970 (2008-2012 5-year est.)

Health Insurance: 50.0% Private; 54.8% Public; 18.3% None. (2008-2012 5-year est.)

Transportation: Commute to work: 80.4% car, 0.0% public transportation, 6.5% walk, 13.0% work from home (2008-2012 5-year est.); Travel time to work: 17.5% less than 15 minutes, 30.0% 15 to 30 minutes, 12.5% 30 to

45 minutes, 32.5% 45 to 60 minutes, 7.5% 60 minutes or more (2008-2012 5-year est.)

GOLCONDA (city). County seat. Covers a land area of 0.491 square miles and a water area of 0.013 square miles. Located at 37.36° N. Lat; 88.49° W. Long. Elevation is 354 feet.

History: Incorporated 1845.

Population: 823 (1990); 726 (2000); 668 (2010); Density: 1,604.4 persons per square mile (2008-2012 5-year est.); Race: 86.8% White, 7.7% Black/African American, 1.5% Asian, 0.0% American Indian/Alaska Native, 0.0% Native Hawaiian/Other Pacific Islander, 4.0% Some other race, 3.8% Two or more races, 0.9% Hispanic of any race (2008-2012 5-year est.); Average household size: 2.18 (2008-2012 5-year est.); Median age: 43.6 (2008-2012 5-year est.); Males per 100 females: 70.6 (2008-2012 5-year est.); Marriage status: 27.7% never married, 38.1% now married, 13.9% widowed, 20.2% divorced (2008-2012 5-year est.); Foreign born: 0.0% (2008-2012 5-year est.); Ancestry (includes multiple ancestries): 28.3% German, 22.1% Irish, 14.2% English, 7.2% American, 4.9% Danish (2008-2012 5-year est.).

Economy: Single-family building permits issued: 0 (2013); Multi-family building permits issued: 0 (2013); Homeowner vacancy rate: 2.4%. Rental vacancy rate: 0.0%. (2008-2012 5-year est.); Employment by occupation: 11.2% management, business, and financial, 0.0% computer, engineering, and science, 4.3% education, legal, community service, arts, and media, 1.5% healthcare practitioners, 32.5% service, 28.3% sales and office, 5.5% natural resources, construction, and maintenance, 16.7% production, transportation, and material moving (2008-2012 5-year est.).

Income: Per capita income: $16,423 (2008-2012 5-year est.); Median household income: $24,904 (2008-2012 5-year est.); Average household income: $33,389 (2008-2012 5-year est.); Percent of households with income of $100,000 or more: 2.4% (2008-2012 5-year est.); Poverty rate: 28.4% (2008-2012 5-year est.).

Education: Percent of population age 25 and over with: High school diploma (including GED) or higher: 87.0% (2008-2012 5-year est.); Bachelor's degree or higher: 6.3% (2008-2012 5-year est.); Master's degree or higher: 2.0% (2008-2012 5-year est.).

School District(s)

Pope County CUD 1 (PK-12)
   2011-12 Enrollment: 549 . . . . (618) 683-2301

Housing: Homeownership rate: 47.2% (2008-2012 5-year est.); Median home value: $68,400 (2008-2012 5-year est.); Median contract rent: $283 per month (2008-2012 5-year est.); Median year structure built: 1954 (2008-2012 5-year est.).

Health Insurance: 41.0% Private; 55.8% Public; 18.7% None. (2008-2012 5-year est.)

Transportation: Commute to work: 97.0% car, 0.9% public transportation, 2.1% walk, 0.0% work from home (2008-2012 5-year est.); Travel time to work: 47.9% less than 15 minutes, 4.0% 15 to 30 minutes, 34.5% 30 to 45 minutes, 7.3% 45 to 60 minutes, 6.4% 60 minutes or more (2008-2012 5-year est.)

Additional Information Contacts

Main Street Golconda . . . . (618) 683-6246
   http://www.mainstreetgolconda.org

HEROD (unincorporated postal area)

Zip Code: 62947

Covers a land area of 68.370 square miles and a water area of 0.159 square miles. Located at 37.52° N. Lat; 88.45° W. Long. Elevation is 423 feet. Population: 539 (2010); Density: 7.9 persons per square mile (2010); Race: 98.3% White, 0.4% Black/African American, 0.2% Asian, 0.0% American Indian/Alaska Native, 0.0% Native Hawaiian/Other Pacific Islander, 1.1% Some other race, 0.9% Two or more races, 0.9% Hispanic of any race (2010); Average household size: 2.29 (2010); Median age: 49.9 (2010); Males per 100 females: 94.6 (2010); Homeownership rate: 91.9% (2010)

Pulaski County

Located in southern Illinois; bounded on the south by the Ohio River and the Kentucky border; drained by the Cache River. Covers a land area of 199.185 square miles, a water area of 4.044 square miles, and is located in the Central Time Zone at 37.22° N. Lat., 89.13° W. Long. The county was founded in 1843. County seat is Mound City.

Population: 7,523 (1990); 7,348 (2000); 6,161 (2010); Race: 64.4% White, 33.4% Black/African American, 0.1% Asian, 0.1% American

Indian/Alaska Native, 0.0% Native Hawaiian/Other Pacific Islander, 2.0% Some other race, 1.9% Two or more races, 1.6% Hispanic of any race (2008-2012 5-year est.); Density: 29.9 persons per square mile (2008-2012 5-year est.); Average household size: 2.46 (2008-2012 5-year est.); Median age: 43.5 (2008-2012 5-year est.); Males per 100 females: 97.5 (2008-2012 5-year est.).

Religion: Six largest groups: 37.2% Baptist, 12.6% Non-denominational Protestant, 10.1% Methodist/Pietist, 6.3% Catholicism, 3.4% Presbyterian-Reformed, 0.9% Lutheran (2010)

Economy: Unemployment rate: 8.6% (April 2014); Total civilian labor force: 2,609 (April 2014); Leading industries: 21.9% health care and social assistance; 12.6% retail trade; 11.7% wholesale trade (2012); Farms: 230 totaling 82,158 acres (2012); Companies that employ 500 or more persons: 0 (2012); Companies that employ 100 to 499 persons: 0 (2012); Companies that employ less than 100 persons: 102 (2012); Black-owned businesses: n/a (2007); Hispanic-owned businesses: n/a (2007); Asian-owned businesses: n/a (2007); Women-owned businesses: n/a (2007); Single-family building permits issued: 3 (2013); Multi-family building permits issued: 0 (2013).

Income: Per capita income: $18,553 (2008-2012 5-year est.); Median household income: $31,795 (2008-2012 5-year est.); Average household income: $44,860 (2008-2012 5-year est.); Percent of households with income of $100,000 or more: 10.4% (2008-2012 5-year est.); Poverty rate: 22.9% (2008-2012 5-year est.); Bankruptcy rate: 8.34% (2013).

Taxes: Total county taxes per capita: $163 (2011); County property taxes per capita: $163 (2011).

Education: Percent of population age 25 and over with: High school diploma (including GED) or higher: 79.0% (2008-2012 5-year est.); Bachelor's degree or higher: 12.2% (2008-2012 5-year est.); Master's degree or higher: 3.9% (2008-2012 5-year est.).

Housing: Homeownership rate: 78.9% (2008-2012 5-year est.); Median home value: $52,700 (2008-2012 5-year est.); Median contract rent: $270 per month (2008-2012 5-year est.); Median year structure built: 1962 (2008-2012 5-year est.)

Health: Birth rate: 99.9 per 10,000 population (2013); Death rate: 106.6 per 10,000 population (2013); Age-adjusted cancer mortality rate: Unreliable deaths per 100,000 population (2011); Number of physicians: 0.0 per 10,000 population (2011); Hospital beds: 0.0 per 10,000 population (2010); Hospital admissions: 0.0 per 10,000 population (2010).

Elections: 2012 Presidential election results: 46.3% Obama, 52.0% Romney

Additional Information Contacts

Pulaski County Government . . . . (618) 748-9360
   http://pulaskicountyil.net

Pulaski County Communities

GRAND CHAIN (unincorporated postal area)

Zip Code: 62941

Covers a land area of 33.934 square miles and a water area of 1.864 square miles. Located at 37.23° N. Lat; 88.98° W. Long. Elevation is 394 feet. Population: 808 (2010); Density: 23.8 persons per square mile (2010); Race: 90.6% White, 6.2% Black/African American, 0.1% Asian, 0.0% American Indian/Alaska Native, 0.0% Native Hawaiian/Other Pacific Islander, 3.1% Some other race, 2.1% Two or more races, 2.5% Hispanic of any race (2010); Average household size: 2.45 (2010); Median age: 44.6 (2010); Males per 100 females: 84.5 (2010); Homeownership rate: 81.2% (2010)

KARNAK (village). Covers a land area of 1.806 square miles and a water area of 0.004 square miles. Located at 37.29° N. Lat; 88.98° W. Long. Elevation is 341 feet.

History: Karnak was established as a company town for a logging and milling industry.

Population: 581 (1990); 619 (2000); 499 (2010); Density: 352.8 persons per square mile (2008-2012 5-year est.); Race: 97.8% White, 0.5% Black/African American, 0.5% Asian, 0.0% American Indian/Alaska Native, 0.0% Native Hawaiian/Other Pacific Islander, 1.2% Some other race, 1.3% Two or more races, 0.0% Hispanic of any race (2008-2012 5-year est.); Average household size: 3.08 (2008-2012 5-year est.); Median age: 36.9 (2008-2012 5-year est.); Males per 100 females: 60.9 (2008-2012 5-year est.); Marriage status: 27.1% never married, 49.6% now married, 12.6% widowed, 10.7% divorced (2008-2012 5-year est.); Foreign born: 1.1% (2008-2012 5-year est.); Ancestry (includes multiple ancestries): 28.4%

German, 14.4% American, 10.7% Irish, 6.0% English, 4.2% French (2008-2012 5-year est.).

Economy: Homeowner vacancy rate: 13.5%. Rental vacancy rate: 14.3%. (2008-2012 5-year est.); Employment by occupation: 6.4% management, business, and financial, 0.0% computer, engineering, and science, 7.3% education, legal, community service, arts, and media, 5.6% healthcare practitioners, 30.0% service, 19.7% sales and office, 16.3% natural resources, construction, and maintenance, 14.6% production, transportation, and material moving (2008-2012 5-year est.).

Income: Per capita income: $16,881 (2008-2012 5-year est.); Median household income: $40,903 (2008-2012 5-year est.); Average household income: $48,934 (2008-2012 5-year est.); Percent of households with income of $100,000 or more: 11.3% (2008-2012 5-year est.); Poverty rate: 17.0% (2008-2012 5-year est.).

Education: Percent of population age 25 and over with: High school diploma (including GED) or higher: 77.0% (2008-2012 5-year est.); Bachelor's degree or higher: 6.8% (2008-2012 5-year est.); Master's degree or higher: 1.5% (2008-2012 5-year est.).

Housing: Homeownership rate: 88.2% (2008-2012 5-year est.); Median home value: $48,300 (2008-2012 5-year est.); Median contract rent: $473 per month (2008-2012 5-year est.); Median year structure built: 1952 (2008-2012 5-year est.).

Health Insurance: 58.7% Private; 49.0% Public; 8.8% None. (2008-2012 5-year est.)

Transportation: Commute to work: 93.0% car, 4.3% public transportation, 0.9% walk, 1.7% work from home (2008-2012 5-year est.); Travel time to work: 14.6% less than 15 minutes, 38.9% 15 to 30 minutes, 30.1% 30 to 45 minutes, 16.4% 45 to 60 minutes, 0.0% 60 minutes or more (2008-2012 5-year est.)

MOUND CITY (city). County seat. Covers a land area of 0.671 square miles and a water area of 0.059 square miles. Located at 37.09° N. Lat; 89.16° W. Long. Elevation is 318 feet.

History: Important Union naval base in Civil War. National cemetery is nearby. City severely damaged in 1937 flood. Incorporated 1857.

Population: 765 (1990); 692 (2000); 588 (2010); Density: 1,178.6 persons per square mile (2008-2012 5-year est.); Race: 56.1% White, 39.1% Black/African American, 0.0% Asian, 0.0% American Indian/Alaska Native, 0.0% Native Hawaiian/Other Pacific Islander, 4.8% Some other race, 4.6% Two or more races, 6.6% Hispanic of any race (2008-2012 5-year est.); Average household size: 3.19 (2008-2012 5-year est.); Median age: 27.9 (2008-2012 5-year est.); Males per 100 females: 99.7 (2008-2012 5-year est.); Marriage status: 40.2% never married, 39.9% now married, 3.0% widowed, 16.9% divorced (2008-2012 5-year est.); Foreign born: 0.0% (2008-2012 5-year est.); Ancestry (includes multiple ancestries): 10.6% German, 6.7% English, 6.7% Irish, 5.8% American, 2.4% French (2008-2012 5-year est.).

Economy: Single-family building permits issued: 0 (2013); Multi-family building permits issued: 0 (2013); Homeowner vacancy rate: 3.1%. Rental vacancy rate: 12.5%. (2008-2012 5-year est.); Employment by occupation: 4.3% management, business, and financial, 0.0% computer, engineering, and science, 4.6% education, legal, community service, arts, and media, 5.0% healthcare practitioners, 32.6% service, 22.0% sales and office, 5.7% natural resources, construction, and maintenance, 25.9% production, transportation, and material moving (2008-2012 5-year est.).

Income: Per capita income: $13,072 (2008-2012 5-year est.); Median household income: $31,071 (2008-2012 5-year est.); Average household income: $36,964 (2008-2012 5-year est.); Percent of households with income of $100,000 or more: 1.6% (2008-2012 5-year est.); Poverty rate: 27.7% (2008-2012 5-year est.).

Education: Percent of population age 25 and over with: High school diploma (including GED) or higher: 74.9% (2008-2012 5-year est.); Bachelor's degree or higher: 8.1% (2008-2012 5-year est.); Master's degree or higher: 2.1% (2008-2012 5-year est.).

Housing: Homeownership rate: 63.3% (2008-2012 5-year est.); Median home value: $34,600 (2008-2012 5-year est.); Median contract rent: $210 per month (2008-2012 5-year est.); Median year structure built: 1965 (2008-2012 5-year est.).

Health Insurance: 46.5% Private; 48.8% Public; 15.4% None. (2008-2012 5-year est.)

Transportation: Commute to work: 92.8% car, 3.6% public transportation, 0.7% walk, 2.9% work from home (2008-2012 5-year est.); Travel time to work: 38.3% less than 15 minutes, 26.0% 15 to 30 minutes, 11.5% 30 to 45 minutes, 11.2% 45 to 60 minutes, 13.0% 60 minutes or more (2008-2012 5-year est.)

MOUNDS (city). Covers a land area of 1.207 square miles and a water area of 0.009 square miles. Located at 37.12° N. Lat; 89.20° W. Long. Elevation is 325 feet.

History: Incorporated 1904.

Population: 1,407 (1990); 1,117 (2000); 810 (2010); Density: 815.1 persons per square mile (2008-2012 5-year est.); Race: 21.1% White, 78.9% Black/African American, 0.0% Asian, 0.0% American Indian/Alaska Native, 0.0% Native Hawaiian/Other Pacific Islander, 0.0% Some other race, 0.0% Two or more races, 0.0% Hispanic of any race (2008-2012 5-year est.); Average household size: 2.23 (2008-2012 5-year est.); Median age: 32.9 (2008-2012 5-year est.); Males per 100 females: 94.5 (2008-2012 5-year est.); Marriage status: 36.8% never married, 25.7% now married, 15.9% widowed, 21.7% divorced (2008-2012 5-year est.); Foreign born: 1.8% (2008-2012 5-year est.); Ancestry (includes multiple ancestries): 7.4% German, 4.8% American, 2.2% Nigerian, 1.7% African, 1.4% Irish (2008-2012 5-year est.).

Economy: Single-family building permits issued: 0 (2013); Multi-family building permits issued: 0 (2013); Homeowner vacancy rate: 4.6%. Rental vacancy rate: 0.0%. (2008-2012 5-year est.); Employment by occupation: 9.0% management, business, and financial, 0.0% computer, engineering, and science, 10.0% education, legal, community service, arts, and media, 2.0% healthcare practitioners, 22.7% service, 30.0% sales and office, 0.0% natural resources, construction, and maintenance, 26.3% production, transportation, and material moving (2008-2012 5-year est.).

Income: Per capita income: $13,088 (2008-2012 5-year est.); Median household income: $17,902 (2008-2012 5-year est.); Average household income: $27,226 (2008-2012 5-year est.); Percent of households with income of $100,000 or more: 3.3% (2008-2012 5-year est.); Poverty rate: 52.3% (2008-2012 5-year est.).

Education: Percent of population age 25 and over with: High school diploma (including GED) or higher: 75.5% (2008-2012 5-year est.); Bachelor's degree or higher: 10.6% (2008-2012 5-year est.); Master's degree or higher: 4.9% (2008-2012 5-year est.).

School District(s)

Meridian CUSD 101 (PK-12)
   2011-12 Enrollment: 615. . . . . (618) 342-6776

Housing: Homeownership rate: 58.5% (2008-2012 5-year est.); Median home value: $33,000 (2008-2012 5-year est.); Median contract rent: $244 per month (2008-2012 5-year est.); Median year structure built: 1953 (2008-2012 5-year est.).

Health Insurance: 31.1% Private; 67.7% Public; 13.2% None. (2008-2012 5-year est.)

Transportation: Commute to work: 87.9% car, 2.3% public transportation, 7.4% walk, 2.3% work from home (2008-2012 5-year est.); Travel time to work: 50.5% less than 15 minutes, 25.8% 15 to 30 minutes, 4.8% 30 to 45 minutes, 11.3% 45 to 60 minutes, 7.6% 60 minutes or more (2008-2012 5-year est.)

NEW GRAND CHAIN (village). Aka Grand Chain. Covers a land area of 1.043 square miles and a water area of 0.015 square miles. Located at 37.25° N. Lat; 89.02° W. Long. Elevation is 410 feet.

History: New Grand Chain was named for a row of rocks in the Ohio River, where the town was first located. It was moved in 1872 to be on the new railroad line.

Population: 273 (1990); 233 (2000); 210 (2010); Density: 217.7 persons per square mile (2008-2012 5-year est.); Race: 93.0% White, 0.0% Black/African American, 0.0% Asian, 0.0% American Indian/Alaska Native, 0.0% Native Hawaiian/Other Pacific Islander, 7.0% Some other race, 3.1% Two or more races, 4.4% Hispanic of any race (2008-2012 5-year est.); Average household size: 2.67 (2008-2012 5-year est.); Median age: 40.7 (2008-2012 5-year est.); Males per 100 females: 122.5 (2008-2012 5-year est.); Marriage status: 14.9% never married, 64.3% now married, 5.8% widowed, 14.9% divorced (2008-2012 5-year est.); Foreign born: 1.8% (2008-2012 5-year est.); Ancestry (includes multiple ancestries): 43.6% German, 18.1% Irish, 7.5% American, 3.5% English, 3.1% Norwegian (2008-2012 5-year est.).

Economy: Homeowner vacancy rate: 0.0%. Rental vacancy rate: 18.2%. (2008-2012 5-year est.); Employment by occupation: 5.6% management, business, and financial, 3.3% computer, engineering, and science, 12.2% education, legal, community service, arts, and media, 7.8% healthcare practitioners, 35.6% service, 20.0% sales and office, 4.4% natural resources, construction, and maintenance, 11.1% production, transportation, and material moving (2008-2012 5-year est.).

Income: Per capita income: $15,876 (2008-2012 5-year est.); Median household income: $22,188 (2008-2012 5-year est.); Average household

income: $39,691 (2008-2012 5-year est.); Percent of households with income of $100,000 or more: 8.2% (2008-2012 5-year est.); Poverty rate: 18.9% (2008-2012 5-year est.).

Education: Percent of population age 25 and over with: High school diploma (including GED) or higher: 78.7% (2008-2012 5-year est.); Bachelor's degree or higher: 17.7% (2008-2012 5-year est.); Master's degree or higher: 5.0% (2008-2012 5-year est.).

Housing: Homeownership rate: 78.8% (2008-2012 5-year est.); Median home value: $56,100 (2008-2012 5-year est.); Median contract rent: $243 per month (2008-2012 5-year est.); Median year structure built: 1961 (2008-2012 5-year est.).

Health Insurance: 54.2% Private; 37.9% Public; 15.4% None. (2008-2012 5-year est.)

Transportation: Commute to work: 81.9% car, 0.0% public transportation, 4.2% walk, 13.9% work from home (2008-2012 5-year est.); Travel time to work: 22.6% less than 15 minutes, 33.9% 15 to 30 minutes, 27.4% 30 to 45 minutes, 11.3% 45 to 60 minutes, 4.8% 60 minutes or more (2008-2012 5-year est.)

OLMSTED (village). Covers a land area of 3.372 square miles and a water area of 0.126 square miles. Located at 37.18° N. Lat; 89.08° W. Long. Elevation is 358 feet.

Population: 358 (1990); 299 (2000); 333 (2010); Density: 128.4 persons per square mile (2008-2012 5-year est.); Race: 85.5% White, 12.5% Black/African American, 0.0% Asian, 0.0% American Indian/Alaska Native, 0.0% Native Hawaiian/Other Pacific Islander, 2.0% Some other race, 2.1% Two or more races, 0.0% Hispanic of any race (2008-2012 5-year est.); Average household size: 2.62 (2008-2012 5-year est.); Median age: 49.1 (2008-2012 5-year est.); Males per 100 females: 96.8 (2008-2012 5-year est.); Marriage status: 19.6% never married, 58.6% now married, 13.0% widowed, 8.8% divorced (2008-2012 5-year est.); Foreign born: 1.2% (2008-2012 5-year est.); Ancestry (includes multiple ancestries): 17.1% English, 15.0% Irish, 8.3% German, 8.1% American, 5.8% French (2008-2012 5-year est.).

Economy: Homeowner vacancy rate: 1.3%. Rental vacancy rate: 0.0%. (2008-2012 5-year est.); Employment by occupation: 4.4% management, business, and financial, 1.8% computer, engineering, and science, 25.4% education, legal, community service, arts, and media, 0.0% healthcare practitioners, 17.5% service, 16.7% sales and office, 8.8% natural resources, construction, and maintenance, 25.4% production, transportation, and material moving (2008-2012 5-year est.).

Income: Per capita income: $19,710 (2008-2012 5-year est.); Median household income: $30,438 (2008-2012 5-year est.); Average household income: $48,089 (2008-2012 5-year est.); Percent of households with income of $100,000 or more: 12.7% (2008-2012 5-year est.); Poverty rate: 27.8% (2008-2012 5-year est.).

Education: Percent of population age 25 and over with: High school diploma (including GED) or higher: 76.4% (2008-2012 5-year est.); Bachelor's degree or higher: 9.5% (2008-2012 5-year est.); Master's degree or higher: 4.9% (2008-2012 5-year est.).

Housing: Homeownership rate: 89.7% (2008-2012 5-year est.); Median home value: $50,600 (2008-2012 5-year est.); Median contract rent: $163 per month (2008-2012 5-year est.); Median year structure built: 1955 (2008-2012 5-year est.).

Health Insurance: 67.9% Private; 58.2% Public; 8.8% None. (2008-2012 5-year est.)

Transportation: Commute to work: 97.2% car, 0.0% public transportation, 0.0% walk, 2.8% work from home (2008-2012 5-year est.); Travel time to work: 20.8% less than 15 minutes, 42.5% 15 to 30 minutes, 4.7% 30 to 45 minutes, 27.4% 45 to 60 minutes, 4.7% 60 minutes or more (2008-2012 5-year est.)

PULASKI (village). Covers a land area of 1.310 square miles and a water area of 0.006 square miles. Located at 37.22° N. Lat; 89.21° W. Long. Elevation is 344 feet.

Population: 361 (1990); 274 (2000); 206 (2010); Density: 171.0 persons per square mile (2008-2012 5-year est.); Race: 42.0% White, 56.3% Black/African American, 0.0% Asian, 0.0% American Indian/Alaska Native, 0.0% Native Hawaiian/Other Pacific Islander, 1.7% Some other race, 1.8% Two or more races, 0.0% Hispanic of any race (2008-2012 5-year est.); Average household size: 2.60 (2008-2012 5-year est.); Median age: 52.3 (2008-2012 5-year est.); Males per 100 females: 119.6 (2008-2012 5-year est.); Marriage status: 41.3% never married, 39.2% now married, 13.2% widowed, 6.3% divorced (2008-2012 5-year est.); Foreign born: 2.2% (2008-2012 5-year est.); Ancestry (includes multiple ancestries): 12.9%

German, 10.7% African, 5.4% Irish, 3.1% Dutch, 3.1% American (2008-2012 5-year est.).

Economy: Single-family building permits issued: 0 (2013); Multi-family building permits issued: 0 (2013); Homeowner vacancy rate: 0.0%. Rental vacancy rate: 7.1%. (2008-2012 5-year est.); Employment by occupation: 3.5% management, business, and financial, 0.0% computer, engineering, and science, 3.5% education, legal, community service, arts, and media, 0.0% healthcare practitioners, 35.1% service, 36.8% sales and office, 10.5% natural resources, construction, and maintenance, 10.5% production, transportation, and material moving (2008-2012 5-year est.).

Income: Per capita income: $14,273 (2008-2012 5-year est.); Median household income: $28,750 (2008-2012 5-year est.); Average household income: $35,571 (2008-2012 5-year est.); Percent of households with income of $100,000 or more: 2.3% (2008-2012 5-year est.); Poverty rate: 16.4% (2008-2012 5-year est.).

Education: Percent of population age 25 and over with: High school diploma (including GED) or higher: 56.6% (2008-2012 5-year est.); Bachelor's degree or higher: 2.9% (2008-2012 5-year est.); Master's degree or higher: 1.2% (2008-2012 5-year est.).

Housing: Homeownership rate: 69.8% (2008-2012 5-year est.); Median home value: $35,800 (2008-2012 5-year est.); Median contract rent: $325 per month (2008-2012 5-year est.); Median year structure built: 1964 (2008-2012 5-year est.).

Health Insurance: 40.6% Private; 60.3% Public; 8.5% None. (2008-2012 5-year est.)

Transportation: Commute to work: 86.0% car, 10.5% public transportation, 0.0% walk, 3.5% work from home (2008-2012 5-year est.); Travel time to work: 43.6% less than 15 minutes, 30.9% 15 to 30 minutes, 1.8% 30 to 45 minutes, 12.7% 45 to 60 minutes, 10.9% 60 minutes or more (2008-2012 5-year est.)

ULLIN (village). Covers a land area of 2.811 square miles and a water area of 0.052 square miles. Located at 37.28° N. Lat; 89.18° W. Long. Elevation is 341 feet.

Population: 402 (1990); 779 (2000); 463 (2010); Density: 217.4 persons per square mile (2008-2012 5-year est.); Race: 59.6% White, 32.7% Black/African American, 0.8% Asian, 0.7% American Indian/Alaska Native, 0.0% Native Hawaiian/Other Pacific Islander, 6.2% Some other race, 6.2% Two or more races, 6.1% Hispanic of any race (2008-2012 5-year est.); Average household size: 2.20 (2008-2012 5-year est.); Median age: 46.1 (2008-2012 5-year est.); Males per 100 females: 105.0 (2008-2012 5-year est.); Marriage status: 30.7% never married, 48.1% now married, 11.8% widowed, 9.4% divorced (2008-2012 5-year est.); Foreign born: 6.9% (2008-2012 5-year est.); Ancestry (includes multiple ancestries): 14.2% German, 10.0% Irish, 4.4% French, 4.4% Dutch, 2.9% American (2008-2012 5-year est.).

Economy: Single-family building permits issued: 0 (2013); Multi-family building permits issued: 0 (2013); Homeowner vacancy rate: 6.6%. Rental vacancy rate: 0.0%. (2008-2012 5-year est.); Employment by occupation: 4.6% management, business, and financial, 0.0% computer, engineering, and science, 13.3% education, legal, community service, arts, and media, 15.6% healthcare practitioners, 32.9% service, 23.7% sales and office, 4.6% natural resources, construction, and maintenance, 5.2% production, transportation, and material moving (2008-2012 5-year est.).

Income: Per capita income: $15,838 (2008-2012 5-year est.); Median household income: $19,762 (2008-2012 5-year est.); Average household income: $40,315 (2008-2012 5-year est.); Percent of households with income of $100,000 or more: 7.8% (2008-2012 5-year est.); Poverty rate: 25.7% (2008-2012 5-year est.).

Education: Percent of population age 25 and over with: High school diploma (including GED) or higher: 73.0% (2008-2012 5-year est.); Bachelor's degree or higher: 11.9% (2008-2012 5-year est.); Master's degree or higher: 2.1% (2008-2012 5-year est.).

School District(s)

Alxndr/john/masc/pulski/unon Roe (06-12)

    2011-12 Enrollment: n/a . . . . (618) 634-2292

Century CUSD 100 (PK-12)

    2011-12 Enrollment: 420 . . . . (618) 845-3447

Two-year College(s)

Shawnee Community College (Public)

    Fall 2012 Enrollment: 1,689 . . . . (618) 634-3200

    2012-13 Tuition: In-state $4,140; Out-of-state $4,620

Housing: Homeownership rate: 64.5% (2008-2012 5-year est.); Median home value: $54,200 (2008-2012 5-year est.); Median contract rent: $464

per month (2008-2012 5-year est.); Median year structure built: 1966 (2008-2012 5-year est.).
Health Insurance: 59.3% Private; 59.9% Public; 6.8% None. (2008-2012 5-year est.)
Transportation: Commute to work: 93.0% car, 0.0% public transportation, 5.7% walk, 1.3% work from home (2008-2012 5-year est.); Travel time to work: 28.8% less than 15 minutes, 44.9% 15 to 30 minutes, 7.7% 30 to 45 minutes, 13.5% 45 to 60 minutes, 5.1% 60 minutes or more (2008-2012 5-year est.)

VILLA RIDGE (unincorporated postal area)
Zip Code: 62996
Covers a land area of 25.355 square miles and a water area of 0.592 square miles. Located at 37.15° N. Lat; 89.15° W. Long. Elevation is 387 feet. Population: 535 (2010); Density: 21.1 persons per square mile (2010); Race: 78.3% White, 17.6% Black/African American, 0.4% Asian, 0.7% American Indian/Alaska Native, 0.6% Native Hawaiian/Other Pacific Islander, 2.4% Some other race, 1.9% Two or more races, 0.2% Hispanic of any race (2010); Average household size: 2.24 (2010); Median age: 47.0 (2010); Males per 100 females: 93.1 (2010); Homeownership rate: 88.3% (2010)

Putnam County

Located in north central Illinois; bounded on the north and west by the Illinois River. Covers a land area of 160.161 square miles, a water area of 12.063 square miles, and is located in the Central Time Zone at 41.20° N. Lat., 89.30° W. Long. The county was founded in 1825. County seat is Hennepin.

Putnam County is part of the Ottawa-Peru, IL Micropolitan Statistical Area. The entire metro area includes: Bureau County, IL; LaSalle County, IL; Putnam County, IL

Weather Station: Hennepin Power Plant   Elevation: 459 feet

	Jan	Feb	Mar	Apr	May	Jun	Jul	Aug	Sep	Oct	Nov	Dec
High	33	37	49	62	74	83	86	85	78	65	50	36
Low	14	17	28	38	48	58	62	60	52	40	30	18
Precip	1.3	1.4	2.0	3.1	3.5	3.8	4.1	4.4	3.5	2.7	2.7	na
Snow	5.0	4.4	na	0.2	0.0	0.0	0.0	0.0	0.0	tr	0.2	5.0

High and Low temperatures in degrees Fahrenheit; Precipitation and Snow in inches

Population: 5,730 (1990); 6,086 (2000); 6,006 (2010); Race: 96.5% White, 0.7% Black/African American, 0.2% Asian, 0.0% American Indian/Alaska Native, 0.0% Native Hawaiian/Other Pacific Islander, 2.6% Some other race, 0.9% Two or more races, 4.4% Hispanic of any race (2008-2012 5-year est.); Density: 36.7 persons per square mile (2008-2012 5-year est.); Average household size: 2.43 (2008-2012 5-year est.); Median age: 44.6 (2008-2012 5-year est.); Males per 100 females: 102.6 (2008-2012 5-year est.).
Religion: Six largest groups: 17.7% Catholicism, 5.2% Methodist/Pietist, 4.1% Presbyterian-Reformed, 3.1% Lutheran, 1.3% Judaism, 1.3% European Free-Church (2010)
Economy: Unemployment rate: 8.6% (April 2014); Total civilian labor force: 2,968 (April 2014); Leading industries: 36.2% manufacturing; 11.9% construction; 10.8% retail trade (2012); Farms: 183 totaling 60,135 acres (2012); Companies that employ 500 or more persons: 0 (2012); Companies that employ 100 to 499 persons: 1 (2012); Companies that employ less than 100 persons: 131 (2012); Black-owned businesses: n/a (2007); Hispanic-owned businesses: n/a (2007); Asian-owned businesses: n/a (2007); Women-owned businesses: n/a (2007); Single-family building permits issued: 20 (2013); Multi-family building permits issued: 0 (2013).
Income: Per capita income: $26,493 (2008-2012 5-year est.); Median household income: $54,467 (2008-2012 5-year est.); Average household income: $65,010 (2008-2012 5-year est.); Percent of households with income of $100,000 or more: 19.0% (2008-2012 5-year est.); Poverty rate: 13.9% (2008-2012 5-year est.); Bankruptcy rate: 3.57% (2013).
Education: Percent of population age 25 and over with: High school diploma (including GED) or higher: 87.2% (2008-2012 5-year est.); Bachelor's degree or higher: 14.5% (2008-2012 5-year est.); Master's degree or higher: 6.0% (2008-2012 5-year est.).
Housing: Homeownership rate: 78.8% (2008-2012 5-year est.); Median home value: $128,600 (2008-2012 5-year est.); Median contract rent: $465 per month (2008-2012 5-year est.); Median year structure built: 1968 (2008-2012 5-year est.)

Health: Birth rate: 74.1 per 10,000 population (2013); Death rate: 108.6 per 10,000 population (2013); Age-adjusted cancer mortality rate: 249.3 deaths per 100,000 population (2011); Number of physicians: 3.4 per 10,000 population (2011); Hospital beds: 0.0 per 10,000 population (2010); Hospital admissions: 0.0 per 10,000 population (2010).
Elections: 2012 Presidential election results: 49.7% Obama, 47.9% Romney
National and State Parks: Donnelley State Fish and Wildlife Area; Fox Run State Conservation Area
Additional Information Contacts
Putnam County Government . . . . (815) 925-7129
  http://www.co.putnam.il.us

Putnam County Communities

GRANVILLE (village). Covers a land area of 0.969 square miles and a water area of 0 square miles. Located at 41.26° N. Lat; 89.23° W. Long. Elevation is 686 feet.
History: Incorporated 1861.
Population: 1,407 (1990); 1,414 (2000); 1,427 (2010); Density: 1,543.1 persons per square mile (2008-2012 5-year est.); Race: 92.6% White, 1.6% Black/African American, 0.0% Asian, 0.0% American Indian/Alaska Native, 0.0% Native Hawaiian/Other Pacific Islander, 5.8% Some other race, 0.0% Two or more races, 7.9% Hispanic of any race (2008-2012 5-year est.); Average household size: 2.10 (2008-2012 5-year est.); Median age: 37.8 (2008-2012 5-year est.); Males per 100 females: 102.0 (2008-2012 5-year est.); Marriage status: 21.9% never married, 51.4% now married, 7.7% widowed, 19.1% divorced (2008-2012 5-year est.); Foreign born: 1.7% (2008-2012 5-year est.); Ancestry (includes multiple ancestries): 42.8% German, 19.5% Irish, 17.7% Italian, 13.3% Polish, 6.5% English (2008-2012 5-year est.).
Economy: Single-family building permits issued: 0 (2013); Multi-family building permits issued: 0 (2013); Homeowner vacancy rate: 0.0%. Rental vacancy rate: 3.7%. (2008-2012 5-year est.); Employment by occupation: 9.8% management, business, and financial, 1.9% computer, engineering, and science, 5.5% education, legal, community service, arts, and media, 6.5% healthcare practitioners, 14.6% service, 27.1% sales and office, 11.7% natural resources, construction, and maintenance, 22.9% production, transportation, and material moving (2008-2012 5-year est.).
Income: Per capita income: $24,089 (2008-2012 5-year est.); Median household income: $41,779 (2008-2012 5-year est.); Average household income: $51,572 (2008-2012 5-year est.); Percent of households with income of $100,000 or more: 9.2% (2008-2012 5-year est.); Poverty rate: 24.0% (2008-2012 5-year est.).
Education: Percent of population age 25 and over with: High school diploma (including GED) or higher: 88.6% (2008-2012 5-year est.); Bachelor's degree or higher: 14.5% (2008-2012 5-year est.); Master's degree or higher: 4.8% (2008-2012 5-year est.).
School District(s)
Putnam County CUSD 535 (PK-12)
    2011-12 Enrollment: 916 . . . . (815) 882-2800
Housing: Homeownership rate: 66.7% (2008-2012 5-year est.); Median home value: $109,700 (2008-2012 5-year est.); Median contract rent: $396 per month (2008-2012 5-year est.); Median year structure built: 1961 (2008-2012 5-year est.).
Health Insurance: 62.2% Private; 41.1% Public; 11.8% None. (2008-2012 5-year est.)
Safety: Violent crime rate: 0.0 per 10,000 population; Property crime rate: 70.5 per 10,000 population (2012).
Transportation: Commute to work: 98.6% car, 0.0% public transportation, 0.5% walk, 0.9% work from home (2008-2012 5-year est.); Travel time to work: 40.0% less than 15 minutes, 43.7% 15 to 30 minutes, 8.6% 30 to 45 minutes, 3.9% 45 to 60 minutes, 3.8% 60 minutes or more (2008-2012 5-year est.)

HENNEPIN (village). County seat. Covers a land area of 5.261 square miles and a water area of 0.365 square miles. Located at 41.25° N. Lat; 89.31° W. Long. Elevation is 502 feet.
History: Hennepin was named for Father Louis Hennepin, an early missionary pilot who guided explorers on the waterways.
Population: 669 (1990); 707 (2000); 757 (2010); Density: 153.6 persons per square mile (2008-2012 5-year est.); Race: 98.4% White, 1.0% Black/African American, 0.0% Asian, 0.0% American Indian/Alaska Native, 0.0% Native Hawaiian/Other Pacific Islander, 0.6% Some other race, 0.0% Two or more races, 12.7% Hispanic of any race (2008-2012 5-year est.);

Average household size: 2.33 (2008-2012 5-year est.); Median age: 39.6 (2008-2012 5-year est.); Males per 100 females: 116.6 (2008-2012 5-year est.); Marriage status: 22.2% never married, 64.2% now married, 5.7% widowed, 8.0% divorced (2008-2012 5-year est.); Foreign born: 3.3% (2008-2012 5-year est.); Ancestry (includes multiple ancestries): 39.0% German, 25.0% Irish, 13.5% Italian, 9.4% English, 6.1% Polish (2008-2012 5-year est.).

Economy: Single-family building permits issued: 2 (2013); Multi-family building permits issued: 0 (2013); Homeowner vacancy rate: 4.5%. Rental vacancy rate: 0.0%. (2008-2012 5-year est.); Employment by occupation: 5.9% management, business, and financial, 3.1% computer, engineering, and science, 8.2% education, legal, community service, arts, and media, 2.8% healthcare practitioners, 15.3% service, 24.6% sales and office, 18.4% natural resources, construction, and maintenance, 21.7% production, transportation, and material moving (2008-2012 5-year est.).

Income: Per capita income: $25,996 (2008-2012 5-year est.); Median household income: $53,681 (2008-2012 5-year est.); Average household income: $61,572 (2008-2012 5-year est.); Percent of households with income of $100,000 or more: 17.5% (2008-2012 5-year est.); Poverty rate: 7.4% (2008-2012 5-year est.).

Education: Percent of population age 25 and over with: High school diploma (including GED) or higher: 87.1% (2008-2012 5-year est.); Bachelor's degree or higher: 10.2% (2008-2012 5-year est.); Master's degree or higher: 3.3% (2008-2012 5-year est.).

School District(s)
Putnam County CUSD 535 (PK-12)
   2011-12 Enrollment: 916 . . . . (815) 882-2800

Housing: Homeownership rate: 73.8% (2008-2012 5-year est.); Median home value: $136,200 (2008-2012 5-year est.); Median contract rent: $600 per month (2008-2012 5-year est.); Median year structure built: 1968 (2008-2012 5-year est.).

Health Insurance: 77.8% Private; 27.4% Public; 10.4% None. (2008-2012 5-year est.)

Transportation: Commute to work: 93.3% car, 0.0% public transportation, 2.1% walk, 4.7% work from home (2008-2012 5-year est.); Travel time to work: 40.7% less than 15 minutes, 37.4% 15 to 30 minutes, 7.3% 30 to 45 minutes, 9.8% 45 to 60 minutes, 4.9% 60 minutes or more (2008-2012 5-year est.)

MAGNOLIA (village). Covers a land area of 0.326 square miles and a water area of 0 square miles. Located at 41.11° N. Lat; 89.20° W. Long. Elevation is 663 feet.

Population: 261 (1990); 279 (2000); 260 (2010); Density: 887.6 persons per square mile (2008-2012 5-year est.); Race: 97.2% White, 1.7% Black/African American, 0.0% Asian, 0.0% American Indian/Alaska Native, 0.0% Native Hawaiian/Other Pacific Islander, 1.1% Some other race, 1.0% Two or more races, 1.4% Hispanic of any race (2008-2012 5-year est.); Average household size: 2.75 (2008-2012 5-year est.); Median age: 34.8 (2008-2012 5-year est.); Males per 100 females: 91.4 (2008-2012 5-year est.); Marriage status: 21.8% never married, 53.1% now married, 3.8% widowed, 21.3% divorced (2008-2012 5-year est.); Foreign born: 0.0% (2008-2012 5-year est.); Ancestry (includes multiple ancestries): 23.5% German, 18.0% Irish, 12.1% Swedish, 10.4% English, 9.3% Dutch (2008-2012 5-year est.).

Economy: Single-family building permits issued: 5 (2013); Multi-family building permits issued: 0 (2013); Homeowner vacancy rate: 5.4%. Rental vacancy rate: 0.0%. (2008-2012 5-year est.); Employment by occupation: 12.2% management, business, and financial, 0.0% computer, engineering, and science, 7.0% education, legal, community service, arts, and media, 0.0% healthcare practitioners, 20.0% service, 11.3% sales and office, 19.1% natural resources, construction, and maintenance, 30.4% production, transportation, and material moving (2008-2012 5-year est.).

Income: Per capita income: $18,088 (2008-2012 5-year est.); Median household income: $43,403 (2008-2012 5-year est.); Average household income: $52,322 (2008-2012 5-year est.); Percent of households with income of $100,000 or more: 7.6% (2008-2012 5-year est.); Poverty rate: 8.3% (2008-2012 5-year est.).

Education: Percent of population age 25 and over with: High school diploma (including GED) or higher: 85.7% (2008-2012 5-year est.); Bachelor's degree or higher: 9.3% (2008-2012 5-year est.); Master's degree or higher: 0.0% (2008-2012 5-year est.).

Housing: Homeownership rate: 66.7% (2008-2012 5-year est.); Median home value: $67,600 (2008-2012 5-year est.); Median contract rent: $383 per month (2008-2012 5-year est.); Median year structure built: Before 1940 (2008-2012 5-year est.).

Health Insurance: 60.6% Private; 48.1% Public; 14.2% None. (2008-2012 5-year est.)

Transportation: Commute to work: 98.2% car, 0.0% public transportation, 1.8% walk, 0.0% work from home (2008-2012 5-year est.); Travel time to work: 17.4% less than 15 minutes, 42.2% 15 to 30 minutes, 31.2% 30 to 45 minutes, 5.5% 45 to 60 minutes, 3.7% 60 minutes or more (2008-2012 5-year est.)

MARK (village). Covers a land area of 1.128 square miles and a water area of 0 square miles. Located at 41.26° N. Lat; 89.26° W. Long. Elevation is 689 feet.

Population: 391 (1990); 491 (2000); 555 (2010); Density: 538.3 persons per square mile (2008-2012 5-year est.); Race: 95.7% White, 0.0% Black/African American, 1.0% Asian, 0.0% American Indian/Alaska Native, 0.0% Native Hawaiian/Other Pacific Islander, 3.3% Some other race, 1.8% Two or more races, 4.3% Hispanic of any race (2008-2012 5-year est.); Average household size: 2.82 (2008-2012 5-year est.); Median age: 35.1 (2008-2012 5-year est.); Males per 100 females: 93.3 (2008-2012 5-year est.); Marriage status: 23.0% never married, 62.8% now married, 6.5% widowed, 7.7% divorced (2008-2012 5-year est.); Foreign born: 2.5% (2008-2012 5-year est.); Ancestry (includes multiple ancestries): 46.1% German, 22.6% Italian, 16.3% Polish, 14.5% Irish, 5.4% English (2008-2012 5-year est.).

Economy: Single-family building permits issued: 1 (2013); Multi-family building permits issued: 0 (2013); Homeowner vacancy rate: 0.0%. Rental vacancy rate: 0.0%. (2008-2012 5-year est.); Employment by occupation: 20.9% management, business, and financial, 0.9% computer, engineering, and science, 10.8% education, legal, community service, arts, and media, 6.6% healthcare practitioners, 14.6% service, 14.2% sales and office, 7.3% natural resources, construction, and maintenance, 24.7% production, transportation, and material moving (2008-2012 5-year est.).

Income: Per capita income: $24,734 (2008-2012 5-year est.); Median household income: $54,107 (2008-2012 5-year est.); Average household income: $70,921 (2008-2012 5-year est.); Percent of households with income of $100,000 or more: 21.3% (2008-2012 5-year est.); Poverty rate: 7.9% (2008-2012 5-year est.).

Education: Percent of population age 25 and over with: High school diploma (including GED) or higher: 89.5% (2008-2012 5-year est.); Bachelor's degree or higher: 14.4% (2008-2012 5-year est.); Master's degree or higher: 6.6% (2008-2012 5-year est.).

Housing: Homeownership rate: 80.0% (2008-2012 5-year est.); Median home value: $105,600 (2008-2012 5-year est.); Median contract rent: $515 per month (2008-2012 5-year est.); Median year structure built: 1971 (2008-2012 5-year est.).

Health Insurance: 81.1% Private; 30.8% Public; 9.6% None. (2008-2012 5-year est.)

Transportation: Commute to work: 100.0% car, 0.0% public transportation, 0.0% walk, 0.0% work from home (2008-2012 5-year est.); Travel time to work: 32.6% less than 15 minutes, 40.5% 15 to 30 minutes, 19.6% 30 to 45 minutes, 0.0% 45 to 60 minutes, 7.3% 60 minutes or more (2008-2012 5-year est.)

MCNABB (village). Covers a land area of 0.199 square miles and a water area of 0 square miles. Located at 41.18° N. Lat; 89.21° W. Long. Elevation is 686 feet.

Population: 310 (1990); 310 (2000); 285 (2010); Density: 1,744.4 persons per square mile (2008-2012 5-year est.); Race: 92.2% White, 0.0% Black/African American, 0.0% Asian, 0.0% American Indian/Alaska Native, 0.0% Native Hawaiian/Other Pacific Islander, 7.8% Some other race, 7.8% Two or more races, 0.6% Hispanic of any race (2008-2012 5-year est.); Average household size: 2.89 (2008-2012 5-year est.); Median age: 37.4 (2008-2012 5-year est.); Males per 100 females: 134.5 (2008-2012 5-year est.); Marriage status: 16.6% never married, 73.0% now married, 5.4% widowed, 5.0% divorced (2008-2012 5-year est.); Foreign born: 0.0% (2008-2012 5-year est.); Ancestry (includes multiple ancestries): 44.7% German, 32.0% Irish, 14.4% Italian, 11.8% American, 6.3% Swedish (2008-2012 5-year est.).

Economy: Single-family building permits issued: 0 (2013); Multi-family building permits issued: 0 (2013); Homeowner vacancy rate: 0.0%. Rental vacancy rate: 6.9%. (2008-2012 5-year est.); Employment by occupation: 6.3% management, business, and financial, 4.4% computer, engineering, and science, 3.1% education, legal, community service, arts, and media, 3.1% healthcare practitioners, 15.6% service, 23.8% sales and office, 10.0% natural resources, construction, and maintenance, 33.8% production, transportation, and material moving (2008-2012 5-year est.).

Income: Per capita income: $19,830 (2008-2012 5-year est.); Median household income: $58,750 (2008-2012 5-year est.); Average household income: $58,395 (2008-2012 5-year est.); Percent of households with income of $100,000 or more: 13.4% (2008-2012 5-year est.); Poverty rate: 20.7% (2008-2012 5-year est.).

Education: Percent of population age 25 and over with: High school diploma (including GED) or higher: 86.9% (2008-2012 5-year est.); Bachelor's degree or higher: 10.3% (2008-2012 5-year est.); Master's degree or higher: 1.4% (2008-2012 5-year est.).

School District(s)

Putnam County CUSD 535 (PK-12)

2011-12 Enrollment: 916. . . . . (815) 882-2800

Housing: Homeownership rate: 79.2% (2008-2012 5-year est.); Median home value: $103,800 (2008-2012 5-year est.); Median contract rent: $445 per month (2008-2012 5-year est.); Median year structure built: 1958 (2008-2012 5-year est.).

Health Insurance: 67.4% Private; 34.3% Public; 6.6% None. (2008-2012 5-year est.)

Transportation: Commute to work: 79.9% car, 0.0% public transportation, 8.4% walk, 2.6% work from home (2008-2012 5-year est.); Travel time to work: 33.3% less than 15 minutes, 45.3% 15 to 30 minutes, 18.7% 30 to 45 minutes, 0.0% 45 to 60 minutes, 2.7% 60 minutes or more (2008-2012 5-year est.)

PUTNAM (unincorporated postal area)

Zip Code: 61560

Covers a land area of 33.121 square miles and a water area of 8.211 square miles. Located at 41.18° N. Lat; 89.41° W. Long. Elevation is 518 feet. Population: 754 (2010); Density: 22.8 persons per square mile (2010); Race: 98.5% White, 0.0% Black/African American, 0.3% Asian, 0.0% American Indian/Alaska Native, 0.0% Native Hawaiian/Other Pacific Islander, 1.2% Some other race, 0.8% Two or more races, 1.9% Hispanic of any race (2010); Average household size: 2.25 (2010); Median age: 54.6 (2010); Males per 100 females: 116.0 (2010); Homeownership rate: 89.2% (2010)

STANDARD (village). Covers a land area of 0.696 square miles and a water area of 0 square miles. Located at 41.26° N. Lat; 89.18° W. Long. Elevation is 679 feet.

Population: 260 (1990); 256 (2000); 220 (2010); Density: 374.9 persons per square mile (2008-2012 5-year est.); Race: 92.0% White, 0.0% Black/African American, 1.5% Asian, 0.0% American Indian/Alaska Native, 0.0% Native Hawaiian/Other Pacific Islander, 6.5% Some other race, 4.6% Two or more races, 3.1% Hispanic of any race (2008-2012 5-year est.); Average household size: 2.35 (2008-2012 5-year est.); Median age: 36.3 (2008-2012 5-year est.); Males per 100 females: 85.1 (2008-2012 5-year est.); Marriage status: 26.1% never married, 55.6% now married, 10.6% widowed, 7.7% divorced (2008-2012 5-year est.); Foreign born: 2.7% (2008-2012 5-year est.); Ancestry (includes multiple ancestries): 36.4% German, 25.3% Italian, 17.6% Irish, 12.6% Polish, 6.9% Welsh (2008-2012 5-year est.).

Economy: Single-family building permits issued: 0 (2013); Multi-family building permits issued: 0 (2013); Homeowner vacancy rate: 0.0%. Rental vacancy rate: 0.0%. (2008-2012 5-year est.); Employment by occupation: 2.2% management, business, and financial, 2.2% computer, engineering, and science, 7.5% education, legal, community service, arts, and media, 0.0% healthcare practitioners, 12.7% service, 37.3% sales and office, 6.0% natural resources, construction, and maintenance, 32.1% production, transportation, and material moving (2008-2012 5-year est.).

Income: Per capita income: $26,888 (2008-2012 5-year est.); Median household income: $49,464 (2008-2012 5-year est.); Average household income: $65,726 (2008-2012 5-year est.); Percent of households with income of $100,000 or more: 13.5% (2008-2012 5-year est.); Poverty rate: 4.6% (2008-2012 5-year est.).

Education: Percent of population age 25 and over with: High school diploma (including GED) or higher: 86.2% (2008-2012 5-year est.); Bachelor's degree or higher: 7.2% (2008-2012 5-year est.); Master's degree or higher: 4.6% (2008-2012 5-year est.).

Housing: Homeownership rate: 70.3% (2008-2012 5-year est.); Median home value: $90,000 (2008-2012 5-year est.); Median contract rent: $521 per month (2008-2012 5-year est.); Median year structure built: 1945 (2008-2012 5-year est.).

Health Insurance: 82.4% Private; 23.8% Public; 10.0% None. (2008-2012 5-year est.)

Transportation: Commute to work: 95.5% car, 0.0% public transportation, 1.5% walk, 3.0% work from home (2008-2012 5-year est.); Travel time to work: 28.9% less than 15 minutes, 48.4% 15 to 30 minutes, 18.8% 30 to 45 minutes, 1.6% 45 to 60 minutes, 2.3% 60 minutes or more (2008-2012 5-year est.)

Randolph County

Located in southwestern Illinois; bounded on the west and south by the Mississippi River and the Missouri border; drained by the Kaskaskia River. Covers a land area of 575.500 square miles, a water area of 21.705 square miles, and is located in the Central Time Zone at 38.06° N. Lat., 89.82° W. Long. The county was founded in 1795. County seat is Chester.

Weather Station: Kaskaskia River Nav Lock   Elevation: 379 feet

	Jan	Feb	Mar	Apr	May	Jun	Jul	Aug	Sep	Oct	Nov	Dec
High	42	47	57	69	79	87	91	90	83	70	57	44
Low	22	25	34	44	54	63	67	65	57	45	35	25
Precip	2.0	2.2	3.3	3.6	5.1	3.8	3.7	3.4	3.5	3.7	3.9	3.3
Snow	1.5	2.1	0.2	0.1	0.0	0.0	0.0	0.0	0.0	0.0	0.4	1.6

High and Low temperatures in degrees Fahrenheit; Precipitation and Snow in inches

Weather Station: Sparta 1 W   Elevation: 535 feet

	Jan	Feb	Mar	Apr	May	Jun	Jul	Aug	Sep	Oct	Nov	Dec
High	41	46	56	67	76	85	89	88	81	70	56	43
Low	23	27	34	44	54	63	67	65	56	46	36	26
Precip	2.6	2.6	4.0	4.1	5.2	3.8	3.8	3.0	2.9	3.6	4.3	3.0
Snow	3.7	3.8	1.1	0.2	0.0	0.0	0.0	0.0	0.0	tr	0.6	3.1

High and Low temperatures in degrees Fahrenheit; Precipitation and Snow in inches

Population: 34,583 (1990); 33,893 (2000); 33,476 (2010); Race: 88.6% White, 9.7% Black/African American, 0.3% Asian, 0.1% American Indian/Alaska Native, 0.1% Native Hawaiian/Other Pacific Islander, 1.2% Some other race, 1.0% Two or more races, 2.6% Hispanic of any race (2008-2012 5-year est.); Density: 57.3 persons per square mile (2008-2012 5-year est.); Average household size: 2.52 (2008-2012 5-year est.); Median age: 41.2 (2008-2012 5-year est.); Males per 100 females: 121.0 (2008-2012 5-year est.).

Religion: Six largest groups: 22.1% Lutheran, 22.0% Catholicism, 9.1% Baptist, 4.9% Presbyterian-Reformed, 4.3% Methodist/Pietist, 2.1% Pentecostal (2010)

Economy: Unemployment rate: 6.1% (April 2014); Total civilian labor force: 15,039 (April 2014); Leading industries: 26.3% manufacturing; 20.8% health care and social assistance; 13.7% retail trade (2012); Farms: 793 totaling 278,596 acres (2012); Companies that employ 500 or more persons: 2 (2012); Companies that employ 100 to 499 persons: 14 (2012); Companies that employ less than 100 persons: 657 (2012); Black-owned businesses: n/a (2007); Hispanic-owned businesses: n/a (2007); Asian-owned businesses: n/a (2007); Women-owned businesses: 757 (2007); Single-family building permits issued: 21 (2013); Multi-family building permits issued: 71 (2013).

Income: Per capita income: $21,600 (2008-2012 5-year est.); Median household income: $48,383 (2008-2012 5-year est.); Average household income: $57,197 (2008-2012 5-year est.); Percent of households with income of $100,000 or more: 15.2% (2008-2012 5-year est.); Poverty rate: 12.4% (2008-2012 5-year est.); Bankruptcy rate: 2.40% (2013).

Education: Percent of population age 25 and over with: High school diploma (including GED) or higher: 81.0% (2008-2012 5-year est.); Bachelor's degree or higher: 11.5% (2008-2012 5-year est.); Master's degree or higher: 3.2% (2008-2012 5-year est.).

Housing: Homeownership rate: 76.1% (2008-2012 5-year est.); Median home value: $89,300 (2008-2012 5-year est.); Median contract rent: $431 per month (2008-2012 5-year est.); Median year structure built: 1966 (2008-2012 5-year est.)

Health: Birth rate: 99.7 per 10,000 population (2013); Death rate: 111.0 per 10,000 population (2013); Age-adjusted cancer mortality rate: 189.0 deaths per 100,000 population (2011); Number of physicians: 8.7 per 10,000 population (2011); Hospital beds: 98.6 per 10,000 population (2010); Hospital admissions: 1,092.4 per 10,000 population (2010).

Environment: Air Quality Index: 92.0% good, 8.0% moderate, 0.0% unhealthy for sensitive individuals, 0.0% unhealthy (percent of days in 2013)

Elections: 2012 Presidential election results: 40.0% Obama, 57.6% Romney

National and State Parks: Baldwin Lake State Fish and Wildlife Area; Fort Chartres State Park; Fort Kaskaskia State Park; Modoc Rock Shelter National Historic Site; Randolph County State Conservation Area
Additional Information Contacts
Randolph County Government . . . . (618) 826-5000
  http://www.randolphco.org/gov

Randolph County Communities

BALDWIN (village). Covers a land area of 0.666 square miles and a water area of 0 square miles. Located at 38.18° N. Lat; 89.85° W. Long. Elevation is 459 feet.
Population: 426 (1990); 3,627 (2000); 373 (2010); Density: 686.4 persons per square mile (2008-2012 5-year est.); Race: 99.3% White, 0.0% Black/African American, 0.0% Asian, 0.0% American Indian/Alaska Native, 0.0% Native Hawaiian/Other Pacific Islander, 0.7% Some other race, 0.7% Two or more races, 3.5% Hispanic of any race (2008-2012 5-year est.); Average household size: 3.07 (2008-2012 5-year est.); Median age: 35.8 (2008-2012 5-year est.); Males per 100 females: 79.2 (2008-2012 5-year est.); Marriage status: 30.4% never married, 54.3% now married, 5.6% widowed, 9.7% divorced (2008-2012 5-year est.); Foreign born: 4.2% (2008-2012 5-year est.); Ancestry (includes multiple ancestries): 49.5% German, 13.8% Irish, 9.4% American, 7.2% Other Arab, 5.3% English (2008-2012 5-year est.).
Economy: Single-family building permits issued: 0 (2013); Multi-family building permits issued: 0 (2013); Homeowner vacancy rate: 0.7%. Rental vacancy rate: 59.1%. (2008-2012 5-year est.); Employment by occupation: 1.2% management, business, and financial, 7.5% computer, engineering, and science, 8.7% education, legal, community service, arts, and media, 4.0% healthcare practitioners, 23.1% service, 16.2% sales and office, 5.2% natural resources, construction, and maintenance, 34.1% production, transportation, and material moving (2008-2012 5-year est.).
Income: Per capita income: $18,420 (2008-2012 5-year est.); Median household income: $43,750 (2008-2012 5-year est.); Average household income: $51,656 (2008-2012 5-year est.); Percent of households with income of $100,000 or more: 8.7% (2008-2012 5-year est.); Poverty rate: 9.2% (2008-2012 5-year est.).
Education: Percent of population age 25 and over with: High school diploma (including GED) or higher: 92.5% (2008-2012 5-year est.); Bachelor's degree or higher: 15.7% (2008-2012 5-year est.); Master's degree or higher: 2.4% (2008-2012 5-year est.).
Housing: Homeownership rate: 94.0% (2008-2012 5-year est.); Median home value: $65,800 (2008-2012 5-year est.); Median contract rent: $413 per month (2008-2012 5-year est.); Median year structure built: 1953 (2008-2012 5-year est.).
Health Insurance: 60.0% Private; 43.8% Public; 10.5% None. (2008-2012 5-year est.)
Transportation: Commute to work: 94.7% car, 0.0% public transportation, 3.6% walk, 1.2% work from home (2008-2012 5-year est.); Travel time to work: 15.6% less than 15 minutes, 35.3% 15 to 30 minutes, 22.8% 30 to 45 minutes, 15.6% 45 to 60 minutes, 10.8% 60 minutes or more (2008-2012 5-year est.)

CHESTER (city). County seat. Covers a land area of 5.809 square miles and a water area of 0.016 square miles. Located at 37.93° N. Lat; 89.83° W. Long. Elevation is 669 feet.
History: Chester was established in 1819 as a commercial rival for Kaskaskia by a land company from Cincinnati.
Population: 8,194 (1990); 5,185 (2000); 8,586 (2010); Density: 1,467.1 persons per square mile (2008-2012 5-year est.); Race: 72.8% White, 25.4% Black/African American, 0.6% Asian, 0.2% American Indian/Alaska Native, 0.0% Native Hawaiian/Other Pacific Islander, 1.0% Some other race, 0.8% Two or more races, 5.0% Hispanic of any race (2008-2012 5-year est.); Average household size: 2.61 (2008-2012 5-year est.); Median age: 36.7 (2008-2012 5-year est.); Males per 100 females: 211.1 (2008-2012 5-year est.); Marriage status: 50.3% never married, 33.5% now married, 5.0% widowed, 11.3% divorced (2008-2012 5-year est.); Foreign born: 2.8% (2008-2012 5-year est.); Ancestry (includes multiple ancestries): 24.2% German, 8.6% English, 5.4% Irish, 4.9% American, 4.3% French (2008-2012 5-year est.).
Economy: Single-family building permits issued: 0 (2013); Multi-family building permits issued: 0 (2013); Homeowner vacancy rate: 5.8%. Rental vacancy rate: 5.2%. (2008-2012 5-year est.); Employment by occupation: 5.6% management, business, and financial, 1.6% computer, engineering, and science, 4.9% education, legal, community service, arts, and media,

6.1% healthcare practitioners, 26.9% service, 14.5% sales and office, 11.9% natural resources, construction, and maintenance, 28.6% production, transportation, and material moving (2008-2012 5-year est.).
Income: Per capita income: $13,671 (2008-2012 5-year est.); Median household income: $47,583 (2008-2012 5-year est.); Average household income: $52,756 (2008-2012 5-year est.); Percent of households with income of $100,000 or more: 12.5% (2008-2012 5-year est.); Poverty rate: 20.2% (2008-2012 5-year est.).
Education: Percent of population age 25 and over with: High school diploma (including GED) or higher: 63.3% (2008-2012 5-year est.); Bachelor's degree or higher: 6.6% (2008-2012 5-year est.); Master's degree or higher: 2.3% (2008-2012 5-year est.).
School District(s)
Chester CUSD 139 (PK-12)
  2011-12 Enrollment: 995. . . . . (618) 826-4509
Housing: Homeownership rate: 66.0% (2008-2012 5-year est.); Median home value: $78,100 (2008-2012 5-year est.); Median contract rent: $435 per month (2008-2012 5-year est.); Median year structure built: 1957 (2008-2012 5-year est.).
Health Insurance: 65.5% Private; 39.8% Public; 8.3% None. (2008-2012 5-year est.)
Hospitals: Memorial Hospital (25 beds)
Safety: Violent crime rate: 10.5 per 10,000 population; Property crime rate: 40.8 per 10,000 population (2012).
Transportation: Commute to work: 93.5% car, 0.1% public transportation, 5.0% walk, 1.4% work from home (2008-2012 5-year est.); Travel time to work: 59.0% less than 15 minutes, 19.2% 15 to 30 minutes, 12.9% 30 to 45 minutes, 2.6% 45 to 60 minutes, 6.3% 60 minutes or more (2008-2012 5-year est.)
Additional Information Contacts
Chester Chamber of Commerce . . . . (618) 826-2721
  http://www.chesterill.com/chamber
City of Chester. . . . . (618) 826-2326
  http://www.chesterill.com

COULTERVILLE (village). Covers a land area of 0.559 square miles and a water area of <.001 square miles. Located at 38.19° N. Lat; 89.60° W. Long. Elevation is 551 feet.
History: Incorporated 1874.
Population: 904 (1990); 1,230 (2000); 945 (2010); Density: 1,048.0 persons per square mile (2008-2012 5-year est.); Race: 98.0% White, 1.6% Black/African American, 0.0% Asian, 0.3% American Indian/Alaska Native, 0.0% Native Hawaiian/Other Pacific Islander, 0.1% Some other race, 0.0% Two or more races, 1.8% Hispanic of any race (2008-2012 5-year est.); Average household size: 2.54 (2008-2012 5-year est.); Median age: 37.3 (2008-2012 5-year est.); Males per 100 females: 71.5 (2008-2012 5-year est.); Marriage status: 33.4% never married, 34.1% now married, 13.7% widowed, 18.8% divorced (2008-2012 5-year est.); Foreign born: 0.7% (2008-2012 5-year est.); Ancestry (includes multiple ancestries): 34.1% German, 13.9% Irish, 10.2% English, 7.1% Polish, 5.2% French (2008-2012 5-year est.).
Economy: Homeowner vacancy rate: 1.4%. Rental vacancy rate: 0.0%. (2008-2012 5-year est.); Employment by occupation: 5.4% management, business, and financial, 4.2% computer, engineering, and science, 5.7% education, legal, community service, arts, and media, 2.1% healthcare practitioners, 39.3% service, 14.2% sales and office, 13.3% natural resources, construction, and maintenance, 15.7% production, transportation, and material moving (2008-2012 5-year est.).
Income: Per capita income: $19,521 (2008-2012 5-year est.); Median household income: $33,750 (2008-2012 5-year est.); Average household income: $45,614 (2008-2012 5-year est.); Percent of households with income of $100,000 or more: 8.2% (2008-2012 5-year est.); Poverty rate: 21.9% (2008-2012 5-year est.).
Education: Percent of population age 25 and over with: High school diploma (including GED) or higher: 82.8% (2008-2012 5-year est.); Bachelor's degree or higher: 10.5% (2008-2012 5-year est.); Master's degree or higher: 2.1% (2008-2012 5-year est.).
School District(s)
Coulterville USD 1 (KG-12)
  2011-12 Enrollment: 224. . . . . (618) 758-2881
Housing: Homeownership rate: 79.5% (2008-2012 5-year est.); Median home value: $72,600 (2008-2012 5-year est.); Median contract rent: $384 per month (2008-2012 5-year est.); Median year structure built: 1964 (2008-2012 5-year est.).

Health Insurance: 55.4% Private; 44.6% Public; 17.6% None. (2008-2012 5-year est.)

Transportation: Commute to work: 92.7% car, 0.0% public transportation, 4.8% walk, 0.6% work from home (2008-2012 5-year est.); Travel time to work: 36.8% less than 15 minutes, 31.6% 15 to 30 minutes, 11.2% 30 to 45 minutes, 3.0% 45 to 60 minutes, 17.3% 60 minutes or more (2008-2012 5-year est.)

ELLIS GROVE (village). Aka Ellisgrove. Covers a land area of 0.491 square miles and a water area of 0.001 square miles. Located at 38.01° N. Lat; 89.91° W. Long. Elevation is 548 feet.

History: Fort Kaskaskia State Historical Site nearby.

Population: 353 (1990); 381 (2000); 363 (2010); Density: 814.9 persons per square mile (2008-2012 5-year est.); Race: 99.5% White, 0.5% Black/African American, 0.0% Asian, 0.0% American Indian/Alaska Native, 0.0% Native Hawaiian/Other Pacific Islander, 0.0% Some other race, 0.0% Two or more races, 5.0% Hispanic of any race (2008-2012 5-year est.); Average household size: 2.78 (2008-2012 5-year est.); Median age: 32.9 (2008-2012 5-year est.); Males per 100 females: 112.8 (2008-2012 5-year est.); Marriage status: 18.2% never married, 60.3% now married, 7.9% widowed, 13.6% divorced (2008-2012 5-year est.); Foreign born: 0.0% (2008-2012 5-year est.); Ancestry (includes multiple ancestries): 45.5% German, 16.0% American, 7.5% Italian, 6.5% English, 6.3% Irish (2008-2012 5-year est.).

Economy: Homeowner vacancy rate: 5.5%. Rental vacancy rate: 0.0%. (2008-2012 5-year est.); Employment by occupation: 9.1% management, business, and financial, 3.4% computer, engineering, and science, 2.3% education, legal, community service, arts, and media, 2.3% healthcare practitioners, 16.5% service, 26.1% sales and office, 12.5% natural resources, construction, and maintenance, 27.8% production, transportation, and material moving (2008-2012 5-year est.).

Income: Per capita income: $21,102 (2008-2012 5-year est.); Median household income: $57,500 (2008-2012 5-year est.); Average household income: $56,574 (2008-2012 5-year est.); Percent of households with income of $100,000 or more: 9.1% (2008-2012 5-year est.); Poverty rate: 4.5% (2008-2012 5-year est.).

Education: Percent of population age 25 and over with: High school diploma (including GED) or higher: 81.5% (2008-2012 5-year est.); Bachelor's degree or higher: 6.7% (2008-2012 5-year est.); Master's degree or higher: 1.5% (2008-2012 5-year est.).

Housing: Homeownership rate: 83.3% (2008-2012 5-year est.); Median home value: $68,600 (2008-2012 5-year est.); Median contract rent: $450 per month (2008-2012 5-year est.); Median year structure built: 1969 (2008-2012 5-year est.).

Health Insurance: 80.3% Private; 34.0% Public; 6.5% None. (2008-2012 5-year est.)

Transportation: Commute to work: 97.7% car, 0.0% public transportation, 1.7% walk, 0.0% work from home (2008-2012 5-year est.); Travel time to work: 18.2% less than 15 minutes, 51.1% 15 to 30 minutes, 10.8% 30 to 45 minutes, 13.1% 45 to 60 minutes, 6.8% 60 minutes or more (2008-2012 5-year est.)

EVANSVILLE (village). Covers a land area of 0.789 square miles and a water area of 0.027 square miles. Located at 38.09° N. Lat; 89.93° W. Long. Elevation is 390 feet.

Population: 844 (1990); 724 (2000); 701 (2010); Density: 807.3 persons per square mile (2008-2012 5-year est.); Race: 99.7% White, 0.2% Black/African American, 0.0% Asian, 0.2% American Indian/Alaska Native, 0.0% Native Hawaiian/Other Pacific Islander, 0.0% Some other race, 0.0% Two or more races, 4.9% Hispanic of any race (2008-2012 5-year est.); Average household size: 2.70 (2008-2012 5-year est.); Median age: 41.8 (2008-2012 5-year est.); Males per 100 females: 84.6 (2008-2012 5-year est.); Marriage status: 27.4% never married, 50.1% now married, 5.3% widowed, 17.1% divorced (2008-2012 5-year est.); Foreign born: 0.5% (2008-2012 5-year est.); Ancestry (includes multiple ancestries): 43.8% German, 14.8% French, 11.8% Irish, 9.1% Italian, 5.8% American (2008-2012 5-year est.).

Economy: Single-family building permits issued: 0 (2013); Multi-family building permits issued: 0 (2013); Homeowner vacancy rate: 0.0%. Rental vacancy rate: 0.0%. (2008-2012 5-year est.); Employment by occupation: 6.4% management, business, and financial, 3.0% computer, engineering, and science, 6.8% education, legal, community service, arts, and media, 1.5% healthcare practitioners, 16.6% service, 22.3% sales and office, 15.1% natural resources, construction, and maintenance, 28.3% production, transportation, and material moving (2008-2012 5-year est.).

Income: Per capita income: $20,646 (2008-2012 5-year est.); Median household income: $50,313 (2008-2012 5-year est.); Average household income: $54,079 (2008-2012 5-year est.); Percent of households with income of $100,000 or more: 7.6% (2008-2012 5-year est.); Poverty rate: 7.8% (2008-2012 5-year est.).

Education: Percent of population age 25 and over with: High school diploma (including GED) or higher: 84.6% (2008-2012 5-year est.); Bachelor's degree or higher: 5.1% (2008-2012 5-year est.); Master's degree or higher: 2.8% (2008-2012 5-year est.).

School District(s)

Sparta CUSD 140 (PK-12)
  2011-12 Enrollment: 1,299 . . . . (618) 443-5331

Housing: Homeownership rate: 81.8% (2008-2012 5-year est.); Median home value: $69,700 (2008-2012 5-year est.); Median contract rent: $406 per month (2008-2012 5-year est.); Median year structure built: 1954 (2008-2012 5-year est.).

Health Insurance: 64.8% Private; 31.2% Public; 13.2% None. (2008-2012 5-year est.)

Transportation: Commute to work: 94.2% car, 0.8% public transportation, 1.5% walk, 0.8% work from home (2008-2012 5-year est.); Travel time to work: 21.3% less than 15 minutes, 28.3% 15 to 30 minutes, 12.8% 30 to 45 minutes, 11.2% 45 to 60 minutes, 26.4% 60 minutes or more (2008-2012 5-year est.)

KASKASKIA (village). Covers a land area of 0.108 square miles and a water area of 0 square miles. Located at 37.92° N. Lat; 89.92° W. Long. Elevation is 381 feet.

History: Second-smallest incorporated community in Illinois.

Population: 32 (1990); 9 (2000); 14 (2010); Density: 36.9 persons per square mile (2008-2012 5-year est.); Race: 100.0% White, 0.0% Black/African American, 0.0% Asian, 0.0% American Indian/Alaska Native, 0.0% Native Hawaiian/Other Pacific Islander, 0.0% Some other race, 0.0% Two or more races, 0.0% Hispanic of any race (2008-2012 5-year est.); Average household size: 2.00 (2008-2012 5-year est.); Median age: 80.5 (2008-2012 5-year est.); Males per 100 females: 100.0 (2008-2012 5-year est.); Marriage status: 0.0% never married, 100.0% now married, 0.0% widowed, 0.0% divorced (2008-2012 5-year est.); Foreign born: 0.0% (2008-2012 5-year est.); Ancestry (includes multiple ancestries): n/a (2008-2012 5-year est.).

Economy: Homeowner vacancy rate: 0.0%. Rental vacancy rate: 0.0%. (2008-2012 5-year est.); Employment by occupation: n/a management, business, and financial, n/a computer, engineering, and science, n/a education, legal, community service, arts, and media, n/a healthcare practitioners, n/a service, n/a sales and office, n/a natural resources, construction, and maintenance, n/a production, transportation, and material moving (2008-2012 5-year est.).

Income: Per capita income: $-1 (2008-2012 5-year est.); Median household income: n/a (2008-2012 5-year est.); Average household income: n/a (2008-2012 5-year est.); Percent of households with income of $100,000 or more: n/a (2008-2012 5-year est.); Poverty rate: 0.0% (2008-2012 5-year est.).

Education: Percent of population age 25 and over with: High school diploma (including GED) or higher: 100.0% (2008-2012 5-year est.); Bachelor's degree or higher: 0.0% (2008-2012 5-year est.); Master's degree or higher: 0.0% (2008-2012 5-year est.).

Housing: Homeownership rate: 100.0% (2008-2012 5-year est.); Median home value: n/a (2008-2012 5-year est.); Median contract rent: n/a per month (2008-2012 5-year est.); Median year structure built: Before 1940 (2008-2012 5-year est.).

Health Insurance: 50.0% Private; 100.0% Public; 0.0% None. (2008-2012 5-year est.)

Transportation: Commute to work: n/a car, n/a public transportation, n/a walk, n/a work from home (2008-2012 5-year est.); Travel time to work: n/a less than 15 minutes, n/a 15 to 30 minutes, n/a 30 to 45 minutes, n/a 45 to 60 minutes, n/a 60 minutes or more (2008-2012 5-year est.)

MODOC (unincorporated postal area)

Zip Code: 62261

Covers a land area of 28.787 square miles and a water area of 2.934 square miles. Located at 37.99° N. Lat; 90.00° W. Long. Elevation is 397 feet. Population: 152 (2010); Density: 5.3 persons per square mile (2010); Race: 100.0% White, 0.0% Black/African American, 0.0% Asian, 0.0% American Indian/Alaska Native, 0.0% Native Hawaiian/Other Pacific Islander, 0.0% Some other race, 0.0% Two or more races, 0.7% Hispanic of any race (2010); Average household size: 2.24 (2010);

Median age: 46.5 (2010); Males per 100 females: 111.1 (2010); Homeownership rate: 88.2% (2010)

PERCY (village).
Covers a land area of 0.927 square miles and a water area of 0.003 square miles. Located at 38.02° N. Lat; 89.62° W. Long. Elevation is 472 feet.

Population: 925 (1990); 942 (2000); 970 (2010); Density: 928.8 persons per square mile (2008-2012 5-year est.); Race: 91.2% White, 0.0% Black/African American, 0.0% Asian, 0.0% American Indian/Alaska Native, 0.0% Native Hawaiian/Other Pacific Islander, 8.8% Some other race, 0.7% Two or more races, 16.1% Hispanic of any race (2008-2012 5-year est.); Average household size: 2.26 (2008-2012 5-year est.); Median age: 40.6 (2008-2012 5-year est.); Males per 100 females: 101.6 (2008-2012 5-year est.); Marriage status: 24.0% never married, 36.9% now married, 8.9% widowed, 30.2% divorced (2008-2012 5-year est.); Foreign born: 9.3% (2008-2012 5-year est.); Ancestry (includes multiple ancestries): 28.1% German, 20.1% English, 13.1% Irish, 4.3% American, 3.8% French (2008-2012 5-year est.).
Economy: Homeowner vacancy rate: 0.0%. Rental vacancy rate: 17.8%. (2008-2012 5-year est.); Employment by occupation: 3.4% management, business, and financial, 0.8% computer, engineering, and science, 3.4% education, legal, community service, arts, and media, 7.3% healthcare practitioners, 14.7% service, 8.8% sales and office, 6.2% natural resources, construction, and maintenance, 55.4% production, transportation, and material moving (2008-2012 5-year est.).
Income: Per capita income: $17,523 (2008-2012 5-year est.); Median household income: $29,904 (2008-2012 5-year est.); Average household income: $36,247 (2008-2012 5-year est.); Percent of households with income of $100,000 or more: 5.8% (2008-2012 5-year est.); Poverty rate: 22.7% (2008-2012 5-year est.).
Education: Percent of population age 25 and over with: High school diploma (including GED) or higher: 77.1% (2008-2012 5-year est.); Bachelor's degree or higher: 4.8% (2008-2012 5-year est.); Master's degree or higher: 1.9% (2008-2012 5-year est.).
Housing: Homeownership rate: 72.0% (2008-2012 5-year est.); Median home value: $51,700 (2008-2012 5-year est.); Median contract rent: $372 per month (2008-2012 5-year est.); Median year structure built: 1965 (2008-2012 5-year est.).
Health Insurance: 60.7% Private; 33.2% Public; 22.5% None. (2008-2012 5-year est.)
Transportation: Commute to work: 93.2% car, 0.0% public transportation, 0.0% walk, 5.4% work from home (2008-2012 5-year est.); Travel time to work: 61.7% less than 15 minutes, 25.6% 15 to 30 minutes, 8.1% 30 to 45 minutes, 1.2% 45 to 60 minutes, 3.3% 60 minutes or more (2008-2012 5-year est.)

PRAIRIE DU ROCHER (village).
Aka Prairie Du Rocher. Covers a land area of 0.571 square miles and a water area of 0 square miles. Located at 38.08° N. Lat; 90.10° W. Long. Elevation is 394 feet.
History: Prairie du Rocher was founded in the early 1700's by people brought to the area by John Law, a Scotch promoter who organized a company and was granted a charter for the Louisiana Territory.
Population: 540 (1990); 613 (2000); 604 (2010); Density: 896.1 persons per square mile (2008-2012 5-year est.); Race: 94.3% White, 0.0% Black/African American, 5.1% Asian, 0.0% American Indian/Alaska Native, 0.0% Native Hawaiian/Other Pacific Islander, 0.6% Some other race, 0.6% Two or more races, 0.0% Hispanic of any race (2008-2012 5-year est.); Average household size: 2.60 (2008-2012 5-year est.); Median age: 35.1 (2008-2012 5-year est.); Males per 100 females: 72.4 (2008-2012 5-year est.); Marriage status: 26.1% never married, 50.9% now married, 9.0% widowed, 14.0% divorced (2008-2012 5-year est.); Foreign born: 1.2% (2008-2012 5-year est.); Ancestry (includes multiple ancestries): 54.3% German, 17.2% French, 13.9% American, 13.3% Irish, 7.6% English (2008-2012 5-year est.).
Economy: Single-family building permits issued: 0 (2013); Multi-family building permits issued: 0 (2013); Homeowner vacancy rate: 5.6%. Rental vacancy rate: 13.5%. (2008-2012 5-year est.); Employment by occupation: 5.8% management, business, and financial, 4.5% computer, engineering, and science, 2.2% education, legal, community service, arts, and media, 4.0% healthcare practitioners, 23.2% service, 23.7% sales and office, 13.8% natural resources, construction, and maintenance, 22.8% production, transportation, and material moving (2008-2012 5-year est.).
Income: Per capita income: $17,598 (2008-2012 5-year est.); Median household income: $38,125 (2008-2012 5-year est.); Average household income: $43,980 (2008-2012 5-year est.); Percent of households with income of $100,000 or more: 6.1% (2008-2012 5-year est.); Poverty rate: 9.4% (2008-2012 5-year est.).
Education: Percent of population age 25 and over with: High school diploma (including GED) or higher: 91.1% (2008-2012 5-year est.); Bachelor's degree or higher: 8.0% (2008-2012 5-year est.); Master's degree or higher: 0.0% (2008-2012 5-year est.).
School District(s)
Prairie Du Rocher CCSD 134 (PK-08)
 2011-12 Enrollment: 169 . . . . (618) 284-3530
Housing: Homeownership rate: 83.8% (2008-2012 5-year est.); Median home value: $71,500 (2008-2012 5-year est.); Median contract rent: $358 per month (2008-2012 5-year est.); Median year structure built: 1955 (2008-2012 5-year est.).
Health Insurance: 72.3% Private; 38.9% Public; 4.9% None. (2008-2012 5-year est.)
Transportation: Commute to work: 95.0% car, 0.0% public transportation, 2.3% walk, 1.4% work from home (2008-2012 5-year est.); Travel time to work: 15.1% less than 15 minutes, 16.0% 15 to 30 minutes, 41.6% 30 to 45 minutes, 16.0% 45 to 60 minutes, 11.4% 60 minutes or more (2008-2012 5-year est.)

RED BUD (city).
Covers a land area of 2.435 square miles and a water area of 0.023 square miles. Located at 38.21° N. Lat; 90.00° W. Long. Elevation is 472 feet.
History: Red Bud was named for the red-bud trees that once covered the town site.
Population: 2,918 (1990); 3,422 (2000); 3,698 (2010); Density: 1,507.2 persons per square mile (2008-2012 5-year est.); Race: 99.1% White, 0.7% Black/African American, 0.0% Asian, 0.2% American Indian/Alaska Native, 0.0% Native Hawaiian/Other Pacific Islander, 0.0% Some other race, 0.0% Two or more races, 1.0% Hispanic of any race (2008-2012 5-year est.); Average household size: 2.41 (2008-2012 5-year est.); Median age: 44.0 (2008-2012 5-year est.); Males per 100 females: 97.2 (2008-2012 5-year est.); Marriage status: 16.7% never married, 62.4% now married, 11.5% widowed, 9.4% divorced (2008-2012 5-year est.); Foreign born: 0.2% (2008-2012 5-year est.); Ancestry (includes multiple ancestries): 49.8% German, 13.1% Irish, 10.6% American, 7.2% French, 5.9% English (2008-2012 5-year est.).
Economy: Single-family building permits issued: 2 (2013); Multi-family building permits issued: 6 (2013); Homeowner vacancy rate: 0.0%. Rental vacancy rate: 15.6%. (2008-2012 5-year est.); Employment by occupation: 11.4% management, business, and financial, 2.0% computer, engineering, and science, 6.8% education, legal, community service, arts, and media, 5.5% healthcare practitioners, 20.1% service, 26.1% sales and office, 6.4% natural resources, construction, and maintenance, 21.7% production, transportation, and material moving (2008-2012 5-year est.).
Income: Per capita income: $27,573 (2008-2012 5-year est.); Median household income: $54,954 (2008-2012 5-year est.); Average household income: $64,747 (2008-2012 5-year est.); Percent of households with income of $100,000 or more: 18.4% (2008-2012 5-year est.); Poverty rate: 4.0% (2008-2012 5-year est.).
Education: Percent of population age 25 and over with: High school diploma (including GED) or higher: 87.6% (2008-2012 5-year est.); Bachelor's degree or higher: 17.3% (2008-2012 5-year est.); Master's degree or higher: 5.4% (2008-2012 5-year est.).
School District(s)
Beck Area Career Center (10-12)
 2011-12 Enrollment: n/a . . . . (618) 473-2222
Monroe/randolph Roe (06-12)
 2011-12 Enrollment: n/a . . . . (618) 939-5650
Red Bud CUSD 132 (PK-12)
 2011-12 Enrollment: 1,090 . . . . (618) 282-3507
Vocational/Technical School(s)
Beck Area Career Center-Red Bud (Public)
 Fall 2012 Enrollment: 102 . . . . (618) 473-2222
 2012-13 Tuition: $14,300
Housing: Homeownership rate: 79.5% (2008-2012 5-year est.); Median home value: $124,600 (2008-2012 5-year est.); Median contract rent: $495 per month (2008-2012 5-year est.); Median year structure built: 1972 (2008-2012 5-year est.).
Health Insurance: 83.7% Private; 27.4% Public; 6.9% None. (2008-2012 5-year est.)
Hospitals: Red Bud Regional Hospital (202 beds)
Safety: Violent crime rate: 40.7 per 10,000 population; Property crime rate: 81.4 per 10,000 population (2012).

Transportation: Commute to work: 89.8% car, 0.0% public transportation, 1.2% walk, 6.7% work from home (2008-2012 5-year est.); Travel time to work: 35.5% less than 15 minutes, 25.1% 15 to 30 minutes, 18.2% 30 to 45 minutes, 9.1% 45 to 60 minutes, 12.1% 60 minutes or more (2008-2012 5-year est.)

Additional Information Contacts
Red Bud Chamber of Commerce . . . . (618) 282-3505
  http://www.redbudchamber.com

ROCKWOOD (village). Covers a land area of 0.212 square miles and a water area of 0 square miles. Located at 37.84° N. Lat; 89.69° W. Long. Elevation is 381 feet.

History: Early settlers in Rockwood provided river steamers with wood for fuel, and built flatboats for transporting cargo.

Population: 45 (1990); 41 (2000); 42 (2010); Density: 392.1 persons per square mile (2008-2012 5-year est.); Race: 100.0% White, 0.0% Black/African American, 0.0% Asian, 0.0% American Indian/Alaska Native, 0.0% Native Hawaiian/Other Pacific Islander, 0.0% Some other race, 0.0% Two or more races, 0.0% Hispanic of any race (2008-2012 5-year est.); Average household size: 3.19 (2008-2012 5-year est.); Median age: 47.1 (2008-2012 5-year est.); Males per 100 females: 72.9 (2008-2012 5-year est.); Marriage status: 45.8% never married, 2.4% now married, 36.1% widowed, 15.7% divorced (2008-2012 5-year est.); Foreign born: 0.0% (2008-2012 5-year est.); Ancestry (includes multiple ancestries): 47.0% German, 34.9% Irish, 18.1% Dutch, 6.0% French, 3.6% American (2008-2012 5-year est.).

Economy: Homeowner vacancy rate: 0.0%. Rental vacancy rate: 0.0%. (2008-2012 5-year est.); Employment by occupation: 0.0% management, business, and financial, 0.0% computer, engineering, and science, 0.0% education, legal, community service, arts, and media, 0.0% healthcare practitioners, 17.6% service, 44.1% sales and office, 5.9% natural resources, construction, and maintenance, 32.4% production, transportation, and material moving (2008-2012 5-year est.).

Income: Per capita income: $16,582 (2008-2012 5-year est.); Median household income: $41,500 (2008-2012 5-year est.); Average household income: $45,150 (2008-2012 5-year est.); Percent of households with income of $100,000 or more: 11.5% (2008-2012 5-year est.); Poverty rate: 36.1% (2008-2012 5-year est.).

Education: Percent of population age 25 and over with: High school diploma (including GED) or higher: 62.7% (2008-2012 5-year est.); Bachelor's degree or higher: 10.4% (2008-2012 5-year est.); Master's degree or higher: 0.0% (2008-2012 5-year est.).

Housing: Homeownership rate: 100.0% (2008-2012 5-year est.); Median home value: $12,500 (2008-2012 5-year est.); Median contract rent: n/a per month (2008-2012 5-year est.); Median year structure built: 1968 (2008-2012 5-year est.).

Health Insurance: 65.1% Private; 12.0% Public; 24.1% None. (2008-2012 5-year est.)

Transportation: Commute to work: 100.0% car, 0.0% public transportation, 0.0% walk, 0.0% work from home (2008-2012 5-year est.); Travel time to work: 17.6% less than 15 minutes, 76.5% 15 to 30 minutes, 0.0% 30 to 45 minutes, 5.9% 45 to 60 minutes, 0.0% 60 minutes or more (2008-2012 5-year est.)

RUMA (village). Covers a land area of 0.740 square miles and a water area of 0 square miles. Located at 38.13° N. Lat; 90.00° W. Long. Elevation is 443 feet.

Population: 256 (1990); 260 (2000); 317 (2010); Density: 458.2 persons per square mile (2008-2012 5-year est.); Race: 100.0% White, 0.0% Black/African American, 0.0% Asian, 0.0% American Indian/Alaska Native, 0.0% Native Hawaiian/Other Pacific Islander, 0.0% Some other race, 0.0% Two or more races, 1.5% Hispanic of any race (2008-2012 5-year est.); Average household size: 3.14 (2008-2012 5-year est.); Median age: 39.2 (2008-2012 5-year est.); Males per 100 females: 99.4 (2008-2012 5-year est.); Marriage status: 25.9% never married, 57.1% now married, 5.0% widowed, 12.0% divorced (2008-2012 5-year est.); Foreign born: 0.6% (2008-2012 5-year est.); Ancestry (includes multiple ancestries): 64.0% German, 9.1% French, 7.4% Irish, 5.0% English, 4.4% American (2008-2012 5-year est.).

Economy: Single-family building permits issued: 1 (2013); Multi-family building permits issued: 0 (2013); Homeowner vacancy rate: 6.7%. Rental vacancy rate: 31.3%. (2008-2012 5-year est.); Employment by occupation: 4.2% management, business, and financial, 9.5% computer, engineering, and science, 1.8% education, legal, community service, arts, and media, 1.2% healthcare practitioners, 12.5% service, 28.6% sales and office,

8.9% natural resources, construction, and maintenance, 33.3% production, transportation, and material moving (2008-2012 5-year est.).

Income: Per capita income: $22,424 (2008-2012 5-year est.); Median household income: $62,813 (2008-2012 5-year est.); Average household income: $63,183 (2008-2012 5-year est.); Percent of households with income of $100,000 or more: 21.3% (2008-2012 5-year est.); Poverty rate: 9.1% (2008-2012 5-year est.).

Education: Percent of population age 25 and over with: High school diploma (including GED) or higher: 91.3% (2008-2012 5-year est.); Bachelor's degree or higher: 2.6% (2008-2012 5-year est.); Master's degree or higher: 1.7% (2008-2012 5-year est.).

School District(s)
Monroe/randolph Roe (06-12)
    2011-12 Enrollment: n/a . . . . (618) 939-5650

Housing: Homeownership rate: 89.8% (2008-2012 5-year est.); Median home value: $91,400 (2008-2012 5-year est.); Median contract rent: $625 per month (2008-2012 5-year est.); Median year structure built: 1990 (2008-2012 5-year est.).

Health Insurance: 75.5% Private; 21.5% Public; 8.0% None. (2008-2012 5-year est.)

Safety: Violent crime rate: 31.6 per 10,000 population; Property crime rate: 94.9 per 10,000 population (2012).

Transportation: Commute to work: 94.6% car, 0.0% public transportation, 4.2% walk, 0.0% work from home (2008-2012 5-year est.); Travel time to work: 23.5% less than 15 minutes, 18.7% 15 to 30 minutes, 22.3% 30 to 45 minutes, 20.5% 45 to 60 minutes, 15.1% 60 minutes or more (2008-2012 5-year est.)

SPARTA (city). Covers a land area of 11.173 square miles and a water area of 0.273 square miles. Located at 38.14° N. Lat; 89.73° W. Long. Elevation is 528 feet.

History: Incorporated 1847.

Population: 4,853 (1990); 4,486 (2000); 4,302 (2010); Density: 385.5 persons per square mile (2008-2012 5-year est.); Race: 78.0% White, 21.1% Black/African American, 0.0% Asian, 0.1% American Indian/Alaska Native, 0.4% Native Hawaiian/Other Pacific Islander, 0.4% Some other race, 0.4% Two or more races, 0.1% Hispanic of any race (2008-2012 5-year est.); Average household size: 2.25 (2008-2012 5-year est.); Median age: 43.3 (2008-2012 5-year est.); Males per 100 females: 95.1 (2008-2012 5-year est.); Marriage status: 23.8% never married, 51.4% now married, 11.3% widowed, 13.5% divorced (2008-2012 5-year est.); Foreign born: 1.6% (2008-2012 5-year est.); Ancestry (includes multiple ancestries): 30.0% German, 14.5% English, 11.9% Irish, 4.4% Italian, 3.9% American (2008-2012 5-year est.).

Economy: Single-family building permits issued: 2 (2013); Multi-family building permits issued: 66 (2013); Homeowner vacancy rate: 6.2%. Rental vacancy rate: 3.6%. (2008-2012 5-year est.); Employment by occupation: 12.0% management, business, and financial, 3.9% computer, engineering, and science, 14.5% education, legal, community service, arts, and media, 6.9% healthcare practitioners, 13.4% service, 13.1% sales and office, 15.1% natural resources, construction, and maintenance, 21.1% production, transportation, and material moving (2008-2012 5-year est.).

Income: Per capita income: $23,194 (2008-2012 5-year est.); Median household income: $43,056 (2008-2012 5-year est.); Average household income: $50,571 (2008-2012 5-year est.); Percent of households with income of $100,000 or more: 12.6% (2008-2012 5-year est.); Poverty rate: 20.3% (2008-2012 5-year est.).

Education: Percent of population age 25 and over with: High school diploma (including GED) or higher: 89.4% (2008-2012 5-year est.); Bachelor's degree or higher: 19.4% (2008-2012 5-year est.); Master's degree or higher: 5.1% (2008-2012 5-year est.).

School District(s)
Sparta CUSD 140 (PK-12)
    2011-12 Enrollment: 1,299 . . . . (618) 443-5331

Housing: Homeownership rate: 64.4% (2008-2012 5-year est.); Median home value: $78,600 (2008-2012 5-year est.); Median contract rent: $395 per month (2008-2012 5-year est.); Median year structure built: 1967 (2008-2012 5-year est.).

Health Insurance: 66.1% Private; 38.5% Public; 8.7% None. (2008-2012 5-year est.)

Hospitals: Sparta Community Hospital (39 beds)

Safety: Violent crime rate: 11.7 per 10,000 population; Property crime rate: 366.1 per 10,000 population (2012).

Transportation: Commute to work: 98.7% car, 0.1% public transportation, 1.1% walk, 0.2% work from home (2008-2012 5-year est.); Travel time to

work: 50.1% less than 15 minutes, 25.0% 15 to 30 minutes, 9.1% 30 to 45 minutes, 4.6% 45 to 60 minutes, 11.2% 60 minutes or more (2008-2012 5-year est.)

Airports: Sparta Community Airport (general aviation)

Additional Information Contacts

Sparta Area Chamber of Commerce . . . . (618) 317-7222
http://spartailchamber.com

STEELEVILLE (village). Covers a land area of 1.520 square miles and a water area of 0.008 square miles. Located at 38.01° N. Lat; 89.66° W. Long. Elevation is 413 feet.

History: Incorporated 1851.

Population: 2,059 (1990); 2,077 (2000); 2,083 (2010); Density: 1,308.4 persons per square mile (2008-2012 5-year est.); Race: 97.0% White, 0.0% Black/African American, 0.0% Asian, 0.0% American Indian/Alaska Native, 0.0% Native Hawaiian/Other Pacific Islander, 3.0% Some other race, 2.6% Two or more races, 0.4% Hispanic of any race (2008-2012 5-year est.); Average household size: 2.43 (2008-2012 5-year est.); Median age: 41.0 (2008-2012 5-year est.); Males per 100 females: 92.0 (2008-2012 5-year est.); Marriage status: 21.9% never married, 54.8% now married, 11.7% widowed, 11.6% divorced (2008-2012 5-year est.); Foreign born: 1.3% (2008-2012 5-year est.); Ancestry (includes multiple ancestries): 52.0% German, 7.9% Irish, 6.9% American, 5.1% French, 4.8% Italian (2008-2012 5-year est.).

Economy: Single-family building permits issued: 2 (2013); Multi-family building permits issued: 0 (2013); Homeowner vacancy rate: 4.4%. Rental vacancy rate: 5.9%. (2008-2012 5-year est.); Employment by occupation: 15.7% management, business, and financial, 1.8% computer, engineering, and science, 5.8% education, legal, community service, arts, and media, 4.0% healthcare practitioners, 15.1% service, 29.7% sales and office, 10.1% natural resources, construction, and maintenance, 17.8% production, transportation, and material moving (2008-2012 5-year est.).

Income: Per capita income: $21,452 (2008-2012 5-year est.); Median household income: $41,458 (2008-2012 5-year est.); Average household income: $49,752 (2008-2012 5-year est.); Percent of households with income of $100,000 or more: 9.4% (2008-2012 5-year est.); Poverty rate: 7.8% (2008-2012 5-year est.).

Education: Percent of population age 25 and over with: High school diploma (including GED) or higher: 87.5% (2008-2012 5-year est.); Bachelor's degree or higher: 10.2% (2008-2012 5-year est.); Master's degree or higher: 2.4% (2008-2012 5-year est.).

School District(s)

Steeleville CUSD 138 (PK-12)
2011-12 Enrollment: 437 . . . . (618) 965-3469

Housing: Homeownership rate: 76.4% (2008-2012 5-year est.); Median home value: $88,800 (2008-2012 5-year est.); Median contract rent: $423 per month (2008-2012 5-year est.); Median year structure built: 1960 (2008-2012 5-year est.).

Health Insurance: 75.4% Private; 33.2% Public; 9.0% None. (2008-2012 5-year est.)

Transportation: Commute to work: 95.0% car, 0.6% public transportation, 1.3% walk, 2.4% work from home (2008-2012 5-year est.); Travel time to work: 48.4% less than 15 minutes, 30.7% 15 to 30 minutes, 8.3% 30 to 45 minutes, 4.6% 45 to 60 minutes, 8.0% 60 minutes or more (2008-2012 5-year est.)

Additional Information Contacts

Steeleville Chamber of Commerce . . . . (618) 965-3134

TILDEN (village). Covers a land area of 0.974 square miles and a water area of 0.011 square miles. Located at 38.21° N. Lat; 89.68° W. Long. Elevation is 525 feet.

Population: 919 (1990); 922 (2000); 934 (2010); Density: 800.6 persons per square mile (2008-2012 5-year est.); Race: 94.4% White, 5.6% Black/African American, 0.0% Asian, 0.0% American Indian/Alaska Native, 0.0% Native Hawaiian/Other Pacific Islander, 0.0% Some other race, 0.0% Two or more races, 1.8% Hispanic of any race (2008-2012 5-year est.); Average household size: 2.81 (2008-2012 5-year est.); Median age: 48.0 (2008-2012 5-year est.); Males per 100 females: 117.9 (2008-2012 5-year est.); Marriage status: 18.6% never married, 63.3% now married, 10.3% widowed, 7.8% divorced (2008-2012 5-year est.); Foreign born: 1.8% (2008-2012 5-year est.); Ancestry (includes multiple ancestries): 27.9% German, 19.1% Irish, 13.5% English, 8.3% American, 7.9% Italian (2008-2012 5-year est.).

Economy: Homeowner vacancy rate: 4.4%. Rental vacancy rate: 10.0%. (2008-2012 5-year est.); Employment by occupation: 3.7% management,

business, and financial, 3.7% computer, engineering, and science, 2.6% education, legal, community service, arts, and media, 2.6% healthcare practitioners, 22.9% service, 25.8% sales and office, 19.6% natural resources, construction, and maintenance, 19.2% production, transportation, and material moving (2008-2012 5-year est.).

Income: Per capita income: $18,935 (2008-2012 5-year est.); Median household income: $33,750 (2008-2012 5-year est.); Average household income: $47,782 (2008-2012 5-year est.); Percent of households with income of $100,000 or more: 8.6% (2008-2012 5-year est.); Poverty rate: 23.6% (2008-2012 5-year est.).

Education: Percent of population age 25 and over with: High school diploma (including GED) or higher: 66.1% (2008-2012 5-year est.); Bachelor's degree or higher: 5.5% (2008-2012 5-year est.); Master's degree or higher: 5.5% (2008-2012 5-year est.).

School District(s)

Perandoe Spec Educ District
2011-12 Enrollment: n/a . . . . (618) 282-6251

Housing: Homeownership rate: 70.9% (2008-2012 5-year est.); Median home value: $61,900 (2008-2012 5-year est.); Median contract rent: $393 per month (2008-2012 5-year est.); Median year structure built: 1975 (2008-2012 5-year est.).

Health Insurance: 50.1% Private; 51.7% Public; 13.3% None. (2008-2012 5-year est.)

Transportation: Commute to work: 100.0% car, 0.0% public transportation, 0.0% walk, 0.0% work from home (2008-2012 5-year est.); Travel time to work: 31.0% less than 15 minutes, 21.0% 15 to 30 minutes, 13.7% 30 to 45 minutes, 11.1% 45 to 60 minutes, 23.2% 60 minutes or more (2008-2012 5-year est.)

WALSH (unincorporated postal area)
Zip Code: 62297

Covers a land area of 23.870 square miles and a water area of 0.216 square miles. Located at 38.05° N. Lat; 89.80° W. Long. Elevation is 479 feet. Population: 452 (2010); Density: 18.9 persons per square mile (2010); Race: 99.8% White, 0.2% Black/African American, 0.0% Asian, 0.0% American Indian/Alaska Native, 0.0% Native Hawaiian/Other Pacific Islander, 0.0% Some other race, 0.0% Two or more races, 0.4% Hispanic of any race (2010); Average household size: 2.39 (2010); Median age: 46.4 (2010); Males per 100 females: 103.6 (2010); Homeownership rate: 84.7% (2010)

Richland County

Located in southeastern Illinois; bounded partly on the west by the Little Wabash River; drained by the Fox River and Bonpas Creek. Covers a land area of 359.990 square miles, a water area of 1.906 square miles, and is located in the Central Time Zone at 38.71° N. Lat., 88.09° W. Long. The county was founded in 1841. County seat is Olney.

Weather Station: Olney 2 S   Elevation: 479 feet

	Jan	Feb	Mar	Apr	May	Jun	Jul	Aug	Sep	Oct	Nov	Dec
High	39	44	54	66	76	85	88	87	81	69	55	42
Low	22	26	34	44	54	63	66	65	57	45	36	26
Precip	3.2	2.7	4.4	4.4	5.6	4.1	4.2	3.3	3.2	4.0	4.5	3.9
Snow	4.3	3.0	1.4	tr	0.0	0.0	0.0	0.0	0.0	tr	0.5	3.7

High and Low temperatures in degrees Fahrenheit; Precipitation and Snow in inches

Population: 16,545 (1990); 16,149 (2000); 16,233 (2010); Race: 97.1% White, 0.4% Black/African American, 1.2% Asian, 0.1% American Indian/Alaska Native, 0.0% Native Hawaiian/Other Pacific Islander, 1.2% Some other race, 1.1% Two or more races, 0.8% Hispanic of any race (2008-2012 5-year est.); Density: 45.0 persons per square mile (2008-2012 5-year est.); Average household size: 2.40 (2008-2012 5-year est.); Median age: 43.6 (2008-2012 5-year est.); Males per 100 females: 96.0 (2008-2012 5-year est.).

Religion: Six largest groups: 16.6% Catholicism, 13.5% Baptist, 7.1% Methodist/Pietist, 6.8% Non-denominational Protestant, 3.4% Lutheran, 2.3% Latter-day Saints (2010)

Economy: Unemployment rate: 7.0% (April 2014); Total civilian labor force: 6,863 (April 2014); Leading industries: 19.6% health care and social assistance; 19.3% transportation & warehousing; 14.1% retail trade (2012); Farms: 554 totaling 188,883 acres (2012); Companies that employ 500 or more persons: 1 (2012); Companies that employ 100 to 499 persons: 3 (2012); Companies that employ less than 100 persons: 452 (2012); Black-owned businesses: n/a (2007); Hispanic-owned businesses: n/a (2007); Asian-owned businesses: n/a (2007); Women-owned

businesses: 320 (2007); Single-family building permits issued: 4 (2013); Multi-family building permits issued: 0 (2013).

Income: Per capita income: $23,236 (2008-2012 5-year est.); Median household income: $43,240 (2008-2012 5-year est.); Average household income: $55,124 (2008-2012 5-year est.); Percent of households with income of $100,000 or more: 13.9% (2008-2012 5-year est.); Poverty rate: 14.0% (2008-2012 5-year est.); Bankruptcy rate: 1.92% (2013).

Education: Percent of population age 25 and over with: High school diploma (including GED) or higher: 89.5% (2008-2012 5-year est.); Bachelor's degree or higher: 19.6% (2008-2012 5-year est.); Master's degree or higher: 5.3% (2008-2012 5-year est.).

Housing: Homeownership rate: 77.4% (2008-2012 5-year est.); Median home value: $79,400 (2008-2012 5-year est.); Median contract rent: $404 per month (2008-2012 5-year est.); Median year structure built: 1970 (2008-2012 5-year est.).

Health: Birth rate: 130.4 per 10,000 population (2013); Death rate: 113.1 per 10,000 population (2013); Age-adjusted cancer mortality rate: 180.9 deaths per 100,000 population (2011); Number of physicians: 19.1 per 10,000 population (2011); Hospital beds: 55.4 per 10,000 population (2010); Hospital admissions: 1,884.4 per 10,000 population (2010).

Elections: 2012 Presidential election results: 32.4% Obama, 65.3% Romney

Additional Information Contacts

Richland County Government . . . . (618) 392-3111

Olney and The Greater Richland County Chamber of Commerce . . . (618) 392-2241

  http://www.olneychamber.com

Richland County Communities

CALHOUN (village). Covers a land area of 1.056 square miles and a water area of 0 square miles. Located at 38.65° N. Lat; 88.04° W. Long. Elevation is 541 feet.

Population: 232 (1990); 222 (2000); 172 (2010); Density: 158.1 persons per square mile (2008-2012 5-year est.); Race: 96.4% White, 0.0% Black/African American, 0.0% Asian, 0.0% American Indian/Alaska Native, 0.0% Native Hawaiian/Other Pacific Islander, 3.6% Some other race, 3.6% Two or more races, 0.0% Hispanic of any race (2008-2012 5-year est.); Average household size: 2.23 (2008-2012 5-year est.); Median age: 56.3 (2008-2012 5-year est.); Males per 100 females: 131.9 (2008-2012 5-year est.); Marriage status: 15.1% never married, 57.2% now married, 7.9% widowed, 19.7% divorced (2008-2012 5-year est.); Foreign born: 0.0% (2008-2012 5-year est.); Ancestry (includes multiple ancestries): 26.3% German, 20.4% Irish, 14.4% American, 12.0% English, 2.4% Scottish (2008-2012 5-year est.).

Economy: Homeowner vacancy rate: 7.7%. Rental vacancy rate: 0.0%. (2008-2012 5-year est.); Employment by occupation: 2.3% management, business, and financial, 2.3% computer, engineering, and science, 0.0% education, legal, community service, arts, and media, 9.1% healthcare practitioners, 8.0% service, 20.5% sales and office, 30.7% natural resources, construction, and maintenance, 27.3% production, transportation, and material moving (2008-2012 5-year est.).

Income: Per capita income: $23,269 (2008-2012 5-year est.); Median household income: $54,375 (2008-2012 5-year est.); Average household income: $52,604 (2008-2012 5-year est.); Percent of households with income of $100,000 or more: 6.7% (2008-2012 5-year est.); Poverty rate: 13.8% (2008-2012 5-year est.).

Education: Percent of population age 25 and over with: High school diploma (including GED) or higher: 91.6% (2008-2012 5-year est.); Bachelor's degree or higher: 4.9% (2008-2012 5-year est.); Master's degree or higher: 1.4% (2008-2012 5-year est.).

Housing: Homeownership rate: 96.0% (2008-2012 5-year est.); Median home value: $56,000 (2008-2012 5-year est.); Median contract rent: n/a per month (2008-2012 5-year est.); Median year structure built: 1973 (2008-2012 5-year est.).

Health Insurance: 67.1% Private; 38.3% Public; 8.4% None. (2008-2012 5-year est.)

Transportation: Commute to work: 90.1% car, 0.0% public transportation, 0.0% walk, 9.9% work from home (2008-2012 5-year est.); Travel time to work: 28.8% less than 15 minutes, 64.4% 15 to 30 minutes, 0.0% 30 to 45 minutes, 2.7% 45 to 60 minutes, 4.1% 60 minutes or more (2008-2012 5-year est.)

CLAREMONT (village). Covers a land area of 1.144 square miles and a water area of 0 square miles. Located at 38.72° N. Lat; 87.97° W. Long. Elevation is 509 feet.

Population: 256 (1990); 212 (2000); 176 (2010); Density: 176.5 persons per square mile (2008-2012 5-year est.); Race: 98.0% White, 0.0% Black/African American, 0.0% Asian, 0.0% American Indian/Alaska Native, 0.0% Native Hawaiian/Other Pacific Islander, 2.0% Some other race, 2.0% Two or more races, 0.0% Hispanic of any race (2008-2012 5-year est.); Average household size: 2.06 (2008-2012 5-year est.); Median age: 52.2 (2008-2012 5-year est.); Males per 100 females: 102.0 (2008-2012 5-year est.); Marriage status: 15.3% never married, 59.0% now married, 7.7% widowed, 18.0% divorced (2008-2012 5-year est.); Foreign born: 0.0% (2008-2012 5-year est.); Ancestry (includes multiple ancestries): 21.3% German, 10.4% English, 8.9% American, 6.9% Irish, 5.9% Dutch (2008-2012 5-year est.).

Economy: Homeowner vacancy rate: 0.0%. Rental vacancy rate: 0.0%. (2008-2012 5-year est.); Employment by occupation: 3.8% management, business, and financial, 0.0% computer, engineering, and science, 6.7% education, legal, community service, arts, and media, 0.0% healthcare practitioners, 21.2% service, 34.6% sales and office, 6.7% natural resources, construction, and maintenance, 26.9% production, transportation, and material moving (2008-2012 5-year est.).

Income: Per capita income: $21,150 (2008-2012 5-year est.); Median household income: $33,750 (2008-2012 5-year est.); Average household income: $42,328 (2008-2012 5-year est.); Percent of households with income of $100,000 or more: 9.2% (2008-2012 5-year est.); Poverty rate: 21.3% (2008-2012 5-year est.).

Education: Percent of population age 25 and over with: High school diploma (including GED) or higher: 85.1% (2008-2012 5-year est.); Bachelor's degree or higher: 16.1% (2008-2012 5-year est.); Master's degree or higher: 4.3% (2008-2012 5-year est.).

Housing: Homeownership rate: 92.9% (2008-2012 5-year est.); Median home value: $53,500 (2008-2012 5-year est.); Median contract rent: $313 per month (2008-2012 5-year est.); Median year structure built: 1962 (2008-2012 5-year est.).

Health Insurance: 68.8% Private; 37.1% Public; 15.8% None. (2008-2012 5-year est.)

Transportation: Commute to work: 95.0% car, 0.0% public transportation, 2.0% walk, 3.0% work from home (2008-2012 5-year est.); Travel time to work: 64.9% less than 15 minutes, 17.5% 15 to 30 minutes, 12.4% 30 to 45 minutes, 2.1% 45 to 60 minutes, 3.1% 60 minutes or more (2008-2012 5-year est.)

DUNDAS (unincorporated postal area)

Zip Code: 62425

  Covers a land area of 41.813 square miles and a water area of 0.057 square miles. Located at 38.83° N. Lat; 88.09° W. Long. Elevation is 472 feet. Population: 649 (2010); Density: 15.5 persons per square mile (2010); Race: 98.2% White, 0.2% Black/African American, 0.3% Asian, 0.6% American Indian/Alaska Native, 0.0% Native Hawaiian/Other Pacific Islander, 0.7% Some other race, 0.5% Two or more races, 0.8% Hispanic of any race (2010); Average household size: 2.54 (2010); Median age: 43.3 (2010); Males per 100 females: 101.6 (2010); Homeownership rate: 87.1% (2010)

NOBLE (village). Covers a land area of 1.024 square miles and a water area of 0.005 square miles. Located at 38.70° N. Lat; 88.22° W. Long. Elevation is 476 feet.

Population: 756 (1990); 746 (2000); 677 (2010); Density: 608.3 persons per square mile (2008-2012 5-year est.); Race: 97.4% White, 0.2% Black/African American, 0.6% Asian, 0.0% American Indian/Alaska Native, 0.0% Native Hawaiian/Other Pacific Islander, 1.8% Some other race, 1.8% Two or more races, 0.0% Hispanic of any race (2008-2012 5-year est.); Average household size: 2.48 (2008-2012 5-year est.); Median age: 38.3 (2008-2012 5-year est.); Males per 100 females: 107.0 (2008-2012 5-year est.); Marriage status: 23.8% never married, 56.9% now married, 10.9% widowed, 8.4% divorced (2008-2012 5-year est.); Foreign born: 0.6% (2008-2012 5-year est.); Ancestry (includes multiple ancestries): 19.9% German, 11.7% American, 9.8% Irish, 5.1% English, 1.9% Dutch (2008-2012 5-year est.).

Economy: Single-family building permits issued: 0 (2013); Multi-family building permits issued: 0 (2013); Homeowner vacancy rate: 0.0%. Rental vacancy rate: 17.5%. (2008-2012 5-year est.); Employment by occupation: 8.3% management, business, and financial, 1.3% computer, engineering, and science, 2.5% education, legal, community service, arts, and media,

5.0% healthcare practitioners, 15.8% service, 27.5% sales and office, 10.8% natural resources, construction, and maintenance, 28.7% production, transportation, and material moving (2008-2012 5-year est.).
Income: Per capita income: $22,819 (2008-2012 5-year est.); Median household income: $31,813 (2008-2012 5-year est.); Average household income: $55,779 (2008-2012 5-year est.); Percent of households with income of $100,000 or more: 8.4% (2008-2012 5-year est.); Poverty rate: 16.5% (2008-2012 5-year est.).
Education: Percent of population age 25 and over with: High school diploma (including GED) or higher: 76.2% (2008-2012 5-year est.); Bachelor's degree or higher: 7.8% (2008-2012 5-year est.); Master's degree or higher: 0.0% (2008-2012 5-year est.).

School District(s)
West Richland CUSD 2 (PK-12)
    2011-12 Enrollment: 381 . . . . (618) 723-2334
Housing: Homeownership rate: 79.3% (2008-2012 5-year est.); Median home value: $47,400 (2008-2012 5-year est.); Median contract rent: $377 per month (2008-2012 5-year est.); Median year structure built: 1962 (2008-2012 5-year est.).
Health Insurance: 49.4% Private; 47.0% Public; 23.9% None. (2008-2012 5-year est.)
Transportation: Commute to work: 94.2% car, 0.0% public transportation, 1.3% walk, 1.7% work from home (2008-2012 5-year est.); Travel time to work: 29.2% less than 15 minutes, 38.1% 15 to 30 minutes, 23.3% 30 to 45 minutes, 3.8% 45 to 60 minutes, 5.5% 60 minutes or more (2008-2012 5-year est.)
Airports: Olney-Noble Airport (general aviation)

OLNEY (city). County seat. Covers a land area of 6.657 square miles and a water area of 0.004 square miles. Located at 38.73° N. Lat; 88.08° W. Long. Elevation is 479 feet.

History: Olney was named for John Olney, lawyer and officer in the Civil War. It developed as a shipping and trading center, and as the seat of Richland County. In 1902 a naturalist brought a pair of albino squirrels to Olney and set them loose. Soon Olney became known as "the home of white squirrels," as thousands of these squirrels took up residence in the parks and gardens.
Population: 8,664 (1990); 8,631 (2000); 9,115 (2010); Density: 1,356.8 persons per square mile (2008-2012 5-year est.); Race: 96.0% White, 0.6% Black/African American, 2.2% Asian, 0.0% American Indian/Alaska Native, 0.0% Native Hawaiian/Other Pacific Islander, 1.2% Some other race, 1.0% Two or more races, 0.6% Hispanic of any race (2008-2012 5-year est.); Average household size: 2.31 (2008-2012 5-year est.); Median age: 40.9 (2008-2012 5-year est.); Males per 100 females: 87.0 (2008-2012 5-year est.); Marriage status: 23.0% never married, 50.1% now married, 11.4% widowed, 15.6% divorced (2008-2012 5-year est.); Foreign born: 3.5% (2008-2012 5-year est.); Ancestry (includes multiple ancestries): 23.9% German, 10.5% English, 9.6% Irish, 8.5% American, 2.2% Dutch (2008-2012 5-year est.).
Economy: Single-family building permits issued: 4 (2013); Multi-family building permits issued: 0 (2013); Homeowner vacancy rate: 3.8%. Rental vacancy rate: 5.8%. (2008-2012 5-year est.); Employment by occupation: 10.6% management, business, and financial, 2.4% computer, engineering, and science, 11.5% education, legal, community service, arts, and media, 6.4% healthcare practitioners, 18.1% service, 20.4% sales and office, 11.1% natural resources, construction, and maintenance, 19.5% production, transportation, and material moving (2008-2012 5-year est.).
Income: Per capita income: $21,396 (2008-2012 5-year est.); Median household income: $36,558 (2008-2012 5-year est.); Average household income: $48,964 (2008-2012 5-year est.); Percent of households with income of $100,000 or more: 12.3% (2008-2012 5-year est.); Poverty rate: 17.3% (2008-2012 5-year est.).
Education: Percent of population age 25 and over with: High school diploma (including GED) or higher: 88.7% (2008-2012 5-year est.); Bachelor's degree or higher: 21.2% (2008-2012 5-year est.); Master's degree or higher: 6.7% (2008-2012 5-year est.).

School District(s)
East Richland CUSD 1 (PK-12)
    2011-12 Enrollment: 2,152 . . . . (618) 395-2324

Two-year College(s)
Illinois Eastern Community Colleges-Olney Central College (Public)
    Fall 2012 Enrollment: 1,477 . . . . (618) 393-2982
    2012-13 Tuition: In-state $8,361; Out-of-state $10,412
Housing: Homeownership rate: 69.4% (2008-2012 5-year est.); Median home value: $68,800 (2008-2012 5-year est.); Median contract rent: $403

per month (2008-2012 5-year est.); Median year structure built: 1964 (2008-2012 5-year est.).
Health Insurance: 65.5% Private; 42.9% Public; 11.7% None. (2008-2012 5-year est.)
Hospitals: Richland Memorial Hospital (135 beds)
Safety: Violent crime rate: 38.4 per 10,000 population; Property crime rate: 324.4 per 10,000 population (2012).
Transportation: Commute to work: 90.8% car, 0.8% public transportation, 2.8% walk, 3.5% work from home (2008-2012 5-year est.); Travel time to work: 64.8% less than 15 minutes, 13.7% 15 to 30 minutes, 11.1% 30 to 45 minutes, 4.9% 45 to 60 minutes, 5.6% 60 minutes or more (2008-2012 5-year est.)
Airports: Olney-Noble Airport (general aviation)
Additional Information Contacts
City of Olney . . . . (618) 395-7302
    http://www.ci.olney.il.us
Olney and The Greater Richland County Chamber of Commerce . . . (618) 392-2241
    http://www.olneychamber.com

PARKERSBURG (village). Covers a land area of 0.751 square miles and a water area of 0 square miles. Located at 38.59° N. Lat; 88.06° W. Long. Elevation is 479 feet.

Population: 211 (1990); 234 (2000); 199 (2010); Density: 331.5 persons per square mile (2008-2012 5-year est.); Race: 100.0% White, 0.0% Black/African American, 0.0% Asian, 0.0% American Indian/Alaska Native, 0.0% Native Hawaiian/Other Pacific Islander, 0.0% Some other race, 0.0% Two or more races, 0.0% Hispanic of any race (2008-2012 5-year est.); Average household size: 2.62 (2008-2012 5-year est.); Median age: 44.6 (2008-2012 5-year est.); Males per 100 females: 100.8 (2008-2012 5-year est.); Marriage status: 28.2% never married, 46.9% now married, 8.9% widowed, 16.0% divorced (2008-2012 5-year est.); Foreign born: 0.0% (2008-2012 5-year est.); Ancestry (includes multiple ancestries): 11.2% German, 10.8% American, 10.0% Irish, 7.2% English, 2.4% Italian (2008-2012 5-year est.).
Economy: Homeowner vacancy rate: 0.0%. Rental vacancy rate: 64.3%. (2008-2012 5-year est.); Employment by occupation: 4.0% management, business, and financial, 0.0% computer, engineering, and science, 2.0% education, legal, community service, arts, and media, 2.0% healthcare practitioners, 10.2% service, 16.2% sales and office, 11.1% natural resources, construction, and maintenance, 45.5% production, transportation, and material moving (2008-2012 5-year est.).
Income: Per capita income: $22,716 (2008-2012 5-year est.); Median household income: $35,208 (2008-2012 5-year est.); Average household income: $54,633 (2008-2012 5-year est.); Percent of households with income of $100,000 or more: 21.1% (2008-2012 5-year est.); Poverty rate: 14.9% (2008-2012 5-year est.).
Education: Percent of population age 25 and over with: High school diploma (including GED) or higher: 77.8% (2008-2012 5-year est.); Bachelor's degree or higher: 0.0% (2008-2012 5-year est.); Master's degree or higher: 0.0% (2008-2012 5-year est.).
Housing: Homeownership rate: 94.7% (2008-2012 5-year est.); Median home value: $36,400 (2008-2012 5-year est.); Median contract rent: $350 per month (2008-2012 5-year est.); Median year structure built: 1968 (2008-2012 5-year est.).
Health Insurance: 41.8% Private; 56.2% Public; 12.9% None. (2008-2012 5-year est.)
Transportation: Commute to work: 92.9% car, 0.0% public transportation, 0.0% walk, 7.1% work from home (2008-2012 5-year est.); Travel time to work: 26.4% less than 15 minutes, 67.0% 15 to 30 minutes, 5.5% 30 to 45 minutes, 0.0% 45 to 60 minutes, 1.1% 60 minutes or more (2008-2012 5-year est.)

Rock Island County

Located in northwestern Illinois; bounded on the north and west by the Mississippi River and the Iowa border, and partly on the east by the Rock River. Covers a land area of 427.636 square miles, a water area of 23.652 square miles, and is located in the Central Time Zone at 41.47° N. Lat., 90.57° W. Long. The county was founded in 1831. County seat is Rock Island.

Rock Island County is part of the Davenport-Moline-Rock Island, IA-IL Metropolitan Statistical Area. The entire metro area includes: Henry County, IL; Mercer County, IL; Rock Island County, IL; Scott County, IA

Weather Station: Moline Quad City Arpt   Elevation: 591 feet

	Jan	Feb	Mar	Apr	May	Jun	Jul	Aug	Sep	Oct	Nov	Dec
High	31	36	49	62	73	82	86	84	77	64	49	35
Low	15	19	29	40	50	60	65	63	54	42	31	19
Precip	1.5	1.6	2.8	3.5	4.3	4.4	4.2	4.6	3.0	3.0	2.5	2.2
Snow	9.2	6.7	4.1	1.2	tr	tr	tr	0.0	tr	0.1	1.2	8.8

High and Low temperatures in degrees Fahrenheit; Precipitation and Snow in inches

Weather Station: Rock Island L&D 15   Elevation: 567 feet

	Jan	Feb	Mar	Apr	May	Jun	Jul	Aug	Sep	Oct	Nov	Dec
High	32	36	49	62	72	81	84	83	77	64	49	35
Low	17	20	31	42	53	64	68	66	57	45	33	20
Precip	1.5	1.6	2.6	3.6	4.9	5.1	4.1	3.9	2.8	2.7	2.4	1.9
Snow	na	na	0.6	0.1	0.0	0.0	0.0	0.0	0.0	tr	0.5	na

High and Low temperatures in degrees Fahrenheit; Precipitation and Snow in inches

Population: 148,723 (1990); 149,374 (2000); 147,546 (2010); Race: 81.6% White, 9.1% Black/African American, 1.7% Asian, 0.3% American Indian/Alaska Native, 0.0% Native Hawaiian/Other Pacific Islander, 7.3% Some other race, 2.7% Two or more races, 11.6% Hispanic of any race (2008-2012 5-year est.); Density: 345.0 persons per square mile (2008-2012 5-year est.); Average household size: 2.36 (2008-2012 5-year est.); Median age: 40.1 (2008-2012 5-year est.); Males per 100 females: 96.2 (2008-2012 5-year est.).

Religion: Six largest groups: 12.4% Catholicism, 6.2% Lutheran, 5.7% Baptist, 3.6% Methodist/Pietist, 3.2% Presbyterian-Reformed, 2.8% Holiness (2010)

Economy: Unemployment rate: 6.3% (April 2014); Total civilian labor force: 75,821 (April 2014); Leading industries: 14.6% health care and social assistance; 13.5% manufacturing; 12.9% retail trade (2012); Farms: 666 totaling 149,186 acres (2012); Companies that employ 500 or more persons: 10 (2012); Companies that employ 100 to 499 persons: 77 (2012); Companies that employ less than 100 persons: 3,198 (2012); Black-owned businesses: 482 (2007); Hispanic-owned businesses: 272 (2007); Asian-owned businesses: n/a (2007); Women-owned businesses: 2,749 (2007); Single-family building permits issued: 74 (2013); Multi-family building permits issued: 83 (2013).

Income: Per capita income: $26,284 (2008-2012 5-year est.); Median household income: $48,205 (2008-2012 5-year est.); Average household income: $62,182 (2008-2012 5-year est.); Percent of households with income of $100,000 or more: 15.3% (2008-2012 5-year est.); Poverty rate: 11.9% (2008-2012 5-year est.); Bankruptcy rate: 2.96% (2013).

Taxes: Total county taxes per capita: $169 (2011); County property taxes per capita: $151 (2011).

Education: Percent of population age 25 and over with: High school diploma (including GED) or higher: 87.1% (2008-2012 5-year est.); Bachelor's degree or higher: 21.5% (2008-2012 5-year est.); Master's degree or higher: 7.3% (2008-2012 5-year est.).

Housing: Homeownership rate: 70.9% (2008-2012 5-year est.); Median home value: $114,000 (2008-2012 5-year est.); Median contract rent: $529 per month (2008-2012 5-year est.); Median year structure built: 1959 (2008-2012 5-year est.)

Health: Birth rate: 123.9 per 10,000 population (2013); Death rate: 96.8 per 10,000 population (2013); Age-adjusted cancer mortality rate: 187.1 deaths per 100,000 population (2011); Number of physicians: 17.0 per 10,000 population (2011); Hospital beds: 28.3 per 10,000 population (2010); Hospital admissions: 1,391.6 per 10,000 population (2010).

Environment: Air Quality Index: 92.7% good, 7.3% moderate, 0.0% unhealthy for sensitive individuals, 0.0% unhealthy (percent of days in 2013)

Elections: 2012 Presidential election results: 60.2% Obama, 38.4% Romney

National and State Parks: Black Hawk State Historical Site; Campbells Island State Park

Additional Information Contacts
Rock Island County Government . . . . (309) 558-3569
    http://www.rockislandcounty.org

Rock Island County Communities

ANDALUSIA (village). Covers a land area of 1.185 square miles and a water area of <.001 square miles. Located at 41.44° N. Lat; 90.72° W. Long. Elevation is 574 feet.

History: Andalusia was the location on the Mississippi River of Clark's Ferry which gave passage to Buffalo, Iowa, to thousands of settlers in the 1830's.

Population: 1,052 (1990); 1,050 (2000); 1,178 (2010); Density: 1,182.7 persons per square mile (2008-2012 5-year est.); Race: 98.9% White, 0.9% Black/African American, 0.2% Asian, 0.0% American Indian/Alaska Native, 0.0% Native Hawaiian/Other Pacific Islander, 0.0% Some other race, 0.0% Two or more races, 0.6% Hispanic of any race (2008-2012 5-year est.); Average household size: 2.73 (2008-2012 5-year est.); Median age: 42.3 (2008-2012 5-year est.); Males per 100 females: 103.9 (2008-2012 5-year est.); Marriage status: 25.1% never married, 57.5% now married, 7.1% widowed, 10.3% divorced (2008-2012 5-year est.); Foreign born: 0.4% (2008-2012 5-year est.); Ancestry (includes multiple ancestries): 42.0% German, 17.0% Irish, 7.9% Swedish, 7.6% English, 5.4% American (2008-2012 5-year est.).

Economy: Single-family building permits issued: 0 (2013); Multi-family building permits issued: 0 (2013); Homeowner vacancy rate: 1.4%. Rental vacancy rate: 7.9%. (2008-2012 5-year est.); Employment by occupation: 12.2% management, business, and financial, 3.7% computer, engineering, and science, 5.3% education, legal, community service, arts, and media, 1.8% healthcare practitioners, 19.8% service, 34.2% sales and office, 9.0% natural resources, construction, and maintenance, 14.1% production, transportation, and material moving (2008-2012 5-year est.).

Income: Per capita income: $27,082 (2008-2012 5-year est.); Median household income: $65,769 (2008-2012 5-year est.); Average household income: $73,381 (2008-2012 5-year est.); Percent of households with income of $100,000 or more: 18.6% (2008-2012 5-year est.); Poverty rate: 4.4% (2008-2012 5-year est.).

Education: Percent of population age 25 and over with: High school diploma (including GED) or higher: 92.2% (2008-2012 5-year est.); Bachelor's degree or higher: 18.8% (2008-2012 5-year est.); Master's degree or higher: 3.6% (2008-2012 5-year est.).

School District(s)
Rockridge CUSD 300 (PK-12)
    2011-12 Enrollment: 1,231 . . . . (309) 793-8001

Housing: Homeownership rate: 93.2% (2008-2012 5-year est.); Median home value: $118,900 (2008-2012 5-year est.); Median contract rent: $498 per month (2008-2012 5-year est.); Median year structure built: 1968 (2008-2012 5-year est.).

Health Insurance: 86.6% Private; 20.7% Public; 5.0% None. (2008-2012 5-year est.)

Transportation: Commute to work: 98.0% car, 0.0% public transportation, 0.4% walk, 1.1% work from home (2008-2012 5-year est.); Travel time to work: 20.3% less than 15 minutes, 51.4% 15 to 30 minutes, 20.5% 30 to 45 minutes, 2.9% 45 to 60 minutes, 4.9% 60 minutes or more (2008-2012 5-year est.)

BARSTOW (unincorporated postal area)
Zip Code: 61236
    Covers a land area of 1.490 square miles and a water area of 0.055 square miles. Located at 41.51° N. Lat; 90.36° W. Long. Elevation is 574 feet. Population: 193 (2010); Density: 129.5 persons per square mile (2010); Race: 89.1% White, 0.0% Black/African American, 0.5% Asian, 3.6% American Indian/Alaska Native, 0.0% Native Hawaiian/Other Pacific Islander, 6.8% Some other race, 5.2% Two or more races, 9.3% Hispanic of any race (2010); Average household size: 2.68 (2010); Median age: 32.4 (2010); Males per 100 females: 109.8 (2010); Homeownership rate: 91.7% (2010)

CARBON CLIFF (village). Covers a land area of 2.048 square miles and a water area of 0 square miles. Located at 41.50° N. Lat; 90.39° W. Long. Elevation is 604 feet.

Population: 1,492 (1990); 1,689 (2000); 2,134 (2010); Density: 1,069.1 persons per square mile (2008-2012 5-year est.); Race: 78.5% White, 10.3% Black/African American, 1.4% Asian, 1.2% American Indian/Alaska Native, 0.0% Native Hawaiian/Other Pacific Islander, 8.6% Some other race, 4.1% Two or more races, 9.0% Hispanic of any race (2008-2012 5-year est.); Average household size: 2.61 (2008-2012 5-year est.); Median age: 32.0 (2008-2012 5-year est.); Males per 100 females: 95.4 (2008-2012 5-year est.); Marriage status: 28.5% never married, 51.7% now married, 5.4% widowed, 14.4% divorced (2008-2012 5-year est.); Foreign born: 4.0% (2008-2012 5-year est.); Ancestry (includes multiple ancestries): 21.4% German, 15.0% Irish, 7.2% Belgian, 6.5% Swedish, 5.8% English (2008-2012 5-year est.).

Economy: Single-family building permits issued: 0 (2013); Multi-family building permits issued: 0 (2013); Homeowner vacancy rate: 2.0%. Rental vacancy rate: 5.3%. (2008-2012 5-year est.); Employment by occupation: 12.0% management, business, and financial, 0.6% computer, engineering,

and science, 3.1% education, legal, community service, arts, and media, 2.3% healthcare practitioners, 21.8% service, 24.6% sales and office, 10.4% natural resources, construction, and maintenance, 25.1% production, transportation, and material moving (2008-2012 5-year est.).
Income: Per capita income: $20,865 (2008-2012 5-year est.); Median household income: $38,333 (2008-2012 5-year est.); Average household income: $54,148 (2008-2012 5-year est.); Percent of households with income of $100,000 or more: 13.3% (2008-2012 5-year est.); Poverty rate: 14.8% (2008-2012 5-year est.).
Education: Percent of population age 25 and over with: High school diploma (including GED) or higher: 85.0% (2008-2012 5-year est.); Bachelor's degree or higher: 10.8% (2008-2012 5-year est.); Master's degree or higher: 3.0% (2008-2012 5-year est.).

School District(s)
Black Hawk Area Sp Ed District (07-12)
    2011-12 Enrollment: n/a . . . . (309) 796-2500
Housing: Homeownership rate: 62.5% (2008-2012 5-year est.); Median home value: $103,800 (2008-2012 5-year est.); Median contract rent: $547 per month (2008-2012 5-year est.); Median year structure built: 1967 (2008-2012 5-year est.).
Health Insurance: 59.4% Private; 46.4% Public; 12.0% None. (2008-2012 5-year est.)
Transportation: Commute to work: 94.5% car, 0.8% public transportation, 2.2% walk, 1.0% work from home (2008-2012 5-year est.); Travel time to work: 24.9% less than 15 minutes, 48.5% 15 to 30 minutes, 20.5% 30 to 45 minutes, 1.4% 45 to 60 minutes, 4.8% 60 minutes or more (2008-2012 5-year est.).

COAL VALLEY (village). Covers a land area of 2.756 square miles and a water area of 0 square miles. Located at 41.45° N. Lat; 90.46° W. Long. Elevation is 623 feet.
Population: 2,683 (1990); 3,606 (2000); 3,743 (2010); Density: 1,354.4 persons per square mile (2008-2012 5-year est.); Race: 96.3% White, 1.8% Black/African American, 0.2% Asian, 0.8% American Indian/Alaska Native, 0.0% Native Hawaiian/Other Pacific Islander, 0.9% Some other race, 0.7% Two or more races, 1.3% Hispanic of any race (2008-2012 5-year est.); Average household size: 2.76 (2008-2012 5-year est.); Median age: 42.5 (2008-2012 5-year est.); Males per 100 females: 100.8 (2008-2012 5-year est.); Marriage status: 18.5% never married, 63.3% now married, 4.1% widowed, 14.1% divorced (2008-2012 5-year est.); Foreign born: 1.1% (2008-2012 5-year est.); Ancestry (includes multiple ancestries): 26.2% German, 20.0% Irish, 10.0% English, 8.4% Swedish, 5.7% Italian (2008-2012 5-year est.).
Economy: Single-family building permits issued: 14 (2013); Multi-family building permits issued: 0 (2013); Homeowner vacancy rate: 0.0%. Rental vacancy rate: 0.0%. (2008-2012 5-year est.); Employment by occupation: 16.4% management, business, and financial, 5.3% computer, engineering, and science, 7.7% education, legal, community service, arts, and media, 7.8% healthcare practitioners, 11.7% service, 28.0% sales and office, 9.6% natural resources, construction, and maintenance, 13.4% production, transportation, and material moving (2008-2012 5-year est.).
Income: Per capita income: $34,671 (2008-2012 5-year est.); Median household income: $72,904 (2008-2012 5-year est.); Average household income: $92,903 (2008-2012 5-year est.); Percent of households with income of $100,000 or more: 34.0% (2008-2012 5-year est.); Poverty rate: 6.8% (2008-2012 5-year est.).
Education: Percent of population age 25 and over with: High school diploma (including GED) or higher: 95.4% (2008-2012 5-year est.); Bachelor's degree or higher: 27.3% (2008-2012 5-year est.); Master's degree or higher: 11.0% (2008-2012 5-year est.).

School District(s)
Moline USD 40 (PK-12)
    2011-12 Enrollment: 7,429 . . . . (309) 743-1600
Housing: Homeownership rate: 94.4% (2008-2012 5-year est.); Median home value: $158,100 (2008-2012 5-year est.); Median contract rent: $603 per month (2008-2012 5-year est.); Median year structure built: 1974 (2008-2012 5-year est.).
Health Insurance: 81.4% Private; 26.8% Public; 5.4% None. (2008-2012 5-year est.)
Safety: Violent crime rate: 8.0 per 10,000 population; Property crime rate: 106.8 per 10,000 population (2012).
Transportation: Commute to work: 95.0% car, 0.0% public transportation, 0.9% walk, 4.1% work from home (2008-2012 5-year est.); Travel time to work: 20.5% less than 15 minutes, 63.5% 15 to 30 minutes, 13.9% 30 to

45 minutes, 1.0% 45 to 60 minutes, 1.1% 60 minutes or more (2008-2012 5-year est.)

CORDOVA (village). Covers a land area of 0.598 square miles and a water area of <.001 square miles. Located at 41.68° N. Lat; 90.32° W. Long. Elevation is 591 feet.
Population: 638 (1990); 633 (2000); 672 (2010); Density: 1,147.3 persons per square mile (2008-2012 5-year est.); Race: 96.9% White, 0.1% Black/African American, 2.5% Asian, 0.4% American Indian/Alaska Native, 0.0% Native Hawaiian/Other Pacific Islander, 0.1% Some other race, 0.0% Two or more races, 0.9% Hispanic of any race (2008-2012 5-year est.); Average household size: 2.46 (2008-2012 5-year est.); Median age: 39.8 (2008-2012 5-year est.); Males per 100 females: 141.5 (2008-2012 5-year est.); Marriage status: 24.7% never married, 56.9% now married, 5.4% widowed, 13.0% divorced (2008-2012 5-year est.); Foreign born: 0.6% (2008-2012 5-year est.); Ancestry (includes multiple ancestries): 28.6% German, 17.6% Irish, 12.4% English, 6.4% Swedish, 5.4% Belgian (2008-2012 5-year est.).
Economy: Single-family building permits issued: 2 (2013); Multi-family building permits issued: 0 (2013); Homeowner vacancy rate: 0.0%. Rental vacancy rate: 0.0%. (2008-2012 5-year est.); Employment by occupation: 10.4% management, business, and financial, 1.6% computer, engineering, and science, 9.3% education, legal, community service, arts, and media, 2.4% healthcare practitioners, 19.4% service, 28.7% sales and office, 12.2% natural resources, construction, and maintenance, 16.0% production, transportation, and material moving (2008-2012 5-year est.).
Income: Per capita income: $32,276 (2008-2012 5-year est.); Median household income: $64,643 (2008-2012 5-year est.); Average household income: $75,994 (2008-2012 5-year est.); Percent of households with income of $100,000 or more: 26.6% (2008-2012 5-year est.); Poverty rate: 5.4% (2008-2012 5-year est.).
Education: Percent of population age 25 and over with: High school diploma (including GED) or higher: 96.0% (2008-2012 5-year est.); Bachelor's degree or higher: 20.2% (2008-2012 5-year est.); Master's degree or higher: 8.1% (2008-2012 5-year est.).
Housing: Homeownership rate: 78.4% (2008-2012 5-year est.); Median home value: $146,300 (2008-2012 5-year est.); Median contract rent: $500 per month (2008-2012 5-year est.); Median year structure built: 1969 (2008-2012 5-year est.).
Health Insurance: 87.6% Private; 20.8% Public; 4.8% None. (2008-2012 5-year est.)
Transportation: Commute to work: 98.6% car, 0.8% public transportation, 0.5% walk, 0.0% work from home (2008-2012 5-year est.); Travel time to work: 27.5% less than 15 minutes, 24.8% 15 to 30 minutes, 27.0% 30 to 45 minutes, 10.4% 45 to 60 minutes, 10.4% 60 minutes or more (2008-2012 5-year est.)

COYNE CENTER (CDP). Covers a land area of 1.624 square miles and a water area of 0 square miles. Located at 41.40° N. Lat; 90.56° W. Long. Elevation is 748 feet.
Population: n/a (1990); 906 (2000); 827 (2010); Density: 580.7 persons per square mile (2008-2012 5-year est.); Race: 92.9% White, 5.4% Black/African American, 0.0% Asian, 0.0% American Indian/Alaska Native, 0.0% Native Hawaiian/Other Pacific Islander, 1.7% Some other race, 1.7% Two or more races, 0.0% Hispanic of any race (2008-2012 5-year est.); Average household size: 2.38 (2008-2012 5-year est.); Median age: 50.3 (2008-2012 5-year est.); Males per 100 females: 92.8 (2008-2012 5-year est.); Marriage status: 22.2% never married, 57.4% now married, 6.0% widowed, 14.4% divorced (2008-2012 5-year est.); Foreign born: 2.7% (2008-2012 5-year est.); Ancestry (includes multiple ancestries): 19.7% American, 18.5% German, 14.5% English, 13.8% Irish, 6.0% Belgian (2008-2012 5-year est.).
Economy: Homeowner vacancy rate: 0.0%. Rental vacancy rate: 0.0%. (2008-2012 5-year est.); Employment by occupation: 7.0% management, business, and financial, 7.0% computer, engineering, and science, 5.5% education, legal, community service, arts, and media, 0.0% healthcare practitioners, 12.3% service, 41.2% sales and office, 4.0% natural resources, construction, and maintenance, 22.9% production, transportation, and material moving (2008-2012 5-year est.).
Income: Per capita income: $26,602 (2008-2012 5-year est.); Median household income: $61,250 (2008-2012 5-year est.); Average household income: $61,512 (2008-2012 5-year est.); Percent of households with income of $100,000 or more: 10.9% (2008-2012 5-year est.); Poverty rate: 3.0% (2008-2012 5-year est.).

Education: Percent of population age 25 and over with: High school diploma (including GED) or higher: 84.4% (2008-2012 5-year est.); Bachelor's degree or higher: 15.3% (2008-2012 5-year est.); Master's degree or higher: 5.5% (2008-2012 5-year est.).
Housing: Homeownership rate: 92.7% (2008-2012 5-year est.); Median home value: $109,000 (2008-2012 5-year est.); Median contract rent: n/a per month (2008-2012 5-year est.); Median year structure built: 1959 (2008-2012 5-year est.).
Health Insurance: 92.5% Private; 26.4% Public; 3.4% None. (2008-2012 5-year est.)
Transportation: Commute to work: 98.1% car, 0.0% public transportation, 0.0% walk, 1.9% work from home (2008-2012 5-year est.); Travel time to work: 31.4% less than 15 minutes, 43.7% 15 to 30 minutes, 19.0% 30 to 45 minutes, 3.2% 45 to 60 minutes, 2.6% 60 minutes or more (2008-2012 5-year est.).

EAST MOLINE (city). Covers a land area of 14.756 square miles and a water area of 0 square miles. Located at 41.52° N. Lat; 90.39° W. Long. Elevation is 702 feet.
History: East Moline was incorporated as a city in 1907, and developed as an industrial center for nearby Moline and Rock Island. An International Harvester plant was a major employer.
Population: 20,147 (1990); 20,333 (2000); 21,302 (2010); Density: 1,462.8 persons per square mile (2008-2012 5-year est.); Race: 71.1% White, 14.8% Black/African American, 3.0% Asian, 0.3% American Indian/Alaska Native, 0.0% Native Hawaiian/Other Pacific Islander, 10.8% Some other race, 3.3% Two or more races, 16.4% Hispanic of any race (2008-2012 5-year est.); Average household size: 2.35 (2008-2012 5-year est.); Median age: 37.9 (2008-2012 5-year est.); Males per 100 females: 99.2 (2008-2012 5-year est.); Marriage status: 31.9% never married, 47.8% now married, 8.3% widowed, 12.0% divorced (2008-2012 5-year est.); Foreign born: 12.5% (2008-2012 5-year est.); Ancestry (includes multiple ancestries): 19.1% German, 11.2% Irish, 5.7% Swedish, 5.5% English, 3.2% American (2008-2012 5-year est.).
Economy: Single-family building permits issued: 6 (2013); Multi-family building permits issued: 6 (2013); Homeowner vacancy rate: 2.3%. Rental vacancy rate: 5.9%. (2008-2012 5-year est.); Employment by occupation: 11.2% management, business, and financial, 5.3% computer, engineering, and science, 7.2% education, legal, community service, arts, and media, 5.2% healthcare practitioners, 19.5% service, 24.1% sales and office, 7.7% natural resources, construction, and maintenance, 19.8% production, transportation, and material moving (2008-2012 5-year est.).
Income: Per capita income: $22,694 (2008-2012 5-year est.); Median household income: $43,037 (2008-2012 5-year est.); Average household income: $53,316 (2008-2012 5-year est.); Percent of households with income of $100,000 or more: 9.1% (2008-2012 5-year est.); Poverty rate: 14.7% (2008-2012 5-year est.).
Taxes: Total city taxes per capita: $390 (2011); City property taxes per capita: $285 (2011).
Education: Percent of population age 25 and over with: High school diploma (including GED) or higher: 83.2% (2008-2012 5-year est.); Bachelor's degree or higher: 17.5% (2008-2012 5-year est.); Master's degree or higher: 5.6% (2008-2012 5-year est.).

School District(s)
East Moline SD 37 (PK-08)
    2011-12 Enrollment: 2,473 . . . . (309) 792-2887
Moline USD 40 (PK-12)
    2011-12 Enrollment: 7,429 . . . . (309) 743-1600
United Twp Area Career Ctr (11-12)
    2011-12 Enrollment: n/a . . . . (309) 752-1691
United Twp HSD 30 (09-12)
    2011-12 Enrollment: 1,712 . . . . (309) 752-1611

Vocational/Technical School(s)
La James International College-East Moline (Private, For-profit)
    Fall 2012 Enrollment: 15 . . . . (309) 755-1313
    2012-13 Tuition: $18,660
Housing: Homeownership rate: 62.6% (2008-2012 5-year est.); Median home value: $112,500 (2008-2012 5-year est.); Median contract rent: $485 per month (2008-2012 5-year est.); Median year structure built: 1964 (2008-2012 5-year est.).
Health Insurance: 67.2% Private; 39.7% Public; 11.2% None. (2008-2012 5-year est.)
Safety: Violent crime rate: 40.8 per 10,000 population; Property crime rate: 259.5 per 10,000 population (2012).

Transportation: Commute to work: 95.6% car, 1.7% public transportation, 0.8% walk, 1.2% work from home (2008-2012 5-year est.); Travel time to work: 35.5% less than 15 minutes, 43.4% 15 to 30 minutes, 16.3% 30 to 45 minutes, 2.0% 45 to 60 minutes, 2.8% 60 minutes or more (2008-2012 5-year est.)
Additional Information Contacts
City of East Moline . . . . (309) 752-1581
    http://www.eastmoline.com
Quad Cities Chamber of Commerce . . . . (309) 757-5416
    http://www.quadcitieschamber.com

HAMPTON (village). Covers a land area of 1.652 square miles and a water area of 0 square miles. Located at 41.56° N. Lat; 90.40° W. Long. Elevation is 587 feet.
Population: 1,601 (1990); 1,626 (2000); 1,863 (2010); Density: 1,329.2 persons per square mile (2008-2012 5-year est.); Race: 89.4% White, 6.3% Black/African American, 0.2% Asian, 0.0% American Indian/Alaska Native, 0.0% Native Hawaiian/Other Pacific Islander, 4.1% Some other race, 2.6% Two or more races, 7.5% Hispanic of any race (2008-2012 5-year est.); Average household size: 2.52 (2008-2012 5-year est.); Median age: 42.5 (2008-2012 5-year est.); Males per 100 females: 130.2 (2008-2012 5-year est.); Marriage status: 28.4% never married, 57.6% now married, 6.1% widowed, 8.0% divorced (2008-2012 5-year est.); Foreign born: 2.0% (2008-2012 5-year est.); Ancestry (includes multiple ancestries): 26.7% German, 14.8% Irish, 7.5% English, 6.7% Swedish, 6.1% Belgian (2008-2012 5-year est.).
Economy: Single-family building permits issued: 1 (2013); Multi-family building permits issued: 0 (2013); Homeowner vacancy rate: 4.5%. Rental vacancy rate: 0.0%. (2008-2012 5-year est.); Employment by occupation: 16.3% management, business, and financial, 5.1% computer, engineering, and science, 8.8% education, legal, community service, arts, and media, 6.5% healthcare practitioners, 14.9% service, 22.7% sales and office, 7.0% natural resources, construction, and maintenance, 18.6% production, transportation, and material moving (2008-2012 5-year est.).
Income: Per capita income: $30,465 (2008-2012 5-year est.); Median household income: $66,908 (2008-2012 5-year est.); Average household income: $81,576 (2008-2012 5-year est.); Percent of households with income of $100,000 or more: 23.5% (2008-2012 5-year est.); Poverty rate: 3.2% (2008-2012 5-year est.).
Education: Percent of population age 25 and over with: High school diploma (including GED) or higher: 89.4% (2008-2012 5-year est.); Bachelor's degree or higher: 23.4% (2008-2012 5-year est.); Master's degree or higher: 8.5% (2008-2012 5-year est.).
School District(s)
Hampton SD 29 (KG-08)
    2011-12 Enrollment: 226 . . . . (309) 755-0693
Housing: Homeownership rate: 87.4% (2008-2012 5-year est.); Median home value: $151,900 (2008-2012 5-year est.); Median contract rent: $475 per month (2008-2012 5-year est.); Median year structure built: 1974 (2008-2012 5-year est.).
Health Insurance: 81.9% Private; 25.5% Public; 7.2% None. (2008-2012 5-year est.)
Safety: Violent crime rate: 26.8 per 10,000 population; Property crime rate: 139.5 per 10,000 population (2012).
Transportation: Commute to work: 95.8% car, 0.4% public transportation, 0.0% walk, 2.5% work from home (2008-2012 5-year est.); Travel time to work: 21.3% less than 15 minutes, 51.6% 15 to 30 minutes, 16.2% 30 to 45 minutes, 5.8% 45 to 60 minutes, 5.0% 60 minutes or more (2008-2012 5-year est.)

HILLSDALE (village). Covers a land area of 0.753 square miles and a water area of 0.029 square miles. Located at 41.61° N. Lat; 90.18° W. Long. Elevation is 581 feet.
Population: 489 (1990); 588 (2000); 523 (2010); Density: 729.0 persons per square mile (2008-2012 5-year est.); Race: 96.0% White, 0.0% Black/African American, 0.0% Asian, 0.2% American Indian/Alaska Native, 0.0% Native Hawaiian/Other Pacific Islander, 3.8% Some other race, 3.8% Two or more races, 3.6% Hispanic of any race (2008-2012 5-year est.); Average household size: 2.25 (2008-2012 5-year est.); Median age: 42.8 (2008-2012 5-year est.); Males per 100 females: 98.9 (2008-2012 5-year est.); Marriage status: 29.1% never married, 50.5% now married, 4.1% widowed, 16.3% divorced (2008-2012 5-year est.); Foreign born: 1.5% (2008-2012 5-year est.); Ancestry (includes multiple ancestries): 24.2% German, 13.1% American, 7.5% Irish, 6.6% Dutch, 5.5% Belgian (2008-2012 5-year est.).

Economy: Homeowner vacancy rate: 0.0%. Rental vacancy rate: 0.0%. (2008-2012 5-year est.); Employment by occupation: 8.7% management, business, and financial, 0.0% computer, engineering, and science, 1.2% education, legal, community service, arts, and media, 1.7% healthcare practitioners, 20.7% service, 19.1% sales and office, 10.8% natural resources, construction, and maintenance, 37.8% production, transportation, and material moving (2008-2012 5-year est.).

Income: Per capita income: $22,129 (2008-2012 5-year est.); Median household income: $40,833 (2008-2012 5-year est.); Average household income: $50,177 (2008-2012 5-year est.); Percent of households with income of $100,000 or more: 7.3% (2008-2012 5-year est.); Poverty rate: 9.8% (2008-2012 5-year est.).

Education: Percent of population age 25 and over with: High school diploma (including GED) or higher: 87.1% (2008-2012 5-year est.); Bachelor's degree or higher: 5.8% (2008-2012 5-year est.); Master's degree or higher: 0.5% (2008-2012 5-year est.).

Housing: Homeownership rate: 72.5% (2008-2012 5-year est.); Median home value: $69,700 (2008-2012 5-year est.); Median contract rent: $475 per month (2008-2012 5-year est.); Median year structure built: 1960 (2008-2012 5-year est.).

Health Insurance: 59.7% Private; 37.2% Public; 23.0% None. (2008-2012 5-year est.)

Transportation: Commute to work: 79.3% car, 0.0% public transportation, 9.5% walk, 9.1% work from home (2008-2012 5-year est.); Travel time to work: 41.1% less than 15 minutes, 34.2% 15 to 30 minutes, 19.2% 30 to 45 minutes, 3.7% 45 to 60 minutes, 1.8% 60 minutes or more (2008-2012 5-year est.)

ILLINOIS CITY (unincorporated postal area)

Zip Code: 61259

Covers a land area of 76.428 square miles and a water area of 8.031 square miles. Located at 41.39° N. Lat; 90.95° W. Long. Elevation is 764 feet. Population: 1,276 (2010); Density: 16.7 persons per square mile (2010); Race: 97.9% White, 0.1% Black/African American, 0.1% Asian, 0.1% American Indian/Alaska Native, 0.0% Native Hawaiian/Other Pacific Islander, 1.8% Some other race, 0.9% Two or more races, 1.6% Hispanic of any race (2010); Average household size: 2.55 (2010); Median age: 46.6 (2010); Males per 100 females: 100.6 (2010); Homeownership rate: 88.6% (2010)

MILAN (village). Covers a land area of 5.870 square miles and a water area of 0.593 square miles. Located at 41.43° N. Lat; 90.56° W. Long. Elevation is 568 feet.

History: Incorporated 1865.

Population: 5,831 (1990); 5,348 (2000); 5,099 (2010); Density: 867.0 persons per square mile (2008-2012 5-year est.); Race: 91.7% White, 4.9% Black/African American, 0.3% Asian, 0.0% American Indian/Alaska Native, 0.0% Native Hawaiian/Other Pacific Islander, 3.1% Some other race, 2.9% Two or more races, 3.5% Hispanic of any race (2008-2012 5-year est.); Average household size: 2.11 (2008-2012 5-year est.); Median age: 44.8 (2008-2012 5-year est.); Males per 100 females: 91.5 (2008-2012 5-year est.); Marriage status: 25.4% never married, 45.3% now married, 9.9% widowed, 19.3% divorced (2008-2012 5-year est.); Foreign born: 1.2% (2008-2012 5-year est.); Ancestry (includes multiple ancestries): 25.2% German, 14.7% Irish, 10.3% English, 9.1% American, 4.3% Swedish (2008-2012 5-year est.).

Economy: Single-family building permits issued: 9 (2013); Multi-family building permits issued: 0 (2013); Homeowner vacancy rate: 0.4%. Rental vacancy rate: 0.0%. (2008-2012 5-year est.); Employment by occupation: 12.2% management, business, and financial, 2.8% computer, engineering, and science, 4.7% education, legal, community service, arts, and media, 3.4% healthcare practitioners, 21.8% service, 21.0% sales and office, 9.9% natural resources, construction, and maintenance, 24.1% production, transportation, and material moving (2008-2012 5-year est.).

Income: Per capita income: $22,105 (2008-2012 5-year est.); Median household income: $39,872 (2008-2012 5-year est.); Average household income: $45,480 (2008-2012 5-year est.); Percent of households with income of $100,000 or more: 9.2% (2008-2012 5-year est.); Poverty rate: 14.6% (2008-2012 5-year est.).

Taxes: Total city taxes per capita: $629 (2011); City property taxes per capita: $617 (2011).

Education: Percent of population age 25 and over with: High school diploma (including GED) or higher: 87.8% (2008-2012 5-year est.); Bachelor's degree or higher: 11.6% (2008-2012 5-year est.); Master's degree or higher: 3.5% (2008-2012 5-year est.).

School District(s)

Rock Island SD 41 (PK-12)

2011-12 Enrollment: 6,622 . . . . (309) 793-5900

Housing: Homeownership rate: 66.5% (2008-2012 5-year est.); Median home value: $96,100 (2008-2012 5-year est.); Median contract rent: $507 per month (2008-2012 5-year est.); Median year structure built: 1964 (2008-2012 5-year est.).

Health Insurance: 63.2% Private; 43.3% Public; 9.1% None. (2008-2012 5-year est.)

Safety: Violent crime rate: 21.6 per 10,000 population; Property crime rate: 296.0 per 10,000 population (2012).

Transportation: Commute to work: 92.5% car, 0.0% public transportation, 3.0% walk, 1.2% work from home (2008-2012 5-year est.); Travel time to work: 35.1% less than 15 minutes, 53.6% 15 to 30 minutes, 8.6% 30 to 45 minutes, 0.9% 45 to 60 minutes, 1.9% 60 minutes or more (2008-2012 5-year est.)

Additional Information Contacts

Milan Chamber of Commerce . . . . (309) 716-8144
http://www.milanilchamber.org
Village of Milan . . . . (309) 787 8500
http://www.milanil.org

MOLINE (city). Covers a land area of 16.427 square miles and a water area of 0.231 square miles. Located at 41.48° N. Lat; 90.49° W. Long. Elevation is 577 feet.

History: Moline was laid out in 1843. An early resident was John Deere, who had been producing plows in Grand Detour, but moved to Moline for the availability of steel for his machinery. The John Deere plants founded here soon became a major employer. Moline was incorporated as a town in 1848, and as a city in 1872.

Population: 43,202 (1990); 43,768 (2000); 43,483 (2010); Density: 2,641.3 persons per square mile (2008-2012 5-year est.); Race: 82.3% White, 5.1% Black/African American, 2.7% Asian, 0.5% American Indian/Alaska Native, 0.0% Native Hawaiian/Other Pacific Islander, 9.4% Some other race, 2.3% Two or more races, 17.1% Hispanic of any race (2008-2012 5-year est.); Average household size: 2.38 (2008-2012 5-year est.); Median age: 38.7 (2008-2012 5-year est.); Males per 100 females: 95.8 (2008-2012 5-year est.); Marriage status: 28.6% never married, 51.1% now married, 7.2% widowed, 13.1% divorced (2008-2012 5-year est.); Foreign born: 10.7% (2008-2012 5-year est.); Ancestry (includes multiple ancestries): 25.2% German, 13.9% Irish, 9.9% English, 6.6% Swedish, 4.9% Belgian (2008-2012 5-year est.).

Economy: Unemployment rate: 6.0% (April 2014); Total civilian labor force: 22,820 (April 2014); Single-family building permits issued: 5 (2013); Multi-family building permits issued: 8 (2013); Homeowner vacancy rate: 3.0%. Rental vacancy rate: 4.9%. (2008-2012 5-year est.); Employment by occupation: 12.0% management, business, and financial, 5.0% computer, engineering, and science, 10.3% education, legal, community service, arts, and media, 4.8% healthcare practitioners, 16.9% service, 26.3% sales and office, 5.9% natural resources, construction, and maintenance, 18.7% production, transportation, and material moving (2008-2012 5-year est.).

Income: Per capita income: $27,854 (2008-2012 5-year est.); Median household income: $49,459 (2008-2012 5-year est.); Average household income: $65,744 (2008-2012 5-year est.); Percent of households with income of $100,000 or more: 16.3% (2008-2012 5-year est.); Poverty rate: 9.2% (2008-2012 5-year est.).

Taxes: Total city taxes per capita: $771 (2011); City property taxes per capita: $415 (2011).

Education: Percent of population age 25 and over with: High school diploma (including GED) or higher: 87.9% (2008-2012 5-year est.); Bachelor's degree or higher: 26.1% (2008-2012 5-year est.); Master's degree or higher: 9.2% (2008-2012 5-year est.).

School District(s)

Moline USD 40 (PK-12)

2011-12 Enrollment: 7,429 . . . . (309) 743-1600

Rock Island Roe

2011-12 Enrollment: n/a . . . . (309) 736-1111

Two-year College(s)

Black Hawk College (Public)

Fall 2012 Enrollment: 6,360 . . . . (309) 796-5000

2012-13 Tuition: In-state $6,495; Out-of-state $6,495

Vocational/Technical School(s)

Midwest Technical Institute (Private, For-profit)

Fall 2012 Enrollment: 274 . . . . (309) 277-7900

2012-13 Tuition: $13,754

Housing: Homeownership rate: 70.0% (2008-2012 5-year est.); Median home value: $112,100 (2008-2012 5-year est.); Median contract rent: $567 per month (2008-2012 5-year est.); Median year structure built: 1954 (2008-2012 5-year est.).

Health Insurance: 72.3% Private; 30.3% Public; 12.3% None. (2008-2012 5-year est.)

Safety: Violent crime rate: 40.5 per 10,000 population; Property crime rate: 311.2 per 10,000 population (2012).

Transportation: Commute to work: 93.4% car, 1.7% public transportation, 1.7% walk, 1.9% work from home (2008-2012 5-year est.); Travel time to work: 42.4% less than 15 minutes, 45.7% 15 to 30 minutes, 7.9% 30 to 45 minutes, 2.0% 45 to 60 minutes, 2.1% 60 minutes or more (2008-2012 5-year est.); Amtrak: Train service available.

Airports: Quad City International Airport (primary service/small hub)

Additional Information Contacts

City of Moline. . . . . (309) 524-2000
    http://www.moline.il.us
Quad Cities Chamber of Commerce . . . . (309) 757-5416
    http://www.quadcitieschamber.com

OAK GROVE (village). Aka Oak Grove Park. Covers a land area of 0.574 square miles and a water area of 0 square miles. Located at 41.41° N. Lat; 90.57° W. Long. Elevation is 722 feet.

Population: 626 (1990); 1,318 (2000); 396 (2010); Density: 1,106.6 persons per square mile (2008-2012 5-year est.); Race: 90.9% White, 5.4% Black/African American, 0.6% Asian, 0.0% American Indian/Alaska Native, 0.0% Native Hawaiian/Other Pacific Islander, 3.1% Some other race, 2.8% Two or more races, 2.7% Hispanic of any race (2008-2012 5-year est.); Average household size: 2.21 (2008-2012 5-year est.); Median age: 31.5 (2008-2012 5-year est.); Males per 100 females: 107.5 (2008-2012 5-year est.); Marriage status: 35.4% never married, 27.8% now married, 5.0% widowed, 31.8% divorced (2008-2012 5-year est.); Foreign born: 2.8% (2008-2012 5-year est.); Ancestry (includes multiple ancestries): 20.9% Irish, 19.7% German, 9.6% American, 4.7% English, 3.9% Italian (2008-2012 5-year est.).

Economy: Homeowner vacancy rate: 0.0%. Rental vacancy rate: 0.0%. (2008-2012 5-year est.); Employment by occupation: 1.3% management, business, and financial, 0.0% computer, engineering, and science, 8.4% education, legal, community service, arts, and media, 0.8% healthcare practitioners, 24.1% service, 25.7% sales and office, 6.8% natural resources, construction, and maintenance, 32.9% production, transportation, and material moving (2008-2012 5-year est.).

Income: Per capita income: $15,384 (2008-2012 5-year est.); Median household income: $24,784 (2008-2012 5-year est.); Average household income: $33,080 (2008-2012 5-year est.); Percent of households with income of $100,000 or more: 3.5% (2008-2012 5-year est.); Poverty rate: 29.0% (2008-2012 5-year est.).

Education: Percent of population age 25 and over with: High school diploma (including GED) or higher: 77.4% (2008-2012 5-year est.); Bachelor's degree or higher: 5.7% (2008-2012 5-year est.); Master's degree or higher: 1.7% (2008-2012 5-year est.).

Housing: Homeownership rate: 77.7% (2008-2012 5-year est.); Median home value: <$10,000 (2008-2012 5-year est.); Median contract rent: $481 per month (2008-2012 5-year est.); Median year structure built: 1973 (2008-2012 5-year est.).

Health Insurance: 44.1% Private; 54.2% Public; 13.7% None. (2008-2012 5-year est.)

Transportation: Commute to work: 100.0% car, 0.0% public transportation, 0.0% walk, 0.0% work from home (2008-2012 5-year est.); Travel time to work: 25.8% less than 15 minutes, 46.2% 15 to 30 minutes, 24.4% 30 to 45 minutes, 0.0% 45 to 60 minutes, 3.6% 60 minutes or more (2008-2012 5-year est.)

PORT BYRON (village). Covers a land area of 2.478 square miles and a water area of 0 square miles. Located at 41.62° N. Lat; 90.33° W. Long. Elevation is 600 feet.

Population: 1,002 (1990); 1,535 (2000); 1,647 (2010); Density: 694.0 persons per square mile (2008-2012 5-year est.); Race: 97.3% White, 0.0% Black/African American, 0.6% Asian, 0.2% American Indian/Alaska Native, 0.0% Native Hawaiian/Other Pacific Islander, 1.9% Some other race, 1.5% Two or more races, 4.6% Hispanic of any race (2008-2012 5-year est.); Average household size: 2.43 (2008-2012 5-year est.); Median age: 44.9 (2008-2012 5-year est.); Males per 100 females: 110.3 (2008-2012 5-year est.); Marriage status: 23.3% never married, 62.9% now married, 3.8% widowed, 10.1% divorced (2008-2012 5-year est.);

Foreign born: 1.1% (2008-2012 5-year est.); Ancestry (includes multiple ancestries): 27.1% German, 17.8% English, 11.7% Irish, 8.7% Swedish, 6.7% American (2008-2012 5-year est.).

Economy: Single-family building permits issued: 3 (2013); Multi-family building permits issued: 0 (2013); Homeowner vacancy rate: 1.5%. Rental vacancy rate: 18.2%. (2008-2012 5-year est.); Employment by occupation: 17.3% management, business, and financial, 5.6% computer, engineering, and science, 4.9% education, legal, community service, arts, and media, 6.2% healthcare practitioners, 14.5% service, 24.9% sales and office, 12.1% natural resources, construction, and maintenance, 14.5% production, transportation, and material moving (2008-2012 5-year est.).

Income: Per capita income: $40,359 (2008-2012 5-year est.); Median household income: $78,967 (2008-2012 5-year est.); Average household income: $96,507 (2008-2012 5-year est.); Percent of households with income of $100,000 or more: 39.0% (2008-2012 5-year est.); Poverty rate: 8.1% (2008-2012 5-year est.).

Education: Percent of population age 25 and over with: High school diploma (including GED) or higher: 96.7% (2008-2012 5-year est.); Bachelor's degree or higher: 30.8% (2008-2012 5-year est.); Master's degree or higher: 10.4% (2008-2012 5-year est.).

School District(s)

Riverdale CUSD 100 (PK-12)
    2011-12 Enrollment: 1,185 . . . . (309) 523-3184

Housing: Homeownership rate: 82.2% (2008-2012 5-year est.); Median home value: $194,100 (2008-2012 5-year est.); Median contract rent: $328 per month (2008-2012 5-year est.); Median year structure built: 1971 (2008-2012 5-year est.).

Health Insurance: 82.0% Private; 24.6% Public; 7.6% None. (2008-2012 5-year est.)

Transportation: Commute to work: 93.0% car, 0.0% public transportation, 1.1% walk, 4.7% work from home (2008-2012 5-year est.); Travel time to work: 15.4% less than 15 minutes, 55.5% 15 to 30 minutes, 24.0% 30 to 45 minutes, 3.5% 45 to 60 minutes, 1.6% 60 minutes or more (2008-2012 5-year est.)

RAPIDS CITY (village). Covers a land area of 1.617 square miles and a water area of 0 square miles. Located at 41.58° N. Lat; 90.34° W. Long. Elevation is 581 feet.

Population: 932 (1990); 953 (2000); 959 (2010); Density: 529.4 persons per square mile (2008-2012 5-year est.); Race: 94.5% White, 0.4% Black/African American, 1.5% Asian, 0.8% American Indian/Alaska Native, 0.0% Native Hawaiian/Other Pacific Islander, 2.8% Some other race, 2.8% Two or more races, 1.2% Hispanic of any race (2008-2012 5-year est.); Average household size: 2.53 (2008-2012 5-year est.); Median age: 45.0 (2008-2012 5-year est.); Males per 100 females: 108.8 (2008-2012 5-year est.); Marriage status: 18.0% never married, 70.5% now married, 5.0% widowed, 6.5% divorced (2008-2012 5-year est.); Foreign born: 3.4% (2008-2012 5-year est.); Ancestry (includes multiple ancestries): 30.3% German, 17.1% Irish, 6.5% Swedish, 6.4% English, 4.0% American (2008-2012 5-year est.).

Economy: Single-family building permits issued: 2 (2013); Multi-family building permits issued: 0 (2013); Homeowner vacancy rate: 4.4%. Rental vacancy rate: 0.0%. (2008-2012 5-year est.); Employment by occupation: 14.5% management, business, and financial, 3.1% computer, engineering, and science, 11.9% education, legal, community service, arts, and media, 9.4% healthcare practitioners, 17.1% service, 13.8% sales and office, 10.4% natural resources, construction, and maintenance, 19.7% production, transportation, and material moving (2008-2012 5-year est.).

Income: Per capita income: $38,889 (2008-2012 5-year est.); Median household income: $80,395 (2008-2012 5-year est.); Average household income: $97,080 (2008-2012 5-year est.); Percent of households with income of $100,000 or more: 37.0% (2008-2012 5-year est.); Poverty rate: 6.9% (2008-2012 5-year est.).

Education: Percent of population age 25 and over with: High school diploma (including GED) or higher: 92.0% (2008-2012 5-year est.); Bachelor's degree or higher: 26.9% (2008-2012 5-year est.); Master's degree or higher: 7.3% (2008-2012 5-year est.).

Housing: Homeownership rate: 90.2% (2008-2012 5-year est.); Median home value: $153,000 (2008-2012 5-year est.); Median contract rent: $450 per month (2008-2012 5-year est.); Median year structure built: 1971 (2008-2012 5-year est.).

Health Insurance: 80.3% Private; 26.8% Public; 5.5% None. (2008-2012 5-year est.)

Transportation: Commute to work: 98.7% car, 0.0% public transportation, 0.8% walk, 0.5% work from home (2008-2012 5-year est.); Travel time to

work: 16.1% less than 15 minutes, 67.3% 15 to 30 minutes, 13.8% 30 to 45 minutes, 2.3% 45 to 60 minutes, 0.5% 60 minutes or more (2008-2012 5-year est.)

REYNOLDS (village).
Covers a land area of 0.371 square miles and a water area of 0 square miles. Located at 41.33° N. Lat; 90.67° W. Long. Elevation is 810 feet.

Population: 583 (1990); 508 (2000); 539 (2010); Density: 1,542.6 persons per square mile (2008-2012 5-year est.); Race: 98.1% White, 0.5% Black/African American, 0.3% Asian, 0.0% American Indian/Alaska Native, 0.0% Native Hawaiian/Other Pacific Islander, 1.1% Some other race, 1.0% Two or more races, 0.0% Hispanic of any race (2008-2012 5-year est.); Average household size: 2.65 (2008-2012 5-year est.); Median age: 32.2 (2008-2012 5-year est.); Males per 100 females: 99.7 (2008-2012 5-year est.); Marriage status: 10.7% never married, 71.9% now married, 5.2% widowed, 12.2% divorced (2008-2012 5-year est.); Foreign born: 0.3% (2008-2012 5-year est.); Ancestry (includes multiple ancestries): 25.8% German, 16.4% Irish, 12.2% English, 10.3% Polish, 9.4% American (2008-2012 5-year est.).
Economy: Single-family building permits issued: 0 (2013); Multi-family building permits issued: 0 (2013); Homeowner vacancy rate: 0.0%. Rental vacancy rate: 0.0%. (2008-2012 5-year est.); Employment by occupation: 25.2% management, business, and financial, 3.7% computer, engineering, and science, 5.9% education, legal, community service, arts, and media, 1.9% healthcare practitioners, 19.6% service, 15.6% sales and office, 3.3% natural resources, construction, and maintenance, 24.8% production, transportation, and material moving (2008-2012 5-year est.).
Income: Per capita income: $23,540 (2008-2012 5-year est.); Median household income: $52,000 (2008-2012 5-year est.); Average household income: $62,166 (2008-2012 5-year est.); Percent of households with income of $100,000 or more: 19.4% (2008-2012 5-year est.); Poverty rate: 17.3% (2008-2012 5-year est.).
Education: Percent of population age 25 and over with: High school diploma (including GED) or higher: 89.8% (2008-2012 5-year est.); Bachelor's degree or higher: 12.9% (2008-2012 5-year est.); Master's degree or higher: 5.2% (2008-2012 5-year est.).

School District(s)
Rockridge CUSD 300 (PK-12)
    2011-12 Enrollment: 1,231 . . . . (309) 793-8001
Housing: Homeownership rate: 89.4% (2008-2012 5-year est.); Median home value: $96,200 (2008-2012 5-year est.); Median contract rent: $477 per month (2008-2012 5-year est.); Median year structure built: 1945 (2008-2012 5-year est.).
Health Insurance: 64.2% Private; 37.5% Public; 9.1% None. (2008-2012 5-year est.)
Transportation: Commute to work: 98.9% car, 0.0% public transportation, 0.0% walk, 0.7% work from home (2008-2012 5-year est.); Travel time to work: 14.2% less than 15 minutes, 41.0% 15 to 30 minutes, 34.0% 30 to 45 minutes, 8.2% 45 to 60 minutes, 2.6% 60 minutes or more (2008-2012 5-year est.)

ROCK ISLAND (city).
Aka Quad Cities. County seat. Covers a land area of 16.846 square miles and a water area of 1.022 square miles. Located at 41.47° N. Lat; 90.59° W. Long. Elevation is 561 feet.
History: Rock Island developed from a community called Stephenson, whose name was changed in 1841. Rock Island was a steamboat port until the Rock Island Railroad Company completed a bridge across the Mississippi in 1855 and rail began to replace water as the means of transportation of goods. The Farmall Works of the International Harvester Company was established in Rock Island. The limestone island that became the location of the Rock Island Arsenal first served as a prison for Confederate soldiers, with more than 12,000 at a time confined here.
Population: 40,552 (1990); 39,684 (2000); 39,018 (2010); Density: 2,303.6 persons per square mile (2008-2012 5-year est.); Race: 74.2% White, 17.3% Black/African American, 0.9% Asian, 0.2% American Indian/Alaska Native, 0.0% Native Hawaiian/Other Pacific Islander, 7.4% Some other race, 3.4% Two or more races, 10.1% Hispanic of any race (2008-2012 5-year est.); Average household size: 2.33 (2008-2012 5-year est.); Median age: 37.0 (2008-2012 5-year est.); Males per 100 females: 88.9 (2008-2012 5-year est.); Marriage status: 35.1% never married, 43.2% now married, 8.0% widowed, 13.6% divorced (2008-2012 5-year est.); Foreign born: 6.1% (2008-2012 5-year est.); Ancestry (includes multiple ancestries): 23.5% German, 12.7% Irish, 7.4% English, 5.3% Swedish, 4.7% American (2008-2012 5-year est.).

Economy: Unemployment rate: 6.6% (April 2014); Total civilian labor force: 19,310 (April 2014); Single-family building permits issued: 7 (2013); Multi-family building permits issued: 67 (2013); Homeowner vacancy rate: 1.0%. Rental vacancy rate: 6.2%. (2008-2012 5-year est.); Employment by occupation: 9.9% management, business, and financial, 3.7% computer, engineering, and science, 11.1% education, legal, community service, arts, and media, 5.0% healthcare practitioners, 22.6% service, 22.6% sales and office, 7.4% natural resources, construction, and maintenance, 17.6% production, transportation, and material moving (2008-2012 5-year est.).
Income: Per capita income: $23,337 (2008-2012 5-year est.); Median household income: $42,613 (2008-2012 5-year est.); Average household income: $56,180 (2008-2012 5-year est.); Percent of households with income of $100,000 or more: 12.7% (2008-2012 5-year est.); Poverty rate: 17.4% (2008-2012 5-year est.).
Education: Percent of population age 25 and over with: High school diploma (including GED) or higher: 84.9% (2008-2012 5-year est.); Bachelor's degree or higher: 22.0% (2008-2012 5-year est.); Master's degree or higher: 6.7% (2008-2012 5-year est.).

School District(s)
Rock Island Roe
    2011-12 Enrollment: n/a . . . . (309) 736-1111
Rock Island SD 41 (PK-12)
    2011-12 Enrollment: 6,622 . . . . (309) 793-5900

Four-year College(s)
Augustana College (Private, Not-for-profit, Evangelical Lutheran Church)
    Fall 2012 Enrollment: 2,551 . . . . (309) 794-7000
    2012-13 Tuition: In-state $34,614; Out-of-state $34,614
Trinity College of Nursing & Health Sciences (Private, Not-for-profit)
    Fall 2012 Enrollment: 232 . . . . (309) 779-7700
    2012-13 Tuition: In-state $24,982; Out-of-state $24,982
Housing: Homeownership rate: 67.6% (2008-2012 5-year est.); Median home value: $98,900 (2008-2012 5-year est.); Median contract rent: $516 per month (2008-2012 5-year est.); Median year structure built: 1950 (2008-2012 5-year est.).
Health Insurance: 67.3% Private; 36.0% Public; 11.6% None. (2008-2012 5-year est.)
Hospitals: Trinity Medical Center (338 beds)
Safety: Violent crime rate: 56.9 per 10,000 population; Property crime rate: 287.9 per 10,000 population (2012).
Transportation: Commute to work: 80.0% car, 2.7% public transportation, 4.9% walk, 4.4% work from home (2008-2012 5-year est.); Travel time to work: 43.0% less than 15 minutes, 42.4% 15 to 30 minutes, 9.1% 30 to 45 minutes, 2.7% 45 to 60 minutes, 2.9% 60 minutes or more (2008-2012 5-year est.); Amtrak: Bus service available.
Additional Information Contacts
City of Rock Island . . . . (309) 732-2000
    http://www.rigov.org

ROCK ISLAND ARSENAL (CDP).
Covers a land area of 1.628 square miles and a water area of 0.938 square miles. Located at 41.52° N. Lat; 90.54° W. Long.
Population: n/a (1990); 145 (2000); 149 (2010); Density: 79.8 persons per square mile (2008-2012 5-year est.); Race: 32.3% White, 23.8% Black/African American, 0.0% Asian, 0.0% American Indian/Alaska Native, 0.0% Native Hawaiian/Other Pacific Islander, 43.9% Some other race, 25.4% Two or more races, 38.5% Hispanic of any race (2008-2012 5-year est.); Average household size: 2.60 (2008-2012 5-year est.); Median age: 29.5 (2008-2012 5-year est.); Males per 100 females: 64.6 (2008-2012 5-year est.); Marriage status: 33.6% never married, 46.7% now married, 9.3% widowed, 10.3% divorced (2008-2012 5-year est.); Foreign born: 30.8% (2008-2012 5-year est.); Ancestry (includes multiple ancestries): 32.3% British, 24.6% Swedish, 3.8% Belgian, 3.1% German, 1.5% Irish (2008-2012 5-year est.).
Economy: Homeowner vacancy rate: 0.0%. Rental vacancy rate: 0.0%. (2008-2012 5-year est.); Employment by occupation: 22.4% management, business, and financial, 19.0% computer, engineering, and science, 17.2% education, legal, community service, arts, and media, 0.0% healthcare practitioners, 0.0% service, 0.0% sales and office, 24.1% natural resources, construction, and maintenance, 17.2% production, transportation, and material moving (2008-2012 5-year est.).
Income: Per capita income: $22,455 (2008-2012 5-year est.); Median household income: $56,250 (2008-2012 5-year est.); Average household income: $59,590 (2008-2012 5-year est.); Percent of households with income of $100,000 or more: 6.0% (2008-2012 5-year est.); Poverty rate: 0.0% (2008-2012 5-year est.).

Education: Percent of population age 25 and over with: High school diploma (including GED) or higher: 71.8% (2008-2012 5-year est.); Bachelor's degree or higher: 58.8% (2008-2012 5-year est.); Master's degree or higher: 14.1% (2008-2012 5-year est.).
Housing: Homeownership rate: 6.0% (2008-2012 5-year est.); Median home value: n/a (2008-2012 5-year est.); Median contract rent: n/a per month (2008-2012 5-year est.); Median year structure built: 1949 (2008-2012 5-year est.).
Health Insurance: 86.7% Private; 21.9% Public; 13.3% None. (2008-2012 5-year est.)
Transportation: Commute to work: 100.0% car, 0.0% public transportation, 0.0% walk, 0.0% work from home (2008-2012 5-year est.); Travel time to work: 49.3% less than 15 minutes, 32.9% 15 to 30 minutes, 17.8% 30 to 45 minutes, 0.0% 45 to 60 minutes, 0.0% 60 minutes or more (2008-2012 5-year est.).

SILVIS (city).
Covers a land area of 4.156 square miles and a water area of 0 square miles. Located at 41.50° N. Lat; 90.41° W. Long. Elevation is 594 feet.
History: Incorporated 1906.
Population: 6,926 (1990); 7,269 (2000); 7,479 (2010); Density: 1,798.4 persons per square mile (2008-2012 5-year est.); Race: 82.5% White, 4.3% Black/African American, 2.5% Asian, 0.0% American Indian/Alaska Native, 0.0% Native Hawaiian/Other Pacific Islander, 10.7% Some other race, 5.4% Two or more races, 11.9% Hispanic of any race (2008-2012 5-year est.); Average household size: 2.17 (2008-2012 5-year est.); Median age: 42.7 (2008-2012 5-year est.); Males per 100 females: 88.0 (2008-2012 5-year est.); Marriage status: 19.6% never married, 49.4% now married, 12.6% widowed, 18.4% divorced (2008-2012 5-year est.); Foreign born: 5.8% (2008-2012 5-year est.); Ancestry (includes multiple ancestries): 23.7% German, 11.5% Irish, 8.2% English, 5.5% Swedish, 5.0% American (2008-2012 5-year est.).
Economy: Single-family building permits issued: 0 (2013); Multi-family building permits issued: 2 (2013); Homeowner vacancy rate: 0.0%. Rental vacancy rate: 0.0%. (2008-2012 5-year est.); Employment by occupation: 7.8% management, business, and financial, 6.3% computer, engineering, and science, 10.1% education, legal, community service, arts, and media, 7.2% healthcare practitioners, 21.2% service, 22.9% sales and office, 10.3% natural resources, construction, and maintenance, 14.3% production, transportation, and material moving (2008-2012 5-year est.).
Income: Per capita income: $24,511 (2008-2012 5-year est.); Median household income: $40,522 (2008-2012 5-year est.); Average household income: $52,343 (2008-2012 5-year est.); Percent of households with income of $100,000 or more: 11.3% (2008-2012 5-year est.); Poverty rate: 10.8% (2008-2012 5-year est.).
Education: Percent of population age 25 and over with: High school diploma (including GED) or higher: 85.2% (2008-2012 5-year est.); Bachelor's degree or higher: 16.8% (2008-2012 5-year est.); Master's degree or higher: 7.5% (2008-2012 5-year est.).

School District(s)
Carbon Cliff-Barstow SD 36 (PK-08)
    2011-12 Enrollment: 232 . . . . (309) 792-2002
East Moline SD 37 (PK-08)
    2011-12 Enrollment: 2,473 . . . . (309) 792-2887
Silvis SD 34 (PK-08)
    2011-12 Enrollment: 630 . . . . (309) 792-9325
Housing: Homeownership rate: 64.3% (2008-2012 5-year est.); Median home value: $122,600 (2008-2012 5-year est.); Median contract rent: $503 per month (2008-2012 5-year est.); Median year structure built: 1966 (2008-2012 5-year est.).
Health Insurance: 68.4% Private; 45.0% Public; 9.0% None. (2008-2012 5-year est.)
Hospitals: Genesis Medical Center-Illini Campus (150 beds)
Safety: Violent crime rate: 26.7 per 10,000 population; Property crime rate: 370.0 per 10,000 population (2012).
Transportation: Commute to work: 98.3% car, 0.0% public transportation, 0.5% walk, 1.2% work from home (2008-2012 5-year est.); Travel time to work: 41.8% less than 15 minutes, 35.5% 15 to 30 minutes, 17.4% 30 to 45 minutes, 3.2% 45 to 60 minutes, 2.1% 60 minutes or more (2008-2012 5-year est.).
Additional Information Contacts
City of Silvis. . . . . (309) 792-9181
    http://www.silvisil.org

TAYLOR RIDGE (unincorporated postal area)
Zip Code: 61284
    Covers a land area of 45.115 square miles and a water area of 0.836 square miles. Located at 41.39° N. Lat; 90.75° W. Long. Elevation is 771 feet. Population: 2,292 (2010); Density: 50.8 persons per square mile (2010); Race: 97.4% White, 0.6% Black/African American, 0.7% Asian, 0.1% American Indian/Alaska Native, 0.0% Native Hawaiian/Other Pacific Islander, 1.2% Some other race, 0.8% Two or more races, 1.7% Hispanic of any race (2010); Average household size: 2.49 (2010); Median age: 46.9 (2010); Males per 100 females: 104.5 (2010); Homeownership rate: 89.1% (2010)

Saline County

Located in southeastern Illinois, partly in the Ozarks; drained by the Saline River; includes part of Shawnee National Forest. Covers a land area of 379.819 square miles, a water area of 6.961 square miles, and is located in the Central Time Zone at 37.75° N. Lat., 88.55° W. Long. The county was founded in 1847. County seat is Harrisburg.

Weather Station: Harrisburg   Elevation: 365 feet

	Jan	Feb	Mar	Apr	May	Jun	Jul	Aug	Sep	Oct	Nov	Dec
High	41	47	57	69	78	86	89	89	82	71	58	46
Low	24	27	35	45	55	64	67	66	57	45	37	28
Precip	3.4	2.8	4.3	4.4	4.9	4.3	3.9	2.9	3.2	3.9	4.1	4.2
Snow	1.3	1.6	0.6	tr	0.0	0.0	0.0	0.0	0.0	tr	0.1	0.6

High and Low temperatures in degrees Fahrenheit; Precipitation and Snow in inches

Population: 26,551 (1990); 26,733 (2000); 24,913 (2010); Race: 93.2% White, 3.8% Black/African American, 0.5% Asian, 0.5% American Indian/Alaska Native, 0.0% Native Hawaiian/Other Pacific Islander, 2.0% Some other race, 1.8% Two or more races, 1.4% Hispanic of any race (2008-2012 5-year est.); Density: 65.8 persons per square mile (2008-2012 5-year est.); Average household size: 2.34 (2008-2012 5-year est.); Median age: 41.8 (2008-2012 5-year est.); Males per 100 females: 94.6 (2008-2012 5-year est.).
Religion: Six largest groups: 43.6% Baptist, 5.1% Methodist/Pietist, 3.7% Non-denominational Protestant, 3.4% Catholicism, 2.0% Presbyterian-Reformed, 1.7% Pentecostal (2010)
Economy: Unemployment rate: 7.5% (April 2014); Total civilian labor force: 12,269 (April 2014); Leading industries: 22.9% health care and social assistance; 16.4% retail trade; 15.2% mining (2012); Farms: 483 totaling 139,854 acres (2012); Companies that employ 500 or more persons: 2 (2012); Companies that employ 100 to 499 persons: 6 (2012); Companies that employ less than 100 persons: 590 (2012); Black-owned businesses: n/a (2007); Hispanic-owned businesses: n/a (2007); Asian-owned businesses: n/a (2007); Women-owned businesses: 497 (2007); Single-family building permits issued: 0 (2013); Multi-family building permits issued: 0 (2013).
Income: Per capita income: $21,341 (2008-2012 5-year est.); Median household income: $37,139 (2008-2012 5-year est.); Average household income: $50,529 (2008-2012 5-year est.); Percent of households with income of $100,000 or more: 10.4% (2008-2012 5-year est.); Poverty rate: 18.6% (2008-2012 5-year est.); Bankruptcy rate: 3.61% (2013).
Education: Percent of population age 25 and over with: High school diploma (including GED) or higher: 83.9% (2008-2012 5-year est.); Bachelor's degree or higher: 13.8% (2008-2012 5-year est.); Master's degree or higher: 4.3% (2008-2012 5-year est.).
Housing: Homeownership rate: 73.2% (2008-2012 5-year est.); Median home value: $71,700 (2008-2012 5-year est.); Median contract rent: $372 per month (2008-2012 5-year est.); Median year structure built: 1967 (2008-2012 5-year est.)
Health: Birth rate: 135.5 per 10,000 population (2013); Death rate: 130.7 per 10,000 population (2013); Age-adjusted cancer mortality rate: 188.0 deaths per 100,000 population (2011); Number of physicians: 12.8 per 10,000 population (2011); Hospital beds: 39.7 per 10,000 population (2010); Hospital admissions: 1,581.5 per 10,000 population (2010).
Elections: 2012 Presidential election results: 34.5% Obama, 63.5% Romney
National and State Parks: Saline County State Conservation Area
Additional Information Contacts
Saline County Government . . . . (618) 252-6905

Saline County Chamber of Commerce . . . . (618) 252-4192
    http://salinecountychamber.org

Saline County Communities

CARRIER MILLS

CARRIER MILLS (village). Aka Carriers Mills. Covers a land area of 1.208 square miles and a water area of 0.011 square miles. Located at 37.69° N. Lat; 88.63° W. Long. Elevation is 387 feet.

History: Carriers (or Carrier) Mills was named for William H. Carrier who built a sawmill here in 1870. The town developed around the mining industry.

Population: n/a (1990); 1,886 (2000); 1,653 (2010); Density: 1,408.5 persons per square mile (2008-2012 5-year est.); Race: 86.4% White, 10.3% Black/African American, 0.0% Asian, 0.4% American Indian/Alaska Native, 0.0% Native Hawaiian/Other Pacific Islander, 2.9% Some other race, 2.1% Two or more races, 0.4% Hispanic of any race (2008-2012 5-year est.); Average household size: 1.99 (2008-2012 5-year est.); Median age: 51.3 (2008-2012 5-year est.); Males per 100 females: 86.4 (2008-2012 5-year est.); Marriage status: 19.3% never married, 54.8% now married, 13.3% widowed, 12.6% divorced (2008-2012 5-year est.); Foreign born: 0.1% (2008-2012 5-year est.); Ancestry (includes multiple ancestries): 21.9% German, 18.6% Irish, 11.3% American, 8.5% English, 4.5% Dutch (2008-2012 5-year est.).

Economy: Homeowner vacancy rate: 2.4%. Rental vacancy rate: 5.9%. (2008-2012 5-year est.); Employment by occupation: 3.7% management, business, and financial, 1.3% computer, engineering, and science, 6.6% education, legal, community service, arts, and media, 10.6% healthcare practitioners, 29.5% service, 27.0% sales and office, 13.7% natural resources, construction, and maintenance, 7.6% production, transportation, and material moving (2008-2012 5-year est.).

Income: Per capita income: $18,968 (2008-2012 5-year est.); Median household income: $30,648 (2008-2012 5-year est.); Average household income: $37,597 (2008-2012 5-year est.); Percent of households with income of $100,000 or more: 5.5% (2008-2012 5-year est.); Poverty rate: 17.4% (2008-2012 5-year est.).

Education: Percent of population age 25 and over with: High school diploma (including GED) or higher: 82.2% (2008-2012 5-year est.); Bachelor's degree or higher: 7.5% (2008-2012 5-year est.); Master's degree or higher: 1.4% (2008-2012 5-year est.).

School District(s)

Carrier Mills-Stonefort CUSD 2 (PK-12)

    2011-12 Enrollment: 462 . . . . (618) 994-2392

Housing: Homeownership rate: 73.1% (2008-2012 5-year est.); Median home value: $52,000 (2008-2012 5-year est.); Median contract rent: $277 per month (2008-2012 5-year est.); Median year structure built: 1959 (2008-2012 5-year est.).

Health Insurance: 54.2% Private; 45.5% Public; 16.1% None. (2008-2012 5-year est.)

Transportation: Commute to work: 97.1% car, 0.7% public transportation, 1.2% walk, 1.0% work from home (2008-2012 5-year est.); Travel time to work: 20.3% less than 15 minutes, 44.7% 15 to 30 minutes, 26.3% 30 to 45 minutes, 7.3% 45 to 60 minutes, 1.4% 60 minutes or more (2008-2012 5-year est.)

ELDORADO

ELDORADO (city). Covers a land area of 2.390 square miles and a water area of 0.041 square miles. Located at 37.81° N. Lat; 88.44° W. Long. Elevation is 394 feet.

History: Incorporated 1873.

Population: 4,536 (1990); 4,534 (2000); 4,122 (2010); Density: 1,812.3 persons per square mile (2008-2012 5-year est.); Race: 95.7% White, 1.7% Black/African American, 0.0% Asian, 0.0% American Indian/Alaska Native, 0.0% Native Hawaiian/Other Pacific Islander, 2.6% Some other race, 2.6% Two or more races, 0.8% Hispanic of any race (2008-2012 5-year est.); Average household size: 2.42 (2008-2012 5-year est.); Median age: 37.2 (2008-2012 5-year est.); Males per 100 females: 75.7 (2008-2012 5-year est.); Marriage status: 25.5% never married, 48.8% now married, 11.6% widowed, 14.1% divorced (2008-2012 5-year est.); Foreign born: 0.6% (2008-2012 5-year est.); Ancestry (includes multiple ancestries): 20.7% Irish, 13.5% American, 13.4% German, 8.1% English, 2.7% Dutch (2008-2012 5-year est.).

Economy: Homeowner vacancy rate: 5.8%. Rental vacancy rate: 0.0%. (2008-2012 5-year est.); Employment by occupation: 12.7% management, business, and financial, 1.3% computer, engineering, and science, 4.9% education, legal, community service, arts, and media, 5.0% healthcare practitioners, 29.1% service, 18.8% sales and office, 11.1% natural resources, construction, and maintenance, 17.2% production, transportation, and material moving (2008-2012 5-year est.).

Income: Per capita income: $15,173 (2008-2012 5-year est.); Median household income: $26,528 (2008-2012 5-year est.); Average household income: $36,714 (2008-2012 5-year est.); Percent of households with income of $100,000 or more: 4.9% (2008-2012 5-year est.); Poverty rate: 26.8% (2008-2012 5-year est.).

Education: Percent of population age 25 and over with: High school diploma (including GED) or higher: 82.5% (2008-2012 5-year est.); Bachelor's degree or higher: 9.6% (2008-2012 5-year est.); Master's degree or higher: 3.1% (2008-2012 5-year est.).

School District(s)

Eldorado CUSD 4 (PK-12)

    2011-12 Enrollment: 1,289 . . . . (618) 273-6394

Housing: Homeownership rate: 71.0% (2008-2012 5-year est.); Median home value: $43,600 (2008-2012 5-year est.); Median contract rent: $313 per month (2008-2012 5-year est.); Median year structure built: 1960 (2008-2012 5-year est.).

Health Insurance: 44.5% Private; 56.4% Public; 12.8% None. (2008-2012 5-year est.)

Hospitals: Ferrell Hospital (51 beds)

Safety: Violent crime rate: 38.7 per 10,000 population; Property crime rate: 428.1 per 10,000 population (2012).

Transportation: Commute to work: 92.8% car, 0.1% public transportation, 3.4% walk, 0.0% work from home (2008-2012 5-year est.); Travel time to work: 46.5% less than 15 minutes, 32.3% 15 to 30 minutes, 10.3% 30 to 45 minutes, 3.9% 45 to 60 minutes, 7.0% 60 minutes or more (2008-2012 5-year est.)

Additional Information Contacts

Saline County Chamber of Commerce . . . . (618) 252-4192
   http://salinecountychamber.org

GALATIA

GALATIA (village). Covers a land area of 1.952 square miles and a water area of 0.029 square miles. Located at 37.84° N. Lat; 88.62° W. Long. Elevation is 420 feet.

Population: 983 (1990); 1,013 (2000); 933 (2010); Density: 481.0 persons per square mile (2008-2012 5-year est.); Race: 98.5% White, 0.0% Black/African American, 0.0% Asian, 0.0% American Indian/Alaska Native, 0.0% Native Hawaiian/Other Pacific Islander, 1.5% Some other race, 1.3% Two or more races, 0.2% Hispanic of any race (2008-2012 5-year est.); Average household size: 2.32 (2008-2012 5-year est.); Median age: 38.3 (2008-2012 5-year est.); Males per 100 females: 90.0 (2000-2012 5-year est.); Marriage status: 20.7% never married, 57.5% now married, 10.0% widowed, 11.8% divorced (2008-2012 5-year est.); Foreign born: 0.4% (2008-2012 5-year est.); Ancestry (includes multiple ancestries): 24.3% Irish, 21.1% German, 10.1% English, 9.8% American, 8.4% Dutch (2008-2012 5-year est.).

Economy: Homeowner vacancy rate: 2.3%. Rental vacancy rate: 0.0%. (2008-2012 5-year est.); Employment by occupation: 2.5% management, business, and financial, 1.2% computer, engineering, and science, 8.9% education, legal, community service, arts, and media, 7.1% healthcare practitioners, 21.8% service, 25.5% sales and office, 17.5% natural resources, construction, and maintenance, 15.4% production, transportation, and material moving (2008-2012 5-year est.).

Income: Per capita income: $18,905 (2008-2012 5-year est.); Median household income: $32,452 (2008-2012 5-year est.); Average household income: $44,362 (2008-2012 5-year est.); Percent of households with income of $100,000 or more: 9.4% (2008-2012 5-year est.); Poverty rate: 21.9% (2008-2012 5-year est.).

Education: Percent of population age 25 and over with: High school diploma (including GED) or higher: 87.9% (2008-2012 5-year est.); Bachelor's degree or higher: 7.4% (2008-2012 5-year est.); Master's degree or higher: 2.5% (2008-2012 5-year est.).

School District(s)

Galatia CUSD 1 (PK-12)

    2011-12 Enrollment: 422 . . . . (618) 268-4194

Housing: Homeownership rate: 71.7% (2008-2012 5-year est.); Median home value: $66,400 (2008-2012 5-year est.); Median contract rent: $282 per month (2008-2012 5-year est.); Median year structure built: 1966 (2008-2012 5-year est.).

Health Insurance: 52.2% Private; 58.0% Public; 10.1% None. (2008-2012 5-year est.)

Transportation: Commute to work: 92.5% car, 0.0% public transportation, 6.0% walk, 1.6% work from home (2008-2012 5-year est.); Travel time to work: 17.3% less than 15 minutes, 52.4% 15 to 30 minutes, 25.6% 30 to 45 minutes, 4.2% 45 to 60 minutes, 0.6% 60 minutes or more (2008-2012 5-year est.)

HARRISBURG (city). County seat. Covers a land area of 6.552 square miles and a water area of 0.209 square miles. Located at 37.74° N. Lat; 88.55° W. Long. Elevation is 397 feet.

History: Harrisburg was platted in 1853 and developed as an industrial center with planing, flour, and woolen mills founded in the late 1800's. Coal mining began in 1905.

Population: 9,289 (1990); 9,860 (2000); 9,017 (2010); Density: 1,367.8 persons per square mile (2008-2012 5-year est.); Race: 89.2% White, 6.8% Black/African American, 1.1% Asian, 1.0% American Indian/Alaska Native, 0.0% Native Hawaiian/Other Pacific Islander, 1.9% Some other race, 1.8% Two or more races, 2.5% Hispanic of any race (2008-2012 5-year est.); Average household size: 2.30 (2008-2012 5-year est.); Median age: 36.9 (2008-2012 5-year est.); Males per 100 females: 101.1 (2008-2012 5-year est.); Marriage status: 28.4% never married, 48.9% now married, 9.5% widowed, 13.1% divorced (2008-2012 5-year est.); Foreign born: 1.5% (2008-2012 5-year est.); Ancestry (includes multiple ancestries): 19.2% Irish, 17.6% German, 12.7% English, 10.6% American, 2.7% Hungarian (2008-2012 5-year est.).

Economy: Homeowner vacancy rate: 1.7%. Rental vacancy rate: 0.2%. (2008-2012 5-year est.); Employment by occupation: 7.5% management, business, and financial, 0.3% computer, engineering, and science, 12.5% education, legal, community service, arts, and media, 6.8% healthcare practitioners, 23.7% service, 24.4% sales and office, 15.6% natural resources, construction, and maintenance, 9.3% production, transportation, and material moving (2008-2012 5-year est.).

Income: Per capita income: $20,002 (2008-2012 5-year est.); Median household income: $34,804 (2008-2012 5-year est.); Average household income: $47,032 (2008-2012 5-year est.); Percent of households with income of $100,000 or more: 9.9% (2008-2012 5-year est.); Poverty rate: 22.3% (2008-2012 5-year est.).

Education: Percent of population age 25 and over with: High school diploma (including GED) or higher: 79.1% (2008-2012 5-year est.); Bachelor's degree or higher: 14.0% (2008-2012 5-year est.); Master's degree or higher: 6.1% (2008-2012 5-year est.).

School District(s)
Edwd/gltn/hdin/pop/slne/wbh/wn/wh (06-12)
   2011-12 Enrollment: n/a . . . . (618) 253-5581
Harrisburg CUSD 3 (PK-12)
   2011-12 Enrollment: 2,178 . . . . (618) 253-7637
Idjj SD 428 (06-12)
   2011-12 Enrollment: 784 . . . . (309) 584-0506

Two-year College(s)
Southeastern Illinois College (Public)
   Fall 2012 Enrollment: 2,087 . . . . (618) 252-5400
   2012-13 Tuition: In-state $4,290; Out-of-state $4,530

Housing: Homeownership rate: 63.6% (2008-2012 5-year est.); Median home value: $65,600 (2008-2012 5-year est.); Median contract rent: $409 per month (2008-2012 5-year est.); Median year structure built: 1956 (2008-2012 5-year est.).

Health Insurance: 55.7% Private; 52.1% Public; 11.9% None. (2008-2012 5-year est.)

Hospitals: Harrisburg Medical Center (86 beds)

Safety: Violent crime rate: 58.6 per 10,000 population; Property crime rate: 205.7 per 10,000 population (2012).

Transportation: Commute to work: 93.6% car, 1.0% public transportation, 1.4% walk, 2.1% work from home (2008-2012 5-year est.); Travel time to work: 54.7% less than 15 minutes, 21.2% 15 to 30 minutes, 13.4% 30 to 45 minutes, 4.8% 45 to 60 minutes, 5.8% 60 minutes or more (2008-2012 5-year est.)

Airports: Harrisburg-Raleigh Airport (general aviation)

Additional Information Contacts
City of Harrisburg . . . . (618) 253-7451
   http://thecityofharrisburgil.com
Saline County Chamber of Commerce . . . . (618) 252-4192
   http://salinecountychamber.org

MUDDY (village). Covers a land area of 0.302 square miles and a water area of 0.001 square miles. Located at 37.77° N. Lat; 88.51° W. Long. Elevation is 371 feet.

Population: 87 (1990); 78 (2000); 68 (2010); Density: 122.5 persons per square mile (2008-2012 5-year est.); Race: 83.8% White, 0.0% Black/African American, 0.0% Asian, 0.0% American Indian/Alaska Native, 0.0% Native Hawaiian/Other Pacific Islander, 16.2% Some other race, 13.5% Two or more races, 8.1% Hispanic of any race (2008-2012 5-year est.); Average household size: 1.68 (2008-2012 5-year est.); Median age:

52.8 (2008-2012 5-year est.); Males per 100 females: 42.3 (2008-2012 5-year est.); Marriage status: 17.1% never married, 20.0% now married, 14.3% widowed, 48.6% divorced (2008-2012 5-year est.); Foreign born: 0.0% (2008-2012 5-year est.); Ancestry (includes multiple ancestries): 18.9% American, 18.9% German, 18.9% Irish, 10.8% Italian, 8.1% English (2008-2012 5-year est.).

Economy: Single-family building permits issued: 0 (2013); Multi-family building permits issued: 0 (2013); Homeowner vacancy rate: 0.0%. Rental vacancy rate: 15.0%. (2008-2012 5-year est.); Employment by occupation: 0.0% management, business, and financial, 0.0% computer, engineering, and science, 16.7% education, legal, community service, arts, and media, 0.0% healthcare practitioners, 45.8% service, 25.0% sales and office, 0.0% natural resources, construction, and maintenance, 12.5% production, transportation, and material moving (2008-2012 5-year est.).

Income: Per capita income: $27,246 (2008-2012 5-year est.); Median household income: $42,500 (2008-2012 5-year est.); Average household income: $44,350 (2008-2012 5-year est.); Percent of households with income of $100,000 or more: n/a (2008-2012 5-year est.); Poverty rate: 5.4% (2008-2012 5-year est.).

Education: Percent of population age 25 and over with: High school diploma (including GED) or higher: 71.0% (2008-2012 5-year est.); Bachelor's degree or higher: 6.5% (2008-2012 5-year est.); Master's degree or higher: 0.0% (2008-2012 5-year est.).

Housing: Homeownership rate: 22.7% (2008-2012 5-year est.); Median home value: $159,400 (2008-2012 5-year est.); Median contract rent: $197 per month (2008-2012 5-year est.); Median year structure built: Before 1940 (2008-2012 5-year est.).

Health Insurance: 59.5% Private; 27.0% Public; 29.7% None. (2008-2012 5-year est.)

Transportation: Commute to work: 90.0% car, 0.0% public transportation, 0.0% walk, 10.0% work from home (2008-2012 5-year est.); Travel time to work: 66.7% less than 15 minutes, 33.3% 15 to 30 minutes, 0.0% 30 to 45 minutes, 0.0% 45 to 60 minutes, 0.0% 60 minutes or more (2008-2012 5-year est.)

RALEIGH (village). Covers a land area of 1.976 square miles and a water area of 0.003 square miles. Located at 37.82° N. Lat; 88.53° W. Long. Elevation is 410 feet.

Population: 305 (1990); 330 (2000); 350 (2010); Density: 159.4 persons per square mile (2008-2012 5-year est.); Race: 100.0% White, 0.0% Black/African American, 0.0% Asian, 0.0% American Indian/Alaska Native, 0.0% Native Hawaiian/Other Pacific Islander, 0.0% Some other race, 0.0% Two or more races, 1.0% Hispanic of any race (2008-2012 5-year est.); Average household size: 2.50 (2008-2012 5-year est.); Median age: 35.0 (2008-2012 5-year est.); Males per 100 females: 110.0 (2008-2012 5-year est.); Marriage status: 19.7% never married, 60.5% now married, 7.0% widowed, 12.7% divorced (2008-2012 5-year est.); Foreign born: 0.0% (2008-2012 5-year est.); Ancestry (includes multiple ancestries): 14.3% American, 14.3% Irish, 10.2% German, 9.5% English, 3.5% Polish (2008-2012 5-year est.).

Economy: Homeowner vacancy rate: 5.9%. Rental vacancy rate: 0.0%. (2008-2012 5-year est.); Employment by occupation: 4.1% management, business, and financial, 0.8% computer, engineering, and science, 0.8% education, legal, community service, arts, and media, 5.0% healthcare practitioners, 14.0% service, 19.0% sales and office, 27.3% natural resources, construction, and maintenance, 28.9% production, transportation, and material moving (2008-2012 5-year est.).

Income: Per capita income: $16,805 (2008-2012 5-year est.); Median household income: $35,000 (2008-2012 5-year est.); Average household income: $41,497 (2008-2012 5-year est.); Percent of households with income of $100,000 or more: 4.0% (2008-2012 5-year est.); Poverty rate: 9.9% (2008-2012 5-year est.).

Education: Percent of population age 25 and over with: High school diploma (including GED) or higher: 87.4% (2008-2012 5-year est.); Bachelor's degree or higher: 3.5% (2008-2012 5-year est.); Master's degree or higher: 0.0% (2008-2012 5-year est.).

Housing: Homeownership rate: 88.1% (2008-2012 5-year est.); Median home value: $51,400 (2008-2012 5-year est.); Median contract rent: $245 per month (2008-2012 5-year est.); Median year structure built: 1962 (2008-2012 5-year est.).

Health Insurance: 51.1% Private; 49.8% Public; 12.1% None. (2008-2012 5-year est.)

Safety: Violent crime rate: 28.5 per 10,000 population; Property crime rate: 227.9 per 10,000 population (2012).

Transportation: Commute to work: 84.8% car, 0.0% public transportation, 0.0% walk, 12.5% work from home (2008-2012 5-year est.); Travel time to work: 42.9% less than 15 minutes, 26.5% 15 to 30 minutes, 7.1% 30 to 45 minutes, 6.1% 45 to 60 minutes, 17.3% 60 minutes or more (2008-2012 5-year est.)

Sangamon County

Located in central Illinois; drained by the Sangamon River and its South Fork; includes Lake Springfield. Covers a land area of 868.302 square miles, a water area of 8.717 square miles, and is located in the Central Time Zone at 39.76° N. Lat., 89.66° W. Long. The county was founded in 1821. County seat is Springfield.

Sangamon County is part of the Springfield, IL Metropolitan Statistical Area. The entire metro area includes: Menard County, IL; Sangamon County, IL

Weather Station: Springfield Capital Arpt   Elevation: 585 feet

	Jan	Feb	Mar	Apr	May	Jun	Jul	Aug	Sep	Oct	Nov	Dec
High	35	40	52	64	75	83	86	85	79	66	52	39
Low	19	23	32	42	53	62	66	64	55	44	34	23
Precip	1.8	1.8	2.7	3.5	4.0	4.3	3.8	3.2	2.8	3.2	3.2	2.5
Snow	6.3	5.6	2.7	0.5	tr	0.0	tr	0.0	0.0	tr	0.8	5.4

High and Low temperatures in degrees Fahrenheit; Precipitation and Snow in inches

Population: 178,386 (1990); 188,951 (2000); 197,465 (2010); Race: 83.7% White, 12.0% Black/African American, 1.6% Asian, 0.2% American Indian/Alaska Native, 0.0% Native Hawaiian/Other Pacific Islander, 2.5% Some other race, 1.9% Two or more races, 1.8% Hispanic of any race (2008-2012 5-year est.); Density: 229.5 persons per square mile (2008-2012 5-year est.); Average household size: 2.35 (2008-2012 5-year est.); Median age: 39.3 (2008-2012 5-year est.); Males per 100 females: 92.4 (2008-2012 5-year est.).
Religion: Six largest groups: 16.1% Catholicism, 11.1% Baptist, 6.8% Methodist/Pietist, 5.7% Lutheran, 5.2% Pentecostal, 2.9% Non-denominational Protestant (2010)
Economy: Unemployment rate: 5.7% (April 2014); Total civilian labor force: 105,901 (April 2014); Leading industries: 25.0% health care and social assistance; 14.6% retail trade; 11.0% accommodation & food services (2012); Farms: 1,002 totaling 514,043 acres (2012); Companies that employ 500 or more persons: 11 (2012); Companies that employ 100 to 499 persons: 112 (2012); Companies that employ less than 100 persons: 4,934 (2012); Black-owned businesses: 1,025 (2007); Hispanic-owned businesses: n/a (2007); Asian-owned businesses: n/a (2007); Women-owned businesses: 4,828 (2007); Single-family building permits issued: 264 (2013); Multi-family building permits issued: 64 (2013).
Income: Per capita income: $29,686 (2008-2012 5-year est.); Median household income: $55,355 (2008-2012 5-year est.); Average household income: $70,417 (2008-2012 5-year est.); Percent of households with income of $100,000 or more: 22.1% (2008-2012 5-year est.); Poverty rate: 13.6% (2008-2012 5-year est.); Bankruptcy rate: 3.36% (2013).
Taxes: Total county taxes per capita: $129 (2011); County property taxes per capita: $125 (2011).
Education: Percent of population age 25 and over with: High school diploma (including GED) or higher: 91.9% (2008-2012 5-year est.); Bachelor's degree or higher: 31.6% (2008-2012 5-year est.); Master's degree or higher: 11.6% (2008-2012 5-year est.).
Housing: Homeownership rate: 71.3% (2008-2012 5-year est.); Median home value: $124,100 (2008-2012 5-year est.); Median contract rent: $552 per month (2008-2012 5-year est.); Median year structure built: 1972 (2008-2012 5-year est.)
Health: Birth rate: 120.6 per 10,000 population (2013); Death rate: 99.4 per 10,000 population (2013); Age-adjusted cancer mortality rate: 193.3 deaths per 100,000 population (2011); Number of physicians: 56.8 per 10,000 population (2011); Hospital beds: 54.7 per 10,000 population (2010); Hospital admissions: 2,365.7 per 10,000 population (2010).
Environment: Air Quality Index: 86.6% good, 13.4% moderate, 0.0% unhealthy for sensitive individuals, 0.0% unhealthy (percent of days in 2013)
Elections: 2012 Presidential election results: 44.6% Obama, 53.3% Romney
National and State Parks: Lincoln Home National Historic Site; Lincolns Tomb State Historic Site; Sangchris Lake State Park
Additional Information Contacts

Sangamon County Government . . . . (217) 753-6600
http://www.co.sangamon.il.us

Sangamon County Communities

AUBURN (city). Covers a land area of 4.075 square miles and a water area of 0 square miles. Located at 39.58° N. Lat; 89.74° W. Long. Elevation is 627 feet.
History: Incorporated 1865.
Population: 3,724 (1990); 4,317 (2000); 4,771 (2010); Density: 1,215.2 persons per square mile (2008-2012 5-year est.); Race: 99.4% White, 0.0% Black/African American, 0.0% Asian, 0.0% American Indian/Alaska Native, 0.6% Native Hawaiian/Other Pacific Islander, 0.0% Some other race, 0.0% Two or more races, 0.5% Hispanic of any race (2008-2012 5-year est.); Average household size: 2.70 (2008-2012 5-year est.); Median age: 34.1 (2008-2012 5-year est.); Males per 100 females: 115.7 (2008-2012 5-year est.); Marriage status: 29.4% never married, 52.9% now married, 6.7% widowed, 11.0% divorced (2008-2012 5-year est.); Foreign born: 1.4% (2008-2012 5-year est.); Ancestry (includes multiple ancestries): 26.1% German, 15.7% Irish, 9.3% American, 7.2% English, 6.6% French (2008-2012 5-year est.).
Economy: Single-family building permits issued: 3 (2013); Multi-family building permits issued: 4 (2013); Homeowner vacancy rate: 0.0%. Rental vacancy rate: 0.0%. (2008-2012 5-year est.); Employment by occupation: 13.9% management, business, and financial, 4.3% computer, engineering, and science, 4.4% education, legal, community service, arts, and media, 4.1% healthcare practitioners, 25.2% service, 27.0% sales and office, 9.8% natural resources, construction, and maintenance, 11.4% production, transportation, and material moving (2008-2012 5-year est.).
Income: Per capita income: $25,932 (2008-2012 5-year est.); Median household income: $60,090 (2008-2012 5-year est.); Average household income: $70,009 (2008-2012 5-year est.); Percent of households with income of $100,000 or more: 22.5% (2008-2012 5-year est.); Poverty rate: 10.9% (2008-2012 5-year est.).
Education: Percent of population age 25 and over with: High school diploma (including GED) or higher: 93.5% (2008-2012 5-year est.); Bachelor's degree or higher: 20.8% (2008-2012 5-year est.); Master's degree or higher: 5.9% (2008-2012 5-year est.).

School District(s)
Auburn CUSD 10 (PK-12)
    2011-12 Enrollment: 1,498 . . . . (217) 438-6164
Housing: Homeownership rate: 72.2% (2008-2012 5-year est.); Median home value: $99,100 (2008-2012 5-year est.); Median contract rent: $511 per month (2008-2012 5-year est.); Median year structure built: 1969 (2008-2012 5-year est.).
Health Insurance: 74.0% Private; 22.9% Public; 12.5% None. (2008-2012 5-year est.)
Transportation: Commute to work: 96.0% car, 0.0% public transportation, 0.3% walk, 1.9% work from home (2008-2012 5-year est.); Travel time to work: 20.5% less than 15 minutes, 37.6% 15 to 30 minutes, 29.2% 30 to 45 minutes, 7.8% 45 to 60 minutes, 4.8% 60 minutes or more (2008-2012 5-year est.)

BERLIN (village). Covers a land area of 0.999 square miles and a water area of 0 square miles. Located at 39.76° N. Lat; 89.90° W. Long. Elevation is 636 feet.
Population: 180 (1990); 140 (2000); 180 (2010); Density: 186.1 persons per square mile (2008-2012 5-year est.); Race: 100.0% White, 0.0% Black/African American, 0.0% Asian, 0.0% American Indian/Alaska Native, 0.0% Native Hawaiian/Other Pacific Islander, 0.0% Some other race, 0.0% Two or more races, 0.0% Hispanic of any race (2008-2012 5-year est.); Average household size: 2.45 (2008-2012 5-year est.); Median age: 50.0 (2008-2012 5-year est.); Males per 100 females: 121.4 (2008-2012 5-year est.); Marriage status: 30.6% never married, 55.6% now married, 5.0% widowed, 8.9% divorced (2008-2012 5-year est.); Foreign born: 0.0% (2008-2012 5-year est.); Ancestry (includes multiple ancestries): 34.9% German, 13.4% Irish, 7.5% American, 4.3% Russian, 3.2% Welsh (2008-2012 5-year est.).
Economy: Homeowner vacancy rate: 0.0%. Rental vacancy rate: 0.0%. (2008-2012 5-year est.); Employment by occupation: 14.2% management, business, and financial, 8.8% computer, engineering, and science, 2.7% education, legal, community service, arts, and media, 0.0% healthcare practitioners, 18.6% service, 24.8% sales and office, 4.4% natural resources, construction, and maintenance, 26.5% production, transportation, and material moving (2008-2012 5-year est.).

Income: Per capita income: $24,607 (2008-2012 5-year est.); Median household income: $51,250 (2008-2012 5-year est.); Average household income: $61,464 (2008-2012 5-year est.); Percent of households with income of $100,000 or more: 10.5% (2008-2012 5-year est.); Poverty rate: 4.8% (2008-2012 5-year est.).

Education: Percent of population age 25 and over with: High school diploma (including GED) or higher: 87.8% (2008-2012 5-year est.); Bachelor's degree or higher: 6.8% (2008-2012 5-year est.); Master's degree or higher: 2.7% (2008-2012 5-year est.).

Housing: Homeownership rate: 82.9% (2008-2012 5-year est.); Median home value: $79,400 (2008-2012 5-year est.); Median contract rent: $309 per month (2008-2012 5-year est.); Median year structure built: 1980 (2008-2012 5-year est.).

Health Insurance: 60.2% Private; 31.7% Public; 18.8% None. (2008-2012 5-year est.)

Transportation: Commute to work: 93.8% car, 0.0% public transportation, 6.2% walk, 0.0% work from home (2008-2012 5-year est.); Travel time to work: 25.7% less than 15 minutes, 24.8% 15 to 30 minutes, 42.5% 30 to 45 minutes, 7.1% 45 to 60 minutes, 0.0% 60 minutes or more (2008-2012 5-year est.)

BUFFALO (village). Covers a land area of 0.365 square miles and a water area of 0 square miles. Located at 39.85° N. Lat; 89.41° W. Long. Elevation is 614 feet.

Population: 503 (1990); 491 (2000); 503 (2010); Density: 1,072.8 persons per square mile (2008-2012 5-year est.); Race: 96.4% White, 0.0% Black/African American, 0.0% Asian, 0.0% American Indian/Alaska Native, 0.0% Native Hawaiian/Other Pacific Islander, 3.6% Some other race, 0.0% Two or more races, 1.5% Hispanic of any race (2008-2012 5-year est.); Average household size: 2.18 (2008-2012 5-year est.); Median age: 49.3 (2008-2012 5-year est.); Males per 100 females: 71.2 (2008-2012 5-year est.); Marriage status: 17.5% never married, 57.8% now married, 10.2% widowed, 14.6% divorced (2008-2012 5-year est.); Foreign born: 3.1% (2008-2012 5-year est.); Ancestry (includes multiple ancestries): 31.4% German, 24.5% Irish, 23.5% English, 8.7% Dutch, 5.1% American (2008-2012 5-year est.).

Economy: Single-family building permits issued: 0 (2013); Multi-family building permits issued: 0 (2013); Homeowner vacancy rate: 8.5%. Rental vacancy rate: 8.9%. (2008-2012 5-year est.); Employment by occupation: 13.5% management, business, and financial, 5.1% computer, engineering, and science, 4.5% education, legal, community service, arts, and media, 0.0% healthcare practitioners, 15.7% service, 25.8% sales and office, 25.3% natural resources, construction, and maintenance, 10.1% production, transportation, and material moving (2008-2012 5-year est.).

Income: Per capita income: $23,990 (2008-2012 5-year est.); Median household income: $42,000 (2008-2012 5-year est.); Average household income: $52,547 (2008-2012 5-year est.); Percent of households with income of $100,000 or more: 16.6% (2008-2012 5-year est.); Poverty rate: 22.2% (2008-2012 5-year est.).

Education: Percent of population age 25 and over with: High school diploma (including GED) or higher: 88.4% (2008-2012 5-year est.); Bachelor's degree or higher: 18.1% (2008-2012 5-year est.); Master's degree or higher: 5.5% (2008-2012 5-year est.).

School District(s)

Tri City CUSD 1 (PK-12)

    2011-12 Enrollment: 582 . . . . (217) 364-4811

Housing: Homeownership rate: 60.0% (2008-2012 5-year est.); Median home value: $84,500 (2008-2012 5-year est.); Median contract rent: $235 per month (2008-2012 5-year est.); Median year structure built: 1967 (2008-2012 5-year est.).

Health Insurance: 63.3% Private; 42.3% Public; 12.2% None. (2008-2012 5-year est.)

Transportation: Commute to work: 97.8% car, 0.0% public transportation, 2.2% walk, 0.0% work from home (2008-2012 5-year est.); Travel time to work: 7.9% less than 15 minutes, 56.2% 15 to 30 minutes, 29.8% 30 to 45 minutes, 3.4% 45 to 60 minutes, 2.8% 60 minutes or more (2008-2012 5-year est.)

CANTRALL (village). Covers a land area of 0.262 square miles and a water area of 0 square miles. Located at 39.94° N. Lat; 89.68° W. Long. Elevation is 594 feet.

Population: 123 (1990); 139 (2000); 139 (2010); Density: 653.2 persons per square mile (2008-2012 5-year est.); Race: 98.8% White, 0.0% Black/African American, 0.0% Asian, 1.2% American Indian/Alaska Native, 0.0% Native Hawaiian/Other Pacific Islander, 0.0% Some other race, 0.0%

Two or more races, 0.0% Hispanic of any race (2008-2012 5-year est.); Average household size: 2.22 (2008-2012 5-year est.); Median age: 45.9 (2008-2012 5-year est.); Males per 100 females: 147.8 (2008-2012 5-year est.); Marriage status: 24.0% never married, 57.5% now married, 3.4% widowed, 15.1% divorced (2008-2012 5-year est.); Foreign born: 5.3% (2008-2012 5-year est.); Ancestry (includes multiple ancestries): 27.5% German, 21.1% Irish, 13.5% American, 8.2% English, 7.6% Dutch (2008-2012 5-year est.).

Economy: Homeowner vacancy rate: 0.0%. Rental vacancy rate: 0.0%. (2008-2012 5-year est.); Employment by occupation: 1.9% management, business, and financial, 10.7% computer, engineering, and science, 6.8% education, legal, community service, arts, and media, 7.8% healthcare practitioners, 24.3% service, 20.4% sales and office, 17.5% natural resources, construction, and maintenance, 10.7% production, transportation, and material moving (2008-2012 5-year est.).

Income: Per capita income: $31,054 (2008-2012 5-year est.); Median household income: $59,375 (2008-2012 5-year est.); Average household income: $69,401 (2008-2012 5-year est.); Percent of households with income of $100,000 or more: 32.5% (2008-2012 5-year est.); Poverty rate: 2.5% (2008-2012 5-year est.).

Education: Percent of population age 25 and over with: High school diploma (including GED) or higher: 98.4% (2008-2012 5-year est.); Bachelor's degree or higher: 15.7% (2008-2012 5-year est.); Master's degree or higher: 2.4% (2008-2012 5-year est.).

School District(s)

Athens CUSD 213 (PK-12)

    2011-12 Enrollment: 1,128 . . . . (217) 636-8761

Housing: Homeownership rate: 85.7% (2008-2012 5-year est.); Median home value: $125,000 (2008-2012 5-year est.); Median contract rent: $469 per month (2008-2012 5-year est.); Median year structure built: 1960 (2008-2012 5-year est.).

Health Insurance: 78.9% Private; 32.2% Public; 18.1% None. (2008-2012 5-year est.)

Transportation: Commute to work: 98.1% car, 0.0% public transportation, 1.0% walk, 1.0% work from home (2008-2012 5-year est.); Travel time to work: 8.8% less than 15 minutes, 64.7% 15 to 30 minutes, 22.5% 30 to 45 minutes, 2.0% 45 to 60 minutes, 2.0% 60 minutes or more (2008-2012 5-year est.)

CHATHAM (village). Covers a land area of 5.720 square miles and a water area of 0.002 square miles. Located at 39.67° N. Lat; 89.70° W. Long. Elevation is 600 feet.

Population: 6,074 (1990); 8,583 (2000); 11,500 (2010); Density: 2,064.3 persons per square mile (2008-2012 5-year est.); Race: 94.7% White, 1.2% Black/African American, 0.9% Asian, 0.1% American Indian/Alaska Native, 0.0% Native Hawaiian/Other Pacific Islander, 3.1% Some other race, 0.6% Two or more races, 3.2% Hispanic of any race (2008-2012 5-year est.); Average household size: 2.75 (2008-2012 5-year est.); Median age: 35.9 (2008-2012 5-year est.); Males per 100 females: 90.5 (2008-2012 5-year est.); Marriage status: 22.8% never married, 64.0% now married, 3.5% widowed, 9.7% divorced (2008-2012 5-year est.); Foreign born: 2.1% (2008-2012 5-year est.); Ancestry (includes multiple ancestries): 33.6% German, 14.8% Irish, 10.9% English, 8.0% Italian, 6.8% American (2008-2012 5-year est.).

Economy: Single-family building permits issued: 65 (2013); Multi-family building permits issued: 12 (2013); Homeowner vacancy rate: 0.0%. Rental vacancy rate: 0.0%. (2008-2012 5-year est.); Employment by occupation: 19.1% management, business, and financial, 8.9% computer, engineering, and science, 11.2% education, legal, community service, arts, and media, 9.2% healthcare practitioners, 12.6% service, 26.1% sales and office, 6.4% natural resources, construction, and maintenance, 6.6% production, transportation, and material moving (2008-2012 5-year est.).

Income: Per capita income: $30,854 (2008-2012 5-year est.); Median household income: $79,659 (2008-2012 5-year est.); Average household income: $84,811 (2008-2012 5-year est.); Percent of households with income of $100,000 or more: 33.8% (2008-2012 5-year est.); Poverty rate: 4.9% (2008-2012 5-year est.).

Education: Percent of population age 25 and over with: High school diploma (including GED) or higher: 97.7% (2008-2012 5-year est.); Bachelor's degree or higher: 41.8% (2008-2012 5-year est.); Master's degree or higher: 16.2% (2008-2012 5-year est.).

School District(s)

Ball Chatham CUSD 5 (PK-12)

    2011-12 Enrollment: 4,518 . . . . (217) 483-2416

Housing: Homeownership rate: 86.7% (2008-2012 5-year est.); Median home value: $161,800 (2008-2012 5-year est.); Median contract rent: $801 per month (2008-2012 5-year est.); Median year structure built: 1991 (2008-2012 5-year est.).
Health Insurance: 89.1% Private; 17.3% Public; 3.0% None. (2008-2012 5-year est.)
Transportation: Commute to work: 95.0% car, 0.0% public transportation, 0.0% walk, 4.8% work from home (2008-2012 5-year est.); Travel time to work: 19.0% less than 15 minutes, 57.9% 15 to 30 minutes, 16.9% 30 to 45 minutes, 2.3% 45 to 60 minutes, 3.9% 60 minutes or more (2008-2012 5-year est.)
Additional Information Contacts
Chatham Area Chamber of Commerce . . . . (217) 483-6450
   http://www.chatham-il-chamber.com
Village of Chatham . . . . (217) 483-2451
   http://www.chathamil.net

CLEAR LAKE (village). Covers a land area of 0.107 square miles and a water area of 0 square miles. Located at 39.81° N. Lat; 89.57° W. Long. Elevation is 574 feet.
Population: 193 (1990); 267 (2000); 229 (2010); Density: 2,326.9 persons per square mile (2008-2012 5-year est.); Race: 91.1% White, 0.0% Black/African American, 0.0% Asian, 0.0% American Indian/Alaska Native, 0.0% Native Hawaiian/Other Pacific Islander, 8.9% Some other race, 0.0% Two or more races, 8.9% Hispanic of any race (2008-2012 5-year est.); Average household size: 2.43 (2008-2012 5-year est.); Median age: 45.6 (2008-2012 5-year est.); Males per 100 females: 85.1 (2008-2012 5-year est.); Marriage status: 24.0% never married, 47.1% now married, 4.4% widowed, 24.5% divorced (2008-2012 5-year est.); Foreign born: 0.0% (2008-2012 5-year est.); Ancestry (includes multiple ancestries): 19.8% German, 13.7% Irish, 11.7% American, 2.8% Polish, 2.4% Scotch-Irish (2008-2012 5-year est.).
Economy: Homeowner vacancy rate: 0.0%. Rental vacancy rate: 0.0%. (2008-2012 5-year est.); Employment by occupation: 6.3% management, business, and financial, 3.9% computer, engineering, and science, 0.0% education, legal, community service, arts, and media, 3.1% healthcare practitioners, 11.7% service, 56.3% sales and office, 5.5% natural resources, construction, and maintenance, 13.3% production, transportation, and material moving (2008-2012 5-year est.).
Income: Per capita income: $22,550 (2008-2012 5-year est.); Median household income: $42,250 (2008-2012 5-year est.); Average household income: $53,594 (2008-2012 5-year est.); Percent of households with income of $100,000 or more: 6.9% (2008-2012 5-year est.); Poverty rate: 8.3% (2008-2012 5-year est.).
Education: Percent of population age 25 and over with: High school diploma (including GED) or higher: 72.6% (2008-2012 5-year est.); Bachelor's degree or higher: 5.1% (2008-2012 5-year est.); Master's degree or higher: 0.0% (2008-2012 5-year est.).
Housing: Homeownership rate: 82.4% (2008-2012 5-year est.); Median home value: $66,000 (2008-2012 5-year est.); Median contract rent: $425 per month (2008-2012 5-year est.); Median year structure built: 1988 (2008-2012 5-year est.).
Health Insurance: 69.0% Private; 33.1% Public; 13.3% None. (2008-2012 5-year est.)
Transportation: Commute to work: 100.0% car, 0.0% public transportation, 0.0% walk, 0.0% work from home (2008-2012 5-year est.); Travel time to work: 29.4% less than 15 minutes, 50.8% 15 to 30 minutes, 15.9% 30 to 45 minutes, 0.0% 45 to 60 minutes, 4.0% 60 minutes or more (2008-2012 5-year est.)

CURRAN (village). Covers a land area of 2.068 square miles and a water area of 0 square miles. Located at 39.74° N. Lat; 89.78° W. Long. Elevation is 623 feet.
History: Incorporated 2005.
Population: n/a (1990); n/a (2000); 212 (2010); Density: 92.3 persons per square mile (2008-2012 5-year est.); Race: 100.0% White, 0.0% Black/African American, 0.0% Asian, 0.0% American Indian/Alaska Native, 0.0% Native Hawaiian/Other Pacific Islander, 0.0% Some other race, 0.0% Two or more races, 1.0% Hispanic of any race (2008-2012 5-year est.); Average household size: 2.30 (2008-2012 5-year est.); Median age: 44.8 (2008-2012 5-year est.); Males per 100 females: 87.3 (2008-2012 5-year est.); Marriage status: 27.0% never married, 47.2% now married, 8.8% widowed, 17.0% divorced (2008-2012 5-year est.); Foreign born: 0.0% (2008-2012 5-year est.); Ancestry (includes multiple ancestries): 47.1%

German, 25.7% Irish, 11.5% French, 8.9% American, 5.8% English (2008-2012 5-year est.).
Economy: Homeowner vacancy rate: 9.6%. Rental vacancy rate: 0.0%. (2008-2012 5-year est.); Employment by occupation: 16.0% management, business, and financial, 0.0% computer, engineering, and science, 2.0% education, legal, community service, arts, and media, 11.0% healthcare practitioners, 15.0% service, 28.0% sales and office, 7.0% natural resources, construction, and maintenance, 21.0% production, transportation, and material moving (2008-2012 5-year est.).
Income: Per capita income: $21,518 (2008-2012 5-year est.); Median household income: $37,250 (2008-2012 5-year est.); Average household income: $48,495 (2008-2012 5-year est.); Percent of households with income of $100,000 or more: 8.4% (2008-2012 5-year est.); Poverty rate: 20.4% (2008-2012 5-year est.).
Education: Percent of population age 25 and over with: High school diploma (including GED) or higher: 83.8% (2008-2012 5-year est.); Bachelor's degree or higher: 2.2% (2008-2012 5-year est.); Master's degree or higher: 2.2% (2008-2012 5-year est.).
Housing: Homeownership rate: 79.5% (2008-2012 5-year est.); Median home value: $70,000 (2008-2012 5-year est.); Median contract rent: $475 per month (2008-2012 5-year est.); Median year structure built: 1960 (2008-2012 5-year est.).
Health Insurance: 68.1% Private; 38.2% Public; 11.5% None. (2008-2012 5-year est.)
Transportation: Commute to work: 92.9% car, 0.0% public transportation, 0.0% walk, 4.1% work from home (2008-2012 5-year est.); Travel time to work: 28.7% less than 15 minutes, 46.8% 15 to 30 minutes, 19.1% 30 to 45 minutes, 2.1% 45 to 60 minutes, 3.2% 60 minutes or more (2008-2012 5-year est.)

DAWSON (village). Covers a land area of 0.885 square miles and a water area of 0 square miles. Located at 39.85° N. Lat; 89.46° W. Long. Elevation is 600 feet.
Population: 536 (1990); 466 (2000); 509 (2010); Density: 603.7 persons per square mile (2008-2012 5-year est.); Race: 100.0% White, 0.0% Black/African American, 0.0% Asian, 0.0% American Indian/Alaska Native, 0.0% Native Hawaiian/Other Pacific Islander, 0.0% Some other race, 0.0% Two or more races, 0.0% Hispanic of any race (2008-2012 5-year est.); Average household size: 2.46 (2008-2012 5-year est.); Median age: 30.9 (2008-2012 5-year est.); Males per 100 females: 82.3 (2000-2012 5-year est.); Marriage status: 28.5% never married, 54.1% now married, 5.9% widowed, 11.5% divorced (2008-2012 5-year est.); Foreign born: 2.1% (2008-2012 5-year est.); Ancestry (includes multiple ancestries): 24.7% German, 18.2% Irish, 14.8% English, 6.9% Italian, 6.0% Scottish (2008-2012 5-year est.).
Economy: Single-family building permits issued: 0 (2013); Multi-family building permits issued: 0 (2013); Homeowner vacancy rate: 0.0%. Rental vacancy rate: 0.0%. (2008-2012 5-year est.); Employment by occupation: 9.6% management, business, and financial, 3.3% computer, engineering, and science, 4.8% education, legal, community service, arts, and media, 4.8% healthcare practitioners, 18.9% service, 30.7% sales and office, 13.3% natural resources, construction, and maintenance, 14.4% production, transportation, and material moving (2008-2012 5-year est.).
Income: Per capita income: $20,520 (2008-2012 5-year est.); Median household income: $45,625 (2008-2012 5-year est.); Average household income: $50,209 (2008-2012 5-year est.); Percent of households with income of $100,000 or more: 12.0% (2008-2012 5-year est.); Poverty rate: 17.8% (2008-2012 5-year est.).
Education: Percent of population age 25 and over with: High school diploma (including GED) or higher: 93.8% (2008-2012 5-year est.); Bachelor's degree or higher: 12.2% (2008-2012 5-year est.); Master's degree or higher: 2.0% (2008-2012 5-year est.).
Housing: Homeownership rate: 79.3% (2008-2012 5-year est.); Median home value: $84,800 (2008-2012 5-year est.); Median contract rent: $452 per month (2008-2012 5-year est.); Median year structure built: 1969 (2008-2012 5-year est.).
Health Insurance: 57.9% Private; 49.4% Public; 9.7% None. (2008-2012 5-year est.)
Transportation: Commute to work: 90.1% car, 0.0% public transportation, 5.7% walk, 4.2% work from home (2008-2012 5-year est.); Travel time to work: 27.4% less than 15 minutes, 48.8% 15 to 30 minutes, 19.8% 30 to 45 minutes, 0.0% 45 to 60 minutes, 4.0% 60 minutes or more (2008-2012 5-year est.)

DIVERNON (village). Covers a land area of 0.790 square miles and a water area of 0.001 square miles. Located at 39.57° N. Lat; 89.65° W. Long. Elevation is 614 feet.

History: Incorporated 1900.

Population: 1,178 (1990); 1,201 (2000); 1,172 (2010); Density: 1,892.0 persons per square mile (2008-2012 5-year est.); Race: 96.3% White, 0.0% Black/African American, 1.1% Asian, 0.6% American Indian/Alaska Native, 0.0% Native Hawaiian/Other Pacific Islander, 2.0% Some other race, 1.9% Two or more races, 0.0% Hispanic of any race (2008-2012 5-year est.); Average household size: 2.78 (2008-2012 5-year est.); Median age: 34.5 (2008-2012 5-year est.); Males per 100 females: 96.5 (2008-2012 5-year est.); Marriage status: 23.3% never married, 53.7% now married, 6.8% widowed, 16.1% divorced (2008-2012 5-year est.); Foreign born: 1.9% (2008-2012 5-year est.); Ancestry (includes multiple ancestries): 26.6% German, 19.6% Irish, 13.4% English, 8.0% American, 5.8% Dutch (2008-2012 5-year est.).

Economy: Single-family building permits issued: 0 (2013); Multi-family building permits issued: 0 (2013); Homeowner vacancy rate: 2.0%. Rental vacancy rate: 0.0%. (2008-2012 5-year est.); Employment by occupation: 9.5% management, business, and financial, 3.3% computer, engineering, and science, 6.8% education, legal, community service, arts, and media, 8.2% healthcare practitioners, 17.6% service, 26.1% sales and office, 13.0% natural resources, construction, and maintenance, 15.5% production, transportation, and material moving (2008-2012 5-year est.).

Income: Per capita income: $23,859 (2008-2012 5-year est.); Median household income: $59,135 (2008-2012 5-year est.); Average household income: $65,674 (2008-2012 5-year est.); Percent of households with income of $100,000 or more: 20.3% (2008-2012 5-year est.); Poverty rate: 11.2% (2008-2012 5-year est.).

Education: Percent of population age 25 and over with: High school diploma (including GED) or higher: 93.6% (2008-2012 5-year est.); Bachelor's degree or higher: 15.0% (2008-2012 5-year est.); Master's degree or higher: 2.4% (2008-2012 5-year est.).

School District(s)

Auburn CUSD 10 (PK-12)

    2011-12 Enrollment: 1,498 . . . . (217) 438-6164

Housing: Homeownership rate: 80.4% (2008-2012 5-year est.); Median home value: $99,100 (2008-2012 5-year est.); Median contract rent: $571 per month (2008-2012 5-year est.); Median year structure built: 1963 (2008-2012 5-year est.).

Health Insurance: 71.2% Private; 32.4% Public; 9.8% None. (2008-2012 5-year est.)

Safety: Violent crime rate: 33.8 per 10,000 population; Property crime rate: 59.2 per 10,000 population (2012).

Transportation: Commute to work: 98.1% car, 0.0% public transportation, 0.9% walk, 0.9% work from home (2008-2012 5-year est.); Travel time to work: 13.2% less than 15 minutes, 44.4% 15 to 30 minutes, 31.9% 30 to 45 minutes, 5.8% 45 to 60 minutes, 4.8% 60 minutes or more (2008-2012 5-year est.)

GLENARM (unincorporated postal area)

Zip Code: 62536

    Covers a land area of 6.911 square miles and a water area of 0.062 square miles. Located at 39.62° N. Lat; 89.65° W. Long. Elevation is 600 feet. Population: 912 (2010); Density: 132.0 persons per square mile (2010); Race: 97.8% White, 0.3% Black/African American, 0.8% Asian, 0.0% American Indian/Alaska Native, 0.0% Native Hawaiian/Other Pacific Islander, 1.1% Some other race, 0.8% Two or more races, 1.2% Hispanic of any race (2010); Average household size: 2.78 (2010); Median age: 44.1 (2010); Males per 100 females: 104.0 (2010); Homeownership rate: 95.1% (2010)

GRANDVIEW (village). Covers a land area of 0.338 square miles and a water area of 0 square miles. Located at 39.82° N. Lat; 89.62° W. Long. Elevation is 597 feet.

History: Incorporated 1939.

Population: 1,647 (1990); 1,537 (2000); 1,441 (2010); Density: 4,534.8 persons per square mile (2008-2012 5-year est.); Race: 86.0% White, 11.9% Black/African American, 0.3% Asian, 0.8% American Indian/Alaska Native, 0.0% Native Hawaiian/Other Pacific Islander, 1.0% Some other race, 0.1% Two or more races, 0.0% Hispanic of any race (2008-2012 5-year est.); Average household size: 2.39 (2008-2012 5-year est.); Median age: 36.2 (2008-2012 5-year est.); Males per 100 females: 78.6 (2008-2012 5-year est.); Marriage status: 29.8% never married, 43.7% now married, 10.8% widowed, 15.7% divorced (2008-2012 5-year est.);

Foreign born: 1.1% (2008-2012 5-year est.); Ancestry (includes multiple ancestries): 23.1% German, 12.2% Irish, 9.8% English, 9.1% American, 4.6% Italian (2008-2012 5-year est.).

Economy: Homeowner vacancy rate: 3.9%. Rental vacancy rate: 4.3%. (2008-2012 5-year est.); Employment by occupation: 10.0% management, business, and financial, 0.4% computer, engineering, and science, 3.5% education, legal, community service, arts, and media, 4.1% healthcare practitioners, 21.4% service, 39.2% sales and office, 10.6% natural resources, construction, and maintenance, 10.7% production, transportation, and material moving (2008-2012 5-year est.).

Income: Per capita income: $21,768 (2008-2012 5-year est.); Median household income: $45,463 (2008-2012 5-year est.); Average household income: $51,034 (2008-2012 5-year est.); Percent of households with income of $100,000 or more: 8.0% (2008-2012 5-year est.); Poverty rate: 18.1% (2008-2012 5-year est.).

Education: Percent of population age 25 and over with: High school diploma (including GED) or higher: 85.8% (2008-2012 5-year est.); Bachelor's degree or higher: 7.9% (2008-2012 5-year est.); Master's degree or higher: 1.3% (2008-2012 5-year est.).

Housing: Homeownership rate: 72.5% (2008-2012 5-year est.); Median home value: $70,800 (2008-2012 5-year est.); Median contract rent: $618 per month (2008-2012 5-year est.); Median year structure built: 1955 (2008-2012 5-year est.).

Health Insurance: 64.0% Private; 38.8% Public; 14.1% None. (2008-2012 5-year est.)

Safety: Violent crime rate: 27.5 per 10,000 population; Property crime rate: 303.0 per 10,000 population (2012).

Transportation: Commute to work: 87.2% car, 4.9% public transportation, 2.6% walk, 2.3% work from home (2008-2012 5-year est.); Travel time to work: 40.5% less than 15 minutes, 40.0% 15 to 30 minutes, 8.5% 30 to 45 minutes, 2.2% 45 to 60 minutes, 8.8% 60 minutes or more (2008-2012 5-year est.)

ILLIOPOLIS (village). Covers a land area of 0.458 square miles and a water area of 0 square miles. Located at 39.85° N. Lat; 89.25° W. Long. Elevation is 604 feet.

Population: 934 (1990); 916 (2000); 891 (2010); Density: 1,902.4 persons per square mile (2008-2012 5-year est.); Race: 99.2% White, 0.3% Black/African American, 0.0% Asian, 0.0% American Indian/Alaska Native, 0.0% Native Hawaiian/Other Pacific Islander, 0.5% Some other race, 0.0% Two or more races, 0.5% Hispanic of any race (2008-2012 5-year est.); Average household size: 2.42 (2008-2012 5-year est.); Median age: 37.2 (2008-2012 5-year est.); Males per 100 females: 97.3 (2008-2012 5-year est.); Marriage status: 21.7% never married, 60.8% now married, 4.0% widowed, 13.5% divorced (2008-2012 5-year est.); Foreign born: 0.0% (2008-2012 5-year est.); Ancestry (includes multiple ancestries): 25.3% German, 16.2% Irish, 13.9% English, 11.7% American, 3.3% Polish (2008-2012 5-year est.).

Economy: Single-family building permits issued: 0 (2013); Multi-family building permits issued: 0 (2013); Homeowner vacancy rate: 0.0%. Rental vacancy rate: 7.0%. (2008-2012 5-year est.); Employment by occupation: 8.6% management, business, and financial, 4.8% computer, engineering, and science, 11.7% education, legal, community service, arts, and media, 5.7% healthcare practitioners, 18.6% service, 22.1% sales and office, 13.6% natural resources, construction, and maintenance, 15.0% production, transportation, and material moving (2008-2012 5-year est.).

Income: Per capita income: $24,541 (2008-2012 5-year est.); Median household income: $50,833 (2008-2012 5-year est.); Average household income: $59,584 (2008-2012 5-year est.); Percent of households with income of $100,000 or more: 13.3% (2008-2012 5-year est.); Poverty rate: 7.5% (2008-2012 5-year est.).

Education: Percent of population age 25 and over with: High school diploma (including GED) or higher: 92.4% (2008-2012 5-year est.); Bachelor's degree or higher: 18.3% (2008-2012 5-year est.); Master's degree or higher: 6.9% (2008-2012 5-year est.).

School District(s)

Sangamon Valley CUSD 9 (PK-12)

    2011-12 Enrollment: 782 . . . . (217) 668-2338

Housing: Homeownership rate: 76.4% (2008-2012 5-year est.); Median home value: $84,800 (2008-2012 5-year est.); Median contract rent: $388 per month (2008-2012 5-year est.); Median year structure built: 1955 (2008-2012 5-year est.).

Health Insurance: 75.2% Private; 26.3% Public; 12.5% None. (2008-2012 5-year est.)

Transportation: Commute to work: 96.3% car, 0.0% public transportation, 1.0% walk, 2.0% work from home (2008-2012 5-year est.); Travel time to work: 26.2% less than 15 minutes, 27.9% 15 to 30 minutes, 35.9% 30 to 45 minutes, 3.7% 45 to 60 minutes, 6.2% 60 minutes or more (2008-2012 5-year est.)

JEROME (village). Covers a land area of 0.451 square miles and a water area of 0 square miles. Located at 39.77° N. Lat; 89.68° W. Long. Elevation is 600 feet.
Population: 1,206 (1990); 1,414 (2000); 1,656 (2010); Density: 3,390.1 persons per square mile (2008-2012 5-year est.); Race: 96.7% White, 2.6% Black/African American, 0.5% Asian, 0.0% American Indian/Alaska Native, 0.0% Native Hawaiian/Other Pacific Islander, 0.2% Some other race, 0.2% Two or more races, 0.6% Hispanic of any race (2008-2012 5-year est.); Average household size: 1.92 (2008-2012 5-year est.); Median age: 47.6 (2008-2012 5-year est.); Males per 100 females: 95.7 (2008-2012 5-year est.); Marriage status: 27.0% never married, 48.5% now married, 8.2% widowed, 16.3% divorced (2008-2012 5-year est.); Foreign born: 2.2% (2008-2012 5-year est.); Ancestry (includes multiple ancestries): 27.7% German, 21.7% English, 19.1% Irish, 12.5% American, 6.1% Italian (2008-2012 5-year est.).
Economy: Single-family building permits issued: 0 (2013); Multi-family building permits issued: 0 (2013); Homeowner vacancy rate: 1.2%. Rental vacancy rate: 0.0%. (2008-2012 5-year est.); Employment by occupation: 14.3% management, business, and financial, 1.8% computer, engineering, and science, 11.1% education, legal, community service, arts, and media, 2.8% healthcare practitioners, 13.8% service, 38.9% sales and office, 10.6% natural resources, construction, and maintenance, 6.7% production, transportation, and material moving (2008-2012 5-year est.).
Income: Per capita income: $31,517 (2008-2012 5-year est.); Median household income: $53,571 (2008-2012 5-year est.); Average household income: $60,173 (2008-2012 5-year est.); Percent of households with income of $100,000 or more: 14.8% (2008-2012 5-year est.); Poverty rate: 4.4% (2008-2012 5-year est.).
Education: Percent of population age 25 and over with: High school diploma (including GED) or higher: 94.0% (2008-2012 5-year est.); Bachelor's degree or higher: 28.1% (2008-2012 5-year est.); Master's degree or higher: 7.3% (2008-2012 5-year est.).
Housing: Homeownership rate: 80.3% (2008-2012 5-year est.); Median home value: $99,100 (2008-2012 5-year est.); Median contract rent: $660 per month (2008-2012 5-year est.); Median year structure built: 1954 (2008-2012 5-year est.).
Health Insurance: 82.1% Private; 30.6% Public; 8.4% None. (2008-2012 5-year est.)
Transportation: Commute to work: 94.4% car, 3.0% public transportation, 0.6% walk, 1.3% work from home (2008-2012 5-year est.); Travel time to work: 46.0% less than 15 minutes, 49.0% 15 to 30 minutes, 1.7% 30 to 45 minutes, 2.6% 45 to 60 minutes, 0.7% 60 minutes or more (2008-2012 5-year est.)

LELAND GROVE (city). Covers a land area of 0.627 square miles and a water area of 0 square miles. Located at 39.78° N. Lat; 89.68° W. Long. Elevation is 600 feet.
Population: 1,679 (1990); 1,592 (2000); 1,503 (2010); Density: 2,773.8 persons per square mile (2008-2012 5-year est.); Race: 91.7% White, 4.3% Black/African American, 1.4% Asian, 0.0% American Indian/Alaska Native, 0.0% Native Hawaiian/Other Pacific Islander, 2.6% Some other race, 1.7% Two or more races, 3.5% Hispanic of any race (2008-2012 5-year est.); Average household size: 2.31 (2008-2012 5-year est.); Median age: 45.7 (2008-2012 5-year est.); Males per 100 females: 84.7 (2008-2012 5-year est.); Marriage status: 22.4% never married, 65.5% now married, 5.5% widowed, 6.6% divorced (2008-2012 5-year est.); Foreign born: 7.9% (2008-2012 5-year est.); Ancestry (includes multiple ancestries): 28.4% German, 21.0% English, 17.9% Irish, 6.8% Scotch-Irish, 6.2% Italian (2008-2012 5-year est.).
Economy: Single-family building permits issued: 0 (2013); Multi-family building permits issued: 0 (2013); Homeowner vacancy rate: 0.0%. Rental vacancy rate: 0.0%. (2008-2012 5-year est.); Employment by occupation: 22.3% management, business, and financial, 5.8% computer, engineering, and science, 26.4% education, legal, community service, arts, and media, 12.5% healthcare practitioners, 4.8% service, 20.5% sales and office, 2.5% natural resources, construction, and maintenance, 5.1% production, transportation, and material moving (2008-2012 5-year est.).
Income: Per capita income: $55,556 (2008-2012 5-year est.); Median household income: $93,558 (2008-2012 5-year est.); Average household

income: $128,614 (2008-2012 5-year est.); Percent of households with income of $100,000 or more: 47.2% (2008-2012 5-year est.); Poverty rate: 6.2% (2008-2012 5-year est.).
Education: Percent of population age 25 and over with: High school diploma (including GED) or higher: 96.8% (2008-2012 5-year est.); Bachelor's degree or higher: 69.7% (2008-2012 5-year est.); Master's degree or higher: 34.7% (2008-2012 5-year est.).
Housing: Homeownership rate: 90.3% (2008-2012 5-year est.); Median home value: $218,300 (2008-2012 5-year est.); Median contract rent: $541 per month (2008-2012 5-year est.); Median year structure built: 1954 (2008-2012 5-year est.).
Health Insurance: 92.8% Private; 23.9% Public; 3.3% None. (2008-2012 5-year est.)
Transportation: Commute to work: 88.9% car, 3.5% public transportation, 0.0% walk, 4.7% work from home (2008-2012 5-year est.); Travel time to work: 52.9% less than 15 minutes, 33.2% 15 to 30 minutes, 3.7% 30 to 45 minutes, 6.0% 45 to 60 minutes, 4.2% 60 minutes or more (2008-2012 5-year est.)

LOAMI (village). Covers a land area of 1.046 square miles and a water area of 0.004 square miles. Located at 39.67° N. Lat; 89.85° W. Long. Elevation is 633 feet.
Population: 802 (1990); 804 (2000); 745 (2010); Density: 763.3 persons per square mile (2008-2012 5-year est.); Race: 90.1% White, 0.0% Black/African American, 1.1% Asian, 3.6% American Indian/Alaska Native, 0.0% Native Hawaiian/Other Pacific Islander, 5.2% Some other race, 3.8% Two or more races, 5.0% Hispanic of any race (2008-2012 5-year est.); Average household size: 2.86 (2008-2012 5-year est.); Median age: 34.3 (2008-2012 5-year est.); Males per 100 females: 98.0 (2008-2012 5-year est.); Marriage status: 23.7% never married, 56.3% now married, 3.6% widowed, 16.4% divorced (2008-2012 5-year est.); Foreign born: 0.5% (2008-2012 5-year est.); Ancestry (includes multiple ancestries): 21.1% German, 15.2% English, 14.0% Irish, 5.9% American, 5.3% French (2008-2012 5-year est.).
Economy: Single-family building permits issued: 2 (2013); Multi-family building permits issued: 0 (2013); Homeowner vacancy rate: 0.0%. Rental vacancy rate: 0.0%. (2008-2012 5-year est.); Employment by occupation: 10.6% management, business, and financial, 4.4% computer, engineering, and science, 3.8% education, legal, community service, arts, and media, 4.4% healthcare practitioners, 18.8% service, 25.3% sales and office, 17.4% natural resources, construction, and maintenance, 15.3% production, transportation, and material moving (2008-2012 5-year est.).
Income: Per capita income: $19,731 (2008-2012 5-year est.); Median household income: $51,875 (2008-2012 5-year est.); Average household income: $55,228 (2008-2012 5-year est.); Percent of households with income of $100,000 or more: 14.0% (2008-2012 5-year est.); Poverty rate: 23.7% (2008-2012 5-year est.).
Education: Percent of population age 25 and over with: High school diploma (including GED) or higher: 89.8% (2008-2012 5-year est.); Bachelor's degree or higher: 9.8% (2008-2012 5-year est.); Master's degree or higher: 3.0% (2008-2012 5-year est.).
Housing: Homeownership rate: 80.6% (2008-2012 5-year est.); Median home value: $79,200 (2008-2012 5-year est.); Median contract rent: $510 per month (2008-2012 5-year est.); Median year structure built: 1974 (2008-2012 5-year est.).
Health Insurance: 66.9% Private; 31.6% Public; 11.0% None. (2008-2012 5-year est.)
Safety: Violent crime rate: 0.0 per 10,000 population; Property crime rate: 160.0 per 10,000 population (2012).
Transportation: Commute to work: 97.1% car, 0.0% public transportation, 0.9% walk, 2.1% work from home (2008-2012 5-year est.); Travel time to work: 9.0% less than 15 minutes, 33.9% 15 to 30 minutes, 43.5% 30 to 45 minutes, 7.5% 45 to 60 minutes, 6.0% 60 minutes or more (2008-2012 5-year est.)

MECHANICSBURG (village). Covers a land area of 1.071 square miles and a water area of 0 square miles. Located at 39.80° N. Lat; 89.41° W. Long. Elevation is 591 feet.
Population: 538 (1990); 456 (2000); 590 (2010); Density: 547.9 persons per square mile (2008-2012 5-year est.); Race: 97.3% White, 1.9% Black/African American, 0.2% Asian, 0.0% American Indian/Alaska Native, 0.0% Native Hawaiian/Other Pacific Islander, 0.6% Some other race, 0.3% Two or more races, 0.0% Hispanic of any race (2008-2012 5-year est.); Average household size: 2.67 (2008-2012 5-year est.); Median age: 39.1 (2008-2012 5-year est.); Males per 100 females: 108.9 (2008-2012 5-year

est.); Marriage status: 28.9% never married, 50.8% now married, 3.3% widowed, 17.0% divorced (2008-2012 5-year est.); Foreign born: 3.7% (2008-2012 5-year est.); Ancestry (includes multiple ancestries): 32.4% German, 15.5% Irish, 13.5% American, 8.0% French, 7.0% Slovak (2008-2012 5-year est.).

Economy: Single-family building permits issued: 3 (2013); Multi-family building permits issued: 0 (2013); Homeowner vacancy rate: 0.0%. Rental vacancy rate: 0.0%. (2008-2012 5-year est.); Employment by occupation: 7.3% management, business, and financial, 6.6% computer, engineering, and science, 3.1% education, legal, community service, arts, and media, 4.2% healthcare practitioners, 23.3% service, 35.1% sales and office, 7.3% natural resources, construction, and maintenance, 13.2% production, transportation, and material moving (2008-2012 5-year est.).

Income: Per capita income: $22,042 (2008-2012 5-year est.); Median household income: $44,886 (2008-2012 5-year est.); Average household income: $58,597 (2008-2012 5-year est.); Percent of households with income of $100,000 or more: 16.8% (2008-2012 5-year est.); Poverty rate: 11.2% (2008-2012 5-year est.).

Education: Percent of population age 25 and over with: High school diploma (including GED) or higher: 84.6% (2008-2012 5-year est.); Bachelor's degree or higher: 8.4% (2008-2012 5-year est.); Master's degree or higher: 1.7% (2008-2012 5-year est.).

Housing: Homeownership rate: 88.6% (2008-2012 5-year est.); Median home value: $89,900 (2008-2012 5-year est.); Median contract rent: $396 per month (2008-2012 5-year est.); Median year structure built: 1955 (2008-2012 5-year est.).

Health Insurance: 53.3% Private; 37.9% Public; 20.6% None. (2008-2012 5-year est.)

Transportation: Commute to work: 96.9% car, 0.0% public transportation, 1.0% walk, 1.4% work from home (2008-2012 5-year est.); Travel time to work: 3.1% less than 15 minutes, 51.7% 15 to 30 minutes, 36.7% 30 to 45 minutes, 5.6% 45 to 60 minutes, 2.8% 60 minutes or more (2008-2012 5-year est.)

NEW BERLIN (village). Covers a land area of 1.145 square miles and a water area of 0 square miles. Located at 39.73° N. Lat; 89.91° W. Long. Elevation is 650 feet.

Population: 797 (1990); 1,030 (2000); 1,346 (2010); Density: 1,119.1 persons per square mile (2008-2012 5-year est.); Race: 99.4% White, 0.6% Black/African American, 0.0% Asian, 0.0% American Indian/Alaska Native, 0.0% Native Hawaiian/Other Pacific Islander, 0.0% Some other race, 0.0% Two or more races, 0.4% Hispanic of any race (2008-2012 5-year est.); Average household size: 2.32 (2008-2012 5-year est.); Median age: 43.6 (2008-2012 5-year est.); Males per 100 females: 92.3 (2008-2012 5-year est.); Marriage status: 27.9% never married, 48.5% now married, 6.0% widowed, 17.5% divorced (2008-2012 5-year est.); Foreign born: 1.7% (2008-2012 5-year est.); Ancestry (includes multiple ancestries): 28.6% German, 16.5% Irish, 11.2% English, 9.4% Italian, 7.3% American (2008-2012 5-year est.).

Economy: Single-family building permits issued: 1 (2013); Multi-family building permits issued: 0 (2013); Homeowner vacancy rate: 0.7%. Rental vacancy rate: 0.0%. (2008-2012 5-year est.); Employment by occupation: 15.4% management, business, and financial, 4.9% computer, engineering, and science, 7.2% education, legal, community service, arts, and media, 11.6% healthcare practitioners, 15.5% service, 32.0% sales and office, 5.5% natural resources, construction, and maintenance, 7.9% production, transportation, and material moving (2008-2012 5-year est.).

Income: Per capita income: $25,166 (2008-2012 5-year est.); Median household income: $52,583 (2008-2012 5-year est.); Average household income: $57,975 (2008-2012 5-year est.); Percent of households with income of $100,000 or more: 15.5% (2008-2012 5-year est.); Poverty rate: 9.1% (2008-2012 5-year est.).

Education: Percent of population age 25 and over with: High school diploma (including GED) or higher: 94.4% (2008-2012 5-year est.); Bachelor's degree or higher: 23.9% (2008-2012 5-year est.); Master's degree or higher: 6.2% (2008-2012 5-year est.).

School District(s)
New Berlin CUSD 16 (PK-12)
    2011-12 Enrollment: 890 . . . . (217) 624-2541

Housing: Homeownership rate: 74.1% (2008-2012 5-year est.); Median home value: $126,800 (2008-2012 5-year est.); Median contract rent: $458 per month (2008-2012 5-year est.); Median year structure built: 1976 (2008-2012 5-year est.).

Health Insurance: 75.4% Private; 25.9% Public; 12.4% None. (2008-2012 5-year est.)

PAWNEE (village). Covers a land area of 1.261 square miles and a water area of 0 square miles. Located at 39.59° N. Lat; 89.58° W. Long. Elevation is 604 feet.

History: Incorporated 1891.

Population: 2,384 (1990); 2,647 (2000); 2,739 (2010); Density: 2,126.0 persons per square mile (2008-2012 5-year est.); Race: 96.8% White, 0.0% Black/African American, 0.6% Asian, 1.2% American Indian/Alaska Native, 0.0% Native Hawaiian/Other Pacific Islander, 1.4% Some other race, 0.5% Two or more races, 1.7% Hispanic of any race (2008-2012 5-year est.); Average household size: 2.38 (2008-2012 5-year est.); Median age: 39.6 (2008-2012 5-year est.); Males per 100 females: 83.8 (2008-2012 5-year est.); Marriage status: 23.9% never married, 55.4% now married, 10.5% widowed, 10.2% divorced (2008-2012 5-year est.); Foreign born: 1.9% (2008-2012 5-year est.); Ancestry (includes multiple ancestries): 29.2% German, 14.4% English, 13.5% Irish, 10.3% American, 6.7% Italian (2008-2012 5-year est.).

Economy: Single-family building permits issued: 1 (2013); Multi-family building permits issued: 0 (2013); Homeowner vacancy rate: 0.0%. Rental vacancy rate: 0.0%. (2008-2012 5-year est.); Employment by occupation: 18.7% management, business, and financial, 2.5% computer, engineering, and science, 10.5% education, legal, community service, arts, and media, 4.5% healthcare practitioners, 14.9% service, 28.3% sales and office, 10.3% natural resources, construction, and maintenance, 10.2% production, transportation, and material moving (2008-2012 5-year est.).

Income: Per capita income: $27,567 (2008-2012 5-year est.); Median household income: $52,574 (2008-2012 5-year est.); Average household income: $64,310 (2008-2012 5-year est.); Percent of households with income of $100,000 or more: 21.3% (2008-2012 5-year est.); Poverty rate: 4.7% (2008-2012 5-year est.).

Education: Percent of population age 25 and over with: High school diploma (including GED) or higher: 91.9% (2008-2012 5-year est.); Bachelor's degree or higher: 21.2% (2008-2012 5-year est.); Master's degree or higher: 5.1% (2008-2012 5-year est.).

School District(s)
Pawnee CUSD 11 (PK-12)
    2011-12 Enrollment: 626 . . . . (217) 625-2471

Housing: Homeownership rate: 80.1% (2008-2012 5-year est.); Median home value: $106,100 (2008-2012 5-year est.); Median contract rent: $558 per month (2008-2012 5-year est.); Median year structure built: 1969 (2008-2012 5-year est.).

Health Insurance: 80.9% Private; 26.3% Public; 6.7% None. (2008-2012 5-year est.)

Safety: Violent crime rate: 0.0 per 10,000 population; Property crime rate: 50.7 per 10,000 population (2012).

Transportation: Commute to work: 92.6% car, 0.0% public transportation, 1.5% walk, 3.2% work from home (2008-2012 5-year est.); Travel time to work: 15.3% less than 15 minutes, 50.6% 15 to 30 minutes, 27.8% 30 to 45 minutes, 4.3% 45 to 60 minutes, 2.0% 60 minutes or more (2008-2012 5-year est.)

Additional Information Contacts
Pawnee Chamber of Commerce . . . . (217) 625-8270
    http://www.pawneechamber.org
Village of Pawnee . . . . (217) 625-2941
    http://www.pawneeil.net

PLEASANT PLAINS (village). Covers a land area of 1.398 square miles and a water area of 0 square miles. Located at 39.87° N. Lat; 89.92° W. Long. Elevation is 610 feet.

Population: 701 (1990); 777 (2000); 802 (2010); Density: 631.7 persons per square mile (2008-2012 5-year est.); Race: 96.8% White, 0.5% Black/African American, 0.3% Asian, 0.0% American Indian/Alaska Native, 0.0% Native Hawaiian/Other Pacific Islander, 2.4% Some other race, 1.6% Two or more races, 0.2% Hispanic of any race (2008-2012 5-year est.); Average household size: 2.68 (2008-2012 5-year est.); Median age: 32.9 (2008-2012 5-year est.); Males per 100 females: 89.9 (2008-2012 5-year est.); Marriage status: 23.8% never married, 60.2% now married, 5.3% widowed, 10.7% divorced (2008-2012 5-year est.); Foreign born: 0.6% (2008-2012 5-year est.); Ancestry (includes multiple ancestries): 30.1%

German, 15.1% Irish, 12.0% American, 8.8% English, 4.3% Italian (2008-2012 5-year est.).

Economy: Single-family building permits issued: 2 (2013); Multi-family building permits issued: 0 (2013); Homeowner vacancy rate: 0.0%. Rental vacancy rate: 0.0%. (2008-2012 5-year est.); Employment by occupation: 12.7% management, business, and financial, 3.0% computer, engineering, and science, 13.7% education, legal, community service, arts, and media, 6.2% healthcare practitioners, 17.8% service, 29.8% sales and office, 12.0% natural resources, construction, and maintenance, 4.7% production, transportation, and material moving (2008-2012 5-year est.).

Income: Per capita income: $25,028 (2008-2012 5-year est.); Median household income: $60,893 (2008-2012 5-year est.); Average household income: $67,502 (2008-2012 5-year est.); Percent of households with income of $100,000 or more: 23.7% (2008-2012 5-year est.); Poverty rate: 7.1% (2008-2012 5-year est.).

Education: Percent of population age 25 and over with: High school diploma (including GED) or higher: 98.4% (2008-2012 5-year est.); Bachelor's degree or higher: 27.8% (2008-2012 5-year est.); Master's degree or higher: 7.8% (2008-2012 5-year est.).

School District(s)

Pleasant Plains CUSD 8 (PK-12)

    2011-12 Enrollment: 1,326 . . . . (217) 626-1041

Housing: Homeownership rate: 88.4% (2008-2012 5-year est.); Median home value: $125,500 (2008-2012 5-year est.); Median contract rent: $467 per month (2008-2012 5-year est.); Median year structure built: 1972 (2008-2012 5-year est.).

Health Insurance: 79.8% Private; 32.7% Public; 4.1% None. (2008-2012 5-year est.)

Safety: Violent crime rate: 0.0 per 10,000 population; Property crime rate: 61.9 per 10,000 population (2012).

Transportation: Commute to work: 98.0% car, 0.0% public transportation, 0.4% walk, 1.5% work from home (2008-2012 5-year est.); Travel time to work: 11.9% less than 15 minutes, 45.9% 15 to 30 minutes, 37.1% 30 to 45 minutes, 2.9% 45 to 60 minutes, 2.2% 60 minutes or more (2008-2012 5-year est.)

RIVERTON (village). Covers a land area of 2.181 square miles and a water area of 0.036 square miles. Located at 39.85° N. Lat; 89.54° W. Long. Elevation is 571 feet.

History: Incorporated 1873.

Population: 2,638 (1990); 3,048 (2000); 3,455 (2010); Density: 1,582.5 persons per square mile (2008-2012 5-year est.); Race: 98.7% White, 0.0% Black/African American, 0.0% Asian, 0.0% American Indian/Alaska Native, 0.0% Native Hawaiian/Other Pacific Islander, 1.3% Some other race, 1.3% Two or more races, 2.6% Hispanic of any race (2008-2012 5-year est.); Average household size: 2.45 (2008-2012 5-year est.); Median age: 38.7 (2008-2012 5-year est.); Males per 100 females: 87.2 (2008-2012 5-year est.); Marriage status: 32.6% never married, 45.4% now married, 7.8% widowed, 14.2% divorced (2008-2012 5-year est.); Foreign born: 4.0% (2008-2012 5-year est.); Ancestry (includes multiple ancestries): 33.6% German, 15.3% Irish, 11.1% Italian, 10.4% American, 7.4% English (2008-2012 5-year est.).

Economy: Single-family building permits issued: 7 (2013); Multi-family building permits issued: 2 (2013); Homeowner vacancy rate: 0.0%. Rental vacancy rate: 9.4%. (2008-2012 5-year est.); Employment by occupation: 15.3% management, business, and financial, 6.8% computer, engineering, and science, 7.8% education, legal, community service, arts, and media, 1.5% healthcare practitioners, 23.4% service, 29.4% sales and office, 10.2% natural resources, construction, and maintenance, 5.6% production, transportation, and material moving (2008-2012 5-year est.).

Income: Per capita income: $22,775 (2008-2012 5-year est.); Median household income: $49,583 (2008-2012 5-year est.); Average household income: $54,984 (2008-2012 5-year est.); Percent of households with income of $100,000 or more: 10.1% (2008-2012 5-year est.); Poverty rate: 23.8% (2008-2012 5-year est.).

Education: Percent of population age 25 and over with: High school diploma (including GED) or higher: 86.2% (2008-2012 5-year est.); Bachelor's degree or higher: 17.5% (2008-2012 5-year est.); Master's degree or higher: 2.3% (2008-2012 5-year est.).

School District(s)

Riverton CUSD 14 (PK-12)

    2011-12 Enrollment: 1,551 . . . . (217) 629-6009

Housing: Homeownership rate: 68.7% (2008-2012 5-year est.); Median home value: $99,500 (2008-2012 5-year est.); Median contract rent: $567 per month (2008-2012 5-year est.); Median year structure built: 1977 (2008-2012 5-year est.).

Health Insurance: 76.8% Private; 32.9% Public; 5.0% None. (2008-2012 5-year est.)

Safety: Violent crime rate: 46.0 per 10,000 population; Property crime rate: 304.4 per 10,000 population (2012).

Transportation: Commute to work: 95.6% car, 0.0% public transportation, 2.9% walk, 1.5% work from home (2008-2012 5-year est.); Travel time to work: 22.8% less than 15 minutes, 60.9% 15 to 30 minutes, 12.2% 30 to 45 minutes, 2.5% 45 to 60 minutes, 1.5% 60 minutes or more (2008-2012 5-year est.)

ROCHESTER (village). Covers a land area of 2.434 square miles and a water area of 0.001 square miles. Located at 39.75° N. Lat; 89.53° W. Long. Elevation is 558 feet.

Population: 2,676 (1990); 2,893 (2000); 3,689 (2010); Density: 1,525.0 persons per square mile (2008-2012 5-year est.); Race: 94.0% White, 0.5% Black/African American, 3.1% Asian, 0.0% American Indian/Alaska Native, 0.0% Native Hawaiian/Other Pacific Islander, 2.4% Some other race, 2.4% Two or more races, 3.4% Hispanic of any race (2008-2012 5-year est.); Average household size: 2.67 (2008-2012 5-year est.); Median age: 40.3 (2008-2012 5-year est.); Males per 100 females: 83.7 (2008-2012 5-year est.); Marriage status: 15.3% never married, 65.6% now married, 6.0% widowed, 13.0% divorced (2008-2012 5-year est.); Foreign born: 3.3% (2008-2012 5-year est.); Ancestry (includes multiple ancestries): 36.7% German, 15.4% English, 15.0% Irish, 9.8% American, 5.2% French (2008-2012 5-year est.).

Economy: Single-family building permits issued: 6 (2013); Multi-family building permits issued: 0 (2013); Homeowner vacancy rate: 2.5%. Rental vacancy rate: 0.0%. (2008-2012 5-year est.); Employment by occupation: 18.1% management, business, and financial, 8.9% computer, engineering, and science, 16.7% education, legal, community service, arts, and media, 13.2% healthcare practitioners, 9.9% service, 25.6% sales and office, 4.1% natural resources, construction, and maintenance, 3.5% production, transportation, and material moving (2008-2012 5-year est.).

Income: Per capita income: $38,374 (2008-2012 5-year est.); Median household income: $89,113 (2008-2012 5-year est.); Average household income: $103,939 (2008-2012 5-year est.); Percent of households with income of $100,000 or more: 40.0% (2008-2012 5-year est.); Poverty rate: 2.8% (2008-2012 5-year est.).

Education: Percent of population age 25 and over with: High school diploma (including GED) or higher: 95.6% (2008-2012 5-year est.); Bachelor's degree or higher: 50.8% (2008-2012 5-year est.); Master's degree or higher: 20.6% (2008-2012 5-year est.).

School District(s)

Rochester CUSD 3a (PK-12)

    2011-12 Enrollment: 2,333 . . . . (217) 498-6210

Housing: Homeownership rate: 90.1% (2008-2012 5-year est.); Median home value: $161,500 (2008-2012 5-year est.); Median contract rent: $682 per month (2008-2012 5-year est.); Median year structure built: 1978 (2008-2012 5-year est.).

Health Insurance: 90.7% Private; 16.7% Public; 5.1% None. (2008-2012 5-year est.)

Transportation: Commute to work: 91.9% car, 0.0% public transportation, 1.2% walk, 5.9% work from home (2008-2012 5-year est.); Travel time to work: 22.2% less than 15 minutes, 64.1% 15 to 30 minutes, 5.5% 30 to 45 minutes, 1.8% 45 to 60 minutes, 6.5% 60 minutes or more (2008-2012 5-year est.)

SHERMAN (village). Covers a land area of 3.187 square miles and a water area of 0.045 square miles. Located at 39.89° N. Lat; 89.61° W. Long. Elevation is 581 feet.

Population: 2,080 (1990); 2,871 (2000); 4,148 (2010); Density: 1,221.6 persons per square mile (2008-2012 5-year est.); Race: 96.2% White, 0.0% Black/African American, 1.7% Asian, 0.0% American Indian/Alaska Native, 0.0% Native Hawaiian/Other Pacific Islander, 2.1% Some other race, 2.1% Two or more races, 0.0% Hispanic of any race (2008-2012 5-year est.); Average household size: 2.49 (2008-2012 5-year est.); Median age: 43.8 (2008-2012 5-year est.); Males per 100 females: 83.6 (2008-2012 5-year est.); Marriage status: 21.5% never married, 64.0% now married, 8.1% widowed, 6.5% divorced (2008-2012 5-year est.); Foreign born: 1.8% (2008-2012 5-year est.); Ancestry (includes multiple ancestries): 36.7% German, 18.7% Irish, 17.5% English, 9.2% Italian, 6.0% American (2008-2012 5-year est.).

Economy: Single-family building permits issued: 44 (2013); Multi-family building permits issued: 0 (2013); Homeowner vacancy rate: 1.8%. Rental vacancy rate: 7.7%. (2008-2012 5-year est.); Employment by occupation: 26.3% management, business, and financial, 8.8% computer, engineering, and science, 13.5% education, legal, community service, arts, and media, 10.8% healthcare practitioners, 11.7% service, 16.1% sales and office, 6.8% natural resources, construction, and maintenance, 6.0% production, transportation, and material moving (2008-2012 5-year est.).

Income: Per capita income: $40,210 (2008-2012 5-year est.); Median household income: $85,269 (2008-2012 5-year est.); Average household income: $103,283 (2008-2012 5-year est.); Percent of households with income of $100,000 or more: 41.3% (2008-2012 5-year est.); Poverty rate: 1.8% (2008-2012 5-year est.).

Education: Percent of population age 25 and over with: High school diploma (including GED) or higher: 95.5% (2008-2012 5-year est.); Bachelor's degree or higher: 45.3% (2008-2012 5-year est.); Master's degree or higher: 16.8% (2008-2012 5-year est.).

School District(s)

Williamsville CUSD 15 (PK-12)

    2011-12 Enrollment: 1,454 . . . . (217) 566-2014

Housing: Homeownership rate: 85.6% (2008-2012 5-year est.); Median home value: $187,300 (2008-2012 5-year est.); Median contract rent: $722 per month (2008-2012 5-year est.); Median year structure built: 1990 (2008-2012 5-year est.).

Health Insurance: 94.4% Private; 14.2% Public; 2.6% None. (2008-2012 5-year est.)

Safety: Violent crime rate: 4.8 per 10,000 population; Property crime rate: 47.9 per 10,000 population (2012).

Transportation: Commute to work: 97.1% car, 0.5% public transportation, 0.0% walk, 1.6% work from home (2008-2012 5-year est.); Travel time to work: 27.5% less than 15 minutes, 58.4% 15 to 30 minutes, 8.2% 30 to 45 minutes, 0.6% 45 to 60 minutes, 5.3% 60 minutes or more (2008-2012 5-year est.)

SOUTHERN VIEW (village). Covers a land area of 0.513 square miles and a water area of 0 square miles. Located at 39.76° N. Lat; 89.65° W. Long. Elevation is 610 feet.

Population: 1,906 (1990); 1,695 (2000); 1,642 (2010); Density: 3,550.0 persons per square mile (2008-2012 5-year est.); Race: 94.8% White, 2.0% Black/African American, 0.4% Asian, 0.0% American Indian/Alaska Native, 0.0% Native Hawaiian/Other Pacific Islander, 2.8% Some other race, 2.6% Two or more races, 2.6% Hispanic of any race (2008-2012 5-year est.); Average household size: 2.33 (2008-2012 5-year est.); Median age: 38.1 (2008-2012 5-year est.); Males per 100 females: 84.6 (2008-2012 5-year est.); Marriage status: 31.9% never married, 42.0% now married, 10.9% widowed, 15.2% divorced (2008-2012 5-year est.); Foreign born: 2.9% (2008-2012 5-year est.); Ancestry (includes multiple ancestries): 31.1% German, 16.7% Irish, 12.3% English, 9.1% American, 5.4% Hungarian (2008-2012 5-year est.).

Economy: Single-family building permits issued: 0 (2013); Multi-family building permits issued: 0 (2013); Homeowner vacancy rate: 0.0%. Rental vacancy rate: 5.5%. (2008-2012 5-year est.); Employment by occupation: 10.6% management, business, and financial, 5.7% computer, engineering, and science, 9.8% education, legal, community service, arts, and media, 5.6% healthcare practitioners, 17.4% service, 29.2% sales and office, 11.6% natural resources, construction, and maintenance, 10.1% production, transportation, and material moving (2008-2012 5-year est.).

Income: Per capita income: $20,249 (2008-2012 5-year est.); Median household income: $42,946 (2008-2012 5-year est.); Average household income: $47,891 (2008-2012 5-year est.); Percent of households with income of $100,000 or more: 3.4% (2008-2012 5-year est.); Poverty rate: 14.6% (2008-2012 5-year est.).

Education: Percent of population age 25 and over with: High school diploma (including GED) or higher: 91.6% (2008-2012 5-year est.); Bachelor's degree or higher: 14.9% (2008-2012 5-year est.); Master's degree or higher: 2.5% (2008-2012 5-year est.).

Housing: Homeownership rate: 77.2% (2008-2012 5-year est.); Median home value: $84,700 (2008-2012 5-year est.); Median contract rent: $578 per month (2008-2012 5-year est.); Median year structure built: 1954 (2008-2012 5-year est.).

Health Insurance: 69.5% Private; 34.3% Public; 10.3% None. (2008-2012 5-year est.)

Transportation: Commute to work: 94.1% car, 0.4% public transportation, 1.9% walk, 2.9% work from home (2008-2012 5-year est.); Travel time to work: 41.2% less than 15 minutes, 50.7% 15 to 30 minutes, 4.7% 30 to 45

minutes, 1.0% 45 to 60 minutes, 2.4% 60 minutes or more (2008-2012 5-year est.)

SPAULDING (village). Covers a land area of 0.789 square miles and a water area of 0.002 square miles. Located at 39.87° N. Lat; 89.55° W. Long. Elevation is 581 feet.

Population: 440 (1990); 559 (2000); 873 (2010); Density: 1,087.3 persons per square mile (2008-2012 5-year est.); Race: 98.6% White, 0.6% Black/African American, 0.0% Asian, 0.0% American Indian/Alaska Native, 0.0% Native Hawaiian/Other Pacific Islander, 0.8% Some other race, 0.8% Two or more races, 0.9% Hispanic of any race (2008-2012 5-year est.); Average household size: 2.90 (2008-2012 5-year est.); Median age: 40.1 (2008-2012 5-year est.); Males per 100 females: 88.6 (2008-2012 5-year est.); Marriage status: 20.5% never married, 71.0% now married, 2.1% widowed, 6.5% divorced (2008-2012 5-year est.); Foreign born: 1.6% (2008-2012 5-year est.); Ancestry (includes multiple ancestries): 43.2% German, 19.3% Irish, 11.2% Italian, 10.1% English, 5.1% American (2008-2012 5-year est.).

Economy: Single-family building permits issued: 2 (2013); Multi-family building permits issued: 0 (2013); Homeowner vacancy rate: 0.0%. Rental vacancy rate: 0.0%. (2008-2012 5-year est.); Employment by occupation: 21.0% management, business, and financial, 5.1% computer, engineering, and science, 5.4% education, legal, community service, arts, and media, 2.4% healthcare practitioners, 15.2% service, 34.9% sales and office, 11.8% natural resources, construction, and maintenance, 4.3% production, transportation, and material moving (2008-2012 5-year est.).

Income: Per capita income: $29,084 (2008-2012 5-year est.); Median household income: $84,773 (2008-2012 5-year est.); Average household income: $85,417 (2008-2012 5-year est.); Percent of households with income of $100,000 or more: 31.4% (2008-2012 5-year est.); Poverty rate: 2.8% (2008-2012 5-year est.).

Education: Percent of population age 25 and over with: High school diploma (including GED) or higher: 91.3% (2008-2012 5-year est.); Bachelor's degree or higher: 17.8% (2008-2012 5-year est.); Master's degree or higher: 6.2% (2008-2012 5-year est.).

Housing: Homeownership rate: 92.9% (2008-2012 5-year est.); Median home value: $175,700 (2008-2012 5-year est.); Median contract rent: $575 per month (2008-2012 5-year est.); Median year structure built: 1990 (2008-2012 5-year est.).

Health Insurance: 92.9% Private; 14.0% Public; 2.1% None. (2008-2012 5-year est.)

Transportation: Commute to work: 98.9% car, 0.0% public transportation, 0.7% walk, 0.4% work from home (2008-2012 5-year est.); Travel time to work: 26.9% less than 15 minutes, 58.4% 15 to 30 minutes, 10.9% 30 to 45 minutes, 1.8% 45 to 60 minutes, 2.0% 60 minutes or more (2008-2012 5-year est.)

SPRINGFIELD (city). Aka Southlawn. County seat. Covers a land area of 59.480 square miles and a water area of 6.284 square miles. Located at 39.76° N. Lat; 89.67° W. Long. Elevation is 597 feet.

History: Springfield's history is closely linked with Abraham Lincoln, who practiced law here from 1837 to 1861. The first settlers here were Elisha Kelly and his brothers, and in 1821 Springfield received its name, from nearby Spring Creek, and became the seat of the new Sangamon County, with the courthouse built in John Kelly's field. Due to Lincoln's leadership, Springfield was chosen for the state capital in 1837, and was incorporated as a city in 1840. Coal mining became an important industry after 1867.

Population: 105,227 (1990); 111,454 (2000); 116,250 (2010); Density: 1,949.9 persons per square mile (2008-2012 5-year est.); Race: 76.2% White, 18.8% Black/African American, 2.0% Asian, 0.3% American Indian/Alaska Native, 0.0% Native Hawaiian/Other Pacific Islander, 2.7% Some other race, 2.2% Two or more races, 2.0% Hispanic of any race (2008-2012 5-year est.); Average household size: 2.25 (2008-2012 5-year est.); Median age: 38.3 (2008-2012 5-year est.); Males per 100 females: 91.2 (2008-2012 5-year est.); Marriage status: 33.2% never married, 45.2% now married, 7.1% widowed, 14.5% divorced (2008-2012 5-year est.); Foreign born: 4.0% (2008-2012 5-year est.); Ancestry (includes multiple ancestries): 24.8% German, 13.5% Irish, 10.4% English, 7.3% American, 5.9% Italian (2008-2012 5-year est.).

Economy: Unemployment rate: 6.0% (April 2014); Total civilian labor force: 61,553 (April 2014); Single-family building permits issued: 81 (2013); Multi-family building permits issued: 46 (2013); Homeowner vacancy rate: 1.4%. Rental vacancy rate: 8.5%. (2008-2012 5-year est.); Employment by occupation: 15.4% management, business, and financial, 5.5% computer, engineering, and science, 11.5% education, legal, community service, arts,

and media, 8.0% healthcare practitioners, 18.4% service, 28.4% sales and office, 5.4% natural resources, construction, and maintenance, 7.4% production, transportation, and material moving (2008-2012 5-year est.).
Income: Per capita income: $29,089 (2008-2012 5-year est.); Median household income: $49,627 (2008-2012 5-year est.); Average household income: $66,350 (2008-2012 5-year est.); Percent of households with income of $100,000 or more: 19.0% (2008-2012 5-year est.); Poverty rate: 16.8% (2008-2012 5-year est.).
Taxes: Total city taxes per capita: $574 (2011); City property taxes per capita: $231 (2011).
Education: Percent of population age 25 and over with: High school diploma (including GED) or higher: 90.7% (2008-2012 5-year est.); Bachelor's degree or higher: 33.1% (2008-2012 5-year est.); Master's degree or higher: 12.7% (2008-2012 5-year est.).

School District(s)
Capital Area Career Center (11-12)
    2011-12 Enrollment: n/a . . . . (217) 529-5431
Sangamon Area Spec Ed Dist (01-12)
    2011-12 Enrollment: n/a . . . . (217) 786-3250
Sangamon Roe (07-12)
    2011-12 Enrollment: n/a . . . . (217) 753-6620
Springfield SD 186 (PK-12)
    2011-12 Enrollment: 14,972 . . . . (217) 525-3002

Four-year College(s)
ITT Technical Institute-Springfield (Private, For-profit)
    Fall 2012 Enrollment: 115 . . . . (217) 547-5700
    2012-13 Tuition: In-state $18,048; Out-of-state $18,048
St Johns College (Private, Not-for-profit, Roman Catholic)
    Fall 2012 Enrollment: 122 . . . . (217) 525-5628
University of Illinois at Springfield (Public)
    Fall 2012 Enrollment: 5,048 . . . . (217) 206-6600
    2012-13 Tuition: In-state $8,952; Out-of-state $16,272

Two-year College(s)
Lincoln Land Community College (Public)
    Fall 2012 Enrollment: 7,193 . . . . (217) 786-2200
    2012-13 Tuition: In-state $4,872; Out-of-state $7,176
Springfield College in Illinois (Private, Not-for-profit, Roman Catholic)
    Fall 2012 Enrollment: n/a . . . . (217) 525-1420

Vocational/Technical School(s)
Capital Area School of Practical Nursing (Public)
    Fall 2012 Enrollment: 131 . . . . (217) 529-5431
    2012-13 Tuition: $8,535
Midwest Technical Institute-Springfield (Private, For-profit)
    Fall 2012 Enrollment: 464 . . . . (217) 527-8324
    2012-13 Tuition: $13,400
St Johns Hospital School of Clinical Lab Science (Private, Not-for-profit, Roman Catholic)
    Fall 2012 Enrollment: 6 . . . . (217) 757-6788
University of Spa & Cosmetology Arts (Private, For-profit)
    Fall 2012 Enrollment: 226 . . . . (217) 753-8990
    2012-13 Tuition: $16,100
Housing: Homeownership rate: 65.0% (2008-2012 5-year est.); Median home value: $115,700 (2008-2012 5-year est.); Median contract rent: $557 per month (2008-2012 5-year est.); Median year structure built: 1971 (2008-2012 5-year est.).
Health Insurance: 69.0% Private; 34.5% Public; 11.2% None. (2008-2012 5-year est.)
Hospitals: Andrew McFarland Mental Health Center (118 beds); Memorial Medical Center (444 beds); St. John's Hospital (742 beds)
Safety: Violent crime rate: 97.2 per 10,000 population; Property crime rate: 592.9 per 10,000 population (2012).
Transportation: Commute to work: 90.4% car, 2.5% public transportation, 2.6% walk, 3.1% work from home (2008-2012 5-year est.); Travel time to work: 43.6% less than 15 minutes, 45.8% 15 to 30 minutes, 6.1% 30 to 45 minutes, 1.8% 45 to 60 minutes, 2.8% 60 minutes or more (2008-2012 5-year est.); Amtrak: Train service available.
Airports: Abraham Lincoln Capital Airport (primary service/non-hub)
Additional Information Contacts
City of Springfield . . . . (217) 789-2200
    http://www.springfield.il.us
Illinois Chamber of Commerce . . . . (217) 522-5512
    http://www.ilchamber.org
Springfield Convention & Visitors Bureau . . . . (217) 789-2360
    http://www.visitspringfieldillinois.com

The Greater Springfield Chamber of Commerce . . . . (217) 525-1173
    http://www.gscc.org

THAYER (village). Covers a land area of 0.606 square miles and a water area of 0 square miles. Located at 39.54° N. Lat; 89.76° W. Long. Elevation is 643 feet.
Population: 730 (1990); 750 (2000); 693 (2010); Density: 916.6 persons per square mile (2008-2012 5-year est.); Race: 97.8% White, 0.0% Black/African American, 1.3% Asian, 0.0% American Indian/Alaska Native, 0.0% Native Hawaiian/Other Pacific Islander, 0.9% Some other race, 0.9% Two or more races, 0.0% Hispanic of any race (2008-2012 5-year est.); Average household size: 2.55 (2008-2012 5-year est.); Median age: 41.2 (2008-2012 5-year est.); Males per 100 females: 120.2 (2008-2012 5-year est.); Marriage status: 28.2% never married, 56.7% now married, 5.8% widowed, 9.3% divorced (2008-2012 5-year est.); Foreign born: 3.4% (2008-2012 5-year est.); Ancestry (includes multiple ancestries): 24.9% German, 11.7% American, 10.6% Irish, 10.5% English, 3.6% Czech (2008-2012 5-year est.).
Economy: Single-family building permits issued: 0 (2013); Multi-family building permits issued: 0 (2013); Homeowner vacancy rate: 1.6%. Rental vacancy rate: 0.0%. (2008-2012 5-year est.); Employment by occupation: 11.8% management, business, and financial, 3.2% computer, engineering, and science, 0.7% education, legal, community service, arts, and media, 10.0% healthcare practitioners, 8.6% service, 30.4% sales and office, 14.6% natural resources, construction, and maintenance, 20.7% production, transportation, and material moving (2008-2012 5-year est.).
Income: Per capita income: $26,098 (2008-2012 5-year est.); Median household income: $55,104 (2008-2012 5-year est.); Average household income: $65,293 (2008-2012 5-year est.); Percent of households with income of $100,000 or more: 22.4% (2008-2012 5-year est.); Poverty rate: 2.9% (2008-2012 5-year est.).
Education: Percent of population age 25 and over with: High school diploma (including GED) or higher: 90.2% (2008-2012 5-year est.); Bachelor's degree or higher: 15.7% (2008-2012 5-year est.); Master's degree or higher: 6.2% (2008-2012 5-year est.).
Housing: Homeownership rate: 85.8% (2008-2012 5-year est.); Median home value: $85,000 (2008-2012 5-year est.); Median contract rent: $525 per month (2008-2012 5-year est.); Median year structure built: 1949 (2008-2012 5-year est.).
Health Insurance: 73.9% Private; 20.7% Public; 13.5% None. (2008-2012 5-year est.)
Transportation: Commute to work: 96.8% car, 0.0% public transportation, 0.7% walk, 2.5% work from home (2008-2012 5-year est.); Travel time to work: 18.1% less than 15 minutes, 16.6% 15 to 30 minutes, 53.1% 30 to 45 minutes, 6.6% 45 to 60 minutes, 5.5% 60 minutes or more (2008-2012 5-year est.)

WILLIAMSVILLE (village). Covers a land area of 1.261 square miles and a water area of 0 square miles. Located at 39.95° N. Lat; 89.55° W. Long. Elevation is 600 feet.
Population: 1,140 (1990); 1,439 (2000); 1,476 (2010); Density: 1,213.1 persons per square mile (2008-2012 5-year est.); Race: 94.9% White, 0.0% Black/African American, 4.2% Asian, 0.0% American Indian/Alaska Native, 0.0% Native Hawaiian/Other Pacific Islander, 0.9% Some other race, 0.3% Two or more races, 2.0% Hispanic of any race (2008-2012 5-year est.); Average household size: 2.59 (2008-2012 5-year est.); Median age: 38.7 (2008-2012 5-year est.); Males per 100 females: 98.2 (2008-2012 5-year est.); Marriage status: 22.0% never married, 62.1% now married, 5.4% widowed, 10.4% divorced (2008-2012 5-year est.); Foreign born: 2.7% (2008-2012 5-year est.); Ancestry (includes multiple ancestries): 32.7% German, 17.7% English, 14.0% American, 12.5% Irish, 7.1% Italian (2008-2012 5-year est.).
Economy: Single-family building permits issued: 2 (2013); Multi-family building permits issued: 0 (2013); Homeowner vacancy rate: 0.0%. Rental vacancy rate: 0.0%. (2008-2012 5-year est.); Employment by occupation: 14.0% management, business, and financial, 4.1% computer, engineering, and science, 12.4% education, legal, community service, arts, and media, 9.8% healthcare practitioners, 16.2% service, 28.3% sales and office, 6.5% natural resources, construction, and maintenance, 8.7% production, transportation, and material moving (2008-2012 5-year est.).
Income: Per capita income: $31,866 (2008-2012 5-year est.); Median household income: $70,875 (2008-2012 5-year est.); Average household income: $82,605 (2008-2012 5-year est.); Percent of households with income of $100,000 or more: 27.6% (2008-2012 5-year est.); Poverty rate: 4.8% (2008-2012 5-year est.).

Education: Percent of population age 25 and over with: High school diploma (including GED) or higher: 95.0% (2008-2012 5-year est.); Bachelor's degree or higher: 24.4% (2008-2012 5-year est.); Master's degree or higher: 5.0% (2008-2012 5-year est.).

School District(s)

Williamsville CUSD 15 (PK-12)

 2011-12 Enrollment: 1,454 . . . . (217) 566-2014

Housing: Homeownership rate: 88.1% (2008-2012 5-year est.); Median home value: $147,700 (2008-2012 5-year est.); Median contract rent: $483 per month (2008-2012 5-year est.); Median year structure built: 1978 (2008-2012 5-year est.).

Health Insurance: 88.3% Private; 19.9% Public; 5.0% None. (2008-2012 5-year est.)

Transportation: Commute to work: 97.0% car, 0.0% public transportation, 1.1% walk, 1.5% work from home (2008-2012 5-year est.); Travel time to work: 20.5% less than 15 minutes, 57.1% 15 to 30 minutes, 19.3% 30 to 45 minutes, 1.9% 45 to 60 minutes, 1.1% 60 minutes or more (2008-2012 5-year est.)

Schuyler County

Located in western Illinois; bounded on the southeast by the Illinois River; drained by the La Moine River. Covers a land area of 437.273 square miles, a water area of 4.059 square miles, and is located in the Central Time Zone at 40.16° N. Lat., 90.61° W. Long. The county was founded in 1825. County seat is Rushville.

Weather Station: Rushville										Elevation: 660 feet		
	Jan	Feb	Mar	Apr	May	Jun	Jul	Aug	Sep	Oct	Nov	Dec
High	34	39	51	63	73	82	86	85	78	66	52	38
Low	18	22	31	42	52	61	66	63	55	44	33	21
Precip	1.7	1.9	2.6	3.9	5.0	4.3	4.0	3.7	3.5	3.2	3.1	2.4
Snow	3.5	3.3	1.2	0.4	0.0	0.0	0.0	0.0	0.0	tr	0.4	3.1

High and Low temperatures in degrees Fahrenheit; Precipitation and Snow in inches

Population: 7,498 (1990); 7,189 (2000); 7,544 (2010); Race: 95.4% White, 1.0% Black/African American, 1.6% Asian, 0.2% American Indian/Alaska Native, 0.0% Native Hawaiian/Other Pacific Islander, 1.8% Some other race, 1.0% Two or more races, 1.4% Hispanic of any race (2008-2012 5-year est.); Density: 17.1 persons per square mile (2008-2012 5-year est.); Average household size: 2.33 (2008-2012 5-year est.); Median age: 43.2 (2008-2012 5-year est.); Males per 100 females: 106.5 (2008-2012 5-year est.).

Religion: Six largest groups: 15.0% Baptist, 12.6% Methodist/Pietist, 3.3% Non-denominational Protestant, 2.8% Catholicism, 2.4% Lutheran, 2.4% Holiness (2010)

Economy: Unemployment rate: 5.5% (April 2014); Total civilian labor force: 4,087 (April 2014); Leading industries: 17.3% retail trade; 10.0% accommodation & food services; 7.7% other services (except public administration) (2012); Farms: 542 totaling 182,093 acres (2012); Companies that employ 500 or more persons: 0 (2012); Companies that employ 100 to 499 persons: 1 (2012); Companies that employ less than 100 persons: 149 (2012); Black-owned businesses: n/a (2007); Hispanic-owned businesses: n/a (2007); Asian-owned businesses: n/a (2007); Women-owned businesses: n/a (2007); Single-family building permits issued: n/a (2013); Multi-family building permits issued: n/a (2013).

Income: Per capita income: $23,075 (2008-2012 5-year est.); Median household income: $46,934 (2008-2012 5-year est.); Average household income: $54,894 (2008-2012 5-year est.); Percent of households with income of $100,000 or more: 11.5% (2008-2012 5-year est.); Poverty rate: 14.7% (2008-2012 5-year est.); Bankruptcy rate: 1.34% (2013).

Education: Percent of population age 25 and over with: High school diploma (including GED) or higher: 89.5% (2008-2012 5-year est.); Bachelor's degree or higher: 18.5% (2008-2012 5-year est.); Master's degree or higher: 3.9% (2008-2012 5-year est.).

Housing: Homeownership rate: 81.1% (2008-2012 5-year est.); Median home value: $75,500 (2008-2012 5-year est.); Median contract rent: $361 per month (2008-2012 5-year est.); Median year structure built: 1958 (2008-2012 5-year est.)

Health: Birth rate: 102.1 per 10,000 population (2013); Death rate: 91.3 per 10,000 population (2013); Age-adjusted cancer mortality rate: 255.9 deaths per 100,000 population (2011); Number of physicians: 4.0 per 10,000 population (2011); Hospital beds: 61.0 per 10,000 population (2010); Hospital admissions: 526.2 per 10,000 population (2010).

Elections: 2012 Presidential election results: 44.5% Obama, 53.1% Romney

National and State Parks: Weinborg-King State Park

Additional Information Contacts

Schuyler County Government . . . . (217) 322-4734
 http://www.schuylercountyillinois.com

Schuyler County Communities

BROWNING (village). Covers a land area of 0.310 square miles and a water area of 0 square miles. Located at 40.13° N. Lat; 90.37° W. Long. Elevation is 449 feet.

Population: 193 (1990); 130 (2000); 137 (2010); Density: 526.5 persons per square mile (2008-2012 5-year est.); Race: 100.0% White, 0.0% Black/African American, 0.0% Asian, 0.0% American Indian/Alaska Native, 0.0% Native Hawaiian/Other Pacific Islander, 0.0% Some other race, 0.0% Two or more races, 3.7% Hispanic of any race (2008-2012 5-year est.); Average household size: 2.40 (2008-2012 5-year est.); Median age: 46.9 (2008-2012 5-year est.); Males per 100 females: 109.0 (2008-2012 5-year est.); Marriage status: 18.5% never married, 65.9% now married, 6.7% widowed, 8.9% divorced (2008-2012 5-year est.); Foreign born: 0.0% (2008-2012 5-year est.); Ancestry (includes multiple ancestries): 28.2% German, 25.8% American, 22.7% Irish, 6.7% Scotch-Irish, 3.7% English (2008-2012 5-year est.).

Economy: Homeowner vacancy rate: 4.8%. Rental vacancy rate: 0.0%. (2008-2012 5-year est.); Employment by occupation: 11.8% management, business, and financial, 0.0% computer, engineering, and science, 9.2% education, legal, community service, arts, and media, 0.0% healthcare practitioners, 15.8% service, 22.4% sales and office, 18.4% natural resources, construction, and maintenance, 22.4% production, transportation, and material moving (2008-2012 5-year est.).

Income: Per capita income: $20,510 (2008-2012 5-year est.); Median household income: $54,500 (2008-2012 5-year est.); Average household income: $48,353 (2008-2012 5-year est.); Percent of households with income of $100,000 or more: n/a (2008-2012 5-year est.); Poverty rate: 9.8% (2008-2012 5-year est.).

Education: Percent of population age 25 and over with: High school diploma (including GED) or higher: 81.3% (2008-2012 5-year est.); Bachelor's degree or higher: 7.3% (2008-2012 5-year est.); Master's degree or higher: 0.0% (2008-2012 5-year est.).

Housing: Homeownership rate: 86.8% (2008-2012 5-year est.); Median home value: $61,000 (2008-2012 5-year est.); Median contract rent: $300 per month (2008-2012 5-year est.); Median year structure built: 1959 (2008-2012 5-year est.).

Health Insurance: 65.6% Private; 30.7% Public; 10.4% None. (2008-2012 5-year est.)

Transportation: Commute to work: 95.9% car, 0.0% public transportation, 1.4% walk, 2.7% work from home (2008-2012 5-year est.); Travel time to work: 1.4% less than 15 minutes, 45.8% 15 to 30 minutes, 2.8% 30 to 45 minutes, 26.4% 45 to 60 minutes, 23.6% 60 minutes or more (2008-2012 5-year est.)

CAMDEN (village). Covers a land area of 0.761 square miles and a water area of 0 square miles. Located at 40.15° N. Lat; 90.77° W. Long. Elevation is 600 feet.

Population: 115 (1990); 97 (2000); 86 (2010); Density: 189.1 persons per square mile (2008-2012 5-year est.); Race: 100.0% White, 0.0% Black/African American, 0.0% Asian, 0.0% American Indian/Alaska Native, 0.0% Native Hawaiian/Other Pacific Islander, 0.0% Some other race, 0.0% Two or more races, 0.0% Hispanic of any race (2008-2012 5-year est.); Average household size: 1.97 (2008-2012 5-year est.); Median age: 54.4 (2008-2012 5-year est.); Males per 100 females: 144.1 (2008-2012 5-year est.); Marriage status: 30.9% never married, 46.3% now married, 8.8% widowed, 14.0% divorced (2008-2012 5-year est.); Foreign born: 0.0% (2008-2012 5-year est.); Ancestry (includes multiple ancestries): 68.1% American, 9.0% German, 6.3% Irish, 4.9% English (2008-2012 5-year est.).

Economy: Homeowner vacancy rate: 3.0%. Rental vacancy rate: 0.0%. (2008-2012 5-year est.); Employment by occupation: 17.0% management, business, and financial, 0.0% computer, engineering, and science, 0.0% education, legal, community service, arts, and media, 0.0% healthcare practitioners, 14.9% service, 29.8% sales and office, 23.4% natural resources, construction, and maintenance, 14.9% production, transportation, and material moving (2008-2012 5-year est.).

Income: Per capita income: $18,297 (2008-2012 5-year est.); Median household income: $22,917 (2008-2012 5-year est.); Average household income: $35,893 (2008-2012 5-year est.); Percent of households with income of $100,000 or more: 5.5% (2008-2012 5-year est.); Poverty rate: 39.0% (2008-2012 5-year est.).
Education: Percent of population age 25 and over with: High school diploma (including GED) or higher: 78.6% (2008-2012 5-year est.); Bachelor's degree or higher: 8.0% (2008-2012 5-year est.); Master's degree or higher: 1.8% (2008-2012 5-year est.).
Housing: Homeownership rate: 87.7% (2008-2012 5-year est.); Median home value: $29,000 (2008-2012 5-year est.); Median contract rent: n/a per month (2008-2012 5-year est.); Median year structure built: 1946 (2008-2012 5-year est.).
Health Insurance: 51.4% Private; 51.4% Public; 17.4% None. (2008-2012 5-year est.)
Transportation: Commute to work: 72.3% car, 0.0% public transportation, 25.5% walk, 2.1% work from home (2008-2012 5-year est.); Travel time to work: 26.1% less than 15 minutes, 69.6% 15 to 30 minutes, 0.0% 30 to 45 minutes, 0.0% 45 to 60 minutes, 4.3% 60 minutes or more (2008-2012 5-year est.)

FREDERICK (unincorporated postal area)

Zip Code: 62639
Covers a land area of 34.010 square miles and a water area of 1.041 square miles. Located at 40.03° N. Lat; 90.48° W. Long. Elevation is 446 feet. Population: 316 (2010); Density: 9.3 persons per square mile (2010); Race: 98.1% White, 0.0% Black/African American, 0.0% Asian, 0.0% American Indian/Alaska Native, 0.0% Native Hawaiian/Other Pacific Islander, 1.9% Some other race, 0.0% Two or more races, 2.5% Hispanic of any race (2010); Average household size: 2.39 (2010); Median age: 42.0 (2010); Males per 100 females: 91.5 (2010); Homeownership rate: 91.7% (2010)

HUNTSVILLE (unincorporated postal area)

Zip Code: 62344
Covers a land area of 35.779 square miles and a water area of 0 square miles. Located at 40.16° N. Lat; 90.83° W. Long. Elevation is 659 feet. Population: 138 (2010); Density: 3.9 persons per square mile (2010); Race: 99.3% White, 0.0% Black/African American, 0.0% Asian, 0.0% American Indian/Alaska Native, 0.0% Native Hawaiian/Other Pacific Islander, 0.7% Some other race, 0.7% Two or more races, 0.0% Hispanic of any race (2010); Average household size: 2.38 (2010); Median age: 45.7 (2010); Males per 100 females: 91.7 (2010); Homeownership rate: 82.7% (2010)

LITTLETON (village). Covers a land area of 1.168 square miles and a water area of 0 square miles. Located at 40.23° N. Lat; 90.62° W. Long. Elevation is 679 feet.

Population: 181 (1990); 197 (2000); 181 (2010); Density: 283.4 persons per square mile (2008-2012 5-year est.); Race: 100.0% White, 0.0% Black/African American, 0.0% Asian, 0.0% American Indian/Alaska Native, 0.0% Native Hawaiian/Other Pacific Islander, 0.0% Some other race, 0.0% Two or more races, 0.9% Hispanic of any race (2008-2012 5-year est.); Average household size: 2.67 (2008-2012 5-year est.); Median age: 43.1 (2008-2012 5-year est.); Males per 100 females: 141.6 (2008-2012 5-year est.); Marriage status: 33.0% never married, 54.1% now married, 3.4% widowed, 9.5% divorced (2008-2012 5-year est.); Foreign born: 0.6% (2008-2012 5-year est.); Ancestry (includes multiple ancestries): 59.2% American, 11.5% German, 9.4% Irish, 6.3% English, 5.7% French (2008-2012 5-year est.).
Economy: Homeowner vacancy rate: 2.5%. Rental vacancy rate: 0.0%. (2008-2012 5-year est.); Employment by occupation: 4.7% management, business, and financial, 0.0% computer, engineering, and science, 1.7% education, legal, community service, arts, and media, 2.1% healthcare practitioners, 8.2% service, 26.6% sales and office, 22.3% natural resources, construction, and maintenance, 34.3% production, transportation, and material moving (2008-2012 5-year est.).
Income: Per capita income: $20,898 (2008-2012 5-year est.); Median household income: $53,750 (2008-2012 5-year est.); Average household income: $55,155 (2008-2012 5-year est.); Percent of households with income of $100,000 or more: 7.3% (2008-2012 5-year est.); Poverty rate: 7.9% (2008-2012 5-year est.).
Education: Percent of population age 25 and over with: High school diploma (including GED) or higher: 89.1% (2008-2012 5-year est.);

Bachelor's degree or higher: 6.6% (2008-2012 5-year est.); Master's degree or higher: 0.9% (2008-2012 5-year est.).
Housing: Homeownership rate: 92.7% (2008-2012 5-year est.); Median home value: $48,700 (2008-2012 5-year est.); Median contract rent: $245 per month (2008-2012 5-year est.); Median year structure built: Before 1940 (2008-2012 5-year est.).
Health Insurance: 62.8% Private; 29.3% Public; 14.2% None. (2008-2012 5-year est.)
Transportation: Commute to work: 99.0% car, 0.0% public transportation, 1.0% walk, 0.0% work from home (2008-2012 5-year est.); Travel time to work: 37.3% less than 15 minutes, 30.1% 15 to 30 minutes, 19.1% 30 to 45 minutes, 5.3% 45 to 60 minutes, 8.1% 60 minutes or more (2008-2012 5-year est.)

RUSHVILLE (city). County seat. Covers a land area of 1.652 square miles and a water area of 0 square miles. Located at 40.12° N. Lat; 90.57° W. Long. Elevation is 676 feet.

History: Rushville was founded in 1825 as Rushton. Both names honor Dr. William Rush, a Philadelphia physician.
Population: 3,229 (1990); 3,212 (2000); 3,192 (2010); Density: 2,060.0 persons per square mile (2008-2012 5-year est.); Race: 93.3% White, 0.7% Black/African American, 3.5% Asian, 0.2% American Indian/Alaska Native, 0.0% Native Hawaiian/Other Pacific Islander, 2.3% Some other race, 2.3% Two or more races, 0.4% Hispanic of any race (2008-2012 5-year est.); Average household size: 2.20 (2008-2012 5-year est.); Median age: 41.5 (2008-2012 5-year est.); Males per 100 females: 100.6 (2008-2012 5-year est.); Marriage status: 22.3% never married, 60.4% now married, 6.4% widowed, 10.9% divorced (2008-2012 5-year est.); Foreign born: 6.4% (2008-2012 5-year est.); Ancestry (includes multiple ancestries): 22.5% American, 13.1% German, 11.5% Irish, 10.1% English, 3.1% Dutch (2008-2012 5-year est.).
Economy: Single-family building permits issued: 0 (2013); Multi-family building permits issued: 0 (2013); Homeowner vacancy rate: 0.0%. Rental vacancy rate: 0.0%. (2008-2012 5-year est.); Employment by occupation: 6.5% management, business, and financial, 2.4% computer, engineering, and science, 10.3% education, legal, community service, arts, and media, 12.3% healthcare practitioners, 17.1% service, 19.3% sales and office, 11.8% natural resources, construction, and maintenance, 20.5% production, transportation, and material moving (2008-2012 5-year est.).
Income: Per capita income: $23,017 (2008-2012 5-year est.); Median household income: $46,162 (2008-2012 5-year est.); Average household income: $50,463 (2008-2012 5-year est.); Percent of households with income of $100,000 or more: 9.7% (2008-2012 5-year est.); Poverty rate: 12.6% (2008-2012 5-year est.).
Education: Percent of population age 25 and over with: High school diploma (including GED) or higher: 89.3% (2008-2012 5-year est.); Bachelor's degree or higher: 25.0% (2008-2012 5-year est.); Master's degree or higher: 5.7% (2008-2012 5-year est.).

School District(s)
Schuyler-Industry CUSD 5 (PK-12)
    2011-12 Enrollment: 1,222 . . . . (217) 322-4311
Housing: Homeownership rate: 76.0% (2008-2012 5-year est.); Median home value: $72,100 (2008-2012 5-year est.); Median contract rent: $375 per month (2008-2012 5-year est.); Median year structure built: 1962 (2008-2012 5-year est.).
Health Insurance: 66.8% Private; 44.5% Public; 8.8% None. (2008-2012 5-year est.)
Hospitals: Culbertson Memorial Hospital (64 beds)
Safety: Violent crime rate: 3.1 per 10,000 population; Property crime rate: 172.9 per 10,000 population (2012).
Transportation: Commute to work: 90.6% car, 0.8% public transportation, 6.7% walk, 1.9% work from home (2008-2012 5-year est.); Travel time to work: 42.2% less than 15 minutes, 29.5% 15 to 30 minutes, 15.5% 30 to 45 minutes, 3.0% 45 to 60 minutes, 9.7% 60 minutes or more (2008-2012 5-year est.)

Scott County

Located in west central Illinois; bounded on the west by the Illinois River; drained by Sandy and Mauvaise Terre Creeks. Covers a land area of 250.913 square miles, a water area of 1.858 square miles, and is located in the Central Time Zone at 39.64° N. Lat., 90.48° W. Long. The county was founded in 1839. County seat is Winchester.

Scott County is part of the Jacksonville, IL Micropolitan Statistical Area. The entire metro area includes: Morgan County, IL; Scott County, IL

Population: 5,644 (1990); 5,537 (2000); 5,355 (2010); Race: 98.1% White, 0.0% Black/African American, 0.1% Asian, 0.0% American Indian/Alaska Native, 0.0% Native Hawaiian/Other Pacific Islander, 1.8% Some other race, 1.4% Two or more races, 0.5% Hispanic of any race (2008-2012 5-year est.); Density: 21.1 persons per square mile (2008-2012 5-year est.); Average household size: 2.49 (2008-2012 5-year est.); Median age: 43.1 (2008-2012 5-year est.); Males per 100 females: 97.5 (2008-2012 5-year est.).
Religion: Six largest groups: 40.8% Baptist, 9.8% Lutheran, 9.3% Methodist/Pietist, 2.6% Catholicism, 0.5% Pentecostal, 0.0% Other Groups (2010)
Economy: Unemployment rate: 6.9% (April 2014); Total civilian labor force: 2,567 (April 2014); Leading industries: 22.0% manufacturing; 15.9% retail trade; 10.2% finance & insurance (2012); Farms: 356 totaling 147,532 acres (2012); Companies that employ 500 or more persons: 0 (2012); Companies that employ 100 to 499 persons: 0 (2012); Companies that employ less than 100 persons: 80 (2012); Black-owned businesses: n/a (2007); Hispanic-owned businesses: n/a (2007); Asian-owned businesses: n/a (2007); Women-owned businesses: n/a (2007); Single-family building permits issued: n/a (2013); Multi-family building permits issued: n/a (2013).
Income: Per capita income: $26,347 (2008-2012 5-year est.); Median household income: $49,746 (2008-2012 5-year est.); Average household income: $64,507 (2008-2012 5-year est.); Percent of households with income of $100,000 or more: 15.7% (2008-2012 5-year est.); Poverty rate: 10.5% (2008-2012 5-year est.); Bankruptcy rate: 3.02% (2013).
Education: Percent of population age 25 and over with: High school diploma (including GED) or higher: 88.7% (2008-2012 5-year est.); Bachelor's degree or higher: 16.6% (2008-2012 5-year est.); Master's degree or higher: 3.2% (2008-2012 5-year est.).
Housing: Homeownership rate: 73.2% (2008-2012 5-year est.); Median home value: $80,800 (2008-2012 5-year est.); Median contract rent: $353 per month (2008-2012 5-year est.); Median year structure built: 1959 (2008-2012 5-year est.)
Health: Birth rate: 99.6 per 10,000 population (2013); Death rate: 84.3 per 10,000 population (2013); Age-adjusted cancer mortality rate: Unreliable deaths per 100,000 population (2011); Number of physicians: 3.8 per 10,000 population (2011); Hospital beds: 0.0 per 10,000 population (2010); Hospital admissions: 0.0 per 10,000 population (2010).
Elections: 2012 Presidential election results: 35.6% Obama, 62.1% Romney
Additional Information Contacts
Scott County Government . . . . (217) 742-3178
   http://scottco.org

Scott County Communities

ALSEY (village). Covers a land area of 0.549 square miles and a water area of 0.010 square miles. Located at 39.56° N. Lat; 90.43° W. Long. Elevation is 630 feet.
Population: 253 (1990); 246 (2000); 227 (2010); Density: 626.1 persons per square mile (2008-2012 5-year est.); Race: 84.6% White, 0.0% Black/African American, 0.0% Asian, 0.0% American Indian/Alaska Native, 0.0% Native Hawaiian/Other Pacific Islander, 15.4% Some other race, 15.4% Two or more races, 0.0% Hispanic of any race (2008-2012 5-year est.); Average household size: 2.75 (2008-2012 5-year est.); Median age: 34.0 (2008-2012 5-year est.); Males per 100 females: 154.8 (2008-2012 5-year est.); Marriage status: 13.6% never married, 55.0% now married, 13.2% widowed, 18.2% divorced (2008-2012 5-year est.); Foreign born: 0.0% (2008-2012 5-year est.); Ancestry (includes multiple ancestries): 43.0% American, 18.6% German, 7.6% English, 6.1% Irish, 3.2% Italian (2008-2012 5-year est.).
Economy: Homeowner vacancy rate: 0.0%. Rental vacancy rate: 0.0%. (2008-2012 5-year est.); Employment by occupation: 16.8% management, business, and financial, 0.0% computer, engineering, and science, 6.1% education, legal, community service, arts, and media, 8.4% healthcare practitioners, 15.3% service, 25.2% sales and office, 14.5% natural resources, construction, and maintenance, 13.7% production, transportation, and material moving (2008-2012 5-year est.).
Income: Per capita income: $19,355 (2008-2012 5-year est.); Median household income: $40,417 (2008-2012 5-year est.); Average household income: $50,550 (2008-2012 5-year est.); Percent of households with

income of $100,000 or more: 7.2% (2008-2012 5-year est.); Poverty rate: 18.9% (2008-2012 5-year est.).
Education: Percent of population age 25 and over with: High school diploma (including GED) or higher: 85.4% (2008-2012 5-year est.); Bachelor's degree or higher: 8.6% (2008-2012 5-year est.); Master's degree or higher: 0.0% (2008-2012 5-year est.).
Housing: Homeownership rate: 76.8% (2008-2012 5-year est.); Median home value: $47,100 (2008-2012 5-year est.); Median contract rent: $398 per month (2008-2012 5-year est.); Median year structure built: Before 1940 (2008-2012 5-year est.).
Health Insurance: 71.8% Private; 28.2% Public; 10.2% None. (2008-2012 5-year est.)
Transportation: Commute to work: 89.9% car, 0.0% public transportation, 3.9% walk, 6.2% work from home (2008-2012 5-year est.); Travel time to work: 19.8% less than 15 minutes, 7.4% 15 to 30 minutes, 30.6% 30 to 45 minutes, 5.8% 45 to 60 minutes, 36.4% 60 minutes or more (2008-2012 5-year est.)

BLUFFS (village). Covers a land area of 0.893 square miles and a water area of 0 square miles. Located at 39.75° N. Lat; 90.54° W. Long. Elevation is 469 feet.
Population: 774 (1990); 748 (2000); 715 (2010); Density: 852.6 persons per square mile (2008-2012 5-year est.); Race: 97.8% White, 0.0% Black/African American, 0.0% Asian, 0.0% American Indian/Alaska Native, 0.0% Native Hawaiian/Other Pacific Islander, 2.2% Some other race, 0.0% Two or more races, 3.5% Hispanic of any race (2008-2012 5-year est.); Average household size: 2.87 (2008-2012 5-year est.); Median age: 40.9 (2008-2012 5-year est.); Males per 100 females: 96.6 (2008-2012 5-year est.); Marriage status: 29.4% never married, 57.6% now married, 2.1% widowed, 10.9% divorced (2008-2012 5-year est.); Foreign born: 3.5% (2008-2012 5-year est.); Ancestry (includes multiple ancestries): 43.2% American, 22.7% German, 14.5% Irish, 10.8% English, 2.1% Italian (2008-2012 5-year est.).
Economy: Homeowner vacancy rate: 3.1%. Rental vacancy rate: 0.0%. (2008-2012 5-year est.); Employment by occupation: 10.0% management, business, and financial, 1.9% computer, engineering, and science, 3.8% education, legal, community service, arts, and media, 3.4% healthcare practitioners, 18.2% service, 32.3% sales and office, 5.6% natural resources, construction, and maintenance, 24.8% production, transportation, and material moving (2008-2012 5-year est.).
Income: Per capita income: $24,340 (2008-2012 5-year est.); Median household income: $46,319 (2008-2012 5-year est.); Average household income: $67,945 (2008-2012 5-year est.); Percent of households with income of $100,000 or more: 11.8% (2008-2012 5-year est.); Poverty rate: 9.5% (2008-2012 5-year est.).
Education: Percent of population age 25 and over with: High school diploma (including GED) or higher: 84.6% (2008-2012 5-year est.); Bachelor's degree or higher: 13.4% (2008-2012 5-year est.); Master's degree or higher: 4.8% (2008-2012 5-year est.).
School District(s)
Scott-Morgan CUSD 2 (PK-12)
   2011-12 Enrollment: 258 . . . . (217) 754-3351
Housing: Homeownership rate: 70.2% (2008-2012 5-year est.); Median home value: $72,700 (2008-2012 5-year est.); Median contract rent: $238 per month (2008-2012 5-year est.); Median year structure built: 1954 (2008-2012 5-year est.).
Health Insurance: 60.1% Private; 44.3% Public; 9.3% None. (2008-2012 5-year est.)
Transportation: Commute to work: 91.3% car, 0.0% public transportation, 2.6% walk, 5.5% work from home (2008-2012 5-year est.); Travel time to work: 28.4% less than 15 minutes, 24.7% 15 to 30 minutes, 38.4% 30 to 45 minutes, 4.1% 45 to 60 minutes, 4.5% 60 minutes or more (2008-2012 5-year est.)

EXETER (village). Covers a land area of 0.690 square miles and a water area of 0 square miles. Located at 39.72° N. Lat; 90.50° W. Long. Elevation is 554 feet.
Population: 59 (1990); 70 (2000); 65 (2010); Density: 179.8 persons per square mile (2008-2012 5-year est.); Race: 100.0% White, 0.0% Black/African American, 0.0% Asian, 0.0% American Indian/Alaska Native, 0.0% Native Hawaiian/Other Pacific Islander, 0.0% Some other race, 0.0% Two or more races, 0.0% Hispanic of any race (2008-2012 5-year est.); Average household size: 2.70 (2008-2012 5-year est.); Median age: 34.7 (2008-2012 5-year est.); Males per 100 females: 153.1 (2008-2012 5-year est.); Marriage status: 43.5% never married, 39.1% now married, 2.6%

widowed, 14.8% divorced (2008-2012 5-year est.); Foreign born: 0.0% (2008-2012 5-year est.); Ancestry (includes multiple ancestries): 45.2% American, 24.2% German, 21.8% English, 18.5% Irish, 5.6% French (2008-2012 5-year est.).

Economy: Homeowner vacancy rate: 0.0%. Rental vacancy rate: 0.0%. (2008-2012 5-year est.); Employment by occupation: 6.3% management, business, and financial, 0.0% computer, engineering, and science, 0.0% education, legal, community service, arts, and media, 2.5% healthcare practitioners, 21.3% service, 32.5% sales and office, 15.0% natural resources, construction, and maintenance, 22.5% production, transportation, and material moving (2008-2012 5-year est.).

Income: Per capita income: $29,242 (2008-2012 5-year est.); Median household income: $74,063 (2008-2012 5-year est.); Average household income: $75,396 (2008-2012 5-year est.); Percent of households with income of $100,000 or more: 19.6% (2008-2012 5-year est.); Poverty rate: 9.1% (2008-2012 5-year est.).

Education: Percent of population age 25 and over with: High school diploma (including GED) or higher: 87.1% (2008-2012 5-year est.); Bachelor's degree or higher: 1.2% (2008-2012 5-year est.); Master's degree or higher: 0.0% (2008-2012 5-year est.)

Housing: Homeownership rate: 93.5% (2008-2012 5-year est.); Median home value: $97,500 (2008-2012 5-year est.); Median contract rent: n/a per month (2008-2012 5-year est.); Median year structure built: 1977 (2008-2012 5-year est.).

Health Insurance: 79.0% Private; 17.7% Public; 13.7% None. (2008-2012 5-year est.)

Transportation: Commute to work: 100.0% car, 0.0% public transportation, 0.0% walk, 0.0% work from home (2008-2012 5-year est.); Travel time to work: 8.8% less than 15 minutes, 55.0% 15 to 30 minutes, 11.3% 30 to 45 minutes, 6.3% 45 to 60 minutes, 18.8% 60 minutes or more (2008-2012 5-year est.)

GLASGOW (village). Covers a land area of 1.011 square miles and a water area of 0 square miles. Located at 39.55° N. Lat; 90.48° W. Long. Elevation is 584 feet.

Population: 163 (1990); 170 (2000); 141 (2010); Density: 157.2 persons per square mile (2008-2012 5-year est.); Race: 98.1% White, 0.0% Black/African American, 0.0% Asian, 0.0% American Indian/Alaska Native, 0.0% Native Hawaiian/Other Pacific Islander, 1.9% Some other race, 1.9% Two or more races, 0.0% Hispanic of any race (2008-2012 5-year est.); Average household size: 2.48 (2008-2012 5-year est.); Median age: 50.2 (2008-2012 5-year est.); Males per 100 females: 103.8 (2008-2012 5-year est.); Marriage status: 24.8% never married, 49.6% now married, 5.1% widowed, 20.4% divorced (2008-2012 5-year est.); Foreign born: 0.0% (2008-2012 5-year est.); Ancestry (includes multiple ancestries): 49.1% American, 15.1% Irish, 10.1% German, 5.7% Welsh, 3.1% English (2008-2012 5-year est.).

Economy: Homeowner vacancy rate: 0.0%. Rental vacancy rate: 0.0%. (2008-2012 5-year est.); Employment by occupation: 13.5% management, business, and financial, 0.0% computer, engineering, and science, 5.4% education, legal, community service, arts, and media, 20.3% healthcare practitioners, 8.1% service, 24.3% sales and office, 10.8% natural resources, construction, and maintenance, 17.6% production, transportation, and material moving (2008-2012 5-year est.).

Income: Per capita income: $24,608 (2008-2012 5-year est.); Median household income: $57,917 (2008-2012 5-year est.); Average household income: $58,145 (2008-2012 5-year est.); Percent of households with income of $100,000 or more: 14.1% (2008-2012 5-year est.); Poverty rate: 11.9% (2008-2012 5-year est.).

Education: Percent of population age 25 and over with: High school diploma (including GED) or higher: 86.8% (2008-2012 5-year est.); Bachelor's degree or higher: 3.9% (2008-2012 5-year est.); Master's degree or higher: 1.6% (2008-2012 5-year est.).

Housing: Homeownership rate: 93.8% (2008-2012 5-year est.); Median home value: $30,000 (2008-2012 5-year est.); Median contract rent: n/a per month (2008-2012 5-year est.); Median year structure built: 1965 (2008-2012 5-year est.).

Health Insurance: 66.0% Private; 23.9% Public; 19.5% None. (2008-2012 5-year est.)

Transportation: Commute to work: 95.9% car, 0.0% public transportation, 0.0% walk, 4.1% work from home (2008-2012 5-year est.); Travel time to work: 14.1% less than 15 minutes, 21.1% 15 to 30 minutes, 57.7% 30 to 45 minutes, 2.8% 45 to 60 minutes, 4.2% 60 minutes or more (2008-2012 5-year est.)

MANCHESTER (village). Covers a land area of 1.062 square miles and a water area of 0 square miles. Located at 39.54° N. Lat; 90.33° W. Long. Elevation is 686 feet.

Population: 347 (1990); 354 (2000); 292 (2010); Density: 427.4 persons per square mile (2008-2012 5-year est.); Race: 94.1% White, 0.0% Black/African American, 1.5% Asian, 0.0% American Indian/Alaska Native, 0.0% Native Hawaiian/Other Pacific Islander, 4.4% Some other race, 4.4% Two or more races, 0.0% Hispanic of any race (2008-2012 5-year est.); Average household size: 2.75 (2008-2012 5-year est.); Median age: 42.5 (2008-2012 5-year est.); Males per 100 females: 93.2 (2008-2012 5-year est.); Marriage status: 17.7% never married, 71.7% now married, 3.6% widowed, 6.9% divorced (2008-2012 5-year est.); Foreign born: 4.6% (2008-2012 5-year est.); Ancestry (includes multiple ancestries): 27.5% German, 26.0% American, 13.9% English, 5.3% Irish, 4.4% Portuguese (2008-2012 5-year est.).

Economy: Homeowner vacancy rate: 0.0%. Rental vacancy rate: 0.0%. (2008-2012 5-year est.); Employment by occupation: 4.7% management, business, and financial, 2.3% computer, engineering, and science, 6.1% education, legal, community service, arts, and media, 4.7% healthcare practitioners, 19.7% service, 30.0% sales and office, 8.5% natural resources, construction, and maintenance, 23.9% production, transportation, and material moving (2008-2012 5-year est.).

Income: Per capita income: $25,081 (2008-2012 5-year est.); Median household income: $49,188 (2008-2012 5-year est.); Average household income: $64,422 (2008-2012 5-year est.); Percent of households with income of $100,000 or more: 14.5% (2008-2012 5-year est.); Poverty rate: 7.7% (2008-2012 5-year est.).

Education: Percent of population age 25 and over with: High school diploma (including GED) or higher: 87.2% (2008-2012 5-year est.); Bachelor's degree or higher: 15.3% (2008-2012 5-year est.); Master's degree or higher: 0.0% (2008-2012 5-year est.).

Housing: Homeownership rate: 79.4% (2008-2012 5-year est.); Median home value: $67,500 (2008-2012 5-year est.); Median contract rent: $222 per month (2008-2012 5-year est.); Median year structure built: Before 1940 (2008-2012 5-year est.).

Health Insurance: 74.0% Private; 35.9% Public; 7.0% None. (2008-2012 5-year est.)

Transportation: Commute to work: 78.9% car, 0.0% public transportation, 6.8% walk, 11.6% work from home (2008-2012 5-year est.); Travel time to work: 15.5% less than 15 minutes, 48.2% 15 to 30 minutes, 16.7% 30 to 45 minutes, 9.5% 45 to 60 minutes, 10.1% 60 minutes or more (2008-2012 5-year est.)

NAPLES (town). Covers a land area of 0.605 square miles and a water area of 0 square miles. Located at 39.75° N. Lat; 90.61° W. Long. Elevation is 440 feet.

History: It was in Naples that the steamboat "Olitippa" was built on the Illinois River, before regular steamboat service began.

Population: 130 (1990); 134 (2000); 130 (2010); Density: 81.0 persons per square mile (2008-2012 5-year est.); Race: 100.0% White, 0.0% Black/African American, 0.0% Asian, 0.0% American Indian/Alaska Native, 0.0% Native Hawaiian/Other Pacific Islander, 0.0% Some other race, 0.0% Two or more races, 0.0% Hispanic of any race (2008-2012 5-year est.); Average household size: 2.72 (2008-2012 5-year est.); Median age: 51.2 (2008-2012 5-year est.); Males per 100 females: 69.0 (2008-2012 5-year est.); Marriage status: 15.6% never married, 77.8% now married, 2.2% widowed, 4.4% divorced (2008-2012 5-year est.); Foreign born: 4.1% (2008-2012 5-year est.); Ancestry (includes multiple ancestries): 22.4% American, 20.4% German, 16.3% Polish, 14.3% Scotch-Irish, 10.2% Irish (2008-2012 5-year est.).

Economy: Homeowner vacancy rate: 0.0%. Rental vacancy rate: 0.0%. (2008-2012 5-year est.); Employment by occupation: 21.4% management, business, and financial, 0.0% computer, engineering, and science, 28.6% education, legal, community service, arts, and media, 10.7% healthcare practitioners, 25.0% service, 7.1% sales and office, 0.0% natural resources, construction, and maintenance, 7.1% production, transportation, and material moving (2008-2012 5-year est.).

Income: Per capita income: $20,278 (2008-2012 5-year est.); Median household income: $55,000 (2008-2012 5-year est.); Average household income: $50,606 (2008-2012 5-year est.); Percent of households with income of $100,000 or more: n/a (2008-2012 5-year est.); Poverty rate: 0.0% (2008-2012 5-year est.).

Education: Percent of population age 25 and over with: High school diploma (including GED) or higher: 100.0% (2008-2012 5-year est.);

Bachelor's degree or higher: 23.7% (2008-2012 5-year est.); Master's degree or higher: 15.8% (2008-2012 5-year est.).
Housing: Homeownership rate: 100.0% (2008-2012 5-year est.); Median home value: $65,000 (2008-2012 5-year est.); Median contract rent: n/a per month (2008-2012 5-year est.); Median year structure built: 1976 (2008-2012 5-year est.).
Health Insurance: 81.6% Private; 16.3% Public; 10.2% None. (2008-2012 5-year est.)
Transportation: Commute to work: 100.0% car, 0.0% public transportation, 0.0% walk, 0.0% work from home (2008-2012 5-year est.); Travel time to work: 45.5% less than 15 minutes, 13.6% 15 to 30 minutes, 27.3% 30 to 45 minutes, 0.0% 45 to 60 minutes, 13.6% 60 minutes or more (2008-2012 5-year est.)

WINCHESTER (city). County seat. Covers a land area of 1.129 square miles and a water area of 0 square miles. Located at 39.63° N. Lat; 90.46° W. Long. Elevation is 541 feet.
History: A grist mill was operating in Winchester in 1824. When the town was platted in 1830, so the story is told, the surveyor allowed a resident from Kentucky to name the townsite in exchange for a jug of whiskey. Stephen A. Douglas taught school and began his legal career here in 1833. Winchester developed as the seat of Scott County.
Population: 1,769 (1990); 1,650 (2000); 1,593 (2010); Density: 1,428.8 persons per square mile (2008-2012 5-year est.); Race: 100.0% White, 0.0% Black/African American, 0.0% Asian, 0.0% American Indian/Alaska Native, 0.0% Native Hawaiian/Other Pacific Islander, 0.0% Some other race, 0.0% Two or more races, 0.0% Hispanic of any race (2008-2012 5-year est.); Average household size: 2.17 (2008-2012 5-year est.); Median age: 44.2 (2008-2012 5-year est.); Males per 100 females: 86.7 (2008-2012 5-year est.); Marriage status: 24.5% never married, 44.5% now married, 9.2% widowed, 21.9% divorced (2008-2012 5-year est.); Foreign born: 0.0% (2008-2012 5-year est.); Ancestry (includes multiple ancestries): 31.0% American, 19.7% German, 15.3% English, 12.3% Irish, 2.8% Dutch (2008-2012 5-year est.).
Economy: Homeowner vacancy rate: 2.1%. Rental vacancy rate: 2.5%. (2008-2012 5-year est.); Employment by occupation: 6.9% management, business, and financial, 1.1% computer, engineering, and science, 10.1% education, legal, community service, arts, and media, 5.2% healthcare practitioners, 20.5% service, 28.7% sales and office, 10.6% natural resources, construction, and maintenance, 16.8% production, transportation, and material moving (2008-2012 5-year est.).
Income: Per capita income: $23,799 (2008-2012 5-year est.); Median household income: $38,125 (2008-2012 5-year est.); Average household income: $49,790 (2008-2012 5-year est.); Percent of households with income of $100,000 or more: 10.6% (2008-2012 5-year est.); Poverty rate: 12.8% (2008-2012 5-year est.).
Education: Percent of population age 25 and over with: High school diploma (including GED) or higher: 89.1% (2008-2012 5-year est.); Bachelor's degree or higher: 18.8% (2008-2012 5-year est.); Master's degree or higher: 6.0% (2008-2012 5-year est.).

School District(s)
Winchester CUSD 1 (PK-12)
    2011-12 Enrollment: 691 . . . . (217) 742-3175
Housing: Homeownership rate: 62.2% (2008-2012 5-year est.); Median home value: $77,200 (2008-2012 5-year est.); Median contract rent: $356 per month (2008-2012 5-year est.); Median year structure built: 1952 (2008-2012 5-year est.).
Health Insurance: 69.8% Private; 37.0% Public; 10.3% None. (2008-2012 5-year est.)
Transportation: Commute to work: 89.3% car, 0.4% public transportation, 5.7% walk, 4.6% work from home (2008-2012 5-year est.); Travel time to work: 31.8% less than 15 minutes, 36.1% 15 to 30 minutes, 17.2% 30 to 45 minutes, 9.7% 45 to 60 minutes, 5.2% 60 minutes or more (2008-2012 5-year est.)

Shelby County

Located in central Illinois; drained by the South Fork of the Sangamon River, and by the Kaskaskia and Little Wabash Rivers. Covers a land area of 758.523 square miles, a water area of 9.547 square miles, and is located in the Central Time Zone at 39.38° N. Lat., 88.80° W. Long. The county was founded in 1827. County seat is Shelbyville.

Weather Station: Windsor   Elevation: 689 feet

	Jan	Feb	Mar	Apr	May	Jun	Jul	Aug	Sep	Oct	Nov	Dec
High	36	41	53	66	76	84	87	86	80	68	53	40
Low	21	24	33	43	54	62	66	64	56	45	35	25
Precip	2.3	2.0	3.1	3.9	4.4	3.7	3.7	3.1	3.1	3.5	4.0	2.9
Snow	6.2	4.1	2.2	0.2	0.0	0.0	0.0	0.0	0.0	tr	1.1	4.8

High and Low temperatures in degrees Fahrenheit; Precipitation and Snow in inches

Population: 22,261 (1990); 22,893 (2000); 22,363 (2010); Race: 98.8% White, 0.3% Black/African American, 0.1% Asian, 0.1% American Indian/Alaska Native, 0.0% Native Hawaiian/Other Pacific Islander, 0.7% Some other race, 0.6% Two or more races, 0.9% Hispanic of any race (2008-2012 5-year est.); Density: 29.3 persons per square mile (2008-2012 5-year est.); Average household size: 2.45 (2008-2012 5-year est.); Median age: 44.0 (2008-2012 5-year est.); Males per 100 females: 98.2 (2008-2012 5-year est.).
Religion: Six largest groups: 17.2% Baptist, 11.8% Catholicism, 8.7% Methodist/Pietist, 7.9% Lutheran, 2.5% Non-denominational Protestant, 1.9% Holiness (2010)
Economy: Unemployment rate: 6.9% (April 2014); Total civilian labor force: 10,177 (April 2014); Leading industries: 25.3% manufacturing; 16.4% health care and social assistance; 15.0% retail trade (2012); Farms: 1,282 totaling 405,783 acres (2012); Companies that employ 500 or more persons: 1 (2012); Companies that employ 100 to 499 persons: 3 (2012); Companies that employ less than 100 persons: 433 (2012); Black-owned businesses: n/a (2007); Hispanic-owned businesses: n/a (2007); Asian-owned businesses: n/a (2007); Women-owned businesses: n/a (2007); Single-family building permits issued: 28 (2013); Multi-family building permits issued: 0 (2013).
Income: Per capita income: $23,233 (2008-2012 5-year est.); Median household income: $46,546 (2008-2012 5-year est.); Average household income: $56,385 (2008-2012 5-year est.); Percent of households with income of $100,000 or more: 12.3% (2008-2012 5-year est.); Poverty rate: 10.1% (2008-2012 5-year est.); Bankruptcy rate: 2.43% (2013).
Education: Percent of population age 25 and over with: High school diploma (including GED) or higher: 88.9% (2008-2012 5-year est.); Bachelor's degree or higher: 14.8% (2008-2012 5-year est.); Master's degree or higher: 4.2% (2008-2012 5-year est.).
Housing: Homeownership rate: 81.4% (2008-2012 5-year est.); Median home value: $87,000 (2008-2012 5-year est.); Median contract rent: $399 per month (2008-2012 5-year est.); Median year structure built: 1960 (2008-2012 5-year est.)
Health: Birth rate: 101.7 per 10,000 population (2013); Death rate: 110.3 per 10,000 population (2013); Age-adjusted cancer mortality rate: 156.9 deaths per 100,000 population (2011); Number of physicians: 5.4 per 10,000 population (2011); Hospital beds: 13.4 per 10,000 population (2010); Hospital admissions: 1,142.1 per 10,000 population (2010).
Elections: 2012 Presidential election results: 32.1% Obama, 65.8% Romney
National and State Parks: Eagle Creek State Park; Hidden Springs State Forest; Wolf Creek State Park
Additional Information Contacts
Shelby County Government . . . . (217) 774-4421
   http://shelbycounty-il.com

Shelby County Communities

COWDEN (village). Covers a land area of 0.402 square miles and a water area of 0 square miles. Located at 39.25° N. Lat; 88.86° W. Long. Elevation is 597 feet.
Population: 599 (1990); 612 (2000); 629 (2010); Density: 1,502.9 persons per square mile (2008-2012 5-year est.); Race: 100.0% White, 0.0% Black/African American, 0.0% Asian, 0.0% American Indian/Alaska Native, 0.0% Native Hawaiian/Other Pacific Islander, 0.0% Some other race, 0.0% Two or more races, 0.8% Hispanic of any race (2008-2012 5-year est.); Average household size: 2.63 (2008-2012 5-year est.); Median age: 40.9 (2008-2012 5-year est.); Males per 100 females: 106.1 (2008-2012 5-year est.); Marriage status: 20.6% never married, 55.7% now married, 9.1% widowed, 14.6% divorced (2008-2012 5-year est.); Foreign born: 0.3% (2008-2012 5-year est.); Ancestry (includes multiple ancestries): 16.1% German, 8.6% Irish, 2.5% English, 2.3% American, 2.2% Dutch (2008-2012 5-year est.).
Economy: Single-family building permits issued: 0 (2013); Multi-family building permits issued: 0 (2013); Homeowner vacancy rate: 0.0%. Rental vacancy rate: 14.5%. (2008-2012 5-year est.); Employment by occupation: 12.9% management, business, and financial, 0.0% computer, engineering,

and science, 6.5% education, legal, community service, arts, and media, 4.4% healthcare practitioners, 16.1% service, 20.6% sales and office, 10.1% natural resources, construction, and maintenance, 29.4% production, transportation, and material moving (2008-2012 5-year est.).
Income: Per capita income: $17,011 (2008-2012 5-year est.); Median household income: $31,346 (2008-2012 5-year est.); Average household income: $42,144 (2008-2012 5-year est.); Percent of households with income of $100,000 or more: 2.6% (2008-2012 5-year est.); Poverty rate: 18.4% (2008-2012 5-year est.).
Education: Percent of population age 25 and over with: High school diploma (including GED) or higher: 87.1% (2008-2012 5-year est.); Bachelor's degree or higher: 8.5% (2008-2012 5-year est.); Master's degree or higher: 1.2% (2008-2012 5-year est.).

School District(s)
Cowden-Herrick CUSD 3a (PK-12)
    2011-12 Enrollment: 423......................(217) 783-2126
Cowden-Herrick CUSD 3a (PK-12)
    2011-12 Enrollment: 423......................(217) 783-2126
Housing: Homeownership rate: 77.0% (2008-2012 5-year est.); Median home value: $58,500 (2008-2012 5-year est.); Median contract rent: $244 per month (2008-2012 5-year est.); Median year structure built: 1966 (2008-2012 5-year est.).
Health Insurance: 48.2% Private; 43.9% Public; 18.4% None. (2008-2012 5-year est.)
Transportation: Commute to work: 98.8% car, 0.0% public transportation, 0.0% walk, 1.2% work from home (2008-2012 5-year est.); Travel time to work: 26.1% less than 15 minutes, 61.6% 15 to 30 minutes, 9.8% 30 to 45 minutes, 0.0% 45 to 60 minutes, 2.4% 60 minutes or more (2008-2012 5-year est.)

FINDLAY (village). Covers a land area of 0.924 square miles and a water area of 0 square miles. Located at 39.52° N. Lat; 88.75° W. Long. Elevation is 679 feet.
Population: 787 (1990); 723 (2000); 683 (2010); Density: 1,035.1 persons per square mile (2008-2012 5-year est.); Race: 99.5% White, 0.0% Black/African American, 0.0% Asian, 0.0% American Indian/Alaska Native, 0.0% Native Hawaiian/Other Pacific Islander, 0.5% Some other race, 0.5% Two or more races, 1.2% Hispanic of any race (2008-2012 5-year est.); Average household size: 2.62 (2008-2012 5-year est.); Median age: 35.4 (2008-2012 5-year est.); Males per 100 females: 97.5 (2008-2012 5-year est.); Marriage status: 23.7% never married, 59.6% now married, 6.7% widowed, 10.0% divorced (2008-2012 5-year est.); Foreign born: 0.0% (2008-2012 5-year est.); Ancestry (includes multiple ancestries): 16.7% German, 12.4% American, 7.7% English, 6.9% Irish, 2.2% French (2008-2012 5-year est.).
Economy: Single-family building permits issued: 0 (2013); Multi-family building permits issued: 0 (2013); Homeowner vacancy rate: 8.7%. Rental vacancy rate: 8.8%. (2008-2012 5-year est.); Employment by occupation: 11.3% management, business, and financial, 0.7% computer, engineering, and science, 4.3% education, legal, community service, arts, and media, 2.0% healthcare practitioners, 21.8% service, 14.5% sales and office, 19.3% natural resources, construction, and maintenance, 26.1% production, transportation, and material moving (2008-2012 5-year est.).
Income: Per capita income: $18,995 (2008-2012 5-year est.); Median household income: $41,146 (2008-2012 5-year est.); Average household income: $48,069 (2008-2012 5-year est.); Percent of households with income of $100,000 or more: 9.5% (2008-2012 5-year est.); Poverty rate: 16.8% (2008-2012 5-year est.).
Education: Percent of population age 25 and over with: High school diploma (including GED) or higher: 94.0% (2008-2012 5-year est.); Bachelor's degree or higher: 10.3% (2008-2012 5-year est.); Master's degree or higher: 3.4% (2008-2012 5-year est.).

School District(s)
Okaw Valley CUSD 302 (PK-12)
    2011-12 Enrollment: 557......................(217) 665-3232
Housing: Homeownership rate: 74.5% (2008-2012 5-year est.); Median home value: $73,100 (2008-2012 5-year est.); Median contract rent: $331 per month (2008-2012 5-year est.); Median year structure built: 1958 (2008-2012 5-year est.).
Health Insurance: 70.4% Private; 29.8% Public; 10.3% None. (2008-2012 5-year est.)
Safety: Violent crime rate: 0.0 per 10,000 population; Property crime rate: 236.0 per 10,000 population (2012).
Transportation: Commute to work: 93.8% car, 0.0% public transportation, 1.4% walk, 4.4% work from home (2008-2012 5-year est.); Travel time to work: 22.3% less than 15 minutes, 31.0% 15 to 30 minutes, 22.0% 30 to 45 minutes, 18.4% 45 to 60 minutes, 6.3% 60 minutes or more (2008-2012 5-year est.)

HERRICK (village). Covers a land area of 0.366 square miles and a water area of 0 square miles. Located at 39.22° N. Lat; 88.98° W. Long. Elevation is 600 feet.
Population: 466 (1990); 524 (2000); 436 (2010); Density: 967.2 persons per square mile (2008-2012 5-year est.); Race: 100.0% White, 0.0% Black/African American, 0.0% Asian, 0.0% American Indian/Alaska Native, 0.0% Native Hawaiian/Other Pacific Islander, 0.0% Some other race, 0.0% Two or more races, 5.1% Hispanic of any race (2008-2012 5-year est.); Average household size: 2.27 (2008-2012 5-year est.); Median age: 44.1 (2008-2012 5-year est.); Males per 100 females: 95.6 (2008-2012 5-year est.); Marriage status: 35.4% never married, 37.4% now married, 17.2% widowed, 10.1% divorced (2008-2012 5-year est.); Foreign born: 0.0% (2008-2012 5-year est.); Ancestry (includes multiple ancestries): 10.7% English, 6.2% German, 4.8% American, 3.7% Irish, 3.1% French (2008-2012 5-year est.).
Economy: Homeowner vacancy rate: 5.3%. Rental vacancy rate: 26.3%. (2008-2012 5-year est.); Employment by occupation: 7.0% management, business, and financial, 3.2% computer, engineering, and science, 6.4% education, legal, community service, arts, and media, 7.0% healthcare practitioners, 21.0% service, 8.9% sales and office, 8.3% natural resources, construction, and maintenance, 38.2% production, transportation, and material moving (2008-2012 5-year est.).
Income: Per capita income: $16,337 (2008-2012 5-year est.); Median household income: $29,821 (2008-2012 5-year est.); Average household income: $38,060 (2008-2012 5-year est.); Percent of households with income of $100,000 or more: 3.2% (2008-2012 5-year est.); Poverty rate: 10.2% (2008-2012 5-year est.).
Education: Percent of population age 25 and over with: High school diploma (including GED) or higher: 72.2% (2008-2012 5-year est.); Bachelor's degree or higher: 5.2% (2008-2012 5-year est.); Master's degree or higher: 3.5% (2008-2012 5-year est.).

School District(s)
Cowden-Herrick CUSD 3a (PK-12)
    2011-12 Enrollment: 423......................(217) 783-2126
Housing: Homeownership rate: 91.0% (2008-2012 5-year est.); Median home value: $61,300 (2008-2012 5-year est.); Median contract rent: $340 per month (2008-2012 5-year est.); Median year structure built: 1961 (2008-2012 5-year est.).
Health Insurance: 60.7% Private; 43.8% Public; 9.6% None. (2008-2012 5-year est.)
Transportation: Commute to work: 85.6% car, 0.0% public transportation, 5.5% walk, 6.8% work from home (2008-2012 5-year est.); Travel time to work: 22.8% less than 15 minutes, 39.7% 15 to 30 minutes, 14.0% 30 to 45 minutes, 3.7% 45 to 60 minutes, 19.9% 60 minutes or more (2008-2012 5-year est.)

MODE (unincorporated postal area)
Zip Code: 62444
    Covers a land area of 29.075 square miles and a water area of 0 square miles. Located at 39.27° N. Lat; 88.73° W. Long. Elevation is 627 feet.
    Population: 387 (2010); Density: 13.3 persons per square mile (2010); Race: 99.0% White, 0.0% Black/African American, 0.5% Asian, 0.3% American Indian/Alaska Native, 0.0% Native Hawaiian/Other Pacific Islander, 0.2% Some other race, 0.3% Two or more races, 0.0% Hispanic of any race (2010); Average household size: 2.55 (2010); Median age: 40.5 (2010); Males per 100 females: 100.5 (2010); Homeownership rate: 86.1% (2010)

MOWEAQUA (village). Covers a land area of 1.769 square miles and a water area of 0 square miles. Located at 39.62° N. Lat; 89.02° W. Long. Elevation is 633 feet.
History: Incorporated 1877.
Population: 1,785 (1990); 1,923 (2000); 1,831 (2010); Density: 1,044.8 persons per square mile (2008-2012 5-year est.); Race: 99.7% White, 0.3% Black/African American, 0.0% Asian, 0.0% American Indian/Alaska Native, 0.0% Native Hawaiian/Other Pacific Islander, 0.0% Some other race, 0.0% Two or more races, 0.0% Hispanic of any race (2008-2012 5-year est.); Average household size: 2.41 (2008-2012 5-year est.); Median age: 40.4 (2008-2012 5-year est.); Males per 100 females: 78.2 (2008-2012 5-year est.); Marriage status: 19.5% never married, 58.1% now married, 11.0% widowed, 11.4% divorced (2008-2012 5-year est.);

Foreign born: 0.0% (2008-2012 5-year est.); Ancestry (includes multiple ancestries): 24.4% German, 14.7% American, 11.7% Irish, 10.0% English, 2.7% Polish (2008-2012 5-year est.).

Economy: Single-family building permits issued: 0 (2013); Multi-family building permits issued: 0 (2013); Homeowner vacancy rate: 3.1%. Rental vacancy rate: 0.0%. (2008-2012 5-year est.); Employment by occupation: 10.2% management, business, and financial, 2.5% computer, engineering, and science, 12.4% education, legal, community service, arts, and media, 9.5% healthcare practitioners, 14.9% service, 22.0% sales and office, 8.8% natural resources, construction, and maintenance, 19.8% production, transportation, and material moving (2008-2012 5-year est.).

Income: Per capita income: $24,583 (2008-2012 5-year est.); Median household income: $48,542 (2008-2012 5-year est.); Average household income: $59,582 (2008-2012 5-year est.); Percent of households with income of $100,000 or more: 16.5% (2008-2012 5-year est.); Poverty rate: 10.4% (2008-2012 5-year est.).

Education: Percent of population age 25 and over with: High school diploma (including GED) or higher: 92.3% (2008-2012 5-year est.); Bachelor's degree or higher: 18.9% (2008-2012 5-year est.); Master's degree or higher: 6.1% (2008-2012 5-year est.).

School District(s)

Central A & M CUD 21 (PK-12)
   2011-12 Enrollment: 892 . . . . (217) 226-4042

Housing: Homeownership rate: 75.5% (2008-2012 5-year est.); Median home value: $86,600 (2008-2012 5-year est.); Median contract rent: $474 per month (2008-2012 5-year est.); Median year structure built: 1959 (2008-2012 5-year est.).

Health Insurance: 76.8% Private; 34.8% Public; 5.7% None. (2008-2012 5-year est.)

Safety: Violent crime rate: 16.5 per 10,000 population; Property crime rate: 99.0 per 10,000 population (2012).

Transportation: Commute to work: 93.6% car, 0.0% public transportation, 1.5% walk, 4.2% work from home (2008-2012 5-year est.); Travel time to work: 27.2% less than 15 minutes, 34.0% 15 to 30 minutes, 30.8% 30 to 45 minutes, 3.5% 45 to 60 minutes, 4.5% 60 minutes or more (2008-2012 5-year est.).

OCONEE (village).

Covers a land area of 0.356 square miles and a water area of 0 square miles. Located at 39.29° N. Lat; 89.11° W. Long. Elevation is 669 feet.

Population: 201 (1990); 202 (2000); 180 (2010); Density: 483.4 persons per square mile (2008-2012 5-year est.); Race: 98.8% White, 0.0% Black/African American, 0.0% Asian, 1.2% American Indian/Alaska Native, 0.0% Native Hawaiian/Other Pacific Islander, 0.0% Some other race, 0.0% Two or more races, 0.0% Hispanic of any race (2008-2012 5-year est.); Average household size: 2.73 (2008-2012 5-year est.); Median age: 33.0 (2008-2012 5-year est.); Males per 100 females: 112.3 (2008-2012 5-year est.); Marriage status: 21.8% never married, 54.6% now married, 10.1% widowed, 13.4% divorced (2008-2012 5-year est.); Foreign born: 0.0% (2008-2012 5-year est.); Ancestry (includes multiple ancestries): 29.7% German, 14.5% American, 4.1% Croatian, 2.9% Irish, 1.7% English (2008-2012 5-year est.).

Economy: Single-family building permits issued: 1 (2013); Multi-family building permits issued: 0 (2013); Homeowner vacancy rate: 0.0%. Rental vacancy rate: 0.0%. (2008-2012 5-year est.); Employment by occupation: 6.3% management, business, and financial, 0.0% computer, engineering, and science, 4.7% education, legal, community service, arts, and media, 1.6% healthcare practitioners, 7.8% service, 29.7% sales and office, 18.8% natural resources, construction, and maintenance, 31.3% production, transportation, and material moving (2008-2012 5-year est.).

Income: Per capita income: $16,187 (2008-2012 5-year est.); Median household income: $37,917 (2008-2012 5-year est.); Average household income: $43,205 (2008-2012 5-year est.); Percent of households with income of $100,000 or more: n/a (2008-2012 5-year est.); Poverty rate: 32.6% (2008-2012 5-year est.).

Education: Percent of population age 25 and over with: High school diploma (including GED) or higher: 88.0% (2008-2012 5-year est.); Bachelor's degree or higher: 13.0% (2008-2012 5-year est.); Master's degree or higher: 3.0% (2008-2012 5-year est.).

Housing: Homeownership rate: 73.0% (2008-2012 5-year est.); Median home value: $78,000 (2008-2012 5-year est.); Median contract rent: $327 per month (2008-2012 5-year est.); Median year structure built: 1963 (2008-2012 5-year est.).

Health Insurance: 61.9% Private; 43.5% Public; 6.5% None. (2008-2012 5-year est.)

Transportation: Commute to work: 92.6% car, 0.0% public transportation, 7.4% walk, 0.0% work from home (2008-2012 5-year est.); Travel time to work: 33.8% less than 15 minutes, 35.3% 15 to 30 minutes, 13.2% 30 to 45 minutes, 11.8% 45 to 60 minutes, 5.9% 60 minutes or more (2008-2012 5-year est.)

SHELBYVILLE (city).

County seat. Covers a land area of 3.826 square miles and a water area of 0.186 square miles. Located at 39.41° N. Lat; 88.80° W. Long. Elevation is 640 feet.

History: Incorporated 1839.

Population: 4,943 (1990); 4,971 (2000); 4,700 (2010); Density: 1,376.5 persons per square mile (2008-2012 5-year est.); Race: 98.6% White, 0.4% Black/African American, 0.0% Asian, 0.3% American Indian/Alaska Native, 0.0% Native Hawaiian/Other Pacific Islander, 0.7% Some other race, 0.8% Two or more races, 1.6% Hispanic of any race (2008-2012 5-year est.); Average household size: 2.25 (2008-2012 5-year est.); Median age: 45.9 (2008-2012 5-year est.); Males per 100 females: 83.5 (2008-2012 5-year est.); Marriage status: 25.6% never married, 54.7% now married, 10.5% widowed, 9.2% divorced (2008-2012 5-year est.); Foreign born: 1.0% (2008-2012 5-year est.); Ancestry (includes multiple ancestries): 22.8% German, 14.4% American, 9.6% Irish, 7.0% English, 4.8% French (2008-2012 5-year est.).

Economy: Single-family building permits issued: 2 (2013); Multi-family building permits issued: 0 (2013); Homeowner vacancy rate: 2.1%. Rental vacancy rate: 12.0%. (2008-2012 5-year est.); Employment by occupation: 11.6% management, business, and financial, 5.9% computer, engineering, and science, 7.2% education, legal, community service, arts, and media, 7.0% healthcare practitioners, 24.1% service, 21.4% sales and office, 4.3% natural resources, construction, and maintenance, 18.4% production, transportation, and material moving (2008-2012 5-year est.).

Income: Per capita income: $22,999 (2008-2012 5-year est.); Median household income: $39,306 (2008-2012 5-year est.); Average household income: $51,870 (2008-2012 5-year est.); Percent of households with income of $100,000 or more: 10.0% (2008-2012 5-year est.); Poverty rate: 10.5% (2008-2012 5-year est.).

Education: Percent of population age 25 and over with: High school diploma (including GED) or higher: 83.2% (2008-2012 5-year est.); Bachelor's degree or higher: 15.0% (2008-2012 5-year est.); Master's degree or higher: 5.7% (2008-2012 5-year est.).

School District(s)

Clk/cls/cmbn/dglas/edgr/mltr/shlb
   2011-12 Enrollment: n/a . . . . (217) 348-0151
Shelbyville CUSD 4 (PK-12)
   2011-12 Enrollment: 1,229 . . . . (217) 774-4626

Housing: Homeownership rate: 74.4% (2008-2012 5-year est.); Median home value: $79,500 (2008-2012 5-year est.); Median contract rent: $397 per month (2008-2012 5-year est.); Median year structure built: 1953 (2008-2012 5-year est.).

Health Insurance: 73.1% Private; 40.2% Public; 6.1% None. (2008-2012 5-year est.)

Hospitals: Shelby Memorial Hospital (54 beds)

Transportation: Commute to work: 91.7% car, 0.2% public transportation, 4.5% walk, 3.6% work from home (2008-2012 5-year est.); Travel time to work: 66.4% less than 15 minutes, 13.6% 15 to 30 minutes, 12.2% 30 to 45 minutes, 4.6% 45 to 60 minutes, 3.1% 60 minutes or more (2008-2012 5-year est.)

Airports: Shelby County Airport (general aviation)

Additional Information Contacts
Greater Shelbyville Chamber of Commerce . . . . (217) 774-2221
   http://www.shelbyvilleillinois.net/shelbyville-chamber-of-commerce/

SIGEL (town).

Covers a land area of 0.280 square miles and a water area of 0.008 square miles. Located at 39.23° N. Lat; 88.49° W. Long. Elevation is 636 feet.

Population: 344 (1990); 386 (2000); 373 (2010); Density: 1,132.0 persons per square mile (2008-2012 5-year est.); Race: 100.0% White, 0.0% Black/African American, 0.0% Asian, 0.0% American Indian/Alaska Native, 0.0% Native Hawaiian/Other Pacific Islander, 0.0% Some other race, 0.0% Two or more races, 4.7% Hispanic of any race (2008-2012 5-year est.); Average household size: 2.60 (2008-2012 5-year est.); Median age: 34.4 (2008-2012 5-year est.); Males per 100 females: 94.5 (2008-2012 5-year est.); Marriage status: 20.9% never married, 50.6% now married, 11.9% widowed, 16.6% divorced (2008-2012 5-year est.); Foreign born: 0.0% (2008-2012 5-year est.); Ancestry (includes multiple ancestries): 66.9%

German, 11.4% Irish, 8.2% American, 7.6% English, 0.3% Polish (2008-2012 5-year est.).

Economy: Single-family building permits issued: 0 (2013); Multi-family building permits issued: 0 (2013); Homeowner vacancy rate: 6.3%. Rental vacancy rate: 0.0%. (2008-2012 5-year est.); Employment by occupation: 13.1% management, business, and financial, 1.5% computer, engineering, and science, 2.2% education, legal, community service, arts, and media, 5.1% healthcare practitioners, 23.4% service, 27.0% sales and office, 6.6% natural resources, construction, and maintenance, 21.2% production, transportation, and material moving (2008-2012 5-year est.).

Income: Per capita income: $18,854 (2008-2012 5-year est.); Median household income: $38,000 (2008-2012 5-year est.); Average household income: $47,340 (2008-2012 5-year est.); Percent of households with income of $100,000 or more: 9.0% (2008-2012 5-year est.); Poverty rate: 15.5% (2008-2012 5-year est.).

Education: Percent of population age 25 and over with: High school diploma (including GED) or higher: 86.5% (2008-2012 5-year est.); Bachelor's degree or higher: 19.2% (2008-2012 5-year est.); Master's degree or higher: 6.3% (2008-2012 5-year est.).

Housing: Homeownership rate: 73.8% (2008-2012 5-year est.); Median home value: $92,000 (2008-2012 5-year est.); Median contract rent: $417 per month (2008-2012 5-year est.); Median year structure built: 1960 (2008-2012 5-year est.).

Health Insurance: 67.2% Private; 39.7% Public; 8.2% None. (2008-2012 5-year est.)

Transportation: Commute to work: 86.8% car, 0.0% public transportation, 4.4% walk, 4.4% work from home (2008-2012 5-year est.); Travel time to work: 36.2% less than 15 minutes, 55.4% 15 to 30 minutes, 7.7% 30 to 45 minutes, 0.0% 45 to 60 minutes, 0.8% 60 minutes or more (2008-2012 5-year est.)

STEWARDSON (village).

Covers a land area of 0.599 square miles and a water area of 0 square miles. Located at 39.26° N. Lat; 88.63° W. Long. Elevation is 643 feet.

Population: 660 (1990); 747 (2000); 734 (2010); Density: 1,294.6 persons per square mile (2008-2012 5-year est.); Race: 100.0% White, 0.0% Black/African American, 0.0% Asian, 0.0% American Indian/Alaska Native, 0.0% Native Hawaiian/Other Pacific Islander, 0.0% Some other race, 0.0% Two or more races, 0.0% Hispanic of any race (2008-2012 5-year est.); Average household size: 2.41 (2008-2012 5-year est.); Median age: 44.4 (2008-2012 5-year est.); Males per 100 females: 93.3 (2008-2012 5-year est.); Marriage status: 17.7% never married, 66.5% now married, 3.9% widowed, 11.9% divorced (2008-2012 5-year est.); Foreign born: 0.0% (2008-2012 5-year est.); Ancestry (includes multiple ancestries): 42.2% German, 9.2% English, 8.5% Irish, 7.6% American, 4.1% Swedish (2008-2012 5-year est.).

Economy: Single-family building permits issued: 0 (2013); Multi-family building permits issued: 0 (2013); Homeowner vacancy rate: 3.4%. Rental vacancy rate: 0.0%. (2008-2012 5-year est.); Employment by occupation: 8.8% management, business, and financial, 5.1% computer, engineering, and science, 6.1% education, legal, community service, arts, and media, 13.6% healthcare practitioners, 14.4% service, 26.3% sales and office, 5.3% natural resources, construction, and maintenance, 20.5% production, transportation, and material moving (2008-2012 5-year est.).

Income: Per capita income: $24,430 (2008-2012 5-year est.); Median household income: $52,500 (2008-2012 5-year est.); Average household income: $57,845 (2008-2012 5-year est.); Percent of households with income of $100,000 or more: 12.4% (2008-2012 5-year est.); Poverty rate: 5.3% (2008-2012 5-year est.).

Education: Percent of population age 25 and over with: High school diploma (including GED) or higher: 92.4% (2008-2012 5-year est.); Bachelor's degree or higher: 17.6% (2008-2012 5-year est.); Master's degree or higher: 6.2% (2008-2012 5-year est.).

Housing: Homeownership rate: 78.6% (2008-2012 5-year est.); Median home value: $82,500 (2008-2012 5-year est.); Median contract rent: $425 per month (2008-2012 5-year est.); Median year structure built: 1960 (2008-2012 5-year est.).

Health Insurance: 78.8% Private; 29.9% Public; 5.8% None. (2008-2012 5-year est.)

Transportation: Commute to work: 85.6% car, 0.0% public transportation, 2.7% walk, 6.5% work from home (2008-2012 5-year est.); Travel time to work: 19.2% less than 15 minutes, 55.2% 15 to 30 minutes, 17.4% 30 to 45 minutes, 1.5% 45 to 60 minutes, 6.7% 60 minutes or more (2008-2012 5-year est.)

STRASBURG (village).

Covers a land area of 0.535 square miles and a water area of 0 square miles. Located at 39.35° N. Lat; 88.62° W. Long. Elevation is 636 feet.

Population: 473 (1990); 603 (2000); 467 (2010); Density: 1,230.7 persons per square mile (2008-2012 5-year est.); Race: 98.0% White, 0.3% Black/African American, 0.0% Asian, 0.0% American Indian/Alaska Native, 0.0% Native Hawaiian/Other Pacific Islander, 1.7% Some other race, 1.7% Two or more races, 0.0% Hispanic of any race (2008-2012 5-year est.); Average household size: 2.44 (2008-2012 5-year est.); Median age: 42.5 (2008-2012 5-year est.); Males per 100 females: 84.3 (2008-2012 5-year est.); Marriage status: 14.7% never married, 63.4% now married, 15.6% widowed, 6.4% divorced (2008-2012 5-year est.); Foreign born: 4.4% (2008-2012 5-year est.); Ancestry (includes multiple ancestries): 44.1% German, 7.8% English, 6.8% American, 4.7% Dutch, 4.0% Irish (2008-2012 5-year est.).

Economy: Single-family building permits issued: 1 (2013); Multi-family building permits issued: 0 (2013); Homeowner vacancy rate: 0.0%. Rental vacancy rate: 0.0%. (2008-2012 5-year est.); Employment by occupation: 6.8% management, business, and financial, 10.8% computer, engineering, and science, 19.0% education, legal, community service, arts, and media, 7.9% healthcare practitioners, 7.5% service, 16.5% sales and office, 10.4% natural resources, construction, and maintenance, 21.1% production, transportation, and material moving (2008-2012 5-year est.).

Income: Per capita income: $22,622 (2008-2012 5-year est.); Median household income: $46,167 (2008-2012 5-year est.); Average household income: $56,858 (2008-2012 5-year est.); Percent of households with income of $100,000 or more: 10.9% (2008-2012 5-year est.); Poverty rate: 14.4% (2008-2012 5-year est.).

Education: Percent of population age 25 and over with: High school diploma (including GED) or higher: 93.5% (2008-2012 5-year est.); Bachelor's degree or higher: 15.8% (2008-2012 5-year est.); Master's degree or higher: 4.4% (2008-2012 5-year est.).

School District(s)

Stewardson-Strasburg CUD 5a (PK-12)

    2011-12 Enrollment: 380 . . . . (217) 682-3355

Housing: Homeownership rate: 89.1% (2008-2012 5-year est.); Median home value: $90,100 (2008-2012 5-year est.); Median contract rent: $369 per month (2008-2012 5-year est.); Median year structure built: 1953 (2008-2012 5-year est.).

Health Insurance: 70.5% Private; 33.7% Public; 11.6% None. (2008-2012 5-year est.)

Transportation: Commute to work: 91.8% car, 0.7% public transportation, 2.9% walk, 3.2% work from home (2008-2012 5-year est.); Travel time to work: 24.4% less than 15 minutes, 55.6% 15 to 30 minutes, 14.1% 30 to 45 minutes, 1.9% 45 to 60 minutes, 4.1% 60 minutes or more (2008-2012 5-year est.)

TOWER HILL (village).

Covers a land area of 1.005 square miles and a water area of 0 square miles. Located at 39.39° N. Lat; 88.96° W. Long. Elevation is 659 feet.

Population: 601 (1990); 609 (2000); 611 (2010); Density: 811.9 persons per square mile (2008-2012 5-year est.); Race: 99.4% White, 0.0% Black/African American, 0.6% Asian, 0.0% American Indian/Alaska Native, 0.0% Native Hawaiian/Other Pacific Islander, 0.0% Some other race, 0.0% Two or more races, 0.5% Hispanic of any race (2008-2012 5-year est.); Average household size: 2.90 (2008-2012 5-year est.); Median age: 43.2 (2008-2012 5-year est.); Males per 100 females: 99.5 (2008-2012 5-year est.); Marriage status: 27.1% never married, 48.2% now married, 7.2% widowed, 17.6% divorced (2008-2012 5-year est.); Foreign born: 0.6% (2008-2012 5-year est.); Ancestry (includes multiple ancestries): 14.1% American, 10.9% Irish, 8.9% German, 5.9% English, 3.1% Scottish (2008-2012 5-year est.).

Economy: Single-family building permits issued: 0 (2013); Multi-family building permits issued: 0 (2013); Homeowner vacancy rate: 0.0%. Rental vacancy rate: 0.0%. (2008-2012 5-year est.); Employment by occupation: 4.3% management, business, and financial, 2.0% computer, engineering, and science, 2.6% education, legal, community service, arts, and media, 2.6% healthcare practitioners, 24.5% service, 25.4% sales and office, 6.6% natural resources, construction, and maintenance, 32.0% production, transportation, and material moving (2008-2012 5-year est.).

Income: Per capita income: $15,617 (2008-2012 5-year est.); Median household income: $43,047 (2008-2012 5-year est.); Average household income: $43,789 (2008-2012 5-year est.); Percent of households with income of $100,000 or more: 2.5% (2008-2012 5-year est.); Poverty rate: 23.9% (2008-2012 5-year est.).

Education: Percent of population age 25 and over with: High school diploma (including GED) or higher: 73.5% (2008-2012 5-year est.); Bachelor's degree or higher: 7.9% (2008-2012 5-year est.); Master's degree or higher: 0.9% (2008-2012 5-year est.).

School District(s)

Pana CUSD 8 (PK-12)

　　2011-12 Enrollment: 1,418 . . . . (217) 562-1500

Housing: Homeownership rate: 78.6% (2008-2012 5-year est.); Median home value: $47,100 (2008-2012 5-year est.); Median contract rent: $369 per month (2008-2012 5-year est.); Median year structure built: 1940 (2008-2012 5-year est.).

Health Insurance: 49.9% Private; 38.4% Public; 20.1% None. (2008-2012 5-year est.)

Transportation: Commute to work: 92.5% car, 1.8% public transportation, 0.0% walk, 3.6% work from home (2008-2012 5-year est.); Travel time to work: 39.9% less than 15 minutes, 44.0% 15 to 30 minutes, 8.0% 30 to 45 minutes, 3.7% 45 to 60 minutes, 4.3% 60 minutes or more (2008-2012 5-year est.)

WESTERVELT (CDP). Covers a land area of 0.086 square miles and a water area of 0 square miles. Located at 39.48° N. Lat; 88.86° W. Long. Elevation is 653 feet.

Population: n/a (1990); n/a (2000); 128 (2010); Density: 1,156.8 persons per square mile (2008-2012 5-year est.); Race: 100.0% White, 0.0% Black/African American, 0.0% Asian, 0.0% American Indian/Alaska Native, 0.0% Native Hawaiian/Other Pacific Islander, 0.0% Some other race, 0.0% Two or more races, 0.0% Hispanic of any race (2008-2012 5-year est.); Average household size: 2.11 (2008-2012 5-year est.); Median age: 31.8 (2008-2012 5-year est.); Males per 100 females: 141.5 (2008-2012 5-year est.); Marriage status: 60.3% never married, 39.7% now married, 0.0% widowed, 0.0% divorced (2008-2012 5-year est.); Foreign born: 0.0% (2008-2012 5-year est.); Ancestry (includes multiple ancestries): 64.6% German, 52.5% Irish (2008-2012 5-year est.).

Economy: Homeowner vacancy rate: 0.0%. Rental vacancy rate: 0.0%. (2008-2012 5-year est.); Employment by occupation: 0.0% management, business, and financial, 0.0% computer, engineering, and science, 0.0% education, legal, community service, arts, and media, 19.0% healthcare practitioners, 0.0% service, 0.0% sales and office, 0.0% natural resources, construction, and maintenance, 81.0% production, transportation, and material moving (2008-2012 5-year est.).

Income: Per capita income: $20,388 (2008-2012 5-year est.); Median household income: $31,679 (2008-2012 5-year est.); Average household income: n/a (2008-2012 5-year est.); Percent of households with income of $100,000 or more: n/a (2008-2012 5-year est.); Poverty rate: 0.0% (2008-2012 5-year est.)

Education: Percent of population age 25 and over with: High school diploma (including GED) or higher: 100.0% (2008-2012 5-year est.); Bachelor's degree or higher: 0.0% (2008-2012 5-year est.); Master's degree or higher: 0.0% (2008-2012 5-year est.).

Housing: Homeownership rate: 100.0% (2008-2012 5-year est.); Median home value: $53,300 (2008-2012 5-year est.); Median contract rent: n/a per month (2008-2012 5-year est.); Median year structure built: 1943 (2008-2012 5-year est.).

Health Insurance: 100.0% Private; 0.0% Public; 0.0% None. (2008-2012 5-year est.)

Transportation: Commute to work: 100.0% car, 0.0% public transportation, 0.0% walk, 0.0% work from home (2008-2012 5-year est.); Travel time to work: 0.0% less than 15 minutes, 74.5% 15 to 30 minutes, 25.5% 30 to 45 minutes, 0.0% 45 to 60 minutes, 0.0% 60 minutes or more (2008-2012 5-year est.)

WINDSOR (city). Covers a land area of 0.630 square miles and a water area of 0 square miles. Located at 39.44° N. Lat; 88.60° W. Long. Elevation is 702 feet.

History: Incorporated 1869.

Population: 1,143 (1990); 1,125 (2000); 1,187 (2010); Density: 2,020.5 persons per square mile (2008-2012 5-year est.); Race: 95.7% White, 2.4% Black/African American, 0.3% Asian, 0.0% American Indian/Alaska Native, 0.0% Native Hawaiian/Other Pacific Islander, 1.6% Some other race, 0.9% Two or more races, 0.4% Hispanic of any race (2008-2012 5-year est.); Average household size: 2.43 (2008-2012 5-year est.); Median age: 31.0 (2008-2012 5-year est.); Males per 100 females: 90.6 (2008-2012 5-year est.); Marriage status: 27.0% never married, 44.7% now married, 13.1% widowed, 15.2% divorced (2008-2012 5-year est.); Foreign born: 0.3% (2008-2012 5-year est.); Ancestry (includes multiple

ancestries): 17.7% German, 13.0% American, 7.1% Irish, 6.0% English, 3.8% Dutch (2008-2012 5-year est.).

Economy: Single-family building permits issued: 2 (2013); Multi-family building permits issued: 0 (2013); Homeowner vacancy rate: 2.0%. Rental vacancy rate: 0.0%. (2008-2012 5-year est.); Employment by occupation: 9.5% management, business, and financial, 0.9% computer, engineering, and science, 6.7% education, legal, community service, arts, and media, 4.5% healthcare practitioners, 15.5% service, 25.4% sales and office, 12.5% natural resources, construction, and maintenance, 24.9% production, transportation, and material moving (2008-2012 5-year est.).

Income: Per capita income: $19,003 (2008-2012 5-year est.); Median household income: $35,694 (2008-2012 5-year est.); Average household income: $45,204 (2008-2012 5-year est.); Percent of households with income of $100,000 or more: 9.6% (2008-2012 5-year est.); Poverty rate: 15.0% (2008-2012 5-year est.).

Education: Percent of population age 25 and over with: High school diploma (including GED) or higher: 91.3% (2008-2012 5-year est.); Bachelor's degree or higher: 11.5% (2008-2012 5-year est.); Master's degree or higher: 3.0% (2008-2012 5-year est.).

School District(s)

Windsor CUSD 1 (PK-12)

　　2011-12 Enrollment: 399. . . . . (217) 459-2636

Housing: Homeownership rate: 74.8% (2008-2012 5-year est.); Median home value: $70,500 (2008-2012 5-year est.); Median contract rent: $366 per month (2008-2012 5-year est.); Median year structure built: 1958 (2008-2012 5-year est.).

Health Insurance: 63.5% Private; 37.2% Public; 14.1% None. (2008-2012 5-year est.)

Transportation: Commute to work: 92.3% car, 0.0% public transportation, 0.4% walk, 6.2% work from home (2008-2012 5-year est.); Travel time to work: 21.4% less than 15 minutes, 49.5% 15 to 30 minutes, 18.1% 30 to 45 minutes, 5.5% 45 to 60 minutes, 5.5% 60 minutes or more (2008-2012 5-year est.)

Saint Clair County

Located in southwestern Illinois; bounded on the northwest by the Mississippi River and the Missouri border; also drained by the Kaskaskia River and Silver Creek. Covers a land area of 657.759 square miles, a water area of 16.274 square miles, and is located in the Central Time Zone at 38.47° N. Lat., 89.93° W. Long. The county was founded in 1790. County seat is Belleville.

Saint Clair County is part of the St. Louis, MO-IL Metropolitan Statistical Area. The entire metro area includes: Bond County, IL; Calhoun County, IL; Clinton County, IL; Jersey County, IL; Macoupin County, IL; Madison County, IL; Monroe County, IL; Saint Clair County, IL; Franklin County, MO; Jefferson County, MO; Lincoln County, MO; Saint Charles County, MO; Saint Louis County, MO; Warren County, MO; Saint Louis city, MO

Weather Station: Belleville Scott AFB										Elevation: 442 feet		
	Jan	Feb	Mar	Apr	May	Jun	Jul	Aug	Sep	Oct	Nov	Dec
High	42	47	58	69	78	86	89	89	82	71	57	44
Low	24	27	36	45	55	63	67	65	56	46	37	27
Precip	2.3	2.2	3.2	3.9	4.8	4.2	3.8	3.2	3.3	3.5	3.8	2.8
Snow	4.5	3.2	1.6	0.4	0.0	0.0	0.0	0.0	0.0	0.0	0.4	3.0

High and Low temperatures in degrees Fahrenheit; Precipitation and Snow in inches

Weather Station: Cahokia										Elevation: 399 feet		
	Jan	Feb	Mar	Apr	May	Jun	Jul	Aug	Sep	Oct	Nov	Dec
High	41	46	56	68	77	85	89	87	81	70	57	44
Low	23	26	34	45	55	64	68	66	58	46	36	25
Precip	2.5	2.6	3.4	3.8	4.5	4.0	4.4	3.5	3.2	3.4	3.7	3.0
Snow	5.0	3.8	1.9	0.2	0.0	0.0	0.0	0.0	0.0	tr	0.6	3.9

High and Low temperatures in degrees Fahrenheit; Precipitation and Snow in inches

Population: 262,852 (1990); 256,082 (2000); 270,056 (2010); Race: 65.2% White, 30.3% Black/African American, 1.1% Asian, 0.2% American Indian/Alaska Native, 0.0% Native Hawaiian/Other Pacific Islander, 3.2% Some other race, 2.5% Two or more races, 3.3% Hispanic of any race (2008-2012 5-year est.); Density: 408.5 persons per square mile (2008-2012 5-year est.); Average household size: 2.57 (2008-2012 5-year est.); Median age: 37.1 (2008-2012 5-year est.); Males per 100 females: 92.9 (2008-2012 5-year est.)

Religion: Six largest groups: 17.2% Catholicism, 12.7% Baptist, 4.6% Methodist/Pietist, 4.1% Non-denominational Protestant, 3.8% Presbyterian-Reformed, 2.5% Lutheran (2010)
Economy: Unemployment rate: 6.9% (April 2014); Total civilian labor force: 124,774 (April 2014); Leading industries: 18.8% health care and social assistance; 17.1% retail trade; 13.6% accommodation & food services (2012); Farms: 732 totaling 251,931 acres (2012); Companies that employ 500 or more persons: 9 (2012); Companies that employ 100 to 499 persons: 96 (2012); Companies that employ less than 100 persons: 5,261 (2012); Black-owned businesses: 2,306 (2007); Hispanic-owned businesses: 253 (2007); Asian-owned businesses: 453 (2007); Women-owned businesses: 5,692 (2007); Single-family building permits issued: 448 (2013); Multi-family building permits issued: 194 (2013).
Income: Per capita income: $25,504 (2008-2012 5-year est.); Median household income: $50,490 (2008-2012 5-year est.); Average household income: $64,053 (2008-2012 5-year est.); Percent of households with income of $100,000 or more: 19.6% (2008-2012 5-year est.); Poverty rate: 17.0% (2008-2012 5-year est.); Bankruptcy rate: 5.19% (2013).
Taxes: Total county taxes per capita: $132 (2011); County property taxes per capita: $129 (2011)
Education: Percent of population age 25 and over with: High school diploma (including GED) or higher: 89.1% (2008-2012 5-year est.); Bachelor's degree or higher: 24.9% (2008-2012 5-year est.); Master's degree or higher: 9.4% (2008-2012 5-year est.).
Housing: Homeownership rate: 66.9% (2008-2012 5-year est.); Median home value: $125,700 (2008-2012 5-year est.); Median contract rent: $562 per month (2008-2012 5-year est.); Median year structure built: 1969 (2008-2012 5-year est.)
Health: Birth rate: 126.5 per 10,000 population (2013); Death rate: 94.8 per 10,000 population (2013); Age-adjusted cancer mortality rate: 187.3 deaths per 100,000 population (2011); Number of physicians: 18.0 per 10,000 population (2011); Hospital beds: 26.4 per 10,000 population (2010); Hospital admissions: 1,296.3 per 10,000 population (2010).
Environment: Air Quality Index: 64.9% good, 35.1% moderate, 0.0% unhealthy for sensitive individuals, 0.0% unhealthy (percent of days in 2013)
Elections: 2012 Presidential election results: 56.4% Obama, 41.9% Romney
National and State Parks: Cahokia Mounds State Park; Holten State Park
Additional Information Contacts
Saint Clair County Government . . . . (618) 277-6600
    http://www.co.st-clair.il.us

Saint Clair County Communities

ALORTON (village). Covers a land area of 1.800 square miles and a water area of 0.030 square miles. Located at 38.59° N. Lat; 90.12° W. Long. Elevation is 417 feet.
History: Incorporated 1944.
Population: 2,960 (1990); 2,749 (2000); 2,002 (2010); Density: 1,031.7 persons per square mile (2008-2012 5-year est.); Race: 1.1% White, 98.2% Black/African American, 0.0% Asian, 0.0% American Indian/Alaska Native, 0.0% Native Hawaiian/Other Pacific Islander, 0.7% Some other race, 0.7% Two or more races, 1.2% Hispanic of any race (2008-2012 5-year est.); Average household size: 2.65 (2008-2012 5-year est.); Median age: 34.2 (2008-2012 5-year est.); Males per 100 females: 86.6 (2008-2012 5-year est.); Marriage status: 53.9% never married, 21.7% now married, 9.4% widowed, 15.0% divorced (2008-2012 5-year est.); Foreign born: 1.0% (2008-2012 5-year est.); Ancestry (includes multiple ancestries): 2.1% African, 1.1% English, 0.6% American, 0.2% Other Subsaharan African (2008-2012 5-year est.).
Economy: Homeowner vacancy rate: 0.0%. Rental vacancy rate: 0.0%. (2008-2012 5-year est.); Employment by occupation: 8.0% management, business, and financial, 0.0% computer, engineering, and science, 4.3% education, legal, community service, arts, and media, 2.2% healthcare practitioners, 32.9% service, 15.3% sales and office, 4.9% natural resources, construction, and maintenance, 32.3% production, transportation, and material moving (2008-2012 5-year est.).
Income: Per capita income: $10,276 (2008-2012 5-year est.); Median household income: $18,495 (2008-2012 5-year est.); Average household income: $25,350 (2008-2012 5-year est.); Percent of households with income of $100,000 or more: 2.0% (2008-2012 5-year est.); Poverty rate: 53.1% (2008-2012 5-year est.).

Education: Percent of population age 25 and over with: High school diploma (including GED) or higher: 68.8% (2008-2012 5-year est.); Bachelor's degree or higher: 4.2% (2008-2012 5-year est.); Master's degree or higher: 2.4% (2008-2012 5-year est.).
School District(s)
East Saint Louis SD 189 (PK-12)
    2011-12 Enrollment: 6,971 . . . . (618) 646-3009
Housing: Homeownership rate: 42.5% (2008-2012 5-year est.); Median home value: $32,100 (2008-2012 5-year est.); Median contract rent: $390 per month (2008-2012 5-year est.); Median year structure built: 1965 (2008-2012 5-year est.).
Health Insurance: 24.1% Private; 59.7% Public; 20.7% None. (2008-2012 5-year est.)
Transportation: Commute to work: 91.1% car, 8.9% public transportation, 0.0% walk, 0.0% work from home (2008-2012 5-year est.); Travel time to work: 35.0% less than 15 minutes, 34.8% 15 to 30 minutes, 18.8% 30 to 45 minutes, 9.7% 45 to 60 minutes, 1.7% 60 minutes or more (2008-2012 5-year est.)

BELLEVILLE (city). County seat. Covers a land area of 22.741 square miles and a water area of 0.269 square miles. Located at 38.52° N. Lat; 89.99° W. Long. Elevation is 515 feet.
History: Named for the French translation of "beautiful city," by George Blair. Settlers came to Belleville early in the 1800's, and in 1814 the settlement became the seat of St. Clair County, succeeding Cahokia. The town was incorporated in 1819. The discovery of coal in 1828 brought many German immigrants to Belleville, which came to be known as Dutch Town.
Population: 42,785 (1990); 41,410 (2000); 44,478 (2010); Density: 1,940.1 persons per square mile (2008-2012 5-year est.); Race: 71.0% White, 23.2% Black/African American, 1.1% Asian, 0.3% American Indian/Alaska Native, 0.0% Native Hawaiian/Other Pacific Islander, 4.4% Some other race, 4.0% Two or more races, 2.5% Hispanic of any race (2008-2012 5-year est.); Average household size: 2.34 (2008-2012 5-year est.); Median age: 37.2 (2008-2012 5-year est.); Males per 100 females: 90.1 (2008-2012 5-year est.); Marriage status: 34.1% never married, 42.7% now married, 7.3% widowed, 15.9% divorced (2008-2012 5-year est.); Foreign born: 2.1% (2008-2012 5-year est.); Ancestry (includes multiple ancestries): 28.1% German, 10.9% Irish, 8.9% European, 6.9% English, 4.8% American (2008-2012 5-year est.).
Economy: Unemployment rate: 6.9% (April 2014); Total civilian labor force: 22,263 (April 2014); Single-family building permits issued: 34 (2013); Multi-family building permits issued: 0 (2013); Homeowner vacancy rate: 2.4%. Rental vacancy rate: 6.5%. (2008-2012 5-year est.); Employment by occupation: 9.1% management, business, and financial, 5.1% computer, engineering, and science, 10.9% education, legal, community service, arts, and media, 6.6% healthcare practitioners, 20.7% service, 27.2% sales and office, 7.6% natural resources, construction, and maintenance, 12.7% production, transportation, and material moving (2008-2012 5-year est.).
Income: Per capita income: $25,466 (2008-2012 5-year est.); Median household income: $48,085 (2008-2012 5-year est.); Average household income: $58,713 (2008-2012 5-year est.); Percent of households with income of $100,000 or more: 15.4% (2008-2012 5-year est.); Poverty rate: 14.7% (2008-2012 5-year est.).
Education: Percent of population age 25 and over with: High school diploma (including GED) or higher: 90.5% (2008-2012 5-year est.); Bachelor's degree or higher: 23.9% (2008-2012 5-year est.); Master's degree or higher: 8.9% (2008-2012 5-year est.).
School District(s)
Belle Valley SD 119 (PK-08)
    2011-12 Enrollment: 932 . . . . (618) 234-7723
Belleville Area Special Services
    2011-12 Enrollment: n/a . . . . (618) 355-4700
Belleville SD 118 (PK-08)
    2011-12 Enrollment: 3,789 . . . . (618) 233-2830
Belleville Twp HSD 201 (09-12)
    2011-12 Enrollment: 4,958 . . . . (618) 222-8241
East Saint Louis SD 189 (PK-12)
    2011-12 Enrollment: 6,971 . . . . (618) 646-3009
Harmony Emge SD 175 (PK-08)
    2011-12 Enrollment: 818 . . . . (618) 397-8444
Saint Clair Roe (PK-12)
    2011-12 Enrollment: n/a . . . . (618) 825-3900
Signal Hill SD 181 (PK-08)
    2011-12 Enrollment: 375 . . . . (618) 397-0325

Whiteside SD 115 (PK-08)
2011-12 Enrollment: 1,391 . . . . (618) 239-0000
Two-year College(s)
Southwestern Illinois College (Public)
Fall 2012 Enrollment: 11,938 . . . . (618) 235-2700
2012-13 Tuition: In-state $6,954; Out-of-state $10,370
Vocational/Technical School(s)
Alvareitas College of Cosmetology-Belleville (Private, For-profit)
Fall 2012 Enrollment: 15 . . . . (618) 257-9193
2012-13 Tuition: $12,600
Housing: Homeownership rate: 62.0% (2008-2012 5-year est.); Median home value: $109,500 (2008-2012 5-year est.); Median contract rent: $530 per month (2008-2012 5-year est.); Median year structure built: 1958 (2008-2012 5-year est.).
Health Insurance: 67.0% Private; 33.0% Public; 12.4% None. (2008-2012 5-year est.)
Hospitals: 375th Medical Group Hospital (161 beds); Memorial Hospital (313 beds); St. Elizabeth's Hospital (498 beds)
Transportation: Commute to work: 90.4% car, 4.2% public transportation, 1.9% walk, 1.9% work from home (2008-2012 5-year est.); Travel time to work: 32.6% less than 15 minutes, 36.7% 15 to 30 minutes, 19.3% 30 to 45 minutes, 7.1% 45 to 60 minutes, 4.3% 60 minutes or more (2008-2012 5-year est.)
Airports: MidAmerica St. Louis Airport (general aviation)
Additional Information Contacts
City of Belleville . . . . (618) 233-6810
  http://www.belleville.net
Greater Belleville Chamber of Commerce . . . . (618) 233-2015
  http://www.bellevillechamber.org

BROOKLYN (village). Aka Lovejoy. Covers a land area of 0.831 square miles and a water area of 0 square miles. Located at 38.65° N. Lat; 90.17° W. Long. Elevation is 413 feet.
History: When it was incorporated in 1874 Brooklyn was called Lovejoy, in honor of Abolitionist editor Elijah P. Lovejoy.
Population: 1,144 (1990); 676 (2000); 749 (2010); Density: 804.8 persons per square mile (2008-2012 5-year est.); Race: 1.3% White, 97.3% Black/African American, 0.0% Asian, 0.0% American Indian/Alaska Native, 0.0% Native Hawaiian/Other Pacific Islander, 1.4% Some other race, 1.3% Two or more races, 0.0% Hispanic of any race (2008-2012 5-year est.); Average household size: 2.69 (2008-2012 5-year est.); Median age: 29.9 (2008-2012 5-year est.); Males per 100 females: 61.6 (2008-2012 5-year est.); Marriage status: 53.1% never married, 26.9% now married, 11.5% widowed, 8.6% divorced (2008-2012 5-year est.); Foreign born: 0.7% (2008-2012 5-year est.); Ancestry (includes multiple ancestries): 3.4% African, 0.7% European, 0.4% English (2008-2012 5-year est.).
Economy: Homeowner vacancy rate: 0.0%. Rental vacancy rate: 0.0%. (2008-2012 5-year est.); Employment by occupation: 15.8% management, business, and financial, 3.8% computer, engineering, and science, 8.7% education, legal, community service, arts, and media, 3.3% healthcare practitioners, 30.4% service, 28.8% sales and office, 0.0% natural resources, construction, and maintenance, 9.2% production, transportation, and material moving (2008-2012 5-year est.).
Income: Per capita income: $12,740 (2008-2012 5-year est.); Median household income: $20,042 (2008-2012 5-year est.); Average household income: $28,916 (2008-2012 5-year est.); Percent of households with income of $100,000 or more: 5.2% (2008-2012 5-year est.); Poverty rate: 43.6% (2008-2012 5-year est.).
Education: Percent of population age 25 and over with: High school diploma (including GED) or higher: 82.0% (2008-2012 5-year est.); Bachelor's degree or higher: 11.3% (2008-2012 5-year est.); Master's degree or higher: 0.0% (2008-2012 5-year est.).
Housing: Homeownership rate: 36.9% (2008-2012 5-year est.); Median home value: $46,700 (2008-2012 5-year est.); Median contract rent: $281 per month (2008-2012 5-year est.); Median year structure built: 1966 (2008-2012 5-year est.).
Health Insurance: 26.3% Private; 61.0% Public; 21.2% None. (2008-2012 5-year est.)
Transportation: Commute to work: 83.7% car, 12.2% public transportation, 4.1% walk, 0.0% work from home (2008-2012 5-year est.); Travel time to work: 22.7% less than 15 minutes, 51.7% 15 to 30 minutes, 20.9% 30 to 45 minutes, 1.7% 45 to 60 minutes, 2.9% 60 minutes or more (2008-2012 5-year est.)

CAHOKIA (village). Aka Maplewood Park. Covers a land area of 9.402 square miles and a water area of 0.500 square miles. Located at 38.57° N. Lat; 90.18° W. Long. Elevation is 407 feet.
History: Named for an Indian tribe of the Illinois Confederacy. Cahokia began with a mission established in 1699 by Jean Francois Buisson de St. Cosme of the Seminary of Foreign Missions, and a trading post developed around the mission. In 1809 county lines were redrawn so that Cahokia served as the seat of a territory that later was divided into 80 northern counties.
Population: 17,550 (1990); 16,391 (2000); 15,241 (2010); Density: 1,613.4 persons per square mile (2008-2012 5-year est.); Race: 34.5% White, 60.7% Black/African American, 0.7% Asian, 0.0% American Indian/Alaska Native, 0.0% Native Hawaiian/Other Pacific Islander, 4.1% Some other race, 2.7% Two or more races, 4.0% Hispanic of any race (2008-2012 5-year est.); Average household size: 3.05 (2008-2012 5-year est.); Median age: 29.9 (2008-2012 5-year est.); Males per 100 females: 90.9 (2008-2012 5-year est.); Marriage status: 46.5% never married, 37.7% now married, 6.6% widowed, 9.2% divorced (2008-2012 5-year est.); Foreign born: 2.0% (2008-2012 5-year est.); Ancestry (includes multiple ancestries): 7.2% German, 6.9% European, 3.8% Irish, 2.9% English, 2.8% American (2008-2012 5-year est.).
Economy: Single-family building permits issued: 0 (2013); Multi-family building permits issued: 0 (2013); Homeowner vacancy rate: 3.0%. Rental vacancy rate: 1.3%. (2008-2012 5-year est.); Employment by occupation: 7.9% management, business, and financial, 2.8% computer, engineering, and science, 6.2% education, legal, community service, arts, and media, 1.3% healthcare practitioners, 31.8% service, 28.7% sales and office, 3.9% natural resources, construction, and maintenance, 17.4% production, transportation, and material moving (2008-2012 5-year est.).
Income: Per capita income: $15,162 (2008-2012 5-year est.); Median household income: $31,892 (2008-2012 5-year est.); Average household income: $43,775 (2008-2012 5-year est.); Percent of households with income of $100,000 or more: 6.3% (2008-2012 5-year est.); Poverty rate: 35.9% (2008-2012 5-year est.).
Education: Percent of population age 25 and over with: High school diploma (including GED) or higher: 83.7% (2008-2012 5-year est.); Bachelor's degree or higher: 7.7% (2008-2012 5-year est.); Master's degree or higher: 2.1% (2008-2012 5-year est.).
School District(s)
Cahokia CUSD 187 (PK-12)
2011-12 Enrollment: 4,221 . . . . (618) 332-3700
Housing: Homeownership rate: 55.3% (2008-2012 5-year est.); Median home value: $64,900 (2008-2012 5-year est.); Median contract rent: $604 per month (2008-2012 5-year est.); Median year structure built: 1960 (2008-2012 5-year est.).
Health Insurance: 41.8% Private; 49.7% Public; 15.9% None. (2008-2012 5-year est.)
Safety: Violent crime rate: 47.8 per 10,000 population; Property crime rate: 495.5 per 10,000 population (2012).
Transportation: Commute to work: 89.2% car, 6.9% public transportation, 1.8% walk, 1.2% work from home (2008-2012 5-year est.); Travel time to work: 21.1% less than 15 minutes, 50.6% 15 to 30 minutes, 20.1% 30 to 45 minutes, 5.2% 45 to 60 minutes, 3.0% 60 minutes or more (2008-2012 5-year est.)
Airports: St. Louis Downtown Airport (reliver airport)
Additional Information Contacts
Cahokia Area Chamber of Commerce . . . . (618) 337-4721
  http://www.cahokiachamber.org
Village of Cahokia . . . . (618) 337-9500
  http://cahokiaillinois.org

CASEYVILLE (village). Covers a land area of 7.008 square miles and a water area of 0.158 square miles. Located at 38.63° N. Lat; 90.03° W. Long. Elevation is 453 feet.
Population: 4,419 (1990); 4,310 (2000); 4,245 (2010); Density: 620.6 persons per square mile (2008-2012 5-year est.); Race: 87.4% White, 6.9% Black/African American, 0.0% Asian, 0.2% American Indian/Alaska Native, 0.0% Native Hawaiian/Other Pacific Islander, 5.5% Some other race, 1.6% Two or more races, 7.7% Hispanic of any race (2008-2012 5-year est.); Average household size: 2.50 (2008-2012 5-year est.); Median age: 37.1 (2008-2012 5-year est.); Males per 100 females: 81.4 (2008-2012 5-year est.); Marriage status: 28.9% never married, 45.8% now married, 10.9% widowed, 14.4% divorced (2008-2012 5-year est.); Foreign born: 3.2% (2008-2012 5-year est.); Ancestry (includes multiple

ancestries): 24.8% German, 14.3% Irish, 7.7% English, 4.8% American, 4.3% European (2008-2012 5-year est.).
Economy: Single-family building permits issued: 5 (2013); Multi-family building permits issued: 0 (2013); Homeowner vacancy rate: 0.0%. Rental vacancy rate: 9.4%. (2008-2012 5-year est.); Employment by occupation: 9.8% management, business, and financial, 1.9% computer, engineering, and science, 5.2% education, legal, community service, arts, and media, 3.9% healthcare practitioners, 22.5% service, 24.7% sales and office, 12.7% natural resources, construction, and maintenance, 19.4% production, transportation, and material moving (2008-2012 5-year est.).
Income: Per capita income: $19,559 (2008-2012 5-year est.); Median household income: $39,531 (2008-2012 5-year est.); Average household income: $49,051 (2008-2012 5-year est.); Percent of households with income of $100,000 or more: 8.9% (2008-2012 5-year est.); Poverty rate: 17.9% (2008-2012 5-year est.).
Education: Percent of population age 25 and over with: High school diploma (including GED) or higher: 80.5% (2008-2012 5-year est.); Bachelor's degree or higher: 8.8% (2008-2012 5-year est.); Master's degree or higher: 2.6% (2008-2012 5-year est.).

School District(s)
Collinsville CUSD 10 (PK-12)
   2011-12 Enrollment: 6,645 . . . . (618) 346-6350
Housing: Homeownership rate: 81.8% (2008-2012 5-year est.); Median home value: $78,800 (2008-2012 5-year est.); Median contract rent: $525 per month (2008-2012 5-year est.); Median year structure built: 1957 (2008-2012 5-year est.).
Health Insurance: 58.8% Private; 42.1% Public; 12.5% None. (2008-2012 5-year est.)
Safety: Violent crime rate: 94.1 per 10,000 population; Property crime rate: 251.8 per 10,000 population (2012).
Transportation: Commute to work: 97.1% car, 0.7% public transportation, 0.5% walk, 0.4% work from home (2008-2012 5-year est.); Travel time to work: 25.4% less than 15 minutes, 48.6% 15 to 30 minutes, 19.1% 30 to 45 minutes, 3.1% 45 to 60 minutes, 3.8% 60 minutes or more (2008-2012 5-year est.)

CENTREVILLE (city). Covers a land area of 4.235 square miles and a water area of 0.057 square miles. Located at 38.57° N. Lat; 90.12° W. Long. Elevation is 413 feet.
Population: 7,489 (1990); 5,951 (2000); 5,309 (2010); Density: 1,253.0 persons per square mile (2008-2012 5-year est.); Race: 0.5% White, 99.4% Black/African American, 0.0% Asian, 0.1% American Indian/Alaska Native, 0.0% Native Hawaiian/Other Pacific Islander, 0.0% Some other race, 0.0% Two or more races, 0.1% Hispanic of any race (2008-2012 5-year est.); Average household size: 2.64 (2008-2012 5-year est.); Median age: 37.5 (2008-2012 5-year est.); Males per 100 females: 84.6 (2008-2012 5-year est.); Marriage status: 46.2% never married, 32.9% now married, 8.5% widowed, 12.4% divorced (2008-2012 5-year est.); Foreign born: 1.2% (2008-2012 5-year est.); Ancestry (includes multiple ancestries): 1.5% African, 0.5% Irish, 0.4% American, 0.3% English, 0.2% Nigerian (2008-2012 5-year est.).
Economy: Single-family building permits issued: 0 (2013); Multi-family building permits issued: 0 (2013); Homeowner vacancy rate: 0.0%. Rental vacancy rate: 0.0%. (2008-2012 5-year est.); Employment by occupation: 5.4% management, business, and financial, 2.5% computer, engineering, and science, 11.8% education, legal, community service, arts, and media, 2.6% healthcare practitioners, 35.1% service, 18.3% sales and office, 3.9% natural resources, construction, and maintenance, 20.3% production, transportation, and material moving (2008-2012 5-year est.).
Income: Per capita income: $15,776 (2008-2012 5-year est.); Median household income: $28,442 (2008-2012 5-year est.); Average household income: $38,546 (2008-2012 5-year est.); Percent of households with income of $100,000 or more: 5.2% (2008-2012 5-year est.); Poverty rate: 31.4% (2008-2012 5-year est.).
Education: Percent of population age 25 and over with: High school diploma (including GED) or higher: 74.0% (2008-2012 5-year est.); Bachelor's degree or higher: 8.5% (2008-2012 5-year est.); Master's degree or higher: 4.5% (2008-2012 5-year est.).

School District(s)
Cahokia CUSD 187 (PK-12)
   2011-12 Enrollment: 4,221 . . . . (618) 332-3700
Housing: Homeownership rate: 53.8% (2008-2012 5-year est.); Median home value: $64,000 (2008-2012 5-year est.); Median contract rent: $376 per month (2008-2012 5-year est.); Median year structure built: 1960 (2008-2012 5-year est.).

Health Insurance: 38.3% Private; 52.5% Public; 17.7% None. (2008-2012 5-year est.)
Hospitals: Touchette Regional Hospital (114 beds)
Transportation: Commute to work: 83.7% car, 9.2% public transportation, 4.4% walk, 0.9% work from home (2008-2012 5-year est.); Travel time to work: 27.6% less than 15 minutes, 39.1% 15 to 30 minutes, 25.3% 30 to 45 minutes, 2.5% 45 to 60 minutes, 5.5% 60 minutes or more (2008-2012 5-year est.)

DUPO (village). Aka Sugar Loaf Heights. Covers a land area of 4.421 square miles and a water area of <.001 square miles. Located at 38.52° N. Lat; 90.21° W. Long. Elevation is 417 feet.
History: The name of Dupo is a shortened form of Prairie du Pont, which is a French term meaning "meadow of the bridge." Oil was discovered near Dupo in 1928 and a brief period of fast growth ensued.
Population: 3,164 (1990); 3,933 (2000); 4,138 (2010); Density: 925.4 persons per square mile (2008-2012 5-year est.); Race: 98.4% White, 0.5% Black/African American, 0.0% Asian, 0.0% American Indian/Alaska Native, 0.0% Native Hawaiian/Other Pacific Islander, 1.1% Some other race, 1.1% Two or more races, 1.0% Hispanic of any race (2008-2012 5-year est.); Average household size: 2.39 (2008-2012 5-year est.); Median age: 38.3 (2008-2012 5-year est.); Males per 100 females: 84.4 (2008-2012 5-year est.); Marriage status: 30.2% never married, 48.9% now married, 7.5% widowed, 13.5% divorced (2008-2012 5-year est.); Foreign born: 0.3% (2008-2012 5-year est.); Ancestry (includes multiple ancestries): 28.8% German, 17.5% Irish, 10.1% English, 7.7% European, 7.7% American (2008-2012 5-year est.).
Economy: Single-family building permits issued: 3 (2013); Multi-family building permits issued: 0 (2013); Homeowner vacancy rate: 9.1%. Rental vacancy rate: 0.0%. (2008-2012 5-year est.); Employment by occupation: 5.9% management, business, and financial, 5.6% computer, engineering, and science, 4.3% education, legal, community service, arts, and media, 7.2% healthcare practitioners, 19.4% service, 29.6% sales and office, 12.5% natural resources, construction, and maintenance, 15.5% production, transportation, and material moving (2008-2012 5-year est.).
Income: Per capita income: $24,070 (2008-2012 5-year est.); Median household income: $44,457 (2008-2012 5-year est.); Average household income: $55,915 (2008-2012 5-year est.); Percent of households with income of $100,000 or more: 14.7% (2008-2012 5-year est.); Poverty rate: 13.4% (2008-2012 5-year est.).
Education: Percent of population age 25 and over with: High school diploma (including GED) or higher: 90.3% (2008-2012 5-year est.); Bachelor's degree or higher: 13.7% (2008-2012 5-year est.); Master's degree or higher: 3.6% (2008-2012 5-year est.).

School District(s)
Dupo CUSD 196 (PK-12)
   2011-12 Enrollment: 1,184 . . . . (618) 286-3812
Housing: Homeownership rate: 84.9% (2008-2012 5-year est.); Median home value: $100,100 (2008-2012 5-year est.); Median contract rent: $576 per month (2008-2012 5-year est.); Median year structure built: 1966 (2008-2012 5-year est.).
Health Insurance: 68.1% Private; 34.0% Public; 10.4% None. (2008-2012 5-year est.)
Safety: Violent crime rate: 77.2 per 10,000 population; Property crime rate: 234.1 per 10,000 population (2012).
Transportation: Commute to work: 91.9% car, 0.0% public transportation, 0.0% walk, 2.9% work from home (2008-2012 5-year est.); Travel time to work: 18.2% less than 15 minutes, 50.4% 15 to 30 minutes, 22.8% 30 to 45 minutes, 5.7% 45 to 60 minutes, 2.8% 60 minutes or more (2008-2012 5-year est.)

EAST CARONDELET (village). Covers a land area of 1.209 square miles and a water area of 0.463 square miles. Located at 38.54° N. Lat; 90.24° W. Long. Elevation is 410 feet.
History: Damaged in floods of 1993.
Population: 630 (1990); 267 (2000); 499 (2010); Density: 361.4 persons per square mile (2008-2012 5-year est.); Race: 91.1% White, 5.5% Black/African American, 0.0% Asian, 0.0% American Indian/Alaska Native, 0.0% Native Hawaiian/Other Pacific Islander, 3.4% Some other race, 3.4% Two or more races, 10.8% Hispanic of any race (2008-2012 5-year est.); Average household size: 3.06 (2008-2012 5-year est.); Median age: 41.0 (2008-2012 5-year est.); Males per 100 females: 82.8 (2008-2012 5-year est.); Marriage status: 33.7% never married, 52.4% now married, 7.1% widowed, 6.8% divorced (2008-2012 5-year est.); Foreign born: 0.0% (2008-2012 5-year est.); Ancestry (includes multiple ancestries): 28.1%

European, 10.1% German, 8.0% Irish, 4.1% Swedish, 2.5% Italian (2008-2012 5-year est.).

Economy: Single-family building permits issued: 0 (2013); Multi-family building permits issued: 0 (2013); Homeowner vacancy rate: 7.3%. Rental vacancy rate: 0.0%. (2008-2012 5-year est.); Employment by occupation: 7.9% management, business, and financial, 1.3% computer, engineering, and science, 1.3% education, legal, community service, arts, and media, 2.6% healthcare practitioners, 33.8% service, 26.5% sales and office, 4.0% natural resources, construction, and maintenance, 22.5% production, transportation, and material moving (2008-2012 5-year est.).

Income: Per capita income: $13,729 (2008-2012 5-year est.); Median household income: $30,179 (2008-2012 5-year est.); Average household income: $38,715 (2008-2012 5-year est.); Percent of households with income of $100,000 or more: 8.4% (2008-2012 5-year est.); Poverty rate: 35.9% (2008-2012 5-year est.).

Education: Percent of population age 25 and over with: High school diploma (including GED) or higher: 79.8% (2008-2012 5-year est.); Bachelor's degree or higher: 4.6% (2008-2012 5-year est.); Master's degree or higher: 0.0% (2008-2012 5-year est.).

Housing: Homeownership rate: 62.2% (2008-2012 5-year est.); Median home value: $54,800 (2008-2012 5-year est.); Median contract rent: $528 per month (2008-2012 5-year est.); Median year structure built: 1975 (2008-2012 5-year est.).

Health Insurance: 39.6% Private; 45.8% Public; 20.8% None. (2008-2012 5-year est.)

Transportation: Commute to work: 98.0% car, 0.0% public transportation, 0.0% walk, 2.0% work from home (2008-2012 5-year est.); Travel time to work: 21.4% less than 15 minutes, 46.9% 15 to 30 minutes, 22.8% 30 to 45 minutes, 6.2% 45 to 60 minutes, 2.8% 60 minutes or more (2008-2012 5-year est.).

EAST SAINT LOUIS (city).

Covers a land area of 13.992 square miles and a water area of 0.380 square miles. Located at 38.62° N. Lat; 90.13° W. Long. Elevation is 417 feet.

History: Settlement across the Mississippi River from St. Louis, Missouri, was achieved by Captain James Piggott who established ferry service here in 1795. A village called Illinoistown was platted near the ferry dock in 1816. When Illinoistown was incorporated in 1859, a town called East St. Louis had been established nearby. In 1861 the charter of Illinoistown was extended to include the new town, and the name was changed to East St. Louis. Near the end of the 19th century, East St. Louis changed from a river town to an industrial center.

Population: 40,944 (1990); 31,542 (2000); 27,006 (2010); Density: 1,938.0 persons per square mile (2008-2012 5-year est.); Race: 1.6% White, 96.7% Black/African American, 0.1% Asian, 0.1% American Indian/Alaska Native, 0.0% Native Hawaiian/Other Pacific Islander, 1.5% Some other race, 0.8% Two or more races, 0.5% Hispanic of any race (2008-2012 5-year est.); Average household size: 2.53 (2008-2012 5-year est.); Median age: 33.1 (2008-2012 5-year est.); Males per 100 females: 86.0 (2008-2012 5-year est.); Marriage status: 56.3% never married, 21.6% now married, 9.5% widowed, 12.6% divorced (2008-2012 5-year est.); Foreign born: 0.1% (2008-2012 5-year est.); Ancestry (includes multiple ancestries): 1.1% African, 0.8% American, 0.5% German, 0.4% Irish, 0.2% English (2008-2012 5-year est.).

Economy: Unemployment rate: 11.9% (April 2014); Total civilian labor force: 8,865 (April 2014); Single-family building permits issued: 5 (2013); Multi-family building permits issued: 164 (2013); Homeowner vacancy rate: 0.0%. Rental vacancy rate: 1.6%. (2008-2012 5-year est.); Employment by occupation: 5.3% management, business, and financial, 1.2% computer, engineering, and science, 9.4% education, legal, community service, arts, and media, 1.7% healthcare practitioners, 42.5% service, 21.2% sales and office, 4.8% natural resources, construction, and maintenance, 13.8% production, transportation, and material moving (2008-2012 5-year est.).

Income: Per capita income: $11,802 (2008-2012 5-year est.); Median household income: $19,278 (2008-2012 5-year est.); Average household income: $27,732 (2008-2012 5-year est.); Percent of households with income of $100,000 or more: 2.0% (2008-2012 5-year est.); Poverty rate: 43.5% (2008-2012 5-year est.).

Taxes: Total city taxes per capita: $528 (2011); City property taxes per capita: $396 (2011).

Education: Percent of population age 25 and over with: High school diploma (including GED) or higher: 76.7% (2008-2012 5-year est.); Bachelor's degree or higher: 8.9% (2008-2012 5-year est.); Master's degree or higher: 2.9% (2008-2012 5-year est.).

School District(s)

East Saint Louis SD 189 (PK-12)
  2011-12 Enrollment: 6,971 . . . . (618) 646-3009
East Saint Louis SD 189 (PK-12)
  2011-12 Enrollment: 6,971 . . . . (618) 646-3009

Vocational/Technical School(s)

Vees School of Beauty Culture (Private, For-profit)
  Fall 2012 Enrollment: 11 . . . . (618) 274-1751
  2012-13 Tuition: $13,000

Housing: Homeownership rate: 47.4% (2008-2012 5-year est.); Median home value: $60,400 (2008-2012 5-year est.); Median contract rent: $317 per month (2008-2012 5-year est.); Median year structure built: 1953 (2008-2012 5-year est.).

Health Insurance: 30.0% Private; 60.6% Public; 18.6% None. (2008-2012 5-year est.)

Safety: Violent crime rate: 499.3 per 10,000 population; Property crime rate: 675.7 per 10,000 population (2012).

Transportation: Commute to work: 78.6% car, 14.2% public transportation, 2.3% walk, 4.1% work from home (2008-2012 5-year est.); Travel time to work: 27.8% less than 15 minutes, 44.0% 15 to 30 minutes, 16.7% 30 to 45 minutes, 3.7% 45 to 60 minutes, 7.8% 60 minutes or more (2008-2012 5-year est.).

Additional Information Contacts

City of East Saint Louis . . . . (618) 482-6600
  http://www.cesl.us
East Saint Louis Business Development Chamber of Commerce . . . . (618) 857-5045
  https://sites.google.com/site/eaststlouischamberofcommerce

FAIRMONT CITY (village).

Covers a land area of 6.201 square miles and a water area of 0.391 square miles. Located at 38.65° N. Lat; 90.10° W. Long. Elevation is 420 feet.

History: Fairmont City came into being in 1910 when the Pennsylvania Railroad built a roundhouse here. First called Willow Town, the name was changed to Fairmont City when it was incorporated in 1914.

Population: 2,140 (1990); 2,436 (2000); 2,635 (2010); Density: 418.6 persons per square mile (2008-2012 5-year est.); Race: 82.5% White, 0.2% Black/African American, 0.0% Asian, 0.0% American Indian/Alaska Native, 0.0% Native Hawaiian/Other Pacific Islander, 17.3% Some other race, 6.1% Two or more races, 76.4% Hispanic of any race (2008-2012 5-year est.); Average household size: 3.27 (2008-2012 5-year est.); Median age: 27.7 (2008-2012 5-year est.); Males per 100 females: 101.1 (2008-2012 5-year est.); Marriage status: 40.0% never married, 48.5% now married, 5.3% widowed, 6.2% divorced (2008-2012 5-year est.); Foreign born: 38.7% (2008-2012 5-year est.); Ancestry (includes multiple ancestries): 6.8% European, 6.2% Irish, 6.1% German, 2.0% Polish, 1.8% French (2008-2012 5-year est.).

Economy: Homeowner vacancy rate: 1.7%. Rental vacancy rate: 0.0%. (2008-2012 5-year est.); Employment by occupation: 3.2% management, business, and financial, 0.6% computer, engineering, and science, 3.7% education, legal, community service, arts, and media, 2.3% healthcare practitioners, 23.8% service, 18.5% sales and office, 18.7% natural resources, construction, and maintenance, 29.1% production, transportation, and material moving (2008-2012 5-year est.).

Income: Per capita income: $12,044 (2008-2012 5-year est.); Median household income: $32,260 (2008-2012 5-year est.); Average household income: $37,266 (2008-2012 5-year est.); Percent of households with income of $100,000 or more: 4.9% (2008-2012 5-year est.); Poverty rate: 39.9% (2008-2012 5-year est.).

Education: Percent of population age 25 and over with: High school diploma (including GED) or higher: 50.5% (2008-2012 5-year est.); Bachelor's degree or higher: 4.5% (2008-2012 5-year est.); Master's degree or higher: 1.1% (2008-2012 5-year est.).

Housing: Homeownership rate: 64.7% (2008-2012 5-year est.); Median home value: $60,600 (2008-2012 5-year est.); Median contract rent: $449 per month (2008-2012 5-year est.); Median year structure built: 1954 (2008-2012 5-year est.).

Health Insurance: 39.1% Private; 42.7% Public; 27.3% None. (2008-2012 5-year est.)

Safety: Violent crime rate: 26.5 per 10,000 population; Property crime rate: 178.1 per 10,000 population (2012).

Transportation: Commute to work: 96.7% car, 0.8% public transportation, 0.8% walk, 1.2% work from home (2008-2012 5-year est.); Travel time to work: 24.1% less than 15 minutes, 48.8% 15 to 30 minutes, 21.0% 30 to

45 minutes, 5.2% 45 to 60 minutes, 1.0% 60 minutes or more (2008-2012 5-year est.)

FAIRVIEW HEIGHTS (city). Aka Fairview. Covers a land area of 11.421 square miles and a water area of 0.077 square miles. Located at 38.60° N. Lat; 90.01° W. Long. Elevation is 584 feet.

History: Named to promote the town as a good place to live. Also known as Fairview. Formerly called Lincoln Heights.

Population: 14,351 (1990); 15,034 (2000); 17,078 (2010); Density: 1,474.4 persons per square mile (2008-2012 5-year est.); Race: 66.9% White, 26.2% Black/African American, 2.9% Asian, 0.8% American Indian/Alaska Native, 0.0% Native Hawaiian/Other Pacific Islander, 3.2% Some other race, 2.2% Two or more races, 3.6% Hispanic of any race (2008-2012 5-year est.); Average household size: 2.39 (2008-2012 5-year est.); Median age: 39.2 (2008-2012 5-year est.); Males per 100 females: 94.0 (2008-2012 5-year est.); Marriage status: 28.4% never married, 54.0% now married, 5.8% widowed, 11.8% divorced (2008-2012 5-year est.); Foreign born: 4.2% (2008-2012 5-year est.); Ancestry (includes multiple ancestries): 25.1% German, 13.6% Irish, 9.0% English, 6.4% American, 4.1% Italian (2008-2012 5-year est.).

Economy: Single-family building permits issued: 70 (2013); Multi-family building permits issued: 3 (2013); Homeowner vacancy rate: 0.4%. Rental vacancy rate: 7.9%. (2008-2012 5-year est.); Employment by occupation: 17.3% management, business, and financial, 6.7% computer, engineering, and science, 9.8% education, legal, community service, arts, and media, 5.9% healthcare practitioners, 19.1% service, 24.3% sales and office, 7.0% natural resources, construction, and maintenance, 9.8% production, transportation, and material moving (2008-2012 5-year est.).

Income: Per capita income: $30,312 (2008-2012 5-year est.); Median household income: $62,495 (2008-2012 5-year est.); Average household income: $70,449 (2008-2012 5-year est.); Percent of households with income of $100,000 or more: 23.0% (2008-2012 5-year est.); Poverty rate: 8.4% (2008-2012 5-year est.).

Education: Percent of population age 25 and over with: High school diploma (including GED) or higher: 93.4% (2008-2012 5-year est.); Bachelor's degree or higher: 31.2% (2008-2012 5-year est.); Master's degree or higher: 11.5% (2008-2012 5-year est.).

School District(s)

Grant CCSD 110 (PK-08)

    2011-12 Enrollment: 683 . . . . (618) 398-5577

Pontiac-W Holliday SD 105 (PK-08)

    2011-12 Enrollment: 754 . . . . (618) 233-2320

Two-year College(s)

Vatterott College-Fairview Heights (Private, For-profit)

    Fall 2012 Enrollment: 292 . . . . (618) 293-0025

    2012-13 Tuition: In-state $11,540; Out-of-state $11,540

Vocational/Technical School(s)

Regency Beauty Institute-Fairview Heights (Private, For-profit)

    Fall 2012 Enrollment: 82 . . . . (800) 787-6456

    2012-13 Tuition: $16,425

Housing: Homeownership rate: 72.5% (2008-2012 5-year est.); Median home value: $135,200 (2008-2012 5-year est.); Median contract rent: $827 per month (2008-2012 5-year est.); Median year structure built: 1975 (2008-2012 5-year est.).

Health Insurance: 72.5% Private; 29.3% Public; 12.7% None. (2008-2012 5-year est.)

Safety: Violent crime rate: 26.3 per 10,000 population; Property crime rate: 602.4 per 10,000 population (2012).

Transportation: Commute to work: 92.6% car, 1.9% public transportation, 1.6% walk, 2.9% work from home (2008-2012 5-year est.); Travel time to work: 25.4% less than 15 minutes, 39.6% 15 to 30 minutes, 22.6% 30 to 45 minutes, 7.9% 45 to 60 minutes, 4.4% 60 minutes or more (2008-2012 5-year est.)

Additional Information Contacts

City of Fairview Heights . . . . (618) 489-2000

    http://www.fairviewheightscity.com

Metro-East Regional Chamber of Commerce . . . . (618) 233-3938

    http://metroeastchamber.org

FAYETTEVILLE (village). Covers a land area of 0.321 square miles and a water area of <.001 square miles. Located at 38.38° N. Lat; 89.80° W. Long. Elevation is 413 feet.

Population: 371 (1990); 384 (2000); 366 (2010); Density: 1,295.1 persons per square mile (2008-2012 5-year est.); Race: 98.3% White, 0.0% Black/African American, 0.2% Asian, 0.0% American Indian/Alaska Native,

0.0% Native Hawaiian/Other Pacific Islander, 1.5% Some other race, 1.4% Two or more races, 0.5% Hispanic of any race (2008-2012 5-year est.); Average household size: 3.13 (2008-2012 5-year est.); Median age: 36.0 (2008-2012 5-year est.); Males per 100 females: 109.0 (2008-2012 5-year est.); Marriage status: 31.4% never married, 52.1% now married, 5.0% widowed, 11.5% divorced (2008-2012 5-year est.); Foreign born: 0.2% (2008-2012 5-year est.); Ancestry (includes multiple ancestries): 59.9% German, 14.4% Irish, 5.3% French, 5.0% Russian, 3.4% Polish (2008-2012 5-year est.).

Economy: Single-family building permits issued: 0 (2013); Multi-family building permits issued: 0 (2013); Homeowner vacancy rate: 0.0%. Rental vacancy rate: 0.0%. (2008-2012 5-year est.); Employment by occupation: 6.4% management, business, and financial, 0.0% computer, engineering, and science, 5.9% education, legal, community service, arts, and media, 3.9% healthcare practitioners, 23.6% service, 28.6% sales and office, 4.9% natural resources, construction, and maintenance, 26.6% production, transportation, and material moving (2008-2012 5-year est.).

Income: Per capita income: $19,977 (2008-2012 5-year est.); Median household income: $55,313 (2008-2012 5-year est.); Average household income: $59,229 (2008-2012 5-year est.); Percent of households with income of $100,000 or more: 15.8% (2008-2012 5-year est.); Poverty rate: 17.1% (2008-2012 5-year est.).

Education: Percent of population age 25 and over with: High school diploma (including GED) or higher: 78.0% (2008-2012 5-year est.); Bachelor's degree or higher: 7.6% (2008-2012 5-year est.); Master's degree or higher: 0.8% (2008-2012 5-year est.).

Housing: Homeownership rate: 79.7% (2008-2012 5-year est.); Median home value: $83,600 (2008-2012 5-year est.); Median contract rent: $517 per month (2008-2012 5-year est.); Median year structure built: 1970 (2008-2012 5-year est.).

Health Insurance: 60.3% Private; 35.1% Public; 16.8% None. (2008-2012 5-year est.)

Safety: Violent crime rate: 0.0 per 10,000 population; Property crime rate: 382.5 per 10,000 population (2012).

Transportation: Commute to work: 98.0% car, 0.0% public transportation, 0.0% walk, 1.5% work from home (2008-2012 5-year est.); Travel time to work: 24.5% less than 15 minutes, 26.5% 15 to 30 minutes, 26.0% 30 to 45 minutes, 9.5% 45 to 60 minutes, 13.5% 60 minutes or more (2008-2012 5-year est.)

FREEBURG (village). Covers a land area of 6.773 square miles and a water area of 0.255 square miles. Located at 38.44° N. Lat; 89.92° W. Long. Elevation is 509 feet.

History: Incorporated 1859.

Population: 3,115 (1990); 3,872 (2000); 4,354 (2010); Density: 671.7 persons per square mile (2008-2012 5-year est.); Race: 98.7% White, 1.1% Black/African American, 0.0% Asian, 0.2% American Indian/Alaska Native, 0.0% Native Hawaiian/Other Pacific Islander, 0.0% Some other race, 0.0% Two or more races, 0.0% Hispanic of any race (2008-2012 5-year est.); Average household size: 2.53 (2008-2012 5-year est.); Median age: 39.9 (2008-2012 5-year est.); Males per 100 females: 92.8 (2008-2012 5-year est.); Marriage status: 27.1% never married, 55.1% now married, 6.6% widowed, 11.2% divorced (2008-2012 5-year est.); Foreign born: 0.6% (2008-2012 5-year est.); Ancestry (includes multiple ancestries): 52.3% German, 14.5% Irish, 12.7% English, 4.9% French, 4.2% American (2008-2012 5-year est.).

Economy: Single-family building permits issued: 7 (2013); Multi-family building permits issued: 0 (2013); Homeowner vacancy rate: 2.7%. Rental vacancy rate: 0.0%. (2008-2012 5-year est.); Employment by occupation: 14.4% management, business, and financial, 6.9% computer, engineering, and science, 13.1% education, legal, community service, arts, and media, 7.5% healthcare practitioners, 12.2% service, 21.6% sales and office, 10.6% natural resources, construction, and maintenance, 13.7% production, transportation, and material moving (2008-2012 5-year est.).

Income: Per capita income: $32,630 (2008-2012 5-year est.); Median household income: $76,611 (2008-2012 5-year est.); Average household income: $82,415 (2008-2012 5-year est.); Percent of households with income of $100,000 or more: 33.0% (2008-2012 5-year est.); Poverty rate: 7.7% (2008-2012 5-year est.).

Education: Percent of population age 25 and over with: High school diploma (including GED) or higher: 91.0% (2008-2012 5-year est.); Bachelor's degree or higher: 25.7% (2008-2012 5-year est.); Master's degree or higher: 11.3% (2008-2012 5-year est.).

School District(s)

Freeburg CCSD 70 (KG-08)
  2011-12 Enrollment: 756. . . . . (618) 539-3188
Freeburg CHSD 77 (09-12)
  2011-12 Enrollment: 637. . . . . (618) 539-5533
Housing: Homeownership rate: 80.0% (2008-2012 5-year est.); Median home value: $178,600 (2008-2012 5-year est.); Median contract rent: $612 per month (2008-2012 5-year est.); Median year structure built: 1990 (2008-2012 5-year est.).
Health Insurance: 84.9% Private; 24.9% Public; 5.5% None. (2008-2012 5-year est.)
Safety: Violent crime rate: 23.0 per 10,000 population; Property crime rate: 103.3 per 10,000 population (2012).
Transportation: Commute to work: 86.3% car, 2.6% public transportation, 6.4% walk, 4.4% work from home (2008-2012 5-year est.); Travel time to work: 19.6% less than 15 minutes, 45.7% 15 to 30 minutes, 23.4% 30 to 45 minutes, 7.1% 45 to 60 minutes, 4.2% 60 minutes or more (2008-2012 5-year est.).

LEBANON (city). Covers a land area of 2.460 square miles and a water area of 0.014 square miles. Located at 38.60° N. Lat; 89.81° W. Long. Elevation is 512 feet.
History: Lebanon was platted in the early 1800's. It grew as the site of McKendree College, organized in 1818 by the Methodist Church. Both Abraham Lincoln and Charles Dickens were guests at the Mermaid Inn, built in 1830 in Lebanon.
Population: 3,688 (1990); 3,523 (2000); 4,418 (2010); Density: 1,634.4 persons per square mile (2008-2012 5-year est.); Race: 75.0% White, 20.8% Black/African American, 1.6% Asian, 0.0% American Indian/Alaska Native, 0.0% Native Hawaiian/Other Pacific Islander, 2.6% Some other race, 1.9% Two or more races, 3.8% Hispanic of any race (2008-2012 5-year est.); Average household size: 2.43 (2008-2012 5-year est.); Median age: 41.2 (2008-2012 5-year est.); Males per 100 females: 78.3 (2008-2012 5-year est.); Marriage status: 28.4% never married, 50.4% now married, 10.1% widowed, 11.2% divorced (2008-2012 5-year est.); Foreign born: 7.3% (2008-2012 5-year est.); Ancestry (includes multiple ancestries): 28.6% German, 14.7% English, 7.2% Irish, 6.9% American, 5.0% Scottish (2008-2012 5-year est.).
Economy: Single-family building permits issued: 4 (2013); Multi-family building permits issued: 27 (2013); Homeowner vacancy rate: 5.0%. Rental vacancy rate: 35.2%. (2008-2012 5-year est.); Employment by occupation: 16.6% management, business, and financial, 4.6% computer, engineering, and science, 19.0% education, legal, community service, arts, and media, 7.4% healthcare practitioners, 9.4% service, 25.1% sales and office, 10.9% natural resources, construction, and maintenance, 7.1% production, transportation, and material moving (2008-2012 5-year est.).
Income: Per capita income: $27,817 (2008-2012 5-year est.); Median household income: $47,604 (2008-2012 5-year est.); Average household income: $70,094 (2008-2012 5-year est.); Percent of households with income of $100,000 or more: 15.5% (2008-2012 5-year est.); Poverty rate: 14.2% (2008-2012 5-year est.).
Education: Percent of population age 25 and over with: High school diploma (including GED) or higher: 95.0% (2008-2012 5-year est.); Bachelor's degree or higher: 34.0% (2008-2012 5-year est.); Master's degree or higher: 14.3% (2008-2012 5-year est.).

School District(s)

Lebanon CUSD 9 (PK-12)
  2011-12 Enrollment: 638. . . . . (618) 537-4611

Four-year College(s)

McKendree University (Private, Not-for-profit, United Methodist)
  Fall 2012 Enrollment: 3,036 . . . . (618) 537-4481
  2012-13 Tuition: In-state $25,340; Out-of-state $25,340
Housing: Homeownership rate: 69.5% (2008-2012 5-year est.); Median home value: $135,100 (2008-2012 5-year est.); Median contract rent: $431 per month (2008-2012 5-year est.); Median year structure built: 1968 (2008-2012 5-year est.).
Health Insurance: 68.8% Private; 37.8% Public; 11.7% None. (2008-2012 5-year est.)
Transportation: Commute to work: 83.5% car, 2.2% public transportation, 6.2% walk, 7.6% work from home (2008-2012 5-year est.); Travel time to work: 35.2% less than 15 minutes, 45.1% 15 to 30 minutes, 8.3% 30 to 45 minutes, 6.0% 45 to 60 minutes, 5.4% 60 minutes or more (2008-2012 5-year est.).
Additional Information Contacts

Lebanon Chamber of Commerce . . . . (618) 537-8420
  http://www.lebanonil.us

LENZBURG (village). Covers a land area of 1.188 square miles and a water area of 0.106 square miles. Located at 38.29° N. Lat; 89.82° W. Long. Elevation is 443 feet.
Population: 510 (1990); 577 (2000); 521 (2010); Density: 357.7 persons per square mile (2008-2012 5-year est.); Race: 95.8% White, 0.0% Black/African American, 0.0% Asian, 0.0% American Indian/Alaska Native, 0.0% Native Hawaiian/Other Pacific Islander, 4.2% Some other race, 2.1% Two or more races, 3.8% Hispanic of any race (2008-2012 5-year est.); Average household size: 2.23 (2008-2012 5-year est.); Median age: 44.9 (2008-2012 5-year est.); Males per 100 females: 90.6 (2008-2012 5-year est.); Marriage status: 24.5% never married, 56.0% now married, 7.1% widowed, 12.4% divorced (2008-2012 5-year est.); Foreign born: 0.9% (2008-2012 5-year est.); Ancestry (includes multiple ancestries): 27.1% German, 16.0% American, 12.5% Irish, 5.6% French, 3.3% English (2008-2012 5-year est.).
Economy: Homeowner vacancy rate: 13.9%. Rental vacancy rate: 31.0%. (2008-2012 5-year est.); Employment by occupation: 10.0% management, business, and financial, 3.6% computer, engineering, and science, 5.0% education, legal, community service, arts, and media, 0.0% healthcare practitioners, 22.1% service, 20.0% sales and office, 20.7% natural resources, construction, and maintenance, 18.6% production, transportation, and material moving (2008-2012 5-year est.).
Income: Per capita income: $15,558 (2008-2012 5-year est.); Median household income: $26,250 (2008-2012 5-year est.); Average household income: $33,489 (2008-2012 5-year est.); Percent of households with income of $100,000 or more: 4.7% (2008-2012 5-year est.); Poverty rate: 21.3% (2008-2012 5-year est.).
Education: Percent of population age 25 and over with: High school diploma (including GED) or higher: 77.9% (2008-2012 5-year est.); Bachelor's degree or higher: 8.8% (2008-2012 5-year est.); Master's degree or higher: 1.0% (2008-2012 5-year est.).
Housing: Homeownership rate: 74.3% (2008-2012 5-year est.); Median home value: $73,300 (2008-2012 5-year est.); Median contract rent: $389 per month (2008-2012 5-year est.); Median year structure built: 1959 (2008-2012 5-year est.).
Health Insurance: 44.5% Private; 59.3% Public; 19.8% None. (2008-2012 5-year est.)
Transportation: Commute to work: 94.2% car, 0.0% public transportation, 2.9% walk, 2.9% work from home (2008-2012 5-year est.); Travel time to work: 17.9% less than 15 minutes, 27.6% 15 to 30 minutes, 33.6% 30 to 45 minutes, 3.7% 45 to 60 minutes, 17.2% 60 minutes or more (2008-2012 5-year est.)

LOVEJOY (unincorporated postal area)
Zip Code: 62059
  Covers a land area of 0.264 square miles and a water area of 0 square miles. Located at 38.65° N. Lat; 90.16° W. Long. Population: 746 (2010); Density: 2,817.3 persons per square mile (2010); Race: 2.5% White, 95.0% Black/African American, 0.0% Asian, 0.0% American Indian/Alaska Native, 0.1% Native Hawaiian/Other Pacific Islander, 2.4% Some other race, 2.0% Two or more races, 1.6% Hispanic of any race (2010); Average household size: 2.49 (2010); Median age: 28.6 (2010); Males per 100 females: 75.1 (2010); Homeownership rate: 33.4% (2010)

MARISSA (village). Covers a land area of 3.353 square miles and a water area of 0.173 square miles. Located at 38.25° N. Lat; 89.76° W. Long. Elevation is 453 feet.
History: Incorporated 1882.
Population: 2,375 (1990); 2,141 (2000); 1,979 (2010); Density: 704.5 persons per square mile (2008-2012 5-year est.); Race: 96.5% White, 1.2% Black/African American, 0.0% Asian, 0.0% American Indian/Alaska Native, 0.0% Native Hawaiian/Other Pacific Islander, 2.3% Some other race, 1.2% Two or more races, 1.0% Hispanic of any race (2008-2012 5-year est.); Average household size: 2.69 (2008-2012 5-year est.); Median age: 36.6 (2008-2012 5-year est.); Males per 100 females: 96.3 (2008-2012 5-year est.); Marriage status: 19.3% never married, 54.9% now married, 9.3% widowed, 16.6% divorced (2008-2012 5-year est.); Foreign born: 0.3% (2008-2012 5-year est.); Ancestry (includes multiple ancestries): 41.7% German, 18.2% Irish, 13.3% American, 9.3% English, 7.2% Polish (2008-2012 5-year est.).

Economy: Single-family building permits issued: 0 (2013); Multi-family building permits issued: 0 (2013); Homeowner vacancy rate: 2.4%. Rental vacancy rate: 0.0%. (2008-2012 5-year est.); Employment by occupation: 10.7% management, business, and financial, 4.8% computer, engineering, and science, 6.5% education, legal, community service, arts, and media, 6.6% healthcare practitioners, 13.5% service, 28.1% sales and office, 11.6% natural resources, construction, and maintenance, 18.1% production, transportation, and material moving (2008-2012 5-year est.).
Income: Per capita income: $20,157 (2008-2012 5-year est.); Median household income: $46,941 (2008-2012 5-year est.); Average household income: $51,630 (2008-2012 5-year est.); Percent of households with income of $100,000 or more: 7.1% (2008-2012 5-year est.); Poverty rate: 19.1% (2008-2012 5-year est.).
Education: Percent of population age 25 and over with: High school diploma (including GED) or higher: 90.2% (2008-2012 5-year est.); Bachelor's degree or higher: 11.0% (2008-2012 5-year est.); Master's degree or higher: 1.8% (2008-2012 5-year est.).

School District(s)

Marissa CUSD 40 (PK-12)
    2011-12 Enrollment: 607 . . . . (618) 295-2313
Housing: Homeownership rate: 76.3% (2008-2012 5-year est.); Median home value: $79,500 (2008-2012 5-year est.); Median contract rent: $435 per month (2008-2012 5-year est.); Median year structure built: 1955 (2008-2012 5-year est.).
Health Insurance: 66.1% Private; 36.9% Public; 13.4% None. (2008-2012 5-year est.)
Transportation: Commute to work: 93.5% car, 0.0% public transportation, 3.3% walk, 0.9% work from home (2008-2012 5-year est.); Travel time to work: 34.8% less than 15 minutes, 28.4% 15 to 30 minutes, 13.2% 30 to 45 minutes, 10.2% 45 to 60 minutes, 13.4% 60 minutes or more (2008-2012 5-year est.)

MASCOUTAH (city).

Covers a land area of 9.497 square miles and a water area of 0.150 square miles. Located at 38.52° N. Lat; 89.80° W. Long. Elevation is 430 feet.
History: Incorporated 1839.
Population: 5,511 (1990); 5,659 (2000); 7,483 (2010); Density: 798.0 persons per square mile (2008-2012 5-year est.); Race: 93.7% White, 4.8% Black/African American, 0.1% Asian, 0.2% American Indian/Alaska Native, 0.0% Native Hawaiian/Other Pacific Islander, 1.2% Some other race, 0.7% Two or more races, 1.9% Hispanic of any race (2008-2012 5-year est.); Average household size: 2.63 (2008-2012 5-year est.); Median age: 36.3 (2008-2012 5-year est.); Males per 100 females: 100.5 (2008-2012 5-year est.); Marriage status: 31.0% never married, 51.4% now married, 6.9% widowed, 10.7% divorced (2008-2012 5-year est.); Foreign born: 1.3% (2008-2012 5-year est.); Ancestry (includes multiple ancestries): 40.5% German, 14.8% Irish, 8.0% English, 6.1% American, 5.5% Polish (2008-2012 5-year est.).
Economy: Single-family building permits issued: 29 (2013); Multi-family building permits issued: 0 (2013); Homeowner vacancy rate: 0.0%. Rental vacancy rate: 9.6%. (2008-2012 5-year est.); Employment by occupation: 16.7% management, business, and financial, 7.1% computer, engineering, and science, 7.5% education, legal, community service, arts, and media, 4.7% healthcare practitioners, 20.3% service, 25.2% sales and office, 5.1% natural resources, construction, and maintenance, 13.3% production, transportation, and material moving (2008-2012 5-year est.).
Income: Per capita income: $27,895 (2008-2012 5-year est.); Median household income: $64,788 (2008-2012 5-year est.); Average household income: $72,098 (2008-2012 5-year est.); Percent of households with income of $100,000 or more: 21.5% (2008-2012 5-year est.); Poverty rate: 8.6% (2008-2012 5-year est.).
Education: Percent of population age 25 and over with: High school diploma (including GED) or higher: 94.1% (2008-2012 5-year est.); Bachelor's degree or higher: 23.7% (2008-2012 5-year est.); Master's degree or higher: 10.4% (2008-2012 5-year est.).

School District(s)

Mascoutah CUD 19 (PK-12)
    2011-12 Enrollment: 3,636 . . . . (618) 566-7414
Housing: Homeownership rate: 69.7% (2008-2012 5-year est.); Median home value: $144,500 (2008-2012 5-year est.); Median contract rent: $595 per month (2008-2012 5-year est.); Median year structure built: 1974 (2008-2012 5-year est.).
Health Insurance: 79.4% Private; 27.9% Public; 6.8% None. (2008-2012 5-year est.)

Safety: Violent crime rate: 1.3 per 10,000 population; Property crime rate: 113.5 per 10,000 population (2012).
Transportation: Commute to work: 89.9% car, 2.9% public transportation, 3.4% walk, 1.3% work from home (2008-2012 5-year est.); Travel time to work: 29.2% less than 15 minutes, 46.4% 15 to 30 minutes, 14.5% 30 to 45 minutes, 5.7% 45 to 60 minutes, 4.1% 60 minutes or more (2008-2012 5-year est.)
Additional Information Contacts
City of Mascoutah . . . . (618) 566-2964
    http://www.mascoutah.com

MILLSTADT (village).

Covers a land area of 3.409 square miles and a water area of 0.166 square miles. Located at 38.46° N. Lat; 90.08° W. Long. Elevation is 617 feet.
History: Incorporated 1878.
Population: 2,566 (1990); 2,794 (2000); 4,011 (2010); Density: 1,157.6 persons per square mile (2008-2012 5-year est.); Race: 99.6% White, 0.4% Black/African American, 0.0% Asian, 0.0% American Indian/Alaska Native, 0.0% Native Hawaiian/Other Pacific Islander, 0.0% Some other race, 0.0% Two or more races, 0.5% Hispanic of any race (2008-2012 5-year est.); Average household size: 2.37 (2008-2012 5-year est.); Median age: 44.4 (2008-2012 5-year est.); Males per 100 females: 82.9 (2008-2012 5-year est.); Marriage status: 16.4% never married, 67.1% now married, 7.8% widowed, 8.8% divorced (2008-2012 5-year est.); Foreign born: 1.8% (2008-2012 5-year est.); Ancestry (includes multiple ancestries): 55.4% German, 14.4% Irish, 9.1% Italian, 7.9% French, 5.2% American (2008-2012 5-year est.).
Economy: Single-family building permits issued: 16 (2013); Multi-family building permits issued: 0 (2013); Homeowner vacancy rate: 0.0%. Rental vacancy rate: 0.0%. (2008-2012 5-year est.); Employment by occupation: 12.0% management, business, and financial, 7.6% computer, engineering, and science, 9.0% education, legal, community service, arts, and media, 8.1% healthcare practitioners, 11.4% service, 28.3% sales and office, 12.3% natural resources, construction, and maintenance, 11.3% production, transportation, and material moving (2008-2012 5-year est.).
Income: Per capita income: $32,258 (2008-2012 5-year est.); Median household income: $63,425 (2008-2012 5-year est.); Average household income: $75,328 (2008-2012 5-year est.); Percent of households with income of $100,000 or more: 26.0% (2008-2012 5-year est.); Poverty rate: 5.2% (2008-2012 5-year est.).
Education: Percent of population age 25 and over with: High school diploma (including GED) or higher: 90.2% (2008-2012 5-year est.); Bachelor's degree or higher: 26.2% (2008-2012 5-year est.); Master's degree or higher: 8.5% (2008-2012 5-year est.).

School District(s)

Millstadt CCSD 160 (PK-08)
    2011-12 Enrollment: 864 . . . . (618) 476-1803
Housing: Homeownership rate: 83.0% (2008-2012 5-year est.); Median home value: $175,100 (2008-2012 5-year est.); Median contract rent: $590 per month (2008-2012 5-year est.); Median year structure built: 1984 (2008-2012 5-year est.).
Health Insurance: 80.2% Private; 27.4% Public; 6.6% None. (2008-2012 5-year est.)
Safety: Violent crime rate: 2.5 per 10,000 population; Property crime rate: 79.7 per 10,000 population (2012).
Transportation: Commute to work: 97.9% car, 0.0% public transportation, 0.0% walk, 2.1% work from home (2008-2012 5-year est.); Travel time to work: 20.4% less than 15 minutes, 41.1% 15 to 30 minutes, 28.9% 30 to 45 minutes, 7.0% 45 to 60 minutes, 2.6% 60 minutes or more (2008-2012 5-year est.)

NEW ATHENS (village).

Covers a land area of 1.916 square miles and a water area of 0.209 square miles. Located at 38.32° N. Lat; 89.88° W. Long. Elevation is 397 feet.
History: Incorporated 1869.
Population: 2,010 (1990); 1,981 (2000); 2,054 (2010); Density: 1,132.3 persons per square mile (2008-2012 5-year est.); Race: 98.1% White, 1.9% Black/African American, 0.0% Asian, 0.0% American Indian/Alaska Native, 0.0% Native Hawaiian/Other Pacific Islander, 0.0% Some other race, 0.0% Two or more races, 2.2% Hispanic of any race (2008-2012 5-year est.); Average household size: 2.79 (2008-2012 5-year est.); Median age: 37.0 (2008-2012 5-year est.); Males per 100 females: 97.8 (2008-2012 5-year est.); Marriage status: 24.4% never married, 60.4% now married, 5.9% widowed, 9.4% divorced (2008-2012 5-year est.); Foreign born: 1.2% (2008-2012 5-year est.); Ancestry (includes multiple

ancestries): 62.1% German, 15.9% Irish, 8.7% English, 7.3% American, 3.8% French (2008-2012 5-year est.).
Economy: Single-family building permits issued: 0 (2013); Multi-family building permits issued: 0 (2013); Homeowner vacancy rate: 7.4%. Rental vacancy rate: 10.5%. (2008-2012 5-year est.); Employment by occupation: 13.0% management, business, and financial, 1.4% computer, engineering, and science, 8.2% education, legal, community service, arts, and media, 6.6% healthcare practitioners, 15.5% service, 26.0% sales and office, 12.7% natural resources, construction, and maintenance, 16.6% production, transportation, and material moving (2008-2012 5-year est.).
Income: Per capita income: $22,715 (2008-2012 5-year est.); Median household income: $55,875 (2008-2012 5-year est.); Average household income: $63,352 (2008-2012 5-year est.); Percent of households with income of $100,000 or more: 14.8% (2008-2012 5-year est.); Poverty rate: 4.2% (2008-2012 5-year est.).
Education: Percent of population age 25 and over with: High school diploma (including GED) or higher: 90.2% (2008-2012 5-year est.); Bachelor's degree or higher: 17.5% (2008-2012 5-year est.); Master's degree or higher: 5.7% (2008-2012 5-year est.).

School District(s)
New Athens CUSD 60 (PK-12)
  2011-12 Enrollment: 558 . . . . (618) 475-2174
Housing: Homeownership rate: 77.7% (2008-2012 5-year est.); Median home value: $99,400 (2008-2012 5-year est.); Median contract rent: $499 per month (2008-2012 5-year est.); Median year structure built: 1956 (2008-2012 5-year est.).
Health Insurance: 72.4% Private; 29.6% Public; 12.1% None. (2008-2012 5-year est.)
Safety: Violent crime rate: 19.4 per 10,000 population; Property crime rate: 155.6 per 10,000 population (2012).
Transportation: Commute to work: 92.3% car, 0.0% public transportation, 3.1% walk, 3.9% work from home (2008-2012 5-year est.); Travel time to work: 20.0% less than 15 minutes, 22.4% 15 to 30 minutes, 35.8% 30 to 45 minutes, 12.2% 45 to 60 minutes, 9.5% 60 minutes or more (2008-2012 5-year est.)

O'FALLON (city).
Covers a land area of 14.354 square miles and a water area of 0.122 square miles. Located at 38.59° N. Lat; 89.92° W. Long. Elevation is 548 feet.
History: O'Fallon developed in 1854 along the railroad route. Named for the owner of the land on which the town was sited, it grew as a residential community.
Population: 16,073 (1990); 21,910 (2000); 28,281 (2010); Density: 1,976.9 persons per square mile (2008-2012 5-year est.); Race: 78.8% White, 15.8% Black/African American, 2.0% Asian, 0.2% American Indian/Alaska Native, 0.0% Native Hawaiian/Other Pacific Islander, 3.2% Some other race, 2.8% Two or more races, 2.8% Hispanic of any race (2008-2012 5-year est.); Average household size: 2.75 (2008-2012 5-year est.); Median age: 34.9 (2008-2012 5-year est.); Males per 100 females: 94.2 (2008-2012 5-year est.); Marriage status: 27.9% never married, 56.8% now married, 4.7% widowed, 10.6% divorced (2008-2012 5-year est.); Foreign born: 3.6% (2008-2012 5-year est.); Ancestry (includes multiple ancestries): 31.5% German, 14.3% Irish, 12.6% English, 5.0% American, 4.3% Polish (2008-2012 5-year est.).
Economy: Unemployment rate: 4.9% (April 2014); Total civilian labor force: 14,571 (April 2014); Single-family building permits issued: 84 (2013); Multi-family building permits issued: 0 (2013); Homeowner vacancy rate: 2.0%. Rental vacancy rate: 1.9%. (2008-2012 5-year est.); Employment by occupation: 19.3% management, business, and financial, 8.5% computer, engineering, and science, 10.1% education, legal, community service, arts, and media, 6.5% healthcare practitioners, 15.3% service, 28.6% sales and office, 5.2% natural resources, construction, and maintenance, 6.5% production, transportation, and material moving (2008-2012 5-year est.).
Income: Per capita income: $33,363 (2008-2012 5-year est.); Median household income: $76,268 (2008-2012 5-year est.); Average household income: $90,073 (2008-2012 5-year est.); Percent of households with income of $100,000 or more: 36.0% (2008-2012 5-year est.); Poverty rate: 7.8% (2008-2012 5-year est.).
Taxes: Total city taxes per capita: $397 (2011); City property taxes per capita: $249 (2011).
Education: Percent of population age 25 and over with: High school diploma (including GED) or higher: 95.4% (2008-2012 5-year est.); Bachelor's degree or higher: 47.3% (2008-2012 5-year est.); Master's degree or higher: 21.0% (2008-2012 5-year est.).

School District(s)
Central SD 104 (PK-08)
  2011-12 Enrollment: 595 . . . . (618) 632-6336
O Fallon CCSD 90 (PK-08)
  2011-12 Enrollment: 3,483 . . . . (618) 632-3666
O Fallon Twp HSD 203 (09-12)
  2011-12 Enrollment: 2,509 . . . . (618) 632-3507
Housing: Homeownership rate: 68.8% (2008-2012 5-year est.); Median home value: $199,900 (2008-2012 5-year est.); Median contract rent: $820 per month (2008-2012 5-year est.); Median year structure built: 1991 (2008-2012 5-year est.).
Health Insurance: 80.1% Private; 24.5% Public; 6.1% None. (2008-2012 5-year est.)
Safety: Violent crime rate: 10.9 per 10,000 population; Property crime rate: 234.4 per 10,000 population (2012).
Transportation: Commute to work: 93.8% car, 1.0% public transportation, 0.8% walk, 3.3% work from home (2008-2012 5-year est.); Travel time to work: 28.0% less than 15 minutes, 40.3% 15 to 30 minutes, 20.0% 30 to 45 minutes, 8.0% 45 to 60 minutes, 3.7% 60 minutes or more (2008-2012 5-year est.)
Additional Information Contacts
City of O'Fallon . . . . (618) 624-4500
  http://www.ofallon.org
O'Fallon-Shiloh Chamber of Commerce . . . . (618) 632-3377
  http://www.ofallonchamber.com

PADERBORN (CDP).
Covers a land area of 0.150 square miles and a water area of 0.003 square miles. Located at 38.36° N. Lat; 90.05° W. Long. Elevation is 495 feet.
Population: n/a (1990); n/a (2000); 43 (2010); Density: 266.6 persons per square mile (2008-2012 5-year est.); Race: 100.0% White, 0.0% Black/African American, 0.0% Asian, 0.0% American Indian/Alaska Native, 0.0% Native Hawaiian/Other Pacific Islander, 0.0% Some other race, 0.0% Two or more races, 0.0% Hispanic of any race (2008-2012 5-year est.); Average household size: 2.67 (2008-2012 5-year est.); Median age: 50.3 (2008-2012 5-year est.); Males per 100 females: 150.0 (2008-2012 5-year est.); Marriage status: 22.5% never married, 77.5% now married, 0.0% widowed, 0.0% divorced (2008-2012 5-year est.); Foreign born: 0.0% (2008-2012 5-year est.); Ancestry (includes multiple ancestries): 100.0% German, 42.5% Irish (2008-2012 5-year est.).
Economy: Homeowner vacancy rate: 0.0%. Rental vacancy rate: 0.0%. (2008-2012 5-year est.); Employment by occupation: 22.6% management, business, and financial, 0.0% computer, engineering, and science, 0.0% education, legal, community service, arts, and media, 0.0% healthcare practitioners, 0.0% service, 0.0% sales and office, 48.4% natural resources, construction, and maintenance, 29.0% production, transportation, and material moving (2008-2012 5-year est.).
Income: Per capita income: $35,968 (2008-2012 5-year est.); Median household income: $95,156 (2008-2012 5-year est.); Average household income: n/a (2008-2012 5-year est.); Percent of households with income of $100,000 or more: n/a (2008-2012 5-year est.); Poverty rate: 0.0% (2008-2012 5-year est.).
Education: Percent of population age 25 and over with: High school diploma (including GED) or higher: 100.0% (2008-2012 5-year est.); Bachelor's degree or higher: 22.6% (2008-2012 5-year est.); Master's degree or higher: 0.0% (2008-2012 5-year est.).
Housing: Homeownership rate: 100.0% (2008-2012 5-year est.); Median home value: $203,100 (2008-2012 5-year est.); Median contract rent: n/a per month (2008-2012 5-year est.); Median year structure built: Before 1940 (2008-2012 5-year est.).
Health Insurance: 100.0% Private; 0.0% Public; 0.0% None. (2008-2012 5-year est.)
Transportation: Commute to work: 100.0% car, 0.0% public transportation, 0.0% walk, 0.0% work from home (2008-2012 5-year est.); Travel time to work: 0.0% less than 15 minutes, 22.6% 15 to 30 minutes, 0.0% 30 to 45 minutes, 54.8% 45 to 60 minutes, 22.6% 60 minutes or more (2008-2012 5-year est.)

SAINT LIBORY (village).
Covers a land area of 0.945 square miles and a water area of <.001 square miles. Located at 38.36° N. Lat; 89.71° W. Long. Elevation is 407 feet.
Population: 525 (1990); 583 (2000); 615 (2010); Density: 655.0 persons per square mile (2008-2012 5-year est.); Race: 98.9% White, 0.0% Black/African American, 0.0% Asian, 0.0% American Indian/Alaska Native, 0.0% Native Hawaiian/Other Pacific Islander, 1.1% Some other race, 1.1%

Two or more races, 0.0% Hispanic of any race (2008-2012 5-year est.); Average household size: 2.19 (2008-2012 5-year est.); Median age: 43.2 (2008-2012 5-year est.); Males per 100 females: 92.8 (2008-2012 5-year est.); Marriage status: 19.9% never married, 60.9% now married, 5.7% widowed, 13.5% divorced (2008-2012 5-year est.); Foreign born: 0.0% (2008-2012 5-year est.); Ancestry (includes multiple ancestries): 64.1% German, 10.8% Irish, 9.7% Polish, 3.1% American, 2.7% English (2008-2012 5-year est.).

Economy: Single-family building permits issued: 2 (2013); Multi-family building permits issued: 0 (2013); Homeowner vacancy rate: 2.7%. Rental vacancy rate: 4.4%. (2008-2012 5-year est.); Employment by occupation: 17.9% management, business, and financial, 5.1% computer, engineering, and science, 12.5% education, legal, community service, arts, and media, 0.6% healthcare practitioners, 20.0% service, 16.7% sales and office, 12.8% natural resources, construction, and maintenance, 14.3% production, transportation, and material moving (2008-2012 5-year est.).

Income: Per capita income: $31,572 (2008-2012 5-year est.); Median household income: $52,639 (2008-2012 5-year est.); Average household income: $67,374 (2008-2012 5-year est.); Percent of households with income of $100,000 or more: 24.3% (2008-2012 5-year est.); Poverty rate: 5.1% (2008-2012 5-year est.).

Education: Percent of population age 25 and over with: High school diploma (including GED) or higher: 89.6% (2008-2012 5-year est.); Bachelor's degree or higher: 12.1% (2008-2012 5-year est.); Master's degree or higher: 1.9% (2008-2012 5-year est.).

School District(s)
Saint Libory CSD 30 (KG-08)
   2011-12 Enrollment: 90 . . . . (618) 768-4923
Housing: Homeownership rate: 77.4% (2008-2012 5-year est.); Median home value: $144,000 (2008-2012 5-year est.); Median contract rent: $432 per month (2008-2012 5-year est.); Median year structure built: 1972 (2008-2012 5-year est.).
Health Insurance: 85.8% Private; 30.2% Public; 1.8% None. (2008-2012 5-year est.)
Transportation: Commute to work: 89.2% car, 2.2% public transportation, 5.2% walk, 2.2% work from home (2008-2012 5-year est.); Travel time to work: 19.2% less than 15 minutes, 23.7% 15 to 30 minutes, 30.0% 30 to 45 minutes, 14.8% 45 to 60 minutes, 12.3% 60 minutes or more (2008-2012 5-year est.)

SAUGET (village). Aka Monsanto. Covers a land area of 4.226 square miles and a water area of 0.364 square miles. Located at 38.59° N. Lat; 90.16° W. Long. Elevation is 410 feet.
History: Formerly called Monsanto.
Population: 197 (1990); 249 (2000); 159 (2010); Density: 52.3 persons per square mile (2008-2012 5-year est.); Race: 86.4% White, 11.8% Black/African American, 0.0% Asian, 0.9% American Indian/Alaska Native, 0.0% Native Hawaiian/Other Pacific Islander, 0.9% Some other race, 0.9% Two or more races, 0.0% Hispanic of any race (2008-2012 5-year est.); Average household size: 2.60 (2008-2012 5-year est.); Median age: 51.3 (2008-2012 5-year est.); Males per 100 females: 140.2 (2008-2012 5-year est.); Marriage status: 37.7% never married, 37.7% now married, 11.3% widowed, 13.2% divorced (2008-2012 5-year est.); Foreign born: 0.0% (2008-2012 5-year est.); Ancestry (includes multiple ancestries): 19.0% German, 17.2% Italian, 14.5% European, 11.8% English, 10.0% French (2008-2012 5-year est.).
Economy: Single-family building permits issued: 0 (2013); Multi-family building permits issued: 0 (2013); Homeowner vacancy rate: 0.0%. Rental vacancy rate: 0.0%. (2008-2012 5-year est.); Employment by occupation: 2.2% management, business, and financial, 0.0% computer, engineering, and science, 0.7% education, legal, community service, arts, and media, 3.7% healthcare practitioners, 34.1% service, 26.7% sales and office, 9.6% natural resources, construction, and maintenance, 23.0% production, transportation, and material moving (2008-2012 5-year est.).
Income: Per capita income: $24,897 (2008-2012 5-year est.); Median household income: $53,625 (2008-2012 5-year est.); Average household income: $59,766 (2008-2012 5-year est.); Percent of households with income of $100,000 or more: 16.5% (2008-2012 5-year est.); Poverty rate: 5.0% (2008-2012 5-year est.).
Education: Percent of population age 25 and over with: High school diploma (including GED) or higher: 81.9% (2008-2012 5-year est.); Bachelor's degree or higher: 3.8% (2008-2012 5-year est.); Master's degree or higher: 0.6% (2008-2012 5-year est.).
Housing: Homeownership rate: 62.4% (2008-2012 5-year est.); Median home value: $68,800 (2008-2012 5-year est.); Median contract rent: $504

per month (2008-2012 5-year est.); Median year structure built: 1958 (2008-2012 5-year est.).
Health Insurance: 75.1% Private; 23.1% Public; 16.3% None. (2008-2012 5-year est.)
Safety: Violent crime rate: 875.0 per 10,000 population; Property crime rate: 5,187.5 per 10,000 population (2012).
Transportation: Commute to work: 92.5% car, 0.0% public transportation, 7.5% walk, 0.0% work from home (2008-2012 5-year est.); Travel time to work: 47.0% less than 15 minutes, 30.6% 15 to 30 minutes, 8.2% 30 to 45 minutes, 14.2% 45 to 60 minutes, 0.0% 60 minutes or more (2008-2012 5-year est.)

SCOTT AFB (CDP). Covers a land area of 4.314 square miles and a water area of 0.028 square miles. Located at 38.54° N. Lat; 89.85° W. Long.
Population: 7,245 (1990); 2,707 (2000); 3,612 (2010); Density: 885.9 persons per square mile (2008-2012 5-year est.); Race: 61.9% White, 27.6% Black/African American, 1.6% Asian, 0.8% American Indian/Alaska Native, 0.0% Native Hawaiian/Other Pacific Islander, 8.1% Some other race, 6.6% Two or more races, 8.3% Hispanic of any race (2008-2012 5-year est.); Average household size: 3.30 (2008-2012 5-year est.); Median age: 22.4 (2008-2012 5-year est.); Males per 100 females: 114.7 (2008-2012 5-year est.); Marriage status: 21.3% never married, 74.0% now married, 0.6% widowed, 4.1% divorced (2008-2012 5-year est.); Foreign born: 3.2% (2008-2012 5-year est.); Ancestry (includes multiple ancestries): 18.9% German, 14.0% Irish, 5.3% American, 4.4% Polish, 3.8% European (2008-2012 5-year est.).
Economy: Homeowner vacancy rate: 0.0%. Rental vacancy rate: 1.8%. (2008-2012 5-year est.); Employment by occupation: 17.5% management, business, and financial, 0.0% computer, engineering, and science, 6.9% education, legal, community service, arts, and media, 6.2% healthcare practitioners, 27.0% service, 27.5% sales and office, 7.7% natural resources, construction, and maintenance, 7.1% production, transportation, and material moving (2008-2012 5-year est.).
Income: Per capita income: $20,397 (2008-2012 5-year est.); Median household income: $53,810 (2008-2012 5-year est.); Average household income: $65,292 (2008-2012 5-year est.); Percent of households with income of $100,000 or more: 16.1% (2008-2012 5-year est.); Poverty rate: 3.3% (2008-2012 5-year est.).
Education: Percent of population age 25 and over with: High school diploma (including GED) or higher: 97.6% (2008-2012 5-year est.); Bachelor's degree or higher: 31.9% (2008-2012 5-year est.); Master's degree or higher: 18.9% (2008-2012 5-year est.).

School District(s)
Mascoutah CUD 19 (PK-12)
   2011-12 Enrollment: 3,636 . . . . (618) 566-7414
Housing: Homeownership rate: 1.7% (2008-2012 5-year est.); Median home value: n/a (2008-2012 5-year est.); Median contract rent: $1,150 per month (2008-2012 5-year est.); Median year structure built: 1994 (2008-2012 5-year est.).
Health Insurance: 87.8% Private; 14.0% Public; 5.7% None. (2008-2012 5-year est.)
Transportation: Commute to work: 88.7% car, 0.0% public transportation, 7.8% walk, 1.6% work from home (2008-2012 5-year est.); Travel time to work: 71.5% less than 15 minutes, 18.8% 15 to 30 minutes, 8.0% 30 to 45 minutes, 1.1% 45 to 60 minutes, 0.6% 60 minutes or more (2008-2012 5-year est.)

SHILOH (village). Covers a land area of 10.865 square miles and a water area of 0.090 square miles. Located at 38.55° N. Lat; 89.92° W. Long. Elevation is 663 feet.
Population: 2,655 (1990); 7,643 (2000); 12,651 (2010); Density: 1,171.3 persons per square mile (2008-2012 5-year est.); Race: 75.0% White, 19.5% Black/African American, 3.3% Asian, 0.1% American Indian/Alaska Native, 0.0% Native Hawaiian/Other Pacific Islander, 2.1% Some other race, 2.1% Two or more races, 3.6% Hispanic of any race (2008-2012 5-year est.); Average household size: 2.64 (2008-2012 5-year est.); Median age: 36.1 (2008-2012 5-year est.); Males per 100 females: 104.5 (2008-2012 5-year est.); Marriage status: 27.0% never married, 59.0% now married, 6.2% widowed, 7.7% divorced (2008-2012 5-year est.); Foreign born: 7.7% (2008-2012 5-year est.); Ancestry (includes multiple ancestries): 25.6% German, 11.1% Irish, 8.2% English, 4.3% Italian, 3.9% American (2008-2012 5-year est.).
Economy: Single-family building permits issued: 60 (2013); Multi-family building permits issued: 0 (2013); Homeowner vacancy rate: 1.3%. Rental

vacancy rate: 3.8%. (2008-2012 5-year est.); Employment by occupation: 15.7% management, business, and financial, 10.5% computer, engineering, and science, 10.2% education, legal, community service, arts, and media, 7.7% healthcare practitioners, 12.8% service, 27.0% sales and office, 8.0% natural resources, construction, and maintenance, 8.0% production, transportation, and material moving (2008-2012 5-year est.).
Income: Per capita income: $35,747 (2008-2012 5-year est.); Median household income: $78,244 (2008-2012 5-year est.); Average household income: $93,921 (2008-2012 5-year est.); Percent of households with income of $100,000 or more: 37.9% (2008-2012 5-year est.); Poverty rate: 4.5% (2008-2012 5-year est.).
Education: Percent of population age 25 and over with: High school diploma (including GED) or higher: 94.5% (2008-2012 5-year est.); Bachelor's degree or higher: 40.3% (2008-2012 5-year est.); Master's degree or higher: 15.4% (2008-2012 5-year est.).

School District(s)
Shiloh Village SD 85 (PK-08)
    2011-12 Enrollment: 592 . . . . (618) 632-7434
Housing: Homeownership rate: 70.3% (2008-2012 5-year est.); Median home value: $207,100 (2008-2012 5-year est.); Median contract rent: $715 per month (2008-2012 5-year est.); Median year structure built: 1995 (2008-2012 5-year est.).
Health Insurance: 86.0% Private; 21.5% Public; 5.6% None. (2008-2012 5-year est.)
Safety: Violent crime rate: 18.1 per 10,000 population; Property crime rate: 173.2 per 10,000 population (2012).
Transportation: Commute to work: 90.0% car, 3.0% public transportation, 2.4% walk, 3.3% work from home (2008-2012 5-year est.); Travel time to work: 34.2% less than 15 minutes, 35.5% 15 to 30 minutes, 14.8% 30 to 45 minutes, 9.5% 45 to 60 minutes, 5.9% 60 minutes or more (2008-2012 5-year est.)

Additional Information Contacts
O'Fallon-Shiloh Chamber of Commerce . . . . (618) 632-3377
    http://www.ofallonchamber.com
Village of Shiloh . . . . (618) 632-1022
    http://www.shilohil.org

SMITHTON (village). Covers a land area of 3.817 square miles and a water area of 0.039 square miles. Located at 38.41° N. Lat; 89.99° W. Long. Elevation is 476 feet.
Population: 1,587 (1990); 2,248 (2000); 3,693 (2010); Density: 955.7 persons per square mile (2008-2012 5-year est.); Race: 97.6% White, 0.9% Black/African American, 1.4% Asian, 0.1% American Indian/Alaska Native, 0.0% Native Hawaiian/Other Pacific Islander, 0.0% Some other race, 0.0% Two or more races, 3.8% Hispanic of any race (2008-2012 5-year est.); Average household size: 2.76 (2008-2012 5-year est.); Median age: 41.2 (2008-2012 5-year est.); Males per 100 females: 71.8 (2008-2012 5-year est.); Marriage status: 19.3% never married, 61.0% now married, 8.5% widowed, 11.2% divorced (2008-2012 5-year est.); Foreign born: 1.4% (2008-2012 5-year est.); Ancestry (includes multiple ancestries): 41.0% German, 10.6% Irish, 10.0% American, 9.5% English, 9.1% French (2008-2012 5-year est.).
Economy: Single-family building permits issued: 17 (2013); Multi-family building permits issued: 0 (2013); Homeowner vacancy rate: 0.2%. Rental vacancy rate: 21.7%. (2008-2012 5-year est.); Employment by occupation: 16.6% management, business, and financial, 4.6% computer, engineering, and science, 8.5% education, legal, community service, arts, and media, 3.9% healthcare practitioners, 14.6% service, 34.7% sales and office, 7.0% natural resources, construction, and maintenance, 10.2% production, transportation, and material moving (2008-2012 5-year est.).
Income: Per capita income: $27,785 (2008-2012 5-year est.); Median household income: $67,202 (2008-2012 5-year est.); Average household income: $75,341 (2008-2012 5-year est.); Percent of households with income of $100,000 or more: 28.9% (2008-2012 5-year est.); Poverty rate: 6.2% (2008-2012 5-year est.).
Education: Percent of population age 25 and over with: High school diploma (including GED) or higher: 89.5% (2008-2012 5-year est.); Bachelor's degree or higher: 24.0% (2008-2012 5-year est.); Master's degree or higher: 7.6% (2008-2012 5-year est.).

School District(s)
Smithton CCSD 130 (PK-08)
    2011-12 Enrollment: 502 . . . . (618) 233-6863
Housing: Homeownership rate: 94.5% (2008-2012 5-year est.); Median home value: $180,300 (2008-2012 5-year est.); Median contract rent: $440

per month (2008-2012 5-year est.); Median year structure built: 1995 (2008-2012 5-year est.).
Health Insurance: 89.3% Private; 25.3% Public; 2.4% None. (2008-2012 5-year est.)
Safety: Violent crime rate: 0.0 per 10,000 population; Property crime rate: 54.1 per 10,000 population (2012).
Transportation: Commute to work: 94.0% car, 2.5% public transportation, 0.8% walk, 2.1% work from home (2008-2012 5-year est.); Travel time to work: 19.0% less than 15 minutes, 38.7% 15 to 30 minutes, 26.4% 30 to 45 minutes, 11.0% 45 to 60 minutes, 5.0% 60 minutes or more (2008-2012 5-year est.)

Additional Information Contacts
Smithton Chamber of Commerce . . . . (618) 473-3366
    http://smithtonchamber.org

SUMMERFIELD (village). Covers a land area of 0.426 square miles and a water area of <.001 square miles. Located at 38.59° N. Lat; 89.74° W. Long. Elevation is 479 feet.
Population: 509 (1990); 472 (2000); 451 (2010); Density: 1,098.2 persons per square mile (2008-2012 5-year est.); Race: 95.9% White, 1.9% Black/African American, 0.6% Asian, 0.0% American Indian/Alaska Native, 0.0% Native Hawaiian/Other Pacific Islander, 1.6% Some other race, 1.1% Two or more races, 0.4% Hispanic of any race (2008-2012 5-year est.); Average household size: 2.61 (2008-2012 5-year est.); Median age: 45.7 (2008-2012 5-year est.); Males per 100 females: 113.7 (2008-2012 5-year est.); Marriage status: 29.3% never married, 52.7% now married, 4.5% widowed, 13.5% divorced (2008-2012 5-year est.); Foreign born: 0.2% (2008-2012 5-year est.); Ancestry (includes multiple ancestries): 39.3% German, 20.3% Irish, 16.7% English, 11.5% American, 8.8% French (2008-2012 5-year est.).
Economy: Single-family building permits issued: 0 (2013); Multi-family building permits issued: 0 (2013); Homeowner vacancy rate: 0.0%. Rental vacancy rate: 0.0%. (2008-2012 5-year est.); Employment by occupation: 6.4% management, business, and financial, 4.1% computer, engineering, and science, 4.6% education, legal, community service, arts, and media, 8.2% healthcare practitioners, 29.2% service, 12.8% sales and office, 13.7% natural resources, construction, and maintenance, 21.0% production, transportation, and material moving (2008-2012 5-year est.).
Income: Per capita income: $21,328 (2008-2012 5-year est.); Median household income: $50,875 (2008-2012 5-year est.); Average household income: $53,130 (2008-2012 5-year est.); Percent of households with income of $100,000 or more: 10.1% (2008-2012 5-year est.); Poverty rate: 12.6% (2008-2012 5-year est.).
Education: Percent of population age 25 and over with: High school diploma (including GED) or higher: 80.8% (2008-2012 5-year est.); Bachelor's degree or higher: 11.0% (2008-2012 5-year est.); Master's degree or higher: 4.1% (2008-2012 5-year est.).
Housing: Homeownership rate: 77.7% (2008-2012 5-year est.); Median home value: $85,900 (2008-2012 5-year est.); Median contract rent: $550 per month (2008-2012 5-year est.); Median year structure built: 1963 (2008-2012 5-year est.).
Health Insurance: 66.7% Private; 24.1% Public; 19.2% None. (2008-2012 5-year est.)
Transportation: Commute to work: 97.6% car, 0.0% public transportation, 0.0% walk, 2.4% work from home (2008-2012 5-year est.); Travel time to work: 16.9% less than 15 minutes, 29.0% 15 to 30 minutes, 23.2% 30 to 45 minutes, 20.8% 45 to 60 minutes, 10.1% 60 minutes or more (2008-2012 5-year est.)

SWANSEA (village). Covers a land area of 6.256 square miles and a water area of 0.174 square miles. Located at 38.55° N. Lat; 89.99° W. Long. Elevation is 545 feet.
History: Incorporated 1895.
Population: 8,201 (1990); 10,579 (2000); 13,430 (2010); Density: 2,157.2 persons per square mile (2008-2012 5-year est.); Race: 75.3% White, 17.3% Black/African American, 1.7% Asian, 0.1% American Indian/Alaska Native, 0.0% Native Hawaiian/Other Pacific Islander, 5.6% Some other race, 4.9% Two or more races, 3.2% Hispanic of any race (2008-2012 5-year est.); Average household size: 2.56 (2008-2012 5-year est.); Median age: 40.7 (2008-2012 5-year est.); Males per 100 females: 84.4 (2008-2012 5-year est.); Marriage status: 28.2% never married, 53.2% now married, 7.2% widowed, 11.4% divorced (2008-2012 5-year est.); Foreign born: 2.7% (2008-2012 5-year est.); Ancestry (includes multiple ancestries): 28.9% German, 12.1% Irish, 10.2% English, 7.4% American, 6.4% European (2008-2012 5-year est.).

Economy: Single-family building permits issued: 31 (2013); Multi-family building permits issued: 0 (2013); Homeowner vacancy rate: 1.1%. Rental vacancy rate: 3.5%. (2008-2012 5-year est.); Employment by occupation: 17.3% management, business, and financial, 5.9% computer, engineering, and science, 11.6% education, legal, community service, arts, and media, 8.6% healthcare practitioners, 15.6% service, 26.6% sales and office, 6.6% natural resources, construction, and maintenance, 7.8% production, transportation, and material moving (2008-2012 5-year est.).
Income: Per capita income: $31,046 (2008-2012 5-year est.); Median household income: $62,760 (2008-2012 5-year est.); Average household income: $78,200 (2008-2012 5-year est.); Percent of households with income of $100,000 or more: 28.0% (2008-2012 5-year est.); Poverty rate: 9.6% (2008-2012 5-year est.).
Education: Percent of population age 25 and over with: High school diploma (including GED) or higher: 94.2% (2008-2012 5-year est.); Bachelor's degree or higher: 34.0% (2008-2012 5-year est.); Master's degree or higher: 14.6% (2008-2012 5-year est.).

School District(s)
High Mount SD 116 (PK-08)
    2011-12 Enrollment: 450 . . . . (618) 233-1054
Wolf Branch SD 113 (KG-08)
    2011-12 Enrollment: 891 . . . . (618) 277-2100
Housing: Homeownership rate: 76.3% (2008-2012 5-year est.); Median home value: $162,500 (2008-2012 5-year est.); Median contract rent: $599 per month (2008-2012 5-year est.); Median year structure built: 1986 (2008-2012 5-year est.).
Health Insurance: 78.6% Private; 29.3% Public; 7.0% None. (2008-2012 5-year est.)
Safety: Violent crime rate: 11.2 per 10,000 population; Property crime rate: 208.2 per 10,000 population (2012).
Transportation: Commute to work: 91.5% car, 4.4% public transportation, 1.1% walk, 2.5% work from home (2008-2012 5-year est.); Travel time to work: 32.7% less than 15 minutes, 32.5% 15 to 30 minutes, 21.8% 30 to 45 minutes, 9.7% 45 to 60 minutes, 3.3% 60 minutes or more (2008-2012 5-year est.)
Additional Information Contacts
Metro-East Regional Chamber of Commerce . . . . (618) 233-3938
    http://metroeastchamber.org
Village of Swansea . . . . (618) 234-0044
    http://www.swanseail.org

WASHINGTON PARK (village). Covers a land area of 2.632 square miles and a water area of 0 square miles. Located at 38.63° N. Lat; 90.09° W. Long. Elevation is 410 feet.
History: Incorporated 1917.
Population: 7,431 (1990); 5,345 (2000); 4,196 (2010); Density: 1,618.0 persons per square mile (2008-2012 5-year est.); Race: 7.0% White, 90.0% Black/African American, 0.3% Asian, 0.0% American Indian/Alaska Native, 0.0% Native Hawaiian/Other Pacific Islander, 2.7% Some other race, 1.0% Two or more races, 2.5% Hispanic of any race (2008-2012 5-year est.); Average household size: 2.91 (2008-2012 5-year est.); Median age: 32.9 (2008-2012 5-year est.); Males per 100 females: 141.1 (2008-2012 5-year est.); Marriage status: 54.9% never married, 30.2% now married, 4.6% widowed, 10.3% divorced (2008-2012 5-year est.); Foreign born: 0.6% (2008-2012 5-year est.); Ancestry (includes multiple ancestries): 3.0% German, 1.4% Polish, 1.2% Irish, 1.1% American, 1.0% Jamaican (2008-2012 5-year est.).
Economy: Single-family building permits issued: 0 (2013); Multi-family building permits issued: 0 (2013); Homeowner vacancy rate: 0.0%. Rental vacancy rate: 0.0%. (2008-2012 5-year est.); Employment by occupation: 4.6% management, business, and financial, 0.0% computer, engineering, and science, 4.1% education, legal, community service, arts, and media, 1.7% healthcare practitioners, 36.4% service, 20.4% sales and office, 11.2% natural resources, construction, and maintenance, 21.6% production, transportation, and material moving (2008-2012 5-year est.).
Income: Per capita income: $10,036 (2008-2012 5-year est.); Median household income: $25,222 (2008-2012 5-year est.); Average household income: $29,901 (2008-2012 5-year est.); Percent of households with income of $100,000 or more: 2.0% (2008-2012 5-year est.); Poverty rate: 45.1% (2008-2012 5-year est.).
Education: Percent of population age 25 and over with: High school diploma (including GED) or higher: 66.7% (2008-2012 5-year est.); Bachelor's degree or higher: 4.3% (2008-2012 5-year est.); Master's degree or higher: 1.6% (2008-2012 5-year est.).

School District(s)
East Saint Louis SD 189 (PK-12)
    2011-12 Enrollment: 6,971 . . . . (618) 646-3009
Housing: Homeownership rate: 51.3% (2008-2012 5-year est.); Median home value: $48,500 (2008-2012 5-year est.); Median contract rent: $428 per month (2008-2012 5-year est.); Median year structure built: 1953 (2008-2012 5-year est.).
Health Insurance: 22.9% Private; 58.6% Public; 22.8% None. (2008-2012 5-year est.)
Safety: Violent crime rate: 309.5 per 10,000 population; Property crime rate: 359.4 per 10,000 population (2012).
Transportation: Commute to work: 77.0% car, 14.3% public transportation, 3.6% walk, 1.3% work from home (2008-2012 5-year est.); Travel time to work: 22.2% less than 15 minutes, 44.6% 15 to 30 minutes, 20.0% 30 to 45 minutes, 5.1% 45 to 60 minutes, 8.1% 60 minutes or more (2008-2012 5-year est.)

Stark County

Located in north central Illinois; drained by the Spoon River and Indian Creek. Covers a land area of 288.079 square miles, a water area of 0.274 square miles, and is located in the Central Time Zone at 41.10° N. Lat., 89.80° W. Long. The county was founded in 1839. County seat is Toulon.

Stark County is part of the Peoria, IL Metropolitan Statistical Area. The entire metro area includes: Marshall County, IL; Peoria County, IL; Stark County, IL; Tazewell County, IL; Woodford County, IL

Population: 6,534 (1990); 6,332 (2000); 5,994 (2010); Race: 97.8% White, 0.3% Black/African American, 0.9% Asian, 0.0% American Indian/Alaska Native, 0.0% Native Hawaiian/Other Pacific Islander, 1.0% Some other race, 0.9% Two or more races, 1.0% Hispanic of any race (2008-2012 5-year est.); Density: 20.6 persons per square mile (2008-2012 5-year est.); Average household size: 2.41 (2008-2012 5-year est.); Median age: 44.0 (2008-2012 5-year est.); Males per 100 females: 96.6 (2008-2012 5-year est.).
Religion: Six largest groups: 11.3% Methodist/Pietist, 8.9% Catholicism, 4.5% European Free-Church, 4.0% Presbyterian-Reformed, 4.0% Holiness, 2.0% Lutheran (2010)
Economy: Unemployment rate: 8.2% (April 2014); Total civilian labor force: 2,702 (April 2014); Leading industries: 23.3% manufacturing; 17.4% retail trade; 10.0% wholesale trade (2012); Farms: 348 totaling 168,127 acres (2012); Companies that employ 500 or more persons: 0 (2012); Companies that employ 100 to 499 persons: 1 (2012); Companies that employ less than 100 persons: 115 (2012); Black-owned businesses: n/a (2007); Hispanic-owned businesses: n/a (2007); Asian-owned businesses: n/a (2007); Women-owned businesses: n/a (2007); Single-family building permits issued: 7 (2013); Multi-family building permits issued: 0 (2013).
Income: Per capita income: $26,157 (2008-2012 5-year est.); Median household income: $51,392 (2008-2012 5-year est.); Average household income: $64,786 (2008-2012 5-year est.); Percent of households with income of $100,000 or more: 13.9% (2008-2012 5-year est.); Poverty rate: 12.1% (2008-2012 5-year est.); Bankruptcy rate: 2.86% (2013).
Education: Percent of population age 25 and over with: High school diploma (including GED) or higher: 88.6% (2008-2012 5-year est.); Bachelor's degree or higher: 15.8% (2008-2012 5-year est.); Master's degree or higher: 3.6% (2008-2012 5-year est.).
Housing: Homeownership rate: 80.4% (2008-2012 5-year est.); Median home value: $86,600 (2008-2012 5-year est.); Median contract rent: $374 per month (2008-2012 5-year est.); Median year structure built: 1945 (2008-2012 5-year est.)
Health: Birth rate: 89.7 per 10,000 population (2013); Death rate: 140.5 per 10,000 population (2013); Age-adjusted cancer mortality rate: Unreliable deaths per 100,000 population (2011); Number of physicians: 1.7 per 10,000 population (2011); Hospital beds: 0.0 per 10,000 population (2010); Hospital admissions: 0.0 per 10,000 population (2010).
Elections: 2012 Presidential election results: 41.1% Obama, 57.4% Romney
Additional Information Contacts
Stark County Government . . . . (309) 286-5911
    http://starkcountyillnois.com

Stark County Communities

BRADFORD (village). Covers a land area of 0.398 square miles and a water area of 0 square miles. Located at 41.18° N. Lat; 89.66° W. Long. Elevation is 807 feet.
Population: 678 (1990); 787 (2000); 768 (2010); Density: 2,161.4 persons per square mile (2008-2012 5-year est.); Race: 98.3% White, 0.8% Black/African American, 0.0% Asian, 0.0% American Indian/Alaska Native, 0.0% Native Hawaiian/Other Pacific Islander, 0.9% Some other race, 0.6% Two or more races, 2.0% Hispanic of any race (2008-2012 5-year est.); Average household size: 2.78 (2008-2012 5-year est.); Median age: 31.6 (2008-2012 5-year est.); Males per 100 females: 83.2 (2008-2012 5-year est.); Marriage status: 28.6% never married, 56.0% now married, 7.9% widowed, 7.5% divorced (2008-2012 5-year est.); Foreign born: 0.2% (2008-2012 5-year est.); Ancestry (includes multiple ancestries): 43.6% German, 14.8% American, 10.8% Irish, 6.2% English, 3.6% Polish (2008-2012 5-year est.).
Economy: Homeowner vacancy rate: 9.1%. Rental vacancy rate: 0.0%. (2008-2012 5-year est.); Employment by occupation: 7.7% management, business, and financial, 4.6% computer, engineering, and science, 9.2% education, legal, community service, arts, and media, 0.4% healthcare practitioners, 22.9% service, 24.6% sales and office, 13.0% natural resources, construction, and maintenance, 17.6% production, transportation, and material moving (2008-2012 5-year est.).
Income: Per capita income: $15,728 (2008-2012 5-year est.); Median household income: $37,721 (2008-2012 5-year est.); Average household income: $44,858 (2008-2012 5-year est.); Percent of households with income of $100,000 or more: 5.5% (2008-2012 5-year est.); Poverty rate: 28.2% (2008-2012 5-year est.).
Education: Percent of population age 25 and over with: High school diploma (including GED) or higher: 88.2% (2008-2012 5-year est.); Bachelor's degree or higher: 12.2% (2008-2012 5-year est.); Master's degree or higher: 3.0% (2008-2012 5-year est.).
School District(s)
Bradford CUSD 1 (PK-08)
  2011-12 Enrollment: 216 . . . . (309) 897-2801
Housing: Homeownership rate: 84.1% (2008-2012 5-year est.); Median home value: $67,700 (2008-2012 5-year est.); Median contract rent: $441 per month (2008-2012 5-year est.); Median year structure built: Before 1940 (2008-2012 5-year est.).
Health Insurance: 52.6% Private; 56.3% Public; 9.8% None. (2008-2012 5-year est.)
Transportation: Commute to work: 89.3% car, 1.4% public transportation, 4.3% walk, 3.2% work from home (2008-2012 5-year est.); Travel time to work: 22.8% less than 15 minutes, 25.4% 15 to 30 minutes, 29.0% 30 to 45 minutes, 16.9% 45 to 60 minutes, 5.9% 60 minutes or more (2008-2012 5-year est.)

CASTLETON (unincorporated postal area)
Zip Code: 61426
  Covers a land area of 3.174 square miles and a water area of 0 square miles. Located at 41.11° N. Lat; 89.70° W. Long. Elevation is 787 feet. Population: 107 (2010); Density: 33.7 persons per square mile (2010); Race: 99.1% White, 0.0% Black/African American, 0.0% Asian, 0.0% American Indian/Alaska Native, 0.0% Native Hawaiian/Other Pacific Islander, 0.9% Some other race, 0.9% Two or more races, 0.0% Hispanic of any race (2010); Average household size: 2.74 (2010); Median age: 35.3 (2010); Males per 100 females: 94.5 (2010); Homeownership rate: 92.3% (2010)

LA FAYETTE (village). Aka Lafayette. Covers a land area of 0.189 square miles and a water area of 0 square miles. Located at 41.11° N. Lat; 89.97° W. Long. Elevation is 797 feet.
Population: 231 (1990); 227 (2000); 223 (2010); Density: 1,429.9 persons per square mile (2008-2012 5-year est.); Race: 99.3% White, 0.7% Black/African American, 0.0% Asian, 0.0% American Indian/Alaska Native, 0.0% Native Hawaiian/Other Pacific Islander, 0.0% Some other race, 0.0% Two or more races, 1.1% Hispanic of any race (2008-2012 5-year est.); Average household size: 2.45 (2008-2012 5-year est.); Median age: 46.5 (2008-2012 5-year est.); Males per 100 females: 107.7 (2008-2012 5-year est.); Marriage status: 37.6% never married, 43.8% now married, 9.7% widowed, 8.8% divorced (2008-2012 5-year est.); Foreign born: 0.7% (2008-2012 5-year est.); Ancestry (includes multiple ancestries): 25.2%

Irish, 24.4% German, 16.3% Swedish, 10.4% English, 5.6% Italian (2008-2012 5-year est.).
Economy: Homeowner vacancy rate: 0.0%. Rental vacancy rate: 22.2%. (2008-2012 5-year est.); Employment by occupation: 8.6% management, business, and financial, 0.0% computer, engineering, and science, 2.9% education, legal, community service, arts, and media, 2.9% healthcare practitioners, 21.9% service, 20.0% sales and office, 4.8% natural resources, construction, and maintenance, 39.0% production, transportation, and material moving (2008-2012 5-year est.).
Income: Per capita income: $16,945 (2008-2012 5-year est.); Median household income: $29,625 (2008-2012 5-year est.); Average household income: $44,025 (2008-2012 5-year est.); Percent of households with income of $100,000 or more: 9.1% (2008-2012 5-year est.); Poverty rate: 9.3% (2008-2012 5-year est.).
Education: Percent of population age 25 and over with: High school diploma (including GED) or higher: 87.0% (2008-2012 5-year est.); Bachelor's degree or higher: 5.6% (2008-2012 5-year est.); Master's degree or higher: 0.0% (2008-2012 5-year est.).
Housing: Homeownership rate: 80.9% (2008-2012 5-year est.); Median home value: $45,000 (2008-2012 5-year est.); Median contract rent: $328 per month (2008-2012 5-year est.); Median year structure built: Before 1940 (2008-2012 5-year est.).
Health Insurance: 38.1% Private; 64.1% Public; 14.4% None. (2008-2012 5-year est.)
Transportation: Commute to work: 95.0% car, 0.0% public transportation, 5.0% walk, 0.0% work from home (2008-2012 5-year est.); Travel time to work: 36.6% less than 15 minutes, 30.7% 15 to 30 minutes, 6.9% 30 to 45 minutes, 14.9% 45 to 60 minutes, 10.9% 60 minutes or more (2008-2012 5-year est.)

SPEER (unincorporated postal area)
Zip Code: 61479
  Covers a land area of 12.010 square miles and a water area of 0 square miles. Located at 41.00° N. Lat; 89.64° W. Long. Elevation is 741 feet. Population: 165 (2010); Density: 13.7 persons per square mile (2010); Race: 96.4% White, 0.0% Black/African American, 0.0% Asian, 0.0% American Indian/Alaska Native, 0.0% Native Hawaiian/Other Pacific Islander, 3.6% Some other race, 1.2% Two or more races, 3.0% Hispanic of any race (2010); Average household size: 2.80 (2010); Median age: 40.3 (2010); Males per 100 females: 123.0 (2010); Homeownership rate: 91.5% (2010)

TOULON (city). County seat. Covers a land area of 1.018 square miles and a water area of 0 square miles. Located at 41.09° N. Lat; 89.86° W. Long. Elevation is 728 feet.
History: Incorporated 1859.
Population: 1,328 (1990); 1,400 (2000); 1,292 (2010); Density: 1,263.5 persons per square mile (2008-2012 5-year est.); Race: 97.0% White, 0.9% Black/African American, 0.6% Asian, 0.0% American Indian/Alaska Native, 0.0% Native Hawaiian/Other Pacific Islander, 1.5% Some other race, 1.2% Two or more races, 0.9% Hispanic of any race (2008-2012 5-year est.); Average household size: 2.38 (2008-2012 5-year est.); Median age: 42.3 (2008-2012 5-year est.); Males per 100 females: 82.7 (2008-2012 5-year est.); Marriage status: 22.8% never married, 51.2% now married, 14.2% widowed, 11.8% divorced (2008-2012 5-year est.); Foreign born: 1.1% (2008-2012 5-year est.); Ancestry (includes multiple ancestries): 32.0% German, 19.1% English, 10.7% Swedish, 10.0% American, 10.0% Irish (2008-2012 5-year est.).
Economy: Homeowner vacancy rate: 2.6%. Rental vacancy rate: 20.5%. (2008-2012 5-year est.); Employment by occupation: 7.5% management, business, and financial, 2.3% computer, engineering, and science, 19.0% education, legal, community service, arts, and media, 3.3% healthcare practitioners, 16.5% service, 21.9% sales and office, 13.8% natural resources, construction, and maintenance, 15.8% production, transportation, and material moving (2008-2012 5-year est.).
Income: Per capita income: $22,107 (2008-2012 5-year est.); Median household income: $43,542 (2008-2012 5-year est.); Average household income: $52,945 (2008-2012 5-year est.); Percent of households with income of $100,000 or more: 10.3% (2008-2012 5-year est.); Poverty rate: 13.9% (2008-2012 5-year est.).
Education: Percent of population age 25 and over with: High school diploma (including GED) or higher: 85.2% (2008-2012 5-year est.); Bachelor's degree or higher: 18.1% (2008-2012 5-year est.); Master's degree or higher: 4.6% (2008-2012 5-year est.).

School District(s)

Stark County CUSD 100 (PK-12)

2011-12 Enrollment: 821. . . . . (309) 695-6123

Housing: Homeownership rate: 74.1% (2008-2012 5-year est.); Median home value: $80,100 (2008-2012 5-year est.); Median contract rent: $362 per month (2008-2012 5-year est.); Median year structure built: 1946 (2008-2012 5-year est.).

Health Insurance: 67.2% Private; 44.1% Public; 11.4% None. (2008-2012 5-year est.)

Transportation: Commute to work: 89.3% car, 0.0% public transportation, 4.1% walk, 5.7% work from home (2008-2012 5-year est.); Travel time to work: 44.6% less than 15 minutes, 16.6% 15 to 30 minutes, 20.1% 30 to 45 minutes, 13.6% 45 to 60 minutes, 5.1% 60 minutes or more (2008-2012 5-year est.)

WYOMING (city). Covers a land area of 0.842 square miles and a water area of 0 square miles. Located at 41.06° N. Lat; 89.77° W. Long. Elevation is 699 feet.

History: Incorporated 1865.

Population: 1,462 (1990); 1,424 (2000); 1,429 (2010); Density: 1,771.5 persons per square mile (2008-2012 5-year est.); Race: 95.9% White, 0.0% Black/African American, 2.5% Asian, 0.0% American Indian/Alaska Native, 0.0% Native Hawaiian/Other Pacific Islander, 1.6% Some other race, 1.5% Two or more races, 1.0% Hispanic of any race (2008-2012 5-year est.); Average household size: 2.47 (2008-2012 5-year est.); Median age: 41.9 (2008-2012 5-year est.); Males per 100 females: 99.6 (2008-2012 5-year est.); Marriage status: 21.6% never married, 61.3% now married, 8.7% widowed, 8.4% divorced (2008-2012 5-year est.); Foreign born: 2.1% (2008-2012 5-year est.); Ancestry (includes multiple ancestries): 21.7% German, 20.5% Irish, 12.5% English, 9.1% American, 4.3% Italian (2008-2012 5-year est.).

Economy: Homeowner vacancy rate: 2.4%. Rental vacancy rate: 7.0%. (2008-2012 5-year est.); Employment by occupation: 11.1% management, business, and financial, 2.8% computer, engineering, and science, 11.1% education, legal, community service, arts, and media, 2.3% healthcare practitioners, 14.2% service, 23.6% sales and office, 10.1% natural resources, construction, and maintenance, 24.8% production, transportation, and material moving (2008-2012 5-year est.).

Income: Per capita income: $20,957 (2008-2012 5-year est.); Median household income: $47,313 (2008-2012 5-year est.); Average household income: $52,194 (2008-2012 5-year est.); Percent of households with income of $100,000 or more: 9.5% (2008-2012 5-year est.); Poverty rate: 14.4% (2008-2012 5-year est.).

Education: Percent of population age 25 and over with: High school diploma (including GED) or higher: 82.8% (2008-2012 5-year est.); Bachelor's degree or higher: 11.2% (2008-2012 5-year est.); Master's degree or higher: 4.2% (2008-2012 5-year est.).

School District(s)

Stark County CUSD 100 (PK-12)

2011-12 Enrollment: 821. . . . . (309) 695-6123

Housing: Homeownership rate: 75.8% (2008-2012 5-year est.); Median home value: $77,800 (2008-2012 5-year est.); Median contract rent: $418 per month (2008-2012 5-year est.); Median year structure built: 1947 (2008-2012 5-year est.).

Health Insurance: 69.2% Private; 43.1% Public; 8.8% None. (2008-2012 5-year est.)

Transportation: Commute to work: 92.0% car, 0.7% public transportation, 3.4% walk, 1.9% work from home (2008-2012 5-year est.); Travel time to work: 34.7% less than 15 minutes, 19.4% 15 to 30 minutes, 24.4% 30 to 45 minutes, 9.0% 45 to 60 minutes, 12.5% 60 minutes or more (2008-2012 5-year est.)

Additional Information Contacts

Wyoming Chamber of Commerce. . . . . (309) 695-3800
http://www.wyoming-chamber.org

Stephenson County

Located in northern Illinois; bounded on the north by Wisconsin; drained by the Pecatonica River. Covers a land area of 564.523 square miles, a water area of 0.535 square miles, and is located in the Central Time Zone at 42.35° N. Lat., 89.67° W. Long. The county was founded in 1837. County seat is Freeport.

Stephenson County is part of the Freeport, IL Micropolitan Statistical Area. The entire metro area includes: Stephenson County, IL

Weather Station: Freeport Waste Wtr Plt   Elevation: 750 feet

	Jan	Feb	Mar	Apr	May	Jun	Jul	Aug	Sep	Oct	Nov	Dec
High	28	33	45	59	70	80	83	81	74	61	47	32
Low	11	15	26	37	48	58	62	60	50	39	29	16
Precip	1.4	1.5	2.0	3.3	4.0	4.5	3.6	4.5	3.8	2.8	2.6	1.8
Snow	8.8	6.4	3.4	1.0	tr	0.0	0.0	0.0	0.0	tr	1.5	9.0

High and Low temperatures in degrees Fahrenheit; Precipitation and Snow in inches

Population: 48,052 (1990); 48,979 (2000); 47,711 (2010); Race: 87.4% White, 9.1% Black/African American, 0.8% Asian, 0.2% American Indian/Alaska Native, 0.0% Native Hawaiian/Other Pacific Islander, 2.5% Some other race, 2.3% Two or more races, 2.9% Hispanic of any race (2008-2012 5-year est.); Density: 83.2 persons per square mile (2008-2012 5-year est.); Average household size: 2.38 (2008-2012 5-year est.); Median age: 43.7 (2008-2012 5-year est.); Males per 100 females: 94.3 (2008-2012 5-year est.).

Religion: Six largest groups: 13.4% Non-denominational Protestant, 12.8% Pentecostal, 11.0% Catholicism, 10.7% Methodist/Pietist, 7.8% Lutheran, 6.1% Presbyterian-Reformed (2010)

Economy: Unemployment rate: 7.9% (April 2014); Total civilian labor force: 22,109 (April 2014); Leading industries: 19.8% manufacturing; 16.3% health care and social assistance; 13.6% retail trade (2012); Farms: 1,087 totaling 352,481 acres (2012); Companies that employ 500 or more persons: 3 (2012); Companies that employ 100 to 499 persons: 24 (2012); Companies that employ less than 100 persons: 1,067 (2012); Black-owned businesses: n/a (2007); Hispanic-owned businesses: 41 (2007); Asian-owned businesses: n/a (2007); Women-owned businesses: n/a (2007); Single-family building permits issued: 18 (2013); Multi-family building permits issued: 0 (2013).

Income: Per capita income: $23,695 (2008-2012 5-year est.); Median household income: $44,572 (2008-2012 5-year est.); Average household income: $55,879 (2008-2012 5-year est.); Percent of households with income of $100,000 or more: 12.8% (2008-2012 5-year est.); Poverty rate: 14.3% (2008-2012 5-year est.); Bankruptcy rate: 4.20% (2013).

Taxes: Total county taxes per capita: $198 (2011); County property taxes per capita: $161 (2011).

Education: Percent of population age 25 and over with: High school diploma (including GED) or higher: 89.3% (2008-2012 5-year est.); Bachelor's degree or higher: 18.3% (2008-2012 5-year est.); Master's degree or higher: 6.2% (2008-2012 5-year est.).

Housing: Homeownership rate: 72.0% (2008-2012 5-year est.); Median home value: $103,400 (2008-2012 5-year est.); Median contract rent: $436 per month (2008-2012 5-year est.); Median year structure built: 1957 (2008-2012 5-year est.).

Health: Birth rate: 102.9 per 10,000 population (2013); Death rate: 113.4 per 10,000 population (2013); Age-adjusted cancer mortality rate: 204.1 deaths per 100,000 population (2011); Number of physicians: 14.3 per 10,000 population (2011); Hospital beds: 25.8 per 10,000 population (2010); Hospital admissions: 1,129.3 per 10,000 population (2010).

Elections: 2012 Presidential election results: 46.7% Obama, 51.3% Romney

National and State Parks: Lake Le-Aqua-Na State Park

Additional Information Contacts

Stephenson County Government . . . . (815) 235-8277
http://www.co.stephenson.il.us

Stephenson County Communities

CEDARVILLE (village). Covers a land area of 0.451 square miles and a water area of 0 square miles. Located at 42.38° N. Lat; 89.64° W. Long. Elevation is 866 feet.

History: Cedarville was the birthplace and burial place of Jane Addams (1860-1935), whose parents built a house here in 1850 and raised their family on the homestead. John Addams operated a mill.

Population: 751 (1990); 719 (2000); 741 (2010); Density: 1,671.4 persons per square mile (2008-2012 5-year est.); Race: 98.4% White, 0.0% Black/African American, 1.6% Asian, 0.0% American Indian/Alaska Native, 0.0% Native Hawaiian/Other Pacific Islander, 0.0% Some other race, 0.0% Two or more races, 0.0% Hispanic of any race (2008-2012 5-year est.); Average household size: 2.42 (2008-2012 5-year est.); Median age: 45.5 (2008-2012 5-year est.); Males per 100 females: 92.1 (2008-2012 5-year est.); Marriage status: 23.0% never married, 61.0% now married, 3.6% widowed, 12.4% divorced (2008-2012 5-year est.); Foreign born: 2.7% (2008-2012 5-year est.); Ancestry (includes multiple ancestries): 64.0% German, 24.3% Irish, 10.6% American, 6.9% English, 3.7% Norwegian (2008-2012 5-year est.).

Economy: Single-family building permits issued: 0 (2013); Multi-family building permits issued: 0 (2013); Homeowner vacancy rate: 0.0%. Rental vacancy rate: 10.3%. (2008-2012 5-year est.); Employment by occupation: 14.8% management, business, and financial, 3.1% computer, engineering, and science, 11.0% education, legal, community service, arts, and media, 2.4% healthcare practitioners, 14.8% service, 22.7% sales and office, 9.1% natural resources, construction, and maintenance, 22.2% production, transportation, and material moving (2008-2012 5-year est.).

Income: Per capita income: $25,633 (2008-2012 5-year est.); Median household income: $58,813 (2008-2012 5-year est.); Average household income: $60,849 (2008-2012 5-year est.); Percent of households with income of $100,000 or more: 8.7% (2008-2012 5-year est.); Poverty rate: 11.0% (2008-2012 5-year est.).

Education: Percent of population age 25 and over with: High school diploma (including GED) or higher: 94.0% (2008-2012 5-year est.); Bachelor's degree or higher: 28.4% (2008-2012 5-year est.); Master's degree or higher: 6.6% (2008-2012 5-year est.).

Housing: Homeownership rate: 83.3% (2008-2012 5-year est.); Median home value: $101,500 (2008-2012 5-year est.); Median contract rent: $463 per month (2008-2012 5-year est.); Median year structure built: 1969 (2008-2012 5-year est.).

Health Insurance: 74.9% Private; 35.5% Public; 5.7% None. (2008-2012 5-year est.)

Transportation: Commute to work: 91.6% car, 0.0% public transportation, 3.4% walk, 4.1% work from home (2008-2012 5-year est.); Travel time to work: 40.5% less than 15 minutes, 48.8% 15 to 30 minutes, 9.0% 30 to 45 minutes, 1.3% 45 to 60 minutes, 0.5% 60 minutes or more (2008-2012 5-year est.)

DAKOTA (village). Covers a land area of 0.287 square miles and a water area of 0 square miles. Located at 42.39° N. Lat; 89.53° W. Long. Elevation is 945 feet.

Population: 549 (1990); 499 (2000); 506 (2010); Density: 2,497.9 persons per square mile (2008-2012 5-year est.); Race: 97.4% White, 0.0% Black/African American, 0.0% Asian, 1.5% American Indian/Alaska Native, 0.0% Native Hawaiian/Other Pacific Islander, 1.1% Some other race, 1.1% Two or more races, 0.6% Hispanic of any race (2008-2012 5-year est.); Average household size: 3.10 (2008-2012 5-year est.); Median age: 32.4 (2008-2012 5-year est.); Males per 100 females: 94.8 (2008-2012 5-year est.); Marriage status: 28.8% never married, 56.5% now married, 1.8% widowed, 12.9% divorced (2008-2012 5-year est.); Foreign born: 0.0% (2008-2012 5-year est.); Ancestry (includes multiple ancestries): 47.4% German, 19.1% English, 11.3% Irish, 8.5% Dutch, 6.0% Italian (2008-2012 5-year est.).

Economy: Single-family building permits issued: 0 (2013); Multi-family building permits issued: 0 (2013); Homeowner vacancy rate: 2.8%. Rental vacancy rate: 0.0%. (2008-2012 5-year est.); Employment by occupation: 3.6% management, business, and financial, 1.8% computer, engineering, and science, 6.9% education, legal, community service, arts, and media, 5.8% healthcare practitioners, 25.7% service, 21.4% sales and office, 6.2% natural resources, construction, and maintenance, 28.6% production, transportation, and material moving (2008-2012 5-year est.).

Income: Per capita income: $17,119 (2008-2012 5-year est.); Median household income: $38,750 (2008-2012 5-year est.); Average household income: $52,044 (2008-2012 5-year est.); Percent of households with income of $100,000 or more: 9.1% (2008-2012 5-year est.); Poverty rate: 3.6% (2008-2012 5-year est.).

Education: Percent of population age 25 and over with: High school diploma (including GED) or higher: 93.4% (2008-2012 5-year est.); Bachelor's degree or higher: 5.6% (2008-2012 5-year est.); Master's degree or higher: 1.5% (2008-2012 5-year est.).

School District(s)

Dakota CUSD 201 (PK-12)

    2011-12 Enrollment: 838 . . . . (815) 449-2832

Housing: Homeownership rate: 74.0% (2008-2012 5-year est.); Median home value: $93,000 (2008-2012 5-year est.); Median contract rent: $424 per month (2008-2012 5-year est.); Median year structure built: 1944 (2008-2012 5-year est.).

Health Insurance: 64.6% Private; 38.6% Public; 12.0% None. (2008-2012 5-year est.)

Transportation: Commute to work: 88.5% car, 0.0% public transportation, 3.3% walk, 3.3% work from home (2008-2012 5-year est.); Travel time to work: 38.3% less than 15 minutes, 39.5% 15 to 30 minutes, 15.7% 30 to 45 minutes, 1.9% 45 to 60 minutes, 4.6% 60 minutes or more (2008-2012 5-year est.)

DAVIS (village). Covers a land area of 0.429 square miles and a water area of 0 square miles. Located at 42.42° N. Lat; 89.42° W. Long. Elevation is 889 feet.

Population: 541 (1990); 662 (2000); 677 (2010); Density: 2,123.5 persons per square mile (2008-2012 5-year est.); Race: 98.7% White, 0.0% Black/African American, 0.8% Asian, 0.0% American Indian/Alaska Native, 0.0% Native Hawaiian/Other Pacific Islander, 0.5% Some other race, 0.5% Two or more races, 0.0% Hispanic of any race (2008-2012 5-year est.); Average household size: 3.06 (2008-2012 5-year est.); Median age: 32.4 (2008-2012 5-year est.); Males per 100 females: 101.8 (2008-2012 5-year est.); Marriage status: 22.7% never married, 64.2% now married, 6.2% widowed, 6.9% divorced (2008-2012 5-year est.); Foreign born: 1.4% (2008-2012 5-year est.); Ancestry (includes multiple ancestries): 45.4% German, 13.7% English, 12.3% Norwegian, 10.2% American, 9.3% Irish (2008-2012 5-year est.).

Economy: Single-family building permits issued: 0 (2013); Multi-family building permits issued: 0 (2013); Homeowner vacancy rate: 0.0%. Rental vacancy rate: 0.0%. (2008-2012 5-year est.); Employment by occupation: 14.9% management, business, and financial, 2.5% computer, engineering, and science, 9.4% education, legal, community service, arts, and media, 8.3% healthcare practitioners, 12.4% service, 22.5% sales and office, 15.1% natural resources, construction, and maintenance, 14.9% production, transportation, and material moving (2008-2012 5-year est.).

Income: Per capita income: $23,342 (2008-2012 5-year est.); Median household income: $55,179 (2008-2012 5-year est.); Average household income: $69,708 (2008-2012 5-year est.); Percent of households with income of $100,000 or more: 26.6% (2008-2012 5-year est.); Poverty rate: 13.7% (2008-2012 5-year est.).

Education: Percent of population age 25 and over with: High school diploma (including GED) or higher: 87.7% (2008-2012 5-year est.); Bachelor's degree or higher: 15.4% (2008-2012 5-year est.); Master's degree or higher: 8.9% (2008-2012 5-year est.).

Housing: Homeownership rate: 71.7% (2008-2012 5-year est.); Median home value: $117,900 (2008-2012 5-year est.); Median contract rent: $563 per month (2008-2012 5-year est.); Median year structure built: 1960 (2008-2012 5-year est.).

Health Insurance: 74.6% Private; 32.9% Public; 6.6% None. (2008-2012 5-year est.)

Safety: Violent crime rate: 0.0 per 10,000 population; Property crime rate: 0.0 per 10,000 population (2012).

Transportation: Commute to work: 90.6% car, 3.2% public transportation, 1.1% walk, 4.6% work from home (2008-2012 5-year est.); Travel time to work: 15.4% less than 15 minutes, 32.2% 15 to 30 minutes, 32.0% 30 to 45 minutes, 13.5% 45 to 60 minutes, 7.0% 60 minutes or more (2008-2012 5-year est.)

ELEROY (unincorporated postal area)

Zip Code: 61027

    Covers a land area of 0.257 square miles and a water area of 0 square miles. Located at 42.33° N. Lat; 89.75° W. Long. Elevation is 909 feet. Population: 52 (2010); Density: 202.0 persons per square mile (2010); Race: 100.0% White, 0.0% Black/African American, 0.0% Asian, 0.0% American Indian/Alaska Native, 0.0% Native Hawaiian/Other Pacific Islander, 0.0% Some other race, 0.0% Two or more races, 0.0% Hispanic of any race (2010); Average household size: 2.08 (2010); Median age: 46.5 (2010); Males per 100 females: 108.0 (2010); Homeownership rate: 88.0% (2010)

FREEPORT (city). County seat. Covers a land area of 11.777 square miles and a water area of 0.010 square miles. Located at 42.29° N. Lat; 89.64° W. Long. Elevation is 778 feet.

History: Freeport was settled in 1835 by William "Tutty" Baker and his wife. The name reportedly came from Baker's generosity in sharing his food with anyone who came along. Miners returning from the Galena lead mines joined the Bakers, and Freeport became the seat of Stephenson County. It was here that the second Lincoln-Douglas debate took place in 1858.

Population: 25,840 (1990); 26,443 (2000); 25,638 (2010); Density: 2,167.7 persons per square mile (2008-2012 5-year est.); Race: 79.3% White, 16.0% Black/African American, 0.8% Asian, 0.2% American Indian/Alaska Native, 0.1% Native Hawaiian/Other Pacific Islander, 3.6% Some other race, 3.5% Two or more races, 4.0% Hispanic of any race (2008-2012 5-year est.); Average household size: 2.28 (2008-2012 5-year est.); Median age: 42.4 (2008-2012 5-year est.); Males per 100 females: 89.1 (2008-2012 5-year est.); Marriage status: 30.3% never married,

45.6% now married, 10.0% widowed, 14.1% divorced (2008-2012 5-year est.); Foreign born: 3.0% (2008-2012 5-year est.); Ancestry (includes multiple ancestries): 36.7% German, 10.9% Irish, 9.1% American, 8.2% English, 4.6% Dutch (2008-2012 5-year est.).

Economy: Unemployment rate: 8.2% (April 2014); Total civilian labor force: 11,237 (April 2014); Single-family building permits issued: 1 (2013); Multi-family building permits issued: 0 (2013); Homeowner vacancy rate: 5.2%. Rental vacancy rate: 6.9%. (2008-2012 5-year est.); Employment by occupation: 10.1% management, business, and financial, 3.2% computer, engineering, and science, 9.6% education, legal, community service, arts, and media, 3.0% healthcare practitioners, 22.1% service, 27.1% sales and office, 4.4% natural resources, construction, and maintenance, 20.7% production, transportation, and material moving (2008-2012 5-year est.).

Income: Per capita income: $21,607 (2008-2012 5-year est.); Median household income: $37,481 (2008-2012 5-year est.); Average household income: $48,743 (2008-2012 5-year est.); Percent of households with income of $100,000 or more: 10.5% (2008-2012 5-year est.); Poverty rate: 19.9% (2008-2012 5-year est.).

Taxes: Total city taxes per capita: $308 (2011); City property taxes per capita: $186 (2011).

Education: Percent of population age 25 and over with: High school diploma (including GED) or higher: 87.5% (2008-2012 5-year est.); Bachelor's degree or higher: 17.9% (2008-2012 5-year est.); Master's degree or higher: 6.3% (2008-2012 5-year est.).

School District(s)

Career & Tech Educ Consortium
  2011-12 Enrollment: n/a . . . . (815) 232-0709
Carroll/jo Daviess/stephenson Roe (PK-12)
  2011-12 Enrollment: n/a . . . . (815) 947-3810
Freeport SD 145 (PK-12)
  2011-12 Enrollment: 4,187 . . . . (815) 232-0300

Two-year College(s)

Highland Community College (Public)
  Fall 2012 Enrollment: 2,064 . . . . (815) 235-6121
  2012-13 Tuition: In-state $3,840; Out-of-state $4,416

Housing: Homeownership rate: 63.6% (2008-2012 5-year est.); Median home value: $80,500 (2008-2012 5-year est.); Median contract rent: $439 per month (2008-2012 5-year est.); Median year structure built: 1955 (2008-2012 5-year est.).

Health Insurance: 59.7% Private; 44.7% Public; 12.7% None. (2008-2012 5-year est.)

Hospitals: FHN Memorial Hospital (194 beds)

Safety: Violent crime rate: 14.5 per 10,000 population; Property crime rate: 367.6 per 10,000 population (2012).

Transportation: Commute to work: 90.2% car, 1.4% public transportation, 3.6% walk, 3.4% work from home (2008-2012 5-year est.); Travel time to work: 63.9% less than 15 minutes, 17.6% 15 to 30 minutes, 8.6% 30 to 45 minutes, 5.7% 45 to 60 minutes, 4.2% 60 minutes or more (2008-2012 5-year est.)

Airports: Albertus Airport (general aviation)

Additional Information Contacts

City of Freeport . . . . (815) 235-8200
  http://www.ci.freeport.il.us
Freeport Area Chamber of Commerce . . . . (815) 233-1350
  http://www.freeportilchamber.com

GERMAN VALLEY (village). Covers a land area of 0.483 square miles and a water area of 0 square miles. Located at 42.21° N. Lat; 89.48° W. Long. Elevation is 823 feet.

Population: 480 (1990); 481 (2000); 463 (2010); Density: 1,165.8 persons per square mile (2008-2012 5-year est.); Race: 98.9% White, 0.0% Black/African American, 0.7% Asian, 0.0% American Indian/Alaska Native, 0.0% Native Hawaiian/Other Pacific Islander, 0.4% Some other race, 0.4% Two or more races, 1.2% Hispanic of any race (2008-2012 5-year est.); Average household size: 3.08 (2008-2012 5-year est.); Median age: 36.4 (2008-2012 5-year est.); Males per 100 females: 112.5 (2008-2012 5-year est.); Marriage status: 21.7% never married, 69.0% now married, 3.5% widowed, 5.7% divorced (2008-2012 5-year est.); Foreign born: 1.1% (2008-2012 5-year est.); Ancestry (includes multiple ancestries): 62.0% German, 15.8% American, 8.0% Irish, 7.3% English, 5.2% Dutch (2008-2012 5-year est.).

Economy: Single-family building permits issued: 0 (2013); Multi-family building permits issued: 0 (2013); Homeowner vacancy rate: 12.6%. Rental vacancy rate: 0.0%. (2008-2012 5-year est.); Employment by occupation: 8.3% management, business, and financial, 3.2% computer, engineering,

and science, 4.3% education, legal, community service, arts, and media, 7.9% healthcare practitioners, 14.0% service, 29.5% sales and office, 11.5% natural resources, construction, and maintenance, 21.2% production, transportation, and material moving (2008-2012 5-year est.).

Income: Per capita income: $21,614 (2008-2012 5-year est.); Median household income: $65,729 (2008-2012 5-year est.); Average household income: $65,174 (2008-2012 5-year est.); Percent of households with income of $100,000 or more: 19.1% (2008-2012 5-year est.); Poverty rate: 2.5% (2008-2012 5-year est.).

Education: Percent of population age 25 and over with: High school diploma (including GED) or higher: 92.6% (2008-2012 5-year est.); Bachelor's degree or higher: 12.9% (2008-2012 5-year est.); Master's degree or higher: 1.7% (2008-2012 5-year est.).

Housing: Homeownership rate: 87.4% (2008-2012 5-year est.); Median home value: $106,000 (2008-2012 5-year est.); Median contract rent: $358 per month (2008-2012 5-year est.); Median year structure built: 1964 (2008-2012 5-year est.).

Health Insurance: 78.9% Private; 26.5% Public; 5.3% None. (2008-2012 5-year est.)

Transportation: Commute to work: 91.5% car, 0.0% public transportation, 3.3% walk, 3.3% work from home (2008-2012 5-year est.); Travel time to work: 21.1% less than 15 minutes, 43.7% 15 to 30 minutes, 25.3% 30 to 45 minutes, 4.6% 45 to 60 minutes, 5.4% 60 minutes or more (2008-2012 5-year est.)

KENT (unincorporated postal area)

Zip Code: 61044

  Covers a land area of 12.578 square miles and a water area of 0 square miles. Located at 42.31° N. Lat; 89.91° W. Long. Elevation is 899 feet. Population: 232 (2010); Density: 18.4 persons per square mile (2010); Race: 95.7% White, 0.4% Black/African American, 0.0% Asian, 0.0% American Indian/Alaska Native, 0.0% Native Hawaiian/Other Pacific Islander, 3.9% Some other race, 3.9% Two or more races, 2.2% Hispanic of any race (2010); Average household size: 2.58 (2010); Median age: 44.4 (2010); Males per 100 females: 90.2 (2010); Homeownership rate: 81.1% (2010)

LENA (village). Covers a land area of 2.608 square miles and a water area of 0 square miles. Located at 42.38° N. Lat; 89.82° W. Long. Elevation is 948 foot.

History: Lena was known as one of the first places in the United States where Camembert and Brie cheeses were made.

Population: 2,605 (1990); 2,887 (2000); 2,912 (2010); Density: 1,091.8 persons per square mile (2008-2012 5-year est.); Race: 97.8% White, 0.0% Black/African American, 0.5% Asian, 0.0% American Indian/Alaska Native, 0.0% Native Hawaiian/Other Pacific Islander, 1.7% Some other race, 1.8% Two or more races, 0.0% Hispanic of any race (2008-2012 5-year est.); Average household size: 2.35 (2008-2012 5-year est.); Median age: 45.0 (2008-2012 5-year est.); Males per 100 females: 91.2 (2008-2012 5-year est.); Marriage status: 20.4% never married, 54.4% now married, 9.7% widowed, 15.5% divorced (2008-2012 5-year est.); Foreign born: 0.6% (2008-2012 5-year est.); Ancestry (includes multiple ancestries): 49.6% German, 17.9% Irish, 10.5% English, 9.3% American, 3.9% Polish (2008-2012 5-year est.).

Economy: Single-family building permits issued: 0 (2013); Multi-family building permits issued: 0 (2013); Homeowner vacancy rate: 3.5%. Rental vacancy rate: 0.0%. (2008-2012 5-year est.); Employment by occupation: 11.3% management, business, and financial, 2.6% computer, engineering, and science, 9.9% education, legal, community service, arts, and media, 5.0% healthcare practitioners, 10.4% service, 25.1% sales and office, 10.1% natural resources, construction, and maintenance, 25.7% production, transportation, and material moving (2008-2012 5-year est.).

Income: Per capita income: $24,261 (2008-2012 5-year est.); Median household income: $47,399 (2008-2012 5-year est.); Average household income: $56,707 (2008-2012 5-year est.); Percent of households with income of $100,000 or more: 13.8% (2008-2012 5-year est.); Poverty rate: 6.9% (2008-2012 5-year est.).

Education: Percent of population age 25 and over with: High school diploma (including GED) or higher: 87.9% (2008-2012 5-year est.); Bachelor's degree or higher: 18.8% (2008-2012 5-year est.); Master's degree or higher: 6.0% (2008-2012 5-year est.).

School District(s)

Lena Winslow CUSD 202 (PK-12)
  2011-12 Enrollment: 889 . . . . (815) 369-3100

Housing: Homeownership rate: 79.7% (2008-2012 5-year est.); Median home value: $116,600 (2008-2012 5-year est.); Median contract rent: $388 per month (2008-2012 5-year est.); Median year structure built: 1970 (2008-2012 5-year est.).
Health Insurance: 79.6% Private; 34.6% Public; 6.6% None. (2008-2012 5-year est.)
Transportation: Commute to work: 97.0% car, 0.0% public transportation, 0.3% walk, 2.4% work from home (2008-2012 5-year est.); Travel time to work: 36.5% less than 15 minutes, 36.6% 15 to 30 minutes, 12.6% 30 to 45 minutes, 7.6% 45 to 60 minutes, 6.6% 60 minutes or more (2008-2012 5-year est.)

MCCONNELL (unincorporated postal area)
Zip Code: 61050

Covers a land area of 9.544 square miles and a water area of 0 square miles. Located at 42.44° N. Lat; 89.73° W. Long. Elevation is 778 feet. Population: 376 (2010); Density: 39.4 persons per square mile (2010); Race: 98.1% White, 0.3% Black/African American, 0.5% Asian, 0.0% American Indian/Alaska Native, 0.0% Native Hawaiian/Other Pacific Islander, 1.1% Some other race, 1.1% Two or more races, 0.5% Hispanic of any race (2010); Average household size: 2.56 (2010); Median age: 41.6 (2010); Males per 100 females: 119.9 (2010); Homeownership rate: 84.3% (2010)

ORANGEVILLE (village). Covers a land area of 0.628 square miles and a water area of 0 square miles. Located at 42.47° N. Lat; 89.65° W. Long. Elevation is 820 feet.
Population: 451 (1990); 751 (2000); 793 (2010); Density: 1,403.8 persons per square mile (2008-2012 5-year est.); Race: 100.0% White, 0.0% Black/African American, 0.0% Asian, 0.0% American Indian/Alaska Native, 0.0% Native Hawaiian/Other Pacific Islander, 0.0% Some other race, 0.0% Two or more races, 2.0% Hispanic of any race (2008-2012 5-year est.); Average household size: 2.53 (2008-2012 5-year est.); Median age: 35.6 (2008-2012 5-year est.); Males per 100 females: 95.3 (2008-2012 5-year est.); Marriage status: 29.9% never married, 53.1% now married, 4.5% widowed, 12.5% divorced (2008-2012 5-year est.); Foreign born: 1.5% (2008-2012 5-year est.); Ancestry (includes multiple ancestries): 60.2% German, 15.2% Irish, 12.0% Norwegian, 11.1% Swiss, 7.9% American (2008-2012 5-year est.).
Economy: Single-family building permits issued: 0 (2013); Multi-family building permits issued: 0 (2013); Homeowner vacancy rate: 0.0%. Rental vacancy rate: 16.0%. (2008-2012 5-year est.); Employment by occupation: 8.1% management, business, and financial, 1.7% computer, engineering, and science, 9.6% education, legal, community service, arts, and media, 4.2% healthcare practitioners, 16.0% service, 29.0% sales and office, 9.2% natural resources, construction, and maintenance, 22.3% production, transportation, and material moving (2008-2012 5-year est.).
Income: Per capita income: $19,348 (2008-2012 5-year est.); Median household income: $38,333 (2008-2012 5-year est.); Average household income: $48,609 (2008-2012 5-year est.); Percent of households with income of $100,000 or more: 6.6% (2008-2012 5-year est.); Poverty rate: 10.0% (2008-2012 5-year est.).
Education: Percent of population age 25 and over with: High school diploma (including GED) or higher: 94.4% (2008-2012 5-year est.); Bachelor's degree or higher: 12.6% (2008-2012 5-year est.); Master's degree or higher: 5.1% (2008-2012 5-year est.).
School District(s)
Orangeville CUSD 203 (PK-12)
2011-12 Enrollment: 414 . . . . (815) 789-4450
Housing: Homeownership rate: 77.3% (2008-2012 5-year est.); Median home value: $96,900 (2008-2012 5-year est.); Median contract rent: $346 per month (2008-2012 5-year est.); Median year structure built: 1957 (2008-2012 5-year est.).
Health Insurance: 76.0% Private; 32.5% Public; 11.4% None. (2008-2012 5-year est.)
Transportation: Commute to work: 92.8% car, 0.0% public transportation, 3.0% walk, 3.0% work from home (2008-2012 5-year est.); Travel time to work: 20.6% less than 15 minutes, 59.7% 15 to 30 minutes, 12.5% 30 to 45 minutes, 1.6% 45 to 60 minutes, 5.6% 60 minutes or more (2008-2012 5-year est.)

PEARL CITY (village). Covers a land area of 0.643 square miles and a water area of 0.009 square miles. Located at 42.27° N. Lat; 89.83° W. Long. Elevation is 833 feet.
Population: 670 (1990); 780 (2000); 838 (2010); Density: 1,366.1 persons per square mile (2008-2012 5-year est.); Race: 97.7% White, 0.0% Black/African American, 0.0% Asian, 0.0% American Indian/Alaska Native, 0.0% Native Hawaiian/Other Pacific Islander, 2.3% Some other race, 1.9% Two or more races, 9.5% Hispanic of any race (2008-2012 5-year est.); Average household size: 2.27 (2008-2012 5-year est.); Median age: 34.3 (2008-2012 5-year est.); Males per 100 females: 114.1 (2008-2012 5-year est.); Marriage status: 27.2% never married, 51.7% now married, 10.8% widowed, 10.3% divorced (2008-2012 5-year est.); Foreign born: 4.6% (2008-2012 5-year est.); Ancestry (includes multiple ancestries): 53.6% German, 9.8% Irish, 7.5% American, 4.4% Swedish, 2.8% European (2008-2012 5-year est.).
Economy: Single-family building permits issued: 2 (2013); Multi-family building permits issued: 0 (2013); Homeowner vacancy rate: 0.0%. Rental vacancy rate: 0.0%. (2008-2012 5-year est.); Employment by occupation: 10.9% management, business, and financial, 3.4% computer, engineering, and science, 9.4% education, legal, community service, arts, and media, 4.7% healthcare practitioners, 12.0% service, 19.9% sales and office, 18.8% natural resources, construction, and maintenance, 20.8% production, transportation, and material moving (2008-2012 5-year est.).
Income: Per capita income: $23,809 (2008-2012 5-year est.); Median household income: $43,988 (2008-2012 5-year est.); Average household income: $53,214 (2008-2012 5-year est.); Percent of households with income of $100,000 or more: 11.6% (2008-2012 5-year est.); Poverty rate: 9.6% (2008-2012 5-year est.).
Education: Percent of population age 25 and over with: High school diploma (including GED) or higher: 89.5% (2008-2012 5-year est.); Bachelor's degree or higher: 19.6% (2008-2012 5-year est.); Master's degree or higher: 2.6% (2008-2012 5-year est.).
School District(s)
Pearl City CUSD 200 (PK-12)
2011-12 Enrollment: 499 . . . . (815) 443-2715
Housing: Homeownership rate: 68.5% (2008-2012 5-year est.); Median home value: $114,800 (2008-2012 5-year est.); Median contract rent: $329 per month (2008-2012 5-year est.); Median year structure built: 1961 (2008-2012 5-year est.).
Health Insurance: 76.0% Private; 24.0% Public; 14.0% None. (2008-2012 5-year est.)
Transportation: Commute to work: 95.0% car, 0.0% public transportation, 3.0% walk, 1.3% work from home (2008-2012 5-year est.); Travel time to work: 32.4% less than 15 minutes, 49.2% 15 to 30 minutes, 6.1% 30 to 45 minutes, 4.8% 45 to 60 minutes, 7.4% 60 minutes or more (2008-2012 5-year est.)

RIDOTT (village). Covers a land area of 0.102 square miles and a water area of 0 square miles. Located at 42.30° N. Lat; 89.48° W. Long. Elevation is 758 feet.
Population: 156 (1990); 159 (2000); 164 (2010); Density: 1,310.2 persons per square mile (2008-2012 5-year est.); Race: 100.0% White, 0.0% Black/African American, 0.0% Asian, 0.0% American Indian/Alaska Native, 0.0% Native Hawaiian/Other Pacific Islander, 0.0% Some other race, 0.0% Two or more races, 0.0% Hispanic of any race (2008-2012 5-year est.); Average household size: 2.53 (2008-2012 5-year est.); Median age: 43.0 (2008-2012 5-year est.); Males per 100 females: 119.7 (2008-2012 5-year est.); Marriage status: 19.8% never married, 67.0% now married, 2.8% widowed, 10.4% divorced (2008-2012 5-year est.); Foreign born: 0.0% (2008-2012 5-year est.); Ancestry (includes multiple ancestries): 29.9% German, 28.4% Swedish, 19.4% Italian, 14.9% Irish, 10.4% American (2008-2012 5-year est.).
Economy: Homeowner vacancy rate: 0.0%. Rental vacancy rate: 0.0%. (2008-2012 5-year est.); Employment by occupation: 8.5% management, business, and financial, 2.1% computer, engineering, and science, 0.0% education, legal, community service, arts, and media, 0.0% healthcare practitioners, 19.1% service, 14.9% sales and office, 12.8% natural resources, construction, and maintenance, 42.6% production, transportation, and material moving (2008-2012 5-year est.).
Income: Per capita income: $18,739 (2008-2012 5-year est.); Median household income: $39,479 (2008-2012 5-year est.); Average household income: $46,970 (2008-2012 5-year est.); Percent of households with income of $100,000 or more: 5.7% (2008-2012 5-year est.); Poverty rate: 6.0% (2008-2012 5-year est.).

Education: Percent of population age 25 and over with: High school diploma (including GED) or higher: 86.7% (2008-2012 5-year est.); Bachelor's degree or higher: 8.9% (2008-2012 5-year est.); Master's degree or higher: 0.0% (2008-2012 5-year est.).
Housing: Homeownership rate: 94.3% (2008-2012 5-year est.); Median home value: $72,700 (2008-2012 5-year est.); Median contract rent: $613 per month (2008-2012 5-year est.); Median year structure built: Before 1940 (2008-2012 5-year est.).
Health Insurance: 47.8% Private; 57.5% Public; 12.7% None. (2008-2012 5-year est.)
Transportation: Commute to work: 89.4% car, 0.0% public transportation, 0.0% walk, 0.0% work from home (2008-2012 5-year est.); Travel time to work: 17.0% less than 15 minutes, 23.4% 15 to 30 minutes, 40.4% 30 to 45 minutes, 14.9% 45 to 60 minutes, 4.3% 60 minutes or more (2008-2012 5-year est.)

ROCK CITY (village). Covers a land area of 0.153 square miles and a water area of 0 square miles. Located at 42.41° N. Lat; 89.47° W. Long. Elevation is 909 feet.
Population: 286 (1990); 313 (2000); 315 (2010); Density: 2,070.9 persons per square mile (2008-2012 5-year est.); Race: 99.7% White, 0.3% Black/African American, 0.0% Asian, 0.0% American Indian/Alaska Native, 0.0% Native Hawaiian/Other Pacific Islander, 0.0% Some other race, 0.0% Two or more races, 0.3% Hispanic of any race (2008-2012 5-year est.); Average household size: 2.41 (2008-2012 5-year est.); Median age: 43.2 (2008-2012 5-year est.); Males per 100 females: 115.0 (2008-2012 5-year est.); Marriage status: 23.9% never married, 58.8% now married, 6.7% widowed, 10.6% divorced (2008-2012 5-year est.); Foreign born: 0.0% (2008-2012 5-year est.); Ancestry (includes multiple ancestries): 50.0% German, 14.6% Irish, 13.6% Swiss, 12.3% Swedish, 7.3% American (2008-2012 5-year est.).
Economy: Single-family building permits issued: 0 (2013); Multi-family building permits issued: 0 (2013); Homeowner vacancy rate: 0.0%. Rental vacancy rate: 0.0%. (2008-2012 5-year est.); Employment by occupation: 14.1% management, business, and financial, 0.0% computer, engineering, and science, 8.2% education, legal, community service, arts, and media, 2.9% healthcare practitioners, 14.1% service, 28.2% sales and office, 5.9% natural resources, construction, and maintenance, 26.5% production, transportation, and material moving (2008-2012 5-year est.).
Income: Per capita income: $27,084 (2008-2012 5-year est.); Median household income: $62,188 (2008-2012 5-year est.); Average household income: $66,759 (2008-2012 5-year est.); Percent of households with income of $100,000 or more: 14.5% (2008-2012 5-year est.); Poverty rate: 5.4% (2008-2012 5-year est.).
Education: Percent of population age 25 and over with: High school diploma (including GED) or higher: 95.0% (2008-2012 5-year est.); Bachelor's degree or higher: 17.4% (2008-2012 5-year est.); Master's degree or higher: 9.1% (2008-2012 5-year est.).
Housing: Homeownership rate: 80.2% (2008-2012 5-year est.); Median home value: $107,500 (2008-2012 5-year est.); Median contract rent: $425 per month (2008-2012 5-year est.); Median year structure built: 1957 (2008-2012 5-year est.).
Health Insurance: 75.0% Private; 33.5% Public; 7.9% None. (2008-2012 5-year est.)
Transportation: Commute to work: 90.5% car, 0.0% public transportation, 4.7% walk, 3.0% work from home (2008-2012 5-year est.); Travel time to work: 16.5% less than 15 minutes, 29.9% 15 to 30 minutes, 38.4% 30 to 45 minutes, 10.4% 45 to 60 minutes, 4.9% 60 minutes or more (2008-2012 5-year est.)

WINSLOW (village). Covers a land area of 0.452 square miles and a water area of 0 square miles. Located at 42.49° N. Lat; 89.79° W. Long. Elevation is 774 feet.
Population: 317 (1990); 345 (2000); 338 (2010); Density: 529.3 persons per square mile (2008-2012 5-year est.); Race: 96.7% White, 0.0% Black/African American, 0.0% Asian, 0.0% American Indian/Alaska Native, 0.0% Native Hawaiian/Other Pacific Islander, 3.3% Some other race, 0.8% Two or more races, 2.5% Hispanic of any race (2008-2012 5-year est.); Average household size: 1.98 (2008-2012 5-year est.); Median age: 46.5 (2008-2012 5-year est.); Males per 100 females: 83.8 (2008-2012 5-year est.); Marriage status: 20.7% never married, 59.6% now married, 9.8% widowed, 9.8% divorced (2008-2012 5-year est.); Foreign born: 2.5% (2008-2012 5-year est.); Ancestry (includes multiple ancestries): 62.8% German, 19.7% Irish, 12.1% Swiss, 8.8% English, 8.8% Norwegian (2008-2012 5-year est.).

Economy: Single-family building permits issued: 0 (2013); Multi-family building permits issued: 0 (2013); Homeowner vacancy rate: 0.0%. Rental vacancy rate: 29.3%. (2008-2012 5-year est.); Employment by occupation: 4.8% management, business, and financial, 0.0% computer, engineering, and science, 6.7% education, legal, community service, arts, and media, 1.0% healthcare practitioners, 35.6% service, 19.2% sales and office, 15.4% natural resources, construction, and maintenance, 17.3% production, transportation, and material moving (2008-2012 5-year est.).
Income: Per capita income: $19,314 (2008-2012 5-year est.); Median household income: $31,750 (2008-2012 5-year est.); Average household income: $39,739 (2008-2012 5-year est.); Percent of households with income of $100,000 or more: 3.3% (2008-2012 5-year est.); Poverty rate: 13.5% (2008-2012 5-year est.).
Education: Percent of population age 25 and over with: High school diploma (including GED) or higher: 90.9% (2008-2012 5-year est.); Bachelor's degree or higher: 6.1% (2008-2012 5-year est.); Master's degree or higher: 0.0% (2008-2012 5-year est.).
Housing: Homeownership rate: 76.0% (2008-2012 5-year est.); Median home value: $75,400 (2008-2012 5-year est.); Median contract rent: $417 per month (2008-2012 5-year est.); Median year structure built: Before 1940 (2008-2012 5-year est.).
Health Insurance: 64.0% Private; 46.9% Public; 12.1% None. (2008-2012 5-year est.)
Transportation: Commute to work: 82.5% car, 0.0% public transportation, 0.0% walk, 15.5% work from home (2008-2012 5-year est.); Travel time to work: 28.0% less than 15 minutes, 43.9% 15 to 30 minutes, 12.2% 30 to 45 minutes, 0.0% 45 to 60 minutes, 15.9% 60 minutes or more (2008-2012 5-year est.)

Tazewell County

Located in central Illinois; bounded on the northwest by the Illinois River; drained by the Mackinaw River. Covers a land area of 648.974 square miles, a water area of 8.962 square miles, and is located in the Central Time Zone at 40.51° N. Lat., 89.52° W. Long. The county was founded in 1827. County seat is Pekin.

Tazewell County is part of the Peoria, IL Metropolitan Statistical Area. The entire metro area includes: Marshall County, IL; Peoria County, IL; Stark County, IL; Tazewell County, IL; Woodford County, IL

Population: 123,692 (1990); 128,485 (2000); 135,394 (2010); Race: 96.4% White, 0.9% Black/African American, 0.7% Asian, 0.1% American Indian/Alaska Native, 0.0% Native Hawaiian/Other Pacific Islander, 1.9% Some other race, 1.5% Two or more races, 1.9% Hispanic of any race (2008-2012 5-year est.); Density: 209.7 persons per square mile (2008-2012 5-year est.); Average household size: 2.44 (2008-2012 5-year est.); Median age: 39.9 (2008-2012 5-year est.); Males per 100 females: 97.1 (2008-2012 5-year est.).
Religion: Six largest groups: 7.9% Catholicism, 6.9% Lutheran, 6.4% Non-denominational Protestant, 6.1% Baptist, 5.8% Methodist/Pietist, 3.0% European Free-Church (2010)
Economy: Unemployment rate: 6.7% (April 2014); Total civilian labor force: 71,050 (April 2014); Leading industries: 18.4% manufacturing; 15.0% retail trade; 13.4% accommodation & food services (2012); Farms: 942 totaling 337,376 acres (2012); Companies that employ 500 or more persons: 8 (2012); Companies that employ 100 to 499 persons: 60 (2012); Companies that employ less than 100 persons: 2,717 (2012); Black-owned businesses: 94 (2007); Hispanic-owned businesses: n/a (2007); Asian-owned businesses: n/a (2007); Women-owned businesses: 2,761 (2007); Single-family building permits issued: 222 (2013); Multi-family building permits issued: 64 (2013).
Income: Per capita income: $27,838 (2008-2012 5-year est.); Median household income: $55,580 (2008-2012 5-year est.); Average household income: $68,293 (2008-2012 5-year est.); Percent of households with income of $100,000 or more: 20.4% (2008-2012 5-year est.); Poverty rate: 8.7% (2008-2012 5-year est.); Bankruptcy rate: 3.83% (2013).
Taxes: Total county taxes per capita: $129 (2011); County property taxes per capita: $73 (2011).
Education: Percent of population age 25 and over with: High school diploma (including GED) or higher: 91.2% (2008-2012 5-year est.); Bachelor's degree or higher: 23.6% (2008-2012 5-year est.); Master's degree or higher: 6.6% (2008-2012 5-year est.).
Housing: Homeownership rate: 77.2% (2008-2012 5-year est.); Median home value: $130,600 (2008-2012 5-year est.); Median contract rent: $519

per month (2008-2012 5-year est.); Median year structure built: 1966 (2008-2012 5-year est.)

Health: Birth rate: 118.5 per 10,000 population (2013); Death rate: 100.0 per 10,000 population (2013); Age-adjusted cancer mortality rate: 206.2 deaths per 100,000 population (2011); Number of physicians: 12.3 per 10,000 population (2011); Hospital beds: 11.1 per 10,000 population (2010); Hospital admissions: 375.1 per 10,000 population (2010).

Environment: Air Quality Index: 81.6% good, 10.8% moderate, 6.1% unhealthy for sensitive individuals, 1.5% unhealthy (percent of days in 2013)

Elections: 2012 Presidential election results: 40.0% Obama, 57.9% Romney

National and State Parks: Fort Creve Coeur State Park

Additional Information Contacts

Tazewell County Government . . . . (309) 477-2272
    http://www.tazewell.com

Tazewell County Communities

ARMINGTON (village). Covers a land area of 0.285 square miles and a water area of 0 square miles. Located at 40.34° N. Lat; 89.31° W. Long. Elevation is 630 feet.

Population: 348 (1990); 368 (2000); 343 (2010); Density: 1,283.4 persons per square mile (2008-2012 5-year est.); Race: 99.5% White, 0.0% Black/African American, 0.0% Asian, 0.0% American Indian/Alaska Native, 0.0% Native Hawaiian/Other Pacific Islander, 0.5% Some other race, 0.0% Two or more races, 3.3% Hispanic of any race (2008-2012 5-year est.); Average household size: 2.60 (2008-2012 5-year est.); Median age: 29.5 (2008-2012 5-year est.); Males per 100 females: 109.1 (2008-2012 5-year est.); Marriage status: 23.9% never married, 57.6% now married, 4.9% widowed, 13.6% divorced (2008-2012 5-year est.); Foreign born: 0.5% (2008-2012 5-year est.); Ancestry (includes multiple ancestries): 29.2% German, 9.3% English, 8.5% American, 7.4% Scottish, 6.3% Irish (2008-2012 5-year est.).

Economy: Single-family building permits issued: 0 (2013); Multi-family building permits issued: 0 (2013); Homeowner vacancy rate: 4.5%. Rental vacancy rate: 0.0%. (2008-2012 5-year est.); Employment by occupation: 9.7% management, business, and financial, 1.4% computer, engineering, and science, 6.2% education, legal, community service, arts, and media, 3.4% healthcare practitioners, 21.4% service, 22.1% sales and office, 15.2% natural resources, construction, and maintenance, 20.7% production, transportation, and material moving (2008-2012 5-year est.).

Income: Per capita income: $18,331 (2008-2012 5-year est.); Median household income: $41,964 (2008-2012 5-year est.); Average household income: $49,682 (2008-2012 5-year est.); Percent of households with income of $100,000 or more: 6.4% (2008-2012 5-year est.); Poverty rate: 26.5% (2008-2012 5-year est.).

Education: Percent of population age 25 and over with: High school diploma (including GED) or higher: 93.3% (2008-2012 5-year est.); Bachelor's degree or higher: 4.8% (2008-2012 5-year est.); Master's degree or higher: 1.9% (2008-2012 5-year est.).

Housing: Homeownership rate: 75.9% (2008-2012 5-year est.); Median home value: $83,400 (2008-2012 5-year est.); Median contract rent: $500 per month (2008-2012 5-year est.); Median year structure built: 1942 (2008-2012 5-year est.).

Health Insurance: 57.1% Private; 39.3% Public; 11.2% None. (2008-2012 5-year est.)

Safety: Violent crime rate: 29.2 per 10,000 population; Property crime rate: 116.6 per 10,000 population (2012).

Transportation: Commute to work: 99.3% car, 0.0% public transportation, 0.0% walk, 0.7% work from home (2008-2012 5-year est.); Travel time to work: 28.2% less than 15 minutes, 19.7% 15 to 30 minutes, 28.9% 30 to 45 minutes, 14.1% 45 to 60 minutes, 9.2% 60 minutes or more (2008-2012 5-year est.)

CREVE COEUR (village). Covers a land area of 4.305 square miles and a water area of 0.365 square miles. Located at 40.64° N. Lat; 89.60° W. Long. Elevation is 686 feet.

History: Incorporated 1921. Nearby is site of old Fort Creve Coeur, built 1680 by La Salle.

Population: 5,938 (1990); 5,448 (2000); 5,451 (2010); Density: 1,268.2 persons per square mile (2008-2012 5-year est.); Race: 97.8% White, 0.8% Black/African American, 0.0% Asian, 0.5% American Indian/Alaska Native, 0.0% Native Hawaiian/Other Pacific Islander, 0.9% Some other race, 1.0% Two or more races, 2.2% Hispanic of any race (2008-2012

5-year est.); Average household size: 2.22 (2008-2012 5-year est.); Median age: 42.8 (2008-2012 5-year est.); Males per 100 females: 94.2 (2008-2012 5-year est.); Marriage status: 26.3% never married, 51.5% now married, 4.3% widowed, 17.9% divorced (2008-2012 5-year est.); Foreign born: 0.0% (2008-2012 5-year est.); Ancestry (includes multiple ancestries): 33.7% German, 17.6% Irish, 14.4% American, 11.5% English, 6.7% Italian (2008-2012 5-year est.).

Economy: Single-family building permits issued: 0 (2013); Multi-family building permits issued: 0 (2013); Homeowner vacancy rate: 0.0%. Rental vacancy rate: 4.5%. (2008-2012 5-year est.); Employment by occupation: 12.6% management, business, and financial, 0.5% computer, engineering, and science, 3.5% education, legal, community service, arts, and media, 2.9% healthcare practitioners, 23.0% service, 27.2% sales and office, 6.9% natural resources, construction, and maintenance, 23.5% production, transportation, and material moving (2008-2012 5-year est.).

Income: Per capita income: $22,491 (2008-2012 5-year est.); Median household income: $41,815 (2008-2012 5-year est.); Average household income: $49,444 (2008-2012 5-year est.); Percent of households with income of $100,000 or more: 4.5% (2008-2012 5-year est.); Poverty rate: 9.9% (2008-2012 5-year est.).

Education: Percent of population age 25 and over with: High school diploma (including GED) or higher: 82.7% (2008-2012 5-year est.); Bachelor's degree or higher: 5.9% (2008-2012 5-year est.); Master's degree or higher: 2.3% (2008-2012 5-year est.).

School District(s)

Creve Coeur SD 76 (PK-08)
    2011-12 Enrollment: 683 . . . . (309) 698-3600
Tazewell Roe (PK-12)
    2011-12 Enrollment: n/a . . . . (309) 477-2290

Housing: Homeownership rate: 71.6% (2008-2012 5-year est.); Median home value: $77,000 (2008-2012 5-year est.); Median contract rent: $505 per month (2008-2012 5-year est.); Median year structure built: 1956 (2008-2012 5-year est.).

Health Insurance: 61.9% Private; 39.4% Public; 15.2% None. (2008-2012 5-year est.)

Transportation: Commute to work: 93.4% car, 0.4% public transportation, 2.3% walk, 1.6% work from home (2008-2012 5-year est.); Travel time to work: 31.5% less than 15 minutes, 45.5% 15 to 30 minutes, 14.7% 30 to 45 minutes, 2.8% 45 to 60 minutes, 5.6% 60 minutes or more (2008-2012 5-year est.)

DEER CREEK (village). Covers a land area of 0.564 square miles and a water area of 0.009 square miles. Located at 40.63° N. Lat; 89.33° W. Long. Elevation is 761 feet.

Population: 630 (1990); 605 (2000); 704 (2010); Density: 1,355.7 persons per square mile (2008-2012 5-year est.); Race: 91.2% White, 0.0% Black/African American, 0.3% Asian, 0.0% American Indian/Alaska Native, 0.0% Native Hawaiian/Other Pacific Islander, 8.5% Some other race, 2.2% Two or more races, 7.8% Hispanic of any race (2008-2012 5-year est.); Average household size: 2.52 (2008-2012 5-year est.); Median age: 34.3 (2008-2012 5-year est.); Males per 100 females: 99.7 (2008-2012 5-year est.); Marriage status: 25.1% never married, 58.4% now married, 6.2% widowed, 10.3% divorced (2008-2012 5-year est.); Foreign born: 1.7% (2008-2012 5-year est.); Ancestry (includes multiple ancestries): 36.2% German, 17.0% Irish, 17.0% English, 10.6% American, 6.0% Polish (2008-2012 5-year est.).

Economy: Single-family building permits issued: 0 (2013); Multi-family building permits issued: 0 (2013); Homeowner vacancy rate: 0.0%. Rental vacancy rate: 0.0%. (2008-2012 5-year est.); Employment by occupation: 14.7% management, business, and financial, 4.7% computer, engineering, and science, 9.8% education, legal, community service, arts, and media, 4.4% healthcare practitioners, 21.6% service, 16.3% sales and office, 8.1% natural resources, construction, and maintenance, 20.5% production, transportation, and material moving (2008-2012 5-year est.).

Income: Per capita income: $25,980 (2008-2012 5-year est.); Median household income: $56,250 (2008-2012 5-year est.); Average household income: $64,539 (2008-2012 5-year est.); Percent of households with income of $100,000 or more: 15.8% (2008-2012 5-year est.); Poverty rate: 3.3% (2008-2012 5-year est.).

Education: Percent of population age 25 and over with: High school diploma (including GED) or higher: 95.2% (2008-2012 5-year est.); Bachelor's degree or higher: 23.9% (2008-2012 5-year est.); Master's degree or higher: 6.0% (2008-2012 5-year est.).

School District(s)

Deer Creek-Mackinaw CUSD 701 (PK-12)

    2011-12 Enrollment: 1,093 . . . . (309) 359-8965

Housing: Homeownership rate: 76.2% (2008-2012 5-year est.); Median home value: $126,800 (2008-2012 5-year est.); Median contract rent: $618 per month (2008-2012 5-year est.); Median year structure built: 1957 (2008-2012 5-year est.).

Health Insurance: 77.5% Private; 29.7% Public; 9.2% None. (2008-2012 5-year est.)

Safety: Violent crime rate: 14.2 per 10,000 population; Property crime rate: 439.7 per 10,000 population (2012).

Transportation: Commute to work: 95.5% car, 0.0% public transportation, 1.0% walk, 2.6% work from home (2008-2012 5-year est.); Travel time to work: 25.7% less than 15 minutes, 37.0% 15 to 30 minutes, 27.9% 30 to 45 minutes, 5.1% 45 to 60 minutes, 4.2% 60 minutes or more (2008-2012 5-year est.)

DELAVAN (city). Covers a land area of 0.712 square miles and a water area of 0 square miles. Located at 40.37° N. Lat; 89.54° W. Long. Elevation is 617 feet.

History: Founded 1837, incorporated 1888.

Population: 1,642 (1990); 1,825 (2000); 1,689 (2010); Density: 2,202.9 persons per square mile (2008-2012 5-year est.); Race: 96.9% White, 1.5% Black/African American, 0.0% Asian, 0.7% American Indian/Alaska Native, 0.0% Native Hawaiian/Other Pacific Islander, 0.9% Some other race, 0.9% Two or more races, 1.7% Hispanic of any race (2008-2012 5-year est.); Average household size: 2.41 (2008-2012 5-year est.); Median age: 40.2 (2008-2012 5-year est.); Males per 100 females: 92.9 (2008-2012 5-year est.); Marriage status: 20.4% never married, 63.7% now married, 6.8% widowed, 9.0% divorced (2008-2012 5-year est.); Foreign born: 0.4% (2008-2012 5-year est.); Ancestry (includes multiple ancestries): 39.9% German, 16.3% Irish, 13.1% American, 8.5% English, 4.1% Italian (2008-2012 5-year est.).

Economy: Single-family building permits issued: 1 (2013); Multi-family building permits issued: 0 (2013); Homeowner vacancy rate: 3.3%. Rental vacancy rate: 0.0%. (2008-2012 5-year est.); Employment by occupation: 10.4% management, business, and financial, 5.5% computer, engineering, and science, 7.8% education, legal, community service, arts, and media, 3.3% healthcare practitioners, 17.6% service, 22.7% sales and office, 12.2% natural resources, construction, and maintenance, 20.6% production, transportation, and material moving (2008-2012 5-year est.).

Income: Per capita income: $26,571 (2008-2012 5-year est.); Median household income: $44,432 (2008-2012 5-year est.); Average household income: $63,559 (2008-2012 5-year est.); Percent of households with income of $100,000 or more: 14.3% (2008-2012 5-year est.); Poverty rate: 11.9% (2008-2012 5-year est.).

Education: Percent of population age 25 and over with: High school diploma (including GED) or higher: 91.3% (2008-2012 5-year est.); Bachelor's degree or higher: 15.9% (2008-2012 5-year est.); Master's degree or higher: 2.9% (2008-2012 5-year est.).

School District(s)

Delavan CUSD 703 (PK-12)

    2011-12 Enrollment: 474 . . . . (309) 244-8283

Housing: Homeownership rate: 77.0% (2008-2012 5-year est.); Median home value: $94,500 (2008-2012 5-year est.); Median contract rent: $407 per month (2008-2012 5-year est.); Median year structure built: 1954 (2008-2012 5-year est.).

Health Insurance: 75.2% Private; 38.1% Public; 7.4% None. (2008-2012 5-year est.)

Safety: Violent crime rate: 11.8 per 10,000 population; Property crime rate: 295.5 per 10,000 population (2012).

Transportation: Commute to work: 95.3% car, 0.0% public transportation, 1.3% walk, 2.1% work from home (2008-2012 5-year est.); Travel time to work: 24.0% less than 15 minutes, 28.1% 15 to 30 minutes, 27.6% 30 to 45 minutes, 13.8% 45 to 60 minutes, 6.5% 60 minutes or more (2008-2012 5-year est.)

EAST PEORIA (city). Covers a land area of 19.957 square miles and a water area of 2.187 square miles. Located at 40.67° N. Lat; 89.54° W. Long. Elevation is 463 feet.

History: East Peoria developed as an industrial and residential neighbor of Peoria. The Caterpillar Tractor Company plant was a major industry.

Population: 21,378 (1990); 22,638 (2000); 23,402 (2010); Density: 1,168.6 persons per square mile (2008-2012 5-year est.); Race: 95.5% White, 0.4% Black/African American, 1.7% Asian, 0.1% American

Indian/Alaska Native, 0.0% Native Hawaiian/Other Pacific Islander, 2.3% Some other race, 2.0% Two or more races, 2.4% Hispanic of any race (2008-2012 5-year est.); Average household size: 2.39 (2008-2012 5-year est.); Median age: 39.1 (2008-2012 5-year est.); Males per 100 females: 96.2 (2008-2012 5-year est.); Marriage status: 26.1% never married, 53.6% now married, 7.7% widowed, 12.5% divorced (2008-2012 5-year est.); Foreign born: 2.1% (2008-2012 5-year est.); Ancestry (includes multiple ancestries): 34.4% German, 13.8% Irish, 13.1% American, 10.5% English, 3.5% Italian (2008-2012 5-year est.).

Economy: Single-family building permits issued: 47 (2013); Multi-family building permits issued: 0 (2013); Homeowner vacancy rate: 1.3%. Rental vacancy rate: 5.9%. (2008-2012 5-year est.); Employment by occupation: 14.5% management, business, and financial, 5.2% computer, engineering, and science, 7.8% education, legal, community service, arts, and media, 6.8% healthcare practitioners, 18.1% service, 22.8% sales and office, 9.3% natural resources, construction, and maintenance, 15.4% production, transportation, and material moving (2008-2012 5-year est.).

Income: Per capita income: $26,373 (2008-2012 5-year est.); Median household income: $52,544 (2008-2012 5-year est.); Average household income: $63,046 (2008-2012 5-year est.); Percent of households with income of $100,000 or more: 18.9% (2008-2012 5-year est.); Poverty rate: 11.2% (2008-2012 5-year est.).

Taxes: Total city taxes per capita: $706 (2011); City property taxes per capita: $345 (2011).

Education: Percent of population age 25 and over with: High school diploma (including GED) or higher: 90.0% (2008-2012 5-year est.); Bachelor's degree or higher: 20.9% (2008-2012 5-year est.); Master's degree or higher: 5.8% (2008-2012 5-year est.).

School District(s)

East Peoria CHSD 309 (09-12)

    2011-12 Enrollment: 1,223 . . . . (309) 694-8300

East Peoria SD 86 (PK-08)

    2011-12 Enrollment: 1,746 . . . . (309) 427-5100

Riverview CCSD 2 (PK-08)

    2011-12 Enrollment: 252 . . . . (309) 822-8550

Robein SD 85 (PK-08)

    2011-12 Enrollment: 173 . . . . (309) 694-1409

Two-year College(s)

Illinois Central College (Public)

    Fall 2012 Enrollment: 11,125 . . . . (309) 694-5422

    2012-13 Tuition: In-state $7,050; Out-of-state $7,050

Vocational/Technical School(s)

Midwest Technical Institute-East Peoria (Private, For-profit)

    Fall 2012 Enrollment: 530 . . . . (309) 427-2750

    2012-13 Tuition: $12,254

Oehrlein School of Cosmetology (Private, For-profit)

    Fall 2012 Enrollment: 68 . . . . (309) 699-1561

    2012-13 Tuition: $14,325

Housing: Homeownership rate: 74.8% (2008-2012 5-year est.); Median home value: $132,100 (2008-2012 5-year est.); Median contract rent: $484 per month (2008-2012 5-year est.); Median year structure built: 1964 (2008-2012 5-year est.).

Health Insurance: 73.2% Private; 29.9% Public; 11.0% None. (2008-2012 5-year est.)

Safety: Violent crime rate: 35.8 per 10,000 population; Property crime rate: 403.3 per 10,000 population (2012).

Transportation: Commute to work: 93.2% car, 0.6% public transportation, 2.0% walk, 3.4% work from home (2008-2012 5-year est.); Travel time to work: 33.1% less than 15 minutes, 52.0% 15 to 30 minutes, 9.6% 30 to 45 minutes, 2.2% 45 to 60 minutes, 3.1% 60 minutes or more (2008-2012 5-year est.)

Additional Information Contacts

City of East Peoria . . . . (309) 698-4715

    http://www.cityofeastpeoria.com

East Peoria Chamber of Commerce . . . . (309) 699-6212

    http://www.epcc.org

GREEN VALLEY (village). Covers a land area of 0.304 square miles and a water area of 0 square miles. Located at 40.41° N. Lat; 89.64° W. Long. Elevation is 538 feet.

Population: 745 (1990); 728 (2000); 709 (2010); Density: 2,368.4 persons per square mile (2008-2012 5-year est.); Race: 95.0% White, 0.0% Black/African American, 0.0% Asian, 0.0% American Indian/Alaska Native, 0.0% Native Hawaiian/Other Pacific Islander, 5.0% Some other race, 4.0% Two or more races, 0.8% Hispanic of any race (2008-2012 5-year est.);

Average household size: 2.91 (2008-2012 5-year est.); Median age: 30.7 (2008-2012 5-year est.); Males per 100 females: 104.8 (2008-2012 5-year est.); Marriage status: 24.9% never married, 62.8% now married, 5.8% widowed, 6.6% divorced (2008-2012 5-year est.); Foreign born: 0.3% (2008-2012 5-year est.); Ancestry (includes multiple ancestries): 28.1% American, 26.6% German, 8.5% Irish, 5.7% English, 1.5% Scotch-Irish (2008-2012 5-year est.).

Economy: Single-family building permits issued: 0 (2013); Multi-family building permits issued: 0 (2013); Homeowner vacancy rate: 0.0%. Rental vacancy rate: 0.0%. (2008-2012 5-year est.); Employment by occupation: 6.5% management, business, and financial, 4.5% computer, engineering, and science, 5.5% education, legal, community service, arts, and media, 5.2% healthcare practitioners, 26.2% service, 21.0% sales and office, 8.7% natural resources, construction, and maintenance, 22.3% production, transportation, and material moving (2008-2012 5-year est.).

Income: Per capita income: $20,613 (2008-2012 5-year est.); Median household income: $48,000 (2008-2012 5-year est.); Average household income: $58,757 (2008-2012 5-year est.); Percent of households with income of $100,000 or more: 12.2% (2008-2012 5-year est.); Poverty rate: 7.7% (2008-2012 5-year est.).

Education: Percent of population age 25 and over with: High school diploma (including GED) or higher: 88.0% (2008-2012 5-year est.); Bachelor's degree or higher: 14.3% (2008-2012 5-year est.); Master's degree or higher: 2.5% (2008-2012 5-year est.).

School District(s)
Midwest Central CUSD 191 (PK-12)
   2011-12 Enrollment: 1,108 . . . . (309) 968-6868

Housing: Homeownership rate: 83.3% (2008-2012 5-year est.); Median home value: $97,800 (2008-2012 5-year est.); Median contract rent: $525 per month (2008-2012 5-year est.); Median year structure built: Before 1940 (2008-2012 5-year est.).

Health Insurance: 65.1% Private; 41.2% Public; 7.7% None. (2008-2012 5-year est.)

Transportation: Commute to work: 97.1% car, 0.0% public transportation, 1.6% walk, 1.3% work from home (2008-2012 5-year est.); Travel time to work: 21.4% less than 15 minutes, 42.4% 15 to 30 minutes, 25.0% 30 to 45 minutes, 7.9% 45 to 60 minutes, 3.3% 60 minutes or more (2008-2012 5-year est.)

GROVELAND (unincorporated postal area)
Zip Code: 61535
   Covers a land area of 8.683 square miles and a water area of 0.063 square miles. Located at 40.57° N. Lat; 89.51° W. Long. Elevation is 771 feet. Population: 1,629 (2010); Density: 187.6 persons per square mile (2010); Race: 98.5% White, 0.2% Black/African American, 0.1% Asian, 0.4% American Indian/Alaska Native, 0.0% Native Hawaiian/Other Pacific Islander, 0.8% Some other race, 0.5% Two or more races, 1.3% Hispanic of any race (2010); Average household size: 2.64 (2010); Median age: 45.7 (2010); Males per 100 females: 103.6 (2010); Homeownership rate: 95.8% (2010)

HERITAGE LAKE (CDP). Covers a land area of 1.131 square miles and a water area of 0.115 square miles. Located at 40.55° N. Lat; 89.33° W. Long.
Population: n/a (1990); n/a (2000); 1,520 (2010); Density: 1,214.7 persons per square mile (2008-2012 5-year est.); Race: 100.0% White, 0.0% Black/African American, 0.0% Asian, 0.0% American Indian/Alaska Native, 0.0% Native Hawaiian/Other Pacific Islander, 0.0% Some other race, 0.0% Two or more races, 0.0% Hispanic of any race (2008-2012 5-year est.); Average household size: 3.09 (2008-2012 5-year est.); Median age: 39.7 (2008-2012 5-year est.); Males per 100 females: 92.4 (2008-2012 5-year est.); Marriage status: 19.1% never married, 68.9% now married, 0.0% widowed, 12.0% divorced (2008-2012 5-year est.); Foreign born: 0.0% (2008-2012 5-year est.); Ancestry (includes multiple ancestries): 38.9% German, 15.9% Irish, 14.1% English, 12.6% American, 5.7% Dutch (2008-2012 5-year est.).

Economy: Homeowner vacancy rate: 3.3%. Rental vacancy rate: 0.0%. (2008-2012 5-year est.); Employment by occupation: 7.3% management, business, and financial, 4.4% computer, engineering, and science, 4.3% education, legal, community service, arts, and media, 15.7% healthcare practitioners, 8.6% service, 24.5% sales and office, 13.3% natural resources, construction, and maintenance, 21.9% production, transportation, and material moving (2008-2012 5-year est.).

Income: Per capita income: $28,509 (2008-2012 5-year est.); Median household income: $90,076 (2008-2012 5-year est.); Average household income: $87,340 (2008-2012 5-year est.); Percent of households with income of $100,000 or more: 39.9% (2008-2012 5-year est.); Poverty rate: 0.0% (2008-2012 5-year est.).

Education: Percent of population age 25 and over with: High school diploma (including GED) or higher: 100.0% (2008-2012 5-year est.); Bachelor's degree or higher: 24.7% (2008-2012 5-year est.); Master's degree or higher: 6.3% (2008-2012 5-year est.).

Housing: Homeownership rate: 100.0% (2008-2012 5-year est.); Median home value: $181,100 (2008-2012 5-year est.); Median contract rent: n/a per month (2008-2012 5-year est.); Median year structure built: 1995 (2008-2012 5-year est.).

Health Insurance: 94.8% Private; 11.1% Public; 2.9% None. (2008-2012 5-year est.)

Transportation: Commute to work: 95.4% car, 0.0% public transportation, 0.0% walk, 0.0% work from home (2008-2012 5-year est.); Travel time to work: 9.0% less than 15 minutes, 29.6% 15 to 30 minutes, 39.8% 30 to 45 minutes, 19.3% 45 to 60 minutes, 2.3% 60 minutes or more (2008-2012 5-year est.)

HOPEDALE (village). Covers a land area of 0.505 square miles and a water area of 0.004 square miles. Located at 40.42° N. Lat; 89.42° W. Long. Elevation is 643 feet.
Population: 805 (1990); 929 (2000); 865 (2010); Density: 2,101.8 persons per square mile (2008-2012 5-year est.); Race: 96.4% White, 2.5% Black/African American, 0.3% Asian, 0.0% American Indian/Alaska Native, 0.0% Native Hawaiian/Other Pacific Islander, 0.8% Some other race, 0.2% Two or more races, 0.6% Hispanic of any race (2008-2012 5-year est.); Average household size: 2.38 (2008-2012 5-year est.); Median age: 42.5 (2008-2012 5-year est.); Males per 100 females: 92.2 (2008-2012 5-year est.); Marriage status: 26.2% never married, 53.7% now married, 10.0% widowed, 10.2% divorced (2008-2012 5-year est.); Foreign born: 1.0% (2008-2012 5-year est.); Ancestry (includes multiple ancestries): 38.5% German, 13.6% English, 10.8% Irish, 10.7% American, 5.7% French (2008-2012 5-year est.).

Economy: Single-family building permits issued: 0 (2013); Multi-family building permits issued: 0 (2013); Homeowner vacancy rate: 0.0%. Rental vacancy rate: 24.0%. (2008-2012 5-year est.); Employment by occupation: 10.6% management, business, and financial, 2.0% computer, engineering, and science, 8.1% education, legal, community service, arts, and media, 12.6% healthcare practitioners, 16.9% service, 24.4% sales and office, 11.5% natural resources, construction, and maintenance, 13.8% production, transportation, and material moving (2008-2012 5-year est.).

Income: Per capita income: $22,106 (2008-2012 5-year est.); Median household income: $49,167 (2008-2012 5-year est.); Average household income: $55,326 (2008-2012 5-year est.); Percent of households with income of $100,000 or more: 11.6% (2008-2012 5-year est.); Poverty rate: 6.4% (2008-2012 5-year est.).

Education: Percent of population age 25 and over with: High school diploma (including GED) or higher: 88.9% (2008-2012 5-year est.); Bachelor's degree or higher: 10.8% (2008-2012 5-year est.); Master's degree or higher: 2.5% (2008-2012 5-year est.).

Housing: Homeownership rate: 69.2% (2008-2012 5-year est.); Median home value: $111,000 (2008-2012 5-year est.); Median contract rent: $443 per month (2008-2012 5-year est.); Median year structure built: 1964 (2008-2012 5-year est.).

Health Insurance: 71.3% Private; 35.9% Public; 10.6% None. (2008-2012 5-year est.)

Hospitals: Hopedale Medical Complex

Safety: Violent crime rate: 0.0 per 10,000 population; Property crime rate: 80.8 per 10,000 population (2012).

Transportation: Commute to work: 86.5% car, 0.0% public transportation, 7.8% walk, 4.0% work from home (2008-2012 5-year est.); Travel time to work: 39.8% less than 15 minutes, 35.3% 15 to 30 minutes, 19.5% 30 to 45 minutes, 4.9% 45 to 60 minutes, 0.5% 60 minutes or more (2008-2012 5-year est.)

MACKINAW (village). Covers a land area of 1.347 square miles and a water area of 0.030 square miles. Located at 40.53° N. Lat; 89.36° W. Long. Elevation is 682 feet.
Population: 1,331 (1990); 1,452 (2000); 1,950 (2010); Density: 1,650.7 persons per square mile (2008-2012 5-year est.); Race: 98.0% White, 0.4% Black/African American, 0.5% Asian, 0.0% American Indian/Alaska Native, 0.0% Native Hawaiian/Other Pacific Islander, 1.1% Some other race, 0.4% Two or more races, 8.4% Hispanic of any race (2008-2012 5-year est.); Average household size: 2.51 (2008-2012 5-year est.);

Median age: 35.2 (2008-2012 5-year est.); Males per 100 females: 93.8 (2008-2012 5-year est.); Marriage status: 22.9% never married, 63.1% now married, 5.6% widowed, 8.4% divorced (2008-2012 5-year est.); Foreign born: 2.2% (2008-2012 5-year est.); Ancestry (includes multiple ancestries): 37.0% German, 14.8% American, 13.9% English, 12.7% Irish, 4.5% Italian (2008-2012 5-year est.).

Economy: Single-family building permits issued: 4 (2013); Multi-family building permits issued: 0 (2013); Homeowner vacancy rate: 0.0%. Rental vacancy rate: 7.7%. (2008-2012 5-year est.); Employment by occupation: 13.6% management, business, and financial, 5.5% computer, engineering, and science, 6.4% education, legal, community service, arts, and media, 7.6% healthcare practitioners, 16.0% service, 21.6% sales and office, 15.5% natural resources, construction, and maintenance, 13.7% production, transportation, and material moving (2008-2012 5-year est.).

Income: Per capita income: $27,099 (2008-2012 5-year est.); Median household income: $61,042 (2008-2012 5-year est.); Average household income: $67,688 (2008-2012 5-year est.); Percent of households with income of $100,000 or more: 19.8% (2008-2012 5-year est.); Poverty rate: 5.3% (2008-2012 5-year est.).

Education: Percent of population age 25 and over with: High school diploma (including GED) or higher: 94.0% (2008-2012 5-year est.); Bachelor's degree or higher: 20.3% (2008-2012 5-year est.); Master's degree or higher: 3.4% (2008-2012 5-year est.).

School District(s)

Deer Creek-Mackinaw CUSD 701 (PK-12)

   2011-12 Enrollment: 1,093 . . . . (309) 359-8965

Housing: Homeownership rate: 71.5% (2008-2012 5-year est.); Median home value: $122,300 (2008-2012 5-year est.); Median contract rent: $511 per month (2008-2012 5-year est.); Median year structure built: 1960 (2008-2012 5-year est.).

Health Insurance: 76.3% Private; 25.3% Public; 9.7% None. (2008-2012 5-year est.)

Transportation: Commute to work: 91.8% car, 0.0% public transportation, 5.1% walk, 2.1% work from home (2008-2012 5-year est.); Travel time to work: 20.0% less than 15 minutes, 33.3% 15 to 30 minutes, 38.6% 30 to 45 minutes, 5.9% 45 to 60 minutes, 2.2% 60 minutes or more (2008-2012 5-year est.)

MARQUETTE HEIGHTS (city). Covers a land area of 0.988 square miles and a water area of 0 square miles. Located at 40.62° N. Lat; 89.60° W. Long. Elevation is 620 feet.

Population: 3,077 (1990); 2,794 (2000); 2,824 (2010); Density: 2,871.7 persons per square mile (2008-2012 5-year est.); Race: 97.1% White, 0.1% Black/African American, 0.5% Asian, 0.0% American Indian/Alaska Native, 0.0% Native Hawaiian/Other Pacific Islander, 2.3% Some other race, 1.9% Two or more races, 4.3% Hispanic of any race (2008-2012 5-year est.); Average household size: 2.75 (2008-2012 5-year est.); Median age: 34.8 (2008-2012 5-year est.); Males per 100 females: 118.3 (2008-2012 5-year est.); Marriage status: 21.2% never married, 63.0% now married, 5.3% widowed, 10.5% divorced (2008-2012 5-year est.); Foreign born: 1.6% (2008-2012 5-year est.); Ancestry (includes multiple ancestries): 26.7% German, 20.7% American, 12.8% Irish, 10.1% English, 4.0% Italian (2008-2012 5-year est.).

Economy: Single-family building permits issued: 1 (2013); Multi-family building permits issued: 0 (2013); Homeowner vacancy rate: 0.0%. Rental vacancy rate: 0.0%. (2008-2012 5-year est.); Employment by occupation: 3.7% management, business, and financial, 2.9% computer, engineering, and science, 5.0% education, legal, community service, arts, and media, 4.4% healthcare practitioners, 17.2% service, 29.9% sales and office, 10.4% natural resources, construction, and maintenance, 26.6% production, transportation, and material moving (2008-2012 5-year est.).

Income: Per capita income: $23,104 (2008-2012 5-year est.); Median household income: $60,602 (2008-2012 5-year est.); Average household income: $62,716 (2008-2012 5-year est.); Percent of households with income of $100,000 or more: 15.9% (2008-2012 5-year est.); Poverty rate: 5.8% (2008-2012 5-year est.).

Education: Percent of population age 25 and over with: High school diploma (including GED) or higher: 89.3% (2008-2012 5-year est.); Bachelor's degree or higher: 12.0% (2008-2012 5-year est.); Master's degree or higher: 3.4% (2008-2012 5-year est.).

School District(s)

N Pekin & Marquette Hght SD 102 (PK-08)

   2011-12 Enrollment: 669 . . . . (309) 382-2172

Housing: Homeownership rate: 90.9% (2008-2012 5-year est.); Median home value: $97,700 (2008-2012 5-year est.); Median contract rent: $734

per month (2008-2012 5-year est.); Median year structure built: 1962 (2008-2012 5-year est.).

Health Insurance: 82.3% Private; 27.3% Public; 6.1% None. (2008-2012 5-year est.)

Transportation: Commute to work: 97.4% car, 0.0% public transportation, 0.7% walk, 1.2% work from home (2008-2012 5-year est.); Travel time to work: 20.6% less than 15 minutes, 63.7% 15 to 30 minutes, 10.3% 30 to 45 minutes, 3.9% 45 to 60 minutes, 1.6% 60 minutes or more (2008-2012 5-year est.)

MINIER (village). Covers a land area of 0.621 square miles and a water area of 0 square miles. Located at 40.43° N. Lat; 89.31° W. Long. Elevation is 636 feet.

Population: 1,155 (1990); 1,244 (2000); 1,252 (2010); Density: 1,769.5 persons per square mile (2008-2012 5-year est.); Race: 97.5% White, 0.0% Black/African American, 0.5% Asian, 0.0% American Indian/Alaska Native, 0.0% Native Hawaiian/Other Pacific Islander, 2.0% Some other race, 0.8% Two or more races, 1.5% Hispanic of any race (2008-2012 5-year est.); Average household size: 2.42 (2008-2012 5-year est.); Median age: 46.3 (2008-2012 5-year est.), Males per 100 females: 98.6 (2008-2012 5-year est.); Marriage status: 28.6% never married, 52.1% now married, 7.6% widowed, 11.8% divorced (2008-2012 5-year est.); Foreign born: 0.4% (2008-2012 5-year est.); Ancestry (includes multiple ancestries): 39.8% German, 15.2% Irish, 12.6% American, 11.9% English, 3.9% Dutch (2008-2012 5-year est.).

Economy: Single-family building permits issued: 1 (2013); Multi-family building permits issued: 0 (2013); Homeowner vacancy rate: 0.0%. Rental vacancy rate: 23.4%. (2008-2012 5-year est.); Employment by occupation: 12.5% management, business, and financial, 5.0% computer, engineering, and science, 7.9% education, legal, community service, arts, and media, 4.8% healthcare practitioners, 15.2% service, 26.2% sales and office, 8.1% natural resources, construction, and maintenance, 20.4% production, transportation, and material moving (2008-2012 5-year est.).

Income: Per capita income: $29,912 (2008-2012 5-year est.); Median household income: $53,393 (2008-2012 5-year est.); Average household income: $71,326 (2008-2012 5-year est.); Percent of households with income of $100,000 or more: 20.3% (2008-2012 5-year est.); Poverty rate: 6.9% (2008-2012 5-year est.).

Education: Percent of population age 25 and over with: High school diploma (including GED) or higher: 87.8% (2008-2012 5-year est.); Bachelor's degree or higher: 20.1% (2008-2012 5-year est.); Master's degree or higher: 4.4% (2008-2012 5-year est.).

School District(s)

Olympia CUSD 16 (PK-12)

   2011-12 Enrollment: 1,940 . . . . (309) 379-6011

Housing: Homeownership rate: 76.9% (2008-2012 5-year est.); Median home value: $110,900 (2008-2012 5-year est.); Median contract rent: $520 per month (2008-2012 5-year est.); Median year structure built: 1966 (2008-2012 5-year est.).

Health Insurance: 78.0% Private; 40.1% Public; 5.6% None. (2008-2012 5-year est.)

Transportation: Commute to work: 94.4% car, 1.2% public transportation, 3.6% walk, 0.2% work from home (2008-2012 5-year est.); Travel time to work: 28.7% less than 15 minutes, 15.0% 15 to 30 minutes, 45.3% 30 to 45 minutes, 7.8% 45 to 60 minutes, 3.2% 60 minutes or more (2008-2012 5-year est.)

MORTON (village). Covers a land area of 12.953 square miles and a water area of 0.044 square miles. Located at 40.61° N. Lat; 89.47° W. Long. Elevation is 715 feet.

History: Incorporated 1877.

Population: 13,799 (1990); 15,198 (2000); 16,267 (2010); Density: 1,254.9 persons per square mile (2008-2012 5-year est.); Race: 97.4% White, 0.9% Black/African American, 0.4% Asian, 0.0% American Indian/Alaska Native, 0.0% Native Hawaiian/Other Pacific Islander, 1.3% Some other race, 1.3% Two or more races, 0.8% Hispanic of any race (2008-2012 5-year est.); Average household size: 2.45 (2008-2012 5-year est.); Median age: 40.1 (2008-2012 5-year est.); Males per 100 females: 101.0 (2008-2012 5-year est.); Marriage status: 23.0% never married, 62.1% now married, 6.7% widowed, 8.2% divorced (2008-2012 5-year est.); Foreign born: 1.9% (2008-2012 5-year est.); Ancestry (includes multiple ancestries): 44.0% German, 14.0% English, 13.5% Irish, 9.3% American, 4.9% Italian (2008-2012 5-year est.).

Economy: Single-family building permits issued: 49 (2013); Multi-family building permits issued: 4 (2013); Homeowner vacancy rate: 2.6%. Rental

vacancy rate: 7.0%. (2008-2012 5-year est.); Employment by occupation: 19.4% management, business, and financial, 7.2% computer, engineering, and science, 9.5% education, legal, community service, arts, and media, 9.5% healthcare practitioners, 13.1% service, 24.8% sales and office, 4.4% natural resources, construction, and maintenance, 12.2% production, transportation, and material moving (2008-2012 5-year est.).

Income: Per capita income: $34,823 (2008-2012 5-year est.); Median household income: $70,510 (2008-2012 5-year est.); Average household income: $85,521 (2008-2012 5-year est.); Percent of households with income of $100,000 or more: 30.0% (2008-2012 5-year est.); Poverty rate: 5.3% (2008-2012 5-year est.).

Taxes: Total city taxes per capita: $276 (2011); City property taxes per capita: $123 (2011).

Education: Percent of population age 25 and over with: High school diploma (including GED) or higher: 94.7% (2008-2012 5-year est.); Bachelor's degree or higher: 43.9% (2008-2012 5-year est.); Master's degree or higher: 12.7% (2008-2012 5-year est.).

School District(s)

Morton CUSD 709 (PK-12)
　　2011-12 Enrollment: 2,817 . . . . (309) 263-2581

Housing: Homeownership rate: 76.5% (2008-2012 5-year est.); Median home value: $175,000 (2008-2012 5-year est.); Median contract rent: $671 per month (2008-2012 5-year est.); Median year structure built: 1973 (2008-2012 5-year est.).

Health Insurance: 87.6% Private; 24.8% Public; 3.9% None. (2008-2012 5-year est.)

Safety: Violent crime rate: 13.5 per 10,000 population; Property crime rate: 105.5 per 10,000 population (2012).

Transportation: Commute to work: 93.0% car, 0.8% public transportation, 1.8% walk, 3.8% work from home (2008-2012 5-year est.); Travel time to work: 34.7% less than 15 minutes, 47.9% 15 to 30 minutes, 13.6% 30 to 45 minutes, 1.9% 45 to 60 minutes, 1.8% 60 minutes or more (2008-2012 5-year est.)

Additional Information Contacts

Morton Chamber of Commerce. . . . . (309) 263-2491
　　http://www.mortonchamber.org
Village of Morton . . . . (309) 266-5361
　　http://www.morton-il.gov

NORTH PEKIN (village). Covers a land area of 1.679 square miles and a water area of 0.028 square miles. Located at 40.61° N. Lat; 89.62° W. Long. Elevation is 482 feet.

Population: 1,556 (1990); 1,574 (2000); 1,573 (2010); Density: 978.7 persons per square mile (2008-2012 5-year est.); Race: 99.0% White, 0.0% Black/African American, 0.2% Asian, 0.2% American Indian/Alaska Native, 0.0% Native Hawaiian/Other Pacific Islander, 0.6% Some other race, 0.5% Two or more races, 0.0% Hispanic of any race (2008-2012 5-year est.); Average household size: 2.52 (2008-2012 5-year est.); Median age: 37.9 (2008-2012 5-year est.); Males per 100 females: 98.4 (2008-2012 5-year est.); Marriage status: 19.7% never married, 61.2% now married, 8.3% widowed, 10.8% divorced (2008-2012 5-year est.); Foreign born: 1.2% (2008-2012 5-year est.); Ancestry (includes multiple ancestries): 38.2% German, 15.6% American, 11.1% Irish, 5.2% English, 5.1% Italian (2008-2012 5-year est.).

Economy: Single-family building permits issued: 3 (2013); Multi-family building permits issued: 0 (2013); Homeowner vacancy rate: 1.3%. Rental vacancy rate: 0.0%. (2008-2012 5-year est.); Employment by occupation: 6.2% management, business, and financial, 1.8% computer, engineering, and science, 8.2% education, legal, community service, arts, and media, 5.2% healthcare practitioners, 18.1% service, 23.5% sales and office, 11.1% natural resources, construction, and maintenance, 25.9% production, transportation, and material moving (2008-2012 5-year est.).

Income: Per capita income: $21,315 (2008-2012 5-year est.); Median household income: $45,208 (2008-2012 5-year est.); Average household income: $53,133 (2008-2012 5-year est.); Percent of households with income of $100,000 or more: 11.7% (2008-2012 5-year est.); Poverty rate: 12.5% (2008-2012 5-year est.).

Education: Percent of population age 25 and over with: High school diploma (including GED) or higher: 81.6% (2008-2012 5-year est.); Bachelor's degree or higher: 9.0% (2008-2012 5-year est.); Master's degree or higher: 1.8% (2008-2012 5-year est.).

School District(s)

N Pekin & Marquette Hght SD 102 (PK-08)
　　2011-12 Enrollment: 669. . . . . (309) 382-2172

Housing: Homeownership rate: 82.4% (2008-2012 5-year est.); Median home value: $90,400 (2008-2012 5-year est.); Median contract rent: $554 per month (2008-2012 5-year est.); Median year structure built: 1956 (2008-2012 5-year est.).

Health Insurance: 68.0% Private; 38.3% Public; 9.7% None. (2008-2012 5-year est.)

Transportation: Commute to work: 97.3% car, 0.0% public transportation, 1.9% walk, 0.9% work from home (2008-2012 5-year est.); Travel time to work: 34.4% less than 15 minutes, 51.2% 15 to 30 minutes, 10.0% 30 to 45 minutes, 1.9% 45 to 60 minutes, 2.5% 60 minutes or more (2008-2012 5-year est.)

PEKIN (city). County seat. Covers a land area of 14.559 square miles and a water area of 0.578 square miles. Located at 40.57° N. Lat; 89.62° W. Long. Elevation is 502 feet.

History: Pekin was settled by pioneers of English descent who came from Virginia, Kentucky, and Tennessee. Abraham Lincoln argued many of his legal cases in the courthouse at Pekin. Incorporated 1948.

Population: 32,254 (1990); 33,857 (2000); 34,094 (2010); Density: 2,314.8 persons per square mile (2008-2012 5-year est.); Race: 95.7% White, 2.4% Black/African American, 0.2% Asian, 0.2% American Indian/Alaska Native, 0.1% Native Hawaiian/Other Pacific Islander, 1.4% Some other race, 1.0% Two or more races, 2.4% Hispanic of any race (2008-2012 5-year est.); Average household size: 2.26 (2008-2012 5-year est.); Median age: 39.7 (2008-2012 5-year est.); Males per 100 females: 94.4 (2008-2012 5-year est.); Marriage status: 26.3% never married, 50.2% now married, 7.8% widowed, 15.8% divorced (2008-2012 5-year est.); Foreign born: 1.0% (2008-2012 5-year est.); Ancestry (includes multiple ancestries): 29.9% German, 15.1% Irish, 14.6% American, 10.3% English, 5.3% Italian (2008-2012 5-year est.).

Economy: Unemployment rate: 7.8% (April 2014); Total civilian labor force: 16,876 (April 2014); Single-family building permits issued: 22 (2013); Multi-family building permits issued: 8 (2013); Homeowner vacancy rate: 1.5%. Rental vacancy rate: 8.0%. (2008-2012 5-year est.); Employment by occupation: 9.9% management, business, and financial, 4.3% computer, engineering, and science, 9.2% education, legal, community service, arts, and media, 5.3% healthcare practitioners, 19.8% service, 25.6% sales and office, 8.5% natural resources, construction, and maintenance, 17.3% production, transportation, and material moving (2008-2012 5-year est.).

Income: Per capita income: $24,451 (2008-2012 5-year est.); Median household income: $46,003 (2008-2012 5-year est.); Average household income: $57,038 (2008-2012 5-year est.); Percent of households with income of $100,000 or more: 13.3% (2008-2012 5-year est.); Poverty rate: 13.5% (2008-2012 5-year est.).

Taxes: Total city taxes per capita: $397 (2011); City property taxes per capita: $188 (2011).

Education: Percent of population age 25 and over with: High school diploma (including GED) or higher: 88.0% (2008-2012 5-year est.); Bachelor's degree or higher: 15.3% (2008-2012 5-year est.); Master's degree or higher: 4.3% (2008-2012 5-year est.).

School District(s)

Pekin CSD 303 (09-12)
　　2011-12 Enrollment: 2,010 . . . . (309) 477-4222
Pekin PSD 108 (PK-08)
　　2011-12 Enrollment: 3,781 . . . . (309) 477-4700
Rankin CSD 98 (KG-08)
　　2011-12 Enrollment: 233. . . . . (309) 346-3182
Tazewell County Area Efe Rds
　　2011-12 Enrollment: n/a . . . . (309) 353-5011
Tazewell-Mason Cntys Sp Ed Assoc (PK-12)
　　2011-12 Enrollment: n/a . . . . (309) 347-5164

Housing: Homeownership rate: 72.1% (2008-2012 5-year est.); Median home value: $99,400 (2008-2012 5-year est.); Median contract rent: $481 per month (2008-2012 5-year est.); Median year structure built: 1960 (2008-2012 5-year est.).

Health Insurance: 69.4% Private; 36.8% Public; 10.1% None. (2008-2012 5-year est.)

Hospitals: Pekin Hospital (125 beds)

Safety: Violent crime rate: 51.5 per 10,000 population; Property crime rate: 267.7 per 10,000 population (2012).

Transportation: Commute to work: 94.8% car, 0.7% public transportation, 2.0% walk, 1.7% work from home (2008-2012 5-year est.); Travel time to work: 42.1% less than 15 minutes, 39.1% 15 to 30 minutes, 14.6% 30 to 45 minutes, 2.6% 45 to 60 minutes, 1.6% 60 minutes or more (2008-2012 5-year est.)

Airports: Pekin Municipal Airport (general aviation)
Additional Information Contacts
City of Pekin . . . . (309) 477-2300
http://www.ci.pekin.il.us
Pekin Area Chamber of Commerce . . . . (309) 346-2106
http://www.pekinchamber.com

SOUTH PEKIN (village). Covers a land area of 0.500 square miles
and a water area of 0 square miles. Located at 40.50° N. Lat; 89.65° W.
Long. Elevation is 515 feet.
History: Incorporated 1917.
Population: 1,184 (1990); 1,162 (2000); 1,146 (2010); Density: 2,450.5
persons per square mile (2008-2012 5-year est.); Race: 96.8% White,
0.0% Black/African American, 0.3% Asian, 0.0% American Indian/Alaska
Native, 0.0% Native Hawaiian/Other Pacific Islander, 2.9% Some other
race, 2.9% Two or more races, 0.8% Hispanic of any race (2008-2012
5-year est.); Average household size: 2.72 (2008-2012 5-year est.);
Median age: 31.7 (2008-2012 5-year est.); Males per 100 females: 101.6
(2008-2012 5-year est.); Marriage status: 32.4% never married, 50.0%
now married, 6.7% widowed, 11.0% divorced (2008-2012 5-year est.);
Foreign born: 0.3% (2008-2012 5-year est.); Ancestry (includes multiple
ancestries): 27.2% German, 20.6% American, 17.8% Irish, 11.7% English,
4.2% Italian (2008-2012 5-year est.).
Economy: Single-family building permits issued: 1 (2013); Multi-family
building permits issued: 0 (2013); Homeowner vacancy rate: 0.0%. Rental
vacancy rate: 16.0%. (2008-2012 5-year est.); Employment by occupation:
4.6% management, business, and financial, 3.7% computer, engineering,
and science, 6.5% education, legal, community service, arts, and media,
4.2% healthcare practitioners, 18.1% service, 28.1% sales and office,
11.6% natural resources, construction, and maintenance, 23.2%
production, transportation, and material moving (2008-2012 5-year est.).
Income: Per capita income: $18,772 (2008-2012 5-year est.); Median
household income: $46,810 (2008-2012 5-year est.); Average household
income: $51,049 (2008-2012 5-year est.); Percent of households with
income of $100,000 or more: 6.0% (2008-2012 5-year est.); Poverty rate:
23.3% (2008-2012 5-year est.).
Education: Percent of population age 25 and over with: High school
diploma (including GED) or higher: 92.0% (2008-2012 5-year est.);
Bachelor's degree or higher: 5.7% (2008-2012 5-year est.); Master's
degree or higher: 1.2% (2008-2012 5-year est.).
School District(s)
South Pekin SD 137 (PK-08)
    2011-12 Enrollment: 221 . . . . (309) 348-3695
Housing: Homeownership rate: 72.7% (2008-2012 5-year est.); Median
home value: $79,700 (2008-2012 5-year est.); Median contract rent: $524
per month (2008-2012 5-year est.); Median year structure built: 1958
(2008-2012 5-year est.).
Health Insurance: 59.8% Private; 39.9% Public; 10.8% None. (2008-2012
5-year est.)
Safety: Violent crime rate: 43.6 per 10,000 population; Property crime rate:
139.4 per 10,000 population (2012).
Transportation: Commute to work: 95.0% car, 0.0% public transportation,
3.6% walk, 1.4% work from home (2008-2012 5-year est.); Travel time to
work: 35.6% less than 15 minutes, 23.8% 15 to 30 minutes, 33.9% 30 to
45 minutes, 6.0% 45 to 60 minutes, 0.7% 60 minutes or more (2008-2012
5-year est.)

TREMONT (village). Covers a land area of 0.944 square miles and a
water area of 0 square miles. Located at 40.52° N. Lat; 89.49° W. Long.
Elevation is 643 feet.
Population: 2,088 (1990); 2,029 (2000); 2,236 (2010); Density: 2,384.4
persons per square mile (2008-2012 5-year est.); Race: 95.2% White,
0.3% Black/African American, 0.5% Asian, 0.0% American Indian/Alaska
Native, 0.0% Native Hawaiian/Other Pacific Islander, 4.0% Some other
race, 3.7% Two or more races, 1.5% Hispanic of any race (2008-2012
5-year est.); Average household size: 2.53 (2008-2012 5-year est.);
Median age: 39.6 (2008-2012 5-year est.); Males per 100 females: 95.3
(2008-2012 5-year est.); Marriage status: 19.3% never married, 69.1%
now married, 6.6% widowed, 5.0% divorced (2008-2012 5-year est.);
Foreign born: 1.5% (2008-2012 5-year est.); Ancestry (includes multiple
ancestries): 45.0% German, 12.8% American, 12.8% Irish, 11.7% English,
5.0% Swiss (2008-2012 5-year est.).
Economy: Single-family building permits issued: 1 (2013); Multi-family
building permits issued: 0 (2013); Homeowner vacancy rate: 0.0%. Rental
vacancy rate: 0.0%. (2008-2012 5-year est.); Employment by occupation:

17.3% management, business, and financial, 4.4% computer, engineering,
and science, 10.8% education, legal, community service, arts, and media,
6.3% healthcare practitioners, 14.1% service, 24.5% sales and office,
6.7% natural resources, construction, and maintenance, 16.0% production,
transportation, and material moving (2008-2012 5-year est.).
Income: Per capita income: $30,181 (2008-2012 5-year est.); Median
household income: $61,438 (2008-2012 5-year est.); Average household
income: $75,732 (2008-2012 5-year est.); Percent of households with
income of $100,000 or more: 20.8% (2008-2012 5-year est.); Poverty rate:
2.3% (2008-2012 5-year est.).
Education: Percent of population age 25 and over with: High school
diploma (including GED) or higher: 94.9% (2008-2012 5-year est.);
Bachelor's degree or higher: 25.4% (2008-2012 5-year est.); Master's
degree or higher: 7.0% (2008-2012 5-year est.).
School District(s)
Tremont CUSD 702 (PK-12)
    2011-12 Enrollment: 980 . . . . (309) 925-3461
Housing: Homeownership rate: 78.0% (2008-2012 5-year est.); Median
home value: $150,200 (2008-2012 5-year est.); Median contract rent: $595
per month (2008-2012 5-year est.); Median year structure built: 1967
(2008-2012 5-year est.).
Health Insurance: 89.6% Private; 20.9% Public; 2.4% None. (2008-2012
5-year est.)
Transportation: Commute to work: 92.4% car, 0.0% public transportation,
2.2% walk, 4.5% work from home (2008-2012 5-year est.); Travel time to
work: 30.0% less than 15 minutes, 40.9% 15 to 30 minutes, 23.5% 30 to
45 minutes, 1.7% 45 to 60 minutes, 3.9% 60 minutes or more (2008-2012
5-year est.)

WASHINGTON (city). Covers a land area of 8.175 square miles and
a water area of 0.012 square miles. Located at 40.70° N. Lat; 89.44° W.
Long. Elevation is 761 feet.
History: Incorporated 1857.
Population: 10,099 (1990); 10,841 (2000); 15,134 (2010); Density:
1,841.2 persons per square mile (2008-2012 5-year est.); Race: 95.3%
White, 0.3% Black/African American, 1.6% Asian, 0.0% American
Indian/Alaska Native, 0.0% Native Hawaiian/Other Pacific Islander, 2.8%
Some other race, 2.4% Two or more races, 1.5% Hispanic of any race
(2008-2012 5-year est.); Average household size: 2.58 (2008-2012 5-year
est.); Median age: 37.4 (2008-2012 5-year est.); Males per 100 females:
93.8 (2008-2012 5-year est.); Marriage status: 19.1% never married,
65.8% now married, 5.6% widowed, 9.5% divorced (2008-2012 5-year
est.); Foreign born: 2.6% (2008-2012 5-year est.); Ancestry (includes
multiple ancestries): 36.2% German, 16.4% Irish, 11.9% English, 10.2%
American, 4.6% Italian (2008-2012 5-year est.).
Economy: Single-family building permits issued: 57 (2013); Multi-family
building permits issued: 52 (2013); Homeowner vacancy rate: 0.5%. Rental
vacancy rate: 4.4%. (2008-2012 5-year est.); Employment by occupation:
17.4% management, business, and financial, 8.0% computer, engineering,
and science, 11.0% education, legal, community service, arts, and media,
7.5% healthcare practitioners, 12.7% service, 24.4% sales and office,
6.8% natural resources, construction, and maintenance, 12.2% production,
transportation, and material moving (2008-2012 5-year est.).
Income: Per capita income: $31,495 (2008-2012 5-year est.); Median
household income: $67,248 (2008-2012 5-year est.); Average household
income: $81,476 (2008-2012 5-year est.); Percent of households with
income of $100,000 or more: 30.3% (2008-2012 5-year est.); Poverty rate:
6.3% (2008-2012 5-year est.).
Education: Percent of population age 25 and over with: High school
diploma (including GED) or higher: 95.8% (2008-2012 5-year est.);
Bachelor's degree or higher: 38.1% (2008-2012 5-year est.); Master's
degree or higher: 11.1% (2008-2012 5-year est.).
School District(s)
Central SD 51 (PK-08)
    2011-12 Enrollment: 1,135 . . . . (309) 444-3943
District 50 Schools (KG-08)
    2011-12 Enrollment: 780 . . . . (309) 745-8914
Washington CHSD 308 (09-12)
    2011-12 Enrollment: 1,189 . . . . (309) 444-7704
Washington SD 52 (PK-08)
    2011-12 Enrollment: 922 . . . . (309) 444-4182
Housing: Homeownership rate: 75.0% (2008-2012 5-year est.); Median
home value: $166,100 (2008-2012 5-year est.); Median contract rent: $584
per month (2008-2012 5-year est.); Median year structure built: 1973
(2008-2012 5-year est.).

Health Insurance: 85.7% Private; 22.7% Public; 5.2% None. (2008-2012 5-year est.)

Safety: Violent crime rate: 14.5 per 10,000 population; Property crime rate: 102.2 per 10,000 population (2012).

Transportation: Commute to work: 96.5% car, 0.2% public transportation, 0.8% walk, 2.4% work from home (2008-2012 5-year est.); Travel time to work: 23.7% less than 15 minutes, 53.6% 15 to 30 minutes, 15.4% 30 to 45 minutes, 4.5% 45 to 60 minutes, 2.8% 60 minutes or more (2008-2012 5-year est.)

Additional Information Contacts

City of Washington . . . . (309) 444-3196
   http://ci.washington.il.us
Washington Chamber of Commerce . . . . (309) 444-9921
   http://washingtonilcoc.com

Union County

Located in southern Illinois; bounded on the west by the Mississippi River and the Missouri border; drained by the Cache River; includes part of Shawnee National Forest. Covers a land area of 413.459 square miles, a water area of 8.689 square miles, and is located in the Central Time Zone at 37.48° N. Lat., 89.25° W. Long. The county was founded in 1818. County seat is Jonesboro.

Weather Station: Anna 2 NNE   Elevation: 600 feet

	Jan	Feb	Mar	Apr	May	Jun	Jul	Aug	Sep	Oct	Nov	Dec
High	43	48	58	69	77	85	89	89	81	70	58	46
Low	25	28	36	45	55	63	67	66	57	46	37	28
Precip	3.7	3.5	4.6	4.5	5.9	4.4	3.4	3.2	3.3	4.3	4.8	4.5
Snow	3.4	3.9	1.1	0.1	0.0	0.0	0.0	0.0	0.0	0.1	0.3	2.6

High and Low temperatures in degrees Fahrenheit; Precipitation and Snow in inches

Population: 17,619 (1990); 18,293 (2000); 17,808 (2010); Race: 95.9% White, 2.0% Black/African American, 0.2% Asian, 0.1% American Indian/Alaska Native, 0.0% Native Hawaiian/Other Pacific Islander, 1.8% Some other race, 0.8% Two or more races, 4.8% Hispanic of any race (2008-2012 5-year est.); Density: 42.7 persons per square mile (2008-2012 5-year est.); Average household size: 2.47 (2008-2012 5-year est.); Median age: 43.3 (2008-2012 5-year est.); Males per 100 females: 100.4 (2008-2012 5-year est.).

Religion: Six largest groups: 45.4% Baptist, 6.7% Catholicism, 6.3% Lutheran, 2.5% Methodist/Pietist, 2.4% Presbyterian-Reformed, 1.0% Holiness (2010)

Economy: Unemployment rate: 8.8% (April 2014); Total civilian labor force: 7,743 (April 2014); Leading industries: 36.4% health care and social assistance; 19.8% retail trade; 10.6% accommodation & food services (2012); Farms: 623 totaling 121,173 acres (2012); Companies that employ 500 or more persons: 0 (2012); Companies that employ 100 to 499 persons: 4 (2012); Companies that employ less than 100 persons: 347 (2012); Black-owned businesses: n/a (2007); Hispanic-owned businesses: 71 (2007); Asian-owned businesses: n/a (2007); Women-owned businesses: n/a (2007); Single-family building permits issued: 18 (2013); Multi-family building permits issued: 6 (2013).

Income: Per capita income: $20,497 (2008-2012 5-year est.); Median household income: $41,869 (2008-2012 5-year est.); Average household income: $50,827 (2008-2012 5-year est.); Percent of households with income of $100,000 or more: 10.2% (2008-2012 5-year est.); Poverty rate: 19.6% (2008-2012 5-year est.); Bankruptcy rate: 4.87% (2013).

Taxes: Total county taxes per capita: $131 (2011); County property taxes per capita: $118 (2011).

Education: Percent of population age 25 and over with: High school diploma (including GED) or higher: 82.5% (2008-2012 5-year est.); Bachelor's degree or higher: 19.1% (2008-2012 5-year est.); Master's degree or higher: 7.6% (2008-2012 5-year est.).

Housing: Homeownership rate: 73.7% (2008-2012 5-year est.); Median home value: $89,700 (2008-2012 5-year est.); Median contract rent: $340 per month (2008-2012 5-year est.); Median year structure built: 1965 (2008-2012 5-year est.)

Health: Birth rate: 93.8 per 10,000 population (2013); Death rate: 123.4 per 10,000 population (2013); Age-adjusted cancer mortality rate: 210.0 deaths per 100,000 population (2011); Number of physicians: 12.4 per 10,000 population (2011); Hospital beds: 70.8 per 10,000 population (2010); Hospital admissions: 771.6 per 10,000 population (2010).

Elections: 2012 Presidential election results: 37.9% Obama, 59.8% Romney

National and State Parks: Larue-Pine Hills National Natural Landmark; Trail of Tears State Forest; Union County State Conservation Area; Union County State Forest

Additional Information Contacts

Union County Government . . . . (618) 833-5711
   http://blog.unioncountyil.gov

Union County Communities

ALTO PASS (village). Covers a land area of 2.134 square miles and a water area of 0.030 square miles. Located at 37.57° N. Lat; 89.32° W. Long. Elevation is 748 feet.

Population: 417 (1990); 388 (2000); 391 (2010); Density: 210.0 persons per square mile (2008-2012 5-year est.); Race: 96.4% White, 1.1% Black/African American, 0.4% Asian, 1.3% American Indian/Alaska Native, 0.0% Native Hawaiian/Other Pacific Islander, 0.8% Some other race, 0.7% Two or more races, 18.1% Hispanic of any race (2008-2012 5-year est.); Average household size: 3.03 (2008-2012 5-year est.); Median age: 39.3 (2008-2012 5-year est.); Males per 100 females: 114.4 (2008-2012 5-year est.); Marriage status: 33.8% never married, 47.0% now married, 5.6% widowed, 13.5% divorced (2008-2012 5-year est.); Foreign born: 14.7% (2008-2012 5-year est.); Ancestry (includes multiple ancestries): 21.4% German, 12.1% Irish, 10.9% English, 4.9% Scottish, 3.6% Dutch (2008-2012 5-year est.)

Economy: Homeowner vacancy rate: 3.2%. Rental vacancy rate: 0.0%. (2008-2012 5-year est.); Employment by occupation: 8.3% management, business, and financial, 0.0% computer, engineering, and science, 1.1% education, legal, community service, arts, and media, 0.0% healthcare practitioners, 18.2% service, 29.8% sales and office, 19.9% natural resources, construction, and maintenance, 22.7% production, transportation, and material moving (2008-2012 5-year est.).

Income: Per capita income: $16,011 (2008-2012 5-year est.); Median household income: $29,375 (2008-2012 5-year est.); Average household income: $43,748 (2008-2012 5-year est.); Percent of households with income of $100,000 or more: 9.5% (2008-2012 5-year est.); Poverty rate: 28.1% (2008-2012 5-year est.).

Education: Percent of population age 25 and over with: High school diploma (including GED) or higher: 80.4% (2008-2012 5-year est.); Bachelor's degree or higher: 7.4% (2008-2012 5-year est.); Master's degree or higher: 1.1% (2008-2012 5-year est.).

Housing: Homeownership rate: 77.0% (2008-2012 5-year est.); Median home value: $76,100 (2008-2012 5-year est.); Median contract rent: $325 per month (2008-2012 5-year est.); Median year structure built: 1978 (2008-2012 5-year est.).

Health Insurance: 49.3% Private; 50.7% Public; 13.6% None. (2008-2012 5-year est.)

Transportation: Commute to work: 91.6% car, 0.0% public transportation, 3.4% walk, 5.0% work from home (2008-2012 5-year est.); Travel time to work: 29.4% less than 15 minutes, 37.1% 15 to 30 minutes, 10.6% 30 to 45 minutes, 10.6% 45 to 60 minutes, 12.4% 60 minutes or more (2008-2012 5-year est.)

ANNA (city). Covers a land area of 3.500 square miles and a water area of 0.019 square miles. Located at 37.47° N. Lat; 89.24° W. Long. Elevation is 630 feet.

History: Incorporated 1865.

Population: 4,805 (1990); 5,136 (2000); 4,442 (2010); Density: 1,277.1 persons per square mile (2008-2012 5-year est.); Race: 96.9% White, 2.3% Black/African American, 0.1% Asian, 0.0% American Indian/Alaska Native, 0.0% Native Hawaiian/Other Pacific Islander, 0.7% Some other race, 0.7% Two or more races, 0.5% Hispanic of any race (2008-2012 5-year est.); Average household size: 2.05 (2008-2012 5-year est.); Median age: 46.4 (2008-2012 5-year est.); Males per 100 females: 96.0 (2008-2012 5-year est.); Marriage status: 22.2% never married, 41.5% now married, 13.6% widowed, 22.7% divorced (2008-2012 5-year est.); Foreign born: 1.2% (2008-2012 5-year est.); Ancestry (includes multiple ancestries): 27.1% German, 9.6% Irish, 9.2% American, 7.1% English, 4.1% Swedish (2008-2012 5-year est.).

Economy: Single-family building permits issued: 1 (2013); Multi-family building permits issued: 0 (2013); Homeowner vacancy rate: 6.1%. Rental vacancy rate: 0.0%. (2008-2012 5-year est.); Employment by occupation: 1.7% management, business, and financial, 0.0% computer, engineering, and science, 10.3% education, legal, community service, arts, and media, 8.7% healthcare practitioners, 30.1% service, 26.2% sales and office,

12.8% natural resources, construction, and maintenance, 10.2% production, transportation, and material moving (2008-2012 5-year est.).
Income: Per capita income: $20,564 (2008-2012 5-year est.); Median household income: $33,779 (2008-2012 5-year est.); Average household income: $43,841 (2008-2012 5-year est.); Percent of households with income of $100,000 or more: 5.9% (2008-2012 5-year est.); Poverty rate: 19.0% (2008-2012 5-year est.).
Education: Percent of population age 25 and over with: High school diploma (including GED) or higher: 75.0% (2008-2012 5-year est.); Bachelor's degree or higher: 13.6% (2008-2012 5-year est.); Master's degree or higher: 7.8% (2008-2012 5-year est.).

School District(s)
Alxndr/john/masc/pulski/unon Roe (06-12)
   2011-12 Enrollment: n/a . . . . (618) 634-2292
Anna CCSD 37 (PK-08)
   2011-12 Enrollment: 765. (618) 833-6812
Anna Jonesboro CHSD 81 (09-12)
   2011-12 Enrollment: 522. (618) 833-8421
Five County Reg Voc System
   2011-12 Enrollment: n/a . . . . (618) 747-2703
Tri-County Sp Ed Jnt Agreement
   2011-12 Enrollment: n/a . . . . (618) 684-2109
Housing: Homeownership rate: 59.2% (2008-2012 5-year est.); Median home value: $74,700 (2008-2012 5-year est.); Median contract rent: $330 per month (2008-2012 5-year est.); Median year structure built: 1953 (2008-2012 5-year est.).
Health Insurance: 48.9% Private; 55.8% Public; 10.9% None. (2008-2012 5-year est.)
Hospitals: Union County Hospital District (58 beds)
Safety: Violent crime rate: 38.4 per 10,000 population; Property crime rate: 294.0 per 10,000 population (2012).
Transportation: Commute to work: 91.3% car, 0.7% public transportation, 8.0% walk, 0.0% work from home (2008-2012 5-year est.); Travel time to work: 62.9% less than 15 minutes, 11.2% 15 to 30 minutes, 19.2% 30 to 45 minutes, 2.8% 45 to 60 minutes, 3.9% 60 minutes or more (2008-2012 5-year est.)
Additional Information Contacts
City of Anna. . . . . (618) 833-8528
   http://www.cityofanna.net

COBDEN (village). Covers a land area of 1.219 square miles and a water area of 0.009 square miles. Located at 37.53° N. Lat; 89.25° W. Long. Elevation is 587 feet.
History: Cobden was named for an English director of the railroad. The town grew as a fruit shipping station on the Illinois Central Railroad.
Population: 1,090 (1990); 1,116 (2000); 1,157 (2010); Density: 1,084.4 persons per square mile (2008-2012 5-year est.); Race: 77.2% White, 11.3% Black/African American, 0.1% Asian, 0.0% American Indian/Alaska Native, 0.0% Native Hawaiian/Other Pacific Islander, 11.4% Some other race, 1.4% Two or more races, 30.0% Hispanic of any race (2008-2012 5-year est.); Average household size: 2.90 (2008-2012 5-year est.); Median age: 38.7 (2008-2012 5-year est.); Males per 100 females: 122.9 (2008-2012 5-year est.); Marriage status: 34.9% never married, 45.2% now married, 11.5% widowed, 8.4% divorced (2008-2012 5-year est.); Foreign born: 16.0% (2008-2012 5-year est.); Ancestry (includes multiple ancestries): 14.6% German, 11.7% Irish, 6.3% English, 5.0% American, 3.6% French (2008-2012 5-year est.).
Economy: Single-family building permits issued: 2 (2013); Multi-family building permits issued: 6 (2013); Homeowner vacancy rate: 3.8%. Rental vacancy rate: 6.2%. (2008-2012 5-year est.); Employment by occupation: 3.5% management, business, and financial, 5.5% computer, engineering, and science, 12.7% education, legal, community service, arts, and media, 7.4% healthcare practitioners, 16.9% service, 24.6% sales and office, 12.9% natural resources, construction, and maintenance, 16.5% production, transportation, and material moving (2008-2012 5-year est.).
Income: Per capita income: $18,092 (2008-2012 5-year est.); Median household income: $40,288 (2008-2012 5-year est.); Average household income: $47,598 (2008-2012 5-year est.); Percent of households with income of $100,000 or more: 9.4% (2008-2012 5-year est.); Poverty rate: 23.3% (2008-2012 5-year est.).
Education: Percent of population age 25 and over with: High school diploma (including GED) or higher: 78.7% (2008-2012 5-year est.); Bachelor's degree or higher: 22.2% (2008-2012 5-year est.); Master's degree or higher: 8.5% (2008-2012 5-year est.).

School District(s)
Cobden Sud 17 (PK-12)
   2011-12 Enrollment: 572. (618) 893-2313
Five County Reg Voc System
   2011-12 Enrollment: n/a . . . . (618) 747-2703
Housing: Homeownership rate: 68.6% (2008-2012 5-year est.); Median home value: $75,900 (2008-2012 5-year est.); Median contract rent: $385 per month (2008-2012 5-year est.); Median year structure built: 1947 (2008-2012 5-year est.).
Health Insurance: 51.7% Private; 35.7% Public; 20.7% None. (2008-2012 5-year est.)
Safety: Violent crime rate: 26.1 per 10,000 population; Property crime rate: 112.9 per 10,000 population (2012).
Transportation: Commute to work: 94.8% car, 0.0% public transportation, 0.0% walk, 5.2% work from home (2008-2012 5-year est.); Travel time to work: 23.4% less than 15 minutes, 29.7% 15 to 30 minutes, 22.6% 30 to 45 minutes, 8.4% 45 to 60 minutes, 16.0% 60 minutes or more (2008-2012 5-year est.)

DONGOLA (village). Covers a land area of 1.089 square miles and a water area of 0.057 square miles. Located at 37.36° N. Lat; 89.16° W. Long. Elevation is 394 feet.
Population: 728 (1990); 806 (2000); 726 (2010); Density: 806.3 persons per square mile (2008-2012 5-year est.); Race: 97.8% White, 1.6% Black/African American, 0.0% Asian, 0.0% American Indian/Alaska Native, 0.0% Native Hawaiian/Other Pacific Islander, 0.6% Some other race, 0.6% Two or more races, 0.6% Hispanic of any race (2008-2012 5-year est.); Average household size: 2.68 (2008-2012 5-year est.); Median age: 36.8 (2008-2012 5-year est.); Males per 100 females: 101.4 (2008-2012 5-year est.); Marriage status: 28.7% never married, 57.5% now married, 6.1% widowed, 7.7% divorced (2008-2012 5-year est.); Foreign born: 0.0% (2008-2012 5-year est.); Ancestry (includes multiple ancestries): 19.8% Irish, 16.3% German, 8.4% Dutch, 5.8% American, 4.9% Polish (2008-2012 5-year est.).
Economy: Homeowner vacancy rate: 4.4%. Rental vacancy rate: 9.8%. (2008-2012 5-year est.); Employment by occupation: 8.5% management, business, and financial, 5.0% computer, engineering, and science, 14.3% education, legal, community service, arts, and media, 5.8% healthcare practitioners, 19.5% service, 15.7% sales and office, 7.6% natural resources, construction, and maintenance, 23.6% production, transportation, and material moving (2008-2012 5-year est.).
Income: Per capita income: $17,750 (2008-2012 5-year est.); Median household income: $40,250 (2008-2012 5-year est.); Average household income: $43,200 (2008-2012 5-year est.); Percent of households with income of $100,000 or more: 6.1% (2008-2012 5-year est.); Poverty rate: 22.9% (2008-2012 5-year est.).
Education: Percent of population age 25 and over with: High school diploma (including GED) or higher: 84.6% (2008-2012 5-year est.); Bachelor's degree or higher: 7.4% (2008-2012 5-year est.); Master's degree or higher: 0.5% (2008-2012 5-year est.).

School District(s)
Dongola USD 66 (PK-12)
   2011-12 Enrollment: 296. (618) 827-3841
Housing: Homeownership rate: 66.2% (2008-2012 5-year est.); Median home value: $64,400 (2008-2012 5-year est.); Median contract rent: $331 per month (2008-2012 5-year est.); Median year structure built: 1955 (2008-2012 5-year est.).
Health Insurance: 43.6% Private; 48.4% Public; 21.1% None. (2008-2012 5-year est.)
Transportation: Commute to work: 87.1% car, 0.0% public transportation, 7.1% walk, 5.9% work from home (2008-2012 5-year est.); Travel time to work: 28.1% less than 15 minutes, 32.2% 15 to 30 minutes, 15.6% 30 to 45 minutes, 10.3% 45 to 60 minutes, 13.8% 60 minutes or more (2008-2012 5-year est.)

JONESBORO (city). County seat. Covers a land area of 2.700 square miles and a water area of 0.006 square miles. Located at 37.45° N. Lat; 89.27° W. Long. Elevation is 564 feet.
History: Jonesboro was platted in 1816 and named for a physician who was a resident there.
Population: 1,728 (1990); 1,853 (2000); 1,821 (2010); Density: 701.7 persons per square mile (2008-2012 5-year est.); Race: 96.5% White, 0.7% Black/African American, 0.0% Asian, 0.4% American Indian/Alaska Native, 0.0% Native Hawaiian/Other Pacific Islander, 2.4% Some other race, 0.6% Two or more races, 4.6% Hispanic of any race (2008-2012

5-year est.); Average household size: 2.60 (2008-2012 5-year est.); Median age: 35.9 (2008-2012 5-year est.); Males per 100 females: 86.1 (2008-2012 5-year est.); Marriage status: 30.4% never married, 46.6% now married, 7.6% widowed, 15.4% divorced (2008-2012 5-year est.); Foreign born: 0.8% (2008-2012 5-year est.); Ancestry (includes multiple ancestries): 30.5% German, 15.7% Irish, 10.6% American, 10.1% English, 2.4% French (2008-2012 5-year est.).

Economy: Single-family building permits issued: 1 (2013); Multi-family building permits issued: 0 (2013); Homeowner vacancy rate: 1.5%. Rental vacancy rate: 13.4%. (2008-2012 5-year est.); Employment by occupation: 7.7% management, business, and financial, 2.2% computer, engineering, and science, 14.9% education, legal, community service, arts, and media, 7.7% healthcare practitioners, 26.1% service, 23.7% sales and office, 5.7% natural resources, construction, and maintenance, 11.9% production, transportation, and material moving (2008-2012 5-year est.).

Income: Per capita income: $18,026 (2008-2012 5-year est.); Median household income: $34,241 (2008-2012 5-year est.); Average household income: $47,412 (2008-2012 5-year est.); Percent of households with income of $100,000 or more: 11.7% (2008-2012 5-year est.); Poverty rate: 25.2% (2008-2012 5-year est.).

Education: Percent of population age 25 and over with: High school diploma (including GED) or higher: 79.3% (2008-2012 5-year est.); Bachelor's degree or higher: 19.2% (2008-2012 5-year est.); Master's degree or higher: 4.2% (2008-2012 5-year est.).

School District(s)
Jonesboro CCSD 43 (PK-08)
   2011-12 Enrollment: 423 . . . . (618) 833-6651

Housing: Homeownership rate: 72.4% (2008-2012 5-year est.); Median home value: $83,900 (2008-2012 5-year est.); Median contract rent: $411 per month (2008-2012 5-year est.); Median year structure built: 1965 (2008-2012 5-year est.).

Health Insurance: 51.1% Private; 52.0% Public; 9.8% None. (2008-2012 5-year est.)

Transportation: Commute to work: 94.2% car, 0.7% public transportation, 0.4% walk, 1.3% work from home (2008-2012 5-year est.); Travel time to work: 43.0% less than 15 minutes, 22.9% 15 to 30 minutes, 22.0% 30 to 45 minutes, 5.8% 45 to 60 minutes, 6.3% 60 minutes or more (2008-2012 5-year est.)

MILL CREEK (village). Aka Millcreek. Covers a land area of 0.376 square miles and a water area of 0.006 square miles. Located at 37.34° N. Lat; 89.25° W. Long. Elevation is 381 feet.

Population: 87 (1990); 76 (2000); 65 (2010); Density: 212.8 persons per square mile (2008-2012 5-year est.); Race: 100.0% White, 0.0% Black/African American, 0.0% Asian, 0.0% American Indian/Alaska Native, 0.0% Native Hawaiian/Other Pacific Islander, 0.0% Some other race, 0.0% Two or more races, 0.0% Hispanic of any race (2008-2012 5-year est.); Average household size: 3.64 (2008-2012 5-year est.); Median age: 30.7 (2008-2012 5-year est.); Males per 100 females: 73.9 (2008-2012 5-year est.); Marriage status: 21.3% never married, 37.7% now married, 13.1% widowed, 27.9% divorced (2008-2012 5-year est.); Foreign born: 0.0% (2008-2012 5-year est.); Ancestry (includes multiple ancestries): 8.8% German, 7.5% Irish, 1.3% Norwegian (2008-2012 5-year est.).

Economy: Homeowner vacancy rate: 0.0%. Rental vacancy rate: 0.0%. (2008-2012 5-year est.); Employment by occupation: 4.9% management, business, and financial, 0.0% computer, engineering, and science, 0.0% education, legal, community service, arts, and media, 0.0% healthcare practitioners, 43.9% service, 12.2% sales and office, 39.0% natural resources, construction, and maintenance, 0.0% production, transportation, and material moving (2008-2012 5-year est.).

Income: Per capita income: $17,201 (2008-2012 5-year est.); Median household income: $51,250 (2008-2012 5-year est.); Average household income: $46,359 (2008-2012 5-year est.); Percent of households with income of $100,000 or more: n/a (2008-2012 5-year est.); Poverty rate: 25.0% (2008-2012 5-year est.).

Education: Percent of population age 25 and over with: High school diploma (including GED) or higher: 57.8% (2008-2012 5-year est.); Bachelor's degree or higher: 13.3% (2008-2012 5-year est.); Master's degree or higher: 0.0% (2008-2012 5-year est.).

Housing: Homeownership rate: 81.8% (2008-2012 5-year est.); Median home value: $65,000 (2008-2012 5-year est.); Median contract rent: n/a per month (2008-2012 5-year est.); Median year structure built: Before 1940 (2008-2012 5-year est.).

Health Insurance: 48.8% Private; 26.3% Public; 27.5% None. (2008-2012 5-year est.)

Transportation: Commute to work: 87.8% car, 0.0% public transportation, 0.0% walk, 2.4% work from home (2008-2012 5-year est.); Travel time to work: 15.0% less than 15 minutes, 17.5% 15 to 30 minutes, 52.5% 30 to 45 minutes, 15.0% 45 to 60 minutes, 0.0% 60 minutes or more (2008-2012 5-year est.)

MILLCREEK (unincorporated postal area)
Zip Code: 62961
   Covers a land area of 0.224 square miles and a water area of 0.005 square miles. Located at 37.33° N. Lat; 89.25° W. Long. Population: 65 (2010); Density: 289.8 persons per square mile (2010); Race: 93.8% White, 0.0% Black/African American, 1.5% Asian, 0.0% American Indian/Alaska Native, 0.0% Native Hawaiian/Other Pacific Islander, 4.7% Some other race, 4.6% Two or more races, 0.0% Hispanic of any race (2010); Average household size: 2.83 (2010); Median age: 31.6 (2010); Males per 100 females: 80.6 (2010); Homeownership rate: 82.6% (2010)

WOLF LAKE (unincorporated postal area)
Zip Code: 62998
   Covers a land area of 46.368 square miles and a water area of 3.953 square miles. Located at 37.51° N. Lat; 89.45° W. Long. Elevation is 354 feet. Population: 419 (2010); Density: 9.0 persons per square mile (2010); Race: 98.8% White, 0.0% Black/African American, 0.2% Asian, 0.0% American Indian/Alaska Native, 0.0% Native Hawaiian/Other Pacific Islander, 1.0% Some other race, 1.0% Two or more races, 0.0% Hispanic of any race (2010); Average household size: 2.41 (2010); Median age: 40.6 (2010); Males per 100 females: 99.5 (2010); Homeownership rate: 76.5% (2010)

Vermilion County

Located in eastern Illinois; bounded on the east by Indiana; drained by the Vermilion and Little Vermilion Rivers; includes Lake Vermilion. Covers a land area of 898.368 square miles, a water area of 2.909 square miles, and is located in the Central Time Zone at 40.19° N. Lat., 87.73° W. Long. The county was founded in 1826. County seat is Danville.

Vermilion County is part of the Danville, IL Metropolitan Statistical Area. The entire metro area includes: Vermilion County, IL

Weather Station: Danville											Elevation: 558 feet	
	Jan	Feb	Mar	Apr	May	Jun	Jul	Aug	Sep	Oct	Nov	Dec
High	35	40	52	65	75	83	86	84	79	66	52	39
Low	19	23	32	42	51	60	65	63	55	44	34	23
Precip	2.2	2.2	3.0	4.0	4.5	4.5	4.6	3.5	2.9	3.6	3.8	2.8
Snow	4.5	4.4	2.1	0.2	tr	0.0	0.0	0.0	0.0	0.2	0.6	4.0

High and Low temperatures in degrees Fahrenheit; Precipitation and Snow in inches

Weather Station: Hoopeston 1 NE											Elevation: 709 feet	
	Jan	Feb	Mar	Apr	May	Jun	Jul	Aug	Sep	Oct	Nov	Dec
High	34	38	50	63	74	83	85	84	78	65	51	37
Low	19	22	31	41	52	61	65	63	55	44	34	23
Precip	1.8	1.9	2.8	3.6	4.4	4.3	4.4	4.0	2.8	3.5	3.1	2.3
Snow	5.5	4.9	1.5	0.4	tr	0.0	0.0	0.0	0.0	0.1	0.6	4.8

High and Low temperatures in degrees Fahrenheit; Precipitation and Snow in inches

Population: 88,257 (1990); 83,919 (2000); 81,625 (2010); Race: 83.1% White, 13.0% Black/African American, 0.6% Asian, 0.2% American Indian/Alaska Native, 0.0% Native Hawaiian/Other Pacific Islander, 3.1% Some other race, 1.9% Two or more races, 4.3% Hispanic of any race (2008-2012 5-year est.); Density: 89.8 persons per square mile (2008-2012 5-year est.); Average household size: 2.50 (2008-2012 5-year est.); Median age: 39.6 (2008-2012 5-year est.); Males per 100 females: 98.1 (2008-2012 5-year est.).

Religion: Six largest groups: 10.7% Baptist, 7.6% Non-denominational Protestant, 5.3% Methodist/Pietist, 4.7% Catholicism, 3.0% Holiness, 2.5% Lutheran (2010)

Economy: Unemployment rate: 8.8% (April 2014); Total civilian labor force: 35,174 (April 2014); Leading industries: 21.8% manufacturing; 21.2% health care and social assistance; 14.5% retail trade (2012); Farms: 956 totaling 434,406 acres (2012); Companies that employ 500 or more persons: 5 (2012); Companies that employ 100 to 499 persons: 35 (2012); Companies that employ less than 100 persons: 1,440 (2012); Black-owned businesses: n/a (2007); Hispanic-owned businesses: n/a (2007); Asian-owned businesses: n/a (2007); Women-owned businesses: 1,661

(2007); Single-family building permits issued: 2 (2013); Multi-family building permits issued: 19 (2013).

Income: Per capita income: $21,169 (2008-2012 5-year est.); Median household income: $40,961 (2008-2012 5-year est.); Average household income: $51,554 (2008-2012 5-year est.); Percent of households with income of $100,000 or more: 10.6% (2008-2012 5-year est.); Poverty rate: 18.9% (2008-2012 5-year est.); Bankruptcy rate: 3.06% (2013).

Taxes: Total county taxes per capita: $153 (2011); County property taxes per capita: $132 (2011).

Education: Percent of population age 25 and over with: High school diploma (including GED) or higher: 85.8% (2008-2012 5-year est.); Bachelor's degree or higher: 13.9% (2008-2012 5-year est.); Master's degree or higher: 4.5% (2008-2012 5-year est.).

Housing: Homeownership rate: 70.8% (2008-2012 5-year est.); Median home value: $77,200 (2008-2012 5-year est.); Median contract rent: $430 per month (2008-2012 5-year est.); Median year structure built: 1955 (2008-2012 5-year est.)

Health: Birth rate: 126.6 per 10,000 population (2013); Death rate: 113.7 per 10,000 population (2013); Age-adjusted cancer mortality rate: 189.2 deaths per 100,000 population (2011); Number of physicians: 11.1 per 10,000 population (2011); Hospital beds: 57.7 per 10,000 population (2010); Hospital admissions: 1,234.8 per 10,000 population (2010).

Elections: 2012 Presidential election results: 41.2% Obama, 56.9% Romney

National and State Parks: Kickapoo State Park; Middle Fork State Fish and Wildlife Areas

Additional Information Contacts
Vermilion County Government . . . . (217) 554-1900
    http://www.co.vermilion.il.us

Vermilion County Communities

ALLERTON (village). Covers a land area of 0.679 square miles and a water area of 0 square miles. Located at 39.92° N. Lat; 87.94° W. Long.

Population: 274 (1990); 293 (2000); 291 (2010); Density: 349.1 persons per square mile (2008-2012 5-year est.); Race: 100.0% White, 0.0% Black/African American, 0.0% Asian, 0.0% American Indian/Alaska Native, 0.0% Native Hawaiian/Other Pacific Islander, 0.0% Some other race, 0.0% Two or more races, 0.0% Hispanic of any race (2008-2012 5-year est.); Average household size: 2.28 (2008-2012 5-year est.); Median age: 45.7 (2008-2012 5-year est.); Males per 100 females: 92.7 (2008-2012 5-year est.); Marriage status: 14.8% never married, 76.2% now married, 2.4% widowed, 6.7% divorced (2008-2012 5-year est.); Foreign born: 0.0% (2008-2012 5-year est.); Ancestry (includes multiple ancestries): 32.1% American, 20.7% German, 19.0% Irish, 13.1% English, 3.0% Scottish (2008-2012 5-year est.).

Economy: Single-family building permits issued: 1 (2013); Multi-family building permits issued: 0 (2013); Homeowner vacancy rate: 4.3%. Rental vacancy rate: 0.0%. (2008-2012 5-year est.); Employment by occupation: 19.3% management, business, and financial, 4.7% computer, engineering, and science, 6.0% education, legal, community service, arts, and media, 5.3% healthcare practitioners, 9.3% service, 24.0% sales and office, 10.7% natural resources, construction, and maintenance, 20.7% production, transportation, and material moving (2008-2012 5-year est.).

Income: Per capita income: $29,047 (2008-2012 5-year est.); Median household income: $65,000 (2008-2012 5-year est.); Average household income: $64,122 (2008-2012 5-year est.); Percent of households with income of $100,000 or more: 11.5% (2008-2012 5-year est.); Poverty rate: 0.0% (2008-2012 5-year est.).

Education: Percent of population age 25 and over with: High school diploma (including GED) or higher: 96.7% (2008-2012 5-year est.); Bachelor's degree or higher: 12.0% (2008-2012 5-year est.); Master's degree or higher: 1.1% (2008-2012 5-year est.).

Housing: Homeownership rate: 86.5% (2008-2012 5-year est.); Median home value: $98,600 (2008-2012 5-year est.); Median contract rent: $475 per month (2008-2012 5-year est.); Median year structure built: 1958 (2008-2012 5-year est.).

Health Insurance: 88.3% Private; 19.0% Public; 3.9% None. (2008-2012 5-year est.)

Transportation: Commute to work: 98.1% car, 0.0% public transportation, 1.9% walk, 0.0% work from home (2008-2012 5-year est.); Travel time to work: 22.4% less than 15 minutes, 30.8% 15 to 30 minutes, 25.0% 30 to 45 minutes, 12.8% 45 to 60 minutes, 9.0% 60 minutes or more (2008-2012 5-year est.)

ALVAN (village). Aka Alvin. Covers a land area of 0.793 square miles and a water area of 0 square miles. Located at 40.31° N. Lat; 87.61° W. Long.

History: Alvin was platted in 1876. The village developed around a grain elevator.

Population: n/a (1990); n/a (2000); 270 (2010); Density: 330.3 persons per square mile (2008-2012 5-year est.); Race: 94.7% White, 0.0% Black/African American, 1.9% Asian, 1.9% American Indian/Alaska Native, 0.0% Native Hawaiian/Other Pacific Islander, 1.5% Some other race, 0.0% Two or more races, 4.6% Hispanic of any race (2008-2012 5-year est.); Average household size: 2.70 (2008-2012 5-year est.); Median age: 44.4 (2008-2012 5-year est.); Males per 100 females: 104.7 (2008-2012 5-year est.); Marriage status: 23.9% never married, 50.5% now married, 6.3% widowed, 19.4% divorced (2008-2012 5-year est.); Foreign born: 2.7% (2008-2012 5-year est.); Ancestry (includes multiple ancestries): 30.5% American, 5.3% German, 5.0% English, 5.0% Irish, 2.3% European (2008-2012 5-year est.).

Economy: Homeowner vacancy rate: 0.0%. Rental vacancy rate: 0.0%. (2008-2012 5-year est.); Employment by occupation: 11.4% management, business, and financial, 1.6% computer, engineering, and science, 1.6% education, legal, community service, arts, and media, 0.8% healthcare practitioners, 21.1% service, 19.5% sales and office, 20.3% natural resources, construction, and maintenance, 23.6% production, transportation, and material moving (2008-2012 5-year est.).

Income: Per capita income: $22,995 (2008-2012 5-year est.); Median household income: $44,063 (2008-2012 5-year est.); Average household income: $54,791 (2008-2012 5-year est.); Percent of households with income of $100,000 or more: 18.6% (2008-2012 5-year est.); Poverty rate: 18.3% (2008-2012 5-year est.).

Education: Percent of population age 25 and over with: High school diploma (including GED) or higher: 86.6% (2008-2012 5-year est.); Bachelor's degree or higher: 4.3% (2008-2012 5-year est.); Master's degree or higher: 0.0% (2008-2012 5-year est.).

Housing: Homeownership rate: 77.3% (2008-2012 5-year est.); Median home value: $67,300 (2008-2012 5-year est.); Median contract rent: $400 per month (2008-2012 5-year est.); Median year structure built: 1958 (2008-2012 5-year est.).

Health Insurance: 70.2% Private; 25.6% Public; 14.5% None. (2008-2012 5-year est.)

Transportation: Commute to work: 98.4% car, 0.0% public transportation, 1.6% walk, 0.0% work from home (2008-2012 5-year est.); Travel time to work: 17.9% less than 15 minutes, 48.0% 15 to 30 minutes, 24.4% 30 to 45 minutes, 1.6% 45 to 60 minutes, 8.1% 60 minutes or more (2008-2012 5-year est.)

ARMSTRONG (unincorporated postal area)
Zip Code: 61812

Covers a land area of 26.674 square miles and a water area of 0 square miles. Located at 40.22° N. Lat; 87.91° W. Long. Elevation is 696 feet. Population: 375 (2010); Density: 14.1 persons per square mile (2010); Race: 96.8% White, 1.9% Black/African American, 0.3% Asian, 0.0% American Indian/Alaska Native, 0.0% Native Hawaiian/Other Pacific Islander, 1.0% Some other race, 0.8% Two or more races, 0.0% Hispanic of any race (2010); Average household size: 2.31 (2010); Median age: 47.6 (2010); Males per 100 females: 109.5 (2010); Homeownership rate: 86.5% (2010)

BELGIUM (village). Covers a land area of 0.434 square miles and a water area of 0 square miles. Located at 40.06° N. Lat; 87.63° W. Long. Elevation is 653 feet.

History: Many of the early residents of Belgium were from the country of Belgium. The village was incorporated in 1909, with coal mining as the major industry.

Population: 511 (1990); 466 (2000); 404 (2010); Density: 1,093.3 persons per square mile (2008-2012 5-year est.); Race: 90.7% White, 5.3% Black/African American, 0.0% Asian, 0.0% American Indian/Alaska Native, 0.0% Native Hawaiian/Other Pacific Islander, 4.0% Some other race, 4.0% Two or more races, 1.3% Hispanic of any race (2008-2012 5-year est.); Average household size: 2.49 (2008-2012 5-year est.); Median age: 40.6 (2008-2012 5-year est.); Males per 100 females: 78.9 (2008-2012 5-year est.); Marriage status: 32.5% never married, 35.8% now married, 7.5% widowed, 24.2% divorced (2008-2012 5-year est.); Foreign born: 0.0% (2008-2012 5-year est.); Ancestry (includes multiple ancestries): 31.0% American, 19.0% Irish, 13.7% German, 13.7% French, 4.2% English (2008-2012 5-year est.).

Economy: Single-family building permits issued: 0 (2013); Multi-family building permits issued: 0 (2013); Homeowner vacancy rate: 0.0%. Rental vacancy rate: 20.0%. (2008-2012 5-year est.); Employment by occupation: 12.0% management, business, and financial, 1.1% computer, engineering, and science, 4.4% education, legal, community service, arts, and media, 1.1% healthcare practitioners, 19.7% service, 29.0% sales and office, 9.8% natural resources, construction, and maintenance, 23.0% production, transportation, and material moving (2008-2012 5-year est.).
Income: Per capita income: $17,610 (2008-2012 5-year est.); Median household income: $33,000 (2008-2012 5-year est.); Average household income: $40,862 (2008-2012 5-year est.); Percent of households with income of $100,000 or more: 3.2% (2008-2012 5-year est.); Poverty rate: 19.2% (2008-2012 5-year est.).
Taxes: Total city taxes per capita: $52 (2011); City property taxes per capita: $15 (2011).
Education: Percent of population age 25 and over with: High school diploma (including GED) or higher: 89.3% (2008-2012 5-year est.); Bachelor's degree or higher: 8.9% (2008-2012 5-year est.); Master's degree or higher: 1.5% (2008-2012 5-year est.).
Housing: Homeownership rate: 68.4% (2008-2012 5-year est.); Median home value: $51,300 (2008-2012 5-year est.); Median contract rent: $393 per month (2008-2012 5-year est.); Median year structure built: 1964 (2008-2012 5-year est.).
Health Insurance: 44.9% Private; 50.8% Public; 20.3% None. (2008-2012 5-year est.)
Safety: Violent crime rate: 0.0 per 10,000 population; Property crime rate: 24.8 per 10,000 population (2012).
Transportation: Commute to work: 96.7% car, 0.0% public transportation, 0.0% walk, 2.2% work from home (2008-2012 5-year est.); Travel time to work: 33.9% less than 15 minutes, 37.9% 15 to 30 minutes, 26.6% 30 to 45 minutes, 1.7% 45 to 60 minutes, 0.0% 60 minutes or more (2008-2012 5-year est.)

BISMARCK (village). Covers a land area of 0.743 square miles and a water area of 0 square miles. Located at 40.26° N. Lat; 87.61° W. Long. Elevation is 646 feet.
Population: n/a (1990); 542 (2000); 579 (2010); Density: 723.6 persons per square mile (2008-2012 5-year est.); Race: 100.0% White, 0.0% Black/African American, 0.0% Asian, 0.0% American Indian/Alaska Native, 0.0% Native Hawaiian/Other Pacific Islander, 0.0% Some other race, 0.0% Two or more races, 0.0% Hispanic of any race (2008-2012 5-year est.); Average household size: 2.38 (2008-2012 5-year est.); Median age: 44.6 (2008-2012 5-year est.); Males per 100 females: 100.0 (2008-2012 5-year est.); Marriage status: 13.4% never married, 71.1% now married, 6.4% widowed, 9.1% divorced (2008-2012 5-year est.); Foreign born: 0.0% (2008-2012 5-year est.); Ancestry (includes multiple ancestries): 27.3% American, 21.0% German, 16.0% Irish, 7.8% English, 2.8% Scotch-Irish (2008-2012 5-year est.).
Economy: Single-family building permits issued: 0 (2013); Multi-family building permits issued: 0 (2013); Homeowner vacancy rate: 0.0%. Rental vacancy rate: 0.0%. (2008-2012 5-year est.); Employment by occupation: 12.5% management, business, and financial, 0.7% computer, engineering, and science, 11.8% education, legal, community service, arts, and media, 5.7% healthcare practitioners, 22.2% service, 28.3% sales and office, 3.2% natural resources, construction, and maintenance, 15.4% production, transportation, and material moving (2008-2012 5-year est.).
Income: Per capita income: $27,680 (2008-2012 5-year est.); Median household income: $55,833 (2008-2012 5-year est.); Average household income: $63,977 (2008-2012 5-year est.); Percent of households with income of $100,000 or more: 16.8% (2008-2012 5-year est.); Poverty rate: 4.1% (2008-2012 5-year est.).
Education: Percent of population age 25 and over with: High school diploma (including GED) or higher: 96.3% (2008-2012 5-year est.); Bachelor's degree or higher: 25.3% (2008-2012 5-year est.); Master's degree or higher: 9.2% (2008-2012 5-year est.).

School District(s)
Bismarck Henning CUSD (KG-12)
    2011-12 Enrollment: 931 . . . . (217) 759-7261
Housing: Homeownership rate: 83.6% (2008-2012 5-year est.); Median home value: $98,500 (2008-2012 5-year est.); Median contract rent: $453 per month (2008-2012 5-year est.); Median year structure built: 1968 (2008-2012 5-year est.).
Health Insurance: 81.6% Private; 32.0% Public; 8.2% None. (2008-2012 5-year est.)

Transportation: Commute to work: 87.3% car, 0.0% public transportation, 2.2% walk, 10.4% work from home (2008-2012 5-year est.); Travel time to work: 22.9% less than 15 minutes, 62.1% 15 to 30 minutes, 6.7% 30 to 45 minutes, 2.1% 45 to 60 minutes, 6.3% 60 minutes or more (2008-2012 5-year est.)

CATLIN (village). Covers a land area of 0.836 square miles and a water area of 0.003 square miles. Located at 40.07° N. Lat; 87.71° W. Long. Elevation is 659 feet.
Population: 2,173 (1990); 2,087 (2000); 2,040 (2010); Density: 2,563.5 persons per square mile (2008-2012 5-year est.); Race: 95.1% White, 4.3% Black/African American, 0.0% Asian, 0.0% American Indian/Alaska Native, 0.0% Native Hawaiian/Other Pacific Islander, 0.6% Some other race, 0.6% Two or more races, 0.5% Hispanic of any race (2008-2012 5-year est.); Average household size: 2.81 (2008-2012 5-year est.); Median age: 35.1 (2008-2012 5-year est.); Males per 100 females: 96.3 (2008-2012 5-year est.); Marriage status: 22.6% never married, 64.5% now married, 5.0% widowed, 8.0% divorced (2008-2012 5-year est.); Foreign born: 0.8% (2008-2012 5-year est.); Ancestry (includes multiple ancestries): 20.1% German, 19.7% American, 16.5% English, 10.9% Irish, 3.5% French (2008-2012 5-year est.).
Economy: Single-family building permits issued: 1 (2013); Multi-family building permits issued: 0 (2013); Homeowner vacancy rate: 0.0%. Rental vacancy rate: 23.4%. (2008-2012 5-year est.); Employment by occupation: 9.0% management, business, and financial, 1.4% computer, engineering, and science, 15.6% education, legal, community service, arts, and media, 10.4% healthcare practitioners, 15.6% service, 25.9% sales and office, 8.0% natural resources, construction, and maintenance, 14.0% production, transportation, and material moving (2008-2012 5-year est.).
Income: Per capita income: $23,297 (2008-2012 5-year est.); Median household income: $58,387 (2008-2012 5-year est.); Average household income: $64,865 (2008-2012 5-year est.); Percent of households with income of $100,000 or more: 17.8% (2008-2012 5-year est.); Poverty rate: 9.6% (2008-2012 5-year est.).
Education: Percent of population age 25 and over with: High school diploma (including GED) or higher: 94.4% (2008-2012 5-year est.); Bachelor's degree or higher: 19.7% (2008-2012 5-year est.); Master's degree or higher: 5.4% (2008-2012 5-year est.).
School District(s)
Catlin CUSD 5 (PK-12)
    2011-12 Enrollment: 533 . . . . (217) 427-2116
Housing: Homeownership rate: 85.4% (2008-2012 5-year est.); Median home value: $95,100 (2008-2012 5-year est.); Median contract rent: $529 per month (2008-2012 5-year est.); Median year structure built: 1964 (2008-2012 5-year est.).
Health Insurance: 84.7% Private; 26.4% Public; 5.8% None. (2008-2012 5-year est.)
Safety: Violent crime rate: 9.8 per 10,000 population; Property crime rate: 186.5 per 10,000 population (2012).
Transportation: Commute to work: 93.2% car, 0.0% public transportation, 3.1% walk, 3.8% work from home (2008-2012 5-year est.); Travel time to work: 20.0% less than 15 minutes, 62.5% 15 to 30 minutes, 9.2% 30 to 45 minutes, 3.1% 45 to 60 minutes, 5.3% 60 minutes or more (2008-2012 5-year est.)

COLLISON (unincorporated postal area)
Zip Code: 61831
    Covers a land area of 11.614 square miles and a water area of 0 square miles. Located at 40.22° N. Lat; 87.79° W. Long. Elevation is 692 feet. Population: 157 (2010); Density: 13.5 persons per square mile (2010); Race: 100.0% White, 0.0% Black/African American, 0.0% Asian, 0.0% American Indian/Alaska Native, 0.0% Native Hawaiian/Other Pacific Islander, 0.0% Some other race, 0.0% Two or more races, 2.5% Hispanic of any race (2010); Average household size: 2.28 (2010); Median age: 50.2 (2010); Males per 100 females: 109.3 (2010); Homeownership rate: 87.0% (2010)

DANVILLE (city). County seat. Covers a land area of 17.888 square miles and a water area of 0.077 square miles. Located at 40.14° N. Lat; 87.61° W. Long. Elevation is 600 feet.
History: Danville had its beginning when a salt works was established in 1824. The town was laid out nearby in 1827 by Dan Beckwith, on land donated by him and Guy W. Smith, and the town was named for Beckwith.
Population: 33,828 (1990); 33,904 (2000); 33,027 (2010); Density: 1,843.5 persons per square mile (2008-2012 5-year est.); Race: 64.1%

White, 30.0% Black/African American, 1.2% Asian, 0.3% American Indian/Alaska Native, 0.0% Native Hawaiian/Other Pacific Islander, 4.4% Some other race, 2.5% Two or more races, 6.1% Hispanic of any race (2008-2012 5-year est.); Average household size: 2.44 (2008-2012 5-year est.); Median age: 36.0 (2008-2012 5-year est.); Males per 100 females: 97.2 (2008-2012 5-year est.); Marriage status: 37.6% never married, 38.7% now married, 8.4% widowed, 15.2% divorced (2008-2012 5-year est.); Foreign born: 3.5% (2008-2012 5-year est.); Ancestry (includes multiple ancestries): 20.7% American, 13.4% German, 7.4% Irish, 5.6% English, 1.7% French (2008-2012 5-year est.).

Economy: Unemployment rate: 9.2% (April 2014); Total civilian labor force: 12,664 (April 2014); Single-family building permits issued: 0 (2013); Multi-family building permits issued: 0 (2013); Homeowner vacancy rate: 6.7%. Rental vacancy rate: 14.5%. (2008-2012 5-year est.); Employment by occupation: 7.9% management, business, and financial, 2.2% computer, engineering, and science, 10.2% education, legal, community service, arts, and media, 5.1% healthcare practitioners, 22.1% service, 23.5% sales and office, 6.2% natural resources, construction, and maintenance, 22.8% production, transportation, and material moving (2008-2012 5-year est.).

Income: Per capita income: $19,464 (2008-2012 5-year est.); Median household income: $35,198 (2008-2012 5-year est.); Average household income: $46,196 (2008-2012 5-year est.); Percent of households with income of $100,000 or more: 8.7% (2008-2012 5-year est.); Poverty rate: 29.1% (2008-2012 5-year est.).

Education: Percent of population age 25 and over with: High school diploma (including GED) or higher: 83.1% (2008-2012 5-year est.); Bachelor's degree or higher: 15.6% (2008-2012 5-year est.); Master's degree or higher: 6.2% (2008-2012 5-year est.).

School District(s)
Danville CCSD 118 (PK-12)
    2011-12 Enrollment: 6,207 . . . . (217) 444-1004
Oakwood CUSD 76 (PK-12)
    2011-12 Enrollment: 1,084 . . . . (217) 354-4355
Vermilion Assoc for Spec Educ
    2011-12 Enrollment: n/a . . . . (217) 443-8273
Vermilion Roe (PK-12)
    2011-12 Enrollment: n/a . . . . (217) 431-2668
Vermilion Voc Ed Deliver System
    2011-12 Enrollment: n/a . . . . (217) 443-8742

Four-year College(s)
Lakeview College of Nursing (Private, Not-for-profit)
    Fall 2012 Enrollment: 294 . . . . (217) 709-0920

Two-year College(s)
Danville Area Community College (Public)
    Fall 2012 Enrollment: 2,967 . . . . (217) 443-3222
    2012-13 Tuition: In-state $6,285; Out-of-state $6,285

Vocational/Technical School(s)
Concept College of Cosmetology (Private, For-profit)
    Fall 2012 Enrollment: 66 . . . . (217) 442-9329
    2012-13 Tuition: $13,675

Housing: Homeownership rate: 58.5% (2008-2012 5-year est.); Median home value: $66,400 (2008-2012 5-year est.); Median contract rent: $435 per month (2008-2012 5-year est.); Median year structure built: 1950 (2008-2012 5-year est.).

Health Insurance: 52.7% Private; 47.6% Public; 13.9% None. (2008-2012 5-year est.)

Hospitals: Danville Veterans Affairs Medical Center (350 beds); Provena United Samaritans Medical Center (210 beds)

Safety: Violent crime rate: 99.4 per 10,000 population; Property crime rate: 600.1 per 10,000 population (2012).

Transportation: Commute to work: 89.3% car, 1.9% public transportation, 4.4% walk, 2.4% work from home (2008-2012 5-year est.); Travel time to work: 64.2% less than 15 minutes, 25.4% 15 to 30 minutes, 6.8% 30 to 45 minutes, 2.1% 45 to 60 minutes, 1.5% 60 minutes or more (2008-2012 5-year est.); Amtrak: Bus service available.

Airports: Vermilion Regional Airport (general aviation)

Additional Information Contacts
City of Danville . . . . (217) 431-2200
    http://www.cityofdanville.org
Vermilion Advantage . . . . (217) 442-6201
    http://www.vermilionadvantage.com

EAST LYNN (unincorporated postal area)
Zip Code: 60932

Covers a land area of 0.740 square miles and a water area of 0 square miles. Located at 40.46° N. Lat; 87.80° W. Long. Elevation is 696 feet.
Population: 78 (2010); Density: 105.3 persons per square mile (2010); Race: 93.6% White, 0.0% Black/African American, 0.0% Asian, 0.0% American Indian/Alaska Native, 0.0% Native Hawaiian/Other Pacific Islander, 6.4% Some other race, 0.0% Two or more races, 14.1% Hispanic of any race (2010); Average household size: 2.69 (2010); Median age: 36.0 (2010); Males per 100 females: 95.0 (2010); Homeownership rate: 75.8% (2010)

FAIRMOUNT (village). Covers a land area of 0.316 square miles and a water area of 0 square miles. Located at 40.05° N. Lat; 87.83° W. Long. Elevation is 666 feet.
Population: 678 (1990); 640 (2000); 642 (2010); Density: 1,760.0 persons per square mile (2008-2012 5-year est.); Race: 99.3% White, 0.0% Black/African American, 0.0% Asian, 0.0% American Indian/Alaska Native, 0.0% Native Hawaiian/Other Pacific Islander, 0.7% Some other race, 0.7% Two or more races, 0.0% Hispanic of any race (2008-2012 5-year est.); Average household size: 2.49 (2008-2012 5-year est.); Median age: 46.0 (2008-2012 5-year est.); Males per 100 females: 89.8 (2008-2012 5-year est.); Marriage status: 20.7% never married, 56.8% now married, 10.8% widowed, 11.7% divorced (2008-2012 5-year est.); Foreign born: 0.0% (2008-2012 5-year est.); Ancestry (includes multiple ancestries): 37.9% American, 14.0% English, 12.6% German, 5.2% Irish, 3.2% Dutch (2008-2012 5-year est.).

Economy: Homeowner vacancy rate: 3.0%. Rental vacancy rate: 16.7%. (2008-2012 5-year est.); Employment by occupation: 4.9% management, business, and financial, 3.4% computer, engineering, and science, 6.5% education, legal, community service, arts, and media, 2.7% healthcare practitioners, 20.2% service, 28.1% sales and office, 12.9% natural resources, construction, and maintenance, 21.3% production, transportation, and material moving (2008-2012 5-year est.).

Income: Per capita income: $21,370 (2008-2012 5-year est.); Median household income: $38,438 (2008-2012 5-year est.); Average household income: $51,203 (2008-2012 5-year est.); Percent of households with income of $100,000 or more: 7.6% (2008-2012 5-year est.); Poverty rate: 11.8% (2008-2012 5-year est.).

Education: Percent of population age 25 and over with: High school diploma (including GED) or higher: 84.8% (2008-2012 5-year est.); Bachelor's degree or higher: 9.0% (2008-2012 5-year est.); Master's degree or higher: 3.0% (2008-2012 5-year est.).

Housing: Homeownership rate: 82.1% (2008-2012 5-year est.); Median home value: $78,000 (2008-2012 5-year est.); Median contract rent: $414 per month (2008-2012 5-year est.); Median year structure built: 1953 (2008-2012 5-year est.).

Health Insurance: 74.6% Private; 36.5% Public; 8.8% None. (2008-2012 5-year est.)

Safety: Violent crime rate: 0.0 per 10,000 population; Property crime rate: 31.2 per 10,000 population (2012).

Transportation: Commute to work: 91.2% car, 0.0% public transportation, 4.4% walk, 3.2% work from home (2008-2012 5-year est.); Travel time to work: 29.0% less than 15 minutes, 37.3% 15 to 30 minutes, 29.0% 30 to 45 minutes, 2.1% 45 to 60 minutes, 2.5% 60 minutes or more (2008-2012 5-year est.)

FITHIAN (village). Covers a land area of 0.383 square miles and a water area of 0 square miles. Located at 40.11° N. Lat; 87.87° W. Long. Elevation is 663 feet.
Population: 512 (1990); 506 (2000); 485 (2010); Density: 1,241.6 persons per square mile (2008-2012 5-year est.); Race: 97.7% White, 0.0% Black/African American, 0.0% Asian, 0.0% American Indian/Alaska Native, 0.0% Native Hawaiian/Other Pacific Islander, 2.3% Some other race, 2.3% Two or more races, 0.0% Hispanic of any race (2008-2012 5-year est.); Average household size: 2.61 (2008-2012 5-year est.); Median age: 40.2 (2008-2012 5-year est.); Males per 100 females: 117.9 (2008-2012 5-year est.); Marriage status: 26.1% never married, 56.8% now married, 2.1% widowed, 15.0% divorced (2008-2012 5-year est.); Foreign born: 0.0% (2008-2012 5-year est.); Ancestry (includes multiple ancestries): 32.2% American, 28.2% German, 17.3% Irish, 5.7% Italian, 4.2% English (2008-2012 5-year est.).

Economy: Single-family building permits issued: 0 (2013); Multi-family building permits issued: 0 (2013); Homeowner vacancy rate: 0.0%. Rental vacancy rate: 0.0%. (2008-2012 5-year est.); Employment by occupation: 5.3% management, business, and financial, 7.2% computer, engineering, and science, 6.4% education, legal, community service, arts, and media,

0.0% healthcare practitioners, 17.4% service, 26.8% sales and office, 15.1% natural resources, construction, and maintenance, 21.9% production, transportation, and material moving (2008-2012 5-year est.).
Income: Per capita income: $24,198 (2008-2012 5-year est.); Median household income: $60,000 (2008-2012 5-year est.); Average household income: $62,558 (2008-2012 5-year est.); Percent of households with income of $100,000 or more: 10.4% (2008-2012 5-year est.); Poverty rate: 4.0% (2008-2012 5-year est.).
Education: Percent of population age 25 and over with: High school diploma (including GED) or higher: 93.2% (2008-2012 5-year est.); Bachelor's degree or higher: 9.1% (2008-2012 5-year est.); Master's degree or higher: 1.9% (2008-2012 5-year est.).

School District(s)
Oakwood CUSD 76 (PK-12)
    2011-12 Enrollment: 1,084 . . . . (217) 354-4355
Housing: Homeownership rate: 89.0% (2008-2012 5-year est.); Median home value: $80,000 (2008-2012 5-year est.); Median contract rent: $541 per month (2008-2012 5-year est.); Median year structure built: 1956 (2008-2012 5-year est.).
Health Insurance: 84.2% Private; 18.9% Public; 6.7% None. (2008-2012 5-year est.)
Safety: Violent crime rate: 0.0 per 10,000 population; Property crime rate: 0.0 per 10,000 population (2012).
Transportation: Commute to work: 95.8% car, 0.0% public transportation, 0.0% walk, 2.7% work from home (2008-2012 5-year est.); Travel time to work: 15.0% less than 15 minutes, 44.7% 15 to 30 minutes, 34.0% 30 to 45 minutes, 4.7% 45 to 60 minutes, 1.6% 60 minutes or more (2008-2012 5-year est.)

GEORGETOWN (city).
Covers a land area of 1.614 square miles and a water area of 0 square miles. Located at 39.98° N. Lat; 87.64° W. Long. Elevation is 669 feet.
History: Georgetown was settled by Quakers from Tennessee and North Carolina. The town was laid out in 1827.
Population: 3,678 (1990); 3,628 (2000); 3,474 (2010); Density: 2,146.8 persons per square mile (2008-2012 5-year est.); Race: 96.4% White, 1.8% Black/African American, 0.0% Asian, 0.0% American Indian/Alaska Native, 0.0% Native Hawaiian/Other Pacific Islander, 1.8% Some other race, 1.7% Two or more races, 0.0% Hispanic of any race (2008-2012 5-year est.); Average household size: 2.62 (2008-2012 5-year est.); Median age: 37.2 (2008-2012 5-year est.); Males per 100 females: 118.0 (2008-2012 5-year est.); Marriage status: 34.3% never married, 41.6% now married, 6.2% widowed, 17.9% divorced (2008-2012 5-year est.); Foreign born: 1.5% (2008-2012 5-year est.); Ancestry (includes multiple ancestries): 37.0% American, 13.6% German, 11.4% English, 5.4% Irish, 3.8% Assyrian/Chaldean/Syriac (2008-2012 5-year est.).
Economy: Single-family building permits issued: 0 (2013); Multi-family building permits issued: 0 (2013); Homeowner vacancy rate: 1.4%. Rental vacancy rate: 8.1%. (2008-2012 5-year est.); Employment by occupation: 4.8% management, business, and financial, 1.9% computer, engineering, and science, 5.8% education, legal, community service, arts, and media, 3.8% healthcare practitioners, 16.7% service, 28.4% sales and office, 7.7% natural resources, construction, and maintenance, 31.0% production, transportation, and material moving (2008-2012 5-year est.).
Income: Per capita income: $17,689 (2008-2012 5-year est.); Median household income: $35,208 (2008-2012 5-year est.); Average household income: $44,737 (2008-2012 5-year est.); Percent of households with income of $100,000 or more: 5.9% (2008-2012 5-year est.); Poverty rate: 19.6% (2008-2012 5-year est.).
Education: Percent of population age 25 and over with: High school diploma (including GED) or higher: 84.0% (2008-2012 5-year est.); Bachelor's degree or higher: 8.4% (2008-2012 5-year est.); Master's degree or higher: 2.3% (2008-2012 5-year est.).

School District(s)
Georgetown-Ridge Farm CUD 4 (PK-12)
    2011-12 Enrollment: 1,135 . . . . (217) 662-8488
Housing: Homeownership rate: 63.0% (2008-2012 5-year est.); Median home value: $63,800 (2008-2012 5-year est.); Median contract rent: $401 per month (2008-2012 5-year est.); Median year structure built: 1955 (2008-2012 5-year est.).
Health Insurance: 56.7% Private; 42.1% Public; 15.8% None. (2008-2012 5-year est.)
Safety: Violent crime rate: 51.9 per 10,000 population; Property crime rate: 181.6 per 10,000 population (2012).

Transportation: Commute to work: 91.9% car, 1.8% public transportation, 5.5% walk, 0.9% work from home (2008-2012 5-year est.); Travel time to work: 21.0% less than 15 minutes, 40.3% 15 to 30 minutes, 25.1% 30 to 45 minutes, 5.6% 45 to 60 minutes, 8.1% 60 minutes or more (2008-2012 5-year est.)

HENNING (village).
Covers a land area of 1.524 square miles and a water area of 0 square miles. Located at 40.31° N. Lat; 87.70° W. Long. Elevation is 686 feet.
Population: 273 (1990); 241 (2000); 251 (2010); Density: 228.3 persons per square mile (2008-2012 5-year est.); Race: 100.0% White, 0.0% Black/African American, 0.0% Asian, 0.0% American Indian/Alaska Native, 0.0% Native Hawaiian/Other Pacific Islander, 0.0% Some other race, 0.0% Two or more races, 1.1% Hispanic of any race (2008-2012 5-year est.); Average household size: 3.52 (2008-2012 5-year est.); Median age: 39.3 (2008-2012 5-year est.); Males per 100 females: 152.2 (2008-2012 5-year est.); Marriage status: 29.5% never married, 69.2% now married, 0.7% widowed, 0.7% divorced (2008-2012 5-year est.); Foreign born: 0.0% (2008-2012 5-year est.); Ancestry (includes multiple ancestries): 19.3% American, 16.4% German, 9.2% Irish, 3.7% Dutch, 3.7% English (2008-2012 5-year est.).
Economy: Single-family building permits issued: 0 (2013); Multi-family building permits issued: 0 (2013); Homeowner vacancy rate: 3.7%. Rental vacancy rate: 0.0%. (2008-2012 5-year est.); Employment by occupation: 8.1% management, business, and financial, 0.7% computer, engineering, and science, 2.2% education, legal, community service, arts, and media, 4.4% healthcare practitioners, 43.0% service, 9.6% sales and office, 4.4% natural resources, construction, and maintenance, 27.4% production, transportation, and material moving (2008-2012 5-year est.).
Income: Per capita income: $14,254 (2008-2012 5-year est.); Median household income: $37,007 (2008-2012 5-year est.); Average household income: $47,364 (2008-2012 5-year est.); Percent of households with income of $100,000 or more: 2.0% (2008-2012 5-year est.); Poverty rate: 2.3% (2008-2012 5-year est.).
Education: Percent of population age 25 and over with: High school diploma (including GED) or higher: 90.9% (2008-2012 5-year est.); Bachelor's degree or higher: 0.9% (2008-2012 5-year est.); Master's degree or higher: 0.0% (2008-2012 5-year est.).
Housing: Homeownership rate: 91.9% (2008-2012 5-year est.); Median home value: $57,000 (2008-2012 5-year est.); Median contract rent: n/a per month (2008-2012 5-year est.); Median year structure built: 1964 (2008-2012 5-year est.).
Health Insurance: 89.9% Private; 22.1% Public; 1.7% None. (2008-2012 5-year est.)
Safety: Violent crime rate: 0.0 per 10,000 population; Property crime rate: 0.0 per 10,000 population (2012).
Transportation: Commute to work: 100.0% car, 0.0% public transportation, 0.0% walk, 0.0% work from home (2008-2012 5-year est.); Travel time to work: 6.7% less than 15 minutes, 62.2% 15 to 30 minutes, 29.6% 30 to 45 minutes, 0.0% 45 to 60 minutes, 1.5% 60 minutes or more (2008-2012 5-year est.)

HOOPESTON (city).
Covers a land area of 3.686 square miles and a water area of 0 square miles. Located at 40.46° N. Lat; 87.66° W. Long. Elevation is 725 feet.
History: Townsites were laid out on the Hoope farm, near the intersection of two railway lines, in 1871. Hoopeston grew rapidly as a canning center.
Population: 5,871 (1990); 5,965 (2000); 5,351 (2010); Density: 1,519.7 persons per square mile (2008-2012 5-year est.); Race: 96.0% White, 0.1% Black/African American, 0.0% Asian, 0.0% American Indian/Alaska Native, 0.0% Native Hawaiian/Other Pacific Islander, 3.9% Some other race, 1.5% Two or more races, 13.9% Hispanic of any race (2008-2012 5-year est.); Average household size: 2.48 (2008-2012 5-year est.); Median age: 39.8 (2008-2012 5-year est.); Males per 100 females: 92.9 (2008-2012 5-year est.); Marriage status: 21.1% never married, 55.6% now married, 10.8% widowed, 12.4% divorced (2008-2012 5-year est.); Foreign born: 2.1% (2008-2012 5-year est.); Ancestry (includes multiple ancestries): 23.8% German, 17.3% American, 10.0% English, 8.6% Irish, 3.3% Italian (2008-2012 5-year est.).
Economy: Single-family building permits issued: 0 (2013); Multi-family building permits issued: 19 (2013); Homeowner vacancy rate: 8.2%. Rental vacancy rate: 0.0%. (2008-2012 5-year est.); Employment by occupation: 5.2% management, business, and financial, 0.5% computer, engineering, and science, 9.2% education, legal, community service, arts, and media, 4.8% healthcare practitioners, 19.1% service, 20.9% sales and office,

12.2% natural resources, construction, and maintenance, 27.9% production, transportation, and material moving (2008-2012 5-year est.).
Income: Per capita income: $18,977 (2008-2012 5-year est.); Median household income: $35,071 (2008-2012 5-year est.); Average household income: $46,692 (2008-2012 5-year est.); Percent of households with income of $100,000 or more: 5.7% (2008-2012 5-year est.); Poverty rate: 22.4% (2008-2012 5-year est.).
Education: Percent of population age 25 and over with: High school diploma (including GED) or higher: 83.8% (2008-2012 5-year est.); Bachelor's degree or higher: 11.3% (2008-2012 5-year est.); Master's degree or higher: 2.0% (2008-2012 5-year est.).

School District(s)
Hoopeston Area CUSD 11 (PK-12)
    2011-12 Enrollment: 1,369 . . . . (217) 283-6668
Housing: Homeownership rate: 69.8% (2008-2012 5-year est.); Median home value: $65,000 (2008-2012 5-year est.); Median contract rent: $421 per month (2008-2012 5-year est.); Median year structure built: 1952 (2008-2012 5-year est.).
Health Insurance: 60.1% Private; 47.3% Public; 11.9% None. (2008-2012 5-year est.)
Hospitals: Hoopeston Community Memorial Hospital (25 beds)
Safety: Violent crime rate: 58.0 per 10,000 population; Property crime rate: 383.5 per 10,000 population (2012).
Transportation: Commute to work: 90.2% car, 0.6% public transportation, 1.9% walk, 7.3% work from home (2008-2012 5-year est.); Travel time to work: 46.1% less than 15 minutes, 6.9% 15 to 30 minutes, 19.5% 30 to 45 minutes, 13.7% 45 to 60 minutes, 13.8% 60 minutes or more (2008-2012 5-year est.)
Additional Information Contacts
City of Hoopeston . . . . (217) 283-5833
    http://www.cityofhoopeston.com
Hoopeston Chamber of Commerce. . . . . (217) 283-7873
    http://www.hoopestonchamber.org

INDIANOLA (village). Covers a land area of 0.388 square miles and a water area of 0 square miles. Located at 39.93° N. Lat; 87.74° W. Long. Elevation is 673 feet.
Population: 336 (1990); 207 (2000); 276 (2010); Density: 805.8 persons per square mile (2008-2012 5-year est.); Race: 100.0% White, 0.0% Black/African American, 0.0% Asian, 0.0% American Indian/Alaska Native, 0.0% Native Hawaiian/Other Pacific Islander, 0.0% Some other race, 0.0% Two or more races, 0.6% Hispanic of any race (2008-2012 5-year est.); Average household size: 2.77 (2008-2012 5-year est.); Median age: 42.3 (2008-2012 5-year est.); Males per 100 females: 92.0 (2008-2012 5-year est.); Marriage status: 27.6% never married, 59.7% now married, 4.9% widowed, 7.8% divorced (2008-2012 5-year est.); Foreign born: 1.9% (2008-2012 5-year est.); Ancestry (includes multiple ancestries): 39.3% American, 11.5% German, 10.5% English, 10.2% Irish, 4.2% French (2008-2012 5-year est.).
Economy: Homeowner vacancy rate: 0.0%. Rental vacancy rate: 0.0%. (2008-2012 5-year est.); Employment by occupation: 7.4% management, business, and financial, 0.0% computer, engineering, and science, 4.1% education, legal, community service, arts, and media, 3.4% healthcare practitioners, 15.5% service, 30.4% sales and office, 18.9% natural resources, construction, and maintenance, 20.3% production, transportation, and material moving (2008-2012 5-year est.).
Income: Per capita income: $21,460 (2008-2012 5-year est.); Median household income: $58,750 (2008-2012 5-year est.); Average household income: $58,435 (2008-2012 5-year est.); Percent of households with income of $100,000 or more: 18.6% (2008-2012 5-year est.); Poverty rate: 13.1% (2008-2012 5-year est.).
Education: Percent of population age 25 and over with: High school diploma (including GED) or higher: 91.0% (2008-2012 5-year est.); Bachelor's degree or higher: 6.7% (2008-2012 5-year est.); Master's degree or higher: 1.4% (2008-2012 5-year est.).
Housing: Homeownership rate: 94.7% (2008-2012 5-year est.); Median home value: $57,900 (2008-2012 5-year est.); Median contract rent: $525 per month (2008-2012 5-year est.); Median year structure built: 1972 (2008-2012 5-year est.).
Health Insurance: 68.1% Private; 39.3% Public; 8.0% None. (2008-2012 5-year est.)
Safety: Violent crime rate: 0.0 per 10,000 population; Property crime rate: 0.0 per 10,000 population (2012).
Transportation: Commute to work: 89.7% car, 0.0% public transportation, 6.2% walk, 3.4% work from home (2008-2012 5-year est.); Travel time to

work: 10.6% less than 15 minutes, 19.9% 15 to 30 minutes, 44.0% 30 to 45 minutes, 7.8% 45 to 60 minutes, 17.7% 60 minutes or more (2008-2012 5-year est.)

MUNCIE (village). Covers a land area of 0.179 square miles and a water area of 0 square miles. Located at 40.12° N. Lat; 87.84° W. Long. Elevation is 646 feet.
Population: 182 (1990); 155 (2000); 146 (2010); Density: 503.4 persons per square mile (2008-2012 5-year est.); Race: 100.0% White, 0.0% Black/African American, 0.0% Asian, 0.0% American Indian/Alaska Native, 0.0% Native Hawaiian/Other Pacific Islander, 0.0% Some other race, 0.0% Two or more races, 0.0% Hispanic of any race (2008-2012 5-year est.); Average household size: 2.09 (2008-2012 5-year est.); Median age: 51.3 (2008-2012 5-year est.); Males per 100 females: 143.2 (2008-2012 5-year est.); Marriage status: 23.2% never married, 45.1% now married, 8.5% widowed, 23.2% divorced (2008-2012 5-year est.); Foreign born: 0.0% (2008-2012 5-year est.); Ancestry (includes multiple ancestries): 30.0% Irish, 26.7% German, 12.2% English, 12.2% French, 10.0% American (2008-2012 5-year est.).
Economy: Single-family building permits issued: 0 (2013); Multi-family building permits issued: 0 (2013); Homeowner vacancy rate: 0.0%. Rental vacancy rate: 0.0%. (2008-2012 5-year est.); Employment by occupation: 10.8% management, business, and financial, 8.1% computer, engineering, and science, 2.7% education, legal, community service, arts, and media, 13.5% healthcare practitioners, 8.1% service, 24.3% sales and office, 13.5% natural resources, construction, and maintenance, 18.9% production, transportation, and material moving (2008-2012 5-year est.).
Income: Per capita income: $23,464 (2008-2012 5-year est.); Median household income: $43,750 (2008-2012 5-year est.); Average household income: $47,949 (2008-2012 5-year est.); Percent of households with income of $100,000 or more: 14.0% (2008-2012 5-year est.); Poverty rate: 12.2% (2008-2012 5-year est.).
Education: Percent of population age 25 and over with: High school diploma (including GED) or higher: 82.6% (2008-2012 5-year est.); Bachelor's degree or higher: 7.2% (2008-2012 5-year est.); Master's degree or higher: 2.9% (2008-2012 5-year est.).
Housing: Homeownership rate: 88.4% (2008-2012 5-year est.); Median home value: $62,000 (2008-2012 5-year est.); Median contract rent: $538 per month (2008-2012 5-year est.); Median year structure built: 1945 (2008-2012 5-year est.).
Health Insurance: 64.4% Private; 41.1% Public; 15.6% None. (2008-2012 5-year est.)
Transportation: Commute to work: 100.0% car, 0.0% public transportation, 0.0% walk, 0.0% work from home (2008-2012 5-year est.); Travel time to work: 8.1% less than 15 minutes, 45.9% 15 to 30 minutes, 37.8% 30 to 45 minutes, 0.0% 45 to 60 minutes, 8.1% 60 minutes or more (2008-2012 5-year est.)

OAKWOOD (village). Covers a land area of 0.928 square miles and a water area of 0 square miles. Located at 40.11° N. Lat; 87.78° W. Long. Elevation is 646 feet.
Population: 1,533 (1990); 1,502 (2000); 1,595 (2010); Density: 1,796.8 persons per square mile (2008-2012 5-year est.); Race: 97.3% White, 0.0% Black/African American, 0.8% Asian, 0.0% American Indian/Alaska Native, 0.0% Native Hawaiian/Other Pacific Islander, 1.9% Some other race, 1.6% Two or more races, 3.1% Hispanic of any race (2008-2012 5-year est.); Average household size: 2.58 (2008-2012 5-year est.); Median age: 39.5 (2008-2012 5-year est.); Males per 100 females: 83.7 (2008-2012 5-year est.); Marriage status: 21.8% never married, 56.1% now married, 6.9% widowed, 15.2% divorced (2008-2012 5-year est.); Foreign born: 0.7% (2008-2012 5-year est.); Ancestry (includes multiple ancestries): 44.7% American, 15.9% German, 9.3% Irish, 8.9% English, 3.4% Welsh (2008-2012 5-year est.).
Economy: Single-family building permits issued: 0 (2013); Multi-family building permits issued: 0 (2013); Homeowner vacancy rate: 0.0%. Rental vacancy rate: 6.2%. (2008-2012 5-year est.); Employment by occupation: 7.4% management, business, and financial, 1.1% computer, engineering, and science, 9.9% education, legal, community service, arts, and media, 4.4% healthcare practitioners, 20.9% service, 25.4% sales and office, 6.2% natural resources, construction, and maintenance, 24.6% production, transportation, and material moving (2008-2012 5-year est.).
Income: Per capita income: $20,591 (2008-2012 5-year est.); Median household income: $39,706 (2008-2012 5-year est.); Average household income: $51,059 (2008-2012 5-year est.); Percent of households with

income of $100,000 or more: 9.2% (2008-2012 5-year est.); Poverty rate: 18.0% (2008-2012 5-year est.).

Education: Percent of population age 25 and over with: High school diploma (including GED) or higher: 89.3% (2008-2012 5-year est.); Bachelor's degree or higher: 10.9% (2008-2012 5-year est.); Master's degree or higher: 1.9% (2008-2012 5-year est.).

School District(s)

Oakwood CUSD 76 (PK-12)

   2011-12 Enrollment: 1,084 . . . . (217) 354-4355

Housing: Homeownership rate: 80.3% (2008-2012 5-year est.); Median home value: $91,000 (2008-2012 5-year est.); Median contract rent: $416 per month (2008-2012 5-year est.); Median year structure built: 1966 (2008-2012 5-year est.).

Health Insurance: 73.7% Private; 33.8% Public; 6.1% None. (2008-2012 5-year est.)

Safety: Violent crime rate: 6.3 per 10,000 population; Property crime rate: 69.0 per 10,000 population (2012).

Transportation: Commute to work: 98.1% car, 0.0% public transportation, 0.0% walk, 1.9% work from home (2008-2012 5-year est.); Travel time to work: 17.4% less than 15 minutes, 51.4% 15 to 30 minutes, 22.6% 30 to 45 minutes, 5.2% 45 to 60 minutes, 3.5% 60 minutes or more (2008-2012 5-year est.)

OLIVET (CDP). Covers a land area of 2.383 square miles and a water area of 0 square miles. Located at 39.94° N. Lat; 87.64° W. Long. Elevation is 666 feet.

Population: n/a (1990); n/a (2000); 428 (2010); Density: 160.7 persons per square mile (2008-2012 5-year est.); Race: 99.7% White, 0.3% Black/African American, 0.0% Asian, 0.0% American Indian/Alaska Native, 0.0% Native Hawaiian/Other Pacific Islander, 0.0% Some other race, 0.0% Two or more races, 0.5% Hispanic of any race (2008-2012 5-year est.); Average household size: 3.02 (2008-2012 5-year est.); Median age: 38.0 (2008-2012 5-year est.); Males per 100 females: 233.0 (2008-2012 5-year est.); Marriage status: 35.0% never married, 61.2% now married, 0.0% widowed, 3.7% divorced (2008-2012 5-year est.); Foreign born: 0.3% (2008-2012 5-year est.); Ancestry (includes multiple ancestries): 53.3% American, 13.8% German, 8.1% Lithuanian, 7.0% Irish, 3.9% Scottish (2008-2012 5-year est.).

Economy: Homeowner vacancy rate: 0.0%. Rental vacancy rate: 0.0%. (2008-2012 5-year est.); Employment by occupation: 9.1% management, business, and financial, 0.0% computer, engineering, and science, 13.4% education, legal, community service, arts, and media, 0.0% healthcare practitioners, 1.1% service, 19.8% sales and office, 12.3% natural resources, construction, and maintenance, 44.4% production, transportation, and material moving (2008-2012 5-year est.).

Income: Per capita income: $21,922 (2008-2012 5-year est.); Median household income: $51,250 (2008-2012 5-year est.); Average household income: $63,164 (2008-2012 5-year est.); Percent of households with income of $100,000 or more: 5.6% (2008-2012 5-year est.); Poverty rate: 1.8% (2008-2012 5-year est.).

Education: Percent of population age 25 and over with: High school diploma (including GED) or higher: 82.6% (2008-2012 5-year est.); Bachelor's degree or higher: 14.7% (2008-2012 5-year est.); Master's degree or higher: 10.6% (2008-2012 5-year est.).

Housing: Homeownership rate: 88.7% (2008-2012 5-year est.); Median home value: $59,700 (2008-2012 5-year est.); Median contract rent: n/a per month (2008-2012 5-year est.); Median year structure built: 1975 (2008-2012 5-year est.).

Health Insurance: 61.1% Private; 20.4% Public; 30.0% None. (2008-2012 5-year est.)

Transportation: Commute to work: 89.3% car, 0.0% public transportation, 7.5% walk, 3.2% work from home (2008-2012 5-year est.); Travel time to work: 18.2% less than 15 minutes, 3.9% 15 to 30 minutes, 59.7% 30 to 45 minutes, 11.6% 45 to 60 minutes, 6.6% 60 minutes or more (2008-2012 5-year est.)

POTOMAC (village). Covers a land area of 0.486 square miles and a water area of 0 square miles. Located at 40.31° N. Lat; 87.80° W. Long. Elevation is 669 feet.

Population: 753 (1990); 681 (2000); 750 (2010); Density: 1,851.7 persons per square mile (2008-2012 5-year est.); Race: 98.7% White, 0.0% Black/African American, 0.0% Asian, 0.6% American Indian/Alaska Native, 0.0% Native Hawaiian/Other Pacific Islander, 0.7% Some other race, 0.7% Two or more races, 1.7% Hispanic of any race (2008-2012 5-year est.); Average household size: 2.68 (2008-2012 5-year est.); Median age: 38.5

(2008-2012 5-year est.); Males per 100 females: 110.8 (2008-2012 5-year est.); Marriage status: 28.4% never married, 54.4% now married, 6.0% widowed, 11.2% divorced (2008-2012 5-year est.); Foreign born: 0.0% (2008-2012 5-year est.); Ancestry (includes multiple ancestries): 35.3% American, 15.0% German, 10.3% Irish, 6.1% English, 3.4% Polish (2008-2012 5-year est.).

Economy: Single-family building permits issued: 0 (2013); Multi-family building permits issued: 0 (2013); Homeowner vacancy rate: 3.6%. Rental vacancy rate: 0.0%. (2008-2012 5-year est.); Employment by occupation: 3.4% management, business, and financial, 2.4% computer, engineering, and science, 11.3% education, legal, community service, arts, and media, 2.1% healthcare practitioners, 21.3% service, 24.9% sales and office, 9.7% natural resources, construction, and maintenance, 24.9% production, transportation, and material moving (2008-2012 5-year est.).

Income: Per capita income: $18,807 (2008-2012 5-year est.); Median household income: $41,250 (2008-2012 5-year est.); Average household income: $48,741 (2008-2012 5-year est.); Percent of households with income of $100,000 or more: 9.2% (2008-2012 5-year est.); Poverty rate: 11.7% (2008-2012 5-year est.).

Education: Percent of population age 25 and over with: High school diploma (including GED) or higher: 82.6% (2008-2012 5-year est.); Bachelor's degree or higher: 10.3% (2008-2012 5-year est.); Master's degree or higher: 3.6% (2008-2012 5-year est.).

School District(s)

Potomac CUSD 10 (PK-08)

   2011-12 Enrollment: 165 . . . . (217) 987-6155

Housing: Homeownership rate: 78.6% (2008-2012 5-year est.); Median home value: $76,600 (2008-2012 5-year est.); Median contract rent: $489 per month (2008-2012 5-year est.); Median year structure built: 1957 (2008-2012 5-year est.).

Health Insurance: 65.7% Private; 35.1% Public; 13.4% None. (2008-2012 5-year est.)

Safety: Violent crime rate: 0.0 per 10,000 population; Property crime rate: 80.1 per 10,000 population (2012).

Transportation: Commute to work: 94.9% car, 0.0% public transportation, 2.4% walk, 1.3% work from home (2008-2012 5-year est.); Travel time to work: 11.1% less than 15 minutes, 37.3% 15 to 30 minutes, 33.2% 30 to 45 minutes, 15.4% 45 to 60 minutes, 3.0% 60 minutes or more (2008-2012 5-year est.)

RANKIN (village). Covers a land area of 0.579 square miles and a water area of 0 square miles. Located at 40.46° N. Lat; 87.90° W. Long. Elevation is 722 feet.

Population: 619 (1990); 617 (2000); 561 (2010); Density: 865.4 persons per square mile (2008-2012 5-year est.); Race: 100.0% White, 0.0% Black/African American, 0.0% Asian, 0.0% American Indian/Alaska Native, 0.0% Native Hawaiian/Other Pacific Islander, 0.0% Some other race, 0.0% Two or more races, 2.4% Hispanic of any race (2008-2012 5-year est.); Average household size: 2.33 (2008-2012 5-year est.); Median age: 39.7 (2008-2012 5-year est.); Males per 100 females: 145.6 (2008-2012 5-year est.); Marriage status: 35.3% never married, 40.8% now married, 6.2% widowed, 17.7% divorced (2008-2012 5-year est.); Foreign born: 0.0% (2008-2012 5-year est.); Ancestry (includes multiple ancestries): 32.3% German, 16.8% American, 16.4% Irish, 7.8% English, 3.0% Polish (2008-2012 5-year est.).

Economy: Single-family building permits issued: 0 (2013); Multi-family building permits issued: 0 (2013); Homeowner vacancy rate: 12.1%. Rental vacancy rate: 13.2%. (2008-2012 5-year est.); Employment by occupation: 4.4% management, business, and financial, 1.6% computer, engineering, and science, 3.8% education, legal, community service, arts, and media, 12.1% healthcare practitioners, 31.3% service, 11.0% sales and office, 16.5% natural resources, construction, and maintenance, 19.2% production, transportation, and material moving (2008-2012 5-year est.).

Income: Per capita income: $17,335 (2008-2012 5-year est.); Median household income: $29,375 (2008-2012 5-year est.); Average household income: $39,273 (2008-2012 5-year est.); Percent of households with income of $100,000 or more: 2.3% (2008-2012 5-year est.); Poverty rate: 28.1% (2008-2012 5-year est.).

Education: Percent of population age 25 and over with: High school diploma (including GED) or higher: 87.1% (2008-2012 5-year est.); Bachelor's degree or higher: 4.8% (2008-2012 5-year est.); Master's degree or higher: 1.8% (2008-2012 5-year est.).

Housing: Homeownership rate: 72.6% (2008-2012 5-year est.); Median home value: $59,300 (2008-2012 5-year est.); Median contract rent: $402

per month (2008-2012 5-year est.); Median year structure built: 1944 (2008-2012 5-year est.).

Health Insurance: 44.7% Private; 55.3% Public; 13.8% None. (2008-2012 5-year est.)

Safety: Violent crime rate: 17.9 per 10,000 population; Property crime rate: 71.4 per 10,000 population (2012).

Transportation: Commute to work: 95.5% car, 2.8% public transportation, 0.0% walk, 1.7% work from home (2008-2012 5-year est.); Travel time to work: 21.6% less than 15 minutes, 43.2% 15 to 30 minutes, 15.3% 30 to 45 minutes, 10.8% 45 to 60 minutes, 9.1% 60 minutes or more (2008-2012 5-year est.)

RIDGE FARM (village). Covers a land area of 3.056 square miles and a water area of 0 square miles. Located at 39.90° N. Lat; 87.65° W. Long. Elevation is 702 feet.

History: Ridge Farm was platted in 1853 and incorporated as a village in 1874. It developed as a trading center.

Population: 939 (1990); 912 (2000); 882 (2010); Density: 306.3 persons per square mile (2008-2012 5-year est.); Race: 99.0% White, 0.0% Black/African American, 0.0% Asian, 0.0% American Indian/Alaska Native, 0.0% Native Hawaiian/Other Pacific Islander, 1.0% Some other race, 1.0% Two or more races, 0.4% Hispanic of any race (2008-2012 5-year est.); Average household size: 2.41 (2008-2012 5-year est.); Median age: 41.2 (2008-2012 5-year est.); Males per 100 females: 98.7 (2008-2012 5-year est.); Marriage status: 25.4% never married, 53.6% now married, 6.4% widowed, 14.6% divorced (2008-2012 5-year est.); Foreign born: 0.0% (2008-2012 5-year est.); Ancestry (includes multiple ancestries): 25.6% American, 16.7% German, 15.7% Irish, 5.9% English, 3.5% Dutch (2008-2012 5-year est.).

Economy: Single-family building permits issued: 0 (2013); Multi-family building permits issued: 0 (2013); Homeowner vacancy rate: 2.9%. Rental vacancy rate: 24.3%. (2008-2012 5-year est.); Employment by occupation: 6.8% management, business, and financial, 3.1% computer, engineering, and science, 3.9% education, legal, community service, arts, and media, 5.6% healthcare practitioners, 9.2% service, 35.6% sales and office, 12.8% natural resources, construction, and maintenance, 23.0% production, transportation, and material moving (2008-2012 5-year est.).

Income: Per capita income: $22,580 (2008-2012 5-year est.); Median household income: $41,328 (2008-2012 5-year est.); Average household income: $53,232 (2008-2012 5-year est.); Percent of households with income of $100,000 or more: 14.4% (2008-2012 5-year est.); Poverty rate: 16.6% (2008-2012 5-year est.).

Education: Percent of population age 25 and over with: High school diploma (including GED) or higher: 84.9% (2008-2012 5-year est.); Bachelor's degree or higher: 7.4% (2008-2012 5-year est.); Master's degree or higher: 1.8% (2008-2012 5-year est.).

School District(s)
Georgetown-Ridge Farm CUD 4 (PK-12)
    2011-12 Enrollment: 1,135 . . . . (217) 662-8488

Housing: Homeownership rate: 79.2% (2008-2012 5-year est.); Median home value: $70,000 (2008-2012 5-year est.); Median contract rent: $267 per month (2008-2012 5-year est.); Median year structure built: 1960 (2008-2012 5-year est.).

Health Insurance: 65.1% Private; 40.4% Public; 9.8% None. (2008-2012 5-year est.)

Safety: Violent crime rate: 11.4 per 10,000 population; Property crime rate: 102.4 per 10,000 population (2012).

Transportation: Commute to work: 97.8% car, 0.0% public transportation, 0.0% walk, 1.5% work from home (2008-2012 5-year est.); Travel time to work: 27.3% less than 15 minutes, 22.5% 15 to 30 minutes, 40.9% 30 to 45 minutes, 0.8% 45 to 60 minutes, 8.6% 60 minutes or more (2008-2012 5-year est.)

ROSSVILLE (village). Covers a land area of 1.397 square miles and a water area of 0 square miles. Located at 40.38° N. Lat; 87.67° W. Long. Elevation is 689 feet.

History: Rossville was laid out in 1857 and named for early settler Jacob Ross. The site at the intersection of two roads had previously been called Henpeck.

Population: 1,334 (1990); 1,217 (2000); 1,331 (2010); Density: 989.6 persons per square mile (2008-2012 5-year est.); Race: 99.6% White, 0.0% Black/African American, 0.0% Asian, 0.4% American Indian/Alaska Native, 0.0% Native Hawaiian/Other Pacific Islander, 0.0% Some other race, 0.0% Two or more races, 0.4% Hispanic of any race (2008-2012 5-year est.); Average household size: 2.70 (2008-2012 5-year est.);

Median age: 32.0 (2008-2012 5-year est.); Males per 100 females: 89.2 (2008-2012 5-year est.); Marriage status: 26.4% never married, 54.1% now married, 7.3% widowed, 12.2% divorced (2008-2012 5-year est.); Foreign born: 0.5% (2008-2012 5-year est.); Ancestry (includes multiple ancestries): 22.1% German, 21.0% American, 15.4% English, 13.4% Irish, 3.3% Italian (2008-2012 5-year est.).

Economy: Single-family building permits issued: 0 (2013); Multi-family building permits issued: 0 (2013); Homeowner vacancy rate: 6.8%. Rental vacancy rate: 6.0%. (2008-2012 5-year est.); Employment by occupation: 11.1% management, business, and financial, 3.4% computer, engineering, and science, 3.3% education, legal, community service, arts, and media, 6.9% healthcare practitioners, 16.5% service, 33.1% sales and office, 6.0% natural resources, construction, and maintenance, 19.7% production, transportation, and material moving (2008-2012 5-year est.).

Income: Per capita income: $22,288 (2008-2012 5-year est.); Median household income: $42,390 (2008-2012 5-year est.); Average household income: $57,783 (2008-2012 5-year est.); Percent of households with income of $100,000 or more: 11.6% (2008-2012 5-year est.); Poverty rate: 11.4% (2008-2012 5-year est.).

Education: Percent of population age 25 and over with: High school diploma (including GED) or higher: 88.6% (2008-2012 5-year est.); Bachelor's degree or higher: 14.6% (2008-2012 5-year est.); Master's degree or higher: 6.2% (2008-2012 5-year est.).

School District(s)
Rossville-Alvin CUSD 7 (PK-08)
    2011-12 Enrollment: 293 . . . . (217) 748-6666

Housing: Homeownership rate: 72.7% (2008-2012 5-year est.); Median home value: $65,000 (2008-2012 5-year est.); Median contract rent: $412 per month (2008-2012 5-year est.); Median year structure built: 1946 (2008-2012 5-year est.).

Health Insurance: 67.2% Private; 37.8% Public; 13.4% None. (2008-2012 5-year est.)

Transportation: Commute to work: 94.2% car, 0.0% public transportation, 1.1% walk, 4.7% work from home (2008-2012 5-year est.); Travel time to work: 23.6% less than 15 minutes, 28.2% 15 to 30 minutes, 40.7% 30 to 45 minutes, 2.9% 45 to 60 minutes, 4.6% 60 minutes or more (2008-2012 5-year est.)

SIDELL (village). Covers a land area of 0.927 square miles and a water area of 0 square miles. Located at 39.91° N. Lat; 87.82° W. Long. Elevation is 682 feet.

Population: 584 (1990); 626 (2000); 617 (2010); Density: 717.6 persons per square mile (2008-2012 5-year est.); Race: 100.0% White, 0.0% Black/African American, 0.0% Asian, 0.0% American Indian/Alaska Native, 0.0% Native Hawaiian/Other Pacific Islander, 0.0% Some other race, 0.0% Two or more races, 0.9% Hispanic of any race (2008-2012 5-year est.); Average household size: 2.89 (2008-2012 5-year est.); Median age: 36.7 (2008-2012 5-year est.); Males per 100 females: 74.1 (2008-2012 5-year est.); Marriage status: 32.6% never married, 51.5% now married, 5.6% widowed, 10.3% divorced (2008-2012 5-year est.); Foreign born: 0.0% (2008-2012 5-year est.); Ancestry (includes multiple ancestries): 43.6% American, 11.3% German, 6.6% Irish, 5.9% English, 1.1% Lithuanian (2008-2012 5-year est.).

Economy: Single-family building permits issued: 0 (2013); Multi-family building permits issued: 0 (2013); Homeowner vacancy rate: 2.8%. Rental vacancy rate: 0.0%. (2008-2012 5-year est.); Employment by occupation: 6.9% management, business, and financial, 2.3% computer, engineering, and science, 8.5% education, legal, community service, arts, and media, 6.6% healthcare practitioners, 26.3% service, 19.7% sales and office, 7.3% natural resources, construction, and maintenance, 22.4% production, transportation, and material moving (2008-2012 5-year est.).

Income: Per capita income: $18,931 (2008-2012 5-year est.); Median household income: $53,438 (2008-2012 5-year est.); Average household income: $53,608 (2008-2012 5-year est.); Percent of households with income of $100,000 or more: 6.0% (2008-2012 5-year est.); Poverty rate: 6.2% (2008-2012 5-year est.).

Education: Percent of population age 25 and over with: High school diploma (including GED) or higher: 88.9% (2008-2012 5-year est.); Bachelor's degree or higher: 7.4% (2008-2012 5-year est.); Master's degree or higher: 1.2% (2008-2012 5-year est.).

School District(s)
Jamaica CUSD 12 (PK-12)
    2011-12 Enrollment: 397 . . . . (217) 288-9306

Housing: Homeownership rate: 84.3% (2008-2012 5-year est.); Median home value: $64,100 (2008-2012 5-year est.); Median contract rent: $310

per month (2008-2012 5-year est.); Median year structure built: Before 1940 (2008-2012 5-year est.).
Health Insurance: 58.8% Private; 44.4% Public; 8.4% None. (2008-2012 5-year est.)
Safety: Violent crime rate: 16.2 per 10,000 population; Property crime rate: 16.2 per 10,000 population (2012).
Transportation: Commute to work: 95.7% car, 0.0% public transportation, 1.2% walk, 3.1% work from home (2008-2012 5-year est.); Travel time to work: 17.4% less than 15 minutes, 17.4% 15 to 30 minutes, 39.7% 30 to 45 minutes, 21.9% 45 to 60 minutes, 3.6% 60 minutes or more (2008-2012 5-year est.)

TILTON (village). Covers a land area of 3.208 square miles and a water area of 0.033 square miles. Located at 40.09° N. Lat; 87.64° W. Long. Elevation is 643 feet.
History: Incorporated 1884.
Population: 2,729 (1990); 2,976 (2000); 2,724 (2010); Density: 846.9 persons per square mile (2008-2012 5-year est.); Race: 92.4% White, 0.0% Black/African American, 0.0% Asian, 0.7% American Indian/Alaska Native, 0.0% Native Hawaiian/Other Pacific Islander, 6.9% Some other race, 1.5% Two or more races, 8.8% Hispanic of any race (2008-2012 5-year est.); Average household size: 2.30 (2008-2012 5-year est.); Median age: 45.5 (2008-2012 5-year est.); Males per 100 females: 82.7 (2008-2012 5-year est.); Marriage status: 17.4% never married, 53.3% now married, 9.3% widowed, 20.0% divorced (2008-2012 5-year est.); Foreign born: 2.4% (2008-2012 5-year est.); Ancestry (includes multiple ancestries): 25.2% American, 12.6% German, 7.3% English, 5.6% Irish, 2.9% Polish (2008-2012 5-year est.).
Economy: Single-family building permits issued: 0 (2013); Multi-family building permits issued: 0 (2013); Homeowner vacancy rate: 2.7%. Rental vacancy rate: 0.0%. (2008-2012 5-year est.); Employment by occupation: 12.4% management, business, and financial, 3.1% computer, engineering, and science, 4.1% education, legal, community service, arts, and media, 4.6% healthcare practitioners, 16.2% service, 26.8% sales and office, 9.3% natural resources, construction, and maintenance, 23.5% production, transportation, and material moving (2008-2012 5-year est.).
Income: Per capita income: $22,627 (2008-2012 5-year est.); Median household income: $45,156 (2008-2012 5-year est.); Average household income: $50,262 (2008-2012 5-year est.); Percent of households with income of $100,000 or more: 7.6% (2008-2012 5-year est.); Poverty rate: 12.9% (2008-2012 5-year est.).
Education: Percent of population age 25 and over with: High school diploma (including GED) or higher: 86.7% (2008-2012 5-year est.); Bachelor's degree or higher: 6.8% (2008-2012 5-year est.); Master's degree or higher: 0.9% (2008-2012 5-year est.).
Housing: Homeownership rate: 75.1% (2008-2012 5-year est.); Median home value: $58,700 (2008-2012 5-year est.); Median contract rent: $454 per month (2008-2012 5-year est.); Median year structure built: 1955 (2008-2012 5-year est.).
Health Insurance: 72.8% Private; 35.7% Public; 14.3% None. (2008-2012 5-year est.)
Safety: Violent crime rate: 40.4 per 10,000 population; Property crime rate: 202.2 per 10,000 population (2012).
Transportation: Commute to work: 98.5% car, 0.1% public transportation, 0.0% walk, 0.0% work from home (2008-2012 5-year est.); Travel time to work: 39.2% less than 15 minutes, 35.0% 15 to 30 minutes, 14.7% 30 to 45 minutes, 3.8% 45 to 60 minutes, 7.4% 60 minutes or more (2008-2012 5-year est.)

WESTVILLE (village). Covers a land area of 1.676 square miles and a water area of 0 square miles. Located at 40.04° N. Lat; 87.64° W. Long. Elevation is 669 feet.
History: Westville was named for W.P. and E.A. West, who laid out the town in 1873. Coal mining was the first major industry.
Population: 3,387 (1990); 3,175 (2000); 3,202 (2010); Density: 1,893.2 persons per square mile (2008-2012 5-year est.); Race: 97.9% White, 0.3% Black/African American, 0.0% Asian, 0.0% American Indian/Alaska Native, 0.0% Native Hawaiian/Other Pacific Islander, 1.8% Some other race, 1.0% Two or more races, 1.8% Hispanic of any race (2008-2012 5-year est.); Average household size: 2.25 (2008-2012 5-year est.); Median age: 43.5 (2008-2012 5-year est.); Males per 100 females: 97.2 (2008-2012 5-year est.); Marriage status: 27.2% never married, 48.7% now married, 11.8% widowed, 12.3% divorced (2008-2012 5-year est.); Foreign born: 1.6% (2008-2012 5-year est.); Ancestry (includes multiple

ancestries): 26.9% American, 18.2% German, 14.9% Irish, 10.6% Italian, 7.5% English (2008-2012 5-year est.).
Economy: Single-family building permits issued: 0 (2013); Multi-family building permits issued: 0 (2013); Homeowner vacancy rate: 4.5%. Rental vacancy rate: 6.2%. (2008-2012 5-year est.); Employment by occupation: 6.9% management, business, and financial, 1.8% computer, engineering, and science, 2.4% education, legal, community service, arts, and media, 4.0% healthcare practitioners, 26.7% service, 25.0% sales and office, 9.0% natural resources, construction, and maintenance, 24.1% production, transportation, and material moving (2008-2012 5-year est.).
Income: Per capita income: $21,268 (2008-2012 5-year est.); Median household income: $38,003 (2008-2012 5-year est.); Average household income: $47,007 (2008-2012 5-year est.); Percent of households with income of $100,000 or more: 8.8% (2008-2012 5-year est.); Poverty rate: 7.2% (2008-2012 5-year est.).
Education: Percent of population age 25 and over with: High school diploma (including GED) or higher: 86.0% (2008-2012 5-year est.); Bachelor's degree or higher: 12.3% (2008-2012 5-year est.); Master's degree or higher: 2.6% (2008-2012 5-year est.).
School District(s)
Westville CUSD 2 (PK-12)
   2011-12 Enrollment: 1,265 . . . . (217) 267-3141
Housing: Homeownership rate: 76.3% (2008-2012 5-year est.); Median home value: $75,000 (2008-2012 5-year est.); Median contract rent: $430 per month (2008-2012 5-year est.); Median year structure built: 1953 (2008-2012 5-year est.).
Health Insurance: 80.1% Private; 29.8% Public; 5.7% None. (2008-2012 5-year est.)
Safety: Violent crime rate: 25.0 per 10,000 population; Property crime rate: 165.7 per 10,000 population (2012).
Transportation: Commute to work: 89.3% car, 0.0% public transportation, 5.3% walk, 4.3% work from home (2008-2012 5-year est.); Travel time to work: 36.3% less than 15 minutes, 42.8% 15 to 30 minutes, 12.0% 30 to 45 minutes, 6.0% 45 to 60 minutes, 2.9% 60 minutes or more (2008-2012 5-year est.)

Wabash County

Located in southeastern Illinois; bounded on the east and south by the Wabash River, and the Indiana border. Covers a land area of 223.252 square miles, a water area of 4.254 square miles, and is located in the Central Time Zone at 38.45° N. Lat., 87.84° W. Long. The county was founded in 1824. County seat is Mount Carmel.

Weather Station: Mount Carmel   Elevation: 430 feet

	Jan	Feb	Mar	Apr	May	Jun	Jul	Aug	Sep	Oct	Nov	Dec
High	41	45	55	67	76	85	89	88	81	70	56	43
Low	22	25	34	44	54	63	66	64	56	44	35	25
Precip	3.0	3.0	4.0	4.3	6.0	4.0	4.0	3.3	3.1	3.6	4.1	3.4
Snow	2.6	3.3	1.0	tr	0.0	0.0	0.0	0.0	0.0	0.1	tr	3.0

High and Low temperatures in degrees Fahrenheit; Precipitation and Snow in inches

Population: 13,111 (1990); 12,937 (2000); 11,947 (2010); Race: 97.1% White, 0.1% Black/African American, 0.8% Asian, 0.0% American Indian/Alaska Native, 0.0% Native Hawaiian/Other Pacific Islander, 2.0% Some other race, 1.6% Two or more races, 1.3% Hispanic of any race (2008-2012 5-year est.); Density: 52.6 persons per square mile (2008-2012 5-year est.); Average household size: 2.48 (2008-2012 5-year est.); Median age: 42.8 (2008-2012 5-year est.); Males per 100 females: 94.3 (2008-2012 5-year est.).
Religion: Six largest groups: 23.1% Baptist, 16.6% Catholicism, 8.7% Methodist/Pietist, 2.4% Holiness, 1.6% Non-denominational Protestant, 1.3% Presbyterian-Reformed (2010)
Economy: Unemployment rate: 5.9% (April 2014); Total civilian labor force: 5,651 (April 2014); Leading industries: 29.5% health care and social assistance; 11.6% retail trade; 10.3% accommodation & food services (2012); Farms: 213 totaling 106,424 acres (2012); Companies that employ 500 or more persons: 0 (2012); Companies that employ 100 to 499 persons: 3 (2012); Companies that employ less than 100 persons: 274 (2012); Black-owned businesses: n/a (2007); Hispanic-owned businesses: n/a (2007); Asian-owned businesses: n/a (2007); Women-owned businesses: 146 (2007); Single-family building permits issued: 2 (2013); Multi-family building permits issued: 0 (2013).
Income: Per capita income: $23,123 (2008-2012 5-year est.); Median household income: $45,011 (2008-2012 5-year est.); Average household income: $57,207 (2008-2012 5-year est.); Percent of households with

income of $100,000 or more: 11.9% (2008-2012 5-year est.); Poverty rate: 12.9% (2008-2012 5-year est.); Bankruptcy rate: 1.45% (2013).

Education: Percent of population age 25 and over with: High school diploma (including GED) or higher: 88.5% (2008-2012 5-year est.); Bachelor's degree or higher: 16.3% (2008-2012 5-year est.); Master's degree or higher: 4.7% (2008-2012 5-year est.).

Housing: Homeownership rate: 78.8% (2008-2012 5-year est.); Median home value: $80,000 (2008-2012 5-year est.); Median contract rent: $365 per month (2008-2012 5-year est.); Median year structure built: 1960 (2008-2012 5-year est.).

Health: Birth rate: 124.3 per 10,000 population (2013); Death rate: 100.3 per 10,000 population (2013); Age-adjusted cancer mortality rate: 245.6 deaths per 100,000 population (2011); Number of physicians: 9.3 per 10,000 population (2011); Hospital beds: 20.9 per 10,000 population (2010); Hospital admissions: 603.5 per 10,000 population (2010).

Environment: Air Quality Index: 93.4% good, 6.0% moderate, 0.5% unhealthy for sensitive individuals, 0.0% unhealthy (percent of days in 2013)

Elections: 2012 Presidential election results: 31.0% Obama, 67.7% Romney

National and State Parks: Beall Woods State Conservation and Natural Area

Additional Information Contacts
Wabash County Government . . . . (618) 262-4561

Wabash County Chamber of Commerce . . . . (618) 262-5116
  http://www.wabashcountychamber.com

Wabash County Communities

ALLENDALE (village). Aka Orio. Covers a land area of 0.309 square miles and a water area of 0 square miles. Located at 38.53° N. Lat; 87.71° W. Long. Elevation is 492 feet.

Population: 476 (1990); 528 (2000); 475 (2010); Density: 1,504.0 persons per square mile (2008-2012 5-year est.); Race: 99.1% White, 0.0% Black/African American, 0.0% Asian, 0.0% American Indian/Alaska Native, 0.0% Native Hawaiian/Other Pacific Islander, 0.9% Some other race, 0.9% Two or more races, 0.2% Hispanic of any race (2008-2012 5-year est.); Average household size: 2.70 (2008-2012 5-year est.); Median age: 38.6 (2008-2012 5-year est.); Males per 100 females: 104.4 (2008-2012 5-year est.); Marriage status: 19.7% never married, 70.4% now married, 2.8% widowed, 7.2% divorced (2008-2012 5-year est.); Foreign born: 0.0% (2008-2012 5-year est.); Ancestry (includes multiple ancestries): 16.6% American, 15.1% German, 7.3% Irish, 6.9% English, 2.2% Dutch (2008-2012 5-year est.).

Economy: Single-family building permits issued: 1 (2013); Multi-family building permits issued: 0 (2013); Homeowner vacancy rate: 0.0%. Rental vacancy rate: 0.0%. (2008-2012 5-year est.); Employment by occupation: 5.3% management, business, and financial, 2.9% computer, engineering, and science, 3.4% education, legal, community service, arts, and media, 7.7% healthcare practitioners, 17.3% service, 24.5% sales and office, 11.5% natural resources, construction, and maintenance, 27.4% production, transportation, and material moving (2008-2012 5-year est.).

Income: Per capita income: $21,131 (2008-2012 5-year est.); Median household income: $51,250 (2008-2012 5-year est.); Average household income: $56,186 (2008-2012 5-year est.); Percent of households with income of $100,000 or more: 4.6% (2008-2012 5-year est.); Poverty rate: 8.8% (2008-2012 5-year est.).

Education: Percent of population age 25 and over with: High school diploma (including GED) or higher: 86.8% (2008-2012 5-year est.); Bachelor's degree or higher: 10.8% (2008-2012 5-year est.); Master's degree or higher: 1.8% (2008-2012 5-year est.).

School District(s)
Allendale CCSD 17 (PK-08)
  2011-12 Enrollment: 126 . . . . (618) 299-3161

Housing: Homeownership rate: 80.2% (2008-2012 5-year est.); Median home value: $74,200 (2008-2012 5-year est.); Median contract rent: $277 per month (2008-2012 5-year est.); Median year structure built: 1973 (2008-2012 5-year est.).

Health Insurance: 76.5% Private; 32.8% Public; 7.1% None. (2008-2012 5-year est.)

Transportation: Commute to work: 100.0% car, 0.0% public transportation, 0.0% walk, 0.0% work from home (2008-2012 5-year est.); Travel time to work: 34.6% less than 15 minutes, 36.1% 15 to 30 minutes,

16.8% 30 to 45 minutes, 4.8% 45 to 60 minutes, 7.7% 60 minutes or more (2008-2012 5-year est.)

BELLMONT (village). Covers a land area of 0.321 square miles and a water area of 0 square miles. Located at 38.38° N. Lat; 87.91° W. Long. Elevation is 446 feet.

Population: 271 (1990); 297 (2000); 276 (2010); Density: 719.2 persons per square mile (2008-2012 5-year est.); Race: 100.0% White, 0.0% Black/African American, 0.0% Asian, 0.0% American Indian/Alaska Native, 0.0% Native Hawaiian/Other Pacific Islander, 0.0% Some other race, 0.0% Two or more races, 0.0% Hispanic of any race (2008-2012 5-year est.); Average household size: 2.43 (2008-2012 5-year est.); Median age: 45.8 (2008-2012 5-year est.); Males per 100 females: 111.9 (2008-2012 5-year est.); Marriage status: 16.2% never married, 56.2% now married, 7.0% widowed, 20.5% divorced (2008-2012 5-year est.); Foreign born: 0.0% (2008-2012 5-year est.); Ancestry (includes multiple ancestries): 6.9% American, 5.2% Irish, 4.8% German, 2.6% English, 2.2% French (2008-2012 5-year est.).

Economy: Homeowner vacancy rate: 0.0%. Rental vacancy rate: 0.0%. (2008-2012 5-year est.); Employment by occupation: 9.5% management, business, and financial, 4.1% computer, engineering, and science, 0.0% education, legal, community service, arts, and media, 4.1% healthcare practitioners, 23.0% service, 13.5% sales and office, 13.5% natural resources, construction, and maintenance, 32.4% production, transportation, and material moving (2008-2012 5-year est.).

Income: Per capita income: $20,569 (2008-2012 5-year est.); Median household income: $31,797 (2008-2012 5-year est.); Average household income: $45,757 (2008-2012 5-year est.); Percent of households with income of $100,000 or more: 13.7% (2008-2012 5-year est.); Poverty rate: 12.6% (2008-2012 5-year est.).

Education: Percent of population age 25 and over with: High school diploma (including GED) or higher: 81.8% (2008-2012 5-year est.); Bachelor's degree or higher: 5.7% (2008-2012 5-year est.); Master's degree or higher: 0.0% (2008-2012 5-year est.).

Housing: Homeownership rate: 96.8% (2008-2012 5-year est.); Median home value: $55,000 (2008-2012 5-year est.); Median contract rent: $275 per month (2008-2012 5-year est.); Median year structure built: 1959 (2008-2012 5-year est.).

Health Insurance: 77.1% Private; 40.7% Public; 3.9% None. (2008-2012 5-year est.)

Transportation: Commute to work: 100.0% car, 0.0% public transportation, 0.0% walk, 0.0% work from home (2008-2012 5-year est.); Travel time to work: 15.1% less than 15 minutes, 43.8% 15 to 30 minutes, 21.9% 30 to 45 minutes, 0.0% 45 to 60 minutes, 19.2% 60 minutes or more (2008-2012 5-year est.)

KEENSBURG (village). Covers a land area of 0.256 square miles and a water area of 0 square miles. Located at 38.35° N. Lat; 87.87° W. Long. Elevation is 436 feet.

Population: 238 (1990); 252 (2000); 210 (2010); Density: 671.8 persons per square mile (2008-2012 5-year est.); Race: 94.8% White, 0.0% Black/African American, 1.7% Asian, 0.0% American Indian/Alaska Native, 0.0% Native Hawaiian/Other Pacific Islander, 3.5% Some other race, 3.5% Two or more races, 0.0% Hispanic of any race (2008-2012 5-year est.); Average household size: 3.02 (2008-2012 5-year est.); Median age: 32.9 (2008-2012 5-year est.); Males per 100 females: 156.7 (2008-2012 5-year est.); Marriage status: 17.4% never married, 64.5% now married, 5.8% widowed, 12.4% divorced (2008-2012 5-year est.); Foreign born: 1.7% (2008-2012 5-year est.); Ancestry (includes multiple ancestries): 16.3% German, 5.8% English, 4.7% Irish, 2.3% French, 1.2% Norwegian (2008-2012 5-year est.).

Economy: Homeowner vacancy rate: 0.0%. Rental vacancy rate: 0.0%. (2008-2012 5-year est.); Employment by occupation: 4.9% management, business, and financial, 4.9% computer, engineering, and science, 4.9% education, legal, community service, arts, and media, 1.2% healthcare practitioners, 16.0% service, 7.4% sales and office, 17.3% natural resources, construction, and maintenance, 43.2% production, transportation, and material moving (2008-2012 5-year est.).

Income: Per capita income: $18,095 (2008-2012 5-year est.); Median household income: $41,750 (2008-2012 5-year est.); Average household income: $49,921 (2008-2012 5-year est.); Percent of households with income of $100,000 or more: 1.8% (2008-2012 5-year est.); Poverty rate: 8.7% (2008-2012 5-year est.).

Education: Percent of population age 25 and over with: High school diploma (including GED) or higher: 80.0% (2008-2012 5-year est.);

Bachelor's degree or higher: 0.0% (2008-2012 5-year est.); Master's degree or higher: 0.0% (2008-2012 5-year est.).
Housing: Homeownership rate: 98.2% (2008-2012 5-year est.); Median home value: $50,000 (2008-2012 5-year est.); Median contract rent: n/a per month (2008-2012 5-year est.); Median year structure built: 1971 (2008-2012 5-year est.).
Health Insurance: 65.7% Private; 25.6% Public; 16.9% None. (2008-2012 5-year est.)
Transportation: Commute to work: 96.3% car, 0.0% public transportation, 0.0% walk, 0.0% work from home (2008-2012 5-year est.); Travel time to work: 19.8% less than 15 minutes, 49.4% 15 to 30 minutes, 27.2% 30 to 45 minutes, 2.5% 45 to 60 minutes, 1.2% 60 minutes or more (2008-2012 5-year est.)

MOUNT CARMEL (city). Aka Sugar Creek. County seat. Covers a land area of 4.855 square miles and a water area of 0.141 square miles. Located at 38.42° N. Lat; 87.77° W. Long. Elevation is 449 feet.
History: Mount Carmel was founded in 1818 by Rev. Thomas S. Hinde of Ohio, who hoped for a "moral, temperate, and industrious village." A mussel and pearl industry began here in 1900.
Population: 8,287 (1990); 7,982 (2000); 7,284 (2010); Density: 1,498.7 persons per square mile (2008-2012 5-year est.); Race: 96.9% White, 0.1% Black/African American, 1.2% Asian, 0.0% American Indian/Alaska Native, 0.0% Native Hawaiian/Other Pacific Islander, 1.8% Some other race, 1.4% Two or more races, 0.8% Hispanic of any race (2008-2012 5-year est.); Average household size: 2.37 (2008-2012 5-year est.); Median age: 42.6 (2008-2012 5-year est.); Males per 100 females: 86.2 (2008-2012 5-year est.); Marriage status: 24.4% never married, 52.9% now married, 8.1% widowed, 14.6% divorced (2008-2012 5-year est.); Foreign born: 1.8% (2008-2012 5-year est.); Ancestry (includes multiple ancestries): 21.4% German, 13.0% English, 11.2% American, 9.7% Irish, 2.4% Dutch (2008-2012 5-year est.).
Economy: Single-family building permits issued: 1 (2013); Multi-family building permits issued: 0 (2013); Homeowner vacancy rate: 6.1%. Rental vacancy rate: 2.2%. (2008-2012 5-year est.); Employment by occupation: 8.7% management, business, and financial, 1.3% computer, engineering, and science, 9.5% education, legal, community service, arts, and media, 5.7% healthcare practitioners, 20.3% service, 20.7% sales and office, 8.2% natural resources, construction, and maintenance, 25.6% production, transportation, and material moving (2008-2012 5-year est.).
Income: Per capita income: $22,317 (2008-2012 5-year est.); Median household income: $41,118 (2008-2012 5-year est.); Average household income: $53,135 (2008-2012 5-year est.); Percent of households with income of $100,000 or more: 9.8% (2008-2012 5-year est.); Poverty rate: 14.8% (2008-2012 5-year est.).
Taxes: Total city taxes per capita: $255 (2011); City property taxes per capita: $203 (2011).
Education: Percent of population age 25 and over with: High school diploma (including GED) or higher: 87.9% (2008-2012 5-year est.); Bachelor's degree or higher: 16.8% (2008-2012 5-year est.); Master's degree or higher: 5.5% (2008-2012 5-year est.).

School District(s)
Wabash CUSD 348 (PK-12)
    2011-12 Enrollment: 1,726 . . . . (618) 262-4181
Two-year College(s)
Illinois Eastern Community Colleges-Wabash Valley College (Public)
    Fall 2012 Enrollment: 4,706 . . . . (618) 393-2982
    2012-13 Tuition: In-state $8,361; Out-of-state $10,412
Housing: Homeownership rate: 73.5% (2008-2012 5-year est.); Median home value: $74,600 (2008-2012 5-year est.); Median contract rent: $374 per month (2008-2012 5-year est.); Median year structure built: 1958 (2008-2012 5-year est.).
Health Insurance: 67.7% Private; 35.4% Public; 11.3% None. (2008-2012 5-year est.)
Hospitals: Wabash General Hospital (56 beds)
Safety: Violent crime rate: 30.5 per 10,000 population; Property crime rate: 324.1 per 10,000 population (2012).
Transportation: Commute to work: 93.0% car, 0.5% public transportation, 1.5% walk, 3.1% work from home (2008-2012 5-year est.); Travel time to work: 59.7% less than 15 minutes, 21.3% 15 to 30 minutes, 11.3% 30 to 45 minutes, 4.2% 45 to 60 minutes, 3.5% 60 minutes or more (2008-2012 5-year est.)
Airports: Mount Carmel Municipal Airport (general aviation)
Additional Information Contacts

City of Mount Carmel. . . . . (618) 262-4822
    http://www.cityofmtcarmel.com
Wabash County Chamber of Commerce . . . . (618) 262-5116
    http://www.wabashcountychamber.com

Warren County

Located in western Illinois; drained by Henderson Creek. Covers a land area of 542.405 square miles, a water area of 0.646 square miles, and is located in the Central Time Zone at 40.85° N. Lat., 90.62° W. Long. The county was founded in 1825. County seat is Monmouth.

Weather Station: Monmouth   Elevation: 745 feet

	Jan	Feb	Mar	Apr	May	Jun	Jul	Aug	Sep	Oct	Nov	Dec
High	33	38	51	64	75	83	86	85	78	66	51	36
Low	16	20	30	41	51	60	64	62	54	43	32	20
Precip	1.6	1.8	2.7	3.8	4.5	4.3	4.1	4.3	3.8	3.0	2.8	2.3
Snow	7.1	5.6	3.0	1.3	0.0	0.0	0.0	0.0	0.0	0.1	1.3	6.5

High and Low temperatures in degrees Fahrenheit; Precipitation and Snow in inches

Population: 19,181 (1990); 18,735 (2000); 17,707 (2010); Race: 90.9% White, 2.6% Black/African American, 0.9% Asian, 0.3% American Indian/Alaska Native, 0.0% Native Hawaiian/Other Pacific Islander, 5.3% Some other race, 1.0% Two or more races, 8.2% Hispanic of any race (2008-2012 5-year est.); Density: 32.8 persons per square mile (2008-2012 5-year est.); Average household size: 2.39 (2008-2012 5-year est.); Median age: 40.0 (2008-2012 5-year est.); Males per 100 females: 95.9 (2008-2012 5-year est.).
Religion: Six largest groups: 11.1% Baptist, 8.1% Methodist/Pietist, 7.7% Catholicism, 6.6% Non-denominational Protestant, 6.4% Presbyterian-Reformed, 2.9% Lutheran (2010)
Economy: Unemployment rate: 5.9% (April 2014); Total civilian labor force: 8,737 (April 2014); Leading industries: 33.9% manufacturing; 9.9% retail trade; 8.9% accommodation & food services (2012); Farms: 605 totaling 338,411 acres (2012); Companies that employ 500 or more persons: 2 (2012); Companies that employ 100 to 499 persons: 3 (2012); Companies that employ less than 100 persons: 351 (2012); Black-owned businesses: n/a (2007); Hispanic-owned businesses: n/a (2007); Asian-owned businesses: n/a (2007); Women-owned businesses: 394 (2007); Single-family building permits issued: 7 (2013); Multi-family building permits issued: 0 (2013).
Income: Per capita income: $20,744 (2008-2012 5-year est.); Median household income: $41,138 (2008-2012 5-year est.); Average household income: $51,674 (2008-2012 5-year est.); Percent of households with income of $100,000 or more: 11.8% (2008-2012 5-year est.); Poverty rate: 15.4% (2008-2012 5-year est.); Bankruptcy rate: 3.05% (2013).
Education: Percent of population age 25 and over with: High school diploma (including GED) or higher: 86.4% (2008-2012 5-year est.); Bachelor's degree or higher: 18.7% (2008-2012 5-year est.); Master's degree or higher: 6.5% (2008-2012 5-year est.).
Housing: Homeownership rate: 71.6% (2008-2012 5-year est.); Median home value: $83,000 (2008-2012 5-year est.); Median contract rent: $405 per month (2008-2012 5-year est.); Median year structure built: 1950 (2008-2012 5-year est.)
Health: Birth rate: 116.2 per 10,000 population (2013); Death rate: 102.7 per 10,000 population (2013); Age-adjusted cancer mortality rate: 224.7 deaths per 100,000 population (2011); Number of physicians: 7.8 per 10,000 population (2011); Hospital beds: 13.0 per 10,000 population (2010); Hospital admissions: 320.8 per 10,000 population (2010).
Elections: 2012 Presidential election results: 52.1% Obama, 46.3% Romney
Additional Information Contacts
Warren County Government . . . . (309) 734-8592
    http://www.warrencountyil.com

Warren County Communities

ALEXIS (village). Covers a land area of 0.475 square miles and a water area of 0 square miles. Located at 41.06° N. Lat; 90.56° W. Long. Elevation is 699 feet.
Population: 908 (1990); 863 (2000); 831 (2010); Density: 2,003.5 persons per square mile (2008-2012 5-year est.); Race: 98.7% White, 0.3% Black/African American, 0.0% Asian, 0.2% American Indian/Alaska Native, 0.0% Native Hawaiian/Other Pacific Islander, 0.8% Some other race, 0.3% Two or more races, 0.6% Hispanic of any race (2008-2012 5-year est.);

Average household size: 2.34 (2008-2012 5-year est.); Median age: 43.9 (2008-2012 5-year est.); Males per 100 females: 83.6 (2008-2012 5-year est.); Marriage status: 17.6% never married, 63.2% now married, 6.8% widowed, 12.4% divorced (2008-2012 5-year est.); Foreign born: 0.8% (2008-2012 5-year est.); Ancestry (includes multiple ancestries): 18.6% Swedish, 18.1% German, 12.4% Irish, 10.5% English, 5.0% American (2008-2012 5-year est.).

Economy: Single-family building permits issued: 0 (2013); Multi-family building permits issued: 0 (2013); Homeowner vacancy rate: 9.1%. Rental vacancy rate: 0.0%. (2008-2012 5-year est.); Employment by occupation: 8.8% management, business, and financial, 3.1% computer, engineering, and science, 8.8% education, legal, community service, arts, and media, 6.7% healthcare practitioners, 11.4% service, 23.7% sales and office, 11.0% natural resources, construction, and maintenance, 26.6% production, transportation, and material moving (2008-2012 5-year est.).

Income: Per capita income: $24,609 (2008-2012 5-year est.); Median household income: $51,750 (2008-2012 5-year est.); Average household income: $58,216 (2008-2012 5-year est.); Percent of households with income of $100,000 or more: 10.1% (2008-2012 5-year est.); Poverty rate: 9.4% (2008-2012 5-year est.).

Education: Percent of population age 25 and over with: High school diploma (including GED) or higher: 93.2% (2008-2012 5-year est.); Bachelor's degree or higher: 12.8% (2008-2012 5-year est.); Master's degree or higher: 2.7% (2008-2012 5-year est.).

School District(s)

United CUSD 304 (PK-12)
    2011-12 Enrollment: 968 . . . . (309) 734-9413

Housing: Homeownership rate: 83.5% (2008-2012 5-year est.); Median home value: $73,600 (2008-2012 5-year est.); Median contract rent: $375 per month (2008-2012 5-year est.); Median year structure built: 1952 (2008-2012 5-year est.).

Health Insurance: 80.4% Private; 37.8% Public; 2.3% None. (2008-2012 5-year est.)

Transportation: Commute to work: 93.3% car, 0.0% public transportation, 3.4% walk, 2.6% work from home (2008-2012 5-year est.); Travel time to work: 16.8% less than 15 minutes, 38.9% 15 to 30 minutes, 27.5% 30 to 45 minutes, 7.3% 45 to 60 minutes, 9.5% 60 minutes or more (2008-2012 5-year est.)

BERWICK (unincorporated postal area)

Zip Code: 61417

Covers a land area of 28.734 square miles and a water area of 0 square miles. Located at 40.77° N. Lat; 90.53° W. Long. Elevation is 709 feet. Population: 259 (2010); Density: 9.0 persons per square mile (2010); Race: 97.7% White, 0.0% Black/African American, 0.0% Asian, 0.0% American Indian/Alaska Native, 0.0% Native Hawaiian/Other Pacific Islander, 2.3% Some other race, 2.3% Two or more races, 0.0% Hispanic of any race (2010); Average household size: 2.31 (2010); Median age: 49.8 (2010); Males per 100 females: 108.9 (2010); Homeownership rate: 80.3% (2010)

CAMERON (unincorporated postal area)

Zip Code: 61423

Covers a land area of 49.079 square miles and a water area of 0 square miles. Located at 40.88° N. Lat; 90.50° W. Long. Elevation is 771 feet. Population: 682 (2010); Density: 13.9 persons per square mile (2010); Race: 97.2% White, 0.4% Black/African American, 0.0% Asian, 0.0% American Indian/Alaska Native, 0.3% Native Hawaiian/Other Pacific Islander, 2.1% Some other race, 1.8% Two or more races, 1.8% Hispanic of any race (2010); Average household size: 2.44 (2010); Median age: 46.0 (2010); Males per 100 females: 101.8 (2010); Homeownership rate: 80.7% (2010)

GERLAW (unincorporated postal area)

Zip Code: 61435

Covers a land area of 9.777 square miles and a water area of 0 square miles. Located at 40.97° N. Lat; 90.54° W. Long. Elevation is 735 feet. Population: 116 (2010); Density: 11.9 persons per square mile (2010); Race: 99.1% White, 0.9% Black/African American, 0.0% Asian, 0.0% American Indian/Alaska Native, 0.0% Native Hawaiian/Other Pacific Islander, 0.0% Some other race, 0.0% Two or more races, 0.9% Hispanic of any race (2010); Average household size: 2.11 (2010); Median age: 58.0 (2010); Males per 100 females: 81.3 (2010); Homeownership rate: 92.8% (2010)

KIRKWOOD (village).

Covers a land area of 0.915 square miles and a water area of 0 square miles. Located at 40.87° N. Lat; 90.75° W. Long. Elevation is 741 feet.

Population: 884 (1990); 794 (2000); 714 (2010); Density: 777.0 persons per square mile (2008-2012 5-year est.); Race: 98.6% White, 0.6% Black/African American, 0.0% Asian, 0.8% American Indian/Alaska Native, 0.0% Native Hawaiian/Other Pacific Islander, 0.0% Some other race, 0.0% Two or more races, 0.3% Hispanic of any race (2008-2012 5-year est.); Average household size: 2.48 (2008-2012 5-year est.); Median age: 33.6 (2008-2012 5-year est.); Males per 100 females: 97.0 (2008-2012 5-year est.); Marriage status: 26.4% never married, 45.6% now married, 7.9% widowed, 20.1% divorced (2008-2012 5-year est.); Foreign born: 0.4% (2008-2012 5-year est.); Ancestry (includes multiple ancestries): 19.7% German, 12.0% Irish, 9.1% Swedish, 7.5% American, 7.2% English (2008-2012 5-year est.).

Economy: Single-family building permits issued: 0 (2013); Multi-family building permits issued: 0 (2013); Homeowner vacancy rate: 4.0%. Rental vacancy rate: 0.0%. (2008-2012 5-year est.); Employment by occupation: 14.4% management, business, and financial, 0.9% computer, engineering, and science, 4.8% education, legal, community service, arts, and media, 2.1% healthcare practitioners, 15.6% service, 26.4% sales and office, 13.2% natural resources, construction, and maintenance, 22.5% production, transportation, and material moving (2008-2012 5-year est.).

Income: Per capita income: $18,759 (2008-2012 5-year est.); Median household income: $39,018 (2008-2012 5-year est.); Average household income: $46,844 (2008-2012 5-year est.); Percent of households with income of $100,000 or more: 9.1% (2008-2012 5-year est.); Poverty rate: 14.1% (2008-2012 5-year est.).

Education: Percent of population age 25 and over with: High school diploma (including GED) or higher: 89.6% (2008-2012 5-year est.); Bachelor's degree or higher: 13.9% (2008-2012 5-year est.); Master's degree or higher: 1.5% (2008-2012 5-year est.).

Housing: Homeownership rate: 74.9% (2008-2012 5-year est.); Median home value: $58,700 (2008-2012 5-year est.); Median contract rent: $421 per month (2008-2012 5-year est.); Median year structure built: Before 1940 (2008-2012 5-year est.).

Health Insurance: 57.7% Private; 46.7% Public; 9.1% None. (2008-2012 5-year est.)

Transportation: Commute to work: 92.3% car, 0.0% public transportation, 2.1% walk, 4.9% work from home (2008-2012 5-year est.); Travel time to work: 33.2% less than 15 minutes, 29.4% 15 to 30 minutes, 23.2% 30 to 45 minutes, 2.3% 45 to 60 minutes, 11.9% 60 minutes or more (2008-2012 5-year est.)

LITTLE YORK (village).

Covers a land area of 0.255 square miles and a water area of 0 square miles. Located at 41.01° N. Lat; 90.75° W. Long. Elevation is 614 feet.

Population: 349 (1990); 269 (2000); 331 (2010); Density: 1,061.3 persons per square mile (2008-2012 5-year est.); Race: 98.9% White, 0.4% Black/African American, 0.0% Asian, 0.0% American Indian/Alaska Native, 0.0% Native Hawaiian/Other Pacific Islander, 0.7% Some other race, 0.7% Two or more races, 0.0% Hispanic of any race (2008-2012 5-year est.); Average household size: 2.34 (2008-2012 5-year est.); Median age: 41.5 (2008-2012 5-year est.); Males per 100 females: 95.0 (2008-2012 5-year est.); Marriage status: 31.5% never married, 42.5% now married, 6.8% widowed, 19.2% divorced (2008-2012 5-year est.); Foreign born: 0.0% (2008-2012 5-year est.); Ancestry (includes multiple ancestries): 32.1% German, 20.3% Irish, 12.5% English, 8.9% Italian, 7.4% American (2008-2012 5-year est.).

Economy: Single-family building permits issued: 0 (2013); Multi-family building permits issued: 0 (2013); Homeowner vacancy rate: 0.0%. Rental vacancy rate: 22.0%. (2008-2012 5-year est.); Employment by occupation: 10.7% management, business, and financial, 0.0% computer, engineering, and science, 0.0% education, legal, community service, arts, and media, 3.8% healthcare practitioners, 26.0% service, 19.8% sales and office, 16.8% natural resources, construction, and maintenance, 22.9% production, transportation, and material moving (2008-2012 5-year est.).

Income: Per capita income: $18,176 (2008-2012 5-year est.); Median household income: $34,167 (2008-2012 5-year est.); Average household income: $42,741 (2008-2012 5-year est.); Percent of households with income of $100,000 or more: 6.9% (2008-2012 5-year est.); Poverty rate: 16.2% (2008-2012 5-year est.).

Education: Percent of population age 25 and over with: High school diploma (including GED) or higher: 88.5% (2008-2012 5-year est.);

Bachelor's degree or higher: 4.4% (2008-2012 5-year est.); Master's degree or higher: 1.6% (2008-2012 5-year est.).
Housing: Homeownership rate: 72.4% (2008-2012 5-year est.); Median home value: $61,700 (2008-2012 5-year est.); Median contract rent: $358 per month (2008-2012 5-year est.); Median year structure built: 1951 (2008-2012 5-year est.).
Health Insurance: 55.4% Private; 41.3% Public; 19.9% None. (2008-2012 5-year est.)
Transportation: Commute to work: 97.5% car, 0.0% public transportation, 1.6% walk, 0.8% work from home (2008-2012 5-year est.); Travel time to work: 18.2% less than 15 minutes, 47.1% 15 to 30 minutes, 15.7% 30 to 45 minutes, 19.0% 45 to 60 minutes, 0.0% 60 minutes or more (2008-2012 5-year est.)

MONMOUTH (city). County seat. Covers a land area of 4.208 square miles and a water area of 0.021 square miles. Located at 40.91° N. Lat; 90.64° W. Long. Elevation is 761 feet.

History: Monmouth was named in remembrance of the Revolutionary War battle that took place at Monmouth, New Jersey. Monmouth was established in 1831, and grew as the seat of Warren County.
Population: 9,489 (1990); 9,841 (2000); 9,444 (2010); Density: 2,295.3 persons per square mile (2008-2012 5-year est.); Race: 85.7% White, 4.2% Black/African American, 0.7% Asian, 0.4% American Indian/Alaska Native, 0.0% Native Hawaiian/Other Pacific Islander, 9.0% Some other race, 1.1% Two or more races, 14.3% Hispanic of any race (2008-2012 5-year est.); Average household size: 2.42 (2008-2012 5-year est.); Median age: 34.5 (2008-2012 5-year est.); Males per 100 females: 96.3 (2008-2012 5-year est.); Marriage status: 38.7% never married, 39.6% now married, 8.1% widowed, 13.6% divorced (2008-2012 5-year est.); Foreign born: 6.7% (2008-2012 5-year est.); Ancestry (includes multiple ancestries): 18.7% German, 13.5% Irish, 8.7% English, 6.2% American, 5.4% Swedish (2008-2012 5-year est.).
Economy: Single-family building permits issued: 0 (2013); Multi-family building permits issued: 0 (2013); Homeowner vacancy rate: 1.8%. Rental vacancy rate: 8.1%. (2008-2012 5-year est.); Employment by occupation: 4.5% management, business, and financial, 2.0% computer, engineering, and science, 11.7% education, legal, community service, arts, and media, 2.6% healthcare practitioners, 30.8% service, 19.7% sales and office, 8.1% natural resources, construction, and maintenance, 20.5% production, transportation, and material moving (2008-2012 5-year est.).
Income: Per capita income: $17,628 (2008-2012 5-year est.); Median household income: $32,695 (2008-2012 5-year est.); Average household income: $46,306 (2008-2012 5-year est.); Percent of households with income of $100,000 or more: 10.7% (2008-2012 5-year est.); Poverty rate: 22.1% (2008-2012 5-year est.).
Taxes: Total city taxes per capita: $197 (2011); City property taxes per capita: $145 (2011).
Education: Percent of population age 25 and over with: High school diploma (including GED) or higher: 81.7% (2008-2012 5-year est.); Bachelor's degree or higher: 16.1% (2008-2012 5-year est.); Master's degree or higher: 6.3% (2008-2012 5-year est.).

School District(s)
Henderson/mercer/warren Roe (07-12)
 2011-12 Enrollment: n/a .... (309) 734-6822
Monmouth-Roseville CUSD 238 (PK-12)
 2011-12 Enrollment: 1,759 .... (309) 734-4712
United CUSD 304 (PK-12)
 2011-12 Enrollment: 968......................... (309) 734-9413

Four-year College(s)
Monmouth College (Private, Not-for-profit, Presbyterian Church (USA))
 Fall 2012 Enrollment: 1,247 .... (309) 457-2311
 2012-13 Tuition: In-state $30,450; Out-of-state $30,450
Housing: Homeownership rate: 62.0% (2008-2012 5-year est.); Median home value: $77,600 (2008-2012 5-year est.); Median contract rent: $417 per month (2008-2012 5-year est.); Median year structure built: 1949 (2008-2012 5-year est.).
Health Insurance: 60.6% Private; 37.0% Public; 15.1% None. (2008-2012 5-year est.)
Hospitals: Community Medical Center (68 beds)
Safety: Violent crime rate: 74.7 per 10,000 population; Property crime rate: 535.6 per 10,000 population (2012).
Transportation: Commute to work: 83.3% car, 0.6% public transportation, 8.6% walk, 4.9% work from home (2008-2012 5-year est.); Travel time to work: 72.4% less than 15 minutes, 13.4% 15 to 30 minutes, 6.0% 30 to 45

minutes, 3.3% 45 to 60 minutes, 4.9% 60 minutes or more (2008-2012 5-year est.)
Airports: Monmouth Municipal Airport (general aviation)
Additional Information Contacts
City of Monmouth .... (309) 734-2141
 http://cityofmonmouth.com
Monmouth Area Chamber of Commerce .... (309) 734-3181
 http://monmouthilchamber.com

ROSEVILLE (village). Covers a land area of 0.812 square miles and a water area of 0 square miles. Located at 40.73° N. Lat; 90.66° W. Long. Elevation is 745 feet.

History: Roseville grew as a trading center and shipping point for oats and soy beans. The town was first called Hat Grove, referring to the shape of a particular grove of trees.
Population: 1,151 (1990); 1,083 (2000); 989 (2010); Density: 1,286.3 persons per square mile (2008-2012 5-year est.); Race: 93.9% White, 3.6% Black/African American, 2.2% Asian, 0.1% American Indian/Alaska Native, 0.0% Native Hawaiian/Other Pacific Islander, 0.2% Some other race, 0.2% Two or more races, 1.8% Hispanic of any race (2008-2012 5-year est.); Average household size: 2.01 (2008-2012 5-year est.); Median age: 47.8 (2008-2012 5-year est.); Males per 100 females: 81.1 (2008-2012 5-year est.); Marriage status: 20.1% never married, 52.7% now married, 10.5% widowed, 16.6% divorced (2008-2012 5-year est.); Foreign born: 2.9% (2008-2012 5-year est.); Ancestry (includes multiple ancestries): 23.7% German, 17.1% Irish, 14.0% English, 11.2% Swedish, 5.9% American (2008-2012 5-year est.).
Economy: Single-family building permits issued: 0 (2013); Multi-family building permits issued: 0 (2013); Homeowner vacancy rate: 0.0%. Rental vacancy rate: 0.0%. (2008-2012 5-year est.); Employment by occupation: 10.5% management, business, and financial, 3.0% computer, engineering, and science, 8.8% education, legal, community service, arts, and media, 4.7% healthcare practitioners, 22.5% service, 22.0% sales and office, 9.6% natural resources, construction, and maintenance, 18.9% production, transportation, and material moving (2008-2012 5-year est.).
Income: Per capita income: $29,930 (2008-2012 5-year est.); Median household income: $40,547 (2008-2012 5-year est.); Average household income: $58,911 (2008-2012 5-year est.); Percent of households with income of $100,000 or more: 13.7% (2008-2012 5-year est.); Poverty rate: 12.6% (2008-2012 5-year est.).
Education: Percent of population age 25 and over with: High school diploma (including GED) or higher: 89.4% (2008-2012 5-year est.); Bachelor's degree or higher: 27.1% (2008-2012 5-year est.); Master's degree or higher: 9.2% (2008-2012 5-year est.).

School District(s)
Monmouth-Roseville CUSD 238 (PK-12)
 2011-12 Enrollment: 1,759 .... (309) 734-4712
Housing: Homeownership rate: 72.4% (2008-2012 5-year est.); Median home value: $74,200 (2008-2012 5-year est.); Median contract rent: $351 per month (2008-2012 5-year est.); Median year structure built: 1947 (2008-2012 5-year est.).
Health Insurance: 62.7% Private; 38.5% Public; 14.6% None. (2008-2012 5-year est.)
Transportation: Commute to work: 88.9% car, 0.6% public transportation, 5.6% walk, 2.3% work from home (2008-2012 5-year est.); Travel time to work: 36.9% less than 15 minutes, 36.1% 15 to 30 minutes, 18.2% 30 to 45 minutes, 4.3% 45 to 60 minutes, 4.5% 60 minutes or more (2008-2012 5-year est.)
Additional Information Contacts
Roseville Chamber of Commerce ....
 http://roseville-il.org

SMITHSHIRE (unincorporated postal area)
Zip Code: 61478
 Covers a land area of 36.387 square miles and a water area of 0 square miles. Located at 40.75° N. Lat; 90.76° W. Long. Elevation is 735 feet. Population: 290 (2010); Density: 8.0 persons per square mile (2010); Race: 99.7% White, 0.0% Black/African American, 0.3% Asian, 0.0% American Indian/Alaska Native, 0.0% Native Hawaiian/Other Pacific Islander, 0.0% Some other race, 0.0% Two or more races, 1.0% Hispanic of any race (2010); Average household size: 2.50 (2010); Median age: 41.0 (2010); Males per 100 females: 93.3 (2010); Homeownership rate: 83.7% (2010)

Washington County

Located in southwestern Illinois; bounded on the north by the Kaskaskia River; drained by the Little Muddy River. Covers a land area of 562.572 square miles, a water area of 1.334 square miles, and is located in the Central Time Zone at 38.35° N. Lat., 89.42° W. Long. The county was founded in 1818. County seat is Nashville.

Weather Station: Nashville 4 NE   Elevation: 515 feet

	Jan	Feb	Mar	Apr	May	Jun	Jul	Aug	Sep	Oct	Nov	Dec
High	39	44	55	67	76	85	88	87	80	69	55	42
Low	23	27	35	45	55	64	68	66	58	47	37	27
Precip	2.3	2.3	3.4	3.7	4.7	3.8	3.9	2.6	3.3	3.4	3.6	2.8
Snow	4.2	4.3	1.0	0.1	0.0	0.0	0.0	0.0	0.0	0.1	0.6	3.5

High and Low temperatures in degrees Fahrenheit; Precipitation and Snow in inches

Population: 14,965 (1990); 15,148 (2000); 14,716 (2010); Race: 97.6% White, 0.9% Black/African American, 0.1% Asian, 0.0% American Indian/Alaska Native, 0.0% Native Hawaiian/Other Pacific Islander, 1.4% Some other race, 0.9% Two or more races, 1.4% Hispanic of any race (2008-2012 5-year est.); Density: 26.0 persons per square mile (2008-2012 5-year est.); Average household size: 2.39 (2008-2012 5-year est.); Median age: 42.4 (2008-2012 5-year est.); Males per 100 females: 100.5 (2008-2012 5-year est.).
Religion: Six largest groups: 29.2% Catholicism, 18.7% Lutheran, 13.8% Presbyterian-Reformed, 3.8% Baptist, 3.8% Methodist/Pietist, 0.6% Non-denominational Protestant (2010)
Economy: Unemployment rate: 5.0% (April 2014); Total civilian labor force: 8,941 (April 2014); Leading industries: 11.1% wholesale trade; 10.8% transportation & warehousing; 10.7% retail trade (2012); Farms: 777 totaling 354,899 acres (2012); Companies that employ 500 or more persons: 1 (2012); Companies that employ 100 to 499 persons: 8 (2012); Companies that employ less than 100 persons: 378 (2012); Black-owned businesses: n/a (2007); Hispanic-owned businesses: n/a (2007); Asian-owned businesses: n/a (2007); Women-owned businesses: n/a (2007); Single-family building permits issued: 16 (2013); Multi-family building permits issued: 2 (2013).
Income: Per capita income: $26,247 (2008-2012 5-year est.); Median household income: $54,407 (2008-2012 5-year est.); Average household income: $63,648 (2008-2012 5-year est.); Percent of households with income of $100,000 or more: 16.2% (2008-2012 5-year est.); Poverty rate: 9.9% (2008-2012 5-year est.); Bankruptcy rate: 2.74% (2013).
Education: Percent of population age 25 and over with: High school diploma (including GED) or higher: 88.6% (2008-2012 5-year est.); Bachelor's degree or higher: 18.8% (2008-2012 5-year est.); Master's degree or higher: 6.8% (2008-2012 5-year est.).
Housing: Homeownership rate: 80.7% (2008-2012 5-year est.); Median home value: $104,800 (2008-2012 5-year est.); Median contract rent: $401 per month (2008-2012 5-year est.); Median year structure built: 1964 (2008-2012 5-year est.)
Health: Birth rate: 99.0 per 10,000 population (2013); Death rate: 93.4 per 10,000 population (2013); Age-adjusted cancer mortality rate: 132.0 deaths per 100,000 population (2011); Number of physicians: 5.5 per 10,000 population (2011); Hospital beds: 34.0 per 10,000 population (2010); Hospital admissions: 252.8 per 10,000 population (2010).
Elections: 2012 Presidential election results: 33.1% Obama, 64.7% Romney
National and State Parks: Washington County State Conservation Area
Additional Information Contacts
Washington County Government . . . . (618) 327-4800
    https://washingtonco.illinois.gov

Washington County Communities

ADDIEVILLE (village). Covers a land area of 1.053 square miles and a water area of 0 square miles. Located at 38.39° N. Lat; 89.49° W. Long. Elevation is 469 feet.
Population: 257 (1990); 267 (2000); 252 (2010); Density: 257.3 persons per square mile (2008-2012 5-year est.); Race: 99.3% White, 0.0% Black/African American, 0.0% Asian, 0.7% American Indian/Alaska Native, 0.0% Native Hawaiian/Other Pacific Islander, 0.0% Some other race, 0.0% Two or more races, 0.0% Hispanic of any race (2008-2012 5-year est.); Average household size: 2.68 (2008-2012 5-year est.); Median age: 38.1 (2008-2012 5-year est.); Males per 100 females: 111.7 (2008-2012 5-year est.); Marriage status: 20.3% never married, 60.4% now married, 5.7% widowed, 13.7% divorced (2008-2012 5-year est.); Foreign born: 0.0%

(2008-2012 5-year est.); Ancestry (includes multiple ancestries): 70.8% German, 11.8% Irish, 3.3% English, 1.8% American, 1.5% Polish (2008-2012 5-year est.).
Economy: Homeowner vacancy rate: 0.0%. Rental vacancy rate: 0.0%. (2008-2012 5-year est.); Employment by occupation: 6.2% management, business, and financial, 3.4% computer, engineering, and science, 3.4% education, legal, community service, arts, and media, 5.5% healthcare practitioners, 19.2% service, 26.0% sales and office, 20.5% natural resources, construction, and maintenance, 15.8% production, transportation, and material moving (2008-2012 5-year est.).
Income: Per capita income: $23,894 (2008-2012 5-year est.); Median household income: $58,375 (2008-2012 5-year est.); Average household income: $62,324 (2008-2012 5-year est.); Percent of households with income of $100,000 or more: 15.8% (2008-2012 5-year est.); Poverty rate: 4.4% (2008-2012 5-year est.).
Education: Percent of population age 25 and over with: High school diploma (including GED) or higher: 83.1% (2008-2012 5-year est.); Bachelor's degree or higher: 12.4% (2008-2012 5-year est.); Master's degree or higher: 1.1% (2008-2012 5-year est.).
Housing: Homeownership rate: 88.1% (2008-2012 5-year est.); Median home value: $86,300 (2008-2012 5-year est.); Median contract rent: $440 per month (2008-2012 5-year est.); Median year structure built: 1945 (2008-2012 5-year est.).
Health Insurance: 74.4% Private; 24.1% Public; 7.8% None. (2008-2012 5-year est.)
Transportation: Commute to work: 94.6% car, 0.0% public transportation, 0.7% walk, 4.8% work from home (2008-2012 5-year est.); Travel time to work: 40.0% less than 15 minutes, 18.6% 15 to 30 minutes, 25.0% 30 to 45 minutes, 9.3% 45 to 60 minutes, 7.1% 60 minutes or more (2008-2012 5-year est.)

ASHLEY (city). Covers a land area of 1.104 square miles and a water area of 0.022 square miles. Located at 38.33° N. Lat; 89.19° W. Long. Elevation is 548 feet.
History: Ashley was named for early settler John Ashley.
Population: 583 (1990); 613 (2000); 536 (2010); Density: 490.8 persons per square mile (2008-2012 5-year est.); Race: 92.4% White, 0.0% Black/African American, 0.0% Asian, 0.0% American Indian/Alaska Native, 0.0% Native Hawaiian/Other Pacific Islander, 7.6% Some other race, 4.4% Two or more races, 3.9% Hispanic of any race (2008-2012 5-year est.); Average household size: 1.96 (2008-2012 5-year est.); Median age: 41.5 (2008-2012 5-year est.); Males per 100 females: 115.1 (2008-2012 5-year est.); Marriage status: 26.1% never married, 48.9% now married, 10.1% widowed, 14.9% divorced (2008-2012 5-year est.); Foreign born: 1.8% (2008-2012 5-year est.); Ancestry (includes multiple ancestries): 32.7% German, 15.9% Polish, 14.9% Irish, 8.7% American, 5.4% English (2008-2012 5-year est.).
Economy: Single-family building permits issued: 0 (2013); Multi-family building permits issued: 0 (2013); Homeowner vacancy rate: 0.0%. Rental vacancy rate: 19.8% (2008-2012 5-year est.); Employment by occupation: 7.9% management, business, and financial, 0.0% computer, engineering, and science, 3.7% education, legal, community service, arts, and media, 2.9% healthcare practitioners, 31.0% service, 23.1% sales and office, 11.6% natural resources, construction, and maintenance, 19.8% production, transportation, and material moving (2008-2012 5-year est.).
Income: Per capita income: $21,304 (2008-2012 5-year est.); Median household income: $36,250 (2008-2012 5-year est.); Average household income: $42,478 (2008-2012 5-year est.); Percent of households with income of $100,000 or more: 6.2% (2008-2012 5-year est.); Poverty rate: 22.9% (2008-2012 5-year est.).
Education: Percent of population age 25 and over with: High school diploma (including GED) or higher: 70.6% (2008-2012 5-year est.); Bachelor's degree or higher: 9.2% (2008-2012 5-year est.); Master's degree or higher: 2.4% (2008-2012 5-year est.).
School District(s)
Ashley CCSD 15 (PK-08)
    2011-12 Enrollment: 157 . . . . (618) 485-6611
Housing: Homeownership rate: 73.6% (2008-2012 5-year est.); Median home value: $61,800 (2008-2012 5-year est.); Median contract rent: $383 per month (2008-2012 5-year est.); Median year structure built: 1964 (2008-2012 5-year est.).
Health Insurance: 62.2% Private; 50.6% Public; 11.1% None. (2008-2012 5-year est.)
Transportation: Commute to work: 98.2% car, 0.0% public transportation, 1.8% walk, 0.0% work from home (2008-2012 5-year est.); Travel time to

work: 24.3% less than 15 minutes, 50.4% 15 to 30 minutes, 14.2% 30 to 45 minutes, 0.9% 45 to 60 minutes, 10.2% 60 minutes or more (2008-2012 5-year est.)

DU BOIS (village). Covers a land area of 1.073 square miles and a water area of 0 square miles. Located at 38.22° N. Lat; 89.21° W. Long. Elevation is 522 feet.

Population: 216 (1990); 222 (2000); 205 (2010); Density: 176.2 persons per square mile (2008-2012 5-year est.); Race: 99.5% White, 0.5% Black/African American, 0.0% Asian, 0.0% American Indian/Alaska Native, 0.0% Native Hawaiian/Other Pacific Islander, 0.0% Some other race, 0.0% Two or more races, 0.0% Hispanic of any race (2008-2012 5-year est.); Average household size: 2.30 (2008-2012 5-year est.); Median age: 43.4 (2008-2012 5-year est.); Males per 100 females: 78.3 (2008-2012 5-year est.); Marriage status: 28.7% never married, 51.2% now married, 11.6% widowed, 8.5% divorced (2008-2012 5-year est.); Foreign born: 0.5% (2008-2012 5-year est.); Ancestry (includes multiple ancestries): 65.1% Polish, 42.3% German, 4.2% Irish, 3.2% American, 2.1% French Canadian (2008-2012 5-year est.).
Economy: Single-family building permits issued: 0 (2013); Multi-family building permits issued: 0 (2013); Homeowner vacancy rate: 7.6%. Rental vacancy rate: 0.0%. (2008-2012 5-year est.); Employment by occupation: 2.4% management, business, and financial, 0.0% computer, engineering, and science, 0.0% education, legal, community service, arts, and media, 2.4% healthcare practitioners, 17.1% service, 18.3% sales and office, 14.6% natural resources, construction, and maintenance, 45.1% production, transportation, and material moving (2008-2012 5-year est.).
Income: Per capita income: $18,597 (2008-2012 5-year est.); Median household income: $45,500 (2008-2012 5-year est.); Average household income: $43,489 (2008-2012 5-year est.); Percent of households with income of $100,000 or more: 3.7% (2008-2012 5-year est.); Poverty rate: 20.6% (2008-2012 5-year est.).
Education: Percent of population age 25 and over with: High school diploma (including GED) or higher: 80.0% (2008-2012 5-year est.); Bachelor's degree or higher: 5.2% (2008-2012 5-year est.); Master's degree or higher: 0.0% (2008-2012 5-year est.).
Housing: Homeownership rate: 89.0% (2008-2012 5-year est.); Median home value: $55,000 (2008-2012 5-year est.); Median contract rent: $275 per month (2008-2012 5-year est.); Median year structure built: 1944 (2008-2012 5-year est.).
Health Insurance: 81.0% Private; 25.4% Public; 10.1% None. (2008-2012 5-year est.)
Transportation: Commute to work: 94.9% car, 1.3% public transportation, 2.5% walk, 1.3% work from home (2008-2012 5-year est.); Travel time to work: 2.6% less than 15 minutes, 28.2% 15 to 30 minutes, 32.1% 30 to 45 minutes, 12.8% 45 to 60 minutes, 24.4% 60 minutes or more (2008-2012 5-year est.)

HOYLETON (village). Covers a land area of 0.751 square miles and a water area of 0 square miles. Located at 38.45° N. Lat; 89.27° W. Long. Elevation is 518 feet.

Population: 508 (1990); 520 (2000); 531 (2010); Density: 662.8 persons per square mile (2008-2012 5-year est.); Race: 79.3% White, 12.2% Black/African American, 0.0% Asian, 0.4% American Indian/Alaska Native, 0.0% Native Hawaiian/Other Pacific Islander, 8.1% Some other race, 0.8% Two or more races, 7.2% Hispanic of any race (2008-2012 5-year est.); Average household size: 2.34 (2008-2012 5-year est.); Median age: 39.3 (2008-2012 5-year est.); Males per 100 females: 132.7 (2008-2012 5-year est.); Marriage status: 22.2% never married, 59.5% now married, 10.4% widowed, 7.8% divorced (2008-2012 5-year est.); Foreign born: 5.8% (2008-2012 5-year est.); Ancestry (includes multiple ancestries): 41.0% German, 7.4% Irish, 4.8% English, 4.4% Scotch-Irish, 4.4% American (2008-2012 5-year est.).
Economy: Single-family building permits issued: 0 (2013); Multi-family building permits issued: 0 (2013); Homeowner vacancy rate: 0.0%. Rental vacancy rate: 10.5%. (2008-2012 5-year est.); Employment by occupation: 7.7% management, business, and financial, 0.0% computer, engineering, and science, 8.3% education, legal, community service, arts, and media, 7.1% healthcare practitioners, 13.7% service, 23.8% sales and office, 11.3% natural resources, construction, and maintenance, 28.0% production, transportation, and material moving (2008-2012 5-year est.).
Income: Per capita income: $21,402 (2008-2012 5-year est.); Median household income: $48,875 (2008-2012 5-year est.); Average household income: $58,740 (2008-2012 5-year est.); Percent of households with

income of $100,000 or more: 11.1% (2008-2012 5-year est.); Poverty rate: 19.1% (2008-2012 5-year est.).
Education: Percent of population age 25 and over with: High school diploma (including GED) or higher: 82.3% (2008-2012 5-year est.); Bachelor's degree or higher: 12.8% (2008-2012 5-year est.); Master's degree or higher: 2.3% (2008-2012 5-year est.).
School District(s)
Hoyleton CSD 29 (KG-08)
   2011-12 Enrollment: 80 . . . . (618) 493-7787
Kaskaskia Spec Educ District
   2011-12 Enrollment: n/a . . . . (618) 532-4721
Housing: Homeownership rate: 80.1% (2008-2012 5-year est.); Median home value: $80,700 (2008-2012 5-year est.); Median contract rent: $396 per month (2008-2012 5-year est.); Median year structure built: 1946 (2008-2012 5-year est.).
Health Insurance: 63.0% Private; 43.0% Public; 11.2% None. (2008-2012 5-year est.)
Transportation: Commute to work: 92.1% car, 0.0% public transportation, 1.8% walk, 3.0% work from home (2008-2012 5-year est.); Travel time to work: 21.4% less than 15 minutes, 47.8% 15 to 30 minutes, 12.6% 30 to 45 minutes, 4.4% 45 to 60 minutes, 13.8% 60 minutes or more (2008-2012 5-year est.)

IRVINGTON (village). Covers a land area of 1.030 square miles and a water area of 0.006 square miles. Located at 38.44° N. Lat; 89.16° W. Long. Elevation is 531 feet.

History: Irvington was a major strawberry-producing center in the 1890's, when special trains took the produce to Chicago.
Population: 827 (1990); 736 (2000); 659 (2010); Density: 652.5 persons per square mile (2008-2012 5-year est.); Race: 97.8% White, 1.2% Black/African American, 0.0% Asian, 0.0% American Indian/Alaska Native, 0.0% Native Hawaiian/Other Pacific Islander, 1.0% Some other race, 1.0% Two or more races, 0.3% Hispanic of any race (2008-2012 5-year est.); Average household size: 2.19 (2008-2012 5-year est.); Median age: 43.7 (2008-2012 5-year est.); Males per 100 females: 110.0 (2008-2012 5-year est.); Marriage status: 25.6% never married, 55.7% now married, 6.0% widowed, 12.7% divorced (2008-2012 5-year est.); Foreign born: 0.0% (2008-2012 5-year est.); Ancestry (includes multiple ancestries): 33.3% German, 18.6% Irish, 15.0% English, 6.5% American, 3.3% Polish (2008-2012 5-year est.).
Economy: Single-family building permits issued: 0 (2013); Multi-family building permits issued: 0 (2013); Homeowner vacancy rate: 8.6%. Rental vacancy rate: 7.6%. (2008-2012 5-year est.); Employment by occupation: 7.3% management, business, and financial, 0.8% computer, engineering, and science, 7.3% education, legal, community service, arts, and media, 5.7% healthcare practitioners, 16.3% service, 19.0% sales and office, 5.2% natural resources, construction, and maintenance, 38.3% production, transportation, and material moving (2008-2012 5-year est.).
Income: Per capita income: $27,582 (2008-2012 5-year est.); Median household income: $53,250 (2008-2012 5-year est.); Average household income: $61,925 (2008-2012 5-year est.); Percent of households with income of $100,000 or more: 15.3% (2008-2012 5-year est.); Poverty rate: 14.0% (2008-2012 5-year est.).
Education: Percent of population age 25 and over with: High school diploma (including GED) or higher: 91.2% (2008-2012 5-year est.); Bachelor's degree or higher: 6.1% (2008-2012 5-year est.); Master's degree or higher: 3.1% (2008-2012 5-year est.).
School District(s)
Irvington CCSD 11 (KG-08)
   2011-12 Enrollment: 75 . . . . (618) 249-6761
Housing: Homeownership rate: 76.2% (2008-2012 5-year est.); Median home value: $70,000 (2008-2012 5-year est.); Median contract rent: $362 per month (2008-2012 5-year est.); Median year structure built: 1969 (2008-2012 5-year est.).
Health Insurance: 64.0% Private; 36.0% Public; 14.9% None. (2008-2012 5-year est.)
Safety: Violent crime rate: 0.0 per 10,000 population; Property crime rate: 245.4 per 10,000 population (2012).
Transportation: Commute to work: 94.3% car, 0.0% public transportation, 0.0% walk, 5.1% work from home (2008-2012 5-year est.); Travel time to work: 25.8% less than 15 minutes, 53.8% 15 to 30 minutes, 15.6% 30 to 45 minutes, 1.2% 45 to 60 minutes, 3.6% 60 minutes or more (2008-2012 5-year est.)

NASHVILLE (city). County seat. Covers a land area of 2.717 square miles and a water area of 0.089 square miles. Located at 38.34° N. Lat; 89.39° W. Long. Elevation is 518 feet.

History: Incorporated 1853.

Population: 3,202 (1990); 3,147 (2000); 3,258 (2010); Density: 1,243.5 persons per square mile (2008-2012 5-year est.); Race: 99.2% White, 0.8% Black/African American, 0.0% Asian, 0.0% American Indian/Alaska Native, 0.0% Native Hawaiian/Other Pacific Islander, 0.0% Some other race, 0.0% Two or more races, 0.4% Hispanic of any race (2008-2012 5-year est.); Average household size: 2.41 (2008-2012 5-year est.); Median age: 37.9 (2008-2012 5-year est.); Males per 100 females: 99.0 (2008-2012 5-year est.); Marriage status: 18.9% never married, 58.2% now married, 11.2% widowed, 11.7% divorced (2008-2012 5-year est.); Foreign born: 0.2% (2008-2012 5-year est.); Ancestry (includes multiple ancestries): 50.1% German, 13.4% Irish, 11.5% English, 11.1% Polish, 5.1% American (2008-2012 5-year est.).

Economy: Single-family building permits issued: 2 (2013); Multi-family building permits issued: 0 (2013); Homeowner vacancy rate: 2.9%. Rental vacancy rate: 0.0%. (2008-2012 5-year est.); Employment by occupation: 11.1% management, business, and financial, 1.7% computer, engineering, and science, 12.2% education, legal, community service, arts, and media, 5.1% healthcare practitioners, 13.7% service, 21.3% sales and office, 12.9% natural resources, construction, and maintenance, 21.9% production, transportation, and material moving (2008-2012 5-year est.).

Income: Per capita income: $23,540 (2008-2012 5-year est.); Median household income: $47,708 (2008-2012 5-year est.); Average household income: $57,456 (2008-2012 5-year est.); Percent of households with income of $100,000 or more: 11.0% (2008-2012 5-year est.); Poverty rate: 17.3% (2008-2012 5-year est.).

Education: Percent of population age 25 and over with: High school diploma (including GED) or higher: 90.1% (2008-2012 5-year est.); Bachelor's degree or higher: 24.4% (2008-2012 5-year est.); Master's degree or higher: 10.9% (2008-2012 5-year est.).

School District(s)

Nashville CCSD 49 (PK-08)

    2011-12 Enrollment: 551 . . . . (618) 327-3055

Nashville CHSD 99 (09-12)

    2011-12 Enrollment: 458 . . . . (618) 327-8286

Housing: Homeownership rate: 74.2% (2008-2012 5-year est.); Median home value: $109,800 (2008-2012 5-year est.); Median contract rent: $429 per month (2008-2012 5-year est.); Median year structure built: 1957 (2008-2012 5-year est.).

Health Insurance: 75.0% Private; 29.9% Public; 6.6% None. (2008-2012 5-year est.)

Hospitals: Washington County Hospital (61 beds)

Transportation: Commute to work: 86.3% car, 0.1% public transportation, 4.2% walk, 9.4% work from home (2008-2012 5-year est.); Travel time to work: 66.3% less than 15 minutes, 7.8% 15 to 30 minutes, 11.4% 30 to 45 minutes, 8.0% 45 to 60 minutes, 6.4% 60 minutes or more (2008-2012 5-year est.)

Additional Information Contacts

Nashville Chamber of Commerce . . . . (618) 327-3700

    http://nashvilleilchamber.com

NEW MINDEN (village). Covers a land area of 0.308 square miles and a water area of 0 square miles. Located at 38.44° N. Lat; 89.37° W. Long. Elevation is 453 feet.

Population: 219 (1990); 204 (2000); 215 (2010); Density: 541.7 persons per square mile (2008-2012 5-year est.); Race: 100.0% White, 0.0% Black/African American, 0.0% Asian, 0.0% American Indian/Alaska Native, 0.0% Native Hawaiian/Other Pacific Islander, 0.0% Some other race, 0.0% Hispanic of any race (2008-2012 5-year est.); Average household size: 2.23 (2008-2012 5-year est.); Median age: 48.1 (2008-2012 5-year est.); Males per 100 females: 106.2 (2008-2012 5-year est.); Marriage status: 28.4% never married, 51.8% now married, 9.9% widowed, 9.9% divorced (2008-2012 5-year est.); Foreign born: 0.0% (2008-2012 5-year est.); Ancestry (includes multiple ancestries): 58.7% German, 10.8% Polish, 9.6% English, 6.6% American, 5.4% Irish (2008-2012 5-year est.).

Economy: Homeowner vacancy rate: 0.0%. Rental vacancy rate: 0.0%. (2008-2012 5-year est.); Employment by occupation: 14.0% management, business, and financial, 1.1% computer, engineering, and science, 3.2% education, legal, community service, arts, and media, 7.5% healthcare practitioners, 7.5% service, 17.2% sales and office, 18.3% natural

resources, construction, and maintenance, 31.2% production, transportation, and material moving (2008-2012 5-year est.).

Income: Per capita income: $30,600 (2008-2012 5-year est.); Median household income: $49,688 (2008-2012 5-year est.); Average household income: $68,259 (2008-2012 5-year est.); Percent of households with income of $100,000 or more: 18.7% (2008-2012 5-year est.); Poverty rate: 3.0% (2008-2012 5-year est.).

Education: Percent of population age 25 and over with: High school diploma (including GED) or higher: 87.9% (2008-2012 5-year est.); Bachelor's degree or higher: 9.8% (2008-2012 5-year est.); Master's degree or higher: 3.0% (2008-2012 5-year est.).

Housing: Homeownership rate: 92.0% (2008-2012 5-year est.); Median home value: $72,800 (2008-2012 5-year est.); Median contract rent: $450 per month (2008-2012 5-year est.); Median year structure built: 1958 (2008-2012 5-year est.).

Health Insurance: 74.9% Private; 39.5% Public; 4.8% None. (2008-2012 5-year est.)

Transportation: Commute to work: 93.3% car, 0.0% public transportation, 0.0% walk, 4.5% work from home (2008-2012 5-year est.); Travel time to work: 45.9% less than 15 minutes, 28.2% 15 to 30 minutes, 7.1% 30 to 45 minutes, 12.9% 45 to 60 minutes, 5.9% 60 minutes or more (2008-2012 5-year est.)

OAKDALE (village). Covers a land area of 1.644 square miles and a water area of 0 square miles. Located at 38.26° N. Lat; 89.50° W. Long. Elevation is 518 feet.

Population: 179 (1990); 213 (2000); 221 (2010); Density: 165.4 persons per square mile (2008-2012 5-year est.); Race: 100.0% White, 0.0% Black/African American, 0.0% Asian, 0.0% American Indian/Alaska Native, 0.0% Native Hawaiian/Other Pacific Islander, 0.0% Some other race, 0.0% Two or more races, 7.0% Hispanic of any race (2008-2012 5-year est.); Average household size: 2.41 (2008-2012 5-year est.); Median age: 40.5 (2008-2012 5-year est.); Males per 100 females: 106.1 (2008-2012 5-year est.); Marriage status: 29.2% never married, 57.1% now married, 5.8% widowed, 8.0% divorced (2008-2012 5-year est.); Foreign born: 1.5% (2008-2012 5-year est.); Ancestry (includes multiple ancestries): 44.5% German, 13.6% Irish, 10.7% American, 9.6% Polish, 7.4% English (2008-2012 5-year est.).

Economy: Homeowner vacancy rate: 0.0%. Rental vacancy rate: 0.0%. (2008-2012 5-year est.); Employment by occupation: 0.0% management, business, and financial, 2.0% computer, engineering, and science, 2.6% education, legal, community service, arts, and media, 10.6% healthcare practitioners, 15.9% service, 18.5% sales and office, 14.6% natural resources, construction, and maintenance, 29.8% production, transportation, and material moving (2008-2012 5-year est.).

Income: Per capita income: $24,807 (2008-2012 5-year est.); Median household income: $48,958 (2008-2012 5-year est.); Average household income: $60,543 (2008-2012 5-year est.); Percent of households with income of $100,000 or more: 11.5% (2008-2012 5-year est.); Poverty rate: 4.4% (2008-2012 5-year est.).

Education: Percent of population age 25 and over with: High school diploma (including GED) or higher: 91.8% (2008-2012 5-year est.); Bachelor's degree or higher: 16.8% (2008-2012 5-year est.); Master's degree or higher: 5.4% (2008-2012 5-year est.).

School District(s)

Oakdale CCSD 1 (KG-08)

    2011-12 Enrollment: 73 . . . . (618) 329-5292

Housing: Homeownership rate: 91.2% (2008-2012 5-year est.); Median home value: $90,000 (2008-2012 5-year est.); Median contract rent: n/a per month (2008-2012 5-year est.); Median year structure built: 1970 (2008-2012 5-year est.).

Health Insurance: 75.0% Private; 38.6% Public; 12.9% None. (2008-2012 5-year est.)

Transportation: Commute to work: 95.8% car, 0.0% public transportation, 1.4% walk, 1.4% work from home (2008-2012 5-year est.); Travel time to work: 29.3% less than 15 minutes, 42.9% 15 to 30 minutes, 4.3% 30 to 45 minutes, 12.1% 45 to 60 minutes, 11.4% 60 minutes or more (2008-2012 5-year est.)

OKAWVILLE (village). Covers a land area of 2.057 square miles and a water area of 0 square miles. Located at 38.43° N. Lat; 89.55° W. Long. Elevation is 440 feet.

Population: 1,274 (1990); 1,355 (2000); 1,434 (2010); Density: 674.3 persons per square mile (2008-2012 5-year est.); Race: 97.1% White, 1.6% Black/African American, 0.0% Asian, 0.2% American Indian/Alaska

Native, 0.0% Native Hawaiian/Other Pacific Islander, 1.1% Some other race, 0.7% Two or more races, 0.5% Hispanic of any race (2008-2012 5-year est.); Average household size: 2.24 (2008-2012 5-year est.); Median age: 39.2 (2008-2012 5-year est.); Males per 100 females: 92.4 (2008-2012 5-year est.); Marriage status: 25.1% never married, 53.7% now married, 10.1% widowed, 11.1% divorced (2008-2012 5-year est.); Foreign born: 0.0% (2008-2012 5-year est.); Ancestry (includes multiple ancestries): 57.9% German, 15.1% Irish, 6.3% American, 4.3% Polish, 3.6% English (2008-2012 5-year est.).
Economy: Single-family building permits issued: 1 (2013); Multi-family building permits issued: 2 (2013); Homeowner vacancy rate: 2.8%. Rental vacancy rate: 5.3%. (2008-2012 5-year est.); Employment by occupation: 13.9% management, business, and financial, 2.6% computer, engineering, and science, 9.8% education, legal, community service, arts, and media, 6.9% healthcare practitioners, 20.2% service, 19.5% sales and office, 14.4% natural resources, construction, and maintenance, 12.7% production, transportation, and material moving (2008-2012 5-year est.).
Income: Per capita income: $25,829 (2008-2012 5-year est.); Median household income: $53,063 (2008-2012 5-year est.); Average household income: $57,825 (2008-2012 5-year est.); Percent of households with income of $100,000 or more: 11.9% (2008-2012 5-year est.); Poverty rate: 10.2% (2008-2012 5-year est.).
Education: Percent of population age 25 and over with: High school diploma (including GED) or higher: 93.4% (2008-2012 5-year est.); Bachelor's degree or higher: 23.0% (2008-2012 5-year est.); Master's degree or higher: 8.1% (2008-2012 5-year est.).

School District(s)
West Washington County CUD 10 (KG-12)
    2011-12 Enrollment: 539 . . . . (618) 243-6454
Housing: Homeownership rate: 72.4% (2008-2012 5-year est.); Median home value: $111,600 (2008-2012 5-year est.); Median contract rent: $488 per month (2008-2012 5-year est.); Median year structure built: 1967 (2008-2012 5-year est.).
Health Insurance: 77.8% Private; 32.9% Public; 5.1% None. (2008-2012 5-year est.)
Safety: Violent crime rate: 7.1 per 10,000 population; Property crime rate: 148.1 per 10,000 population (2012).
Transportation: Commute to work: 93.8% car, 0.1% public transportation, 3.6% walk, 0.7% work from home (2008-2012 5-year est.); Travel time to work: 33.4% less than 15 minutes, 25.3% 15 to 30 minutes, 24.9% 30 to 45 minutes, 9.4% 45 to 60 minutes, 7.0% 60 minutes or more (2008-2012 5-year est.).
Additional Information Contacts
Okawville Chamber of Commerce & Tourism . . . . (618) 243-5694
    http://www.okawvillecc.com

RADOM (village). Covers a land area of 1.041 square miles and a water area of 0 square miles. Located at 38.28° N. Lat; 89.19° W. Long. Elevation is 535 feet.
Population: 174 (1990); 395 (2000); 220 (2010); Density: 202.7 persons per square mile (2008-2012 5-year est.); Race: 99.5% White, 0.0% Black/African American, 0.0% Asian, 0.0% American Indian/Alaska Native, 0.0% Native Hawaiian/Other Pacific Islander, 0.5% Some other race, 0.0% Two or more races, 0.9% Hispanic of any race (2008-2012 5-year est.); Average household size: 2.18 (2008-2012 5-year est.); Median age: 50.3 (2008-2012 5-year est.); Males per 100 females: 119.8 (2008-2012 5-year est.); Marriage status: 23.9% never married, 57.4% now married, 12.7% widowed, 6.1% divorced (2008-2012 5-year est.); Foreign born: 0.0% (2008-2012 5-year est.); Ancestry (includes multiple ancestries): 58.3% Polish, 17.5% German, 7.6% Italian, 7.1% Irish, 5.7% English (2008-2012 5-year est.).
Economy: Homeowner vacancy rate: 0.0%. Rental vacancy rate: 0.0%. (2008-2012 5-year est.); Employment by occupation: 9.9% management, business, and financial, 2.7% computer, engineering, and science, 5.4% education, legal, community service, arts, and media, 2.7% healthcare practitioners, 13.5% service, 12.6% sales and office, 30.6% natural resources, construction, and maintenance, 22.5% production, transportation, and material moving (2008-2012 5-year est.).
Income: Per capita income: $21,995 (2008-2012 5-year est.); Median household income: $38,393 (2008-2012 5-year est.); Average household income: $47,457 (2008-2012 5-year est.); Percent of households with income of $100,000 or more: 4.1% (2008-2012 5-year est.); Poverty rate: 2.4% (2008-2012 5-year est.).
Education: Percent of population age 25 and over with: High school diploma (including GED) or higher: 77.9% (2008-2012 5-year est.);

Bachelor's degree or higher: 7.4% (2008-2012 5-year est.); Master's degree or higher: 1.8% (2008-2012 5-year est.).
Housing: Homeownership rate: 86.6% (2008-2012 5-year est.); Median home value: $79,300 (2008-2012 5-year est.); Median contract rent: n/a per month (2008-2012 5-year est.); Median year structure built: 1971 (2008-2012 5-year est.).
Health Insurance: 74.9% Private; 31.8% Public; 9.5% None. (2008-2012 5-year est.)
Transportation: Commute to work: 90.8% car, 0.0% public transportation, 0.0% walk, 7.3% work from home (2008-2012 5-year est.); Travel time to work: 7.9% less than 15 minutes, 59.4% 15 to 30 minutes, 17.8% 30 to 45 minutes, 0.0% 45 to 60 minutes, 14.9% 60 minutes or more (2008-2012 5-year est.).

RICHVIEW (village). Covers a land area of 1.120 square miles and a water area of 0 square miles. Located at 38.38° N. Lat; 89.18° W. Long. Elevation is 541 feet.
Population: 307 (1990); 308 (2000); 253 (2010); Density: 183.1 persons per square mile (2008-2012 5-year est.); Race: 99.5% White, 0.0% Black/African American, 0.0% Asian, 0.0% American Indian/Alaska Native, 0.0% Native Hawaiian/Other Pacific Islander, 0.5% Some other race, 0.5% Two or more races, 0.0% Hispanic of any race (2008-2012 5-year est.); Average household size: 1.99 (2008-2012 5-year est.); Median age: 43.9 (2008-2012 5-year est.); Males per 100 females: 93.4 (2008-2012 5-year est.); Marriage status: 33.3% never married, 52.9% now married, 6.3% widowed, 7.5% divorced (2008-2012 5-year est.); Foreign born: 0.0% (2008-2012 5-year est.); Ancestry (includes multiple ancestries): 41.0% German, 15.6% English, 13.7% Irish, 13.7% Polish, 6.8% American (2008-2012 5-year est.).
Economy: Single-family building permits issued: 0 (2013); Multi-family building permits issued: 0 (2013); Homeowner vacancy rate: 5.1%. Rental vacancy rate: 0.0%. (2008-2012 5-year est.); Employment by occupation: 14.2% management, business, and financial, 0.0% computer, engineering, and science, 5.7% education, legal, community service, arts, and media, 8.5% healthcare practitioners, 18.9% service, 10.4% sales and office, 14.2% natural resources, construction, and maintenance, 28.3% production, transportation, and material moving (2008-2012 5-year est.).
Income: Per capita income: $19,015 (2008-2012 5-year est.); Median household income: $27,969 (2008-2012 5-year est.); Average household income: $36,950 (2008-2012 5-year est.); Percent of households with income of $100,000 or more: 3.9% (2008-2012 5-year est.); Poverty rate: 25.4% (2008-2012 5-year est.).
Education: Percent of population age 25 and over with: High school diploma (including GED) or higher: 78.3% (2008-2012 5-year est.); Bachelor's degree or higher: 3.6% (2008-2012 5-year est.); Master's degree or higher: 2.9% (2008-2012 5-year est.).
Housing: Homeownership rate: 71.8% (2008-2012 5-year est.); Median home value: $49,200 (2008-2012 5-year est.); Median contract rent: $362 per month (2008-2012 5-year est.); Median year structure built: 1969 (2008-2012 5-year est.).
Health Insurance: 60.0% Private; 27.8% Public; 20.5% None. (2008-2012 5-year est.)
Transportation: Commute to work: 98.1% car, 0.0% public transportation, 1.9% walk, 0.0% work from home (2008-2012 5-year est.); Travel time to work: 20.8% less than 15 minutes, 67.0% 15 to 30 minutes, 9.4% 30 to 45 minutes, 0.0% 45 to 60 minutes, 2.8% 60 minutes or more (2008-2012 5-year est.).

VENEDY (village). Covers a land area of 0.286 square miles and a water area of 0 square miles. Located at 38.40° N. Lat; 89.65° W. Long. Elevation is 453 feet.
Population: 158 (1990); 137 (2000); 138 (2010); Density: 377.9 persons per square mile (2008-2012 5-year est.); Race: 98.1% White, 1.9% Black/African American, 0.0% Asian, 0.0% American Indian/Alaska Native, 0.0% Native Hawaiian/Other Pacific Islander, 0.0% Some other race, 0.0% Two or more races, 1.9% Hispanic of any race (2008-2012 5-year est.); Average household size: 2.08 (2008-2012 5-year est.); Median age: 52.3 (2008-2012 5-year est.); Males per 100 females: 107.7 (2008-2012 5-year est.); Marriage status: 17.8% never married, 63.3% now married, 13.3% widowed, 5.6% divorced (2008-2012 5-year est.); Foreign born: 0.9% (2008-2012 5-year est.); Ancestry (includes multiple ancestries): 64.8% German, 16.7% Italian, 8.3% Irish, 3.7% Portuguese, 1.9% Scottish (2008-2012 5-year est.).
Economy: Homeowner vacancy rate: 0.0%. Rental vacancy rate: 0.0%. (2008-2012 5-year est.); Employment by occupation: 17.8% management,

business, and financial, 0.0% computer, engineering, and science, 0.0% education, legal, community service, arts, and media, 2.2% healthcare practitioners, 13.3% service, 24.4% sales and office, 22.2% natural resources, construction, and maintenance, 20.0% production, transportation, and material moving (2008-2012 5-year est.).
Income: Per capita income: $28,717 (2008-2012 5-year est.); Median household income: $42,500 (2008-2012 5-year est.); Average household income: $58,400 (2008-2012 5-year est.); Percent of households with income of $100,000 or more: 11.5% (2008-2012 5-year est.); Poverty rate: 16.1% (2008-2012 5-year est.).
Education: Percent of population age 25 and over with: High school diploma (including GED) or higher: 77.1% (2008-2012 5-year est.); Bachelor's degree or higher: 4.8% (2008-2012 5-year est.); Master's degree or higher: 0.0% (2008-2012 5-year est.).
Housing: Homeownership rate: 84.6% (2008-2012 5-year est.); Median home value: $91,400 (2008-2012 5-year est.); Median contract rent: $350 per month (2008-2012 5-year est.); Median year structure built: 1959 (2008-2012 5-year est.).
Health Insurance: 61.1% Private; 24.1% Public; 32.4% None. (2008-2012 5-year est.)
Transportation: Commute to work: 97.8% car, 0.0% public transportation, 0.0% walk, 2.2% work from home (2008-2012 5-year est.); Travel time to work: 18.2% less than 15 minutes, 50.0% 15 to 30 minutes, 13.6% 30 to 45 minutes, 11.4% 45 to 60 minutes, 6.8% 60 minutes or more (2008-2012 5-year est.)

Wayne County

Located in southeastern Illinois; drained by the Little Wabash River. Covers a land area of 713.814 square miles, a water area of 1.672 square miles, and is located in the Central Time Zone at 38.43° N. Lat., 88.43° W. Long. The county was founded in 1819. County seat is Fairfield.

Weather Station: Fairfield Radio Wfiw										Elevation: 430 feet		
	Jan	Feb	Mar	Apr	May	Jun	Jul	Aug	Sep	Oct	Nov	Dec
High	39	44	55	67	76	85	88	87	81	68	55	42
Low	23	26	34	44	53	62	66	64	56	44	35	26
Precip	3.0	2.8	4.5	4.4	4.9	3.7	3.6	3.1	2.7	4.0	4.1	3.5
Snow	3.7	4.0	1.6	0.1	0.0	0.0	0.0	0.0	0.0	0.1	0.3	3.7

High and Low temperatures in degrees Fahrenheit; Precipitation and Snow in inches

Population: 17,241 (1990); 17,151 (2000); 16,760 (2010); Race: 98.3% White, 0.4% Black/African American, 0.5% Asian, 0.0% American Indian/Alaska Native, 0.0% Native Hawaiian/Other Pacific Islander, 0.8% Some other race, 0.6% Two or more races, 1.1% Hispanic of any race (2008-2012 5-year est.); Density: 23.3 persons per square mile (2008-2012 5-year est.); Average household size: 2.32 (2008-2012 5-year est.); Median age: 42.6 (2008-2012 5-year est.); Males per 100 females: 95.2 (2008-2012 5-year est.).
Religion: Six largest groups: 36.2% Baptist, 5.6% Methodist/Pietist, 3.4% Presbyterian-Reformed, 2.3% European Free-Church, 1.9% Pentecostal, 1.8% Catholicism (2010)
Economy: Unemployment rate: 6.8% (April 2014); Total civilian labor force: 7,508 (April 2014); Leading industries: 23.4% health care and social assistance; 17.7% retail trade; 8.8% accommodation & food services (2012); Farms: 1,187 totaling 368,518 acres (2012); Companies that employ 500 or more persons: 1 (2012); Companies that employ 100 to 499 persons: 4 (2012); Companies that employ less than 100 persons: 368 (2012); Black-owned businesses: n/a (2007); Hispanic-owned businesses: n/a (2007); Asian-owned businesses: n/a (2007); Women-owned businesses: 393 (2007); Single-family building permits issued: 0 (2013); Multi-family building permits issued: 0 (2013).
Income: Per capita income: $23,242 (2008-2012 5-year est.); Median household income: $41,446 (2008-2012 5-year est.); Average household income: $53,225 (2008-2012 5-year est.); Percent of households with income of $100,000 or more: 9.6% (2008-2012 5-year est.); Poverty rate: 13.0% (2008-2012 5-year est.); Bankruptcy rate: 2.23% (2013).
Taxes: Total county taxes per capita: $144 (2011); County property taxes per capita: $87 (2011).
Education: Percent of population age 25 and over with: High school diploma (including GED) or higher: 85.4% (2008-2012 5-year est.); Bachelor's degree or higher: 12.7% (2008-2012 5-year est.); Master's degree or higher: 3.1% (2008-2012 5-year est.).
Housing: Homeownership rate: 77.6% (2008-2012 5-year est.); Median home value: $72,500 (2008-2012 5-year est.); Median contract rent: $323

per month (2008-2012 5-year est.); Median year structure built: 1968 (2008-2012 5-year est.)
Health: Birth rate: 129.4 per 10,000 population (2013); Death rate: 122.2 per 10,000 population (2013); Age-adjusted cancer mortality rate: 175.7 deaths per 100,000 population (2011); Number of physicians: 7.2 per 10,000 population (2011); Hospital beds: 94.9 per 10,000 population (2010); Hospital admissions: 627.1 per 10,000 population (2010).
Elections: 2012 Presidential election results: 19.7% Obama, 78.0% Romney
National and State Parks: Sam Dale Lake State Conservation Area
Additional Information Contacts
Wayne County Government . . . . (618) 842-5182

Wayne County Communities

BARNHILL (unincorporated postal area)
Zip Code: 62809
Covers a land area of 11.735 square miles and a water area of 0.031 square miles. Located at 38.27° N. Lat; 88.29° W. Long. Elevation is 397 feet. Population: 142 (2010); Density: 12.1 persons per square mile (2010); Race: 98.6% White, 0.0% Black/African American, 0.7% Asian, 0.0% American Indian/Alaska Native, 0.0% Native Hawaiian/Other Pacific Islander, 0.7% Some other race, 0.0% Two or more races, 0.7% Hispanic of any race (2010); Average household size: 2.41 (2010); Median age: 44.5 (2010); Males per 100 females: 108.8 (2010); Homeownership rate: 86.5% (2010)

CISNE (village). Covers a land area of 0.635 square miles and a water area of 0 square miles. Located at 38.51° N. Lat; 88.44° W. Long. Elevation is 459 feet.
Population: 645 (1990); 673 (2000); 672 (2010); Density: 1,190.6 persons per square mile (2008-2012 5-year est.); Race: 96.0% White, 0.0% Black/African American, 3.0% Asian, 0.0% American Indian/Alaska Native, 0.0% Native Hawaiian/Other Pacific Islander, 1.0% Some other race, 0.0% Two or more races, 1.6% Hispanic of any race (2008-2012 5-year est.); Average household size: 2.41 (2008-2012 5-year est.); Median age: 40.7 (2008-2012 5-year est.); Males per 100 females: 107.7 (2008-2012 5-year est.); Marriage status: 23.1% never married, 57.5% now married, 10.1% widowed, 9.3% divorced (2008-2012 5-year est.); Foreign born: 3.0% (2008-2012 5-year est.); Ancestry (includes multiple ancestries): 10.8% German, 6.1% American, 3.4% Irish, 3.4% English, 2.5% Polish (2008-2012 5-year est.).
Economy: Homeowner vacancy rate: 5.3%. Rental vacancy rate: 11.5%. (2008-2012 5-year est.); Employment by occupation: 3.7% management, business, and financial, 1.8% computer, engineering, and science, 5.2% education, legal, community service, arts, and media, 4.1% healthcare practitioners, 18.8% service, 30.6% sales and office, 14.4% natural resources, construction, and maintenance, 21.4% production, transportation, and material moving (2008-2012 5-year est.).
Income: Per capita income: $17,705 (2008-2012 5-year est.); Median household income: $35,724 (2008-2012 5-year est.); Average household income: $45,021 (2008-2012 5-year est.); Percent of households with income of $100,000 or more: 8.7% (2008-2012 5-year est.); Poverty rate: 6.6% (2008-2012 5-year est.).
Education: Percent of population age 25 and over with: High school diploma (including GED) or higher: 87.0% (2008-2012 5-year est.); Bachelor's degree or higher: 11.4% (2008-2012 5-year est.); Master's degree or higher: 3.6% (2008-2012 5-year est.).
School District(s)
North Wayne CUSD 200 (PK-12)
2011-12 Enrollment: 428 . . . . (618) 673-2151
Wayne City CUSD 100 (KG-12)
2011-12 Enrollment: 556 . . . . (618) 895-3103
Housing: Homeownership rate: 81.9% (2008-2012 5-year est.); Median home value: $58,900 (2008-2012 5-year est.); Median contract rent: $248 per month (2008-2012 5-year est.); Median year structure built: 1958 (2008-2012 5-year est.).
Health Insurance: 63.2% Private; 37.8% Public; 12.6% None. (2008-2012 5-year est.)
Transportation: Commute to work: 93.9% car, 0.0% public transportation, 0.0% walk, 6.1% work from home (2008-2012 5-year est.); Travel time to work: 27.8% less than 15 minutes, 56.1% 15 to 30 minutes, 10.0% 30 to 45 minutes, 0.0% 45 to 60 minutes, 6.1% 60 minutes or more (2008-2012 5-year est.)

FAIRFIELD (city). Aka Thomas Prairie. County seat. Covers a land area of 4.016 square miles and a water area of 0.034 square miles. Located at 38.38° N. Lat; 88.37° W. Long. Elevation is 440 feet.

History: Fairfield was established in 1819, and developed as the seat of Wayne County. Clothing and automobile parts manufacturing were early industries.

Population: 5,439 (1990); 5,421 (2000); 5,154 (2010); Density: 1,315.8 persons per square mile (2008-2012 5-year est.); Race: 97.5% White, 0.9% Black/African American, 0.3% Asian, 0.0% American Indian/Alaska Native, 0.0% Native Hawaiian/Other Pacific Islander, 1.3% Some other race, 1.3% Two or more races, 1.2% Hispanic of any race (2008-2012 5-year est.); Average household size: 2.03 (2008-2012 5-year est.); Median age: 43.3 (2008-2012 5-year est.); Males per 100 females: 84.8 (2008-2012 5-year est.); Marriage status: 19.6% never married, 49.1% now married, 13.2% widowed, 18.1% divorced (2008-2012 5-year est.); Foreign born: 0.7% (2008-2012 5-year est.); Ancestry (includes multiple ancestries): 14.5% American, 14.1% German, 12.4% English, 8.8% Irish, 2.3% Scotch-Irish (2008-2012 5-year est.).

Economy: Single-family building permits issued: 0 (2013); Multi-family building permits issued: 0 (2013); Homeowner vacancy rate: 2.1%. Rental vacancy rate: 5.1%. (2008-2012 5-year est.); Employment by occupation: 3.3% management, business, and financial, 3.3% computer, engineering, and science, 9.0% education, legal, community service, arts, and media, 5.5% healthcare practitioners, 16.8% service, 22.8% sales and office, 14.2% natural resources, construction, and maintenance, 25.2% production, transportation, and material moving (2008-2012 5-year est.).

Income: Per capita income: $20,795 (2008-2012 5-year est.); Median household income: $31,006 (2008-2012 5-year est.); Average household income: $41,798 (2008-2012 5-year est.); Percent of households with income of $100,000 or more: 5.5% (2008-2012 5-year est.); Poverty rate: 23.3% (2008-2012 5-year est.).

Taxes: Total city taxes per capita: $248 (2011); City property taxes per capita: $214 (2011).

Education: Percent of population age 25 and over with: High school diploma (including GED) or higher: 84.3% (2008-2012 5-year est.); Bachelor's degree or higher: 12.7% (2008-2012 5-year est.); Master's degree or higher: 3.3% (2008-2012 5-year est.).

School District(s)

Fairfield Community HSD 225 (09-12)
    2011-12 Enrollment: 421 . . . . (618) 842-7448
Fairfield PSD 112 (PK-08)
    2011-12 Enrollment: 716 . . . . (618) 842-6501
Jasper CCSD 17 (KG-08)
    2011-12 Enrollment: 169 . . . . (618) 842-3048
New Hope CCSD 6 (PK-08)
    2011-12 Enrollment: 196 . . . . (618) 842-3296

Two-year College(s)

Illinois Eastern Community Colleges-Frontier Community Coll (Public)
    Fall 2012 Enrollment: 2,597 . . . . (618) 393-2982
    2012-13 Tuition: In-state $8,361; Out-of-state $10,412

Housing: Homeownership rate: 62.1% (2008-2012 5-year est.); Median home value: $62,900 (2008-2012 5-year est.); Median contract rent: $351 per month (2008-2012 5-year est.); Median year structure built: 1959 (2008-2012 5-year est.).

Health Insurance: 60.2% Private; 47.2% Public; 12.6% None. (2008-2012 5-year est.)

Hospitals: Fairfield Memorial Hospital (80 beds)

Safety: Violent crime rate: 66.3 per 10,000 population; Property crime rate: 325.9 per 10,000 population (2012).

Transportation: Commute to work: 92.7% car, 0.0% public transportation, 3.4% walk, 1.8% work from home (2008-2012 5-year est.); Travel time to work: 65.1% less than 15 minutes, 14.9% 15 to 30 minutes, 11.8% 30 to 45 minutes, 4.4% 45 to 60 minutes, 3.8% 60 minutes or more (2008-2012 5-year est.).

Airports: Fairfield Municipal Airport (general aviation)

Additional Information Contacts

City of Fairfield . . . . (618) 842-3871
    http://www.fairfield-il.com
Greater Fairfield Area Chamber of Commerce . . . . (618) 842-6116
    http://fairfieldillinoischamber.com

GEFF (unincorporated postal area)

Zip Code: 62842
    Covers a land area of 43.998 square miles and a water area of 0.009 square miles. Located at 38.46° N. Lat; 88.37° W. Long. Elevation is

459 feet. Population: 835 (2010); Density: 19.0 persons per square mile (2010); Race: 98.6% White, 0.1% Black/African American, 0.1% Asian, 0.2% American Indian/Alaska Native, 0.0% Native Hawaiian/Other Pacific Islander, 1.0% Some other race, 0.4% Two or more races, 1.2% Hispanic of any race (2010); Average household size: 2.45 (2010); Median age: 39.6 (2010); Males per 100 females: 100.7 (2010); Homeownership rate: 82.4% (2010)

GOLDEN GATE (village). Aka Goldengate. Covers a land area of 0.076 square miles and a water area of 0 square miles. Located at 38.36° N. Lat; 88.20° W. Long. Elevation is 397 feet.

Population: 71 (1990); 100 (2000); 68 (2010); Density: 987.8 persons per square mile (2008-2012 5-year est.); Race: 100.0% White, 0.0% Black/African American, 0.0% Asian, 0.0% American Indian/Alaska Native, 0.0% Native Hawaiian/Other Pacific Islander, 0.0% Some other race, 0.0% Two or more races, 0.0% Hispanic of any race (2008-2012 5-year est.); Average household size: 1.74 (2008-2012 5-year est.); Median age: 55.3 (2008-2012 5-year est.); Males per 100 females: 114.3 (2008-2012 5-year est.); Marriage status: 11.6% never married, 65.2% now married, 21.7% widowed, 1.4% divorced (2008-2012 5-year est.); Foreign born: 0.0% (2008-2012 5-year est.); Ancestry (includes multiple ancestries): 18.7% German, 14.7% English, 5.3% Irish (2008-2012 5-year est.).

Economy: Homeowner vacancy rate: 0.0%. Rental vacancy rate: 100.0%. (2008-2012 5-year est.); Employment by occupation: 0.0% management, business, and financial, 10.0% computer, engineering, and science, 0.0% education, legal, community service, arts, and media, 0.0% healthcare practitioners, 0.0% service, 10.0% sales and office, 10.0% natural resources, construction, and maintenance, 70.0% production, transportation, and material moving (2008-2012 5-year est.).

Income: Per capita income: $18,203 (2008-2012 5-year est.); Median household income: $25,750 (2008-2012 5-year est.); Average household income: $31,579 (2008-2012 5-year est.); Percent of households with income of $100,000 or more: n/a (2008-2012 5-year est.); Poverty rate: 29.3% (2008-2012 5-year est.).

Education: Percent of population age 25 and over with: High school diploma (including GED) or higher: 76.8% (2008-2012 5-year est.); Bachelor's degree or higher: 11.6% (2008-2012 5-year est.); Master's degree or higher: 7.2% (2008-2012 5-year est.).

Housing: Homeownership rate: 100.0% (2008-2012 5-year est.); Median home value: $56,300 (2008-2012 5-year est.); Median contract rent: n/a per month (2008-2012 5-year est.); Median year structure built: 1951 (2008-2012 5-year est.).

Health Insurance: 52.0% Private; 45.3% Public; 12.0% None. (2008-2012 5-year est.)

Transportation: Commute to work: 100.0% car, 0.0% public transportation, 0.0% walk, 0.0% work from home (2008-2012 5-year est.); Travel time to work: 10.0% less than 15 minutes, 90.0% 15 to 30 minutes, 0.0% 30 to 45 minutes, 0.0% 45 to 60 minutes, 0.0% 60 minutes or more (2008-2012 5-year est.)

JEFFERSONVILLE (village). Aka Geff. Covers a land area of 1.020 square miles and a water area of 0 square miles. Located at 38.44° N. Lat; 88.40° W. Long.

History: Also known as Geff.

Population: 311 (1990); 366 (2000); 367 (2010); Density: 482.4 persons per square mile (2008-2012 5-year est.); Race: 99.4% White, 0.0% Black/African American, 0.6% Asian, 0.0% American Indian/Alaska Native, 0.0% Native Hawaiian/Other Pacific Islander, 0.0% Some other race, 0.0% Two or more races, 0.0% Hispanic of any race (2008-2012 5-year est.); Average household size: 2.54 (2008-2012 5-year est.); Median age: 31.5 (2008-2012 5-year est.); Males per 100 females: 65.1 (2008-2012 5-year est.); Marriage status: 18.4% never married, 46.0% now married, 10.7% widowed, 24.9% divorced (2008-2012 5-year est.); Foreign born: 0.6% (2008-2012 5-year est.); Ancestry (includes multiple ancestries): 14.6% German, 12.0% American, 4.7% Irish, 4.5% Hungarian, 2.6% English (2008-2012 5-year est.).

Economy: Homeowner vacancy rate: 0.0%. Rental vacancy rate: 0.0%. (2008-2012 5-year est.); Employment by occupation: 3.9% management, business, and financial, 0.9% computer, engineering, and science, 1.7% education, legal, community service, arts, and media, 16.9% healthcare practitioners, 18.6% service, 22.1% sales and office, 12.6% natural resources, construction, and maintenance, 23.4% production, transportation, and material moving (2008-2012 5-year est.).

Income: Per capita income: $16,561 (2008-2012 5-year est.); Median household income: $30,714 (2008-2012 5-year est.); Average household

income: $40,233 (2008-2012 5-year est.); Percent of households with income of $100,000 or more: 4.6% (2008-2012 5-year est.); Poverty rate: 11.2% (2008-2012 5-year est.).

Education: Percent of population age 25 and over with: High school diploma (including GED) or higher: 77.5% (2008-2012 5-year est.); Bachelor's degree or higher: 7.6% (2008-2012 5-year est.); Master's degree or higher: 1.1% (2008-2012 5-year est.).

Housing: Homeownership rate: 67.5% (2008-2012 5-year est.); Median home value: $39,200 (2008-2012 5-year est.); Median contract rent: $237 per month (2008-2012 5-year est.); Median year structure built: 1979 (2008-2012 5-year est.).

Health Insurance: 47.0% Private; 53.0% Public; 9.3% None. (2008-2012 5-year est.)

Transportation: Commute to work: 98.3% car, 0.0% public transportation, 1.3% walk, 0.4% work from home (2008-2012 5-year est.); Travel time to work: 67.0% less than 15 minutes, 20.4% 15 to 30 minutes, 3.0% 30 to 45 minutes, 3.9% 45 to 60 minutes, 5.7% 60 minutes or more (2008-2012 5-year est.)

JOHNSONVILLE (village). Covers a land area of 0.212 square miles and a water area of 0 square miles. Located at 38.52° N. Lat; 88.54° W. Long. Elevation is 541 feet.

Population: 68 (1990); 69 (2000); 77 (2010); Density: 363.7 persons per square mile (2008-2012 5-year est.); Race: 100.0% White, 0.0% Black/African American, 0.0% Asian, 0.0% American Indian/Alaska Native, 0.0% Native Hawaiian/Other Pacific Islander, 0.0% Some other race, 0.0% Two or more races, 0.0% Hispanic of any race (2008-2012 5-year est.); Average household size: 3.21 (2008-2012 5-year est.); Median age: 34.8 (2008-2012 5-year est.); Males per 100 females: 75.0 (2008-2012 5-year est.); Marriage status: 42.4% never married, 28.8% now married, 8.5% widowed, 20.3% divorced (2008-2012 5-year est.); Foreign born: 0.0% (2008-2012 5-year est.); Ancestry (includes multiple ancestries): 7.8% German, 3.9% Irish, 1.3% English (2008-2012 5-year est.).

Economy: Homeowner vacancy rate: 0.0%. Rental vacancy rate: 0.0%. (2008-2012 5-year est.); Employment by occupation: 13.9% management, business, and financial, 0.0% computer, engineering, and science, 13.9% education, legal, community service, arts, and media, 5.6% healthcare practitioners, 0.0% service, 16.7% sales and office, 22.2% natural resources, construction, and maintenance, 27.8% production, transportation, and material moving (2008-2012 5-year est.).

Income: Per capita income: $15,214 (2008-2012 5-year est.); Median household income: $31,429 (2008-2012 5-year est.); Average household income: $44,292 (2008-2012 5-year est.); Percent of households with income of $100,000 or more: 16.7% (2008-2012 5-year est.); Poverty rate: 15.6% (2008-2012 5-year est.).

Education: Percent of population age 25 and over with: High school diploma (including GED) or higher: 94.1% (2008-2012 5-year est.); Bachelor's degree or higher: 15.7% (2008-2012 5-year est.); Master's degree or higher: 5.9% (2008-2012 5-year est.).

School District(s)

North Wayne CUSD 200 (PK-12)

 2011-12 Enrollment: 428 . . . . (618) 673-2151

Housing: Homeownership rate: 100.0% (2008-2012 5-year est.); Median home value: $50,000 (2008-2012 5-year est.); Median contract rent: n/a per month (2008-2012 5-year est.); Median year structure built: 1983 (2008-2012 5-year est.).

Health Insurance: 83.1% Private; 32.5% Public; 0.0% None. (2008-2012 5-year est.)

Transportation: Commute to work: 80.6% car, 5.6% public transportation, 8.3% walk, 5.6% work from home (2008-2012 5-year est.); Travel time to work: 17.6% less than 15 minutes, 64.7% 15 to 30 minutes, 17.6% 30 to 45 minutes, 0.0% 45 to 60 minutes, 0.0% 60 minutes or more (2008-2012 5-year est.)

KEENES (village). Covers a land area of 0.128 square miles and a water area of 0 square miles. Located at 38.34° N. Lat; 88.64° W. Long. Elevation is 449 feet.

Population: 62 (1990); 99 (2000); 83 (2010); Density: 500.6 persons per square mile (2008-2012 5-year est.); Race: 82.8% White, 17.2% Black/African American, 0.0% Asian, 0.0% American Indian/Alaska Native, 0.0% Native Hawaiian/Other Pacific Islander, 0.0% Some other race, 0.0% Two or more races, 0.0% Hispanic of any race (2008-2012 5-year est.); Average household size: 1.88 (2008-2012 5-year est.); Median age: 57.5 (2008-2012 5-year est.); Males per 100 females: 128.6 (2008-2012 5-year est.); Marriage status: 21.1% never married, 64.9% now married, 5.3%

widowed, 8.8% divorced (2008-2012 5-year est.); Foreign born: 0.0% (2008-2012 5-year est.); Ancestry (includes multiple ancestries): 10.9% American, 3.1% English, 3.1% French (2008-2012 5-year est.).

Economy: Homeowner vacancy rate: 0.0%. Rental vacancy rate: 0.0%. (2008-2012 5-year est.); Employment by occupation: 0.0% management, business, and financial, 0.0% computer, engineering, and science, 8.7% education, legal, community service, arts, and media, 0.0% healthcare practitioners, 21.7% service, 17.4% sales and office, 13.0% natural resources, construction, and maintenance, 39.1% production, transportation, and material moving (2008-2012 5-year est.).

Income: Per capita income: $19,400 (2008-2012 5-year est.); Median household income: $32,500 (2008-2012 5-year est.); Average household income: $36,094 (2008-2012 5-year est.); Percent of households with income of $100,000 or more: n/a (2008-2012 5-year est.); Poverty rate: 0.0% (2008-2012 5-year est.).

Education: Percent of population age 25 and over with: High school diploma (including GED) or higher: 80.4% (2008-2012 5-year est.); Bachelor's degree or higher: 3.9% (2008-2012 5-year est.); Master's degree or higher: 0.0% (2008-2012 5-year est.).

Housing: Homeownership rate: 91.2% (2008-2012 5-year est.); Median home value: $74,100 (2008-2012 5-year est.); Median contract rent: n/a per month (2008-2012 5-year est.); Median year structure built: 1973 (2008-2012 5-year est.).

Health Insurance: 68.8% Private; 32.8% Public; 20.3% None. (2008-2012 5-year est.)

Transportation: Commute to work: 100.0% car, 0.0% public transportation, 0.0% walk, 0.0% work from home (2008-2012 5-year est.); Travel time to work: 21.7% less than 15 minutes, 39.1% 15 to 30 minutes, 4.3% 30 to 45 minutes, 34.8% 45 to 60 minutes, 0.0% 60 minutes or more (2008-2012 5-year est.)

MOUNT ERIE (village). Covers a land area of 0.396 square miles and a water area of 0 square miles. Located at 38.51° N. Lat; 88.23° W. Long. Elevation is 499 feet.

Population: 137 (1990); 105 (2000); 88 (2010); Density: 323.6 persons per square mile (2008-2012 5-year est.); Race: 96.9% White, 0.0% Black/African American, 3.1% Asian, 0.0% American Indian/Alaska Native, 0.0% Native Hawaiian/Other Pacific Islander, 0.0% Some other race, 0.0% Two or more races, 0.0% Hispanic of any race (2008-2012 5-year est.); Average household size: 2.91 (2000-2012 5-year est.), Median age: 35.5 (2008-2012 5-year est.); Males per 100 females: 77.8 (2008-2012 5-year est.); Marriage status: 36.4% never married, 50.9% now married, 4.5% widowed, 8.2% divorced (2008-2012 5-year est.); Foreign born: 3.1% (2008-2012 5-year est.); Ancestry (includes multiple ancestries): 13.3% English, 6.3% German, 5.5% American, 3.1% French, 1.6% Norwegian (2008-2012 5-year est.).

Economy: Homeowner vacancy rate: 0.0%. Rental vacancy rate: 0.0%. (2008-2012 5-year est.); Employment by occupation: 0.0% management, business, and financial, 0.0% computer, engineering, and science, 12.5% education, legal, community service, arts, and media, 0.0% healthcare practitioners, 14.1% service, 32.8% sales and office, 10.9% natural resources, construction, and maintenance, 29.7% production, transportation, and material moving (2008-2012 5-year est.).

Income: Per capita income: $17,045 (2008-2012 5-year est.); Median household income: $45,833 (2008-2012 5-year est.); Average household income: $47,589 (2008-2012 5-year est.); Percent of households with income of $100,000 or more: n/a (2008-2012 5-year est.); Poverty rate: 8.0% (2008-2012 5-year est.).

Education: Percent of population age 25 and over with: High school diploma (including GED) or higher: 75.3% (2008-2012 5-year est.); Bachelor's degree or higher: 6.2% (2008-2012 5-year est.); Master's degree or higher: 0.0% (2008-2012 5-year est.).

School District(s)

North Wayne CUSD 200 (PK-12)

 2011-12 Enrollment: 428 . . . . (618) 673-2151

Housing: Homeownership rate: 81.8% (2008-2012 5-year est.); Median home value: $60,000 (2008-2012 5-year est.); Median contract rent: n/a per month (2008-2012 5-year est.); Median year structure built: 1973 (2008-2012 5-year est.).

Health Insurance: 76.6% Private; 18.8% Public; 12.5% None. (2008-2012 5-year est.)

Transportation: Commute to work: 91.8% car, 0.0% public transportation, 4.9% walk, 0.0% work from home (2008-2012 5-year est.); Travel time to work: 14.8% less than 15 minutes, 52.5% 15 to 30 minutes, 24.6% 30 to

45 minutes, 3.3% 45 to 60 minutes, 4.9% 60 minutes or more (2008-2012 5-year est.)

RINARD (unincorporated postal area)
Zip Code: 62878

Covers a land area of 35.256 square miles and a water area of 0.010 square miles. Located at 38.57° N. Lat; 88.50° W. Long. Elevation is 459 feet. Population: 410 (2010); Density: 11.6 persons per square mile (2010); Race: 99.3% White, 0.0% Black/African American, 0.0% Asian, 0.0% American Indian/Alaska Native, 0.0% Native Hawaiian/Other Pacific Islander, 0.7% Some other race, 0.7% Two or more races, 0.2% Hispanic of any race (2010); Average household size: 2.53 (2010); Median age: 43.5 (2010); Males per 100 females: 106.0 (2010); Homeownership rate: 88.3% (2010)

SIMS (village). Covers a land area of 1.202 square miles and a water area of 0 square miles. Located at 38.36° N. Lat; 88.54° W. Long. Elevation is 410 feet.
Population: 338 (1990); 273 (2000); 252 (2010); Density: 287.8 persons per square mile (2008-2012 5-year est.); Race: 100.0% White, 0.0% Black/African American, 0.0% Asian, 0.0% American Indian/Alaska Native, 0.0% Native Hawaiian/Other Pacific Islander, 0.0% Some other race, 0.0% Two or more races, 0.0% Hispanic of any race (2008-2012 5-year est.); Average household size: 2.98 (2008-2012 5-year est.); Median age: 36.6 (2008-2012 5-year est.); Males per 100 females: 121.8 (2008-2012 5-year est.); Marriage status: 35.2% never married, 43.0% now married, 12.1% widowed, 9.8% divorced (2008-2012 5-year est.); Foreign born: 0.0% (2008-2012 5-year est.); Ancestry (includes multiple ancestries): 6.6% English, 5.8% Irish, 5.2% American, 3.2% German, 1.7% Scottish (2008-2012 5-year est.).
Economy: Homeowner vacancy rate: 0.0%. Rental vacancy rate: 0.0%. (2008-2012 5-year est.); Employment by occupation: 10.5% management, business, and financial, 15.0% computer, engineering, and science, 0.0% education, legal, community service, arts, and media, 7.8% healthcare practitioners, 17.6% service, 19.6% sales and office, 4.6% natural resources, construction, and maintenance, 24.8% production, transportation, and material moving (2008-2012 5-year est.).
Income: Per capita income: $17,695 (2008-2012 5-year est.); Median household income: $45,000 (2008-2012 5-year est.); Average household income: $52,438 (2008-2012 5-year est.); Percent of households with income of $100,000 or more: 12.9% (2008-2012 5-year est.); Poverty rate: 11.6% (2008-2012 5-year est.).
Education: Percent of population age 25 and over with: High school diploma (including GED) or higher: 86.7% (2008-2012 5-year est.); Bachelor's degree or higher: 6.0% (2008-2012 5-year est.); Master's degree or higher: 0.0% (2008-2012 5-year est.).
Housing: Homeownership rate: 95.7% (2008-2012 5-year est.); Median home value: $43,200 (2008-2012 5-year est.); Median contract rent: n/a per month (2008-2012 5-year est.); Median year structure built: 1970 (2008-2012 5-year est.).
Health Insurance: 76.9% Private; 20.2% Public; 18.5% None. (2008-2012 5-year est.)
Transportation: Commute to work: 92.6% car, 0.0% public transportation, 0.0% walk, 4.1% work from home (2008-2012 5-year est.); Travel time to work: 40.8% less than 15 minutes, 37.3% 15 to 30 minutes, 14.1% 30 to 45 minutes, 4.2% 45 to 60 minutes, 3.5% 60 minutes or more (2008-2012 5-year est.)

WAYNE CITY (village). Covers a land area of 1.715 square miles and a water area of 0 square miles. Located at 38.35° N. Lat; 88.59° W. Long. Elevation is 433 feet.
Population: 1,099 (1990); 1,089 (2000); 1,032 (2010); Density: 692.7 persons per square mile (2008-2012 5-year est.); Race: 99.4% White, 0.0% Black/African American, 0.0% Asian, 0.4% American Indian/Alaska Native, 0.0% Native Hawaiian/Other Pacific Islander, 0.2% Some other race, 0.2% Two or more races, 5.8% Hispanic of any race (2008-2012 5-year est.); Average household size: 2.54 (2008-2012 5-year est.); Median age: 43.1 (2008-2012 5-year est.); Males per 100 females: 88.9 (2008-2012 5-year est.); Marriage status: 27.2% never married, 51.3% now married, 13.6% widowed, 7.9% divorced (2008-2012 5-year est.); Foreign born: 0.7% (2008-2012 5-year est.); Ancestry (includes multiple ancestries): 9.5% German, 9.5% Irish, 7.7% English, 3.3% American, 2.4% Swedish (2008-2012 5-year est.).
Economy: Homeowner vacancy rate: 0.0%. Rental vacancy rate: 10.0%. (2008-2012 5-year est.); Employment by occupation: 17.5% management,

business, and financial, 0.0% computer, engineering, and science, 8.2% education, legal, community service, arts, and media, 2.7% healthcare practitioners, 13.2% service, 24.1% sales and office, 12.8% natural resources, construction, and maintenance, 21.6% production, transportation, and material moving (2008-2012 5-year est.).
Income: Per capita income: $19,998 (2008-2012 5-year est.); Median household income: $44,219 (2008-2012 5-year est.); Average household income: $49,329 (2008-2012 5-year est.); Percent of households with income of $100,000 or more: 8.7% (2008-2012 5-year est.); Poverty rate: 10.3% (2008-2012 5-year est.).
Education: Percent of population age 25 and over with: High school diploma (including GED) or higher: 83.2% (2008-2012 5-year est.); Bachelor's degree or higher: 13.3% (2008-2012 5-year est.); Master's degree or higher: 1.4% (2008-2012 5-year est.).

School District(s)
Wayne City CUSD 100 (KG-12)
    2011-12 Enrollment: 556 . . . . (618) 895-3103
Housing: Homeownership rate: 81.2% (2008-2012 5-year est.); Median home value: $72,600 (2008-2012 5-year est.); Median contract rent: $342 per month (2008-2012 5-year est.); Median year structure built: 1961 (2008-2012 5-year est.).
Health Insurance: 66.0% Private; 40.6% Public; 12.5% None. (2008-2012 5-year est.)
Transportation: Commute to work: 95.1% car, 0.0% public transportation, 3.1% walk, 1.9% work from home (2008-2012 5-year est.); Travel time to work: 33.5% less than 15 minutes, 43.0% 15 to 30 minutes, 15.1% 30 to 45 minutes, 2.7% 45 to 60 minutes, 5.7% 60 minutes or more (2008-2012 5-year est.)

White County

Located in southeastern Illinois; bounded on the east by the Wabash River and the Indiana border; drained by the Little Wabash River. Covers a land area of 494.766 square miles, a water area of 7.095 square miles, and is located in the Central Time Zone at 38.09° N. Lat., 88.18° W. Long. The county was founded in 1815. County seat is Carmi.

Weather Station: Fulton L&D #13 — Elevation: 591 feet

	Jan	Feb	Mar	Apr	May	Jun	Jul	Aug	Sep	Oct	Nov	Dec
High	29	33	45	59	70	80	83	82	75	62	47	33
Low	13	16	27	39	50	60	64	63	54	42	31	18
Precip	1.2	1.4	2.3	3.1	3.6	4.2	3.2	4.1	2.9	2.9	2.5	1.8
Snow	3.1	1.7	0.4	0.5	0.0	0.0	0.0	0.0	0.0	0.0	0.2	1.5

High and Low temperatures in degrees Fahrenheit; Precipitation and Snow in inches

Weather Station: Morrison — Elevation: 603 feet

	Jan	Feb	Mar	Apr	May	Jun	Jul	Aug	Sep	Oct	Nov	Dec
High	31	35	47	61	73	82	85	83	76	64	49	35
Low	12	16	27	37	49	58	62	60	51	39	29	17
Precip	1.5	1.6	2.6	3.3	4.1	4.4	3.9	4.8	3.0	2.9	2.8	2.1
Snow	10.0	6.9	3.3	1.0	0.0	0.0	0.0	0.0	0.0	tr	1.5	8.5

High and Low temperatures in degrees Fahrenheit; Precipitation and Snow in inches

Population: 16,522 (1990); 15,371 (2000); 14,665 (2010); Race: 98.3% White, 0.7% Black/African American, 0.2% Asian, 0.0% American Indian/Alaska Native, 0.0% Native Hawaiian/Other Pacific Islander, 0.8% Some other race, 0.7% Two or more races, 1.1% Hispanic of any race (2008-2012 5-year est.); Density: 29.5 persons per square mile (2008-2012 5-year est.); Average household size: 2.29 (2008-2012 5-year est.); Median age: 44.5 (2008-2012 5-year est.); Males per 100 females: 92.5 (2008-2012 5-year est.).
Religion: Six largest groups: 27.7% Baptist, 8.5% Methodist/Pietist, 6.5% Catholicism, 3.6% Non-denominational Protestant, 2.5% Pentecostal, 1.9% Presbyterian-Reformed (2010)
Economy: Unemployment rate: 6.4% (April 2014); Total civilian labor force: 7,100 (April 2014); Leading industries: 18.5% health care and social assistance; 14.9% retail trade; 9.3% accommodation & food services (2012); Farms: 582 totaling 310,890 acres (2012); Companies that employ 500 or more persons: 0 (2012); Companies that employ 100 to 499 persons: 5 (2012); Companies that employ less than 100 persons: 373 (2012); Black-owned businesses: n/a (2007); Hispanic-owned businesses: n/a (2007); Asian-owned businesses: n/a (2007); Women-owned businesses: n/a (2007); Single-family building permits issued: 0 (2013); Multi-family building permits issued: 0 (2013).
Income: Per capita income: $24,150 (2008-2012 5-year est.); Median household income: $43,151 (2008-2012 5-year est.); Average household

income: $55,735 (2008-2012 5-year est.); Percent of households with income of $100,000 or more: 12.1% (2008-2012 5-year est.); Poverty rate: 15.5% (2008-2012 5-year est.); Bankruptcy rate: 1.99% (2013).
Education: Percent of population age 25 and over with: High school diploma (including GED) or higher: 85.0% (2008-2012 5-year est.); Bachelor's degree or higher: 13.1% (2008-2012 5-year est.); Master's degree or higher: 4.9% (2008-2012 5-year est.).
Housing: Homeownership rate: 79.0% (2008-2012 5-year est.); Median home value: $67,700 (2008-2012 5-year est.); Median contract rent: $318 per month (2008-2012 5-year est.); Median year structure built: 1959 (2008-2012 5-year est.)
Health: Birth rate: 115.5 per 10,000 population (2013); Death rate: 146.4 per 10,000 population (2013); Age-adjusted cancer mortality rate: 214.0 deaths per 100,000 population (2011); Number of physicians: 2.7 per 10,000 population (2011); Hospital beds: 0.0 per 10,000 population (2010); Hospital admissions: 0.0 per 10,000 population (2010).
Elections: 2012 Presidential election results: 31.0% Obama, 67.0% Romney
Additional Information Contacts
White County Government . . . . (618) 382-7211
   http://www.whitecounty-il.gov

White County Communities

BURNT PRAIRIE (village). Aka Liberty. Covers a land area of 0.078 square miles and a water area of 0 square miles. Located at 38.25° N. Lat; 88.26° W. Long. Elevation is 446 feet.
Population: 71 (1990); 58 (2000); 52 (2010); Density: 860.1 persons per square mile (2008-2012 5-year est.); Race: 100.0% White, 0.0% Black/African American, 0.0% Asian, 0.0% American Indian/Alaska Native, 0.0% Native Hawaiian/Other Pacific Islander, 0.0% Some other race, 0.0% Two or more races, 0.0% Hispanic of any race (2008-2012 5-year est.); Average household size: 2.39 (2008-2012 5-year est.); Median age: 53.3 (2008-2012 5-year est.); Males per 100 females: 81.1 (2008-2012 5-year est.); Marriage status: 5.5% never married, 81.8% now married, 7.3% widowed, 5.5% divorced (2008-2012 5-year est.); Foreign born: 0.0% (2008-2012 5-year est.); Ancestry (includes multiple ancestries): 25.4% German, 11.9% American, 10.4% Irish, 7.5% English, 6.0% Polish (2008-2012 5-year est.).
Economy: Homeowner vacancy rate: 0.0%. Rental vacancy rate: 0.0%. (2008-2012 5-year est.); Employment by occupation: 8.0% management, business, and financial, 0.0% computer, engineering, and science, 8.0% education, legal, community service, arts, and media, 16.0% healthcare practitioners, 16.0% service, 32.0% sales and office, 12.0% natural resources, construction, and maintenance, 8.0% production, transportation, and material moving (2008-2012 5-year est.).
Income: Per capita income: $20,533 (2008-2012 5-year est.); Median household income: $53,125 (2008-2012 5-year est.); Average household income: $48,750 (2008-2012 5-year est.); Percent of households with income of $100,000 or more: n/a (2008-2012 5-year est.); Poverty rate: 26.9% (2008-2012 5-year est.).
Education: Percent of population age 25 and over with: High school diploma (including GED) or higher: 87.5% (2008-2012 5-year est.); Bachelor's degree or higher: 2.1% (2008-2012 5-year est.); Master's degree or higher: 2.1% (2008-2012 5-year est.).
Housing: Homeownership rate: 100.0% (2008-2012 5-year est.); Median home value: $28,800 (2008-2012 5-year est.); Median contract rent: n/a per month (2008-2012 5-year est.); Median year structure built: Before 1940 (2008-2012 5-year est.).
Health Insurance: 52.2% Private; 62.7% Public; 9.0% None. (2008-2012 5-year est.)
Transportation: Commute to work: 84.0% car, 0.0% public transportation, 8.0% walk, 8.0% work from home (2008-2012 5-year est.); Travel time to work: 30.4% less than 15 minutes, 47.8% 15 to 30 minutes, 8.7% 30 to 45 minutes, 13.0% 45 to 60 minutes, 0.0% 60 minutes or more (2008-2012 5-year est.)

CARMI (city). County seat. Covers a land area of 2.496 square miles and a water area of 0.031 square miles. Located at 38.09° N. Lat; 88.17° W. Long. Elevation is 394 feet.
History: Carmi, platted in 1816, developed as the seat of White County.
Population: 5,564 (1990); 5,422 (2000); 5,240 (2010); Density: 2,143.4 persons per square mile (2008-2012 5-year est.); Race: 97.1% White, 0.8% Black/African American, 0.5% Asian, 0.0% American Indian/Alaska Native, 0.0% Native Hawaiian/Other Pacific Islander, 1.6% Some other

race, 1.1% Two or more races, 0.5% Hispanic of any race (2008-2012 5-year est.); Average household size: 2.23 (2008-2012 5-year est.); Median age: 45.5 (2008-2012 5-year est.); Males per 100 females: 78.2 (2008-2012 5-year est.); Marriage status: 23.5% never married, 53.0% now married, 11.5% widowed, 12.0% divorced (2008-2012 5-year est.); Foreign born: 1.6% (2008-2012 5-year est.); Ancestry (includes multiple ancestries): 20.1% German, 17.8% American, 12.2% English, 9.7% Irish, 2.0% Polish (2008-2012 5-year est.).
Economy: Single-family building permits issued: 0 (2013); Multi-family building permits issued: 0 (2013); Homeowner vacancy rate: 3.4%. Rental vacancy rate: 4.9%. (2008-2012 5-year est.); Employment by occupation: 8.3% management, business, and financial, 0.3% computer, engineering, and science, 9.4% education, legal, community service, arts, and media, 2.8% healthcare practitioners, 28.1% service, 25.1% sales and office, 9.9% natural resources, construction, and maintenance, 16.1% production, transportation, and material moving (2008-2012 5-year est.).
Income: Per capita income: $20,760 (2008-2012 5-year est.); Median household income: $35,446 (2008-2012 5-year est.); Average household income: $46,980 (2008-2012 5-year est.); Percent of households with income of $100,000 or more: 7.9% (2008-2012 5-year est.); Poverty rate: 19.2% (2008-2012 5-year est.).
Education: Percent of population age 25 and over with: High school diploma (including GED) or higher: 82.6% (2008-2012 5-year est.); Bachelor's degree or higher: 11.6% (2008-2012 5-year est.); Master's degree or higher: 5.6% (2008-2012 5-year est.).
School District(s)
Carmi-White County CUSD 5 (PK-12)
   2011-12 Enrollment: 1,373 . . . . (618) 382-2341
Housing: Homeownership rate: 72.8% (2008-2012 5-year est.); Median home value: $65,600 (2008-2012 5-year est.); Median contract rent: $353 per month (2008-2012 5-year est.); Median year structure built: 1956 (2008-2012 5-year est.).
Health Insurance: 55.1% Private; 47.1% Public; 16.0% None. (2008-2012 5-year est.)
Hospitals: White County Medical Center (49 beds)
Transportation: Commute to work: 92.2% car, 1.2% public transportation, 2.8% walk, 2.4% work from home (2008-2012 5-year est.); Travel time to work: 51.0% less than 15 minutes, 13.7% 15 to 30 minutes, 15.0% 30 to 45 minutes, 5.6% 45 to 60 minutes, 14.7% 60 minutes or more (2008-2012 5-year est.)
Airports: Carmi Municipal Airport (general aviation)
Additional Information Contacts
City of Carmi . . . . (618) 384-2001
   http://www.cityofcarmi.com

CROSSVILLE (village). Covers a land area of 0.641 square miles and a water area of 0 square miles. Located at 38.16° N. Lat; 88.06° W. Long. Elevation is 410 feet.
Population: 805 (1990); 782 (2000); 745 (2010); Density: 1,195.5 persons per square mile (2008-2012 5-year est.); Race: 98.8% White, 0.0% Black/African American, 0.1% Asian, 0.0% American Indian/Alaska Native, 0.0% Native Hawaiian/Other Pacific Islander, 1.1% Some other race, 1.0% Two or more races, 1.8% Hispanic of any race (2008-2012 5-year est.); Average household size: 2.39 (2008-2012 5-year est.); Median age: 35.6 (2008-2012 5-year est.); Males per 100 females: 95.9 (2008-2012 5-year est.); Marriage status: 19.6% never married, 57.6% now married, 7.3% widowed, 15.6% divorced (2008-2012 5-year est.); Foreign born: 0.1% (2008-2012 5-year est.); Ancestry (includes multiple ancestries): 23.4% German, 19.2% Irish, 12.5% American, 7.7% French, 7.6% English (2008-2012 5-year est.).
Economy: Single-family building permits issued: 0 (2013); Multi-family building permits issued: 0 (2013); Homeowner vacancy rate: 3.8%. Rental vacancy rate: 0.0%. (2008-2012 5-year est.); Employment by occupation: 7.9% management, business, and financial, 0.0% computer, engineering, and science, 6.8% education, legal, community service, arts, and media, 0.0% healthcare practitioners, 24.1% service, 25.5% sales and office, 11.5% natural resources, construction, and maintenance, 24.1% production, transportation, and material moving (2008-2012 5-year est.).
Income: Per capita income: $17,423 (2008-2012 5-year est.); Median household income: $29,107 (2008-2012 5-year est.); Average household income: $41,831 (2008-2012 5-year est.); Percent of households with income of $100,000 or more: 5.3% (2008-2012 5-year est.); Poverty rate: 22.3% (2008-2012 5-year est.).
Education: Percent of population age 25 and over with: High school diploma (including GED) or higher: 76.0% (2008-2012 5-year est.);

Bachelor's degree or higher: 6.2% (2008-2012 5-year est.); Master's degree or higher: 1.0% (2008-2012 5-year est.).

School District(s)

Carmi-White County CUSD 5 (PK-12)
    2011-12 Enrollment: 1,373 . . . . (618) 382-2341
Housing: Homeownership rate: 72.0% (2008-2012 5-year est.); Median home value: $39,300 (2008-2012 5-year est.); Median contract rent: $278 per month (2008-2012 5-year est.); Median year structure built: 1955 (2008-2012 5-year est.).
Health Insurance: 45.2% Private; 60.1% Public; 9.1% None. (2008-2012 5-year est.)
Transportation: Commute to work: 88.6% car, 0.0% public transportation, 3.3% walk, 8.2% work from home (2008-2012 5-year est.); Travel time to work: 40.9% less than 15 minutes, 20.0% 15 to 30 minutes, 19.1% 30 to 45 minutes, 11.1% 45 to 60 minutes, 8.9% 60 minutes or more (2008-2012 5-year est.)

ENFIELD (village). Covers a land area of 1.186 square miles and a water area of 0 square miles. Located at 38.10° N. Lat; 88.34° W. Long. Elevation is 486 feet.
History: Enfield was settled in 1813.
Population: 683 (1990); 625 (2000); 596 (2010); Density: 587.5 persons per square mile (2008-2012 5-year est.); Race: 100.0% White, 0.0% Black/African American, 0.0% Asian, 0.0% American Indian/Alaska Native, 0.0% Native Hawaiian/Other Pacific Islander, 0.0% Some other race, 0.0% Two or more races, 0.0% Hispanic of any race (2008-2012 5-year est.); Average household size: 2.54 (2008-2012 5-year est.); Median age: 35.8 (2008-2012 5-year est.); Males per 100 females: 90.4 (2008-2012 5-year est.); Marriage status: 25.5% never married, 55.9% now married, 4.2% widowed, 14.4% divorced (2008-2012 5-year est.); Foreign born: 0.0% (2008-2012 5-year est.); Ancestry (includes multiple ancestries): 26.1% German, 22.4% Irish, 18.9% English, 11.0% American, 1.9% Danish (2008-2012 5-year est.).
Economy: Homeowner vacancy rate: 0.0%. Rental vacancy rate: 0.0%. (2008-2012 5-year est.); Employment by occupation: 6.5% management, business, and financial, 1.4% computer, engineering, and science, 6.1% education, legal, community service, arts, and media, 5.0% healthcare practitioners, 22.7% service, 21.2% sales and office, 18.0% natural resources, construction, and maintenance, 19.1% production, transportation, and material moving (2008-2012 5-year est.).
Income: Per capita income: $17,541 (2008-2012 5-year est.); Median household income: $29,306 (2008-2012 5-year est.); Average household income: $44,270 (2008-2012 5-year est.); Percent of households with income of $100,000 or more: 6.8% (2008-2012 5-year est.); Poverty rate: 26.7% (2008-2012 5-year est.).
Education: Percent of population age 25 and over with: High school diploma (including GED) or higher: 85.5% (2008-2012 5-year est.); Bachelor's degree or higher: 9.4% (2008-2012 5-year est.); Master's degree or higher: 4.7% (2008-2012 5-year est.).

School District(s)

Norris City-Omaha-Enfield CUSD 3 (PK-12)
    2011-12 Enrollment: 736 . . . . (618) 378-3222
Housing: Homeownership rate: 83.3% (2008-2012 5-year est.); Median home value: $42,000 (2008-2012 5-year est.); Median contract rent: $321 per month (2008-2012 5-year est.); Median year structure built: 1955 (2008-2012 5-year est.).
Health Insurance: 36.2% Private; 58.1% Public; 14.3% None. (2008-2012 5-year est.)
Transportation: Commute to work: 96.3% car, 0.7% public transportation, 0.0% walk, 1.9% work from home (2008-2012 5-year est.); Travel time to work: 39.3% less than 15 minutes, 47.3% 15 to 30 minutes, 3.4% 30 to 45 minutes, 6.5% 45 to 60 minutes, 3.4% 60 minutes or more (2008-2012 5-year est.)

GRAYVILLE (city). Covers a land area of 2.134 square miles and a water area of 0.043 square miles. Located at 38.26° N. Lat; 88.00° W. Long.
Population: 2,043 (1990); 1,725 (2000); 1,666 (2010); Density: 781.5 persons per square mile (2008-2012 5-year est.); Race: 98.5% White, 0.4% Black/African American, 0.0% Asian, 0.0% American Indian/Alaska Native, 0.0% Native Hawaiian/Other Pacific Islander, 1.1% Some other race, 1.1% Two or more races, 0.4% Hispanic of any race (2008-2012 5-year est.); Average household size: 2.13 (2008-2012 5-year est.); Median age: 49.5 (2008-2012 5-year est.); Males per 100 females: 83.5 (2008-2012 5-year est.); Marriage status: 26.5% never married, 52.3%

now married, 9.4% widowed, 11.8% divorced (2008-2012 5-year est.); Foreign born: 0.8% (2008-2012 5-year est.); Ancestry (includes multiple ancestries): 20.1% German, 11.9% English, 11.1% Irish, 10.9% American, 3.5% Scottish (2008-2012 5-year est.).
Economy: Single-family building permits issued: 0 (2013); Multi-family building permits issued: 0 (2013); Homeowner vacancy rate: 7.4%. Rental vacancy rate: 3.9%. (2008-2012 5-year est.); Employment by occupation: 14.4% management, business, and financial, 0.7% computer, engineering, and science, 7.2% education, legal, community service, arts, and media, 4.2% healthcare practitioners, 26.4% service, 17.1% sales and office, 7.1% natural resources, construction, and maintenance, 22.9% production, transportation, and material moving (2008-2012 5-year est.).
Income: Per capita income: $19,659 (2008-2012 5-year est.); Median household income: $31,799 (2008-2012 5-year est.); Average household income: $41,809 (2008-2012 5-year est.); Percent of households with income of $100,000 or more: 7.0% (2008-2012 5-year est.); Poverty rate: 21.0% (2008-2012 5-year est.).
Education: Percent of population age 25 and over with: High school diploma (including GED) or higher: 85.1% (2008-2012 5-year est.); Bachelor's degree or higher: 11.0% (2008-2012 5-year est.); Master's degree or higher: 5.4% (2008-2012 5-year est.).

School District(s)

Grayville CUSD 1 (PK-12)
    2011-12 Enrollment: 317 . . . . (618) 375-7214
Housing: Homeownership rate: 73.6% (2008-2012 5-year est.); Median home value: $51,300 (2008-2012 5-year est.); Median contract rent: $329 per month (2008-2012 5-year est.); Median year structure built: 1951 (2008-2012 5-year est.).
Health Insurance: 64.9% Private; 46.9% Public; 13.3% None. (2008-2012 5-year est.)
Transportation: Commute to work: 93.0% car, 0.0% public transportation, 3.3% walk, 2.5% work from home (2008-2012 5-year est.); Travel time to work: 50.2% less than 15 minutes, 26.6% 15 to 30 minutes, 13.8% 30 to 45 minutes, 4.3% 45 to 60 minutes, 5.0% 60 minutes or more (2008-2012 5-year est.)
Additional Information Contacts
Grayville Chamber of Commerce . . . . (618) 375-7518

MAUNIE (village). Covers a land area of 0.159 square miles and a water area of 0 square miles. Located at 38.04° N. Lat; 88.05° W. Long. Elevation is 371 feet.
Population: 119 (1990); 177 (2000); 139 (2010); Density: 903.4 persons per square mile (2008-2012 5-year est.); Race: 97.9% White, 0.0% Black/African American, 0.0% Asian, 2.1% American Indian/Alaska Native, 0.0% Native Hawaiian/Other Pacific Islander, 0.0% Some other race, 0.0% Two or more races, 0.0% Hispanic of any race (2008-2012 5-year est.); Average household size: 2.57 (2008-2012 5-year est.); Median age: 40.5 (2008-2012 5-year est.); Males per 100 females: 105.7 (2008-2012 5-year est.); Marriage status: 23.1% never married, 47.0% now married, 9.4% widowed, 20.5% divorced (2008-2012 5-year est.); Foreign born: 2.8% (2008-2012 5-year est.); Ancestry (includes multiple ancestries): 66.0% Irish, 47.2% German, 16.0% English, 6.9% French, 5.6% Dutch (2008-2012 5-year est.).
Economy: Homeowner vacancy rate: 0.0%. Rental vacancy rate: 0.0%. (2008-2012 5-year est.); Employment by occupation: 9.7% management, business, and financial, 0.0% computer, engineering, and science, 6.5% education, legal, community service, arts, and media, 6.5% healthcare practitioners, 41.9% service, 0.0% sales and office, 9.7% natural resources, construction, and maintenance, 25.8% production, transportation, and material moving (2008-2012 5-year est.).
Income: Per capita income: $14,753 (2008-2012 5-year est.); Median household income: $33,333 (2008-2012 5-year est.); Average household income: $34,921 (2008-2012 5-year est.); Percent of households with income of $100,000 or more: n/a (2008-2012 5-year est.); Poverty rate: 31.9% (2008-2012 5-year est.).
Education: Percent of population age 25 and over with: High school diploma (including GED) or higher: 65.2% (2008-2012 5-year est.); Bachelor's degree or higher: 0.0% (2008-2012 5-year est.); Master's degree or higher: 0.0% (2008-2012 5-year est.).
Housing: Homeownership rate: 89.3% (2008-2012 5-year est.); Median home value: $19,400 (2008-2012 5-year est.); Median contract rent: n/a per month (2008-2012 5-year est.); Median year structure built: 1964 (2008-2012 5-year est.).
Health Insurance: 34.0% Private; 76.4% Public; 12.5% None. (2008-2012 5-year est.)

Transportation: Commute to work: 100.0% car, 0.0% public transportation, 0.0% walk, 0.0% work from home (2008-2012 5-year est.); Travel time to work: 25.8% less than 15 minutes, 51.6% 15 to 30 minutes, 12.9% 30 to 45 minutes, 9.7% 45 to 60 minutes, 0.0% 60 minutes or more (2008-2012 5-year est.)

MILL SHOALS (village). Covers a land area of 0.791 square miles and a water area of 0 square miles. Located at 38.25° N. Lat; 88.35° W. Long. Elevation is 381 feet.

Population: 247 (1990); 235 (2000); 215 (2010); Density: 274.5 persons per square mile (2008-2012 5-year est.); Race: 100.0% White, 0.0% Black/African American, 0.0% Asian, 0.0% American Indian/Alaska Native, 0.0% Native Hawaiian/Other Pacific Islander, 0.0% Some other race, 0.0% Two or more races, 3.7% Hispanic of any race (2008-2012 5-year est.); Average household size: 2.47 (2008-2012 5-year est.); Median age: 42.3 (2008-2012 5-year est.); Males per 100 females: 102.8 (2008-2012 5-year est.); Marriage status: 22.0% never married, 61.3% now married, 5.4% widowed, 11.3% divorced (2008-2012 5-year est.); Foreign born: 0.5% (2008-2012 5-year est.); Ancestry (includes multiple ancestries): 25.3% German, 21.2% Irish, 20.3% American, 10.1% English, 2.3% Scottish (2008-2012 5-year est.).
Economy: Homeowner vacancy rate: 0.0%. Rental vacancy rate: 0.0%. (2008-2012 5-year est.); Employment by occupation: 8.8% management, business, and financial; 5.3% computer, engineering, and science, 1.8% education, legal, community service, arts, and media, 4.4% healthcare practitioners, 26.3% service, 15.8% sales and office, 13.2% natural resources, construction, and maintenance, 24.6% production, transportation, and material moving (2008-2012 5-year est.).
Income: Per capita income: $21,147 (2008-2012 5-year est.); Median household income: $44,444 (2008-2012 5-year est.); Average household income: $52,606 (2008-2012 5-year est.); Percent of households with income of $100,000 or more: 7.9% (2008-2012 5-year est.); Poverty rate: 18.6% (2008-2012 5-year est.).
Education: Percent of population age 25 and over with: High school diploma (including GED) or higher: 85.1% (2008-2012 5-year est.); Bachelor's degree or higher: 6.7% (2008-2012 5-year est.); Master's degree or higher: 0.0% (2008-2012 5-year est.).

School District(s)

Edwd/gltn/hdin/pop/slne/wbh/wn/wh (06-12)

     2011-12 Enrollment: n/a . . . . (618) 253-5581
Housing: Homeownership rate: 79.5% (2008-2012 5-year est.); Median home value: $41,400 (2008-2012 5-year est.); Median contract rent: $261 per month (2008-2012 5-year est.); Median year structure built: 1966 (2008-2012 5-year est.).
Health Insurance: 58.5% Private; 45.2% Public; 20.3% None. (2008-2012 5-year est.)
Transportation: Commute to work: 90.3% car, 4.4% public transportation, 1.8% walk, 3.5% work from home (2008-2012 5-year est.); Travel time to work: 22.9% less than 15 minutes, 44.0% 15 to 30 minutes, 10.1% 30 to 45 minutes, 18.3% 45 to 60 minutes, 4.6% 60 minutes or more (2008-2012 5-year est.)

NORRIS CITY (village). Covers a land area of 1.183 square miles and a water area of 0.002 square miles. Located at 37.98° N. Lat; 88.33° W. Long. Elevation is 420 feet.

History: Norris City was named for pioneer settler William Norris. It developed as an agricultural and coal mining trading area.
Population: 1,341 (1990); 1,057 (2000); 1,275 (2010); Density: 1,075.0 persons per square mile (2008-2012 5-year est.); Race: 98.4% White, 1.6% Black/African American, 0.0% Asian, 0.0% American Indian/Alaska Native, 0.0% Native Hawaiian/Other Pacific Islander, 0.0% Some other race, 0.0% Two or more races, 1.3% Hispanic of any race (2008-2012 5-year est.); Average household size: 2.27 (2008-2012 5-year est.); Median age: 33.5 (2008-2012 5-year est.); Males per 100 females: 108.5 (2008-2012 5-year est.); Marriage status: 30.6% never married, 50.2% now married, 5.2% widowed, 14.0% divorced (2008-2012 5-year est.); Foreign born: 0.0% (2008-2012 5-year est.); Ancestry (includes multiple ancestries): 36.3% German, 26.3% Irish, 15.3% English, 5.0% American, 4.7% Dutch (2008-2012 5-year est.).
Economy: Homeowner vacancy rate: 4.5%. Rental vacancy rate: 5.5%. (2008-2012 5-year est.); Employment by occupation: 1.7% management, business, and financial, 4.1% computer, engineering, and science, 14.7% education, legal, community service, arts, and media, 2.8% healthcare practitioners, 21.8% service, 23.3% sales and office, 13.1% natural

resources, construction, and maintenance, 18.5% production, transportation, and material moving (2008-2012 5-year est.).
Income: Per capita income: $20,806 (2008-2012 5-year est.); Median household income: $30,288 (2008-2012 5-year est.); Average household income: $47,621 (2008-2012 5-year est.); Percent of households with income of $100,000 or more: 9.0% (2008-2012 5-year est.); Poverty rate: 20.5% (2008-2012 5-year est.).
Education: Percent of population age 25 and over with: High school diploma (including GED) or higher: 88.2% (2008-2012 5-year est.); Bachelor's degree or higher: 15.1% (2008-2012 5-year est.); Master's degree or higher: 6.2% (2008-2012 5-year est.).

School District(s)

Norris City-Omaha-Enfield CUSD 3 (PK-12)

     2011-12 Enrollment: 736. . . . . (618) 378-3222
Ohio & Wabash Valley Reg Voc Sys

     2011-12 Enrollment: n/a . . . . (618) 378-2274
Wabash & Ohio Valley Sp Ed Dist (KG-12)

     2011-12 Enrollment: n/a . . . . (618) 378-2131
Housing: Homeownership rate: 72.4% (2008-2012 5-year est.); Median home value: $53,200 (2008-2012 5-year est.); Median contract rent: $280 per month (2008-2012 5-year est.); Median year structure built: 1957 (2008-2012 5-year est.).
Health Insurance: 63.5% Private; 45.4% Public; 9.8% None. (2008-2012 5-year est.)
Safety: Violent crime rate: 31.3 per 10,000 population; Property crime rate: 54.9 per 10,000 population (2012).
Transportation: Commute to work: 93.3% car, 4.1% public transportation, 0.5% walk, 1.6% work from home (2008-2012 5-year est.); Travel time to work: 41.9% less than 15 minutes, 23.7% 15 to 30 minutes, 18.3% 30 to 45 minutes, 8.7% 45 to 60 minutes, 7.5% 60 minutes or more (2008-2012 5-year est.)

PHILLIPSTOWN (village). Covers a land area of 0.273 square miles and a water area of 0 square miles. Located at 38.14° N. Lat; 88.02° W. Long. Elevation is 545 feet.

Population: 48 (1990); 28 (2000); 44 (2010); Density: 253.1 persons per square mile (2008-2012 5-year est.); Race: 100.0% White, 0.0% Black/African American, 0.0% Asian, 0.0% American Indian/Alaska Native, 0.0% Native Hawaiian/Other Pacific Islander, 0.0% Some other race, 0.0% Two or more races, 0.0% Hispanic of any race (2008-2012 5-year est.); Average household size: 4.06 (2008-2012 5-year est.); Median age: 37.1 (2008-2012 5-year est.); Males per 100 females: 50.0 (2008-2012 5-year est.); Marriage status: 28.8% never married, 71.2% now married, 0.0% widowed, 0.0% divorced (2008-2012 5-year est.); Foreign born: 0.0% (2008-2012 5-year est.); Ancestry (includes multiple ancestries): 72.5% German, 63.8% Irish, 7.2% American, 4.3% Dutch, 4.3% English (2008-2012 5-year est.).
Economy: Homeowner vacancy rate: 0.0%. Rental vacancy rate: 0.0%. (2008-2012 5-year est.); Employment by occupation: 7.7% management, business, and financial, 11.5% computer, engineering, and science, 0.0% education, legal, community service, arts, and media, 57.7% healthcare practitioners, 0.0% service, 7.7% sales and office, 15.4% natural resources, construction, and maintenance, 0.0% production, transportation, and material moving (2008-2012 5-year est.).
Income: Per capita income: $18,829 (2008-2012 5-year est.); Median household income: $76,250 (2008-2012 5-year est.); Average household income: $69,576 (2008-2012 5-year est.); Percent of households with income of $100,000 or more: 5.9% (2008-2012 5-year est.); Poverty rate: 0.0% (2008-2012 5-year est.).
Education: Percent of population age 25 and over with: High school diploma (including GED) or higher: 100.0% (2008-2012 5-year est.); Bachelor's degree or higher: 0.0% (2008-2012 5-year est.); Master's degree or higher: 0.0% (2008-2012 5-year est.).
Housing: Homeownership rate: 100.0% (2008-2012 5-year est.); Median home value: $94,200 (2008-2012 5-year est.); Median contract rent: n/a per month (2008-2012 5-year est.); Median year structure built: 2002 (2008-2012 5-year est.).
Health Insurance: 95.7% Private; 24.6% Public; 4.3% None. (2008-2012 5-year est.)
Transportation: Commute to work: 88.5% car, 0.0% public transportation, 0.0% walk, 11.5% work from home (2008-2012 5-year est.); Travel time to work: 8.7% less than 15 minutes, 39.1% 15 to 30 minutes, 17.4% 30 to 45 minutes, 34.8% 45 to 60 minutes, 0.0% 60 minutes or more (2008-2012 5-year est.)

SPRINGERTON (village). Aka Springer. Covers a land area of 0.125 square miles and a water area of 0 square miles. Located at 38.18° N. Lat; 88.35° W. Long. Elevation is 394 feet.
Population: 166 (1990); 134 (2000); 110 (2010); Density: 754.2 persons per square mile (2008-2012 5-year est.); Race: 100.0% White, 0.0% Black/African American, 0.0% Asian, 0.0% American Indian/Alaska Native, 0.0% Native Hawaiian/Other Pacific Islander, 0.0% Some other race, 0.0% Two or more races, 0.0% Hispanic of any race (2008-2012 5-year est.); Average household size: 2.76 (2008-2012 5-year est.); Median age: 46.0 (2008-2012 5-year est.); Males per 100 females: 80.8 (2008-2012 5-year est.); Marriage status: 18.8% never married, 55.1% now married, 4.3% widowed, 21.7% divorced (2008-2012 5-year est.); Foreign born: 0.0% (2008-2012 5-year est.); Ancestry (includes multiple ancestries): 19.1% Irish, 17.0% American, 16.0% German, 13.8% English, 4.3% Dutch (2008-2012 5-year est.).
Economy: Homeowner vacancy rate: 27.3%. Rental vacancy rate: 0.0%. (2008-2012 5-year est.); Employment by occupation: 0.0% management, business, and financial, 0.0% computer, engineering, and science, 0.0% education, legal, community service, arts, and media, 2.9% healthcare practitioners, 20.6% service, 41.2% sales and office, 0.0% natural resources, construction, and maintenance, 35.3% production, transportation, and material moving (2008-2012 5-year est.).
Income: Per capita income: $19,104 (2008-2012 5-year est.); Median household income: $42,500 (2008-2012 5-year est.); Average household income: $46,609 (2008-2012 5-year est.); Percent of households with income of $100,000 or more: 2.9% (2008-2012 5-year est.); Poverty rate: 6.4% (2008-2012 5-year est.).
Education: Percent of population age 25 and over with: High school diploma (including GED) or higher: 86.2% (2008-2012 5-year est.); Bachelor's degree or higher: 6.2% (2008-2012 5-year est.); Master's degree or higher: 0.0% (2008-2012 5-year est.).
Housing: Homeownership rate: 94.1% (2008-2012 5-year est.); Median home value: $26,300 (2008-2012 5-year est.); Median contract rent: n/a per month (2008-2012 5-year est.); Median year structure built: 1948 (2008-2012 5-year est.).
Health Insurance: 61.7% Private; 42.6% Public; 18.1% None. (2008-2012 5-year est.)
Transportation: Commute to work: 100.0% car, 0.0% public transportation, 0.0% walk, 0.0% work from home (2008-2012 5-year est.); Travel time to work: 26.5% less than 15 minutes, 26.5% 15 to 30 minutes, 17.6% 30 to 45 minutes, 17.6% 45 to 60 minutes, 11.8% 60 minutes or more (2008-2012 5-year est.)

Whiteside County

Located in northwestern Illinois; bounded on the northwest by the Mississippi River and the Iowa border; drained by the Rock River. Covers a land area of 684.250 square miles, a water area of 12.277 square miles, and is located in the Central Time Zone at 41.75° N. Lat., 89.91° W. Long. The county was founded in 1836. County seat is Morrison.

Whiteside County is part of the Sterling, IL Micropolitan Statistical Area. The entire metro area includes: Whiteside County, IL

Weather Station: Fulton L&D #13 — Elevation: 591 feet

	Jan	Feb	Mar	Apr	May	Jun	Jul	Aug	Sep	Oct	Nov	Dec
High	29	33	45	59	70	80	83	82	75	62	47	33
Low	13	16	27	39	50	60	64	63	54	42	31	18
Precip	1.2	1.4	2.3	3.1	3.6	4.2	3.2	4.1	2.9	2.9	2.5	1.8
Snow	3.1	1.7	0.4	0.5	0.0	0.0	0.0	0.0	0.0	0.0	0.2	1.5

High and Low temperatures in degrees Fahrenheit; Precipitation and Snow in inches

Weather Station: Morrison — Elevation: 603 feet

	Jan	Feb	Mar	Apr	May	Jun	Jul	Aug	Sep	Oct	Nov	Dec
High	31	35	47	61	73	82	85	83	76	64	49	35
Low	12	16	27	37	49	58	62	60	51	39	29	17
Precip	1.5	1.6	2.6	3.3	4.1	4.4	3.9	4.8	3.0	2.9	2.8	2.1
Snow	10.0	6.9	3.3	1.0	0.0	0.0	0.0	0.0	0.0	tr	1.5	8.5

High and Low temperatures in degrees Fahrenheit; Precipitation and Snow in inches

Population: 60,186 (1990); 60,653 (2000); 58,498 (2010); Race: 92.6% White, 1.4% Black/African American, 0.5% Asian, 0.5% American Indian/Alaska Native, 0.1% Native Hawaiian/Other Pacific Islander, 4.9% Some other race, 2.0% Two or more races, 11.1% Hispanic of any race (2008-2012 5-year est.); Density: 84.5 persons per square mile (2008-2012 5-year est.); Average household size: 2.45 (2008-2012 5-year

est.); Median age: 42.0 (2008-2012 5-year est.); Males per 100 females: 96.6 (2008-2012 5-year est.).
Religion: Six largest groups: 17.5% Catholicism, 9.4% Lutheran, 8.2% Presbyterian-Reformed, 7.2% Methodist/Pietist, 6.5% Baptist, 6.4% Non-denominational Protestant (2010)
Economy: Unemployment rate: 6.9% (April 2014); Total civilian labor force: 29,014 (April 2014); Leading industries: 22.8% manufacturing; 17.9% health care and social assistance; 15.3% retail trade (2012); Farms: 1,110 totaling 403,242 acres (2012); Companies that employ 500 or more persons: 3 (2012); Companies that employ 100 to 499 persons: 21 (2012); Companies that employ less than 100 persons: 1,222 (2012); Black-owned businesses: n/a (2007); Hispanic-owned businesses: n/a (2007); Asian-owned businesses: n/a (2007); Women-owned businesses: 961 (2007); Single-family building permits issued: 82 (2013); Multi-family building permits issued: 48 (2013).
Income: Per capita income: $24,062 (2008-2012 5-year est.); Median household income: $46,193 (2008-2012 5-year est.); Average household income: $58,342 (2008-2012 5-year est.); Percent of households with income of $100,000 or more: 12.8% (2008-2012 5-year est.); Poverty rate: 12.2% (2008-2012 5-year est.); Bankruptcy rate: 3.20% (2013).
Taxes: Total county taxes per capita: $152 (2011); County property taxes per capita: $147 (2011).
Education: Percent of population age 25 and over with: High school diploma (including GED) or higher: 86.5% (2008-2012 5-year est.); Bachelor's degree or higher: 15.4% (2008-2012 5-year est.); Master's degree or higher: 5.0% (2008-2012 5-year est.).
Housing: Homeownership rate: 75.7% (2008-2012 5-year est.); Median home value: $99,400 (2008-2012 5-year est.); Median contract rent: $465 per month (2008-2012 5-year est.); Median year structure built: 1959 (2008-2012 5-year est.).
Health: Birth rate: 109.8 per 10,000 population (2013); Death rate: 104.6 per 10,000 population (2013); Age-adjusted cancer mortality rate: 204.8 deaths per 100,000 population (2011); Number of physicians: 12.7 per 10,000 population (2011); Hospital beds: 27.2 per 10,000 population (2010); Hospital admissions: 1,129.6 per 10,000 population (2010).
Elections: 2012 Presidential election results: 57.7% Obama, 40.4% Romney
National and State Parks: Big Bend State Conservation Area; Morrison-Rockwood State Park; Prophetstown State Park
Additional Information Contacts
Whiteside County Government . . . . (815) 772-5100
   http://www.whiteside.org

Whiteside County Communities

ALBANY (village). Covers a land area of 1.072 square miles and a water area of 0 square miles. Located at 41.79° N. Lat; 90.22° W. Long. Elevation is 614 feet.
Population: 835 (1990); 895 (2000); 891 (2010); Density: 817.5 persons per square mile (2008-2012 5-year est.); Race: 95.5% White, 0.0% Black/African American, 2.9% Asian, 0.0% American Indian/Alaska Native, 0.0% Native Hawaiian/Other Pacific Islander, 1.6% Some other race, 0.0% Two or more races, 3.0% Hispanic of any race (2008-2012 5-year est.); Average household size: 2.32 (2008-2012 5-year est.); Median age: 44.4 (2008-2012 5-year est.); Males per 100 females: 95.5 (2008-2012 5-year est.); Marriage status: 20.7% never married, 55.2% now married, 11.8% widowed, 12.3% divorced (2008-2012 5-year est.); Foreign born: 3.2% (2008-2012 5-year est.); Ancestry (includes multiple ancestries): 32.2% German, 13.7% Irish, 10.6% Dutch, 7.2% English, 6.6% American (2008-2012 5-year est.).
Economy: Single-family building permits issued: 4 (2013); Multi-family building permits issued: 0 (2013); Homeowner vacancy rate: 2.0%. Rental vacancy rate: 28.6%. (2008-2012 5-year est.); Employment by occupation: 5.1% management, business, and financial, 6.0% computer, engineering, and science, 7.0% education, legal, community service, arts, and media, 3.6% healthcare practitioners, 12.6% service, 31.6% sales and office, 14.5% natural resources, construction, and maintenance, 19.6% production, transportation, and material moving (2008-2012 5-year est.).
Income: Per capita income: $28,518 (2008-2012 5-year est.); Median household income: $61,500 (2008-2012 5-year est.); Average household income: $64,252 (2008-2012 5-year est.); Percent of households with income of $100,000 or more: 16.9% (2008-2012 5-year est.); Poverty rate: 5.4% (2008-2012 5-year est.).
Taxes: Total city taxes per capita: $222 (2011); City property taxes per capita: $168 (2011).

Education: Percent of population age 25 and over with: High school diploma (including GED) or higher: 87.7% (2008-2012 5-year est.); Bachelor's degree or higher: 14.8% (2008-2012 5-year est.); Master's degree or higher: 2.7% (2008-2012 5-year est.).
Housing: Homeownership rate: 92.1% (2008-2012 5-year est.); Median home value: $114,600 (2008-2012 5-year est.); Median contract rent: $431 per month (2008-2012 5-year est.); Median year structure built: 1961 (2008-2012 5-year est.).
Health Insurance: 79.2% Private; 32.9% Public; 7.6% None. (2008-2012 5-year est.)
Safety: Violent crime rate: 0.0 per 10,000 population; Property crime rate: 135.0 per 10,000 population (2012).
Transportation: Commute to work: 98.5% car, 0.0% public transportation, 0.0% walk, 0.7% work from home (2008-2012 5-year est.); Travel time to work: 20.6% less than 15 minutes, 52.2% 15 to 30 minutes, 10.9% 30 to 45 minutes, 5.7% 45 to 60 minutes, 10.4% 60 minutes or more (2008-2012 5-year est.)

COLETA (village). Covers a land area of 0.596 square miles and a water area of 0 square miles. Located at 41.00° N. Lat; 89.80° W. Long. Elevation is 817 feet.
Population: 154 (1990); 155 (2000); 164 (2010); Density: 309.0 persons per square mile (2008-2012 5-year est.); Race: 97.3% White, 0.0% Black/African American, 2.7% Asian, 0.0% American Indian/Alaska Native, 0.0% Native Hawaiian/Other Pacific Islander, 0.0% Some other race, 0.0% Two or more races, 1.6% Hispanic of any race (2008-2012 5-year est.); Average household size: 2.75 (2008-2012 5-year est.); Median age: 31.7 (2008-2012 5-year est.); Males per 100 females: 139.0 (2008-2012 5-year est.); Marriage status: 28.5% never married, 46.2% now married, 3.8% widowed, 21.5% divorced (2008-2012 5-year est.); Foreign born: 0.0% (2008-2012 5-year est.); Ancestry (includes multiple ancestries): 34.8% German, 17.9% Irish, 3.3% American, 1.6% Scotch-Irish, 1.6% Italian (2008-2012 5-year est.).
Economy: Homeowner vacancy rate: 0.0%. Rental vacancy rate: 0.0%. (2008-2012 5-year est.); Employment by occupation: 2.7% management, business, and financial, 0.0% computer, engineering, and science, 6.8% education, legal, community service, arts, and media, 10.8% healthcare practitioners, 21.6% service, 25.7% sales and office, 29.7% natural resources, construction, and maintenance, 2.7% production, transportation, and material moving (2008-2012 5-year est.).
Income: Per capita income: $19,239 (2008-2012 5-year est.); Median household income: $33,750 (2008-2012 5-year est.); Average household income: $51,494 (2008-2012 5-year est.); Percent of households with income of $100,000 or more: 13.4% (2008-2012 5-year est.); Poverty rate: 21.9% (2008-2012 5-year est.).
Education: Percent of population age 25 and over with: High school diploma (including GED) or higher: 83.8% (2008-2012 5-year est.); Bachelor's degree or higher: 20.0% (2008-2012 5-year est.); Master's degree or higher: 1.9% (2008-2012 5-year est.).
Housing: Homeownership rate: 89.6% (2008-2012 5-year est.); Median home value: $59,200 (2008-2012 5-year est.); Median contract rent: $417 per month (2008-2012 5-year est.); Median year structure built: Before 1940 (2008-2012 5-year est.).
Health Insurance: 48.4% Private; 46.7% Public; 13.0% None. (2008-2012 5-year est.)
Transportation: Commute to work: 94.5% car, 0.0% public transportation, 4.1% walk, 1.4% work from home (2008-2012 5-year est.); Travel time to work: 20.8% less than 15 minutes, 52.8% 15 to 30 minutes, 16.7% 30 to 45 minutes, 4.2% 45 to 60 minutes, 5.6% 60 minutes or more (2008-2012 5-year est.)

COMO (CDP). Covers a land area of 1.068 square miles and a water area of 0.087 square miles. Located at 41.77° N. Lat; 89.77° W. Long. Elevation is 630 feet.
Population: n/a (1990); n/a (2000); 567 (2010); Density: 401.6 persons per square mile (2008-2012 5-year est.); Race: 100.0% White, 0.0% Black/African American, 0.0% Asian, 0.0% American Indian/Alaska Native, 0.0% Native Hawaiian/Other Pacific Islander, 0.0% Some other race, 0.0% Two or more races, 0.0% Hispanic of any race (2008-2012 5-year est.); Average household size: 2.17 (2008-2012 5-year est.); Median age: 41.5 (2008-2012 5-year est.); Males per 100 females: 79.5 (2008-2012 5-year est.); Marriage status: 27.9% never married, 41.1% now married, 13.4% widowed, 17.5% divorced (2008-2012 5-year est.); Foreign born: 0.0% (2008-2012 5-year est.); Ancestry (includes multiple ancestries): 25.2%

German, 22.8% Irish, 17.5% American, 8.9% English, 2.1% Portuguese (2008-2012 5-year est.).
Economy: Homeowner vacancy rate: 0.0%. Rental vacancy rate: 0.0%. (2008-2012 5-year est.); Employment by occupation: 7.3% management, business, and financial, 3.2% computer, engineering, and science, 11.0% education, legal, community service, arts, and media, 10.1% healthcare practitioners, 8.3% service, 28.4% sales and office, 7.8% natural resources, construction, and maintenance, 23.9% production, transportation, and material moving (2008-2012 5-year est.).
Income: Per capita income: $32,869 (2008-2012 5-year est.); Median household income: $56,500 (2008-2012 5-year est.); Average household income: $69,604 (2008-2012 5-year est.); Percent of households with income of $100,000 or more: 20.7% (2008-2012 5-year est.); Poverty rate: 4.7% (2008-2012 5-year est.).
Education: Percent of population age 25 and over with: High school diploma (including GED) or higher: 78.5% (2008-2012 5-year est.); Bachelor's degree or higher: 16.0% (2008-2012 5-year est.); Master's degree or higher: 6.1% (2008-2012 5-year est.).
Housing: Homeownership rate: 90.4% (2008-2012 5-year est.); Median home value: $118,100 (2008-2012 5-year est.); Median contract rent: $498 per month (2008-2012 5-year est.); Median year structure built: 1972 (2008-2012 5-year est.).
Health Insurance: 95.3% Private; 27.0% Public; 0.0% None. (2008-2012 5-year est.)
Transportation: Commute to work: 96.8% car, 0.0% public transportation, 0.0% walk, 0.0% work from home (2008-2012 5-year est.); Travel time to work: 46.8% less than 15 minutes, 32.6% 15 to 30 minutes, 0.0% 30 to 45 minutes, 16.1% 45 to 60 minutes, 4.6% 60 minutes or more (2008-2012 5-year est.)

DEER GROVE (village). Covers a land area of 0.455 square miles and a water area of 0 square miles. Located at 41.61° N. Lat; 89.69° W. Long. Elevation is 646 feet.
Population: 44 (1990); 48 (2000); 48 (2010); Density: 177.9 persons per square mile (2008-2012 5-year est.); Race: 100.0% White, 0.0% Black/African American, 0.0% Asian, 0.0% American Indian/Alaska Native, 0.0% Native Hawaiian/Other Pacific Islander, 0.0% Some other race, 0.0% Two or more races, 0.0% Hispanic of any race (2008-2012 5-year est.); Average household size: 2.89 (2008-2012 5-year est.); Median age: 31.1 (2008-2012 5-year est.); Males per 100 females: 76.1 (2008-2012 5-year est.); Marriage status: 12.8% never married, 76.6% now married, 6.4% widowed, 4.3% divorced (2008-2012 5-year est.); Foreign born: 0.0% (2008-2012 5-year est.); Ancestry (includes multiple ancestries): 48.1% German, 43.2% Irish, 22.2% Dutch, 7.4% Polish, 7.4% French (2008-2012 5-year est.).
Economy: Homeowner vacancy rate: 0.0%. Rental vacancy rate: 0.0%. (2008-2012 5-year est.); Employment by occupation: 8.3% management, business, and financial, 0.0% computer, engineering, and science, 0.0% education, legal, community service, arts, and media, 0.0% healthcare practitioners, 8.3% service, 45.8% sales and office, 12.5% natural resources, construction, and maintenance, 25.0% production, transportation, and material moving (2008-2012 5-year est.).
Income: Per capita income: $13,881 (2008-2012 5-year est.); Median household income: $41,250 (2008-2012 5-year est.); Average household income: $40,157 (2008-2012 5-year est.); Percent of households with income of $100,000 or more: n/a (2008-2012 5-year est.); Poverty rate: 46.9% (2008-2012 5-year est.).
Education: Percent of population age 25 and over with: High school diploma (including GED) or higher: 80.9% (2008-2012 5-year est.); Bachelor's degree or higher: 4.3% (2008-2012 5-year est.); Master's degree or higher: 4.3% (2008-2012 5-year est.).
Housing: Homeownership rate: 57.1% (2008-2012 5-year est.); Median home value: $90,000 (2008-2012 5-year est.); Median contract rent: $525 per month (2008-2012 5-year est.); Median year structure built: 1970 (2008-2012 5-year est.).
Health Insurance: 71.6% Private; 27.2% Public; 3.7% None. (2008-2012 5-year est.)
Transportation: Commute to work: 91.7% car, 0.0% public transportation, 0.0% walk, 0.0% work from home (2008-2012 5-year est.); Travel time to work: 16.7% less than 15 minutes, 83.3% 15 to 30 minutes, 0.0% 30 to 45 minutes, 0.0% 45 to 60 minutes, 0.0% 60 minutes or more (2008-2012 5-year est.)

ERIE (village). Covers a land area of 1.443 square miles and a water area of 0.009 square miles. Located at 41.66° N. Lat; 90.08° W. Long. Elevation is 591 feet.

History: Incorporated 1872.

Population: 1,572 (1990); 1,589 (2000); 1,602 (2010); Density: 1,160.9 persons per square mile (2008-2012 5-year est.); Race: 96.3% White, 1.1% Black/African American, 0.2% Asian, 0.9% American Indian/Alaska Native, 0.0% Native Hawaiian/Other Pacific Islander, 1.5% Some other race, 1.4% Two or more races, 5.4% Hispanic of any race (2008-2012 5-year est.); Average household size: 2.43 (2008-2012 5-year est.); Median age: 39.8 (2008-2012 5-year est.); Males per 100 females: 102.5 (2008-2012 5-year est.); Marriage status: 21.9% never married, 63.1% now married, 6.2% widowed, 8.9% divorced (2008-2012 5-year est.); Foreign born: 1.4% (2008-2012 5-year est.); Ancestry (includes multiple ancestries): 25.4% German, 16.1% Irish, 11.8% English, 7.9% American, 7.6% Swedish (2008-2012 5-year est.).

Economy: Single-family building permits issued: 2 (2013); Multi-family building permits issued: 0 (2013); Homeowner vacancy rate: 5.8%. Rental vacancy rate: 6.4%. (2008-2012 5-year est.); Employment by occupation: 8.6% management, business, and financial, 5.2% computer, engineering, and science, 10.6% education, legal, community service, arts, and media, 3.5% healthcare practitioners, 11.1% service, 29.5% sales and office, 8.0% natural resources, construction, and maintenance, 23.5% production, transportation, and material moving (2008-2012 5-year est.).

Income: Per capita income: $25,484 (2008-2012 5-year est.); Median household income: $49,773 (2008-2012 5-year est.); Average household income: $60,592 (2008-2012 5-year est.); Percent of households with income of $100,000 or more: 16.2% (2008-2012 5-year est.); Poverty rate: 5.2% (2008-2012 5-year est.).

Education: Percent of population age 25 and over with: High school diploma (including GED) or higher: 89.0% (2008-2012 5-year est.); Bachelor's degree or higher: 20.2% (2008-2012 5-year est.); Master's degree or higher: 7.0% (2008-2012 5-year est.).

School District(s)

Erie CUSD 1 (PK-12)

    2011-12 Enrollment: 706 . . . . (309) 659-2239

Housing: Homeownership rate: 82.4% (2008-2012 5-year est.); Median home value: $116,200 (2008-2012 5-year est.); Median contract rent: $465 per month (2008-2012 5-year est.); Median year structure built: 1962 (2008-2012 5-year est.).

Health Insurance: 83.4% Private; 31.1% Public; 6.9% None. (2008-2012 5-year est.)

Transportation: Commute to work: 95.0% car, 0.0% public transportation, 1.2% walk, 2.9% work from home (2008-2012 5-year est.); Travel time to work: 29.0% less than 15 minutes, 22.1% 15 to 30 minutes, 30.1% 30 to 45 minutes, 14.3% 45 to 60 minutes, 4.5% 60 minutes or more (2008-2012 5-year est.)

FENTON (unincorporated postal area)

Zip Code: 61251

    Covers a land area of 17.779 square miles and a water area of 0 square miles. Located at 41.73° N. Lat; 90.07° W. Long. Elevation is 620 feet. Population: 347 (2010); Density: 19.5 persons per square mile (2010); Race: 98.6% White, 0.0% Black/African American, 0.6% Asian, 0.3% American Indian/Alaska Native, 0.0% Native Hawaiian/Other Pacific Islander, 0.5% Some other race, 0.6% Two or more races, 0.9% Hispanic of any race (2010); Average household size: 2.53 (2010); Median age: 43.8 (2010); Males per 100 females: 106.5 (2010); Homeownership rate: 95.6% (2010)

FULTON (city). Covers a land area of 2.274 square miles and a water area of 0.064 square miles. Located at 41.86° N. Lat; 90.16° W. Long. Elevation is 650 feet.

History: The name of Fulton honors the inventor of the steamboat, and the city itself owes its early development to river commerce. Later it became the center of an agricultural area, producing tomatoes and cucumbers.

Population: 3,698 (1990); 3,881 (2000); 3,481 (2010); Density: 1,577.6 persons per square mile (2008-2012 5-year est.); Race: 95.2% White, 1.3% Black/African American, 1.0% Asian, 0.3% American Indian/Alaska Native, 0.0% Native Hawaiian/Other Pacific Islander, 2.2% Some other race, 2.3% Two or more races, 0.4% Hispanic of any race (2008-2012 5-year est.); Average household size: 2.12 (2008-2012 5-year est.); Median age: 46.2 (2008-2012 5-year est.); Males per 100 females: 99.4 (2008-2012 5-year est.); Marriage status: 24.7% never married, 57.7% now married, 4.5% widowed, 13.1% divorced (2008-2012 5-year est.);

Foreign born: 2.4% (2008-2012 5-year est.); Ancestry (includes multiple ancestries): 33.1% Dutch, 29.0% German, 13.1% Irish, 6.4% American, 3.8% English (2008-2012 5-year est.).

Economy: Single-family building permits issued: 2 (2013); Multi-family building permits issued: 0 (2013); Homeowner vacancy rate: 5.0%. Rental vacancy rate: 20.4%. (2008-2012 5-year est.); Employment by occupation: 8.1% management, business, and financial, 2.9% computer, engineering, and science, 6.9% education, legal, community service, arts, and media, 6.2% healthcare practitioners, 11.9% service, 26.8% sales and office, 10.8% natural resources, construction, and maintenance, 26.4% production, transportation, and material moving (2008-2012 5-year est.).

Income: Per capita income: $27,426 (2008-2012 5-year est.); Median household income: $51,314 (2008-2012 5-year est.); Average household income: $57,325 (2008-2012 5-year est.); Percent of households with income of $100,000 or more: 13.0% (2008-2012 5-year est.); Poverty rate: 7.1% (2008-2012 5-year est.).

Education: Percent of population age 25 and over with: High school diploma (including GED) or higher: 93.4% (2008-2012 5-year est.); Bachelor's degree or higher: 17.1% (2008-2012 5-year est.); Master's degree or higher: 6.8% (2008-2012 5-year est.).

School District(s)

River Bend CUSD 2 (PK-12)

    2011-12 Enrollment: 1,003 . . . . (815) 589-2711

Housing: Homeownership rate: 80.5% (2008-2012 5-year est.); Median home value: $105,600 (2008-2012 5-year est.); Median contract rent: $427 per month (2008-2012 5-year est.); Median year structure built: 1957 (2008-2012 5-year est.).

Health Insurance: 79.9% Private; 33.3% Public; 8.3% None. (2008-2012 5-year est.)

Safety: Violent crime rate: 11.5 per 10,000 population; Property crime rate: 120.8 per 10,000 population (2012).

Transportation: Commute to work: 93.0% car, 0.0% public transportation, 1.9% walk, 2.9% work from home (2008-2012 5-year est.); Travel time to work: 51.7% less than 15 minutes, 37.0% 15 to 30 minutes, 4.8% 30 to 60 minutes, 3.0% 45 to 60 minutes, 3.5% 60 minutes or more (2008-2012 5-year est.)

Additional Information Contacts

Fulton Chamber of Commerce . . . . (815) 589-4545

    http://www.cityoffulton.us/business/chamber/chamber-of-commerce.html

GALT (unincorporated postal area)

Zip Code: 61037

    Covers a land area of 0.167 square miles and a water area of 0 square miles. Located at 41.78° N. Lat; 89.76° W. Long. Elevation is 640 feet. Population: 140 (2010); Density: 833.3 persons per square mile (2010); Race: 95.0% White, 0.0% Black/African American, 0.0% Asian, 2.9% American Indian/Alaska Native, 0.0% Native Hawaiian/Other Pacific Islander, 2.1% Some other race, 0.7% Two or more races, 7.1% Hispanic of any race (2010); Average household size: 2.50 (2010); Median age: 40.5 (2010); Males per 100 females: 89.2 (2010); Homeownership rate: 82.2% (2010)

LYNDON (village). Covers a land area of 0.777 square miles and a water area of 0.001 square miles. Located at 41.72° N. Lat; 89.92° W. Long. Elevation is 614 feet.

Population: 615 (1990); 566 (2000); 648 (2010); Density: 845.5 persons per square mile (2008-2012 5-year est.); Race: 96.5% White, 2.0% Black/African American, 0.5% Asian, 0.0% American Indian/Alaska Native, 0.0% Native Hawaiian/Other Pacific Islander, 1.0% Some other race, 1.1% Two or more races, 3.3% Hispanic of any race (2008-2012 5-year est.); Average household size: 2.71 (2008-2012 5-year est.); Median age: 37.5 (2008-2012 5-year est.); Males per 100 females: 82.0 (2008-2012 5-year est.); Marriage status: 20.9% never married, 56.7% now married, 4.3% widowed, 18.1% divorced (2008-2012 5-year est.); Foreign born: 0.5% (2008-2012 5-year est.); Ancestry (includes multiple ancestries): 24.2% German, 22.1% Irish, 13.7% American, 10.8% English, 5.9% Dutch (2008-2012 5-year est.).

Economy: Single-family building permits issued: 0 (2013); Multi-family building permits issued: 0 (2013); Homeowner vacancy rate: 3.9%. Rental vacancy rate: 0.0%. (2008-2012 5-year est.); Employment by occupation: 5.5% management, business, and financial, 3.8% computer, engineering, and science, 6.5% education, legal, community service, arts, and media, 6.2% healthcare practitioners, 21.2% service, 15.1% sales and office, 12.0% natural resources, construction, and maintenance, 29.8% production, transportation, and material moving (2008-2012 5-year est.).

Income: Per capita income: $21,095 (2008-2012 5-year est.); Median household income: $50,625 (2008-2012 5-year est.); Average household income: $54,537 (2008-2012 5-year est.); Percent of households with income of $100,000 or more: 9.9% (2008-2012 5-year est.); Poverty rate: 11.3% (2008-2012 5-year est.).
Education: Percent of population age 25 and over with: High school diploma (including GED) or higher: 84.6% (2008-2012 5-year est.); Bachelor's degree or higher: 13.8% (2008-2012 5-year est.); Master's degree or higher: 6.8% (2008-2012 5-year est.).
Housing: Homeownership rate: 80.6% (2008-2012 5-year est.); Median home value: $84,700 (2008-2012 5-year est.); Median contract rent: $439 per month (2008-2012 5-year est.); Median year structure built: 1960 (2008-2012 5-year est.).
Health Insurance: 63.8% Private; 28.5% Public; 14.3% None. (2008-2012 5-year est.)
Transportation: Commute to work: 97.5% car, 0.0% public transportation, 0.0% walk, 1.4% work from home (2008-2012 5-year est.); Travel time to work: 25.1% less than 15 minutes, 35.6% 15 to 30 minutes, 18.9% 30 to 45 minutes, 13.8% 45 to 60 minutes, 6.5% 60 minutes or more (2008-2012 5-year est.)

MORRISON (city). County seat. Covers a land area of 2.463 square miles and a water area of 0 square miles. Located at 41.81° N. Lat; 89.96° W. Long. Elevation is 679 feet.
History: Morrison developed when the Chicago & North Western Railway built its station here. It was in Morrison in 1874 that James Sargent installed the first time lock in the First National Bank of Morrison.
Population: 4,363 (1990); 4,447 (2000); 4,188 (2010); Density: 1,645.2 persons per square mile (2008-2012 5-year est.); Race: 95.5% White, 2.1% Black/African American, 0.0% Asian, 0.5% American Indian/Alaska Native, 1.8% Native Hawaiian/Other Pacific Islander, 0.1% Some other race, 0.0% Two or more races, 4.2% Hispanic of any race (2008-2012 5-year est.); Average household size: 2.31 (2008-2012 5-year est.); Median age: 43.1 (2008-2012 5-year est.); Males per 100 females: 99.4 (2008-2012 5-year est.); Marriage status: 26.7% never married, 49.1% now married, 10.3% widowed, 14.0% divorced (2008-2012 5-year est.); Foreign born: 1.4% (2008-2012 5-year est.); Ancestry (includes multiple ancestries): 33.7% German, 18.2% Dutch, 16.6% Irish, 9.1% English, 8.0% American (2008-2012 5-year est.).
Economy: Single-family building permits issued: 40 (2013); Multi-family building permits issued: 0 (2013); Homeowner vacancy rate: 0.0%. Rental vacancy rate: 6.0%. (2008-2012 5-year est.); Employment by occupation: 14.6% management, business, and financial, 4.4% computer, engineering, and science, 6.7% education, legal, community service, arts, and media, 4.8% healthcare practitioners, 22.4% service, 13.1% sales and office, 13.2% natural resources, construction, and maintenance, 20.9% production, transportation, and material moving (2008-2012 5-year est.).
Income: Per capita income: $23,364 (2008-2012 5-year est.); Median household income: $46,279 (2008-2012 5-year est.); Average household income: $56,204 (2008-2012 5-year est.); Percent of households with income of $100,000 or more: 13.0% (2008-2012 5-year est.); Poverty rate: 12.3% (2008-2012 5-year est.).
Education: Percent of population age 25 and over with: High school diploma (including GED) or higher: 89.0% (2008-2012 5-year est.); Bachelor's degree or higher: 15.1% (2008-2012 5-year est.); Master's degree or higher: 3.3% (2008-2012 5-year est.).
School District(s)
Morrison CUSD 6 (PK-12)
    2011-12 Enrollment: 1,123 . . . . (815) 772-2064
Two-year College(s)
Morrison Institute of Technology (Private, Not-for-profit)
    Fall 2012 Enrollment: 83 . . . . (815) 772-7218
    2012-13 Tuition: In-state $15,100; Out-of-state $15,100
Housing: Homeownership rate: 71.9% (2008-2012 5-year est.); Median home value: $87,600 (2008-2012 5-year est.); Median contract rent: $434 per month (2008-2012 5-year est.); Median year structure built: 1953 (2008-2012 5-year est.).
Health Insurance: 72.7% Private; 40.6% Public; 8.9% None. (2008-2012 5-year est.)
Hospitals: Morrison Community Hospital (76 beds)
Safety: Violent crime rate: 21.5 per 10,000 population; Property crime rate: 114.8 per 10,000 population (2012).
Transportation: Commute to work: 92.1% car, 0.0% public transportation, 3.4% walk, 1.0% work from home (2008-2012 5-year est.); Travel time to work: 39.4% less than 15 minutes, 31.2% 15 to 30 minutes, 17.4% 30 to

45 minutes, 6.0% 45 to 60 minutes, 5.9% 60 minutes or more (2008-2012 5-year est.)
Additional Information Contacts
Morrison Chamber of Commerce . . . . (815) 772-3757
    http://www.morrisonchamber.com

PROPHETSTOWN (city). Covers a land area of 1.371 square miles and a water area of 0.024 square miles. Located at 41.67° N. Lat; 89.94° W. Long. Elevation is 620 feet.
History: The name of Prophetstown refers to the Indian prophet White Cloud, who warned his people about the loss of their lands. The town was founded on the Rock River, where White Cloud had lived.
Population: 1,749 (1990); 2,023 (2000); 2,080 (2010); Density: 1,555.8 persons per square mile (2008-2012 5-year est.); Race: 97.6% White, 0.5% Black/African American, 0.9% Asian, 0.0% American Indian/Alaska Native, 0.0% Native Hawaiian/Other Pacific Islander, 1.0% Some other race, 0.9% Two or more races, 5.1% Hispanic of any race (2008-2012 5-year est.); Average household size: 2.46 (2008-2012 5-year est.); Median age: 40.6 (2008-2012 5-year est.); Males per 100 females: 85.2 (2008-2012 5-year est.); Marriage status: 26.2% never married, 52.8% now married, 11.3% widowed, 9.7% divorced (2008-2012 5-year est.); Foreign born: 1.4% (2008-2012 5-year est.); Ancestry (includes multiple ancestries): 34.6% German, 16.7% Irish, 11.7% English, 10.3% American, 7.5% Dutch (2008-2012 5-year est.).
Economy: Single-family building permits issued: 0 (2013); Multi-family building permits issued: 0 (2013); Homeowner vacancy rate: 0.0%. Rental vacancy rate: 0.0%. (2008-2012 5-year est.); Employment by occupation: 6.6% management, business, and financial, 1.5% computer, engineering, and science, 13.4% education, legal, community service, arts, and media, 4.1% healthcare practitioners, 22.2% service, 23.2% sales and office, 7.2% natural resources, construction, and maintenance, 21.8% production, transportation, and material moving (2008-2012 5-year est.).
Income: Per capita income: $21,191 (2008-2012 5-year est.); Median household income: $45,667 (2008-2012 5-year est.); Average household income: $52,743 (2008-2012 5-year est.); Percent of households with income of $100,000 or more: 7.9% (2008-2012 5-year est.); Poverty rate: 9.2% (2008-2012 5-year est.).
Education: Percent of population age 25 and over with: High school diploma (including GED) or higher: 88.9% (2008-2012 5-year est.); Bachelor's degree or higher: 16.5% (2008-2012 5-year est.); Master's degree or higher: 7.3% (2008-2012 5-year est.).
School District(s)
Prophetstown-Lyndon-Tampico Cusd3 (PK-12)
    2011-12 Enrollment: 951 . . . . (815) 537-5101
Housing: Homeownership rate: 76.1% (2008-2012 5-year est.); Median home value: $90,700 (2008-2012 5-year est.); Median contract rent: $465 per month (2008-2012 5-year est.); Median year structure built: 1950 (2008-2012 5-year est.).
Health Insurance: 68.7% Private; 44.5% Public; 7.3% None. (2008-2012 5-year est.)
Transportation: Commute to work: 89.3% car, 0.8% public transportation, 6.3% walk, 0.9% work from home (2008-2012 5-year est.); Travel time to work: 47.3% less than 15 minutes, 31.3% 15 to 30 minutes, 14.0% 30 to 45 minutes, 2.7% 45 to 60 minutes, 4.8% 60 minutes or more (2008-2012 5-year est.)
Additional Information Contacts
Prophetstown Main Street . . . . (815) 537-5139
    http://prophetstownil.com/

ROCK FALLS (city). Covers a land area of 3.655 square miles and a water area of 0.135 square miles. Located at 41.77° N. Lat; 89.69° W. Long. Elevation is 646 feet.
History: Rock Falls was platted in 1837. Development came when a dam was built across the river, and later when a feeder canal connected Rock Falls and the Rock River with the Illinois & Mississippi Canal.
Population: 9,654 (1990); 9,580 (2000); 9,266 (2010); Density: 2,482.9 persons per square mile (2008-2012 5-year est.); Race: 91.7% White, 1.2% Black/African American, 0.4% Asian, 0.1% American Indian/Alaska Native, 0.0% Native Hawaiian/Other Pacific Islander, 6.6% Some other race, 2.7% Two or more races, 14.0% Hispanic of any race (2008-2012 5-year est.); Average household size: 2.31 (2008-2012 5-year est.); Median age: 39.7 (2008-2012 5-year est.); Males per 100 females: 97.8 (2008-2012 5-year est.); Marriage status: 33.0% never married, 45.2% now married, 9.1% widowed, 12.7% divorced (2008-2012 5-year est.); Foreign born: 4.2% (2008-2012 5-year est.); Ancestry (includes multiple

ancestries): 26.2% German, 13.5% Irish, 10.0% American, 8.0% English, 4.8% Swedish (2008-2012 5-year est.).

Economy: Single-family building permits issued: 0 (2013); Multi-family building permits issued: 0 (2013); Homeowner vacancy rate: 3.4%. Rental vacancy rate: 5.9%. (2008-2012 5-year est.); Employment by occupation: 4.4% management, business, and financial, 3.2% computer, engineering, and science, 6.2% education, legal, community service, arts, and media, 3.0% healthcare practitioners, 24.3% service, 28.0% sales and office, 6.3% natural resources, construction, and maintenance, 24.6% production, transportation, and material moving (2008-2012 5-year est.).

Income: Per capita income: $18,856 (2008-2012 5-year est.); Median household income: $35,432 (2008-2012 5-year est.); Average household income: $42,533 (2008-2012 5-year est.); Percent of households with income of $100,000 or more: 5.3% (2008-2012 5-year est.); Poverty rate: 18.8% (2008-2012 5-year est.).

Education: Percent of population age 25 and over with: High school diploma (including GED) or higher: 81.2% (2008-2012 5-year est.); Bachelor's degree or higher: 8.3% (2008-2012 5-year est.); Master's degree or higher: 2.6% (2008-2012 5-year est.).

School District(s)

East Coloma SD 12 (PK-08)
  2011-12 Enrollment: 256 . . . . (815) 625-4400
Montmorency CCSD 145 (PK-08)
  2011-12 Enrollment: 318 . . . . (815) 625-6616
Riverdale SD 14 (PK-08)
  2011-12 Enrollment: 72 . . . . (815) 625-5280
Rock Falls ESD 13 (PK-08)
  2011-12 Enrollment: 1,055 . . . . (815) 626-2604
Rock Falls Twp HSD 301 (09-12)
  2011-12 Enrollment: 665 . . . . (815) 625-3886

Housing: Homeownership rate: 62.6% (2008-2012 5-year est.); Median home value: $79,000 (2008-2012 5-year est.); Median contract rent: $457 per month (2008-2012 5-year est.); Median year structure built: 1957 (2008-2012 5-year est.).

Health Insurance: 55.4% Private; 45.2% Public; 14.8% None. (2008-2012 5-year est.)

Safety: Violent crime rate: 31.3 per 10,000 population; Property crime rate: 482.0 per 10,000 population (2012).

Transportation: Commute to work: 94.0% car, 1.0% public transportation, 2.3% walk, 0.7% work from home (2008-2012 5-year est.); Travel time to work: 54.4% less than 15 minutes, 31.5% 15 to 30 minutes, 9.6% 30 to 45 minutes, 2.2% 45 to 60 minutes, 2.2% 60 minutes or more (2008-2012 5-year est.)

Airports: Whiteside County Airport (general aviation)

Additional Information Contacts
City of Rock Falls . . . . (815) 622-1100
  http://www.rockfalls61071.com
Rock Falls Chamber of Commerce . . . . (815) 625-4500
  http://www.rockfallschamber.com

STERLING (city).
Covers a land area of 5.709 square miles and a water area of 0.233 square miles. Located at 41.80° N. Lat; 89.70° W. Long. Elevation is 659 feet.

History: Sterling originated in 1839 from the union of Chatham and Harrisburg in the hopes that the new town would become the seat of Whiteside County. Though Sterling was chosen, it soon lost the honor to Morrison.

Population: 15,132 (1990); 15,451 (2000); 15,370 (2010); Density: 2,691.7 persons per square mile (2008-2012 5-year est.); Race: 85.9% White, 2.3% Black/African American, 0.2% Asian, 0.1% American Indian/Alaska Native, 0.0% Native Hawaiian/Other Pacific Islander, 10.6% Some other race, 3.1% Two or more races, 23.9% Hispanic of any race (2008-2012 5-year est.); Average household size: 2.51 (2008-2012 5-year est.); Median age: 38.5 (2008-2012 5-year est.); Males per 100 females: 92.0 (2008-2012 5-year est.); Marriage status: 28.7% never married, 47.9% now married, 8.6% widowed, 14.8% divorced (2008-2012 5-year est.); Foreign born: 4.8% (2008-2012 5-year est.); Ancestry (includes multiple ancestries): 26.4% German, 14.8% Irish, 7.0% English, 6.4% American, 3.5% Italian (2008-2012 5-year est.).

Economy: Single-family building permits issued: 2 (2013); Multi-family building permits issued: 48 (2013); Homeowner vacancy rate: 1.0%. Rental vacancy rate: 12.3%. (2008-2012 5-year est.); Employment by occupation: 9.2% management, business, and financial, 2.0% computer, engineering, and science, 9.3% education, legal, community service, arts, and media, 6.5% healthcare practitioners, 20.4% service, 26.0% sales and office,

4.5% natural resources, construction, and maintenance, 22.1% production, transportation, and material moving (2008-2012 5-year est.).

Income: Per capita income: $20,448 (2008-2012 5-year est.); Median household income: $39,749 (2008-2012 5-year est.); Average household income: $50,822 (2008-2012 5-year est.); Percent of households with income of $100,000 or more: 8.3% (2008-2012 5-year est.); Poverty rate: 17.3% (2008-2012 5-year est.).

Taxes: Total city taxes per capita: $376 (2011); City property taxes per capita: $249 (2011).

Education: Percent of population age 25 and over with: High school diploma (including GED) or higher: 81.7% (2008-2012 5-year est.); Bachelor's degree or higher: 17.1% (2008-2012 5-year est.); Master's degree or higher: 5.5% (2008-2012 5-year est.).

School District(s)

Bi-County Special Educ Coop (PK-PK)
  2011-12 Enrollment: n/a . . . . (815) 622-0858
Sterling CUSD 5 (PK-12)
  2011-12 Enrollment: 3,441 . . . . (815) 626-5050
Whiteside Area Career (11-12)
  2011-12 Enrollment: n/a . . . . (815) 626-5810
Whiteside Roe (07-11)
  2011-12 Enrollment: n/a . . . . (815) 625-1495

Vocational/Technical School(s)

Educators of Beauty-Sterling (Private, For-profit)
  Fall 2012 Enrollment: 46 . . . . (815) 625-0247
  2012-13 Tuition: $17,175

Housing: Homeownership rate: 65.7% (2008-2012 5-year est.); Median home value: $86,100 (2008-2012 5-year est.); Median contract rent: $494 per month (2008-2012 5-year est.); Median year structure built: 1956 (2008-2012 5-year est.).

Health Insurance: 59.2% Private; 42.9% Public; 13.7% None. (2008-2012 5-year est.)

Hospitals: CGH Medical Center (139 beds)

Safety: Violent crime rate: 27.9 per 10,000 population; Property crime rate: 391.1 per 10,000 population (2012).

Transportation: Commute to work: 92.1% car, 1.0% public transportation, 1.8% walk, 1.4% work from home (2008-2012 5-year est.); Travel time to work: 58.0% less than 15 minutes, 26.8% 15 to 30 minutes, 6.6% 30 to 45 minutes, 3.7% 45 to 60 minutes, 4.9% 60 minutes or more (2008-2012 5-year est.)

Airports: Whiteside County Airport (general aviation)

Additional Information Contacts
City of Sterling . . . . (815) 632-6621
  http://ci.sterling.il.us
Sauk Valley Area Chamber of Commerce . . . . (815) 625-2400
  http://www.saukvalleyareachamber.com

TAMPICO (village).
Covers a land area of 0.388 square miles and a water area of 0 square miles. Located at 41.63° N. Lat; 89.79° W. Long. Elevation is 640 feet.

History: Birthplace of Ronald Reagan.

Population: 833 (1990); 772 (2000); 790 (2010); Density: 2,236.4 persons per square mile (2008-2012 5-year est.); Race: 99.3% White, 0.0% Black/African American, 0.7% Asian, 0.0% American Indian/Alaska Native, 0.0% Native Hawaiian/Other Pacific Islander, 0.0% Some other race, 0.0% Two or more races, 4.3% Hispanic of any race (2008-2012 5-year est.); Average household size: 2.90 (2008-2012 5-year est.); Median age: 31.0 (2008-2012 5-year est.); Males per 100 females: 84.5 (2008-2012 5-year est.); Marriage status: 32.7% never married, 53.1% now married, 7.0% widowed, 7.2% divorced (2008-2012 5-year est.); Foreign born: 0.9% (2008-2012 5-year est.); Ancestry (includes multiple ancestries): 23.0% German, 13.8% American, 13.4% Irish, 9.8% Dutch, 4.8% English (2008-2012 5-year est.).

Economy: Single-family building permits issued: 0 (2013); Multi-family building permits issued: 0 (2013); Homeowner vacancy rate: 0.0%. Rental vacancy rate: 10.3%. (2008-2012 5-year est.); Employment by occupation: 10.9% management, business, and financial, 1.0% computer, engineering, and science, 10.4% education, legal, community service, arts, and media, 1.9% healthcare practitioners, 14.8% service, 31.1% sales and office, 13.1% natural resources, construction, and maintenance, 16.7% production, transportation, and material moving (2008-2012 5-year est.).

Income: Per capita income: $18,106 (2008-2012 5-year est.); Median household income: $40,446 (2008-2012 5-year est.); Average household income: $51,518 (2008-2012 5-year est.); Percent of households with

income of $100,000 or more: 11.7% (2008-2012 5-year est.); Poverty rate: 11.4% (2008-2012 5-year est.).

Education: Percent of population age 25 and over with: High school diploma (including GED) or higher: 86.7% (2008-2012 5-year est.); Bachelor's degree or higher: 9.2% (2008-2012 5-year est.); Master's degree or higher: 3.5% (2008-2012 5-year est.).

School District(s)

Prophetstown-Lyndon-Tampico Cusd3 (PK-12)

2011-12 Enrollment: 951 . . . . (815) 537-5101

Housing: Homeownership rate: 67.9% (2008-2012 5-year est.); Median home value: $83,200 (2008-2012 5-year est.); Median contract rent: $441 per month (2008-2012 5-year est.); Median year structure built: 1941 (2008-2012 5-year est.).

Health Insurance: 66.1% Private; 37.0% Public; 11.8% None. (2008-2012 5-year est.)

Transportation: Commute to work: 92.7% car, 0.0% public transportation, 2.7% walk, 1.5% work from home (2008-2012 5-year est.); Travel time to work: 24.5% less than 15 minutes, 45.8% 15 to 30 minutes, 19.8% 30 to 45 minutes, 4.2% 45 to 60 minutes, 5.7% 60 minutes or more (2008-2012 5-year est.)

Will County

Located in northeastern Illinois; bounded on the east by Indiana; drained by the Des Plaines, Du Page, and Kankakee Rivers. Covers a land area of 836.908 square miles, a water area of 12.318 square miles, and is located in the Central Time Zone at 41.45° N. Lat., 87.98° W. Long. The county was founded in 1836. County seat is Joliet.

Will County is part of the Chicago-Naperville-Elgin, IL-IN-WI Metropolitan Statistical Area. The entire metro area includes: Chicago-Naperville-Arlington Heights, IL Metropolitan Division (Cook County, IL; DuPage County, IL; Grundy County, IL; Kendall County, IL; McHenry County, IL; Will County, IL); Elgin, IL Metropolitan Division (DeKalb County, IL; Kane County, IL); Gary, IN Metropolitan Division (Jasper County, IN; Lake County, IN; Newton County, IN; Porter County, IN); Lake County-Kenosha County, IL-WI Metropolitan Division (Lake County, IL; Kenosha County, WI)

Weather Station: Joliet Brandon Rd Dam									Elevation: 542 feet		
	Jan	Feb	Mar	Apr	May	Jun	Jul	Aug	Sep	Oct	Nov	Dec
High	31	36	47	60	71	81	84	83	76	63	49	35
Low	16	19	29	39	49	59	64	62	54	42	32	20
Precip	1.7	1.7	2.3	3.5	4.0	3.7	4.3	3.9	3.2	3.0	3.0	2.2
Snow	na	na	1.0	0.1	0.0	0.0	0.0	0.0	0.0	0.0	0.1	3.3

High and Low temperatures in degrees Fahrenheit; Precipitation and Snow in inches

Population: 357,313 (1990); 502,266 (2000); 677,560 (2010); Race: 77.1% White, 10.9% Black/African American, 4.5% Asian, 0.2% American Indian/Alaska Native, 0.0% Native Hawaiian/Other Pacific Islander, 7.3% Some other race, 2.3% Two or more races, 15.6% Hispanic of any race (2008-2012 5-year est.); Density: 814.4 persons per square mile (2008-2012 5-year est.); Average household size: 3.02 (2008-2012 5-year est.); Median age: 35.5 (2008-2012 5-year est.); Males per 100 females: 98.9 (2008-2012 5-year est.).

Religion: Six largest groups: 31.3% Catholicism, 3.1% Lutheran, 2.3% Baptist, 2.1% Non-denominational Protestant, 2.0% Methodist/Pietist, 1.6% Presbyterian-Reformed (2010)

Economy: Unemployment rate: 7.8% (April 2014); Total civilian labor force: 366,040 (April 2014); Leading industries: 14.2% retail trade; 12.2% health care and social assistance; 10.4% accommodation & food services (2012); Farms: 882 totaling 234,249 acres (2012); Companies that employ 500 or more persons: 31 (2012); Companies that employ 100 to 499 persons: 304 (2012); Companies that employ less than 100 persons: 13,807 (2012); Black-owned businesses: 3,671 (2007); Hispanic-owned businesses: 2,819 (2007); Asian-owned businesses: 2,765 (2007); Women-owned businesses: 15,591 (2007); Single-family building permits issued: 955 (2013); Multi-family building permits issued: 22 (2013).

Income: Per capita income: $30,407 (2008-2012 5-year est.); Median household income: $76,352 (2008-2012 5-year est.); Average household income: $90,888 (2008-2012 5-year est.); Percent of households with income of $100,000 or more: 35.1% (2008-2012 5-year est.); Poverty rate: 7.7% (2008-2012 5-year est.); Bankruptcy rate: 5.72% (2013).

Taxes: Total county taxes per capita: $215 (2011); County property taxes per capita: $210 (2011).

Education: Percent of population age 25 and over with: High school diploma (including GED) or higher: 90.4% (2008-2012 5-year est.); Bachelor's degree or higher: 32.1% (2008-2012 5-year est.); Master's degree or higher: 11.3% (2008-2012 5-year est.).

Housing: Homeownership rate: 83.6% (2008-2012 5-year est.); Median home value: $228,900 (2008-2012 5-year est.); Median contract rent: $809 per month (2008-2012 5-year est.); Median year structure built: 1990 (2008-2012 5-year est.)

Health: Birth rate: 115.7 per 10,000 population (2013); Death rate: 59.3 per 10,000 population (2013); Age-adjusted cancer mortality rate: 174.4 deaths per 100,000 population (2011); Number of physicians: 14.0 per 10,000 population (2011); Hospital beds: 12.7 per 10,000 population (2010); Hospital admissions: 667.0 per 10,000 population (2010).

Environment: Air Quality Index: 81.6% good, 18.4% moderate, 0.0% unhealthy for sensitive individuals, 0.0% unhealthy (percent of days in 2013)

Elections: 2012 Presidential election results: 51.1% Obama, 47.4% Romney

National and State Parks: Channahon Parkway State Park; Des Plaines State Conservation Area; Kankakee River State Park; Midewin National Tallgrass Prairie

Additional Information Contacts

Will County Government . . . . (815) 722-5515
 http://www.willcountyillinois.com
Will County Center for Economic Development . . . . (815) 723-1800
 http://www.willcountyced.com

Will County Communities

BEECHER (village). Covers a land area of 2.961 square miles and a water area of 0 square miles. Located at 41.35° N. Lat; 87.62° W. Long. Elevation is 735 feet.

History: Beecher was platted in 1870 when the Chicago & Eastern Illinois Railway was being built here. The village was named for Henry Ward Beecher.

Population: 2,032 (1990); 2,033 (2000); 4,359 (2010); Density: 1,573.1 persons per square mile (2008-2012 5-year est.); Race: 86.6% White, 8.1% Black/African American, 2.9% Asian, 0.0% American Indian/Alaska Native, 0.0% Native Hawaiian/Other Pacific Islander, 2.4% Some other race, 2.0% Two or more races, 4.4% Hispanic of any race (2000-2012 5-year est.); Average household size: 2.94 (2008-2012 5-year est.); Median age: 39.4 (2008-2012 5-year est.); Males per 100 females: 91.3 (2008-2012 5-year est.); Marriage status: 21.5% never married, 59.4% now married, 6.1% widowed, 13.0% divorced (2008-2012 5-year est.); Foreign born: 5.6% (2008-2012 5-year est.); Ancestry (includes multiple ancestries): 32.7% German, 27.8% Irish, 16.4% Italian, 14.2% Polish, 7.9% English (2008-2012 5-year est.).

Economy: Single-family building permits issued: 6 (2013); Multi-family building permits issued: 0 (2013); Homeowner vacancy rate: 1.9%. Rental vacancy rate: 5.3%. (2008-2012 5-year est.); Employment by occupation: 11.9% management, business, and financial, 3.2% computer, engineering, and science, 15.2% education, legal, community service, arts, and media, 10.9% healthcare practitioners, 16.9% service, 20.4% sales and office, 7.1% natural resources, construction, and maintenance, 14.4% production, transportation, and material moving (2008-2012 5-year est.).

Income: Per capita income: $29,161 (2008-2012 5-year est.); Median household income: $84,115 (2008-2012 5-year est.); Average household income: $86,226 (2008-2012 5-year est.); Percent of households with income of $100,000 or more: 36.9% (2008-2012 5-year est.); Poverty rate: 6.7% (2008-2012 5-year est.).

Education: Percent of population age 25 and over with: High school diploma (including GED) or higher: 92.9% (2008-2012 5-year est.); Bachelor's degree or higher: 21.3% (2008-2012 5-year est.); Master's degree or higher: 6.5% (2008-2012 5-year est.).

School District(s)

Beecher CUSD 200u (KG-12)

2011-12 Enrollment: 1,079 . . . . (708) 946-2266

Housing: Homeownership rate: 83.9% (2008-2012 5-year est.); Median home value: $207,600 (2008-2012 5-year est.); Median contract rent: $767 per month (2008-2012 5-year est.); Median year structure built: 1988 (2008-2012 5-year est.).

Health Insurance: 92.7% Private; 12.8% Public; 5.1% None. (2008-2012 5-year est.)

Safety: Violent crime rate: 4.6 per 10,000 population; Property crime rate: 95.8 per 10,000 population (2012).

Transportation: Commute to work: 95.4% car, 0.9% public transportation, 0.0% walk, 2.3% work from home (2008-2012 5-year est.); Travel time to work: 25.2% less than 15 minutes, 13.0% 15 to 30 minutes, 32.7% 30 to 45 minutes, 16.6% 45 to 60 minutes, 12.4% 60 minutes or more (2008-2012 5-year est.)

BOLINGBROOK (village). Covers a land area of 24.049 square miles and a water area of 0.207 square miles. Located at 41.69° N. Lat; 88.10° W. Long. Elevation is 702 feet.

Population: 40,843 (1990); 56,321 (2000); 73,366 (2010); Density: 3,051.4 persons per square mile (2008-2012 5-year est.); Race: 56.4% White, 20.8% Black/African American, 10.1% Asian, 0.4% American Indian/Alaska Native, 0.0% Native Hawaiian/Other Pacific Islander, 12.3% Some other race, 2.9% Two or more races, 24.5% Hispanic of any race (2008-2012 5-year est.); Average household size: 3.36 (2008-2012 5-year est.); Median age: 33.1 (2008-2012 5-year est.); Males per 100 females: 100.5 (2008-2012 5-year est.); Marriage status: 33.0% never married, 55.8% now married, 3.2% widowed, 8.0% divorced (2008-2012 5-year est.); Foreign born: 22.2% (2008-2012 5-year est.); Ancestry (includes multiple ancestries): 14.3% German, 10.7% Irish, 8.4% Polish, 6.8% Italian, 3.3% English (2008-2012 5-year est.).

Economy: Unemployment rate: 7.2% (April 2014); Total civilian labor force: 41,531 (April 2014); Single-family building permits issued: 108 (2013); Multi-family building permits issued: 0 (2013); Homeowner vacancy rate: 1.8%. Rental vacancy rate: 6.3%. (2008-2012 5-year est.); Employment by occupation: 15.6% management, business, and financial, 4.7% computer, engineering, and science, 7.4% education, legal, community service, arts, and media, 6.0% healthcare practitioners, 17.1% service, 28.6% sales and office, 7.0% natural resources, construction, and maintenance, 13.7% production, transportation, and material moving (2008-2012 5-year est.).

Income: Per capita income: $27,420 (2008-2012 5-year est.); Median household income: $80,112 (2008-2012 5-year est.); Average household income: $89,432 (2008-2012 5-year est.); Percent of households with income of $100,000 or more: 36.9% (2008-2012 5-year est.); Poverty rate: 8.4% (2008-2012 5-year est.).

Taxes: Total city taxes per capita: $636 (2011); City property taxes per capita: $249 (2011).

Education: Percent of population age 25 and over with: High school diploma (including GED) or higher: 88.2% (2008-2012 5-year est.); Bachelor's degree or higher: 33.7% (2008-2012 5-year est.); Master's degree or higher: 10.3% (2008-2012 5-year est.).

School District(s)

Indian Prairie CUSD 204 (PK-12)
    2011-12 Enrollment: 29,286 . . . . (630) 375-3000
Plainfield SD 202 (PK-12)
    2011-12 Enrollment: 28,904 . . . . (815) 577-4000
Valley View CUSD 365u (PK-12)
    2011-12 Enrollment: 17,838 . . . . (815) 886-2700
Will Roe (06-12)
    2011-12 Enrollment: n/a . . . . (815) 740-8360

Housing: Homeownership rate: 84.1% (2008-2012 5-year est.); Median home value: $224,700 (2008-2012 5-year est.); Median contract rent: $935 per month (2008-2012 5-year est.); Median year structure built: 1986 (2008-2012 5-year est.).

Health Insurance: 72.0% Private; 20.9% Public; 12.9% None. (2008-2012 5-year est.)

Safety: Violent crime rate: 24.4 per 10,000 population; Property crime rate: 154.3 per 10,000 population (2012).

Transportation: Commute to work: 89.9% car, 2.9% public transportation, 1.0% walk, 4.3% work from home (2008-2012 5-year est.); Travel time to work: 18.3% less than 15 minutes, 29.1% 15 to 30 minutes, 24.0% 30 to 45 minutes, 13.5% 45 to 60 minutes, 15.1% 60 minutes or more (2008-2012 5-year est.)

Airports: Bolingbrook's Clow International Airport (general aviation)

Additional Information Contacts

Bolingbrook Area Chamber of Commerce . . . . (630) 226-8420
    http://www.bolingbrook.org
Village of Bolingbrook . . . . (630) 226-8400
    http://www.bolingbrook.com

BRAIDWOOD (city). Covers a land area of 4.580 square miles and a water area of 0.184 square miles. Located at 41.27° N. Lat; 88.22° W. Long. Elevation is 574 feet.

History: Braidwood was a crowded coal-mining town in the 1880's, with many mining syndicates operating. The first coal vein was discovered in 1865 by settler William Henneberry. By 1873 Braidwood was incorporated as a city.

Population: 3,584 (1990); 5,203 (2000); 6,191 (2010); Density: 1,320.4 persons per square mile (2008-2012 5-year est.); Race: 97.2% White, 0.9% Black/African American, 0.3% Asian, 0.3% American Indian/Alaska Native, 0.0% Native Hawaiian/Other Pacific Islander, 1.3% Some other race, 1.2% Two or more races, 2.8% Hispanic of any race (2008-2012 5-year est.); Average household size: 2.58 (2008-2012 5-year est.); Median age: 41.5 (2008-2012 5-year est.); Males per 100 females: 99.0 (2008-2012 5-year est.); Marriage status: 30.4% never married, 50.4% now married, 8.2% widowed, 11.0% divorced (2008-2012 5-year est.); Foreign born: 1.6% (2008-2012 5-year est.); Ancestry (includes multiple ancestries): 26.3% German, 23.7% Irish, 12.3% Polish, 11.1% Italian, 8.4% English (2008-2012 5-year est.).

Economy: Single-family building permits issued: 6 (2013); Multi-family building permits issued: 0 (2013); Homeowner vacancy rate: 4.2%. Rental vacancy rate: 15.4%. (2008-2012 5-year est.); Employment by occupation: 10.5% management, business, and financial, 1.1% computer, engineering, and science, 6.1% education, legal, community service, arts, and media, 2.8% healthcare practitioners, 18.0% service, 24.9% sales and office, 12.4% natural resources, construction, and maintenance, 24.1% production, transportation, and material moving (2008-2012 5-year est.).

Income: Per capita income: $25,524 (2008-2012 5-year est.); Median household income: $56,524 (2008-2012 5-year est.); Average household income: $64,449 (2008-2012 5-year est.); Percent of households with income of $100,000 or more: 19.4% (2008-2012 5-year est.); Poverty rate: 14.6% (2008-2012 5-year est.).

Education: Percent of population age 25 and over with: High school diploma (including GED) or higher: 87.1% (2008-2012 5-year est.); Bachelor's degree or higher: 12.0% (2008-2012 5-year est.); Master's degree or higher: 4.6% (2008-2012 5-year est.).

School District(s)

Reed Custer CUSD 255u (PK-12)
    2011-12 Enrollment: 1,743 . . . . (815) 458-2307

Housing: Homeownership rate: 86.0% (2008-2012 5-year est.); Median home value: $165,900 (2008-2012 5-year est.); Median contract rent: $667 per month (2008-2012 5-year est.); Median year structure built: 1991 (2008-2012 5-year est.).

Health Insurance: 73.6% Private; 24.6% Public; 12.1% None. (2008-2012 5-year est.)

Safety: Violent crime rate: 19.3 per 10,000 population; Property crime rate: 184.6 per 10,000 population (2012).

Transportation: Commute to work: 98.2% car, 0.1% public transportation, 0.0% walk, 0.3% work from home (2008-2012 5-year est.); Travel time to work: 23.3% less than 15 minutes, 31.2% 15 to 30 minutes, 17.9% 30 to 45 minutes, 12.1% 45 to 60 minutes, 15.4% 60 minutes or more (2008-2012 5-year est.)

Additional Information Contacts

City of Braidwood . . . . (815) 458-2333
    http://www.braidwood.us

CHANNAHON (village). Covers a land area of 14.990 square miles and a water area of 1.427 square miles. Located at 41.42° N. Lat; 88.26° W. Long. Elevation is 528 feet.

History: Channahon was settled in 1832 and developed when the Illinois & Michigan Canal was built. Early industries included grain shipping, quarrying, and the manufacture of farm equipment.

Population: 4,266 (1990); 7,344 (2000); 12,560 (2010); Density: 825.7 persons per square mile (2008-2012 5-year est.); Race: 97.9% White, 0.4% Black/African American, 0.3% Asian, 0.0% American Indian/Alaska Native, 0.0% Native Hawaiian/Other Pacific Islander, 1.4% Some other race, 0.4% Two or more races, 3.2% Hispanic of any race (2008-2012 5-year est.); Average household size: 3.26 (2008-2012 5-year est.); Median age: 33.5 (2008-2012 5-year est.); Males per 100 females: 97.7 (2008-2012 5-year est.); Marriage status: 23.5% never married, 65.2% now married, 3.2% widowed, 8.2% divorced (2008-2012 5-year est.); Foreign born: 2.0% (2008-2012 5-year est.); Ancestry (includes multiple ancestries): 30.4% German, 26.6% Irish, 16.4% Italian, 15.6% Polish, 10.0% English (2008-2012 5-year est.).

Economy: Single-family building permits issued: 10 (2013); Multi-family building permits issued: 0 (2013); Homeowner vacancy rate: 0.0%. Rental vacancy rate: 5.5%. (2008-2012 5-year est.); Employment by occupation: 10.0% management, business, and financial, 5.0% computer, engineering, and science, 9.9% education, legal, community service, arts, and media, 7.8% healthcare practitioners, 11.8% service, 27.2% sales and office, 14.4% natural resources, construction, and maintenance, 14.0% production, transportation, and material moving (2008-2012 5-year est.).
Income: Per capita income: $30,565 (2008-2012 5-year est.); Median household income: $89,559 (2008-2012 5-year est.); Average household income: $98,045 (2008-2012 5-year est.); Percent of households with income of $100,000 or more: 44.1% (2008-2012 5-year est.); Poverty rate: 1.7% (2008-2012 5-year est.).
Education: Percent of population age 25 and over with: High school diploma (including GED) or higher: 95.7% (2008-2012 5-year est.); Bachelor's degree or higher: 26.3% (2008-2012 5-year est.); Master's degree or higher: 7.7% (2008-2012 5-year est.).

School District(s)
Channahon SD 17 (PK-08)
   2011-12 Enrollment: 1,488 . . . . (815) 467-4315
Housing: Homeownership rate: 90.4% (2008-2012 5-year est.); Median home value: $219,600 (2008-2012 5-year est.); Median contract rent: $888 per month (2008-2012 5-year est.); Median year structure built: 1997 (2008-2012 5-year est.).
Health Insurance: 90.8% Private; 12.6% Public; 4.2% None. (2008-2012 5-year est.)
Safety: Violent crime rate: 1.6 per 10,000 population; Property crime rate: 69.7 per 10,000 population (2012).
Transportation: Commute to work: 93.6% car, 1.3% public transportation, 0.8% walk, 3.7% work from home (2008-2012 5-year est.); Travel time to work: 21.3% less than 15 minutes, 33.7% 15 to 30 minutes, 24.2% 30 to 45 minutes, 7.4% 45 to 60 minutes, 13.4% 60 minutes or more (2008-2012 5-year est.)
Additional Information Contacts
Channahon Minooka Chamber of Commerce . . . . (815) 942-0113
   http://www.grundychamber.com/cm_chamber/index.html
Village of Channahon . . . . (815) 467-6644
   http://www.channahon.org

CREST HILL (city). Covers a land area of 0.034 square miles and a water area of 0.136 square miles. Located at 41.57° N. Lat; 88.11° W. Long. Elevation is 643 feet.
Population: 10,643 (1990); 13,329 (2000); 20,837 (2010); Density: 2,294.0 persons per square mile (2008-2012 5-year est.); Race: 73.0% White, 15.6% Black/African American, 3.0% Asian, 0.5% American Indian/Alaska Native, 0.0% Native Hawaiian/Other Pacific Islander, 7.9% Some other race, 3.0% Two or more races, 17.2% Hispanic of any race (2008-2012 5-year est.); Average household size: 2.41 (2008-2012 5-year est.); Median age: 36.6 (2008-2012 5-year est.); Males per 100 females: 117.2 (2008-2012 5-year est.); Marriage status: 36.8% never married, 43.5% now married, 6.1% widowed, 13.7% divorced (2008-2012 5-year est.); Foreign born: 8.6% (2008-2012 5-year est.); Ancestry (includes multiple ancestries): 19.8% German, 14.2% Polish, 12.2% Irish, 11.5% Italian, 4.7% English (2008-2012 5-year est.).
Economy: Single-family building permits issued: 1 (2013); Multi-family building permits issued: 0 (2013); Homeowner vacancy rate: 2.1%. Rental vacancy rate: 3.7%. (2008-2012 5-year est.); Employment by occupation: 13.4% management, business, and financial, 4.1% computer, engineering, and science, 6.7% education, legal, community service, arts, and media, 3.4% healthcare practitioners, 19.9% service, 28.1% sales and office, 8.8% natural resources, construction, and maintenance, 15.5% production, transportation, and material moving (2008-2012 5-year est.).
Income: Per capita income: $22,367 (2008-2012 5-year est.); Median household income: $48,745 (2008-2012 5-year est.); Average household income: $58,707 (2008-2012 5-year est.); Percent of households with income of $100,000 or more: 15.1% (2008-2012 5-year est.); Poverty rate: 10.1% (2008-2012 5-year est.).
Education: Percent of population age 25 and over with: High school diploma (including GED) or higher: 85.0% (2008-2012 5-year est.); Bachelor's degree or higher: 16.2% (2008-2012 5-year est.); Master's degree or higher: 4.3% (2008-2012 5-year est.).

School District(s)
Chaney-Monge SD 88 (KG-08)
   2011-12 Enrollment: 481 . . . . (815) 722-6673

Richland Gsd 88a (PK-08)
   2011-12 Enrollment: 976 . . . . (815) 744-7288
Housing: Homeownership rate: 70.3% (2008-2012 5-year est.); Median home value: $172,500 (2008-2012 5-year est.); Median contract rent: $831 per month (2008-2012 5-year est.); Median year structure built: 1991 (2008-2012 5-year est.).
Health Insurance: 68.9% Private; 30.4% Public; 13.9% None. (2008-2012 5-year est.)
Safety: Violent crime rate: 15.8 per 10,000 population; Property crime rate: 180.4 per 10,000 population (2012).
Transportation: Commute to work: 96.2% car, 2.0% public transportation, 0.2% walk, 1.6% work from home (2008-2012 5-year est.); Travel time to work: 26.7% less than 15 minutes, 33.1% 15 to 30 minutes, 17.2% 30 to 45 minutes, 11.8% 45 to 60 minutes, 11.2% 60 minutes or more (2008-2012 5-year est.)
Additional Information Contacts
City of Crest Hill . . . . (815) 741-5100
   http://www.cityofcresthill.com
Crest Hill Chamber of Commerce . . . . (815) 414-2204
   http://www.cresthillchamberofcommerce.com

CRETE (village). Covers a land area of 9.611 square miles and a water area of 0.017 square miles. Located at 41.44° N. Lat; 87.62° W. Long. Elevation is 728 feet.
History: Crete was laid out in 1849 by William Wood, operator of a tavern for travelers on the Chicago-Vincennes Road.
Population: 6,773 (1990); 7,346 (2000); 8,259 (2010); Density: 867.3 persons per square mile (2008-2012 5-year est.); Race: 69.4% White, 24.4% Black/African American, 3.2% Asian, 0.4% American Indian/Alaska Native, 0.0% Native Hawaiian/Other Pacific Islander, 2.6% Some other race, 2.2% Two or more races, 2.1% Hispanic of any race (2008-2012 5-year est.); Average household size: 2.61 (2008-2012 5-year est.); Median age: 39.7 (2008-2012 5-year est.); Males per 100 females: 92.5 (2008-2012 5-year est.); Marriage status: 27.0% never married, 57.7% now married, 7.9% widowed, 7.4% divorced (2008-2012 5-year est.); Foreign born: 5.2% (2008-2012 5-year est.); Ancestry (includes multiple ancestries): 26.5% German, 13.0% Irish, 10.7% Polish, 9.7% English, 9.7% Italian (2008-2012 5-year est.).
Economy: Single-family building permits issued: 0 (2013); Multi-family building permits issued: 0 (2013); Homeowner vacancy rate: 4.0%. Rental vacancy rate: 12.4%. (2008-2012 5-year est.); Employment by occupation: 16.8% management, business, and financial, 3.7% computer, engineering, and science, 10.1% education, legal, community service, arts, and media, 9.3% healthcare practitioners, 16.6% service, 24.6% sales and office, 10.6% natural resources, construction, and maintenance, 8.2% production, transportation, and material moving (2008-2012 5-year est.).
Income: Per capita income: $31,851 (2008-2012 5-year est.); Median household income: $70,963 (2008-2012 5-year est.); Average household income: $83,028 (2008-2012 5-year est.); Percent of households with income of $100,000 or more: 29.4% (2008-2012 5-year est.); Poverty rate: 6.5% (2008-2012 5-year est.).
Education: Percent of population age 25 and over with: High school diploma (including GED) or higher: 94.5% (2008-2012 5-year est.); Bachelor's degree or higher: 38.3% (2008-2012 5-year est.); Master's degree or higher: 15.6% (2008-2012 5-year est.).

School District(s)
Crete Monee CUSD 201u (PK-12)
   2011-12 Enrollment: 5,136 . . . . (708) 367-8300
Housing: Homeownership rate: 84.8% (2008-2012 5-year est.); Median home value: $194,200 (2008-2012 5-year est.); Median contract rent: $1,111 per month (2008-2012 5-year est.); Median year structure built: 1980 (2008-2012 5-year est.).
Health Insurance: 82.5% Private; 24.3% Public; 8.0% None. (2008-2012 5-year est.)
Safety: Violent crime rate: 19.3 per 10,000 population; Property crime rate: 225.0 per 10,000 population (2012).
Transportation: Commute to work: 90.0% car, 4.3% public transportation, 0.5% walk, 4.6% work from home (2008-2012 5-year est.); Travel time to work: 29.8% less than 15 minutes, 29.2% 15 to 30 minutes, 18.5% 30 to 45 minutes, 7.9% 45 to 60 minutes, 14.5% 60 minutes or more (2008-2012 5-year est.)
Additional Information Contacts
Crete Area Chamber of Commerce . . . . (708) 672-9216
   http://www.cretechamber.com

Village of Crete . . . . (708) 672-5431
http://www.villageofcrete.org

CRYSTAL LAWNS (CDP). Covers a land area of 0.629 square miles and a water area of 0 square miles. Located at 41.57° N. Lat; 88.16° W. Long. Elevation is 604 feet.

Population: 3,037 (1990); 2,933 (2000); 1,872 (2010); Density: 3,087.8 persons per square mile (2008-2012 5-year est.); Race: 99.9% White, 0.0% Black/African American, 0.1% Asian, 0.0% American Indian/Alaska Native, 0.0% Native Hawaiian/Other Pacific Islander, 0.0% Some other race, 0.0% Two or more races, 11.5% Hispanic of any race (2008-2012 5-year est.); Average household size: 2.75 (2008-2012 5-year est.); Median age: 41.9 (2008-2012 5-year est.); Males per 100 females: 98.5 (2008-2012 5-year est.); Marriage status: 25.1% never married, 50.9% now married, 5.7% widowed, 18.2% divorced (2008-2012 5-year est.); Foreign born: 0.1% (2008-2012 5-year est.); Ancestry (includes multiple ancestries): 33.8% Irish, 33.4% German, 16.4% Polish, 15.6% Italian, 6.7% American (2008-2012 5-year est.).

Economy: Homeowner vacancy rate: 0.0%. Rental vacancy rate: 0.0%. (2008-2012 5-year est.); Employment by occupation: 9.9% management, business, and financial, 2.2% computer, engineering, and science, 4.5% education, legal, community service, arts, and media, 6.4% healthcare practitioners, 14.0% service, 30.9% sales and office, 10.3% natural resources, construction, and maintenance, 21.9% production, transportation, and material moving (2008-2012 5-year est.).

Income: Per capita income: $31,316 (2008-2012 5-year est.); Median household income: $73,887 (2008-2012 5-year est.); Average household income: $84,318 (2008-2012 5-year est.); Percent of households with income of $100,000 or more: 32.8% (2008-2012 5-year est.); Poverty rate: 3.7% (2008-2012 5-year est.).

Education: Percent of population age 25 and over with: High school diploma (including GED) or higher: 92.8% (2008-2012 5-year est.); Bachelor's degree or higher: 13.9% (2008-2012 5-year est.); Master's degree or higher: 7.8% (2008-2012 5-year est.).

Housing: Homeownership rate: 88.2% (2008-2012 5-year est.); Median home value: $181,400 (2008-2012 5-year est.); Median contract rent: n/a per month (2008-2012 5-year est.); Median year structure built: 1964 (2008-2012 5-year est.).

Health Insurance: 85.4% Private; 20.1% Public; 5.9% None. (2008-2012 5-year est.)

Transportation: Commute to work: 96.4% car, 0.7% public transportation, 0.0% walk, 2.9% work from home (2008-2012 5-year est.); Travel time to work: 32.9% less than 15 minutes, 37.6% 15 to 30 minutes, 12.5% 30 to 45 minutes, 8.8% 45 to 60 minutes, 8.2% 60 minutes or more (2008-2012 5-year est.)

ELWOOD (village). Covers a land area of 6.528 square miles and a water area of 0 square miles. Located at 41.41° N. Lat; 88.13° W. Long. Elevation is 646 feet.

Population: 951 (1990); 1,620 (2000); 2,279 (2010); Density: 339.4 persons per square mile (2008-2012 5-year est.); Race: 98.1% White, 1.7% Black/African American, 0.0% Asian, 0.0% American Indian/Alaska Native, 0.0% Native Hawaiian/Other Pacific Islander, 0.2% Some other race, 0.0% Two or more races, 2.4% Hispanic of any race (2008-2012 5-year est.); Average household size: 2.62 (2008-2012 5-year est.); Median age: 38.7 (2008-2012 5-year est.); Males per 100 females: 98.7 (2008-2012 5-year est.); Marriage status: 15.9% never married, 67.9% now married, 7.2% widowed, 9.1% divorced (2008-2012 5-year est.); Foreign born: 0.0% (2008-2012 5-year est.); Ancestry (includes multiple ancestries): 29.4% Irish, 28.1% German, 17.3% Italian, 13.6% Polish, 7.4% English (2008-2012 5-year est.).

Economy: Single-family building permits issued: 1 (2013); Multi-family building permits issued: 0 (2013); Homeowner vacancy rate: 2.1%. Rental vacancy rate: 0.0%. (2008-2012 5-year est.); Employment by occupation: 8.5% management, business, and financial, 2.4% computer, engineering, and science, 10.9% education, legal, community service, arts, and media, 5.0% healthcare practitioners, 12.6% service, 32.6% sales and office, 8.2% natural resources, construction, and maintenance, 19.9% production, transportation, and material moving (2008-2012 5-year est.).

Income: Per capita income: $28,870 (2008-2012 5-year est.); Median household income: $68,942 (2008-2012 5-year est.); Average household income: $73,689 (2008-2012 5-year est.); Percent of households with income of $100,000 or more: 26.0% (2008-2012 5-year est.); Poverty rate: 12.7% (2008-2012 5-year est.).

Taxes: Total city taxes per capita: $4,090 (2011); City property taxes per capita: $3,806 (2011).

Education: Percent of population age 25 and over with: High school diploma (including GED) or higher: 94.4% (2008-2012 5-year est.); Bachelor's degree or higher: 16.2% (2008-2012 5-year est.); Master's degree or higher: 7.2% (2008-2012 5-year est.).

School District(s)

Elwood CCSD 203 (KG-08)
    2011-12 Enrollment: 427 . . . . (815) 423-5588

Housing: Homeownership rate: 86.3% (2008-2012 5-year est.); Median home value: $186,300 (2008-2012 5-year est.); Median contract rent: $633 per month (2008-2012 5-year est.); Median year structure built: 1994 (2008-2012 5-year est.).

Health Insurance: 80.3% Private; 24.9% Public; 5.5% None. (2008-2012 5-year est.)

Safety: Violent crime rate: 17.4 per 10,000 population; Property crime rate: 161.4 per 10,000 population (2012).

Transportation: Commute to work: 96.1% car, 1.5% public transportation, 0.0% walk, 2.3% work from home (2008-2012 5-year est.); Travel time to work: 20.0% less than 15 minutes, 31.9% 15 to 30 minutes, 30.1% 30 to 45 minutes, 8.5% 45 to 60 minutes, 9.5% 60 minutes or more (2008-2012 5-year est.)

FAIRMONT (CDP). Covers a land area of 1.364 square miles and a water area of 0 square miles. Located at 41.56° N. Lat; 88.06° W. Long. Elevation is 633 feet.

Population: 2,894 (1990); 2,563 (2000); 2,459 (2010); Density: 1,668.8 persons per square mile (2008-2012 5-year est.); Race: 38.0% White, 46.9% Black/African American, 5.6% Asian, 0.0% American Indian/Alaska Native, 0.0% Native Hawaiian/Other Pacific Islander, 9.5% Some other race, 4.2% Two or more races, 25.5% Hispanic of any race (2008-2012 5-year est.); Average household size: 2.66 (2008-2012 5-year est.); Median age: 39.9 (2008-2012 5-year est.); Males per 100 females: 102.6 (2008-2012 5-year est.); Marriage status: 32.4% never married, 45.7% now married, 8.9% widowed, 13.0% divorced (2008-2012 5-year est.); Foreign born: 15.0% (2008-2012 5-year est.); Ancestry (includes multiple ancestries): 10.2% Polish, 8.3% Irish, 8.0% German, 3.6% Italian, 2.3% English (2008-2012 5-year est.).

Economy: Homeowner vacancy rate: 3.6%. Rental vacancy rate: 8.5%. (2008-2012 5-year est.); Employment by occupation: 11.7% management, business, and financial, 0.0% computer, engineering, and science, 6.8% education, legal, community service, arts, and media, 0.0% healthcare practitioners, 17.4% service, 27.8% sales and office, 7.5% natural resources, construction, and maintenance, 28.8% production, transportation, and material moving (2008-2012 5-year est.).

Income: Per capita income: $22,824 (2008-2012 5-year est.); Median household income: $51,875 (2008-2012 5-year est.); Average household income: $59,362 (2008-2012 5-year est.); Percent of households with income of $100,000 or more: 19.2% (2008-2012 5-year est.); Poverty rate: 21.2% (2008-2012 5-year est.).

Education: Percent of population age 25 and over with: High school diploma (including GED) or higher: 76.8% (2008-2012 5-year est.); Bachelor's degree or higher: 13.6% (2008-2012 5-year est.); Master's degree or higher: 7.3% (2008-2012 5-year est.).

Housing: Homeownership rate: 73.4% (2008-2012 5-year est.); Median home value: $131,800 (2008-2012 5-year est.); Median contract rent: $679 per month (2008-2012 5-year est.); Median year structure built: 1958 (2008-2012 5-year est.).

Health Insurance: 56.5% Private; 36.0% Public; 18.6% None. (2008-2012 5-year est.)

Transportation: Commute to work: 93.0% car, 4.5% public transportation, 0.0% walk, 0.7% work from home (2008-2012 5-year est.); Travel time to work: 22.2% less than 15 minutes, 34.0% 15 to 30 minutes, 23.2% 30 to 45 minutes, 2.1% 45 to 60 minutes, 18.5% 60 minutes or more (2008-2012 5-year est.)

FRANKFORT (village). Covers a land area of 14.982 square miles and a water area of 0 square miles. Located at 41.49° N. Lat; 87.84° W. Long. Elevation is 761 feet.

History: Frankfort's name was never spelled "Frankfurt" even though it was named after Frankfurt am Main in Germany. It was commonly known as "Frankfort Station" after the opening of the Joliet & Northern Indiana Railroad through the township in 1855. The local residents incorporated as a village in 1879. After that it was simply known as "Frankfort."

Population: 7,180 (1990); 10,391 (2000); 17,782 (2010); Density: 1,187.2 persons per square mile (2008-2012 5-year est.); Race: 89.8% White, 6.8% Black/African American, 1.4% Asian, 0.0% American Indian/Alaska Native, 0.1% Native Hawaiian/Other Pacific Islander, 1.9% Some other race, 1.7% Two or more races, 3.2% Hispanic of any race (2008-2012 5-year est.); Average household size: 3.17 (2008-2012 5-year est.); Median age: 39.5 (2008-2012 5-year est.); Males per 100 females: 91.8 (2008-2012 5-year est.); Marriage status: 22.2% never married, 69.2% now married, 3.9% widowed, 4.7% divorced (2008-2012 5-year est.); Foreign born: 3.8% (2008-2012 5-year est.); Ancestry (includes multiple ancestries): 26.8% German, 22.9% Irish, 18.0% Polish, 14.3% Italian, 7.0% English (2008-2012 5-year est.).
Economy: Single-family building permits issued: 96 (2013); Multi-family building permits issued: 0 (2013); Homeowner vacancy rate: 1.2%. Rental vacancy rate: 0.0%. (2008-2012 5-year est.); Employment by occupation: 25.6% management, business, and financial, 4.7% computer, engineering, and science, 14.8% education, legal, community service, arts, and media, 8.6% healthcare practitioners, 7.0% service, 24.7% sales and office, 5.9% natural resources, construction, and maintenance, 8.7% production, transportation, and material moving (2008-2012 5-year est.).
Income: Per capita income: $44,997 (2008-2012 5-year est.); Median household income: $114,972 (2008-2012 5-year est.); Average household income: $142,056 (2008-2012 5-year est.); Percent of households with income of $100,000 or more: 59.4% (2008-2012 5-year est.); Poverty rate: 3.7% (2008-2012 5-year est.).
Education: Percent of population age 25 and over with: High school diploma (including GED) or higher: 97.7% (2008-2012 5-year est.); Bachelor's degree or higher: 55.8% (2008-2012 5-year est.); Master's degree or higher: 23.2% (2008-2012 5-year est.).

School District(s)

Frankfort CCSD 157c (PK-08)
    2011-12 Enrollment: 2,434 . . . . (815) 469-5922
Lincoln Way CHSD 210 (09-12)
    2011-12 Enrollment: 7,346 . . . . (815) 462-2100
Lincoln-Way Area Spec Ed Ja Dist (PK-12)
    2011-12 Enrollment: n/a . . . . (815) 806-4600
Peotone CUSD 207u (PK-12)
    2011-12 Enrollment: 1,887 . . . . (708) 258-6061
Summit Hill SD 161 (PK-08)
    2011-12 Enrollment: 3,527 . . . . (815) 469-9103

Housing: Homeownership rate: 95.2% (2008-2012 5-year est.); Median home value: $383,600 (2008-2012 5-year est.); Median contract rent: $896 per month (2008-2012 5-year est.); Median year structure built: 1994 (2008-2012 5-year est.).
Health Insurance: 91.8% Private; 15.7% Public; 2.7% None. (2008-2012 5-year est.)
Safety: Violent crime rate: 5.6 per 10,000 population; Property crime rate: 108.4 per 10,000 population (2012).
Transportation: Commute to work: 85.2% car, 8.3% public transportation, 0.3% walk, 5.7% work from home (2008-2012 5-year est.); Travel time to work: 20.7% less than 15 minutes, 23.0% 15 to 30 minutes, 23.6% 30 to 45 minutes, 13.1% 45 to 60 minutes, 19.5% 60 minutes or more (2008-2012 5-year est.)
Additional Information Contacts
Frankfort Chamber of Commerce . . . . (815) 469-3356
    http://www.frankfortchamber.com
Village of Frankfort . . . . (815) 469-2177
    http://www.villageoffrankfort.com

FRANKFORT SQUARE (CDP). Covers a land area of 2.530 square miles and a water area of 0 square miles. Located at 41.52° N. Lat; 87.80° W. Long. Elevation is 709 feet.

Population: 6,227 (1990); 7,766 (2000); 9,276 (2010); Density: 3,606.3 persons per square mile (2008-2012 5-year est.); Race: 92.4% White, 2.0% Black/African American, 0.8% Asian, 0.3% American Indian/Alaska Native, 0.0% Native Hawaiian/Other Pacific Islander, 4.5% Some other race, 1.9% Two or more races, 6.7% Hispanic of any race (2008-2012 5-year est.); Average household size: 3.08 (2008-2012 5-year est.); Median age: 35.5 (2008-2012 5-year est.); Males per 100 females: 94.1 (2008-2012 5-year est.); Marriage status: 25.5% never married, 65.7% now married, 3.4% widowed, 5.4% divorced (2008-2012 5-year est.); Foreign born: 3.0% (2008-2012 5-year est.); Ancestry (includes multiple ancestries): 31.2% German, 25.9% Polish, 25.1% Irish, 20.4% Italian, 6.7% English (2008-2012 5-year est.).

Economy: Homeowner vacancy rate: 1.5%. Rental vacancy rate: 14.6%. (2008-2012 5-year est.); Employment by occupation: 11.5% management, business, and financial, 4.6% computer, engineering, and science, 11.4% education, legal, community service, arts, and media, 7.4% healthcare practitioners, 12.2% service, 27.7% sales and office, 13.7% natural resources, construction, and maintenance, 11.5% production, transportation, and material moving (2008-2012 5-year est.).
Income: Per capita income: $29,801 (2008-2012 5-year est.); Median household income: $83,289 (2008-2012 5-year est.); Average household income: $90,995 (2008-2012 5-year est.); Percent of households with income of $100,000 or more: 35.1% (2008-2012 5-year est.); Poverty rate: 2.8% (2008-2012 5-year est.).
Education: Percent of population age 25 and over with: High school diploma (including GED) or higher: 93.5% (2008-2012 5-year est.); Bachelor's degree or higher: 30.9% (2008-2012 5-year est.); Master's degree or higher: 9.9% (2008-2012 5-year est.).
Housing: Homeownership rate: 94.9% (2008-2012 5-year est.); Median home value: $237,200 (2008-2012 5-year est.); Median contract rent: $901 per month (2008-2012 5-year est.); Median year structure built: 1986 (2008-2012 5-year est.).
Health Insurance: 86.2% Private; 15.2% Public; 4.7% None. (2008-2012 5-year est.)
Transportation: Commute to work: 88.8% car, 7.9% public transportation, 0.3% walk, 2.6% work from home (2008-2012 5-year est.); Travel time to work: 26.9% less than 15 minutes, 25.6% 15 to 30 minutes, 20.0% 30 to 45 minutes, 12.2% 45 to 60 minutes, 15.3% 60 minutes or more (2008-2012 5-year est.)

GODLEY (village). Covers a land area of 1.088 square miles and a water area of <.001 square miles. Located at 41.24° N. Lat; 88.24° W. Long. Elevation is 587 feet.

History: Godley began as a coal town settled by Scotch, Irish, and Welsh miners in the 1880's. The population declined when the mines closed in the early 1900's.
Population: 322 (1990); 594 (2000); 601 (2010); Density: 694.1 persons per square mile (2008-2012 5-year est.); Race: 93.6% White, 0.0% Black/African American, 0.4% Asian, 0.1% American Indian/Alaska Native, 0.0% Native Hawaiian/Other Pacific Islander, 5.9% Some other race, 5.4% Two or more races, 7.9% Hispanic of any race (2008-2012 5-year est.); Average household size: 3.19 (2008-2012 5-year est.); Median age: 29.8 (2008-2012 5-year est.); Males per 100 females: 87.8 (2008-2012 5-year est.); Marriage status: 42.5% never married, 35.7% now married, 8.9% widowed, 12.9% divorced (2008-2012 5-year est.); Foreign born: 0.8% (2008-2012 5-year est.); Ancestry (includes multiple ancestries): 32.5% Irish, 30.6% German, 7.0% Italian, 6.4% English, 5.8% French (2008-2012 5-year est.).
Economy: Single-family building permits issued: 5 (2013); Multi-family building permits issued: 0 (2013); Homeowner vacancy rate: 0.0%. Rental vacancy rate: 0.0%. (2008-2012 5-year est.); Employment by occupation: 11.7% management, business, and financial, 0.0% computer, engineering, and science, 2.1% education, legal, community service, arts, and media, 0.0% healthcare practitioners, 28.3% service, 19.1% sales and office, 14.5% natural resources, construction, and maintenance, 24.4% production, transportation, and material moving (2008-2012 5-year est.).
Income: Per capita income: $14,903 (2008-2012 5-year est.); Median household income: $38,750 (2008-2012 5-year est.); Average household income: $46,119 (2008-2012 5-year est.); Percent of households with income of $100,000 or more: 9.3% (2008-2012 5-year est.); Poverty rate: 27.5% (2008-2012 5-year est.).
Education: Percent of population age 25 and over with: High school diploma (including GED) or higher: 84.4% (2008-2012 5-year est.); Bachelor's degree or higher: 8.4% (2008-2012 5-year est.); Master's degree or higher: 0.7% (2008-2012 5-year est.).
Housing: Homeownership rate: 68.8% (2008-2012 5-year est.); Median home value: $109,900 (2008-2012 5-year est.); Median contract rent: $879 per month (2008-2012 5-year est.); Median year structure built: 1990 (2008-2012 5-year est.).
Health Insurance: 61.9% Private; 38.4% Public; 10.5% None. (2008-2012 5-year est.)
Safety: Violent crime rate: 49.6 per 10,000 population; Property crime rate: 214.9 per 10,000 population (2012).
Transportation: Commute to work: 97.9% car, 0.7% public transportation, 0.0% walk, 0.0% work from home (2008-2012 5-year est.); Travel time to work: 18.8% less than 15 minutes, 21.3% 15 to 30 minutes, 45.7% 30 to

45 minutes, 2.8% 45 to 60 minutes, 11.3% 60 minutes or more (2008-2012 5-year est.)

HOMER GLEN (village). Covers a land area of 22.173 square miles and a water area of 0.040 square miles. Located at 41.61° N. Lat; 87.95° W. Long. Elevation is 738 feet.

Population: n/a (1990); n/a (2000); 24,220 (2010); Density: 1,101.7 persons per square mile (2008-2012 5-year est.); Race: 94.1% White, 2.0% Black/African American, 1.4% Asian, 0.3% American Indian/Alaska Native, 0.0% Native Hawaiian/Other Pacific Islander, 2.2% Some other race, 0.6% Two or more races, 7.7% Hispanic of any race (2008-2012 5-year est.); Average household size: 3.07 (2008-2012 5-year est.); Median age: 41.3 (2008-2012 5-year est.); Males per 100 females: 99.2 (2008-2012 5-year est.); Marriage status: 25.4% never married, 64.9% now married, 4.0% widowed, 5.7% divorced (2008-2012 5-year est.); Foreign born: 12.4% (2008-2012 5-year est.); Ancestry (includes multiple ancestries): 24.6% Polish, 20.7% Irish, 18.2% German, 15.6% Italian, 6.6% Lithuanian (2008-2012 5-year est.).

Economy: Unemployment rate: 6.6% (April 2014); Total civilian labor force: 13,625 (April 2014); Single-family building permits issued: 28 (2013); Multi-family building permits issued: 0 (2013); Homeowner vacancy rate: 1.8%. Rental vacancy rate: 0.0%. (2008-2012 5-year est.); Employment by occupation: 18.6% management, business, and financial, 5.1% computer, engineering, and science, 9.2% education, legal, community service, arts, and media, 6.2% healthcare practitioners, 13.1% service, 26.7% sales and office, 9.8% natural resources, construction, and maintenance, 11.3% production, transportation, and material moving (2008-2012 5-year est.).

Income: Per capita income: $36,000 (2008-2012 5-year est.); Median household income: $97,848 (2008-2012 5-year est.); Average household income: $108,708 (2008-2012 5-year est.); Percent of households with income of $100,000 or more: 48.6% (2008-2012 5-year est.); Poverty rate: 2.8% (2008-2012 5-year est.).

Education: Percent of population age 25 and over with: High school diploma (including GED) or higher: 94.3% (2008-2012 5-year est.); Bachelor's degree or higher: 36.2% (2008-2012 5-year est.); Master's degree or higher: 13.9% (2008-2012 5-year est.).

School District(s)

Homer CCSD 33c (PK-08)
   2011-12 Enrollment: 3,681 . . . . (708) 226-7600
Will County SD 92 (PK-08)
   2011-12 Enrollment: 1,796 . . . . (815) 838-8031

Housing: Homeownership rate: 93.6% (2008-2012 5-year est.); Median home value: $337,100 (2008-2012 5-year est.); Median contract rent: $1,643 per month (2008-2012 5-year est.); Median year structure built: 1989 (2008-2012 5-year est.).

Health Insurance: 85.0% Private; 19.1% Public; 5.9% None. (2008-2012 5-year est.)

Safety: Violent crime rate: 2.5 per 10,000 population; Property crime rate: 76.3 per 10,000 population (2012).

Transportation: Commute to work: 91.6% car, 4.2% public transportation, 0.4% walk, 2.9% work from home (2008-2012 5-year est.); Travel time to work: 14.3% less than 15 minutes, 25.0% 15 to 30 minutes, 27.6% 30 to 45 minutes, 15.5% 45 to 60 minutes, 17.7% 60 minutes or more (2008-2012 5-year est.)

INGALLS PARK (CDP). Covers a land area of 1.127 square miles and a water area of 0 square miles. Located at 41.52° N. Lat; 88.03° W. Long. Elevation is 610 feet.

Population: 3,173 (1990); 3,082 (2000); 3,314 (2010); Density: 3,041.2 persons per square mile (2008-2012 5-year est.); Race: 77.5% White, 7.8% Black/African American, 2.1% Asian, 0.0% American Indian/Alaska Native, 0.0% Native Hawaiian/Other Pacific Islander, 12.6% Some other race, 1.7% Two or more races, 31.3% Hispanic of any race (2008-2012 5-year est.); Average household size: 2.75 (2008-2012 5-year est.); Median age: 30.4 (2008-2012 5-year est.); Males per 100 females: 110.6 (2008-2012 5-year est.); Marriage status: 29.8% never married, 48.8% now married, 5.4% widowed, 16.0% divorced (2008-2012 5-year est.); Foreign born: 9.7% (2008-2012 5-year est.); Ancestry (includes multiple ancestries): 23.9% Irish, 23.8% German, 6.4% Italian, 5.5% Polish, 5.3% French (2008-2012 5-year est.).

Economy: Homeowner vacancy rate: 0.0%. Rental vacancy rate: 7.2%. (2008-2012 5-year est.); Employment by occupation: 8.4% management, business, and financial, 2.1% computer, engineering, and science, 3.0% education, legal, community service, arts, and media, 6.3% healthcare practitioners, 34.8% service, 15.2% sales and office, 9.4% natural

resources, construction, and maintenance, 20.9% production, transportation, and material moving (2008-2012 5-year est.).

Income: Per capita income: $19,786 (2008-2012 5-year est.); Median household income: $53,800 (2008-2012 5-year est.); Average household income: $54,209 (2008-2012 5-year est.); Percent of households with income of $100,000 or more: 7.9% (2008-2012 5-year est.); Poverty rate: 20.8% (2008-2012 5-year est.).

Education: Percent of population age 25 and over with: High school diploma (including GED) or higher: 86.5% (2008-2012 5-year est.); Bachelor's degree or higher: 9.2% (2008-2012 5-year est.); Master's degree or higher: 3.5% (2008-2012 5-year est.).

Housing: Homeownership rate: 70.9% (2008-2012 5-year est.); Median home value: $135,700 (2008-2012 5-year est.); Median contract rent: $835 per month (2008-2012 5-year est.); Median year structure built: 1952 (2008-2012 5-year est.).

Health Insurance: 53.5% Private; 35.8% Public; 19.7% None. (2008-2012 5-year est.)

Transportation: Commute to work: 93.4% car, 0.0% public transportation, 0.0% walk, 2.4% work from home (2008-2012 5-year est.); Travel time to work: 30.5% less than 15 minutes, 30.0% 15 to 30 minutes, 19.0% 30 to 45 minutes, 9.5% 45 to 60 minutes, 11.0% 60 minutes or more (2008-2012 5-year est.)

JOLIET (city). County seat. Covers a land area of 62.114 square miles and a water area of 0.658 square miles. Located at 41.52° N. Lat; 88.16° W. Long. Elevation is 541 feet.

History: Named for Louis Joliet (1645-1700), French-Canadian explorer. The town of Joliet was laid out in 1834 with the name of Juliet (a neighboring village was Romeo) and incorporated in 1837 as the seat of Will County. Industry bloomed in Joliet when the Illinois & Michigan Canal was completed here in 1848. Limestone from the Joliet quarries was shipped across the country. Steel manufacturing in the late 1800's was replaced by the production of wallpaper as a leading industry.

Population: 76,836 (1990); 106,221 (2000); 147,433 (2010); Density: 2,368.2 persons per square mile (2008-2012 5-year est.); Race: 70.9% White, 15.3% Black/African American, 2.3% Asian, 0.2% American Indian/Alaska Native, 0.0% Native Hawaiian/Other Pacific Islander, 11.3% Some other race, 2.4% Two or more races, 27.2% Hispanic of any race (2008-2012 5-year est.); Average household size: 3.08 (2008-2012 5-year est.); Median age: 31.6 (2008-2012 5-year est.); Males per 100 females: 96.4 (2008-2012 5-year est.); Marriage status: 33.6% never married, 51.6% now married, 5.1% widowed, 9.6% divorced (2008-2012 5-year est.); Foreign born: 14.9% (2008-2012 5-year est.); Ancestry (includes multiple ancestries): 16.6% German, 15.4% Irish, 9.3% Polish, 9.2% Italian, 4.5% English (2008-2012 5-year est.).

Economy: Unemployment rate: 10.2% (April 2014); Total civilian labor force: 73,293 (April 2014); Single-family building permits issued: 74 (2013); Multi-family building permits issued: 0 (2013); Homeowner vacancy rate: 1.9%. Rental vacancy rate: 7.4%. (2008-2012 5-year est.); Employment by occupation: 10.7% management, business, and financial, 3.3% computer, engineering, and science, 8.3% education, legal, community service, arts, and media, 4.8% healthcare practitioners, 19.8% service, 26.5% sales and office, 9.6% natural resources, construction, and maintenance, 17.0% production, transportation, and material moving (2008-2012 5-year est.).

Income: Per capita income: $23,600 (2008-2012 5-year est.); Median household income: $61,948 (2008-2012 5-year est.); Average household income: $71,654 (2008-2012 5-year est.); Percent of households with income of $100,000 or more: 23.6% (2008-2012 5-year est.); Poverty rate: 12.4% (2008-2012 5-year est.).

Taxes: Total city taxes per capita: $494 (2011); City property taxes per capita: $290 (2011).

Education: Percent of population age 25 and over with: High school diploma (including GED) or higher: 83.9% (2008-2012 5-year est.); Bachelor's degree or higher: 23.6% (2008-2012 5-year est.); Master's degree or higher: 7.0% (2008-2012 5-year est.).

School District(s)

Idjj SD 428 (06-12)
   2011-12 Enrollment: 784 . . . . (309) 584-0506
Joliet PSD 86 (PK-08)
   2011-12 Enrollment: 11,308 . . . . (815) 740-3196
Joliet Twp HSD 204 (09-12)
   2011-12 Enrollment: 5,930 . . . . (815) 727-6970
Laraway CCSD 70c (PK-08)
   2011-12 Enrollment: 383 . . . . (815) 727-5196

Minooka CCSD 201 (PK-08)
   2011-12 Enrollment: 3,963 . . . . (815) 467-6121
Plainfield SD 202 (PK-12)
   2011-12 Enrollment: 28,904 . . . . (815) 577-4000
Plainfield SD 202 (PK-12)
   2011-12 Enrollment: 28,904 . . . . (815) 577-4000
S Will County Coop for Spec Ed (KG-12)
   2011-12 Enrollment: n/a . . . . (815) 741-7777
Troy CCSD 30c (PK-08)
   2011-12 Enrollment: 4,564 . . . . (815) 577-6760
Union SD 81 (KG-08)
   2011-12 Enrollment: 124 . . . . (815) 726-5218
Will Roe (06-12)
   2011-12 Enrollment: n/a . . . . (815) 740-8360

Four-year College(s)
University of St Francis (Private, Not-for-profit, Roman Catholic)
   Fall 2012 Enrollment: 3,455 . . . . (815) 740-3360
   2012-13 Tuition: In-state $26,924; Out-of-state $26,924

Two-year College(s)
Joliet Junior College (Public)
   Fall 2012 Enrollment: 15,589 . . . . (815) 729-9020
   2012-13 Tuition: In-state $7,871; Out-of-state $8,543

Vocational/Technical School(s)
Professionals Choice Hair Design Academy (Private, For-profit)
   Fall 2012 Enrollment: 47 . . . . (815) 741-8224
   2012-13 Tuition: $15,000
Regency Beauty Institute-Joliet (Private, For-profit)
   Fall 2012 Enrollment: 47 . . . . (800) 787-6456
   2012-13 Tuition: $16,425

Housing: Homeownership rate: 73.5% (2008-2012 5-year est.); Median home value: $181,300 (2008-2012 5-year est.); Median contract rent: $717 per month (2008-2012 5-year est.); Median year structure built: 1978 (2008-2012 5-year est.).
Health Insurance: 67.8% Private; 26.1% Public; 13.6% None. (2008-2012 5-year est.)
Hospitals: Silver Cross Hospital (297 beds); St. Joseph Medical Center (452 beds); Stateville Correctional Center Hospital (32 beds)
Safety: Violent crime rate: 34.1 per 10,000 population; Property crime rate: 258.3 per 10,000 population (2012).
Transportation: Commute to work: 91.4% car, 2.4% public transportation, 1.4% walk, 2.8% work from home (2008-2012 5-year est.); Travel time to work: 22.2% less than 15 minutes, 30.2% 15 to 30 minutes, 20.0% 30 to 45 minutes, 12.2% 45 to 60 minutes, 15.4% 60 minutes or more (2008-2012 5-year est.); Amtrak: Train service available.
Airports: Joliet Regional Airport (general aviation)

Additional Information Contacts
City of Joliet . . . . (815) 724-4000
   http://www.cityofjoliet.info
Joliet Region Chamber of Commerce & Industry . . . . (815) 727-5371
   http://www.jolietchamber.com
Will County Center for Economic Development . . . . (815) 723-1800
   http://www.willcountyced.com

LAKEWOOD SHORES (CDP). Covers a land area of 2.287 square miles and a water area of 0.220 square miles. Located at 41.27° N. Lat; 88.14° W. Long. Elevation is 564 feet.

Population: 1,606 (1990); 1,487 (2000); 1,347 (2010); Density: 544.8 persons per square mile (2008-2012 5-year est.); Race: 95.1% White, 0.0% Black/African American, 0.0% Asian, 0.0% American Indian/Alaska Native, 0.0% Native Hawaiian/Other Pacific Islander, 4.9% Some other race, 4.9% Two or more races, 1.2% Hispanic of any race (2008-2012 5-year est.); Average household size: 2.63 (2008-2012 5-year est.); Median age: 42.5 (2008-2012 5-year est.); Males per 100 females: 103.6 (2008-2012 5-year est.); Marriage status: 24.5% never married, 59.6% now married, 7.8% widowed, 8.1% divorced (2008-2012 5-year est.); Foreign born: 1.9% (2008-2012 5-year est.); Ancestry (includes multiple ancestries): 30.6% German, 18.9% Polish, 16.9% Irish, 16.5% Italian, 7.1% English (2008-2012 5-year est.).
Economy: Homeowner vacancy rate: 0.0%. Rental vacancy rate: 0.0%. (2008-2012 5-year est.); Employment by occupation: 2.5% management, business, and financial, 1.6% computer, engineering, and science, 2.7% education, legal, community service, arts, and media, 0.0% healthcare practitioners, 12.5% service, 36.6% sales and office, 21.3% natural resources, construction, and maintenance, 22.9% production, transportation, and material moving (2008-2012 5-year est.).

Income: Per capita income: $25,528 (2008-2012 5-year est.); Median household income: $66,118 (2008-2012 5-year est.); Average household income: $66,504 (2008-2012 5-year est.); Percent of households with income of $100,000 or more: 16.7% (2008-2012 5-year est.); Poverty rate: 10.0% (2008-2012 5-year est.).
Education: Percent of population age 25 and over with: High school diploma (including GED) or higher: 89.7% (2008-2012 5-year est.); Bachelor's degree or higher: 5.4% (2008-2012 5-year est.); Master's degree or higher: 1.2% (2008-2012 5-year est.).
Housing: Homeownership rate: 91.5% (2008-2012 5-year est.); Median home value: $143,900 (2008-2012 5-year est.); Median contract rent: n/a per month (2008-2012 5-year est.); Median year structure built: 1964 (2008-2012 5-year est.).
Health Insurance: 76.4% Private; 32.4% Public; 2.5% None. (2008-2012 5-year est.)
Transportation: Commute to work: 96.9% car, 0.0% public transportation, 0.0% walk, 3.1% work from home (2008-2012 5-year est.); Travel time to work: 8.6% less than 15 minutes, 20.9% 15 to 30 minutes, 39.6% 30 to 45 minutes, 20.4% 45 to 60 minutes, 10.5% 60 minutes or more (2008-2012 5-year est.)

LOCKPORT (city). Covers a land area of 11.399 square miles and a water area of 0 square miles. Located at 41.59° N. Lat; 88.03° W. Long. Elevation is 594 feet.

History: Named for the locks on the Illinois and Michigan Canal. Lockport developed as a shipping and transfer point on the Illinois & Michigan Canal. This was the location of the lock that controlled the volume of water from Lake Michigan. The canal company offices were located here also.
Population: 9,401 (1990); 15,191 (2000); 24,839 (2010); Density: 2,164.4 persons per square mile (2008-2012 5-year est.); Race: 94.3% White, 2.0% Black/African American, 1.5% Asian, 0.0% American Indian/Alaska Native, 0.0% Native Hawaiian/Other Pacific Islander, 2.2% Some other race, 1.3% Two or more races, 7.0% Hispanic of any race (2008-2012 5-year est.); Average household size: 2.80 (2008-2012 5-year est.); Median age: 33.8 (2008-2012 5-year est.); Males per 100 females: 98.6 (2008-2012 5-year est.); Marriage status: 25.9% never married, 60.7% now married, 4.9% widowed, 8.5% divorced (2008-2012 5-year est.); Foreign born: 8.1% (2008-2012 5-year est.); Ancestry (includes multiple ancestries): 26.9% German, 25.0% Polish, 21.6% Irish, 17.5% Italian, 5.6% English (2008-2012 5-year est.).
Economy: Unemployment rate: 7.7% (April 2014); Total civilian labor force: 14,122 (April 2014); Single-family building permits issued: 29 (2013); Multi-family building permits issued: 0 (2013); Homeowner vacancy rate: 2.8%. Rental vacancy rate: 10.2%. (2008-2012 5-year est.); Employment by occupation: 14.0% management, business, and financial, 5.6% computer, engineering, and science, 9.6% education, legal, community service, arts, and media, 6.5% healthcare practitioners, 14.1% service, 25.5% sales and office, 11.5% natural resources, construction, and maintenance, 13.2% production, transportation, and material moving (2008-2012 5-year est.).
Income: Per capita income: $31,143 (2008-2012 5-year est.); Median household income: $77,220 (2008-2012 5-year est.); Average household income: $86,084 (2008-2012 5-year est.); Percent of households with income of $100,000 or more: 32.3% (2008-2012 5-year est.); Poverty rate: 4.3% (2008-2012 5-year est.).
Taxes: Total city taxes per capita: $310 (2011); City property taxes per capita: $240 (2011).
Education: Percent of population age 25 and over with: High school diploma (including GED) or higher: 93.3% (2008-2012 5-year est.); Bachelor's degree or higher: 29.8% (2008-2012 5-year est.); Master's degree or higher: 8.3% (2008-2012 5-year est.).

School District(s)
Fairmont SD 89 (PK-08)
   2011-12 Enrollment: 291 . . . . (815) 726-6318
Homer CCSD 33c (PK-08)
   2011-12 Enrollment: 3,681 . . . . (708) 226-7600
Lockport SD 91 (PK-08)
   2011-12 Enrollment: 652 . . . . (815) 838-0737
Lockport Twp HSD 205 (09-12)
   2011-12 Enrollment: 3,748 . . . . (815) 588-8100
Taft SD 90 (PK-08)
   2011-12 Enrollment: 351 . . . . (815) 838-0408
Will County SD 92 (PK-08)
   2011-12 Enrollment: 1,796 . . . . (815) 838-8031

Housing: Homeownership rate: 87.6% (2008-2012 5-year est.); Median home value: $222,600 (2008-2012 5-year est.); Median contract rent: $737 per month (2008-2012 5-year est.); Median year structure built: 1995 (2008-2012 5-year est.).

Health Insurance: 85.7% Private; 17.5% Public; 6.2% None. (2008-2012 5-year est.)

Safety: Violent crime rate: 6.0 per 10,000 population; Property crime rate: 126.8 per 10,000 population (2012).

Transportation: Commute to work: 92.3% car, 4.0% public transportation, 0.4% walk, 2.6% work from home (2008-2012 5-year est.); Travel time to work: 17.8% less than 15 minutes, 26.2% 15 to 30 minutes, 26.3% 30 to 45 minutes, 14.7% 45 to 60 minutes, 15.0% 60 minutes or more (2008-2012 5-year est.).

Additional Information Contacts

City of Lockport . . . . (815) 838-0549
  http://www.cityoflockport.net
Lockport Area Chamber of Commerce . . . . (815) 838-3357
  http://www.lockportchamber.com

MANHATTAN (village). Covers a land area of 6.568 square miles and a water area of 0 square miles. Located at 41.42° N. Lat; 87.98° W. Long. Elevation is 682 feet.

Population: 2,059 (1990); 3,330 (2000); 7,051 (2010); Density: 983.0 persons per square mile (2008-2012 5-year est.); Race: 98.7% White, 0.1% Black/African American, 0.4% Asian, 0.2% American Indian/Alaska Native, 0.0% Native Hawaiian/Other Pacific Islander, 0.6% Some other race, 0.3% Two or more races, 4.5% Hispanic of any race (2008-2012 5-year est.); Average household size: 2.83 (2008-2012 5-year est.); Median age: 32.1 (2008-2012 5-year est.); Males per 100 females: 104.8 (2008-2012 5-year est.); Marriage status: 23.9% never married, 61.1% now married, 3.5% widowed, 11.4% divorced (2008-2012 5-year est.); Foreign born: 0.5% (2008-2012 5-year est.); Ancestry (includes multiple ancestries): 32.2% German, 27.4% Irish, 19.1% Italian, 11.4% Polish, 5.6% French (2008-2012 5-year est.).

Economy: Single-family building permits issued: 46 (2013); Multi-family building permits issued: 0 (2013); Homeowner vacancy rate: 6.0%. Rental vacancy rate: 0.0%. (2008-2012 5-year est.); Employment by occupation: 15.2% management, business, and financial, 3.4% computer, engineering, and science, 14.6% education, legal, community service, arts, and media, 6.3% healthcare practitioners, 13.6% service, 21.7% sales and office, 18.5% natural resources, construction, and maintenance, 6.7% production, transportation, and material moving (2008-2012 5-year est.).

Income: Per capita income: $30,055 (2008-2012 5-year est.); Median household income: $76,474 (2008-2012 5-year est.); Average household income: $83,890 (2008-2012 5-year est.); Percent of households with income of $100,000 or more: 32.4% (2008-2012 5-year est.); Poverty rate: 3.5% (2008-2012 5-year est.).

Education: Percent of population age 25 and over with: High school diploma (including GED) or higher: 98.2% (2008-2012 5-year est.); Bachelor's degree or higher: 32.1% (2008-2012 5-year est.); Master's degree or higher: 13.4% (2008-2012 5-year est.).

School District(s)

Manhattan SD 114 (PK-08)
  2011-12 Enrollment: 1,249 . . . . (815) 478-0191
Peotone CUSD 207u (PK-12)
  2011-12 Enrollment: 1,887 . . . . (708) 258-6061

Housing: Homeownership rate: 88.7% (2008-2012 5-year est.); Median home value: $217,100 (2008-2012 5-year est.); Median contract rent: $953 per month (2008-2012 5-year est.); Median year structure built: 1998 (2008-2012 5-year est.).

Health Insurance: 87.5% Private; 12.5% Public; 7.4% None. (2008-2012 5-year est.)

Safety: Violent crime rate: 7.0 per 10,000 population; Property crime rate: 80.3 per 10,000 population (2012).

Transportation: Commute to work: 89.6% car, 7.8% public transportation, 0.6% walk, 1.9% work from home (2008-2012 5-year est.); Travel time to work: 14.3% less than 15 minutes, 24.1% 15 to 30 minutes, 27.2% 30 to 45 minutes, 14.7% 45 to 60 minutes, 19.8% 60 minutes or more (2008-2012 5-year est.).

Additional Information Contacts

Manhattan Chamber of Commerce . . . . (815) 478-3811
  http://www.manhattan-il.com
Village of Manhattan . . . . (815) 418-2100
  http://www.villageofmanhattan.org

MOKENA (village). Covers a land area of 8.890 square miles and a water area of 0.003 square miles. Located at 41.53° N. Lat; 87.88° W. Long. Elevation is 705 feet.

Population: 6,128 (1990); 14,583 (2000); 18,740 (2010); Density: 2,072.3 persons per square mile (2008-2012 5-year est.); Race: 94.9% White, 0.8% Black/African American, 0.8% Asian, 0.0% American Indian/Alaska Native, 0.0% Native Hawaiian/Other Pacific Islander, 3.5% Some other race, 1.3% Two or more races, 6.1% Hispanic of any race (2008-2012 5-year est.); Average household size: 3.04 (2008-2012 5-year est.); Median age: 39.5 (2008-2012 5-year est.); Males per 100 females: 99.8 (2008-2012 5-year est.); Marriage status: 31.5% never married, 57.3% now married, 4.4% widowed, 6.7% divorced (2008-2012 5-year est.); Foreign born: 4.6% (2008-2012 5-year est.); Ancestry (includes multiple ancestries): 29.3% Irish, 26.9% German, 18.4% Polish, 15.1% Italian, 5.6% English (2008-2012 5-year est.).

Economy: Single-family building permits issued: 86 (2013); Multi-family building permits issued: 22 (2013); Homeowner vacancy rate: 0.6%. Rental vacancy rate: 3.0%. (2008-2012 5-year est.); Employment by occupation: 18.8% management, business, and financial, 3.4% computer, engineering, and science, 10.7% education, legal, community service, arts, and media, 8.4% healthcare practitioners, 13.8% service, 26.8% sales and office, 7.1% natural resources, construction, and maintenance, 11.0% production, transportation, and material moving (2008-2012 5-year est.).

Income: Per capita income: $37,990 (2008-2012 5-year est.); Median household income: $103,678 (2008-2012 5-year est.); Average household income: $113,458 (2008-2012 5-year est.); Percent of households with income of $100,000 or more: 53.2% (2008-2012 5-year est.); Poverty rate: 3.0% (2008-2012 5-year est.).

Education: Percent of population age 25 and over with: High school diploma (including GED) or higher: 96.4% (2008-2012 5-year est.); Bachelor's degree or higher: 37.5% (2008-2012 5-year est.); Master's degree or higher: 12.2% (2008-2012 5-year est.).

School District(s)

Mokena SD 159 (PK-08)
  2011-12 Enrollment: 1,808 . . . . (708) 342-4900
Summit Hill SD 161 (PK-08)
  2011-12 Enrollment: 3,527 . . . . (815) 469-9103

Housing: Homeownership rate: 89.3% (2008-2012 5-year est.); Median home value: $307,900 (2008-2012 5-year est.); Median contract rent: $926 per month (2008-2012 5-year est.); Median year structure built: 1994 (2008-2012 5-year est.).

Health Insurance: 91.5% Private; 14.5% Public; 3.5% None. (2008-2012 5-year est.)

Safety: Violent crime rate: 5.8 per 10,000 population; Property crime rate: 115.0 per 10,000 population (2012).

Transportation: Commute to work: 88.1% car, 8.2% public transportation, 0.8% walk, 1.7% work from home (2008-2012 5-year est.); Travel time to work: 20.7% less than 15 minutes, 29.4% 15 to 30 minutes, 21.1% 30 to 45 minutes, 12.8% 45 to 60 minutes, 16.0% 60 minutes or more (2008-2012 5-year est.).

Additional Information Contacts

Mokena Chamber of Commerce . . . . (708) 479-2468
  http://www.mokena.com
Village of Mokena . . . . (708) 479-3900
  http://www.mokena.org

MONEE (village). Covers a land area of 4.425 square miles and a water area of 0 square miles. Located at 41.42° N. Lat; 87.75° W. Long. Elevation is 797 feet.

Population: 1,044 (1990); 2,924 (2000); 5,148 (2010); Density: 1,152.4 persons per square mile (2008-2012 5-year est.); Race: 85.3% White, 7.6% Black/African American, 0.7% Asian, 0.0% American Indian/Alaska Native, 0.0% Native Hawaiian/Other Pacific Islander, 6.4% Some other race, 5.5% Two or more races, 11.2% Hispanic of any race (2008-2012 5-year est.); Average household size: 2.60 (2008-2012 5-year est.); Median age: 37.6 (2008-2012 5-year est.); Males per 100 females: 99.4 (2008-2012 5-year est.); Marriage status: 15.6% never married, 70.0% now married, 6.1% widowed, 8.3% divorced (2008-2012 5-year est.); Foreign born: 2.0% (2008-2012 5-year est.); Ancestry (includes multiple ancestries): 27.9% German, 20.0% Irish, 17.6% Polish, 8.8% English, 7.9% Italian (2008-2012 5-year est.).

Economy: Single-family building permits issued: 1 (2013); Multi-family building permits issued: 0 (2013); Homeowner vacancy rate: 2.2%. Rental vacancy rate: 0.0%. (2008-2012 5-year est.); Employment by occupation: 19.1% management, business, and financial, 1.6% computer, engineering,

and science, 5.1% education, legal, community service, arts, and media, 6.5% healthcare practitioners, 16.7% service, 26.1% sales and office, 11.8% natural resources, construction, and maintenance, 13.1% production, transportation, and material moving (2008-2012 5-year est.).
Income: Per capita income: $34,558 (2008-2012 5-year est.); Median household income: $67,371 (2008-2012 5-year est.); Average household income: $88,594 (2008-2012 5-year est.); Percent of households with income of $100,000 or more: 28.7% (2008-2012 5-year est.); Poverty rate: 3.7% (2008-2012 5-year est.).
Education: Percent of population age 25 and over with: High school diploma (including GED) or higher: 93.2% (2008-2012 5-year est.); Bachelor's degree or higher: 22.1% (2008-2012 5-year est.); Master's degree or higher: 6.3% (2008-2012 5-year est.).

School District(s)
Crete Monee CUSD 201u (PK-12)
   2011-12 Enrollment: 5,136 . . . . (708) 367-8300
Will Roe (06-12)
   2011-12 Enrollment: n/a . . . . (815) 740-8360
Housing: Homeownership rate: 90.5% (2008-2012 5-year est.); Median home value: $179,800 (2008-2012 5-year est.); Median contract rent: $705 per month (2008-2012 5-year est.); Median year structure built: 1997 (2008-2012 5-year est.).
Health Insurance: 80.6% Private; 31.1% Public; 4.6% None. (2008-2012 5-year est.)
Safety: Violent crime rate: 3.9 per 10,000 population; Property crime rate: 133.2 per 10,000 population (2012).
Transportation: Commute to work: 83.9% car, 7.3% public transportation, 0.0% walk, 3.8% work from home (2008-2012 5-year est.); Travel time to work: 12.0% less than 15 minutes, 30.6% 15 to 30 minutes, 25.5% 30 to 45 minutes, 13.0% 45 to 60 minutes, 18.8% 60 minutes or more (2008-2012 5-year est.)
Airports: Bult Field (general aviation)
Additional Information Contacts
Monee Area Chamber of Commerce . . . . (708) 421-1786
   http://www.moneechamber.org

NEW LENOX (village).
Covers a land area of 15.661 square miles and a water area of 0.023 square miles. Located at 41.51° N. Lat; 87.97° W. Long. Elevation is 669 feet.
History: New Lenox was first settled in the 1820's along Hickory Creek.
Population: 9,627 (1990); 17,771 (2000); 24,394 (2010); Density: 1,556.1 persons per square mile (2008-2012 5-year est.); Race: 93.9% White, 0.6% Black/African American, 1.7% Asian, 0.0% American Indian/Alaska Native, 0.0% Native Hawaiian/Other Pacific Islander, 3.8% Some other race, 1.4% Two or more races, 7.0% Hispanic of any race (2008-2012 5-year est.); Average household size: 3.00 (2008-2012 5-year est.); Median age: 36.2 (2008-2012 5-year est.); Males per 100 females: 89.9 (2008-2012 5-year est.); Marriage status: 24.3% never married, 64.6% now married, 5.2% widowed, 5.9% divorced (2008-2012 5-year est.); Foreign born: 3.6% (2008-2012 5-year est.); Ancestry (includes multiple ancestries): 27.8% Irish, 27.4% German, 18.8% Polish, 18.0% Italian, 7.9% English (2008-2012 5-year est.).
Economy: Single-family building permits issued: 174 (2013); Multi-family building permits issued: 0 (2013); Homeowner vacancy rate: 0.7%. Rental vacancy rate: 7.0%. (2008-2012 5-year est.); Employment by occupation: 16.8% management, business, and financial, 5.9% computer, engineering, and science, 11.6% education, legal, community service, arts, and media, 6.4% healthcare practitioners, 12.6% service, 26.7% sales and office, 11.0% natural resources, construction, and maintenance, 9.0% production, transportation, and material moving (2008-2012 5-year est.).
Income: Per capita income: $33,581 (2008-2012 5-year est.); Median household income: $90,833 (2008-2012 5-year est.); Average household income: $99,781 (2008-2012 5-year est.); Percent of households with income of $100,000 or more: 42.6% (2008-2012 5-year est.); Poverty rate: 2.3% (2008-2012 5-year est.).
Taxes: Total city taxes per capita: $286 (2011); City property taxes per capita: $114 (2011).
Education: Percent of population age 25 and over with: High school diploma (including GED) or higher: 97.3% (2008-2012 5-year est.); Bachelor's degree or higher: 35.1% (2008-2012 5-year est.); Master's degree or higher: 13.6% (2008-2012 5-year est.).

School District(s)
Lincoln Way CHSD 210 (09-12)
   2011-12 Enrollment: 7,346 . . . . (815) 462-2100

Lincoln-Way Area Spec Ed Ja Dist (PK-12)
   2011-12 Enrollment: n/a . . . . (815) 806-4600
New Lenox SD 122 (PK-08)
   2011-12 Enrollment: 5,565 . . . . (815) 485-2169
Vocational/Technical School(s)
Capri Beauty College (Private, For-profit)
   Fall 2012 Enrollment: 54 . . . . (815) 485-3020
   2012-13 Tuition: $18,300
Housing: Homeownership rate: 87.5% (2008-2012 5-year est.); Median home value: $291,700 (2008-2012 5-year est.); Median contract rent: $895 per month (2008-2012 5-year est.); Median year structure built: 1993 (2008-2012 5-year est.).
Health Insurance: 92.0% Private; 12.9% Public; 3.5% None. (2008-2012 5-year est.)
Safety: Violent crime rate: 7.7 per 10,000 population; Property crime rate: 123.0 per 10,000 population (2012).
Transportation: Commute to work: 87.4% car, 6.4% public transportation, 0.3% walk, 5.0% work from home (2008-2012 5-year est.); Travel time to work: 19.8% less than 15 minutes, 30.1% 15 to 30 minutes, 22.8% 30 to 45 minutes, 9.3% 45 to 60 minutes, 18.0% 60 minutes or more (2008-2012 5-year est.)
Additional Information Contacts
New Lenox Chamber of Commerce . . . . (815) 485-4241
   http://www.newlenoxchamber.com
Village of New Lenox. . . . . (815) 462-6400
   http://www.newlenox.net

PEOTONE (village).
Covers a land area of 1.875 square miles and a water area of 0.003 square miles. Located at 41.33° N. Lat; 87.79° W. Long. Elevation is 705 feet.
History: Incorporated 1869.
Population: 2,947 (1990); 3,385 (2000); 4,142 (2010); Density: 2,508.3 persons per square mile (2008-2012 5-year est.); Race: 99.8% White, 0.1% Black/African American, 0.0% Asian, 0.0% American Indian/Alaska Native, 0.0% Native Hawaiian/Other Pacific Islander, 0.1% Some other race, 0.1% Two or more races, 0.2% Hispanic of any race (2008-2012 5-year est.); Average household size: 2.69 (2008-2012 5-year est.); Median age: 40.1 (2008-2012 5-year est.); Males per 100 females: 110.2 (2008-2012 5-year est.); Marriage status: 21.2% never married, 67.8% now married, 5.0% widowed, 6.1% divorced (2008-2012 5-year est.); Foreign born: 0.0% (2008-2012 5-year est.); Ancestry (includes multiple ancestries): 35.3% German, 18.1% Irish, 15.3% Polish, 12.4% English, 10.6% Italian (2008-2012 5-year est.).
Economy: Single-family building permits issued: 4 (2013); Multi-family building permits issued: 0 (2013); Homeowner vacancy rate: 0.0%. Rental vacancy rate: 6.9%. (2008-2012 5-year est.); Employment by occupation: 8.9% management, business, and financial, 4.3% computer, engineering, and science, 11.8% education, legal, community service, arts, and media, 3.0% healthcare practitioners, 17.3% service, 33.9% sales and office, 14.1% natural resources, construction, and maintenance, 6.7% production, transportation, and material moving (2008-2012 5-year est.).
Income: Per capita income: $29,618 (2008-2012 5-year est.); Median household income: $77,398 (2008-2012 5-year est.); Average household income: $79,163 (2008-2012 5-year est.); Percent of households with income of $100,000 or more: 27.2% (2008-2012 5-year est.); Poverty rate: 3.1% (2008-2012 5-year est.).
Education: Percent of population age 25 and over with: High school diploma (including GED) or higher: 95.7% (2008-2012 5-year est.); Bachelor's degree or higher: 28.4% (2008-2012 5-year est.); Master's degree or higher: 10.2% (2008-2012 5-year est.).
School District(s)
Peotone CUSD 207u (PK-12)
   2011-12 Enrollment: 1,887 . . . . (708) 258-6061
Housing: Homeownership rate: 85.1% (2008-2012 5-year est.); Median home value: $204,600 (2008-2012 5-year est.); Median contract rent: $748 per month (2008-2012 5-year est.); Median year structure built: 1971 (2008-2012 5-year est.).
Health Insurance: 90.2% Private; 20.4% Public; 2.5% None. (2008-2012 5-year est.)
Safety: Violent crime rate: 16.8 per 10,000 population; Property crime rate: 117.5 per 10,000 population (2012).
Transportation: Commute to work: 92.6% car, 2.6% public transportation, 0.9% walk, 3.9% work from home (2008-2012 5-year est.); Travel time to work: 22.6% less than 15 minutes, 24.4% 15 to 30 minutes, 28.2% 30 to

45 minutes, 7.9% 45 to 60 minutes, 17.0% 60 minutes or more (2008-2012 5-year est.)

Additional Information Contacts
Peotone Chamber of Commerce . . . . (708) 258-9450
  http://www.peotonechamber.com

PLAINFIELD (village).
Covers a land area of 23.224 square miles and a water area of 0.979 square miles. Located at 41.63° N. Lat; 88.25° W. Long. Elevation is 617 feet.

History: Plainfield began as a trading post founded by the Frenchman Du Pazhe about 1790, and later operated by Vetel Vermette for the American Fur Trading Company. The town grew around a cabin built by Captain James Walker in 1829, and was first known as Walker's Grove. The name of Plainfield refers to the flat prairie setting.

Population: 4,557 (1990); 13,038 (2000); 39,581 (2010); Density: 1,680.6 persons per square mile (2008-2012 5-year est.); Race: 83.1% White, 4.8% Black/African American, 7.2% Asian, 0.0% American Indian/Alaska Native, 0.1% Native Hawaiian/Other Pacific Islander, 4.8% Some other race, 2.6% Two or more races, 10.5% Hispanic of any race (2008-2012 5-year est.); Average household size: 3.37 (2008-2012 5-year est.); Median age: 33.4 (2008-2012 5-year est.); Males per 100 females: 98.7 (2008-2012 5-year est.); Marriage status: 25.0% never married, 65.3% now married, 2.8% widowed, 6.9% divorced (2008-2012 5-year est.); Foreign born: 10.7% (2008-2012 5-year est.); Ancestry (includes multiple ancestries): 22.9% Irish, 21.7% German, 15.1% Italian, 12.0% Polish, 6.0% English (2008-2012 5-year est.).

Economy: Unemployment rate: 6.4% (April 2014); Total civilian labor force: 21,599 (April 2014); Single-family building permits issued: 136 (2013); Multi-family building permits issued: 0 (2013); Homeowner vacancy rate: 2.6%. Rental vacancy rate: 4.8%. (2008-2012 5-year est.); Employment by occupation: 25.4% management, business, and financial, 6.5% computer, engineering, and science, 12.4% education, legal, community service, arts, and media, 6.8% healthcare practitioners, 10.3% service, 25.7% sales and office, 4.7% natural resources, construction, and maintenance, 8.1% production, transportation, and material moving (2008-2012 5-year est.).

Income: Per capita income: $35,312 (2008-2012 5-year est.); Median household income: $111,637 (2008-2012 5-year est.); Average household income: $117,234 (2008-2012 5-year est.); Percent of households with income of $100,000 or more: 57.0% (2008-2012 5-year est.); Poverty rate: 4.0% (2008-2012 5-year est.).

Taxes: Total city taxes per capita: $390 (2011); City property taxes per capita: $186 (2011).

Education: Percent of population age 25 and over with: High school diploma (including GED) or higher: 96.9% (2008-2012 5-year est.); Bachelor's degree or higher: 48.3% (2008-2012 5-year est.); Master's degree or higher: 17.7% (2008-2012 5-year est.).

School District(s)

Oswego CUSD 308 (PK-12)
  2011-12 Enrollment: 17,150 . . . . (630) 636-3080
Plainfield SD 202 (PK-12)
  2011-12 Enrollment: 28,904 . . . . (815) 577-4000
Plainfield SD 202 (PK-12)
  2011-12 Enrollment: 28,904 . . . . (815) 577-4000
Troy CCSD 30c (PK-08)
  2011-12 Enrollment: 4,564 . . . . (815) 577-6760

Housing: Homeownership rate: 90.1% (2008-2012 5-year est.); Median home value: $299,500 (2008-2012 5-year est.); Median contract rent: $1,256 per month (2008-2012 5-year est.); Median year structure built: 2002 (2008-2012 5-year est.).

Health Insurance: 87.8% Private; 12.1% Public; 6.1% None. (2008-2012 5-year est.)

Safety: Violent crime rate: 8.8 per 10,000 population; Property crime rate: 125.2 per 10,000 population (2012).

Transportation: Commute to work: 88.4% car, 3.2% public transportation, 0.9% walk, 5.9% work from home (2008-2012 5-year est.); Travel time to work: 13.9% less than 15 minutes, 25.9% 15 to 30 minutes, 22.4% 30 to 45 minutes, 15.5% 45 to 60 minutes, 22.3% 60 minutes or more (2008-2012 5-year est.)

Additional Information Contacts
Plainfield Area Chamber of Commerce . . . . (815) 436-4431
  http://www.plainfieldchamber.com
Village of Plainfield . . . . (815) 436-7093
  http://www.plainfield-il.org

PRESTON HEIGHTS (CDP).
Covers a land area of 0.954 square miles and a water area of 0 square miles. Located at 41.49° N. Lat; 88.08° W. Long. Elevation is 630 feet.

Population: 2,750 (1990); 2,527 (2000); 2,575 (2010); Density: 2,912.4 persons per square mile (2008-2012 5-year est.); Race: 26.7% White, 63.1% Black/African American, 0.0% Asian, 0.0% American Indian/Alaska Native, 0.0% Native Hawaiian/Other Pacific Islander, 10.2% Some other race, 4.1% Two or more races, 16.9% Hispanic of any race (2008-2012 5-year est.); Average household size: 2.85 (2008-2012 5-year est.); Median age: 39.6 (2008-2012 5-year est.); Males per 100 females: 116.4 (2008-2012 5-year est.); Marriage status: 41.4% never married, 41.3% now married, 7.3% widowed, 10.0% divorced (2008-2012 5-year est.); Foreign born: 4.8% (2008-2012 5-year est.); Ancestry (includes multiple ancestries): 5.3% German, 3.7% American, 3.6% Irish, 2.0% Polish, 1.8% Italian (2008-2012 5-year est.).

Economy: Homeowner vacancy rate: 2.4%. Rental vacancy rate: 0.0%. (2008-2012 5-year est.); Employment by occupation: 1.6% management, business, and financial, 0.4% computer, engineering, and science, 5.4% education, legal, community service, arts, and media, 4.2% healthcare practitioners, 33.8% service, 20.0% sales and office, 5.9% natural resources, construction, and maintenance, 28.8% production, transportation, and material moving (2008-2012 5-year est.).

Income: Per capita income: $25,975 (2008-2012 5-year est.); Median household income: $45,714 (2008-2012 5-year est.); Average household income: $68,882 (2008-2012 5-year est.); Percent of households with income of $100,000 or more: 18.2% (2008-2012 5-year est.); Poverty rate: 18.7% (2008-2012 5-year est.).

Education: Percent of population age 25 and over with: High school diploma (including GED) or higher: 78.6% (2008-2012 5-year est.); Bachelor's degree or higher: 6.4% (2008-2012 5-year est.); Master's degree or higher: 1.8% (2008-2012 5-year est.).

Housing: Homeownership rate: 63.2% (2008-2012 5-year est.); Median home value: $145,800 (2008-2012 5-year est.); Median contract rent: $738 per month (2008-2012 5-year est.); Median year structure built: 1964 (2008-2012 5-year est.).

Health Insurance: 58.3% Private; 34.2% Public; 14.9% None. (2008-2012 5-year est.)

Transportation: Commute to work: 91.8% car, 3.2% public transportation, 0.5% walk, 1.6% work from home (2008-2012 5-year est.); Travel time to work: 26.9% less than 15 minutes, 44.7% 15 to 30 minutes, 13.0% 30 to 45 minutes, 7.4% 45 to 60 minutes, 8.0% 60 minutes or more (2008-2012 5-year est.)

ROCKDALE (village).
Covers a land area of 0.795 square miles and a water area of 0 square miles. Located at 41.51° N. Lat; 88.12° W. Long. Elevation is 551 feet.

History: Incorporated 1903.

Population: 1,709 (1990); 1,888 (2000); 1,976 (2010); Density: 2,402.2 persons per square mile (2008-2012 5-year est.); Race: 82.5% White, 1.8% Black/African American, 0.0% Asian, 0.2% American Indian/Alaska Native, 0.0% Native Hawaiian/Other Pacific Islander, 15.5% Some other race, 4.1% Two or more races, 34.0% Hispanic of any race (2008-2012 5-year est.); Average household size: 2.37 (2008-2012 5-year est.); Median age: 37.7 (2008-2012 5-year est.); Males per 100 females: 87.5 (2008-2012 5-year est.); Marriage status: 29.8% never married, 44.5% now married, 6.4% widowed, 19.2% divorced (2008-2012 5-year est.); Foreign born: 11.5% (2008-2012 5-year est.); Ancestry (includes multiple ancestries): 20.6% German, 14.2% Irish, 13.9% Italian, 9.5% Polish, 3.2% Slovene (2008-2012 5-year est.).

Economy: Single-family building permits issued: 0 (2013); Multi-family building permits issued: 0 (2013); Homeowner vacancy rate: 0.9%. Rental vacancy rate: 0.0%. (2008-2012 5-year est.); Employment by occupation: 6.1% management, business, and financial, 2.5% computer, engineering, and science, 9.0% education, legal, community service, arts, and media, 3.4% healthcare practitioners, 22.1% service, 30.0% sales and office, 9.7% natural resources, construction, and maintenance, 17.1% production, transportation, and material moving (2008-2012 5-year est.).

Income: Per capita income: $26,134 (2008-2012 5-year est.); Median household income: $51,898 (2008-2012 5-year est.); Average household income: $60,544 (2008-2012 5-year est.); Percent of households with income of $100,000 or more: 11.1% (2008-2012 5-year est.); Poverty rate: 9.1% (2008-2012 5-year est.).

Education: Percent of population age 25 and over with: High school diploma (including GED) or higher: 80.6% (2008-2012 5-year est.);

Bachelor's degree or higher: 8.3% (2008-2012 5-year est.); Master's degree or higher: 1.0% (2008-2012 5-year est.).
School District(s)
Rockdale SD 84 (PK-08)
   2011-12 Enrollment: 286. . . . . (815) 725-5321
Housing: Homeownership rate: 51.7% (2008-2012 5-year est.); Median home value: $152,500 (2008-2012 5-year est.); Median contract rent: $716 per month (2008-2012 5-year est.); Median year structure built: 1953 (2008-2012 5-year est.).
Health Insurance: 62.7% Private; 30.2% Public; 19.4% None. (2008-2012 5-year est.)
Safety: Violent crime rate: 10.1 per 10,000 population; Property crime rate: 135.7 per 10,000 population (2012).
Transportation: Commute to work: 90.0% car, 4.5% public transportation, 3.0% walk, 1.1% work from home (2008-2012 5-year est.); Travel time to work: 36.0% less than 15 minutes, 30.4% 15 to 30 minutes, 16.3% 30 to 45 minutes, 9.3% 45 to 60 minutes, 7.9% 60 minutes or more (2008-2012 5-year est.).

ROMEOVILLE (village). Aka Romeo. Covers a land area of 18.437 square miles and a water area of 0.319 square miles. Located at 41.64° N. Lat; 88.10° W. Long. Elevation is 617 feet.
History: Named for the hero of Shakespeare's "Romeo and Juliet". Romeoville developed along the Illinois & Michigan Canal. An early industry was the Globe Oil Refinery.
Population: 14,074 (1990); 21,153 (2000); 39,680 (2010); Density: 2,124.8 persons per square mile (2008-2012 5-year est.); Race: 68.8% White, 10.5% Black/African American, 7.0% Asian, 0.5% American Indian/Alaska Native, 0.0% Native Hawaiian/Other Pacific Islander, 13.2% Some other race, 3.8% Two or more races, 32.4% Hispanic of any race (2008-2012 5-year est.); Average household size: 3.28 (2008-2012 5-year est.); Median age: 31.9 (2008-2012 5-year est.); Males per 100 females: 97.3 (2008-2012 5-year est.); Marriage status: 32.7% never married, 54.9% now married, 3.9% widowed, 8.4% divorced (2008-2012 5-year est.); Foreign born: 21.4% (2008-2012 5-year est.); Ancestry (includes multiple ancestries): 13.4% German, 13.2% Irish, 10.9% Polish, 9.6% Italian, 3.3% English (2008-2012 5-year est.).
Economy: Unemployment rate: 7.7% (April 2014); Total civilian labor force: 23,171 (April 2014); Single-family building permits issued: 24 (2013); Multi-family building permits issued: 0 (2013); Homeowner vacancy rate: 1.0%. Rental vacancy rate: 15.3%. (2008-2012 5-year est.); Employment by occupation: 12.0% management, business, and financial, 4.4% computer, engineering, and science, 7.2% education, legal, community service, arts, and media, 6.1% healthcare practitioners, 17.0% service, 25.4% sales and office, 8.6% natural resources, construction, and maintenance, 19.2% production, transportation, and material moving (2008-2012 5-year est.).
Income: Per capita income: $23,116 (2008-2012 5-year est.); Median household income: $70,541 (2008-2012 5-year est.); Average household income: $75,658 (2008-2012 5-year est.); Percent of households with income of $100,000 or more: 26.8% (2008-2012 5-year est.); Poverty rate: 9.4% (2008-2012 5-year est.).
Taxes: Total city taxes per capita: $790 (2011); City property taxes per capita: $399 (2011).
Education: Percent of population age 25 and over with: High school diploma (including GED) or higher: 85.8% (2008-2012 5-year est.); Bachelor's degree or higher: 23.8% (2008-2012 5-year est.); Master's degree or higher: 5.7% (2008-2012 5-year est.).
School District(s)
Valley View CUSD 365u (PK-12)
   2011-12 Enrollment: 17,838 . . . . (815) 886-2700
Wilco Area Career Center (11-12)
   2011-12 Enrollment: n/a . . . . (815) 838-6941
Four-year College(s)
Lewis University (Private, Not-for-profit, Roman Catholic)
   Fall 2012 Enrollment: 6,539 . . . . (815) 838-0500
   2012-13 Tuition: In-state $25,770; Out-of-state $25,770
Housing: Homeownership rate: 86.3% (2008-2012 5-year est.); Median home value: $187,300 (2008-2012 5-year est.); Median contract rent: $1,085 per month (2008-2012 5-year est.); Median year structure built: 1997 (2008-2012 5-year est.).
Health Insurance: 70.1% Private; 24.2% Public; 12.7% None. (2008-2012 5-year est.)
Safety: Violent crime rate: 7.5 per 10,000 population; Property crime rate: 207.9 per 10,000 population (2012).

Transportation: Commute to work: 91.4% car, 3.3% public transportation, 1.6% walk, 3.0% work from home (2008-2012 5-year est.); Travel time to work: 15.9% less than 15 minutes, 24.5% 15 to 30 minutes, 27.6% 30 to 45 minutes, 13.2% 45 to 60 minutes, 18.9% 60 minutes or more (2008-2012 5-year est.)
Airports: Lewis University Airport (reliver airport)
Additional Information Contacts
Romeoville Area Chamber of Commerce . . . . (815) 886-2076
   http://www.romeovillechamber.org
Village of Romeoville. . . . . (815) 866-7200
   http://www.romeoville.org

SHOREWOOD (village). Covers a land area of 7.773 square miles and a water area of 0.114 square miles. Located at 41.52° N. Lat; 88.22° W. Long. Elevation is 577 feet.
Population: 6,264 (1990); 7,686 (2000); 15,615 (2010); Density: 2,008.3 persons per square mile (2008-2012 5-year est.); Race: 84.2% White, 7.2% Black/African American, 3.4% Asian, 0.1% American Indian/Alaska Native, 0.0% Native Hawaiian/Other Pacific Islander, 5.1% Some other race, 1.7% Two or more races, 12.5% Hispanic of any race (2008-2012 5-year est.); Average household size: 2.98 (2008-2012 5-year est.); Median age: 38.3 (2008-2012 5-year est.); Males per 100 females: 102.9 (2008-2012 5-year est.); Marriage status: 24.8% never married, 63.3% now married, 4.1% widowed, 7.8% divorced (2008-2012 5-year est.); Foreign born: 7.6% (2008-2012 5-year est.); Ancestry (includes multiple ancestries): 22.6% German, 18.8% Irish, 13.0% Polish, 12.7% Italian, 6.3% English (2008-2012 5-year est.).
Economy: Single-family building permits issued: 92 (2013); Multi-family building permits issued: 0 (2013); Homeowner vacancy rate: 1.8%. Rental vacancy rate: 0.0%. (2008-2012 5-year est.); Employment by occupation: 18.1% management, business, and financial, 7.4% computer, engineering, and science, 12.7% education, legal, community service, arts, and media, 6.4% healthcare practitioners, 9.9% service, 25.9% sales and office, 9.7% natural resources, construction, and maintenance, 9.9% production, transportation, and material moving (2008-2012 5-year est.).
Income: Per capita income: $32,104 (2008-2012 5-year est.); Median household income: $87,263 (2008-2012 5-year est.); Average household income: $94,101 (2008-2012 5-year est.); Percent of households with income of $100,000 or more: 42.8% (2008-2012 5-year est.); Poverty rate: 6.7% (2008-2012 5-year est.)
Education: Percent of population age 25 and over with: High school diploma (including GED) or higher: 91.8% (2008-2012 5-year est.); Bachelor's degree or higher: 38.4% (2008-2012 5-year est.); Master's degree or higher: 12.8% (2008-2012 5-year est.).
School District(s)
Minooka CCSD 201 (PK-08)
   2011-12 Enrollment: 3,963 . . . . (815) 467-6121
Troy CCSD 30c (PK-08)
   2011-12 Enrollment: 4,564 . . . . (815) 577-6760
Vocational/Technical School(s)
Salon Professional Academy (The) (Private, For-profit)
   Fall 2012 Enrollment: 63 . . . . (815) 609-6880
   2012-13 Tuition: $17,000
Housing: Homeownership rate: 91.9% (2008-2012 5-year est.); Median home value: $241,800 (2008-2012 5-year est.); Median contract rent: $1,350 per month (2008-2012 5-year est.); Median year structure built: 1998 (2008-2012 5-year est.).
Health Insurance: 83.5% Private; 16.0% Public; 9.6% None. (2008-2012 5-year est.)
Safety: Violent crime rate: 5.7 per 10,000 population; Property crime rate: 120.9 per 10,000 population (2012).
Transportation: Commute to work: 95.7% car, 1.4% public transportation, 0.0% walk, 2.7% work from home (2008-2012 5-year est.); Travel time to work: 16.6% less than 15 minutes, 31.8% 15 to 30 minutes, 18.9% 30 to 45 minutes, 17.4% 45 to 60 minutes, 15.2% 60 minutes or more (2008-2012 5-year est.)
Additional Information Contacts
Shorewood Area Chamber of Commerce . . . . (815) 725-2900
   http://www.shorewoodchamber.com
Village of Shorewood . . . . (815) 725-2150
   http://www.vil.shorewood.il.us

STEGER (village). Covers a land area of 3.454 square miles and a water area of 0 square miles. Located at 41.47° N. Lat; 87.62° W. Long. Elevation is 712 feet.

History: Steger grew up around the piano factory founded by John V. Steger.

Population: 8,584 (1990); 9,682 (2000); 9,570 (2010); Density: 2,787.9 persons per square mile (2008-2012 5-year est.); Race: 67.9% White, 16.9% Black/African American, 1.3% Asian, 0.5% American Indian/Alaska Native, 0.0% Native Hawaiian/Other Pacific Islander, 13.4% Some other race, 8.1% Two or more races, 17.6% Hispanic of any race (2008-2012 5-year est.); Average household size: 2.42 (2008-2012 5-year est.); Median age: 35.7 (2008-2012 5-year est.); Males per 100 females: 97.2 (2008-2012 5-year est.); Marriage status: 30.0% never married, 49.8% now married, 8.3% widowed, 11.9% divorced (2008-2012 5-year est.); Foreign born: 6.1% (2008-2012 5-year est.); Ancestry (includes multiple ancestries): 17.9% German, 14.4% Italian, 13.1% Irish, 10.1% Polish, 5.4% English (2008-2012 5-year est.).

Economy: Single-family building permits issued: 0 (2013); Multi-family building permits issued: 0 (2013); Homeowner vacancy rate: 5.5%. Rental vacancy rate: 9.3%. (2008-2012 5-year est.); Employment by occupation: 10.0% management, business, and financial, 2.8% computer, engineering, and science, 7.4% education, legal, community service, arts, and media, 3.5% healthcare practitioners, 18.3% service, 26.1% sales and office, 11.4% natural resources, construction, and maintenance, 20.6% production, transportation, and material moving (2008-2012 5-year est.).

Income: Per capita income: $22,152 (2008-2012 5-year est.); Median household income: $43,024 (2008-2012 5-year est.); Average household income: $52,561 (2008-2012 5-year est.); Percent of households with income of $100,000 or more: 13.6% (2008-2012 5-year est.); Poverty rate: 17.6% (2008-2012 5-year est.).

Education: Percent of population age 25 and over with: High school diploma (including GED) or higher: 82.4% (2008-2012 5-year est.); Bachelor's degree or higher: 14.3% (2008-2012 5-year est.); Master's degree or higher: 5.9% (2008-2012 5-year est.).

School District(s)
Steger SD 194 (PK-08)

    2011-12 Enrollment: 1,569 . . . . (708) 755-0022

Housing: Homeownership rate: 57.5% (2008-2012 5-year est.); Median home value: $124,200 (2008-2012 5-year est.); Median contract rent: $709 per month (2008-2012 5-year est.); Median year structure built: 1965 (2008-2012 5-year est.).

Health Insurance: 63.9% Private; 37.3% Public; 13.3% None. (2008-2012 5-year est.)

Safety: Violent crime rate: 14.5 per 10,000 population; Property crime rate: 350.1 per 10,000 population (2012).

Transportation: Commute to work: 89.6% car, 3.6% public transportation, 1.1% walk, 2.0% work from home (2008-2012 5-year est.); Travel time to work: 23.0% less than 15 minutes, 35.2% 15 to 30 minutes, 21.3% 30 to 45 minutes, 7.5% 45 to 60 minutes, 13.0% 60 minutes or more (2008-2012 5-year est.)

Additional Information Contacts

Chicago Southland Convention & Visitors Bureau . . . . (708) 895-8200
    http://www.visitchicagosouthland.com

Village of Steger . . . . (708) 754-3395
    http://www.villageofsteger.com

SYMERTON (village). Covers a land area of 0.046 square miles and a water area of 0 square miles. Located at 41.33° N. Lat; 88.05° W. Long. Elevation is 640 feet.

Population: 110 (1990); 106 (2000); 87 (2010); Density: 1,468.9 persons per square mile (2008-2012 5-year est.); Race: 100.0% White, 0.0% Black/African American, 0.0% Asian, 0.0% American Indian/Alaska Native, 0.0% Native Hawaiian/Other Pacific Islander, 0.0% Some other race, 0.0% Two or more races, 13.4% Hispanic of any race (2008-2012 5-year est.); Average household size: 2.23 (2008-2012 5-year est.); Median age: 41.5 (2008-2012 5-year est.); Males per 100 females: 148.1 (2008-2012 5-year est.); Marriage status: 27.9% never married, 42.6% now married, 9.8% widowed, 19.7% divorced (2008-2012 5-year est.); Foreign born: 0.0% (2008-2012 5-year est.); Ancestry (includes multiple ancestries): 19.4% German, 6.0% Belgian, 6.0% English, 6.0% French, 6.0% French Canadian (2008-2012 5-year est.).

Economy: Single-family building permits issued: 0 (2013); Multi-family building permits issued: 0 (2013); Homeowner vacancy rate: 0.0%. Rental vacancy rate: 0.0%. (2008-2012 5-year est.); Employment by occupation: 4.3% management, business, and financial, 4.3% computer, engineering,

and science, 0.0% education, legal, community service, arts, and media, 0.0% healthcare practitioners, 13.0% service, 13.0% sales and office, 43.5% natural resources, construction, and maintenance, 21.7% production, transportation, and material moving (2008-2012 5-year est.).

Income: Per capita income: $22,336 (2008-2012 5-year est.); Median household income: $50,000 (2008-2012 5-year est.); Average household income: $49,780 (2008-2012 5-year est.); Percent of households with income of $100,000 or more: n/a (2008-2012 5-year est.); Poverty rate: 7.5% (2008-2012 5-year est.).

Education: Percent of population age 25 and over with: High school diploma (including GED) or higher: 76.1% (2008-2012 5-year est.); Bachelor's degree or higher: 4.3% (2008-2012 5-year est.); Master's degree or higher: 4.3% (2008-2012 5-year est.).

Housing: Homeownership rate: 93.3% (2008-2012 5-year est.); Median home value: $150,000 (2008-2012 5-year est.); Median contract rent: n/a per month (2008-2012 5-year est.); Median year structure built: Before 1940 (2008-2012 5-year est.).

Health Insurance: 73.1% Private; 20.9% Public; 14.9% None. (2008-2012 5-year est.)

Transportation: Commute to work: 100.0% car, 0.0% public transportation, 0.0% walk, 0.0% work from home (2008-2012 5-year est.); Travel time to work: 0.0% less than 15 minutes, 17.4% 15 to 30 minutes, 34.8% 30 to 45 minutes, 39.1% 45 to 60 minutes, 8.7% 60 minutes or more (2008-2012 5-year est.)

UNIVERSITY PARK (village). Aka Park Forest South. Covers a land area of 10.837 square miles and a water area of 0.002 square miles. Located at 41.45° N. Lat; 87.71° W. Long. Elevation is 771 feet.

History: Seat of Governors State University.

Population: 6,204 (1990); 6,662 (2000); 7,129 (2010); Density: 649.1 persons per square mile (2008-2012 5-year est.); Race: 6.6% White, 88.8% Black/African American, 0.0% Asian, 0.0% American Indian/Alaska Native, 0.0% Native Hawaiian/Other Pacific Islander, 4.6% Some other race, 3.5% Two or more races, 3.2% Hispanic of any race (2008-2012 5-year est.); Average household size: 2.95 (2008-2012 5-year est.); Median age: 27.3 (2008-2012 5-year est.); Males per 100 females: 86.1 (2008-2012 5-year est.); Marriage status: 46.5% never married, 36.2% now married, 5.5% widowed, 11.8% divorced (2008-2012 5-year est.); Foreign born: 2.3% (2008-2012 5-year est.); Ancestry (includes multiple ancestries): 2.2% Italian, 2.1% African, 1.3% Irish, 1.3% German, 1.2% Jamaican (2008-2012 5-year est.).

Economy: Single-family building permits issued: 0 (2013); Multi-family building permits issued: 0 (2013); Homeowner vacancy rate: 7.0%. Rental vacancy rate: 9.4%. (2008-2012 5-year est.); Employment by occupation: 6.3% management, business, and financial, 1.5% computer, engineering, and science, 13.0% education, legal, community service, arts, and media, 3.8% healthcare practitioners, 23.6% service, 24.4% sales and office, 7.3% natural resources, construction, and maintenance, 20.2% production, transportation, and material moving (2008-2012 5-year est.).

Income: Per capita income: $19,838 (2008-2012 5-year est.); Median household income: $48,173 (2008-2012 5-year est.); Average household income: $56,341 (2008-2012 5-year est.); Percent of households with income of $100,000 or more: 15.0% (2008-2012 5-year est.); Poverty rate: 21.0% (2008-2012 5-year est.).

Education: Percent of population age 25 and over with: High school diploma (including GED) or higher: 95.8% (2008-2012 5-year est.); Bachelor's degree or higher: 23.8% (2008-2012 5-year est.); Master's degree or higher: 7.0% (2008-2012 5-year est.).

School District(s)
Crete Monee CUSD 201u (PK-12)

    2011-12 Enrollment: 5,136 . . . . (708) 367-8300

Four-year College(s)
Governors State University (Public)

    Fall 2012 Enrollment: 5,601 . . . . (708) 534-5000

Housing: Homeownership rate: 55.3% (2008-2012 5-year est.); Median home value: $133,400 (2008-2012 5-year est.); Median contract rent: $776 per month (2008-2012 5-year est.); Median year structure built: 1975 (2008-2012 5-year est.).

Health Insurance: 56.9% Private; 34.2% Public; 14.6% None. (2008-2012 5-year est.)

Transportation: Commute to work: 76.8% car, 12.9% public transportation, 4.3% walk, 3.3% work from home (2008-2012 5-year est.); Travel time to work: 13.6% less than 15 minutes, 27.4% 15 to 30 minutes, 19.5% 30 to 45 minutes, 12.4% 45 to 60 minutes, 27.1% 60 minutes or more (2008-2012 5-year est.)

Additional Information Contacts
Matteson Area Chamber of Commerce . . . . (708) 747-6000
  http://www.macclink.com
Village of University Park . . . . (708) 534-6451
  http://www.university-park-il.com

WILLOWBROOK (CDP).

WILLOWBROOK (CDP). Covers a land area of 3.335 square miles and a water area of 0.016 square miles. Located at 41.45° N. Lat; 87.54° W. Long. Elevation is 715 feet.

Population: 1,808 (1990); 2,130 (2000); 2,076 (2010); Density: 631.8 persons per square mile (2008-2012 5-year est.); Race: 63.8% White, 33.3% Black/African American, 1.2% Asian, 0.4% American Indian/Alaska Native, 0.0% Native Hawaiian/Other Pacific Islander, 1.3% Some other race, 1.2% Two or more races, 1.6% Hispanic of any race (2008-2012 5-year est.); Average household size: 2.58 (2008-2012 5-year est.); Median age: 51.5 (2008-2012 5-year est.); Males per 100 females: 89.8 (2008-2012 5-year est.); Marriage status: 27.6% never married, 56.3% now married, 8.4% widowed, 7.8% divorced (2008-2012 5-year est.); Foreign born: 4.8% (2008-2012 5-year est.); Ancestry (includes multiple ancestries): 13.5% German, 9.9% Dutch, 8.8% Polish, 5.8% Irish, 5.6% English (2008-2012 5-year est.).

Economy: Homeowner vacancy rate: 0.0%. Rental vacancy rate: 0.0%. (2008-2012 5-year est.); Employment by occupation: 17.8% management, business, and financial, 10.2% computer, engineering, and science, 9.4% education, legal, community service, arts, and media, 4.1% healthcare practitioners, 10.5% service, 35.2% sales and office, 8.9% natural resources, construction, and maintenance, 3.9% production, transportation, and material moving (2008-2012 5-year est.).

Income: Per capita income: $41,471 (2008-2012 5-year est.); Median household income: $95,938 (2008-2012 5-year est.); Average household income: $104,687 (2008-2012 5-year est.); Percent of households with income of $100,000 or more: 45.0% (2008-2012 5-year est.); Poverty rate: 4.0% (2008-2012 5-year est.).

Education: Percent of population age 25 and over with: High school diploma (including GED) or higher: 93.9% (2008-2012 5-year est.); Bachelor's degree or higher: 36.7% (2008-2012 5-year est.); Master's degree or higher: 8.3% (2008-2012 5-year est.).

School District(s)
CCSD 180 (PK-08)
  2011-12 Enrollment: 666 . . . . (630) 734-6600
Gower SD 62 (PK-08)
  2011-12 Enrollment: 852 . . . . (630) 986-5383
Maercker SD 60 (PK-08)
  2011-12 Enrollment: 1,341 . . . . (630) 515-4840

Housing: Homeownership rate: 96.7% (2008-2012 5-year est.); Median home value: $283,300 (2008-2012 5-year est.); Median contract rent: n/a per month (2008-2012 5-year est.); Median year structure built: 1983 (2008-2012 5-year est.).

Health Insurance: 76.2% Private; 21.9% Public; 14.9% None. (2008-2012 5-year est.)

Transportation: Commute to work: 82.6% car, 6.8% public transportation, 0.0% walk, 10.6% work from home (2008-2012 5-year est.); Travel time to work: 5.4% less than 15 minutes, 37.8% 15 to 30 minutes, 20.9% 30 to 45 minutes, 10.7% 45 to 60 minutes, 25.2% 60 minutes or more (2008-2012 5-year est.)

WILLMINGTON (city).

WILMINGTON (city). Covers a land area of 9.398 square miles and a water area of 0.650 square miles. Located at 41.32° N. Lat; 88.14° W. Long. Elevation is 545 feet.

History: Wilmington was laid out in the 1840's by Thomas Fox, who called it Winchester. In 1854 it was incorporated as a village with the name of Wilmington. The village grew around grist, saw, and carding mills operated by Fox.

Population: 4,743 (1990); 5,134 (2000); 5,724 (2010); Density: 629.7 persons per square mile (2008-2012 5-year est.); Race: 95.4% White, 1.7% Black/African American, 0.0% Asian, 0.0% American Indian/Alaska Native, 0.0% Native Hawaiian/Other Pacific Islander, 2.9% Some other race, 2.2% Two or more races, 5.8% Hispanic of any race (2008-2012 5-year est.); Average household size: 2.46 (2008-2012 5-year est.); Median age: 38.9 (2008-2012 5-year est.); Males per 100 females: 109.7 (2008-2012 5-year est.); Marriage status: 31.7% never married, 47.1% now married, 8.1% widowed, 13.0% divorced (2008-2012 5-year est.); Foreign born: 2.5% (2008-2012 5-year est.); Ancestry (includes multiple ancestries): 27.6% German, 27.0% Irish, 13.6% English, 10.2% Polish, 7.8% Italian (2008-2012 5-year est.).

Economy: Single-family building permits issued: 3 (2013); Multi-family building permits issued: 0 (2013); Homeowner vacancy rate: 0.0%. Rental vacancy rate: 4.0%. (2008-2012 5-year est.); Employment by occupation: 12.0% management, business, and financial, 1.7% computer, engineering, and science, 6.5% education, legal, community service, arts, and media, 3.3% healthcare practitioners, 17.8% service, 21.7% sales and office, 13.0% natural resources, construction, and maintenance, 24.0% production, transportation, and material moving (2008-2012 5-year est.).

Income: Per capita income: $27,067 (2008-2012 5-year est.); Median household income: $58,488 (2008-2012 5-year est.); Average household income: $66,409 (2008-2012 5-year est.); Percent of households with income of $100,000 or more: 21.2% (2008-2012 5-year est.); Poverty rate: 8.5% (2008-2012 5-year est.).

Education: Percent of population age 25 and over with: High school diploma (including GED) or higher: 89.5% (2008-2012 5-year est.); Bachelor's degree or higher: 14.1% (2008-2012 5-year est.); Master's degree or higher: 4.9% (2008-2012 5-year est.).

School District(s)
S Will County Coop for Spec Ed (KG-12)
  2011-12 Enrollment: n/a . . . . (815) 741-7777
Wilmington CUSD 209u (PK-12)
  2011-12 Enrollment: 1,474 . . . . (815) 926-1751

Housing: Homeownership rate: 72.2% (2008-2012 5-year est.); Median home value: $173,600 (2008-2012 5-year est.); Median contract rent: $445 per month (2008-2012 5-year est.); Median year structure built: 1971 (2008-2012 5-year est.).

Health Insurance: 75.6% Private; 28.4% Public; 7.6% None. (2008-2012 5-year est.)

Safety: Violent crime rate: 34.7 per 10,000 population; Property crime rate: 211.8 per 10,000 population (2012).

Transportation: Commute to work: 94.4% car, 1.0% public transportation, 1.7% walk, 1.4% work from home (2008-2012 5-year est.); Travel time to work: 28.8% less than 15 minutes, 19.4% 15 to 30 minutes, 27.1% 30 to 45 minutes, 4.1% 45 to 60 minutes, 20.6% 60 minutes or more (2008-2012 5-year est.)

Additional Information Contacts
City of Wilmington . . . . (815) 476-2175
  http://www.wilmington-il.com
Wilmington Chamber of Commerce . . . . (815) 476-5991
  http://wilmingtonilchamber.org

Williamson County

Located in southern Illinois; drained by the Big Muddy and South Fork of the Saline River; includes Crab Orchard Lake. Covers a land area of 420.149 square miles, a water area of 24.203 square miles, and is located in the Central Time Zone at 37.73° N. Lat., 88.93° W. Long. The county was founded in 1839. County seat is Marion.

Williamson County is part of the Carbondale-Marion, IL Metropolitan Statistical Area. The entire metro area includes: Jackson County, IL; Williamson County, IL

Population: 57,733 (1990); 61,296 (2000); 66,357 (2010); Race: 93.0% White, 3.9% Black/African American, 0.7% Asian, 0.4% American Indian/Alaska Native, 0.0% Native Hawaiian/Other Pacific Islander, 2.0% Some other race, 1.6% Two or more races, 2.0% Hispanic of any race (2008-2012 5-year est.); Density: 158.8 persons per square mile (2008-2012 5-year est.); Average household size: 2.40 (2008-2012 5-year est.); Median age: 40.4 (2008-2012 5-year est.); Males per 100 females: 98.0 (2008-2012 5-year est.).

Religion: Six largest groups: 23.2% Baptist, 7.2% Catholicism, 4.9% Methodist/Pietist, 3.8% Non-denominational Protestant, 1.2% Pentecostal, 1.1% Holiness (2010)

Economy: Unemployment rate: 6.7% (April 2014); Total civilian labor force: 34,211 (April 2014); Leading industries: 27.9% health care and social assistance; 16.7% retail trade; 11.6% accommodation & food services (2012); Farms: 702 totaling 103,421 acres (2012); Companies that employ 500 or more persons: 4 (2012); Companies that employ 100 to 499 persons: 27 (2012); Companies that employ less than 100 persons: 1,579 (2012); Black-owned businesses: n/a (2007); Hispanic-owned businesses: 56 (2007); Asian-owned businesses: n/a (2007); Women-owned businesses: 1,632 (2007); Single-family building permits issued: 85 (2013); Multi-family building permits issued: 73 (2013).

Income: Per capita income: $22,840 (2008-2012 5-year est.); Median household income: $41,596 (2008-2012 5-year est.); Average household income: $54,527 (2008-2012 5-year est.); Percent of households with income of $100,000 or more: 12.9% (2008-2012 5-year est.); Poverty rate: 16.5% (2008-2012 5-year est.); Bankruptcy rate: 4.89% (2013).

Taxes: Total county taxes per capita: $132 (2011); County property taxes per capita: $126 (2011).

Education: Percent of population age 25 and over with: High school diploma (including GED) or higher: 88.4% (2008-2012 5-year est.); Bachelor's degree or higher: 21.7% (2008-2012 5-year est.); Master's degree or higher: 8.4% (2008-2012 5-year est.).

Housing: Homeownership rate: 71.3% (2008-2012 5-year est.); Median home value: $90,300 (2008-2012 5-year est.); Median contract rent: $450 per month (2008-2012 5-year est.); Median year structure built: 1974 (2008-2012 5-year est.).

Health: Birth rate: 108.3 per 10,000 population (2013); Death rate: 111.0 per 10,000 population (2013); Age-adjusted cancer mortality rate: 203.8 deaths per 100,000 population (2011); Number of physicians: 22.3 per 10,000 population (2011); Hospital beds: 46.9 per 10,000 population (2010); Hospital admissions: 2,285.1 per 10,000 population (2010).

Elections: 2012 Presidential election results: 36.5% Obama, 61.5% Romney

National and State Parks: Crab Orchard National Wildlife Refuge

Additional Information Contacts

Williamson County Government . . . . (618) 997-1301
   http://www.williamsoncountycourthouse.com

Williamson County Communities

BUSH (village). Covers a land area of 0.455 square miles and a water area of 0.006 square miles. Located at 37.84° N. Lat; 89.13° W. Long. Elevation is 410 feet.

Population: 351 (1990); 257 (2000); 275 (2010); Density: 585.0 persons per square mile (2008-2012 5-year est.); Race: 98.5% White, 0.0% Black/African American, 0.4% Asian, 0.0% American Indian/Alaska Native, 0.0% Native Hawaiian/Other Pacific Islander, 1.1% Some other race, 1.1% Two or more races, 0.0% Hispanic of any race (2008-2012 5-year est.); Average household size: 2.61 (2008-2012 5-year est.); Median age: 46.0 (2008-2012 5-year est.); Males per 100 females: 76.2 (2008-2012 5-year est.); Marriage status: 27.5% never married, 46.3% now married, 5.7% widowed, 20.5% divorced (2008-2012 5-year est.); Foreign born: 0.4% (2008-2012 5-year est.); Ancestry (includes multiple ancestries): 27.4% Irish, 16.9% English, 11.3% American, 9.8% German, 9.0% Welsh (2008-2012 5-year est.).

Economy: Homeowner vacancy rate: 4.2%. Rental vacancy rate: 0.0%. (2008-2012 5-year est.); Employment by occupation: 1.1% management, business, and financial, 0.0% computer, engineering, and science, 8.0% education, legal, community service, arts, and media, 0.0% healthcare practitioners, 18.4% service, 42.5% sales and office, 11.5% natural resources, construction, and maintenance, 18.4% production, transportation, and material moving (2008-2012 5-year est.).

Income: Per capita income: $14,386 (2008-2012 5-year est.); Median household income: $29,167 (2008-2012 5-year est.); Average household income: $35,250 (2008-2012 5-year est.); Percent of households with income of $100,000 or more: 1.0% (2008-2012 5-year est.); Poverty rate: 25.8% (2008-2012 5-year est.).

Education: Percent of population age 25 and over with: High school diploma (including GED) or higher: 75.2% (2008-2012 5-year est.); Bachelor's degree or higher: 6.4% (2008-2012 5-year est.); Master's degree or higher: 1.0% (2008-2012 5-year est.).

Housing: Homeownership rate: 90.2% (2008-2012 5-year est.); Median home value: $30,800 (2008-2012 5-year est.); Median contract rent: $344 per month (2008-2012 5-year est.); Median year structure built: 1948 (2008-2012 5-year est.).

Health Insurance: 59.0% Private; 46.6% Public; 13.9% None. (2008-2012 5-year est.)

Transportation: Commute to work: 98.8% car, 0.0% public transportation, 0.0% walk, 1.2% work from home (2008-2012 5-year est.); Travel time to work: 16.5% less than 15 minutes, 51.8% 15 to 30 minutes, 25.9% 30 to 45 minutes, 3.5% 45 to 60 minutes, 2.4% 60 minutes or more (2008-2012 5-year est.)

CAMBRIA (village). Covers a land area of 1.363 square miles and a water area of 0.043 square miles. Located at 37.78° N. Lat; 89.12° W. Long. Elevation is 423 feet.

Population: 1,230 (1990); 1,330 (2000); 1,228 (2010); Density: 957.4 persons per square mile (2008-2012 5-year est.); Race: 95.5% White, 0.9% Black/African American, 0.9% Asian, 0.0% American Indian/Alaska Native, 0.0% Native Hawaiian/Other Pacific Islander, 2.7% Some other race, 2.7% Two or more races, 1.5% Hispanic of any race (2008-2012 5-year est.); Average household size: 2.56 (2008-2012 5-year est.); Median age: 37.9 (2008-2012 5-year est.); Males per 100 females: 106.2 (2008-2012 5-year est.); Marriage status: 29.0% never married, 48.9% now married, 8.2% widowed, 13.9% divorced (2008-2012 5-year est.); Foreign born: 1.3% (2008-2012 5-year est.); Ancestry (includes multiple ancestries): 24.0% Irish, 23.7% English, 19.0% German, 4.8% French, 4.1% Welsh (2008-2012 5-year est.).

Economy: Single-family building permits issued: 3 (2013); Multi-family building permits issued: 0 (2013); Homeowner vacancy rate: 0.0%. Rental vacancy rate: 7.2%. (2008-2012 5-year est.); Employment by occupation: 7.0% management, business, and financial, 0.9% computer, engineering, and science, 11.9% education, legal, community service, arts, and media, 3.8% healthcare practitioners, 26.4% service, 18.1% sales and office, 18.1% natural resources, construction, and maintenance, 13.8% production, transportation, and material moving (2008-2012 5-year est.).

Income: Per capita income: $13,371 (2008-2012 5-year est.); Median household income: $22,361 (2008-2012 5-year est.); Average household income: $32,387 (2008-2012 5-year est.); Percent of households with income of $100,000 or more: 2.8% (2008-2012 5-year est.); Poverty rate: 34.4% (2008-2012 5-year est.).

Education: Percent of population age 25 and over with: High school diploma (including GED) or higher: 81.3% (2008-2012 5-year est.); Bachelor's degree or higher: 13.3% (2008-2012 5-year est.); Master's degree or higher: 5.5% (2008-2012 5-year est.).

Housing: Homeownership rate: 64.5% (2008-2012 5-year est.); Median home value: $56,300 (2008-2012 5-year est.); Median contract rent: $455 per month (2008-2012 5-year est.); Median year structure built: 1975 (2008-2012 5-year est.).

Health Insurance: 42.0% Private; 45.7% Public; 24.0% None. (2008-2012 5-year est.)

Transportation: Commute to work: 97.7% car, 0.0% public transportation, 0.6% walk, 1.7% work from home (2008-2012 5-year est.); Travel time to work: 33.1% less than 15 minutes, 60.5% 15 to 30 minutes, 6.5% 30 to 45 minutes, 0.0% 45 to 60 minutes, 0.0% 60 minutes or more (2008-2012 5-year est.)

CARTERVILLE (city). Covers a land area of 5.190 square miles and a water area of 0.092 square miles. Located at 37.76° N. Lat; 89.08° W. Long. Elevation is 449 feet.

History: Incorporated 1892.

Population: 3,630 (1990); 4,616 (2000); 5,496 (2010); Density: 1,056.9 persons per square mile (2008-2012 5-year est.); Race: 95.0% White, 1.9% Black/African American, 0.3% Asian, 0.0% American Indian/Alaska Native, 0.0% Native Hawaiian/Other Pacific Islander, 2.8% Some other race, 2.6% Two or more races, 2.2% Hispanic of any race (2008-2012 5-year est.); Average household size: 2.42 (2008-2012 5-year est.); Median age: 37.2 (2008-2012 5-year est.); Males per 100 females: 89.7 (2008-2012 5-year est.); Marriage status: 24.0% never married, 52.4% now married, 4.8% widowed, 18.8% divorced (2008-2012 5-year est.); Foreign born: 0.3% (2008-2012 5-year est.); Ancestry (includes multiple ancestries): 23.5% German, 16.5% English, 12.7% Irish, 8.2% American, 7.3% Italian (2008-2012 5-year est.).

Economy: Single-family building permits issued: 20 (2013); Multi-family building permits issued: 38 (2013); Homeowner vacancy rate: 0.0%. Rental vacancy rate: 11.8%. (2008-2012 5-year est.); Employment by occupation: 15.7% management, business, and financial, 2.4% computer, engineering, and science, 19.8% education, legal, community service, arts, and media, 8.7% healthcare practitioners, 13.5% service, 29.7% sales and office, 5.4% natural resources, construction, and maintenance, 4.7% production, transportation, and material moving (2008-2012 5-year est.).

Income: Per capita income: $29,667 (2008-2012 5-year est.); Median household income: $46,282 (2008-2012 5-year est.); Average household income: $69,160 (2008-2012 5-year est.); Percent of households with income of $100,000 or more: 21.3% (2008-2012 5-year est.); Poverty rate: 17.7% (2008-2012 5-year est.).

Education: Percent of population age 25 and over with: High school diploma (including GED) or higher: 94.1% (2008-2012 5-year est.);

Bachelor's degree or higher: 38.1% (2008-2012 5-year est.); Master's degree or higher: 17.9% (2008-2012 5-year est.).

School District(s)

Carterville CUSD 5 (KG-12)

  2011-12 Enrollment: 1,909 . . . . (618) 985-4826

Two-year College(s)

John A Logan College (Public)

  Fall 2012 Enrollment: 7,437 . . . . (618) 985-3741

  2012-13 Tuition: In-state $6,480; Out-of-state $8,340

Housing: Homeownership rate: 69.5% (2008-2012 5-year est.); Median home value: $112,400 (2008-2012 5-year est.); Median contract rent: $472 per month (2008-2012 5-year est.); Median year structure built: 1977 (2008-2012 5-year est.).

Health Insurance: 71.3% Private; 34.9% Public; 8.0% None. (2008-2012 5-year est.)

Transportation: Commute to work: 94.3% car, 0.2% public transportation, 0.0% walk, 3.8% work from home (2008-2012 5-year est.); Travel time to work: 23.6% less than 15 minutes, 62.1% 15 to 30 minutes, 7.9% 30 to 45 minutes, 0.4% 45 to 60 minutes, 6.0% 60 minutes or more (2008-2012 5-year est.)

Additional Information Contacts

Carterville Chamber of Commerce . . . . (618) 985-6942

  http://www.cartervillechamber.com

COLP (village). Covers a land area of 0.139 square miles and a water area of <.001 square miles. Located at 37.81° N. Lat; 89.08° W. Long. Elevation is 400 feet.

Population: 235 (1990); 224 (2000); 225 (2010); Density: 1,694.6 persons per square mile (2008-2012 5-year est.); Race: 57.2% White, 42.8% Black/African American, 0.0% Asian, 0.0% American Indian/Alaska Native, 0.0% Native Hawaiian/Other Pacific Islander, 0.0% Some other race, 0.0% Two or more races, 0.8% Hispanic of any race (2008-2012 5-year est.); Average household size: 3.15 (2008-2012 5-year est.); Median age: 25.3 (2008-2012 5-year est.); Males per 100 females: 90.3 (2008-2012 5-year est.); Marriage status: 32.9% never married, 48.3% now married, 6.7% widowed, 12.1% divorced (2008-2012 5-year est.); Foreign born: 0.0% (2008-2012 5-year est.); Ancestry (includes multiple ancestries): 15.3% Irish, 13.6% American, 13.6% German, 8.5% English, 8.1% Italian (2008-2012 5-year est.).

Economy: Homeowner vacancy rate: 7.0%. Rental vacancy rate: 0.0%. (2008-2012 5-year est.); Employment by occupation: 3.0% management, business, and financial, 0.0% computer, engineering, and science, 10.6% education, legal, community service, arts, and media, 0.0% healthcare practitioners, 22.7% service, 24.2% sales and office, 15.2% natural resources, construction, and maintenance, 24.2% production, transportation, and material moving (2008-2012 5-year est.).

Income: Per capita income: $10,120 (2008-2012 5-year est.); Median household income: $25,625 (2008-2012 5-year est.); Average household income: $28,227 (2008-2012 5-year est.); Percent of households with income of $100,000 or more: 2.7% (2008-2012 5-year est.); Poverty rate: 45.3% (2008-2012 5-year est.).

Education: Percent of population age 25 and over with: High school diploma (including GED) or higher: 84.3% (2008-2012 5-year est.); Bachelor's degree or higher: 10.7% (2008-2012 5-year est.); Master's degree or higher: 1.7% (2008-2012 5-year est.).

Housing: Homeownership rate: 70.7% (2008-2012 5-year est.); Median home value: $47,900 (2008-2012 5-year est.); Median contract rent: $375 per month (2008-2012 5-year est.); Median year structure built: 1975 (2008-2012 5-year est.).

Health Insurance: 29.2% Private; 76.7% Public; 12.7% None. (2008-2012 5-year est.)

Transportation: Commute to work: 96.7% car, 0.0% public transportation, 0.0% walk, 0.0% work from home (2008-2012 5-year est.); Travel time to work: 36.7% less than 15 minutes, 53.3% 15 to 30 minutes, 10.0% 30 to 45 minutes, 0.0% 45 to 60 minutes, 0.0% 60 minutes or more (2008-2012 5-year est.)

CRAB ORCHARD (CDP). Covers a land area of 1.395 square miles and a water area of 0.035 square miles. Located at 37.72° N. Lat; 88.81° W. Long. Elevation is 482 feet.

Population: n/a (1990); n/a (2000); 333 (2010); Density: 209.2 persons per square mile (2008-2012 5-year est.); Race: 95.5% White, 0.0% Black/African American, 0.0% Asian, 4.5% American Indian/Alaska Native, 0.0% Native Hawaiian/Other Pacific Islander, 0.0% Some other race, 0.0% Two or more races, 0.0% Hispanic of any race (2008-2012 5-year est.);

Average household size: 1.74 (2008-2012 5-year est.); Median age: 56.4 (2008-2012 5-year est.); Males per 100 females: 113.1 (2008-2012 5-year est.); Marriage status: 12.0% never married, 62.7% now married, 4.0% widowed, 21.4% divorced (2008-2012 5-year est.); Foreign born: 2.1% (2008-2012 5-year est.); Ancestry (includes multiple ancestries): 21.6% American, 18.5% English, 15.8% Irish, 11.6% German, 6.8% Italian (2008-2012 5-year est.).

Economy: Homeowner vacancy rate: 0.0%. Rental vacancy rate: 0.0%. (2008-2012 5-year est.); Employment by occupation: 15.2% management, business, and financial, 0.0% computer, engineering, and science, 8.1% education, legal, community service, arts, and media, 10.1% healthcare practitioners, 0.0% service, 35.4% sales and office, 12.1% natural resources, construction, and maintenance, 19.2% production, transportation, and material moving (2008-2012 5-year est.).

Income: Per capita income: $27,091 (2008-2012 5-year est.); Median household income: $41,196 (2008-2012 5-year est.); Average household income: $46,328 (2008-2012 5-year est.); Percent of households with income of $100,000 or more: 10.7% (2008-2012 5-year est.); Poverty rate: 0.0% (2008-2012 5-year est.).

Education: Percent of population age 25 and over with: High school diploma (including GED) or higher: 88.2% (2008-2012 5-year est.); Bachelor's degree or higher: 7.4% (2008-2012 5-year est.); Master's degree or higher: 0.0% (2008-2012 5-year est.).

Housing: Homeownership rate: 91.7% (2008-2012 5-year est.); Median home value: $107,600 (2008-2012 5-year est.); Median contract rent: n/a per month (2008-2012 5-year est.); Median year structure built: 1974 (2008-2012 5-year est.).

Health Insurance: 68.8% Private; 43.2% Public; 7.9% None. (2008-2012 5-year est.)

Transportation: Commute to work: 89.9% car, 0.0% public transportation, 4.0% walk, 6.1% work from home (2008-2012 5-year est.); Travel time to work: 16.1% less than 15 minutes, 78.5% 15 to 30 minutes, 0.0% 30 to 45 minutes, 0.0% 45 to 60 minutes, 5.4% 60 minutes or more (2008-2012 5-year est.)

CRAINVILLE (village). Covers a land area of 1.593 square miles and a water area of 0.007 square miles. Located at 37.75° N. Lat; 89.06° W. Long. Elevation is 469 feet.

Population: 1,019 (1990); 992 (2000); 1,254 (2010); Density: 772.3 persons per square mile (2008-2012 5-year est.); Race: 96.9% White, 3.6% Black/African American, 0.0% Asian, 0.0% American Indian/Alaska Native, 0.0% Native Hawaiian/Other Pacific Islander, 0.5% Some other race, 0.5% Two or more races, 1.2% Hispanic of any race (2008-2012 5-year est.); Average household size: 2.24 (2008-2012 5-year est.); Median age: 35.0 (2008-2012 5-year est.); Males per 100 females: 83.3 (2008-2012 5-year est.); Marriage status: 29.5% never married, 55.3% now married, 7.1% widowed, 8.1% divorced (2008-2012 5-year est.); Foreign born: 1.7% (2008-2012 5-year est.); Ancestry (includes multiple ancestries): 20.5% German, 16.5% English, 15.0% Irish, 5.9% Dutch, 5.1% Italian (2008-2012 5-year est.).

Economy: Single-family building permits issued: 10 (2013); Multi-family building permits issued: 0 (2013); Homeowner vacancy rate: 0.0%. Rental vacancy rate: 0.0%. (2008-2012 5-year est.); Employment by occupation: 15.0% management, business, and financial, 3.6% computer, engineering, and science, 15.0% education, legal, community service, arts, and media, 2.5% healthcare practitioners, 8.8% service, 34.6% sales and office, 8.0% natural resources, construction, and maintenance, 12.4% production, transportation, and material moving (2008-2012 5-year est.).

Income: Per capita income: $25,104 (2008-2012 5-year est.); Median household income: $46,597 (2008-2012 5-year est.); Average household income: $54,390 (2008-2012 5-year est.); Percent of households with income of $100,000 or more: 12.6% (2008-2012 5-year est.); Poverty rate: 11.8% (2008-2012 5-year est.).

Education: Percent of population age 25 and over with: High school diploma (including GED) or higher: 92.5% (2008-2012 5-year est.); Bachelor's degree or higher: 33.3% (2008-2012 5-year est.); Master's degree or higher: 12.6% (2008-2012 5-year est.).

Housing: Homeownership rate: 66.8% (2008-2012 5-year est.); Median home value: $119,300 (2008-2012 5-year est.); Median contract rent: $511 per month (2008-2012 5-year est.); Median year structure built: 1979 (2008-2012 5-year est.).

Health Insurance: 81.1% Private; 29.3% Public; 7.6% None. (2008-2012 5-year est.)

Transportation: Commute to work: 95.5% car, 0.7% public transportation, 0.3% walk, 3.0% work from home (2008-2012 5-year est.); Travel time to

work: 39.9% less than 15 minutes, 44.0% 15 to 30 minutes, 7.5% 30 to 45 minutes, 2.8% 45 to 60 minutes, 5.9% 60 minutes or more (2008-2012 5-year est.)

CREAL SPRINGS (city). Covers a land area of 0.992 square miles and a water area of 0.006 square miles. Located at 37.62° N. Lat; 88.84° W. Long. Elevation is 509 feet.

Population: 791 (1990); 702 (2000); 543 (2010); Density: 697.5 persons per square mile (2008-2012 5-year est.); Race: 93.8% White, 0.0% Black/African American, 1.4% Asian, 1.0% American Indian/Alaska Native, 0.0% Native Hawaiian/Other Pacific Islander, 3.8% Some other race, 3.8% Two or more races, 4.2% Hispanic of any race (2008-2012 5-year est.); Average household size: 2.22 (2008-2012 5-year est.); Median age: 44.0 (2008-2012 5-year est.); Males per 100 females: 96.0 (2008-2012 5-year est.); Marriage status: 24.2% never married, 50.4% now married, 7.7% widowed, 17.7% divorced (2008-2012 5-year est.); Foreign born: 3.9% (2008-2012 5-year est.); Ancestry (includes multiple ancestries): 23.6% German, 14.9% English, 12.4% Italian, 9.1% Irish, 5.1% American (2008-2012 5-year est.).
Economy: Homeowner vacancy rate: 0.0%. Rental vacancy rate: 17.7%. (2008-2012 5-year est.); Employment by occupation: 2.8% management, business, and financial, 2.1% computer, engineering, and science, 2.4% education, legal, community service, arts, and media, 2.8% healthcare practitioners, 25.2% service, 12.2% sales and office, 19.9% natural resources, construction, and maintenance, 32.5% production, transportation, and material moving (2008-2012 5-year est.).
Income: Per capita income: $15,502 (2008-2012 5-year est.); Median household income: $29,091 (2008-2012 5-year est.); Average household income: $34,999 (2008-2012 5-year est.); Percent of households with income of $100,000 or more: 4.0% (2008-2012 5-year est.); Poverty rate: 15.7% (2008-2012 5-year est.).
Education: Percent of population age 25 and over with: High school diploma (including GED) or higher: 70.6% (2008-2012 5-year est.); Bachelor's degree or higher: 2.9% (2008-2012 5-year est.); Master's degree or higher: 1.7% (2008-2012 5-year est.).

School District(s)
Marion CUSD 2 (PK-12)
   2011-12 Enrollment: 4,006 . . . . (618) 993-2321
Housing: Homeownership rate: 83.1% (2008-2012 5-year est.); Median home value: $41,100 (2008-2012 5-year est.); Median contract rent: $313 per month (2008-2012 5-year est.); Median year structure built: 1965 (2008-2012 5-year est.).
Health Insurance: 48.1% Private; 46.5% Public; 17.7% None. (2008-2012 5-year est.)
Transportation: Commute to work: 98.3% car, 0.0% public transportation, 1.0% walk, 0.7% work from home (2008-2012 5-year est.); Travel time to work: 10.2% less than 15 minutes, 55.3% 15 to 30 minutes, 20.8% 30 to 45 minutes, 3.5% 45 to 60 minutes, 10.2% 60 minutes or more (2008-2012 5-year est.)

ENERGY (village). Covers a land area of 1.176 square miles and a water area of 0.018 square miles. Located at 37.78° N. Lat; 89.02° W. Long. Elevation is 459 feet.

Population: 1,106 (1990); 1,175 (2000); 1,146 (2010); Density: 664.0 persons per square mile (2008-2012 5-year est.); Race: 95.0% White, 2.0% Black/African American, 1.9% Asian, 0.0% American Indian/Alaska Native, 0.0% Native Hawaiian/Other Pacific Islander, 1.1% Some other race, 1.0% Two or more races, 0.0% Hispanic of any race (2008-2012 5-year est.); Average household size: 1.88 (2008-2012 5-year est.); Median age: 50.2 (2008-2012 5-year est.); Males per 100 females: 90.0 (2008-2012 5-year est.); Marriage status: 25.3% never married, 44.9% now married, 15.5% widowed, 14.3% divorced (2008-2012 5-year est.); Foreign born: 1.8% (2008-2012 5-year est.); Ancestry (includes multiple ancestries): 14.7% Irish, 13.8% English, 13.2% German, 10.6% Italian, 4.5% American (2008-2012 5-year est.).
Economy: Single-family building permits issued: 3 (2013); Multi-family building permits issued: 0 (2013); Homeowner vacancy rate: 0.0%. Rental vacancy rate: 12.9%. (2008-2012 5-year est.); Employment by occupation: 13.9% management, business, and financial, 0.0% computer, engineering, and science, 7.9% education, legal, community service, arts, and media, 4.0% healthcare practitioners, 24.6% service, 34.6% sales and office, 4.2% natural resources, construction, and maintenance, 10.8% production, transportation, and material moving (2008-2012 5-year est.).
Income: Per capita income: $21,771 (2008-2012 5-year est.); Median household income: $31,000 (2008-2012 5-year est.); Average household

income: $40,709 (2008-2012 5-year est.); Percent of households with income of $100,000 or more: 5.2% (2008-2012 5-year est.); Poverty rate: 19.8% (2008-2012 5-year est.).
Education: Percent of population age 25 and over with: High school diploma (including GED) or higher: 89.5% (2008-2012 5-year est.); Bachelor's degree or higher: 22.7% (2008-2012 5-year est.); Master's degree or higher: 4.6% (2008-2012 5-year est.).
Housing: Homeownership rate: 44.5% (2008-2012 5-year est.); Median home value: $104,300 (2008-2012 5-year est.); Median contract rent: $338 per month (2008-2012 5-year est.); Median year structure built: 1979 (2008-2012 5-year est.).
Health Insurance: 69.2% Private; 41.5% Public; 7.9% None. (2008-2012 5-year est.)
Transportation: Commute to work: 95.4% car, 2.9% public transportation, 0.0% walk, 0.9% work from home (2008-2012 5-year est.); Travel time to work: 51.6% less than 15 minutes, 30.6% 15 to 30 minutes, 15.2% 30 to 45 minutes, 2.6% 45 to 60 minutes, 0.0% 60 minutes or more (2008-2012 5-year est.)

FREEMAN SPUR (village). Covers a land area of 0.399 square miles and a water area of 0.003 square miles. Located at 37.86° N. Lat; 89.00° W. Long. Elevation is 397 feet.

Population: 290 (1990); 273 (2000); 287 (2010); Density: 771.1 persons per square mile (2008-2012 5-year est.); Race: 96.8% White, 1.9% Black/African American, 0.0% Asian, 0.0% American Indian/Alaska Native, 0.0% Native Hawaiian/Other Pacific Islander, 1.3% Some other race, 1.3% Two or more races, 0.0% Hispanic of any race (2008-2012 5-year est.); Average household size: 2.46 (2008-2012 5-year est.); Median age: 33.9 (2008-2012 5-year est.); Males per 100 females: 121.6 (2008-2012 5-year est.); Marriage status: 26.8% never married, 60.2% now married, 3.3% widowed, 9.8% divorced (2008-2012 5-year est.); Foreign born: 0.0% (2008-2012 5-year est.); Ancestry (includes multiple ancestries): 20.1% English, 15.9% Italian, 13.3% German, 7.5% Irish, 4.9% French (2008-2012 5-year est.).
Economy: Homeowner vacancy rate: 0.0%. Rental vacancy rate: 0.0%. (2008-2012 5-year est.); Employment by occupation: 6.9% management, business, and financial, 0.8% computer, engineering, and science, 1.5% education, legal, community service, arts, and media, 0.8% healthcare practitioners, 36.9% service, 11.5% sales and office, 7.7% natural resources, construction, and maintenance, 33.8% production, transportation, and material moving (2008-2012 5-year est.).
Income: Per capita income: $17,328 (2008-2012 5-year est.); Median household income: $35,341 (2008-2012 5-year est.); Average household income: $40,777 (2008-2012 5-year est.); Percent of households with income of $100,000 or more: 10.4% (2008-2012 5-year est.); Poverty rate: 19.7% (2008-2012 5-year est.).
Education: Percent of population age 25 and over with: High school diploma (including GED) or higher: 86.4% (2008-2012 5-year est.); Bachelor's degree or higher: 5.1% (2008-2012 5-year est.); Master's degree or higher: 3.0% (2008-2012 5-year est.).
Housing: Homeownership rate: 81.6% (2008-2012 5-year est.); Median home value: $41,300 (2008-2012 5-year est.); Median contract rent: $341 per month (2008-2012 5-year est.); Median year structure built: 1960 (2008-2012 5-year est.).
Health Insurance: 48.1% Private; 42.9% Public; 22.7% None. (2008-2012 5-year est.)
Transportation: Commute to work: 96.0% car, 0.0% public transportation, 0.0% walk, 0.0% work from home (2008-2012 5-year est.); Travel time to work: 14.4% less than 15 minutes, 61.6% 15 to 30 minutes, 21.6% 30 to 45 minutes, 2.4% 45 to 60 minutes, 0.0% 60 minutes or more (2008-2012 5-year est.)

HERRIN (city). Covers a land area of 9.235 square miles and a water area of 0.231 square miles. Located at 37.80° N. Lat; 89.03° W. Long. Elevation is 420 feet.

History: Coal mining began in Herrin in 1895. It was incorporated as a village in 1898 and as a city in 1900.
Population: 10,857 (1990); 11,298 (2000); 12,501 (2010); Density: 1,356.2 persons per square mile (2008-2012 5-year est.); Race: 94.4% White, 3.2% Black/African American, 0.2% Asian, 0.0% American Indian/Alaska Native, 0.1% Native Hawaiian/Other Pacific Islander, 2.1% Some other race, 1.2% Two or more races, 1.5% Hispanic of any race (2008-2012 5-year est.); Average household size: 2.38 (2008-2012 5-year est.); Median age: 37.0 (2008-2012 5-year est.); Males per 100 females: 98.3 (2008-2012 5-year est.); Marriage status: 25.8% never married,

51.5% now married, 8.6% widowed, 14.1% divorced (2008-2012 5-year est.); Foreign born: 0.8% (2008-2012 5-year est.); Ancestry (includes multiple ancestries): 23.4% German, 15.9% English, 14.7% Irish, 11.9% American, 10.8% Italian (2008-2012 5-year est.).

Economy: Single-family building permits issued: 30 (2013); Multi-family building permits issued: 6 (2013); Homeowner vacancy rate: 2.9%. Rental vacancy rate: 11.4%. (2008-2012 5-year est.); Employment by occupation: 11.2% management, business, and financial, 2.0% computer, engineering, and science, 12.1% education, legal, community service, arts, and media, 7.2% healthcare practitioners, 21.3% service, 26.8% sales and office, 8.6% natural resources, construction, and maintenance, 10.7% production, transportation, and material moving (2008-2012 5-year est.).

Income: Per capita income: $21,671 (2008-2012 5-year est.); Median household income: $39,123 (2008-2012 5-year est.); Average household income: $50,957 (2008-2012 5-year est.); Percent of households with income of $100,000 or more: 11.4% (2008-2012 5-year est.); Poverty rate: 15.9% (2008-2012 5-year est.).

Education: Percent of population age 25 and over with: High school diploma (including GED) or higher: 87.9% (2008-2012 5-year est.); Bachelor's degree or higher: 23.1% (2008-2012 5-year est.); Master's degree or higher: 6.8% (2008-2012 5-year est.).

School District(s)
Herrin CUSD 4 (PK-12)
    2011-12 Enrollment: 2,528 . . . . (618) 988-8024

Housing: Homeownership rate: 66.7% (2008-2012 5-year est.); Median home value: $75,600 (2008-2012 5-year est.); Median contract rent: $440 per month (2008-2012 5-year est.); Median year structure built: 1964 (2008-2012 5-year est.).

Health Insurance: 62.6% Private; 39.6% Public; 13.6% None. (2008-2012 5-year est.)

Hospitals: Herrin Hospital (92 beds)

Safety: Violent crime rate: 128.0 per 10,000 population; Property crime rate: 337.9 per 10,000 population (2012).

Transportation: Commute to work: 92.6% car, 0.7% public transportation, 1.5% walk, 3.5% work from home (2008-2012 5-year est.); Travel time to work: 36.0% less than 15 minutes, 38.5% 15 to 30 minutes, 18.9% 30 to 45 minutes, 3.9% 45 to 60 minutes, 2.7% 60 minutes or more (2008-2012 5-year est.)

Additional Information Contacts
City of Herrin . . . . (618) 942-3175
    http://www.cityofherrin.com
Herrin Chamber of Commerce . . . . (618) 942-5163
    http://www.herrinchamber.com

HURST (city). Covers a land area of 0.855 square miles and a water area of 0.002 square miles. Located at 37.84° N. Lat; 89.15° W. Long. Elevation is 390 feet.

Population: 842 (1990); 805 (2000); 795 (2010); Density: 955.1 persons per square mile (2008-2012 5-year est.); Race: 100.0% White, 0.0% Black/African American, 0.0% Asian, 0.0% American Indian/Alaska Native, 0.0% Native Hawaiian/Other Pacific Islander, 0.0% Some other race, 0.0% Two or more races, 0.0% Hispanic of any race (2008-2012 5-year est.); Average household size: 2.33 (2008-2012 5-year est.); Median age: 39.3 (2008-2012 5-year est.); Males per 100 females: 102.7 (2008-2012 5-year est.); Marriage status: 17.9% never married, 53.4% now married, 7.0% widowed, 21.7% divorced (2008-2012 5-year est.); Foreign born: 0.0% (2008-2012 5-year est.); Ancestry (includes multiple ancestries): 35.1% German, 24.6% English, 23.1% Irish, 4.4% Scottish, 3.2% Italian (2008-2012 5-year est.).

Economy: Single-family building permits issued: 2 (2013); Multi-family building permits issued: 0 (2013); Homeowner vacancy rate: 3.2%. Rental vacancy rate: 0.0%. (2008-2012 5-year est.); Employment by occupation: 9.9% management, business, and financial, 0.9% computer, engineering, and science, 3.1% education, legal, community service, arts, and media, 9.9% healthcare practitioners, 17.4% service, 16.5% sales and office, 19.6% natural resources, construction, and maintenance, 22.7% production, transportation, and material moving (2008-2012 5-year est.).

Income: Per capita income: $17,656 (2008-2012 5-year est.); Median household income: $35,208 (2008-2012 5-year est.); Average household income: $39,460 (2008-2012 5-year est.); Percent of households with income of $100,000 or more: 1.4% (2008-2012 5-year est.); Poverty rate: 20.2% (2008-2012 5-year est.).

Education: Percent of population age 25 and over with: High school diploma (including GED) or higher: 87.7% (2008-2012 5-year est.);

Bachelor's degree or higher: 7.3% (2008-2012 5-year est.); Master's degree or higher: 1.3% (2008-2012 5-year est.).

Housing: Homeownership rate: 76.6% (2008-2012 5-year est.); Median home value: $50,000 (2008-2012 5-year est.); Median contract rent: $296 per month (2008-2012 5-year est.); Median year structure built: 1962 (2008-2012 5-year est.).

Health Insurance: 48.3% Private; 49.6% Public; 15.3% None. (2008-2012 5-year est.)

Transportation: Commute to work: 96.3% car, 0.0% public transportation, 3.1% walk, 0.0% work from home (2008-2012 5-year est.); Travel time to work: 9.3% less than 15 minutes, 63.4% 15 to 30 minutes, 19.3% 30 to 45 minutes, 3.1% 45 to 60 minutes, 5.0% 60 minutes or more (2008-2012 5-year est.)

JOHNSTON CITY (city). Covers a land area of 2.065 square miles and a water area of 0.060 square miles. Located at 37.82° N. Lat; 88.93° W. Long. Elevation is 430 feet.

History: Incorporated 1896.

Population: 3,706 (1990); 3,557 (2000); 3,543 (2010); Density: 1,722.7 persons per square mile (2008-2012 5-year est.); Race: 92.9% White, 0.0% Black/African American, 0.8% Asian, 1.0% American Indian/Alaska Native, 0.0% Native Hawaiian/Other Pacific Islander, 5.3% Some other race, 5.3% Two or more races, 2.4% Hispanic of any race (2008-2012 5-year est.); Average household size: 2.54 (2008-2012 5-year est.); Median age: 33.1 (2008-2012 5-year est.); Males per 100 females: 95.3 (2008-2012 5-year est.); Marriage status: 28.0% never married, 50.8% now married, 6.0% widowed, 15.3% divorced (2008-2012 5-year est.); Foreign born: 0.8% (2008-2012 5-year est.); Ancestry (includes multiple ancestries): 20.1% English, 15.8% Irish, 15.6% German, 10.6% American, 3.6% Scotch-Irish (2008-2012 5-year est.).

Economy: Single-family building permits issued: 0 (2013); Multi-family building permits issued: 0 (2013); Homeowner vacancy rate: 0.0%. Rental vacancy rate: 0.0%. (2008-2012 5-year est.); Employment by occupation: 1.1% management, business, and financial, 0.6% computer, engineering, and science, 6.8% education, legal, community service, arts, and media, 4.9% healthcare practitioners, 24.9% service, 33.1% sales and office, 5.7% natural resources, construction, and maintenance, 22.8% production, transportation, and material moving (2008-2012 5-year est.).

Income: Per capita income: $16,284 (2008-2012 5-year est.); Median household income: $38,164 (2008-2012 5-year est.); Average household income: $40,772 (2008-2012 5-year est.); Percent of households with income of $100,000 or more: 3.0% (2008-2012 5-year est.); Poverty rate: 27.4% (2008-2012 5-year est.).

Education: Percent of population age 25 and over with: High school diploma (including GED) or higher: 79.8% (2008-2012 5-year est.); Bachelor's degree or higher: 6.2% (2008-2012 5-year est.); Master's degree or higher: 2.3% (2008-2012 5-year est.).

School District(s)
Franklin/williamson Roe (PK-12)
    2011-12 Enrollment: n/a . . . . (618) 438-9711
Johnston City CUSD 1 (PK-12)
    2011-12 Enrollment: 1,215 . . . . (618) 983-8021

Housing: Homeownership rate: 69.4% (2008-2012 5-year est.); Median home value: $54,600 (2008-2012 5-year est.); Median contract rent: $406 per month (2008-2012 5-year est.); Median year structure built: 1949 (2008-2012 5-year est.).

Health Insurance: 53.2% Private; 44.7% Public; 13.7% None. (2008-2012 5-year est.)

Transportation: Commute to work: 99.4% car, 0.0% public transportation, 0.0% walk, 0.6% work from home (2008-2012 5-year est.); Travel time to work: 28.5% less than 15 minutes, 57.5% 15 to 30 minutes, 8.1% 30 to 45 minutes, 2.4% 45 to 60 minutes, 3.6% 60 minutes or more (2008-2012 5-year est.)

MARION (city). County seat. Covers a land area of 15.987 square miles and a water area of 0.227 square miles. Located at 37.72° N. Lat; 88.93° W. Long. Elevation is 423 feet.

History: Marion was established in the mid-1800's. Early residents were Robert G. Ingersoll and John A. Logan, both of whom became colonels serving in the Civil War.

Population: 14,545 (1990); 16,035 (2000); 17,193 (2010); Density: 1,075.8 persons per square mile (2008-2012 5-year est.); Race: 89.3% White, 6.6% Black/African American, 1.2% Asian, 0.6% American Indian/Alaska Native, 0.0% Native Hawaiian/Other Pacific Islander, 2.3% Some other race, 2.1% Two or more races, 2.4% Hispanic of any race

(2008-2012 5-year est.); Average household size: 2.24 (2008-2012 5-year est.); Median age: 40.8 (2008-2012 5-year est.); Males per 100 females: 85.4 (2008-2012 5-year est.); Marriage status: 26.8% never married, 48.4% now married, 9.9% widowed, 14.8% divorced (2008-2012 5-year est.); Foreign born: 2.3% (2008-2012 5-year est.); Ancestry (includes multiple ancestries): 24.3% German, 15.8% Irish, 13.5% English, 9.8% American, 4.4% Italian (2008-2012 5-year est.).

Economy: Single-family building permits issued: 17 (2013); Multi-family building permits issued: 29 (2013); Homeowner vacancy rate: 2.2%. Rental vacancy rate: 9.8%. (2008-2012 5-year est.); Employment by occupation: 11.6% management, business, and financial, 2.3% computer, engineering, and science, 13.1% education, legal, community service, arts, and media, 8.7% healthcare practitioners, 23.0% service, 26.0% sales and office, 7.3% natural resources, construction, and maintenance, 8.0% production, transportation, and material moving (2008-2012 5-year est.).

Income: Per capita income: $24,054 (2008-2012 5-year est.); Median household income: $38,260 (2008-2012 5-year est.); Average household income: $53,490 (2008-2012 5-year est.); Percent of households with income of $100,000 or more: 12.4% (2008-2012 5-year est.); Poverty rate: 19.4% (2008-2012 5-year est.).

Taxes: Total city taxes per capita: $744 (2011); City property taxes per capita: $341 (2011).

Education: Percent of population age 25 and over with: High school diploma (including GED) or higher: 89.7% (2008-2012 5-year est.); Bachelor's degree or higher: 23.8% (2008-2012 5-year est.); Master's degree or higher: 9.4% (2008-2012 5-year est.).

School District(s)
Crab Orchard CUSD 3 (PK-12)
    2011-12 Enrollment: 463 . . . . (618) 982-2181
Marion CUSD 2 (PK-12)
    2011-12 Enrollment: 4,006 . . . . (618) 993-2321
Williamson County Spec Educ District (PK-12)
    2011-12 Enrollment: n/a . . . . (618) 993-2138

Housing: Homeownership rate: 60.5% (2008-2012 5-year est.); Median home value: $100,800 (2008-2012 5-year est.); Median contract rent: $472 per month (2008-2012 5-year est.); Median year structure built: 1974 (2008-2012 5-year est.).

Health Insurance: 61.8% Private; 41.0% Public; 14.4% None. (2008-2012 5-year est.)

Hospitals: Heartland Regional Medical Center (92 beds); US Penitentiary Infirmary; Veterans Affairs Medical Center (39 beds)

Transportation: Commute to work: 94.9% car, 0.2% public transportation, 2.2% walk, 2.0% work from home (2008-2012 5-year est.); Travel time to work: 50.5% less than 15 minutes, 28.8% 15 to 30 minutes, 13.5% 30 to 45 minutes, 4.0% 45 to 60 minutes, 3.2% 60 minutes or more (2008-2012 5-year est.)

Airports: Williamson County Regional Airport (commercial service–non-primary)

Additional Information Contacts
City of Marion . . . . (618) 997-6281
    http://www.cityofmarionil.gov
Marion Chamber of Commerce . . . . (618) 997-6311
    http://www.marionillinois.com

PITTSBURG (village). Covers a land area of 2.074 square miles and a water area of 0.030 square miles. Located at 37.78° N. Lat; 88.85° W. Long. Elevation is 466 feet.

Population: 602 (1990); 575 (2000); 572 (2010); Density: 352.0 persons per square mile (2008-2012 5-year est.); Race: 96.3% White, 0.0% Black/African American, 0.3% Asian, 0.0% American Indian/Alaska Native, 0.0% Native Hawaiian/Other Pacific Islander, 3.4% Some other race, 2.6% Two or more races, 0.8% Hispanic of any race (2008-2012 5-year est.); Average household size: 2.38 (2008-2012 5-year est.); Median age: 37.5 (2008-2012 5-year est.); Males per 100 females: 127.4 (2008-2012 5-year est.); Marriage status: 17.3% never married, 67.3% now married, 6.2% widowed, 9.2% divorced (2008-2012 5-year est.); Foreign born: 1.4% (2008-2012 5-year est.); Ancestry (includes multiple ancestries): 27.7% German, 15.1% Irish, 8.5% English, 8.4% American, 5.9% French (2008-2012 5-year est.).

Economy: Homeowner vacancy rate: 0.0%. Rental vacancy rate: 0.0%. (2008-2012 5-year est.); Employment by occupation: 7.3% management, business, and financial, 0.0% computer, engineering, and science, 6.8% education, legal, community service, arts, and media, 7.3% healthcare practitioners, 23.2% service, 26.3% sales and office, 11.3% natural

resources, construction, and maintenance, 17.8% production, transportation, and material moving (2008-2012 5-year est.).

Income: Per capita income: $19,098 (2008-2012 5-year est.); Median household income: $37,321 (2008-2012 5-year est.); Average household income: $44,277 (2008-2012 5-year est.); Percent of households with income of $100,000 or more: 3.3% (2008-2012 5-year est.); Poverty rate: 13.2% (2008-2012 5-year est.).

Education: Percent of population age 25 and over with: High school diploma (including GED) or higher: 76.8% (2008-2012 5-year est.); Bachelor's degree or higher: 9.7% (2008-2012 5-year est.); Master's degree or higher: 2.5% (2008-2012 5-year est.).

School District(s)
Johnston City CUSD 1 (PK-12)
    2011-12 Enrollment: 1,215 . . . . (618) 983-8021

Housing: Homeownership rate: 80.5% (2008-2012 5-year est.); Median home value: $59,800 (2008-2012 5-year est.); Median contract rent: $382 per month (2008-2012 5-year est.); Median year structure built: 1943 (2008-2012 5-year est.).

Health Insurance: 56.7% Private; 35.8% Public; 18.8% None. (2008-2012 5-year est.)

Transportation: Commute to work: 94.8% car, 0.0% public transportation, 0.0% walk, 2.0% work from home (2008-2012 5-year est.); Travel time to work: 16.5% less than 15 minutes, 58.2% 15 to 30 minutes, 11.5% 30 to 45 minutes, 6.2% 45 to 60 minutes, 7.6% 60 minutes or more (2008-2012 5-year est.)

SPILLERTOWN (village). Covers a land area of 0.360 square miles and a water area of 0.009 square miles. Located at 37.76° N. Lat; 88.92° W. Long. Elevation is 482 feet.

Population: 249 (1990); 220 (2000); 203 (2010); Density: 574.3 persons per square mile (2008-2012 5-year est.); Race: 92.8% White, 0.0% Black/African American, 4.8% Asian, 0.0% American Indian/Alaska Native, 0.0% Native Hawaiian/Other Pacific Islander, 2.4% Some other race, 2.4% Two or more races, 6.8% Hispanic of any race (2008-2012 5-year est.); Average household size: 2.38 (2008-2012 5-year est.); Median age: 43.8 (2008-2012 5-year est.); Males per 100 females: 95.3 (2008-2012 5-year est.); Marriage status: 24.6% never married, 62.6% now married, 7.0% widowed, 5.8% divorced (2008-2012 5-year est.); Foreign born: 0.0% (2008-2012 5-year est.); Ancestry (includes multiple ancestries): 24.2% Irish, 16.9% German, 14.0% American, 13.0% English, 8.2% French (2008-2012 5-year est.).

Economy: Homeowner vacancy rate: 0.0%. Rental vacancy rate: 0.0%. (2008-2012 5-year est.); Employment by occupation: 6.0% management, business, and financial, 0.0% computer, engineering, and science, 8.3% education, legal, community service, arts, and media, 3.6% healthcare practitioners, 28.6% service, 26.2% sales and office, 9.5% natural resources, construction, and maintenance, 17.9% production, transportation, and material moving (2008-2012 5-year est.).

Income: Per capita income: $17,364 (2008-2012 5-year est.); Median household income: $29,821 (2008-2012 5-year est.); Average household income: $39,214 (2008-2012 5-year est.); Percent of households with income of $100,000 or more: 5.7% (2008-2012 5-year est.); Poverty rate: 16.3% (2008-2012 5-year est.).

Education: Percent of population age 25 and over with: High school diploma (including GED) or higher: 73.0% (2008-2012 5-year est.); Bachelor's degree or higher: 10.8% (2008-2012 5-year est.); Master's degree or higher: 2.0% (2008-2012 5-year est.).

Housing: Homeownership rate: 89.7% (2008-2012 5-year est.); Median home value: $61,100 (2008-2012 5-year est.); Median contract rent: $250 per month (2008-2012 5-year est.); Median year structure built: 1973 (2008-2012 5-year est.).

Health Insurance: 53.6% Private; 46.9% Public; 16.4% None. (2008-2012 5-year est.)

Transportation: Commute to work: 95.1% car, 2.4% public transportation, 0.0% walk, 2.4% work from home (2008-2012 5-year est.); Travel time to work: 26.3% less than 15 minutes, 47.5% 15 to 30 minutes, 16.3% 30 to 45 minutes, 10.0% 45 to 60 minutes, 0.0% 60 minutes or more (2008-2012 5-year est.)

STONEFORT (village). Covers a land area of 1.454 square miles and a water area of 0.006 square miles. Located at 37.62° N. Lat; 88.70° W. Long. Elevation is 410 feet.

History: Stonefort was built on the ruins of an old stone fort, a prehistoric structure on a cliff with a stone barricade on the approachable side. In 1872 the town was moved to take advantage of the arrival of the railroad.

Population: 311 (1990); 292 (2000); 297 (2010); Density: 200.9 persons per square mile (2008-2012 5-year est.); Race: 97.9% White, 2.1% Black/African American, 0.0% Asian, 0.0% American Indian/Alaska Native, 0.0% Native Hawaiian/Other Pacific Islander, 0.0% Some other race, 0.0% Two or more races, 0.0% Hispanic of any race (2008-2012 5-year est.); Average household size: 2.68 (2008-2012 5-year est.); Median age: 40.9 (2008-2012 5-year est.); Males per 100 females: 101.4 (2008-2012 5-year est.); Marriage status: 19.6% never married, 57.0% now married, 4.3% widowed, 19.1% divorced (2008-2012 5-year est.); Foreign born: 0.0% (2008-2012 5-year est.); Ancestry (includes multiple ancestries): 21.6% English, 20.5% German, 16.8% Irish, 6.8% American, 3.1% Welsh (2008-2012 5-year est.).

Economy: Homeowner vacancy rate: 4.3%. Rental vacancy rate: 0.0%. (2008-2012 5-year est.); Employment by occupation: 6.9% management, business, and financial, 0.0% computer, engineering, and science, 5.9% education, legal, community service, arts, and media, 3.0% healthcare practitioners, 34.7% service, 30.7% sales and office, 13.9% natural resources, construction, and maintenance, 5.0% production, transportation, and material moving (2008-2012 5-year est.).

Income: Per capita income: $17,152 (2008-2012 5-year est.); Median household income: $36,750 (2008-2012 5-year est.); Average household income: $44,643 (2008-2012 5-year est.); Percent of households with income of $100,000 or more: 7.3% (2008-2012 5-year est.); Poverty rate: 14.4% (2008-2012 5-year est.).

Education: Percent of population age 25 and over with: High school diploma (including GED) or higher: 85.1% (2008-2012 5-year est.); Bachelor's degree or higher: 1.5% (2008-2012 5-year est.); Master's degree or higher: 0.0% (2008-2012 5-year est.).

Housing: Homeownership rate: 80.7% (2008-2012 5-year est.); Median home value: $31,700 (2008-2012 5-year est.); Median contract rent: $355 per month (2008-2012 5-year est.); Median year structure built: 1954 (2008-2012 5-year est.).

Health Insurance: 50.3% Private; 54.5% Public; 7.2% None. (2008-2012 5-year est.)

Transportation: Commute to work: 98.0% car, 0.0% public transportation, 0.0% walk, 2.0% work from home (2008-2012 5-year est.); Travel time to work: 19.2% less than 15 minutes, 32.3% 15 to 30 minutes, 30.3% 30 to 45 minutes, 9.1% 45 to 60 minutes, 9.1% 60 minutes or more (2008-2012 5-year est.)

WHITEASH (village). Covers a land area of 0.864 square miles and a water area of 0.024 square miles. Located at 37.78° N. Lat; 88.93° W. Long. Elevation is 440 feet.

Population: 249 (1990); 268 (2000); 241 (2010); Density: 326.5 persons per square mile (2008-2012 5-year est.); Race: 100.0% White, 0.0% Black/African American, 0.0% Asian, 0.0% American Indian/Alaska Native, 0.0% Native Hawaiian/Other Pacific Islander, 0.0% Some other race, 0.0% Two or more races, 0.7% Hispanic of any race (2008-2012 5-year est.); Average household size: 2.69 (2008-2012 5-year est.); Median age: 38.7 (2008-2012 5-year est.); Males per 100 females: 131.1 (2008-2012 5-year est.); Marriage status: 20.0% never married, 59.1% now married, 6.2% widowed, 14.7% divorced (2008-2012 5-year est.); Foreign born: 0.0% (2008-2012 5-year est.); Ancestry (includes multiple ancestries): 21.3% English, 21.3% Irish, 11.0% German, 6.4% Italian, 3.9% European (2008-2012 5-year est.).

Economy: Homeowner vacancy rate: 0.0%. Rental vacancy rate: 0.0%. (2008-2012 5-year est.); Employment by occupation: 6.0% management, business, and financial, 1.5% computer, engineering, and science, 8.2% education, legal, community service, arts, and media, 2.2% healthcare practitioners, 32.1% service, 24.6% sales and office, 9.0% natural resources, construction, and maintenance, 16.4% production, transportation, and material moving (2008-2012 5-year est.).

Income: Per capita income: $22,735 (2008-2012 5-year est.); Median household income: $41,979 (2008-2012 5-year est.); Average household income: $57,130 (2008-2012 5-year est.); Percent of households with income of $100,000 or more: 12.5% (2008-2012 5-year est.); Poverty rate: 15.3% (2008-2012 5-year est.).

Education: Percent of population age 25 and over with: High school diploma (including GED) or higher: 90.7% (2008-2012 5-year est.); Bachelor's degree or higher: 16.6% (2008-2012 5-year est.); Master's degree or higher: 2.9% (2008-2012 5-year est.).

Housing: Homeownership rate: 77.1% (2008-2012 5-year est.); Median home value: $79,500 (2008-2012 5-year est.); Median contract rent: $450 per month (2008-2012 5-year est.); Median year structure built: 1983 (2008-2012 5-year est.).

Health Insurance: 68.4% Private; 34.4% Public; 10.3% None. (2008-2012 5-year est.)

Transportation: Commute to work: 95.3% car, 0.0% public transportation, 0.0% walk, 0.8% work from home (2008-2012 5-year est.); Travel time to work: 35.7% less than 15 minutes, 44.4% 15 to 30 minutes, 4.8% 30 to 45 minutes, 2.4% 45 to 60 minutes, 12.7% 60 minutes or more (2008-2012 5-year est.)

Winnebago County

Located in northern Illinois; bounded on the north by Wisconsin; drained by the Rock, Pecatonica, and Kishwaukee Rivers. Covers a land area of 513.362 square miles, a water area of 5.888 square miles, and is located in the Central Time Zone at 42.34° N. Lat., 89.16° W. Long. The county was founded in 1836. County seat is Rockford.

Winnebago County is part of the Rockford, IL Metropolitan Statistical Area. The entire metro area includes: Boone County, IL; Winnebago County, IL

Weather Station: Rockford Greater Rockford Arpt   Elevation: 680 feet

	Jan	Feb	Mar	Apr	May	Jun	Jul	Aug	Sep	Oct	Nov	Dec
High	29	34	46	60	71	80	84	82	75	62	47	33
Low	13	17	27	37	48	58	63	61	52	40	30	18
Precip	1.4	1.4	2.3	3.3	3.9	4.7	3.8	4.7	3.5	2.6	2.6	2.0
Snow	10.3	7.6	5.0	1.1	tr	tr	tr	tr	tr	0.1	1.7	10.8

High and Low temperatures in degrees Fahrenheit; Precipitation and Snow in inches

Population: 252,913 (1990); 278,418 (2000); 295,266 (2010); Race: 80.4% White, 12.3% Black/African American, 2.3% Asian, 0.3% American Indian/Alaska Native, 0.0% Native Hawaiian/Other Pacific Islander, 4.7% Some other race, 2.4% Two or more races, 11.0% Hispanic of any race (2008-2012 5-year est.); Density: 568.5 persons per square mile (2008-2012 5-year est.); Average household size: 2.56 (2008-2012 5-year est.); Median age: 38.4 (2008-2012 5-year est.); Males per 100 females: 95.5 (2008-2012 5-year est.).

Religion: Six largest groups: 20.1% Catholicism, 9.7% Non-denominational Protestant, 6.5% Lutheran, 4.7% Baptist, 4.4% Methodist/Pietist, 2.1% Pentecostal (2010)

Economy: Unemployment rate: 9.1% (April 2014); Total civilian labor force: 137,108 (April 2014); Leading industries: 21.0% manufacturing; 10.7% health care and social assistance, 12.2% retail trade (2012); Farms: 807 totaling 182,905 acres (2012); Companies that employ 500 or more persons: 19 (2012); Companies that employ 100 to 499 persons: 171 (2012); Companies that employ less than 100 persons: 6,363 (2012); Black-owned businesses: 1,665 (2007); Hispanic-owned businesses: 563 (2007); Asian-owned businesses: 650 (2007); Women-owned businesses: 6,844 (2007); Single-family building permits issued: 53 (2013); Multi-family building permits issued: 0 (2013).

Income: Per capita income: $24,404 (2008-2012 5-year est.); Median household income: $47,573 (2008-2012 5-year est.); Average household income: $61,452 (2008-2012 5-year est.); Percent of households with income of $100,000 or more: 15.6% (2008-2012 5-year est.); Poverty rate: 17.0% (2008-2012 5-year est.); Bankruptcy rate: 5.37% (2013).

Taxes: Total county taxes per capita: $230 (2011); County property taxes per capita: $136 (2011).

Education: Percent of population age 25 and over with: High school diploma (including GED) or higher: 85.6% (2008-2012 5-year est.); Bachelor's degree or higher: 20.9% (2008-2012 5-year est.); Master's degree or higher: 7.4% (2008-2012 5-year est.).

Housing: Homeownership rate: 67.6% (2008-2012 5-year est.); Median home value: $127,500 (2008-2012 5-year est.); Median contract rent: $576 per month (2008-2012 5-year est.); Median year structure built: 1968 (2008-2012 5-year est.).

Health: Birth rate: 122.5 per 10,000 population (2013); Death rate: 90.3 per 10,000 population (2013); Age-adjusted cancer mortality rate: 214.6 deaths per 100,000 population (2011); Number of physicians: 24.1 per 10,000 population (2011); Hospital beds: 36.3 per 10,000 population (2010); Hospital admissions: 1,470.9 per 10,000 population (2010).

Environment: Air Quality Index: 92.9% good, 7.1% moderate, 0.0% unhealthy for sensitive individuals, 0.0% unhealthy (percent of days in 2013)

Elections: 2012 Presidential election results: 52.0% Obama, 46.3% Romney

National and State Parks: Rock Cut State Park

Additional Information Contacts

Winnebago County Government . . . . (815) 319-4250
http://www.co.winnebago.il.us

Winnebago County Communities

CHERRY VALLEY (village). Covers a land area of 8.442 square miles and a water area of 0.257 square miles. Located at 42.24° N. Lat; 88.97° W. Long. Elevation is 728 feet.
Population: 1,615 (1990); 2,191 (2000); 3,162 (2010); Density: 379.4 persons per square mile (2008-2012 5-year est.); Race: 92.0% White, 3.2% Black/African American, 2.8% Asian, 0.0% American Indian/Alaska Native, 0.0% Native Hawaiian/Other Pacific Islander, 2.0% Some other race, 1.5% Two or more races, 1.8% Hispanic of any race (2008-2012 5-year est.); Average household size: 2.25 (2008-2012 5-year est.); Median age: 43.1 (2008-2012 5-year est.); Males per 100 females: 97.2 (2008-2012 5-year est.); Marriage status: 24.1% never married, 58.3% now married, 7.1% widowed, 10.6% divorced (2008-2012 5-year est.); Foreign born: 3.9% (2008-2012 5-year est.); Ancestry (includes multiple ancestries): 22.9% German, 17.0% American, 12.7% Swedish, 11.8% Irish, 10.1% English (2008-2012 5-year est.).
Economy: Homeowner vacancy rate: 2.2%. Rental vacancy rate: 0.0%. (2008-2012 5-year est.); Employment by occupation: 14.8% management, business, and financial, 4.5% computer, engineering, and science, 10.5% education, legal, community service, arts, and media, 3.0% healthcare practitioners, 19.7% service, 24.9% sales and office, 12.3% natural resources, construction, and maintenance, 10.4% production, transportation, and material moving (2008-2012 5-year est.).
Income: Per capita income: $34,657 (2008-2012 5-year est.); Median household income: $61,588 (2008-2012 5-year est.); Average household income: $77,166 (2008-2012 5-year est.); Percent of households with income of $100,000 or more: 27.4% (2008-2012 5-year est.); Poverty rate: 2.8% (2008-2012 5-year est.).
Education: Percent of population age 25 and over with: High school diploma (including GED) or higher: 92.5% (2008-2012 5-year est.); Bachelor's degree or higher: 32.1% (2008-2012 5-year est.); Master's degree or higher: 7.2% (2008-2012 5-year est.).
School District(s)
Rockford SD 205 (PK-12)
    2011-12 Enrollment: 28,118 . . . . (815) 966-3101
Housing: Homeownership rate: 74.8% (2008-2012 5-year est.); Median home value: $175,500 (2008-2012 5-year est.); Median contract rent: $614 per month (2008-2012 5-year est.); Median year structure built: 1993 (2008-2012 5-year est.).
Health Insurance: 86.8% Private; 19.2% Public; 6.1% None. (2008-2012 5-year est.)
Safety: Violent crime rate: 22.2 per 10,000 population; Property crime rate: 976.8 per 10,000 population (2012).
Transportation: Commute to work: 92.7% car, 0.2% public transportation, 0.0% walk, 5.5% work from home (2008-2012 5-year est.); Travel time to work: 30.8% less than 15 minutes, 42.2% 15 to 30 minutes, 10.8% 30 to 45 minutes, 5.6% 45 to 60 minutes, 10.6% 60 minutes or more (2008-2012 5-year est.)

DURAND (village). Covers a land area of 0.936 square miles and a water area of 0 square miles. Located at 42.43° N. Lat; 89.33° W. Long. Elevation is 771 feet.
Population: 1,100 (1990); 1,081 (2000); 1,443 (2010); Density: 1,473.0 persons per square mile (2008-2012 5-year est.); Race: 91.4% White, 0.7% Black/African American, 0.7% Asian, 0.7% American Indian/Alaska Native, 2.2% Native Hawaiian/Other Pacific Islander, 4.3% Some other race, 4.1% Two or more races, 1.4% Hispanic of any race (2008-2012 5-year est.); Average household size: 2.52 (2008-2012 5-year est.); Median age: 39.8 (2008-2012 5-year est.); Males per 100 females: 106.4 (2008-2012 5-year est.); Marriage status: 27.1% never married, 50.3% now married, 10.4% widowed, 12.2% divorced (2008-2012 5-year est.); Foreign born: 1.6% (2008-2012 5-year est.); Ancestry (includes multiple ancestries): 38.7% German, 12.0% Irish, 10.3% American, 6.9% Italian, 6.6% English (2008-2012 5-year est.).
Economy: Single-family building permits issued: 0 (2013); Multi-family building permits issued: 0 (2013); Homeowner vacancy rate: 2.3%. Rental vacancy rate: 5.8%. (2008-2012 5-year est.); Employment by occupation: 11.4% management, business, and financial, 4.7% computer, engineering, and science, 5.9% education, legal, community service, arts, and media, 7.4% healthcare practitioners, 16.0% service, 26.6% sales and office,

10.5% natural resources, construction, and maintenance, 17.5% production, transportation, and material moving (2008-2012 5-year est.).
Income: Per capita income: $22,933 (2008-2012 5-year est.); Median household income: $51,481 (2008-2012 5-year est.); Average household income: $57,176 (2008-2012 5-year est.); Percent of households with income of $100,000 or more: 14.5% (2008-2012 5-year est.); Poverty rate: 9.9% (2008-2012 5-year est.).
Education: Percent of population age 25 and over with: High school diploma (including GED) or higher: 87.7% (2008-2012 5-year est.); Bachelor's degree or higher: 15.7% (2008-2012 5-year est.); Master's degree or higher: 3.1% (2008-2012 5-year est.).
School District(s)
Durand CUSD 322 (PK-12)
    2011-12 Enrollment: 641 . . . . (815) 248-2171
Housing: Homeownership rate: 74.4% (2008-2012 5-year est.); Median home value: $116,800 (2008-2012 5-year est.); Median contract rent: $483 per month (2008-2012 5-year est.); Median year structure built: 1969 (2008-2012 5-year est.).
Health Insurance: 69.6% Private; 27.7% Public; 14.1% None. (2008-2012 5-year est.)
Transportation: Commute to work: 96.2% car, 0.8% public transportation, 0.5% walk, 1.3% work from home (2008-2012 5-year est.); Travel time to work: 20.0% less than 15 minutes, 18.5% 15 to 30 minutes, 40.3% 30 to 45 minutes, 15.8% 45 to 60 minutes, 5.5% 60 minutes or more (2008-2012 5-year est.)

LAKE SUMMERSET (CDP). Covers a land area of 2.058 square miles and a water area of 0.437 square miles. Located at 42.45° N. Lat; 89.39° W. Long. Elevation is 860 feet.
Population: 1,296 (1990); 2,061 (2000); 2,048 (2010); Density: 922.5 persons per square mile (2008-2012 5-year est.); Race: 98.3% White, 0.0% Black/African American, 0.0% Asian, 1.7% American Indian/Alaska Native, 0.0% Native Hawaiian/Other Pacific Islander, 0.0% Some other race, 0.0% Two or more races, 4.3% Hispanic of any race (2008-2012 5-year est.); Average household size: 2.43 (2008-2012 5-year est.); Median age: 57.6 (2008-2012 5-year est.); Males per 100 females: 93.1 (2008-2012 5-year est.); Marriage status: 11.0% never married, 74.8% now married, 6.1% widowed, 8.0% divorced (2008-2012 5-year est.); Foreign born: 4.3% (2008-2012 5-year est.); Ancestry (includes multiple ancestries): 28.2% German, 21.4% Irish, 9.9% English, 9.2% Polish, 8.9% Italian (2008-2012 5-year est.).
Economy: Homeowner vacancy rate: 1.3%. Rental vacancy rate: 0.0%. (2008-2012 5-year est.); Employment by occupation: 13.7% management, business, and financial, 0.8% computer, engineering, and science, 9.6% education, legal, community service, arts, and media, 13.7% healthcare practitioners, 7.2% service, 24.3% sales and office, 12.2% natural resources, construction, and maintenance, 18.6% production, transportation, and material moving (2008-2012 5-year est.).
Income: Per capita income: $29,039 (2008-2012 5-year est.); Median household income: $59,934 (2008-2012 5-year est.); Average household income: $70,247 (2008-2012 5-year est.); Percent of households with income of $100,000 or more: 18.4% (2008-2012 5-year est.); Poverty rate: 1.7% (2008-2012 5-year est.).
Education: Percent of population age 25 and over with: High school diploma (including GED) or higher: 94.5% (2008-2012 5-year est.); Bachelor's degree or higher: 31.3% (2008-2012 5-year est.); Master's degree or higher: 10.3% (2008-2012 5-year est.).
Housing: Homeownership rate: 97.6% (2008-2012 5-year est.); Median home value: $172,400 (2008-2012 5-year est.); Median contract rent: n/a per month (2008-2012 5-year est.); Median year structure built: 1988 (2008-2012 5-year est.).
Health Insurance: 83.2% Private; 41.8% Public; 1.7% None. (2008-2012 5-year est.)
Transportation: Commute to work: 84.3% car, 0.0% public transportation, 5.8% walk, 5.5% work from home (2008-2012 5-year est.); Travel time to work: 12.6% less than 15 minutes, 19.4% 15 to 30 minutes, 40.7% 30 to 45 minutes, 12.0% 45 to 60 minutes, 15.3% 60 minutes or more (2008-2012 5-year est.)

LOVES PARK (city). Covers a land area of 16.031 square miles and a water area of 0.416 square miles. Located at 42.34° N. Lat; 89.00° W. Long. Elevation is 728 feet.
History: Incorporated 1947.
Population: 15,462 (1990); 20,044 (2000); 23,996 (2010); Density: 1,495.1 persons per square mile (2008-2012 5-year est.); Race: 91.4%

White, 4.0% Black/African American, 2.4% Asian, 0.0% American Indian/Alaska Native, 0.0% Native Hawaiian/Other Pacific Islander, 2.2% Some other race, 1.7% Two or more races, 6.6% Hispanic of any race (2008-2012 5-year est.); Average household size: 2.54 (2008-2012 5-year est.); Median age: 37.6 (2008-2012 5-year est.); Males per 100 females: 93.1 (2008-2012 5-year est.); Marriage status: 28.2% never married, 50.5% now married, 6.9% widowed, 14.4% divorced (2008-2012 5-year est.); Foreign born: 5.1% (2008-2012 5-year est.); Ancestry (includes multiple ancestries): 27.4% German, 15.8% Irish, 11.0% American, 10.0% Italian, 9.8% English (2008-2012 5-year est.).

Economy: Single-family building permits issued: 9 (2013); Multi-family building permits issued: 0 (2013); Homeowner vacancy rate: 0.8%. Rental vacancy rate: 3.2%. (2008-2012 5-year est.); Employment by occupation: 13.0% management, business, and financial, 4.5% computer, engineering, and science, 8.6% education, legal, community service, arts, and media, 5.5% healthcare practitioners, 16.0% service, 28.6% sales and office, 6.4% natural resources, construction, and maintenance, 17.5% production, transportation, and material moving (2008-2012 5-year est.).

Income: Per capita income: $25,817 (2008-2012 5-year est.); Median household income: $50,901 (2008-2012 5-year est.); Average household income: $64,489 (2008-2012 5-year est.); Percent of households with income of $100,000 or more: 15.6% (2008-2012 5-year est.); Poverty rate: 9.2% (2008-2012 5-year est.).

Education: Percent of population age 25 and over with: High school diploma (including GED) or higher: 90.9% (2008-2012 5-year est.); Bachelor's degree or higher: 23.5% (2008-2012 5-year est.); Master's degree or higher: 8.1% (2008-2012 5-year est.).

School District(s)

Boone/winnebago Roe (PK-12)
    2011-12 Enrollment: n/a . . . . (815) 636-3060
Harlem Ud 122 (PK-12)
    2011-12 Enrollment: 7,218 . . . . (815) 654-4500

Housing: Homeownership rate: 72.1% (2008-2012 5-year est.); Median home value: $121,600 (2008-2012 5-year est.); Median contract rent: $634 per month (2008-2012 5-year est.); Median year structure built: 1983 (2008-2012 5-year est.).

Health Insurance: 71.0% Private; 28.7% Public; 12.9% None. (2008-2012 5-year est.)

Safety: Violent crime rate: 23.0 per 10,000 population; Property crime rate: 339.1 per 10,000 population (2012).

Transportation: Commute to work: 95.2% car, 0.4% public transportation, 0.9% walk, 3.0% work from home (2008-2012 5-year est.); Travel time to work: 33.0% less than 15 minutes, 48.9% 15 to 30 minutes, 8.8% 30 to 45 minutes, 3.7% 45 to 60 minutes, 5.6% 60 minutes or more (2008-2012 5-year est.)

Additional Information Contacts

City of Loves Park . . . . (815) 654-5034
    http://www.loves-park.il.us
The Parks Chamber of Commerce . . . . (815) 633-3999
    http://www.parkschamber.com

MACHESNEY PARK (village). Covers a land area of 12.678 square miles and a water area of 0.325 square miles. Located at 42.37° N. Lat; 89.02° W. Long. Elevation is 741 feet.

Population: 19,033 (1990); 20,759 (2000); 23,499 (2010); Density: 1,832.4 persons per square mile (2008-2012 5-year est.); Race: 94.2% White, 1.9% Black/African American, 1.3% Asian, 0.7% American Indian/Alaska Native, 0.1% Native Hawaiian/Other Pacific Islander, 1.8% Some other race, 1.3% Two or more races, 5.0% Hispanic of any race (2008-2012 5-year est.); Average household size: 2.71 (2008-2012 5-year est.); Median age: 39.1 (2008-2012 5-year est.); Males per 100 females: 97.2 (2008-2012 5-year est.); Marriage status: 30.4% never married, 50.8% now married, 5.4% widowed, 13.3% divorced (2008-2012 5-year est.); Foreign born: 4.0% (2008-2012 5-year est.); Ancestry (includes multiple ancestries): 35.6% German, 17.0% Irish, 11.8% English, 9.8% American, 8.8% Italian (2008-2012 5-year est.).

Economy: Single-family building permits issued: 7 (2013); Multi-family building permits issued: 0 (2013); Homeowner vacancy rate: 0.0%. Rental vacancy rate: 5.6%. (2008-2012 5-year est.); Employment by occupation: 9.0% management, business, and financial, 3.8% computer, engineering, and science, 6.4% education, legal, community service, arts, and media, 5.2% healthcare practitioners, 14.3% service, 29.4% sales and office, 9.6% natural resources, construction, and maintenance, 22.4% production, transportation, and material moving (2008-2012 5-year est.).

Income: Per capita income: $23,988 (2008-2012 5-year est.); Median household income: $55,365 (2008-2012 5-year est.); Average household income: $62,320 (2008-2012 5-year est.); Percent of households with income of $100,000 or more: 14.6% (2008-2012 5-year est.); Poverty rate: 9.0% (2008-2012 5-year est.).

Education: Percent of population age 25 and over with: High school diploma (including GED) or higher: 86.0% (2008-2012 5-year est.); Bachelor's degree or higher: 12.5% (2008-2012 5-year est.); Master's degree or higher: 4.0% (2008-2012 5-year est.).

School District(s)

Harlem Ud 122 (PK-12)
    2011-12 Enrollment: 7,218 . . . . (815) 654-4500

Housing: Homeownership rate: 79.0% (2008-2012 5-year est.); Median home value: $121,300 (2008-2012 5-year est.); Median contract rent: $673 per month (2008-2012 5-year est.); Median year structure built: 1974 (2008-2012 5-year est.).

Health Insurance: 68.2% Private; 29.5% Public; 13.4% None. (2008-2012 5-year est.)

Safety: Violent crime rate: 32.5 per 10,000 population; Property crime rate: 250.0 per 10,000 population (2012).

Transportation: Commute to work: 96.0% car, 0.4% public transportation, 0.5% walk, 2.5% work from home (2008-2012 5-year est.); Travel time to work: 27.4% less than 15 minutes, 47.1% 15 to 30 minutes, 15.8% 30 to 45 minutes, 2.5% 45 to 60 minutes, 7.2% 60 minutes or more (2008-2012 5-year est.)

Additional Information Contacts

The Parks Chamber of Commerce . . . . (815) 633-3999
    http://www.parkschamber.com
Village of Machesney Park . . . . (815) 877-5432
    http://machesneypark.org

NEW MILFORD (village). Covers a land area of 1.449 square miles and a water area of 0.028 square miles. Located at 42.18° N. Lat; 89.06° W. Long. Elevation is 735 feet.

Population: 463 (1990); 541 (2000); 697 (2010); Density: 545.2 persons per square mile (2008-2012 5-year est.); Race: 84.4% White, 3.8% Black/African American, 11.8% Asian, 0.0% American Indian/Alaska Native, 0.0% Native Hawaiian/Other Pacific Islander, 0.0% Some other race, 0.0% Two or more races, 2.2% Hispanic of any race (2008-2012 5-year est.); Average household size: 2.70 (2008-2012 5-year est.); Median age: 38.4 (2008-2012 5-year est.); Males per 100 females: 106.3 (2008-2012 5-year est.); Marriage status: 24.1% never married, 55.5% now married, 6.1% widowed, 14.3% divorced (2008-2012 5-year est.); Foreign born: 8.9% (2008-2012 5-year est.); Ancestry (includes multiple ancestries): 16.2% German, 10.1% Irish, 9.9% English, 9.0% Finnish, 5.9% American (2008-2012 5-year est.).

Economy: Homeowner vacancy rate: 0.0%. Rental vacancy rate: 0.0%. (2008-2012 5-year est.); Employment by occupation: 6.7% management, business, and financial, 7.8% computer, engineering, and science, 2.6% education, legal, community service, arts, and media, 8.4% healthcare practitioners, 21.4% service, 22.9% sales and office, 4.9% natural resources, construction, and maintenance, 25.2% production, transportation, and material moving (2008-2012 5-year est.).

Income: Per capita income: $25,268 (2008-2012 5-year est.); Median household income: $57,917 (2008-2012 5-year est.); Average household income: $68,956 (2008-2012 5-year est.); Percent of households with income of $100,000 or more: 18.7% (2008-2012 5-year est.); Poverty rate: 17.1% (2008-2012 5-year est.).

Education: Percent of population age 25 and over with: High school diploma (including GED) or higher: 87.4% (2008-2012 5-year est.); Bachelor's degree or higher: 10.2% (2008-2012 5-year est.); Master's degree or higher: 1.9% (2008-2012 5-year est.).

Housing: Homeownership rate: 80.6% (2008-2012 5-year est.); Median home value: $76,300 (2008-2012 5-year est.); Median contract rent: $926 per month (2008-2012 5-year est.); Median year structure built: 1992 (2008-2012 5-year est.).

Health Insurance: 67.3% Private; 26.3% Public; 14.7% None. (2008-2012 5-year est.)

Transportation: Commute to work: 93.8% car, 0.0% public transportation, 1.2% walk, 5.0% work from home (2008-2012 5-year est.); Travel time to work: 38.8% less than 15 minutes, 43.8% 15 to 30 minutes, 13.7% 30 to 45 minutes, 0.6% 45 to 60 minutes, 3.1% 60 minutes or more (2008-2012 5-year est.)

PECATONICA (village). Covers a land area of 1.282 square miles and a water area of 0.015 square miles. Located at 42.31° N. Lat; 89.36° W. Long. Elevation is 771 feet.

History: Incorporated 1869.

Population: 1,760 (1990); 1,997 (2000); 2,195 (2010); Density: 1,746.4 persons per square mile (2008-2012 5-year est.); Race: 91.9% White, 0.0% Black/African American, 0.0% Asian, 0.0% American Indian/Alaska Native, 0.0% Native Hawaiian/Other Pacific Islander, 8.1% Some other race, 7.5% Two or more races, 2.8% Hispanic of any race (2008-2012 5-year est.); Average household size: 2.60 (2008-2012 5-year est.); Median age: 34.4 (2008-2012 5-year est.); Males per 100 females: 85.1 (2008-2012 5-year est.); Marriage status: 24.2% never married, 54.8% now married, 8.1% widowed, 12.9% divorced (2008-2012 5-year est.); Foreign born: 0.7% (2008-2012 5-year est.); Ancestry (includes multiple ancestries): 41.0% German, 16.0% American, 14.4% Irish, 10.5% Swedish, 8.6% English (2008-2012 5-year est.).

Economy: Single-family building permits issued: 0 (2013); Multi-family building permits issued: 0 (2013); Homeowner vacancy rate: 0.0%. Rental vacancy rate: 0.0%. (2008-2012 5-year est.); Employment by occupation: 10.7% management, business, and financial, 3.8% computer, engineering, and science, 6.4% education, legal, community service, arts, and media, 4.3% healthcare practitioners, 19.2% service, 30.3% sales and office, 8.1% natural resources, construction, and maintenance, 17.3% production, transportation, and material moving (2008-2012 5-year est.).

Income: Per capita income: $24,337 (2008-2012 5-year est.); Median household income: $53,674 (2008-2012 5-year est.); Average household income: $62,017 (2008-2012 5-year est.); Percent of households with income of $100,000 or more: 16.7% (2008-2012 5-year est.); Poverty rate: 6.2% (2008-2012 5-year est.).

Education: Percent of population age 25 and over with: High school diploma (including GED) or higher: 93.6% (2008-2012 5-year est.); Bachelor's degree or higher: 18.5% (2008-2012 5-year est.); Master's degree or higher: 4.0% (2008-2012 5-year est.).

School District(s)

Pecatonica CUSD 321 (PK-12)

    2011-12 Enrollment: 957 . . . . (815) 239-1639

Housing: Homeownership rate: 82.3% (2008-2012 5-year est.); Median home value: $117,300 (2008-2012 5-year est.); Median contract rent: $460 per month (2008-2012 5-year est.); Median year structure built: 1959 (2008-2012 5-year est.).

Health Insurance: 80.3% Private; 29.8% Public; 4.1% None. (2008-2012 5-year est.)

Transportation: Commute to work: 90.6% car, 0.0% public transportation, 4.1% walk, 3.7% work from home (2008-2012 5-year est.); Travel time to work: 31.0% less than 15 minutes, 24.4% 15 to 30 minutes, 39.4% 30 to 45 minutes, 0.4% 45 to 60 minutes, 4.8% 60 minutes or more (2008-2012 5-year est.).

ROCKFORD (city). County seat. Covers a land area of 61.081 square miles and a water area of 0.869 square miles. Located at 42.26° N. Lat; 89.06° W. Long. Elevation is 715 feet.

History: Rockford was named for the ford across the Rock River where the stagecoach crossed before the town was built. Rockford was settled by New Englanders after Germanicus Kent and Thatcher Blake of Galena laid out the town and opened a sawmill. The availability of water power accounted for Rockford's growth, and it was incorporated in 1839 along with a village that had grown up on the other side of the river. In the 1850's both the Rockford Water Power Company and the Manny Company, producer of reaper-mower machines, were founded. After 1852, when the Chicago & Galena Union Railroad arrived, many people of Swedish descent settled here.

Population: 139,426 (1990); 150,115 (2000); 152,871 (2010); Density: 2,504.0 persons per square mile (2008-2012 5-year est.); Race: 69.2% White, 20.9% Black/African American, 2.8% Asian, 0.3% American Indian/Alaska Native, 0.0% Native Hawaiian/Other Pacific Islander, 6.8% Some other race, 3.3% Two or more races, 16.3% Hispanic of any race (2008-2012 5-year est.); Average household size: 2.51 (2008-2012 5-year est.); Median age: 35.6 (2008-2012 5-year est.); Males per 100 females: 93.7 (2008-2012 5-year est.); Marriage status: 35.5% never married, 43.6% now married, 7.4% widowed, 13.5% divorced (2008-2012 5-year est.); Foreign born: 10.4% (2008-2012 5-year est.); Ancestry (includes multiple ancestries): 19.0% German, 10.4% Irish, 7.5% Swedish, 6.8% American, 6.5% Italian (2008-2012 5-year est.).

Economy: Unemployment rate: 10.2% (April 2014); Total civilian labor force: 66,640 (April 2014); Single-family building permits issued: 11 (2013);

Multi-family building permits issued: 0 (2013); Homeowner vacancy rate: 2.0%. Rental vacancy rate: 5.1%. (2008-2012 5-year est.); Employment by occupation: 9.8% management, business, and financial, 3.5% computer, engineering, and science, 9.5% education, legal, community service, arts, and media, 5.7% healthcare practitioners, 20.2% service, 24.1% sales and office, 6.9% natural resources, construction, and maintenance, 20.4% production, transportation, and material moving (2008-2012 5-year est.).

Income: Per capita income: $21,579 (2008-2012 5-year est.); Median household income: $38,157 (2008-2012 5-year est.); Average household income: $53,257 (2008-2012 5-year est.); Percent of households with income of $100,000 or more: 11.7% (2008-2012 5-year est.); Poverty rate: 25.1% (2008-2012 5-year est.).

Taxes: Total city taxes per capita: $469 (2011); City property taxes per capita: $375 (2011).

Education: Percent of population age 25 and over with: High school diploma (including GED) or higher: 81.6% (2008-2012 5-year est.); Bachelor's degree or higher: 20.7% (2008-2012 5-year est.); Master's degree or higher: 7.9% (2008-2012 5-year est.).

School District(s)

Boone/winnebago Roe (PK-12)

    2011-12 Enrollment: n/a . . . . (815) 636-3060

Rockford SD 205 (PK-12)

    2011-12 Enrollment: 28,118 . . . . (815) 966-3101

Four-year College(s)

Rasmussen College-Illinois (Private, For-profit)

    Fall 2012 Enrollment: 1,721 . . . . (815) 316-4800

    2012-13 Tuition: In-state $12,650; Out-of-state $12,650

Rockford University (Private, Not-for-profit)

    Fall 2012 Enrollment: 1,243 . . . . (815) 226-4186

    2012-13 Tuition: In-state $26,310; Out-of-state $26,310

Saint Anthony College of Nursing (Private, Not-for-profit, Roman Catholic)

    Fall 2012 Enrollment: 283 . . . . (815) 395-5091

Two-year College(s)

Rock Valley College (Public)

    Fall 2012 Enrollment: 8,317 . . . . (815) 921-7821

    2012-13 Tuition: In-state $8,234; Out-of-state $14,994

Rockford Career College (Private, For-profit)

    Fall 2012 Enrollment: 537 . . . . (815) 965-8616

    2012-13 Tuition: In-state $9,632; Out-of-state $9,632

Vocational/Technical School(s)

Educators of Beauty-Rockford (Private, For-profit)

    Fall 2012 Enrollment: 57 . . . . (815) 639-9200

    2012-13 Tuition: $17,175

Regency Beauty Institute-Rockford (Private, For-profit)

    Fall 2012 Enrollment: 96 . . . . (800) 787-6456

    2012-13 Tuition: $16,425

Tricoci University of Beauty Culture-Rockford (Private, For-profit)

    Fall 2012 Enrollment: 142 . . . . (630) 528-3336

    2012-13 Tuition: $18,050

Housing: Homeownership rate: 57.0% (2008-2012 5-year est.); Median home value: $106,600 (2008-2012 5-year est.); Median contract rent: $562 per month (2008-2012 5-year est.); Median year structure built: 1960 (2008-2012 5-year est.).

Health Insurance: 55.0% Private; 41.5% Public; 15.4% None. (2008-2012 5-year est.)

Hospitals: H. Douglas Singer Mental Health & Development Center (80 beds); Rockford Memorial Hospital (396 beds); St. Anthony Medical Center (254 beds); Swedish American Hospital (357 beds)

Safety: Violent crime rate: 136.8 per 10,000 population; Property crime rate: 499.6 per 10,000 population (2012).

Transportation: Commute to work: 91.6% car, 1.8% public transportation, 1.6% walk, 3.5% work from home (2008-2012 5-year est.); Travel time to work: 36.2% less than 15 minutes, 45.0% 15 to 30 minutes, 10.4% 30 to 45 minutes, 3.3% 45 to 60 minutes, 5.1% 60 minutes or more (2008-2012 5-year est.); Amtrak: Train service available.

Airports: Chicago Rockford International Airport (primary service/non-hub)

Additional Information Contacts

City of Rockford . . . . (815) 987-5700

    http://www.rockfordil.gov

Rockford Chamber of Commerce . . . . (815) 987-8100

    http://www.rockfordchamber.com

ROCKTON (village). Covers a land area of 5.499 square miles and a water area of 0.208 square miles. Located at 42.45° N. Lat; 89.06° W. Long. Elevation is 738 feet.

History: Incorporated 1847.

Population: 2,928 (1990); 5,296 (2000); 7,685 (2010); Density: 1,340.3 persons per square mile (2008-2012 5-year est.); Race: 96.6% White, 0.2% Black/African American, 2.7% Asian, 0.3% American Indian/Alaska Native, 0.0% Native Hawaiian/Other Pacific Islander, 0.2% Some other race, 0.0% Two or more races, 1.6% Hispanic of any race (2008-2012 5-year est.); Average household size: 2.75 (2008-2012 5-year est.); Median age: 38.1 (2008-2012 5-year est.); Males per 100 females: 100.9 (2008-2012 5-year est.); Marriage status: 23.3% never married, 59.5% now married, 7.2% widowed, 9.9% divorced (2008-2012 5-year est.); Foreign born: 3.0% (2008-2012 5-year est.); Ancestry (includes multiple ancestries): 39.9% German, 19.8% Irish, 10.2% English, 8.3% Italian, 7.6% Norwegian (2008-2012 5-year est.).

Economy: Homeowner vacancy rate: 0.0%. Rental vacancy rate: 3.0%. (2008-2012 5-year est.); Employment by occupation: 17.1% management, business, and financial, 6.2% computer, engineering, and science, 8.2% education, legal, community service, arts, and media, 6.9% healthcare practitioners, 17.6% service, 25.9% sales and office, 9.2% natural resources, construction, and maintenance, 8.8% production, transportation, and material moving (2008-2012 5-year est.).

Income: Per capita income: $30,444 (2008-2012 5-year est.); Median household income: $78,023 (2008-2012 5-year est.); Average household income: $82,609 (2008-2012 5-year est.); Percent of households with income of $100,000 or more: 31.5% (2008-2012 5-year est.); Poverty rate: 4.5% (2008-2012 5-year est.).

Education: Percent of population age 25 and over with: High school diploma (including GED) or higher: 94.8% (2008-2012 5-year est.); Bachelor's degree or higher: 29.3% (2008-2012 5-year est.); Master's degree or higher: 10.0% (2008-2012 5-year est.).

School District(s)

Hononegah Chd 207 (09-12)

    2011-12 Enrollment: 2,130 . . . . (815) 624-5010

Rockton SD 140 (PK-08)

    2011-12 Enrollment: 1,534 . . . . (815) 624-7143

Housing: Homeownership rate: 77.8% (2008-2012 5-year est.); Median home value: $170,300 (2008-2012 5-year est.); Median contract rent: $562 per month (2008-2012 5-year est.); Median year structure built: 1990 (2008-2012 5-year est.).

Health Insurance: 80.6% Private; 18.6% Public; 9.6% None. (2008-2012 5-year est.)

Safety: Violent crime rate: 11.8 per 10,000 population; Property crime rate: 156.7 per 10,000 population (2012).

Transportation: Commute to work: 94.6% car, 0.6% public transportation, 0.9% walk, 3.0% work from home (2008-2012 5-year est.); Travel time to work: 24.7% less than 15 minutes, 35.1% 15 to 30 minutes, 23.2% 30 to 45 minutes, 7.8% 45 to 60 minutes, 9.2% 60 minutes or more (2008-2012 5-year est.)

Additional Information Contacts

Rockton Chamber of Commerce . . . . (815) 624-7625

    http://www.rocktonchamber.com

Village of Rockton . . . . (815) 624-7600

    http://rocktonvillage.com

ROSCOE (village). Covers a land area of 10.360 square miles and a water area of 0.075 square miles. Located at 42.43° N. Lat; 89.01° W. Long. Elevation is 738 feet.

Population: 2,079 (1990); 6,244 (2000); 10,785 (2010); Density: 1,030.8 persons per square mile (2008-2012 5-year est.); Race: 91.8% White, 2.9% Black/African American, 3.2% Asian, 0.1% American Indian/Alaska Native, 0.0% Native Hawaiian/Other Pacific Islander, 2.0% Some other race, 1.5% Two or more races, 3.8% Hispanic of any race (2008-2012 5-year est.); Average household size: 2.92 (2008-2012 5-year est.); Median age: 34.5 (2008-2012 5-year est.); Males per 100 females: 92.6 (2008-2012 5-year est.); Marriage status: 24.2% never married, 63.4% now married, 3.3% widowed, 9.0% divorced (2008-2012 5-year est.); Foreign born: 6.4% (2008-2012 5-year est.); Ancestry (includes multiple ancestries): 31.6% German, 14.3% Irish, 13.5% American, 10.4% English, 8.4% Italian (2008-2012 5-year est.).

Economy: Homeowner vacancy rate: 0.0%. Rental vacancy rate: 4.3%. (2008-2012 5-year est.); Employment by occupation: 12.4% management, business, and financial, 7.3% computer, engineering, and science, 7.4% education, legal, community service, arts, and media, 6.3% healthcare practitioners, 14.5% service, 27.0% sales and office, 8.9% natural resources, construction, and maintenance, 16.3% production, transportation, and material moving (2008-2012 5-year est.).

Income: Per capita income: $26,491 (2008-2012 5-year est.); Median household income: $69,122 (2008-2012 5-year est.); Average household income: $76,036 (2008-2012 5-year est.); Percent of households with income of $100,000 or more: 23.6% (2008-2012 5-year est.); Poverty rate: 5.8% (2008-2012 5-year est.).

Taxes: Total city taxes per capita: $190 (2011); City property taxes per capita: $137 (2011).

Education: Percent of population age 25 and over with: High school diploma (including GED) or higher: 91.7% (2008-2012 5-year est.); Bachelor's degree or higher: 27.9% (2008-2012 5-year est.); Master's degree or higher: 9.2% (2008-2012 5-year est.).

School District(s)

Kinnikinnick CCSD 131 (PK-08)

    2011-12 Enrollment: 2,045 . . . . (815) 623-2837

Housing: Homeownership rate: 67.5% (2008-2012 5-year est.); Median home value: $172,000 (2008-2012 5-year est.); Median contract rent: $832 per month (2008-2012 5-year est.); Median year structure built: 1990 (2008-2012 5-year est.).

Health Insurance: 81.5% Private; 21.9% Public; 6.4% None. (2008-2012 5-year est.)

Transportation: Commute to work: 95.2% car, 0.2% public transportation, 0.8% walk, 2.4% work from home (2008-2012 5-year est.); Travel time to work: 17.0% less than 15 minutes, 52.8% 15 to 30 minutes, 18.1% 30 to 45 minutes, 3.6% 45 to 60 minutes, 8.5% 60 minutes or more (2008-2012 5-year est.)

Additional Information Contacts

Roscoe Area Chamber of Commerce . . . . (815) 623-9065

    http://www.roscoechamber.com

Village of Roscoe . . . . (815) 623-2829

    http://www.villageofroscoe.com

SEWARD (unincorporated postal area)

Zip Code: 61077

    Covers a land area of 0.031 square miles and a water area of 0 square miles. Located at 42.23° N. Lat; 89.35° W. Long. Elevation is 896 feet. Population: 73 (2010); Density: 2,282.3 persons per square mile (2010); Race: 100.0% White, 0.0% Black/African American, 0.0% Asian, 0.0% American Indian/Alaska Native, 0.0% Native Hawaiian/Other Pacific Islander, 0.0% Some other race, 0.0% Two or more races, 2.7% Hispanic of any race (2010); Average household size: 2.21 (2010); Median age: 45.5 (2010); Males per 100 females: 82.5 (2010); Homeownership rate: 57.6% (2010)

SHIRLAND (unincorporated postal area)

Zip Code: 61079

    Covers a land area of 1.764 square miles and a water area of 0.035 square miles. Located at 42.43° N. Lat; 89.21° W. Long. Elevation is 738 feet. Population: 188 (2010); Density: 106.5 persons per square mile (2010); Race: 99.5% White, 0.5% Black/African American, 0.0% Asian, 0.0% American Indian/Alaska Native, 0.0% Native Hawaiian/Other Pacific Islander, 0.0% Some other race, 0.0% Two or more races, 0.5% Hispanic of any race (2010); Average household size: 2.81 (2010); Median age: 40.3 (2010); Males per 100 females: 123.8 (2010); Homeownership rate: 77.6% (2010)

SOUTH BELOIT (city). Covers a land area of 5.901 square miles and a water area of 0.230 square miles. Located at 42.48° N. Lat; 89.03° W. Long. Elevation is 738 feet.

History: Incorporated 1917.

Population: 4,072 (1990); 5,397 (2000); 7,892 (2010); Density: 1,341.6 persons per square mile (2008-2012 5-year est.); Race: 92.4% White, 3.4% Black/African American, 1.9% Asian, 0.0% American Indian/Alaska Native, 0.0% Native Hawaiian/Other Pacific Islander, 2.3% Some other race, 2.1% Two or more races, 8.3% Hispanic of any race (2008-2012 5-year est.); Average household size: 2.89 (2008-2012 5-year est.); Median age: 32.8 (2008-2012 5-year est.); Males per 100 females: 83.0 (2008-2012 5-year est.); Marriage status: 28.0% never married, 54.6% now married, 4.0% widowed, 13.5% divorced (2008-2012 5-year est.); Foreign born: 2.5% (2008-2012 5-year est.); Ancestry (includes multiple ancestries): 27.5% German, 16.8% Irish, 11.9% American, 10.8% Italian, 8.9% Norwegian (2008-2012 5-year est.).

Economy: Homeowner vacancy rate: 1.8%. Rental vacancy rate: 7.6%. (2008-2012 5-year est.); Employment by occupation: 8.8% management, business, and financial, 5.7% computer, engineering, and science, 4.3% education, legal, community service, arts, and media, 3.1% healthcare practitioners, 15.6% service, 32.6% sales and office, 7.9% natural resources, construction, and maintenance, 21.9% production, transportation, and material moving (2008-2012 5-year est.).
Income: Per capita income: $21,547 (2008-2012 5-year est.); Median household income: $49,472 (2008-2012 5-year est.); Average household income: $61,142 (2008-2012 5-year est.); Percent of households with income of $100,000 or more: 15.4% (2008-2012 5-year est.); Poverty rate: 14.4% (2008-2012 5-year est.).
Education: Percent of population age 25 and over with: High school diploma (including GED) or higher: 86.9% (2008-2012 5-year est.); Bachelor's degree or higher: 14.6% (2008-2012 5-year est.); Master's degree or higher: 2.6% (2008-2012 5-year est.).

School District(s)
County of Winnebago SD 320 (PK-12)
 2011-12 Enrollment: 1,061 . . . . (815) 389-3478
Prairie Hill CCSD 133 (KG-08)
 2011-12 Enrollment: 777. . . . . (815) 389-3957
Housing: Homeownership rate: 71.4% (2008-2012 5-year est.); Median home value: $126,200 (2008-2012 5-year est.); Median contract rent: $571 per month (2008-2012 5-year est.); Median year structure built: 1990 (2008-2012 5-year est.).
Health Insurance: 72.1% Private; 25.9% Public; 10.1% None. (2008-2012 5-year est.)
Safety: Violent crime rate: 21.6 per 10,000 population; Property crime rate: 207.4 per 10,000 population (2012).
Transportation: Commute to work: 95.3% car, 0.0% public transportation, 2.3% walk, 1.9% work from home (2008-2012 5-year est.); Travel time to work: 43.0% less than 15 minutes, 28.7% 15 to 30 minutes, 16.9% 30 to 45 minutes, 5.1% 45 to 60 minutes, 6.2% 60 minutes or more (2008-2012 5-year est.); Amtrak: Bus service available.
Additional Information Contacts
City of South Beloit . . . . (815) 389-3023
 http://www.southbeloit.org

WINNEBAGO (village).
Covers a land area of 1.948 square miles and a water area of 0 square miles. Located at 42.27° N. Lat; 89.23° W. Long. Elevation is 869 feet.
Population: 1,840 (1990); 2,958 (2000); 3,101 (2010); Density: 1,783.3 persons per square mile (2008-2012 5-year est.); Race: 94.2% White, 2.7% Black/African American, 0.0% Asian, 0.0% American Indian/Alaska Native, 0.0% Native Hawaiian/Other Pacific Islander, 3.1% Some other race, 2.9% Two or more races, 3.6% Hispanic of any race (2008-2012 5-year est.); Average household size: 2.96 (2008-2012 5-year est.); Median age: 38.6 (2008-2012 5-year est.); Males per 100 females: 97.0 (2008-2012 5-year est.); Marriage status: 21.7% never married, 65.9% now married, 3.5% widowed, 8.8% divorced (2008-2012 5-year est.); Foreign born: 2.0% (2008-2012 5-year est.); Ancestry (includes multiple ancestries): 44.3% German, 20.8% Irish, 11.7% American, 10.3% English, 7.5% Italian (2008-2012 5-year est.).
Economy: Single-family building permits issued: 1 (2013); Multi-family building permits issued: 0 (2013); Homeowner vacancy rate: 2.7%. Rental vacancy rate: 8.6%. (2008-2012 5-year est.); Employment by occupation: 11.1% management, business, and financial, 6.6% computer, engineering, and science, 12.4% education, legal, community service, arts, and media, 7.6% healthcare practitioners, 12.7% service, 26.3% sales and office, 9.4% natural resources, construction, and maintenance, 13.9% production, transportation, and material moving (2008-2012 5-year est.).
Income: Per capita income: $29,062 (2008-2012 5-year est.); Median household income: $78,782 (2008-2012 5-year est.); Average household income: $84,415 (2008-2012 5-year est.); Percent of households with income of $100,000 or more: 31.2% (2008-2012 5-year est.); Poverty rate: 5.5% (2008-2012 5-year est.).
Education: Percent of population age 25 and over with: High school diploma (including GED) or higher: 96.8% (2008-2012 5-year est.); Bachelor's degree or higher: 26.9% (2008-2012 5-year est.); Master's degree or higher: 10.6% (2008-2012 5-year est.).

School District(s)
Winnebago CUSD 323 (PK-12)
 2011-12 Enrollment: 1,593 . . . . (815) 335-2456
Housing: Homeownership rate: 84.7% (2008-2012 5-year est.); Median home value: $151,600 (2008-2012 5-year est.); Median contract rent: $591

per month (2008-2012 5-year est.); Median year structure built: 1983 (2008-2012 5-year est.).
Health Insurance: 85.9% Private; 23.4% Public; 4.3% None. (2008-2012 5-year est.)
Safety: Violent crime rate: 9.7 per 10,000 population; Property crime rate: 194.3 per 10,000 population (2012).
Transportation: Commute to work: 94.7% car, 0.3% public transportation, 0.3% walk, 4.7% work from home (2008-2012 5-year est.); Travel time to work: 21.0% less than 15 minutes, 52.7% 15 to 30 minutes, 18.6% 30 to 45 minutes, 3.3% 45 to 60 minutes, 4.5% 60 minutes or more (2008-2012 5-year est.)

Woodford County

Located in central Illinois; bounded on the west by the Illinois River; drained by the Mackinaw River. Covers a land area of 527.799 square miles, a water area of 14.843 square miles, and is located in the Central Time Zone at 40.79° N. Lat., 89.21° W. Long. The county was founded in 1841. County seat is Eureka.

Woodford County is part of the Peoria, IL Metropolitan Statistical Area. The entire metro area includes: Marshall County, IL; Peoria County, IL; Stark County, IL; Tazewell County, IL; Woodford County, IL

Weather Station: Minonk									Elevation: 750 feet			
	Jan	Feb	Mar	Apr	May	Jun	Jul	Aug	Sep	Oct	Nov	Dec
High	32	37	49	62	73	83	86	84	78	65	50	36
Low	15	19	28	39	49	59	63	60	52	41	31	19
Precip	2.0	1.9	2.9	3.6	4.2	3.7	3.8	3.5	3.4	3.0	3.5	2.4
Snow	6.5	6.7	2.9	0.9	tr	0.0	0.0	0.0	0.0	tr	0.8	6.2

High and Low temperatures in degrees Fahrenheit; Precipitation and Snow in inches

Population: 32,653 (1990); 35,469 (2000); 38,664 (2010); Race: 97.2% White, 0.6% Black/African American, 0.6% Asian, 0.1% American Indian/Alaska Native, 0.0% Native Hawaiian/Other Pacific Islander, 1.5% Some other race, 1.0% Two or more races, 1.4% Hispanic of any race (2008-2012 5-year est.); Density: 73.8 persons per square mile (2008-2012 5-year est.); Average household size: 2.64 (2008-2012 5-year est.); Median age: 40.1 (2008-2012 5-year est.); Males per 100 females: 97.1 (2008-2012 5-year est.).
Religion: Six largest groups: 10.7% European Free-Church, 9.8% Catholicism, 5.1% Methodist/Pietist, 4.7% Lutheran, 4.1% Non-denominational Protestant, 3.3% Baptist (2010)
Economy: Unemployment rate: 5.6% (April 2014); Total civilian labor force: 20,456 (April 2014); Leading industries: 24.5% manufacturing; 20.8% health care and social assistance; 9.8% retail trade (2012); Farms: 958 totaling 322,983 acres (2012); Companies that employ 500 or more persons: 1 (2012); Companies that employ 100 to 499 persons: 16 (2012); Companies that employ less than 100 persons: 739 (2012); Black-owned businesses: n/a (2007); Hispanic-owned businesses: n/a (2007); Asian-owned businesses: n/a (2007); Women-owned businesses: n/a (2007); Single-family building permits issued: 82 (2013); Multi-family building permits issued: 10 (2013).
Income: Per capita income: $30,401 (2008-2012 5-year est.); Median household income: $68,552 (2008-2012 5-year est.); Average household income: $81,294 (2008-2012 5-year est.); Percent of households with income of $100,000 or more: 29.3% (2008-2012 5-year est.); Poverty rate: 7.4% (2008-2012 5-year est.); Bankruptcy rate: 3.05% (2013).
Taxes: Total county taxes per capita: $83 (2011); County property taxes per capita: $83 (2011).
Education: Percent of population age 25 and over with: High school diploma (including GED) or higher: 93.0% (2008-2012 5-year est.); Bachelor's degree or higher: 26.3% (2008-2012 5-year est.); Master's degree or higher: 8.5% (2008-2012 5-year est.).
Housing: Homeownership rate: 82.4% (2008-2012 5-year est.); Median home value: $156,600 (2008-2012 5-year est.); Median contract rent: $493 per month (2008-2012 5-year est.); Median year structure built: 1971 (2008-2012 5-year est.)
Health: Birth rate: 115.6 per 10,000 population (2013); Death rate: 98.0 per 10,000 population (2013); Age-adjusted cancer mortality rate: 175.0 deaths per 100,000 population (2011); Number of physicians: 11.3 per 10,000 population (2011); Hospital beds: 4.7 per 10,000 population (2010); Hospital admissions: 138.1 per 10,000 population (2010).
Elections: 2012 Presidential election results: 29.5% Obama, 68.7% Romney
National and State Parks: Woodford County State Conservation Area

Additional Information Contacts
Woodford County Government . . . . (309) 467-2822
　http://www.woodford-county.org

Woodford County Communities

BAY VIEW GARDENS (village). Covers a land area of 0.435 square miles and a water area of 0 square miles. Located at 40.81° N. Lat; 89.52° W. Long. Elevation is 525 feet.
Population: 418 (1990); 366 (2000); 378 (2010); Density: 945.4 persons per square mile (2008-2012 5-year est.); Race: 99.0% White, 0.0% Black/African American, 0.0% Asian, 0.2% American Indian/Alaska Native, 0.0% Native Hawaiian/Other Pacific Islander, 0.8% Some other race, 0.7% Two or more races, 1.5% Hispanic of any race (2008-2012 5-year est.); Average household size: 2.42 (2008-2012 5-year est.); Median age: 42.6 (2008-2012 5-year est.); Males per 100 females: 115.2 (2008-2012 5-year est.); Marriage status: 27.4% never married, 53.9% now married, 7.9% widowed, 10.8% divorced (2008-2012 5-year est.); Foreign born: 0.5% (2008-2012 5-year est.); Ancestry (includes multiple ancestries): 19.7% American, 18.2% German, 15.1% Dutch, 10.5% French, 8.0% English (2008-2012 5-year est.).
Economy: Single-family building permits issued: 3 (2013); Multi-family building permits issued: 0 (2013); Homeowner vacancy rate: 0.0%. Rental vacancy rate: 0.0%. (2008-2012 5-year est.); Employment by occupation: 6.3% management, business, and financial, 1.4% computer, engineering, and science, 3.9% education, legal, community service, arts, and media, 0.5% healthcare practitioners, 28.0% service, 29.5% sales and office, 7.2% natural resources, construction, and maintenance, 23.2% production, transportation, and material moving (2008-2012 5-year est.).
Income: Per capita income: $23,201 (2008-2012 5-year est.); Median household income: $43,929 (2008-2012 5-year est.); Average household income: $56,632 (2008-2012 5-year est.); Percent of households with income of $100,000 or more: 15.3% (2008-2012 5-year est.); Poverty rate: 10.5% (2008-2012 5-year est.).
Education: Percent of population age 25 and over with: High school diploma (including GED) or higher: 81.4% (2008-2012 5-year est.); Bachelor's degree or higher: 3.8% (2008-2012 5-year est.); Master's degree or higher: 1.5% (2008-2012 5-year est.).
Housing: Homeownership rate: 80.0% (2008-2012 5-year est.); Median home value: $94,500 (2008-2012 5-year est.); Median contract rent: $186 per month (2008-2012 5-year est.); Median year structure built: 1962 (2008-2012 5-year est.).
Health Insurance: 66.7% Private; 24.6% Public; 20.7% None. (2008-2012 5-year est.)
Transportation: Commute to work: 97.5% car, 0.0% public transportation, 0.0% walk, 1.5% work from home (2008-2012 5-year est.); Travel time to work: 19.9% less than 15 minutes, 63.2% 15 to 30 minutes, 10.0% 30 to 45 minutes, 6.0% 45 to 60 minutes, 1.0% 60 minutes or more (2008-2012 5-year est.)

BENSON (village). Covers a land area of 0.168 square miles and a water area of 0 square miles. Located at 40.85° N. Lat; 89.12° W. Long. Elevation is 764 feet.
Population: 410 (1990); 408 (2000); 423 (2010); Density: 2,658.7 persons per square mile (2008-2012 5-year est.); Race: 98.0% White, 0.0% Black/African American, 0.0% Asian, 0.0% American Indian/Alaska Native, 0.0% Native Hawaiian/Other Pacific Islander, 2.0% Some other race, 2.0% Two or more races, 0.4% Hispanic of any race (2008-2012 5-year est.); Average household size: 2.24 (2008-2012 5-year est.); Median age: 40.3 (2008-2012 5-year est.); Males per 100 females: 93.9 (2008-2012 5-year est.); Marriage status: 19.6% never married, 62.2% now married, 5.8% widowed, 12.4% divorced (2008-2012 5-year est.); Foreign born: 0.2% (2008-2012 5-year est.); Ancestry (includes multiple ancestries): 56.5% German, 17.0% Irish, 10.5% English, 7.4% American, 4.7% Italian (2008-2012 5-year est.).
Economy: Single-family building permits issued: 0 (2013); Multi-family building permits issued: 0 (2013); Homeowner vacancy rate: 1.2%. Rental vacancy rate: 0.0%. (2008-2012 5-year est.); Employment by occupation: 6.8% management, business, and financial, 2.3% computer, engineering, and science, 3.7% education, legal, community service, arts, and media, 5.9% healthcare practitioners, 20.5% service, 25.1% sales and office, 12.8% natural resources, construction, and maintenance, 22.8% production, transportation, and material moving (2008-2012 5-year est.).
Income: Per capita income: $25,307 (2008-2012 5-year est.); Median household income: $46,250 (2008-2012 5-year est.); Average household

income: $55,457 (2008-2012 5-year est.); Percent of households with income of $100,000 or more: 13.6% (2008-2012 5-year est.); Poverty rate: 11.0% (2008-2012 5-year est.).
Education: Percent of population age 25 and over with: High school diploma (including GED) or higher: 92.5% (2008-2012 5-year est.); Bachelor's degree or higher: 12.3% (2008-2012 5-year est.); Master's degree or higher: 2.5% (2008-2012 5-year est.).
School District(s)
Roanoke Benson CUSD 60 (PK-12)
　2011-12 Enrollment: 581 . . . . (309) 923-8921
Housing: Homeownership rate: 80.9% (2008-2012 5-year est.); Median home value: $82,000 (2008-2012 5-year est.); Median contract rent: $500 per month (2008-2012 5-year est.); Median year structure built: 1941 (2008-2012 5-year est.).
Health Insurance: 73.0% Private; 34.9% Public; 7.0% None. (2008-2012 5-year est.)
Transportation: Commute to work: 92.4% car, 0.0% public transportation, 4.8% walk, 1.9% work from home (2008-2012 5-year est.); Travel time to work: 33.5% less than 15 minutes, 30.1% 15 to 30 minutes, 20.4% 30 to 45 minutes, 11.2% 45 to 60 minutes, 4.9% 60 minutes or more (2008-2012 5-year est.)

CONGERVILLE (village). Covers a land area of 1.116 square miles and a water area of 0.004 square miles. Located at 40.62° N. Lat; 89.20° W. Long. Elevation is 748 feet.
Population: 397 (1990); 466 (2000); 474 (2010); Density: 464.3 persons per square mile (2008-2012 5-year est.); Race: 99.4% White, 0.0% Black/African American, 0.2% Asian, 0.0% American Indian/Alaska Native, 0.0% Native Hawaiian/Other Pacific Islander, 0.4% Some other race, 0.4% Two or more races, 0.6% Hispanic of any race (2008-2012 5-year est.); Average household size: 3.10 (2008-2012 5-year est.); Median age: 30.1 (2008-2012 5-year est.); Males per 100 females: 109.7 (2008-2012 5-year est.); Marriage status: 20.2% never married, 70.3% now married, 2.8% widowed, 6.7% divorced (2008-2012 5-year est.); Foreign born: 0.0% (2008-2012 5-year est.); Ancestry (includes multiple ancestries): 61.6% German, 20.3% Swiss, 9.8% American, 8.7% Irish, 5.8% English (2008-2012 5-year est.).
Economy: Single-family building permits issued: 2 (2013); Multi-family building permits issued: 0 (2013); Homeowner vacancy rate: 0.0%. Rental vacancy rate: 0.0%. (2008-2012 5-year est.); Employment by occupation: 19.2% management, business, and financial, 5.5% computer, engineering, and science, 4.3% education, legal, community service, arts, and media, 11.8% healthcare practitioners, 10.6% service, 22.4% sales and office, 16.9% natural resources, construction, and maintenance, 9.4% production, transportation, and material moving (2008-2012 5-year est.).
Income: Per capita income: $27,957 (2008-2012 5-year est.); Median household income: $69,250 (2008-2012 5-year est.); Average household income: $88,178 (2008-2012 5-year est.); Percent of households with income of $100,000 or more: 26.4% (2008-2012 5-year est.); Poverty rate: 2.7% (2008-2012 5-year est.).
Education: Percent of population age 25 and over with: High school diploma (including GED) or higher: 96.0% (2008-2012 5-year est.); Bachelor's degree or higher: 25.3% (2008-2012 5-year est.); Master's degree or higher: 4.0% (2008-2012 5-year est.).
School District(s)
Eureka CUD 140 (PK-12)
　2011-12 Enrollment: 1,595 . . . . (309) 467-3737
Housing: Homeownership rate: 76.6% (2008-2012 5-year est.); Median home value: $136,700 (2008-2012 5-year est.); Median contract rent: $550 per month (2008-2012 5-year est.); Median year structure built: 1971 (2008-2012 5-year est.).
Health Insurance: 91.5% Private; 11.6% Public; 4.8% None. (2008-2012 5-year est.)
Transportation: Commute to work: 92.5% car, 0.0% public transportation, 3.6% walk, 4.0% work from home (2008-2012 5-year est.); Travel time to work: 34.3% less than 15 minutes, 32.2% 15 to 30 minutes, 28.5% 30 to 45 minutes, 3.7% 45 to 60 minutes, 1.2% 60 minutes or more (2008-2012 5-year est.)

EL PASO (city). Covers a land area of 2.133 square miles and a water area of 0 square miles. Located at 40.74° N. Lat; 89.02° W. Long. Elevation is 751 feet.
History: El Paso was the home of Lester Pfister who developed a hybrid corn that gave a high yield.

Population: 2,499 (1990); 2,695 (2000); 2,810 (2010); Density: 1,193.5 persons per square mile (2008-2012 5-year est.); Race: 97.5% White, 1.1% Black/African American, 0.2% Asian, 0.6% American Indian/Alaska Native, 0.0% Native Hawaiian/Other Pacific Islander, 0.6% Some other race, 0.7% Two or more races, 1.8% Hispanic of any race (2008-2012 5-year est.); Average household size: 2.49 (2008-2012 5-year est.); Median age: 41.3 (2008-2012 5-year est.); Males per 100 females: 76.4 (2008-2012 5-year est.); Marriage status: 29.6% never married, 51.4% now married, 8.4% widowed, 10.6% divorced (2008-2012 5-year est.); Foreign born: 1.1% (2008-2012 5-year est.); Ancestry (includes multiple ancestries): 40.7% German, 15.9% English, 14.1% Irish, 7.3% American, 2.4% Italian (2008-2012 5-year est.).
Economy: Single-family building permits issued: 1 (2013); Multi-family building permits issued: 0 (2013); Homeowner vacancy rate: 3.4%. Rental vacancy rate: 8.8%. (2008-2012 5-year est.); Employment by occupation: 7.9% management, business, and financial, 1.9% computer, engineering, and science, 6.8% education, legal, community service, arts, and media, 5.2% healthcare practitioners, 15.7% service, 28.6% sales and office, 16.5% natural resources, construction, and maintenance, 17.5% production, transportation, and material moving (2008-2012 5-year est.).
Income: Per capita income: $26,086 (2008-2012 5-year est.); Median household income: $52,452 (2008-2012 5-year est.); Average household income: $65,834 (2008-2012 5-year est.); Percent of households with income of $100,000 or more: 23.8% (2008-2012 5-year est.); Poverty rate: 6.4% (2008-2012 5-year est.).
Education: Percent of population age 25 and over with: High school diploma (including GED) or higher: 91.0% (2008-2012 5-year est.); Bachelor's degree or higher: 12.6% (2008-2012 5-year est.); Master's degree or higher: 4.9% (2008-2012 5-year est.).

School District(s)
El Paso-Gridley CUSD 11 (PK-12)
    2011-12 Enrollment: 1,278 . . . . (309) 527-4410
Housing: Homeownership rate: 77.3% (2008-2012 5-year est.); Median home value: $115,000 (2008-2012 5-year est.); Median contract rent: $520 per month (2008-2012 5-year est.); Median year structure built: 1960 (2008-2012 5-year est.).
Health Insurance: 71.2% Private; 34.6% Public; 7.2% None. (2008-2012 5-year est.)
Safety: Violent crime rate: 21.2 per 10,000 population; Property crime rate: 198.2 per 10,000 population (2012).
Transportation: Commute to work: 94.5% car, 0.2% public transportation, 2.0% walk, 1.8% work from home (2008-2012 5-year est.); Travel time to work: 41.1% less than 15 minutes, 28.6% 15 to 30 minutes, 23.3% 30 to 45 minutes, 4.1% 45 to 60 minutes, 3.0% 60 minutes or more (2008-2012 5-year est.)

EUREKA (city). County seat. Covers a land area of 3.023 square miles and a water area of 0.048 square miles. Located at 40.71° N. Lat; 89.28° W. Long. Elevation is 768 feet.
History: Eureka was settled in the 1830's, and developed around Eureka College, which began in 1848 as a seminary founded by the Disciples of Christ. Eureka was named the seat of Woodford County in 1896.
Population: 4,435 (1990); 4,871 (2000); 5,295 (2010); Density: 1,793.5 persons per square mile (2008-2012 5-year est.); Race: 96.3% White, 1.5% Black/African American, 0.1% Asian, 0.2% American Indian/Alaska Native, 0.0% Native Hawaiian/Other Pacific Islander, 1.9% Some other race, 0.8% Two or more races, 1.9% Hispanic of any race (2008-2012 5-year est.); Average household size: 2.54 (2008-2012 5-year est.); Median age: 37.2 (2008-2012 5-year est.); Males per 100 females: 95.9 (2008-2012 5-year est.); Marriage status: 26.4% never married, 55.0% now married, 9.7% widowed, 8.9% divorced (2008-2012 5-year est.); Foreign born: 1.9% (2008-2012 5-year est.); Ancestry (includes multiple ancestries): 46.6% German, 18.8% Irish, 9.4% English, 5.6% American, 5.4% Swiss (2008-2012 5-year est.).
Economy: Single-family building permits issued: 6 (2013); Multi-family building permits issued: 6 (2013); Homeowner vacancy rate: 0.0%. Rental vacancy rate: 7.7%. (2008-2012 5-year est.); Employment by occupation: 16.9% management, business, and financial, 4.9% computer, engineering, and science, 12.6% education, legal, community service, arts, and media, 5.2% healthcare practitioners, 18.7% service, 23.0% sales and office, 7.6% natural resources, construction, and maintenance, 11.3% production, transportation, and material moving (2008-2012 5-year est.).
Income: Per capita income: $24,113 (2008-2012 5-year est.); Median household income: $53,950 (2008-2012 5-year est.); Average household income: $65,263 (2008-2012 5-year est.); Percent of households with

income of $100,000 or more: 22.9% (2008-2012 5-year est.); Poverty rate: 17.1% (2008-2012 5-year est.).
Education: Percent of population age 25 and over with: High school diploma (including GED) or higher: 93.2% (2008-2012 5-year est.); Bachelor's degree or higher: 25.9% (2008-2012 5-year est.); Master's degree or higher: 11.8% (2008-2012 5-year est.).

School District(s)
Eureka CUD 140 (PK-12)
    2011-12 Enrollment: 1,595 . . . . (309) 467-3737
Four-year College(s)
Eureka College (Private, Not-for-profit, Christian Church (Disciples of Christ))
    Fall 2012 Enrollment: 754 . . . . (309) 467-3721
    2012-13 Tuition: In-state $19,480; Out-of-state $19,480
Housing: Homeownership rate: 65.1% (2008-2012 5-year est.); Median home value: $142,700 (2008-2012 5-year est.); Median contract rent: $444 per month (2008-2012 5-year est.); Median year structure built: 1972 (2008-2012 5-year est.).
Health Insurance: 72.0% Private; 37.9% Public; 5.3% None. (2008-2012 5-year est.)
Hospitals: Eureka Community Hospital (25 beds)
Safety: Violent crime rate: 9.4 per 10,000 population; Property crime rate: 105.2 per 10,000 population (2012).
Transportation: Commute to work: 85.0% car, 0.0% public transportation, 8.0% walk, 4.9% work from home (2008-2012 5-year est.); Travel time to work: 40.3% less than 15 minutes, 29.7% 15 to 30 minutes, 23.2% 30 to 45 minutes, 5.9% 45 to 60 minutes, 0.9% 60 minutes or more (2008-2012 5-year est.)

GERMANTOWN HILLS (village). Aka Oak Grove Park. Covers a land area of 1.626 square miles and a water area of 0.047 square miles. Located at 40.77° N. Lat; 89.46° W. Long. Elevation is 804 feet.
Population: 1,195 (1990); 2,111 (2000); 3,438 (2010); Density: 2,094.1 persons per square mile (2008-2012 5-year est.); Race: 97.6% White, 0.0% Black/African American, 2.2% Asian, 0.0% American Indian/Alaska Native, 0.0% Native Hawaiian/Other Pacific Islander, 0.2% Some other race, 0.0% Two or more races, 0.8% Hispanic of any race (2008-2012 5-year est.); Average household size: 2.98 (2008-2012 5-year est.); Median age: 36.4 (2008-2012 5-year est.); Males per 100 females: 94.5 (2008-2012 5-year est.); Marriage status: 26.1% never married, 63.5% now married, 2.7% widowed, 7.8% divorced (2008-2012 5-year est.); Foreign born: 1.5% (2008-2012 5-year est.); Ancestry (includes multiple ancestries): 35.7% German, 21.3% Irish, 11.0% English, 6.8% American, 4.1% European (2008-2012 5-year est.).
Economy: Single-family building permits issued: 7 (2013); Multi-family building permits issued: 4 (2013); Homeowner vacancy rate: 1.2%. Rental vacancy rate: 22.7%. (2008-2012 5-year est.); Employment by occupation: 20.1% management, business, and financial, 10.3% computer, engineering, and science, 11.4% education, legal, community service, arts, and media, 6.3% healthcare practitioners, 11.4% service, 24.7% sales and office, 11.0% natural resources, construction, and maintenance, 4.8% production, transportation, and material moving (2008-2012 5-year est.).
Income: Per capita income: $35,962 (2008-2012 5-year est.); Median household income: $96,055 (2008-2012 5-year est.); Average household income: $107,450 (2008-2012 5-year est.); Percent of households with income of $100,000 or more: 45.3% (2008-2012 5-year est.); Poverty rate: 3.6% (2008-2012 5-year est.).
Education: Percent of population age 25 and over with: High school diploma (including GED) or higher: 98.4% (2008-2012 5-year est.); Bachelor's degree or higher: 42.7% (2008-2012 5-year est.); Master's degree or higher: 11.2% (2008-2012 5-year est.).

School District(s)
Germantown Hills SD 69 (PK-08)
    2011-12 Enrollment: 894 . . . . (309) 383-2121
Housing: Homeownership rate: 91.1% (2008-2012 5-year est.); Median home value: $215,600 (2008-2012 5-year est.); Median contract rent: $832 per month (2008-2012 5-year est.); Median year structure built: 1996 (2008-2012 5-year est.).
Health Insurance: 87.5% Private; 14.4% Public; 6.6% None. (2008-2012 5-year est.)
Transportation: Commute to work: 95.8% car, 0.0% public transportation, 0.0% walk, 3.8% work from home (2008-2012 5-year est.); Travel time to work: 16.2% less than 15 minutes, 59.5% 15 to 30 minutes, 19.6% 30 to 45 minutes, 2.2% 45 to 60 minutes, 2.5% 60 minutes or more (2008-2012 5-year est.)

GOODFIELD (village). Covers a land area of 1.688 square miles and a water area of 0.008 square miles. Located at 40.63° N. Lat; 89.26° W. Long. Elevation is 741 feet.
Population: 454 (1990); 686 (2000); 860 (2010); Density: 615.6 persons per square mile (2008-2012 5-year est.); Race: 93.7% White, 0.0% Black/African American, 0.0% Asian, 0.0% American Indian/Alaska Native, 0.0% Native Hawaiian/Other Pacific Islander, 6.3% Some other race, 6.3% Two or more races, 0.2% Hispanic of any race (2008-2012 5-year est.); Average household size: 3.06 (2008-2012 5-year est.); Median age: 33.2 (2008-2012 5-year est.); Males per 100 females: 99.8 (2008-2012 5-year est.); Marriage status: 24.0% never married, 66.6% now married, 5.6% widowed, 3.8% divorced (2008-2012 5-year est.); Foreign born: 0.0% (2008-2012 5-year est.); Ancestry (includes multiple ancestries): 45.1% German, 13.0% Irish, 8.2% English, 6.5% European, 6.3% Swiss (2008-2012 5-year est.).
Economy: Single-family building permits issued: 7 (2013); Multi-family building permits issued: 0 (2013); Homeowner vacancy rate: 0.0%. Rental vacancy rate: 0.0%. (2008-2012 5-year est.); Employment by occupation: 13.8% management, business, and financial, 6.0% computer, engineering, and science, 9.9% education, legal, community service, arts, and media, 6.4% healthcare practitioners, 23.8% service, 18.1% sales and office, 8.0% natural resources, construction, and maintenance, 13.8% production, transportation, and material moving (2008-2012 5-year est.).
Income: Per capita income: $30,995 (2008-2012 5-year est.); Median household income: $84,432 (2008-2012 5-year est.); Average household income: $94,032 (2008-2012 5-year est.); Percent of households with income of $100,000 or more: 35.6% (2008-2012 5-year est.); Poverty rate: 3.0% (2008-2012 5-year est.).
Taxes: Total city taxes per capita: $500 (2011); City property taxes per capita: $363 (2011).
Education: Percent of population age 25 and over with: High school diploma (including GED) or higher: 98.2% (2008-2012 5-year est.); Bachelor's degree or higher: 29.1% (2008-2012 5-year est.); Master's degree or higher: 7.6% (2008-2012 5-year est.).
School District(s)
Eureka CUD 140 (PK-12)
    2011-12 Enrollment: 1,595 . . . . (309) 467-3737
Housing: Homeownership rate: 95.9% (2008-2012 5-year est.); Median home value: $210,200 (2008-2012 5-year est.); Median contract rent: $375 per month (2000-2012 5-year est.); Median year structure built: 1979 (2008-2012 5-year est.).
Health Insurance: 90.1% Private; 15.5% Public; 5.6% None. (2008-2012 5-year est.)
Safety: Violent crime rate: 0.0 per 10,000 population; Property crime rate: 695.2 per 10,000 population (2012).
Transportation: Commute to work: 93.9% car, 0.0% public transportation, 2.0% walk, 3.5% work from home (2008-2012 5-year est.); Travel time to work: 41.2% less than 15 minutes, 33.1% 15 to 30 minutes, 18.8% 30 to 45 minutes, 5.1% 45 to 60 minutes, 1.8% 60 minutes or more (2008-2012 5-year est.)

KAPPA (village). Covers a land area of 0.338 square miles and a water area of 0 square miles. Located at 40.68° N. Lat; 89.01° W. Long. Elevation is 738 feet.
Population: 134 (1990); 170 (2000); 227 (2010); Density: 1,218.3 persons per square mile (2008-2012 5-year est.); Race: 100.0% White, 0.0% Black/African American, 0.0% Asian, 0.0% American Indian/Alaska Native, 0.0% Native Hawaiian/Other Pacific Islander, 0.0% Some other race, 0.0% Two or more races, 1.0% Hispanic of any race (2008-2012 5-year est.); Average household size: 3.19 (2008-2012 5-year est.); Median age: 25.3 (2008-2012 5-year est.); Males per 100 females: 127.6 (2008-2012 5-year est.); Marriage status: 36.0% never married, 51.1% now married, 0.0% widowed, 12.9% divorced (2008-2012 5-year est.); Foreign born: 0.0% (2008-2012 5-year est.); Ancestry (includes multiple ancestries): 33.3% Irish, 23.5% German, 20.6% American, 5.6% English, 3.6% Canadian (2008-2012 5-year est.).
Economy: Single-family building permits issued: 1 (2013); Multi-family building permits issued: 0 (2013); Homeowner vacancy rate: 0.0%. Rental vacancy rate: 0.0%. (2008-2012 5-year est.); Employment by occupation: 14.7% management, business, and financial, 1.0% computer, engineering, and science, 16.8% education, legal, community service, arts, and media, 5.8% healthcare practitioners, 9.9% service, 22.0% sales and office, 14.1% natural resources, construction, and maintenance, 15.7% production, transportation, and material moving (2008-2012 5-year est.).

Income: Per capita income: $30,259 (2008-2012 5-year est.); Median household income: $57,750 (2008-2012 5-year est.); Average household income: $96,052 (2008-2012 5-year est.); Percent of households with income of $100,000 or more: 24.8% (2008-2012 5-year est.); Poverty rate: 24.1% (2008-2012 5-year est.).
Education: Percent of population age 25 and over with: High school diploma (including GED) or higher: 91.9% (2008-2012 5-year est.); Bachelor's degree or higher: 33.5% (2008-2012 5-year est.); Master's degree or higher: 4.3% (2008-2012 5-year est.).
Housing: Homeownership rate: 86.0% (2008-2012 5-year est.); Median home value: $156,900 (2008-2012 5-year est.); Median contract rent: $375 per month (2008-2012 5-year est.); Median year structure built: 1997 (2008-2012 5-year est.).
Health Insurance: 67.2% Private; 34.0% Public; 5.1% None. (2008-2012 5-year est.)
Transportation: Commute to work: 93.6% car, 0.0% public transportation, 5.9% walk, 0.0% work from home (2008-2012 5-year est.); Travel time to work: 20.2% less than 15 minutes, 34.0% 15 to 30 minutes, 26.6% 30 to 45 minutes, 16.5% 45 to 60 minutes, 2.7% 60 minutes or more (2008-2012 5-year est.)

LOWPOINT (unincorporated postal area)
Zip Code: 61545
    Covers a land area of 30.488 square miles and a water area of 0 square miles. Located at 40.87° N. Lat; 89.35° W. Long. Population: 646 (2010); Density: 21.2 persons per square mile (2010); Race: 98.0% White, 0.6% Black/African American, 0.5% Asian, 0.0% American Indian/Alaska Native, 0.0% Native Hawaiian/Other Pacific Islander, 0.9% Some other race, 0.3% Two or more races, 0.6% Hispanic of any race (2010); Average household size: 2.57 (2010); Median age: 44.3 (2010); Males per 100 females: 101.9 (2010); Homeownership rate: 87.3% (2010)

METAMORA (village). Covers a land area of 2.199 square miles and a water area of 0.004 square miles. Located at 40.80° N. Lat; 89.37° W. Long. Elevation is 817 feet.
History: Former capital of Woodford county. Old courthouse is now state memorial to Lincoln, who often argued cases here. Incorporated 1845.
Population: 2,520 (1990); 2,700 (2000); 3,636 (2010); Density: 1,544.3 persons per square mile (2008-2012 5-year est.); Race: 99.9% White, 0.0% Black/African American, 0.0% Asian, 0.0% American Indian/Alaska Native, 0.0% Native Hawaiian/Other Pacific Islander, 0.1% Some other race, 0.0% Two or more races, 0.2% Hispanic of any race (2008-2012 5-year est.); Average household size: 2.56 (2008-2012 5-year est.); Median age: 39.1 (2008-2012 5-year est.); Males per 100 females: 94.2 (2008-2012 5-year est.); Marriage status: 20.2% never married, 59.4% now married, 10.0% widowed, 10.4% divorced (2008-2012 5-year est.); Foreign born: 0.2% (2008-2012 5-year est.); Ancestry (includes multiple ancestries): 53.8% German, 14.0% Irish, 8.2% American, 8.2% English, 6.4% Italian (2008-2012 5-year est.).
Economy: Single-family building permits issued: 11 (2013); Multi-family building permits issued: 0 (2013); Homeowner vacancy rate: 2.6%. Rental vacancy rate: 0.0%. (2008-2012 5-year est.); Employment by occupation: 22.0% management, business, and financial, 6.5% computer, engineering, and science, 6.9% education, legal, community service, arts, and media, 4.5% healthcare practitioners, 17.7% service, 21.9% sales and office, 4.7% natural resources, construction, and maintenance, 15.8% production, transportation, and material moving (2008-2012 5-year est.).
Income: Per capita income: $29,294 (2008-2012 5-year est.); Median household income: $58,793 (2008-2012 5-year est.); Average household income: $74,783 (2008-2012 5-year est.); Percent of households with income of $100,000 or more: 21.3% (2008-2012 5-year est.); Poverty rate: 2.3% (2008-2012 5-year est.).
Education: Percent of population age 25 and over with: High school diploma (including GED) or higher: 91.4% (2008-2012 5-year est.); Bachelor's degree or higher: 31.5% (2008-2012 5-year est.); Master's degree or higher: 7.9% (2008-2012 5-year est.).
School District(s)
Central II Voc Ed Coop
    2011-12 Enrollment: n/a . . . . (309) 367-2783
County of Woodford School (09-12)
    2011-12 Enrollment: 982 . . . . (309) 367-4151
Metamora CCSD 1 (PK-08)
    2011-12 Enrollment: 894 . . . . (309) 367-2361

Housing: Homeownership rate: 82.1% (2008-2012 5-year est.); Median home value: $132,200 (2008-2012 5-year est.); Median contract rent: $483 per month (2008-2012 5-year est.); Median year structure built: 1972 (2008-2012 5-year est.).

Health Insurance: 90.4% Private; 23.6% Public; 5.9% None. (2008-2012 5-year est.)

Transportation: Commute to work: 89.1% car, 0.0% public transportation, 2.0% walk, 3.2% work from home (2008-2012 5-year est.); Travel time to work: 36.6% less than 15 minutes, 29.6% 15 to 30 minutes, 25.3% 30 to 45 minutes, 2.8% 45 to 60 minutes, 5.8% 60 minutes or more (2008-2012 5-year est.)

MINONK (city). Covers a land area of 2.422 square miles and a water area of 0 square miles. Located at 40.91° N. Lat; 89.04° W. Long. Elevation is 741 feet.

History: Incorporated 1867.

Population: 1,982 (1990); 2,168 (2000); 2,078 (2010); Density: 920.4 persons per square mile (2008-2012 5-year est.); Race: 99.6% White, 0.0% Black/African American, 0.4% Asian, 0.0% American Indian/Alaska Native, 0.0% Native Hawaiian/Other Pacific Islander, 0.0% Some other race, 0.0% Two or more races, 1.3% Hispanic of any race (2008-2012 5-year est.); Average household size: 2.30 (2008-2012 5-year est.); Median age: 39.0 (2008-2012 5-year est.); Males per 100 females: 86.2 (2008-2012 5-year est.); Marriage status: 18.4% never married, 57.2% now married, 13.7% widowed, 10.8% divorced (2008-2012 5-year est.); Foreign born: 0.9% (2008-2012 5-year est.); Ancestry (includes multiple ancestries): 48.8% German, 13.0% Irish, 8.3% American, 6.5% English, 5.2% Polish (2008-2012 5-year est.).

Economy: Single-family building permits issued: 0 (2013); Multi-family building permits issued: 0 (2013); Homeowner vacancy rate: 0.0%. Rental vacancy rate: 0.0%. (2008-2012 5-year est.); Employment by occupation: 6.4% management, business, and financial, 2.8% computer, engineering, and science, 5.6% education, legal, community service, arts, and media, 3.4% healthcare practitioners, 23.7% service, 28.6% sales and office, 5.0% natural resources, construction, and maintenance, 24.4% production, transportation, and material moving (2008-2012 5-year est.).

Income: Per capita income: $23,481 (2008-2012 5-year est.); Median household income: $46,413 (2008-2012 5-year est.); Average household income: $54,590 (2008-2012 5-year est.); Percent of households with income of $100,000 or more: 15.3% (2008-2012 5-year est.); Poverty rate: 11.6% (2008-2012 5-year est.).

Education: Percent of population age 25 and over with: High school diploma (including GED) or higher: 85.1% (2008-2012 5-year est.); Bachelor's degree or higher: 12.0% (2008-2012 5-year est.); Master's degree or higher: 4.1% (2008-2012 5-year est.).

School District(s)

Fieldcrest CUSD 6 (PK-12)

    2011-12 Enrollment: 1,226 . . . . (309) 432-2177

Housing: Homeownership rate: 77.1% (2008-2012 5-year est.); Median home value: $95,300 (2008-2012 5-year est.); Median contract rent: $396 per month (2008-2012 5-year est.); Median year structure built: 1953 (2008-2012 5-year est.).

Health Insurance: 77.9% Private; 32.4% Public; 8.1% None. (2008-2012 5-year est.)

Transportation: Commute to work: 97.8% car, 0.0% public transportation, 0.1% walk, 1.2% work from home (2008-2012 5-year est.); Travel time to work: 34.7% less than 15 minutes, 22.9% 15 to 30 minutes, 23.4% 30 to 45 minutes, 12.7% 45 to 60 minutes, 6.2% 60 minutes or more (2008-2012 5-year est.)

PANOLA (village). Covers a land area of 0.204 square miles and a water area of 0 square miles. Located at 40.78° N. Lat; 89.02° W. Long. Elevation is 735 feet.

Population: 43 (1990); 33 (2000); 45 (2010); Density: 250.0 persons per square mile (2008-2012 5-year est.); Race: 92.2% White, 0.0% Black/African American, 0.0% Asian, 0.0% American Indian/Alaska Native, 0.0% Native Hawaiian/Other Pacific Islander, 7.8% Some other race, 7.8% Two or more races, 9.8% Hispanic of any race (2008-2012 5-year est.); Average household size: 2.55 (2008-2012 5-year est.); Median age: 45.8 (2008-2012 5-year est.); Males per 100 females: 96.2 (2008-2012 5-year est.); Marriage status: 9.1% never married, 79.5% now married, 0.0% widowed, 11.4% divorced (2008-2012 5-year est.); Foreign born: 0.0% (2008-2012 5-year est.); Ancestry (includes multiple ancestries): 80.4% German, 13.7% English, 7.8% Irish, 3.9% Swedish, 3.9% Scottish (2008-2012 5-year est.).

Economy: Homeowner vacancy rate: 0.0%. Rental vacancy rate: 0.0%. (2008-2012 5-year est.); Employment by occupation: 60.0% management, business, and financial, 0.0% computer, engineering, and science, 0.0% education, legal, community service, arts, and media, 0.0% healthcare practitioners, 16.0% service, 24.0% sales and office, 0.0% natural resources, construction, and maintenance, 0.0% production, transportation, and material moving (2008-2012 5-year est.).

Income: Per capita income: $27,173 (2008-2012 5-year est.); Median household income: $75,000 (2008-2012 5-year est.); Average household income: $70,335 (2008-2012 5-year est.); Percent of households with income of $100,000 or more: 10.0% (2008-2012 5-year est.); Poverty rate: 9.8% (2008-2012 5-year est.).

Education: Percent of population age 25 and over with: High school diploma (including GED) or higher: 97.6% (2008-2012 5-year est.); Bachelor's degree or higher: 35.7% (2008-2012 5-year est.); Master's degree or higher: 23.8% (2008-2012 5-year est.).

Housing: Homeownership rate: 100.0% (2008-2012 5-year est.); Median home value: $134,400 (2008-2012 5-year est.); Median contract rent: n/a per month (2008-2012 5-year est.); Median year structure built: 1968 (2008-2012 5-year est.).

Health Insurance: 90.2% Private; 17.6% Public; 9.8% None. (2008-2012 5-year est.)

Transportation: Commute to work: 100.0% car, 0.0% public transportation, 0.0% walk, 0.0% work from home (2008-2012 5-year est.); Travel time to work: 32.0% less than 15 minutes, 4.0% 15 to 30 minutes, 48.0% 30 to 45 minutes, 16.0% 45 to 60 minutes, 0.0% 60 minutes or more (2008-2012 5-year est.)

ROANOKE (village). Covers a land area of 0.924 square miles and a water area of 0.037 square miles. Located at 40.80° N. Lat; 89.20° W. Long. Elevation is 732 feet.

History: Incorporated 1874.

Population: 1,910 (1990); 1,994 (2000); 2,065 (2010); Density: 2,192.7 persons per square mile (2008-2012 5-year est.); Race: 98.4% White, 0.0% Black/African American, 0.0% Asian, 0.0% American Indian/Alaska Native, 0.0% Native Hawaiian/Other Pacific Islander, 1.6% Some other race, 1.6% Two or more races, 2.8% Hispanic of any race (2008-2012 5-year est.); Average household size: 2.29 (2008-2012 5-year est.); Median age: 41.2 (2008-2012 5-year est.); Males per 100 females: 102.9 (2008-2012 5-year est.); Marriage status: 15.0% never married, 63.8% now married, 9.9% widowed, 11.4% divorced (2008-2012 5-year est.); Foreign born: 0.0% (2008-2012 5-year est.); Ancestry (includes multiple ancestries): 58.5% German, 8.6% Irish, 8.3% Swiss, 6.7% Italian, 6.2% American (2008-2012 5-year est.).

Economy: Single-family building permits issued: 0 (2013); Multi-family building permits issued: 0 (2013); Homeowner vacancy rate: 1.4%. Rental vacancy rate: 0.0%. (2008-2012 5-year est.); Employment by occupation: 9.6% management, business, and financial, 8.2% computer, engineering, and science, 5.0% education, legal, community service, arts, and media, 4.5% healthcare practitioners, 21.4% service, 23.5% sales and office, 11.7% natural resources, construction, and maintenance, 16.1% production, transportation, and material moving (2008-2012 5-year est.).

Income: Per capita income: $34,100 (2008-2012 5-year est.); Median household income: $55,952 (2008-2012 5-year est.); Average household income: $78,642 (2008-2012 5-year est.); Percent of households with income of $100,000 or more: 24.2% (2008-2012 5-year est.); Poverty rate: 5.9% (2008-2012 5-year est.).

Education: Percent of population age 25 and over with: High school diploma (including GED) or higher: 95.8% (2008-2012 5-year est.); Bachelor's degree or higher: 17.5% (2008-2012 5-year est.); Master's degree or higher: 3.9% (2008-2012 5-year est.).

School District(s)

Roanoke Benson CUSD 60 (PK-12)

    2011-12 Enrollment: 581 . . . . (309) 923-8921

Housing: Homeownership rate: 80.8% (2008-2012 5-year est.); Median home value: $121,200 (2008-2012 5-year est.); Median contract rent: $542 per month (2008-2012 5-year est.); Median year structure built: 1958 (2008-2012 5-year est.).

Health Insurance: 89.8% Private; 26.8% Public; 1.8% None. (2008-2012 5-year est.)

Transportation: Commute to work: 93.6% car, 0.0% public transportation, 3.8% walk, 1.3% work from home (2008-2012 5-year est.); Travel time to work: 43.4% less than 15 minutes, 24.4% 15 to 30 minutes, 25.3% 30 to 45 minutes, 5.6% 45 to 60 minutes, 1.4% 60 minutes or more (2008-2012 5-year est.)

SECOR (village). Covers a land area of 0.295 square miles and a water area of 0 square miles. Located at 40.74° N. Lat; 89.14° W. Long. Elevation is 732 feet.

Population: 389 (1990); 379 (2000); 373 (2010); Density: 1,530.1 persons per square mile (2008-2012 5-year est.); Race: 94.9% White, 0.0% Black/African American, 0.0% Asian, 0.0% American Indian/Alaska Native, 0.0% Native Hawaiian/Other Pacific Islander, 5.1% Some other race, 2.9% Two or more races, 5.5% Hispanic of any race (2008-2012 5-year est.); Average household size: 2.55 (2008-2012 5-year est.); Median age: 36.3 (2008-2012 5-year est.); Males per 100 females: 75.2 (2008-2012 5-year est.); Marriage status: 25.6% never married, 47.6% now married, 5.7% widowed, 21.1% divorced (2008-2012 5-year est.); Foreign born: 2.9% (2008-2012 5-year est.); Ancestry (includes multiple ancestries): 45.8% German, 17.9% American, 7.5% English, 6.2% French, 4.4% Irish (2008-2012 5-year est.).

Economy: Single-family building permits issued: 0 (2013); Multi-family building permits issued: 0 (2013); Homeowner vacancy rate: 5.4%. Rental vacancy rate: 0.0%. (2008-2012 5-year est.); Employment by occupation: 10.4% management, business, and financial, 5.5% computer, engineering, and science, 6.0% education, legal, community service, arts, and media, 1.0% healthcare practitioners, 11.4% service, 17.4% sales and office, 8.5% natural resources, construction, and maintenance, 39.8% production, transportation, and material moving (2008-2012 5-year est.).

Income: Per capita income: $20,029 (2008-2012 5-year est.); Median household income: $54,773 (2008-2012 5-year est.); Average household income: $54,522 (2008-2012 5-year est.); Percent of households with income of $100,000 or more: 3.6% (2008-2012 5-year est.); Poverty rate: 22.5% (2008-2012 5-year est.).

Education: Percent of population age 25 and over with: High school diploma (including GED) or higher: 92.4% (2008-2012 5-year est.); Bachelor's degree or higher: 8.3% (2008-2012 5-year est.); Master's degree or higher: 3.5% (2008-2012 5-year est.).

Housing: Homeownership rate: 83.7% (2008-2012 5-year est.); Median home value: $83,400 (2008-2012 5-year est.); Median contract rent: $425 per month (2008-2012 5-year est.); Median year structure built: 1946 (2008-2012 5-year est.).

Health Insurance: 65.3% Private; 32.1% Public; 10.6% None. (2008-2012 5-year est.)

Transportation: Commute to work: 92.0% car, 0.0% public transportation, 0.5% walk, 7.0% work from home (2008-2012 5-year est.); Travel time to work: 23.8% less than 15 minutes, 40.5% 15 to 30 minutes, 16.8% 30 to 45 minutes, 18.9% 45 to 60 minutes, 0.0% 60 minutes or more (2008-2012 5-year est.)

SPRING BAY (village). Covers a land area of 0.815 square miles and a water area of 0.329 square miles. Located at 40.82° N. Lat; 89.53° W. Long. Elevation is 469 feet.

Population: 439 (1990); 436 (2000); 452 (2010); Density: 726.1 persons per square mile (2008-2012 5-year est.); Race: 98.1% White, 0.3% Black/African American, 0.0% Asian, 0.0% American Indian/Alaska Native, 0.0% Native Hawaiian/Other Pacific Islander, 1.6% Some other race, 0.5% Two or more races, 1.2% Hispanic of any race (2008-2012 5-year est.); Average household size: 2.81 (2008-2012 5-year est.); Median age: 35.0 (2008-2012 5-year est.); Males per 100 females: 104.8 (2008-2012 5-year est.); Marriage status: 24.5% never married, 52.3% now married, 3.3% widowed, 19.9% divorced (2008-2012 5-year est.); Foreign born: 0.2% (2008-2012 5-year est.); Ancestry (includes multiple ancestries): 41.6% German, 19.6% Irish, 12.2% American, 11.0% English, 6.6% Polish (2008-2012 5-year est.).

Economy: Single-family building permits issued: 0 (2013); Multi-family building permits issued: 0 (2013); Homeowner vacancy rate: 2.2%. Rental vacancy rate: 0.0%. (2008-2012 5-year est.); Employment by occupation: 5.8% management, business, and financial, 1.8% computer, engineering, and science, 5.1% education, legal, community service, arts, and media, 5.4% healthcare practitioners, 17.0% service, 28.9% sales and office, 13.0% natural resources, construction, and maintenance, 23.1% production, transportation, and material moving (2008-2012 5-year est.).

Income: Per capita income: $22,263 (2008-2012 5-year est.); Median household income: $55,625 (2008-2012 5-year est.); Average household income: $61,366 (2008-2012 5-year est.); Percent of households with income of $100,000 or more: 16.6% (2008-2012 5-year est.); Poverty rate: 12.7% (2008-2012 5-year est.).

Education: Percent of population age 25 and over with: High school diploma (including GED) or higher: 88.5% (2008-2012 5-year est.);

Bachelor's degree or higher: 9.1% (2008-2012 5-year est.); Master's degree or higher: 2.7% (2008-2012 5-year est.).

Housing: Homeownership rate: 80.6% (2008-2012 5-year est.); Median home value: $111,000 (2008-2012 5-year est.); Median contract rent: $527 per month (2008-2012 5-year est.); Median year structure built: 1971 (2008-2012 5-year est.).

Health Insurance: 66.0% Private; 28.4% Public; 15.4% None. (2008-2012 5-year est.)

Transportation: Commute to work: 94.9% car, 0.0% public transportation, 3.2% walk, 0.4% work from home (2008-2012 5-year est.); Travel time to work: 13.0% less than 15 minutes, 45.3% 15 to 30 minutes, 33.3% 30 to 45 minutes, 4.7% 45 to 60 minutes, 3.6% 60 minutes or more (2008-2012 5-year est.)

WASHBURN (village). Covers a land area of 0.766 square miles and a water area of 0 square miles. Located at 40.92° N. Lat; 89.29° W. Long. Elevation is 686 feet.

Population: 1,075 (1990); 1,147 (2000); 1,155 (2010); Density: 1,528.9 persons per square mile (2008-2012 5-year est.); Race: 96.4% White, 0.2% Black/African American, 0.0% Asian, 0.0% American Indian/Alaska Native, 0.0% Native Hawaiian/Other Pacific Islander, 3.4% Some other race, 0.8% Two or more races, 2.1% Hispanic of any race (2008-2012 5-year est.); Average household size: 2.63 (2008-2012 5-year est.); Median age: 33.4 (2008-2012 5-year est.); Males per 100 females: 106.9 (2008-2012 5-year est.); Marriage status: 27.9% never married, 55.8% now married, 5.1% widowed, 11.1% divorced (2008-2012 5-year est.); Foreign born: 0.2% (2008-2012 5-year est.); Ancestry (includes multiple ancestries): 38.9% German, 18.9% Irish, 14.2% English, 7.9% American, 4.4% Italian (2008-2012 5-year est.).

Economy: Single-family building permits issued: 0 (2013); Multi-family building permits issued: 0 (2013); Homeowner vacancy rate: 0.0%. Rental vacancy rate: 12.1%. (2008-2012 5-year est.); Employment by occupation: 12.3% management, business, and financial, 6.2% computer, engineering, and science, 12.3% education, legal, community service, arts, and media, 2.9% healthcare practitioners, 8.4% service, 17.4% sales and office, 10.8% natural resources, construction, and maintenance, 29.5% production, transportation, and material moving (2008-2012 5-year est.).

Income: Per capita income: $22,308 (2008-2012 5-year est.); Median household income: $52,826 (2008-2012 5-year est.); Average household income: $58,630 (2008-2012 5-year est.); Percent of households with income of $100,000 or more: 17.0% (2008-2012 5-year est.); Poverty rate: 9.0% (2008-2012 5-year est.).

Education: Percent of population age 25 and over with: High school diploma (including GED) or higher: 91.2% (2008-2012 5-year est.); Bachelor's degree or higher: 15.3% (2008-2012 5-year est.); Master's degree or higher: 5.6% (2008-2012 5-year est.).

School District(s)
Lowpoint-Washburn CUSD 21 (PK-12)
    2011-12 Enrollment: 388 . . . . (309) 248-7522

Housing: Homeownership rate: 75.6% (2008-2012 5-year est.); Median home value: $90,100 (2008-2012 5-year est.); Median contract rent: $445 per month (2008-2012 5-year est.); Median year structure built: 1954 (2008-2012 5-year est.).

Health Insurance: 72.0% Private; 22.9% Public; 13.6% None. (2008-2012 5-year est.)

Transportation: Commute to work: 98.5% car, 0.0% public transportation, 0.0% walk, 1.1% work from home (2008-2012 5-year est.); Travel time to work: 24.1% less than 15 minutes, 19.6% 15 to 30 minutes, 34.2% 30 to 45 minutes, 17.4% 45 to 60 minutes, 4.7% 60 minutes or more (2008-2012 5-year est.);

A

Abingdon city *Knox County*, 275
Adair CDP *McDonough County*, 366
Adams County, 35 - 39
Addieville village *Washington County*, 513
Addison village *DuPage County*, 158
Adeline village *Ogle County*, 410
Albany village *Whiteside County*, 524
Albers village *Clinton County*, 84
Albion city *Edwards County*, 175
Aledo city *Mercer County*, 391
Alexander County, 40 - 41
Alexander postal area *Morgan County*, 404
Alexis village *Warren County*, 510
Algonquin village *McHenry County*, 370
Alhambra village *Madison County*, 341
Allendale village *Wabash County*, 509
Allenville village *Moultrie County*, 407
Allerton village *Vermilion County*, 501
Alma village *Marion County*, 352
Alorton village *Saint Clair County*, 475
Alpha village *Henry County*, 221
Alsey village *Scott County*, 468
Alsip village *Cook County*, 92
Altamont city *Effingham County*, 176
Alto Pass village *Union County*, 498
Alton city *Madison County*, 341
Altona village *Knox County*, 275
Alvan village *Vermilion County*, 501
Amboy city *Lee County*, 312
Anchor village *McLean County*, 381
Ancona postal area *Livingston County*, 317
Andalusia village *Rock Island County*, 448
Andover village *Henry County*, 221
Anna city *Union County*, 498
Annapolis CDP *Crawford County*, 143
Annawan town *Henry County*, 221
Antioch village *Lake County*, 290
Apple Canyon Lake CDP *Jo Daviess Co.*, 247
Apple River village *Jo Daviess County*, 248
Arcola city *Douglas County*, 155
Arenzville village *Cass County*, 63
Argenta village *Macon County*, 327
Arlington Heights village *Cook County*, 92
Arlington village *Bureau County*, 50
Armington village *Tazewell County*, 492
Armstrong postal area *Vermilion County*, 501
Aroma Park village *Kankakee County*, 264
Arrowsmith village *McLean County*, 381
Arthur village *Douglas County*, 155
Ashkum village *Iroquois County*, 226
Ashland village *Cass County*, 63
Ashley city *Washington County*, 513
Ashmore village *Coles County*, 89
Ashton village *Lee County*, 313
Assumption city *Christian County*, 74
Astoria town *Fulton County*, 192
Athens city *Menard County*, 388
Atkinson town *Henry County*, 222
Atlanta city *Logan County*, 322
Atwood village *Piatt County*, 425
Auburn city *Sangamon County*, 457
Augusta village *Hancock County*, 211
Aurora city *Kane County*, 255
Ava city *Jackson County*, 233
Aviston village *Clinton County*, 84
Avon village *Fulton County*, 192

B

Baileyville postal area *Ogle County*, 410
Baldwin village *Randolph County*, 441
Banner village *Fulton County*, 192
Bannockburn village *Lake County*, 290
Bardolph village *McDonough County*, 366
Barnhill postal area *Wayne County*, 517
Barrington Hills village *Cook County*, 93
Barrington village *Cook County*, 92
Barry city *Pike County*, 428
Barstow postal area *Rock Island County*, 448
Bartelso village *Clinton County*, 85
Bartlett village *DuPage County*, 159
Bartonville village *Peoria County*, 416
Basco village *Hancock County*, 211
Batavia city *Kane County*, 255
Batchtown village *Calhoun County*, 58
Bath village *Mason County*, 360
Bay View Gardens village *Woodford County*, 553
Baylis village *Pike County*, 429
Beach Park village *Lake County*, 291
Beardstown city *Cass County*, 63
Beason CDP *Logan County*, 323
Beaverville village *Iroquois County*, 226
Beckemeyer village *Clinton County*, 85
Bedford Park village *Cook County*, 93
Beecher City village *Effingham County*, 177
Beecher village *Will County*, 529
Belgium village *Vermilion County*, 501
Belknap village *Johnson County*, 252
Belle Prairie City town *Hamilton County*, 209
Belle Rive village *Jefferson County*, 241
Belleville city *Saint Clair County*, 475
Bellevue village *Peoria County*, 416
Bellflower village *McLean County*, 381
Bellmont village *Wabash County*, 509
Bellwood village *Cook County*, 94
Belvidere city *Boone County*, 46
Bement village *Piatt County*, 425
Benld city *Macoupin County*, 332
Bensenville village *DuPage County*, 159
Benson village *Woodford County*, 553
Bentley town *Hancock County*, 211
Benton city *Franklin County*, 186
Berkeley village *Cook County*, 94
Berlin village *Sangamon County*, 457
Berwick postal area *Warren County*, 511
Berwyn city *Cook County*, 94
Bethalto village *Madison County*, 342
Bethany village *Moultrie County*, 408
Big Rock village *Kane County*, 256
Biggsville village *Henderson County*, 217
Bingham village *Fayette County*, 180
Bishop Hill village *Henry County*, 222
Bismarck village *Vermilion County*, 502
Blackstone postal area *Livingston County*, 317
Blandinsville village *McDonough County*, 366
Bloomingdale village *DuPage County*, 159
Bloomington city *McLean County*, 381
Blue Island city *Cook County*, 95
Blue Mound village *Macon County*, 327
Bluff Springs postal area *Cass County*, 64
Bluffs village *Scott County*, 468
Bluford village *Jefferson County*, 241
Bolingbrook village *Will County*, 530
Bond County, 42 - 44
Bondville village *Champaign County*, 65
Bone Gap village *Edwards County*, 175

Bonfield village *Kankakee County*, 265
Bonnie village *Jefferson County*, 241
Boody CDP *Macon County*, 328
Boone County, 45 - 47
Boulder Hill CDP *Kendall County*, 271
Bourbonnais village *Kankakee County*, 265
Bowen village *Hancock County*, 212
Braceville village *Grundy County*, 205
Bradford village *Stark County*, 486
Bradley village *Kankakee County*, 265
Braidwood city *Will County*, 530
Breese city *Clinton County*, 85
Bridgeport city *Lawrence County*, 310
Bridgeview village *Cook County*, 95
Brighton village *Macoupin County*, 332
Brimfield village *Peoria County*, 416
Bristol postal area *Kendall County*, 271
Broadlands village *Champaign County*, 65
Broadview village *Cook County*, 96
Broadwell village *Logan County*, 323
Brocton village *Edgar County*, 172
Brookfield village *Cook County*, 96
Brooklyn village *Saint Clair County*, 476
Brookport city *Massac County*, 364
Broughton village *Hamilton County*, 209
Brown County, 48
Browning village *Schuyler County*, 466
Browns village *Edwards County*, 175
Brownstown village *Fayette County*, 180
Brussels village *Calhoun County*, 58
Bryant village *Fulton County*, 193
Buckingham village *Kankakee County*, 266
Buckley village *Iroquois County*, 227
Buckner village *Franklin County*, 186
Buda village *Bureau County*, 50
Buffalo Grove village *Lake County*, 291
Buffalo village *Sangamon County*, 458
Bull Valley village *McHenry County*, 370
Bulpitt village *Christian County*, 75
Buncombe village *Johnson County*, 252
Bunker Hill city *Macoupin County*, 333
Burbank city *Cook County*, 97
Bureau County, 49 - 56
Bureau Junction village *Bureau County*, 51
Burlington village *Kane County*, 256
Burnham village *Cook County*, 97
Burnt Prairie village *White County*, 521
Burr Ridge village *DuPage County*, 160
Bush village *Williamson County*, 542
Bushnell city *McDonough County*, 366
Butler village *Montgomery County*, 397
Byron city *Ogle County*, 410

C

Cabery village *Ford County*, 183
Cahokia village *Saint Clair County*, 476
Cairo city *Alexander County*, 40
Caledonia village *Boone County*, 46
Calhoun County, 57 - 59
Calhoun village *Richland County*, 446
Calumet City city *Cook County*, 97
Calumet Park village *Cook County*, 98
Camargo village *Douglas County*, 156
Cambria village *Williamson County*, 542
Cambridge village *Henry County*, 222
Camden village *Schuyler County*, 466
Cameron postal area *Warren County*, 511
Camp Grove postal area *Marshall County*, 357
Camp Point village *Adams County*, 35
Campbell Hill village *Jackson County*, 234

CDP = Census Designated Place

CDP = Census Designated Place

CDP = Census Designated Place

CDP = Census Designated Place

Lena village *Stephenson County*, 489

Lenzburg village *Saint Clair County*, 480

Leonore village *LaSalle County*, 283

Lerna village *Coles County*, 90

Lewistown city *Fulton County*, 195

Lexington city *McLean County*, 386

Liberty village *Adams County*, 37

Libertyville village *Lake County*, 300

Lily Lake village *Kane County*, 260

Lima village *Adams County*, 37

Limestone village *Kankakee County*, 268

Lincoln city *Logan County*, 325

Lincolnshire village *Lake County*, 301

Lincolnwood village *Cook County*, 117

Lindenhurst village *Lake County*, 301

Lindenwood postal area *Ogle County*, 413

Lisbon village *Kendall County*, 272

Lisle village *DuPage County*, 164

Litchfield city *Montgomery County*, 400

Little York village *Warren County*, 511

Littleton village *Schuyler County*, 467

Liverpool village *Fulton County*, 196

Livingston County, 317 - 321

Livingston village *Madison County*, 347

Loami village *Sangamon County*, 461

Lockport city *Will County*, 535

Loda village *Iroquois County*, 230

Logan County, 322 - 326

Logan postal area *Franklin County*, 188

Lomax village *Henderson County*, 218

Lombard village *DuPage County*, 165

London Mills village *Fulton County*, 196

Long Creek village *Macon County*, 329

Long Grove village *Lake County*, 302

Long Lake CDP *Lake County*, 302

Long Point village *Livingston County*, 320

Longview village *Champaign County*, 68

Loraine village *Adams County*, 38

Lost Nation CDP *Ogle County*, 413

Lostant village *LaSalle County*, 284

Louisville village *Clay County*, 83

Lovejoy postal area *Saint Clair County*, 480

Loves Park city *Winnebago County*, 548

Lovington village *Moultrie County*, 409

Lowpoint postal area *Woodford County*, 555

Ludlow village *Champaign County*, 69

Lyndon village *Whiteside County*, 526

Lynn Center postal area *Henry County*, 225

Lynnville village *Morgan County*, 405

Lynwood village *Cook County*, 117

Lyons village *Cook County*, 118

M

Macedonia village *Franklin County*, 188

Machesney Park village *Winnebago County*, 549

Mackinaw village *Tazewell County*, 494

Macomb city *McDonough County*, 368

Macon County, 327 - 331

Macon city *Macon County*, 330

Macoupin County, 332 - 340

Madison County, 341 - 351

Madison city *Madison County*, 347

Maeystown village *Monroe County*, 396

Magnolia village *Putnam County*, 439

Mahomet village *Champaign County*, 69

Makanda village *Jackson County*, 236

Malden village *Bureau County*, 53

Malta village *DeKalb County*, 152

Manchester village *Scott County*, 469

Manhattan village *Will County*, 536

Manito village *Mason County*, 362

Manlius village *Bureau County*, 53

Mansfield village *Piatt County*, 427

Manteno village *Kankakee County*, 268

Maple Park village *Kane County*, 260

Mapleton village *Peoria County*, 419

Maquon village *Knox County*, 277

Marengo city *McHenry County*, 375

Marietta village *Fulton County*, 196

Marine village *Madison County*, 347

Marion County, 352 - 356

Marion city *Williamson County*, 545

Marissa village *Saint Clair County*, 480

Mark village *Putnam County*, 439

Markham city *Cook County*, 118

Maroa city *Macon County*, 330

Marquette Heights city *Tazewell County*, 495

Marseilles city *LaSalle County*, 284

Marshall County, 357 - 359

Marshall city *Clark County*, 80

Martinsville city *Clark County*, 80

Martinton village *Iroquois County*, 230

Maryville village *Madison County*, 348

Mascoutah city *Saint Clair County*, 481

Mason City city *Mason County*, 363

Mason County, 360 - 363

Mason town *Effingham County*, 178

Massac County, 364

Matherville village *Mercer County*, 392

Matteson village *Cook County*, 118

Mattoon city *Coles County*, 90

Maunie village *White County*, 522

Maywood village *Cook County*, 119

Mazon village *Grundy County*, 207

McClure village *Alexander County*, 41

McConnell postal area *Stephenson County*, 490

McCook village *Cook County*, 119

McCullom Lake village *McHenry County*, 376

McDonough County, 365 - 368

McHenry County, 369 - 379

McHenry city *McHenry County*, 376

McLean County, 380 - 387

McLean village *McLean County*, 386

McLeansboro city *Hamilton County*, 210

McNabb village *Putnam County*, 439

Mechanicsburg village *Sangamon County*, 461

Media village *Henderson County*, 219

Medinah postal area *Du Page County*, 165

Medora village *Macoupin County*, 336

Melrose Park village *Cook County*, 120

Melvin village *Ford County*, 184

Menard County, 388 - 389

Mendon village *Adams County*, 38

Mendota city *LaSalle County*, 284

Menominee village *Jo Daviess County*, 249

Mercer County, 390 - 393

Meredosia village *Morgan County*, 405

Merrionette Park village *Cook County*, 120

Metamora village *Woodford County*, 555

Metcalf village *Edgar County*, 173

Metropolis city *Massac County*, 365

Mettawa village *Lake County*, 302

Michael postal area *Calhoun County*, 59

Middletown village *Logan County*, 326

Midlothian village *Cook County*, 120

Milan village *Rock Island County*, 451

Milford village *Iroquois County*, 230

Mill Creek village *Union County*, 500

Mill Shoals village *White County*, 523

Millbrook village *Kendall County*, 272

Millcreek postal area *Union County*, 500

Milledgeville village *Carroll County*, 61

Miller City postal area *Alexander County*, 41

Millington village *LaSalle County*, 285

Millstadt village *Saint Clair County*, 481

Milmine postal area *Piatt County*, 427

Milton village *Pike County*, 431

Mineral village *Bureau County*, 54

Minier village *Tazewell County*, 495

Minonk city *Woodford County*, 556

Minooka village *Grundy County*, 207

Mitchell CDP *Madison County*, 348

Mode postal area *Shelby County*, 471

Modesto village *Macoupin County*, 336

Modoc postal area *Randolph County*, 442

Mokena village *Will County*, 536

Moline city *Rock Island County*, 451

Momence city *Kankakee County*, 269

Monee village *Will County*, 536

Monmouth city *Warren County*, 512

Monroe Center village *Ogle County*, 413

Monroe County, 394 - 396

Montgomery County, 397 - 402

Montgomery village *Kendall County*, 272

Monticello city *Piatt County*, 427

Montrose village *Effingham County*, 178

Mooseheart postal area *Kane County*, 260

Morgan County, 403 - 406

Moro postal area *Madison County*, 348

Morris city *Grundy County*, 207

Morrison city *Whiteside County*, 527

Morrisonville village *Christian County*, 76

Morton Grove village *Cook County*, 121

Morton village *Tazewell County*, 495

Mossville postal area *Peoria County*, 419

Moultrie County, 407 - 408

Mound City city *Pulaski County*, 436

Mound Station village *Brown County*, 48

Mounds city *Pulaski County*, 436

Mount Auburn village *Christian County*, 76

Mount Carmel city *Wabash County*, 510

Mount Carroll city *Carroll County*, 61

Mount Clare village *Macoupin County*, 336

Mount Erie village *Wayne County*, 519

Mount Morris village *Ogle County*, 413

Mount Olive city *Macoupin County*, 337

Mount Prospect village *Cook County*, 121

Mount Pulaski city *Logan County*, 326

Mount Sterling city *Brown County*, 48

Mount Vernon city *Jefferson County*, 242

Mount Zion village *Macon County*, 330

Moweaqua village *Shelby County*, 471

Mozier postal area *Calhoun County*, 60

Muddy village *Saline County*, 456

Mulberry Grove village *Bond County*, 43

Mulkeytown CDP *Franklin County*, 188

Muncie village *Vermilion County*, 505

Mundelein village *Lake County*, 303

Murdock postal area *Douglas County*, 157

Murphysboro city *Jackson County*, 237

Murrayville village *Morgan County*, 406

N

Nachusa postal area *Lee County*, 315

Naperville city *DuPage County*, 165

Naplate village *LaSalle County*, 285

Naples town *Scott County*, 469

CDP = Census Designated Place

CDP = Census Designated Place

CDP = Census Designated Place

Comparative
Statistics

Population

Place	1990 Census	2000 Census	2010 Census
Addison village *Du Page Co.*	32,058	35,914	36,942
Algonquin village *McHenry Co.*	11,663	23,276	30,046
Alton city *Madison Co.*	32,905	30,496	27,865
Arlington Heights village *Cook Co.*	75,460	76,031	75,101
Aurora city *Kane Co.*	99,581	142,990	197,899
Bartlett village *Du Page Co.*	19,373	36,706	41,208
Batavia city *Kane Co.*	17,076	23,866	26,045
Belleville city *Saint Clair Co.*	42,785	41,410	44,478
Belvidere city *Boone Co.*	15,958	20,820	25,585
Berwyn city *Cook Co.*	45,426	54,016	56,657
Bloomington city *McLean Co.*	51,972	64,808	76,610
Bolingbrook village *Will Co.*	40,843	56,321	73,366
Buffalo Grove village *Lake Co.*	36,427	42,909	41,496
Burbank city *Cook Co.*	27,600	27,902	28,925
Calumet City city *Cook Co.*	37,840	39,071	37,042
Carbondale city *Jackson Co.*	27,033	20,681	25,902
Carol Stream village *Du Page Co.*	31,716	40,438	39,711
Carpentersville village *Kane Co.*	23,049	30,586	37,691
Champaign city *Champaign Co.*	63,502	67,518	81,055
Chicago city *Cook Co.*	2,783,726	2,896,016	2,695,598
Chicago Heights city *Cook Co.*	33,072	32,776	30,276
Cicero town *Cook Co.*	67,436	85,616	83,891
Collinsville city *Madison Co.*	22,446	24,707	25,579
Crystal Lake city *McHenry Co.*	24,512	38,000	40,743
Danville city *Vermilion Co.*	33,828	33,904	33,027
DeKalb city *De Kalb Co.*	34,925	39,018	43,862
Decatur city *Macon Co.*	83,885	81,860	76,122
Des Plaines city *Cook Co.*	53,223	58,720	58,364
Downers Grove village *Du Page Co.*	46,858	48,724	47,833
East Saint Louis city *Saint Clair Co.*	40,944	31,542	27,006
Edwardsville city *Madison Co.*	14,579	21,491	24,293
Elgin city *Kane Co.*	77,010	94,487	108,188
Elk Grove Village village *Cook Co.*	33,429	34,727	33,127
Elmhurst city *Du Page Co.*	42,029	42,762	44,121
Elmwood Park village *Cook Co.*	23,206	25,405	24,883
Evanston city *Cook Co.*	73,233	74,239	74,486
Freeport city *Stephenson Co.*	25,840	26,443	25,638
Galesburg city *Knox Co.*	33,530	33,706	32,195
Glen Ellyn village *Du Page Co.*	24,944	26,999	27,450
Glendale Heights village *Du Page Co.*	27,973	31,765	34,208
Glenview village *Cook Co.*	37,093	41,847	44,692
Granite City city *Madison Co.*	32,862	31,301	29,849
Gurnee village *Lake Co.*	13,701	28,834	31,295
Hanover Park village *Cook Co.*	32,895	38,278	37,973
Harvey city *Cook Co.*	29,771	30,000	25,282
Highland Park city *Lake Co.*	30,575	31,365	29,763
Hoffman Estates village *Cook Co.*	46,561	49,495	51,895
Homer Glen village *Will Co.*	n/a	n/a	24,220
Huntley village *McHenry Co.*	2,453	5,730	24,291
Joliet city *Will Co.*	76,836	106,221	147,433

Place	1990 Census	2000 Census	2010 Census
Kankakee city Kankakee Co.	27,575	27,491	27,537
Lake in the Hills village McHenry Co.	5,866	23,152	28,965
Lansing village Cook Co.	28,086	28,332	28,331
Lockport city Will Co.	9,401	15,191	24,839
Lombard village Du Page Co.	39,408	42,322	43,165
McHenry city McHenry Co.	16,177	21,501	26,992
Melrose Park village Cook Co.	20,859	23,171	25,411
Moline city Rock Island Co.	43,202	43,768	43,483
Mount Prospect village Cook Co.	53,170	56,265	54,167
Mundelein village Lake Co.	21,215	30,935	31,064
Naperville city Du Page Co.	85,351	128,358	141,853
New Lenox village Will Co.	9,627	17,771	24,394
Niles village Cook Co.	28,284	30,068	29,803
Normal town McLean Co.	40,023	45,386	52,497
North Chicago city Lake Co.	34,978	35,918	32,574
Northbrook village Cook Co.	32,308	33,435	33,170
O'Fallon city Saint Clair Co.	16,073	21,910	28,281
Oak Forest city Cook Co.	26,203	28,051	27,962
Oak Lawn village Cook Co.	56,182	55,245	56,690
Oak Park village Cook Co.	53,648	52,524	51,878
Orland Park village Cook Co.	35,720	51,077	56,767
Oswego village Kendall Co.	3,876	13,326	30,355
Palatine village Cook Co.	39,253	65,479	68,557
Park Ridge city Cook Co.	36,175	37,775	37,480
Pekin city Tazewell Co.	32,254	33,857	34,094
Peoria city Peoria Co.	113,504	112,936	115,007
Plainfield village Will Co.	4,557	13,038	39,581
Quincy city Adams Co.	39,681	40,366	40,633
Rock Island city Rock Island Co.	40,552	39,684	39,018
Rockford city Winnebago Co.	139,426	150,115	152,871
Rolling Meadows city Cook Co.	22,591	24,604	24,099
Romeoville village Will Co.	14,074	21,153	39,680
Round Lake Beach village Lake Co.	16,434	25,859	28,175
Saint Charles city Kane Co.	22,501	27,896	32,974
Schaumburg village Cook Co.	68,586	75,386	74,227
Skokie village Cook Co.	59,432	63,348	64,784
Springfield city Sangamon Co.	105,227	111,454	116,250
Streamwood village Cook Co.	30,987	36,407	39,858
Tinley Park village Cook Co.	37,121	48,401	56,703
Urbana city Champaign Co.	36,344	36,395	41,250
Vernon Hills village Lake Co.	15,319	20,120	25,113
Waukegan city Lake Co.	69,392	87,901	89,078
West Chicago city Du Page Co.	14,796	23,469	27,086
Westmont village Du Page Co.	21,228	24,554	24,685
Wheaton city Du Page Co.	51,464	55,416	52,894
Wheeling village Cook Co.	29,911	34,496	37,648
Wilmette village Cook Co.	26,690	27,651	27,087
Woodridge village Du Page Co.	26,256	30,934	32,971
Woodstock city McHenry Co.	14,353	20,151	24,770
Zion city Lake Co.	19,775	22,866	24,413

SOURCE: U.S. Census Bureau, Census 2010, Census 2000, 1990 Census

Physical Characteristics

Place	Density (persons per square mile)	Land Area (square miles)	Water Area (square miles)	Elevation (feet)
Addison village *Du Page Co.*	3,781.9	9.76	0.20	689
Algonquin village *McHenry Co.*	2,457.6	12.22	0.18	741
Alton city *Madison Co.*	1,801.2	15.47	1.26	499
Arlington Heights village *Cook Co.*	4,521.9	16.60	0.02	702
Aurora city *Kane Co.*	4,404.0	44.93	0.85	679
Bartlett village *Du Page Co.*	2,637.1	15.62	0.23	n/a
Batavia city *Kane Co.*	2,702.6	9.63	0.06	715
Belleville city *Saint Clair Co.*	1,955.9	22.74	0.26	515
Belvidere city *Boone Co.*	2,118.2	12.07	0.23	781
Berwyn city *Cook Co.*	14,508.8	3.90	0.00	617
Bloomington city *McLean Co.*	2,814.7	27.21	0.00	797
Bolingbrook village *Will Co.*	3,050.7	24.04	0.20	702
Buffalo Grove village *Lake Co.*	4,367.8	9.50	0.02	679
Burbank city *Cook Co.*	6,932.4	4.17	0.00	620
Calumet City city *Cook Co.*	5,155.2	7.18	0.12	591
Carbondale city *Jackson Co.*	1,516.0	17.08	0.42	413
Carol Stream village *Du Page Co.*	4,366.8	9.09	0.32	758
Carpentersville village *Kane Co.*	4,768.9	7.90	0.19	889
Champaign city *Champaign Co.*	3,613.2	22.43	0.02	738
Chicago city *Cook Co.*	11,841.8	227.63	6.47	587
Chicago Heights city *Cook Co.*	3,005.1	10.07	0.01	659
Cicero town *Cook Co.*	14,304.8	5.86	0.00	604
Collinsville city *Madison Co.*	1,742.4	14.68	0.19	561
Crystal Lake city *McHenry Co.*	2,220.1	18.35	0.60	915
Danville city *Vermilion Co.*	1,846.3	17.88	0.07	600
DeKalb city *De Kalb Co.*	2,993.8	14.65	0.16	879
Decatur city *Macon Co.*	1,802.8	42.22	4.69	673
Des Plaines city *Cook Co.*	4,086.2	14.28	0.13	633
Downers Grove village *Du Page Co.*	3,343.8	14.30	0.14	741
East Saint Louis city *Saint Clair Co.*	1,930.1	13.99	0.37	417
Edwardsville city *Madison Co.*	1,241.7	19.56	0.60	541
Elgin city *Kane Co.*	2,911.1	37.16	0.54	745
Elk Grove Village village *Cook Co.*	2,920.5	11.34	0.06	686
Elmhurst city *Du Page Co.*	4,303.0	10.25	0.05	686
Elmwood Park village *Cook Co.*	13,045.7	1.90	0.00	643
Evanston city *Cook Co.*	9,575.0	7.77	0.02	614
Freeport city *Stephenson Co.*	2,177.0	11.77	0.01	778
Galesburg city *Knox Co.*	1,813.8	17.74	0.17	771
Glen Ellyn village *Du Page Co.*	4,152.1	6.61	0.16	741
Glendale Heights village *Du Page Co.*	6,367.3	5.37	0.13	761
Glenview village *Cook Co.*	3,204.2	13.94	0.04	653
Granite City city *Madison Co.*	1,547.5	19.28	1.41	423
Gurnee village *Lake Co.*	2,318.6	13.49	0.07	679
Hanover Park village *Cook Co.*	5,999.9	6.32	0.10	804
Harvey city *Cook Co.*	4,011.1	6.30	0.00	604
Highland Park city *Lake Co.*	2,439.8	12.19	0.03	696
Hoffman Estates village *Cook Co.*	2,495.5	20.79	0.18	784
Homer Glen village *Will Co.*	1,092.3	22.17	0.03	738
Huntley village *McHenry Co.*	1,726.5	14.06	0.03	889
Joliet city *Will Co.*	2,373.6	62.11	0.65	541

Place	Density (persons per square mile)	Land Area (square miles)	Water Area (square miles)	Elevation (feet)
Kankakee city *Kankakee Co.*	1,947.9	14.13	0.47	656
Lake in the Hills village *McHenry Co.*	2,791.3	10.37	0.23	866
Lansing village *Cook Co.*	4,174.4	6.78	0.05	630
Lockport city *Will Co.*	2,179.1	11.39	0.00	594
Lombard village *Du Page Co.*	4,210.3	10.25	0.19	719
McHenry city *McHenry Co.*	1,831.1	14.74	0.43	797
Melrose Park village *Cook Co.*	5,996.3	4.23	0.00	633
Moline city *Rock Island Co.*	2,647.0	16.42	0.23	577
Mount Prospect village *Cook Co.*	5,239.4	10.33	0.03	669
Mundelein village *Lake Co.*	3,247.7	9.56	0.39	735
Naperville city *Du Page Co.*	3,658.9	38.76	0.55	709
New Lenox village *Will Co.*	1,557.7	15.66	0.02	669
Niles village *Cook Co.*	5,097.3	5.84	0.00	636
Normal town *McLean Co.*	2,861.2	18.34	0.06	801
North Chicago city *Lake Co.*	4,123.9	7.89	0.01	659
Northbrook village *Cook Co.*	2,514.9	13.18	0.06	646
O'Fallon city *Saint Clair Co.*	1,970.2	14.35	0.12	548
Oak Forest city *Cook Co.*	4,698.3	5.95	0.04	673
Oak Lawn village *Cook Co.*	6,596.1	8.59	0.00	597
Oak Park village *Cook Co.*	11,037.1	4.70	0.00	620
Orland Park village *Cook Co.*	2,594.7	21.87	0.28	705
Oswego village *Kendall Co.*	1,954.9	15.52	0.10	640
Palatine village *Cook Co.*	5,034.8	13.61	0.14	741
Park Ridge city *Cook Co.*	5,286.5	7.08	0.04	643
Pekin city *Tazewell Co.*	2,341.8	14.55	0.57	502
Peoria city *Peoria Co.*	2,395.6	48.00	2.21	502
Plainfield village *Will Co.*	1,704.3	23.22	0.97	617
Quincy city *Adams Co.*	2,554.1	15.90	0.03	568
Rock Island city *Rock Island Co.*	2,316.1	16.84	1.02	561
Rockford city *Winnebago Co.*	2,502.7	61.08	0.86	715
Rolling Meadows city *Cook Co.*	4,278.9	5.63	0.00	719
Romeoville village *Will Co.*	2,152.2	18.43	0.31	617
Round Lake Beach village *Lake Co.*	5,565.2	5.06	0.15	764
Saint Charles city *Kane Co.*	2,257.7	14.60	0.32	732
Schaumburg village *Cook Co.*	3,862.3	19.21	0.11	794
Skokie village *Cook Co.*	6,437.9	10.06	0.00	607
Springfield city *Sangamon Co.*	1,954.5	59.47	6.28	597
Streamwood village *Cook Co.*	5,100.0	7.81	0.03	807
Tinley Park village *Cook Co.*	3,539.3	16.02	0.01	699
Urbana city *Champaign Co.*	3,539.6	11.65	0.04	728
Vernon Hills village *Lake Co.*	3,258.2	7.70	0.20	735
Waukegan city *Lake Co.*	3,762.8	23.67	0.20	653
West Chicago city *Du Page Co.*	1,830.4	14.79	0.34	784
Westmont village *Du Page Co.*	4,907.9	5.02	0.10	748
Wheaton city *Du Page Co.*	4,700.8	11.25	0.18	758
Wheeling village *Cook Co.*	4,326.8	8.70	0.05	650
Wilmette village *Cook Co.*	5,013.1	5.40	0.00	636
Woodridge village *Du Page Co.*	3,499.2	9.42	0.16	732
Woodstock city *McHenry Co.*	1,827.9	13.55	0.00	945
Zion city *Lake Co.*	2,489.2	9.80	0.00	650

SOURCE: U.S. Census Bureau, Census 2010

Population by Race/Hispanic Origin

Place	White[1] (%)	Black[1] (%)	Asian[1] (%)	AIAN[1,2] (%)	NHOPI[1,3] (%)	Other (%)	Hispanic[4] (%)
Addison village *Du Page Co.*	81.6	3.4	6.6	0.2	0.0	8.2	38.8
Algonquin village *McHenry Co.*	84.9	2.7	8.3	0.1	0.0	4.0	8.6
Alton city *Madison Co.*	71.0	24.1	0.6	0.6	0.0	3.7	2.0
Arlington Heights village *Cook Co.*	87.0	1.8	7.8	0.2	0.0	3.2	6.4
Aurora city *Kane Co.*	55.5	9.4	6.9	0.3	0.0	27.9	41.5
Bartlett village *Du Page Co.*	79.2	2.6	13.1	0.1	0.0	5.0	10.6
Batavia city *Kane Co.*	90.4	3.6	1.6	0.1	0.0	4.3	6.4
Belleville city *Saint Clair Co.*	71.0	23.2	1.1	0.3	0.0	4.4	2.5
Belvidere city *Boone Co.*	86.7	2.5	1.4	0.0	0.0	9.4	33.4
Berwyn city *Cook Co.*	62.3	6.7	1.8	0.4	0.0	28.8	58.4
Bloomington city *McLean Co.*	78.9	10.0	7.0	0.2	0.0	3.9	5.2
Bolingbrook village *Will Co.*	56.4	20.8	10.1	0.4	0.0	12.3	24.5
Buffalo Grove village *Lake Co.*	80.6	1.2	15.6	0.1	0.0	2.5	5.5
Burbank city *Cook Co.*	83.7	0.6	3.1	0.5	0.0	12.1	27.2
Calumet City city *Cook Co.*	23.2	68.8	0.2	0.1	0.0	7.7	16.6
Carbondale city *Jackson Co.*	62.9	25.7	5.9	0.4	0.1	5.0	5.8
Carol Stream village *Du Page Co.*	76.7	5.5	13.8	0.2	0.0	3.8	14.4
Carpentersville village *Kane Co.*	67.5	7.9	3.9	0.3	0.0	20.4	48.9
Champaign city *Champaign Co.*	69.0	15.3	12.1	0.2	0.0	3.4	5.5
Chicago city *Cook Co.*	47.0	32.9	5.6	0.3	0.0	14.2	28.4
Chicago Heights city *Cook Co.*	40.6	42.0	0.2	0.5	0.0	16.7	34.2
Cicero town *Cook Co.*	36.8	3.5	0.3	0.4	0.1	58.9	86.7
Collinsville city *Madison Co.*	83.5	13.1	0.4	0.1	0.0	2.9	3.7
Crystal Lake city *McHenry Co.*	90.2	2.0	2.2	0.0	0.0	5.6	12.0
Danville city *Vermilion Co.*	64.1	30.0	1.2	0.3	0.0	4.4	6.1
DeKalb city *De Kalb Co.*	73.7	12.4	4.0	0.1	0.1	9.7	12.5
Decatur city *Macon Co.*	72.3	22.8	1.1	0.1	0.0	3.7	2.1
Des Plaines city *Cook Co.*	78.1	1.0	12.1	0.3	0.0	8.5	18.1
Downers Grove village *Du Page Co.*	89.7	2.9	5.5	0.1	0.0	1.8	4.6
East Saint Louis city *Saint Clair Co.*	1.6	96.7	0.1	0.1	0.0	1.5	0.5
Edwardsville city *Madison Co.*	87.3	8.0	2.4	0.1	0.0	2.2	2.1
Elgin city *Kane Co.*	66.1	6.7	5.3	0.4	0.0	21.5	45.0
Elk Grove Village village *Cook Co.*	82.3	1.3	8.9	0.4	0.1	7.0	10.4
Elmhurst city *Du Page Co.*	89.5	1.7	5.7	0.0	0.0	3.1	6.1
Elmwood Park village *Cook Co.*	82.1	0.9	3.1	0.7	0.0	13.2	22.3
Evanston city *Cook Co.*	67.7	18.3	8.6	0.0	0.0	5.4	10.0
Freeport city *Stephenson Co.*	79.3	16.0	0.8	0.2	0.1	3.6	4.0
Galesburg city *Knox Co.*	82.6	12.5	1.1	0.1	0.0	3.7	7.5
Glen Ellyn village *Du Page Co.*	89.7	3.4	4.9	0.2	0.1	1.7	4.3
Glendale Heights village *Du Page Co.*	62.5	7.1	23.0	0.8	0.1	6.5	30.7
Glenview village *Cook Co.*	83.6	1.4	12.3	0.1	0.0	2.6	6.4
Granite City city *Madison Co.*	90.7	5.1	0.4	0.3	0.0	3.5	4.5
Gurnee village *Lake Co.*	72.9	9.2	12.3	0.0	0.0	5.6	10.6
Hanover Park village *Cook Co.*	51.5	7.8	17.9	0.0	0.0	22.8	36.4
Harvey city *Cook Co.*	13.4	76.0	0.4	0.0	0.0	10.2	16.7
Highland Park city *Lake Co.*	93.8	2.2	2.0	0.0	0.0	2.0	5.1
Hoffman Estates village *Cook Co.*	62.8	3.7	22.3	0.1	0.0	11.1	15.3
Homer Glen village *Will Co.*	94.1	2.0	1.4	0.3	0.0	2.2	7.7
Huntley village *McHenry Co.*	88.6	1.6	6.3	0.2	0.0	3.3	6.3
Joliet city *Will Co.*	70.9	15.3	2.3	0.2	0.0	11.3	27.2

Place	White[1] (%)	Black[1] (%)	Asian[1] (%)	AIAN[1,2] (%)	NHOPI[1,3] (%)	Other (%)	Hispanic[4] (%)
Kankakee city Kankakee Co.	52.2	38.9	0.1	0.0	0.0	8.8	18.8
Lake in the Hills village McHenry Co.	90.0	1.4	4.5	0.2	0.0	3.9	9.0
Lansing village Cook Co.	61.5	31.4	0.8	0.0	0.0	6.3	13.9
Lockport city Will Co.	94.3	2.0	1.5	0.0	0.0	2.2	7.0
Lombard village Du Page Co.	81.8	5.1	8.9	0.1	0.0	4.1	7.9
McHenry city McHenry Co.	90.3	0.2	1.9	0.2	0.0	7.4	11.0
Melrose Park village Cook Co.	52.5	6.6	1.1	0.0	0.0	39.8	71.1
Moline city Rock Island Co.	82.3	5.1	2.7	0.5	0.0	9.4	17.1
Mount Prospect village Cook Co.	74.6	1.8	11.7	0.2	0.0	11.7	16.2
Mundelein village Lake Co.	82.8	1.3	8.1	0.2	0.0	7.6	30.8
Naperville city Du Page Co.	76.2	4.8	15.5	0.1	0.1	3.3	5.9
New Lenox village Will Co.	93.9	0.6	1.7	0.0	0.0	3.8	7.0
Niles village Cook Co.	75.1	1.1	18.9	0.3	0.0	4.6	9.5
Normal town McLean Co.	84.2	8.1	3.3	0.2	0.0	4.2	5.0
North Chicago city Lake Co.	44.9	31.5	4.1	0.5	0.0	19.0	28.0
Northbrook village Cook Co.	84.4	1.0	12.9	0.0	0.0	1.7	1.9
O'Fallon city Saint Clair Co.	78.8	15.8	2.0	0.2	0.0	3.2	2.8
Oak Forest city Cook Co.	87.0	4.7	2.9	0.5	0.0	4.9	14.7
Oak Lawn village Cook Co.	89.5	3.8	1.1	0.3	0.0	5.3	15.7
Oak Park village Cook Co.	68.4	21.0	5.2	0.2	0.0	5.2	6.1
Orland Park village Cook Co.	90.9	2.0	4.7	0.0	0.0	2.4	5.4
Oswego village Kendall Co.	86.7	5.7	3.2	0.1	0.0	4.3	10.3
Palatine village Cook Co.	79.8	3.2	11.1	0.0	0.1	5.8	17.4
Park Ridge city Cook Co.	93.5	1.2	3.4	0.0	0.0	1.9	5.4
Pekin city Tazewell Co.	95.7	2.4	0.2	0.2	0.1	1.4	2.4
Peoria city Peoria Co.	63.9	26.6	4.6	0.4	0.0	4.5	5.0
Plainfield village Will Co.	83.1	4.8	7.2	0.0	0.1	4.8	10.5
Quincy city Adams Co.	90.2	5.5	1.2	0.1	0.0	3.0	1.5
Rock Island city Rock Island Co.	74.2	17.3	0.9	0.2	0.0	7.4	10.1
Rockford city Winnebago Co.	69.2	20.9	2.8	0.3	0.0	6.8	16.3
Rolling Meadows city Cook Co.	71.9	2.9	8.5	0.4	0.0	16.3	25.2
Romeoville village Will Co.	68.8	10.5	7.0	0.5	0.0	13.2	32.4
Round Lake Beach village Lake Co.	85.0	3.4	2.7	0.6	0.0	8.3	51.1
Saint Charles city Kane Co.	92.0	1.5	2.4	0.1	0.1	3.9	9.7
Schaumburg village Cook Co.	70.9	4.1	19.0	0.1	0.0	5.9	9.0
Skokie village Cook Co.	64.1	7.4	24.8	0.1	0.0	3.6	8.6
Springfield city Sangamon Co.	76.2	18.8	2.0	0.3	0.0	2.7	2.0
Streamwood village Cook Co.	61.2	4.3	15.0	0.2	0.0	19.3	28.7
Tinley Park village Cook Co.	88.3	3.2	3.9	0.0	0.0	4.6	8.4
Urbana city Champaign Co.	62.7	17.7	16.2	0.3	0.0	3.1	5.2
Vernon Hills village Lake Co.	76.3	0.8	17.8	0.0	0.0	5.1	11.4
Waukegan city Lake Co.	50.8	16.8	4.0	0.2	0.0	28.2	53.1
West Chicago city Du Page Co.	83.8	2.7	5.2	0.0	0.0	8.3	48.4
Westmont village Du Page Co.	70.8	8.1	13.1	0.4	0.0	7.6	9.3
Wheaton city Du Page Co.	86.9	3.4	6.3	0.1	0.0	3.3	4.9
Wheeling village Cook Co.	74.3	1.4	14.1	0.1	0.0	10.1	32.4
Wilmette village Cook Co.	84.6	1.1	12.4	0.1	0.0	1.8	4.5
Woodridge village Du Page Co.	69.5	9.0	12.9	0.2	0.0	8.4	13.3
Woodstock city McHenry Co.	86.4	1.5	2.3	0.5	0.0	9.3	22.3
Zion city Lake Co.	48.9	33.2	2.3	0.3	0.1	15.2	22.5

NOTE: (1) Exclude multiple race combinations; (2) American Indian/Alaska Native; (3) Native Hawaiian/Other Pacific Islander; (4) May be of any race
SOURCE: U.S. Census Bureau, American Community Survey, 2008-2012 Five-Year Estimates

Avg. Household Size, Median Age, Male/Female Ratio & Foreign Born

Place	Average Household Size (persons)	Median Age (years)	Males per 100 Females	Foreign Born (%)
Addison village *Du Page Co.*	3.08	34.3	95.9	34.5
Algonquin village *McHenry Co.*	2.88	38.8	100.3	12.6
Alton city *Madison Co.*	2.39	33.9	91.2	1.5
Arlington Heights village *Cook Co.*	2.47	42.1	93.1	18.2
Aurora city *Kane Co.*	3.13	31.0	99.7	25.4
Bartlett village *Du Page Co.*	2.96	36.7	98.2	17.3
Batavia city *Kane Co.*	2.77	39.7	91.4	4.9
Belleville city *Saint Clair Co.*	2.34	37.2	90.1	2.1
Belvidere city *Boone Co.*	2.99	33.4	101.0	16.3
Berwyn city *Cook Co.*	3.05	33.1	94.5	25.1
Bloomington city *McLean Co.*	2.43	33.9	94.9	8.5
Bolingbrook village *Will Co.*	3.36	33.1	100.5	22.2
Buffalo Grove village *Lake Co.*	2.55	42.1	91.9	26.8
Burbank city *Cook Co.*	3.21	36.9	95.2	30.7
Calumet City city *Cook Co.*	2.57	35.9	78.3	8.8
Carbondale city *Jackson Co.*	2.18	23.3	106.3	10.0
Carol Stream village *Du Page Co.*	2.70	36.4	96.3	19.9
Carpentersville village *Kane Co.*	3.41	29.8	104.0	28.5
Champaign city *Champaign Co.*	2.25	26.3	104.8	13.7
Chicago city *Cook Co.*	2.57	33.1	93.9	21.2
Chicago Heights city *Cook Co.*	3.09	30.7	96.9	12.5
Cicero town *Cook Co.*	3.89	28.0	103.8	42.6
Collinsville city *Madison Co.*	2.27	37.0	96.8	1.9
Crystal Lake city *McHenry Co.*	2.86	35.2	98.2	11.3
Danville city *Vermilion Co.*	2.44	36.0	97.2	3.5
DeKalb city *De Kalb Co.*	2.43	23.5	100.0	9.1
Decatur city *Macon Co.*	2.31	38.8	89.1	2.0
Des Plaines city *Cook Co.*	2.57	41.5	94.5	28.5
Downers Grove village *Du Page Co.*	2.56	41.8	92.4	8.9
East Saint Louis city *Saint Clair Co.*	2.53	33.1	86.0	0.1
Edwardsville city *Madison Co.*	2.52	31.2	99.5	4.1
Elgin city *Kane Co.*	3.05	32.5	98.4	26.2
Elk Grove Village village *Cook Co.*	2.51	42.9	98.2	19.7
Elmhurst city *Du Page Co.*	2.82	39.5	95.0	9.7
Elmwood Park village *Cook Co.*	2.70	39.8	89.8	29.7
Evanston city *Cook Co.*	2.36	34.4	94.5	17.8
Freeport city *Stephenson Co.*	2.28	42.4	89.1	3.0
Galesburg city *Knox Co.*	2.12	39.8	101.1	3.8
Glen Ellyn village *Du Page Co.*	2.62	40.2	90.3	9.5
Glendale Heights village *Du Page Co.*	3.06	31.6	104.3	34.4
Glenview village *Cook Co.*	2.64	45.7	90.6	20.7
Granite City city *Madison Co.*	2.42	37.7	96.2	2.1
Gurnee village *Lake Co.*	2.74	39.0	88.0	15.8
Hanover Park village *Cook Co.*	3.49	32.1	98.7	36.6
Harvey city *Cook Co.*	3.22	30.6	80.8	8.5
Highland Park city *Lake Co.*	2.55	45.4	93.3	11.4
Hoffman Estates village *Cook Co.*	2.90	36.5	97.0	29.8
Homer Glen village *Will Co.*	3.07	41.3	99.2	12.4
Huntley village *McHenry Co.*	2.43	44.1	88.8	8.4
Joliet city *Will Co.*	3.08	31.6	96.4	14.9

Place	Average Household Size (persons)	Median Age (years)	Males per 100 Females	Foreign Born (%)
Kankakee city *Kankakee Co.*	2.71	32.3	101.6	9.5
Lake in the Hills village *McHenry Co.*	2.95	36.3	102.9	10.9
Lansing village *Cook Co.*	2.50	39.3	85.2	6.4
Lockport city *Will Co.*	2.80	33.8	98.6	8.1
Lombard village *Du Page Co.*	2.41	39.9	93.2	13.6
McHenry city *McHenry Co.*	2.69	37.7	99.1	8.3
Melrose Park village *Cook Co.*	3.31	30.3	105.5	38.4
Moline city *Rock Island Co.*	2.38	38.7	95.8	10.7
Mount Prospect village *Cook Co.*	2.66	39.4	97.4	32.0
Mundelein village *Lake Co.*	2.93	36.6	107.3	29.3
Naperville city *Du Page Co.*	2.86	38.0	95.2	16.9
New Lenox village *Will Co.*	3.00	36.2	89.9	3.6
Niles village *Cook Co.*	2.52	48.5	92.6	44.2
Normal town *McLean Co.*	2.57	23.7	90.6	4.5
North Chicago city *Lake Co.*	3.02	24.1	157.8	18.0
Northbrook village *Cook Co.*	2.67	46.5	92.8	19.2
O'Fallon city *Saint Clair Co.*	2.75	34.9	94.2	3.6
Oak Forest city *Cook Co.*	2.92	35.3	95.1	7.9
Oak Lawn village *Cook Co.*	2.58	40.8	90.2	15.0
Oak Park village *Cook Co.*	2.36	38.5	86.3	10.4
Orland Park village *Cook Co.*	2.63	45.0	88.8	13.2
Oswego village *Kendall Co.*	3.09	33.7	99.0	6.2
Palatine village *Cook Co.*	2.65	36.3	97.1	22.2
Park Ridge city *Cook Co.*	2.64	44.4	91.7	15.2
Pekin city *Tazewell Co.*	2.26	39.7	94.4	1.0
Peoria city *Peoria Co.*	2.33	33.7	91.7	6.5
Plainfield village *Will Co.*	3.37	33.4	98.7	10.7
Quincy city *Adams Co.*	2.35	38.5	88.4	1.6
Rock Island city *Rock Island Co.*	2.33	37.0	88.9	6.1
Rockford city *Winnebago Co.*	2.51	35.6	93.7	10.4
Rolling Meadows city *Cook Co.*	2.59	36.6	97.0	27.8
Romeoville village *Will Co.*	3.28	31.9	97.3	21.4
Round Lake Beach village *Lake Co.*	3.45	29.4	96.2	29.9
Saint Charles city *Kane Co.*	2.62	39.6	101.5	10.0
Schaumburg village *Cook Co.*	2.40	37.2	95.6	25.7
Skokie village *Cook Co.*	2.75	43.7	92.5	41.1
Springfield city *Sangamon Co.*	2.25	38.3	91.2	4.0
Streamwood village *Cook Co.*	3.01	34.5	97.1	29.4
Tinley Park village *Cook Co.*	2.67	38.8	94.2	8.2
Urbana city *Champaign Co.*	2.12	24.0	98.8	18.9
Vernon Hills village *Lake Co.*	2.68	37.9	96.7	27.9
Waukegan city *Lake Co.*	3.03	30.7	100.2	31.3
West Chicago city *Du Page Co.*	3.45	30.8	105.1	32.1
Westmont village *Du Page Co.*	2.28	40.5	86.8	22.8
Wheaton city *Du Page Co.*	2.61	37.8	94.8	11.4
Wheeling village *Cook Co.*	2.60	35.8	94.4	42.0
Wilmette village *Cook Co.*	2.84	43.5	102.0	16.9
Woodridge village *Du Page Co.*	2.59	36.6	98.5	20.4
Woodstock city *McHenry Co.*	2.62	35.4	92.9	15.2
Zion city *Lake Co.*	2.96	30.8	91.9	12.1

SOURCE: U.S. Census Bureau, American Community Survey, 2008-2012 Five-Year Estimates

Five Largest Ancestry Groups

Place	Group 1	Group 2	Group 3	Group 4	Group 5
Addison village *Du Page Co.*	Italian (13.4%)	German (12.4%)	Polish (12.4%)	Irish (8.4%)	Greek (2.5%)
Algonquin village *McHenry Co.*	German (28.3%)	Polish (17.1%)	Irish (14.6%)	Italian (13.2%)	English (6.8%)
Alton city *Madison Co.*	German (24.9%)	Irish (12.3%)	English (9.5%)	American (4.8%)	Italian (4.3%)
Arlington Heights village *Cook Co.*	German (26.7%)	Irish (18.0%)	Polish (16.0%)	Italian (11.2%)	English (6.1%)
Aurora city *Kane Co.*	German (14.8%)	Irish (9.3%)	Polish (4.9%)	English (4.7%)	Italian (4.5%)
Bartlett village *Du Page Co.*	German (27.5%)	Italian (17.4%)	Irish (15.7%)	Polish (15.7%)	English (4.4%)
Batavia city *Kane Co.*	German (32.5%)	Irish (18.4%)	Polish (13.1%)	English (11.6%)	Italian (11.6%)
Belleville city *Saint Clair Co.*	German (28.1%)	Irish (10.9%)	European (8.9%)	English (6.9%)	American (4.8%)
Belvidere city *Boone Co.*	German (18.5%)	Irish (13.0%)	American (7.7%)	English (7.1%)	Swedish (5.7%)
Berwyn city *Cook Co.*	Italian (8.1%)	German (7.4%)	Irish (7.2%)	Polish (6.8%)	Czech (3.4%)
Bloomington city *McLean Co.*	German (26.8%)	Irish (14.3%)	English (10.2%)	American (9.5%)	Italian (3.4%)
Bolingbrook village *Will Co.*	German (14.3%)	Irish (10.7%)	Polish (8.4%)	Italian (6.8%)	English (3.3%)
Buffalo Grove village *Lake Co.*	Russian (14.4%)	German (13.5%)	Polish (10.1%)	Irish (7.6%)	American (6.9%)
Burbank city *Cook Co.*	Polish (30.5%)	Irish (11.2%)	German (10.9%)	Italian (5.5%)	Palestinian (3.2%)
Calumet City city *Cook Co.*	Polish (5.4%)	German (2.3%)	Irish (2.0%)	Italian (2.0%)	African (1.4%)
Carbondale city *Jackson Co.*	German (18.6%)	Irish (9.5%)	English (7.8%)	Italian (3.6%)	Polish (3.2%)
Carol Stream village *Du Page Co.*	German (23.0%)	Irish (13.6%)	Italian (13.4%)	Polish (11.7%)	English (5.9%)
Carpentersville village *Kane Co.*	German (15.2%)	Polish (6.8%)	Irish (6.7%)	Italian (6.2%)	English (2.9%)
Champaign city *Champaign Co.*	German (19.0%)	Irish (11.4%)	American (11.3%)	English (7.6%)	Italian (4.1%)
Chicago city *Cook Co.*	German (7.6%)	Irish (7.6%)	Polish (6.2%)	Italian (3.9%)	English (2.3%)
Chicago Heights city *Cook Co.*	Italian (8.4%)	German (6.9%)	Polish (4.3%)	Irish (4.3%)	American (1.8%)
Cicero town *Cook Co.*	Polish (2.4%)	Irish (2.4%)	German (2.3%)	Italian (2.0%)	Czech (0.9%)
Collinsville city *Madison Co.*	German (27.1%)	Irish (13.2%)	English (9.9%)	Italian (8.6%)	American (5.2%)
Crystal Lake city *McHenry Co.*	German (29.9%)	Irish (19.0%)	Polish (14.4%)	Italian (11.9%)	English (7.5%)
Danville city *Vermilion Co.*	American (20.7%)	German (13.4%)	Irish (7.4%)	English (5.6%)	French (1.7%)
DeKalb city *De Kalb Co.*	German (23.5%)	Irish (14.4%)	English (7.2%)	Polish (7.2%)	Italian (6.3%)
Decatur city *Macon Co.*	German (19.2%)	American (16.3%)	Irish (11.9%)	English (9.3%)	Polish (2.1%)
Des Plaines city *Cook Co.*	German (19.9%)	Polish (15.1%)	Irish (13.7%)	Italian (9.1%)	English (3.8%)
Downers Grove village *Du Page Co.*	German (26.5%)	Irish (20.7%)	Italian (13.9%)	Polish (13.7%)	English (8.2%)
East Saint Louis city *Saint Clair Co.*	African (1.1%)	American (0.8%)	German (0.5%)	Irish (0.4%)	English (0.2%)
Edwardsville city *Madison Co.*	German (34.8%)	Irish (13.4%)	English (12.2%)	Italian (6.4%)	American (6.1%)
Elgin city *Kane Co.*	German (17.0%)	Irish (7.8%)	English (5.4%)	Polish (5.4%)	Italian (5.3%)
Elk Grove Village village *Cook Co.*	German (25.1%)	Polish (20.1%)	Irish (18.2%)	Italian (12.4%)	English (5.6%)
Elmhurst city *Du Page Co.*	German (27.8%)	Irish (25.7%)	Italian (16.2%)	Polish (10.7%)	English (6.0%)
Elmwood Park village *Cook Co.*	Polish (24.5%)	Italian (19.7%)	German (12.6%)	Irish (11.5%)	Ukrainian (3.1%)
Evanston city *Cook Co.*	German (16.1%)	Irish (12.6%)	English (7.9%)	Polish (6.3%)	Italian (4.7%)
Freeport city *Stephenson Co.*	German (36.7%)	Irish (10.9%)	American (9.1%)	English (8.2%)	Dutch (4.6%)
Galesburg city *Knox Co.*	German (19.1%)	Irish (12.7%)	English (9.1%)	Swedish (9.0%)	American (6.7%)
Glen Ellyn village *Du Page Co.*	German (28.3%)	Irish (24.3%)	English (11.9%)	Polish (11.6%)	Italian (10.2%)
Glendale Heights village *Du Page Co.*	German (12.5%)	Polish (8.6%)	Italian (6.6%)	Irish (6.3%)	English (2.5%)
Glenview village *Cook Co.*	German (19.6%)	Irish (14.6%)	Polish (10.9%)	Italian (9.4%)	Russian (6.2%)
Granite City city *Madison Co.*	German (20.4%)	Irish (19.1%)	English (10.7%)	American (9.6%)	Italian (4.9%)
Gurnee village *Lake Co.*	German (21.3%)	Irish (15.1%)	Polish (10.1%)	Italian (8.6%)	English (7.7%)
Hanover Park village *Cook Co.*	German (13.3%)	Polish (9.8%)	Irish (8.5%)	Italian (5.8%)	English (2.8%)
Harvey city *Cook Co.*	African (1.0%)	Polish (1.0%)	American (0.7%)	English (0.6%)	German (0.6%)
Highland Park city *Lake Co.*	German (18.3%)	Russian (18.2%)	American (9.8%)	Polish (9.4%)	Irish (8.0%)
Hoffman Estates village *Cook Co.*	German (16.8%)	Polish (13.2%)	Irish (10.4%)	Italian (8.6%)	English (5.2%)
Homer Glen village *Will Co.*	Polish (24.6%)	Irish (20.7%)	German (18.2%)	Italian (15.6%)	Lithuanian (6.6%)
Huntley village *McHenry Co.*	German (29.6%)	Polish (17.4%)	Irish (16.0%)	Italian (14.8%)	English (7.2%)
Joliet city *Will Co.*	German (16.6%)	Irish (15.4%)	Polish (9.3%)	Italian (9.2%)	English (4.5%)

Place	Group 1	Group 2	Group 3	Group 4	Group 5
Kankakee city *Kankakee Co.*	German (13.3%)	Irish (7.5%)	French (6.8%)	English (4.0%)	Italian (2.7%)
Lake in the Hills village *McHenry Co.*	German (28.5%)	Irish (19.0%)	Polish (17.5%)	Italian (14.1%)	English (5.5%)
Lansing village *Cook Co.*	German (14.3%)	Polish (13.1%)	Irish (10.3%)	Dutch (8.1%)	Italian (7.0%)
Lockport city *Will Co.*	German (26.9%)	Polish (25.0%)	Irish (21.6%)	Italian (17.5%)	English (5.6%)
Lombard village *Du Page Co.*	German (28.0%)	Irish (19.6%)	Italian (14.4%)	Polish (12.8%)	English (7.3%)
McHenry city *McHenry Co.*	German (38.1%)	Irish (18.7%)	Polish (15.9%)	Italian (8.4%)	English (6.9%)
Melrose Park village *Cook Co.*	Italian (12.2%)	German (4.1%)	Polish (3.2%)	Irish (2.8%)	American (0.8%)
Moline city *Rock Island Co.*	German (25.2%)	Irish (13.9%)	English (9.9%)	Swedish (6.6%)	Belgian (4.9%)
Mount Prospect village *Cook Co.*	German (20.9%)	Polish (18.2%)	Irish (12.5%)	Italian (9.5%)	English (4.1%)
Mundelein village *Lake Co.*	German (19.2%)	Polish (9.6%)	Irish (9.5%)	American (7.0%)	Italian (5.6%)
Naperville city *Du Page Co.*	German (22.2%)	Irish (16.6%)	Italian (10.4%)	Polish (10.0%)	English (7.6%)
New Lenox village *Will Co.*	Irish (27.8%)	German (27.4%)	Polish (18.8%)	Italian (18.0%)	English (7.9%)
Niles village *Cook Co.*	Polish (21.0%)	German (11.3%)	Irish (7.0%)	Italian (6.7%)	Greek (4.0%)
Normal town *McLean Co.*	German (27.8%)	Irish (15.9%)	English (9.8%)	American (9.6%)	Italian (5.1%)
North Chicago city *Lake Co.*	German (9.0%)	Irish (8.9%)	Italian (3.9%)	Polish (2.8%)	English (2.6%)
Northbrook village *Cook Co.*	German (16.9%)	Irish (11.3%)	Russian (11.1%)	Polish (9.3%)	American (6.6%)
O'Fallon city *Saint Clair Co.*	German (31.5%)	Irish (14.3%)	English (12.6%)	American (5.0%)	Polish (4.3%)
Oak Forest city *Cook Co.*	German (24.4%)	Irish (24.3%)	Polish (14.8%)	Italian (13.0%)	Dutch (3.7%)
Oak Lawn village *Cook Co.*	Irish (24.9%)	Polish (19.8%)	German (17.8%)	Italian (10.2%)	Lithuanian (4.0%)
Oak Park village *Cook Co.*	German (18.6%)	Irish (18.4%)	English (9.4%)	Italian (8.2%)	Polish (7.6%)
Orland Park village *Cook Co.*	Irish (23.9%)	German (18.4%)	Polish (17.1%)	Italian (14.4%)	English (4.4%)
Oswego village *Kendall Co.*	German (28.5%)	Irish (20.3%)	Italian (12.2%)	Polish (9.7%)	English (8.3%)
Palatine village *Cook Co.*	German (21.0%)	Irish (14.6%)	Polish (14.0%)	Italian (9.9%)	English (5.6%)
Park Ridge city *Cook Co.*	Irish (22.3%)	German (22.2%)	Polish (20.3%)	Italian (14.2%)	English (6.3%)
Pekin city *Tazewell Co.*	German (29.9%)	Irish (15.1%)	American (14.6%)	English (10.3%)	Italian (5.3%)
Peoria city *Peoria Co.*	German (22.6%)	Irish (12.2%)	English (8.1%)	American (4.2%)	Italian (3.7%)
Plainfield village *Will Co.*	Irish (22.9%)	German (21.7%)	Italian (15.1%)	Polish (12.0%)	English (6.0%)
Quincy city *Adams Co.*	German (40.1%)	Irish (11.8%)	American (10.0%)	English (9.7%)	French (2.1%)
Rock Island city *Rock Island Co.*	German (23.5%)	Irish (12.7%)	English (7.4%)	Swedish (5.3%)	American (4.7%)
Rockford city *Winnebago Co.*	German (19.0%)	Irish (10.4%)	Swedish (7.5%)	American (6.8%)	Italian (6.5%)
Rolling Meadows city *Cook Co.*	German (20.4%)	Polish (13.8%)	Irish (11.3%)	Italian (10.3%)	English (4.6%)
Romeoville village *Will Co.*	German (13.4%)	Irish (13.2%)	Polish (10.9%)	Italian (9.6%)	English (3.3%)
Round Lake Beach village *Lake Co.*	German (14.4%)	Irish (9.2%)	Polish (8.8%)	Italian (3.6%)	English (3.3%)
Saint Charles city *Kane Co.*	German (31.4%)	Irish (18.9%)	Italian (12.4%)	English (10.4%)	Polish (10.3%)
Schaumburg village *Cook Co.*	German (21.1%)	Polish (14.6%)	Irish (12.8%)	Italian (11.1%)	English (4.6%)
Skokie village *Cook Co.*	German (8.8%)	Russian (6.2%)	Irish (5.8%)	Polish (5.8%)	(a) (5.6%)
Springfield city *Sangamon Co.*	German (24.8%)	Irish (13.5%)	English (10.4%)	American (7.3%)	Italian (5.9%)
Streamwood village *Cook Co.*	German (16.3%)	Polish (13.2%)	Irish (9.4%)	Italian (8.2%)	English (3.8%)
Tinley Park village *Cook Co.*	Irish (26.2%)	German (22.0%)	Polish (20.4%)	Italian (12.4%)	English (4.7%)
Urbana city *Champaign Co.*	German (16.4%)	American (10.5%)	Irish (9.0%)	English (7.7%)	European (4.1%)
Vernon Hills village *Lake Co.*	German (16.0%)	Irish (10.3%)	Russian (9.3%)	Polish (8.4%)	American (6.5%)
Waukegan city *Lake Co.*	German (7.9%)	Irish (5.2%)	Polish (2.7%)	Italian (2.7%)	English (2.6%)
West Chicago city *Du Page Co.*	German (12.3%)	Irish (8.8%)	Polish (7.2%)	Italian (6.6%)	English (3.9%)
Westmont village *Du Page Co.*	German (19.0%)	Irish (13.1%)	Polish (12.5%)	Italian (8.1%)	English (4.8%)
Wheaton city *Du Page Co.*	German (25.4%)	Irish (17.3%)	English (12.1%)	Italian (11.0%)	Polish (10.0%)
Wheeling village *Cook Co.*	German (12.2%)	Polish (9.6%)	Irish (7.4%)	Russian (6.3%)	Italian (4.9%)
Wilmette village *Cook Co.*	German (23.1%)	Irish (17.7%)	English (10.5%)	Polish (6.6%)	Italian (6.4%)
Woodridge village *Du Page Co.*	German (19.8%)	Irish (12.4%)	Polish (11.7%)	Italian (11.0%)	English (5.2%)
Woodstock city *McHenry Co.*	German (27.9%)	Irish (16.5%)	Polish (9.9%)	English (6.9%)	Italian (6.6%)
Zion city *Lake Co.*	German (12.3%)	Irish (10.9%)	American (4.1%)	English (3.5%)	Polish (3.1%)

NOTE: (a) Assyrian/Chaldean/Syriac; "French" excludes Basque; Please refer to the Explanation of Data for more information.
SOURCE: U.S. Census Bureau, American Community Survey, 2008-2012 Five-Year Estimates

Marriage Status

Place	Never Married (%)	Now Married (%)	Widowed (%)	Divorced (%)
Addison village *Du Page Co.*	31.5	55.6	6.0	6.9
Algonquin village *McHenry Co.*	23.8	65.6	3.9	6.6
Alton city *Madison Co.*	34.8	42.5	6.7	16.0
Arlington Heights village *Cook Co.*	25.5	59.9	6.4	8.2
Aurora city *Kane Co.*	34.0	53.7	3.7	8.7
Bartlett village *Du Page Co.*	26.4	64.3	3.6	5.7
Batavia city *Kane Co.*	25.7	61.4	5.1	7.8
Belleville city *Saint Clair Co.*	34.1	42.7	7.3	15.9
Belvidere city *Boone Co.*	29.5	54.8	5.8	10.0
Berwyn city *Cook Co.*	38.9	46.0	5.8	9.3
Bloomington city *McLean Co.*	33.9	49.3	4.9	11.9
Bolingbrook village *Will Co.*	33.0	55.8	3.2	8.0
Buffalo Grove village *Lake Co.*	22.6	64.0	4.9	8.6
Burbank city *Cook Co.*	32.6	52.6	7.2	7.6
Calumet City city *Cook Co.*	42.1	35.3	8.3	14.3
Carbondale city *Jackson Co.*	69.6	20.3	3.3	6.8
Carol Stream village *Du Page Co.*	29.8	57.9	4.3	8.0
Carpentersville village *Kane Co.*	35.8	51.3	4.1	8.8
Champaign city *Champaign Co.*	53.2	36.2	3.0	7.6
Chicago city *Cook Co.*	47.9	37.6	5.7	8.8
Chicago Heights city *Cook Co.*	43.3	40.4	7.4	8.8
Cicero town *Cook Co.*	39.0	50.8	3.8	6.4
Collinsville city *Madison Co.*	34.2	45.7	6.1	14.0
Crystal Lake city *McHenry Co.*	29.4	55.6	5.2	9.8
Danville city *Vermilion Co.*	37.6	38.7	8.4	15.2
DeKalb city *De Kalb Co.*	57.8	31.3	3.9	7.0
Decatur city *Macon Co.*	32.9	44.4	7.9	14.9
Des Plaines city *Cook Co.*	28.6	54.2	8.5	8.7
Downers Grove village *Du Page Co.*	27.9	57.7	6.3	8.1
East Saint Louis city *Saint Clair Co.*	56.3	21.6	9.5	12.6
Edwardsville city *Madison Co.*	40.2	47.8	3.1	8.9
Elgin city *Kane Co.*	32.5	52.6	5.7	9.2
Elk Grove Village village *Cook Co.*	26.7	57.0	5.4	10.9
Elmhurst city *Du Page Co.*	27.5	57.7	7.1	7.8
Elmwood Park village *Cook Co.*	33.6	49.5	8.2	8.7
Evanston city *Cook Co.*	42.7	43.7	5.2	8.3
Freeport city *Stephenson Co.*	30.3	45.6	10.0	14.1
Galesburg city *Knox Co.*	37.4	39.4	8.2	15.0
Glen Ellyn village *Du Page Co.*	25.0	59.9	5.6	9.5
Glendale Heights village *Du Page Co.*	34.1	53.4	3.2	9.3
Glenview village *Cook Co.*	22.9	62.1	8.3	6.6
Granite City city *Madison Co.*	27.0	48.3	8.8	15.9
Gurnee village *Lake Co.*	27.9	56.4	5.2	10.4
Hanover Park village *Cook Co.*	31.3	58.6	3.0	7.1
Harvey city *Cook Co.*	48.9	32.4	8.2	10.4
Highland Park city *Lake Co.*	19.9	64.8	6.6	8.8
Hoffman Estates village *Cook Co.*	28.3	59.9	4.2	7.7
Homer Glen village *Will Co.*	25.4	64.9	4.0	5.7
Huntley village *McHenry Co.*	14.3	70.5	7.6	7.6
Joliet city *Will Co.*	33.6	51.6	5.1	9.6

Place	Never Married (%)	Now Married (%)	Widowed (%)	Divorced (%)
Kankakee city *Kankakee Co.*	43.2	37.4	6.7	12.6
Lake in the Hills village *McHenry Co.*	23.2	62.2	3.3	11.3
Lansing village *Cook Co.*	34.3	46.9	7.4	11.4
Lockport city *Will Co.*	25.9	60.7	4.9	8.5
Lombard village *Du Page Co.*	32.2	51.2	7.3	9.4
McHenry city *McHenry Co.*	28.4	56.5	6.7	8.4
Melrose Park village *Cook Co.*	37.6	48.5	5.0	8.9
Moline city *Rock Island Co.*	28.6	51.1	7.2	13.1
Mount Prospect village *Cook Co.*	28.6	58.1	6.6	6.6
Mundelein village *Lake Co.*	29.1	59.8	4.0	7.2
Naperville city *Du Page Co.*	26.2	63.1	3.6	7.1
New Lenox village *Will Co.*	24.3	64.6	5.2	5.9
Niles village *Cook Co.*	28.1	53.2	12.0	6.8
Normal town *McLean Co.*	54.0	36.0	3.0	7.1
North Chicago city *Lake Co.*	58.1	32.0	3.0	7.0
Northbrook village *Cook Co.*	20.6	64.3	7.6	7.5
O'Fallon city *Saint Clair Co.*	27.9	56.8	4.7	10.6
Oak Forest city *Cook Co.*	32.3	53.3	5.0	9.4
Oak Lawn village *Cook Co.*	30.6	50.7	9.0	9.7
Oak Park village *Cook Co.*	33.0	53.6	4.0	9.4
Orland Park village *Cook Co.*	27.3	56.8	8.8	7.0
Oswego village *Kendall Co.*	22.6	67.8	3.6	6.1
Palatine village *Cook Co.*	30.7	56.1	4.5	8.7
Park Ridge city *Cook Co.*	26.6	59.0	7.0	7.5
Pekin city *Tazewell Co.*	26.3	50.2	7.8	15.8
Peoria city *Peoria Co.*	40.2	42.2	6.2	11.4
Plainfield village *Will Co.*	25.0	65.3	2.8	6.9
Quincy city *Adams Co.*	30.3	47.6	9.4	12.7
Rock Island city *Rock Island Co.*	35.1	43.2	8.0	13.6
Rockford city *Winnebago Co.*	35.5	43.6	7.4	13.5
Rolling Meadows city *Cook Co.*	29.1	55.9	5.7	9.4
Romeoville village *Will Co.*	32.7	54.9	3.9	8.4
Round Lake Beach village *Lake Co.*	32.9	55.0	4.1	8.0
Saint Charles city *Kane Co.*	25.7	59.7	5.1	9.5
Schaumburg village *Cook Co.*	30.6	54.1	5.5	9.8
Skokie village *Cook Co.*	28.0	56.4	7.2	8.4
Springfield city *Sangamon Co.*	33.2	45.2	7.1	14.5
Streamwood village *Cook Co.*	29.6	58.0	4.6	7.8
Tinley Park village *Cook Co.*	28.3	55.5	6.6	9.6
Urbana city *Champaign Co.*	64.6	26.1	3.2	6.1
Vernon Hills village *Lake Co.*	26.0	61.6	4.6	7.8
Waukegan city *Lake Co.*	37.4	48.7	4.8	9.1
West Chicago city *Du Page Co.*	32.8	55.7	2.9	8.6
Westmont village *Du Page Co.*	28.9	52.1	8.7	10.3
Wheaton city *Du Page Co.*	32.0	55.7	4.7	7.7
Wheeling village *Cook Co.*	27.8	56.6	6.6	8.9
Wilmette village *Cook Co.*	23.5	64.0	6.3	6.2
Woodridge village *Du Page Co.*	31.9	56.2	2.9	9.0
Woodstock city *McHenry Co.*	28.5	53.0	5.8	12.7
Zion city *Lake Co.*	36.1	47.0	4.5	12.4

SOURCE: U.S. Census Bureau, American Community Survey, 2008-2012 Five-Year Estimates

Employment and Building Permits Issued

Place	Unemployment Rate (%)	Total Civilian Labor Force	Single-Family Building Permits	Multi-Family Building Permits
Addison village *Du Page Co.*	8.1	19,987	3	0
Algonquin village *McHenry Co.*	6.3	16,558	4	0
Alton city *Madison Co.*	8.0	12,720	1	12
Arlington Heights village *Cook Co.*	5.5	42,203	55	0
Aurora city *Kane Co.*	7.4	106,605	154	0
Bartlett village *Du Page Co.*	6.1	23,706	3	0
Batavia city *Kane Co.*	6.4	14,412	7	0
Belleville city *Saint Clair Co.*	6.9	22,263	34	0
Belvidere city *Boone Co.*	11.3	11,908	12	0
Berwyn city *Cook Co.*	7.7	28,330	0	0
Bloomington city *McLean Co.*	5.6	40,759	197	172
Bolingbrook village *Will Co.*	7.2	41,531	108	0
Buffalo Grove village *Lake Co.*	5.4	23,497	6	0
Burbank city *Cook Co.*	7.3	15,053	14	0
Calumet City city *Cook Co.*	10.1	18,081	0	0
Carbondale city *Jackson Co.*	5.4	13,532	7	34
Carol Stream village *Du Page Co.*	6.2	23,014	32	0
Carpentersville village *Kane Co.*	9.9	18,900	39	0
Champaign city *Champaign Co.*	5.6	41,336	73	288
Chicago city *Cook Co.*	8.4	1,253,780	448	2,577
Chicago Heights city *Cook Co.*	11.3	13,036	0	0
Cicero town *Cook Co.*	9.4	33,280	0	0
Collinsville city *Madison Co.*	5.9	13,687	5	0
Crystal Lake city *McHenry Co.*	6.3	21,482	24	68
Danville city *Vermilion Co.*	9.2	12,664	0	0
DeKalb city *De Kalb Co.*	6.8	23,644	3	0
Decatur city *Macon Co.*	10.2	33,910	13	0
Des Plaines city *Cook Co.*	7.1	31,005	31	0
Downers Grove village *Du Page Co.*	5.3	27,269	74	0
East Saint Louis city *Saint Clair Co.*	11.9	8,865	5	164
Edwardsville city *Madison Co.*	n/a	n/a	47	72
Elgin city *Kane Co.*	9.0	59,470	343	0
Elk Grove Village village *Cook Co.*	5.9	19,924	0	0
Elmhurst city *Du Page Co.*	5.2	24,383	118	0
Elmwood Park village *Cook Co.*	6.6	13,456	0	0
Evanston city *Cook Co.*	5.5	41,256	7	77
Freeport city *Stephenson Co.*	8.2	11,237	1	0
Galesburg city *Knox Co.*	6.8	13,895	4	2
Glen Ellyn village *Du Page Co.*	5.1	14,711	29	0
Glendale Heights village *Du Page Co.*	7.3	20,406	0	0
Glenview village *Cook Co.*	4.6	23,228	124	434
Granite City city *Madison Co.*	7.0	14,213	12	0
Gurnee village *Lake Co.*	5.4	17,215	4	0
Hanover Park village *Cook Co.*	7.9	21,524	14	0
Harvey city *Cook Co.*	12.4	9,897	0	0
Highland Park city *Lake Co.*	4.6	15,575	18	0
Hoffman Estates village *Cook Co.*	5.5	30,000	2	0
Homer Glen village *Will Co.*	6.6	13,625	28	0
Huntley village *McHenry Co.*	n/a	n/a	176	0
Joliet city *Will Co.*	10.2	73,293	74	0

Place	Unemployment Rate (%)	Total Civilian Labor Force	Single-Family Building Permits	Multi-Family Building Permits
Kankakee city *Kankakee Co.*	11.2	11,511	1	0
Lake in the Hills village *McHenry Co.*	7.0	16,801	18	0
Lansing village *Cook Co.*	7.8	15,002	0	0
Lockport city *Will Co.*	7.7	14,122	29	0
Lombard village *Du Page Co.*	6.1	24,767	37	4
McHenry city *McHenry Co.*	7.2	15,072	7	12
Melrose Park village *Cook Co.*	8.0	12,305	0	0
Moline city *Rock Island Co.*	6.0	22,820	5	8
Mount Prospect village *Cook Co.*	5.3	30,430	8	92
Mundelein village *Lake Co.*	7.3	16,777	84	0
Naperville city *Du Page Co.*	5.7	76,735	297	298
New Lenox village *Will Co.*	n/a	n/a	174	0
Niles village *Cook Co.*	6.1	14,636	5	0
Normal town *McLean Co.*	5.5	26,744	117	109
North Chicago city *Lake Co.*	10.1	8,345	0	0
Northbrook village *Cook Co.*	5.0	16,872	39	0
O'Fallon city *Saint Clair Co.*	4.9	14,571	84	0
Oak Forest city *Cook Co.*	7.1	15,935	1	0
Oak Lawn village *Cook Co.*	7.8	28,137	6	0
Oak Park village *Cook Co.*	5.2	31,442	1	0
Orland Park village *Cook Co.*	6.1	29,736	68	0
Oswego village *Kendall Co.*	6.8	17,646	226	0
Palatine village *Cook Co.*	5.8	41,546	51	0
Park Ridge city *Cook Co.*	5.6	19,520	24	0
Pekin city *Tazewell Co.*	7.8	16,876	22	8
Peoria city *Peoria Co.*	7.8	55,077	147	6
Plainfield village *Will Co.*	6.4	21,599	136	0
Quincy city *Adams Co.*	4.8	21,473	43	0
Rock Island city *Rock Island Co.*	6.6	19,310	7	67
Rockford city *Winnebago Co.*	10.2	66,640	11	0
Rolling Meadows city *Cook Co.*	n/a	n/a	7	0
Romeoville village *Will Co.*	7.7	23,171	24	0
Round Lake Beach village *Lake Co.*	10.4	14,992	0	0
Saint Charles city *Kane Co.*	5.7	19,304	37	0
Schaumburg village *Cook Co.*	5.5	46,378	1	31
Skokie village *Cook Co.*	6.2	33,083	3	0
Springfield city *Sangamon Co.*	6.0	61,553	81	46
Streamwood village *Cook Co.*	7.1	23,646	14	0
Tinley Park village *Cook Co.*	6.6	31,421	23	0
Urbana city *Champaign Co.*	6.3	20,027	15	64
Vernon Hills village *Lake Co.*	4.7	15,147	26	96
Waukegan city *Lake Co.*	9.6	42,772	29	8
West Chicago city *Du Page Co.*	7.3	14,899	5	0
Westmont village *Du Page Co.*	6.5	13,507	25	0
Wheaton city *Du Page Co.*	5.4	28,808	49	0
Wheeling village *Cook Co.*	6.1	22,725	15	0
Wilmette village *Cook Co.*	5.1	13,095	44	0
Woodridge village *Du Page Co.*	6.7	19,748	20	0
Woodstock city *McHenry Co.*	n/a	n/a	48	0
Zion city *Lake Co.*	9.4	11,538	0	0

NOTE: n/a not available.
SOURCE: U.S. Department of Labor, Bureau of Labor Statistics, Local Area Unemployment Statistics, April 2014 (unemployment rate and civilian labor force);
U.S. Census Bureau, Manufacturing and Construction Division, 2013 (building permit data)

Employment by Occupation

Place	MBF[1] (%)	CES[2] (%)	ELCAM[3] (%)	HPT[4] (%)	S[5] (%)	SO[6] (%)	NRCM[7] (%)	PTMM[8] (%)
Addison village *Du Page Co.*	11.6	3.2	6.1	4.9	15.1	29.3	8.5	21.3
Algonquin village *McHenry Co.*	20.5	9.5	9.8	6.1	10.9	29.2	5.7	8.3
Alton city *Madison Co.*	8.8	3.8	12.8	5.0	22.4	23.1	8.6	15.6
Arlington Heights village *Cook Co.*	24.4	8.5	12.6	5.2	10.5	26.2	5.0	7.6
Aurora city *Kane Co.*	13.8	6.0	8.6	3.8	16.3	25.4	6.5	19.6
Bartlett village *Du Page Co.*	22.7	6.8	8.9	5.4	10.7	30.7	5.3	9.3
Batavia city *Kane Co.*	24.6	7.2	13.5	5.7	11.6	24.7	4.2	8.3
Belleville city *Saint Clair Co.*	9.1	5.1	10.9	6.6	20.7	27.2	7.6	12.7
Belvidere city *Boone Co.*	8.6	2.7	5.3	3.6	12.8	27.0	10.1	29.8
Berwyn city *Cook Co.*	8.4	3.1	9.0	3.8	22.0	27.1	8.9	17.7
Bloomington city *McLean Co.*	17.3	11.5	11.4	4.5	15.7	25.9	5.3	8.3
Bolingbrook village *Will Co.*	15.6	4.7	7.4	6.0	17.1	28.6	7.0	13.7
Buffalo Grove village *Lake Co.*	25.8	11.7	14.5	5.8	9.5	24.0	3.2	5.4
Burbank city *Cook Co.*	8.1	2.6	4.6	3.1	19.9	26.3	12.5	22.8
Calumet City city *Cook Co.*	8.1	1.6	6.7	5.4	20.6	29.5	6.9	21.3
Carbondale city *Jackson Co.*	7.4	4.0	27.1	3.7	26.4	24.2	1.8	5.3
Carol Stream village *Du Page Co.*	14.0	5.8	9.3	5.1	15.8	30.0	6.6	13.5
Carpentersville village *Kane Co.*	11.0	6.9	5.2	3.0	17.4	23.2	8.8	24.5
Champaign city *Champaign Co.*	12.1	9.5	20.7	4.8	19.5	21.1	3.9	8.3
Chicago city *Cook Co.*	15.3	4.7	12.8	4.6	20.1	23.5	5.9	13.1
Chicago Heights city *Cook Co.*	7.8	1.9	8.7	5.6	24.1	22.5	9.9	19.6
Cicero town *Cook Co.*	6.2	1.2	4.1	1.6	21.6	22.4	11.8	31.1
Collinsville city *Madison Co.*	11.9	6.6	9.5	4.5	17.4	27.8	9.5	12.8
Crystal Lake city *McHenry Co.*	16.9	7.2	12.2	3.9	16.0	28.6	4.3	10.9
Danville city *Vermilion Co.*	7.9	2.2	10.2	5.1	22.1	23.5	6.2	22.8
DeKalb city *De Kalb Co.*	9.7	3.0	16.9	4.0	21.5	27.9	5.1	11.8
Decatur city *Macon Co.*	10.0	4.9	9.2	4.8	21.5	25.0	8.2	16.4
Des Plaines city *Cook Co.*	17.2	5.4	8.7	6.2	15.3	26.8	8.1	12.3
Downers Grove village *Du Page Co.*	23.1	7.2	14.5	6.2	10.7	28.1	4.7	5.5
East Saint Louis city *Saint Clair Co.*	5.3	1.2	9.4	1.7	42.5	21.2	4.8	13.8
Edwardsville city *Madison Co.*	18.2	7.8	13.3	7.3	16.7	24.1	5.6	6.9
Elgin city *Kane Co.*	11.1	4.4	8.2	3.3	17.9	24.3	9.4	21.3
Elk Grove Village village *Cook Co.*	17.7	5.3	10.2	4.1	14.3	30.7	6.8	10.9
Elmhurst city *Du Page Co.*	22.1	6.4	14.3	7.3	10.8	27.4	5.7	6.0
Elmwood Park village *Cook Co.*	12.1	2.9	6.5	6.0	18.2	32.0	10.3	12.0
Evanston city *Cook Co.*	20.3	10.3	25.3	5.7	11.7	19.2	3.2	4.3
Freeport city *Stephenson Co.*	10.1	3.2	9.6	3.0	22.1	27.1	4.4	20.7
Galesburg city *Knox Co.*	8.0	1.4	11.5	7.3	21.8	26.3	7.1	16.5
Glen Ellyn village *Du Page Co.*	28.8	5.4	15.3	4.6	10.7	24.9	3.6	6.7
Glendale Heights village *Du Page Co.*	10.6	5.9	4.8	4.9	16.4	29.4	7.6	20.4
Glenview village *Cook Co.*	27.0	6.5	15.1	7.7	8.5	25.7	4.8	4.8
Granite City city *Madison Co.*	10.0	2.2	8.2	5.1	21.0	25.5	8.0	20.1
Gurnee village *Lake Co.*	21.1	10.1	10.3	6.1	12.4	27.4	4.8	7.8
Hanover Park village *Cook Co.*	11.0	5.7	5.4	3.1	20.8	27.1	7.3	19.6
Harvey city *Cook Co.*	5.4	1.0	7.7	4.2	29.7	22.8	8.6	20.6
Highland Park city *Lake Co.*	25.7	4.7	19.6	6.7	10.2	26.1	3.1	4.0
Hoffman Estates village *Cook Co.*	19.1	9.7	9.2	4.8	14.2	28.3	3.8	10.9
Homer Glen village *Will Co.*	18.6	5.1	9.2	6.2	13.1	26.7	9.8	11.3
Huntley village *McHenry Co.*	23.4	5.0	8.7	5.4	10.5	28.7	7.3	11.0
Joliet city *Will Co.*	10.7	3.3	8.3	4.8	19.8	26.5	9.6	17.0

Place	MBF[1] (%)	CES[2] (%)	ELCAM[3] (%)	HPT[4] (%)	S[5] (%)	SO[6] (%)	NRCM[7] (%)	PTMM[8] (%)
Kankakee city Kankakee Co.	6.9	1.9	7.9	5.8	26.9	19.2	7.0	24.4
Lake in the Hills village McHenry Co.	19.1	5.3	7.6	4.5	11.5	29.2	9.1	13.7
Lansing village Cook Co.	9.6	3.4	10.7	5.3	16.1	31.4	10.2	13.3
Lockport city Will Co.	14.0	5.6	9.6	6.5	14.1	25.5	11.5	13.2
Lombard village Du Page Co.	17.5	7.3	10.7	7.1	14.1	28.8	6.7	7.8
McHenry city McHenry Co.	11.6	4.8	10.0	4.4	18.9	28.6	8.7	13.0
Melrose Park village Cook Co.	6.3	1.5	3.6	2.7	20.8	23.7	9.2	32.2
Moline city Rock Island Co.	12.0	5.0	10.3	4.8	16.9	26.3	5.9	18.7
Mount Prospect village Cook Co.	16.2	6.0	9.8	6.4	15.5	24.7	6.4	15.0
Mundelein village Lake Co.	15.2	8.2	10.3	2.7	16.6	27.3	6.8	13.0
Naperville city Du Page Co.	25.3	10.8	13.5	6.5	9.7	26.9	2.4	4.9
New Lenox village Will Co.	16.8	5.9	11.6	6.4	12.6	26.7	11.0	9.0
Niles village Cook Co.	12.3	5.1	6.0	7.1	20.0	26.3	9.2	14.1
Normal town McLean Co.	14.4	6.5	15.4	3.4	21.4	28.2	3.4	7.4
North Chicago city Lake Co.	8.6	4.3	8.9	3.6	24.4	22.0	8.4	19.7
Northbrook village Cook Co.	27.3	6.8	16.9	8.4	8.1	27.8	2.0	2.8
O'Fallon city Saint Clair Co.	19.3	8.5	10.1	6.5	15.3	28.6	5.2	6.5
Oak Forest city Cook Co.	11.2	4.6	12.2	4.4	18.2	26.8	11.4	11.3
Oak Lawn village Cook Co.	12.5	2.3	10.3	5.5	17.1	28.8	9.7	13.8
Oak Park village Cook Co.	21.6	8.9	25.5	7.8	9.0	21.3	2.0	3.9
Orland Park village Cook Co.	19.0	3.5	11.9	7.8	13.5	28.8	6.3	9.3
Oswego village Kendall Co.	19.7	7.4	14.2	7.2	9.7	26.1	6.0	9.8
Palatine village Cook Co.	20.6	8.2	11.2	4.2	14.8	26.3	4.8	9.9
Park Ridge city Cook Co.	24.3	6.4	13.5	8.1	11.5	26.3	4.6	5.2
Pekin city Tazewell Co.	9.9	4.3	9.2	5.3	19.8	25.6	8.5	17.3
Peoria city Peoria Co.	13.7	7.8	11.2	7.5	19.7	24.6	4.4	11.2
Plainfield village Will Co.	25.4	6.5	12.4	6.8	10.3	25.7	4.7	8.1
Quincy city Adams Co.	11.8	2.5	8.9	4.8	22.6	27.2	5.5	16.6
Rock Island city Rock Island Co.	9.9	3.7	11.1	5.0	22.6	22.6	7.4	17.6
Rockford city Winnebago Co.	9.8	3.5	9.5	5.7	20.2	24.1	6.9	20.4
Rolling Meadows city Cook Co.	14.8	6.5	8.1	3.4	20.6	26.4	7.7	12.6
Romeoville village Will Co.	12.0	4.4	7.2	6.1	17.0	25.4	8.6	19.2
Round Lake Beach village Lake Co.	8.5	4.0	6.0	2.9	21.9	26.7	9.5	20.6
Saint Charles city Kane Co.	21.9	6.3	14.3	4.8	13.1	27.7	4.4	7.6
Schaumburg village Cook Co.	21.6	11.1	9.7	3.8	9.8	28.3	5.6	10.1
Skokie village Cook Co.	16.9	5.5	14.2	8.8	14.3	25.7	5.1	9.6
Springfield city Sangamon Co.	15.4	5.5	11.5	8.0	18.4	28.4	5.4	7.4
Streamwood village Cook Co.	13.3	7.3	6.8	4.5	15.7	31.4	7.2	13.8
Tinley Park village Cook Co.	14.7	4.8	10.1	8.5	12.9	28.2	8.2	12.5
Urbana city Champaign Co.	7.3	10.8	29.5	3.8	18.8	21.7	3.2	4.9
Vernon Hills village Lake Co.	23.2	11.9	11.0	6.0	9.7	27.3	2.9	8.1
Waukegan city Lake Co.	9.7	4.0	5.7	2.6	22.8	22.8	8.2	24.2
West Chicago city Du Page Co.	13.1	4.8	6.8	2.5	18.6	24.4	7.1	22.7
Westmont village Du Page Co.	17.6	9.5	10.1	6.6	16.5	23.7	6.3	9.7
Wheaton city Du Page Co.	21.3	9.7	18.6	5.3	10.8	24.4	3.9	6.0
Wheeling village Cook Co.	13.0	9.1	6.3	2.5	18.8	27.1	5.4	17.9
Wilmette village Cook Co.	28.9	6.7	24.3	8.5	6.5	19.8	2.1	3.2
Woodridge village Du Page Co.	15.9	9.8	9.5	6.8	14.2	29.7	5.4	8.7
Woodstock city McHenry Co.	12.8	4.2	12.3	5.4	15.7	24.5	8.3	16.8
Zion city Lake Co.	8.8	3.2	8.2	4.5	18.6	29.3	8.3	18.9

NOTES: (1) Management, business, and financial occupations; (2) Computer, engineering, and science occupations; (3) Education, legal, community service, arts, and media occupations; (4) Healthcare practitioners and technical occupations; (5) Service occupations; (6) Sales and office occupations; (7) Natural resources, construction, and maintenance occupations; (8) Production, transportation, and material moving occupations
SOURCE: U.S. Census Bureau, American Community Survey, 2008-2012 Five-Year Estimates

Educational Attainment

Place	Percent of Population 25 Years and Over with:		
	High School Diploma including Equivalency	Bachelor's Degree or Higher	Master's Degree or Higher
Addison village *Du Page Co.*	78.0	20.6	5.0
Algonquin village *McHenry Co.*	95.5	46.9	16.9
Alton city *Madison Co.*	88.4	18.3	6.8
Arlington Heights village *Cook Co.*	95.6	51.7	20.1
Aurora city *Kane Co.*	77.3	30.9	11.5
Bartlett village *Du Page Co.*	93.2	42.9	14.9
Batavia city *Kane Co.*	95.3	49.8	20.6
Belleville city *Saint Clair Co.*	90.5	23.9	8.9
Belvidere city *Boone Co.*	76.4	13.5	4.2
Berwyn city *Cook Co.*	76.8	18.6	5.5
Bloomington city *McLean Co.*	93.8	45.4	14.1
Bolingbrook village *Will Co.*	88.2	33.7	10.3
Buffalo Grove village *Lake Co.*	96.3	60.9	25.0
Burbank city *Cook Co.*	76.3	12.1	2.9
Calumet City city *Cook Co.*	84.7	15.2	4.8
Carbondale city *Jackson Co.*	92.9	52.1	27.1
Carol Stream village *Du Page Co.*	90.2	35.9	11.0
Carpentersville village *Kane Co.*	73.7	20.7	6.2
Champaign city *Champaign Co.*	94.6	49.9	25.2
Chicago city *Cook Co.*	80.5	33.6	13.5
Chicago Heights city *Cook Co.*	79.5	14.1	5.7
Cicero town *Cook Co.*	63.1	7.6	1.4
Collinsville city *Madison Co.*	91.6	23.8	7.3
Crystal Lake city *McHenry Co.*	92.6	40.0	13.2
Danville city *Vermilion Co.*	83.1	15.6	6.2
DeKalb city *De Kalb Co.*	90.5	35.2	14.3
Decatur city *Macon Co.*	85.4	20.0	7.1
Des Plaines city *Cook Co.*	87.4	32.4	10.5
Downers Grove village *Du Page Co.*	96.1	52.3	20.5
East Saint Louis city *Saint Clair Co.*	76.7	8.9	2.9
Edwardsville city *Madison Co.*	95.9	50.4	19.6
Elgin city *Kane Co.*	77.2	23.6	7.6
Elk Grove Village village *Cook Co.*	93.5	35.5	9.5
Elmhurst city *Du Page Co.*	94.9	56.1	21.8
Elmwood Park village *Cook Co.*	86.9	25.3	10.3
Evanston city *Cook Co.*	93.9	65.4	37.0
Freeport city *Stephenson Co.*	87.5	17.9	6.3
Galesburg city *Knox Co.*	82.8	16.1	7.2
Glen Ellyn village *Du Page Co.*	94.9	61.6	24.7
Glendale Heights village *Du Page Co.*	82.1	28.8	7.3
Glenview village *Cook Co.*	95.9	61.3	27.5
Granite City city *Madison Co.*	85.8	11.9	3.4
Gurnee village *Lake Co.*	94.5	47.0	16.2
Hanover Park village *Cook Co.*	79.9	24.7	5.8
Harvey city *Cook Co.*	76.7	10.5	2.0
Highland Park city *Lake Co.*	96.6	68.0	33.3
Hoffman Estates village *Cook Co.*	91.2	44.8	15.4
Homer Glen village *Will Co.*	94.3	36.2	13.9
Huntley village *McHenry Co.*	96.1	32.5	10.1
Joliet city *Will Co.*	83.9	23.6	7.0

Place	Percent of Population 25 Years and Over with:		
	High School Diploma including Equivalency	Bachelor's Degree or Higher	Master's Degree or Higher
Kankakee city *Kankakee Co.*	75.8	11.1	3.2
Lake in the Hills village *McHenry Co.*	94.6	30.6	8.3
Lansing village *Cook Co.*	89.6	20.4	5.6
Lockport city *Will Co.*	93.3	29.8	8.3
Lombard village *Du Page Co.*	93.0	42.1	13.9
McHenry city *McHenry Co.*	91.1	25.1	6.2
Melrose Park village *Cook Co.*	67.4	9.5	2.6
Moline city *Rock Island Co.*	87.9	26.1	9.2
Mount Prospect village *Cook Co.*	88.7	38.0	13.0
Mundelein village *Lake Co.*	85.6	40.5	14.5
Naperville city *Du Page Co.*	96.5	66.1	29.1
New Lenox village *Will Co.*	97.3	35.1	13.6
Niles village *Cook Co.*	81.0	27.9	9.1
Normal town *McLean Co.*	95.2	47.1	15.7
North Chicago city *Lake Co.*	78.4	19.3	5.0
Northbrook village *Cook Co.*	97.0	68.3	31.3
O'Fallon city *Saint Clair Co.*	95.4	47.3	21.0
Oak Forest city *Cook Co.*	89.7	23.2	7.8
Oak Lawn village *Cook Co.*	87.7	26.4	9.4
Oak Park village *Cook Co.*	96.5	67.2	35.3
Orland Park village *Cook Co.*	94.1	37.9	14.5
Oswego village *Kendall Co.*	96.0	44.7	16.0
Palatine village *Cook Co.*	91.0	47.9	17.1
Park Ridge city *Cook Co.*	95.4	53.4	23.0
Pekin city *Tazewell Co.*	88.0	15.3	4.3
Peoria city *Peoria Co.*	88.9	32.7	13.0
Plainfield village *Will Co.*	96.9	48.3	17.7
Quincy city *Adams Co.*	89.4	21.8	7.1
Rock Island city *Rock Island Co.*	84.9	22.0	6.7
Rockford city *Winnebago Co.*	81.6	20.7	7.9
Rolling Meadows city *Cook Co.*	86.1	30.7	10.7
Romeoville village *Will Co.*	85.8	23.8	5.7
Round Lake Beach village *Lake Co.*	72.8	15.4	5.7
Saint Charles city *Kane Co.*	94.3	48.1	17.7
Schaumburg village *Cook Co.*	94.7	44.2	15.1
Skokie village *Cook Co.*	88.9	45.8	18.8
Springfield city *Sangamon Co.*	90.7	33.1	12.7
Streamwood village *Cook Co.*	86.1	32.3	9.2
Tinley Park village *Cook Co.*	93.8	32.8	9.9
Urbana city *Champaign Co.*	92.5	54.3	32.0
Vernon Hills village *Lake Co.*	94.5	57.7	24.2
Waukegan city *Lake Co.*	70.3	17.3	5.6
West Chicago city *Du Page Co.*	74.0	25.4	7.4
Westmont village *Du Page Co.*	92.4	41.9	16.3
Wheaton city *Du Page Co.*	95.3	61.0	25.8
Wheeling village *Cook Co.*	86.4	37.0	11.0
Wilmette village *Cook Co.*	98.1	79.0	44.1
Woodridge village *Du Page Co.*	93.9	44.4	15.6
Woodstock city *McHenry Co.*	87.3	30.1	10.1
Zion city *Lake Co.*	82.7	14.2	4.9

SOURCE: U.S. Census Bureau, American Community Survey, 2008-2012 Five-Year Estimates

Income and Poverty

Place	Average Household Income ($)	Median Household Income ($)	Per Capita Income ($)	Households w/$100,000+ Income (%)	Poverty Rate (%)
Addison village *Du Page Co.*	73,917	59,104	24,666	25.0	12.2
Algonquin village *McHenry Co.*	112,325	100,269	39,368	50.2	3.0
Alton city *Madison Co.*	45,833	35,776	19,217	7.2	23.5
Arlington Heights village *Cook Co.*	99,707	77,121	40,645	37.8	4.1
Aurora city *Kane Co.*	80,228	62,589	26,091	26.9	13.6
Bartlett village *Du Page Co.*	106,173	96,127	36,403	47.0	5.3
Batavia city *Kane Co.*	106,739	90,060	38,565	44.1	7.1
Belleville city *Saint Clair Co.*	58,713	48,085	25,466	15.4	14.7
Belvidere city *Boone Co.*	61,179	51,340	20,915	15.8	13.6
Berwyn city *Cook Co.*	61,487	51,192	21,101	16.0	13.8
Bloomington city *McLean Co.*	79,875	59,956	32,593	26.2	11.2
Bolingbrook village *Will Co.*	89,432	80,112	27,420	36.9	8.4
Buffalo Grove village *Lake Co.*	113,459	93,567	45,057	45.4	3.9
Burbank city *Cook Co.*	65,599	56,617	21,516	18.2	11.7
Calumet City city *Cook Co.*	51,358	41,244	20,723	9.3	20.3
Carbondale city *Jackson Co.*	36,495	17,743	14,779	9.5	48.0
Carol Stream village *Du Page Co.*	81,427	73,705	30,577	32.7	9.1
Carpentersville village *Kane Co.*	69,166	55,000	20,850	22.4	16.5
Champaign city *Champaign Co.*	61,071	41,403	24,855	17.5	26.3
Chicago city *Cook Co.*	71,020	47,408	28,202	20.6	22.1
Chicago Heights city *Cook Co.*	52,413	42,959	17,452	12.4	28.8
Cicero town *Cook Co.*	54,480	45,656	14,935	11.3	18.7
Collinsville city *Madison Co.*	60,347	47,229	26,957	15.6	16.6
Crystal Lake city *McHenry Co.*	88,510	78,311	31,172	34.4	6.2
Danville city *Vermilion Co.*	46,196	35,198	19,464	8.7	29.1
DeKalb city *De Kalb Co.*	53,355	39,412	19,464	14.5	30.3
Decatur city *Macon Co.*	53,890	39,635	23,056	11.3	21.4
Des Plaines city *Cook Co.*	78,317	65,194	31,007	26.5	7.0
Downers Grove village *Du Page Co.*	107,573	82,181	41,949	41.9	4.3
East Saint Louis city *Saint Clair Co.*	27,732	19,278	11,802	2.0	43.5
Edwardsville city *Madison Co.*	91,595	73,759	33,023	34.5	11.6
Elgin city *Kane Co.*	70,870	58,487	23,601	22.3	13.0
Elk Grove Village village *Cook Co.*	82,852	67,983	33,828	30.1	4.7
Elmhurst city *Du Page Co.*	122,418	94,424	42,706	47.9	3.4
Elmwood Park village *Cook Co.*	70,106	56,396	26,709	23.2	7.1
Evanston city *Cook Co.*	105,497	68,051	41,725	35.7	12.8
Freeport city *Stephenson Co.*	48,743	37,481	21,607	10.5	19.9
Galesburg city *Knox Co.*	45,150	33,109	19,339	8.1	21.1
Glen Ellyn village *Du Page Co.*	130,754	90,640	50,590	46.3	6.8
Glendale Heights village *Du Page Co.*	71,440	62,208	24,159	21.0	12.1
Glenview village *Cook Co.*	137,996	99,841	52,227	49.9	3.7
Granite City city *Madison Co.*	50,138	41,799	20,798	10.0	18.8
Gurnee village *Lake Co.*	101,120	83,750	37,231	41.7	4.1
Hanover Park village *Cook Co.*	78,395	70,067	23,338	25.3	12.9
Harvey city *Cook Co.*	40,597	28,123	13,678	8.5	34.4
Highland Park city *Lake Co.*	171,884	115,321	67,267	56.0	5.7
Hoffman Estates village *Cook Co.*	95,279	81,105	33,456	37.9	5.7
Homer Glen village *Will Co.*	108,708	97,848	36,000	48.6	2.8
Huntley village *McHenry Co.*	85,295	70,524	35,289	31.3	3.4
Joliet city *Will Co.*	71,654	61,948	23,600	23.6	12.4

Place	Average Household Income ($)	Median Household Income ($)	Per Capita Income ($)	Households w/$100,000+ Income (%)	Poverty Rate (%)
Kankakee city *Kankakee Co.*	41,637	32,064	15,482	7.5	32.3
Lake in the Hills village *McHenry Co.*	95,017	85,429	32,560	38.2	5.6
Lansing village *Cook Co.*	61,426	51,637	25,215	17.6	11.5
Lockport city *Will Co.*	86,084	77,220	31,143	32.3	4.3
Lombard village *Du Page Co.*	82,293	71,721	34,246	31.4	5.6
McHenry city *McHenry Co.*	80,610	67,740	30,302	26.8	8.7
Melrose Park village *Cook Co.*	55,028	44,691	17,597	14.6	14.1
Moline city *Rock Island Co.*	65,744	49,459	27,854	16.3	9.2
Mount Prospect village *Cook Co.*	86,088	68,375	33,054	29.8	5.9
Mundelein village *Lake Co.*	102,584	80,082	35,422	39.2	5.4
Naperville city *Du Page Co.*	134,222	108,252	46,598	53.5	3.8
New Lenox village *Will Co.*	99,781	90,833	33,581	42.6	2.3
Niles village *Cook Co.*	64,462	45,546	26,127	19.7	10.3
Normal town *McLean Co.*	66,020	51,994	23,708	22.0	24.8
North Chicago city *Lake Co.*	55,008	45,684	18,012	12.9	23.5
Northbrook village *Cook Co.*	150,016	109,241	56,077	54.4	4.0
O'Fallon city *Saint Clair Co.*	90,073	76,268	33,363	36.0	7.8
Oak Forest city *Cook Co.*	78,729	69,048	27,745	28.9	6.7
Oak Lawn village *Cook Co.*	72,429	57,428	28,781	23.7	8.8
Oak Park village *Cook Co.*	108,800	75,118	46,386	38.2	8.0
Orland Park village *Cook Co.*	94,385	77,863	36,374	36.1	4.9
Oswego village *Kendall Co.*	105,031	96,819	34,046	47.3	3.8
Palatine village *Cook Co.*	93,179	73,811	35,738	35.5	8.5
Park Ridge city *Cook Co.*	113,035	86,621	43,003	43.9	3.6
Pekin city *Tazewell Co.*	57,038	46,003	24,451	13.3	13.5
Peoria city *Peoria Co.*	68,130	45,772	28,752	18.5	22.2
Plainfield village *Will Co.*	117,234	111,637	35,312	57.0	4.0
Quincy city *Adams Co.*	55,275	41,239	23,493	11.0	16.9
Rock Island city *Rock Island Co.*	56,180	42,613	23,337	12.7	17.4
Rockford city *Winnebago Co.*	53,257	38,157	21,579	11.7	25.1
Rolling Meadows city *Cook Co.*	78,758	60,409	30,919	24.3	9.3
Romeoville village *Will Co.*	75,658	70,541	23,116	26.8	9.4
Round Lake Beach village *Lake Co.*	68,382	60,864	20,266	19.7	16.9
Saint Charles city *Kane Co.*	109,303	80,310	41,627	41.3	4.1
Schaumburg village *Cook Co.*	84,336	70,060	35,689	29.2	6.4
Skokie village *Cook Co.*	88,225	67,030	32,868	30.8	9.5
Springfield city *Sangamon Co.*	66,350	49,627	29,089	19.0	16.8
Streamwood village *Cook Co.*	86,356	71,306	29,326	31.3	5.5
Tinley Park village *Cook Co.*	86,166	77,989	32,782	34.1	5.8
Urbana city *Champaign Co.*	47,079	30,313	19,052	11.7	35.5
Vernon Hills village *Lake Co.*	113,335	90,161	42,544	43.6	2.9
Waukegan city *Lake Co.*	61,035	46,256	20,324	16.1	18.8
West Chicago city *Du Page Co.*	87,548	65,111	25,862	30.4	15.1
Westmont village *Du Page Co.*	80,364	60,149	35,294	25.6	7.5
Wheaton city *Du Page Co.*	112,657	86,074	41,153	43.8	6.4
Wheeling village *Cook Co.*	69,237	57,364	27,362	22.2	10.4
Wilmette village *Cook Co.*	194,261	130,088	68,612	60.6	2.6
Woodridge village *Du Page Co.*	92,026	76,218	35,929	33.5	5.9
Woodstock city *McHenry Co.*	68,238	56,479	26,168	21.4	13.3
Zion city *Lake Co.*	60,099	50,807	20,512	16.9	15.1

SOURCE: *U.S. Census Bureau, American Community Survey, 2008-2012 Five-Year Estimates*

Taxes

Place	Total City Taxes Per Capita ($)	City Property Taxes Per Capita ($)
Addison village *Du Page Co.*	566	325
Algonquin village *McHenry Co.*	399	197
Alton city *Madison Co.*	353	138
Arlington Heights village *Cook Co.*	859	560
Aurora city *Kane Co.*	795	550
Bartlett village *Du Page Co.*	n/a	n/a
Batavia city *Kane Co.*	471	265
Belleville city *Saint Clair Co.*	n/a	n/a
Belvidere city *Boone Co.*	n/a	n/a
Berwyn city *Cook Co.*	751	552
Bloomington city *McLean Co.*	759	352
Bolingbrook village *Will Co.*	636	249
Buffalo Grove village *Lake Co.*	501	317
Burbank city *Cook Co.*	316	167
Calumet City city *Cook Co.*	825	513
Carbondale city *Jackson Co.*	478	37
Carol Stream village *Du Page Co.*	222	15
Carpentersville village *Kane Co.*	n/a	n/a
Champaign city *Champaign Co.*	643	314
Chicago city *Cook Co.*	821	266
Chicago Heights city *Cook Co.*	686	531
Cicero town *Cook Co.*	777	458
Collinsville city *Madison Co.*	251	164
Crystal Lake city *McHenry Co.*	n/a	n/a
Danville city *Vermilion Co.*	n/a	n/a
DeKalb city *De Kalb Co.*	683	351
Decatur city *Macon Co.*	431	174
Des Plaines city *Cook Co.*	1,004	622
Downers Grove village *Du Page Co.*	721	433
East Saint Louis city *Saint Clair Co.*	528	396
Edwardsville city *Madison Co.*	n/a	n/a
Elgin city *Kane Co.*	602	522
Elk Grove Village village *Cook Co.*	1,033	590
Elmhurst city *Du Page Co.*	788	460
Elmwood Park village *Cook Co.*	n/a	n/a
Evanston city *Cook Co.*	1,055	620
Freeport city *Stephenson Co.*	308	186
Galesburg city *Knox Co.*	n/a	n/a
Glen Ellyn village *Du Page Co.*	n/a	n/a
Glendale Heights village *Du Page Co.*	n/a	n/a
Glenview village *Cook Co.*	1,233	884
Granite City city *Madison Co.*	n/a	n/a
Gurnee village *Lake Co.*	n/a	n/a
Hanover Park village *Cook Co.*	525	356
Harvey city *Cook Co.*	n/a	n/a
Highland Park city *Lake Co.*	904	479
Hoffman Estates village *Cook Co.*	1,066	837
Homer Glen village *Will Co.*	n/a	n/a
Huntley village *McHenry Co.*	398	270
Joliet city *Will Co.*	494	290

Place	Total City Taxes Per Capita ($)	City Property Taxes Per Capita ($)
Kankakee city *Kankakee Co.*	777	612
Lake in the Hills village *McHenry Co.*	n/a	n/a
Lansing village *Cook Co.*	691	472
Lockport city *Will Co.*	310	240
Lombard village *Du Page Co.*	461	193
McHenry city *McHenry Co.*	n/a	n/a
Melrose Park village *Cook Co.*	960	751
Moline city *Rock Island Co.*	771	415
Mount Prospect village *Cook Co.*	775	511
Mundelein village *Lake Co.*	n/a	n/a
Naperville city *Du Page Co.*	566	367
New Lenox village *Will Co.*	286	114
Niles village *Cook Co.*	797	262
Normal town *McLean Co.*	570	203
North Chicago city *Lake Co.*	328	203
Northbrook village *Cook Co.*	717	485
O'Fallon city *Saint Clair Co.*	397	249
Oak Forest city *Cook Co.*	n/a	n/a
Oak Lawn village *Cook Co.*	532	401
Oak Park village *Cook Co.*	1,098	818
Orland Park village *Cook Co.*	560	329
Oswego village *Kendall Co.*	184	50
Palatine village *Cook Co.*	646	438
Park Ridge city *Cook Co.*	803	508
Pekin city *Tazewell Co.*	397	188
Peoria city *Peoria Co.*	670	303
Plainfield village *Will Co.*	390	186
Quincy city *Adams Co.*	340	77
Rock Island city *Rock Island Co.*	n/a	n/a
Rockford city *Winnebago Co.*	469	375
Rolling Meadows city *Cook Co.*	963	594
Romeoville village *Will Co.*	790	399
Round Lake Beach village *Lake Co.*	375	303
Saint Charles city *Kane Co.*	791	422
Schaumburg village *Cook Co.*	962	370
Skokie village *Cook Co.*	859	487
Springfield city *Sangamon Co.*	574	231
Streamwood village *Cook Co.*	409	251
Tinley Park village *Cook Co.*	n/a	n/a
Urbana city *Champaign Co.*	582	298
Vernon Hills village *Lake Co.*	n/a	n/a
Waukegan city *Lake Co.*	485	289
West Chicago city *Du Page Co.*	321	177
Westmont village *Du Page Co.*	n/a	n/a
Wheaton city *Du Page Co.*	598	423
Wheeling village *Cook Co.*	784	527
Wilmette village *Cook Co.*	821	502
Woodridge village *Du Page Co.*	412	214
Woodstock city *McHenry Co.*	468	419
Zion city *Lake Co.*	483	254

NOTE: n/a not available.
SOURCE: U.S. Census Bureau, State and Local Government Finances, 2011

Housing

Place	Homeownership Rate (%)	Median Home Value ($)	Median Year Structure Built	Median Rent ($/month)
Addison village *Du Page Co.*	71.2	$262,500	1973	$847
Algonquin village *McHenry Co.*	88.3	$264,000	1992	$1,312
Alton city *Madison Co.*	62.4	$85,000	1948	$516
Arlington Heights village *Cook Co.*	76.9	$343,500	1971	$1,057
Aurora city *Kane Co.*	69.0	$194,300	1980	$848
Bartlett village *Du Page Co.*	88.2	$293,700	1991	$1,030
Batavia city *Kane Co.*	77.0	$286,600	1984	$900
Belleville city *Saint Clair Co.*	62.0	$109,500	1958	$530
Belvidere city *Boone Co.*	75.7	$124,200	1970	$566
Berwyn city *Cook Co.*	60.5	$216,200	Before 1940	$778
Bloomington city *McLean Co.*	63.9	$159,800	1979	$603
Bolingbrook village *Will Co.*	84.1	$224,700	1986	$935
Buffalo Grove village *Lake Co.*	81.9	$314,400	1982	$1,177
Burbank city *Cook Co.*	80.0	$210,600	1963	$873
Calumet City city *Cook Co.*	59.1	$122,400	1965	$749
Carbondale city *Jackson Co.*	28.6	$115,000	1975	$564
Carol Stream village *Du Page Co.*	68.2	$248,100	1983	$914
Carpentersville village *Kane Co.*	74.3	$172,700	1979	$811
Champaign city *Champaign Co.*	47.8	$151,300	1974	$687
Chicago city *Cook Co.*	46.1	$247,800	1945	$806
Chicago Heights city *Cook Co.*	61.2	$127,300	1956	$683
Cicero town *Cook Co.*	52.5	$171,000	Before 1940	$706
Collinsville city *Madison Co.*	61.7	$119,800	1966	$605
Crystal Lake city *McHenry Co.*	77.1	$223,600	1983	$981
Danville city *Vermilion Co.*	58.5	$66,400	1950	$435
DeKalb city *De Kalb Co.*	44.3	$171,200	1974	$676
Decatur city *Macon Co.*	62.6	$80,100	1958	$487
Des Plaines city *Cook Co.*	80.2	$258,100	1964	$903
Downers Grove village *Du Page Co.*	80.6	$340,700	1972	$979
East Saint Louis city *Saint Clair Co.*	47.4	$60,400	1953	$317
Edwardsville city *Madison Co.*	69.9	$196,300	1976	$705
Elgin city *Kane Co.*	70.8	$190,700	1974	$818
Elk Grove Village village *Cook Co.*	76.0	$274,800	1974	$914
Elmhurst city *Du Page Co.*	81.4	$377,200	1959	$1,060
Elmwood Park village *Cook Co.*	70.5	$241,900	1952	$814
Evanston city *Cook Co.*	56.6	$367,800	1942	$1,039
Freeport city *Stephenson Co.*	63.6	$80,500	1955	$439
Galesburg city *Knox Co.*	58.7	$73,900	1951	$419
Glen Ellyn village *Du Page Co.*	75.6	$399,100	1969	$854
Glendale Heights village *Du Page Co.*	72.0	$198,900	1977	$916
Glenview village *Cook Co.*	83.6	$494,500	1973	$1,439
Granite City city *Madison Co.*	71.0	$83,600	1954	$466
Gurnee village *Lake Co.*	74.6	$273,400	1990	$966
Hanover Park village *Cook Co.*	80.1	$196,000	1975	$939
Harvey city *Cook Co.*	51.6	$95,000	1956	$718
Highland Park city *Lake Co.*	82.8	$521,700	1963	$1,249
Hoffman Estates village *Cook Co.*	77.3	$270,100	1976	$988
Homer Glen village *Will Co.*	93.6	$337,100	1989	$1,643
Huntley village *McHenry Co.*	93.5	$237,800	2003	$1,295
Joliet city *Will Co.*	73.5	$181,300	1978	$717

Place	Homeownership Rate (%)	Median Home Value ($)	Median Year Structure Built	Median Rent ($/month)
Kankakee city *Kankakee Co.*	50.0	$102,200	1956	$554
Lake in the Hills village *McHenry Co.*	91.0	$223,300	1995	$1,126
Lansing village *Cook Co.*	74.2	$143,600	1965	$814
Lockport city *Will Co.*	87.6	$222,600	1995	$737
Lombard village *Du Page Co.*	71.5	$254,200	1969	$1,055
McHenry city *McHenry Co.*	77.5	$205,200	1984	$900
Melrose Park village *Cook Co.*	54.4	$213,900	1955	$769
Moline city *Rock Island Co.*	70.0	$112,100	1954	$567
Mount Prospect village *Cook Co.*	71.9	$316,300	1967	$875
Mundelein village *Lake Co.*	79.5	$241,600	1982	$986
Naperville city *Du Page Co.*	77.0	$384,500	1987	$1,111
New Lenox village *Will Co.*	87.5	$291,700	1993	$895
Niles village *Cook Co.*	76.7	$290,700	1963	$911
Normal town *McLean Co.*	56.8	$159,500	1981	$632
North Chicago city *Lake Co.*	37.0	$135,700	1971	$860
Northbrook village *Cook Co.*	88.6	$528,400	1972	$1,668
O'Fallon city *Saint Clair Co.*	68.8	$199,900	1991	$820
Oak Forest city *Cook Co.*	80.5	$210,300	1972	$855
Oak Lawn village *Cook Co.*	82.9	$213,300	1966	$846
Oak Park village *Cook Co.*	62.2	$369,200	Before 1940	$933
Orland Park village *Cook Co.*	89.3	$289,200	1987	$925
Oswego village *Kendall Co.*	87.4	$244,900	2001	$1,368
Palatine village *Cook Co.*	70.7	$290,200	1977	$986
Park Ridge city *Cook Co.*	84.7	$421,800	1957	$1,083
Pekin city *Tazewell Co.*	72.1	$99,400	1960	$481
Peoria city *Peoria Co.*	58.4	$124,400	1962	$555
Plainfield village *Will Co.*	90.1	$299,500	2002	$1,256
Quincy city *Adams Co.*	66.2	$96,400	1956	$432
Rock Island city *Rock Island Co.*	67.6	$98,900	1950	$516
Rockford city *Winnebago Co.*	57.0	$106,600	1960	$562
Rolling Meadows city *Cook Co.*	72.7	$254,500	1972	$966
Romeoville village *Will Co.*	86.3	$187,300	1997	$1,085
Round Lake Beach village *Lake Co.*	81.7	$155,000	1985	$862
Saint Charles city *Kane Co.*	73.1	$289,000	1983	$975
Schaumburg village *Cook Co.*	66.8	$252,300	1977	$1,085
Skokie village *Cook Co.*	73.7	$315,700	1958	$968
Springfield city *Sangamon Co.*	65.0	$115,700	1971	$557
Streamwood village *Cook Co.*	87.6	$205,500	1980	$1,230
Tinley Park village *Cook Co.*	85.5	$240,800	1986	$891
Urbana city *Champaign Co.*	34.2	$151,100	1973	$640
Vernon Hills village *Lake Co.*	76.0	$325,100	1985	$1,235
Waukegan city *Lake Co.*	54.9	$152,600	1963	$739
West Chicago city *Du Page Co.*	66.7	$243,100	1981	$806
Westmont village *Du Page Co.*	51.9	$288,200	1977	$892
Wheaton city *Du Page Co.*	72.2	$344,900	1974	$1,080
Wheeling village *Cook Co.*	65.1	$211,100	1977	$927
Wilmette village *Cook Co.*	84.4	$643,600	1953	$1,422
Woodridge village *Du Page Co.*	66.7	$267,500	1978	$959
Woodstock city *McHenry Co.*	68.1	$190,300	1985	$816
Zion city *Lake Co.*	56.6	$157,500	1973	$739

SOURCE: U.S. Census Bureau, American Community Survey, 2008-2012 Five-Year Estimates

Commute to Work

Place	Automobile (%)	Public Transportation (%)	Walk (%)	Work from Home (%)
Addison village *Du Page Co.*	93.1	3.5	0.8	1.5
Algonquin village *McHenry Co.*	87.9	3.4	0.4	7.0
Alton city *Madison Co.*	93.7	1.5	1.4	2.1
Arlington Heights village *Cook Co.*	86.6	5.9	1.6	5.0
Aurora city *Kane Co.*	87.6	5.0	1.1	3.7
Bartlett village *Du Page Co.*	88.5	4.3	0.7	5.7
Batavia city *Kane Co.*	84.6	3.2	1.2	7.8
Belleville city *Saint Clair Co.*	90.4	4.2	1.9	1.9
Belvidere city *Boone Co.*	92.1	0.1	2.3	2.5
Berwyn city *Cook Co.*	80.9	11.1	4.7	2.3
Bloomington city *McLean Co.*	90.5	1.9	3.1	2.9
Bolingbrook village *Will Co.*	89.9	2.9	1.0	4.3
Buffalo Grove village *Lake Co.*	88.8	4.4	0.5	5.0
Burbank city *Cook Co.*	91.4	4.7	1.4	1.6
Calumet City city *Cook Co.*	85.9	8.7	2.3	1.3
Carbondale city *Jackson Co.*	76.2	1.2	15.1	2.7
Carol Stream village *Du Page Co.*	91.6	3.0	1.0	3.4
Carpentersville village *Kane Co.*	93.6	1.2	0.8	2.5
Champaign city *Champaign Co.*	74.0	5.8	12.1	4.7
Chicago city *Cook Co.*	59.9	26.7	6.4	4.2
Chicago Heights city *Cook Co.*	89.4	5.9	1.7	0.6
Cicero town *Cook Co.*	83.3	10.5	3.5	1.1
Collinsville city *Madison Co.*	93.1	2.4	0.4	2.5
Crystal Lake city *McHenry Co.*	88.1	3.9	1.4	5.9
Danville city *Vermilion Co.*	89.3	1.9	4.4	2.4
DeKalb city *De Kalb Co.*	80.4	4.9	8.5	4.2
Decatur city *Macon Co.*	92.4	1.7	2.5	1.5
Des Plaines city *Cook Co.*	88.4	6.5	1.0	3.0
Downers Grove village *Du Page Co.*	79.6	11.3	2.2	5.7
East Saint Louis city *Saint Clair Co.*	78.6	14.2	2.3	4.1
Edwardsville city *Madison Co.*	90.3	2.1	3.1	3.1
Elgin city *Kane Co.*	91.6	2.6	2.1	2.5
Elk Grove Village village *Cook Co.*	91.1	3.3	1.2	3.6
Elmhurst city *Du Page Co.*	81.6	9.6	2.1	5.7
Elmwood Park village *Cook Co.*	85.3	8.6	2.7	2.6
Evanston city *Cook Co.*	55.9	20.3	11.6	8.1
Freeport city *Stephenson Co.*	90.2	1.4	3.6	3.4
Galesburg city *Knox Co.*	88.2	0.8	5.8	2.6
Glen Ellyn village *Du Page Co.*	77.1	10.9	3.1	8.1
Glendale Heights village *Du Page Co.*	93.4	1.6	1.3	2.5
Glenview village *Cook Co.*	80.1	11.0	1.3	6.8
Granite City city *Madison Co.*	93.4	1.7	0.7	3.1
Gurnee village *Lake Co.*	88.5	3.7	0.4	6.5
Hanover Park village *Cook Co.*	90.3	2.9	1.1	2.6
Harvey city *Cook Co.*	81.0	11.5	3.6	2.5
Highland Park city *Lake Co.*	74.9	10.1	1.8	11.3
Hoffman Estates village *Cook Co.*	90.2	3.3	0.8	3.7
Homer Glen village *Will Co.*	91.6	4.2	0.4	2.9
Huntley village *McHenry Co.*	92.8	1.8	0.0	4.8
Joliet city *Will Co.*	91.4	2.4	1.4	2.8

Place	Automobile (%)	Public Transportation (%)	Walk (%)	Work from Home (%)
Kankakee city *Kankakee Co.*	88.1	3.2	2.6	4.1
Lake in the Hills village *McHenry Co.*	92.5	1.7	0.3	4.8
Lansing village *Cook Co.*	90.2	6.5	0.8	1.5
Lockport city *Will Co.*	92.3	4.0	0.4	2.6
Lombard village *Du Page Co.*	88.2	5.2	1.9	3.1
McHenry city *McHenry Co.*	91.7	2.0	1.7	3.8
Melrose Park village *Cook Co.*	88.4	4.8	3.5	1.7
Moline city *Rock Island Co.*	93.4	1.7	1.7	1.9
Mount Prospect village *Cook Co.*	85.8	6.8	2.7	2.9
Mundelein village *Lake Co.*	89.3	2.8	0.8	5.0
Naperville city *Du Page Co.*	80.7	9.3	1.3	7.6
New Lenox village *Will Co.*	87.4	6.4	0.3	5.0
Niles village *Cook Co.*	84.3	8.6	1.6	3.4
Normal town *McLean Co.*	81.6	2.2	10.6	3.6
North Chicago city *Lake Co.*	48.1	2.5	32.2	15.8
Northbrook village *Cook Co.*	79.5	9.9	1.7	8.1
O'Fallon city *Saint Clair Co.*	93.8	1.0	0.8	3.3
Oak Forest city *Cook Co.*	89.5	7.9	0.2	1.7
Oak Lawn village *Cook Co.*	87.8	6.9	2.4	1.7
Oak Park village *Cook Co.*	64.1	22.5	3.7	7.0
Orland Park village *Cook Co.*	87.1	7.6	1.3	3.7
Oswego village *Kendall Co.*	90.6	4.2	0.4	4.0
Palatine village *Cook Co.*	88.2	5.0	1.4	4.6
Park Ridge city *Cook Co.*	79.0	10.4	3.8	5.8
Pekin city *Tazewell Co.*	94.8	0.7	2.0	1.7
Peoria city *Peoria Co.*	89.7	2.9	2.7	3.0
Plainfield village *Will Co.*	88.4	3.2	0.9	5.9
Quincy city *Adams Co.*	90.9	0.7	4.1	2.9
Rock Island city *Rock Island Co.*	86.0	2.7	4.9	4.4
Rockford city *Winnebago Co.*	91.6	1.8	1.6	3.5
Rolling Meadows city *Cook Co.*	89.6	3.9	2.5	3.1
Romeoville village *Will Co.*	91.4	3.3	1.6	3.0
Round Lake Beach village *Lake Co.*	93.7	2.5	1.7	1.8
Saint Charles city *Kane Co.*	86.3	3.8	2.3	7.2
Schaumburg village *Cook Co.*	91.5	3.6	0.7	2.9
Skokie village *Cook Co.*	84.1	9.3	1.6	3.9
Springfield city *Sangamon Co.*	90.4	2.5	2.6	3.1
Streamwood village *Cook Co.*	91.2	3.7	0.6	3.4
Tinley Park village *Cook Co.*	86.8	9.1	1.2	2.2
Urbana city *Champaign Co.*	55.4	16.0	16.6	5.8
Vernon Hills village *Lake Co.*	87.3	4.0	0.3	6.6
Waukegan city *Lake Co.*	90.3	3.8	1.4	3.3
West Chicago city *Du Page Co.*	90.3	3.0	1.6	3.0
Westmont village *Du Page Co.*	82.3	9.0	2.3	5.0
Wheaton city *Du Page Co.*	79.2	7.7	4.8	7.4
Wheeling village *Cook Co.*	92.2	2.4	1.0	3.0
Wilmette village *Cook Co.*	66.8	19.2	3.4	9.5
Woodridge village *Du Page Co.*	86.7	5.2	2.3	3.7
Woodstock city *McHenry Co.*	90.1	2.9	1.9	3.7
Zion city *Lake Co.*	91.8	2.5	0.8	3.6

SOURCE: U.S. Census Bureau, American Community Survey, 2008-2012 Five-Year Estimates

Travel Time to Work

Place	Less than 15 Minutes (%)	15 to 30 Minutes (%)	30 to 45 Minutes (%)	45 to 60 Minutes (%)	60 Minutes or More (%)
Addison village *Du Page Co.*	24.1	36.4	22.6	7.4	9.6
Algonquin village *McHenry Co.*	16.7	22.9	23.2	15.7	21.5
Alton city *Madison Co.*	34.5	33.9	19.1	8.0	4.6
Arlington Heights village *Cook Co.*	21.9	33.0	24.4	10.1	10.6
Aurora city *Kane Co.*	22.9	35.5	20.0	8.7	12.9
Bartlett village *Du Page Co.*	14.4	28.4	29.8	13.1	14.3
Batavia city *Kane Co.*	29.8	29.8	22.0	8.1	10.4
Belleville city *Saint Clair Co.*	32.6	36.7	19.3	7.1	4.3
Belvidere city *Boone Co.*	29.4	25.5	20.4	9.7	15.0
Berwyn city *Cook Co.*	17.0	29.7	29.6	11.4	12.2
Bloomington city *McLean Co.*	54.8	34.1	4.5	3.5	3.1
Bolingbrook village *Will Co.*	18.3	29.1	24.0	13.5	15.1
Buffalo Grove village *Lake Co.*	18.7	33.9	27.1	9.1	11.3
Burbank city *Cook Co.*	22.0	28.4	23.9	12.9	12.7
Calumet City city *Cook Co.*	14.5	28.4	25.3	13.1	18.8
Carbondale city *Jackson Co.*	72.1	19.4	6.2	1.3	1.0
Carol Stream village *Du Page Co.*	24.1	30.3	25.5	8.8	11.3
Carpentersville village *Kane Co.*	14.7	32.3	31.9	12.1	9.0
Champaign city *Champaign Co.*	51.5	40.3	4.2	2.1	2.0
Chicago city *Cook Co.*	13.4	28.3	29.4	14.0	14.9
Chicago Heights city *Cook Co.*	31.1	30.2	19.9	8.4	10.4
Cicero town *Cook Co.*	14.1	30.4	31.2	12.1	12.1
Collinsville city *Madison Co.*	24.5	36.5	28.0	7.4	3.6
Crystal Lake city *McHenry Co.*	28.4	27.5	13.9	11.2	19.0
Danville city *Vermilion Co.*	64.2	25.4	6.8	2.1	1.5
DeKalb city *De Kalb Co.*	52.4	22.8	9.8	6.4	8.5
Decatur city *Macon Co.*	51.8	35.4	5.9	3.5	3.4
Des Plaines city *Cook Co.*	18.8	36.0	27.5	9.1	8.6
Downers Grove village *Du Page Co.*	25.3	32.2	20.5	11.0	11.1
East Saint Louis city *Saint Clair Co.*	27.8	44.0	16.7	3.7	7.8
Edwardsville city *Madison Co.*	37.9	25.4	24.5	8.3	3.8
Elgin city *Kane Co.*	24.1	31.6	23.6	9.9	10.8
Elk Grove Village village *Cook Co.*	29.0	36.0	20.0	8.2	6.8
Elmhurst city *Du Page Co.*	26.3	29.5	23.5	9.1	11.6
Elmwood Park village *Cook Co.*	18.0	26.1	31.5	11.5	12.8
Evanston city *Cook Co.*	25.8	26.0	21.3	16.0	10.9
Freeport city *Stephenson Co.*	63.9	17.6	8.6	5.7	4.2
Galesburg city *Knox Co.*	63.6	22.4	3.7	6.0	4.3
Glen Ellyn village *Du Page Co.*	26.5	31.9	19.7	8.4	13.4
Glendale Heights village *Du Page Co.*	24.5	34.3	25.4	6.2	9.5
Glenview village *Cook Co.*	22.1	27.7	27.6	10.6	12.1
Granite City city *Madison Co.*	31.4	35.6	24.2	5.9	2.9
Gurnee village *Lake Co.*	19.6	35.8	22.9	10.0	11.7
Hanover Park village *Cook Co.*	19.3	36.6	25.9	8.9	9.3
Harvey city *Cook Co.*	21.2	27.3	29.3	9.9	12.3
Highland Park city *Lake Co.*	23.6	33.5	19.3	8.3	15.4
Hoffman Estates village *Cook Co.*	18.5	35.7	23.9	10.7	11.1
Homer Glen village *Will Co.*	14.3	25.0	27.6	15.5	17.7
Huntley village *McHenry Co.*	15.9	22.6	20.0	20.7	20.8
Joliet city *Will Co.*	22.2	30.2	20.0	12.2	15.4

Place	Less than 15 Minutes (%)	15 to 30 Minutes (%)	30 to 45 Minutes (%)	45 to 60 Minutes (%)	60 Minutes or More (%)
Kankakee city Kankakee Co.	46.8	29.9	11.9	3.6	7.8
Lake in the Hills village McHenry Co.	17.2	25.7	18.8	18.1	20.3
Lansing village Cook Co.	24.0	26.2	22.7	12.5	14.7
Lockport city Will Co.	17.8	26.2	26.3	14.7	15.0
Lombard village Du Page Co.	25.1	34.1	21.3	10.3	9.1
McHenry city McHenry Co.	28.7	30.8	15.6	10.4	14.5
Melrose Park village Cook Co.	32.3	33.4	21.5	7.0	5.8
Moline city Rock Island Co.	42.4	45.7	7.9	2.0	2.1
Mount Prospect village Cook Co.	20.7	34.7	26.1	8.9	9.6
Mundelein village Lake Co.	26.3	26.8	23.1	11.6	12.2
Naperville city Du Page Co.	20.5	29.4	19.2	11.2	19.6
New Lenox village Will Co.	19.8	30.1	22.8	9.3	18.0
Niles village Cook Co.	18.8	34.6	26.4	10.7	9.5
Normal town McLean Co.	53.1	34.8	5.7	3.4	3.0
North Chicago city Lake Co.	55.4	25.6	10.2	4.4	4.4
Northbrook village Cook Co.	27.5	26.0	21.8	11.5	13.2
O'Fallon city Saint Clair Co.	28.0	40.3	20.0	8.0	3.7
Oak Forest city Cook Co.	18.7	29.7	24.6	13.0	14.0
Oak Lawn village Cook Co.	23.2	24.4	27.2	12.2	13.0
Oak Park village Cook Co.	16.1	22.4	34.9	17.8	8.7
Orland Park village Cook Co.	19.1	27.0	24.6	10.6	18.7
Oswego village Kendall Co.	22.9	27.4	21.4	10.9	17.4
Palatine village Cook Co.	21.6	33.7	26.8	8.7	9.1
Park Ridge city Cook Co.	26.5	27.5	25.0	11.7	9.2
Pekin city Tazewell Co.	42.1	39.1	14.6	2.6	1.6
Peoria city Peoria Co.	40.3	48.3	6.4	2.5	2.5
Plainfield village Will Co.	13.9	25.9	22.4	15.5	22.3
Quincy city Adams Co.	63.9	29.4	3.5	1.3	2.0
Rock Island city Rock Island Co.	43.0	42.4	9.1	2.7	2.9
Rockford city Winnebago Co.	36.2	45.0	10.4	3.3	5.1
Rolling Meadows city Cook Co.	28.1	36.8	21.5	6.7	6.9
Romeoville village Will Co.	15.9	24.5	27.6	13.2	18.9
Round Lake Beach village Lake Co.	16.4	30.6	26.4	12.5	14.1
Saint Charles city Kane Co.	30.1	24.9	20.1	12.2	12.7
Schaumburg village Cook Co.	23.3	33.5	23.6	9.9	9.7
Skokie village Cook Co.	21.4	33.1	21.6	11.1	12.8
Springfield city Sangamon Co.	43.6	45.8	6.1	1.8	2.8
Streamwood village Cook Co.	14.7	37.8	25.4	9.3	12.8
Tinley Park village Cook Co.	20.0	26.7	22.9	12.1	18.3
Urbana city Champaign Co.	55.3	35.9	5.9	0.8	2.1
Vernon Hills village Lake Co.	24.4	32.1	25.8	8.3	9.3
Waukegan city Lake Co.	23.7	37.5	24.0	7.0	7.8
West Chicago city Du Page Co.	28.7	34.1	17.9	10.6	8.6
Westmont village Du Page Co.	23.1	31.7	20.6	11.7	12.9
Wheaton city Du Page Co.	30.4	30.5	17.6	8.6	12.8
Wheeling village Cook Co.	23.8	37.4	25.3	6.7	6.8
Wilmette village Cook Co.	21.9	24.3	22.3	14.1	17.4
Woodridge village Du Page Co.	16.4	34.8	22.4	13.3	13.1
Woodstock city McHenry Co.	32.2	33.0	12.0	6.4	16.4
Zion city Lake Co.	19.1	37.4	23.4	11.2	8.9

SOURCE: U.S. Census Bureau, American Community Survey, 2008-2012 Five-Year Estimates

Crime

Place	Violent Crime Rate (crimes per 10,000 population)	Property Crime Rate (crimes per 10,000 population)
Addison village *Du Page Co.*	19.9	194.0
Algonquin village *McHenry Co.*	9.6	166.5
Alton city *Madison Co.*	45.0	442.5
Arlington Heights village *Cook Co.*	5.4	129.6
Aurora city *Kane Co.*	28.2	178.5
Bartlett village *Du Page Co.*	7.5	76.4
Batavia city *Kane Co.*	12.5	182.1
Belleville city *Saint Clair Co.*	n/a	n/a
Belvidere city *Boone Co.*	n/a	n/a
Berwyn city *Cook Co.*	19.8	251.3
Bloomington city *McLean Co.*	48.2	233.1
Bolingbrook village *Will Co.*	24.4	154.3
Buffalo Grove village *Lake Co.*	1.2	89.2
Burbank city *Cook Co.*	17.9	197.8
Calumet City city *Cook Co.*	n/a	n/a
Carbondale city *Jackson Co.*	100.1	420.5
Carol Stream village *Du Page Co.*	9.0	120.0
Carpentersville village *Kane Co.*	8.1	140.0
Champaign city *Champaign Co.*	91.1	332.0
Chicago city *Cook Co.*	n/a	415.3
Chicago Heights city *Cook Co.*	82.8	361.3
Cicero town *Cook Co.*	45.0	263.5
Collinsville city *Madison Co.*	16.1	297.0
Crystal Lake city *McHenry Co.*	15.2	197.1
Danville city *Vermilion Co.*	99.4	600.1
DeKalb city *De Kalb Co.*	44.8	298.2
Decatur city *Macon Co.*	46.2	321.6
Des Plaines city *Cook Co.*	11.1	160.5
Downers Grove village *Du Page Co.*	6.0	206.3
East Saint Louis city *Saint Clair Co.*	499.3	675.7
Edwardsville city *Madison Co.*	8.3	180.8
Elgin city *Kane Co.*	23.5	181.6
Elk Grove Village village *Cook Co.*	6.3	205.2
Elmhurst city *Du Page Co.*	7.2	139.9
Elmwood Park village *Cook Co.*	11.6	179.2
Evanston city *Cook Co.*	30.5	274.5
Freeport city *Stephenson Co.*	14.5	367.6
Galesburg city *Knox Co.*	38.2	340.9
Glen Ellyn village *Du Page Co.*	5.8	131.2
Glendale Heights village *Du Page Co.*	7.8	171.2
Glenview village *Cook Co.*	8.7	106.7
Granite City city *Madison Co.*	57.8	282.1
Gurnee village *Lake Co.*	8.6	459.9
Hanover Park village *Cook Co.*	11.8	114.9
Harvey city *Cook Co.*	137.4	583.8
Highland Park city *Lake Co.*	12.0	121.1
Hoffman Estates village *Cook Co.*	12.7	136.2
Homer Glen village *Will Co.*	2.5	76.3
Huntley village *McHenry Co.*	2.5	87.8
Joliet city *Will Co.*	34.1	258.3

Place	Violent Crime Rate (crimes per 10,000 population)	Property Crime Rate (crimes per 10,000 population)
Kankakee city *Kankakee Co.*	85.8	435.0
Lake in the Hills village *McHenry Co.*	n/a	n/a
Lansing village *Cook Co.*	32.7	467.8
Lockport city *Will Co.*	6.0	126.8
Lombard village *Du Page Co.*	12.4	262.6
McHenry city *McHenry Co.*	13.0	154.3
Melrose Park village *Cook Co.*	22.7	195.8
Moline city *Rock Island Co.*	40.5	311.2
Mount Prospect village *Cook Co.*	5.9	136.9
Mundelein village *Lake Co.*	8.3	108.0
Naperville city *Du Page Co.*	8.3	143.1
New Lenox village *Will Co.*	7.7	123.0
Niles village *Cook Co.*	8.0	250.5
Normal town *McLean Co.*	21.6	247.4
North Chicago city *Lake Co.*	24.5	58.4
Northbrook village *Cook Co.*	3.0	159.9
O'Fallon city *Saint Clair Co.*	10.9	234.4
Oak Forest city *Cook Co.*	10.3	159.8
Oak Lawn village *Cook Co.*	14.4	199.6
Oak Park village *Cook Co.*	n/a	n/a
Orland Park village *Cook Co.*	2.8	238.2
Oswego village *Kendall Co.*	5.2	162.6
Palatine village *Cook Co.*	4.2	129.3
Park Ridge city *Cook Co.*	5.8	121.9
Pekin city *Tazewell Co.*	51.5	267.7
Peoria city *Peoria Co.*	79.7	435.6
Plainfield village *Will Co.*	8.8	125.2
Quincy city *Adams Co.*	46.2	320.5
Rock Island city *Rock Island Co.*	56.9	287.0
Rockford city *Winnebago Co.*	136.8	499.6
Rolling Meadows city *Cook Co.*	8.7	149.1
Romeoville village *Will Co.*	7.5	207.9
Round Lake Beach village *Lake Co.*	12.4	267.8
Saint Charles city *Kane Co.*	5.4	150.7
Schaumburg village *Cook Co.*	9.1	333.4
Skokie village *Cook Co.*	20.6	242.3
Springfield city *Sangamon Co.*	97.2	592.9
Streamwood village *Cook Co.*	8.5	175.5
Tinley Park village *Cook Co.*	7.5	147.2
Urbana city *Champaign Co.*	35.6	347.4
Vernon Hills village *Lake Co.*	7.1	228.4
Waukegan city *Lake Co.*	46.9	300.4
West Chicago city *Du Page Co.*	8.8	127.9
Westmont village *Du Page Co.*	10.9	156.4
Wheaton city *Du Page Co.*	2.3	108.9
Wheeling village *Cook Co.*	8.2	142.7
Wilmette village *Cook Co.*	4.0	154.3
Woodridge village *Du Page Co.*	11.4	157.5
Woodstock city *McHenry Co.*	14.9	153.6
Zion city *Lake Co.*	59.1	422.9

NOTE: n/a not available.
SOURCE: Federal Bureau of Investigation, Uniform Crime Reports, 2012

Education

Illinois Public School Educational Profile

Category	Value	Category	Value
Schools *(2011-2012)*	4,336	**Diploma Recipients** *(2009-2010)*	139,035
Instructional Level		White, Non-Hispanic	83,547
Primary	2,546	Black, Non-Hispanic	24,859
Middle	773	Asian/Pacific Islander, Non-Hispanic	5,827
High	815	American Indian/Alaskan Native, Non-Hispanic	284
Other/Not Reported	202	Hawaiian Native/Pacific Islander, Non-Hispanic	n/a
Curriculum		Two or More Races, Non-Hispanic	n/a
Regular	3,994	Hispanic of Any Race	22,320
Special Education	141	**Staff** *(2011-2012)*	
Vocational	51	Teachers (FTE)	131,431.9
Alternative	150	Salary[1] ($)	60,124
Type		Librarians/Media Specialists (FTE)	1,919.8
Magnet	108	Guidance Counselors (FTE)	3,132.4
Charter	52	**Ratios** *(2011-2012)*	
Title I Eligible	3,277	Number of Students per Teacher	15.8 to 1
School-wide Title I	1,647	Number of Students per Librarian	1,085.1 to 1
Students *(2011-2012)*	2,083,097	Number of Students per Guidance Counselor	665.0 to 1
Gender (%)		**Finances** *(2010-2011)*	
Male	51.4	Current Expenditures ($ per student)	
Female	48.6	Total	11,742
Race/Ethnicity (%)		Instruction	7,025
White, Non-Hispanic	50.8	Support Services	4,360
Black, Non-Hispanic	18.0	Other	357
Asian, Non-Hispanic	4.2	General Revenue ($ per student)	
American Indian/Alaskan Native, Non-Hisp.	0.3	Total	13,818
Hawaiian Native/Pacific Islander, Non-Hisp.	0.1	From Federal Sources	1,387
Two or More Races, Non-Hispanic	2.8	From State Sources	4,449
Hispanic of Any Race	23.7	From Local Sources	7,982
Special Programs (%)		Long-Term Debt Outstanding ($ per student)	
Individual Education Program (IEP)	14.3	At Beginning of Fiscal Year	9,055
English Language Learner (ELL)	8.2	Issued During Fiscal Year	1,069
Eligible for Free Lunch Program	21.5	Retired During Fiscal Year	605
Eligible for Reduced-Price Lunch Program	27.4	At End of Fiscal Year	9,309
Average Freshman Grad. Rate (%) *(2009-2010)*	81.9	**College Entrance Exam Scores**	
White, Non-Hispanic	88.1	SAT Reasoning Test™ *(2013)*	
Black, Non-Hispanic	68.7	Participation Rate (%)	5
Asian/Pacific Islander, Non-Hispanic	97.1	Mean Critical Reading Score	600
American Indian/Alaskan Native, Non-Hispanic	82.1	Mean Math Score	617
Hispanic of Any Race	76.0	Mean Writing Score	590
High School Drop-out Rate (%) *(2009-2010)*	2.9	ACT *(2013)*	
White, Non-Hispanic	1.8	Participation Rate (%)	100
Black, Non-Hispanic	5.7	Mean Composite Score	20.6
Asian/Pacific Islander, Non-Hispanic	0.9	Mean English Score	20.2
American Indian/Alaskan Native, Non-Hispanic	3.0	Mean Math Score	20.7
Hawaiian Native/Pacific Islander, Non-Hispanic	n/a	Mean Reading Score	20.4
Two or More Races, Non-Hispanic	n/a	Mean Science Score	20.5
Hispanic of Any Race	3.8		

Note: For an explanation of data, please refer to the User's Guide in the front of the book; (1) Average salary for classroom teachers in 2013-14

Number of Schools

Rank	Number	District Name	City
1	641	City of Chicago SD 299	Chicago
2	57	SD U-46	Elgin
3	50	Rockford SD 205	Rockford
4	37	Springfield SD 186	Springfield
5	33	Indian Prairie CUSD 204	Aurora
6	32	Peoria SD 150	Peoria
7	30	Plainfield SD 202	Plainfield
8	27	CUSD 300	Carpentersville
8	27	Schaumburg CCSD 54	Schaumburg
10	24	E Saint Louis SD 189	E Saint Louis
10	24	Mclean County USD 5	Normal
10	24	Waukegan CUSD 60	Waukegan
13	23	Decatur SD 61	Decatur
14	22	Joliet PSD 86	Joliet
14	22	Naperville CUSD 203	Naperville
14	22	Oswego CUSD 308	Oswego
17	20	CUSD 200	Wheaton
17	20	Palatine CCSD 15	Palatine
17	20	Valley View CUSD 365u	Romeoville
20	18	Aurora East USD 131	Aurora
20	18	Champaign CUSD 4	Champaign
20	18	Moline USD 40	Moline
23	17	Aurora West USD 129	Aurora
23	17	Evanston CCSD 65	Evanston
23	17	Saint Charles CUSD 303	Saint Charles
26	16	Cicero SD 99	Cicero
27	14	Community CSD 59	Arlington Hgts
27	14	Edwardsville CUSD 7	Edwardsville
27	14	Rock Island SD 41	Rock Island
30	13	Cook County SD 130	Blue Island
30	13	Downers Grove GSD 58	Downers Grove
30	13	Elmhurst SD 205	Elmhurst
30	13	Wheeling CCSD 21	Wheeling
34	12	Barrington CUSD 220	Barrington
34	12	Belvidere CUSD 100	Belvidere
34	12	Crystal Lake CCSD 47	Crystal Lake
34	12	Jacksonville SD 117	Jacksonville
34	12	Kankakee SD 111	Kankakee
34	12	New Lenox SD 122	New Lenox
34	12	North Shore SD 112	Highland Park
34	12	Quincy SD 172	Quincy
34	12	Woodstock CUSD 200	Woodstock
43	11	Alton CUSD 11	Alton
43	11	Belleville SD 118	Belleville
43	11	Cahokia CUSD 187	Cahokia
43	11	CCSD 62	Des Plaines
43	11	Collinsville CUSD 10	Collinsville
43	11	Danville CCSD 118	Danville
43	11	Dekalb CUSD 428	Dekalb
43	11	Granite City CUSD 9	Granite City
43	11	Harlem Ud 122	Machesney Park
43	11	Pekin PSD 108	Pekin
53	10	Chicago Heights SD 170	Chicago Heights
53	10	Crete Monee CUSD 201u	Crete
53	10	Dolton SD 148	Riverdale
53	10	Freeport SD 145	Freeport
53	10	Galesburg CUSD 205	Galesburg
53	10	Geneva CUSD 304	Geneva
53	10	Maywood-Melrose Park-Broadview 89	Melrose Park
53	10	Oak Park ESD 97	Oak Park
53	10	Orland SD 135	Orland Park
53	10	Township HSD 214	Arlington Hgts
63	9	Arlington Hgts SD 25	Arlington Hgts
63	9	Bloomington SD 87	Bloomington
63	9	Grayslake CCSD 46	Grayslake
63	9	Hinsdale CCSD 181	Burr Ridge
63	9	North Chicago SD 187	North Chicago
63	9	Round Lake CUSD 116	Round Lake
63	9	Urbana SD 116	Urbana
63	9	Yorkville CUSD 115	Yorkville
71	8	Addison SD 4	Addison
71	8	Batavia USD 101	Batavia
71	8	Berwyn South SD 100	Berwyn
71	8	Burbank SD 111	Burbank
71	8	CCSD 93	Bloomingdale
71	8	CSD 158	Algonquin
71	8	Glenview CCSD 34	Glenview
71	8	Harvey SD 152	Harvey
71	8	Lake Zurich CUSD 95	Lake Zurich
71	8	Mchenry CCSD 15	Mchenry
71	8	Park Ridge CCSD 64	Park Ridge
71	8	Prairie-Hills ESD 144	Markham
71	8	SD 45 Dupage County	Villa Park
71	8	West Chicago ESD 33	West Chicago
85	7	Bellwood SD 88	Bellwood
85	7	Central CUSD 301	Burlington
85	7	Dunlap CUSD 323	Peoria
85	7	East Maine SD 63	Des Plaines
85	7	East Peoria SD 86	East Peoria
85	7	Effingham CUSD 40	Effingham
85	7	Hawthorn CCSD 73	Vernon Hills
85	7	Highland CUSD 5	Highland
85	7	Jersey CUSD 100	Jerseyville
85	7	Kewanee CUSD 229	Kewanee
85	7	Kildeer Countryside CCSD 96	Buffalo Grove
85	7	Kirby SD 140	Tinley Park
85	7	Lombard SD 44	Lombard
85	7	Marion CUSD 2	Marion
85	7	Massac Ud 1	Metropolis
85	7	Matteson ESD 162	Richton Park
85	7	Minooka CCSD 201	Minooka
85	7	O Fallon CCSD 90	O Fallon
85	7	Prairie Central CUSD 8	Fairbury
85	7	Summit Hill SD 161	Frankfort
85	7	Sycamore CUSD 427	Sycamore
85	7	Township HSD 211	Palatine
85	7	Troy CCSD 30c	Plainfield
85	7	Woodridge SD 68	Woodridge
85	7	Zion ESD 6	Zion
110	6	Ball Chatham CUSD 5	Chatham
110	6	Berkeley SD 87	Berkeley
110	6	Bethalto CUSD 8	Bethalto
110	6	Bourbonnais SD 53	Bourbonnais
110	6	Charleston CUSD 1	Charleston
110	6	Clinton CUSD 15	Clinton
110	6	Deerfield SD 109	Deerfield
110	6	Dolton SD 149	Calumet City
110	6	Geneseo CUSD 228	Geneseo
110	6	Homer CCSD 33c	Homer Glen
110	6	Il Valley Central USD 321	Chillicothe
110	6	Indian Springs SD 109	Justice
110	6	Kaneland CUSD 302	Maple Park
110	6	La Grange SD 102	La Grange Park
110	6	Litchfield CUSD 12	Litchfield
110	6	Lyons SD 103	Lyons
110	6	Morton CUSD 709	Morton
110	6	North Boone CUSD 200	Poplar Grove
110	6	Oak Lawn-Hometown SD 123	Oak Lawn
110	6	Park Forest SD 163	Park Forest
110	6	Peotone CUSD 207u	Peotone
110	6	Sandwich CUSD 430	Sandwich
110	6	Southwestern CUSD 9	Piasa
110	6	Sterling CUSD 5	Sterling
110	6	Taylorville CUSD 3	Taylorville
110	6	Triad CUSD 2	Troy
110	6	Wauconda CUSD 118	Wauconda
110	6	Wilmette SD 39	Wilmette
138	5	Antioch CCSD 34	Antioch
138	5	Beach Park CCSD 3	Beach Park
138	5	Beardstown CUSD 15	Beardstown
138	5	Bensenville SD 2	Bensenville
138	5	Bond County CUSD 2	Greenville
138	5	Canton Union SD 66	Canton
138	5	CCSD 89	Glen Ellyn
138	5	Coal City CUSD 1	Coal City
138	5	Dixon USD 170	Dixon
138	5	East Moline SD 37	East Moline
138	5	Elmwood Park CUSD 401	Elmwood Park
138	5	ESD 159	Matteson
138	5	Eureka CUD 140	Eureka
138	5	Evergreen Park ESD 124	Evergreen Park
138	5	Flossmoor SD 161	Chicago Heights
138	5	Genoa Kingston CUSD 424	Genoa
138	5	Glen Ellyn SD 41	Glen Ellyn
138	5	Harvard CUSD 50	Harvard
138	5	Herscher CUSD 2	Herscher
138	5	Lake Forest SD 67	Lake Forest
138	5	Lake Villa CCSD 41	Lake Villa
138	5	Lansing SD 158	Lansing
138	5	Libertyville SD 70	Libertyville
138	5	Macomb USD 185	Macomb
138	5	Mahomet-Seymour CUSD 3	Mahomet
138	5	Maine Township HSD 207	Park Ridge
138	5	Mannheim SD 83	Franklin Park
138	5	Marquardt SD 15	Glendale Hgts
138	5	Mattoon CUSD 2	Mattoon
138	5	Monmouth-Roseville CUSD 238	Monmouth
138	5	Monticello CUSD 25	Monticello
138	5	Mt Zion CUSD 3	Mount Zion
138	5	North Palos SD 117	Palos Hills
138	5	Olympia CUSD 16	Stanford
138	5	Ottawa ESD 141	Ottawa
138	5	Plano CUSD 88	Plano
138	5	Posen-Robbins ESD 143-5	Posen
138	5	Rantoul City SD 137	Rantoul
138	5	Ridgeland SD 122	Oak Lawn
138	5	Riverside SD 96	Riverside
138	5	Rochelle CCSD 231	Rochelle
138	5	Rochester CUSD 3a	Rochester
138	5	Sherrard CUSD 200	Sherrard
138	5	Streator ESD 44	Streator
138	5	Summit SD 104	Summit
138	5	Tinley Park CCSD 146	Tinley Park
138	5	Waterloo CUSD 5	Waterloo
138	5	Winnetka SD 36	Winnetka
186	4	Alsip-Hazlgrn-Oaklwn SD 126	Alsip
186	4	Aptakisic-Tripp CCSD 102	Buffalo Grove
186	4	Berwyn North SD 98	Berwyn
186	4	Bremen CHSD 228	Midlothian
186	4	Cary CCSD 26	Cary
186	4	CHSD 117	Lake Villa
186	4	CHSD 155	Crystal Lake
186	4	CHSD 218	Oak Lawn
186	4	Columbia CUSD 4	Columbia
186	4	Forest Ridge SD 142	Oak Forest
186	4	Frankfort CUSD 168	West Frankfort
186	4	Glenbard Twp HSD 87	Glen Ellyn
186	4	Gurnee SD 56	Gurnee
186	4	Harrisburg CUSD 3	Harrisburg
186	4	Herrin CUSD 4	Herrin
186	4	Hillsboro CUSD 3	Hillsboro
186	4	Homewood SD 153	Homewood
186	4	J S Morton HSD 201	Cicero
186	4	Johnsburg CUSD 12	Johnsburg
186	4	Kinnikinnick CCSD 131	Roscoe
186	4	Lincoln Way CHSD 210	New Lenox
186	4	Lisle CUSD 202	Lisle
186	4	Manteno CUSD 5	Manteno
186	4	Mascoutah CUD 19	Mascoutah
186	4	Meridian CUSD 223	Stillman Valley
186	4	Midlothian SD 143	Midlothian
186	4	Mount Prospect SD 57	Mount Prospect
186	4	Mount Vernon SD 80	Mount Vernon
186	4	Murphysboro CUSD 186	Murphysboro
186	4	North Mac CUSD 34	Girard
186	4	Northbrook SD 28	Northbrook
186	4	Northfield Twp HSD 225	Glenview
186	4	Queen Bee SD 16	Glendale Hgts
186	4	Reed Custer CUSD 255u	Braidwood
186	4	Robinson CUSD 2	Robinson
186	4	Roxana CUSD 1	Roxana
186	4	Skokie SD 68	Skokie
186	4	Steger SD 194	Steger
186	4	Tolono CUSD 7	Tolono
186	4	Vandalia CUSD 203	Vandalia
186	4	Wabash CUSD 348	Mount Carmel
186	4	Will County SD 92	Lockport
186	4	Winnebago CUSD 323	Winnebago
186	4	Woodland CCSD 50	Gurnee
230	3	Belleville Twp HSD 201	Belleville
230	3	Big Hollow SD 38	Ingleside
230	3	Bloom Twp HSD 206	Chicago Heights
230	3	Bradley SD 61	Bradley
230	3	Byron CUSD 226	Byron
230	3	Carterville CUSD 5	Carterville
230	3	CCSD 168	Sauk Village
230	3	Cons HSD 230	Orland Park
230	3	Darien SD 61	Darien
230	3	Duquoin CUSD 300	Du Quoin
230	3	East Richland CUSD 1	Olney
230	3	Frankfort CCSD 157c	Frankfort
230	3	Fremont SD 79	Mundelein
230	3	Joliet Twp HSD 204	Joliet
230	3	Keeneyville SD 20	Hanover Park
230	3	Lemont-Bromberek CSD 113a	Lemont
230	3	Lincolnshire-Prairieview SD 103	Lincolnshire
230	3	Mokena SD 159	Mokena
230	3	Mundelein ESD 75	Mundelein
230	3	Niles Twp CHSD 219	Skokie
230	3	Oregon CUSD 220	Oregon
230	3	Palos CCSD 118	Palos Park
230	3	Proviso Twp HSD 209	Forest Park
230	3	Rich Twp HSD 227	Olympia Fields
230	3	Riverton CUSD 14	Spaulding
230	3	Rockton SD 140	Rockton

Note: This section only includes districts with 1,500 or more students; All categories are ranked from high to low

230	3	Skokie SD 69	Skokie
230	3	Thornton Twp HSD 205	South Holland
258	2	CHSD 128	Vernon Hills
258	2	CHSD 99	Downers Grove
258	2	Dupage HSD 88	Addison
258	2	Grayslake CHSD 127	Grayslake
258	2	Hinsdale Twp HSD 86	Hinsdale
258	2	Leyden CHSD 212	Franklin Park
258	2	Mchenry CHSD 156	Mchenry
258	2	Millburn CCSD 24	Old Mill Creek
258	2	New Trier Twp HSD 203	Northfield
258	2	Thornton Fractional Twp HSD 215	Calumet City
258	2	Twp HSD 113	Highland Park
258	2	United Twp HSD 30	East Moline
258	2	Zion-Benton Twp HSD 126	Zion
271	1	Adlai E Stevenson HSD 125	Lincolnshire
271	1	Argo CHSD 217	Summit
271	1	Bradley Bourbonnais CHSD 307	Bradley
271	1	CHSD 94	West Chicago
271	1	Evanston Twp HSD 202	Evanston
271	1	Fenton CHSD 100	Bensenville
271	1	Grant CHSD 124	Fox Lake
271	1	Homewood Flossmoor CHSD 233	Flossmoor
271	1	Hononegah Chd 207	Rockton
271	1	Lake Forest CHSD 115	Lake Forest
271	1	Lake Park CHSD 108	Roselle
271	1	Lemont Twp HSD 210	Lemont
271	1	Lockport Twp HSD 205	Lockport
271	1	Lyons Twp HSD 204	La Grange
271	1	Minooka CHSD 111	Minooka
271	1	Mundelein Cons HSD 120	Mundelein
271	1	O Fallon Twp HSD 203	O Fallon
271	1	Oak Lawn CHSD 229	Oak Lawn
271	1	Oak Park - River Forest SD 200	Oak Park
271	1	Pekin CSD 303	Pekin
271	1	Reavis Twp HSD 220	Burbank
271	1	Warren Twp HSD 121	Gurnee

Number of Teachers

Rank	Number	District Name	City
1	22,459.6	City of Chicago SD 299	Chicago
2	2,048.5	SD U-46	Elgin
3	1,767.2	Indian Prairie CUSD 204	Aurora
4	1,674.6	Rockford SD 205	Rockford
5	1,623.5	Plainfield SD 202	Plainfield
6	1,106.5	Springfield SD 186	Springfield
7	1,098.3	CUSD 300	Carpentersville
8	1,070.3	Waukegan CUSD 60	Waukegan
9	1,054.2	Valley View CUSD 365u	Romeoville
10	1,048.2	Naperville CUSD 203	Naperville
11	1,021.2	Schaumburg CCSD 54	Schaumburg
12	985.8	Peoria SD 150	Peoria
13	889.0	Oswego CUSD 308	Oswego
14	847.8	CUSD 200	Wheaton
15	837.2	Saint Charles CUSD 303	Saint Charles
16	804.3	Mclean County USD 5	Normal
17	793.4	Township HSD 211	Palatine
18	780.0	Aurora East USD 131	Aurora
19	767.7	Cicero SD 99	Cicero
20	733.6	Township HSD 214	Arlington Hgts
21	710.9	Palatine CCSD 15	Palatine
22	710.2	Aurora West USD 129	Aurora
23	697.7	Champaign CUSD 4	Champaign
24	629.5	Joliet PSD 86	Joliet
25	593.8	Evanston CCSD 65	Evanston
26	572.0	Barrington CUSD 220	Barrington
27	531.2	CSD 158	Algonquin
28	518.1	Elmhurst SD 205	Elmhurst
29	513.0	Crystal Lake CCSD 47	Crystal Lake
30	510.6	Harlem Ud 122	Machesney Park
31	510.3	Glenbard Twp HSD 87	Glen Ellyn
32	509.7	Belvidere CUSD 100	Belvidere
33	505.8	Cons HSD 230	Orland Park
34	477.6	Wheeling CCSD 21	Wheeling
35	454.2	Alton CUSD 11	Alton
36	450.2	Community CSD 59	Arlington Hgts
37	441.3	Edwardsville CUSD 7	Edwardsville
38	438.9	Decatur SD 61	Decatur
39	434.9	E Saint Louis SD 189	E Saint Louis
40	433.4	Moline USD 40	Moline
41	431.5	Woodland CCSD 50	Gurnee
42	420.7	Maine Township HSD 207	Park Ridge
43	416.6	Lincoln Way CHSD 210	New Lenox
44	409.0	Quincy SD 172	Quincy
45	402.7	Oak Park ESD 97	Oak Park
46	399.1	CHSD 155	Crystal Lake
47	395.6	Collinsville CUSD 10	Collinsville
48	392.9	Lake Zurich CUSD 95	Lake Zurich
49	390.6	Round Lake CUSD 116	Round Lake
50	386.0	Danville CCSD 118	Danville
51	383.5	Thornton Twp HSD 205	South Holland
52	382.3	Woodstock CUSD 200	Woodstock
53	378.5	Rock Island SD 41	Rock Island
54	364.0	Granite City CUSD 9	Granite City
55	362.6	CHSD 218	Oak Lawn
56	360.5	North Shore SD 112	Highland Park
57	358.4	Bloomington SD 87	Bloomington
58	355.4	Niles Twp CHSD 219	Skokie
59	355.1	Geneva CUSD 304	Geneva
60	354.9	J S Morton HSD 201	Cicero
61	354.8	Northfield Twp HSD 225	Glenview
62	347.4	Glenview CCSD 34	Glenview
63	343.7	Kankakee SD 111	Kankakee
64	342.9	Arlington Hgts SD 25	Arlington Hgts
65	342.1	Batavia USD 101	Batavia
66	340.5	CCSD 62	Des Plaines
67	339.2	Dekalb CUSD 428	Dekalb
68	338.5	New Trier Twp HSD 203	Northfield
69	335.4	Joliet Twp HSD 204	Joliet
70	328.7	Orland SD 135	Orland Park
71	328.1	Park Ridge CCSD 64	Park Ridge
72	327.6	Yorkville CUSD 115	Yorkville
73	327.4	Freeport SD 145	Freeport
74	322.7	Urbana SD 116	Urbana
75	320.6	CHSD 99	Downers Grove
76	306.4	Bremen CHSD 228	Midlothian
77	294.6	Ball Chatham CUSD 5	Chatham
78	293.0	Hinsdale Twp HSD 86	Hinsdale
79	286.1	CCSD 93	Bloomingdale
80	284.5	Mchenry CCSD 15	Mchenry
81	284.4	Kaneland CUSD 302	Maple Park
82	284.1	Crete Monee CUSD 201u	Crete
83	280.2	Maywood-Melrose Park-Broadview 89	Melrose Park
84	278.8	Berwyn South SD 100	Berwyn
85	277.3	Cook County SD 130	Blue Island
86	277.0	Cahokia CUSD 187	Cahokia
86	277.0	Troy CCSD 30c	Plainfield
88	276.5	Downers Grove GSD 58	Downers Grove
89	275.1	Hinsdale CCSD 181	Burr Ridge
90	274.6	Wilmette SD 39	Wilmette
91	273.5	New Lenox SD 122	New Lenox
92	270.8	Wauconda CUSD 118	Wauconda
93	270.3	Galesburg CUSD 205	Galesburg
94	269.3	Rich Twp HSD 227	Olympia Fields
95	268.3	Grayslake CCSD 46	Grayslake
96	262.2	Belleville Twp HSD 201	Belleville
97	260.5	Hawthorn CCSD 73	Vernon Hills
98	258.0	Kirby SD 140	Tinley Park
99	251.9	Warren Twp HSD 121	Gurnee
100	251.0	Adlai E Stevenson HSD 125	Lincolnshire
101	248.6	North Chicago SD 187	North Chicago
102	244.3	Pekin PSD 108	Pekin
103	242.4	West Chicago ESD 33	West Chicago
104	242.2	Addison SD 4	Addison
104	242.2	Jacksonville SD 117	Jacksonville
106	241.3	Lyons Twp HSD 204	La Grange
107	241.0	Twp HSD 113	Highland Park
108	239.0	Proviso Twp HSD 209	Forest Park
109	236.2	Dupage HSD 88	Addison
110	232.0	Glen Ellyn SD 41	Glen Ellyn
111	231.7	Homer CCSD 33c	Homer Glen
112	230.6	Deerfield SD 109	Deerfield
113	227.6	Sycamore CUSD 427	Sycamore
114	226.2	La Grange SD 102	La Grange Park
115	224.7	Kildeer Countryside CCSD 96	Buffalo Grove
116	223.7	Lombard SD 44	Lombard
117	221.0	Triad CUSD 2	Troy
118	220.0	Leyden CHSD 212	Franklin Park
119	217.9	Belleville SD 118	Belleville
120	215.1	Chicago Heights SD 170	Chicago Heights
121	214.5	East Maine SD 63	Des Plaines
121	214.5	Evanston Twp HSD 202	Evanston
123	214.2	CHSD 128	Vernon Hills
124	213.3	Central CUSD 301	Burlington
124	213.3	Marion CUSD 2	Marion
126	213.1	Mattoon CUSD 2	Mattoon
127	212.6	SD 45 Dupage County	Villa Park
128	208.6	Mascoutah CUD 19	Mascoutah
129	208.1	Matteson ESD 162	Richton Park
130	206.8	Dunlap CUSD 323	Peoria
131	205.9	Oak Lawn-Hometown SD 123	Oak Lawn
132	205.0	Summit Hill SD 161	Frankfort
133	204.0	Burbank SD 111	Burbank
134	203.1	Grayslake CHSD 127	Grayslake
134	203.1	Lockport Twp HSD 205	Lockport
136	202.8	Sterling CUSD 5	Sterling
137	201.7	Indian Springs SD 109	Justice
138	198.5	Oak Park - River Forest SD 200	Oak Park
139	197.6	Mannheim SD 83	Franklin Park
140	194.6	O Fallon CCSD 90	O Fallon
141	192.4	Antioch CCSD 34	Antioch
141	192.4	Lake Villa CCSD 41	Lake Villa
143	192.0	Minooka CCSD 201	Minooka
144	189.2	Dolton SD 148	Riverdale
145	188.3	Berwyn North SD 98	Berwyn
146	186.4	Thornton Fractional Twp HSD 215	Calumet City
147	186.2	Prairie-Hills ESD 144	Markham
148	181.6	Highland CUSD 5	Highland
148	181.6	North Palos SD 117	Palos Hills
150	181.2	Woodridge SD 68	Woodridge
151	176.4	East Moline SD 37	East Moline
152	175.4	CHSD 117	Lake Villa
153	174.5	Elmwood Park CUSD 401	Elmwood Park
154	173.1	Lyons SD 103	Lyons
155	171.2	Canton Union SD 66	Canton
156	171.0	Bloom Twp HSD 206	Chicago Heights
157	170.7	Winnetka SD 36	Winnetka
158	169.9	Mahomet-Seymour CUSD 3	Mahomet
159	168.9	Marquardt SD 15	Glendale Hgts
160	167.8	Charleston CUSD 1	Charleston
161	166.6	Flossmoor SD 161	Chicago Heights
162	166.0	Zion ESD 6	Zion
162	166.0	Zion-Benton Twp HSD 126	Zion
164	165.6	Lake Forest SD 67	Lake Forest
165	165.3	Homewood Flossmoor CHSD 233	Flossmoor
166	165.0	Berkeley SD 87	Berkeley
167	164.0	Waterloo CUSD 5	Waterloo
168	163.0	Effingham CUSD 40	Effingham
169	162.9	Jersey CUSD 100	Jerseyville
169	162.9	Tinley Park CCSD 146	Tinley Park
171	162.0	Dolton SD 149	Calumet City
172	161.8	Bethalto CUSD 8	Bethalto
173	160.7	Dixon USD 170	Dixon
174	160.0	Sandwich CUSD 430	Sandwich
175	159.4	Bellwood SD 88	Bellwood
176	158.2	Morton CUSD 709	Morton
177	157.6	Libertyville SD 70	Libertyville
178	156.8	Northbrook SD 28	Northbrook
179	155.7	Beach Park CCSD 3	Beach Park
180	154.5	Geneseo CUSD 228	Geneseo
181	153.7	Plano CUSD 88	Plano
182	153.2	Johnsburg CUSD 12	Johnsburg
183	153.1	Bourbonnais SD 53	Bourbonnais
184	153.0	Manteno CUSD 5	Manteno
185	152.3	Aptakisic-Tripp CCSD 102	Buffalo Grove
186	151.0	Lansing SD 158	Lansing
187	150.5	Gurnee SD 56	Gurnee
188	150.3	Harvard CUSD 50	Harvard
189	149.2	Prairie Central CUSD 8	Fairbury
190	148.0	Frankfort CCSD 157c	Frankfort
191	146.5	Lake Park CHSD 108	Roselle
192	146.1	Bensenville SD 2	Bensenville
193	144.0	Ottawa ESD 141	Ottawa
194	142.4	Mchenry CHSD 156	Mchenry
195	140.8	Taylorville CUSD 3	Taylorville
196	139.8	Homewood SD 153	Homewood
196	139.8	Rochester CUSD 3a	Rochester
198	139.4	Massac Ud 1	Metropolis
199	139.3	CCSD 89	Glen Ellyn
200	139.1	Skokie SD 68	Skokie
201	139.0	Herscher CUSD 2	Herscher
202	137.8	Harrisburg CUSD 3	Harrisburg
203	137.6	Il Valley Central USD 321	Chillicothe
204	136.0	Clinton CUSD 15	Clinton
205	135.6	Coal City CUSD 1	Coal City
206	134.9	Evergreen Park ESD 124	Evergreen Park
207	133.9	Murphysboro CUSD 186	Murphysboro
208	133.0	Harvey SD 152	Harvey
209	132.6	ESD 159	Matteson
210	132.5	O Fallon Twp HSD 203	O Fallon
211	132.0	Midlothian SD 143	Midlothian
212	131.7	Fremont SD 79	Mundelein
213	131.1	East Richland CUSD 1	Olney
214	129.2	Mt Zion CUSD 3	Mount Zion
215	127.8	Macomb CUSD 185	Macomb
216	127.0	Herrin CUSD 4	Herrin
217	126.4	Streator ESD 44	Streator

Note: This section only includes districts with 1,500 or more students; All categories are ranked from high to low

218	124.5	Mount Prospect SD 57	Mount Prospect
219	124.4	Ridgeland SD 122	Oak Lawn
220	124.2	Minooka CHSD 111	Minooka
221	123.2	Lake Forest CHSD 115	Lake Forest
222	122.6	Pekin CSD 303	Pekin
223	122.0	Lincolnshire-Prairieview SD 103	Lincolnshire
224	121.5	Byron CUSD 226	Byron
225	121.3	Genoa Kingston CUSD 424	Genoa
226	121.2	CHSD 94	West Chicago
227	120.4	Palos CCSD 118	Palos Park
228	120.1	Roxana CUSD 1	Roxana
229	120.0	Cary CCSD 26	Cary
229	120.0	Hononegah Chd 207	Rockton
231	119.5	Olympia CUSD 16	Stanford
232	118.9	Rochelle CCSD 231	Rochelle
233	116.2	Queen Bee SD 16	Glendale Hgts
234	116.0	East Peoria SD 86	East Peoria
235	115.8	Bond County CUSD 2	Greenville
236	115.1	Mundelein ESD 75	Mundelein
237	115.0	Mundelein Cons HSD 120	Mundelein
238	114.1	Tolono CUSD 7	Tolono
239	113.6	Steger SD 194	Steger
240	113.3	Alsip-Hazlgrn-Oaklwn SD 126	Alsip
241	112.6	Will County SD 92	Lockport
242	112.2	Meridian CUSD 223	Stillman Valley
243	112.1	Park Forest SD 163	Park Forest
244	111.1	Bradley Bourbonnais CHSD 307	Bradley
245	110.9	Beardstown CUSD 15	Beardstown
246	110.8	Big Hollow SD 38	Ingleside
247	110.7	Reed Custer CUSD 255u	Braidwood
248	110.0	CCSD 168	Sauk Village
249	109.7	Peotone CUSD 207u	Peotone
250	109.3	Carterville CUSD 5	Carterville
251	108.9	Sherrard CUSD 200	Sherrard
252	108.7	Monmouth-Roseville CUSD 238	Monmouth
253	108.4	Kewanee CUSD 229	Kewanee
253	108.4	Rantoul City SD 137	Rantoul
255	107.8	Lisle CUSD 202	Lisle
255	107.8	Oak Lawn CHSD 229	Oak Lawn
257	107.3	Kinnikinnick CCSD 131	Roscoe
258	107.1	Vandalia CUSD 203	Vandalia
259	106.5	Columbia CUSD 4	Columbia
259	106.5	Monticello CUSD 25	Monticello
259	106.5	Wabash CUSD 348	Mount Carmel
262	106.2	Frankfort CUSD 168	West Frankfort
263	106.0	Darien SD 61	Darien
264	105.8	North Boone CUSD 200	Poplar Grove
265	105.6	Bradley SD 61	Bradley
266	105.0	Robinson CUSD 2	Robinson
267	104.5	Argo CHSD 217	Summit
268	104.4	Winnebago CUSD 323	Winnebago
269	104.0	Posen-Robbins ESD 143-5	Posen
270	103.9	Eureka CUD 140	Eureka
271	102.9	Mount Vernon SD 80	Mount Vernon
271	102.9	Riverside SD 96	Riverside
273	102.4	Grant CHSD 124	Fox Lake
274	102.1	Duquoin CUSD 300	Du Quoin
274	102.1	Hillsboro CUSD 3	Hillsboro
276	99.7	Skokie SD 69	Skokie
277	98.0	Lemont-Bromberek CSD 113a	Lemont
277	98.0	Summit SD 104	Summit
279	97.7	Forest Ridge SD 142	Oak Forest
279	97.7	Southwestern CUSD 9	Piasa
281	97.5	Reavis Twp HSD 220	Burbank
282	96.1	Oregon CUSD 220	Oregon
283	95.0	Fenton CHSD 100	Bensenville
284	94.5	Rockton SD 140	Rockton
285	94.1	Keeneyville SD 20	Hanover Park
286	92.5	Lemont Twp HSD 210	Lemont
287	90.9	North Mac CUSD 34	Girard
288	88.5	Millburn CCSD 24	Old Mill Creek
289	84.5	United Twp HSD 30	East Moline
290	83.6	Riverton CUSD 14	Spaulding
291	83.0	Litchfield CUSD 12	Litchfield
291	83.0	Mokena SD 159	Mokena

Number of Students

Rank	Number	District Name	City
1	403,004	City of Chicago SD 299	Chicago
2	40,687	SD U-46	Elgin
3	29,286	Indian Prairie CUSD 204	Aurora
4	28,904	Plainfield SD 202	Plainfield
5	28,118	Rockford SD 205	Rockford
6	20,810	CUSD 300	Carpentersville
7	17,838	Valley View CUSD 365u	Romeoville
8	17,768	Naperville CUSD 203	Naperville
9	17,150	Oswego CUSD 308	Oswego
10	16,597	Waukegan CUSD 60	Waukegan
11	14,972	Springfield SD 186	Springfield
12	14,502	Aurora East USD 131	Aurora
13	14,083	Schaumburg CCSD 54	Schaumburg
14	14,057	Peoria SD 150	Peoria
15	13,672	Saint Charles CUSD 303	Saint Charles
16	13,423	CUSD 200	Wheaton
17	13,367	Cicero SD 99	Cicero
18	13,309	Mclean County USD 5	Normal
19	12,663	Palatine CCSD 15	Palatine
20	12,593	Township HSD 211	Palatine
21	12,467	Aurora West USD 129	Aurora
22	12,305	Township HSD 214	Arlington Hgts
23	11,308	Joliet PSD 86	Joliet
24	9,492	Champaign CUSD 4	Champaign
25	9,285	CSD 158	Algonquin
26	9,088	Barrington CUSD 220	Barrington
27	9,007	Decatur SD 61	Decatur
28	8,891	Glenbard Twp HSD 87	Glen Ellyn
29	8,622	Belvidere CUSD 100	Belvidere
30	8,344	J S Morton HSD 201	Cicero
31	8,340	Elmhurst SD 205	Elmhurst
32	8,301	Cons HSD 230	Orland Park
33	8,214	Crystal Lake CCSD 47	Crystal Lake
34	7,480	Edwardsville CUSD 7	Edwardsville
35	7,429	Moline USD 40	Moline
36	7,346	Lincoln Way CHSD 210	New Lenox
37	7,271	Evanston CCSD 65	Evanston
38	7,218	Harlem Ud 122	Machesney Park
39	7,217	Round Lake CUSD 116	Round Lake
40	7,176	Quincy SD 172	Quincy
41	7,009	CHSD 155	Crystal Lake
42	6,971	E Saint Louis SD 189	E Saint Louis
43	6,873	Granite City CUSD 9	Granite City
44	6,866	Wheeling CCSD 21	Wheeling
45	6,645	Collinsville CUSD 10	Collinsville
46	6,622	Rock Island SD 41	Rock Island
47	6,537	Community CSD 59	Arlington Hgts
48	6,522	Woodland CCSD 50	Gurnee
49	6,408	Alton CUSD 11	Alton
49	6,408	Woodstock CUSD 200	Woodstock
51	6,307	Batavia USD 101	Batavia
52	6,207	Danville CCSD 118	Danville
53	6,104	Dekalb CUSD 428	Dekalb
54	5,959	Geneva CUSD 304	Geneva
55	5,958	Lake Zurich CUSD 95	Lake Zurich
56	5,930	Joliet Twp HSD 204	Joliet
57	5,671	CHSD 218	Oak Lawn
58	5,670	Kankakee SD 111	Kankakee
59	5,631	Oak Park ESD 97	Oak Park
60	5,586	Bloomington SD 87	Bloomington
61	5,565	New Lenox SD 122	New Lenox
62	5,491	Bremen CHSD 228	Midlothian
63	5,470	Yorkville CUSD 115	Yorkville
64	5,362	Maywood-Melrose Park-Broadview 89	Melrose Park
65	5,283	Thornton Twp HSD 205	South Holland
66	5,213	Orland SD 135	Orland Park
67	5,196	CHSD 99	Downers Grove
68	5,192	Arlington Hgts SD 25	Arlington Hgts
69	5,136	Crete Monee CUSD 201u	Crete
70	5,122	Proviso Twp HSD 209	Forest Park
71	5,097	Maine Township HSD 207	Park Ridge
72	5,047	Downers Grove GSD 58	Downers Grove
73	4,958	Belleville Twp HSD 201	Belleville
74	4,901	Glenview CCSD 34	Glenview
75	4,845	Mchenry CCSD 15	Mchenry
76	4,835	Kaneland CUSD 302	Maple Park
77	4,810	Niles Twp CHSD 219	Skokie
78	4,750	Northfield Twp HSD 225	Glenview
79	4,679	CCSD 62	Des Plaines
80	4,592	Galesburg CUSD 205	Galesburg
81	4,564	Troy CCSD 30c	Plainfield
82	4,531	Hinsdale Twp HSD 86	Hinsdale
83	4,522	Warren Twp HSD 121	Gurnee
84	4,518	Ball Chatham CUSD 5	Chatham
85	4,492	Wauconda CUSD 118	Wauconda
86	4,475	North Shore SD 112	Highland Park
87	4,406	West Chicago ESD 33	West Chicago
88	4,324	Urbana SD 116	Urbana
89	4,317	Park Ridge CCSD 64	Park Ridge
90	4,296	Addison SD 4	Addison
91	4,234	New Trier Twp HSD 203	Northfield
92	4,221	Cahokia CUSD 187	Cahokia
93	4,187	Freeport SD 145	Freeport
94	4,125	Grayslake CCSD 46	Grayslake
95	4,118	Adlai E Stevenson HSD 125	Lincolnshire
96	4,077	Dupage HSD 88	Addison
97	4,006	Marion CUSD 2	Marion
98	3,982	Hinsdale CCSD 181	Burr Ridge
99	3,981	Lyons Twp HSD 204	La Grange
100	3,968	Hawthorn CCSD 73	Vernon Hills
101	3,963	Berwyn South SD 100	Berwyn
101	3,963	Minooka CCSD 201	Minooka
103	3,905	Rich Twp HSD 227	Olympia Fields
104	3,879	CCSD 93	Bloomingdale
105	3,869	Cook County SD 130	Blue Island
106	3,840	Sycamore CUSD 427	Sycamore
107	3,837	North Chicago SD 187	North Chicago
108	3,789	Belleville SD 118	Belleville
109	3,785	Dunlap CUSD 323	Peoria
110	3,781	Pekin PSD 108	Pekin
111	3,748	Lockport Twp HSD 205	Lockport
112	3,735	Kirby SD 140	Tinley Park
113	3,693	Twp HSD 113	Highland Park
114	3,681	Homer CCSD 33c	Homer Glen
115	3,679	Wilmette SD 39	Wilmette
116	3,658	Jacksonville SD 117	Jacksonville
117	3,652	Triad CUSD 2	Troy
118	3,642	Glen Ellyn SD 41	Glen Ellyn
119	3,636	Mascoutah CUD 19	Mascoutah
120	3,628	East Maine SD 63	Des Plaines
121	3,567	Thornton Fractional Twp HSD 215	Calumet City
122	3,527	Summit Hill SD 161	Frankfort
123	3,500	Leyden CHSD 212	Franklin Park
124	3,483	O Fallon CCSD 90	O Fallon
125	3,470	Central CUSD 301	Burlington
126	3,441	Sterling CUSD 5	Sterling
127	3,436	Mattoon CUSD 2	Mattoon
128	3,406	Bloom Twp HSD 206	Chicago Heights
129	3,404	CHSD 128	Vernon Hills
130	3,389	Berwyn North SD 98	Berwyn
131	3,356	Burbank SD 111	Burbank
132	3,315	SD 45 Dupage County	Villa Park
133	3,273	Oak Park - River Forest SD 200	Oak Park
134	3,232	Chicago Heights SD 170	Chicago Heights
135	3,180	Matteson ESD 162	Richton Park
136	3,142	Evanston Twp HSD 202	Evanston
137	3,138	Lombard SD 44	Lombard
138	3,135	Dolton SD 149	Calumet City
139	3,134	Kildeer Countryside CCSD 96	Buffalo Grove
140	3,126	La Grange SD 102	La Grange Park
141	3,124	Deerfield SD 109	Deerfield
142	3,108	Indian Springs SD 109	Justice
142	3,108	Lake Villa CCSD 41	Lake Villa
144	3,088	Antioch CCSD 34	Antioch
145	3,080	Highland CUSD 5	Highland
146	3,057	Oak Lawn-Hometown SD 123	Oak Lawn
147	3,005	North Palos SD 117	Palos Hills
148	2,990	Woodridge SD 68	Woodridge
149	2,983	Elmwood Park CUSD 401	Elmwood Park
150	2,968	Grayslake CHSD 127	Grayslake
151	2,904	Mahomet-Seymour CUSD 3	Mahomet
152	2,879	Bellwood SD 88	Bellwood
153	2,841	Homewood Flossmoor CHSD 233	Flossmoor
154	2,838	Berkeley SD 87	Berkeley
155	2,825	Lake Park CHSD 108	Roselle
156	2,821	CHSD 117	Lake Villa
157	2,817	Morton CUSD 709	Morton
158	2,810	Zion-Benton Twp HSD 126	Zion
159	2,796	Cary CCSD 26	Cary
159	2,796	Prairie-Hills ESD 144	Markham
161	2,795	Charleston CUSD 1	Charleston
162	2,768	Taylorville CUSD 3	Taylorville
163	2,767	Dixon USD 170	Dixon
164	2,766	Zion ESD 6	Zion
165	2,764	Jersey CUSD 100	Jerseyville
166	2,760	Effingham CUSD 40	Effingham
167	2,741	Waterloo CUSD 5	Waterloo
168	2,732	Marquardt SD 15	Glendale Hgts
169	2,646	Geneseo CUSD 228	Geneseo
170	2,636	Canton Union SD 66	Canton
171	2,604	Mannheim SD 83	Franklin Park
172	2,603	Bethalto CUSD 8	Bethalto
173	2,555	Bourbonnais SD 53	Bourbonnais
174	2,543	Minooka CHSD 111	Minooka
175	2,537	Mchenry CHSD 156	Mchenry
176	2,534	Libertyville SD 70	Libertyville
177	2,528	Herrin CUSD 4	Herrin
178	2,509	O Fallon Twp HSD 203	O Fallon
179	2,503	Mt Zion CUSD 3	Mount Zion

Note: This section only includes districts with 1,500 or more students; All categories are ranked from high to low

180	2,486	Lyons SD 103	Lyons
181	2,473	East Moline SD 37	East Moline
182	2,459	Harvey SD 152	Harvey
183	2,448	Beach Park CCSD 3	Beach Park
184	2,446	Dolton SD 148	Riverdale
185	2,438	Harvard CUSD 50	Harvard
186	2,434	Frankfort CCSD 157c	Frankfort
187	2,408	Tinley Park CCSD 146	Tinley Park
188	2,398	Lemont-Bromberek CSD 113a	Lemont
189	2,389	Flossmoor SD 161	Chicago Heights
190	2,372	Lansing SD 158	Lansing
191	2,364	Sandwich CUSD 430	Sandwich
192	2,342	Ridgeland SD 122	Oak Lawn
193	2,334	Johnsburg CUSD 12	Johnsburg
194	2,333	Rochester CUSD 3a	Rochester
195	2,320	Plano CUSD 88	Plano
196	2,305	Manteno CUSD 5	Manteno
197	2,251	Mundelein Cons HSD 120	Mundelein
198	2,206	Fremont SD 79	Mundelein
199	2,189	Il Valley Central USD 321	Chillicothe
200	2,178	Harrisburg CUSD 3	Harrisburg
201	2,159	Prairie Central CUSD 8	Fairbury
202	2,153	CHSD 94	West Chicago
203	2,152	East Richland CUSD 1	Olney
204	2,135	Massac Ud 1	Metropolis
205	2,133	Mount Prospect SD 57	Mount Prospect
205	2,133	Murphysboro CUSD 186	Murphysboro
207	2,130	Hononegah Chd 207	Rockton
208	2,122	Gurnee SD 56	Gurnee
209	2,109	Bradley Bourbonnais CHSD 307	Bradley
210	2,105	Bensenville SD 2	Bensenville
211	2,082	Coal City CUSD 1	Coal City
211	2,082	Ottawa ESD 141	Ottawa
213	2,060	Columbia CUSD 4	Columbia
214	2,053	Aptakisic-Tripp CCSD 102	Buffalo Grove
215	2,045	Kinnikinnick CCSD 131	Roscoe
216	2,039	Lake Forest SD 67	Lake Forest
217	2,010	Pekin CSD 303	Pekin
218	2,000	CCSD 89	Glen Ellyn
219	1,997	Macomb CUSD 185	Macomb
219	1,997	Streator ESD 44	Streator
221	1,995	Bond County CUSD 2	Greenville
222	1,984	Midlothian SD 143	Midlothian
223	1,980	Herscher CUSD 2	Herscher
223	1,980	Meridian CUSD 223	Stillman Valley
225	1,970	Clinton CUSD 15	Clinton
226	1,967	ESD 159	Matteson
227	1,957	Park Forest SD 163	Park Forest
228	1,955	Queen Bee SD 16	Glendale Hgts
229	1,940	Olympia CUSD 16	Stanford
230	1,926	Hillsboro CUSD 3	Hillsboro
231	1,909	Carterville CUSD 5	Carterville
232	1,905	Frankfort CUSD 168	West Frankfort
232	1,905	Genoa Kingston CUSD 424	Genoa
234	1,904	Kewanee CUSD 229	Kewanee
235	1,891	Roxana CUSD 1	Roxana
236	1,889	Oak Lawn CHSD 229	Oak Lawn
237	1,888	Homewood SD 153	Homewood
238	1,887	Peotone CUSD 207u	Peotone
239	1,877	Argo CHSD 217	Summit
240	1,874	Grant CHSD 124	Fox Lake
241	1,873	Palos CCSD 118	Palos Park
242	1,850	Posen-Robbins ESD 143-5	Posen
243	1,838	Evergreen Park ESD 124	Evergreen Park
244	1,832	Summit SD 104	Summit
245	1,810	Winnetka SD 36	Winnetka
246	1,808	Mokena SD 159	Mokena
247	1,796	Will County SD 92	Lockport
248	1,785	Reavis Twp HSD 220	Burbank
249	1,777	Big Hollow SD 38	Ingleside
250	1,773	Skokie SD 68	Skokie
251	1,759	Monmouth-Roseville CUSD 238	Monmouth
252	1,749	Rochelle CCSD 231	Rochelle
253	1,746	East Peoria SD 86	East Peoria
254	1,743	Reed Custer CUSD 255u	Braidwood
255	1,739	Mount Vernon SD 80	Mount Vernon
256	1,730	CCSD 168	Sauk Village
257	1,726	Wabash CUSD 348	Mount Carmel
258	1,725	Lake Forest CHSD 115	Lake Forest
259	1,722	North Boone CUSD 200	Poplar Grove
260	1,721	Skokie SD 69	Skokie
261	1,720	Mundelein ESD 75	Mundelein
262	1,712	United Twp HSD 30	East Moline
263	1,694	Monticello CUSD 25	Monticello
264	1,691	Northbrook SD 28	Northbrook
265	1,690	Tolono CUSD 7	Tolono
266	1,665	Forest Ridge SD 142	Oak Forest
267	1,663	Robinson CUSD 2	Robinson
267	1,663	Southwestern CUSD 9	Piasa
269	1,661	Bradley SD 61	Bradley
270	1,648	Darien SD 61	Darien
271	1,643	North Mac CUSD 34	Girard
272	1,633	Lincolnshire-Prairieview SD 103	Lincolnshire
273	1,620	Keeneyville SD 20	Hanover Park
274	1,618	Lisle CUSD 202	Lisle
275	1,605	Beardstown CUSD 15	Beardstown
276	1,596	Alsip-Hazlgrn-Oaklwn SD 126	Alsip
277	1,595	Eureka CUD 140	Eureka
277	1,595	Sherrard CUSD 200	Sherrard
279	1,593	Winnebago CUSD 323	Winnebago
280	1,588	Rantoul City SD 137	Rantoul
281	1,579	Fenton CHSD 100	Bensenville
281	1,579	Riverside SD 96	Riverside
283	1,569	Steger SD 194	Steger
284	1,562	Byron CUSD 226	Byron
285	1,559	Oregon CUSD 220	Oregon
286	1,557	Vandalia CUSD 203	Vandalia
287	1,556	Duquoin CUSD 300	Du Quoin
288	1,551	Riverton CUSD 14	Spaulding
289	1,541	Millburn CCSD 24	Old Mill Creek
290	1,534	Rockton SD 140	Rockton
291	1,528	Litchfield CUSD 12	Litchfield
292	1,507	Lemont Twp HSD 210	Lemont

Male Students

Rank	Percent	District Name	City
1	54.7	Sandwich CUSD 430	Sandwich
2	54.1	Central CUSD 301	Burlington
3	54.0	Antioch CCSD 34	Antioch
3	54.0	Collinsville CUSD 10	Collinsville
5	53.8	Mundelein ESD 75	Mundelein
6	53.7	CHSD 117	Lake Villa
7	53.5	Coal City CUSD 1	Coal City
7	53.5	East Moline SD 37	East Moline
7	53.5	Mount Prospect SD 57	Mount Prospect
10	53.4	Evergreen Park ESD 124	Evergreen Park
10	53.4	Frankfort CUSD 168	West Frankfort
10	53.4	Herscher CUSD 2	Herscher
13	53.3	Bethalto CUSD 8	Bethalto
13	53.3	Kaneland CUSD 302	Maple Park
13	53.3	Will County SD 92	Lockport
16	53.2	Harvard CUSD 50	Harvard
16	53.2	Winnebago CUSD 323	Winnebago
18	53.1	Columbia CUSD 4	Columbia
18	53.1	Cook County SD 130	Blue Island
18	53.1	Oak Lawn-Hometown SD 123	Oak Lawn
18	53.1	Peotone CUSD 207u	Peotone
22	53.0	Grant CHSD 124	Fox Lake
22	53.0	Lake Villa CCSD 41	Lake Villa
24	52.9	Alton CUSD 11	Alton
24	52.9	Argo CHSD 217	Summit
24	52.9	ESD 159	Matteson
24	52.9	O Fallon CCSD 90	O Fallon
24	52.9	Roxana CUSD 1	Roxana
24	52.9	Zion ESD 6	Zion
30	52.8	Carterville CUSD 5	Carterville
30	52.8	CCSD 93	Bloomingdale
30	52.8	CHSD 218	Oak Lawn
30	52.8	Effingham CUSD 40	Effingham
30	52.8	Il Valley Central USD 321	Chillicothe
30	52.8	Wauconda CUSD 118	Wauconda
30	52.8	Yorkville CUSD 115	Yorkville
37	52.7	Morton CUSD 709	Morton
37	52.7	Prairie Central CUSD 8	Fairbury
37	52.7	Warren Twp HSD 121	Gurnee
40	52.6	CCSD 62	Des Plaines
40	52.6	Crete Monee CUSD 201u	Crete
40	52.6	Duquoin CUSD 300	Du Quoin
40	52.6	Elmwood Park CUSD 401	Elmwood Park
40	52.6	Harlem Ud 122	Machesney Park
40	52.6	Marion CUSD 2	Marion
40	52.6	Mascoutah CUD 19	Mascoutah
40	52.6	Mount Vernon SD 80	Mount Vernon
40	52.6	New Trier Twp HSD 203	Northfield
49	52.5	Alsip-Hazlgrn-Oaklwn SD 126	Alsip
49	52.5	Dolton SD 148	Riverdale
49	52.5	East Peoria SD 86	East Peoria
49	52.5	Edwardsville CUSD 7	Edwardsville
49	52.5	Fremont SD 79	Mundelein
49	52.5	Glen Ellyn SD 41	Glen Ellyn
49	52.5	Mt Zion CUSD 3	Mount Zion
49	52.5	Queen Bee SD 16	Glendale Hgts
49	52.5	Woodstock CUSD 200	Woodstock
58	52.4	Bond County CUSD 2	Greenville
58	52.4	Burbank SD 111	Burbank
58	52.4	Charleston CUSD 1	Charleston
58	52.4	Lemont Twp HSD 210	Lemont
58	52.4	Mattoon CUSD 2	Mattoon
58	52.4	Maywood-Melrose Park-Broadview 89	Melrose Park
58	52.4	Southwestern CUSD 9	Piasa
58	52.4	Twp HSD 113	Highland Park
58	52.4	Waterloo CUSD 5	Waterloo
67	52.3	Aptakisic-Tripp CCSD 102	Buffalo Grove
67	52.3	CCSD 89	Glen Ellyn
67	52.3	Chicago Heights SD 170	Chicago Heigh
67	52.3	Clinton CUSD 15	Clinton
67	52.3	Evanston Twp HSD 202	Evanston
67	52.3	Granite City CUSD 9	Granite City
67	52.3	Grayslake CHSD 127	Grayslake
67	52.3	Homer CCSD 33c	Homer Glen
67	52.3	Kirby SD 140	Tinley Park
67	52.3	Northfield Twp HSD 225	Glenview
67	52.3	Olympia CUSD 16	Stanford
67	52.3	Oregon CUSD 220	Oregon
67	52.3	Skokie SD 69	Skokie
80	52.2	Bloom Twp HSD 206	Chicago Heigh
80	52.2	Bloomington SD 87	Bloomington
80	52.2	Flossmoor SD 161	Chicago Heigh
80	52.2	Galesburg CUSD 205	Galesburg
80	52.2	Grayslake CCSD 46	Grayslake
80	52.2	Jacksonville SD 117	Jacksonville
80	52.2	Lyons SD 103	Lyons
80	52.2	Macomb CUSD 185	Macomb
80	52.2	North Chicago SD 187	North Chicago
80	52.2	Oak Lawn CHSD 229	Oak Lawn
80	52.2	Round Lake CUSD 116	Round Lake
80	52.2	Taylorville CUSD 3	Taylorville
92	52.1	Downers Grove GSD 58	Downers Grov
92	52.1	Hillsboro CUSD 3	Hillsboro
92	52.1	Joliet PSD 86	Joliet
92	52.1	Mannheim SD 83	Franklin Park
92	52.1	Midlothian SD 143	Midlothian
92	52.1	SD 45 Dupage County	Villa Park
98	52.0	CHSD 155	Crystal Lake
98	52.0	Lake Zurich CUSD 95	Lake Zurich
98	52.0	Minooka CCSD 201	Minooka
98	52.0	North Mac CUSD 34	Girard
98	52.0	Rich Twp HSD 227	Olympia Fields
98	52.0	Rochelle CCSD 231	Rochelle
98	52.0	Rochester CUSD 3a	Rochester
98	52.0	Rockton SD 140	Rockton
98	52.0	SD U-46	Elgin
98	52.0	Summit Hill SD 161	Frankfort
108	51.9	Berwyn North SD 98	Berwyn
108	51.9	Champaign CUSD 4	Champaign
108	51.9	Crystal Lake CCSD 47	Crystal Lake
108	51.9	Dupage HSD 88	Addison
108	51.9	Highland CUSD 5	Highland
108	51.9	J S Morton HSD 201	Cicero
108	51.9	Lake Forest SD 67	Lake Forest
108	51.9	Lemont-Bromberek CSD 113a	Lemont
108	51.9	Lisle CUSD 202	Lisle
108	51.9	Lyons Twp HSD 204	La Grange
108	51.9	New Lenox SD 122	New Lenox
108	51.9	Oswego CUSD 308	Oswego
108	51.9	Park Ridge CCSD 64	Park Ridge
108	51.9	Plainfield SD 202	Plainfield
108	51.9	Reed Custer CUSD 255u	Braidwood
108	51.9	Saint Charles CUSD 303	Saint Charles
108	51.9	Schaumburg CCSD 54	Schaumburg
125	51.8	Bremen CHSD 228	Midlothian
125	51.8	Community CSD 59	Arlington Hgts
125	51.8	East Maine SD 63	Des Plaines
125	51.8	Glenbard Twp HSD 87	Glen Ellyn
125	51.8	Hawthorn CCSD 73	Vernon Hills
125	51.8	Indian Springs SD 109	Justice
125	51.8	Manteno CUSD 5	Manteno
125	51.8	Sherrard CUSD 200	Sherrard
125	51.8	Tinley Park CCSD 146	Tinley Park
125	51.8	Township HSD 211	Palatine
125	51.8	Triad CUSD 2	Troy
125	51.8	Wabash CUSD 348	Mount Carmel
125	51.8	West Chicago ESD 33	West Chicago
138	51.7	Berkeley SD 87	Berkeley
138	51.7	Deerfield SD 109	Deerfield
138	51.7	Eureka CUD 140	Eureka
138	51.7	Gurnee SD 56	Gurnee

Note: This section only includes districts with 1,500 or more students; All categories are ranked from high to low

Rank	Percent	District Name	City
138	51.7	Joliet Twp HSD 204	Joliet
138	51.7	Naperville CUSD 203	Naperville
138	51.7	North Boone CUSD 200	Poplar Grove
138	51.7	Riverside SD 96	Riverside
138	51.7	Wheeling CCSD 21	Wheeling
147	51.6	Elmhurst SD 205	Elmhurst
147	51.6	Fenton CHSD 100	Bensenville
147	51.6	Frankfort CCSD 157c	Frankfort
147	51.6	La Grange SD 102	La Grange Park
147	51.6	Libertyville SD 70	Libertyville
147	51.6	Lincoln Way CHSD 210	New Lenox
147	51.6	Lombard SD 44	Lombard
147	51.6	Monticello CUSD 25	Monticello
147	51.6	Orland SD 135	Orland Park
147	51.6	Plano CUSD 88	Plano
147	51.6	Posen-Robbins ESD 143-5	Posen
147	51.6	Ridgeland SD 122	Oak Lawn
159	51.5	Berwyn South SD 100	Berwyn
159	51.5	Bradley SD 61	Bradley
159	51.5	CUSD 200	Wheaton
159	51.5	Johnsburg CUSD 12	Johnsburg
159	51.5	Mchenry CCSD 15	Mchenry
159	51.5	Niles Twp CHSD 219	Skokie
159	51.5	Oak Park - River Forest SD 200	Oak Park
159	51.5	Township HSD 214	Arlington Hgts
159	51.5	Woodland CCSD 50	Gurnee
168	51.4	Barrington CUSD 220	Barrington
168	51.4	Beardstown CUSD 15	Beardstown
168	51.4	Big Hollow SD 38	Ingleside
168	51.4	Bourbonnais SD 53	Bourbonnais
168	51.4	CUSD 300	Carpentersville
168	51.4	Dekalb CUSD 428	Dekalb
168	51.4	Dolton SD 149	Calumet City
168	51.4	Indian Prairie CUSD 204	Aurora
168	51.4	Leyden CHSD 212	Franklin Park
168	51.4	Lockport Twp HSD 205	Lockport
168	51.4	Maine Township HSD 207	Park Ridge
168	51.4	Murphysboro CUSD 186	Murphysboro
168	51.4	North Palos SD 117	Palos Hills
168	51.4	Northbrook SD 28	Northbrook
168	51.4	Palos CCSD 118	Palos Park
168	51.4	Winnetka SD 36	Winnetka
184	51.3	Batavia USD 101	Batavia
184	51.3	Bensenville SD 2	Bensenville
184	51.3	CHSD 99	Downers Grove
184	51.3	Cons HSD 230	Orland Park
184	51.3	CSD 158	Algonquin
184	51.3	Darien SD 61	Darien
184	51.3	Dunlap CUSD 323	Peoria
184	51.3	East Richland CUSD 1	Olney
184	51.3	Evanston CCSD 65	Evanston
184	51.3	Matteson ESD 162	Richton Park
184	51.3	Mclean County USD 5	Normal
184	51.3	Prairie-Hills ESD 144	Markham
184	51.3	Valley View CUSD 365u	Romeoville
197	51.2	Bellwood SD 88	Bellwood
197	51.2	Canton Union SD 66	Canton
197	51.2	Geneseo CUSD 228	Geneseo
197	51.2	Genoa Kingston CUSD 424	Genoa
197	51.2	Glenview CCSD 34	Glenview
197	51.2	North Shore SD 112	Highland Park
197	51.2	Sterling CUSD 5	Sterling
197	51.2	Vandalia CUSD 203	Vandalia
205	51.1	Aurora East USD 131	Aurora
205	51.1	Belleville Twp HSD 201	Belleville
205	51.1	Bradley Bourbonnais CHSD 307	Bradley
205	51.1	Hinsdale CCSD 181	Burr Ridge
205	51.1	Lincolnshire-Prairieview SD 103	Lincolnshire
205	51.1	Pekin CSD 303	Pekin
205	51.1	Quincy SD 172	Quincy
205	51.1	Rockford SD 205	Rockford
205	51.1	Springfield SD 186	Springfield
205	51.1	Waukegan CUSD 60	Waukegan
205	51.1	Woodridge SD 68	Woodridge
216	51.0	Belleville SD 118	Belleville
216	51.0	Cary CCSD 26	Cary
216	51.0	Kankakee SD 111	Kankakee
216	51.0	Kildeer Countryside CCSD 96	Buffalo Grove
216	51.0	Palatine CCSD 15	Palatine
216	51.0	Park Forest SD 163	Park Forest
216	51.0	Rantoul City SD 137	Rantoul
216	51.0	Reavis Twp HSD 220	Burbank
216	51.0	Thornton Fractional Twp HSD 215	Calumet City
225	50.9	Byron CUSD 226	Byron
225	50.9	Cicero SD 99	Cicero
225	50.9	Lansing SD 158	Lansing
225	50.9	Mchenry CHSD 156	Mchenry
225	50.9	Millburn CCSD 24	Old Mill Creek
225	50.9	Mokena SD 159	Mokena
225	50.9	Peoria SD 150	Peoria
225	50.9	Tolono CUSD 7	Tolono
233	50.8	Belvidere CUSD 100	Belvidere
233	50.8	CHSD 128	Vernon Hills
233	50.8	Geneva CUSD 304	Geneva
233	50.8	Harrisburg CUSD 3	Harrisburg
233	50.8	Homewood SD 153	Homewood
233	50.8	Minooka CHSD 111	Minooka
233	50.8	Proviso Twp HSD 209	Forest Park
233	50.8	Streator ESD 44	Streator
241	50.7	Arlington Hgts SD 25	Arlington Hgts
241	50.7	Cahokia CUSD 187	Cahokia
241	50.7	Freeport SD 145	Freeport
241	50.7	Jersey CUSD 100	Jerseyville
241	50.7	Rock Island SD 41	Rock Island
246	50.6	Aurora West USD 129	Aurora
246	50.6	Mundelein Cons HSD 120	Mundelein
246	50.6	Oak Park ESD 97	Oak Park
246	50.6	Robinson CUSD 2	Robinson
250	50.5	Ball Chatham CUSD 5	Chatham
250	50.5	Decatur SD 61	Decatur
250	50.5	Forest Ridge SD 142	Oak Forest
250	50.5	Kinnikinnick CCSD 131	Roscoe
250	50.5	Moline USD 40	Moline
250	50.5	Ottawa ESD 141	Ottawa
250	50.5	Summit SD 104	Summit
250	50.5	Sycamore CUSD 427	Sycamore
250	50.5	Zion-Benton Twp HSD 126	Zion
259	50.4	Addison SD 4	Addison
259	50.4	City of Chicago SD 299	Chicago
259	50.4	Lake Park CHSD 108	Roselle
259	50.4	Marquardt SD 15	Glendale Hgts
259	50.4	United Twp HSD 30	East Moline
264	50.3	Kewanee CUSD 229	Kewanee
264	50.3	Meridian CUSD 223	Stillman Valley
266	50.2	Beach Park CCSD 3	Beach Park
266	50.2	O Fallon Twp HSD 203	O Fallon
266	50.2	Steger SD 194	Steger
266	50.2	Troy CCSD 30c	Plainfield
266	50.2	Urbana SD 116	Urbana
271	50.1	Harvey SD 152	Harvey
271	50.1	Keeneyville SD 20	Hanover Park
271	50.1	Mahomet-Seymour CUSD 3	Mahomet
274	50.0	Adlai E Stevenson HSD 125	Lincolnshire
274	50.0	Monmouth-Roseville CUSD 238	Monmouth
274	50.0	Pekin PSD 108	Pekin
274	50.0	Riverton CUSD 14	Spaulding
278	49.9	Herrin CUSD 4	Herrin
278	49.9	Homewood Flossmoor CHSD 233	Flossmoor
278	49.9	Skokie SD 68	Skokie
281	49.7	Hinsdale Twp HSD 86	Hinsdale
281	49.7	Lake Forest CHSD 115	Lake Forest
283	49.6	CCSD 168	Sauk Village
284	49.5	Litchfield CUSD 12	Litchfield
284	49.5	Thornton Twp HSD 205	South Holland
286	49.4	Hononegah Chd 207	Rockton
286	49.4	Wilmette SD 39	Wilmette
288	49.3	Dixon USD 170	Dixon
288	49.3	E Saint Louis SD 189	E Saint Louis
288	49.3	Massac Ud 1	Metropolis
291	49.0	CHSD 94	West Chicago
291	49.0	Danville CCSD 118	Danville

Female Students

Rank	Percent	District Name	City
1	51.0	CHSD 94	West Chicago
1	51.0	Danville CCSD 118	Danville
3	50.7	Dixon USD 170	Dixon
3	50.7	E Saint Louis SD 189	E Saint Louis
3	50.7	Massac Ud 1	Metropolis
6	50.6	Hononegah Chd 207	Rockton
6	50.6	Wilmette SD 39	Wilmette
8	50.5	Litchfield CUSD 12	Litchfield
8	50.5	Thornton Twp HSD 205	South Holland
10	50.4	CCSD 168	Sauk Village
11	50.3	Hinsdale Twp HSD 86	Hinsdale
11	50.3	Lake Forest CHSD 115	Lake Forest
13	50.1	Herrin CUSD 4	Herrin
13	50.1	Homewood Flossmoor CHSD 233	Flossmoor
13	50.1	Skokie SD 68	Skokie
16	50.0	Adlai E Stevenson HSD 125	Lincolnshire
16	50.0	Monmouth-Roseville CUSD 238	Monmouth
16	50.0	Pekin PSD 108	Pekin
16	50.0	Riverton CUSD 14	Spaulding
20	49.9	Harvey SD 152	Harvey
20	49.9	Keeneyville SD 20	Hanover Park
20	49.9	Mahomet-Seymour CUSD 3	Mahomet
23	49.8	Beach Park CCSD 3	Beach Park
23	49.8	O Fallon Twp HSD 203	O Fallon
23	49.8	Steger SD 194	Steger
23	49.8	Troy CCSD 30c	Plainfield
23	49.8	Urbana SD 116	Urbana
28	49.7	Kewanee CUSD 229	Kewanee
28	49.7	Meridian CUSD 223	Stillman Valley
30	49.6	Addison SD 4	Addison
30	49.6	City of Chicago SD 299	Chicago
30	49.6	Lake Park CHSD 108	Roselle
30	49.6	Marquardt SD 15	Glendale Hgts
30	49.6	United Twp HSD 30	East Moline
35	49.5	Ball Chatham CUSD 5	Chatham
35	49.5	Decatur SD 61	Decatur
35	49.5	Forest Ridge SD 142	Oak Forest
35	49.5	Kinnikinnick CCSD 131	Roscoe
35	49.5	Moline USD 40	Moline
35	49.5	Ottawa ESD 141	Ottawa
35	49.5	Summit SD 104	Summit
35	49.5	Sycamore CUSD 427	Sycamore
35	49.5	Zion-Benton Twp HSD 126	Zion
44	49.4	Aurora West USD 129	Aurora
44	49.4	Mundelein Cons HSD 120	Mundelein
44	49.4	Oak Park ESD 97	Oak Park
44	49.4	Robinson CUSD 2	Robinson
48	49.3	Arlington Hgts SD 25	Arlington Hgts
48	49.3	Cahokia CUSD 187	Cahokia
48	49.3	Freeport SD 145	Freeport
48	49.3	Jersey CUSD 100	Jerseyville
48	49.3	Rock Island SD 41	Rock Island
53	49.2	Belvidere CUSD 100	Belvidere
53	49.2	CHSD 128	Vernon Hills
53	49.2	Geneva CUSD 304	Geneva
53	49.2	Harrisburg CUSD 3	Harrisburg
53	49.2	Homewood SD 153	Homewood
53	49.2	Minooka CHSD 111	Minooka
53	49.2	Proviso Twp HSD 209	Forest Park
53	49.2	Streator ESD 44	Streator
61	49.1	Byron CUSD 226	Byron
61	49.1	Cicero SD 99	Cicero
61	49.1	Lansing SD 158	Lansing
61	49.1	Mchenry CHSD 156	Mchenry
61	49.1	Millburn CCSD 24	Old Mill Creek
61	49.1	Mokena SD 159	Mokena
61	49.1	Peoria SD 150	Peoria
61	49.1	Tolono CUSD 7	Tolono
69	49.0	Belleville SD 118	Belleville
69	49.0	Cary CCSD 26	Cary
69	49.0	Kankakee SD 111	Kankakee
69	49.0	Kildeer Countryside CCSD 96	Buffalo Grove
69	49.0	Palatine CCSD 15	Palatine
69	49.0	Park Forest SD 163	Park Forest
69	49.0	Rantoul City SD 137	Rantoul
69	49.0	Reavis Twp HSD 220	Burbank
69	49.0	Thornton Fractional Twp HSD 215	Calumet City
78	48.9	Aurora East USD 131	Aurora
78	48.9	Belleville Twp HSD 201	Belleville
78	48.9	Bradley Bourbonnais CHSD 307	Bradley
78	48.9	Hinsdale CCSD 181	Burr Ridge
78	48.9	Lincolnshire-Prairieview SD 103	Lincolnshire
78	48.9	Pekin CSD 303	Pekin
78	48.9	Quincy SD 172	Quincy
78	48.9	Rockford SD 205	Rockford
78	48.9	Springfield SD 186	Springfield
78	48.9	Waukegan CUSD 60	Waukegan
78	48.9	Woodridge SD 68	Woodridge
89	48.8	Bellwood SD 88	Bellwood
89	48.8	Canton Union SD 66	Canton
89	48.8	Geneseo CUSD 228	Geneseo
89	48.8	Genoa Kingston CUSD 424	Genoa
89	48.8	Glenview CCSD 34	Glenview
89	48.8	North Shore SD 112	Highland Park
89	48.8	Sterling CUSD 5	Sterling
89	48.8	Vandalia CUSD 203	Vandalia
97	48.7	Batavia USD 101	Batavia
97	48.7	Bensenville SD 2	Bensenville
97	48.7	CHSD 99	Downers Grove
97	48.7	Cons HSD 230	Orland Park
97	48.7	CSD 158	Algonquin
97	48.7	Darien SD 61	Darien
97	48.7	Dunlap CUSD 323	Peoria

Note: This section only includes districts with 1,500 or more students; All categories are ranked from high to low

97	48.7	East Richland CUSD 1	Olney
97	48.7	Evanston CCSD 65	Evanston
97	48.7	Matteson ESD 162	Richton Park
97	48.7	Mclean County USD 5	Normal
97	48.7	Prairie-Hills ESD 144	Markham
97	48.7	Valley View CUSD 365u	Romeoville
110	48.6	Barrington CUSD 220	Barrington
110	48.6	Beardstown CUSD 15	Beardstown
110	48.6	Big Hollow SD 38	Ingleside
110	48.6	Bourbonnais SD 53	Bourbonnais
110	48.6	CUSD 300	Carpentersville
110	48.6	Dekalb CUSD 428	Dekalb
110	48.6	Dolton SD 149	Calumet City
110	48.6	Indian Prairie CUSD 204	Aurora
110	48.6	Leyden CHSD 212	Franklin Park
110	48.6	Lockport Twp HSD 205	Lockport
110	48.6	Maine Township HSD 207	Park Ridge
110	48.6	Murphysboro CUSD 186	Murphysboro
110	48.6	North Palos SD 117	Palos Hills
110	48.6	Northbrook SD 28	Northbrook
110	48.6	Palos CCSD 118	Palos Park
110	48.6	Winnetka SD 36	Winnetka
126	48.5	Berwyn South SD 100	Berwyn
126	48.5	Bradley SD 61	Bradley
126	48.5	CUSD 200	Wheaton
126	48.5	Johnsburg CUSD 12	Johnsburg
126	48.5	Mchenry CCSD 15	Mchenry
126	48.5	Niles Twp CHSD 219	Skokie
126	48.5	Oak Park - River Forest SD 200	Oak Park
126	48.5	Township HSD 214	Arlington Hgts
126	48.5	Woodland CCSD 50	Gurnee
135	48.4	Elmhurst SD 205	Elmhurst
135	48.4	Fenton CHSD 100	Bensenville
135	48.4	Frankfort CCSD 157c	Frankfort
135	48.4	La Grange SD 102	La Grange Park
135	48.4	Libertyville SD 70	Libertyville
135	48.4	Lincoln Way CHSD 210	New Lenox
135	48.4	Lombard SD 44	Lombard
135	48.4	Monticello CUSD 25	Monticello
135	48.4	Orland SD 135	Orland Park
135	48.4	Plano CUSD 88	Plano
135	48.4	Posen-Robbins ESD 143-5	Posen
135	48.4	Ridgeland SD 122	Oak Lawn
147	48.3	Berkeley SD 87	Berkeley
147	48.3	Deerfield SD 109	Deerfield
147	48.3	Eureka CUD 140	Eureka
147	48.3	Gurnee SD 56	Gurnee
147	48.3	Joliet Twp HSD 204	Joliet
147	48.3	Naperville CUSD 203	Naperville
147	48.3	North Boone CUSD 200	Poplar Grove
147	48.3	Riverside SD 96	Riverside
147	48.3	Wheeling CCSD 21	Wheeling
156	48.2	Bremen CHSD 228	Midlothian
156	48.2	Community CSD 59	Arlington Hgts
156	48.2	East Maine SD 63	Des Plaines
156	48.2	Glenbard Twp HSD 87	Glen Ellyn
156	48.2	Hawthorn CCSD 73	Vernon Hills
156	48.2	Indian Springs SD 109	Justice
156	48.2	Manteno CUSD 5	Manteno
156	48.2	Sherrard CUSD 200	Sherrard
156	48.2	Tinley Park CCSD 146	Tinley Park
156	48.2	Township HSD 211	Palatine
156	48.2	Triad CUSD 2	Troy
156	48.2	Wabash CUSD 348	Mount Carmel
156	48.2	West Chicago ESD 33	West Chicago
169	48.1	Berwyn North SD 98	Berwyn
169	48.1	Champaign CUSD 4	Champaign
169	48.1	Crystal Lake CCSD 47	Crystal Lake
169	48.1	Dupage HSD 88	Addison
169	48.1	Highland CUSD 5	Highland
169	48.1	J S Morton HSD 201	Cicero
169	48.1	Lake Forest SD 67	Lake Forest
169	48.1	Lemont-Bromberek CSD 113a	Lemont
169	48.1	Lisle CUSD 202	Lisle
169	48.1	Lyons Twp HSD 204	La Grange
169	48.1	New Lenox SD 122	New Lenox
169	48.1	Oswego CUSD 308	Oswego
169	48.1	Park Ridge CCSD 64	Park Ridge
169	48.1	Plainfield SD 202	Plainfield
169	48.1	Reed Custer CUSD 255u	Braidwood
169	48.1	Saint Charles CUSD 303	Saint Charles
169	48.1	Schaumburg CCSD 54	Schaumburg
186	48.0	CHSD 155	Crystal Lake
186	48.0	Lake Zurich CUSD 95	Lake Zurich
186	48.0	Minooka CCSD 201	Minooka
186	48.0	North Mac CUSD 34	Girard
186	48.0	Rich Twp HSD 227	Olympia Fields
186	48.0	Rochelle CCSD 231	Rochelle
186	48.0	Rochester CUSD 3a	Rochester
186	48.0	Rockton SD 140	Rockton
186	48.0	SD U-46	Elgin
186	48.0	Summit Hill SD 161	Frankfort
196	47.9	Downers Grove GSD 58	Downers Grove
196	47.9	Hillsboro CUSD 3	Hillsboro
196	47.9	Joliet PSD 86	Joliet
196	47.9	Mannheim SD 83	Franklin Park
196	47.9	Midlothian SD 143	Midlothian
196	47.9	SD 45 Dupage County	Villa Park
202	47.8	Bloom Twp HSD 206	Chicago Heights
202	47.8	Bloomington SD 87	Bloomington
202	47.8	CCSD 89	Glen Ellyn
202	47.8	Flossmoor SD 161	Chicago Heights
202	47.8	Galesburg CUSD 205	Galesburg
202	47.8	Grayslake CCSD 46	Grayslake
202	47.8	Jacksonville SD 117	Jacksonville
202	47.8	Lyons SD 103	Lyons
202	47.8	Macomb CUSD 185	Macomb
202	47.8	North Chicago SD 187	North Chicago
202	47.8	Oak Lawn CHSD 229	Oak Lawn
202	47.8	Round Lake CUSD 116	Round Lake
202	47.8	Taylorville CUSD 3	Taylorville
215	47.7	Aptakisic-Tripp CCSD 102	Buffalo Grove
215	47.7	Chicago Heights SD 170	Chicago Heights
215	47.7	Clinton CUSD 15	Clinton
215	47.7	Evanston Twp HSD 202	Evanston
215	47.7	Granite City CUSD 9	Granite City
215	47.7	Grayslake CHSD 127	Grayslake
215	47.7	Homer CCSD 33c	Homer Glen
215	47.7	Kirby SD 140	Tinley Park
215	47.7	Northfield Twp HSD 225	Glenview
215	47.7	Olympia CUSD 16	Stanford
215	47.7	Oregon CUSD 220	Oregon
215	47.7	Skokie SD 69	Skokie
227	47.6	Bond County CUSD 2	Greenville
227	47.6	Burbank SD 111	Burbank
227	47.6	Charleston CUSD 1	Charleston
227	47.6	Lemont Twp HSD 210	Lemont
227	47.6	Mattoon CUSD 2	Mattoon
227	47.6	Maywood-Melrose Park-Broadview 89	Melrose Park
227	47.6	Southwestern CUSD 9	Piasa
227	47.6	Twp HSD 113	Highland Park
227	47.6	Waterloo CUSD 5	Waterloo
236	47.5	Alsip-Hazlgrn-Oaklwn SD 126	Alsip
236	47.5	Dolton SD 148	Riverdale
236	47.5	East Peoria SD 86	East Peoria
236	47.5	Edwardsville CUSD 7	Edwardsville
236	47.5	Fremont SD 79	Mundelein
236	47.5	Glen Ellyn SD 41	Glen Ellyn
236	47.5	Mt Zion CUSD 3	Mount Zion
236	47.5	Queen Bee SD 16	Glendale Hgts
236	47.5	Woodstock CUSD 200	Woodstock
245	47.4	CCSD 62	Des Plaines
245	47.4	Crete Monee CUSD 201u	Crete
245	47.4	Duquoin CUSD 300	Du Quoin
245	47.4	Elmwood Park CUSD 401	Elmwood Park
245	47.4	Harlem Ud 122	Machesney Park
245	47.4	Marion CUSD 2	Marion
245	47.4	Mascoutah CUD 19	Mascoutah
245	47.4	Mount Vernon SD 80	Mount Vernon
245	47.4	New Trier Twp HSD 203	Northfield
254	47.3	Morton CUSD 709	Morton
254	47.3	Prairie Central CUSD 8	Fairbury
254	47.3	Warren Twp HSD 121	Gurnee
257	47.2	Carterville CUSD 5	Carterville
257	47.2	CCSD 93	Bloomingdale
257	47.2	CHSD 218	Oak Lawn
257	47.2	Effingham CUSD 40	Effingham
257	47.2	Il Valley Central USD 321	Chillicothe
257	47.2	Wauconda CUSD 118	Wauconda
257	47.2	Yorkville CUSD 115	Yorkville
264	47.1	Alton CUSD 11	Alton
264	47.1	Argo CHSD 217	Summit
264	47.1	ESD 159	Matteson
264	47.1	O Fallon CCSD 90	O Fallon
264	47.1	Roxana CUSD 1	Roxana
264	47.1	Zion ESD 6	Zion
270	47.0	Grant CHSD 124	Fox Lake
270	47.0	Lake Villa CCSD 41	Lake Villa
272	46.9	Columbia CUSD 4	Columbia
272	46.9	Cook County SD 130	Blue Island
272	46.9	Oak Lawn-Hometown SD 123	Oak Lawn
272	46.9	Peotone CUSD 207u	Peotone
276	46.8	Harvard CUSD 50	Harvard
276	46.8	Winnebago CUSD 323	Winnebago
278	46.7	Bethalto CUSD 8	Bethalto
278	46.7	Kaneland CUSD 302	Maple Park
278	46.7	Will County SD 92	Lockport
281	46.6	Evergreen Park ESD 124	Evergreen Park
281	46.6	Frankfort CUSD 168	West Frankfort
281	46.6	Herscher CUSD 2	Herscher
284	46.5	Coal City CUSD 1	Coal City
284	46.5	East Moline SD 37	East Moline
284	46.5	Mount Prospect SD 57	Mount Prospect
287	46.3	CHSD 117	Lake Villa
288	46.2	Mundelein ESD 75	Mundelein
289	46.0	Antioch CCSD 34	Antioch
289	46.0	Collinsville CUSD 10	Collinsville
291	45.9	Central CUSD 301	Burlington
292	45.3	Sandwich CUSD 430	Sandwich

Individual Education Program Students

Rank	Percent	District Name	City
1	22.5	Springfield SD 186	Springfield
2	22.1	Charleston CUSD 1	Charleston
3	22.0	Alton CUSD 11	Alton
4	21.6	Cahokia CUSD 187	Cahokia
5	20.8	Riverton CUSD 14	Spaulding
6	20.5	Thornton Twp HSD 205	South Holland
7	20.2	Belleville SD 118	Belleville
8	20.1	Maine Township HSD 207	Park Ridge
8	20.1	North Mac CUSD 34	Girard
10	20.0	Cary CCSD 26	Cary
10	20.0	Highland CUSD 5	Highland
12	19.9	Belleville Twp HSD 201	Belleville
13	19.8	Murphysboro CUSD 186	Murphysboro
13	19.8	Streator ESD 44	Streator
15	19.7	Jacksonville SD 117	Jacksonville
15	19.7	Urbana SD 116	Urbana
17	19.5	Evergreen Park ESD 124	Evergreen Park
17	19.5	Granite City CUSD 9	Granite City
19	19.3	Prairie Central CUSD 8	Fairbury
20	19.2	Frankfort CUSD 168	West Frankfort
20	19.2	Pekin PSD 108	Pekin
22	19.1	Elmwood Park CUSD 401	Elmwood Park
22	19.1	Riverside SD 96	Riverside
24	19.0	Proviso Twp HSD 209	Forest Park
25	18.9	Effingham CUSD 40	Effingham
25	18.9	Park Forest SD 163	Park Forest
27	18.8	Bloom Twp HSD 206	Chicago Heights
28	18.7	Peoria SD 150	Peoria
29	18.4	CCSD 168	Sauk Village
29	18.4	Crete Monee CUSD 201u	Crete
29	18.4	Sterling CUSD 5	Sterling
32	18.3	Clinton CUSD 15	Clinton
32	18.3	East Peoria SD 86	East Peoria
34	18.2	Lisle CUSD 202	Lisle
35	18.1	Joliet Twp HSD 204	Joliet
36	18.0	Beardstown CUSD 15	Beardstown
36	18.0	Harrisburg CUSD 3	Harrisburg
38	17.9	Duquoin CUSD 300	Du Quoin
38	17.9	Ottawa ESD 141	Ottawa
40	17.7	Collinsville CUSD 10	Collinsville
40	17.7	Macomb CUSD 185	Macomb
40	17.7	Mundelein ESD 75	Mundelein
40	17.7	Quincy SD 172	Quincy
40	17.7	Wabash CUSD 348	Mount Carmel
45	17.6	Kewanee CUSD 229	Kewanee
45	17.6	Rich Twp HSD 227	Olympia Fields
47	17.3	Alsip-Hazlgrn-Oaklwn SD 126	Alsip
47	17.3	Decatur SD 61	Decatur
47	17.3	Mount Vernon SD 80	Mount Vernon
47	17.3	Rantoul City SD 137	Rantoul
47	17.3	Vandalia CUSD 203	Vandalia
52	17.2	Beach Park CCSD 3	Beach Park
53	17.1	Mchenry CCSD 15	Mchenry
53	17.1	O Fallon CCSD 90	O Fallon
53	17.1	Orland SD 135	Orland Park
56	16.9	Canton Union SD 66	Canton
56	16.9	CCSD 62	Des Plaines
56	16.9	Lansing SD 158	Lansing
56	16.9	Marion CUSD 2	Marion
56	16.9	Mattoon CUSD 2	Mattoon
56	16.9	Midlothian SD 143	Midlothian
62	16.8	Tinley Park CCSD 146	Tinley Park
63	16.7	Bond County CUSD 2	Greenville
63	16.7	Herrin CUSD 4	Herrin
63	16.7	Lake Forest CHSD 115	Lake Forest

Note: This section only includes districts with 1,500 or more students; All categories are ranked from high to low

63	16.7	North Chicago SD 187	North Chicago
63	16.7	Ridgeland SD 122	Oak Lawn
68	16.6	Bremen CHSD 228	Midlothian
68	16.6	Oak Park - River Forest SD 200	Oak Park
68	16.6	Robinson CUSD 2	Robinson
71	16.5	Taylorville CUSD 3	Taylorville
72	16.4	Dixon USD 170	Dixon
72	16.4	Mundelein Cons HSD 120	Mundelein
74	16.3	Berwyn North SD 98	Berwyn
74	16.3	Bradley SD 61	Bradley
74	16.3	Carterville CUSD 5	Carterville
74	16.3	Olympia CUSD 16	Stanford
74	16.3	Skokie SD 68	Skokie
74	16.3	Woodridge SD 68	Woodridge
80	16.2	Gurnee SD 56	Gurnee
80	16.2	Lyons SD 103	Lyons
82	16.1	East Moline SD 37	East Moline
82	16.1	Homewood SD 153	Homewood
82	16.1	New Trier Twp HSD 203	Northfield
82	16.1	Oak Lawn-Hometown SD 123	Oak Lawn
82	16.1	Palos CCSD 118	Palos Park
87	16.0	Big Hollow SD 38	Ingleside
87	16.0	CUSD 200	Wheaton
87	16.0	Prairie-Hills ESD 144	Markham
90	15.9	Bethalto CUSD 8	Bethalto
90	15.9	Il Valley Central USD 321	Chillicothe
90	15.9	Jersey CUSD 100	Jerseyville
90	15.9	Park Ridge CCSD 64	Park Ridge
90	15.9	SD 45 Dupage County	Villa Park
95	15.8	Evanston Twp HSD 202	Evanston
95	15.8	Lake Villa CCSD 41	Lake Villa
97	15.7	Arlington Hgts SD 25	Arlington Hgts
97	15.7	Bradley Bourbonnais CHSD 307	Bradley
97	15.7	Grayslake CCSD 46	Grayslake
97	15.7	Kankakee SD 111	Kankakee
97	15.7	Leyden CHSD 212	Franklin Park
97	15.7	North Shore SD 112	Highland Park
97	15.7	Twp HSD 113	Highland Park
104	15.6	Cook County SD 130	Blue Island
104	15.6	Homer CCSD 33c	Homer Glen
104	15.6	Kinnikinnick CCSD 131	Roscoe
104	15.6	Plano CUSD 88	Plano
104	15.6	Round Lake CUSD 116	Round Lake
109	15.5	Bloomington SD 87	Bloomington
109	15.5	Keeneyville SD 20	Hanover Park
109	15.5	Oak Park ESD 97	Oak Park
109	15.5	Southwestern CUSD 9	Piasa
113	15.4	Barrington CUSD 220	Barrington
113	15.4	Litchfield CUSD 12	Litchfield
113	15.4	Triad CUSD 2	Troy
116	15.3	Lake Zurich CUSD 95	Lake Zurich
116	15.3	Pekin CSD 303	Pekin
116	15.3	Rochelle CCSD 231	Rochelle
116	15.3	Sandwich CUSD 430	Sandwich
120	15.2	CCSD 93	Bloomingdale
120	15.2	Champaign CUSD 4	Champaign
120	15.2	Rockford SD 205	Rockford
123	15.1	Galesburg CUSD 205	Galesburg
123	15.1	Matteson ESD 162	Richton Park
125	15.0	Addison SD 4	Addison
125	15.0	Hillsboro CUSD 3	Hillsboro
125	15.0	Mokena SD 159	Mokena
125	15.0	Reed Custer CUSD 255u	Braidwood
125	15.0	Roxana CUSD 1	Roxana
130	14.9	North Boone CUSD 200	Poplar Grove
130	14.9	Thornton Fractional Twp HSD 215	Calumet City
132	14.8	Grant CHSD 124	Fox Lake
132	14.8	Harlem Ud 122	Machesney Park
132	14.8	Joliet PSD 86	Joliet
132	14.8	Manteno CUSD 5	Manteno
136	14.7	Byron CUSD 226	Byron
136	14.7	Darien SD 61	Darien
136	14.7	ESD 159	Matteson
136	14.7	Geneva CUSD 304	Geneva
136	14.7	La Grange SD 102	La Grange Park
136	14.7	Mascoutah CUD 19	Mascoutah
136	14.7	Niles Twp CHSD 219	Skokie
136	14.7	Zion-Benton Twp HSD 126	Zion
144	14.6	Belvidere CUSD 100	Belvidere
144	14.6	Elmhurst SD 205	Elmhurst
144	14.6	Lockport Twp HSD 205	Lockport
144	14.6	Mannheim SD 83	Franklin Park
144	14.6	Maywood-Melrose Park-Broadview 89	Melrose Park
144	14.6	Mclean County USD 5	Normal
144	14.6	Rock Island SD 41	Rock Island
144	14.6	Saint Charles CUSD 303	Saint Charles
144	14.6	Winnetka SD 36	Winnetka
153	14.5	Chicago Heights SD 170	Chicago Heights
153	14.5	Glenview CCSD 34	Glenview
155	14.4	Dupage HSD 88	Addison
155	14.4	East Richland CUSD 1	Olney
157	14.3	CHSD 218	Oak Lawn
157	14.3	Cons HSD 230	Orland Park
157	14.3	Downers Grove GSD 58	Downers Grove
157	14.3	Morton CUSD 709	Morton
161	14.2	Burbank SD 111	Burbank
161	14.2	Danville CCSD 118	Danville
161	14.2	Dekalb CUSD 428	Dekalb
161	14.2	Kirby SD 140	Tinley Park
161	14.2	Massac Ud 1	Metropolis
161	14.2	Mchenry CHSD 156	Mchenry
167	14.1	CUSD 300	Carpentersville
167	14.1	E Saint Louis SD 189	E Saint Louis
167	14.1	Valley View CUSD 365u	Romeoville
167	14.1	Winnebago CUSD 323	Winnebago
167	14.1	Woodland CCSD 50	Gurnee
172	14.0	CHSD 99	Downers Grove
172	14.0	Community CSD 59	Arlington Hgts
172	14.0	Summit Hill SD 161	Frankfort
172	14.0	United Twp HSD 30	East Moline
172	14.0	Zion ESD 6	Zion
177	13.9	Aurora East USD 131	Aurora
177	13.9	Forest Ridge SD 142	Oak Forest
177	13.9	Freeport SD 145	Freeport
177	13.9	Hawthorn CCSD 73	Vernon Hills
177	13.9	Monticello CUSD 25	Monticello
182	13.8	CSD 158	Algonquin
182	13.8	Fenton CHSD 100	Bensenville
182	13.8	Kildeer Countryside CCSD 96	Buffalo Grove
182	13.8	Woodstock CUSD 200	Woodstock
186	13.7	Herscher CUSD 2	Herscher
186	13.7	Peotone CUSD 207u	Peotone
186	13.7	Rochester CUSD 3a	Rochester
186	13.7	Tolono CUSD 7	Tolono
186	13.7	Wauconda CUSD 118	Wauconda
191	13.6	East Maine SD 63	Des Plaines
191	13.6	Lake Forest SD 67	Lake Forest
191	13.6	Oregon CUSD 220	Oregon
194	13.5	Argo CHSD 217	Summit
194	13.5	Yorkville CUSD 115	Yorkville
196	13.4	Eureka CUD 140	Eureka
196	13.4	Frankfort CCSD 157c	Frankfort
196	13.4	J S Morton HSD 201	Cicero
196	13.4	Lombard SD 44	Lombard
196	13.4	Minooka CCSD 201	Minooka
196	13.4	Waterloo CUSD 5	Waterloo
202	13.3	Glenbard Twp HSD 87	Glen Ellyn
202	13.3	Summit SD 104	Summit
204	13.2	Bourbonnais SD 53	Bourbonnais
204	13.2	Evanston CCSD 65	Evanston
204	13.2	Oswego CUSD 308	Oswego
207	13.1	New Lenox SD 122	New Lenox
207	13.1	North Palos SD 117	Palos Hills
207	13.1	Wilmette SD 39	Wilmette
210	13.0	Berkeley SD 87	Berkeley
210	13.0	Deerfield SD 109	Deerfield
210	13.0	Homewood Flossmoor CHSD 233	Flossmoor
210	13.0	Monmouth-Roseville CUSD 238	Monmouth
214	12.9	CHSD 117	Lake Villa
214	12.9	Fremont SD 79	Mundelein
214	12.9	Indian Springs SD 109	Justice
214	12.9	Lincolnshire-Prairieview SD 103	Lincolnshire
214	12.9	Plainfield SD 202	Plainfield
214	12.9	Steger SD 194	Steger
214	12.9	Township HSD 214	Arlington Hgts
221	12.8	Palatine CCSD 15	Palatine
221	12.8	Rockton SD 140	Rockton
223	12.7	Harvard CUSD 50	Harvard
223	12.7	Moline USD 40	Moline
223	12.7	SD U-46	Elgin
226	12.6	Aurora West USD 129	Aurora
226	12.6	Berwyn South SD 100	Berwyn
226	12.6	CCSD 89	Glen Ellyn
226	12.6	Coal City CUSD 1	Coal City
226	12.6	Millburn CCSD 24	Old Mill Creek
226	12.6	O Fallon Twp HSD 203	O Fallon
226	12.6	West Chicago ESD 33	West Chicago
226	12.6	Will County SD 92	Lockport
234	12.5	Aptakisic-Tripp CCSD 102	Buffalo Grove
234	12.5	Central CUSD 301	Burlington
234	12.5	City of Chicago SD 299	Chicago
234	12.5	Hinsdale CCSD 181	Burr Ridge
234	12.5	Mount Prospect SD 57	Mount Prospect
234	12.5	Reavis Twp HSD 220	Burbank
240	12.4	CHSD 155	Crystal Lake
240	12.4	Dolton SD 148	Riverdale
240	12.4	Kaneland CUSD 302	Maple Park
240	12.4	Skokie SD 69	Skokie
244	12.2	CHSD 94	West Chicago
244	12.2	Dolton SD 149	Calumet City
244	12.2	Dunlap CUSD 323	Peoria
244	12.2	Oak Lawn CHSD 229	Oak Lawn
244	12.2	Township HSD 211	Palatine
249	12.1	Crystal Lake CCSD 47	Crystal Lake
249	12.1	Grayslake CHSD 127	Grayslake
249	12.1	Johnsburg CUSD 12	Johnsburg
249	12.1	Waukegan CUSD 60	Waukegan
253	12.0	Hononegah Chd 207	Rockton
253	12.0	Sherrard CUSD 200	Sherrard
255	11.9	Lake Park CHSD 108	Roselle
256	11.8	Adlai E Stevenson HSD 125	Lincolnshire
256	11.8	Antioch CCSD 34	Antioch
256	11.8	Meridian CUSD 223	Stillman Valley
256	11.8	Northbrook SD 28	Northbrook
256	11.8	Northfield Twp HSD 225	Glenview
256	11.8	Troy CCSD 30c	Plainfield
262	11.7	Batavia USD 101	Batavia
262	11.7	Lincoln Way CHSD 210	New Lenox
264	11.6	Cicero SD 99	Cicero
264	11.6	Lyons Twp HSD 204	La Grange
264	11.6	Minooka CHSD 111	Minooka
267	11.5	Ball Chatham CUSD 5	Chatham
267	11.5	Flossmoor SD 161	Chicago Heights
269	11.4	Bellwood SD 88	Bellwood
270	11.3	Mahomet-Seymour CUSD 3	Mahomet
270	11.3	Schaumburg CCSD 54	Schaumburg
270	11.3	Warren Twp HSD 121	Gurnee
273	11.2	Queen Bee SD 16	Glendale Hgts
274	11.0	Glen Ellyn SD 41	Glen Ellyn
274	11.0	Sycamore CUSD 427	Sycamore
276	10.9	Harvey SD 152	Harvey
277	10.7	Hinsdale Twp HSD 86	Hinsdale
278	10.6	Geneseo CUSD 228	Geneseo
279	10.5	Mt Zion CUSD 3	Mount Zion
280	10.3	CHSD 128	Vernon Hills
280	10.3	Naperville CUSD 203	Naperville
282	10.1	Bensenville SD 2	Bensenville
282	10.1	Indian Prairie CUSD 204	Aurora
282	10.1	Wheeling CCSD 21	Wheeling
285	9.9	Lemont-Bromberek CSD 113a	Lemont
285	9.9	Posen-Robbins ESD 143-5	Posen
287	9.5	Edwardsville CUSD 7	Edwardsville
288	9.4	Genoa Kingston CUSD 424	Genoa
289	9.0	Columbia CUSD 4	Columbia
290	8.0	Lemont Twp HSD 210	Lemont
291	7.9	Libertyville SD 70	Libertyville
292	6.7	Marquardt SD 15	Glendale Hgts

English Language Learner Students

Rank	Percent	District Name	City
1	51.1	Cicero SD 99	Cicero
2	48.3	West Chicago ESD 33	West Chicago
3	34.5	Wheeling CCSD 21	Wheeling
4	32.7	Aurora East USD 131	Aurora
5	31.9	East Maine SD 63	Des Plaines
6	31.2	Mannheim SD 83	Franklin Park
7	31.0	Community CSD 59	Arlington Hgts
8	30.8	Bensenville SD 2	Bensenville
9	30.6	Queen Bee SD 16	Glendale Hgts
10	29.3	Addison SD 4	Addison
11	29.0	CCSD 62	Des Plaines
12	28.8	Berkeley SD 87	Berkeley
13	28.7	Summit SD 104	Summit
14	27.7	Waukegan CUSD 60	Waukegan
15	26.9	Maywood-Melrose Park-Broadview 89	Melrose Park
16	26.0	Round Lake CUSD 116	Round Lake
17	25.8	Harvard CUSD 50	Harvard
18	25.4	Beardstown CUSD 15	Beardstown
19	24.9	Burbank SD 111	Burbank
20	24.8	Marquardt SD 15	Glendale Hgts
21	24.4	Berwyn South SD 100	Berwyn
22	23.2	Posen-Robbins ESD 143-5	Posen
23	22.9	North Chicago SD 187	North Chicago
24	22.5	Bellwood SD 88	Bellwood
24	22.5	Cook County SD 130	Blue Island
26	22.3	Mundelein ESD 75	Mundelein
27	21.7	Berwyn North SD 98	Berwyn

Note: This section only includes districts with 1,500 or more students; All categories are ranked from high to low

Rank		District	City	Rank		District	City	Rank		District	City
28	20.0	Rochelle CCSD 231	Rochelle	114	4.7	Elmhurst SD 205	Elmhurst	197	1.1	Grant CHSD 124	Fox Lake
29	19.7	Ridgeland SD 122	Oak Lawn	114	4.7	Township HSD 214	Arlington Hgts	201	1.0	Frankfort CCSD 157c	Frankfort
30	19.3	Palatine CCSD 15	Palatine	116	4.6	Argo CHSD 217	Summit	201	1.0	Homer CCSD 33c	Homer Glen
31	19.0	Indian Springs SD 109	Justice	117	4.5	Bloomington SD 87	Bloomington	203	0.9	East Peoria SD 86	East Peoria
32	18.8	SD 45 Dupage County	Villa Park	118	4.4	Dunlap CUSD 323	Peoria	203	0.9	Effingham CUSD 40	Effingham
33	18.7	SD U-46	Elgin	119	4.3	Mount Prospect SD 57	Mount Prospect	203	0.9	Lemont Twp HSD 210	Lemont
34	18.6	North Palos SD 117	Palos Hills	120	4.2	Palos CUSD 118	Palos Park	206	0.8	CHSD 155	Crystal Lake
35	18.3	Joliet PSD 86	Joliet	121	4.1	Northbrook SD 28	Northbrook	206	0.8	Minooka CHSD 111	Minooka
36	18.0	Woodridge SD 68	Woodridge	121	4.1	Orland SD 135	Orland Park	206	0.8	Rochester CUSD 3a	Rochester
37	17.9	Chicago Heights SD 170	Chicago Heights	121	4.1	Peoria SD 150	Peoria	206	0.8	Thornton Fractional Twp HSD 215	Calumet City
37	17.9	Lyons SD 103	Lyons	124	4.0	Lansing SD 158	Lansing	210	0.7	Bradley Bourbonnais CHSD 307	Bradley
39	17.3	Hawthorn CCSD 73	Vernon Hills	125	3.9	Downers Grove GSD 58	Downers Grove	210	0.7	Decatur SD 61	Decatur
40	17.2	Keeneyville SD 20	Hanover Park	125	3.9	La Grange SD 102	La Grange Park	210	0.7	Il Valley Central USD 321	Chillicothe
41	16.9	Skokie SD 69	Skokie	125	3.9	Leyden CHSD 212	Franklin Park	210	0.7	Jacksonville SD 117	Jacksonville
42	16.3	Plano CUSD 88	Plano	125	3.9	Meridian CUSD 223	Stillman Valley	210	0.7	Lake Park CHSD 108	Roselle
43	16.2	CCSD 93	Bloomingdale	129	3.8	CHSD 218	Oak Lawn	210	0.7	Manteno CUSD 5	Manteno
44	16.0	Schaumburg CCSD 54	Schaumburg	129	3.8	Dupage HSD 88	Addison	210	0.7	Springfield SD 186	Springfield
45	15.8	Zion ESD 6	Zion	129	3.8	Lake Zurich CUSD 95	Lake Zurich	217	0.6	Bethalto CUSD 8	Bethalto
46	14.9	Skokie SD 68	Skokie	132	3.7	Mundelein Cons HSD 120	Mundelein	217	0.6	Carterville CUSD 5	Carterville
47	14.7	Aptakisic-Tripp CCSD 102	Buffalo Grove	133	3.6	Naperville CUSD 203	Naperville	217	0.6	Edwardsville CUSD 7	Edwardsville
48	14.6	Aurora West USD 129	Aurora	134	3.5	Glenbard Twp HSD 87	Glen Ellyn	217	0.6	Kinnikinnick CCSD 131	Roscoe
49	13.3	City of Chicago SD 299	Chicago	134	3.5	Oswego CUSD 308	Oswego	217	0.6	Marion CUSD 2	Marion
49	13.3	North Shore SD 112	Highland Park	134	3.5	Township HSD 211	Palatine	217	0.6	Midlothian SD 143	Midlothian
51	12.9	East Moline SD 37	East Moline	137	3.4	Lisle CUSD 202	Lisle	217	0.6	Morton CUSD 709	Morton
52	12.7	Glenview CCSD 34	Glenview	138	3.3	Joliet Twp HSD 204	Joliet	217	0.6	New Trier Twp HSD 203	Northfield
53	12.4	Beach Park CCSD 3	Beach Park	138	3.3	Oak Lawn CHSD 229	Oak Lawn	217	0.6	Winnetka SD 36	Winnetka
53	12.4	Valley View CUSD 365u	Romeoville	138	3.3	Winnebago CUSD 323	Winnebago	226	0.5	Charleston CUSD 1	Charleston
55	12.3	Alsip-Hazlgrn-Oaklwn SD 126	Alsip	141	3.2	Batavia USD 101	Batavia	226	0.5	Clinton CUSD 15	Clinton
56	12.1	Woodland CCSD 50	Gurnee	141	3.2	Park Ridge CCSD 64	Park Ridge	226	0.5	E Saint Louis SD 189	E Saint Louis
57	12.0	CUSD 300	Carpentersville	141	3.2	Saint Charles CUSD 303	Saint Charles	226	0.5	Highland CUSD 5	Highland
58	11.9	Gurnee SD 56	Gurnee	141	3.2	Yorkville CUSD 115	Yorkville	226	0.5	Lincoln Way CHSD 210	New Lenox
59	11.7	Darien SD 61	Darien	145	3.1	CCSD 168	Sauk Village	231	0.4	Byron CUSD 226	Byron
60	11.2	Woodstock CUSD 200	Woodstock	145	3.1	Harlem Ud 122	Machesney Park	231	0.4	CHSD 128	Vernon Hills
61	11.0	Rantoul City SD 137	Rantoul	147	3.0	Minooka CCSD 201	Minooka	231	0.4	Homewood SD 153	Homewood
62	10.9	Proviso Twp HSD 209	Forest Park	148	2.9	Antioch CCSD 34	Antioch	231	0.4	Lake Forest SD 67	Lake Forest
63	10.8	Grayslake CCSD 46	Grayslake	148	2.9	Bloom Twp HSD 206	Chicago Heights	231	0.4	Mascoutah CUD 19	Mascoutah
64	10.7	Glen Ellyn SD 41	Glen Ellyn	148	2.9	Kirby SD 140	Tinley Park	231	0.4	New Lenox SD 122	New Lenox
64	10.7	Mchenry CCSD 15	Mchenry	151	2.8	Sycamore CUSD 427	Sycamore	231	0.4	Park Forest SD 163	Park Forest
66	10.5	Rockford SD 205	Rockford	152	2.7	Danville CCSD 118	Danville	231	0.4	Southwestern CUSD 9	Piasa
67	10.4	Belvidere CUSD 100	Belvidere	152	2.7	Mclean County USD 5	Normal	231	0.4	Triad CUSD 2	Troy
67	10.4	Elmwood Park CUSD 401	Elmwood Park	152	2.7	Prairie-Hills ESD 144	Markham	240	0.3	Alton CUSD 11	Alton
69	10.2	Evanston CCSD 65	Evanston	155	2.6	Flossmoor SD 161	Chicago Heights	240	0.3	Ball Chatham CUSD 5	Chatham
70	9.7	J S Morton HSD 201	Cicero	156	2.5	Grayslake CHSD 127	Grayslake	240	0.3	Belleville Twp HSD 201	Belleville
71	9.6	Kildeer Countryside CCSD 96	Buffalo Grove	156	2.5	Sandwich CUSD 430	Sandwich	240	0.3	Bond County CUSD 2	Greenville
72	9.4	Wauconda CUSD 118	Wauconda	156	2.5	Will County SD 92	Lockport	240	0.3	Canton Union SD 66	Canton
73	9.3	Fremont SD 79	Mundelein	159	2.3	CSD 158	Algonquin	240	0.3	Litchfield CUSD 12	Litchfield
73	9.3	Lombard SD 44	Lombard	159	2.3	Mokena SD 159	Mokena	240	0.3	Mahomet-Seymour CUSD 3	Mahomet
75	8.5	Cary CCSD 26	Cary	159	2.3	Northfield Twp HSD 225	Glenview	240	0.3	Mattoon CUSD 2	Mattoon
75	8.5	Kankakee SD 111	Kankakee	159	2.3	Summit Hill SD 161	Frankfort	240	0.3	Mount Vernon SD 80	Mount Vernon
77	8.3	Rock Island SD 41	Rock Island	163	2.2	Evanston Twp HSD 202	Evanston	240	0.3	Rich Twp HSD 227	Olympia Fields
77	8.3	Tinley Park CCSD 146	Tinley Park	163	2.2	Galesburg CUSD 205	Galesburg	240	0.3	Tolono CUSD 7	Tolono
79	8.1	CUSD 200	Wheaton	163	2.2	Kaneland CUSD 302	Maple Park	251	0.2	Hononegah Chd 207	Rockton
80	8.0	Moline USD 40	Moline	166	2.1	Wilmette SD 39	Wilmette	251	0.2	Monticello CUSD 25	Monticello
80	8.0	Urbana SD 116	Urbana	167	2.0	Ottawa ESD 141	Ottawa	251	0.2	Oak Park - River Forest SD 200	Oak Park
82	7.6	Dekalb CUSD 428	Dekalb	167	2.0	Warren Twp HSD 121	Gurnee	251	0.2	Olympia CUSD 16	Stanford
83	7.5	North Boone CUSD 200	Poplar Grove	167	2.0	Zion-Benton Twp HSD 126	Zion	251	0.2	Pekin PSD 108	Pekin
84	7.4	CHSD 94	West Chicago	170	1.9	Freeport SD 145	Freeport	251	0.2	Quincy SD 172	Quincy
85	7.1	Oak Lawn-Hometown SD 123	Oak Lawn	170	1.9	Granite City CUSD 9	Granite City	251	0.2	Roxana CUSD 1	Roxana
86	7.0	Forest Ridge SD 142	Oak Forest	170	1.9	Millburn CCSD 24	Old Mill Creek	258	0.1	Cahokia CUSD 187	Cahokia
86	7.0	Monmouth-Roseville CUSD 238	Monmouth	173	1.8	Macomb CUSD 185	Macomb	258	0.1	Coal City CUSD 1	Coal City
88	6.9	Steger SD 194	Steger	174	1.7	Bremen CHSD 228	Midlothian	258	0.1	Columbia CUSD 4	Columbia
89	6.7	Crystal Lake CCSD 47	Crystal Lake	174	1.7	Cons HSD 230	Orland Park	258	0.1	Dolton SD 149	Calumet City
89	6.7	Lemont-Bromberek CSD 113a	Lemont	174	1.7	Harvey SD 152	Harvey	258	0.1	Duquoin CUSD 300	Du Quoin
91	6.6	Bradley SD 61	Bradley	174	1.7	Twp HSD 113	Highland Park	258	0.1	Hillsboro CUSD 3	Hillsboro
92	6.5	CCSD 89	Glen Ellyn	178	1.6	Adlai E Stevenson HSD 125	Lincolnshire	258	0.1	O Fallon CCSD 90	O Fallon
93	6.4	Lake Villa CCSD 41	Lake Villa	178	1.6	Hinsdale CCSD 181	Burr Ridge	258	0.1	O Fallon Twp HSD 203	O Fallon
93	6.4	Reavis Twp HSD 220	Burbank	178	1.6	Oregon CUSD 220	Oregon	258	0.1	Peotone CUSD 207u	Peotone
95	6.3	Lincolnshire-Prairieview SD 103	Lincolnshire	178	1.6	Thornton Twp HSD 205	South Holland	258	0.1	Riverton CUSD 14	Spaulding
95	6.3	Plainfield SD 202	Plainfield	182	1.5	Mchenry CHSD 156	Mchenry	258	0.1	Wabash CUSD 348	Mount Carmel
97	6.2	Arlington Hgts SD 25	Arlington Hgts	182	1.5	Oak Park ESD 97	Oak Park	269	0.0	Belleville SD 118	Belleville
98	6.1	Kewanee CUSD 229	Kewanee	182	1.5	United Twp HSD 30	East Moline	269	0.0	CHSD 117	Lake Villa
99	6.0	Barrington CUSD 220	Barrington	185	1.4	CHSD 99	Downers Grove	269	0.0	East Richland CUSD 1	Olney
99	6.0	Big Hollow SD 38	Ingleside	185	1.4	Crete Monee CUSD 201u	Crete	269	0.0	Eureka CUD 140	Eureka
99	6.0	Fenton CHSD 100	Bensenville	185	1.4	ESD 159	Matteson	269	0.0	Frankfort CUSD 168	West Frankfort
99	6.0	Troy CCSD 30c	Plainfield	185	1.4	Hinsdale Twp HSD 86	Hinsdale	269	0.0	Geneseo CUSD 228	Geneseo
103	5.8	Collinsville CUSD 10	Collinsville	185	1.4	Murphysboro CUSD 186	Murphysboro	269	0.0	Harrisburg CUSD 3	Harrisburg
104	5.7	Champaign CUSD 4	Champaign	185	1.4	Rockton SD 140	Rockton	269	0.0	Herrin CUSD 4	Herrin
105	5.5	Evergreen Park ESD 124	Evergreen Park	191	1.3	Libertyville SD 70	Libertyville	269	0.0	Herscher CUSD 2	Herscher
106	5.3	Riverside SD 96	Riverside	191	1.3	Lockport Twp HSD 205	Lockport	269	0.0	Homewood Flossmoor CHSD 233	Flossmoor
107	5.2	Niles Twp CHSD 219	Skokie	191	1.3	Lyons Twp HSD 204	La Grange	269	0.0	Jersey CUSD 100	Jerseyville
108	5.1	Genoa Kingston CUSD 424	Genoa	191	1.3	Matteson ESD 162	Richton Park	269	0.0	Johnsburg CUSD 12	Johnsburg
108	5.1	Maine Township HSD 207	Park Ridge	195	1.2	Dixon USD 170	Dixon	269	0.0	Lake Forest CHSD 115	Lake Forest
108	5.1	Sterling CUSD 5	Sterling	195	1.2	Geneva CUSD 304	Geneva	269	0.0	Massac Ud 1	Metropolis
108	5.1	Streator ESD 44	Streator	197	1.1	Bourbonnais SD 53	Bourbonnais	269	0.0	Mt Zion CUSD 3	Mount Zion
112	5.0	Central CUSD 301	Burlington	197	1.1	Deerfield SD 109	Deerfield	269	0.0	North Mac CUSD 34	Girard
112	5.0	Indian Prairie CUSD 204	Aurora	197	1.1	Dolton SD 148	Riverdale	269	0.0	Pekin CSD 303	Pekin

Note: This section only includes districts with 1,500 or more students; All categories are ranked from high to low

Rank	Percent	District Name	City
269	0.0	Prairie Central CUSD 8	Fairbury
269	0.0	Reed Custer CUSD 255u	Braidwood
269	0.0	Robinson CUSD 2	Robinson
269	0.0	Sherrard CUSD 200	Sherrard
269	0.0	Taylorville CUSD 3	Taylorville
269	0.0	Vandalia CUSD 203	Vandalia
269	0.0	Waterloo CUSD 5	Waterloo

Students Eligible for Free Lunch

Rank	Percent	District Name	City
1	58.1	E Saint Louis SD 189	E Saint Louis
2	54.0	Cahokia CUSD 187	Cahokia
3	47.3	Mount Vernon SD 80	Mount Vernon
4	47.1	Danville CCSD 118	Danville
5	46.6	Harvey SD 152	Harvey
6	46.4	Dolton SD 148	Riverdale
7	44.1	CCSD 168	Sauk Village
8	42.9	Park Forest SD 163	Park Forest
9	41.9	Maywood-Melrose Park-Broadview 89	Melrose Park
10	41.5	Posen-Robbins ESD 143-5	Posen
11	41.1	Dolton SD 149	Calumet City
12	40.8	Kankakee SD 111	Kankakee
13	40.8	Peoria SD 150	Peoria
14	40.5	City of Chicago SD 299	Chicago
15	40.4	Rantoul City SD 137	Rantoul
16	40.2	Chicago Heights SD 170	Chicago Heights
17	39.1	Rockford SD 205	Rockford
18	38.5	Zion ESD 6	Zion
19	37.8	Cicero SD 99	Cicero
20	37.7	Joliet PSD 86	Joliet
21	36.8	Freeport SD 145	Freeport
22	36.7	Decatur SD 61	Decatur
23	35.6	Bellwood SD 88	Bellwood
24	35.4	Springfield SD 186	Springfield
25	35.3	Prairie-Hills ESD 144	Markham
26	35.2	Murphysboro CUSD 186	Murphysboro
27	33.8	Berwyn North SD 98	Berwyn
28	33.6	North Chicago SD 187	North Chicago
29	33.1	Urbana SD 116	Urbana
30	32.8	Galesburg CUSD 205	Galesburg
31	32.7	Frankfort CUSD 168	West Frankfort
32	32.5	Cook County SD 130	Blue Island
32	32.5	Streator ESD 44	Streator
34	32.2	Harrisburg CUSD 3	Harrisburg
35	32.1	Granite City CUSD 9	Granite City
36	31.2	Alton CUSD 11	Alton
37	31.1	Thornton Twp HSD 205	South Holland
38	31.0	Kewanee CUSD 229	Kewanee
39	30.6	Herrin CUSD 4	Herrin
40	30.4	Midlothian SD 143	Midlothian
41	30.1	Aurora East USD 131	Aurora
41	30.1	Massac Ud 1	Metropolis
43	30.0	Bloomington SD 87	Bloomington
43	30.0	Rock Island SD 41	Rock Island
45	29.7	Waukegan CUSD 60	Waukegan
46	29.6	Summit SD 104	Summit
47	29.4	East Moline SD 37	East Moline
48	29.1	Mattoon CUSD 2	Mattoon
49	29.0	Bloom Twp HSD 206	Chicago Heights
49	29.0	Pekin PSD 108	Pekin
51	28.8	Jacksonville SD 117	Jacksonville
52	28.6	Litchfield CUSD 12	Litchfield
53	28.4	Steger SD 194	Steger
54	28.1	Berkeley SD 87	Berkeley
54	28.1	Matteson ESD 162	Richton Park
56	27.7	Vandalia CUSD 203	Vandalia
57	27.5	Bradley SD 61	Bradley
58	27.3	Ottawa ESD 141	Ottawa
59	27.0	Belleville SD 118	Belleville
60	26.8	Quincy SD 172	Quincy
61	26.6	Champaign CUSD 4	Champaign
62	26.3	J S Morton HSD 201	Cicero
63	26.0	Berwyn South SD 100	Berwyn
64	25.9	ESD 159	Matteson
64	25.9	Indian Springs SD 109	Justice
64	25.9	Taylorville CUSD 3	Taylorville
67	25.4	Marquardt SD 15	Glendale Hgts
67	25.4	Rich Twp HSD 227	Olympia Fields
69	25.3	Hillsboro CUSD 3	Hillsboro
69	25.3	Marion CUSD 2	Marion
71	25.0	Ridgeland SD 122	Oak Lawn
71	25.0	Rochelle CCSD 231	Rochelle
73	24.8	Lansing SD 158	Lansing
74	24.7	Collinsville CUSD 10	Collinsville
75	24.5	East Richland CUSD 1	Olney
76	24.4	Canton Union SD 66	Canton
76	24.4	Mannheim SD 83	Franklin Park
78	24.1	West Chicago ESD 33	West Chicago
79	23.9	Robinson CUSD 2	Robinson
80	23.8	Burbank SD 111	Burbank
80	23.8	Roxana CUSD 1	Roxana
82	23.7	Lyons SD 103	Lyons
82	23.7	North Mac CUSD 34	Girard
84	23.6	Round Lake CUSD 116	Round Lake
85	23.5	Crete Monee CUSD 201u	Crete
86	23.2	Aurora West USD 129	Aurora
86	23.2	Proviso Twp HSD 209	Forest Park
88	23.1	Riverton CUSD 14	Spaulding
89	22.9	Skokie SD 69	Skokie
90	22.5	Dekalb CUSD 428	Dekalb
90	22.5	Jersey CUSD 100	Jerseyville
92	22.3	Addison SD 4	Addison
93	22.2	Duquoin CUSD 300	Du Quoin
93	22.2	Joliet Twp HSD 204	Joliet
95	22.0	Clinton CUSD 15	Clinton
96	21.7	Effingham CUSD 40	Effingham
96	21.7	Macomb CUSD 185	Macomb
98	21.6	Monmouth-Roseville CUSD 238	Monmouth
99	21.3	Plano CUSD 88	Plano
100	21.2	Bond County CUSD 2	Greenville
100	21.2	CHSD 218	Oak Lawn
102	20.6	Argo CHSD 217	Summit
102	20.6	Oregon CUSD 220	Oregon
102	20.6	Sterling CUSD 5	Sterling
105	20.5	Alsip-Hazlgrn-Oaklwn SD 126	Alsip
105	20.5	Moline USD 40	Moline
107	20.4	North Palos SD 117	Palos Hills
108	20.3	Bensenville SD 2	Bensenville
109	19.7	East Peoria SD 86	East Peoria
110	19.5	Beardstown CUSD 15	Beardstown
111	19.4	Wabash CUSD 348	Mount Carmel
112	19.2	Beach Park CCSD 3	Beach Park
112	19.2	Carterville CUSD 5	Carterville
112	19.2	Dixon USD 170	Dixon
115	18.9	Charleston CUSD 1	Charleston
116	18.7	Bourbonnais SD 53	Bourbonnais
117	18.4	Skokie SD 68	Skokie
117	18.4	Wheeling CCSD 21	Wheeling
119	18.2	Harvard CUSD 50	Harvard
120	18.0	Bethalto CUSD 8	Bethalto
121	17.8	Zion-Benton Twp HSD 126	Zion
122	17.6	United Twp HSD 30	East Moline
123	17.5	Bremen CHSD 228	Midlothian
123	17.5	SD 45 Dupage County	Villa Park
123	17.5	SD U-46	Elgin
126	17.4	Evanston CCSD 65	Evanston
127	17.0	Valley View CUSD 365u	Romeoville
128	16.6	Leyden CHSD 212	Franklin Park
128	16.6	Queen Bee SD 16	Glendale Hgts
130	16.3	Belvidere CUSD 100	Belvidere
131	16.1	Harlem Ud 122	Machesney Park
132	16.0	CCSD 62	Des Plaines
133	15.7	East Maine SD 63	Des Plaines
134	15.5	Oak Lawn CHSD 229	Oak Lawn
135	15.2	Prairie Central CUSD 8	Fairbury
136	15.1	Pekin CSD 303	Pekin
137	15.0	Elmwood Park CUSD 401	Elmwood Park
137	15.0	Oak Lawn-Hometown SD 123	Oak Lawn
139	14.9	Bradley Bourbonnais CHSD 307	Bradley
139	14.9	Evergreen Park ESD 124	Evergreen Park
141	14.4	Keeneyville SD 20	Hanover Park
141	14.4	Reavis Twp HSD 220	Burbank
143	14.3	Manteno CUSD 5	Manteno
144	14.0	Mclean County USD 5	Normal
145	13.8	Mchenry CUSD 15	Mchenry
146	13.7	Woodridge SD 68	Woodridge
147	13.6	Belleville Twp HSD 201	Belleville
147	13.6	Forest Ridge SD 142	Oak Forest
149	13.3	Palatine CUSD 15	Palatine
150	13.2	Woodstock CUSD 200	Woodstock
151	13.1	Fenton CHSD 100	Bensenville
151	13.1	Flossmoor SD 161	Chicago Heights
151	13.1	Sandwich CUSD 430	Sandwich
154	12.8	CUSD 300	Carpentersville
155	12.6	Dupage HSD 88	Addison
155	12.6	Olympia CUSD 16	Stanford
155	12.6	Tinley Park CCSD 146	Tinley Park
158	12.5	Reed Custer CUSD 255u	Braidwood
159	12.3	Meridian CUSD 223	Stillman Valley
160	11.9	Southwestern CUSD 9	Piasa
161	11.8	CCSD 93	Bloomingdale
162	11.7	Evanston Twp HSD 202	Evanston
163	11.5	Grant CHSD 124	Fox Lake
164	11.4	Darien SD 61	Darien
165	11.2	Sherrard CUSD 200	Sherrard
166	10.8	Homewood SD 153	Homewood
166	10.8	Lombard SD 44	Lombard
166	10.8	Mundelein ESD 75	Mundelein
169	10.7	Thornton Fractional Twp HSD 215	Calumet City
169	10.7	Troy CCSD 30c	Plainfield
171	10.6	Genoa Kingston CUSD 424	Genoa
171	10.6	Herscher CUSD 2	Herscher
171	10.6	Niles Twp CHSD 219	Skokie
174	10.4	Il Valley Central USD 321	Chillicothe
174	10.4	North Boone CUSD 200	Poplar Grove
176	10.1	Woodland CCSD 50	Gurnee
177	10.0	Highland CUSD 5	Highland
177	10.0	Schaumburg CCSD 54	Schaumburg
179	9.9	Tolono CUSD 7	Tolono
180	9.8	Winnebago CUSD 323	Winnebago
181	9.6	Antioch CCSD 34	Antioch
181	9.6	CUSD 200	Wheaton
181	9.6	Lisle CUSD 202	Lisle
184	9.5	Sycamore CUSD 427	Sycamore
185	9.3	Gurnee SD 56	Gurnee
186	9.1	Eureka CUD 140	Eureka
186	9.1	Minooka CCSD 201	Minooka
188	8.8	Mundelein Cons HSD 120	Mundelein
189	8.7	Glenbard Twp HSD 87	Glen Ellyn
189	8.7	Mchenry CHSD 156	Mchenry
191	8.5	Coal City CUSD 1	Coal City
191	8.5	Glen Ellyn SD 41	Glen Ellyn
193	8.4	Wauconda CUSD 118	Wauconda
194	8.3	Byron CUSD 226	Byron
194	8.3	CCSD 89	Glen Ellyn
194	8.3	Rockton SD 140	Rockton
197	8.2	Hawthorn CCSD 73	Vernon Hills
198	8.0	Homewood Flossmoor CHSD 233	Flossmoor
198	8.0	Mahomet-Seymour CUSD 3	Mahomet
200	7.9	Oak Park ESD 97	Oak Park
201	7.8	Grayslake CCSD 46	Grayslake
201	7.8	O Fallon CCSD 90	O Fallon
201	7.8	Oak Park - River Forest SD 200	Oak Park
204	7.7	Crystal Lake CCSD 47	Crystal Lake
204	7.7	Plainfield SD 202	Plainfield
206	7.6	Cary CCSD 26	Cary
206	7.6	Kinnikinnick CCSD 131	Roscoe
208	7.4	Johnsburg CUSD 12	Johnsburg
208	7.4	Oswego CUSD 308	Oswego
210	7.2	Edwardsville CUSD 7	Edwardsville
210	7.2	Glenview CCSD 34	Glenview
210	7.2	Lake Park CHSD 108	Roselle
210	7.2	Maine Township HSD 207	Park Ridge
210	7.2	Yorkville CUSD 115	Yorkville
215	7.1	Palos CCSD 118	Palos Park
216	7.0	Big Hollow SD 38	Ingleside
216	7.0	Cons HSD 230	Orland Park
218	6.9	Peotone CUSD 207u	Peotone
219	6.8	Lake Villa CCSD 41	Lake Villa
219	6.8	Township HSD 214	Arlington Hgts
221	6.6	Mt Zion CUSD 3	Mount Zion
221	6.6	Triad CUSD 2	Troy
223	6.5	Ball Chatham CUSD 5	Chatham
223	6.5	CHSD 99	Downers Grove
225	6.4	Township HSD 211	Palatine
225	6.4	Waterloo CUSD 5	Waterloo
225	6.4	Will County SD 92	Lockport
228	6.1	Lyons Twp HSD 204	La Grange
229	5.8	CHSD 117	Lake Villa
230	5.5	O Fallon Twp HSD 203	O Fallon
231	5.4	Geneseo CUSD 228	Geneseo
232	5.3	CHSD 94	West Chicago
232	5.3	Orland SD 135	Orland Park
234	5.2	Batavia USD 101	Batavia
234	5.2	Riverside SD 96	Riverside
236	5.1	Elmhurst SD 205	Elmhurst
236	5.1	Hinsdale Twp HSD 86	Hinsdale
236	5.1	La Grange SD 102	La Grange Park
236	5.1	Warren Twp HSD 121	Gurnee
240	4.7	North Shore SD 112	Highland Park
241	4.6	Mokena SD 159	Mokena
241	4.6	Morton CUSD 709	Morton
243	4.5	Barrington CUSD 220	Barrington
243	4.5	Grayslake CHSD 127	Grayslake
243	4.5	Homer CCSD 33c	Homer Glen
243	4.5	Kaneland CUSD 302	Maple Park
243	4.5	New Lenox SD 122	New Lenox

Note: This section only includes districts with 1,500 or more students; All categories are ranked from high to low

248	4.4	Indian Prairie CUSD 204	Aurora
248	4.4	Lockport Twp HSD 205	Lockport
248	4.4	Monticello CUSD 25	Monticello
248	4.4	Saint Charles CUSD 303	Saint Charles
252	4.1	Central CUSD 301	Burlington
252	4.1	CHSD 155	Crystal Lake
254	3.9	Naperville CUSD 203	Naperville
255	3.8	Downers Grove GSD 58	Downers Grove
256	3.7	Rochester CUSD 3a	Rochester
257	3.6	Mascoutah CUD 19	Mascoutah
257	3.6	Minooka CHSD 111	Minooka
259	3.4	Aptakisic-Tripp CCSD 102	Buffalo Grove
259	3.4	Columbia CUSD 4	Columbia
259	3.4	Summit Hill SD 161	Frankfort
262	3.3	Lincoln Way CHSD 210	New Lenox
263	3.2	Dunlap CUSD 323	Peoria
264	3.1	Lemont-Bromberek CSD 113a	Lemont
264	3.1	Mount Prospect SD 57	Mount Prospect
266	3.0	Hononegah Chd 207	Rockton
266	3.0	Lake Zurich CUSD 95	Lake Zurich
266	3.0	Park Ridge CCSD 64	Park Ridge
269	2.9	Northfield Twp HSD 225	Glenview
270	2.8	Lemont Twp HSD 210	Lemont
271	2.7	Arlington Hgts SD 25	Arlington Hgts
272	2.4	Geneva CUSD 304	Geneva
273	2.2	Kildeer Countryside CCSD 96	Buffalo Grove
274	2.1	Frankfort CCSD 157c	Frankfort
274	2.1	Fremont SD 79	Mundelein
276	1.8	Kirby SD 140	Tinley Park
277	1.6	CHSD 128	Vernon Hills
278	1.5	Libertyville SD 70	Libertyville
278	1.5	Twp HSD 113	Highland Park
280	1.4	Northbrook SD 28	Northbrook
281	1.3	Lake Forest CHSD 115	Lake Forest
282	1.2	Community CSD 59	Arlington Hgts
282	1.2	CSD 158	Algonquin
282	1.2	Hinsdale CCSD 181	Burr Ridge
285	1.1	Adlai E Stevenson HSD 125	Lincolnshire
286	1.0	Millburn CCSD 24	Old Mill Creek
287	0.6	New Trier Twp HSD 203	Northfield
287	0.6	Wilmette SD 39	Wilmette
289	0.3	Lake Forest SD 67	Lake Forest
290	0.2	Lincolnshire-Prairieview SD 103	Lincolnshire
291	0.1	Deerfield SD 109	Deerfield
291	0.1	Winnetka SD 36	Winnetka

Students Eligible for Reduced-Price Lunch

Rank	Percent	District Name	City
1	61.1	J S Morton HSD 201	Cicero
2	58.2	Bellwood SD 88	Bellwood
3	57.7	Dolton SD 149	Calumet City
4	55.3	Beardstown CUSD 15	Beardstown
5	54.0	Chicago Heights SD 170	Chicago Heights
6	53.8	Berwyn North SD 98	Berwyn
7	52.6	Cicero SD 99	Cicero
7	52.6	West Chicago ESD 33	West Chicago
9	52.3	Prairie-Hills ESD 144	Markham
10	51.2	Posen-Robbins ESD 143-5	Posen
11	50.6	Aurora East USD 131	Aurora
12	50.0	Thornton Twp HSD 205	South Holland
13	49.9	Berwyn South SD 100	Berwyn
14	49.6	Maywood-Melrose Park-Broadview 89	Melrose Park
15	49.3	Rich Twp HSD 227	Olympia Fields
16	48.5	Bloom Twp HSD 206	Chicago Heights
17	47.2	Monmouth-Roseville CUSD 238	Monmouth
18	46.7	Cook County SD 130	Blue Island
19	46.0	City of Chicago SD 299	Chicago
20	45.7	Summit SD 104	Summit
21	45.5	Round Lake CUSD 116	Round Lake
22	44.6	North Chicago SD 187	North Chicago
23	44.5	Berkeley SD 87	Berkeley
24	44.3	Park Forest SD 163	Park Forest
25	44.0	Harvey SD 152	Harvey
25	44.0	Mannheim SD 83	Franklin Park
27	43.7	Lyons SD 103	Lyons
28	43.2	Joliet Twp HSD 204	Joliet
29	43.0	Argo CHSD 217	Summit
30	42.8	Harvard CUSD 50	Harvard
31	42.6	Zion ESD 6	Zion
32	42.4	Addison SD 4	Addison
33	42.2	Marquardt SD 15	Glendale Hgts
34	41.3	Bensenville SD 2	Bensenville
35	40.7	Crete Monee CUSD 201u	Crete
36	40.3	Kewanee CUSD 229	Kewanee
37	40.2	Dolton SD 148	Riverdale
38	40.1	E Saint Louis SD 189	E Saint Louis
38	40.1	ESD 159	Matteson
40	39.6	Joliet PSD 86	Joliet
41	39.4	Rockford SD 205	Rockford
42	39.3	Matteson ESD 162	Richton Park
43	39.2	Midlothian SD 143	Midlothian
44	39.1	Kankakee SD 111	Kankakee
44	39.1	Rantoul City SD 137	Rantoul
46	38.8	Valley View CUSD 365u	Romeoville
47	38.7	Steger SD 194	Steger
48	38.1	Burbank SD 111	Burbank
49	37.4	SD U-46	Elgin
50	37.1	Aurora West USD 129	Aurora
51	36.7	East Moline SD 37	East Moline
52	36.1	Fenton CHSD 100	Bensenville
53	35.6	CHSD 218	Oak Lawn
53	35.6	Indian Springs SD 109	Justice
55	35.4	Lansing SD 158	Lansing
55	35.4	Urbana SD 116	Urbana
57	33.8	Rock Island SD 41	Rock Island
58	33.6	CCSD 168	Sauk Village
59	33.2	United Twp HSD 30	East Moline
60	33.1	Bradley SD 61	Bradley
60	33.1	Zion-Benton Twp HSD 126	Zion
62	33.0	Mount Vernon SD 80	Mount Vernon
62	33.0	Rochelle CCSD 231	Rochelle
62	33.0	Wheeling CCSD 21	Wheeling
65	32.9	Belleville SD 118	Belleville
66	32.7	Roxana CUSD 1	Roxana
67	32.3	Proviso Twp HSD 209	Forest Park
68	32.2	Ridgeland SD 122	Oak Lawn
68	32.2	Waukegan CUSD 60	Waukegan
70	32.0	Streator ESD 44	Streator
71	31.2	East Maine SD 63	Des Plaines
71	31.2	Leyden CHSD 212	Franklin Park
73	31.1	Collinsville CUSD 10	Collinsville
73	31.1	Sterling CUSD 5	Sterling
75	30.8	Dupage HSD 88	Addison
76	30.5	Queen Bee SD 16	Glendale Hgts
77	30.2	Beach Park CCSD 3	Beach Park
77	30.2	Champaign CUSD 4	Champaign
79	30.0	Keeneyville SD 20	Hanover Park
79	30.0	Skokie SD 69	Skokie
81	29.7	Pekin PSD 108	Pekin
81	29.7	Woodstock CUSD 200	Woodstock
83	29.6	Skokie SD 68	Skokie
84	29.4	Alsip-Hazlgrn-Oaklwn SD 126	Alsip
85	29.3	Galesburg CUSD 205	Galesburg
85	29.3	Quincy SD 172	Quincy
87	29.2	Plano CUSD 88	Plano
88	29.1	Alton CUSD 11	Alton
88	29.1	Evanston Twp HSD 202	Evanston
90	29.0	Belvidere CUSD 100	Belvidere
90	29.0	CCSD 62	Des Plaines
90	29.0	Danville CCSD 118	Danville
93	28.8	Frankfort CUSD 168	West Frankfort
94	28.6	Freeport SD 145	Freeport
95	28.5	Harlem Ud 122	Machesney Park
96	28.1	Decatur SD 61	Decatur
96	28.1	Jacksonville SD 117	Jacksonville
98	28.0	Peoria SD 150	Peoria
98	28.0	Woodridge SD 68	Woodridge
100	27.9	Dekalb CUSD 428	Dekalb
101	27.8	North Boone CUSD 200	Poplar Grove
102	27.6	Bethalto CUSD 8	Bethalto
102	27.6	SD 45 Dupage County	Villa Park
104	27.2	Moline USD 40	Moline
105	27.0	Elmwood Park CUSD 401	Elmwood Park
105	27.0	Herrin CUSD 4	Herrin
107	26.9	Evergreen Park ESD 124	Evergreen Park
107	26.9	Granite City CUSD 9	Granite City
109	26.7	CUSD 300	Carpentersville
110	25.9	Vandalia CUSD 203	Vandalia
111	25.7	Murphysboro CUSD 186	Murphysboro
112	25.6	Dixon USD 170	Dixon
112	25.6	East Richland CUSD 1	Olney
114	25.2	Oak Lawn-Hometown SD 123	Oak Lawn
115	25.1	Canton Union SD 66	Canton
115	25.1	Evanston CCSD 65	Evanston
115	25.1	Harrisburg CUSD 3	Harrisburg
118	24.9	Bloomington SD 87	Bloomington
119	24.8	Mundelein Cons HSD 120	Mundelein
120	24.7	Taylorville CUSD 3	Taylorville
121	24.6	Reed Custer CUSD 255u	Braidwood
122	24.2	Wabash CUSD 348	Mount Carmel
123	24.1	Bradley Bourbonnais CHSD 307	Bradley
123	24.1	Mattoon CUSD 2	Mattoon
125	24.0	Troy CCSD 30c	Plainfield
126	23.9	Massac Ud 1	Metropolis
127	23.8	Belleville Twp HSD 201	Belleville
128	23.7	Hillsboro CUSD 3	Hillsboro
129	23.5	Pekin CSD 303	Pekin
130	23.4	Bond County CUSD 2	Greenville
130	23.4	Genoa Kingston CUSD 424	Genoa
130	23.4	Prairie Central CUSD 8	Fairbury
133	23.3	North Mac CUSD 34	Girard
134	23.2	Riverton CUSD 14	Spaulding
135	23.1	Litchfield CUSD 12	Litchfield
136	22.7	Robinson CUSD 2	Robinson
137	22.6	Cahokia CUSD 187	Cahokia
138	22.2	North Palos SD 117	Palos Hills
139	22.1	East Peoria SD 86	East Peoria
140	22.0	Springfield SD 186	Springfield
141	21.9	Macomb CUSD 185	Macomb
141	21.9	Southwestern CUSD 9	Piasa
143	21.5	Clinton CUSD 15	Clinton
143	21.5	Niles Twp CHSD 219	Skokie
143	21.5	Wauconda CUSD 118	Wauconda
146	21.4	Marion CUSD 2	Marion
147	21.2	Flossmoor SD 161	Chicago Heigh
147	21.2	Jersey CUSD 100	Jerseyville
149	21.1	Duquoin CUSD 300	Du Quoin
149	21.1	Ottawa ESD 141	Ottawa
151	21.0	CHSD 94	West Chicago
152	20.9	Oak Lawn CHSD 229	Oak Lawn
153	20.7	Bremen CHSD 228	Midlothian
154	20.6	Bourbonnais SD 53	Bourbonnais
155	20.5	Effingham CUSD 40	Effingham
155	20.5	Maine Township HSD 207	Park Ridge
157	20.2	Charleston CUSD 1	Charleston
158	20.1	Palatine CCSD 15	Palatine
159	20.0	Grant CHSD 124	Fox Lake
160	19.9	Forest Ridge SD 142	Oak Forest
161	19.8	Oregon CUSD 220	Oregon
161	19.8	Thornton Fractional Twp HSD 215	Calumet City
163	19.5	Mundelein ESD 75	Mundelein
164	19.3	Tolono CUSD 7	Tolono
165	18.9	Sycamore CUSD 427	Sycamore
165	18.9	Tinley Park CCSD 146	Tinley Park
167	18.8	Hawthorn CCSD 73	Vernon Hills
167	18.8	Lombard SD 44	Lombard
167	18.8	Woodland CCSD 50	Gurnee
170	18.7	Mchenry CCSD 15	Mchenry
171	18.6	Geneseo CUSD 228	Geneseo
172	18.1	Olympia CUSD 16	Stanford
172	18.1	Sandwich CUSD 430	Sandwich
174	17.7	CCSD 93	Bloomingdale
174	17.7	CUSD 200	Wheaton
174	17.7	North Shore SD 112	Highland Park
177	17.6	Highland CUSD 5	Highland
178	17.5	Darien SD 61	Darien
179	17.3	Reavis Twp HSD 220	Burbank
180	17.1	Il Valley Central USD 321	Chillicothe
181	17.0	Lake Villa CCSD 41	Lake Villa
182	16.6	Sherrard CUSD 200	Sherrard
183	16.5	Glenbard Twp HSD 87	Glen Ellyn
183	16.5	Mchenry CHSD 156	Mchenry
185	16.4	Carterville CUSD 5	Carterville
186	16.3	Lisle CUSD 202	Lisle
187	16.2	Crystal Lake CCSD 47	Crystal Lake
188	16.1	Manteno CUSD 5	Manteno
189	16.0	Herscher CUSD 2	Herscher
190	15.9	Township HSD 214	Arlington Hgts
191	15.7	Grayslake CCSD 46	Grayslake
192	15.6	Oswego CUSD 308	Oswego
193	15.3	Mascoutah CUD 19	Mascoutah
194	15.2	Winnebago CUSD 323	Winnebago
195	15.0	Antioch CCSD 34	Antioch
196	14.8	Township HSD 211	Palatine
197	14.7	CHSD 99	Downers Grove
198	14.6	Mclean County USD 5	Normal
198	14.6	Minooka CCSD 201	Minooka
200	14.5	Rockton SD 140	Rockton
201	14.2	Homewood SD 153	Homewood
202	14.1	Big Hollow SD 38	Ingleside
203	13.8	Eureka CUD 140	Eureka
203	13.8	Waterloo CUSD 5	Waterloo
205	13.7	Homewood Flossmoor CHSD 233	Flossmoor
206	13.6	Coal City CUSD 1	Coal City
206	13.6	Meridian CUSD 223	Stillman Valley
206	13.6	Yorkville CUSD 115	Yorkville

Note: This section only includes districts with 1,500 or more students; All categories are ranked from high to low

Rank	Number	District Name	City
209	13.0	Barrington CUSD 220	Barrington
209	13.0	Cary CCSD 26	Cary
211	12.7	O Fallon CCSD 90	O Fallon
212	12.6	Glenview CCSD 34	Glenview
212	12.6	Oak Park - River Forest SD 200	Oak Park
214	12.5	Plainfield SD 202	Plainfield
215	12.4	Gurnee SD 56	Gurnee
216	12.2	CCSD 89	Glen Ellyn
216	12.2	Kinnikinnick CCSD 131	Roscoe
218	12.0	Johnsburg CUSD 12	Johnsburg
219	11.9	CHSD 117	Lake Villa
219	11.9	Triad CUSD 2	Troy
221	11.5	Northfield Twp HSD 225	Glenview
222	11.4	Oak Park ESD 97	Oak Park
223	11.3	Byron CUSD 226	Byron
224	10.7	Monticello CUSD 25	Monticello
225	10.6	O Fallon Twp HSD 203	O Fallon
225	10.6	Peotone CUSD 207u	Peotone
227	10.5	Glen Ellyn SD 41	Glen Ellyn
228	10.4	Will County SD 92	Lockport
229	10.3	Mahomet-Seymour CUSD 3	Mahomet
230	10.2	CHSD 155	Crystal Lake
231	10.0	Cons HSD 230	Orland Park
231	10.0	Minooka CHSD 111	Minooka
233	9.9	Indian Prairie CUSD 204	Aurora
234	9.6	Hononegah Chd 207	Rockton
234	9.6	Kaneland CUSD 302	Maple Park
236	9.3	Mokena SD 159	Mokena
237	9.2	Ball Chatham CUSD 5	Chatham
238	9.1	Warren Twp HSD 121	Gurnee
239	9.0	Edwardsville CUSD 7	Edwardsville
240	8.7	Lincoln Way CHSD 210	New Lenox
240	8.7	Morton CUSD 709	Morton
240	8.7	Saint Charles CUSD 303	Saint Charles
243	8.5	Elmhurst SD 205	Elmhurst
244	8.4	Lemont-Bromberek CSD 113a	Lemont
245	8.2	La Grange SD 102	La Grange Park
246	8.1	Schaumburg CCSD 54	Schaumburg
247	8.0	New Lenox SD 122	New Lenox
248	7.9	Lake Park CHSD 108	Roselle
248	7.9	Lyons Twp HSD 204	La Grange
250	7.8	Mt Zion CUSD 3	Mount Zion
251	7.5	Grayslake CHSD 127	Grayslake
252	7.3	Columbia CUSD 4	Columbia
253	7.2	Batavia USD 101	Batavia
253	7.2	Palos CCSD 118	Palos Park
255	7.1	Twp HSD 113	Highland Park
256	7.0	Naperville CUSD 203	Naperville
256	7.0	Orland SD 135	Orland Park
258	6.9	Central CUSD 301	Burlington
258	6.9	Hinsdale Twp HSD 86	Hinsdale
258	6.9	Lake Zurich CUSD 95	Lake Zurich
258	6.9	Lockport Twp HSD 205	Lockport
262	6.7	CSD 158	Algonquin
262	6.7	Homer CCSD 33c	Homer Glen
264	6.2	Rochester CUSD 3a	Rochester
265	6.1	CHSD 128	Vernon Hills
265	6.1	Fremont SD 79	Mundelein
267	5.5	Dunlap CUSD 323	Peoria
268	5.2	Riverside SD 96	Riverside
269	5.1	Aptakisic-Tripp CCSD 102	Buffalo Grove
269	5.1	Kildeer Countryside CCSD 96	Buffalo Grove
271	5.0	Downers Grove GSD 58	Downers Grove
272	4.9	Mount Prospect SD 57	Mount Prospect
273	4.8	Arlington Hgts SD 25	Arlington Hgts
274	4.5	Lemont Twp HSD 210	Lemont
275	4.2	Libertyville SD 70	Libertyville
276	3.7	Geneva CUSD 304	Geneva
277	3.6	Summit Hill SD 161	Frankfort
278	3.4	Lake Forest CHSD 115	Lake Forest
279	3.2	Adlai E Stevenson HSD 125	Lincolnshire
280	2.8	Frankfort CCSD 157c	Frankfort
280	2.8	Millburn CUSD 24	Old Mill Creek
282	2.6	Hinsdale CCSD 181	Burr Ridge
282	2.6	Park Ridge CCSD 64	Park Ridge
284	2.5	New Trier Twp HSD 203	Northfield
285	2.4	Community CSD 59	Arlington Hgts
286	1.9	Wilmette SD 39	Wilmette
287	1.7	Kirby SD 140	Tinley Park
287	1.7	Northbrook SD 28	Northbrook
289	1.1	Lake Forest SD 67	Lake Forest
290	0.6	Lincolnshire-Prairieview SD 103	Lincolnshire
291	0.4	Deerfield SD 109	Deerfield
292	0.1	Winnetka SD 36	Winnetka

Student/Teacher Ratio

(number of students per teacher)

Rank	Number	District Name	City
1	10.6	Winnetka SD 36	Winnetka
2	10.8	Northbrook SD 28	Northbrook
3	12.1	Maine Township HSD 207	Park Ridge
4	12.2	Evanston CCSD 65	Evanston
5	12.3	Lake Forest SD 67	Lake Forest
6	12.4	North Shore SD 112	Highland Park
7	12.5	New Trier Twp HSD 203	Northfield
8	12.7	Skokie SD 68	Skokie
9	12.8	Freeport SD 145	Freeport
10	12.9	Byron CUSD 226	Byron
10	12.9	Dolton SD 148	Riverdale
12	13.2	Mannheim SD 83	Franklin Park
12	13.2	Park Ridge CCSD 64	Park Ridge
14	13.4	Lincolnshire-Prairieview SD 103	Lincolnshire
14	13.4	Northfield Twp HSD 225	Glenview
14	13.4	Urbana SD 116	Urbana
14	13.4	Wilmette SD 39	Wilmette
18	13.5	Aptakisic-Tripp CCSD 102	Buffalo Grove
18	13.5	Deerfield SD 109	Deerfield
18	13.5	Homewood SD 153	Homewood
18	13.5	Niles Twp CHSD 219	Skokie
18	13.5	Springfield SD 186	Springfield
23	13.6	CCSD 93	Bloomingdale
23	13.6	Champaign CUSD 4	Champaign
23	13.6	Evergreen Park ESD 124	Evergreen Park
26	13.7	CCSD 62	Des Plaines
27	13.8	La Grange SD 102	La Grange Park
27	13.8	Schaumburg CCSD 54	Schaumburg
27	13.8	Steger SD 194	Steger
27	13.8	Thornton Twp HSD 205	South Holland
31	13.9	Kildeer Countryside CCSD 96	Buffalo Grove
32	14.0	Cook County SD 130	Blue Island
32	14.0	East Moline SD 37	East Moline
32	14.0	Lake Forest CHSD 115	Lake Forest
32	14.0	Lombard SD 44	Lombard
32	14.0	Oak Park ESD 97	Oak Park
37	14.1	Alsip-Hazlgrn-Oaklwn SD 126	Alsip
37	14.1	Alton CUSD 11	Alton
37	14.1	Glenview CCSD 34	Glenview
37	14.1	Gurnee SD 56	Gurnee
37	14.1	Harlem Ud 122	Machesney Park
42	14.2	Berwyn South SD 100	Berwyn
42	14.2	Herscher CUSD 2	Herscher
44	14.3	Flossmoor SD 161	Chicago Heights
44	14.3	Peoria SD 150	Peoria
46	14.4	Bensenville SD 2	Bensenville
46	14.4	CCSD 89	Glen Ellyn
46	14.4	Lyons SD 103	Lyons
46	14.4	Wheeling CCSD 21	Wheeling
50	14.5	Beardstown CUSD 15	Beardstown
50	14.5	Clinton CUSD 15	Clinton
50	14.5	Community CSD 59	Arlington Hgts
50	14.5	Hinsdale CCSD 181	Burr Ridge
50	14.5	Kirby SD 140	Tinley Park
50	14.5	Ottawa ESD 141	Ottawa
50	14.5	Prairie Central CUSD 8	Fairbury
50	14.5	Rich Twp HSD 227	Olympia Fields
50	14.5	Vandalia CUSD 203	Vandalia
59	14.6	Evanston Twp HSD 202	Evanston
59	14.6	Grayslake CHSD 127	Grayslake
59	14.6	Rantoul City SD 137	Rantoul
59	14.6	Sherrard CUSD 200	Sherrard
63	14.7	Rochelle CCSD 231	Rochelle
64	14.8	ESD 159	Matteson
64	14.8	Oak Lawn-Hometown SD 123	Oak Lawn
64	14.8	Sandwich CUSD 430	Sandwich
64	14.8	Tinley Park CCSD 146	Tinley Park
64	14.8	Tolono CUSD 7	Tolono
69	14.9	Mundelein ESD 75	Mundelein
70	15.0	Chicago Heights SD 170	Chicago Heights
70	15.0	Lisle CUSD 202	Lisle
70	15.0	Midlothian SD 143	Midlothian
70	15.0	Prairie-Hills ESD 144	Markham
74	15.1	Arlington Hgts SD 25	Arlington Hgts
74	15.1	East Peoria SD 86	East Peoria
74	15.1	Jacksonville SD 117	Jacksonville
74	15.1	Manteno CUSD 5	Manteno
74	15.1	Plano CUSD 88	Plano
74	15.1	Woodland CCSD 50	Gurnee
80	15.2	Cahokia CUSD 187	Cahokia
80	15.2	Duquoin CUSD 300	Du Quoin
80	15.2	Hawthorn CCSD 73	Vernon Hills
80	15.2	Johnsburg CUSD 12	Johnsburg
80	15.2	Lake Zurich CUSD 95	Lake Zurich
85	15.3	Ball Chatham CUSD 5	Chatham
85	15.3	Massac Ud 1	Metropolis
85	15.3	Matteson ESD 162	Richton Park
85	15.3	Riverside SD 96	Riverside
85	15.3	Twp HSD 113	Highland Park
85	15.3	Winnebago CUSD 323	Winnebago
91	15.4	Canton Union SD 66	Canton
91	15.4	Coal City CUSD 1	Coal City
91	15.4	Eureka CUD 140	Eureka
91	15.4	Grayslake CCSD 46	Grayslake
91	15.4	Indian Springs SD 109	Justice
91	15.4	North Chicago SD 187	North Chicago
97	15.5	Darien SD 61	Darien
97	15.5	Hinsdale Twp HSD 86	Hinsdale
97	15.5	Pekin PSD 108	Pekin
97	15.5	Waukegan CUSD 60	Waukegan
101	15.6	Bloomington SD 87	Bloomington
101	15.6	CHSD 218	Oak Lawn
101	15.6	Macomb CUSD 185	Macomb
101	15.6	Palos CCSD 118	Palos Park
101	15.6	SD 45 Dupage County	Villa Park
106	15.7	Beach Park CCSD 3	Beach Park
106	15.7	Bradley SD 61	Bradley
106	15.7	CCSD 168	Sauk Village
106	15.7	Genoa Kingston CUSD 424	Genoa
106	15.7	Glen Ellyn SD 41	Glen Ellyn
106	15.7	Lansing SD 158	Lansing
106	15.7	Reed Custer CUSD 255u	Braidwood
106	15.7	Roxana CUSD 1	Roxana
114	15.8	CUSD 200	Wheaton
114	15.8	Harrisburg CUSD 3	Harrisburg
114	15.8	Robinson CUSD 2	Robinson
114	15.8	Streator ESD 44	Streator
118	15.9	Barrington CUSD 220	Barrington
118	15.9	CHSD 128	Vernon Hills
118	15.9	Homer CCSD 33c	Homer Glen
118	15.9	Il Valley Central USD 321	Chillicothe
118	15.9	Leyden CHSD 212	Franklin Park
118	15.9	Monticello CUSD 25	Monticello
118	15.9	Murphysboro CUSD 186	Murphysboro
118	15.9	Orland SD 135	Orland Park
118	15.9	Township HSD 211	Palatine
127	16.0	Big Hollow SD 38	Ingleside
127	16.0	Crystal Lake CCSD 47	Crystal Lake
127	16.0	E Saint Louis SD 189	E Saint Louis
127	16.0	Will County SD 92	Lockport
131	16.1	Antioch CCSD 34	Antioch
131	16.1	Bethalto CUSD 8	Bethalto
131	16.1	CHSD 117	Lake Villa
131	16.1	Danville CCSD 118	Danville
131	16.1	Elmhurst SD 205	Elmhurst
131	16.1	Libertyville SD 70	Libertyville
131	16.1	Mattoon CUSD 2	Mattoon
138	16.2	CHSD 99	Downers Grove
138	16.2	Harvard CUSD 50	Harvard
138	16.2	Lake Villa CCSD 41	Lake Villa
138	16.2	Marquardt SD 15	Glendale Hgts
138	16.2	Monmouth-Roseville CUSD 238	Monmouth
138	16.2	Olympia CUSD 16	Stanford
138	16.2	Oregon CUSD 220	Oregon
138	16.2	Rockton SD 140	Rockton
138	16.2	Wabash CUSD 348	Mount Carmel
147	16.3	Central CUSD 301	Burlington
147	16.3	Lemont Twp HSD 210	Lemont
147	16.3	North Boone CUSD 200	Poplar Grove
147	16.3	Saint Charles CUSD 303	Saint Charles
151	16.4	Adlai E Stevenson HSD 125	Lincolnshire
151	16.4	Cons HSD 230	Orland Park
151	16.4	East Richland CUSD 1	Olney
151	16.4	Frankfort CCSD 157c	Frankfort
151	16.4	Pekin CUSD 303	Pekin
156	16.5	Burbank SD 111	Burbank
156	16.5	Kankakee SD 111	Kankakee
156	16.5	Lyons Twp HSD 204	La Grange
156	16.5	Mclean County USD 5	Normal
156	16.5	North Palos SD 117	Palos Hills
156	16.5	Oak Park - River Forest SD 200	Oak Park
156	16.5	Triad CUSD 2	Troy
156	16.5	Troy CCSD 30c	Plainfield
156	16.5	Woodridge SD 68	Woodridge
165	16.6	Fenton CHSD 100	Bensenville
165	16.6	Indian Prairie CUSD 204	Aurora
165	16.6	Wauconda CUSD 118	Wauconda
168	16.7	Bourbonnais SD 53	Bourbonnais

Note: This section only includes districts with 1,500 or more students; All categories are ranked from high to low

168	16.7	Charleston CUSD 1	Charleston
168	16.7	Rochester CUSD 3a	Rochester
168	16.7	Waterloo CUSD 5	Waterloo
168	16.7	Yorkville CUSD 115	Yorkville
168	16.7	Zion ESD 6	Zion
174	16.8	Collinsville CUSD 10	Collinsville
174	16.8	Fremont SD 79	Mundelein
174	16.8	Geneva CUSD 304	Geneva
174	16.8	Queen Bee SD 16	Glendale Hgts
174	16.8	Rockford SD 205	Rockford
174	16.8	Township HSD 214	Arlington Hgts
174	16.8	Woodstock CUSD 200	Woodstock
181	16.9	Belvidere CUSD 100	Belvidere
181	16.9	East Maine SD 63	Des Plaines
181	16.9	Effingham CUSD 40	Effingham
181	16.9	Mount Vernon SD 80	Mount Vernon
181	16.9	Sycamore CUSD 427	Sycamore
181	16.9	Valley View CUSD 365u	Romeoville
181	16.9	Zion-Benton Twp HSD 126	Zion
188	17.0	Edwardsville CUSD 7	Edwardsville
188	17.0	Galesburg CUSD 205	Galesburg
188	17.0	Highland CUSD 5	Highland
188	17.0	Jersey CUSD 100	Jerseyville
188	17.0	Kaneland CUSD 302	Maple Park
188	17.0	Mchenry CCSD 15	Mchenry
188	17.0	Naperville CUSD 203	Naperville
188	17.0	Southwestern CUSD 9	Piasa
188	17.0	Sterling CUSD 5	Sterling
197	17.1	Elmwood Park CUSD 401	Elmwood Park
197	17.1	Forest Ridge SD 142	Oak Forest
197	17.1	Geneseo CUSD 228	Geneseo
197	17.1	Mahomet-Seymour CUSD 3	Mahomet
197	17.1	Moline USD 40	Moline
197	17.1	Mount Prospect SD 57	Mount Prospect
203	17.2	Berkeley SD 87	Berkeley
203	17.2	Bond County CUSD 2	Greenville
203	17.2	Dixon USD 170	Dixon
203	17.2	Homewood Flossmoor CHSD 233	Flossmoor
203	17.2	Keeneyville SD 20	Hanover Park
203	17.2	Peotone CUSD 207u	Peotone
203	17.2	Summit Hill SD 161	Frankfort
210	17.3	Dupage HSD 88	Addison
210	17.3	Skokie SD 69	Skokie
212	17.4	Belleville SD 118	Belleville
212	17.4	Cicero SD 99	Cicero
212	17.4	Glenbard Twp HSD 87	Glen Ellyn
212	17.4	Mascoutah CUD 19	Mascoutah
212	17.4	Millburn CCSD 24	Old Mill Creek
217	17.5	Carterville CUSD 5	Carterville
217	17.5	CSD 158	Algonquin
217	17.5	Oak Lawn CHSD 229	Oak Lawn
217	17.5	Park Forest SD 163	Park Forest
217	17.5	Quincy SD 172	Quincy
217	17.5	Rock Island SD 41	Rock Island
223	17.6	Aurora West USD 129	Aurora
223	17.6	CHSD 155	Crystal Lake
223	17.6	Kewanee CUSD 229	Kewanee
223	17.6	Lincoln Way CHSD 210	New Lenox
223	17.6	Meridian CUSD 223	Stillman Valley
228	17.7	Addison SD 4	Addison
228	17.7	Joliet Twp HSD 204	Joliet
230	17.8	CHSD 94	West Chicago
230	17.8	Hononegah Chd 207	Rockton
230	17.8	Mchenry CHSD 156	Mchenry
230	17.8	Morton CUSD 709	Morton
230	17.8	Palatine CCSD 15	Palatine
230	17.8	Plainfield SD 202	Plainfield
230	17.8	Posen-Robbins ESD 143-5	Posen
237	17.9	Bremen CHSD 228	Midlothian
237	17.9	City of Chicago SD 299	Chicago
237	17.9	Frankfort CUSD 168	West Frankfort
237	17.9	O Fallon CCSD 90	O Fallon
241	18.0	Argo CHSD 217	Summit
241	18.0	Berwyn North SD 98	Berwyn
241	18.0	Dekalb CUSD 428	Dekalb
241	18.0	Joliet PSD 86	Joliet
241	18.0	Warren Twp HSD 121	Gurnee
246	18.1	Bellwood SD 88	Bellwood
246	18.1	Crete Monee CUSD 201u	Crete
246	18.1	North Mac CUSD 34	Girard
249	18.2	West Chicago ESD 33	West Chicago
250	18.3	Downers Grove GSD 58	Downers Grove
250	18.3	Dunlap CUSD 323	Peoria
250	18.3	Grant CHSD 124	Fox Lake
250	18.3	Reavis Twp HSD 220	Burbank
254	18.4	Batavia USD 101	Batavia
254	18.4	Litchfield CUSD 12	Litchfield
256	18.5	Harvey SD 152	Harvey
256	18.5	Lockport Twp HSD 205	Lockport
256	18.5	Round Lake CUSD 116	Round Lake
259	18.6	Aurora East USD 131	Aurora
259	18.6	Riverton CUSD 14	Spaulding
261	18.7	Summit SD 104	Summit
262	18.8	Marion CUSD 2	Marion
262	18.8	Ridgeland SD 122	Oak Lawn
264	18.9	Belleville Twp HSD 201	Belleville
264	18.9	CUSD 300	Carpentersville
264	18.9	Granite City CUSD 9	Granite City
264	18.9	Hillsboro CUSD 3	Hillsboro
264	18.9	O Fallon Twp HSD 203	O Fallon
269	19.0	Bradley Bourbonnais CHSD 307	Bradley
270	19.1	Kinnikinnick CCSD 131	Roscoe
270	19.1	Maywood-Melrose Park-Broadview 89	Melrose Park
270	19.1	Thornton Fractional Twp HSD 215	Calumet City
273	19.3	Columbia CUSD 4	Columbia
273	19.3	Lake Park CHSD 108	Roselle
273	19.3	Oswego CUSD 308	Oswego
276	19.4	Dolton SD 149	Calumet City
276	19.4	Mt Zion CUSD 3	Mount Zion
278	19.6	Mundelein Cons HSD 120	Mundelein
279	19.7	Taylorville CUSD 3	Taylorville
280	19.9	Bloom Twp HSD 206	Chicago Heights
280	19.9	Herrin CUSD 4	Herrin
280	19.9	SD U-46	Elgin
283	20.3	New Lenox SD 122	New Lenox
283	20.3	United Twp HSD 30	East Moline
285	20.5	Decatur SD 61	Decatur
285	20.5	Minooka CHSD 111	Minooka
287	20.6	Minooka CCSD 201	Minooka
288	21.4	Proviso Twp HSD 209	Forest Park
289	21.8	Mokena SD 159	Mokena
290	23.3	Cary CCSD 26	Cary
291	23.5	J S Morton HSD 201	Cicero
292	24.5	Lemont-Bromberek CSD 113a	Lemont

Student/Librarian Ratio

(number of students per librarian)

Rank	Number	District Name	City
1	351.8	Monmouth-Roseville CUSD 238	Monmouth
2	377.6	Homewood SD 153	Homewood
3	388.2	Downers Grove GSD 58	Downers Grove
4	393.4	ESD 159	Matteson
5	399.0	Alsip-Hazlgrn-Oaklwn SD 126	Alsip
6	400.0	CCSD 89	Glen Ellyn
7	404.5	Lisle CUSD 202	Lisle
8	406.8	North Shore SD 112	Highland Park
9	421.0	Bensenville SD 2	Bensenville
10	422.8	Northbrook SD 28	Northbrook
11	425.4	CCSD 62	Des Plaines
12	427.1	Woodridge SD 68	Woodridge
13	442.4	Hinsdale CCSD 181	Burr Ridge
14	449.0	Will County SD 92	Lockport
15	452.5	Winnetka SD 36	Winnetka
16	466.9	Community CSD 59	Arlington Hgts
17	481.6	Tinley Park CCSD 146	Tinley Park
18	483.6	Cook County SD 130	Blue Island
19	484.7	Evanston CCSD 65	Evanston
20	484.9	CCSD 93	Bloomingdale
21	489.2	Matteson ESD 162	Richton Park
22	492.3	New Trier Twp HSD 203	Northfield
23	494.6	East Moline SD 37	East Moline
24	506.8	Libertyville SD 70	Libertyville
25	511.0	Bourbonnais SD 53	Bourbonnais
26	511.9	Oak Park ESD 97	Oak Park
27	513.3	Aptakisic-Tripp CCSD 102	Buffalo Grove
28	517.0	Riverton CUSD 14	Spaulding
29	518.3	East Maine SD 63	Des Plaines
30	520.7	Deerfield SD 109	Deerfield
31	521.3	Orland SD 135	Orland Park
32	521.6	Schaumburg CCSD 54	Schaumburg
33	522.8	Lake Forest SD 67	Lake Forest
34	533.6	Kirby SD 140	Tinley Park
35	539.8	Prairie Central CUSD 8	Fairbury
36	540.5	Urbana SD 116	Urbana
37	544.3	Lincolnshire-Prairieview SD 103	Lincolnshire
38	544.5	Harrisburg CUSD 3	Harrisburg
39	546.4	Marquardt SD 15	Glendale Hgts
40	547.7	North Mac CUSD 34	Girard
41	554.3	Robinson CUSD 2	Robinson
42	559.0	Charleston CUSD 1	Charleston
43	563.3	Tolono CUSD 7	Tolono
44	564.7	Monticello CUSD 25	Monticello
45	572.2	Wheeling CCSD 21	Wheeling
46	573.3	Mundelein ESD 75	Mundelein
47	575.6	Park Ridge CCSD 64	Park Ridge
48	576.9	Arlington Hgts SD 25	Arlington Hgts
49	582.5	Woodstock CUSD 200	Woodstock
50	583.5	Johnsburg CUSD 12	Johnsburg
51	593.3	Champaign CUSD 4	Champaign
52	601.5	Harlem Ud 122	Machesney Park
53	605.6	Mchenry CCSD 15	Mchenry
54	612.6	Glenview CCSD 34	Glenview
55	613.2	Wilmette SD 39	Wilmette
56	613.3	Mclean County USD 5	Normal
57	617.7	Palatine CCSD 15	Palatine
58	624.3	Palos CCSD 118	Palos Park
59	625.2	La Grange SD 102	La Grange Park
60	625.8	Mt Zion CUSD 3	Mount Zion
61	626.8	Kildeer Countryside CCSD 96	Buffalo Grove
62	641.5	Elmhurst SD 205	Elmhurst
63	656.7	Clinton CUSD 15	Clinton
64	660.0	Herscher CUSD 2	Herscher
65	662.1	Geneva CUSD 304	Geneva
66	671.2	CUSD 200	Wheaton
67	682.2	Lombard SD 44	Lombard
68	684.5	Crystal Lake CCSD 47	Crystal Lake
69	692.6	Skokie SD 68	Skokie
70	698.3	Bloomington SD 87	Bloomington
71	707.3	Gurnee SD 56	Gurnee
72	710.2	Twp HSD 113	Highland Park
73	726.0	Mahomet-Seymour CUSD 3	Mahomet
74	728.9	Galesburg CUSD 205	Galesburg
75	735.3	Fremont SD 79	Mundelein
76	744.8	Lake Zurich CUSD 95	Lake Zurich
77	748.7	Wauconda CUSD 118	Wauconda
78	751.3	North Palos SD 117	Palos Hills
79	753.0	Ball Chatham CUSD 5	Chatham
80	757.3	Barrington CUSD 220	Barrington
81	759.6	Saint Charles CUSD 303	Saint Charles
82	764.3	Oak Lawn-Hometown SD 123	Oak Lawn
83	779.2	Aurora West USD 129	Aurora
84	788.4	Batavia USD 101	Batavia
85	789.5	Fenton CHSD 100	Bensenville
85	789.5	Riverside SD 96	Riverside
87	791.7	Northfield Twp HSD 225	Glenview
88	795.0	New Lenox SD 122	New Lenox
89	811.7	Naperville CUSD 203	Naperville
90	812.7	Harvard CUSD 50	Harvard
91	815.3	Dolton SD 148	Riverdale
92	825.4	Moline USD 40	Moline
93	859.0	Mattoon CUSD 2	Mattoon
94	862.5	Lake Forest CHSD 115	Lake Forest
95	868.0	Mannheim SD 83	Franklin Park
96	875.0	Leyden CHSD 212	Franklin Park
97	880.5	Thornton Twp HSD 205	South Holland
98	885.0	Winnebago CUSD 323	Winnebago
99	896.8	Valley View CUSD 365u	Romeoville
100	899.5	Township HSD 211	Palatine
101	902.6	Oswego CUSD 308	Oswego
102	909.0	Mascoutah CUD 19	Mascoutah
103	939.0	Morton CUSD 709	Morton
104	944.5	Oak Lawn CHSD 229	Oak Lawn
105	944.7	Indian Prairie CUSD 204	Aurora
106	945.5	Roxana CUSD 1	Roxana
107	962.0	Niles Twp CHSD 219	Skokie
108	967.0	Kaneland CUSD 302	Maple Park
109	970.0	Olympia CUSD 16	Stanford
110	985.0	Hinsdale Twp HSD 86	Hinsdale
111	987.9	Glenbard Twp HSD 87	Glen Ellyn
112	990.0	Meridian CUSD 223	Stillman Valley
113	992.0	Hawthorn CCSD 73	Vernon Hills
114	998.5	Macomb CUSD 185	Macomb
115	1,028.2	Cicero SD 99	Cicero
116	1,031.3	Grayslake CCSD 46	Grayslake
117	1,039.2	CHSD 99	Downers Grove
118	1,040.6	Glen Ellyn SD 41	Glen Ellyn
119	1,066.5	Murphysboro CUSD 186	Murphysboro
120	1,068.0	Alton CUSD 11	Alton
121	1,076.0	East Richland CUSD 1	Olney
122	1,076.5	CHSD 94	West Chicago
123	1,078.2	Joliet Twp HSD 204	Joliet
124	1,091.0	Oak Park - River Forest SD 200	Oak Park
125	1,094.0	Yorkville CUSD 115	Yorkville
126	1,098.2	Bremen CHSD 228	Midlothian
127	1,129.7	Berwyn North SD 98	Berwyn
128	1,132.3	Minooka CCSD 201	Minooka

Note: This section only includes districts with 1,500 or more students; All categories are ranked from high to low

129	1,134.7	CHSD 128	Vernon Hills
130	1,146.1	City of Chicago SD 299	Chicago
131	1,151.7	Springfield SD 186	Springfield
132	1,186.0	Lansing SD 158	Lansing
133	1,243.0	Lyons SD 103	Lyons
134	1,254.5	O Fallon Twp HSD 203	O Fallon
135	1,264.0	Herrin CUSD 4	Herrin
136	1,268.5	Mchenry CHSD 156	Mchenry
137	1,271.5	Minooka CHSD 111	Minooka
138	1,301.5	Bethalto CUSD 8	Bethalto
139	1,301.7	Rich Twp HSD 227	Olympia Fields
140	1,323.0	Geneseo CUSD 228	Geneseo
141	1,335.3	Marion CUSD 2	Marion
142	1,370.5	Waterloo CUSD 5	Waterloo
143	1,376.4	Plainfield SD 202	Plainfield
144	1,380.0	Effingham CUSD 40	Effingham
145	1,382.0	Jersey CUSD 100	Jerseyville
146	1,383.5	Cons HSD 230	Orland Park
147	1,384.0	Taylorville CUSD 3	Taylorville
148	1,395.7	Freeport SD 145	Freeport
149	1,410.5	CHSD 117	Lake Villa
150	1,412.5	Lake Park CHSD 108	Roselle
151	1,417.8	CHSD 218	Oak Lawn
152	1,420.5	Homewood Flossmoor CHSD 233	Flossmoor
153	1,437.0	Belvidere CUSD 100	Belvidere
154	1,484.0	Grayslake CHSD 127	Grayslake
155	1,486.4	CUSD 300	Carpentersville
156	1,507.0	Lemont Twp HSD 210	Lemont
157	1,534.0	Rockton SD 140	Rockton
158	1,540.0	Highland CUSD 5	Highland
159	1,541.0	Millburn CCSD 24	Old Mill Creek
160	1,544.0	Antioch CCSD 34	Antioch
161	1,554.0	Indian Springs SD 109	Justice
162	1,557.0	Vandalia CUSD 203	Vandalia
163	1,559.0	Oregon CUSD 220	Oregon
164	1,562.0	Byron CUSD 226	Byron
165	1,569.0	Steger SD 194	Steger
166	1,571.0	Evanston Twp HSD 202	Evanston
167	1,595.0	Eureka CUD 140	Eureka
167	1,595.0	Sherrard CUSD 200	Sherrard
169	1,605.0	Beardstown CUSD 15	Beardstown
170	1,620.0	Keeneyville SD 20	Hanover Park
171	1,648.0	Darien SD 61	Darien
172	1,652.7	Belleville Twp HSD 201	Belleville
173	1,661.0	Bradley SD 61	Bradley
174	1,663.0	Southwestern CUSD 9	Piasa
175	1,665.0	Forest Ridge SD 142	Oak Forest
176	1,699.0	Maine Township HSD 207	Park Ridge
177	1,703.0	Bloom Twp HSD 206	Chicago Heights
178	1,707.3	Proviso Twp HSD 209	Forest Park
179	1,712.0	United Twp HSD 30	East Moline
180	1,721.0	Skokie SD 69	Skokie
181	1,722.0	North Boone CUSD 200	Poplar Grove
182	1,726.0	Wabash CUSD 348	Mount Carmel
183	1,735.0	Central CUSD 301	Burlington
184	1,742.8	E Saint Louis SD 189	E Saint Louis
185	1,743.0	Reed Custer CUSD 255u	Braidwood
186	1,746.0	East Peoria SD 86	East Peoria
187	1,749.0	Rochelle CCSD 231	Rochelle
188	1,752.3	CHSD 155	Crystal Lake
189	1,783.5	Thornton Fractional Twp HSD 215	Calumet City
190	1,785.0	Reavis Twp HSD 220	Burbank
191	1,829.0	Jacksonville SD 117	Jacksonville
192	1,850.0	Posen-Robbins ESD 143-5	Posen
193	1,874.0	Grant CHSD 124	Fox Lake
193	1,874.0	Lockport Twp HSD 205	Lockport
195	1,887.0	Peotone CUSD 207u	Peotone
196	1,892.5	Dunlap CUSD 323	Peoria
197	1,904.0	Kewanee CUSD 229	Kewanee
198	1,905.0	Genoa Kingston CUSD 424	Genoa
199	1,926.0	Hillsboro CUSD 3	Hillsboro
200	1,955.0	Queen Bee SD 16	Glendale Hgts
201	1,990.5	Lyons Twp HSD 204	La Grange
202	1,995.0	Bond County CUSD 2	Greenville
203	1,997.0	Streator ESD 44	Streator
204	2,010.0	Pekin CSD 303	Pekin
205	2,040.6	Lincoln Way CHSD 210	New Lenox
206	2,059.0	Adlai E Stevenson HSD 125	Lincolnshire
207	2,060.0	Columbia CUSD 4	Columbia
208	2,074.6	Waukegan CUSD 60	Waukegan
209	2,082.0	Coal City CUSD 1	Coal City
209	2,082.0	Ottawa ESD 141	Ottawa
211	2,109.0	Bradley Bourbonnais CHSD 307	Bradley
212	2,130.0	Hononegah Chd 207	Rockton
213	2,133.0	Mount Prospect SD 57	Mount Prospect
214	2,135.0	Massac Ud 1	Metropolis
215	2,173.0	Rockford SD 205	Rockford
216	2,174.0	Woodland CCSD 50	Gurnee
217	2,210.0	SD 45 Dupage County	Villa Park
218	2,251.0	Mundelein Cons HSD 120	Mundelein
219	2,261.0	Warren Twp HSD 121	Gurnee
220	2,305.0	Manteno CUSD 5	Manteno
221	2,320.0	Plano CUSD 88	Plano
222	2,321.3	CSD 158	Algonquin
223	2,333.0	Rochester CUSD 3a	Rochester
224	2,364.0	Sandwich CUSD 430	Sandwich
225	2,389.0	Flossmoor SD 161	Chicago Heights
226	2,398.0	Lemont-Bromberek CSD 113a	Lemont
227	2,448.0	Beach Park CCSD 3	Beach Park
228	2,461.0	Township HSD 214	Arlington Hgts
229	2,636.0	Canton Union SD 66	Canton
230	2,766.0	Zion ESD 6	Zion
231	2,767.0	Dixon USD 170	Dixon
232	2,781.3	J S Morton HSD 201	Cicero
233	2,796.0	Cary CCSD 26	Cary
233	2,796.0	Prairie-Hills ESD 144	Markham
235	2,810.0	Zion-Benton Twp HSD 126	Zion
236	2,835.0	Kankakee SD 111	Kankakee
237	2,983.0	Elmwood Park CUSD 401	Elmwood Park
238	3,002.3	Decatur SD 61	Decatur
239	3,108.0	Lake Villa CCSD 41	Lake Villa
240	3,198.9	Bellwood SD 88	Bellwood
241	3,322.5	Collinsville CUSD 10	Collinsville
242	3,441.0	Sterling CUSD 5	Sterling
243	3,483.0	O Fallon CCSD 90	O Fallon
244	3,527.0	Summit Hill SD 161	Frankfort
245	3,625.5	Aurora East USD 131	Aurora
246	3,652.0	Triad CUSD 2	Troy
247	3,676.0	Evergreen Park ESD 124	Evergreen Park
248	3,781.0	Pekin PSD 108	Pekin
249	3,840.0	Sycamore CUSD 427	Sycamore
250	4,077.0	Dupage HSD 88	Addison
251	4,221.0	Cahokia CUSD 187	Cahokia
252	4,296.0	Addison SD 4	Addison
253	4,378.0	Il Valley Central USD 321	Chillicothe
254	4,406.0	West Chicago ESD 33	West Chicago
255	4,520.8	SD U-46	Elgin
256	4,564.0	Troy CCSD 30c	Plainfield
257	4,685.7	Peoria SD 150	Peoria
258	5,136.0	Crete Monee CUSD 201u	Crete
259	5,654.0	Joliet PSD 86	Joliet
260	6,104.0	Dekalb CUSD 428	Dekalb
261	6,207.0	Danville CCSD 118	Danville
262	6,622.0	Rock Island SD 41	Rock Island
263	6,873.0	Granite City CUSD 9	Granite City
264	7,176.0	Quincy SD 172	Quincy
265	7,480.0	Edwardsville CUSD 7	Edwardsville
n/a	n/a	Argo CHSD 217	Summit
n/a	n/a	Belleville SD 118	Belleville
n/a	n/a	Berkeley SD 87	Berkeley
n/a	n/a	Berwyn South SD 100	Berwyn
n/a	n/a	Big Hollow SD 38	Ingleside
n/a	n/a	Burbank SD 111	Burbank
n/a	n/a	Carterville CUSD 5	Carterville
n/a	n/a	CCSD 168	Sauk Village
n/a	n/a	Chicago Heights SD 170	Chicago Heights
n/a	n/a	Dolton SD 149	Calumet City
n/a	n/a	Duquoin CUSD 300	Du Quoin
n/a	n/a	Frankfort CCSD 157c	Frankfort
n/a	n/a	Frankfort CUSD 168	West Frankfort
n/a	n/a	Harvey SD 152	Harvey
n/a	n/a	Homer CCSD 33c	Homer Glen
n/a	n/a	Kinnikinnick CCSD 131	Roscoe
n/a	n/a	Litchfield CUSD 12	Litchfield
n/a	n/a	Maywood-Melrose Park-Broadview 89	Melrose Park
n/a	n/a	Midlothian SD 143	Midlothian
n/a	n/a	Mokena SD 159	Mokena
n/a	n/a	Mount Vernon SD 80	Mount Vernon
n/a	n/a	North Chicago SD 187	North Chicago
n/a	n/a	Park Forest SD 163	Park Forest
n/a	n/a	Rantoul City SD 137	Rantoul
n/a	n/a	Ridgeland SD 122	Oak Lawn
n/a	n/a	Round Lake CUSD 116	Round Lake
n/a	n/a	Summit SD 104	Summit

Student/Counselor Ratio

(number of students per counselor)

Rank	Number	District Name	City
1	192.8	Maine Township HSD 207	Park Ridge
2	205.2	Twp HSD 113	Highland Park
3	209.5	Evanston Twp HSD 202	Evanston
4	217.9	Northfield Twp HSD 225	Glenview
5	225.4	Hinsdale Twp HSD 86	Hinsdale
6	226.3	Adlai E Stevenson HSD 125	Lincolnshire
7	239.4	Township HSD 214	Arlington Hgts
8	240.1	Thornton Twp HSD 205	South Holland
9	242.9	Niles Twp CHSD 219	Skokie
10	243.1	CHSD 128	Vernon Hills
11	246.4	Lake Forest CHSD 115	Lake Forest
12	246.6	CHSD 218	Oak Lawn
13	246.7	Fenton CHSD 100	Bensenville
14	250.0	Leyden CHSD 212	Franklin Park
15	250.1	Mundelein Cons HSD 120	Mundelein
16	250.4	Lyons Twp HSD 204	La Grange
17	256.7	Grayslake CHSD 127	Grayslake
18	258.3	Homewood Flossmoor CHSD 233	Flossmoor
19	268.1	Argo CHSD 217	Summit
20	269.9	Oak Lawn CHSD 229	Oak Lawn
21	270.4	Cons HSD 230	Orland Park
22	272.8	Oak Park - River Forest SD 200	Oak Park
23	274.4	Township HSD 211	Palatine
24	278.9	Rich Twp HSD 227	Olympia Fields
25	281.5	Bloom Twp HSD 206	Chicago Heights
26	282.5	Lake Park CHSD 108	Roselle
27	284.1	Glenbard Twp HSD 87	Glen Ellyn
28	287.1	Pekin CSD 303	Pekin
29	288.3	Lockport Twp HSD 205	Lockport
30	288.7	CHSD 99	Downers Grove
31	293.2	Monmouth-Roseville CUSD 238	Monmouth
32	297.5	Reavis Twp HSD 220	Burbank
33	301.3	Bradley Bourbonnais CHSD 307	Bradley
33	301.3	Proviso Twp HSD 209	Forest Park
35	308.2	Lemont Twp HSD 210	Lemont
36	309.0	J S Morton HSD 201	Cicero
37	311.8	Oregon CUSD 220	Oregon
38	313.6	Dupage HSD 88	Addison
39	317.1	Mchenry CHSD 156	Mchenry
40	319.4	Lincoln Way CHSD 210	New Lenox
41	320.1	Sterling CUSD 5	Sterling
42	324.3	Thornton Fractional Twp HSD 215	Calumet City
43	339.8	Joliet Twp HSD 204	Joliet
44	342.4	United Twp HSD 30	East Moline
45	351.3	Zion-Benton Twp HSD 126	Zion
46	352.6	CHSD 117	Lake Villa
47	353.3	East Moline SD 37	East Moline
48	355.0	Hononegah Chd 207	Rockton
49	363.3	Minooka CHSD 111	Minooka
50	374.8	Grant CHSD 124	Fox Lake
51	376.8	Warren Twp HSD 121	Gurnee
52	382.0	Litchfield CUSD 12	Litchfield
53	389.4	CHSD 155	Crystal Lake
54	390.5	Byron CUSD 226	Byron
55	390.8	Bremen CHSD 228	Midlothian
56	396.0	Meridian CUSD 223	Stillman Valley
57	399.2	Vandalia CUSD 203	Vandalia
58	415.8	Robinson CUSD 2	Robinson
59	416.4	Ottawa ESD 141	Ottawa
60	418.2	O Fallon Twp HSD 203	O Fallon
61	419.7	Sherrard CUSD 200	Sherrard
62	421.3	CHSD 94	West Chicago
63	437.3	Rochelle CCSD 231	Rochelle
64	450.7	Belleville Twp HSD 201	Belleville
65	460.0	Effingham CUSD 40	Effingham
66	461.2	Dixon USD 170	Dixon
67	463.3	Elmhurst SD 205	Elmhurst
68	471.3	Marion CUSD 2	Marion
69	477.3	Carterville CUSD 5	Carterville
70	480.2	Naperville CUSD 203	Naperville
71	485.9	Macomb CUSD 185	Macomb
72	489.9	City of Chicago SD 299	Chicago
73	497.9	E Saint Louis SD 189	E Saint Louis
74	502.0	Ball Chatham CUSD 5	Chatham
75	506.5	CUSD 200	Wheaton
76	517.0	Riverton CUSD 14	Spaulding
77	529.2	Geneseo CUSD 228	Geneseo
78	529.3	New Trier Twp HSD 203	Northfield
79	529.6	Clinton CUSD 15	Clinton
80	533.3	Murphysboro CUSD 186	Murphysboro
81	534.6	Barrington CUSD 220	Barrington
82	539.3	Lisle CUSD 202	Lisle
83	547.7	North Mac CUSD 34	Girard
84	555.2	Harlem Ud 122	Machesney Park
85	558.4	Champaign CUSD 4	Champaign
86	559.0	Charleston CUSD 1	Charleston
87	563.3	Tolono CUSD 7	Tolono
88	574.8	Belvidere CUSD 100	Belvidere

Note: This section only includes districts with 1,500 or more students; All categories are ranked from high to low

89	578.9	Rockford SD 205	Rockford
90	581.1	Decatur SD 61	Decatur
91	583.5	Johnsburg CUSD 12	Johnsburg
92	588.4	Woodstock CUSD 200	Woodstock
93	598.1	Freeport SD 145	Freeport
94	599.0	Indian Prairie CUSD 204	Aurora
95	604.4	Kaneland CUSD 302	Maple Park
96	609.7	Jacksonville SD 117	Jacksonville
97	610.4	Dekalb CUSD 428	Dekalb
98	617.7	Urbana SD 116	Urbana
99	621.5	Saint Charles CUSD 303	Saint Charles
100	625.8	Mt Zion CUSD 3	Mount Zion
101	626.3	Waukegan CUSD 60	Waukegan
102	627.3	Geneva CUSD 304	Geneva
103	630.2	Pekin PSD 108	Pekin
104	632.0	Herrin CUSD 4	Herrin
105	659.0	Canton Union SD 66	Canton
106	662.0	Lake Zurich CUSD 95	Lake Zurich
107	665.0	Bond County CUSD 2	Greenville
108	669.4	Peoria SD 150	Peoria
109	686.7	Columbia CUSD 4	Columbia
110	687.2	Mattoon CUSD 2	Mattoon
111	689.0	Valley View CUSD 365u	Romeoville
112	694.0	Coal City CUSD 1	Coal City
113	704.3	Morton CUSD 709	Morton
114	709.5	Berkeley SD 87	Berkeley
115	717.3	East Richland CUSD 1	Olney
116	727.2	Mascoutah CUD 19	Mascoutah
117	729.7	Il Valley Central USD 321	Chillicothe
118	732.7	Genoa Kingston CUSD 424	Genoa
119	733.7	Crete Monee CUSD 201u	Crete
120	736.2	Homer CCSD 33c	Homer Glen
121	739.4	Mclean County USD 5	Normal
122	742.9	Moline USD 40	Moline
123	757.0	Dunlap CUSD 323	Peoria
124	757.8	Olympia CUSD 16	Stanford
125	767.4	North Chicago SD 187	North Chicago
126	768.0	Sycamore CUSD 427	Sycamore
127	770.0	Highland CUSD 5	Highland
128	770.7	CUSD 300	Carpentersville
129	773.3	Plano CUSD 88	Plano
130	778.0	Duquoin CUSD 300	Du Quoin
131	788.0	Sandwich CUSD 430	Sandwich
132	791.4	Oswego CUSD 308	Oswego
133	796.5	Winnebago CUSD 323	Winnebago
134	797.3	Quincy SD 172	Quincy
135	797.5	Eureka CUD 140	Eureka
136	798.0	Bloomington SD 87	Bloomington
137	799.4	Batavia USD 101	Batavia
138	802.5	Beardstown CUSD 15	Beardstown
139	805.7	Aurora East USD 131	Aurora
140	827.8	Rock Island SD 41	Rock Island
141	863.0	Wabash CUSD 348	Mount Carmel
142	869.5	Mount Vernon SD 80	Mount Vernon
143	871.5	Reed Custer CUSD 255u	Braidwood
144	890.0	Manteno CUSD 5	Manteno
145	898.4	Wauconda CUSD 118	Wauconda
146	911.1	North Boone CUSD 200	Poplar Grove
147	911.7	Yorkville CUSD 115	Yorkville
148	913.0	Triad CUSD 2	Troy
149	913.7	Waterloo CUSD 5	Waterloo
150	921.3	Jersey CUSD 100	Jerseyville
151	935.0	Edwardsville CUSD 7	Edwardsville
152	943.5	Peotone CUSD 207u	Peotone
153	945.0	Kankakee SD 111	Kankakee
154	945.5	Roxana CUSD 1	Roxana
155	952.0	Kewanee CUSD 229	Kewanee
156	963.0	Hillsboro CUSD 3	Hillsboro
157	968.0	Mahomet-Seymour CUSD 3	Mahomet
158	990.0	Herscher CUSD 2	Herscher
159	1,031.7	CSD 158	Algonquin
160	1,034.5	Danville CCSD 118	Danville
161	1,052.5	Bensenville SD 2	Bensenville
162	1,067.5	Massac Ud 1	Metropolis
163	1,079.5	Prairie Central CUSD 8	Fairbury
164	1,080.5	Galesburg CUSD 205	Galesburg
165	1,089.0	Harrisburg CUSD 3	Harrisburg
166	1,156.7	Central CUSD 301	Burlington
167	1,166.5	Rochester CUSD 3a	Rochester
168	1,196.7	SD U-46	Elgin
169	1,202.8	Round Lake CUSD 116	Round Lake
170	1,214.0	Glen Ellyn SD 41	Glen Ellyn
171	1,219.0	Harvard CUSD 50	Harvard
172	1,228.6	Mundelein ESD 75	Mundelein
173	1,275.0	Plainfield SD 202	Plainfield
174	1,281.6	Alton CUSD 11	Alton
175	1,289.7	Cook County SD 130	Blue Island
176	1,301.5	Bethalto CUSD 8	Bethalto
177	1,343.7	Elmwood Park CUSD 401	Elmwood Park
178	1,374.6	Granite City CUSD 9	Granite City
179	1,384.0	Taylorville CUSD 3	Taylorville
180	1,402.4	Aurora West USD 129	Aurora
181	1,407.0	Cahokia CUSD 187	Cahokia
182	1,521.3	Troy CCSD 30c	Plainfield
183	1,562.0	Deerfield SD 109	Deerfield
184	1,567.0	Kildeer Countryside CCSD 96	Buffalo Grove
185	1,567.5	Dolton SD 149	Calumet City
186	1,569.0	Lombard SD 44	Lombard
187	1,657.5	SD 45 Dupage County	Villa Park
188	1,661.3	Collinsville CUSD 10	Collinsville
189	1,663.0	Southwestern CUSD 9	Piasa
190	1,665.0	Forest Ridge SD 142	Oak Forest
191	1,682.3	Downers Grove GSD 58	Downers Grove
192	1,694.0	Monticello CUSD 25	Monticello
193	1,746.0	East Peoria SD 86	East Peoria
194	1,905.0	Frankfort CUSD 168	West Frankfort
195	1,955.0	Queen Bee SD 16	Glendale Hgts
196	1,981.5	Berwyn South SD 100	Berwyn
197	2,000.0	CCSD 89	Glen Ellyn
198	2,045.0	Kinnikinnick CCSD 131	Roscoe
199	2,158.5	Park Ridge CCSD 64	Park Ridge
200	2,203.0	West Chicago ESD 33	West Chicago
201	2,260.9	Summit Hill SD 161	Frankfort
202	2,555.0	Bourbonnais SD 53	Bourbonnais
203	2,606.5	Orland SD 135	Orland Park
204	2,990.0	Woodridge SD 68	Woodridge
205	3,088.0	Antioch CCSD 34	Antioch
206	3,165.8	Palatine CCSD 15	Palatine
207	3,735.0	Kirby SD 140	Tinley Park
208	3,982.0	Hinsdale CCSD 181	Burr Ridge
209	14,083.0	Schaumburg CCSD 54	Schaumburg
n/a	n/a	Addison SD 4	Addison
n/a	n/a	Alsip-Hazlgrn-Oaklwn SD 126	Alsip
n/a	n/a	Aptakisic-Tripp CCSD 102	Buffalo Grove
n/a	n/a	Arlington Hgts SD 25	Arlington Hgts
n/a	n/a	Beach Park CCSD 3	Beach Park
n/a	n/a	Belleville SD 118	Belleville
n/a	n/a	Bellwood SD 88	Bellwood
n/a	n/a	Berwyn North SD 98	Berwyn
n/a	n/a	Big Hollow SD 38	Ingleside
n/a	n/a	Bradley SD 61	Bradley
n/a	n/a	Burbank SD 111	Burbank
n/a	n/a	Cary CCSD 26	Cary
n/a	n/a	CCSD 168	Sauk Village
n/a	n/a	CCSD 62	Des Plaines
n/a	n/a	CCSD 93	Bloomingdale
n/a	n/a	Chicago Heights SD 170	Chicago Heights
n/a	n/a	Cicero SD 99	Cicero
n/a	n/a	Community CSD 59	Arlington Hgts
n/a	n/a	Crystal Lake CCSD 47	Crystal Lake
n/a	n/a	Darien SD 61	Darien
n/a	n/a	Dolton SD 148	Riverdale
n/a	n/a	East Maine SD 63	Des Plaines
n/a	n/a	ESD 159	Matteson
n/a	n/a	Evanston CCSD 65	Evanston
n/a	n/a	Evergreen Park ESD 124	Evergreen Park
n/a	n/a	Flossmoor SD 161	Chicago Heights
n/a	n/a	Frankfort CCSD 157c	Frankfort
n/a	n/a	Fremont SD 79	Mundelein
n/a	n/a	Glenview CCSD 34	Glenview
n/a	n/a	Grayslake CCSD 46	Grayslake
n/a	n/a	Gurnee SD 56	Gurnee
n/a	n/a	Harvey SD 152	Harvey
n/a	n/a	Hawthorn CCSD 73	Vernon Hills
n/a	n/a	Homewood SD 153	Homewood
n/a	n/a	Indian Springs SD 109	Justice
n/a	n/a	Joliet PSD 86	Joliet
n/a	n/a	Keeneyville SD 20	Hanover Park
n/a	n/a	La Grange SD 102	La Grange Park
n/a	n/a	Lake Forest SD 67	Lake Forest
n/a	n/a	Lake Villa CCSD 41	Lake Villa
n/a	n/a	Lansing SD 158	Lansing
n/a	n/a	Lemont-Bromberek CSD 113a	Lemont
n/a	n/a	Libertyville SD 70	Libertyville
n/a	n/a	Lincolnshire-Prairieview SD 103	Lincolnshire
n/a	n/a	Lyons SD 103	Lyons
n/a	n/a	Mannheim SD 83	Franklin Park
n/a	n/a	Marquardt SD 15	Glendale Hgts
n/a	n/a	Matteson ESD 162	Richton Park
n/a	n/a	Maywood-Melrose Park-Broadview 89	Melrose Park
n/a	n/a	Mchenry CCSD 15	Mchenry
n/a	n/a	Midlothian SD 143	Midlothian
n/a	n/a	Millburn CCSD 24	Old Mill Creek
n/a	n/a	Minooka CCSD 201	Minooka
n/a	n/a	Mokena SD 159	Mokena
n/a	n/a	Mount Prospect SD 57	Mount Prospect
n/a	n/a	New Lenox SD 122	New Lenox
n/a	n/a	North Palos SD 117	Palos Hills
n/a	n/a	North Shore SD 112	Highland Park
n/a	n/a	Northbrook SD 28	Northbrook
n/a	n/a	O Fallon CCSD 90	O Fallon
n/a	n/a	Oak Lawn-Hometown SD 123	Oak Lawn
n/a	n/a	Oak Park ESD 97	Oak Park
n/a	n/a	Palos CCSD 118	Palos Park
n/a	n/a	Park Forest SD 163	Park Forest
n/a	n/a	Posen-Robbins ESD 143-5	Posen
n/a	n/a	Prairie-Hills ESD 144	Markham
n/a	n/a	Rantoul City SD 137	Rantoul
n/a	n/a	Ridgeland SD 122	Oak Lawn
n/a	n/a	Riverside SD 96	Riverside
n/a	n/a	Rockton SD 140	Rockton
n/a	n/a	Skokie SD 68	Skokie
n/a	n/a	Skokie SD 69	Skokie
n/a	n/a	Springfield SD 186	Springfield
n/a	n/a	Steger SD 194	Steger
n/a	n/a	Streator ESD 44	Streator
n/a	n/a	Summit SD 104	Summit
n/a	n/a	Tinley Park CCSD 146	Tinley Park
n/a	n/a	Wheeling CCSD 21	Wheeling
n/a	n/a	Will County SD 92	Lockport
n/a	n/a	Wilmette SD 39	Wilmette
n/a	n/a	Winnetka SD 36	Winnetka
n/a	n/a	Woodland CCSD 50	Gurnee
n/a	n/a	Zion ESD 6	Zion

Current Expenditures per Student

Rank	Dollars	District Name	City
1	23,036	Niles Twp CHSD 219	Skokie
2	22,107	New Trier Twp HSD 203	Northfield
3	21,710	Lake Forest CHSD 115	Lake Forest
4	21,602	Evanston Twp HSD 202	Evanston
5	21,476	CCSD 62	Des Plaines
6	20,816	Township HSD 211	Palatine
7	20,746	Northfield Twp HSD 225	Glenview
8	20,175	Twp HSD 113	Highland Park
9	19,156	CHSD 128	Vernon Hills
10	18,200	Leyden CHSD 212	Franklin Park
11	18,194	Northbrook SD 28	Northbrook
12	18,156	Hinsdale Twp HSD 86	Hinsdale
13	18,110	Township HSD 214	Arlington Hgts
14	17,980	Adlai E Stevenson HSD 125	Lincolnshire
15	17,887	Oak Park - River Forest SD 200	Oak Park
16	17,792	Maine Township HSD 207	Park Ridge
17	17,562	Winnetka SD 36	Winnetka
18	17,244	Fenton CHSD 100	Bensenville
19	16,597	Rich Twp HSD 227	Olympia Fields
20	16,373	Argo CHSD 217	Summit
21	16,213	Lyons Twp HSD 204	La Grange
22	15,948	Evanston CCSD 65	Evanston
23	15,820	Lisle CUSD 202	Lisle
24	15,803	Aptakisic-Tripp CCSD 102	Buffalo Grove
25	15,768	Lincolnshire-Prairieview SD 103	Lincolnshire
26	15,558	Homewood Flossmoor CHSD 233	Flossmoor
27	15,358	E Saint Louis SD 189	E Saint Louis
28	15,346	Lake Forest SD 67	Lake Forest
29	15,300	Lake Park CHSD 108	Roselle
30	15,191	Skokie SD 68	Skokie
31	15,103	North Shore SD 112	Highland Park
32	14,765	Reavis Twp HSD 220	Burbank
33	14,728	Hinsdale CCSD 181	Burr Ridge
34	14,611	Dupage HSD 88	Addison
35	14,602	Byron CUSD 226	Byron
36	14,599	Champaign CUSD 4	Champaign
37	14,567	CHSD 99	Downers Grove
38	14,529	Lemont Twp HSD 210	Lemont
39	14,528	CHSD 218	Oak Lawn
40	14,457	Bloom Twp HSD 206	Chicago Heights
41	14,453	Community CSD 59	Arlington Hgts
42	14,415	Park Ridge CCSD 64	Park Ridge
43	14,342	Mannheim SD 83	Franklin Park
44	14,323	Joliet Twp HSD 204	Joliet
45	14,189	Cons HSD 230	Orland Park
46	14,136	Oak Lawn CHSD 229	Oak Lawn
47	14,092	Barrington CUSD 220	Barrington
48	14,082	Glenbard Twp HSD 87	Glen Ellyn
49	14,061	CHSD 117	Lake Villa
50	13,930	Grayslake CHSD 127	Grayslake

Note: This section only includes districts with 1,500 or more students; All categories are ranked from high to low

51	13,914	Cahokia CUSD 187	Cahokia
52	13,908	CCSD 93	Bloomingdale
53	13,903	Tinley Park CCSD 146	Tinley Park
54	13,885	Lombard SD 44	Lombard
55	13,745	Oak Park ESD 97	Oak Park
56	13,719	Park Forest SD 163	Park Forest
57	13,694	Wilmette SD 39	Wilmette
58	13,632	Deerfield SD 109	Deerfield
59	13,581	Orland SD 135	Orland Park
60	13,407	Kildeer Countryside CCSD 96	Buffalo Grove
61	13,371	Naperville CUSD 203	Naperville
62	13,330	Bremen CHSD 228	Midlothian
63	13,301	Glenview CCSD 34	Glenview
64	13,196	Dolton SD 148	Riverdale
65	13,193	Proviso Twp HSD 209	Forest Park
66	13,064	Schaumburg CCSD 54	Schaumburg
67	12,844	Prairie-Hills ESD 144	Markham
68	12,839	Bensenville SD 2	Bensenville
69	12,827	Zion-Benton Twp HSD 126	Zion
70	12,817	Springfield SD 186	Springfield
71	12,769	Elmhurst SD 205	Elmhurst
72	12,725	Wheeling CCSD 21	Wheeling
73	12,643	ESD 159	Matteson
74	12,598	CHSD 155	Crystal Lake
75	12,564	Palos CCSD 118	Palos Park
76	12,483	Urbana SD 116	Urbana
77	12,407	Riverside SD 96	Riverside
78	12,394	CHSD 94	West Chicago
79	12,286	Lockport Twp HSD 205	Lockport
80	12,247	Mundelein Cons HSD 120	Mundelein
81	12,243	Matteson ESD 162	Richton Park
82	12,214	Reed Custer CUSD 255u	Braidwood
83	12,150	CCSD 89	Glen Ellyn
84	12,135	Woodridge SD 68	Woodridge
85	12,122	Evergreen Park ESD 124	Evergreen Park
86	12,115	Minooka CHSD 111	Minooka
87	12,109	East Maine SD 63	Des Plaines
88	12,080	Arlington Hgts SD 25	Arlington Hgts
89	12,035	Chicago Heights SD 170	Chicago Heights
90	12,032	North Chicago SD 187	North Chicago
91	11,931	City of Chicago SD 299	Chicago
92	11,917	Rockford SD 205	Rockford
93	11,911	Palatine CCSD 15	Palatine
94	11,909	Lincoln Way CHSD 210	New Lenox
95	11,869	Downers Grove GSD 58	Downers Grove
96	11,826	Dolton SD 149	Calumet City
97	11,810	Woodstock CUSD 200	Woodstock
98	11,776	Lake Zurich CUSD 95	Lake Zurich
99	11,746	Central CUSD 301	Burlington
100	11,741	CCSD 168	Sauk Village
101	11,730	Homewood SD 153	Homewood
102	11,726	Oak Lawn-Hometown SD 123	Oak Lawn
103	11,710	Coal City CUSD 1	Coal City
104	11,708	Harlem Ud 122	Machesney Park
105	11,704	Hawthorn CCSD 73	Vernon Hills
106	11,670	Sycamore CUSD 427	Sycamore
107	11,661	Flossmoor SD 161	Chicago Heights
108	11,645	Valley View CUSD 365u	Romeoville
109	11,644	CUSD 200	Wheaton
110	11,635	SD 45 Dupage County	Villa Park
111	11,625	Alsip-Hazlgrn-Oaklwn SD 126	Alsip
112	11,621	Glen Ellyn SD 41	Glen Ellyn
113	11,619	Saint Charles CUSD 303	Saint Charles
114	11,602	Geneva CUSD 304	Geneva
115	11,509	Dekalb CUSD 428	Dekalb
116	11,507	Freeport SD 145	Freeport
117	11,494	Cook County SD 130	Blue Island
118	11,485	Gurnee SD 56	Gurnee
119	11,477	Marquardt SD 15	Glendale Hgts
120	11,427	Mchenry CHSD 156	Mchenry
121	11,405	Skokie SD 69	Skokie
122	11,379	Peoria SD 150	Peoria
123	11,348	Zion ESD 6	Zion
124	11,334	Batavia USD 101	Batavia
124	11,334	Harvey SD 152	Harvey
126	11,311	Thornton Fractional Twp HSD 215	Calumet City
127	11,255	Ottawa ESD 141	Ottawa
128	11,245	Woodland CCSD 50	Gurnee
129	11,220	Libertyville SD 70	Libertyville
130	11,172	Johnsburg CUSD 12	Johnsburg
131	11,166	Kirby SD 140	Tinley Park
132	11,162	Homer CCSD 33c	Homer Glen
133	11,146	West Chicago ESD 33	West Chicago
134	11,125	Crete Monee CUSD 201u	Crete
134	11,125	Kankakee SD 111	Kankakee
136	11,067	La Grange SD 102	La Grange Park
137	11,014	Bloomington SD 87	Bloomington
138	10,997	Keeneyville SD 20	Hanover Park
139	10,951	East Moline SD 37	East Moline
140	10,940	Herscher CUSD 2	Herscher
141	10,927	Danville CCSD 118	Danville
142	10,883	Waukegan CUSD 60	Waukegan
143	10,829	Mount Vernon SD 80	Mount Vernon
144	10,747	Elmwood Park CUSD 401	Elmwood Park
145	10,728	Belleville Twp HSD 201	Belleville
146	10,720	Lyons SD 103	Lyons
147	10,655	Streator ESD 44	Streator
148	10,650	Moline USD 40	Moline
149	10,636	Mount Prospect SD 57	Mount Prospect
150	10,609	Wauconda CUSD 118	Wauconda
151	10,572	J S Morton HSD 201	Cicero
152	10,561	Will County SD 92	Lockport
153	10,558	Summit SD 104	Summit
154	10,533	United Twp HSD 30	East Moline
155	10,532	Grant CHSD 124	Fox Lake
156	10,460	North Palos SD 117	Palos Hills
157	10,394	Belleville SD 118	Belleville
158	10,358	Winnebago CUSD 323	Winnebago
159	10,348	Rock Island SD 41	Rock Island
160	10,345	Sandwich CUSD 430	Sandwich
161	10,304	Indian Prairie CUSD 204	Aurora
162	10,300	Macomb CUSD 185	Macomb
163	10,289	Alton CUSD 11	Alton
164	10,285	Aurora West USD 129	Aurora
165	10,276	Beach Park CCSD 3	Beach Park
166	10,264	Warren Twp HSD 121	Gurnee
167	10,239	Grayslake CCSD 46	Grayslake
168	10,223	Frankfort CCSD 157c	Frankfort
169	10,209	Kaneland CUSD 302	Maple Park
170	10,203	Pekin CSD 303	Pekin
171	10,179	Olympia CUSD 16	Stanford
172	10,120	Vandalia CUSD 203	Vandalia
173	10,113	Oregon CUSD 220	Oregon
174	10,105	Berwyn South SD 100	Berwyn
175	10,098	Queen Bee SD 16	Glendale Hgts
176	10,087	Bradley SD 61	Bradley
177	10,071	Mascoutah CUD 19	Mascoutah
178	10,065	Steger SD 194	Steger
179	10,052	Burbank SD 111	Burbank
180	10,013	Roxana CUSD 1	Roxana
181	9,990	O Fallon Twp HSD 203	O Fallon
182	9,969	Fremont SD 79	Mundelein
183	9,917	Crystal Lake CCSD 47	Crystal Lake
184	9,888	Mundelein ESD 75	Mundelein
185	9,881	Joliet PSD 86	Joliet
186	9,843	Hononegah Chd 207	Rockton
187	9,805	Robinson CUSD 2	Robinson
188	9,773	East Peoria SD 86	East Peoria
189	9,767	Morton CUSD 709	Morton
190	9,754	Troy CCSD 30c	Plainfield
191	9,730	Decatur SD 61	Decatur
192	9,724	Millburn CCSD 24	Old Mill Creek
193	9,712	Mclean County USD 5	Normal
193	9,712	Quincy SD 172	Quincy
195	9,678	Genoa Kingston CUSD 424	Genoa
196	9,652	Belvidere CUSD 100	Belvidere
197	9,647	Prairie Central CUSD 8	Fairbury
198	9,635	Rockton SD 140	Rockton
199	9,624	Dixon USD 170	Dixon
200	9,620	Round Lake CUSD 116	Round Lake
201	9,612	Mchenry CCSD 15	Mchenry
202	9,584	Rantoul City SD 137	Rantoul
203	9,564	SD U-46	Elgin
204	9,525	Darien SD 61	Darien
205	9,486	CUSD 300	Carpentersville
206	9,467	Harvard CUSD 50	Harvard
207	9,431	Mattoon CUSD 2	Mattoon
208	9,407	Pekin PSD 108	Pekin
209	9,400	Bradley Bourbonnais CHSD 307	Bradley
210	9,399	Edwardsville CUSD 7	Edwardsville
211	9,332	Cicero SD 99	Cicero
212	9,310	Aurora East USD 131	Aurora
213	9,304	Highland CUSD 5	Highland
214	9,290	Ridgeland SD 122	Oak Lawn
215	9,284	Tolono CUSD 7	Tolono
216	9,283	Duquoin CUSD 300	Du Quoin
217	9,279	Jacksonville SD 117	Jacksonville
218	9,257	Antioch CCSD 34	Antioch
219	9,173	Beardstown CUSD 15	Beardstown
220	9,143	Jersey CUSD 100	Jerseyville
221	9,126	Cary CCSD 26	Cary
222	9,113	Berwyn North SD 98	Berwyn
223	9,086	Clinton CUSD 15	Clinton
224	9,082	Effingham CUSD 40	Effingham
225	9,067	Murphysboro CUSD 186	Murphysboro
226	9,051	Sherrard CUSD 200	Sherrard
227	9,034	Forest Ridge SD 142	Oak Forest
228	9,023	Il Valley Central USD 321	Chillicothe
229	9,014	Meridian CUSD 223	Stillman Valley
229	9,014	Plainfield SD 202	Plainfield
231	9,012	Sterling CUSD 5	Sterling
232	8,985	Ball Chatham CUSD 5	Chatham
233	8,974	Bethalto CUSD 8	Bethalto
234	8,949	Indian Springs SD 109	Justice
235	8,927	Canton Union SD 66	Canton
236	8,860	Lansing SD 158	Lansing
237	8,858	Marion CUSD 2	Marion
238	8,855	Yorkville CUSD 115	Yorkville
239	8,801	Eureka CUD 140	Eureka
240	8,799	North Boone CUSD 200	Poplar Grove
241	8,795	Granite City CUSD 9	Granite City
242	8,790	Berkeley SD 87	Berkeley
243	8,789	Plano CUSD 88	Plano
244	8,783	Waterloo CUSD 5	Waterloo
245	8,781	Mahomet-Seymour CUSD 3	Mahomet
246	8,780	New Lenox SD 122	New Lenox
247	8,765	Litchfield CUSD 12	Litchfield
248	8,726	Addison SD 4	Addison
249	8,709	Rochelle CCSD 231	Rochelle
250	8,694	Bond County CUSD 2	Greenville
251	8,691	Harrisburg CUSD 3	Harrisburg
252	8,636	East Richland CUSD 1	Olney
253	8,631	Massac Ud 1	Metropolis
254	8,604	CSD 158	Algonquin
255	8,588	Lake Villa CCSD 41	Lake Villa
256	8,575	Galesburg CUSD 205	Galesburg
257	8,520	Bourbonnais SD 53	Bourbonnais
258	8,509	Frankfort CUSD 168	West Frankfort
259	8,496	Triad CUSD 2	Troy
260	8,479	Monticello CUSD 25	Monticello
261	8,462	Hillsboro CUSD 3	Hillsboro
262	8,445	North Mac CUSD 34	Girard
263	8,416	Peotone CUSD 207u	Peotone
264	8,412	Geneseo CUSD 228	Geneseo
265	8,403	Lemont-Bromberek CSD 113a	Lemont
266	8,367	Kinnikinnick CCSD 131	Roscoe
267	8,341	Midlothian SD 143	Midlothian
268	8,322	Big Hollow SD 38	Ingleside
268	8,322	Charleston CUSD 1	Charleston
270	8,314	Manteno CUSD 5	Manteno
271	8,250	Collinsville CUSD 10	Collinsville
272	8,193	Oswego CUSD 308	Oswego
273	8,137	O Fallon CCSD 90	O Fallon
274	8,105	Herrin CUSD 4	Herrin
275	8,024	Posen-Robbins ESD 143-5	Posen
276	8,005	Carterville CUSD 5	Carterville
277	7,898	Mokena SD 159	Mokena
278	7,892	Monmouth-Roseville CUSD 238	Monmouth
279	7,890	Southwestern CUSD 9	Piasa
280	7,818	Summit Hill SD 161	Frankfort
281	7,783	Dunlap CUSD 323	Peoria
282	7,751	Kewanee CUSD 229	Kewanee
283	7,742	Mt Zion CUSD 3	Mount Zion
284	7,732	Wabash CUSD 348	Mount Carmel
285	7,540	Columbia CUSD 4	Columbia
286	7,422	Taylorville CUSD 3	Taylorville
287	7,225	Riverton CUSD 14	Spaulding
288	6,844	Minooka CCSD 201	Minooka
289	6,802	Rochester CUSD 3a	Rochester
n/a	n/a	Bellwood SD 88	Bellwood
n/a	n/a	Maywood-Melrose Park-Broadview 89	Melrose Park
n/a	n/a	Thornton Twp HSD 205	South Holland

Total General Revenue per Student

Rank	Dollars	District Name	City
1	31,321	Niles Twp CHSD 219	Skokie
2	28,202	Lake Forest CHSD 115	Lake Forest
3	27,567	Twp HSD 113	Highland Park
4	26,058	CHSD 128	Vernon Hills
5	25,831	Oak Park - River Forest SD 200	Oak Park
6	25,514	Evanston Twp HSD 202	Evanston
7	25,512	New Trier Twp HSD 203	Northfield
8	24,768	Adlai E Stevenson HSD 125	Lincolnshire
9	24,709	Northfield Twp HSD 225	Glenview
10	23,256	Township HSD 211	Palatine
11	22,817	Winnetka SD 36	Winnetka
12	22,661	Leyden CHSD 212	Franklin Park

Note: This section only includes districts with 1,500 or more students; All categories are ranked from high to low

13	20,957	Northbrook SD 28	Northbrook
14	20,908	Fenton CHSD 100	Bensenville
15	20,544	Township HSD 214	Arlington Hgts
16	20,538	Lisle CUSD 202	Lisle
17	20,415	Ottawa ESD 141	Ottawa
18	20,193	Maine Township HSD 207	Park Ridge
19	19,962	Hinsdale Twp HSD 86	Hinsdale
20	19,885	Carterville CUSD 5	Carterville
21	19,838	Homewood Flossmoor CHSD 233	Flossmoor
22	19,722	Mannheim SD 83	Franklin Park
23	19,602	Rich Twp HSD 227	Olympia Fields
24	19,554	Lincolnshire-Prairieview SD 103	Lincolnshire
25	19,472	Park Ridge CCSD 64	Park Ridge
26	19,190	Skokie SD 68	Skokie
27	19,177	Argo CHSD 217	Summit
28	19,086	Grayslake CHSD 127	Grayslake
29	19,082	Lyons Twp HSD 204	La Grange
30	18,949	CHSD 117	Lake Villa
31	18,764	Lake Park CHSD 108	Roselle
32	18,321	North Shore SD 112	Highland Park
33	18,253	CCSD 62	Des Plaines
34	18,135	Aptakisic-Tripp CCSD 102	Buffalo Grove
35	18,008	Evanston CCSD 65	Evanston
36	17,991	Byron CUSD 226	Byron
37	17,918	Lake Forest SD 67	Lake Forest
38	17,835	CHSD 99	Downers Grove
39	17,794	CHSD 218	Oak Lawn
40	17,612	Cons HSD 230	Orland Park
41	17,559	Skokie SD 69	Skokie
42	17,482	Lemont Twp HSD 210	Lemont
43	17,453	CCSD 93	Bloomingdale
44	17,444	Kildeer Countryside CCSD 96	Buffalo Grove
45	17,327	Dupage HSD 88	Addison
46	17,209	Lombard SD 44	Lombard
47	17,155	Deerfield SD 109	Deerfield
48	17,070	Grant CHSD 124	Fox Lake
49	17,005	ESD 159	Matteson
50	16,913	Hinsdale CCSD 181	Burr Ridge
51	16,882	Riverside SD 96	Riverside
52	16,873	Bensenville SD 2	Bensenville
53	16,833	Alsip-Hazlgrn-Oaklwn SD 126	Alsip
54	16,780	Reavis Twp HSD 220	Burbank
55	16,768	Barrington CUSD 220	Barrington
56	16,711	Joliet Twp HSD 204	Joliet
57	16,694	Glenbard Twp HSD 87	Glen Ellyn
58	16,638	Oak Lawn CHSD 229	Oak Lawn
59	16,559	Bloom Twp HSD 206	Chicago Heights
59	16,559	Community CSD 59	Arlington Hgts
61	16,435	Tinley Park CCSD 146	Tinley Park
62	16,415	Bremen CHSD 228	Midlothian
63	16,407	Mundelein Cons HSD 120	Mundelein
64	16,228	Dekalb CUSD 428	Dekalb
65	16,101	Proviso Twp HSD 209	Forest Park
66	15,926	Dolton SD 148	Riverdale
67	15,901	E Saint Louis SD 189	E Saint Louis
68	15,835	Park Forest SD 163	Park Forest
69	15,703	Geneva CUSD 304	Geneva
70	15,700	Lockport Twp HSD 205	Lockport
71	15,699	Orland SD 135	Orland Park
72	15,589	Central CUSD 301	Burlington
73	15,549	Zion-Benton Twp HSD 126	Zion
74	15,430	Urbana SD 116	Urbana
75	15,421	Lansing SD 158	Lansing
75	15,421	Thornton Fractional Twp HSD 215	Calumet City
77	15,406	Minooka CHSD 111	Minooka
78	15,390	Naperville CUSD 203	Naperville
79	15,366	Chicago Heights SD 170	Chicago Heights
80	15,285	Cahokia CUSD 187	Cahokia
81	15,195	Woodridge SD 68	Woodridge
82	15,134	Lake Zurich CUSD 95	Lake Zurich
83	15,045	CHSD 94	West Chicago
84	15,012	Glenview CCSD 34	Glenview
85	14,964	Harvey SD 152	Harvey
86	14,859	Elmhurst SD 205	Elmhurst
87	14,851	Schaumburg CCSD 54	Schaumburg
88	14,769	Oak Park ESD 97	Oak Park
89	14,659	Wheeling CCSD 21	Wheeling
90	14,601	Frankfort CCSD 157c	Frankfort
91	14,595	Gurnee SD 56	Gurnee
92	14,509	Lincoln Way CHSD 210	New Lenox
93	14,452	Palos CCSD 118	Palos Park
94	14,437	Coal City CUSD 1	Coal City
95	14,435	Marquardt SD 15	Glendale Hgts
96	14,362	Libertyville SD 70	Libertyville
97	14,312	Flossmoor SD 161	Chicago Heights
98	14,291	Arlington Hgts SD 25	Arlington Hgts
99	14,285	Wilmette SD 39	Wilmette
100	14,275	Elmwood Park CUSD 401	Elmwood Park
101	14,238	CHSD 155	Crystal Lake
102	14,191	Glen Ellyn SD 41	Glen Ellyn
103	14,148	Evergreen Park ESD 124	Evergreen Park
104	14,107	Crete Monee CUSD 201u	Crete
104	14,107	Saint Charles CUSD 303	Saint Charles
106	14,094	Woodstock CUSD 200	Woodstock
107	14,086	East Maine SD 63	Des Plaines
108	14,084	Will County SD 92	Lockport
109	14,041	SD 45 Dupage County	Villa Park
110	14,032	CCSD 89	Glen Ellyn
111	13,998	Hawthorn CCSD 73	Vernon Hills
112	13,957	City of Chicago SD 299	Chicago
113	13,898	Reed Custer CUSD 255u	Braidwood
114	13,873	North Boone CUSD 200	Poplar Grove
115	13,853	Prairie-Hills ESD 144	Markham
116	13,799	North Palos SD 117	Palos Hills
117	13,767	Dolton SD 149	Calumet City
118	13,758	Springfield SD 186	Springfield
119	13,726	Mchenry CHSD 156	Mchenry
120	13,721	Oak Lawn-Hometown SD 123	Oak Lawn
121	13,632	Peoria SD 150	Peoria
122	13,602	North Chicago SD 187	North Chicago
123	13,589	J S Morton HSD 201	Cicero
124	13,549	Rockford SD 205	Rockford
125	13,472	Sycamore CUSD 427	Sycamore
126	13,448	CUSD 200	Wheaton
126	13,448	Zion ESD 6	Zion
128	13,431	Joliet PSD 86	Joliet
129	13,385	CCSD 168	Sauk Village
130	13,334	Valley View CUSD 365u	Romeoville
131	13,331	Homewood SD 153	Homewood
132	13,266	Homer CCSD 33c	Homer Glen
133	13,166	Wauconda CUSD 118	Wauconda
134	13,161	Warren Twp HSD 121	Gurnee
135	13,155	Champaign CUSD 4	Champaign
136	13,133	Matteson ESD 162	Richton Park
137	13,083	Murphysboro CUSD 186	Murphysboro
138	13,070	Hononegah Chd 207	Rockton
139	13,060	Cook County SD 130	Blue Island
140	13,018	Kaneland CUSD 302	Maple Park
141	13,009	Ridgeland SD 122	Oak Lawn
142	12,958	Rantoul City SD 137	Rantoul
143	12,951	Batavia USD 101	Batavia
144	12,915	Fremont SD 79	Mundelein
145	12,868	Belleville Twp HSD 201	Belleville
146	12,843	Queen Bee SD 16	Glendale Hgts
147	12,813	Waukegan CUSD 60	Waukegan
148	12,812	Kirby SD 140	Tinley Park
149	12,793	Pekin CSD 303	Pekin
150	12,759	Belleville SD 118	Belleville
151	12,745	Palatine CCSD 15	Palatine
152	12,738	Harlem Ud 122	Machesney Park
153	12,737	Mount Vernon SD 80	Mount Vernon
154	12,713	West Chicago ESD 33	West Chicago
155	12,693	Downers Grove GSD 58	Downers Grove
156	12,679	Lyons SD 103	Lyons
157	12,618	La Grange SD 102	La Grange Park
158	12,583	Beach Park CCSD 3	Beach Park
159	12,571	Mchenry CCSD 15	Mchenry
160	12,567	Aurora West USD 129	Aurora
161	12,539	Woodland CCSD 50	Gurnee
162	12,538	Johnsburg CUSD 12	Johnsburg
163	12,513	Burbank SD 111	Burbank
164	12,490	Bloomington SD 87	Bloomington
165	12,485	United Twp HSD 30	East Moline
166	12,459	Mundelein ESD 75	Mundelein
167	12,430	Freeport SD 145	Freeport
168	12,420	Summit SD 104	Summit
169	12,399	Troy CCSD 30c	Plainfield
170	12,397	Vandalia CUSD 203	Vandalia
171	12,374	Kankakee SD 111	Kankakee
172	12,366	O Fallon Twp HSD 203	O Fallon
173	12,361	Olympia CUSD 16	Stanford
174	12,353	Cicero SD 99	Cicero
175	12,346	Duquoin CUSD 300	Du Quoin
176	12,345	Danville CCSD 118	Danville
177	12,327	Round Lake CUSD 116	Round Lake
178	12,171	Grayslake CCSD 46	Grayslake
179	12,168	East Moline SD 37	East Moline
180	12,160	Macomb CUSD 185	Macomb
181	12,133	Alton CUSD 11	Alton
182	12,128	Keeneyville SD 20	Hanover Park
183	12,100	Rock Island SD 41	Rock Island
184	12,090	Winnebago CUSD 323	Winnebago
185	12,064	Aurora East USD 131	Aurora
186	12,026	Decatur SD 61	Decatur
187	12,020	Berwyn North SD 98	Berwyn
188	11,998	SD U-46	Elgin
189	11,923	Darien SD 61	Darien
190	11,908	Indian Prairie CUSD 204	Aurora
191	11,890	Roxana CUSD 1	Roxana
192	11,832	Herscher CUSD 2	Herscher
193	11,824	Big Hollow SD 38	Ingleside
194	11,787	Manteno CUSD 5	Manteno
195	11,745	Plano CUSD 88	Plano
196	11,719	Yorkville CUSD 115	Yorkville
197	11,694	Steger SD 194	Steger
198	11,689	Mount Prospect SD 57	Mount Prospec
199	11,676	Highland CUSD 5	Highland
200	11,663	Oregon CUSD 220	Oregon
201	11,662	Morton CUSD 709	Morton
202	11,640	Mclean County USD 5	Normal
203	11,639	Moline USD 40	Moline
204	11,625	Tolono CUSD 7	Tolono
205	11,618	Bradley Bourbonnais CHSD 307	Bradley
206	11,597	Quincy SD 172	Quincy
207	11,503	Streator ESD 44	Streator
208	11,454	Peotone CUSD 207u	Peotone
209	11,432	Antioch CCSD 34	Antioch
210	11,406	Sandwich CUSD 430	Sandwich
211	11,396	CUSD 300	Carpentersville
212	11,385	Mascoutah CUD 19	Mascoutah
213	11,380	Bradley SD 61	Bradley
214	11,375	Clinton CUSD 15	Clinton
215	11,374	Hillsboro CUSD 3	Hillsboro
216	11,350	Dunlap CUSD 323	Peoria
217	11,339	Bethalto CUSD 8	Bethalto
218	11,315	Berkeley SD 87	Berkeley
219	11,308	Cary CCSD 26	Cary
220	11,292	Forest Ridge SD 142	Oak Forest
221	11,287	New Lenox SD 122	New Lenox
222	11,273	Prairie Central CUSD 8	Fairbury
222	11,273	Robinson CUSD 2	Robinson
224	11,272	North Mac CUSD 34	Girard
225	11,270	Berwyn South SD 100	Berwyn
226	11,249	East Peoria SD 86	East Peoria
227	11,226	Sherrard CUSD 200	Sherrard
228	11,180	Dixon USD 170	Dixon
229	11,132	Effingham CUSD 40	Effingham
230	11,076	Harvard CUSD 50	Harvard
231	11,066	Addison SD 4	Addison
232	11,038	Crystal Lake CCSD 47	Crystal Lake
233	11,023	Genoa Kingston CUSD 424	Genoa
233	11,023	Rochelle CCSD 231	Rochelle
235	11,002	Monticello CUSD 25	Monticello
236	10,994	Belvidere CUSD 100	Belvidere
237	10,929	Summit Hill SD 161	Frankfort
238	10,924	Oswego CUSD 308	Oswego
239	10,912	Meridian CUSD 223	Stillman Valley
240	10,877	Triad CUSD 2	Troy
241	10,868	Sterling CUSD 5	Sterling
242	10,823	Granite City CUSD 9	Granite City
243	10,783	Ball Chatham CUSD 5	Chatham
244	10,779	Mahomet-Seymour CUSD 3	Mahomet
245	10,768	Millburn CCSD 24	Old Mill Creek
246	10,738	Galesburg CUSD 205	Galesburg
247	10,717	Harrisburg CUSD 3	Harrisburg
248	10,688	CSD 158	Algonquin
249	10,673	Herrin CUSD 4	Herrin
250	10,667	Plainfield SD 202	Plainfield
251	10,659	Jacksonville SD 117	Jacksonville
252	10,650	Lemont-Bromberek CSD 113a	Lemont
253	10,641	Lake Villa CCSD 41	Lake Villa
254	10,640	Bond County CUSD 2	Greenville
255	10,588	Indian Springs SD 109	Justice
256	10,584	Pekin PSD 108	Pekin
257	10,545	Charleston CUSD 1	Charleston
258	10,542	Edwardsville CUSD 7	Edwardsville
259	10,516	Jersey CUSD 100	Jerseyville
260	10,510	Beardstown CUSD 15	Beardstown
261	10,500	Southwestern CUSD 9	Piasa
262	10,487	Marion CUSD 2	Marion
263	10,481	Kewanee CUSD 229	Kewanee
264	10,463	Mokena SD 159	Mokena
265	10,431	Posen-Robbins ESD 143-5	Posen
266	10,395	Il Valley Central USD 321	Chillicothe
267	10,302	Rockton SD 140	Rockton
268	10,301	Canton Union SD 66	Canton
269	10,280	Geneseo CUSD 228	Geneseo
270	10,269	Litchfield CUSD 12	Litchfield

Note: This section only includes districts with 1,500 or more students; All categories are ranked from high to low

271	10,232	Waterloo CUSD 5	Waterloo
272	10,122	Mattoon CUSD 2	Mattoon
273	10,094	Bourbonnais SD 53	Bourbonnais
274	10,069	Riverton CUSD 14	Spaulding
275	10,019	Collinsville CUSD 10	Collinsville
276	9,992	Frankfort CUSD 168	West Frankfort
277	9,955	Columbia CUSD 4	Columbia
278	9,923	Monmouth-Roseville CUSD 238	Monmouth
279	9,875	Eureka CUD 140	Eureka
280	9,838	Massac Ud 1	Metropolis
281	9,829	East Richland CUSD 1	Olney
282	9,807	Midlothian SD 143	Midlothian
283	9,784	O Fallon CCSD 90	O Fallon
284	9,656	Taylorville CUSD 3	Taylorville
285	9,374	Wabash CUSD 348	Mount Carmel
286	9,239	Kinnikinnick CCSD 131	Roscoe
287	9,123	Mt Zion CUSD 3	Mount Zion
288	9,075	Minooka CCSD 201	Minooka
289	8,868	Rochester CUSD 3a	Rochester
n/a	n/a	Bellwood SD 88	Bellwood
n/a	n/a	Maywood-Melrose Park-Broadview 89	Melrose Park
n/a	n/a	Thornton Twp HSD 205	South Holland

Long-Term Debt per Student (end of FY)

Rank	Dollars	District Name	City
1	35,406	Niles Twp CHSD 219	Skokie
2	33,482	Lake Forest CHSD 115	Lake Forest
3	32,958	Lemont Twp HSD 210	Lemont
4	31,887	Winnetka SD 36	Winnetka
5	28,837	Dupage HSD 88	Addison
6	27,887	Lincoln Way CHSD 210	New Lenox
7	26,607	Geneva CUSD 304	Geneva
8	26,184	Minooka CHSD 111	Minooka
9	23,896	Kaneland CUSD 302	Maple Park
10	23,490	Oswego CUSD 308	Oswego
11	22,841	Woodstock CUSD 200	Woodstock
12	22,396	New Lenox SD 122	New Lenox
13	21,321	Northfield Twp HSD 225	Glenview
14	21,278	Crete Monee CUSD 201u	Crete
15	21,148	Hinsdale CCSD 181	Burr Ridge
16	20,971	O Fallon Twp HSD 203	O Fallon
17	20,771	Gurnee SD 56	Gurnee
18	20,665	Minooka CCSD 201	Minooka
19	20,514	Byron CUSD 226	Byron
20	20,000	Carterville CUSD 5	Carterville
21	19,853	Troy CCSD 30c	Plainfield
22	19,401	Warren Twp HSD 121	Gurnee
23	19,259	Wauconda CUSD 118	Wauconda
24	19,177	Summit Hill SD 161	Frankfort
25	18,600	Coal City CUSD 1	Coal City
26	18,574	Bensenville SD 2	Bensenville
27	18,515	Grant CHSD 124	Fox Lake
28	18,225	CCSD 62	Des Plaines
29	18,114	Sycamore CUSD 427	Sycamore
30	17,964	Triad CUSD 2	Troy
31	17,963	Summit SD 104	Summit
32	17,902	Grayslake CCSD 46	Grayslake
33	17,757	Lake Park CHSD 108	Roselle
34	17,727	Rochester CUSD 3a	Rochester
35	17,652	Yorkville CUSD 115	Yorkville
36	17,649	Edwardsville CUSD 7	Edwardsville
37	17,605	ESD 159	Matteson
38	17,589	Dekalb CUSD 428	Dekalb
39	17,268	Frankfort CCSD 157c	Frankfort
40	17,257	Big Hollow SD 38	Ingleside
41	17,112	Waterloo CUSD 5	Waterloo
42	16,828	Oak Lawn-Hometown SD 123	Oak Lawn
43	16,738	CUSD 300	Carpentersville
44	16,549	Valley View CUSD 365u	Romeoville
45	16,198	Batavia USD 101	Batavia
46	16,041	Elmhurst SD 205	Elmhurst
47	15,474	Mascoutah CUD 19	Mascoutah
48	15,260	Dunlap CUSD 323	Peoria
49	15,201	Mclean County USD 5	Normal
50	15,040	Plano CUSD 88	Plano
51	14,957	Manteno CUSD 5	Manteno
52	14,921	CUSD 200	Wheaton
53	14,886	Joliet Twp HSD 204	Joliet
54	14,472	Peotone CUSD 207u	Peotone
55	14,199	CHSD 99	Downers Grove
56	14,193	Columbia CUSD 4	Columbia
57	13,976	CSD 158	Algonquin
58	13,816	Central CUSD 301	Burlington
59	13,793	Prairie-Hills ESD 144	Markham
60	13,755	City of Chicago SD 299	Chicago
61	13,666	Belleville Twp HSD 201	Belleville
62	13,654	Cary CCSD 26	Cary
63	13,653	Rich Twp HSD 227	Olympia Fields
64	13,488	Dolton SD 148	Riverdale
65	13,161	Millburn CCSD 24	Old Mill Creek
66	13,148	Robinson CUSD 2	Robinson
67	13,141	Matteson ESD 162	Richton Park
68	12,665	Mannheim SD 83	Franklin Park
69	12,600	Fremont SD 79	Mundelein
70	12,396	Plainfield SD 202	Plainfield
71	12,218	CCSD 89	Glen Ellyn
72	11,945	Tinley Park CCSD 146	Tinley Park
73	11,934	Woodland CCSD 50	Gurnee
74	11,886	North Chicago SD 187	North Chicago
75	11,885	Mchenry CHSD 156	Mchenry
76	11,845	Hawthorn CCSD 73	Vernon Hills
77	11,668	Ridgeland SD 122	Oak Lawn
78	11,340	O Fallon CCSD 90	O Fallon
79	11,124	Peoria SD 150	Peoria
80	11,097	Champaign CUSD 4	Champaign
81	11,096	Mundelein Cons HSD 120	Mundelein
82	11,062	Duquoin CUSD 300	Du Quoin
83	11,011	Park Forest SD 163	Park Forest
84	10,893	La Grange SD 102	La Grange Park
85	10,885	Indian Prairie CUSD 204	Aurora
86	10,831	Roxana CUSD 1	Roxana
87	10,737	Proviso Twp HSD 209	Forest Park
88	10,729	Twp HSD 113	Highland Park
89	10,606	SD U-46	Elgin
90	10,377	Saint Charles CUSD 303	Saint Charles
91	10,250	Urbana SD 116	Urbana
92	10,049	Barrington CUSD 220	Barrington
93	9,912	Berwyn South SD 100	Berwyn
94	9,740	Skokie SD 69	Skokie
95	9,631	Harvard CUSD 50	Harvard
96	9,585	Rantoul City SD 137	Rantoul
97	9,555	CHSD 128	Vernon Hills
98	9,546	Highland CUSD 5	Highland
99	9,464	Lake Zurich CUSD 95	Lake Zurich
100	9,348	Tolono CUSD 7	Tolono
101	9,347	Aurora West USD 129	Aurora
102	9,260	CHSD 117	Lake Villa
103	9,233	SD 45 Dupage County	Villa Park
104	9,117	North Boone CUSD 200	Poplar Grove
105	9,038	East Richland CUSD 1	Olney
106	8,980	Alton CUSD 11	Alton
107	8,680	Argo CHSD 217	Summit
108	8,615	West Chicago ESD 33	West Chicago
109	8,585	Aurora East USD 131	Aurora
110	8,534	Vandalia CUSD 203	Vandalia
111	8,526	Marion CUSD 2	Marion
112	8,512	Bond County CUSD 2	Greenville
113	8,478	Herrin CUSD 4	Herrin
114	8,424	Belvidere CUSD 100	Belvidere
115	8,284	Elmwood Park CUSD 401	Elmwood Park
116	8,221	Cons HSD 230	Orland Park
117	8,172	Lockport Twp HSD 205	Lockport
118	8,061	Homewood SD 153	Homewood
119	8,039	Evanston Twp HSD 202	Evanston
120	8,012	Thornton Fractional Twp HSD 215	Calumet City
121	7,965	Ball Chatham CUSD 5	Chatham
122	7,795	Jersey CUSD 100	Jerseyville
123	7,748	Southwestern CUSD 9	Piasa
124	7,691	Bloomington SD 87	Bloomington
125	7,660	Reavis Twp HSD 220	Burbank
126	7,612	CHSD 94	West Chicago
127	7,452	Lake Forest SD 67	Lake Forest
128	7,423	Forest Ridge SD 142	Oak Forest
129	7,392	Queen Bee SD 16	Glendale Hgts
130	7,356	Olympia CUSD 16	Stanford
131	7,274	Mundelein ESD 75	Mundelein
132	7,164	Mahomet-Seymour CUSD 3	Mahomet
133	7,150	Evanston CCSD 65	Evanston
134	7,092	Adlai E Stevenson HSD 125	Lincolnshire
135	7,062	Lisle CUSD 202	Lisle
136	6,896	Mchenry CCSD 15	Mchenry
137	6,864	Meridian CUSD 223	Stillman Valley
138	6,855	Mount Prospect SD 57	Mount Prospect
139	6,843	Oak Park - River Forest SD 200	Oak Park
140	6,769	Bradley Bourbonnais CHSD 307	Bradley
141	6,605	Harlem Ud 122	Machesney Park
142	6,586	Lake Villa CCSD 41	Lake Villa
143	6,556	Lemont-Bromberek CSD 113a	Lemont
144	6,513	Wheeling CCSD 21	Wheeling
145	6,428	North Palos SD 117	Palos Hills
146	6,401	Monticello CUSD 25	Monticello
147	6,343	J S Morton HSD 201	Cicero
148	6,255	Libertyville SD 70	Libertyville
148	6,255	Springfield SD 186	Springfield
150	6,231	Hononegah Chd 207	Rockton
151	6,206	Johnsburg CUSD 12	Johnsburg
152	6,099	Galesburg CUSD 205	Galesburg
153	6,097	Riverton CUSD 14	Spaulding
154	6,056	Rock Island SD 41	Rock Island
155	6,045	Orland SD 135	Orland Park
156	5,927	New Trier Twp HSD 203	Northfield
157	5,882	Berkeley SD 87	Berkeley
158	5,875	CHSD 218	Oak Lawn
159	5,853	Freeport SD 145	Freeport
160	5,788	Bremen CHSD 228	Midlothian
161	5,773	Beach Park CCSD 3	Beach Park
162	5,713	Joliet PSD 86	Joliet
163	5,678	Herscher CUSD 2	Herscher
164	5,595	East Maine SD 63	Des Plaines
165	5,583	Homewood Flossmoor CHSD 233	Flossmoor
166	5,530	Oak Park ESD 97	Oak Park
167	5,488	Deerfield SD 109	Deerfield
168	5,422	Zion-Benton Twp HSD 126	Zion
169	5,405	Ottawa ESD 141	Ottawa
170	5,266	East Peoria SD 86	East Peoria
171	5,255	Bloom Twp HSD 206	Chicago Heights
172	5,248	Lombard SD 44	Lombard
173	5,187	E Saint Louis SD 189	E Saint Louis
174	5,175	Addison SD 4	Addison
175	5,135	Wilmette SD 39	Wilmette
176	5,096	CCSD 93	Bloomingdale
177	5,044	Sterling CUSD 5	Sterling
178	4,987	Glenbard Twp HSD 87	Glen Ellyn
179	4,881	Homer CCSD 33c	Homer Glen
180	4,853	Crystal Lake CCSD 47	Crystal Lake
181	4,801	Zion ESD 6	Zion
182	4,741	Winnebago CUSD 323	Winnebago
183	4,675	Township HSD 214	Arlington Hgts
184	4,607	Leyden CHSD 212	Franklin Park
185	4,551	Cicero SD 99	Cicero
186	4,544	Glenview CCSD 34	Glenview
187	4,539	Danville CCSD 118	Danville
188	4,533	Glen Ellyn SD 41	Glen Ellyn
189	4,476	Antioch CCSD 34	Antioch
190	4,448	Mattoon CUSD 2	Mattoon
191	4,361	Alsip-Hazlgrn-Oaklwn SD 126	Alsip
192	4,333	Bourbonnais SD 53	Bourbonnais
193	4,308	Keeneyville SD 20	Hanover Park
194	4,267	Evergreen Park ESD 124	Evergreen Park
195	4,198	North Shore SD 112	Highland Park
196	4,177	Pekin CSD 303	Pekin
197	4,143	Genoa Kingston CUSD 424	Genoa
198	4,099	Mokena SD 159	Mokena
199	4,096	Kinnikinnick CCSD 131	Roscoe
200	4,074	Quincy SD 172	Quincy
201	4,019	Collinsville CUSD 10	Collinsville
202	3,954	Il Valley Central USD 321	Chillicothe
203	3,903	Moline USD 40	Moline
204	3,896	Effingham CUSD 40	Effingham
205	3,891	Lyons SD 103	Lyons
206	3,837	Massac Ud 1	Metropolis
207	3,836	Bethalto CUSD 8	Bethalto
208	3,822	Waukegan CUSD 60	Waukegan
209	3,818	Lincolnshire-Prairieview SD 103	Lincolnshire
210	3,810	Burbank SD 111	Burbank
211	3,668	Geneseo CUSD 228	Geneseo
212	3,656	Cook County SD 130	Blue Island
213	3,598	Litchfield CUSD 12	Litchfield
214	3,547	Sandwich CUSD 430	Sandwich
215	3,528	Indian Springs SD 109	Justice
216	3,498	Palatine CCSD 15	Palatine
217	3,444	Aptakisic-Tripp CCSD 102	Buffalo Grove
217	3,444	Macomb CUSD 185	Macomb
219	3,438	Park Ridge CCSD 64	Park Ridge
220	3,411	Cahokia CUSD 187	Cahokia
221	3,378	Rochelle CCSD 231	Rochelle
222	3,359	Dolton SD 149	Calumet City
223	3,328	Belleville SD 118	Belleville
224	3,295	Prairie Central CUSD 8	Fairbury
225	3,201	Hillsboro CUSD 3	Hillsboro
226	3,179	Murphysboro CUSD 186	Murphysboro
227	3,169	Mt Zion CUSD 3	Mount Zion
228	3,102	Taylorville CUSD 3	Taylorville
229	3,072	Sherrard CUSD 200	Sherrard
230	3,059	Fenton CHSD 100	Bensenville
231	3,051	Community CSD 59	Arlington Hgts
232	3,012	Will County SD 92	Lockport

Note: This section only includes districts with 1,500 or more students; All categories are ranked from high to low

Rank	Number	District Name	City
233	3,004	Beardstown CUSD 15	Beardstown
234	2,973	North Mac CUSD 34	Girard
235	2,954	Arlington Hgts SD 25	Arlington Hgts
236	2,927	Harrisburg CUSD 3	Harrisburg
237	2,888	Lansing SD 158	Lansing
238	2,864	Steger SD 194	Steger
239	2,806	Rockford SD 205	Rockford
240	2,798	Oak Lawn CHSD 229	Oak Lawn
241	2,791	CHSD 155	Crystal Lake
242	2,632	Marquardt SD 15	Glendale Hgts
243	2,516	Kildeer Countryside CCSD 96	Buffalo Grove
244	2,490	Chicago Heights SD 170	Chicago Heights
245	2,414	Palos CCSD 118	Palos Park
246	2,368	Downers Grove GSD 58	Downers Grove
247	2,328	Township HSD 211	Palatine
248	2,319	Naperville CUSD 203	Naperville
249	2,287	Mount Vernon SD 80	Mount Vernon
249	2,287	Posen-Robbins ESD 143-5	Posen
251	2,249	Darien SD 61	Darien
252	2,221	Canton Union SD 66	Canton
253	2,211	Kirby SD 140	Tinley Park
254	2,146	Rockton SD 140	Rockton
255	2,083	Hinsdale Twp HSD 86	Hinsdale
256	1,991	East Moline SD 37	East Moline
257	1,951	Lyons Twp HSD 204	La Grange
258	1,855	Kankakee SD 111	Kankakee
259	1,844	Maine Township HSD 207	Park Ridge
260	1,796	Charleston CUSD 1	Charleston
261	1,794	Frankfort CUSD 168	West Frankfort
262	1,774	Granite City CUSD 9	Granite City
263	1,702	Woodridge SD 68	Woodridge
264	1,566	Dixon USD 170	Dixon
265	1,503	Pekin PSD 108	Pekin
266	1,340	Skokie SD 68	Skokie
267	1,325	Oregon CUSD 220	Oregon
268	1,302	Decatur SD 61	Decatur
269	1,249	Kewanee CUSD 229	Kewanee
270	1,244	Streator ESD 44	Streator
271	1,169	Harvey SD 152	Harvey
272	1,116	Monmouth-Roseville CUSD 238	Monmouth
273	1,038	Berwyn North SD 98	Berwyn
274	982	Clinton CUSD 15	Clinton
275	976	Wabash CUSD 348	Mount Carmel
276	965	Midlothian SD 143	Midlothian
277	774	Bradley SD 61	Bradley
278	607	Schaumburg CCSD 54	Schaumburg
279	545	Flossmoor SD 161	Chicago Heights
280	465	Eureka CUD 140	Eureka
281	385	Morton CUSD 709	Morton
282	282	United Twp HSD 30	East Moline
283	6	Northbrook SD 28	Northbrook
284	1	Round Lake CUSD 116	Round Lake
285	0	Bellwood SD 88	Bellwood
285	0	CCSD 168	Sauk Village
285	0	Grayslake CHSD 127	Grayslake
285	0	Jacksonville SD 117	Jacksonville
285	0	Maywood-Melrose Park-Broadview 89	Melrose Park
285	0	Reed Custer CUSD 255u	Braidwood
285	0	Riverside SD 96	Riverside
285	0	Thornton Twp HSD 205	South Holland

Number of Diploma Recipients

Rank	Number	District Name	City
1	20,082	City of Chicago SD 299	Chicago
2	2,895	Township HSD 211	Palatine
3	2,894	Township HSD 214	Arlington Hgts
4	2,455	SD U-46	Elgin
5	2,207	Cons HSD 230	Orland Park
6	2,054	Glenbard Twp HSD 87	Glen Ellyn
7	1,643	Plainfield SD 202	Plainfield
8	1,636	Lincoln Way CHSD 210	New Lenox
9	1,611	CHSD 155	Crystal Lake
10	1,579	Naperville CUSD 203	Naperville
11	1,538	J S Morton HSD 201	Cicero
12	1,453	Maine Township HSD 207	Park Ridge
13	1,367	Rockford SD 205	Rockford
14	1,326	CUSD 300	Carpentersville
15	1,229	CHSD 99	Downers Grove
16	1,174	Niles Twp CHSD 219	Skokie
17	1,171	Belleville Twp HSD 201	Belleville
18	1,152	Northfield Twp HSD 225	Glenview
19	1,140	Valley View CUSD 365u	Romeoville
20	1,130	Thornton Twp HSD 205	South Holland
21	1,129	Adlai E Stevenson HSD 125	Lincolnshire
22	1,116	CHSD 218	Oak Lawn
23	1,110	CUSD 200	Wheaton
24	1,081	Bremen CHSD 228	Midlothian
25	1,059	Hinsdale Twp HSD 86	Hinsdale
26	1,037	Saint Charles CUSD 303	Saint Charles
27	1,022	New Trier Twp HSD 203	Northfield
28	998	Rich Twp HSD 227	Olympia Fields
29	897	Dupage HSD 88	Addison
30	893	Proviso Twp HSD 209	Forest Park
31	887	Lyons Twp HSD 204	La Grange
32	871	Joliet Twp HSD 204	Joliet
33	859	Twp HSD 113	Highland Park
34	848	Warren Twp HSD 121	Gurnee
35	846	CHSD 128	Vernon Hills
36	843	Lockport Twp HSD 205	Lockport
37	833	Peoria SD 150	Peoria
38	811	Waukegan CUSD 60	Waukegan
39	795	Oswego CUSD 308	Oswego
40	771	Mclean County USD 5	Normal
41	725	Lake Park CHSD 108	Roselle
42	711	Oak Park - River Forest SD 200	Oak Park
43	699	Leyden CHSD 212	Franklin Park
44	692	Barrington CUSD 220	Barrington
45	684	Springfield SD 186	Springfield
46	636	CHSD 117	Lake Villa
46	636	Homewood Flossmoor CHSD 233	Flossmoor
48	635	Evanston Twp HSD 202	Evanston
49	623	Aurora West USD 129	Aurora
50	620	Thornton Fractional Twp HSD 215	Calumet City
51	606	Mchenry CHSD 156	Mchenry
52	599	Elmhurst SD 205	Elmhurst
53	596	Grayslake CHSD 127	Grayslake
54	594	Bloom Twp HSD 206	Chicago Heights
55	578	Champaign CUSD 4	Champaign
56	563	Edwardsville CUSD 7	Edwardsville
56	563	O Fallon Twp HSD 203	O Fallon
58	525	Minooka CHSD 111	Minooka
59	509	Aurora East USD 131	Aurora
60	499	Lake Zurich CUSD 95	Lake Zurich
61	490	Harlem Ud 122	Machesney Park
62	488	Zion-Benton Twp HSD 126	Zion
63	484	Mundelein Cons HSD 120	Mundelein
64	478	Geneva CUSD 304	Geneva
65	472	Moline USD 40	Moline
66	467	Alton CUSD 11	Alton
66	467	Quincy SD 172	Quincy
68	455	E Saint Louis SD 189	E Saint Louis
69	448	Pekin CSD 303	Pekin
70	447	Decatur SD 61	Decatur
71	446	Bradley Bourbonnais CHSD 307	Bradley
72	443	Batavia USD 101	Batavia
73	441	Belvidere CUSD 100	Belvidere
74	440	Woodstock CUSD 200	Woodstock
75	436	CHSD 94	West Chicago
76	428	Collinsville CUSD 10	Collinsville
77	427	Hononegah Chd 207	Rockton
78	418	Granite City CUSD 9	Granite City
79	414	Lake Forest CHSD 115	Lake Forest
80	407	Oak Lawn CHSD 229	Oak Lawn
81	402	Reavis Twp HSD 220	Burbank
82	392	CSD 158	Algonquin
82	392	Grant CHSD 124	Fox Lake
84	367	United Twp HSD 30	East Moline
85	365	Argo CHSD 217	Summit
86	354	Lemont Twp HSD 210	Lemont
87	350	Ball Chatham CUSD 5	Chatham
87	350	Dekalb CUSD 428	Dekalb
89	348	Crete Monee CUSD 201u	Crete
90	321	Triad CUSD 2	Troy
91	310	Rock Island SD 41	Rock Island
91	310	Round Lake CUSD 116	Round Lake
93	307	Fenton CHSD 100	Bensenville
94	306	Bloomington SD 87	Bloomington
95	305	Wauconda CUSD 118	Wauconda
96	302	Yorkville CUSD 115	Yorkville
97	294	Sycamore CUSD 427	Sycamore
98	290	Freeport SD 145	Freeport
99	284	Jacksonville SD 117	Jacksonville
100	277	Danville CCSD 118	Danville
101	272	Kaneland CUSD 302	Maple Park
102	261	Galesburg CUSD 205	Galesburg
103	243	Marion CUSD 2	Marion
104	240	Kankakee SD 111	Kankakee
105	233	Highland CUSD 5	Highland
106	232	Mattoon CUSD 2	Mattoon
107	231	Jersey CUSD 100	Jerseyville
108	230	Central CUSD 301	Burlington
109	228	Dunlap CUSD 323	Peoria
110	225	Sterling CUSD 5	Sterling
111	224	Effingham CUSD 40	Effingham
112	222	Cahokia CUSD 187	Cahokia
112	222	Urbana SD 116	Urbana
112	222	Waterloo CUSD 5	Waterloo
115	218	Geneseo CUSD 228	Geneseo
116	213	Mahomet-Seymour CUSD 3	Mahomet
117	209	Johnsburg CUSD 12	Johnsburg
118	207	Mascoutah CUD 19	Mascoutah
118	207	Taylorville CUSD 3	Taylorville
120	205	Morton CUSD 709	Morton
121	202	Elmwood Park CUSD 401	Elmwood Park
122	194	Dixon USD 170	Dixon
123	190	Mt Zion CUSD 3	Mount Zion
124	188	Charleston CUSD 1	Charleston
124	188	Sandwich CUSD 430	Sandwich
126	181	Bethalto CUSD 8	Bethalto
127	172	Peotone CUSD 207u	Peotone
128	171	Manteno CUSD 5	Manteno
129	164	Reed Custer CUSD 255u	Braidwood
130	162	Il Valley Central USD 321	Chillicothe
131	161	Canton Union SD 66	Canton
132	158	Prairie Central CUSD 8	Fairbury
133	157	Olympia CUSD 16	Stanford
134	153	Harvard CUSD 50	Harvard
135	152	Herscher CUSD 2	Herscher
136	151	North Chicago SD 187	North Chicago
136	151	Rochester CUSD 3a	Rochester
138	150	Murphysboro CUSD 186	Murphysboro
138	150	Winnebago CUSD 323	Winnebago
140	148	Coal City CUSD 1	Coal City
140	148	Massac Ud 1	Metropolis
140	148	Oregon CUSD 220	Oregon
143	144	Wabash CUSD 348	Mount Carmel
144	143	East Richland CUSD 1	Olney
145	142	Byron CUSD 226	Byron
145	142	Herrin CUSD 4	Herrin
147	141	Columbia CUSD 4	Columbia
148	138	Macomb CUSD 185	Macomb
149	133	Meridian CUSD 223	Stillman Valley
149	133	Vandalia CUSD 203	Vandalia
151	132	Plano CUSD 88	Plano
151	132	Roxana CUSD 1	Roxana
153	131	Lisle CUSD 202	Lisle
154	126	Eureka CUD 140	Eureka
155	125	Harrisburg CUSD 3	Harrisburg
156	122	Tolono CUSD 7	Tolono
157	121	Carterville CUSD 5	Carterville
158	117	Genoa Kingston CUSD 424	Genoa
158	117	Monticello CUSD 25	Monticello
160	116	Bond County CUSD 2	Greenville
161	113	Robinson CUSD 2	Robinson
162	108	Hillsboro CUSD 3	Hillsboro
162	108	Sherrard CUSD 200	Sherrard
162	108	Southwestern CUSD 9	Piasa
165	105	Kewanee CUSD 229	Kewanee
166	104	North Boone CUSD 200	Poplar Grove
167	103	Duquoin CUSD 300	Du Quoin
168	101	Monmouth-Roseville CUSD 238	Monmouth
169	95	Frankfort CUSD 168	West Frankfort
170	94	Riverton CUSD 14	Spaulding
171	92	Litchfield CUSD 12	Litchfield
172	88	Beardstown CUSD 15	Beardstown
173	25	Indian Prairie CUSD 204	Aurora
n/a	n/a	Addison SD 4	Addison
n/a	n/a	Alsip-Hazlgrn-Oaklwn SD 126	Alsip
n/a	n/a	Antioch CCSD 34	Antioch
n/a	n/a	Aptakisic-Tripp CCSD 102	Buffalo Grove
n/a	n/a	Arlington Hgts SD 25	Arlington Hgts
n/a	n/a	Beach Park CCSD 3	Beach Park
n/a	n/a	Belleville SD 118	Belleville
n/a	n/a	Bellwood SD 88	Bellwood
n/a	n/a	Bensenville SD 2	Bensenville
n/a	n/a	Berkeley SD 87	Berkeley
n/a	n/a	Berwyn North SD 98	Berwyn
n/a	n/a	Berwyn South SD 100	Berwyn
n/a	n/a	Big Hollow SD 38	Ingleside
n/a	n/a	Bourbonnais SD 53	Bourbonnais
n/a	n/a	Bradley SD 61	Bradley
n/a	n/a	Burbank SD 111	Burbank
n/a	n/a	Cary CCSD 26	Cary
n/a	n/a	CCSD 168	Sauk Village
n/a	n/a	CCSD 62	Des Plaines
n/a	n/a	CCSD 89	Glen Ellyn
n/a	n/a	CCSD 93	Bloomingdale

Note: This section only includes districts with 1,500 or more students; All categories are ranked from high to low

		District	City
n/a	n/a	Chicago Heights SD 170	Chicago Heights
n/a	n/a	Cicero SD 99	Cicero
n/a	n/a	Clinton CUSD 15	Clinton
n/a	n/a	Community CSD 59	Arlington Hgts
n/a	n/a	Cook County SD 130	Blue Island
n/a	n/a	Crystal Lake CCSD 47	Crystal Lake
n/a	n/a	Darien SD 61	Darien
n/a	n/a	Deerfield SD 109	Deerfield
n/a	n/a	Dolton SD 148	Riverdale
n/a	n/a	Dolton SD 149	Calumet City
n/a	n/a	Downers Grove GSD 58	Downers Grove
n/a	n/a	East Maine SD 63	Des Plaines
n/a	n/a	East Moline SD 37	East Moline
n/a	n/a	East Peoria SD 86	East Peoria
n/a	n/a	ESD 159	Matteson
n/a	n/a	Evanston CCSD 65	Evanston
n/a	n/a	Evergreen Park ESD 124	Evergreen Park
n/a	n/a	Flossmoor SD 161	Chicago Heights
n/a	n/a	Forest Ridge SD 142	Oak Forest
n/a	n/a	Frankfort CCSD 157c	Frankfort
n/a	n/a	Fremont SD 79	Mundelein
n/a	n/a	Glen Ellyn SD 41	Glen Ellyn
n/a	n/a	Glenview CCSD 34	Glenview
n/a	n/a	Grayslake CCSD 46	Grayslake
n/a	n/a	Gurnee SD 56	Gurnee
n/a	n/a	Harvey SD 152	Harvey
n/a	n/a	Hawthorn CCSD 73	Vernon Hills
n/a	n/a	Hinsdale CCSD 181	Burr Ridge
n/a	n/a	Homer CCSD 33c	Homer Glen
n/a	n/a	Homewood SD 153	Homewood
n/a	n/a	Indian Springs SD 109	Justice
n/a	n/a	Joliet PSD 86	Joliet
n/a	n/a	Keeneyville SD 20	Hanover Park
n/a	n/a	Kildeer Countryside CCSD 96	Buffalo Grove
n/a	n/a	Kinnikinnick CCSD 131	Roscoe
n/a	n/a	Kirby SD 140	Tinley Park
n/a	n/a	La Grange SD 102	La Grange Park
n/a	n/a	Lake Forest SD 67	Lake Forest
n/a	n/a	Lake Villa CCSD 41	Lake Villa
n/a	n/a	Lansing SD 158	Lansing
n/a	n/a	Lemont-Bromberek CSD 113a	Lemont
n/a	n/a	Libertyville SD 70	Libertyville
n/a	n/a	Lincolnshire-Prairieview SD 103	Lincolnshire
n/a	n/a	Lombard SD 44	Lombard
n/a	n/a	Lyons SD 103	Lyons
n/a	n/a	Mannheim SD 83	Franklin Park
n/a	n/a	Marquardt SD 15	Glendale Hgts
n/a	n/a	Matteson ESD 162	Richton Park
n/a	n/a	Maywood-Melrose Park-Broadview 89	Melrose Park
n/a	n/a	Mchenry CCSD 15	Mchenry
n/a	n/a	Midlothian SD 143	Midlothian
n/a	n/a	Millburn CCSD 24	Old Mill Creek
n/a	n/a	Minooka CCSD 201	Minooka
n/a	n/a	Mokena SD 159	Mokena
n/a	n/a	Mount Prospect SD 57	Mount Prospect
n/a	n/a	Mount Vernon SD 80	Mount Vernon
n/a	n/a	Mundelein ESD 75	Mundelein
n/a	n/a	New Lenox SD 122	New Lenox
n/a	n/a	North Mac CUSD 34	Girard
n/a	n/a	North Palos SD 117	Palos Hills
n/a	n/a	North Shore SD 112	Highland Park
n/a	n/a	Northbrook SD 28	Northbrook
n/a	n/a	O Fallon CCSD 90	O Fallon
n/a	n/a	Oak Lawn-Hometown SD 123	Oak Lawn
n/a	n/a	Oak Park ESD 97	Oak Park
n/a	n/a	Orland SD 135	Orland Park
n/a	n/a	Ottawa ESD 141	Ottawa
n/a	n/a	Palatine CCSD 15	Palatine
n/a	n/a	Palos CCSD 118	Palos Park
n/a	n/a	Park Forest SD 163	Park Forest
n/a	n/a	Park Ridge CCSD 64	Park Ridge
n/a	n/a	Pekin PSD 108	Pekin
n/a	n/a	Posen-Robbins ESD 143-5	Posen
n/a	n/a	Prairie-Hills ESD 144	Markham
n/a	n/a	Queen Bee SD 16	Glendale Hgts
n/a	n/a	Rantoul City SD 137	Rantoul
n/a	n/a	Ridgeland SD 122	Oak Lawn
n/a	n/a	Riverside SD 96	Riverside
n/a	n/a	Rochelle CCSD 231	Rochelle
n/a	n/a	Rockton SD 140	Rockton
n/a	n/a	Schaumburg CCSD 54	Schaumburg
n/a	n/a	SD 45 Dupage County	Villa Park
n/a	n/a	Skokie SD 68	Skokie
n/a	n/a	Skokie SD 69	Skokie
n/a	n/a	Steger SD 194	Steger
n/a	n/a	Streator ESD 44	Streator

		District	City
n/a	n/a	Summit Hill SD 161	Frankfort
n/a	n/a	Summit SD 104	Summit
n/a	n/a	Tinley Park CCSD 146	Tinley Park
n/a	n/a	Troy CCSD 30c	Plainfield
n/a	n/a	West Chicago ESD 33	West Chicago
n/a	n/a	Wheeling CCSD 21	Wheeling
n/a	n/a	Will County SD 92	Lockport
n/a	n/a	Wilmette SD 39	Wilmette
n/a	n/a	Winnetka SD 36	Winnetka
n/a	n/a	Woodland CCSD 50	Gurnee
n/a	n/a	Woodridge SD 68	Woodridge
n/a	n/a	Zion ESD 6	Zion

High School Drop-out Rate

Rank	Percent	District Name	City
1	30.3	E Saint Louis SD 189	E Saint Louis
2	30.1	Decatur SD 61	Decatur
3	28.1	Cahokia CUSD 187	Cahokia
4	27.4	Rock Island SD 41	Rock Island
5	26.8	North Chicago SD 187	North Chicago
6	26.0	Adlai E Stevenson HSD 125	Lincolnshire
7	25.4	North Boone CUSD 200	Poplar Grove
8	22.7	Lockport Twp HSD 205	Lockport
8	22.7	Rockford SD 205	Rockford
10	22.0	Kankakee SD 111	Kankakee
10	22.0	Thornton Twp HSD 205	South Holland
12	21.5	Aurora East USD 131	Aurora
13	19.8	Peoria SD 150	Peoria
14	18.9	Danville CCSD 118	Danville
15	18.4	Champaign CUSD 4	Champaign
16	17.8	Waukegan CUSD 60	Waukegan
17	17.3	Thornton Fractional Twp HSD 215	Calumet City
18	16.9	Freeport SD 145	Freeport
19	16.7	Kewanee CUSD 229	Kewanee
20	16.3	Frankfort CUSD 168	West Frankfort
21	15.8	Bloom Twp HSD 206	Chicago Heights
22	15.5	Beardstown CUSD 15	Beardstown
22	15.5	Crete Monee CUSD 201u	Crete
24	15.3	Round Lake CUSD 116	Round Lake
25	15.2	Granite City CUSD 9	Granite City
25	15.2	Monticello CUSD 25	Monticello
27	15.0	City of Chicago SD 299	Chicago
28	14.7	Galesburg CUSD 205	Galesburg
29	14.1	Riverton CUSD 14	Spaulding
30	13.9	Urbana SD 110	Urbana
31	13.7	Valley View CUSD 365u	Romeoville
32	13.6	Bloomington SD 87	Bloomington
33	13.4	Alton CUSD 11	Alton
33	13.4	Aurora West USD 129	Aurora
33	13.4	Vandalia CUSD 203	Vandalia
36	13.1	J S Morton HSD 201	Cicero
37	12.5	Dixon USD 170	Dixon
38	12.3	Harlem Ud 122	Machesney Park
38	12.3	Moline USD 40	Moline
38	12.3	Rich Twp HSD 227	Olympia Fields
41	12.0	Harvard CUSD 50	Harvard
41	12.0	Proviso Twp HSD 209	Forest Park
43	11.9	Belvidere CUSD 100	Belvidere
44	11.8	Herrin CUSD 4	Herrin
45	11.7	Roxana CUSD 1	Roxana
46	11.5	Mascoutah CUD 19	Mascoutah
47	11.4	Effingham CUSD 40	Effingham
47	11.4	Joliet Twp HSD 204	Joliet
49	11.3	United Twp HSD 30	East Moline
50	11.2	Dekalb CUSD 428	Dekalb
50	11.2	Robinson CUSD 2	Robinson
52	11.1	Sterling CUSD 5	Sterling
53	11.0	Springfield SD 186	Springfield
54	10.8	Plano CUSD 88	Plano
55	10.7	Mattoon CUSD 2	Mattoon
56	10.6	Collinsville CUSD 10	Collinsville
57	10.5	Marion CUSD 2	Marion
58	10.4	Murphysboro CUSD 186	Murphysboro
59	10.3	Hillsboro CUSD 3	Hillsboro
59	10.3	Zion-Benton Twp HSD 126	Zion
61	10.1	Canton Union SD 66	Canton
61	10.1	Charleston CUSD 1	Charleston
61	10.1	Lake Park CHSD 108	Roselle
61	10.1	Taylorville CUSD 3	Taylorville
65	10.0	Manteno CUSD 5	Manteno
66	9.9	Massac Ud 1	Metropolis
67	9.6	Duquoin CUSD 300	Du Quoin
68	9.5	Pekin CSD 303	Pekin
69	9.3	Argo CHSD 217	Summit
69	9.3	Evanston Twp HSD 202	Evanston
71	9.1	Harrisburg CUSD 3	Harrisburg
71	9.1	Leyden CHSD 212	Franklin Park
71	9.1	SD U-46	Elgin
74	9.0	Bethalto CUSD 8	Bethalto
74	9.0	Litchfield CUSD 12	Litchfield
74	9.0	Wauconda CUSD 118	Wauconda
77	8.9	Elmwood Park CUSD 401	Elmwood Park
78	8.8	CUSD 300	Carpentersville
78	8.8	Jacksonville SD 117	Jacksonville
78	8.8	Sherrard CUSD 200	Sherrard
81	8.7	Quincy SD 172	Quincy
82	8.6	Wabash CUSD 348	Mount Carmel
83	8.3	Homewood Flossmoor CHSD 233	Flossmoor
83	8.3	Macomb CUSD 185	Macomb
85	8.1	Belleville Twp HSD 201	Belleville
85	8.1	East Richland CUSD 1	Olney
85	8.1	Meridian CUSD 223	Stillman Valley
85	8.1	O Fallon Twp HSD 203	O Fallon
85	8.1	Plainfield SD 202	Plainfield
85	8.1	Woodstock CUSD 200	Woodstock
91	8.0	CHSD 94	West Chicago
91	8.0	Mclean County USD 5	Normal
91	8.0	Monmouth-Roseville CUSD 238	Monmouth
94	7.8	Bond County CUSD 2	Greenville
94	7.8	Bremen CHSD 228	Midlothian
94	7.8	Peotone CUSD 207u	Peotone
97	7.7	Hononegah Chd 207	Rockton
98	7.5	Sandwich CUSD 430	Sandwich
99	7.1	Grant CHSD 124	Fox Lake
100	6.9	Genoa Kingston CUSD 424	Genoa
100	6.9	Prairie Central CUSD 8	Fairbury
102	6.8	Mt Zion CUSD 3	Mount Zion
103	6.7	Rochester CUSD 3a	Rochester
104	6.6	Bradley Bourbonnais CHSD 307	Bradley
104	6.6	Olympia CUSD 16	Stanford
106	6.5	Ball Chatham CUSD 5	Chatham
107	6.3	Fenton CHSD 100	Bensenville
107	6.3	Highland CUSD 5	Highland
107	6.3	Il Valley Central USD 321	Chillicothe
107	6.3	Oregon CUSD 220	Oregon
107	6.3	Reavis Twp HSD 220	Burbank
107	6.3	Reed Custer CUSD 255u	Braidwood
113	6.1	CHSD 218	Oak Lawn
113	6.1	Dupage HSD 88	Addison
115	6.0	Jersey CUSD 100	Jerseyville
115	6.0	Oswego CUSD 308	Oswego
117	5.9	Clinton CUSD 15	Clinton
117	5.9	Mundelein Cons HSD 120	Mundelein
117	5.9	Southwestern CUSD 9	Piasa
117	5.9	Yorkville CUSD 115	Yorkville
121	5.8	Carterville CUSD 5	Carterville
121	5.8	Oak Park - River Forest SD 200	Oak Park
123	5.7	Mchenry CHSD 156	Mchenry
124	5.6	Batavia USD 101	Batavia
124	5.6	Coal City CUSD 1	Coal City
126	5.5	Eureka CUD 140	Eureka
126	5.5	Indian Prairie CUSD 204	Aurora
126	5.5	Johnsburg CUSD 12	Johnsburg
126	5.5	Lisle CUSD 202	Lisle
126	5.5	Oak Lawn CHSD 229	Oak Lawn
131	5.4	CHSD 117	Lake Villa
131	5.4	Naperville CUSD 203	Naperville
133	5.3	Dunlap CUSD 323	Peoria
134	5.2	Herscher CUSD 2	Herscher
134	5.2	Triad CUSD 2	Troy
134	5.2	Warren Twp HSD 121	Gurnee
137	5.1	Central CUSD 301	Burlington
137	5.1	CUSD 200	Wheaton
137	5.1	Glenbard Twp HSD 87	Glen Ellyn
140	5.0	CHSD 155	Crystal Lake
141	4.8	Grayslake CHSD 127	Grayslake
141	4.8	Morton CUSD 709	Morton
143	4.7	CSD 158	Algonquin
143	4.7	Saint Charles CUSD 303	Saint Charles
145	4.5	Byron CUSD 226	Byron
145	4.5	Maine Township HSD 207	Park Ridge
147	4.3	Edwardsville CUSD 7	Edwardsville
147	4.3	Mahomet-Seymour CUSD 3	Mahomet
147	4.3	Township HSD 211	Palatine
150	4.2	Winnebago CUSD 323	Winnebago
151	4.1	CHSD 99	Downers Grove
152	3.8	Kaneland CUSD 302	Maple Park
153	3.7	Lyons Twp HSD 204	La Grange
153	3.7	Waterloo CUSD 5	Waterloo
155	3.6	Lake Zurich CUSD 95	Lake Zurich
156	3.5	Geneseo CUSD 228	Geneseo

Note: This section only includes districts with 1,500 or more students; All categories are ranked from high to low

Rank	Value	District	City
156	3.5	Hinsdale Twp HSD 86	Hinsdale
158	3.4	Lemont Twp HSD 210	Lemont
158	3.4	Township HSD 214	Arlington Hgts
160	3.2	Lincoln Way CHSD 210	New Lenox
160	3.2	Niles Twp CHSD 219	Skokie
162	3.1	Barrington CUSD 220	Barrington
162	3.1	Sycamore CUSD 427	Sycamore
164	3.0	Columbia CUSD 4	Columbia
165	2.9	Elmhurst SD 205	Elmhurst
165	2.9	Tolono CUSD 7	Tolono
167	2.8	Geneva CUSD 304	Geneva
168	2.6	CHSD 128	Vernon Hills
169	2.5	Cons HSD 230	Orland Park
170	2.4	Lake Forest CHSD 115	Lake Forest
170	2.4	Twp HSD 113	Highland Park
172	2.1	New Trier Twp HSD 203	Northfield
173	2.0	Northfield Twp HSD 225	Glenview
n/a	n/a	Minooka CHSD 111	Minooka
n/a	n/a	North Mac CUSD 34	Girard
n/a	n/a	Addison SD 4	Addison
n/a	n/a	Alsip-Hazlgrn-Oaklwn SD 126	Alsip
n/a	n/a	Antioch CCSD 34	Antioch
n/a	n/a	Aptakisic-Tripp CCSD 102	Buffalo Grove
n/a	n/a	Arlington Hgts SD 25	Arlington Hgts
n/a	n/a	Beach Park CCSD 3	Beach Park
n/a	n/a	Belleville SD 118	Belleville
n/a	n/a	Bellwood SD 88	Bellwood
n/a	n/a	Bensenville SD 2	Bensenville
n/a	n/a	Berkeley SD 87	Berkeley
n/a	n/a	Berwyn North SD 98	Berwyn
n/a	n/a	Berwyn South SD 100	Berwyn
n/a	n/a	Big Hollow SD 38	Ingleside
n/a	n/a	Bourbonnais SD 53	Bourbonnais
n/a	n/a	Bradley SD 61	Bradley
n/a	n/a	Burbank SD 111	Burbank
n/a	n/a	Cary CCSD 26	Cary
n/a	n/a	CCSD 168	Sauk Village
n/a	n/a	CCSD 62	Des Plaines
n/a	n/a	CCSD 89	Glen Ellyn
n/a	n/a	CCSD 93	Bloomingdale
n/a	n/a	Chicago Heights SD 170	Chicago Heights
n/a	n/a	Cicero SD 99	Cicero
n/a	n/a	Community CSD 59	Arlington Hgts
n/a	n/a	Cook County SD 130	Blue Island
n/a	n/a	Crystal Lake CCSD 47	Crystal Lake
n/a	n/a	Darien SD 61	Darien
n/a	n/a	Deerfield SD 109	Deerfield
n/a	n/a	Dolton SD 148	Riverdale
n/a	n/a	Dolton SD 149	Calumet City
n/a	n/a	Downers Grove GSD 58	Downers Grove
n/a	n/a	East Maine SD 63	Des Plaines
n/a	n/a	East Moline SD 37	East Moline
n/a	n/a	East Peoria SD 86	East Peoria
n/a	n/a	ESD 159	Matteson
n/a	n/a	Evanston CCSD 65	Evanston
n/a	n/a	Evergreen Park ESD 124	Evergreen Park
n/a	n/a	Flossmoor SD 161	Chicago Heights
n/a	n/a	Forest Ridge SD 142	Oak Forest
n/a	n/a	Frankfort CCSD 157c	Frankfort
n/a	n/a	Fremont SD 79	Mundelein
n/a	n/a	Glen Ellyn SD 41	Glen Ellyn
n/a	n/a	Glenview CCSD 34	Glenview
n/a	n/a	Grayslake CCSD 46	Grayslake
n/a	n/a	Gurnee SD 56	Gurnee
n/a	n/a	Harvey SD 152	Harvey
n/a	n/a	Hawthorn CCSD 73	Vernon Hills
n/a	n/a	Hinsdale CCSD 181	Burr Ridge
n/a	n/a	Homer CCSD 33c	Homer Glen
n/a	n/a	Homewood SD 153	Homewood
n/a	n/a	Indian Springs SD 109	Justice
n/a	n/a	Joliet PSD 86	Joliet
n/a	n/a	Keeneyville SD 20	Hanover Park
n/a	n/a	Kildeer Countryside CCSD 96	Buffalo Grove
n/a	n/a	Kinnikinnick CCSD 131	Roscoe
n/a	n/a	Kirby SD 140	Tinley Park
n/a	n/a	La Grange SD 102	La Grange
n/a	n/a	Lake Forest SD 67	Lake Forest
n/a	n/a	Lake Villa CCSD 41	Lake Villa
n/a	n/a	Lansing SD 158	Lansing
n/a	n/a	Lemont-Bromberek CSD 113a	Lemont
n/a	n/a	Libertyville SD 70	Libertyville
n/a	n/a	Lincolnshire-Prairieview SD 103	Lincolnshire
n/a	n/a	Lombard SD 44	Lombard
n/a	n/a	Lyons SD 103	Lyons
n/a	n/a	Mannheim SD 83	Franklin Park
n/a	n/a	Marquardt SD 15	Glendale Hgts
n/a	n/a	Matteson ESD 162	Richton Park
n/a	n/a	Maywood-Melrose Park-Broadview 89	Melrose Park
n/a	n/a	Mchenry CCSD 15	Mchenry
n/a	n/a	Midlothian SD 143	Midlothian
n/a	n/a	Millburn CCSD 24	Old Mill Creek
n/a	n/a	Minooka CCSD 201	Minooka
n/a	n/a	Mokena SD 159	Mokena
n/a	n/a	Mount Prospect SD 57	Mount Prospect
n/a	n/a	Mount Vernon SD 80	Mount Vernon
n/a	n/a	Mundelein ESD 75	Mundelein
n/a	n/a	New Lenox SD 122	New Lenox
n/a	n/a	North Palos SD 117	Palos Hills
n/a	n/a	North Shore SD 112	Highland Park
n/a	n/a	Northbrook SD 28	Northbrook
n/a	n/a	O Fallon CCSD 90	O Fallon
n/a	n/a	Oak Lawn-Hometown SD 123	Oak Lawn
n/a	n/a	Oak Park ESD 97	Oak Park
n/a	n/a	Orland SD 135	Orland Park
n/a	n/a	Ottawa ESD 141	Ottawa
n/a	n/a	Palatine CCSD 15	Palatine
n/a	n/a	Palos CCSD 118	Palos Park
n/a	n/a	Park Forest SD 163	Park Forest
n/a	n/a	Park Ridge CCSD 64	Park Ridge
n/a	n/a	Pekin PSD 108	Pekin
n/a	n/a	Posen-Robbins ESD 143-5	Posen
n/a	n/a	Prairie-Hills ESD 144	Markham
n/a	n/a	Queen Bee SD 16	Glendale Hgts
n/a	n/a	Rantoul City SD 137	Rantoul
n/a	n/a	Ridgeland SD 122	Oak Lawn
n/a	n/a	Riverside SD 96	Riverside
n/a	n/a	Rochelle CCSD 231	Rochelle
n/a	n/a	Rockton SD 140	Rockton
n/a	n/a	Schaumburg CCSD 54	Schaumburg
n/a	n/a	SD 45 Dupage County	Villa Park
n/a	n/a	Skokie SD 68	Skokie
n/a	n/a	Skokie SD 69	Skokie
n/a	n/a	Steger SD 194	Steger
n/a	n/a	Streator ESD 44	Streator
n/a	n/a	Summit Hill SD 161	Frankfort
n/a	n/a	Summit SD 104	Summit
n/a	n/a	Tinley Park CCSD 146	Tinley Park
n/a	n/a	Troy CCSD 30c	Plainfield
n/a	n/a	West Chicago ESD 33	West Chicago
n/a	n/a	Wheeling CCSD 21	Wheeling
n/a	n/a	Will County SD 92	Lockport
n/a	n/a	Wilmette SD 39	Wilmette
n/a	n/a	Winnetka SD 36	Winnetka
n/a	n/a	Woodland CCSD 50	Gurnee
n/a	n/a	Woodridge SD 68	Woodridge
n/a	n/a	Zion ESD 6	Zion

Average Freshman Graduation Rate

Rank	Percent	District Name	City
1	100.0	Central CUSD 301	Burlington
1	100.0	CHSD 117	Lake Villa
1	100.0	Dunlap CUSD 323	Peoria
1	100.0	Maine Township HSD 207	Park Ridge
1	100.0	Naperville CUSD 203	Naperville
1	100.0	Tolono CUSD 7	Tolono
1	100.0	Yorkville CUSD 115	Yorkville
8	99.2	Ball Chatham CUSD 5	Chatham
9	98.1	Johnsburg CUSD 12	Johnsburg
10	98.0	Elmhurst SD 205	Elmhurst
10	98.0	Sycamore CUSD 427	Sycamore
12	97.8	Plano CUSD 88	Plano
13	97.6	Reed Custer CUSD 255u	Braidwood
14	97.3	Mahomet-Seymour CUSD 3	Mahomet
15	97.2	Columbia CUSD 4	Columbia
15	97.2	Peotone CUSD 207u	Peotone
15	97.2	Saint Charles CUSD 303	Saint Charles
18	96.9	Lake Zurich CUSD 95	Lake Zurich
18	96.9	Plainfield SD 202	Plainfield
20	96.8	Barrington CUSD 220	Barrington
20	96.8	Geneva CUSD 304	Geneva
22	96.7	CUSD 200	Wheaton
23	96.6	Byron CUSD 226	Byron
24	96.5	Kaneland CUSD 302	Maple Park
25	96.2	Edwardsville CUSD 7	Edwardsville
26	96.1	Coal City CUSD 1	Coal City
27	95.9	Monticello CUSD 25	Monticello
28	95.8	Triad CUSD 2	Troy
29	95.1	CSD 158	Algonquin
30	94.5	Effingham CUSD 40	Effingham
31	94.4	Jacksonville SD 117	Jacksonville
31	94.4	Rochester CUSD 3a	Rochester
33	94.3	Winnebago CUSD 323	Winnebago
34	93.6	Morton CUSD 709	Morton
35	93.3	Oswego CUSD 308	Oswego
36	92.6	Eureka CUD 140	Eureka
37	92.5	Waterloo CUSD 5	Waterloo
38	91.6	Mascoutah CUD 19	Mascoutah
39	91.4	CUSD 300	Carpentersville
39	91.4	Genoa Kingston CUSD 424	Genoa
41	90.9	Jersey CUSD 100	Jerseyville
42	90.8	Geneseo CUSD 228	Geneseo
43	90.5	Il Valley Central USD 321	Chillicothe
44	90.3	Lisle CUSD 202	Lisle
45	90.2	Oregon CUSD 220	Oregon
46	89.9	East Richland CUSD 1	Olney
47	89.4	Herscher CUSD 2	Herscher
48	89.0	Carterville CUSD 5	Carterville
49	88.8	Crete Monee CUSD 201u	Crete
50	88.7	Olympia CUSD 16	Stanford
51	88.4	Wauconda CUSD 118	Wauconda
52	88.1	Manteno CUSD 5	Manteno
53	87.9	Batavia USD 101	Batavia
53	87.9	Macomb CUSD 185	Macomb
55	87.4	Sandwich CUSD 430	Sandwich
56	86.8	Mt Zion CUSD 3	Mount Zion
56	86.8	Woodstock CUSD 200	Woodstock
58	86.3	Roxana CUSD 1	Roxana
59	86.2	Alton CUSD 11	Alton
59	86.2	Wabash CUSD 348	Mount Carmel
61	85.6	Mclean County USD 5	Normal
62	85.3	Highland CUSD 5	Highland
63	85.1	Duquoin CUSD 300	Du Quoin
64	84.7	Mattoon CUSD 2	Mattoon
64	84.7	Meridian CUSD 223	Stillman Valley
66	84.6	Valley View CUSD 365u	Romeoville
67	83.2	Prairie Central CUSD 8	Fairbury
68	83.1	Robinson CUSD 2	Robinson
69	82.9	Collinsville CUSD 10	Collinsville
70	82.5	Dekalb CUSD 428	Dekalb
71	81.5	Beardstown CUSD 15	Beardstown
72	81.4	Charleston CUSD 1	Charleston
73	81.1	Murphysboro CUSD 186	Murphysboro
74	80.6	Champaign CUSD 4	Champaign
75	80.5	Elmwood Park CUSD 401	Elmwood Park
76	80.2	SD U-46	Elgin
76	80.2	Taylorville CUSD 3	Taylorville
78	80.0	Moline USD 40	Moline
78	80.0	Sherrard CUSD 200	Sherrard
80	79.6	Massac Ud 1	Metropolis
80	79.6	Vandalia CUSD 203	Vandalia
82	79.4	North Boone CUSD 200	Poplar Grove
83	78.6	Marion CUSD 2	Marion
84	78.4	Freeport SD 145	Freeport
85	78.2	Canton Union SD 66	Canton
86	77.8	Quincy SD 172	Quincy
87	77.7	Harvard CUSD 50	Harvard
88	77.0	Riverton CUSD 14	Spaulding
89	76.7	Dixon USD 170	Dixon
90	76.5	Sterling CUSD 5	Sterling
91	76.1	Southwestern CUSD 9	Piasa
92	75.8	Bond County CUSD 2	Greenville
93	75.5	Kewanee CUSD 229	Kewanee
94	75.4	Frankfort CUSD 168	West Frankfort
95	74.9	Harrisburg CUSD 3	Harrisburg
96	74.5	Bethalto CUSD 8	Bethalto
97	74.2	Harlem Ud 122	Machesney Park
97	74.2	Litchfield CUSD 12	Litchfield
99	72.8	Herrin CUSD 4	Herrin
100	71.4	Peoria SD 150	Peoria
101	68.8	Hillsboro CUSD 3	Hillsboro
102	67.4	Round Lake CUSD 116	Round Lake
103	65.7	Granite City CUSD 9	Granite City
104	65.5	Bloomington SD 87	Bloomington
105	65.3	Galesburg CUSD 205	Galesburg
106	65.2	Waukegan CUSD 60	Waukegan
107	65.0	Belvidere CUSD 100	Belvidere
108	64.8	Aurora West USD 129	Aurora
109	64.2	Rock Island SD 41	Rock Island
110	63.2	Urbana SD 116	Urbana
111	60.8	City of Chicago SD 299	Chicago
112	59.6	Springfield SD 186	Springfield
113	59.1	Aurora East USD 131	Aurora
114	58.4	Danville CCSD 118	Danville
115	58.0	Cahokia CUSD 187	Cahokia
116	57.3	Decatur SD 61	Decatur
117	55.2	Kankakee SD 111	Kankakee
118	55.0	Rockford SD 205	Rockford

Note: This section only includes districts with 1,500 or more students; All categories are ranked from high to low

Rank	Value	District	City
119	54.0	E Saint Louis SD 189	E Saint Louis
120	52.4	North Chicago SD 187	North Chicago
121	1.2	Indian Prairie CUSD 204	Aurora
n/a	n/a	Addison SD 4	Addison
n/a	n/a	Adlai E Stevenson HSD 125	Lincolnshire
n/a	n/a	Alsip-Hazlgrn-Oaklwn SD 126	Alsip
n/a	n/a	Antioch CCSD 34	Antioch
n/a	n/a	Aptakisic-Tripp CCSD 102	Buffalo Grove
n/a	n/a	Argo CHSD 217	Summit
n/a	n/a	Arlington Hgts SD 25	Arlington Hgts
n/a	n/a	Beach Park CCSD 3	Beach Park
n/a	n/a	Belleville SD 118	Belleville
n/a	n/a	Belleville Twp HSD 201	Belleville
n/a	n/a	Bellwood SD 88	Bellwood
n/a	n/a	Bensenville SD 2	Bensenville
n/a	n/a	Berkeley SD 87	Berkeley
n/a	n/a	Berwyn North SD 98	Berwyn
n/a	n/a	Berwyn South SD 100	Berwyn
n/a	n/a	Big Hollow SD 38	Ingleside
n/a	n/a	Bloom Twp HSD 206	Chicago Heights
n/a	n/a	Bourbonnais SD 53	Bourbonnais
n/a	n/a	Bradley Bourbonnais CHSD 307	Bradley
n/a	n/a	Bradley SD 61	Bradley
n/a	n/a	Bremen CHSD 228	Midlothian
n/a	n/a	Burbank SD 111	Burbank
n/a	n/a	Cary CCSD 26	Cary
n/a	n/a	CCSD 168	Sauk Village
n/a	n/a	CCSD 62	Des Plaines
n/a	n/a	CCSD 89	Glen Ellyn
n/a	n/a	CCSD 93	Bloomingdale
n/a	n/a	Chicago Heights SD 170	Chicago Heights
n/a	n/a	CHSD 128	Vernon Hills
n/a	n/a	CHSD 155	Crystal Lake
n/a	n/a	CHSD 218	Oak Lawn
n/a	n/a	CHSD 94	West Chicago
n/a	n/a	CHSD 99	Downers Grove
n/a	n/a	Cicero SD 99	Cicero
n/a	n/a	Clinton CUSD 15	Clinton
n/a	n/a	Community CSD 59	Arlington Hgts
n/a	n/a	Cons HSD 230	Orland Park
n/a	n/a	Cook County SD 130	Blue Island
n/a	n/a	Crystal Lake CCSD 47	Crystal Lake
n/a	n/a	Darien SD 61	Darien
n/a	n/a	Deerfield SD 109	Deerfield
n/a	n/a	Dolton SD 148	Riverdale
n/a	n/a	Dolton SD 149	Calumet City
n/a	n/a	Downers Grove GSD 58	Downers Grove
n/a	n/a	Dupage HSD 88	Addison
n/a	n/a	East Maine SD 63	Des Plaines
n/a	n/a	East Moline SD 37	East Moline
n/a	n/a	East Peoria SD 86	East Peoria
n/a	n/a	ESD 159	Matteson
n/a	n/a	Evanston CCSD 65	Evanston
n/a	n/a	Evanston Twp HSD 202	Evanston
n/a	n/a	Evergreen Park ESD 124	Evergreen Park
n/a	n/a	Fenton CHSD 100	Bensenville
n/a	n/a	Flossmoor SD 161	Chicago Heights
n/a	n/a	Forest Ridge SD 142	Oak Forest
n/a	n/a	Frankfort CCSD 157c	Frankfort
n/a	n/a	Fremont SD 79	Mundelein
n/a	n/a	Glen Ellyn SD 41	Glen Ellyn
n/a	n/a	Glenbard Twp HSD 87	Glen Ellyn
n/a	n/a	Glenview CCSD 34	Glenview
n/a	n/a	Grant CHSD 124	Fox Lake
n/a	n/a	Grayslake CCSD 46	Grayslake
n/a	n/a	Grayslake CHSD 127	Grayslake
n/a	n/a	Gurnee SD 56	Gurnee
n/a	n/a	Harvey SD 152	Harvey
n/a	n/a	Hawthorn CCSD 73	Vernon Hills
n/a	n/a	Hinsdale CCSD 181	Burr Ridge
n/a	n/a	Hinsdale Twp HSD 86	Hinsdale
n/a	n/a	Homer CCSD 33c	Homer Glen
n/a	n/a	Homewood Flossmoor CHSD 233	Flossmoor
n/a	n/a	Homewood SD 153	Homewood
n/a	n/a	Hononegah Chd 207	Rockton
n/a	n/a	Indian Springs SD 109	Justice
n/a	n/a	J S Morton HSD 201	Cicero
n/a	n/a	Joliet PSD 86	Joliet
n/a	n/a	Joliet Twp HSD 204	Joliet
n/a	n/a	Keeneyville SD 20	Hanover Park
n/a	n/a	Kildeer Countryside CCSD 96	Buffalo Grove
n/a	n/a	Kinnikinnick CCSD 131	Roscoe
n/a	n/a	Kirby SD 140	Tinley Park
n/a	n/a	La Grange SD 102	La Grange Park
n/a	n/a	Lake Forest CHSD 115	Lake Forest
n/a	n/a	Lake Forest SD 67	Lake Forest
n/a	n/a	Lake Park CHSD 108	Roselle
n/a	n/a	Lake Villa CCSD 41	Lake Villa
n/a	n/a	Lansing SD 158	Lansing
n/a	n/a	Lemont Twp HSD 210	Lemont
n/a	n/a	Lemont-Bromberek CSD 113a	Lemont
n/a	n/a	Leyden CHSD 212	Franklin Park
n/a	n/a	Libertyville SD 70	Libertyville
n/a	n/a	Lincoln Way CHSD 210	New Lenox
n/a	n/a	Lincolnshire-Prairieview SD 103	Lincolnshire
n/a	n/a	Lockport Twp HSD 205	Lockport
n/a	n/a	Lombard SD 44	Lombard
n/a	n/a	Lyons SD 103	Lyons
n/a	n/a	Lyons Twp HSD 204	La Grange
n/a	n/a	Mannheim SD 83	Franklin Park
n/a	n/a	Marquardt SD 15	Glendale Hgts
n/a	n/a	Matteson ESD 162	Richton Park
n/a	n/a	Maywood-Melrose Park-Broadview 89	Melrose Park
n/a	n/a	Mchenry CCSD 15	Mchenry
n/a	n/a	Mchenry CHSD 156	Mchenry
n/a	n/a	Midlothian SD 143	Midlothian
n/a	n/a	Millburn CCSD 24	Old Mill Creek
n/a	n/a	Minooka CCSD 201	Minooka
n/a	n/a	Minooka CHSD 111	Minooka
n/a	n/a	Mokena SD 159	Mokena
n/a	n/a	Monmouth-Roseville CUSD 238	Monmouth
n/a	n/a	Mount Prospect SD 57	Mount Prospect
n/a	n/a	Mount Vernon SD 80	Mount Vernon
n/a	n/a	Mundelein Cons HSD 120	Mundelein
n/a	n/a	Mundelein ESD 75	Mundelein
n/a	n/a	New Lenox SD 122	New Lenox
n/a	n/a	New Trier Twp HSD 203	Northfield
n/a	n/a	Niles Twp CHSD 219	Skokie
n/a	n/a	North Mac CUSD 34	Girard
n/a	n/a	North Palos SD 117	Palos Hills
n/a	n/a	North Shore SD 112	Highland Park
n/a	n/a	Northbrook SD 28	Northbrook
n/a	n/a	Northfield Twp HSD 225	Glenview
n/a	n/a	O Fallon CCSD 90	O Fallon
n/a	n/a	O Fallon Twp HSD 203	O Fallon
n/a	n/a	Oak Lawn CHSD 229	Oak Lawn
n/a	n/a	Oak Lawn-Hometown SD 123	Oak Lawn
n/a	n/a	Oak Park - River Forest SD 200	Oak Park
n/a	n/a	Oak Park ESD 97	Oak Park
n/a	n/a	Orland SD 135	Orland Park
n/a	n/a	Ottawa ESD 141	Ottawa
n/a	n/a	Palatine CCSD 15	Palatine
n/a	n/a	Palos CCSD 118	Palos Park
n/a	n/a	Park Forest SD 163	Park Forest
n/a	n/a	Park Ridge CCSD 64	Park Ridge
n/a	n/a	Pekin CSD 303	Pekin
n/a	n/a	Pekin PSD 108	Pekin
n/a	n/a	Posen-Robbins ESD 143-5	Posen
n/a	n/a	Prairie-Hills ESD 144	Markham
n/a	n/a	Proviso Twp HSD 209	Forest Park
n/a	n/a	Queen Bee SD 16	Glendale Hgts
n/a	n/a	Rantoul City SD 137	Rantoul
n/a	n/a	Reavis Twp HSD 220	Burbank
n/a	n/a	Rich Twp HSD 227	Olympia Fields
n/a	n/a	Ridgeland SD 122	Oak Lawn
n/a	n/a	Riverside SD 96	Riverside
n/a	n/a	Rochelle CCSD 231	Rochelle
n/a	n/a	Rockton SD 140	Rockton
n/a	n/a	Schaumburg CCSD 54	Schaumburg
n/a	n/a	SD 45 Dupage County	Villa Park
n/a	n/a	Skokie SD 68	Skokie
n/a	n/a	Skokie SD 69	Skokie
n/a	n/a	Steger SD 194	Steger
n/a	n/a	Streator ESD 44	Streator
n/a	n/a	Summit Hill SD 161	Frankfort
n/a	n/a	Summit SD 104	Summit
n/a	n/a	Thornton Fractional Twp HSD 215	Calumet City
n/a	n/a	Thornton Twp HSD 205	South Holland
n/a	n/a	Tinley Park CCSD 146	Tinley Park
n/a	n/a	Township HSD 211	Palatine
n/a	n/a	Township HSD 214	Arlington Hgts
n/a	n/a	Troy CCSD 30c	Plainfield
n/a	n/a	Twp HSD 113	Highland Park
n/a	n/a	United Twp HSD 30	East Moline
n/a	n/a	Warren Twp HSD 121	Gurnee
n/a	n/a	West Chicago ESD 33	West Chicago
n/a	n/a	Wheeling CCSD 21	Wheeling
n/a	n/a	Will County SD 92	Lockport
n/a	n/a	Wilmette SD 39	Wilmette
n/a	n/a	Winnetka SD 36	Winnetka
n/a	n/a	Woodland CCSD 50	Gurnee
n/a	n/a	Woodridge SD 68	Woodridge
n/a	n/a	Zion ESD 6	Zion
n/a	n/a	Zion-Benton Twp HSD 126	Zion

Note: This section only includes districts with 1,500 or more students; All categories are ranked from high to low

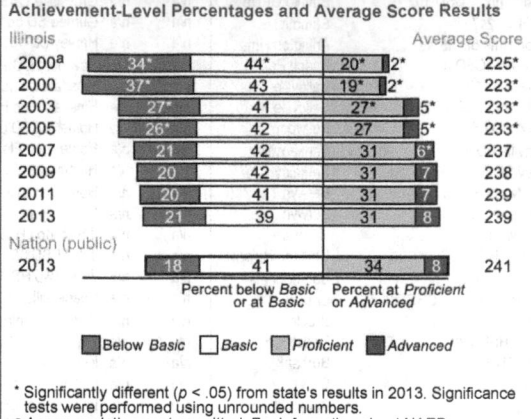

The Nation's Report Card
Mathematics
2013 State Snapshot Report

Illinois
Grade 4
Public Schools

Overall Results

- In 2013, the average score of fourth-grade students in Illinois was 239. This was not significantly different from the average score of 241 for public school students in the nation.
- The average score for students in Illinois in 2013 (239) was not significantly different from their average score in 2011 (239) and was higher than their average score in 2000 (223).
- The score gap between higher performing students in Illinois (those at the 75th percentile) and lower performing students (those at the 25th percentile) was 43 points in 2013. This performance gap was not significantly different from that in 2000 (42 points).
- The percentage of students in Illinois who performed at or above the NAEP *Proficient* level was 39 percent in 2013. This percentage was not significantly different from that in 2011 (38 percent) and was greater than that in 2000 (20 percent).
- The percentage of students in Illinois who performed at or above the NAEP *Basic* level was 79 percent in 2013. This percentage was not significantly different from that in 2011 (80 percent) and was greater than that in 2000 (63 percent).

Achievement-Level Percentages and Average Score Results

Illinois	Below Basic	Basic	Proficient	Advanced	Average Score
2000ᵃ	34*	44*	20*	2*	225*
2000	37*	43	19*	2*	223*
2003	27*	41	27*	5*	233*
2005	26*	42	27	5*	233*
2007	21	42	31	6*	237
2009	20	42	31	7	238
2011	20	41	31	7	239
2013	21	39	31	8	239
Nation (public)					
2013	18	41	34	8	241

Percent below *Basic* or at *Basic*   Percent at *Proficient* or *Advanced*

■ Below *Basic*   ☐ *Basic*   ▨ *Proficient*   ■ *Advanced*

* Significantly different (*p* < .05) from state's results in 2013. Significance tests were performed using unrounded numbers.
ᵃ Accommodations not permitted. For information about NAEP accommodations, see http://nces.ed.gov/nationsreportcard/about/inclusion.aspx.

NOTE: Detail may not sum to totals because of rounding.

Compare the Average Score in 2013 to Other States/Jurisdictions

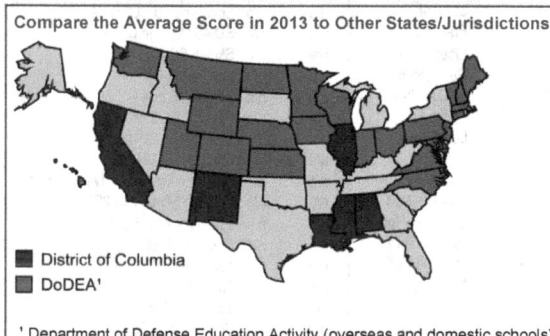

■ District of Columbia
■ DoDEA¹

¹ Department of Defense Education Activity (overseas and domestic schools).

In 2013, the average score in **Illinois** (239) was
- lower than those in 26 states/jurisdictions
- higher than those in 6 states/jurisdictions
- not significantly different from those in 19 states/jurisdictions

Average Scores for State/Jurisdiction and Nation (public)

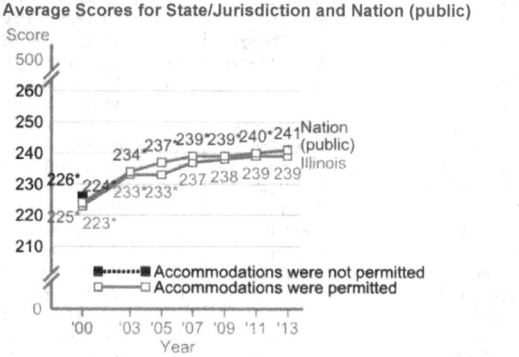

Nation (public): 234, 237*, 239*, 239*, 240*, 241
Illinois: 226*, 224, 223*, 233*, 233*, 237, 238, 239, 239

■ Accommodations were not permitted
☐ Accommodations were permitted

* Significantly different (*p* < .05) from 2013. Significance tests were performed using unrounded numbers.

NOTE: For information about NAEP accommodations, see http://nces.ed.gov/nationsreportcard/about/inclusion.aspx.

Results for Student Groups in 2013

Reporting Groups	Percent of students	Avg. score	Percentages at or above		Percent at Advanced
			Basic	Proficient	
Race/Ethnicity					
White	48	248	88	51	11
Black	17	220	59	16	1
Hispanic	27	229	71	25	3
Asian	5	266	96	73	31
American Indian/Alaska Native	#	‡	‡	‡	‡
Native Hawaiian/Pacific Islander	#	‡	‡	‡	‡
Two or more races	3	246	87	46	12
Gender					
Male	51	239	78	39	9
Female	49	239	79	39	8
National School Lunch Program					
Eligible	51	226	67	22	2
Not eligible	49	252	90	57	15

Rounds to zero.   ‡ Reporting standards not met.

NOTE: Detail may not sum to totals because of rounding, and because the "Information not available" category for the National School Lunch Program, which provides free/reduced-price lunches, is not displayed. Black includes African American and Hispanic includes Latino. Race categories exclude Hispanic origin.

Score Gaps for Student Groups

- In 2013, Black students had an average score that was 28 points lower than White students. This performance gap was not significantly different from that in 2000 (33 points).
- In 2013, Hispanic students had an average score that was 19 points lower than White students. This performance gap was not significantly different from that in 2000 (24 points).
- In 2013, male students in Illinois had an average score that was not significantly different from female students.
- In 2013, students who were eligible for free/reduced-price school lunch, an indicator of low family income, had an average score that was 26 points lower than students who were not eligible for free/reduced-price school lunch. This performance gap was not significantly different from that in 2000 (25 points).

NOTE: Statistical comparisons are calculated on the basis of unrounded scale scores or percentages.
SOURCE: U.S. Department of Education, Institute of Education Sciences, National Center for Education Statistics, National Assessment of Educational Progress (NAEP), various years, 2000–2013 Mathematics Assessments.

The Nation's Report Card — **Mathematics** 2013 State Snapshot Report

Illinois
Grade 8
Public Schools

Overall Results

- In 2013, the average score of eighth-grade students in Illinois was 285. This was not significantly different from the average score of 284 for public school students in the nation.
- The average score for students in Illinois in 2013 (285) was not significantly different from their average score in 2011 (283) and was higher than their average score in 1990 (261).
- The score gap between higher performing students in Illinois (those at the 75th percentile) and lower performing students (those at the 25th percentile) was 50 points in 2013. This performance gap was not significantly different from that in 1990 (49 points).
- The percentage of students in Illinois who performed at or above the NAEP *Proficient* level was 36 percent in 2013. This percentage was not significantly different from that in 2011 (33 percent) and was greater than that in 1990 (15 percent).
- The percentage of students in Illinois who performed at or above the NAEP *Basic* level was 74 percent in 2013. This percentage was not significantly different from that in 2011 (73 percent) and was greater than that in 1990 (50 percent).

Achievement-Level Percentages and Average Score Results

Illinois	Below Basic	Basic	Proficient	Advanced	Average Score
1990[a]	50*	36	13*	2*	261*
2000[a]	32*	41	23*	4*	277*
2000	33*	40	22*	4*	275*
2003	34*	37	23*	6*	277*
2005	32*	40	23*	5*	278*
2007	30	40	24*	7*	280*
2009	27	40	26	7	282
2011	27	40	25	8	283
2013	26	37	27	9	285
Nation (public)					
2013	27	39	26	8	284

Percent below *Basic* or at *Basic*   Percent at *Proficient* or *Advanced*

■ Below *Basic* ☐ *Basic* ▨ *Proficient* ■ *Advanced*

* Significantly different (*p* < .05) from state's results in 2013. Significance tests were performed using unrounded numbers.
[a] Accommodations not permitted. For information about NAEP accommodations, see http://nces.ed.gov/nationsreportcard/about/inclusion.aspx.

NOTE: Detail may not sum to totals because of rounding.

Compare the Average Score in 2013 to Other States/Jurisdictions

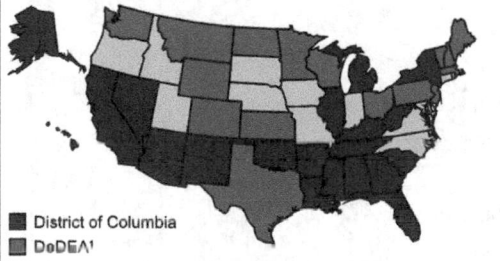

■ District of Columbia
▨ DoDEA[1]

[1] Department of Defense Education Activity (overseas and domestic schools).

In 2013, the average score in Illinois (285) was
- lower than those in 17 states/jurisdictions
- higher than those in 20 states/jurisdictions
- not significantly different from those in 14 states/jurisdictions

Average Scores for State/Jurisdiction and Nation (public)

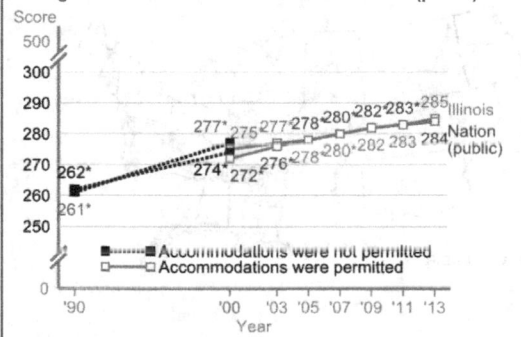

Illinois: 262*, 275*, 277*, 278*, 280*, 282*, 283*, 285
Nation (public): 261*, 274*, 272*, 276*, 278*, 280*, 282, 283, 284

■ Accommodations were not permitted
☐ Accommodations were permitted

* Significantly different (*p* < .05) from 2013. Significance tests were performed using unrounded numbers.

NOTE: For information about NAEP accommodations, see http://nces.ed.gov/nationsreportcard/about/inclusion.aspx.

Results for Student Groups in 2013

Reporting Groups	Percent of students	Avg. score	Percentages at or above Basic	Percentages at or above Proficient	Percent at Advanced
Race/Ethnicity					
White	52	296	85	48	13
Black	17	260	49	12	1
Hispanic	24	272	64	22	2
Asian	5	313	90	70	34
American Indian/Alaska Native	#	‡	‡	‡	‡
Native Hawaiian/Pacific Islander	#	‡	‡	‡	‡
Two or more races	3	285	74	33	12
Gender					
Male	51	285	73	37	10
Female	49	285	74	36	9
National School Lunch Program					
Eligible	46	268	58	18	2
Not eligible	54	299	87	52	15

\# Rounds to zero.   ‡ Reporting standards not met.

NOTE: Detail may not sum to totals because of rounding, and because the "Information not available" category for the National School Lunch Program, which provides free/reduced-price lunches, is not displayed. Black includes African American and Hispanic includes Latino. Race categories exclude Hispanic origin.

Score Gaps for Student Groups

- In 2013, Black students had an average score that was 35 points lower than White students. This performance gap was not significantly different from that in 1990 (38 points).
- In 2013, Hispanic students had an average score that was 24 points lower than White students. This performance gap was not significantly different from that in 1990 (33 points).
- In 2013, male students in Illinois had an average score that was not significantly different from female students.
- In 2013, students who were eligible for free/reduced-price school lunch, an indicator of low family income, had an average score that was 32 points lower than students who were not eligible for free/reduced-price school lunch. This performance gap was not significantly different from that in 2000 (30 points).

 NATIONAL CENTER FOR EDUCATION STATISTICS — Institute of Education Sciences

NOTE: Statistical comparisons are calculated on the basis of unrounded scale scores or percentages.
SOURCE: U.S. Department of Education, Institute of Education Sciences, National Center for Education Statistics, National Assessment of Educational Progress (NAEP), various years, 1990–2013 Mathematics Assessments.

The Nation's Report Card **Mathematics**
2013 State Snapshot Report

Illinois
Grade 12
Public Schools

Overall Results

- In 2013, the average score of twelfth-grade students in Illinois was 154. This was not significantly different from the average score of 152 for public school students in the nation.
- The average score for students in Illinois in 2013 (154) was not significantly different from their average score in 2009 (154).
- The score gap between higher performing students in Illinois (those at the 75th percentile) and lower performing students (those at the 25th percentile) was 47 points in 2013. This performance gap was not significantly different from that in 2009 (45 points).
- The percentage of students in Illinois who performed at or above the NAEP *Proficient* level was 27 percent in 2013. This percentage was not significantly different from that in 2009 (26 percent).
- The percentage of students in Illinois who performed at or above the NAEP *Basic* level was 65 percent in 2013. This percentage was not significantly different from that in 2009 (67 percent).

Achievement-Level Percentages and Average Score Results

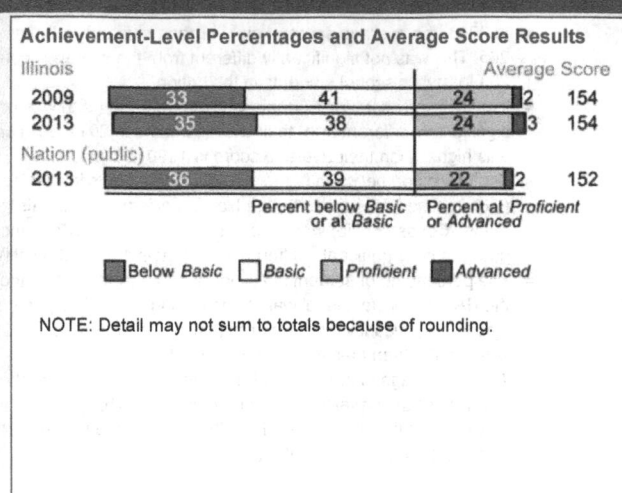

Illinois					Average Score
2009	33	41	24	2	154
2013	35	38	24	3	154
Nation (public)					
2013	36	39	22	2	152

Percent below *Basic* or at *Basic*   Percent at *Proficient* or *Advanced*

◼ Below *Basic*   ◻ *Basic*   ◻ *Proficient*   ◼ *Advanced*

NOTE: Detail may not sum to totals because of rounding.

Compare the Average Score in 2013 to Other States/Jurisdictions

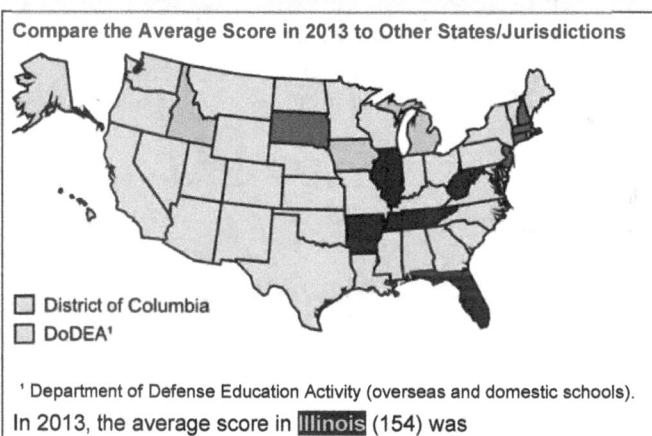

☐ District of Columbia
☐ DoDEA[1]

[1] Department of Defense Education Activity (overseas and domestic schools).

In 2013, the average score in Illinois (154) was
- lower than those in 5 states/jurisdictions
- higher than those in 4 states/jurisdictions
- not significantly different from those in 3 states/jurisdictions

Average Scores for State/Jurisdiction and Nation (public)

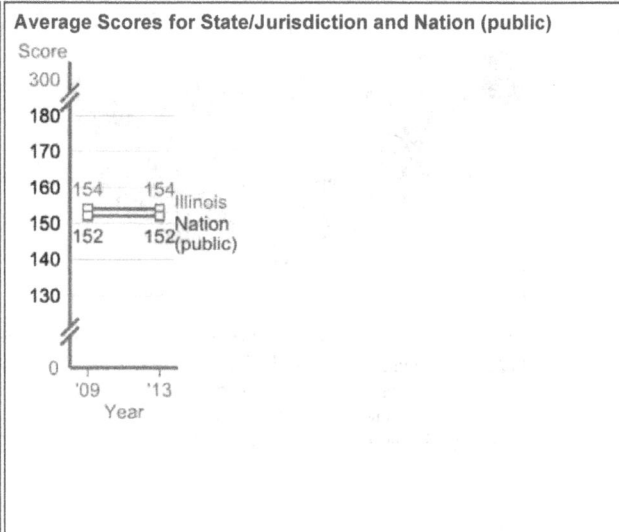

Results for Student Groups in 2013

Reporting Groups	Percent of students	Avg. score	Percentages at or above *Basic*	Percentages at or above *Proficient*	Percent at *Advanced*
Race/Ethnicity					
White	56	165	79	37	4
Black	17	123	28	5	#
Hispanic	21	143	53	12	1
Asian	4	181	89	57	14
American Indian/Alaska Native	#	‡	‡	‡	‡
Native Hawaiian/Pacific Islander	#	‡	‡	‡	‡
Two or more races	2	‡	‡	‡	‡
Gender					
Male	51	155	64	29	4
Female	49	153	66	25	2

\# Rounds to zero.   ‡ Reporting standards not met.

NOTE: Detail may not sum to totals because of rounding. Black includes African American and Hispanic includes Latino. Race categories exclude Hispanic origin.

Score Gaps for Student Groups

- In 2013, Black students had an average score that was 42 points lower than White students. This performance gap was not significantly different from that in 2009 (32 points).
- In 2013, Hispanic students had an average score that was 22 points lower than White students. This performance gap was not significantly different from that in 2009 (20 points).
- In 2013, male students in Illinois had an average score that was not significantly different from female students.

NOTE: Statistical comparisons are calculated on the basis of unrounded scale scores or percentages.
SOURCE: U.S. Department of Education, Institute of Education Sciences, National Center for Education Statistics, National Assessment of Educational Progress (NAEP), 2009 and 2013 Mathematics Assessments.

The Nation's Report Card Reading
2013 State Snapshot Report

Illinois
Grade 4
Public Schools

Overall Results

- In 2013, the average score of fourth-grade students in Illinois was 219. This was not significantly different from the average score of 221 for public school students in the nation.
- The average score for students in Illinois in 2013 (219) was not significantly different from their average score in 2011 (219) and in 2003 (216).
- The score gap between higher performing students in Illinois (those at the 75th percentile) and lower performing students (those at the 25th percentile) was 51 points in 2013. This performance gap was not significantly different from that in 2003 (53 points).
- The percentage of students in Illinois who performed at or above the NAEP *Proficient* level was 34 percent in 2013. This percentage was not significantly different from that in 2011 (33 percent) and in 2003 (31 percent).
- The percentage of students in Illinois who performed at or above the NAEP *Basic* level was 64 percent in 2013. This percentage was not significantly different from that in 2011 (65 percent) and in 2003 (61 percent).

Achievement-Level Percentages and Average Score Results

Illinois					Average Score
2003	39	30	23	8	216
2005	38	33	23	7	216
2007	35	33	24	8	219
2009	35	32	24	9	219
2011	35	32	25	9	219
2013	36	31	25	8	219

Nation (public)					
2013	33	33	26	8	221

Percent below *Basic* or at *Basic*   Percent at *Proficient* or *Advanced*

■ Below *Basic* □ *Basic* □ *Proficient* ■ *Advanced*

NOTE: Detail may not sum to totals because of rounding.

Compare the Average Score in 2013 to Other States/Jurisdictions

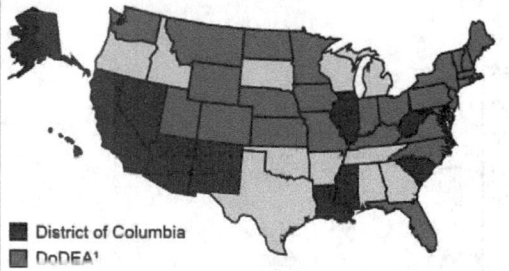

■ District of Columbia
■ DoDEA[1]

[1] Department of Defense Education Activity (overseas and domestic schools).

In 2013, the average score in Illinois (219) was
- lower than those in 29 states/jurisdictions
- higher than those in 11 states/jurisdictions
- not significantly different from those in 11 states/jurisdictions

Average Scores for State/Jurisdiction and Nation (public)

Score: 216, 217, 220*, 220*, 220, 221 Nation (public)
Illinois: 216, 216, 219, 219, 219, 219

Year: '03 '05 '07 '09 '11 '13

* Significantly different (*p* < .05) from 2013. Significance tests were performed using unrounded numbers.

Results for Student Groups in 2013

Reporting Groups	Percent of students	Avg. score	Percentages at or above Basic	Percentages at or above Proficient	Percent at Advanced
Race/Ethnicity					
White	48	231	78	46	12
Black	17	199	42	14	2
Hispanic	27	204	50	18	2
Asian	5	242	86	59	23
American Indian/Alaska Native	#	‡	‡	‡	‡
Native Hawaiian/Pacific Islander	#	‡	‡	‡	‡
Two or more races	3	221	66	37	10
Gender					
Male	51	215	61	30	7
Female	49	222	68	37	10
National School Lunch Program					
Eligible	51	202	48	16	2
Not eligible	49	235	82	52	15

Rounds to zero.   ‡ Reporting standards not met.

NOTE: Detail may not sum to totals because of rounding, and because the "Information not available" category for the National School Lunch Program, which provides free/reduced-price lunches, is not displayed. Black includes African American and Hispanic includes Latino. Race categories exclude Hispanic origin.

Score Gaps for Student Groups

- In 2013, Black students had an average score that was 32 points lower than White students. This performance gap was not significantly different from that in 2003 (34 points).
- In 2013, Hispanic students had an average score that was 27 points lower than White students. This performance gap was not significantly different from that in 2003 (31 points).
- In 2013, female students in Illinois had an average score that was higher than male students by 8 points.
- In 2013, students who were eligible for free/reduced-price school lunch, an indicator of low family income, had an average score that was 33 points lower than students who were not eligible for free/reduced-price school lunch. This performance gap was not significantly different from that in 2003 (35 points).

Overall Results

- In 2013, the average score of eighth-grade students in Illinois was 267. This was not significantly different from the average score of 266 for public school students in the nation.
- The average score for students in Illinois in 2013 (267) was not significantly different from their average score in 2011 (266) and in 2003 (266).
- The score gap between higher performing students in Illinois (those at the 75th percentile) and lower performing students (those at the 25th percentile) was 45 points in 2013. This performance gap was not significantly different from that in 2003 (44 points).
- The percentage of students in Illinois who performed at or above the NAEP *Proficient* level was 36 percent in 2013. This percentage was not significantly different from that in 2011 (34 percent) and in 2003 (35 percent).
- The percentage of students in Illinois who performed at or above the NAEP *Basic* level was 77 percent in 2013. This percentage was not significantly different from that in 2011 (77 percent) and in 2003 (77 percent).

Achievement-Level Percentages and Average Score Results

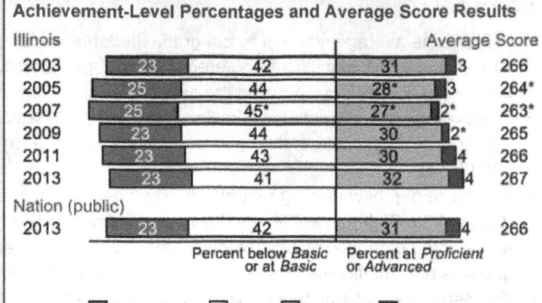

Illinois				Average Score
2003	23	42	31	3	266
2005	25	44	28*	3	264*
2007	25	45*	27*	2*	263*
2009	23	44	30	2*	265
2011	23	43	30	4	266
2013	23	41	32	4	267

Nation (public)
| 2013 | 23 | 42 | 31 | 4 | 266 |

Percent below *Basic* or at *Basic* — Percent at *Proficient* or *Advanced*

■ Below *Basic* □ *Basic* ■ *Proficient* ■ *Advanced*

* Significantly different (*p* < .05) from state's results in 2013. Significance tests were performed using unrounded numbers.

NOTE: Detail may not sum to totals because of rounding.

Compare the Average Score in 2013 to Other States/Jurisdictions

■ District of Columbia
■ DoDEA[1]

[1] Department of Defense Education Activity (overseas and domestic schools).

In 2013, the average score in Illinois (267) was
- lower than those in 15 states/jurisdictions
- higher than those in 15 states/jurisdictions
- not significantly different from those in 21 states/jurisdictions

Average Scores for State/Jurisdiction and Nation (public)

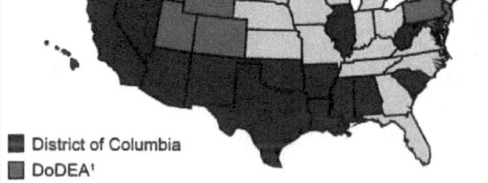

Score
500
290
280
270 — 266 264* 263* 265 266 267 Illinois
260 — 261* 260* 261 262 264* 266 Nation (public)
250
240
0

'03 '05 '07 '09 '11 '13
Year

* Significantly different (*p* < .05) from 2013. Significance tests were performed using unrounded numbers.

Results for Student Groups in 2013

Reporting Groups	Percent of students	Avg. score	Percentages at or above Basic	Percentages at or above Proficient	Percent at Advanced
Race/Ethnicity					
White	52	276	87	47	5
Black	17	246	56	14	1
Hispanic	24	257	69	24	1
Asian	5	285	91	59	12
American Indian/Alaska Native	#	‡	‡	‡	‡
Native Hawaiian/Pacific Islander	#	‡	‡	‡	‡
Two or more races	3	270	79	42	4
Gender					
Male	51	263	74	32	3
Female	49	271	81	41	5
National School Lunch Program					
Eligible	46	252	64	20	1
Not eligible	54	280	89	50	6

Rounds to zero.   ‡ Reporting standards not met.

NOTE: Detail may not sum to totals because of rounding, and because the "Information not available" category for the National School Lunch Program, which provides free/reduced-price lunches, is not displayed. Black includes African American and Hispanic includes Latino. Race categories exclude Hispanic origin.

Score Gaps for Student Groups

- In 2013, Black students had an average score that was 30 points lower than White students. This performance gap was not significantly different from that in 2003 (29 points).
- In 2013, Hispanic students had an average score that was 20 points lower than White students. This performance gap was narrower than that in 2003 (26 points).
- In 2013, female students in Illinois had an average score that was higher than male students by 8 points.
- In 2013, students who were eligible for free/reduced-price school lunch, an indicator of low family income, had an average score that was 28 points lower than students who were not eligible for free/reduced-price school lunch. This performance gap was not significantly different from that in 2003 (27 points).

 NATIONAL CENTER FOR EDUCATION STATISTICS
Institute of Education Sciences

NOTE: Statistical comparisons are calculated on the basis of unrounded scale scores or percentages.
SOURCE: U.S. Department of Education, Institute of Education Sciences, National Center for Education Statistics, National Assessment of Educational Progress (NAEP), various years, 2003–2013 Reading Assessments.

Illinois
Grade 12
Public Schools

The Nation's Report Card — Reading — 2013 State Snapshot Report

Overall Results

- In 2013, the average score of twelfth-grade students in Illinois was 289. This was not significantly different from the average score of 287 for public school students in the nation.
- The average score for students in Illinois in 2013 (289) was not significantly different from their average score in 2009 (292).
- The score gap between higher performing students in Illinois (those at the 75th percentile) and lower performing students (those at the 25th percentile) was 49 points in 2013. This performance gap was not significantly different from that in 2009 (47 points).
- The percentage of students in Illinois who performed at or above the NAEP *Proficient* level was 39 percent in 2013. This percentage was not significantly different from that in 2009 (40 percent).
- The percentage of students in Illinois who performed at or above the NAEP *Basic* level was 76 percent in 2013. This percentage was not significantly different from that in 2009 (78 percent).

Achievement-Level Percentages and Average Score Results

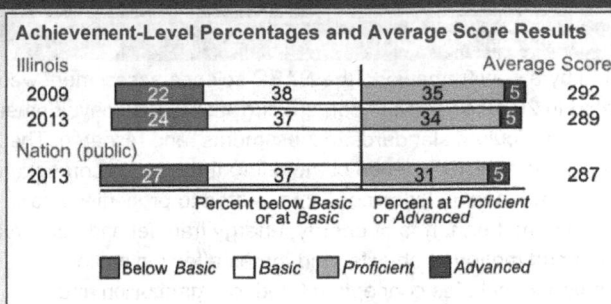

				Average Score
Illinois				
2009	22	38	35	5 → 292
2013	24	37	34	5 → 289
Nation (public)				
2013	27	37	31	5 → 287

Percent below *Basic* or at *Basic* | Percent at *Proficient* or *Advanced*

■ Below *Basic* □ *Basic* ▨ *Proficient* ■ *Advanced*

NOTE: Detail may not sum to totals because of rounding.

Compare the Average Score in 2013 to Other States/Jurisdictions

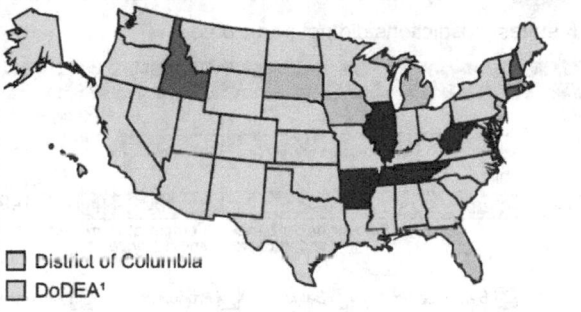

□ District of Columbia
□ DoDEA[1]

[1] Department of Defense Education Activity (overseas and domestic schools).

In 2013, the average score in Illinois (289) was
- lower than those in 3 states/jurisdictions
- higher than those in 3 states/jurisdictions
- not significantly different from those in 6 states/jurisdictions

Average Scores for State/Jurisdiction and Nation (public)

Illinois: 292 ('09) → 289 ('13)
Nation (public): 287 ('09) → 287 ('13)

Results for Student Groups in 2013

Reporting Groups	Percent of students	Avg. score	Percentages at or above Basic	Proficient	Percent at Advanced
Race/Ethnicity					
White	56	299	84	50	7
Black	17	267	54	15	1
Hispanic	21	278	68	24	1
Asian	4	303	85	57	11
American Indian/Alaska Native	#	‡	‡	‡	‡
Native Hawaiian/Pacific Islander	#	‡	‡	‡	‡
Two or more races	2	‡	‡	‡	‡
Gender					
Male	51	285	72	34	4
Female	49	294	80	44	6

Rounds to zero.   ‡ Reporting standards not met.

NOTE: Detail may not sum to totals because of rounding. Black includes African American and Hispanic includes Latino. Race categories exclude Hispanic origin.

Score Gaps for Student Groups

- In 2013, Black students had an average score that was 32 points lower than White students. This performance gap was not significantly different from that in 2009 (26 points).
- In 2013, Hispanic students had an average score that was 21 points lower than White students. This performance gap was not significantly different from that in 2009 (22 points).
- In 2013, female students in Illinois had an average score that was higher than male students by 10 points.

NOTE: Statistical comparisons are calculated on the basis of unrounded scale scores or percentages.
SOURCE: U.S. Department of Education, Institute of Education Sciences, National Center for Education Statistics, National Assessment of Educational Progress (NAEP), 2009 and 2013 Reading Assessments.

2009 Science Assessment Content

Guided by a new framework, the NAEP science assessment was updated in 2009 to keep the content current with key developments in science, curriculum standards, assessments, and research. The 2009 framework organizes science content into three broad content areas. **Physical science** includes concepts related to properties and changes of matter, forms of energy, energy transfer and conservation, position and motion of objects, and forces affecting motion. **Life science** includes concepts related to organization and development, matter and energy transformations, interdependence, heredity and reproduction, and evolution and diversity. **Earth and space sciences** includes concepts related to objects in the universe, the history of the Earth, properties of Earth materials, tectonics, energy in Earth systems, climate and weather, and biogeochemical cycles.

The 2009 science assessment was composed of 143 questions at grade 4, 162 at grade 8, and 179 at grade 12. Students responded to only a portion of the questions, which included both multiple-choice questions and questions that required a written response.

Compare the Average Score in 2009 to Other States/Jurisdictions

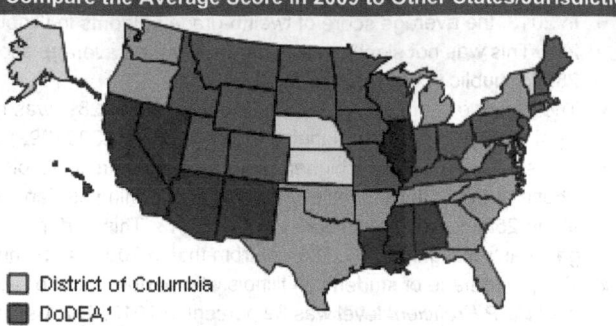

☐ District of Columbia
■ DoDEA[1]

[1] Department of Defense Education Activity (overseas and domestic schools).

In 2009, the average score in **Illinois** was
- lower than those in 23 states/jurisdictions
- higher than those in 8 states/jurisdictions
- not significantly different from those in 15 states/jurisdictions
- 5 states/jurisdictions did not participate

Overall Results

- In 2009, the average score of fourth-grade students in Illinois was 148. This was not significantly different from the average score of 149 for public school students in the nation.
- The percentage of students in Illinois who performed at or above the NAEP *Proficient* level was 32 percent in 2009. This percentage was not significantly different from the nation (32 percent).
- The percentage of students in Illinois who performed at or above the NAEP *Basic* level was 69 percent in 2009. This percentage was not significantly different from the nation (71 percent).

Achievement-Level Percentages and Average Score Results

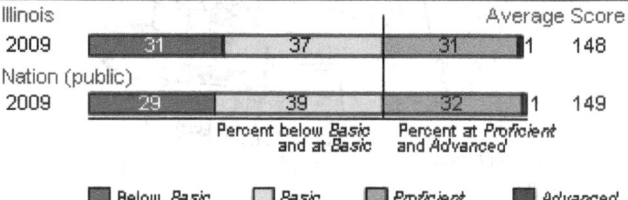

NOTE: Detail may not sum to totals because of rounding.

Results for Student Groups in 2009

Reporting Groups	Percent of students	Avg. score	Percentages at or above Basic	Percentages at or above Proficient	Percent at Advanced
Gender					
Male	50	148	69	34	1
Female	50	147	69	30	1
Race/Ethnicity					
White	51	164	87	48	1
Black	19	120	37	9	#
Hispanic	22	129	51	10	#
Asian/Pacific Islander	5	166	86	51	3
American Indian/Alaska Native	#	‡	‡	‡	‡
National School Lunch Program					
Eligible	46	129	50	14	#
Not eligible	53	163	86	48	1

Rounds to zero.   ‡ Reporting standards not met.

NOTE: Detail may not sum to totals because of rounding, and because the "Information not available" category for the National School Lunch Program, which provides free/reduced-price lunches, and the "Unclassified" category for race/ethnicity are not displayed.

Score Gaps for Student Groups

- In 2009, male students in Illinois had an average score that was not significantly different from female students.
- In 2009, Black students had an average score that was 44 points lower than White students. This performance gap was wider than the nation (35 points).
- In 2009, Hispanic students had an average score that was 35 points lower than White students. This performance gap was not significantly different from the nation (32 points).
- In 2009, students who were eligible for free/reduced-price school lunch, an indicator of low family income, had an average score that was 34 points lower than students who were not eligible for free/reduced-price school lunch. This performance gap was wider than the nation (29 points).

NOTE: Statistical comparisons are calculated on the basis of unrounded scale scores or percentages.
SOURCE: U.S. Department of Education, Institute of Education Sciences, National Center for Education Statistics, National Assessment of Educational Progress (NAEP), 2009 Science Assessment.

Overall Results

- In 2011, the average score of eighth-grade students in Illinois was 147. This was lower than the average score of 151 for public school students in the nation.
- The average score for students in Illinois in 2011 (147) was not significantly different from their average score in 2009 (148).
- In 2011, the score gap between students in Illinois at the 75th percentile and students at the 25th percentile was 45 points. This performance gap was not significantly different from that of 2009 (48 points).
- The percentage of students in Illinois who performed at or above the NAEP *Proficient* level was 26 percent in 2011. This percentage was not significantly different from that in 2009 (28 percent).
- The percentage of students in Illinois who performed at or above the NAEP *Basic* level was 60 percent in 2011. This percentage was not significantly different from that in 2009 (61 percent).

Achievement-Level Percentages and Average Score Results

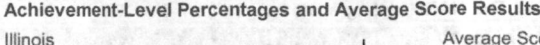
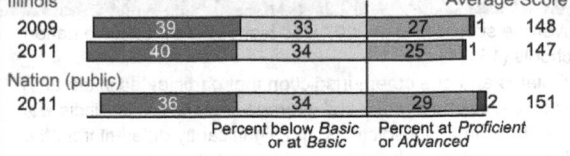

NOTE: Detail may not sum to totals because of rounding.

Compare the Average Score in 2011 to Other States/Jurisdictions

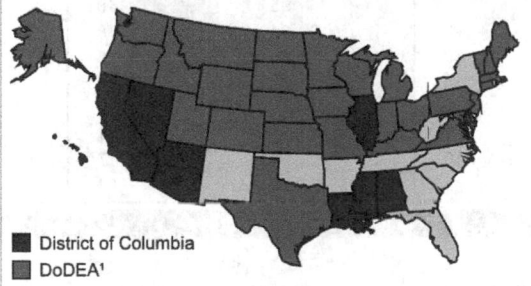

- District of Columbia
- DoDEA[1]

[1] Department of Defense Education Activity (overseas and domestic schools).

In 2011, the average score in Illinois (147) was
- lower than those in 32 states/jurisdictions
- higher than those in 8 states/jurisdictions
- not significantly different from those in 11 states/jurisdictions

Average Scores for State/Jurisdiction and Nation (public)

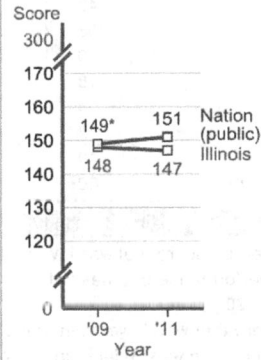

* Significantly different ($p < .05$) from 2011. Significance tests were performed using unrounded numbers.

Results for Student Groups in 2011

Reporting Groups	Percent of students	Avg. score	Percentages at or above Basic	Percentages at or above Proficient	Percent at Advanced
Race/Ethnicity					
White	51	161	78	39	2
Black	18	120	25	4	#
Hispanic	23	135	44	11	#
Asian	5	163	80	42	5
American Indian/Alaska Native	#	‡	‡	‡	‡
Native Hawaiian/Pacific Islander	#	‡	‡	‡	‡
Two or more races	2	‡	‡	‡	‡
Gender					
Male	51	150	63	30	2
Female	49	144	57	21	1
National School Lunch Program					
Eligible	48	132	41	10	#
Not eligible	52	162	78	41	2

Rounds to zero.   ‡ Reporting standards not met.

NOTE: Detail may not sum to totals because of rounding, and because the "Information not available" category for the National School Lunch Program, which provides free/reduced-price lunches, is not displayed. Black includes African American and Hispanic includes Latino. Race categories exclude Hispanic origin.

Score Gaps for Student Groups

- In 2011, Black students had an average score that was 41 points lower than White students. This performance gap was not significantly different from that in 2009 (44 points).
- In 2011, Hispanic students had an average score that was 26 points lower than White students. This performance gap was not significantly different from that in 2009 (30 points).
- In 2011, male students in Illinois had an average score that was higher than female students by 6 points.
- In 2011, students who were eligible for free/reduced-price school lunch, an indicator of low family income, had an average score that was 30 points lower than students who were not eligible for free/reduced-price school lunch. This performance gap was not significantly different from that in 2009 (34 points).

NOTE: Statistical comparisons are calculated on the basis of unrounded scale scores or percentages.
SOURCE: U.S. Department of Education, Institute of Education Sciences, National Center for Education Statistics, National Assessment of Educational Progress (NAEP), 2009 and 2011 Science Assessments.

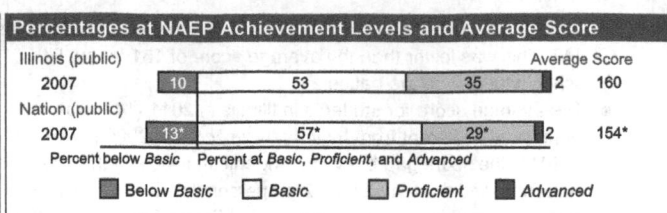

Illinois
Grade 8
Public Schools

The National Assessment of Educational Progress (NAEP) assesses writing for three purposes identified in the NAEP framework: narrative, informative, and persuasive. The NAEP writing scale ranges from 0 to 300.

Overall Writing Results for Illinois

- Illinois' average score (160) in 2007 was higher than that of the nation's public schools (154).[1]
- Of the 45 states and one other jurisdiction that participated in the 2007 eighth-grade assessment, students' average scale score in Illinois was higher than those in 27 jurisdictions, not significantly different from those in 14 jurisdictions, and lower than those in 4 jurisdictions.[2]
- The percentage of students in Illinois who performed at or above the NAEP *Proficient* level was 37 percent in 2007. This percentage was greater than that in the nation (31 percent).
- The percentage of students in Illinois who performed at or above the NAEP *Basic* level was 90 percent in 2007. This percentage was greater than that in the nation (87 percent).

Percentages at NAEP Achievement Levels and Average Score

				Average Score
Illinois (public) 2007	10	53	35	2	160
Nation (public) 2007	13*	57*	29*	2	154*

Percent below *Basic*   Percent at *Basic*, *Proficient*, and *Advanced*

■ Below *Basic*   □ *Basic*   ▨ *Proficient*   ■ *Advanced*

NOTE: The NAEP grade 8 writing achievement levels correspond to the following scale points: Below *Basic*, 113 or lower; *Basic*, 114–172; *Proficient*, 173–223; *Advanced*, 224 or above.

Performance of NAEP Reporting Groups in Illinois: 2007

Reporting groups	Percent of students	Average score	Percent below *Basic*	Percent of students at or above *Basic*	*Proficient*	Percent *Advanced*
Male	51	150↑	15↓	85↑	27↑	1
Female	49	170↑	5↓	95↑	48↑	4
White	58	169↑	6↓	94↑	48↑	3
Black	19	142	19	81	18	#
Hispanic	18	143	18	82	17	#
Asian/Pacific Islander	4	180↑	2	98	60↑	8
American Indian/Alaska Native	#↓	‡	‡	‡	‡	‡
Eligible for National School Lunch Program	40	142	19	81	17	#
Not eligible for National School Lunch Program	60	172↑	5↓	95↑	51↑	4

Average Score Gaps Between Selected Groups

- In 2007, male students in Illinois had an average score that was lower than that of female students by 19 points. This performance gap was not significantly different from that of the nation (20 points).
- In 2007, Black students had an average score that was lower than that of White students by 27 points. This performance gap was wider than that of the nation (22 points).
- In 2007, Hispanic students had an average score that was lower than that of White students by 26 points. This performance gap was not significantly different from that of the nation (21 points).
- In 2007, students who were eligible for free/reduced-price school lunch, an indicator of poverty, had an average score that was lower than that of students who were not eligible for free/reduced-price school lunch by 29 points. This performance gap was wider than that of the nation (23 points).
- In 2007, the score gap between students at the 75th percentile and students at the 25th percentile was 47 points. This performance gap was not significantly different from that of the nation (46 points).

Writing Scores at Selected Percentiles: 2007

Jurisdiction	25th Percentile	50th Percentile	75th Percentile
Illinois	138	162	185
Nation (public)	132*	156*	178*

NOTE: Scores at selected percentiles on the NAEP writing scale indicate how well students at lower, middle, and higher levels performed. For example, the data above show that 75 percent of students in public schools nationally scored below 178, while 75 percent of students in Illinois scored below 185.

Rounds to zero.   ‡ Reporting standards not met.
* Significantly different from Illinois.   ↑ Significantly higher than nation (public). ↓ Significantly lower than nation (public).
[1] Comparisons (higher/lower/narrower/wider/not different) are based on statistical tests. The .05 level with appropriate adjustments for multiple comparisons was used for testing statistical significance. Statistical comparisons are calculated on the basis of unrounded scale scores or percentages. Comparisons across jurisdictions and comparisons with the nation or within a jurisdiction across years may be affected by differences in exclusion rates for students with disabilities (SD) and English language learners (ELL). The exclusion rates for SD and ELL in Illinois were 2 percent and 1 percent in 2007, respectively. For more information on NAEP significance testing, see http://nces.ed.gov/nationsreportcard/writing/interpret-results.asp#statistical.
[2] "Jurisdiction" refers to states, the District of Columbia, and the Department of Defense Education Activity schools.
NOTE: Detail may not sum to totals because of rounding and because the "Information not available" category for the National School Lunch Program, which provides free and reduced-price lunches, and the "Unclassified" category for race/ethnicity are not displayed. Visit http://nces.ed.gov/nationsreportcard/states/ for additional results and detailed information.
SOURCE: U.S. Department of Education, Institute of Education Sciences, National Center for Education Statistics, National Assessment of Educational Progress (NAEP), 2007 Writing Assessment.

ILLINOIS STATE REPORT CARD

State and federal laws require public school districts to release report cards to the public each year.

This year, we have updated the report card to provide a full picture of school performance beyond just test scores. A display of this data designed with parents and communities in mind is available on illinoisreportcard.com. All of the metrics posted on illinoisreportcard.com are also included in this report.

STUDENTS

RACIAL/ETHNIC BACKGROUND AND OTHER INFORMATION

White	Black	Hispanic	Asian	Native Hawaiian/ Pacific Islander	American Indian	Two or More Races	Percent Low- Income	Percent Limited- English- Proficient	Percent IEP	Percent Homeless	Total Enrollment
50.6	17.6	24.1	4.3	0.1	0.3	3.0	49.9	9.5	13.6	2.0	2,054,155

Low-income students come from families receiving public aid; live in institutions for neglected or delinquent children; are supported in foster homes with public funds; or are eligible to receive free or reduced-price lunches.
IEP Students are those students eligible to receive special education services.

Limited-English-proficient students are those students eligible for transitional bilingual programs.
Total Enrollment is based on Home School.
Homeless students are students who do not have permanent and adequate homes.

RACIAL/ETHNIC BACKGROUND AND OTHER INFORMATION

High Sch. Dropout Rate	Chronic Truancy Rate	Mobility Rate	Attendance Rate
2.4	9.8	12.8	94.2

Mobility rate is based on the number of times students enroll in or leave a school during the school year.
Chronic truants are students who are absent from school without valid cause for 0 or more of the last 180 school days.

INSTRUCTIONAL SETTING

PARENTAL CONTACT*	
	Percent
	95.5

TOTAL SCHOOL DAY	
	Days
	176

* Parental contact includes parent-teacher conferences, parental visits to school, school visits to home, telephone conversations, and written correspondence.

AVERAGE CLASS SIZE (as of the first school day in May)											
Grades	K	1	2	3	4	5	6	7	8	9-12	Overall
	21.1	21.5	21.5	21.9	22.5	22.5	23.1	22.3	22.2	19.3	21.2

TIME DEVOTED TO TEACHING CORE SUBJECTS (Minutes Per Day)

Grades	Mathematics			Science			English/Language Arts			Social Science		
	3	6	8	3	6	8	3	6	8	3	6	8
	62	58	55	31	44	46	142	103	92	30	43	45

TEACHER INFORMATION

	% of Classes Not Taught by Highly Qualified Teachers
All Schools	0.2
High Poverty Schools	0.5
Low Poverty Schools	0.0

The No Child Left Behind Act requires that information for certain data elements be disaggregated by high- and low-poverty schools. Poverty (low-income) is defined on page 1 of all report cards. High- and low-poverty schools include those in the top and bottom quarters of the poverty distribution of schools in the state.

SCHOOL DISTRICT FINANCES

EXPENDITURE BY FUNCTION 2011-12 (Percentages)

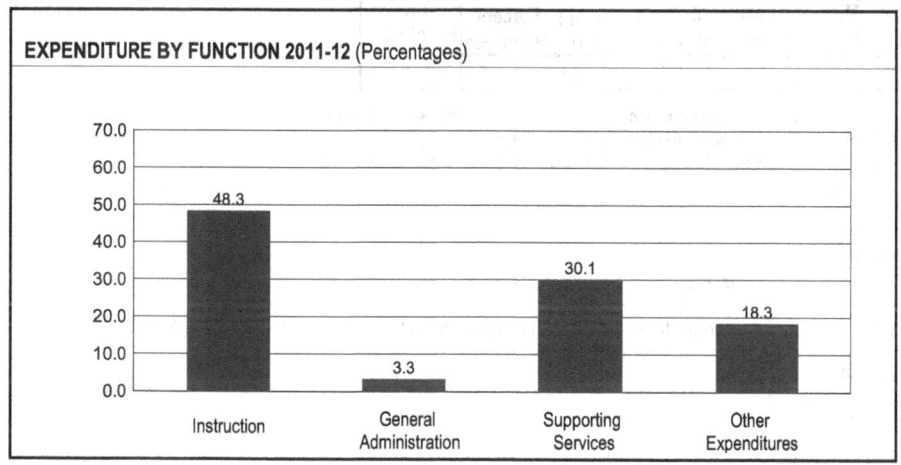

REVENUE BY SOURCE 2011-12

	Percent
Local Property Taxes	61.1
Other Local Funding	4.8
General State Aid	16.4
Other State Funding	9.7
Federal Funding	8.1

EXPENDITURE BY FUND 2011-12

	Percent
Education	73.4
Operations & Maintenance	6.2
Transportation	3.7
Debt Service	7.6
Tort	1.2
Municipal Retirement/ Social Security	2.0
Fire Prevention & Safety	0.7
Capital Projects	5.2

OTHER FINANCIAL INDICATORS

	2011-12 Instructional Expenditure per Pupil	2011-12 Operating Expenditure per Pupil
	$6,974	$11,842

Instructional expenditure per pupil includes the direct costs of teaching pupils or the interaction between teachers and pupils.
Operating expenditure per pupil includes the gross operating cost of a school district excluding summer school, adult education, bond principal retired, and capital expenditures.

ACADEMIC PERFORMANCE

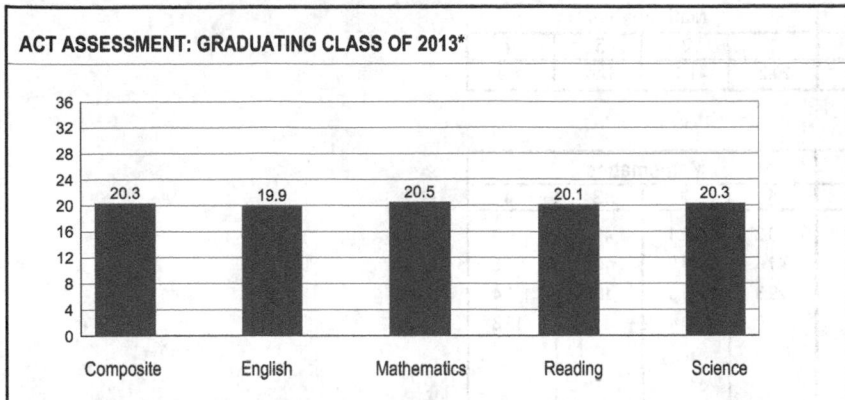

ACT ASSESSMENT: GRADUATING CLASS OF 2013*

	Composite	English	Mathematics	Reading	Science
	20.3	19.9	20.5	20.1	20.3

The number and percent of students taking the ACT are no longer reported since virtually every eleventh grade student takes the ACT as part of the PSAE.

* Includes graduating students' most recent ACT Assessment scores from an ACT national test date or PSAE testing. All students whose scores are college reportable, both standard and extended time tests, are now included. State averages for ACT data are based on regular public schools and do not include private and special purpose schools.

READY FOR COLLEGE COURSE WORK
45.7

HIGH SCHOOL 4-YEAR GRADUATION RATE

	Gender		Race / Ethnicity										
All	Male	Female	White	Black	Hispanic	Asian	Native Hawaiian/ Pacific Islander	American Indian	Two or More Races	LEP	Migrant	Students with Disabilities	Economically Disadvantaged
83.2	80.3	86.1	89.3	70.9	76.3	92.0	78.0	78.2	83.1	63.7	48.7	70.1	73.0

HIGH SCHOOL 5-YEAR GRADUATION RATE

	Gender		Race / Ethnicity										
All	Male	Female	White	Black	Hispanic	Asian	Native Hawaiian/ Pacific Islander	American Indian	Two or More Races	LEP	Migrant	Students with Disabilities	Economically Disadvantaged
87.0	84.9	89.1	90.7	78.4	83.2	94.9	89.2	83.0	86.5	76.5	76.0	76.8	80.6

2011 NATIONAL ASSESSMENT OF EDUCATIONAL PROGRESS (NAEP)

NAEP is sponsored by the U.S. Department of Education and administered to students in grade 4, 8, and 12. Only grade 4 and 8 results are required to be reported.

Achievement levels reflect what students should know and be able to do. Based on recommendations from policymakers, educators, and members of the general public, the Governing Board sets specific achievement levels for each subject area and grade. To provide a context for interpreting student performance, NAEP results are reported as percentages of students performing below the *Basic* level, at or above the *Basic* and *Proficient* levels, and at the *Advanced* level.

Basic denotes partial mastery of prerequisite knowledge and skills that are fundamental for proficient work at a given grade.

Proficient represents solid academic performance. Students reaching this level have demonstrated competency over challenging subject matter.

Advanced represents superior performance.

The four achievement levels (below basic, basic, proficient, and advanced) are reported as level 1 through level 4, respectively.

Grade 4

Grade 4 - All

Levels	Reading				Mathematics			
	1	2	3	4	1	2	3	4
	34.7	32.0	24.7	8.6	20.2	41.5	31.4	6.9

Grade 4 - Racial/Ethnic Background

Levels	Reading				Mathematics			
	1	2	3	4	1	2	3	4
White	21.8	33.6	32.2	12.3	10.2	38.4	41.6	9.9
Black	57.7	29.9	10.9	1.6	41.8	43.9	12.8	1.5
Hispanic	51.2	30.7	15.7	2.4	29.6	50.5	18.5	1.4
Asian	16.1	31.3	35.5	17.1	5.9	29.4	44.8	19.8
Native Hawaiian/Pacific Islander								
American Indian								

Grade 4 - Limited-English-Proficient

Levels	Reading				Mathematics			
	1	2	3	4	1	2	3	4
	77.4	18.1	4.2	0.0	46.4	41.6	11.3	0.8

Grade 4 - Students with Disabilities

Levels	Reading				Mathematics			
	1	2	3	4	1	2	3	4
	67.6	19.4	11.0	2.0	43.2	37.6	17.5	1.6

Grade 4 - Economically Disadvantaged

Levels	Reading				Mathematics			
	1	2	3	4	1	2	3	4
	52.0	31.6	14.3	2.1	33.1	47.2	18.1	1.5

Grade 4

NAEP PARTICIPATION RATES	Reading	Mathematics
Limited English Proficient Students	92.4	93.5
Student with Disabilities	91.1	86.1

Grade 8

Grade 8 - All

Levels	Reading				Mathematics			
	1	2	3	4	1	2	3	4
	23.2	43.0	30.3	3.6	26.9	40.2	24.7	8.1

Grade 8 - Racial/Ethnic Background

Levels	Reading				Mathematics			
	1	2	3	4	1	2	3	4
White	15.3	41.2	38.8	4.7	15.7	40.2	32.8	11.2
Black	38.0	46.6	14.4	1.0	51.7	38.4	9.4	0.5
Hispanic	30.6	45.9	21.9	1.6	35.8	45.1	16.4	2.7
Asian	11.3	34.3	43.1	11.3	7.5	24.0	36.8	31.7
Native Hawaiian/Pacific Islander								
American Indian								

Grade 8 - Limited-English-Proficient

Levels	Reading				Mathematics			
	1	2	3	4	1	2	3	4
	67.9	29.9	2.2	0.0	69.5	27.0	3.2	0.0

Grade 8 - Students with Disabilities

Levels	Reading				Mathematics			
	1	2	3	4	1	2	3	4
	63.6	28.5	7.5	0.0	63.6	26.8	7.8	1.7

Grade 8 - Economically Disadvantaged

Levels	Reading				Mathematics			
	1	2	3	4	1	2	3	4
	34.4	47.0	17.8	0.9	39.3	43.7	15.0	2.1

Grade 8

NAEP PARTICIPATION RATES	Reading	Mathematics
Limited English Proficient Students	91.2	89.9
Student with Disabilities	90.2	84.6

OVERALL STUDENT PERFORMANCE

These charts present the overall percentages of state test scores categorized as meeting or exceeding the Illinois Learning Standards for the state. They represent performance in reading and mathematics. Starting in 2013, Illinois raised the performance cut scores in reading and math to align with college and career ready expectations.

OVERALL PERFORMANCE - ALL STATE TESTS

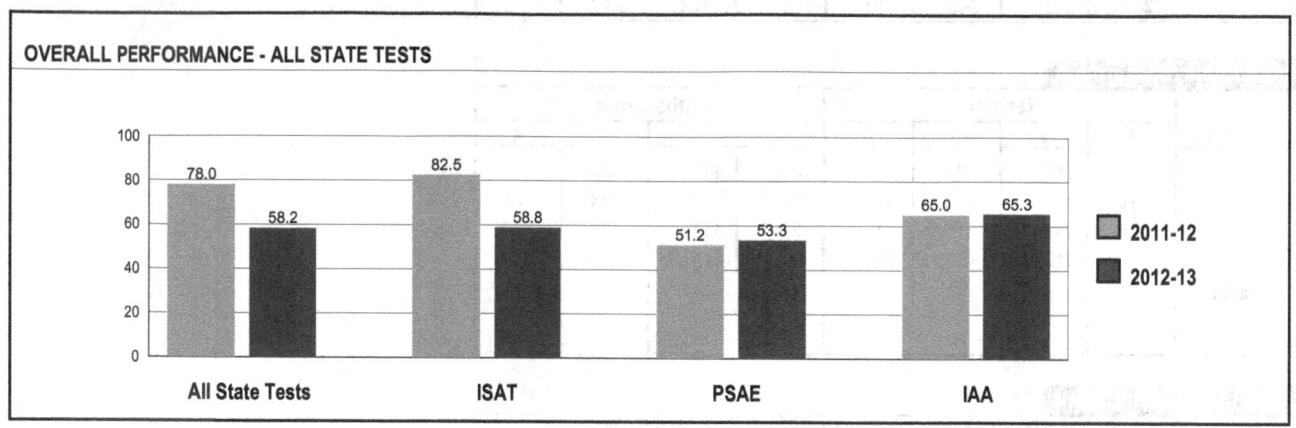

ILLINOIS STANDARDS ACHIEVEMENT TEST (ISAT) PERFORMANCE

These charts provide information on attainment of the Illinois Learning Standards. They show the percents of student scores meeting or exceeding Standards for the grades and subjects tested on ISAT.

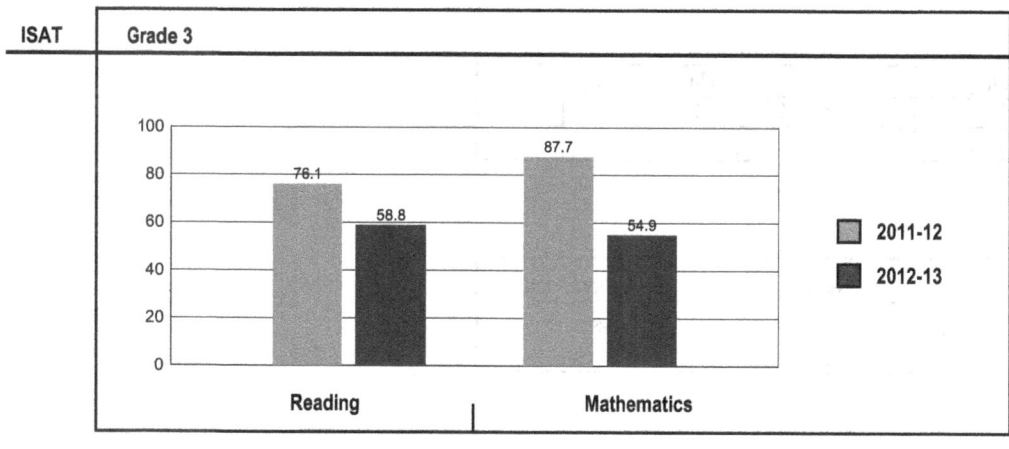

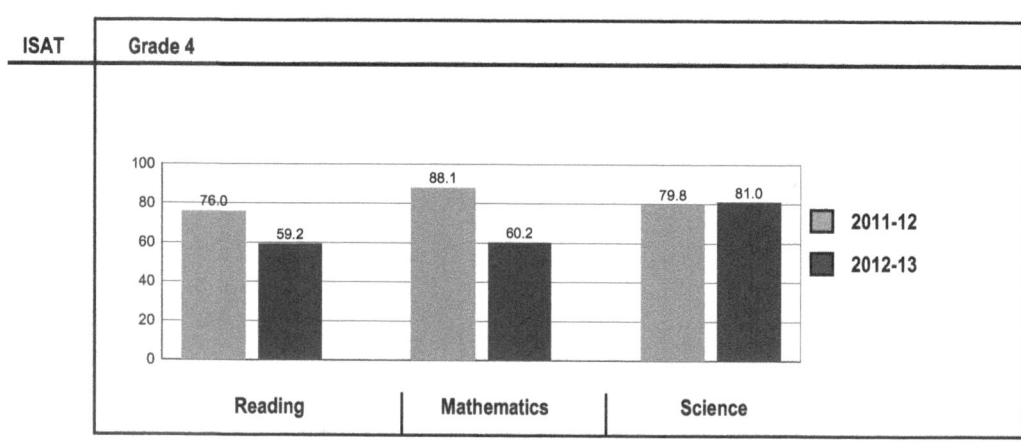

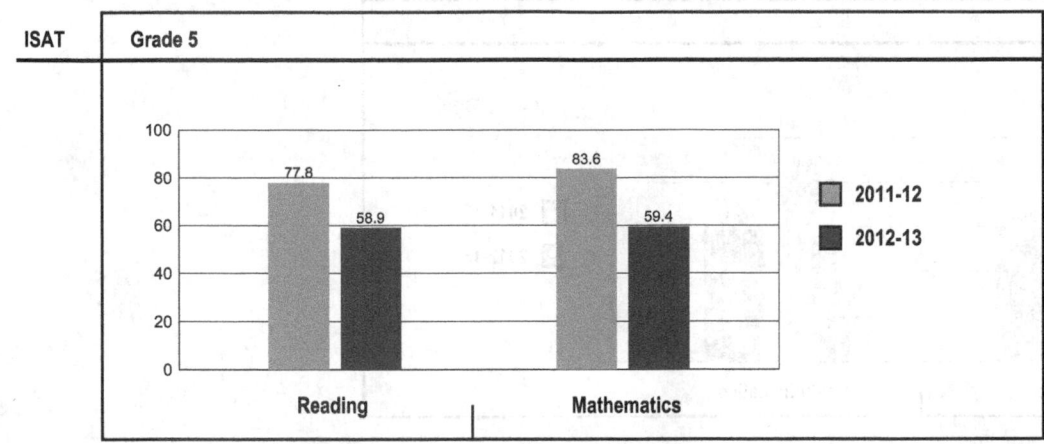

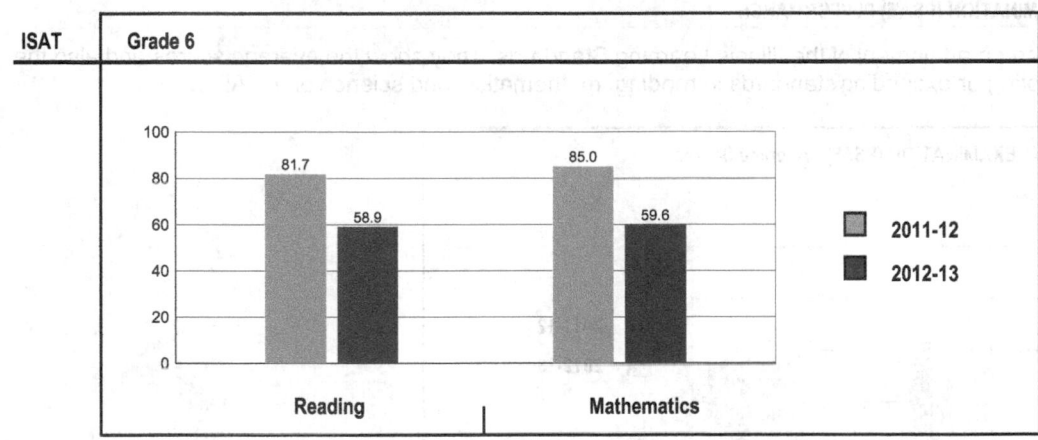

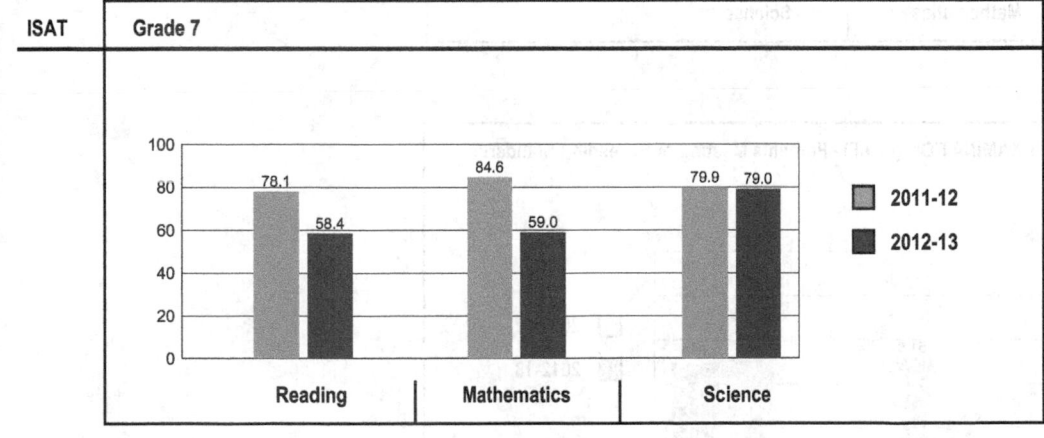

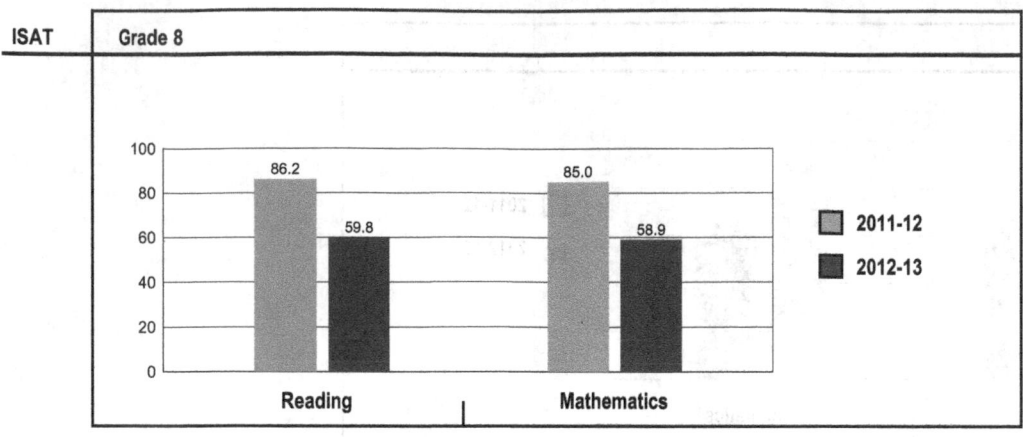

| ISAT | Grade 8 |

PRAIRIE STATE ACHIEVEMENT EXAMINATION (PSAE) PERFORMANCE

These charts provide information on attainment of the Illinois Learning Standards. They show the average scores and also the percents of student scores meeting or exceeding standards in reading, mathematics, and science on PSAE.

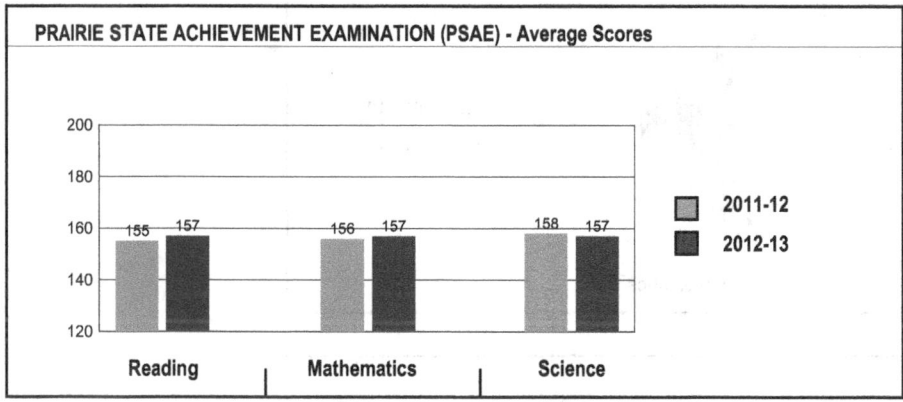

PSAE scores range from 120 to 200.

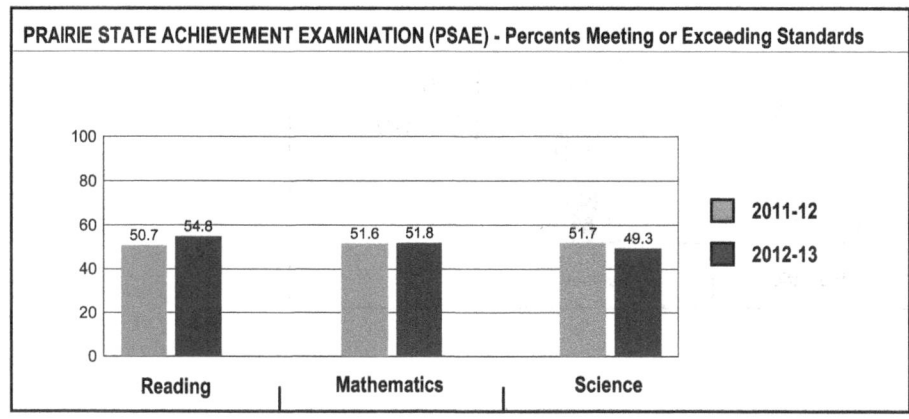

Number of students in the State with PSAE scores in 2013:   142,758

| ILLINOIS ALTERNATE ASSESSMENT (IAA) PERFORMANCE |

These charts provide information on attainment of the Illinois Learning Standards. They show the percents of student scores meeting or exceeding Standards for the grades and subjects tested on IAA.

IAA

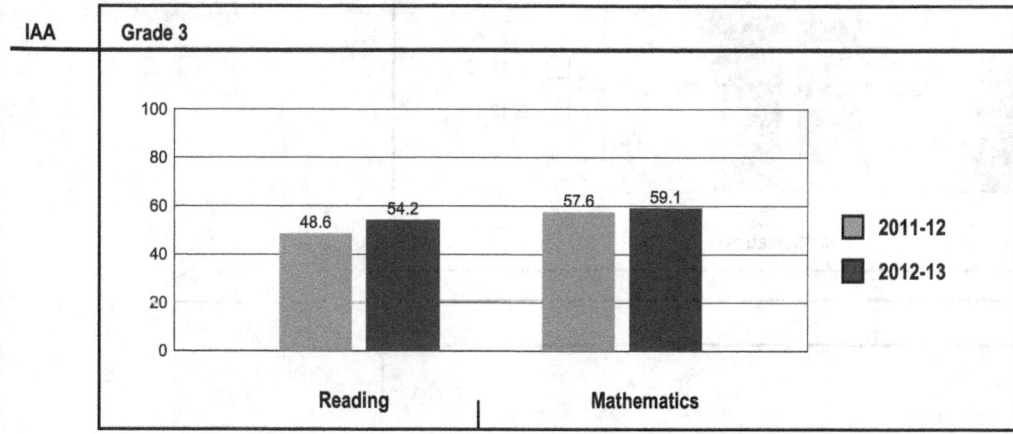

IAA

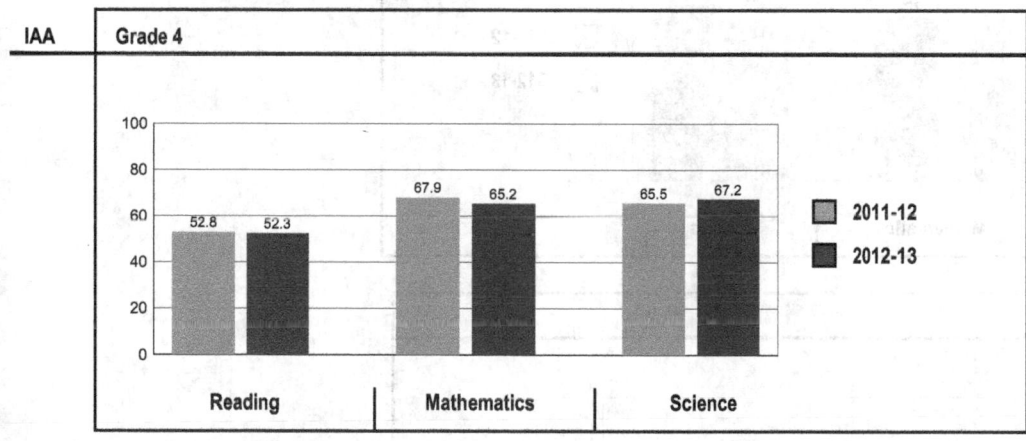

IAA

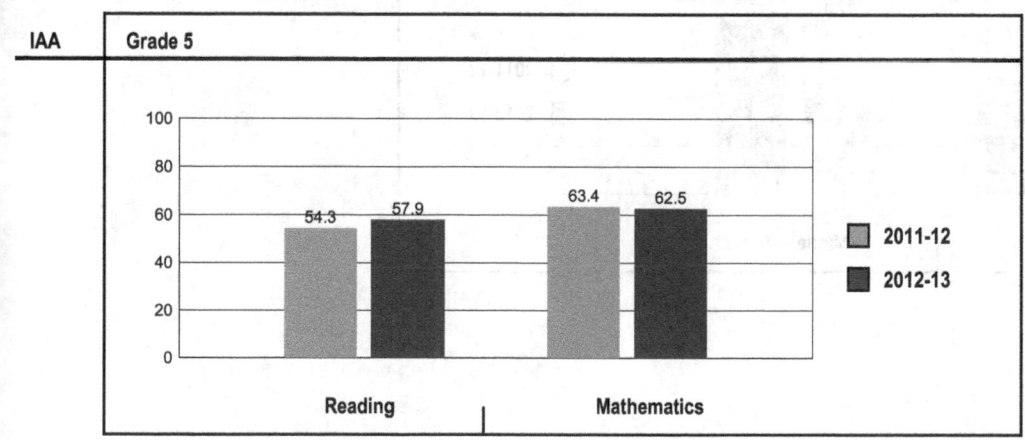

IAA   Grade 6

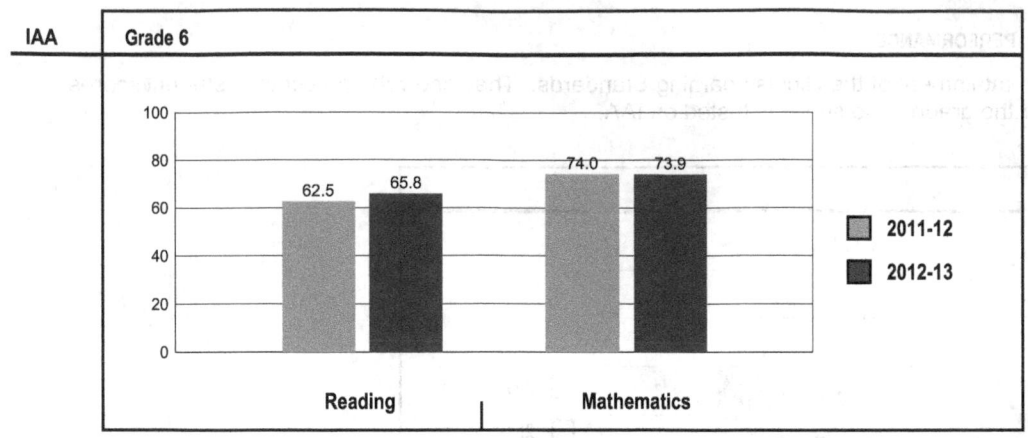

IAA   Grade 7

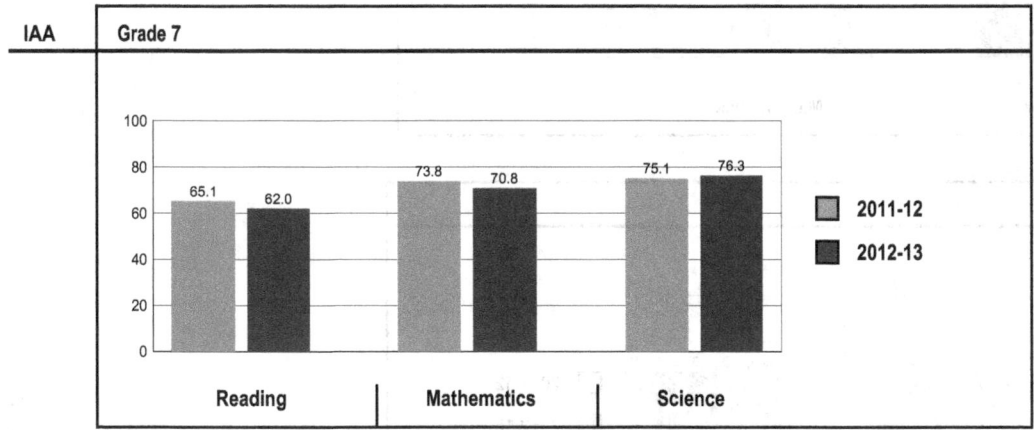

IAA   Grade 8

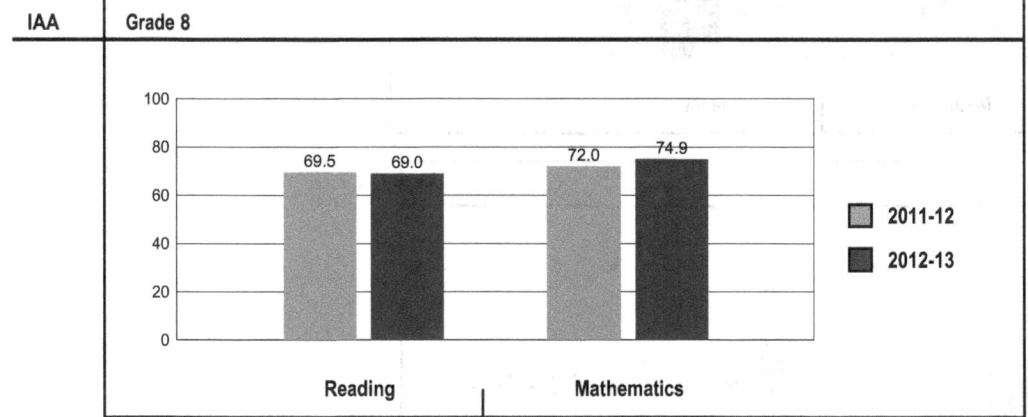

IAA   Grade 11

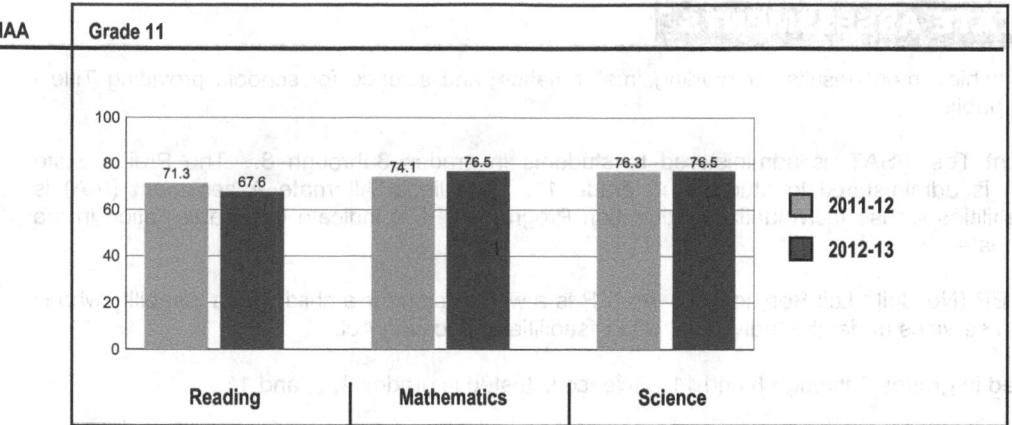

PERFORMANCE ON STATE ASSESSMENTS

Federal law requires that student achievement results for reading, mathematics, and science for schools providing Title I services be reported to the general public.

The Illinois Standards Achievement Test (ISAT) is administered to students in grades 3 through 8.   The Prairie State Achievement Examination (PSAE) is administered to students in grade 11. The Illinois Alternate Assessment (IAA) is administered to students with disabilities whose Individualized Education Programs (IEPs) indicate that participation in the ISAT or PSAE would not be appropriate.

Students with disabilities have an IEP (No Child Left Behind Act). An IEP is a written plan for a child with a disability who is eligible to receive special education services under the Individuals with Disabilities Education Act.

Reading and Mathematics are tested in grades 3 through 8 and 11. Science is tested in grades 4, 7, and 11.

In order to protect students' identities, test data for groups of fewer than ten students are not reported.

PERCENTAGE OF STUDENTS NOT TESTED IN STATE TESTING PROGRAMS FOR READING

		Gender		Racial/Ethnic Background									Students with Disabilities	Economically Disadvantaged
	All	Male	Female	White	Black	Hispanic	Asian	Native Hawaiian /Pacific Islander	American Indian	Two or More Races	LEP	Migrant		
*Enrollment	1,067,095	545,884	521,053	542,053	188,403	253,427	46,751	1,561	3,694	30,704	73,555	276	143,695	542,427
Reading	0.4	0.4	0.3	0.3	0.6	0.3	0.2	0.3	0.4	0.4	0.6	1.1	0.8	0.5

* Enrollment as reported during the testing windows for grades 3 - 8 and 11.

Number of LEP Students who have attended schools in the U.S. for less than 12 months and are not assessed on the State's reading/language arts test: 1606

PERCENTAGE OF STUDENTS NOT TESTED IN STATE TESTING PROGRAMS FOR MATHEMATICS

		Gender		Racial/Ethnic Background									Students with Disabilities	Economically Disadvantaged
	All	Male	Female	White	Black	Hispanic	Asian	Native Hawaiian /Pacific Islander	American Indian	Two or More Races	LEP	Migrant		
*Enrollment	1,068,846	546,846	521,842	542,440	188,509	254,061	47,334	1,565	3,709	30,726	75,331	278	143,714	543,668
Mathematics	0.4	0.4	0.3	0.3	0.6	0.3	0.2	0.3	0.3	0.4	0.3	0.7	0.9	0.5

* Enrollment as reported during the testing windows for grades 3 - 8 and 11.

PERCENTAGE OF STUDENTS NOT TESTED IN STATE TESTING PROGRAMS FOR SCIENCE

		Gender		Racial/Ethnic Background									Students with Disabilities	Economically Disadvantaged
	All	Male	Female	White	Black	Hispanic	Asian	Native Hawaiian /Pacific Islander	American Indian	Two or More Races	LEP	Migrant		
*Enrollment	455,414	232,478	222,882	234,340	79,949	105,892	20,304	615	1,520	12,626	25,072	106	60,808	223,602
Science	0.6	0.7	0.5	0.5	1.1	0.6	0.3	0.7	0.7	0.7	0.7	0.9	1.4	0.8

* Enrollment as reported during the testing windows for grades 4, 7, and 11.

ILLINOIS STANDARDS ACHIEVEMENT TEST (ISAT)

The following tables show the percentages of student scores in each of four performance levels. These levels were established with the help of Illinois educators who teach the grade levels and learning areas tested. Due to rounding, the sum of the percentages in the four performance levels may not always equal 100.

Level 1 -- Academic Warning -   Student work demonstrates limited knowledge and skills in the subject. Because of major gaps in learning, students apply knowledge and skills ineffectively.

Level 2 -- Below Standards -   Student work demonstrates basic knowledge and skills in the subject. However, because of gaps in learning, students apply knowledge and skills in limited ways.

Level 3 -- Meets Standards -   Student work demonstrates proficient knowledge and skills in the subject. Students effectively apply knowledge and skills to solve problems.

Level 4 -- Exceeds Standards -   Student work demonstrates advanced knowledge and skills in the subject. Students creatively apply knowledge and skills to solve problems and evaluate the results.

Grade 3

Grade 3 - All

Levels	Reading				Mathematics			
	1	2	3	4	1	2	3	4
	6.7	34.5	39.4	19.4	6.9	38.2	43.7	11.1

Grade 3 - Gender

Levels	Reading				Mathematics			
	1	2	3	4	1	2	3	4
Male	8.2	37.6	38.2	16.0	7.2	37.1	43.9	11.8
Female	5.1	31.3	40.7	23.0	6.6	39.4	43.5	10.4

Grade 3 - Racial/Ethnic Background

Levels	Reading				Mathematics			
	1	2	3	4	1	2	3	4
White	3.3	25.2	44.7	26.8	3.0	28.8	53.2	15.0
Black	11.8	47.7	32.4	8.1	15.5	53.5	27.9	3.1
Hispanic	10.8	46.7	33.2	9.3	9.6	50.0	35.5	4.9
Asian	2.2	18.1	42.5	37.1	2.2	18.0	47.4	32.4
Native Hawaiian/Pacific Islander	7.5	34.0	38.5	20.0	6.5	35.8	45.3	12.4
American Indian	8.7	41.6	36.7	13.0	7.2	46.8	38.9	7.2
Two or More Races	4.7	30.3	41.6	23.4	5.9	35.7	44.8	13.6

Grade 3 - Limited-English-Proficient

Levels	Reading				Mathematics			
	1	2	3	4	1	2	3	4
	15.6	59.5	22.4	2.4	12.9	58.1	26.6	2.3

Grade 3 - Migrant

Levels	Reading				Mathematics			
	1	2	3	4	1	2	3	4
	16.7	61.9	19.0	2.4	16.3	60.5	18.6	4.7

Grade 3 - Students with Disabilities

Levels	Reading				Mathematics			
	1	2	3	4	1	2	3	4
IEP	25.5	49.1	19.7	5.8	19.6	50.5	26.1	3.8
Non-IEP	4.0	32.4	42.2	21.4	5.2	36.5	46.2	12.2

Grade 3 - Economically Disadvantaged

Levels	Reading				Mathematics			
	1	2	3	4	1	2	3	4
Free/Reduced Price Lunch	10.6	46.1	34.4	8.9	11.1	50.0	34.6	4.3
Not Eligible	2.1	20.9	45.3	31.7	2.1	24.5	54.4	19.1

Grade 4

Grade 4 - All

Levels	Reading				Mathematics				Science			
	1	2	3	4	1	2	3	4	1	2	3	4
	6.2	34.6	44.3	14.9	6.6	33.2	48.4	11.8	2.1	17.0	59.9	21.0

Grade 4 - Gender

Levels	Reading				Mathematics				Science			
	1	2	3	4	1	2	3	4	1	2	3	4
Male	7.9	36.1	43.0	13.0	7.3	32.8	47.5	12.4	2.4	16.8	58.2	22.6
Female	4.4	32.9	45.7	17.0	5.9	33.5	49.4	11.2	1.7	17.1	61.7	19.4

Grade 4 - Racial/Ethnic Background

Levels	Reading				Mathematics				Science			
	1	2	3	4	1	2	3	4	1	2	3	4
White	3.2	25.4	50.8	20.6	3.5	25.4	55.4	15.7	0.8	9.5	60.7	29.0
Black	12.3	48.9	33.3	5.6	13.8	47.4	35.4	3.4	4.9	31.8	55.7	7.7
Hispanic	8.8	46.8	37.7	6.6	8.8	42.5	43.6	5.1	2.8	23.8	62.8	10.6
Asian	2.2	16.3	49.6	31.9	2.4	13.4	48.5	35.8	1.1	6.8	51.4	40.6
Native Hawaiian/Pacific Islander	3.9	31.2	47.3	17.6	5.4	32.7	48.3	13.7	1.5	12.2	62.4	23.9
American Indian	9.1	42.5	37.6	10.9	9.8	41.2	39.4	9.6	3.6	21.7	61.6	13.1
Two or More Races	5.1	30.5	46.3	18.1	6.2	32.6	47.5	13.7	1.9	14.7	60.1	23.2

Grade 4 - Limited-English-Proficient

Levels	Reading				Mathematics				Science			
	1	2	3	4	1	2	3	4	1	2	3	4
	22.1	64.2	13.1	0.6	20.1	56.2	22.5	1.2	7.3	44.4	46.6	1.6

Grade 4 - Migrant

Levels	Reading				Mathematics				Science			
	1	2	3	4	1	2	3	4	1	2	3	4
	8.1	62.2	27.0	2.7	13.2	50.0	36.8	0.0	2.6	50.0	42.1	5.3

Grade 4 - Students with Disabilities

Levels	Reading				Mathematics				Science			
	1	2	3	4	1	2	3	4	1	2	3	4
IEP	28.0	48.4	19.8	3.9	24.1	47.3	25.2	3.4	6.9	35.6	50.0	7.6
Non-IEP	3.0	32.6	47.9	16.5	4.1	31.1	51.8	13.0	1.4	14.3	61.4	23.0

Grade 4 - Economically Disadvantaged

Levels	Reading				Mathematics				Science			
	1	2	3	4	1	2	3	4	1	2	3	4
Free/Reduced Price Lunch	9.7	46.6	37.3	6.4	10.3	43.9	41.3	4.5	3.3	25.4	61.0	10.3
Not Eligible	2.2	21.0	52.2	24.6	2.5	21.0	56.4	20.1	0.7	7.4	58.7	33.2

Grade 5

Grade 5 - All

Levels	Reading				Mathematics			
	1	2	3	4	1	2	3	4
	6.3	34.8	42.7	16.2	7.2	33.4	47.7	11.7

Grade 5 - Gender

Levels	Reading				Mathematics			
	1	2	3	4	1	2	3	4
Male	7.9	36.4	41.6	14.1	8.2	33.0	46.3	12.5
Female	4.7	33.1	43.8	18.4	6.1	33.9	49.2	10.9

Grade 5 - Racial/Ethnic Background

Levels	Reading				Mathematics			
	1	2	3	4	1	2	3	4
White	3.1	25.1	49.4	22.3	3.9	26.0	54.7	15.5
Black	12.4	50.4	31.8	5.5	15.2	48.1	33.8	2.9
Hispanic	9.4	46.7	36.2	7.6	9.1	41.9	43.7	5.3
Asian	2.3	17.7	44.9	35.1	2.4	14.1	46.7	36.9
Native Hawaiian/Pacific Islander	4.3	32.9	50.7	12.1	4.8	27.8	56.0	11.5
American Indian	9.4	43.3	38.7	8.7	8.4	41.0	44.7	5.9
Two or More Races	5.2	31.6	43.9	19.3	6.9	32.0	46.1	15.0

Grade 5 - Limited-English-Proficient

Levels	Reading				Mathematics			
	1	2	3	4	1	2	3	4
	29.8	61.5	8.2	0.5	23.9	56.0	19.2	0.9

Grade 5 - Migrant

Levels	Reading				Mathematics			
	1	2	3	4	1	2	3	4
	21.1	60.5	18.4	0.0	21.1	52.6	26.3	0.0

Grade 5 - Students with Disabilities

Levels	Reading				Mathematics			
	1	2	3	4	1	2	3	4
IEP	28.4	50.6	17.5	3.5	26.2	47.7	23.3	2.7
Non-IEP	3.1	32.5	46.3	18.0	4.4	31.3	51.2	13.0

Grade 5 - Economically Disadvantaged

Levels	Reading				Mathematics			
	1	2	3	4	1	2	3	4
Free/Reduced Price Lunch	10.2	47.1	35.9	6.8	11.0	44.1	40.6	4.2
Not Eligible	2.1	21.2	50.2	26.5	2.9	21.6	55.5	19.9

Grade 6

Grade 6 - All

Levels	Reading				Mathematics			
	1	2	3	4	1	2	3	4
	6.1	35.0	42.7	16.2	7.2	33.1	47.0	12.6

Grade 6 - Gender

Levels	Reading				Mathematics			
	1	2	3	4	1	2	3	4
Male	8.0	37.9	41.2	13.0	8.4	33.6	45.0	13.0
Female	4.1	31.9	44.4	19.5	6.0	32.7	49.2	12.2

Grade 6 - Racial/Ethnic Background

Levels	Reading				Mathematics			
	1	2	3	4	1	2	3	4
White	3.5	27.1	47.8	21.6	4.1	25.6	53.7	16.7
Black	11.7	48.5	33.6	6.3	15.3	47.7	33.6	3.4
Hispanic	8.1	45.1	38.7	8.1	8.7	41.9	43.4	5.9
Asian	2.2	17.5	43.4	36.8	2.5	14.2	45.2	38.1
Native Hawaiian/Pacific Islander	10.6	32.4	42.1	14.8	8.3	36.1	43.5	12.0
American Indian	7.7	45.4	36.9	10.0	9.3	43.8	39.1	7.9
Two or More Races	5.0	30.5	44.3	20.2	6.9	30.1	47.3	15.7

Grade 6 - Limited-English-Proficient

Levels	Reading				Mathematics			
	1	2	3	4	1	2	3	4
	28.6	61.2	9.5	0.7	25.8	57.8	15.3	1.0

Grade 6 - Migrant

Levels	Reading				Mathematics			
	1	2	3	4	1	2	3	4
	10.9	56.5	21.7	10.9	17.0	46.8	36.2	0.0

Grade 6 - Students with Disabilities

Levels	Reading				Mathematics			
	1	2	3	4	1	2	3	4
IEP	29.0	52.7	15.6	2.8	29.4	49.4	18.9	2.3
Non-IEP	2.9	32.5	46.6	18.1	4.1	30.9	51.0	14.1

Grade 6 - Economically Disadvantaged

Levels	Reading				Mathematics			
	1	2	3	4	1	2	3	4
Free/Reduced Price Lunch	9.6	46.2	37.1	7.2	11.1	43.9	40.0	5.0
Not Eligible	2.3	22.9	48.9	25.9	3.0	21.4	54.7	20.9

Grade 7

Grade 7 - All

Levels	Reading				Mathematics				Science			
	1	2	3	4	1	2	3	4	1	2	3	4
	6.5	35.0	43.6	14.9	7.0	34.0	46.7	12.4	6.9	14.1	54.3	24.7

Grade 7 - Gender

Levels	Reading				Mathematics				Science			
	1	2	3	4	1	2	3	4	1	2	3	4
Male	8.5	37.4	42.1	11.9	8.5	34.5	44.2	12.8	8.3	14.6	50.6	26.5
Female	4.4	32.5	45.1	18.0	5.4	33.4	49.3	11.9	5.4	13.5	58.2	22.8

Grade 7 - Racial/Ethnic Background

Levels	Reading				Mathematics				Science			
	1	2	3	4	1	2	3	4	1	2	3	4
White	4.0	28.2	48.4	19.4	4.1	27.3	52.5	16.1	3.6	9.0	53.2	34.2
Black	12.3	47.6	34.2	5.9	14.2	47.5	35.0	3.3	14.3	24.0	54.0	7.7
Hispanic	8.3	43.8	39.6	8.3	8.6	42.2	43.3	6.0	9.1	19.3	59.0	12.6
Asian	2.3	16.7	47.7	33.3	2.3	13.4	46.0	38.4	2.8	5.3	45.7	46.2
Native Hawaiian/Pacific Islander	5.2	36.6	43.3	14.9	6.7	34.9	44.6	13.8	6.0	15.3	55.6	23.1
American Indian	9.7	39.2	39.3	11.8	9.4	40.5	41.3	8.7	9.5	17.7	53.0	19.8
Two or More Races	6.1	31.3	43.7	18.9	6.9	31.6	45.5	15.9	6.4	12.4	51.2	29.9

Grade 7 - Limited-English-Proficient

Levels	Reading				Mathematics				Science			
	1	2	3	4	1	2	3	4	1	2	3	4
	28.3	62.6	8.8	0.4	25.4	58.6	15.2	0.8	27.3	38.5	33.2	1.0

Grade 7 - Migrant

Levels	Reading				Mathematics				Science			
	1	2	3	4	1	2	3	4	1	2	3	4
	28.2	53.8	15.4	2.6	17.5	60.0	22.5	0.0	22.5	25.0	52.5	0.0

Grade 7 - Students with Disabilities

Levels	Reading				Mathematics				Science			
	1	2	3	4	1	2	3	4	1	2	3	4
IEP	30.7	52.7	14.7	1.9	30.8	51.2	16.2	1.7	24.0	31.3	39.0	5.7
Non-IEP	3.1	32.5	47.7	16.7	3.6	31.5	51.0	13.9	4.5	11.7	56.5	27.4

Grade 7 - Economically Disadvantaged

Levels	Reading				Mathematics				Science			
	1	2	3	4	1	2	3	4	1	2	3	4
Free/Reduced Price Lunch	10.3	45.9	37.1	6.8	10.8	44.8	39.6	4.8	10.8	20.7	56.7	11.7
Not Eligible	2.6	23.8	50.3	23.3	3.0	22.8	54.0	20.2	2.8	7.2	51.8	38.2

Grade 8

Grade 8 - All

Levels	Reading				Mathematics			
	1	2	3	4	1	2	3	4
	5.9	34.4	41.7	18.1	5.4	35.7	45.7	13.2

Grade 8 - Gender

Levels	Reading				Mathematics			
	1	2	3	4	1	2	3	4
Male	8.0	36.9	39.5	15.6	6.5	36.1	44.0	13.4
Female	3.7	31.7	43.9	20.7	4.2	35.4	47.4	12.9

Grade 8 - Racial/Ethnic Background

Levels	Reading				Mathematics			
	1	2	3	4	1	2	3	4
White	3.8	26.5	45.2	24.5	3.5	28.5	50.6	17.3
Black	11.1	48.9	33.9	6.1	11.2	51.9	33.6	3.3
Hispanic	7.1	44.0	39.5	9.4	5.5	43.4	44.6	6.5
Asian	2.5	17.0	43.6	36.8	1.9	14.2	44.6	39.3
Native Hawaiian/Pacific Islander	8.3	38.4	40.7	12.6	4.0	39.3	47.9	8.9
American Indian	6.8	40.2	42.8	10.2	7.5	41.7	41.1	9.7
Two or More Races	5.6	31.5	40.5	22.4	5.5	34.8	43.0	16.7

Grade 8 - Limited-English-Proficient

Levels	Reading				Mathematics			
	1	2	3	4	1	2	3	4
	25.7	65.0	8.9	0.4	17.0	64.7	17.1	1.2

Grade 8 - Migrant

Levels	Reading				Mathematics			
	1	2	3	4	1	2	3	4
	17.5	55.0	25.0	2.5	19.5	48.8	29.3	2.4

Grade 8 - Students with Disabilities

Levels	Reading				Mathematics			
	1	2	3	4	1	2	3	4
IEP	29.7	53.6	14.2	2.5	26.3	56.7	15.1	1.9
Non-IEP	2.5	31.6	45.5	20.3	2.5	32.8	50.0	14.7

Grade 8 - Economically Disadvantaged

Levels	Reading				Mathematics			
	1	2	3	4	1	2	3	4
Free/Reduced Price Lunch	9.1	46.0	36.8	8.0	8.3	47.3	39.3	5.1
Not Eligible	2.7	22.8	46.5	28.1	2.5	24.3	52.0	21.1

PRAIRIE STATE ACHIEVEMENT EXAMINATION (PSAE)

The following tables show the percentages of student scores in each of four performance levels. These levels were established with the help of Illinois educators who teach the grade levels and learning areas tested. Due to rounding, the sum of the percentages in the four performance levels may not always equal 100.

Level 1 -- Academic Warning -   Student work demonstrates limited knowledge and skills in the subject. Because of major gaps in learning, students apply knowledge and skills ineffectively.

Level 2 -- Below Standards -   Student work demonstrates basic knowledge and skills in the subject. However, because of gaps in learning, students apply knowledge and skills in limited ways.

Level 3 -- Meets Standards -   Student work demonstrates proficient knowledge and skills in the subject. Students effectively apply knowledge and skills to solve problems.

Level 4 -- Exceeds Standards -   Student work demonstrates advanced knowledge and skills in the subject. Students creatively apply knowledge and skills to solve problems and evaluate the results.

Grade 11

Grade 11 - All

Levels	Reading				Mathematics				Science			
	1	2	3	4	1	2	3	4	1	2	3	4
	8.2	37.1	42.9	11.9	9.9	38.3	42.4	9.4	9.2	41.4	38.0	11.4

Grade 11 - Gender

Levels	Reading				Mathematics				Science			
	1	2	3	4	1	2	3	4	1	2	3	4
Male	10.6	37.1	40.5	11.9	10.0	36.4	42.7	10.9	9.5	38.0	38.7	13.9
Female	5.7	37.1	45.3	11.9	9.9	40.2	42.1	7.8	9.0	44.8	37.3	8.9

Grade 11 - Racial/Ethnic Background

Levels	Reading				Mathematics				Science			
	1	2	3	4	1	2	3	4	1	2	3	4
White	4.8	27.5	50.9	16.9	4.9	30.0	52.1	12.9	4.3	31.3	47.9	16.5
Black	15.7	55.4	27.0	1.9	24.2	54.7	20.3	0.8	22.5	59.8	16.6	1.1
Hispanic	11.7	50.8	33.4	4.1	13.0	50.8	33.5	2.7	12.8	56.4	27.4	3.4
Asian	4.8	23.3	48.7	23.2	3.5	20.4	48.5	27.5	4.4	25.9	46.3	23.4
Native Hawaiian/Pacific Islander	8.9	35.8	44.7	10.6	7.3	38.2	47.2	7.3	5.7	42.3	43.9	8.1
American Indian	8.6	42.1	39.2	10.1	14.0	41.6	39.5	4.9	10.9	43.7	37.5	8.0
Two or More Races	7.2	32.8	44.3	15.7	8.4	37.3	42.2	12.1	7.3	39.1	39.2	14.4

Grade 11 - Limited-English-Proficient

Levels	Reading				Mathematics				Science			
	1	2	3	4	1	2	3	4	1	2	3	4
	49.0	46.3	4.7	0.1	43.6	47.6	8.3	0.5	49.9	45.6	4.3	0.2

Grade 11 - Migrant

Levels	Reading				Mathematics				Science			
	1	2	3	4	1	2	3	4	1	2	3	4
	36.0	40.0	24.0	0.0	36.0	32.0	32.0	0.0	24.0	52.0	24.0	0.0

Grade 11 - Students with Disabilities

Levels	Reading				Mathematics				Science			
	1	2	3	4	1	2	3	4	1	2	3	4
IEP	32.3	49.9	15.5	2.3	41.0	44.8	12.7	1.4	38.8	44.8	13.5	2.9
Non-IEP	5.2	35.5	46.3	13.1	6.1	37.5	46.1	10.3	5.6	41.0	41.0	12.4

Grade 11 - Economically Disadvantaged

Levels	Reading				Mathematics				Science			
	1	2	3	4	1	2	3	4	1	2	3	4
Free/Reduced Price Lunch	13.8	51.1	31.6	3.5	17.3	51.5	29.3	2.0	16.5	56.2	24.4	2.8
Not Eligible	4.1	26.9	51.0	17.9	4.6	28.8	51.9	14.7	4.0	30.7	47.7	17.5

ILLINOIS ALTERNATE ASSESSMENT (IAA)

The Illinois Alternate Assessment (IAA) is administered to students with disabilities whose Individualized Education Programs (IEPs) indicate that participation in the ISAT or PSAE would not be appropriate. The table below presents the percentages of student scores in each of four performance levels.

Level 1 -- Entry -   Students do not demonstrate knowledge and skills in the subject through links to the Illinois Learning Standards.

Level 2 --Foundational -   Students demonstrate emerging knowledge and skills in the subject as linked to the Illinois Learning Standards. Students exhibit an ability to reproduce knowledge and skills.

Level 3 -- Satisfactory -   Students demonstrate basic knowledge and skills in the subject through links to the Illinois Learning Standards. Students exhibit an ability to associate their knowledge and skills.

Level 4 -- Mastery -   Students demonstrate knowledge and skills in the subject through links to the Illinois Learning Standards. Students exhibit the ability to apply their knowledge and skills.

Grade 3

Grade 3 - All

Levels	Reading				Mathematics			
	1	2	3	4	1	2	3	4
	17.7	28.1	46.5	7.7	22.4	18.4	36.6	22.5

Grade 3 - Gender

Levels	Reading				Mathematics			
	1	2	3	4	1	2	3	4
Male	17.1	28.3	46.0	8.6	21.7	18.4	35.8	24.1
Female	18.9	28.1	47.2	5.8	24.0	18.7	37.8	19.5

Grade 3 - Racial/Ethnic Background

Levels	Reading				Mathematics			
	1	2	3	4	1	2	3	4
White	14.6	28.1	49.0	8.3	18.7	17.9	38.8	24.6
Black	19.8	26.7	45.7	7.9	24.8	19.6	33.7	22.0
Hispanic	20.7	26.8	44.7	7.8	25.6	17.9	33.6	22.8
Asian	25.4	40.3	32.8	1.5	32.8	14.9	40.3	11.9
Native Hawaiian/Pacific Islander								
American Indian								
Two or More Races	13.0	38.9	42.6	5.6	18.5	29.6	38.9	13.0

Grade 3 - Limited-English-Proficient

Levels	Reading				Mathematics			
	1	2	3	4	1	2	3	4
	21.3	25.4	46.3	7.0	23.2	17.6	36.4	22.8

Grade 3 - Economically Disadvantaged

Levels	Reading				Mathematics			
	1	2	3	4	1	2	3	4
Free/Reduced Price Lunch	15.4	26.4	49.5	8.7	20.3	17.9	37.1	24.6
Not Eligible	21.0	30.7	42.1	6.1	25.5	19.2	35.9	19.4

Grade 4

Grade 4 - All

Levels	Reading				Mathematics				Science			
	1	2	3	4	1	2	3	4	1	2	3	4
	20.0	27.7	36.1	16.1	16.8	18.0	50.2	15.0	12.7	20.2	28.0	39.1

Grade 4 - Gender

Levels	Reading				Mathematics				Science			
	1	2	3	4	1	2	3	4	1	2	3	4
Male	19.7	26.4	36.6	17.3	16.8	17.1	49.1	17.0	12.4	20.1	26.5	41.0
Female	20.6	30.2	35.4	13.8	16.9	19.7	52.4	11.1	13.4	20.0	31.1	35.5

Grade 4 - Racial/Ethnic Background

Levels	Reading				Mathematics				Science			
	1	2	3	4	1	2	3	4	1	2	3	4
White	18.8	25.8	36.2	19.2	14.3	17.8	52.1	15.8	10.3	20.8	26.2	42.7
Black	21.1	26.2	37.0	15.7	19.0	13.9	52.8	14.4	14.6	17.2	29.5	38.7
Hispanic	21.8	30.4	35.1	12.7	18.6	20.0	46.7	14.7	13.9	21.8	29.3	35.0
Asian	21.1	36.6	36.6	5.6	22.5	29.6	39.4	8.5	20.0	22.9	28.6	28.6
Native Hawaiian/Pacific Islander												
American Indian	20.0	20.0	60.0	0.0	20.0	0.0	60.0	20.0	10.0	30.0	30.0	30.0
Two or More Races	16.1	33.9	32.3	17.7	16.1	22.6	45.2	16.1	16.1	12.9	32.3	38.7

Grade 4 - Limited-English-Proficient

Levels	Reading				Mathematics				Science			
	1	2	3	4	1	2	3	4	1	2	3	4
	21.1	29.1	41.1	8.7	18.5	19.9	50.0	11.6	13.9	21.5	31.8	32.8

Grade 4 - Economically Disadvantaged

Levels	Reading				Mathematics				Science			
	1	2	3	4	1	2	3	4	1	2	3	4
Free/Reduced Price Lunch	19.2	27.3	36.8	16.8	16.5	16.7	51.0	15.9	12.0	18.5	27.9	41.7
Not Eligible	21.3	28.3	35.2	15.2	17.3	19.9	49.1	13.7	13.7	22.7	28.3	35.3

Grade 5

Grade 5 - All

Levels	Reading				Mathematics			
	1	2	3	4	1	2	3	4
	25.2	16.9	18.0	39.8	14.3	23.2	49.5	13.0

Grade 5 - Gender

Levels	Reading				Mathematics			
	1	2	3	4	1	2	3	4
Male	24.9	18.2	17.4	39.5	14.3	23.4	48.9	13.5
Female	25.3	14.4	19.3	41.0	14.0	22.6	51.2	12.2

Grade 5 - Racial/Ethnic Background

Levels	Reading				Mathematics			
	1	2	3	4	1	2	3	4
White	24.1	15.8	18.6	41.5	13.2	23.3	49.3	14.2
Black	25.4	16.1	16.1	42.4	14.2	22.9	49.6	13.3
Hispanic	27.6	19.7	18.9	33.9	16.3	25.0	48.2	10.5
Asian	26.1	21.7	18.8	33.3	15.9	23.2	53.6	7.2
Native Hawaiian/Pacific Islander								
American Indian								
Two or More Races	19.6	15.7	15.7	49.0	13.7	9.8	60.8	15.7

Grade 5 - Limited-English-Proficient

Levels	Reading				Mathematics			
	1	2	3	4	1	2	3	4
	23.3	24.2	19.9	32.6	14.0	22.5	52.5	11.0

Grade 5 - Economically Disadvantaged

Levels	Reading				Mathematics			
	1	2	3	4	1	2	3	4
Free/Reduced Price Lunch	22.4	15.7	18.9	43.0	12.5	20.7	52.4	14.4
Not Eligible	29.3	18.6	16.8	35.4	16.9	26.8	45.2	11.1

Grade 6

Grade 6 - All

Levels	Reading				Mathematics			
	1	2	3	4	1	2	3	4
	13.4	20.8	41.2	24.6	11.3	14.8	35.4	38.4

Grade 6 - Gender

Levels	Reading				Mathematics			
	1	2	3	4	1	2	3	4
Male	13.9	21.4	40.4	24.4	10.9	15.6	34.7	38.8
Female	12.7	19.7	42.7	24.9	12.1	13.3	36.9	37.7

Grade 6 - Racial/Ethnic Background

Levels	Reading				Mathematics			
	1	2	3	4	1	2	3	4
White	12.4	19.3	41.9	26.4	9.8	14.7	34.3	41.2
Black	15.3	19.5	39.6	25.6	12.1	15.5	36.7	35.8
Hispanic	13.9	23.7	41.8	20.5	13.5	14.0	35.9	36.7
Asian	13.3	29.3	42.7	14.7	10.7	20.0	40.0	29.3
Native Hawaiian/Pacific Islander								
American Indian								
Two or More Races	11.9	22.0	39.0	27.1	13.6	10.2	35.6	40.7

Grade 6 - Limited-English-Proficient

Levels	Reading				Mathematics			
	1	2	3	4	1	2	3	4
	10.7	23.2	45.1	21.0	12.6	13.9	34.5	39.0

Grade 6 - Economically Disadvantaged

Levels	Reading				Mathematics			
	1	2	3	4	1	2	3	4
Free/Reduced Price Lunch	12.1	18.8	43.0	26.1	10.7	13.6	35.0	40.6
Not Eligible	15.7	23.9	38.2	22.1	12.4	16.7	36.1	34.8

Grade 7

Grade 7 - All

Levels	Reading				Mathematics				Science			
	1	2	3	4	1	2	3	4	1	2	3	4
	15.2	22.8	46.7	15.3	15.0	14.2	48.3	22.5	6.5	17.2	33.7	42.7

Grade 7 - Gender

Levels	Reading				Mathematics				Science			
	1	2	3	4	1	2	3	4	1	2	3	4
Male	15.1	23.1	46.3	15.6	14.1	14.4	47.7	23.8	6.4	16.6	33.1	43.9
Female	15.5	22.2	47.5	14.9	16.8	13.9	49.4	19.8	6.5	18.4	34.8	40.2

Grade 7 - Racial/Ethnic Background

Levels	Reading				Mathematics				Science			
	1	2	3	4	1	2	3	4	1	2	3	4
White	14.2	24.2	46.5	15.1	14.9	13.7	48.2	23.2	5.5	18.0	32.4	44.1
Black	15.8	20.8	47.6	15.8	15.4	13.7	48.6	22.2	7.3	16.5	35.1	41.1
Hispanic	17.7	20.4	48.1	13.7	15.3	15.9	48.1	20.7	8.4	15.4	34.8	41.5
Asian	15.3	36.1	37.5	11.1	15.5	19.7	45.1	19.7	5.6	28.2	38.0	28.2
Native Hawaiian/Pacific Islander												
American Indian												
Two or More Races	13.8	13.8	46.6	25.9	12.1	12.1	46.6	29.3	5.2	10.3	29.3	55.2

Grade 7- Limited-English-Proficient

Levels	Reading				Mathematics				Science			
	1	2	3	4	1	2	3	4	1	2	3	4
	10.2	23.5	49.0	17.3	11.7	12.2	46.9	29.1	5.1	13.8	32.3	48.7

Grade 7 - Economically Disadvantaged

Levels	Reading				Mathematics				Science			
	1	2	3	4	1	2	3	4	1	2	3	4
Free/Reduced Price Lunch	13.6	20.7	49.1	16.6	13.2	13.4	49.1	24.4	5.8	15.0	31.9	47.4
Not Eligible	17.5	25.7	43.3	13.5	17.6	15.4	47.2	19.7	7.5	20.4	36.2	35.9

Grade 8

Grade 8 - All

Levels	Reading				Mathematics			
	1	2	3	4	1	2	3	4
	15.9	15.1	43.7	25.3	10.6	14.5	44.0	30.9

Grade 8 - Gender

Levels	Reading				Mathematics			
	1	2	3	4	1	2	3	4
Male	14.8	16.7	44.2	24.4	10.3	15.3	42.9	31.5
Female	17.8	12.4	43.0	26.8	11.0	13.3	45.6	30.1

Grade 8 - Racial/Ethnic Background

Levels	Reading				Mathematics			
	1	2	3	4	1	2	3	4
White	13.8	13.0	47.0	26.2	9.5	13.1	45.5	31.9
Black	15.8	15.2	42.4	26.6	10.5	15.2	44.9	29.5
Hispanic	18.2	19.4	40.2	22.3	12.0	16.9	40.4	30.7
Asian	23.2	10.1	37.5	23.2	12.5	14.3	48.2	25.0
Native Hawaiian/Pacific Islander								
American Indian								
Two or More Races	23.8	19.0	35.7	21.4	16.7	16.7	31.0	35.7

Grade 8 - Limited-English-Proficient

Levels	Reading				Mathematics			
	1	2	3	4	1	2	3	4
	15.6	22.1	40.2	22.1	9.5	16.1	45.2	29.1

Grade 8 - Economically Disadvantaged

Levels	Reading				Mathematics			
	1	2	3	4	1	2	3	4
Free/Reduced Price Lunch	13.4	13.7	45.0	28.0	8.8	13.7	44.0	33.5
Not Eligible	19.3	17.2	42.0	21.5	13.0	15.7	43.9	27.4

Grade 11

Grade 11 - All

Levels	Reading				Mathematics				Science			
	1	2	3	4	1	2	3	4	1	2	3	4
	15.4	17.0	52.6	15.0	13.2	10.3	58.4	18.1	11.8	11.7	27.5	49.0

Grade 11 - Gender

Levels	Reading				Mathematics				Science			
	1	2	3	4	1	2	3	4	1	2	3	4
Male	14.2	17.3	53.0	15.5	12.2	10.4	57.5	19.9	11.1	11.4	27.0	50.5
Female	17.1	16.4	52.2	14.3	14.9	9.7	60.2	15.2	12.9	12.2	28.0	46.9

Grade 11 - Racial/Ethnic Background

Levels	Reading				Mathematics				Science			
	1	2	3	4	1	2	3	4	1	2	3	4
White	14.5	16.7	52.5	16.3	11.8	10.1	60.1	18.0	10.1	12.6	24.5	52.8
Black	15.7	14.7	53.0	16.6	14.2	11.4	55.8	18.5	12.7	10.9	29.1	47.2
Hispanic	13.8	21.8	53.8	10.8	12.3	8.5	60.5	18.8	11.8	10.8	32.3	45.3
Asian	32.8	19.0	37.9	10.3	29.3	12.1	43.1	15.5	27.6	17.2	25.9	29.3
Native Hawaiian/Pacific Islander												
American Indian												
Two or More Races	17.2	10.3	58.6	13.8	17.2	6.9	58.6	17.2	10.3	3.4	24.1	62.1

Grade 11 - Limited-English-Proficient

Levels	Reading				Mathematics				Science			
	1	2	3	4	1	2	3	4	1	2	3	4
	16.9	19.2	54.1	9.9	13.4	9.3	57.6	19.8	14.0	11.6	34.3	40.1

Grade 11 - Economically Disadvantaged

Levels	Reading				Mathematics				Science			
	1	2	3	4	1	2	3	4	1	2	3	4
Free/Reduced Price Lunch	14.2	15.8	53.4	16.6	12.8	8.8	58.4	20.1	11.4	10.2	27.3	51.1
Not Eligible	16.9	18.4	51.6	13.1	13.8	12.1	58.4	15.7	12.3	13.5	27.7	46.5

2013 ADEQUATE YEARLY PROGRESS (AYP) STATUS REPORT - STATE

Is the state making Adequate Yearly Progress (AYP)?	No
Is the state making AYP in Reading?	No
Is the state making AYP in Mathematics?	No

	Percent Tested on State Tests				Percent Meeting/Exceeding Standards *						Other Indicators			
	Reading		Mathematics		Reading			Mathematics			Attendance Rate		Graduation Rate	
	%	Met AYP	%	Met AYP	%	Safe Harbor Target **	Met AYP	%	Safe Harbor Target **	Met AYP	%	Met AYP	%	Met AYP
State AYP Minimum Target	95.0		95.0		92.5			92.5			92.0		85.0	
All	99.6	Yes	99.6	Yes	58.6	62.0	No	58.1	62.7	No	94.2	Yes	83.2	No
White	99.7	Yes	99.7	Yes	69.8	72.4	No	68.9	72.9	No	95.4		89.3	
Black	99.4	Yes	99.4	Yes	38.7	43.4	No	35.3	42.1	No	93.6		70.9	
Hispanic	99.7	Yes	99.7	Yes	44.9	49.8	No	46.9	52.2	No	95.3		76.3	
Asian	99.8	Yes	99.8	Yes	79.3	80.1	No	82.8	84.6	No	96.4		92.0	
Native Hawaiian/ Pacific Islander	99.7	Yes	99.7	Yes	58.9	69.9	No	59.7	70.90	No	95.5		78.0	
American Indian	99.6	Yes	99.7	Yes	49.8	56.3	No	49.2	57.7	No	96.8		78.2	
Two or More Races	99.6	Yes	99.6	Yes	63.5	66.8	No	60.4	65.4	No	94.3		83.1	
LEP	99.4	Yes	99.7	Yes	27.0	34.3	No	33.9	40.9	No	95.5		63.7	
Students with Disabilities	99.2	Yes	99.1	Yes	23.9	31.4	No	26.7	34.7	No	93.8		70.1	
Economically Disadvantaged	99.5	Yes	99.5	Yes	43.2	47.8	No	43.1	48.8	No	94.3		73.0	

Four Conditions Are Required For Making Adequate Yearly Progress (AYP):

1. At least 95% tested in reading and mathematics for every student group. If the current year participation rate is less than 95%, this condition may be met if the average of the current and preceding year rates is at least 95%, or if the average of the current and two preceding years is at least 95%. Only actual participation rates are printed. If the participation rate printed is less than 95% and yet this school makes AYP, it means that the 95% condition was met by averaging.

2. At least 92.5% meeting/exceeding standards in reading and mathematics for every group. For any group with less than 92.5% meeting/exceeding standards, a 95% confidence interval was applied. Subgroups may meet this condition through Safe Harbor provisions.***

3. At least 92% attendance rate.

4. At least 85.0% graduation rate for high schools. The State would first examine whether the school met the target for the four-year graduation rate. If it did not, the State would then determine whether the school met the five-year graduation rate target. If either of those rates were met, this would indicate that the school met the other academic indicator for AYP. The largest number among the 4-year and 5-year graduation rates would be printed.

* The Full Academic Year provision does not apply at the state level.

** Safe Harbor Targets of 92.5% or above are not printed.

***Subgroups with fewer than 45 students are not reported. Safe Harbor only applies to subgroups of 45 or more. In order for Safe Harbor to apply, a subgroup must decrease by 10% the percentage of scores that did not meet standards from the previous year plus meet the other indicators (attendance rate for non-high schools and graduation rate for high schools) for the subgroup. For subgroups that do not meet their Safe Harbor Targets, a 75% confidence interval is applied. Safe Harbor allows schools an alternate method to meet subgroup minimum targets on achievement.

2013 STUDENT ACADEMIC GROWTH

Average Growth Value		
	Reading	Math
State	102.1	101.4

Illinois has chosen to use a value table methodology to determine the school and district growth metric based on student performance on large-scale assessments (the ISAT). The numbers contained in the value table represent the number of students in each cell.

The average of all students' academic growth over two year's performance will be used to determine the growth metric.

Reading

			Performance Level in Year 2							
			Academic Warning		Below Standards		Meets Standards		Exceeds Standards	
			1A	1B	2A	2B	3A	3B	4A	4B
Performance Level in Year 1	Academic Warning	1A	2,006	3,915	1,748	300	34	4	1	
		1B	4,094	15,159	14,252	4,042	471	63	10	1
	Below Standards	2A	1,345	11,522	35,103	27,366	4,773	468	52	3
		2B	352	3,706	29,113	79,854	44,863	8,184	1,062	75
	Meets Standards	3A	54	510	5,179	41,996	78,378	39,528	10,562	1,161
		3B	18	76	678	8,210	41,035	51,105	29,034	6,963
	Exceeds Standards	4A	4	18	90	1,025	8,968	23,214	24,432	11,091
		4B	1	2	7	154	1,923	9,149	17,477	15,406

Math

			Performance Level in Year 2							
			Academic Warning		Below Standards		Meets Standards		Exceeds Standards	
			1A	1B	2A	2B	3A	3B	4A	4B
Performance Level in Year 1	Academic Warning	1A	1,396	3,423	1,444	203	52	6	1	
		1B	3,164	17,107	17,377	3,855	671	54	5	1
	Below Standards	2A	1,284	14,028	43,372	26,477	6,277	359	24	3
		2B	306	4,188	32,721	63,102	41,558	3,429	143	10
	Meets Standards	3A	71	803	8,015	40,869	108,447	38,810	3,016	184
		3B	13	88	557	3,942	41,946	74,186	24,715	3,773
	Exceeds Standards	4A		3	24	159	2,978	21,250	26,646	11,469
		4B	2	2	3	20	213	2,745	9,111	11,529

Ancestry and Ethnicity

State Profile

Place Type: State
Population: 12,830,632

Ancestry	Population	%
Afghan (988)	1,058	0.01
African, Sub-Saharan (67,978)	80,211	0.63
African (42,006)	50,756	0.40
Cape Verdean (80)	197	<0.01
Ethiopian (3,090)	3,306	0.03
Ghanaian (3,842)	3,934	0.03
Kenyan (760)	863	0.01
Liberian (365)	439	<0.01
Nigerian (11,674)	13,217	0.10
Senegalese (62)	62	<0.01
Sierra Leonean (485)	497	<0.01
Somalian (708)	839	0.01
South African (1,058)	1,623	0.01
Sudanese (541)	585	<0.01
Ugandan (79)	117	<0.01
Zimbabwean (132)	146	<0.01
Other Sub-Saharan African (3,096)	3,630	0.03
Albanian (7,385)	8,794	0.07
Alsatian (172)	669	0.01
American (587,066)	587,066	4.61
Arab (55,460)	71,622	0.56
Arab (16,645)	19,609	0.15
Egyptian (4,415)	5,053	0.04
Iraqi (3,513)	4,332	0.03
Jordanian (4,208)	4,755	0.04
Lebanese (5,524)	11,409	0.09
Moroccan (2,566)	3,159	0.02
Palestinian (8,695)	9,810	0.08
Syrian (2,905)	4,734	0.04
Other Arab (6,989)	8,761	0.07
Armenian (4,519)	8,357	0.07
Assyrian/Chaldean/Syriac (13,746)	17,225	0.14
Australian (1,125)	2,719	0.02
Austrian (9,169)	41,675	0.33
Basque (186)	569	<0.01
Belgian (10,999)	33,847	0.27
Brazilian (3,373)	5,648	0.04
British (16,707)	36,600	0.29
Bulgarian (12,183)	14,058	0.11
Cajun (224)	612	<0.01
Canadian (6,813)	15,620	0.12
Carpatho Rusyn (26)	91	<0.01
Celtic (403)	980	0.01
Croatian (15,769)	44,065	0.35
Cypriot (159)	171	<0.01
Czech (34,757)	128,879	1.01
Czechoslovakian (7,590)	17,974	0.14
Danish (11,332)	53,218	0.42
Dutch (50,239)	201,329	1.58
Eastern European (16,848)	18,969	0.15
English (233,152)	836,287	6.56
Estonian (538)	947	0.01
European (96,902)	107,785	0.85
Finnish (4,814)	18,771	0.15
French, ex. Basque (38,474)	272,074	2.13
French Canadian (11,475)	37,197	0.29
German (885,614)	2,634,885	20.67
German Russian (160)	523	<0.01
Greek (56,674)	105,569	0.83
Guyanese (577)	897	0.01
Hungarian (14,609)	55,195	0.43
Icelander (433)	1,165	0.01
Iranian (7,390)	9,708	0.08
Irish (416,169)	1,648,856	12.94
Israeli (2,829)	4,197	0.03
Italian (288,615)	810,398	6.36
Latvian (3,359)	6,982	0.05
Lithuanian (38,465)	92,913	0.73
Luxemburger (1,664)	6,688	0.05
Macedonian (3,137)	4,372	0.03
Maltese (127)	356	<0.01
New Zealander (351)	542	<0.01
Northern European (5,809)	6,547	0.05
Norwegian (45,991)	173,334	1.36
Pennsylvania German (3,049)	5,327	0.04
Polish (436,077)	979,781	7.69
Portuguese (2,738)	9,579	0.08
Romanian (22,091)	34,691	0.27
Russian (60,501)	136,208	1.07
Scandinavian (7,294)	16,473	0.13
Scotch-Irish (48,149)	142,246	1.12
Scottish (40,521)	160,166	1.26
Serbian (13,999)	21,258	0.17
Slavic (2,087)	5,900	0.05
Slovak (13,847)	41,893	0.33
Slovene (4,953)	14,745	0.12
Soviet Union (88)	102	<0.01
Swedish (73,449)	302,369	2.37
Swiss (7,416)	41,435	0.33
Turkish (4,062)	5,949	0.05
Ukrainian (28,637)	50,346	0.40
Welsh (9,118)	52,576	0.41
West Indian, ex. Hispanic (21,918)	29,090	0.23
Bahamian (186)	333	<0.01
Barbadian (354)	506	<0.01
Belizean (3,784)	4,851	0.04
Bermudan (0)	59	<0.01
British West Indian (194)	345	<0.01
Dutch West Indian (123)	259	<0.01
Haitian (6,376)	7,639	0.06
Jamaican (8,824)	11,721	0.09
Trinidadian/Tobagonian (683)	1,069	0.01
U.S. Virgin Islander (151)	157	<0.01
West Indian (1,234)	2,142	0.02
Other West Indian (9)	9	<0.01
Yugoslavian (14,105)	20,954	0.16

Hispanic Origin	Population	%
Hispanic or Latino (of any race)	2,027,578	15.80
Central American, ex. Mexican	70,000	0.55
Costa Rican	1,874	0.01
Guatemalan	35,321	0.28
Honduran	12,023	0.09
Nicaraguan	3,078	0.02
Panamanian	2,843	0.02
Salvadoran	14,217	0.11
Other Central American	644	0.01
Cuban	22,541	0.18
Dominican Republic	5,691	0.04
Mexican	1,602,403	12.49
Puerto Rican	182,989	1.43
South American	67,862	0.53
Argentinean	5,294	0.04
Bolivian	2,304	0.02
Chilean	2,753	0.02
Colombian	19,345	0.15
Ecuadorian	22,816	0.18
Paraguayan	423	<0.01
Peruvian	10,213	0.08
Uruguayan	737	0.01
Venezuelan	3,283	0.03
Other South American	694	0.01
Other Hispanic or Latino	76,092	0.59

Race*	Population	%
African-American/Black (1,866,414)	1,974,113	15.39
Not Hispanic (1,832,924)	1,919,384	14.96
Hispanic (33,490)	54,729	0.43
American Indian/Alaska Native (43,963)	101,451	0.79
Not Hispanic (18,849)	60,948	0.48
Hispanic (25,114)	40,503	0.32
Alaska Athabascan (Ala. Nat.) (44)	86	<0.01
Aleut (Alaska Native) (53)	97	<0.01
Apache (536)	1,521	0.01
Arapaho (30)	93	<0.01
Blackfeet (361)	2,752	0.02
Canadian/French Am. Ind. (103)	279	<0.01
Central American Ind. (211)	424	<0.01
Cherokee (3,462)	17,033	0.1
Cheyenne (59)	224	<0.0
Chickasaw (88)	351	<0.0
Chippewa (1,352)	2,740	0.0
Choctaw (530)	1,934	0.0
Colville (7)	16	<0.0
Comanche (88)	251	<0.0
Cree (59)	197	<0.0
Creek (189)	599	<0.0
Crow (34)	147	<0.0
Delaware (70)	186	<0.0
Hopi (41)	99	<0.0
Houma (19)	28	<0.0
Inupiat (Alaska Native) (89)	173	<0.0
Iroquois (569)	1,336	0.0
Kiowa (57)	95	<0.0
Lumbee (106)	205	<0.0
Menominee (205)	390	<0.0
Mexican American Ind. (5,153)	7,421	0.0
Navajo (506)	1,063	0.0
Osage (69)	238	<0.0
Ottawa (124)	222	<0.0
Paiute (30)	55	<0.0
Pima (46)	85	<0.0
Potawatomi (294)	625	<0.0
Pueblo (124)	230	<0.0
Puget Sound Salish (32)	56	<0.0
Seminole (58)	316	<0.0
Shoshone (26)	107	<0.0
Sioux (829)	2,270	0.0
South American Ind. (559)	1,402	0.0
Spanish American Ind. (357)	535	<0.0
Tlingit-Haida (Alaska Native) (49)	86	<0.0
Tohono O'Odham (36)	47	<0.0
Tsimshian (Alaska Native) (4)	7	<0.0
Ute (18)	72	<0.0
Yakama (8)	17	<0.0
Yaqui (100)	193	<0.0
Yuman (20)	33	<0.0
Yup'ik (Alaska Native) (26)	49	<0.0
Asian (586,934)	668,694	5.2
Not Hispanic (580,586)	652,951	5.0
Hispanic (6,348)	15,743	0.1
Bangladeshi (1,895)	2,088	0.0
Bhutanese (467)	559	<0.0
Burmese (2,675)	2,950	0.0
Cambodian (3,526)	4,366	0.0
Chinese, ex. Taiwanese (98,269)	112,951	0.8
Filipino (114,724)	139,090	1.0
Hmong (572)	651	0.0
Indian (188,328)	203,669	1.5
Indonesian (1,144)	1,665	0.0
Japanese (17,542)	28,623	0.2
Korean (61,469)	70,263	0.5
Laotian (5,822)	7,102	0.0
Malaysian (635)	939	0.0
Nepalese (1,277)	1,459	0.0
Pakistani (29,646)	33,000	0.2
Sri Lankan (1,148)	1,320	0.0
Taiwanese (5,600)	6,705	0.0
Thai (7,430)	9,800	0.0
Vietnamese (25,036)	29,101	0.2
Hawaii Native/Pacific Islander (4,050)	13,546	0.1
Not Hispanic (2,977)	9,816	0.0
Hispanic (1,073)	3,730	0.0
Fijian (80)	133	<0.0
Guamanian/Chamorro (1,100)	1,928	0.0
Marshallese (32)	41	<0.0
Native Hawaiian (1,122)	3,636	0.0
Samoan (492)	1,191	0.0
Tongan (44)	82	<0.0
White (9,177,877)	9,423,048	73.4
Not Hispanic (8,167,753)	8,324,628	64.8
Hispanic (1,010,124)	1,098,420	8.5

Notes: † The Census 2010 population figure is used to calculate the percentages in the Hispanic Origin and Race categories. Ancestry percentages are based on the 2006-2010 American Communit
Survey population (not shown); ‡ Numbers in parentheses indicate the number of people reporting a single ancestry; * Numbers in parentheses indicate the number of persons reporting this race alor
not in combination with any other race; Please refer to the Explanation of Data for more information.

County Profiles

Champaign County

Population: 201,081

Ancestry	Population	%
Afghan (0)	0	<0.01
African, Sub-Saharan (5,147)	5,202	2.63
African (4,779)	4,801	2.43
Cape Verdean (0)	0	<0.01
Ethiopian (0)	0	<0.01
Ghanaian (83)	83	0.04
Kenyan (22)	22	0.01
Liberian (0)	0	<0.01
Nigerian (114)	147	0.07
Senegalese (0)	0	<0.01
Sierra Leonean (0)	0	<0.01
Somalian (0)	0	<0.01
South African (21)	21	0.01
Sudanese (0)	0	<0.01
Ugandan (0)	0	<0.01
Zimbabwean (25)	25	0.01
Other Sub-Saharan African (103)	103	0.05
Albanian (122)	122	0.06
Alsatian (0)	0	<0.01
American (22,670)	22,670	11.46
Arab (701)	882	0.45
Arab (52)	76	0.04
Egyptian (149)	165	0.08
Iraqi (79)	87	0.04
Jordanian (58)	82	0.04
Lebanese (30)	97	0.05
Moroccan (66)	66	0.03
Palestinian (79)	79	0.04
Syrian (0)	10	0.01
Other Arab (188)	220	0.11
Armenian (43)	43	0.02
Assyrian/Chaldean/Syriac (0)	34	0.02
Australian (42)	46	0.02
Austrian (220)	570	0.29
Basque (0)	20	0.01
Belgian (120)	320	0.10
Brazilian (240)	341	0.17
British (525)	1,158	0.59
Bulgarian (44)	79	0.04
Cajun (7)	9	<0.01
Canadian (127)	289	0.15
Carpatho Rusyn (0)	0	<0.01
Celtic (27)	27	0.01
Croatian (57)	181	0.09
Cypriot (0)	0	<0.01
Czech (204)	952	0.48
Czechoslovakian (110)	204	0.10
Danish (220)	670	0.34
Dutch (612)	3,249	1.64
Eastern European (174)	212	0.11
English (5,048)	17,598	8.89
Estonian (0)	17	0.01
European (5,150)	5,415	2.74
Finnish (45)	168	0.08
French, ex. Basque (595)	4,085	2.06
French Canadian (199)	523	0.26
German (18,527)	47,200	23.85
German Russian (0)	0	<0.01
Greek (458)	940	0.48
Guyanese (0)	18	0.01
Hungarian (159)	479	0.24
Icelander (105)	114	0.06
Iranian (239)	314	0.16
Irish (6,049)	24,099	12.18
Israeli (160)	160	0.08
Italian (1,797)	6,809	3.44
Latvian (27)	50	0.03
Lithuanian (240)	698	0.35
Luxemburger (3)	68	0.03
Macedonian (0)	0	<0.01
Maltese (24)	24	0.01
New Zealander (0)	0	<0.01

Ancestry	Population	%
Northern European (91)	91	0.05
Norwegian (681)	2,668	1.35
Pennsylvania German (62)	159	0.08
Polish (2,344)	7,051	3.56
Portuguese (59)	182	0.09
Romanian (164)	256	0.13
Russian (899)	2,160	1.09
Scandinavian (135)	344	0.17
Scotch-Irish (933)	2,924	1.48
Scottish (1,085)	3,747	1.89
Serbian (37)	68	0.03
Slavic (48)	75	0.04
Slovak (132)	366	0.18
Slovene (29)	50	0.03
Soviet Union (0)	0	<0.01
Swedish (1,005)	4,090	2.07
Swiss (172)	947	0.48
Turkish (333)	459	0.23
Ukrainian (331)	554	0.28
Welsh (209)	1,172	0.59
West Indian, ex. Hispanic (258)	368	0.19
Bahamian (0)	0	<0.01
Barbadian (0)	0	<0.01
Belizean (0)	0	<0.01
Bermudan (0)	0	<0.01
British West Indian (0)	0	<0.01
Dutch West Indian (0)	0	<0.01
Haitian (68)	114	0.06
Jamaican (77)	141	0.07
Trinidadian/Tobagonian (19)	19	0.01
U.S. Virgin Islander (81)	81	0.04
West Indian (13)	13	0.01
Other West Indian (0)	0	<0.01
Yugoslavian (113)	196	0.10

Hispanic Origin	Population	%
Hispanic or Latino (of any race)	10,607	5.27
Central American, ex. Mexican	792	0.39
Costa Rican	74	0.04
Guatemalan	437	0.22
Honduran	96	0.05
Nicaraguan	45	0.02
Panamanian	53	0.03
Salvadoran	83	0.04
Other Central American	4	<0.01
Cuban	232	0.12
Dominican Republic	67	0.03
Mexican	6,782	3.37
Puerto Rican	924	0.46
South American	939	0.47
Argentinean	138	0.07
Bolivian	57	0.03
Chilean	69	0.03
Colombian	272	0.14
Ecuadorian	112	0.06
Paraguayan	18	0.01
Peruvian	162	0.08
Uruguayan	17	0.01
Venezuelan	82	0.04
Other South American	12	0.01
Other Hispanic or Latino	871	0.43

Race*	Population	%
African-American/Black (24,946)	27,573	13.71
Not Hispanic (24,553)	26,910	13.38
Hispanic (393)	663	0.33
American Indian/Alaska Native (549)	1,540	0.77
Not Hispanic (360)	1,188	0.59
Hispanic (189)	352	0.18
Alaska Athabascan (Ala. Nat.) (0)	0	<0.01
Aleut (Alaska Native) (5)	5	<0.01
Apache (8)	17	0.01
Arapaho (2)	2	<0.01
Blackfeet (4)	55	0.03
Canadian/French Am. Ind. (0)	2	<0.01
Central American Ind. (4)	11	0.01

	Population	%
Cherokee (83)	369	0.18
Cheyenne (0)	8	<0.01
Chickasaw (11)	16	0.01
Chippewa (17)	35	0.02
Choctaw (15)	46	0.02
Colville (0)	0	<0.01
Comanche (1)	2	<0.01
Cree (0)	4	<0.01
Creek (7)	16	0.01
Crow (0)	1	<0.01
Delaware (5)	8	<0.01
Hopi (1)	4	<0.01
Houma (0)	0	<0.01
Inupiat (Alaska Native) (1)	2	<0.01
Iroquois (6)	22	0.01
Kiowa (1)	1	<0.01
Lumbee (4)	4	<0.01
Menominee (1)	1	<0.01
Mexican American Ind. (48)	71	0.04
Navajo (13)	18	0.01
Osage (3)	7	<0.01
Ottawa (3)	5	<0.01
Paiute (0)	0	<0.01
Pima (1)	3	<0.01
Potawatomi (6)	15	0.01
Pueblo (7)	8	<0.01
Puget Sound Salish (1)	2	<0.01
Seminole (1)	3	<0.01
Shoshone (0)	0	<0.01
Sioux (8)	33	0.02
South American Ind. (11)	21	0.01
Spanish American Ind. (0)	1	<0.01
Tlingit-Haida (Alaska Native) (0)	0	<0.01
Tohono O'Odham (1)	1	<0.01
Tsimshian (Alaska Native) (0)	0	<0.01
Ute (0)	1	<0.01
Yakama (1)	1	<0.01
Yaqui (0)	3	<0.01
Yuman (0)	0	<0.01
Yup'ik (Alaska Native) (0)	0	<0.01
Asian (17,969)	19,990	9.94
Not Hispanic (17,879)	19,802	9.85
Hispanic (90)	188	0.09
Bangladeshi (77)	88	0.04
Bhutanese (0)	0	<0.01
Burmese (22)	26	0.01
Cambodian (79)	107	0.05
Chinese, ex. Taiwanese (5,378)	5,848	2.91
Filipino (996)	1,372	0.68
Hmong (11)	12	0.01
Indian (3,806)	4,065	2.02
Indonesian (87)	108	0.05
Japanese (458)	786	0.39
Korean (3,993)	4,241	2.11
Laotian (231)	278	0.14
Malaysian (79)	84	0.04
Nepalese (53)	58	0.03
Pakistani (330)	365	0.18
Sri Lankan (59)	65	0.03
Taiwanese (663)	749	0.37
Thai (225)	278	0.14
Vietnamese (932)	1,059	0.53
Hawaii Native/Pacific Islander (134)	354	0.18
Not Hispanic (129)	316	0.16
Hispanic (5)	38	0.02
Fijian (0)	2	<0.01
Guamanian/Chamorro (7)	20	0.01
Marshallese (1)	2	<0.01
Native Hawaiian (30)	83	0.04
Samoan (13)	30	0.01
Tongan (1)	2	<0.01
White (147,600)	152,407	75.79
Not Hispanic (142,470)	146,617	72.91
Hispanic (5,130)	5,790	2.88

Cook County

Population: 5,194,675

Ancestry	Population	%
Afghan (298)	347	0.01
African, Sub-Saharan (42,790)	49,787	0.96
African (24,877)	30,022	0.58
Cape Verdean (27)	54	<0.01
Ethiopian (2,370)	2,474	0.05
Ghanaian (2,241)	2,288	0.04
Kenyan (610)	623	0.01
Liberian (209)	279	0.01
Nigerian (8,837)	9,691	0.19
Senegalese (39)	39	<0.01
Sierra Leonean (316)	328	0.01
Somalian (510)	637	0.01
South African (426)	651	0.01
Sudanese (288)	332	0.01
Ugandan (66)	80	<0.01
Zimbabwean (107)	121	<0.01
Other Sub-Saharan African (1,867)	2,168	0.04
Albanian (3,569)	4,123	0.08
Alsatian (72)	296	0.01
American (81,737)	81,737	1.58
Arab (38,445)	46,630	0.90
Arab (11,795)	13,717	0.27
Egyptian (2,456)	2,859	0.06
Iraqi (2,859)	3,583	0.07
Jordanian (3,388)	3,670	0.07
Lebanese (2,391)	4,489	0.09
Moroccan (1,538)	1,932	0.04
Palestinian (6,916)	7,600	0.15
Syrian (1,742)	2,357	0.05
Other Arab (5,360)	6,423	0.12
Armenian (2,746)	4,516	0.09
Assyrian/Chaldean/Syriac (12,714)	14,987	0.29
Australian (364)	977	0.02
Austrian (3,880)	18,467	0.36
Basque (86)	283	0.01
Belgian (1,543)	6,170	0.12
Brazilian (1,504)	2,617	0.05
British (5,025)	10,719	0.21
Bulgarian (8,965)	9,665	0.19
Cajun (70)	189	<0.01
Canadian (2,372)	4,905	0.09
Carpatho Rusyn (0)	47	<0.01
Celtic (137)	362	0.01
Croatian (7,987)	18,706	0.36
Cypriot (122)	134	<0.01
Czech (14,075)	49,346	0.95
Czechoslovakian (2,795)	6,729	0.13
Danish (2,772)	14,533	0.28
Dutch (16,379)	48,081	0.93
Eastern European (10,191)	11,307	0.22
English (33,140)	170,223	3.29
Estonian (343)	528	0.01
European (28,856)	32,210	0.62
Finnish (1,507)	5,880	0.11
French, ex. Basque (6,910)	62,151	1.20
French Canadian (2,952)	11,045	0.21
German (144,579)	581,493	11.24
German Russian (89)	231	<0.01
Greek (35,962)	56,997	1.10
Guyanese (230)	419	0.01
Hungarian (6,304)	21,499	0.42
Icelander (162)	475	0.01
Iranian (4,022)	5,319	0.10
Irish (150,659)	523,319	10.12
Israeli (1,868)	2,827	0.05
Italian (120,842)	307,056	5.94
Latvian (1,907)	3,469	0.07
Lithuanian (18,443)	41,978	0.81
Luxemburger (611)	2,600	0.05
Macedonian (1,354)	1,896	0.04
Maltese (34)	82	<0.01
New Zealander (190)	241	<0.01
Northern European (2,630)	3,014	0.06
Norwegian (9,594)	42,318	0.82
Pennsylvania German (221)	548	0.01

Ancestry	Population	%
Polish (265,594)	488,352	9.44
Portuguese (789)	2,483	0.05
Romanian (15,331)	20,601	0.40
Russian (34,187)	72,968	1.41
Scandinavian (1,995)	4,342	0.08
Scotch-Irish (10,716)	33,082	0.64
Scottish (8,867)	40,342	0.78
Serbian (9,183)	12,802	0.25
Slavic (1,105)	2,244	0.04
Slovak (5,448)	14,558	0.28
Slovene (1,585)	4,356	0.08
Soviet Union (78)	92	<0.01
Swedish (16,665)	78,000	1.51
Swiss (1,554)	8,432	0.16
Turkish (2,194)	2,944	0.06
Ukrainian (18,192)	29,108	0.56
Welsh (1,609)	13,391	0.26
West Indian, ex. Hispanic (15,959)	20,401	0.39
Bahamian (83)	119	<0.01
Barbadian (204)	292	<0.01
Belizean (2,598)	3,267	0.06
Bermudan (0)	35	<0.01
British West Indian (60)	151	<0.01
Dutch West Indian (16)	24	<0.01
Haitian (5,136)	6,057	0.12
Jamaican (6,436)	8,312	0.16
Trinidadian/Tobagonian (528)	735	0.01
U.S. Virgin Islander (43)	43	<0.01
West Indian (855)	1,366	0.03
Other West Indian (0)	0	<0.01
Yugoslavian (9,821)	11,984	0.23

Hispanic Origin	Population	%
Hispanic or Latino (of any race)	1,244,762	23.96
Central American, ex. Mexican	45,028	0.87
Costa Rican	1,064	0.02
Guatemalan	24,931	0.48
Honduran	6,569	0.13
Nicaraguan	1,987	0.04
Panamanian	1,399	0.03
Salvadoran	8,671	0.17
Other Central American	407	0.01
Cuban	13,679	0.26
Dominican Republic	3,893	0.07
Mexican	961,963	18.52
Puerto Rican	133,882	2.58
South American	47,583	0.92
Argentinean	3,380	0.07
Bolivian	1,244	0.02
Chilean	1,538	0.03
Colombian	12,114	0.23
Ecuadorian	19,450	0.37
Paraguayan	231	<0.01
Peruvian	6,771	0.13
Uruguayan	515	0.01
Venezuelan	1,821	0.04
Other South American	519	0.01
Other Hispanic or Latino	38,734	0.75

Race*	Population	%
African-American/Black (1,287,767)	1,331,016	25.62
Not Hispanic (1,265,778)	1,297,101	24.97
Hispanic (21,989)	33,915	0.65
American Indian/Alaska Native (21,559)	45,040	0.87
Not Hispanic (6,682)	21,781	0.42
Hispanic (14,877)	23,259	0.45
Alaska Athabascan (Ala. Nat.) (5)	20	<0.01
Aleut (Alaska Native) (7)	17	<0.01
Apache (216)	577	0.01
Arapaho (20)	42	<0.01
Blackfeet (94)	914	0.02
Canadian/French Am. Ind. (34)	87	<0.01
Central American Ind. (137)	278	0.01
Cherokee (806)	4,880	0.09
Cheyenne (18)	50	<0.01
Chickasaw (19)	111	<0.01
Chippewa (567)	1,115	0.02
Choctaw (190)	854	0.02
Colville (2)	8	<0.01

Race*	Population	%
Comanche (24)	60	<0.01
Cree (25)	74	<0.01
Creek (44)	240	<0.01
Crow (5)	37	<0.01
Delaware (8)	37	<0.01
Hopi (12)	37	<0.01
Houma (1)	4	<0.01
Inupiat (Alaska Native) (30)	48	<0.01
Iroquois (254)	562	0.01
Kiowa (22)	34	<0.01
Lumbee (35)	60	<0.01
Menominee (98)	188	<0.01
Mexican American Ind. (3,058)	4,414	0.08
Navajo (223)	446	0.01
Osage (18)	64	<0.01
Ottawa (52)	103	<0.01
Paiute (9)	16	<0.01
Pima (15)	30	<0.01
Potawatomi (88)	196	<0.01
Pueblo (54)	105	<0.01
Puget Sound Salish (7)	12	<0.01
Seminole (20)	138	<0.01
Shoshone (9)	30	<0.01
Sioux (255)	710	0.01
South American Ind. (381)	999	0.02
Spanish American Ind. (192)	298	0.01
Tlingit-Haida (Alaska Native) (18)	23	<0.01
Tohono O'Odham (11)	15	<0.01
Tsimshian (Alaska Native) (1)	1	<0.01
Ute (7)	19	<0.01
Yakama (0)	3	<0.01
Yaqui (39)	86	<0.01
Yuman (17)	25	<0.01
Yup'ik (Alaska Native) (8)	12	<0.01
Asian (322,672)	362,929	6.99
Not Hispanic (318,869)	353,882	6.81
Hispanic (3,803)	9,047	0.17
Bangladeshi (1,123)	1,235	0.02
Bhutanese (282)	345	0.01
Burmese (838)	963	0.02
Cambodian (1,901)	2,302	0.04
Chinese, ex. Taiwanese (59,732)	67,586	1.30
Filipino (64,349)	75,425	1.45
Hmong (138)	159	<0.01
Indian (93,730)	101,873	1.96
Indonesian (581)	789	0.02
Japanese (11,446)	16,814	0.32
Korean (37,008)	41,004	0.79
Laotian (1,523)	1,849	0.04
Malaysian (251)	396	0.01
Nepalese (750)	863	0.02
Pakistani (16,438)	18,349	0.35
Sri Lankan (533)	605	0.01
Taiwanese (2,514)	2,982	0.06
Thai (4,727)	5,748	0.11
Vietnamese (13,522)	15,435	0.30
Hawaii Native/Pacific Islander (1,724)	6,393	0.12
Not Hispanic (1,043)	4,090	0.08
Hispanic (681)	2,303	0.04
Fijian (31)	48	<0.01
Guamanian/Chamorro (542)	878	0.02
Marshallese (11)	16	<0.01
Native Hawaiian (430)	1,352	0.03
Samoan (202)	504	0.01
Tongan (10)	28	<0.01
White (2,877,212)	2,982,285	57.41
Not Hispanic (2,278,358)	2,333,942	44.93
Hispanic (598,854)	648,343	12.48

*Notes: † The Census 2010 population figure is used to calculate the percentages in the Hispanic Origin and Race categories. Ancestry percentages are based on the 2006-2010 American Community Survey population (not shown); ‡ Numbers in parentheses indicate the number of people reporting a single ancestry; * Numbers in parentheses indicate the number of persons reporting this race alone, not in combination with any other race; Please refer to the Explanation of Data for more information.*

DeKalb County

Population: 105,160

Ancestry	Population	%
Afghan (0)	0	<0.01
African, Sub-Saharan (193)	354	0.34
African (148)	214	0.21
Cape Verdean (0)	0	<0.01
Ethiopian (0)	0	<0.01
Ghanaian (0)	0	<0.01
Kenyan (25)	46	0.04
Liberian (0)	0	<0.01
Nigerian (4)	78	0.07
Senegalese (0)	0	<0.01
Sierra Leonean (0)	0	<0.01
Somalian (0)	0	<0.01
South African (0)	0	<0.01
Sudanese (16)	16	0.02
Ugandan (0)	0	<0.01
Zimbabwean (0)	0	<0.01
Other Sub-Saharan African (0)	0	<0.01
Albanian (203)	228	0.22
Alsatian (0)	0	<0.01
American (3,947)	3,947	3.79
Arab (123)	282	0.27
Arab (0)	0	<0.01
Egyptian (0)	0	<0.01
Iraqi (0)	0	<0.01
Jordanian (48)	48	0.05
Lebanese (40)	49	0.05
Moroccan (0)	0	<0.01
Palestinian (11)	11	0.01
Syrian (0)	32	0.03
Other Arab (24)	142	0.14
Armenian (45)	110	0.11
Assyrian/Chaldean/Syriac (0)	0	<0.01
Australian (35)	53	0.05
Austrian (109)	475	0.46
Basque (0)	8	0.01
Belgian (24)	410	0.39
Brazilian (0)	0	<0.01
British (127)	387	0.37
Bulgarian (75)	75	0.07
Cajun (10)	10	0.01
Canadian (44)	193	0.19
Carpatho Rusyn (0)	0	<0.01
Celtic (0)	0	<0.01
Croatian (48)	231	0.22
Cypriot (0)	0	<0.01
Czech (223)	1,188	1.14
Czechoslovakian (23)	72	0.07
Danish (311)	980	0.94
Dutch (374)	1,919	1.84
Eastern European (54)	54	0.05
English (1,941)	9,032	8.68
Estonian (0)	0	<0.01
European (805)	965	0.93
Finnish (76)	308	0.30
French, ex. Basque (323)	2,957	2.84
French Canadian (149)	443	0.43
German (10,081)	33,865	32.55
German Russian (0)	0	<0.01
Greek (421)	837	0.80
Guyanese (0)	0	<0.01
Hungarian (100)	404	0.39
Icelander (0)	0	<0.01
Iranian (22)	227	0.22
Irish (4,276)	18,210	17.51
Israeli (18)	18	0.02
Italian (1,860)	6,685	6.43
Latvian (27)	67	0.06
Lithuanian (289)	704	0.68
Luxemburger (58)	137	0.13
Macedonian (0)	0	<0.01
Maltese (0)	0	<0.01
New Zealander (0)	0	<0.01
Northern European (79)	94	0.09
Norwegian (1,637)	4,915	4.72
Pennsylvania German (25)	132	0.13

Ancestry	Population	%
Polish (2,085)	7,317	7.03
Portuguese (0)	95	0.09
Romanian (10)	249	0.24
Russian (169)	841	0.81
Scandinavian (138)	320	0.31
Scotch-Irish (401)	1,532	1.47
Scottish (285)	1,689	1.62
Serbian (134)	257	0.25
Slavic (0)	20	0.02
Slovak (68)	260	0.25
Slovene (24)	51	0.05
Soviet Union (0)	0	<0.01
Swedish (1,224)	6,563	6.31
Swiss (43)	379	0.36
Turkish (0)	13	0.01
Ukrainian (118)	354	0.34
Welsh (25)	539	0.52
West Indian, ex. Hispanic (23)	60	0.06
Bahamian (0)	0	<0.01
Barbadian (0)	0	<0.01
Belizean (0)	15	0.01
Bermudan (0)	0	<0.01
British West Indian (0)	0	<0.01
Dutch West Indian (0)	0	<0.01
Haitian (23)	31	0.03
Jamaican (0)	14	0.01
Trinidadian/Tobagonian (0)	0	<0.01
U.S. Virgin Islander (0)	0	<0.01
West Indian (0)	0	<0.01
Other West Indian (0)	0	<0.01
Yugoslavian (124)	175	0.17

Hispanic Origin	Population	%
Hispanic or Latino (of any race)	10,647	10.12
Central American, ex. Mexican	203	0.19
Costa Rican	13	0.01
Guatemalan	109	0.10
Honduran	32	0.03
Nicaraguan	15	0.01
Panamanian	18	0.02
Salvadoran	14	0.01
Other Central American	2	<0.01
Cuban	140	0.13
Dominican Republic	25	0.02
Mexican	8,886	8.45
Puerto Rican	643	0.61
South American	240	0.23
Argentinean	22	0.02
Bolivian	5	<0.01
Chilean	16	0.02
Colombian	78	0.07
Ecuadorian	46	0.04
Paraguayan	2	<0.01
Peruvian	53	0.05
Uruguayan	0	<0.01
Venezuelan	18	0.02
Other South American	0	<0.01
Other Hispanic or Latino	510	0.48

Race*	Population	%
African-American/Black (6,732)	7,508	7.14
Not Hispanic (6,579)	7,242	6.89
Hispanic (153)	266	0.25
American Indian/Alaska Native (267)	762	0.72
Not Hispanic (127)	501	0.48
Hispanic (140)	261	0.25
Alaska Athabascan (Ala. Nat.) (1)	1	<0.01
Aleut (Alaska Native) (0)	0	<0.01
Apache (1)	8	0.01
Arapaho (0)	0	<0.01
Blackfeet (6)	25	0.02
Canadian/French Am. Ind. (0)	0	<0.01
Central American Ind. (0)	0	<0.01
Cherokee (24)	151	0.14
Cheyenne (0)	2	<0.01
Chickasaw (1)	2	<0.01
Chippewa (12)	34	0.03
Choctaw (3)	14	0.01
Colville (0)	0	<0.01

Race*	Population	%
Comanche (0)	0	<0.01
Cree (0)	0	<0.01
Creek (0)	3	<0.01
Crow (0)	0	<0.01
Delaware (3)	4	<0.01
Hopi (0)	0	<0.01
Houma (0)	0	<0.01
Inupiat (Alaska Native) (0)	1	<0.01
Iroquois (12)	16	0.02
Kiowa (0)	0	<0.01
Lumbee (6)	6	0.01
Menominee (0)	1	<0.01
Mexican American Ind. (48)	66	0.06
Navajo (7)	17	0.02
Osage (1)	1	<0.01
Ottawa (0)	0	<0.01
Paiute (0)	0	<0.01
Pima (0)	6	0.01
Potawatomi (3)	7	0.01
Pueblo (0)	2	<0.01
Puget Sound Salish (0)	0	<0.01
Seminole (0)	4	<0.01
Shoshone (0)	3	<0.01
Sioux (8)	35	0.03
South American Ind. (1)	6	0.01
Spanish American Ind. (1)	1	<0.01
Tlingit-Haida (Alaska Native) (0)	0	<0.01
Tohono O'Odham (0)	0	<0.01
Tsimshian (Alaska Native) (0)	0	<0.01
Ute (0)	0	<0.01
Yakama (0)	0	<0.01
Yaqui (0)	2	<0.01
Yuman (0)	0	<0.01
Yup'ik (Alaska Native) (0)	0	<0.01
Asian (2,438)	2,972	2.83
Not Hispanic (2,400)	2,892	2.75
Hispanic (38)	80	0.08
Bangladeshi (10)	11	0.01
Bhutanese (0)	0	<0.01
Burmese (9)	9	0.01
Cambodian (38)	45	0.04
Chinese, ex. Taiwanese (484)	577	0.55
Filipino (319)	466	0.44
Hmong (0)	0	<0.01
Indian (686)	743	0.71
Indonesian (22)	25	0.02
Japanese (74)	155	0.15
Korean (285)	359	0.34
Laotian (53)	67	0.06
Malaysian (14)	22	0.02
Nepalese (9)	9	0.01
Pakistani (130)	137	0.13
Sri Lankan (10)	10	0.01
Taiwanese (25)	32	0.03
Thai (37)	53	0.05
Vietnamese (156)	182	0.17
Hawaii Native/Pacific Islander (23)	84	0.08
Not Hispanic (19)	64	0.06
Hispanic (4)	20	0.02
Fijian (0)	0	<0.01
Guamanian/Chamorro (2)	5	<0.01
Marshallese (0)	0	<0.01
Native Hawaiian (7)	43	0.04
Samoan (3)	5	<0.01
Tongan (2)	3	<0.01
White (89,453)	91,322	86.84
Not Hispanic (83,825)	85,143	80.97
Hispanic (5,628)	6,179	5.88

Notes: † The Census 2010 population figure is used to calculate the percentages in the Hispanic Origin and Race categories. Ancestry percentages are based on the 2006-2010 American Community Survey population (not shown); ‡ Numbers in parentheses indicate the number of people reporting a single ancestry; * Numbers in parentheses indicate the number of persons reporting this race alone, not in combination with any other race; Please refer to the Explanation of Data for more information.

DuPage County

Population: 916,924

Ancestry	Population	%
Afghan (428)	445	0.05
African, Sub-Saharan (3,025)	3,386	0.37
African (1,001)	1,188	0.13
Cape Verdean (0)	0	<0.01
Ethiopian (216)	216	0.02
Ghanaian (662)	662	0.07
Kenyan (9)	9	<0.01
Liberian (0)	0	<0.01
Nigerian (329)	453	0.05
Senegalese (0)	0	<0.01
Sierra Leonean (8)	8	<0.01
Somalian (134)	134	0.01
South African (78)	114	0.01
Sudanese (193)	193	0.02
Ugandan (0)	0	<0.01
Zimbabwean (0)	0	<0.01
Other Sub-Saharan African (395)	409	0.04
Albanian (1,984)	2,179	0.24
Alsatian (32)	90	0.01
American (19,903)	19,903	2.18
Arab (5,196)	6,983	0.77
Arab (1,327)	1,550	0.17
Egyptian (990)	998	0.11
Iraqi (138)	150	0.02
Jordanian (488)	488	0.05
Lebanese (732)	1,687	0.19
Moroccan (270)	402	0.04
Palestinian (397)	485	0.05
Syrian (435)	626	0.07
Other Arab (419)	597	0.07
Armenian (322)	700	0.08
Assyrian/Chaldean/Syriac (185)	469	0.05
Australian (93)	226	0.02
Austrian (922)	4,399	0.48
Basque (10)	10	<0.01
Belgian (714)	2,196	0.24
Brazilian (655)	1,039	0.11
British (2,301)	5,651	0.62
Bulgarian (1,178)	1,366	0.15
Cajun (19)	64	0.01
Canadian (841)	2,078	0.23
Carpatho Rusyn (0)	5	<0.01
Celtic (16)	51	0.01
Croatian (1,700)	4,943	0.54
Cypriot (0)	0	<0.01
Czech (7,533)	23,297	2.56
Czechoslovakian (1,391)	2,864	0.31
Danish (981)	5,854	0.64
Dutch (4,957)	15,824	1.74
Eastern European (800)	922	0.10
English (12,062)	62,476	6.85
Estonian (42)	131	0.01
European (8,074)	9,176	1.01
Finnish (333)	1,872	0.21
French, ex. Basque (2,090)	19,308	2.12
French Canadian (758)	2,942	0.32
German (52,242)	210,328	23.08
German Russian (0)	0	<0.01
Greek (5,852)	12,833	1.41
Guyanese (284)	284	0.03
Hungarian (1,302)	5,252	0.58
Icelander (27)	83	0.01
Iranian (1,256)	1,383	0.15
Irish (35,192)	150,770	16.54
Israeli (64)	158	0.02
Italian (38,867)	110,215	12.09
Latvian (427)	981	0.11
Lithuanian (6,414)	12,881	1.41
Luxemburger (94)	621	0.07
Macedonian (1,100)	1,280	0.14
Maltese (0)	12	<0.01
New Zealander (13)	13	<0.01
Northern European (760)	812	0.09
Norwegian (3,341)	16,584	1.82
Pennsylvania German (82)	152	0.02

	Population	%
Polish (44,241)	110,757	12.15
Portuguese (304)	840	0.09
Romanian (1,754)	2,902	0.32
Russian (3,688)	9,829	1.08
Scandinavian (883)	2,305	0.25
Scotch-Irish (3,346)	11,280	1.24
Scottish (2,696)	13,599	1.49
Serbian (1,591)	2,422	0.27
Slavic (128)	406	0.04
Slovak (1,771)	5,262	0.58
Slovene (426)	1,296	0.14
Soviet Union (0)	0	<0.01
Swedish (5,161)	27,151	2.98
Swiss (393)	3,278	0.36
Turkish (388)	551	0.06
Ukrainian (2,468)	5,471	0.60
Welsh (560)	4,401	0.48
West Indian, ex. Hispanic (783)	998	0.11
Bahamian (10)	21	<0.01
Barbadian (77)	116	0.01
Belizean (100)	110	0.01
Bermudan (0)	0	<0.01
British West Indian (16)	40	<0.01
Dutch West Indian (0)	0	<0.01
Haitian (119)	136	0.01
Jamaican (373)	433	0.05
Trinidadian/Tobagonian (35)	89	0.01
U.S. Virgin Islander (0)	0	<0.01
West Indian (53)	53	0.01
Other West Indian (0)	0	<0.01
Yugoslavian (1,353)	2,091	0.23

Hispanic Origin	Population	%
Hispanic or Latino (of any race)	121,506	13.25
Central American, ex. Mexican	5,055	0.55
Costa Rican	143	0.02
Guatemalan	3,322	0.36
Honduran	505	0.06
Nicaraguan	177	0.02
Panamanian	206	0.02
Salvadoran	659	0.07
Other Central American	43	<0.01
Cuban	2,345	0.26
Dominican Republic	256	0.03
Mexican	96,039	10.47
Puerto Rican	7,736	0.84
South American	5,184	0.57
Argentinean	537	0.06
Bolivian	305	0.03
Chilean	324	0.04
Colombian	1,629	0.18
Ecuadorian	993	0.11
Paraguayan	51	0.01
Peruvian	869	0.09
Uruguayan	42	<0.01
Venezuelan	389	0.04
Other South American	45	<0.01
Other Hispanic or Latino	4,891	0.53

Race*	Population	%
African-American/Black (42,346)	47,708	5.20
Not Hispanic (41,024)	45,299	4.94
Hispanic (1,322)	2,409	0.26
American Indian/Alaska Native (2,415)	5,776	0.63
Not Hispanic (992)	3,420	0.37
Hispanic (1,423)	2,356	0.26
Alaska Athabascan (Ala. Nat.) (3)	9	<0.01
Aleut (Alaska Native) (4)	8	<0.01
Apache (21)	65	0.01
Arapaho (0)	7	<0.01
Blackfeet (12)	108	0.01
Canadian/French Am. Ind. (5)	17	<0.01
Central American Ind. (9)	21	<0.01
Cherokee (161)	955	0.10
Cheyenne (0)	2	<0.01
Chickasaw (4)	18	<0.01
Chippewa (68)	179	0.02
Choctaw (49)	101	0.01
Colville (0)	0	<0.01

	Population	%
Comanche (3)	12	<0.01
Cree (1)	10	<0.01
Creek (6)	36	<0.01
Crow (3)	10	<0.01
Delaware (2)	11	<0.01
Hopi (0)	2	<0.01
Houma (2)	2	<0.01
Inupiat (Alaska Native) (5)	9	<0.01
Iroquois (51)	109	0.01
Kiowa (0)	0	<0.01
Lumbee (13)	20	<0.01
Menominee (8)	26	<0.01
Mexican American Ind. (304)	443	0.05
Navajo (21)	57	0.01
Osage (3)	24	<0.01
Ottawa (5)	13	<0.01
Paiute (1)	2	<0.01
Pima (1)	4	<0.01
Potawatomi (10)	25	<0.01
Pueblo (8)	18	<0.01
Puget Sound Salish (1)	2	<0.01
Seminole (1)	13	<0.01
Shoshone (0)	4	<0.01
Sioux (32)	95	0.01
South American Ind. (28)	74	0.01
Spanish American Ind. (28)	43	<0.01
Tlingit-Haida (Alaska Native) (1)	2	<0.01
Tohono O'Odham (2)	4	<0.01
Tsimshian (Alaska Native) (0)	0	<0.01
Ute (1)	15	<0.01
Yakama (0)	0	<0.01
Yaqui (11)	17	<0.01
Yuman (0)	0	<0.01
Yup'ik (Alaska Native) (4)	6	<0.01
Asian (92,304)	101,542	11.07
Not Hispanic (91,793)	100,232	10.93
Hispanic (511)	1,310	0.14
Bangladeshi (252)	270	0.03
Bhutanese (87)	87	0.01
Burmese (595)	639	0.07
Cambodian (505)	622	0.07
Chinese, ex. Taiwanese (11,708)	13,459	1.47
Filipino (15,254)	18,004	1.96
Hmong (77)	87	0.01
Indian (42,233)	44,823	4.89
Indonesian (123)	189	0.02
Japanese (1,369)	2,400	0.26
Korean (4,758)	5,481	0.60
Laotian (187)	277	0.03
Malaysian (76)	118	0.01
Nepalese (107)	114	0.01
Pakistani (6,511)	7,180	0.78
Sri Lankan (202)	236	0.03
Taiwanese (1,308)	1,575	0.17
Thai (555)	775	0.08
Vietnamese (3,747)	4,089	0.45
Hawaii Native/Pacific Islander (217)	958	0.10
Not Hispanic (171)	754	0.08
Hispanic (46)	204	0.02
Fijian (15)	27	<0.01
Guamanian/Chamorro (47)	103	0.01
Marshallese (3)	3	<0.01
Native Hawaiian (50)	236	0.03
Samoan (28)	61	0.01
Tongan (2)	4	<0.01
White (714,140)	730,865	79.71
Not Hispanic (646,130)	657,493	71.71
Hispanic (68,010)	73,372	8.00

*Notes: † The Census 2010 population figure is used to calculate the percentages in the Hispanic Origin and Race categories. Ancestry percentages are based on the 2006-2010 American Community Survey population (not shown); ‡ Numbers in parentheses indicate the number of people reporting a single ancestry; * Numbers in parentheses indicate the number of persons reporting this race alone, not in combination with any other race; Please refer to the Explanation of Data for more information.*

Kane County

Population: 515,269

Ancestry	Population	%
Afghan (179)	179	0.04
African, Sub-Saharan (1,349)	1,696	0.34
African (543)	870	0.17
Cape Verdean (0)	0	<0.01
Ethiopian (79)	79	0.02
Ghanaian (47)	47	0.01
Kenyan (0)	0	<0.01
Liberian (0)	0	<0.01
Nigerian (312)	312	0.06
Senegalese (0)	0	<0.01
Sierra Leonean (0)	0	<0.01
Somalian (0)	0	<0.01
South African (79)	99	0.02
Sudanese (0)	0	<0.01
Ugandan (0)	0	<0.01
Zimbabwean (0)	0	<0.01
Other Sub-Saharan African (289)	289	0.06
Albanian (354)	492	0.10
Alsatian (0)	0	<0.01
American (11,997)	11,997	2.39
Arab (658)	1,348	0.27
Arab (105)	197	0.04
Egyptian (22)	45	0.01
Iraqi (0)	0	<0.01
Jordanian (13)	109	0.02
Lebanese (129)	404	0.08
Moroccan (0)	0	<0.01
Palestinian (55)	198	0.04
Syrian (179)	216	0.04
Other Arab (155)	179	0.04
Armenian (101)	142	0.03
Assyrian/Chaldean/Syriac (291)	437	0.09
Australian (0)	43	0.01
Austrian (730)	2,298	0.46
Basque (45)	58	0.01
Belgian (395)	1,536	0.31
Brazilian (164)	261	0.05
British (679)	1,386	0.28
Bulgarian (149)	321	0.06
Cajun (8)	32	0.01
Canadian (306)	916	0.18
Carpatho Rusyn (14)	14	<0.01
Celtic (14)	51	0.01
Croatian (270)	1,151	0.23
Cypriot (0)	0	<0.01
Czech (1,348)	6,114	1.22
Czechoslovakian (368)	955	0.19
Danish (596)	3,478	0.69
Dutch (1,305)	6,754	1.34
Eastern European (308)	388	0.08
English (7,356)	35,570	7.08
Estonian (8)	18	<0.01
European (3,901)	4,650	0.93
Finnish (106)	1,075	0.21
French, ex. Basque (1,205)	11,999	2.39
French Canadian (545)	2,064	0.41
German (34,749)	121,934	24.26
German Russian (0)	0	<0.01
Greek (1,422)	3,261	0.65
Guyanese (0)	0	<0.01
Hungarian (699)	3,221	0.64
Icelander (7)	61	0.01
Iranian (71)	164	0.03
Irish (12,184)	65,521	13.04
Israeli (35)	35	0.01
Italian (11,807)	37,057	7.37
Latvian (68)	339	0.07
Lithuanian (959)	3,016	0.60
Luxemburger (352)	1,255	0.25
Macedonian (61)	118	0.02
Maltese (0)	23	<0.01
New Zealander (0)	0	<0.01
Northern European (132)	132	0.03
Norwegian (2,793)	11,639	2.32
Pennsylvania German (44)	106	0.02

Ancestry	Population	%
Polish (12,957)	39,862	7.93
Portuguese (151)	366	0.07
Romanian (445)	1,918	0.38
Russian (1,082)	3,562	0.71
Scandinavian (253)	702	0.14
Scotch-Irish (1,507)	5,913	1.18
Scottish (1,493)	7,775	1.55
Serbian (249)	408	0.08
Slavic (70)	184	0.04
Slovak (392)	1,459	0.29
Slovene (108)	354	0.07
Soviet Union (0)	0	<0.01
Swedish (3,990)	18,166	3.61
Swiss (340)	1,914	0.38
Turkish (0)	40	0.01
Ukrainian (851)	1,992	0.40
Welsh (547)	2,658	0.53
West Indian, ex. Hispanic (132)	322	0.06
Bahamian (13)	13	<0.01
Barbadian (0)	0	<0.01
Belizean (0)	0	<0.01
Bermudan (0)	12	<0.01
British West Indian (0)	0	<0.01
Dutch West Indian (0)	0	<0.01
Haitian (0)	22	<0.01
Jamaican (76)	141	0.03
Trinidadian/Tobagonian (22)	85	0.02
U.S. Virgin Islander (0)	0	<0.01
West Indian (21)	49	0.01
Other West Indian (0)	0	<0.01
Yugoslavian (236)	492	0.10

Hispanic Origin	Population	%
Hispanic or Latino (of any race)	158,390	30.74
Central American, ex. Mexican	2,939	0.57
Costa Rican	81	0.02
Guatemalan	1,094	0.21
Honduran	360	0.07
Nicaraguan	153	0.03
Panamanian	100	0.02
Salvadoran	1,115	0.22
Other Central American	36	0.01
Cuban	843	0.16
Dominican Republic	197	0.04
Mexican	139,009	26.98
Puerto Rican	8,540	1.66
South American	2,072	0.40
Argentinean	233	0.05
Bolivian	128	0.02
Chilean	118	0.02
Colombian	692	0.13
Ecuadorian	397	0.08
Paraguayan	8	<0.01
Peruvian	346	0.07
Uruguayan	10	<0.01
Venezuelan	130	0.03
Other South American	10	<0.01
Other Hispanic or Latino	4,790	0.93

Race*	Population	%
African-American/Black (29,422)	33,594	6.52
Not Hispanic (27,819)	30,657	5.95
Hispanic (1,603)	2,937	0.57
American Indian/Alaska Native (2,887)	5,055	0.98
Not Hispanic (591)	1,760	0.34
Hispanic (2,296)	3,295	0.64
Alaska Athabascan (Ala. Nat.) (0)	1	<0.01
Aleut (Alaska Native) (2)	6	<0.01
Apache (26)	60	0.01
Arapaho (0)	2	<0.01
Blackfeet (10)	75	0.01
Canadian/French Am. Ind. (1)	8	<0.01
Central American Ind. (8)	14	<0.01
Cherokee (99)	453	0.09
Cheyenne (0)	4	<0.01
Chickasaw (4)	7	<0.01
Chippewa (52)	106	0.02
Choctaw (14)	34	0.01
Colville (0)	0	<0.01

	Population	%
Comanche (4)	22	<0.01
Cree (4)	6	<0.01
Creek (6)	23	<0.01
Crow (1)	5	<0.01
Delaware (5)	6	<0.01
Hopi (8)	14	<0.01
Houma (0)	0	<0.01
Inupiat (Alaska Native) (8)	17	<0.01
Iroquois (20)	62	0.01
Kiowa (2)	4	<0.01
Lumbee (8)	10	<0.01
Menominee (2)	15	<0.01
Mexican American Ind. (466)	608	0.12
Navajo (23)	30	0.01
Osage (1)	15	<0.01
Ottawa (5)	11	<0.01
Paiute (3)	3	<0.01
Pima (4)	7	<0.01
Potawatomi (13)	37	0.01
Pueblo (5)	11	<0.01
Puget Sound Salish (0)	0	<0.01
Seminole (3)	5	<0.01
Shoshone (0)	0	<0.01
Sioux (24)	90	0.02
South American Ind. (27)	51	0.01
Spanish American Ind. (42)	60	0.01
Tlingit-Haida (Alaska Native) (1)	1	<0.01
Tohono O'Odham (4)	5	<0.01
Tsimshian (Alaska Native) (0)	0	<0.01
Ute (0)	0	<0.01
Yakama (1)	1	<0.01
Yaqui (16)	21	<0.01
Yuman (0)	0	<0.01
Yup'ik (Alaska Native) (1)	1	<0.01
Asian (17,895)	21,080	4.09
Not Hispanic (17,505)	20,122	3.91
Hispanic (390)	958	0.19
Bangladeshi (23)	23	<0.01
Bhutanese (61)	81	0.02
Burmese (248)	255	0.05
Cambodian (126)	168	0.03
Chinese, ex. Taiwanese (1,627)	2,137	0.41
Filipino (4,988)	6,133	1.19
Hmong (121)	127	0.02
Indian (4,695)	5,200	1.01
Indonesian (31)	59	0.01
Japanese (358)	724	0.14
Korean (1,095)	1,434	0.28
Laotian (1,545)	1,779	0.35
Malaysian (8)	16	<0.01
Nepalese (35)	44	0.01
Pakistani (940)	1,047	0.20
Sri Lankan (31)	38	0.01
Taiwanese (84)	107	0.02
Thai (219)	311	0.06
Vietnamese (883)	1,073	0.21
Hawaii Native/Pacific Islander (193)	481	0.09
Not Hispanic (130)	296	0.06
Hispanic (63)	185	0.04
Fijian (2)	2	<0.01
Guamanian/Chamorro (35)	59	0.01
Marshallese (5)	5	<0.01
Native Hawaiian (58)	139	0.03
Samoan (12)	26	0.01
Tongan (6)	8	<0.01
White (384,548)	396,290	76.91
Not Hispanic (304,051)	309,682	60.10
Hispanic (80,497)	86,608	16.81

*Notes: † The Census 2010 population figure is used to calculate the percentages in the Hispanic Origin and Race categories. Ancestry percentages are based on the 2006-2010 American Community Survey population (not shown); ‡ Numbers in parentheses indicate the number of people reporting a single ancestry; * Numbers in parentheses indicate the number of persons reporting this race alone, not in combination with any other race; Please refer to the Explanation of Data for more information.*

Kankakee County

Population: 113,449

Ancestry	Population	%
Afghan (0)	0	<0.01
African, Sub-Saharan (244)	279	0.25
African (174)	189	0.17
Cape Verdean (0)	0	<0.01
Ethiopian (15)	35	0.03
Ghanaian (0)	0	<0.01
Kenyan (0)	0	<0.01
Liberian (0)	0	<0.01
Nigerian (3)	3	<0.01
Senegalese (0)	0	<0.01
Sierra Leonean (0)	0	<0.01
Somalian (0)	0	<0.01
South African (0)	0	<0.01
Sudanese (0)	0	<0.01
Ugandan (0)	0	<0.01
Zimbabwean (0)	0	<0.01
Other Sub-Saharan African (52)	52	0.05
Albanian (0)	0	<0.01
Alsatian (0)	0	<0.01
American (4,001)	4,001	3.57
Arab (101)	121	0.11
Arab (5)	5	<0.01
Egyptian (18)	29	0.03
Iraqi (0)	0	<0.01
Jordanian (0)	0	<0.01
Lebanese (65)	65	0.06
Moroccan (13)	13	0.01
Palestinian (0)	0	<0.01
Syrian (0)	0	<0.01
Other Arab (0)	9	0.01
Armenian (0)	35	0.03
Assyrian/Chaldean/Syriac (0)	4	<0.01
Australian (0)	0	<0.01
Austrian (28)	139	0.12
Basque (0)	0	<0.01
Belgian (49)	272	0.24
Brazilian (25)	25	0.02
British (73)	240	0.21
Bulgarian (0)	13	0.01
Cajun (0)	0	<0.01
Canadian (57)	182	0.16
Carpatho Rusyn (0)	0	<0.01
Celtic (0)	0	<0.01
Croatian (5)	148	0.13
Cypriot (0)	0	<0.01
Czech (111)	686	0.61
Czechoslovakian (3)	52	0.05
Danish (210)	884	0.79
Dutch (1,245)	3,874	3.46
Eastern European (31)	49	0.04
English (2,120)	8,244	7.35
Estonian (0)	0	<0.01
European (497)	542	0.48
Finnish (44)	50	0.04
French, ex. Basque (2,594)	10,512	9.38
French Canadian (894)	1,754	1.56
German (9,024)	29,663	26.46
German Russian (0)	21	0.02
Greek (224)	589	0.53
Guyanese (0)	0	<0.01
Hungarian (68)	279	0.25
Icelander (0)	0	<0.01
Iranian (10)	10	0.01
Irish (3,008)	15,942	14.22
Israeli (0)	0	<0.01
Italian (2,664)	7,562	6.75
Latvian (25)	32	0.03
Lithuanian (193)	734	0.65
Luxemburger (0)	17	0.02
Macedonian (0)	26	0.02
Maltese (0)	0	<0.01
New Zealander (0)	0	<0.01
Northern European (22)	22	0.02
Norwegian (340)	1,270	1.13
Pennsylvania German (13)	38	0.03

Ancestry (cont.)	Population	%
Polish (2,328)	6,448	5.75
Portuguese (16)	113	0.10
Romanian (15)	75	0.07
Russian (13)	118	0.11
Scandinavian (19)	86	0.08
Scotch-Irish (352)	1,309	1.17
Scottish (342)	1,396	1.25
Serbian (24)	99	0.09
Slavic (9)	101	0.09
Slovak (87)	266	0.24
Slovene (42)	87	0.08
Soviet Union (0)	0	<0.01
Swedish (495)	2,591	2.31
Swiss (15)	165	0.15
Turkish (0)	9	0.01
Ukrainian (19)	112	0.10
Welsh (153)	566	0.50
West Indian, ex. Hispanic (55)	99	0.09
Bahamian (17)	17	0.02
Barbadian (0)	0	<0.01
Belizean (0)	0	<0.01
Bermudan (0)	0	<0.01
British West Indian (0)	0	<0.01
Dutch West Indian (0)	0	<0.01
Haitian (18)	27	0.02
Jamaican (11)	46	0.04
Trinidadian/Tobagonian (9)	9	0.01
U.S. Virgin Islander (0)	0	<0.01
West Indian (0)	0	<0.01
Other West Indian (0)	0	<0.01
Yugoslavian (0)	19	0.02

Hispanic Origin	Population	%
Hispanic or Latino (of any race)	10,167	8.96
Central American, ex. Mexican	119	0.10
Costa Rican	4	<0.01
Guatemalan	53	0.05
Honduran	16	0.01
Nicaraguan	4	<0.01
Panamanian	21	0.02
Salvadoran	21	0.02
Other Central American	0	<0.01
Cuban	80	0.07
Dominican Republic	10	0.01
Mexican	8,824	7.78
Puerto Rican	435	0.38
South American	130	0.11
Argentinean	6	0.01
Bolivian	8	0.01
Chilean	10	0.01
Colombian	33	0.03
Ecuadorian	48	0.04
Paraguayan	2	<0.01
Peruvian	16	0.01
Uruguayan	0	<0.01
Venezuelan	7	0.01
Other South American	0	<0.01
Other Hispanic or Latino	569	0.50

Race*	Population	%
African-American/Black (17,187)	18,489	16.30
Not Hispanic (16,998)	18,134	15.98
Hispanic (189)	355	0.31
American Indian/Alaska Native (286)	859	0.76
Not Hispanic (187)	651	0.57
Hispanic (99)	208	0.18
Alaska Athabascan (Ala. Nat.) (3)	3	<0.01
Aleut (Alaska Native) (0)	0	<0.01
Apache (11)	22	0.02
Arapaho (0)	1	<0.01
Blackfeet (6)	36	0.03
Canadian/French Am. Ind. (2)	4	<0.01
Central American Ind. (0)	0	<0.01
Cherokee (34)	207	0.18
Cheyenne (1)	3	<0.01
Chickasaw (0)	2	<0.01
Chippewa (5)	23	0.02
Choctaw (10)	30	0.03
Colville (0)	0	<0.01

Race* (cont.)	Population	%
Comanche (0)	0	<0.0
Cree (0)	2	<0.0
Creek (0)	4	<0.0
Crow (0)	2	<0.0
Delaware (1)	5	<0.0
Hopi (0)	0	<0.0
Houma (1)	2	<0.0
Inupiat (Alaska Native) (0)	1	<0.0
Iroquois (6)	24	<0.0
Kiowa (0)	0	<0.0
Lumbee (0)	1	<0.0
Menominee (5)	5	<0.0
Mexican American Ind. (23)	29	0.0
Navajo (1)	5	<0.0
Osage (0)	3	<0.0
Ottawa (1)	1	<0.0
Paiute (0)	0	<0.0
Pima (0)	0	<0.0
Potawatomi (5)	17	0.0
Pueblo (0)	3	<0.0
Puget Sound Salish (0)	0	<0.0
Seminole (1)	1	<0.0
Shoshone (1)	3	<0.0
Sioux (10)	31	0.0
South American Ind. (0)	2	<0.0
Spanish American Ind. (2)	2	<0.0
Tlingit-Haida (Alaska Native) (0)	0	<0.0
Tohono O'Odham (0)	0	<0.0
Tsimshian (Alaska Native) (0)	0	<0.0
Ute (0)	2	<0.0
Yakama (0)	0	<0.0
Yaqui (5)	6	0.0
Yuman (0)	0	<0.0
Yup'ik (Alaska Native) (1)	1	<0.0
Asian (1,052)	1,365	1.2
Not Hispanic (1,030)	1,295	1.1
Hispanic (22)	70	0.0
Bangladeshi (0)	0	<0.0
Bhutanese (0)	0	<0.0
Burmese (8)	8	<0.0
Cambodian (2)	2	<0.0
Chinese, ex. Taiwanese (167)	198	0.1
Filipino (302)	404	0.3
Hmong (6)	6	0.0
Indian (309)	367	0.3
Indonesian (0)	1	<0.0
Japanese (21)	58	0.0
Korean (101)	145	0.1
Laotian (3)	8	0.0
Malaysian (0)	0	<0.0
Nepalese (0)	0	<0.0
Pakistani (20)	27	0.0
Sri Lankan (5)	5	<0.0
Taiwanese (2)	6	<0.0
Thai (12)	18	0.0
Vietnamese (64)	79	0.0
Hawaii Native/Pacific Islander (34)	77	0.0
Not Hispanic (32)	65	0.0
Hispanic (2)	12	0.0
Fijian (0)	0	<0.0
Guamanian/Chamorro (2)	2	<0.0
Marshallese (0)	0	<0.0
Native Hawaiian (13)	37	0.0
Samoan (9)	11	0.0
Tongan (0)	0	<0.0
White (87,986)	90,149	79.4
Not Hispanic (83,218)	84,788	74.7
Hispanic (4,768)	5,361	4.7

*Notes: † The Census 2010 population figure is used to calculate the percentages in the Hispanic Origin and Race categories. Ancestry percentages are based on the 2006-2010 American Communit Survey population (not shown); ‡ Numbers in parentheses indicate the number of people reporting a single ancestry; * Numbers in parentheses indicate the number of persons reporting this race alon not in combination with any other race; Please refer to the Explanation of Data for more information.*

Kendall County

Population: 114,736

Ancestry	Population	%
Afghan (0)	0	<0.01
African, Sub-Saharan (154)	411	0.39
African (11)	64	0.06
Cape Verdean (44)	134	0.13
Ethiopian (28)	28	0.03
Ghanaian (0)	0	<0.01
Kenyan (0)	0	<0.01
Liberian (0)	4	<0.01
Nigerian (0)	18	0.02
Senegalese (0)	0	<0.01
Sierra Leonean (0)	0	<0.01
Somalian (0)	0	<0.01
South African (71)	163	0.15
Sudanese (0)	0	<0.01
Ugandan (0)	0	<0.01
Zimbabwean (0)	0	<0.01
Other Sub-Saharan African (0)	0	<0.01
Albanian (14)	28	0.03
Alsatian (0)	0	<0.01
American (3,430)	3,430	3.25
Arab (128)	194	0.18
Arab (16)	16	0.02
Egyptian (12)	12	0.01
Iraqi (0)	0	<0.01
Jordanian (0)	0	<0.01
Lebanese (0)	66	0.06
Moroccan (0)	0	<0.01
Palestinian (91)	91	0.09
Syrian (9)	9	0.01
Other Arab (0)	0	<0.01
Armenian (26)	37	0.04
Assyrian/Chaldean/Syriac (26)	38	0.04
Australian (0)	0	<0.01
Austrian (56)	190	0.18
Basque (14)	28	0.03
Belgian (80)	266	0.25
Brazilian (0)	9	0.01
British (127)	326	0.31
Bulgarian (0)	0	<0.01
Cajun (0)	14	0.01
Canadian (59)	103	0.10
Carpatho Rusyn (0)	0	<0.01
Celtic (12)	15	0.01
Croatian (90)	350	0.33
Cypriot (0)	0	<0.01
Czech (685)	2,096	1.98
Czechoslovakian (89)	211	0.20
Danish (83)	460	0.44
Dutch (476)	1,638	1.55
Eastern European (67)	76	0.07
English (1,758)	7,934	7.51
Estonian (0)	0	<0.01
European (965)	1,019	0.96
Finnish (56)	261	0.25
French, ex. Basque (359)	3,338	3.16
French Canadian (67)	329	0.31
German (8,647)	29,618	28.05
German Russian (0)	46	0.04
Greek (383)	820	0.78
Guyanese (0)	15	0.01
Hungarian (233)	976	0.92
Icelander (0)	0	<0.01
Iranian (25)	25	0.02
Irish (2,731)	16,924	16.03
Israeli (15)	15	0.01
Italian (2,592)	9,931	9.40
Latvian (12)	116	0.11
Lithuanian (255)	700	0.66
Luxemburger (71)	219	0.21
Macedonian (0)	0	<0.01
Maltese (0)	0	<0.01
New Zealander (0)	0	<0.01
Northern European (5)	5	<0.01
Norwegian (1,359)	3,928	3.72
Pennsylvania German (11)	30	0.03

Ancestry	Population	%
Polish (2,655)	10,018	9.49
Portuguese (0)	59	0.06
Romanian (148)	543	0.51
Russian (292)	755	0.71
Scandinavian (62)	221	0.21
Scotch-Irish (347)	1,392	1.32
Scottish (433)	1,614	1.53
Serbian (0)	79	0.07
Slavic (0)	16	0.02
Slovak (186)	461	0.44
Slovene (60)	278	0.26
Soviet Union (0)	0	<0.01
Swedish (705)	3,305	3.13
Swiss (80)	453	0.43
Turkish (0)	27	0.03
Ukrainian (211)	414	0.39
Welsh (77)	675	0.64
West Indian, ex. Hispanic (0)	55	0.05
Bahamian (0)	0	<0.01
Barbadian (0)	0	<0.01
Belizean (0)	0	<0.01
Bermudan (0)	0	<0.01
British West Indian (0)	10	0.01
Dutch West Indian (0)	23	0.02
Haitian (0)	22	0.02
Jamaican (0)	0	<0.01
Trinidadian/Tobagonian (0)	0	<0.01
U.S. Virgin Islander (0)	0	<0.01
West Indian (0)	0	<0.01
Other West Indian (0)	0	<0.01
Yugoslavian (45)	302	0.29

Hispanic Origin	Population	%
Hispanic or Latino (of any race)	17,898	15.60
Central American, ex. Mexican	367	0.32
Costa Rican	13	0.01
Guatemalan	195	0.17
Honduran	30	0.03
Nicaraguan	45	0.04
Panamanian	20	0.02
Salvadoran	60	0.05
Other Central American	4	<0.01
Cuban	191	0.17
Dominican Republic	36	0.03
Mexican	14,461	12.60
Puerto Rican	1,687	1.47
South American	564	0.49
Argentinean	47	0.04
Bolivian	42	0.04
Chilean	23	0.02
Colombian	200	0.17
Ecuadorian	131	0.11
Paraguayan	7	0.01
Peruvian	65	0.06
Uruguayan	2	<0.01
Venezuelan	37	0.03
Other South American	10	0.01
Other Hispanic or Latino	592	0.52

Race*	Population	%
African-American/Black (6,585)	7,546	6.58
Not Hispanic (6,343)	7,088	6.18
Hispanic (242)	458	0.40
American Indian/Alaska Native (316)	736	0.64
Not Hispanic (129)	431	0.38
Hispanic (187)	305	0.27
Alaska Athabascan (Ala. Nat.) (0)	0	<0.01
Aleut (Alaska Native) (1)	5	<0.01
Apache (0)	6	0.01
Arapaho (0)	0	<0.01
Blackfeet (2)	16	0.01
Canadian/French Am. Ind. (1)	1	<0.01
Central American Ind. (2)	4	<0.01
Cherokee (37)	135	0.12
Cheyenne (2)	3	<0.01
Chickasaw (0)	4	<0.01
Chippewa (17)	31	0.03
Choctaw (1)	20	0.02
Colville (0)	0	<0.01

Race*	Population	%
Comanche (0)	1	<0.01
Cree (0)	5	<0.01
Creek (7)	9	0.01
Crow (0)	1	<0.01
Delaware (0)	3	<0.01
Hopi (0)	0	<0.01
Houma (1)	1	<0.01
Inupiat (Alaska Native) (0)	5	<0.01
Iroquois (3)	10	0.01
Kiowa (0)	0	<0.01
Lumbee (1)	4	<0.01
Menominee (0)	0	<0.01
Mexican American Ind. (27)	46	0.04
Navajo (1)	5	<0.01
Osage (0)	0	<0.01
Ottawa (0)	1	<0.01
Paiute (0)	0	<0.01
Pima (1)	1	<0.01
Potawatomi (0)	0	<0.01
Pueblo (0)	1	<0.01
Puget Sound Salish (0)	0	<0.01
Seminole (0)	0	<0.01
Shoshone (0)	0	<0.01
Sioux (5)	18	0.02
South American Ind. (0)	3	<0.01
Spanish American Ind. (4)	7	0.01
Tlingit-Haida (Alaska Native) (1)	1	<0.01
Tohono O'Odham (3)	3	<0.01
Tsimshian (Alaska Native) (0)	0	<0.01
Ute (0)	1	<0.01
Yakama (0)	0	<0.01
Yaqui (1)	1	<0.01
Yuman (0)	1	<0.01
Yup'ik (Alaska Native) (3)	12	0.01
Asian (3,467)	4,339	3.78
Not Hispanic (3,403)	4,163	3.63
Hispanic (64)	176	0.15
Bangladeshi (3)	3	<0.01
Bhutanese (0)	0	<0.01
Burmese (0)	3	<0.01
Cambodian (33)	42	0.04
Chinese, ex. Taiwanese (351)	474	0.41
Filipino (983)	1,296	1.13
Hmong (19)	19	0.02
Indian (1,152)	1,254	1.09
Indonesian (5)	13	0.01
Japanese (47)	176	0.15
Korean (187)	296	0.26
Laotian (64)	79	0.07
Malaysian (8)	10	<0.01
Nepalese (2)	2	<0.01
Pakistani (192)	233	0.20
Sri Lankan (6)	11	0.01
Taiwanese (15)	25	0.02
Thai (39)	56	0.05
Vietnamese (233)	297	0.26
Hawaii Native/Pacific Islander (33)	78	0.07
Not Hispanic (28)	65	0.06
Hispanic (5)	13	0.01
Fijian (0)	0	<0.01
Guamanian/Chamorro (6)	13	0.01
Marshallese (0)	0	<0.01
Native Hawaiian (4)	17	0.01
Samoan (4)	5	<0.01
Tongan (0)	0	<0.01
White (95,891)	98,329	85.70
Not Hispanic (85,156)	86,696	75.56
Hispanic (10,735)	11,633	10.14

Notes: † The Census 2010 population figure is used to calculate the percentages in the Hispanic Origin and Race categories. Ancestry percentages are based on the 2006-2010 American Community Survey population (not shown); ‡ Numbers in parentheses indicate the number of people reporting a single ancestry; * Numbers in parentheses indicate the number of persons reporting this race alone, not in combination with any other race; Please refer to the Explanation of Data for more information.

LaSalle County

Population: 113,924

Ancestry	Population	%
Afghan (0)	0	<0.01
African, Sub-Saharan (210)	239	0.21
African (210)	225	0.20
Cape Verdean (0)	0	<0.01
Ethiopian (0)	14	0.01
Ghanaian (0)	0	<0.01
Kenyan (0)	0	<0.01
Liberian (0)	0	<0.01
Nigerian (0)	0	<0.01
Senegalese (0)	0	<0.01
Sierra Leonean (0)	0	<0.01
Somalian (0)	0	<0.01
South African (0)	0	<0.01
Sudanese (0)	0	<0.01
Ugandan (0)	0	<0.01
Zimbabwean (0)	0	<0.01
Other Sub-Saharan African (0)	0	<0.01
Albanian (0)	0	<0.01
Alsatian (0)	9	0.01
American (6,821)	6,821	5.99
Arab (106)	165	0.15
Arab (7)	7	0.01
Egyptian (0)	0	<0.01
Iraqi (16)	16	0.01
Jordanian (7)	13	0.01
Lebanese (69)	116	0.10
Moroccan (0)	0	<0.01
Palestinian (0)	0	<0.01
Syrian (0)	0	<0.01
Other Arab (7)	13	0.01
Armenian (12)	57	0.05
Assyrian/Chaldean/Syriac (0)	43	0.04
Australian (0)	9	0.01
Austrian (77)	330	0.29
Basque (0)	0	<0.01
Belgian (40)	277	0.24
Brazilian (13)	19	0.02
British (109)	244	0.21
Bulgarian (0)	12	0.01
Cajun (0)	0	<0.01
Canadian (35)	82	0.07
Carpatho Rusyn (0)	0	<0.01
Celtic (0)	3	<0.01
Croatian (148)	344	0.30
Cypriot (14)	14	0.01
Czech (199)	998	0.88
Czechoslovakian (92)	342	0.30
Danish (178)	593	0.52
Dutch (407)	2,767	2.43
Eastern European (103)	114	0.10
English (2,772)	11,101	9.76
Estonian (24)	24	0.02
European (653)	721	0.63
Finnish (25)	88	0.08
French, ex. Basque (443)	3,709	3.26
French Canadian (44)	347	0.30
German (10,678)	38,302	33.66
German Russian (0)	0	<0.01
Greek (123)	466	0.41
Guyanese (0)	0	<0.01
Hungarian (62)	301	0.26
Icelander (0)	0	<0.01
Iranian (4)	4	<0.01
Irish (4,682)	21,580	18.96
Israeli (0)	0	<0.01
Italian (3,817)	10,510	9.24
Latvian (0)	7	0.01
Lithuanian (234)	832	0.73
Luxemburger (0)	36	0.03
Macedonian (0)	0	<0.01
Maltese (0)	0	<0.01
New Zealander (0)	0	<0.01
Northern European (9)	9	0.01
Norwegian (2,193)	6,243	5.49
Pennsylvania German (59)	118	0.10

Ancestry	Population	%
Polish (2,655)	8,925	7.84
Portuguese (13)	167	0.15
Romanian (154)	332	0.29
Russian (77)	386	0.34
Scandinavian (112)	202	0.18
Scotch-Irish (407)	1,811	1.59
Scottish (477)	1,880	1.65
Serbian (6)	6	0.01
Slavic (18)	191	0.17
Slovak (968)	3,186	2.80
Slovene (198)	525	0.46
Soviet Union (0)	0	<0.01
Swedish (477)	3,216	2.83
Swiss (32)	275	0.24
Turkish (25)	25	0.02
Ukrainian (60)	195	0.17
Welsh (124)	556	0.49
West Indian, ex. Hispanic (0)	10	0.01
Bahamian (0)	10	0.01
Barbadian (0)	0	<0.01
Belizean (0)	0	<0.01
Bermudan (0)	0	<0.01
British West Indian (0)	0	<0.01
Dutch West Indian (0)	0	<0.01
Haitian (0)	0	<0.01
Jamaican (0)	0	<0.01
Trinidadian/Tobagonian (0)	0	<0.01
U.S. Virgin Islander (0)	0	<0.01
West Indian (0)	0	<0.01
Other West Indian (0)	0	<0.01
Yugoslavian (37)	208	0.18

Hispanic Origin	Population	%
Hispanic or Latino (of any race)	9,135	8.02
Central American, ex. Mexican	94	0.08
Costa Rican	7	0.01
Guatemalan	54	0.05
Honduran	13	0.01
Nicaraguan	1	<0.01
Panamanian	2	<0.01
Salvadoran	16	0.01
Other Central American	1	<0.01
Cuban	31	0.03
Dominican Republic	5	<0.01
Mexican	7,883	6.92
Puerto Rican	533	0.47
South American	82	0.07
Argentinean	10	0.01
Bolivian	6	0.01
Chilean	6	0.01
Colombian	47	0.04
Ecuadorian	2	<0.01
Paraguayan	0	<0.01
Peruvian	4	<0.01
Uruguayan	0	<0.01
Venezuelan	7	0.01
Other South American	0	<0.01
Other Hispanic or Latino	507	0.45

Race*	Population	%
African-American/Black (2,186)	2,789	2.45
Not Hispanic (2,104)	2,635	2.31
Hispanic (82)	154	0.14
American Indian/Alaska Native (289)	730	0.64
Not Hispanic (200)	568	0.50
Hispanic (89)	162	0.14
Alaska Athabascan (Ala. Nat.) (0)	0	<0.01
Aleut (Alaska Native) (1)	1	<0.01
Apache (4)	16	0.01
Arapaho (0)	0	<0.01
Blackfeet (7)	26	0.02
Canadian/French Am. Ind. (0)	5	<0.01
Central American Ind. (0)	0	<0.01
Cherokee (55)	176	0.15
Cheyenne (1)	1	<0.01
Chickasaw (3)	5	<0.01
Chippewa (7)	16	0.01
Choctaw (4)	14	0.01
Colville (0)	0	<0.01

Race*	Population	%
Comanche (0)	0	<0.01
Cree (0)	0	<0.01
Creek (2)	4	<0.01
Crow (0)	0	<0.01
Delaware (3)	3	<0.01
Hopi (0)	0	<0.01
Houma (0)	0	<0.01
Inupiat (Alaska Native) (2)	4	<0.01
Iroquois (3)	11	0.01
Kiowa (0)	0	<0.01
Lumbee (0)	0	<0.01
Menominee (0)	0	<0.01
Mexican American Ind. (14)	30	0.03
Navajo (4)	6	0.01
Osage (1)	1	<0.01
Ottawa (0)	1	<0.01
Paiute (1)	1	<0.01
Pima (2)	3	<0.01
Potawatomi (3)	11	0.01
Pueblo (4)	5	<0.01
Puget Sound Salish (0)	0	<0.01
Seminole (2)	2	<0.01
Shoshone (0)	0	<0.01
Sioux (28)	37	0.03
South American Ind. (0)	0	<0.01
Spanish American Ind. (4)	4	<0.01
Tlingit-Haida (Alaska Native) (4)	4	<0.01
Tohono O'Odham (1)	3	<0.01
Tsimshian (Alaska Native) (0)	0	<0.01
Ute (0)	1	<0.01
Yakama (0)	0	<0.01
Yaqui (0)	1	<0.01
Yuman (0)	0	<0.01
Yup'ik (Alaska Native) (1)	3	<0.01
Asian (762)	1,035	0.91
Not Hispanic (755)	993	0.87
Hispanic (7)	42	0.04
Bangladeshi (5)	5	<0.01
Bhutanese (0)	0	<0.01
Burmese (0)	0	<0.01
Cambodian (13)	16	0.01
Chinese, ex. Taiwanese (140)	165	0.14
Filipino (169)	284	0.25
Hmong (0)	0	<0.01
Indian (150)	171	0.15
Indonesian (0)	7	0.01
Japanese (55)	95	0.08
Korean (56)	93	0.08
Laotian (18)	25	0.02
Malaysian (0)	0	<0.01
Nepalese (0)	0	<0.01
Pakistani (20)	20	0.02
Sri Lankan (0)	0	<0.01
Taiwanese (4)	5	<0.01
Thai (29)	40	0.04
Vietnamese (70)	86	0.08
Hawaii Native/Pacific Islander (16)	54	0.05
Not Hispanic (13)	43	0.04
Hispanic (3)	11	0.01
Fijian (0)	0	<0.01
Guamanian/Chamorro (4)	8	0.01
Marshallese (0)	0	<0.01
Native Hawaiian (8)	29	0.03
Samoan (1)	4	<0.01
Tongan (1)	1	<0.01
White (106,187)	107,771	94.60
Not Hispanic (100,545)	101,646	89.22
Hispanic (5,642)	6,125	5.38

*Notes: † The Census 2010 population figure is used to calculate the percentages in the Hispanic Origin and Race categories. Ancestry percentages are based on the 2006-2010 American Community Survey population (not shown); ‡ Numbers in parentheses indicate the number of people reporting a single ancestry; * Numbers in parentheses indicate the number of persons reporting this race alone, not in combination with any other race; Please refer to the Explanation of Data for more information.*

Lake County

Population: 703,462

Ancestry	Population	%
Afghan (0)	0	<0.01
African, Sub-Saharan (1,418)	2,058	0.30
African (1,053)	1,622	0.23
Cape Verdean (0)	0	<0.01
Ethiopian (42)	42	0.01
Ghanaian (27)	27	<0.01
Kenyan (5)	5	<0.01
Liberian (0)	0	<0.01
Nigerian (112)	157	0.02
Senegalese (0)	0	<0.01
Sierra Leonean (0)	0	<0.01
Somalian (13)	13	<0.01
South African (110)	136	0.02
Sudanese (0)	0	<0.01
Ugandan (0)	0	<0.01
Zimbabwean (0)	0	<0.01
Other Sub-Saharan African (56)	56	0.01
Albanian (40)	94	0.01
Alsatian (0)	11	<0.01
American (27,837)	27,837	3.99
Arab (1,407)	2,167	0.31
Arab (211)	272	0.04
Egyptian (272)	299	0.04
Iraqi (152)	152	0.02
Jordanian (99)	99	0.01
Lebanese (98)	424	0.06
Moroccan (91)	121	0.02
Palestinian (161)	190	0.03
Syrian (156)	394	0.06
Other Arab (167)	216	0.03
Armenian (694)	1,229	0.18
Assyrian/Chaldean/Syriac (165)	455	0.07
Australian (111)	171	0.02
Austrian (729)	3,560	0.51
Basque (17)	76	0.01
Belgian (566)	2,038	0.29
Brazilian (217)	289	0.04
British (952)	2,575	0.37
Bulgarian (828)	929	0.13
Cajun (0)	0	<0.01
Canadian (477)	1,280	0.18
Carpatho Rusyn (0)	0	<0.01
Celtic (20)	77	0.01
Croatian (1,008)	2,707	0.39
Cypriot (8)	8	<0.01
Czech (1,814)	6,920	0.99
Czechoslovakian (390)	860	0.12
Danish (1,029)	5,382	0.77
Dutch (1,510)	9,046	1.30
Eastern European (3,422)	3,691	0.53
English (9,665)	45,343	6.50
Estonian (23)	78	0.01
European (7,372)	8,139	1.17
Finnish (1,457)	3,997	0.57
French, ex. Basque (1,399)	13,610	1.95
French Canadian (777)	2,837	0.41
German (37,407)	142,717	20.47
German Russian (43)	55	0.01
Greek (3,942)	7,647	1.10
Guyanese (0)	50	0.01
Hungarian (1,178)	4,636	0.66
Icelander (36)	126	0.02
Iranian (748)	920	0.13
Irish (19,599)	89,892	12.89
Israeli (354)	520	0.07
Italian (16,462)	48,323	6.93
Latvian (553)	971	0.14
Lithuanian (1,718)	5,442	0.78
Luxemburger (112)	563	0.08
Macedonian (51)	87	0.01
Maltese (40)	65	0.01
New Zealander (30)	30	<0.01
Northern European (438)	512	0.07
Norwegian (3,232)	14,053	2.02
Pennsylvania German (53)	119	0.02

	Population	%
Polish (23,954)	65,403	9.38
Portuguese (101)	754	0.11
Romanian (1,848)	3,416	0.49
Russian (13,790)	26,710	3.83
Scandinavian (655)	1,392	0.20
Scotch-Irish (2,548)	7,975	1.14
Scottish (2,553)	10,760	1.54
Serbian (1,351)	1,782	0.26
Slavic (124)	524	0.08
Slovak (587)	2,335	0.33
Slovene (566)	1,637	0.23
Soviet Union (10)	10	<0.01
Swedish (4,046)	20,711	2.97
Swiss (393)	2,317	0.33
Turkish (413)	691	0.10
Ukrainian (3,215)	4,695	0.67
Welsh (438)	3,046	0.44
West Indian, ex. Hispanic (2,542)	3,129	0.45
Bahamian (0)	0	<0.01
Barbadian (0)	0	<0.01
Belizean (896)	1,146	0.16
Bermudan (0)	0	<0.01
British West Indian (85)	85	0.01
Dutch West Indian (6)	6	<0.01
Haitian (216)	254	0.04
Jamaican (1,247)	1,509	0.22
Trinidadian/Tobagonian (14)	14	<0.01
U.S. Virgin Islander (0)	0	<0.01
West Indian (78)	115	0.02
Other West Indian (0)	0	<0.01
Yugoslavian (433)	1,038	0.15

Hispanic Origin	Population	%
Hispanic or Latino (of any race)	139,987	19.90
Central American, ex. Mexican	7,674	1.09
Costa Rican	96	0.01
Guatemalan	1,647	0.23
Honduran	3,313	0.47
Nicaraguan	203	0.03
Panamanian	232	0.03
Salvadoran	2,081	0.30
Other Central American	102	0.01
Cuban	1,324	0.19
Dominican Republic	393	0.06
Mexican	111,952	15.91
Puerto Rican	9,510	1.35
South American	3,931	0.56
Argentinean	347	0.05
Bolivian	142	0.02
Chilean	174	0.02
Colombian	1,793	0.25
Ecuadorian	546	0.08
Paraguayan	32	<0.01
Peruvian	619	0.09
Uruguayan	42	0.01
Venezuelan	208	0.03
Other South American	28	<0.01
Other Hispanic or Latino	5,203	0.74

Race*	Population	%
African-American/Black (49,033)	54,533	7.75
Not Hispanic (46,989)	51,155	7.27
Hispanic (2,044)	3,378	0.48
American Indian/Alaska Native (3,279)	6,334	0.90
Not Hispanic (1,058)	3,091	0.44
Hispanic (2,221)	3,243	0.46
Alaska Athabascan (Ala. Nat.) (2)	3	<0.01
Aleut (Alaska Native) (3)	10	<0.01
Apache (42)	108	0.02
Arapaho (1)	4	<0.01
Blackfeet (24)	124	0.02
Canadian/French Am. Ind. (8)	21	<0.01
Central American Ind. (21)	35	<0.01
Cherokee (161)	861	0.12
Cheyenne (3)	16	<0.01
Chickasaw (5)	25	<0.01
Chippewa (126)	260	0.04
Choctaw (37)	126	0.02
Colville (0)	0	<0.01

	Population	%
Comanche (3)	16	<0.01
Cree (7)	10	<0.01
Creek (17)	43	0.01
Crow (3)	9	<0.01
Delaware (4)	10	<0.01
Hopi (5)	9	<0.01
Houma (1)	1	<0.01
Inupiat (Alaska Native) (3)	9	<0.01
Iroquois (29)	69	0.01
Kiowa (6)	8	<0.01
Lumbee (9)	17	<0.01
Menominee (22)	38	0.01
Mexican American Ind. (434)	574	0.08
Navajo (43)	71	0.01
Osage (4)	9	<0.01
Ottawa (5)	11	<0.01
Paiute (0)	2	<0.01
Pima (1)	4	<0.01
Potawatomi (14)	23	<0.01
Pueblo (7)	13	<0.01
Puget Sound Salish (1)	3	<0.01
Seminole (0)	18	<0.01
Shoshone (2)	6	<0.01
Sioux (34)	120	0.02
South American Ind. (42)	86	0.01
Spanish American Ind. (54)	63	0.01
Tlingit-Haida (Alaska Native) (3)	4	<0.01
Tohono O'Odham (3)	4	<0.01
Tsimshian (Alaska Native) (1)	1	<0.01
Ute (3)	10	<0.01
Yakama (1)	1	<0.01
Yaqui (10)	14	<0.01
Yuman (0)	1	<0.01
Yup'ik (Alaska Native) (1)	3	<0.01
Asian (44,358)	50,622	7.20
Not Hispanic (43,954)	49,433	7.03
Hispanic (404)	1,189	0.17
Bangladeshi (103)	114	0.02
Bhutanese (0)	0	<0.01
Burmese (38)	43	0.01
Cambodian (404)	481	0.07
Chinese, ex. Taiwanese (7,692)	8,948	1.27
Filipino (10,565)	12,928	1.84
Hmong (71)	83	0.01
Indian (12,660)	13,629	1.94
Indonesian (63)	107	0.02
Japanese (1,496)	2,487	0.35
Korean (7,334)	8,102	1.15
Laotian (50)	76	0.01
Malaysian (52)	83	0.01
Nepalese (49)	53	0.01
Pakistani (1,022)	1,157	0.16
Sri Lankan (94)	113	0.02
Taiwanese (333)	418	0.06
Thai (303)	459	0.07
Vietnamese (857)	1,112	0.16
Hawaii Native/Pacific Islander (294)	1,056	0.15
Not Hispanic (228)	838	0.12
Hispanic (66)	218	0.03
Fijian (7)	11	<0.01
Guamanian/Chamorro (92)	166	0.02
Marshallese (1)	4	<0.01
Native Hawaiian (58)	277	0.04
Samoan (53)	123	0.02
Tongan (3)	7	<0.01
White (528,204)	543,803	77.30
Not Hispanic (458,701)	468,205	66.56
Hispanic (69,503)	75,598	10.75

Notes: † The Census 2010 population figure is used to calculate the percentages in the Hispanic Origin and Race categories. Ancestry percentages are based on the 2006-2010 American Community Survey population (not shown); ‡ Numbers in parentheses indicate the number of people reporting a single ancestry; * Numbers in parentheses indicate the number of persons reporting this race alone, not in combination with any other race; Please refer to the Explanation of Data for more information.

Macon County
Population: 110,768

Ancestry	Population	%
Afghan (0)	0	<0.01
African, Sub-Saharan (167)	191	0.17
African (145)	169	0.15
Cape Verdean (0)	0	<0.01
Ethiopian (0)	0	<0.01
Ghanaian (22)	22	0.02
Kenyan (0)	0	<0.01
Liberian (0)	0	<0.01
Nigerian (0)	0	<0.01
Senegalese (0)	0	<0.01
Sierra Leonean (0)	0	<0.01
Somalian (0)	0	<0.01
South African (0)	0	<0.01
Sudanese (0)	0	<0.01
Ugandan (0)	0	<0.01
Zimbabwean (0)	0	<0.01
Other Sub-Saharan African (0)	0	<0.01
Albanian (0)	0	<0.01
Alsatian (0)	0	<0.01
American (18,788)	18,788	16.97
Arab (192)	206	0.19
Arab (161)	161	0.15
Egyptian (11)	11	0.01
Iraqi (0)	0	<0.01
Jordanian (0)	0	<0.01
Lebanese (0)	14	0.01
Moroccan (20)	20	0.02
Palestinian (0)	0	<0.01
Syrian (0)	0	<0.01
Other Arab (0)	0	<0.01
Armenian (0)	10	0.01
Assyrian/Chaldean/Syriac (0)	0	<0.01
Australian (0)	45	0.04
Austrian (55)	188	0.17
Basque (0)	0	<0.01
Belgian (63)	144	0.13
Brazilian (0)	11	0.01
British (135)	298	0.27
Bulgarian (0)	16	0.01
Cajun (0)	0	<0.01
Canadian (59)	176	0.16
Carpatho Rusyn (0)	0	<0.01
Celtic (0)	0	<0.01
Croatian (17)	114	0.10
Cypriot (0)	0	<0.01
Czech (77)	257	0.23
Czechoslovakian (20)	25	0.02
Danish (94)	211	0.19
Dutch (372)	2,198	1.99
Eastern European (86)	86	0.08
English (4,911)	11,985	10.82
Estonian (0)	0	<0.01
European (913)	982	0.89
Finnish (6)	17	0.02
French, ex. Basque (529)	2,529	2.28
French Canadian (83)	260	0.23
German (9,631)	24,055	21.73
German Russian (0)	0	<0.01
Greek (186)	535	0.48
Guyanese (0)	0	<0.01
Hungarian (77)	333	0.30
Icelander (0)	0	<0.01
Iranian (40)	40	0.04
Irish (4,005)	14,304	12.92
Israeli (0)	3	<0.01
Italian (753)	2,611	2.36
Latvian (0)	0	<0.01
Lithuanian (31)	170	0.15
Luxemburger (0)	21	0.02
Macedonian (0)	0	<0.01
Maltese (0)	11	0.01
New Zealander (0)	0	<0.01
Northern European (9)	9	0.01
Norwegian (226)	796	0.72
Pennsylvania German (91)	105	0.09
Polish (810)	2,349	2.12
Portuguese (75)	107	0.10
Romanian (0)	8	0.01
Russian (116)	188	0.17
Scandinavian (94)	122	0.11
Scotch-Irish (864)	1,812	1.64
Scottish (696)	1,821	1.64
Serbian (9)	9	0.01
Slavic (21)	28	0.03
Slovak (22)	101	0.09
Slovene (0)	12	0.01
Soviet Union (0)	0	<0.01
Swedish (342)	1,218	1.10
Swiss (58)	225	0.20
Turkish (0)	0	<0.01
Ukrainian (23)	86	0.08
Welsh (113)	488	0.44
West Indian, ex. Hispanic (75)	100	0.09
Bahamian (0)	0	<0.01
Barbadian (0)	0	<0.01
Belizean (0)	0	<0.01
Bermudan (0)	0	<0.01
British West Indian (0)	0	<0.01
Dutch West Indian (0)	0	<0.01
Haitian (65)	65	0.06
Jamaican (10)	24	0.02
Trinidadian/Tobagonian (0)	11	0.01
U.S. Virgin Islander (0)	0	<0.01
West Indian (0)	0	<0.01
Other West Indian (0)	0	<0.01
Yugoslavian (4)	14	0.01

Hispanic Origin	Population	%
Hispanic or Latino (of any race)	2,072	1.87
Central American, ex. Mexican	96	0.09
Costa Rican	10	0.01
Guatemalan	28	0.03
Honduran	13	0.01
Nicaraguan	21	0.02
Panamanian	15	0.01
Salvadoran	7	0.01
Other Central American	2	<0.01
Cuban	75	0.07
Dominican Republic	19	0.02
Mexican	1,320	1.19
Puerto Rican	200	0.18
South American	88	0.08
Argentinean	9	0.01
Bolivian	4	<0.01
Chilean	9	0.01
Colombian	20	0.02
Ecuadorian	9	0.01
Paraguayan	0	<0.01
Peruvian	18	0.02
Uruguayan	0	<0.01
Venezuelan	19	0.02
Other South American	0	<0.01
Other Hispanic or Latino	274	0.25

Race*	Population	%
African-American/Black (18,027)	19,971	18.03
Not Hispanic (17,916)	19,755	17.83
Hispanic (111)	216	0.20
American Indian/Alaska Native (226)	792	0.72
Not Hispanic (199)	714	0.64
Hispanic (27)	78	0.07
Alaska Athabascan (Ala. Nat.) (1)	1	<0.01
Aleut (Alaska Native) (0)	3	<0.01
Apache (8)	18	0.02
Arapaho (0)	0	<0.01
Blackfeet (3)	37	0.03
Canadian/French Am. Ind. (1)	2	<0.01
Central American Ind. (0)	0	<0.01
Cherokee (33)	219	0.20
Cheyenne (0)	4	<0.01
Chickasaw (0)	3	<0.01
Chippewa (9)	14	0.01
Choctaw (7)	12	0.01
Colville (0)	0	<0.01

Comanche (0)	1	<0.01
Cree (0)	2	<0.01
Creek (1)	8	0.01
Crow (0)	0	<0.01
Delaware (0)	2	<0.01
Hopi (0)	0	<0.01
Houma (1)	1	<0.01
Inupiat (Alaska Native) (0)	0	<0.01
Iroquois (1)	7	0.01
Kiowa (0)	0	<0.01
Lumbee (0)	0	<0.01
Menominee (1)	1	<0.01
Mexican American Ind. (6)	12	0.01
Navajo (8)	17	0.02
Osage (0)	1	<0.01
Ottawa (0)	0	<0.01
Paiute (3)	7	<0.01
Pima (0)	0	<0.01
Potawatomi (4)	4	<0.01
Pueblo (0)	0	<0.01
Puget Sound Salish (1)	1	<0.01
Seminole (1)	1	<0.01
Shoshone (0)	2	<0.01
Sioux (6)	23	0.02
South American Ind. (0)	2	<0.01
Spanish American Ind. (0)	1	<0.01
Tlingit-Haida (Alaska Native) (0)	0	<0.01
Tohono O'Odham (0)	0	<0.01
Tsimshian (Alaska Native) (0)	0	<0.01
Ute (0)	0	<0.01
Yakama (0)	0	<0.01
Yaqui (0)	0	<0.01
Yuman (0)	0	<0.01
Yup'ik (Alaska Native) (0)	0	<0.01
Asian (1,118)	1,424	1.29
Not Hispanic (1,107)	1,383	1.25
Hispanic (11)	41	0.04
Bangladeshi (3)	3	<0.01
Bhutanese (0)	0	<0.01
Burmese (1)	1	<0.01
Cambodian (2)	3	<0.01
Chinese, ex. Taiwanese (152)	182	0.16
Filipino (166)	238	0.21
Hmong (0)	0	<0.01
Indian (468)	497	0.45
Indonesian (5)	17	0.02
Japanese (26)	65	0.06
Korean (84)	113	0.10
Laotian (2)	4	<0.01
Malaysian (1)	1	<0.01
Nepalese (0)	0	<0.01
Pakistani (87)	91	0.08
Sri Lankan (7)	7	0.01
Taiwanese (4)	4	<0.01
Thai (12)	17	0.02
Vietnamese (69)	94	0.08
Hawaii Native/Pacific Islander (32)	117	0.11
Not Hispanic (26)	99	0.09
Hispanic (6)	18	0.02
Fijian (0)	0	<0.01
Guamanian/Chamorro (2)	10	0.01
Marshallese (0)	0	<0.01
Native Hawaiian (11)	24	0.02
Samoan (5)	11	0.01
Tongan (0)	0	<0.01
White (87,855)	90,401	81.61
Not Hispanic (86,822)	89,148	80.48
Hispanic (1,033)	1,253	1.13

*Notes: † The Census 2010 population figure is used to calculate the percentages in the Hispanic Origin and Race categories. Ancestry percentages are based on the 2006-2010 American Community Survey population (not shown); ‡ Numbers in parentheses indicate the number of people reporting a single ancestry; * Numbers in parentheses indicate the number of persons reporting this race alone, not in combination with any other race; Please refer to the Explanation of Data for more information.*

Madison County

Population: 269,282

Ancestry	Population	%
Afghan (0)	0	<0.01
African, Sub-Saharan (701)	810	0.30
African (551)	636	0.24
Cape Verdean (0)	0	<0.01
Ethiopian (12)	12	<0.01
Ghanaian (39)	51	0.02
Kenyan (0)	0	<0.01
Liberian (0)	0	<0.01
Nigerian (75)	87	0.03
Senegalese (0)	0	<0.01
Sierra Leonean (0)	0	<0.01
Somalian (0)	0	<0.01
South African (0)	0	<0.01
Sudanese (0)	0	<0.01
Ugandan (0)	0	<0.01
Zimbabwean (0)	0	<0.01
Other Sub-Saharan African (24)	24	0.01
Albanian (0)	11	<0.01
Alsatian (0)	0	<0.01
American (20,063)	20,063	7.49
Arab (410)	444	0.17
Arab (141)	149	0.06
Egyptian (108)	108	0.04
Iraqi (0)	0	<0.01
Jordanian (23)	23	0.01
Lebanese (9)	35	0.01
Moroccan (38)	38	0.01
Palestinian (77)	77	0.03
Syrian (0)	0	<0.01
Other Arab (14)	14	0.01
Armenian (129)	255	0.10
Assyrian/Chaldean/Syriac (0)	0	<0.01
Australian (0)	77	0.03
Austrian (181)	521	0.19
Basque (0)	0	<0.01
Belgian (87)	272	0.10
Brazilian (94)	94	0.04
British (387)	749	0.28
Bulgarian (265)	510	0.19
Cajun (0)	12	<0.01
Canadian (77)	152	0.06
Carpatho Rusyn (0)	0	<0.01
Celtic (0)	4	<0.01
Croatian (530)	1,500	0.56
Cypriot (0)	0	<0.01
Czech (531)	1,724	0.64
Czechoslovakian (234)	468	0.17
Danish (106)	526	0.20
Dutch (1,047)	6,001	2.24
Eastern European (32)	87	0.03
English (9,702)	28,078	10.48
Estonian (0)	0	<0.01
European (4,016)	4,401	1.64
Finnish (56)	322	0.12
French, ex. Basque (1,781)	10,290	3.84
French Canadian (330)	607	0.23
German (40,106)	87,661	32.71
German Russian (16)	27	0.01
Greek (637)	1,383	0.52
Guyanese (0)	0	<0.01
Hungarian (501)	1,601	0.60
Icelander (0)	14	0.01
Iranian (10)	10	<0.01
Irish (10,893)	39,878	14.88
Israeli (0)	0	<0.01
Italian (5,911)	15,311	5.71
Latvian (0)	0	<0.01
Lithuanian (391)	1,069	0.40
Luxemburger (0)	0	<0.01
Macedonian (95)	238	0.09
Maltese (9)	9	<0.01
New Zealander (0)	0	<0.01
Northern European (140)	179	0.07
Norwegian (506)	1,404	0.52
Pennsylvania German (37)	63	0.02

Ancestry (cont.)	Population	%
Polish (2,922)	8,422	3.14
Portuguese (31)	147	0.05
Romanian (149)	278	0.10
Russian (523)	1,165	0.43
Scandinavian (165)	277	0.10
Scotch-Irish (1,886)	4,475	1.67
Scottish (1,026)	3,649	1.36
Serbian (10)	101	0.04
Slavic (36)	237	0.09
Slovak (162)	715	0.27
Slovene (8)	31	0.01
Soviet Union (0)	0	<0.01
Swedish (528)	2,358	0.88
Swiss (284)	1,750	0.65
Turkish (153)	206	0.08
Ukrainian (245)	464	0.17
Welsh (416)	1,891	0.71
West Indian, ex. Hispanic (24)	51	0.02
Bahamian (0)	0	<0.01
Barbadian (0)	0	<0.01
Belizean (10)	10	<0.01
Bermudan (0)	0	<0.01
British West Indian (0)	0	<0.01
Dutch West Indian (0)	0	<0.01
Haitian (0)	0	<0.01
Jamaican (14)	35	0.01
Trinidadian/Tobagonian (0)	6	<0.01
U.S. Virgin Islander (0)	0	<0.01
West Indian (0)	0	<0.01
Other West Indian (0)	0	<0.01
Yugoslavian (119)	262	0.10

Hispanic Origin	Population	%
Hispanic or Latino (of any race)	7,313	2.72
Central American, ex. Mexican	295	0.11
Costa Rican	22	0.01
Guatemalan	85	0.03
Honduran	62	0.02
Nicaraguan	22	0.01
Panamanian	69	0.03
Salvadoran	28	0.01
Other Central American	7	<0.01
Cuban	104	0.04
Dominican Republic	37	0.01
Mexican	5,335	1.98
Puerto Rican	445	0.17
South American	200	0.07
Argentinean	16	0.01
Bolivian	5	<0.01
Chilean	23	0.01
Colombian	61	0.02
Ecuadorian	20	0.01
Paraguayan	0	<0.01
Peruvian	46	0.02
Uruguayan	0	<0.01
Venezuelan	28	0.01
Other South American	1	<0.01
Other Hispanic or Latino	897	0.33

Race*	Population	%
African-American/Black (21,235)	23,799	8.84
Not Hispanic (21,066)	23,491	8.72
Hispanic (169)	308	0.11
American Indian/Alaska Native (659)	2,031	0.75
Not Hispanic (556)	1,815	0.67
Hispanic (103)	216	0.08
Alaska Athabascan (Ala. Nat.) (0)	1	<0.01
Aleut (Alaska Native) (1)	3	<0.01
Apache (8)	31	0.01
Arapaho (2)	7	<0.01
Blackfeet (15)	101	0.04
Canadian/French Am. Ind. (3)	10	<0.01
Central American Ind. (0)	2	<0.01
Cherokee (180)	703	0.26
Cheyenne (4)	9	<0.01
Chickasaw (5)	13	<0.01
Chippewa (24)	44	0.02
Choctaw (20)	74	0.03
Colville (0)	0	<0.01

Race* (cont.)	Population	%
Comanche (3)	5	<0.01
Cree (2)	2	<0.01
Creek (11)	22	0.01
Crow (0)	3	<0.01
Delaware (1)	6	<0.01
Hopi (1)	4	<0.01
Houma (0)	0	<0.01
Inupiat (Alaska Native) (1)	2	<0.01
Iroquois (3)	12	<0.01
Kiowa (6)	6	<0.01
Lumbee (2)	11	<0.01
Menominee (8)	9	<0.01
Mexican American Ind. (30)	40	0.01
Navajo (7)	20	0.01
Osage (1)	3	<0.01
Ottawa (0)	1	<0.01
Paiute (3)	3	<0.01
Pima (0)	0	<0.01
Potawatomi (3)	10	<0.01
Pueblo (0)	1	<0.01
Puget Sound Salish (5)	6	<0.01
Seminole (2)	14	0.01
Shoshone (2)	9	<0.01
Sioux (34)	80	0.03
South American Ind. (2)	3	<0.01
Spanish American Ind. (2)	5	<0.01
Tlingit-Haida (Alaska Native) (0)	0	<0.01
Tohono O'Odham (0)	0	<0.01
Tsimshian (Alaska Native) (0)	0	<0.01
Ute (0)	0	<0.01
Yakama (0)	0	<0.01
Yaqui (1)	6	<0.01
Yuman (0)	0	<0.01
Yup'ik (Alaska Native) (0)	0	<0.01
Asian (2,254)	3,216	1.19
Not Hispanic (2,211)	3,103	1.15
Hispanic (43)	113	0.04
Bangladeshi (9)	11	<0.01
Bhutanese (0)	0	<0.01
Burmese (11)	16	0.01
Cambodian (2)	4	<0.01
Chinese, ex. Taiwanese (401)	515	0.19
Filipino (332)	626	0.23
Hmong (0)	0	<0.01
Indian (529)	636	0.24
Indonesian (4)	12	<0.01
Japanese (128)	299	0.11
Korean (340)	483	0.18
Laotian (27)	52	0.02
Malaysian (1)	4	<0.01
Nepalese (33)	38	0.01
Pakistani (68)	77	0.03
Sri Lankan (5)	5	<0.01
Taiwanese (36)	42	0.02
Thai (83)	122	0.05
Vietnamese (123)	152	0.06
Hawaii Native/Pacific Islander (107)	253	0.09
Not Hispanic (92)	216	0.08
Hispanic (15)	37	0.01
Fijian (1)	4	<0.01
Guamanian/Chamorro (25)	40	0.01
Marshallese (0)	0	<0.01
Native Hawaiian (48)	102	0.04
Samoan (9)	29	0.01
Tongan (0)	0	<0.01
White (237,641)	242,239	89.96
Not Hispanic (233,515)	237,577	88.23
Hispanic (4,126)	4,662	1.73

Notes: † The Census 2010 population figure is used to calculate the percentages in the Hispanic Origin and Race categories. Ancestry percentages are based on the 2006-2010 American Community Survey population (not shown); ‡ Numbers in parentheses indicate the number of people reporting a single ancestry; * Numbers in parentheses indicate the number of persons reporting this race alone, not in combination with any other race; Please refer to the Explanation of Data for more information.

McHenry County
Population: 308,760

Ancestry	Population	%
Afghan (0)	0	<0.01
African, Sub-Saharan (721)	920	0.30
African (265)	421	0.14
Cape Verdean (0)	0	<0.01
Ethiopian (0)	0	<0.01
Ghanaian (0)	0	<0.01
Kenyan (0)	0	<0.01
Liberian (0)	0	<0.01
Nigerian (444)	444	0.15
Senegalese (0)	0	<0.01
Sierra Leonean (0)	0	<0.01
Somalian (0)	0	<0.01
South African (12)	40	0.01
Sudanese (0)	0	<0.01
Ugandan (0)	0	<0.01
Zimbabwean (0)	0	<0.01
Other Sub-Saharan African (0)	15	<0.01
Albanian (33)	33	0.01
Alsatian (18)	62	0.02
American (11,233)	11,233	3.67
Arab (272)	506	0.17
Arab (67)	107	0.03
Egyptian (9)	9	<0.01
Iraqi (0)	0	<0.01
Jordanian (0)	56	0.02
Lebanese (62)	173	0.06
Moroccan (5)	8	<0.01
Palestinian (22)	29	0.01
Syrian (0)	17	0.01
Other Arab (107)	107	0.03
Armenian (47)	243	0.08
Assyrian/Chaldean/Syriac (131)	234	0.08
Australian (8)	53	0.02
Austrian (396)	1,926	0.63
Basque (0)	25	0.01
Belgian (201)	754	0.25
Brazilian (147)	221	0.07
British (483)	939	0.31
Bulgarian (6)	78	0.03
Cajun (26)	60	0.02
Canadian (398)	753	0.25
Carpatho Rusyn (0)	0	<0.01
Celtic (0)	0	<0.01
Croatian (241)	1,180	0.39
Cypriot (0)	0	<0.01
Czech (1,204)	5,622	1.84
Czechoslovakian (274)	642	0.21
Danish (514)	2,359	0.77
Dutch (1,273)	5,999	1.96
Eastern European (313)	423	0.14
English (5,213)	23,733	7.75
Estonian (29)	51	0.02
European (2,579)	2,998	0.98
Finnish (75)	709	0.23
French, ex. Basque (542)	8,269	2.70
French Canadian (435)	1,715	0.56
German (30,738)	105,348	34.42
German Russian (0)	0	<0.01
Greek (705)	2,415	0.79
Guyanese (0)	0	<0.01
Hungarian (449)	2,489	0.81
Icelander (16)	42	0.01
Iranian (54)	66	0.02
Irish (11,180)	57,350	18.74
Israeli (10)	26	0.01
Italian (9,829)	32,920	10.76
Latvian (65)	113	0.04
Lithuanian (507)	2,316	0.76
Luxemburger (42)	213	0.07
Macedonian (0)	42	0.01
Maltese (0)	0	<0.01
New Zealander (0)	0	<0.01
Northern European (128)	128	0.04
Norwegian (2,338)	10,035	3.28
Pennsylvania German (23)	74	0.02

Ancestry	Population	%
Polish (13,693)	43,429	14.19
Portuguese (43)	403	0.13
Romanian (766)	1,079	0.35
Russian (1,035)	3,456	1.13
Scandinavian (547)	1,070	0.35
Scotch-Irish (1,288)	4,074	1.33
Scottish (1,126)	5,010	1.64
Serbian (87)	390	0.13
Slavic (18)	49	0.02
Slovak (271)	745	0.24
Slovene (125)	316	0.10
Soviet Union (0)	0	<0.01
Swedish (2,658)	13,397	4.38
Swiss (245)	919	0.30
Turkish (23)	26	0.01
Ukrainian (474)	1,511	0.49
Welsh (188)	1,494	0.49
West Indian, ex. Hispanic (98)	179	0.06
Bahamian (0)	0	<0.01
Barbadian (15)	40	0.01
Belizean (18)	25	0.01
Bermudan (0)	0	<0.01
British West Indian (0)	14	<0.01
Dutch West Indian (0)	0	<0.01
Haitian (27)	38	0.01
Jamaican (15)	22	0.01
Trinidadian/Tobagonian (0)	0	<0.01
U.S. Virgin Islander (14)	14	<0.01
West Indian (9)	26	0.01
Other West Indian (0)	0	<0.01
Yugoslavian (372)	729	0.24

Hispanic Origin	Population	%
Hispanic or Latino (of any race)	35,249	11.42
Central American, ex. Mexican	931	0.30
Costa Rican	54	0.02
Guatemalan	415	0.13
Honduran	136	0.04
Nicaraguan	41	0.01
Panamanian	46	0.01
Salvadoran	237	0.08
Other Central American	2	<0.01
Cuban	439	0.14
Dominican Republic	61	0.02
Mexican	28,796	9.33
Puerto Rican	2,156	0.70
South American	1,204	0.39
Argentinean	82	0.03
Bolivian	50	0.02
Chilean	70	0.02
Colombian	395	0.13
Ecuadorian	223	0.07
Paraguayan	6	<0.01
Peruvian	267	0.09
Uruguayan	2	<0.01
Venezuelan	93	0.03
Other South American	16	0.01
Other Hispanic or Latino	1,662	0.54

Race*	Population	%
African-American/Black (3,283)	4,579	1.48
Not Hispanic (3,045)	4,111	1.33
Hispanic (238)	468	0.15
American Indian/Alaska Native (939)	2,095	0.68
Not Hispanic (455)	1,338	0.43
Hispanic (484)	757	0.25
Alaska Athabascan (Ala. Nat.) (1)	1	<0.01
Aleut (Alaska Native) (3)	3	<0.01
Apache (19)	33	0.01
Arapaho (0)	3	<0.01
Blackfeet (7)	57	0.02
Canadian/French Am. Ind. (3)	6	<0.01
Central American Ind. (4)	4	<0.01
Cherokee (75)	380	0.12
Cheyenne (4)	9	<0.01
Chickasaw (2)	4	<0.01
Chippewa (85)	158	0.05
Choctaw (5)	14	<0.01
Colville (0)	0	<0.01

Race*	Population	%
Comanche (1)	6	<0.0
Cree (1)	3	<0.0
Creek (1)	6	<0.0
Crow (0)	1	<0.0
Delaware (0)	8	<0.0
Hopi (0)	0	<0.0
Houma (1)	2	<0.0
Inupiat (Alaska Native) (1)	7	<0.0
Iroquois (18)	44	0.0
Kiowa (0)	0	<0.0
Lumbee (5)	6	<0.0
Menominee (6)	20	0.0
Mexican American Ind. (72)	116	0.0
Navajo (10)	29	0.0
Osage (1)	2	<0.0
Ottawa (12)	14	<0.0
Paiute (0)	0	<0.0
Pima (0)	0	<0.0
Potawatomi (14)	39	0.0
Pueblo (4)	8	<0.0
Puget Sound Salish (1)	1	<0.0
Seminole (1)	7	<0.0
Shoshone (1)	7	<0.0
Sioux (32)	69	0.0
South American Ind. (15)	25	0.0
Spanish American Ind. (0)	1	<0.0
Tlingit-Haida (Alaska Native) (0)	1	<0.0
Tohono O'Odham (0)	1	<0.0
Tsimshian (Alaska Native) (0)	0	<0.0
Ute (0)	0	<0.0
Yakama (0)	0	<0.0
Yaqui (0)	3	<0.0
Yuman (0)	0	<0.0
Yup'ik (Alaska Native) (0)	0	<0.0
Asian (7,807)	9,552	3.0
Not Hispanic (7,712)	9,319	3.0
Hispanic (95)	233	0.0
Bangladeshi (22)	33	0.0
Bhutanese (0)	0	<0.0
Burmese (11)	12	<0.0
Cambodian (17)	29	0.0
Chinese, ex. Taiwanese (851)	1,144	0.3
Filipino (2,215)	2,849	0.9
Hmong (5)	7	<0.0
Indian (2,517)	2,741	0.8
Indonesian (20)	40	0.0
Japanese (219)	496	0.1
Korean (674)	876	0.2
Laotian (120)	148	0.0
Malaysian (14)	17	0.0
Nepalese (3)	5	<0.0
Pakistani (358)	415	0.1
Sri Lankan (20)	23	0.0
Taiwanese (37)	42	0.0
Thai (110)	170	0.0
Vietnamese (319)	373	0.1
Hawaii Native/Pacific Islander (80)	244	0.0
Not Hispanic (68)	192	0.0
Hispanic (12)	52	0.0
Fijian (1)	1	<0.0
Guamanian/Chamorro (23)	47	0.0
Marshallese (0)	0	<0.0
Native Hawaiian (27)	85	0.0
Samoan (7)	19	0.0
Tongan (0)	0	<0.0
White (278,257)	283,049	91.6
Not Hispanic (258,584)	261,775	84.7
Hispanic (19,673)	21,274	6.8

*Notes: † The Census 2010 population figure is used to calculate the percentages in the Hispanic Origin and Race categories. Ancestry percentages are based on the 2006-2010 American Communi Survey population (not shown); ‡ Numbers in parentheses indicate the number of people reporting a single ancestry; * Numbers in parentheses indicate the number of persons reporting this race alo not in combination with any other race; Please refer to the Explanation of Data for more information.*

McLean County
Population: 169,572

Ancestry	Population	%
Afghan (0)	0	<0.01
African, Sub-Saharan (661)	753	0.45
African (423)	472	0.28
Cape Verdean (0)	0	<0.01
Ethiopian (41)	64	0.04
Ghanaian (18)	18	0.01
Kenyan (10)	10	0.01
Liberian (0)	0	<0.01
Nigerian (78)	78	0.05
Senegalese (0)	0	<0.01
Sierra Leonean (0)	0	<0.01
Somalian (0)	0	<0.01
South African (0)	9	0.01
Sudanese (0)	0	<0.01
Ugandan (0)	0	<0.01
Zimbabwean (0)	0	<0.01
Other Sub-Saharan African (91)	102	0.06
Albanian (61)	61	0.04
Alsatian (0)	33	0.02
American (18,928)	18,928	11.35
Arab (52)	316	0.19
Arab (11)	22	0.01
Egyptian (0)	0	<0.01
Iraqi (0)	0	<0.01
Jordanian (0)	0	<0.01
Lebanese (41)	171	0.10
Moroccan (0)	0	<0.01
Palestinian (0)	8	<0.01
Syrian (0)	83	0.05
Other Arab (0)	32	0.02
Armenian (27)	58	0.03
Assyrian/Chaldean/Syriac (0)	0	<0.01
Australian (12)	18	0.01
Austrian (36)	336	0.20
Basque (0)	0	<0.01
Belgian (83)	409	0.25
Brazilian (0)	13	0.01
British (214)	671	0.40
Bulgarian (14)	14	0.01
Cajun (0)	0	<0.01
Canadian (42)	162	0.10
Carpatho Rusyn (0)	0	<0.01
Celtic (15)	15	0.01
Croatian (53)	354	0.21
Cypriot (0)	0	<0.01
Czech (207)	1,033	0.62
Czechoslovakian (78)	165	0.10
Danish (134)	714	0.43
Dutch (675)	2,954	1.77
Eastern European (96)	103	0.06
English (6,135)	18,293	10.97
Estonian (12)	12	0.01
European (1,721)	1,902	1.14
Finnish (20)	170	0.10
French, ex. Basque (621)	4,264	2.56
French Canadian (135)	389	0.23
German (20,761)	52,068	31.23
German Russian (0)	11	0.01
Greek (229)	514	0.31
Guyanese (0)	0	<0.01
Hungarian (214)	661	0.40
Icelander (0)	0	<0.01
Iranian (48)	48	0.03
Irish (6,935)	25,700	15.42
Israeli (5)	40	0.02
Italian (1,748)	7,045	4.23
Latvian (16)	45	0.03
Lithuanian (80)	364	0.22
Luxemburger (0)	11	0.01
Macedonian (0)	9	0.01
Maltese (0)	0	<0.01
New Zealander (0)	0	<0.01
Northern European (66)	66	0.04
Norwegian (893)	2,746	1.65
Pennsylvania German (14)	104	0.06

	Population	%
Polish (1,464)	5,867	3.52
Portuguese (30)	147	0.09
Romanian (61)	131	0.08
Russian (188)	571	0.34
Scandinavian (68)	164	0.10
Scotch-Irish (1,175)	3,149	1.89
Scottish (980)	3,349	2.01
Serbian (0)	0	<0.01
Slavic (3)	36	0.02
Slovak (152)	611	0.37
Slovene (15)	164	0.10
Soviet Union (0)	0	<0.01
Swedish (1,126)	3,820	2.29
Swiss (162)	1,197	0.72
Turkish (83)	152	0.09
Ukrainian (192)	327	0.20
Welsh (408)	1,248	0.75
West Indian, ex. Hispanic (81)	111	0.07
Bahamian (0)	0	<0.01
Barbadian (13)	13	0.01
Belizean (0)	14	0.01
Bermudan (0)	0	<0.01
British West Indian (11)	11	0.01
Dutch West Indian (11)	11	0.01
Haitian (10)	17	0.01
Jamaican (8)	17	0.01
Trinidadian/Tobagonian (0)	0	<0.01
U.S. Virgin Islander (13)	13	0.01
West Indian (15)	15	0.01
Other West Indian (0)	0	<0.01
Yugoslavian (3)	18	0.01

Hispanic Origin	Population	%
Hispanic or Latino (of any race)	7,434	4.38
Central American, ex. Mexican	562	0.33
Costa Rican	12	0.01
Guatemalan	374	0.22
Honduran	52	0.03
Nicaraguan	7	<0.01
Panamanian	29	0.02
Salvadoran	87	0.05
Other Central American	1	<0.01
Cuban	155	0.09
Dominican Republic	37	0.02
Mexican	5,253	3.10
Puerto Rican	559	0.33
South American	330	0.19
Argentinean	24	0.01
Bolivian	17	0.01
Chilean	45	0.03
Colombian	122	0.07
Ecuadorian	28	0.02
Paraguayan	10	0.01
Peruvian	57	0.03
Uruguayan	1	<0.01
Venezuelan	26	0.02
Other South American	0	<0.01
Other Hispanic or Latino	538	0.32

Race*	Population	%
African-American/Black (12,426)	14,531	8.57
Not Hispanic (12,246)	14,170	8.36
Hispanic (180)	361	0.21
American Indian/Alaska Native (383)	1,150	0.68
Not Hispanic (290)	952	0.56
Hispanic (93)	198	0.12
Alaska Athabascan (Ala. Nat.) (0)	0	<0.01
Aleut (Alaska Native) (3)	3	<0.01
Apache (8)	25	0.01
Arapaho (0)	0	<0.01
Blackfeet (3)	33	0.02
Canadian/French Am. Ind. (4)	4	<0.01
Central American Ind. (1)	6	<0.01
Cherokee (64)	305	0.18
Cheyenne (0)	9	0.01
Chickasaw (2)	6	<0.01
Chippewa (12)	29	0.02
Choctaw (9)	38	0.02
Colville (1)	1	<0.01

	Population	%
Comanche (1)	4	<0.01
Cree (2)	3	<0.01
Creek (3)	13	0.01
Crow (0)	0	<0.01
Delaware (0)	0	<0.01
Hopi (0)	1	<0.01
Houma (0)	0	<0.01
Inupiat (Alaska Native) (2)	2	<0.01
Iroquois (3)	12	0.01
Kiowa (0)	0	<0.01
Lumbee (0)	0	<0.01
Menominee (0)	0	<0.01
Mexican American Ind. (25)	42	0.02
Navajo (2)	6	<0.01
Osage (0)	5	<0.01
Ottawa (0)	0	<0.01
Paiute (0)	0	<0.01
Pima (0)	0	<0.01
Potawatomi (12)	20	0.01
Pueblo (0)	1	<0.01
Puget Sound Salish (1)	1	<0.01
Seminole (1)	9	0.01
Shoshone (0)	3	<0.01
Sioux (15)	42	0.02
South American Ind. (3)	7	<0.01
Spanish American Ind. (0)	0	<0.01
Tlingit-Haida (Alaska Native) (0)	0	<0.01
Tohono O'Odham (1)	1	<0.01
Tsimshian (Alaska Native) (0)	0	<0.01
Ute (0)	0	<0.01
Yakama (1)	1	<0.01
Yaqui (1)	1	<0.01
Yuman (0)	1	<0.01
Yup'ik (Alaska Native) (1)	1	<0.01
Asian (7,227)	8,232	4.85
Not Hispanic (7,180)	8,111	4.78
Hispanic (47)	121	0.07
Bangladeshi (21)	22	0.01
Bhutanese (0)	0	<0.01
Burmese (13)	15	0.01
Cambodian (8)	15	0.01
Chinese, ex. Taiwanese (783)	947	0.56
Filipino (388)	642	0.38
Hmong (0)	0	<0.01
Indian (4,794)	4,974	2.93
Indonesian (12)	28	0.02
Japanese (175)	337	0.20
Korean (374)	516	0.30
Laotian (6)	11	0.01
Malaysian (1)	10	0.01
Nepalese (27)	27	0.02
Pakistani (126)	148	0.09
Sri Lankan (16)	22	0.01
Taiwanese (39)	47	0.03
Thai (58)	90	0.05
Vietnamese (259)	319	0.19
Hawaii Native/Pacific Islander (55)	143	0.08
Not Hispanic (48)	112	0.07
Hispanic (7)	31	0.02
Fijian (4)	4	<0.01
Guamanian/Chamorro (11)	17	0.01
Marshallese (0)	0	<0.01
Native Hawaiian (19)	40	0.02
Samoan (8)	17	0.01
Tongan (2)	2	<0.01
White (142,940)	146,519	86.41
Not Hispanic (138,835)	141,905	83.68
Hispanic (4,105)	4,614	2.72

Notes: † The Census 2010 population figure is used to calculate the percentages in the Hispanic Origin and Race categories. Ancestry percentages are based on the 2006-2010 American Community Survey population (not shown); ‡ Numbers in parentheses indicate the number of people reporting a single ancestry; * Numbers in parentheses indicate the number of persons reporting this race alone, not in combination with any other race; Please refer to the Explanation of Data for more information.

Peoria County

Population: 186,494

Ancestry	Population	%
Afghan (71)	71	0.04
African, Sub-Saharan (529)	616	0.33
African (176)	263	0.14
Cape Verdean (0)	0	<0.01
Ethiopian (0)	0	<0.01
Ghanaian (236)	236	0.13
Kenyan (0)	0	<0.01
Liberian (0)	0	<0.01
Nigerian (94)	94	0.05
Senegalese (0)	0	<0.01
Sierra Leonean (0)	0	<0.01
Somalian (0)	0	<0.01
South African (13)	13	0.01
Sudanese (10)	10	0.01
Ugandan (0)	0	<0.01
Zimbabwean (0)	0	<0.01
Other Sub-Saharan African (0)	0	<0.01
Albanian (0)	15	0.01
Alsatian (0)	13	0.01
American (10,194)	10,194	5.51
Arab (819)	1,252	0.68
Arab (110)	110	0.06
Egyptian (0)	0	<0.01
Iraqi (0)	0	<0.01
Jordanian (18)	18	0.01
Lebanese (682)	1,115	0.60
Moroccan (9)	9	<0.01
Palestinian (0)	0	<0.01
Syrian (0)	0	<0.01
Other Arab (0)	0	<0.01
Armenian (0)	0	<0.01
Assyrian/Chaldean/Syriac (0)	0	<0.01
Australian (6)	14	0.01
Austrian (36)	424	0.23
Basque (0)	0	<0.01
Belgian (236)	772	0.42
Brazilian (71)	144	0.08
British (288)	603	0.33
Bulgarian (54)	91	0.05
Cajun (0)	12	0.01
Canadian (77)	170	0.09
Carpatho Rusyn (0)	0	<0.01
Celtic (0)	15	0.01
Croatian (138)	285	0.15
Cypriot (0)	0	<0.01
Czech (236)	1,086	0.59
Czechoslovakian (43)	115	0.06
Danish (151)	704	0.38
Dutch (398)	3,265	1.76
Eastern European (97)	124	0.07
English (5,842)	19,170	10.36
Estonian (17)	17	0.01
European (1,468)	1,599	0.86
Finnish (14)	120	0.06
French, ex. Basque (1,021)	5,955	3.22
French Canadian (373)	801	0.43
German (19,821)	52,390	28.30
German Russian (0)	0	<0.01
Greek (342)	611	0.33
Guyanese (11)	22	0.01
Hungarian (178)	575	0.31
Icelander (0)	0	<0.01
Iranian (56)	86	0.05
Irish (7,043)	27,364	14.78
Israeli (3)	14	0.01
Italian (2,531)	6,542	3.53
Latvian (21)	21	0.01
Lithuanian (220)	456	0.25
Luxemburger (0)	102	0.06
Macedonian (18)	18	0.01
Maltese (0)	0	<0.01
New Zealander (0)	0	<0.01
Northern European (10)	23	0.01
Norwegian (651)	2,052	1.11
Pennsylvania German (18)	58	0.03

Ancestry	Population	%
Polish (1,039)	4,026	2.17
Portuguese (14)	103	0.06
Romanian (62)	144	0.08
Russian (197)	704	0.38
Scandinavian (229)	376	0.20
Scotch-Irish (1,023)	2,901	1.57
Scottish (943)	3,142	1.70
Serbian (78)	239	0.13
Slavic (31)	62	0.03
Slovak (68)	425	0.23
Slovene (65)	145	0.08
Soviet Union (0)	0	<0.01
Swedish (1,060)	4,828	2.61
Swiss (281)	1,594	0.86
Turkish (0)	0	<0.01
Ukrainian (205)	309	0.17
Welsh (240)	1,236	0.67
West Indian, ex. Hispanic (339)	359	0.19
Bahamian (0)	0	<0.01
Barbadian (0)	0	<0.01
Belizean (0)	0	<0.01
Bermudan (0)	0	<0.01
British West Indian (0)	0	<0.01
Dutch West Indian (0)	9	<0.01
Haitian (326)	326	0.18
Jamaican (13)	24	0.01
Trinidadian/Tobagonian (0)	0	<0.01
U.S. Virgin Islander (0)	0	<0.01
West Indian (0)	0	<0.01
Other West Indian (0)	0	<0.01
Yugoslavian (55)	168	0.09

Hispanic Origin	Population	%
Hispanic or Latino (of any race)	7,102	3.81
Central American, ex. Mexican	220	0.12
Costa Rican	7	<0.01
Guatemalan	99	0.05
Honduran	32	0.02
Nicaraguan	14	0.01
Panamanian	27	0.01
Salvadoran	39	0.02
Other Central American	2	<0.01
Cuban	149	0.08
Dominican Republic	32	0.02
Mexican	5,561	2.98
Puerto Rican	389	0.21
South American	257	0.14
Argentinean	21	0.01
Bolivian	23	0.01
Chilean	26	0.01
Colombian	98	0.05
Ecuadorian	20	0.01
Paraguayan	3	<0.01
Peruvian	25	0.01
Uruguayan	11	0.01
Venezuelan	29	0.02
Other South American	1	<0.01
Other Hispanic or Latino	494	0.26

Race*	Population	%
African-American/Black (33,030)	36,487	19.56
Not Hispanic (32,720)	35,884	19.24
Hispanic (310)	603	0.32
American Indian/Alaska Native (526)	1,474	0.79
Not Hispanic (373)	1,210	0.65
Hispanic (153)	264	0.14
Alaska Athabascan (Ala. Nat.) (2)	3	<0.01
Aleut (Alaska Native) (1)	1	<0.01
Apache (7)	18	0.01
Arapaho (1)	2	<0.01
Blackfeet (8)	55	0.03
Canadian/French Am. Ind. (0)	1	<0.01
Central American Ind. (2)	4	<0.01
Cherokee (83)	349	0.19
Cheyenne (0)	4	<0.01
Chickasaw (0)	11	0.01
Chippewa (8)	34	0.02
Choctaw (13)	35	0.02
Colville (0)	0	<0.01

Race*	Population	%
Comanche (0)	1	<0.01
Cree (1)	5	<0.01
Creek (2)	5	<0.01
Crow (0)	4	<0.01
Delaware (3)	4	<0.01
Hopi (0)	0	<0.01
Houma (2)	2	<0.01
Inupiat (Alaska Native) (6)	6	<0.01
Iroquois (4)	8	<0.01
Kiowa (2)	2	<0.01
Lumbee (3)	7	<0.01
Menominee (2)	4	<0.01
Mexican American Ind. (22)	32	0.02
Navajo (8)	28	0.02
Osage (2)	4	<0.01
Ottawa (8)	11	0.01
Paiute (1)	1	<0.01
Pima (2)	2	<0.01
Potawatomi (15)	15	0.01
Pueblo (0)	0	<0.01
Puget Sound Salish (4)	4	<0.01
Seminole (0)	4	<0.01
Shoshone (0)	1	<0.01
Sioux (18)	44	0.02
South American Ind. (2)	3	<0.01
Spanish American Ind. (1)	1	<0.01
Tlingit-Haida (Alaska Native) (1)	5	<0.01
Tohono O'Odham (0)	0	<0.01
Tsimshian (Alaska Native) (0)	0	<0.01
Ute (0)	0	<0.01
Yakama (0)	0	<0.01
Yaqui (2)	3	<0.01
Yuman (0)	0	<0.01
Yup'ik (Alaska Native) (2)	2	<0.01
Asian (5,856)	6,762	3.63
Not Hispanic (5,819)	6,667	3.57
Hispanic (37)	95	0.05
Bangladeshi (50)	51	0.03
Bhutanese (0)	0	<0.01
Burmese (20)	21	0.01
Cambodian (3)	7	<0.01
Chinese, ex. Taiwanese (1,138)	1,294	0.69
Filipino (476)	679	0.36
Hmong (2)	2	<0.01
Indian (2,657)	2,829	1.52
Indonesian (29)	34	0.02
Japanese (125)	271	0.15
Korean (357)	481	0.26
Laotian (59)	81	0.04
Malaysian (14)	17	0.01
Nepalese (19)	19	0.01
Pakistani (234)	254	0.14
Sri Lankan (26)	27	0.01
Taiwanese (44)	53	0.03
Thai (35)	68	0.04
Vietnamese (423)	520	0.28
Hawaii Native/Pacific Islander (62)	199	0.11
Not Hispanic (59)	183	0.10
Hispanic (3)	16	0.01
Fijian (1)	1	<0.01
Guamanian/Chamorro (9)	35	0.02
Marshallese (0)	0	<0.01
Native Hawaiian (31)	80	0.04
Samoan (6)	18	0.01
Tongan (0)	0	<0.01
White (138,800)	143,538	76.97
Not Hispanic (135,620)	139,738	74.93
Hispanic (3,180)	3,800	2.04

*Notes: † The Census 2010 population figure is used to calculate the percentages in the Hispanic Origin and Race categories. Ancestry percentages are based on the 2006-2010 American Community Survey population (not shown); ‡ Numbers in parentheses indicate the number of people reporting a single ancestry; * Numbers in parentheses indicate the number of persons reporting this race alone, not in combination with any other race; Please refer to the Explanation of Data for more information.*

Rock Island County

Population: 147,546

Ancestry	Population	%
Afghan (0)	0	<0.01
African, Sub-Saharan (1,053)	1,249	0.85
African (877)	965	0.65
Cape Verdean (0)	0	<0.01
Ethiopian (0)	0	<0.01
Ghanaian (0)	0	<0.01
Kenyan (0)	0	<0.01
Liberian (11)	11	0.01
Nigerian (99)	99	0.07
Senegalese (6)	6	<0.01
Sierra Leonean (0)	0	<0.01
Somalian (12)	12	0.01
South African (0)	0	<0.01
Sudanese (0)	0	<0.01
Ugandan (0)	0	<0.01
Zimbabwean (0)	0	<0.01
Other Sub-Saharan African (48)	156	0.11
Albanian (20)	35	0.02
Alsatian (0)	0	<0.01
American (7,647)	7,647	5.18
Arab (319)	389	0.26
Arab (39)	80	0.05
Egyptian (13)	13	0.01
Iraqi (0)	0	<0.01
Jordanian (0)	0	<0.01
Lebanese (7)	10	0.01
Moroccan (260)	260	0.18
Palestinian (0)	0	<0.01
Syrian (0)	26	0.02
Other Arab (0)	0	<0.01
Armenian (3)	102	0.07
Assyrian/Chaldean/Syriac (2)	2	<0.01
Australian (10)	10	0.01
Austrian (70)	265	0.18
Basque (0)	0	<0.01
Belgian (3,236)	7,459	5.06
Brazilian (0)	36	0.02
British (157)	426	0.29
Bulgarian (13)	13	0.01
Cajun (0)	0	<0.01
Canadian (80)	226	0.15
Carpatho Rusyn (0)	0	<0.01
Celtic (20)	30	0.02
Croatian (252)	484	0.33
Cypriot (0)	0	<0.01
Czech (345)	991	0.67
Czechoslovakian (30)	127	0.09
Danish (167)	844	0.57
Dutch (475)	3,042	2.06
Eastern European (97)	97	0.07
English (3,164)	12,796	8.67
Estonian (0)	0	<0.01
European (895)	1,030	0.70
Finnish (105)	284	0.19
French, ex. Basque (544)	3,727	2.53
French Canadian (150)	485	0.33
German (13,432)	38,224	25.91
German Russian (0)	0	<0.01
Greek (353)	797	0.54
Guyanese (0)	0	<0.01
Hungarian (17)	176	0.12
Icelander (0)	13	0.01
Iranian (16)	49	0.03
Irish (5,690)	21,002	14.24
Israeli (0)	0	<0.01
Italian (1,722)	5,220	3.54
Latvian (0)	17	0.01
Lithuanian (94)	327	0.22
Luxemburger (11)	42	0.03
Macedonian (0)	0	<0.01
Maltese (0)	0	<0.01
New Zealander (14)	14	0.01
Northern European (65)	65	0.04
Norwegian (752)	2,268	1.54
Pennsylvania German (114)	172	0.12

Ancestry	Population	%
Polish (1,123)	3,231	2.19
Portuguese (35)	44	0.03
Romanian (105)	178	0.12
Russian (253)	550	0.37
Scandinavian (36)	199	0.13
Scotch-Irish (936)	2,578	1.75
Scottish (519)	2,392	1.62
Serbian (67)	116	0.08
Slavic (0)	34	0.02
Slovak (40)	169	0.11
Slovene (10)	33	0.02
Soviet Union (0)	0	<0.01
Swedish (2,842)	10,093	6.84
Swiss (73)	517	0.35
Turkish (0)	14	0.01
Ukrainian (29)	43	0.03
Welsh (63)	632	0.43
West Indian, ex. Hispanic (44)	52	0.04
Bahamian (0)	0	<0.01
Barbadian (0)	0	<0.01
Belizean (19)	19	0.01
Bermudan (0)	0	<0.01
British West Indian (0)	0	<0.01
Dutch West Indian (0)	0	<0.01
Haitian (6)	14	0.01
Jamaican (19)	19	0.01
Trinidadian/Tobagonian (0)	0	<0.01
U.S. Virgin Islander (0)	0	<0.01
West Indian (0)	0	<0.01
Other West Indian (0)	0	<0.01
Yugoslavian (135)	266	0.18

Hispanic Origin	Population	%
Hispanic or Latino (of any race)	17,118	11.60
Central American, ex. Mexican	191	0.13
Costa Rican	9	0.01
Guatemalan	46	0.03
Honduran	60	0.04
Nicaraguan	8	0.01
Panamanian	17	0.01
Salvadoran	48	0.03
Other Central American	3	<0.01
Cuban	00	0.00
Dominican Republic	7	<0.01
Mexican	15,598	10.57
Puerto Rican	301	0.20
South American	118	0.08
Argentinean	17	0.01
Bolivian	5	<0.01
Chilean	13	0.01
Colombian	38	0.03
Ecuadorian	14	0.01
Paraguayan	1	<0.01
Peruvian	16	0.01
Uruguayan	0	<0.01
Venezuelan	13	0.01
Other South American	1	<0.01
Other Hispanic or Latino	815	0.55

Race*	Population	%
African-American/Black (13,289)	15,607	10.58
Not Hispanic (12,911)	14,823	10.05
Hispanic (378)	784	0.53
American Indian/Alaska Native (395)	1,532	1.04
Not Hispanic (283)	970	0.66
Hispanic (112)	562	0.38
Alaska Athabascan (Ala. Nat.) (0)	1	<0.01
Aleut (Alaska Native) (0)	1	<0.01
Apache (12)	31	0.02
Arapaho (0)	1	<0.01
Blackfeet (11)	81	0.05
Canadian/French Am. Ind. (1)	3	<0.01
Central American Ind. (2)	2	<0.01
Cherokee (57)	317	0.21
Cheyenne (0)	4	<0.01
Chickasaw (2)	5	<0.01
Chippewa (21)	36	0.02
Choctaw (1)	26	0.02
Colville (0)	0	<0.01

	Population	%
Comanche (1)	3	<0.01
Cree (1)	7	<0.01
Creek (4)	5	<0.01
Crow (3)	3	<0.01
Delaware (5)	8	0.01
Hopi (0)	0	<0.01
Houma (0)	0	<0.01
Inupiat (Alaska Native) (0)	0	<0.01
Iroquois (3)	9	0.01
Kiowa (0)	2	<0.01
Lumbee (0)	1	<0.01
Menominee (2)	4	<0.01
Mexican American Ind. (16)	39	0.03
Navajo (8)	12	0.01
Osage (0)	7	<0.01
Ottawa (0)	0	<0.01
Paiute (0)	0	<0.01
Pima (1)	3	<0.01
Potawatomi (7)	8	0.01
Pueblo (0)	0	<0.01
Puget Sound Salish (0)	2	<0.01
Seminole (1)	3	<0.01
Shoshone (0)	1	<0.01
Sioux (23)	57	0.04
South American Ind. (0)	3	<0.01
Spanish American Ind. (1)	2	<0.01
Tlingit-Haida (Alaska Native) (3)	6	<0.01
Tohono O'Odham (0)	0	<0.01
Tsimshian (Alaska Native) (0)	0	<0.01
Ute (0)	3	<0.01
Yakama (0)	0	<0.01
Yaqui (1)	2	<0.01
Yuman (0)	0	<0.01
Yup'ik (Alaska Native) (0)	0	<0.01
Asian (2,419)	2,988	2.03
Not Hispanic (2,383)	2,883	1.95
Hispanic (36)	105	0.07
Bangladeshi (5)	5	<0.01
Bhutanese (30)	39	0.03
Burmese (377)	410	0.28
Cambodian (9)	18	0.01
Chinese, ex. Taiwanese (175)	253	0.17
Filipino (168)	272	0.18
Hmong (0)	0	<0.01
Indian (980)	1,064	0.72
Indonesian (4)	5	<0.01
Japanese (46)	100	0.07
Korean (114)	205	0.14
Laotian (51)	79	0.05
Malaysian (3)	4	<0.01
Nepalese (75)	92	0.06
Pakistani (24)	32	0.02
Sri Lankan (3)	3	<0.01
Taiwanese (1)	2	<0.01
Thai (48)	78	0.05
Vietnamese (183)	240	0.16
Hawaii Native/Pacific Islander (48)	132	0.09
Not Hispanic (44)	120	0.08
Hispanic (4)	12	0.01
Fijian (1)	1	<0.01
Guamanian/Chamorro (7)	17	0.01
Marshallese (0)	0	<0.01
Native Hawaiian (4)	25	0.02
Samoan (21)	36	0.02
Tongan (0)	0	<0.01
White (120,382)	124,187	84.17
Not Hispanic (111,764)	114,456	77.57
Hispanic (8,618)	9,731	6.60

*Notes: † The Census 2010 population figure is used to calculate the percentages in the Hispanic Origin and Race categories. Ancestry percentages are based on the 2006-2010 American Community Survey population (not shown); ‡ Numbers in parentheses indicate the number of people reporting a single ancestry; * Numbers in parentheses indicate the number of persons reporting this race alone, not in combination with any other race; Please refer to the Explanation of Data for more information.*

Sangamon County

Population: 197,465

Ancestry	Population	%
Afghan (0)	0	<0.01
African, Sub-Saharan (769)	937	0.48
African (473)	611	0.31
Cape Verdean (0)	0	<0.01
Ethiopian (0)	0	<0.01
Ghanaian (58)	58	0.03
Kenyan (0)	0	<0.01
Liberian (83)	83	0.04
Nigerian (155)	185	0.09
Senegalese (0)	0	<0.01
Sierra Leonean (0)	0	<0.01
Somalian (0)	0	<0.01
South African (0)	0	<0.01
Sudanese (0)	0	<0.01
Ugandan (0)	0	<0.01
Zimbabwean (0)	0	<0.01
Other Sub-Saharan African (0)	0	<0.01
Albanian (0)	0	<0.01
Alsatian (0)	0	<0.01
American (18,588)	18,588	9.52
Arab (401)	635	0.33
Arab (104)	120	0.06
Egyptian (15)	29	0.01
Iraqi (0)	0	<0.01
Jordanian (22)	22	0.01
Lebanese (48)	56	0.03
Moroccan (7)	7	<0.01
Palestinian (0)	0	<0.01
Syrian (158)	274	0.14
Other Arab (47)	127	0.07
Armenian (0)	0	<0.01
Assyrian/Chaldean/Syriac (15)	15	0.01
Australian (55)	100	0.05
Austrian (164)	505	0.26
Basque (0)	0	<0.01
Belgian (219)	459	0.24
Brazilian (0)	19	0.01
British (397)	758	0.39
Bulgarian (4)	19	0.01
Cajun (0)	0	<0.01
Canadian (73)	143	0.07
Carpatho Rusyn (0)	0	<0.01
Celtic (0)	42	0.02
Croatian (75)	486	0.25
Cypriot (0)	0	<0.01
Czech (266)	830	0.43
Czechoslovakian (70)	214	0.11
Danish (114)	520	0.27
Dutch (371)	3,475	1.78
Eastern European (54)	83	0.04
English (7,955)	23,715	12.14
Estonian (10)	10	0.01
European (1,654)	1,768	0.91
Finnish (25)	38	0.02
French, ex. Basque (1,249)	6,333	3.24
French Canadian (94)	271	0.14
German (22,253)	57,464	29.43
German Russian (0)	11	0.01
Greek (232)	584	0.30
Guyanese (0)	0	<0.01
Hungarian (226)	767	0.39
Icelander (12)	12	0.01
Iranian (19)	35	0.02
Irish (7,365)	28,917	14.81
Israeli (0)	0	<0.01
Italian (4,920)	12,313	6.31
Latvian (0)	44	0.02
Lithuanian (881)	1,595	0.82
Luxemburger (0)	23	0.01
Macedonian (10)	10	0.01
Maltese (0)	0	<0.01
New Zealander (19)	19	0.01
Northern European (111)	181	0.09
Norwegian (505)	1,465	0.75
Pennsylvania German (58)	92	0.05

	Population	%
Polish (1,299)	4,350	2.23
Portuguese (213)	618	0.32
Romanian (13)	47	0.02
Russian (174)	678	0.35
Scandinavian (135)	248	0.13
Scotch-Irish (1,298)	4,110	2.10
Scottish (997)	3,893	1.99
Serbian (14)	54	0.03
Slavic (60)	201	0.10
Slovak (193)	712	0.36
Slovene (90)	166	0.09
Soviet Union (0)	0	<0.01
Swedish (619)	2,407	1.23
Swiss (99)	589	0.30
Turkish (19)	21	0.01
Ukrainian (104)	280	0.14
Welsh (289)	1,561	0.80
West Indian, ex. Hispanic (77)	191	0.10
Bahamian (0)	0	<0.01
Barbadian (0)	0	<0.01
Belizean (0)	0	<0.01
Bermudan (0)	0	<0.01
British West Indian (0)	0	<0.01
Dutch West Indian (0)	14	0.01
Haitian (17)	24	0.01
Jamaican (46)	115	0.06
Trinidadian/Tobagonian (0)	9	<0.01
U.S. Virgin Islander (0)	0	<0.01
West Indian (14)	29	0.01
Other West Indian (0)	0	<0.01
Yugoslavian (50)	160	0.08

Hispanic Origin	Population	%
Hispanic or Latino (of any race)	3,480	1.76
Central American, ex. Mexican	234	0.12
Costa Rican	17	0.01
Guatemalan	67	0.03
Honduran	44	0.02
Nicaraguan	35	0.02
Panamanian	41	0.02
Salvadoran	29	0.01
Other Central American	1	<0.01
Cuban	82	0.04
Dominican Republic	25	0.01
Mexican	1,956	0.99
Puerto Rican	495	0.25
South American	271	0.14
Argentinean	18	0.01
Bolivian	29	0.01
Chilean	30	0.02
Colombian	59	0.03
Ecuadorian	48	0.02
Paraguayan	0	<0.01
Peruvian	61	0.03
Uruguayan	5	<0.01
Venezuelan	18	0.01
Other South American	3	<0.01
Other Hispanic or Latino	417	0.21

Race*	Population	%
African-American/Black (23,335)	26,157	13.25
Not Hispanic (23,146)	25,830	13.08
Hispanic (189)	327	0.17
American Indian/Alaska Native (394)	1,389	0.70
Not Hispanic (343)	1,248	0.63
Hispanic (51)	141	0.07
Alaska Athabascan (Ala. Nat.) (2)	2	<0.01
Aleut (Alaska Native) (4)	4	<0.01
Apache (5)	18	0.01
Arapaho (0)	0	<0.01
Blackfeet (9)	74	0.04
Canadian/French Am. Ind. (5)	6	<0.01
Central American Ind. (2)	2	<0.01
Cherokee (83)	435	0.22
Cheyenne (0)	5	<0.01
Chickasaw (5)	9	<0.01
Chippewa (6)	14	0.01
Choctaw (4)	43	0.02
Colville (0)	0	<0.01

	Population	%
Comanche (1)	2	<0.01
Cree (0)	1	<0.01
Creek (4)	7	<0.01
Crow (2)	6	<0.01
Delaware (1)	1	<0.01
Hopi (0)	0	<0.01
Houma (0)	0	<0.01
Inupiat (Alaska Native) (1)	1	<0.01
Iroquois (8)	12	0.01
Kiowa (0)	0	<0.01
Lumbee (1)	7	<0.01
Menominee (16)	19	0.01
Mexican American Ind. (8)	19	0.01
Navajo (4)	6	<0.01
Osage (2)	2	<0.01
Ottawa (1)	1	<0.01
Paiute (0)	0	<0.01
Pima (0)	1	<0.01
Potawatomi (5)	7	<0.01
Pueblo (5)	6	<0.01
Puget Sound Salish (0)	0	<0.01
Seminole (1)	6	<0.01
Shoshone (0)	0	<0.01
Sioux (19)	39	0.02
South American Ind. (3)	3	<0.01
Spanish American Ind. (0)	0	<0.01
Tlingit-Haida (Alaska Native) (0)	0	<0.01
Tohono O'Odham (0)	0	<0.01
Tsimshian (Alaska Native) (0)	0	<0.01
Ute (1)	2	<0.01
Yakama (0)	0	<0.01
Yaqui (0)	2	<0.01
Yuman (0)	0	<0.01
Yup'ik (Alaska Native) (0)	0	<0.01
Asian (3,220)	3,964	2.01
Not Hispanic (3,198)	3,899	1.97
Hispanic (22)	65	0.03
Bangladeshi (11)	11	0.01
Bhutanese (0)	0	<0.01
Burmese (12)	16	0.01
Cambodian (11)	18	0.01
Chinese, ex. Taiwanese (611)	704	0.36
Filipino (347)	525	0.27
Hmong (2)	3	<0.01
Indian (1,160)	1,273	0.64
Indonesian (9)	9	<0.01
Japanese (87)	185	0.09
Korean (249)	382	0.19
Laotian (42)	60	0.03
Malaysian (9)	12	0.01
Nepalese (14)	14	0.01
Pakistani (146)	164	0.08
Sri Lankan (7)	7	<0.01
Taiwanese (74)	89	0.05
Thai (52)	83	0.04
Vietnamese (271)	308	0.16
Hawaii Native/Pacific Islander (47)	153	0.08
Not Hispanic (44)	131	0.07
Hispanic (3)	22	0.01
Fijian (4)	7	<0.01
Guamanian/Chamorro (13)	24	0.01
Marshallese (0)	0	<0.01
Native Hawaiian (9)	49	0.02
Samoan (12)	25	0.01
Tongan (0)	0	<0.01
White (165,103)	169,052	85.61
Not Hispanic (162,987)	166,649	84.39
Hispanic (2,116)	2,403	1.22

*Notes: † The Census 2010 population figure is used to calculate the percentages in the Hispanic Origin and Race categories. Ancestry percentages are based on the 2006-2010 American Community Survey population (not shown); ‡ Numbers in parentheses indicate the number of people reporting a single ancestry; * Numbers in parentheses indicate the number of persons reporting this race alone, not in combination with any other race; Please refer to the Explanation of Data for more information.*

St. Clair County

Population: 270,056

Ancestry	Population	%
Afghan (0)	4	<0.01
African, Sub-Saharan (1,082)	1,400	0.52
African (911)	1,166	0.44
Cape Verdean (9)	9	<0.01
Ethiopian (21)	21	0.01
Ghanaian (0)	0	<0.01
Kenyan (40)	60	0.02
Liberian (0)	0	<0.01
Nigerian (38)	81	0.03
Senegalese (17)	17	0.01
Sierra Leonean (0)	0	<0.01
Somalian (0)	0	<0.01
South African (0)	0	<0.01
Sudanese (0)	0	<0.01
Ugandan (0)	0	<0.01
Zimbabwean (0)	0	<0.01
Other Sub-Saharan African (46)	46	0.02
Albanian (0)	0	<0.01
Alsatian (0)	0	<0.01
American (12,374)	12,374	4.64
Arab (42)	176	0.07
Arab (0)	0	<0.01
Egyptian (8)	8	<0.01
Iraqi (0)	0	<0.01
Jordanian (9)	9	<0.01
Lebanese (14)	88	0.03
Moroccan (9)	9	<0.01
Palestinian (0)	0	<0.01
Syrian (2)	38	0.01
Other Arab (0)	24	0.01
Armenian (157)	195	0.07
Assyrian/Chaldean/Syriac (12)	12	<0.01
Australian (98)	350	0.13
Austrian (108)	569	0.21
Basque (13)	53	0.02
Belgian (48)	175	0.07
Brazilian (15)	15	0.01
British (440)	866	0.32
Bulgarian (77)	167	0.06
Cajun (0)	15	0.01
Canadian (99)	236	0.09
Carpatho Rusyn (0)	0	<0.01
Celtic (5)	11	<0.01
Croatian (162)	517	0.19
Cypriot (0)	0	<0.01
Czech (294)	1,393	0.52
Czechoslovakian (124)	294	0.11
Danish (180)	771	0.29
Dutch (570)	3,663	1.37
Eastern European (47)	47	0.02
English (5,459)	19,669	7.37
Estonian (0)	0	<0.01
European (7,212)	7,636	2.86
Finnish (39)	115	0.04
French, ex. Basque (1,356)	9,981	3.74
French Canadian (285)	767	0.29
German (33,583)	73,392	27.52
German Russian (0)	0	<0.01
Greek (213)	989	0.37
Guyanese (0)	0	<0.01
Hungarian (94)	837	0.31
Icelander (54)	54	0.02
Iranian (0)	0	<0.01
Irish (6,659)	29,492	11.06
Israeli (0)	0	<0.01
Italian (2,743)	8,794	3.30
Latvian (0)	17	0.01
Lithuanian (273)	688	0.26
Luxemburger (0)	0	<0.01
Macedonian (13)	42	0.02
Maltese (0)	0	<0.01
New Zealander (0)	0	<0.01
Northern European (25)	25	0.01
Norwegian (733)	2,001	0.75
Pennsylvania German (59)	116	0.04

Ancestry	Population	%
Polish (1,727)	6,702	2.51
Portuguese (40)	160	0.06
Romanian (25)	256	0.10
Russian (266)	752	0.28
Scandinavian (44)	283	0.11
Scotch-Irish (993)	3,068	1.15
Scottish (1,173)	3,469	1.30
Serbian (25)	102	0.04
Slavic (50)	124	0.05
Slovak (159)	389	0.15
Slovene (12)	28	0.01
Soviet Union (0)	0	<0.01
Swedish (681)	2,129	0.80
Swiss (58)	853	0.32
Turkish (67)	109	0.04
Ukrainian (142)	311	0.12
Welsh (202)	1,491	0.56
West Indian, ex. Hispanic (228)	415	0.16
Bahamian (0)	0	<0.01
Barbadian (0)	0	<0.01
Belizean (0)	0	<0.01
Bermudan (0)	0	<0.01
British West Indian (0)	0	<0.01
Dutch West Indian (0)	0	<0.01
Haitian (0)	27	0.01
Jamaican (122)	192	0.07
Trinidadian/Tobagonian (37)	37	0.01
U.S. Virgin Islander (0)	0	<0.01
West Indian (69)	159	0.06
Other West Indian (0)	0	<0.01
Yugoslavian (0)	57	0.02

Hispanic Origin	Population	%
Hispanic or Latino (of any race)	8,785	3.25
Central American, ex. Mexican	382	0.14
Costa Rican	32	0.01
Guatemalan	105	0.04
Honduran	34	0.01
Nicaraguan	25	0.01
Panamanian	133	0.05
Salvadoran	53	0.02
Other Central American	0	<0.01
Cuban	156	0.06
Dominican Republic	56	0.02
Mexican	6,048	2.24
Puerto Rican	896	0.33
South American	232	0.09
Argentinean	15	0.01
Bolivian	21	0.01
Chilean	22	0.01
Colombian	88	0.03
Ecuadorian	21	0.01
Paraguayan	0	<0.01
Peruvian	37	0.01
Uruguayan	0	<0.01
Venezuelan	26	0.01
Other South American	2	<0.01
Other Hispanic or Latino	1,015	0.38

Race*	Population	%
African-American/Black (82,302)	85,623	31.71
Not Hispanic (81,860)	84,934	31.45
Hispanic (442)	689	0.26
American Indian/Alaska Native (652)	2,037	0.75
Not Hispanic (539)	1,801	0.67
Hispanic (113)	236	0.09
Alaska Athabascan (Ala. Nat.) (6)	9	<0.01
Aleut (Alaska Native) (5)	5	<0.01
Apache (6)	16	0.01
Arapaho (0)	3	<0.01
Blackfeet (10)	80	0.03
Canadian/French Am. Ind. (4)	9	<0.01
Central American Ind. (2)	3	<0.01
Cherokee (122)	560	0.21
Cheyenne (2)	2	<0.01
Chickasaw (2)	9	<0.01
Chippewa (12)	31	0.01
Choctaw (15)	53	0.02
Colville (0)	0	<0.01

	Population	%
Comanche (15)	25	0.01
Cree (0)	3	<0.01
Creek (4)	11	<0.01
Crow (0)	2	<0.01
Delaware (1)	1	<0.01
Hopi (1)	2	<0.01
Houma (1)	3	<0.01
Inupiat (Alaska Native) (2)	2	<0.01
Iroquois (8)	13	<0.01
Kiowa (1)	6	<0.01
Lumbee (1)	7	<0.01
Menominee (6)	6	<0.01
Mexican American Ind. (20)	29	0.01
Navajo (24)	44	0.02
Osage (5)	8	<0.01
Ottawa (1)	1	<0.01
Paiute (0)	0	<0.01
Pima (0)	0	<0.01
Potawatomi (6)	11	<0.01
Pueblo (6)	6	<0.01
Puget Sound Salish (0)	0	<0.01
Seminole (6)	13	<0.01
Shoshone (3)	4	<0.01
Sioux (16)	54	0.02
South American Ind. (1)	2	<0.01
Spanish American Ind. (4)	6	<0.01
Tlingit-Haida (Alaska Native) (3)	12	<0.01
Tohono O'Odham (0)	0	<0.01
Tsimshian (Alaska Native) (0)	0	<0.01
Ute (0)	0	<0.01
Yakama (0)	3	<0.01
Yaqui (2)	2	<0.01
Yuman (1)	1	<0.01
Yup'ik (Alaska Native) (0)	3	<0.01
Asian (3,276)	5,005	1.85
Not Hispanic (3,213)	4,810	1.78
Hispanic (63)	195	0.07
Bangladeshi (6)	11	<0.01
Bhutanese (0)	0	<0.01
Burmese (0)	1	<0.01
Cambodian (18)	28	0.01
Chinese, ex. Taiwanese (392)	580	0.21
Filipino (854)	1,516	0.56
Hmong (0)	2	<0.01
Indian (527)	641	0.24
Indonesian (8)	11	<0.01
Japanese (198)	457	0.17
Korean (546)	867	0.32
Laotian (20)	39	0.01
Malaysian (0)	9	<0.01
Nepalese (11)	14	0.01
Pakistani (79)	88	0.03
Sri Lankan (3)	5	<0.01
Taiwanese (28)	43	0.02
Thai (183)	311	0.12
Vietnamese (220)	319	0.12
Hawaii Native/Pacific Islander (227)	517	0.19
Not Hispanic (213)	466	0.17
Hispanic (14)	51	0.02
Fijian (1)	2	<0.01
Guamanian/Chamorro (87)	152	0.06
Marshallese (3)	3	<0.01
Native Hawaiian (60)	171	0.06
Samoan (31)	76	0.03
Tongan (1)	1	<0.01
White (174,458)	179,605	66.51
Not Hispanic (169,858)	174,402	64.58
Hispanic (4,600)	5,203	1.93

Notes: † The Census 2010 population figure is used to calculate the percentages in the Hispanic Origin and Race categories. Ancestry percentages are based on the 2006-2010 American Community Survey population (not shown); ‡ Numbers in parentheses indicate the number of people reporting a single ancestry; * Numbers in parentheses indicate the number of persons reporting this race alone, not in combination with any other race; Please refer to the Explanation of Data for more information.

Tazewell County

Population: 135,394

Ancestry	Population	%
Afghan (12)	12	0.01
African, Sub-Saharan (85)	136	0.10
African (70)	112	0.08
Cape Verdean (0)	0	<0.01
Ethiopian (15)	15	0.01
Ghanaian (0)	0	<0.01
Kenyan (0)	0	<0.01
Liberian (0)	0	<0.01
Nigerian (0)	9	0.01
Senegalese (0)	0	<0.01
Sierra Leonean (0)	0	<0.01
Somalian (0)	0	<0.01
South African (0)	0	<0.01
Sudanese (0)	0	<0.01
Ugandan (0)	0	<0.01
Zimbabwean (0)	0	<0.01
Other Sub-Saharan African (0)	0	<0.01
Albanian (0)	0	<0.01
Alsatian (9)	9	0.01
American (20,860)	20,860	15.58
Arab (413)	686	0.51
Arab (28)	28	0.02
Egyptian (0)	0	<0.01
Iraqi (0)	0	<0.01
Jordanian (0)	0	<0.01
Lebanese (312)	585	0.44
Moroccan (40)	40	0.03
Palestinian (11)	11	0.01
Syrian (0)	0	<0.01
Other Arab (22)	22	0.02
Armenian (7)	7	0.01
Assyrian/Chaldean/Syriac (0)	0	<0.01
Australian (64)	64	0.05
Austrian (22)	94	0.07
Basque (0)	0	<0.01
Belgian (178)	302	0.23
Brazilian (0)	0	<0.01
British (249)	393	0.29
Bulgarian (25)	57	0.04
Cajun (0)	0	<0.01
Canadian (53)	150	0.11
Carpatho Rusyn (0)	0	<0.01
Celtic (0)	0	<0.01
Croatian (120)	289	0.22
Cypriot (0)	0	<0.01
Czech (166)	605	0.45
Czechoslovakian (19)	95	0.07
Danish (147)	519	0.39
Dutch (595)	2,732	2.04
Eastern European (10)	10	0.01
English (5,744)	16,047	11.99
Estonian (0)	0	<0.01
European (1,207)	1,390	1.04
Finnish (66)	132	0.10
French, ex. Basque (674)	4,424	3.30
French Canadian (113)	335	0.25
German (22,880)	47,667	35.61
German Russian (0)	0	<0.01
Greek (72)	266	0.20
Guyanese (0)	0	<0.01
Hungarian (109)	319	0.24
Icelander (0)	0	<0.01
Iranian (0)	0	<0.01
Irish (5,482)	19,248	14.38
Israeli (0)	0	<0.01
Italian (2,631)	5,679	4.24
Latvian (0)	0	<0.01
Lithuanian (236)	353	0.26
Luxemburger (0)	17	0.01
Macedonian (0)	0	<0.01
Maltese (0)	0	<0.01
New Zealander (0)	0	<0.01
Northern European (32)	32	0.02
Norwegian (632)	1,526	1.14
Pennsylvania German (70)	105	0.08

Ancestry (cont.)	Population	%
Polish (729)	2,692	2.01
Portuguese (51)	94	0.07
Romanian (46)	84	0.06
Russian (149)	330	0.25
Scandinavian (92)	133	0.10
Scotch-Irish (916)	2,517	1.88
Scottish (829)	2,851	2.13
Serbian (30)	32	0.02
Slavic (4)	50	0.04
Slovak (72)	148	0.11
Slovene (0)	37	0.03
Soviet Union (0)	0	<0.01
Swedish (824)	2,723	2.03
Swiss (224)	1,336	1.00
Turkish (0)	10	0.01
Ukrainian (59)	88	0.07
Welsh (125)	556	0.42
West Indian, ex. Hispanic (19)	43	0.03
Bahamian (0)	0	<0.01
Barbadian (0)	0	<0.01
Belizean (0)	0	<0.01
Bermudan (0)	0	<0.01
British West Indian (0)	12	0.01
Dutch West Indian (0)	0	<0.01
Haitian (0)	0	<0.01
Jamaican (19)	19	0.01
Trinidadian/Tobagonian (0)	12	0.01
U.S. Virgin Islander (0)	0	<0.01
West Indian (0)	0	<0.01
Other West Indian (0)	0	<0.01
Yugoslavian (69)	179	0.13

Hispanic Origin	Population	%
Hispanic or Latino (of any race)	2,514	1.86
Central American, ex. Mexican	98	0.07
Costa Rican	3	<0.01
Guatemalan	34	0.03
Honduran	6	<0.01
Nicaraguan	8	0.01
Panamanian	27	0.02
Salvadoran	20	0.01
Other Central American	0	<0.01
Cuban	47	0.03
Dominican Republic	8	0.01
Mexican	1,733	1.28
Puerto Rican	226	0.17
South American	97	0.07
Argentinean	9	0.01
Bolivian	2	<0.01
Chilean	12	0.01
Colombian	30	0.02
Ecuadorian	17	0.01
Paraguayan	0	<0.01
Peruvian	20	0.01
Uruguayan	2	<0.01
Venezuelan	2	<0.01
Other South American	3	<0.01
Other Hispanic or Latino	305	0.23

Race*	Population	%
African-American/Black (1,374)	1,972	1.46
Not Hispanic (1,351)	1,914	1.41
Hispanic (23)	58	0.04
American Indian/Alaska Native (365)	943	0.70
Not Hispanic (307)	836	0.62
Hispanic (58)	107	0.08
Alaska Athabascan (Ala. Nat.) (1)	1	<0.01
Aleut (Alaska Native) (1)	2	<0.01
Apache (4)	10	0.01
Arapaho (1)	1	<0.01
Blackfeet (4)	35	0.03
Canadian/French Am. Ind. (1)	3	<0.01
Central American Ind. (3)	4	<0.01
Cherokee (59)	240	0.18
Cheyenne (0)	1	<0.01
Chickasaw (2)	5	<0.01
Chippewa (33)	43	0.03
Choctaw (5)	25	0.02
Colville (0)	0	<0.01

Race* (cont.)	Population	%
Comanche (5)	13	0.0
Cree (3)	4	<0.0
Creek (2)	6	<0.0
Crow (0)	1	<0.0
Delaware (0)	0	<0.0
Hopi (1)	1	<0.0
Houma (0)	0	<0.0
Inupiat (Alaska Native) (2)	4	<0.0
Iroquois (3)	19	0.0
Kiowa (0)	0	<0.0
Lumbee (0)	0	<0.0
Menominee (7)	7	<0.0
Mexican American Ind. (12)	21	0.0
Navajo (2)	6	<0.0
Osage (1)	2	<0.0
Ottawa (5)	5	<0.0
Paiute (0)	0	<0.0
Pima (0)	0	<0.0
Potawatomi (11)	12	0.0
Pueblo (1)	2	<0.0
Puget Sound Salish (0)	0	<0.0
Seminole (3)	12	0.0
Shoshone (0)	0	<0.0
Sioux (21)	39	0.0
South American Ind. (0)	2	<0.0
Spanish American Ind. (1)	1	<0.0
Tlingit-Haida (Alaska Native) (4)	6	<0.0
Tohono O'Odham (0)	0	<0.0
Tsimshian (Alaska Native) (0)	3	<0.0
Ute (0)	1	<0.0
Yakama (0)	0	<0.0
Yaqui (0)	0	<0.0
Yuman (0)	0	<0.0
Yup'ik (Alaska Native) (3)	3	<0.0
Asian (999)	1,381	1.0
Not Hispanic (990)	1,345	0.9
Hispanic (9)	36	0.0
Bangladeshi (0)	0	<0.0
Bhutanese (0)	0	<0.0
Burmese (5)	6	<0.0
Cambodian (3)	7	0.0
Chinese, ex. Taiwanese (196)	236	0.1
Filipino (171)	285	0.2
Hmong (13)	13	0.0
Indian (207)	249	0.1
Indonesian (1)	4	<0.0
Japanese (43)	103	0.0
Korean (140)	202	0.1
Laotian (12)	19	0.0
Malaysian (1)	1	<0.0
Nepalese (0)	0	<0.0
Pakistani (20)	20	0.0
Sri Lankan (1)	1	<0.0
Taiwanese (5)	5	<0.0
Thai (16)	30	0.0
Vietnamese (123)	164	0.1
Hawaii Native/Pacific Islander (33)	101	0.0
Not Hispanic (30)	82	0.0
Hispanic (3)	19	0.0
Fijian (0)	0	<0.0
Guamanian/Chamorro (9)	17	0.0
Marshallese (0)	0	<0.0
Native Hawaiian (13)	48	0.0
Samoan (4)	11	0.0
Tongan (1)	1	<0.0
White (130,225)	131,880	97.4
Not Hispanic (128,625)	130,035	96.0
Hispanic (1,600)	1,845	1.3

*Notes: † The Census 2010 population figure is used to calculate the percentages in the Hispanic Origin and Race categories. Ancestry percentages are based on the 2006-2010 American Communi Survey population (not shown); ‡ Numbers in parentheses indicate the number of people reporting a single ancestry; * Numbers in parentheses indicate the number of persons reporting this race alo not in combination with any other race; Please refer to the Explanation of Data for more information.*

Will County

Population: 677,560

Ancestry	Population	%
Afghan (0)	0	<0.01
African, Sub-Saharan (3,567)	4,524	0.68
African (1,983)	2,647	0.40
Cape Verdean (0)	0	<0.01
Ethiopian (208)	208	0.03
Ghanaian (391)	418	0.06
Kenyan (18)	67	0.01
Liberian (0)	0	<0.01
Nigerian (611)	698	0.10
Senegalese (0)	0	<0.01
Sierra Leonean (148)	148	0.02
Somalian (0)	0	<0.01
South African (126)	214	0.03
Sudanese (0)	0	<0.01
Ugandan (0)	13	<0.01
Zimbabwean (0)	0	<0.01
Other Sub-Saharan African (82)	111	0.02
Albanian (225)	433	0.06
Alsatian (14)	29	<0.01
American (14,005)	14,005	2.10
Arab (3,722)	4,874	0.73
Arab (1,809)	2,230	0.33
Egyptian (172)	224	0.03
Iraqi (110)	110	0.02
Jordanian (0)	56	0.01
Lebanese (466)	781	0.12
Moroccan (115)	115	0.02
Palestinian (752)	876	0.13
Syrian (71)	183	0.03
Other Arab (227)	299	0.04
Armenian (38)	321	0.05
Assyrian/Chaldean/Syriac (69)	260	0.04
Australian (27)	77	0.01
Austrian (551)	2,685	0.40
Basque (0)	0	<0.01
Belgian (253)	1,151	0.17
Brazilian (127)	291	0.04
British (728)	1,767	0.26
Bulgarian (321)	336	0.05
Cajun (0)	1	<0.01
Canadian (498)	1,090	0.16
Carpatho Rusyn (8)	21	<0.01
Celtic (10)	37	0.01
Croatian (1,558)	6,484	0.97
Cypriot (0)	0	<0.01
Czech (2,663)	12,766	1.91
Czechoslovakian (462)	1,103	0.17
Danish (453)	2,959	0.44
Dutch (4,225)	14,237	2.13
Eastern European (493)	612	0.09
English (7,288)	39,447	5.91
Estonian (12)	12	<0.01
European (3,803)	4,092	0.61
Finnish (266)	839	0.13
French, ex. Basque (1,402)	15,656	2.34
French Canadian (652)	2,911	0.44
German (31,435)	144,456	21.63
German Russian (0)	29	<0.01
Greek (2,856)	7,188	1.08
Guyanese (40)	60	0.01
Hungarian (895)	4,081	0.61
Icelander (0)	89	0.01
Iranian (329)	465	0.07
Irish (26,893)	123,997	18.56
Israeli (241)	255	0.04
Italian (19,381)	73,930	11.07
Latvian (56)	357	0.05
Lithuanian (4,309)	10,878	1.63
Luxemburger (31)	169	0.03
Macedonian (195)	253	0.04
Maltese (13)	52	0.01
New Zealander (47)	150	0.02
Northern European (132)	148	0.02
Norwegian (1,983)	8,884	1.33
Pennsylvania German (19)	100	0.01

Ancestry	Population	%
Polish (30,087)	89,171	13.35
Portuguese (88)	447	0.07
Romanian (578)	996	0.15
Russian (1,200)	4,571	0.68
Scandinavian (292)	694	0.10
Scotch-Irish (2,120)	7,827	1.17
Scottish (1,538)	7,593	1.14
Serbian (686)	1,390	0.21
Slavic (97)	515	0.08
Slovak (1,777)	5,803	0.87
Slovene (1,236)	4,153	0.62
Soviet Union (0)	0	<0.01
Swedish (3,270)	17,455	2.61
Swiss (206)	1,472	0.22
Turkish (95)	222	0.03
Ukrainian (631)	1,706	0.26
Welsh (344)	2,372	0.36
West Indian, ex. Hispanic (518)	883	0.13
Bahamian (21)	21	<0.01
Barbadian (45)	45	0.01
Belizean (0)	83	0.01
Bermudan (0)	0	<0.01
British West Indian (9)	9	<0.01
Dutch West Indian (0)	10	<0.01
Haitian (243)	319	0.05
Jamaican (110)	257	0.04
Trinidadian/Tobagonian (14)	26	<0.01
U.S. Virgin Islander (0)	0	<0.01
West Indian (67)	104	0.02
Other West Indian (9)	9	<0.01
Yugoslavian (260)	658	0.10

Hispanic Origin	Population	%
Hispanic or Latino (of any race)	105,817	15.62
Central American, ex. Mexican	1,963	0.29
Costa Rican	80	0.01
Guatemalan	1,079	0.16
Honduran	234	0.03
Nicaraguan	96	0.01
Panamanian	137	0.02
Salvadoran	324	0.05
Other Central American	13	<0.01
Cuban	844	0.12
Dominican Republic	206	0.03
Mexican	90,355	13.34
Puerto Rican	6,842	1.01
South American	2,231	0.33
Argentinean	190	0.03
Bolivian	113	0.02
Chilean	69	0.01
Colombian	761	0.11
Ecuadorian	428	0.06
Paraguayan	15	<0.01
Peruvian	414	0.06
Uruguayan	29	<0.01
Venezuelan	196	0.03
Other South American	16	<0.01
Other Hispanic or Latino	3,376	0.50

Race*	Population	%
African-American/Black (75,743)	81,225	11.99
Not Hispanic (74,419)	78,769	11.63
Hispanic (1,324)	2,456	0.36
American Indian/Alaska Native (1,703)	4,515	0.67
Not Hispanic (814)	2,903	0.43
Hispanic (889)	1,612	0.24
Alaska Athabascan (Ala. Nat.) (4)	4	<0.01
Aleut (Alaska Native) (0)	1	<0.01
Apache (31)	98	0.01
Arapaho (1)	9	<0.01
Blackfeet (12)	145	0.02
Canadian/French Am. Ind. (8)	24	<0.01
Central American Ind. (2)	6	<0.01
Cherokee (163)	877	0.13
Cheyenne (6)	14	<0.01
Chickasaw (6)	24	<0.01
Chippewa (65)	143	0.02
Choctaw (11)	75	0.01
Colville (1)	1	<0.01

Race*	Population	%
Comanche (5)	15	<0.01
Cree (2)	11	<0.01
Creek (16)	34	0.01
Crow (1)	6	<0.01
Delaware (3)	5	<0.01
Hopi (7)	12	<0.01
Houma (1)	1	<0.01
Inupiat (Alaska Native) (5)	13	<0.01
Iroquois (32)	72	0.01
Kiowa (2)	3	<0.01
Lumbee (6)	16	<0.01
Menominee (0)	6	<0.01
Mexican American Ind. (198)	288	0.04
Navajo (26)	50	0.01
Osage (3)	9	<0.01
Ottawa (4)	14	<0.01
Paiute (2)	2	<0.01
Pima (2)	2	<0.01
Potawatomi (34)	63	0.01
Pueblo (3)	7	<0.01
Puget Sound Salish (0)	0	<0.01
Seminole (1)	10	<0.01
Shoshone (0)	6	<0.01
Sioux (28)	98	0.01
South American Ind. (23)	47	0.01
Spanish American Ind. (15)	22	<0.01
Tlingit-Haida (Alaska Native) (0)	2	<0.01
Tohono O'Odham (1)	1	<0.01
Tsimshian (Alaska Native) (0)	0	<0.01
Ute (5)	5	<0.01
Yakama (4)	5	<0.01
Yaqui (4)	6	<0.01
Yuman (0)	1	<0.01
Yup'ik (Alaska Native) (0)	1	<0.01
Asian (30,833)	35,379	5.22
Not Hispanic (30,458)	34,487	5.09
Hispanic (375)	892	0.13
Bangladeshi (116)	130	0.02
Bhutanese (0)	0	<0.01
Burmese (28)	49	0.01
Cambodian (278)	336	0.05
Chinese, ex. Taiwanese (3,507)	4,264	0.63
Filipino (8,191)	9,895	1.46
Hmong (29)	36	0.01
Indian (11,100)	11,932	1.76
Indonesian (60)	83	0.01
Japanese (342)	847	0.13
Korean (1,824)	2,274	0.34
Laotian (353)	423	0.06
Malaysian (25)	32	<0.01
Nepalese (24)	32	<0.01
Pakistani (2,408)	2,618	0.39
Sri Lankan (42)	55	0.01
Taiwanese (209)	259	0.04
Thai (271)	436	0.06
Vietnamese (1,086)	1,298	0.19
Hawaii Native/Pacific Islander (136)	529	0.08
Not Hispanic (104)	378	0.06
Hispanic (32)	151	0.02
Fijian (7)	11	<0.01
Guamanian/Chamorro (30)	57	0.01
Marshallese (2)	2	<0.01
Native Hawaiian (36)	166	0.02
Samoan (14)	38	0.01
Tongan (5)	10	<0.01
White (514,664)	527,954	77.92
Not Hispanic (455,577)	463,912	68.47
Hispanic (59,087)	64,042	9.45

Notes: † The Census 2010 population figure is used to calculate the percentages in the Hispanic Origin and Race categories. Ancestry percentages are based on the 2006-2010 American Community Survey population (not shown); ‡ Numbers in parentheses indicate the number of people reporting a single ancestry; * Numbers in parentheses indicate the number of persons reporting this race alone, not in combination with any other race; Please refer to the Explanation of Data for more information.

Winnebago County

Population: 295,266

Ancestry	Population	%
Afghan (0)	0	<0.01
African, Sub-Saharan (480)	582	0.20
African (375)	421	0.14
Cape Verdean (0)	0	<0.01
Ethiopian (9)	45	0.02
Ghanaian (10)	10	<0.01
Kenyan (0)	0	<0.01
Liberian (14)	14	<0.01
Nigerian (0)	9	<0.01
Senegalese (0)	0	<0.01
Sierra Leonean (13)	13	<0.01
Somalian (0)	0	<0.01
South African (14)	14	<0.01
Sudanese (11)	11	<0.01
Ugandan (13)	24	0.01
Zimbabwean (0)	0	<0.01
Other Sub-Saharan African (21)	21	0.01
Albanian (167)	217	0.07
Alsatian (0)	9	<0.01
American (27,680)	27,680	9.42
Arab (659)	884	0.30
Arab (400)	400	0.14
Egyptian (0)	0	<0.01
Iraqi (125)	125	0.04
Jordanian (9)	27	0.01
Lebanese (34)	143	0.05
Moroccan (0)	0	<0.01
Palestinian (91)	95	0.03
Syrian (0)	79	0.03
Other Arab (0)	15	0.01
Armenian (16)	77	0.03
Assyrian/Chaldean/Syriac (0)	0	<0.01
Australian (0)	0	<0.01
Austrian (126)	504	0.17
Basque (1)	1	<0.01
Belgian (128)	641	0.22
Brazilian (25)	34	0.01
British (442)	832	0.28
Bulgarian (16)	16	0.01
Cajun (12)	35	0.01
Canadian (140)	264	0.09
Carpatho Rusyn (0)	0	<0.01
Celtic (0)	21	0.01
Croatian (135)	355	0.12
Cypriot (0)	0	<0.01
Czech (314)	1,633	0.56
Czechoslovakian (95)	315	0.11
Danish (509)	2,079	0.71
Dutch (887)	5,511	1.87
Eastern European (27)	27	0.01
English (5,387)	24,511	8.34
Estonian (7)	25	0.01
European (1,627)	1,836	0.62
Finnish (131)	742	0.25
French, ex. Basque (701)	7,453	2.54
French Canadian (379)	985	0.34
German (22,758)	75,251	25.60
German Russian (0)	68	0.02
Greek (285)	711	0.24
Guyanese (0)	0	<0.01
Hungarian (179)	769	0.26
Icelander (0)	9	<0.01
Iranian (16)	26	0.01
Irish (7,744)	39,682	13.50
Israeli (0)	0	<0.01
Italian (8,670)	21,624	7.36
Latvian (53)	123	0.04
Lithuanian (578)	1,594	0.54
Luxemburger (41)	95	0.03
Macedonian (116)	116	0.04
Maltese (3)	3	<0.01
New Zealander (0)	0	<0.01
Northern European (179)	210	0.07
Norwegian (2,846)	11,387	3.87
Pennsylvania German (110)	197	0.07

Ancestry (cont.)	Population	%
Polish (3,519)	10,901	3.71
Portuguese (0)	75	0.03
Romanian (24)	195	0.07
Russian (454)	1,136	0.39
Scandinavian (442)	799	0.27
Scotch-Irish (1,012)	3,193	1.09
Scottish (882)	3,923	1.33
Serbian (275)	421	0.14
Slavic (35)	114	0.04
Slovak (104)	251	0.09
Slovene (31)	69	0.02
Soviet Union (0)	0	<0.01
Swedish (8,608)	25,721	8.75
Swiss (309)	1,829	0.62
Turkish (49)	66	0.02
Ukrainian (214)	524	0.18
Welsh (241)	1,387	0.47
West Indian, ex. Hispanic (64)	157	0.05
Bahamian (21)	21	0.01
Barbadian (0)	0	<0.01
Belizean (0)	0	<0.01
Bermudan (0)	0	<0.01
British West Indian (0)	0	<0.01
Dutch West Indian (0)	0	<0.01
Haitian (0)	0	<0.01
Jamaican (10)	62	0.02
Trinidadian/Tobagonian (0)	0	<0.01
U.S. Virgin Islander (0)	0	<0.01
West Indian (33)	74	0.03
Other West Indian (0)	0	<0.01
Yugoslavian (430)	550	0.19

Hispanic Origin	Population	%
Hispanic or Latino (of any race)	32,177	10.90
Central American, ex. Mexican	682	0.23
Costa Rican	43	0.01
Guatemalan	324	0.11
Honduran	106	0.04
Nicaraguan	34	0.01
Panamanian	35	0.01
Salvadoran	137	0.05
Other Central American	3	<0.01
Cuban	570	0.19
Dominican Republic	73	0.02
Mexican	26,414	8.95
Puerto Rican	1,908	0.65
South American	801	0.27
Argentinean	60	0.02
Bolivian	37	0.01
Chilean	56	0.02
Colombian	347	0.12
Ecuadorian	95	0.03
Paraguayan	4	<0.01
Peruvian	110	0.04
Uruguayan	48	0.02
Venezuelan	40	0.01
Other South American	4	<0.01
Other Hispanic or Latino	1,729	0.59

Race*	Population	%
African-American/Black (36,108)	40,317	13.65
Not Hispanic (35,358)	38,936	13.19
Hispanic (750)	1,381	0.47
American Indian/Alaska Native (963)	2,734	0.93
Not Hispanic (563)	1,922	0.65
Hispanic (400)	812	0.28
Alaska Athabascan (Ala. Nat.) (4)	8	<0.01
Aleut (Alaska Native) (0)	1	<0.01
Apache (10)	38	0.01
Arapaho (1)	2	<0.01
Blackfeet (6)	87	0.03
Canadian/French Am. Ind. (0)	12	<0.01
Central American Ind. (1)	10	<0.01
Cherokee (96)	472	0.16
Cheyenne (1)	5	<0.01
Chickasaw (0)	1	<0.01
Chippewa (51)	114	0.04
Choctaw (3)	43	0.01
Colville (0)	0	<0.01

Race* (cont.)	Population	%
Comanche (4)	15	0.01
Cree (2)	3	<0.01
Creek (3)	21	0.01
Crow (7)	13	<0.01
Delaware (0)	5	<0.01
Hopi (0)	0	<0.01
Houma (2)	2	<0.01
Inupiat (Alaska Native) (2)	8	<0.01
Iroquois (24)	43	0.01
Kiowa (0)	1	<0.01
Lumbee (1)	1	<0.01
Menominee (3)	3	<0.01
Mexican American Ind. (74)	118	0.04
Navajo (19)	42	0.01
Osage (2)	3	<0.01
Ottawa (3)	4	<0.01
Paiute (0)	6	<0.01
Pima (4)	4	<0.01
Potawatomi (2)	10	<0.01
Pueblo (1)	1	<0.01
Puget Sound Salish (0)	10	<0.01
Seminole (1)	7	<0.01
Shoshone (5)	5	<0.01
Sioux (36)	76	0.03
South American Ind. (2)	17	0.01
Spanish American Ind. (5)	5	<0.01
Tlingit-Haida (Alaska Native) (0)	0	<0.01
Tohono O'Odham (0)	0	<0.01
Tsimshian (Alaska Native) (1)	1	<0.01
Ute (0)	1	<0.01
Yakama (0)	1	<0.01
Yaqui (2)	3	<0.01
Yuman (0)	0	<0.01
Yup'ik (Alaska Native) (0)	0	<0.01
Asian (6,810)	8,289	2.81
Not Hispanic (6,722)	8,051	2.73
Hispanic (88)	238	0.08
Bangladeshi (21)	24	0.01
Bhutanese (1)	1	<0.01
Burmese (404)	418	0.14
Cambodian (21)	42	0.01
Chinese, ex. Taiwanese (598)	796	0.27
Filipino (1,027)	1,416	0.48
Hmong (33)	40	0.01
Indian (1,200)	1,397	0.47
Indonesian (22)	32	0.01
Japanese (182)	382	0.13
Korean (500)	655	0.22
Laotian (1,237)	1,423	0.48
Malaysian (8)	13	<0.01
Nepalese (0)	3	<0.01
Pakistani (191)	216	0.07
Sri Lankan (21)	21	0.01
Taiwanese (24)	35	0.01
Thai (134)	207	0.07
Vietnamese (762)	904	0.31
Hawaii Native/Pacific Islander (71)	272	0.09
Not Hispanic (61)	206	0.07
Hispanic (10)	66	0.02
Fijian (0)	0	<0.01
Guamanian/Chamorro (12)	22	0.01
Marshallese (2)	2	<0.01
Native Hawaiian (30)	114	0.04
Samoan (5)	26	0.01
Tongan (0)	0	<0.01
White (228,652)	236,143	79.98
Not Hispanic (214,196)	219,580	74.37
Hispanic (14,456)	16,563	5.61

*Notes: † The Census 2010 population figure is used to calculate the percentages in the Hispanic Origin and Race categories. Ancestry percentages are based on the 2006-2010 American Community Survey population (not shown); ‡ Numbers in parentheses indicate the number of people reporting a single ancestry; * Numbers in parentheses indicate the number of persons reporting this race alone, not in combination with any other race; Please refer to the Explanation of Data for more information.*

Place Profiles

Arlington Heights

Place Type: Village
County: Cook
Population: 75,101

Ancestry	Population	%
Afghan (0)	0	<0.01
African, Sub-Saharan (91)	113	0.15
African (44)	44	0.06
Cape Verdean (0)	0	<0.01
Ethiopian (0)	0	<0.01
Ghanaian (0)	0	<0.01
Kenyan (0)	0	<0.01
Liberian (0)	0	<0.01
Nigerian (35)	57	0.08
Senegalese (0)	0	<0.01
Sierra Leonean (0)	0	<0.01
Somalian (0)	0	<0.01
South African (0)	0	<0.01
Sudanese (0)	0	<0.01
Ugandan (0)	0	<0.01
Zimbabwean (0)	0	<0.01
Other Sub-Saharan African (12)	12	0.02
Albanian (142)	176	0.23
Alsatian (0)	12	0.02
American (2,097)	2,097	2.80
Arab (58)	157	0.21
Arab (22)	82	0.11
Egyptian (7)	22	0.03
Iraqi (0)	0	<0.01
Jordanian (0)	0	<0.01
Lebanese (0)	9	0.01
Moroccan (0)	0	<0.01
Palestinian (18)	18	0.02
Syrian (11)	11	0.01
Other Arab (0)	15	0.02
Armenian (112)	156	0.21
Assyrian/Chaldean/Syriac (19)	58	0.08
Australian (0)	0	<0.01
Austrian (150)	732	0.98
Basque (0)	0	<0.01
Belgian (16)	173	0.23
Brazilian (0)	57	0.08
British (205)	459	0.61
Bulgarian (675)	754	1.01
Cajun (0)	0	<0.01
Canadian (38)	46	0.06
Carpatho Rusyn (0)	0	<0.01
Celtic (0)	0	<0.01
Croatian (126)	323	0.43
Cypriot (0)	0	<0.01
Czech (218)	1,161	1.55
Czechoslovakian (95)	117	0.16
Danish (121)	645	0.86
Dutch (277)	929	1.24
Eastern European (145)	161	0.21
English (965)	5,336	7.12
Estonian (34)	34	0.05
European (908)	982	1.31
Finnish (22)	153	0.20
French, ex. Basque (120)	1,500	2.00
French Canadian (39)	173	0.23
German (5,600)	20,088	26.80
German Russian (0)	0	<0.01
Greek (986)	1,599	2.13
Guyanese (0)	0	<0.01
Hungarian (130)	475	0.63
Icelander (0)	15	0.02
Iranian (10)	106	0.14
Irish (3,424)	14,141	18.86
Israeli (60)	74	0.10
Italian (3,379)	8,782	11.71
Latvian (0)	27	0.04
Lithuanian (201)	510	0.68
Luxemburger (20)	122	0.16
Macedonian (0)	10	0.01

Ancestry	Population	%
Maltese (0)	0	<0.01
New Zealander (0)	0	<0.01
Northern European (48)	48	0.06
Norwegian (383)	1,657	2.21
Pennsylvania German (0)	37	0.05
Polish (6,196)	12,420	16.57
Portuguese (34)	81	0.11
Romanian (417)	548	0.73
Russian (943)	1,800	2.40
Scandinavian (89)	117	0.16
Scotch-Irish (266)	952	1.27
Scottish (381)	1,440	1.92
Serbian (225)	307	0.41
Slavic (0)	0	<0.01
Slovak (81)	388	0.52
Slovene (99)	150	0.20
Soviet Union (0)	0	<0.01
Swedish (895)	3,191	4.26
Swiss (0)	191	0.25
Turkish (0)	27	0.04
Ukrainian (320)	626	0.84
Welsh (71)	369	0.49
West Indian, ex. Hispanic (61)	71	0.09
Bahamian (0)	0	<0.01
Barbadian (0)	0	<0.01
Belizean (9)	9	0.01
Bermudan (0)	0	<0.01
British West Indian (0)	0	<0.01
Dutch West Indian (0)	0	<0.01
Haitian (52)	52	0.07
Jamaican (0)	0	<0.01
Trinidadian/Tobagonian (0)	0	<0.01
U.S. Virgin Islander (0)	0	<0.01
West Indian (0)	10	0.01
Other West Indian (0)	0	<0.01
Yugoslavian (65)	81	0.11

Hispanic Origin	Population	%
Hispanic or Latino (of any race)	4,306	5.73
Central American, ex. Mexican	202	0.27
Costa Rican	7	0.01
Guatemalan	90	0.12
Honduran	32	0.04
Nicaraguan	17	0.02
Panamanian	15	0.02
Salvadoran	40	0.05
Other Central American	1	<0.01
Cuban	162	0.22
Dominican Republic	36	0.05
Mexican	2,850	3.79
Puerto Rican	375	0.50
South American	443	0.59
Argentinean	53	0.07
Bolivian	7	0.01
Chilean	13	0.02
Colombian	138	0.18
Ecuadorian	115	0.15
Paraguayan	4	0.01
Peruvian	69	0.09
Uruguayan	9	0.01
Venezuelan	32	0.04
Other South American	3	<0.01
Other Hispanic or Latino	238	0.32

Race*	Population	%
African-American/Black (984)	1,176	1.57
Not Hispanic (936)	1,083	1.44
Hispanic (48)	93	0.12
American Indian/Alaska Native (95)	237	0.32
Not Hispanic (48)	158	0.21
Hispanic (47)	79	0.11
Alaska Athabascan (Ala. Nat.) (0)	0	<0.01
Aleut (Alaska Native) (0)	0	<0.01
Apache (0)	1	<0.01
Arapaho (0)	0	<0.01
Blackfeet (0)	6	0.01

Race*	Population	%
Canadian/French Am. Ind. (0)	2	<0.01
Central American Ind. (1)	2	<0.01
Cherokee (13)	42	0.06
Cheyenne (0)	0	<0.01
Chickasaw (0)	0	<0.01
Chippewa (6)	19	0.03
Choctaw (1)	4	0.01
Colville (0)	0	<0.01
Comanche (0)	0	<0.01
Cree (0)	0	<0.01
Creek (0)	0	<0.01
Crow (0)	0	<0.01
Delaware (0)	0	<0.01
Hopi (0)	0	<0.01
Houma (0)	0	<0.01
Inupiat (Alaska Native) (0)	0	<0.01
Iroquois (1)	3	<0.01
Kiowa (1)	1	<0.01
Lumbee (0)	0	<0.01
Menominee (0)	0	<0.01
Mexican American Ind. (6)	17	0.02
Navajo (2)	3	<0.01
Osage (0)	0	<0.01
Ottawa (2)	2	<0.01
Paiute (0)	0	<0.01
Pima (0)	0	<0.01
Potawatomi (0)	0	<0.01
Pueblo (0)	0	<0.01
Puget Sound Salish (0)	0	<0.01
Seminole (0)	0	<0.01
Shoshone (0)	0	<0.01
Sioux (1)	9	0.01
South American Ind. (4)	8	0.01
Spanish American Ind. (0)	0	<0.01
Tlingit-Haida (Alaska Native) (0)	0	<0.01
Tohono O'Odham (0)	0	<0.01
Tsimshian (Alaska Native) (0)	0	<0.01
Ute (0)	0	<0.01
Yakama (0)	0	<0.01
Yaqui (0)	0	<0.01
Yuman (0)	0	<0.01
Yup'ik (Alaska Native) (0)	0	<0.01
Asian (5,349)	5,992	7.98
Not Hispanic (5,320)	5,930	7.90
Hispanic (29)	62	0.08
Bangladeshi (6)	6	0.01
Bhutanese (0)	0	<0.01
Burmese (0)	0	<0.01
Cambodian (7)	10	0.01
Chinese, ex. Taiwanese (673)	813	1.08
Filipino (748)	955	1.27
Hmong (0)	0	<0.01
Indian (1,586)	1,677	2.23
Indonesian (14)	20	0.03
Japanese (670)	819	1.09
Korean (1,104)	1,193	1.59
Laotian (7)	14	0.02
Malaysian (8)	16	0.02
Nepalese (0)	0	<0.01
Pakistani (109)	118	0.16
Sri Lankan (0)	0	<0.01
Taiwanese (70)	82	0.11
Thai (45)	59	0.08
Vietnamese (160)	191	0.25
Hawaii Native/Pacific Islander (8)	44	0.06
Not Hispanic (7)	40	0.05
Hispanic (1)	4	0.01
Fijian (0)	0	<0.01
Guamanian/Chamorro (4)	5	0.01
Marshallese (0)	0	<0.01
Native Hawaiian (2)	17	0.02
Samoan (1)	2	<0.01
Tongan (0)	0	<0.01
White (66,266)	67,261	89.56
Not Hispanic (63,532)	64,320	85.64
Hispanic (2,734)	2,941	3.92

Notes: † The Census 2010 population figure is used to calculate the percentages in the Hispanic Origin and Race categories. Ancestry percentages are based on the 2006-2010 American Community Survey population (not shown); ‡ Numbers in parentheses indicate the number of people reporting a single ancestry; * Numbers in parentheses indicate the number of persons reporting this race alone, not in combination with any other race; Please refer to the Explanation of Data for more information.

Aurora

Place Type: City
County: Kane
Population: 197,899

Ancestry	Population	%
Afghan (261)	261	0.14
African, Sub-Saharan (800)	977	0.51
African (236)	395	0.21
Cape Verdean (0)	0	<0.01
Ethiopian (0)	0	<0.01
Ghanaian (0)	0	<0.01
Kenyan (0)	0	<0.01
Liberian (0)	0	<0.01
Nigerian (354)	372	0.20
Senegalese (0)	0	<0.01
Sierra Leonean (8)	8	<0.01
Somalian (0)	0	<0.01
South African (0)	0	<0.01
Sudanese (0)	0	<0.01
Ugandan (0)	0	<0.01
Zimbabwean (0)	0	<0.01
Other Sub-Saharan African (202)	202	0.11
Albanian (369)	467	0.25
Alsatian (0)	15	0.01
American (2,674)	2,674	1.40
Arab (326)	570	0.30
Arab (118)	118	0.06
Egyptian (45)	77	0.04
Iraqi (0)	0	<0.01
Jordanian (13)	26	0.01
Lebanese (35)	126	0.07
Moroccan (0)	0	<0.01
Palestinian (115)	115	0.06
Syrian (0)	12	0.01
Other Arab (0)	96	0.05
Armenian (23)	23	0.01
Assyrian/Chaldean/Syriac (26)	37	0.02
Australian (0)	12	0.01
Austrian (151)	389	0.20
Basque (0)	0	<0.01
Belgian (102)	290	0.15
Brazilian (12)	186	0.10
British (259)	619	0.33
Bulgarian (39)	54	0.03
Cajun (0)	0	<0.01
Canadian (141)	357	0.19
Carpatho Rusyn (0)	0	<0.01
Celtic (0)	0	<0.01
Croatian (31)	246	0.13
Cypriot (0)	0	<0.01
Czech (456)	1,429	0.75
Czechoslovakian (113)	244	0.13
Danish (119)	707	0.37
Dutch (344)	1,799	0.94
Eastern European (248)	297	0.16
English (2,025)	9,343	4.91
Estonian (0)	10	0.01
European (1,287)	1,374	0.72
Finnish (0)	193	0.10
French, ex. Basque (445)	2,674	1.40
French Canadian (161)	565	0.30
German (8,935)	31,118	16.34
German Russian (0)	6	<0.01
Greek (410)	1,065	0.56
Guyanese (0)	20	0.01
Hungarian (209)	924	0.49
Icelander (0)	11	0.01
Iranian (188)	188	0.10
Irish (3,076)	18,380	9.65
Israeli (0)	0	<0.01
Italian (2,974)	9,132	4.80
Latvian (17)	116	0.06
Lithuanian (280)	979	0.51
Luxemburger (168)	608	0.32
Macedonian (14)	14	0.01
Maltese (0)	0	<0.01
New Zealander (0)	0	<0.01
Northern European (68)	68	0.04

Ancestry (cont.)	Population	%
Norwegian (483)	2,157	1.13
Pennsylvania German (7)	25	0.01
Polish (2,715)	9,369	4.92
Portuguese (89)	276	0.14
Romanian (437)	1,266	0.66
Russian (509)	1,340	0.70
Scandinavian (37)	202	0.11
Scotch-Irish (317)	1,361	0.71
Scottish (364)	2,105	1.11
Serbian (39)	138	0.07
Slavic (24)	36	0.02
Slovak (102)	421	0.22
Slovene (16)	77	0.04
Soviet Union (0)	0	<0.01
Swedish (601)	3,178	1.67
Swiss (65)	397	0.21
Turkish (23)	109	0.06
Ukrainian (292)	509	0.27
Welsh (233)	954	0.50
West Indian, ex. Hispanic (55)	133	0.07
Bahamian (0)	0	<0.01
Barbadian (0)	0	<0.01
Belizean (0)	0	<0.01
Bermudan (0)	0	<0.01
British West Indian (0)	0	<0.01
Dutch West Indian (0)	0	<0.01
Haitian (32)	32	0.02
Jamaican (16)	94	0.05
Trinidadian/Tobagonian (0)	0	<0.01
U.S. Virgin Islander (0)	0	<0.01
West Indian (7)	7	<0.01
Other West Indian (0)	0	<0.01
Yugoslavian (63)	212	0.11

Hispanic Origin	Population	%
Hispanic or Latino (of any race)	81,809	41.34
Central American, ex. Mexican	1,086	0.55
Costa Rican	13	0.01
Guatemalan	386	0.20
Honduran	211	0.11
Nicaraguan	98	0.05
Panamanian	60	0.03
Salvadoran	289	0.15
Other Central American	29	0.01
Cuban	318	0.16
Dominican Republic	110	0.06
Mexican	72,924	36.85
Puerto Rican	3,867	1.95
South American	1,010	0.51
Argentinean	133	0.07
Bolivian	96	0.05
Chilean	42	0.02
Colombian	311	0.16
Ecuadorian	135	0.07
Paraguayan	3	<0.01
Peruvian	187	0.09
Uruguayan	5	<0.01
Venezuelan	94	0.05
Other South American	4	<0.01
Other Hispanic or Latino	2,494	1.26

Race*	Population	%
African-American/Black (21,202)	23,545	11.90
Not Hispanic (20,348)	21,960	11.10
Hispanic (854)	1,585	0.80
American Indian/Alaska Native (1,004)	1,868	0.94
Not Hispanic (246)	738	0.37
Hispanic (758)	1,130	0.57
Alaska Athabascan (Ala. Nat.) (0)	0	<0.01
Aleut (Alaska Native) (1)	1	<0.01
Apache (7)	25	0.01
Arapaho (0)	0	<0.01
Blackfeet (5)	31	0.02
Canadian/French Am. Ind. (2)	3	<0.01
Central American Ind. (1)	6	<0.01
Cherokee (42)	187	0.09
Cheyenne (0)	3	<0.01
Chickasaw (2)	4	<0.01
Chippewa (10)	23	0.01

Race* (cont.)	Population	%
Choctaw (5)	16	0.01
Colville (0)	0	<0.01
Comanche (1)	4	<0.01
Cree (0)	2	<0.01
Creek (1)	6	<0.01
Crow (2)	3	<0.01
Delaware (0)	0	<0.01
Hopi (8)	14	0.01
Houma (0)	0	<0.01
Inupiat (Alaska Native) (4)	10	0.01
Iroquois (9)	15	0.01
Kiowa (0)	0	<0.01
Lumbee (4)	4	<0.01
Menominee (0)	1	<0.01
Mexican American Ind. (164)	222	0.11
Navajo (20)	26	0.01
Osage (0)	0	<0.01
Ottawa (0)	2	<0.01
Paiute (0)	0	<0.01
Pima (3)	5	<0.01
Potawatomi (7)	11	0.01
Pueblo (0)	5	<0.01
Puget Sound Salish (0)	0	<0.01
Seminole (0)	0	<0.01
Shoshone (0)	0	<0.01
Sioux (11)	29	0.01
South American Ind. (8)	17	0.01
Spanish American Ind. (19)	28	0.01
Tlingit-Haida (Alaska Native) (1)	1	<0.01
Tohono O'Odham (0)	0	<0.01
Tsimshian (Alaska Native) (0)	0	<0.01
Ute (0)	2	<0.01
Yakama (0)	0	<0.01
Yaqui (7)	12	0.01
Yuman (0)	0	<0.01
Yup'ik (Alaska Native) (0)	0	<0.01
Asian (13,248)	14,809	7.48
Not Hispanic (13,105)	14,444	7.30
Hispanic (143)	365	0.18
Bangladeshi (93)	95	0.05
Bhutanese (61)	81	0.04
Burmese (198)	206	0.10
Cambodian (51)	76	0.04
Chinese, ex. Taiwanese (1,388)	1,636	0.83
Filipino (2,058)	2,529	1.28
Hmong (92)	97	0.05
Indian (6,464)	6,828	3.45
Indonesian (39)	55	0.03
Japanese (110)	264	0.13
Korean (648)	801	0.40
Laotian (128)	151	0.08
Malaysian (23)	25	0.01
Nepalese (23)	31	0.02
Pakistani (755)	829	0.42
Sri Lankan (70)	72	0.04
Taiwanese (67)	80	0.04
Thai (86)	143	0.07
Vietnamese (533)	601	0.30
Hawaii Native/Pacific Islander (65)	202	0.10
Not Hispanic (53)	152	0.08
Hispanic (12)	50	0.03
Fijian (1)	4	<0.01
Guamanian/Chamorro (19)	38	0.02
Marshallese (0)	0	<0.01
Native Hawaiian (10)	44	0.02
Samoan (2)	9	<0.01
Tongan (2)	2	<0.01
White (118,172)	123,599	62.46
Not Hispanic (78,924)	81,537	41.20
Hispanic (39,248)	42,062	21.25

*Notes: † The Census 2010 population figure is used to calculate the percentages in the Hispanic Origin and Race categories. Ancestry percentages are based on the 2006-2010 American Community Survey population (not shown); ‡ Numbers in parentheses indicate the number of people reporting a single ancestry; * Numbers in parentheses indicate the number of persons reporting this race alone, not in combination with any other race; Please refer to the Explanation of Data for more information.*

Berwyn

Place Type: City
County: Cook
Population: 56,657

Ancestry	Population	%
Afghan (0)	0	<0.01
African, Sub-Saharan (131)	155	0.28
African (115)	139	0.25
Cape Verdean (0)	0	<0.01
Ethiopian (0)	0	<0.01
Ghanaian (0)	0	<0.01
Kenyan (0)	0	<0.01
Liberian (0)	0	<0.01
Nigerian (0)	0	<0.01
Senegalese (0)	0	<0.01
Sierra Leonean (0)	0	<0.01
Somalian (0)	0	<0.01
South African (16)	16	0.03
Sudanese (0)	0	<0.01
Ugandan (0)	0	<0.01
Zimbabwean (0)	0	<0.01
Other Sub-Saharan African (0)	0	<0.01
Albanian (0)	9	0.02
Alsatian (0)	0	<0.01
American (481)	481	0.87
Arab (191)	204	0.37
Arab (64)	64	0.12
Egyptian (14)	14	0.03
Iraqi (0)	0	<0.01
Jordanian (31)	31	0.06
Lebanese (0)	13	0.02
Moroccan (82)	82	0.15
Palestinian (0)	0	<0.01
Syrian (0)	0	<0.01
Other Arab (0)	0	<0.01
Armenian (9)	9	0.02
Assyrian/Chaldean/Syriac (0)	0	<0.01
Australian (0)	0	<0.01
Austrian (34)	151	0.27
Basque (0)	0	<0.01
Belgian (17)	49	0.09
Brazilian (10)	22	0.04
British (0)	0	<0.01
Bulgarian (0)	0	<0.01
Cajun (0)	0	<0.01
Canadian (13)	26	0.05
Carpatho Rusyn (0)	0	<0.01
Celtic (0)	0	<0.01
Croatian (134)	231	0.42
Cypriot (0)	0	<0.01
Czech (746)	1,864	3.35
Czechoslovakian (163)	346	0.62
Danish (20)	72	0.13
Dutch (63)	243	0.44
Eastern European (13)	13	0.02
English (173)	1,153	2.07
Estonian (12)	12	0.02
European (25)	25	0.04
Finnish (10)	33	0.06
French, ex. Basque (55)	637	1.15
French Canadian (31)	109	0.20
German (927)	4,978	8.96
German Russian (0)	0	<0.01
Greek (147)	321	0.58
Guyanese (0)	0	<0.01
Hungarian (28)	61	0.11
Icelander (0)	0	<0.01
Iranian (0)	8	0.01
Irish (1,033)	4,905	8.82
Israeli (0)	0	<0.01
Italian (1,722)	4,694	8.44
Latvian (0)	0	<0.01
Lithuanian (196)	441	0.79
Luxemburger (0)	0	<0.01
Macedonian (0)	0	<0.01
Maltese (0)	0	<0.01
New Zealander (0)	0	<0.01
Northern European (0)	0	<0.01

	Population	%
Norwegian (41)	388	0.70
Pennsylvania German (24)	50	0.09
Polish (1,586)	4,633	8.34
Portuguese (9)	9	0.02
Romanian (13)	32	0.06
Russian (39)	217	0.39
Scandinavian (0)	6	0.01
Scotch-Irish (50)	258	0.46
Scottish (70)	467	0.84
Serbian (34)	54	0.10
Slavic (0)	11	0.02
Slovak (52)	93	0.17
Slovene (17)	57	0.10
Soviet Union (0)	0	<0.01
Swedish (18)	333	0.60
Swiss (0)	47	0.08
Turkish (8)	8	0.01
Ukrainian (137)	194	0.35
Welsh (10)	64	0.12
West Indian, ex. Hispanic (81)	159	0.29
Bahamian (0)	0	<0.01
Barbadian (0)	0	<0.01
Belizean (0)	0	<0.01
Bermudan (0)	0	<0.01
British West Indian (0)	0	<0.01
Dutch West Indian (0)	0	<0.01
Haitian (32)	32	0.06
Jamaican (23)	101	0.18
Trinidadian/Tobagonian (26)	26	0.05
U.S. Virgin Islander (0)	0	<0.01
West Indian (0)	0	<0.01
Other West Indian (0)	0	<0.01
Yugoslavian (89)	166	0.30

Hispanic Origin	Population	%
Hispanic or Latino (of any race)	33,676	59.44
Central American, ex. Mexican	825	1.46
Costa Rican	15	0.03
Guatemalan	476	0.84
Honduran	95	0.17
Nicaraguan	41	0.07
Panamanian	16	0.03
Salvadoran	182	0.32
Other Central American	0	<0.01
Cuban	167	0.29
Dominican Republic	47	0.08
Mexican	28,185	49.75
Puerto Rican	2,918	5.15
South American	856	1.51
Argentinean	79	0.14
Bolivian	34	0.06
Chilean	36	0.06
Colombian	276	0.49
Ecuadorian	257	0.45
Paraguayan	7	0.01
Peruvian	128	0.23
Uruguayan	16	0.03
Venezuelan	18	0.03
Other South American	5	0.01
Other Hispanic or Latino	678	1.20

Race*	Population	%
African-American/Black (3,627)	4,007	7.07
Not Hispanic (3,373)	3,564	6.29
Hispanic (254)	443	0.78
American Indian/Alaska Native (335)	605	1.07
Not Hispanic (66)	205	0.36
Hispanic (269)	400	0.71
Alaska Athabascan (Ala. Nat.) (0)	1	<0.01
Aleut (Alaska Native) (0)	0	<0.01
Apache (13)	18	0.03
Arapaho (0)	0	<0.01
Blackfeet (1)	11	0.02
Canadian/French Am. Ind. (0)	1	<0.01
Central American Ind. (5)	7	0.01
Cherokee (9)	51	0.09
Cheyenne (0)	0	<0.01
Chickasaw (0)	0	<0.01
Chippewa (9)	22	0.04

	Population	%
Choctaw (4)	14	0.02
Colville (0)	0	<0.01
Comanche (0)	1	<0.01
Cree (0)	0	<0.01
Creek (0)	1	<0.01
Crow (0)	0	<0.01
Delaware (0)	0	<0.01
Hopi (0)	0	<0.01
Houma (0)	0	<0.01
Inupiat (Alaska Native) (1)	1	<0.01
Iroquois (4)	6	0.01
Kiowa (3)	3	0.01
Lumbee (0)	3	0.01
Menominee (3)	6	0.01
Mexican American Ind. (74)	102	0.18
Navajo (6)	7	0.01
Osage (0)	0	<0.01
Ottawa (2)	2	<0.01
Paiute (0)	0	<0.01
Pima (1)	1	<0.01
Potawatomi (0)	0	<0.01
Pueblo (0)	0	<0.01
Puget Sound Salish (0)	0	<0.01
Seminole (0)	0	<0.01
Shoshone (0)	0	<0.01
Sioux (3)	16	0.03
South American Ind. (12)	26	0.05
Spanish American Ind. (0)	5	<0.01
Tlingit-Haida (Alaska Native) (0)	0	<0.01
Tohono O'Odham (0)	0	<0.01
Tsimshian (Alaska Native) (0)	0	<0.01
Ute (0)	0	<0.01
Yakama (0)	0	<0.01
Yaqui (0)	3	0.01
Yuman (0)	0	<0.01
Yup'ik (Alaska Native) (1)	1	<0.01
Asian (1,425)	1,766	3.12
Not Hispanic (1,362)	1,586	2.80
Hispanic (63)	180	0.32
Bangladeshi (0)	0	<0.01
Bhutanese (0)	0	<0.01
Burmese (3)	3	0.01
Cambodian (10)	20	0.04
Chinese, ex. Taiwanese (133)	192	0.34
Filipino (802)	923	1.63
Hmong (1)	1	<0.01
Indian (130)	182	0.32
Indonesian (6)	6	0.01
Japanese (19)	53	0.09
Korean (32)	44	0.08
Laotian (7)	8	0.01
Malaysian (2)	2	<0.01
Nepalese (0)	0	<0.01
Pakistani (49)	65	0.11
Sri Lankan (1)	1	<0.01
Taiwanese (1)	1	<0.01
Thai (49)	55	0.10
Vietnamese (138)	159	0.28
Hawaii Native/Pacific Islander (17)	80	0.14
Not Hispanic (2)	33	0.06
Hispanic (15)	47	0.08
Fijian (1)	4	0.01
Guamanian/Chamorro (4)	4	0.01
Marshallese (0)	0	<0.01
Native Hawaiian (0)	8	0.01
Samoan (1)	8	0.01
Tongan (0)	0	<0.01
White (34,270)	35,893	63.35
Not Hispanic (17,592)	18,019	31.80
Hispanic (16,678)	17,874	31.55

Notes: † The Census 2010 population figure is used to calculate the percentages in the Hispanic Origin and Race categories. Ancestry percentages are based on the 2006-2010 American Community Survey population (not shown); ‡ Numbers in parentheses indicate the number of people reporting a single ancestry; * Numbers in parentheses indicate the number of persons reporting this race alone, not in combination with any other race; Please refer to the Explanation of Data for more information.

Bloomington

Place Type: City
County: McLean
Population: 76,610

Ancestry	Population	%
Afghan (0)	0	<0.01
African, Sub-Saharan (331)	365	0.49
African (264)	264	0.35
Cape Verdean (0)	0	<0.01
Ethiopian (18)	41	0.05
Ghanaian (17)	17	0.02
Kenyan (10)	10	0.01
Liberian (0)	0	<0.01
Nigerian (10)	10	0.01
Senegalese (0)	0	<0.01
Sierra Leonean (0)	0	<0.01
Somalian (0)	0	<0.01
South African (0)	0	<0.01
Sudanese (0)	0	<0.01
Ugandan (0)	0	<0.01
Zimbabwean (0)	0	<0.01
Other Sub-Saharan African (12)	23	0.03
Albanian (0)	0	<0.01
Alsatian (0)	8	0.01
American (8,005)	8,005	10.69
Arab (24)	203	0.27
Arab (0)	11	0.01
Egyptian (0)	0	<0.01
Iraqi (0)	0	<0.01
Jordanian (0)	0	<0.01
Lebanese (24)	69	0.09
Moroccan (0)	0	<0.01
Palestinian (0)	8	0.01
Syrian (0)	83	0.11
Other Arab (0)	32	0.04
Armenian (8)	8	0.01
Assyrian/Chaldean/Syriac (0)	0	<0.01
Australian (12)	12	0.02
Austrian (7)	126	0.17
Basque (0)	0	<0.01
Belgian (52)	185	0.25
Brazilian (0)	0	<0.01
British (155)	380	0.51
Bulgarian (14)	14	0.02
Cajun (0)	0	<0.01
Canadian (0)	89	0.12
Carpatho Rusyn (0)	0	<0.01
Celtic (15)	15	0.02
Croatian (17)	194	0.26
Cypriot (0)	0	<0.01
Czech (89)	437	0.58
Czechoslovakian (50)	90	0.12
Danish (61)	273	0.36
Dutch (322)	1,285	1.72
Eastern European (62)	69	0.09
English (2,777)	8,376	11.19
Estonian (12)	12	0.02
European (769)	905	1.21
Finnish (0)	102	0.14
French, ex. Basque (226)	1,815	2.42
French Canadian (58)	171	0.23
German (7,694)	20,952	27.99
German Russian (0)	11	0.01
Greek (113)	154	0.21
Guyanese (0)	0	<0.01
Hungarian (129)	190	0.25
Icelander (0)	0	<0.01
Iranian (0)	0	<0.01
Irish (2,941)	11,242	15.02
Israeli (0)	10	0.01
Italian (801)	2,707	3.62
Latvian (16)	28	0.04
Lithuanian (44)	202	0.27
Luxemburger (0)	11	0.01
Macedonian (0)	9	0.01
Maltese (0)	0	<0.01
New Zealander (0)	0	<0.01
Northern European (31)	31	0.04

Ancestry (cont.)	Population	%
Norwegian (363)	1,211	1.62
Pennsylvania German (0)	44	0.06
Polish (561)	2,344	3.13
Portuguese (20)	132	0.18
Romanian (31)	31	0.04
Russian (64)	192	0.26
Scandinavian (29)	68	0.09
Scotch-Irish (506)	1,404	1.88
Scottish (356)	1,576	2.11
Serbian (0)	0	<0.01
Slavic (0)	19	0.03
Slovak (88)	300	0.40
Slovene (15)	63	0.08
Soviet Union (0)	0	<0.01
Swedish (447)	1,505	2.01
Swiss (40)	421	0.56
Turkish (65)	96	0.13
Ukrainian (173)	192	0.26
Welsh (229)	581	0.78
West Indian, ex. Hispanic (45)	75	0.10
Bahamian (0)	0	<0.01
Barbadian (0)	0	<0.01
Belizean (0)	14	0.02
Bermudan (0)	0	<0.01
British West Indian (11)	11	0.01
Dutch West Indian (11)	11	0.01
Haitian (10)	17	0.02
Jamaican (0)	9	0.01
Trinidadian/Tobagonian (0)	0	<0.01
U.S. Virgin Islander (13)	13	0.02
West Indian (0)	0	<0.01
Other West Indian (0)	0	<0.01
Yugoslavian (0)	8	0.01

Hispanic Origin	Population	%
Hispanic or Latino (of any race)	4,308	5.62
Central American, ex. Mexican	413	0.54
Costa Rican	2	<0.01
Guatemalan	301	0.39
Honduran	26	0.03
Nicaraguan	2	<0.01
Panamanian	17	0.02
Salvadoran	64	0.08
Other Central American	1	<0.01
Cuban	81	0.11
Dominican Republic	12	0.02
Mexican	3,077	4.02
Puerto Rican	259	0.34
South American	160	0.21
Argentinean	9	0.01
Bolivian	11	0.01
Chilean	18	0.02
Colombian	53	0.07
Ecuadorian	15	0.02
Paraguayan	7	0.01
Peruvian	30	0.04
Uruguayan	0	<0.01
Venezuelan	17	0.02
Other South American	0	<0.01
Other Hispanic or Latino	306	0.40

Race*	Population	%
African-American/Black (7,770)	9,050	11.81
Not Hispanic (7,663)	8,833	11.53
Hispanic (107)	217	0.28
American Indian/Alaska Native (231)	608	0.79
Not Hispanic (170)	493	0.64
Hispanic (61)	115	0.15
Alaska Athabascan (Ala. Nat.) (0)	0	<0.01
Aleut (Alaska Native) (3)	3	<0.01
Apache (3)	6	0.01
Arapaho (0)	0	<0.01
Blackfeet (1)	17	0.02
Canadian/French Am. Ind. (0)	0	<0.01
Central American Ind. (0)	2	<0.01
Cherokee (26)	131	0.17
Cheyenne (0)	2	<0.01
Chickasaw (2)	6	0.01
Chippewa (6)	13	0.02

Race* (cont.)	Population	%
Choctaw (5)	15	0.0
Colville (1)	1	<0.0
Comanche (1)	1	<0.0
Cree (1)	2	<0.0
Creek (1)	5	0.0
Crow (0)	0	<0.0
Delaware (0)	0	<0.0
Hopi (0)	0	<0.0
Houma (0)	0	<0.0
Inupiat (Alaska Native) (0)	0	<0.0
Iroquois (2)	4	0.0
Kiowa (0)	0	<0.0
Lumbee (0)	0	<0.0
Menominee (0)	0	<0.0
Mexican American Ind. (21)	32	0.0
Navajo (1)	3	0.0
Osage (0)	1	<0.0
Ottawa (0)	0	<0.0
Paiute (0)	0	<0.0
Pima (0)	0	<0.0
Potawatomi (8)	14	0.0
Pueblo (0)	0	<0.0
Puget Sound Salish (1)	1	<0.0
Seminole (0)	0	<0.0
Shoshone (0)	1	<0.0
Sioux (13)	30	0.0
South American Ind. (3)	3	<0.0
Spanish American Ind. (0)	0	<0.0
Tlingit-Haida (Alaska Native) (0)	0	<0.0
Tohono O'Odham (0)	0	<0.0
Tsimshian (Alaska Native) (0)	0	<0.0
Ute (0)	0	<0.0
Yakama (1)	1	<0.0
Yaqui (0)	0	<0.0
Yuman (0)	0	<0.0
Yup'ik (Alaska Native) (1)	1	<0.0
Asian (5,343)	5,890	7.6
Not Hispanic (5,315)	5,815	7.5
Hispanic (28)	75	0.1
Bangladeshi (14)	15	0.0
Bhutanese (0)	0	<0.0
Burmese (5)	5	0.0
Cambodian (5)	8	0.0
Chinese, ex. Taiwanese (428)	526	0.6
Filipino (234)	362	0.4
Hmong (0)	0	<0.0
Indian (3,968)	4,090	5.3
Indonesian (8)	18	0.0
Japanese (96)	167	0.2
Korean (176)	250	0.3
Laotian (1)	4	0.0
Malaysian (0)	8	0.0
Nepalese (5)	5	0.0
Pakistani (82)	98	0.1
Sri Lankan (0)	1	<0.0
Taiwanese (27)	34	0.0
Thai (30)	47	0.0
Vietnamese (172)	207	0.2
Hawaii Native/Pacific Islander (28)	74	0.1
Not Hispanic (23)	52	0.0
Hispanic (5)	22	0.0
Fijian (2)	2	<0.0
Guamanian/Chamorro (8)	10	0.0
Marshallese (0)	0	<0.0
Native Hawaiian (10)	20	0.0
Samoan (2)	5	0.0
Tongan (2)	2	<0.0
White (59,353)	61,325	80.0
Not Hispanic (57,141)	58,841	76.8
Hispanic (2,212)	2,484	3.2

*Notes: † The Census 2010 population figure is used to calculate the percentages in the Hispanic Origin and Race categories. Ancestry percentages are based on the 2006-2010 American Communit Survey population (not shown); ‡ Numbers in parentheses indicate the number of people reporting a single ancestry; * Numbers in parentheses indicate the number of persons reporting this race alo not in combination with any other race; Please refer to the Explanation of Data for more information.*

Bolingbrook

Place Type: Village
County: Will
Population: 73,366

Ancestry	Population	%
Afghan (0)	0	<0.01
African, Sub-Saharan (1,195)	1,497	2.06
African (664)	870	1.20
Cape Verdean (0)	0	<0.01
Ethiopian (0)	0	<0.01
Ghanaian (287)	314	0.43
Kenyan (0)	12	0.02
Liberian (0)	0	<0.01
Nigerian (160)	171	0.24
Senegalese (0)	0	<0.01
Sierra Leonean (43)	43	0.06
Somalian (0)	0	<0.01
South African (0)	17	0.02
Sudanese (0)	0	<0.01
Ugandan (0)	0	<0.01
Zimbabwean (0)	0	<0.01
Other Sub-Saharan African (41)	70	0.10
Albanian (48)	54	0.07
Alsatian (0)	0	<0.01
American (1,296)	1,296	1.78
Arab (75)	172	0.24
Arab (7)	20	0.03
Egyptian (0)	0	<0.01
Iraqi (0)	0	<0.01
Jordanian (0)	0	<0.01
Lebanese (13)	84	0.12
Moroccan (55)	55	0.08
Palestinian (0)	0	<0.01
Syrian (0)	0	<0.01
Other Arab (0)	13	0.02
Armenian (22)	35	0.05
Assyrian/Chaldean/Syriac (69)	172	0.24
Australian (0)	0	<0.01
Austrian (40)	159	0.22
Basque (0)	0	<0.01
Belgian (28)	131	0.18
Brazilian (44)	44	0.06
British (107)	262	0.36
Bulgarian (90)	90	0.12
Cajun (0)	0	<0.01
Canadian (63)	193	0.27
Carpatho Rusyn (0)	0	<0.01
Celtic (0)	0	<0.01
Croatian (39)	158	0.22
Cypriot (0)	0	<0.01
Czech (417)	1,080	1.49
Czechoslovakian (28)	63	0.09
Danish (0)	191	0.26
Dutch (139)	817	1.12
Eastern European (11)	37	0.05
English (531)	3,042	4.19
Estonian (0)	0	<0.01
European (234)	282	0.39
Finnish (101)	196	0.27
French, ex. Basque (98)	1,041	1.43
French Canadian (26)	169	0.23
German (2,178)	10,413	14.33
German Russian (0)	0	<0.01
Greek (178)	498	0.69
Guyanese (0)	0	<0.01
Hungarian (62)	443	0.61
Icelander (0)	0	<0.01
Iranian (98)	122	0.17
Irish (1,622)	8,387	11.54
Israeli (0)	0	<0.01
Italian (1,156)	4,612	6.35
Latvian (0)	26	0.04
Lithuanian (304)	640	0.88
Luxemburger (0)	12	0.02
Macedonian (0)	0	<0.01
Maltese (0)	0	<0.01
New Zealander (18)	68	0.09
Northern European (0)	0	<0.01

Ancestry	Population	%
Norwegian (196)	798	1.10
Pennsylvania German (0)	0	<0.01
Polish (2,137)	7,074	9.74
Portuguese (0)	18	0.02
Romanian (133)	142	0.20
Russian (31)	166	0.23
Scandinavian (21)	27	0.04
Scotch-Irish (218)	605	0.83
Scottish (209)	807	1.11
Serbian (129)	224	0.31
Slavic (0)	47	0.06
Slovak (64)	234	0.32
Slovene (26)	114	0.16
Soviet Union (0)	0	<0.01
Swedish (198)	1,093	1.50
Swiss (9)	78	0.11
Turkish (26)	39	0.05
Ukrainian (22)	102	0.14
Welsh (73)	307	0.42
West Indian, ex. Hispanic (106)	197	0.27
Bahamian (0)	0	<0.01
Barbadian (18)	18	0.02
Belizean (0)	64	0.09
Bermudan (0)	0	<0.01
British West Indian (9)	9	0.01
Dutch West Indian (0)	0	<0.01
Haitian (0)	0	<0.01
Jamaican (79)	96	0.13
Trinidadian/Tobagonian (0)	0	<0.01
U.S. Virgin Islander (0)	0	<0.01
West Indian (0)	10	0.01
Other West Indian (0)	0	<0.01
Yugoslavian (8)	86	0.12

Hispanic Origin	Population	%
Hispanic or Latino (of any race)	17,957	24.48
Central American, ex. Mexican	460	0.63
Costa Rican	14	0.02
Guatemalan	262	0.36
Honduran	46	0.06
Nicaraguan	25	0.03
Panamanian	41	0.06
Salvadoran	71	0.10
Other Central American	1	<0.01
Cuban	117	0.16
Dominican Republic	29	0.04
Mexican	15,256	20.79
Puerto Rican	1,254	1.71
South American	405	0.55
Argentinean	23	0.03
Bolivian	29	0.04
Chilean	4	0.01
Colombian	140	0.19
Ecuadorian	75	0.10
Paraguayan	3	<0.01
Peruvian	99	0.13
Uruguayan	3	<0.01
Venezuelan	28	0.04
Other South American	1	<0.01
Other Hispanic or Latino	436	0.59

Race*	Population	%
African-American/Black (14,999)	15,996	21.80
Not Hispanic (14,735)	15,519	21.15
Hispanic (264)	477	0.65
American Indian/Alaska Native (230)	581	0.79
Not Hispanic (94)	353	0.48
Hispanic (136)	228	0.31
Alaska Athabascan (Ala. Nat.) (0)	0	<0.01
Aleut (Alaska Native) (0)	0	<0.01
Apache (6)	14	0.02
Arapaho (0)	6	0.01
Blackfeet (0)	8	0.01
Canadian/French Am. Ind. (1)	1	<0.01
Central American Ind. (1)	5	0.01
Cherokee (21)	107	0.15
Cheyenne (0)	0	<0.01
Chickasaw (0)	3	<0.01
Chippewa (7)	12	0.02

Race*	Population	%
Choctaw (0)	4	0.01
Colville (0)	0	<0.01
Comanche (1)	1	<0.01
Cree (0)	0	<0.01
Creek (2)	4	0.01
Crow (0)	1	<0.01
Delaware (0)	0	<0.01
Hopi (0)	0	<0.01
Houma (0)	0	<0.01
Inupiat (Alaska Native) (0)	0	<0.01
Iroquois (4)	12	0.02
Kiowa (0)	0	<0.01
Lumbee (3)	3	<0.01
Menominee (0)	0	<0.01
Mexican American Ind. (25)	36	0.05
Navajo (3)	3	<0.01
Osage (0)	0	<0.01
Ottawa (0)	2	<0.01
Paiute (0)	0	<0.01
Pima (0)	0	<0.01
Potawatomi (5)	8	0.01
Pueblo (0)	0	<0.01
Puget Sound Salish (0)	0	<0.01
Seminole (0)	0	<0.01
Shoshone (0)	2	<0.01
Sioux (2)	12	0.02
South American Ind. (1)	4	0.01
Spanish American Ind. (0)	0	<0.01
Tlingit-Haida (Alaska Native) (0)	0	<0.01
Tohono O'Odham (0)	0	<0.01
Tsimshian (Alaska Native) (0)	0	<0.01
Ute (0)	0	<0.01
Yakama (0)	0	<0.01
Yaqui (1)	1	<0.01
Yuman (0)	1	<0.01
Yup'ik (Alaska Native) (0)	0	<0.01
Asian (8,357)	9,178	12.51
Not Hispanic (8,264)	8,979	12.24
Hispanic (93)	199	0.27
Bangladeshi (36)	37	0.05
Bhutanese (0)	0	<0.01
Burmese (0)	0	<0.01
Cambodian (100)	125	0.17
Chinese, ex. Taiwanese (754)	887	1.21
Filipino (2,878)	3,222	4.39
Hmong (6)	7	0.01
Indian (2,791)	2,996	4.08
Indonesian (9)	13	0.02
Japanese (55)	115	0.16
Korean (278)	327	0.45
Laotian (35)	49	0.07
Malaysian (3)	5	0.01
Nepalese (14)	20	0.03
Pakistani (792)	835	1.14
Sri Lankan (14)	16	0.02
Taiwanese (37)	40	0.05
Thai (67)	111	0.15
Vietnamese (227)	277	0.38
Hawaii Native/Pacific Islander (15)	78	0.11
Not Hispanic (9)	55	0.07
Hispanic (6)	23	0.03
Fijian (1)	1	<0.01
Guamanian/Chamorro (3)	6	0.01
Marshallese (1)	1	<0.01
Native Hawaiian (3)	23	0.03
Samoan (1)	6	0.01
Tongan (0)	0	<0.01
White (39,819)	41,835	57.02
Not Hispanic (30,587)	31,853	43.42
Hispanic (9,232)	9,982	13.61

Notes: † The Census 2010 population figure is used to calculate the percentages in the Hispanic Origin and Race categories. Ancestry percentages are based on the 2006-2010 American Community Survey population (not shown); ‡ Numbers in parentheses indicate the number of people reporting a single ancestry; * Numbers in parentheses indicate the number of persons reporting this race alone, not in combination with any other race; Please refer to the Explanation of Data for more information.

Champaign

Place Type: City
County: Champaign
Population: 81,055

Ancestry	Population	%
Afghan (0)	0	<0.01
African, Sub-Saharan (3,180)	3,208	4.04
African (3,030)	3,045	3.83
Cape Verdean (0)	0	<0.01
Ethiopian (0)	0	<0.01
Ghanaian (0)	0	<0.01
Kenyan (0)	0	<0.01
Liberian (0)	0	<0.01
Nigerian (63)	76	0.10
Senegalese (0)	0	<0.01
Sierra Leonean (0)	0	<0.01
Somalian (0)	0	<0.01
South African (0)	0	<0.01
Sudanese (0)	0	<0.01
Ugandan (0)	0	<0.01
Zimbabwean (0)	0	<0.01
Other Sub-Saharan African (87)	87	0.11
Albanian (0)	0	<0.01
Alsatian (0)	0	<0.01
American (8,172)	8,172	10.29
Arab (188)	247	0.31
Arab (33)	33	0.04
Egyptian (65)	65	0.08
Iraqi (22)	30	0.04
Jordanian (0)	24	0.03
Lebanese (20)	39	0.05
Moroccan (0)	0	<0.01
Palestinian (0)	0	<0.01
Syrian (0)	8	0.01
Other Arab (48)	48	0.06
Armenian (0)	0	<0.01
Assyrian/Chaldean/Syriac (0)	16	0.02
Australian (15)	15	0.02
Austrian (70)	313	0.39
Basque (0)	0	<0.01
Belgian (47)	121	0.15
Brazilian (167)	239	0.30
British (256)	501	0.63
Bulgarian (0)	0	<0.01
Cajun (0)	0	<0.01
Canadian (51)	137	0.17
Carpatho Rusyn (0)	0	<0.01
Celtic (6)	6	0.01
Croatian (28)	86	0.11
Cypriot (0)	0	<0.01
Czech (141)	491	0.62
Czechoslovakian (81)	126	0.16
Danish (15)	144	0.18
Dutch (180)	1,045	1.32
Eastern European (124)	162	0.20
English (1,790)	6,475	8.15
Estonian (0)	17	0.02
European (2,322)	2,373	2.99
Finnish (22)	65	0.08
French, ex. Basque (141)	1,291	1.63
French Canadian (68)	199	0.25
German (5,713)	16,461	20.72
German Russian (0)	0	<0.01
Greek (292)	489	0.62
Guyanese (0)	0	<0.01
Hungarian (90)	319	0.40
Icelander (0)	9	0.01
Iranian (123)	149	0.19
Irish (2,520)	9,671	12.18
Israeli (51)	51	0.06
Italian (764)	3,146	3.96
Latvian (0)	23	0.03
Lithuanian (136)	342	0.43
Luxemburger (0)	50	0.06
Macedonian (0)	0	<0.01
Maltese (24)	24	0.03
New Zealander (0)	0	<0.01
Northern European (6)	6	0.01

Ancestry	Population	%
Norwegian (286)	986	1.24
Pennsylvania German (33)	81	0.10
Polish (1,269)	3,632	4.57
Portuguese (42)	90	0.11
Romanian (100)	156	0.20
Russian (386)	1,127	1.42
Scandinavian (71)	136	0.17
Scotch-Irish (195)	1,009	1.27
Scottish (392)	1,389	1.75
Serbian (8)	8	0.01
Slavic (15)	22	0.03
Slovak (35)	169	0.21
Slovene (14)	35	0.04
Soviet Union (0)	0	<0.01
Swedish (390)	1,659	2.09
Swiss (39)	332	0.42
Turkish (177)	263	0.33
Ukrainian (233)	373	0.47
Welsh (116)	433	0.55
West Indian, ex. Hispanic (174)	198	0.25
Bahamian (0)	0	<0.01
Barbadian (0)	0	<0.01
Belizean (0)	0	<0.01
Bermudan (0)	0	<0.01
British West Indian (0)	0	<0.01
Dutch West Indian (0)	0	<0.01
Haitian (0)	0	<0.01
Jamaican (74)	98	0.12
Trinidadian/Tobagonian (19)	19	0.02
U.S. Virgin Islander (81)	81	0.10
West Indian (0)	0	<0.01
Other West Indian (0)	0	<0.01
Yugoslavian (18)	31	0.04

Hispanic Origin	Population	%
Hispanic or Latino (of any race)	5,111	6.31
Central American, ex. Mexican	344	0.42
Costa Rican	29	0.04
Guatemalan	217	0.27
Honduran	23	0.03
Nicaraguan	17	0.02
Panamanian	18	0.02
Salvadoran	39	0.05
Other Central American	1	<0.01
Cuban	125	0.15
Dominican Republic	34	0.04
Mexican	3,310	4.08
Puerto Rican	415	0.51
South American	481	0.59
Argentinean	73	0.09
Bolivian	25	0.03
Chilean	41	0.05
Colombian	132	0.16
Ecuadorian	59	0.07
Paraguayan	8	0.01
Peruvian	91	0.11
Uruguayan	8	0.01
Venezuelan	41	0.05
Other South American	3	<0.01
Other Hispanic or Latino	402	0.50

Race*	Population	%
African-American/Black (12,680)	13,834	17.07
Not Hispanic (12,474)	13,520	16.68
Hispanic (206)	314	0.39
American Indian/Alaska Native (205)	593	0.73
Not Hispanic (143)	453	0.56
Hispanic (62)	140	0.17
Alaska Athabascan (Ala. Nat.) (0)	0	<0.01
Aleut (Alaska Native) (1)	1	<0.01
Apache (7)	10	0.01
Arapaho (0)	0	<0.01
Blackfeet (0)	19	0.02
Canadian/French Am. Ind. (0)	0	<0.01
Central American Ind. (2)	2	<0.01
Cherokee (30)	139	0.17
Cheyenne (0)	3	<0.01
Chickasaw (7)	8	0.01
Chippewa (4)	11	0.01

Race*	Population	%
Choctaw (4)	13	0.02
Colville (0)	0	<0.01
Comanche (0)	0	<0.01
Cree (0)	4	<0.01
Creek (1)	6	0.01
Crow (0)	0	<0.01
Delaware (2)	4	<0.01
Hopi (1)	4	<0.01
Houma (0)	0	<0.01
Inupiat (Alaska Native) (1)	2	<0.01
Iroquois (1)	7	0.01
Kiowa (1)	1	<0.01
Lumbee (0)	0	<0.01
Menominee (1)	1	<0.01
Mexican American Ind. (11)	25	0.03
Navajo (8)	12	0.01
Osage (3)	3	<0.01
Ottawa (1)	3	<0.01
Paiute (0)	0	<0.01
Pima (1)	3	<0.01
Potawatomi (2)	7	0.01
Pueblo (5)	5	0.01
Puget Sound Salish (0)	0	<0.01
Seminole (0)	0	<0.01
Shoshone (0)	0	<0.01
Sioux (3)	10	0.01
South American Ind. (8)	13	0.02
Spanish American Ind. (0)	1	<0.01
Tlingit-Haida (Alaska Native) (0)	0	<0.01
Tohono O'Odham (0)	0	<0.01
Tsimshian (Alaska Native) (0)	0	<0.01
Ute (0)	0	<0.01
Yakama (0)	0	<0.01
Yaqui (0)	2	<0.01
Yuman (0)	0	<0.01
Yup'ik (Alaska Native) (0)	0	<0.01
Asian (8,566)	9,544	11.77
Not Hispanic (8,510)	9,442	11.65
Hispanic (56)	102	0.13
Bangladeshi (47)	56	0.07
Bhutanese (0)	0	<0.01
Burmese (16)	18	0.02
Cambodian (15)	26	0.03
Chinese, ex. Taiwanese (2,068)	2,302	2.84
Filipino (572)	755	0.93
Hmong (8)	9	0.01
Indian (2,162)	2,308	2.85
Indonesian (9)	15	0.02
Japanese (214)	379	0.47
Korean (1,930)	2,060	2.54
Laotian (74)	89	0.11
Malaysian (44)	46	0.06
Nepalese (34)	39	0.05
Pakistani (154)	174	0.21
Sri Lankan (27)	31	0.04
Taiwanese (234)	272	0.34
Thai (99)	126	0.16
Vietnamese (618)	687	0.85
Hawaii Native/Pacific Islander (58)	173	0.21
Not Hispanic (56)	151	0.19
Hispanic (2)	22	0.03
Fijian (0)	2	<0.01
Guamanian/Chamorro (1)	7	0.01
Marshallese (0)	0	<0.01
Native Hawaiian (19)	37	0.05
Samoan (10)	23	0.03
Tongan (1)	2	<0.01
White (54,918)	56,978	70.30
Not Hispanic (52,533)	54,308	67.00
Hispanic (2,385)	2,670	3.29

*Notes: † The Census 2010 population figure is used to calculate the percentages in the Hispanic Origin and Race categories. Ancestry percentages are based on the 2006-2010 American Community Survey population (not shown); ‡ Numbers in parentheses indicate the number of people reporting a single ancestry; * Numbers in parentheses indicate the number of persons reporting this race alone, not in combination with any other race; Please refer to the Explanation of Data for more information.*

Chicago

Place Type: City
County: Cook
Population: 2,695,598

Ancestry	Population	%
Afghan (223)	234	0.01
African, Sub-Saharan (31,194)	36,226	1.34
African (18,104)	21,971	0.81
Cape Verdean (22)	22	<0.01
Ethiopian (2,136)	2,224	0.08
Ghanaian (1,826)	1,873	0.07
Kenyan (456)	456	0.02
Liberian (58)	102	<0.01
Nigerian (5,645)	6,193	0.23
Senegalese (0)	0	<0.01
Sierra Leonean (209)	221	0.01
Somalian (510)	637	0.02
South African (211)	375	0.01
Sudanese (195)	225	0.01
Ugandan (39)	39	<0.01
Zimbabwean (107)	107	<0.01
Other Sub-Saharan African (1,676)	1,781	0.07
Albanian (1,499)	1,699	0.06
Alsatian (39)	96	<0.01
American (34,496)	34,496	1.28
Arab (13,702)	16,946	0.63
Arab (3,850)	4,311	0.16
Egyptian (827)	1,010	0.04
Iraqi (1,318)	1,592	0.06
Jordanian (899)	948	0.04
Lebanese (990)	1,936	0.07
Moroccan (836)	1,014	0.04
Palestinian (1,874)	2,219	0.08
Syrian (784)	1,029	0.04
Other Arab (2,324)	2,887	0.11
Armenian (706)	1,256	0.05
Assyrian/Chaldean/Syriac (3,653)	4,646	0.17
Australian (212)	561	0.02
Austrian (1,166)	7,125	0.26
Basque (72)	259	0.01
Belgian (705)	2,597	0.10
Brazilian (984)	1,439	0.05
British (2,697)	5,392	0.20
Bulgarian (2,922)	3,223	0.12
Cajun (42)	99	<0.01
Canadian (1,176)	2,179	0.08
Carpatho Rusyn (0)	25	<0.01
Celtic (42)	155	0.01
Croatian (3,116)	7,104	0.26
Cypriot (122)	122	<0.01
Czech (3,306)	12,642	0.47
Czechoslovakian (884)	2,450	0.09
Danish (1,099)	5,565	0.21
Dutch (3,430)	14,116	0.52
Eastern European (5,362)	5,967	0.22
English (12,819)	64,585	2.39
Estonian (131)	202	0.01
European (15,353)	17,169	0.64
Finnish (853)	2,609	0.10
French, ex. Basque (3,518)	25,053	0.93
French Canadian (1,564)	4,592	0.17
German (51,511)	205,863	7.61
German Russian (46)	106	<0.01
Greek (11,174)	17,672	0.65
Guyanese (94)	272	0.01
Hungarian (2,700)	8,760	0.32
Icelander (71)	207	0.01
Iranian (1,735)	2,222	0.08
Irish (63,543)	201,693	7.46
Israeli (822)	1,411	0.05
Italian (39,947)	102,842	3.80
Latvian (842)	1,505	0.06
Lithuanian (5,099)	12,503	0.46
Luxemburger (234)	657	0.02
Macedonian (304)	495	0.02
Maltese (22)	70	<0.01
New Zealander (181)	205	0.01
Northern European (1,402)	1,551	0.06

Ancestry	Population	%
Norwegian (3,187)	14,090	0.52
Pennsylvania German (131)	200	0.01
Polish (100,880)	176,295	6.52
Portuguese (354)	1,187	0.04
Romanian (7,237)	9,121	0.34
Russian (12,700)	28,264	1.05
Scandinavian (805)	1,792	0.07
Scotch-Irish (4,221)	13,218	0.49
Scottish (3,852)	16,230	0.60
Serbian (3,708)	5,286	0.20
Slavic (535)	1,157	0.04
Slovak (1,859)	4,761	0.18
Slovene (540)	1,432	0.05
Soviet Union (19)	19	<0.01
Swedish (5,864)	26,075	0.96
Swiss (715)	3,481	0.13
Turkish (1,281)	1,598	0.06
Ukrainian (8,223)	12,513	0.46
Welsh (651)	5,904	0.22
West Indian, ex. Hispanic (8,397)	11,174	0.41
Bahamian (22)	22	<0.01
Barbadian (75)	154	0.01
Belizean (1,847)	2,273	0.08
Bermudan (0)	24	<0.01
British West Indian (57)	103	<0.01
Dutch West Indian (0)	0	<0.01
Haitian (2,288)	2,734	0.10
Jamaican (3,412)	4,601	0.17
Trinidadian/Tobagonian (341)	533	0.02
U.S. Virgin Islander (32)	32	<0.01
West Indian (323)	698	0.03
Other West Indian (0)	0	<0.01
Yugoslavian (5,621)	6,612	0.24

Hispanic Origin	Population	%
Hispanic or Latino (of any race)	778,862	28.89
Central American, ex. Mexican	31,263	1.16
Costa Rican	681	0.03
Guatemalan	17,973	0.67
Honduran	5,021	0.19
Nicaraguan	1,239	0.05
Panamanian	883	0.03
Salvadoran	5,204	0.19
Other Central American	262	0.01
Cuban	8,331	0.31
Dominican Republic	2,737	0.10
Mexican	578,100	21.45
Puerto Rican	102,703	3.81
South American	32,129	1.19
Argentinean	1,743	0.06
Bolivian	626	0.02
Chilean	876	0.03
Colombian	7,547	0.28
Ecuadorian	15,466	0.57
Paraguayan	101	<0.01
Peruvian	4,075	0.15
Uruguayan	267	0.01
Venezuelan	1,121	0.04
Other South American	307	0.01
Other Hispanic or Latino	23,599	0.88

Race*	Population	%
African-American/Black (887,608)	913,009	33.87
Not Hispanic (872,286)	889,783	33.01
Hispanic (15,322)	23,226	0.86
American Indian/Alaska Native (13,337)	26,933	1.00
Not Hispanic (4,097)	12,449	0.46
Hispanic (9,240)	14,484	0.54
Alaska Athabascan (Ala. Nat.) (4)	11	<0.01
Aleut (Alaska Native) (4)	8	<0.01
Apache (135)	350	0.01
Arapaho (9)	20	<0.01
Blackfeet (65)	590	0.02
Canadian/French Am. Ind. (22)	55	<0.01
Central American Ind. (92)	203	0.01
Cherokee (458)	2,639	0.10
Cheyenne (11)	27	<0.01
Chickasaw (10)	56	<0.01
Chippewa (382)	659	0.02

Race*	Population	%
Choctaw (120)	513	0.02
Colville (2)	5	<0.01
Comanche (21)	47	<0.01
Cree (16)	54	<0.01
Creek (22)	139	0.01
Crow (4)	17	<0.01
Delaware (3)	25	<0.01
Hopi (6)	26	<0.01
Houma (1)	3	<0.01
Inupiat (Alaska Native) (18)	30	<0.01
Iroquois (170)	359	0.01
Kiowa (13)	23	<0.01
Lumbee (13)	25	<0.01
Menominee (66)	117	<0.01
Mexican American Ind. (1,924)	2,810	0.10
Navajo (122)	261	0.01
Osage (9)	31	<0.01
Ottawa (21)	41	<0.01
Paiute (6)	9	<0.01
Pima (6)	16	<0.01
Potawatomi (56)	115	<0.01
Pueblo (36)	71	<0.01
Puget Sound Salish (5)	8	<0.01
Seminole (10)	80	<0.01
Shoshone (6)	17	<0.01
Sioux (163)	385	0.01
South American Ind. (290)	743	0.03
Spanish American Ind. (156)	225	0.01
Tlingit-Haida (Alaska Native) (13)	15	<0.01
Tohono O'Odham (1)	4	<0.01
Tsimshian (Alaska Native) (1)	1	<0.01
Ute (5)	8	<0.01
Yakama (0)	3	<0.01
Yaqui (34)	58	<0.01
Yuman (11)	15	<0.01
Yup'ik (Alaska Native) (7)	10	<0.01
Asian (147,164)	166,770	6.19
Not Hispanic (144,903)	161,439	5.99
Hispanic (2,261)	5,331	0.20
Bangladeshi (624)	679	0.03
Bhutanese (276)	339	0.01
Burmese (648)	711	0.03
Cambodian (1,204)	1,404	0.05
Chinese, ex. Taiwanese (42,060)	46,446	1.72
Filipino (29,664)	35,188	1.31
Hmong (85)	97	<0.01
Indian (29,948)	33,528	1.24
Indonesian (294)	430	0.02
Japanese (4,347)	7,044	0.26
Korean (11,422)	13,418	0.50
Laotian (414)	529	0.02
Malaysian (110)	165	0.01
Nepalese (534)	627	0.02
Pakistani (7,008)	7,926	0.29
Sri Lankan (335)	376	0.01
Taiwanese (1,111)	1,319	0.05
Thai (2,658)	3,168	0.12
Vietnamese (8,930)	10,118	0.38
Hawaii Native/Pacific Islander (1,013)	3,770	0.14
Not Hispanic (557)	2,186	0.08
Hispanic (456)	1,584	0.06
Fijian (12)	18	<0.01
Guamanian/Chamorro (361)	592	0.02
Marshallese (2)	5	<0.01
Native Hawaiian (242)	731	0.03
Samoan (94)	281	0.01
Tongan (5)	10	<0.01
White (1,212,835)	1,270,097	47.12
Not Hispanic (854,717)	881,920	32.72
Hispanic (358,118)	388,177	14.40

*Notes: † The Census 2010 population figure is used to calculate the percentages in the Hispanic Origin and Race categories. Ancestry percentages are based on the 2006-2010 American Community Survey population (not shown); ‡ Numbers in parentheses indicate the number of people reporting a single ancestry; * Numbers in parentheses indicate the number of persons reporting this race alone, not in combination with any other race; Please refer to the Explanation of Data for more information.*

Cicero

Place Type: Town
County: Cook
Population: 83,891

Ancestry	Population	%
Afghan (0)	0	<0.01
African, Sub-Saharan (0)	0	<0.01
African (0)	0	<0.01
Cape Verdean (0)	0	<0.01
Ethiopian (0)	0	<0.01
Ghanaian (0)	0	<0.01
Kenyan (0)	0	<0.01
Liberian (0)	0	<0.01
Nigerian (0)	0	<0.01
Senegalese (0)	0	<0.01
Sierra Leonean (0)	0	<0.01
Somalian (0)	0	<0.01
South African (0)	0	<0.01
Sudanese (0)	0	<0.01
Ugandan (0)	0	<0.01
Zimbabwean (0)	0	<0.01
Other Sub-Saharan African (0)	0	<0.01
Albanian (0)	0	<0.01
Alsatian (0)	0	<0.01
American (233)	233	0.28
Arab (195)	220	0.26
Arab (110)	135	0.16
Egyptian (0)	0	<0.01
Iraqi (0)	0	<0.01
Jordanian (0)	0	<0.01
Lebanese (0)	0	<0.01
Moroccan (14)	14	0.02
Palestinian (55)	55	0.07
Syrian (0)	0	<0.01
Other Arab (16)	16	0.02
Armenian (0)	0	<0.01
Assyrian/Chaldean/Syriac (0)	0	<0.01
Australian (0)	0	<0.01
Austrian (5)	47	0.06
Basque (0)	0	<0.01
Belgian (0)	0	<0.01
Brazilian (0)	0	<0.01
British (0)	49	0.06
Bulgarian (46)	46	0.06
Cajun (0)	0	<0.01
Canadian (23)	23	0.03
Carpatho Rusyn (0)	0	<0.01
Celtic (0)	14	0.02
Croatian (11)	68	0.08
Cypriot (0)	0	<0.01
Czech (400)	863	1.04
Czechoslovakian (50)	75	0.09
Danish (39)	55	0.07
Dutch (0)	127	0.15
Eastern European (32)	32	0.04
English (58)	451	0.54
Estonian (27)	27	0.03
European (66)	66	0.08
Finnish (0)	0	<0.01
French, ex. Basque (17)	429	0.51
French Canadian (31)	55	0.07
German (400)	1,951	2.34
German Russian (0)	0	<0.01
Greek (26)	36	0.04
Guyanese (0)	0	<0.01
Hungarian (0)	51	0.06
Icelander (0)	0	<0.01
Iranian (0)	0	<0.01
Irish (360)	2,168	2.60
Israeli (0)	0	<0.01
Italian (609)	1,690	2.03
Latvian (9)	9	0.01
Lithuanian (106)	130	0.16
Luxemburger (0)	0	<0.01
Macedonian (23)	23	0.03
Maltese (0)	0	<0.01
New Zealander (0)	0	<0.01
Northern European (0)	0	<0.01

Ancestry	Population	%
Norwegian (0)	31	0.04
Pennsylvania German (0)	0	<0.01
Polish (1,032)	2,065	2.48
Portuguese (99)	231	0.28
Romanian (46)	75	0.09
Russian (0)	73	0.09
Scandinavian (0)	0	<0.01
Scotch-Irish (33)	69	0.08
Scottish (24)	183	0.22
Serbian (36)	45	0.05
Slavic (0)	0	<0.01
Slovak (80)	89	0.11
Slovene (0)	0	<0.01
Soviet Union (0)	0	<0.01
Swedish (7)	138	0.17
Swiss (0)	16	0.02
Turkish (0)	0	<0.01
Ukrainian (31)	107	0.13
Welsh (0)	52	0.06
West Indian, ex. Hispanic (32)	100	0.12
Bahamian (0)	0	<0.01
Barbadian (0)	0	<0.01
Belizean (0)	68	0.08
Bermudan (0)	0	<0.01
British West Indian (0)	0	<0.01
Dutch West Indian (0)	0	<0.01
Haitian (0)	0	<0.01
Jamaican (32)	32	0.04
Trinidadian/Tobagonian (0)	0	<0.01
U.S. Virgin Islander (0)	0	<0.01
West Indian (0)	0	<0.01
Other West Indian (0)	0	<0.01
Yugoslavian (54)	91	0.11

Hispanic Origin	Population	%
Hispanic or Latino (of any race)	72,609	86.55
Central American, ex. Mexican	1,293	1.54
Costa Rican	21	0.03
Guatemalan	650	0.77
Honduran	205	0.24
Nicaraguan	105	0.13
Panamanian	22	0.03
Salvadoran	278	0.33
Other Central American	12	0.01
Cuban	137	0.16
Dominican Republic	150	0.18
Mexican	65,694	78.31
Puerto Rican	2,782	3.32
South American	719	0.86
Argentinean	48	0.06
Bolivian	13	0.02
Chilean	12	0.01
Colombian	145	0.17
Ecuadorian	365	0.44
Paraguayan	3	<0.01
Peruvian	85	0.10
Uruguayan	6	0.01
Venezuelan	35	0.04
Other South American	7	0.01
Other Hispanic or Latino	1,834	2.19

Race*	Population	%
African-American/Black (3,154)	3,508	4.18
Not Hispanic (2,690)	2,781	3.32
Hispanic (464)	727	0.87
American Indian/Alaska Native (693)	1,024	1.22
Not Hispanic (56)	102	0.12
Hispanic (637)	922	1.10
Alaska Athabascan (Ala. Nat.) (0)	4	<0.01
Aleut (Alaska Native) (0)	0	<0.01
Apache (6)	9	<0.01
Arapaho (1)	1	<0.01
Blackfeet (1)	1	<0.01
Canadian/French Am. Ind. (0)	2	<0.01
Central American Ind. (6)	6	0.01
Cherokee (11)	22	0.03
Cheyenne (0)	5	<0.01
Chickasaw (0)	0	<0.01
Chippewa (5)	8	0.01

Race*	Population	%
Choctaw (4)	4	<0.01
Colville (0)	0	<0.01
Comanche (0)	1	<0.01
Cree (0)	0	<0.01
Creek (0)	2	<0.01
Crow (0)	0	<0.01
Delaware (1)	2	<0.01
Hopi (0)	0	<0.01
Houma (0)	0	<0.01
Inupiat (Alaska Native) (0)	0	<0.01
Iroquois (2)	4	<0.01
Kiowa (0)	0	<0.01
Lumbee (0)	0	<0.01
Menominee (6)	6	0.01
Mexican American Ind. (169)	256	0.31
Navajo (9)	17	0.02
Osage (0)	0	<0.01
Ottawa (0)	0	<0.01
Paiute (1)	1	<0.01
Pima (0)	0	<0.01
Potawatomi (1)	1	<0.01
Pueblo (2)	2	<0.01
Puget Sound Salish (0)	0	<0.01
Seminole (0)	0	<0.01
Shoshone (0)	0	<0.01
Sioux (5)	5	0.01
South American Ind. (4)	16	0.02
Spanish American Ind. (6)	6	0.01
Tlingit-Haida (Alaska Native) (0)	0	<0.01
Tohono O'Odham (0)	0	<0.01
Tsimshian (Alaska Native) (0)	0	<0.01
Ute (0)	0	<0.01
Yakama (0)	0	<0.01
Yaqui (0)	0	<0.01
Yuman (0)	0	<0.01
Yup'ik (Alaska Native) (0)	1	<0.01
Asian (510)	718	0.86
Not Hispanic (467)	574	0.68
Hispanic (43)	144	0.17
Bangladeshi (3)	3	<0.01
Bhutanese (0)	0	<0.01
Burmese (0)	0	<0.01
Cambodian (13)	16	0.02
Chinese, ex. Taiwanese (60)	73	0.09
Filipino (247)	320	0.38
Hmong (0)	0	<0.01
Indian (38)	65	0.08
Indonesian (5)	5	0.01
Japanese (6)	18	0.02
Korean (13)	23	0.03
Laotian (0)	0	<0.01
Malaysian (0)	2	<0.01
Nepalese (0)	0	<0.01
Pakistani (10)	23	0.03
Sri Lankan (2)	5	0.01
Taiwanese (0)	0	<0.01
Thai (24)	25	0.03
Vietnamese (50)	64	0.08
Hawaii Native/Pacific Islander (53)	118	0.14
Not Hispanic (26)	31	0.04
Hispanic (27)	87	0.10
Fijian (0)	0	<0.01
Guamanian/Chamorro (22)	29	0.03
Marshallese (0)	0	<0.01
Native Hawaiian (10)	18	0.02
Samoan (12)	13	0.02
Tongan (0)	0	<0.01
White (43,579)	46,142	55.00
Not Hispanic (7,696)	7,917	9.44
Hispanic (35,883)	38,225	45.57

*Notes: † The Census 2010 population figure is used to calculate the percentages in the Hispanic Origin and Race categories. Ancestry percentages are based on the 2006-2010 American Community Survey population (not shown); ‡ Numbers in parentheses indicate the number of people reporting a single ancestry; * Numbers in parentheses indicate the number of persons reporting this race alone, not in combination with any other race; Please refer to the Explanation of Data for more information.*

Decatur

Place Type: City
County: Macon
Population: 76,122

Ancestry	Population	%
Afghan (0)	0	<0.01
African, Sub-Saharan (145)	169	0.22
African (145)	169	0.22
Cape Verdean (0)	0	<0.01
Ethiopian (0)	0	<0.01
Ghanaian (0)	0	<0.01
Kenyan (0)	0	<0.01
Liberian (0)	0	<0.01
Nigerian (0)	0	<0.01
Senegalese (0)	0	<0.01
Sierra Leonean (0)	0	<0.01
Somalian (0)	0	<0.01
South African (0)	0	<0.01
Sudanese (0)	0	<0.01
Ugandan (0)	0	<0.01
Zimbabwean (0)	0	<0.01
Other Sub-Saharan African (0)	0	<0.01
Albanian (0)	0	<0.01
Alsatian (0)	0	<0.01
American (11,484)	11,484	15.03
Arab (172)	172	0.23
Arab (152)	152	0.20
Egyptian (11)	11	0.01
Iraqi (0)	0	<0.01
Jordanian (0)	0	<0.01
Lebanese (0)	0	<0.01
Moroccan (9)	9	0.01
Palestinian (0)	0	<0.01
Syrian (0)	0	<0.01
Other Arab (0)	0	<0.01
Armenian (0)	0	<0.01
Assyrian/Chaldean/Syriac (0)	0	<0.01
Australian (0)	45	0.06
Austrian (41)	149	0.19
Basque (0)	0	<0.01
Belgian (59)	105	0.14
Brazilian (0)	0	<0.01
British (126)	231	0.30
Bulgarian (0)	0	<0.01
Cajun (0)	0	<0.01
Canadian (44)	125	0.16
Carpatho Rusyn (0)	0	<0.01
Celtic (0)	0	<0.01
Croatian (17)	94	0.12
Cypriot (0)	0	<0.01
Czech (67)	194	0.25
Czechoslovakian (0)	0	<0.01
Danish (36)	118	0.15
Dutch (225)	1,233	1.61
Eastern European (10)	10	0.01
English (2,879)	7,427	9.72
Estonian (0)	0	<0.01
European (483)	548	0.72
Finnish (0)	11	0.01
French, ex. Basque (317)	1,477	1.93
French Canadian (58)	209	0.27
German (5,963)	15,437	20.20
German Russian (0)	0	<0.01
Greek (128)	341	0.45
Guyanese (0)	0	<0.01
Hungarian (66)	231	0.30
Icelander (0)	0	<0.01
Iranian (29)	29	0.04
Irish (2,614)	9,737	12.74
Israeli (0)	0	<0.01
Italian (511)	1,740	2.28
Latvian (0)	0	<0.01
Lithuanian (0)	36	0.05
Luxemburger (0)	21	0.03
Macedonian (0)	0	<0.01
Maltese (0)	11	0.01
New Zealander (0)	0	<0.01
Northern European (9)	9	0.01

Ancestry	Population	%
Norwegian (187)	555	0.73
Pennsylvania German (51)	51	0.07
Polish (467)	1,558	2.04
Portuguese (75)	90	0.12
Romanian (0)	0	<0.01
Russian (23)	60	0.08
Scandinavian (0)	28	0.04
Scotch-Irish (606)	1,194	1.56
Scottish (485)	1,176	1.54
Serbian (6)	6	0.01
Slavic (21)	28	0.04
Slovak (9)	77	0.10
Slovene (0)	0	<0.01
Soviet Union (0)	0	<0.01
Swedish (219)	706	0.92
Swiss (53)	176	0.23
Turkish (0)	0	<0.01
Ukrainian (23)	83	0.11
Welsh (102)	368	0.48
West Indian, ex. Hispanic (75)	100	0.13
Bahamian (0)	0	<0.01
Barbadian (0)	0	<0.01
Belizean (0)	0	<0.01
Bermudan (0)	0	<0.01
British West Indian (0)	0	<0.01
Dutch West Indian (0)	0	<0.01
Haitian (65)	65	0.09
Jamaican (10)	24	0.03
Trinidadian/Tobagonian (0)	11	0.01
U.S. Virgin Islander (0)	0	<0.01
West Indian (0)	0	<0.01
Other West Indian (0)	0	<0.01
Yugoslavian (0)	10	0.01

Hispanic Origin	Population	%
Hispanic or Latino (of any race)	1,650	2.17
Central American, ex. Mexican	80	0.11
Costa Rican	10	0.01
Guatemalan	17	0.02
Honduran	10	0.01
Nicaraguan	21	0.03
Panamanian	14	0.02
Salvadoran	7	0.01
Other Central American	1	<0.01
Cuban	50	0.07
Dominican Republic	16	0.02
Mexican	1,055	1.39
Puerto Rican	163	0.21
South American	55	0.07
Argentinean	4	0.01
Bolivian	2	<0.01
Chilean	4	0.01
Colombian	18	0.02
Ecuadorian	3	<0.01
Paraguayan	0	<0.01
Peruvian	15	0.02
Uruguayan	0	<0.01
Venezuelan	9	0.01
Other South American	0	<0.01
Other Hispanic or Latino	231	0.30

Race*	Population	%
African-American/Black (17,704)	19,491	25.60
Not Hispanic (17,600)	19,291	25.34
Hispanic (104)	200	0.26
American Indian/Alaska Native (173)	621	0.82
Not Hispanic (155)	561	0.74
Hispanic (18)	60	0.08
Alaska Athabascan (Ala. Nat.) (1)	1	<0.01
Aleut (Alaska Native) (0)	3	<0.01
Apache (8)	16	0.02
Arapaho (0)	0	<0.01
Blackfeet (3)	31	0.04
Canadian/French Am. Ind. (0)	0	<0.01
Central American Ind. (0)	0	<0.01
Cherokee (24)	161	0.21
Cheyenne (0)	2	<0.01
Chickasaw (0)	3	<0.01
Chippewa (9)	13	0.02

Race*	Population	%
Choctaw (5)	9	0.01
Colville (0)	0	<0.01
Comanche (0)	0	<0.01
Cree (0)	1	<0.01
Creek (0)	7	0.01
Crow (0)	0	<0.01
Delaware (0)	2	<0.01
Hopi (0)	0	<0.01
Houma (0)	0	<0.01
Inupiat (Alaska Native) (0)	0	<0.01
Iroquois (1)	3	<0.01
Kiowa (0)	0	<0.01
Lumbee (0)	0	<0.01
Menominee (0)	0	<0.01
Mexican American Ind. (1)	7	0.01
Navajo (8)	17	0.02
Osage (0)	1	<0.01
Ottawa (0)	0	<0.01
Paiute (3)	5	0.01
Pima (0)	0	<0.01
Potawatomi (4)	4	0.01
Pueblo (0)	0	<0.01
Puget Sound Salish (0)	0	<0.01
Seminole (0)	1	<0.01
Shoshone (0)	0	<0.01
Sioux (6)	22	0.03
South American Ind. (0)	2	<0.01
Spanish American Ind. (0)	1	<0.01
Tlingit-Haida (Alaska Native) (0)	0	<0.01
Tohono O'Odham (0)	0	<0.01
Tsimshian (Alaska Native) (0)	0	<0.01
Ute (0)	0	<0.01
Yakama (0)	0	<0.01
Yaqui (0)	0	<0.01
Yuman (0)	0	<0.01
Yup'ik (Alaska Native) (0)	0	<0.01
Asian (704)	904	1.19
Not Hispanic (695)	873	1.15
Hispanic (9)	31	0.04
Bangladeshi (0)	0	<0.01
Bhutanese (0)	0	<0.01
Burmese (1)	1	<0.01
Cambodian (2)	3	<0.01
Chinese, ex. Taiwanese (78)	94	0.12
Filipino (131)	183	0.24
Hmong (0)	0	<0.01
Indian (302)	318	0.42
Indonesian (4)	12	0.02
Japanese (14)	30	0.04
Korean (55)	61	0.08
Laotian (2)	4	0.01
Malaysian (1)	1	<0.01
Nepalese (0)	0	<0.01
Pakistani (32)	34	0.04
Sri Lankan (1)	1	<0.01
Taiwanese (2)	2	<0.01
Thai (9)	11	0.01
Vietnamese (49)	68	0.09
Hawaii Native/Pacific Islander (23)	91	0.12
Not Hispanic (18)	76	0.10
Hispanic (5)	15	0.02
Fijian (0)	0	<0.01
Guamanian/Chamorro (1)	9	0.01
Marshallese (0)	0	<0.01
Native Hawaiian (4)	11	0.01
Samoan (4)	9	0.01
Tongan (0)	0	<0.01
White (54,509)	56,669	74.44
Not Hispanic (53,749)	55,734	73.22
Hispanic (760)	935	1.23

Notes: † The Census 2010 population figure is used to calculate the percentages in the Hispanic Origin and Race categories. Ancestry percentages are based on the 2006-2010 American Community Survey population (not shown); ‡ Numbers in parentheses indicate the number of people reporting a single ancestry; * Numbers in parentheses indicate the number of persons reporting this race alone, not in combination with any other race; Please refer to the Explanation of Data for more information.

Des Plaines

Place Type: City
County: Cook
Population: 58,364

Ancestry	Population	%
Afghan (0)	0	<0.01
African, Sub-Saharan (49)	49	0.09
African (37)	37	0.06
Cape Verdean (0)	0	<0.01
Ethiopian (0)	0	<0.01
Ghanaian (0)	0	<0.01
Kenyan (0)	0	<0.01
Liberian (0)	0	<0.01
Nigerian (12)	12	0.02
Senegalese (0)	0	<0.01
Sierra Leonean (0)	0	<0.01
Somalian (0)	0	<0.01
South African (0)	0	<0.01
Sudanese (0)	0	<0.01
Ugandan (0)	0	<0.01
Zimbabwean (0)	0	<0.01
Other Sub-Saharan African (0)	0	<0.01
Albanian (147)	234	0.41
Alsatian (0)	0	<0.01
American (1,236)	1,236	2.15
Arab (213)	354	0.62
Arab (31)	114	0.20
Egyptian (44)	66	0.12
Iraqi (25)	61	0.11
Jordanian (0)	0	<0.01
Lebanese (0)	0	<0.01
Moroccan (100)	100	0.17
Palestinian (6)	6	0.01
Syrian (0)	0	<0.01
Other Arab (7)	7	0.01
Armenian (33)	44	0.08
Assyrian/Chaldean/Syriac (461)	614	1.07
Australian (9)	57	0.10
Austrian (104)	295	0.51
Basque (0)	0	<0.01
Belgian (24)	69	0.12
Brazilian (0)	0	<0.01
British (19)	44	0.08
Bulgarian (383)	389	0.68
Cajun (0)	11	0.02
Canadian (27)	121	0.21
Carpatho Rusyn (0)	0	<0.01
Celtic (5)	5	0.01
Croatian (235)	351	0.61
Cypriot (0)	0	<0.01
Czech (289)	742	1.29
Czechoslovakian (10)	92	0.16
Danish (61)	279	0.49
Dutch (83)	425	0.74
Eastern European (32)	32	0.06
English (347)	2,086	3.64
Estonian (10)	10	0.02
European (244)	267	0.47
Finnish (9)	110	0.19
French, ex. Basque (108)	1,019	1.78
French Canadian (0)	150	0.26
German (3,866)	11,836	20.64
German Russian (0)	0	<0.01
Greek (1,221)	1,559	2.72
Guyanese (0)	0	<0.01
Hungarian (111)	251	0.44
Icelander (14)	14	0.02
Iranian (11)	61	0.11
Irish (2,008)	7,675	13.38
Israeli (0)	0	<0.01
Italian (2,610)	5,675	9.89
Latvian (54)	54	0.09
Lithuanian (118)	400	0.70
Luxemburger (59)	144	0.25
Macedonian (8)	23	0.04
Maltese (0)	0	<0.01
New Zealander (0)	0	<0.01
Northern European (12)	12	0.02

Ancestry	Population	%
Norwegian (294)	1,002	1.75
Pennsylvania German (0)	19	0.03
Polish (6,110)	9,648	16.82
Portuguese (0)	7	0.01
Romanian (676)	867	1.51
Russian (310)	545	0.95
Scandinavian (22)	22	0.04
Scotch-Irish (38)	322	0.56
Scottish (126)	443	0.77
Serbian (172)	282	0.49
Slavic (22)	22	0.04
Slovak (84)	198	0.35
Slovene (45)	56	0.10
Soviet Union (0)	0	<0.01
Swedish (459)	1,901	3.31
Swiss (0)	101	0.18
Turkish (82)	155	0.27
Ukrainian (238)	401	0.70
Welsh (0)	177	0.31
West Indian, ex. Hispanic (0)	0	<0.01
Bahamian (0)	0	<0.01
Barbadian (0)	0	<0.01
Belizean (0)	0	<0.01
Bermudan (0)	0	<0.01
British West Indian (0)	0	<0.01
Dutch West Indian (0)	0	<0.01
Haitian (0)	0	<0.01
Jamaican (0)	0	<0.01
Trinidadian/Tobagonian (0)	0	<0.01
U.S. Virgin Islander (0)	0	<0.01
West Indian (0)	0	<0.01
Other West Indian (0)	0	<0.01
Yugoslavian (320)	381	0.66

Hispanic Origin	Population	%
Hispanic or Latino (of any race)	10,053	17.22
Central American, ex. Mexican	445	0.76
Costa Rican	28	0.05
Guatemalan	184	0.32
Honduran	29	0.05
Nicaraguan	24	0.04
Panamanian	10	0.02
Salvadoran	165	0.28
Other Central American	5	0.01
Cuban	149	0.26
Dominican Republic	19	0.03
Mexican	8,001	13.71
Puerto Rican	615	1.05
South American	492	0.84
Argentinean	27	0.05
Bolivian	27	0.05
Chilean	28	0.05
Colombian	139	0.24
Ecuadorian	165	0.28
Paraguayan	1	<0.01
Peruvian	70	0.12
Uruguayan	3	0.01
Venezuelan	23	0.04
Other South American	9	0.02
Other Hispanic or Latino	332	0.57

Race*	Population	%
African-American/Black (1,039)	1,285	2.20
Not Hispanic (963)	1,160	1.99
Hispanic (76)	125	0.21
American Indian/Alaska Native (369)	588	1.01
Not Hispanic (63)	199	0.34
Hispanic (306)	389	0.67
Alaska Athabascan (Ala. Nat.) (0)	0	<0.01
Aleut (Alaska Native) (1)	5	0.01
Apache (1)	6	0.01
Arapaho (0)	0	<0.01
Blackfeet (0)	4	0.01
Canadian/French Am. Ind. (1)	2	0.01
Central American Ind. (1)	1	<0.01
Cherokee (6)	39	0.07
Cheyenne (0)	0	<0.01
Chickasaw (0)	1	<0.01
Chippewa (5)	11	0.02

Race*	Population	%
Choctaw (1)	3	0.0
Colville (0)	0	<0.0
Comanche (0)	0	<0.0
Cree (0)	0	<0.0
Creek (1)	1	<0.0
Crow (0)	0	<0.0
Delaware (0)	1	<0.0
Hopi (0)	0	<0.0
Houma (0)	0	<0.0
Inupiat (Alaska Native) (0)	2	<0.0
Iroquois (4)	10	0.0
Kiowa (0)	0	<0.0
Lumbee (0)	0	<0.0
Menominee (1)	5	0.0
Mexican American Ind. (59)	75	0.1
Navajo (0)	2	<0.0
Osage (0)	0	<0.0
Ottawa (0)	0	<0.0
Paiute (0)	0	<0.0
Pima (0)	0	<0.0
Potawatomi (2)	3	0.0
Pueblo (0)	2	<0.0
Puget Sound Salish (0)	0	<0.0
Seminole (0)	2	<0.0
Shoshone (0)	0	<0.0
Sioux (2)	12	0.0
South American Ind. (2)	3	0.0
Spanish American Ind. (12)	13	0.0
Tlingit-Haida (Alaska Native) (0)	0	<0.0
Tohono O'Odham (3)	3	0.0
Tsimshian (Alaska Native) (0)	0	<0.0
Ute (0)	0	<0.0
Yakama (0)	0	<0.0
Yaqui (0)	0	<0.0
Yuman (0)	0	<0.0
Yup'ik (Alaska Native) (0)	0	<0.0
Asian (6,674)	7,292	12.4
Not Hispanic (6,613)	7,146	12.2
Hispanic (61)	146	0.2
Bangladeshi (5)	6	0.0
Bhutanese (0)	0	<0.0
Burmese (4)	5	0.0
Cambodian (103)	105	0.1
Chinese, ex. Taiwanese (370)	432	0.7
Filipino (1,689)	1,851	3.1
Hmong (0)	0	<0.0
Indian (2,995)	3,214	5.5
Indonesian (2)	4	0.0
Japanese (151)	212	0.3
Korean (621)	664	1.1
Laotian (11)	13	0.0
Malaysian (1)	1	<0.0
Nepalese (8)	8	0.0
Pakistani (314)	375	0.6
Sri Lankan (8)	10	0.0
Taiwanese (26)	27	0.0
Thai (38)	53	0.0
Vietnamese (159)	171	0.2
Hawaii Native/Pacific Islander (9)	78	0.1
Not Hispanic (9)	63	0.1
Hispanic (0)	15	0.0
Fijian (0)	0	<0.0
Guamanian/Chamorro (0)	0	<0.0
Marshallese (1)	1	<0.0
Native Hawaiian (4)	16	0.0
Samoan (0)	9	0.0
Tongan (0)	0	<0.0
White (45,133)	46,247	79.2
Not Hispanic (39,689)	40,347	69.1
Hispanic (5,444)	5,900	10.1

Notes: † The Census 2010 population figure is used to calculate the percentages in the Hispanic Origin and Race categories. Ancestry percentages are based on the 2006-2010 American Communit
Survey population (not shown); ‡ Numbers in parentheses indicate the number of people reporting a single ancestry; * Numbers in parentheses indicate the number of persons reporting this race alon
not in combination with any other race; Please refer to the Explanation of Data for more information.

Elgin

Place Type: City
County: Kane
Population: 108,188

Ancestry	Population	%
Afghan (0)	0	<0.01
African, Sub-Saharan (278)	351	0.33
African (118)	191	0.18
Cape Verdean (0)	0	<0.01
Ethiopian (130)	130	0.12
Ghanaian (0)	0	<0.01
Kenyan (0)	0	<0.01
Liberian (0)	0	<0.01
Nigerian (28)	28	0.03
Senegalese (0)	0	<0.01
Sierra Leonean (0)	0	<0.01
Somalian (0)	0	<0.01
South African (0)	0	<0.01
Sudanese (0)	0	<0.01
Ugandan (0)	0	<0.01
Zimbabwean (0)	0	<0.01
Other Sub-Saharan African (2)	2	<0.01
Albanian (0)	0	<0.01
Alsatian (0)	0	<0.01
American (1,704)	1,704	1.59
Arab (173)	301	0.28
Arab (0)	16	0.01
Egyptian (22)	45	0.04
Iraqi (0)	0	<0.01
Jordanian (0)	0	<0.01
Lebanese (50)	139	0.13
Moroccan (0)	0	<0.01
Palestinian (0)	0	<0.01
Syrian (91)	91	0.09
Other Arab (10)	10	0.01
Armenian (89)	89	0.08
Assyrian/Chaldean/Syriac (220)	263	0.25
Australian (0)	12	0.01
Austrian (175)	316	0.30
Basque (45)	58	0.05
Belgian (22)	201	0.19
Brazilian (15)	23	0.02
British (76)	269	0.25
Bulgarian (30)	30	0.03
Cajun (0)	0	<0.01
Canadian (75)	130	0.12
Carpatho Rusyn (0)	0	<0.01
Celtic (0)	0	<0.01
Croatian (57)	189	0.18
Cypriot (0)	0	<0.01
Czech (268)	969	0.91
Czechoslovakian (74)	83	0.08
Danish (21)	477	0.45
Dutch (117)	950	0.89
Eastern European (24)	57	0.05
English (888)	5,690	5.33
Estonian (0)	0	<0.01
European (531)	573	0.54
Finnish (21)	131	0.12
French, ex. Basque (129)	2,594	2.43
French Canadian (111)	254	0.24
German (5,227)	20,264	18.97
German Russian (0)	0	<0.01
Greek (219)	551	0.52
Guyanese (0)	0	<0.01
Hungarian (151)	544	0.51
Icelander (0)	18	0.02
Iranian (0)	0	<0.01
Irish (1,667)	9,498	8.89
Israeli (35)	35	0.03
Italian (2,051)	6,096	5.71
Latvian (0)	42	0.04
Lithuanian (81)	209	0.20
Luxemburger (25)	106	0.10
Macedonian (0)	24	0.02
Maltese (0)	0	<0.01
New Zealander (0)	0	<0.01
Northern European (19)	19	0.02

	Population	%
Norwegian (328)	1,798	1.68
Pennsylvania German (24)	39	0.04
Polish (2,146)	6,145	5.75
Portuguese (0)	17	0.02
Romanian (0)	62	0.06
Russian (190)	606	0.57
Scandinavian (77)	294	0.28
Scotch-Irish (259)	1,228	1.15
Scottish (365)	1,285	1.20
Serbian (65)	87	0.08
Slavic (0)	0	<0.01
Slovak (36)	113	0.11
Slovene (11)	22	0.02
Soviet Union (0)	0	<0.01
Swedish (278)	2,441	2.28
Swiss (61)	450	0.42
Turkish (0)	9	0.01
Ukrainian (108)	230	0.22
Welsh (68)	340	0.32
West Indian, ex. Hispanic (31)	31	0.03
Bahamian (0)	0	<0.01
Barbadian (0)	0	<0.01
Belizean (0)	0	<0.01
Bermudan (0)	0	<0.01
British West Indian (0)	0	<0.01
Dutch West Indian (0)	0	<0.01
Haitian (0)	0	<0.01
Jamaican (17)	17	0.02
Trinidadian/Tobagonian (0)	0	<0.01
U.S. Virgin Islander (0)	0	<0.01
West Indian (14)	14	0.01
Other West Indian (0)	0	<0.01
Yugoslavian (31)	31	0.03

Hispanic Origin	Population	%
Hispanic or Latino (of any race)	47,121	43.55
Central American, ex. Mexican	888	0.82
Costa Rican	15	0.01
Guatemalan	356	0.33
Honduran	87	0.08
Nicaraguan	20	0.02
Panamanian	21	0.02
Salvadoran	307	0.30
Other Central American	2	<0.01
Cuban	204	0.19
Dominican Republic	66	0.06
Mexican	41,265	38.14
Puerto Rican	2,973	2.75
South American	637	0.59
Argentinean	30	0.03
Bolivian	11	0.01
Chilean	27	0.02
Colombian	253	0.23
Ecuadorian	152	0.14
Paraguayan	0	<0.01
Peruvian	117	0.11
Uruguayan	3	<0.01
Venezuelan	41	0.04
Other South American	3	<0.01
Other Hispanic or Latino	1,088	1.01

Race*	Population	%
African-American/Black (7,982)	9,269	8.57
Not Hispanic (7,467)	8,299	7.67
Hispanic (515)	970	0.90
American Indian/Alaska Native (1,468)	2,220	2.05
Not Hispanic (144)	405	0.37
Hispanic (1,324)	1,815	1.68
Alaska Athabascan (Ala. Nat.) (0)	0	<0.01
Aleut (Alaska Native) (0)	0	<0.01
Apache (12)	14	0.01
Arapaho (0)	0	<0.01
Blackfeet (1)	16	0.01
Canadian/French Am. Ind. (1)	5	<0.01
Central American Ind. (4)	4	<0.01
Cherokee (23)	101	0.09
Cheyenne (0)	0	<0.01
Chickasaw (0)	0	<0.01
Chippewa (14)	30	0.03

	Population	%
Choctaw (8)	11	0.01
Colville (0)	0	<0.01
Comanche (0)	0	<0.01
Cree (3)	3	<0.01
Creek (1)	8	0.01
Crow (0)	2	<0.01
Delaware (0)	0	<0.01
Hopi (0)	0	<0.01
Houma (0)	0	<0.01
Inupiat (Alaska Native) (0)	1	<0.01
Iroquois (3)	10	0.01
Kiowa (1)	3	<0.01
Lumbee (2)	3	<0.01
Menominee (2)	5	<0.01
Mexican American Ind. (245)	292	0.27
Navajo (4)	6	0.01
Osage (0)	7	0.01
Ottawa (3)	5	<0.01
Paiute (3)	3	<0.01
Pima (0)	1	<0.01
Potawatomi (2)	14	0.01
Pueblo (0)	0	<0.01
Puget Sound Salish (0)	0	<0.01
Seminole (3)	9	0.01
Shoshone (0)	0	<0.01
Sioux (11)	32	0.03
South American Ind. (11)	35	0.03
Spanish American Ind. (16)	18	0.02
Tlingit-Haida (Alaska Native) (0)	0	<0.01
Tohono O'Odham (1)	2	<0.01
Tsimshian (Alaska Native) (0)	0	<0.01
Ute (0)	0	<0.01
Yakama (0)	0	<0.01
Yaqui (0)	0	<0.01
Yuman (0)	0	<0.01
Yup'ik (Alaska Native) (0)	0	<0.01
Asian (5,809)	6,551	6.06
Not Hispanic (5,675)	6,250	5.78
Hispanic (134)	301	0.28
Bangladeshi (0)	0	<0.01
Bhutanese (0)	0	<0.01
Burmese (10)	13	0.01
Cambodian (57)	72	0.07
Chinese, ex. Taiwanese (338)	492	0.45
Filipino (1,453)	1,699	1.57
Hmong (19)	20	0.02
Indian (1,425)	1,559	1.44
Indonesian (7)	15	0.01
Japanese (97)	164	0.15
Korean (181)	260	0.24
Laotian (1,304)	1,445	1.34
Malaysian (4)	14	0.01
Nepalese (7)	7	0.01
Pakistani (267)	301	0.28
Sri Lankan (1)	1	<0.01
Taiwanese (13)	16	0.01
Thai (85)	109	0.10
Vietnamese (275)	320	0.30
Hawaii Native/Pacific Islander (37)	139	0.13
Not Hispanic (19)	71	0.07
Hispanic (18)	68	0.06
Fijian (1)	1	<0.01
Guamanian/Chamorro (1)	13	0.01
Marshallese (1)	1	<0.01
Native Hawaiian (9)	31	0.03
Samoan (13)	22	0.02
Tongan (0)	0	<0.01
White (71,347)	74,584	68.94
Not Hispanic (46,089)	47,429	43.84
Hispanic (25,258)	27,155	25.10

Notes: † The Census 2010 population figure is used to calculate the percentages in the Hispanic Origin and Race categories. Ancestry percentages are based on the 2006-2010 American Community Survey population (not shown); ‡ Numbers in parentheses indicate the number of people reporting a single ancestry; * Numbers in parentheses indicate the number of persons reporting this race alone, not in combination with any other race; Please refer to the Explanation of Data for more information.

Evanston

Place Type: City
County: Cook
Population: 74,486

Ancestry	Population	%
Afghan (0)	0	<0.01
African, Sub-Saharan (579)	686	0.93
African (347)	430	0.58
Cape Verdean (0)	0	<0.01
Ethiopian (11)	11	0.01
Ghanaian (0)	0	<0.01
Kenyan (0)	0	<0.01
Liberian (0)	0	<0.01
Nigerian (120)	130	0.18
Senegalese (0)	0	<0.01
Sierra Leonean (0)	0	<0.01
Somalian (0)	0	<0.01
South African (27)	27	0.04
Sudanese (0)	0	<0.01
Ugandan (27)	41	0.06
Zimbabwean (0)	0	<0.01
Other Sub-Saharan African (47)	47	0.06
Albanian (0)	0	<0.01
Alsatian (0)	0	<0.01
American (2,009)	2,009	2.72
Arab (153)	375	0.51
Arab (20)	37	0.05
Egyptian (44)	44	0.06
Iraqi (0)	14	0.02
Jordanian (0)	0	<0.01
Lebanese (59)	178	0.24
Moroccan (17)	17	0.02
Palestinian (0)	17	0.02
Syrian (13)	42	0.06
Other Arab (0)	26	0.04
Armenian (89)	174	0.24
Assyrian/Chaldean/Syriac (29)	54	0.07
Australian (22)	35	0.05
Austrian (75)	528	0.71
Basque (14)	14	0.02
Belgian (51)	369	0.50
Brazilian (47)	118	0.16
British (205)	732	0.99
Bulgarian (55)	84	0.11
Cajun (0)	0	<0.01
Canadian (98)	169	0.23
Carpatho Rusyn (0)	0	<0.01
Celtic (0)	0	<0.01
Croatian (68)	135	0.18
Cypriot (0)	0	<0.01
Czech (139)	631	0.85
Czechoslovakian (25)	79	0.11
Danish (35)	343	0.46
Dutch (304)	1,150	1.56
Eastern European (787)	854	1.16
English (1,009)	6,226	8.43
Estonian (60)	73	0.10
European (1,341)	1,549	2.10
Finnish (0)	97	0.13
French, ex. Basque (179)	1,878	2.54
French Canadian (109)	286	0.39
German (2,850)	12,775	17.29
German Russian (0)	62	0.08
Greek (310)	886	1.20
Guyanese (0)	0	<0.01
Hungarian (198)	576	0.78
Icelander (0)	11	0.01
Iranian (58)	86	0.12
Irish (2,111)	9,193	12.44
Israeli (99)	129	0.17
Italian (896)	3,687	4.99
Latvian (11)	86	0.12
Lithuanian (99)	524	0.71
Luxemburger (82)	132	0.18
Macedonian (0)	23	0.03
Maltese (0)	0	<0.01
New Zealander (0)	15	0.02
Northern European (97)	181	0.24

Ancestry	Population	%
Norwegian (357)	1,725	2.33
Pennsylvania German (0)	0	<0.01
Polish (1,266)	4,765	6.45
Portuguese (34)	112	0.15
Romanian (362)	499	0.68
Russian (1,325)	3,244	4.39
Scandinavian (83)	122	0.17
Scotch-Irish (541)	1,417	1.92
Scottish (394)	1,848	2.50
Serbian (92)	101	0.14
Slavic (28)	53	0.07
Slovak (64)	247	0.33
Slovene (14)	137	0.19
Soviet Union (0)	14	0.02
Swedish (491)	2,448	3.31
Swiss (72)	388	0.53
Turkish (141)	152	0.21
Ukrainian (147)	547	0.74
Welsh (77)	501	0.68
West Indian, ex. Hispanic (1,938)	2,476	3.35
Bahamian (8)	44	0.06
Barbadian (0)	0	<0.01
Belizean (318)	358	0.48
Bermudan (0)	0	<0.01
British West Indian (0)	25	0.03
Dutch West Indian (0)	0	<0.01
Haitian (551)	781	1.06
Jamaican (1,029)	1,181	1.60
Trinidadian/Tobagonian (0)	0	<0.01
U.S. Virgin Islander (0)	0	<0.01
West Indian (32)	87	0.12
Other West Indian (0)	0	<0.01
Yugoslavian (15)	52	0.07

Hispanic Origin	Population	%
Hispanic or Latino (of any race)	6,739	9.05
Central American, ex. Mexican	438	0.59
Costa Rican	24	0.03
Guatemalan	181	0.24
Honduran	33	0.04
Nicaraguan	30	0.04
Panamanian	52	0.07
Salvadoran	108	0.14
Other Central American	10	0.01
Cuban	278	0.37
Dominican Republic	59	0.08
Mexican	4,310	5.79
Puerto Rican	483	0.65
South American	708	0.95
Argentinean	134	0.18
Bolivian	22	0.03
Chilean	81	0.11
Colombian	179	0.24
Ecuadorian	94	0.13
Paraguayan	8	0.01
Peruvian	103	0.14
Uruguayan	12	0.02
Venezuelan	63	0.08
Other South American	12	0.02
Other Hispanic or Latino	463	0.62

Race*	Population	%
African-American/Black (13,474)	14,878	19.97
Not Hispanic (13,139)	14,338	19.25
Hispanic (335)	540	0.72
American Indian/Alaska Native (175)	671	0.90
Not Hispanic (96)	486	0.65
Hispanic (79)	185	0.25
Alaska Athabascan (Ala. Nat.) (0)	0	<0.01
Aleut (Alaska Native) (0)	0	<0.01
Apache (3)	12	0.02
Arapaho (1)	1	<0.01
Blackfeet (0)	25	0.03
Canadian/French Am. Ind. (0)	3	<0.01
Central American Ind. (1)	6	0.01
Cherokee (13)	131	0.18
Cheyenne (0)	0	<0.01
Chickasaw (1)	6	0.01
Chippewa (3)	16	0.02

	Population	%
Choctaw (1)	25	0.03
Colville (0)	0	<0.01
Comanche (0)	0	<0.01
Cree (4)	4	0.01
Creek (0)	1	<0.01
Crow (0)	0	<0.01
Delaware (1)	2	<0.01
Hopi (0)	2	<0.01
Houma (0)	0	<0.01
Inupiat (Alaska Native) (0)	0	<0.01
Iroquois (0)	12	0.02
Kiowa (0)	0	<0.01
Lumbee (0)	2	<0.01
Menominee (1)	1	<0.01
Mexican American Ind. (29)	54	0.07
Navajo (1)	3	<0.01
Osage (0)	0	<0.01
Ottawa (0)	3	<0.01
Paiute (0)	0	<0.01
Pima (0)	0	<0.01
Potawatomi (1)	1	<0.01
Pueblo (1)	4	0.01
Puget Sound Salish (0)	0	<0.01
Seminole (0)	11	0.01
Shoshone (0)	1	<0.01
Sioux (5)	13	0.02
South American Ind. (3)	13	0.02
Spanish American Ind. (0)	2	<0.01
Tlingit-Haida (Alaska Native) (1)	4	0.01
Tohono O'Odham (1)	1	<0.01
Tsimshian (Alaska Native) (0)	0	<0.01
Ute (1)	2	<0.01
Yakama (0)	0	<0.01
Yaqui (2)	3	<0.01
Yuman (0)	0	<0.01
Yup'ik (Alaska Native) (0)	0	<0.01
Asian (6,416)	7,576	10.17
Not Hispanic (6,355)	7,436	9.98
Hispanic (61)	140	0.19
Bangladeshi (19)	20	0.03
Bhutanese (5)	5	0.01
Burmese (2)	2	<0.01
Cambodian (9)	17	0.02
Chinese, ex. Taiwanese (1,981)	2,322	3.12
Filipino (496)	748	1.00
Hmong (2)	2	<0.01
Indian (1,467)	1,678	2.25
Indonesian (17)	26	0.03
Japanese (341)	560	0.75
Korean (1,100)	1,239	1.66
Laotian (4)	6	0.01
Malaysian (7)	20	0.03
Nepalese (10)	10	0.01
Pakistani (197)	245	0.33
Sri Lankan (6)	6	0.01
Taiwanese (252)	290	0.39
Thai (102)	138	0.19
Vietnamese (124)	159	0.21
Hawaii Native/Pacific Islander (16)	106	0.14
Not Hispanic (13)	95	0.13
Hispanic (3)	11	0.01
Fijian (1)	2	<0.01
Guamanian/Chamorro (5)	8	0.01
Marshallese (0)	0	<0.01
Native Hawaiian (5)	32	0.04
Samoan (1)	3	<0.01
Tongan (0)	0	<0.01
White (48,872)	51,233	68.78
Not Hispanic (45,551)	47,492	63.76
Hispanic (3,321)	3,741	5.02

*Notes: † The Census 2010 population figure is used to calculate the percentages in the Hispanic Origin and Race categories. Ancestry percentages are based on the 2006-2010 American Community Survey population (not shown); ‡ Numbers in parentheses indicate the number of people reporting a single ancestry; * Numbers in parentheses indicate the number of persons reporting this race alone, not in combination with any other race; Please refer to the Explanation of Data for more information.*

Hoffman Estates

Place Type: Village
County: Cook
Population: 51,895

Ancestry	Population	%
Afghan (0)	0	<0.01
African, Sub-Saharan (175)	175	0.34
African (175)	175	0.34
Cape Verdean (0)	0	<0.01
Ethiopian (0)	0	<0.01
Ghanaian (0)	0	<0.01
Kenyan (0)	0	<0.01
Liberian (0)	0	<0.01
Nigerian (0)	0	<0.01
Senegalese (0)	0	<0.01
Sierra Leonean (0)	0	<0.01
Somalian (0)	0	<0.01
South African (0)	0	<0.01
Sudanese (0)	0	<0.01
Ugandan (0)	0	<0.01
Zimbabwean (0)	0	<0.01
Other Sub-Saharan African (0)	0	<0.01
Albanian (65)	65	0.13
Alsatian (0)	0	<0.01
American (715)	715	1.40
Arab (219)	239	0.47
Arab (11)	11	0.02
Egyptian (164)	164	0.32
Iraqi (0)	0	<0.01
Jordanian (0)	0	<0.01
Lebanese (37)	57	0.11
Moroccan (0)	0	<0.01
Palestinian (0)	0	<0.01
Syrian (0)	0	<0.01
Other Arab (7)	7	0.01
Armenian (77)	89	0.17
Assyrian/Chaldean/Syriac (114)	114	0.22
Australian (0)	0	<0.01
Austrian (11)	189	0.37
Basque (0)	0	<0.01
Belgian (0)	110	0.21
Brazilian (0)	0	<0.01
British (0)	65	0.13
Bulgarian (36)	49	0.10
Cajun (0)	0	<0.01
Canadian (11)	83	0.16
Carpatho Rusyn (0)	0	<0.01
Celtic (0)	0	<0.01
Croatian (14)	77	0.15
Cypriot (0)	0	<0.01
Czech (216)	623	1.22
Czechoslovakian (21)	29	0.06
Danish (43)	344	0.67
Dutch (100)	335	0.65
Eastern European (74)	74	0.14
English (468)	2,170	4.24
Estonian (0)	0	<0.01
European (291)	299	0.58
Finnish (19)	65	0.13
French, ex. Basque (104)	978	1.91
French Canadian (76)	328	0.64
German (2,168)	8,675	16.94
German Russian (0)	0	<0.01
Greek (631)	863	1.69
Guyanese (0)	0	<0.01
Hungarian (49)	124	0.24
Icelander (0)	0	<0.01
Iranian (234)	293	0.57
Irish (1,476)	5,754	11.24
Israeli (0)	0	<0.01
Italian (1,561)	4,281	8.36
Latvian (0)	50	0.10
Lithuanian (184)	461	0.90
Luxemburger (21)	86	0.17
Macedonian (12)	12	0.02
Maltese (0)	0	<0.01
New Zealander (0)	0	<0.01
Northern European (74)	74	0.14

Ancestry	Population	%
Norwegian (221)	986	1.93
Pennsylvania German (7)	7	0.01
Polish (3,474)	7,198	14.06
Portuguese (15)	24	0.05
Romanian (240)	333	0.65
Russian (301)	694	1.36
Scandinavian (71)	102	0.20
Scotch-Irish (246)	462	0.90
Scottish (97)	417	0.81
Serbian (69)	69	0.13
Slavic (0)	13	0.03
Slovak (28)	296	0.58
Slovene (21)	21	0.04
Soviet Union (0)	0	<0.01
Swedish (243)	1,473	2.88
Swiss (41)	101	0.20
Turkish (92)	92	0.18
Ukrainian (257)	343	0.67
Welsh (14)	197	0.38
West Indian, ex. Hispanic (18)	18	0.04
Bahamian (0)	0	<0.01
Barbadian (0)	0	<0.01
Belizean (0)	0	<0.01
Bermudan (0)	0	<0.01
British West Indian (0)	0	<0.01
Dutch West Indian (0)	0	<0.01
Haitian (0)	0	<0.01
Jamaican (18)	18	0.04
Trinidadian/Tobagonian (0)	0	<0.01
U.S. Virgin Islander (0)	0	<0.01
West Indian (0)	0	<0.01
Other West Indian (0)	0	<0.01
Yugoslavian (85)	85	0.17

Hispanic Origin	Population	%
Hispanic or Latino (of any race)	7,297	14.06
Central American, ex. Mexican	326	0.63
Costa Rican	7	0.01
Guatemalan	133	0.26
Honduran	31	0.06
Nicaraguan	17	0.03
Panamanian	13	0.03
Salvadoran	125	0.24
Other Central American	0	<0.01
Cuban	114	0.22
Dominican Republic	30	0.06
Mexican	5,522	10.64
Puerto Rican	584	1.13
South American	439	0.85
Argentinean	23	0.04
Bolivian	17	0.03
Chilean	15	0.03
Colombian	115	0.22
Ecuadorian	130	0.25
Paraguayan	0	<0.01
Peruvian	111	0.21
Uruguayan	11	0.02
Venezuelan	16	0.03
Other South American	1	<0.01
Other Hispanic or Latino	282	0.54

Race*	Population	%
African-American/Black (2,478)	2,765	5.33
Not Hispanic (2,393)	2,624	5.06
Hispanic (85)	141	0.27
American Indian/Alaska Native (120)	288	0.55
Not Hispanic (60)	185	0.36
Hispanic (60)	103	0.20
Alaska Athabascan (Ala. Nat.) (0)	0	<0.01
Aleut (Alaska Native) (0)	0	<0.01
Apache (0)	1	<0.01
Arapaho (1)	2	<0.01
Blackfeet (1)	10	0.02
Canadian/French Am. Ind. (1)	1	<0.01
Central American Ind. (0)	0	<0.01
Cherokee (4)	29	0.06
Cheyenne (0)	0	<0.01
Chickasaw (0)	5	0.01
Chippewa (2)	4	0.01

Race*	Population	%
Choctaw (5)	10	0.02
Colville (0)	0	<0.01
Comanche (0)	0	<0.01
Cree (0)	0	<0.01
Creek (0)	0	<0.01
Crow (0)	0	<0.01
Delaware (0)	0	<0.01
Hopi (0)	0	<0.01
Houma (0)	0	<0.01
Inupiat (Alaska Native) (0)	0	<0.01
Iroquois (1)	1	<0.01
Kiowa (0)	0	<0.01
Lumbee (0)	0	<0.01
Menominee (0)	0	<0.01
Mexican American Ind. (11)	21	0.04
Navajo (1)	4	<0.01
Osage (0)	0	<0.01
Ottawa (0)	0	<0.01
Paiute (0)	0	<0.01
Pima (2)	2	<0.01
Potawatomi (3)	3	0.01
Pueblo (3)	3	0.01
Puget Sound Salish (0)	0	<0.01
Seminole (0)	1	<0.01
Shoshone (0)	0	<0.01
Sioux (6)	6	0.01
South American Ind. (0)	3	0.01
Spanish American Ind. (0)	0	<0.01
Tlingit-Haida (Alaska Native) (0)	0	<0.01
Tohono O'Odham (0)	0	<0.01
Tsimshian (Alaska Native) (0)	0	<0.01
Ute (0)	0	<0.01
Yakama (0)	0	<0.01
Yaqui (1)	1	<0.01
Yuman (0)	2	<0.01
Yup'ik (Alaska Native) (0)	0	<0.01
Asian (11,760)	12,555	24.19
Not Hispanic (11,701)	12,439	23.97
Hispanic (59)	116	0.22
Bangladeshi (19)	20	0.04
Bhutanese (0)	0	<0.01
Burmese (3)	3	0.01
Cambodian (18)	26	0.05
Chinese, ex. Taiwanese (1,039)	1,160	2.24
Filipino (1,369)	1,541	2.97
Hmong (8)	8	0.02
Indian (5,738)	5,985	11.53
Indonesian (10)	15	0.03
Japanese (786)	885	1.71
Korean (1,514)	1,602	3.09
Laotian (44)	51	0.10
Malaysian (2)	15	0.03
Nepalese (4)	4	0.01
Pakistani (651)	712	1.37
Sri Lankan (3)	5	0.01
Taiwanese (104)	137	0.26
Thai (78)	101	0.19
Vietnamese (113)	125	0.24
Hawaii Native/Pacific Islander (8)	83	0.16
Not Hispanic (4)	66	0.13
Hispanic (4)	17	0.03
Fijian (0)	0	<0.01
Guamanian/Chamorro (2)	2	<0.01
Marshallese (0)	0	<0.01
Native Hawaiian (2)	25	0.05
Samoan (0)	1	<0.01
Tongan (0)	0	<0.01
White (33,270)	34,214	65.93
Not Hispanic (29,357)	30,014	57.84
Hispanic (3,913)	4,200	8.09

Joliet

Place Type: City
County: Will
Population: 147,433

Ancestry	Population	%
Afghan (0)	0	<0.01
African, Sub-Saharan (678)	955	0.66
African (581)	837	0.58
Cape Verdean (0)	0	<0.01
Ethiopian (0)	0	<0.01
Ghanaian (26)	26	0.02
Kenyan (0)	0	<0.01
Liberian (0)	0	<0.01
Nigerian (42)	63	0.04
Senegalese (0)	0	<0.01
Sierra Leonean (0)	0	<0.01
Somalian (0)	0	<0.01
South African (29)	29	0.02
Sudanese (0)	0	<0.01
Ugandan (0)	0	<0.01
Zimbabwean (0)	0	<0.01
Other Sub-Saharan African (0)	0	<0.01
Albanian (48)	48	0.03
Alsatian (0)	15	0.01
American (2,512)	2,512	1.73
Arab (608)	694	0.48
Arab (320)	331	0.23
Egyptian (119)	133	0.09
Iraqi (0)	0	<0.01
Jordanian (0)	14	0.01
Lebanese (105)	105	0.07
Moroccan (9)	9	0.01
Palestinian (33)	80	0.06
Syrian (9)	9	0.01
Other Arab (13)	13	0.01
Armenian (7)	32	0.02
Assyrian/Chaldean/Syriac (0)	28	0.02
Australian (0)	0	<0.01
Austrian (65)	306	0.21
Basque (0)	0	<0.01
Belgian (39)	88	0.06
Brazilian (0)	53	0.04
British (106)	289	0.20
Bulgarian (10)	10	0.01
Cajun (0)	0	<0.01
Canadian (32)	80	0.06
Carpatho Rusyn (0)	0	<0.01
Celtic (0)	27	0.02
Croatian (259)	1,196	0.82
Cypriot (0)	0	<0.01
Czech (254)	1,474	1.02
Czechoslovakian (48)	84	0.06
Danish (59)	464	0.32
Dutch (225)	1,311	0.90
Eastern European (33)	55	0.04
English (1,024)	6,635	4.58
Estonian (0)	0	<0.01
European (625)	694	0.48
Finnish (30)	81	0.06
French, ex. Basque (200)	2,385	1.64
French Canadian (107)	304	0.21
German (4,859)	23,053	15.90
German Russian (0)	29	0.02
Greek (445)	1,225	0.84
Guyanese (19)	19	0.01
Hungarian (159)	782	0.54
Icelander (0)	34	0.02
Iranian (0)	0	<0.01
Irish (4,615)	21,088	14.54
Israeli (0)	0	<0.01
Italian (3,491)	13,198	9.10
Latvian (0)	0	<0.01
Lithuanian (594)	1,678	1.16
Luxemburger (14)	33	0.02
Macedonian (34)	34	0.02
Maltese (0)	0	<0.01
New Zealander (0)	0	<0.01
Northern European (0)	0	<0.01

Ancestry	Population	%
Norwegian (387)	1,862	1.28
Pennsylvania German (0)	34	0.02
Polish (4,763)	14,334	9.89
Portuguese (33)	201	0.14
Romanian (118)	294	0.20
Russian (189)	621	0.43
Scandinavian (52)	220	0.15
Scotch-Irish (280)	1,214	0.84
Scottish (318)	1,556	1.07
Serbian (87)	305	0.21
Slavic (58)	153	0.11
Slovak (506)	1,601	1.10
Slovene (487)	1,830	1.26
Soviet Union (0)	0	<0.01
Swedish (342)	2,493	1.72
Swiss (38)	180	0.12
Turkish (0)	0	<0.01
Ukrainian (48)	145	0.10
Welsh (86)	459	0.32
West Indian, ex. Hispanic (69)	94	0.06
Bahamian (0)	0	<0.01
Barbadian (0)	0	<0.01
Belizean (0)	0	<0.01
Bermudan (0)	0	<0.01
British West Indian (0)	0	<0.01
Dutch West Indian (0)	13	0.01
Haitian (55)	55	0.04
Jamaican (0)	12	0.01
Trinidadian/Tobagonian (14)	14	0.01
U.S. Virgin Islander (0)	0	<0.01
West Indian (0)	0	<0.01
Other West Indian (0)	0	<0.01
Yugoslavian (11)	26	0.02

Hispanic Origin	Population	%
Hispanic or Latino (of any race)	41,042	27.84
Central American, ex. Mexican	588	0.40
Costa Rican	17	0.01
Guatemalan	323	0.22
Honduran	69	0.05
Nicaraguan	26	0.02
Panamanian	42	0.03
Salvadoran	109	0.07
Other Central American	2	<0.01
Cuban	151	0.10
Dominican Republic	88	0.06
Mexican	36,570	24.80
Puerto Rican	2,084	1.41
South American	485	0.33
Argentinean	25	0.02
Bolivian	23	0.02
Chilean	15	0.01
Colombian	167	0.11
Ecuadorian	95	0.06
Paraguayan	9	0.01
Peruvian	102	0.07
Uruguayan	10	0.01
Venezuelan	39	0.03
Other South American	0	<0.01
Other Hispanic or Latino	1,076	0.73

Race*	Population	%
African-American/Black (23,562)	25,255	17.13
Not Hispanic (23,025)	24,271	16.46
Hispanic (537)	984	0.67
American Indian/Alaska Native (475)	1,176	0.80
Not Hispanic (192)	636	0.43
Hispanic (283)	540	0.37
Alaska Athabascan (Ala. Nat.) (1)	1	<0.01
Aleut (Alaska Native) (0)	2	<0.01
Apache (7)	28	0.02
Arapaho (0)	0	<0.01
Blackfeet (5)	31	0.02
Canadian/French Am. Ind. (3)	3	<0.01
Central American Ind. (0)	0	<0.01
Cherokee (34)	194	0.13
Cheyenne (2)	4	<0.01
Chickasaw (3)	4	<0.01
Chippewa (16)	29	0.02

Race*	Population	%
Choctaw (1)	23	0.02
Colville (0)	0	<0.01
Comanche (1)	1	<0.01
Cree (0)	1	<0.01
Creek (12)	17	0.01
Crow (1)	1	<0.01
Delaware (0)	0	<0.01
Hopi (1)	2	<0.01
Houma (0)	0	<0.01
Inupiat (Alaska Native) (1)	3	<0.01
Iroquois (9)	18	0.01
Kiowa (0)	0	<0.01
Lumbee (0)	0	<0.01
Menominee (0)	0	<0.01
Mexican American Ind. (67)	110	0.07
Navajo (9)	24	0.02
Osage (0)	0	<0.01
Ottawa (0)	2	<0.01
Paiute (0)	0	<0.01
Pima (0)	0	<0.01
Potawatomi (6)	11	0.01
Pueblo (0)	1	<0.01
Puget Sound Salish (0)	0	<0.01
Seminole (0)	1	<0.01
Shoshone (0)	0	<0.01
Sioux (6)	25	0.02
South American Ind. (4)	13	0.01
Spanish American Ind. (10)	14	0.01
Tlingit-Haida (Alaska Native) (0)	0	<0.01
Tohono O'Odham (0)	0	<0.01
Tsimshian (Alaska Native) (0)	0	<0.01
Ute (4)	4	<0.01
Yakama (0)	0	<0.01
Yaqui (0)	0	<0.01
Yuman (0)	0	<0.01
Yup'ik (Alaska Native) (0)	0	<0.01
Asian (2,841)	3,584	2.43
Not Hispanic (2,747)	3,347	2.27
Hispanic (94)	237	0.16
Bangladeshi (5)	9	0.01
Bhutanese (0)	0	<0.01
Burmese (11)	12	0.01
Cambodian (100)	110	0.07
Chinese, ex. Taiwanese (154)	247	0.17
Filipino (990)	1,269	0.86
Hmong (22)	24	0.02
Indian (617)	706	0.48
Indonesian (8)	12	0.01
Japanese (50)	146	0.10
Korean (134)	212	0.14
Laotian (201)	221	0.15
Malaysian (5)	9	0.01
Nepalese (0)	0	<0.01
Pakistani (190)	214	0.15
Sri Lankan (0)	5	<0.01
Taiwanese (17)	18	0.01
Thai (38)	58	0.04
Vietnamese (211)	246	0.17
Hawaii Native/Pacific Islander (30)	116	0.08
Not Hispanic (18)	59	0.04
Hispanic (12)	57	0.04
Fijian (0)	2	<0.01
Guamanian/Chamorro (7)	12	0.01
Marshallese (1)	1	<0.01
Native Hawaiian (5)	22	0.01
Samoan (9)	13	0.01
Tongan (2)	2	<0.01
White (99,494)	103,279	70.05
Not Hispanic (78,159)	80,019	54.27
Hispanic (21,335)	23,260	15.78

*Notes: † The Census 2010 population figure is used to calculate the percentages in the Hispanic Origin and Race categories. Ancestry percentages are based on the 2006-2010 American Community Survey population (not shown); ‡ Numbers in parentheses indicate the number of people reporting a single ancestry; * Numbers in parentheses indicate the number of persons reporting this race alone, not in combination with any other race; Please refer to the Explanation of Data for more information.*

Mount Prospect

Place Type: Village
County: Cook
Population: 54,167

Ancestry	Population	%
Afghan (0)	0	<0.01
African, Sub-Saharan (91)	120	0.22
African (81)	110	0.20
Cape Verdean (0)	0	<0.01
Ethiopian (0)	0	<0.01
Ghanaian (0)	0	<0.01
Kenyan (0)	0	<0.01
Liberian (0)	0	<0.01
Nigerian (0)	0	<0.01
Senegalese (0)	0	<0.01
Sierra Leonean (0)	0	<0.01
Somalian (0)	0	<0.01
South African (0)	0	<0.01
Sudanese (0)	0	<0.01
Ugandan (0)	0	<0.01
Zimbabwean (0)	0	<0.01
Other Sub-Saharan African (10)	10	0.02
Albanian (84)	95	0.18
Alsatian (14)	29	0.05
American (1,106)	1,106	2.05
Arab (139)	191	0.35
Arab (53)	80	0.15
Egyptian (18)	18	0.03
Iraqi (0)	0	<0.01
Jordanian (0)	0	<0.01
Lebanese (45)	54	0.10
Moroccan (0)	0	<0.01
Palestinian (0)	16	0.03
Syrian (0)	0	<0.01
Other Arab (23)	23	0.04
Armenian (111)	223	0.41
Assyrian/Chaldean/Syriac (307)	355	0.66
Australian (0)	0	<0.01
Austrian (71)	361	0.67
Basque (0)	0	<0.01
Belgian (11)	39	0.07
Brazilian (14)	30	0.06
British (42)	131	0.24
Bulgarian (902)	926	1.72
Cajun (0)	0	<0.01
Canadian (11)	85	0.16
Carpatho Rusyn (0)	0	<0.01
Celtic (0)	0	<0.01
Croatian (129)	301	0.56
Cypriot (0)	0	<0.01
Czech (176)	831	1.54
Czechoslovakian (67)	81	0.15
Danish (27)	314	0.58
Dutch (125)	667	1.24
Eastern European (67)	73	0.14
English (401)	1,958	3.64
Estonian (0)	0	<0.01
European (357)	357	0.66
Finnish (9)	9	0.02
French, ex. Basque (65)	891	1.65
French Canadian (37)	114	0.21
German (3,286)	11,827	21.97
German Russian (0)	0	<0.01
Greek (846)	1,303	2.42
Guyanese (0)	0	<0.01
Hungarian (142)	353	0.66
Icelander (0)	9	0.02
Iranian (65)	82	0.15
Irish (1,474)	6,885	12.79
Israeli (0)	0	<0.01
Italian (2,263)	5,061	9.40
Latvian (26)	34	0.06
Lithuanian (207)	369	0.69
Luxemburger (0)	23	0.04
Macedonian (8)	8	0.01
Maltese (0)	0	<0.01
New Zealander (0)	0	<0.01
Northern European (61)	61	0.11

Ancestry	Population	%
Norwegian (173)	983	1.83
Pennsylvania German (0)	13	0.02
Polish (5,687)	9,709	18.03
Portuguese (13)	13	0.02
Romanian (319)	474	0.88
Russian (119)	712	1.32
Scandinavian (33)	46	0.09
Scotch-Irish (149)	456	0.85
Scottish (106)	510	0.95
Serbian (103)	111	0.21
Slavic (0)	22	0.04
Slovak (80)	161	0.30
Slovene (0)	33	0.06
Soviet Union (0)	0	<0.01
Swedish (438)	1,525	2.83
Swiss (10)	83	0.15
Turkish (160)	160	0.30
Ukrainian (199)	335	0.62
Welsh (29)	386	0.72
West Indian, ex. Hispanic (318)	331	0.61
Bahamian (0)	0	<0.01
Barbadian (0)	0	<0.01
Belizean (0)	0	<0.01
Bermudan (0)	0	<0.01
British West Indian (0)	0	<0.01
Dutch West Indian (0)	0	<0.01
Haitian (295)	308	0.57
Jamaican (23)	23	0.04
Trinidadian/Tobagonian (0)	0	<0.01
U.S. Virgin Islander (0)	0	<0.01
West Indian (0)	0	<0.01
Other West Indian (0)	0	<0.01
Yugoslavian (207)	244	0.45

Hispanic Origin	Population	%
Hispanic or Latino (of any race)	8,408	15.52
Central American, ex. Mexican	310	0.57
Costa Rican	4	0.01
Guatemalan	137	0.25
Honduran	18	0.03
Nicaraguan	17	0.03
Panamanian	13	0.02
Salvadoran	115	0.21
Other Central American	6	0.01
Cuban	170	0.31
Dominican Republic	14	0.03
Mexican	6,932	12.80
Puerto Rican	452	0.83
South American	319	0.59
Argentinean	22	0.04
Bolivian	10	0.02
Chilean	15	0.03
Colombian	93	0.17
Ecuadorian	89	0.16
Paraguayan	2	<0.01
Peruvian	65	0.12
Uruguayan	2	<0.01
Venezuelan	16	0.03
Other South American	5	0.01
Other Hispanic or Latino	211	0.39

Race*	Population	%
African-American/Black (1,282)	1,506	2.78
Not Hispanic (1,230)	1,409	2.60
Hispanic (52)	97	0.18
American Indian/Alaska Native (196)	359	0.66
Not Hispanic (47)	169	0.31
Hispanic (149)	190	0.35
Alaska Athabascan (Ala. Nat.) (0)	0	<0.01
Aleut (Alaska Native) (0)	0	<0.01
Apache (1)	1	<0.01
Arapaho (0)	0	<0.01
Blackfeet (0)	5	0.01
Canadian/French Am. Ind. (0)	0	<0.01
Central American Ind. (0)	1	<0.01
Cherokee (1)	28	0.05
Cheyenne (0)	0	<0.01
Chickasaw (0)	0	<0.01
Chippewa (2)	9	0.02

Race*	Population	%
Choctaw (0)	2	<0.01
Colville (0)	0	<0.01
Comanche (1)	1	<0.01
Cree (0)	0	<0.01
Creek (0)	1	<0.01
Crow (0)	1	<0.01
Delaware (0)	0	<0.01
Hopi (0)	0	<0.01
Houma (0)	0	<0.01
Inupiat (Alaska Native) (0)	0	<0.01
Iroquois (3)	6	0.01
Kiowa (0)	0	<0.01
Lumbee (0)	0	<0.01
Menominee (1)	1	<0.01
Mexican American Ind. (12)	20	0.04
Navajo (0)	1	<0.01
Osage (0)	0	<0.01
Ottawa (1)	1	<0.01
Paiute (0)	0	<0.01
Pima (0)	0	<0.01
Potawatomi (2)	3	0.01
Pueblo (0)	0	<0.01
Puget Sound Salish (0)	0	<0.01
Seminole (0)	1	<0.01
Shoshone (0)	0	<0.01
Sioux (1)	3	0.01
South American Ind. (3)	4	0.01
Spanish American Ind. (0)	1	<0.01
Tlingit-Haida (Alaska Native) (0)	0	<0.01
Tohono O'Odham (0)	0	<0.01
Tsimshian (Alaska Native) (0)	0	<0.01
Ute (0)	0	<0.01
Yakama (0)	0	<0.01
Yaqui (0)	3	0.01
Yuman (0)	0	<0.01
Yup'ik (Alaska Native) (0)	0	<0.01
Asian (6,339)	6,844	12.63
Not Hispanic (6,312)	6,782	12.52
Hispanic (27)	62	0.11
Bangladeshi (9)	10	0.02
Bhutanese (0)	0	<0.01
Burmese (4)	4	0.01
Cambodian (18)	21	0.04
Chinese, ex. Taiwanese (384)	474	0.88
Filipino (857)	1,007	1.86
Hmong (1)	1	<0.01
Indian (3,183)	3,314	6.12
Indonesian (9)	10	0.02
Japanese (229)	306	0.56
Korean (1,047)	1,101	2.03
Laotian (11)	12	0.02
Malaysian (6)	6	0.01
Nepalese (8)	8	0.01
Pakistani (147)	173	0.32
Sri Lankan (0)	0	<0.01
Taiwanese (20)	22	0.04
Thai (28)	37	0.07
Vietnamese (141)	157	0.29
Hawaii Native/Pacific Islander (16)	67	0.12
Not Hispanic (11)	49	0.09
Hispanic (5)	18	0.03
Fijian (0)	0	<0.01
Guamanian/Chamorro (6)	18	0.03
Marshallese (0)	0	<0.01
Native Hawaiian (6)	19	0.04
Samoan (1)	2	<0.01
Tongan (0)	0	<0.01
White (41,715)	42,591	78.63
Not Hispanic (37,355)	37,930	70.02
Hispanic (4,360)	4,661	8.60

Notes: † The Census 2010 population figure is used to calculate the percentages in the Hispanic Origin and Race categories. Ancestry percentages are based on the 2006-2010 American Community Survey population (not shown); ‡ Numbers in parentheses indicate the number of people reporting a single ancestry; * Numbers in parentheses indicate the number of persons reporting this race alone, not in combination with any other race; Please refer to the Explanation of Data for more information.

Naperville

Place Type: City
County: DuPage
Population: 141,853

Ancestry	Population	%
Afghan (0)	0	<0.01
African, Sub-Saharan (460)	634	0.45
African (108)	135	0.10
Cape Verdean (0)	0	<0.01
Ethiopian (0)	0	<0.01
Ghanaian (110)	110	0.08
Kenyan (18)	55	0.04
Liberian (0)	0	<0.01
Nigerian (91)	133	0.09
Senegalese (0)	0	<0.01
Sierra Leonean (0)	0	<0.01
Somalian (0)	0	<0.01
South African (125)	179	0.13
Sudanese (0)	0	<0.01
Ugandan (0)	0	<0.01
Zimbabwean (0)	0	<0.01
Other Sub-Saharan African (8)	22	0.02
Albanian (60)	60	0.04
Alsatian (32)	59	0.04
American (3,568)	3,568	2.53
Arab (1,209)	1,759	1.25
Arab (157)	266	0.19
Egyptian (143)	157	0.11
Iraqi (0)	0	<0.01
Jordanian (0)	42	0.03
Lebanese (209)	367	0.26
Moroccan (182)	235	0.17
Palestinian (294)	336	0.24
Syrian (15)	89	0.06
Other Arab (209)	267	0.19
Armenian (23)	108	0.08
Assyrian/Chaldean/Syriac (56)	74	0.05
Australian (65)	114	0.08
Austrian (44)	666	0.47
Basque (0)	0	<0.01
Belgian (66)	443	0.31
Brazilian (119)	313	0.22
British (389)	1,104	0.78
Bulgarian (55)	62	0.04
Cajun (0)	14	0.01
Canadian (480)	734	0.52
Carpatho Rusyn (0)	0	<0.01
Celtic (0)	9	0.01
Croatian (290)	1,020	0.72
Cypriot (0)	0	<0.01
Czech (809)	3,566	2.53
Czechoslovakian (116)	266	0.19
Danish (107)	1,049	0.74
Dutch (508)	2,210	1.57
Eastern European (210)	278	0.20
English (2,285)	12,476	8.86
Estonian (0)	0	<0.01
European (2,330)	2,659	1.89
Finnish (78)	379	0.27
French, ex. Basque (481)	3,333	2.37
French Canadian (129)	768	0.55
German (7,562)	32,930	23.38
German Russian (0)	0	<0.01
Greek (931)	1,872	1.33
Guyanese (116)	116	0.08
Hungarian (256)	798	0.57
Icelander (9)	31	0.02
Iranian (461)	510	0.36
Irish (5,996)	25,848	18.35
Israeli (0)	0	<0.01
Italian (3,586)	14,744	10.47
Latvian (46)	283	0.20
Lithuanian (879)	2,734	1.94
Luxemburger (24)	92	0.07
Macedonian (282)	295	0.21
Maltese (13)	64	0.05
New Zealander (13)	13	0.01
Northern European (71)	71	0.05
Norwegian (470)	2,831	2.01
Pennsylvania German (10)	18	0.01
Polish (4,945)	15,623	11.09
Portuguese (25)	169	0.12
Romanian (91)	331	0.24
Russian (730)	1,979	1.41
Scandinavian (182)	324	0.23
Scotch-Irish (767)	2,240	1.59
Scottish (504)	2,657	1.89
Serbian (92)	301	0.21
Slavic (0)	20	0.01
Slovak (340)	1,015	0.72
Slovene (0)	178	0.13
Soviet Union (0)	0	<0.01
Swedish (861)	4,354	3.09
Swiss (62)	647	0.46
Turkish (102)	112	0.08
Ukrainian (459)	915	0.65
Welsh (129)	847	0.60
West Indian, ex. Hispanic (63)	121	0.09
Bahamian (21)	21	0.01
Barbadian (0)	0	<0.01
Belizean (0)	0	<0.01
Bermudan (0)	0	<0.01
British West Indian (0)	0	<0.01
Dutch West Indian (0)	0	<0.01
Haitian (0)	0	<0.01
Jamaican (30)	46	0.03
Trinidadian/Tobagonian (12)	54	0.04
U.S. Virgin Islander (0)	0	<0.01
West Indian (0)	0	<0.01
Other West Indian (0)	0	<0.01
Yugoslavian (21)	77	0.05

Hispanic Origin	Population	%
Hispanic or Latino (of any race)	7,574	5.34
Central American, ex. Mexican	320	0.23
Costa Rican	26	0.02
Guatemalan	135	0.10
Honduran	42	0.03
Nicaraguan	31	0.02
Panamanian	35	0.02
Salvadoran	49	0.03
Other Central American	2	<0.01
Cuban	286	0.20
Dominican Republic	66	0.05
Mexican	4,767	3.36
Puerto Rican	853	0.60
South American	798	0.56
Argentinean	111	0.08
Bolivian	27	0.02
Chilean	65	0.05
Colombian	262	0.18
Ecuadorian	96	0.07
Paraguayan	9	0.01
Peruvian	109	0.08
Uruguayan	9	0.01
Venezuelan	108	0.08
Other South American	2	<0.01
Other Hispanic or Latino	484	0.34

Race*	Population	%
African-American/Black (6,612)	7,463	5.26
Not Hispanic (6,504)	7,225	5.09
Hispanic (108)	238	0.17
American Indian/Alaska Native (212)	688	0.49
Not Hispanic (122)	497	0.35
Hispanic (90)	191	0.13
Alaska Athabascan (Ala. Nat.) (1)	1	<0.01
Aleut (Alaska Native) (0)	0	<0.01
Apache (3)	15	0.01
Arapaho (0)	1	<0.01
Blackfeet (0)	10	0.01
Canadian/French Am. Ind. (0)	2	<0.01
Central American Ind. (6)	8	0.01
Cherokee (31)	161	0.11
Cheyenne (0)	0	<0.01
Chickasaw (0)	4	<0.01
Chippewa (2)	21	0.01

Choctaw (5)	12	0.0
Colville (0)	0	<0.0
Comanche (0)	0	<0.0
Cree (0)	0	<0.0
Creek (0)	3	<0.0
Crow (0)	0	<0.0
Delaware (0)	0	<0.0
Hopi (0)	0	<0.0
Houma (0)	0	<0.0
Inupiat (Alaska Native) (2)	2	<0.0
Iroquois (4)	12	<0.0
Kiowa (0)	0	<0.0
Lumbee (0)	3	<0.0
Menominee (0)	0	<0.0
Mexican American Ind. (11)	27	0.0
Navajo (4)	17	0.0
Osage (3)	7	<0.0
Ottawa (0)	0	<0.0
Paiute (0)	0	<0.0
Pima (0)	0	<0.0
Potawatomi (4)	4	<0.0
Pueblo (3)	3	<0.0
Puget Sound Salish (0)	1	<0.0
Seminole (1)	6	<0.0
Shoshone (0)	0	<0.0
Sioux (7)	20	0.0
South American Ind. (2)	7	<0.0
Spanish American Ind. (1)	1	<0.0
Tlingit-Haida (Alaska Native) (0)	0	<0.0
Tohono O'Odham (0)	0	<0.0
Tsimshian (Alaska Native) (0)	0	<0.0
Ute (0)	5	<0.0
Yakama (0)	0	<0.0
Yaqui (0)	0	<0.0
Yuman (0)	0	<0.0
Yup'ik (Alaska Native) (0)	1	<0.0
Asian (21,170)	23,042	16.2
Not Hispanic (21,094)	22,868	16.1
Hispanic (76)	174	0.1
Bangladeshi (71)	77	0.0
Bhutanese (1)	1	<0.0
Burmese (17)	25	0.0
Cambodian (13)	24	0.0
Chinese, ex. Taiwanese (4,966)	5,487	3.8
Filipino (1,287)	1,716	1.2
Hmong (2)	2	<0.0
Indian (10,469)	10,917	7.7
Indonesian (31)	49	0.0
Japanese (252)	480	0.3
Korean (1,661)	1,864	1.3
Laotian (14)	28	0.0
Malaysian (13)	16	0.0
Nepalese (15)	15	0.0
Pakistani (968)	1,060	0.7
Sri Lankan (53)	62	0.0
Taiwanese (503)	597	0.4
Thai (73)	116	0.0
Vietnamese (277)	332	0.2
Hawaii Native/Pacific Islander (32)	146	0.1
Not Hispanic (32)	136	0.1
Hispanic (0)	10	0.1
Fijian (4)	7	<0.0
Guamanian/Chamorro (5)	14	0.0
Marshallese (0)	0	<0.0
Native Hawaiian (6)	43	0.0
Samoan (1)	10	0.0
Tongan (1)	3	<0.0
White (108,447)	111,144	78.3
Not Hispanic (103,603)	105,833	74.6
Hispanic (4,844)	5,311	3.7

Notes: † *The Census 2010 population figure is used to calculate the percentages in the Hispanic Origin and Race categories. Ancestry percentages are based on the 2006-2010 American Communi... Survey population (not shown); ‡ Numbers in parentheses indicate the number of people reporting a single ancestry; * Numbers in parentheses indicate the number of persons reporting this race alo... not in combination with any other race; Please refer to the Explanation of Data for more information.*

Normal

Place Type: Town
County: McLean
Population: 52,497

Ancestry	Population	%
Afghan (0)	0	<0.01
African, Sub-Saharan (330)	388	0.75
African (159)	208	0.40
Cape Verdean (0)	0	<0.01
Ethiopian (23)	23	0.04
Ghanaian (1)	1	<0.01
Kenyan (0)	0	<0.01
Liberian (0)	0	<0.01
Nigerian (68)	68	0.13
Senegalese (0)	0	<0.01
Sierra Leonean (0)	0	<0.01
Somalian (0)	0	<0.01
South African (0)	9	0.02
Sudanese (0)	0	<0.01
Ugandan (0)	0	<0.01
Zimbabwean (0)	0	<0.01
Other Sub-Saharan African (79)	79	0.15
Albanian (38)	38	0.07
Alsatian (0)	13	0.03
American (4,384)	4,384	8.49
Arab (17)	95	0.18
Arab (0)	0	<0.01
Egyptian (0)	0	<0.01
Iraqi (0)	0	<0.01
Jordanian (0)	0	<0.01
Lebanese (17)	95	0.18
Moroccan (0)	0	<0.01
Palestinian (0)	0	<0.01
Syrian (0)	0	<0.01
Other Arab (0)	0	<0.01
Armenian (19)	46	0.09
Assyrian/Chaldean/Syriac (0)	0	<0.01
Australian (0)	0	<0.01
Austrian (26)	145	0.28
Basque (0)	0	<0.01
Belgian (27)	162	0.31
Brazilian (0)	0	<0.01
British (39)	185	0.36
Bulgarian (0)	0	<0.01
Cajun (0)	0	<0.01
Canadian (29)	58	0.11
Carpatho Rusyn (0)	0	<0.01
Celtic (0)	0	<0.01
Croatian (29)	143	0.28
Cypriot (0)	0	<0.01
Czech (69)	455	0.88
Czechoslovakian (21)	63	0.12
Danish (47)	289	0.56
Dutch (242)	932	1.81
Eastern European (25)	25	0.05
English (1,446)	4,945	9.58
Estonian (0)	0	<0.01
European (449)	494	0.96
Finnish (14)	47	0.09
French, ex. Basque (180)	1,299	2.52
French Canadian (52)	141	0.27
German (6,093)	16,582	32.13
German Russian (0)	0	<0.01
Greek (116)	314	0.61
Guyanese (0)	0	<0.01
Hungarian (19)	210	0.41
Icelander (0)	0	<0.01
Iranian (48)	48	0.09
Irish (2,206)	8,434	16.34
Israeli (0)	25	0.05
Italian (574)	3,057	5.92
Latvian (0)	17	0.03
Lithuanian (24)	110	0.21
Luxemburger (0)	0	<0.01
Macedonian (0)	0	<0.01
Maltese (0)	0	<0.01
New Zealander (0)	0	<0.01
Northern European (14)	14	0.03

Ancestry (cont.)	Population	%
Norwegian (351)	988	1.91
Pennsylvania German (0)	34	0.07
Polish (589)	2,606	5.05
Portuguese (0)	0	<0.01
Romanian (17)	81	0.16
Russian (105)	285	0.55
Scandinavian (16)	52	0.10
Scotch-Irish (312)	905	1.75
Scottish (388)	1,129	2.19
Serbian (0)	0	<0.01
Slavic (0)	12	0.02
Slovak (22)	201	0.39
Slovene (0)	101	0.20
Soviet Union (0)	0	<0.01
Swedish (341)	1,314	2.55
Swiss (61)	392	0.76
Turkish (18)	44	0.09
Ukrainian (16)	75	0.15
Welsh (86)	342	0.66
West Indian, ex. Hispanic (36)	36	0.07
Bahamian (0)	0	<0.01
Barbadian (13)	13	0.03
Belizean (0)	0	<0.01
Bermudan (0)	0	<0.01
British West Indian (0)	0	<0.01
Dutch West Indian (0)	0	<0.01
Haitian (0)	0	<0.01
Jamaican (8)	8	0.02
Trinidadian/Tobagonian (0)	0	<0.01
U.S. Virgin Islander (0)	0	<0.01
West Indian (15)	15	0.03
Other West Indian (0)	0	<0.01
Yugoslavian (0)	0	<0.01

Hispanic Origin	Population	%
Hispanic or Latino (of any race)	2,133	4.06
Central American, ex. Mexican	110	0.21
Costa Rican	9	0.02
Guatemalan	54	0.10
Honduran	14	0.03
Nicaraguan	0	<0.01
Panamanian	10	0.02
Salvadoran	23	0.04
Other Central American	0	<0.01
Cuban	62	0.12
Dominican Republic	22	0.04
Mexican	1,418	2.70
Puerto Rican	230	0.44
South American	140	0.27
Argentinean	15	0.03
Bolivian	6	0.01
Chilean	21	0.04
Colombian	51	0.10
Ecuadorian	13	0.02
Paraguayan	3	0.01
Peruvian	23	0.04
Uruguayan	1	<0.01
Venezuelan	7	0.01
Other South American	0	<0.01
Other Hispanic or Latino	151	0.29

Race*	Population	%
African-American/Black (4,257)	4,918	9.37
Not Hispanic (4,201)	4,796	9.14
Hispanic (56)	122	0.23
American Indian/Alaska Native (79)	273	0.52
Not Hispanic (59)	220	0.42
Hispanic (20)	53	0.10
Alaska Athabascan (Ala. Nat.) (0)	0	<0.01
Aleut (Alaska Native) (0)	0	<0.01
Apache (4)	8	0.02
Arapaho (0)	0	<0.01
Blackfeet (2)	7	0.01
Canadian/French Am. Ind. (4)	4	0.01
Central American Ind. (1)	4	0.01
Cherokee (22)	82	0.16
Cheyenne (0)	0	<0.01
Chickasaw (0)	0	<0.01
Chippewa (3)	5	0.01

Race* (cont.)	Population	%
Choctaw (1)	11	0.02
Colville (0)	0	<0.01
Comanche (0)	0	<0.01
Cree (1)	1	<0.01
Creek (1)	6	0.01
Crow (0)	0	<0.01
Delaware (0)	0	<0.01
Hopi (0)	0	<0.01
Houma (0)	0	<0.01
Inupiat (Alaska Native) (0)	0	<0.01
Iroquois (1)	2	<0.01
Kiowa (0)	0	<0.01
Lumbee (0)	0	<0.01
Menominee (0)	0	<0.01
Mexican American Ind. (2)	7	0.01
Navajo (1)	3	0.01
Osage (0)	0	<0.01
Ottawa (0)	0	<0.01
Paiute (0)	0	<0.01
Pima (0)	0	<0.01
Potawatomi (2)	4	0.01
Pueblo (0)	1	<0.01
Puget Sound Salish (0)	0	<0.01
Seminole (0)	3	0.01
Shoshone (0)	2	<0.01
Sioux (0)	1	<0.01
South American Ind. (0)	4	0.01
Spanish American Ind. (0)	0	<0.01
Tlingit-Haida (Alaska Native) (0)	0	<0.01
Tohono O'Odham (1)	1	<0.01
Tsimshian (Alaska Native) (0)	0	<0.01
Ute (0)	0	<0.01
Yakama (0)	0	<0.01
Yaqui (1)	1	<0.01
Yuman (0)	1	<0.01
Yup'ik (Alaska Native) (0)	0	<0.01
Asian (1,687)	2,043	3.89
Not Hispanic (1,673)	2,002	3.81
Hispanic (14)	41	0.08
Bangladeshi (7)	7	0.01
Bhutanese (0)	0	<0.01
Burmese (7)	9	0.02
Cambodian (2)	6	0.01
Chinese, ex. Taiwanese (317)	378	0.72
Filipino (128)	226	0.43
Hmong (0)	0	<0.01
Indian (763)	806	1.54
Indonesian (1)	7	0.01
Japanese (66)	131	0.25
Korean (167)	216	0.41
Laotian (5)	7	0.01
Malaysian (1)	2	<0.01
Nepalese (22)	22	0.04
Pakistani (38)	42	0.08
Sri Lankan (16)	21	0.04
Taiwanese (11)	12	0.02
Thai (24)	35	0.07
Vietnamese (81)	101	0.19
Hawaii Native/Pacific Islander (23)	51	0.10
Not Hispanic (21)	42	0.08
Hispanic (2)	9	0.02
Fijian (2)	2	<0.01
Guamanian/Chamorro (3)	6	0.01
Marshallese (0)	0	<0.01
Native Hawaiian (9)	16	0.03
Samoan (6)	11	0.02
Tongan (0)	0	<0.01
White (44,660)	45,768	87.18
Not Hispanic (43,313)	44,263	84.32
Hispanic (1,347)	1,505	2.87

Notes: † The Census 2010 population figure is used to calculate the percentages in the Hispanic Origin and Race categories. Ancestry percentages are based on the 2006-2010 American Community Survey population (not shown); ‡ Numbers in parentheses indicate the number of people reporting a single ancestry; * Numbers in parentheses indicate the number of persons reporting this race alone, not in combination with any other race; Please refer to the Explanation of Data for more information.

Oak Lawn

Place Type: Village
County: Cook
Population: 56,690

Ancestry	Population	%
Afghan (0)	0	<0.01
African, Sub-Saharan (111)	178	0.32
African (24)	91	0.16
Cape Verdean (0)	0	<0.01
Ethiopian (77)	77	0.14
Ghanaian (0)	0	<0.01
Kenyan (0)	0	<0.01
Liberian (0)	0	<0.01
Nigerian (0)	0	<0.01
Senegalese (0)	0	<0.01
Sierra Leonean (0)	0	<0.01
Somalian (0)	0	<0.01
South African (0)	0	<0.01
Sudanese (10)	10	0.02
Ugandan (0)	0	<0.01
Zimbabwean (0)	0	<0.01
Other Sub-Saharan African (0)	0	<0.01
Albanian (52)	52	0.09
Alsatian (0)	0	<0.01
American (860)	860	1.54
Arab (2,517)	2,764	4.95
Arab (1,246)	1,415	2.53
Egyptian (88)	88	0.16
Iraqi (0)	0	<0.01
Jordanian (220)	254	0.45
Lebanese (28)	28	0.05
Moroccan (118)	137	0.25
Palestinian (725)	739	1.32
Syrian (10)	21	0.04
Other Arab (82)	82	0.15
Armenian (0)	0	<0.01
Assyrian/Chaldean/Syriac (0)	0	<0.01
Australian (0)	0	<0.01
Austrian (193)	411	0.74
Basque (0)	0	<0.01
Belgian (0)	49	0.09
Brazilian (0)	9	0.02
British (30)	45	0.08
Bulgarian (15)	27	0.05
Cajun (0)	0	<0.01
Canadian (27)	43	0.08
Carpatho Rusyn (0)	0	<0.01
Celtic (11)	11	0.02
Croatian (265)	577	1.03
Cypriot (0)	0	<0.01
Czech (155)	1,005	1.80
Czechoslovakian (78)	145	0.26
Danish (44)	284	0.51
Dutch (349)	1,045	1.87
Eastern European (4)	4	0.01
English (296)	1,738	3.11
Estonian (0)	15	0.03
European (160)	172	0.31
Finnish (0)	44	0.08
French, ex. Basque (82)	806	1.44
French Canadian (83)	252	0.45
German (1,731)	10,189	18.25
German Russian (0)	0	<0.01
Greek (870)	1,162	2.08
Guyanese (11)	11	0.02
Hungarian (36)	438	0.78
Icelander (0)	0	<0.01
Iranian (0)	8	0.01
Irish (5,081)	14,106	25.27
Israeli (103)	122	0.22
Italian (2,067)	6,249	11.19
Latvian (0)	0	<0.01
Lithuanian (1,098)	2,267	4.06
Luxemburger (14)	48	0.09
Macedonian (24)	24	0.04
Maltese (0)	0	<0.01
New Zealander (0)	0	<0.01
Northern European (13)	13	0.02

Ancestry	Population	%
Norwegian (172)	620	1.11
Pennsylvania German (0)	0	<0.01
Polish (5,809)	11,843	21.21
Portuguese (0)	0	<0.01
Romanian (258)	315	0.56
Russian (66)	204	0.37
Scandinavian (0)	11	0.02
Scotch-Irish (95)	296	0.53
Scottish (67)	547	0.98
Serbian (79)	79	0.14
Slavic (0)	76	0.14
Slovak (159)	616	1.10
Slovene (26)	46	0.08
Soviet Union (0)	0	<0.01
Swedish (245)	897	1.61
Swiss (50)	79	0.14
Turkish (0)	0	<0.01
Ukrainian (98)	326	0.58
Welsh (0)	226	0.40
West Indian, ex. Hispanic (11)	23	0.04
Bahamian (0)	0	<0.01
Barbadian (0)	0	<0.01
Belizean (0)	0	<0.01
Bermudan (0)	0	<0.01
British West Indian (0)	12	0.02
Dutch West Indian (0)	0	<0.01
Haitian (11)	11	0.02
Jamaican (0)	0	<0.01
Trinidadian/Tobagonian (0)	0	<0.01
U.S. Virgin Islander (0)	0	<0.01
West Indian (0)	0	<0.01
Other West Indian (0)	0	<0.01
Yugoslavian (9)	9	0.02

Hispanic Origin	Population	%
Hispanic or Latino (of any race)	8,108	14.30
Central American, ex. Mexican	169	0.30
Costa Rican	8	0.01
Guatemalan	86	0.15
Honduran	24	0.04
Nicaraguan	9	0.02
Panamanian	6	0.01
Salvadoran	36	0.06
Other Central American	0	<0.01
Cuban	58	0.10
Dominican Republic	13	0.02
Mexican	6,856	12.09
Puerto Rican	580	1.02
South American	213	0.38
Argentinean	16	0.03
Bolivian	23	0.04
Chilean	10	0.02
Colombian	73	0.13
Ecuadorian	55	0.10
Paraguayan	0	<0.01
Peruvian	21	0.04
Uruguayan	3	0.01
Venezuelan	10	0.02
Other South American	2	<0.01
Other Hispanic or Latino	219	0.39

Race*	Population	%
African-American/Black (2,946)	3,152	5.56
Not Hispanic (2,893)	3,055	5.39
Hispanic (53)	97	0.17
American Indian/Alaska Native (139)	308	0.54
Not Hispanic (54)	168	0.30
Hispanic (85)	140	0.25
Alaska Athabascan (Ala. Nat.) (0)	0	<0.01
Aleut (Alaska Native) (0)	0	<0.01
Apache (4)	13	0.02
Arapaho (0)	0	<0.01
Blackfeet (0)	4	0.01
Canadian/French Am. Ind. (0)	0	<0.01
Central American Ind. (0)	0	<0.01
Cherokee (7)	51	0.09
Cheyenne (0)	0	<0.01
Chickasaw (1)	1	<0.01
Chippewa (0)	0	<0.01

Race* (cont.)	Population	%
Choctaw (0)	2	<0.01
Colville (0)	0	<0.01
Comanche (0)	0	<0.01
Cree (0)	0	<0.01
Creek (0)	0	<0.01
Crow (0)	0	<0.01
Delaware (0)	0	<0.01
Hopi (0)	0	<0.01
Houma (0)	0	<0.01
Inupiat (Alaska Native) (2)	2	<0.01
Iroquois (1)	9	0.02
Kiowa (0)	0	<0.01
Lumbee (0)	0	<0.01
Menominee (0)	0	<0.01
Mexican American Ind. (27)	36	0.06
Navajo (2)	6	0.01
Osage (0)	0	<0.01
Ottawa (0)	0	<0.01
Paiute (0)	0	<0.01
Pima (0)	1	<0.01
Potawatomi (0)	0	<0.01
Pueblo (0)	0	<0.01
Puget Sound Salish (0)	0	<0.01
Seminole (0)	0	<0.01
Shoshone (1)	2	<0.01
Sioux (0)	8	0.01
South American Ind. (1)	3	0.01
Spanish American Ind. (0)	0	<0.01
Tlingit-Haida (Alaska Native) (0)	0	<0.01
Tohono O'Odham (0)	0	<0.01
Tsimshian (Alaska Native) (0)	0	<0.01
Ute (0)	0	<0.01
Yakama (0)	0	<0.01
Yaqui (0)	0	<0.01
Yuman (0)	0	<0.01
Yup'ik (Alaska Native) (0)	0	<0.01
Asian (1,234)	1,624	2.86
Not Hispanic (1,207)	1,558	2.75
Hispanic (27)	66	0.12
Bangladeshi (4)	4	<0.01
Bhutanese (0)	0	<0.01
Burmese (7)	11	0.02
Cambodian (0)	0	<0.01
Chinese, ex. Taiwanese (73)	96	0.17
Filipino (553)	646	1.14
Hmong (0)	0	<0.01
Indian (228)	265	0.47
Indonesian (2)	5	0.01
Japanese (23)	56	0.10
Korean (44)	67	0.12
Laotian (4)	6	0.01
Malaysian (0)	0	<0.01
Nepalese (0)	0	<0.01
Pakistani (80)	85	0.15
Sri Lankan (0)	0	<0.01
Taiwanese (0)	0	<0.01
Thai (39)	41	0.07
Vietnamese (107)	119	0.21
Hawaii Native/Pacific Islander (19)	55	0.10
Not Hispanic (14)	45	0.08
Hispanic (5)	10	0.02
Fijian (0)	0	<0.01
Guamanian/Chamorro (5)	6	0.01
Marshallese (0)	0	<0.01
Native Hawaiian (4)	10	0.02
Samoan (1)	4	0.01
Tongan (0)	0	<0.01
White (48,279)	49,247	86.87
Not Hispanic (43,680)	44,283	78.11
Hispanic (4,599)	4,964	8.76

*Notes: † The Census 2010 population figure is used to calculate the percentages in the Hispanic Origin and Race categories. Ancestry percentages are based on the 2006-2010 American Community Survey population (not shown); ‡ Numbers in parentheses indicate the number of people reporting a single ancestry; * Numbers in parentheses indicate the number of persons reporting this race alone, not in combination with any other race; Please refer to the Explanation of Data for more information.*

Oak Park

Place Type: Village
County: Cook
Population: 51,878

Ancestry	Population	%
Afghan (0)	9	0.02
African, Sub-Saharan (291)	448	0.87
African (224)	376	0.73
Cape Verdean (0)	0	<0.01
Ethiopian (0)	5	0.01
Ghanaian (17)	17	0.03
Kenyan (0)	0	<0.01
Liberian (0)	0	<0.01
Nigerian (50)	50	0.10
Senegalese (0)	0	<0.01
Sierra Leonean (0)	0	<0.01
Somalian (0)	0	<0.01
South African (0)	0	<0.01
Sudanese (0)	0	<0.01
Ugandan (0)	0	<0.01
Zimbabwean (0)	0	<0.01
Other Sub-Saharan African (0)	0	<0.01
Albanian (0)	17	0.03
Alsatian (0)	40	0.08
American (1,122)	1,122	2.18
Arab (150)	265	0.52
Arab (58)	83	0.16
Egyptian (24)	41	0.08
Iraqi (0)	10	0.02
Jordanian (0)	0	<0.01
Lebanese (13)	43	0.08
Moroccan (0)	0	<0.01
Palestinian (0)	0	<0.01
Syrian (0)	10	0.02
Other Arab (55)	78	0.15
Armenian (22)	45	0.09
Assyrian/Chaldean/Syriac (7)	16	0.03
Australian (5)	5	0.01
Austrian (41)	203	0.39
Basque (0)	0	<0.01
Belgian (32)	48	0.09
Brazilian (0)	15	0.03
British (193)	385	0.75
Bulgarian (18)	50	0.10
Cajun (0)	0	<0.01
Canadian (93)	153	0.30
Carpatho Rusyn (0)	0	<0.01
Celtic (0)	0	<0.01
Croatian (32)	111	0.22
Cypriot (0)	12	0.02
Czech (210)	895	1.74
Czechoslovakian (0)	21	0.04
Danish (23)	224	0.44
Dutch (234)	842	1.64
Eastern European (310)	328	0.64
English (982)	5,023	9.77
Estonian (0)	0	<0.01
European (680)	789	1.53
Finnish (39)	174	0.34
French, ex. Basque (217)	1,472	2.86
French Canadian (60)	365	0.71
German (2,325)	10,013	19.47
German Russian (0)	0	<0.01
Greek (242)	581	1.13
Guyanese (0)	11	0.02
Hungarian (34)	210	0.41
Icelander (0)	0	<0.01
Iranian (19)	74	0.14
Irish (2,638)	9,760	18.98
Israeli (12)	12	0.02
Italian (1,359)	4,437	8.63
Latvian (133)	190	0.37
Lithuanian (112)	375	0.73
Luxemburger (0)	5	0.01
Macedonian (0)	0	<0.01
Maltese (12)	12	0.02
New Zealander (0)	0	<0.01
Northern European (118)	134	0.26

	Population	%
Norwegian (138)	779	1.51
Pennsylvania German (0)	0	<0.01
Polish (1,299)	3,986	7.75
Portuguese (0)	39	0.08
Romanian (98)	248	0.48
Russian (451)	1,231	2.39
Scandinavian (7)	83	0.16
Scotch-Irish (301)	882	1.72
Scottish (226)	1,042	2.03
Serbian (141)	236	0.46
Slavic (14)	34	0.07
Slovak (66)	268	0.52
Slovene (62)	208	0.40
Soviet Union (0)	0	<0.01
Swedish (213)	1,349	2.62
Swiss (17)	207	0.40
Turkish (21)	39	0.08
Ukrainian (73)	232	0.45
Welsh (18)	432	0.84
West Indian, ex. Hispanic (236)	304	0.59
Bahamian (7)	7	0.01
Barbadian (0)	0	<0.01
Belizean (0)	0	<0.01
Bermudan (0)	0	<0.01
British West Indian (0)	0	<0.01
Dutch West Indian (0)	0	<0.01
Haitian (42)	64	0.12
Jamaican (80)	113	0.22
Trinidadian/Tobagonian (0)	0	<0.01
U.S. Virgin Islander (0)	0	<0.01
West Indian (107)	120	0.23
Other West Indian (0)	0	<0.01
Yugoslavian (57)	65	0.13

Hispanic Origin	Population	%
Hispanic or Latino (of any race)	3,521	6.79
Central American, ex. Mexican	198	0.38
Costa Rican	6	0.01
Guatemalan	87	0.17
Honduran	23	0.04
Nicaraguan	22	0.04
Panamanian	34	0.07
Salvadoran	22	0.04
Other Central American	4	0.01
Cuban	134	0.26
Dominican Republic	47	0.09
Mexican	1,858	3.58
Puerto Rican	555	1.07
South American	477	0.92
Argentinean	77	0.15
Bolivian	20	0.04
Chilean	49	0.09
Colombian	116	0.22
Ecuadorian	58	0.11
Paraguayan	10	0.02
Peruvian	91	0.18
Uruguayan	15	0.03
Venezuelan	31	0.06
Other South American	10	0.02
Other Hispanic or Latino	252	0.49

Race*	Population	%
African-American/Black (11,233)	12,235	23.58
Not Hispanic (11,023)	11,872	22.88
Hispanic (210)	363	0.70
American Indian/Alaska Native (93)	416	0.80
Not Hispanic (65)	303	0.58
Hispanic (28)	113	0.22
Alaska Athabascan (Ala. Nat.) (0)	0	<0.01
Aleut (Alaska Native) (0)	0	<0.01
Apache (3)	4	0.01
Arapaho (0)	0	<0.01
Blackfeet (0)	10	0.02
Canadian/French Am. Ind. (0)	1	<0.01
Central American Ind. (1)	1	<0.01
Cherokee (3)	84	0.16
Cheyenne (0)	0	<0.01
Chickasaw (0)	0	<0.01
Chippewa (2)	12	0.02

	Population	%
Choctaw (1)	10	0.02
Colville (0)	0	<0.01
Comanche (1)	5	0.01
Cree (0)	1	<0.01
Creek (0)	2	<0.01
Crow (0)	1	<0.01
Delaware (0)	1	<0.01
Hopi (0)	0	<0.01
Houma (0)	0	<0.01
Inupiat (Alaska Native) (0)	0	<0.01
Iroquois (1)	4	0.01
Kiowa (0)	0	<0.01
Lumbee (1)	2	<0.01
Menominee (0)	3	0.01
Mexican American Ind. (7)	18	0.03
Navajo (2)	3	0.01
Osage (1)	2	<0.01
Ottawa (2)	3	0.01
Paiute (0)	0	<0.01
Pima (0)	0	<0.01
Potawatomi (0)	0	<0.01
Pueblo (0)	0	<0.01
Puget Sound Salish (0)	0	<0.01
Seminole (1)	1	<0.01
Shoshone (0)	0	<0.01
Sioux (1)	5	0.01
South American Ind. (4)	19	0.04
Spanish American Ind. (0)	1	<0.01
Tlingit-Haida (Alaska Native) (1)	1	<0.01
Tohono O'Odham (0)	0	<0.01
Tsimshian (Alaska Native) (0)	0	<0.01
Ute (0)	0	<0.01
Yakama (0)	0	<0.01
Yaqui (0)	0	<0.01
Yuman (0)	0	<0.01
Yup'ik (Alaska Native) (0)	0	<0.01
Asian (2,511)	3,219	6.20
Not Hispanic (2,474)	3,142	6.06
Hispanic (37)	77	0.15
Bangladeshi (7)	8	0.02
Bhutanese (0)	0	<0.01
Burmese (6)	6	0.01
Cambodian (5)	9	0.02
Chinese, ex. Taiwanese (614)	793	1.53
Filipino (430)	601	1.16
Hmong (0)	0	<0.01
Indian (669)	845	1.63
Indonesian (9)	12	0.02
Japanese (186)	314	0.61
Korean (205)	275	0.53
Laotian (12)	19	0.04
Malaysian (9)	11	0.02
Nepalese (13)	14	0.03
Pakistani (38)	55	0.11
Sri Lankan (18)	21	0.04
Taiwanese (31)	45	0.09
Thai (66)	93	0.18
Vietnamese (75)	102	0.20
Hawaii Native/Pacific Islander (16)	52	0.10
Not Hispanic (15)	44	0.08
Hispanic (1)	8	0.02
Fijian (0)	0	<0.01
Guamanian/Chamorro (3)	5	0.01
Marshallese (0)	0	<0.01
Native Hawaiian (7)	22	0.04
Samoan (3)	5	0.01
Tongan (0)	0	<0.01
White (35,121)	36,676	70.70
Not Hispanic (33,076)	34,374	66.26
Hispanic (2,045)	2,302	4.44

Notes: † The Census 2010 population figure is used to calculate the percentages in the Hispanic Origin and Race categories. Ancestry percentages are based on the 2006-2010 American Community Survey population (not shown); ‡ Numbers in parentheses indicate the number of people reporting a single ancestry; * Numbers in parentheses indicate the number of persons reporting this race alone, not in combination with any other race; Please refer to the Explanation of Data for more information.

Orland Park

Place Type: Village
County: Cook
Population: 56,767

Ancestry	Population	%
Afghan (0)	0	<0.01
African, Sub-Saharan (45)	56	0.10
African (45)	56	0.10
Cape Verdean (0)	0	<0.01
Ethiopian (0)	0	<0.01
Ghanaian (0)	0	<0.01
Kenyan (0)	0	<0.01
Liberian (0)	0	<0.01
Nigerian (0)	0	<0.01
Senegalese (0)	0	<0.01
Sierra Leonean (0)	0	<0.01
Somalian (0)	0	<0.01
South African (0)	0	<0.01
Sudanese (0)	0	<0.01
Ugandan (0)	0	<0.01
Zimbabwean (0)	0	<0.01
Other Sub-Saharan African (0)	0	<0.01
Albanian (170)	170	0.31
Alsatian (0)	0	<0.01
American (1,155)	1,155	2.10
Arab (2,258)	2,393	4.34
Arab (1,023)	1,104	2.00
Egyptian (22)	22	0.04
Iraqi (18)	18	0.03
Jordanian (316)	316	0.57
Lebanese (66)	86	0.16
Moroccan (0)	0	<0.01
Palestinian (563)	563	1.02
Syrian (38)	55	0.10
Other Arab (212)	229	0.42
Armenian (12)	12	0.02
Assyrian/Chaldean/Syriac (0)	0	<0.01
Australian (0)	15	0.03
Austrian (126)	387	0.70
Basque (0)	0	<0.01
Belgian (11)	88	0.16
Brazilian (25)	25	0.05
British (15)	30	0.05
Bulgarian (13)	13	0.02
Cajun (0)	0	<0.01
Canadian (46)	78	0.14
Carpatho Rusyn (0)	0	<0.01
Celtic (0)	0	<0.01
Croatian (239)	840	1.52
Cypriot (0)	0	<0.01
Czech (231)	1,159	2.10
Czechoslovakian (79)	149	0.27
Danish (66)	373	0.68
Dutch (815)	1,504	2.73
Eastern European (24)	24	0.04
English (487)	2,409	4.37
Estonian (0)	0	<0.01
European (195)	265	0.48
Finnish (31)	69	0.13
French, ex. Basque (16)	768	1.39
French Canadian (50)	163	0.30
German (2,043)	10,706	19.43
German Russian (0)	0	<0.01
Greek (1,345)	1,744	3.17
Guyanese (0)	0	<0.01
Hungarian (109)	364	0.66
Icelander (10)	10	0.02
Iranian (28)	28	0.05
Irish (4,845)	14,774	26.81
Israeli (0)	0	<0.01
Italian (2,867)	7,670	13.92
Latvian (23)	23	0.04
Lithuanian (866)	1,425	2.59
Luxemburger (0)	23	0.04
Macedonian (75)	75	0.14
Maltese (0)	0	<0.01
New Zealander (0)	0	<0.01
Northern European (19)	19	0.03

Ancestry	Population	%
Norwegian (161)	570	1.03
Pennsylvania German (0)	0	<0.01
Polish (4,567)	10,058	18.25
Portuguese (0)	0	<0.01
Romanian (12)	54	0.10
Russian (276)	607	1.10
Scandinavian (0)	65	0.12
Scotch-Irish (113)	392	0.71
Scottish (135)	542	0.98
Serbian (156)	457	0.83
Slavic (15)	35	0.06
Slovak (35)	198	0.36
Slovene (12)	98	0.18
Soviet Union (0)	0	<0.01
Swedish (215)	1,277	2.32
Swiss (10)	118	0.21
Turkish (37)	37	0.07
Ukrainian (105)	294	0.53
Welsh (0)	112	0.20
West Indian, ex. Hispanic (18)	37	0.07
Bahamian (0)	0	<0.01
Barbadian (0)	0	<0.01
Belizean (18)	37	0.07
Bermudan (0)	0	<0.01
British West Indian (0)	0	<0.01
Dutch West Indian (0)	0	<0.01
Haitian (0)	0	<0.01
Jamaican (0)	0	<0.01
Trinidadian/Tobagonian (0)	0	<0.01
U.S. Virgin Islander (0)	0	<0.01
West Indian (0)	0	<0.01
Other West Indian (0)	0	<0.01
Yugoslavian (13)	33	0.06

Hispanic Origin	Population	%
Hispanic or Latino (of any race)	3,528	6.21
Central American, ex. Mexican	83	0.15
Costa Rican	0	<0.01
Guatemalan	56	0.10
Honduran	18	0.03
Nicaraguan	2	<0.01
Panamanian	0	<0.01
Salvadoran	6	0.01
Other Central American	1	<0.01
Cuban	51	0.09
Dominican Republic	3	0.01
Mexican	2,883	5.08
Puerto Rican	181	0.32
South American	140	0.25
Argentinean	10	0.02
Bolivian	15	0.03
Chilean	11	0.02
Colombian	49	0.09
Ecuadorian	24	0.04
Paraguayan	3	0.01
Peruvian	14	0.02
Uruguayan	2	<0.01
Venezuelan	9	0.02
Other South American	3	0.01
Other Hispanic or Latino	187	0.33

Race*	Population	%
African-American/Black (945)	1,050	1.85
Not Hispanic (936)	1,034	1.82
Hispanic (9)	16	0.03
American Indian/Alaska Native (51)	163	0.29
Not Hispanic (20)	110	0.19
Hispanic (31)	53	0.09
Alaska Athabascan (Ala. Nat.) (0)	0	<0.01
Aleut (Alaska Native) (0)	0	<0.01
Apache (0)	1	<0.01
Arapaho (0)	1	<0.01
Blackfeet (0)	0	<0.01
Canadian/French Am. Ind. (0)	0	<0.01
Central American Ind. (2)	2	<0.01
Cherokee (2)	33	0.06
Cheyenne (0)	0	<0.01
Chickasaw (0)	0	<0.01
Chippewa (1)	6	0.01

Race*	Population	%
Choctaw (0)	4	0.01
Colville (0)	0	<0.01
Comanche (0)	0	<0.01
Cree (0)	0	<0.01
Creek (1)	1	<0.01
Crow (0)	0	<0.01
Delaware (0)	0	<0.01
Hopi (0)	0	<0.01
Houma (0)	0	<0.01
Inupiat (Alaska Native) (0)	0	<0.01
Iroquois (4)	4	0.01
Kiowa (0)	0	<0.01
Lumbee (0)	0	<0.01
Menominee (0)	2	<0.01
Mexican American Ind. (5)	9	0.02
Navajo (0)	2	<0.01
Osage (0)	3	0.01
Ottawa (3)	6	0.01
Paiute (0)	0	<0.01
Pima (0)	0	<0.01
Potawatomi (0)	4	0.01
Pueblo (0)	0	<0.01
Puget Sound Salish (0)	0	<0.01
Seminole (0)	0	<0.01
Shoshone (0)	0	<0.01
Sioux (0)	2	<0.01
South American Ind. (0)	0	<0.01
Spanish American Ind. (0)	0	<0.01
Tlingit-Haida (Alaska Native) (0)	0	<0.01
Tohono O'Odham (0)	0	<0.01
Tsimshian (Alaska Native) (0)	0	<0.01
Ute (0)	0	<0.01
Yakama (0)	0	<0.01
Yaqui (0)	0	<0.01
Yuman (0)	0	<0.01
Yup'ik (Alaska Native) (0)	0	<0.01
Asian (2,788)	3,238	5.70
Not Hispanic (2,777)	3,199	5.64
Hispanic (11)	39	0.07
Bangladeshi (3)	7	0.01
Bhutanese (0)	0	<0.01
Burmese (1)	1	<0.01
Cambodian (1)	3	0.01
Chinese, ex. Taiwanese (238)	267	0.47
Filipino (843)	939	1.65
Hmong (0)	0	<0.01
Indian (906)	988	1.74
Indonesian (3)	7	0.01
Japanese (21)	39	0.07
Korean (339)	395	0.70
Laotian (2)	2	<0.01
Malaysian (3)	5	0.01
Nepalese (0)	0	<0.01
Pakistani (197)	219	0.39
Sri Lankan (0)	0	<0.01
Taiwanese (21)	24	0.04
Thai (39)	49	0.09
Vietnamese (87)	98	0.17
Hawaii Native/Pacific Islander (5)	38	0.07
Not Hispanic (3)	35	0.06
Hispanic (2)	3	0.01
Fijian (0)	0	<0.01
Guamanian/Chamorro (3)	5	0.01
Marshallese (0)	0	<0.01
Native Hawaiian (2)	9	0.02
Samoan (0)	1	<0.01
Tongan (0)	0	<0.01
White (51,234)	51,944	91.50
Not Hispanic (48,851)	49,389	87.00
Hispanic (2,383)	2,555	4.50

Notes: † The Census 2010 population figure is used to calculate the percentages in the Hispanic Origin and Race categories. Ancestry percentages are based on the 2006-2010 American Community Survey population (not shown); ‡ Numbers in parentheses indicate the number of people reporting a single ancestry; * Numbers in parentheses indicate the number of persons reporting this race alone, not in combination with any other race; Please refer to the Explanation of Data for more information.

Palatine

Place Type: Village
County: Cook
Population: 68,557

Ancestry	Population	%
Afghan (0)	0	<0.01
African, Sub-Saharan (298)	322	0.48
African (100)	111	0.16
Cape Verdean (0)	0	<0.01
Ethiopian (0)	0	<0.01
Ghanaian (28)	28	0.04
Kenyan (19)	32	0.05
Liberian (0)	0	<0.01
Nigerian (151)	151	0.22
Senegalese (0)	0	<0.01
Sierra Leonean (0)	0	<0.01
Somalian (0)	0	<0.01
South African (0)	0	<0.01
Sudanese (0)	0	<0.01
Ugandan (0)	0	<0.01
Zimbabwean (0)	0	<0.01
Other Sub-Saharan African (0)	0	<0.01
Albanian (67)	67	0.10
Alsatian (9)	9	0.01
American (1,365)	1,365	2.02
Arab (124)	149	0.22
Arab (17)	31	0.05
Egyptian (20)	31	0.05
Iraqi (42)	42	0.06
Jordanian (0)	0	<0.01
Lebanese (31)	31	0.05
Moroccan (0)	0	<0.01
Palestinian (14)	14	0.02
Syrian (0)	0	<0.01
Other Arab (0)	0	<0.01
Armenian (66)	82	0.12
Assyrian/Chaldean/Syriac (22)	36	0.05
Australian (18)	38	0.06
Austrian (57)	362	0.54
Basque (0)	0	<0.01
Belgian (0)	135	0.20
Brazilian (37)	91	0.13
British (79)	242	0.36
Bulgarian (267)	267	0.40
Cajun (0)	0	<0.01
Canadian (81)	131	0.19
Carpatho Rusyn (0)	0	<0.01
Celtic (0)	0	<0.01
Croatian (33)	159	0.24
Cypriot (0)	0	<0.01
Czech (111)	650	0.96
Czechoslovakian (13)	59	0.09
Danish (65)	722	1.07
Dutch (231)	966	1.43
Eastern European (194)	194	0.29
English (807)	3,707	5.50
Estonian (0)	0	<0.01
European (278)	314	0.47
Finnish (14)	144	0.21
French, ex. Basque (99)	1,409	2.09
French Canadian (14)	126	0.19
German (3,805)	14,535	21.56
German Russian (0)	0	<0.01
Greek (418)	709	1.05
Guyanese (0)	0	<0.01
Hungarian (106)	400	0.59
Icelander (0)	0	<0.01
Iranian (11)	59	0.09
Irish (2,523)	10,714	15.89
Israeli (45)	45	0.07
Italian (2,440)	7,027	10.42
Latvian (35)	65	0.10
Lithuanian (155)	378	0.56
Luxemburger (19)	73	0.11
Macedonian (24)	40	0.06
Maltese (0)	0	<0.01
New Zealander (0)	0	<0.01
Northern European (0)	0	<0.01

	Population	%
Norwegian (197)	1,230	1.82
Pennsylvania German (0)	0	<0.01
Polish (4,475)	9,622	14.27
Portuguese (13)	54	0.08
Romanian (139)	170	0.25
Russian (731)	1,452	2.15
Scandinavian (32)	154	0.23
Scotch-Irish (197)	723	1.07
Scottish (143)	906	1.34
Serbian (86)	109	0.16
Slavic (39)	51	0.08
Slovak (98)	341	0.51
Slovene (15)	115	0.17
Soviet Union (0)	0	<0.01
Swedish (536)	2,447	3.63
Swiss (63)	212	0.31
Turkish (29)	29	0.04
Ukrainian (435)	620	0.92
Welsh (57)	300	0.45
West Indian, ex. Hispanic (118)	126	0.19
Bahamian (0)	0	<0.01
Barbadian (0)	0	<0.01
Belizean (0)	0	<0.01
Bermudan (0)	0	<0.01
British West Indian (0)	8	0.01
Dutch West Indian (0)	0	<0.01
Haitian (45)	45	0.07
Jamaican (62)	62	0.09
Trinidadian/Tobagonian (0)	0	<0.01
U.S. Virgin Islander (0)	0	<0.01
West Indian (11)	11	0.02
Other West Indian (0)	0	<0.01
Yugoslavian (26)	33	0.05

Hispanic Origin	Population	%
Hispanic or Latino (of any race)	12,347	18.01
Central American, ex. Mexican	484	0.71
Costa Rican	22	0.03
Guatemalan	165	0.24
Honduran	101	0.15
Nicaraguan	18	0.03
Panamanian	16	0.02
Salvadoran	153	0.22
Other Central American	9	0.01
Cuban	109	0.16
Dominican Republic	14	0.02
Mexican	10,256	14.96
Puerto Rican	484	0.71
South American	532	0.78
Argentinean	37	0.05
Bolivian	7	0.01
Chilean	23	0.03
Colombian	162	0.24
Ecuadorian	74	0.11
Paraguayan	10	0.01
Peruvian	189	0.28
Uruguayan	1	<0.01
Venezuelan	24	0.04
Other South American	5	0.01
Other Hispanic or Latino	468	0.68

Race*	Population	%
African-American/Black (1,869)	2,208	3.22
Not Hispanic (1,798)	2,055	3.00
Hispanic (71)	153	0.22
American Indian/Alaska Native (190)	455	0.66
Not Hispanic (61)	216	0.32
Hispanic (129)	239	0.35
Alaska Athabascan (Ala. Nat.) (0)	0	<0.01
Aleut (Alaska Native) (0)	0	<0.01
Apache (3)	5	0.01
Arapaho (0)	0	<0.01
Blackfeet (2)	9	0.01
Canadian/French Am. Ind. (0)	0	<0.01
Central American Ind. (0)	0	<0.01
Cherokee (8)	59	0.09
Cheyenne (0)	0	<0.01
Chickasaw (1)	1	<0.01
Chippewa (11)	21	0.03

	Population	%
Choctaw (3)	8	0.01
Colville (0)	0	<0.01
Comanche (0)	0	<0.01
Cree (0)	0	<0.01
Creek (1)	7	0.01
Crow (0)	1	<0.01
Delaware (0)	0	<0.01
Hopi (0)	1	<0.01
Houma (0)	0	<0.01
Inupiat (Alaska Native) (1)	1	<0.01
Iroquois (2)	6	0.01
Kiowa (4)	4	0.01
Lumbee (0)	0	<0.01
Menominee (0)	1	<0.01
Mexican American Ind. (27)	47	0.07
Navajo (1)	1	<0.01
Osage (0)	0	<0.01
Ottawa (4)	6	0.01
Paiute (0)	0	<0.01
Pima (0)	0	<0.01
Potawatomi (6)	7	0.01
Pueblo (0)	0	<0.01
Puget Sound Salish (1)	1	<0.01
Seminole (0)	1	<0.01
Shoshone (0)	0	<0.01
Sioux (1)	9	0.01
South American Ind. (8)	22	0.03
Spanish American Ind. (0)	6	0.01
Tlingit-Haida (Alaska Native) (0)	0	<0.01
Tohono O'Odham (0)	0	<0.01
Tsimshian (Alaska Native) (0)	0	<0.01
Ute (0)	0	<0.01
Yakama (0)	0	<0.01
Yaqui (0)	0	<0.01
Yuman (0)	0	<0.01
Yup'ik (Alaska Native) (0)	0	<0.01
Asian (7,077)	7,704	11.24
Not Hispanic (7,043)	7,623	11.12
Hispanic (34)	81	0.12
Bangladeshi (16)	16	0.02
Bhutanese (0)	0	<0.01
Burmese (9)	11	0.02
Cambodian (12)	19	0.03
Chinese, ex. Taiwanese (1,112)	1,249	1.82
Filipino (702)	874	1.27
Hmong (1)	3	<0.01
Indian (2,695)	2,836	4.14
Indonesian (17)	18	0.03
Japanese (567)	683	1.00
Korean (1,094)	1,175	1.71
Laotian (11)	14	0.02
Malaysian (8)	15	0.02
Nepalese (6)	6	0.01
Pakistani (379)	422	0.62
Sri Lankan (11)	12	0.02
Taiwanese (77)	88	0.13
Thai (27)	37	0.05
Vietnamese (142)	167	0.24
Hawaii Native/Pacific Islander (23)	68	0.10
Not Hispanic (19)	57	0.08
Hispanic (4)	11	0.02
Fijian (0)	0	<0.01
Guamanian/Chamorro (5)	11	0.02
Marshallese (0)	0	<0.01
Native Hawaiian (2)	14	0.02
Samoan (1)	13	0.02
Tongan (1)	3	<0.01
White (52,736)	54,068	78.87
Not Hispanic (46,246)	47,024	68.59
Hispanic (6,490)	7,044	10.27

Peoria

Place Type: City
County: Peoria
Population: 115,007

Ancestry	Population	%
Afghan (71)	71	0.06
African, Sub-Saharan (413)	489	0.43
African (136)	212	0.19
Cape Verdean (0)	0	<0.01
Ethiopian (0)	0	<0.01
Ghanaian (236)	236	0.21
Kenyan (0)	0	<0.01
Liberian (0)	0	<0.01
Nigerian (18)	18	0.02
Senegalese (0)	0	<0.01
Sierra Leonean (0)	0	<0.01
Somalian (0)	0	<0.01
South African (13)	13	0.01
Sudanese (10)	10	0.01
Ugandan (0)	0	<0.01
Zimbabwean (0)	0	<0.01
Other Sub-Saharan African (0)	0	<0.01
Albanian (0)	15	0.01
Alsatian (0)	13	0.01
American (4,712)	4,712	4.14
Arab (692)	1,002	0.88
Arab (110)	110	0.10
Egyptian (0)	0	<0.01
Iraqi (0)	0	<0.01
Jordanian (18)	18	0.02
Lebanese (564)	874	0.77
Moroccan (0)	0	<0.01
Palestinian (0)	0	<0.01
Syrian (0)	0	<0.01
Other Arab (0)	0	<0.01
Armenian (0)	0	<0.01
Assyrian/Chaldean/Syriac (0)	0	<0.01
Australian (0)	0	<0.01
Austrian (17)	217	0.19
Basque (0)	0	<0.01
Belgian (152)	465	0.41
Brazilian (71)	144	0.13
British (140)	341	0.30
Bulgarian (0)	0	<0.01
Cajun (0)	0	<0.01
Canadian (27)	77	0.07
Carpatho Rusyn (0)	0	<0.01
Celtic (0)	12	0.01
Croatian (54)	162	0.14
Cypriot (0)	0	<0.01
Czech (135)	749	0.66
Czechoslovakian (10)	72	0.06
Danish (77)	386	0.34
Dutch (134)	1,746	1.53
Eastern European (77)	101	0.09
English (2,566)	10,009	8.79
Estonian (0)	0	<0.01
European (926)	1,028	0.90
Finnish (14)	64	0.06
French, ex. Basque (664)	3,579	3.14
French Canadian (301)	515	0.45
German (8,867)	26,263	23.07
German Russian (0)	0	<0.01
Greek (230)	352	0.31
Guyanese (11)	22	0.02
Hungarian (131)	436	0.38
Icelander (0)	0	<0.01
Iranian (56)	86	0.08
Irish (3,834)	15,136	13.29
Israeli (0)	0	<0.01
Italian (1,641)	4,211	3.70
Latvian (12)	12	0.01
Lithuanian (160)	319	0.28
Luxemburger (62)	62	0.05
Macedonian (18)	18	0.02
Maltese (0)	0	<0.01
New Zealander (0)	0	<0.01
Northern European (0)	13	0.01

Ancestry	Population	%
Norwegian (408)	1,408	1.24
Pennsylvania German (11)	28	0.02
Polish (649)	2,654	2.33
Portuguese (14)	103	0.09
Romanian (53)	95	0.08
Russian (122)	391	0.34
Scandinavian (105)	227	0.20
Scotch-Irish (585)	1,755	1.54
Scottish (558)	1,670	1.47
Serbian (72)	222	0.19
Slavic (31)	57	0.05
Slovak (64)	276	0.24
Slovene (65)	105	0.09
Soviet Union (0)	0	<0.01
Swedish (566)	2,798	2.46
Swiss (158)	729	0.64
Turkish (0)	0	<0.01
Ukrainian (51)	120	0.11
Welsh (127)	669	0.59
West Indian, ex. Hispanic (326)	346	0.30
Bahamian (0)	0	<0.01
Barbadian (0)	0	<0.01
Belizean (0)	0	<0.01
Bermudan (0)	0	<0.01
British West Indian (0)	0	<0.01
Dutch West Indian (0)	9	0.01
Haitian (313)	313	0.27
Jamaican (13)	24	0.02
Trinidadian/Tobagonian (0)	0	<0.01
U.S. Virgin Islander (0)	0	<0.01
West Indian (0)	0	<0.01
Other West Indian (0)	0	<0.01
Yugoslavian (22)	115	0.10

Hispanic Origin	Population	%
Hispanic or Latino (of any race)	5,628	4.89
Central American, ex. Mexican	185	0.16
Costa Rican	6	0.01
Guatemalan	79	0.07
Honduran	31	0.03
Nicaraguan	9	0.01
Panamanian	21	0.02
Salvadoran	37	0.03
Other Central American	2	<0.01
Cuban	122	0.11
Dominican Republic	24	0.02
Mexican	4,422	3.84
Puerto Rican	299	0.26
South American	197	0.17
Argentinean	18	0.02
Bolivian	16	0.01
Chilean	20	0.02
Colombian	76	0.07
Ecuadorian	16	0.01
Paraguayan	2	<0.01
Peruvian	16	0.01
Uruguayan	5	<0.01
Venezuelan	27	0.02
Other South American	1	<0.01
Other Hispanic or Latino	379	0.33

Race*	Population	%
African-American/Black (30,991)	33,877	29.46
Not Hispanic (30,705)	33,328	28.98
Hispanic (286)	549	0.48
American Indian/Alaska Native (360)	1,021	0.89
Not Hispanic (233)	815	0.71
Hispanic (127)	206	0.18
Alaska Athabascan (Ala. Nat.) (2)	3	<0.01
Aleut (Alaska Native) (0)	0	<0.01
Apache (4)	10	0.01
Arapaho (1)	2	<0.01
Blackfeet (3)	30	0.03
Canadian/French Am. Ind. (0)	0	<0.01
Central American Ind. (1)	3	<0.01
Cherokee (51)	215	0.19
Cheyenne (0)	0	<0.01
Chickasaw (0)	11	0.01
Chippewa (4)	24	0.02

	Population	%
Choctaw (8)	21	0.0
Colville (0)	0	<0.0
Comanche (0)	0	<0.0
Cree (1)	5	<0.0
Creek (2)	4	<0.0
Crow (0)	4	<0.0
Delaware (3)	4	<0.0
Hopi (0)	0	<0.0
Houma (2)	2	<0.0
Inupiat (Alaska Native) (1)	1	<0.0
Iroquois (2)	5	<0.0
Kiowa (0)	0	<0.0
Lumbee (2)	6	0.0
Menominee (1)	3	<0.0
Mexican American Ind. (13)	17	0.0
Navajo (3)	16	0.0
Osage (1)	2	<0.0
Ottawa (4)	7	0.0
Paiute (0)	0	<0.0
Pima (2)	2	<0.0
Potawatomi (1)	1	<0.0
Pueblo (0)	0	<0.0
Puget Sound Salish (4)	4	<0.0
Seminole (0)	4	<0.0
Shoshone (0)	1	<0.0
Sioux (11)	26	0.0
South American Ind. (0)	0	<0.0
Spanish American Ind. (0)	1	<0.0
Tlingit-Haida (Alaska Native) (0)	0	<0.0
Tohono O'Odham (0)	0	<0.0
Tsimshian (Alaska Native) (0)	0	<0.0
Ute (0)	0	<0.0
Yakama (0)	0	<0.0
Yaqui (2)	2	<0.0
Yuman (0)	0	<0.0
Yup'ik (Alaska Native) (1)	1	<0.0
Asian (5,240)	5,927	5.1
Not Hispanic (5,214)	5,864	5.1
Hispanic (26)	63	0.0
Bangladeshi (50)	51	0.0
Bhutanese (0)	0	<0.0
Burmese (20)	21	0.0
Cambodian (1)	1	<0.0
Chinese, ex. Taiwanese (959)	1,081	0.9
Filipino (371)	521	0.4
Hmong (1)	1	<0.0
Indian (2,528)	2,673	2.3
Indonesian (28)	31	0.0
Japanese (106)	201	0.1
Korean (288)	361	0.3
Laotian (57)	76	0.0
Malaysian (14)	17	0.0
Nepalese (19)	19	0.0
Pakistani (226)	246	0.2
Sri Lankan (26)	27	0.0
Taiwanese (35)	43	0.0
Thai (28)	54	0.0
Vietnamese (366)	439	0.3
Hawaii Native/Pacific Islander (29)	125	0.1
Not Hispanic (27)	112	0.1
Hispanic (2)	13	0.0
Fijian (0)	0	<0.0
Guamanian/Chamorro (4)	24	0.0
Marshallese (0)	0	<0.0
Native Hawaiian (15)	46	0.0
Samoan (3)	9	0.0
Tongan (0)	0	<0.0
White (71,740)	75,399	65.5
Not Hispanic (69,454)	72,633	63.1
Hispanic (2,286)	2,766	2.4

Notes: † The Census 2010 population figure is used to calculate the percentages in the Hispanic Origin and Race categories. Ancestry percentages are based on the 2006-2010 American Communit
*Survey population (not shown); ‡ Numbers in parentheses indicate the number of people reporting a single ancestry; * Numbers in parentheses indicate the number of persons reporting this race alon*
not in combination with any other race; Please refer to the Explanation of Data for more information.

Rockford

Place Type: City
County: Winnebago
Population: 152,871

Ancestry	Population	%
Afghan (0)	0	<0.01
African, Sub-Saharan (388)	474	0.31
African (331)	372	0.24
Cape Verdean (0)	0	<0.01
Ethiopian (9)	45	0.03
Ghanaian (10)	10	0.01
Kenyan (0)	0	<0.01
Liberian (0)	0	<0.01
Nigerian (0)	9	0.01
Senegalese (0)	0	<0.01
Sierra Leonean (13)	13	0.01
Somalian (0)	0	<0.01
South African (14)	14	0.01
Sudanese (11)	11	0.01
Ugandan (0)	0	<0.01
Zimbabwean (0)	0	<0.01
Other Sub-Saharan African (0)	0	<0.01
Albanian (0)	40	0.03
Alsatian (0)	0	<0.01
American (12,203)	12,203	7.90
Arab (554)	697	0.45
Arab (397)	397	0.26
Egyptian (0)	0	<0.01
Iraqi (125)	125	0.08
Jordanian (9)	27	0.02
Lebanese (10)	71	0.05
Moroccan (0)	0	<0.01
Palestinian (13)	17	0.01
Syrian (0)	60	0.04
Other Arab (0)	0	<0.01
Armenian (0)	0	<0.01
Assyrian/Chaldean/Syriac (0)	0	<0.01
Australian (0)	0	<0.01
Austrian (100)	235	0.15
Basque (1)	1	<0.01
Belgian (79)	269	0.17
Brazilian (0)	9	0.01
British (180)	369	0.24
Bulgarian (0)	0	<0.01
Cajun (0)	0	<0.01
Canadian (42)	95	0.06
Carpatho Rusyn (0)	0	<0.01
Celtic (0)	0	<0.01
Croatian (70)	116	0.08
Cypriot (0)	0	<0.01
Czech (119)	629	0.41
Czechoslovakian (58)	133	0.09
Danish (327)	1,067	0.69
Dutch (395)	2,584	1.67
Eastern European (16)	16	0.01
English (2,200)	10,118	6.55
Estonian (7)	25	0.02
European (517)	588	0.38
Finnish (55)	336	0.22
French, ex. Basque (327)	3,268	2.11
French Canadian (200)	485	0.31
German (8,977)	29,971	19.40
German Russian (0)	68	0.04
Greek (91)	315	0.20
Guyanese (0)	0	<0.01
Hungarian (71)	412	0.27
Icelander (0)	0	<0.01
Iranian (16)	26	0.02
Irish (2,946)	16,387	10.61
Israeli (0)	0	<0.01
Italian (4,622)	10,137	6.56
Latvian (24)	58	0.04
Lithuanian (275)	827	0.54
Luxemburger (8)	18	0.01
Macedonian (116)	116	0.08
Maltese (0)	0	<0.01
New Zealander (0)	0	<0.01
Northern European (66)	85	0.06

Ancestry	Population	%
Norwegian (1,140)	4,532	2.93
Pennsylvania German (87)	113	0.07
Polish (1,775)	4,787	3.10
Portuguese (0)	51	0.03
Romanian (13)	78	0.05
Russian (183)	433	0.28
Scandinavian (324)	588	0.38
Scotch-Irish (422)	1,348	0.87
Scottish (340)	1,513	0.98
Serbian (66)	155	0.10
Slavic (16)	64	0.04
Slovak (76)	131	0.08
Slovene (0)	0	<0.01
Soviet Union (0)	0	<0.01
Swedish (4,608)	12,535	8.11
Swiss (141)	625	0.40
Turkish (49)	66	0.04
Ukrainian (157)	317	0.21
Welsh (98)	569	0.37
West Indian, ex. Hispanic (64)	157	0.10
Bahamian (21)	21	0.01
Barbadian (0)	0	<0.01
Belizean (0)	0	<0.01
Bermudan (0)	0	<0.01
British West Indian (0)	0	<0.01
Dutch West Indian (0)	0	<0.01
Haitian (0)	0	<0.01
Jamaican (10)	62	0.04
Trinidadian/Tobagonian (0)	0	<0.01
U.S. Virgin Islander (0)	0	<0.01
West Indian (33)	74	0.05
Other West Indian (0)	0	<0.01
Yugoslavian (277)	375	0.24

Hispanic Origin	Population	%
Hispanic or Latino (of any race)	24,085	15.76
Central American, ex. Mexican	510	0.33
Costa Rican	29	0.02
Guatemalan	240	0.16
Honduran	92	0.06
Nicaraguan	23	0.02
Panamanian	23	0.02
Salvadoran	100	0.07
Other Central American	3	<0.01
Cuban	418	0.27
Dominican Republic	42	0.03
Mexican	20,019	13.10
Puerto Rican	1,323	0.87
South American	494	0.32
Argentinean	38	0.02
Bolivian	26	0.02
Chilean	29	0.02
Colombian	211	0.14
Ecuadorian	53	0.03
Paraguayan	1	<0.01
Peruvian	81	0.05
Uruguayan	32	0.02
Venezuelan	21	0.01
Other South American	2	<0.01
Other Hispanic or Latino	1,279	0.84

Race*	Population	%
African-American/Black (31,359)	34,438	22.53
Not Hispanic (30,695)	33,293	21.78
Hispanic (664)	1,145	0.75
American Indian/Alaska Native (614)	1,703	1.11
Not Hispanic (308)	1,100	0.72
Hispanic (306)	603	0.39
Alaska Athabascan (Ala. Nat.) (1)	1	<0.01
Aleut (Alaska Native) (0)	1	<0.01
Apache (6)	22	0.01
Arapaho (1)	2	<0.01
Blackfeet (4)	58	0.04
Canadian/French Am. Ind. (0)	5	<0.01
Central American Ind. (1)	6	<0.01
Cherokee (52)	259	0.17
Cheyenne (1)	3	<0.01
Chickasaw (0)	0	<0.01
Chippewa (17)	42	0.03

	Population	%
Choctaw (2)	25	0.02
Colville (0)	0	<0.01
Comanche (3)	13	0.01
Cree (2)	3	<0.01
Creek (3)	11	0.01
Crow (7)	10	0.01
Delaware (0)	5	<0.01
Hopi (0)	0	<0.01
Houma (0)	0	<0.01
Inupiat (Alaska Native) (1)	4	<0.01
Iroquois (13)	23	0.02
Kiowa (0)	1	<0.01
Lumbee (1)	1	<0.01
Menominee (1)	1	<0.01
Mexican American Ind. (65)	88	0.06
Navajo (7)	21	0.01
Osage (0)	0	<0.01
Ottawa (2)	2	<0.01
Paiute (0)	4	<0.01
Pima (4)	4	<0.01
Potawatomi (2)	8	0.01
Pueblo (0)	0	<0.01
Puget Sound Salish (0)	4	<0.01
Seminole (0)	3	<0.01
Shoshone (0)	0	<0.01
Sioux (20)	46	0.03
South American Ind. (2)	12	0.01
Spanish American Ind. (4)	4	<0.01
Tlingit-Haida (Alaska Native) (0)	0	<0.01
Tohono O'Odham (0)	0	<0.01
Tsimshian (Alaska Native) (1)	1	<0.01
Ute (0)	0	<0.01
Yakama (0)	0	<0.01
Yaqui (1)	1	<0.01
Yuman (0)	0	<0.01
Yup'ik (Alaska Native) (0)	0	<0.01
Asian (4,443)	5,272	3.45
Not Hispanic (4,390)	5,115	3.35
Hispanic (53)	157	0.10
Bangladeshi (20)	22	0.01
Bhutanese (1)	1	<0.01
Burmese (389)	403	0.26
Cambodian (6)	18	0.01
Chinese, ex. Taiwanese (333)	453	0.30
Filipino (581)	768	0.50
Hmong (26)	30	0.02
Indian (825)	948	0.62
Indonesian (12)	14	0.01
Japanese (100)	208	0.14
Korean (240)	303	0.20
Laotian (903)	1,027	0.67
Malaysian (4)	9	0.01
Nepalese (0)	3	<0.01
Pakistani (133)	153	0.10
Sri Lankan (10)	10	0.01
Taiwanese (11)	13	0.01
Thai (85)	122	0.08
Vietnamese (490)	586	0.38
Hawaii Native/Pacific Islander (41)	163	0.11
Not Hispanic (36)	117	0.08
Hispanic (5)	46	0.03
Fijian (0)	0	<0.01
Guamanian/Chamorro (8)	17	0.01
Marshallese (0)	0	<0.01
Native Hawaiian (19)	56	0.04
Samoan (2)	16	0.01
Tongan (0)	0	<0.01
White (99,517)	104,370	68.27
Not Hispanic (89,349)	92,788	60.70
Hispanic (10,168)	11,582	7.58

Notes: † The Census 2010 population figure is used to calculate the percentages in the Hispanic Origin and Race categories. Ancestry percentages are based on the 2006-2010 American Community Survey population (not shown); ‡ Numbers in parentheses indicate the number of people reporting a single ancestry; * Numbers in parentheses indicate the number of persons reporting this race alone, not in combination with any other race; Please refer to the Explanation of Data for more information.

Schaumburg

Place Type: Village
County: Cook
Population: 74,227

Ancestry	Population	%
Afghan (0)	0	<0.01
African, Sub-Saharan (324)	334	0.46
African (39)	49	0.07
Cape Verdean (0)	0	<0.01
Ethiopian (0)	0	<0.01
Ghanaian (0)	0	<0.01
Kenyan (88)	88	0.12
Liberian (0)	0	<0.01
Nigerian (105)	105	0.14
Senegalese (39)	39	0.05
Sierra Leonean (53)	53	0.07
Somalian (0)	0	<0.01
South African (0)	0	<0.01
Sudanese (0)	0	<0.01
Ugandan (0)	0	<0.01
Zimbabwean (0)	0	<0.01
Other Sub-Saharan African (0)	0	<0.01
Albanian (27)	27	0.04
Alsatian (0)	0	<0.01
American (1,210)	1,210	1.65
Arab (528)	684	0.93
Arab (0)	80	0.11
Egyptian (14)	14	0.02
Iraqi (217)	217	0.30
Jordanian (10)	10	0.01
Lebanese (110)	177	0.24
Moroccan (48)	48	0.07
Palestinian (0)	0	<0.01
Syrian (83)	92	0.13
Other Arab (46)	46	0.06
Armenian (101)	130	0.18
Assyrian/Chaldean/Syriac (35)	59	0.08
Australian (28)	42	0.06
Austrian (25)	265	0.36
Basque (0)	0	<0.01
Belgian (34)	241	0.33
Brazilian (0)	11	0.02
British (162)	332	0.45
Bulgarian (207)	207	0.28
Cajun (0)	24	0.03
Canadian (52)	125	0.17
Carpatho Rusyn (0)	0	<0.01
Celtic (0)	0	<0.01
Croatian (87)	273	0.37
Cypriot (0)	0	<0.01
Czech (322)	1,159	1.58
Czechoslovakian (42)	86	0.12
Danish (38)	259	0.35
Dutch (132)	963	1.31
Eastern European (33)	46	0.06
English (603)	3,875	5.28
Estonian (0)	17	0.02
European (595)	639	0.87
Finnish (45)	144	0.20
French, ex. Basque (167)	1,472	2.01
French Canadian (69)	232	0.32
German (4,694)	16,982	23.16
German Russian (0)	0	<0.01
Greek (721)	1,317	1.80
Guyanese (41)	41	0.06
Hungarian (215)	631	0.86
Icelander (0)	0	<0.01
Iranian (170)	224	0.31
Irish (1,649)	10,048	13.70
Israeli (33)	41	0.06
Italian (3,155)	8,459	11.54
Latvian (8)	43	0.06
Lithuanian (65)	357	0.49
Luxemburger (15)	69	0.09
Macedonian (0)	0	<0.01
Maltese (0)	0	<0.01
New Zealander (0)	0	<0.01
Northern European (77)	90	0.12

Ancestry	Population	%
Norwegian (376)	1,676	2.29
Pennsylvania German (0)	0	<0.01
Polish (5,853)	11,923	16.26
Portuguese (15)	15	0.02
Romanian (182)	262	0.36
Russian (388)	1,071	1.46
Scandinavian (45)	113	0.15
Scotch-Irish (357)	889	1.21
Scottish (260)	810	1.10
Serbian (69)	151	0.21
Slavic (0)	18	0.02
Slovak (73)	161	0.22
Slovene (79)	154	0.21
Soviet Union (0)	0	<0.01
Swedish (342)	2,209	3.01
Swiss (18)	189	0.26
Turkish (25)	51	0.07
Ukrainian (211)	435	0.59
Welsh (23)	258	0.35
West Indian, ex. Hispanic (0)	10	0.01
Bahamian (0)	0	<0.01
Barbadian (0)	0	<0.01
Belizean (0)	0	<0.01
Bermudan (0)	0	<0.01
British West Indian (0)	0	<0.01
Dutch West Indian (0)	0	<0.01
Haitian (0)	0	<0.01
Jamaican (0)	10	0.01
Trinidadian/Tobagonian (0)	0	<0.01
U.S. Virgin Islander (0)	0	<0.01
West Indian (0)	0	<0.01
Other West Indian (0)	0	<0.01
Yugoslavian (133)	180	0.25

Hispanic Origin	Population	%
Hispanic or Latino (of any race)	6,554	8.83
Central American, ex. Mexican	356	0.48
Costa Rican	10	0.01
Guatemalan	150	0.20
Honduran	46	0.06
Nicaraguan	26	0.04
Panamanian	20	0.03
Salvadoran	92	0.12
Other Central American	12	0.02
Cuban	148	0.20
Dominican Republic	38	0.05
Mexican	4,375	5.89
Puerto Rican	715	0.96
South American	590	0.79
Argentinean	60	0.08
Bolivian	9	0.01
Chilean	31	0.04
Colombian	211	0.28
Ecuadorian	132	0.18
Paraguayan	2	<0.01
Peruvian	106	0.14
Uruguayan	3	<0.01
Venezuelan	24	0.03
Other South American	12	0.02
Other Hispanic or Latino	332	0.45

Race*	Population	%
African-American/Black (3,123)	3,563	4.80
Not Hispanic (2,987)	3,359	4.53
Hispanic (136)	204	0.27
American Indian/Alaska Native (162)	423	0.57
Not Hispanic (112)	306	0.41
Hispanic (50)	117	0.16
Alaska Athabascan (Ala. Nat.) (0)	0	<0.01
Aleut (Alaska Native) (0)	0	<0.01
Apache (2)	2	<0.01
Arapaho (0)	0	<0.01
Blackfeet (1)	10	0.01
Canadian/French Am. Ind. (0)	0	<0.01
Central American Ind. (2)	2	<0.01
Cherokee (8)	57	0.08
Cheyenne (0)	0	<0.01
Chickasaw (0)	1	<0.01
Chippewa (3)	9	0.01

Race*	Population	%
Choctaw (6)	13	0.02
Colville (0)	0	<0.01
Comanche (0)	0	<0.01
Cree (0)	0	<0.01
Creek (4)	10	0.01
Crow (0)	0	<0.01
Delaware (3)	3	<0.01
Hopi (0)	0	<0.01
Houma (0)	0	<0.01
Inupiat (Alaska Native) (0)	0	<0.01
Iroquois (2)	5	0.01
Kiowa (0)	0	<0.01
Lumbee (1)	1	<0.01
Menominee (0)	1	<0.01
Mexican American Ind. (11)	14	0.02
Navajo (0)	3	<0.01
Osage (0)	1	<0.01
Ottawa (1)	1	<0.01
Paiute (0)	3	<0.01
Pima (0)	0	<0.01
Potawatomi (1)	2	<0.01
Pueblo (0)	0	<0.01
Puget Sound Salish (0)	0	<0.01
Seminole (0)	0	<0.01
Shoshone (0)	0	<0.01
Sioux (3)	12	0.02
South American Ind. (3)	6	0.01
Spanish American Ind. (0)	0	<0.01
Tlingit-Haida (Alaska Native) (0)	0	<0.01
Tohono O'Odham (0)	0	<0.01
Tsimshian (Alaska Native) (0)	0	<0.01
Ute (1)	1	<0.01
Yakama (0)	0	<0.01
Yaqui (0)	0	<0.01
Yuman (0)	0	<0.01
Yup'ik (Alaska Native) (0)	0	<0.01
Asian (14,731)	15,744	21.21
Not Hispanic (14,675)	15,608	21.03
Hispanic (56)	136	0.18
Bangladeshi (34)	36	0.05
Bhutanese (0)	0	<0.01
Burmese (12)	13	0.02
Cambodian (32)	33	0.04
Chinese, ex. Taiwanese (1,168)	1,306	1.76
Filipino (1,339)	1,597	2.15
Hmong (3)	3	<0.01
Indian (7,988)	8,303	11.19
Indonesian (30)	36	0.05
Japanese (1,044)	1,216	1.64
Korean (1,892)	1,994	2.69
Laotian (12)	18	0.02
Malaysian (14)	21	0.03
Nepalese (16)	16	0.02
Pakistani (515)	550	0.74
Sri Lankan (18)	20	0.03
Taiwanese (97)	104	0.14
Thai (104)	131	0.18
Vietnamese (109)	125	0.17
Hawaii Native/Pacific Islander (23)	93	0.13
Not Hispanic (18)	74	0.10
Hispanic (5)	19	0.03
Fijian (1)	3	<0.01
Guamanian/Chamorro (5)	6	0.01
Marshallese (0)	0	<0.01
Native Hawaiian (6)	30	0.04
Samoan (6)	11	0.01
Tongan (0)	3	<0.01
White (52,281)	53,580	72.18
Not Hispanic (48,385)	49,375	66.52
Hispanic (3,896)	4,205	5.67

*Notes: † The Census 2010 population figure is used to calculate the percentages in the Hispanic Origin and Race categories. Ancestry percentages are based on the 2006-2010 American Community Survey population (not shown); ‡ Numbers in parentheses indicate the number of people reporting a single ancestry; * Numbers in parentheses indicate the number of persons reporting this race alone, not in combination with any other race; Please refer to the Explanation of Data for more information.*

Skokie

Place Type: Village
County: Cook
Population: 64,784

Ancestry	Population	%
Afghan (0)	0	<0.01
African, Sub-Saharan (371)	433	0.68
African (176)	208	0.33
Cape Verdean (0)	0	<0.01
Ethiopian (23)	23	0.04
Ghanaian (0)	0	<0.01
Kenyan (0)	0	<0.01
Liberian (35)	35	0.05
Nigerian (74)	74	0.12
Senegalese (0)	0	<0.01
Sierra Leonean (0)	0	<0.01
Somalian (0)	0	<0.01
South African (63)	79	0.12
Sudanese (0)	14	0.02
Ugandan (0)	0	<0.01
Zimbabwean (0)	0	<0.01
Other Sub-Saharan African (0)	0	<0.01
Albanian (135)	135	0.21
Alsatian (0)	0	<0.01
American (2,241)	2,241	3.51
Arab (1,282)	1,643	2.57
Arab (101)	128	0.20
Egyptian (0)	20	0.03
Iraqi (709)	898	1.41
Jordanian (16)	16	0.03
Lebanese (132)	221	0.35
Moroccan (0)	0	<0.01
Palestinian (63)	63	0.10
Syrian (131)	158	0.25
Other Arab (130)	139	0.22
Armenian (341)	372	0.58
Assyrian/Chaldean/Syriac (3,620)	3,833	6.01
Australian (0)	0	<0.01
Austrian (95)	212	0.33
Basque (0)	0	<0.01
Belgian (8)	64	0.10
Brazilian (13)	13	0.02
British (93)	139	0.22
Bulgarian (205)	205	0.32
Cajun (0)	0	<0.01
Canadian (35)	51	0.08
Carpatho Rusyn (0)	0	<0.01
Celtic (0)	0	<0.01
Croatian (227)	337	0.53
Cypriot (0)	0	<0.01
Czech (57)	312	0.49
Czechoslovakian (7)	19	0.03
Danish (24)	165	0.26
Dutch (98)	333	0.52
Eastern European (584)	592	0.93
English (441)	1,670	2.62
Estonian (0)	0	<0.01
European (504)	570	0.89
Finnish (11)	21	0.03
French, ex. Basque (125)	515	0.81
French Canadian (0)	58	0.09
German (1,867)	6,040	9.46
German Russian (0)	0	<0.01
Greek (1,378)	1,666	2.61
Guyanese (43)	43	0.07
Hungarian (304)	668	1.05
Icelander (0)	0	<0.01
Iranian (248)	294	0.46
Irish (1,084)	3,563	5.58
Israeli (321)	497	0.78
Italian (435)	1,594	2.50
Latvian (64)	140	0.22
Lithuanian (176)	550	0.86
Luxemburger (0)	33	0.05
Macedonian (188)	229	0.36
Maltese (0)	0	<0.01
New Zealander (0)	0	<0.01
Northern European (30)	30	0.05

Ancestry	Population	%
Norwegian (34)	255	0.40
Pennsylvania German (0)	0	<0.01
Polish (1,797)	4,292	6.72
Portuguese (0)	11	0.02
Romanian (1,248)	1,582	2.48
Russian (2,347)	4,794	7.51
Scandinavian (28)	73	0.11
Scotch-Irish (58)	288	0.45
Scottish (39)	325	0.51
Serbian (242)	325	0.51
Slavic (11)	11	0.02
Slovak (52)	61	0.10
Slovene (16)	38	0.06
Soviet Union (20)	20	0.03
Swedish (189)	746	1.17
Swiss (11)	149	0.23
Turkish (0)	0	<0.01
Ukrainian (943)	1,223	1.92
Welsh (14)	123	0.19
West Indian, ex. Hispanic (1,059)	1,073	1.68
Bahamian (0)	0	<0.01
Barbadian (0)	0	<0.01
Belizean (22)	36	0.06
Bermudan (0)	0	<0.01
British West Indian (0)	0	<0.01
Dutch West Indian (0)	0	<0.01
Haitian (891)	891	1.40
Jamaican (146)	146	0.23
Trinidadian/Tobagonian (0)	0	<0.01
U.S. Virgin Islander (0)	0	<0.01
West Indian (0)	0	<0.01
Other West Indian (0)	0	<0.01
Yugoslavian (223)	281	0.44

Hispanic Origin	Population	%
Hispanic or Latino (of any race)	5,728	8.84
Central American, ex. Mexican	497	0.77
Costa Rican	15	0.02
Guatemalan	284	0.44
Honduran	51	0.08
Nicaraguan	26	0.04
Panamanian	25	0.04
Salvadoran	87	0.13
Other Central American	9	0.01
Cuban	476	0.73
Dominican Republic	33	0.05
Mexican	2,854	4.41
Puerto Rican	754	1.16
South American	822	1.27
Argentinean	74	0.11
Bolivian	59	0.09
Chilean	29	0.04
Colombian	220	0.34
Ecuadorian	195	0.30
Paraguayan	2	<0.01
Peruvian	161	0.25
Uruguayan	12	0.02
Venezuelan	40	0.06
Other South American	30	0.05
Other Hispanic or Latino	292	0.45

Race*	Population	%
African-American/Black (4,701)	5,294	8.17
Not Hispanic (4,566)	5,028	7.76
Hispanic (135)	266	0.41
American Indian/Alaska Native (120)	349	0.54
Not Hispanic (70)	246	0.38
Hispanic (50)	103	0.16
Alaska Athabascan (Ala. Nat.) (1)	2	<0.01
Aleut (Alaska Native) (0)	0	<0.01
Apache (3)	4	0.01
Arapaho (0)	0	<0.01
Blackfeet (1)	6	0.01
Canadian/French Am. Ind. (0)	0	<0.01
Central American Ind. (3)	6	0.01
Cherokee (4)	54	0.08
Cheyenne (0)	1	<0.01
Chickasaw (0)	0	<0.01
Chippewa (5)	10	0.02

Race*	Population	%
Choctaw (1)	6	0.01
Colville (0)	0	<0.01
Comanche (0)	0	<0.01
Cree (0)	0	<0.01
Creek (0)	6	0.01
Crow (0)	5	0.01
Delaware (0)	0	<0.01
Hopi (0)	0	<0.01
Houma (0)	0	<0.01
Inupiat (Alaska Native) (0)	0	<0.01
Iroquois (1)	2	<0.01
Kiowa (0)	0	<0.01
Lumbee (0)	0	<0.01
Menominee (0)	0	<0.01
Mexican American Ind. (11)	17	0.03
Navajo (5)	8	0.01
Osage (0)	0	<0.01
Ottawa (0)	0	<0.01
Paiute (0)	0	<0.01
Pima (0)	0	<0.01
Potawatomi (1)	2	<0.01
Pueblo (0)	1	<0.01
Puget Sound Salish (0)	0	<0.01
Seminole (0)	1	<0.01
Shoshone (0)	0	<0.01
Sioux (6)	8	0.01
South American Ind. (0)	12	0.02
Spanish American Ind. (1)	1	<0.01
Tlingit-Haida (Alaska Native) (1)	1	<0.01
Tohono O'Odham (0)	0	<0.01
Tsimshian (Alaska Native) (0)	0	<0.01
Ute (0)	0	<0.01
Yakama (0)	0	<0.01
Yaqui (0)	0	<0.01
Yuman (0)	0	<0.01
Yup'ik (Alaska Native) (0)	0	<0.01
Asian (16,549)	17,996	27.78
Not Hispanic (16,437)	17,752	27.40
Hispanic (112)	244	0.38
Bangladeshi (91)	98	0.15
Bhutanese (0)	0	<0.01
Burmese (12)	14	0.02
Cambodian (136)	162	0.25
Chinese, ex. Taiwanese (1,503)	1,726	2.66
Filipino (4,505)	4,896	7.56
Hmong (8)	10	0.02
Indian (4,283)	4,624	7.14
Indonesian (36)	41	0.06
Japanese (304)	431	0.67
Korean (1,771)	1,880	2.90
Laotian (23)	37	0.06
Malaysian (22)	37	0.06
Nepalese (43)	48	0.07
Pakistani (1,990)	2,121	3.27
Sri Lankan (46)	52	0.08
Taiwanese (69)	78	0.12
Thai (208)	234	0.36
Vietnamese (717)	794	1.23
Hawaii Native/Pacific Islander (13)	139	0.21
Not Hispanic (13)	122	0.19
Hispanic (0)	17	0.03
Fijian (2)	3	<0.01
Guamanian/Chamorro (0)	4	0.01
Marshallese (4)	4	0.01
Native Hawaiian (2)	11	0.02
Samoan (0)	0	<0.01
Tongan (0)	0	<0.01
White (39,045)	40,807	62.99
Not Hispanic (35,955)	37,310	57.59
Hispanic (3,090)	3,497	5.40

Notes: † The Census 2010 population figure is used to calculate the percentages in the Hispanic Origin and Race categories. Ancestry percentages are based on the 2006-2010 American Community Survey population (not shown); ‡ Numbers in parentheses indicate the number of people reporting a single ancestry; * Numbers in parentheses indicate the number of persons reporting this race alone, not in combination with any other race; Please refer to the Explanation of Data for more information.

Springfield

Place Type: City
County: Sangamon
Population: 116,250

Ancestry	Population	%
Afghan (0)	0	<0.01
African, Sub-Saharan (591)	749	0.65
African (409)	537	0.47
Cape Verdean (0)	0	<0.01
Ethiopian (0)	0	<0.01
Ghanaian (58)	58	0.05
Kenyan (0)	0	<0.01
Liberian (0)	0	<0.01
Nigerian (124)	154	0.13
Senegalese (0)	0	<0.01
Sierra Leonean (0)	0	<0.01
Somalian (0)	0	<0.01
South African (0)	0	<0.01
Sudanese (0)	0	<0.01
Ugandan (0)	0	<0.01
Zimbabwean (0)	0	<0.01
Other Sub-Saharan African (0)	0	<0.01
Albanian (0)	0	<0.01
Alsatian (0)	0	<0.01
American (9,384)	9,384	8.15
Arab (389)	567	0.49
Arab (104)	108	0.09
Egyptian (15)	29	0.03
Iraqi (0)	0	<0.01
Jordanian (22)	22	0.02
Lebanese (42)	42	0.04
Moroccan (7)	7	0.01
Palestinian (0)	0	<0.01
Syrian (155)	235	0.20
Other Arab (44)	124	0.11
Armenian (0)	0	<0.01
Assyrian/Chaldean/Syriac (15)	15	0.01
Australian (0)	0	<0.01
Austrian (76)	239	0.21
Basque (0)	0	<0.01
Belgian (110)	289	0.25
Brazilian (0)	19	0.02
British (192)	384	0.33
Bulgarian (4)	19	0.02
Cajun (0)	0	<0.01
Canadian (29)	66	0.06
Carpatho Rusyn (0)	0	<0.01
Celtic (0)	0	<0.01
Croatian (39)	258	0.22
Cypriot (0)	0	<0.01
Czech (130)	445	0.39
Czechoslovakian (47)	183	0.16
Danish (34)	255	0.22
Dutch (188)	1,655	1.44
Eastern European (31)	37	0.03
English (4,232)	13,247	11.51
Estonian (10)	10	0.01
European (617)	691	0.60
Finnish (25)	25	0.02
French, ex. Basque (571)	3,255	2.83
French Canadian (23)	144	0.13
German (10,961)	30,854	26.80
German Russian (0)	11	0.01
Greek (157)	255	0.22
Guyanese (0)	0	<0.01
Hungarian (106)	393	0.34
Icelander (0)	0	<0.01
Iranian (19)	19	0.02
Irish (4,182)	16,364	14.21
Israeli (0)	0	<0.01
Italian (3,061)	7,362	6.40
Latvian (0)	44	0.04
Lithuanian (548)	973	0.85
Luxemburger (0)	19	0.02
Macedonian (0)	0	<0.01
Maltese (0)	0	<0.01
New Zealander (0)	0	<0.01
Northern European (45)	115	0.10

Ancestry	Population	%
Norwegian (349)	963	0.84
Pennsylvania German (47)	59	0.05
Polish (892)	2,578	2.24
Portuguese (125)	282	0.24
Romanian (13)	36	0.03
Russian (158)	464	0.40
Scandinavian (107)	152	0.13
Scotch-Irish (763)	2,407	2.09
Scottish (594)	2,251	1.96
Serbian (14)	14	0.01
Slavic (38)	129	0.11
Slovak (80)	430	0.37
Slovene (56)	96	0.08
Soviet Union (0)	0	<0.01
Swedish (332)	1,351	1.17
Swiss (71)	366	0.32
Turkish (19)	19	0.02
Ukrainian (75)	180	0.16
Welsh (141)	877	0.76
West Indian, ex. Hispanic (60)	154	0.13
Bahamian (0)	0	<0.01
Barbadian (0)	0	<0.01
Belizean (0)	0	<0.01
Bermudan (0)	0	<0.01
British West Indian (0)	0	<0.01
Dutch West Indian (0)	14	0.01
Haitian (0)	7	0.01
Jamaican (46)	115	0.10
Trinidadian/Tobagonian (0)	0	<0.01
U.S. Virgin Islander (0)	0	<0.01
West Indian (14)	18	0.02
Other West Indian (0)	0	<0.01
Yugoslavian (0)	70	0.06

Hispanic Origin	Population	%
Hispanic or Latino (of any race)	2,325	2.00
Central American, ex. Mexican	153	0.13
Costa Rican	14	0.01
Guatemalan	41	0.04
Honduran	28	0.02
Nicaraguan	25	0.02
Panamanian	28	0.02
Salvadoran	17	0.01
Other Central American	0	<0.01
Cuban	47	0.04
Dominican Republic	21	0.02
Mexican	1,287	1.11
Puerto Rican	374	0.32
South American	179	0.15
Argentinean	5	<0.01
Bolivian	20	0.02
Chilean	27	0.02
Colombian	37	0.03
Ecuadorian	30	0.03
Paraguayan	0	<0.01
Peruvian	45	0.04
Uruguayan	0	<0.01
Venezuelan	12	0.01
Other South American	3	<0.01
Other Hispanic or Latino	264	0.23

Race*	Population	%
African-American/Black (21,510)	23,683	20.37
Not Hispanic (21,344)	23,404	20.13
Hispanic (166)	279	0.24
American Indian/Alaska Native (239)	889	0.76
Not Hispanic (205)	797	0.69
Hispanic (34)	92	0.08
Alaska Athabascan (Ala. Nat.) (1)	1	<0.01
Aleut (Alaska Native) (0)	0	<0.01
Apache (3)	11	0.01
Arapaho (0)	0	<0.01
Blackfeet (6)	55	0.05
Canadian/French Am. Ind. (3)	4	<0.01
Central American Ind. (1)	1	<0.01
Cherokee (36)	248	0.21
Cheyenne (0)	2	<0.01
Chickasaw (2)	6	0.01
Chippewa (3)	11	0.01

Race*	Population	%
Choctaw (1)	27	0.02
Colville (0)	0	<0.01
Comanche (0)	1	<0.01
Cree (0)	1	<0.01
Creek (4)	7	0.01
Crow (1)	5	<0.01
Delaware (1)	1	<0.01
Hopi (0)	0	<0.01
Houma (0)	0	<0.01
Inupiat (Alaska Native) (0)	0	<0.01
Iroquois (7)	9	0.01
Kiowa (0)	0	<0.01
Lumbee (1)	7	0.01
Menominee (11)	12	0.01
Mexican American Ind. (7)	17	0.01
Navajo (3)	4	<0.01
Osage (0)	1	<0.01
Ottawa (1)	1	<0.01
Paiute (0)	0	<0.01
Pima (0)	1	<0.01
Potawatomi (4)	5	<0.01
Pueblo (2)	2	<0.01
Puget Sound Salish (0)	0	<0.01
Seminole (1)	5	<0.01
Shoshone (0)	0	<0.01
Sioux (12)	26	0.02
South American Ind. (2)	2	<0.01
Spanish American Ind. (0)	0	<0.01
Tlingit-Haida (Alaska Native) (0)	0	<0.01
Tohono O'Odham (0)	0	<0.01
Tsimshian (Alaska Native) (0)	0	<0.01
Ute (1)	1	<0.01
Yakama (0)	1	<0.01
Yaqui (0)	1	<0.01
Yuman (0)	0	<0.01
Yup'ik (Alaska Native) (0)	0	<0.01
Asian (2,555)	3,047	2.62
Not Hispanic (2,538)	3,002	2.58
Hispanic (17)	45	0.04
Bangladeshi (11)	11	0.01
Bhutanese (0)	0	<0.01
Burmese (12)	16	0.01
Cambodian (9)	13	0.01
Chinese, ex. Taiwanese (485)	549	0.47
Filipino (244)	363	0.31
Hmong (2)	3	<0.01
Indian (1,005)	1,091	0.94
Indonesian (8)	8	0.01
Japanese (53)	118	0.10
Korean (174)	251	0.22
Laotian (32)	43	0.04
Malaysian (5)	6	0.01
Nepalese (14)	14	0.01
Pakistani (110)	122	0.10
Sri Lankan (6)	6	0.01
Taiwanese (54)	62	0.05
Thai (36)	61	0.05
Vietnamese (218)	240	0.21
Hawaii Native/Pacific Islander (25)	85	0.07
Not Hispanic (23)	78	0.07
Hispanic (2)	7	0.01
Fijian (3)	4	<0.01
Guamanian/Chamorro (3)	7	0.01
Marshallese (0)	0	<0.01
Native Hawaiian (4)	21	0.02
Samoan (6)	14	0.01
Tongan (0)	0	<0.01
White (88,092)	90,846	78.15
Not Hispanic (86,781)	89,342	76.85
Hispanic (1,311)	1,504	1.29

Notes: † The Census 2010 population figure is used to calculate the percentages in the Hispanic Origin and Race categories. Ancestry percentages are based on the 2006-2010 American Community Survey population (not shown); ‡ Numbers in parentheses indicate the number of people reporting a single ancestry; * Numbers in parentheses indicate the number of persons reporting this race alone not in combination with any other race; Please refer to the Explanation of Data for more information.

Tinley Park

Place Type: Village
County: Cook
Population: 56,703

Ancestry	Population	%
Afghan (0)	0	<0.01
African, Sub-Saharan (193)	193	0.35
African (193)	193	0.35
Cape Verdean (0)	0	<0.01
Ethiopian (0)	0	<0.01
Ghanaian (0)	0	<0.01
Kenyan (0)	0	<0.01
Liberian (0)	0	<0.01
Nigerian (0)	0	<0.01
Senegalese (0)	0	<0.01
Sierra Leonean (0)	0	<0.01
Somalian (0)	0	<0.01
South African (0)	0	<0.01
Sudanese (0)	0	<0.01
Ugandan (0)	0	<0.01
Zimbabwean (0)	0	<0.01
Other Sub-Saharan African (0)	0	<0.01
Albanian (10)	10	0.02
Alsatian (0)	0	<0.01
American (1,190)	1,190	2.17
Arab (1,274)	1,358	2.47
Arab (884)	902	1.64
Egyptian (0)	0	<0.01
Iraqi (0)	0	<0.01
Jordanian (101)	101	0.18
Lebanese (29)	29	0.05
Moroccan (0)	0	<0.01
Palestinian (62)	95	0.17
Syrian (0)	0	<0.01
Other Arab (198)	231	0.42
Armenian (28)	67	0.12
Assyrian/Chaldean/Syriac (0)	0	<0.01
Australian (0)	0	<0.01
Austrian (185)	566	1.03
Basque (0)	0	<0.01
Belgian (15)	42	0.08
Brazilian (0)	0	<0.01
British (0)	50	0.09
Bulgarian (28)	28	0.05
Cajun (0)	0	<0.01
Canadian (12)	37	0.07
Carpatho Rusyn (0)	0	<0.01
Celtic (22)	42	0.08
Croatian (166)	394	0.72
Cypriot (0)	0	<0.01
Czech (334)	1,409	2.56
Czechoslovakian (12)	104	0.19
Danish (36)	207	0.38
Dutch (746)	1,517	2.76
Eastern European (49)	49	0.09
English (508)	3,135	5.71
Estonian (0)	0	<0.01
European (201)	315	0.57
Finnish (0)	78	0.14
French, ex. Basque (71)	1,228	2.24
French Canadian (38)	193	0.35
German (2,606)	12,421	22.61
German Russian (0)	0	<0.01
Greek (448)	1,065	1.94
Guyanese (0)	0	<0.01
Hungarian (49)	233	0.42
Icelander (0)	0	<0.01
Iranian (0)	0	<0.01
Irish (3,462)	13,718	24.97
Israeli (37)	37	0.07
Italian (2,134)	7,333	13.35
Latvian (35)	35	0.06
Lithuanian (489)	1,503	2.74
Luxemburger (0)	0	<0.01
Macedonian (0)	0	<0.01
Maltese (0)	0	<0.01
New Zealander (0)	0	<0.01
Northern European (0)	0	<0.01

Ancestry	Population	%
Norwegian (99)	451	0.82
Pennsylvania German (11)	11	0.02
Polish (3,838)	10,148	18.47
Portuguese (0)	0	<0.01
Romanian (0)	0	<0.01
Russian (65)	485	0.88
Scandinavian (42)	56	0.10
Scotch-Irish (246)	686	1.25
Scottish (83)	452	0.82
Serbian (61)	74	0.13
Slavic (0)	0	<0.01
Slovak (78)	487	0.89
Slovene (5)	24	0.04
Soviet Union (0)	0	<0.01
Swedish (228)	1,818	3.31
Swiss (49)	175	0.32
Turkish (15)	15	0.03
Ukrainian (190)	619	1.13
Welsh (17)	96	0.17
West Indian, ex. Hispanic (146)	169	0.31
Bahamian (0)	0	<0.01
Barbadian (0)	0	<0.01
Belizean (7)	7	0.01
Bermudan (0)	0	<0.01
British West Indian (0)	0	<0.01
Dutch West Indian (0)	0	<0.01
Haitian (12)	35	0.06
Jamaican (0)	0	<0.01
Trinidadian/Tobagonian (0)	0	<0.01
U.S. Virgin Islander (0)	0	<0.01
West Indian (127)	127	0.23
Other West Indian (0)	0	<0.01
Yugoslavian (45)	45	0.08

Hispanic Origin	Population	%
Hispanic or Latino (of any race)	3,898	6.87
Central American, ex. Mexican	70	0.12
Costa Rican	9	0.02
Guatemalan	43	0.08
Honduran	7	0.01
Nicaraguan	7	0.01
Panamanian	0	<0.01
Salvadoran	3	0.01
Other Central American	1	<0.01
Cuban	37	0.07
Dominican Republic	15	0.03
Mexican	3,220	5.68
Puerto Rican	255	0.45
South American	107	0.19
Argentinean	17	0.03
Bolivian	5	0.01
Chilean	0	<0.01
Colombian	30	0.05
Ecuadorian	27	0.05
Paraguayan	2	<0.01
Peruvian	16	0.03
Uruguayan	1	<0.01
Venezuelan	9	0.02
Other South American	0	<0.01
Other Hispanic or Latino	194	0.34

Race*	Population	%
African-American/Black (2,085)	2,223	3.92
Not Hispanic (2,062)	2,176	3.84
Hispanic (23)	47	0.08
American Indian/Alaska Native (80)	212	0.37
Not Hispanic (52)	158	0.28
Hispanic (28)	54	0.10
Alaska Athabascan (Ala. Nat.) (0)	0	<0.01
Aleut (Alaska Native) (0)	0	<0.01
Apache (0)	5	0.01
Arapaho (0)	0	<0.01
Blackfeet (1)	8	0.01
Canadian/French Am. Ind. (0)	0	<0.01
Central American Ind. (0)	0	<0.01
Cherokee (7)	33	0.06
Cheyenne (0)	0	<0.01
Chickasaw (0)	0	<0.01
Chippewa (3)	5	0.01

Race*	Population	%
Choctaw (1)	3	0.01
Colville (0)	0	<0.01
Comanche (0)	0	<0.01
Cree (0)	0	<0.01
Creek (0)	1	<0.01
Crow (0)	0	<0.01
Delaware (0)	0	<0.01
Hopi (0)	0	<0.01
Houma (0)	0	<0.01
Inupiat (Alaska Native) (0)	0	<0.01
Iroquois (0)	1	<0.01
Kiowa (0)	0	<0.01
Lumbee (0)	0	<0.01
Menominee (1)	1	<0.01
Mexican American Ind. (7)	9	0.02
Navajo (6)	8	0.01
Osage (0)	0	<0.01
Ottawa (0)	0	<0.01
Paiute (0)	0	<0.01
Pima (0)	0	<0.01
Potawatomi (1)	1	<0.01
Pueblo (0)	0	<0.01
Puget Sound Salish (0)	0	<0.01
Seminole (0)	0	<0.01
Shoshone (0)	3	0.01
Sioux (2)	3	0.01
South American Ind. (0)	0	<0.01
Spanish American Ind. (0)	0	<0.01
Tlingit-Haida (Alaska Native) (1)	1	<0.01
Tohono O'Odham (0)	0	<0.01
Tsimshian (Alaska Native) (0)	0	<0.01
Ute (0)	1	<0.01
Yakama (0)	0	<0.01
Yaqui (0)	0	<0.01
Yuman (0)	0	<0.01
Yup'ik (Alaska Native) (0)	0	<0.01
Asian (2,208)	2,602	4.59
Not Hispanic (2,199)	2,571	4.53
Hispanic (9)	31	0.05
Bangladeshi (5)	6	0.01
Bhutanese (0)	0	<0.01
Burmese (10)	15	0.03
Cambodian (2)	2	<0.01
Chinese, ex. Taiwanese (223)	266	0.47
Filipino (783)	887	1.56
Hmong (0)	0	<0.01
Indian (711)	785	1.38
Indonesian (2)	2	<0.01
Japanese (21)	48	0.08
Korean (101)	127	0.22
Laotian (20)	27	0.05
Malaysian (3)	3	0.01
Nepalese (0)	3	0.01
Pakistani (108)	128	0.23
Sri Lankan (9)	9	0.02
Taiwanese (4)	7	0.01
Thai (50)	60	0.11
Vietnamese (101)	109	0.19
Hawaii Native/Pacific Islander (10)	45	0.08
Not Hispanic (6)	37	0.07
Hispanic (4)	8	0.01
Fijian (0)	0	<0.01
Guamanian/Chamorro (5)	7	0.01
Marshallese (0)	0	<0.01
Native Hawaiian (0)	12	0.02
Samoan (4)	5	0.01
Tongan (0)	0	<0.01
White (50,332)	51,088	90.10
Not Hispanic (47,858)	48,383	85.33
Hispanic (2,474)	2,705	4.77

Notes: † The Census 2010 population figure is used to calculate the percentages in the Hispanic Origin and Race categories. Ancestry percentages are based on the 2006-2010 American Community Survey population (not shown); ‡ Numbers in parentheses indicate the number of people reporting a single ancestry; * Numbers in parentheses indicate the number of persons reporting this race alone, not in combination with any other race; Please refer to the Explanation of Data for more information.

Waukegan

Place Type: City
County: Lake
Population: 89,078

Ancestry	Population	%
Afghan (0)	0	<0.01
African, Sub-Saharan (507)	574	0.64
African (481)	548	0.61
Cape Verdean (0)	0	<0.01
Ethiopian (0)	0	<0.01
Ghanaian (16)	16	0.02
Kenyan (0)	0	<0.01
Liberian (0)	0	<0.01
Nigerian (0)	0	<0.01
Senegalese (0)	0	<0.01
Sierra Leonean (0)	0	<0.01
Somalian (0)	0	<0.01
South African (10)	10	0.01
Sudanese (0)	0	<0.01
Ugandan (0)	0	<0.01
Zimbabwean (0)	0	<0.01
Other Sub-Saharan African (0)	0	<0.01
Albanian (0)	0	<0.01
Alsatian (0)	0	<0.01
American (920)	920	1.03
Arab (58)	58	0.06
Arab (31)	31	0.03
Egyptian (0)	0	<0.01
Iraqi (0)	0	<0.01
Jordanian (0)	0	<0.01
Lebanese (0)	0	<0.01
Moroccan (27)	27	0.03
Palestinian (0)	0	<0.01
Syrian (0)	0	<0.01
Other Arab (0)	0	<0.01
Armenian (105)	172	0.19
Assyrian/Chaldean/Syriac (0)	0	<0.01
Australian (0)	0	<0.01
Austrian (0)	103	0.12
Basque (0)	0	<0.01
Belgian (39)	219	0.25
Brazilian (0)	0	<0.01
British (27)	97	0.11
Bulgarian (20)	27	0.03
Cajun (0)	0	<0.01
Canadian (0)	13	0.01
Carpatho Rusyn (0)	0	<0.01
Celtic (0)	17	0.02
Croatian (66)	253	0.28
Cypriot (0)	0	<0.01
Czech (28)	204	0.23
Czechoslovakian (18)	29	0.03
Danish (78)	264	0.30
Dutch (84)	511	0.57
Eastern European (46)	77	0.09
English (538)	2,197	2.46
Estonian (0)	0	<0.01
European (290)	395	0.44
Finnish (272)	886	0.99
French, ex. Basque (76)	813	0.91
French Canadian (5)	108	0.12
German (1,543)	6,744	7.55
German Russian (0)	0	<0.01
Greek (157)	340	0.38
Guyanese (0)	0	<0.01
Hungarian (30)	62	0.07
Icelander (14)	23	0.03
Iranian (0)	33	0.04
Irish (873)	4,124	4.61
Israeli (0)	0	<0.01
Italian (851)	2,273	2.54
Latvian (0)	0	<0.01
Lithuanian (135)	436	0.49
Luxemburger (0)	31	0.03
Macedonian (40)	49	0.05
Maltese (0)	0	<0.01
New Zealander (0)	0	<0.01
Northern European (0)	0	<0.01

Ancestry (cont.)	Population	%
Norwegian (168)	855	0.96
Pennsylvania German (0)	10	0.01
Polish (841)	2,391	2.68
Portuguese (0)	0	<0.01
Romanian (143)	150	0.17
Russian (42)	125	0.14
Scandinavian (13)	49	0.05
Scotch-Irish (234)	507	0.57
Scottish (102)	631	0.71
Serbian (225)	225	0.25
Slavic (30)	73	0.08
Slovak (67)	117	0.13
Slovene (61)	304	0.34
Soviet Union (0)	0	<0.01
Swedish (315)	1,267	1.42
Swiss (9)	103	0.12
Turkish (58)	58	0.06
Ukrainian (77)	206	0.23
Welsh (0)	144	0.16
West Indian, ex. Hispanic (887)	1,126	1.26
Bahamian (0)	0	<0.01
Barbadian (0)	0	<0.01
Belizean (475)	536	0.60
Bermudan (0)	0	<0.01
British West Indian (0)	0	<0.01
Dutch West Indian (0)	0	<0.01
Haitian (43)	43	0.05
Jamaican (351)	529	0.59
Trinidadian/Tobagonian (0)	0	<0.01
U.S. Virgin Islander (0)	0	<0.01
West Indian (18)	18	0.02
Other West Indian (0)	0	<0.01
Yugoslavian (21)	98	0.11

Hispanic Origin	Population	%
Hispanic or Latino (of any race)	47,612	53.45
Central American, ex. Mexican	3,653	4.10
Costa Rican	3	<0.01
Guatemalan	340	0.38
Honduran	2,311	2.59
Nicaraguan	39	0.04
Panamanian	29	0.03
Salvadoran	887	1.00
Other Central American	44	0.05
Cuban	136	0.15
Dominican Republic	103	0.12
Mexican	38,636	43.37
Puerto Rican	2,918	3.28
South American	546	0.61
Argentinean	8	0.01
Bolivian	12	0.01
Chilean	21	0.02
Colombian	358	0.40
Ecuadorian	76	0.09
Paraguayan	5	0.01
Peruvian	44	0.05
Uruguayan	5	0.01
Venezuelan	16	0.02
Other South American	1	<0.01
Other Hispanic or Latino	1,620	1.82

Race*	Population	%
African-American/Black (17,081)	18,333	20.58
Not Hispanic (16,240)	17,078	19.17
Hispanic (841)	1,255	1.41
American Indian/Alaska Native (1,042)	1,628	1.83
Not Hispanic (173)	470	0.53
Hispanic (869)	1,158	1.30
Alaska Athabascan (Ala. Nat.) (0)	0	<0.01
Aleut (Alaska Native) (0)	0	<0.01
Apache (12)	21	0.02
Arapaho (0)	1	<0.01
Blackfeet (8)	32	0.04
Canadian/French Am. Ind. (0)	1	<0.01
Central American Ind. (10)	23	0.03
Cherokee (19)	130	0.15
Cheyenne (0)	1	<0.01
Chickasaw (0)	0	<0.01
Chippewa (21)	37	0.04

Race* (cont.)	Population	%
Choctaw (5)	20	0.02
Colville (0)	0	<0.01
Comanche (0)	4	<0.01
Cree (0)	0	<0.01
Creek (0)	4	<0.01
Crow (0)	0	<0.01
Delaware (0)	0	<0.01
Hopi (1)	1	<0.01
Houma (0)	0	<0.01
Inupiat (Alaska Native) (0)	0	<0.01
Iroquois (1)	5	0.01
Kiowa (0)	1	<0.01
Lumbee (1)	1	<0.01
Menominee (0)	1	<0.01
Mexican American Ind. (154)	192	0.22
Navajo (7)	16	0.02
Osage (0)	0	<0.01
Ottawa (0)	0	<0.01
Paiute (0)	0	<0.01
Pima (0)	0	<0.01
Potawatomi (0)	3	<0.01
Pueblo (3)	3	<0.01
Puget Sound Salish (0)	0	<0.01
Seminole (0)	2	<0.01
Shoshone (0)	0	<0.01
Sioux (1)	3	<0.01
South American Ind. (17)	32	0.04
Spanish American Ind. (29)	36	0.04
Tlingit-Haida (Alaska Native) (0)	1	<0.01
Tohono O'Odham (2)	2	<0.01
Tsimshian (Alaska Native) (0)	0	<0.01
Ute (2)	2	<0.01
Yakama (1)	1	<0.01
Yaqui (5)	7	0.01
Yuman (0)	0	<0.01
Yup'lk (Alaska Native) (0)	0	<0.01
Asian (3,825)	4,401	4.9
Not Hispanic (3,722)	4,123	4.6
Hispanic (103)	278	0.3
Bangladeshi (3)	3	<0.0
Bhutanese (0)	0	<0.0
Burmese (1)	1	<0.0
Cambodian (36)	50	0.0
Chinese, ex. Taiwanese (247)	310	0.3
Filipino (1,958)	2,230	2.5
Hmong (10)	11	0.0
Indian (1,084)	1,184	1.3
Indonesian (7)	11	0.0
Japanese (38)	84	0.0
Korean (157)	220	0.2
Laotian (10)	11	0.0
Malaysian (1)	5	0.0
Nepalese (9)	9	0.0
Pakistani (78)	93	0.1
Sri Lankan (3)	6	0.0
Taiwanese (21)	21	0.0
Thai (24)	41	0.0
Vietnamese (54)	72	0.0
Hawaii Native/Pacific Islander (52)	156	0.1
Not Hispanic (26)	82	0.0
Hispanic (26)	74	0.0
Fijian (0)	0	<0.0
Guamanian/Chamorro (28)	35	0.0
Marshallese (0)	0	<0.0
Native Hawaiian (4)	35	0.0
Samoan (2)	3	<0.0
Tongan (1)	2	<0.0
White (41,552)	44,475	49.9
Not Hispanic (19,370)	20,407	22.9
Hispanic (22,182)	24,068	27.0

Notes: † The Census 2010 population figure is used to calculate the percentages in the Hispanic Origin and Race categories. Ancestry percentages are based on the 2006-2010 American Communit Survey population (not shown); ‡ Numbers in parentheses indicate the number of people reporting a single ancestry; * Numbers in parentheses indicate the number of persons reporting this race alon not in combination with any other race; Please refer to the Explanation of Data for more information.

Wheaton

Place Type: City
County: DuPage
Population: 52,894.

Ancestry	Population	%
Afghan (0)	0	<0.01
African, Sub-Saharan (230)	239	0.45
African (21)	30	0.06
Cape Verdean (0)	0	<0.01
Ethiopian (0)	0	<0.01
Ghanaian (0)	0	<0.01
Kenyan (9)	9	0.02
Liberian (0)	0	<0.01
Nigerian (30)	30	0.06
Senegalese (0)	0	<0.01
Sierra Leonean (0)	0	<0.01
Somalian (134)	134	0.25
South African (0)	0	<0.01
Sudanese (36)	36	0.07
Ugandan (0)	0	<0.01
Zimbabwean (0)	0	<0.01
Other Sub-Saharan African (0)	0	<0.01
Albanian (199)	212	0.40
Alsatian (0)	0	<0.01
American (1,206)	1,206	2.27
Arab (76)	199	0.37
Arab (0)	0	<0.01
Egyptian (14)	14	0.03
Iraqi (0)	0	<0.01
Jordanian (0)	0	<0.01
Lebanese (40)	155	0.29
Moroccan (0)	0	<0.01
Palestinian (9)	9	0.02
Syrian (0)	8	0.02
Other Arab (13)	13	0.02
Armenian (162)	224	0.42
Assyrian/Chaldean/Syriac (9)	50	0.09
Australian (0)	34	0.06
Austrian (107)	313	0.59
Basque (0)	0	<0.01
Belgian (102)	213	0.40
Brazilian (0)	11	0.02
British (319)	601	1.13
Bulgarian (0)	0	<0.01
Cajun (0)	0	<0.01
Canadian (35)	85	0.16
Carpatho Rusyn (0)	0	<0.01
Celtic (0)	0	<0.01
Croatian (49)	146	0.27
Cypriot (0)	0	<0.01
Czech (251)	791	1.49
Czechoslovakian (78)	172	0.32
Danish (82)	538	1.01
Dutch (327)	1,202	2.26
Eastern European (30)	30	0.06
English (1,317)	6,664	12.54
Estonian (0)	0	<0.01
European (925)	1,145	2.15
Finnish (58)	145	0.27
French, ex. Basque (288)	1,566	2.95
French Canadian (37)	302	0.57
German (3,674)	14,873	27.99
German Russian (0)	0	<0.01
Greek (272)	657	1.24
Guyanese (7)	7	0.01
Hungarian (50)	342	0.64
Icelander (0)	16	0.03
Iranian (0)	0	<0.01
Irish (2,089)	9,656	18.17
Israeli (53)	53	0.10
Italian (1,902)	5,622	10.58
Latvian (0)	103	0.19
Lithuanian (344)	835	1.57
Luxemburger (0)	62	0.12
Macedonian (0)	12	0.02
Maltese (0)	0	<0.01
New Zealander (0)	0	<0.01
Northern European (126)	135	0.25

Ancestry	Population	%
Norwegian (331)	1,598	3.01
Pennsylvania German (0)	0	<0.01
Polish (1,653)	5,226	9.83
Portuguese (0)	14	0.03
Romanian (94)	159	0.30
Russian (595)	986	1.86
Scandinavian (154)	330	0.62
Scotch-Irish (411)	1,284	2.42
Scottish (222)	1,270	2.39
Serbian (84)	163	0.31
Slavic (0)	43	0.08
Slovak (106)	306	0.58
Slovene (27)	47	0.09
Soviet Union (0)	0	<0.01
Swedish (620)	2,653	4.99
Swiss (0)	322	0.61
Turkish (147)	147	0.28
Ukrainian (136)	338	0.64
Welsh (26)	378	0.71
West Indian, ex. Hispanic (36)	91	0.17
Bahamian (0)	0	<0.01
Barbadian (0)	0	<0.01
Belizean (0)	10	0.02
Bermudan (0)	0	<0.01
British West Indian (0)	0	<0.01
Dutch West Indian (0)	0	<0.01
Haitian (14)	23	0.04
Jamaican (22)	58	0.11
Trinidadian/Tobagonian (0)	0	<0.01
U.S. Virgin Islander (0)	0	<0.01
West Indian (0)	0	<0.01
Other West Indian (0)	0	<0.01
Yugoslavian (219)	285	0.54

Hispanic Origin	Population	%
Hispanic or Latino (of any race)	2,617	4.95
Central American, ex. Mexican	150	0.28
Costa Rican	13	0.02
Guatemalan	71	0.13
Honduran	18	0.03
Nicaraguan	15	0.03
Panamanian	11	0.02
Salvadoran	21	0.04
Other Central American	1	<0.01
Cuban	149	0.28
Dominican Republic	11	0.02
Mexican	1,503	2.84
Puerto Rican	290	0.55
South American	358	0.68
Argentinean	42	0.08
Bolivian	40	0.08
Chilean	29	0.05
Colombian	129	0.24
Ecuadorian	47	0.09
Paraguayan	0	<0.01
Peruvian	39	0.07
Uruguayan	4	0.01
Venezuelan	28	0.05
Other South American	0	<0.01
Other Hispanic or Latino	156	0.29

Race*	Population	%
African-American/Black (2,357)	2,644	5.00
Not Hispanic (2,324)	2,565	4.85
Hispanic (33)	79	0.15
American Indian/Alaska Native (97)	268	0.51
Not Hispanic (55)	186	0.35
Hispanic (42)	82	0.16
Alaska Athabascan (Ala. Nat.) (0)	0	<0.01
Aleut (Alaska Native) (0)	0	<0.01
Apache (0)	4	0.01
Arapaho (0)	0	<0.01
Blackfeet (1)	11	0.02
Canadian/French Am. Ind. (0)	7	0.01
Central American Ind. (1)	1	<0.01
Cherokee (4)	49	0.09
Cheyenne (0)	0	<0.01
Chickasaw (0)	0	<0.01
Chippewa (2)	17	0.03

Race*	Population	%
Choctaw (1)	4	0.01
Colville (0)	0	<0.01
Comanche (0)	1	<0.01
Cree (1)	1	<0.01
Creek (0)	0	<0.01
Crow (1)	1	<0.01
Delaware (1)	1	<0.01
Hopi (1)	1	<0.01
Houma (0)	0	<0.01
Inupiat (Alaska Native) (0)	0	<0.01
Iroquois (4)	6	0.01
Kiowa (0)	0	<0.01
Lumbee (0)	0	<0.01
Menominee (0)	0	<0.01
Mexican American Ind. (14)	21	0.04
Navajo (0)	2	<0.01
Osage (0)	0	<0.01
Ottawa (0)	0	<0.01
Paiute (0)	0	<0.01
Pima (0)	0	<0.01
Potawatomi (0)	0	<0.01
Pueblo (0)	1	<0.01
Puget Sound Salish (0)	0	<0.01
Seminole (0)	0	<0.01
Shoshone (0)	2	<0.01
Sioux (2)	11	0.02
South American Ind. (2)	3	0.01
Spanish American Ind. (2)	2	<0.01
Tlingit-Haida (Alaska Native) (0)	0	<0.01
Tohono O'Odham (0)	0	<0.01
Tsimshian (Alaska Native) (0)	0	<0.01
Ute (0)	0	<0.01
Yakama (0)	0	<0.01
Yaqui (0)	0	<0.01
Yuman (0)	0	<0.01
Yup'ik (Alaska Native) (1)	1	<0.01
Asian (2,721)	3,313	6.26
Not Hispanic (2,708)	3,267	6.18
Hispanic (13)	46	0.09
Bangladeshi (0)	3	0.01
Bhutanese (68)	68	0.13
Burmese (230)	245	0.46
Cambodian (33)	43	0.08
Chinese, ex. Taiwanese (398)	574	1.09
Filipino (302)	446	0.84
Hmong (8)	10	0.02
Indian (616)	715	1.35
Indonesian (6)	11	0.02
Japanese (73)	150	0.28
Korean (332)	393	0.74
Laotian (3)	3	0.01
Malaysian (3)	5	0.01
Nepalese (26)	27	0.05
Pakistani (154)	176	0.33
Sri Lankan (0)	1	<0.01
Taiwanese (48)	75	0.14
Thai (21)	33	0.06
Vietnamese (288)	327	0.62
Hawaii Native/Pacific Islander (13)	57	0.11
Not Hispanic (12)	51	0.10
Hispanic (1)	6	0.01
Fijian (0)	0	<0.01
Guamanian/Chamorro (2)	2	<0.01
Marshallese (0)	0	<0.01
Native Hawaiian (3)	18	0.03
Samoan (2)	3	0.01
Tongan (0)	0	<0.01
White (46,165)	47,131	89.10
Not Hispanic (44,232)	45,045	85.16
Hispanic (1,933)	2,086	3.94

Notes: † The Census 2010 population figure is used to calculate the percentages in the Hispanic Origin and Race categories. Ancestry percentages are based on the 2006-2010 American Community Survey population (not shown); ‡ Numbers in parentheses indicate the number of people reporting a single ancestry; * Numbers in parentheses indicate the number of persons reporting this race alone, not in combination with any other race; Please refer to the Explanation of Data for more information.

Ancestry Group Rankings

Afghan

Top 10 Places Sorted by Population
Based on all places, regardless of total population

Place	Population	%
Glen Ellyn (village) DuPage County	305	1.11
Aurora (city) Kane County	261	0.14
Chicago (city) Cook County	234	0.01
Peoria (city) Peoria County	71	0.06
Flossmoor (village) Cook County	47	0.51
Hickory Hills (city) Cook County	44	0.31
Downers Grove (village) DuPage County	33	0.07
St. Charles (city) Kane County	25	0.08
Chicago Ridge (village) Cook County	13	0.09
Morton (village) Tazewell County	12	0.08

Top 10 Places Sorted by Percent of Total Population
Based on all places, regardless of total population

Place	Population	%
Glen Ellyn (village) DuPage County	305	1.11
Flossmoor (village) Cook County	47	0.51
Hickory Hills (city) Cook County	44	0.31
Aurora (city) Kane County	261	0.14
Chicago Ridge (village) Cook County	13	0.09
St. Charles (city) Kane County	25	0.08
Morton (village) Tazewell County	12	0.08
Downers Grove (village) DuPage County	33	0.07
Peoria (city) Peoria County	71	0.06
Oak Park (village) Cook County	9	0.02

Top 10 Places Sorted by Percent of Total Population
Based on places with total population of 50,000 or more

Place	Population	%
Aurora (city) Kane County	261	0.14
Peoria (city) Peoria County	71	0.06
Oak Park (village) Cook County	9	0.02
Chicago (city) Cook County	234	0.01
Arlington Heights (village) Cook County	0	0.00
Berwyn (city) Cook County	0	0.00
Bloomington (city) McLean County	0	0.00
Bolingbrook (village) Will County	0	0.00
Champaign (city) Champaign County	0	0.00
Cicero (town) Cook County	0	0.00

African, Sub-Saharan

Top 10 Places Sorted by Population
Based on all places, regardless of total population

Place	Population	%
Chicago (city) Cook County	36,226	1.34
Champaign (city) Champaign County	3,208	4.04
Urbana (city) Champaign County	1,594	3.91
Bolingbrook (village) Will County	1,497	2.06
Aurora (city) Kane County	977	0.51
Joliet (city) Will County	955	0.66
Springfield (city) Sangamon County	749	0.65
Evanston (city) Cook County	686	0.93
Naperville (city) DuPage County	634	0.45
Galesburg (city) Knox County	627	1.95

Top 10 Places Sorted by Percent of Total Population
Based on all places, regardless of total population

Place	Population	%
Sciota (village) McDonough County	8	21.05
Royal Lakes (village) Macoupin County	15	10.27
Creston (village) Ogle County	70	8.96
Mettawa (village) Lake County	34	5.70
Pulaski (village) Pulaski County	13	5.53
Leland Grove (city) Sangamon County	83	5.14
Champaign (city) Champaign County	3,208	4.04
Urbana (city) Champaign County	1,594	3.91
Elsah (village) Jersey County	21	3.79
Flossmoor (village) Cook County	334	3.62

Top 10 Places Sorted by Percent of Total Population
Based on places with total population of 50,000 or more

Place	Population	%
Champaign (city) Champaign County	3,208	4.04
Bolingbrook (village) Will County	1,497	2.06
Chicago (city) Cook County	36,226	1.34
Evanston (city) Cook County	686	0.93
Oak Park (village) Cook County	448	0.87
Normal (town) McLean County	388	0.75
Skokie (village) Cook County	433	0.68
Joliet (city) Will County	955	0.66
Springfield (city) Sangamon County	749	0.65
Waukegan (city) Lake County	574	0.64

African, Sub-Saharan: African

Top 10 Places Sorted by Population
Based on all places, regardless of total population

Place	Population	%
Chicago (city) Cook County	21,971	0.81
Champaign (city) Champaign County	3,045	3.83
Urbana (city) Champaign County	1,356	3.32
Bolingbrook (village) Will County	870	1.20
Joliet (city) Will County	837	0.58
Galesburg (city) Knox County	600	1.86
Waukegan (city) Lake County	548	0.61
Danville (city) Vermilion County	539	1.62
Springfield (city) Sangamon County	537	0.47
East St. Louis (city) St. Clair County	484	1.74

Top 10 Places Sorted by Percent of Total Population
Based on all places, regardless of total population

Place	Population	%
Sciota (village) McDonough County	8	21.05
Royal Lakes (village) Macoupin County	15	10.27
Creston (village) Ogle County	70	8.96
Pulaski (village) Pulaski County	13	5.53
Champaign (city) Champaign County	3,045	3.83
Brooklyn (village) St. Clair County	18	3.44
Olympia Fields (village) Cook County	162	3.43
Urbana (city) Champaign County	1,356	3.32
Thornton (village) Cook County	78	3.18
Mounds (city) Pulaski County	26	3.03

Top 10 Places Sorted by Percent of Total Population
Based on places with total population of 50,000 or more

Place	Population	%
Champaign (city) Champaign County	3,045	3.83
Bolingbrook (village) Will County	870	1.20
Chicago (city) Cook County	21,971	0.81
Oak Park (village) Cook County	376	0.73
Waukegan (city) Lake County	548	0.61
Joliet (city) Will County	837	0.58
Evanston (city) Cook County	430	0.58
Springfield (city) Sangamon County	537	0.47
Normal (town) McLean County	208	0.40
Bloomington (city) McLean County	264	0.35

African, Sub-Saharan: Cape Verdean

Top 10 Places Sorted by Population
Based on all places, regardless of total population

Place	Population	%
Montgomery (village) Kendall County	134	0.84
Chicago (city) Cook County	22	<0.01
Roselle (village) DuPage County	15	0.07
Lemont (village) Cook County	12	0.08
O'Fallon (city) St. Clair County	9	0.03
Glenwood (village) Cook County	5	0.06
Abingdon (city) Knox County	0	0.00
Adair (cdp) McDonough County	0	0.00
Addieville (village) Washington County	0	0.00
Addison (village) DuPage County	0	0.00

Top 10 Places Sorted by Percent of Total Population
Based on all places, regardless of total population

Place	Population	%
Montgomery (village) Kendall County	134	0.84
Lemont (village) Cook County	12	0.08
Roselle (village) DuPage County	15	0.07
Glenwood (village) Cook County	5	0.06
O'Fallon (city) St. Clair County	9	0.03
Chicago (city) Cook County	22	<0.01
Abingdon (city) Knox County	0	0.00
Adair (cdp) McDonough County	0	0.00
Addieville (village) Washington County	0	0.00
Addison (village) DuPage County	0	0.00

Top 10 Places Sorted by Percent of Total Population
Based on places with total population of 50,000 or more

Place	Population	%
Chicago (city) Cook County	22	<0.01
Arlington Heights (village) Cook County	0	0.00
Aurora (city) Kane County	0	0.00
Berwyn (city) Cook County	0	0.00
Bloomington (city) McLean County	0	0.00
Bolingbrook (village) Will County	0	0.00
Champaign (city) Champaign County	0	0.00
Cicero (town) Cook County	0	0.00
Decatur (city) Macon County	0	0.00
Des Plaines (city) Cook County	0	0.00

African, Sub-Saharan: Ethiopian

Top 10 Places Sorted by Population
Based on all places, regardless of total population

Place	Population	%
Chicago (city) Cook County	2,224	0.08
Romeoville (village) Will County	192	0.51
Elgin (city) Kane County	130	0.12
Woodridge (village) DuPage County	97	0.30
Oak Lawn (village) Cook County	77	0.14
Carol Stream (village) DuPage County	70	0.18
Rockford (city) Winnebago County	45	0.03
Bloomington (city) McLean County	41	0.05
Bourbonnais (village) Kankakee County	35	0.19
Glendale Heights (village) DuPage County	35	0.10

Top 10 Places Sorted by Percent of Total Population
Based on all places, regardless of total population

Place	Population	%
Indian Creek (village) Lake County	4	0.75
Romeoville (village) Will County	192	0.51
Evansville (village) Randolph County	3	0.46
Orion (village) Henry County	8	0.43
Woodridge (village) DuPage County	97	0.30
West Dundee (village) Kane County	17	0.24
Bourbonnais (village) Kankakee County	35	0.19
Yorkville (city) Kendall County	28	0.19
Carol Stream (village) DuPage County	70	0.18
Richton Park (village) Cook County	22	0.17

Top 10 Places Sorted by Percent of Total Population
Based on places with total population of 50,000 or more

Place	Population	%
Oak Lawn (village) Cook County	77	0.14
Elgin (city) Kane County	130	0.12
Chicago (city) Cook County	2,224	0.08
Bloomington (city) McLean County	41	0.05
Normal (town) McLean County	23	0.04
Skokie (village) Cook County	23	0.04
Rockford (city) Winnebago County	45	0.03
Evanston (city) Cook County	11	0.01
Oak Park (village) Cook County	5	0.01
Arlington Heights (village) Cook County	0	0.00

African, Sub-Saharan: Ghanaian

Top 10 Places Sorted by Population
Based on all places, regardless of total population

Place	Population	%
Chicago (city) Cook County	1,873	0.07
Bolingbrook (village) Will County	314	0.43
Woodridge (village) DuPage County	276	0.85
Peoria (city) Peoria County	236	0.21
Hanover Park (village) Cook County	233	0.62
Burr Ridge (village) DuPage County	122	1.16
Harvey (city) Cook County	110	0.43
Naperville (city) DuPage County	110	0.08
Urbana (city) Champaign County	83	0.20
Romeoville (village) Will County	78	0.21

Top 10 Places Sorted by Percent of Total Population
Based on all places, regardless of total population

Place	Population	%
Burr Ridge (village) DuPage County	122	1.16
Orland Hills (village) Cook County	73	1.04
Woodridge (village) DuPage County	276	0.85
Forsyth (village) Macon County	22	0.67
Hanover Park (village) Cook County	233	0.62
Bolingbrook (village) Will County	314	0.43
Harvey (city) Cook County	110	0.43
Montgomery (village) Kendall County	36	0.23
Peoria (city) Peoria County	236	0.21
Romeoville (village) Will County	78	0.21

Top 10 Places Sorted by Percent of Total Population
Based on places with total population of 50,000 or more

Place	Population	%
Bolingbrook (village) Will County	314	0.43
Peoria (city) Peoria County	236	0.21
Naperville (city) DuPage County	110	0.08
Chicago (city) Cook County	1,873	0.07
Springfield (city) Sangamon County	58	0.05
Palatine (village) Cook County	28	0.04
Oak Park (village) Cook County	17	0.03
Joliet (city) Will County	26	0.02
Bloomington (city) McLean County	17	0.02
Waukegan (city) Lake County	16	0.02

African, Sub-Saharan: Kenyan

Top 10 Places Sorted by Population
Based on all places, regardless of total population

Place	Population	%
Chicago (city) Cook County	456	0.02
Schaumburg (village) Cook County	88	0.12
Naperville (city) DuPage County	55	0.04
Prospect Heights (city) Cook County	47	0.29
Sycamore (city) DeKalb County	46	0.27
O'Fallon (city) St. Clair County	32	0.12
Palatine (village) Cook County	32	0.05
Collinsville (city) Madison County	28	0.11
Urbana (city) Champaign County	22	0.05
Elsah (village) Jersey County	21	3.79

Top 10 Places Sorted by Percent of Total Population
Based on all places, regardless of total population

Place	Population	%
Elsah (village) Jersey County	21	3.79
Prospect Heights (city) Cook County	47	0.29
Sycamore (city) DeKalb County	46	0.27
Schaumburg (village) Cook County	88	0.12
O'Fallon (city) St. Clair County	32	0.12
Collinsville (city) Madison County	28	0.11
Palatine (village) Cook County	32	0.05
Urbana (city) Champaign County	22	0.05
Naperville (city) DuPage County	55	0.04
Round Lake (village) Lake County	5	0.03

Top 10 Places Sorted by Percent of Total Population
Based on places with total population of 50,000 or more

Place	Population	%
Schaumburg (village) Cook County	88	0.12
Palatine (village) Cook County	32	0.05
Naperville (city) DuPage County	55	0.04
Chicago (city) Cook County	456	0.02

Bolingbrook (village) Will County	12	0.02
Wheaton (city) DuPage County	9	0.02
Bloomington (city) McLean County	10	0.01
Arlington Heights (village) Cook County	0	0.00
Aurora (city) Kane County	0	0.00
Berwyn (city) Cook County	0	0.00

African, Sub-Saharan: Liberian

Top 10 Places Sorted by Population
Based on all places, regardless of total population

Place	Population	%
Chicago (city) Cook County	102	<0.01
Leland Grove (city) Sangamon County	83	5.14
Posen (village) Cook County	71	1.25
Maywood (village) Cook County	45	0.18
Skokie (village) Cook County	35	0.05
Cairo (city) Alexander County	27	0.91
Lynwood (village) Cook County	26	0.30
Macomb (city) McDonough County	12	0.06
Rock Island (city) Rock Island County	11	0.03
Abingdon (city) Knox County	0	0.00

Top 10 Places Sorted by Percent of Total Population
Based on all places, regardless of total population

Place	Population	%
Leland Grove (city) Sangamon County	83	5.14
Posen (village) Cook County	71	1.25
Cairo (city) Alexander County	27	0.91
Lynwood (village) Cook County	26	0.30
Maywood (village) Cook County	45	0.18
Macomb (city) McDonough County	12	0.06
Skokie (village) Cook County	35	0.05
Rock Island (city) Rock Island County	11	0.03
Chicago (city) Cook County	102	<0.01
Abingdon (city) Knox County	0	0.00

Top 10 Places Sorted by Percent of Total Population
Based on places with total population of 50,000 or more

Place	Population	%
Skokie (village) Cook County	35	0.05
Chicago (city) Cook County	102	<0.01
Arlington Heights (village) Cook County	0	0.00
Aurora (city) Kane County	0	0.00
Berwyn (city) Cook County	0	0.00
Bloomington (city) McLean County	0	0.00
Bolingbrook (village) Will County	0	0.00
Champaign (city) Champaign County	0	0.00
Cicero (town) Cook County	0	0.00
Decatur (city) Macon County	0	0.00

African, Sub-Saharan: Nigerian

Top 10 Places Sorted by Population
Based on all places, regardless of total population

Place	Population	%
Chicago (city) Cook County	6,193	0.23
Aurora (city) Kane County	372	0.20
Calumet City (city) Cook County	352	0.95
Huntley (village) McHenry County	340	1.60
Frankfort (village) Will County	276	1.62
Hazel Crest (village) Cook County	234	1.64
Flossmoor (village) Cook County	221	2.40
Country Club Hills (city) Cook County	194	1.19
Homewood (village) Will County	180	0.93
Bolingbrook (village) Will County	171	0.24

Top 10 Places Sorted by Percent of Total Population
Based on all places, regardless of total population

Place	Population	%
Mettawa (village) Lake County	34	5.70
Flossmoor (village) Cook County	221	2.40
Posen (village) Cook County	127	2.23
Hazel Crest (village) Cook County	234	1.64
Frankfort (village) Will County	276	1.62
Huntley (village) McHenry County	340	1.60
Country Club Hills (city) Cook County	194	1.19
Carbon Cliff (village) Rock Island County	24	1.13
Lynwood (village) Cook County	96	1.10
Spring Grove (village) McHenry County	52	1.00

Top 10 Places Sorted by Percent of Total Population
Based on places with total population of 50,000 or more

Place	Population	%
Bolingbrook (village) Will County	171	0.24
Chicago (city) Cook County	6,193	0.23
Palatine (village) Cook County	151	0.22
Aurora (city) Kane County	372	0.20
Evanston (city) Cook County	130	0.18
Schaumburg (village) Cook County	105	0.14
Springfield (city) Sangamon County	154	0.13
Normal (town) McLean County	68	0.13
Skokie (village) Cook County	74	0.12
Champaign (city) Champaign County	76	0.10

African, Sub-Saharan: Senegalese

Top 10 Places Sorted by Population
Based on all places, regardless of total population

Place	Population	%
Schaumburg (village) Cook County	39	0.05
Fairview Heights (city) St. Clair County	17	0.10
Moline (city) Rock Island County	6	0.01
Abingdon (city) Knox County	0	0.00
Adair (cdp) McDonough County	0	0.00
Addieville (village) Washington County	0	0.00
Addison (village) DuPage County	0	0.00
Adeline (village) Ogle County	0	0.00
Albany (village) Whiteside County	0	0.00
Albers (village) Clinton County	0	0.00

Top 10 Places Sorted by Percent of Total Population
Based on all places, regardless of total population

Place	Population	%
Fairview Heights (city) St. Clair County	17	0.10
Schaumburg (village) Cook County	39	0.05
Moline (city) Rock Island County	6	0.01
Abingdon (city) Knox County	0	0.00
Adair (cdp) McDonough County	0	0.00
Addieville (village) Washington County	0	0.00
Addison (village) DuPage County	0	0.00
Adeline (village) Ogle County	0	0.00
Albany (village) Whiteside County	0	0.00
Albers (village) Clinton County	0	0.00

Top 10 Places Sorted by Percent of Total Population
Based on places with total population of 50,000 or more

Place	Population	%
Schaumburg (village) Cook County	39	0.05
Arlington Heights (village) Cook County	0	0.00
Aurora (city) Kane County	0	0.00
Berwyn (city) Cook County	0	0.00
Bloomington (city) McLean County	0	0.00
Bolingbrook (village) Will County	0	0.00
Champaign (city) Champaign County	0	0.00
Chicago (city) Cook County	0	0.00
Cicero (town) Cook County	0	0.00
Decatur (city) Macon County	0	0.00

African, Sub-Saharan: Sierra Leonean

Top 10 Places Sorted by Population
Based on all places, regardless of total population

Place	Population	%
Chicago (city) Cook County	221	0.01
Romeoville (village) Will County	105	0.28
South Holland (village) Cook County	54	0.25
Schaumburg (village) Cook County	53	0.07
Bolingbrook (village) Will County	43	0.06
Rockford (city) Winnebago County	13	0.01
Aurora (city) Kane County	8	<0.01
Abingdon (city) Knox County	0	0.00
Adair (cdp) McDonough County	0	0.00
Addieville (village) Washington County	0	0.00

Top 10 Places Sorted by Percent of Total Population
Based on all places, regardless of total population

Place	Population	%
Romeoville (village) Will County	105	0.28
South Holland (village) Cook County	54	0.25
Schaumburg (village) Cook County	53	0.07

Place	Population	%
Bolingbrook (village) Will County	43	0.06
Chicago (city) Cook County	221	0.01
Rockford (city) Winnebago County	13	0.01
Aurora (city) Kane County	8	<0.01
Abingdon (city) Knox County	0	0.00
Adair (cdp) McDonough County	0	0.00
Addieville (village) Washington County	0	0.00

Top 10 Places Sorted by Percent of Total Population
Based on places with total population of 50,000 or more

Place	Population	%
Schaumburg (village) Cook County	53	0.07
Bolingbrook (village) Will County	43	0.06
Chicago (city) Cook County	221	0.01
Rockford (city) Winnebago County	13	0.01
Aurora (city) Kane County	8	<0.01
Arlington Heights (village) Cook County	0	0.00
Berwyn (city) Cook County	0	0.00
Bloomington (city) McLean County	0	0.00
Champaign (city) Champaign County	0	0.00
Cicero (town) Cook County	0	0.00

African, Sub-Saharan: Somalian

Top 10 Places Sorted by Population
Based on all places, regardless of total population

Place	Population	%
Chicago (city) Cook County	637	0.02
Wheaton (city) DuPage County	134	0.25
Salem (city) Marion County	39	0.52
Lake Forest (city) Lake County	13	0.07
East Moline (city) Rock Island County	12	0.06
Manchester (village) Scott County	4	0.89
Abingdon (city) Knox County	0	0.00
Adair (cdp) McDonough County	0	0.00
Addieville (village) Washington County	0	0.00
Addison (village) DuPage County	0	0.00

Top 10 Places Sorted by Percent of Total Population
Based on all places, regardless of total population

Place	Population	%
Manchester (village) Scott County	4	0.89
Salem (city) Marion County	39	0.52
Wheaton (city) DuPage County	134	0.25
Lake Forest (city) Lake County	13	0.07
East Moline (city) Rock Island County	12	0.06
Chicago (city) Cook County	637	0.02
Abingdon (city) Knox County	0	0.00
Adair (cdp) McDonough County	0	0.00
Addieville (village) Washington County	0	0.00
Addison (village) DuPage County	0	0.00

Top 10 Places Sorted by Percent of Total Population
Based on places with total population of 50,000 or more

Place	Population	%
Wheaton (city) DuPage County	134	0.25
Chicago (city) Cook County	637	0.02
Arlington Heights (village) Cook County	0	0.00
Aurora (city) Kane County	0	0.00
Berwyn (city) Cook County	0	0.00
Bloomington (city) McLean County	0	0.00
Bolingbrook (village) Will County	0	0.00
Champaign (city) Champaign County	0	0.00
Cicero (town) Cook County	0	0.00
Decatur (city) Macon County	0	0.00

African, Sub-Saharan: South African

Top 10 Places Sorted by Population
Based on all places, regardless of total population

Place	Population	%
Chicago (city) Cook County	375	0.01
Naperville (city) DuPage County	179	0.13
Montgomery (village) Kendall County	163	1.02
Skokie (village) Cook County	79	0.12
Plainfield (village) Will County	52	0.15
Prospect Heights (city) Cook County	49	0.30
Highland Park (city) Lake County	48	0.16
North Aurora (village) Kane County	42	0.27
Northbrook (village) Cook County	33	0.10
Joliet (city) Will County	29	0.02

Top 10 Places Sorted by Percent of Total Population
Based on all places, regardless of total population

Place	Population	%
Montgomery (village) Kendall County	163	1.02
Davis Junction (village) Ogle County	22	1.01
Hopewell (village) Marshall County	3	0.72
Knollwood (cdp) Lake County	10	0.60
Sleepy Hollow (village) Kane County	20	0.59
Bannockburn (village) Lake County	8	0.58
Wayne (village) DuPage County	13	0.47
Lincolnshire (village) Lake County	26	0.37
Prospect Heights (city) Cook County	49	0.30
North Aurora (village) Kane County	42	0.27

Top 10 Places Sorted by Percent of Total Population
Based on places with total population of 50,000 or more

Place	Population	%
Naperville (city) DuPage County	179	0.13
Skokie (village) Cook County	79	0.12
Evanston (city) Cook County	27	0.04
Berwyn (city) Cook County	16	0.03
Joliet (city) Will County	29	0.02
Bolingbrook (village) Will County	17	0.02
Normal (town) McLean County	9	0.02
Chicago (city) Cook County	375	0.01
Rockford (city) Winnebago County	14	0.01
Peoria (city) Peoria County	13	0.01

African, Sub-Saharan: Sudanese

Top 10 Places Sorted by Population
Based on all places, regardless of total population

Place	Population	%
Chicago (city) Cook County	225	0.01
Glen Ellyn (village) DuPage County	157	0.57
Chicago Ridge (village) Cook County	54	0.38
Wheaton (city) DuPage County	36	0.07
Melrose Park (village) Cook County	29	0.12
DeKalb (city) DeKalb County	16	0.04
Pontiac (city) Livingston County	15	0.12
Skokie (village) Cook County	14	0.02
Rockford (city) Winnebago County	11	0.01
Oak Lawn (village) Cook County	10	0.02

Top 10 Places Sorted by Percent of Total Population
Based on all places, regardless of total population

Place	Population	%
Glen Ellyn (village) DuPage County	157	0.57
Chicago Ridge (village) Cook County	54	0.38
Melrose Park (village) Cook County	29	0.12
Pontiac (city) Livingston County	15	0.12
Wheaton (city) DuPage County	36	0.07
Kewanee (city) Henry County	8	0.06
DeKalb (city) DeKalb County	16	0.04
Skokie (village) Cook County	14	0.02
Oak Lawn (village) Cook County	10	0.02
Chicago (city) Cook County	225	0.01

Top 10 Places Sorted by Percent of Total Population
Based on places with total population of 50,000 or more

Place	Population	%
Wheaton (city) DuPage County	36	0.07
Skokie (village) Cook County	14	0.02
Oak Lawn (village) Cook County	10	0.02
Chicago (city) Cook County	225	0.01
Rockford (city) Winnebago County	11	0.01
Peoria (city) Peoria County	10	0.01
Arlington Heights (village) Cook County	0	0.00
Aurora (city) Kane County	0	0.00
Berwyn (city) Cook County	0	0.00
Bloomington (city) McLean County	0	0.00

African, Sub-Saharan: Ugandan

Top 10 Places Sorted by Population
Based on all places, regardless of total population

Place	Population	%
Evanston (city) Cook County	41	0.06
Chicago (city) Cook County	39	<0.01
Roscoe (village) Winnebago County	24	0.24

Place	Population	%
Abingdon (city) Knox County	0	0.00
Adair (cdp) McDonough County	0	0.00
Addieville (village) Washington County	0	0.00
Addison (village) DuPage County	0	0.00
Adeline (village) Ogle County	0	0.00
Albany (village) Whiteside County	0	0.00
Albers (village) Clinton County	0	0.00

Top 10 Places Sorted by Percent of Total Population
Based on all places, regardless of total population

Place	Population	%
Roscoe (village) Winnebago County	24	0.24
Evanston (city) Cook County	41	0.06
Chicago (city) Cook County	39	<0.01
Abingdon (city) Knox County	0	0.00
Adair (cdp) McDonough County	0	0.00
Addieville (village) Washington County	0	0.00
Addison (village) DuPage County	0	0.00
Adeline (village) Ogle County	0	0.00
Albany (village) Whiteside County	0	0.00
Albers (village) Clinton County	0	0.00

Top 10 Places Sorted by Percent of Total Population
Based on places with total population of 50,000 or more

Place	Population	%
Evanston (city) Cook County	41	0.06
Chicago (city) Cook County	39	<0.01
Arlington Heights (village) Cook County	0	0.00
Aurora (city) Kane County	0	0.00
Berwyn (city) Cook County	0	0.00
Bloomington (city) McLean County	0	0.00
Bolingbrook (village) Will County	0	0.00
Champaign (city) Champaign County	0	0.00
Cicero (town) Cook County	0	0.00
Decatur (city) Macon County	0	0.00

African, Sub-Saharan: Zimbabwean

Top 10 Places Sorted by Population
Based on all places, regardless of total population

Place	Population	%
Chicago (city) Cook County	107	<0.01
Urbana (city) Champaign County	25	0.06
Buffalo Grove (village) Lake County	14	0.01
Abingdon (city) Knox County	0	0.00
Adair (cdp) McDonough County	0	0.00
Addieville (village) Washington County	0	0.00
Addison (village) DuPage County	0	0.00
Adeline (village) Ogle County	0	0.00
Albany (village) Whiteside County	0	0.00
Albers (village) Clinton County	0	0.00

Top 10 Places Sorted by Percent of Total Population
Based on all places, regardless of total population

Place	Population	%
Urbana (city) Champaign County	25	0.06
Buffalo Grove (village) Lake County	14	0.01
Chicago (city) Cook County	107	<0.01
Abingdon (city) Knox County	0	0.00
Adair (cdp) McDonough County	0	0.00
Addieville (village) Washington County	0	0.00
Addison (village) DuPage County	0	0.00
Adeline (village) Ogle County	0	0.00
Albany (village) Whiteside County	0	0.00
Albers (village) Clinton County	0	0.00

Top 10 Places Sorted by Percent of Total Population
Based on places with total population of 50,000 or more

Place	Population	%
Chicago (city) Cook County	107	<0.01
Arlington Heights (village) Cook County	0	0.00
Aurora (city) Kane County	0	0.00
Berwyn (city) Cook County	0	0.00
Bloomington (city) McLean County	0	0.00
Bolingbrook (village) Will County	0	0.00
Champaign (city) Champaign County	0	0.00
Cicero (town) Cook County	0	0.00
Decatur (city) Macon County	0	0.00
Des Plaines (city) Cook County	0	0.00

Please refer to the Explanation of Data in the front of the book for more detailed information.

African, Sub-Saharan: Other

Top 10 Places Sorted by Population
Based on all places, regardless of total population

Place	Population	%
Chicago (city) Cook County	1,781	0.07
Aurora (city) Kane County	202	0.11
Morton Grove (village) Cook County	146	0.64
Glen Ellyn (village) DuPage County	122	0.45
Moline (city) Rock Island County	117	0.27
Montgomery (village) Kendall County	105	0.66
Champaign (city) Champaign County	87	0.11
Normal (town) McLean County	79	0.15
Bolingbrook (village) Will County	70	0.10
Hanover Park (village) Cook County	69	0.18

Top 10 Places Sorted by Percent of Total Population
Based on all places, regardless of total population

Place	Population	%
Beardstown (city) Cass County	56	0.93
Gainesville (village) Lake County	27	0.81
Montgomery (village) Kendall County	105	0.66
Morton Grove (village) Cook County	146	0.64
Glen Ellyn (village) DuPage County	122	0.45
Shiloh (village) St. Clair County	46	0.38
Barrington Hills (village) Cook County	15	0.36
Homewood (village) Cook County	54	0.28
Moline (city) Rock Island County	117	0.27
Hanover Park (village) Cook County	69	0.18

Top 10 Places Sorted by Percent of Total Population
Based on places with total population of 50,000 or more

Place	Population	%
Normal (town) McLean County	79	0.15
Aurora (city) Kane County	202	0.11
Champaign (city) Champaign County	87	0.11
Bolingbrook (village) Will County	70	0.10
Chicago (city) Cook County	1,781	0.07
Evanston (city) Cook County	47	0.06
Bloomington (city) McLean County	23	0.03
Naperville (city) DuPage County	22	0.02
Arlington Heights (village) Cook County	12	0.02
Mount Prospect (village) Cook County	10	0.02

Albanian

Top 10 Places Sorted by Population
Based on all places, regardless of total population

Place	Population	%
Chicago (city) Cook County	1,699	0.06
Addison (village) DuPage County	526	1.43
Aurora (city) Kane County	467	0.25
Willow Springs (village) Cook County	258	4.83
Des Plaines (city) Cook County	234	0.41
Wheaton (city) DuPage County	212	0.40
Cortland (town) DeKalb County	186	4.89
Arlington Heights (village) Cook County	176	0.23
Lombard (village) DuPage County	173	0.40
Orland Park (village) Cook County	170	0.31

Top 10 Places Sorted by Percent of Total Population
Based on all places, regardless of total population

Place	Population	%
Forreston (village) Ogle County	91	5.86
Cortland (town) DeKalb County	186	4.89
Willow Springs (village) Cook County	258	4.83
Vergennes (village) Jackson County	7	1.87
Henry (city) Marshall County	42	1.70
Cedarville (village) Stephenson County	15	1.69
Rossville (village) Vermilion County	21	1.66
Addison (village) DuPage County	526	1.43
Wadsworth (village) Lake County	54	1.40
Gridley (village) McLean County	20	1.32

Top 10 Places Sorted by Percent of Total Population
Based on places with total population of 50,000 or more

Place	Population	%
Des Plaines (city) Cook County	234	0.41
Wheaton (city) DuPage County	212	0.40
Orland Park (village) Cook County	170	0.31
Aurora (city) Kane County	467	0.25

Arlington Heights (village) Cook County	176	0.23
Skokie (village) Cook County	135	0.21
Mount Prospect (village) Cook County	95	0.18
Hoffman Estates (village) Cook County	65	0.13
Palatine (village) Cook County	67	0.10
Oak Lawn (village) Cook County	52	0.09

Alsatian

Top 10 Places Sorted by Population
Based on all places, regardless of total population

Place	Population	%
Chicago (city) Cook County	96	<0.01
Naperville (city) DuPage County	59	0.04
Elk Grove Village (village) Cook County	54	0.16
Jacksonville (city) Morgan County	40	0.21
Oak Park (village) Cook County	40	0.08
Mount Prospect (village) Cook County	29	0.05
Maywood (village) Cook County	20	0.08
Downers Grove (village) DuPage County	16	0.03
Northbrook (village) Cook County	15	0.05
Aurora (city) Kane County	15	0.01

Top 10 Places Sorted by Percent of Total Population
Based on all places, regardless of total population

Place	Population	%
Apple Canyon Lake (cdp) Jo Daviess County	6	1.07
Congerville (village) Woodford County	5	0.90
Murrayville (village) Morgan County	3	0.50
Somonauk (village) DeKalb County	9	0.45
Pecatonica (village) Winnebago County	9	0.36
Beecher (village) Will County	14	0.30
Jacksonville (city) Morgan County	40	0.21
Elk Grove Village (village) Cook County	54	0.16
Aledo (city) Mercer County	6	0.16
Gages Lake (cdp) Lake County	11	0.11

Top 10 Places Sorted by Percent of Total Population
Based on places with total population of 50,000 or more

Place	Population	%
Oak Park (village) Cook County	40	0.08
Mount Prospect (village) Cook County	29	0.05
Naperville (city) DuPage County	59	0.04
Normal (town) McLean County	13	0.03
Arlington Heights (village) Cook County	12	0.02
Aurora (city) Kane County	15	0.01
Joliet (city) Will County	15	0.01
Peoria (city) Peoria County	13	0.01
Palatine (village) Cook County	9	0.01
Bloomington (city) McLean County	8	0.01

American

Top 10 Places Sorted by Population
Based on all places, regardless of total population

Place	Population	%
Chicago (city) Cook County	34,496	1.28
Rockford (city) Winnebago County	12,203	7.90
Decatur (city) Macon County	11,484	15.03
Springfield (city) Sangamon County	9,384	8.15
Champaign (city) Champaign County	8,172	10.29
Bloomington (city) McLean County	8,005	10.69
Pekin (city) Tazewell County	5,931	17.58
Danville (city) Vermilion County	5,369	16.15
Peoria (city) Peoria County	4,712	4.14
Quincy (city) Adams County	4,580	11.31

Top 10 Places Sorted by Percent of Total Population
Based on all places, regardless of total population

Place	Population	%
Boody (cdp) Macon County	163	85.34
Camden (village) Schuyler County	75	78.95
Hollowayville (village) Bureau County	41	68.33
Foosland (village) Champaign County	66	64.08
Middletown (village) Logan County	198	60.55
Alsey (village) Scott County	180	52.94
Littleton (village) Schuyler County	170	52.63
Kenney (village) De Witt County	199	50.64
Kilbourne (village) Mason County	147	50.34
Broadwell (village) Logan County	54	45.38

Top 10 Places Sorted by Percent of Total Population
Based on places with total population of 50,000 or more

Place	Population	%
Decatur (city) Macon County	11,484	15.03
Bloomington (city) McLean County	8,005	10.69
Champaign (city) Champaign County	8,172	10.29
Normal (town) McLean County	4,384	8.49
Springfield (city) Sangamon County	9,384	8.15
Rockford (city) Winnebago County	12,203	7.90
Peoria (city) Peoria County	4,712	4.14
Skokie (village) Cook County	2,241	3.51
Arlington Heights (village) Cook County	2,097	2.80
Evanston (city) Cook County	2,009	2.72

Arab: Total

Top 10 Places Sorted by Population
Based on all places, regardless of total population

Place	Population	%
Chicago (city) Cook County	16,946	0.63
Oak Lawn (village) Cook County	2,764	4.95
Orland Park (village) Cook County	2,393	4.34
Bridgeview (village) Cook County	2,010	12.45
Naperville (city) DuPage County	1,759	1.25
Skokie (village) Cook County	1,643	2.57
Chicago Ridge (village) Cook County	1,605	11.35
Hickory Hills (city) Cook County	1,595	11.39
Burbank (city) Cook County	1,558	5.48
Palos Hills (city) Cook County	1,536	8.84

Top 10 Places Sorted by Percent of Total Population
Based on all places, regardless of total population

Place	Population	%
Bridgeview (village) Cook County	2,010	12.45
Hickory Hills (city) Cook County	1,595	11.39
Chicago Ridge (village) Cook County	1,605	11.35
Orland Hills (village) Cook County	796	11.35
Palos Hills (city) Cook County	1,536	8.84
Baldwin (village) Randolph County	32	8.82
Garden Prairie (village) Boone County	15	8.11
Rutland (village) LaSalle County	26	7.54
Burbank (city) Cook County	1,558	5.48
Justice (village) Cook County	671	5.31

Top 10 Places Sorted by Percent of Total Population
Based on places with total population of 50,000 or more

Place	Population	%
Oak Lawn (village) Cook County	2,764	4.95
Orland Park (village) Cook County	2,393	4.34
Skokie (village) Cook County	1,643	2.57
Tinley Park (village) Cook County	1,358	2.47
Naperville (city) DuPage County	1,759	1.25
Schaumburg (village) Cook County	684	0.93
Peoria (city) Peoria County	1,002	0.88
Chicago (city) Cook County	16,946	0.63
Des Plaines (city) Cook County	354	0.62
Oak Park (village) Cook County	265	0.52

Arab: Arab

Top 10 Places Sorted by Population
Based on all places, regardless of total population

Place	Population	%
Chicago (city) Cook County	4,311	0.16
Oak Lawn (village) Cook County	1,415	2.53
Orland Park (village) Cook County	1,104	2.00
Tinley Park (village) Cook County	902	1.64
Bridgeview (village) Cook County	786	4.87
Chicago Ridge (village) Cook County	766	5.42
Hickory Hills (city) Cook County	727	5.19
Palos Hills (city) Cook County	637	3.67
Burbank (city) Cook County	532	1.87
Lockport (city) Will County	407	1.71

Top 10 Places Sorted by Percent of Total Population
Based on all places, regardless of total population

Place	Population	%
Chicago Ridge (village) Cook County	766	5.42
Hickory Hills (city) Cook County	727	5.19
Orland Hills (village) Cook County	357	5.09

Place	Population	%
Bridgeview (village) Cook County	786	4.87
Noble (village) Richland County	28	4.61
Hardin (village) Calhoun County	48	4.13
Palos Hills (city) Cook County	637	3.67
Monee (village) Will County	160	3.25
Oak Lawn (village) Cook County	1,415	2.53
Justice (village) Cook County	281	2.22

Top 10 Places Sorted by Percent of Total Population
Based on places with total population of 50,000 or more

Place	Population	%
Oak Lawn (village) Cook County	1,415	2.53
Orland Park (village) Cook County	1,104	2.00
Tinley Park (village) Cook County	902	1.64
Rockford (city) Winnebago County	397	0.26
Joliet (city) Will County	331	0.23
Decatur (city) Macon County	152	0.20
Skokie (village) Cook County	128	0.20
Des Plaines (city) Cook County	114	0.20
Naperville (city) DuPage County	266	0.19
Chicago (city) Cook County	4,311	0.16

Arab: Egyptian

Top 10 Places Sorted by Population
Based on all places, regardless of total population

Place	Population	%
Chicago (city) Cook County	1,010	0.04
Justice (village) Cook County	262	2.07
Bridgeview (village) Cook County	224	1.39
Hickory Hills (city) Cook County	209	1.49
Addison (village) DuPage County	167	0.46
Hoffman Estates (village) Cook County	164	0.32
Westmont (village) DuPage County	160	0.65
Naperville (city) DuPage County	157	0.11
Joliet (city) Will County	133	0.09
Woodridge (village) DuPage County	120	0.37

Top 10 Places Sorted by Percent of Total Population
Based on all places, regardless of total population

Place	Population	%
Justice (village) Cook County	262	2.07
Strasburg (village) Shelby County	16	2.06
Hickory Hills (city) Cook County	209	1.49
Bridgeview (village) Cook County	224	1.39
Burr Ridge (village) DuPage County	100	0.95
Oakbrook Terrace (city) DuPage County	18	0.81
New Baden (village) Clinton County	27	0.80
Glen Carbon (village) Madison County	88	0.72
Westmont (village) DuPage County	160	0.65
Harwood Heights (village) Cook County	52	0.61

Top 10 Places Sorted by Percent of Total Population
Based on places with total population of 50,000 or more

Place	Population	%
Hoffman Estates (village) Cook County	164	0.32
Oak Lawn (village) Cook County	88	0.16
Des Plaines (city) Cook County	66	0.12
Naperville (city) DuPage County	157	0.11
Joliet (city) Will County	133	0.09
Champaign (city) Champaign County	65	0.08
Oak Park (village) Cook County	41	0.08
Evanston (city) Cook County	44	0.06
Palatine (village) Cook County	31	0.05
Chicago (city) Cook County	1,010	0.04

Arab: Iraqi

Top 10 Places Sorted by Population
Based on all places, regardless of total population

Place	Population	%
Chicago (city) Cook County	1,592	0.06
Skokie (village) Cook County	898	1.41
Niles (village) Cook County	391	1.33
Schaumburg (village) Cook County	217	0.30
Highland Park (city) Lake County	132	0.44
Rockford (city) Winnebago County	125	0.08
West Chicago (city) DuPage County	91	0.35
Glenview (village) Cook County	82	0.19
Morton Grove (village) Cook County	72	0.31
Danville (city) Vermilion County	66	0.20

Top 10 Places Sorted by Percent of Total Population
Based on all places, regardless of total population

Place	Population	%
Skokie (village) Cook County	898	1.41
Niles (village) Cook County	391	1.33
Highland Park (city) Lake County	132	0.44
Lake Holiday (cdp) LaSalle County	16	0.36
West Chicago (city) DuPage County	91	0.35
Morton Grove (village) Cook County	72	0.31
Schaumburg (village) Cook County	217	0.30
Clarendon Hills (village) DuPage County	17	0.21
Danville (city) Vermilion County	66	0.20
Glenview (village) Cook County	82	0.19

Top 10 Places Sorted by Percent of Total Population
Based on places with total population of 50,000 or more

Place	Population	%
Skokie (village) Cook County	898	1.41
Schaumburg (village) Cook County	217	0.30
Des Plaines (city) Cook County	61	0.11
Rockford (city) Winnebago County	125	0.08
Chicago (city) Cook County	1,592	0.06
Palatine (village) Cook County	42	0.06
Champaign (city) Champaign County	30	0.04
Orland Park (village) Cook County	18	0.03
Evanston (city) Cook County	14	0.02
Oak Park (village) Cook County	10	0.02

Arab: Jordanian

Top 10 Places Sorted by Population
Based on all places, regardless of total population

Place	Population	%
Chicago (city) Cook County	948	0.04
Orland Park (village) Cook County	316	0.57
Bensenville (village) DuPage County	307	1.65
Oak Lawn (village) Cook County	254	0.45
Bridgeview (village) Cook County	225	1.39
Oak Forest (city) Cook County	201	0.73
Hickory Hills (city) Cook County	180	1.29
Park Ridge (city) Cook County	168	0.45
Crestwood (village) Cook County	143	1.31
Chicago Ridge (village) Cook County	130	0.92

Top 10 Places Sorted by Percent of Total Population
Based on all places, regardless of total population

Place	Population	%
Rutland (village) LaSalle County	13	3.77
Pingree Grove (village) Kane County	83	2.20
Bensenville (village) DuPage County	307	1.65
Bridgeview (village) Cook County	225	1.39
Crestwood (village) Cook County	143	1.31
Hickory Hills (city) Cook County	180	1.29
Hainesville (village) Lake County	38	1.14
Chicago Ridge (village) Cook County	130	0.92
Willow Springs (village) Cook County	43	0.80
Oak Forest (city) Cook County	201	0.73

Top 10 Places Sorted by Percent of Total Population
Based on places with total population of 50,000 or more

Place	Population	%
Orland Park (village) Cook County	316	0.57
Oak Lawn (village) Cook County	254	0.45
Tinley Park (village) Cook County	101	0.18
Berwyn (city) Cook County	31	0.06
Chicago (city) Cook County	948	0.04
Naperville (city) DuPage County	42	0.03
Champaign (city) Champaign County	24	0.03
Skokie (village) Cook County	16	0.03
Rockford (city) Winnebago County	27	0.02
Springfield (city) Sangamon County	22	0.02

Arab: Lebanese

Top 10 Places Sorted by Population
Based on all places, regardless of total population

Place	Population	%
Chicago (city) Cook County	1,936	0.07
Peoria (city) Peoria County	874	0.77
Naperville (city) DuPage County	367	0.26

Place	Population	%
Washington (city) Tazewell County	274	1
West Chicago (city) DuPage County	258	1
Western Springs (village) Cook County	251	1
East Peoria (city) Tazewell County	224	1
Skokie (village) Cook County	221	0
Evanston (city) Cook County	178	0
Schaumburg (village) Cook County	177	0

Top 10 Places Sorted by Percent of Total Populati
Based on all places, regardless of total population

Place	Population	
Garden Prairie (village) Boone County	15	8
Millington (village) LaSalle County	44	5
Prestbury (cdp) Kane County	46	2
Western Springs (village) Cook County	251	1
Washington (city) Tazewell County	274	1
Orland Hills (village) Cook County	120	1
Burlington (village) Kane County	9	1
Spring Bay (village) Woodford County	9	1
Homer (village) Champaign County	15	1
Goreville (village) Johnson County	14	1

Top 10 Places Sorted by Percent of Total Populati
Based on places with total population of 50,000 or more

Place	Population	
Peoria (city) Peoria County	874	
Skokie (village) Cook County	221	
Wheaton (city) DuPage County	155	
Naperville (city) DuPage County	367	
Evanston (city) Cook County	178	0
Schaumburg (village) Cook County	177	0
Normal (town) McLean County	95	
Orland Park (village) Cook County	86	
Elgin (city) Kane County	139	
Bolingbrook (village) Will County	84	

Arab: Moroccan

Top 10 Places Sorted by Population
Based on all places, regardless of total population

Place	Population	
Chicago (city) Cook County	1,014	0
Naperville (city) DuPage County	235	0
East Moline (city) Rock Island County	172	0
Oak Lawn (village) Cook County	137	0
Lansing (village) Cook County	123	0
Des Plaines (city) Cook County	100	0
Moline (city) Rock Island County	88	0
Prospect Heights (city) Cook County	85	0
Berwyn (city) Cook County	82	0
Hickory Hills (city) Cook County	69	0

Top 10 Places Sorted by Percent of Total Populatio
Based on all places, regardless of total population

Place	Population	
Merrionette Park (village) Cook County	20	0
East Moline (city) Rock Island County	172	0
Prospect Heights (city) Cook County	85	0
Savoy (village) Champaign County	32	0
Hickory Hills (city) Cook County	69	0
Oak Brook (village) DuPage County	36	0
Lansing (village) Cook County	123	0
Bridgeview (village) Cook County	65	0
Forsyth (village) Macon County	11	0
River Grove (village) Cook County	29	0

Top 10 Places Sorted by Percent of Total Populatie
Based on places with total population of 50,000 or more

Place	Population	
Oak Lawn (village) Cook County	137	0
Naperville (city) DuPage County	235	0
Des Plaines (city) Cook County	100	0
Berwyn (city) Cook County	82	0
Bolingbrook (village) Will County	55	0
Schaumburg (village) Cook County	48	0
Chicago (city) Cook County	1,014	0
Waukegan (city) Lake County	27	0
Evanston (city) Cook County	17	0
Cicero (town) Cook County	14	0

Arab: Palestinian

Top 10 Places Sorted by Population
Based on all places, regardless of total population

Place	Population	%
Chicago (city) Cook County	2,219	0.08
Oak Lawn (village) Cook County	739	1.32
Burbank (city) Cook County	620	2.18
Chicago Ridge (village) Cook County	598	4.23
Orland Park (village) Cook County	563	1.02
Naperville (city) DuPage County	336	0.24
Palos Hills (city) Cook County	330	1.90
Bridgeview (village) Cook County	284	1.76
Hickory Hills (city) Cook County	274	1.96
Worth (village) Cook County	249	2.33

Top 10 Places Sorted by Percent of Total Population
Based on all places, regardless of total population

Place	Population	%
Chicago Ridge (village) Cook County	598	4.23
Rosemont (village) Cook County	117	2.94
Orland Hills (village) Cook County	178	2.54
Worth (village) Cook County	249	2.33
Pingree Grove (village) Kane County	83	2.20
Burbank (city) Cook County	620	2.18
Hickory Hills (city) Cook County	274	1.96
Elkhart (village) Logan County	7	1.92
Palos Hills (city) Cook County	330	1.90
Bridgeview (village) Cook County	284	1.76

Top 10 Places Sorted by Percent of Total Population
Based on places with total population of 50,000 or more

Place	Population	%
Oak Lawn (village) Cook County	739	1.32
Orland Park (village) Cook County	563	1.02
Naperville (city) DuPage County	336	0.24
Tinley Park (village) Cook County	95	0.17
Skokie (village) Cook County	63	0.10
Chicago (city) Cook County	2,219	0.08
Cicero (town) Cook County	55	0.07
Aurora (city) Kane County	115	0.06
Joliet (city) Will County	80	0.06
Mount Prospect (village) Cook County	16	0.03

Arab: Syrian

Top 10 Places Sorted by Population
Based on all places, regardless of total population

Place	Population	%
Chicago (city) Cook County	1,029	0.04
Springfield (city) Sangamon County	235	0.20
Skokie (village) Cook County	158	0.25
South Elgin (village) Kane County	151	0.71
Carol Stream (village) DuPage County	136	0.34
Schiller Park (village) Cook County	108	0.93
Addison (village) DuPage County	108	0.29
Schaumburg (village) Cook County	92	0.13
Elgin (city) Kane County	91	0.09
Naperville (city) DuPage County	89	0.06

Top 10 Places Sorted by Percent of Total Population
Based on all places, regardless of total population

Place	Population	%
Foosland (village) Champaign County	2	1.94
Westville (village) Vermilion County	53	1.66
Cairo (city) Alexander County	43	1.45
Riverwoods (village) Lake County	51	1.30
Winthrop Harbor (village) Lake County	85	1.25
Barrington Hills (village) Cook County	51	1.22
Port Byron (village) Rock Island County	20	1.20
Athens (city) Menard County	23	1.00
Schiller Park (village) Cook County	108	0.93
Cordova (village) Rock Island County	6	0.92

Top 10 Places Sorted by Percent of Total Population
Based on places with total population of 50,000 or more

Place	Population	%
Skokie (village) Cook County	158	0.25
Springfield (city) Sangamon County	235	0.20
Schaumburg (village) Cook County	92	0.13
Bloomington (city) McLean County	83	0.11

Place	Population	%
Orland Park (village) Cook County	55	0.10
Elgin (city) Kane County	91	0.09
Naperville (city) DuPage County	89	0.06
Evanston (city) Cook County	42	0.06
Chicago (city) Cook County	1,029	0.04
Rockford (city) Winnebago County	60	0.04

Arab: Other

Top 10 Places Sorted by Population
Based on all places, regardless of total population

Place	Population	%
Chicago (city) Cook County	2,887	0.11
Palos Hills (city) Cook County	455	2.62
Bridgeview (village) Cook County	426	2.64
Burbank (city) Cook County	339	1.19
Naperville (city) DuPage County	267	0.19
Tinley Park (village) Cook County	231	0.42
Orland Park (village) Cook County	229	0.42
Urbana (city) Champaign County	151	0.37
Orland Hills (village) Cook County	141	2.01
Skokie (village) Cook County	139	0.22

Top 10 Places Sorted by Percent of Total Population
Based on all places, regardless of total population

Place	Population	%
Baldwin (village) Randolph County	32	8.82
Rutland (village) LaSalle County	13	3.77
Bridgeview (village) Cook County	426	2.64
Palos Hills (city) Cook County	455	2.62
Orland Hills (village) Cook County	141	2.01
Vandalia (city) Fayette County	109	1.87
Burbank (city) Cook County	339	1.19
Hickory Hills (city) Cook County	136	0.97
South Barrington (village) Cook County	41	0.94
Hawthorn Woods (village) Lake County	60	0.81

Top 10 Places Sorted by Percent of Total Population
Based on places with total population of 50,000 or more

Place	Population	%
Tinley Park (village) Cook County	231	0.42
Orland Park (village) Cook County	229	0.42
Skokie (village) Cook County	139	0.22
Naperville (city) DuPage County	267	0.19
Oak Lawn (village) Cook County	82	0.15
Oak Park (village) Cook County	78	0.15
Chicago (city) Cook County	2,887	0.11
Springfield (city) Sangamon County	124	0.11
Champaign (city) Champaign County	48	0.06
Schaumburg (village) Cook County	46	0.06

Armenian

Top 10 Places Sorted by Population
Based on all places, regardless of total population

Place	Population	%
Chicago (city) Cook County	1,256	0.05
Skokie (village) Cook County	372	0.58
Wheaton (city) DuPage County	224	0.42
Mount Prospect (village) Cook County	223	0.41
Libertyville (village) Lake County	193	0.94
Norridge (village) Cook County	186	1.29
Evanston (city) Cook County	174	0.24
Waukegan (city) Lake County	172	0.19
Arlington Heights (village) Cook County	156	0.21
Glenview (village) Cook County	153	0.35

Top 10 Places Sorted by Percent of Total Population
Based on all places, regardless of total population

Place	Population	%
Wadsworth (village) Lake County	86	2.23
Indian Creek (village) Lake County	11	2.06
Valmeyer (village) Monroe County	28	1.68
Indian Head Park (village) Cook County	55	1.45
Manhattan (village) Will County	89	1.37
Norridge (village) Cook County	186	1.29
Crete (village) Will County	104	1.23
Hawthorn Woods (village) Lake County	91	1.23
Port Barrington (village) McHenry County	20	1.15
Hampton (village) Rock Island County	20	1.04

Top 10 Places Sorted by Percent of Total Population
Based on places with total population of 50,000 or more

Place	Population	%
Skokie (village) Cook County	372	0.58
Wheaton (city) DuPage County	224	0.42
Mount Prospect (village) Cook County	223	0.41
Evanston (city) Cook County	174	0.24
Arlington Heights (village) Cook County	156	0.21
Waukegan (city) Lake County	172	0.19
Schaumburg (village) Cook County	130	0.18
Hoffman Estates (village) Cook County	89	0.17
Palatine (village) Cook County	82	0.12
Tinley Park (village) Cook County	67	0.12

Assyrian/Chaldean/Syriac

Top 10 Places Sorted by Population
Based on all places, regardless of total population

Place	Population	%
Chicago (city) Cook County	4,646	0.17
Skokie (village) Cook County	3,833	6.01
Niles (village) Cook County	1,483	5.03
Lincolnwood (village) Cook County	905	7.29
Des Plaines (city) Cook County	614	1.07
Morton Grove (village) Cook County	533	2.33
Mount Prospect (village) Cook County	355	0.66
Glenview (village) Cook County	303	0.69
Elgin (city) Kane County	263	0.25
Park Ridge (city) Cook County	255	0.69

Top 10 Places Sorted by Percent of Total Population
Based on all places, regardless of total population

Place	Population	%
Lincolnwood (village) Cook County	905	7.29
Skokie (village) Cook County	3,833	6.01
Niles (village) Cook County	1,483	5.03
Millington (village) LaSalle County	43	4.90
Georgetown (city) Vermilion County	134	3.84
Morton Grove (village) Cook County	533	2.33
Sleepy Hollow (village) Kane County	40	1.17
Venetian Village (cdp) Lake County	33	1.08
Des Plaines (city) Cook County	614	1.07
Johnsburg (village) McHenry County	64	1.02

Top 10 Places Sorted by Percent of Total Population
Based on places with total population of 50,000 or more

Place	Population	%
Skokie (village) Cook County	3,833	6.01
Des Plaines (city) Cook County	614	1.07
Mount Prospect (village) Cook County	355	0.66
Elgin (city) Kane County	263	0.25
Bolingbrook (village) Will County	172	0.24
Hoffman Estates (village) Cook County	114	0.22
Chicago (city) Cook County	4,646	0.17
Wheaton (city) DuPage County	50	0.09
Schaumburg (village) Cook County	59	0.08
Arlington Heights (village) Cook County	58	0.08

Australian

Top 10 Places Sorted by Population
Based on all places, regardless of total population

Place	Population	%
Chicago (city) Cook County	561	0.02
Shiloh (village) St. Clair County	250	2.08
Naperville (city) DuPage County	114	0.08
Lake Forest (city) Lake County	65	0.34
Des Plaines (city) Cook County	57	0.10
Troy (city) Madison County	54	0.55
Park Ridge (city) Cook County	48	0.13
Monticello (city) Piatt County	45	0.87
Decatur (city) Macon County	45	0.06
Schaumburg (village) Cook County	42	0.06

Top 10 Places Sorted by Percent of Total Population
Based on all places, regardless of total population

Place	Population	%
Cooksville (village) McLean County	6	3.95
Shiloh (village) St. Clair County	250	2.08
Beaverville (village) Iroquois County	8	1.97

Place	Population	%
Bannockburn (village) Lake County	17	1.24
Roodhouse (city) Greene County	23	1.18
Pleasant Plains (village) Sangamon County	10	1.11
New Baden (village) Clinton County	34	1.01
Lake Ka-Ho (village) Macoupin County	2	0.93
Brimfield (village) Peoria County	8	0.88
Monticello (city) Piatt County	45	0.87

Top 10 Places Sorted by Percent of Total Population
Based on places with total population of 50,000 or more

Place	Population	%
Des Plaines (city) Cook County	57	0.10
Naperville (city) DuPage County	114	0.08
Decatur (city) Macon County	45	0.06
Schaumburg (village) Cook County	42	0.06
Palatine (village) Cook County	38	0.06
Wheaton (city) DuPage County	34	0.06
Evanston (city) Cook County	35	0.05
Orland Park (village) Cook County	15	0.03
Chicago (city) Cook County	561	0.02
Champaign (city) Champaign County	15	0.02

Austrian

Top 10 Places Sorted by Population
Based on all places, regardless of total population

Place	Population	%
Chicago (city) Cook County	7,125	0.26
Arlington Heights (village) Cook County	732	0.98
Naperville (city) DuPage County	666	0.47
Tinley Park (village) Cook County	566	1.03
Evanston (city) Cook County	528	0.71
St. Charles (city) Kane County	426	1.32
Oak Lawn (village) Cook County	411	0.74
Glenview (village) Cook County	406	0.93
Aurora (city) Kane County	389	0.20
Orland Park (village) Cook County	387	0.70

Top 10 Places Sorted by Percent of Total Population
Based on all places, regardless of total population

Place	Population	%
Ripley (village) Brown County	3	5.36
Hennepin (village) Putnam County	27	3.74
Merrionette Park (village) Cook County	81	3.60
North City (village) Franklin County	26	3.31
Gilberts (village) Kane County	192	3.27
Eldred (village) Greene County	3	3.23
Channel Lake (cdp) Lake County	57	3.18
Twin Grove (cdp) McLean County	45	3.13
Hardin (village) Calhoun County	35	3.01
Deer Grove (village) Whiteside County	2	2.56

Top 10 Places Sorted by Percent of Total Population
Based on places with total population of 50,000 or more

Place	Population	%
Tinley Park (village) Cook County	566	1.03
Arlington Heights (village) Cook County	732	0.98
Oak Lawn (village) Cook County	411	0.74
Evanston (city) Cook County	528	0.71
Orland Park (village) Cook County	387	0.70
Mount Prospect (village) Cook County	361	0.67
Wheaton (city) DuPage County	313	0.59
Palatine (village) Cook County	362	0.54
Des Plaines (city) Cook County	295	0.51
Naperville (city) DuPage County	666	0.47

Basque

Top 10 Places Sorted by Population
Based on all places, regardless of total population

Place	Population	%
Chicago (city) Cook County	259	0.01
Elgin (city) Kane County	58	0.05
Libertyville (village) Lake County	41	0.20
Mundelein (village) Lake County	31	0.10
Oswego (village) Kendall County	28	0.10
Cary (village) McHenry County	25	0.14
Urbana (city) Champaign County	20	0.05
Evanston (city) Cook County	14	0.02
Belleville (city) St. Clair County	13	0.03
Glen Ellyn (village) DuPage County	10	0.04

Top 10 Places Sorted by Percent of Total Population
Based on all places, regardless of total population

Place	Population	%
Cortland (town) DeKalb County	8	0.21
Libertyville (village) Lake County	41	0.20
Cary (village) McHenry County	25	0.14
Mundelein (village) Lake County	31	0.10
Oswego (village) Kendall County	28	0.10
Riverwoods (village) Lake County	4	0.10
Elgin (city) Kane County	58	0.05
Urbana (city) Champaign County	20	0.05
Glen Ellyn (village) DuPage County	10	0.04
Belleville (city) St. Clair County	13	0.03

Top 10 Places Sorted by Percent of Total Population
Based on places with total population of 50,000 or more

Place	Population	%
Elgin (city) Kane County	58	0.05
Evanston (city) Cook County	14	0.02
Chicago (city) Cook County	259	0.01
Rockford (city) Winnebago County	1	<0.01
Arlington Heights (village) Cook County	0	0.00
Aurora (city) Kane County	0	0.00
Berwyn (city) Cook County	0	0.00
Bloomington (city) McLean County	0	0.00
Bolingbrook (village) Will County	0	0.00
Champaign (city) Champaign County	0	0.00

Belgian

Top 10 Places Sorted by Population
Based on all places, regardless of total population

Place	Population	%
Moline (city) Rock Island County	2,722	6.28
Chicago (city) Cook County	2,597	0.10
Rock Island (city) Rock Island County	1,408	3.63
East Moline (city) Rock Island County	816	3.82
Geneseo (city) Henry County	628	9.70
Kewanee (city) Henry County	560	4.30
Peoria (city) Peoria County	465	0.41
Naperville (city) DuPage County	443	0.31
Silvis (city) Rock Island County	433	5.82
Evanston (city) Cook County	369	0.50

Top 10 Places Sorted by Percent of Total Population
Based on all places, regardless of total population

Place	Population	%
Atkinson (town) Henry County	248	26.41
Annawan (town) Henry County	214	22.86
Geneseo (city) Henry County	628	9.70
Mineral (village) Bureau County	21	8.79
Coyne Center (cdp) Rock Island County	63	8.74
Cleveland (village) Henry County	14	8.70
Sheffield (village) Bureau County	84	8.55
Coal Valley (village) Rock Island County	284	8.22
Orion (village) Henry County	145	7.74
Hillsdale (village) Rock Island County	37	7.37

Top 10 Places Sorted by Percent of Total Population
Based on places with total population of 50,000 or more

Place	Population	%
Evanston (city) Cook County	369	0.50
Peoria (city) Peoria County	465	0.41
Wheaton (city) DuPage County	213	0.40
Schaumburg (village) Cook County	241	0.33
Naperville (city) DuPage County	443	0.31
Normal (town) McLean County	162	0.31
Springfield (city) Sangamon County	289	0.25
Waukegan (city) Lake County	219	0.25
Bloomington (city) McLean County	185	0.25
Arlington Heights (village) Cook County	173	0.23

Brazilian

Top 10 Places Sorted by Population
Based on all places, regardless of total population

Place	Population	%
Chicago (city) Cook County	1,439	0.05
Naperville (city) DuPage County	313	0.22
Champaign (city) Champaign County	239	0.30

Place	Population	%
Bensenville (village) DuPage County	227	1.22
Aurora (city) Kane County	186	0.10
Woodstock (city) McHenry County	178	0.73
Harwood Heights (village) Cook County	169	2.00
Carol Stream (village) DuPage County	161	0.41
Peoria (city) Peoria County	144	0.13
Crestwood (village) Cook County	128	1.17

Top 10 Places Sorted by Percent of Total Population
Based on all places, regardless of total population

Place	Population	%
Elsah (village) Jersey County	14	2.53
Harwood Heights (village) Cook County	169	2.00
Bensenville (village) DuPage County	227	1.22
Crestwood (village) Cook County	128	1.17
Fisher (village) Champaign County	23	1.17
Highwood (city) Lake County	49	0.90
Long Creek (village) Macon County	11	0.81
Lyons (village) Cook County	82	0.78
Woodstock (city) McHenry County	178	0.73
Carol Stream (village) DuPage County	161	0.41

Top 10 Places Sorted by Percent of Total Population
Based on places with total population of 50,000 or more

Place	Population	%
Champaign (city) Champaign County	239	0.30
Naperville (city) DuPage County	313	0.22
Evanston (city) Cook County	118	0.16
Peoria (city) Peoria County	144	0.13
Palatine (village) Cook County	91	0.13
Aurora (city) Kane County	186	0.10
Arlington Heights (village) Cook County	57	0.08
Bolingbrook (village) Will County	44	0.06
Mount Prospect (village) Cook County	30	0.06
Chicago (city) Cook County	1,439	0.05

British

Top 10 Places Sorted by Population
Based on all places, regardless of total population

Place	Population	%
Chicago (city) Cook County	5,392	0.20
Naperville (city) DuPage County	1,104	0.78
Evanston (city) Cook County	732	0.99
Elmhurst (city) DuPage County	637	1.46
Aurora (city) Kane County	619	0.33
Wheaton (city) DuPage County	601	1.13
Champaign (city) Champaign County	501	0.63
Arlington Heights (village) Cook County	459	0.61
Downers Grove (village) DuPage County	414	0.86
Oak Park (village) Cook County	385	0.75

Top 10 Places Sorted by Percent of Total Population
Based on all places, regardless of total population

Place	Population	%
Hume (village) Edgar County	25	4.77
Clarendon Hills (village) DuPage County	373	4.51
McCook (village) Cook County	16	4.38
LaPlace (cdp) Piatt County	9	4.17
Kaneville (village) Kane County	15	4.09
Banner (village) Fulton County	5	3.70
Hartsburg (village) Logan County	8	2.72
Grandview (village) Sangamon County	37	2.50
Flora (city) Clay County	124	2.44
Omaha (village) Gallatin County	8	2.43

Top 10 Places Sorted by Percent of Total Population
Based on places with total population of 50,000 or more

Place	Population	%
Wheaton (city) DuPage County	601	1.13
Evanston (city) Cook County	732	0.99
Naperville (city) DuPage County	1,104	0.78
Oak Park (village) Cook County	385	0.75
Champaign (city) Champaign County	501	0.63
Arlington Heights (village) Cook County	459	0.61
Bloomington (city) McLean County	380	0.45
Schaumburg (village) Cook County	332	0.45
Bolingbrook (village) Will County	262	0.36
Palatine (village) Cook County	242	0.36

Bulgarian

Top 10 Places Sorted by Population
Based on all places, regardless of total population

Place	Population	%
Chicago (city) Cook County	3,223	0.12
Mount Prospect (village) Cook County	926	1.72
Arlington Heights (village) Cook County	754	1.01
Des Plaines (city) Cook County	389	0.68
Wheeling (village) Cook County	351	0.95
Schiller Park (village) Cook County	318	2.73
Palatine (village) Cook County	267	0.40
Rolling Meadows (city) Cook County	246	1.04
Glendale Heights (village) DuPage County	212	0.63
Schaumburg (village) Cook County	207	0.28

Top 10 Places Sorted by Percent of Total Population
Based on all places, regardless of total population

Place	Population	%
Bishop Hill (village) Henry County	6	5.66
Forest Lake (cdp) Lake County	63	3.47
Rosemont (village) Cook County	131	3.29
Hanna City (village) Peoria County	37	2.82
Schiller Park (village) Cook County	318	2.73
Knollwood (cdp) Lake County	38	2.27
Willowbrook (village) DuPage County	162	1.90
Mount Prospect (village) Cook County	926	1.72
Harwood Heights (village) Cook County	121	1.43
Sleepy Hollow (village) Kane County	48	1.41

Top 10 Places Sorted by Percent of Total Population
Based on places with total population of 50,000 or more

Place	Population	%
Mount Prospect (village) Cook County	926	1.72
Arlington Heights (village) Cook County	754	1.01
Des Plaines (city) Cook County	389	0.68
Palatine (village) Cook County	267	0.40
Skokie (village) Cook County	205	0.32
Schaumburg (village) Cook County	207	0.28
Chicago (city) Cook County	3,223	0.12
Bolingbrook (village) Will County	90	0.12
Evanston (city) Cook County	84	0.11
Oak Park (village) Cook County	50	0.10

Cajun

Top 10 Places Sorted by Population
Based on all places, regardless of total population

Place	Population	%
Chicago (city) Cook County	99	<0.01
Fairfield (city) Wayne County	56	0.99
Machesney Park (village) Winnebago County	35	0.15
North Aurora (village) Kane County	32	0.20
Danville (city) Vermilion County	32	0.10
Rolling Meadows (city) Cook County	27	0.11
Schaumburg (village) Cook County	24	0.03
Paris (city) Edgar County	15	0.17
Kewanee (city) Henry County	15	0.12
Harvard (city) McHenry County	14	0.16

Top 10 Places Sorted by Percent of Total Population
Based on all places, regardless of total population

Place	Population	%
Ludlow (village) Champaign County	7	1.57
Fairfield (city) Wayne County	56	0.99
Sadorus (village) Champaign County	2	0.37
North Aurora (village) Kane County	32	0.20
Peoria Heights (village) Peoria County	12	0.19
Paris (city) Edgar County	15	0.17
Maryville (village) Madison County	12	0.17
Harvard (city) McHenry County	14	0.16
Machesney Park (village) Winnebago County	35	0.15
Sandwich (city) DeKalb County	10	0.13

Top 10 Places Sorted by Percent of Total Population
Based on places with total population of 50,000 or more

Place	Population	%
Schaumburg (village) Cook County	24	0.03
Des Plaines (city) Cook County	11	0.02
Naperville (city) DuPage County	14	0.01
Chicago (city) Cook County	99	<0.01

Place	Population	%
Arlington Heights (village) Cook County	0	0.00
Aurora (city) Kane County	0	0.00
Berwyn (city) Cook County	0	0.00
Bloomington (city) McLean County	0	0.00
Bolingbrook (village) Will County	0	0.00
Champaign (city) Champaign County	0	0.00

Canadian

Top 10 Places Sorted by Population
Based on all places, regardless of total population

Place	Population	%
Chicago (city) Cook County	2,179	0.08
Naperville (city) DuPage County	734	0.52
Aurora (city) Kane County	357	0.19
Bolingbrook (village) Will County	193	0.27
Hanover Park (village) Cook County	189	0.50
Crystal Lake (city) McHenry County	177	0.43
Evanston (city) Cook County	169	0.23
Highland Park (city) Lake County	166	0.55
Huntley (village) McHenry County	157	0.74
Oak Park (village) Cook County	153	0.30

Top 10 Places Sorted by Percent of Total Population
Based on all places, regardless of total population

Place	Population	%
Simpson (village) Johnson County	2	8.70
Garden Prairie (village) Boone County	10	5.41
St. Anne (village) Kankakee County	63	5.04
Kappa (village) Woodford County	11	3.64
Plainville (village) Adams County	11	3.50
Grafton (city) Jersey County	23	3.09
New Burnside (village) Johnson County	7	2.70
Christopher (city) Franklin County	65	2.45
Forest Lake (cdp) Lake County	44	2.43
Hindsboro (village) Douglas County	8	2.23

Top 10 Places Sorted by Percent of Total Population
Based on places with total population of 50,000 or more

Place	Population	%
Naperville (city) DuPage County	734	0.52
Oak Park (village) Cook County	153	0.30
Bolingbrook (village) Will County	193	0.27
Evanston (city) Cook County	169	0.23
Des Plaines (city) Cook County	121	0.21
Aurora (city) Kane County	357	0.19
Palatine (village) Cook County	131	0.19
Champaign (city) Champaign County	137	0.17
Schaumburg (village) Cook County	125	0.17
Decatur (city) Macon County	125	0.16

Carpatho Rusyn

Top 10 Places Sorted by Population
Based on all places, regardless of total population

Place	Population	%
Chicago (city) Cook County	25	<0.01
Batavia (city) Kane County	14	0.05
Romeoville (village) Will County	13	0.03
South Barrington (village) Cook County	12	0.27
Flossmoor (village) Cook County	10	0.11
Addison (village) DuPage County	5	0.01
Abingdon (city) Knox County	0	0.00
Adair (cdp) McDonough County	0	0.00
Addieville (village) Washington County	0	0.00
Adeline (village) Ogle County	0	0.00

Top 10 Places Sorted by Percent of Total Population
Based on all places, regardless of total population

Place	Population	%
South Barrington (village) Cook County	12	0.27
Flossmoor (village) Cook County	10	0.11
Batavia (city) Kane County	14	0.05
Romeoville (village) Will County	13	0.03
Addison (village) DuPage County	5	0.01
Chicago (city) Cook County	25	<0.01
Abingdon (city) Knox County	0	0.00
Adair (cdp) McDonough County	0	0.00
Addieville (village) Washington County	0	0.00
Adeline (village) Ogle County	0	0.00

Top 10 Places Sorted by Percent of Total Population
Based on places with total population of 50,000 or more

Place	Population	%
Chicago (city) Cook County	25	<0.01
Arlington Heights (village) Cook County	0	0.00
Aurora (city) Kane County	0	0.00
Berwyn (city) Cook County	0	0.00
Bloomington (city) McLean County	0	0.00
Bolingbrook (village) Will County	0	0.00
Champaign (city) Champaign County	0	0.00
Cicero (town) Cook County	0	0.00
Decatur (city) Macon County	0	0.00
Des Plaines (city) Cook County	0	0.00

Celtic

Top 10 Places Sorted by Population
Based on all places, regardless of total population

Place	Population	%
Chicago (city) Cook County	155	0.01
Chatham (village) Sangamon County	42	0.38
Tinley Park (village) Cook County	42	0.08
Antioch (village) Lake County	29	0.21
Joliet (city) Will County	27	0.02
Geneva (city) Kane County	26	0.12
Wilmette (village) Cook County	26	0.10
Tuscola (city) Douglas County	25	0.59
Machesney Park (village) Winnebago County	21	0.09
Jacksonville (city) Morgan County	20	0.10

Top 10 Places Sorted by Percent of Total Population
Based on all places, regardless of total population

Place	Population	%
Nelson (village) Lee County	3	1.42
Stewardson (village) Shelby County	6	0.87
Hull (village) Pike County	3	0.74
Tuscola (city) Douglas County	25	0.59
Lerna (village) Coles County	2	0.48
Chatham (village) Sangamon County	42	0.38
Sullivan (city) Moultrie County	16	0.37
Coal Valley (village) Rock Island County	11	0.32
Smithton (village) St. Clair County	11	0.32
Athens (city) Menard County	7	0.31

Top 10 Places Sorted by Percent of Total Population
Based on places with total population of 50,000 or more

Place	Population	%
Tinley Park (village) Cook County	42	0.08
Joliet (city) Will County	27	0.02
Waukegan (city) Lake County	17	0.02
Bloomington (city) McLean County	15	0.02
Cicero (town) Cook County	14	0.02
Oak Lawn (village) Cook County	11	0.02
Chicago (city) Cook County	155	0.01
Peoria (city) Peoria County	12	0.01
Naperville (city) DuPage County	9	0.01
Champaign (city) Champaign County	6	0.01

Croatian

Top 10 Places Sorted by Population
Based on all places, regardless of total population

Place	Population	%
Chicago (city) Cook County	7,104	0.26
Joliet (city) Will County	1,196	0.82
Naperville (city) DuPage County	1,020	0.72
Orland Park (village) Cook County	840	1.52
Oak Lawn (village) Cook County	577	1.03
Lansing (village) Cook County	471	1.68
Channahon (village) Will County	446	3.65
Downers Grove (village) DuPage County	446	0.93
New Lenox (village) Will County	407	1.70
Tinley Park (village) Cook County	394	0.72

Top 10 Places Sorted by Percent of Total Population
Based on all places, regardless of total population

Place	Population	%
McCook (village) Cook County	66	18.08
Gilson (cdp) Knox County	9	9.09
White City (village) Macoupin County	18	7.26

Place		Population	%
Wilsonville (village) Macoupin County		35	6.89
Essex (village) Kankakee County		38	6.53
Ellisville (village) Fulton County		6	6.32
St. David (village) Fulton County		31	6.08
Hometown (city) Cook County		237	5.48
Nason (city) Jefferson County		10	5.35
Sawyerville (village) Macoupin County		14	5.32

Top 10 Places Sorted by Percent of Total Population
Based on places with total population of 50,000 or more

Place	Population	%
Orland Park (village) Cook County	840	1.52
Oak Lawn (village) Cook County	577	1.03
Joliet (city) Will County	1,196	0.82
Naperville (city) DuPage County	1,020	0.72
Tinley Park (village) Cook County	394	0.72
Des Plaines (city) Cook County	351	0.61
Mount Prospect (village) Cook County	301	0.56
Skokie (village) Cook County	337	0.53
Arlington Heights (village) Cook County	323	0.43
Berwyn (city) Cook County	231	0.42

Cypriot

Top 10 Places Sorted by Population
Based on all places, regardless of total population

Place	Population	%
Chicago (city) Cook County	122	<0.01
Carbondale (city) Jackson County	15	0.06
Marseilles (city) LaSalle County	14	0.27
Oak Park (village) Cook County	12	0.02
Highland Park (city) Lake County	8	0.03
Abingdon (city) Knox County	0	0.00
Adair (cdp) McDonough County	0	0.00
Addieville (village) Washington County	0	0.00
Addison (village) DuPage County	0	0.00
Adeline (village) Ogle County	0	0.00

Top 10 Places Sorted by Percent of Total Population
Based on all places, regardless of total population

Place	Population	%
Marseilles (city) LaSalle County	14	0.27
Carbondale (city) Jackson County	15	0.06
Highland Park (city) Lake County	8	0.03
Oak Park (village) Cook County	12	0.02
Chicago (city) Cook County	122	<0.01
Abingdon (city) Knox County	0	0.00
Adair (cdp) McDonough County	0	0.00
Addieville (village) Washington County	0	0.00
Addison (village) DuPage County	0	0.00
Adeline (village) Ogle County	0	0.00

Top 10 Places Sorted by Percent of Total Population
Based on places with total population of 50,000 or more

Place	Population	%
Oak Park (village) Cook County	12	0.02
Chicago (city) Cook County	122	<0.01
Arlington Heights (village) Cook County	0	0.00
Aurora (city) Kane County	0	0.00
Berwyn (city) Cook County	0	0.00
Bloomington (city) McLean County	0	0.00
Bolingbrook (village) Will County	0	0.00
Champaign (city) Champaign County	0	0.00
Cicero (town) Cook County	0	0.00
Decatur (city) Macon County	0	0.00

Czech

Top 10 Places Sorted by Population
Based on all places, regardless of total population

Place	Population	%
Chicago (city) Cook County	12,642	0.47
Naperville (city) DuPage County	3,566	2.53
Downers Grove (village) DuPage County	2,278	4.75
Berwyn (city) Cook County	1,864	3.35
Brookfield (village) Cook County	1,651	8.78
Joliet (city) Will County	1,474	1.02
Aurora (city) Kane County	1,429	0.75
Tinley Park (village) Cook County	1,409	2.56
Darien (city) DuPage County	1,274	5.75
Arlington Heights (village) Cook County	1,161	1.55

Top 10 Places Sorted by Percent of Total Population
Based on all places, regardless of total population

Place	Population	%
Forest View (village) Cook County	174	20.86
Verona (village) Grundy County	28	11.43
North Riverside (village) Cook County	738	11.08
Nora (village) Jo Daviess County	10	10.42
Lily Lake (village) Kane County	93	9.54
Brookfield (village) Cook County	1,651	8.78
Riverside (village) Cook County	725	8.30
Stickney (village) Cook County	510	7.72
La Grange Park (village) Cook County	966	7.22
Indian Head Park (village) Cook County	273	7.19

Top 10 Places Sorted by Percent of Total Population
Based on places with total population of 50,000 or more

Place	Population	%
Berwyn (city) Cook County	1,864	3.35
Tinley Park (village) Cook County	1,409	2.56
Naperville (city) DuPage County	3,566	2.53
Orland Park (village) Cook County	1,159	2.10
Oak Lawn (village) Cook County	1,005	1.80
Oak Park (village) Cook County	895	1.74
Schaumburg (village) Cook County	1,159	1.58
Arlington Heights (village) Cook County	1,161	1.55
Mount Prospect (village) Cook County	831	1.54
Bolingbrook (village) Will County	1,080	1.49

Czechoslovakian

Top 10 Places Sorted by Population
Based on all places, regardless of total population

Place	Population	%
Chicago (city) Cook County	2,450	0.09
Berwyn (city) Cook County	346	0.62
Downers Grove (village) DuPage County	291	0.61
Naperville (city) DuPage County	266	0.19
Aurora (city) Kane County	244	0.13
Westchester (village) Cook County	213	1.29
Darien (city) DuPage County	198	0.89
Geneva (city) Kane County	190	0.89
Springfield (city) Sangamon County	183	0.16
Woodridge (village) DuPage County	176	0.54

Top 10 Places Sorted by Percent of Total Population
Based on all places, regardless of total population

Place	Population	%
Irvington (village) Washington County	54	8.91
Sawyerville (village) Macoupin County	20	7.60
Williamson (village) Madison County	8	3.21
Oakbrook Terrace (city) DuPage County	56	2.52
Versailles (village) Brown County	9	2.18
Lily Lake (village) Kane County	21	2.15
Stickney (village) Cook County	141	2.13
Crystal Lawns (cdp) Will County	38	1.90
Elsah (village) Jersey County	10	1.81
New Boston (city) Mercer County	13	1.77

Top 10 Places Sorted by Percent of Total Population
Based on places with total population of 50,000 or more

Place	Population	%
Berwyn (city) Cook County	346	0.62
Wheaton (city) DuPage County	172	0.32
Orland Park (village) Cook County	149	0.27
Oak Lawn (village) Cook County	145	0.26
Naperville (city) DuPage County	266	0.19
Tinley Park (village) Cook County	104	0.19
Springfield (city) Sangamon County	183	0.16
Champaign (city) Champaign County	126	0.16
Arlington Heights (village) Cook County	117	0.16
Des Plaines (city) Cook County	92	0.16

Danish

Top 10 Places Sorted by Population
Based on all places, regardless of total population

Place	Population	%
Chicago (city) Cook County	5,565	0.21
Rockford (city) Winnebago County	1,067	0.69
Naperville (city) DuPage County	1,049	0.74

Place	Population	%
Palatine (village) Cook County	722	1.0
Aurora (city) Kane County	707	0.3
Arlington Heights (village) Cook County	645	0.8
Wheaton (city) DuPage County	538	1.0
Downers Grove (village) DuPage County	482	1.0
Elgin (city) Kane County	477	0.4
Joliet (city) Will County	464	0.3

Top 10 Places Sorted by Percent of Total Population
Based on all places, regardless of total population

Place	Population	%
Chemung (cdp) McHenry County	35	15.5
Georgetown (cdp) McDonough County	61	12.1
Standard (village) Putnam County	23	9.3
Kinsman (village) Grundy County	13	9.1
Gardner (village) Grundy County	86	7.1
Campus (village) Livingston County	8	5.7
East Brooklyn (village) Grundy County	6	5.6
Dwight (village) Livingston County	213	5.0
Long Lake (cdp) Lake County	136	4.4
Mineral (village) Bureau County	10	4.1

Top 10 Places Sorted by Percent of Total Population
Based on places with total population of 50,000 or more

Place	Population	%
Palatine (village) Cook County	722	1.0
Wheaton (city) DuPage County	538	1.0
Arlington Heights (village) Cook County	645	0.8
Naperville (city) DuPage County	1,049	0.7
Rockford (city) Winnebago County	1,067	0.6
Orland Park (village) Cook County	373	0.6
Hoffman Estates (village) Cook County	344	0.6
Mount Prospect (village) Cook County	314	0.5
Normal (town) McLean County	289	0.5
Oak Lawn (village) Cook County	284	0.5

Dutch

Top 10 Places Sorted by Population
Based on all places, regardless of total population

Place	Population	%
Chicago (city) Cook County	14,116	0.5
Lansing (village) Cook County	2,662	9.5
Rockford (city) Winnebago County	2,584	1.6
Naperville (city) DuPage County	2,210	1.5
Aurora (city) Kane County	1,799	0.9
Peoria (city) Peoria County	1,746	1.5
Springfield (city) Sangamon County	1,655	1.4
Tinley Park (village) Cook County	1,517	2.7
Orland Park (village) Cook County	1,504	2.7
Downers Grove (village) DuPage County	1,495	3.1

Top 10 Places Sorted by Percent of Total Population
Based on all places, regardless of total population

Place	Population	%
Fulton (city) Whiteside County	1,189	33.2
Morrison (city) Whiteside County	777	19.5
Deer Grove (village) Whiteside County	15	19.2
Sammons Point (village) Kankakee County	47	18.6
Liverpool (village) Fulton County	13	18.0
Rockwood (village) Randolph County	9	16.6
Lima (village) Adams County	33	16.2
Bay View Gardens (village) Woodford County	61	15.8
Annapolis (cdp) Crawford County	9	15.0
Eddyville (village) Pope County	13	14.9

Top 10 Places Sorted by Percent of Total Population
Based on places with total population of 50,000 or more

Place	Population	%
Tinley Park (village) Cook County	1,517	2.7
Orland Park (village) Cook County	1,504	2.7
Wheaton (city) DuPage County	1,202	2.2
Oak Lawn (village) Cook County	1,045	1.8
Normal (town) McLean County	932	1.8
Bloomington (city) McLean County	1,285	1.7
Rockford (city) Winnebago County	2,584	1.6
Oak Park (village) Cook County	842	1.6
Decatur (city) Macon County	1,233	1.6
Naperville (city) DuPage County	2,210	1.5

Eastern European

Top 10 Places Sorted by Population
Based on all places, regardless of total population

Place	Population	%
Chicago (city) Cook County	5,967	0.22
Highland Park (city) Lake County	980	3.26
Evanston (city) Cook County	854	1.16
Deerfield (village) Lake County	618	3.36
Glenview (village) Cook County	596	1.37
Skokie (village) Cook County	592	0.93
Northbrook (village) Cook County	578	1.76
Buffalo Grove (village) Lake County	577	1.38
Wilmette (village) Cook County	349	1.30
Oak Park (village) Cook County	328	0.64

Top 10 Places Sorted by Percent of Total Population
Based on all places, regardless of total population

Place	Population	%
Deerfield (village) Lake County	618	3.36
Highland Park (city) Lake County	980	3.26
Bull Valley (village) McHenry County	35	3.03
Glencoe (village) Cook County	201	2.33
Lincolnshire (village) Lake County	162	2.29
Riverwoods (village) Lake County	89	2.27
Holiday Hills (village) McHenry County	13	1.93
Indian Creek (village) Lake County	10	1.88
Northbrook (village) Cook County	578	1.76
Long Grove (village) Lake County	128	1.63

Top 10 Places Sorted by Percent of Total Population
Based on places with total population of 50,000 or more

Place	Population	%
Evanston (city) Cook County	854	1.16
Skokie (village) Cook County	592	0.93
Oak Park (village) Cook County	328	0.64
Palatine (village) Cook County	194	0.29
Chicago (city) Cook County	5,967	0.22
Arlington Heights (village) Cook County	161	0.21
Naperville (city) DuPage County	278	0.20
Champaign (city) Champaign County	162	0.20
Aurora (city) Kane County	297	0.16
Coffman Estates (village) Cook County	74	0.14

English

Top 10 Places Sorted by Population
Based on all places, regardless of total population

Place	Population	%
Chicago (city) Cook County	64,585	2.39
Springfield (city) Sangamon County	13,247	11.51
Naperville (city) DuPage County	12,476	8.86
Rockford (city) Winnebago County	10,118	6.55
Peoria (city) Peoria County	10,009	8.79
Aurora (city) Kane County	9,343	4.91
Bloomington (city) McLean County	8,376	11.19
Decatur (city) Macon County	7,427	9.72
Wheaton (city) DuPage County	6,664	12.54
Joliet (city) Will County	6,635	4.58

Top 10 Places Sorted by Percent of Total Population
Based on all places, regardless of total population

Place	Population	%
Time (village) Pike County	5	50.00
Golden Gate (village) Wayne County	27	43.55
LaPlace (cdp) Piatt County	85	39.35
Sciota (village) McDonough County	14	36.84
Redmon (village) Edgar County	65	34.39
Powell (village) Jackson County	105	33.76
Wellington (village) Iroquois County	71	33.18
Freeman Spur (village) Williamson County	86	31.50
Bush (village) Williamson County	77	31.17
Whiteash (village) Williamson County	89	31.01

Top 10 Places Sorted by Percent of Total Population
Based on places with total population of 50,000 or more

Place	Population	%
Wheaton (city) DuPage County	6,664	12.54
Springfield (city) Sangamon County	13,247	11.51
Bloomington (city) McLean County	8,376	11.19
Oak Park (village) Cook County	5,023	9.77

Decatur (city) Macon County	7,427	9.72
Normal (town) McLean County	4,945	9.58
Naperville (city) DuPage County	12,476	8.86
Peoria (city) Peoria County	10,009	8.79
Evanston (city) Cook County	6,226	8.43
Champaign (city) Champaign County	6,475	8.15

Estonian

Top 10 Places Sorted by Population
Based on all places, regardless of total population

Place	Population	%
Chicago (city) Cook County	202	0.01
Evanston (city) Cook County	73	0.10
La Grange (village) Cook County	50	0.32
Bloomingdale (village) DuPage County	36	0.16
Northbrook (village) Cook County	34	0.10
Arlington Heights (village) Cook County	34	0.05
Vernon Hills (village) Lake County	31	0.13
Cicero (town) Cook County	27	0.03
Rockford (city) Winnebago County	25	0.02
Peru (city) LaSalle County	24	0.23

Top 10 Places Sorted by Percent of Total Population
Based on all places, regardless of total population

Place	Population	%
Third Lake (village) Lake County	15	1.00
Hanover (village) Jo Daviess County	4	0.46
La Grange (village) Cook County	50	0.32
Peoria Heights (village) Peoria County	17	0.27
Harvard (city) McHenry County	22	0.26
Peru (city) LaSalle County	24	0.23
Summit (village) Cook County	21	0.19
Bloomingdale (village) DuPage County	36	0.16
Lakemoor (village) Lake County	8	0.14
Vernon Hills (village) Lake County	31	0.13

Top 10 Places Sorted by Percent of Total Population
Based on places with total population of 50,000 or more

Place	Population	%
Evanston (city) Cook County	73	0.10
Arlington Heights (village) Cook County	34	0.05
Cicero (town) Cook County	27	0.03
Oak Lawn (village) Cook County	15	0.03
Rockford (city) Winnebago County	25	0.02
Champaign (city) Champaign County	17	0.02
Schaumburg (village) Cook County	17	0.02
Berwyn (city) Cook County	12	0.02
Bloomington (city) McLean County	12	0.02
Des Plaines (city) Cook County	10	0.02

European

Top 10 Places Sorted by Population
Based on all places, regardless of total population

Place	Population	%
Chicago (city) Cook County	17,169	0.64
Naperville (city) DuPage County	2,659	1.89
Champaign (city) Champaign County	2,373	2.99
Belleville (city) St. Clair County	2,261	5.15
Evanston (city) Cook County	1,549	2.10
Aurora (city) Kane County	1,374	0.72
Wheaton (city) DuPage County	1,145	2.15
Cahokia (village) St. Clair County	1,138	7.39
Peoria (city) Peoria County	1,028	0.90
Arlington Heights (village) Cook County	982	1.31

Top 10 Places Sorted by Percent of Total Population
Based on all places, regardless of total population

Place	Population	%
Bentley (town) Hancock County	10	52.63
Sauget (village) St. Clair County	38	15.64
LaPlace (cdp) Piatt County	33	15.28
Madison (city) Madison County	540	12.33
Union Hill (village) Kankakee County	7	12.28
Huey (village) Clinton County	17	9.88
Concord (village) Morgan County	9	8.49
Tolono (village) Champaign County	287	7.94
Beckemeyer (village) Clinton County	85	7.60
Cahokia (village) St. Clair County	1,138	7.39

Top 10 Places Sorted by Percent of Total Population
Based on places with total population of 50,000 or more

Place	Population	%
Champaign (city) Champaign County	2,373	2.99
Wheaton (city) DuPage County	1,145	2.15
Evanston (city) Cook County	1,549	2.10
Naperville (city) DuPage County	2,659	1.89
Oak Park (village) Cook County	789	1.53
Arlington Heights (village) Cook County	982	1.31
Bloomington (city) McLean County	905	1.21
Normal (town) McLean County	494	0.96
Peoria (city) Peoria County	1,028	0.90
Skokie (village) Cook County	570	0.89

Finnish

Top 10 Places Sorted by Population
Based on all places, regardless of total population

Place	Population	%
Chicago (city) Cook County	2,609	0.10
Waukegan (city) Lake County	886	0.99
Beach Park (village) Lake County	421	3.16
Naperville (city) DuPage County	379	0.27
Rockford (city) Winnebago County	336	0.22
Streamwood (village) Cook County	317	0.81
Zion (city) Lake County	293	1.20
Buffalo Grove (village) Lake County	278	0.66
Glenview (village) Cook County	208	0.48
DeKalb (city) DeKalb County	197	0.45

Top 10 Places Sorted by Percent of Total Population
Based on all places, regardless of total population

Place	Population	%
Cornell (village) Livingston County	27	5.14
Liberty (village) Adams County	24	4.75
Mitchell (cdp) Madison County	46	4.17
Maple Park (village) Kane County	51	3.46
Beach Park (village) Lake County	421	3.16
Arlington (village) Bureau County	6	3.14
Wadsworth (village) Lake County	115	2.98
Elsah (village) Jersey County	14	2.53
Knollwood (cdp) Lake County	37	2.21
Venetian Village (cdp) Lake County	67	2.19

Top 10 Places Sorted by Percent of Total Population
Based on places with total population of 50,000 or more

Place	Population	%
Waukegan (city) Lake County	886	0.99
Oak Park (village) Cook County	174	0.34
Naperville (city) DuPage County	379	0.27
Bolingbrook (village) Will County	196	0.27
Wheaton (city) DuPage County	145	0.27
Rockford (city) Winnebago County	336	0.22
Palatine (village) Cook County	144	0.21
Arlington Heights (village) Cook County	153	0.20
Schaumburg (village) Cook County	144	0.20
Des Plaines (city) Cook County	110	0.19

French, except Basque

Top 10 Places Sorted by Population
Based on all places, regardless of total population

Place	Population	%
Chicago (city) Cook County	25,053	0.93
Peoria (city) Peoria County	3,579	3.14
Naperville (city) DuPage County	3,333	2.37
Rockford (city) Winnebago County	3,268	2.11
Springfield (city) Sangamon County	3,255	2.83
Aurora (city) Kane County	2,674	1.40
Elgin (city) Kane County	2,594	2.43
Joliet (city) Will County	2,385	1.64
Bradley (village) Kankakee County	2,150	13.97
Belleville (city) St. Clair County	1,893	4.31

Top 10 Places Sorted by Percent of Total Population
Based on all places, regardless of total population

Place	Population	%
Martinton (village) Iroquois County	100	27.40
Beaverville (village) Iroquois County	104	25.55
Papineau (village) Iroquois County	38	24.36

Place	Population	%
Ashkum (village) Iroquois County	123	21.77
Prairie du Rocher (village) Randolph County	105	21.17
Sawyerville (village) Macoupin County	54	20.53
North City (village) Franklin County	155	19.72
Chebanse (village) Iroquois County	237	19.04
St. Anne (village) Kankakee County	228	18.24
Clifton (village) Iroquois County	263	17.65

Top 10 Places Sorted by Percent of Total Population
Based on places with total population of 50,000 or more

Place	Population	%
Peoria (city) Peoria County	3,579	3.14
Wheaton (city) DuPage County	1,566	2.95
Oak Park (village) Cook County	1,472	2.86
Springfield (city) Sangamon County	3,255	2.83
Evanston (city) Cook County	1,878	2.54
Normal (town) McLean County	1,299	2.52
Elgin (city) Kane County	2,594	2.43
Bloomington (city) McLean County	1,815	2.42
Naperville (city) DuPage County	3,333	2.37
Tinley Park (village) Cook County	1,228	2.24

French Canadian

Top 10 Places Sorted by Population
Based on all places, regardless of total population

Place	Population	%
Chicago (city) Cook County	4,592	0.17
Naperville (city) DuPage County	768	0.55
Aurora (city) Kane County	565	0.30
Peoria (city) Peoria County	515	0.45
Rockford (city) Winnebago County	485	0.31
Oak Park (village) Cook County	365	0.71
Bradley (village) Kankakee County	343	2.23
Hoffman Estates (village) Cook County	328	0.64
Crystal Lake (city) McHenry County	304	0.74
Joliet (city) Will County	304	0.21

Top 10 Places Sorted by Percent of Total Population
Based on all places, regardless of total population

Place	Population	%
Eddyville (village) Pope County	20	22.99
St. Augustine (village) Knox County	7	7.29
Beaverville (village) Iroquois County	26	6.39
Aroma Park (village) Kankakee County	46	5.65
Sammons Point (village) Kankakee County	13	5.16
Irwin (village) Kankakee County	4	4.82
St. Anne (village) Kankakee County	46	3.68
Naplate (village) LaSalle County	22	3.52
Ferris (village) Hancock County	5	3.38
Bryant (village) Fulton County	8	3.24

Top 10 Places Sorted by Percent of Total Population
Based on places with total population of 50,000 or more

Place	Population	%
Oak Park (village) Cook County	365	0.71
Hoffman Estates (village) Cook County	328	0.64
Wheaton (city) DuPage County	302	0.57
Naperville (city) DuPage County	768	0.55
Peoria (city) Peoria County	515	0.45
Oak Lawn (village) Cook County	252	0.45
Evanston (city) Cook County	286	0.39
Tinley Park (village) Cook County	193	0.35
Schaumburg (village) Cook County	232	0.32
Rockford (city) Winnebago County	485	0.31

German

Top 10 Places Sorted by Population
Based on all places, regardless of total population

Place	Population	%
Chicago (city) Cook County	205,863	7.61
Naperville (city) DuPage County	32,930	23.38
Aurora (city) Kane County	31,118	16.34
Springfield (city) Sangamon County	30,854	26.80
Rockford (city) Winnebago County	29,971	19.40
Peoria (city) Peoria County	26,263	23.07
Joliet (city) Will County	23,053	15.90
Bloomington (city) McLean County	20,952	27.99
Elgin (city) Kane County	20,264	18.97
Arlington Heights (village) Cook County	20,088	26.80

Top 10 Places Sorted by Percent of Total Population
Based on all places, regardless of total population

Place	Population	%
Paderborn (cdp) St. Clair County	59	100.00
Time (village) Pike County	10	100.00
La Prairie (village) Adams County	16	84.21
Maeystown (village) Monroe County	228	82.01
Bartelso (village) Clinton County	473	77.80
Germantown (village) Clinton County	899	77.37
Venedy (village) Washington County	89	76.72
St. Libory (village) St. Clair County	335	75.62
Ruma (village) Randolph County	219	73.00
Belle Prairie City (town) Hamilton County	74	70.48

Top 10 Places Sorted by Percent of Total Population
Based on places with total population of 50,000 or more

Place	Population	%
Normal (town) McLean County	16,582	32.13
Bloomington (city) McLean County	20,952	27.99
Wheaton (city) DuPage County	14,873	27.99
Springfield (city) Sangamon County	30,854	26.80
Arlington Heights (village) Cook County	20,088	26.80
Naperville (city) DuPage County	32,930	23.38
Schaumburg (village) Cook County	16,982	23.16
Peoria (city) Peoria County	26,263	23.07
Tinley Park (village) Cook County	12,421	22.61
Mount Prospect (village) Cook County	11,827	21.97

German Russian

Top 10 Places Sorted by Population
Based on all places, regardless of total population

Place	Population	%
Chicago (city) Cook County	106	<0.01
Rockford (city) Winnebago County	68	0.04
Evanston (city) Cook County	62	0.08
Boulder Hill (cdp) Kendall County	40	0.46
Matteson (village) Cook County	33	0.19
Flossmoor (village) Cook County	30	0.33
Joliet (city) Will County	29	0.02
Zion (city) Lake County	23	0.09
Gurnee (village) Lake County	22	0.07
Kankakee (city) Kankakee County	21	0.08

Top 10 Places Sorted by Percent of Total Population
Based on all places, regardless of total population

Place	Population	%
Boulder Hill (cdp) Kendall County	40	0.46
Flossmoor (village) Cook County	30	0.33
Matteson (village) Cook County	33	0.19
Princeton (city) Bureau County	12	0.15
Eureka (city) Woodford County	6	0.11
Gages Lake (cdp) Lake County	10	0.10
Zion (city) Lake County	23	0.09
Evanston (city) Cook County	62	0.08
Kankakee (city) Kankakee County	21	0.08
Gurnee (village) Lake County	22	0.07

Top 10 Places Sorted by Percent of Total Population
Based on places with total population of 50,000 or more

Place	Population	%
Evanston (city) Cook County	62	0.08
Rockford (city) Winnebago County	68	0.04
Joliet (city) Will County	29	0.02
Bloomington (city) McLean County	11	0.01
Springfield (city) Sangamon County	11	0.01
Chicago (city) Cook County	106	<0.01
Aurora (city) Kane County	6	<0.01
Arlington Heights (village) Cook County	0	0.00
Berwyn (city) Cook County	0	0.00
Bolingbrook (village) Will County	0	0.00

Greek

Top 10 Places Sorted by Population
Based on all places, regardless of total population

Place	Population	%
Chicago (city) Cook County	17,672	0.65
Naperville (city) DuPage County	1,872	1.33
Orland Park (village) Cook County	1,744	3.17

Place	Population	%
Skokie (village) Cook County	1,666	2
Arlington Heights (village) Cook County	1,599	2
Des Plaines (city) Cook County	1,559	2
Glenview (village) Cook County	1,332	2
Schaumburg (village) Cook County	1,317	2
Mount Prospect (village) Cook County	1,303	2
Palos Hills (city) Cook County	1,289	7

Top 10 Places Sorted by Percent of Total Populati
Based on all places, regardless of total population

Place	Population	%
South Barrington (village) Cook County	403	9
Inverness (village) Cook County	591	8
Lincolnwood (village) Cook County	964	7
Palos Hills (city) Cook County	1,289	7
Bedford Park (village) Cook County	34	5
Bannockburn (village) Lake County	77	5
Norridge (village) Cook County	719	4
Morton Grove (village) Cook County	1,109	4
Deer Park (village) Lake County	153	4
Forest View (village) Cook County	38	4

Top 10 Places Sorted by Percent of Total Populatic
Based on places with total population of 50,000 or more

Place	Population	%
Orland Park (village) Cook County	1,744	3
Des Plaines (city) Cook County	1,559	2
Skokie (village) Cook County	1,666	2
Mount Prospect (village) Cook County	1,303	2
Arlington Heights (village) Cook County	1,599	2
Oak Lawn (village) Cook County	1,162	2
Tinley Park (village) Cook County	1,065	1
Schaumburg (village) Cook County	1,317	1
Hoffman Estates (village) Cook County	863	1
Naperville (city) DuPage County	1,872	1

Guyanese

Top 10 Places Sorted by Population
Based on all places, regardless of total population

Place	Population	
Chicago (city) Cook County	272	0
Naperville (city) DuPage County	116	0
Downers Grove (village) DuPage County	82	0
Elmhurst (city) DuPage County	79	0
North Chicago (city) Lake County	50	0
Skokie (village) Cook County	43	0
Schaumburg (village) Cook County	41	0
Peoria (city) Peoria County	22	0
Crest Hill (city) Will County	21	0
Aurora (city) Kane County	20	0

Top 10 Places Sorted by Percent of Total Populatic
Based on all places, regardless of total population

Place	Population	
St. Joseph (village) Champaign County	18	0
Westville (village) Vermilion County	12	0
Henry (city) Marshall County	5	0
Elmhurst (city) DuPage County	79	0
Downers Grove (village) DuPage County	82	0
North Chicago (city) Lake County	50	0
Hazel Crest (village) Cook County	17	0
Richton Park (village) Cook County	14	0
Crest Hill (city) Will County	21	0
Naperville (city) DuPage County	116	0

Top 10 Places Sorted by Percent of Total Populatic
Based on places with total population of 50,000 or more

Place	Population	
Naperville (city) DuPage County	116	0
Skokie (village) Cook County	43	0
Schaumburg (village) Cook County	41	0
Peoria (city) Peoria County	22	0
Oak Lawn (village) Cook County	11	0
Oak Park (village) Cook County	11	0
Chicago (city) Cook County	272	0
Aurora (city) Kane County	20	0
Joliet (city) Will County	19	0
Wheaton (city) DuPage County	7	0

Please refer to the Explanation of Data in the front of the book for more detailed information.

Hungarian

Top 10 Places Sorted by Population
Based on all places, regardless of total population

Place	Population	%
Chicago (city) Cook County	8,760	0.32
Aurora (city) Kane County	924	0.49
Naperville (city) DuPage County	798	0.57
Joliet (city) Will County	782	0.54
Skokie (village) Cook County	668	1.05
Schaumburg (village) Cook County	631	0.86
Evanston (city) Cook County	576	0.78
Elgin (city) Kane County	544	0.51
Glenview (village) Cook County	514	1.18
Buffalo Grove (village) Lake County	499	1.19

Top 10 Places Sorted by Percent of Total Population
Based on all places, regardless of total population

Place	Population	%
Leaf River (village) Ogle County	33	8.57
Mount Clare (village) Macoupin County	66	6.15
Holiday Shores (cdp) Madison County	137	5.60
Buckley (village) Iroquois County	28	5.47
Lake Catherine (cdp) Lake County	51	4.70
Stillman Valley (village) Ogle County	51	4.64
Jeffersonville (village) Wayne County	22	4.58
Leland (village) LaSalle County	35	4.50
Grand Detour (cdp) Ogle County	20	4.33
Dowell (village) Jackson County	13	4.18

Top 10 Places Sorted by Percent of Total Population
Based on places with total population of 50,000 or more

Place	Population	%
Skokie (village) Cook County	668	1.05
Schaumburg (village) Cook County	631	0.86
Evanston (city) Cook County	576	0.78
Oak Lawn (village) Cook County	438	0.78
Orland Park (village) Cook County	364	0.66
Mount Prospect (village) Cook County	353	0.66
Wheaton (city) DuPage County	342	0.64
Arlington Heights (village) Cook County	475	0.63
Bolingbrook (village) Will County	443	0.61
Palatine (village) Cook County	400	0.59

Icelander

Top 10 Places Sorted by Population
Based on all places, regardless of total population

Place	Population	%
Chicago (city) Cook County	207	0.01
Urbana (city) Champaign County	105	0.26
Niles (village) Cook County	78	0.26
New Lenox (village) Will County	55	0.23
Belleville (city) St. Clair County	54	0.12
Olney (city) Richland County	40	0.46
Lake Zurich (village) Lake County	34	0.17
Joliet (city) Will County	34	0.02
Naperville (city) DuPage County	31	0.02
Park Forest (village) Cook County	24	0.11

Top 10 Places Sorted by Percent of Total Population
Based on all places, regardless of total population

Place	Population	%
Channel Lake (cdp) Lake County	13	0.73
Olney (city) Richland County	40	0.46
Spring Grove (village) McHenry County	23	0.44
Lakemoor (village) Lake County	22	0.38
Rochester (village) Sangamon County	12	0.33
Northfield (village) Cook County	17	0.31
Riverwoods (village) Lake County	12	0.31
Urbana (city) Champaign County	105	0.26
Niles (village) Cook County	78	0.26
New Lenox (village) Will County	55	0.23

Top 10 Places Sorted by Percent of Total Population
Based on places with total population of 50,000 or more

Place	Population	%
Waukegan (city) Lake County	23	0.03
Wheaton (city) DuPage County	16	0.03
Joliet (city) Will County	34	0.02
Naperville (city) DuPage County	31	0.02

Place	Population	%
Elgin (city) Kane County	18	0.02
Arlington Heights (village) Cook County	15	0.02
Des Plaines (city) Cook County	14	0.02
Orland Park (village) Cook County	10	0.02
Mount Prospect (village) Cook County	9	0.02
Chicago (city) Cook County	207	0.01

Iranian

Top 10 Places Sorted by Population
Based on all places, regardless of total population

Place	Population	%
Chicago (city) Cook County	2,222	0.08
Naperville (city) DuPage County	510	0.36
Skokie (village) Cook County	294	0.46
Hoffman Estates (village) Cook County	293	0.57
Glenview (village) Cook County	261	0.60
Oak Brook (village) DuPage County	244	3.09
Schaumburg (village) Cook County	224	0.31
Northbrook (village) Cook County	207	0.63
Aurora (city) Kane County	188	0.10
DeKalb (city) DeKalb County	173	0.39

Top 10 Places Sorted by Percent of Total Population
Based on all places, regardless of total population

Place	Population	%
Golf (village) Cook County	58	9.78
Lomax (village) Henderson County	17	3.46
Bannockburn (village) Lake County	47	3.43
Oak Brook (village) DuPage County	244	3.09
Hinckley (village) DeKalb County	36	1.67
Highwood (city) Lake County	79	1.45
Oak Run (cdp) Knox County	6	1.29
Wadsworth (village) Lake County	47	1.22
Tuscola (city) Douglas County	44	1.04
River Forest (village) Cook County	102	0.91

Top 10 Places Sorted by Percent of Total Population
Based on places with total population of 50,000 or more

Place	Population	%
Hoffman Estates (village) Cook County	293	0.57
Skokie (village) Cook County	294	0.46
Naperville (city) DuPage County	510	0.36
Schaumburg (village) Cook County	224	0.31
Champaign (city) Champaign County	149	0.19
Bolingbrook (village) Will County	122	0.17
Mount Prospect (village) Cook County	82	0.15
Arlington Heights (village) Cook County	106	0.14
Oak Park (village) Cook County	74	0.14
Evanston (city) Cook County	86	0.12

Irish

Top 10 Places Sorted by Population
Based on all places, regardless of total population

Place	Population	%
Chicago (city) Cook County	201,693	7.46
Naperville (city) DuPage County	25,848	18.35
Joliet (city) Will County	21,088	14.54
Aurora (city) Kane County	18,380	9.65
Rockford (city) Winnebago County	16,387	10.61
Springfield (city) Sangamon County	16,364	14.21
Peoria (city) Peoria County	15,136	13.29
Orland Park (village) Cook County	14,774	26.81
Arlington Heights (village) Cook County	14,141	18.86
Oak Lawn (village) Cook County	14,106	25.27

Top 10 Places Sorted by Percent of Total Population
Based on all places, regardless of total population

Place	Population	%
El Dara (village) Pike County	88	70.97
Phillipstown (village) White County	43	55.84
Lynnville (village) Morgan County	70	53.03
Maunie (village) White County	71	51.82
Reddick (village) Kankakee County	132	50.38
Browning (village) Schuyler County	65	45.14
Strawn (village) Livingston County	58	43.61
Campus (village) Livingston County	61	43.57
Menominee (village) Jo Daviess County	71	39.89
Symerton (village) Will County	37	39.36

Top 10 Places Sorted by Percent of Total Population
Based on places with total population of 50,000 or more

Place	Population	%
Orland Park (village) Cook County	14,774	26.81
Oak Lawn (village) Cook County	14,106	25.27
Tinley Park (village) Cook County	13,718	24.97
Oak Park (village) Cook County	9,760	18.98
Arlington Heights (village) Cook County	14,141	18.86
Naperville (city) DuPage County	25,848	18.35
Wheaton (city) DuPage County	9,656	18.17
Normal (town) McLean County	8,434	16.34
Palatine (village) Cook County	10,714	15.89
Bloomington (city) McLean County	11,242	15.02

Israeli

Top 10 Places Sorted by Population
Based on all places, regardless of total population

Place	Population	%
Chicago (city) Cook County	1,411	0.05
Skokie (village) Cook County	497	0.78
Homer Glen (village) Will County	241	0.97
Highland Park (city) Lake County	143	0.48
Evanston (city) Cook County	129	0.17
Oak Lawn (village) Cook County	122	0.22
Northbrook (village) Cook County	118	0.36
Lincolnwood (village) Cook County	75	0.60
Arlington Heights (village) Cook County	74	0.10
Urbana (city) Champaign County	73	0.18

Top 10 Places Sorted by Percent of Total Population
Based on all places, regardless of total population

Place	Population	%
Indian Creek (village) Lake County	15	2.81
Tower Hill (village) Shelby County	8	1.00
Homer Glen (village) Will County	241	0.97
Skokie (village) Cook County	497	0.78
Lincolnshire (village) Lake County	47	0.66
Glencoe (village) Cook County	53	0.61
Lincolnwood (village) Cook County	75	0.60
Savoy (village) Champaign County	36	0.56
Lakewood Shores (cdp) Will County	8	0.55
Bellevue (village) Peoria County	11	0.52

Top 10 Places Sorted by Percent of Total Population
Based on places with total population of 50,000 or more

Place	Population	%
Skokie (village) Cook County	497	0.78
Oak Lawn (village) Cook County	122	0.22
Evanston (city) Cook County	129	0.17
Arlington Heights (village) Cook County	74	0.10
Wheaton (city) DuPage County	53	0.10
Palatine (village) Cook County	45	0.07
Tinley Park (village) Cook County	37	0.07
Champaign (city) Champaign County	51	0.06
Schaumburg (village) Cook County	41	0.06
Chicago (city) Cook County	1,411	0.05

Italian

Top 10 Places Sorted by Population
Based on all places, regardless of total population

Place	Population	%
Chicago (city) Cook County	102,842	3.80
Naperville (city) DuPage County	14,744	10.47
Joliet (city) Will County	13,198	9.10
Rockford (city) Winnebago County	10,137	6.56
Aurora (city) Kane County	9,132	4.80
Arlington Heights (village) Cook County	8,782	11.71
Schaumburg (village) Cook County	8,459	11.54
Orland Park (village) Cook County	7,670	13.92
Springfield (city) Sangamon County	7,362	6.40
Tinley Park (village) Cook County	7,333	13.35

Top 10 Places Sorted by Percent of Total Population
Based on all places, regardless of total population

Place	Population	%
Dalzell (village) Bureau County	236	34.01
Annapolis (cdp) Crawford County	16	26.67
South Wilmington (village) Grundy County	156	26.17

Place	Population	%
Standard (village) Putnam County	64	26.12
Bloomingdale (village) DuPage County	5,683	25.98
Emington (village) Livingston County	28	24.35
Naplate (village) LaSalle County	151	24.16
Norridge (village) Cook County	3,448	23.92
Sawyerville (village) Macoupin County	62	23.57
Elmwood Park (village) Cook County	5,806	23.50

Top 10 Places Sorted by Percent of Total Population
Based on places with total population of 50,000 or more

Place	Population	%
Orland Park (village) Cook County	7,670	13.92
Tinley Park (village) Cook County	7,333	13.35
Arlington Heights (village) Cook County	8,782	11.71
Schaumburg (village) Cook County	8,459	11.54
Oak Lawn (village) Cook County	6,249	11.19
Wheaton (city) DuPage County	5,622	10.58
Naperville (city) DuPage County	14,744	10.47
Palatine (village) Cook County	7,027	10.42
Des Plaines (city) Cook County	5,675	9.89
Mount Prospect (village) Cook County	5,061	9.40

Latvian

Top 10 Places Sorted by Population
Based on all places, regardless of total population

Place	Population	%
Chicago (city) Cook County	1,505	0.06
Naperville (city) DuPage County	283	0.20
Mundelein (village) Lake County	229	0.74
Oak Park (village) Cook County	190	0.37
Northbrook (village) Cook County	183	0.56
Buffalo Grove (village) Lake County	170	0.41
Elk Grove Village (village) Cook County	162	0.49
Skokie (village) Cook County	140	0.22
Elmhurst (city) DuPage County	137	0.31
Aurora (city) Kane County	116	0.06

Top 10 Places Sorted by Percent of Total Population
Based on all places, regardless of total population

Place	Population	%
Big Rock (village) Kane County	36	3.13
Makanda (village) Jackson County	7	1.30
Volo (village) Lake County	23	1.24
German Valley (village) Stephenson County	7	1.05
Lily Lake (village) Kane County	9	0.92
Golf (village) Cook County	5	0.84
Lincolnwood (village) Cook County	101	0.81
Lincolnshire (village) Lake County	57	0.81
Carbon Cliff (village) Rock Island County	17	0.80
Mundelein (village) Lake County	229	0.74

Top 10 Places Sorted by Percent of Total Population
Based on places with total population of 50,000 or more

Place	Population	%
Oak Park (village) Cook County	190	0.37
Skokie (village) Cook County	140	0.22
Naperville (city) DuPage County	283	0.20
Wheaton (city) DuPage County	103	0.19
Evanston (city) Cook County	86	0.12
Palatine (village) Cook County	65	0.10
Hoffman Estates (village) Cook County	50	0.10
Des Plaines (city) Cook County	54	0.09
Chicago (city) Cook County	1,505	0.06
Aurora (city) Kane County	116	0.06

Lithuanian

Top 10 Places Sorted by Population
Based on all places, regardless of total population

Place	Population	%
Chicago (city) Cook County	12,503	0.46
Naperville (city) DuPage County	2,734	1.94
Oak Lawn (village) Cook County	2,267	4.06
Joliet (city) Will County	1,678	1.16
Tinley Park (village) Cook County	1,503	2.74
Orland Park (village) Cook County	1,425	2.59
Woodridge (village) DuPage County	1,229	3.78
Homer Glen (village) Will County	1,167	4.72
Lemont (village) Cook County	1,131	7.38
Palos Hills (city) Cook County	1,012	5.83

Top 10 Places Sorted by Percent of Total Population
Based on all places, regardless of total population

Place	Population	%
Palos Park (village) Cook County	392	8.19
Willow Springs (village) Cook County	416	7.78
Lemont (village) Cook County	1,131	7.38
Indian Head Park (village) Cook County	272	7.17
Olivet (cdp) Vermilion County	29	7.00
Merrionette Park (village) Cook County	138	6.14
Palos Hills (city) Cook County	1,012	5.83
Virgil (village) Kane County	19	5.23
Worth (village) Cook County	540	5.06
Herscher (village) Kankakee County	83	5.02

Top 10 Places Sorted by Percent of Total Population
Based on places with total population of 50,000 or more

Place	Population	%
Oak Lawn (village) Cook County	2,267	4.06
Tinley Park (village) Cook County	1,503	2.74
Orland Park (village) Cook County	1,425	2.59
Naperville (city) DuPage County	2,734	1.94
Wheaton (city) DuPage County	835	1.57
Joliet (city) Will County	1,678	1.16
Hoffman Estates (village) Cook County	461	0.90
Bolingbrook (village) Will County	640	0.88
Skokie (village) Cook County	550	0.86
Springfield (city) Sangamon County	973	0.85

Luxemburger

Top 10 Places Sorted by Population
Based on all places, regardless of total population

Place	Population	%
Chicago (city) Cook County	657	0.02
Aurora (city) Kane County	608	0.32
Des Plaines (city) Cook County	144	0.25
Evanston (city) Cook County	132	0.18
Elmhurst (city) DuPage County	129	0.29
Arlington Heights (village) Cook County	122	0.16
Elgin (city) Kane County	106	0.10
Roselle (village) DuPage County	104	0.46
Naperville (city) DuPage County	92	0.07
Hoffman Estates (village) Cook County	86	0.17

Top 10 Places Sorted by Percent of Total Population
Based on all places, regardless of total population

Place	Population	%
Kaneville (village) Kane County	13	3.54
Prestbury (cdp) Kane County	29	1.60
Rapids City (village) Rock Island County	11	1.33
Cortland (town) DeKalb County	49	1.29
East Dubuque (city) Jo Daviess County	21	1.22
Forest Lake (cdp) Lake County	21	1.16
Holiday Hills (village) McHenry County	7	1.04
Lake Summerset (cdp) Winnebago County	17	0.97
Cuba (city) Fulton County	13	0.94
Winnetka (village) Cook County	79	0.65

Top 10 Places Sorted by Percent of Total Population
Based on places with total population of 50,000 or more

Place	Population	%
Aurora (city) Kane County	608	0.32
Des Plaines (city) Cook County	144	0.25
Evanston (city) Cook County	132	0.18
Hoffman Estates (village) Cook County	86	0.17
Arlington Heights (village) Cook County	122	0.16
Wheaton (city) DuPage County	62	0.12
Palatine (village) Cook County	73	0.11
Elgin (city) Kane County	106	0.10
Schaumburg (village) Cook County	69	0.09
Oak Lawn (village) Cook County	48	0.09

Macedonian

Top 10 Places Sorted by Population
Based on all places, regardless of total population

Place	Population	%
Chicago (city) Cook County	495	0.02
Naperville (city) DuPage County	295	0.21
Skokie (village) Cook County	229	0.36

Place	Population	%
Willowbrook (village) DuPage County	214	2.50
Streamwood (village) Cook County	204	0.52
Darien (city) DuPage County	169	0.76
Granite City (city) Madison County	148	0.49
Woodridge (village) DuPage County	139	0.43
La Grange (village) Cook County	128	0.83
Downers Grove (village) DuPage County	125	0.26

Top 10 Places Sorted by Percent of Total Population
Based on all places, regardless of total population

Place	Population	%
Willowbrook (village) DuPage County	214	2.50
Ashley (city) Washington County	8	1.48
Shannon (village) Carroll County	13	1.42
White City (village) Macoupin County	3	1.21
Third Lake (village) Lake County	15	1.00
Stickney (village) Cook County	64	0.97
Lewistown (city) Fulton County	21	0.94
Countryside (city) Cook County	53	0.91
La Grange (village) Cook County	128	0.83
Fulton (city) Whiteside County	29	0.81

Top 10 Places Sorted by Percent of Total Population
Based on places with total population of 50,000 or more

Place	Population	%
Skokie (village) Cook County	229	0.36
Naperville (city) DuPage County	295	0.21
Orland Park (village) Cook County	75	0.14
Rockford (city) Winnebago County	116	0.08
Palatine (village) Cook County	40	0.06
Waukegan (city) Lake County	49	0.05
Oak Lawn (village) Cook County	24	0.04
Des Plaines (city) Cook County	23	0.04
Cicero (town) Cook County	23	0.03
Evanston (city) Cook County	23	0.03

Maltese

Top 10 Places Sorted by Population
Based on all places, regardless of total population

Place	Population	%
Chicago (city) Cook County	70	<0.01
Naperville (city) DuPage County	64	0.05
Anna (city) Union County	53	1.15
Highland Park (city) Lake County	25	0.08
Champaign (city) Champaign County	24	0.03
St. Charles (city) Kane County	23	0.07
Round Lake (village) Lake County	18	0.11
Galesburg (city) Knox County	15	0.05
Mundelein (village) Lake County	14	0.04
Oak Park (village) Cook County	12	0.02

Top 10 Places Sorted by Percent of Total Population
Based on all places, regardless of total population

Place	Population	%
Anna (city) Union County	53	1.15
Cuba (city) Fulton County	4	0.29
Durand (village) Winnebago County	3	0.21
Pontoon Beach (village) Madison County	9	0.15
Round Lake (village) Lake County	18	0.11
Highland Park (city) Lake County	25	0.08
St. Charles (city) Kane County	23	0.07
Naperville (city) DuPage County	64	0.05
Galesburg (city) Knox County	15	0.05
Mundelein (village) Lake County	14	0.04

Top 10 Places Sorted by Percent of Total Population
Based on places with total population of 50,000 or more

Place	Population	%
Naperville (city) DuPage County	64	0.05
Champaign (city) Champaign County	24	0.03
Oak Park (village) Cook County	12	0.02
Decatur (city) Macon County	11	0.01
Chicago (city) Cook County	70	<0.01
Arlington Heights (village) Cook County	0	0.00
Aurora (city) Kane County	0	0.00
Berwyn (city) Cook County	0	0.00
Bloomington (city) McLean County	0	0.00
Bolingbrook (village) Will County	0	0.00

Please refer to the Explanation of Data in the front of the book for more detailed information.

New Zealander

Top 10 Places Sorted by Population
Based on all places, regardless of total population

Place	Population	%
Chicago (city) Cook County	205	0.01
Bolingbrook (village) Will County	68	0.09
Mount Pulaski (city) Logan County	38	2.38
Lake Summerset (cdp) Winnebago County	21	1.19
Long Grove (village) Lake County	16	0.20
Evanston (city) Cook County	15	0.02
Libertyville (village) Lake County	14	0.07
Rock Island (city) Rock Island County	14	0.04
Taylorville (city) Christian County	13	0.10
Naperville (city) DuPage County	13	0.01

Top 10 Places Sorted by Percent of Total Population
Based on all places, regardless of total population

Place	Population	%
Mount Pulaski (city) Logan County	38	2.38
Lake Summerset (cdp) Winnebago County	21	1.19
Williamsfield (village) Knox County	3	0.49
Long Grove (village) Lake County	16	0.20
Steger (village) Will County	12	0.12
Taylorville (city) Christian County	13	0.10
Bolingbrook (village) Will County	68	0.09
Libertyville (village) Lake County	14	0.07
Hickory Hills (city) Cook County	9	0.06
Morton Grove (village) Cook County	12	0.05

Top 10 Places Sorted by Percent of Total Population
Based on places with total population of 50,000 or more

Place	Population	%
Bolingbrook (village) Will County	68	0.09
Evanston (city) Cook County	15	0.02
Chicago (city) Cook County	205	0.01
Naperville (city) DuPage County	13	0.01
Arlington Heights (village) Cook County	0	0.00
Aurora (city) Kane County	0	0.00
Berwyn (city) Cook County	0	0.00
Bloomington (city) McLean County	0	0.00
Champaign (city) Champaign County	0	0.00
Cicero (town) Cook County	0	0.00

Northern European

Top 10 Places Sorted by Population
Based on all places, regardless of total population

Place	Population	%
Chicago (city) Cook County	1,551	0.06
Evanston (city) Cook County	181	0.24
Wheaton (city) DuPage County	135	0.25
Oak Park (village) Cook County	134	0.26
Springfield (city) Sangamon County	115	0.10
Schaumburg (village) Cook County	90	0.12
Oak Brook (village) DuPage County	85	1.08
Rockford (city) Winnebago County	85	0.06
Lake Forest (city) Lake County	74	0.38
Hoffman Estates (village) Cook County	74	0.14

Top 10 Places Sorted by Percent of Total Population
Based on all places, regardless of total population

Place	Population	%
Millbrook (village) Kendall County	5	2.19
Concord (village) Morgan County	2	1.89
Mettawa (village) Lake County	11	1.84
Kirkwood (village) Warren County	11	1.53
Kenilworth (village) Cook County	35	1.39
Virden (city) Macoupin County	44	1.28
Tower Lakes (village) Lake County	16	1.09
Oak Brook (village) DuPage County	85	1.08
Waterman (village) DeKalb County	15	1.08
Teutopolis (village) Effingham County	17	1.02

Top 10 Places Sorted by Percent of Total Population
Based on places with total population of 50,000 or more

Place	Population	%
Oak Park (village) Cook County	134	0.26
Wheaton (city) DuPage County	135	0.25
Evanston (city) Cook County	181	0.24
Hoffman Estates (village) Cook County	74	0.14

Schaumburg (village) Cook County	90	0.12
Mount Prospect (village) Cook County	61	0.11
Springfield (city) Sangamon County	115	0.10
Chicago (city) Cook County	1,551	0.06
Rockford (city) Winnebago County	85	0.06
Arlington Heights (village) Cook County	48	0.06

Norwegian

Top 10 Places Sorted by Population
Based on all places, regardless of total population

Place	Population	%
Chicago (city) Cook County	14,090	0.52
Rockford (city) Winnebago County	4,532	2.93
Naperville (city) DuPage County	2,831	2.01
Aurora (city) Kane County	2,157	1.13
Joliet (city) Will County	1,862	1.28
Elgin (city) Kane County	1,798	1.68
Evanston (city) Cook County	1,725	2.33
Schaumburg (village) Cook County	1,676	2.29
Arlington Heights (village) Cook County	1,657	2.21
Ottawa (city) LaSalle County	1,807	8.34

Top 10 Places Sorted by Percent of Total Population
Based on all places, regardless of total population

Place	Population	%
Rock Island Arsenal (cdp) Rock Island County	30	38.46
Chemung (cdp) McHenry County	68	30.22
Lisbon (village) Kendall County	87	29.79
Newark (village) Kendall County	184	20.49
Creston (village) Ogle County	143	18.31
Leland (village) LaSalle County	140	18.02
Dana (village) LaSalle County	40	15.56
Kinsman (village) Grundy County	22	15.49
Davis (village) Stephenson County	97	12.11
Orangeville (village) Stephenson County	106	11.90

Top 10 Places Sorted by Percent of Total Population
Based on places with total population of 50,000 or more

Place	Population	%
Wheaton (city) DuPage County	1,598	3.01
Rockford (city) Winnebago County	4,532	2.93
Evanston (city) Cook County	1,725	2.33
Schaumburg (village) Cook County	1,676	2.29
Arlington Heights (village) Cook County	1,657	2.21
Naperville (city) DuPage County	2,831	2.01
Hoffman Estates (village) Cook County	986	1.93
Normal (town) McLean County	988	1.91
Mount Prospect (village) Cook County	983	1.83
Palatine (village) Cook County	1,230	1.82

Pennsylvania German

Top 10 Places Sorted by Population
Based on all places, regardless of total population

Place	Population	%
Chicago (city) Cook County	200	0.01
Rockford (city) Winnebago County	113	0.07
Champaign (city) Champaign County	81	0.10
Springfield (city) Sangamon County	59	0.05
Midlothian (village) Cook County	57	0.39
Sycamore (city) DeKalb County	54	0.32
Decatur (city) Macon County	51	0.07
Freeport (city) Stephenson County	50	0.19
Berwyn (city) Cook County	50	0.09
Lena (village) Stephenson County	46	1.72

Top 10 Places Sorted by Percent of Total Population
Based on all places, regardless of total population

Place	Population	%
Russellville (village) Lawrence County	2	3.85
Hurst (city) Williamson County	23	2.84
Wapella (village) De Witt County	13	2.05
Columbus (village) Adams County	2	1.85
Cedarville (village) Stephenson County	16	1.81
Lena (village) Stephenson County	46	1.72
Buda (village) Bureau County	9	1.68
Westfield (village) Clark County	11	1.61
Milledgeville (village) Carroll County	20	1.58
Muncie (village) Vermilion County	2	1.52

Top 10 Places Sorted by Percent of Total Population
Based on places with total population of 50,000 or more

Place	Population	%
Champaign (city) Champaign County	81	0.10
Berwyn (city) Cook County	50	0.09
Rockford (city) Winnebago County	113	0.07
Decatur (city) Macon County	51	0.07
Normal (town) McLean County	34	0.07
Bloomington (city) McLean County	44	0.06
Springfield (city) Sangamon County	59	0.05
Arlington Heights (village) Cook County	37	0.05
Elgin (city) Kane County	39	0.04
Des Plaines (city) Cook County	19	0.03

Polish

Top 10 Places Sorted by Population
Based on all places, regardless of total population

Place	Population	%
Chicago (city) Cook County	176,295	6.52
Naperville (city) DuPage County	15,623	11.09
Joliet (city) Will County	14,334	9.89
Arlington Heights (village) Cook County	12,420	16.57
Schaumburg (village) Cook County	11,923	16.26
Oak Lawn (village) Cook County	11,843	21.21
Tinley Park (village) Cook County	10,148	18.47
Orland Park (village) Cook County	10,058	18.25
Mount Prospect (village) Cook County	9,709	18.03
Des Plaines (city) Cook County	9,648	16.82

Top 10 Places Sorted by Percent of Total Population
Based on all places, regardless of total population

Place	Population	%
Du Bois (village) Washington County	149	73.04
Radom (village) Washington County	122	59.22
Norridge (village) Cook County	5,070	35.17
Burbank (city) Cook County	9,415	33.12
River Grove (village) Cook County	3,374	33.08
Lemont (village) Cook County	4,685	30.58
Wood Dale (city) DuPage County	4,061	29.69
Pingree Grove (village) Kane County	1,104	29.21
Justice (village) Cook County	3,666	29.02
Hickory Hills (city) Cook County	4,052	28.93

Top 10 Places Sorted by Percent of Total Population
Based on places with total population of 50,000 or more

Place	Population	%
Oak Lawn (village) Cook County	11,843	21.21
Tinley Park (village) Cook County	10,148	18.47
Orland Park (village) Cook County	10,058	18.25
Mount Prospect (village) Cook County	9,709	18.03
Des Plaines (city) Cook County	9,648	16.82
Arlington Heights (village) Cook County	12,420	16.57
Schaumburg (village) Cook County	11,923	16.26
Palatine (village) Cook County	9,622	14.27
Hoffman Estates (village) Cook County	7,198	14.06
Naperville (city) DuPage County	15,623	11.09

Portuguese

Top 10 Places Sorted by Population
Based on all places, regardless of total population

Place	Population	%
Chicago (city) Cook County	1,187	0.04
North Chicago (city) Lake County	294	0.89
Springfield (city) Sangamon County	282	0.24
Aurora (city) Kane County	276	0.14
Jacksonville (city) Morgan County	274	1.41
Cicero (town) Cook County	231	0.28
Joliet (city) Will County	201	0.14
Naperville (city) DuPage County	169	0.12
Bloomington (city) McLean County	132	0.18
Gurnee (village) Lake County	120	0.39

Top 10 Places Sorted by Percent of Total Population
Based on all places, regardless of total population

Place	Population	%
Clear Lake (village) Sangamon County	10	6.67
Woodson (village) Morgan County	30	5.77
Manchester (village) Scott County	19	4.22

Place			
Grand Detour (cdp) Ogle County		17	3.68
Scottville (village) Macoupin County		5	3.52
Venedy (village) Washington County		4	3.45
Murrayville (village) Morgan County		16	2.66
Como (cdp) Whiteside County		15	2.62
Loami (village) Sangamon County		21	2.57
Virginia (city) Cass County		40	2.37

Top 10 Places Sorted by Percent of Total Population
Based on places with total population of 50,000 or more

Place	Population	%
Cicero (town) Cook County	231	0.28
Springfield (city) Sangamon County	282	0.24
Bloomington (city) McLean County	132	0.18
Evanston (city) Cook County	112	0.15
Aurora (city) Kane County	276	0.14
Joliet (city) Will County	201	0.14
Naperville (city) DuPage County	169	0.12
Decatur (city) Macon County	90	0.12
Champaign (city) Champaign County	90	0.11
Arlington Heights (village) Cook County	81	0.11

Romanian

Top 10 Places Sorted by Population
Based on all places, regardless of total population

Place	Population	%
Chicago (city) Cook County	9,121	0.34
Skokie (village) Cook County	1,582	2.48
Aurora (city) Kane County	1,266	0.66
Des Plaines (city) Cook County	867	1.51
Morton Grove (village) Cook County	624	2.73
Lincolnwood (village) Cook County	605	4.87
Arlington Heights (village) Cook County	548	0.73
Highland Park (city) Lake County	530	1.76
Evanston (city) Cook County	499	0.68
Mount Prospect (village) Cook County	474	0.88

Top 10 Places Sorted by Percent of Total Population
Based on all places, regardless of total population

Place	Population	%
Kaneville (village) Kane County	21	5.72
Lincolnwood (village) Cook County	605	4.87
Millbrook (village) Kendall County	11	4.82
Forest Lake (cdp) Lake County	83	4.58
Big Rock (village) Kane County	43	3.74
East Dundee (village) Kane County	90	3.07
Morton Grove (village) Cook County	624	2.73
Topeka (village) Mason County	1	2.63
Knollwood (cdp) Lake County	42	2.51
Skokie (village) Cook County	1,582	2.48

Top 10 Places Sorted by Percent of Total Population
Based on places with total population of 50,000 or more

Place	Population	%
Skokie (village) Cook County	1,582	2.48
Des Plaines (city) Cook County	867	1.51
Mount Prospect (village) Cook County	474	0.88
Arlington Heights (village) Cook County	548	0.73
Evanston (city) Cook County	499	0.68
Aurora (city) Kane County	1,266	0.66
Hoffman Estates (village) Cook County	333	0.65
Oak Lawn (village) Cook County	315	0.56
Oak Park (village) Cook County	248	0.48
Schaumburg (village) Cook County	262	0.36

Russian

Top 10 Places Sorted by Population
Based on all places, regardless of total population

Place	Population	%
Chicago (city) Cook County	28,264	1.05
Buffalo Grove (village) Lake County	6,299	15.05
Highland Park (city) Lake County	6,049	20.11
Skokie (village) Cook County	4,794	7.51
Northbrook (village) Cook County	4,261	12.94
Deerfield (village) Lake County	3,318	18.03
Evanston (city) Cook County	3,244	4.39
Wheeling (village) Cook County	2,904	7.84
Glenview (village) Cook County	2,477	5.67
Vernon Hills (village) Lake County	2,089	8.57

Top 10 Places Sorted by Percent of Total Population
Based on all places, regardless of total population

Place	Population	%
Highland Park (city) Lake County	6,049	20.11
Deerfield (village) Lake County	3,318	18.03
Glencoe (village) Cook County	1,479	17.14
Riverwoods (village) Lake County	651	16.61
Buffalo Grove (village) Lake County	6,299	15.05
Northbrook (village) Cook County	4,261	12.94
Indian Creek (village) Lake County	49	9.19
Long Grove (village) Lake County	704	8.95
Lincolnshire (village) Lake County	610	8.62
Vernon Hills (village) Lake County	2,089	8.57

Top 10 Places Sorted by Percent of Total Population
Based on places with total population of 50,000 or more

Place	Population	%
Skokie (village) Cook County	4,794	7.51
Evanston (city) Cook County	3,244	4.39
Arlington Heights (village) Cook County	1,800	2.40
Oak Park (village) Cook County	1,231	2.39
Palatine (village) Cook County	1,452	2.15
Wheaton (city) DuPage County	986	1.86
Schaumburg (village) Cook County	1,071	1.46
Champaign (city) Champaign County	1,127	1.42
Naperville (city) DuPage County	1,979	1.41
Hoffman Estates (village) Cook County	694	1.36

Scandinavian

Top 10 Places Sorted by Population
Based on all places, regardless of total population

Place	Population	%
Chicago (city) Cook County	1,792	0.07
Rockford (city) Winnebago County	588	0.38
Wheaton (city) DuPage County	330	0.62
Naperville (city) DuPage County	324	0.23
Elgin (city) Kane County	294	0.28
Glenview (village) Cook County	238	0.55
Peoria (city) Peoria County	227	0.20
Joliet (city) Will County	220	0.15
Aurora (city) Kane County	202	0.11
Downers Grove (village) DuPage County	162	0.34

Top 10 Places Sorted by Percent of Total Population
Based on all places, regardless of total population

Place	Population	%
Rockbridge (village) Greene County	8	4.85
Georgetown (cdp) McDonough County	22	4.37
Rock City (village) Stephenson County	10	2.58
Elsah (village) Jersey County	14	2.53
Grand Detour (cdp) Ogle County	11	2.38
Old Mill Creek (village) Lake County	3	2.11
Crossville (village) White County	15	2.01
Pesotum (village) Champaign County	10	1.97
Saunemin (village) Livingston County	7	1.94
Third Lake (village) Lake County	29	1.93

Top 10 Places Sorted by Percent of Total Population
Based on places with total population of 50,000 or more

Place	Population	%
Wheaton (city) DuPage County	330	0.62
Rockford (city) Winnebago County	588	0.38
Elgin (city) Kane County	294	0.28
Naperville (city) DuPage County	324	0.23
Palatine (village) Cook County	154	0.23
Peoria (city) Peoria County	227	0.20
Hoffman Estates (village) Cook County	102	0.20
Champaign (city) Champaign County	136	0.17
Evanston (city) Cook County	122	0.17
Arlington Heights (village) Cook County	117	0.16

Scotch-Irish

Top 10 Places Sorted by Population
Based on all places, regardless of total population

Place	Population	%
Chicago (city) Cook County	13,218	0.49
Springfield (city) Sangamon County	2,407	2.09
Naperville (city) DuPage County	2,240	1.59

Place	Population	%
Peoria (city) Peoria County	1,755	1.54
Evanston (city) Cook County	1,417	1.92
Bloomington (city) McLean County	1,404	1.8
Aurora (city) Kane County	1,361	0.7
Rockford (city) Winnebago County	1,348	0.87
Wheaton (city) DuPage County	1,284	2.42
Elgin (city) Kane County	1,228	1.15

Top 10 Places Sorted by Percent of Total Population
Based on all places, regardless of total population

Place	Population	%
Leonore (village) LaSalle County	18	20.93
Time (village) Pike County	2	20.00
Naples (town) Scott County	15	18.99
West Union (cdp) Clark County	79	18.76
La Prairie (village) Adams County	3	15.79
Shipman (town) Macoupin County	118	14.34
Browning (village) Schuyler County	16	11.11
Glasgow (village) Scott County	16	10.67
Alma (village) Marion County	32	10.22
Summerfield (village) St. Clair County	35	10.17

Top 10 Places Sorted by Percent of Total Population
Based on places with total population of 50,000 or more

Place	Population	%
Wheaton (city) DuPage County	1,284	2.42
Springfield (city) Sangamon County	2,407	2.09
Evanston (city) Cook County	1,417	1.92
Bloomington (city) McLean County	1,404	1.8
Normal (town) McLean County	905	1.75
Oak Park (village) Cook County	882	1.7
Naperville (city) DuPage County	2,240	1.59
Decatur (city) Macon County	1,194	1.5
Peoria (city) Peoria County	1,755	1.5
Champaign (city) Champaign County	1,009	1.2

Scottish

Top 10 Places Sorted by Population
Based on all places, regardless of total population

Place	Population	%
Chicago (city) Cook County	16,230	0.6
Naperville (city) DuPage County	2,657	1.8
Springfield (city) Sangamon County	2,251	1.9
Aurora (city) Kane County	2,105	1.1
Evanston (city) Cook County	1,848	2.5
Peoria (city) Peoria County	1,670	1.5
Bloomington (city) McLean County	1,576	2.1
Joliet (city) Will County	1,556	1.07
Rockford (city) Winnebago County	1,513	0.9
Arlington Heights (village) Cook County	1,440	1.92

Top 10 Places Sorted by Percent of Total Population
Based on all places, regardless of total population

Place	Population	%
New Bedford (village) Bureau County	13	20.6
Broughton (village) Hamilton County	47	18.7
Georgetown (cdp) McDonough County	83	16.4
Pearl (village) Pike County	27	16.2
Standard City (village) Macoupin County	22	14.8
Panola (village) Woodford County	5	12.5
Stonefort (village) Williamson County	23	11.8
East Gillespie (village) Macoupin County	21	10.5
Crystal Lawns (cdp) Will County	197	9.8
Stoy (village) Crawford County	6	9.5

Top 10 Places Sorted by Percent of Total Population
Based on places with total population of 50,000 or more

Place	Population	%
Evanston (city) Cook County	1,848	2.5
Wheaton (city) DuPage County	1,270	2.3
Normal (town) McLean County	1,129	2.1
Bloomington (city) McLean County	1,576	2.1
Oak Park (village) Cook County	1,042	2.0
Springfield (city) Sangamon County	2,251	1.9
Arlington Heights (village) Cook County	1,440	1.9
Naperville (city) DuPage County	2,657	1.8
Champaign (city) Champaign County	1,389	1.7
Decatur (city) Macon County	1,176	1.5

Serbian

Top 10 Places Sorted by Population
Based on all places, regardless of total population

Place	Population	%
Chicago (city) Cook County	5,286	0.20
Niles (village) Cook County	498	1.69
Orland Park (village) Cook County	457	0.83
Lansing (village) Cook County	441	1.57
Countryside (city) Cook County	351	6.03
Skokie (village) Cook County	325	0.51
Harwood Heights (village) Cook County	319	3.77
Arlington Heights (village) Cook County	307	0.41
Joliet (city) Will County	305	0.21
Naperville (city) DuPage County	301	0.21

Top 10 Places Sorted by Percent of Total Population
Based on all places, regardless of total population

Place	Population	%
Countryside (city) Cook County	351	6.03
Manchester (village) Scott County	22	4.89
Indian Head Park (village) Cook County	153	4.03
Harwood Heights (village) Cook County	319	3.77
Armington (village) Tazewell County	13	3.32
Tower Lakes (village) Lake County	41	2.78
Knollwood (cdp) Lake County	41	2.45
Orient (city) Franklin County	7	1.85
Niles (village) Cook County	498	1.69
Lincolnwood (village) Cook County	206	1.66

Top 10 Places Sorted by Percent of Total Population
Based on places with total population of 50,000 or more

Place	Population	%
Orland Park (village) Cook County	457	0.83
Skokie (village) Cook County	325	0.51
Des Plaines (city) Cook County	282	0.49
Oak Park (village) Cook County	236	0.46
Arlington Heights (village) Cook County	307	0.41
Bolingbrook (village) Will County	224	0.31
Wheaton (city) DuPage County	163	0.31
Waukegan (city) Lake County	225	0.25
Joliet (city) Will County	305	0.21
Naperville (city) DuPage County	301	0.21

Slavic

Top 10 Places Sorted by Population
Based on all places, regardless of total population

Place	Population	%
Chicago (city) Cook County	1,157	0.04
Joliet (city) Will County	153	0.11
Springfield (city) Sangamon County	129	0.11
Niles (village) Cook County	120	0.41
Lemont (village) Cook County	117	0.76
Granite City (city) Madison County	110	0.36
Crest Hill (city) Will County	76	0.37
Oak Lawn (village) Cook County	76	0.14
Gurnee (village) Lake County	75	0.24
Waukegan (city) Lake County	73	0.08

Top 10 Places Sorted by Percent of Total Population
Based on all places, regardless of total population

Place	Population	%
Rutland (village) LaSalle County	6	1.74
Sherrard (village) Mercer County	12	1.45
Cooksville (village) McLean County	2	1.32
Odell (village) Livingston County	14	1.28
Staunton (city) Macoupin County	60	1.23
Wolf (village) Cook County	7	1.18
Taylor Springs (village) Montgomery County	5	1.13
Alto Pass (village) Union County	4	1.09
Oglesby (city) LaSalle County	30	0.89
Annawan (town) Henry County	8	0.85

Top 10 Places Sorted by Percent of Total Population
Based on places with total population of 50,000 or more

Place	Population	%
Oak Lawn (village) Cook County	76	0.14
Joliet (city) Will County	153	0.11
Springfield (city) Sangamon County	129	0.11
Waukegan (city) Lake County	73	0.08

Place	Population	%
Palatine (village) Cook County	51	0.08
Wheaton (city) DuPage County	43	0.08
Evanston (city) Cook County	53	0.07
Oak Park (village) Cook County	34	0.07
Bolingbrook (village) Will County	47	0.06
Orland Park (village) Cook County	35	0.06

Slovak

Top 10 Places Sorted by Population
Based on all places, regardless of total population

Place	Population	%
Chicago (city) Cook County	4,761	0.18
Joliet (city) Will County	1,601	1.10
Streator (city) LaSalle County	1,596	12.10
Naperville (city) DuPage County	1,015	0.72
Oak Lawn (village) Cook County	616	1.10
Downers Grove (village) DuPage County	526	1.10
Tinley Park (village) Cook County	487	0.89
Lombard (village) DuPage County	470	1.10
Springfield (city) Sangamon County	430	0.37
Aurora (city) Kane County	421	0.22

Top 10 Places Sorted by Percent of Total Population
Based on all places, regardless of total population

Place	Population	%
Streator (city) LaSalle County	1,596	12.10
Grand Ridge (village) LaSalle County	42	8.35
Mechanicsburg (village) Sangamon County	48	8.11
Magnolia (village) Putnam County	19	7.57
Kangley (village) LaSalle County	32	7.34
Sawyerville (village) Macoupin County	15	5.70
Walshville (village) Montgomery County	4	5.13
Ransom (village) LaSalle County	18	5.10
Huey (village) Clinton County	8	4.65
Butler (village) Montgomery County	7	4.55

Top 10 Places Sorted by Percent of Total Population
Based on places with total population of 50,000 or more

Place	Population	%
Joliet (city) Will County	1,601	1.10
Oak Lawn (village) Cook County	616	1.10
Tinley Park (village) Cook County	487	0.89
Naperville (city) DuPage County	1,015	0.72
Wheaton (city) DuPage County	306	0.58
Hoffman Estates (village) Cook County	296	0.58
Arlington Heights (village) Cook County	388	0.52
Oak Park (village) Cook County	268	0.52
Palatine (village) Cook County	341	0.51
Bloomington (city) McLean County	300	0.40

Slovene

Top 10 Places Sorted by Population
Based on all places, regardless of total population

Place	Population	%
Joliet (city) Will County	1,830	1.26
Chicago (city) Cook County	1,432	0.05
Shorewood (village) Will County	352	2.39
Crest Hill (city) Will County	346	1.70
Waukegan (city) Lake County	304	0.34
Lemont (village) Cook County	303	1.98
Channahon (village) Will County	268	2.19
LaSalle (city) LaSalle County	209	2.16
Oak Park (village) Cook County	208	0.40
Buffalo Grove (village) Lake County	201	0.48

Top 10 Places Sorted by Percent of Total Population
Based on all places, regardless of total population

Place	Population	%
Mount Clare (village) Macoupin County	85	7.92
North Utica (village) LaSalle County	38	3.20
Rockdale (village) Will County	62	3.17
Shorewood (village) Will County	352	2.39
Channahon (village) Will County	268	2.19
LaSalle (city) LaSalle County	209	2.16
Lemont (village) Cook County	303	1.98
Wadsworth (village) Lake County	74	1.92
Deer Park (village) Lake County	61	1.89
London Mills (village) Fulton County	8	1.82

Top 10 Places Sorted by Percent of Total Population
Based on places with total population of 50,000 or more

Place	Population	%
Joliet (city) Will County	1,830	1.26
Oak Park (village) Cook County	208	0.40
Waukegan (city) Lake County	304	0.34
Schaumburg (village) Cook County	154	0.21
Arlington Heights (village) Cook County	150	0.20
Normal (town) McLean County	101	0.20
Evanston (city) Cook County	137	0.19
Orland Park (village) Cook County	98	0.18
Palatine (village) Cook County	115	0.17
Bolingbrook (village) Will County	114	0.16

Soviet Union

Top 10 Places Sorted by Population
Based on all places, regardless of total population

Place	Population	%
Morton Grove (village) Cook County	21	0.09
Skokie (village) Cook County	20	0.03
Chicago (city) Cook County	19	<0.01
Buffalo Grove (village) Lake County	18	0.04
Evanston (city) Cook County	14	0.02
Vernon Hills (village) Lake County	10	0.04
Abingdon (city) Knox County	0	0.00
Adair (cdp) McDonough County	0	0.00
Addieville (village) Washington County	0	0.00
Addison (village) DuPage County	0	0.00

Top 10 Places Sorted by Percent of Total Population
Based on all places, regardless of total population

Place	Population	%
Morton Grove (village) Cook County	21	0.09
Buffalo Grove (village) Lake County	18	0.04
Vernon Hills (village) Lake County	10	0.04
Skokie (village) Cook County	20	0.03
Evanston (city) Cook County	14	0.02
Chicago (city) Cook County	19	<0.01
Abingdon (city) Knox County	0	0.00
Adair (cdp) McDonough County	0	0.00
Addieville (village) Washington County	0	0.00
Addison (village) DuPage County	0	0.00

Top 10 Places Sorted by Percent of Total Population
Based on places with total population of 50,000 or more

Place	Population	%
Skokie (village) Cook County	20	0.03
Evanston (city) Cook County	14	0.02
Chicago (city) Cook County	19	<0.01
Arlington Heights (village) Cook County	0	0.00
Aurora (city) Kane County	0	0.00
Berwyn (city) Cook County	0	0.00
Bloomington (city) McLean County	0	0.00
Bolingbrook (village) Will County	0	0.00
Champaign (city) Champaign County	0	0.00
Cicero (town) Cook County	0	0.00

Swedish

Top 10 Places Sorted by Population
Based on all places, regardless of total population

Place	Population	%
Chicago (city) Cook County	26,075	0.96
Rockford (city) Winnebago County	12,535	8.11
Naperville (city) DuPage County	4,354	3.09
Moline (city) Rock Island County	3,277	7.56
Arlington Heights (village) Cook County	3,191	4.26
Aurora (city) Kane County	3,178	1.67
Galesburg (city) Knox County	3,141	9.76
Peoria (city) Peoria County	2,798	2.46
Wheaton (city) DuPage County	2,653	4.99
Joliet (city) Will County	2,493	1.72

Top 10 Places Sorted by Percent of Total Population
Based on all places, regardless of total population

Place	Population	%
Rock Island Arsenal (cdp) Rock Island County	30	38.46
Bishop Hill (village) Henry County	36	33.96
Andover (village) Henry County	176	31.15

Place	Population	%
Alpha (village) Henry County	169	27.84
Chemung (cdp) McHenry County	53	23.56
Orion (village) Henry County	426	22.73
La Fayette (village) Stark County	56	22.05
Woodhull (village) Henry County	175	21.93
Ridott (village) Stephenson County	24	21.62
Caledonia (village) Boone County	45	20.93

Top 10 Places Sorted by Percent of Total Population
Based on places with total population of 50,000 or more

Place	Population	%
Rockford (city) Winnebago County	12,535	8.11
Wheaton (city) DuPage County	2,653	4.99
Arlington Heights (village) Cook County	3,191	4.26
Palatine (village) Cook County	2,447	3.63
Evanston (city) Cook County	2,448	3.31
Des Plaines (city) Cook County	1,901	3.31
Tinley Park (village) Cook County	1,818	3.31
Naperville (city) DuPage County	4,354	3.09
Schaumburg (village) Cook County	2,209	3.01
Hoffman Estates (village) Cook County	1,473	2.88

Swiss

Top 10 Places Sorted by Population
Based on all places, regardless of total population

Place	Population	%
Chicago (city) Cook County	3,481	0.13
Peoria (city) Peoria County	729	0.64
Naperville (city) DuPage County	647	0.46
Rockford (city) Winnebago County	625	0.40
Highland (city) Madison County	576	6.12
Elgin (city) Kane County	450	0.42
Bloomington (city) McLean County	421	0.56
Freeport (city) Stephenson County	406	1.58
Aurora (city) Kane County	397	0.21
Normal (town) McLean County	392	0.76

Top 10 Places Sorted by Percent of Total Population
Based on all places, regardless of total population

Place	Population	%
Yale (village) Jasper County	11	16.42
Congerville (village) Woodford County	87	15.70
Orangeville (village) Stephenson County	110	12.35
Rock City (village) Stephenson County	44	11.37
Winslow (village) Stephenson County	27	10.63
Fairbury (city) Livingston County	341	8.88
Plattville (village) Kendall County	13	8.55
Goodfield (village) Woodford County	91	8.15
Eureka (city) Woodford County	389	7.45
Roanoke (village) Woodford County	153	7.35

Top 10 Places Sorted by Percent of Total Population
Based on places with total population of 50,000 or more

Place	Population	%
Normal (town) McLean County	392	0.76
Peoria (city) Peoria County	729	0.64
Wheaton (city) DuPage County	322	0.61
Bloomington (city) McLean County	421	0.56
Evanston (city) Cook County	388	0.53
Naperville (city) DuPage County	647	0.46
Elgin (city) Kane County	450	0.42
Champaign (city) Champaign County	332	0.42
Rockford (city) Winnebago County	625	0.40
Oak Park (village) Cook County	207	0.40

Turkish

Top 10 Places Sorted by Population
Based on all places, regardless of total population

Place	Population	%
Chicago (city) Cook County	1,598	0.06
Champaign (city) Champaign County	263	0.33
Gages Lake (cdp) Lake County	167	1.64
Mount Prospect (village) Cook County	160	0.30
Urbana (city) Champaign County	155	0.38
Des Plaines (city) Cook County	155	0.27
Evanston (city) Cook County	152	0.21
Wheaton (city) DuPage County	147	0.28
Naperville (city) DuPage County	112	0.08
Aurora (city) Kane County	109	0.06

Top 10 Places Sorted by Percent of Total Population
Based on all places, regardless of total population

Place	Population	%
Marietta (village) Fulton County	18	14.17
Dunfermline (village) Fulton County	11	5.42
Benson (village) Woodford County	11	2.78
Saybrook (village) McLean County	12	1.88
Gages Lake (cdp) Lake County	167	1.64
Fulton (city) Whiteside County	45	1.26
Chicago Ridge (village) Cook County	97	0.69
Mahomet (village) Champaign County	41	0.60
Cedarville (village) Stephenson County	5	0.56
North Pekin (village) Tazewell County	10	0.55

Top 10 Places Sorted by Percent of Total Population
Based on places with total population of 50,000 or more

Place	Population	%
Champaign (city) Champaign County	263	0.33
Mount Prospect (village) Cook County	160	0.30
Wheaton (city) DuPage County	147	0.28
Des Plaines (city) Cook County	155	0.27
Evanston (city) Cook County	152	0.21
Hoffman Estates (village) Cook County	92	0.18
Bloomington (city) McLean County	96	0.13
Normal (town) McLean County	44	0.09
Naperville (city) DuPage County	112	0.08
Oak Park (village) Cook County	39	0.08

Ukrainian

Top 10 Places Sorted by Population
Based on all places, regardless of total population

Place	Population	%
Chicago (city) Cook County	12,513	0.46
Buffalo Grove (village) Lake County	1,311	3.13
Skokie (village) Cook County	1,223	1.92
Naperville (city) DuPage County	915	0.65
Glenview (village) Cook County	741	1.70
Northbrook (village) Cook County	655	1.99
Arlington Heights (village) Cook County	626	0.84
Palatine (village) Cook County	620	0.92
Tinley Park (village) Cook County	619	1.13
Wheeling (village) Cook County	610	1.65

Top 10 Places Sorted by Percent of Total Population
Based on all places, regardless of total population

Place	Population	%
Macedonia (village) Franklin County	6	25.00
Smithfield (village) Fulton County	46	15.81
Norris (village) Fulton County	9	5.96
Lakewood (village) McHenry County	141	3.76
Deer Park (village) Lake County	110	3.41
Symerton (village) Will County	3	3.19
Buffalo Grove (village) Lake County	1,311	3.13
Northfield (village) Cook County	170	3.13
Lake Catherine (cdp) Lake County	32	2.95
Harwood Heights (village) Cook County	224	2.65

Top 10 Places Sorted by Percent of Total Population
Based on places with total population of 50,000 or more

Place	Population	%
Skokie (village) Cook County	1,223	1.92
Tinley Park (village) Cook County	619	1.13
Palatine (village) Cook County	620	0.92
Arlington Heights (village) Cook County	626	0.84
Evanston (city) Cook County	547	0.74
Des Plaines (city) Cook County	401	0.70
Hoffman Estates (village) Cook County	343	0.67
Naperville (city) DuPage County	915	0.65
Wheaton (city) DuPage County	338	0.64
Mount Prospect (village) Cook County	335	0.62

Welsh

Top 10 Places Sorted by Population
Based on all places, regardless of total population

Place	Population	%
Chicago (city) Cook County	5,904	0.22
Aurora (city) Kane County	954	0.50
Springfield (city) Sangamon County	877	0.76

Place	Population	%
Naperville (city) DuPage County	847	0
Peoria (city) Peoria County	669	0
Bloomington (city) McLean County	581	0
Rockford (city) Winnebago County	569	0
Evanston (city) Cook County	501	0
Joliet (city) Will County	459	0
Champaign (city) Champaign County	433	0

Top 10 Places Sorted by Percent of Total Populati
Based on all places, regardless of total population

Place	Population	
Eagarville (village) Macoupin County	10	12
Bush (village) Williamson County	22	8
Hidalgo (village) Jasper County	11	8
Oakdale (village) Washington County	22	7
West Union (cdp) Clark County	30	6
Jewett (village) Cumberland County	17	6
Norris City (village) White County	66	6
Elizabethtown (village) Hardin County	24	6
Nashville (city) Washington County	200	6
Glasgow (village) Scott County	9	6

Top 10 Places Sorted by Percent of Total Populati
Based on places with total population of 50,000 or more

Place	Population	
Oak Park (village) Cook County	432	
Bloomington (city) McLean County	581	
Springfield (city) Sangamon County	877	
Mount Prospect (village) Cook County	386	
Wheaton (city) DuPage County	378	
Evanston (city) Cook County	501	
Normal (town) McLean County	342	
Naperville (city) DuPage County	847	
Peoria (city) Peoria County	669	
Champaign (city) Champaign County	433	

West Indian, excluding Hispanic

Top 10 Places Sorted by Population
Based on all places, regardless of total population

Place	Population	
Chicago (city) Cook County	11,174	0
Evanston (city) Cook County	2,476	3
Waukegan (city) Lake County	1,126	1
Skokie (village) Cook County	1,073	1
Calumet City (city) Cook County	809	2
North Chicago (city) Lake County	706	2
Round Lake (village) Lake County	361	2
Peoria (city) Peoria County	346	0
Mount Prospect (village) Cook County	331	0
Oak Park (village) Cook County	304	0

Top 10 Places Sorted by Percent of Total Populati
Based on all places, regardless of total population

Place	Population	
Golf (village) Cook County	33	5
Franklin Grove (village) Lee County	61	4
Sun River Terrace (village) Kankakee County	18	3
Evanston (city) Cook County	2,476	3
Henning (village) Vermilion County	7	2
Round Lake (village) Lake County	361	2
Calumet City (city) Cook County	809	2
North Chicago (city) Lake County	706	2
Thompsonville (village) Franklin County	12	2
Preston Heights (cdp) Will County	57	2

Top 10 Places Sorted by Percent of Total Populati
Based on places with total population of 50,000 or more

Place	Population	
Evanston (city) Cook County	2,476	3
Skokie (village) Cook County	1,073	1
Waukegan (city) Lake County	1,126	1
Mount Prospect (village) Cook County	331	0
Oak Park (village) Cook County	304	0
Chicago (city) Cook County	11,174	0
Tinley Park (village) Cook County	169	0
Peoria (city) Peoria County	346	0
Berwyn (city) Cook County	159	0
Bolingbrook (village) Will County	197	0

Please refer to the Explanation of Data in the front of the book for more detailed information.

West Indian: Bahamian, excluding Hispanic

Top 10 Places Sorted by Population
Based on all places, regardless of total population

Place	Population	%
Galesburg (city) Knox County	97	0.30
Evanston (city) Cook County	44	0.06
Lansing (village) Cook County	35	0.12
Chicago (city) Cook County	22	<0.01
Naperville (city) DuPage County	21	0.01
Rockford (city) Winnebago County	21	0.01
Bourbonnais (village) Kankakee County	17	0.09
Macomb (city) McDonough County	14	0.07
Markham (city) Cook County	11	0.09
LaSalle (city) LaSalle County	10	0.10

Top 10 Places Sorted by Percent of Total Population
Based on all places, regardless of total population

Place	Population	%
Galesburg (city) Knox County	97	0.30
Lansing (village) Cook County	35	0.12
LaSalle (city) LaSalle County	10	0.10
Bourbonnais (village) Kankakee County	17	0.09
Markham (city) Cook County	11	0.09
Macomb (city) McDonough County	14	0.07
Evanston (city) Cook County	44	0.06
Naperville (city) DuPage County	21	0.01
Rockford (city) Winnebago County	21	0.01
Oak Park (village) Cook County	7	0.01

Top 10 Places Sorted by Percent of Total Population
Based on places with total population of 50,000 or more

Place	Population	%
Evanston (city) Cook County	44	0.06
Naperville (city) DuPage County	21	0.01
Rockford (city) Winnebago County	21	0.01
Oak Park (village) Cook County	7	0.01
Chicago (city) Cook County	22	<0.01
Arlington Heights (village) Cook County	0	0.00
Aurora (city) Kane County	0	0.00
Berwyn (city) Cook County	0	0.00
Bloomington (city) McLean County	0	0.00
Bolingbrook (village) Will County	0	0.00

West Indian: Barbadian, excluding Hispanic

Top 10 Places Sorted by Population
Based on all places, regardless of total population

Place	Population	%
Chicago (city) Cook County	154	0.01
Maywood (village) Cook County	129	0.53
Crest Hill (city) Will County	27	0.13
Glendale Heights (village) DuPage County	26	0.08
Fox River Grove (village) McHenry County	25	0.49
Bolingbrook (village) Will County	18	0.02
Crystal Lake (city) McHenry County	15	0.04
Normal (town) McLean County	13	0.03
Darien (city) DuPage County	9	0.04
Elmwood Park (village) Cook County	9	0.04

Top 10 Places Sorted by Percent of Total Population
Based on all places, regardless of total population

Place	Population	%
Maywood (village) Cook County	129	0.53
Fox River Grove (village) McHenry County	25	0.49
Crest Hill (city) Will County	27	0.13
Glendale Heights (village) DuPage County	26	0.08
Crystal Lake (city) McHenry County	15	0.04
Darien (city) DuPage County	9	0.04
Elmwood Park (village) Cook County	9	0.04
Normal (town) McLean County	13	0.03
Bolingbrook (village) Will County	18	0.02
Chicago (city) Cook County	154	0.01

Top 10 Places Sorted by Percent of Total Population
Based on places with total population of 50,000 or more

Place	Population	%
Normal (town) McLean County	13	0.03

Bolingbrook (village) Will County	18	0.02
Chicago (city) Cook County	154	0.01
Arlington Heights (village) Cook County	0	0.00
Aurora (city) Kane County	0	0.00
Berwyn (city) Cook County	0	0.00
Bloomington (city) McLean County	0	0.00
Champaign (city) Champaign County	0	0.00
Cicero (town) Cook County	0	0.00
Decatur (city) Macon County	0	0.00

West Indian: Belizean, excluding Hispanic

Top 10 Places Sorted by Population
Based on all places, regardless of total population

Place	Population	%
Chicago (city) Cook County	2,273	0.08
Waukegan (city) Lake County	536	0.60
Evanston (city) Cook County	358	0.48
North Chicago (city) Lake County	217	0.66
Gurnee (village) Lake County	122	0.39
Zion (city) Lake County	102	0.42
Harwood Heights (village) Cook County	75	0.89
Westmont (village) DuPage County	72	0.29
Cicero (town) Cook County	68	0.08
Bolingbrook (village) Will County	64	0.09

Top 10 Places Sorted by Percent of Total Population
Based on all places, regardless of total population

Place	Population	%
Franklin Grove (village) Lee County	61	4.39
Long Lake (cdp) Lake County	53	1.73
Harwood Heights (village) Cook County	75	0.89
North Chicago (city) Lake County	217	0.66
Waukegan (city) Lake County	536	0.60
Park City (city) Lake County	40	0.53
Evanston (city) Cook County	358	0.48
Zion (city) Lake County	102	0.42
Gurnee (village) Lake County	122	0.39
Kewanee (city) Henry County	50	0.38

Top 10 Places Sorted by Percent of Total Population
Based on places with total population of 50,000 or more

Place	Population	%
Waukegan (city) Lake County	536	0.60
Evanston (city) Cook County	358	0.48
Bolingbrook (village) Will County	64	0.09
Chicago (city) Cook County	2,273	0.08
Cicero (town) Cook County	68	0.08
Orland Park (village) Cook County	37	0.07
Skokie (village) Cook County	36	0.06
Bloomington (city) McLean County	14	0.02
Wheaton (city) DuPage County	10	0.02
Arlington Heights (village) Cook County	9	0.01

West Indian: Bermudan, excluding Hispanic

Top 10 Places Sorted by Population
Based on all places, regardless of total population

Place	Population	%
Chicago (city) Cook County	24	<0.01
Thompsonville (village) Franklin County	12	2.13
Glenview (village) Cook County	11	0.03
Abingdon (city) Knox County	0	0.00
Adair (cdp) McDonough County	0	0.00
Addieville (village) Washington County	0	0.00
Addison (village) DuPage County	0	0.00
Adeline (village) Ogle County	0	0.00
Albany (village) Whiteside County	0	0.00
Albers (village) Clinton County	0	0.00

Top 10 Places Sorted by Percent of Total Population
Based on all places, regardless of total population

Place	Population	%
Thompsonville (village) Franklin County	12	2.13
Glenview (village) Cook County	11	0.03
Chicago (city) Cook County	24	<0.01
Abingdon (city) Knox County	0	0.00
Adair (cdp) McDonough County	0	0.00
Addieville (village) Washington County	0	0.00
Addison (village) DuPage County	0	0.00

Adeline (village) Ogle County	0	0.00
Albany (village) Whiteside County	0	0.00
Albers (village) Clinton County	0	0.00

Top 10 Places Sorted by Percent of Total Population
Based on places with total population of 50,000 or more

Place	Population	%
Chicago (city) Cook County	24	<0.01
Arlington Heights (village) Cook County	0	0.00
Aurora (city) Kane County	0	0.00
Berwyn (city) Cook County	0	0.00
Bloomington (city) McLean County	0	0.00
Bolingbrook (village) Will County	0	0.00
Champaign (city) Champaign County	0	0.00
Cicero (town) Cook County	0	0.00
Decatur (city) Macon County	0	0.00
Des Plaines (city) Cook County	0	0.00

West Indian: British West Indian, excluding Hispanic

Top 10 Places Sorted by Population
Based on all places, regardless of total population

Place	Population	%
Chicago (city) Cook County	103	<0.01
North Chicago (city) Lake County	43	0.13
Round Lake Beach (village) Lake County	38	0.14
Evanston (city) Cook County	25	0.03
Woodstock (city) McHenry County	14	0.06
Creve Coeur (village) Tazewell County	12	0.23
Oak Lawn (village) Cook County	12	0.02
Bloomington (city) McLean County	11	0.01
Boulder Hill (cdp) Kendall County	10	0.12
Bolingbrook (village) Will County	9	0.01

Top 10 Places Sorted by Percent of Total Population
Based on all places, regardless of total population

Place	Population	%
Creve Coeur (village) Tazewell County	12	0.23
Round Lake Beach (village) Lake County	38	0.14
North Chicago (city) Lake County	43	0.13
Boulder Hill (cdp) Kendall County	10	0.12
Woodstock (city) McHenry County	11	0.06
Evanston (city) Cook County	25	0.03
Bensenville (village) DuPage County	5	0.03
Oak Lawn (village) Cook County	12	0.02
Bloomington (city) McLean County	11	0.01
Bolingbrook (village) Will County	9	0.01

Top 10 Places Sorted by Percent of Total Population
Based on places with total population of 50,000 or more

Place	Population	%
Evanston (city) Cook County	25	0.03
Oak Lawn (village) Cook County	12	0.02
Bloomington (city) McLean County	11	0.01
Bolingbrook (village) Will County	9	0.01
Palatine (village) Cook County	8	0.01
Chicago (city) Cook County	103	<0.01
Arlington Heights (village) Cook County	0	0.00
Aurora (city) Kane County	0	0.00
Berwyn (city) Cook County	0	0.00
Champaign (city) Champaign County	0	0.00

West Indian: Dutch West Indian, excluding Hispanic

Top 10 Places Sorted by Population
Based on all places, regardless of total population

Place	Population	%
Trenton (city) Clinton County	20	0.74
Clinton (city) De Witt County	17	0.23
Sauk Village (village) Cook County	16	0.15
Springfield (city) Sangamon County	14	0.01
Joliet (city) Will County	13	0.01
Eldorado (city) Saline County	11	0.25
Bloomington (city) McLean County	11	0.01
Boulder Hill (cdp) Kendall County	10	0.12
Romeoville (village) Will County	10	0.03
Peoria (city) Peoria County	9	0.01

Top 10 Places Sorted by Percent of Total Population
Based on all places, regardless of total population

Place	Population	%
Henning (village) Vermilion County	7	2.73
Vergennes (village) Jackson County	7	1.87
Ridott (village) Stephenson County	2	1.80
Golconda (city) Pope County	8	0.99
Trenton (city) Clinton County	20	0.74
Ramsey (village) Fayette County	6	0.63
Vienna (city) Johnson County	8	0.53
Kirkwood (village) Warren County	3	0.42
Shipman (town) Macoupin County	3	0.36
Knoxville (city) Knox County	8	0.28

Top 10 Places Sorted by Percent of Total Population
Based on places with total population of 50,000 or more

Place	Population	%
Springfield (city) Sangamon County	14	0.01
Joliet (city) Will County	13	0.01
Bloomington (city) McLean County	11	0.01
Peoria (city) Peoria County	9	0.01
Arlington Heights (village) Cook County	0	0.00
Aurora (city) Kane County	0	0.00
Berwyn (city) Cook County	0	0.00
Bolingbrook (village) Will County	0	0.00
Champaign (city) Champaign County	0	0.00
Chicago (city) Cook County	0	0.00

West Indian: Haitian, excluding Hispanic

Top 10 Places Sorted by Population
Based on all places, regardless of total population

Place	Population	%
Chicago (city) Cook County	2,734	0.10
Skokie (village) Cook County	891	1.40
Evanston (city) Cook County	781	1.06
Peoria (city) Peoria County	313	0.27
Mount Prospect (village) Cook County	308	0.57
Calumet City (city) Cook County	223	0.60
Romeoville (village) Will County	137	0.37
South Holland (village) Cook County	120	0.55
Lynwood (village) Cook County	112	1.28
Rantoul (village) Champaign County	79	0.63

Top 10 Places Sorted by Percent of Total Population
Based on all places, regardless of total population

Place	Population	%
Golf (village) Cook County	33	5.56
Sun River Terrace (village) Kankakee County	18	3.65
Preston Heights (cdp) Will County	57	2.04
Creston (village) Ogle County	14	1.79
Ullin (village) Pulaski County	10	1.62
Knollwood (cdp) Lake County	24	1.43
Skokie (village) Cook County	891	1.40
Lynwood (village) Cook County	112	1.28
Edinburg (village) Christian County	13	1.10
Evanston (city) Cook County	781	1.06

Top 10 Places Sorted by Percent of Total Population
Based on places with total population of 50,000 or more

Place	Population	%
Skokie (village) Cook County	891	1.40
Evanston (city) Cook County	781	1.06
Mount Prospect (village) Cook County	308	0.57
Peoria (city) Peoria County	313	0.27
Oak Park (village) Cook County	64	0.12
Chicago (city) Cook County	2,734	0.10
Decatur (city) Macon County	65	0.09
Arlington Heights (village) Cook County	52	0.07
Palatine (village) Cook County	45	0.07
Tinley Park (village) Cook County	35	0.06

West Indian: Jamaican, excluding Hispanic

Top 10 Places Sorted by Population
Based on all places, regardless of total population

Place	Population	%
Chicago (city) Cook County	4,601	0.17
Evanston (city) Cook County	1,181	1.60

Place	Population	%
Waukegan (city) Lake County	529	0.59
Calumet City (city) Cook County	468	1.27
North Chicago (city) Lake County	374	1.13
Round Lake (village) Lake County	334	2.07
Woodridge (village) DuPage County	271	0.83
Skokie (village) Cook County	146	0.23
Evergreen Park (village) Cook County	130	0.66
Lincolnwood (village) Cook County	119	0.96

Top 10 Places Sorted by Percent of Total Population
Based on all places, regardless of total population

Place	Population	%
Round Lake (village) Lake County	334	2.07
Evanston (city) Cook County	1,181	1.60
East Hazel Crest (village) Cook County	23	1.34
Calumet City (city) Cook County	468	1.27
Washington Park (village) St. Clair County	57	1.27
North Chicago (city) Lake County	374	1.13
Biggsville (village) Henderson County	4	1.10
Cairo (city) Alexander County	30	1.01
Lincolnwood (village) Cook County	119	0.96
East Carondelet (village) St. Clair County	4	0.91

Top 10 Places Sorted by Percent of Total Population
Based on places with total population of 50,000 or more

Place	Population	%
Evanston (city) Cook County	1,181	1.60
Waukegan (city) Lake County	529	0.59
Skokie (village) Cook County	146	0.23
Oak Park (village) Cook County	113	0.22
Berwyn (city) Cook County	101	0.18
Chicago (city) Cook County	4,601	0.17
Bolingbrook (village) Will County	96	0.13
Champaign (city) Champaign County	98	0.12
Wheaton (city) DuPage County	58	0.11
Springfield (city) Sangamon County	115	0.10

West Indian: Trinidadian and Tobagonian, excluding Hispanic

Top 10 Places Sorted by Population
Based on all places, regardless of total population

Place	Population	%
Chicago (city) Cook County	533	0.02
Lansing (village) Cook County	85	0.30
Gilberts (village) Kane County	82	1.40
Naperville (city) DuPage County	54	0.04
Elk Grove Village (village) Cook County	42	0.13
O'Fallon (city) St. Clair County	37	0.14
Berwyn (city) Cook County	26	0.05
Maywood (village) Cook County	24	0.10
Champaign (city) Champaign County	19	0.02
Downers Grove (village) DuPage County	14	0.03

Top 10 Places Sorted by Percent of Total Population
Based on all places, regardless of total population

Place	Population	%
Gilberts (village) Kane County	82	1.40
Bradford (village) Stark County	5	0.70
Hennepin (village) Putnam County	5	0.69
Knollwood (cdp) Lake County	7	0.42
Oakbrook Terrace (city) DuPage County	9	0.40
Lansing (village) Cook County	85	0.30
Rochester (village) Sangamon County	9	0.25
Creve Coeur (village) Tazewell County	12	0.23
O'Fallon (city) St. Clair County	37	0.14
Elk Grove Village (village) Cook County	42	0.13

Top 10 Places Sorted by Percent of Total Population
Based on places with total population of 50,000 or more

Place	Population	%
Berwyn (city) Cook County	26	0.05
Naperville (city) DuPage County	54	0.04
Chicago (city) Cook County	533	0.02
Champaign (city) Champaign County	19	0.02
Joliet (city) Will County	14	0.01
Decatur (city) Macon County	11	0.01
Arlington Heights (village) Cook County	0	0.00
Aurora (city) Kane County	0	0.00
Bloomington (city) McLean County	0	0.00
Bolingbrook (village) Will County	0	0.00

West Indian: U.S. Virgin Islander, excluding Hispanic

Top 10 Places Sorted by Population
Based on all places, regardless of total population

Place	Population	%
Champaign (city) Champaign County	81	0.10
Chicago (city) Cook County	32	<0.01
Bloomington (city) McLean County	13	0.02
Park Ridge (city) Cook County	11	0.03
Abingdon (city) Knox County	0	0.00
Adair (cdp) McDonough County	0	0.00
Addieville (village) Washington County	0	0.00
Addison (village) DuPage County	0	0.00
Adeline (village) Ogle County	0	0.00
Albany (village) Whiteside County	0	0.00

Top 10 Places Sorted by Percent of Total Population
Based on all places, regardless of total population

Place	Population	%
Champaign (city) Champaign County	81	0.10
Park Ridge (city) Cook County	11	0.03
Bloomington (city) McLean County	13	0.02
Chicago (city) Cook County	32	<0.01
Abingdon (city) Knox County	0	0.00
Adair (cdp) McDonough County	0	0.00
Addieville (village) Washington County	0	0.00
Addison (village) DuPage County	0	0.00
Adeline (village) Ogle County	0	0.00
Albany (village) Whiteside County	0	0.00

Top 10 Places Sorted by Percent of Total Population
Based on places with total population of 50,000 or more

Place	Population	%
Champaign (city) Champaign County	81	0.10
Bloomington (city) McLean County	13	0.02
Chicago (city) Cook County	32	<0.01
Arlington Heights (village) Cook County	0	0.00
Aurora (city) Kane County	0	0.00
Berwyn (city) Cook County	0	0.00
Bolingbrook (village) Will County	0	0.00
Cicero (town) Cook County	0	0.00
Decatur (city) Macon County	0	0.00
Des Plaines (city) Cook County	0	0.00

West Indian: West Indian, excluding Hispanic

Top 10 Places Sorted by Population
Based on all places, regardless of total population

Place	Population	%
Chicago (city) Cook County	698	0.03
Tinley Park (village) Cook County	127	0.23
Shiloh (village) St. Clair County	126	1.05
Oak Park (village) Cook County	120	0.23
Calumet City (city) Cook County	94	0.25
Murphysboro (city) Jackson County	90	1.07
Evanston (city) Cook County	87	0.12
Robbins (village) Cook County	76	1.44
Rockford (city) Winnebago County	74	0.05
Antioch (village) Lake County	57	0.42

Top 10 Places Sorted by Percent of Total Population
Based on all places, regardless of total population

Place	Population	%
Robbins (village) Cook County	76	1.44
Murphysboro (city) Jackson County	90	1.07
Shiloh (village) St. Clair County	126	1.05
Willowbrook (cdp) Will County	14	0.58
Pawnee (village) Sangamon County	11	0.43
Antioch (village) Lake County	57	0.42
Mound City (city) Pulaski County	3	0.36
Calumet City (city) Cook County	94	0.25
Bellwood (village) Cook County	46	0.24
Tinley Park (village) Cook County	127	0.23

Top 10 Places Sorted by Percent of Total Population
Based on places with total population of 50,000 or more

Place	Population	%
Tinley Park (village) Cook County	127	0.23

Place	Population	%
Oak Park (village) Cook County	120	0.23
Evanston (city) Cook County	87	0.12
Rockford (city) Winnebago County	74	0.05
Chicago (city) Cook County	698	0.03
Normal (town) McLean County	15	0.03
Springfield (city) Sangamon County	18	0.02
Waukegan (city) Lake County	18	0.02
Palatine (village) Cook County	11	0.02
Elgin (city) Kane County	14	0.01

West Indian: Other, excluding Hispanic

Top 10 Places Sorted by Population
Based on all places, regardless of total population

Place	Population	%
Abingdon (city) Knox County	0	0.00
Adair (cdp) McDonough County	0	0.00
Addieville (village) Washington County	0	0.00
Addison (village) DuPage County	0	0.00
Adeline (village) Ogle County	0	0.00
Albany (village) Whiteside County	0	0.00
Albers (village) Clinton County	0	0.00
Albion (city) Edwards County	0	0.00
Aledo (city) Mercer County	0	0.00
Alexis (village) Warren County	0	0.00

Top 10 Places Sorted by Percent of Total Population
Based on all places, regardless of total population

Place	Population	%
Abingdon (city) Knox County	0	0.00
Adair (cdp) McDonough County	0	0.00
Addieville (village) Washington County	0	0.00
Addison (village) DuPage County	0	0.00
Adeline (village) Ogle County	0	0.00
Albany (village) Whiteside County	0	0.00
Albers (village) Clinton County	0	0.00
Albion (city) Edwards County	0	0.00
Aledo (city) Mercer County	0	0.00
Alexis (village) Warren County	0	0.00

Top 10 Places Sorted by Percent of Total Population
Based on places with total population of 50,000 or more

Place	Population	%
Arlington Heights (village) Cook County	0	0.00
Aurora (city) Kane County	0	0.00
Berwyn (city) Cook County	0	0.00
Bloomington (city) McLean County	0	0.00
Bolingbrook (village) Will County	0	0.00
Champaign (city) Champaign County	0	0.00
Chicago (city) Cook County	0	0.00
Cicero (town) Cook County	0	0.00
Decatur (city) Macon County	0	0.00
Des Plaines (city) Cook County	0	0.00

Yugoslavian

Top 10 Places Sorted by Population
Based on all places, regardless of total population

Place	Population	%
Chicago (city) Cook County	6,612	0.24
Des Plaines (city) Cook County	381	0.66
Rockford (city) Winnebago County	375	0.24
Niles (village) Cook County	327	1.11
Wheaton (city) DuPage County	285	0.54
Skokie (village) Cook County	281	0.44
Brookfield (village) Cook County	279	1.48
Hanover Park (village) Cook County	265	0.70
Oswego (village) Kendall County	263	0.95
Villa Park (village) DuPage County	251	1.13

Top 10 Places Sorted by Percent of Total Population
Based on all places, regardless of total population

Place	Population	%
Ridott (village) Stephenson County	8	7.21
De Witt (village) De Witt County	8	3.85
Dunfermline (village) Fulton County	7	3.45
Witt (city) Montgomery County	31	3.18
Dongola (village) Union County	18	2.30
Buckingham (village) Kankakee County	6	2.21
Newman (city) Douglas County	22	2.09
London Mills (village) Fulton County	8	1.82

Place	Population	%
Matherville (village) Mercer County	11	1.53
Brookfield (village) Cook County	279	1.48

Top 10 Places Sorted by Percent of Total Population
Based on places with total population of 50,000 or more

Place	Population	%
Des Plaines (city) Cook County	381	0.66
Wheaton (city) DuPage County	285	0.54
Mount Prospect (village) Cook County	244	0.45
Skokie (village) Cook County	281	0.44
Berwyn (city) Cook County	166	0.30
Schaumburg (village) Cook County	180	0.25
Chicago (city) Cook County	6,612	0.24
Rockford (city) Winnebago County	375	0.24
Hoffman Estates (village) Cook County	85	0.17
Oak Park (village) Cook County	65	0.13

Hispanic Origin Rankings

Hispanic or Latino (of any race)

Top 10 Places Sorted by Population
Based on all places, regardless of total population

Place	Population	%
Chicago (city) Cook County	778,862	28.89
Aurora (city) Kane County	81,809	41.34
Cicero (town) Cook County	72,609	86.55
Waukegan (city) Lake County	47,612	53.45
Elgin (city) Kane County	47,121	43.55
Joliet (city) Will County	41,042	27.84
Berwyn (city) Cook County	33,676	59.44
Rockford (city) Winnebago County	24,085	15.76
Carpentersville (village) Kane County	18,877	50.08
Bolingbrook (village) Will County	17,957	24.48

Top 10 Places Sorted by Percent of Total Population
Based on all places, regardless of total population

Place	Population	%
Stone Park (village) Cook County	4,359	88.13
Cicero (town) Cook County	72,609	86.55
Fairmont City (village) St. Clair County	1,882	71.42
Melrose Park (village) Cook County	17,675	69.56
Park City (city) Lake County	4,933	65.17
Summit (village) Cook County	7,042	63.71
Berwyn (city) Cook County	33,676	59.44
Highwood (city) Lake County	3,074	56.87
De Pue (village) Bureau County	1,005	54.68
Waukegan (city) Lake County	47,612	53.45

Top 10 Places Sorted by Percent of Total Population
Based on places with total population of 50,000 or more

Place	Population	%
Cicero (town) Cook County	72,609	86.55
Berwyn (city) Cook County	33,676	59.44
Waukegan (city) Lake County	47,612	53.45
Elgin (city) Kane County	47,121	43.55
Aurora (city) Kane County	81,809	41.34
Chicago (city) Cook County	778,862	28.89
Joliet (city) Will County	41,042	27.84
Bolingbrook (village) Will County	17,957	24.48
Palatine (village) Cook County	12,347	18.01
Des Plaines (city) Cook County	10,053	17.22

Central American, excluding Mexican

Top 10 Places Sorted by Population
Based on all places, regardless of total population

Place	Population	%
Chicago (city) Cook County	31,263	1.16
Waukegan (city) Lake County	3,653	4.10
Cicero (town) Cook County	1,293	1.54
Aurora (city) Kane County	1,086	0.55
Bensenville (village) DuPage County	1,072	5.84
Elgin (city) Kane County	888	0.82
Berwyn (city) Cook County	825	1.46
Carpentersville (village) Kane County	748	1.98
Joliet (city) Will County	588	0.40
Addison (village) DuPage County	561	1.52

Top 10 Places Sorted by Percent of Total Population
Based on all places, regardless of total population

Place	Population	%
Bensenville (village) DuPage County	1,072	5.84
Pontoosuc (village) Hancock County	6	4.11
Waukegan (city) Lake County	3,653	4.10
Round Lake Heights (village) Lake County	81	3.03
Northlake (city) Cook County	361	2.93
Stone Park (village) Cook County	144	2.91
Park City (city) Lake County	217	2.87
Highwood (city) Lake County	149	2.76
Franklin Park (village) Cook County	387	2.11
Carpentersville (village) Kane County	748	1.98

Top 10 Places Sorted by Percent of Total Population
Based on places with total population of 50,000 or more

Place	Population	%
Waukegan (city) Lake County	3,653	4.10
Cicero (town) Cook County	1,293	1.54
Berwyn (city) Cook County	825	1.46
Chicago (city) Cook County	31,263	1.16
Elgin (city) Kane County	888	0.82
Skokie (village) Cook County	497	0.77
Des Plaines (city) Cook County	445	0.76
Palatine (village) Cook County	484	0.71
Bolingbrook (village) Will County	460	0.63
Hoffman Estates (village) Cook County	326	0.63

Central American: Costa Rican

Top 10 Places Sorted by Population
Based on all places, regardless of total population

Place	Population	%
Chicago (city) Cook County	681	0.03
Champaign (city) Champaign County	29	0.04
Rockford (city) Winnebago County	29	0.02
Des Plaines (city) Cook County	28	0.05
Naperville (city) DuPage County	26	0.02
Evanston (city) Cook County	24	0.03
Palatine (village) Cook County	22	0.03
Cicero (town) Cook County	21	0.03
Carpentersville (village) Kane County	18	0.05
Cary (village) McHenry County	17	0.09

Top 10 Places Sorted by Percent of Total Population
Based on all places, regardless of total population

Place	Population	%
Spillertown (village) Williamson County	2	0.99
Crainville (village) Williamson County	5	0.40
Edgewood (village) Effingham County	1	0.23
Carterville (city) Williamson County	10	0.18
Carrollton (city) Greene County	4	0.16
Findlay (village) Shelby County	1	0.15
Prestbury (cdp) Kane County	2	0.12
Southern View (village) Sangamon County	2	0.12
Lincolnshire (village) Lake County	8	0.11
Prairie Grove (village) McHenry County	2	0.11

Top 10 Places Sorted by Percent of Total Population
Based on places with total population of 50,000 or more

Place	Population	%
Des Plaines (city) Cook County	28	0.05
Champaign (city) Champaign County	29	0.04
Chicago (city) Cook County	681	0.03
Evanston (city) Cook County	24	0.03
Palatine (village) Cook County	22	0.03
Cicero (town) Cook County	21	0.03
Berwyn (city) Cook County	15	0.03
Rockford (city) Winnebago County	29	0.02
Naperville (city) DuPage County	26	0.02
Skokie (village) Cook County	15	0.02

Central American: Guatemalan

Top 10 Places Sorted by Population
Based on all places, regardless of total population

Place	Population	%
Chicago (city) Cook County	17,973	0.67
Bensenville (village) DuPage County	969	5.28
Cicero (town) Cook County	650	0.77
Berwyn (city) Cook County	476	0.84
Addison (village) DuPage County	418	1.13
Aurora (city) Kane County	386	0.20
Glendale Heights (village) DuPage County	357	1.04
Elgin (city) Kane County	356	0.33
Waukegan (city) Lake County	340	0.38
Joliet (city) Will County	323	0.22

Top 10 Places Sorted by Percent of Total Population
Based on all places, regardless of total population

Place	Population	%
Bensenville (village) DuPage County	969	5.28
Pontoosuc (village) Hancock County	6	4.11
Northlake (city) Cook County	285	2.31
Stone Park (village) Cook County	107	2.10
Franklin Park (village) Cook County	273	1.49
Cedar Point (village) LaSalle County	4	1.44
Cantrall (village) Sangamon County	2	1.44
Highwood (city) Lake County	74	1.37
Melrose Park (village) Cook County	297	1.17
Addison (village) DuPage County	418	1.13

Top 10 Places Sorted by Percent of Total Population
Based on places with total population of 50,000 or more

Place	Population	%
Berwyn (city) Cook County	476	0.84
Cicero (town) Cook County	650	0.77
Chicago (city) Cook County	17,973	0.67
Skokie (village) Cook County	284	0.4
Bloomington (city) McLean County	301	0.39
Waukegan (city) Lake County	340	0.38
Bolingbrook (village) Will County	262	0.36
Elgin (city) Kane County	356	0.33
Des Plaines (city) Cook County	184	0.31
Champaign (city) Champaign County	217	0.2

Central American: Honduran

Top 10 Places Sorted by Population
Based on all places, regardless of total population

Place	Population	%
Chicago (city) Cook County	5,021	0.19
Waukegan (city) Lake County	2,311	2.59
Aurora (city) Kane County	211	0.1
Cicero (town) Cook County	205	0.24
Zion (city) Lake County	184	0.75
North Chicago (city) Lake County	157	0.44
Palatine (village) Cook County	101	0.15
Park City (city) Lake County	95	1.25
Berwyn (city) Cook County	95	0.17
Gurnee (village) Lake County	94	0.36

Top 10 Places Sorted by Percent of Total Population
Based on all places, regardless of total population

Place	Population	%
Waukegan (city) Lake County	2,311	2.59
Arlington (village) Bureau County	3	1.5
Park City (city) Lake County	95	1.25
Percy (village) Randolph County	8	0.82
Highwood (city) Lake County	43	0.8
Zion (city) Lake County	184	0.75
East Hazel Crest (village) Cook County	10	0.6
South Chicago Heights (village) Cook County	24	0.5
Beach Park (village) Lake County	73	0.5
Makanda (village) Jackson County	3	0.5

Top 10 Places Sorted by Percent of Total Population
Based on places with total population of 50,000 or more

Place	Population	%
Waukegan (city) Lake County	2,311	2.59
Cicero (town) Cook County	205	0.24
Chicago (city) Cook County	5,021	0.19
Berwyn (city) Cook County	95	0.1
Palatine (village) Cook County	101	0.15
Aurora (city) Kane County	211	0.11
Elgin (city) Kane County	87	0.08
Skokie (village) Cook County	51	0.08
Rockford (city) Winnebago County	92	0.06
Bolingbrook (village) Will County	46	0.06

Central American: Nicaraguan

Top 10 Places Sorted by Population
Based on all places, regardless of total population

Place	Population	%
Chicago (city) Cook County	1,239	0.05
Cicero (town) Cook County	105	0.13
Aurora (city) Kane County	98	0.05
Berwyn (city) Cook County	41	0.07
Waukegan (city) Lake County	39	0.04
Naperville (city) DuPage County	31	0.02
Evanston (city) Cook County	30	0.04
Schaumburg (village) Cook County	26	0.04
Skokie (village) Cook County	26	0.04
Joliet (city) Will County	26	0.02

Top 10 Places Sorted by Percent of Total Population
Based on all places, regardless of total population

Place	Population	%
Indian Creek (village) Lake County	3	0.65
North City (village) Franklin County	3	0.49
McCook (village) Cook County	1	0.44
Newman (city) Douglas County	3	0.35
Burlington (village) Kane County	2	0.32
New Boston (city) Mercer County	2	0.29
Jerome (village) Sangamon County	4	0.24
Port Barrington (village) McHenry County	3	0.20
Stone Park (village) Cook County	9	0.18
Park City (city) Lake County	12	0.16

Top 10 Places Sorted by Percent of Total Population
Based on places with total population of 50,000 or more

Place	Population	%
Cicero (town) Cook County	105	0.13
Berwyn (city) Cook County	41	0.07
Chicago (city) Cook County	1,239	0.05
Aurora (city) Kane County	98	0.05
Waukegan (city) Lake County	39	0.04
Evanston (city) Cook County	30	0.04
Schaumburg (village) Cook County	26	0.04
Skokie (village) Cook County	26	0.04
Des Plaines (city) Cook County	24	0.04
Oak Park (village) Cook County	22	0.04

Central American: Panamanian

Top 10 Places Sorted by Population
Based on all places, regardless of total population

Place	Population	%
Chicago (city) Cook County	883	0.03
Aurora (city) Kane County	60	0.03
Evanston (city) Cook County	52	0.07
Joliet (city) Will County	42	0.03
Bolingbrook (village) Will County	41	0.06
Naperville (city) DuPage County	35	0.02
Oak Park (village) Cook County	34	0.07
O'Fallon (city) St. Clair County	32	0.11
Waukegan (city) Lake County	29	0.03
Springfield (city) Sangamon County	28	0.02

Top 10 Places Sorted by Percent of Total Population
Based on all places, regardless of total population

Place	Population	%
Whiteash (village) Williamson County	2	0.83
Chestnut (cdp) Logan County	2	0.81
Thayer (village) Sangamon County	4	0.58
Creal Springs (city) Williamson County	3	0.55
Scott AFB (cdp) St. Clair County	18	0.50
Buckley (village) Iroquois County	3	0.50
Du Bois (village) Washington County	1	0.49
McCook (village) Cook County	1	0.44
Kempton (village) Ford County	1	0.43
Thompsonville (village) Franklin County	2	0.37

Top 10 Places Sorted by Percent of Total Population
Based on places with total population of 50,000 or more

Place	Population	%
Evanston (city) Cook County	52	0.07
Oak Park (village) Cook County	34	0.07
Bolingbrook (village) Will County	41	0.06
Skokie (village) Cook County	25	0.04

Place	Population	%
Chicago (city) Cook County	883	0.03
Aurora (city) Kane County	60	0.03
Joliet (city) Will County	42	0.03
Waukegan (city) Lake County	29	0.03
Cicero (town) Cook County	22	0.03
Schaumburg (village) Cook County	20	0.03

Central American: Salvadoran

Top 10 Places Sorted by Population
Based on all places, regardless of total population

Place	Population	%
Chicago (city) Cook County	5,204	0.19
Waukegan (city) Lake County	887	1.00
Carpentersville (village) Kane County	478	1.27
Elgin (city) Kane County	387	0.36
Aurora (city) Kane County	289	0.15
Cicero (town) Cook County	278	0.33
Streamwood (village) Cook County	234	0.59
Berwyn (city) Cook County	182	0.32
Wheeling (village) Cook County	167	0.44
Des Plaines (city) Cook County	165	0.28

Top 10 Places Sorted by Percent of Total Population
Based on all places, regardless of total population

Place	Population	%
Round Lake Heights (village) Lake County	46	1.72
Carpentersville (village) Kane County	478	1.27
Waukegan (city) Lake County	887	1.00
De Pue (village) Bureau County	16	0.87
Bedford Park (village) Cook County	5	0.86
Summit (village) Cook County	87	0.79
Hainesville (village) Lake County	28	0.78
Beardstown (city) Cass County	43	0.70
Rolling Meadows (city) Cook County	153	0.63
Park City (city) Lake County	46	0.61

Top 10 Places Sorted by Percent of Total Population
Based on places with total population of 50,000 or more

Place	Population	%
Waukegan (city) Lake County	887	1.00
Elgin (city) Kane County	387	0.36
Cicero (town) Cook County	278	0.33
Berwyn (city) Cook County	182	0.32
Des Plaines (city) Cook County	165	0.28
Hoffman Estates (village) Cook County	125	0.24
Palatine (village) Cook County	153	0.22
Mount Prospect (village) Cook County	115	0.21
Chicago (city) Cook County	5,204	0.19
Aurora (city) Kane County	289	0.15

Central American: Other Central American

Top 10 Places Sorted by Population
Based on all places, regardless of total population

Place	Population	%
Chicago (city) Cook County	262	0.01
Waukegan (city) Lake County	44	0.05
Aurora (city) Kane County	29	0.01
Park City (city) Lake County	13	0.17
Addison (village) DuPage County	12	0.03
Schaumburg (village) Cook County	12	0.02
Cicero (town) Cook County	12	0.01
Maywood (village) Cook County	10	0.04
Evanston (city) Cook County	10	0.01
Justice (village) Cook County	9	0.07

Top 10 Places Sorted by Percent of Total Population
Based on all places, regardless of total population

Place	Population	%
Worden (village) Madison County	5	0.48
Owaneco (village) Christian County	1	0.42
Park City (city) Lake County	13	0.17
East Dundee (village) Kane County	4	0.14
Assumption (city) Christian County	1	0.09
Justice (village) Cook County	9	0.07
Waukegan (city) Lake County	44	0.05
Northlake (city) Cook County	6	0.05
Island Lake (village) McHenry County	4	0.05
Maywood (village) Cook County	10	0.04

Central American: Other

Top 10 Places Sorted by Percent of Total Population
Based on places with total population of 50,000 or more

Place	Population	%
Waukegan (city) Lake County	44	0.05
Schaumburg (village) Cook County	12	0.02
Chicago (city) Cook County	262	0.01
Aurora (city) Kane County	29	0.01
Cicero (town) Cook County	12	0.01
Evanston (city) Cook County	10	0.01
Palatine (village) Cook County	9	0.01
Skokie (village) Cook County	9	0.01
Mount Prospect (village) Cook County	6	0.01
Des Plaines (city) Cook County	5	0.01

Cuban

Top 10 Places Sorted by Population
Based on all places, regardless of total population

Place	Population	%
Chicago (city) Cook County	8,331	0.31
Skokie (village) Cook County	476	0.73
Rockford (city) Winnebago County	418	0.27
Aurora (city) Kane County	318	0.16
Naperville (city) DuPage County	286	0.20
Evanston (city) Cook County	278	0.37
Melrose Park (village) Cook County	237	0.93
Elgin (city) Kane County	204	0.19
West Chicago (city) DuPage County	182	0.67
Elmhurst (city) DuPage County	174	0.39

Top 10 Places Sorted by Percent of Total Population
Based on all places, regardless of total population

Place	Population	%
Rock Island Arsenal (cdp) Rock Island County	3	2.01
Beardstown (city) Cass County	98	1.60
Shumway (village) Effingham County	3	1.49
Stone Park (village) Cook County	57	1.15
Northlake (city) Cook County	122	0.99
Melrose Park (village) Cook County	237	0.93
Rio (village) Knox County	2	0.91
Lee (village) Lee County	3	0.89
Lincolnwood (village) Cook County	93	0.74
Skokie (village) Cook County	476	0.73

Top 10 Places Sorted by Percent of Total Population
Based on places with total population of 50,000 or more

Place	Population	%
Skokie (village) Cook County	476	0.73
Evanston (city) Cook County	278	0.37
Chicago (city) Cook County	8,331	0.31
Mount Prospect (village) Cook County	170	0.31
Berwyn (city) Cook County	167	0.29
Wheaton (city) DuPage County	149	0.28
Rockford (city) Winnebago County	418	0.27
Des Plaines (city) Cook County	149	0.26
Oak Park (village) Cook County	134	0.26
Arlington Heights (village) Cook County	162	0.22

Dominican Republic

Top 10 Places Sorted by Population
Based on all places, regardless of total population

Place	Population	%
Chicago (city) Cook County	2,737	0.10
Cicero (town) Cook County	150	0.18
Aurora (city) Kane County	110	0.06
Waukegan (city) Lake County	103	0.12
Joliet (city) Will County	88	0.06
Elgin (city) Kane County	66	0.06
Naperville (city) DuPage County	66	0.05
Beardstown (city) Cass County	64	1.05
North Chicago (city) Lake County	63	0.19
Evanston (city) Cook County	59	0.08

Top 10 Places Sorted by Percent of Total Population
Based on all places, regardless of total population

Place	Population	%
Secor (village) Woodford County	4	1.07
Beardstown (city) Cass County	64	1.05
Ellis Grove (village) Randolph County	2	0.55

Place	Population	%
Shannon (village) Carroll County	3	0.40
Garden Prairie (village) Boone County	1	0.28
Melrose Park (village) Cook County	54	0.21
Stone Park (village) Cook County	10	0.20
East Carondelet (village) St. Clair County	1	0.20
North Chicago (city) Lake County	63	0.19
Bannockburn (village) Lake County	3	0.19

Top 10 Places Sorted by Percent of Total Population
Based on places with total population of 50,000 or more

Place	Population	%
Cicero (town) Cook County	150	0.18
Waukegan (city) Lake County	103	0.12
Chicago (city) Cook County	2,737	0.10
Oak Park (village) Cook County	47	0.09
Evanston (city) Cook County	59	0.08
Berwyn (city) Cook County	47	0.08
Aurora (city) Kane County	110	0.06
Joliet (city) Will County	88	0.06
Elgin (city) Kane County	66	0.06
Hoffman Estates (village) Cook County	30	0.06

Mexican

Top 10 Places Sorted by Population
Based on all places, regardless of total population

Place	Population	%
Chicago (city) Cook County	578,100	21.45
Aurora (city) Kane County	72,924	36.85
Cicero (town) Cook County	65,694	78.31
Elgin (city) Kane County	41,265	38.14
Waukegan (city) Lake County	38,636	43.37
Joliet (city) Will County	36,570	24.80
Berwyn (city) Cook County	28,185	49.75
Rockford (city) Winnebago County	20,019	13.10
Carpentersville (village) Kane County	16,794	44.56
Bolingbrook (village) Will County	15,256	20.79

Top 10 Places Sorted by Percent of Total Population
Based on all places, regardless of total population

Place	Population	%
Stone Park (village) Cook County	3,887	78.59
Cicero (town) Cook County	65,694	78.31
Fairmont City (village) St. Clair County	1,755	66.60
Melrose Park (village) Cook County	15,141	59.58
Summit (village) Cook County	6,500	58.80
Park City (city) Lake County	4,279	56.53
Highwood (city) Lake County	2,777	51.38
Posen (village) Cook County	3,025	50.53
De Pue (village) Bureau County	915	49.78
Berwyn (city) Cook County	28,185	49.75

Top 10 Places Sorted by Percent of Total Population
Based on places with total population of 50,000 or more

Place	Population	%
Cicero (town) Cook County	65,694	78.31
Berwyn (city) Cook County	28,185	49.75
Waukegan (city) Lake County	38,636	43.37
Elgin (city) Kane County	41,265	38.14
Aurora (city) Kane County	72,924	36.85
Joliet (city) Will County	36,570	24.80
Chicago (city) Cook County	578,100	21.45
Bolingbrook (village) Will County	15,256	20.79
Palatine (village) Cook County	10,256	14.96
Des Plaines (city) Cook County	8,001	13.71

Puerto Rican

Top 10 Places Sorted by Population
Based on all places, regardless of total population

Place	Population	%
Chicago (city) Cook County	102,703	3.81
Aurora (city) Kane County	3,867	1.95
Elgin (city) Kane County	2,973	2.75
Berwyn (city) Cook County	2,918	5.15
Waukegan (city) Lake County	2,918	3.28
Cicero (town) Cook County	2,782	3.32
Joliet (city) Will County	2,084	1.41
Elmwood Park (village) Cook County	1,735	6.97
Rockford (city) Winnebago County	1,323	0.87
Bolingbrook (village) Will County	1,254	1.71

Top 10 Places Sorted by Percent of Total Population
Based on all places, regardless of total population

Place	Population	%
Kaskaskia (village) Randolph County	4	28.57
Elmwood Park (village) Cook County	1,735	6.97
River Grove (village) Cook County	562	5.50
Berwyn (city) Cook County	2,918	5.15
Franklin Park (village) Cook County	829	4.52
Melrose Park (village) Cook County	1,095	4.31
Northlake (city) Cook County	522	4.24
Chicago (city) Cook County	102,703	3.81
Stickney (village) Cook County	255	3.76
Zion (city) Lake County	870	3.56

Top 10 Places Sorted by Percent of Total Population
Based on places with total population of 50,000 or more

Place	Population	%
Berwyn (city) Cook County	2,918	5.15
Chicago (city) Cook County	102,703	3.81
Cicero (town) Cook County	2,782	3.32
Waukegan (city) Lake County	2,918	3.28
Elgin (city) Kane County	2,973	2.75
Aurora (city) Kane County	3,867	1.95
Bolingbrook (village) Will County	1,254	1.71
Joliet (city) Will County	2,084	1.41
Skokie (village) Cook County	754	1.16
Hoffman Estates (village) Cook County	584	1.13

South American

Top 10 Places Sorted by Population
Based on all places, regardless of total population

Place	Population	%
Chicago (city) Cook County	32,129	1.19
Aurora (city) Kane County	1,010	0.51
Berwyn (city) Cook County	856	1.51
Skokie (village) Cook County	822	1.27
Naperville (city) DuPage County	798	0.56
Cicero (town) Cook County	719	0.86
Evanston (city) Cook County	708	0.95
Elgin (city) Kane County	637	0.59
Schaumburg (village) Cook County	590	0.79
Waukegan (city) Lake County	546	0.61

Top 10 Places Sorted by Percent of Total Population
Based on all places, regardless of total population

Place	Population	%
Elmwood Park (village) Cook County	489	1.97
Lynnville (village) Morgan County	2	1.71
Pingree Grove (village) Kane County	73	1.61
Forest View (village) Cook County	11	1.58
Camargo (village) Douglas County	7	1.57
Lincolnwood (village) Cook County	197	1.56
Berwyn (city) Cook County	856	1.51
Harwood Heights (village) Cook County	126	1.46
Niles (village) Cook County	402	1.35
Schiller Park (village) Cook County	152	1.29

Top 10 Places Sorted by Percent of Total Population
Based on places with total population of 50,000 or more

Place	Population	%
Berwyn (city) Cook County	856	1.51
Skokie (village) Cook County	822	1.27
Chicago (city) Cook County	32,129	1.19
Evanston (city) Cook County	708	0.95
Oak Park (village) Cook County	477	0.92
Cicero (town) Cook County	719	0.86
Hoffman Estates (village) Cook County	439	0.85
Des Plaines (city) Cook County	492	0.84
Schaumburg (village) Cook County	590	0.79
Palatine (village) Cook County	532	0.78

South American: Argentinean

Top 10 Places Sorted by Population
Based on all places, regardless of total population

Place	Population	%
Chicago (city) Cook County	1,743	0.06
Evanston (city) Cook County	134	0.18
Aurora (city) Kane County	133	0.07

Place	Population	%
Naperville (city) DuPage County	111	0
Elmwood Park (village) Cook County	81	0
Berwyn (city) Cook County	79	0
Oak Park (village) Cook County	77	0
Skokie (village) Cook County	74	0
Champaign (city) Champaign County	73	0
Schaumburg (village) Cook County	60	0

Top 10 Places Sorted by Percent of Total Populati
Based on all places, regardless of total population

Place	Population	
Cypress (village) Johnson County	1	0
Braceville (village) Grundy County	3	0
Mettawa (village) Lake County	2	0
Elmwood Park (village) Cook County	81	0
South Wilmington (village) Grundy County	2	0
Hawthorn Woods (village) Lake County	19	0
Stickney (village) Cook County	16	0
Willowbrook (cdp) Will County	5	0
Sadorus (village) Champaign County	1	0
Schiller Park (village) Cook County	23	0

Top 10 Places Sorted by Percent of Total Populati
Based on places with total population of 50,000 or more

Place	Population	
Evanston (city) Cook County	134	0
Oak Park (village) Cook County	77	0
Berwyn (city) Cook County	79	0
Skokie (village) Cook County	74	0
Champaign (city) Champaign County	73	0
Naperville (city) DuPage County	111	0
Schaumburg (village) Cook County	60	0
Wheaton (city) DuPage County	42	0
Aurora (city) Kane County	133	0
Arlington Heights (village) Cook County	53	0

South American: Bolivian

Top 10 Places Sorted by Population
Based on all places, regardless of total population

Place	Population	
Chicago (city) Cook County	626	0
Aurora (city) Kane County	96	0
Skokie (village) Cook County	59	0
Wheaton (city) DuPage County	40	0
Berwyn (city) Cook County	34	0
Wilmette (village) Cook County	31	0
Bolingbrook (village) Will County	29	0
Elmhurst (city) DuPage County	28	0
Des Plaines (city) Cook County	27	0
Naperville (city) DuPage County	27	0

Top 10 Places Sorted by Percent of Total Populatic
Based on all places, regardless of total population

Place	Population	
Golf (village) Cook County	2	0
Grandwood Park (cdp) Lake County	13	0
River Forest (village) Cook County	25	0
Oak Brook (village) DuPage County	16	0
Greenfield (city) Greene County	2	0
Riverside (village) Cook County	13	0
Willowbrook (cdp) Will County	3	0
Kenilworth (village) Cook County	3	0
Wilmette (village) Cook County	31	0
Lincolnwood (village) Cook County	14	0

Top 10 Places Sorted by Percent of Total Populati
Based on places with total population of 50,000 or more

Place	Population	
Skokie (village) Cook County	59	0
Wheaton (city) DuPage County	40	0
Berwyn (city) Cook County	34	0
Aurora (city) Kane County	96	0
Des Plaines (city) Cook County	27	0
Bolingbrook (village) Will County	29	0
Oak Lawn (village) Cook County	23	0
Oak Park (village) Cook County	20	0
Champaign (city) Champaign County	25	0
Evanston (city) Cook County	22	0

South American: Chilean

Top 10 Places Sorted by Population
Based on all places, regardless of total population

Place	Population	%
Chicago (city) Cook County	876	0.03
Evanston (city) Cook County	81	0.11
Naperville (city) DuPage County	65	0.05
Oak Park (village) Cook County	49	0.09
Aurora (city) Kane County	42	0.02
Champaign (city) Champaign County	41	0.05
Berwyn (city) Cook County	36	0.06
Schaumburg (village) Cook County	31	0.04
Wheaton (city) DuPage County	29	0.05
Skokie (village) Cook County	29	0.04

Top 10 Places Sorted by Percent of Total Population
Based on all places, regardless of total population

Place	Population	%
Lynnville (village) Morgan County	2	1.71
Bull Valley (village) McHenry County	5	0.46
Indian Creek (village) Lake County	2	0.43
Golf (village) Cook County	2	0.40
Fairmont City (village) St. Clair County	10	0.38
Coulterville (village) Randolph County	3	0.32
Wyoming (city) Stark County	4	0.28
Windsor (city) Shelby County	3	0.25
Hopewell (village) Marshall County	1	0.24
Oak Brook (village) DuPage County	15	0.19

Top 10 Places Sorted by Percent of Total Population
Based on places with total population of 50,000 or more

Place	Population	%
Evanston (city) Cook County	81	0.11
Oak Park (village) Cook County	49	0.09
Berwyn (city) Cook County	36	0.06
Naperville (city) DuPage County	65	0.05
Champaign (city) Champaign County	41	0.05
Wheaton (city) DuPage County	29	0.05
Des Plaines (city) Cook County	28	0.05
Schaumburg (village) Cook County	31	0.04
Skokie (village) Cook County	29	0.04
Normal (town) McLean County	21	0.04

South American: Colombian

Top 10 Places Sorted by Population
Based on all places, regardless of total population

Place	Population	%
Chicago (city) Cook County	7,547	0.28
Waukegan (city) Lake County	358	0.40
Aurora (city) Kane County	311	0.16
Berwyn (city) Cook County	276	0.49
Naperville (city) DuPage County	262	0.18
Elgin (city) Kane County	253	0.23
Skokie (village) Cook County	220	0.34
Schaumburg (village) Cook County	211	0.28
Rockford (city) Winnebago County	211	0.14
Evanston (city) Cook County	179	0.24

Top 10 Places Sorted by Percent of Total Population
Based on all places, regardless of total population

Place	Population	%
Forest View (village) Cook County	8	1.15
Congerville (village) Woodford County	5	1.05
Tennessee (village) McDonough County	1	0.87
Pingree Grove (village) Kane County	31	0.68
Woodhull (village) Henry County	5	0.62
Elmwood Park (village) Cook County	142	0.57
Schiller Park (village) Cook County	62	0.53
Berwyn (city) Cook County	276	0.49
Du Bois (village) Washington County	1	0.49
Grand Detour (cdp) Ogle County	2	0.47

Top 10 Places Sorted by Percent of Total Population
Based on places with total population of 50,000 or more

Place	Population	%
Berwyn (city) Cook County	276	0.49
Waukegan (city) Lake County	358	0.40
Skokie (village) Cook County	220	0.34
Chicago (city) Cook County	7,547	0.28

Place	Population	%
Schaumburg (village) Cook County	211	0.28
Evanston (city) Cook County	179	0.24
Palatine (village) Cook County	162	0.24
Des Plaines (city) Cook County	139	0.24
Wheaton (city) DuPage County	129	0.24
Elgin (city) Kane County	253	0.23

South American: Ecuadorian

Top 10 Places Sorted by Population
Based on all places, regardless of total population

Place	Population	%
Chicago (city) Cook County	15,466	0.57
Cicero (town) Cook County	365	0.44
Berwyn (city) Cook County	257	0.45
Niles (village) Cook County	203	0.68
Skokie (village) Cook County	195	0.30
Des Plaines (city) Cook County	165	0.28
Elgin (city) Kane County	152	0.14
Elmwood Park (village) Cook County	137	0.55
Aurora (city) Kane County	135	0.07
Schaumburg (village) Cook County	132	0.18

Top 10 Places Sorted by Percent of Total Population
Based on all places, regardless of total population

Place	Population	%
Camargo (village) Douglas County	5	1.12
Niles (village) Cook County	203	0.68
Chicago (city) Cook County	15,466	0.57
Harwood Heights (village) Cook County	48	0.56
Elmwood Park (village) Cook County	137	0.55
Berwyn (city) Cook County	257	0.45
Rosemont (village) Cook County	19	0.45
Cicero (town) Cook County	365	0.44
River Grove (village) Cook County	45	0.44
Lincolnwood (village) Cook County	54	0.43

Top 10 Places Sorted by Percent of Total Population
Based on places with total population of 50,000 or more

Place	Population	%
Chicago (city) Cook County	15,466	0.57
Berwyn (city) Cook County	257	0.45
Cicero (town) Cook County	365	0.44
Skokie (village) Cook County	195	0.30
Des Plaines (city) Cook County	165	0.28
Hoffman Estates (village) Cook County	130	0.25
Schaumburg (village) Cook County	132	0.18
Mount Prospect (village) Cook County	89	0.16
Arlington Heights (village) Cook County	115	0.15
Elgin (city) Kane County	152	0.14

South American: Paraguayan

Top 10 Places Sorted by Population
Based on all places, regardless of total population

Place	Population	%
Chicago (city) Cook County	101	<0.01
Brookfield (village) Cook County	13	0.07
Oak Park (village) Cook County	10	0.02
Palatine (village) Cook County	10	0.01
Joliet (city) Will County	9	0.01
Naperville (city) DuPage County	9	0.01
Carthage (city) Hancock County	8	0.31
Urbana (city) Champaign County	8	0.02
Champaign (city) Champaign County	8	0.01
Evanston (city) Cook County	8	0.01

Top 10 Places Sorted by Percent of Total Population
Based on all places, regardless of total population

Place	Population	%
Forest View (village) Cook County	3	0.43
Carthage (city) Hancock County	8	0.31
Braceville (village) Grundy County	2	0.25
Rosemont (village) Cook County	4	0.10
Hainesville (village) Lake County	3	0.08
Brookfield (village) Cook County	13	0.07
Posen (village) Cook County	3	0.05
Riverwoods (village) Lake County	2	0.05
Morris (city) Grundy County	6	0.04
Burr Ridge (village) DuPage County	4	0.04

Top 10 Places Sorted by Percent of Total Population
Based on places with total population of 50,000 or more

Place	Population	%
Oak Park (village) Cook County	10	0.02
Palatine (village) Cook County	10	0.01
Joliet (city) Will County	9	0.01
Naperville (city) DuPage County	9	0.01
Champaign (city) Champaign County	8	0.01
Evanston (city) Cook County	8	0.01
Berwyn (city) Cook County	7	0.01
Bloomington (city) McLean County	7	0.01
Waukegan (city) Lake County	5	0.01
Arlington Heights (village) Cook County	4	0.01

South American: Peruvian

Top 10 Places Sorted by Population
Based on all places, regardless of total population

Place	Population	%
Chicago (city) Cook County	4,075	0.15
Palatine (village) Cook County	189	0.28
Aurora (city) Kane County	187	0.09
Skokie (village) Cook County	161	0.25
Berwyn (city) Cook County	128	0.23
Elgin (city) Kane County	117	0.11
Hoffman Estates (village) Cook County	111	0.21
Naperville (city) DuPage County	109	0.08
Schaumburg (village) Cook County	106	0.14
Evanston (city) Cook County	103	0.14

Top 10 Places Sorted by Percent of Total Population
Based on all places, regardless of total population

Place	Population	%
Mettawa (village) Lake County	4	0.73
Redmon (village) Edgar County	1	0.58
Lily Lake (village) Kane County	5	0.50
Seaton (village) Mercer County	1	0.45
McCook (village) Cook County	1	0.44
Pingree Grove (village) Kane County	18	0.40
Melrose Park (village) Cook County	90	0.35
Elmwood Park (village) Cook County	77	0.31
Stone Park (village) Cook County	15	0.30
Golconda (city) Pope County	2	0.30

Top 10 Places Sorted by Percent of Total Population
Based on places with total population of 50,000 or more

Place	Population	%
Palatine (village) Cook County	189	0.28
Skokie (village) Cook County	161	0.25
Berwyn (city) Cook County	128	0.23
Hoffman Estates (village) Cook County	111	0.21
Oak Park (village) Cook County	91	0.18
Chicago (city) Cook County	4,075	0.15
Schaumburg (village) Cook County	106	0.14
Evanston (city) Cook County	103	0.14
Bolingbrook (village) Will County	99	0.13
Des Plaines (city) Cook County	70	0.12

South American: Uruguayan

Top 10 Places Sorted by Population
Based on all places, regardless of total population

Place	Population	%
Chicago (city) Cook County	267	0.01
Rockford (city) Winnebago County	32	0.02
Berwyn (city) Cook County	16	0.03
South Chicago Heights (village) Cook County	15	0.36
Oak Park (village) Cook County	15	0.03
Morton Grove (village) Cook County	12	0.05
Chicago Heights (city) Cook County	12	0.04
Evanston (city) Cook County	12	0.02
Skokie (village) Cook County	12	0.02
Hoffman Estates (village) Cook County	11	0.02

Top 10 Places Sorted by Percent of Total Population
Based on all places, regardless of total population

Place	Population	%
South Chicago Heights (village) Cook County	15	0.36
Millbrook (village) Kendall County	1	0.30
Elsah (village) Jersey County	1	0.15

Place	Population	%
New Milford (village) Winnebago County	1	0.14
Savoy (village) Champaign County	6	0.08
Poplar Grove (village) Boone County	4	0.08
Rosemont (village) Cook County	3	0.07
Summit (village) Cook County	7	0.06
Knollwood (cdp) Lake County	1	0.06
Morton Grove (village) Cook County	12	0.05

Top 10 Places Sorted by Percent of Total Population
Based on places with total population of 50,000 or more

Place	Population	%
Berwyn (city) Cook County	16	0.03
Oak Park (village) Cook County	15	0.03
Rockford (city) Winnebago County	32	0.02
Evanston (city) Cook County	12	0.02
Skokie (village) Cook County	12	0.02
Hoffman Estates (village) Cook County	11	0.02
Chicago (city) Cook County	267	0.01
Joliet (city) Will County	10	0.01
Arlington Heights (village) Cook County	9	0.01
Naperville (city) DuPage County	9	0.01

South American: Venezuelan

Top 10 Places Sorted by Population
Based on all places, regardless of total population

Place	Population	%
Chicago (city) Cook County	1,121	0.04
Naperville (city) DuPage County	108	0.08
Aurora (city) Kane County	94	0.05
Evanston (city) Cook County	63	0.08
Champaign (city) Champaign County	41	0.05
Elgin (city) Kane County	41	0.04
Skokie (village) Cook County	40	0.06
Joliet (city) Will County	39	0.03
Cicero (town) Cook County	35	0.04
Plainfield (village) Will County	32	0.08

Top 10 Places Sorted by Percent of Total Population
Based on all places, regardless of total population

Place	Population	%
Karnak (village) Pulaski County	3	0.60
Port Barrington (village) McHenry County	8	0.53
New Grand Chain (village) Pulaski County	1	0.48
Camargo (village) Douglas County	2	0.45
Steward (village) Lee County	1	0.39
Olmsted (village) Pulaski County	1	0.30
Forsyth (village) Macon County	9	0.26
Elkville (village) Jackson County	2	0.22
Oakbrook Terrace (city) DuPage County	4	0.19
Maryville (village) Madison County	12	0.16

Top 10 Places Sorted by Percent of Total Population
Based on places with total population of 50,000 or more

Place	Population	%
Naperville (city) DuPage County	108	0.08
Evanston (city) Cook County	63	0.08
Skokie (village) Cook County	40	0.06
Oak Park (village) Cook County	31	0.06
Aurora (city) Kane County	94	0.05
Champaign (city) Champaign County	41	0.05
Wheaton (city) DuPage County	28	0.05
Chicago (city) Cook County	1,121	0.04
Elgin (city) Kane County	41	0.04
Cicero (town) Cook County	35	0.04

South American: Other South American

Top 10 Places Sorted by Population
Based on all places, regardless of total population

Place	Population	%
Chicago (city) Cook County	307	0.01
Skokie (village) Cook County	30	0.05
Burnham (village) Cook County	14	0.33
Evanston (city) Cook County	12	0.02
Schaumburg (village) Cook County	12	0.02
Addison (village) DuPage County	10	0.03
Oak Park (village) Cook County	10	0.02
Des Plaines (city) Cook County	9	0.02
Algonquin (village) McHenry County	8	0.03
Glenview (village) Cook County	8	0.02

Top 10 Places Sorted by Percent of Total Population
Based on all places, regardless of total population

Place	Population	%
Burnham (village) Cook County	14	0.33
McCullom Lake (village) McHenry County	2	0.19
Hainesville (village) Lake County	4	0.11
Fairmont City (village) St. Clair County	2	0.08
Plano (city) Kendall County	6	0.06
Virginia (city) Cass County	1	0.06
Skokie (village) Cook County	30	0.05
Harwood Heights (village) Cook County	4	0.05
Oak Brook (village) DuPage County	4	0.05
La Grange (village) Cook County	6	0.04

Top 10 Places Sorted by Percent of Total Population
Based on places with total population of 50,000 or more

Place	Population	%
Skokie (village) Cook County	30	0.05
Evanston (city) Cook County	12	0.02
Schaumburg (village) Cook County	12	0.02
Oak Park (village) Cook County	10	0.02
Des Plaines (city) Cook County	9	0.02
Chicago (city) Cook County	307	0.01
Cicero (town) Cook County	7	0.01
Berwyn (city) Cook County	5	0.01
Mount Prospect (village) Cook County	5	0.01
Palatine (village) Cook County	5	0.01

Other Hispanic or Latino

Top 10 Places Sorted by Population
Based on all places, regardless of total population

Place	Population	%
Chicago (city) Cook County	23,599	0.88
Aurora (city) Kane County	2,494	1.26
Cicero (town) Cook County	1,834	2.19
Waukegan (city) Lake County	1,620	1.82
Rockford (city) Winnebago County	1,279	0.84
Elgin (city) Kane County	1,088	1.01
Joliet (city) Will County	1,076	0.73
Berwyn (city) Cook County	678	1.20
North Chicago (city) Lake County	526	1.61
Naperville (city) DuPage County	484	0.34

Top 10 Places Sorted by Percent of Total Population
Based on all places, regardless of total population

Place	Population	%
Sumner (city) Lawrence County	215	6.77
Ina (village) Jefferson County	118	5.05
Sheridan (village) LaSalle County	108	5.05
De Pue (village) Bureau County	66	3.59
Hillcrest (village) Ogle County	45	3.39
Harmon (village) Lee County	4	3.33
Fairmont City (village) St. Clair County	79	3.00
Pinckneyville (city) Perry County	157	2.78
Oakdale (village) Washington County	6	2.71
Broughton (village) Hamilton County	5	2.58

Top 10 Places Sorted by Percent of Total Population
Based on places with total population of 50,000 or more

Place	Population	%
Cicero (town) Cook County	1,834	2.19
Waukegan (city) Lake County	1,620	1.82
Aurora (city) Kane County	2,494	1.26
Berwyn (city) Cook County	678	1.20
Elgin (city) Kane County	1,088	1.01
Chicago (city) Cook County	23,599	0.88
Rockford (city) Winnebago County	1,279	0.84
Joliet (city) Will County	1,076	0.73
Palatine (village) Cook County	468	0.68
Evanston (city) Cook County	463	0.62

Racial Group Rankings

African-American/Black

Top 10 Places Sorted by Population
Based on all places, regardless of total population

Place	Population	%
Chicago (city) Cook County	913,009	33.87
Rockford (city) Winnebago County	34,438	22.53
Peoria (city) Peoria County	33,877	29.46
East St. Louis (city) St. Clair County	26,665	98.74
Calumet City (city) Cook County	26,633	71.90
Joliet (city) Will County	25,255	17.13
Springfield (city) Sangamon County	23,683	20.37
Aurora (city) Kane County	23,545	11.90
Dolton (village) Cook County	21,318	92.07
Harvey (city) Cook County	19,506	77.15

Top 10 Places Sorted by Percent of Total Population
Based on all places, regardless of total population

Place	Population	%
Alorton (village) St. Clair County	1,980	98.90
East St. Louis (city) St. Clair County	26,665	98.74
Centreville (city) St. Clair County	5,180	97.57
Brooklyn (village) St. Clair County	727	97.06
Ford Heights (village) Cook County	2,679	96.96
Venice (city) Madison County	1,810	95.77
Riverdale (village) Cook County	12,852	94.86
Robbins (village) Cook County	5,051	94.64
Hopkins Park (village) Kankakee County	568	94.20
Phoenix (village) Cook County	1,836	93.48

Top 10 Places Sorted by Percent of Total Population
Based on places with total population of 50,000 or more

Place	Population	%
Chicago (city) Cook County	913,009	33.87
Peoria (city) Peoria County	33,877	29.46
Decatur (city) Macon County	19,491	25.60
Oak Park (village) Cook County	12,235	23.58
Rockford (city) Winnebago County	34,438	22.53
Bolingbrook (village) Will County	15,996	21.80
Waukegan (city) Lake County	18,333	20.58
Springfield (city) Sangamon County	23,683	20.37
Evanston (city) Cook County	14,878	19.97
Joliet (city) Will County	25,255	17.13

African-American/Black: Not Hispanic

Top 10 Places Sorted by Population
Based on all places, regardless of total population

Place	Population	%
Chicago (city) Cook County	889,783	33.01
Peoria (city) Peoria County	33,328	28.98
Rockford (city) Winnebago County	33,293	21.78
East St. Louis (city) St. Clair County	26,574	98.40
Calumet City (city) Cook County	26,282	70.95
Joliet (city) Will County	24,271	16.46
Springfield (city) Sangamon County	23,404	20.13
Aurora (city) Kane County	21,960	11.10
Dolton (village) Cook County	21,164	91.41
Harvey (city) Cook County	19,293	76.31

Top 10 Places Sorted by Percent of Total Population
Based on all places, regardless of total population

Place	Population	%
Alorton (village) St. Clair County	1,976	98.70
East St. Louis (city) St. Clair County	26,574	98.40
Centreville (city) St. Clair County	5,169	97.36
Ford Heights (village) Cook County	2,668	96.56
Brooklyn (village) St. Clair County	718	95.86
Venice (city) Madison County	1,792	94.81
Robbins (village) Cook County	5,023	94.12
Riverdale (village) Cook County	12,749	94.10
Hopkins Park (village) Kankakee County	567	94.03
Phoenix (village) Cook County	1,811	92.21

Top 10 Places Sorted by Percent of Total Population
Based on places with total population of 50,000 or more

Place	Population	%
Chicago (city) Cook County	889,783	33.01
Peoria (city) Peoria County	33,328	28.98
Decatur (city) Macon County	19,291	25.34
Oak Park (village) Cook County	11,872	22.88
Rockford (city) Winnebago County	33,293	21.78
Bolingbrook (village) Will County	15,519	21.15
Springfield (city) Sangamon County	23,404	20.13
Evanston (city) Cook County	14,338	19.25
Waukegan (city) Lake County	17,078	19.17
Champaign (city) Champaign County	13,520	16.68

African-American/Black: Hispanic

Top 10 Places Sorted by Population
Based on all places, regardless of total population

Place	Population	%
Chicago (city) Cook County	23,226	0.86
Aurora (city) Kane County	1,585	0.80
Waukegan (city) Lake County	1,255	1.41
Rockford (city) Winnebago County	1,145	0.75
Joliet (city) Will County	984	0.67
Elgin (city) Kane County	970	0.90
Cicero (town) Cook County	727	0.87
Peoria (city) Peoria County	549	0.48
Evanston (city) Cook County	540	0.72
Bolingbrook (village) Will County	477	0.65

Top 10 Places Sorted by Percent of Total Population
Based on all places, regardless of total population

Place	Population	%
Shumway (village) Effingham County	5	2.48
Old Mill Creek (village) Lake County	4	2.25
Alsey (village) Scott County	4	1.76
Chemung (cdp) McHenry County	5	1.62
South Chicago Heights (village) Cook County	64	1.55
Mounds (city) Pulaski County	12	1.48
New Grand Chain (village) Pulaski County	3	1.43
Waukegan (city) Lake County	1,255	1.41
Zion (city) Lake County	333	1.36
North Chicago (city) Lake County	427	1.31

Top 10 Places Sorted by Percent of Total Population
Based on places with total population of 50,000 or more

Place	Population	%
Waukegan (city) Lake County	1,255	1.41
Elgin (city) Kane County	970	0.90
Cicero (town) Cook County	727	0.87
Chicago (city) Cook County	23,226	0.86
Aurora (city) Kane County	1,585	0.80
Berwyn (city) Cook County	443	0.78
Rockford (city) Winnebago County	1,145	0.75
Evanston (city) Cook County	540	0.72
Oak Park (village) Cook County	363	0.70
Joliet (city) Will County	984	0.67

American Indian/Alaska Native

Top 10 Places Sorted by Population
Based on all places, regardless of total population

Place	Population	%
Chicago (city) Cook County	26,933	1.00
Elgin (city) Kane County	2,220	2.05
Aurora (city) Kane County	1,868	0.94
Rockford (city) Winnebago County	1,703	1.11
Waukegan (city) Lake County	1,628	1.83
Joliet (city) Will County	1,176	0.80
Cicero (town) Cook County	1,024	1.22
Peoria (city) Peoria County	1,021	0.89
Springfield (city) Sangamon County	889	0.76
Naperville (city) DuPage County	688	0.49

Top 10 Places Sorted by Percent of Total Population
Based on all places, regardless of total population

Place	Population	%
Ripley (village) Brown County	6	6.98
Johnsonville (village) Wayne County	5	6.49
Burnt Prairie (village) White County	3	5.77
Mill Creek (village) Union County	3	4.62
La Fayette (village) Stark County	10	4.48
Fidelity (village) Jersey County	5	4.39
Cantrall (village) Sangamon County	6	4.32
Russellville (village) Lawrence County	4	4.26
Cedar Point (village) LaSalle County	11	3.97
Shumway (village) Effingham County	8	3.96

Top 10 Places Sorted by Percent of Total Population
Based on places with total population of 50,000 or more

Place	Population	%
Elgin (city) Kane County	2,220	2.05
Waukegan (city) Lake County	1,628	1.83
Cicero (town) Cook County	1,024	1.22
Rockford (city) Winnebago County	1,703	1.11
Berwyn (city) Cook County	605	1.07
Des Plaines (city) Cook County	588	1.01
Chicago (city) Cook County	26,933	1.00
Aurora (city) Kane County	1,868	0.94
Evanston (city) Cook County	671	0.90
Peoria (city) Peoria County	1,021	0.89

American Indian/Alaska Native: Not Hispanic

Top 10 Places Sorted by Population
Based on all places, regardless of total population

Place	Population	%
Chicago (city) Cook County	12,449	0.46
Rockford (city) Winnebago County	1,100	0.72
Peoria (city) Peoria County	815	0.71
Springfield (city) Sangamon County	797	0.69
Aurora (city) Kane County	738	0.37
Joliet (city) Will County	630	0.43
Decatur (city) Macon County	561	0.74
Naperville (city) DuPage County	497	0.35
Bloomington (city) McLean County	493	0.64
Evanston (city) Cook County	486	0.65

Top 10 Places Sorted by Percent of Total Population
Based on all places, regardless of total population

Place	Population	%
Ripley (village) Brown County	6	6.98
Johnsonville (village) Wayne County	5	6.49
Burnt Prairie (village) White County	3	5.77
Mill Creek (village) Union County	3	4.62
La Fayette (village) Stark County	10	4.48
Fidelity (village) Jersey County	5	4.39
Russellville (village) Lawrence County	4	4.26
Fults (village) Monroe County	1	3.85
Yale (village) Jasper County	3	3.49
Dunfermline (village) Fulton County	10	3.33

Top 10 Places Sorted by Percent of Total Population
Based on places with total population of 50,000 or more

Place	Population	%
Decatur (city) Macon County	561	0.74
Rockford (city) Winnebago County	1,100	0.72
Peoria (city) Peoria County	815	0.71
Springfield (city) Sangamon County	797	0.69
Evanston (city) Cook County	486	0.65
Bloomington (city) McLean County	493	0.64
Oak Park (village) Cook County	303	0.58
Champaign (city) Champaign County	453	0.56
Waukegan (city) Lake County	470	0.53
Bolingbrook (village) Will County	353	0.48

American Indian/Alaska Native: Hispanic

Top 10 Places Sorted by Population
Based on all places, regardless of total population

Place	Population	%
Chicago (city) Cook County	14,484	0.54
Elgin (city) Kane County	1,815	1.68
Waukegan (city) Lake County	1,158	1.30
Aurora (city) Kane County	1,130	0.57
Cicero (town) Cook County	922	1.10
Rockford (city) Winnebago County	603	0.39
Joliet (city) Will County	540	0.37
Streamwood (village) Cook County	430	1.08
Hanover Park (village) Cook County	417	1.10
Berwyn (city) Cook County	400	0.71

Top 10 Places Sorted by Percent of Total Population
Based on all places, regardless of total population

Place	Population	%
Cypress (village) Johnson County	7	2.99
Cantrall (village) Sangamon County	4	2.88
Shumway (village) Effingham County	5	2.48
Verona (village) Grundy County	5	2.33
Donnellson (village) Montgomery County	4	1.90
Kinderhook (village) Pike County	4	1.85
Garden Prairie (village) Boone County	6	1.70
Elgin (city) Kane County	1,815	1.68
Round Lake Park (village) Lake County	126	1.68
Cedar Point (village) LaSalle County	4	1.44

Top 10 Places Sorted by Percent of Total Population
Based on places with total population of 50,000 or more

Place	Population	%
Elgin (city) Kane County	1,815	1.68
Waukegan (city) Lake County	1,158	1.30
Cicero (town) Cook County	922	1.10
Berwyn (city) Cook County	400	0.71
Des Plaines (city) Cook County	389	0.67
Aurora (city) Kane County	1,130	0.57
Chicago (city) Cook County	14,484	0.54
Rockford (city) Winnebago County	603	0.39
Joliet (city) Will County	540	0.37
Palatine (village) Cook County	239	0.35

Alaska Native: Alaska Athabascan

Top 10 Places Sorted by Population
Based on all places, regardless of total population

Place	Population	%
Chicago (city) Cook County	11	<0.01
Belleville (city) St. Clair County	4	0.01
Cicero (town) Cook County	4	<0.01
Carmi (city) White County	3	0.06
Fairfield (city) Wayne County	3	0.06
Bourbonnais (village) Kankakee County	3	0.02
Herrin (city) Williamson County	3	0.02
Shorewood (village) Will County	3	0.02
Bartlett (village) DuPage County	3	0.01
O'Fallon (city) St. Clair County	3	0.01

Top 10 Places Sorted by Percent of Total Population
Based on all places, regardless of total population

Place	Population	%
Grandview (village) Sangamon County	1	0.07
Carmi (city) White County	3	0.06
Fairfield (city) Wayne County	3	0.06
Knoxville (city) Knox County	1	0.03
Bourbonnais (village) Kankakee County	3	0.02
Herrin (city) Williamson County	3	0.02
Shorewood (village) Will County	3	0.02
Barrington Hills (village) Cook County	1	0.02
Breese (city) Clinton County	1	0.02
Belleville (city) St. Clair County	4	0.01

Top 10 Places Sorted by Percent of Total Population
Based on places with total population of 50,000 or more

Place	Population	%
Chicago (city) Cook County	11	<0.01
Cicero (town) Cook County	4	<0.01
Peoria (city) Peoria County	3	<0.01
Skokie (village) Cook County	2	<0.01

Place	Population	%
Berwyn (city) Cook County	1	<0.01
Decatur (city) Macon County	1	<0.01
Joliet (city) Will County	1	<0.01
Naperville (city) DuPage County	1	<0.01
Rockford (city) Winnebago County	1	<0.01
Springfield (city) Sangamon County	1	<0.01

Alaska Native: Aleut

Top 10 Places Sorted by Population
Based on all places, regardless of total population

Place	Population	%
Chicago (city) Cook County	8	<0.01
Des Plaines (city) Cook County	5	0.01
Riverton (village) Sangamon County	4	0.12
Beach Park (village) Lake County	4	0.03
Rantoul (village) Champaign County	4	0.03
Woodridge (village) DuPage County	4	0.01
Granite City (city) Madison County	3	0.01
Huntley (village) McHenry County	3	0.01
Bloomington (city) McLean County	3	<0.01
Decatur (city) Macon County	3	<0.01

Top 10 Places Sorted by Percent of Total Population
Based on all places, regardless of total population

Place	Population	%
Waltonville (village) Jefferson County	2	0.46
Nebo (village) Pike County	1	0.29
Enfield (village) White County	1	0.17
Riverton (village) Sangamon County	4	0.12
Oquawka (village) Henderson County	1	0.07
Beach Park (village) Lake County	4	0.03
Rantoul (village) Champaign County	4	0.03
Winthrop Harbor (village) Lake County	2	0.03
Braidwood (city) Will County	1	0.02
Lawrenceville (city) Lawrence County	1	0.02

Top 10 Places Sorted by Percent of Total Population
Based on places with total population of 50,000 or more

Place	Population	%
Des Plaines (city) Cook County	5	0.01
Chicago (city) Cook County	8	<0.01
Bloomington (city) McLean County	3	<0.01
Decatur (city) Macon County	3	<0.01
Joliet (city) Will County	2	<0.01
Aurora (city) Kane County	1	<0.01
Champaign (city) Champaign County	1	<0.01
Rockford (city) Winnebago County	1	<0.01
Arlington Heights (village) Cook County	0	0.00
Berwyn (city) Cook County	0	0.00

American Indian: Apache

Top 10 Places Sorted by Population
Based on all places, regardless of total population

Place	Population	%
Chicago (city) Cook County	350	0.01
Joliet (city) Will County	28	0.02
Aurora (city) Kane County	25	0.01
Rockford (city) Winnebago County	22	0.01
Waukegan (city) Lake County	21	0.02
Berwyn (city) Cook County	18	0.03
Decatur (city) Macon County	16	0.02
Naperville (city) DuPage County	15	0.01
Bolingbrook (village) Will County	14	0.02
Elgin (city) Kane County	14	0.01

Top 10 Places Sorted by Percent of Total Population
Based on all places, regardless of total population

Place	Population	%
Johnsonville (village) Wayne County	5	6.49
Springerton (village) White County	2	1.82
Neponset (village) Bureau County	3	0.63
Cisne (village) Wayne County	3	0.45
Owaneco (village) Christian County	1	0.42
Chestnut (cdp) Logan County	1	0.41
Gardner (village) Grundy County	5	0.34
Lake Catherine (cdp) Lake County	4	0.29
St. Anne (village) Kankakee County	3	0.24
Rockdale (village) Will County	4	0.20

Top 10 Places Sorted by Percent of Total Population
Based on places with total population of 50,000 or more

Place	Population	%
Berwyn (city) Cook County	18	0.03
Joliet (city) Will County	28	0.02
Waukegan (city) Lake County	21	0.02
Decatur (city) Macon County	16	0.02
Bolingbrook (village) Will County	14	0.02
Oak Lawn (village) Cook County	13	0.02
Evanston (city) Cook County	12	0.02
Normal (town) McLean County	8	0.02
Chicago (city) Cook County	350	0.01
Aurora (city) Kane County	25	0.01

American Indian: Arapaho

Top 10 Places Sorted by Population
Based on all places, regardless of total population

Place	Population	%
Chicago (city) Cook County	20	<0.01
Bolingbrook (village) Will County	6	0.01
Harwood Heights (village) Cook County	5	0.06
Collinsville (city) Madison County	4	0.02
Park Forest (village) Cook County	4	0.03
Johnston City (city) Williamson County	2	0.04
Algonquin (village) McHenry County	2	0.01
Bridgeview (village) Cook County	2	0.01
Fairview Heights (city) St. Clair County	2	0.01
Frankfort (village) Will County	2	0.01

Top 10 Places Sorted by Percent of Total Population
Based on all places, regardless of total population

Place	Population	%
Cordova (village) Rock Island County	1	0.18
Palmyra (village) Macoupin County	1	0.14
Harwood Heights (village) Cook County	5	0.06
Johnston City (city) Williamson County	2	0.04
Phoenix (village) Cook County	1	0.05
Madison (city) Madison County	1	0.04
Tolono (village) Champaign County	1	0.03
Collinsville (city) Madison County	4	0.02
Park Forest (village) Cook County	4	0.02
Lakemoor (village) Lake County	1	0.02

Top 10 Places Sorted by Percent of Total Population
Based on places with total population of 50,000 or more

Place	Population	%
Bolingbrook (village) Will County	6	0.01
Chicago (city) Cook County	20	<0.01
Hoffman Estates (village) Cook County	2	<0.01
Peoria (city) Peoria County	2	<0.01
Rockford (city) Winnebago County	2	<0.01
Cicero (town) Cook County	1	<0.01
Evanston (city) Cook County	1	<0.01
Naperville (city) DuPage County	1	<0.01
Orland Park (village) Cook County	1	<0.01
Waukegan (city) Lake County	1	<0.01

American Indian: Blackfeet

Top 10 Places Sorted by Population
Based on all places, regardless of total population

Place	Population	%
Chicago (city) Cook County	590	0.02
Rockford (city) Winnebago County	58	0.04
Springfield (city) Sangamon County	55	0.05
Rock Island (city) Rock Island County	50	0.13
Waukegan (city) Lake County	32	0.04
Decatur (city) Macon County	31	0.04
Aurora (city) Kane County	31	0.02
Joliet (city) Will County	31	0.02
Peoria (city) Peoria County	30	0.03
Evanston (city) Cook County	25	0.03

Top 10 Places Sorted by Percent of Total Population
Based on all places, regardless of total population

Place	Population	%
Walnut Hill (village) Marion County	2	1.85
Rose Hill (village) Jasper County	1	1.25
Adeline (village) Ogle County	1	1.18

Cabery (village) Ford County	3	1.13
Godley (village) Will County	6	1.00
Keensburg (village) Wabash County	2	0.95
Old Ripley (village) Bond County	1	0.93
Junction City (village) Marion County	4	0.83
Thawville (village) Iroquois County	2	0.83
LaPlace (cdp) Piatt County	2	0.77

Top 10 Places Sorted by Percent of Total Population
Based on places with total population of 50,000 or more

Place	Population	%
Springfield (city) Sangamon County	55	0.05
Rockford (city) Winnebago County	58	0.04
Waukegan (city) Lake County	32	0.04
Decatur (city) Macon County	31	0.04
Peoria (city) Peoria County	30	0.03
Evanston (city) Cook County	25	0.03
Chicago (city) Cook County	590	0.02
Aurora (city) Kane County	31	0.02
Joliet (city) Will County	31	0.02
Champaign (city) Champaign County	19	0.02

American Indian: Canadian/French American Indian

Top 10 Places Sorted by Population
Based on all places, regardless of total population

Place	Population	%
Chicago (city) Cook County	55	<0.01
Granite City (city) Madison County	8	0.03
Romeoville (village) Will County	7	0.02
Wheaton (city) DuPage County	7	0.01
Louisville (village) Clay County	5	0.44
Elgin (city) Kane County	5	<0.01
Rockford (city) Winnebago County	5	<0.01
Wilmington (city) Will County	4	0.07
Roscoe (village) Winnebago County	4	0.04
Centralia (city) Marion County	4	0.03

Top 10 Places Sorted by Percent of Total Population
Based on all places, regardless of total population

Place	Population	%
Camden (village) Schuyler County	1	1.16
Eldred (village) Greene County	1	0.50
Louisville (village) Clay County	5	0.44
Cypress (village) Johnson County	1	0.43
Third Lake (village) Lake County	3	0.25
Capron (village) Boone County	3	0.22
Divernon (village) Sangamon County	2	0.17
Seneca (village) LaSalle County	3	0.13
Ashmore (village) Coles County	1	0.13
Hanover (village) Jo Daviess County	1	0.12

Top 10 Places Sorted by Percent of Total Population
Based on places with total population of 50,000 or more

Place	Population	%
Wheaton (city) DuPage County	7	0.01
Normal (town) McLean County	4	0.01
Chicago (city) Cook County	55	<0.01
Elgin (city) Kane County	5	<0.01
Rockford (city) Winnebago County	5	<0.01
Springfield (city) Sangamon County	4	<0.01
Aurora (city) Kane County	3	<0.01
Evanston (city) Cook County	3	<0.01
Joliet (city) Will County	3	<0.01
Arlington Heights (village) Cook County	2	<0.01

American Indian: Central American Indian

Top 10 Places Sorted by Population
Based on all places, regardless of total population

Place	Population	%
Chicago (city) Cook County	203	0.01
Waukegan (city) Lake County	23	0.03
Naperville (city) DuPage County	8	0.01
Northlake (city) Cook County	7	0.06
Berwyn (city) Cook County	7	0.01
Cicero (town) Cook County	6	0.01
Evanston (city) Cook County	6	0.01
Skokie (village) Cook County	6	0.01
Aurora (city) Kane County	6	<0.01

Rockford (city) Winnebago County	6	<0.01

Top 10 Places Sorted by Percent of Total Population
Based on all places, regardless of total population

Place	Population	%
Channel Lake (cdp) Lake County	2	0.12
Stone Park (village) Cook County	5	0.10
Rosemont (village) Cook County	3	0.07
Northlake (city) Cook County	7	0.06
Forest Lake (cdp) Lake County	1	0.06
Fisher (village) Champaign County	1	0.05
Waukegan (city) Lake County	23	0.03
Homewood (village) Cook County	4	0.02
Markham (city) Cook County	2	0.02
Eureka (city) Woodford County	1	0.02

Top 10 Places Sorted by Percent of Total Population
Based on places with total population of 50,000 or more

Place	Population	%
Waukegan (city) Lake County	23	0.03
Chicago (city) Cook County	203	0.01
Naperville (city) DuPage County	8	0.01
Berwyn (city) Cook County	7	0.01
Cicero (town) Cook County	6	0.01
Evanston (city) Cook County	6	0.01
Skokie (village) Cook County	6	0.01
Bolingbrook (village) Will County	5	0.01
Normal (town) McLean County	4	0.01
Aurora (city) Kane County	6	<0.01

American Indian: Cherokee

Top 10 Places Sorted by Population
Based on all places, regardless of total population

Place	Population	%
Chicago (city) Cook County	2,639	0.10
Rockford (city) Winnebago County	259	0.17
Springfield (city) Sangamon County	248	0.21
Peoria (city) Peoria County	215	0.19
Joliet (city) Will County	194	0.13
Aurora (city) Kane County	187	0.09
Decatur (city) Macon County	161	0.21
Naperville (city) DuPage County	161	0.11
Champaign (city) Champaign County	139	0.17
Evanston (city) Cook County	131	0.18

Top 10 Places Sorted by Percent of Total Population
Based on all places, regardless of total population

Place	Population	%
Fidelity (village) Jersey County	5	4.39
Burnt Prairie (village) White County	2	3.85
Johnsonville (village) Wayne County	2	2.60
Donnellson (village) Montgomery County	4	1.90
Jeisyville (village) Christian County	2	1.87
Garrett (village) Douglas County	3	1.85
La Fayette (village) Stark County	4	1.79
Chesterfield (village) Macoupin County	3	1.60
West York (cdp) Crawford County	2	1.55
Ullin (village) Pulaski County	7	1.51

Top 10 Places Sorted by Percent of Total Population
Based on places with total population of 50,000 or more

Place	Population	%
Springfield (city) Sangamon County	248	0.21
Decatur (city) Macon County	161	0.21
Peoria (city) Peoria County	215	0.19
Evanston (city) Cook County	131	0.18
Rockford (city) Winnebago County	259	0.17
Champaign (city) Champaign County	139	0.17
Bloomington (city) McLean County	131	0.17
Oak Park (village) Cook County	84	0.16
Normal (town) McLean County	82	0.16
Waukegan (city) Lake County	130	0.15

American Indian: Cheyenne

Top 10 Places Sorted by Population
Based on all places, regardless of total population

Place	Population	%
Chicago (city) Cook County	27	<0.01

Heyworth (village) McLean County	7	0.25
Bement (village) Piatt County	6	0.35
St. Joseph (village) Champaign County	5	0.13
Vandalia (city) Fayette County	5	0.07
Riverside (village) Cook County	5	0.06
Cicero (town) Cook County	5	0.01
Rockdale (village) Will County	4	0.20
Murphysboro (city) Jackson County	4	0.05
Joliet (city) Will County	4	<0.01

Top 10 Places Sorted by Percent of Total Population
Based on all places, regardless of total population

Place	Population	%
Keensburg (village) Wabash County	1	0.48
Jewett (village) Cumberland County	1	0.45
Bement (village) Piatt County	6	0.35
Heyworth (village) McLean County	7	0.25
Third Lake (village) Lake County	3	0.25
Rockdale (village) Will County	4	0.20
Worden (village) Madison County	2	0.19
Zeigler (city) Franklin County	3	0.17
Rosiclare (city) Hardin County	2	0.17
Noble (village) Richland County	1	0.15

Top 10 Places Sorted by Percent of Total Population
Based on places with total population of 50,000 or more

Place	Population	%
Cicero (town) Cook County	5	0.01
Chicago (city) Cook County	27	<0.01
Joliet (city) Will County	4	<0.01
Aurora (city) Kane County	3	<0.01
Champaign (city) Champaign County	3	<0.01
Rockford (city) Winnebago County	3	<0.01
Bloomington (city) McLean County	2	<0.01
Decatur (city) Macon County	2	<0.01
Springfield (city) Sangamon County	2	<0.01
Skokie (village) Cook County	1	<0.01

American Indian: Chickasaw

Top 10 Places Sorted by Population
Based on all places, regardless of total population

Place	Population	%
Chicago (city) Cook County	56	<0.01
Peoria (city) Peoria County	11	0.01
Crete (village) Will County	9	0.11
Champaign (city) Champaign County	8	0.01
Flossmoor (village) Cook County	7	0.07
Campton Hills (village) Kane County	7	0.06
Carbondale (city) Jackson County	7	0.03
Highland Park (city) Lake County	6	0.02
Bloomington (city) McLean County	6	0.01
Evanston (city) Cook County	6	0.01

Top 10 Places Sorted by Percent of Total Population
Based on all places, regardless of total population

Place	Population	%
La Fayette (village) Stark County	1	0.45
Homer (village) Champaign County	2	0.17
Williamsfield (village) Knox County	1	0.17
Elsah (village) Jersey County	1	0.15
Grafton (city) Jersey County	1	0.15
South Wilmington (village) Grundy County	1	0.15
Westville (village) Vermilion County	4	0.12
Crete (village) Will County	9	0.11
Elkville (village) Jackson County	1	0.11
South Barrington (village) Cook County	4	0.09

Top 10 Places Sorted by Percent of Total Population
Based on places with total population of 50,000 or more

Place	Population	%
Peoria (city) Peoria County	11	0.01
Champaign (city) Champaign County	8	0.01
Bloomington (city) McLean County	6	0.01
Evanston (city) Cook County	6	0.01
Springfield (city) Sangamon County	6	0.01
Hoffman Estates (village) Cook County	5	0.01
Chicago (city) Cook County	56	<0.01
Aurora (city) Kane County	4	<0.01
Joliet (city) Will County	4	<0.01
Naperville (city) DuPage County	4	<0.01

Please refer to the Explanation of Data in the front of the book for more detailed information.

American Indian: Chippewa

Top 10 Places Sorted by Population
Based on all places, regardless of total population

Place	Population	%
Chicago (city) Cook County	659	0.02
Rockford (city) Winnebago County	42	0.03
Waukegan (city) Lake County	37	0.04
Elgin (city) Kane County	30	0.03
Joliet (city) Will County	29	0.02
Pekin (city) Tazewell County	28	0.08
Crystal Lake (city) McHenry County	24	0.06
Peoria (city) Peoria County	24	0.02
Aurora (city) Kane County	23	0.01
Berwyn (city) Cook County	22	0.04

Top 10 Places Sorted by Percent of Total Population
Based on all places, regardless of total population

Place	Population	%
La Fayette (village) Stark County	5	2.24
Dunfermline (village) Fulton County	4	1.33
Naplate (village) LaSalle County	5	1.01
Holiday Hills (village) McHenry County	4	0.66
Grant Park (village) Kankakee County	8	0.60
Nelson (village) Lee County	1	0.59
Golden (village) Adams County	3	0.47
Lake Petersburg (cdp) Menard County	3	0.42
Mount Auburn (village) Christian County	2	0.42
Wonder Lake (village) McHenry County	16	0.40

Top 10 Places Sorted by Percent of Total Population
Based on places with total population of 50,000 or more

Place	Population	%
Waukegan (city) Lake County	37	0.04
Berwyn (city) Cook County	22	0.04
Rockford (city) Winnebago County	42	0.03
Elgin (city) Kane County	30	0.03
Palatine (village) Cook County	21	0.03
Arlington Heights (village) Cook County	19	0.03
Wheaton (city) DuPage County	17	0.03
Chicago (city) Cook County	659	0.02
Joliet (city) Will County	29	0.02
Peoria (city) Peoria County	24	0.02

American Indian: Choctaw

Top 10 Places Sorted by Population
Based on all places, regardless of total population

Place	Population	%
Chicago (city) Cook County	513	0.02
Springfield (city) Sangamon County	27	0.02
Evanston (city) Cook County	25	0.03
Rockford (city) Winnebago County	25	0.02
Joliet (city) Will County	23	0.02
Peoria (city) Peoria County	21	0.02
Park Forest (village) Cook County	20	0.09
Waukegan (city) Lake County	20	0.02
North Chicago (city) Lake County	16	0.05
Aurora (city) Kane County	16	0.01

Top 10 Places Sorted by Percent of Total Population
Based on all places, regardless of total population

Place	Population	%
Golden Gate (village) Wayne County	1	1.47
St. Johns (village) Perry County	2	0.91
Mounds (city) Pulaski County	4	0.49
Ullin (village) Pulaski County	2	0.43
Green Valley (village) Tazewell County	3	0.42
LaPlace (cdp) Piatt County	1	0.39
Manito (village) Mason County	6	0.37
Germantown (village) Clinton County	4	0.32
Dieterich (village) Effingham County	2	0.32
Mulberry Grove (village) Bond County	2	0.32

Top 10 Places Sorted by Percent of Total Population
Based on places with total population of 50,000 or more

Place	Population	%
Evanston (city) Cook County	25	0.03
Chicago (city) Cook County	513	0.02
Springfield (city) Sangamon County	27	0.02
Rockford (city) Winnebago County	25	0.02

Place	Population	%
Joliet (city) Will County	23	0.02
Peoria (city) Peoria County	21	0.02
Waukegan (city) Lake County	20	0.02
Bloomington (city) McLean County	15	0.02
Berwyn (city) Cook County	14	0.02
Champaign (city) Champaign County	13	0.02

American Indian: Colville

Top 10 Places Sorted by Population
Based on all places, regardless of total population

Place	Population	%
Chicago (city) Cook County	5	<0.01
Loda (village) Iroquois County	2	0.49
Mount Carmel (city) Wabash County	2	0.03
Lansing (village) Cook County	2	0.01
Braidwood (city) Will County	1	0.02
Lemont (village) Cook County	1	0.01
Bloomington (city) McLean County	1	<0.01
Abingdon (city) Knox County	0	0.00
Adair (cdp) McDonough County	0	0.00
Addieville (village) Washington County	0	0.00

Top 10 Places Sorted by Percent of Total Population
Based on all places, regardless of total population

Place	Population	%
Loda (village) Iroquois County	2	0.49
Mount Carmel (city) Wabash County	2	0.03
Braidwood (city) Will County	1	0.02
Lansing (village) Cook County	2	0.01
Lemont (village) Cook County	1	0.01
Chicago (city) Cook County	5	<0.01
Bloomington (city) McLean County	1	<0.01
Abingdon (city) Knox County	0	0.00
Adair (cdp) McDonough County	0	0.00
Addieville (village) Washington County	0	0.00

Top 10 Places Sorted by Percent of Total Population
Based on places with total population of 50,000 or more

Place	Population	%
Chicago (city) Cook County	5	<0.01
Bloomington (city) McLean County	1	<0.01
Arlington Heights (village) Cook County	0	0.00
Aurora (city) Kane County	0	0.00
Berwyn (city) Cook County	0	0.00
Bolingbrook (village) Will County	0	0.00
Champaign (city) Champaign County	0	0.00
Cicero (town) Cook County	0	0.00
Decatur (city) Macon County	0	0.00
Des Plaines (city) Cook County	0	0.00

American Indian: Comanche

Top 10 Places Sorted by Population
Based on all places, regardless of total population

Place	Population	%
Chicago (city) Cook County	47	<0.01
Rockford (city) Winnebago County	13	0.01
West Dundee (village) Kane County	8	0.11
Pekin (city) Tazewell County	7	0.02
Carpentersville (village) Kane County	6	0.02
Lebanon (city) St. Clair County	5	0.11
Crystal Lake (city) McHenry County	5	0.01
Oak Park (village) Cook County	5	0.01
Mascoutah (city) St. Clair County	4	0.05
Monmouth (city) Warren County	4	0.04

Top 10 Places Sorted by Percent of Total Population
Based on all places, regardless of total population

Place	Population	%
South Wilmington (village) Grundy County	2	0.29
Evansville (village) Randolph County	1	0.14
Henry (city) Marshall County	3	0.12
West Dundee (village) Kane County	8	0.11
Lebanon (city) St. Clair County	5	0.11
Rockdale (village) Will County	2	0.10
Thomasboro (village) Champaign County	1	0.09
Le Roy (city) McLean County	3	0.08
Scott AFB (cdp) St. Clair County	3	0.08
Dupo (village) St. Clair County	3	0.07

American Indian: Colville *(Top Percent — 50,000+)*

Top 10 Places Sorted by Percent of Total Population
Based on places with total population of 50,000 or more

Place	Population	%
Rockford (city) Winnebago County	13	0
Oak Park (village) Cook County	5	0
Chicago (city) Cook County	47	<0
Aurora (city) Kane County	4	<0
Waukegan (city) Lake County	4	<0
Berwyn (city) Cook County	1	<0
Bloomington (city) McLean County	1	<0
Bolingbrook (village) Will County	1	<0
Cicero (town) Cook County	1	<0
Joliet (city) Will County	1	<0

American Indian: Cree

Top 10 Places Sorted by Population
Based on all places, regardless of total population

Place	Population	%
Chicago (city) Cook County	54	<0
Danville (city) Vermilion County	7	0
Romeoville (village) Will County	6	0
Minooka (village) Grundy County	5	0
Peoria (city) Peoria County	5	0
Millbrook (village) Kendall County	4	1
Evanston (city) Cook County	4	0
Glendale Heights (village) DuPage County	4	0
Champaign (city) Champaign County	4	<0
Bement (village) Piatt County	3	0

Top 10 Places Sorted by Percent of Total Population
Based on all places, regardless of total population

Place	Population	%
Millbrook (village) Kendall County	4	1
Belgium (village) Vermilion County	2	0
Fieldon (village) Jersey County	1	0
Bement (village) Piatt County	3	0
Hanover (village) Jo Daviess County	1	0
Bridgeport (city) Lawrence County	2	0
South Pekin (village) Tazewell County	1	0
Wyoming (city) Stark County	1	0
Stone Park (village) Cook County	3	0
Delavan (city) Tazewell County	1	0

Top 10 Places Sorted by Percent of Total Population
Based on places with total population of 50,000 or more

Place	Population	%
Evanston (city) Cook County	4	0
Chicago (city) Cook County	54	<0
Peoria (city) Peoria County	5	<0
Champaign (city) Champaign County	4	<0
Elgin (city) Kane County	3	<0
Rockford (city) Winnebago County	3	<0
Aurora (city) Kane County	2	<0
Bloomington (city) McLean County	2	<0
Decatur (city) Macon County	1	<0
Joliet (city) Will County	1	<0

American Indian: Creek

Top 10 Places Sorted by Population
Based on all places, regardless of total population

Place	Population
Chicago (city) Cook County	139	0
Joliet (city) Will County	17	0
Rockford (city) Winnebago County	11	0
Schaumburg (village) Cook County	10	0
Elgin (city) Kane County	8	0
Decatur (city) Macon County	7	0
Palatine (village) Cook County	7	0
Springfield (city) Sangamon County	7	0
Elk Grove Village (village) Cook County	6	0
Highland Park (city) Lake County	6	0

Top 10 Places Sorted by Percent of Total Populati
Based on all places, regardless of total population

Place	Population
Modesto (village) Macoupin County	1	0
Royal Lakes (village) Macoupin County	1	0
Gladstone (village) Henderson County	1	0

Please refer to the Explanation of Data in the front of the book for more detailed information.

Place	Population	%
Lovington (village) Moultrie County	3	0.27
Latham (village) Logan County	1	0.26
Varna (village) Marshall County	1	0.26
Ashland (village) Cass County	3	0.23
St. Jacob (village) Madison County	2	0.18
Tolono (village) Champaign County	5	0.15
Lake Summerset (cdp) Winnebago County	3	0.15

Top 10 Places Sorted by Percent of Total Population
Based on places with total population of 50,000 or more

Place	Population	%
Chicago (city) Cook County	139	0.01
Joliet (city) Will County	17	0.01
Rockford (city) Winnebago County	11	0.01
Schaumburg (village) Cook County	10	0.01
Elgin (city) Kane County	8	0.01
Decatur (city) Macon County	7	0.01
Palatine (village) Cook County	7	0.01
Springfield (city) Sangamon County	7	0.01
Champaign (city) Champaign County	6	0.01
Normal (town) McLean County	6	0.01

American Indian: Crow

Top 10 Places Sorted by Population
Based on all places, regardless of total population

Place	Population	%
Chicago (city) Cook County	17	<0.01
Rockford (city) Winnebago County	10	0.01
Skokie (village) Cook County	5	0.01
Springfield (city) Sangamon County	5	<0.01
Peoria (city) Peoria County	4	<0.01
Roanoke (village) Woodford County	3	0.15
Georgetown (city) Vermilion County	3	0.09
Peotone (village) Will County	3	0.07
Lyons (village) Cook County	3	0.03
Paris (city) Edgar County	3	0.03

Top 10 Places Sorted by Percent of Total Population
Based on all places, regardless of total population

Place	Population	%
Emington (village) Livingston County	1	0.85
New Salem (village) Pike County	1	0.73
Hopkins Park (village) Kankakee County	2	0.33
Coalton (village) Montgomery County	1	0.33
Belle Rive (village) Jefferson County	1	0.28
Roanoke (village) Woodford County	3	0.15
Elkville (village) Jackson County	1	0.11
Paw Paw (village) Lee County	1	0.11
Georgetown (city) Vermilion County	3	0.09
Peotone (village) Will County	3	0.07

Top 10 Places Sorted by Percent of Total Population
Based on places with total population of 50,000 or more

Place	Population	%
Rockford (city) Winnebago County	10	0.01
Skokie (village) Cook County	5	0.01
Chicago (city) Cook County	17	<0.01
Springfield (city) Sangamon County	5	<0.01
Peoria (city) Peoria County	4	<0.01
Aurora (city) Kane County	3	<0.01
Elgin (city) Kane County	2	<0.01
Bolingbrook (village) Will County	1	<0.01
Joliet (city) Will County	1	<0.01
Mount Prospect (village) Cook County	1	<0.01

American Indian: Delaware

Top 10 Places Sorted by Population
Based on all places, regardless of total population

Place	Population	%
Chicago (city) Cook County	25	<0.01
Sheldon (village) Iroquois County	5	0.47
Carpentersville (village) Kane County	5	0.01
Rockford (city) Winnebago County	5	<0.01
Manteno (village) Kankakee County	4	0.04
Lisle (village) DuPage County	4	0.02
Lake in the Hills (village) McHenry County	4	<0.01
Champaign (city) Champaign County	4	<0.01
Peoria (city) Peoria County	4	<0.01
Watson (village) Effingham County	3	0.40

Top 10 Places Sorted by Percent of Total Population
Based on all places, regardless of total population

Place	Population	%
Keensburg (village) Wabash County	2	0.95
Sheldon (village) Iroquois County	5	0.47
Watson (village) Effingham County	3	0.40
Washburn (village) Woodford County	3	0.26
Warsaw (city) Hancock County	3	0.19
Crossville (village) White County	1	0.13
Carthage (city) Hancock County	3	0.12
Oakland (city) Coles County	1	0.11
West Salem (village) Edwards County	1	0.11
Lawrenceville (city) Lawrence County	3	0.07

Top 10 Places Sorted by Percent of Total Population
Based on places with total population of 50,000 or more

Place	Population	%
Chicago (city) Cook County	25	<0.01
Rockford (city) Winnebago County	5	<0.01
Champaign (city) Champaign County	4	<0.01
Peoria (city) Peoria County	4	<0.01
Schaumburg (village) Cook County	3	<0.01
Cicero (town) Cook County	2	<0.01
Decatur (city) Macon County	2	<0.01
Evanston (city) Cook County	2	<0.01
Des Plaines (city) Cook County	1	<0.01
Oak Park (village) Cook County	1	<0.01

American Indian: Hopi

Top 10 Places Sorted by Population
Based on all places, regardless of total population

Place	Population	%
Chicago (city) Cook County	26	<0.01
Aurora (city) Kane County	14	0.01
Champaign (city) Champaign County	4	<0.01
Frankfort Square (cdp) Will County	3	0.03
Lemont (village) Cook County	3	0.02
Elk Grove Village (village) Cook County	3	0.01
Granite City (city) Madison County	3	0.01
Bay View Gardens (village) Woodford County	2	0.53
Lindenhurst (village) Lake County	2	0.01
New Lenox (village) Will County	2	0.01

Top 10 Places Sorted by Percent of Total Population
Based on all places, regardless of total population

Place	Population	%
Bay View Gardens (village) Woodford County	2	0.53
Arrowsmith (village) McLean County	1	0.34
Albany (village) Whiteside County	1	0.11
Carrier Mills (village) Saline County	1	0.06
Warsaw (city) Hancock County	1	0.06
Fairmont (cdp) Will County	1	0.04
Round Lake Heights (village) Lake County	1	0.04
Frankfort Square (cdp) Will County	3	0.03
Lemont (village) Cook County	3	0.02
Eureka (city) Woodford County	1	0.02

Top 10 Places Sorted by Percent of Total Population
Based on places with total population of 50,000 or more

Place	Population	%
Aurora (city) Kane County	14	0.01
Chicago (city) Cook County	26	<0.01
Champaign (city) Champaign County	4	<0.01
Evanston (city) Cook County	2	<0.01
Joliet (city) Will County	2	<0.01
Palatine (village) Cook County	1	<0.01
Waukegan (city) Lake County	1	<0.01
Wheaton (city) DuPage County	1	<0.01
Arlington Heights (village) Cook County	0	0.00
Berwyn (city) Cook County	0	0.00

American Indian: Houma

Top 10 Places Sorted by Population
Based on all places, regardless of total population

Place	Population	%
Toluca (city) Marshall County	3	0.21
Chicago (city) Cook County	3	<0.01
Bradley (village) Kankakee County	2	0.01

Place	Population	%
Loves Park (city) Winnebago County	2	0.01
Peoria (city) Peoria County	2	<0.01
Vergennes (village) Jackson County	1	0.34
Ridge Farm (village) Vermilion County	1	0.11
De Soto (village) Jackson County	1	0.06
McLeansboro (city) Hamilton County	1	0.03
Bensenville (village) DuPage County	1	0.01

Top 10 Places Sorted by Percent of Total Population
Based on all places, regardless of total population

Place	Population	%
Vergennes (village) Jackson County	1	0.34
Toluca (city) Marshall County	3	0.21
Ridge Farm (village) Vermilion County	1	0.11
De Soto (village) Jackson County	1	0.06
McLeansboro (city) Hamilton County	1	0.03
Bradley (village) Kankakee County	2	0.01
Loves Park (city) Winnebago County	2	0.01
Bensenville (village) DuPage County	1	0.01
Crete (village) Will County	1	0.01
Montgomery (village) Kendall County	1	0.01

Top 10 Places Sorted by Percent of Total Population
Based on places with total population of 50,000 or more

Place	Population	%
Chicago (city) Cook County	3	<0.01
Peoria (city) Peoria County	2	<0.01
Arlington Heights (village) Cook County	0	0.00
Aurora (city) Kane County	0	0.00
Berwyn (city) Cook County	0	0.00
Bloomington (city) McLean County	0	0.00
Bolingbrook (village) Will County	0	0.00
Champaign (city) Champaign County	0	0.00
Cicero (town) Cook County	0	0.00
Decatur (city) Macon County	0	0.00

Alaska Native: Inupiat (Eskimo)

Top 10 Places Sorted by Population
Based on all places, regardless of total population

Place	Population	%
Chicago (city) Cook County	30	<0.01
Aurora (city) Kane County	10	0.01
West Peoria (city) Peoria County	5	0.11
Glenview (village) Cook County	5	0.01
Marseilles (city) LaSalle County	4	0.08
Benton (city) Franklin County	4	0.06
Lincoln (city) Logan County	4	0.03
Loves Park (city) Winnebago County	4	0.02
Crystal Lake (city) McHenry County	4	0.01
Rockford (city) Winnebago County	4	<0.01

Top 10 Places Sorted by Percent of Total Population
Based on all places, regardless of total population

Place	Population	%
Richview (village) Washington County	1	0.40
Steward (village) Lee County	1	0.39
Rossville (village) Vermilion County	2	0.15
Gridley (village) McLean County	2	0.14
Kansas (village) Edgar County	1	0.13
West Peoria (city) Peoria County	5	0.11
Richmond (village) McHenry County	2	0.11
Mackinaw (village) Tazewell County	2	0.10
Washburn (village) Woodford County	1	0.09
Marseilles (city) LaSalle County	4	0.08

Top 10 Places Sorted by Percent of Total Population
Based on places with total population of 50,000 or more

Place	Population	%
Aurora (city) Kane County	10	0.01
Chicago (city) Cook County	30	<0.01
Rockford (city) Winnebago County	4	<0.01
Joliet (city) Will County	3	<0.01
Champaign (city) Champaign County	2	<0.01
Des Plaines (city) Cook County	2	<0.01
Naperville (city) DuPage County	2	<0.01
Oak Lawn (village) Cook County	2	<0.01
Berwyn (city) Cook County	1	<0.01
Elgin (city) Kane County	1	<0.01

American Indian: Iroquois

Top 10 Places Sorted by Population
Based on all places, regardless of total population

Place	Population	%
Chicago (city) Cook County	359	0.01
Rockford (city) Winnebago County	23	0.02
Joliet (city) Will County	18	0.01
Aurora (city) Kane County	15	0.01
Round Lake Beach (village) Lake County	12	0.04
Carpentersville (village) Kane County	12	0.03
Crystal Lake (city) McHenry County	12	0.03
Bolingbrook (village) Will County	12	0.02
Evanston (city) Cook County	12	0.02
Naperville (city) DuPage County	12	0.01

Top 10 Places Sorted by Percent of Total Population
Based on all places, regardless of total population

Place	Population	%
Sawyerville (village) Macoupin County	4	1.43
Iola (village) Clay County	1	0.71
Sheffield (village) Bureau County	6	0.65
Garden Prairie (village) Boone County	2	0.57
East Cape Girardeau (village) Alexander County	2	0.52
Colp (village) Williamson County	1	0.44
Kappa (village) Woodford County	1	0.44
McCook (village) Cook County	1	0.44
Chestnut (cdp) Logan County	1	0.41
Stanford (village) McLean County	2	0.34

Top 10 Places Sorted by Percent of Total Population
Based on places with total population of 50,000 or more

Place	Population	%
Rockford (city) Winnebago County	23	0.02
Bolingbrook (village) Will County	12	0.02
Evanston (city) Cook County	12	0.02
Des Plaines (city) Cook County	10	0.02
Oak Lawn (village) Cook County	9	0.02
Chicago (city) Cook County	359	0.01
Joliet (city) Will County	18	0.01
Aurora (city) Kane County	15	0.01
Naperville (city) DuPage County	12	0.01
Elgin (city) Kane County	10	0.01

American Indian: Kiowa

Top 10 Places Sorted by Population
Based on all places, regardless of total population

Place	Population	%
Chicago (city) Cook County	23	<0.01
Gurnee (village) Lake County	6	0.02
Palatine (village) Cook County	4	0.01
Marine (village) Madison County	3	0.31
Effingham (city) Effingham County	3	0.02
Herrin (city) Williamson County	3	0.02
Berwyn (city) Cook County	3	0.01
O'Fallon (city) St. Clair County	3	0.01
Elgin (city) Kane County	3	<0.01
Hanna City (village) Peoria County	2	0.16

Top 10 Places Sorted by Percent of Total Population
Based on all places, regardless of total population

Place	Population	%
Broughton (village) Hamilton County	1	0.52
Marine (village) Madison County	3	0.31
Hanna City (village) Peoria County	2	0.16
Orion (village) Henry County	1	0.05
Flora (city) Clay County	2	0.04
East Alton (village) Madison County	2	0.03
Gurnee (village) Lake County	6	0.02
Effingham (city) Effingham County	3	0.02
Herrin (city) Williamson County	3	0.02
Minooka (village) Grundy County	2	0.02

Top 10 Places Sorted by Percent of Total Population
Based on places with total population of 50,000 or more

Place	Population	%
Palatine (village) Cook County	4	0.01
Berwyn (city) Cook County	3	0.01
Chicago (city) Cook County	23	<0.01
Elgin (city) Kane County	3	<0.01

Place	Population	%
Arlington Heights (village) Cook County	1	<0.01
Champaign (city) Champaign County	1	<0.01
Rockford (city) Winnebago County	1	<0.01
Waukegan (city) Lake County	1	<0.01
Aurora (city) Kane County	0	0.00
Bloomington (city) McLean County	0	0.00

American Indian: Lumbee

Top 10 Places Sorted by Population
Based on all places, regardless of total population

Place	Population	%
Chicago (city) Cook County	25	<0.01
Springfield (city) Sangamon County	7	0.01
Sandwich (city) DeKalb County	6	0.08
Gurnee (village) Lake County	6	0.02
Peoria (city) Peoria County	6	0.01
Markham (city) Cook County	5	0.04
Granite City (city) Madison County	5	0.02
Harrison (cdp) Jackson County	4	0.41
Newark (village) Kendall County	4	0.40
Orland Hills (village) Cook County	4	0.06

Top 10 Places Sorted by Percent of Total Population
Based on all places, regardless of total population

Place	Population	%
Harrison (cdp) Jackson County	4	0.41
Newark (village) Kendall County	4	0.40
Ogden (village) Champaign County	2	0.25
Germantown Hills (village) Woodford County	3	0.09
Sandwich (city) DeKalb County	6	0.08
Volo (village) Lake County	2	0.07
Orland Hills (village) Cook County	4	0.06
Bellevue (village) Peoria County	1	0.05
Markham (city) Cook County	5	0.04
Monticello (city) Piatt County	2	0.04

Top 10 Places Sorted by Percent of Total Population
Based on places with total population of 50,000 or more

Place	Population	%
Springfield (city) Sangamon County	7	0.01
Peoria (city) Peoria County	6	0.01
Berwyn (city) Cook County	3	0.01
Chicago (city) Cook County	25	<0.01
Aurora (city) Kane County	4	<0.01
Bolingbrook (village) Will County	3	<0.01
Elgin (city) Kane County	3	<0.01
Naperville (city) DuPage County	3	<0.01
Evanston (city) Cook County	2	<0.01
Oak Park (village) Cook County	2	<0.01

American Indian: Menominee

Top 10 Places Sorted by Population
Based on all places, regardless of total population

Place	Population	%
Chicago (city) Cook County	117	<0.01
Springfield (city) Sangamon County	12	0.01
Crystal Lake (city) McHenry County	10	0.02
Elmhurst (city) DuPage County	8	0.02
Monmouth (city) Warren County	7	0.07
Carpentersville (village) Kane County	7	0.02
Pekin (city) Tazewell County	7	0.02
Carlinville (city) Macoupin County	6	0.10
Berwyn (city) Cook County	6	0.01
Cicero (town) Cook County	6	0.01

Top 10 Places Sorted by Percent of Total Population
Based on all places, regardless of total population

Place	Population	%
Golconda (city) Pope County	1	0.15
Lyndon (village) Whiteside County	1	0.15
Grandview (village) Sangamon County	2	0.14
Channel Lake (cdp) Lake County	2	0.12
Tiskilwa (village) Bureau County	1	0.12
Timberlane (village) Boone County	1	0.11
Carlinville (city) Macoupin County	6	0.10
Malta (village) DeKalb County	1	0.09
La Harpe (city) Hancock County	1	0.08
Monmouth (city) Warren County	7	0.07

Top 10 Places Sorted by Percent of Total Population
Based on places with total population of 50,000 or more

Place	Population	%
Springfield (city) Sangamon County	12	0.01
Berwyn (city) Cook County	6	0.01
Cicero (town) Cook County	6	0.01
Des Plaines (city) Cook County	5	0.01
Oak Park (village) Cook County	3	0.01
Chicago (city) Cook County	117	<0.01
Elgin (city) Kane County	5	<0.01
Peoria (city) Peoria County	3	<0.01
Orland Park (village) Cook County	2	<0.01
Aurora (city) Kane County	1	<0.01

American Indian: Mexican American Indian

Top 10 Places Sorted by Population
Based on all places, regardless of total population

Place	Population	%
Chicago (city) Cook County	2,810	0.10
Elgin (city) Kane County	292	0.27
Cicero (town) Cook County	256	0.31
Aurora (city) Kane County	222	0.11
Waukegan (city) Lake County	192	0.22
Joliet (city) Will County	110	0.07
Berwyn (city) Cook County	102	0.18
Rockford (city) Winnebago County	88	0.06
Des Plaines (city) Cook County	75	0.13
Streamwood (village) Cook County	68	0.17

Top 10 Places Sorted by Percent of Total Population
Based on all places, regardless of total population

Place	Population	%
Cedar Point (village) LaSalle County	4	1.44
Alto Pass (village) Union County	5	1.28
Berlin (village) Sangamon County	2	1.11
Cobden (village) Union County	12	1.04
Good Hope (village) McDonough County	4	1.01
Marietta (village) Fulton County	1	0.89
Beecher City (village) Effingham County	4	0.86
Bluford (village) Jefferson County	5	0.73
Glasford (village) Peoria County	6	0.59
Keensburg (village) Wabash County	1	0.48

Top 10 Places Sorted by Percent of Total Population
Based on places with total population of 50,000 or more

Place	Population	%
Cicero (town) Cook County	256	0.31
Elgin (city) Kane County	292	0.27
Waukegan (city) Lake County	192	0.22
Berwyn (city) Cook County	102	0.18
Des Plaines (city) Cook County	75	0.13
Aurora (city) Kane County	222	0.11
Chicago (city) Cook County	2,810	0.10
Joliet (city) Will County	110	0.07
Evanston (city) Cook County	54	0.07
Palatine (village) Cook County	47	0.07

American Indian: Navajo

Top 10 Places Sorted by Population
Based on all places, regardless of total population

Place	Population	%
Chicago (city) Cook County	261	0.01
Aurora (city) Kane County	26	0.01
Joliet (city) Will County	24	0.02
Rockford (city) Winnebago County	21	0.01
Cicero (town) Cook County	17	0.02
Decatur (city) Macon County	17	0.02
Naperville (city) DuPage County	17	0.01
North Chicago (city) Lake County	16	0.05
Waukegan (city) Lake County	16	0.02
Peoria (city) Peoria County	16	0.01

Top 10 Places Sorted by Percent of Total Population
Based on all places, regardless of total population

Place	Population	%
Springerton (village) White County	2	1.82
Russellville (village) Lawrence County	1	1.06

Place	Population	%
Maunie (village) White County	1	0.72
Galatia (village) Saline County	5	0.54
Deer Creek (village) Tazewell County	3	0.43
Raleigh (village) Saline County	1	0.29
Edinburg (village) Christian County	3	0.28
Essex (village) Kankakee County	2	0.25
Rome (cdp) Peoria County	4	0.23
Zeigler (city) Franklin County	4	0.22

Top 10 Places Sorted by Percent of Total Population
Based on places with total population of 50,000 or more

Place	Population	%
Joliet (city) Will County	24	0.02
Cicero (town) Cook County	17	0.02
Decatur (city) Macon County	17	0.02
Waukegan (city) Lake County	16	0.02
Chicago (city) Cook County	261	0.01
Aurora (city) Kane County	26	0.01
Rockford (city) Winnebago County	21	0.01
Naperville (city) DuPage County	17	0.01
Peoria (city) Peoria County	16	0.01
Champaign (city) Champaign County	12	0.01

American Indian: Osage

Top 10 Places Sorted by Population
Based on all places, regardless of total population

Place	Population	%
Chicago (city) Cook County	31	<0.01
Elgin (city) Kane County	7	0.01
Naperville (city) DuPage County	7	<0.01
Tamms (village) Alexander County	5	0.79
Big Rock (village) Kane County	5	0.44
Itasca (village) DuPage County	5	0.06
Sauk Village (village) Cook County	5	0.05
Glendale Heights (village) DuPage County	5	0.01
Vandalia (city) Fayette County	4	0.06
Streamwood (village) Cook County	4	0.01

Top 10 Places Sorted by Percent of Total Population
Based on all places, regardless of total population

Place	Population	%
Tamms (village) Alexander County	5	0.79
Raritan (village) Henderson County	1	0.72
Huey (village) Clinton County	1	0.59
Royal Lakes (village) Macoupin County	1	0.51
Big Rock (village) Kane County	5	0.44
Bardolph (village) McDonough County	1	0.40
Stronghurst (village) Henderson County	3	0.34
Tilden (village) Randolph County	3	0.32
Rutland (village) LaSalle County	1	0.31
East Cape Girardeau (village) Alexander County	1	0.26

Top 10 Places Sorted by Percent of Total Population
Based on places with total population of 50,000 or more

Place	Population	%
Elgin (city) Kane County	7	0.01
Orland Park (village) Cook County	3	0.01
Chicago (city) Cook County	31	<0.01
Naperville (city) DuPage County	7	<0.01
Champaign (city) Champaign County	3	<0.01
Oak Park (village) Cook County	2	<0.01
Peoria (city) Peoria County	2	<0.01
Bloomington (city) McLean County	1	<0.01
Decatur (city) Macon County	1	<0.01
Schaumburg (village) Cook County	1	<0.01

American Indian: Ottawa

Top 10 Places Sorted by Population
Based on all places, regardless of total population

Place	Population	%
Chicago (city) Cook County	41	<0.01
South Holland (village) Cook County	8	0.04
Peoria (city) Peoria County	7	0.01
Hanover Park (village) Cook County	6	0.02
Orland Park (village) Cook County	6	0.01
Palatine (village) Cook County	6	0.01
North Riverside (village) Cook County	5	0.07
Crete (village) Will County	5	0.06
Lemont (village) Cook County	5	0.03

Place	Population	%
Elgin (city) Kane County	5	<0.01

Top 10 Places Sorted by Percent of Total Population
Based on all places, regardless of total population

Place	Population	%
Thomson (village) Carroll County	2	0.34
Marquette Heights (city) Tazewell County	4	0.14
Yates City (village) Knox County	1	0.14
Prairie Grove (village) McHenry County	2	0.11
North Riverside (village) Cook County	5	0.07
Lake Catherine (cdp) Lake County	1	0.07
Crete (village) Will County	5	0.06
Earlville (city) LaSalle County	1	0.06
Fisher (village) Champaign County	1	0.05
Lake Summerset (cdp) Winnebago County	1	0.05

Top 10 Places Sorted by Percent of Total Population
Based on places with total population of 50,000 or more

Place	Population	%
Peoria (city) Peoria County	7	0.01
Orland Park (village) Cook County	6	0.01
Palatine (village) Cook County	6	0.01
Oak Park (village) Cook County	3	0.01
Chicago (city) Cook County	41	<0.01
Elgin (city) Kane County	5	<0.01
Champaign (city) Champaign County	3	<0.01
Evanston (city) Cook County	3	<0.01
Arlington Heights (village) Cook County	2	<0.01
Aurora (city) Kane County	2	<0.01

American Indian: Paiute

Top 10 Places Sorted by Population
Based on all places, regardless of total population

Place	Population	%
Chicago (city) Cook County	9	<0.01
Decatur (city) Macon County	5	0.01
Monmouth (city) Warren County	4	0.04
Rockford (city) Winnebago County	4	<0.01
Coulterville (village) Randolph County	3	0.32
Granite City (city) Madison County	3	0.01
Elgin (city) Kane County	3	<0.01
Schaumburg (village) Cook County	3	<0.01
North Chicago (city) Lake County	2	0.01
Dayton (cdp) LaSalle County	1	0.19

Top 10 Places Sorted by Percent of Total Population
Based on all places, regardless of total population

Place	Population	%
Coulterville (village) Randolph County	3	0.32
Dayton (cdp) LaSalle County	1	0.19
Monmouth (city) Warren County	4	0.04
Peoria Heights (village) Peoria County	1	0.02
Decatur (city) Macon County	5	0.01
Granite City (city) Madison County	3	0.01
North Chicago (city) Lake County	2	0.01
Kewanee (city) Henry County	1	0.01
Midlothian (village) Cook County	1	0.01
Chicago (city) Cook County	9	<0.01

Top 10 Places Sorted by Percent of Total Population
Based on places with total population of 50,000 or more

Place	Population	%
Decatur (city) Macon County	5	0.01
Chicago (city) Cook County	9	<0.01
Rockford (city) Winnebago County	4	<0.01
Elgin (city) Kane County	3	<0.01
Schaumburg (village) Cook County	3	<0.01
Cicero (town) Cook County	1	<0.01
Arlington Heights (village) Cook County	0	0.00
Aurora (city) Kane County	0	0.00
Berwyn (city) Cook County	0	0.00
Bloomington (city) McLean County	0	0.00

American Indian: Pima

Top 10 Places Sorted by Population
Based on all places, regardless of total population

Place	Population	%
Chicago (city) Cook County	16	<0.01

Place	Population	%
Cortland (town) DeKalb County	6	0.14
Lansing (village) Cook County	5	0.02
Aurora (city) Kane County	5	<0.01
Poplar Grove (village) Boone County	4	0.08
Rockford (city) Winnebago County	4	<0.01
Charleston (city) Coles County	3	0.01
Gurnee (village) Lake County	3	0.01
Lombard (village) DuPage County	3	0.01
Champaign (city) Champaign County	3	<0.01

Top 10 Places Sorted by Percent of Total Population
Based on all places, regardless of total population

Place	Population	%
Cortland (town) DeKalb County	6	0.14
Poplar Grove (village) Boone County	4	0.08
Silvis (city) Rock Island County	2	0.03
Lansing (village) Cook County	5	0.02
Carterville (city) Williamson County	1	0.02
Lake Holiday (cdp) LaSalle County	1	0.02
Marseilles (city) LaSalle County	1	0.02
Charleston (city) Coles County	3	0.01
Gurnee (village) Lake County	3	0.01
Lombard (village) DuPage County	3	0.01

Top 10 Places Sorted by Percent of Total Population
Based on places with total population of 50,000 or more

Place	Population	%
Chicago (city) Cook County	16	<0.01
Aurora (city) Kane County	5	<0.01
Rockford (city) Winnebago County	4	<0.01
Champaign (city) Champaign County	3	<0.01
Hoffman Estates (village) Cook County	2	<0.01
Peoria (city) Peoria County	2	<0.01
Berwyn (city) Cook County	1	<0.01
Elgin (city) Kane County	1	<0.01
Oak Lawn (village) Cook County	1	<0.01
Springfield (city) Sangamon County	1	<0.01

American Indian: Potawatomi

Top 10 Places Sorted by Population
Based on all places, regardless of total population

Place	Population	%
Chicago (city) Cook County	115	<0.01
Bloomington (city) McLean County	14	0.02
Elgin (city) Kane County	14	0.01
South Elgin (village) Kane County	11	0.05
Aurora (city) Kane County	11	0.01
Joliet (city) Will County	11	0.01
Harvard (city) McHenry County	9	0.10
East Peoria (city) Tazewell County	8	0.03
Bolingbrook (village) Will County	8	0.01
Rockford (city) Winnebago County	8	0.01

Top 10 Places Sorted by Percent of Total Population
Based on all places, regardless of total population

Place	Population	%
Yale (village) Jasper County	3	3.49
Willow Hill (village) Jasper County	4	1.74
Longview (village) Champaign County	1	0.65
Norwood (village) Peoria County	3	0.63
Beaverville (village) Iroquois County	2	0.55
Banner (village) Fulton County	1	0.53
Irving (village) Montgomery County	2	0.40
Edgewood (village) Effingham County	1	0.23
Buckner (village) Franklin County	1	0.22
Summerfield (village) St. Clair County	1	0.22

Top 10 Places Sorted by Percent of Total Population
Based on places with total population of 50,000 or more

Place	Population	%
Bloomington (city) McLean County	14	0.02
Elgin (city) Kane County	14	0.01
Aurora (city) Kane County	11	0.01
Joliet (city) Will County	11	0.01
Bolingbrook (village) Will County	8	0.01
Rockford (city) Winnebago County	8	0.01
Champaign (city) Champaign County	7	0.01
Palatine (village) Cook County	7	0.01
Decatur (city) Macon County	4	0.01
Normal (town) McLean County	4	0.01

American Indian: Pueblo

Top 10 Places Sorted by Population
Based on all places, regardless of total population

Place	Population	%
Chicago (city) Cook County	71	<0.01
Beardstown (city) Cass County	7	0.11
Westchester (village) Cook County	7	0.04
Champaign (city) Champaign County	5	0.01
Aurora (city) Kane County	5	<0.01
Campton Hills (village) Kane County	4	0.04
Bartlett (village) DuPage County	4	0.01
Evanston (city) Cook County	4	0.01
North Chicago (city) Lake County	4	0.01
Patoka (village) Marion County	3	0.51

Top 10 Places Sorted by Percent of Total Population
Based on all places, regardless of total population

Place	Population	%
Patoka (village) Marion County	3	0.51
Galatia (village) Saline County	2	0.21
Athens (city) Menard County	3	0.15
Beardstown (city) Cass County	7	0.11
New Athens (village) St. Clair County	2	0.10
Thomasboro (village) Champaign County	1	0.09
Bannockburn (village) Lake County	1	0.06
Posen (village) Cook County	3	0.05
Westchester (village) Cook County	7	0.04
Campton Hills (village) Kane County	4	0.04

Top 10 Places Sorted by Percent of Total Population
Based on places with total population of 50,000 or more

Place	Population	%
Champaign (city) Champaign County	5	0.01
Evanston (city) Cook County	4	0.01
Hoffman Estates (village) Cook County	3	0.01
Chicago (city) Cook County	71	<0.01
Aurora (city) Kane County	5	<0.01
Naperville (city) DuPage County	3	<0.01
Waukegan (city) Lake County	3	<0.01
Cicero (town) Cook County	2	<0.01
Des Plaines (city) Cook County	2	<0.01
Springfield (city) Sangamon County	2	<0.01

American Indian: Puget Sound Salish

Top 10 Places Sorted by Population
Based on all places, regardless of total population

Place	Population	%
Chicago (city) Cook County	8	<0.01
Glen Carbon (village) Madison County	5	0.04
Peoria (city) Peoria County	4	<0.01
Rockford (city) Winnebago County	4	<0.01
Coal City (village) Grundy County	3	0.05
Roscoe (village) Winnebago County	3	0.03
Machesney Park (village) Winnebago County	3	0.01
North Chicago (city) Lake County	3	0.01
Coal Valley (village) Rock Island County	2	0.05
Barrington (village) Cook County	2	0.02

Top 10 Places Sorted by Percent of Total Population
Based on all places, regardless of total population

Place	Population	%
Coal City (village) Grundy County	3	0.05
Coal Valley (village) Rock Island County	2	0.05
Glen Carbon (village) Madison County	5	0.04
Roscoe (village) Winnebago County	3	0.03
Aledo (city) Mercer County	1	0.03
Forsyth (village) Macon County	1	0.03
Barrington (village) Cook County	2	0.02
Machesney Park (village) Winnebago County	3	0.01
North Chicago (city) Lake County	3	0.01
Belvidere (city) Boone County	2	0.01

Top 10 Places Sorted by Percent of Total Population
Based on places with total population of 50,000 or more

Place	Population	%
Chicago (city) Cook County	8	<0.01
Peoria (city) Peoria County	4	<0.01
Rockford (city) Winnebago County	4	<0.01
Bloomington (city) McLean County	1	<0.01

Naperville (city) DuPage County	1	<0.01
Palatine (village) Cook County	1	<0.01
Arlington Heights (village) Cook County	0	0.00
Aurora (city) Kane County	0	0.00
Berwyn (city) Cook County	0	0.00
Bolingbrook (village) Will County	0	0.00

American Indian: Seminole

Top 10 Places Sorted by Population
Based on all places, regardless of total population

Place	Population	%
Chicago (city) Cook County	80	<0.01
Evanston (city) Cook County	11	0.01
East Peoria (city) Tazewell County	9	0.04
Elgin (city) Kane County	9	0.01
Hainesville (village) Lake County	7	0.19
Franklin Park (village) Cook County	7	0.04
Country Club Hills (city) Cook County	6	0.04
Park Ridge (city) Cook County	6	0.02
Naperville (city) DuPage County	6	<0.01
Geneseo (city) Henry County	5	0.08

Top 10 Places Sorted by Percent of Total Population
Based on all places, regardless of total population

Place	Population	%
Greenview (village) Menard County	2	0.26
Hainesville (village) Lake County	7	0.19
Lenzburg (village) St. Clair County	1	0.19
Bethany (village) Moultrie County	2	0.15
Brownstown (village) Fayette County	1	0.13
Channel Lake (cdp) Lake County	2	0.12
Byron (city) Ogle County	4	0.11
Oakland (city) Coles County	1	0.11
Prophetstown (city) Whiteside County	2	0.10
Leland (village) LaSalle County	1	0.10

Top 10 Places Sorted by Percent of Total Population
Based on places with total population of 50,000 or more

Place	Population	%
Evanston (city) Cook County	11	0.01
Elgin (city) Kane County	9	0.01
Normal (town) McLean County	3	0.01
Chicago (city) Cook County	80	<0.01
Naperville (city) DuPage County	6	<0.01
Springfield (city) Sangamon County	5	<0.01
Peoria (city) Peoria County	4	<0.01
Rockford (city) Winnebago County	3	<0.01
Des Plaines (city) Cook County	2	<0.01
Waukegan (city) Lake County	2	<0.01

American Indian: Shoshone

Top 10 Places Sorted by Population
Based on all places, regardless of total population

Place	Population	%
Chicago (city) Cook County	17	<0.01
Loves Park (city) Winnebago County	5	0.02
Frankfort (village) Will County	4	0.02
Bourbonnais (village) Kankakee County	3	0.02
Cahokia (village) St. Clair County	3	0.02
Deerfield (village) Lake County	3	0.02
Godfrey (village) Madison County	3	0.02
DeKalb (city) DeKalb County	3	0.01
Oak Forest (city) Cook County	3	0.01
Tinley Park (village) Cook County	3	0.01

Top 10 Places Sorted by Percent of Total Population
Based on all places, regardless of total population

Place	Population	%
Ellis Grove (village) Randolph County	2	0.55
Williamsfield (village) Knox County	2	0.35
Athens (city) Menard County	1	0.05
Venetian Village (cdp) Lake County	1	0.04
Byron (city) Ogle County	1	0.03
Loves Park (city) Winnebago County	5	0.02
Frankfort (village) Will County	4	0.02
Bourbonnais (village) Kankakee County	3	0.02
Cahokia (village) St. Clair County	3	0.02
Deerfield (village) Lake County	3	0.02

Top 10 Places Sorted by Percent of Total Population
Based on places with total population of 50,000 or more

Place	Population	%
Tinley Park (village) Cook County	3	0.0
Chicago (city) Cook County	17	<0.0
Bolingbrook (village) Will County	2	<0.0
Normal (town) McLean County	2	<0.0
Oak Lawn (village) Cook County	2	<0.0
Wheaton (city) DuPage County	2	<0.0
Bloomington (city) McLean County	1	<0.0
Evanston (city) Cook County	1	<0.0
Peoria (city) Peoria County	1	<0.0
Arlington Heights (village) Cook County	0	0.00

American Indian: Sioux

Top 10 Places Sorted by Population
Based on all places, regardless of total population

Place	Population	%
Chicago (city) Cook County	385	0.0
Rockford (city) Winnebago County	46	0.0
Elgin (city) Kane County	32	0.0
Bloomington (city) McLean County	30	0.04
Aurora (city) Kane County	29	0.0
Peoria (city) Peoria County	26	0.0
Springfield (city) Sangamon County	26	0.0
Joliet (city) Will County	25	0.0
Moline (city) Rock Island County	24	0.0
Decatur (city) Macon County	22	0.0

Top 10 Places Sorted by Percent of Total Population
Based on all places, regardless of total population

Place	Population	%
McClure (village) Alexander County	5	1.2
Parkersburg (village) Richland County	2	1.0
Marietta (village) Fulton County	1	0.8
Ohlman (village) Montgomery County	1	0.74
Raritan (village) Henderson County	1	0.7
Coalton (village) Montgomery County	2	0.6
Donovan (village) Iroquois County	2	0.6
Hanaford (village) Franklin County	2	0.6
Oconee (village) Shelby County	1	0.5
Broughton (village) Hamilton County	1	0.5

Top 10 Places Sorted by Percent of Total Population
Based on places with total population of 50,000 or more

Place	Population	%
Bloomington (city) McLean County	30	0.04
Rockford (city) Winnebago County	46	0.0
Elgin (city) Kane County	32	0.0
Decatur (city) Macon County	22	0.0
Berwyn (city) Cook County	16	0.0
Peoria (city) Peoria County	26	0.0
Springfield (city) Sangamon County	26	0.0
Joliet (city) Will County	25	0.0
Evanston (city) Cook County	13	0.0
Bolingbrook (village) Will County	12	0.0

American Indian: South American Indian

Top 10 Places Sorted by Population
Based on all places, regardless of total population

Place	Population	%
Chicago (city) Cook County	743	0.0
Elgin (city) Kane County	35	0.0
Waukegan (city) Lake County	32	0.0
Berwyn (city) Cook County	26	0.0
Palatine (village) Cook County	22	0.0
Oak Park (village) Cook County	19	0.0
Aurora (city) Kane County	17	0.0
Cicero (town) Cook County	16	0.0
Elmhurst (city) DuPage County	15	0.0
Hanover Park (village) Cook County	14	0.0

Top 10 Places Sorted by Percent of Total Population
Based on all places, regardless of total population

Place	Population	%
Matherville (village) Mercer County	2	0.28
Onarga (village) Iroquois County	3	0.2
Braceville (village) Grundy County	1	0.1

Please refer to the Explanation of Data in the front of the book for more detailed information.

Place	Population	%
Chatsworth (town) Livingston County	1	0.08
Third Lake (village) Lake County	1	0.08
River Grove (village) Cook County	7	0.07
South Chicago Heights (village) Cook County	3	0.07
Berwyn (city) Cook County	26	0.05
Wood Dale (city) DuPage County	7	0.05
Schiller Park (village) Cook County	6	0.05

Top 10 Places Sorted by Percent of Total Population
Based on places with total population of 50,000 or more

Place	Population	%
Berwyn (city) Cook County	26	0.05
Waukegan (city) Lake County	32	0.04
Oak Park (village) Cook County	19	0.04
Chicago (city) Cook County	743	0.03
Elgin (city) Kane County	35	0.03
Palatine (village) Cook County	22	0.03
Cicero (town) Cook County	16	0.02
Champaign (city) Champaign County	13	0.02
Evanston (city) Cook County	13	0.02
Skokie (village) Cook County	12	0.02

American Indian: Spanish American Indian

Top 10 Places Sorted by Population
Based on all places, regardless of total population

Place	Population	%
Chicago (city) Cook County	225	0.01
Waukegan (city) Lake County	36	0.04
Aurora (city) Kane County	28	0.01
Elgin (city) Kane County	18	0.02
Round Lake Beach (village) Lake County	17	0.06
Carol Stream (village) DuPage County	14	0.04
Joliet (city) Will County	14	0.01
Des Plaines (city) Cook County	13	0.02
Burbank (city) Cook County	7	0.02
West Chicago (city) DuPage County	6	0.02

Top 10 Places Sorted by Percent of Total Population
Based on all places, regardless of total population

Place	Population	%
Summerfield (village) St. Clair County	1	0.22
Minier (village) Tazewell County	1	0.08
Round Lake Beach (village) Lake County	17	0.06
Crystal Lawns (cdp) Will County	1	0.05
Waukegan (city) Lake County	36	0.04
Carol Stream (village) DuPage County	14	0.04
Highwood (city) Lake County	2	0.04
Fairmont City (village) St. Clair County	1	0.04
Bensenville (village) DuPage County	5	0.03
Sterling (city) Whiteside County	4	0.03

Top 10 Places Sorted by Percent of Total Population
Based on places with total population of 50,000 or more

Place	Population	%
Waukegan (city) Lake County	36	0.04
Elgin (city) Kane County	18	0.02
Des Plaines (city) Cook County	13	0.02
Chicago (city) Cook County	225	0.01
Aurora (city) Kane County	28	0.01
Joliet (city) Will County	14	0.01
Cicero (town) Cook County	6	0.01
Palatine (village) Cook County	6	0.01
Berwyn (city) Cook County	5	0.01
Rockford (city) Winnebago County	4	<0.01

Alaska Native: Tlingit-Haida

Top 10 Places Sorted by Population
Based on all places, regardless of total population

Place	Population	%
Chicago (city) Cook County	15	<0.01
O'Fallon (city) St. Clair County	7	0.02
Belleville (city) St. Clair County	5	0.01
Bartonville (village) Peoria County	4	0.06
Silvis (city) Rock Island County	4	0.05
Evanston (city) Cook County	4	0.01
Hamilton (city) Hancock County	3	0.10
Gillespie (city) Macoupin County	3	0.09
Shelbyville (city) Shelby County	3	0.06

Place	Population	%
Delavan (city) Tazewell County	2	0.12

Top 10 Places Sorted by Percent of Total Population
Based on all places, regardless of total population

Place	Population	%
Kilbourne (village) Mason County	1	0.33
Delavan (city) Tazewell County	2	0.12
Hamilton (city) Hancock County	3	0.10
Gillespie (city) Macoupin County	3	0.09
Hanna City (village) Peoria County	1	0.08
Bartonville (village) Peoria County	4	0.06
Shelbyville (city) Shelby County	3	0.06
Silvis (city) Rock Island County	4	0.05
O'Fallon (city) St. Clair County	7	0.02
Herrin (city) Williamson County	2	0.02

Top 10 Places Sorted by Percent of Total Population
Based on places with total population of 50,000 or more

Place	Population	%
Evanston (city) Cook County	4	0.01
Chicago (city) Cook County	15	<0.01
Aurora (city) Kane County	1	<0.01
Oak Park (village) Cook County	1	<0.01
Skokie (village) Cook County	1	<0.01
Tinley Park (village) Cook County	1	<0.01
Waukegan (city) Lake County	1	<0.01
Arlington Heights (village) Cook County	0	0.00
Berwyn (city) Cook County	0	0.00
Bloomington (city) McLean County	0	0.00

American Indian: Tohono O'Odham

Top 10 Places Sorted by Population
Based on all places, regardless of total population

Place	Population	%
Summit (village) Cook County	4	0.04
Chicago (city) Cook County	4	<0.01
Mendota (city) LaSalle County	3	0.04
West Dundee (village) Kane County	3	0.04
Danville (city) Vermilion County	3	0.01
Des Plaines (city) Cook County	3	0.01
Itasca (village) DuPage County	2	0.02
Carbondale (city) Jackson County	2	0.01
Yorkville (city) Kendall County	2	0.01
Elgin (city) Kane County	2	<0.01

Top 10 Places Sorted by Percent of Total Population
Based on all places, regardless of total population

Place	Population	%
Summit (village) Cook County	4	0.04
Mendota (city) LaSalle County	3	0.04
West Dundee (village) Kane County	3	0.04
Itasca (village) DuPage County	2	0.02
Braidwood (city) Will County	1	0.02
Danville (city) Vermilion County	3	0.01
Des Plaines (city) Cook County	3	0.01
Carbondale (city) Jackson County	2	0.01
Yorkville (city) Kendall County	2	0.01
Boulder Hill (cdp) Kendall County	1	0.01

Top 10 Places Sorted by Percent of Total Population
Based on places with total population of 50,000 or more

Place	Population	%
Des Plaines (city) Cook County	3	0.01
Chicago (city) Cook County	4	<0.01
Elgin (city) Kane County	2	<0.01
Waukegan (city) Lake County	2	<0.01
Evanston (city) Cook County	1	<0.01
Normal (town) McLean County	1	<0.01
Arlington Heights (village) Cook County	0	0.00
Aurora (city) Kane County	0	0.00
Berwyn (city) Cook County	0	0.00
Bloomington (city) McLean County	0	0.00

Alaska Native: Tsimshian

Top 10 Places Sorted by Population
Based on all places, regardless of total population

Place	Population	%
Creve Coeur (village) Tazewell County	2	0.04

Place	Population	%
Effingham (city) Effingham County	1	0.01
Chicago (city) Cook County	1	<0.01
East Peoria (city) Tazewell County	1	<0.01
Rockford (city) Winnebago County	1	<0.01
Abingdon (city) Knox County	0	0.00
Adair (cdp) McDonough County	0	0.00
Addieville (village) Washington County	0	0.00
Addison (village) DuPage County	0	0.00
Adeline (village) Ogle County	0	0.00

Top 10 Places Sorted by Percent of Total Population
Based on all places, regardless of total population

Place	Population	%
Creve Coeur (village) Tazewell County	2	0.04
Effingham (city) Effingham County	1	0.01
Chicago (city) Cook County	1	<0.01
East Peoria (city) Tazewell County	1	<0.01
Rockford (city) Winnebago County	1	<0.01
Abingdon (city) Knox County	0	0.00
Adair (cdp) McDonough County	0	0.00
Addieville (village) Washington County	0	0.00
Addison (village) DuPage County	0	0.00
Adeline (village) Ogle County	0	0.00

Top 10 Places Sorted by Percent of Total Population
Based on places with total population of 50,000 or more

Place	Population	%
Chicago (city) Cook County	1	<0.01
Rockford (city) Winnebago County	1	<0.01
Arlington Heights (village) Cook County	0	0.00
Aurora (city) Kane County	0	0.00
Berwyn (city) Cook County	0	0.00
Bloomington (city) McLean County	0	0.00
Bolingbrook (village) Will County	0	0.00
Champaign (city) Champaign County	0	0.00
Cicero (town) Cook County	0	0.00
Decatur (city) Macon County	0	0.00

American Indian: Ute

Top 10 Places Sorted by Population
Based on all places, regardless of total population

Place	Population	%
Chicago (city) Cook County	8	<0.01
Villa Park (village) DuPage County	5	0.02
Naperville (city) DuPage County	5	<0.01
Grayslake (village) Lake County	4	0.02
Danville (city) Vermilion County	4	0.01
Joliet (city) Will County	4	<0.01
Lansing (village) Cook County	3	0.01
Round Lake Heights (village) Lake County	2	0.07
Momence (city) Kankakee County	2	0.06
Mount Vernon (city) Jefferson County	2	0.01

Top 10 Places Sorted by Percent of Total Population
Based on all places, regardless of total population

Place	Population	%
Round Lake Heights (village) Lake County	2	0.07
Momence (city) Kankakee County	2	0.06
Villa Park (village) DuPage County	5	0.02
Grayslake (village) Lake County	4	0.02
Creve Coeur (village) Tazewell County	1	0.02
Danville (city) Vermilion County	4	0.01
Lansing (village) Cook County	3	0.01
Mount Vernon (city) Jefferson County	2	0.01
North Chicago (city) Lake County	2	0.01
Rock Island (city) Rock Island County	2	0.01

Top 10 Places Sorted by Percent of Total Population
Based on places with total population of 50,000 or more

Place	Population	%
Chicago (city) Cook County	8	<0.01
Naperville (city) DuPage County	5	<0.01
Joliet (city) Will County	4	<0.01
Aurora (city) Kane County	2	<0.01
Evanston (city) Cook County	2	<0.01
Waukegan (city) Lake County	2	<0.01
Schaumburg (village) Cook County	1	<0.01
Springfield (city) Sangamon County	1	<0.01
Tinley Park (village) Cook County	1	<0.01
Arlington Heights (village) Cook County	0	0.00

American Indian: Yakama

Top 10 Places Sorted by Population
Based on all places, regardless of total population

Place	Population	%
Manhattan (village) Will County	4	0.06
Mascoutah (city) St. Clair County	3	0.04
Chicago (city) Cook County	3	<0.01
Centralia (city) Marion County	1	0.01
Rockton (village) Winnebago County	1	0.01
Bloomington (city) McLean County	1	<0.01
Carpentersville (village) Kane County	1	<0.01
Waukegan (city) Lake County	1	<0.01
Abingdon (city) Knox County	0	0.00
Adair (cdp) McDonough County	0	0.00

Top 10 Places Sorted by Percent of Total Population
Based on all places, regardless of total population

Place	Population	%
Manhattan (village) Will County	4	0.06
Mascoutah (city) St. Clair County	3	0.04
Centralia (city) Marion County	1	0.01
Rockton (village) Winnebago County	1	0.01
Chicago (city) Cook County	3	<0.01
Bloomington (city) McLean County	1	<0.01
Carpentersville (village) Kane County	1	<0.01
Waukegan (city) Lake County	1	<0.01
Abingdon (city) Knox County	0	0.00
Adair (cdp) McDonough County	0	0.00

Top 10 Places Sorted by Percent of Total Population
Based on places with total population of 50,000 or more

Place	Population	%
Chicago (city) Cook County	3	<0.01
Bloomington (city) McLean County	1	<0.01
Waukegan (city) Lake County	1	<0.01
Arlington Heights (village) Cook County	0	0.00
Aurora (city) Kane County	0	0.00
Berwyn (city) Cook County	0	0.00
Bolingbrook (village) Will County	0	0.00
Champaign (city) Champaign County	0	0.00
Cicero (town) Cook County	0	0.00
Decatur (city) Macon County	0	0.00

American Indian: Yaqui

Top 10 Places Sorted by Population
Based on all places, regardless of total population

Place	Population	%
Chicago (city) Cook County	58	<0.01
Aurora (city) Kane County	12	0.01
Waukegan (city) Lake County	7	0.01
North Riverside (village) Cook County	5	0.07
Bensenville (village) DuPage County	5	0.03
Beach Park (village) Lake County	4	0.03
Bradley (village) Kankakee County	4	0.03
Godfrey (village) Madison County	4	0.02
Oak Forest (city) Cook County	4	0.01
Greenview (village) Menard County	3	0.39

Top 10 Places Sorted by Percent of Total Population
Based on all places, regardless of total population

Place	Population	%
Greenview (village) Menard County	3	0.39
Irving (village) Montgomery County	1	0.20
Pocahontas (village) Bond County	1	0.13
North Riverside (village) Cook County	5	0.07
Southern View (village) Sangamon County	1	0.06
Bellevue (village) Peoria County	1	0.05
Bensenville (village) DuPage County	5	0.03
Beach Park (village) Lake County	4	0.03
Bradley (village) Kankakee County	4	0.03
Calumet Park (village) Cook County	2	0.03

Top 10 Places Sorted by Percent of Total Population
Based on places with total population of 50,000 or more

Place	Population	%
Aurora (city) Kane County	12	0.01
Waukegan (city) Lake County	7	0.01
Berwyn (city) Cook County	3	0.01
Mount Prospect (village) Cook County	3	0.01

Place	Population	%
Chicago (city) Cook County	58	<0.01
Evanston (city) Cook County	3	<0.01
Champaign (city) Champaign County	2	<0.01
Peoria (city) Peoria County	2	<0.01
Bolingbrook (village) Will County	1	<0.01
Hoffman Estates (village) Cook County	1	<0.01

American Indian: Yuman

Top 10 Places Sorted by Population
Based on all places, regardless of total population

Place	Population	%
Chicago (city) Cook County	15	<0.01
Lansing (village) Cook County	4	0.01
Buffalo Grove (village) Lake County	3	0.01
Morris (city) Grundy County	2	0.01
Hoffman Estates (village) Cook County	2	<0.01
Volo (village) Lake County	1	0.03
Boulder Hill (cdp) Kendall County	1	0.01
Shiloh (village) St. Clair County	1	0.01
Bolingbrook (village) Will County	1	<0.01
Chicago Heights (city) Cook County	1	<0.01

Top 10 Places Sorted by Percent of Total Population
Based on all places, regardless of total population

Place	Population	%
Volo (village) Lake County	1	0.03
Lansing (village) Cook County	4	0.01
Buffalo Grove (village) Lake County	3	0.01
Morris (city) Grundy County	2	0.01
Boulder Hill (cdp) Kendall County	1	0.01
Shiloh (village) St. Clair County	1	0.01
Chicago (city) Cook County	15	<0.01
Hoffman Estates (village) Cook County	2	<0.01
Bolingbrook (village) Will County	1	<0.01
Chicago Heights (city) Cook County	1	<0.01

Top 10 Places Sorted by Percent of Total Population
Based on places with total population of 50,000 or more

Place	Population	%
Chicago (city) Cook County	15	<0.01
Hoffman Estates (village) Cook County	2	<0.01
Bolingbrook (village) Will County	1	<0.01
Normal (town) McLean County	1	<0.01
Arlington Heights (village) Cook County	0	0.00
Aurora (city) Kane County	0	0.00
Berwyn (city) Cook County	0	0.00
Bloomington (city) McLean County	0	0.00
Champaign (city) Champaign County	0	0.00
Cicero (town) Cook County	0	0.00

Alaska Native: Yup'ik

Top 10 Places Sorted by Population
Based on all places, regardless of total population

Place	Population	%
Chicago (city) Cook County	10	<0.01
Oswego (village) Kendall County	8	0.03
Boulder Hill (cdp) Kendall County	4	0.05
Smithton (village) St. Clair County	3	0.08
Ottawa (city) LaSalle County	3	0.02
East Peoria (city) Tazewell County	3	0.01
North Chicago (city) Lake County	3	0.01
Forreston (village) Ogle County	1	0.07
Bradley (village) Kankakee County	1	0.01
Sugar Grove (village) Kane County	1	0.01

Top 10 Places Sorted by Percent of Total Population
Based on all places, regardless of total population

Place	Population	%
Smithton (village) St. Clair County	3	0.08
Forreston (village) Ogle County	1	0.07
Boulder Hill (cdp) Kendall County	4	0.05
Oswego (village) Kendall County	8	0.03
Ottawa (city) LaSalle County	3	0.02
East Peoria (city) Tazewell County	3	0.01
North Chicago (city) Lake County	3	0.01
Bradley (village) Kankakee County	1	0.01
Sugar Grove (village) Kane County	1	0.01
Chicago (city) Cook County	10	<0.01

Top 10 Places Sorted by Percent of Total Populati
Based on places with total population of 50,000 or more

Place	Population	
Chicago (city) Cook County	10	<0
Berwyn (city) Cook County	1	<0
Bloomington (city) McLean County	1	<0
Cicero (town) Cook County	1	<0
Naperville (city) DuPage County	1	<0
Peoria (city) Peoria County	1	<0
Wheaton (city) DuPage County	1	<0
Arlington Heights (village) Cook County	0	0
Aurora (city) Kane County	0	0
Bolingbrook (village) Will County	0	0

Asian

Top 10 Places Sorted by Population
Based on all places, regardless of total population

Place	Population	
Chicago (city) Cook County	166,770	6
Naperville (city) DuPage County	23,042	16
Skokie (village) Cook County	17,996	27
Schaumburg (village) Cook County	15,744	21
Aurora (city) Kane County	14,809	7
Hoffman Estates (village) Cook County	12,555	24
Champaign (city) Champaign County	9,544	11
Bolingbrook (village) Will County	9,178	12
Glendale Heights (village) DuPage County	8,024	23
Urbana (city) Champaign County	7,895	19

Top 10 Places Sorted by Percent of Total Populati
Based on all places, regardless of total population

Place	Population	
Morton Grove (village) Cook County	6,933	29
Lincolnwood (village) Cook County	3,639	28
South Barrington (village) Cook County	1,298	28
Skokie (village) Cook County	17,996	27
Oak Brook (village) DuPage County	1,974	25
Hoffman Estates (village) Cook County	12,555	24
Glendale Heights (village) DuPage County	8,024	23
Schaumburg (village) Cook County	15,744	21
Vernon Hills (village) Lake County	5,162	20
Urbana (city) Champaign County	7,895	19

Top 10 Places Sorted by Percent of Total Populati
Based on places with total population of 50,000 or more

Place	Population	
Skokie (village) Cook County	17,996	27
Hoffman Estates (village) Cook County	12,555	24
Schaumburg (village) Cook County	15,744	21
Naperville (city) DuPage County	23,042	16
Mount Prospect (village) Cook County	6,844	12
Bolingbrook (village) Will County	9,178	12
Des Plaines (city) Cook County	7,292	12
Champaign (city) Champaign County	9,544	11
Palatine (village) Cook County	7,704	11
Evanston (city) Cook County	7,576	10

Asian: Not Hispanic

Top 10 Places Sorted by Population
Based on all places, regardless of total population

Place	Population	
Chicago (city) Cook County	161,439	5
Naperville (city) DuPage County	22,868	16
Skokie (village) Cook County	17,752	27
Schaumburg (village) Cook County	15,608	21
Aurora (city) Kane County	14,444	7
Hoffman Estates (village) Cook County	12,439	23
Champaign (city) Champaign County	9,442	11
Bolingbrook (village) Will County	8,979	12
Glendale Heights (village) DuPage County	7,940	23
Urbana (city) Champaign County	7,843	19

Top 10 Places Sorted by Percent of Total Populatic
Based on all places, regardless of total population

Place	Population	
Morton Grove (village) Cook County	6,884	29
Lincolnwood (village) Cook County	3,596	28
South Barrington (village) Cook County	1,295	28

Place	Population	%
Skokie (village) Cook County	17,752	27.40
Oak Brook (village) DuPage County	1,966	24.94
Hoffman Estates (village) Cook County	12,439	23.97
Glendale Heights (village) DuPage County	7,940	23.21
Schaumburg (village) Cook County	15,608	21.03
Vernon Hills (village) Lake County	5,130	20.43
Urbana (city) Champaign County	7,843	19.01

Top 10 Places Sorted by Percent of Total Population
Based on places with total population of 50,000 or more

Place	Population	%
Skokie (village) Cook County	17,752	27.40
Hoffman Estates (village) Cook County	12,439	23.97
Schaumburg (village) Cook County	15,608	21.03
Naperville (city) DuPage County	22,868	16.12
Mount Prospect (village) Cook County	6,782	12.52
Bolingbrook (village) Will County	8,979	12.24
Des Plaines (city) Cook County	7,146	12.24
Champaign (city) Champaign County	9,442	11.65
Palatine (village) Cook County	7,623	11.12
Evanston (city) Cook County	7,436	9.98

Asian: Hispanic

Top 10 Places Sorted by Population
Based on all places, regardless of total population

Place	Population	%
Chicago (city) Cook County	5,331	0.20
Aurora (city) Kane County	365	0.18
Elgin (city) Kane County	301	0.28
Waukegan (city) Lake County	278	0.31
Skokie (village) Cook County	244	0.38
Joliet (city) Will County	237	0.16
Bolingbrook (village) Will County	199	0.27
Berwyn (city) Cook County	180	0.32
Naperville (city) DuPage County	174	0.12
Rockford (city) Winnebago County	157	0.10

Top 10 Places Sorted by Percent of Total Population
Based on all places, regardless of total population

Place	Population	%
Shumway (village) Effingham County	5	2.48
Congerville (village) Woodford County	5	1.05
Caledonia (village) Boone County	2	1.02
New Milford (village) Winnebago County	6	0.86
Murrayville (village) Morgan County	5	0.85
Cypress (village) Johnson County	2	0.85
Gilberts (village) Kane County	55	0.80
Bondville (village) Champaign County	3	0.68
Seymour (cdp) Champaign County	2	0.66
Middletown (village) Logan County	2	0.62

Top 10 Places Sorted by Percent of Total Population
Based on places with total population of 50,000 or more

Place	Population	%
Skokie (village) Cook County	244	0.38
Berwyn (city) Cook County	180	0.32
Waukegan (city) Lake County	278	0.31
Elgin (city) Kane County	301	0.28
Bolingbrook (village) Will County	199	0.27
Des Plaines (city) Cook County	146	0.25
Hoffman Estates (village) Cook County	116	0.22
Chicago (city) Cook County	5,331	0.20
Evanston (city) Cook County	140	0.19
Aurora (city) Kane County	365	0.18

Asian: Bangladeshi

Top 10 Places Sorted by Population
Based on all places, regardless of total population

Place	Population	%
Chicago (city) Cook County	679	0.03
Skokie (village) Cook County	98	0.15
Aurora (city) Kane County	95	0.05
Naperville (city) DuPage County	77	0.05
Champaign (city) Champaign County	56	0.07
Peoria (city) Peoria County	51	0.04
Bolingbrook (village) Will County	37	0.05
Schaumburg (village) Cook County	36	0.05
Lincolnwood (village) Cook County	34	0.27
Wheeling (village) Cook County	27	0.07

Top 10 Places Sorted by Percent of Total Population
Based on all places, regardless of total population

Place	Population	%
Round Lake Heights (village) Lake County	10	0.37
Lincolnwood (village) Cook County	34	0.27
South Barrington (village) Cook County	8	0.18
Skokie (village) Cook County	98	0.15
Itasca (village) DuPage County	13	0.15
Bridgeview (village) Cook County	23	0.14
Morton Grove (village) Cook County	23	0.10
Lena (village) Stephenson County	3	0.10
Oak Brook (village) DuPage County	7	0.09
Forsyth (village) Macon County	3	0.09

Top 10 Places Sorted by Percent of Total Population
Based on places with total population of 50,000 or more

Place	Population	%
Skokie (village) Cook County	98	0.15
Champaign (city) Champaign County	56	0.07
Aurora (city) Kane County	95	0.05
Naperville (city) DuPage County	77	0.05
Bolingbrook (village) Will County	37	0.05
Schaumburg (village) Cook County	36	0.05
Peoria (city) Peoria County	51	0.04
Hoffman Estates (village) Cook County	20	0.04
Chicago (city) Cook County	679	0.03
Evanston (city) Cook County	20	0.03

Asian: Bhutanese

Top 10 Places Sorted by Population
Based on all places, regardless of total population

Place	Population	%
Chicago (city) Cook County	339	0.01
Aurora (city) Kane County	81	0.04
Wheaton (city) DuPage County	68	0.13
Rock Island (city) Rock Island County	29	0.07
Glendale Heights (village) DuPage County	14	0.04
Moline (city) Rock Island County	10	0.02
Evanston (city) Cook County	5	0.01
Glen Ellyn (village) DuPage County	4	0.01
Sauk Village (village) Cook County	1	0.01
Naperville (city) DuPage County	1	<0.01

Top 10 Places Sorted by Percent of Total Population
Based on all places, regardless of total population

Place	Population	%
Wheaton (city) DuPage County	68	0.13
Rock Island (city) Rock Island County	29	0.07
Aurora (city) Kane County	81	0.04
Glendale Heights (village) DuPage County	14	0.04
Moline (city) Rock Island County	10	0.02
Chicago (city) Cook County	339	0.01
Evanston (city) Cook County	5	0.01
Glen Ellyn (village) DuPage County	4	0.01
Sauk Village (village) Cook County	1	0.01
Naperville (city) DuPage County	1	<0.01

Top 10 Places Sorted by Percent of Total Population
Based on places with total population of 50,000 or more

Place	Population	%
Wheaton (city) DuPage County	68	0.13
Aurora (city) Kane County	81	0.04
Chicago (city) Cook County	339	0.01
Evanston (city) Cook County	5	0.01
Naperville (city) DuPage County	1	<0.01
Rockford (city) Winnebago County	1	<0.01
Arlington Heights (village) Cook County	0	0.00
Berwyn (city) Cook County	0	0.00
Bloomington (city) McLean County	0	0.00
Bolingbrook (village) Will County	0	0.00

Asian: Burmese

Top 10 Places Sorted by Population
Based on all places, regardless of total population

Place	Population	%
Chicago (city) Cook County	711	0.03
Rockford (city) Winnebago County	403	0.26
Rock Island (city) Rock Island County	282	0.72
Wheaton (city) DuPage County	245	0.46
Glen Ellyn (village) DuPage County	226	0.82
Aurora (city) Kane County	206	0.10
Moline (city) Rock Island County	94	0.22
East Moline (city) Rock Island County	34	0.16
Carol Stream (village) DuPage County	30	0.08
Wheeling (village) Cook County	28	0.07

Top 10 Places Sorted by Percent of Total Population
Based on all places, regardless of total population

Place	Population	%
Glen Ellyn (village) DuPage County	226	0.82
Rock Island (city) Rock Island County	282	0.72
Wheaton (city) DuPage County	245	0.46
Rockford (city) Winnebago County	403	0.26
Minier (village) Tazewell County	3	0.24
Moline (city) Rock Island County	94	0.22
East Moline (city) Rock Island County	34	0.16
Clarendon Hills (village) DuPage County	11	0.13
Aurora (city) Kane County	206	0.10
South Beloit (city) Winnebago County	7	0.09

Top 10 Places Sorted by Percent of Total Population
Based on places with total population of 50,000 or more

Place	Population	%
Wheaton (city) DuPage County	245	0.46
Rockford (city) Winnebago County	403	0.26
Aurora (city) Kane County	206	0.10
Chicago (city) Cook County	711	0.03
Tinley Park (village) Cook County	15	0.03
Naperville (city) DuPage County	25	0.02
Peoria (city) Peoria County	21	0.02
Champaign (city) Champaign County	18	0.02
Skokie (village) Cook County	14	0.02
Schaumburg (village) Cook County	13	0.02

Asian: Cambodian

Top 10 Places Sorted by Population
Based on all places, regardless of total population

Place	Population	%
Chicago (city) Cook County	1,404	0.05
Skokie (village) Cook County	162	0.25
Glendale Heights (village) DuPage County	128	0.37
Hanover Park (village) Cook County	125	0.33
Bolingbrook (village) Will County	125	0.17
Joliet (city) Will County	110	0.07
Des Plaines (city) Cook County	105	0.18
Carol Stream (village) DuPage County	81	0.20
Aurora (city) Kane County	76	0.04
Elgin (city) Kane County	72	0.07

Top 10 Places Sorted by Percent of Total Population
Based on all places, regardless of total population

Place	Population	%
Hainesville (village) Lake County	32	0.89
Emington (village) Livingston County	1	0.85
Park City (city) Lake County	54	0.71
Volo (village) Lake County	14	0.48
Lostant (village) LaSalle County	2	0.40
Glendale Heights (village) DuPage County	128	0.37
Hanover Park (village) Cook County	125	0.33
Beach Park (village) Lake County	37	0.27
Round Lake Heights (village) Lake County	7	0.26
Skokie (village) Cook County	162	0.25

Top 10 Places Sorted by Percent of Total Population
Based on places with total population of 50,000 or more

Place	Population	%
Skokie (village) Cook County	162	0.25
Des Plaines (city) Cook County	105	0.18
Bolingbrook (village) Will County	125	0.17
Wheaton (city) DuPage County	43	0.08
Joliet (city) Will County	110	0.07
Elgin (city) Kane County	72	0.07
Waukegan (city) Lake County	50	0.06
Chicago (city) Cook County	1,404	0.05
Hoffman Estates (village) Cook County	26	0.05
Aurora (city) Kane County	76	0.04

Asian: Chinese, except Taiwanese

Top 10 Places Sorted by Population
Based on all places, regardless of total population

Place	Population	%
Chicago (city) Cook County	46,446	1.72
Naperville (city) DuPage County	5,487	3.87
Urbana (city) Champaign County	3,067	7.44
Evanston (city) Cook County	2,322	3.12
Champaign (city) Champaign County	2,302	2.84
Skokie (village) Cook County	1,726	2.66
Aurora (city) Kane County	1,636	0.83
Buffalo Grove (village) Lake County	1,552	3.74
Schaumburg (village) Cook County	1,306	1.76
Vernon Hills (village) Lake County	1,265	5.04

Top 10 Places Sorted by Percent of Total Population
Based on all places, regardless of total population

Place	Population	%
Urbana (city) Champaign County	3,067	7.44
South Barrington (village) Cook County	235	5.15
Vernon Hills (village) Lake County	1,265	5.04
Lisle (village) DuPage County	943	4.21
Long Grove (village) Lake County	318	3.95
Naperville (city) DuPage County	5,487	3.87
Bannockburn (village) Lake County	60	3.79
Kildeer (village) Lake County	150	3.78
Buffalo Grove (village) Lake County	1,552	3.74
Georgetown (cdp) McDonough County	15	3.71

Top 10 Places Sorted by Percent of Total Population
Based on places with total population of 50,000 or more

Place	Population	%
Naperville (city) DuPage County	5,487	3.87
Evanston (city) Cook County	2,322	3.12
Champaign (city) Champaign County	2,302	2.84
Skokie (village) Cook County	1,726	2.66
Hoffman Estates (village) Cook County	1,160	2.24
Palatine (village) Cook County	1,249	1.82
Schaumburg (village) Cook County	1,306	1.76
Chicago (city) Cook County	46,446	1.72
Oak Park (village) Cook County	793	1.53
Bolingbrook (village) Will County	887	1.21

Asian: Filipino

Top 10 Places Sorted by Population
Based on all places, regardless of total population

Place	Population	%
Chicago (city) Cook County	35,188	1.31
Skokie (village) Cook County	4,896	7.56
Bolingbrook (village) Will County	3,222	4.39
Aurora (city) Kane County	2,529	1.28
Waukegan (city) Lake County	2,230	2.50
Glendale Heights (village) DuPage County	2,027	5.93
Des Plaines (city) Cook County	1,851	3.17
Morton Grove (village) Cook County	1,835	7.89
Streamwood (village) Cook County	1,786	4.48
Naperville (city) DuPage County	1,716	1.21

Top 10 Places Sorted by Percent of Total Population
Based on all places, regardless of total population

Place	Population	%
Rentchler (cdp) St. Clair County	4	11.76
Morton Grove (village) Cook County	1,835	7.89
Skokie (village) Cook County	4,896	7.56
Gilberts (village) Kane County	429	6.24
Glendale Heights (village) DuPage County	2,027	5.93
Hainesville (village) Lake County	209	5.81
Round Lake (village) Lake County	1,021	5.58
Emington (village) Livingston County	6	5.13
Niles (village) Cook County	1,461	4.90
Pingree Grove (village) Kane County	218	4.81

Top 10 Places Sorted by Percent of Total Population
Based on places with total population of 50,000 or more

Place	Population	%
Skokie (village) Cook County	4,896	7.56
Bolingbrook (village) Will County	3,222	4.39
Des Plaines (city) Cook County	1,851	3.17
Hoffman Estates (village) Cook County	1,541	2.97

Waukegan (city) Lake County	2,230	2.50
Schaumburg (village) Cook County	1,597	2.15
Mount Prospect (village) Cook County	1,007	1.86
Orland Park (village) Cook County	939	1.65
Berwyn (city) Cook County	923	1.63
Elgin (city) Kane County	1,699	1.57

Asian: Hmong

Top 10 Places Sorted by Population
Based on all places, regardless of total population

Place	Population	%
Aurora (city) Kane County	97	0.05
Chicago (city) Cook County	97	<0.01
Hanover Park (village) Cook County	37	0.10
Rockford (city) Winnebago County	30	0.02
Joliet (city) Will County	24	0.02
Elgin (city) Kane County	20	0.02
Round Lake Beach (village) Lake County	19	0.07
Danville (city) Vermilion County	19	0.06
North Chicago (city) Lake County	18	0.06
Mattoon (city) Coles County	15	0.08

Top 10 Places Sorted by Percent of Total Population
Based on all places, regardless of total population

Place	Population	%
Indian Creek (village) Lake County	3	0.65
Tiskilwa (village) Bureau County	4	0.48
Round Lake Heights (village) Lake County	10	0.37
Bannockburn (village) Lake County	4	0.25
Volo (village) Lake County	5	0.17
De Pue (village) Bureau County	2	0.11
Hanover Park (village) Cook County	37	0.10
Mattoon (city) Coles County	15	0.08
North Aurora (village) Kane County	14	0.08
Round Lake Beach (village) Lake County	19	0.07

Top 10 Places Sorted by Percent of Total Population
Based on places with total population of 50,000 or more

Place	Population	%
Aurora (city) Kane County	97	0.05
Rockford (city) Winnebago County	30	0.02
Joliet (city) Will County	24	0.02
Elgin (city) Kane County	20	0.02
Skokie (village) Cook County	10	0.02
Wheaton (city) DuPage County	10	0.02
Hoffman Estates (village) Cook County	8	0.02
Waukegan (city) Lake County	11	0.01
Champaign (city) Champaign County	9	0.01
Bolingbrook (village) Will County	7	0.01

Asian: Indian

Top 10 Places Sorted by Population
Based on all places, regardless of total population

Place	Population	%
Chicago (city) Cook County	33,528	1.24
Naperville (city) DuPage County	10,917	7.70
Schaumburg (village) Cook County	8,303	11.19
Aurora (city) Kane County	6,828	3.45
Hoffman Estates (village) Cook County	5,985	11.53
Skokie (village) Cook County	4,624	7.14
Bloomington (city) McLean County	4,090	5.34
Mount Prospect (village) Cook County	3,314	6.12
Glendale Heights (village) DuPage County	3,215	9.40
Des Plaines (city) Cook County	3,214	5.51

Top 10 Places Sorted by Percent of Total Population
Based on all places, regardless of total population

Place	Population	%
South Barrington (village) Cook County	702	15.38
Oak Brook (village) DuPage County	1,116	14.16
Hoffman Estates (village) Cook County	5,985	11.53
Schaumburg (village) Cook County	8,303	11.19
Morton Grove (village) Cook County	2,309	9.92
Glendale Heights (village) DuPage County	3,215	9.40
Burr Ridge (village) DuPage County	968	9.17
Lincolnwood (village) Cook County	1,151	9.14
Hanover Park (village) Cook County	3,151	8.30
Naperville (city) DuPage County	10,917	7.70

Top 10 Places Sorted by Percent of Total Population
Based on places with total population of 50,000 or more

Place	Population	%
Hoffman Estates (village) Cook County	5,985	11.53
Schaumburg (village) Cook County	8,303	11.19
Naperville (city) DuPage County	10,917	7.70
Skokie (village) Cook County	4,624	7.14
Mount Prospect (village) Cook County	3,314	6.12
Des Plaines (city) Cook County	3,214	5.51
Bloomington (city) McLean County	4,090	5.34
Palatine (village) Cook County	2,836	4.14
Bolingbrook (village) Will County	2,996	4.08
Aurora (city) Kane County	6,828	3.45

Asian: Indonesian

Top 10 Places Sorted by Population
Based on all places, regardless of total population

Place	Population	%
Chicago (city) Cook County	430	0.02
Urbana (city) Champaign County	80	0.19
Aurora (city) Kane County	55	0.03
Naperville (city) DuPage County	49	0.03
Skokie (village) Cook County	41	0.06
Schaumburg (village) Cook County	36	0.05
Peoria (city) Peoria County	31	0.03
Evanston (city) Cook County	26	0.03
Arlington Heights (village) Cook County	20	0.03
Palatine (village) Cook County	18	0.03

Top 10 Places Sorted by Percent of Total Population
Based on all places, regardless of total population

Place	Population	%
Neponset (village) Bureau County	2	0.42
Kenney (village) De Witt County	1	0.31
Urbana (city) Champaign County	80	0.19
Grand Ridge (village) LaSalle County	1	0.18
Savoy (village) Champaign County	11	0.15
Venetian Village (cdp) Lake County	4	0.14
Hennepin (village) Putnam County	1	0.13
Olney (city) Richland County	11	0.12
Rosemont (village) Cook County	5	0.12
South Barrington (village) Cook County	5	0.11

Top 10 Places Sorted by Percent of Total Population
Based on places with total population of 50,000 or more

Place	Population	%
Skokie (village) Cook County	41	0.06
Schaumburg (village) Cook County	36	0.05
Aurora (city) Kane County	55	0.03
Naperville (city) DuPage County	49	0.03
Peoria (city) Peoria County	31	0.03
Evanston (city) Cook County	26	0.03
Arlington Heights (village) Cook County	20	0.03
Palatine (village) Cook County	18	0.03
Hoffman Estates (village) Cook County	15	0.03
Chicago (city) Cook County	430	0.02

Asian: Japanese

Top 10 Places Sorted by Population
Based on all places, regardless of total population

Place	Population	%
Chicago (city) Cook County	7,044	0.26
Schaumburg (village) Cook County	1,216	1.64
Hoffman Estates (village) Cook County	885	1.71
Arlington Heights (village) Cook County	819	1.09
Palatine (village) Cook County	683	1.00
Elk Grove Village (village) Cook County	589	1.78
Evanston (city) Cook County	560	0.75
Buffalo Grove (village) Lake County	498	1.20
Naperville (city) DuPage County	480	0.34
Skokie (village) Cook County	431	0.67

Top 10 Places Sorted by Percent of Total Population
Based on all places, regardless of total population

Place	Population	%
Mill Creek (village) Union County	3	4.62
Elk Grove Village (village) Cook County	589	1.78
Hoffman Estates (village) Cook County	885	1.71

Please refer to the Explanation of Data in the front of the book for more detailed information.

Place	Population	%
Whiteash (village) Williamson County	4	1.66
Schaumburg (village) Cook County	1,216	1.64
Buffalo Grove (village) Lake County	498	1.20
Millbrook (village) Kendall County	4	1.19
Arlington Heights (village) Cook County	819	1.09
Wilmette (village) Cook County	294	1.09
Tower Lakes (village) Lake County	13	1.01

Top 10 Places Sorted by Percent of Total Population
Based on places with total population of 50,000 or more

Place	Population	%
Hoffman Estates (village) Cook County	885	1.71
Schaumburg (village) Cook County	1,216	1.64
Arlington Heights (village) Cook County	819	1.09
Palatine (village) Cook County	683	1.00
Evanston (city) Cook County	560	0.75
Skokie (village) Cook County	431	0.67
Oak Park (village) Cook County	314	0.61
Mount Prospect (village) Cook County	306	0.56
Champaign (city) Champaign County	379	0.47
Des Plaines (city) Cook County	212	0.36

Asian: Korean

Top 10 Places Sorted by Population
Based on all places, regardless of total population

Place	Population	%
Chicago (city) Cook County	13,418	0.50
Glenview (village) Cook County	2,321	5.19
Champaign (city) Champaign County	2,060	2.54
Northbrook (village) Cook County	2,005	6.04
Schaumburg (village) Cook County	1,994	2.69
Skokie (village) Cook County	1,880	2.90
Naperville (city) DuPage County	1,864	1.31
Buffalo Grove (village) Lake County	1,780	4.29
Hoffman Estates (village) Cook County	1,602	3.09
Urbana (city) Champaign County	1,598	3.87

Top 10 Places Sorted by Percent of Total Population
Based on all places, regardless of total population

Place	Population	%
Bannockburn (village) Lake County	134	8.46
Northbrook (village) Cook County	2,005	6.04
Vernon Hills (village) Lake County	1,429	5.69
Savoy (village) Champaign County	386	5.30
Glenview (village) Cook County	2,321	5.19
Indian Creek (village) Lake County	24	5.19
Morton Grove (village) Cook County	1,069	4.59
Buffalo Grove (village) Lake County	1,780	4.29
Urbana (city) Champaign County	1,598	3.87
Long Grove (village) Lake County	294	3.66

Top 10 Places Sorted by Percent of Total Population
Based on places with total population of 50,000 or more

Place	Population	%
Hoffman Estates (village) Cook County	1,602	3.09
Skokie (village) Cook County	1,880	2.90
Schaumburg (village) Cook County	1,994	2.69
Champaign (city) Champaign County	2,060	2.54
Mount Prospect (village) Cook County	1,101	2.03
Palatine (village) Cook County	1,175	1.71
Evanston (city) Cook County	1,239	1.66
Arlington Heights (village) Cook County	1,193	1.59
Naperville (city) DuPage County	1,864	1.31
Des Plaines (city) Cook County	664	1.14

Asian: Laotian

Top 10 Places Sorted by Population
Based on all places, regardless of total population

Place	Population	%
Elgin (city) Kane County	1,445	1.34
Rockford (city) Winnebago County	1,027	0.67
Chicago (city) Cook County	529	0.02
South Elgin (village) Kane County	402	1.83
Joliet (city) Will County	221	0.15
Aurora (city) Kane County	151	0.08
Urbana (city) Champaign County	93	0.23
North Aurora (village) Kane County	90	0.54
Bartlett (village) DuPage County	90	0.22
Champaign (city) Champaign County	89	0.11

Top 10 Places Sorted by Percent of Total Population
Based on all places, regardless of total population

Place	Population	%
New Milford (village) Winnebago County	22	3.16
South Elgin (village) Kane County	402	1.83
De Pue (village) Bureau County	25	1.36
Elgin (city) Kane County	1,445	1.34
Cherry Valley (village) Winnebago County	36	1.14
Gilberts (village) Kane County	64	0.93
Golden (village) Adams County	5	0.78
Rockford (city) Winnebago County	1,027	0.67
Burlington (village) Kane County	4	0.65
Malden (village) Bureau County	2	0.55

Top 10 Places Sorted by Percent of Total Population
Based on places with total population of 50,000 or more

Place	Population	%
Elgin (city) Kane County	1,445	1.34
Rockford (city) Winnebago County	1,027	0.67
Joliet (city) Will County	221	0.15
Champaign (city) Champaign County	89	0.11
Hoffman Estates (village) Cook County	51	0.10
Aurora (city) Kane County	151	0.08
Peoria (city) Peoria County	76	0.07
Bolingbrook (village) Will County	49	0.07
Skokie (village) Cook County	37	0.06
Tinley Park (village) Cook County	27	0.05

Asian: Malaysian

Top 10 Places Sorted by Population
Based on all places, regardless of total population

Place	Population	%
Chicago (city) Cook County	165	0.01
Carbondale (city) Jackson County	52	0.20
Champaign (city) Champaign County	46	0.06
Skokie (village) Cook County	37	0.06
Urbana (city) Champaign County	35	0.08
Aurora (city) Kane County	25	0.01
Schaumburg (village) Cook County	21	0.03
Evanston (city) Cook County	20	0.03
Bartlett (village) DuPage County	19	0.05
Gurnee (village) Lake County	17	0.05

Top 10 Places Sorted by Percent of Total Population
Based on all places, regardless of total population

Place	Population	%
Congerville (village) Woodford County	5	1.05
Kampsville (village) Calhoun County	1	0.30
Carbondale (city) Jackson County	52	0.20
Northfield (village) Cook County	7	0.13
North Barrington (village) Lake County	4	0.13
Green Oaks (village) Lake County	4	0.10
Urbana (city) Champaign County	35	0.08
Valmeyer (village) Monroe County	1	0.08
Gages Lake (cdp) Lake County	7	0.07
East Dundee (village) Kane County	2	0.07

Top 10 Places Sorted by Percent of Total Population
Based on places with total population of 50,000 or more

Place	Population	%
Champaign (city) Champaign County	46	0.06
Skokie (village) Cook County	37	0.06
Schaumburg (village) Cook County	21	0.03
Evanston (city) Cook County	20	0.03
Hoffman Estates (village) Cook County	15	0.03
Arlington Heights (village) Cook County	16	0.02
Palatine (village) Cook County	15	0.02
Oak Park (village) Cook County	11	0.02
Chicago (city) Cook County	165	0.01
Aurora (city) Kane County	25	0.01

Asian: Nepalese

Top 10 Places Sorted by Population
Based on all places, regardless of total population

Place	Population	%
Chicago (city) Cook County	627	0.02
Skokie (village) Cook County	48	0.07
Rock Island (city) Rock Island County	47	0.12

Place	Population	%
Champaign (city) Champaign County	39	0.05
Carbondale (city) Jackson County	31	0.12
Aurora (city) Kane County	31	0.02
Wheaton (city) DuPage County	27	0.05
Normal (town) McLean County	22	0.04
Niles (village) Cook County	20	0.07
Bolingbrook (village) Will County	20	0.03

Top 10 Places Sorted by Percent of Total Population
Based on all places, regardless of total population

Place	Population	%
Annawan (town) Henry County	3	0.34
Maryville (village) Madison County	17	0.23
Carbon Cliff (village) Rock Island County	4	0.19
Silvis (city) Rock Island County	11	0.15
Rock Island (city) Rock Island County	47	0.12
Carbondale (city) Jackson County	31	0.12
Lebanon (city) St. Clair County	5	0.11
Colona (city) Henry County	5	0.10
Troy (city) Madison County	8	0.08
Lakewood (village) McHenry County	3	0.08

Top 10 Places Sorted by Percent of Total Population
Based on places with total population of 50,000 or more

Place	Population	%
Skokie (village) Cook County	48	0.07
Champaign (city) Champaign County	39	0.05
Wheaton (city) DuPage County	27	0.05
Normal (town) McLean County	22	0.04
Bolingbrook (village) Will County	20	0.03
Oak Park (village) Cook County	14	0.03
Chicago (city) Cook County	627	0.02
Aurora (city) Kane County	31	0.02
Peoria (city) Peoria County	19	0.02
Schaumburg (village) Cook County	16	0.02

Asian: Pakistani

Top 10 Places Sorted by Population
Based on all places, regardless of total population

Place	Population	%
Chicago (city) Cook County	7,926	0.29
Skokie (village) Cook County	2,121	3.27
Naperville (city) DuPage County	1,060	0.75
Glendale Heights (village) DuPage County	877	2.56
Bolingbrook (village) Will County	835	1.14
Aurora (city) Kane County	829	0.42
Hoffman Estates (village) Cook County	712	1.37
Lombard (village) DuPage County	710	1.64
Hanover Park (village) Cook County	631	1.66
Lincolnwood (village) Cook County	580	4.61

Top 10 Places Sorted by Percent of Total Population
Based on all places, regardless of total population

Place	Population	%
Lincolnwood (village) Cook County	580	4.61
Skokie (village) Cook County	2,121	3.27
Oak Brook (village) DuPage County	215	2.73
Glendale Heights (village) DuPage County	877	2.56
Morton Grove (village) Cook County	466	2.00
Hanover Park (village) Cook County	631	1.66
Burr Ridge (village) DuPage County	174	1.65
Lombard (village) DuPage County	710	1.64
South Barrington (village) Cook County	69	1.51
Forsyth (village) Macon County	49	1.40

Top 10 Places Sorted by Percent of Total Population
Based on places with total population of 50,000 or more

Place	Population	%
Skokie (village) Cook County	2,121	3.27
Hoffman Estates (village) Cook County	712	1.37
Bolingbrook (village) Will County	835	1.14
Naperville (city) DuPage County	1,060	0.75
Schaumburg (village) Cook County	550	0.74
Des Plaines (city) Cook County	375	0.64
Palatine (village) Cook County	422	0.62
Aurora (city) Kane County	829	0.42
Orland Park (village) Cook County	219	0.39
Evanston (city) Cook County	245	0.33

Asian: Sri Lankan

Top 10 Places Sorted by Population
Based on all places, regardless of total population

Place	Population	%
Chicago (city) Cook County	376	0.01
Aurora (city) Kane County	72	0.04
Naperville (city) DuPage County	62	0.04
Skokie (village) Cook County	52	0.08
Champaign (city) Champaign County	31	0.04
Peoria (city) Peoria County	27	0.02
Carbondale (city) Jackson County	25	0.10
Urbana (city) Champaign County	23	0.06
Normal (town) McLean County	21	0.04
Oak Park (village) Cook County	21	0.04

Top 10 Places Sorted by Percent of Total Population
Based on all places, regardless of total population

Place	Population	%
Ste. Marie (village) Jasper County	4	1.64
Oak Brook (village) DuPage County	15	0.19
Prairie Grove (village) McHenry County	3	0.16
Grandwood Park (cdp) Lake County	8	0.15
Bannockburn (village) Lake County	2	0.13
Hainesville (village) Lake County	4	0.11
Carbondale (city) Jackson County	25	0.10
River Forest (village) Cook County	11	0.10
Lisle (village) DuPage County	20	0.09
Round Lake (village) Lake County	16	0.09

Top 10 Places Sorted by Percent of Total Population
Based on places with total population of 50,000 or more

Place	Population	%
Skokie (village) Cook County	52	0.08
Aurora (city) Kane County	72	0.04
Naperville (city) DuPage County	62	0.04
Champaign (city) Champaign County	31	0.04
Normal (town) McLean County	21	0.04
Oak Park (village) Cook County	21	0.04
Schaumburg (village) Cook County	20	0.03
Peoria (city) Peoria County	27	0.02
Bolingbrook (village) Will County	16	0.02
Palatine (village) Cook County	12	0.02

Asian: Taiwanese

Top 10 Places Sorted by Population
Based on all places, regardless of total population

Place	Population	%
Chicago (city) Cook County	1,319	0.05
Naperville (city) DuPage County	597	0.42
Urbana (city) Champaign County	422	1.02
Evanston (city) Cook County	290	0.39
Champaign (city) Champaign County	272	0.34
Hoffman Estates (village) Cook County	137	0.26
Lisle (village) DuPage County	117	0.52
Westmont (village) DuPage County	108	0.44
Wilmette (village) Cook County	107	0.40
Schaumburg (village) Cook County	104	0.14

Top 10 Places Sorted by Percent of Total Population
Based on all places, regardless of total population

Place	Population	%
Indian Creek (village) Lake County	5	1.08
Urbana (city) Champaign County	422	1.02
Oak Brook (village) DuPage County	79	1.00
Georgetown (cdp) McDonough County	4	0.99
Golf (village) Cook County	4	0.80
Willowbrook (village) DuPage County	59	0.69
Lisle (village) DuPage County	117	0.52
Savoy (village) Champaign County	33	0.45
Westmont (village) DuPage County	108	0.44
Inverness (village) Cook County	32	0.43

Top 10 Places Sorted by Percent of Total Population
Based on places with total population of 50,000 or more

Place	Population	%
Naperville (city) DuPage County	597	0.42
Evanston (city) Cook County	290	0.39
Champaign (city) Champaign County	272	0.34
Hoffman Estates (village) Cook County	137	0.26

Schaumburg (village) Cook County	104	0.14
Wheaton (city) DuPage County	75	0.14
Palatine (village) Cook County	88	0.13
Skokie (village) Cook County	78	0.12
Arlington Heights (village) Cook County	82	0.11
Oak Park (village) Cook County	45	0.09

Asian: Thai

Top 10 Places Sorted by Population
Based on all places, regardless of total population

Place	Population	%
Chicago (city) Cook County	3,168	0.12
Skokie (village) Cook County	234	0.36
Aurora (city) Kane County	143	0.07
Evanston (city) Cook County	138	0.19
Schaumburg (village) Cook County	131	0.18
Champaign (city) Champaign County	126	0.16
Rockford (city) Winnebago County	122	0.08
Naperville (city) DuPage County	116	0.08
Wilmette (village) Cook County	111	0.41
Bolingbrook (village) Will County	111	0.15

Top 10 Places Sorted by Percent of Total Population
Based on all places, regardless of total population

Place	Population	%
Kingston Mines (village) Peoria County	3	0.99
Dahlgren (village) Hamilton County	5	0.95
Colp (village) Williamson County	2	0.89
Lincolnwood (village) Cook County	77	0.61
Carbon Hill (village) Grundy County	2	0.58
Roberts (village) Ford County	2	0.55
Elsah (village) Jersey County	3	0.45
Scott AFB (cdp) St. Clair County	15	0.42
Wilmette (village) Cook County	111	0.41
Windsor (village) Mercer County	3	0.40

Top 10 Places Sorted by Percent of Total Population
Based on places with total population of 50,000 or more

Place	Population	%
Skokie (village) Cook County	234	0.36
Evanston (city) Cook County	138	0.19
Hoffman Estates (village) Cook County	101	0.19
Schaumburg (village) Cook County	131	0.18
Oak Park (village) Cook County	93	0.18
Champaign (city) Champaign County	126	0.16
Bolingbrook (village) Will County	111	0.15
Chicago (city) Cook County	3,168	0.12
Tinley Park (village) Cook County	60	0.11
Elgin (city) Kane County	109	0.10

Asian: Vietnamese

Top 10 Places Sorted by Population
Based on all places, regardless of total population

Place	Population	%
Chicago (city) Cook County	10,118	0.38
Glendale Heights (village) DuPage County	1,077	3.15
Carol Stream (village) DuPage County	804	2.02
Skokie (village) Cook County	794	1.23
Champaign (city) Champaign County	687	0.85
Aurora (city) Kane County	601	0.30
Rockford (city) Winnebago County	586	0.38
Peoria (city) Peoria County	439	0.38
Naperville (city) DuPage County	332	0.23
Wheaton (city) DuPage County	327	0.62

Top 10 Places Sorted by Percent of Total Population
Based on all places, regardless of total population

Place	Population	%
Glendale Heights (village) DuPage County	1,077	3.15
Lincolnwood (village) Cook County	278	2.21
Carol Stream (village) DuPage County	804	2.02
Skokie (village) Cook County	794	1.23
Penfield (cdp) Champaign County	2	1.04
Morton Grove (village) Cook County	237	1.02
New Milford (village) Winnebago County	7	1.00
Jerome (village) Sangamon County	16	0.97
Virgil (village) Kane County	3	0.91
Lee (village) Lee County	3	0.89

Top 10 Places Sorted by Percent of Total Population
Based on places with total population of 50,000 or more

Place	Population	%
Skokie (village) Cook County	794	1.2
Champaign (city) Champaign County	687	0.8
Wheaton (city) DuPage County	327	0.6
Chicago (city) Cook County	10,118	0.3
Rockford (city) Winnebago County	586	0.3
Peoria (city) Peoria County	439	0.3
Bolingbrook (village) Will County	277	0.3
Aurora (city) Kane County	601	0.3
Elgin (city) Kane County	320	0.30
Des Plaines (city) Cook County	171	0.2

Hawaii Native/Pacific Islander

Top 10 Places Sorted by Population
Based on all places, regardless of total population

Place	Population	%
Chicago (city) Cook County	3,770	0.14
North Chicago (city) Lake County	223	0.6
Aurora (city) Kane County	202	0.10
Champaign (city) Champaign County	173	0.2
Rockford (city) Winnebago County	163	0.1
Waukegan (city) Lake County	156	0.18
Naperville (city) DuPage County	146	0.1
Skokie (village) Cook County	139	0.2
Elgin (city) Kane County	139	0.1
Peoria (city) Peoria County	125	0.1

Top 10 Places Sorted by Percent of Total Population
Based on all places, regardless of total population

Place	Population	%
Shumway (village) Effingham County	5	2.4
Garden Prairie (village) Boone County	6	1.7
Irwin (village) Kankakee County	1	1.3
Johnsonville (village) Wayne County	1	1.3
Scott AFB (cdp) St. Clair County	44	1.2
Millbrook (village) Kendall County	4	1.1
Mapleton (village) Peoria County	3	1.1
Cleveland (village) Henry County	2	1.0
Russellville (village) Lawrence County	1	1.0
McClure (village) Alexander County	4	1.0

Top 10 Places Sorted by Percent of Total Population
Based on places with total population of 50,000 or more

Place	Population	%
Champaign (city) Champaign County	173	0.2
Skokie (village) Cook County	139	0.2
Waukegan (city) Lake County	156	0.18
Hoffman Estates (village) Cook County	83	0.1
Chicago (city) Cook County	3,770	0.14
Cicero (town) Cook County	118	0.14
Evanston (city) Cook County	106	0.14
Berwyn (city) Cook County	80	0.14
Elgin (city) Kane County	139	0.13
Schaumburg (village) Cook County	93	0.13

Hawaii Native/Pacific Islander: Not Hispanic

Top 10 Places Sorted by Population
Based on all places, regardless of total population

Place	Population	%
Chicago (city) Cook County	2,186	0.08
North Chicago (city) Lake County	183	0.56
Aurora (city) Kane County	152	0.08
Champaign (city) Champaign County	151	0.19
Naperville (city) DuPage County	136	0.10
Skokie (village) Cook County	122	0.19
Rockford (city) Winnebago County	117	0.08
Peoria (city) Peoria County	112	0.10
Urbana (city) Champaign County	100	0.24
Evanston (city) Cook County	95	0.13

Top 10 Places Sorted by Percent of Total Population
Based on all places, regardless of total population

Place	Population	%
Garden Prairie (village) Boone County	6	1.70
Irwin (village) Kankakee County	1	1.38

Please refer to the Explanation of Data in the front of the book for more detailed information.

Place	Population	%
Johnsonville (village) Wayne County	1	1.30
Millbrook (village) Kendall County	4	1.19
Scott AFB (cdp) St. Clair County	41	1.14
Mapleton (village) Peoria County	3	1.11
Cleveland (village) Henry County	2	1.06
Russellville (village) Lawrence County	1	1.06
McClure (village) Alexander County	4	1.00
Kingston Mines (village) Peoria County	3	0.99

Top 10 Places Sorted by Percent of Total Population
Based on places with total population of 50,000 or more

Place	Population	%
Champaign (city) Champaign County	151	0.19
Skokie (village) Cook County	122	0.19
Evanston (city) Cook County	95	0.13
Hoffman Estates (village) Cook County	66	0.13
Des Plaines (city) Cook County	63	0.11
Naperville (city) DuPage County	136	0.10
Peoria (city) Peoria County	112	0.10
Decatur (city) Macon County	76	0.10
Schaumburg (village) Cook County	74	0.10
Wheaton (city) DuPage County	51	0.10

Hawaii Native/Pacific Islander: Hispanic

Top 10 Places Sorted by Population
Based on all places, regardless of total population

Place	Population	%
Chicago (city) Cook County	1,584	0.06
Cicero (town) Cook County	87	0.10
Waukegan (city) Lake County	74	0.08
Elgin (city) Kane County	68	0.06
Joliet (city) Will County	57	0.04
Aurora (city) Kane County	50	0.03
Berwyn (city) Cook County	47	0.08
Rockford (city) Winnebago County	46	0.03
North Chicago (city) Lake County	40	0.12
Carpentersville (village) Kane County	27	0.07

Top 10 Places Sorted by Percent of Total Population
Based on all places, regardless of total population

Place	Population	%
Shumway (village) Effingham County	5	2.48
Damiansville (village) Clinton County	4	0.81
Brocton (village) Edgar County	2	0.62
Pulaski (village) Pulaski County	1	0.49
Whiteash (village) Williamson County	1	0.41
Hometown (city) Cook County	12	0.28
London Mills (village) Fulton County	1	0.26
Albers (village) Clinton County	3	0.25
Percy (village) Randolph County	2	0.21
Rosemont (village) Cook County	8	0.19

Top 10 Places Sorted by Percent of Total Population
Based on places with total population of 50,000 or more

Place	Population	%
Cicero (town) Cook County	87	0.10
Waukegan (city) Lake County	74	0.08
Berwyn (city) Cook County	47	0.08
Chicago (city) Cook County	1,584	0.06
Elgin (city) Kane County	68	0.06
Joliet (city) Will County	57	0.04
Aurora (city) Kane County	50	0.03
Rockford (city) Winnebago County	46	0.03
Bolingbrook (village) Will County	23	0.03
Bloomington (city) McLean County	22	0.03

Hawaii Native/Pacific Islander: Fijian

Top 10 Places Sorted by Population
Based on all places, regardless of total population

Place	Population	%
Chicago (city) Cook County	18	<0.01
Glendale Heights (village) DuPage County	9	0.03
Naperville (city) DuPage County	7	<0.01
North Chicago (city) Lake County	5	0.02
Roselle (village) DuPage County	5	0.02
Crete (village) Will County	4	0.05
Collinsville (city) Madison County	4	0.02
Berwyn (city) Cook County	4	0.01
Calumet City (city) Cook County	4	0.01

Place	Population	%
Aurora (city) Kane County	4	<0.01

Top 10 Places Sorted by Percent of Total Population
Based on all places, regardless of total population

Place	Population	%
Cleveland (village) Henry County	2	1.06
Chatsworth (town) Livingston County	3	0.25
Hull (village) Pike County	1	0.22
Williamsville (village) Sangamon County	2	0.14
Colona (city) Henry County	3	0.06
Forest Lake (cdp) Lake County	1	0.06
Crete (village) Will County	4	0.05
Glendale Heights (village) DuPage County	9	0.03
North Chicago (city) Lake County	5	0.02
Roselle (village) DuPage County	5	0.02

Top 10 Places Sorted by Percent of Total Population
Based on places with total population of 50,000 or more

Place	Population	%
Berwyn (city) Cook County	4	0.01
Chicago (city) Cook County	18	<0.01
Naperville (city) DuPage County	7	<0.01
Aurora (city) Kane County	4	<0.01
Springfield (city) Sangamon County	4	<0.01
Schaumburg (village) Cook County	3	<0.01
Skokie (village) Cook County	3	<0.01
Bloomington (city) McLean County	2	<0.01
Champaign (city) Champaign County	2	<0.01
Evanston (city) Cook County	2	<0.01

Hawaii Native/Pacific Islander: Guamanian or Chamorro

Top 10 Places Sorted by Population
Based on all places, regardless of total population

Place	Population	%
Chicago (city) Cook County	592	0.02
Aurora (city) Kane County	38	0.02
Waukegan (city) Lake County	35	0.04
Cicero (town) Cook County	29	0.03
Blue Island (city) Cook County	24	0.10
Belleville (city) St. Clair County	24	0.05
Peoria (city) Peoria County	24	0.02
O'Fallon (city) St. Clair County	22	0.08
North Chicago (city) Lake County	19	0.06
Swansea (village) St. Clair County	18	0.13

Top 10 Places Sorted by Percent of Total Population
Based on all places, regardless of total population

Place	Population	%
Venedy (village) Washington County	1	0.72
Scott AFB (cdp) St. Clair County	15	0.42
Toluca (city) Marshall County	5	0.35
Brocton (village) Edgar County	1	0.31
Percy (village) Randolph County	2	0.21
Hammond (village) Piatt County	1	0.20
Hoffman (village) Clinton County	1	0.20
Cherry Valley (village) Winnebago County	6	0.19
Trout Valley (village) McHenry County	1	0.19
Princeville (village) Peoria County	3	0.17

Top 10 Places Sorted by Percent of Total Population
Based on places with total population of 50,000 or more

Place	Population	%
Waukegan (city) Lake County	35	0.04
Cicero (town) Cook County	29	0.03
Mount Prospect (village) Cook County	18	0.03
Chicago (city) Cook County	592	0.02
Aurora (city) Kane County	38	0.02
Peoria (city) Peoria County	24	0.02
Palatine (village) Cook County	11	0.02
Rockford (city) Winnebago County	17	0.01
Naperville (city) DuPage County	14	0.01
Elgin (city) Kane County	13	0.01

Hawaii Native/Pacific Islander: Marshallese

Top 10 Places Sorted by Population
Based on all places, regardless of total population

Place	Population	%
Chicago (city) Cook County	5	<0.01
Posen (village) Cook County	4	0.07
Libertyville (village) Lake County	4	0.02
Skokie (village) Cook County	4	0.01
Wayne (village) DuPage County	3	0.12
East Dubuque (city) Jo Daviess County	2	0.12
West Chicago (city) DuPage County	2	0.01
Georgetown (cdp) McDonough County	1	0.25
Palos Hills (city) Cook County	1	0.01
Swansea (village) St. Clair County	1	0.01

Top 10 Places Sorted by Percent of Total Population
Based on all places, regardless of total population

Place	Population	%
Georgetown (cdp) McDonough County	1	0.25
Wayne (village) DuPage County	3	0.12
East Dubuque (city) Jo Daviess County	2	0.12
Posen (village) Cook County	4	0.07
Libertyville (village) Lake County	4	0.02
Skokie (village) Cook County	4	0.01
West Chicago (city) DuPage County	2	0.01
Palos Hills (city) Cook County	1	0.01
Swansea (village) St. Clair County	1	0.01
Winfield (village) DuPage County	1	0.01

Top 10 Places Sorted by Percent of Total Population
Based on places with total population of 50,000 or more

Place	Population	%
Skokie (village) Cook County	4	0.01
Chicago (city) Cook County	5	<0.01
Bolingbrook (village) Will County	1	<0.01
Des Plaines (city) Cook County	1	<0.01
Elgin (city) Kane County	1	<0.01
Joliet (city) Will County	1	<0.01
Arlington Heights (village) Cook County	0	0.00
Aurora (city) Kane County	0	0.00
Berwyn (city) Cook County	0	0.00
Bloomington (city) McLean County	0	0.00

Hawaii Native/Pacific Islander: Native Hawaiian

Top 10 Places Sorted by Population
Based on all places, regardless of total population

Place	Population	%
Chicago (city) Cook County	731	0.03
North Chicago (city) Lake County	56	0.17
Rockford (city) Winnebago County	56	0.04
Peoria (city) Peoria County	46	0.04
Aurora (city) Kane County	44	0.02
Naperville (city) DuPage County	43	0.03
Champaign (city) Champaign County	37	0.05
Waukegan (city) Lake County	35	0.04
Evanston (city) Cook County	32	0.04
Elgin (city) Kane County	31	0.03

Top 10 Places Sorted by Percent of Total Population
Based on all places, regardless of total population

Place	Population	%
Garden Prairie (village) Boone County	6	1.70
Johnsonville (village) Wayne County	1	1.30
Mapleton (village) Peoria County	3	1.11
Russellville (village) Lawrence County	1	1.06
Avon (village) Fulton County	7	0.88
Menominee (village) Jo Daviess County	2	0.81
Hennepin (village) Putnam County	5	0.66
Junction City (village) Marion County	3	0.62
Brocton (village) Edgar County	2	0.62
London Mills (village) Fulton County	2	0.51

Top 10 Places Sorted by Percent of Total Population
Based on places with total population of 50,000 or more

Place	Population	%
Champaign (city) Champaign County	37	0.05

Place	Population	%
Hoffman Estates (village) Cook County	25	0.05
Rockford (city) Winnebago County	56	0.04
Peoria (city) Peoria County	46	0.04
Waukegan (city) Lake County	35	0.04
Evanston (city) Cook County	32	0.04
Schaumburg (village) Cook County	30	0.04
Oak Park (village) Cook County	22	0.04
Mount Prospect (village) Cook County	19	0.04
Chicago (city) Cook County	731	0.03

Hawaii Native/Pacific Islander: Samoan

Top 10 Places Sorted by Population
Based on all places, regardless of total population

Place	Population	%
Chicago (city) Cook County	281	0.01
North Chicago (city) Lake County	27	0.08
Champaign (city) Champaign County	23	0.03
Elgin (city) Kane County	22	0.02
Rockford (city) Winnebago County	16	0.01
Scott AFB (cdp) St. Clair County	14	0.39
East Moline (city) Rock Island County	14	0.07
Springfield (city) Sangamon County	14	0.01
Cicero (town) Cook County	13	0.02
Palatine (village) Cook County	13	0.02

Top 10 Places Sorted by Percent of Total Population
Based on all places, regardless of total population

Place	Population	%
McClure (village) Alexander County	4	1.00
St. Libory (village) St. Clair County	4	0.65
Lyndon (village) Whiteside County	4	0.62
Pulaski (village) Pulaski County	1	0.49
Livingston (village) Madison County	4	0.47
Nilwood (town) Macoupin County	1	0.42
Scott AFB (cdp) St. Clair County	14	0.39
Long Lake (cdp) Lake County	8	0.23
Carbon Cliff (village) Rock Island County	5	0.23
South Chicago Heights (village) Cook County	8	0.19

Top 10 Places Sorted by Percent of Total Population
Based on places with total population of 50,000 or more

Place	Population	%
Champaign (city) Champaign County	23	0.03
Elgin (city) Kane County	22	0.02
Cicero (town) Cook County	13	0.02
Palatine (village) Cook County	13	0.02
Normal (town) McLean County	11	0.02
Des Plaines (city) Cook County	9	0.02
Chicago (city) Cook County	281	0.01
Rockford (city) Winnebago County	16	0.01
Springfield (city) Sangamon County	14	0.01
Joliet (city) Will County	13	0.01

Hawaii Native/Pacific Islander: Tongan

Top 10 Places Sorted by Population
Based on all places, regardless of total population

Place	Population	%
Chicago (city) Cook County	10	<0.01
Mount Carmel (city) Wabash County	6	0.08
Morton Grove (village) Cook County	5	0.02
St. Charles (city) Kane County	5	0.02
Litchfield (city) Montgomery County	4	0.06
Antioch (village) Lake County	4	0.03
Plainfield (village) Will County	4	0.03
Naperville (city) DuPage County	3	<0.01
Palatine (village) Cook County	3	<0.01
Schaumburg (village) Cook County	3	<0.01

Top 10 Places Sorted by Percent of Total Population
Based on all places, regardless of total population

Place	Population	%
Nauvoo (city) Hancock County	1	0.09
Mount Carmel (city) Wabash County	6	0.08
Litchfield (city) Montgomery County	4	0.06
Antioch (village) Lake County	4	0.03
Long Lake (cdp) Lake County	1	0.03
Morton Grove (village) Cook County	5	0.02
St. Charles (city) Kane County	5	0.02
Warrenville (city) DuPage County	2	0.02

Place	Population	%
Burnham (village) Cook County	1	0.02
Lebanon (city) St. Clair County	1	0.02

Top 10 Places Sorted by Percent of Total Population
Based on places with total population of 50,000 or more

Place	Population	%
Chicago (city) Cook County	10	<0.01
Naperville (city) DuPage County	3	<0.01
Palatine (village) Cook County	3	<0.01
Schaumburg (village) Cook County	3	<0.01
Aurora (city) Kane County	2	<0.01
Bloomington (city) McLean County	2	<0.01
Champaign (city) Champaign County	2	<0.01
Joliet (city) Will County	2	<0.01
Waukegan (city) Lake County	2	<0.01
Arlington Heights (village) Cook County	0	0.00

White

Top 10 Places Sorted by Population
Based on all places, regardless of total population

Place	Population	%
Chicago (city) Cook County	1,270,097	47.12
Aurora (city) Kane County	123,599	62.46
Naperville (city) DuPage County	111,144	78.35
Rockford (city) Winnebago County	104,370	68.27
Joliet (city) Will County	103,279	70.05
Springfield (city) Sangamon County	90,846	78.15
Peoria (city) Peoria County	75,399	65.56
Elgin (city) Kane County	74,584	68.94
Arlington Heights (village) Cook County	67,261	89.56
Bloomington (city) McLean County	61,325	80.05

Top 10 Places Sorted by Percent of Total Population
Based on all places, regardless of total population

Place	Population	%
Coffeen (city) Montgomery County	685	100.00
Farina (village) Fayette County	518	100.00
Plymouth (village) Hancock County	505	100.00
Herrick (village) Shelby County	436	100.00
Waynesville (village) De Witt County	434	100.00
New Haven (village) Gallatin County	433	100.00
Dowell (village) Jackson County	408	100.00
Sparland (village) Marshall County	406	100.00
London Mills (village) Fulton County	392	100.00
Orient (city) Franklin County	358	100.00

Top 10 Places Sorted by Percent of Total Population
Based on places with total population of 50,000 or more

Place	Population	%
Orland Park (village) Cook County	51,944	91.50
Tinley Park (village) Cook County	51,088	90.10
Arlington Heights (village) Cook County	67,261	89.56
Wheaton (city) DuPage County	47,131	89.10
Normal (town) McLean County	45,768	87.18
Oak Lawn (village) Cook County	49,247	86.87
Bloomington (city) McLean County	61,325	80.05
Des Plaines (city) Cook County	46,247	79.24
Palatine (village) Cook County	54,068	78.87
Mount Prospect (village) Cook County	42,591	78.63

White: Not Hispanic

Top 10 Places Sorted by Population
Based on all places, regardless of total population

Place	Population	%
Chicago (city) Cook County	881,920	32.72
Naperville (city) DuPage County	105,833	74.61
Rockford (city) Winnebago County	92,788	60.70
Springfield (city) Sangamon County	89,342	76.85
Aurora (city) Kane County	81,537	41.20
Joliet (city) Will County	80,019	54.27
Peoria (city) Peoria County	72,633	63.16
Arlington Heights (village) Cook County	64,320	85.64
Bloomington (city) McLean County	58,841	76.81
Decatur (city) Macon County	55,734	73.22

Top 10 Places Sorted by Percent of Total Population
Based on all places, regardless of total population

Place	Population	%
Farina (village) Fayette County	518	100.
Herrick (village) Shelby County	436	100.
Waynesville (village) De Witt County	434	100.
West Union (cdp) Clark County	288	100.
Mount Clare (village) Macoupin County	278	100.
Plainville (village) Adams County	264	100.
Addieville (village) Washington County	252	100.
Harvel (village) Montgomery County	223	100.
New Minden (village) Washington County	215	100.
Norris (village) Fulton County	213	100.

Top 10 Places Sorted by Percent of Total Population
Based on places with total population of 50,000 or more

Place	Population	%
Orland Park (village) Cook County	49,389	87.
Arlington Heights (village) Cook County	64,320	85.
Tinley Park (village) Cook County	48,383	85.
Wheaton (city) DuPage County	45,045	85.
Normal (town) McLean County	44,263	84.
Oak Lawn (village) Cook County	44,283	78.
Springfield (city) Sangamon County	89,342	76.
Bloomington (city) McLean County	58,841	76.
Naperville (city) DuPage County	105,833	74.
Decatur (city) Macon County	55,734	73.

White: Hispanic

Top 10 Places Sorted by Population
Based on all places, regardless of total population

Place	Population	%
Chicago (city) Cook County	388,177	14.
Aurora (city) Kane County	42,062	21.
Cicero (town) Cook County	38,225	45
Elgin (city) Kane County	27,155	25.
Waukegan (city) Lake County	24,068	27
Joliet (city) Will County	23,260	15.
Berwyn (city) Cook County	17,874	31.
Rockford (city) Winnebago County	11,582	7.
Carpentersville (village) Kane County	10,566	28.
Bolingbrook (village) Will County	9,982	13

Top 10 Places Sorted by Percent of Total Population
Based on all places, regardless of total population

Place	Population	
Cicero (town) Cook County	38,225	45
Stone Park (village) Cook County	2,020	40
Melrose Park (village) Cook County	9,291	36.
Summit (village) Cook County	3,989	36
Highwood (city) Lake County	1,796	33.
Berwyn (city) Cook County	17,874	31
Posen (village) Cook County	1,860	31
Fairmont City (village) St. Clair County	789	29.
West Chicago (city) DuPage County	7,950	29
Northlake (city) Cook County	3,501	28

Top 10 Places Sorted by Percent of Total Population
Based on places with total population of 50,000 or more

Place	Population	
Cicero (town) Cook County	38,225	45
Berwyn (city) Cook County	17,874	31
Waukegan (city) Lake County	24,068	27
Elgin (city) Kane County	27,155	25
Aurora (city) Kane County	42,062	21
Joliet (city) Will County	23,260	15
Chicago (city) Cook County	388,177	14
Bolingbrook (village) Will County	9,982	13
Palatine (village) Cook County	7,044	10
Des Plaines (city) Cook County	5,900	10

Climate

Illinois Physical Features and Climate Narrative

PHYSICAL FEATURES. Illinois lies midway between the Continental Divide and the Atlantic Ocean and some 500 miles north of the Gulf of Mexico. Its climate is typically continental with cold winters, warm summers, and frequent short period fluctuations in temperature, humidity, cloudiness, and wind direction.

The irregular shape of the State has a width of less than 200 miles at most points, but extends for 385 miles in the north-south direction. Except for a few low hills in the extreme south and a small unglaciated area in the extreme northwest, the terrain is flat. Differences in elevation have no significant influence on the climate. River drainage is mainly toward the Mississippi River, which forms the entire western boundary of the State. From north to south the principal rivers entering the Mississippi are the Rock, Illinois, Kaskaskia, and the Big Muddy. Approximately one-seventh of the State area drains southeastward into the Wabash and Ohio Rivers. Only a small area drains into Lake Michigan.

GENERAL CLIMATE. Without the protection of natural barriers, such as mountain ranges, Illinois experiences the full sweep of the winds which are constantly bringing in the climates of other areas. Southeast and easterly winds bring mild and wet weather; southerly winds are warm and showery; westerly winds are dry with moderate temperatures; and winds from the northwest and north are cool and dry. Winds are controlled by the storm systems and weather fronts which move eastward and northeastward through this area.

Storm systems move through the State most frequently during the winter and spring months and cause a maximum of cloudiness during those seasons. Summer-season storm systems tend to be weaker and to stay farther north, leaving Illinois with much sunshine interspersed with thunderstorm situations of comparatively short duration. The retreat of the sun in autumn is associated with variable periods of pleasant dry weather of the Indian summer variety. This season ends rather abruptly with the returning storminess which usually begins in November.

TEMPERATURE. Because Illinois extends so far in a north-south direction, the contrasts in winter temperature conditions are rather strong. The extreme north has frequent snow and temperatures drop to below zero several times each winter. The soil freezes to a depth of about three feet and occasionally remains snow-covered for weeks at a time. In the extreme south snow falls only occasionally and leaves after a few days, while temperatures drop to zero on an average of only about one day each winter. The soil freezes, but only to a depth of eight to 12 inches, with great variation in the duration of soil-frost periods. The north-south range in winter mean temperatures is approximately 14°F.

During the summer season the sun heats the entire State quite strongly and uniformly. The north-south range of mean temperatures in July is only about 6°F. The annual average of days with temperatures of 90°F. or higher is near 20 in the north and near 50 in the south and west-central. Summer also brings periods of uncomfortably hot and humid weather, which are most persistent in the south. In the north the heat is usually broken after a few days by the arrival of cool air from Canada, but this cooling does not always penetrate to the southern portions of the State.

PRECIPITATION. Latitude is the principal control for both temperature and precipitation, with the northern counties averaging cooler and drier than the south. Distance from the Gulf of Mexico and lower airmass temperatures both tend to reduce the amounts of precipitation in the northern portion. Annual precipitation is approximately one and one-half times as great in the extreme south as in the extreme north, but most of the excess in the southern portion falls during winter and early spring. Mean total precipitation for the four-month period of December through March ranges from near seven inches in the extreme northwest to more than 14 inches in the extreme southeast. Precipitation during the warm season is more uniform. Totals for the six-month period of April through September range from 21 to 24 inches throughout the State. The driest month is February. The wettest months are May and June.

Precipitation during fall, winter, and spring tends to fall uniformly over large areas. In contrast, summer rainfall occurs principally as brief showers affecting relatively small areas. The erratic occurrence of summer showers results in uneven distribution. The high rates of summer rainfall also cause runoff and soil erosion. Summer showers are usually accompanied by thunder and, sometimes, by hail or destructive windstorms.

Floods occur nearly every year in at least some part of the State. The spring and early summer flood season results from a tendency for heavy general rainfall at that time of the year. The extreme north frequently has late winter or early spring flooding with the breakup of river ice, especially if there is an appreciable snow cover which is taken off by rain. River stages tend to decline during late summer, but local flash floods in minor streams, due to heavy thunderstorm rains, are common throughout the warm season. The interior rivers in the central and south have flat beds and sluggish currents so that they rise slowly and remain in flood conditions for relatively long periods.

SNOWFALL. The annual average of snowfall ranges from near 30 inches in the extreme north to only 10 inches in the extreme south. In the extreme north the most likely form of winter precipitation is snow. In contrast, more than 90% of Cairo's winter precipitation falls as rain. In a large number of winter storm situations, only a slight change in the temperature pattern would suffice to change rain to snow or vice versa. For this reason, Illinois snowfall records show great variability. Snowfalls of one inch or more occur on an average of 10 to 12 days per year in the extreme north and decrease to three or four in the far south. The two northern divisions average about 50 days annually when the ground is covered with one inch or more of snow, and this average decreases to about 15 days in the two southern divisions.

STORMS. Heavy snows of four to six inches or more average one or two per year in the north and less frequently in the south. Strong winds will drift snow and make driving hazardous. Moderate to heavy ice storms average about once every four or five years and can be quite damaging. Thunderstorms average about 35 to 50 annually, but most are quite harmless. On occasion they provide the source for hail, damaging winds, and tornadoes. Hail falls on an average of two or three days annually in the same locality, but usually causes little damage.

More than 65 percent of Illinois tornadoes occur during the months of March, April, May, and June. This "tornado season" is marked by a rapid increase in activity during March, a peak in April and May, and a decline during June. Tornadoes have occurred during each of the twelve months of the year.

INFLUENCE OF LAKE MICHIGAN. Because prevailing winds are westerly and storm systems move from the same direction, the influence of the lake on Illinois weather is not large. When the wind blows from the lake toward the shore, which it does for approximately one-fourth of the time during spring and summer and for about one-eighth of the time during fall and winter, the result is a moderation of temperature. In addition to the general occurrence of onshore winds, there is the local "sea breeze" effect on summer afternoons which is usually observable in a narrow strip near the lake shore.

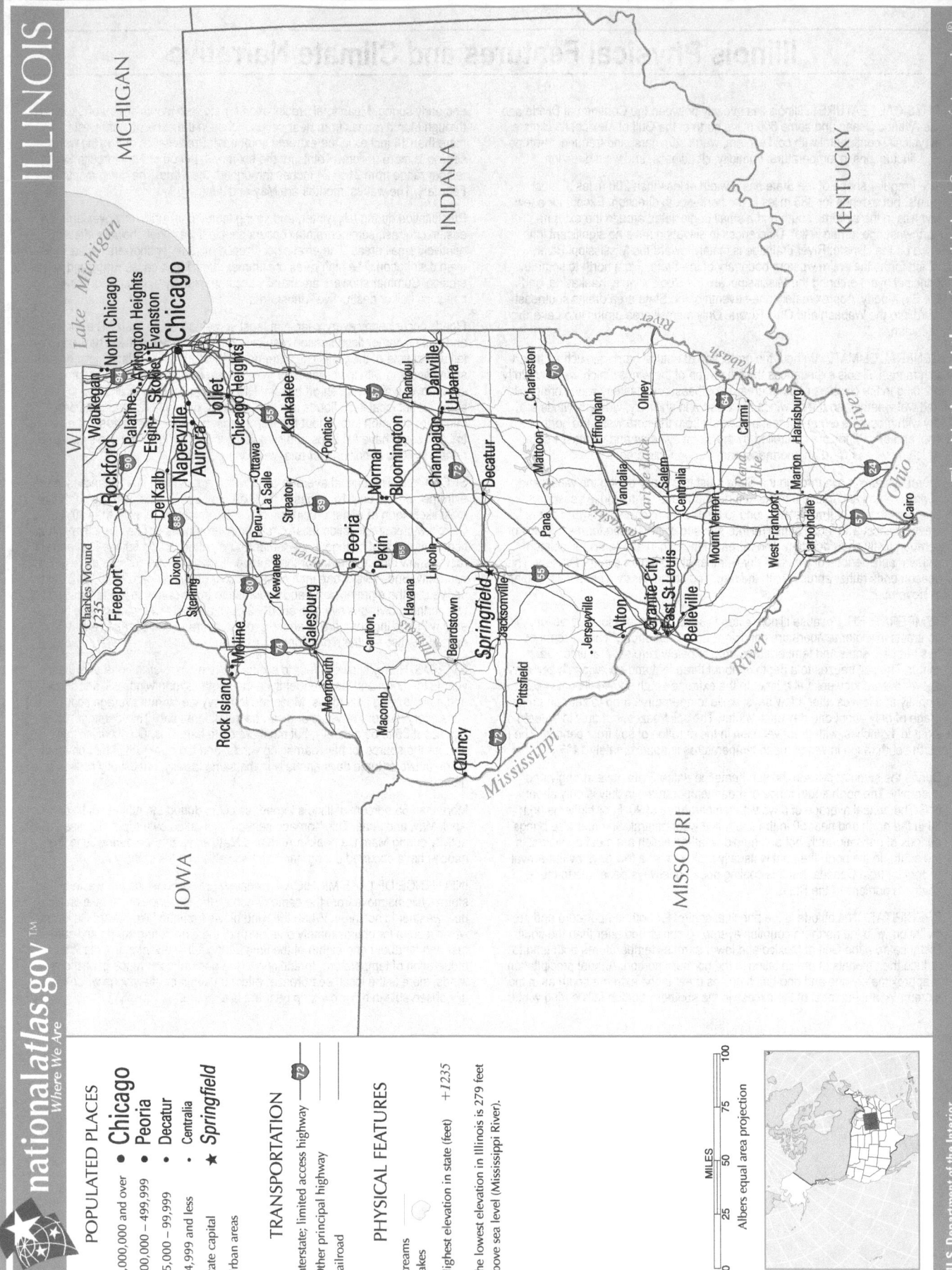

Illinois Physical Features and Climate Narrative

ILLINOIS

nationalatlas.gov™
Where We Are

POPULATED PLACES

1,000,000 and over   ● Chicago
100,000 – 499,999   ● Peoria
25,000 – 99,999   ● Decatur
24,999 and less   · Centralia
State capital   ★ Springfield
Urban areas

TRANSPORTATION

Interstate; limited access highway   ──72──
Other principal highway
Railroad

PHYSICAL FEATURES

Streams
Lakes
Highest elevation in state (feet)   +1235
The lowest elevation in Illinois is 279 feet
above sea level (Mississippi River).

MILES
0   25   50   75   100

Albers equal area projection

U.S. Department of the Interior
U.S. Geological Survey

The National Atlas of the United States of America®

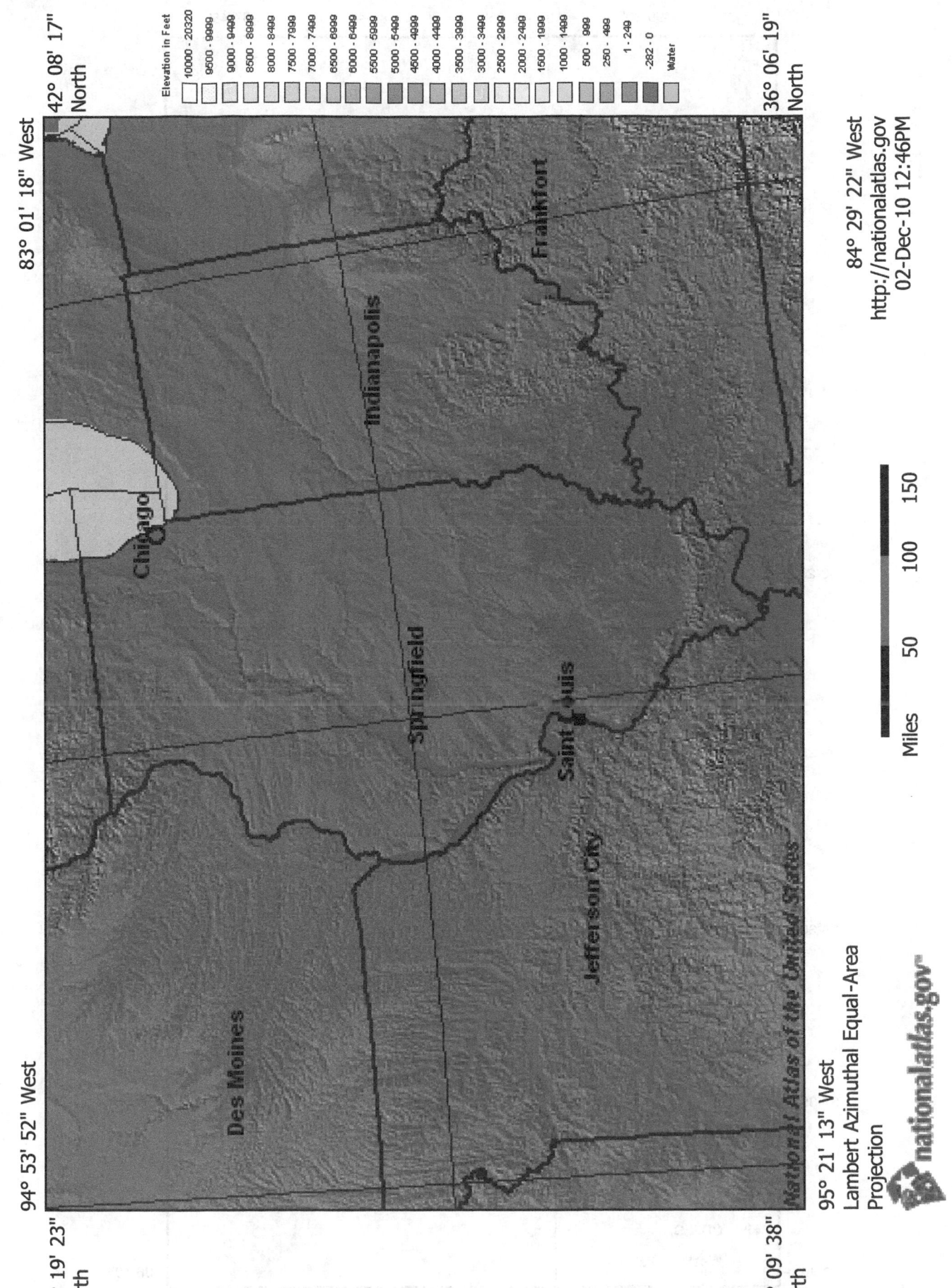

Elevation in Feet

10000 - 20320	
9500 - 9999	
9000 - 9499	
8500 - 8999	
8000 - 8499	
7500 - 7999	
7000 - 7499	
6500 - 6999	
6000 - 6499	
5500 - 5999	
5000 - 5499	
4500 - 4999	
4000 - 4499	
3500 - 3999	
3000 - 3499	
2500 - 2999	
2000 - 2499	
1500 - 1999	
1000 - 1499	
500 - 999	
250 - 499	
1 - 249	
-282 - 0	
Water	

94° 53' 52" West

83° 01' 18" West

42° 08' 17" North

43° 19' 23" North

36° 06' 19" North

37° 09' 38" North

Chicago

Des Moines

Springfield

Indianapolis

Frankfort

Saint Louis

Jefferson City

National Atlas of the United States

95° 21' 13" West
Lambert Azimuthal Equal-Area
Projection

84° 29' 22" West
http://nationalatlas.gov
02-Dec-10 12:46PM

Miles   50   100   150

nationalatlas.gov™

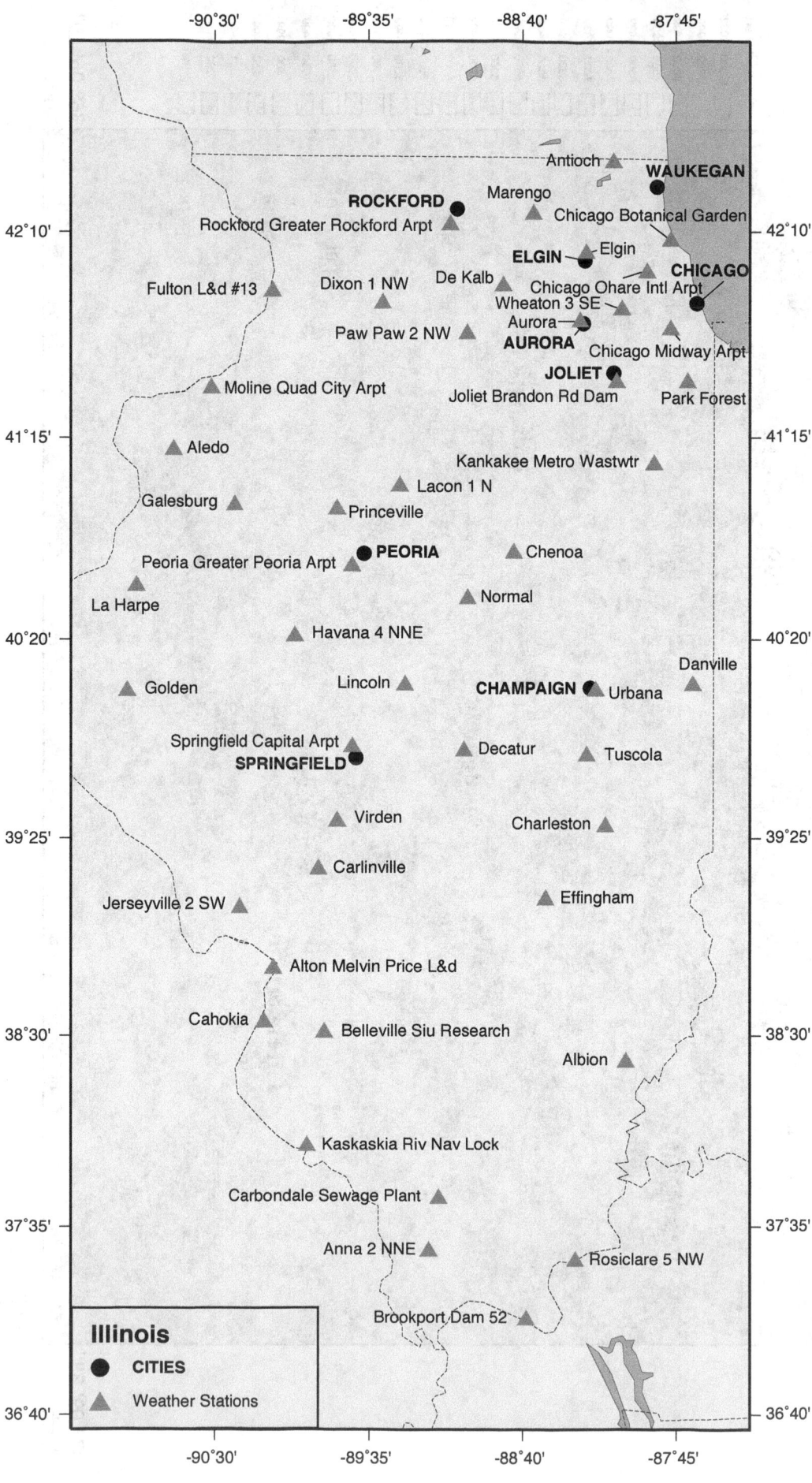

Antioch

WAUKEGAN

Marengo

ROCKFORD

Rockford Greater Rockford Arpt

Chicago Botanical Garden

ELGIN   Elgin

Fulton L&d #13   Dixon 1 NW   De Kalb   **CHICAGO**

Chicago Ohare Intl Arpt

Wheaton 3 SE

Paw Paw 2 NW   Aurora

AURORA   Chicago Midway Arpt

JOLIET

Moline Quad City Arpt   Joliet Brandon Rd Dam   Park Forest

Aledo

Kankakee Metro Wastwtr

Galesburg   Lacon 1 N

Princeville

Chenoa

Peoria Greater Peoria Arpt   **PEORIA**

La Harpe   Normal

Havana 4 NNE

Danville

Golden   Lincoln   **CHAMPAIGN**   Urbana

Springfield Capital Arpt   Decatur   Tuscola

SPRINGFIELD

Virden   Charleston

Carlinville

Jerseyville 2 SW   Effingham

Alton Melvin Price L&d

Cahokia   Belleville Siu Research

Albion

Kaskaskia Riv Nav Lock

Carbondale Sewage Plant

Anna 2 NNE   Rosiclare 5 NW

Brookport Dam 52

Illinois

● **CITIES**

▲ Weather Stations

-90°30'   -89°35'   -88°40'   -87°45'

42°10'

41°15'

40°20'

39°25'

38°30'

37°35'

36°40'

Illinois Weather Stations by County

County	Station Name
Adams	Golden
Champaign	Urbana
Coles	Charleston
Cook	Chicago Botanical Garden Chicago Midway Arpt Chicago Ohare Intl Arpt Park Forest
Dekalb	De Kalb
Douglas	Tuscola
Dupage	Wheaton 3 SE
Edwards	Albion
Effingham	Effingham
Hancock	La Harpe
Hardin	Rosiclare 5 NW
Jackson	Carbondale Sewage Plant
Jersey	Jerseyville 2 SW
Kane	Aurora Elgin
Kankakee	Kankakee Metro Wastwater
Knox	Galesburg
Lake	Antioch
Lee	Dixon 1 NW Paw Paw 2 NW
Logan	Lincoln
Macon	Decatur
Macoupin	Carlinville Virden
Madison	Alton Melvin Price L&D
Marshall	Lacon 1 N
Mason	Havana 4 NNE
Massac	Brookport Dam 52
Mchenry	Marengo
Mclean	Chenoa Normal
Mercer	Aledo
Peoria	Peoria Greater Peoria Arpt

County	Station Name
Peoria (cont.)	Princeville
Randolph	Kaskaskia River Nav Lock
Rock Island	Moline Quad City Arpt
Sangamon	Springfield Capital Arpt
St. Clair	Belleville Siu Research Cahokia
Union	Anna 2 NNE
Vermilion	Danville
Whiteside	Fulton L&D #13
Will	Joliet Brandon Rd Dam
Winnebago	Rockford Greater Rockford Arpt

See User Guide for station inclusion criteria.

Illinois Weather Stations by City

City	Station Name	Miles
Arlington Heights	Chicago Botanical Garden	10.5
	Chicago Ohare Intl Arpt	8.3
	Elgin	15.6
	Wheaton 3 SE	19.6
Aurora	Aurora	1.2
	Chicago Ohare Intl Arpt	24.9
	Elgin	21.3
	Joliet Brandon Rd Dam	20.5
	Wheaton 3 SE	12.5
Berwyn	Chicago Botanical Garden	19.9
	Chicago Ohare Intl Arpt	11.5
	Chicago Midway Arpt	7.8
	Park Forest	24.5
	Wheaton 3 SE	14.4
Bloomington	Chenoa	22.0
	Normal	2.9
Bolingbrook	Aurora	12.8
	Chicago Ohare Intl Arpt	21.3
	Chicago Midway Arpt	15.6
	Joliet Brandon Rd Dam	14.0
	Park Forest	24.9
	Wheaton 3 SE	8.0
Buffalo Grove	Antioch	23.4
	Chicago Botanical Garden	9.6
	Chicago Ohare Intl Arpt	12.7
	Elgin	17.6
	Wheaton 3 SE	24.5
Carol Stream	Aurora	14.1
	Chicago Botanical Garden	23.4
	Chicago Ohare Intl Arpt	12.1
	Chicago Midway Arpt	22.3
	Elgin	12.6
	Wheaton 3 SE	8.0
Champaign	Tuscola	21.5
	Urbana	1.6
Chicago	Chicago Botanical Garden	19.4
	Chicago Ohare Intl Arpt	14.6
	Chicago Midway Arpt	10.3
	Wheaton 3 SE	20.0
Cicero	Chicago Botanical Garden	19.8
	Chicago Ohare Intl Arpt	12.3
	Chicago Midway Arpt	8.0
	Park Forest	24.4
	Wheaton 3 SE	15.9
Crystal Lake	Antioch	21.3
	Elgin	11.1
	Marengo	13.5
DeKalb	De Kalb	1.2
	Marengo	23.2
	Paw Paw 2 NW	19.5
Decatur	Decatur	4.3

City	Station Name	Miles
Des Plaines	Chicago Botanical Garden	9.2
	Chicago Ohare Intl Arpt	3.6
	Chicago Midway Arpt	21.7
	Elgin	19.6
	Wheaton 3 SE	17.2
Downers Grove	Aurora	15.7
	Chicago Ohare Intl Arpt	14.5
	Chicago Midway Arpt	12.4
	Elgin	23.8
	Joliet Brandon Rd Dam	20.3
	Wheaton 3 SE	3.4
Elgin	Aurora	18.8
	Chicago Ohare Intl Arpt	19.4
	Elgin	2.0
	Marengo	21.7
	Wheaton 3 SE	19.1
Elmhurst	Aurora	21.1
	Chicago Botanical Garden	18.5
	Chicago Ohare Intl Arpt	6.4
	Chicago Midway Arpt	13.7
	Elgin	21.2
	Wheaton 3 SE	8.3
Evanston	Chicago Botanical Garden	7.8
	Chicago Ohare Intl Arpt	12.3
	Chicago Midway Arpt	22.0
	Wheaton 3 SE	24.9
Glenview	Chicago Botanical Garden	4.1
	Chicago Ohare Intl Arpt	8.3
	Chicago Midway Arpt	24.0
	Elgin	23.8
	Wheaton 3 SE	22.2
Hoffman Estates	Aurora	23.1
	Chicago Botanical Garden	17.5
	Chicago Ohare Intl Arpt	11.4
	Elgin	8.9
	Wheaton 3 SE	17.3
Joliet	Aurora	18.8
	Chicago Midway Arpt	22.1
	Joliet Brandon Rd Dam	2.8
	Park Forest	22.8
	Wheaton 3 SE	19.5
Lombard	Aurora	17.2
	Chicago Botanical Garden	21.5
	Chicago Ohare Intl Arpt	9.1
	Chicago Midway Arpt	15.3
	Elgin	19.2
	Wheaton 3 SE	4.7
Moline	Aledo	24.0
	Moline Quad City Arpt	2.0
	Clinton No 1, IA	24.4
	Le Claire L & D 14, IA	7.2
Mount Prospect	Chicago Botanical Garden	9.4
	Chicago Ohare Intl Arpt	5.5
	Chicago Midway Arpt	24.0

See User Guide for station inclusion criteria.

City	Station Name	Miles
Mt Prospect *(cont.)*	Elgin	17.6
	Wheaton 3 SE	18.1
Naperville	Aurora	8.4
	Chicago Ohare Intl Arpt	20.4
	Chicago Midway Arpt	19.2
	Elgin	23.0
	Joliet Brandon Rd Dam	17.3
	Wheaton 3 SE	6.6
Normal	Chenoa	20.7
	Normal	0.7
Oak Lawn	Chicago Ohare Intl Arpt	20.5
	Chicago Midway Arpt	2.1
	Joliet Brandon Rd Dam	23.3
	Park Forest	15.2
	Wheaton 3 SE	17.7
Oak Park	Chicago Botanical Garden	17.1
	Chicago Ohare Intl Arpt	9.4
	Chicago Midway Arpt	10.5
	Wheaton 3 SE	15.0
Orland Park	Chicago Midway Arpt	9.1
	Joliet Brandon Rd Dam	15.1
	Park Forest	11.5
	Wheaton 3 SE	18.1
Palatine	Chicago Botanical Garden	12.9
	Chicago Ohare Intl Arpt	11.5
	Elgin	13.3
	Wheaton 3 SE	21.3
Peoria	Lacon 1 N	23.9
	Peoria Greater Peoria Arpt	5.6
	Princeville	16.3
Rockford	Marengo	23.7
	Rockford Greater Rockford Arpt	5.6
	Beloit, WI	15.9
Schaumburg	Aurora	21.8
	Chicago Botanical Garden	17.0
	Chicago Ohare Intl Arpt	9.2
	Elgin	10.5
	Wheaton 3 SE	14.8
Skokie	Chicago Botanical Garden	7.1
	Chicago Ohare Intl Arpt	9.8
	Chicago Midway Arpt	21.1
	Wheaton 3 SE	22.6
Springfield	Springfield Capital Arpt	4.4
	Virden	20.8
Tinley Park	Chicago Midway Arpt	10.8
	Joliet Brandon Rd Dam	16.2
	Park Forest	8.3
	Wheaton 3 SE	21.3
Waukegan	Antioch	15.4
	Chicago Botanical Garden	16.7
	Kenosha, WI	13.8
	Racine, WI	23.2

City	Station Name	Miles
Wheaton	Aurora	12.5
	Chicago Ohare Intl Arpt	13.1
	Chicago Midway Arpt	18.6
	Elgin	17.2
	Joliet Brandon Rd Dam	24.6
	Wheaton 3 SE	3.4

Note: Miles is the distance between the geographic center of the city and the weather station.

Illinois Weather Stations by Elevation

Feet	Station Name
950	Paw Paw 2 NW
873	De Kalb
819	Marengo
785	Normal
771	Galesburg
763	Elgin
750	Antioch
743	Urbana
734	Princeville
725	Golden
720	Aledo
709	Chenoa
709	Park Forest
700	Dixon 1 NW
700	La Harpe
680	Charleston
680	Rockford Greater Rockford Arpt
680	Wheaton 3 SE
674	Virden
658	Chicago Ohare Intl Arpt
652	Tuscola
651	Peoria Greater Peoria Arpt
640	Aurora
640	Kankakee Metro Wastwater
629	Carlinville
629	Chicago Botanical Garden
629	Jerseyville 2 SW
620	Chicago Midway Arpt
620	Decatur
600	Anna 2 NNE
595	Effingham
591	Fulton L&D #13
591	Moline Quad City Arpt
585	Springfield Capital Arpt
583	Lincoln
558	Danville
542	Joliet Brandon Rd Dam
529	Albion
459	Havana 4 NNE
459	Lacon 1 N
450	Belleville Siu Research
430	Alton Melvin Price L&D
399	Cahokia
399	Rosiclare 5 NW
390	Carbondale Sewage Plant
379	Kaskaskia River Nav Lock
330	Brookport Dam 52

See User Guide for station inclusion criteria.

Chicago O'Hare Int'l Airport

Chicago is located along the southwest shore of Lake Michigan and occupies a plain which, for the most part, is only some tens of feet above the lake. Lake Michigan averages 579 feet above sea level. Natural water drainage over most of the city would be into Lake Michigan, and from areas west of the city is into the Mississippi River System. But actual drainage over most of the city is artificially channeled also into the Mississippi system.

Chicago is in a region of frequently changeable weather. The climate is predominately continental, ranging from relatively warm in summer to relatively cold in winter. In late autumn and winter however, air masses that are initially very cold often reach the city only after being tempered by passage over one or more of the lakes. Similarly, in late spring and summer, air masses reaching the city from the north, northeast, or east are cooler because of movement over the Great Lakes. Very low winter temperatures most often occur in air that flows southward to the west of Lake Superior before reaching the Chicago area. In summer the higher temperatures are with south or southwest flow and are therefore not influenced by the lakes, the only modifying effect being a local lake breeze.

During the warm season, when the lake is cold relative to land, there is frequently a lake breeze that reduces daytime temperature near the shore. When the breeze off the lake is light this effect usually reaches inland only a mile or two, but with stronger on-shore winds the whole city is cooled. On the other hand, temperatures at night are warmer near the lake.

At the O'Hare International Airport temperatures of 96 degrees or higher occur in about half the summers, while about half the winters have a minimum as low as -15 degrees. The average occurrence of the first temperature as low as 32 degrees in the fall is mid-October and the average occurrence of the last temperature as low as 32 degrees in the spring is late April.

Precipitation falls mostly from air that has passed over the Gulf of Mexico. But in winter there is sometimes snowfall, light inland but locally heavy near the lakeshore, with Lake Michigan as the principal moisture source. The effect of Lake Michigan, both on winter temperatures and lake-produced snowfall, is enhanced by non-freezing of much of the lake during the winter, even though areas and harbors are often ice-choked.

Summer thunderstorms are often locally heavy and variable, parts of the city may receive substantial rainfall and other parts none. Longer periods of continuous precipitation are mostly in autumn, winter, and spring.

Chicago O'Hare Int'l Airport *Cook County*   Elevation: 658 ft.   Latitude: 41° 59' N   Longitude: 87° 55' W

	JAN	FEB	MAR	APR	MAY	JUN	JUL	AUG	SEP	OCT	NOV	DEC	YEAR
Mean Maximum Temp. (°F)	31.2	35.2	46.3	58.7	70.0	79.6	84.1	81.9	74.8	62.0	48.2	35.0	58.9
Mean Temp. (°F)	23.7	27.5	37.5	48.6	59.0	68.7	73.9	72.3	64.5	52.2	40.2	27.9	49.7
Mean Minimum Temp. (°F)	16.3	19.8	28.6	38.4	48.0	57.7	63.6	62.7	54.2	42.4	32.3	20.7	40.4
Extreme Maximum Temp. (°F)	65	72	88	91	92	104	104	101	99	88	75	71	104
Extreme Minimum Temp. (°F)	-27	-19	-7	7	27	37	45	42	29	17	6	-25	-27
Days Maximum Temp. ≥ 90°F	0	0	0	0	0	4	7	4	1	0	0	0	16
Days Maximum Temp. ≤ 32°F	16	11	4	0	0	0	0	0	0	0	2	12	45
Days Minimum Temp. ≤ 32°F	28	25	21	7	0	0	0	0	0	4	15	27	127
Days Minimum Temp. ≤ 0°F	4	2	0	0	0	0	0	0	0	0	0	2	8
Heating Degree Days (base 65°F)	1,272	1,054	848	495	224	48	4	8	102	399	737	1,144	6,335
Cooling Degree Days (base 65°F)	0	0	1	9	45	166	286	242	94	10	0	0	853
Mean Precipitation (in.)	1.72	1.77	2.51	3.39	3.62	3.37	3.52	5.12	3.30	3.19	3.10	2.29	36.90
Maximum Precipitation (in.)*	4.1	3.5	5.9	7.7	7.1	10.0	8.3	17.1	11.4	7.4	8.2	8.6	49.3
Minimum Precipitation (in.)*	0.1	0.1	0.6	1.0	0.3	0.9	1.2	0.5	trace	0.2	0.6	0.2	21.8
Extreme Maximum Daily Precip. (in.)	1.24	3.44	1.75	2.37	3.45	3.97	2.90	6.49	6.64	3.79	2.93	4.47	6.64
Days With ≥ 0.1" Precipitation	5	4	6	7	7	6	6	7	6	6	6	5	71
Days With ≥ 0.5" Precipitation	1	1	1	2	2	2	2	3	2	2	2	1	21
Days With ≥ 1.0" Precipitation	0	0	0	1	1	1	1	2	1	1	1	0	9
Mean Snowfall (in.)	11.4	8.6	5.9	1.4	trace	trace	trace	trace	trace	0.3	1.4	8.3	37.3
Maximum Snowfall (in.)*	34	26	25	11	2	0	0	0	0	7	10	35	75
Maximum 24-hr. Snowfall (in.)*	15	10	9	11	2	0	0	0	0	4	5	10	15
Maximum Snow Depth (in.)	18	15	12	6	trace	trace	trace	trace	trace	3	4	17	18
Days With ≥ 1.0" Snow Depth	17	11	4	1	0	0	0	0	0	0	1	9	43
Thunderstorm Days*	< 1	< 1	2	4	5	6	6	6	4	2	1	1	37
Foggy Days*	12	11	12	10	10	8	9	12	11	11	12	13	131
Predominant Sky Cover*	OVR	OVR	OVR	OVR	OVR	OVR	SCT	SCT	OVR	OVR	OVR	OVR	OVR
Mean Relative Humidity 6am (%)*	77	78	79	77	77	78	82	85	85	82	81	80	80
Mean Relative Humidity 3pm (%)*	66	63	59	53	51	52	54	55	55	53	62	68	58
Mean Dewpoint (°F)*	14	18	27	36	46	56	62	61	54	42	31	21	39
Prevailing Wind Direction*	W	W	W	NNE	NNE	SSW	SW	SSW	S	S	SSW	WNW	SSW
Prevailing Wind Speed (mph)*	12	10	12	13	12	10	9	9	9	10	13	12	10
Maximum Wind Gust (mph)*	58	54	84	69	58	63	76	64	58	58	62	62	84

Note: (*) Period of record is 1958-1995

Moline Quad City Airport

The locality is in the heart of the Corn Belt. Agricultural crops include many important staple products in addition to corn. Cattle, hogs, horses, and poultry produced in Iowa and Illinois rank high in the nation. Close to the Mississippi River there is large scale truck gardening and considerable dairying. Field production of grains and livestock attains greater development farther away from the large streams, where the countryside is rolling prairie. Damaging droughts are not common. This, together with the variety of agricultural products, has led to designating the section as the Bread Basket of America.

The climate is favorable for many industries as evidenced by the large number and variety of manufacturing and other enterprises which have located and developed in the community. Among these are some of the largest producers of agricultural machinery in the world.

This area has a temperate continental climate, with a wide temperature range throughout the year. There are some intensely hot, unusually humid, periods in summer and severely cold periods in winter. Maxima of 90 degrees or more have occurred in summer as frequently as 55 days and zero or lower readings have occurred during every winter.

Freezing temperatures have occurred as late in spring as late May and as early in autumn as late September. Precipitation is usually well distributed throughout the year with the greatest amounts falling during the 177-day average crop growing season. Substantial weather changes frequently occur at three or four day intervals, as a direct result of proximity to some of the most important storm tracks.

Moline Quad City Airport *Rock Island County*   Elevation: 591 ft.   Latitude: 41° 28' N   Longitude: 90° 31' W

	JAN	FEB	MAR	APR	MAY	JUN	JUL	AUG	SEP	OCT	NOV	DEC	YEAR
Mean Maximum Temp. (°F)	31.4	35.9	48.7	62.2	73.2	82.4	85.9	83.7	76.8	63.7	49.1	34.8	60.6
Mean Temp. (°F)	23.2	27.4	38.9	51.0	61.7	71.2	75.3	73.2	65.2	52.7	40.1	26.9	50.6
Mean Minimum Temp. (°F)	14.8	18.9	29.1	39.8	50.2	60.0	64.7	62.7	53.5	41.7	31.1	19.0	40.5
Extreme Maximum Temp. (°F)	69	71	88	93	95	104	103	103	98	95	80	71	104
Extreme Minimum Temp. (°F)	-29	-28	-9	7	25	39	48	40	30	16	4	-24	-29
Days Maximum Temp. ≥ 90°F	0	0	0	0	1	5	9	6	2	0	0	0	23
Days Maximum Temp. ≤ 32°F	16	11	3	0	0	0	0	0	0	0	2	11	43
Days Minimum Temp. ≤ 32°F	29	24	20	7	0	0	0	0	0	6	17	27	130
Days Minimum Temp. ≤ 0°F	5	3	0	0	0	0	0	0	0	0	0	3	11
Heating Degree Days (base 65°F)	1,291	1,056	803	427	159	19	1	7	94	387	741	1,175	6,160
Cooling Degree Days (base 65°F)	0	0	2	14	63	213	328	268	106	14	0	0	1,008
Mean Precipitation (in.)	1.46	1.62	2.82	3.53	4.29	4.37	4.22	4.63	3.04	2.95	2.54	2.21	37.68
Maximum Precipitation (in.)*	4.4	2.8	7.4	11.3	11.4	13.2	11.8	15.2	8.5	6.8	5.0	56.4
Minimum Precipitation (in.)*	0.3	0.2	0.3	0.7	0.3	1.0	0.4	0.3	trace	trace	0.5	0.3	20.2
Extreme Maximum Daily Precip. (in.)	1.51	1.30	2.16	2.18	2.92	3.71	3.56	3.55	4.26	4.14	2.04	3.11	4.26
Days With ≥ 0.1" Precipitation	4	4	6	7	7	7	6	7	5	5	5	5	68
Days With ≥ 0.5" Precipitation	1	1	2	3	3	3	3	3	2	2	2	1	26
Days With ≥ 1.0" Precipitation	0	0	1	1	1	1	1	2	1	1	0	0	9
Mean Snowfall (in.)	9.2	6.7	4.1	1.2	trace	trace	trace	0.0	trace	0.1	1.2	8.8	31.3
Maximum Snowfall (in.)*	27	21	20	13	trace	0	0	0	0	7	16	22	63
Maximum 24-hr. Snowfall (in.)*	16	9	10	8	trace	0	0	0	0	7	8	9	16
Maximum Snow Depth (in.)	na	na	na	na	na	na	na	na	na	na	na	na	na
Days With ≥ 1.0" Snow Depth	na	na	na	na	na	na	na	na	na	na	na	na	na
Thunderstorm Days*	< 1	< 1	2	5	7	8	8	7	5	2	1	< 1	45
Foggy Days*	12	11	13	10	11	9	12	15	14	13	12	13	145
Predominant Sky Cover*	OVR	OVR	OVR	OVR	OVR	OVR	CLR	CLR	CLR	CLR	OVR	OVR	OVR
Mean Relative Humidity 6am (%)*	76	78	79	78	79	81	85	89	87	82	80	79	81
Mean Relative Humidity 3pm (%)*	66	63	57	50	49	50	54	55	52	49	59	67	56
Mean Dewpoint (°F)*	13	18	27	37	48	59	64	63	54	42	30	19	40
Prevailing Wind Direction*	WNW	WNW	WNW	WNW	S	S	S	S	S	S	WNW	WNW	WNW
Prevailing Wind Speed (mph)*	14	14	14	15	12	10	9	9	10	12	14	14	13
Maximum Wind Gust (mph)*	59	54	69	81	66	79	66	81	59	61	60	69	81

Note: (*) Period of record is 1943-1995

Greater Peoria Airport

The airport station is situated on a rather level tableland surrounded by well-drained and gently rolling terrain. It is set back a mile from the rim of the Illinois River Valley and is almost 200 feet above the river bed. Exposures of all instruments are good. The climate of this area is typically continental as shown by its changeable weather and the wide range of temperature extremes.

June and September are usually the most pleasant months of the year. Then during October or the first of November, Indian Summer is often experienced with an extended period of warm, dry weather.

Precipitation is normally heaviest during the growing season and lowest during midwinter.

The earliest snowfalls have occurred in September and the latest in the spring have occurred as late as May. Heavy snowfalls have rarely exceeded 20 inches.

Based on the 1951-1980 period, the average first occurrence of 32 degrees Fahrenheit in the fall is October 20 and the average last occurrence in the spring is April 24.

Greater Peoria Airport *Peoria County*   Elevation: 651 ft.   Latitude: 40° 40' N   Longitude: 89° 41' W

	JAN	FEB	MAR	APR	MAY	JUN	JUL	AUG	SEP	OCT	NOV	DEC	YEAR
Mean Maximum Temp. (°F)	32.9	37.6	50.0	62.7	73.2	82.1	85.6	83.8	77.1	64.2	50.2	36.3	61.3
Mean Temp. (°F)	25.1	29.3	40.4	52.0	62.4	71.6	75.6	73.8	66.2	53.8	41.5	28.8	51.7
Mean Minimum Temp. (°F)	17.1	20.9	30.7	41.2	51.5	61.1	65.5	63.8	55.2	43.3	32.8	21.2	42.0
Extreme Maximum Temp. (°F)	70	71	86	92	94	105	104	103	97	93	80	71	105
Extreme Minimum Temp. (°F)	-22	-19	-4	14	28	39	50	41	29	21	5	-23	-23
Days Maximum Temp. ≥ 90°F	0	0	0	0	1	5	9	6	2	0	0	0	23
Days Maximum Temp. ≤ 32°F	15	9	3	0	0	0	0	0	0	0	2	10	39
Days Minimum Temp. ≤ 32°F	28	24	18	5	0	0	0	0	0	4	15	26	120
Days Minimum Temp. ≤ 0°F	4	2	0	0	0	0	0	0	0	0	0	2	8
Heating Degree Days (base 65°F)	1,232	1,004	758	399	142	17	1	5	80	356	698	1,116	5,808
Cooling Degree Days (base 65°F)	0	0	2	14	69	222	336	285	121	15	0	0	1,064
Mean Precipitation (in.)	1.74	1.76	2.78	3.61	4.13	3.61	3.74	3.36	3.12	2.87	3.09	2.36	36.17
Maximum Precipitation (in.)*	8.1	4.9	6.9	8.7	11.5	11.7	10.1	8.6	13.1	10.5	7.6	6.3	55.3
Minimum Precipitation (in.)*	0.1	0.1	0.4	0.7	0.5	0.4	0.3	0.3	trace	trace	0.1	0.3	22.2
Extreme Maximum Daily Precip. (in.)	2.35	1.81	1.92	3.05	2.99	4.42	3.36	2.63	3.05	2.68	4.26	2.34	4.42
Days With ≥ 0.1" Precipitation	4	4	6	7	8	6	6	6	5	6	6	5	69
Days With ≥ 0.5" Precipitation	1	1	2	2	2	2	2	3	2	2	2	1	22
Days With ≥ 1.0" Precipitation	0	0	1	1	1	1	1	1	1	1	0	1	9
Mean Snowfall (in.)	6.8	5.9	2.9	0.9	trace	trace	trace	0.0	trace	trace	1.3	6.5	24.3
Maximum Snowfall (in.)*	25	15	18	13	trace	0	0	0	1	3	11	22	52
Maximum 24-hr. Snowfall (in.)*	12	9	9	6	trace	0	0	0	1	3	8	7	12
Maximum Snow Depth (in.)	16	10	7	10	trace	trace	trace	0	trace	trace	4	13	16
Days With ≥ 1.0" Snow Depth	14	9	3	0	0	0	0	0	0	0	1	9	36
Thunderstorm Days*	< 1	1	3	5	7	9	8	7	5	2	1	1	49
Foggy Days*	11	10	9	7	7	6	7	9	9	10	10	12	107
Predominant Sky Cover*	OVR	OVR	OVR	OVR	OVR	OVR	SCT	CLR	CLR	OVR	OVR	OVR	OVR
Mean Relative Humidity 6am (%)*	80	81	81	78	80	82	86	89	87	84	83	83	83
Mean Relative Humidity 3pm (%)*	67	64	58	52	52	52	55	56	52	52	61	69	57
Mean Dewpoint (°F)*	10	20	29	00	40	50	04	00	54	40	00	00	41
Prevailing Wind Direction*	S	S	S	S	S	S	S	S	S	S	S	S	S
Prevailing Wind Speed (mph)*	12	12	13	12	10	10	9	8	9	10	12	12	10
Maximum Wind Gust (mph)*	54	53	68	69	61	75	85	54	75	48	62	59	85

Note: (*) Period of record is 1948-1995

Rockford Greater Rockford Arpt.

The climate of Rockford is characterized by hot summers and cold winters.

When winter northeasterly winds blow across Lake Michigan, cloudiness often is increased in the Rockford area, and temperatures are somewhat higher than those westward around the Mississippi River. Conversely, in summer, the cooling effect of Lake Michigan sometimes is felt as far westward as Rockford.

While 34 percent of the precipitation occurs in the three summer months of June to August, and 64 percent in the six months, April to September, no month averages less than four percent of the annual total.

Though summers may be described as hot, seldom does oppressive heat prevail for extended periods. In general, the summers are pleasant.

Winters are cold. Snow cover is adequate for diversified winter sports, and usually is continuous from late December through February.

Based on the 1951-1980 period, the average first occurrence of 32 degrees Fahrenheit in the fall is October 11 and the average last occurrence in the spring is April 29.

Rockford Greater Rockford Arpt. *Winnebago County*   Elevation: 680 ft.   Latitude: 42° 12' N   Longitude: 89° 07' W

	JAN	FEB	MAR	APR	MAY	JUN	JUL	AUG	SEP	OCT	NOV	DEC	YEAR
Mean Maximum Temp. (°F)	28.9	33.5	45.8	59.8	71.2	80.4	83.9	81.7	74.7	61.7	46.9	32.7	58.4
Mean Temp. (°F)	21.0	25.3	36.3	48.7	59.6	69.3	73.3	71.4	63.4	50.9	38.3	25.1	48.6
Mean Minimum Temp. (°F)	13.0	17.0	26.8	37.5	48.0	58.0	62.7	61.0	52.0	40.1	29.8	17.6	38.6
Extreme Maximum Temp. (°F)	63	70	85	91	93	101	102	104	95	90	76	67	104
Extreme Minimum Temp. (°F)	-27	-24	-11	5	26	37	47	41	27	18	1	-24	-27
Days Maximum Temp. ≥ 90°F	0	0	0	0	0	4	6	4	1	0	0	0	15
Days Maximum Temp. ≤ 32°F	19	13	4	0	0	0	0	0	0	0	3	14	53
Days Minimum Temp. ≤ 32°F	30	26	23	8	1	0	0	0	0	7	19	28	142
Days Minimum Temp. ≤ 0°F	6	4	0	0	0	0	0	0	0	0	0	4	14
Heating Degree Days (base 65°F)	1,358	1,117	882	491	206	34	3	12	120	437	793	1,229	6,682
Cooling Degree Days (base 65°F)	0	0	1	8	45	169	268	217	79	8	0	0	795
Mean Precipitation (in.)	1.37	1.43	2.30	3.34	3.90	4.65	3.75	4.70	3.49	2.61	2.55	2.01	36.10
Maximum Precipitation (in.)*	4.7	3.0	5.6	9.9	7.0	11.8	11.8	13.5	10.7	8.3	5.5	5.0	56.5
Minimum Precipitation (in.)*	0.2	trace	0.6	1.0	0.5	0.5	0.8	0.7	0	trace	0.4	0.4	23.3
Extreme Maximum Daily Precip. (in.)	1.34	1.39	2.15	1.71	4.77	4.20	3.87	5.70	3.26	2.18	2.06	2.00	5.70
Days With ≥ 0.1" Precipitation	4	4	5	6	7	7	6	7	5	5	5	5	66
Days With ≥ 0.5" Precipitation	1	1	1	2	2	3	3	3	2	2	2	1	23
Days With ≥ 1.0" Precipitation	0	0	0	1	1	1	1	1	1	0	0	0	6
Mean Snowfall (in.)	10.3	7.6	5.0	1.0	trace	trace	trace	trace	trace	0.1	1.7	10.8	36.5
Maximum Snowfall (in.)*	26	30	23	8	1	0	0	0	0	2	15	25	59
Maximum 24-hr. Snowfall (in.)*	10	8	10	6	1	0	0	0	0	2	7	11	11
Maximum Snow Depth (in.)	19	14	*9*	5	*trace*	*trace*	*trace*	trace	trace	*trace*	*7*	*18*	*19*
Days With ≥ 1.0" Snow Depth	21	15	*5*	1	*0*	*0*	*0*	0	0	*0*	*1*	*15*	*58*
Thunderstorm Days*	< 1	< 1	2	4	5	8	8	6	5	2	1	< 1	41
Foggy Days*	12	11	12	11	11	8	12	16	14	12	13	14	146
Predominant Sky Cover*	OVR	OVR	OVR	OVR	OVR	OVR	OVR	OVR	OVR	OVR	OVR	OVR	OVR
Mean Relative Humidity 6am (%)*	80	81	82	80	80	81	86	90	90	86	83	83	84
Mean Relative Humidity 3pm (%)*	69	64	60	51	50	51	53	56	54	53	63	70	58
Mean Dewpoint (°F)*	13	17	26	36	47	57	62	62	53	41	30	19	39
Prevailing Wind Direction*	WNW	WNW	WNW	ENE	S	S	S	S	S	S	S	WNW	S
Prevailing Wind Speed (mph)*	13	13	13	13	10	9	8	8	8	9	10	13	10
Maximum Wind Gust (mph)*	56	54	54	64	81	67	79	67	58	59	59	62	81

Note: (*) Period of record is 1951-1995

Springfield Capital Airport

The location of Springfield near the center of North America gives it a typical continental climate with warm summers and fairly cold winters. The surrounding country is nearly level. There are no large hills in the vicinity, but rolling terrain is found near the Sangamon River and Spring Creek.

Monthly temperatures range from the upper 20s for January to the upper 70s for July. Considerable variation may take place within the seasons. Temperatures of 70 degrees or higher may occur in winter and temperatures near 50 degrees are sometimes recorded during the summer months.

There are no wet and dry seasons. Monthly precipitation ranges from a little over four inches in May and June to about two inches in January. There is some variation in rainfall totals from year to year. Thunderstorms are common during hot weather, and these are sometimes locally severe with brief but heavy showers. The average year has about fifty thunderstorms of which two-thirds occur during the months of May through August. Damaging hail accompanies only a few of the thunderstorms and the areas affected are usually small.

Sunshine is particularly abundant during the summer months when days are long and not very cloudy. January is the cloudiest month, with only about a third as much sunshine as July or August. March is the windiest month, and August the month with the least wind. Velocities of more than 40 mph are not unusual for brief periods in most months of the year. The prevailing wind direction is southerly during most of the year with northwesterly winds during the late fall and early spring months.

An overall description of the climate of Springfield would be one indicating pleasant conditions with sharp seasonal changes, but no extended periods of severely cold weather. Summer weather is often uncomfortably warm and humid.

Based on the 1951-1980 period, the average first occurrence of 32 degrees Fahrenheit in the fall is October 19 and the average last occurrence in the spring is April 17.

Springfield Capital Airport *Sangamon County* Elevation: 585 ft. Latitude: 39° 51' N Longitude: 89° 41' W

	JAN	FEB	MAR	APR	MAY	JUN	JUL	AUG	SEP	OCT	NOV	DEC	YEAR
Mean Maximum Temp. (°F)	35.1	39.7	51.7	64.2	74.8	83.1	86.3	85.0	78.9	66.2	52.1	38.5	63.0
Mean Temp. (°F)	27.1	31.3	42.0	53.4	63.8	72.6	76.1	74.5	66.9	55.2	43.2	30.7	53.1
Mean Minimum Temp. (°F)	19.2	22.8	32.3	42.5	52.9	62.0	65.8	63.9	54.9	44.1	34.2	22.9	43.1
Extreme Maximum Temp. (°F)	69	74	87	90	94	101	102	102	101	93	81	74	102
Extreme Minimum Temp. (°F)	-21	-19	-2	19	30	39	49	43	32	19	1	-21	-21
Days Maximum Temp. ≥ 90°F	0	0	0	0	1	6	10	7	3	0	0	0	27
Days Maximum Temp. ≤ 32°F	13	8	2	0	0	0	0	0	0	0	1	9	33
Days Minimum Temp. ≤ 32°F	27	22	16	4	0	0	0	0	0	4	14	25	112
Days Minimum Temp. ≤ 0°F	3	2	0	0	0	0	0	0	0	0	0	2	7
Heating Degree Days (base 65°F)	1,167	947	708	362	118	14	0	4	72	322	648	1,055	5,417
Cooling Degree Days (base 65°F)	0	0	3	20	89	248	351	304	137	24	1	0	1,177
Mean Precipitation (in.)	1.80	1.78	2.69	3.46	4.02	4.30	3.82	3.22	2.80	3.16	3.16	2.53	36.74
Maximum Precipitation (in.)*	6.2	4.9	7.9	9.9	10.6	10.8	10.8	8.4	15.2	13.4	6.9	8.9	54.5
Minimum Precipitation (in.)*	trace	0.3	0.2	0.7	0.3	0.2	0.3	0.1	trace	0.1	trace	0.1	22.8
Extreme Maximum Daily Precip. (in.)	1.68	2.37	2.18	2.95	3.54	4.71	4.33	4.40	4.23	3.24	2.05	4.70	4.71
Days With ≥ 0.1" Precipitation	4	4	6	7	7	6	6	5	5	6	6	5	67
Days With ≥ 0.5" Precipitation	1	1	2	2	2	3	3	2	2	2	2	1	23
Days With ≥ 1.0" Precipitation	0	0	1	1	1	1	1	1	1	1	1	1	10
Mean Snowfall (in.)	6.3	5.6	2.7	0.5	trace	0.0	trace	0.0	0.0	trace	0.8	5.4	21.3
Maximum Snowfall (in.)*	21	18	23	8	1	0	0	0	0	3	9	23	48
Maximum 24-hr. Snowfall (in.)*	8	10	9	6	1	0	0	0	0	3	8	11	11
Maximum Snow Depth (in.)	12	11	6	4	trace	0	trace	0	0	trace	4	9	12
Days With ≥ 1.0" Snow Depth	10	8	2	0	0	0	0	0	0	0	0	7	27
Thunderstorm Days*	< 1	1	3	5	7	9	8	7	5	2	2	< 1	49
Foggy Days*	9	8	8	6	6	5	6	9	8	8	8	10	91
Predominant Sky Cover*	OVR	OVR	OVR	OVR	OVR	OVR	SCT	CLR	CLR	CLR	OVR	OVR	OVR
Mean Relative Humidity 6am (%)*	80	81	81	79	81	82	85	89	87	83	82	82	83
Mean Relative Humidity 3pm (%)*	67	65	59	52	51	51	54	56	50	50	60	69	57
Mean Dewpoint (°F)*	18	22	31	41	51	61	65	64	56	44	33	24	43
Prevailing Wind Direction*	S	S	S	S	S	S	S	S	S	S	S	S	S
Prevailing Wind Speed (mph)*	15	14	15	15	13	12	9	9	10	13	14	15	13
Maximum Wind Gust (mph)*	55	53	71	63	67	59	60	69	61	53	76	73	76

Note: (*) Period of record is 1948-1995

Albion *Edwards County*   Elevation: 529 ft.   Latitude: 38° 23' N   Longitude: 88° 03' W

	JAN	FEB	MAR	APR	MAY	JUN	JUL	AUG	SEP	OCT	NOV	DEC	YEAR
Mean Maximum Temp. (°F)	39.4	45.0	54.8	67.3	76.9	85.5	89.9	88.5	82.0	70.6	55.3	42.6	66.5
Mean Temp. (°F)	31.5	36.3	45.1	56.5	66.4	75.1	79.2	77.6	70.4	59.1	46.2	34.5	56.5
Mean Minimum Temp. (°F)	23.9	27.3	35.3	45.7	55.8	64.6	68.4	66.5	58.8	47.5	37.2	26.4	46.5
Extreme Maximum Temp. (°F)	73	75	85	89	97	101	105	104	100	93	81	75	105
Extreme Minimum Temp. (°F)	-20	-11	2	23	32	42	50	47	31	24	11	-18	-20
Days Maximum Temp. ≥ 90°F	0	0	0	0	2	10	16	13	6	0	0	0	47
Days Maximum Temp. ≤ 32°F	7	5	1	0	0	0	0	0	0	0	0	6	19
Days Minimum Temp. ≤ 32°F	23	18	12	2	0	0	0	0	0	1	10	21	87
Days Minimum Temp. ≤ 0°F	1	0	0	0	0	0	0	0	0	0	0	1	2
Heating Degree Days (base 65°F)	1,032	806	612	280	76	6	0	1	36	218	559	937	4,563
Cooling Degree Days (base 65°F)	0	0	4	32	127	315	447	397	206	42	2	0	1,572
Mean Precipitation (in.)	2.62	2.47	4.03	4.86	5.43	3.66	3.55	3.17	2.76	3.66	4.07	3.04	43.32
Extreme Maximum Daily Precip. (in.)	2.90	na	3.80	4.50	na	na	4.20	6.80	4.50	3.20	4.20	4.90	na
Days With ≥ 0.1" Precipitation	4	4	5	7	7	6	4	4	4	5	5	5	60
Days With ≥ 0.5" Precipitation	2	2	3	3	4	2	2	2	2	3	3	2	30
Days With ≥ 1.0" Precipitation	1	1	1	1	1	1	1	1	1	1	1	1	12
Mean Snowfall (in.)	2.0	2.4	1.0	0.0	0.0	0.0	0.0	0.0	0.0	0.1	trace	2.6	8.1
Maximum Snow Depth (in.)	6	10	9	0	0	0	0	0	0	1	trace	7	10
Days With ≥ 1.0" Snow Depth	2	2	0	0	0	0	0	0	0	0	0	0	4

Aledo *Mercer County*   Elevation: 720 ft.   Latitude: 41° 12' N   Longitude: 90° 45' W

	JAN	FEB	MAR	APR	MAY	JUN	JUL	AUG	SEP	OCT	NOV	DEC	YEAR
Mean Maximum Temp. (°F)	31.1	35.6	48.3	62.0	72.5	81.1	84.7	83.0	76.0	63.4	48.7	34.4	60.0
Mean Temp. (°F)	22.8	26.9	38.2	50.5	61.1	70.3	73.9	72.6	64.5	52.5	39.6	26.5	49.9
Mean Minimum Temp. (°F)	14.5	18.2	28.1	39.0	49.8	59.5	63.3	62.1	53.0	41.6	30.5	18.5	39.8
Extreme Maximum Temp. (°F)	69	68	87	91	93	103	103	102	97	91	78	70	103
Extreme Minimum Temp. (°F)	-25	-28	-8	10	23	42	49	45	30	18	0	-20	-28
Days Maximum Temp. ≥ 90°F	0	0	0	0	0	3	7	5	1	0	0	0	16
Days Maximum Temp. ≤ 32°F	16	11	4	0	0	0	0	0	0	0	2	12	45
Days Minimum Temp. ≤ 32°F	29	25	21	7	0	0	0	0	0	5	18	28	133
Days Minimum Temp. ≤ 0°F	5	3	0	0	0	0	0	0	0	0	0	3	11
Heating Degree Days (base 65°F)	1,300	1,072	825	440	167	23	2	7	102	390	755	1,189	6,272
Cooling Degree Days (base 65°F)	0	0	1	11	54	190	285	249	94	10	0	0	894
Mean Precipitation (in.)	1.35	1.53	2.44	3.70	4.34	4.47	3.95	4.53	3.28	2.98	2.34	2.01	36.92
Extreme Maximum Daily Precip. (in.)	2.10	1.75	1.78	1.72	4.80	3.12	3.10	6.27	4.15	3.40	1.60	2.70	6.27
Days With ≥ 0.1" Precipitation	4	4	5	7	8	7	6	7	5	6	5	5	69
Days With ≥ 0.5" Precipitation	1	1	2	3	3	3	3	3	2	2	1	1	25
Days With ≥ 1.0" Precipitation	0	0	1	1	1	1	1	1	1	1	0	0	8
Mean Snowfall (in.)	6.8	4.5	2.7	0.8	trace	0.0	0.0	0.0	0.0	0.1	0.6	5.2	20.7
Maximum Snow Depth (in.)	15	na	4	4	trace	0	0	0	0	trace	2	10	na
Days With ≥ 1.0" Snow Depth	5	3	1	0	0	0	0	0	0	0	0	3	12

Alton Melvin Price L&D *Madison County*   Elevation: 430 ft.   Latitude: 38° 49' N   Longitude: 90° 09' W

	JAN	FEB	MAR	APR	MAY	JUN	JUL	AUG	SEP	OCT	NOV	DEC	YEAR
Mean Maximum Temp. (°F)	37.6	42.4	52.7	64.7	74.5	83.5	87.6	86.5	79.5	67.3	54.4	41.6	64.4
Mean Temp. (°F)	29.7	33.8	43.7	55.1	65.2	74.4	78.5	77.1	69.6	57.3	45.7	34.0	55.3
Mean Minimum Temp. (°F)	21.9	25.1	34.6	45.5	55.7	65.1	69.3	67.6	59.5	47.3	37.0	26.4	46.3
Extreme Maximum Temp. (°F)	71	76	85	90	93	98	106	103	98	97	81	73	106
Extreme Minimum Temp. (°F)	-16	-15	3	20	37	44	52	46	38	25	9	-16	-16
Days Maximum Temp. ≥ 90°F	0	0	0	0	0	6	12	10	3	0	0	0	31
Days Maximum Temp. ≤ 32°F	10	6	1	0	0	0	0	0	0	0	1	6	24
Days Minimum Temp. ≤ 32°F	26	21	13	2	0	0	0	0	0	1	9	21	93
Days Minimum Temp. ≤ 0°F	1	1	0	0	0	0	0	0	0	0	0	1	3
Heating Degree Days (base 65°F)	1,086	877	658	313	87	8	0	2	40	263	572	951	4,857
Cooling Degree Days (base 65°F)	0	0	4	22	99	296	425	382	183	25	1	0	1,437
Mean Precipitation (in.)	2.44	2.25	3.22	4.23	5.09	3.62	3.76	3.27	3.13	3.17	3.78	2.91	40.87
Extreme Maximum Daily Precip. (in.)	2.65	2.10	2.75	7.70	4.70	4.23	3.27	2.97	2.63	3.50	3.00	2.71	7.70
Days With ≥ 0.1" Precipitation	5	5	7	7	8	6	5	6	5	6	6	6	72
Days With ≥ 0.5" Precipitation	2	1	2	3	4	2	2	2	2	2	3	2	27
Days With ≥ 1.0" Precipitation	1	0	1	1	2	1	1	1	1	1	1	1	12
Mean Snowfall (in.)	1.4	1.8	0.8	0.2	0.0	0.0	0.0	0.0	0.0	trace	0.1	0.5	4.8
Maximum Snow Depth (in.)	10	21	6	5	0	0	0	0	0	0	7	5	21
Days With ≥ 1.0" Snow Depth	2	2	0	0	0	0	0	0	0	0	0	1	6

Anna 2 NNE *Union County*   Elevation: 600 ft.   Latitude: 37° 28' N   Longitude: 89° 14' W

	JAN	FEB	MAR	APR	MAY	JUN	JUL	AUG	SEP	OCT	NOV	DEC	YEAR
Mean Maximum Temp. (°F)	43.1	48.4	58.5	69.1	77.2	85.3	88.7	88.6	81.4	70.4	57.8	45.6	67.8
Mean Temp. (°F)	34.0	38.3	47.2	57.2	65.9	74.2	78.1	77.2	69.4	58.3	47.5	36.7	57.0
Mean Minimum Temp. (°F)	24.8	28.1	35.9	45.3	54.5	63.1	67.3	65.7	57.4	46.2	37.1	27.7	46.1
Extreme Maximum Temp. (°F)	69	77	84	90	92	100	104	103	101	90	83	76	104
Extreme Minimum Temp. (°F)	-17	-10	5	20	31	44	49	46	32	20	10	-14	-17
Days Maximum Temp. ≥ 90°F	0	0	0	0	0	8	15	14	4	0	0	0	41
Days Maximum Temp. ≤ 32°F	5	3	0	0	0	0	0	0	0	0	0	4	12
Days Minimum Temp. ≤ 32°F	24	19	13	3	0	0	0	0	0	2	11	21	93
Days Minimum Temp. ≤ 0°F	1	0	0	0	0	0	0	0	0	0	0	1	2
Heating Degree Days (base 65°F)	954	750	548	256	73	4	0	1	38	231	520	872	4,247
Cooling Degree Days (base 65°F)	0	0	3	30	108	287	412	386	178	32	2	0	1,438
Mean Precipitation (in.)	3.66	3.48	4.58	4.50	5.87	4.37	3.36	3.23	3.32	4.29	4.76	4.48	49.90
Extreme Maximum Daily Precip. (in.)	6.70	2.34	7.74	3.22	4.76	4.86	3.26	3.71	4.45	3.42	6.24	4.43	7.74
Days With ≥ 0.1" Precipitation	6	6	7	8	8	6	6	5	5	7	7	7	78
Days With ≥ 0.5" Precipitation	2	3	3	3	4	3	2	2	2	3	3	3	33
Days With ≥ 1.0" Precipitation	1	1	1	1	2	1	1	1	1	1	1	1	13
Mean Snowfall (in.)	3.3	3.9	1.0	0.1	0.0	0.0	0.0	0.0	0.0	0.1	0.3	2.6	11.3
Maximum Snow Depth (in.)	7	10	6	trace	0	0	0	0	0	trace	4	14	14
Days With ≥ 1.0" Snow Depth	4	4	1	0	0	0	0	0	0	0	0	3	12

The period of record for all cooperative weather station data is 1980 – 2009. See User Guide for detailed explanation of data.

Antioch Lake County   Elevation: 750 ft.   Latitude: 42° 29' N   Longitude: 88° 07' W

	JAN	FEB	MAR	APR	MAY	JUN	JUL	AUG	SEP	OCT	NOV	DEC	YEAR
Mean Maximum Temp. (°F)	29.6	33.1	43.6	57.0	68.0	77.7	82.1	80.9	73.6	61.0	46.7	33.6	57.2
Mean Temp. (°F)	21.5	24.7	34.8	47.0	57.2	67.1	71.9	70.9	63.1	50.9	38.5	26.3	47.8
Mean Minimum Temp. (°F)	13.5	16.3	25.9	36.8	46.4	56.5	61.8	60.9	52.7	40.7	30.3	18.8	38.4
Extreme Maximum Temp. (°F)	63	70	78	90	91	96	102	104	95	89	74	68	104
Extreme Minimum Temp. (°F)	-28	-17	-10	6	27	36	42	40	29	18	4	-24	-28
Days Maximum Temp. ≥ 90°F	0	0	0	0	0	2	4	3	1	0	0	0	10
Days Maximum Temp. ≤ 32°F	18	13	5	0	0	0	0	0	0	0	3	13	52
Days Minimum Temp. ≤ 32°F	29	26	23	9	1	0	0	0	0	6	17	28	139
Days Minimum Temp. ≤ 0°F	6	5	1	0	0	0	0	0	0	0	0	3	15
Heating Degree Days (base 65°F)	1,342	1,132	931	542	267	61	10	15	125	438	787	1,193	6,843
Cooling Degree Days (base 65°F)	0	0	1	7	33	132	232	206	77	7	0	0	695
Mean Precipitation (in.)	1.58	1.54	1.85	3.20	4.08	4.05	3.80	4.26	3.58	2.87	2.87	2.09	35.77
Extreme Maximum Daily Precip. (in.)	1.59	1.62	1.87	1.85	2.60	4.64	8.10	3.31	3.81	2.30	1.64	na	na
Days With ≥ 0.1" Precipitation	4	4	4	6	7	7	6	6	6	6	5	5	66
Days With ≥ 0.5" Precipitation	1	1	1	2	3	2	3	3	2	2	2	1	23
Days With ≥ 1.0" Precipitation	0	0	0	1	1	1	1	1	1	1	1	0	8
Mean Snowfall (in.)	11.1	9.1	5.6	1.5	trace	0.0	0.0	0.0	0.0	0.1	1.7	10.1	39.2
Maximum Snow Depth (in.)	21	22	16	8	trace	0	0	0	0	1	4	17	22
Days With ≥ 1.0" Snow Depth	18	15	6	1	0	0	0	0	0	0	1	10	51

Aurora Kane County   Elevation: 640 ft.   Latitude: 41° 46' N   Longitude: 88° 19' W

	JAN	FEB	MAR	APR	MAY	JUN	JUL	AUG	SEP	OCT	NOV	DEC	YEAR
Mean Maximum Temp. (°F)	31.4	36.0	47.7	60.6	71.9	81.2	84.7	82.7	75.9	62.8	48.5	34.7	59.8
Mean Temp. (°F)	22.8	27.0	37.8	49.5	60.1	69.7	73.8	72.1	64.4	51.8	39.8	26.6	49.6
Mean Minimum Temp. (°F)	14.2	17.9	27.7	38.4	48.2	58.1	62.8	61.5	52.9	40.8	30.8	18.5	39.3
Extreme Maximum Temp. (°F)	66	72	83	91	94	103	102	101	95	89	77	69	103
Extreme Minimum Temp. (°F)	-26	-20	-8	8	26	39	42	43	28	15	5	-22	-26
Days Maximum Temp. ≥ 90°F	0	0	0	0	1	5	7	4	2	0	0	0	19
Days Maximum Temp. ≤ 32°F	16	10	3	0	0	0	0	0	0	0	2	11	42
Days Minimum Temp. ≤ 32°F	29	26	22	7	1	0	0	0	0	6	17	28	136
Days Minimum Temp. ≤ 0°F	5	3	0	0	0	0	0	0	0	0	0	3	11
Heating Degree Days (base 65°F)	1,303	1,066	838	466	196	34	3	8	105	414	751	1,186	6,370
Cooling Degree Days (base 65°F)	0	0	1	8	49	181	282	235	94	10	0	0	860
Mean Precipitation (in.)	1.64	1.74	2.34	3.67	3.88	4.02	4.20	4.26	3.57	3.04	3.27	2.27	37.90
Extreme Maximum Daily Precip. (in.)	1.82	3.26	2.47	2.09	3.59	4.38	16.91	3.01	4.00	2.81	2.74	2.83	16.91
Days With ≥ 0.1" Precipitation	4	4	5	7	7	7	6	7	5	6	6	5	69
Days With ≥ 0.5" Precipitation	1	1	1	3	3	2	2	3	2	2	2	1	23
Days With ≥ 1.0" Precipitation	0	0	0	1	1	1	1	1	1	1	1	0	8
Mean Snowfall (in.)	9.6	6.8	2.8	0.6	0.0	0.0	0.0	0.0	0.0	trace	0.9	7.6	28.3
Maximum Snow Depth (in.)	25	18	14	6	0	0	0	0	0	1	4	20	25
Days With ≥ 1.0" Snow Depth	18	13	3	0	0	0	0	0	0	0	1	10	45

Belleville Siu Research St. Clair County   Elevation: 450 ft.   Latitude: 38° 31' N   Longitude: 89° 51' W

	JAN	FEB	MAR	APR	MAY	JUN	JUL	AUG	SEP	OCT	NOV	DEC	YEAR
Mean Maximum Temp. (°F)	41.9	47.1	57.8	68.9	77.6	86.0	89.5	88.5	81.9	71.0	57.4	44.3	67.7
Mean Temp. (°F)	32.9	37.3	46.8	57.1	66.2	74.6	78.3	76.6	69.1	58.3	47.3	35.7	56.7
Mean Minimum Temp. (°F)	23.9	27.4	35.6	45.2	54.8	63.2	67.1	64.7	56.3	45.6	37.1	27.0	45.7
Extreme Maximum Temp. (°F)	73	81	89	91	94	101	105	105	101	94	83	75	105
Extreme Minimum Temp. (°F)	-16	-21	2	18	32	41	49	39	26	20	2	-19	-21
Days Maximum Temp. ≥ 90°F	0	0	0	0	1	10	16	14	5	1	0	0	47
Days Maximum Temp. ≤ 32°F	7	4	1	0	0	0	0	0	0	0	0	5	17
Days Minimum Temp. ≤ 32°F	24	19	13	4	0	0	0	0	0	4	11	22	97
Days Minimum Temp. ≤ 0°F	1	1	0	0	0	0	0	0	0	0	0	1	3
Heating Degree Days (base 65°F)	988	779	565	266	76	5	0	2	45	239	529	903	4,397
Cooling Degree Days (base 65°F)	0	1	7	34	120	300	419	369	175	37	3	0	1,465
Mean Precipitation (in.)	2.25	2.20	3.23	3.85	4.79	4.18	3.81	3.19	3.27	3.50	3.83	2.82	40.92
Extreme Maximum Daily Precip. (in.)	2.17	4.48	2.68	4.58	4.57	3.22	3.48	3.00	3.75	3.45	3.23	3.97	4.58
Days With ≥ 0.1" Precipitation	4	4	6	7	8	7	5	5	5	6	6	5	68
Days With ≥ 0.5" Precipitation	1	1	2	3	3	3	3	2	2	3	3	2	28
Days With ≥ 1.0" Precipitation	1	1	1	1	1	1	1	1	1	1	1	1	12
Mean Snowfall (in.)	4.5	3.2	1.6	0.4	0.0	0.0	0.0	0.0	0.0	0.0	0.4	3.0	13.1
Maximum Snow Depth (in.)	15	19	8	30	0	0	0	0	0	0	3	8	30
Days With ≥ 1.0" Snow Depth	5	3	1	0	0	0	0	0	0	0	0	4	13

Brookport Dam 52 Massac County   Elevation: 330 ft.   Latitude: 37° 08' N   Longitude: 88° 39' W

	JAN	FEB	MAR	APR	MAY	JUN	JUL	AUG	SEP	OCT	NOV	DEC	YEAR
Mean Maximum Temp. (°F)	43.6	48.2	58.1	68.9	77.4	85.5	89.3	88.8	81.7	70.3	58.1	46.1	68.0
Mean Temp. (°F)	35.0	39.0	47.7	57.9	66.8	74.9	79.0	77.8	70.4	58.9	48.3	37.6	57.8
Mean Minimum Temp. (°F)	26.3	29.7	37.3	46.7	56.2	64.3	68.6	66.8	58.9	47.3	38.4	29.0	47.5
Extreme Maximum Temp. (°F)	72	74	83	89	94	100	105	103	99	92	85	74	105
Extreme Minimum Temp. (°F)	-21	-9	9	21	34	43	52	42	29	18	9	-13	-21
Days Maximum Temp. ≥ 90°F	0	0	0	0	1	8	16	14	5	0	0	0	44
Days Maximum Temp. ≤ 32°F	5	3	0	0	0	0	0	0	0	0	0	4	12
Days Minimum Temp. ≤ 32°F	22	17	12	2	0	0	0	0	0	2	9	19	83
Days Minimum Temp. ≤ 0°F	1	0	0	0	0	0	0	0	0	0	0	0	1
Heating Degree Days (base 65°F)	924	730	532	238	60	3	0	1	34	223	498	844	4,087
Cooling Degree Days (base 65°F)	0	0	4	29	123	309	441	405	201	40	3	0	1,555
Mean Precipitation (in.)	3.49	3.92	4.14	4.64	4.97	4.13	4.15	2.82	3.49	3.97	4.16	4.56	48.44
Extreme Maximum Daily Precip. (in.)	2.60	5.32	3.88	5.20	3.66	3.20	3.60	2.93	3.88	3.50	3.40	3.50	5.32
Days With ≥ 0.1" Precipitation	6	6	7	8	8	6	5	4	5	6	7	7	75
Days With ≥ 0.5" Precipitation	2	3	2	3	3	3	3	2	3	3	3	4	34
Days With ≥ 1.0" Precipitation	1	1	1	1	1	1	1	1	1	1	1	1	12
Mean Snowfall (in.)	2.1	2.4	0.5	trace	0.0	0.0	0.0	0.0	0.0	0.0	0.0	1.7	6.7
Maximum Snow Depth (in.)	8	7	10	trace	0	0	0	0	0	0	0	13	13
Days With ≥ 1.0" Snow Depth	3	3	0	0	0	0	0	0	0	0	0	2	8

The period of record for all cooperative weather station data is 1980 – 2009. See User Guide for detailed explanation of data.

Cahokia *St. Clair County*   Elevation: 399 ft.   Latitude: 38° 34' N   Longitude: 90° 12' W

	JAN	FEB	MAR	APR	MAY	JUN	JUL	AUG	SEP	OCT	NOV	DEC	YEAR
Mean Maximum Temp. (°F)	41.2	46.1	56.4	67.9	76.5	85.1	88.6	87.3	80.6	69.6	56.7	43.6	66.6
Mean Temp. (°F)	32.0	35.9	45.3	56.4	65.6	74.7	78.5	76.8	69.1	57.6	46.4	34.5	56.1
Mean Minimum Temp. (°F)	22.6	25.7	34.5	44.9	54.7	64.1	68.3	66.1	57.5	45.5	35.9	25.4	45.4
Extreme Maximum Temp. (°F)	78	81	89	93	94	102	106	105	102	94	85	74	106
Extreme Minimum Temp. (°F)	-17	-16	4	18	32	42	54	41	32	22	10	-19	-19
Days Maximum Temp. ≥ 90°F	0	0	0	0	1	9	15	11	4	0	0	0	40
Days Maximum Temp. ≤ 32°F	7	4	1	0	0	0	0	0	0	0	0	5	17
Days Minimum Temp. ≤ 32°F	26	21	14	3	0	0	0	0	0	3	12	23	102
Days Minimum Temp. ≤ 0°F	1	1	0	0	0	0	0	0	0	0	0	0	2
Heating Degree Days (base 65°F)	1,017	816	603	283	85	6	0	2	44	257	555	939	4,607
Cooling Degree Days (base 65°F)	0	0	6	31	111	302	427	374	173	33	3	0	1,460
Mean Precipitation (in.)	2.45	2.55	3.39	3.81	4.52	4.02	4.44	3.51	3.23	3.43	3.67	2.99	42.01
Extreme Maximum Daily Precip. (in.)	2.39	2.47	2.83	3.00	4.37	2.68	3.47	4.27	3.15	2.52	2.30	2.55	4.37
Days With ≥ 0.1" Precipitation	5	5	7	8	8	7	6	6	5	6	7	6	76
Days With ≥ 0.5" Precipitation	1	2	2	3	3	3	2	2	3	3	3	2	29
Days With ≥ 1.0" Precipitation	1	1	1	1	1	1	2	1	1	1	1	1	13
Mean Snowfall (in.)	5.0	3.8	1.9	0.2	0.0	0.0	0.0	0.0	0.0	trace	0.6	3.9	15.4
Maximum Snow Depth (in.)	8	10	11	3	0	0	0	0	0	trace	4	9	11
Days With ≥ 1.0" Snow Depth	6	3	1	0	0	0	0	0	0	0	0	4	14

Carbondale Sewage Plant *Jackson County*   Elevation: 390 ft.   Latitude: 37° 44' N   Longitude: 89° 10' W

	JAN	FEB	MAR	APR	MAY	JUN	JUL	AUG	SEP	OCT	NOV	DEC	YEAR
Mean Maximum Temp. (°F)	41.5	46.4	56.1	67.2	76.3	84.8	88.4	88.3	81.2	69.3	56.9	44.9	66.8
Mean Temp. (°F)	32.4	36.2	45.1	55.5	65.0	73.9	77.6	76.2	68.2	56.1	46.2	35.5	55.7
Mean Minimum Temp. (°F)	23.2	25.9	34.1	43.7	53.7	62.9	66.8	64.1	55.2	42.9	35.4	26.1	44.5
Extreme Maximum Temp. (°F)	70	79	84	90	95	102	103	105	99	93	83	77	105
Extreme Minimum Temp. (°F)	-21	-11	5	21	31	41	51	43	30	18	10	-14	-21
Days Maximum Temp. ≥ 90°F	0	0	0	0	1	8	13	13	4	0	0	0	39
Days Maximum Temp. ≤ 32°F	7	4	1	0	0	0	0	0	0	0	0	4	16
Days Minimum Temp. ≤ 32°F	25	21	15	4	0	0	0	0	0	5	13	22	105
Days Minimum Temp. ≤ 0°F	1	1	0	0	0	0	0	0	0	0	0	1	3
Heating Degree Days (base 65°F)	1,006	809	612	305	90	7	0	2	53	293	559	908	4,644
Cooling Degree Days (base 65°F)	0	0	4	27	99	280	399	355	156	25	2	0	1,347
Mean Precipitation (in.)	3.15	3.06	4.25	4.47	5.47	4.60	3.68	3.10	3.10	3.72	4.43	4.07	47.10
Extreme Maximum Daily Precip. (in.)	3.52	3.75	6.10	4.96	4.14	6.90	4.35	3.19	4.22	3.47	5.35	3.57	6.90
Days With ≥ 0.1" Precipitation	6	6	7	8	8	6	5	5	5	5	7	6	74
Days With ≥ 0.5" Precipitation	2	2	3	3	4	3	2	2	2	3	3	3	32
Days With ≥ 1.0" Precipitation	1	1	1	1	2	1	1	1	1	1	1	1	13
Mean Snowfall (in.)	2.9	3.6	1.1	trace	0.0	0.0	0.0	0.0	0.0	0.1	0.3	2.7	10.7
Maximum Snow Depth (in.)	7	11	10	trace	0	0	0	0	0	0	2	7	13	13
Days With ≥ 1.0" Snow Depth	4	4	1	0	0	0	0	0	0	0	0	3	12

Carlinville *Macoupin County*   Elevation: 629 ft.   Latitude: 39° 17' N   Longitude: 89° 53' W

	JAN	FEB	MAR	APR	MAY	JUN	JUL	AUG	SEP	OCT	NOV	DEC	YEAR
Mean Maximum Temp. (°F)	36.5	42.4	53.4	65.4	75.3	83.7	86.9	85.7	79.3	67.1	53.5	39.9	64.1
Mean Temp. (°F)	28.5	33.6	43.4	54.3	64.4	73.2	76.7	74.9	67.7	56.0	44.5	32.2	54.1
Mean Minimum Temp. (°F)	20.6	24.8	33.4	43.2	53.5	62.7	66.4	64.1	56.0	44.8	35.4	24.5	44.1
Extreme Maximum Temp. (°F)	70	75	86	90	92	99	103	105	99	92	79	74	105
Extreme Minimum Temp. (°F)	-19	-17	-2	18	30	42	49	41	31	20	1	-15	-19
Days Maximum Temp. ≥ 90°F	0	0	0	0	0	6	11	9	3	0	0	0	29
Days Maximum Temp. ≤ 32°F	11	7	1	0	0	0	0	0	0	0	1	7	27
Days Minimum Temp. ≤ 32°F	27	21	15	4	0	0	0	0	0	4	12	24	107
Days Minimum Temp. ≤ 0°F	2	1	0	0	0	0	0	0	0	0	0	1	4
Heating Degree Days (base 65°F)	1,124	882	667	334	103	10	1	4	60	296	610	1,009	5,100
Cooling Degree Days (base 65°F)	0	0	4	20	92	263	369	319	147	24	1	0	1,239
Mean Precipitation (in.)	2.11	2.05	3.11	3.96	3.98	3.54	3.57	3.19	3.22	3.24	3.70	2.82	38.49
Extreme Maximum Daily Precip. (in.)	2.18	2.84	2.10	2.84	2.74	3.38	2.49	3.49	3.21	2.38	2.98	3.75	3.75
Days With ≥ 0.1" Precipitation	4	4	7	7	7	7	6	5	5	6	6	5	69
Days With ≥ 0.5" Precipitation	1	1	2	3	3	3	3	2	2	2	3	2	27
Days With ≥ 1.0" Precipitation	0	0	1	1	1	1	1	1	1	1	1	1	10
Mean Snowfall (in.)	5.9	4.4	2.7	0.4	trace	0.0	0.0	0.0	0.0	trace	0.9	3.4	17.7
Maximum Snow Depth (in.)	12	12	7	5	0	0	0	0	0	trace	4	8	12
Days With ≥ 1.0" Snow Depth	8	5	2	0	0	0	0	0	0	0	0	5	20

Charleston *Coles County*   Elevation: 680 ft.   Latitude: 39° 29' N   Longitude: 88° 10' W

	JAN	FEB	MAR	APR	MAY	JUN	JUL	AUG	SEP	OCT	NOV	DEC	YEAR
Mean Maximum Temp. (°F)	36.6	41.4	52.7	65.4	75.1	83.6	86.5	85.0	79.0	66.8	53.1	39.9	63.8
Mean Temp. (°F)	28.7	32.9	43.0	54.5	64.3	72.9	76.4	74.8	67.7	56.2	44.4	32.2	54.0
Mean Minimum Temp. (°F)	20.7	24.3	33.2	43.6	53.3	62.2	66.2	64.5	56.4	45.5	35.6	24.5	44.2
Extreme Maximum Temp. (°F)	69	74	84	89	94	102	101	102	97	91	80	71	102
Extreme Minimum Temp. (°F)	-27	-18	-1	17	29	38	50	42	32	20	6	-20	-27
Days Maximum Temp. ≥ 90°F	0	0	0	0	1	6	9	8	3	0	0	0	27
Days Maximum Temp. ≤ 32°F	11	7	1	0	0	0	0	0	0	0	1	7	27
Days Minimum Temp. ≤ 32°F	26	21	15	4	0	0	0	0	0	3	12	23	104
Days Minimum Temp. ≤ 0°F	2	1	0	0	0	0	0	0	0	0	0	1	4
Heating Degree Days (base 65°F)	1,120	900	678	329	106	11	0	3	59	293	613	1,010	5,122
Cooling Degree Days (base 65°F)	0	0	4	22	90	256	360	314	147	26	1	0	1,220
Mean Precipitation (in.)	2.35	2.39	3.02	4.15	4.47	3.86	4.18	3.31	3.22	3.85	3.96	3.09	41.85
Extreme Maximum Daily Precip. (in.)	1.76	2.70	2.24	3.55	4.66	3.23	3.46	2.75	4.95	3.61	2.49	2.87	4.95
Days With ≥ 0.1" Precipitation	5	5	7	8	8	6	6	5	5	6	7	6	74
Days With ≥ 0.5" Precipitation	1	1	2	3	3	3	3	2	2	3	3	2	28
Days With ≥ 1.0" Precipitation	1	0	0	1	1	1	1	1	1	1	1	1	10
Mean Snowfall (in.)	8.5	3.8	2.1	0.2	trace	0.0	0.0	0.0	0.0	trace	1.0	5.1	20.7
Maximum Snow Depth (in.)	24	21	9	2	trace	0	0	0	0	trace	8	9	24
Days With ≥ 1.0" Snow Depth	11	8	3	0	0	0	0	0	0	0	1	7	30

The period of record for all cooperative weather station data is 1980 – 2009. See User Guide for detailed explanation of data.

Chenoa *Mclean County*   Elevation: 709 ft.   Latitude: 40° 44' N   Longitude: 88° 43' W

	JAN	FEB	MAR	APR	MAY	JUN	JUL	AUG	SEP	OCT	NOV	DEC	YEAR
Mean Maximum Temp. (°F)	33.4	38.0	50.2	63.7	74.5	83.0	85.2	83.6	78.0	65.2	50.5	36.6	61.8
Mean Temp. (°F)	25.0	29.2	40.0	52.0	62.8	71.8	74.6	72.8	66.0	54.1	41.7	28.8	51.6
Mean Minimum Temp. (°F)	16.6	20.4	29.7	40.4	50.9	60.5	64.0	61.9	53.9	43.0	32.8	21.0	41.3
Extreme Maximum Temp. (°F)	66	73	85	91	95	102	101	103	98	91	79	70	103
Extreme Minimum Temp. (°F)	-25	-19	-6	7	26	38	45	40	28	17	5	-26	-26
Days Maximum Temp. ≥ 90°F	0	0	0	0	1	6	7	5	2	0	0	0	21
Days Maximum Temp. ≤ 32°F	14	9	2	0	0	0	0	0	0	0	1	10	36
Days Minimum Temp. ≤ 32°F	29	25	20	6	0	0	0	0	0	4	16	26	126
Days Minimum Temp. ≤ 0°F	4	2	0	0	0	0	0	0	0	0	0	2	8
Heating Degree Days (base 65°F)	1,232	1,006	771	397	137	16	1	7	80	348	693	1,114	5,802
Cooling Degree Days (base 65°F)	0	0	2	15	74	227	307	255	117	17	0	0	1,014
Mean Precipitation (in.)	1.72	1.34	2.90	3.28	3.95	3.79	3.54	3.21	2.86	3.10	2.87	2.23	34.79
Extreme Maximum Daily Precip. (in.)	1.89	1.80	3.73	1.79	2.45	3.63	2.81	3.93	3.59	5.66	2.21	5.07	5.66
Days With ≥ 0.1" Precipitation	4	3	6	7	7	6	6	5	5	6	6	4	65
Days With ≥ 0.5" Precipitation	1	1	2	3	3	3	3	2	2	2	2	1	25
Days With ≥ 1.0" Precipitation	0	0	0	1	1	1	1	1	1	1	1	0	8
Mean Snowfall (in.)	5.0	5.5	1.8	0.9	trace	0.0	0.0	0.0	0.0	0.0	1.0	4.2	18.4
Maximum Snow Depth (in.)	14	20	5	5	0	0	0	0	0	trace	4	14	20
Days With ≥ 1.0" Snow Depth	9	9	2	0	0	0	0	0	0	0	1	6	27

Chicago Botanical Garden *Cook County*   Elevation: 629 ft.   Latitude: 42° 08' N   Longitude: 87° 47' W

	JAN	FEB	MAR	APR	MAY	JUN	JUL	AUG	SEP	OCT	NOV	DEC	YEAR
Mean Maximum Temp. (°F)	31.9	35.7	45.2	56.3	67.3	77.7	82.5	81.2	74.5	62.4	48.5	35.8	58.3
Mean Temp. (°F)	24.1	27.5	36.7	47.1	57.3	67.3	72.8	71.7	64.2	52.4	40.7	28.2	49.2
Mean Minimum Temp. (°F)	16.2	19.2	28.2	37.8	47.2	56.8	63.0	62.2	53.8	42.3	32.8	20.6	40.0
Extreme Maximum Temp. (°F)	65	74	83	90	93	102	105	101	97	89	76	70	105
Extreme Minimum Temp. (°F)	-27	-20	-5	10	28	37	45	42	30	24	6	-20	-27
Days Maximum Temp. ≥ 90°F	0	0	0	0	1	4	6	4	1	0	0	0	16
Days Maximum Temp. ≤ 32°F	16	10	4	0	0	0	0	0	0	0	2	10	42
Days Minimum Temp. ≤ 32°F	28	25	21	8	0	0	0	0	0	4	14	27	127
Days Minimum Temp. ≤ 0°F	4	2	0	0	0	0	0	0	0	0	0	2	8
Heating Degree Days (base 65°F)	1,262	1,054	872	541	272	70	8	12	108	394	724	1,134	6,451
Cooling Degree Days (base 65°F)	0	0	1	10	40	145	257	228	90	10	0	0	781
Mean Precipitation (in.)	1.95	1.71	2.45	3.53	4.01	3.55	3.51	4.72	3.52	3.31	3.06	2.40	37.72
Extreme Maximum Daily Precip. (in.)	2.14	3.20	2.00	2.58	2.97	4.50	3.03	5.54	3.35	3.59	2.33	2.79	5.54
Days With ≥ 0.1" Precipitation	5	4	6	7	8	6	6	7	6	6	6	6	73
Days With ≥ 0.5" Precipitation	1	1	2	3	3	2	2	3	2	2	2	1	24
Days With ≥ 1.0" Precipitation	0	0	0	1	1	1	1	1	1	1	1	0	8
Mean Snowfall (in.)	10.2	8.1	5.2	0.9	trace	0.0	0.0	0.0	0.0	0.1	1.5	7.8	33.8
Maximum Snow Depth (in.)	15	15	13	9	trace	0	0	0	0	trace	5	18	18
Days With ≥ 1.0" Snow Depth	19	14	6	1	0	0	0	0	0	0	1	10	51

Chicago Midway Arpt *Cook County*   Elevation: 620 ft.   Latitude: 41° 44' N   Longitude: 87° 47' W

	JAN	FEB	MAR	APR	MAY	JUN	JUL	AUG	SEP	OCT	NOV	DEC	YEAR
Mean Maximum Temp. (°F)	32.2	36.4	47.3	59.7	70.9	80.6	84.8	82.6	75.9	63.0	49.0	36.0	59.9
Mean Temp. (°F)	25.4	29.2	39.1	50.4	61.0	70.9	75.8	74.1	66.7	54.2	41.8	29.4	51.5
Mean Minimum Temp. (°F)	18.4	21.9	30.9	41.0	51.1	61.2	66.8	65.6	57.5	45.3	34.6	22.8	43.1
Extreme Maximum Temp. (°F)	67	73	86	91	94	104	106	102	98	89	77	69	106
Extreme Minimum Temp. (°F)	-25	-17	-4	10	28	39	48	46	34	20	7	-20	-25
Days Maximum Temp. ≥ 90°F	0	0	0	0	1	5	8	5	2	0	0	0	21
Days Maximum Temp. ≤ 32°F	15	10	3	0	0	0	0	0	0	0	2	11	41
Days Minimum Temp. ≤ 32°F	27	23	18	5	0	0	0	0	0	2	12	25	112
Days Minimum Temp. ≤ 0°F	3	1	0	0	0	0	0	0	0	0	0	1	5
Heating Degree Days (base 65°F)	1,222	1,008	797	446	182	29	1	4	71	346	689	1,097	5,892
Cooling Degree Days (base 65°F)	0	0	2	12	65	213	342	293	128	16	0	0	1,071
Mean Precipitation (in.)	2.04	1.92	2.70	3.60	4.13	3.91	3.85	4.09	3.42	3.26	3.38	2.57	38.87
Extreme Maximum Daily Precip. (in.)	1.59	3.25	2.02	1.84	2.80	3.16	5.72	3.90	4.16	3.80	3.49	2.78	5.72
Days With ≥ 0.1" Precipitation	5	5	6	7	7	6	6	6	5	6	6	5	70
Days With ≥ 0.5" Precipitation	1	1	2	2	3	3	3	3	2	2	2	1	25
Days With ≥ 1.0" Precipitation	0	0	0	1	1	1	1	1	1	1	1	1	9
Mean Snowfall (in.)	11.6	9.3	5.6	1.1	trace	0.0	trace	0.0	trace	0.1	1.4	8.5	37.6
Maximum Snow Depth (in.)	21	17	13	10	0	0	trace	0	trace	2	4	20	21
Days With ≥ 1.0" Snow Depth	18	13	5	1	0	0	0	0	0	0	1	10	48

Danville *Vermilion County*   Elevation: 558 ft.   Latitude: 40° 08' N   Longitude: 87° 39' W

	JAN	FEB	MAR	APR	MAY	JUN	JUL	AUG	SEP	OCT	NOV	DEC	YEAR
Mean Maximum Temp. (°F)	35.4	40.2	51.7	64.8	75.0	83.2	85.7	84.2	78.5	66.2	52.3	38.7	63.0
Mean Temp. (°F)	27.4	31.4	41.6	53.3	63.1	71.9	75.2	73.7	66.8	54.9	43.4	31.1	52.8
Mean Minimum Temp. (°F)	19.3	22.6	31.5	41.7	51.2	60.4	64.6	63.1	55.0	43.6	34.5	23.5	42.6
Extreme Maximum Temp. (°F)	68	74	84	90	93	102	102	102	96	89	79	72	102
Extreme Minimum Temp. (°F)	-26	-22	-6	12	29	39	46	41	29	19	8	-25	-26
Days Maximum Temp. ≥ 90°F	0	0	0	0	1	5	7	5	2	0	0	0	20
Days Maximum Temp. ≤ 32°F	13	8	2	0	0	0	0	0	0	0	1	9	33
Days Minimum Temp. ≤ 32°F	26	23	17	6	0	0	0	0	0	4	14	24	114
Days Minimum Temp. ≤ 0°F	3	2	0	0	0	0	0	0	0	0	0	2	7
Heating Degree Days (base 65°F)	1,161	944	719	363	128	16	1	4	66	325	642	1,045	5,414
Cooling Degree Days (base 65°F)	0	0	2	18	76	228	324	279	126	20	1	0	1,074
Mean Precipitation (in.)	2.17	2.22	3.03	3.95	4.52	4.52	4.61	3.53	2.93	3.60	3.77	2.79	41.64
Extreme Maximum Daily Precip. (in.)	1.91	2.45	2.59	3.92	3.46	3.86	2.94	3.34	3.70	2.54	3.71	1.71	3.92
Days With ≥ 0.1" Precipitation	5	5	7	8	8	7	7	6	5	6	7	7	78
Days With ≥ 0.5" Precipitation	1	1	2	3	3	3	4	2	2	3	3	2	29
Days With ≥ 1.0" Precipitation	0	0	1	1	1	1	1	1	1	1	1	0	9
Mean Snowfall (in.)	4.5	4.4	2.1	0.2	trace	0.0	0.0	0.0	0.0	0.1	0.6	4.0	15.9
Maximum Snow Depth (in.)	13	14	7	2	trace	0	0	0	0	trace	5	11	14
Days With ≥ 1.0" Snow Depth	8	7	2	0	0	0	0	0	0	0	1	6	23

The period of record for all cooperative weather station data is 1980 – 2009. See User Guide for detailed explanation of data.

De Kalb *Dekalb County*   Elevation: 873 ft.   Latitude: 41° 56' N   Longitude: 88° 47' W

	JAN	FEB	MAR	APR	MAY	JUN	JUL	AUG	SEP	OCT	NOV	DEC	YEAR
Mean Maximum Temp. (°F)	28.2	33.2	45.2	59.2	70.7	80.3	83.6	81.6	75.4	62.1	46.9	33.0	58.3
Mean Temp. (°F)	20.5	25.2	36.0	48.5	59.5	69.6	73.2	71.4	64.1	51.3	38.5	25.7	48.6
Mean Minimum Temp. (°F)	12.8	17.1	26.9	37.6	48.2	58.8	62.9	61.0	52.8	40.5	30.1	18.3	38.9
Extreme Maximum Temp. (°F)	62	69	81	91	95	101	102	103	94	89	76	65	103
Extreme Minimum Temp. (°F)	-27	-23	-13	8	24	34	46	42	27	13	5	-22	-27
Days Maximum Temp. ≥ 90°F	0	0	0	0	0	4	5	4	1	0	0	0	14
Days Maximum Temp. ≤ 32°F	20	13	5	0	0	0	0	0	0	0	3	14	55
Days Minimum Temp. ≤ 32°F	30	26	23	8	1	0	0	0	0	7	18	28	141
Days Minimum Temp. ≤ 0°F	6	4	0	0	0	0	0	0	0	0	0	3	13
Heating Degree Days (base 65°F)	1,373	1,121	892	498	209	36	4	14	111	427	787	1,213	6,685
Cooling Degree Days (base 65°F)	0	0	1	9	44	180	267	218	91	9	0	0	819
Mean Precipitation (in.)	1.43	1.55	2.25	3.27	4.48	4.09	4.27	4.67	3.38	2.90	2.67	2.19	37.15
Extreme Maximum Daily Precip. (in.)	1.46	2.60	1.72	2.08	2.81	2.79	8.09	5.71	3.47	2.82	2.20	2.03	8.09
Days With ≥ 0.1" Precipitation	4	4	5	7	8	7	6	6	6	6	5	5	69
Days With ≥ 0.5" Precipitation	0	1	1	2	3	3	2	3	2	2	2	1	22
Days With ≥ 1.0" Precipitation	0	0	0	1	1	1	1	1	1	1	1	0	8
Mean Snowfall (in.)	9.9	7.4	4.3	1.0	trace	0.0	0.0	0.0	0.0	0.1	1.2	9.6	33.5
Maximum Snow Depth (in.)	17	17	10	5	trace	0	0	0	0	1	5	17	17
Days With ≥ 1.0" Snow Depth	21	15	5	1	0	0	0	0	0	0	1	12	55

Decatur *Macon County*   Elevation: 620 ft.   Latitude: 39° 49' N   Longitude: 89° 01' W

	JAN	FEB	MAR	APR	MAY	JUN	JUL	AUG	SEP	OCT	NOV	DEC	YEAR
Mean Maximum Temp. (°F)	36.2	41.4	52.8	65.7	75.9	84.5	87.6	86.1	80.1	67.5	53.1	39.9	64.2
Mean Temp. (°F)	27.7	32.3	42.5	54.1	64.0	73.0	76.5	74.9	67.9	55.9	43.8	31.8	53.7
Mean Minimum Temp. (°F)	19.2	23.2	32.3	42.5	52.0	61.5	65.4	63.6	55.7	44.3	34.5	23.6	43.2
Extreme Maximum Temp. (°F)	67	73	86	93	95	103	104	106	100	95	80	71	106
Extreme Minimum Temp. (°F)	-22	-20	-4	15	27	39	48	42	29	18	0	-22	-22
Days Maximum Temp. ≥ 90°F	0	0	0	0	1	7	11	8	4	0	0	0	31
Days Maximum Temp. ≤ 32°F	11	6	2	0	0	0	0	0	0	0	1	7	27
Days Minimum Temp. ≤ 32°F	27	23	16	5	0	0	0	0	0	4	13	24	112
Days Minimum Temp. ≤ 0°F	3	2	0	0	0	0	0	0	0	0	0	1	6
Heating Degree Days (base 65°F)	1,148	918	692	339	110	11	0	4	59	300	630	1,024	5,235
Cooling Degree Days (base 65°F)	0	0	2	20	86	258	363	317	153	25	1	0	1,225
Mean Precipitation (in.)	2.21	2.04	2.73	3.70	4.59	4.02	3.80	3.69	3.06	3.38	3.39	2.68	39.29
Extreme Maximum Daily Precip. (in.)	2.12	2.70	1.80	2.54	3.78	3.77	5.11	3.38	5.84	4.09	2.00	2.16	5.84
Days With ≥ 0.1" Precipitation	4	4	6	7	7	6	6	5	5	6	6	6	68
Days With ≥ 0.5" Precipitation	1	1	2	3	3	3	3	3	2	2	2	2	27
Days With ≥ 1.0" Precipitation	1	1	0	1	1	1	1	1	1	1	1	0	10
Mean Snowfall (in.)	6.0	4.3	1.9	0.2	trace	0.0	0.0	0.0	0.0	trace	0.7	5.0	18.1
Maximum Snow Depth (in.)	10	14	10	3	trace	0	0	0	0	trace	9	12	14
Days With ≥ 1.0" Snow Depth	10	7	2	0	0	0	0	0	0	0	1	5	25

Dixon 1 NW *Lee County*   Elevation: 700 ft.   Latitude: 41° 51' N   Longitude: 89° 30' W

	JAN	FEB	MAR	APR	MAY	JUN	JUL	AUG	SEP	OCT	NOV	DEC	YEAR
Mean Maximum Temp. (°F)	29.1	33.7	45.9	60.1	70.8	79.5	82.9	81.4	74.7	62.3	47.6	33.2	58.4
Mean Temp. (°F)	20.4	24.6	36.3	48.9	59.7	68.9	72.7	71.0	63.0	50.8	38.5	25.1	48.3
Mean Minimum Temp. (°F)	11.6	15.5	26.6	37.6	48.5	58.2	62.4	60.5	51.3	39.3	29.3	17.0	38.2
Extreme Maximum Temp. (°F)	65	71	87	93	93	100	101	103	97	91	78	68	103
Extreme Minimum Temp. (°F)	-32	-26	-13	8	24	38	45	40	28	17	4	-25	-32
Days Maximum Temp. ≥ 90°F	0	0	0	0	0	2	5	4	1	0	0	0	12
Days Maximum Temp. ≤ 32°F	18	12	4	0	0	0	0	0	0	0	3	13	50
Days Minimum Temp. ≤ 32°F	30	26	23	9	1	0	0	0	0	8	19	28	144
Days Minimum Temp. ≤ 0°F	7	5	0	0	0	0	0	0	0	0	0	4	16
Heating Degree Days (base 65°F)	1,377	1,136	884	486	204	37	6	15	129	442	789	1,230	6,735
Cooling Degree Days (base 65°F)	0	0	1	9	47	161	251	207	75	10	0	0	761
Mean Precipitation (in.)	1.51	1.59	2.43	3.51	4.33	4.71	4.07	4.62	3.49	2.86	2.67	2.13	37.92
Extreme Maximum Daily Precip. (in.)	1.76	1.79	2.19	2.64	4.16	4.54	4.36	4.08	4.95	3.33	1.92	3.12	4.95
Days With ≥ 0.1" Precipitation	4	4	5	7	8	8	6	7	5	5	5	5	69
Days With ≥ 0.5" Precipitation	1	1	2	2	3	3	3	3	2	2	2	1	25
Days With ≥ 1.0" Precipitation	0	0	0	1	1	1	1	1	1	1	0	0	7
Mean Snowfall (in.)	10.3	6.9	3.7	0.8	0.0	0.0	0.0	0.0	0.0	0.1	1.3	8.5	31.6
Maximum Snow Depth (in.)	24	13	11	4	0	0	0	0	0	trace	7	19	24
Days With ≥ 1.0" Snow Depth	18	14	4	0	0	0	0	0	0	0	1	11	48

Effingham *Effingham County*   Elevation: 595 ft.   Latitude: 39° 08' N   Longitude: 88° 32' W

	JAN	FEB	MAR	APR	MAY	JUN	JUL	AUG	SEP	OCT	NOV	DEC	YEAR
Mean Maximum Temp. (°F)	36.4	40.6	52.1	64.4	74.3	83.7	87.2	86.1	79.1	66.6	53.7	39.9	63.7
Mean Temp. (°F)	28.2	31.4	42.0	53.4	63.3	72.7	76.5	74.8	67.0	55.0	44.1	31.6	53.4
Mean Minimum Temp. (°F)	19.9	22.2	31.9	42.4	52.3	61.8	65.8	63.5	54.9	43.3	34.5	23.2	43.0
Extreme Maximum Temp. (°F)	69	74	84	89	94	102	102	103	98	93	81	71	103
Extreme Minimum Temp. (°F)	-22	-19	-2	21	30	39	50	44	33	20	7	-16	-22
Days Maximum Temp. ≥ 90°F	0	0	0	0	1	7	11	10	3	0	0	0	32
Days Maximum Temp. ≤ 32°F	11	7	2	0	0	0	0	0	0	0	1	8	29
Days Minimum Temp. ≤ 32°F	27	23	17	4	0	0	0	0	0	4	14	24	113
Days Minimum Temp. ≤ 0°F	2	2	0	0	0	0	0	0	0	0	0	2	6
Heating Degree Days (base 65°F)	1,134	943	708	360	122	14	1	4	70	325	621	1,029	5,331
Cooling Degree Days (base 65°F)	0	0	3	19	78	253	364	316	138	21	1	0	1,193
Mean Precipitation (in.)	2.43	2.72	3.23	3.87	5.07	4.21	4.34	2.88	3.09	3.74	4.05	3.30	42.93
Extreme Maximum Daily Precip. (in.)	2.24	2.78	2.50	2.61	3.79	5.70	5.25	2.90	3.39	4.45	3.17	3.27	5.70
Days With ≥ 0.1" Precipitation	5	5	7	8	9	7	7	5	5	6	7	6	77
Days With ≥ 0.5" Precipitation	2	2	2	2	4	3	3	2	2	3	3	2	30
Days With ≥ 1.0" Precipitation	1	1	1	1	1	1	1	1	1	1	1	1	12
Mean Snowfall (in.)	5.7	5.1	2.1	0.1	0.0	0.0	0.0	0.0	0.0	trace	1.0	3.8	17.8
Maximum Snow Depth (in.)	10	16	8	trace	0	0	0	0	0	trace	10	8	16
Days With ≥ 1.0" Snow Depth	7	7	2	0	0	0	0	0	0	0	1	5	22

The period of record for all cooperative weather station data is 1980 – 2009. See User Guide for detailed explanation of data.

Elgin Kane County   Elevation: 763 ft.   Latitude: 42° 04' N   Longitude: 88° 17' W

	JAN	FEB	MAR	APR	MAY	JUN	JUL	AUG	SEP	OCT	NOV	DEC	YEAR
Mean Maximum Temp. (°F)	29.4	33.8	45.0	58.3	69.7	79.5	83.3	81.6	74.8	61.7	47.3	33.3	58.1
Mean Temp. (°F)	21.4	25.3	35.6	47.7	58.7	68.4	73.1	71.4	63.5	50.8	38.8	25.6	48.4
Mean Minimum Temp. (°F)	13.4	16.7	26.2	37.1	47.7	57.3	62.8	61.0	52.1	39.8	30.3	18.1	38.5
Extreme Maximum Temp. (°F)	63	70	82	91	92	101	101	98	95	88	75	67	101
Extreme Minimum Temp. (°F)	-27	-22	-8	11	28	36	45	40	29	18	4	-24	-27
Days Maximum Temp. ≥ 90°F	0	0	0	0	0	4	5	4	1	0	0	0	14
Days Maximum Temp. ≤ 32°F	18	12	5	0	0	0	0	0	0	0	3	13	51
Days Minimum Temp. ≤ 32°F	29	26	23	9	0	0	0	0	0	7	19	28	141
Days Minimum Temp. ≤ 0°F	5	4	0	0	0	0	0	0	0	0	0	3	12
Heating Degree Days (base 65°F)	1,346	1,116	904	520	228	47	6	12	117	442	779	1,214	6,731
Cooling Degree Days (base 65°F)	0	0	1	7	41	157	264	217	78	8	0	0	773
Mean Precipitation (in.)	1.51	1.47	2.08	3.70	4.19	3.83	3.70	5.08	3.53	2.95	3.09	2.10	37.23
Extreme Maximum Daily Precip. (in.)	1.63	3.17	1.81	2.14	2.35	3.25	3.11	4.93	3.75	3.02	2.25	2.60	4.93
Days With ≥ 0.1" Precipitation	4	4	5	7	8	7	6	7	6	6	6	5	71
Days With ≥ 0.5" Precipitation	1	1	1	3	3	3	3	3	2	2	2	1	25
Days With ≥ 1.0" Precipitation	0	0	0	1	1	1	1	2	1	1	1	0	9
Mean Snowfall (in.)	9.4	6.8	3.6	0.5	0.0	0.0	0.0	0.0	0.0	trace	0.7	8.1	29.1
Maximum Snow Depth (in.)	24	16	10	2	0	0	0	0	0	trace	4	19	24
Days With ≥ 1.0" Snow Depth	13	8	3	0	0	0	0	0	0	0	1	9	34

Fulton L&D #13 Whiteside County   Elevation: 591 ft.   Latitude: 41° 54' N   Longitude: 90° 09' W

	JAN	FEB	MAR	APR	MAY	JUN	JUL	AUG	SEP	OCT	NOV	DEC	YEAR
Mean Maximum Temp. (°F)	29.5	33.2	44.8	59.0	70.3	79.5	83.5	81.9	74.6	62.2	47.3	32.9	58.2
Mean Temp. (°F)	21.2	24.8	36.0	49.2	60.2	69.6	73.7	72.2	64.2	52.1	39.2	25.4	49.0
Mean Minimum Temp. (°F)	13.0	16.3	27.2	39.3	50.0	59.6	63.8	62.5	53.7	41.9	30.9	17.8	39.7
Extreme Maximum Temp. (°F)	62	66	82	91	92	98	102	102	96	90	82	66	102
Extreme Minimum Temp. (°F)	-33	-26	-5	13	30	40	46	42	30	16	8	-22	-33
Days Maximum Temp. ≥ 90°F	0	0	0	0	0	3	6	4	1	0	0	0	14
Days Maximum Temp. ≤ 32°F	18	12	5	0	0	0	0	0	0	0	2	13	50
Days Minimum Temp. ≤ 32°F	30	26	23	6	0	0	0	0	0	4	17	28	134
Days Minimum Temp. ≤ 0°F	6	4	0	0	0	0	0	0	0	0	0	4	14
Heating Degree Days (base 65°F)	1,350	1,131	892	478	186	33	4	8	106	404	769	1,221	6,582
Cooling Degree Days (base 65°F)	0	0	0	10	44	177	280	238	88	10	0	0	847
Mean Precipitation (in.)	1.20	1.39	2.32	3.06	3.57	4.16	3.24	4.05	2.87	2.87	2.52	1.80	33.05
Extreme Maximum Daily Precip. (in.)	1.43	1.72	1.86	1.64	2.55	4.11	2.12	4.71	2.56	2.37	2.23	1.64	4.71
Days With ≥ 0.1" Precipitation	3	4	5	6	7	7	6	6	5	5	5	4	63
Days With ≥ 0.5" Precipitation	1	1	2	2	3	3	2	3	2	2	2	1	24
Days With ≥ 1.0" Precipitation	0	0	0	1	1	1	1	1	1	1	0	0	7
Mean Snowfall (in.)	3.1	1.7	0.4	0.5	0.0	0.0	0.0	0.0	0.0	0.0	0.1	1.5	7.3
Maximum Snow Depth (in.)	15	15	4	7	0	0	0	0	0	0	4	8	15
Days With ≥ 1.0" Snow Depth	6	7	2	0	0	0	0	0	0	0	0	3	18

Galesburg Knox County   Elevation: 771 ft.   Latitude: 40° 57' N   Longitude: 90° 23' W

	JAN	FEB	MAR	APR	MAY	JUN	JUL	AUG	SEP	OCT	NOV	DEC	YEAR
Mean Maximum Temp. (°F)	31.2	35.8	48.6	61.9	72.6	81.4	84.7	82.6	75.8	63.0	48.7	34.4	60.1
Mean Temp. (°F)	23.5	27.8	39.2	51.4	62.2	71.4	75.2	73.2	65.5	53.1	40.2	27.1	50.8
Mean Minimum Temp. (°F)	15.7	19.7	29.7	40.9	51.7	61.4	65.7	63.8	55.2	43.1	31.6	19.7	41.5
Extreme Maximum Temp. (°F)	66	69	86	91	93	101	102	101	97	94	78	68	102
Extreme Minimum Temp. (°F)	-27	-24	-6	9	29	41	49	42	29	21	1	-21	-27
Days Maximum Temp. ≥ 90°F	0	0	0	0	1	4	7	5	1	0	0	0	18
Days Maximum Temp. ≤ 32°F	17	11	3	0	0	0	0	0	0	0	2	12	45
Days Minimum Temp. ≤ 32°F	29	25	20	6	0	0	0	0	0	4	17	27	128
Days Minimum Temp. ≤ 0°F	4	3	0	0	0	0	0	0	0	0	0	3	10
Heating Degree Days (base 65°F)	1,281	1,045	796	416	149	19	2	7	88	377	738	1,167	6,085
Cooling Degree Days (base 65°F)	0	0	2	14	68	218	325	268	111	14	0	0	1,020
Mean Precipitation (in.)	1.46	1.63	2.74	3.66	4.28	4.04	4.32	4.20	3.49	2.73	2.85	2.38	37.78
Extreme Maximum Daily Precip. (in.)	1.23	2.76	3.90	3.01	3.62	3.92	6.13	3.40	3.06	2.18	2.15	3.28	6.13
Days With ≥ 0.1" Precipitation	4	4	6	7	8	7	6	7	5	6	6	5	71
Days With ≥ 0.5" Precipitation	1	1	2	2	3	3	2	3	2	2	2	2	25
Days With ≥ 1.0" Precipitation	0	0	0	1	1	1	1	1	1	1	1	1	9
Mean Snowfall (in.)	7.4	5.2	2.0	1.3	trace	0.0	0.0	0.0	0.0	trace	0.8	6.0	22.7
Maximum Snow Depth (in.)	20	11	9	11	trace	0	0	0	0	1	6	13	20
Days With ≥ 1.0" Snow Depth	14	10	3	0	0	0	0	0	0	0	1	7	35

Golden Adams County   Elevation: 725 ft.   Latitude: 40° 06' N   Longitude: 91° 01' W

	JAN	FEB	MAR	APR	MAY	JUN	JUL	AUG	SEP	OCT	NOV	DEC	YEAR
Mean Maximum Temp. (°F)	33.9	38.1	50.7	62.7	73.5	82.8	86.6	85.2	78.1	66.0	50.4	37.1	62.1
Mean Temp. (°F)	25.7	29.1	40.7	51.7	62.7	72.2	75.9	74.2	66.3	54.5	41.2	29.0	51.9
Mean Minimum Temp. (°F)	17.4	20.1	30.7	40.7	51.8	61.6	65.2	63.1	54.4	42.9	32.0	20.9	41.7
Extreme Maximum Temp. (°F)	68	73	84	93	93	101	102	103	98	95	78	71	103
Extreme Minimum Temp. (°F)	-23	-18	-5	13	31	43	50	43	30	20	-2	-22	-23
Days Maximum Temp. ≥ 90°F	0	0	0	0	1	5	10	9	3	0	0	0	28
Days Maximum Temp. ≤ 32°F	13	10	3	0	0	0	0	0	0	0	2	10	38
Days Minimum Temp. ≤ 32°F	28	24	19	6	0	0	0	0	0	4	17	27	125
Days Minimum Temp. ≤ 0°F	3	3	0	0	0	0	0	0	0	0	0	3	9
Heating Degree Days (base 65°F)	1,213	1,009	747	406	137	15	1	6	85	339	708	1,109	5,775
Cooling Degree Days (base 65°F)	0	0	2	14	73	239	346	298	129	19	0	0	1,120
Mean Precipitation (in.)	1.48	1.82	2.46	3.47	5.02	4.54	4.22	3.98	3.11	3.07	3.02	2.14	38.33
Extreme Maximum Daily Precip. (in.)	1.73	3.00	2.30	3.00	3.60	5.00	4.85	4.36	3.00	3.50	2.65	3.10	5.00
Days With ≥ 0.1" Precipitation	3	4	6	7	8	7	6	6	5	6	6	4	68
Days With ≥ 0.5" Precipitation	1	1	2	3	3	3	3	3	2	2	2	2	27
Days With ≥ 1.0" Precipitation	0	0	1	1	1	1	1	1	1	1	1	1	10
Mean Snowfall (in.)	5.1	4.2	1.4	0.5	0.0	0.0	0.0	0.0	0.0	trace	0.7	3.8	15.7
Maximum Snow Depth (in.)	9	8	3	2	0	0	0	0	0	trace	5	11	11
Days With ≥ 1.0" Snow Depth	2	2	0	0	0	0	0	0	0	0	0	3	7

The period of record for all cooperative weather station data is 1980 – 2009. See User Guide for detailed explanation of data.

Havana 4 NNE *Mason County* Elevation: 459 ft. Latitude: 40° 21' N Longitude: 90° 01' W

	JAN	FEB	MAR	APR	MAY	JUN	JUL	AUG	SEP	OCT	NOV	DEC	YEAR
Mean Maximum Temp. (°F)	34.0	38.9	50.7	63.7	74.1	83.5	88.2	86.1	79.5	67.0	51.7	37.7	62.9
Mean Temp. (°F)	25.1	29.3	40.2	51.9	62.5	72.1	76.5	74.1	66.0	53.8	41.5	28.8	51.8
Mean Minimum Temp. (°F)	16.2	19.7	29.6	40.1	50.9	60.5	64.7	62.1	52.4	40.6	31.2	19.8	40.7
Extreme Maximum Temp. (°F)	69	74	88	95	95	104	106	106	100	95	82	72	106
Extreme Minimum Temp. (°F)	-30	-19	-3	16	27	40	50	38	28	19	1	-23	-30
Days Maximum Temp. ≥ 90°F	0	0	0	0	1	7	13	9	4	0	0	0	34
Days Maximum Temp. ≤ 32°F	14	9	2	0	0	0	0	0	0	0	2	9	36
Days Minimum Temp. ≤ 32°F	29	25	20	6	0	0	0	0	0	7	18	27	132
Days Minimum Temp. ≤ 0°F	4	3	0	0	0	0	0	0	0	0	0	3	10
Heating Degree Days (base 65°F)	1,229	1,002	765	400	142	20	1	5	87	358	699	1,116	5,824
Cooling Degree Days (base 65°F)	0	0	2	14	72	239	364	296	124	17	0	0	1,128
Mean Precipitation (in.)	2.11	2.09	2.79	3.63	4.45	4.19	3.87	3.76	3.17	3.04	3.24	2.80	39.14
Extreme Maximum Daily Precip. (in.)	2.85	2.71	1.90	2.45	4.35	3.10	3.86	3.75	3.40	2.75	2.52	2.60	4.35
Days With ≥ 0.1" Precipitation	5	4	6	7	8	7	7	6	5	6	6	5	72
Days With ≥ 0.5" Precipitation	1	1	2	3	3	3	3	2	2	2	2	2	26
Days With ≥ 1.0" Precipitation	1	0	1	1	1	1	1	1	1	1	1	1	11
Mean Snowfall (in.)	9.3	7.5	3.1	1.1	trace	0.0	0.0	0.0	0.0	trace	1.0	7.5	29.5
Maximum Snow Depth (in.)	18	12	8	8	trace	0	0	0	0	trace	4	13	18
Days With ≥ 1.0" Snow Depth	14	8	2	0	0	0	0	0	0	0	1	7	32

Jerseyville 2 SW *Jersey County* Elevation: 629 ft. Latitude: 39° 06' N Longitude: 90° 21' W

	JAN	FEB	MAR	APR	MAY	JUN	JUL	AUG	SEP	OCT	NOV	DEC	YEAR
Mean Maximum Temp. (°F)	37.1	41.8	52.5	64.8	74.3	83.1	87.5	86.2	79.4	67.1	53.6	40.3	64.0
Mean Temp. (°F)	28.3	32.2	42.3	53.6	63.5	72.4	76.7	74.7	66.9	55.0	43.8	31.5	53.4
Mean Minimum Temp. (°F)	19.4	22.6	32.0	42.3	52.5	61.8	65.8	63.1	54.3	42.8	33.9	22.6	42.8
Extreme Maximum Temp. (°F)	71	76	86	91	92	100	104	104	101	92	80	73	104
Extreme Minimum Temp. (°F)	-20	-22	-3	20	29	42	48	38	27	17	-2	-19	-22
Days Maximum Temp. ≥ 90°F	0	0	0	0	0	5	12	10	3	0	0	0	30
Days Maximum Temp. ≤ 32°F	11	7	2	0	0	0	0	0	0	0	1	7	28
Days Minimum Temp. ≤ 32°F	28	23	17	5	0	0	0	0	0	5	14	25	117
Days Minimum Temp. ≤ 0°F	2	2	0	0	0	0	0	0	0	0	0	2	6
Heating Degree Days (base 65°F)	1,131	921	700	356	120	15	1	5	73	323	631	1,033	5,309
Cooling Degree Days (base 65°F)	0	0	3	20	80	244	369	312	135	20	1	0	1,184
Mean Precipitation (in.)	2.19	2.23	3.26	3.87	4.59	3.69	3.46	3.17	3.33	3.36	3.98	2.85	39.98
Extreme Maximum Daily Precip. (in.)	2.63	2.21	2.40	2.70	4.53	3.57	2.61	3.62	3.78	2.76	3.52	5.12	5.12
Days With ≥ 0.1" Precipitation	4	4	7	7	7	6	6	5	5	6	6	5	68
Days With ≥ 0.5" Precipitation	1	1	2	3	3	3	2	2	2	2	3	2	26
Days With ≥ 1.0" Precipitation	0	0	1	1	1	1	1	1	1	1	1	1	10
Mean Snowfall (in.)	4.0	3.4	2.0	0.2	0.0	0.0	0.0	0.0	0.0	trace	0.8	3.1	13.5
Maximum Snow Depth (in.)	15	16	12	4	0	0	0	0	0	trace	7	10	16
Days With ≥ 1.0" Snow Depth	8	5	2	0	0	0	0	0	0	0	1	5	21

Joliet Brandon Rd Dam *Will County* Elevation: 542 ft. Latitude: 41° 30' N Longitude: 88° 06' W

	JAN	FEB	MAR	APR	MAY	JUN	JUL	AUG	SEP	OCT	NOV	DEC	YEAR
Mean Maximum Temp. (°F)	31.4	35.8	47.0	60.2	71.1	80.9	84.3	82.5	76.3	63.5	49.3	35.5	59.8
Mean Temp. (°F)	23.6	27.6	37.8	49.7	60.0	70.0	74.0	72.5	65.2	52.9	40.9	28.0	50.2
Mean Minimum Temp. (°F)	15.8	19.3	28.5	39.1	48.8	59.1	63.6	62.4	54.1	42.4	32.4	20.4	40.5
Extreme Maximum Temp. (°F)	65	73	86	92	93	104	103	102	95	88	77	70	104
Extreme Minimum Temp. (°F)	-26	-19	-7	11	30	35	47	39	32	21	6	-20	-26
Days Maximum Temp. ≥ 90°F	0	0	0	0	1	4	6	4	2	0	0	0	17
Days Maximum Temp. ≤ 32°F	16	11	4	0	0	0	0	0	0	0	2	11	44
Days Minimum Temp. ≤ 32°F	28	25	22	7	0	0	0	0	0	4	16	27	129
Days Minimum Temp. ≤ 0°F	4	2	0	0	0	0	0	0	0	0	0	2	8
Heating Degree Days (base 65°F)	1,276	1,052	837	463	195	32	3	6	89	379	717	1,142	6,191
Cooling Degree Days (base 65°F)	0	0	1	10	47	189	288	245	103	12	0	0	895
Mean Precipitation (in.)	1.66	1.73	2.31	3.49	4.02	3.72	4.29	3.93	3.16	2.96	3.00	2.20	36.47
Extreme Maximum Daily Precip. (in.)	2.45	2.75	2.25	2.12	3.30	5.13	13.60	3.86	2.74	2.92	2.54	3.34	13.60
Days With ≥ 0.1" Precipitation	4	5	6	7	8	6	6	6	5	6	6	5	70
Days With ≥ 0.5" Precipitation	1	1	1	2	3	2	3	3	2	2	2	1	23
Days With ≥ 1.0" Precipitation	0	0	0	1	1	1	1	1	1	1	1	0	8
Mean Snowfall (in.)	na	na	1.0	0.1	0.0	0.0	0.0	0.0	0.0	0.0	0.1	3.2	na
Maximum Snow Depth (in.)	na	na	na	na	na	na	0	0	0	na	na	na	na
Days With ≥ 1.0" Snow Depth	na	na	1	0	0	0	0	0	0	0	0	5	na

Kankakee Metro Wastwater *Kankakee County* Elevation: 640 ft. Latitude: 41° 08' N Longitude: 87° 53' W

	JAN	FEB	MAR	APR	MAY	JUN	JUL	AUG	SEP	OCT	NOV	DEC	YEAR
Mean Maximum Temp. (°F)	32.6	36.8	48.3	61.2	72.5	82.3	85.3	83.5	77.7	64.8	50.5	36.7	61.0
Mean Temp. (°F)	23.9	27.6	38.2	49.8	60.8	70.6	74.4	72.3	65.1	52.7	41.1	28.3	50.4
Mean Minimum Temp. (°F)	15.1	18.4	28.0	38.3	49.0	58.8	63.4	61.1	52.4	40.6	31.6	19.9	39.7
Extreme Maximum Temp. (°F)	66	74	84	91	94	103	103	107	99	90	78	70	107
Extreme Minimum Temp. (°F)	-29	-19	-7	8	27	38	46	39	30	18	4	-26	-29
Days Maximum Temp. ≥ 90°F	0	0	0	0	1	6	8	5	2	0	0	0	22
Days Maximum Temp. ≤ 32°F	15	9	3	0	0	0	0	0	0	0	1	10	38
Days Minimum Temp. ≤ 32°F	29	26	22	7	0	0	0	0	0	5	16	27	132
Days Minimum Temp. ≤ 0°F	5	3	0	0	0	0	0	0	0	0	0	3	11
Heating Degree Days (base 65°F)	1,268	1,049	825	459	181	28	2	8	95	386	712	1,131	6,144
Cooling Degree Days (base 65°F)	0	0	1	8	56	202	300	243	105	12	0	0	927
Mean Precipitation (in.)	1.91	1.83	2.58	3.46	4.77	3.91	4.66	3.33	2.97	3.13	3.45	2.48	38.48
Extreme Maximum Daily Precip. (in.)	2.78	1.93	3.00	2.85	3.95	3.88	4.36	3.30	3.44	2.52	3.36	3.65	4.36
Days With ≥ 0.1" Precipitation	5	4	6	7	8	6	6	5	5	6	6	5	69
Days With ≥ 0.5" Precipitation	1	1	2	2	3	3	4	2	2	2	2	1	25
Days With ≥ 1.0" Precipitation	0	0	0	1	1	1	1	1	1	1	1	1	9
Mean Snowfall (in.)	7.7	6.5	2.8	0.9	trace	0.0	0.0	0.0	0.0	trace	0.7	5.5	24.1
Maximum Snow Depth (in.)	18	15	12	6	trace	0	0	0	0	0	1	13	18
Days With ≥ 1.0" Snow Depth	15	11	3	0	0	0	0	0	0	0	1	8	38

The period of record for all cooperative weather station data is 1980 – 2009. See User Guide for detailed explanation of data.

Kaskaskia River Nav Lock *Randolph County* Elevation: 379 ft. Latitude: 37° 59' N Longitude: 89° 57' W

	JAN	FEB	MAR	APR	MAY	JUN	JUL	AUG	SEP	OCT	NOV	DEC	YEAR
Mean Maximum Temp. (°F)	42.3	46.7	57.1	68.6	78.7	87.2	91.4	90.4	82.7	70.4	57.5	44.1	68.1
Mean Temp. (°F)	32.4	35.9	45.5	56.2	66.4	75.1	79.4	77.7	69.7	57.6	46.5	34.4	56.4
Mean Minimum Temp. (°F)	22.5	25.0	33.7	43.8	54.1	63.0	67.2	64.9	56.5	44.7	35.4	24.7	44.6
Extreme Maximum Temp. (°F)	74	83	89	99	98	105	108	109	105	96	87	77	109
Extreme Minimum Temp. (°F)	-18	-14	1	22	32	44	51	41	32	23	9	-18	-18
Days Maximum Temp. ≥ 90°F	0	0	0	0	3	12	20	18	8	1	0	0	62
Days Maximum Temp. ≤ 32°F	7	4	1	0	0	0	0	0	0	0	0	5	17
Days Minimum Temp. ≤ 32°F	27	22	14	3	0	0	0	0	0	3	13	24	106
Days Minimum Temp. ≤ 0°F	1	1	0	0	0	0	0	0	0	0	0	1	3
Heating Degree Days (base 65°F)	1,003	817	604	287	72	5	0	2	44	256	552	941	4,583
Cooling Degree Days (base 65°F)	0	0	4	31	123	317	452	402	191	33	2	0	1,555
Mean Precipitation (in.)	1.98	2.21	3.32	3.56	5.10	3.78	3.70	3.38	3.47	3.66	3.86	3.27	41.29
Extreme Maximum Daily Precip. (in.)	3.00	2.60	4.00	2.42	3.58	3.85	3.97	2.42	3.62	3.26	3.19	2.82	4.00
Days With ≥ 0.1" Precipitation	4	5	7	7	8	6	5	5	5	6	6	6	70
Days With ≥ 0.5" Precipitation	1	2	2	2	3	2	3	3	2	3	3	2	28
Days With ≥ 1.0" Precipitation	1	0	1	1	1	1	1	1	1	1	1	1	11
Mean Snowfall (in.)	1.5	2.1	0.2	0.1	0.0	0.0	0.0	0.0	0.0	0.0	0.4	1.6	5.9
Maximum Snow Depth (in.)	10	24	4	0	0	0	0	0	0	0	8	4	24
Days With ≥ 1.0" Snow Depth	1	2	0	0	0	0	0	0	0	0	0	1	4

La Harpe *Hancock County* Elevation: 700 ft. Latitude: 40° 35' N Longitude: 90° 58' W

	JAN	FEB	MAR	APR	MAY	JUN	JUL	AUG	SEP	OCT	NOV	DEC	YEAR
Mean Maximum Temp. (°F)	33.8	38.7	50.4	63.1	73.7	82.8	86.7	85.0	77.7	65.4	51.0	37.1	62.1
Mean Temp. (°F)	24.2	28.6	39.3	51.0	61.8	71.2	75.0	73.2	65.0	52.9	40.5	27.7	50.9
Mean Minimum Temp. (°F)	14.6	18.4	28.2	38.9	49.9	59.6	63.3	61.3	52.3	40.4	30.0	18.2	39.6
Extreme Maximum Temp. (°F)	66	72	87	92	95	105	104	105	99	96	80	72	105
Extreme Minimum Temp. (°F)	-23	-22	-8	13	28	40	49	40	29	18	-1	-23	-23
Days Maximum Temp. ≥ 90°F	0	0	0	0	1	6	11	8	3	0	0	0	29
Days Maximum Temp. ≤ 32°F	14	9	2	0	0	0	0	0	0	0	2	10	37
Days Minimum Temp. ≤ 32°F	30	25	22	7	0	0	0	0	0	7	19	28	138
Days Minimum Temp. ≤ 0°F	5	3	0	0	0	0	0	0	0	0	0	3	11
Heating Degree Days (base 65°F)	1,258	1,024	790	424	153	20	2	6	98	380	728	1,150	6,033
Cooling Degree Days (base 65°F)	0	0	1	12	60	212	320	266	106	13	0	0	990
Mean Precipitation (in.)	1.47	1.74	2.66	3.81	4.63	4.66	4.43	3.74	3.90	3.04	2.93	2.35	39.36
Extreme Maximum Daily Precip. (in.)	1.64	3.41	5.08	2.62	3.22	4.10	4.32	4.11	4.34	4.74	3.20	3.37	5.08
Days With ≥ 0.1" Precipitation	4	4	6	8	8	7	7	6	6	6	6	5	73
Days With ≥ 0.5" Precipitation	1	1	2	3	3	3	3	2	2	2	2	1	25
Days With ≥ 1.0" Precipitation	0	0	0	1	1	1	1	1	1	1	1	1	9
Mean Snowfall (in.)	6.0	3.7	2.7	0.8	0.0	0.0	0.0	0.0	0.0	trace	0.9	5.0	19.1
Maximum Snow Depth (in.)	17	9	8	5	0	0	0	0	0	trace	4	15	17
Days With ≥ 1.0" Snow Depth	15	10	3	0	0	0	0	0	0	0	1	10	39

Lacon 1 N *Marshall County* Elevation: 459 ft. Latitude: 41° 02' N Longitude: 89° 24' W

	JAN	FEB	MAR	APR	MAY	JUN	JUL	AUG	SEP	OCT	NOV	DEC	YEAR
Mean Maximum Temp. (°F)	33.6	38.5	50.6	64.3	74.8	83.7	87.1	85.5	78.8	66.3	51.5	37.5	62.7
Mean Temp. (°F)	26.2	29.9	40.6	52.8	62.9	72.1	75.9	74.3	66.6	54.8	42.4	29.7	52.3
Mean Minimum Temp. (°F)	18.2	21.2	30.5	41.2	50.9	60.4	64.6	62.9	54.4	43.2	33.1	21.9	41.9
Extreme Maximum Temp. (°F)	70	71	81	91	93	102	103	102	98	90	81	70	103
Extreme Minimum Temp. (°F)	-27	-19	-5	11	26	36	45	44	28	18	2	-24	-27
Days Maximum Temp. ≥ 90°F	0	0	0	0	1	6	11	8	3	0	0	0	29
Days Maximum Temp. ≤ 32°F	14	9	2	0	0	0	0	0	0	0	1	9	35
Days Minimum Temp. ≤ 32°F	27	24	19	6	0	0	0	0	0	4	15	26	121
Days Minimum Temp. ≤ 0°F	3	2	0	0	0	0	0	0	0	0	0	2	7
Heating Degree Days (base 65°F)	1,197	988	752	378	131	14	0	5	73	329	673	1,086	5,626
Cooling Degree Days (base 65°F)	0	0	2	18	71	232	345	298	129	20	0	0	1,115
Mean Precipitation (in.)	1.88	1.81	3.09	3.89	4.36	3.84	3.78	3.69	3.21	3.18	3.15	2.28	38.16
Extreme Maximum Daily Precip. (in.)	2.50	3.52	3.12	2.65	2.35	3.60	3.91	3.25	4.88	2.78	2.77	2.13	4.88
Days With ≥ 0.1" Precipitation	4	4	6	8	7	6	6	7	5	6	6	5	70
Days With ≥ 0.5" Precipitation	1	1	2	3	3	3	2	3	2	2	2	1	25
Days With ≥ 1.0" Precipitation	1	0	1	1	1	1	1	1	1	1	1	1	11
Mean Snowfall (in.)	6.5	5.0	2.8	0.8	trace	0.0	0.0	0.0	0.0	trace	0.8	6.1	22.0
Maximum Snow Depth (in.)	14	9	11	5	trace	0	0	0	0	trace	3	14	14
Days With ≥ 1.0" Snow Depth	14	11	3	1	0	0	0	0	0	0	1	9	39

Lincoln *Logan County* Elevation: 583 ft. Latitude: 40° 08' N Longitude: 89° 22' W

	JAN	FEB	MAR	APR	MAY	JUN	JUL	AUG	SEP	OCT	NOV	DEC	YEAR
Mean Maximum Temp. (°F)	34.0	38.9	50.9	63.8	74.5	83.2	86.2	84.5	79.0	66.1	51.8	38.4	62.6
Mean Temp. (°F)	25.6	29.9	40.5	52.2	62.9	72.1	75.2	73.2	66.1	53.8	42.1	30.0	52.0
Mean Minimum Temp. (°F)	17.1	20.8	30.1	40.5	51.3	60.8	64.2	61.8	53.1	41.5	32.3	21.5	41.2
Extreme Maximum Temp. (°F)	68	75	86	91	95	102	103	104	97	92	81	72	104
Extreme Minimum Temp. (°F)	-25	-20	-2	15	25	39	49	39	28	21	5	-19	-25
Days Maximum Temp. ≥ 90°F	0	0	0	0	1	6	9	7	3	0	0	0	26
Days Maximum Temp. ≤ 32°F	13	8	2	0	0	0	0	0	0	0	1	9	33
Days Minimum Temp. ≤ 32°F	28	24	19	6	0	0	0	0	0	6	16	26	125
Days Minimum Temp. ≤ 0°F	3	2	0	0	0	0	0	0	0	0	0	2	7
Heating Degree Days (base 65°F)	1,217	986	754	394	133	18	1	7	79	357	680	1,080	5,706
Cooling Degree Days (base 65°F)	0	0	2	15	76	236	324	267	118	17	0	0	1,055
Mean Precipitation (in.)	1.95	1.61	2.70	3.65	4.06	3.87	4.95	3.92	3.04	3.32	3.27	2.58	38.92
Extreme Maximum Daily Precip. (in.)	2.73	1.56	1.98	3.96	4.11	3.17	4.76	3.70	3.55	3.73	1.89	5.18	5.18
Days With ≥ 0.1" Precipitation	4	4	6	7	8	6	6	6	5	6	6	6	70
Days With ≥ 0.5" Precipitation	1	1	2	2	2	3	3	3	2	2	2	1	24
Days With ≥ 1.0" Precipitation	0	0	0	1	1	1	1	1	1	1	1	1	9
Mean Snowfall (in.)	6.1	4.9	1.8	0.5	0.0	0.0	0.0	0.0	0.0	trace	0.7	5.4	19.4
Maximum Snow Depth (in.)	14	11	4	5	0	0	0	0	0	trace	6	12	14
Days With ≥ 1.0" Snow Depth	10	6	1	0	0	0	0	0	0	0	0	6	23

The period of record for all cooperative weather station data is 1980 – 2009. See User Guide for detailed explanation of data.

Marengo *Mchenry County*   Elevation: 819 ft.   Latitude: 42° 15' N   Longitude: 88° 36' W

	JAN	FEB	MAR	APR	MAY	JUN	JUL	AUG	SEP	OCT	NOV	DEC	YEAR
Mean Maximum Temp. (°F)	29.5	33.0	44.8	58.7	70.8	81.1	84.2	82.3	75.8	62.3	47.1	33.1	58.6
Mean Temp. (°F)	20.6	23.6	35.0	47.4	58.5	68.7	72.7	70.8	63.0	50.2	37.8	24.9	47.8
Mean Minimum Temp. (°F)	11.8	14.2	25.2	36.0	46.2	56.3	61.1	59.2	50.2	38.1	28.5	16.6	36.9
Extreme Maximum Temp. (°F)	61	70	84	91	94	105	105	103	98	90	76	64	105
Extreme Minimum Temp. (°F)	-28	-23	-10	6	26	36	43	39	26	14	1	-23	-28
Days Maximum Temp. ≥ 90°F	0	0	0	0	1	5	7	4	1	0	0	0	18
Days Maximum Temp. ≤ 32°F	17	13	4	0	0	0	0	0	0	0	2	13	49
Days Minimum Temp. ≤ 32°F	29	27	23	11	1	0	0	0	1	9	20	29	150
Days Minimum Temp. ≤ 0°F	7	5	1	0	0	0	0	0	0	0	0	4	17
Heating Degree Days (base 65°F)	1,371	1,163	923	530	236	44	7	18	130	460	808	1,237	6,927
Cooling Degree Days (base 65°F)	0	0	0	8	42	163	252	204	77	9	0	0	755
Mean Precipitation (in.)	1.30	1.31	2.03	3.23	4.01	4.01	3.70	4.81	2.97	2.85	2.58	1.87	34.67
Extreme Maximum Daily Precip. (in.)	2.90	1.30	1.94	1.94	2.75	5.15	3.30	8.20	3.34	2.32	1.96	2.21	8.20
Days With ≥ 0.1" Precipitation	3	3	4	7	8	6	6	7	6	6	6	4	66
Days With ≥ 0.5" Precipitation	1	1	1	2	3	3	2	3	2	2	2	1	23
Days With ≥ 1.0" Precipitation	0	0	0	1	1	1	1	1	1	1	0	0	7
Mean Snowfall (in.)	9.3	8.0	3.3	1.1	0.1	0.0	0.0	0.0	0.0	0.1	1.7	7.6	31.2
Maximum Snow Depth (in.)	17	19	14	6	2	0	0	0	0	1	5	12	19
Days With ≥ 1.0" Snow Depth	15	13	5	1	0	0	0	0	0	0	2	9	45

Normal *Mclean County*   Elevation: 785 ft.   Latitude: 40° 31' N   Longitude: 89° 00' W

	JAN	FEB	MAR	APR	MAY	JUN	JUL	AUG	SEP	OCT	NOV	DEC	YEAR
Mean Maximum Temp. (°F)	33.7	38.9	49.7	62.9	73.9	83.2	85.9	84.4	78.2	65.7	50.8	37.1	62.0
Mean Temp. (°F)	25.3	29.8	39.5	51.4	62.5	72.0	75.4	73.5	66.2	54.2	41.6	28.9	51.7
Mean Minimum Temp. (°F)	16.9	20.6	29.3	39.9	51.0	60.9	64.8	62.6	54.1	42.7	32.4	20.7	41.3
Extreme Maximum Temp. (°F)	66	71	85	91	93	103	102	103	96	90	80	71	103
Extreme Minimum Temp. (°F)	-23	-20	-3	10	26	35	48	41	31	18	2	-22	-23
Days Maximum Temp. ≥ 90°F	0	0	0	0	1	6	9	7	2	0	0	0	25
Days Maximum Temp. ≤ 32°F	14	9	3	0	0	0	0	0	0	0	2	10	38
Days Minimum Temp. ≤ 32°F	28	24	20	7	0	0	0	0	0	5	16	27	127
Days Minimum Temp. ≤ 0°F	4	2	0	0	0	0	0	0	0	0	0	2	8
Heating Degree Days (base 65°F)	1,223	991	785	417	150	19	1	7	84	347	695	1,112	5,831
Cooling Degree Days (base 65°F)	0	0	2	15	79	237	330	278	126	19	0	0	1,086
Mean Precipitation (in.)	2.08	1.92	2.75	3.71	4.41	3.95	4.06	3.95	3.02	3.27	3.22	2.46	38.80
Extreme Maximum Daily Precip. (in.)	2.35	2.27	1.65	3.15	3.21	3.50	5.63	2.63	5.21	3.53	1.94	2.64	5.63
Days With ≥ 0.1" Precipitation	5	5	6	7	8	7	6	7	5	6	6	6	74
Days With ≥ 0.5" Precipitation	1	1	2	3	3	3	3	3	2	2	2	2	27
Days With ≥ 1.0" Precipitation	0	0	0	1	1	1	1	1	1	1	1	0	8
Mean Snowfall (in.)	6.1	5.3	1.8	0.8	trace	0.0	0.0	0.0	0.0	0.1	0.7	4.9	19.7
Maximum Snow Depth (in.)	18	11	7	4	trace	0	0	0	0	trace	6	12	18
Days With ≥ 1.0" Snow Depth	14	8	3	0	0	0	0	0	0	0	1	8	34

Park Forest *Cook County*   Elevation: 709 ft.   Latitude: 41° 30' N   Longitude: 87° 41' W

	JAN	FEB	MAR	APR	MAY	JUN	JUL	AUG	SEP	OCT	NOV	DEC	YEAR
Mean Maximum Temp. (°F)	30.9	35.1	45.8	59.0	69.9	79.9	83.7	81.8	75.1	62.5	48.7	35.1	59.0
Mean Temp. (°F)	23.3	27.1	37.2	49.1	59.6	69.6	74.0	72.2	64.8	52.3	40.7	27.8	49.8
Mean Minimum Temp. (°F)	15.7	19.1	28.5	39.2	49.3	59.2	64.3	62.6	54.4	42.1	32.7	20.5	40.6
Extreme Maximum Temp. (°F)	65	71	83	89	94	102	102	103	95	89	75	70	103
Extreme Minimum Temp. (°F)	-27	-18	-6	9	28	37	46	41	29	18	4	-21	-27
Days Maximum Temp. ≥ 90°F	0	0	0	0	1	4	6	4	1	0	0	0	16
Days Maximum Temp. ≤ 32°F	17	11	4	0	0	0	0	0	0	0	2	11	45
Days Minimum Temp. ≤ 32°F	29	25	21	6	0	0	0	0	0	4	15	27	127
Days Minimum Temp. ≤ 0°F	4	2	0	0	0	0	0	0	0	0	0	2	8
Heating Degree Days (base 65°F)	1,287	1,063	857	480	212	41	5	10	100	398	721	1,146	6,320
Cooling Degree Days (base 65°F)	0	0	1	10	52	185	291	242	101	12	0	0	894
Mean Precipitation (in.)	2.06	1.81	2.57	3.78	4.41	4.35	4.27	4.11	3.27	3.25	3.52	2.56	39.96
Extreme Maximum Daily Precip. (in.)	3.48	2.27	1.97	3.88	6.43	3.61	6.55	3.13	4.04	3.18	3.40	3.87	6.55
Days With ≥ 0.1" Precipitation	5	4	6	7	7	6	6	6	6	6	6	6	71
Days With ≥ 0.5" Precipitation	1	1	1	3	3	3	3	3	2	2	2	1	25
Days With ≥ 1.0" Precipitation	0	0	0	1	1	1	1	2	1	1	1	0	9
Mean Snowfall (in.)	9.4	7.8	4.9	0.8	trace	0.0	0.0	0.0	0.0	0.3	0.9	6.7	30.8
Maximum Snow Depth (in.)	17	16	14	7	trace	0	0	0	0	2	4	17	17
Days With ≥ 1.0" Snow Depth	19	13	5	0	0	0	0	0	0	0	1	10	48

Paw Paw 2 NW *Lee County*   Elevation: 950 ft.   Latitude: 41° 43' N   Longitude: 89° 00' W

	JAN	FEB	MAR	APR	MAY	JUN	JUL	AUG	SEP	OCT	NOV	DEC	YEAR
Mean Maximum Temp. (°F)	27.8	32.1	44.1	58.4	69.6	79.5	82.2	80.0	74.1	61.4	46.2	31.7	57.2
Mean Temp. (°F)	20.0	24.0	34.8	47.2	58.4	68.6	71.8	69.7	62.7	50.2	37.5	24.1	47.4
Mean Minimum Temp. (°F)	12.2	15.9	25.5	36.0	47.1	57.6	61.4	59.4	51.2	39.0	28.7	16.4	37.5
Extreme Maximum Temp. (°F)	62	66	83	92	91	101	100	99	92	90	75	65	101
Extreme Minimum Temp. (°F)	-25	-33	-16	9	24	38	41	37	29	17	3	-23	-33
Days Maximum Temp. ≥ 90°F	0	0	0	0	0	3	4	2	1	0	0	0	10
Days Maximum Temp. ≤ 32°F	20	14	5	0	0	0	0	0	0	0	4	15	58
Days Minimum Temp. ≤ 32°F	30	27	25	10	1	0	0	0	0	7	20	29	149
Days Minimum Temp. ≤ 0°F	7	4	0	0	0	0	0	0	0	0	0	4	15
Heating Degree Days (base 65°F)	1,388	1,152	930	532	234	40	9	19	129	458	818	1,262	6,971
Cooling Degree Days (base 65°F)	0	0	0	5	37	153	227	172	66	6	0	0	666
Mean Precipitation (in.)	1.28	1.42	2.07	3.07	4.45	4.00	4.14	4.25	3.62	2.78	2.96	1.98	36.02
Extreme Maximum Daily Precip. (in.)	1.43	2.95	1.86	2.02	2.95	6.92	5.46	3.15	5.24	2.94	2.55	3.77	6.92
Days With ≥ 0.1" Precipitation	3	3	5	7	8	7	6	6	6	5	6	5	67
Days With ≥ 0.5" Precipitation	1	1	1	2	3	2	3	3	2	2	2	1	23
Days With ≥ 1.0" Precipitation	0	0	0	0	1	1	1	1	1	1	1	0	7
Mean Snowfall (in.)	8.8	6.5	3.9	0.8	trace	0.0	0.0	0.0	0.0	0.2	1.2	8.5	29.9
Maximum Snow Depth (in.)	25	11	12	7	trace	0	0	0	0	3	3	24	25
Days With ≥ 1.0" Snow Depth	17	12	4	0	0	0	0	0	0	0	1	12	46

The period of record for all cooperative weather station data is 1980 – 2009. See User Guide for detailed explanation of data.

Princeville *Peoria County*   Elevation: 734 ft.   Latitude: 40° 56' N   Longitude: 89° 46' W

	JAN	FEB	MAR	APR	MAY	JUN	JUL	AUG	SEP	OCT	NOV	DEC	YEAR
Mean Maximum Temp. (°F)	32.0	37.0	49.3	62.9	73.4	81.5	85.2	83.3	76.9	64.5	50.3	35.6	61.0
Mean Temp. (°F)	22.4	26.8	37.9	49.9	60.7	69.5	73.0	70.9	63.4	51.6	39.5	26.2	49.3
Mean Minimum Temp. (°F)	12.8	16.6	26.3	36.9	48.0	57.4	60.8	58.6	49.7	38.7	28.7	16.8	37.6
Extreme Maximum Temp. (°F)	66	72	87	93	95	101	104	105	99	92	82	70	105
Extreme Minimum Temp. (°F)	-26	-26	-8	5	22	35	44	36	26	12	0	-26	-26
Days Maximum Temp. ≥ 90°F	0	0	0	0	1	5	8	6	2	0	0	0	22
Days Maximum Temp. ≤ 32°F	15	10	3	0	0	0	0	0	0	0	2	11	41
Days Minimum Temp. ≤ 32°F	30	26	24	10	1	0	0	0	1	9	20	29	150
Days Minimum Temp. ≤ 0°F	6	4	0	0	0	0	0	0	0	0	0	4	14
Heating Degree Days (base 65°F)	1,314	1,072	836	457	179	34	5	17	124	419	759	1,194	6,410
Cooling Degree Days (base 65°F)	0	0	1	11	53	175	261	208	81	11	0	0	801
Mean Precipitation (in.)	2.08	1.85	2.92	3.55	4.46	3.71	3.86	3.87	3.39	2.77	3.01	2.35	37.82
Extreme Maximum Daily Precip. (in.)	5.00	1.84	3.02	1.71	4.60	3.74	4.45	3.15	3.50	3.95	2.81	3.10	5.00
Days With ≥ 0.1" Precipitation	4	4	6	8	8	7	6	7	5	6	6	5	72
Days With ≥ 0.5" Precipitation	1	1	2	3	3	3	3	3	2	2	2	2	27
Days With ≥ 1.0" Precipitation	0	0	1	1	1	1	1	1	1	0	1	0	9
Mean Snowfall (in.)	6.1	5.9	2.3	0.4	trace	0.0	0.0	0.0	0.0	trace	1.0	5.9	21.6
Maximum Snow Depth (in.)	14	11	5	12	trace	0	0	0	0	trace	3	15	15
Days With ≥ 1.0" Snow Depth	8	6	2	0	0	0	0	0	0	0	0	5	21

Rosiclare 5 NW *Hardin County*   Elevation: 399 ft.   Latitude: 37° 25' N   Longitude: 88° 21' W

	JAN	FEB	MAR	APR	MAY	JUN	JUL	AUG	SEP	OCT	NOV	DEC	YEAR
Mean Maximum Temp. (°F)	42.7	47.9	58.1	68.8	76.6	84.2	87.7	87.8	81.3	70.2	58.1	45.8	67.4
Mean Temp. (°F)	32.8	36.9	46.1	55.8	64.3	72.8	76.6	75.8	68.2	56.7	46.6	35.9	55.7
Mean Minimum Temp. (°F)	22.8	25.9	34.1	42.8	52.4	61.3	65.5	63.9	55.2	43.2	35.1	25.9	44.0
Extreme Maximum Temp. (°F)	70	77	85	90	92	100	102	104	100	90	84	76	104
Extreme Minimum Temp. (°F)	-22	-12	6	16	31	39	47	36	32	18	3	-17	-22
Days Maximum Temp. ≥ 90°F	0	0	0	0	0	6	13	13	4	0	0	0	36
Days Maximum Temp. ≤ 32°F	6	3	1	0	0	0	0	0	0	0	0	4	14
Days Minimum Temp. ≤ 32°F	25	21	15	5	0	0	0	0	0	5	13	23	107
Days Minimum Temp. ≤ 0°F	1	1	0	0	0	0	0	0	0	0	0	0	2
Heating Degree Days (base 65°F)	992	788	586	292	100	8	0	2	51	275	546	896	4,536
Cooling Degree Days (base 65°F)	0	0	6	24	87	247	367	344	155	24	2	0	1,256
Mean Precipitation (in.)	3.58	3.81	4.61	4.63	5.51	4.36	4.32	3.18	3.46	3.80	4.19	4.46	49.91
Extreme Maximum Daily Precip. (in.)	2.66	3.31	5.87	3.55	3.38	2.65	4.42	6.14	3.02	4.60	2.87	4.96	6.14
Days With ≥ 0.1" Precipitation	6	6	8	7	8	6	6	4	5	5	7	7	75
Days With ≥ 0.5" Precipitation	2	3	3	3	4	3	3	2	3	3	3	4	36
Days With ≥ 1.0" Precipitation	1	1	1	1	2	1	1	1	1	1	1	1	13
Mean Snowfall (in.)	2.4	2.2	0.5	trace	0.0	0.0	0.0	0.0	0.0	0.2	trace	1.2	6.5
Maximum Snow Depth (in.)	8	10	7	trace	0	0	0	0	0	1	trace	8	10
Days With ≥ 1.0" Snow Depth	4	4	0	0	0	0	0	0	0	0	0	2	10

Tuscola *Douglas County*   Elevation: 652 ft.   Latitude: 39° 48' N   Longitude: 88° 17' W

	JAN	FEB	MAR	APR	MAY	JUN	JUL	AUG	SEP	OCT	NOV	DEC	YEAR
Mean Maximum Temp. (°F)	35.5	39.8	51.7	65.1	75.6	84.5	87.3	85.6	80.1	67.2	52.6	39.7	63.7
Mean Temp. (°F)	27.2	30.9	41.6	53.4	64.2	73.2	76.2	74.3	67.6	55.4	43.2	31.8	53.3
Mean Minimum Temp. (°F)	19.0	22.0	31.4	41.8	52.6	61.9	65.1	62.9	55.1	43.5	33.9	23.9	42.7
Extreme Maximum Temp. (°F)	68	73	86	90	95	104	104	104	99	91	79	70	104
Extreme Minimum Temp. (°F)	-23	-18	0	15	30	39	49	43	31	20	1	-26	-26
Days Maximum Temp. ≥ 90°F	0	0	0	0	2	8	11	9	4	0	0	0	34
Days Maximum Temp. ≤ 32°F	12	8	2	0	0	0	0	0	0	0	1	7	30
Days Minimum Temp. ≤ 32°F	27	23	17	5	0	0	0	0	0	4	14	25	115
Days Minimum Temp. ≤ 0°F	3	2	0	0	0	0	0	0	0	0	0	1	6
Heating Degree Days (base 65°F)	1,165	956	721	357	111	13	0	4	59	314	647	1,021	5,368
Cooling Degree Days (base 65°F)	0	0	2	17	92	266	355	299	143	23	0	0	1,197
Mean Precipitation (in.)	2.22	2.20	2.75	4.01	4.14	4.08	4.47	3.37	3.15	3.35	3.83	2.88	40.45
Extreme Maximum Daily Precip. (in.)	1.68	2.30	2.02	2.40	3.75	3.72	3.89	4.07	3.72	2.60	3.02	3.00	4.07
Days With ≥ 0.1" Precipitation	5	5	6	8	8	7	6	5	5	6	7	6	74
Days With ≥ 0.5" Precipitation	2	1	2	3	3	3	3	2	2	2	3	2	28
Days With ≥ 1.0" Precipitation	0	0	0	1	1	1	1	1	1	1	1	1	9
Mean Snowfall (in.)	6.3	5.1	2.2	0.2	trace	0.0	0.0	0.0	0.0	trace	1.0	4.7	19.5
Maximum Snow Depth (in.)	15	19	7	2	trace	0	0	0	0	trace	8	10	19
Days With ≥ 1.0" Snow Depth	9	8	2	0	0	0	0	0	0	0	0	5	24

Urbana *Champaign County*   Elevation: 743 ft.   Latitude: 40° 06' N   Longitude: 88° 14' W

	JAN	FEB	MAR	APR	MAY	JUN	JUL	AUG	SEP	OCT	NOV	DEC	YEAR
Mean Maximum Temp. (°F)	33.7	38.1	50.1	62.9	73.7	82.6	85.2	83.8	78.2	65.2	50.7	37.1	61.8
Mean Temp. (°F)	25.9	30.0	40.6	52.0	62.7	71.9	75.0	73.5	66.4	54.2	41.9	29.7	52.0
Mean Minimum Temp. (°F)	18.2	21.8	31.0	41.0	51.7	61.2	64.8	63.0	54.5	43.0	33.1	22.3	42.1
Extreme Maximum Temp. (°F)	67	72	84	91	94	103	101	102	97	92	79	71	103
Extreme Minimum Temp. (°F)	-25	-17	1	16	29	41	48	40	30	19	7	-20	-25
Days Maximum Temp. ≥ 90°F	0	0	0	0	1	6	7	6	2	0	0	0	22
Days Maximum Temp. ≤ 32°F	14	9	2	0	0	0	0	0	0	0	1	10	36
Days Minimum Temp. ≤ 32°F	28	24	18	5	0	0	0	0	0	4	15	26	120
Days Minimum Temp. ≤ 0°F	3	2	0	0	0	0	0	0	0	0	0	2	7
Heating Degree Days (base 65°F)	1,204	983	752	397	136	17	1	4	74	346	685	1,086	5,685
Cooling Degree Days (base 65°F)	0	0	1	12	72	231	319	274	123	17	0	0	1,049
Mean Precipitation (in.)	2.01	2.13	2.90	3.69	4.90	4.15	4.62	3.96	3.22	3.11	3.58	2.69	40.96
Extreme Maximum Daily Precip. (in.)	1.45	2.30	2.92	2.96	2.98	3.89	4.43	5.32	3.30	3.72	3.53	2.41	5.32
Days With ≥ 0.1" Precipitation	5	4	6	8	8	6	7	6	5	6	7	6	74
Days With ≥ 0.5" Precipitation	1	1	2	2	3	3	3	3	2	2	2	2	26
Days With ≥ 1.0" Precipitation	0	0	1	1	1	1	1	1	1	1	1	0	9
Mean Snowfall (in.)	6.8	5.9	2.5	0.5	trace	0.0	0.0	0.0	0.0	0.1	1.2	5.8	22.8
Maximum Snow Depth (in.)	17	19	10	3	trace	0	0	0	0	trace	8	13	19
Days With ≥ 1.0" Snow Depth	12	8	2	0	0	0	0	0	0	0	1	7	30

The period of record for all cooperative weather station data is 1980 – 2009. See User Guide for detailed explanation of data.

Virden *Macoupin County*   Elevation: 674 ft.   Latitude: 39° 30' N   Longitude: 89° 46' W

	JAN	FEB	MAR	APR	MAY	JUN	JUL	AUG	SEP	OCT	NOV	DEC	YEAR
Mean Maximum Temp. (°F)	36.6	40.9	52.6	66.1	75.7	83.7	87.2	86.0	79.8	67.5	53.0	39.6	64.1
Mean Temp. (°F)	28.8	33.0	43.0	55.2	65.1	73.6	77.1	75.4	68.3	56.8	44.3	32.0	54.4
Mean Minimum Temp. (°F)	20.9	24.6	33.3	44.3	54.4	63.4	66.9	64.7	56.7	46.0	35.7	24.3	44.6
Extreme Maximum Temp. (°F)	70	72	85	90	93	100	102	105	99	91	81	72	105
Extreme Minimum Temp. (°F)	-19	-19	0	19	33	43	50	39	31	20	-1	-20	-20
Days Maximum Temp. ≥ 90°F	0	0	0	0	1	6	10	9	3	0	0	0	29
Days Maximum Temp. ≤ 32°F	11	7	1	0	0	0	0	0	0	0	1	8	28
Days Minimum Temp. ≤ 32°F	26	21	14	3	0	0	0	0	0	3	12	24	103
Days Minimum Temp. ≤ 0°F	2	1	0	0	0	0	0	0	0	0	0	1	4
Heating Degree Days (base 65°F)	1,117	899	679	313	92	9	0	2	55	277	614	1,017	5,074
Cooling Degree Days (base 65°F)	0	0	2	26	102	272	381	329	161	29	1	0	1,303
Mean Precipitation (in.)	1.85	2.11	2.77	3.52	4.16	3.84	3.51	2.74	2.94	3.11	3.45	2.53	36.53
Extreme Maximum Daily Precip. (in.)	2.24	1.72	1.92	3.98	3.77	4.30	4.30	2.27	4.38	3.05	2.63	4.25	4.38
Days With ≥ 0.1" Precipitation	4	4	6	6	7	6	5	5	5	6	6	4	64
Days With ≥ 0.5" Precipitation	1	1	2	2	3	2	2	2	2	2	2	2	23
Days With ≥ 1.0" Precipitation	0	0	0	1	1	1	1	1	1	1	1	1	9
Mean Snowfall (in.)	5.1	5.6	3.0	0.4	0.0	0.0	0.0	0.0	0.0	trace	0.8	4.6	19.5
Maximum Snow Depth (in.)	12	8	8	4	0	0	0	0	0	trace	4	12	12
Days With ≥ 1.0" Snow Depth	9	6	2	0	0	0	0	0	0	0	0	5	22

Wheaton 3 SE *Dupage County*   Elevation: 680 ft.   Latitude: 41° 49' N   Longitude: 88° 04' W

	JAN	FEB	MAR	APR	MAY	JUN	JUL	AUG	SEP	OCT	NOV	DEC	YEAR
Mean Maximum Temp. (°F)	33.6	38.4	49.8	63.2	74.1	83.4	86.8	85.0	78.0	*65.7*	50.6	37.3	*62.2*
Mean Temp. (°F)	25.2	29.1	39.0	50.8	61.0	70.5	75.1	73.6	65.8	*53.7*	41.5	29.3	*51.2*
Mean Minimum Temp. (°F)	16.9	19.7	28.1	38.4	47.9	57.5	63.4	62.1	53.4	*41.7*	32.4	21.3	*40.2*
Extreme Maximum Temp. (°F)	65	74	85	90	94	103	105	100	96	*89*	77	70	*105*
Extreme Minimum Temp. (°F)	-26	-20	-7	4	26	34	44	42	28	*14*	5	-21	*-26*
Days Maximum Temp. ≥ 90°F	0	0	0	0	1	7	10	7	2	*0*	0	0	*27*
Days Maximum Temp. ≤ 32°F	14	8	2	0	0	0	0	0	0	*0*	1	9	*34*
Days Minimum Temp. ≤ 32°F	28	24	21	8	1	0	0	0	0	*6*	16	25	*129*
Days Minimum Temp. ≤ 0°F	4	3	0	0	0	0	0	0	0	*0*	0	2	*9*
Heating Degree Days (base 65°F)	1,226	1,010	801	433	178	29	2	5	85	*357*	697	1,098	*5,921*
Cooling Degree Days (base 65°F)	0	0	1	13	61	200	324	278	114	*15*	0	0	*1,006*
Mean Precipitation (in.)	1.88	1.66	2.37	3.52	4.00	3.98	4.10	4.44	3.36	*3.13*	3.49	2.13	*38.06*
Extreme Maximum Daily Precip. (in.)	1.75	2.85	2.58	2.00	3.79	3.22	9.24	6.01	3.35	*4.43*	2.98	3.04	*9.24*
Days With ≥ 0.1" Precipitation	5	4	6	7	7	7	6	*6*	6	*5*	6	5	*70*
Days With ≥ 0.5" Precipitation	1	1	1	2	3	3	3	*3*	2	*2*	2	1	*24*
Days With ≥ 1.0" Precipitation	0	0	0	1	1	1	1	*1*	1	*1*	1	0	*8*
Mean Snowfall (in.)	9.4	6.9	4.2	0.7	trace	0.0	0.0	0.0	0.0	*trace*	1.0	5.7	*27.9*
Maximum Snow Depth (in.)	*16*	*16*	*10*	*3*	*trace*	*0*	*0*	*0*	*0*	na	*4*	*21*	na
Days With ≥ 1.0" Snow Depth	*14*	*10*	3	0	0	0	0	0	0	*0*	1	7	*35*

The period of record for all cooperative weather station data is 1980 – 2009. See User Guide for detailed explanation of data.

Illinois Weather Station Rankings

Annual Extreme Maximum Temperature

Rank	Highest — Station Name	°F	Rank	Lowest — Station Name	°F
1	Kaskaskia River Nav Lock	109	1	Elgin	101
2	Kankakee Metro Wastwater	107	1	Paw Paw 2 NW	101
3	Alton Melvin Price L&D	106	3	Charleston	102
3	Cahokia	106	3	Danville	102
3	Chicago Midway Arpt	106	3	Fulton L&D #13	102
3	Decatur	106	3	Galesburg	102
3	Havana 4 NNE	106	3	Springfield Capital Arpt	102
8	Albion	105	8	Aledo	103
8	Belleville Siu Research	105	8	Aurora	103
8	Brookport Dam 52	105	8	Chenoa	103
8	Carbondale Sewage Plant	105	8	De Kalb	103
8	Carlinville	105	8	Dixon 1 NW	103
8	Chicago Botanical Garden	105	8	Effingham	103
8	La Harpe	105	8	Golden	103
8	Marengo	105	8	Lacon 1 N	103
8	Peoria Greater Peoria Arpt	105	8	Normal	103
8	Princeville	105	8	Park Forest	103
8	Virden	105	8	Urbana	103
8	Wheaton 3 SE	105	19	Anna 2 NNE	104
20	Anna 2 NNE	104	19	Antioch	104
20	Antioch	104	19	Chicago Ohare Intl Arpt	104
20	Chicago Ohare Intl Arpt	104	19	Jerseyville 2 SW	104
20	Jerseyville 2 SW	104	19	Joliet Brandon Rd Dam	104
20	Joliet Brandon Rd Dam	104	19	Lincoln	104
20	Lincoln	104	19	Moline Quad City Arpt	104

Annual Mean Maximum Temperature

Rank	Highest — Station Name	°F	Rank	Lowest — Station Name	°F
1	Kaskaskia River Nav Lock	68.1	1	Antioch	57.3
2	Brookport Dam 52	68.0	1	Paw Paw 2 NW	57.3
3	Anna 2 NNE	67.9	3	Elgin	58.1
4	Belleville Siu Research	67.7	4	Fulton L&D #13	58.2
5	Rosiclare 5 NW	67.4	5	Chicago Botanical Garden	58.3
6	Carbondale Sewage Plant	66.8	5	De Kalb	58.3
7	Cahokia	66.6	7	Dixon 1 NW	58.4
8	Albion	66.5	7	Rockford Greater Rockford Arpt	58.4
9	Alton Melvin Price L&D	64.4	9	Marengo	58.6
10	Decatur	64.2	10	Chicago Ohare Intl Arpt	58.9
11	Carlinville	64.1	11	Park Forest	59.0
11	Virden	64.1	12	Aurora	59.8
13	Jerseyville 2 SW	64.0	12	Joliet Brandon Rd Dam	59.8
14	Charleston	63.8	14	Chicago Midway Arpt	59.9
15	Effingham	63.7	15	Aledo	60.0
15	Tuscola	63.7	16	Galesburg	60.1
17	Danville	63.0	17	Moline Quad City Arpt	60.7
17	Springfield Capital Arpt	63.0	18	Kankakee Metro Wastwater	61.0
19	Havana 4 NNE	62.9	18	Princeville	61.0
20	Lacon 1 N	62.7	20	Peoria Greater Peoria Arpt	61.3
21	Lincoln	62.6	21	Chenoa	61.8
22	Wheaton 3 SE	62.2	21	Urbana	61.8
23	Golden	62.1	23	Normal	62.0
23	La Harpe	62.1	24	Golden	62.1
25	Normal	62.0	24	La Harpe	62.1

Rankings include 25 highest/lowest stations. If state has less than 25 stations, all stations are included. The period of record is 1980–2009. See User Guide for detailed explanation of data.

Annual Mean Temperature

	Highest				Lowest	
Rank	Station Name	°F		Rank	Station Name	°F
1	Brookport Dam 52	57.8		1	Paw Paw 2 NW	47.4
2	Anna 2 NNE	57.0		2	Antioch	*47.8*
3	Belleville Siu Research	56.7		2	Marengo	*47.8*
4	Albion	*56.5*		4	Dixon 1 NW	48.3
5	Kaskaskia River Nav Lock	*56.4*		5	Elgin	*48.4*
6	Cahokia	*56.1*		6	De Kalb	48.6
7	Carbondale Sewage Plant	55.7		6	Rockford Greater Rockford Arpt	48.6
7	Rosiclare 5 NW	55.7		8	Fulton L&D #13	49.0
9	Alton Melvin Price L&D	55.3		9	Chicago Botanical Garden	49.2
10	Virden	54.4		10	Princeville	49.3
11	Carlinville	*54.1*		11	Aurora	49.6
12	Charleston	54.0		12	Chicago Ohare Intl Arpt	49.7
13	Decatur	53.7		13	Park Forest	49.8
14	Effingham	53.4		14	Aledo	50.0
14	Jerseyville 2 SW	53.4		15	Joliet Brandon Rd Dam	50.2
16	Tuscola	53.3		16	Kankakee Metro Wastwater	50.4
17	Springfield Capital Arpt	53.1		17	Moline Quad City Arpt	50.6
18	Danville	52.8		18	Galesburg	50.8
19	Lacon 1 N	52.3		19	La Harpe	50.9
20	Lincoln	52.0		20	Wheaton 3 SE	*51.2*
20	Urbana	52.0		21	Chicago Midway Arpt	51.5
22	Golden	*51.9*		22	Chenoa	51.6
23	Havana 4 NNE	51.8		23	Normal	51.7
24	Normal	51.7		23	Peoria Greater Peoria Arpt	51.7
24	Peoria Greater Peoria Arpt	51.7		25	Havana 4 NNE	51.8

Annual Mean Minimum Temperature

	Highest				Lowest	
Rank	Station Name	°F		Rank	Station Name	°F
1	Brookport Dam 52	47.5		1	Marengo	*37.0*
2	Albion	*46.5*		2	Paw Paw 2 NW	37.5
3	Alton Melvin Price L&D	46.3		3	Princeville	37.6
4	Anna 2 NNE	46.1		4	Dixon 1 NW	38.2
5	Belleville Siu Research	45.7		5	Antioch	*38.4*
6	Cahokia	*45.5*		6	Elgin	38.5
7	Kaskaskia River Nav Lock	*44.6*		7	Rockford Greater Rockford Arpt	38.6
7	Virden	44.6		8	De Kalb	38.9
9	Carbondale Sewage Plant	44.5		9	Aurora	39.3
10	Charleston	44.2		10	La Harpe	39.6
11	Carlinville	*44.1*		11	Fulton L&D #13	39.7
12	Rosiclare 5 NW	44.0		11	Kankakee Metro Wastwater	39.7
13	Decatur	43.2		13	Aledo	39.8
14	Chicago Midway Arpt	43.1		14	Chicago Botanical Garden	40.0
14	Springfield Capital Arpt	43.1		15	Wheaton 3 SE	*40.2*
16	Effingham	43.0		16	Chicago Ohare Intl Arpt	40.4
17	Jerseyville 2 SW	42.8		17	Joliet Brandon Rd Dam	40.5
18	Tuscola	42.7		17	Moline Quad City Arpt	40.5
19	Danville	42.6		19	Park Forest	40.6
20	Urbana	42.1		20	Havana 4 NNE	40.7
21	Peoria Greater Peoria Arpt	42.0		21	Lincoln	41.2
22	Lacon 1 N	41.9		22	Chenoa	41.3
23	Golden	*41.7*		22	Normal	41.3
24	Galesburg	41.5		24	Galesburg	41.5
25	Chenoa	41.3		25	Golden	*41.7*

Rankings include 25 highest/lowest stations. If state has less than 25 stations, all stations are included. The period of record is 1980–2009. See User Guide for detailed explanation of data.

Annual Extreme Minimum Temperature

	Highest				Lowest	
Rank	Station Name	°F		Rank	Station Name	°F
1	Alton Melvin Price L&D	*-16*		1	Fulton L&D #13	-33
2	Anna 2 NNE	-17		1	Paw Paw 2 NW	-33
3	Kaskaskia River Nav Lock	*-18*		3	Dixon 1 NW	-32
4	Cahokia	*-19*		4	Havana 4 NNE	-30
4	Carlinville	*-19*		5	Kankakee Metro Wastwater	-29
6	Albion	*-20*		5	Moline Quad City Arpt	-29
6	Virden	-20		7	Aledo	-28
8	Belleville Siu Research	-21		7	Antioch	*-28*
8	Brookport Dam 52	-21		7	Marengo	*-28*
8	Carbondale Sewage Plant	-21		10	Charleston	-27
8	Springfield Capital Arpt	-21		10	Chicago Botanical Garden	-27
12	Decatur	-22		10	Chicago Ohare Intl Arpt	-27
12	Effingham	*-22*		10	De Kalb	-27
12	Jerseyville 2 SW	-22		10	Elgin	-27
12	Rosiclare 5 NW	-22		10	Galesburg	-27
16	Golden	*-23*		10	Lacon 1 N	-27
16	La Harpe	-23		10	Park Forest	-27
16	Normal	-23		10	Rockford Greater Rockford Arpt	-27
16	Peoria Greater Peoria Arpt	-23		19	Aurora	-26
20	Chicago Midway Arpt	-25		19	Chenoa	-26
20	Lincoln	-25		19	Danville	-26
20	Urbana	-25		19	Joliet Brandon Rd Dam	-26
23	Aurora	-26		19	Princeville	-26
23	Chenoa	-26		19	Tuscola	-26
23	Danville	-26		19	Wheaton 3 SE	*-26*

July Mean Maximum Temperature

	Highest				Lowest	
Rank	Station Name	°F		Rank	Station Name	°F
1	Kaskaskia River Nav Lock	91.4		1	Antioch	*82.1*
2	Albion	*89.9*		2	Paw Paw 2 NW	82.2
3	Belleville Siu Research	89.5		3	Chicago Botanical Garden	82.5
4	Brookport Dam 52	89.3		4	Dixon 1 NW	82.9
5	Anna 2 NNE	88.7		5	Elgin	83.3
5	Cahokia	88.7		6	Fulton L&D #13	83.5
7	Carbondale Sewage Plant	88.4		7	De Kalb	83.6
8	Havana 4 NNE	88.2		8	Park Forest	83.7
9	Rosiclare 5 NW	87.7		9	Rockford Greater Rockford Arpt	83.9
10	Alton Melvin Price L&D	87.6		10	Chicago Ohare Intl Arpt	84.1
10	Decatur	87.6		11	Marengo	84.2
12	Jerseyville 2 SW	87.5		12	Joliet Brandon Rd Dam	84.3
13	Tuscola	87.3		13	Aledo	84.7
14	Effingham	87.2		13	Aurora	84.7
14	Virden	87.2		13	Galesburg	84.7
16	Lacon 1 N	87.1		16	Chicago Midway Arpt	84.8
17	Carlinville	86.9		17	Chenoa	85.2
18	Wheaton 3 SE	86.8		17	Princeville	85.2
19	La Harpe	86.7		19	Kankakee Metro Wastwater	85.3
20	Golden	*86.6*		19	Urbana	85.3
21	Charleston	86.5		21	Danville	85.7
22	Springfield Capital Arpt	86.3		21	Peoria Greater Peoria Arpt	85.7
23	Lincoln	86.2		23	Moline Quad City Arpt	85.9
24	Moline Quad City Arpt	85.9		23	Normal	85.9
24	Normal	85.9		25	Lincoln	86.2

Rankings include 25 highest/lowest stations. If state has less than 25 stations, all stations are included. The period of record is 1980–2009. See User Guide for detailed explanation of data.

January Mean Minimum Temperature

Highest			Lowest		
Rank	Station Name	°F	Rank	Station Name	°F
1	Brookport Dam 52	26.3	1	Dixon 1 NW	11.6
2	Anna 2 NNE	24.8	2	Marengo	11.8
3	Albion	23.9	3	Paw Paw 2 NW	12.2
3	Belleville Siu Research	23.9	4	De Kalb	12.8
5	Carbondale Sewage Plant	23.2	4	Princeville	12.8
6	Rosiclare 5 NW	22.8	6	Fulton L&D #13	13.0
7	Cahokia	22.6	6	Rockford Greater Rockford Arpt	13.0
8	Kaskaskia River Nav Lock	22.5	8	Elgin	13.4
9	Alton Melvin Price L&D	21.9	9	Antioch	13.5
10	Virden	20.9	10	Aurora	14.2
11	Charleston	20.7	11	Aledo	14.5
12	Carlinville	20.6	12	La Harpe	14.6
13	Effingham	19.9	13	Moline Quad City Arpt	14.8
14	Jerseyville 2 SW	19.4	14	Kankakee Metro Wastwater	15.1
15	Danville	19.3	15	Galesburg	15.7
16	Decatur	19.2	15	Park Forest	15.7
16	Springfield Capital Arpt	19.2	17	Joliet Brandon Rd Dam	15.8
18	Tuscola	19.0	18	Chicago Botanical Garden	16.2
19	Chicago Midway Arpt	18.4	18	Havana 4 NNE	16.2
20	Lacon 1 N	18.2	20	Chicago Ohare Intl Arpt	16.3
20	Urbana	18.2	21	Chenoa	16.6
22	Golden	17.4	22	Normal	16.9
23	Lincoln	17.1	22	Wheaton 3 SE	16.9
23	Peoria Greater Peoria Arpt	17.1	24	Lincoln	17.1
25	Normal	16.9	24	Peoria Greater Peoria Arpt	17.1

Number of Days Annually Maximum Temperature ≥ 90°F

Highest			Lowest		
Rank	Station Name	Days	Rank	Station Name	Days
1	Kaskaskia River Nav Lock	62	1	Antioch	10
2	Albion	47	1	Paw Paw 2 NW	10
2	Belleville Siu Research	47	3	Dixon 1 NW	12
4	Brookport Dam 52	44	4	De Kalb	14
5	Anna 2 NNE	41	4	Elgin	14
6	Cahokia	40	4	Fulton L&D #13	14
7	Carbondale Sewage Plant	39	7	Rockford Greater Rockford Arpt	15
8	Rosiclare 5 NW	36	8	Aledo	16
9	Havana 4 NNE	34	8	Chicago Botanical Garden	16
9	Tuscola	34	8	Chicago Ohare Intl Arpt	16
11	Effingham	32	8	Park Forest	16
12	Alton Melvin Price L&D	31	12	Joliet Brandon Rd Dam	17
12	Decatur	31	13	Galesburg	18
14	Jerseyville 2 SW	30	13	Marengo	18
15	Carlinville	29	15	Aurora	19
15	La Harpe	29	16	Danville	20
15	Lacon 1 N	29	17	Chenoa	21
15	Virden	29	17	Chicago Midway Arpt	21
19	Golden	28	19	Kankakee Metro Wastwater	22
20	Charleston	27	19	Princeville	22
20	Springfield Capital Arpt	27	19	Urbana	22
20	Wheaton 3 SE	27	22	Moline Quad City Arpt	23
23	Lincoln	26	22	Peoria Greater Peoria Arpt	23
24	Normal	25	24	Normal	25
25	Moline Quad City Arpt	23	25	Lincoln	26

Rankings include 25 highest/lowest stations. If state has less than 25 stations, all stations are included. The period of record is 1980–2009. See User Guide for detailed explanation of data.

Number of Days Annually Maximum Temperature ≤ 32°F

Highest			Lowest		
Rank	**Station Name**	**Days**	**Rank**	**Station Name**	**Days**
1	Paw Paw 2 NW	58	1	Anna 2 NNE	12
2	De Kalb	55	1	Brookport Dam 52	12
3	Rockford Greater Rockford Arpt	53	3	Rosiclare 5 NW	14
4	Antioch	*52*	4	Carbondale Sewage Plant	16
5	Elgin	51	5	Belleville Siu Research	17
6	Dixon 1 NW	50	5	Cahokia	*17*
6	Fulton L&D #13	50	5	Kaskaskia River Nav Lock	*17*
8	Marengo	*49*	8	Albion	*19*
9	Aledo	45	9	Alton Melvin Price L&D	24
9	Chicago Ohare Intl Arpt	45	10	Carlinville	*27*
9	Galesburg	45	10	Charleston	27
9	Park Forest	45	10	Decatur	27
13	Joliet Brandon Rd Dam	44	13	Jerseyville 2 SW	28
14	Moline Quad City Arpt	43	13	Virden	28
15	Aurora	42	15	Effingham	29
15	Chicago Botanical Garden	42	16	Tuscola	30
17	Chicago Midway Arpt	41	17	Danville	33
17	Princeville	41	17	Lincoln	33
19	Peoria Greater Peoria Arpt	39	17	Springfield Capital Arpt	33
20	Golden	*38*	20	Wheaton 3 SE	*34*
20	Kankakee Metro Wastwater	38	21	Lacon 1 N	35
20	Normal	38	22	Chenoa	36
23	La Harpe	37	22	Havana 4 NNE	36
24	Chenoa	36	22	Urbana	36
24	Havana 4 NNE	36	25	La Harpe	37

Number of Days Annually Minimum Temperature ≤ 32°F

Highest			Lowest		
Rank	**Station Name**	**Days**	**Rank**	**Station Name**	**Days**
1	Marengo	*150*	1	Brookport Dam 52	83
1	Princeville	150	2	Albion	*87*
3	Paw Paw 2 NW	149	3	Alton Melvin Price L&D	93
4	Dixon 1 NW	144	3	Anna 2 NNE	93
5	Rockford Greater Rockford Arpt	142	5	Belleville Siu Research	97
6	De Kalb	141	6	Cahokia	*102*
6	Elgin	141	7	Virden	103
8	Antioch	*139*	8	Charleston	104
9	La Harpe	138	9	Carbondale Sewage Plant	105
10	Aurora	136	10	Kaskaskia River Nav Lock	*106*
11	Fulton L&D #13	134	11	Carlinville	*107*
12	Aledo	133	11	Rosiclare 5 NW	107
13	Havana 4 NNE	132	13	Chicago Midway Arpt	112
13	Kankakee Metro Wastwater	132	13	Decatur	112
15	Moline Quad City Arpt	130	13	Springfield Capital Arpt	112
16	Joliet Brandon Rd Dam	129	16	Effingham	113
16	Wheaton 3 SE	*129*	17	Danville	114
18	Galesburg	128	18	Tuscola	115
19	Chicago Botanical Garden	127	19	Jerseyville 2 SW	117
19	Chicago Ohare Intl Arpt	127	20	Peoria Greater Peoria Arpt	120
19	Normal	127	20	Urbana	120
19	Park Forest	127	22	Lacon 1 N	121
23	Chenoa	126	23	Golden	*125*
24	Golden	*125*	23	Lincoln	125
24	Lincoln	125	25	Chenoa	126

Rankings include 25 highest/lowest stations. If state has less than 25 stations, all stations are included. The period of record is 1980–2009. See User Guide for detailed explanation of data.

Number of Days Annually Minimum Temperature ≤ 0°F

Highest			Lowest		
Rank	Station Name	Days	Rank	Station Name	Days
1	Marengo	*17*	1	Brookport Dam 52	1
2	Dixon 1 NW	16	2	Albion	*2*
3	Antioch	*15*	2	Anna 2 NNE	2
3	Paw Paw 2 NW	15	2	Cahokia	*2*
5	Fulton L&D #13	14	2	Rosiclare 5 NW	2
5	Princeville	14	6	Alton Melvin Price L&D	3
5	Rockford Greater Rockford Arpt	14	6	Belleville Siu Research	3
8	De Kalb	13	6	Carbondale Sewage Plant	3
9	Elgin	12	6	Kaskaskia River Nav Lock	*3*
10	Aledo	11	10	Carlinville	*4*
10	Aurora	11	10	Charleston	4
10	Kankakee Metro Wastwater	11	10	Virden	4
10	La Harpe	11	13	Chicago Midway Arpt	5
10	Moline Quad City Arpt	11	14	Decatur	6
15	Galesburg	10	14	Effingham	6
15	Havana 4 NNE	10	14	Jerseyville 2 SW	6
17	Golden	*9*	14	Tuscola	6
17	Wheaton 3 SE	*9*	18	Danville	7
19	Chenoa	8	18	Lacon 1 N	7
19	Chicago Botanical Garden	8	18	Lincoln	7
19	Chicago Ohare Intl Arpt	8	18	Springfield Capital Arpt	7
19	Joliet Brandon Rd Dam	8	18	Urbana	7
19	Normal	8	23	Chenoa	8
19	Park Forest	8	23	Chicago Botanical Garden	8
19	Peoria Greater Peoria Arpt	8	23	Chicago Ohare Intl Arpt	8

Number of Annual Heating Degree Days

Highest			Lowest		
Rank	Station Name	Num.	Rank	Station Name	Num.
1	Paw Paw 2 NW	6,971	1	Brookport Dam 52	4,087
2	Marengo	*6,927*	2	Anna 2 NNE	4,247
3	Antioch	*6,843*	3	Belleville Siu Research	4,397
4	Dixon 1 NW	6,735	4	Rosiclare 5 NW	4,536
5	Elgin	*6,731*	5	Albion	*4,563*
6	De Kalb	6,685	6	Kaskaskia River Nav Lock	*4,583*
7	Rockford Greater Rockford Arpt	6,682	7	Cahokia	*4,607*
8	Fulton L&D #13	6,582	8	Carbondale Sewage Plant	4,644
9	Chicago Botanical Garden	6,451	9	Alton Melvin Price L&D	*4,857*
10	Princeville	6,410	10	Virden	5,074
11	Aurora	6,370	11	Carlinville	*5,100*
12	Chicago Ohare Intl Arpt	6,335	12	Charleston	5,122
13	Park Forest	6,320	13	Decatur	5,235
14	Aledo	6,272	14	Jerseyville 2 SW	5,309
15	Joliet Brandon Rd Dam	6,191	15	Effingham	5,331
16	Moline Quad City Arpt	6,160	16	Tuscola	5,368
17	Kankakee Metro Wastwater	6,144	17	Danville	5,414
18	Galesburg	6,085	18	Springfield Capital Arpt	5,417
19	La Harpe	6,033	19	Lacon 1 N	5,626
20	Wheaton 3 SE	*5,921*	20	Urbana	5,685
21	Chicago Midway Arpt	5,892	21	Lincoln	5,706
22	Normal	5,831	22	Golden	*5,775*
23	Havana 4 NNE	5,824	23	Chenoa	5,802
24	Peoria Greater Peoria Arpt	5,808	24	Peoria Greater Peoria Arpt	5,808
25	Chenoa	5,802	25	Havana 4 NNE	5,824

Rankings include 25 highest/lowest stations. If state has less than 25 stations, all stations are included. The period of record is 1980–2009. See User Guide for detailed explanation of data.

Number of Annual Cooling Degree Days

	Highest			Lowest	
Rank	Station Name	Num.	Rank	Station Name	Num.
1	Albion	1,572	1	Paw Paw 2 NW	666
2	Brookport Dam 52	1,555	2	Antioch	695
2	Kaskaskia River Nav Lock	1,555	3	Marengo	755
4	Belleville Siu Research	1,465	4	Dixon 1 NW	761
5	Cahokia	1,460	5	Elgin	773
6	Anna 2 NNE	1,438	6	Chicago Botanical Garden	781
7	Alton Melvin Price L&D	1,437	7	Rockford Greater Rockford Arpt	795
8	Carbondale Sewage Plant	1,347	8	Princeville	801
9	Virden	1,303	9	De Kalb	819
10	Rosiclare 5 NW	1,256	10	Fulton L&D #13	847
11	Carlinville	1,239	11	Chicago Ohare Intl Arpt	853
12	Decatur	1,225	12	Aurora	860
13	Charleston	1,220	13	Aledo	894
14	Tuscola	1,197	13	Park Forest	894
15	Effingham	1,193	15	Joliet Brandon Rd Dam	895
16	Jerseyville 2 SW	1,184	16	Kankakee Metro Wastwater	927
17	Springfield Capital Arpt	1,177	17	La Harpe	990
18	Havana 4 NNE	1,128	18	Wheaton 3 SE	1,006
19	Golden	1,120	19	Moline Quad City Arpt	1,008
20	Lacon 1 N	1,115	20	Chenoa	1,014
21	Normal	1,086	21	Galesburg	1,020
22	Danville	1,074	22	Urbana	1,049
23	Chicago Midway Arpt	1,071	23	Lincoln	1,055
24	Peoria Greater Peoria Arpt	1,064	24	Peoria Greater Peoria Arpt	1,064
25	Lincoln	1,055	25	Chicago Midway Arpt	1,071

Annual Precipitation

	Highest			Lowest	
Rank	Station Name	Inches	Rank	Station Name	Inches
1	Rosiclare 5 NW	49.91	1	Fulton L&D #13	33.05
2	Anna 2 NNE	49.90	2	Marengo	34.67
3	Brookport Dam 52	48.44	3	Chenoa	34.79
4	Carbondale Sewage Plant	47.10	4	Antioch	35.77
5	Albion	43.32	5	Paw Paw 2 NW	36.02
6	Effingham	42.93	6	Rockford Greater Rockford Arpt	36.10
7	Cahokia	42.01	7	Peoria Greater Peoria Arpt	36.17
8	Charleston	41.85	8	Joliet Brandon Rd Dam	36.47
9	Danville	41.64	9	Virden	36.53
10	Kaskaskia River Nav Lock	41.29	10	Springfield Capital Arpt	36.74
11	Urbana	40.96	11	Chicago Ohare Intl Arpt	36.90
12	Belleville Siu Research	40.92	12	Aledo	36.92
13	Alton Melvin Price L&D	40.87	13	De Kalb	37.15
14	Tuscola	40.45	14	Elgin	37.23
15	Jerseyville 2 SW	39.98	15	Moline Quad City Arpt	37.68
16	Park Forest	39.96	16	Chicago Botanical Garden	37.72
17	La Harpe	39.36	17	Galesburg	37.78
18	Decatur	39.29	18	Princeville	37.82
19	Havana 4 NNE	39.14	19	Aurora	37.90
20	Lincoln	38.92	20	Dixon 1 NW	37.92
21	Chicago Midway Arpt	38.87	21	Wheaton 3 SE	38.06
22	Normal	38.80	22	Lacon 1 N	38.16
23	Carlinville	38.49	23	Golden	38.33
24	Kankakee Metro Wastwater	38.48	24	Kankakee Metro Wastwater	38.48
25	Golden	38.33	25	Carlinville	38.49

Rankings include 25 highest/lowest stations. If state has less than 25 stations, all stations are included. The period of record is 1980–2009. See User Guide for detailed explanation of data.

Annual Extreme Maximum Daily Precipitation

Highest			Lowest		
Rank	Station Name	Inches	Rank	Station Name	Inches
1	Aurora	16.91	1	Carlinville	3.75
2	Joliet Brandon Rd Dam	13.60	2	Danville	3.92
3	Wheaton 3 SE	9.24	3	Kaskaskia River Nav Lock	4.00
4	Marengo	8.20	4	Tuscola	4.07
5	De Kalb	8.09	5	Moline Quad City Arpt	4.26
6	Anna 2 NNE	7.74	6	Havana 4 NNE	4.35
7	Alton Melvin Price L&D	7.70	7	Kankakee Metro Wastwater	4.36
8	Paw Paw 2 NW	6.92	8	Cahokia	4.37
9	Carbondale Sewage Plant	6.90	9	Virden	4.38
10	Chicago Ohare Intl Arpt	6.64	10	Peoria Greater Peoria Arpt	4.42
11	Park Forest	6.55	11	Belleville Siu Research	4.58
12	Aledo	6.27	12	Fulton L&D #13	4.71
13	Rosiclare 5 NW	6.14	12	Springfield Capital Arpt	4.71
14	Galesburg	6.13	14	Lacon 1 N	4.88
15	Decatur	5.84	15	Elgin	4.93
16	Chicago Midway Arpt	5.72	16	Charleston	4.95
17	Effingham	5.70	16	Dixon 1 NW	4.95
17	Rockford Greater Rockford Arpt	5.70	18	Golden	5.00
19	Chenoa	5.66	18	Princeville	5.00
20	Normal	5.63	20	La Harpe	5.08
21	Chicago Botanical Garden	5.54	21	Jerseyville 2 SW	5.12
22	Brookport Dam 52	5.32	22	Lincoln	5.18
22	Urbana	5.32	23	Brookport Dam 52	5.32
24	Lincoln	5.18	23	Urbana	5.32
25	Jerseyville 2 SW	5.12	25	Chicago Botanical Garden	5.54

Number of Days Annually With ≥ 0.1 Inches of Precipitation

Highest			Lowest		
Rank	Station Name	Days	Rank	Station Name	Days
1	Anna 2 NNE	78	1	Albion	60
1	Danville	78	2	Fulton L&D #13	63
3	Effingham	77	3	Virden	64
4	Cahokia	76	4	Chenoa	65
5	Brookport Dam 52	75	5	Antioch	66
5	Rosiclare 5 NW	75	5	Marengo	66
7	Carbondale Sewage Plant	74	5	Rockford Greater Rockford Arpt	66
7	Charleston	74	8	Paw Paw 2 NW	67
7	Normal	74	8	Springfield Capital Arpt	67
7	Tuscola	74	10	Belleville Siu Research	68
7	Urbana	74	10	Decatur	68
12	Chicago Botanical Garden	73	10	Golden	68
12	La Harpe	73	10	Jerseyville 2 SW	68
14	Alton Melvin Price L&D	72	10	Moline Quad City Arpt	68
14	Havana 4 NNE	72	15	Aledo	69
14	Princeville	72	15	Aurora	69
17	Chicago Ohare Intl Arpt	71	15	Carlinville	69
17	Elgin	71	15	De Kalb	69
17	Galesburg	71	15	Dixon 1 NW	69
17	Park Forest	71	15	Kankakee Metro Wastwater	69
21	Chicago Midway Arpt	70	15	Peoria Greater Peoria Arpt	69
21	Joliet Brandon Rd Dam	70	22	Chicago Midway Arpt	70
21	Kaskaskia River Nav Lock	70	22	Joliet Brandon Rd Dam	70
21	Lacon 1 N	70	22	Kaskaskia River Nav Lock	70
21	Lincoln	70	22	Lacon 1 N	70

Rankings include 25 highest/lowest stations. If state has less than 25 stations, all stations are included. The period of record is 1980–2009. See User Guide for detailed explanation of data.

Number of Days Annually With ≥ 0.5 Inches of Precipitation

	Highest			Lowest	
Rank	Station Name	Days	Rank	Station Name	Days
1	Rosiclare 5 NW	36	1	Chicago Ohare Intl Arpt	21
2	Brookport Dam 52	34	2	De Kalb	22
3	Anna 2 NNE	33	2	Peoria Greater Peoria Arpt	22
4	Carbondale Sewage Plant	32	4	Antioch	23
5	Albion	30	4	Aurora	23
5	Effingham	30	4	Joliet Brandon Rd Dam	23
7	Cahokia	29	4	Marengo	23
7	Danville	29	4	Paw Paw 2 NW	23
9	Belleville Siu Research	28	4	Rockford Greater Rockford Arpt	23
9	Charleston	28	4	Springfield Capital Arpt	23
9	Kaskaskia River Nav Lock	28	4	Virden	23
9	Tuscola	28	12	Chicago Botanical Garden	24
13	Alton Melvin Price L&D	27	12	Fulton L&D #13	24
13	Carlinville	27	12	Lincoln	24
13	Decatur	27	12	Wheaton 3 SE	24
13	Golden	27	16	Aledo	25
13	Normal	27	16	Chenoa	25
13	Princeville	27	16	Chicago Midway Arpt	25
19	Havana 4 NNE	26	16	Dixon 1 NW	25
19	Jerseyville 2 SW	26	16	Elgin	25
19	Moline Quad City Arpt	26	16	Galesburg	25
19	Urbana	26	16	Kankakee Metro Wastwater	25
23	Aledo	25	16	La Harpe	25
23	Chenoa	25	16	Lacon 1 N	25
23	Chicago Midway Arpt	25	16	Park Forest	25

Number of Days Annually With > 1.0 Inches of Precipitation

	Highest			Lowest	
Rank	Station Name	Days	Rank	Station Name	Days
1	Anna 2 NNE	13	1	Rockford Greater Rockford Arpt	6
1	Cahokia	13	2	Dixon 1 NW	7
1	Carbondale Sewage Plant	13	2	Fulton L&D #13	7
1	Rosiclare 5 NW	13	2	Marengo	7
5	Albion	12	2	Paw Paw 2 NW	7
5	Alton Melvin Price L&D	12	6	Aledo	8
5	Belleville Siu Research	12	6	Antioch	8
5	Brookport Dam 52	12	6	Aurora	8
5	Effingham	12	6	Chenoa	8
10	Havana 4 NNE	11	6	Chicago Botanical Garden	8
10	Kaskaskia River Nav Lock	11	6	De Kalb	8
10	Lacon 1 N	11	6	Joliet Brandon Rd Dam	8
13	Carlinville	10	6	Normal	8
13	Charleston	10	6	Wheaton 3 SE	8
13	Decatur	10	15	Chicago Midway Arpt	9
13	Golden	10	15	Chicago Ohare Intl Arpt	9
13	Jerseyville 2 SW	10	15	Danville	9
13	Springfield Capital Arpt	10	15	Elgin	9
19	Chicago Midway Arpt	9	15	Galesburg	9
19	Chicago Ohare Intl Arpt	9	15	Kankakee Metro Wastwater	9
19	Danville	9	15	La Harpe	9
19	Elgin	9	15	Lincoln	9
19	Galesburg	9	15	Moline Quad City Arpt	9
19	Kankakee Metro Wastwater	9	15	Park Forest	9
19	La Harpe	9	15	Peoria Greater Peoria Arpt	9

Rankings include 25 highest/lowest stations. If state has less than 25 stations, all stations are included. The period of record is 1980–2009. See User Guide for detailed explanation of data.

Annual Snowfall

	Highest			Lowest	
Rank	**Station Name**	**Inches**	**Rank**	**Station Name**	**Inches**
1	Antioch	*39.2*	1	Alton Melvin Price L&D	*4.8*
2	Chicago Midway Arpt	37.6	2	Kaskaskia River Nav Lock	*5.9*
3	Chicago Ohare Intl Arpt	37.3	3	Rosiclare 5 NW	6.5
4	Rockford Greater Rockford Arpt	36.5	4	Brookport Dam 52	6.7
5	Chicago Botanical Garden	33.8	5	Fulton L&D #13	*7.3*
6	De Kalb	33.5	6	Albion	*8.1*
7	Dixon 1 NW	31.6	7	Carbondale Sewage Plant	10.7
8	Moline Quad City Arpt	31.3	8	Anna 2 NNE	11.3
9	Marengo	*31.2*	9	Belleville Siu Research	13.1
10	Park Forest	30.8	10	Jerseyville 2 SW	13.5
11	Paw Paw 2 NW	29.9	11	Cahokia	*15.4*
12	Havana 4 NNE	29.5	12	Golden	*15.7*
13	Elgin	29.1	13	Danville	15.9
14	Aurora	28.3	14	Carlinville	*17.7*
15	Wheaton 3 SE	*27.9*	15	Effingham	17.8
16	Peoria Greater Peoria Arpt	24.3	16	Decatur	18.1
17	Kankakee Metro Wastwater	24.1	17	Chenoa	18.4
18	Urbana	22.8	18	La Harpe	19.1
19	Galesburg	22.7	19	Lincoln	19.4
20	Lacon 1 N	22.0	20	Tuscola	19.5
21	Princeville	21.6	20	Virden	19.5
22	Springfield Capital Arpt	21.3	22	Normal	19.7
23	Aledo	20.7	23	Aledo	20.7
23	Charleston	20.7	23	Charleston	20.7
25	Normal	19.7	25	Springfield Capital Arpt	21.3

Annual Maximum Snow Depth

	Highest			Lowest	
Rank	**Station Name**	**Inches**	**Rank**	**Station Name**	**Inches**
1	Belleville Siu Research	30	1	Albion	*10*
2	Aurora	25	1	Rosiclare 5 NW	10
2	Paw Paw 2 NW	25	3	Cahokia	*11*
4	Charleston	24	3	Golden	*11*
4	Dixon 1 NW	24	5	Carlinville	*12*
4	Elgin	*24*	5	Springfield Capital Arpt	12
4	Kaskaskia River Nav Lock	*24*	5	Virden	12
8	Antioch	*22*	8	Brookport Dam 52	13
9	Alton Melvin Price L&D	*21*	8	Carbondale Sewage Plant	13
9	Chicago Midway Arpt	21	10	Anna 2 NNE	14
11	Chenoa	20	10	Danville	14
11	Galesburg	20	10	Decatur	14
13	Marengo	*19*	10	Lacon 1 N	*14*
13	Rockford Greater Rockford Arpt	*19*	10	Lincoln	*14*
13	Tuscola	19	15	Fulton L&D #13	*15*
13	Urbana	19	15	Princeville	*15*
17	Chicago Botanical Garden	18	17	Effingham	*16*
17	Chicago Ohare Intl Arpt	18	17	Jerseyville 2 SW	16
17	Havana 4 NNE	18	17	Peoria Greater Peoria Arpt	16
17	Kankakee Metro Wastwater	18	20	De Kalb	*17*
17	Normal	18	20	La Harpe	17
22	De Kalb	*17*	20	Park Forest	17
22	La Harpe	17	23	Chicago Botanical Garden	18
22	Park Forest	17	23	Chicago Ohare Intl Arpt	18
25	Effingham	*16*	23	Havana 4 NNE	18

Rankings include 25 highest/lowest stations. If state has less than 25 stations, all stations are included. The period of record is 1980–2009. See User Guide for detailed explanation of data.

Number of Days Annually With ≥ 1.0 Inch Snow Depth

	Highest			Lowest	
Rank	Station Name	Days	Rank	Station Name	Days
1	Rockford Greater Rockford Arpt	**58**	1	Albion	**4**
2	De Kalb	55	1	Kaskaskia River Nav Lock	**4**
3	Antioch	**51**	3	Alton Melvin Price L&D	**6**
3	Chicago Botanical Garden	51	4	Golden	**7**
5	Chicago Midway Arpt	48	5	Brookport Dam 52	8
5	Dixon 1 NW	48	6	Rosiclare 5 NW	10
5	Park Forest	48	7	Aledo	**12**
8	Paw Paw 2 NW	46	7	Anna 2 NNE	12
9	Aurora	45	7	Carbondale Sewage Plant	12
9	Marengo	**45**	10	Belleville Siu Research	13
11	Chicago Ohare Intl Arpt	43	11	Cahokia	**14**
12	La Harpe	39	12	Fulton L&D #13	**18**
12	Lacon 1 N	39	13	Carlinville	**20**
14	Kankakee Metro Wastwater	38	14	Jerseyville 2 SW	21
15	Peoria Greater Peoria Arpt	36	14	Princeville	**21**
16	Galesburg	35	16	Effingham	**22**
16	Wheaton 3 SE	**35**	16	Virden	22
18	Elgin	**34**	18	Danville	23
18	Normal	34	18	Lincoln	**23**
20	Havana 4 NNE	32	20	Tuscola	24
21	Charleston	30	21	Decatur	25
21	Urbana	30	22	Chenoa	27
23	Chenoa	27	22	Springfield Capital Arpt	27
23	Springfield Capital Arpt	27	24	Charleston	30
25	Decatur	25	24	Urbana	30

Rankings include 25 highest/lowest stations. If state has less than 25 stations, all stations are included. The period of record is 1980–2009. See User Guide for detailed explanation of data.

Significant Storm Events in Illinois: 2000 – 2009

Location or County	Date	Type	Mag.	Deaths	Injuries	Property Damage ($mil.)	Crop Damage ($mil.)
Vermilion	07/08/01	Thunderstorm Wind	85 mph	0	0	8.5	0.0
Cook	07/21/01	Excessive Heat	na	10	0	0.0	0.0
Cook	07/29/01	Excessive Heat	na	6	0	0.0	0.0
Cook	08/02/01	Flash Flood	na	0	0	37.0	0.0
Cook	08/06/01	Excessive Heat	na	14	0	0.0	0.0
Wayne	04/21/02	Tornado	F3	1	42	4.0	0.0
Sangamon	05/27/02	Hail	2.00 in.	0	0	9.0	0.0
Cook	06/21/02	Excessive Heat	na	7	0	0.0	0.0
Cook	07/01/02	Excessive Heat	na	12	0	0.0	0.0
Cook	07/15/02	Excessive Heat	na	11	0	0.0	0.0
Mercer	04/30/03	Flash Flood	na	0	0	10.0	0.0
Henry	04/30/03	Flash Flood	na	0	0	10.0	0.0
Massac	05/06/03	Tornado	F4	1	20	10.0	0.0
Pulaski	05/06/03	Tornado	F4	1	13	3.5	0.0
Henderson	05/08/03	Hail	4.00 in.	0	0	10.0	0.0
Tazewell	05/10/03	Tornado	F3	0	32	10.0	0.0
De Witt	05/30/03	Tornado	F2	0	4	9.3	0.0
Mercer	07/20/03	Thunderstorm Wind	81 mph	0	0	10.0	3.0
Henry	07/21/03	Thunderstorm Wind	92 mph	0	0	50.0	25.0
Will	07/27/03	Flash Flood	na	0	0	14.0	0.0
Coles	09/26/03	Tornado	F1	0	1	10.0	0.0
Putnam	04/20/04	Tornado	F2	0	5	8.0	0.0
La Salle	04/20/04	Tornado	F3	8	7	0.0	0.0
St. Clair	04/02/06	Tornado	F2	1	11	0.0	0.0
Cook	07/15/06	Excessive Heat	na	9	0	0.0	0.0
Jefferson	07/21/06	Thunderstorm Wind	90 mph	0	5	13.0	0.0
Cook	08/01/06	Excessive Heat	na	24	0	0.0	0.0
Winnebago	09/04/06	Flash Flood	na	0	0	20.0	0.0
Cook	12/02/06	Extreme Cold/Wind Chill	na	7	5	0.0	0.0
Cook	02/01/07	Extreme Cold/Wind Chill	na	10	0	0.0	0.0
Du Page	03/31/07	Thunderstorm Wind	96 mph	0	11	1.0	0.0
Cook	01/22/08	Extreme Cold/Wind Chill	na	5	0	0.0	0.0
Saline	03/18/08	Flood	na	0	0	16.8	0.0
Cook	09/13/08	Flash Flood	na	1	0	35.0	0.0
Cook	09/14/08	Flash Flood	na	0	0	20.0	0.0
Du Page	09/14/08	Flash Flood	na	0	0	8.0	0.0
Cook	12/21/08	Cold/Wind Chill	na	5	0	0.0	0.0
Williamson	05/08/09	Thunderstorm Wind	100 mph	0	1	175.0	0.0
Jackson	05/08/09	Thunderstorm Wind	106 mph	1	6	100.0	0.0
Sangamon	08/19/09	Tornado	F3	0	17	11.0	0.0
Logan	08/19/09	Tornado	F3	0	2	7.2	1.0

Note: Deaths, injuries, and damages are date and location specific.

2014 Title List

Visit **www.GreyHouse.com** for Product Information, Table of Contents and Sample Pages

General Reference

America's College Museums
American Environmental Leaders: From Colonial Times to the Present
An African Biographical Dictionary
An Encyclopedia of Human Rights in the United States
Constitutional Amendments
Encyclopedia of African-American Writing
Encyclopedia of the Continental Congress
Encyclopedia of Gun Control & Gun Rights
Encyclopedia of Invasions & Conquests
Encyclopedia of Prisoners of War & Internment
Encyclopedia of Religion & Law in America
Encyclopedia of Rural America
Encyclopedia of the United States Cabinet, 1789-2010
Encyclopedia of War Journalism
Encyclopedia of Warrior Peoples & Fighting Groups
From Suffrage to the Senate: America's Political Women
Nations of the World
Political Corruption in America
Speakers of the House of Representatives, 1789-2009
The Environmental Debate: A Documentary History
The Evolution Wars: A Guide to the Debates
The Religious Right: A Reference Handbook
The Value of a Dollar: 1860-2009
The Value of a Dollar: Colonial Era
This is Who We Were: A Companion to the 1940 Census
This is Who We Were: The 1920s
This is Who We Were: The 1950s
This is Who We Were: The 1960s
US Land & Natural Resource Policy
Working Americans 1770-1869 Vol. IX: Revolutionary War to the Civil War
Working Americans 1880-1999 Vol. I: The Working Class
Working Americans 1880-1999 Vol. II: The Middle Class
Working Americans 1880-1999 Vol. III: The Upper Class
Working Americans 1880-1999 Vol. IV: Their Children
Working Americans 1880-2003 Vol. V: At War
Working Americans 1880-2005 Vol. VI: Women at Work
Working Americans 1880-2006 Vol. VII: Social Movements
Working Americans 1880-2007 Vol. VIII: Immigrants
Working Americans 1880-2009 Vol. X: Sports & Recreation
Working Americans 1880-2010 Vol. XI: Inventors & Entrepreneurs
Working Americans 1880-2011 Vol. XII: Our History through Music
Working Americans 1880-2012 Vol. XIII: Education & Educators
World Cultural Leaders of the 20th & 21st Centuries

Business Information

Complete Television, Radio & Cable Industry Directory
Directory of Business Information Resources
Directory of Mail Order Catalogs
Directory of Venture Capital & Private Equity Firms
Environmental Resource Handbook
Food & Beverage Market Place
Grey House Homeland Security Directory
Grey House Performing Arts Directory
Hudson's Washington News Media Contacts Directory
New York State Directory
Sports Market Place Directory

Education Information

Charter School Movement
Comparative Guide to American Elementary & Secondary Schools
Complete Learning Disabilities Directory
Educators Resource Directory
Special Education

Health Information

Comparative Guide to American Hospitals
Complete Directory for Pediatric Disorders
Complete Directory for People with Chronic Illness
Complete Directory for People with Disabilities
Complete Mental Health Directory
Diabetes in America: A Geographic & Demographic Analysis
Directory of Health Care Group Purchasing Organizations
Directory of Hospital Personnel
HMO/PPO Directory
Medical Device Register
Older Americans Information Directory

Statistics & Demographics

America's Top-Rated Cities
America's Top-Rated Small Towns & Cities
America's Top-Rated Smaller Cities
American Tally
Ancestry & Ethnicity in America
Comparative Guide to American Hospitals
Comparative Guide to American Suburbs
Profiles of America
Profiles of... Series – State Handbooks
The Hispanic Databook
Weather America

Financial Ratings Series

TheStreet.com Ratings Guide to Bond & Money Market Mutual Funds
TheStreet.com Ratings Guide to Common Stocks
TheStreet.com Ratings Guide to Exchange-Traded Funds
TheStreet.com Ratings Guide to Stock Mutual Funds
TheStreet.com Ratings Ultimate Guided Tour of Stock Investing
Weiss Ratings Consumer Guides
Weiss Ratings Guide to Banks & Thrifts
Weiss Ratings Guide to Credit Unions
Weiss Ratings Guide to Health Insurers
Weiss Ratings Guide to Life & Annuity Insurers
Weiss Ratings Guide to Property & Casualty Insurers

Bowker's Books In Print®Titles

Books In Print®
Books In Print® Supplement
American Book Publishing Record® Annual
American Book Publishing Record® Monthly
Books Out Loud™
Bowker's Complete Video Directory™
Children's Books In Print®
El-Hi Textbooks & Serials In Print®
Forthcoming Books®
Law Books & Serials In Print™
Medical & Health Care Books In Print™
Publishers, Distributors & Wholesalers of the US™
Subject Guide to Books In Print®
Subject Guide to Children's Books In Print®

Canadian General Reference

Associations Canada
Canadian Almanac & Directory
Canadian Environmental Resource Guide
Canadian Parliamentary Guide
Financial Services Canada
Governments Canada
Health Services Canada
Libraries Canada
Major Canadian Cities
The History of Canada

Grey House Publishing | Salem Press | H.W. Wilson
4919 Route, 22 PO Box 56, Amenia NY 12501-0056

2014 Title List

Visit **www.SalemPress.com** for Product Information, Table of Contents and Sample Pages

Literature

American Ethnic Writers
Critical Insights: Authors
Critical Insights: New Literary Collection Bundles
Critical Insights: Themes
Critical Insights: Works
Critical Survey of Drama
Critical Survey of Graphic Novels: Heroes & Super Heroes
Critical Survey of Graphic Novels: History, Theme & Technique
Critical Survey of Graphic Novels: Independents & Underground Classics
Critical Survey of Graphic Novels: Manga
Critical Survey of Long Fiction
Critical Survey of Mystery & Detective Fiction
Critical Survey of Mythology and Folklore: Heroes and Heroines
Critical Survey of Mythology and Folklore: Love, Sexuality & Desire
Critical Survey of Mythology and Folklore: World Mythology
Critical Survey of Poetry
Critical Survey of Poetry: American Poetry
Critical Survey of Poetry: British, Irish & Commonwealth Poets
Critical Survey of Poetry: European Poets
Critical Survey of Poetry: European Poets
Critical Survey of Poetry: Topical Essays
Critical Survey of Poetry: World Poets
Critical Survey of Science Fiction & Fantasy Literature
Critical Survey of Shakespeare's Sonnets
Critical Survey of Short Fiction
Critical Survey of Short Fiction: American Writers
Critical Survey of Short Fiction: British, Irish & Commonwealth Poets
Critical Survey of Short Fiction: European Writers
Critical Survey of Short Fiction: Topical Essays
Critical Survey of Short Fiction: World Writers
Cyclopedia of Literary Characters
Introduction to Literary Context: American Post-Modernist Novels
Introduction to Literary Context: American Short Fiction
Introduction to Literary Context: English Literature
Introduction to Literary Context: World Literature
Magill's Literary Annual 2014
Magill's Survey of American Literature
Magill's Survey of World Literature
Masterplots
Masterplots II: African American Literature
Masterplots II: Christian Literature
Masterplots II: Drama Series
Masterplots II: Short Story Series
Notable African American Writers
Notable American Novelists
Notable Playwrights
Short Story Writers

Science, Careers & Mathematics

Applied Science
Applied Science: Engineering & Mathematics
Applied Science: Science & Medicine
Applied Science: Technology
Biomes and Ecosystems
Careers in Chemistry
Careers in Communications & Media
Careers in Healthcare
Careers in Hospitality & Tourism
Careers in Law & Criminology
Careers in Physics
Computer Technology Inventors
Contemporary Biographies in Chemistry
Contemporary Biographies in Communications & Media
Contemporary Biographies in Healthcare
Contemporary Biographies in Hospitality & Tourism
Contemporary Biographies in Law & Criminology
Contemporary Biographies in Physics
Earth Science
Earth Science: Earth Materials & Resources
Earth Science: Earth's Surface and History
Earth Science: Physics & Chemistry of the Earth
Earth Science: Weather, Water & Atmosphere
Encyclopedia of Energy
Encyclopedia of Environmental Issues
Encyclopedia of Global Resources
Encyclopedia of Global Warming
Encyclopedia of Mathematics and Society
Encyclopedia of the Ancient World
Forensic Science
Internet Innovators
Introduction to Chemistry
Magill's Encyclopedia of Science: Animal Life
Magill's Encyclopedia of Science: Plant life
Magill's Medical Guide
Notable Natural Disasters
Solar System

Health

Addictions & Substance Abuse
Cancer
Complementary & Alternative Medicine
Genetics & Inherited Conditions
Infectious Diseases & Conditions
Magill's Medical Guide
Psychology & Mental Health
Psychology Basics

Grey House Publishing | Salem Press | H.W. Wilson
4919 Route, 22 PO Box 56, Amenia NY 12501-0056

2014 Title List

Visit **www.SalemPress.com** for Product Information, Table of Contents and Sample Pages

story and Social Science

Grey House Publishing | Salem Press | H.W. Wilson
4919 Route, 22 PO Box 56, Amenia NY 12501-0056

2014 Title List
Visit **www.HwWilsonInPrint.com** for Product Information, Table of Contents and Sample Pages

Current Biography
Current Biography Cumulative Index 1946-2013
Current Biography Magazine
Current Biography Yearbook-2004
Current Biography Yearbook-2005
Current Biography Yearbook-2006
Current Biography Yearbook-2007
Current Biography Yearbook-2008
Current Biography Yearbook-2009
Current Biography Yearbook-2010
Current Biography Yearbook-2011
Current Biography Yearbook-2012
Current Biography Yearbook-2013
Current Biography Yearbook-2014

Core Collections
Senior High Core Collection
Middle & Junior High School Core
Children's Core Collection
Fiction Core Collection
Public Library Core Collection: Nonfiction

Sears List
Sears List of Subject Headings
Sears: Lista de Encabezamientos de Materia

The Reference Shelf
Aging in America
Revisiting Gender
The U.S. National Debate Topic, 2014/2015
Embracing New Paradigms in education
Marijuana Reform
Representative American Speeches 2013-2014
Reality Television
The Business of Food
The Future of U.S. Economic Relations: Mexico, Cuba, and Venezuela
Sports in America
Global Climate Change
Representative American Speeches, 2012-2013
Conspiracy Theories
The Arab Spring
U.S. National Debate Topic: Transportation Infrastructure
Families: Traditional and New Structures
Faith & Science
Representative American Speeches 2011-2012
Social Networking
Dinosaurs
Space Exploration & Development
U.S. Infrastructure
Politics of the Ocean
Representative American Speeches 2010-2011
Robotics
The News and its Future
American Military Presence Overseas
Russia
Graphic Novels and Comic Books
Representative American Speeches 2009-2010

Readers' Guide
Readers Guide to Periodicals Literature
Abridged Readers' Guide to Periodical Literature
Short Story Index

Indexes
Short Story Index
Index to Legal Periodicals & Books

Facts About Series
Facts About the Presidents, Eighth Edition
Facts About China
Facts About the 20th Century
Facts About American Immigration
Facts About World's Languages

Nobel Prize Winners
Nobel Prize Winners, 2002-2013

World Authors
World Authors 2000-2005
World Authors 2006-2013

Famous First Facts
Famous First Facts, Seventh Edition
Famous First Facts About American Politics
Famous First Facts About Sports
Famous First Facts About the Environment
Famous First Facts, International Edition

American Book of Days
The American Book of Days, Fifth Edition
The International Book of Days

Junior Authors & Illustrators
Tenth Book of Junior Authors & Illustrations

Monographs
The Barnhart Dictionary of Etymology
Celebrate the World
Indexing from A to Z
Radical Change: Books for Youth in a Digital Age
The Poetry Break
Guide to the Ancient World

Wilson Chronology
Wilson Chronology of Asia and the Pacific
Wilson Chronology of Human Rights
Wilson Chronology of Ideas
Wilson Chronology of the Arts
Wilson Chronology of the World's Religions
Wilson Chronology of Women's Achievements

Book Review Digest
Book Review Digest, 2014

Grey House Publishing | Salem Press | H.W. Wilson
4919 Route, 22 PO Box 56, Amenia NY 12501-0056